2007 EDITION

FEDERAL CRIMINAL CODE and RULES

As received to February 2, 2007

Rules of Criminal Procedure
Rules Governing Habeas Corpus Cases
Rules Governing Motion Attacking Sentence
Rules for the Alien Terrorist Removal Court
Rules of Evidence
Rules of Appellate Procedure
Rules of Supreme Court of the United States

Includes legislation through Public Law 109-482, approved January 15, 2007

Mat #40521485

This publication was created to provide you with accurate and authoritative information concerning the subject matter covered; however, this publication was not necessarily prepared by persons licensed to practice law in a particular jurisdiction. The publisher is not engaged in rendering legal or other professional advice and this publication is not a substitute for the advice of an attorney. If you require legal or other expert advice, you should seek the services of a competent attorney or other professional

ISBN 978–0–314–96960–6

PREFACE

This 2007 Edition supercedes the 2006 Edition and its supplement. This Edition updates the rules as received to February 2, 2007, and includes legislation through Pub.L. 109–482, approved January 15, 2007.

Reference should also be made to Supreme Court Reporter, Federal Reporter, Federal Supplement, and Federal Rules Decisions advance sheets, as well as Westlaw, for any interim changes affecting the court rules in this Pamphlet.

This convenient reference Pamphlet, in form suitable for courtroom and office use, contains the text of the following:

Federal Rules of Criminal Procedure.

Rules Governing Cases under Sections 2254 and 2255 of Title 28, United States Code (Habeas Corpus Cases and Motion Attacking Sentence).

Rules for the Alien Terrorist Removal Court.

Federal Rules of Evidence.

Federal Rules of Appellate Procedure.

Rules of the Supreme Court of the United States.

Title 18, U.S. Code, Crimes and Criminal Procedure.

Constitution of the United States.

Title 8, Chapter 12, Immigration and Nationality, Subchapter II, Part VIII, General Penalty Provisions.

Title 15, U.S. Code, Chapter 41, Consumer Credit Protection, Section 1644, Fraudulent Use of Credit Cards; Penalties.

Title 21, U.S. Code, Chapter 13, Drug Abuse Prevention and Control.

Title 26, Chapter 53, Machine Guns, Destructive Devices, and Certain Other Firearms and Chapter 75, Crimes, Other Offenses, and Forfeitures, Subchapter A, Part I, General Provisions.

Title 28, U.S. Code, Chapter 58, United States Sentencing Commission; Chapter 83, Court of Appeals, Section 1291, Final Decisions of District Courts; Chapter 153, Habeas Corpus; Chapter 154, Special Habeas Corpus Procedures in Capital Cases; and Chapter 175, Civil Commitment and Rehabilitation of Narcotic Addicts [Repealed].

Title 31, U.S. Code, Chapter 53, Monetary Transactions, Subchapter II, Records and Reports on Monetary Instruments Transactions; Subchapter III, Money Laundering and Related Financial Crimes.

Title 41, Chapter 1, General Provisions, Sections 51 to 58, Anti-kickback Act of 1986.

Title 46, U.S. Code, Chapter 705, Maritime Drug Law Enforcement.

Title 49, U.S. Code, Chapter 11, National Transportation and Safety Board, Section 1155, Aviation Penalties; Chapter 463, Penalties, Sections 46306 to 46319; Chapter 465, Special Aircraft Jurisdiction of the United States.

Following the text of Title 18, the unlawful possession or receipt of firearms repealed provisions from Pub.L. 90–351, Title VII, §§ 1201 to 1203, are summarized in Appendix I; the

PREFACE

Interstate Agreement on Detainers Act from Pub.L. 91–538 is set out in Appendix II; and the Classified Information Procedures Act from Pub.L. 96–456 is set out in Appendix III.

As a regular feature in this Pamphlet, Advisory Committee Notes for the rules have been set out immediately following each rule.

A combined Time Table for Lawyers under the Federal Rules of Criminal Procedure, the Federal Rules of Appellate Procedure, and the Rules of the Supreme Court also appears herein. This Table indicates the time for each of the various procedural steps required by the Rules.

A detailed, consolidated Index appears in the back of this Pamphlet.

March, 2007

THE PUBLISHER

RELATED PRODUCTS IN FEDERAL LAW FROM WEST

FEDERAL PRACTICE

COURTROOM HANDBOOK ON FEDERAL EVIDENCE
Steven Goode and Olin Guy Wellborn III

FEDERAL CIVIL RULES HANDBOOK
Steven Baicker–McKee, William Janssen and John B. Corr

FEDERAL CRIMINAL RULES HANDBOOK
Laurie L. Levenson

MODERN SCIENTIFIC EVIDENCE
David L. Faigman, David H. Kaye, Michael J. Saks and Joseph Sanders

FEDERAL JURY PRACTICE AND INSTRUCTIONS
Kevin F. O'Malley, Jay E. Grenig and William C. Lee

[Also available in CD–ROM]

FEDERAL PRACTICE AND PROCEDURE
Charles Alan Wright, Arthur R. Miller, Mary Kay Kane, Edward H. Cooper, Richard L. Marcus, Kenneth W. Graham, Victor James Gold, Richard D. Freer, Patrick J. Schlitz, Vikram David Amar, Joan E. Steinman, Andrew D. Leipold, Peter J. Henning, Sarah H. Welling, Nancy J. King, Susan R. Klein, Charles H. Koch, Jr., and Michael H. Graham

[Also available in CD–ROM]

POLICE MISCONDUCT AND CIVIL RIGHTS—FEDERAL JURY PRACTICE AND INSTRUCTIONS
Stephen Yagman and Harold S. Lewis, Jr.

[Includes Instructions on Disk]

WEST'S FEDERAL ADMINISTRATIVE PRACTICE
Authored by Federal Practice Experts

WEST'S FEDERAL FORMS
Authored by Federal Practice Experts
[Also available in CD–ROM]

FEDERAL COURT OF APPEALS MANUAL
David G. Knibb

FEDERAL PRACTICE AND PROCEDURE—FEDERAL PRACTICE DESKBOOK
Charles Alan Wright and Mary Kay Kane

HANDBOOK OF FEDERAL EVIDENCE
Michael H. Graham

TREATISE ON CONSTITUTIONAL LAW
Ronald D. Rotunda and John E. Nowak

RELATED PRODUCTS

THE JUDGE'S EVIDENCE BENCHBOOK
Leo H. Whinery, Theodore P. Roberts, and Robert B. Smith

ADMINISTRATIVE LAW AND PRACTICE
Charles H. Koch, Jr.

FEDERAL RULES OF EVIDENCE WITH TRIAL OBJECTIONS
Charles B. Gibbons

BUSINESS AND COMMERCIAL LITIGATION IN FEDERAL COURTS
Robert L. Haig, Editor–In–Chief

NEWBERG ON CLASS ACTIONS, 3rd
Herbert Newberg and Alba Conte

HANDBOOK OF FEDERAL CIVIL DISCOVERY AND DISCLOSURE
Jay E. Grenig and Jeffrey S. Kinsler
[Includes forms on Disk]

ANNOTATED MANUAL FOR COMPLEX LITIGATION
David F. Herr

MULTIDISTRICT LITIGATION MANUAL
David F. Herr

United States Code Annotated
West's Federal Practice Digest 4th
United States Code Congressional and Administrative News

CRIMINAL PRACTICE

SEARCH AND SEIZURE
Wayne R. LaFave

SUBSTANTIVE CRIMINAL LAW
Wayne R. LaFave

CRIMINAL LAW DEFENSES
Paul H. Robinson

CRIMINAL PROCEDURE
Wayne R. LaFave, Jerold H. Israel, and Nancy J. King

FEDERAL SENTENCING LAW AND PRACTICE
Thomas W. Hutchison, Peter B. Hoffman, Deborah Young, and Sigmund G. Popko

FEDERAL SENTENCING GUIDELINES HANDBOOK
Roger W. Haines, Jr., Frank O. Bowman III, and Jennifer C. Woll

---

RELATED PRODUCTS

Corpus Juris Secundum
West's Federal Case News
Federal Civil Judicial Procedure and Rules
Federal Criminal Code and Rules
Federal Environmental Laws
Federal Immigration Laws and Regulations
Federal Labor Laws
Federal Sentencing Guidelines
Federal Social Security Laws, Selected Statutes and Regulations
Federal Intellectual Property Laws and Regulations
Federal Litigator
Reference Manual on Scientific Evidence, 2d

TAX PUBLICATIONS

Federal Tax Regulations
Internal Revenue Code
Internal Revenue Acts

To order any of these Federal practice tools, call your West Representative or **1–800–328–9352**.

INTERNET ACCESS

Contact the West Editorial Department directly with your questions and suggestions by e-mail at west.editor@thomson.com.
Visit West's home page at
west.thomson.com.

*

WESTLAW ELECTRONIC RESEARCH GUIDE

Westlaw—Expanding the Reach of Your Library

Westlaw is West's online legal research service. With Westlaw, you experience the same quality and integrity that you have come to expect from West books, plus quick, easy access to West's vast collection of statutes, case law materials, public records, and other legal resources, in addition to current news articles and business information. For the most current and comprehensive legal research, combine the strengths of West books and Westlaw.

When you research with westlaw.com you get the convenience of the Internet combined with comprehensive and accurate Westlaw content, including exclusive editorial enhancements, plus features found only in westlaw.com such as ResultsPlus™ or StatutesPlus.™

Accessing Databases Using the Westlaw Directory

The Westlaw Directory lists all databases on Westlaw and contains links to detailed information relating to the content of each database. Click **Directory** on the westlaw.com toolbar. There are several ways to access a database even when you don't know the database identifier. Browse a directory view. Scan the directory. Type all or part of a database name in the Search these Databases box. The Find a Database Wizard can help you select relevant databases for your search. You can access up to ten databases at one time for user-defined multibase searching.

Retrieving a Specific Document

To retrieve a specific document by citation or title on westlaw.com click **Find&Print** on the toolbar to display the Find a Document page. If you are unsure of the correct citation format, type the publication abbreviation, e.g., **xx st** (where xx is a state's two-letter postal abbreviation), in the Find this document by citation box and click **Go** to display a fill-in-the-blank template. To retrieve a specific case when you know one or more parties' names, click **Find a Case by Party Name**.

KeyCite®

KeyCite, the citation research service on Westlaw, makes it easy to trace the history of your case, statute, administrative decision or regulation to determine if there are recent updates, and to find other documents that cite your document. KeyCite will also find pending legislation relating to federal or state statutes. Access the powerful features of KeyCite from the westlaw.com toolbar, the **Links** tab, or KeyCite flags in a document display. KeyCite's red and yellow warning flags tell you at a glance whether your document has negative history. Depth-of-treatment stars help you focus on the most important citing references. KeyCite Alert allows you to monitor the status of your case, statute or rule, and automatically sends you updates at the frequency you specify.

ResultsPlus™

ResultsPlus is a Westlaw technology that automatically suggests additional information related to your search. The suggested materials are accessible by a set of links that appear to the right of your westlaw.com search results:

- Go directly to relevant ALR® articles and Am Jur® annotations.
- Find on-point resources by key number.
- See information from related treatises and law reviews.

StatutesPlus™

When you access a statutes database in westlaw.com you are brought to a powerful Search Center which collects, on one toolbar, the tools that are most useful for fast, efficient retrieval of statutes documents:

- Have a few key terms? Click **Statutes Index**.
- Know the common name? Click **Popular Name Table**.
- Familiar with the subject matter? Click **Table of Contents**.
- Have a citation or section number? Click **Find by Citation**.
- Interested in topical surveys providing citations across multiple state statutes? Click **50 State Surveys**.
- Or, simply search with **Natural Language** or **Terms and Connectors.**

When you access a statutes section, click on the **Links** tab for all relevant links for the current document that will also include a KeyCite section with a description of the KeyCite status flag. Depending on your document, links may also include administrative, bill text, and other sources that were previously only available by accessing and searching other databases.

Additional Information

Westlaw is available on the Web at www.westlaw.com.

For search assistance, call the West Reference Attorneys at 1–800–REF–ATTY (1–800–733–2889).

For technical assistance, call West Customer Technical Support at 1–800–WESTLAW (1–800–937–8529).

TABLE OF CONTENTS

TABLE OF CONTENTS

PROCEDURES FOR THE CONDUCT OF BUSINESS BY THE JUDICIAL CONFERENCE COMMITTEES ON RULES OF PRACTICE AND PROCEDURE

Scope

These procedures govern the operations of the Judicial Conference Committee on Rules of Practice, Procedure, and Evidence (Standing Committee) and the various Judicial Conference Advisory Committees on Rules of Practice and Procedure in drafting and recommending new rules of practice, procedure, and evidence and amendments to existing rules.

Part I—Advisory Committees

1. Functions

   Each Advisory Committee shall carry on "a continuous study of the operation and effect of the general rules of practice and procedure now or hereafter in use" in its particular field, taking into consideration suggestions and recommendations received from any source, new statutes and court decisions affecting the rules, and legal commentary.

2. Suggestions and Recommendations

   Suggestions and recommendations with respect to the rules should be sent to the Secretary, Committee on Rules of Practice and Procedure, Administrative Office of the United States Courts, Washington, D.C. 20544, who shall, to the extent feasible, acknowledge in writing every written suggestion or recommendation so received and shall refer all suggestions and recommendations to the appropriate Advisory Committee. To the extent feasible, the Secretary, in consultation with the Chairman of the Advisory Committee, shall advise the person making a recommendation or suggestion of the action taken thereon by the Advisory Committee.

3. Drafting Rules Changes

   a. An Advisory Committee shall meet at such times and places as the Chairman may authorize. All Advisory Committee meetings shall be open to the public, except when the committee so meeting, in open session and with a majority present, determines that it is in the public interest that all or part of the remainder of the meeting on that day shall be closed to the public and states the reason for closing the meeting. Each meeting shall be preceded by notice of the time and place of the meeting, including publication in the Federal Register, sufficient to permit interested persons to attend.

   b. The reporter assigned to each Advisory Committee shall, under the direction of the Committee or its Chairman, prepare initial draft rules changes, "Committee Notes" explaining their purpose and intent, copies or summaries of all written recommendations and suggestions received by the Advisory Committee, and shall forward them to the Advisory Committee.

   c. The Advisory Committee shall then meet to consider the draft proposed new rules and rules amendments, together with Committee Notes, make revisions therein, and submit them for approval of publication to the Standing Committee, or its Chairman, with a written report explaining the Committee's action, including any minority or other separate views.

4. Publication and Public Hearings

a. When publication is approved by the Standing Committee, the Secretary shall arrange for the printing and circulation of the proposed rules changes to the bench and bar, and to the public generally. Publication shall be as wide as practicable. Notice of the proposed rule shall be published in the Federal Register and copies provided to appropriate legal publishing firms with a request that they be timely included in their publications. The Secretary shall also provide copies to the chief justice of the highest court of each state and, insofar as is practicable, to all individuals and organizations that request them.

b. In order to provide full notice and opportunity for comment on proposed rule changes, a period of at least six months from the time of publication of notice in the Federal Register shall be permitted, unless a shorter period is approved under the provisions of subparagraph d of this paragraph.

c. An Advisory Committee shall conduct public hearings on all proposed rules changes unless elimination of such hearings is approved under the provisions of subparagraph d of this paragraph. The hearings shall be held at such times and places as determined by the chairman of the Advisory Committee and shall be preceded by adequate notice, including publication in the Federal Register. Proceedings shall be recorded and a transcript prepared. Subject to the provisions of paragraph six, such transcript shall be available for public inspection.

d. Exceptions to the time period for public comment and the public hearing requirement may be granted by the Standing Committee or its chairman when the Standing Committee or its chairman determines that the administration of justice requires that a proposed rule change should be expedited and that appropriate public notice and comment may be achieved by a shortened comment period, without public hearings, or both. The Standing Committee may eliminate the public notice and comment requirement if, in the case of a technical or conforming amendment, it determines that notice and comment are not appropriate or necessary. Whenever such an exception is made, the Standing Committee shall advise the Judicial Conference of the exception and the reasons for the exception.

5. Subsequent Procedures

a. At the conclusion of the comment period the reporter shall prepare a summary of the written comments received and the testimony presented at public hearings. The Advisory Committee shall review the proposed rules changes in the light of the comments and testimony. If the Advisory Committee makes any substantial change, an additional period for public notice and comment may be provided.

b. The Advisory Committee shall submit proposed rules changes and Committee Notes, as finally agreed upon, to the Standing Committee. Each submission shall be accompanied by a separate report of the comments received and shall explain any changes made subsequent to the original publication. The submission shall also include minority views of Advisory Committee members who wish to have separate views recorded.

6. Records

a. The Chairman of the Advisory Committee shall arrange for the preparation of minutes of all Advisory Committee meetings.

b. The records of an Advisory Committee shall consist of the written suggestions received from the public; the written comments received on drafts of proposed rules, responses thereto, transcripts of public hearings, and summaries prepared by the reporter; all correspondence relating to proposed rules changes; minutes of Advisory Committee meetings; approved drafts of rules changes; and reports to the Standing Committee. The records shall be maintained at the Administrative Office of the United States Courts for a minimum of two years and shall be available for public inspection during reasonable office hours. Thereafter the records may be transferred to a Government Records Center in accordance with applicable Government retention and disposition schedules.

c. Any portion of minutes, relating to a closed meeting and made available to the public, may contain such deletions as may be necessary to avoid frustrating the purposes of closing the meeting as provided in subparagraph 3a.

d. Copies of records shall be furnished to any person upon payment of a reasonable fee for the cost of reproduction.

PART II—Standing Committee

7. Functions

The Standing Committee shall coordinate the work of the several Advisory Committees, make suggestions of proposals to be studied by them, consider proposals recommended by the Advisory Committees, and transmit such proposals with its recommendation to the Judicial Conference, or recommit them to the appropriate Advisory Committee for further study and consideration.

8. Procedures

a. The Standing Committee shall meet at such times and places as the Chairman may authorize. All Committee meetings shall be open to the public, except when the committee so meeting, in open session and with a majority present, determines that it is in the public interest that all or part of the remainder of the meeting on that day shall be closed to the public and states the reason for closing the meeting. Each meeting shall be preceded by notice of the time and place of the meeting, including publication in the Federal Register, sufficient to permit interested persons to attend.

b. When an Advisory Committee's final recommendations for rules changes have been submitted, the Chairman and Reporter of the Advisory Committee shall attend the Standing Committee meeting to present the proposed rules changes and Committee Notes.

c. The Standing Committee may accept, reject, or modify a proposal. If a modification effects a substantial change, the proposal will be returned to the Advisory Committee with appropriate instructions.

d. The Standing Committee shall transmit to the Judicial Conference the proposed rules changes and Committee Notes approved by it, together with the Advisory Committee report. The Standing Committee's report to the Judicial Conference shall include its recommendations and explain any changes it has made.

9. Records

a. The Secretary shall prepare minutes of all Standing Committee meetings.

b. The records of the Standing Committee shall consist of the minutes of Standing and Advisory Committee meetings, reports to the Judicial Conference, and correspondence concerning rules changes including correspondence with Advisory Committee Chairmen. The records shall be maintained at the Administrative Office of the United States

Courts for a minimum of two years and shall be available for public inspection during reasonable office hours. Thereafter the records may be transferred to a Government Records Center in accordance with applicable Government retention and disposition schedules.

c. Copies of records shall be furnished to any person upon payment of a reasonable fee for the cost of reproduction.

STANDING COMMITTEE ON RULES OF PRACTICE AND PROCEDURE

As Constituted December 11, 2006

Chair:
HONORABLE DAVID F. LEVI
Members:

HONORABLE HARRIS L HARTZ
HONORABLE SIDNEY A. FITZWATER
HONORABLE THOMAS W. THRASH, JR.
HONORABLE MARK R. KRAVITZ
HONORABLE JAMES A. TEILBORG
HONORABLE RONALD M. GEORGE
PROFESSOR DANIEL J. MELTZER
DAVID J. BECK, ESQUIRE
JOHN G. KESTER, ESQUIRE
WILLIAM J. MALEDON, ESQUIRE
DOUGLAS R. COX, ESQUIRE
DEPUTY ATTORNEY GENERAL (EX OFFICIO)
HONORABLE PAUL J. MCNULTY

Reporter:

PROFESSOR DANIEL R. COQUILLETTE

Advisors and Consultants:

PROFESSOR GEOFFREY C. HAZARD, JR.
PROFESSOR R. JOSEPH KIMBLE
JOSEPH F. SPANIOL, JR., ESQUIRE

Secretary:

PETER G. MCCABE

ADVISORY COMMITTEE ON APPELLATE RULES

As Constituted December 11, 2006

Chair:
HONORABLE CARL E. STEWART
Members:

HONORABLE JEFFREY S. SUTTON
HONORABLE KERMIT EDWARD BYE
HONORABLE T.S. ELLIS III
HONORABLE RANDY J. HOLLAND
DEAN STEPHEN R. MCALLISTER
MARK I. LEVY, ESQUIRE
MAUREEN E. MAHONEY, ESQUIRE
JAMES F BENNETT, ESQUIRE
SOLICITOR GENERAL (EX OFFICIO)
HONORABLE PAUL D. CLEMENT
APPELLATE LITIGATION COUNSEL
DOUGLAS LETTER

Reporter:

PROFESSOR CATHERINE T. STRUVE

Advisors and Consultants:

CHARLES R. FULBRUGE, III

Liaison Member:

(OPEN)

Secretary:

PETER G. MCCABE

ADVISORY COMMITTEE ON BANKRUPTCY RULES

As Constituted December 11, 2006

Chair:
HONORABLE A. THOMAS S. ZILLY
Members:

HONORABLE R. GUY COLE, JR.
HONORABLE IRENE M. KEELEY
HONORABLE LAURA TAYLOR SWAIN
HONORABLE RICHARD A. SCHELL
HONORABLE WILLIAM H. PAULEY III
HONORABLE MARK B. MCFEELEY
HONORABLE EUGENE R. WEDOFF
HONORABLE KENNETH J. MEYERS, JR.
HONORABLE CHRISTOPHER M. KLEIN
DEAN LAWRENCE PONOROFF
J. MICHAEL LAMBERTH, ESQUIRE
G. ERIC BRUNSTAD, JR., ESQUIRE
JOHN RAO, ESQUIRE
DIRECTOR, COMMERCIAL LITIGATION BRANCH, CIVIL DIVISION, U.S. DEPT. OF JUSTICE (EX OFFICIO)
J. CHRISTOPHER KOHN, ESQUIRE

Reporter:
PROFESSOR JEFFREY W. MORRIS

Advisors and Consultants:
JAMES J. WALDRON
DONALD WALTON, ACTING DEPUTY DIRECTOR
PATRICIA S. KETCHUM, ESQUIRE

Liaison Member:
HONORABLE HARRIS L HARTZ

Liaison from Committee on the Administration of the Bankruptcy System:
(OPEN)

Secretary:
PETER G. MCCABE

ADVISORY COMMITTEE ON CIVIL RULES

As Constituted December 11, 2006

Chair:
Honorable Lee H. Rosenthal
Members:

Honorable Paul J. Kelly, Jr.
Honorable Jose A. Cabranes
Honorable Vaughn R. Walker
Honorable Michael M. Baylson
Honorable David G. Campbell
Honorable C. Christopher Hagy
Honorable Randall T. Shepard
Professor Steven S. Gensler
Robert C. Heim, Esquire
Chilton Davis Varner, Esquire
Daniel C. Girard, Esquire
Anton R. Valukas, Esquire
Assistant Attorney General for the Civil Division (ex officio)
Honorable Peter D. Keisler
Ted Hirt, Assistant Director
Federal Programs Branch
Civil Division

Liaison Members:

Honorable Sidney A. Fitzwater
Honorable Eugene R. Wedoff

Reporter:

Professor Edward H. Cooper

Advisors and Consultants:

Professor Richard L. Marcus
Professor Thomas D. Rowe, Jr.

Secretary:

Peter G. McCabe

ADVISORY COMMITTEE ON CRIMINAL RULES

As Constituted December 11, 2006

Chair:
Honorable Susan C. Bucklew
Members:

Honorable Richard C. Tallman
Honorable Harvey Bartle III
Judge Mark L. Wolf
Honorable James P. Jones
Honorable David G. Trager
Honorable Anthony J. Battaglia
Honorable Robert H. Edmunds, Jr.
Professor Nancy J. King
Leo P. Cunningham, Esquire
Rachel Brill, Esquire
Federal Public Defender
Thomas P. McNamara
Assistant Attorney General for the Criminal Division (ex officio)
Honorable Alice S. Fisher
Counselor to Assistant Attorney General
Criminal Division
Benton J. Campbell

Reporter:

Professor Sara Sun Beale

Liaison Member:

Honorable Mark R. Kravitz

Secretary:

Peter G. McCabe

ADVISORY COMMITTEE ON EVIDENCE RULES

As Constituted December 11, 2006

Chair:
HONORABLE JERRY E. SMITH
Members:

HONORABLE JOSEPH F. ANDERSON, JR.
HONORABLE ROBERT L. HINKLE
HONORABLE JOAN N. ERICKSON
HONORABLE ANDREW D. HURWITZ
WILLIAM W. TAYLOR, III, ESQUIRE
WILLIAM T. HANGLEY, ESQUIRE
MARJORIE A. MEYERS
FEDERAL PUBLIC DEFENDER
RONALD J. TENPAS
ASSOCIATE DEPUTY ATTORNEY GENERAL
ELIZABETH J. SHAPIRO
ASSISTANT DIRECTOR, CIVIL DIVISION

Liaison Members:
HONORABLE THOMAS W. THRASH, JR.
HONORABLE CHRISTOPHER M. KLEIN
HONORABLE MICHAEL M. BAYLSON
HONORABLE DAVID G. TRAGER

Reporter:
PROFESSOR DANIEL J. CAPRA

Advisors and Consultants:
PROFESSOR KENNETH S. BROUN

Secretary:
PETER G. MCCABE

FEDERAL RULES

CRIMINAL PROCEDURE

HABEAS CORPUS CASES

MOTION ATTACKING SENTENCE

ALIEN TERRORIST REMOVAL COURT

EVIDENCE

APPELLATE PROCEDURE

SUPREME COURT

*

FEDERAL RULES OF CRIMINAL PROCEDURE FOR THE UNITED STATES DISTRICT COURTS

Amendments received to February 2, 2007

TIME TABLE FOR LAWYERS IN FEDERAL CRIMINAL CASES

Amended to February 2, 2007

This table, prepared by the Publisher's editorial staff as a guide to the user, indicates the time for the various steps in a criminal action as provided by the Federal Rules of Criminal Procedure, the Federal Rules of Appellate Procedure, the Rules of the Supreme Court, and, where applicable, Titles 18 and 28. The user should always consult the actual text of the rule. Most of these time limitations may be enlarged by the court under the conditions and with the exceptions indicated under "Enlargement of time" in the table. Citations are to the supporting Rules and are in the form "Crim.R. —" for the Rules of Criminal Procedure; "App.R. —" for the Rules of Appellate Procedure; "28 U.S.C.A. § —" for statutes; and "Supreme Court Rule —".

ACQUITTAL

Motion for judgment of	After evidence on either side is closed. Court may reserve decision on motion, proceed with trial, where the motion is made before the close of all the evidence, submit the case to the jury and decide motion either before verdict is returned or after jury returns verdict of guilty or is discharged without verdict. If court reserves decision, motion must be decided on basis of evidence at the time ruling was reserved. Motion may be made or renewed within 7 days after discharge of jury. Crim.R. 29.

ALIBI

Notice by defense	Defendant to serve within 10 days of written request from government, or at some other time the court sets. Crim.R. 12.1(a). Exceptions for good cause. Crim.R. 12.1(d).
Disclosure by government	Within 10 days after defendant serves notice of alibi, unless the court directs otherwise, government to disclose witnesses government intends to rely upon to establish defendant's presence at scene of offense and rebuttal witnesses to the alibi defense. Disclosure must be made no later than 10 days before trial. Crim.R. 12.1(b). Exceptions for good cause. Crim.R. 12.1(d).
Continuing duty to disclose	Either party to disclose promptly if party learns before or during trial of additional witness who should have been disclosed under Crim.R. 12.1(a) or (b). Crim.R. 12.1(c). Exceptions for good cause. Crim.R. 12.1(d).

ALLOCUTION	Before imposing sentence, court must provide defendant's counsel an opportunity to speak on defendant's behalf, and must address defendant personally in order to permit defendant to speak or present information to mitigate sentence. Crim.R. 32(c)(4)(A).

APPEAL

	See, also, "CERTIORARI", this table.
Notification of right	After imposing sentence in any case of any right to appeal the sentence. Crim.R. 32(j)(1)(B).
	After imposing sentence in case which has gone to trial on a plea of not guilty. Crim.R. 32(j)(1)(A).
From magistrate judge's order or judgment	Interlocutory appeal or appeal from conviction or sentence to district judge within 10 days after entry of order, or judgment. Crim.R. 58(g)(2).
By Defendant	Within 10 days after the later of the entry either of the judgment or order appealed from or of the filing of a notice of appeal by the Government. If a timely motion is made for judgment of acquittal under Rule 29, for arrest of judgment under Rule 34, for a new trial under Rule 33 on any ground other than newly discovered evidence, or for a new trial based on the ground of newly discovered evidence if the motion is made no later than 10 days after entry of the judgment, appeal from a judgment of conviction must be taken within 10 days after entry of the order disposing of the last such motion outstanding, or within 10 days after the entry of the judgment of conviction, whichever is later. Time may be extended for not more than 30 additional days on a showing of excusable neglect or good cause. App.R. 4(b)(1), (3) and (4).
By government	Within 30 days after the later of the entry of judgment or order appealed from or the filing of a notice of appeal by any defendant. Time may be enlarged for not more than 30 additional days on a showing of excusable neglect or good cause. App.R. 4(b)(1) and (4).
Appeal by inmate confined in institution	When deposited in the institution's internal mail system on or before the last day for filing. Timely filing may be shown by a notarized statement or by a declaration (in compliance with 28 U.S.C.A. § 1746) setting forth the date of deposit and stating that first-class postage had been prepaid. 30-day period for the government to file its notice of appeal runs from entry of judgment or order appealed from or from the district court's docketing of the defendant's notice of appeal, whichever is later. App.R. 4(c).
Representation statement	Within 10 days after filing a notice of appeal, unless another time is designated by the court of appeals, attorney who filed notice of appeal must file, with clerk of the court of appeals, a statement naming each party represented on appeal by that attorney. App.R. 12(b).
Record (appellant)	Within 10 days after filing notice of appeal or entry of order disposing of last timely remaining motion of a type specified in App.R. 4(a)(4)(A), whichever is later: Appellant to place written order for transcript and file copy of order with clerk; if none to be ordered, file a certificate to that effect; unless entire transcript to be included, file a statement of issues and serve appellee a copy of order or certificate and of statement. App.R. 10(b).
Record (appellee)	Within 10 days after service of appellant's order or certificate and statement, appellee to file and serve on appellant a designation of additional parts of transcript to be included. Unless within 10 days

APPEAL	
	after designation appellant has ordered such parts and so notified appellee, appellee may within following 10 days either order the parts or move in district court for order requiring appellant to do so. App.R. 10(b).
Record (costs)	At time of ordering, party to make satisfactory arrangements with reporter for payment of cost of transcript. App.R. 10(b)(4).
Record (reporter)	If transcript cannot be completed within 30 days of receipt of order, reporter shall request extension of time from circuit clerk. App.R. 11(b).
Setting appeal for argument	The clerk must advise the parties. A request for postponement of argument or for allowance of additional time must be made by motion filed reasonably in advance of the date fixed for hearing. App.R. 34(b).
APPEARANCE	See, also, "ARRESTED persons", this table.
Before magistrate judge	Without unnecessary delay after an arrest within the United States and also after an arrest outside the United States unless a statute provides otherwise. Crim.R. 5(a)(1).
ARREST of judgment	Defendant must move within 7 days after verdict or finding of guilty, or after plea of guilty or nolo contendere. Crim.R. 34.
ARRESTED persons	See, also, "CUSTODY", this table.
Initial appearance generally	To be taken without unnecessary delay before a magistrate judge, after an arrest within the United States and also after an arrest outside the United States unless a statute provides otherwise. Crim.R. 5(a)(1).
Exceptions	Arrests upon charges of interstate flight or failing to appear in another district, or for violations of probation or supervised release, appearances without unnecessary delay, see Crim.R. 5(a)(2), 32.1, 40.
	If a the arrest is in the district where the offense was allegedly committed and a magistrate judge is not reasonably available, initial appearance may be before a state or local judicial officer. Crim.R. 5(c)(1)(B).
	If person is arrested without warrant, complaint must be promptly filed. Crim.R. 5(b).
BILL of particulars	Before arraignment. Crim.R. 7(f).
Amendment	At any time subject to such conditions as justice requires. Crim.R. 7(f).
Motion for	Before arraignment or within 10 days after arraignment or at such later time as court may permit. Crim.R. 7(f).
CERTIORARI	
Petition for writ	See 28 U.S.C.A. Rules, Supreme Court Rule 13.
CHANGE of venue	See "TRANSFER", this table.
CLERICAL error	Corrected at any time after court gives such notice it considers appropriate. Crim.R. 36
CLERK'S office	Open during business hours on all days except Saturdays, Sundays, legal holidays and on days on

which weather or other conditions have made office of clerk inaccessible. Crim.R. 56; App.R. 45(a).

COMMITMENT to another district

Person arrested (1) in a district other than that in which the offense is alleged to have been committed, or (2) for a violation of probation or supervised release in a district other than the district having jurisdiction, or (3) on a warrant (issued for failure to appear pursuant to subpoena or terms of release) in a district other than that in which the warrant was issued, is to be taken without unnecessary delay before the nearest available magistrate judge. Crim.R. 40.

COMPLAINT

When a person arrested without a warrant is brought before a magistrate judge, a complaint must be promptly filed. Crim.R. 5(b).

COMPUTATION of time

Exclude day of the act, event, or default that begins the period of time. Include last day of the period unless it is a Saturday, Sunday, legal holiday, or other conditions make the clerk's office inaccessible. When last day is excluded, period runs until end of the next day which is not one of the aforementioned days. Crim.R. 45(a); App.R. 26(a).

Intermediate Saturdays, Sundays, and legal holidays are excluded if the period is less than 11 days. Crim.R. 45(a).

Intermediate Saturdays, Sundays, and legal holidays are excluded if the period is less than 11 days, unless stated in calendar days. App.R. 26(a).

Service by mail adds three days to a period computed from the time of said service. Crim.R. 45(e). When a party is required or permitted to act within a prescribed period after service of a notice or a paper upon that party, three calendar days are added to the prescribed period unless the paper is delivered on the date of service stated in the proof of service. Crim.R. 45(c); App.R. 26(c). A paper served electronically is not treated as delivered on the day of service stated in the proof of service. App.R. 26(c).

Supreme Court matters, see 28 U.S.C.A. Rules, Supreme Court Rule 30.

CORPORATE disclosure

Generally

Nongovernmental corporate parties must file, upon defendant's initial appearance, statement identifying a parent corporation or any corporation owning 10% or more of its stock or stating that there is no such corporation. Crim.R. 12.4(a)(1), (b)(1).

Organizational victim

Government must file, upon defendant's initial appearance, statement identifying the victim and, if victim is a corporation, statement identifying a parent corporation or any corporation owning 10% or more of victim corporation's stock or stating that there is no such corporation, to the extent information can be obtained through due diligence. Crim.R. 12.4(a)(2), (b)(1).

Supplemental statement

Party must file supplemental statement upon any change in the information that the original statement requires. Crim.R. 12.4(b)(2).

COUNSEL	
Joint representation	Court must promptly inquire about the propriety of joint representation and shall personally advise each defendant of right to effective assistance of counsel, including separate representation. Crim.R. 44(c)(2).
COURTS	Always open except when weather or other conditions make court inaccessible. Crim.R. 45(a).
	District courts always open. Crim.R. 56(a).
CUSTODY	
	See, also, "ARRESTED PERSONS", this table.
Release before trial	Provisions of 18 U.S.C.A. §§ 3142 and 3144 govern. Crim.R. 46(a).
Release during trial	Person released before trial continues on release during trial unless court determines otherwise. Crim.R. 46(b).
Release pending sentencing or appeal	Provisions of 18 U.S.C.A. § 3143 govern. Crim.R. 46(c).
Witness	Witness who has been detained pursuant to 18 U.S.C.A. § 3144 and whose deposition is taken pursuant to Crim.R. 15(a) may be discharged by court after witness has signed deposition transcript under oath. Crim.R. 15(a)(2).
Reports	Attorney for government must report biweekly to court listing witnesses held in excess of 10 days; shall state why each witness should not be released with or without a deposition being taken. Crim.R. 46(h)(2).
DEFENSES and objections	
Raising of motion	Deadline for making pretrial motions or requests may be set by court at time of arraignment or as soon thereafter as practicable. Crim.R. 12(c). Defenses and objections which may be, and those which must be, raised before trial, see Crim.R. 12(b)(3).
Ruling on motion	Court must decide all pretrial motions before trial unless court finds good cause to defer a ruling. Crim.R. 12(d).
Alibi	See "ALIBI", this table.
Insanity	Defendant intending to assert insanity defense must notify attorney for government and file copy with clerk within time provided for filing of pretrial motions or at later time court sets. Court may for good cause allow late filing, grant additional time, or make other appropriate orders. Crim.R. 12.2(a).
Mental condition	Defendant intending to introduce expert evidence relating to any mental condition must notify attorney for government and file copy with clerk within time provided for filing of pretrial motions or at any other time the court sets. Court may for good cause allow late filing, grant additional time, or make other appropriate orders. Crim.R. 12.2(b).
Public authority	Notice of defense—Defendant intending to assert public-authority defense must notify attorney for government and file copy with clerk within time provided for filing of pretrial motions or at any other time the court sets. Crim.R. 12.3(a)(1).
	Response to notice—Government attorney must serve response within 10 days after receiving no-

DEFENSES and objections

tice, but no later than 20 days before trial. Crim.R. 12.3(a)(3).

Witness disclosure—Government attorney, no later than 20 days before trial, may request statement of names, etc. of witnesses relied upon to establish defense. Within 7 days after request, defendant must serve statement. Within 7 days after receiving statement, government attorney must serve statement of witnesses upon which the government intends to rely. Crim.R. 12.3(a)(4). Additional witness information must be disclosed promptly after disclosing party learns of the witness. Crim.R. 12.3(b).

Additional time—Court may for good cause allow a party additional time to comply with rule. Crim.R. 12.3(a)(5).

DEPOSITIONS

Notice of taking	The court for good cause may change the date of deposition. Crim.R. 15(b)(1).
Taking of	By order of court due to exceptional circumstances and in interest of justice. Crim.R. 15(a)(1).

DISCOVERY or inspection

Motion	Motion for discovery under Crim.R. 16 must be raised prior to trial. Crim.R. 12(b)(3).
Notice by government of intention to use evidence	At arraignment or as soon thereafter as practicable, defendant may request notice of government's intention to use (in evidence-in-chief at trial) any evidence defendant may be entitled to discover under Crim.R. 16. Crim.R. 12(b)(4).
Statements or report by government witnesses	Shall not be subject of subpoena, discovery, or inspection until witness has testified on direct examination in the trial of the case. 18 U.S.C.A. § 3500(a).
Continuing duty to disclose	Party who, prior to or during trial, discovers additional evidence or material previously requested or ordered, which is subject to discovery or inspection, shall promptly notify other party or attorney or the court. Crim.R. 16(c).

DISMISSAL — By court of indictment, information, or complaint if unnecessary delay occurs in presenting charge to grand jury, filing an information against defendant, or bringing defendant to trial. Crim.R. 48(b).

EVIDENCE

Suppression	Motion must be raised prior to trial. Crim.R. 12(b)(3).
Notice by government of intention to use evidence	At arraignment or as soon thereafter as practicable, either at discretion of government respecting specified evidence or at request of defendant respecting intention to use (in evidence-in-chief at trial) any evidence defendant may (under Crim.R. 16) be entitled to discover. Crim.R. 12(b)(4).
Notice by defendant of intention to introduce expert testimony of mental condition	Defendant intending to introduce expert evidence relating to any mental condition must notify attorney for government and file copy with clerk within time provided for filing of pretrial motions or at any other time the court sets. Court may for good cause allow late filing, grant additional time, or make other appropriate orders. Crim.R. 12.2(b).

EXTENDING time	
Last day of period	Computation of time when last day is Saturday, Sunday, holiday, or day on which weather or other conditions have made office of clerk inaccessible. Crim.R. 45(a)(3).
Generally	When act must be done at or within a specified period, court on its own may extend the time, or for good cause may do so on party's motion made before the originally prescribed or previously extended time expires, or after the time expires if the party failed to act because of excusable neglect. Exceptions: see "Motion for judgment of acquittal", "Motion for new trial", "Motion to arrest judgment", and "Correcting a sentence", this heading. Crim.R. 45(b).
Appeal	Extension of time for filing notice of appeal for period not to exceed 30 days from expiration of time otherwise prescribed by App.R. 4(b), upon a finding of excusable neglect or good cause, before or after time has expired. App.R. 4(b). In cases on appeal, for good cause, court may extend time prescribed by rules of appellate procedure or by its order to perform any act, or may permit an act to be done after expiration of such time. Court may not, however, extend time for filing notice of appeal (but see provision in App.R. 4(b) for extension of time), or petition for permission to appeal. App.R. 26(b).
Supreme Court	See 28 U.S.C.A. Rules, Supreme Court Rule 30.
Motion for judgment of acquittal	No extension of the 7–day period. Crim.R. 29.
Motion for new trial	No extension of the 7–day period. Crim.R. 33.
Motion to arrest judgment	No extension of the 7–day period. Crim.R. 34.
Correcting a sentence	No extension. Crim.R. 35, 45(b).
FOREIGN law	**Reasonable written notice required of party intending to raise an issue concerning the law of a foreign country. Crim.R. 26.1.**
GRAND jury	
Challenges	A Challenge to the grand jury or based on an individual juror's lack of qualification may be made before the voir dire examination begins, or within 7 days after the grounds of challenge are discovered or could have been discovered, whichever is earlier. 28 U.S.C.A. § 1867(a), (b).
Excuse of juror	At any time for cause court may excuse a juror either temporarily or permanently. Crim.R. 6(h).
Summoning	Grand juries must be summoned when the public interest requires. Crim.R. 6(a)(1).
Tenure	Until discharged by court but more than 18 months only if court determines that an extension is in the public interest. Extensions may be granted for no more than 6 months except as otherwise provided by statute. Crim.R. 6(g).
HOLIDAYS	New Year's Day, Birthday of Martin Luther King, Jr., Washington's Birthday, Memorial Day, Independence Day, Labor Day, Columbus Day, Veterans' Day, Thanksgiving Day, Christmas Day, and any other day declared a holiday by the President, Congress or the state in which is located either the district court that rendered the challenged judg-

	ment or order, or the circuit clerk's principal office. Crim.R. 45(a); App.R. 26(a).
	Exclusion in computation of time when the period is less than 11 days. Crim.R. 45(a); App.R. 26(a).
INDICTMENT	
Defects	Defenses and objections based on defects (other than failure to invoke the court's jurisdiction or to state an offense, which the court may hear at any time while case is pending) must be raised prior to trial. Crim.R. 12(b).
Failure to find	If complaint or information is pending, failure for 12 jurors to vote to indict must be reported to magistrate judge promptly. Crim.R. 6(f).
Sealing and secrecy	Magistrate judge to whom an indictment is returned may direct that indictment shall be kept secret until defendant is in custody or has been released pending trial; clerk thereupon to seal and no person to disclose except when necessary for issuance and execution of warrant or summons. Crim.R. 6(e)(4).
INFORMATION	
Amendment	At any time before verdict or finding unless an additional or different offense is charged or a substantial right is prejudiced. Crim.R. 7(e).
Defects	Defenses and objections based on defects (other than failure to show jurisdiction in the court or to charge an offense which objections shall be noticed by the court at any time during pendency of proceedings) must be raised prior to trial. Crim.R. 12(b)(3).
INSTRUCTIONS	
Requests for	At close of evidence or at any earlier time during trial as court reasonably sets. When request is made, requesting party must furnish a copy of request to every other party. Crim.R. 30(a).
Ruling on requests	Court must inform parties before closing arguments how it intends to rule on requested instructions. Crim.R. 30(b).
Time for giving	Court may instruct jury before or after arguments are completed or at both times. Crim.R. 30(c).
Objections	Before jury retires to deliberate. Failure to object in accordance with rule precludes review, except as permitted under Crim.R. 52(b). Crim.R. 30(d).
JUDGMENT of acquittal	
Before submission to jury	After government closes its evidence or after the close of all the evidence, on defendant's motion. Crim.R. 29(a).
After jury verdict or discharge	Defendant may move for judgment of acquittal or renew such motion within 7 days after guilty verdict or after court discharges jury, whichever is later. Defendant is not required to move for judgment of acquittal before court submits case to jury as a prerequisite for making such motion after jury discharge. Crim.R. 29(c).
JURY	
	See, also, "GRAND JURY", this table.
Alternate jurors	The court may retain alternate jurors after the jury retires to deliberate. Crim.R. 24(c)(3).

JURY	
Array, challenge of	Must be made before voir dire examination begins, or within 7 days after the grounds for the challenge are discovered or could have been discovered, whichever is earlier. 28 U.S.C.A. § 1867(a), (b).
Order for jury of 11	After jury has retired to deliberate, court may permit jury of 11 persons to return verdict, if court finds good cause to excuse a juror. Crim.R. 23(b)(3).
Poll of jury	After verdict is returned but before jury is discharged, at request of any party or on court's own motion. Crim.R. 31(d).
LEGAL holidays	See "HOLIDAYS", this table.
MAIL	Service by mail adds three days to a period computed from the time of such service. Crim.R. 45(c).
	When a party is required or permitted to act within a prescribed period after service of a paper upon that party, three calendar days are added to the prescribed period unless the paper is delivered on the date of service stated in the proof of service. A paper served electronically is not treated as delivered on the day of service stated in the proof of service. App.R. 26(c).
MENTAL condition (defense)	Defendant intending to introduce expert evidence relating to any mental condition must notify attorney for government and file copy with clerk within time provided for filing of pretrial motions or at any other time the court sets. Court may for good cause allow late filing, grant additional time, or make other appropriate orders. Crim.R. 12.2(b).
MOTIONS	
Service of	Written motions (other than motions court may hear ex parte) with supporting affidavits, and any hearing notice: at least 5 days before hearing date, unless rule or court order sets a different period. For good cause, court may set a different period upon ex parte application. Crim.R. 47(c), (d).
	Responding party must serve opposing affidavits at least one day before hearing, unless court permits later service. Crim.R. 47(d).
NEW trial	
Motion generally	Within 7 days after verdict or finding of guilt. Crim.R. 33(b)(2).
Newly discovered evidence	Only within three years after the verdict or finding of guilty. If appeal is pending, court may not grant motion until appellate court remands case. Crim.R. 33(b)(1).
OBJECTIONS	See "DEFENSES AND OBJECTIONS", this table.
PLEA of guilty or nolo contendere	
Agreement procedure	Disclosure of plea agreement required when plea is offered. Crim.R. 11(e)(2).
Appeal	Notification following sentence of any right to appeal sentence. Crim.R. 32(j)(1)(B).
Withdrawal	Before court accepts plea, for any reason or no reason. After court accepts plea, but before court imposes sentence, if court rejects a plea agreement under Crim.R. 11(c)(5) or defendant can show a fair

PLEA of guilty or nolo contendere	and just reason for request. After court imposes sentence, defendant may not withdraw; plea may be set aside only on direct appeal or collateral attack. Crim.R. 11(d), (e).
PRELIMINARY hearing	
Defendant in custody	Preliminary hearing within a reasonable time but not later than 10 days after initial appearance. Crim.R. 5.1(c). See, also, 18 U.S.C.A. § 3060.
Defendant not in custody	Preliminary hearing within a reasonable time but not later than 20 days after initial appearance. Crim.R. 5.1(c). See, also, 18 U.S.C.A. § 3060.
Extension	With consent of defendant, one or more times, by judge or magistrate judge. Without consent of defendant, by magistrate judge only upon showing that extraordinary circumstances exist and that justice requires the delay. Crim.R. 5.1(d). See, also, 18 U.S.C.A. § 3060(c).
PRESENTENCE investigation and report	
When made	Before imposition of sentence unless 18 U.S.C.A. or another statute requires otherwise, or court finds that record information enables it to meaningfully exercise its sentencing authority, and court explains finding on the record. Crim.R. 32(c)(1)(A).
Notice	At least 35 days before sentencing hearing, unless the defendant waives this minimum period, probation officer must give report to defendant, defendant's counsel, and an attorney for the Government. Crim.R. 32(e)(2).
Objections	Within 14 days after the receiving report, parties must state in writing any objections, and provide a copy of objections to opposing party and probation officer. Crim.R. 32(f).
Submission to court	At least 7 days before sentencing, probation officer must submit to court and parties report and addendum containing unresolved objections, grounds for those objections, and officer's comments on objections. Crim.R. 32(g).
PROBATION or supervised release	
Hearings relating to revocation	Initial appearance—Without unnecessary delay before a magistrate judge who must inform the person of the alleged violation and certain rights. Crim.R. 32.1(a).
	Preliminary hearing—Magistrate judge must promptly conduct a hearing to determine probable cause to believe a violation has occurred. Crim.R. 32.1(b)(1).
	Revocation hearing—Unless waived, within a reasonable time in the district having jurisdiction. Crim.R. 32.1(b)(2).
REMOVAL proceedings	See "COMMITMENT TO ANOTHER DISTRICT", this table.
SATURDAYS AND SUNDAYS	Exclusion in computation of time when period is less than 11 days (unless stated in calendar days [App.R. 26(a)]. Crim.R. 45(a); App.R. 26(a).

SEARCH warrant	
Issuance	Warrant must command officer to execute it within a specified time no longer than 10 days. Crim.R. 41(c)(2).
Execution and return	Officer executing the warrant must promptly return it, with a copy of inventory, to magistrate judge. Crim.R. 41(f)(4).
SENTENCE	
	See, also, "PRESENTENCE INVESTIGATION AND REPORT", this table.
Changing time limits	Court may for good cause change any time limits prescribed by Crim.R. 32. Crim.R. 32(b)(2).
Correction or reduction	Assistance to government. Upon government motion made within one year of sentencing, if defendant after sentencing provided substantial assistance in investigating or prosecuting another person, and reduction accords with sentencing guidelines. If motion made more than one year after sentencing, if assistance involved information not known to defendant or not useful to government until one year or more after imposition, or was promptly provided to government after its usefulness was reasonably apparent to defendant. Crim.R. 35(b).
	Clear error. Within 7 days after sentencing, court may correct sentence resulting from arithmetical, technical, or other clear error. Crim.R. 35(a).
Imposition	Without unnecessary delay. Crim.R. 32(b)(1).
Vacation, setting aside, or correction, motion for	At any time. 28 U.S.C.A. § 2255.
	One year period of limitation commencing as provided in 28 U.S.C.A. § 2255.
SEVERANCE	A Crim.R. 14 motion to sever charges or defendants must be raised prior to trial. Crim.R. 12(b)(3).
SUBPOENA	Court may direct that books, papers, documents, or objects designated in subpoena be produced before court prior to trial or prior to time they are to be offered in evidence and may upon their production permit them to be inspected by parties or their attorneys. Crim.R. 17(c).
SUMMONS	
Return	On or before the return day. Crim.R. 4(c)(4)(B).
SUPERVISED RELEASE	See "PROBATION OR SUPERVISED RELEASE", this Table.
TERM of court	Terms of court have been abolished. 28 U.S.C.A. § 138.
TRANSFER	
Motion for	At or before arraignment or at such other time as the court or the rules prescribe. Crim.R. 21(d).
WARRANT (arrest)	
	See, also, "ARRESTED PERSONS", this table.
Showing to defendant	Officer who does not have warrant in possession at time of arrest must show it to defendant as soon as possible upon request. Crim.R. 4(c)(3)(A).

ORDERS OF THE SUPREME COURT OF THE UNITED STATES ADOPTING AND AMENDING RULES

ORDER OF DECEMBER 26, 1944

It is ordered that Rules of Criminal Procedure for the District Courts of the United States governing proceedings in criminal cases prior to and including verdict, finding of guilty or not guilty by the court, or plea of guilty, be prescribed pursuant to the Act of June 29, 1940, c. 445, 54 Stat. 688, 18 U.S.C.A. § 687. And the Chief Justice is authorized and directed to transmit the Rules as prescribed to the Attorney General and to request him, as provided in that Act, to report these Rules to the Congress at the beginning of the regular session in January 1945.

Mr. Justice Black states that he does not approve of the adoption of the Rules.

Mr. Justice Frankfurter does not join in the Court's action for reasons stated in a memorandum opinion.

MR. JUSTICE FRANKFURTER:

That the federal courts have power, or may be empowered, to make rules of procedure for the conduct of litigation has been settled for a century and a quarter (*Wayman* v. *Southard*, 10 Wheat. 1, 6 L.Ed. 253). And experience proves that justice profits if the responsibility for such rule making be vested in a small, standing rule-making body rather than be left to legislation generated by particular controversies. These views make me regret all the more not to be able to join my brethren in the adoption of the Rules of Criminal Procedure of the District Courts of the United States.

By withholding approval of the adoption of the rules I do not imply disapproval. I express no opinion on their merits. With all respect to contrary views, I believe that this Court is not an appropriate agency for formulating the rules of criminal procedure for the district courts.

From the beginning of the nation down to the Evarts Act of 1891, 26 Stat. 826, though less and less after the Civil War, the members of this Court rode circuit. They thus had intimate, first-hand experience with the duties and demands of trial courts. For the last fifty years the Justices have become necessarily removed from direct, day-by-day contact with trials in the district courts. To that extent they are largely denied the first-hand opportunities for realizing vividly what rules of procedure are best calculated to promote the largest measure of justice. These considerations are especially relevant to the formulation of rules for the conduct of criminal trials. These closely concern the public security as well as the liberties of citizens.

And this leads to another strong reason for not charging this Court with the duty of approving in advance a code of criminal procedure. Such a code can hardly escape provisions in which lurk serious questions for future adjudication by this Court. Every lawyer knows the difference between passing on a question concretely raised by specific litigation and the formulation of abstract rules, however fully considered by members of the lower courts and the bar. I deem it unwise to prejudge, however unintentionally, questions that may in due course of litigation come before this Court by having this Court lay down rules in the abstract rather than deciding issues coming here with the impact of actuality and duly contested.

And there is one more important consideration. The business of this Court is increasing in volume and complexity. In the years ahead the number of cases will not decrease nor their difficulties lessen. The jurisdiction of this Court has already been cut almost to the bone. If the Court is not to be swamped, as it has been in the past, and is to do its best work, it must exercise rigorously its discretionary jurisdiction. Every additional duty, such as responsibility for fashioning progressive codes of procedure and keeping them current, makes inroads upon the discharge of functions which no one else can exercise.

Brief as is this statement, it can leave no room for doubt that the reasons which have constrained me to withhold approval of adoption of the rules completely transcend judgment of their merits.

ORDER OF FEBRUARY 8, 1946

It is ordered on this 8th day of February, 1946 that the annexed Rules governing proceedings in criminal cases after verdict, finding of guilty or not guilty by the court, or pleas of guilty, be prescribed pursuant to the Act of February 24, 1933, c. 119 as amended [47 Stat. 904, U.S.Code Title 18 § 3772] for the District Courts of the United States, the United States Circuit Courts of Appeals, the United States Court of Appeals for the District of Columbia and the Supreme Court of the United States, and that said rules shall become effective on the 21st day of March, 1946.

It is further ordered that these Rules and the Rules heretofore promulgated by order dated December 26, 1944 governing proceedings prior to and including verdict, finding of guilty or not guilty by the court, or plea of guilty, shall be consecutively numbered as indicated and shall be known as the Federal Rules of Criminal Procedure.

ORDER OF DECEMBER 27, 1948

The following order was adopted by the Supreme Court on December 27, 1948.

1. That the title of the Federal Rules of Criminal Procedure be, and it hereby is, amended to read as follows:

Rules of Criminal Procedure for the United States District Courts.

2. That Rules 17(e)(2), 41(b)(3), 41(g), 54(a)(1), 54(b), 54(c), 55, 56, and Rule 57(a), of the Federal Rules of Criminal Procedure be, and they hereby are, amended as hereinafter set forth.

[See the amendments made thereby under the respective rules, post]

3. That Forms 1 to 27, inclusive, contained in the Appendix of Forms to the Federal Rules of Criminal Procedure be, and they hereby are, amended as hereinafter specified.

4. That these amendments to the Federal Rules of Criminal Procedure shall take effect on the day following the final adjournment of the first regular session of the 81st Congress.

5. That The Chief Justice be authorized to transmit these amendments to the Attorney General with the request that he report them to the Congress at the beginning of the regular session of the 81st Congress in January, 1949.

ORDER OF DECEMBER 27, 1948

1. That the first sentence of Rule 37(a)(1) of the Federal Rules of Criminal Procedure be, and it hereby is, amended to read as follows:

[See the amendment made thereby under Rule 37, post]

2. That the first sentence of Rule 38(a)(3) of the Federal Rules of Criminal Procedure be, and it hereby is, amended to read as follows:

[See the amendment made thereby under Rule 38, post]

3. That Rule 38(c) of the Federal Rules of Criminal Procedure be, and it hereby is, amended to read as follows:

[See the amendment made thereby under Rule 38, post]

4. That Rule 39(b)(2) of the Federal Rules of Criminal Procedure be, and it hereby is, amended to read as follows:

[See the amendment made thereby under Rule 39, post]

5. That the foregoing amendments to the Federal Rules of Criminal Procedure shall take effect on January 1, 1949.

ORDER OF APRIL 12, 1954

That Rule 37 of the Federal Rules of Criminal Procedure be, and it hereby is, amended to read as follows:

[See the amendment made thereby under Rule 37, post]

That the foregoing amendment to the Federal Rules of Criminal Procedure shall take effect on July 1, 1954.

ORDER OF APRIL 9, 1956

1. That Rules 41(a), 46(a)(2), 54(a)(1), and 54(c) of the Rules of Criminal Procedure for the United States District Courts be, and they hereby are, amended as hereinafter set forth.

[See the amendments made thereby under the respective rules, post]

2. That the Chief Justice be authorized to report these amendments to Congress in accordance with the provisions of Title 18 U.S.C.A. § 3771.

ORDER OF FEBRUARY 28, 1966

1. That the Rules of Criminal Procedure for the United States District Courts be, and they hereby are, amended by including therein Rules 17.1 and 26.1 and amendments to Rules 4, 5, 6, 7, 11, 14, 16, 17, 18, 20, 21, 23, 24, 25, 28, 29, 30, 32, 33, 34, 35, 37, 38, 40, 44, 45, 46, 49, 54, 55, and 56, and to Form 26, as hereinafter set forth:

[See amendments made thereby under respective rules, post]

2. That the foregoing amendments and additions to the Rules of Criminal Procedure shall take effect on July 1, 1966, and shall govern all criminal proceedings thereafter commenced and so far as just and practicable all proceedings then pending.

3. That the Chief Justice be, and he hereby is, authorized to transmit to the Congress the foregoing amendments and additions to the Rules of Criminal Procedure in accordance with the provisions of title 18, U.S.C., section 3771.

4. That Rule 19 and subdivision (c) of Rule 45 of the Rules of Criminal Procedure for the United States District Courts, promulgated by this court on December 26, 1944, effective March 21, 1946, are hereby rescinded, effective July 1, 1966.

MR. JUSTICE BLACK, dissenting.

The Amendments to the Federal Rules of Civil and Criminal Procedure today transmitted to the Congress are the work of very capable advisory committees. Those committees, not the Court, wrote the rules. Whether by this transmittal the individual members of the Court who voted to transmit the rules intended to express approval of the varied policy decisions the rules embody I am not sure. I am reasonably certain, however, that the Court's transmittal does not carry with it a decision that the amended rules are all constitutional. For such a decision would be the equivalent of an advisory opinion which, I assume the Court would unanimously agree, we are without constitutional power to give. And I agree with my Brother DOUGLAS that some of the proposed criminal rules go to the very border line if they do not actually transgress the constitutional right of a defendant not to be compelled to be a witness against himself. This phase of the criminal rules in itself so infects the whole collection of proposals that, without mentioning other objections, I am opposed to transmittal of the proposed amendments to the criminal rules.

I am likewise opposed to transmittal of the proposed revision of the civil rules. In the first place I think the provisions of 28 U.S.C. § 2072 (1964 ed.), under which these rules are transmitted and the corresponding section, 18 U.S.C. § 3771 (1964 ed.), relating to the criminal rules, both of which provide for giving transmitted rules the effect of law as though they had been properly enacted by Congress are unconstitutional for reasons I have previously stated.[1] And in prior dissents I have stated some of the basic reasons for my objections to repeated rules revisions [2] that tend to upset established meanings and need not repeat those grounds of objection here. The confusion created by the adoption of the present rules, over my objection, has been partially dispelled by judicial interpretations of them by this Court and others. New rules and extensive amendments to present rules will mean renewed confusion resulting in new challenges and new reversals and prejudicial "pretrial" dismissals of cases before a trial on the merits for failure of lawyers to understand and comply with new rules of uncertain meaning. Despite my continuing objection to the old rules, it seems to me that since they have at least gained some degree of certainty it would be wiser to "bear those ills we have than fly to others we know not of," unless, of course, we are reasonably sure that the proposed reforms of the old rules are badly needed. But I am not. The new proposals, at least some of them, have, as I view them, objectionable possibilities that cause me to believe our judicial system could get along much better without them.

1 In a statement accompanying a previous transmittal of the civil rules, MR. JUSTICE DOUGLAS and I said:

"MR. JUSTICE BLACK and MR. JUSTICE DOUGLAS are opposed to the submission of these rules to the Congress under a statute which permits them to 'take effect' and to repeal 'all laws in conflict with such rules' without requiring any affirmative consideration, action, or approval of the rules by Congress or by the President. We believe that while some of the Rules of Civil Procedure are simply housekeeping details, many determine matters so substantially affecting the rights of litigants in lawsuits that in practical effect they are the equivalent of new legislation which, in our judgment, the Constitution requires to be initiated in and enacted by the Congress and approved by the President. The Constitution, as we read it, provides that all laws shall be enacted by the House, the Senate, and the President, not by the mere failure of Congress to reject proposals of an outside agency. * * *'" (Footnotes omitted.) 374 U.S. 865–866.

2 346 U.S. 946, 374 U.S. 865. And see 368 U.S. 1011 and 1012.

The momentum given the proposed revision of the old rules by this Court's transmittal makes it practically certain that Congress, just as has this Court, will permit the rules to take effect exactly as they were written by the Advisory Committee on Rules. Nevertheless, I am including here a memorandum I submitted to the Court expressing objections to the Committee's proposals and suggesting changes should they be transmitted. These suggestions chiefly center around rules that grant broad discretion to trial judges with reference to class suits, pretrial procedures, and dismissal of cases with prejudice. Cases coming before the federal courts over the years now filling nearly 40 volumes of Federal Rules Decisions show an accumulation of grievances by lawyers and litigants about the way many trial judges exercise their almost unlimited discretionary powers to use pretrial procedures to dismiss cases without trials. In fact, many of these cases indicate a belief of many judges and legal commentators that the cause of justice is best served in the long run not by trials on the merits but by summary dismissals based on out of court affidavits, pretrial depositions, and other pretrial techniques. My belief is that open court trials on the merits where litigants have the right to prove their case or defense best comports with due process of law.

The proposed rules revisions, instead of introducing changes designed to prevent the continued abuse of pretrial power to dismiss cases summarily without trials, move in the opposite direction. Of course, each such dismissal results in removal of one more case from our congested court dockets, but that factor should not weigh more heavily in our system of justice than assuring a full-fledged due process trial of every bona fide lawsuit brought to vindicate an honest, substantial claim. It is to protect this ancient right of a person to have his case tried rather than summarily thrown out of court that I suggested to the Court that it recommend changes in the Committee's proposals of the nature set out in the following memorandum.

"Dear Brethren:

"I have gone over all the proposed amendments carefully and while there are probably some good suggestions, it is my belief that the bad results that can come from the adoption of these amendments predominate over any good they can bring about. I particularly think that every member of the Court should examine with great care the amendments relating to class suits. It seems to me that they place too much power in the hands of the trial judges and that the rules might almost as well simply provide that 'class suits can be maintained either for or against particular groups whenever in the discretion of a judge he thinks it is wise.' The power given to the judge to dismiss such suits or to divide them up into groups at will subjects members of classes to dangers that could not follow from carefully prescribed legal standards enacted to control class suits.

"In addition, the rules as amended, in my judgment, greatly aggravate the evil of vesting judges with practically uncontrolled power to dismiss with prejudice cases brought by plaintiffs or defenses interposed by defendants. The power to dismiss a plaintiff's case or to render judgments by default against defendants can work great harm to both parties. There are many inherent urges in existence which may subconsciously incline a judge towards disposing of the cases before him without having to go through the burden of a trial. Mr. Chief Justice White, before he became Chief Justice, wrote an opinion in the case of *Hovey* v. *Elliot*, 167 U.S. 409 [17 S.Ct. 841, 42 L.Ed. 215], which pointed out grave constitutional questions raised by attempting to punish the parties by depriving them of the right to try their law suits or to defend against law suits brought against them by others.

"Rule 41 entitled 'Dismissal of Actions' points up the great power of judges to dismiss actions and provides an automatic method under which a dismissal must be construed as a dismissal 'with prejudice' unless the judge specifically states otherwise. For that reason I suggest to the Conference that if the Rules are accepted, including that one, the last sentence of Rule 41(b) be amended so as to provide that a simple order of dismissal by a judge instead of operating 'as an adjudication upon the merits,' as the amended rule reads, shall provide that such a dismissal 'does not operate as an adjudication upon the merits.'

"As a further guarantee against oppressive dismissals I suggest the addition of the following as subdivision (c) of Rule 41.

" 'No plaintiff's case shall be dismissed or defendant's right to defend be cut off because of the neglect, misfeasance, malfeasance, or failure of their counsel to obey any order of the court, until and unless such plaintiff or defendant shall have been personally served with notice of their counsel's delinquency, and not then unless the parties themselves do or fail to do something on their own part that can legally justify dismissal of the plaintiff's case or of the defendant's defense.'

"This proposed amendment is suggested in order to protect litigants, both plaintiffs and defendants, against being thrown out of court as a penalty for their lawyer's neglect or misconduct. The necessity for such a rule is shown, I think, by the dismissal in the plaintiff's case in *Link* v. *Wabash R. Co.*, 370 U.S. 626 [82 S.Ct. 1386, 8 L.Ed.2d 734]. The usual argument against this suggestion is that a party to a law suit hires his lawyer and should therefore be responsible for everything his lawyer does in the conduct of his case. This may be a good argument with reference to affluent litigants who not only know the best lawyers but are able to hire them. It is a wholly unrealistic argument, however, to make with reference to individual persons who do not know the ability of various lawyers or who are not financially able to hire those at the top of the bar and who are compelled to rely on the assumption that a lawyer licensed by the State is competent. It seems to me to be an uncivilized practice to punish clients by throwing their cases out of court because of their lawyers' conduct. It may be supportable by good, sound, formal logic but I think has no support whatever in a procedural system supposed to work as far as humanly possible to the end of obtaining equal and exact justice.

"H. L. B."

For all the reasons stated above and in my previous objections to the transmittals of rules I dissent from the transmittals here.

MR. JUSTICE DOUGLAS, dissenting in part.

I reiterate today what I stated on an earlier occasion (374 U.S. 865, 869–870) (statement of Black and Douglas, JJ.), that the responsibility for promulgating Rules of the kind we send to Congress today should rest with the Judicial Conference and not the Court. It is the Judicial Conference, not the Court, which appoints the Advisory Committee on Criminal Rules which makes the actual recommendations.[1] Members of the Judicial Conference, being in large part judges of the lower courts and attorneys who are using the Rules day in and day out, are in a far better position to make a practical judgment upon their utility or inutility than we.

But since under the statute [2] the Rules go to Congress only on the initiative of the Court, I cannot be only a conduit. I think that placing our imprimatur on the amendments to the Rules entails a large degree of responsibility of judgment concerning them. Some of the Criminal Rules which we forward to Congress today are very bothersome—not in the sense that they may be unwieldy or unworkable—but in the sense that they may entrench on important constitutional rights of defendants.

In my judgment, the amendments to Rule 16 dealing with discovery require further reflection. To the extent that they expand the defendant's opportunities for discovery, they accord with the views of a great many commentators who have concluded that a civilized society ought not to tolerate the conduct of a criminal prosecution as a "game." [3] But the proposed changes in the Rule go further. Rule 16(c) would permit a trial judge to condition granting the defendant discovery on the defendant's willingness to permit the prosecution to discover "scientific or medical reports, books, papers, documents, tangible objects, or copies or portions thereof" which (1) are in the defendant's possession; (2) he intends to produce at trial; and (3) are shown to be material to the preparation of the prosecution's case.[4]

The extent to which a court may compel the defendant to disclose information or evidence pertaining to his case without infringing the privilege against self-incrimination is a source of current controversy among judges, prosecutors, defense lawyers, and other legal commentators. A distinguished state court has concluded—although not without a strong dissent—that the privilege is not violated by discovery of the names of expert medical witnesses whose appearance at trial is contemplated by the defense.[5] I mean to imply no views on the point, except to note that a serious constitutional question lurks here.

The prosecution's opportunity to discover evidence in the possession of the defense is somewhat limited in the proposal with which we deal in that it is tied to the exercise by the defense of the right to discover from the prosecution. But *if* discovery, by itself, of information in the possession of the defendant would violate the privilege against self-incrimination, is it any less a violation if conditioned on the defendant's exercise of the opportunity to discover evidence? May benefits be conditioned on the abandonment of constitutional rights? See, e. g., *Sherbert* v. *Verner*, 374 U.S. 398, 403–406, 83 S.Ct. 1790, 1793–1795, 10 L.Ed.2d 965. To deny a defendant the opportunity to discovery—an opportunity not withheld from defendants who agree to prosecutorial discovery or from whom discovery is not sought—merely because the defendant chooses to exercise the constitutional right to refrain from self-incrimination arguably imposes a penalty upon the exercise of that fundamental privilege. It is said, however, that fairness may require disclosure by a defendant who obtains information from the prosecution. Perhaps—but the proposed rule establishes no such standards. Its application is mechanical: if the defendant is allowed discovery, so, too, is the prosecution. No requirement is imposed, for example, that the subject matter of the material sought to be discovered by the prosecution be limited to that relating to the subject of the defendant's discovery.

The proposed addition of Rule 17.1 also suggests difficulties, perhaps of constitutional dimension. This rule would establish a pretrial conference procedure. The language of the rule and the Advisory Committee's comments suggest that under some circumstances, the conference might even take place in the absence of the defendants! Cf. *Lewis* v. *United States*, 146 U.S. 370, 13 S.Ct. 136, 36 L.Ed. 1011; Fed.Rules Crim.Proc. Rule 43.

The proposed amendment to Rule 32(c)(2) states that the trial judge "may" disclose to the defendant or his counsel the contents of a presentence report on which he is relying in fixing sentence. The imposition of sentence is of critical importance to a man convicted of crime. Trial judges need presentence reports so that they may have at their disposal the fullest possible information. See *Williams* v. *People of State of New York*, 337 U.S. 241, 69 S.Ct. 1079, 93 L.Ed. 1337. But while the formal rules of evidence do not apply to restrict the factors which the sentencing judge may consider, fairness would, in my opinion, require that the defendant be advised of the facts—perhaps very damaging to him—on which the judge intends to rely. The presentence report may be inaccurate, a flaw which may be of constitutional dimension. Cf. *Townsend* v. *Burke*, 334 U.S. 736, 68 S.Ct. 1252, 92 L.Ed. 1690. It may exaggerate the gravity of the defendant's prior offenses. The investigator may have made an incomplete investigation. See Tappan, Crime, Justice and Correction 556 (1960). There may be countervailing factors not disclosed by the probation report. In many areas we can rely on the sound exercise of discretion by the trial judge; but how can a judge know whether or not the presentence report calls for a reply by the defendant? Its faults may not appear on the face of the document.

Some States require full disclosure of the report to the defense.[6] The proposed Model Penal Code takes the middle-ground and requires the sentencing judge to disclose to the defense the factual contents of the report so that there is an opportunity to reply.[7] Whatever should be the rule for the federal courts, it ought not to be one which permits a judge to impose sentence on the basis of information of which the defendant may be unaware and to which he has not been afforded an opportunity to reply.

I do not think we should approve Rules 16, 17.1, and 32(c)(2). Instead, we should refer them back to the Judicial Conference and the Advisory Committee for further consideration and reflection, where I believe they were approved only by the narrowest majority.

WILLIAM O. DOUGLAS.

1 28 U.S.C. § 331 (1964 ed.) which establishes the Judicial Conference of the United States, provides that the Conference shall "carry on

a continuous study of the operation and effect of the general rules of practice and procedure * * * prescribed by the Supreme Court * * *." The Conference has resolved that a standing Committee on Rules of Practice and Procedure be appointed by the Chief Justice and that, in addition, five advisory committees be established to recommend to the Judicial Conference changes in the rules of practice and procedure for the federal courts. See Annual Report of the Proceedings of the Judicial Conference of the United States 6–7 (1958).

2 18 U.S.C. § 3771 (1964 ed.).

3 See, *e. g.*, Brennan, The Criminal Prosecution: Sporting Event or Quest for Truth?, 1963 Wash.U.L.Q. 279; Louisell, Criminal Discovery: Dilemma Real or Apparent?, 49 Calif.L.Rev. 56 (1961); Traynor, Ground Lost and Found in Criminal Discovery, 39 N.Y.U.L.Rev. 228 (1964).

4 The proposed rule explicitly provides that the prosecution may not discover nonmedical documents or reports "made by the defendant, or his attorneys or agents in connection with the investigation or defense of the case, or of statements made by the defendant, or by government or defense witnesses, or by prospective government or defense witnesses, to the defendant, his agents or attorneys."

5 *Jones* v. *Superior Court of Nevada County*, 58 Cal.2d 56, 22 Cal. Rptr. 879, 372 P.2d 919, 96 A.L.R.2d 1213. See Comment, 51 Calif.L.Rev. 135; Note, 76 Harv.L.Rev. 838 (1963). The case is more extensively treated in Louisell, Criminal Discovery and Self-Incrimination, 53 Calif.L.Rev. 89 (1965).

6 *E. g.*, Calif.Penal Code § 12003.

7 Model Penal Code § 7.07(5) (Proposed Official Draft, 1962). The Code provides that the sources of confidential information need not be disclosed. "Less disclosure than this hardly comports with elementary fairness." Comment to § 7.07 (Tent.Draft No. 2, 1954), at 55. A discarded draft of the amendment to Fed.Rules Crim.Proc. Rule 32 would have allowed disclosure to defense counsel of the report, from which the confidential sources would be removed. A defendant not represented by counsel would be told of the "essential facts" in the report. See 8 Moore's Federal Practice ¶¶ 32.03[4], 32.09 (1965).

ORDER OF DECEMBER 4, 1967

1. That the following rules, to be known as the Federal Rules of Appellate Procedure, be, and they hereby are, prescribed, pursuant to sections 3771 and 3772 of Title 18, United States Code, and sections 2072 and 2075 of Title 28, United States Code, to govern the procedure in appeals to United States courts of appeals from the United States district courts, in the review by United States courts of appeals of decisions of the Tax Court of the United States, in proceedings in the United States courts of appeals for the review or enforcement of orders of administrative agencies, boards, commissions and officers, and in applications for writs or other relief which a United States court of appeals or judge thereof is competent to give:

[See text of Rules of Appellate Procedure, post]

2. That the foregoing rules shall take effect on July 1, 1968, and shall govern all proceedings in appeals and petitions for review or enforcement of orders thereafter brought and in all such proceedings then pending, except to the extent that in the opinion of the court of appeals their application in a particular proceeding then pending would not be feasible or would work injustice, in which case the former procedure may be followed.

3. *[Certain Rules of Civil Procedure for the United States District Courts, amended]*

4. *[Certain Rules of Civil Procedure for the United States District Courts, and Form 27, abrogated]*

5. That Rules 45, 49, 56 and 57 of the Rules of Criminal Procedure for the United States District Courts be, and they hereby are, amended, effective July 1, 1968, as hereinafter set forth:

[See amendments made thereby under the respective rules, post]

6. That the chapter heading "VIII. APPEAL", all of Rules 37 and 39, and subdivisions (b) and (c) of Rule 38 of the Rules of Criminal Procedure for the United States District Courts, and Forms 26 and 27 annexed to the said rules, be, and they hereby are, abrogated, effective July 1, 1968.

7. That the Chief Justice be, and he hereby is, authorized to transmit to the Congress the foregoing new rules and amendments to and abrogation of existing rules, in accordance with the provisions of Title 18, U.S.C., § 3771, and Title 28, U.S.C., §§ 2072 and 2075.

ORDER OF MARCH 1, 1971

1. *[Certain Rules of Civil Procedure for the United States District Courts amended]*

2. That subdivision (a) of Rule 45 and all of Rule 56 of the Federal Rules of Criminal Procedure be, and they hereby are, amended, effective July 1, 1971, to read as follows:

[See amendments made thereby under the respective rules, post]

3. That subdivision (a) of Rule 26 and subdivision (a) of Rule 45 of the Federal Rules of Appellate Procedure be, and they hereby are, amended, effective July 1, 1971, to read as follows:

[See amendments made thereby under the respective rules, post]

4. That THE CHIEF JUSTICE be, and he hereby is, authorized to transmit to the Congress the foregoing amendments to the Rules of Civil, Criminal and Appellate Procedure, in accordance with the provisions of Title 18 U.S.C. § 3771, and Title 28 U.S.C. §§ 2072 and 2075.

Mr. Justice Black and Mr. Justice Douglas dissent.

ORDER OF APRIL 24, 1972

1. That Rules 1, 3, 4(b) & (c), 5, 5.1, 6(b), 7(c), 9(b), (c) & (d), 17(a) & (g), 31(e), 32(b), 38(a), 40, 41, 44, 46, 50, 54 and 55 of the Federal Rules of Criminal Procedure be, and they hereby are, amended effective October 1, 1972, to read as follows:

[See amendments made thereby under the respective rules, post]

2. That Rule 9(c) of the Federal Rules of Appellate Procedure be, and hereby is amended, effective October 1, 1972, to read as follows:

[See amendments made thereby under the respective rules, post]

3. That THE CHIEF JUSTICE be, and he hereby is, authorized to transmit to the Congress the foregoing amendments to Rules of Criminal and Appellate Procedure, in accordance with the provisions of Title 18, U.S.Code, § 3771 and § 3772.

Mr. Justice Douglas dissented to adoption of Rule 50(b) of the Federal Rules of Criminal Procedure.

ORDER OF NOVEMBER 20, 1972

1. That the rules hereinafter set forth, to be known as the Federal Rules of Evidence, be, and they hereby are, prescribed pursuant to Sections 3402, 3771, and 3772, Title 18, United States Code, and Sections 2072 and 2075, Title 28, United States Code, to govern procedure, in the proceedings and to the extent set forth therein, in the United States courts of appeals, the United States district courts, the District Court for the District of the Canal Zone and the district courts of Guam and the Virgin Islands, and before United States magistrates.

2. That the aforementioned Federal Rules of Evidence shall take effect on July 1, 1973, and shall be applicable to actions and proceedings brought thereafter and also to further procedure in actions and proceedings then pending, except to the extent that in the opinion of the court their application in a particular action or proceeding then pending would not be feasible or would work injustice in which event the former procedure applies.

3. *[Certain Rules of Civil Procedure for the United State District Courts amended]*

4. That subdivision (c) of Rule 32 of the Federal Rules of Civil Procedure be, and it hereby is, abrogated, effective July 1, 1973.

5. That Rules 26, 26.1 and 28 of the Federal Rules of Criminal Procedure be, and they hereby are, amended effective July 1, 1973, to read as hereinafter set forth.

[See amendments made thereby under the respective rules, post]

6. That the Chief Justice be, and he hereby is, authorized to transmit the foregoing new rules and amendments to and abrogation of existing rules to the Congress at the beginning of its next regular session, in accordance with the provisions of Title 18 U.S.C. § 3771 and Title 28 U.S.C. §§ 2072 and 2075.

CONGRESSIONAL ACTION ON PROPOSED RULES OF EVIDENCE AND 1972 AMENDMENTS TO FEDERAL RULES OF CIVIL PROCEDURE AND FEDERAL RULES OF CRIMINAL PROCEDURE

Pub.L. 93–12, Mar. 30, 1973, 87 Stat. 9, provided: "That notwithstanding any other provisions of law, the Rules of Evidence for United States Courts and Magistrates, the Amendments to the Federal Rules of Civil Procedure, and the Amendments to the Federal Rules of Criminal Procedure, which are embraced by the orders entered by the Supreme Court of the United States on Monday, November 20, 1972, and Monday, December 18, 1972, shall have no force or effect except to the extent, and with such amendments, as they may be expressly approved by Act of Congress."

Pub.L. 93–595, § 3, Jan. 2, 1975, 88 Stat. 1959, provided that: "The Congress expressly approves the amendments to the Federal Rules of Civil Procedure, and the amendments to the Federal Rules of Criminal Procedure, which are embraced by the orders entered by the Supreme Court of the United States on November 20, 1972, and December 18, 1972, and such amendments shall take effect on the one hundred and eightieth day beginning after the date of the enactment of this Act [Jan. 2, 1975]."

ORDER OF MARCH 18, 1974

1. *[Amended subdivision 14 of Official Bankruptcy Form 7]*

2. That subdivision (a) of Rule 41 and the first paragraph of Rule 50 of the Federal Rules of Criminal Procedure be, and they hereby are, amended, effective July 1, 1974, to read as follows:

[See amendments made thereby under the respective rules, post]

3. That THE CHIEF JUSTICE be, and he hereby is, authorized to transmit the foregoing amendments to Official Bankruptcy Form 7 and Rules 41 and 50 of the Federal Rules of Criminal Procedure to the Congress in accordance with Title 28, U.S.C. § 2075, and Title 18, § 3771.

ORDER OF APRIL 22, 1974

1. That the Rules of Criminal Procedure for the United States District Courts be, and they hereby are, amended by including therein Rules 12.1, 12.2, and 29.1 and amendments to Rules 4, 9(a), 11, 12, 15, 16, 17(f), 20, 32(a), 32(c), 32(e) and 43 as hereinafter set forth:

[See amendments made thereby under the respective rules, post]

2. That the foregoing amendments and additions to the Rules of Criminal Procedure shall take effect on August 1, 1974, and shall govern all criminal proceedings thereafter commenced and, insofar as just and practicable, in proceedings then pending.

3. That The Chief Justice be, and he hereby is, authorized to transmit to the Congress the foregoing amendments and additions to the Rules of Criminal Procedure in accordance with the provisions of title 18, United States Code, sections 3771 and 3772.

Mr. Justice Douglas is opposed to the Court being a mere conduit of Rules to Congress since the Court has had no hand in drafting them and has no competence to design them in keeping with the titles and spirit of the Constitution.

CONGRESSIONAL ACTION ON AMENDMENTS TO RULES PROPOSED APRIL 22, 1974

Pub.L. 93–361, July 30, 1974, 88 Stat. 397, provided: "That, notwithstanding the provisions of sections 3771 and 3772 of title 18 of the United States Code, the effective date of the proposed amendments to the Federal Rules of Criminal Procedure which are embraced by the order entered by the United States Supreme Court on April 22, 1974, and which were transmitted to the Congress by the Chief Justice on April 22, 1974, is postponed until August 1, 1975."

Pub.L. 94–64, § 2, July 31, 1975, 89 Stat. 370, provided that: "The amendments proposed by the United States Supreme Court to the Federal Rules of Criminal Procedure which are embraced in the order of that Court on April 22, 1974, are approved except as otherwise provided in this Act and shall take effect on December 1, 1975. Except with respect to the amendment of Rule 11, insofar as it adds Rule 11(e)(6), which shall take effect on August 1, 1975, the amendments made by section 3 of this Act shall also take effect on December 1, 1975."

ORDER OF APRIL 26, 1976

1. That the Rules of Criminal Procedure for the United States District Courts be, and they hereby are, amended by including therein Rule 40.1 and amendments to Rules 6(e), 6(f), 23(b), 23(c), 24(b), 41(a), 41(c), and 50(b) as hereinafter set forth:

[See amendments made thereby under the respective rules, post, and Congressional Action on Amendments to Rules hereunder]

2. That the foregoing amendments and additions to the rules of procedure shall take effect on August 1, 1976, and shall govern all criminal proceedings thereafter commenced and, insofar as just and practicable, in proceedings then pending.

3. That The Chief Justice be, and he hereby is, authorized to transmit to the Congress the foregoing amendments and addition to the Rules of Criminal Procedure in accordance with the provisions of Title 18, United States Code, Sections 3771 and 3772.

CONGRESSIONAL ACTION ON AMENDMENTS TO RULES PROPOSED APRIL 26, 1976

Pub.L. 94–349, § 1, July 8, 1976, 90 Stat. 822, provided: "That, notwithstanding the provisions of sections 3771 and 3772 of title 18 of the United States Code, the amendments to rules 6(e), 23, 24, 40.1 and 41(c)(2) of the Rules of Criminal Procedure for the United States district courts which are embraced by the order entered by the United States Supreme Court on April 26, 1976, and which were transmitted to the Congress on or about April 26, 1976, shall not take effect until August 1, 1977, or until and to the extent approved by Act of Congress, whichever is earlier. The remainder of the proposed amendments to the Federal Rules of Criminal Procedure [to rules 6(f), 41(a), 41(c)(1), and 50(b)] shall become effective August 1, 1976, pursuant to law."

Pub.L. 95–78, § 1, July 30, 1977, 91 Stat. 319, provided: "That notwithstanding the first section of the Act entitled 'An Act to delay the effective date of certain proposed amendments to the Federal Rules of Criminal Procedure and certain other rules promulgated by the United States Supreme Court' (Public Law 94–349, approved July 8, 1976) the amendments to rules 6(e), 23, 24, 40.1 and 41(c)(2) of the Rules of Criminal Procedure for the United States district courts which are embraced by the order entered by the United States Supreme Court on April 26, 1976, shall take effect only as provided in this Act."

Section 2(a) of Pub.L. 95–78 provided in part that "The amendment proposed by the Supreme Court to subdivision (e) of rule 6 of such Rules of Criminal Procedure is approved in modified form".

Section 2(b) of Pub.L. 95–78 provided "The amendments proposed by the Supreme Court to subdivisions (b) and (c) of rule 23 of such Rules of Criminal Procedure are approved."

Section 2(c) of Pub.L. 95–78 provided "The amendment proposed by the Supreme Court to rule 24 of such Rules of Criminal Procedure is disapproved and shall not take effect."

Section 2(d) of Pub.L. 95–78 provided "The amendment proposed by the Supreme Court to such Rules of Criminal Procedure, adding a new rule designated as rule 40.1, is disapproved and shall not take effect."

Section 2(e) of Pub.L. 95–78 provided in part that "The amendment proposed by the Supreme Court to subdivision (c) of rule 41 of such Rules of Criminal Procedure is approved in a modified form".

Section 4(b) of Pub.L. 95–78 provided that the amendments to the Federal Rules of Criminal Procedure shall take effect October 1, 1977.

ORDER OF APRIL 30, 1979

1. That the Rules of Criminal Procedure for the United States District Courts be, and they hereby are, amended by including therein Rules 26.2 and 32.1 and amendments to Rules 6(e), 7(c)(2), 9(a), 11(e)(2) and (6), 17(h), 18, 32(c)(3)(E) and 32(f), 35, 40, 41(a), (b) and (c), and 44(c) as hereinafter set forth:

[See amendments made thereby under the respective rules, post]

2. That the foregoing amendments and additions to the rules of procedure shall take effect on August 1, 1979, and shall govern all criminal proceedings thereafter commenced and, insofar as just and practicable, all proceedings then pending.

3. That THE CHIEF JUSTICE be, and he hereby is, authorized to transmit to the Congress the foregoing amendments and additions to the Rules of Criminal Procedure in accordance with the provisions of Title 18, United States Code, Sections 3771 and 3772.

CONGRESSIONAL ACTION ON AMENDMENTS TO RULES PROPOSED APRIL 30, 1979

Pub.L. 96–42, July 31, 1979, 93 Stat. 326, provided: "That notwithstanding any provision of section 3771 or 3772 of title 18 of the United States Code or of section 2072, 2075, or 2076 of title 28 of the United States Code to the contrary—

"(1) the amendments proposed by the United States Supreme Court and transmitted by the Chief Justice on April 30, 1979, to the Federal Rules of Criminal Procedure affecting rules 11(e)(6), 17(h), 32(f), and 44(c), and adding new rules 26.2 and 32.1, and the amendment so proposed and transmitted to the Federal Rules of Evidence affecting rule 410, shall not take effect until December 1, 1980, or until and then only to the extent approved by Act of Congress, whichever is earlier; and

"(2) the amendment proposed by the United States Supreme Court and transmitted by the Chief Justice on April 30, 1979, affecting rule 40 of the Federal Rules of Criminal Procedure shall take effect on August 1, 1979, with the following amendments:

"(A) In the matter designated as paragraph (1) of subdivision (d), strike out 'in accordance with Rule 32.1(a)'.

"(B) In the matter designated as paragraph (2) of subdivision (d), strike out 'in accordance with Rule 32.1(a)(1)'."

ORDER OF APRIL 28, 1982

1. That the Federal Rules of Criminal Procedure be, and they hereby are, amended by including therein amendments to Rule 1, 5(b), 9(a), 9(b)(1), 9(b)(2), 9(c)(1), 9(c)(2), 11(c)(1), 11(c)(4), 11(c)(5), 20(b), 40(d)(1), 40(d)(2), 45(a), 54(a), 54(b)(4) and 54(c) as hereinafter set forth:

[See amendments made thereby under the respective rules, post]

2. That subdivision (d) of Rule 9 of the Federal Rules of Criminal Procedure is hereby abrogated.

3. That the foregoing amendments to the Federal Rules of Criminal Procedure shall take effect on August 1, 1982, and shall govern all criminal proceedings thereafter commenced and, insofar as just and practicable, all proceedings then pending.

4. That THE CHIEF JUSTICE be, and he hereby is, authorized to transmit to the Congress the foregoing amendments to the Federal Rules of Criminal Procedure in accordance with the provisions of Sections 3771 and 3772 of Title 18, United States Code.

ORDER OF APRIL 28, 1983

1. That the Federal Rules of Criminal Procedure for the United States District Courts be, and they hereby are, amended by including therein new Rules 11(h), 12(i) and 12.2(e), and amendments to Rules 6(e) and (g), 11(a), 12.2(b), (c) and (d), 16(a), 23(b), 32(a), (c) and (d), 35(b) and 55, as hereinafter set forth:

[See amendments made thereby under the respective rules, post]

2. That Rule 58 of the Federal Rules of Criminal Procedure and the Appendix of Forms are hereby abrogated.

3. That the foregoing additions and amendments to the Federal Rules of Criminal Procedure, together with the abrogation of Rule 58 and the Official Forms, shall take effect on August 1, 1983 and shall govern all criminal proceedings thereafter commenced and, insofar as just and practicable, in proceedings then pending.

4. That THE CHIEF JUSTICE be, and he hereby is, authorized to transmit to the Congress the foregoing additions to and changes in the Federal Rules of Criminal Procedure in accordance with the provisions of Sections 3771 and 3772 of Title 18, United States Code.

JUSTICE O'CONNOR, dissenting.

With one minor reservation, I join the Court in its adoption of the proposed amendments. They represent the product of considerable effort by the Advisory Committee, and they will institute desirable reforms. My sole disagreement with the Court's action today lies in its failure to recommend correction of an apparent error in the drafting of Proposed Rule 12.2(e).

As proposed, Rule 12.2(e) reads:

"Evidence of an intention as to which notice was given under subdivision (a) or (b), later withdrawn, is not admissible in any civil or criminal proceeding against the person who gave notice of the intention."

Identical language formerly appeared in Fed. Rules Crim. Proc. 11(e)(6) and Fed. Rules Evid. 410, each of which stated that

"[Certain material] is not admissible in any civil or criminal proceeding against the defendant."

Those rules were amended, Supreme Court Order April 30, 1979, 441 U.S. 970, 987, 1007, Pub. Law 96–42, approved July 31, 1979, 93 Stat. 326. After the amendments, the relevant language read,

"[Certain material] is not, in any civil or criminal proceeding, admissible against the defendant."

As the Advisory Committee explained, this minor change was necessary to eliminate an ambiguity. Before the amendment, the word "against" could be read as referring either to the kind of proceeding in which the evidence was offered or to the purpose for which it was offered. Thus, for instance, if a person was a witness in a suit but not a party, it was unclear whether the evidence could be used to impeach him. In such a case, the *use* would be against the person, but the *proceeding* would not be against him. Similarly, if the person wished to introduce the evidence in a proceeding in which he was the defendant, the use, but not the proceeding, would be against him. To eliminate the ambiguity, the Advisory Committee proposed the amendment clarifying that the evidence was inadmissible against the person, regardless of whether the particular proceeding was against the person. See Adv. Comm. Note to Fed. Rules Crim. Proc. 11(e)(6); Adv. Comm. Note to Fed. Rules Evid. 410.

The same ambiguity inheres in the proposed version of Rule 12.2(e). We should recommend that it be eliminated now. To that extent, I respectfully dissent.

ORDER OF APRIL 29, 1985

1. That the Federal Rules of Criminal Procedure for the United States District Courts be, and they hereby are, amended by including therein a new Rule 49(e) and amendments to Rules 6(e)(3)(A)(ii), 6(e)(3)(B) and (C), 11(c)(1), 12.1(f), 12.2(e), 35(b), 45(a) and 57, as hereinafter set forth:

[See amendments made thereby under the respective rules, post]

2. That the foregoing amendments to the Federal Rules of Criminal Procedure shall take effect on August 1, 1985 and shall govern all proceedings in criminal cases thereafter commenced and, insofar as just and practicable, all proceedings in criminal cases then pending. The amendment to Rule 35(b) shall be effective until November 1, 1986 when Section 215(b) of the Comprehensive Crime Control Act of 1984, Pub.L. 98–473, approved October 12, 1984, 98 Stat. 2015, goes into effect.

3. That THE CHIEF JUSTICE be, and he hereby is, authorized to transmit to the Congress the foregoing addition to and changes in the Federal Rules of Criminal Procedure in accordance with the provisions of Sections 3771 and 3772 of Title 18, United States Code.

ORDER OF MARCH 9, 1987

That the Federal Rules of Criminal Procedure for the United States District Courts be, and they hereby are, amended by including therein amendments to Criminal Rules 4, 5, 5.1, 6, 7, 10, 11, 12, 12.1, 12.2, 15, 16, 17, 17.1, 20, 21, 24, 25, 26.2, 30, 32, 32.1, 33, 38, 40, 41, 42, 43, 44, 45, 46, 49, and 51, as hereinafter set forth:

[See amendments made thereby under respective rules, post]

2. That the foregoing amendments to the Federal Rules of Criminal Procedure shall take effect on August 1, 1987 and shall govern all proceedings in criminal cases thereafter commenced and, insofar as just and practicable, all proceedings in criminal cases then pending.

3. That THE CHIEF JUSTICE be, and he hereby is, authorized to transmit to the Congress the foregoing amendments to the Federal Rules of Criminal Procedure in accordance with the provisions of Sections 3771 and 3772 of Title 18, United States Code.

ORDER OF APRIL 25, 1988

That the Federal Rules of Criminal Procedure for the United States District Courts be, and they hereby are, amended by including therein amendments to Criminal Rules 30 and 56, as hereinafter set forth:

[See amendments made thereby under respective rules, post]

2. That the foregoing amendments to the Federal Rules of Criminal Procedure shall take effect on August 1, 1988 and shall govern all proceedings in criminal cases thereafter commenced and, insofar as just and practicable, all proceedings in criminal cases then pending.

3. That THE CHIEF JUSTICE be, and he hereby is, authorized to transmit to the Congress the foregoing amendments to the Federal Rules of Criminal Procedure in accordance with the provisions of Sections 3771 and 3772 of Title 18, United States Code.

ORDER OF APRIL 25, 1989

1. That the Federal Rules of Criminal Procedure for the United States District Courts be, and they hereby are, amended by including therein amendments to Criminal Rules 11(c), 32(a) and (c), 32.1(a) and (b), 40(d) and 41(e) as hereinafter set forth:

[See amendments made thereby under respective rules, post]

2. That the foregoing amendments to the Federal Rules of Criminal Procedure shall take effect on December 1, 1989 and shall govern all proceedings in criminal cases thereafter commenced and, insofar as just and practicable, all proceedings in criminal cases then pending.

That THE CHIEF JUSTICE be, and he hereby is, authorized to transmit to the Congress the foregoing amendments to the Federal Rules of Criminal Procedure in accordance with the provisions of Section 2072 of Title 28, United States Code.

ORDER OF MAY 1, 1990

1. That the Federal Rules of Criminal Procedure for the United States District Courts be, and they hereby are, amended by including therein amendments to Criminal Rules 5(b), 41(a), 54(b)(4), and (c), and new Rule 58 as hereinafter set forth:

[See amendments made thereby under respective rules, post.]

2. That the foregoing amendments to the Federal Rules of Criminal Procedure shall take effect on December 1, 1990 and shall govern all proceedings in criminal cases thereafter commenced and, insofar as just and practicable, all proceedings in criminal cases then pending.

3. That the Rules of Procedure for the Trial of Misdemeanors before United States Magistrates, promulgated April 14, 1980, as amended, are hereby abrogated, effective December 1, 1990.

4. That THE CHIEF JUSTICE be, and he hereby is, authorized to transmit to the Congress the foregoing amendments to the Federal Rules of Criminal Procedure and the abrogation of the Rules of Procedure for the Trial of Misdemeanors before United States Magistrates in accordance with the provisions of Section 2072 of Title 28, United States Code.

ORDER OF APRIL 30, 1991

1. That the Federal Rules of Criminal Procedure for the United States District Courts be, and they hereby are, amended by including therein amendments to Criminal Rules 16(a), 32(c), 32.1(a), 35(b) and (c), 46(h), 54(a), and 58(b) and (d).

[See amendments made thereby under respective rules, post.]

2. That the foregoing amendments to the Federal Rules of Criminal Procedure shall take effect on December 1, 1991, and shall govern all proceedings in criminal cases thereafter commenced and, insofar as just and practicable, all proceedings in criminal cases then pending.

3. That THE CHIEF JUSTICE be, and he hereby is, authorized to transmit to the Congress the foregoing amendments to the Federal Rules of Criminal Procedure in accordance with the provisions of Section 2072 of Title 28, United States Code.

ORDER OF APRIL 22, 1993

1. That the Federal Rules of Criminal Procedure for the United States District Courts be, and they hereby are, amended by including therein amendments to Criminal Rules 1, 3, 4, 5, 5.1, 6, 9, 12, 16, 17, 26.2, 32, 32.1, 40, 41, 44, 46, 49, 50, 54, 55, 57, and 58, and new Rule 26.3, and an amendment to Rule 8 of the Rules Governing Section 2255 Proceedings.

[See addition and amendments made thereby under the respective rules, post.]

2. That the foregoing amendments to the Federal Rules of Criminal Procedure shall take effect on December 1, 1993, and shall govern all proceedings in criminal cases thereafter commenced and, insofar as just and practicable, all proceedings in criminal cases then pending.

3. That THE CHIEF JUSTICE be, and he hereby is, authorized to transmit to the Congress the foregoing amendments to the Federal Rules of Criminal Procedure in accordance with the provisions of Section 2072 of Title 28, United States Code.

ORDER OF APRIL 29, 1994

1. That the Federal Rules of Criminal Procedure for the United States District Courts be, and they hereby are, amended by including therein amendments to Criminal Rules 16, 29, 32, and 40.

[See amendments made thereby under the respective rules, post]

2. That the foregoing amendments to the Federal Rules of Criminal Procedure shall take effect on December 1, 1994, and shall govern all proceedings in criminal cases thereafter commenced and, insofar as just and practicable, all proceedings in criminal cases then pending.

3. That THE CHIEF JUSTICE be, and he hereby is, authorized to transmit to the Congress the foregoing amendments to the Federal Rules of Criminal Procedure in accordance with the provisions of Section 2072 of Title 28, United States Code.

ORDER OF APRIL 27, 1995

1. That the Federal Rules of Criminal Procedure for the United States District Courts be, and they hereby are, amended by including therein amendments to Criminal Rules 5, 40, 43, 49, and 57.

[See amendments made thereby under the respective rules, post]

2. That the foregoing amendments to the Federal Rules of Criminal Procedure shall take effect on December 1, 1995, and shall govern all proceedings in criminal cases thereafter commenced and, insofar as just and practicable, all proceedings in criminal cases then pending.

3. That THE CHIEF JUSTICE be, and hereby is, authorized to transmit to the Congress the foregoing amendments to the Federal Rules of Criminal Procedure in accordance with the provisions of Section 2072 of Title 28, United States Code.

ORDER OF APRIL 23, 1996

1. That the Federal Rules of Criminal Procedure for the United States District Courts be, and they hereby are, amended by including therein amendments to Criminal Rule 32.

[See amendments made thereby under respective rule, post]

2. That the foregoing amendments to the Federal Rules of Criminal Procedure shall take effect on December 1, 1996, and shall govern all proceedings in criminal cases thereafter commenced and, insofar as just and practicable, all proceedings in criminal cases then pending.

3. That THE CHIEF JUSTICE be, and hereby is, authorized to transmit to the Congress the foregoing amendments to the Federal Rules of Criminal Procedure in accordance with the provisions of Section 2072 of Title 28, United States Code.

ORDER OF APRIL 11, 1997

1. That the Federal Rules of Criminal Procedure for the United States District Courts be, and they hereby are, amended by including therein amendments to Criminal Rules 16 and 58.

[See amendments made thereby under respective rules, post]

2. That the foregoing amendments to the Federal Rules of Criminal Procedure shall take effect on December 1, 1997, and shall govern all proceedings in criminal cases thereafter commenced and, insofar as just and practicable, all proceedings in criminal cases then pending.

3. That THE CHIEF JUSTICE be, and hereby is, authorized to transmit to the Congress the foregoing amendments to the Federal Rules of Criminal Procedure in accordance with the provisions of Section 2072 of Title 28, United States Code.

ORDER OF APRIL 24, 1998

1. That the Federal Rules of Criminal Procedure for the United States District Courts be, and they hereby are, amended by including therein amendments to Criminal Rules 5.1, 26.2, 31, 33, 35, and 43.

[See amendments made thereby under respective rules, post]

2. That the foregoing amendments to the Federal Rules of Criminal Procedure shall take effect on December 1, 1998, and shall govern all proceedings in criminal cases thereafter commenced and, insofar as just and practicable, all proceedings in criminal cases then pending.

3. That THE CHIEF JUSTICE be, and hereby is, authorized to transmit to the Congress the foregoing amendments to the Federal Rules of Criminal Procedure in accordance with the provisions of Section 2072 of Title 28, United States Code.

ORDER OF APRIL 26, 1999

1. That the Federal Rules of Criminal Procedure for the United States District Courts be, and they hereby are, amended by including therein amendments to Criminal Rules 6, 11, 24, and 54.

[See amendments made thereby under respective rules, post.]

2. That the foregoing amendments to the Federal Rules of Criminal Procedure shall take effect on December 1, 1999, and shall govern all proceedings in criminal cases thereafter commenced and, insofar as just and practicable, all proceedings in criminal cases then pending.

3. That THE CHIEF JUSTICE be, and hereby is, authorized to transmit to the Congress the foregoing amendments to the Federal Rules of Criminal Procedure in accordance with the provisions of Section 2072 of Title 28, United States Code.

ORDER OF APRIL 17, 2000

1. That the Federal Rules of Criminal Procedure for the United States District Courts be, and they hereby are, amended by including therein amendments to Criminal Rules 7, 31, 32, and 38, and new Rule 32.2.

[See amendments made thereby under respective rules, post.]

2. That the foregoing amendments to the Federal Rules of Criminal Procedure shall take effect on December 1, 2000, and shall govern in all proceedings in criminal cases thereafter commenced and, insofar as just and practicable, all proceedings then pending.

3. That THE CHIEF JUSTICE be, and hereby is, authorized to transmit to the Congress the foregoing amendments to the Federal Rules of Criminal Procedure in accordance with the provisions of Section 2072 of Title 28, United States Code.

ORDER OF APRIL 29, 2002

1. That the Federal Rules of Criminal Procedure be, and they hereby are, amended by including therein amendments to Criminal Rules 1 through 60.

[See amendments made thereby under respective rules, post.]

2. That the foregoing amendments to the Federal Rules of Criminal Procedure shall take effect on December 1, 2002, and shall govern in all proceedings in criminal cases thereafter commenced and, insofar as just and practicable, all proceedings then pending.

3. That THE CHIEF JUSTICE be, and hereby is, authorized to transmit to the Congress the foregoing amendments to the Federal Rules of Criminal Procedure in accordance with the provisions of Section 2072 of Title 28, United States Code.

ORDER OF APRIL 26, 2004

1. That the Federal Rules of Criminal Procedure be, and they hereby are, amended by including therein an amendment to Criminal Rule 35.

2. That the rules and forms governing cases in the United States District Courts under Section 2254 and Section 2255 of Title 28, United States Code, be, and they hereby are, amended by including therein amendments to Rules 1 through 11 of the Rules Governing Section 2254 Cases in the United States District Courts, Rules 1 through 12 of the Rules Governing Section 2255 Cases in the United States District Courts, and forms for use in applications under Section 2254 and motions under Section 2255.

[See amendments made thereby under respective rules, post.]

3. That the foregoing amendments to the Federal Rules of Criminal Procedure, the Rules Governing Section 2254 Cases in the United States District Courts, and the Rules Governing Section 2255 Cases in the United States District Courts shall take effect on December 1, 2004, and shall govern in all proceedings thereafter commenced and, insofar as just and practicable, all proceedings then pending.

4. That the CHIEF JUSTICE be, and hereby is, authorized to transmit to the Congress the foregoing amendments to the Federal Rules of Criminal Procedure, the Rules Governing Section 2254 Cases in the United States District Courts, and the Rules Governing Section 2255 Cases in the United States District Courts in accordance with the provisions of Section 2072 of Title 28, United States Code.

ORDER OF APRIL 25, 2005

1. That the Federal Rules of Criminal Procedure be, and they hereby are, amended by including therein amendments to Criminal Rules 12.2, 29, 32.1, 33, 34, 45, and new Rule 59.

[See amendments made thereby under respective rules, post.]

2. That the foregoing amendments to the Federal Rules of Criminal Procedure shall take effect on December 1, 2005, and shall govern in all proceedings thereafter commenced and, insofar as just and practicable, all proceedings then pending.

3. That the CHIEF JUSTICE be, and hereby is, authorized to transmit to the Congress the foregoing amendments to the Federal Rules of Criminal Procedure in accordance with the provisions of Section 2072 of Title 28, United States Code.

ORDER OF APRIL 12, 2006

1. That the Federal Rules of Criminal Procedure be, and they hereby are, amended by including therein amendments to Criminal Rules 5, 6, 32.1, 40, 41, and 58.

[See amendments made thereby under respective rules, post.]

2. That the foregoing amendments to the Federal Rules of Criminal Procedure shall take effect on December 1, 2006, and shall govern in all proceedings thereafter commenced and, insofar as just and practicable, all proceedings then pending.

3. That the CHIEF JUSTICE be, and hereby is, authorized to transmit to the Congress the foregoing amendments to the Federal Rules of Criminal Procedure in accordance with the provisions of Section 2072 of Title 28, United States Code.

HISTORICAL NOTES

The original Rules of Criminal Procedure for the District Courts were adopted by order of the Supreme Court on Dec. 26, 1944, transmitted to the Congress by the Attorney General on Jan. 3, 1945, and became effective Mar. 21, 1946.

These Rules have been amended Dec. 27, 1948, eff. Jan. 1, 1949; Dec. 27, 1948, eff. Oct. 20, 1949; Apr. 12, 1954, eff. July 1, 1954; Apr. 9, 1956, eff. July 8, 1956; Feb. 28, 1966, eff. July 1, 1966; Dec. 4, 1967, eff. July 1, 1968; Mar. 1, 1971, eff. July 1, 1971; Apr. 24, 1972, eff. Oct. 1, 1972; Nov. 20, 1972, eff. July 1, 1975, pursuant to Pub.L. 93–595; Mar. 18, 1974, eff. July 1, 1974; Apr. 22, 1974, eff. in part Aug. 1, 1975, and Dec. 1, 1975, pursuant to Pub.L. 93–361 and Pub.L. 94–64; Dec. 12, 1975, Pub.L. 94–149, § 5, 89 Stat. 806; Apr. 26, 1976, eff. in part Aug. 1, 1976, and Oct. 1, 1977, pursuant to Pub.L. 94–349 and Pub.L. 95–78; Apr. 30, 1979, eff. in part Aug. 1, 1979, and Dec. 1, 1980, pursuant to Pub.L. 96–42; Apr. 28, 1982, eff. Aug. 1, 1982; Oct. 12, 1982, Pub.L. 97–291, § 3, 96 Stat. 1249; Apr. 28, 1983, eff. Aug. 1, 1983; Oct. 12, 1984, Pub.L. 98–473, title II, §§ 209, 215, 404, 98 Stat. 1986, 2014, 2067; Pub.L. 98–596, § 11(a), (b), Oct. 30, 1984, 98 Stat. 3138; Apr. 29, 1985, eff. Aug. 1, 1985; Oct. 27, 1986, Pub.L. 99–570, Title I, § 1009(a), 100 Stat. 3207–8; Nov. 10, 1986, Pub.L. 99–646, §§ 12(b), 24, 25(a), 54(a), 100 Stat. 3594, 3597, 3607; Mar. 9, 1987, eff. Aug. 1, 1987; Apr. 25, 1988, eff. Aug. 1, 1988; Nov. 18, 1988, Pub.L. 100–690, Title VI, § 6483, Title VII, §§ 7076, 7089(c), 102 Stat. 4382, 4406, 4409; Apr. 25, 1989, eff. Dec. 1, 1989; May 1, 1990, eff. Dec. 1, 1990; Apr. 30, 1991, eff. Dec. 1, 1991; Apr. 22, 1993, eff. Dec. 1, 1993; Apr. 29, 1994, eff. Dec. 1, 1994; Apr. 27, 1995, eff. Dec. 1, 1995; Apr. 23, 1996, eff. Dec. 1, 1996; Apr. 11, 1997, eff. Dec. 1, 1997; Apr. 24, 1998, eff. Dec. 1, 1998; Apr. 26, 1999, eff. Dec. 1, 1999; Apr. 17, 2000, eff. Dec. 1, 2000; Apr. 29, 2002, eff. Dec. 1, 2002; Apr. 26, 2004, eff. Dec. 1, 2004; Apr. 25, 2005, eff. Dec. 1, 2005; Apr. 12, 2006, eff. Dec. 1, 2006.

I. APPLICABILITY

Rule 1. Scope; Definitions

(a) Scope.

(1) In General. These rules govern the procedure in all criminal proceedings in the United States district courts, the United States courts of appeals, and the Supreme Court of the United States.

(2) State or Local Judicial Officer. When a rule so states, it applies to a proceeding before a state or local judicial officer.

(3) Territorial Courts. These rules also govern the procedure in all criminal proceedings in the following courts:

(A) the district court of Guam;

(B) the district court for the Northern Mariana Islands, except as otherwise provided by law; and

(C) the district court of the Virgin Islands, except that the prosecution of offenses in that court must be by indictment or information as otherwise provided by law.

(4) Removed Proceedings. Although these rules govern all proceedings after removal from a state court, state law governs a dismissal by the prosecution.

(5) Excluded Proceedings. Proceedings not governed by these rules include:

(A) the extradition and rendition of a fugitive;

(B) a civil property forfeiture for violating a federal statute;

(C) the collection of a fine or penalty;

(D) a proceeding under a statute governing juvenile delinquency to the extent the procedure is inconsistent with the statute, unless Rule 20(d) provides otherwise;

(E) a dispute between seamen under 22 U.S.C. §§ 256–258; and

(F) a proceeding against a witness in a foreign country under 28 U.S.C. § 1784.

(b) Definitions. The following definitions apply to these rules:

(1) "Attorney for the government" means:

(A) the Attorney General or an authorized assistant;

(B) a United States attorney or an authorized assistant;

(C) when applicable to cases arising under Guam law, the Guam Attorney General or other person whom Guam law authorizes to act in the matter; and

(D) any other attorney authorized by law to conduct proceedings under these rules as a prosecutor.

(2) "Court" means a federal judge performing functions authorized by law.

(3) "Federal judge" means:

(A) a justice or judge of the United States as these terms are defined in 28 U.S.C. § 451;

(B) a magistrate judge; and

(C) a judge confirmed by the United States Senate and empowered by statute in any commonwealth, territory, or possession to perform a function to which a particular rule relates.

(4) "Judge" means a federal judge or a state or local judicial officer.

(5) "Magistrate judge" means a United States magistrate judge as defined in 28 U.S.C. §§ 631–639.

(6) "Oath" includes an affirmation.

(7) "Organization" is defined in 18 U.S.C. § 18.

(8) "Petty offense" is defined in 18 U.S.C. § 19.

(9) "State" includes the District of Columbia, and any commonwealth, territory, or possession of the United States.

(10) "State or local judicial officer" means:

(A) a state or local officer authorized to act under 18 U.S.C. § 3041; and

(B) a judicial officer empowered by statute in the District of Columbia or in any commonwealth, territory, or possession to perform a function to which a particular rule relates.

(c) Authority of a Justice or Judge of the United States. When these rules authorize a magistrate judge to act, any other federal judge may also act.

(As amended Apr. 24, 1972, eff. Oct. 1, 1972; Apr. 28, 1982, eff. Aug. 1, 1982; Apr. 22, 1993, eff. Dec. 1, 1993; Apr. 29, 2002, eff. Dec. 1, 2002.)

ADVISORY COMMITTEE NOTES

1944 Adoption

1. These rules are prescribed under the authority of two acts of Congress, namely: the Act of June 29, 1940, c. 445, 18 U.S.C. former § 687 [now § 3771] (Proceedings in criminal cases prior to and including verdict; power of Supreme Court to prescribe rules) and the Act of November 21, 1941, c. 492, 18 U.S.C. former § 689 [now §§ 3771 and 3772] (Proceedings to punish for criminal contempt of court; application to §§ 687 and 688).

2. The courts of the United States covered by the rules are enumerated in Rule 54(a). In addition to Federal courts in the continental United States they include district courts in Alaska, Hawaii, Puerto Rico and the Virgin Islands. In the Canal Zone only the rules governing proceedings after verdict, finding or plea of guilty are applicable.

3. While the rules apply to proceedings before commissioners when acting as committing magistrates, they do not govern when a commissioner acts as a trial magistrate for the trial of petty offenses committed on Federal reservations. That procedure is governed by rules adopted by order promulgated by the Supreme Court on January 6, 1941 (311 U.S. 733, 61 S.Ct. clv), pursuant to the Act of October 9, 1940, c. 785, secs. 1 to 5. See 18 U.S.C. former §§ 576–576d [now §§ 3401, 3402] (relating to trial of petty offenses on Federal reservations by United States commissioners).

1972 Amendment

The rule is amended to make clear that the rules are applicable to courts of the United States and, where the rule so provides, to proceedings before United States magistrates and state or local judicial officers.

Primarily these rules are intended to govern proceedings in criminal cases triable in the United States District Court. Special rules have been promulgated, pursuant to the authority set forth in 28 U.S.C. § 636(c) [now (d)], for the trial of "minor offenses" before United States magistrates. (See Rules of Procedure for the Trial of Minor Offenses Before United States Magistrates (January 27, 1971).)

However, there is inevitably some overlap between the two sets of rules. The Rules of Criminal Procedure for the United States District Courts deal with preliminary, supplementary, and special proceedings which will often be conducted before United States magistrates. This is true, for example, with regard to rule 3—The Complaint; rule 4—Arrest Warrant or Summons Upon Complaint; rule 5—Initial Appearance Before the Magistrate; and rule 5.1—Preliminary Examination. It is also true, for example, of supplementary and special proceedings such as rule 40—Commitment to Another District, Removal; rule 41—Search and Seizure; and rule 46—Release from Custody. Other of these rules, where applicable, also apply to proceedings before United States magistrates. See Rules of Procedure for the Trial of Minor Offenses Before United States Magistrates, rule 1—Scope:

These rules govern the procedure and practice for the trial of minor offenses (including petty offenses) before United States magistrates under Title 18, U.S.C.. § 3401, and for appeals in such cases to judges of the district courts. To the extent that pretrial and trial procedure and practice are not specifically covered by these rules, the Federal Rules of Criminal Procedure apply as to minor offenses other than petty offenses. All other proceedings in criminal matters, other than petty offenses, before United States magistrates are governed by the Federal Rules of Criminal Procedure.

State and local judicial officers are governed by these rules, but only when the rule specifically so provides. This is the case of rule 3—The Complaint; rule 4—Arrest Warrant or Summons Upon Complaint; and rule 5—Initial Appearance Before the Magistrate. These rules confer authority upon the "magistrate," a term which is defined in new rule 54 as follows:

"Magistrate" includes a United States magistrate as defined in 28 U.S.C. §§ 631–639, a judge of the United States, another judge or judicial officer specifically empowered by statute in force in any territory or possession, the commonwealth of Puerto Rico, or the District of Columbia, to perform a function to which a particular rule relates, and a state or local judicial officer, authorized by 18 U.S.C. § 3041 to perform the functions prescribed in rules 3, 4, and 5.

Rule 41 provides that a search warrant may be issued by "a judge of a state court of record" and thus confers that authority upon appropriate state judicial officers.

The scope of rules 1 and 54 is discussed in C. Wright, Federal Practice and Procedure: Criminal §§ 21, 871–874 (1969, Supp.1971), and 8 and 8A J. Moore, Federal Practice chapters 1 and 54 (2d ed. Cipes 1970, Supp.1971).

1982 Amendment

The amendment corrects an erroneous cross reference, from Rule 54(c) to Rule 54(a), and replaces the word "defined" with the more appropriate word "provided."

1993 Amendment

The Rule is amended to conform to the Judicial Improvements Act of 1990 [P.L. 101–650, Title III, Section 321] which provides that each United States magistrate appointed under section 631 of title 28, United States Code, shall be known as a United States magistrate judge.

2002 Amendments

Rule 1 is entirely revised and expanded to incorporate Rule 54, which deals with the application of the rules. Consistent with the title of the existing rule, the Committee believed that a statement of the scope of the rules should be placed at the beginning to show readers which proceedings are governed by these rules. The Committee also revised the rule to incorporate the definitions found in Rule 54(c) as a new Rule 1(b).

Rule 1(a) contains language from Rule 54(b). But language in current Rule 54(b)(2)-(4) has been deleted for several reasons: First, Rule 54(b)(2) refers to a venue statute that governs an offense committed on the high seas or somewhere outside the jurisdiction of a particular district; it is unnecessary and has been deleted because once venue has been established, the Rules of Criminal Procedure automatically apply. Second, Rule 54(b)(3) currently deals with peace bonds; that provision is inconsistent with the governing statute and has therefore been deleted. Finally, Rule 54(b)(4) references proceedings conducted before United States Magistrate Judges, a topic now covered in Rule 58.

Rule 1(a)(5) consists of material currently located in Rule 54(b)(5), with the exception of the references to the navigation laws and to fishery offenses. Those provisions were considered obsolete. But if those proceedings were to arise, they would be governed by the Rules of Criminal Procedure.

Rule 1(b) is composed of material currently located in Rule 54(c), with several exceptions. First, the reference to an "Act of Congress" has been deleted from the restyled rules; instead the rules use the self-explanatory term "federal statute." Second, the language concerning demurrers, pleas in abatement, etc., has been deleted as being anachronistic. Third, the definitions of "civil action" and "district court" have been deleted. Fourth, the term "attorney for the government" has been expanded to include reference to those attorneys who may serve as special or independent counsel under applicable federal statutes. The term "attorney for the government" contemplates an attorney of record in the case.

Fifth, the Committee added a definition for the term "court" in Rule 1(b)(2). Although that term originally was almost always synonymous with the term "district judge," the term might be misleading or unduly narrow because it may not cover the many functions performed by magistrate judges. *See generally* 28 U.S.C. §§ 132, 636. Additionally, the term does not cover circuit judges who may be authorized to hold a district court. *See* 28 U.S.C. § 291. The proposed definition continues the traditional view that "court" means district judge, but also reflects the current understanding that magistrate judges act as the "court" in many proceedings. Finally, the Committee intends that the term "court" be used principally to describe a judicial officer, except where a rule uses the term in a spatial sense, such as describing proceedings in "open court."

Sixth, the term "Judge of the United States" has been replaced with the term "Federal judge." That term includes Article III judges and magistrate judges and, as noted in Rule 1(b)(3)(C), federal judges other than Article III judges who may be authorized by statute to perform a particular act specified in the Rules of Criminal Procedure. The term does not include local judges in the District of Columbia. Seventh, the definition of "Law" has been deleted as being superfluous and possibly misleading because it suggests that administrative regulations are excluded.

Eighth, the current rules include three definitions of "magistrate judge." The term used in amended Rule 1(b)(5) is limited to United States magistrate judges. In the current rules the term magistrate judge includes not only United States magistrate judges, but also district court judges, court of appeals judges, Supreme Court justices, and where authorized, state and local officers. The Committee believed that the rules should reflect current practice, i.e., the wider and almost exclusive use of United States magistrate judges, especially in preliminary matters. The definition, however, is not intended to restrict the use of other federal judicial officers to perform those functions. Thus, Rule 1(c) has been added to make it clear that where the rules authorize a magistrate judge to act, any other federal judge or justice may act.

Finally, the term "organization" has been added to the list of definitions.

The remainder of the rule has been amended as part of the general restyling of the rules to make them more easily understood. In addition to changes made to improve the clarity, the Committee has changed language to make style and terminology consistent throughout the Criminal Rules. These changes are intended to be stylistic only.

HISTORICAL NOTES

Change of Name

United States magistrate appointed under section 631 of Title 28, Judiciary and Judicial Procedure, to be known as United States magistrate judge after Dec. 1, 1990, with any reference to United States magistrate or magistrate in Title 28, in any other Federal statute, etc., deemed a reference to United States magistrate judge appointed under section 631 of Title 28, see section 321 of Pub.L. 101–650, set out as a note under section 631 of Title 28.

Rule 2. Interpretation

These rules are to be interpreted to provide for the just determination of every criminal proceeding, to secure simplicity in procedure and fairness in administration, and to eliminate unjustifiable expense and delay.

(As amended Apr. 29, 2002, eff. Dec. 1, 2002.)

ADVISORY COMMITTEE NOTES

1944 Adoption

Compare Federal Rules of Civil Procedure, 28 U.S.C. following section 2072, Rule 1 (Scope of Rules), last sentence: "They [the Federal Rules of Civil Procedure] shall be construed to secure the just, speedy, and inexpensive determination of every action."

2002 Amendments

The language of Rule 2 has been amended as part of the general restyling of the Criminal Rules to make them more easily understood and to make style and terminology consistent throughout the rules. These changes are intended to be stylistic. No substantive change is intended.

In particular, Rule 2 has been amended to clarify the purpose of the Rules of Criminal Procedure. The words "are intended" have been changed to read "are to be interpreted." The Committee believed that that was the original intent of the drafters and more accurately reflects the purpose of the rules.

II. PRELIMINARY PROCEEDINGS

Rule 3. The Complaint

The complaint is a written statement of the essential facts constituting the offense charged. It must be made under oath before a magistrate judge or, if none is reasonably available, before a state or local judicial officer.

(As amended Apr. 24, 1972, eff. Oct. 1, 1972; Apr. 22, 1993, eff. Dec. 1, 1993; Apr. 29, 2002, eff. Dec. 1, 2002.)

ADVISORY COMMITTEE NOTES

1944 Adoption

The rule generally states existing law and practice, 18 U.S.C. former § 591 (now § 3041) (Arrest and removal for trial); *United States v. Simon*, D.C.E.D.Pa., 248 F. 980; *United States v. Maresca*, D.C.S.D.N.Y., 266 F. 713, 719–721. It eliminates, however, the requirement of conformity to State law as to the form and sufficiency of the complaint. See, also, Rule 57(b).

1972 Amendment

The amendment deletes the reference to "commissioner or other officer empowered to commit persons charged with offenses against the United States" and substitutes therefor "magistrate".

The change is editorial in nature to conform the language of the rule to the recently enacted Federal Magistrates Act. The term "magistrate" is defined in rule 54.

1993 Amendment

The Rule is amended to conform to the Judicial Improvements Act of 1990 [P.L. 101–650, Title III, Section 321] which provides that each United States magistrate appointed under section 631 of title 28, United States Code, shall be known as a United States magistrate judge.

2002 Amendments

The language of Rule 3 is amended as part of the general restyling of the Criminal Rules to make them more easily understood and to make style and terminology consistent throughout the rules. These changes are intended to be stylistic and no substantive change is intended, except as described below.

The amendment makes one change in practice. Currently, Rule 3 requires the complaint to be sworn before a "magistrate judge," which under current Rule 54 could include a state or local judicial officer. Revised Rule 1 no longer includes state and local officers in the definition of magistrate judges for the purposes of these rules. Instead, the definition includes only United States magistrate judges. Rule 3 requires that the complaint be made before a United States magistrate judge or before a state or local officer. The revised rule does, however, make a change to reflect prevailing practice and the outcome desired by the Committee—that the procedure take place before a *federal* judicial officer if one is reasonably available. As noted in Rule 1(c), where the rules, such as Rule 3, authorize a magistrate judge to act, any other federal judge may act.

HISTORICAL NOTES

Change of Name

United States magistrate appointed under section 631 of Title 28, Judiciary and Judicial Procedure, to be known as United States magistrate judge after Dec. 1, 1990, with any reference to United States magistrate or magistrate in Title 28, in any other Federal statute, etc., deemed a reference to United States magistrate judge appointed under section 631 of Title 28, see section 321 of Pub.L. 101–650, set out as a note under section 631 of Title 28.

Rule 4. Arrest Warrant or Summons on a Complaint

(a) Issuance. If the complaint or one or more affidavits filed with the complaint establish probable cause to believe that an offense has been committed and that the defendant committed it, the judge must issue an arrest warrant to an officer authorized to execute it. At the request of an attorney for the government, the judge must issue a summons, instead of a warrant, to a person authorized to serve it. A judge may issue more than one warrant or summons on the same complaint. If a defendant fails to appear in response to a summons, a judge may, and upon request of an attorney for the government must, issue a warrant.

(b) Form.

(1) Warrant. A warrant must:

(A) contain the defendant's name or, if it is unknown, a name or description by which the defendant can be identified with reasonable certainty;

(B) describe the offense charged in the complaint;

(C) command that the defendant be arrested and brought without unnecessary delay before a magistrate judge or, if none is reasonably available, before a state or local judicial officer; and

(D) be signed by a judge.

(2) Summons. A summons must be in the same form as a warrant except that it must require the defendant to appear before a magistrate judge at a stated time and place.

(c) Execution or Service, and Return.

(1) By Whom. Only a marshal or other authorized officer may execute a warrant. Any person authorized to serve a summons in a federal civil action may serve a summons.

(2) Location. A warrant may be executed, or a summons served, within the jurisdiction of the United States or anywhere else a federal statute authorizes an arrest.

(3) Manner.

(A) A warrant is executed by arresting the defendant. Upon arrest, an officer possessing the warrant must show it to the defendant. If the officer does not possess the warrant, the officer must inform the defendant of the warrant's existence and of the offense charged and, at the defendant's request, must show the warrant to the defendant as soon as possible.

(B) A summons is served on an individual defendant:

(i) by delivering a copy to the defendant personally; or

(ii) by leaving a copy at the defendant's residence or usual place of abode with a person of suitable age and discretion residing at that location and by mailing a copy to the defendant's last known address.

(C) A summons is served on an organization by delivering a copy to an officer, to a managing or general agent, or to another agent appointed or legally authorized to receive service of process. A copy must also be mailed to the organization's last known address within the district or to its principal place of business elsewhere in the United States.

(4) Return.

(A) After executing a warrant, the officer must return it to the judge before whom the defendant is brought in accordance with Rule 5. At the request of an attorney for the government, an unexecuted warrant must be brought back to and canceled by a magistrate judge or, if none is reasonably available, by a state or local judicial officer.

(B) The person to whom a summons was delivered for service must return it on or before the return day.

(C) At the request of an attorney for the government, a judge may deliver an unexecuted warrant, an unserved summons, or a copy of the warrant or summons to the marshal or other authorized person for execution or service.

(As amended Feb. 28, 1966, eff. July 1, 1966; Apr. 24, 1972, eff. Oct. 1, 1972; Apr. 22, 1974, eff. Dec. 1, 1975; July 31, 1975, Pub.L. 94–64, § 3(1)–(3), 89 Stat. 370; Mar. 9, 1987, eff. Aug. 1, 1987; Apr. 22, 1993, eff. Dec. 1, 1993; Apr. 29, 2002, eff. Dec. 1, 2002.)

ADVISORY COMMITTEE NOTES

1944 Adoption

Note to Subdivision (a). 1. The rule states the existing law relating to warrants issued by commissioner or other magistrate. United States Constitution, Amendment IV; 18 U.S.C. § 591 [now § 3041] (Arrest and removal for trial).

2. The provision for summons is new, although a summons has been customarily used against corporate defendants, 28 U.S.C. former § 377 [now § 1651] (Power to issue writs); *United States v. John Kelso Co.*, D.C.N.D.Cal.1898, 86 F. 304. See also, *Albrecht v. United States*, 1927, 273 U.S. 1, 8, 47 S.Ct. 250, 71 L.Ed. 505. The use of the summons in criminal cases is sanctioned by many States, among them Indiana, Maryland, Massachusetts, New York, New Jersey, Ohio, and others. See A.L.I. Code of Criminal Procedure (1931), Commentaries to secs. 12, 13, and 14. The use of the summons is permitted in England by 11 & 12 Vict., c. 42, sec. 1 (1848). More general use of a summons in place of a warrant was recommended by the National Commission on Law Observance and Enforcement, Report on Criminal Procedure (1931) 47. The Uniform Arrest Act, proposed by the Interstate Commission on Crime, provides for a summons. Warner, 28 Va.L.R. 315. See also, Medalie, 4 Lawyers Guild R. 1, 6.

3. The provision for the issuance of additional warrants on the same complaint embodies the practice heretofore followed in some districts. It is desirable from a practical standpoint, since when a complaint names several defendants, it may be preferable to issue a separate warrant as to each in order to facilitate service and return, especially if the defendants are apprehended at different times and places. Berge, 42 Mich.L.R. 353, 356.

4. Failure to respond to a summons is not a contempt of court, but is ground for issuing a warrant.

Note to Subdivision (b). Compare Rule 9(b) and forms of warrant and summons, Appendix of Forms [Abrogated].

Note to Subdivision (c)(2). This rule and Rule 9(c)(1) modify the existing practice under which a warrant may be served only within the district in which it is issued. *Mitchell v. Dexter*, 1 Cir., 1917, 244 Fed. 926 (C.C.A. 1st, 1917); *Palmer v. Thompson*, 1902, 20 App.D.C. 273 (1902); but see *In re Christian*, 82 F. 885 (C.C.W.D.Ark. 1897); 2 Op.Atty. Gen. 564. When a defendant is apprehended in a district other than that in which the prosecution has been instituted, this change will eliminate some of the steps that are at present followed: the issuance of a warrant in the district where the prosecution is pending; the return of the warrant non est inventus; the filing of a complaint on the basis of the warrant and its return in the district in which the defendant is found; and the issuance of another warrant in the latter district. The warrant originally issued will have efficacy throughout the United States and will constitute authority for arresting the defendant wherever found. Waite, 27 Jour. of Am.Judicature Soc. 101, 103. The change will not modify or affect the rights of the defendant as to removal. See Rule 40. The authority of the marshal to serve process is not limited to the district for which he is appointed, 28 U.S.C.A. § 503 [now § 569].

Note to Subdivision (c)(3). 1. The provision that the arresting officer need not have the warrant in his possession at the time of the arrest is rendered necessary by the fact that a fugitive may be discovered and apprehended by any one of many officers. It is obviously impossible for a warrant to be in the possession of every officer who is searching for a fugitive or who unexpectedly might find himself in a position to apprehend the fugitive. The rule sets forth the customary practice in such matters, which has the sanction of the courts. "It would be a strong proposition in an ordinary felony case to say that a fugitive from justice for whom a capias or warrant was outstanding could not be apprehended until the apprehending officer had physical possession of the capias or the warrant. If such were the law, criminals could circulate freely from one end of the land to the other, because they could always keep ahead of an officer with the warrant." *In re Kosopud*, N.D.Ohio, 272 F. 330, 336. Waite, 27 Jour. of Am.Judicature Soc. 101, 103. The rule, however, safeguards the defendant's rights in such case.

2. Service of summons under the rule is substantially the same as in civil actions under Federal Rules of Civil Procedure, Rule 4(d)(1), 28 U.S.C., Appendix.

Note to Subdivision (c)(4). Return of a warrant or summons to the commissioner or other officer is provided by 18 U.S.C. § 603 [now § 4084] (Writs; copy as jailer's authority). The return of all "copies of process" by the commissioner to the clerk of the court is provided by 18 U.S.C. former § 591 [now § 3041]; and see Rule 5(c), *infra.*

1966 Amendments

In *Giordenello v. United States*, 357 U.S. 480 (1958) it was held that to support the issuance of a warrant the complaint must contain in addition to a statement "of the essential facts constituting the offense" (Rule 3) a statement of the fact relied upon by the complainant to establish probable cause. The amendment permits the complainant to state the facts constituting probable cause in a separate affidavit in lieu of spelling them out in the complaint. See also *Jaben v. United States*, 381 U.S. 214 (1965).

1972 Amendments

Throughout the rule the term "magistrate" is substituted for the term "commissioner." Magistrate is defined in rule 54 to include a judge of the United States, a United States magistrate, and those state and local judicial officers specified in 18 U.S.C. § 3041.

1974 Amendments

The amendments are designed to achieve several objectives: (1) to make explicit the fact that the determination of probable cause may be based upon hearsay evidence; (2) to make clear that probable cause is a prerequisite to the issuance of a summons; and (3) to give priority to the issuance of a summons rather than a warrant.

Subdivision (a) makes clear that the normal situation is to issue a summons.

Subdivision (b) provides for the issuance of an arrest warrant in lieu of or in addition to the issuance of a summons.

Subdivision (b)(1) restates the provision of the old rule mandating the issuance of a warrant when a defendant fails to appear in response to a summons.

Subdivision (b)(2) provides for the issuance of an arrest warrant rather than a summons whenever "a valid reason is shown" for the issuance of a warrant. The reason may be apparent from the face of the complaint or may be provided by the federal law enforcement officer or attorney for the government. See comparable provision in rule 9.

Subdivision (b)(3) deals with the situation in which conditions change after a summons has issued. It affords the government an opportunity to demonstrate the need for an arrest warrant. This may be done in the district in which the defendant is located if this is the convenient place to do so.

Subdivision (c) provides that a warrant or summons may issue on the basis of hearsay evidence. What constitutes probable cause is left to be dealt with on a case-to-case basis, taking account of the unlimited variations in source of information and in the opportunity of the informant to perceive accurately the factual data which he furnishes. See, *e.g., Giordenello v. United States*, 357 U.S. 480, 78 S.Ct. 1245, 2 L.Ed.2d 1503 (1958); *Aguilar v. Texas*, 378 U.S. 108, 84 S.Ct. 1509, 12 L.Ed.2d 723 (1964); *United States v. Ventresca*, 380 U.S. 102, 85 S.Ct. 741, 13 L.Ed.2d 684 (1965); *Jaben v. United States*, 381 U.S. 214, 85 S.Ct. 1365, 14 L.Ed.2d 345 (1965); *McCray v. Illinois*, 386 U.S. 300, 87 S.Ct. 1056, 18 L.Ed.2d 62 (1967); *Spinelli v. United States*, 393 U.S. 410, 89 S.Ct. 584, 21 L.Ed.2d 637 (1969); *United States v. Harris*, 403 U.S. 573, 91 S.Ct. 2075, 29 L.Ed.2d 723 (1971); Note, The Informer's Tip as Probable Cause for Search or Arrest, 54 Cornell L.Rev. 958 (1969); C. Wright, Federal Practice and Procedure: Criminal § 52 (1969, Supp.1971); 8 S.J. Moore, Federal Practice ¶ 4.03 (2d ed. Cipes 1970, Supp. 1971).

1975 Enactment

A. Amendments Proposed by the Supreme Court. Rule 4 of the Federal Rules of Criminal Procedure deals with arrest procedures when a criminal complaint has been filed. It provides in pertinent part:

> If it appears ... that there is probable cause ... a warrant for the arrest of the defendant shall issue to any officer authorized by law to execute it. Upon the *request* of the attorney for the government a summons instead of a warrant *shall* issue. [emphasis added]

The Supreme Court's amendments make a basic change in Rule 4. As proposed to be amended, Rule 4 gives priority to the issuance of a summons instead of an arrest warrant. In order for the magistrate to issue an arrest warrant, the attorney for the government must show a "valid reason."

B. Committee Action. The Committee agrees with and approves the basic change in Rule 4. The decision to take a citizen into custody is a very important one with farreaching consequences. That decision ought to be made by a neutral official (a magistrate) rather than by an interested party (the prosecutor).

It has been argued that undesirable consequences will result if this change is adopted—including an increase in the number of fugitives and the introduction of substantial delays in our system of criminal justice. [See testimony of Assistant Attorney General W. Vincent Rakestraw in Hearings on Proposed Amendments to Federal Rules of Criminal Procedure Before the Subcommittee on Criminal Justice of the House Committee on the Judiciary, 93d Cong., 2d Sess., Serial No. 61, at 41–43 (1974) [hereinafter cited as "Hearing I"].] The Committee has carefully considered these arguments and finds them to be wanting. [The Advisory Committee on Criminal Rules has thoroughly analyzed the arguments raised by Mr. Rakestraw and convincingly demonstrated that the undesirable consequences predicted will not necessarily result. See Hearings on Proposed Amendments to Federal Rules of Criminal Procedure Before the Subcommittee on Criminal Justice of the House Committee on the Judiciary, 94th Congress, 1st Session, Serial No. 6, at 208–09 (1975) [hereinafter cited "Hearings II"].] The present rule permits the use of a summons in lieu of a warrant. The major difference between the present rule and the proposed rule is that the present rule vests the decision to issue a summons or a warrant in the prosecutor, while the proposed rule vests that decision in a judicial officer. Thus, the basic premise underlying the arguments against the proposed rule is the notion that only the prosecutor can be trusted to act responsibly in deciding whether a summons or a warrant shall issue.

The Committee rejects the notion that the federal judiciary cannot be trusted to exercise discretion wisely and in the public interest.

The Committee recast the language of Rule 4(b). No change in substance is intended. The phrase "valid reason" was changed to "good cause," a phrase with which lawyers are more familiar. [Rule 4, both as proposed by the Supreme Court and as changed by the Committee, does not in any way authorize a magistrate to issue a summons or a warrant sua sponte, nor does it enlarge, limit or change in any way the law governing warrantless arrests.]

The Committee deleted two sentences from Rule 4(c). These sentences permitted a magistrate to question the complainant and other witnesses under oath and required the magistrate to keep a record or summary of such a proceeding. The Committee does not intend this change to discontinue or discourage the practice of having the complainant appear personally or the practice of making a record or summary of such an appearance. Rather, the Committee intended to leave Rule 4(c) neutral on this matter, neither encouraging nor discouraging these practices.

The Committee added a new section that provides that the determination of good cause for the issuance of a warrant in lieu of a summons shall not be grounds for a motion to suppress evidence. This provision does not apply when the issue is whether there was probable cause to believe an offense has been committed. This provision does not in any way expand or limit the so-called "exclusionary rule."

House Report No. 94–247.

Rule 4(e)(3) deals with the manner in which warrants and summonses may be served. The House version provides two methods for serving a summons: (1) personal service upon the defendant, or (2) service by leaving it with someone of suitable age at the defendant's dwelling *and* by mailing it to the defendant's last known address. The Senate version provides three methods: (1) personal service, (2) service by leaving it with someone of suitable age at the defendant's dwelling, or (3) service by mailing it to defendant's last known address.

House Report No. 94–414.

1987 Amendments

The amendments are technical. No substantive change is intended.

1993 Amendments

The Rule is amended to conform to the Judicial Improvements Act of 1990 [P.L. 101–650, Title III, Section 321] which provides that each United States magistrate appointed under section 631 of title 28, United States Code, shall be known as a United States magistrate judge.

2002 Amendments

The language of Rule 4 has been amended as part of the general restyling of the Criminal Rules to make them more easily understood and to make style and terminology consistent throughout the rules. These changes are intended to be stylistic, except as noted below.

The first non-stylistic change is in Rule 4(a), which has been amended to provide an element of discretion in those situations when the defendant fails to respond to a summons. Under the current rule, the judge must in all cases issue an arrest warrant. The revised rule provides discretion to the judge to issue an arrest warrant if the attorney for the government does not request that an arrest warrant be issued for a failure to appear.

Current Rule 4(b), which refers to the fact that hearsay evidence may be used to support probable cause, has been deleted. That language was added to the rule in 1974, apparently to reflect emerging federal case law. *See* Advisory Committee Note to 1974 Amendments to Rule 4 (citing cases). A similar amendment was made to Rule 41 in 1972. In the intervening years, however, the case law has become perfectly clear on that proposition. Thus, the Committee believed that the reference to hearsay was no longer necessary. Furthermore, the limited reference to hearsay evidence was misleading to the extent that it might have suggested that other forms of inadmissible evidence could not be considered. For example, the rule made no reference to considering a defendant's prior criminal record, which clearly may be considered in deciding whether probable cause exists. *See, e.g., Brinegar v. United States*, 338 U.S. 160 (1949) (officer's knowledge of defendant's prior criminal activity). Rather than address that issue, or any other similar issues, the Committee believed that the matter was best addressed in Rule 1101(d)(3), Federal Rules of Evidence. That rule explicitly provides that the Federal Rules of Evidence do not apply to "preliminary examinations in criminal cases, . . . issuance of warrants for arrest, criminal summonses, and search warrants." The Advisory Committee Note accompanying that rule recognizes that: "The nature of the proceedings makes application of the formal rules of evidence inappropriate and impracticable." The Committee did not intend to make any substantive changes in practice by deleting the reference to hearsay evidence.

New Rule 4(b), which is currently Rule 4(c), addresses the form of an arrest warrant and a summons and includes two non-stylistic changes. First, Rule 4(b)(1)(C) mandates that the warrant require that the defendant be brought "without unnecessary delay" before a judge. The Committee believed that this was a more appropriate standard than the current requirement that the defendant be brought before the "nearest available" magistrate judge. This new language accurately reflects the thrust of the original rule, that time is of the essence and that the defendant should be brought with dispatch before a judicial officer in the district. Second, the revised rule states a preference that the defendant be brought before a federal judicial officer.

Rule 4(b)(2) has been amended to require that if a summons is issued, the defendant must appear before a magistrate judge. The current rule requires the appearance before a "magistrate," which could include a state or local judicial officer. This change is consistent with the preference for requiring defendants to appear before federal judicial officers stated in revised Rule 4(b)(1).

Rule 4(c) (currently Rule 4(d)) includes three changes. First, current Rule 4(d)(2) states the traditional rule recognizing the territorial limits for executing warrants. Rule 4(c)(2) includes new language that reflects the recent enactment of the Military Extraterritorial Jurisdiction Act (Pub. L. No. 106–523, 114 Stat. 2488) that permits arrests of certain military and Department of Defense personnel overseas. *See also* 14 U.S.C. § 89 (Coast Guard authority to effect arrests outside territorial limits of United States). Second, current Rule 4(d)(3) provides that the arresting officer is only required to inform the defendant of the offense charged and that a warrant exists if the officer does not have a copy of the warrant. As revised, Rule 4(c)(3)(A) explicitly requires the arresting officer in all instances to inform the defendant of the offense charged and of the fact that an arrest warrant exists. The new rule continues the current provision that the arresting officer need not have a copy of the warrant, but if the defendant requests to see it, the officer must show the warrant to the defendant as soon as possible. The rule does not attempt to define any particular time limits for showing the warrant to the defendant.

Third, Rule 4(c)(3)(C) is taken from former Rule 9(c)(1). That provision specifies the manner of serving a summons on an organization. The Committee believed that Rule 4 was the more appropriate location for general provisions addressing the mechanics of arrest warrants and summonses. Revised Rule 9 liberally cross-references the basic provisions appearing in Rule 4. Under the amended rule, in all cases in which a summons is being served on an organization, a copy of the summons must be mailed to the organization.

Fourth, a change is made in Rule 4(c)(4). Currently, Rule 4(d)(4) requires that an unexecuted warrant must be returned to the judicial officer or judge who issued it. As amended, Rule 4(c)(4)(A) provides that after a warrant is executed, the officer must return it to the judge before whom the defendant will appear under Rule 5. At the government's request, however, an unexecuted warrant must be canceled by a magistrate judge. The change recognizes the possibility that at the time the warrant is returned, the issuing judicial officer may not be available.

HISTORICAL NOTES

Approval and Effective Date of Amendments Proposed Apr. 22, 1974; Effective Date of 1975 Amendments

Section 2 of Pub.L. 94–64 provided that: "The amendments proposed by the United States Supreme Court to the Federal Rules of Criminal Procedure [adding rules 12.1, 12.2 and 29.1 and amending rules 4, 9, 11, 12, 15, 16, 17, 20, 32 and 43 of these rules] which are embraced in the order of that Court on April 22, 1974, are approved except as otherwise provided in this Act and shall take effect on December 1, 1975. Except with respect to the amendment to Rule 11, insofar as it adds Rule 11(e)(6), which shall take effect on August 1, 1975, the amendments made by section 3 of this Act [to rules 4, 9, 11, 12, 12.1, 12.2, 15, 16, 17, 20, 32 and 43 of these rules] shall also take effect on December 1, 1975."

Change of Name

United States magistrate appointed under section 631 of Title 28, Judiciary and Judicial Procedure, to be known as United States magistrate judge after Dec. 1, 1990, with any reference to United States magistrate or magistrate in Title 28, in any other Federal statute, etc., deemed a reference to United States magistrate judge appointed under section 631 of Title 28, see section 321 of Pub.L. 101–650, set out as a note under section 631 of Title 28.

Rule 5. Initial Appearance

(a) In General.

(1) Appearance Upon an Arrest.

(A) A person making an arrest within the United States must take the defendant without unnecessary delay before a magistrate judge, or before a state or local judicial officer as Rule 5(c) provides, unless a statute provides otherwise.

(B) A person making an arrest outside the United States must take the defendant without unnecessary delay before a magistrate judge, unless a statute provides otherwise.

(2) Exceptions.

(A) An officer making an arrest under a warrant issued upon a complaint charging solely a violation of 18 U.S.C. § 1073 need not comply with this rule if:

(i) the person arrested is transferred without unnecessary delay to the custody of appropriate state or local authorities in the district of arrest; and

(ii) an attorney for the government moves promptly, in the district where the warrant was issued, to dismiss the complaint.

(B) If a defendant is arrested for violating probation or supervised release, Rule 32.1 applies.

(C) If a defendant is arrested for failing to appear in another district, Rule 40 applies.

(3) Appearance Upon a Summons. When a defendant appears in response to a summons under Rule 4, a magistrate judge must proceed under Rule 5(d) or (e), as applicable.

(b) Arrest Without a Warrant. If a defendant is arrested without a warrant, a complaint meeting Rule 4(a)'s requirement of probable cause must be promptly filed in the district where the offense was allegedly committed.

(c) Place of Initial Appearance; Transfer to Another District.

(1) Arrest in the District Where the Offense Was Allegedly Committed. If the defendant is arrested in the district where the offense was allegedly committed:

(A) the initial appearance must be in that district; and

(B) if a magistrate judge is not reasonably available, the initial appearance may be before a state or local judicial officer.

(2) Arrest in a District Other Than Where the Offense Was Allegedly Committed. If the defendant was arrested in a district other than where the offense was allegedly committed, the initial appearance must be:

(A) in the district of arrest; or

(B) in an adjacent district if:

(i) the appearance can occur more promptly there; or

(ii) the offense was allegedly committed there and the initial appearance will occur on the day of arrest.

(3) Procedures in a District Other Than Where the Offense Was Allegedly Committed. If the initial appearance occurs in a district other than where the offense was allegedly committed, the following procedures apply:

(A) the magistrate judge must inform the defendant about the provisions of Rule 20;

(B) if the defendant was arrested without a warrant, the district court where the offense was allegedly committed must first issue a warrant before the magistrate judge transfers the defendant to that district;

(C) the magistrate judge must conduct a preliminary hearing if required by Rule 5.1;

(D) the magistrate judge must transfer the defendant to the district where the offense was allegedly committed if:

(i) the government produces the warrant, a certified copy of the warrant, or a reliable electronic form of either; and

(ii) the judge finds that the defendant is the same person named in the indictment, information, or warrant; and

(E) when a defendant is transferred and discharged, the clerk must promptly transmit the papers and any bail to the clerk in the district where the offense was allegedly committed.

(d) Procedure in a Felony Case.

(1) Advice. If the defendant is charged with a felony, the judge must inform the defendant of the following:

(A) the complaint against the defendant, and any affidavit filed with it;

(B) the defendant's right to retain counsel or to request that counsel be appointed if the defendant cannot obtain counsel;

(C) the circumstances, if any, under which the defendant may secure pretrial release;

(D) any right to a preliminary hearing; and

(E) the defendant's right not to make a statement, and that any statement made may be used against the defendant.

(2) Consulting with Counsel. The judge must allow the defendant reasonable opportunity to consult with counsel.

(3) Detention or Release. The judge must detain or release the defendant as provided by statute or these rules.

(4) Plea. A defendant may be asked to plead only under Rule 10.

(e) Procedure in a Misdemeanor Case. If the defendant is charged with a misdemeanor only, the judge must inform the defendant in accordance with Rule 58(b)(2).

(f) Video Teleconferencing. Video teleconferencing may be used to conduct an appearance under this rule if the defendant consents.

(As amended Feb. 28, 1966, eff. July 1, 1966; Apr. 24, 1972, eff. Oct. 1, 1972; Apr. 28, 1982, eff. Aug. 1, 1982; Oct. 12, 1984, Pub.L. 98–473, Title II, § 209(a), 98 Stat. 1986; Mar. 9, 1987, eff. Aug. 1, 1987; May 1, 1990, eff. Dec. 1, 1990; Apr. 22, 1993, eff. Dec. 1, 1993; Apr. 27, 1995, eff. Dec. 1, 1995; Apr. 29, 2002, eff. Dec. 1, 2002; Apr. 12, 2006 eff. Dec. 1, 2006.)

ADVISORY COMMITTEE NOTES

1944 Adoption

Note to Subdivision (a).1. The time within which a prisoner must be brought before a committing magistrate is defined differently in different statutes. The rule supersedes all statutory provisions on this point and fixes a single standard, i.e., "without unnecessary delay", 18 U.S.C. former § 593 (Operating illicit distillery; arrest; bail); § 595 (Persons arrested taken before nearest officer for hearing); 5 U.S.C. former § 300a [now 18 U.S.C. §§ 3052, 3107] (Division of Investigation; authority of officers to serve warrants and make arrests); 16 U.S.C. former § 10 (Arrests by employees of park service for violations of laws and regulations); 16 U.S.C. § 706 (Migratory Bird Treaty Act; arrests; search warrants); D.C.Code (1940), Title 4, sec. 140 (Arrests without warrant); see, also, 33 U.S.C. former § 436, §§ 446, 452; 46 U.S.C. former § 708 (now 18 U.S.C. § 2279). What constitutes "unnecessary delay", i.e., reasonable time within which the prisoner should be brought before a committing magistrate, must be determined in the light of all the facts and circumstances of the case. The following authorities discuss the question what constitutes reasonable time for this purpose in various situations: *Carroll v. Parry*, 48 App.D.C. 453; *Janus v. United States*, 9 Cir., 38 F.2d 431, C.C.A.9th; *Commonwealth v. Di Stasio*, 294 Mass. 273, 1 N.E.2d 189; *State v. Freeman*, 86 N.C. 683; *Peloquin v. Hibner*, 231 Wis. 77, 285 N.W. 380; see, also, Warner, 28 Va.L.R. 315, 339–341.

2. The rule also states the prevailing state practice, A.L.I. Code of Criminal Procedure (1931), Commentaries to secs. 35, 36.

Note to Subdivisions (b) and (c).1. These rules prescribe a uniform procedure to be followed at preliminary hearings before a commissioner. They supersede the general provisions of 18 U.S.C. § 591 [now 18 U.S.C. § 3041] (Arrest and removal for trial). The procedure prescribed by the rules is that generally prevailing. See *Wood v. United States*, 128 F. 265, 271–272, App.D.C.; A.L.I. Code of Criminal Procedure (1931), secs. 39–60 and Commentaries thereto; Manual for United States Commissioners, pp. 6–10, published by Administrative Office of the United States Courts.

2. Pleas before a commissioner are excluded, as a plea of guilty at this stage has no legal status or function except to serve as a waiver of preliminary examination. It has been held inadmissible in evidence at the trial, if the defendant was not represented by counsel when the plea was entered. *Wood v. United States*, 128 F.2d 265, App.D.C. The rule expressly provides for a waiver of examination, thereby eliminating any necessity for a provision as to plea.

1966 Amendments

The first change is designed to insure that under the revision made in Rule 4(a) the defendant arrested on a warrant will receive the same information concerning the basis for the issuance of the warrant as would previously have been given him by the complaint itself.

The second change obligates the commissioner [now magistrate] to inform the defendant of his right to request the assignment of counsel if he is unable to obtain counsel. Cf. the amendment to Rule 44, and the Advisory Committee's Note thereon.

1972 Amendment

There are a number of changes made in rule 5 which are designed to improve the editorial clarity of the rule; to conform the rule to the Federal Magistrates Act [28 U.S.C. § 631 et seq.]; and to deal explicitly in the rule with issues as to which the rule was silent and the law uncertain.

The principal editorial change is to deal separately with the initial appearance before the magistrate and the preliminary examination. They are dealt with together in old rule 5. They are separated in order to prevent confusion as to whether they constitute a single or two separate proceedings. Although the preliminary examination can be held at the time of the initial appearance, in practice this ordinarily does not occur. Usually counsel need time to prepare for the preliminary examination and as a consequence a separate date is typically set for the preliminary examination.

Because federal magistrates are reasonably available to conduct initial appearances, the rule is drafted on the assumption that the initial appearance is before a federal magistrate. If experience under the act indicates that there must be frequent appearances before state or local judicial officers it may be desirable to draft an additional rule, such as the following, detailing the procedure for an initial appearance before a state or local judicial officer:

Initial Appearance Before a State or Local Judicial Officer. If a United States magistrate is not reasonably available under rule 5(a), the arrested person shall be brought before a state or local judicial officer authorized by 18 U.S.C. § 3041, and such officer shall inform the person of the rights specified in rule 5(c) and shall authorize the release of the arrested person under the terms provided for by these rules and by 18 U.S.C. § 3146. The judicial officer shall immediately transmit any written order of release and any papers filed before him to the appropriate United States magistrate of the district and order the arrested person to appear before such United States magistrate within three days if not in custody or at the next regular hour of business of the United States magistrate if the arrested person is retained in custody. Upon his appearance before the United States magistrate, the procedure shall be that prescribed in rule 5.

Several changes are made to conform the language of the rule to the Federal Magistrates Act [28 U.S.C. § 631 et seq.].

(1) The term "magistrate," which is defined in new rule 54, is substituted for the term "commissioner." As defined, "magistrate" includes those state and local judicial officers specified in 18 U.S.C. § 3041, and thus the initial appearance may be before a state or local judicial officer when a federal magistrate is not reasonably available. This is made explicit in subdivision (a).

(2) Subdivision (b) conforms the rule to the procedure prescribed in the Federal Magistrate Act [28 U.S.C. § 631 et seq.] when a defendant appears before a magistrate charged with a "minor offense" as defined in 18 U.S.C. § 3401(f): "misdemeanors punishable under the laws of the United States, the penalty for which does not exceed imprisonment for a period of one year, or a fine of not more than $1,000, or both, except that such term does not include ... [specified exceptions]."

If the "minor offense" is tried before a United States magistrate, the procedure must be in accordance with the Rules of Procedure for the Trial of Minor Offenses Before United States Magistrates, (January 27, 1971).

(3) Subdivision (d) makes clear that a defendant is not entitled to a preliminary examination if he has been indicted by a grand jury prior to the date set for the preliminary examination or, in appropriate cases, if any information is filed in the district court prior to that date. See C. Wright, Federal Practice and Procedure: Criminal § 80, pp. 137–140 (1969, Supp.1971). This is also provided in the Federal Magistrates Act, 18 U.S.C. § 3060(e).

Rule 5 is also amended to deal with several issues not dealt with in old rule 5:

Subdivision (a) is amended to make clear that a complaint, complying with the requirements of rule 4(a), must be filed whenever a person has been arrested without a warrant. This means that the complaint, or an affidavit or affidavits filed with the complaint, must show probable cause. As provided in rule 4(a) the showing of probable cause "may be based upon hearsay evidence in whole or in part."

Subdivision (c) provides that defendant should be notified of the general circumstances under which he is entitled to pretrial release under the Bail Reform Act of 1966 (18 U.S.C. §§ 3141 to 3152). Defendants often do not in fact have counsel at the initial appearance and thus, unless told by the magistrate, may be unaware of their right to pretrial release. See C. Wright, Federal Practice and Procedure: Criminal § 78 N. 61 (1969).

Subdivision (c) makes clear that a defendant who does not waive his right to trial before a judge of the district court is entitled to a preliminary examination to determine probable cause for any offense except a petty offense. It also, by necessary implication, makes clear that a defendant is not entitled to a preliminary examination if he consents to be tried on the issue of guilt or innocence by the United States magistrate, even though the offense may be one not heretofore triable by the United States commissioner and therefore one as to which the defendant had a right to a preliminary examination. The rationale is that the preliminary examination serves only to justify holding the defendant in custody or on bail during the period of time it takes to bind the defendant over to the district court for trial. See *State v. Solomon,* 158 Wis. 146, 147 N.W. 640 (1914). A similar conclusion is reached in the New York Proposed Criminal Procedure Law. See McKinney's Session Law News, April 10, 1969, at p. A–119.

Subdivision (c) also contains time limits within which the preliminary examination must be held. These are taken from 18 U.S.C. § 3060. The provisions for the extension of the prescribed time limits are the same as the provisions of 18 U.S.C. § 3060 with two exceptions: The new language allows delay consented to by the defendant only if there is "a showing of good cause, taking into account the public interest in the prompt disposition of criminal cases." This reflects the view of the Advisory Committee that delay, whether prosecution or defense induced, ought to be avoided whenever possible. The second difference between the new rule and 18 U.S.C. § 3060 is that the rule allows the decision to grant a continuance to be made by a United States magistrate as well as by a judge of the United States. This reflects the view of the Advisory Committee that the United States magistrate should have sufficient judicial competence to make decisions such as that contemplated in subdivision (c).

1982 Amendments

Subdivision (b). The amendment of subdivision (b) reflects the recent amendment of 18 U.S.C. § 3401(a), by the Federal Magistrate Act of 1979, to read: "When specially designated to exercise such jurisdiction by the district court or courts he serves, any United States magistrate shall have jurisdiction to try persons accused of, and sentence persons convicted of, misdemeanors committed within that judicial district."

1987 Amendments

The amendments are technical. No substantive change is intended.

1993 Amendments

The Rule is amended to conform to the Judicial Improvements Act of 1990 [P.L. 101–650, Title III, Section 321] which provides that each United States magistrate appointed under section 631 of title 28, United States Code, shall be known as a United States magistrate judge.

1995 Amendments

The amendment to Rule 5 is intended to address the interplay between the requirements for a prompt appearance before a magistrate judge and the processing of persons arrested for the offense of unlawfully fleeing to avoid prosecution under 18 U.S.C. § 1073, when no federal prosecution is intended. Title 18 U.S.C. § 1073 provides in part:

> Whoever moves or travels in interstate or foreign commerce with intent . . . to avoid prosecution, or custody or confinement after conviction, under the laws of the place from which he flees . . . shall be fined not more than $5,000 or imprisoned not more than five years, or both.
>
> Violations of this section may be prosecuted . . . only upon formal approval in writing by the Attorney General, the Deputy Attorney General, the Associate Attorney General, or an Assistant Attorney General of the United States, which function of approving prosecutions may not be delegated.

In enacting § 1073, Congress apparently intended to provide assistance to state criminal justice authorities in an effort to apprehend and prosecute state offenders. It also appears that by requiring permission of high ranking officials, Congress intended that prosecutions be limited in number. In fact, prosecutions under this section have been rare. The purpose of the statute is fulfilled when the person is apprehended and turned over to state or local authorities. In such cases the requirement of Rule 5 that any person arrested under a federal warrant must be brought before a federal magistrate judge becomes a largely meaningless exercise and a needless demand upon federal judicial resources.

In addressing this problem, several options are available to federal authorities when no federal prosecution is intended to ensue after the arrest. First, once federal authorities locate a fugitive, they may contact local law enforcement officials who make the arrest based upon the underlying out-of-state warrant. In that instance, Rule 5 is not implicated and the United States Attorney in the district issuing the § 1073 complaint and warrant can take action to dismiss both. In a second scenario, the fugitive is arrested by federal authorities who, in compliance with Rule 5, bring the person before a federal magistrate judge. If local law enforcement officers are present, they can take custody, once the United States Attorney informs the magistrate judge that there will be no prosecution under § 1073. Depending on the availability of state or local officers, there may be some delay in the Rule 5 proceedings; any delays following release to local officials, however, would not be a function of Rule 5. In a third situation, federal authorities arrest the fugitive but local law enforcement authorities are not present at the Rule 5 appearance. Depending on a variety of practices, the magistrate judge may calendar a removal hearing under Rule 40, or order that the person be held in federal custody pending further action by the local authorities.

Under the amendment, officers arresting a fugitive charged only with violating § 1073 need not bring the person before a magistrate judge under Rule 5(a) if there is no intent to actually prosecute the person under that charge. Two requirements, however, must be met. First, the arrested fugitive must be transferred without unnecessary delay to the custody of state officials. Second, steps must be taken in the appropriate district to dismiss the complaint alleging a violation of § 1073. The rule continues to contemplate that persons arrested by federal officials are entitled to prompt handling of federal charges, if prosecution is intended, and prompt transfer to state custody if federal prosecution is not contemplated.

2002 Amendments

The language of Rule 5 has been amended as part of the general restyling of the Criminal Rules to make them more easily understood and to make style and terminology consistent throughout the rules. These changes are intended to be stylistic, except as noted below.

Rule 5 has been completely revised to more clearly set out the procedures for initial appearances and to recognize that such appearances may be required at various stages of a criminal proceeding, for example, where a defendant has been arrested for violating the terms of probation.

Rule 5(a), which governs initial appearances by an arrested defendant before a magistrate judge, includes several changes. The first is a clarifying change; revised Rule 5(a)(1) provides that a person making the arrest must bring the defendant "without unnecessary delay" before a magistrate judge, instead of the current reference to "nearest available" magistrate judge. This language parallels changes in Rule 4 and reflects the view that time is of the essence. The Committee intends no change in practice. In using the term, the Committee recognizes that on occasion there may be necessary delay in presenting the defendant, for example, due to weather conditions or other natural causes. A second change is non-stylistic, and reflects the stated preference (as in other provisions throughout the rules) that the defendant be brought before a federal judicial officer. Only if a magistrate judge is not available should the defendant be taken before a state or local officer.

The third sentence in current Rule 5(a), which states that a magistrate judge must proceed in accordance with the rule where a defendant is arrested without a warrant or given a summons, has been deleted because it is unnecessary.

Rule 5(a)(1)(B) codifies the caselaw reflecting that the right to an initial appearance applies not only when a person is arrested within the United States but also when an arrest occurs outside the United States. *See, e.g., United States v. Purvis*, 768 F.2d 1237 (11th Cir. 1985); *United States v. Yunis*, 859 F.2d 953 (D.C. Cir. 1988). In these circumstances, the Committee believes—and the rule so provides—that the initial appearance should be before a federal magistrate judge rather than a state or local judicial officer. Rule 5(a)(1)(B) has also been amended by adding the words, "unless a federal statute provides otherwise," to reflect recent enactment of the Military Extraterritorial Jurisdiction Act (Pub. L. No. 106–523, 114 Stat. 2488) that permits certain persons overseas to appear before a magistrate judge by telephonic communication.

Rule 5(a)(2)(A) consists of language currently located in Rule 5 that addresses the procedure to be followed where a defendant has been arrested under a warrant issued on a complaint charging solely a violation of 18 U.S.C. § 1073 (unlawful flight to avoid prosecution). Rule 5(a)(2)(B) and 5(a)(2)(C) are new provisions. They are intended to make it clear that when a defendant is arrested for violating probation or supervised release, or for failing to appear in another district, Rules 32.1 or 40 apply. No change in practice is intended.

Rule 5(a)(3) is new and fills a perceived gap in the rules. It recognizes that a defendant may be subjected to an initial appearance under this rule if a summons was issued under Rule 4, instead of an arrest warrant. If the defendant is appearing pursuant to a summons in a felony case, Rule 5(d) applies, and if the defendant is appearing in a misdemeanor case, Rule 5(e) applies.

Rule 5(b) carries forward the requirement in former Rule 5(a) that if the defendant is arrested without a warrant, a complaint must be promptly filed.

Rule 5(c) is a new provision and sets out where an initial appearance is to take place. If the defendant is arrested in the district where the offense was allegedly committed, under Rule 5(c)(1) the defendant must be taken to a magistrate judge in that district. If no magistrate judge is reasonably available, a state or local judicial officer may conduct the initial appearance. On the other hand, if the defendant is arrested in a district other than the district where the offense was allegedly committed, Rule 5(c)(2) governs. In those instances, the defendant must be taken to a magistrate judge within the district of arrest, unless the appearance can take place more promptly in an adjacent district. The Committee recognized that in some cases, the nearest magistrate judge may actually be across a district's lines. The remainder of Rule 5(c)(2) includes material formerly located in Rule 40.

Rule 5(d), derived from current Rule 5(c), has been retitled to more clearly reflect the subject of that subdivision and the procedure to be used if the defendant is charged with a felony. Rule 5(d)(4) has been added to make clear that a defendant may only be called upon to enter a plea under the provisions of Rule 10. That language is intended to reflect and reaffirm current practice.

The remaining portions of current Rule 5(c) have been moved to Rule 5.1, which deals with preliminary hearings in felony cases.

The major substantive change is in new Rule 5(f), which permits video teleconferencing for an appearance under this rule if the defendant consents. This change reflects the growing practice among state courts to use video teleconferencing to conduct initial proceedings. A similar amendment has been made to Rule 10 concerning arraignments.

In amending Rules 5, 10, and 43 (which generally requires the defendant's presence at all proceedings), the Committee carefully considered the argument that permitting a defendant to appear by video teleconferencing might be considered an erosion of an important element of the judicial process. Much can be lost when video teleconferencing occurs. First, the setting itself may not promote the public's confidence in the integrity and solemnity of a federal criminal proceeding; that is the view of some who have witnessed the use of such proceedings in some state jurisdictions. While it is difficult to quantify the intangible benefits and impact of requiring a defendant to be brought before a federal judicial officer in a federal courtroom, the Committee realizes that something is lost when a defendant is not required to make a personal appearance. A related consideration is that the defendant may be located in a room that bears no resemblance whatsoever to a judicial forum and the equipment may be inadequate for high-quality transmissions. Second, using video teleconferencing can interfere with counsel's ability to meet personally with his or her client at what, at least in that jurisdiction, might be an important appearance before a magistrate judge. Third, the defendant may miss an opportunity to meet with family or friends, and others who might be able to assist the defendant, especially in any attempts to obtain bail. Finally, the magistrate judge may miss an opportunity to accurately assess the physical, emotional, and mental condition of a defendant—a factor that may weigh on pretrial decisions, such as release from detention.

On the other hand, the Committee considered that in some jurisdictions, the court systems face a high volume of criminal proceedings. In other jurisdictions, counsel may not be appointed until after the initial appearance and thus there is no real problem with a defendant being able to consult with counsel before or during that proceeding. The Committee was also persuaded to adopt the amendment because in some jurisdictions delays may occur in travel time from one location to another—in some cases requiring either the magistrate judge or the participants to travel long distances. In those instances, it is not unusual for a defense counsel to recognize the benefit of conducting a video teleconferenced proceeding, which will eliminate lengthy and sometimes expensive travel or permit the initial appearance to be conducted much sooner. Finally, the Committee was aware that in some jurisdictions, courtrooms now contain high quality technology for conducting such procedures, and that some courts are already using video teleconferencing—with the consent of the parties.

The Committee believed that, on balance and in appropriate circumstances, the court and the defendant should have the option of using video teleconferencing, as long as the defendant consents to that procedure. The question of when it would be appropriate for a defendant to consent is not spelled out in the rule. That is left to the defendant and the court in each case. Although the rule does not specify any particular technical requirements regarding the system to be used, if the equipment or technology is deficient, the public may lose confidence in the integrity and dignity of the proceedings.

The amendment does not require a court to adopt or use video teleconferencing. In deciding whether to use such procedures, a court may wish to consider establishing clearly articulated standards and procedures. For example, the court would normally want to insure that the location used for televising the video teleconferencing is conducive to the solemnity of a federal criminal proceeding. That might require additional coordination, for example, with the detention facility to insure that the room, furniture, and furnishings reflect the dignity associated with a federal courtroom. Provision should also be made to insure that the judge, or a surrogate, is in a position to carefully assess the defendant's condition. And the court should also consider establishing procedures for insuring that counsel and the defendant (and even the defendant's immediate family) are provided an ample opportunity to confer in private.

2006 Amendments

Subdivisions (c)(3)(C) and (D). The amendment to Rule 5(c)(3)(C) parallels an amendment to Rule 58(b)(2)(G), which in turn has been amended to remove a conflict between that rule and Rule 5.1(a), concerning the right to a preliminary hearing.

Rule 5(c)(3)(D) has been amended to permit the magistrate judge to accept a warrant by reliable electronic means. Currently, the rule requires the government to produce the original warrant, a certified copy of the warrant, or a facsimile copy of either of those documents. This amendment parallels similar changes to Rules 32.1(a)(5)(B)(i) and 41. The reference to a facsimile version of the warrant was removed because the Committee believed that the broader term "electronic form" includes facsimiles.

The amendment reflects a number of significant improvements in technology. First, more courts are now equipped to receive filings by electronic means, and indeed, some courts encourage or require that certain documents be filed by electronic means. Second, the technology has advanced to the state where such filings could be sent from, and received at, locations outside the courthouse. Third, electronic media can now provide improved quality of transmission and security measures. In short, in a particular case, using electronic media to transmit a document might be just as reliable and efficient as using a facsimile.

The term "electronic" is used to provide some flexibility to the rule and make allowance for further technological advances in transmitting data.

The rule requires that if electronic means are to be used to transmit a warrant to the magistrate judge, that the means used be "reliable." While the rule does not further define that term, the Committee envisions that a court or magistrate judge would make that determination as a local matter. In deciding whether a particular electronic means, or media, would be reliable, the court might consider first, the expected quality and clarity of the transmission. For example, is it possible to read the contents of the warrant in its entirety, as though it were the original or a clean photocopy? Second, the court may consider whether security measures are available to insure that the transmission is not compromised. In this regard, most courts are now equipped to require that certain documents contain a digital signature, or some other similar system for restricting access. Third, the court may consider whether there are reliable means of preserving the document for later use.

HISTORICAL NOTES

Change of Name

United States magistrate appointed under section 631 of Title 28, Judiciary and Judicial Procedure, to be known as United States magistrate judge after Dec. 1, 1990, with any reference to United States magistrate or magistrate in Title 28, in any other Federal statute, etc., deemed a reference to United States magistrate judge appointed under section 631 of Title 28, see section 321 of Pub.L. 101–650, set out as a note under section 631 of Title 28.

Rule 5.1. Preliminary Hearing

(a) In General. If a defendant is charged with an offense other than a petty offense, a magistrate judge must conduct a preliminary hearing unless:

(1) the defendant waives the hearing;

(2) the defendant is indicted;

(3) the government files an information under Rule 7(b) charging the defendant with a felony;

(4) the government files an information charging the defendant with a misdemeanor; or

(5) the defendant is charged with a misdemeanor and consents to trial before a magistrate judge.

(b) Selecting a District. A defendant arrested in a district other than where the offense was allegedly committed may elect to have the preliminary hearing conducted in the district where the prosecution is pending.

(c) Scheduling. The magistrate judge must hold the preliminary hearing within a reasonable time, but no later than 10 days after the initial appearance if the defendant is in custody and no later than 20 days if not in custody.

(d) Extending the Time. With the defendant's consent and upon a showing of good cause—taking into account the public interest in the prompt disposition of criminal cases—a magistrate judge may extend the time limits in Rule 5.1(c) one or more times. If the defendant does not consent, the magistrate judge may extend the time limits only on a showing that extraordinary circumstances exist and justice requires the delay.

(e) Hearing and Finding. At the preliminary hearing, the defendant may cross-examine adverse witnesses and may introduce evidence but may not object to evidence on the ground that it was unlawfully acquired. If the magistrate judge finds probable cause to believe an offense has been committed and the defendant committed it, the magistrate judge must promptly require the defendant to appear for further proceedings.

(f) Discharging the Defendant. If the magistrate judge finds no probable cause to believe an offense has been committed or the defendant committed it, the magistrate judge must dismiss the complaint and discharge the defendant. A discharge does not preclude the government from later prosecuting the defendant for the same offense.

(g) Recording the Proceedings. The preliminary hearing must be recorded by a court reporter or by a suitable recording device. A recording of the proceeding may be made available to any party upon request. A copy of the recording and a transcript may be provided to any party upon request and upon any payment required by applicable Judicial Conference regulations.

(h) Producing a Statement.

(1) In General. Rule 26.2(a)–(d) and (f) applies at any hearing under this rule, unless the magistrate judge for good cause rules otherwise in a particular case.

(2) Sanctions for Not Producing a Statement. If a party disobeys a Rule 26.2 order to deliver a statement to the moving party, the magistrate judge must not consider the testimony of a witness whose statement is withheld.

(Added Apr. 24, 1972, eff. Oct. 1, 1972, and amended Mar. 9, 1987, eff. Aug. 1, 1987; Apr. 22, 1993, eff. Dec. 1, 1993; Apr. 24, 1998, eff. Dec. 1, 1998; Apr. 29, 2002, eff. Dec. 1, 2002.)

ADVISORY COMMITTEE NOTES

1972 Addition

Rule 5.1 is, for the most part, a clarification of old rule 5(c).

Under the new rule, the preliminary examination must be conducted before a "federal magistrate" as defined in rule 54. Giving state or local judicial officers authority to conduct a preliminary examination does not seem necessary. There are not likely to be situations in which a "federal magistrate" is not "reasonably available" to conduct the preliminary examination, which is usually not held until several days after the initial appearance provided for in rule 5.

Subdivision (a) makes clear that a finding of probable cause may be based on "hearsay evidence in whole or in part." The propriety of relying upon hearsay at the preliminary examination has been a matter of some uncertainty in the federal system. See C. Wright, Federal Practice and Procedure: Criminal § 80 (1969, Supp.1971); 8 J. Moore, Federal Practice ¶ 504[4] (2d ed. Cipes 1970, Supp.1971); *Washington v. Clemmer*, 339 F.2d 715, 719 (D.C.Cir.1964); *Washington v. Clemmer*, 339 F.2d 725, 728 (D.C.Cir.1964); *Ross v. Sirica*, 380 F.2d 557, 565 (D.C.Cir.1967); *Howard v. United States*, 389 F.2d 287, 292 (D.C.Cir.1967); Weinberg and Weinberg, The Congressional Invitation to Avoid the Preliminary Hearing: An Analysis of Section 303 of the Federal Magistrates Act of 1968, 67 Mich.L.Rev. 1361, especially n. 92 at 1383 (1969); D. Wright, The Rules of Evidence Applicable to Hearings in Probable Cause, 37 Conn.B.J. 561 (1963); Comment, Preliminary Examination—Evidence and Due Process, 15 Kan.L.Rev. 374, 379–381 (1967).

A grand jury indictment may properly be based upon hearsay evidence. *Costello v. United States*, 350 U.S. 359 (1956); 8 J. Moore, Federal Practice ¶ 6.03[2] (2d ed. Cipes 1970, Supp.1971). This being so, there is practical advantage in making the evidentiary requirements for the preliminary examination as flexible as they are for the grand jury. Otherwise there will be increased pressure upon United States Attorneys to abandon the preliminary examination in favor of the grand jury indictment. See C. Wright, Federal Practice and Procedure: Criminal § 80 at p. 143 (1969). New York State, which also utilizes both the preliminary examination and the grand jury, has under consideration a new Code of Criminal Procedure which would allow the use of hearsay at the preliminary examination. See McKinney's Session Law News, April 10, 1969, pp. A119–A120.

For the same reason, subdivision (a) also provides that the preliminary examination is not the proper place to raise the issue of illegally obtained evidence. This is current law. In *Giordenello v. United States*, 357 U.S. 480, 484 (1958), the Supreme Court said:

[T]he Commissioner [now magistrate] here had no authority to adjudicate the admissibility at petitioner's later trial of the heroin taken from his person. That issue was for the trial court. This is specifically recognized by Rule 41(e) of the Criminal Rules, which provides that a defendant aggrieved by an unlawful search and seizure may " * * * move the district court * * * to suppress for use as evidence anything so obtained on the ground that * * * " the arrest warrant was defective on any of several grounds.

Dicta in *Costello v. United States*, 350 U.S. 359, 363–364 (1956), and *United States v. Blue*, 384 U.S. 251, 255 (1966), also support the proposed rule. In *United States ex rel. Almeida v. Rundle*, 383 F.2d 421, 424 (3d Cir.1967), the court, in considering the adequacy of an indictment, said:

On this score, it is settled law that (1) "[an] indictment returned by a legally constituted nonbiased grand jury, * * * is enough to call for a trial of the charge on the merits and satisfies the requirements of the Fifth Amendment.", *Lawn v. United States*, 355 U.S. 339, 349, 78 S.Ct. 311, 317, 2 L.Ed.2d 321 (1958); (2) an indictment cannot be challenged "on the ground that there was inadequate or incompetent evidence before the grand jury", *Costello v. United States*, 350 U.S. 359, 363, 76 S.Ct. 406, 408, 100 L.Ed. 397 (1956); and (3) a prosecution is not abated, nor barred, even where "tainted evidence" has been submitted to a grand jury. *United States v. Blue*, 384 U.S. 251, 86 S.Ct. 1416, 16 L.Ed.2d 510 (1966).

See also C. Wright, Federal Practice and Procedure: Criminal § 80 at 143 n. 5 (1969, Supp.1971) 8 J. Moore, Federal Practice ¶ 6.03[3] (2d ed. Cipes 1970, Supp.1971). The Manual for United States Commissioners (Administrative Office of United States Courts, 1948) provides at pp. 24–25: "Motions for this purpose [to suppress illegally obtained evidence] may be made and heard only before a district judge. Commissioners [now magistrates] are not empowered to consider or act upon such motions."

It has been urged that the rules of evidence at the preliminary examination should be those applicable at the trial because the purpose of the preliminary examination should be, not to review the propriety of the arrest or prior detention, but rather to determine whether there is evidence sufficient to justify subjecting the defendant to the expense and inconvenience of trial. See Weinberg and Weinberg, The Congressional Invitation to Avoid the Preliminary Hearing: An Analysis of Section 303 of the Federal Magistrates Act of 1968, 67 Mich.L.Rev. 1361, 1396–1399 (1969). The rule rejects this view for reasons largely of administrative necessity and the efficient administration of justice. The Congress has decided that a preliminary examination shall not be required when there is a grand jury indictment (18 U.S.C. § 3060). Increasing the procedural and evidentiary requirements applicable to the preliminary examination will therefore add to the administrative pressure to avoid the preliminary examination. Allowing objections to evidence on the ground that evidence has been illegally obtained would require two determinations of admissibility, one before the United States magistrate and one in the district court. The objective is to reduce, not increase, the number of preliminary motions.

To provide that a probable cause finding may be based upon hearsay does not preclude the magistrate from requiring a showing that admissible evidence will be available at the time of trial. See Comment, Criminal Procedure—Grand Jury—Validity of Indictment Based Solely on Hearsay Questioned When Direct Testimony Is Readily Available, 43 N.Y.U.L.Rev. 578 (1968); *United States v. Umans*, 368 F.2d

725 (2d Cir.1966), cert. dismissed as improvidently granted 389 U.S. 80 (1967); *United States v. Andrews*, 381 F.2d 377, 378 (2d Cir.1967); *United States v. Messina*, 388 F.2d 393, 394 n. 1 (2d Cir.1968); *United States v. Beltram*, 388 F.2d 449 (2d Cir.1968); and *United States v. Arcuri*, 282 F.Supp. 347 (E.D.N.Y.1968). The fact that a defendant is not entitled to object to evidence alleged to have been illegally obtained does not deprive him of an opportunity for a pretrial determination of the admissibility of evidence. He can raise such an objection prior to trial in accordance with the provisions of rule 12.

Subdivision (b) makes it clear that the United States magistrate may not only discharge the defendant but may also dismiss the complaint. Current federal law authorizes the magistrate to discharge the defendant but he must await authorization from the United States Attorney before he can close his records on the case by dismissing the complaint. Making dismissal of the complaint a separate procedure accomplishes no worthwhile objective, and the new rule makes it clear that the magistrate can both discharge the defendant and file the record with the clerk.

Subdivision (b) also deals with the legal effect of a discharge of a defendant at a preliminary examination. This issue is not dealt with explicitly in the old rule. Existing federal case law is limited. What cases there are seem to support the right of the government to issue a new complaint and start over. See e.g., *Collins v. Loisel*, 262 U.S. 426 (1923); *Morse v. United States*, 267 U.S. 80 (1925). State law is similar. See *People v. Dillon*, 197 N.Y. 254, 90 N.E. 820 (1910); *Tell v. Wolke*, 21 Wis.2d 613, 124 N.W.2d 655 (1963). In the Tell case the Wisconsin court stated the common rationale for allowing the prosecutor to issue a new complaint and start over:

> The state has no appeal from errors of law committed by a magistrate upon preliminary examination and the discharge on a preliminary would operate as an unchallengeable acquittal. * * * The only way an error of law committed on the preliminary examination prejudicial to the state may be challenged or corrected is by a preliminary examination on a second complaint. (21 Wis.2d at 619–620.)

Subdivision (c) is based upon old rule 5(c) and upon the Federal Magistrates Act, 18 U.S.C. § 3060(f). It provides methods for making available to counsel the record of the preliminary examination. See C. Wright, Federal Practice and Procedure: Criminal § 82 (1969, Supp.1971). The new rule is designed to eliminate delay and expense occasioned by preparation of transcripts where listening to the tape recording would be sufficient. Ordinarily the recording should be made available pursuant to subdivision (c)(1). A written transcript may be provided under subdivision (c)(2) at the discretion of the court, a discretion which must be exercised in accordance with *Britt v. North Carolina*, 404 U.S. 226, 30 L.Ed.2d 400, 405 (1971):

> A defendant who claims the right to a free transcript does not, under our cases, bear the burden of proving inadequate such alternatives as may be suggested by the State or conjured up by a court in hindsight. In this case, however, petitioner has conceded that he had available an informal alternative which appears to be substantially equivalent to a transcript. Accordingly, we cannot conclude that the court below was in error in rejecting his claim.

1987 Amendments

The amendments are technical. No substantive change is intended.

1993 Amendments

The Rule is amended to conform to the Judicial Improvements Act of 1990 [P.L. 101–650, Title III, Section 321] which provides that each United States magistrate appointed under section 631 of title 28, United States Code, shall be known as a United States magistrate judge.

1998 Amendments

The addition of subdivision (d) mirrors similar amendments made in 1993 which extend the scope of Rule 26.2 to Rules 32, 32.1, 46 and Rule 8 of the Rules Governing Proceedings under 28 U.S.C. § 2255. As indicated in the Committee Notes accompanying those amendments, the primary reason for extending the coverage of Rule 26.2 rested heavily upon the compelling need for accurate information affecting a witness' credibility. That need, the Committee believes, extends to a preliminary examination under this rule where both the prosecution and the defense have high interests at stake.

A witness' statement must be produced only after the witness has personally testified.

2002 Amendments

The language of Rule 5.1 has been amended as part of the general restyling of the Criminal Rules to make them more easily understood and to make style and terminology consistent throughout the rules. These changes are intended to be stylistic, except as noted below.

First, the title of the rule has been changed. Although the underlying statute, 18 U.S.C. § 3060, uses the phrase *preliminary examination*, the Committee believes that the phrase *preliminary hearing* is more accurate. What happens at this proceeding is more than just an examination; it includes an evidentiary hearing, argument, and a judicial ruling. Further, the phrase *preliminary hearing* predominates in actual usage.

Rule 5.1(a) is composed of the first sentence of the second paragraph of current Rule 5(c). Rule 5.1(b) addresses the ability of a defendant to elect where a preliminary hearing will be held. That provision is taken from current Rule 40(a).

Rule 5.1(c) and (d) include material currently located in Rule 5(c): scheduling and extending the time limits for the hearing. The Committee is aware that in most districts, magistrate judges perform these functions. That point is also reflected in the definition of "court" in Rule 1(b), which in turn recognizes that magistrate judges may be authorized to act.

Rule 5.1(d) contains a significant change in practice. The revised rule includes language that expands the authority of a United States magistrate judge to grant a continuance for a preliminary hearing conducted under the rule. Currently, the rule authorizes a magistrate judge to grant a continuance only in those cases in which the defendant has consented to the continuance. If the defendant does not consent, then the government must present the matter to a district judge, usually on the same day. The proposed amendment conflicts with 18 U.S.C. § 3060, which tracks the original language of the rule and permits only district judges to grant continuances when the defendant objects. The Committee believes that this restriction is an anomaly and that it can lead to needless consumption of judicial and other resources. Magistrate judges are routinely required to make probable cause determinations and other difficult decisions regarding the defendant's liberty interests, reflecting that the magistrate judge's role has developed toward a higher level of responsibility for preindictment matters. The Committee believes that the change in the rule will provide greater judicial economy and that it is entirely appropriate to seek this change to the rule through the Rules Enabling Act procedures. *See* 28 U.S.C. § 2072(b). Under those procedures, approval by Congress of this rule change would supersede the parallel provisions in 18 U.S.C. § 3060.

Rule 5.1(e), addressing the issue of probable cause, contains the language currently located in Rule 5.1(a), with the exception of the sentence, "The finding of probable cause may be based upon hearsay evidence in whole or in part." That language was included in the original promulgation of the rule in 1972. Similar language was added to Rule 4 in 1974. In the Committee Note on the 1974 amendment, the Advisory Committee explained that the language was included to make it clear that a finding of probable cause may be based upon hearsay, noting that there had been some uncertainty in the federal system about the propriety of relying upon hearsay at the preliminary hearing. *See* Advisory Committee Note to Rule 5.1 (citing cases and commentary). Federal law is now clear on that proposition. Thus, the Committee believed that the reference to hearsay was no longer necessary. Further, the Committee believed that the matter was best addressed in Rule 1101(d)(3), Federal Rules of Evidence. That rule explicitly states that the Federal Rules of Evidence do not apply to "preliminary examinations in criminal cases, . . . issuance of warrants for arrest, criminal summonses, and search warrants." The Advisory Committee Note accompanying that rule recognizes that: "The nature of the proceedings makes application of the formal rules of evidence inappropriate and impracticable." The Committee did not intend to make any substantive changes in practice by deleting the reference to hearsay evidence.

Rule 5.1(f), which deals with the discharge of a defendant, consists of former Rule 5.1(b).

Rule 5.1(g) is a revised version of the material in current Rule 5.1(c). Instead of including detailed information in the rule itself concerning records of preliminary hearings, the Committee opted simply to direct the reader to the applicable Judicial Conference regulations governing records. The Committee did not intend to make any substantive changes in the way in which those records are currently made available.

Finally, although the rule speaks in terms of initial appearances being conducted before a magistrate judge, Rule 1(c) makes clear that a district judge may perform any function in these rules that a magistrate judge may perform.

III. THE GRAND JURY, THE INDICTMENT, AND THE INFORMATION

Rule 6. The Grand Jury

(a) Summoning a Grand Jury.

(1) In General. When the public interest so requires, the court must order that one or more grand juries be summoned. A grand jury must have 16 to 23 members, and the court must order that enough legally qualified persons be summoned to meet this requirement.

(2) Alternate Jurors. When a grand jury is selected, the court may also select alternate jurors. Alternate jurors must have the same qualifications and be selected in the same manner as any other juror. Alternate jurors replace jurors in the same sequence in which the alternates were selected. An alternate juror who replaces a juror is subject to the same challenges, takes the same oath, and has the same authority as the other jurors.

(b) Objection to the Grand Jury or to a Grand Juror.

(1) Challenges. Either the government or a defendant may challenge the grand jury on the ground that it was not lawfully drawn, summoned, or selected, and may challenge an individual juror on the ground that the juror is not legally qualified.

(2) Motion to Dismiss an Indictment. A party may move to dismiss the indictment based on an objection to the grand jury or on an individual juror's lack of legal qualification, unless the court has previously ruled on the same objection under Rule 6(b)(1). The motion to dismiss is governed by 28 U.S.C. § 1867(e). The court must not dismiss the indictment on the ground that a grand juror was not legally qualified if the record shows that at least 12 qualified jurors concurred in the indictment.

(c) Foreperson and Deputy Foreperson. The court will appoint one juror as the foreperson and another as the deputy foreperson. In the foreperson's absence, the deputy foreperson will act as the foreperson. The foreperson may administer oaths and affirmations and will sign all indictments. The foreperson—or another juror designated by the foreperson—will record the number of jurors concurring in every indictment and will file the record with the clerk, but the record may not be made public unless the court so orders.

(d) Who May Be Present.

(1) While the Grand Jury Is in Session. The following persons may be present while the grand jury is in session: attorneys for the government, the witness being questioned, interpreters when needed, and a court reporter or an operator of a recording device.

(2) During Deliberations and Voting. No person other than the jurors, and any interpreter needed to assist a hearing-impaired or speech-impaired juror, may be present while the grand jury is deliberating or voting.

(e) Recording and Disclosing the Proceedings.

(1) Recording the Proceedings. Except while the grand jury is deliberating or voting, all proceedings must be recorded by a court reporter or by a suitable recording device. But the validity of a prosecution is not affected by the unintentional failure to make a recording. Unless the court orders otherwise, an attorney for the government will retain control of the recording, the reporter's notes, and any transcript prepared from those notes.

(2) Secrecy.

(A) No obligation of secrecy may be imposed on any person except in accordance with Rule 6(e)(2)(B).

(B) Unless these rules provide otherwise, the following persons must not disclose a matter occurring before the grand jury:

(i) a grand juror;

(ii) an interpreter;

(iii) a court reporter;

(iv) an operator of a recording device;

(v) a person who transcribes recorded testimony;

(vi) an attorney for the government; or

(vii) a person to whom disclosure is made under Rule 6(e)(3)(A)(ii) or (iii).

(3) Exceptions.

(A) Disclosure of a grand-jury matter—other than the grand jury's deliberations or any grand juror's vote—may be made to:

(i) an attorney for the government for use in performing that attorney's duty;

(ii) any government personnel—including those of a state, state subdivision, Indian tribe, or foreign government—that an attorney for the government considers necessary to assist in performing that attorney's duty to enforce federal criminal law; or

(iii) a person authorized by 18 U.S.C. § 3322.

(B) A person to whom information is disclosed under Rule 6(e)(3)(A)(ii) may use that information only to assist an attorney for the government in performing that attorney's duty to enforce federal criminal law. An attorney for the government must promptly provide the court that impaneled the grand jury with the names of all persons to whom a disclosure has been made, and must certify that the attorney has advised those persons of their obligation of secrecy under this rule.

(C) An attorney for the government may disclose any grand-jury matter to another federal grand jury.

(D) An attorney for the government may disclose any grand-jury matter involving foreign intelligence, counterintelligence (as defined in 50 U.S.C. § 401a), or foreign intelligence information (as defined in Rule 6(e)(3)(D)(iii)) to any federal law enforcement, intelligence, protective, immigration, national defense, or national security official to assist the official receiving the information in the performance of that official's duties. An attorney for the government may also disclose any grand-jury matter involving, within the United States or elsewhere, a threat of attack or other grave hostile acts of a foreign power or its agent, a threat of domestic or international sabotage or terrorism, or clandestine intelligence gathering activities by an intelligence service or network of a foreign power or by its agent, to any appropriate federal, state, state subdivision, Indian tribal, or foreign government official, for the purpose of preventing or responding to such threat or activities.

(i) Any official who receives information under Rule 6(e)(3)(D) may use the information only as necessary in the conduct of that person's official duties subject to any limitations on the unauthorized disclosure of such information. Any state, state subdivision, Indian tribal, or foreign government official who receives information under Rule 6(e)(3)(D) may use the information only in a manner consistent with any guidelines issued by the Attorney General and the Director of National Intelligence.

(ii) Within a reasonable time after disclosure is made under Rule 6(e)(3)(D), an attorney for the government must file, under seal, a notice with the court in the district where the grand jury convened stating that such information was disclosed and the departments, agencies, or entities to which the disclosure was made.

(iii) As used in Rule 6(e)(3)(D), the term "foreign intelligence information" means:

(a) information, whether or not it concerns a United States person, that relates to the ability of the United States to protect against—

- actual or potential attack or other grave hostile acts of a foreign power or its agent;
- sabotage or international terrorism by a foreign power or its agent; or
- clandestine intelligence activities by an intelligence service or network of a foreign power or by its agent; or

(b) information, whether or not it concerns a United States person, with respect to a foreign power or foreign territory that relates to—

• the national defense or the security of the United States; or

• the conduct of the foreign affairs of the United States.

(E) The court may authorize disclosure—at a time, in a manner, and subject to any other conditions that it directs—of a grand-jury matter:

(i) preliminarily to or in connection with a judicial proceeding;

(ii) at the request of a defendant who shows that a ground may exist to dismiss the indictment because of a matter that occurred before the grand jury;

(iii) at the request of the government, when sought by a foreign court or prosecutor for use in an official criminal investigation;

(iv) at the request of the government if it shows that the matter may disclose a violation of State, Indian tribal, or foreign criminal law, as long as the disclosure is to an appropriate state, state-subdivision, Indian tribal, or foreign government official for the purpose of enforcing that law; or

(v) at the request of the government if it shows that the matter may disclose a violation of military criminal law under the Uniform Code of Military Justice, as long as the disclosure is to an appropriate military official for the purpose of enforcing that law.

(F) A petition to disclose a grand-jury matter under Rule 6(e)(3)(E)(i) must be filed in the district where the grand jury convened. Unless the hearing is ex parte—as it may be when the government is the petitioner—the petitioner must serve the petition on, and the court must afford a reasonable opportunity to appear and be heard to:

(i) an attorney for the government;

(ii) the parties to the judicial proceeding; and

(iii) any other person whom the court may designate.

(G) If the petition to disclose arises out of a judicial proceeding in another district, the petitioned court must transfer the petition to the other court unless the petitioned court can reasonably determine whether disclosure is proper. If the petitioned court decides to transfer, it must send to the transferee court the material sought to be disclosed, if feasible, and a written evaluation of the need for continued grand-jury secrecy. The transferee court must afford those persons identified in Rule 6(e)(3)(F) a reasonable opportunity to appear and be heard.

(4) **Sealed Indictment.** The magistrate judge to whom an indictment is returned may direct that the indictment be kept secret until the defendant is in custody or has been released pending trial. The clerk must then seal the indictment, and no person may disclose the indictment's existence except as necessary to issue or execute a warrant or summons.

(5) **Closed Hearing.** Subject to any right to an open hearing in a contempt proceeding, the court must close any hearing to the extent necessary to prevent disclosure of a matter occurring before a grand jury.

(6) **Sealed Records.** Records, orders, and subpoenas relating to grand-jury proceedings must be kept under seal to the extent and as long as necessary to prevent the unauthorized disclosure of a matter occurring before a grand jury.

(7) **Contempt.** A knowing violation of Rule 6, or of any guidelines jointly issued by the Attorney General and the Director of National Intelligence under Rule 6, may be punished as a contempt of court.

(f) Indictment and Return. A grand jury may indict only if at least 12 jurors concur. The grand jury—or its foreperson or deputy foreperson—must return the indictment to a magistrate judge in open court. If a complaint or information is pending against the defendant and 12 jurors do not concur in the indictment, the foreperson must promptly and in writing report the lack of concurrence to the magistrate judge.

(g) Discharging the Grand Jury. A grand jury must serve until the court discharges it, but it may serve more than 18 months only if the court, having determined that an extension is in the public interest, extends the grand jury's service. An extension may be granted for no more than 6 months, except as otherwise provided by statute.

(h) Excusing a Juror. At any time, for good cause, the court may excuse a juror either temporarily or permanently, and if permanently, the court may impanel an alternate juror in place of the excused juror.

(i) "Indian Tribe" Defined. "Indian tribe" means an Indian tribe recognized by the Secretary of the Interior on a list published in the Federal Register under 25 U.S.C. § 479a–1.

(As amended Feb. 28, 1966, eff. July 1, 1966; Apr. 24, 1972, eff. Oct. 1, 1972; Apr. 26, 1976, eff. Aug. 1, 1976; July 30, 1977, Pub.L. 95–78, § 2(a), 91 Stat. 319; Apr. 30, 1979, eff. Aug. 1, 1979; Apr. 28, 1983, eff. Aug. 1, 1983; Apr. 29, 1985, eff. Aug. 1, 1985; Oct. 12, 1984, Pub.L. 98–473, Title II, § 215(f), 98 Stat. 2016; Apr. 29, 1985, eff. Aug. 1, 1985; Mar. 9, 1987, eff. Aug. 1, 1987; Apr. 22, 1993, eff. Dec. 1, 1993;

Apr. 29, 1999, eff. Dec. 1, 1999; Oct. 26, 2001, Pub.L. 107–56, Title II, § 203(a), 115 Stat. 278; Apr. 29, 2002; eff. Dec. 1, 2002; Nov. 25, 2002, Pub.L. 107–296, Title VIII, § 895, 116 Stat. 2256; Dec. 17, 2004, Pub.L. 108–458, Title VI, § 6501(a), 118 Stat. 3760; Apr.12, 2006, eff. Dec. 1, 2006.)

ADVISORY COMMITTEE NOTES

1944 Adoption

* * * * * * *

Note to Subdivision (a). **1.** The first sentence of this rule vests in the court full discretion as to the number of grand juries to be summoned and as to the times when they should be convened. This provision supersedes the existing law, which limits the authority of the court to summon more than one grand jury at the same time. At present two grand juries may be convened simultaneously only in a district which has a city or borough of at least 300,000 inhabitants, and three grand juries only in the Southern District of New York, 28 U.S.C. former § 421 (Grand juries; when, how and by whom summoned; length of service). This statute has been construed, however, as only limiting the authority of the court to summon more than one grand jury for a single place of holding court, and as not circumscribing the power to convene simultaneously several grand juries at different points within the same district. *Morris v. United States*, 128 F.2d 912, C.C.A.5th; *United States v. Perlstein*, 39 F.Supp. 965, D.N.J.

2. The provision that the grand jury shall consist of not less than 16 and not more than 23 members continues existing law, 28 U.S.C. former § 419 [now 18 U.S.C. § 3321] (Grand jurors; number when less than required number).

3. The rule does not affect or deal with the method of summoning and selecting grand juries. Existing statutes on the subjects are not superseded. See 28 U.S.C. former §§ 411–426 [now §§ 1861 to 1870]. As these provisions of law relate to jurors for both criminal and civil cases, it seemed best not to deal with this subject.

Note to Subdivision (b)(1). Challenges to the array and to individual jurors, although rarely invoked in connection with the selection of grand juries, are nevertheless permitted in the Federal courts and are continued by this rule. *United States v. Gale*, 3 S.Ct. 1, 109 U.S. 65, 69–70, 27 L.Ed. 857; *Clawson v. United States*, 5 S.Ct. 949, 114 U.S. 477, 29 L.Ed. 179; *Agnew v. United States*, 17 S.Ct. 235, 165 U.S. 36, 44, 41 L.Ed. 624. It is not contemplated, however, that defendants held for action of the grand jury shall receive notice of the time and place of the impaneling of a grand jury, or that defendants in custody shall be brought to court to attend at the selection of the grand jury. Failure to challenge is not a waiver of any objection. The objection may still be interposed by motion under Rule 6(b)(2).

Note to Subdivision (b)(2). **1.** The motion provided by this rule takes the place of a plea in abatement, or motion to quash, *Crowley v. United States*, 24 S.Ct. 731, 194 U.S. 461, 469–474, 48 L.Ed. 1075; *United States v. Gale, supra.*

2. The second sentence of the rule is a restatement of 18 U.S.C. former § 554a (Indictments and presentments; objection on ground of unqualified juror barred where twelve qualified jurors concurred; record of number concurring), and introduces no change in existing law.

Note to Subdivision (c). **1.** This rule generally is a restatement of existing law, 18 U.S.C. former § 554a and 28 U.S.C. former § 420. Failure of the foreman to sign or endorse the indictment is an irregularity and is not fatal. *Frisbie v. United States*, 15 S.Ct. 586, 157 U.S. 160, 163–165, 39 L.Ed. 657.

2. The provision for the appointment of a deputy foreman is new. Its purpose is to facilitate the transaction of business if the foreman is absent. Such a provision is found in the law of at least one State, N.Y.Code Criminal Procedure, sec. 244.

Note to Subdivision (d). This rule generally continues existing law. See 18 U.S.C. former § 556 (Indictments and presentments; defects of form); and 5 U.S.C. § 310 [now 28 U.S.C. § 515(a)] (Conduct of legal proceedings).

Note to Subdivision (e). **1.** This rule continues the traditional practice of secrecy on the part of members of the grand jury, except when the court permits a disclosure, *Schmidt v. United States*, 6 Cir., 115 F.2d 394; *United States v. American Medical Association*, D.C., 26 F.Supp. 429; Cf. *Atwell v. United States*, 4 Cir., 162 F. 97; and see 18 U.S.C. § 554a (Indictments and presentments; objection on ground of unqualified juror barred where twelve qualified jurors concurred; record of number concurring). Government attorneys are entitled to disclosure of grand jury proceedings, other than the deliberations and the votes of the jurors, inasmuch as they may be present in the grand jury room during the presentation of evidence. The rule continues this practice.

2. The rule does not impose any obligation of secrecy on witnesses. The existing practice on this point varies among the districts. The seal of secrecy on witnesses seems an unnecessary hardship and may lead to injustice if a witness is not permitted to make a disclosure to counsel or to an associate.

3. The last sentence authorizing the court to seal indictments continues present practice.

Note to Subdivision (f). This rule continues existing law, 18 U.S.C. former § 554 (Indictments and presentments; by twelve grand jurors). The purpose of the last sentence is to provide means for a prompt release of a defendant if in custody, or exoneration of bail if he is on bail, in the event that the grand jury considers the case of a defendant held for its action and finds no indictment.

Note to Subdivision (g). Under existing law a grand jury serves only during the term for which it is summoned, but the court may extend its period of service for as long as 18 months, 28 U.S.C. former § 421. During the extended period, however, a grand jury may conduct only investigations commenced during the original term. The rule continues the 18 months' maximum for the period of service of a grand jury, but provides for such service as a matter of course, unless the court terminates it at an earlier date. The matter is left in the discretion of the court, as it is under existing law. The expiration of a term of court as a time limitation is elsewhere entirely eliminated (Rule 45(c)) and specific time limitations are substituted therefor. This was previously done by the Federal Rules of Civil Procedure for the civil side of the courts (Federal Rules of Civil Procedure, Rule 6(c)). The elimination of the requirement that at an extended period the grand jury may continue only investigations previously commenced, will obviate such a controversy as was presented in *United States v. Johnson,* 63 S.Ct. 1233, 319 U.S. 503, 87 L.Ed. 1546, rehearing denied 320 U.S. 808, 64 S.Ct. 25, 88 L.Ed. 488.

1966 Amendments

Subdivision (d). The amendment makes it clear that recording devices may be used to take evidence at grand jury sessions.

Subdivision (e). The amendment makes it clear that the operator of a recording device and a typist who transcribes recorded testimony are bound to the obligation of secrecy.

Subdivision (f). A minor change conforms the language to what doubtless is the practice. The need for a report to the court that no indictment has been found may be present even though the defendant has not been "held to answer." If the defendant is in custody or has given bail, some official record should be made of the grand jury action so that the defendant can be released or his bail exonerated.

1972 Amendments

Subdivision (b)(2) is amended to incorporate by express reference the provisions of the Jury Selection and Service Act of 1968. That act provides in part:

The procedures prescribed by this section shall be the exclusive means by which a person accused of a Federal crime [or] the Attorney General of the United States * * * may challenge any jury on the ground that such jury was not selected in conformity with the provisions of this title. [28 U.S.C. § 1867(c)]

Under rule 12(e) the judge shall decide the motion before trial or order it deferred until after verdict. The authority which the judge has to delay his ruling until after verdict gives him an option which can be exercised to prevent the unnecessary delay of a trial in the event that a motion attacking a grand jury is made on the eve of the trial. In addition, rule 12(c) gives the judge authority to fix the time at which pretrial motions must be made. Failure to make a pretrial motion at the appropriate time may constitute a waiver under rule 12(f).

1976 Amendments

Under the proposed amendment to rule 6(f), an indictment may be returned to a federal magistrate. ("Federal magistrate" is defined in rule 54(c) as including a United States magistrate as defined in 28 U.S.C. §§ 631–639 and a judge of the United States.) This change will foreclose the possibility of noncompliance with the Speedy Trial Act timetable because of the nonavailability of a judge. Upon the effective date of certain provisions of the Speedy Trial Act of 1974, the timely return of indictments will become a matter of critical importance; for the year commencing July 1, 1976, indictments must be returned within 60 days of arrest or summons, for the year following within 45 days, and thereafter within 30 days. 18 U.S.C. §§ 3161(b) and (f), 3163(a). The problem is acute in a one-judge district where, if the judge is holding court in another part of the district, or is otherwise absent, the return of the indictment must await the later reappearance of the judge at the place where the grand jury is sitting.

A corresponding change has been made to that part of subdivision (f) which concerns the reporting of a "no bill," and to that part of subdivision (e) which concerns keeping an indictment secret.

The change in the third sentence of rule 6(f) is made so as to cover all situations in which by virtue of a pending complaint or information the defendant is in custody or released under some form of conditional release.

1977 Amendments

The proposed definition of "attorneys for the government" in subdivision (e) is designed to facilitate an increasing need, on the part of government attorneys, to make use of outside expertise in complex litigation. The phrase "other government personnel" includes, but is not limited to, employees of administrative agencies and government departments.

Present subdivision (e) provides for disclosure "to the attorneys for the government for use in the performance of their duties." This limitation is designed to further "the long established policy that maintains the secrecy of the grand jury in federal courts." United States v. Procter and Gamble Co., 356 U.S. 677 (1958).

As defined in rule 54(c), " 'Attorney for the government' means the Attorney General, an authorized assistant of the Attorney General, a United States Attorney, an authorized assistant of a United States Attorney and when applicable to cases arising under the laws of Guam * * *." The limited nature of this definition is pointed out in In re Grand Jury Proceedings, 309 F.2d 440 (3d Cir. 1962) at 443:

The term attorneys for the government is restrictive in its application. * * * If it had been intended that the attorneys for the administrative agencies were to have free access to matters occurring before a grand jury, the rule would have so provided.

The proposed amendment reflects the fact that there is often government personnel assisting the Justice Department in grand jury proceedings. In re Grand Jury Investigation of William H. Pflaumer & Sons, Inc., 53 F.R.D. 464 (E.D.Pa.1971), the opinion quoted the United States Attorney:

It is absolutely necessary in grand jury investigations involving analysis of books and records, for the government attorneys to rely upon investigative personnel (from the government agencies) for assistance.

See also 8 J. Moore, Federal Practice ¶6.05 at 6–28 (2d ed. Cipes, 1969):

The rule [6(e)] has presented a problem, however, with respect to attorneys and nonattorneys who are assisting in preparation of a case for the grand jury. * * * These assistants often cannot properly perform their work without having access to grand jury minutes.

Although case law is limited, the trend seems to be in the direction of allowing disclosure to government personnel who assist attorneys for the government in situations where their expertise is required. This is subject to the qualification that the matters disclosed be used only for the purposes of the grand jury investigation. The court may inquire as to the good faith of the assisting personnel, to ensure that access to material is not merely a subterfuge to gather evidence unattainable by means other than the grand jury. This approach was taken in In re Grand Jury Investigation of William H. Pflaumer & Sons, Inc., 53 F.R.D. 464 (E.D.Pa. 1971); In re April 1956 Term Grand Jury, 239 F.2d 263 (7th Cir.1956); United States v. Anzelimo, 319 F.Supp. 1106

(D.C.La.1970). Another case, Application of Kelly, 19 F.R.D. 269 (S.D.N.Y.1956), assumed, without deciding, that assistance given the attorney for the government by IRS and FBI agents was authorized.

The change at line 27 reflects the fact that under the Bail Reform Act of 1966 some persons will be released without requiring bail. See 18 U.S.C. §§ 3146, 3148.

Under the proposed amendment to rule 6(f), an indictment may be returned to a federal magistrate. ("Federal magistrate" is defined in rule 54(c) as including a United States magistrate as defined in 28 U.S.C. §§ 631–639 and a judge of the United States.) This change will foreclose the possibility of noncompliance with the Speedy Trial Act timetable because of the nonavailability of a judge. Upon the effective date of certain provisions of the Speedy Trial Act of 1974, the timely return of indictments will become a matter of critical importance; for the year commencing July 1, 1976, indictments must be returned within 60 days of arrest or summons, for the year following within 45 days, and thereafter within 30 days. 18 U.S.C. §§ 3161(b) and (f), 3163(a). The problem is acute in a one-judge district where, if the judge is holding court in another part of the district, or is otherwise absent, the return of the indictment must await the later reappearance of the judge at the place where the grand jury is sitting.

A corresponding change has been made to that part of subdivision (f) which concerns the reporting of a "no bill," and to that part of subdivision (e) which concerns keeping an indictment secret.

The change in the third sentence of rule 6(f) is made so as to cover all situations in which by virtue of a pending complaint or information the defendant is in custody or released under some form of conditional release.

1977 Enactment

Rule 6(e) currently provides that "disclosure of matters occurring before the grand jury other than its deliberations and the vote of any juror may be made to the attorneys for the government for use in the performance of their duties." Rule 54(c) defines attorneys for the government to mean "the Attorney General, an authorized assistant to the Attorney General, a United States attorney, and an authorized assistant of the United States attorney, and when applicable to cases arising under the laws of Guam, means the Attorney General of Guam. . . ."

The Supreme Court proposal would change Rule 6(e) by adding the following new language:

> For purposes of this subdivision, "attorneys for the government" includes those enumerated in Rule 54(c); it also includes such other government personnel as are necessary to assist the attorneys for the government in the performance of their duties.

It would also make a series of changes in the rule designed to make its provisions consistent with other provisions in the Rules and the Bail Reform Act of 1966.

The Advisory Committee note states that the proposed amendment is intended "to facilitate an increasing need, on the part of Government attorneys to make use of outside expertise in complex litigation". The note indicated that:

> Although case law is limited, the trend seems to be in the direction of allowing disclosure to Government personnel who assist attorneys for the Government in situations where their expertise is required. This is subject to the qualification that the matter disclosed be used only for the purposes of the grand jury investigation.

It is past history at this point that the Supreme Court proposal attracted substantial criticism, which seemed to stem more from the lack of precision in defining, and consequent confusion and uncertainty concerning, the intended scope of the proposed change than from a fundamental disagreement with the objective.

Attorneys for the Government in the performance of their duties with a grand jury must possess the authority to utilize the services of other government employees. Federal crimes are "investigated" by the FBI, the IRS, or by Treasury agents and not by government prosecutors or the citizens who sit on grand juries. Federal agents gather and present information relating to criminal behavior to prosecutors who analyze and evaluate it and present it to grand juries. Often the prosecutors need the assistance of the agents in evaluating evidence. Also, if further investigation is required during or after grand jury proceedings, or even during the course of criminal trials, the Federal agents must do it. There is no reason for a barrier of secrecy to exist between the facets of the criminal justice system upon which we all depend to enforce the criminal laws.

The parameters of the authority of an attorney for the government to disclose grand jury information in the course of performing his own duties is not defined by Rule 6. However, a commonsense interpretation prevails, permitting "Representatives of other government agencies actively assisting United States attorneys in a grand jury investigation . . . access to grand jury material in the performance of their duties." Yet projected against this current practice, and the weight of case law, is the anomalous language of Rule 6(e) itself, which, in its present state of uncertainty, is spawning some judicial decisions highly restrictive of the use of government experts that require the government to "show the necessity (to the Court) for each particular person's aid rather than showing merely a general necessity for assistance, expert or otherwise" and that make Rule 6(e) orders subject to interlocutory appeal.

In this state of uncertainty, the Committee believes it is timely to redraft subdivision (e) of Rule 6 to make it clear.

Paragraph (1) as proposed by the Committee states the general rule that a grand jury, an interpreter, a stenographer, an operator of a recording device, a typist who transcribes recorded testimony, an attorney for the government, or government personnel to whom disclosure is made under paragraph (2)(A)(ii) shall not disclose matters occurring before the grand jury, except as otherwise provided in these rules. It also expressly provides that a knowing violation of Rule 6 may be punished as a contempt of court. In addition, it carries forward the current provision that no obligation of secrecy may be imposed on any person except in accordance with this Rule.

Having stated the general rule of nondisclosure, paragraph (2) sets forth exemptions from nondisclosure. Subparagraph (A) of paragraph (2) provides that disclosure otherwise prohibited, other than the grand jury deliberations and the vote of any grand juror, may be made to an attorney for the government for use in the performance of his duty and to such personnel as are deemed necessary by an attorney for the government to assist an attorney for the government in the performance of such attorney's duty to enforce Federal criminal law. In order to facilitate resolution of subsequent claims of improper disclosure, subparagraph (B) further provides that the names of government personnel designated to assist the attorney for the government shall be promptly provided to the district court and such personnel shall not utilize grand jury material for any purpose other than assisting the attorney for the government in the performance of such attorney's duty to enforce Federal criminal law. Although not expressly required by the rule, the Committee contemplates that the names of such personnel will generally be furnished to the court before disclosure is made to them. Subparagraph (C) permits disclosure as directed by a court preliminarily to or in connection with a judicial proceeding or, at the request of the defendant, upon a showing that grounds may exist for dismissing the indictment because of matters occurring before the grand jury. Paragraph (3) carries forward the last sentence of current Rule 6(e) with the technical changes recommended by the Supreme Court.

The Rule as redrafted is designed to accommodate the belief on the one hand that Federal prosecutors should be able, without the time-consuming requirement of prior judicial interposition, to make such disclosures of grand jury information to other government personnel as they deem necessary to facilitate the performance of their duties relating to criminal law enforcement. On the other hand, the Rule seeks to allay the concerns of those who fear that such prosecutorial power will lead to misuse of the grand jury to enforce non-criminal Federal laws by (1) providing a clear prohibition, subject to the penalty of contempt and (2) requiring that a court order under paragraph (C) be obtained to authorize such a disclosure. There is, however, no intent to preclude the use of grand jury-developed evidence for civil law enforcement purposes. On the contrary, there is no reason why such use is improper, assuming that the grand jury was utilized for the legitimate purpose of a criminal investigation. Accordingly, the Committee believes and intends that the basis for a court's refusal to issue an order under paragraph (C) to enable the government to disclose grand jury information in a non-criminal proceeding should be no more restrictive than is the case today under prevailing court decisions. It is contemplated that the judicial hearing in connection with an application for a court order by the government under subparagraph (3) (C) (i) should be *ex parte* so as to preserve, to the maximum extent possible, grand jury secrecy. Senate Report No. 95–354.

1979 Amendments

Note to Subdivision (e) (1). Proposed subdivision (e) (1) requires that all proceedings, except when the grand jury is deliberating or voting, be recorded. The existing rule does not require that grand jury proceedings be recorded. The provision in rule 6(d) that "a stenographer or operator of a recording device may be present while the grand jury is in session" has been taken to mean that recordation is permissive and not mandatory; see *United States v. Aloisio*, 440 F.2d 705 (7th Cir. 1971), collecting the cases. However, the cases rather frequently state that recordation of the proceedings is the better practice; see *United States v. Aloisio, supra*; *United States v. Cramer*, 447 F.2d 210 (2d Cir. 1971); *Schlinsky v. United States*, 379 F.2d 735 (1st Cir. 1967); and some cases require the district court, after a demand to exercise discretion as to whether the proceedings should be recorded. *United States v. Price*, 474 F.2d 1223 (9th Cir. 1973); *United States v. Thoresen*, 428 F.2d 654 (9th Cir. 1970). Some district courts have adopted a recording requirement. See, e.g. *United States v. Aloisio, supra*; *United States v. Gramolini*, 301 F.Supp. 39 (D.R.I. 1969). Recording of grand jury proceedings is currently a requirement in a number of states. See, e.g., Cal.Pen. Code §§ 938–938.3; Iowa Code Ann. § 772.4; Ky.Rev.Stat.Ann. § 28.460; and Ky.R.Crim.P. § 5.16(2).

The assumption underlying the proposal is that the cost of such recording is justified by the contribution made to the improved administration of criminal justice. See United States v. Gramolini, supra, noting: "Nor can it be claimed that the cost of recordation is prohibitive; in an electronic age, the cost of recordation must be categorized as miniscule." For a discussion of the success of electronic recording in Alaska, see Reynolds, Alaska's Ten Years of Electronic Reporting, 56 A.B.A.J. 1080 (1970).

Among the benefits to be derived from a recordation requirement are the following:

(1) Ensuring that the defendant may impeach a prosecution witness on the basis of his prior inconsistent statements before the grand jury. As noted in the opinion of Oakes, J., in *United States v. Cramer*: "First, since *Dennis v. United States*, 384 U.S. 855, 86 S.Ct. 1840, 16 L.Ed.2d 973 (1966), a defendant has been entitled to examine the grand jury testimony of witnesses against him. On this point, the Court was unanimous, holding that there was 'no justification' for the District of Columbia Court of Appeals' 'relying upon [the] "assumption" ' that 'no inconsistencies would have come to light.' The Court's decision was based on the general proposition that '[i]n our adversary system for determining guilt or innocence, it is rarely justifiable for the prosecution to have exclusive access to a storehouse of relevant facts.' In the case at bar the prosecution *did* have exclusive access to the grand jury testimony of the witness Sager, by virtue of being present, and the defense had none—to determine whether there were any inconsistencies with, say, his subsequent testimony as to damaging admissions by the defendant and his attorney Richard Thaler. The Government claims, and it is supported by the majority here, that there is no problem since defendants were given the benefit of Sager's subsequent statements including these admissions as Jencks Act materials. But assuming this to be true, it does not cure the basic infirmity that the defense could not know whether the witness testified inconsistently before the grand jury."

(2) Ensuring that the testimony received by the grand jury is trustworthy. In *United States v. Cramer*, Oakes, J., also observed: "The recording of testimony is in a very real sense a circumstantial guaranty of trustworthiness. Without the restraint of being subject to prosecution for perjury, a restraint which is wholly meaningless or nonexistent if the testimony is unrecorded, a witness may make baseless accusations founded on hearsay or false accusations, all resulting in the indictment of a fellow citizen for a crime."

(3) Restraining prosecutorial abuses before the grand jury. As noted in *United States v. Gramolini*: "In no way does recordation inhibit the grand jury's investigation. True, recordation restrains certain prosecutorial practices which might, in its absence be used, but that is no reason not to record. Indeed, a sophisticated prosecutor must acknowledge that there develops between a grand jury and the prosecutor with whom the jury is closeted a rapport—a dependency relationship—which can easily be turned into an instrument of influence on grand jury deliberations. Recordation is the most effective restraint upon such potential abuses."

(4) Supporting the case made by the prosecution at trial. Oakes, J., observed in *United States v. Cramer*: "The benefits of having grand jury testimony recorded do not all inure to the defense. See, e.g., *United States v. DeSisto*, 329 F.2d 929, 934: (2nd Cir.), cert. denied, 377 U.S. 979, 84 S.Ct. 1885, 12 L.Ed.2d 747 (1964) (conviction sustained in part on basis of witnesses's prior sworn testimony before grand jury)." Fed.R.Evid. 801(d) (1) (A) excludes from the category of hearsay the prior inconsistent testimony of a witness given before a grand jury. *United States v. Morgan*, 555 F.2d 238 (9th Cir. 1977). See also *United States v. Carlson*, 547 F.2d 1346 (8th Cir.1976), admitting under Fed.R.Evid. 804(b) (5) the grand jury testimony of a witness who refused to testify at trial because of threats by the defendant.

Commentators have also supported a recording requirement. 8 Moore, Federal Practice par. 6.02[2] [d] (2d ed. 1972) states: "Fairness to the defendant would seem to compel a change in the practice, particularly in view of the 1970 amendment to 18 U.S.C. § 3500 making grand jury testimony of government witnesses available at trial for purposes of impeachment. The requirement of a record may also prove salutary in controlling overreaching or improper examination of witnesses by the prosecutor." Similarly, 1 Wright, Federal Practice and Procedure—Criminal § 103 (1969), states that the present rule "ought to be changed, either by amendment or by judicial construction. The Supreme Court has emphasized the importance to the defense of access to the transcript of the grand jury proceedings [citing *Dennis*]. A defendant cannot have that advantage if the proceedings go unrecorded." American Bar Association, Report of the Special Committee on Federal Rules of Procedure, 52 F.R.D. 87, 94–95 (1971), renews the committee's 1965 recommendation "that all accusatorial grand jury proceedings either be transcribed by a reporter or recorded by electronic means."

Under proposed subdivision (e) (1), if the failure to record is unintentional, the failure to record would not invalidate subsequent judicial proceedings. Under present law, the failure to compel production of grand jury testimony where there is no record is not reversible error. See *Wyatt v. United States*, 388 F.2d 395 (10th Cir. 1968).

The provision that the recording or reporter's notes or any transcript prepared therefrom are to remain in the custody or control (as where the notes are in the immediate possession of a contract reporter employed by the Department of Justice) of the attorney for the government is in accord with present practice. It is specifically recognized, however, that the court in a particular case may have reason to order otherwise.

It must be emphasized that the proposed changes in rule 6(e) deal only with the recording requirement, and in no way expand the circumstances in which disclosure of the grand jury proceedings is permitted or required. "Secrecy of grand jury proceedings is not jeopardized by recordation. The making of a record cannot be equated with disclosure of its contents, and disclosure is controlled by other means." *United States v. Price*, 474 F.2d 1223 (9th Cir. 1973). Specifically, the proposed changes do not provide for copies of the grand jury minutes to defendants as a matter of right, as is the case in some states. See, e.g., Cal.Pen. Code § 938.1; Iowa Code Ann. § 772.4. The matter of disclosure continues to be governed by other provisions, such as rule 16(a) (recorded statements of the defendant), 18 U.S.C. § 3500 (statements of government witnesses), and the unchanged portions of rule 6(e), and the cases interpreting these provisions. See, e.g., *United States v. Howard*, 433 F.2d 1 (5th Cir. 1970), and *Beatrice Foods Co. v. United States*, 312 F.2d 29 (8th Cir. 1963), concerning the showing which must be made of improper matters occurring before the grand jury before disclosure is required.

Likewise, the proposed changes in rule 6(e) are not intended to make any change regarding whether a defendant may challenge a grand jury indictment. The Supreme Court has declined to hold that defendants may challenge indictments on the ground that they are not supported by sufficient or competent evidence. *Costello v. United States*, 350 U.S. 359 (1956); *Lawn v. United States*, 355 U.S. 339 (1958); *United States v. Blue*, 384 U.S. 251 (1966). Nor are the changes intended to permit the defendant to challenge the conduct of the attorney for the government before the grand jury absent a preliminary factual showing of serious misconduct.

Note to Subdivision (e) (3) (C). The sentence added to subdivision (e) (3) (C) gives express recognition to the fact that if the court orders disclosure, it may determine the circumstances of the disclosure. For example, if the proceedings are electronically recorded, the court would have discretion in an appropriate case to deny defendant the right to a transcript at government expense. While it takes special skills to make a stenographic record understandable, an electronic recording can be understood by merely listening to it, thus avoiding the expense of transcription.

1983 Amendments

* * * * * *

Rule 6(e)(3)(C). New subdivision (e)(3)(C)(iii) recognizes that it is permissible for the attorney for the government to make disclosure of matters occurring before one grand jury to another federal grand jury. Even absent a specific provision to that effect, the courts have permitted such disclosure in some circumstances. See, e.g., *United States v. Socony-Vacuum Oil Co.*, 310 U.S. 150 (1940); *United States v. Garcia*, 420 F.2d 309 (2d Cir.1970). In this kind of situation, "[s]ecrecy of grand jury materials should be protected almost as well by the safeguards at the second grand jury proceeding, including the oath of the jurors, as by judicial supervision of the disclosure of such materials." *United States v. Malatesta*, 583 F.2d 748 (5th Cir.1978).

Rule 6(e)(3)(D). In *Douglas Oil Co. v. Petrol Stops Northwest*, 441 U.S. 211 (1979), the Court held on the facts there presented that it was an abuse of discretion for the district judge to order disclosure of grand jury transcripts for use in civil proceedings in another district where that judge had insufficient knowledge of those proceedings to make a determination of the need for disclosure. The Court suggested a "better practice" on those facts, but declared that "procedures to deal with the many variations are best left to the rulemaking procedures established by Congress."

The first sentence of subdivision (e)(3)(D) makes it clear that when disclosure is sought under subdivision (e)(2)(C)(i), the petition is to be filed in the district where the grand jury was convened, whether or not it is the district of the "judicial proceeding" giving rise to the petition. Courts which have addressed the question have generally taken this view, e.g., *Illinois v. Sarbaugh*, 522 F.2d 768 [552 F.2d 768] (7th Cir.1977). As stated in Douglas Oil,

* * * * * * *

> those who seek grand jury transcripts have little choice other than to file a request with the court that supervised the grand jury, as it is the only court with control over the transcripts.
>
> Quite apart from the practical necessity, the policies underlying Rule 6(e) dictate that the grand jury's supervisory court participate in reviewing such requests, as it is in the best position to determine the continuing need for grand jury secrecy. Ideally, the judge who supervised the grand jury should review the request for disclosure, as he will have firsthand knowledge of the grand jury's activities. But even other judges of the district where the grand jury sat may be able to discover facts affecting the need for secrecy more easily than would judges from elsewhere around the country. The records are in the custody of the District Court, and therefore are readily available for references. Moreover, the personnel of that court—particularly those of the United States Attorney's Office who worked with the grand jury—are more likely to be informed about the grand jury proceedings than those in a district that had no prior experience with the subject of the request.

The second sentence requires the petitioner to serve notice of his petition upon several persons who, by the third sentence, are recognized as entitled to appear and be heard on the matter. The notice requirement ensures that all interested parties, if they wish, may make a timely appearance. Absent such notice, these persons, who then might only learn of the order made in response to the motion after it was entered, have had to resort to the cumbersome and inefficient procedure of a motion to vacate the order. *In re Special February 1971 Grand Jury v. Conlisk*, 490 F.2d 894 (7th Cir.1973).

Though some authority is to be found that parties to the judicial proceeding giving rise to the motion are not entitled to intervene, in that "the order to produce was not directed to" them, *United States v. American Oil Co.*, 456 F.2d 1043 (3d Cir.1972), that position was rejected in Douglas Oil, where it was noted that such persons have standing "to object to the disclosure order, as release of the transcripts to their civil adversaries could result in substantial injury to them." As noted in *Illinois v. Sarbaugh*, supra, while present rule 6(e) "omits to state whether any one is entitled to object to disclosure," the rule

> seems to contemplate a proceeding of some kind, judicial proceedings are not normally *ex parte*, and persons in the situation of the intervenors [parties to the civil proceeding] are likely to be the only ones to object to an order for disclosure. If they are not allowed to appear, the advantages of an adversary proceeding are lost.

If the judicial proceeding is a class action, notice to the representative is sufficient.

The amendment also recognizes that the attorney for the government in the district where the grand jury convened also has an interest in the matter and should be allowed to be heard. It may sometimes be the case, as in *Douglas Oil*, that the prosecutor will have relatively little concern for secrecy, at least as compared with certain parties to the civil proceeding. Nonetheless, it is appropriate to recognize that generally the attorney for the government is entitled to be heard so that he may represent what *Douglas Oil* characterizes as "the public interest in secrecy," including the government's legitimate concern about "the possible effect upon the functioning of future grand juries" of unduly liberal disclosure.

The second sentence leaves it to the court to decide whether any other persons should receive notice and be allowed to intervene. This is appropriate, for the necessity for and feasibility of involving others may vary substantially from case to case. In *Douglas Oil*, it was noted that the individual who produced before the grand jury the information now sought has an interest in the matter:

> Fear of future retribution or social stigma may act as powerful deterrents to those who would come forward and aid the grand jury in the performance of its duties. Concern as to the future consequences of frank and full testimony is heightened where the witness is an employee of a company under investigation.

Notice to such persons, however is by no means inevitably necessary, and in some cases the information sought may have reached the grand jury from such a variety of sources that it is not practicable to involve these sources in the disclosure proceeding. Similarly, while *Douglas Oil* notes that rule 6(e) secrecy affords "protection of the innocent accused from disclosure of the accusation made against him before the grand jury," it is appropriate to leave to the court whether that interest requires representation directly by the grand jury target at this time. When deemed necessary to protect the identity of such other persons, it would be a permissible alternative for the government or the court directly to give notice to these other persons, and thus the rule does not foreclose such action.

The notice requirement in the second sentence is inapplicable if the hearing is to be *ex parte*. The legislative history of rule 6(e) states: "It is contemplated that the judicial hearing in connection with an application for a court order by the government, under subparagraph (3)(C)(i) should be *ex parte* so as to preserve, to the maximum extent possible, grand jury secrecy." S.Rep. No. 95–354, 1977 U.S.Code Cong. & Admin.News p. 532. Although such cases are distinguishable from other cases arising under this subdivision because internal regulations limit further disclosure of information disclosed to the government, the rule provides only that the hearing "may" be *ex parte* when the petitioner is the government. This allows the court to decide that matter based upon the circumstances of the particular case. For example, an *ex parte* proceeding is much less likely to be appropriate if the government acts as petitioner as an accommodation to, e.g., a state agency.

Rule 6(e)(3)(E). Under the first sentence in new subdivision (e)(3)(E), the petitioner or any intervenor might seek to have the matter transferred to the federal district court where the judicial proceeding giving rise to the petition is pending. Usually it will be the petitioner, who is seeking disclosure, who will desire the transfer, but this is not inevitably the case. An intervenor might seek transfer on the ground that the other court, with greater knowledge of the extent of the need, would be less likely to conclude "that the material * * * is needed to avoid a possible injustice" (the test under *Douglas Oil*). The court may transfer on its own motion, for as noted in *Douglas Oil*, if transfer is the better course of action it should not be foreclosed "merely because the parties have failed to specify the relief to which they are entitled."

It must be emphasized that transfer is proper only if the proceeding giving rise to the petition "is in federal district court in another district." If, for example, the proceeding is located in another district but is at the state level, a situation encompassed within rule 6(e)(3)(C)(i), *In re Special February 1971 Grand Jury v. Conlisk*, supra, there is no occasion to transfer. Ultimate resolution of the matter cannot be placed in the hands of the state court, and in such a case the federal court in that place would lack what *Douglas Oil* recognizes as the benefit to be derived from transfer: "first-hand knowledge of the litigation in which the transcripts allegedly are needed." Formal transfer is unnecessary in intradistrict cases, even when the grand jury court and judicial proceeding court are not in the same division.

As stated in the first sentence, transfer by the court is appropriate "unless it can reasonably obtain sufficient knowledge of the proceeding to determine whether disclosure is proper." (As reflected by the "whether disclosure is proper" language, the amendment makes no effort to define the disclosure standard; that matter is currently governed by *Douglas Oil* and the authorities cited therein, and is best left to elaboration by future case law.) The amendment expresses a preference for having the disclosure issue decided by the grand jury court. Yet, it must be recognized, as stated in *Douglas Oil*, that often this will not be possible because

> the judges of the court having custody of the grand jury transcripts will have no first-hand knowledge of the litigation in which the transcripts allegedly are needed, and no practical means by which such knowledge can be obtained. In such a case, a judge in the district of the grand jury cannot weigh in an informed manner the need for disclosure against the need for maintaining grand jury secrecy.

The penultimate sentence provides that upon transfer the transferring court shall order transmitted the material sought to be disclosed and also a written evaluation of the need for continuing grand jury secrecy. Because the transferring court is in the best position to assess the interest in continued grand jury secrecy in the particular instance, it is important that the court which will now have to balance that interest against the need for disclosure receive the benefit of the transferring court's assessment. Transmittal of the material sought to be disclosed will not only facilitate timely disclosure if it is thereafter ordered, but will also assist the other court in deciding how great the need for disclosure actually is. For example, with that material at hand the other court will be able to determine if there is any inconsistency between certain grand jury testimony and testimony received in the other judicial proceeding. The rule recognizes, however, that there may be instances in which transfer of everything sought to be disclosed is not feasible. See, e.g., *In re 1975–2 Grand Jury Investigation*, 566 F.2d 1293 (5th Cir.1978) (court ordered transmittal of "an inventory of the grand jury subpoenas, transcripts, and documents," as the materials in question were "exceedingly voluminous, filling no less than 55 large file boxes and one metal filing cabinet").

The last sentence makes it clear that in a case in which the matter is transferred to another court, that court should permit the various interested parties specified in the rule to be heard. Even if those persons were previously heard before the court which ordered the transfer, this will not suffice. The order of transfer did not decide the ultimate issue of "whether a particularized need for disclosure outweighs the interest in continued grand jury secrecy," *Douglas Oil*, supra, which is what now remains to be resolved by the court to which transfer was made. Cf. *In re 1975–2 Grand Jury Investigation*, supra, holding that a transfer order is not appealable because it does not determine the ultimate question of disclosure, and thus "[n]o one has yet been aggrieved and no one will become aggrieved until [the court to which the matter was transferred] acts."

Rule 6(e)(5). This addition to rule 6 would make it clear that certain hearings which would reveal matters which have previously occurred before a grand jury or are likely to occur before a grand jury with respect to a pending or ongoing investigation must be conducted in camera in whole or in part in order to prevent public disclosure of such secret information. One such hearing is that conducted under subdivision (e)(3)(D), for it will at least sometimes be necessary to consider and assess some of the "matters occurring before the grand jury" in order to decide the disclosure issue. Two other kinds of hearings at which information about a particular grand jury investigation might need to be discussed are those at which the question is whether to grant a grand jury witness immunity or whether to order a grand jury witness to comply fully with the terms of a subpoena directed to him.

A recent GAO study established that there is considerable variety in the practice as to whether such hearings are closed or open, and that open hearings often seriously jeopardize grand jury secrecy:

> For judges to decide these matters, the witness' relationship to the case under investigation must be discussed. Accordingly, the identities of witnesses and targets, the nature of expected testimony, and the extent to which the witness is cooperating are often revealed during preindictment proceedings. Because the matters discussed can compromise the purposes of grand jury secrecy, some judges close the preindictment proceedings to the public and the press; others do not. When the proceeding is open, information that may otherwise be kept secret under rule 6(e) becomes available to the public and the press. . . .
>
> Open preindictment proceedings are a major source of information which can compromise the purposes of grand jury secrecy. In 25 cases we were able to establish links between open proceedings and later newspaper articles containing information about the identities of witnesses and targets and the nature of grand jury investigations.

Comptroller General, More Guidance and Supervision Needed over Federal Grand Jury Proceedings 8–9 (Oct. 16, 1980).

The provisions of rule 6(e)(5) do not violate any constitutional right of the public or media to attend such pretrial hearings. There is no Sixth Amendment right in the public to attend pretrial proceedings, *Gannett Co., Inc. v. DePasquale*, 443 U.S. 368 (1979), and *Richmond Newspapers, Inc. v. Virginia*, 448 U.S. 555, (1980), only recognizes a First Amendment "right to attend criminal trials." *Richmond Newspapers* was based largely upon the "*unbroken, uncontradicted history*" of public trials, while in *Gannett* it was noted "there exists no persuasive evidence that at common law members of the public had any right to attend pretrial proceedings." Moreover, even assuming some public right to attend certain pretrial proceedings, see *United States v.*

Criden, 675 F.2d 550 (3d Cir.1982), that right is not absolute; it must give way, as stated in *Richmond Newspapers*, to "an overriding interest" in a particular case in favor of a closed proceeding. By permitting closure only "to the extent necessary to prevent disclosure of matters occurring before a grand jury," rule 6(e)(5) recognizes the longstanding interest in the secrecy of grand jury proceedings. Counsel or others allowed to be present at the closed hearing may be put under a protective order by the court.

Subdivision (e)(5) is expressly made "subject to any right to an open hearing in contempt proceedings." This will accommodate any First Amendment right which might be deemed applicable in that context because of the proceedings' similarities to a criminal trial, cf. *United States v. Criden*, supra, and also any Fifth or Sixth Amendment right of the contemnor. The latter right clearly exists as to a criminal contempt proceeding, *In re Oliver*, 333 U.S. 257 (1948), and some authority is to be found recognizing such a right in civil contempt proceedings as well. *In re Rosahn*, 671 F.2d 690 (2d Cir.1982). This right of the contemnor must be requested by him and, in any event, does not require that the entire contempt proceedings, including recitation of the substance of the questions he has refused to answer, be public. *Levine v. United States*, 362 U.S. 610 (1960).

Rule 6(e)(6). Subdivision (e)(6) provides that records, orders and subpoenas relating to grand jury proceedings shall be kept under seal to the extent and for so long as is necessary to prevent disclosure of matters occurring before a grand jury. By permitting such documents as grand jury subpoenas and immunity orders to be kept under seal, this provision addresses a serious problem of grand jury secrecy and expressly authorizes a procedure now in use in many but not all districts. As reported in Comptroller General, More Guidance and Supervision Needed over Federal Grand Jury Proceedings 10, 14 (Oct. 16, 1980):

> In 262 cases, documents presented at open preindictment proceedings and filed in public files revealed details of grand jury investigations. These documents are, of course, available to anyone who wants them, including targets of investigations. [There are] two documents commonly found in public files which usually reveal the identities of witnesses and targets. The first document is a Department of Justice authorization to a U.S. attorney to apply to the court for a grant of immunity for a witness. The second document is the court's order granting the witness immunity from prosecution and compelling him to testify and produce requested information. * * *
>
> Subpoenas are the fundamental documents used during a grand jury's investigation because through subpoenas, grand juries can require witnesses to testify and produce documentary evidence for their consideration. Subpoenas can identify witnesses, potential targets, and the nature of an investigation. Rule 6(e) does not provide specific guidance on whether a grand jury's subpoena should be kept secret. Additionally, case law has not consistently stated whether the subpoenas are protected by rule 6(e).
>
> District courts still have different opinions about whether grand jury subpoenas should be kept secret. Out of 40 Federal District Courts we contacted, 36 consider these documents to be secret. However, 4 districts do make them available to the public.

Rule 6(g). In its present form, subdivision 6(g) permits a grand jury to serve no more than 18 months after its members have been sworn, and absolutely no exceptions are permitted. (By comparison, under the Organized Crime Control Act of 1970, Title I, 18 U.S.C. §§ 3331–3334, special grand juries may be extended beyond their basic terms of 18 months if their business has not been completed.) The purpose of the amendment is to permit some degree of flexibility as to the discharge of grand juries where the public interest would be served by an extension.

As noted in *United States v. Fein*, 504 F.2d 1170 (2d Cir.1974), upholding the dismissal of an indictment returned 9 days after the expiration of the 18-month period but during an attempted extension, under the present inflexible rule "it may well be that criminal proceedings which would be in the public interest will be frustrated and that those who might be found guilty will escape trial and conviction." The present inflexible rule can produce several undesirable consequences, especially when complex fraud, organized crime, tax or antitrust cases are under investigation: (i) wastage of a significant amount of time and resources by the necessity of presenting the case once again to a successor grand jury simply because the matter could not be concluded before the term of the first grand jury expired; (ii) precipitous action to conclude the investigation before the expiration date of the grand jury; and (iii) potential defendants may be kept under investigation for a longer time because of the necessity to present the matter again to another grand jury.

The amendment to subdivision 6(g) permits extension of a regular grand jury only "upon a determination that such extension is in the public interest." This permits some flexibility, but reflects the fact that extension of regular grand juries beyond 18 months is to be the exception and not the norm. The intention of the amendment is to make it possible for a grand jury to have sufficient extra time to wind up an investigation when, for example, such extension becomes necessary because of the unusual nature of the case or unforeseen developments.

Because terms of court have been abolished, 28 U.S.C. § 138, the second sentence of subdivision 6(g) has been deleted.

1985 Amendments

Rule 6 (e)(3)(A)(ii). Rule 6(e)(3)(A)(ii) currently provides that an attorney for the government may disclose grand jury information, without prior judicial approval, to other government personnel whose assistance the attorney for the government deems necessary in conducting the grand jury investigation. Courts have differed over whether employees of state and local governments are "government personnel" within the meaning of the rule. Compare *In re Miami Federal Grand Jury No. 79-9*, 478 F.Supp. 490 (S.D.Fla. 1979), and *In re Grand Jury Proceedings*, 445 F.Supp. 349 (D.R.I.1978) (state and local personnel not included); with *In re 1979 Grand Jury Proceedings*, 479 F.Supp. 93 (E.D.N.Y. 1979) (state and local personnel included). The amendment clarifies the rule to include state and local personnel.

It is clearly desirable that federal and state authorities cooperate, as they often do, in organized crime and racketeering investigations, in public corruption and major fraud cases, and in various other situations where federal and state criminal jurisdictions overlap. Because of such cooperation, government attorneys in complex grand jury investigations frequently find it necessary to enlist the help of a team of government agents. While the agents are usually federal personnel, it is not uncommon in certain types of investigations that federal prosecutors wish to obtain the assistance of state law enforcement personnel, which could be uniquely beneficial. The amendment permits disclosure to those personnel in the circumstances stated.

It must be emphasized that the disclosure permitted is limited. The disclosure under this subdivision is permissible only in connection with the attorney for the government's "duty to enforce federal criminal law" and only to those personnel "deemed necessary . . . to assist" in the performance of that duty. Under subdivision (e)(3)(B), the material disclosed may not be used for any other purpose, and the names of persons to whom disclosure is made must be promptly provided to the court.

Rule 6 (e)(3)(B). The amendment to subdivision (e)(3)(B) imposes upon the attorney for the government the responsibility to certify to the district court that he has advised those persons to whom disclosure was made under subdivision (e)(3)(A)(ii) of their obligation of secrecy under Rule 6. Especially with the amendment of subdivision (e)(3)(A)(ii) to include personnel of a state or subdivision of a state, who otherwise would likely be unaware of this obligation of secrecy, the giving of such advice is an important step in ensuring against inadvertent breach of grand jury secrecy. But because not all federal government personnel will otherwise know of this obligation, the giving of the advice and certification thereof is required as to *all* persons receiving disclosure under subdivision (e)(3)(A)(ii).

Rule 6 (e)(3)(C). It sometimes happens that during a federal grand jury investigation evidence will be developed tending to show a violation of state law. When this occurs, it is very frequently the case that this evidence cannot be communicated to the appropriate state officials for further investigation. For one thing, any state officials who might seek this information must show particularized need. *Illinois v. Abbott & Associates,* 103 S.Ct. 1356 (1983). For another, and more significant, it is often the case that the information relates to a state crime outside the context of any pending or even contemplated state judicial proceeding, so that the "preliminarily to or in connection with a judicial proceeding" requirement of subdivision (e)(3)(C)(i) cannot be met.

This inability lawfully to disclose evidence of a state criminal violation—evidence legitimately obtained by the grand jury—constitutes an unreasonable barrier to the effective enforcement of our two-tiered system of criminal laws. It would be removed by new subdivision (e)(3)(C)(iv), which would allow a court to permit disclosure to a state or local official for the purpose of enforcing state law when an attorney for the government so requests and makes the requisite showing.

The federal court has been given control over any disclosure which is authorized, for subdivision (e)(3)(C) presently states that "the disclosure shall be made in such manner, at such time, and under such conditions as the court may direct." The Committee is advised that it will be the policy of the Department of Justice under this amendment to seek such disclosure only upon approval of the Assistant Attorney General in charge of the Criminal Division. There is no intention, by virtue of this amendment, to have federal grand juries act as an arm of the state.

1987 Amendments

Subdivision (a)(2). New subdivision (a)(2) gives express recognition to a practice now followed in some district courts, namely, that of designating alternate grand jurors at the time the grand jury is selected. (A person so designated does not attend court and is not paid the jury attendance fees and expenses authorized by 28 U.S.C. § 1871 unless subsequently impanelled pursuant to Rule 6(g).) Because such designation may be a more efficient procedure than election of additional grand jurors later as need arises under subdivision (g), the amendment makes it clear that it is a permissible step in the grand jury selection process.

This amendment is not intended to work any change in subdivision (g). In particular, the fact that one or more alternate jurors either have or have not been previously designated does not limit the district court's discretion under subdivision (g) to decide whether, if a juror is excused temporarily or permanently, another person should replace him to assure the continuity of the grand jury and its ability to obtain a quorum in order to complete its business.

Subdivisions (c), (f). The amendments are technical. No substantive change is intended.

1993 Amendments

The Rule is amended to conform to the Judicial Improvements Act of 1990 [P.L. 101–650, Title III, Section 321] which provides that each United States magistrate appointed under section 631 of title 28, United States Code, shall be known as a United States magistrate judge.

1999 Amendments

Subdivision 6(d). As currently written, Rule 6(d) absolutely bars any person, other than the jurors themselves, from being present during the jury's deliberations and voting. Accordingly, interpreters are barred from attending the deliberations and voting by the grand jury, even though they may have been present during the taking of testimony. The amendment is intended to permit interpreters to assist persons who are speech or hearing impaired and are serving on a grand jury. Although the Committee believes that the need for secrecy of grand jury deliberations and voting is paramount, permitting interpreters to assist hearing and speech impaired jurors in the process seems a reasonable accommodation. *See also United States v. Dempsey,* 830 F.2d 1084 (10th Cir. 1987) (constitutionally rooted prohibition of non-jurors being present during deliberations was not violated by interpreter for deaf petit jury member).

The subdivision has also been restyled and reorganized.

Subdivision 6(f). The amendment to Rule 6(f) is intended to avoid the problems associated with bringing the entire jury to the court for the purpose of returning an indictment. Although the practice is long-standing, in *Breese v. United States,* 226 U.S. 1 (1912), the Court rejected the argument that the requirement was rooted in the Constitution and observed that if there were ever any strong reasons for the requirement, "they have disappeared, at least in part." 226 U.S. at 9. The Court added that grand jury's presence at the time the indictment was presented was a defect, if at all, in form only. *Id.* at 11. Given the problems of space, in some jurisdictions the grand jury sits in a building completely separated from the courtrooms. In those cases, moving the entire jury to the courtroom for the simple process of presenting the indictment may prove difficult and time consuming. Even where the jury is in the same location, having all of the jurors present can be unnecessarily cumbersome in light of the fact that filing of the indictment requires a certification as to how the jurors voted.

The amendment provides that the indictment must be presented either by the jurors themselves, as currently provided for in the rule, or by the foreperson or the deputy foreperson, acting on behalf of the jurors. In an appropriate case, the court might require all of the jurors to be present if it had inquiries about the indictment.

GAP Report—Rule 6.

The Committee modified Rule 6(d) to permit only interpreters assisting hearing or speech impaired grand jurors to be present during deliberations and voting.

2002 Amendments

The language of Rule 6 has been amended as part of the general restyling of the Criminal Rules to make them more easily understood and to make style and terminology consistent throughout the rules. These changes are intended to be stylistic, except as noted below.

The first change is in Rule 6(b)(1). The last sentence of current Rule 6(b)(1) provides that "Challenges shall be made before the administration of the oath to the jurors and shall be tried by the court." That language has been deleted from the amended rule. The remainder of this subdivision rests on the assumption that formal proceedings have begun against a person, i.e., an indictment has been returned. The Committee believed that although the first sentence reflects current practice of a defendant being able to challenge the composition or qualifications of the grand jurors after the indictment is returned, the second sentence does not comport with modern practice. That is, a defendant will normally not know the composition of the grand jury or identity of the grand jurors before they are administered their oath. Thus, there is no opportunity to challenge them and have the court decide the issue before the oath is given.

In Rule 6(d)(1), the term "court stenographer" has been changed to "court reporter." Similar changes have been made in Rule 6(e)(1) and (2).

Rule 6(e) continues to spell out the general rule of secrecy of grand-jury proceedings and the exceptions to that general rule. The last sentence in current Rule 6(e)(2), concerning contempt for violating Rule 6, now appears in Rule 6(e)(7). No change in substance is intended.

Rule 6(e)(3)(A)(ii) includes a new provision recognizing the sovereignty of Indian Tribes and the possibility that it would be necessary to disclose grand-jury information to appropriate tribal officials in order to enforce federal law. Similar language has been added to Rule 6(e)(3)(E)(iii).

Rule 6(e)(3)(A)(iii) is a new provision that recognizes that disclosure may be made to a person under 18 U.S.C. § 3322 (authorizing disclosures to an attorney for the government and banking regulators for enforcing civil forfeiture and civil banking laws). This reference was added to avoid the possibility of the amendments to Rule 6 superseding that particular statute.

Rule 6(e)(3)(C) consists of language located in current Rule 6(e)(3)(C)(iii). The Committee believed that this provision, which recognizes that prior court approval is not required for disclosure of a grand-jury matter to another grand jury, should be treated as a separate subdivision in revised Rule 6(e)(3). No change in practice is intended.

Rule 6(e)(3)(D) is new and reflects changes made to Rule 6 in the Uniting and Strengthening America by Providing Appropriate Tools Required to Intercept and Obstruct Terrorism (USA PATRIOT ACT) Act of 2001. The new provision permits an attorney for the government to disclose grand-jury matters involving foreign intelligence or counterintelligence to other Federal officials, in order to assist those officials in performing their duties. Under Rule 6(e)(3)(D)(i), the federal official receiving the information may only use the information as necessary and may be otherwise limited in making further disclosures. Any disclosures made under this provision must be reported under seal, within a reasonable time, to the court. The term "foreign intelligence information" is defined in Rule 6(e)(3)(D)(iii).

Rule 6(e)(3)(E)(iv) is a new provision that addresses disclosure of grand-jury information to armed forces personnel where the disclosure is for the purpose of enforcing military criminal law under the Uniform Code of Military Justice, 10 U.S.C. §§ 801–946. *See, e.g.,* Department of Defense Directive 5525.7 (January 22, 1985); 1984 Memorandum of Understanding Between Department of Justice and the Department of Defense Relating to the Investigation and Prosecution of Certain Crimes; Memorandum of Understanding Between the Departments of Justice and Transportation (Coast Guard) Relating to the Investigations and Prosecution of Crimes Over Which the Two Departments Have Concurrent Jurisdiction (October 9, 1967).

In Rule 6(e)(3)(F)(ii), the Committee considered whether to amend the language relating to "parties to the judicial proceeding" and determined that in the context of the rule it is understood that the parties referred to are the parties in the same judicial proceeding identified in Rule 6(e)(3)(E)(i).

The Committee decided to leave in subdivision (e) the provision stating that a "knowing violation of Rule 6" may be punished by contempt notwithstanding that, due to its apparent application to the entirety of the Rule, the provision seemingly is misplaced in subdivision (e). Research shows that Congress added the provision in 1977 and that it was crafted solely to deal with violations of the secrecy prohibitions in subdivision (e). *See* S. Rep. No. 95–354, p. 8 (1977). Supporting this narrow construction, the Committee found no reported decision involving an application or attempted use of the contempt sanction to a violation other than of the disclosure restrictions in subdivision (e). On the other hand, the Supreme Court in dicta did indicate on one occasion its arguable understanding that the contempt sanction would be available also for a violation of Rule 6(d) relating to who may be present during the grand jury's deliberations. *Bank of Nova Scotia v. United States*, 487 U.S. 250, 263 (1988).

In sum, it appears that the scope of the contempt sanction in Rule 6 is unsettled. Because the provision creates an offense, altering its scope may be beyond the authority bestowed by the Rules Enabling Act, 28 U.S.C. §§ 2071 et seq. *See* 28 U.S.C. § 2072(b) (Rules must not "abridge, enlarge, or modify any substantive right"). The Committee decided to leave the contempt provision in its present location in subdivision (e), because breaking it out into a separate subdivision could be construed to support the interpretation that the sanction may be applied to a knowing violation of any of the Rule's provisions rather than just those in subdivision (e). Whether or not that is a correct interpretation of the provision—a matter on which the Committee takes no position—must be determined by case law, or resolved by Congress.

Current Rule 6(g) has been divided into two new subdivisions, Rule 6(g), Discharge, and Rule 6(h), Excuse. The Committee added the phrase in Rule 6(g) "except as otherwise provided by statute," to recognize the provisions of 18 U.S.C. § 3331 relating to special grand juries.

Rule 6(i) is a new provision defining the term "Indian Tribe," a term used only in this rule.

2006 Amendments

Subdivision (e)(3) and (7). This amendment makes technical changes to the language added to Rule 6 by the Intelligence Reform and Terrorism Prevention Act of 2004, Pub.L. 108–458, Title VI, § 6501(a), 118 Stat. 3760, in order to bring the new language into conformity with the conventions introduced in the general restyling of the Criminal Rules. No substantive change is intended.

HISTORICAL NOTES

Codifications

Section 895 of Pub.L. 107–296, which purported to amend subd. (e) of this rule, failed to take into account the amendment of this rule by Order of the Supreme Court of the United States dated April 29, 2002, effective December 1, 2002, and was therefore incapable of execution. Section 895 of Pub.L. 107–296 provided:

"Rule 6(e) of the Federal Rules of Criminal Procedure is amended—

"**(1)** in paragraph (2), by inserting ', or of guidelines jointly issued by the Attorney General and Director of Central Intelligence pursuant to Rule 6,' after 'Rule 6'; and

"**(2)** in paragraph (3)—

"**(A)** in subparagraph (A)(ii), by inserting 'or of a foreign government' after '(including personnel of a state or subdivision of a state';

"**(B)** in subparagraph (C)(i)—

"**(i)** in subclause (I), by inserting before the semicolon the following: 'or, upon a request by an attorney for the government, when sought by a foreign court or prosecutor for use in an official criminal investigation';

"**(ii)** in subclause (IV)—

"**(I)** by inserting 'or foreign' after 'may disclose a violation of State';

"**(II)** by inserting 'or of a foreign government' after 'to an appropriate official of a State or subdivision of a State'; and

"**(III)** by striking 'or' at the end;

"**(iii)** by striking the period at the end of subclause (V) and inserting '; or'; and

"**(iv)** by adding at the end the following:

" '**(VI)** when matters involve a threat of actual or potential attack or other grave hostile acts of a foreign power or an agent of a foreign power, domestic or international sabotage, domestic or international terrorism, or clandestine intelligence gathering activities by an intelligence service or network of a foreign power or by an agent of a foreign power, within the United States or elsewhere, to any appropriate federal, state, local, or foreign government official for the purpose of preventing or responding to such a threat.'; and

"**(C)** in subparagraph (C)(iii)—

"**(i)** by striking 'Federal';

"**(ii)** by inserting 'or clause (i)(VI)' after 'clause (i)(V)'; and

"**(iii)** by adding at the end the following: 'Any state, local, or foreign official who receives information pursuant to clause (i)(VI) shall use that information only consistent with such guidelines as the Attorney General and Director of Central Intelligence shall jointly issue.'."

Pub.L. 98–473, Title II, §§ 215(f), 235, Oct. 12, 1984, 98 Stat. 2016, 2031, as amended by Pub.L. 99–217, § 4, Dec. 26, 1985, 99 Stat. 1728, provided that, effective Nov. 1, 1987, subd. (e)(3)(C) of this rule is amended by adding the following subdivision:

"**(iv)** when permitted by a court at the request of an attorney for the government, upon a showing that such matters may disclose a violation of state criminal law, to an appropriate official of a state or subdivision of a state for the purpose of enforcing such law".

Such amendment duplicates amendment made by Supreme Court of the United States order dated Apr. 29, 1985, eff. Aug. 1, 1985.

References in Text

The Uniform Code of Military Justice, referred to in subd. (e)(3)(E)(iv), is classified to chapter 47 of Title 10, 10 U.S.C.A. § 801 et seq.

Effective and Applicability Provisions

2002 Acts. Amendment to this Rule by Pub.L. 107–296 effective 60 days after Nov. 25, 2002, see Pub.L. 107–296, § 4, set out as a note under 6 U.S.C.A. § 101. Amendment was not executed to the text due to conflict with Court amendment, see Codifications note above.

1977 Acts. Amendment of this rule by order of the United States Supreme Court on Apr. 26, 1976, modified and approved by Pub.L. 95–78, effective Oct. 1, 1977, under section 4 of Pub.L. 95–78.

1976 Acts. Amendment of subd. (f) by the order of the United States Supreme Court of Apr. 26, 1976, effective Aug. 1, 1976, under section 1 of Pub.L. 94–349, July 8, 1976, 90 Stat. 822.

1984 Acts. Amendment by Pub.L. 98–473 effective on the first day of first calendar month beginning thirty six months after Oct. 12, 1984, applicable only to offenses committed after taking effect of sections 211 to 239 of Pub.L. 98–473, and except as otherwise provided for therein, see section 235 of Pub.L. 98–473, as amended, set out as a note under section 3551 of Title 18, Crimes and Criminal Procedure.

Change of Name

United States magistrate appointed under section 631 of Title 28, Judiciary and Judicial Procedure, to be known as United States magistrate judge after Dec. 1, 1990, with any reference to United States magistrate or magistrate in Title 28, in any other Federal statute, etc., deemed a reference to United States magistrate judge appointed under section 631 of Title 28, see section 321 of Pub.L. 101–650, set out as a note under section 631 of Title 28.

Rule 7. The Indictment and the Information

(a) When Used.

(1) Felony. An offense (other than criminal contempt) must be prosecuted by an indictment if it is punishable:

(A) by death; or

(B) by imprisonment for more than one year.

(2) Misdemeanor. An offense punishable by imprisonment for one year or less may be prosecuted in accordance with Rule 58(b)(1).

(b) Waiving Indictment. An offense punishable by imprisonment for more than one year may be prosecuted by information if the defendant—in open court and after being advised of the nature of the charge and of the defendant's rights—waives prosecution by indictment.

(c) Nature and Contents.

(1) In General. The indictment or information must be a plain, concise, and definite written statement of the essential facts constituting the offense charged and must be signed by an attorney for the government. It need not contain a formal introduction or conclusion. A count may incorporate by reference an allegation made in another count. A count may allege that the means by which the defendant committed the offense are unknown or that the defendant committed it by one or more specified means. For each count, the indictment or information must give the official or customary citation of the statute, rule, regulation, or other provision of law that the defendant is alleged to have violated. For purposes of an indictment referred to in section 3282 of title 18, United States Code, for which the identity of the defendant is unknown, it shall be sufficient for the indictment to describe the defendant as an individual whose name is unknown, but who has a particular DNA profile, as that term is defined in that section 3282.

(2) Criminal Forfeiture. No judgment of forfeiture may be entered in a criminal proceeding unless the indictment or the information provides notice that the defendant has an interest in property that is subject to forfeiture in accordance with the applicable statute.

(3) Citation Error. Unless the defendant was misled and thereby prejudiced, neither an error in a citation nor a citation's omission is a ground to dismiss the indictment or information or to reverse a conviction.

(d) Surplusage. Upon the defendant's motion, the court may strike surplusage from the indictment or information.

(e) Amending an Information. Unless an additional or different offense is charged or a substantial right of the defendant is prejudiced, the court may permit an information to be amended at any time before the verdict or finding.

(f) Bill of Particulars. The court may direct the government to file a bill of particulars. The defendant may move for a bill of particulars before or within 10 days after arraignment or at a later time if the court permits. The government may amend a bill of particulars subject to such conditions as justice requires.

(As amended Feb. 28, 1966, eff. July 1, 1966; Apr. 24, 1972, eff. Oct. 1, 1972; Apr. 30, 1979, eff. Aug. 1, 1979; Mar. 9, 1987, eff. Aug. 1, 1987; Apr. 17, 2000, eff. Dec. 1, 2000; Apr. 29, 2002, eff. Dec. 1, 2002; Apr. 30, 2003, Pub.L. 108–21, Title VI, § 610(b), 117 Stat. 692.)

ADVISORY COMMITTEE NOTES

1944 Adoption

Note to Subdivision (a). 1. This rule gives effect to the following provision of the Fifth Amendment to the Constitution of the United States: "No person shall be held to answer for a capital, or otherwise infamous crime, unless on a presentment or indictment of a Grand Jury * * * ". An infamous crime has been defined as a crime punishable by death or by imprisonment in a penitentiary or at hard labor, *Ex parte Wilson*, 114 U.S. 417, 427, 5 S.Ct. 935, 29 L.Ed. 89; *United States v. Moreland*, 258 U.S. 433, 42 S.Ct. 368, 66 L.Ed. 100, 24 A.L.R. 992. Any sentence of imprisonment for a term of over one year may be served in a penitentiary, if so directed by the Attorney General, 18 U.S.C. former § 753f [now 18 U.S.C. §§ 4082, 4083] (Commitment of persons by any court of the United States and the juvenile court of the District of Columbia; place of confinement; transfers). Consequently any offense punishable by imprisonment for a term of over one year is an infamous crime.

2. Petty offenses and misdemeanors for which no infamous punishment is prescribed may now be prosecuted by information, 18 U.S.C. former § 541 (now § 1) (Felonies and misdemeanors); *Duke v. United States*, 301 U.S. 492, 57 S.Ct. 835, 81 L.Ed. 1243.

3. For a discussion of the provision for waiver of indictment, see Note to Rule 7(b), *infra*.

4. Presentment is not included as an additional type of formal accusation, since presentments as a method of instituting prosecutions are obsolete, at least as concerns the Federal courts.

Note to Subdivision (b). 1. Opportunity to waive indictment and to consent to prosecution by information will be a substantial aid to defendants, especially those who, because of inability to give bail, are incarcerated pending action of the grand jury, but desire to plead guilty. This rule is particularly important in those districts in which considerable intervals occur between sessions of the grand jury. In many districts where the grand jury meets infrequently a defendant unable to give bail and desiring to plead guilty is compelled to spend many days, and sometimes many weeks, and even months, in jail before he can begin the service of his sentence, whatever it may be, awaiting the action of a grand jury. Homer Cummings, 29 A.B.A.Jour. 654–655; Vanderbilt, 29 A.B.A.Jour. 376, 377; Robinson, 27 Jour. of the Am. Judicature Soc. 38, 45; Medalie, 4 Lawyers Guild R. (3) 1, 3. The rule contains safeguards against improvident waivers.

The Judicial Conference of Senior Circuit Judges, in September 1941, recommended that "existing law or established procedure be so changed that a defendant may waive indictment and plead guilty to an information filed by a United States attorney in all cases except capital felonies." Report of the Judicial Conference of Senior Circuit Judges (1941) 13. In September 1942 the Judicial Conference recommended that provision be made "for waiver of indictment and jury trial, so that persons accused of crime may not be held in jail needlessly pending trial." Id. (1942) 8.

Attorneys General of the United States have from time to time recommended legislation to permit defendants to waive indictment and to consent to prosecution by information. See Annual Report of the Attorney General of the United States (Mitchell) (1931) 3; Id. (Mitchell) (1932) 6; Id. (Cummings) (1933) 1, (1936) 2, (1937) 11, (1938) 9; Id. (Murphy) (1939) 7.

The Federal Juvenile Delinquency Act now permits a juvenile charged with an offense not punishable by death or life imprisonment to consent to prosecution by information on a charge of juvenile delinquency, 18 U.S.C. former § 922 (now §§ 5032, 5033).

2. On the constitutionality of this rule, see United States v. Gill, D.C.N.M., 55 F.2d 399, holding that the constitutional guaranty of indictment by grand jury may be waived by defendant. It has also been held that other constitutional guaranties may be waived by the defendant, e.g., *Patton v. United States*, 281 U.S. 276, 50 S.Ct. 253, 74 L.Ed. 854, 70 A.L.R. 263 (trial by jury); *Johnson v. Zerbst*, 304 U.S. 458, 465, 58 S.Ct. 1019, 82 L.Ed. 1461, 146 A.L.R. 357 (right of counsel); *Trono v. United States*, 199 U.S. 521, 534, 26 S.Ct. 121, 50 L.Ed. 292, 4 Ann.Cas. 773 (protection against double jeopardy); *United States v. Murdock*, 284 U.S. 141, 148, 52 S.Ct. 63, 76 L.Ed. 210, 82 A.L.R. 1376 (privilege against self-incrimination); *Diaz v. United States*, 223 U.S. 442, 450, 32 S.Ct. 250, 56 L.Ed. 500, Ann.Cas.1913C, 1138 (right of confrontation).

Note to Subdivision (c). 1. This rule introduces a simple form of indictment, illustrated by Forms 1 to 11 in the Appendix of Forms [now abrogated]. Cf. Rule 8(a) of the Federal Rules of Civil Procedure, 28 U.S.C. following § 2072. For discussion of the effect of this rule and a comparison between the present form of indictment and the simple form introduced by this rule, see Vanderbilt, 29 A.B.A.Jour. 376, 377; Homer Cummings, 29 A.B.A.Jour. 654, 655; Holtzoff, 3 F.R.D. 445, 448–449; Holtzoff, 12 Geo.Washington L.R. 119, 123–126; Medalie, 4 Lawyers Guild R. (3) 1, 3.

2. The provision contained in the fifth sentence that it may be alleged in a single count that the means by which the defendant committed the offense are unknown, or that he committed it by one or more specified means, is intended to eliminate the use of multiple counts for the purpose of alleging the commission of the offense by different means or in different ways. Cf. Federal Rules of Civil Procedure, Rule 8(e)(2).

3. The law at present regards citations to statutes or regulations as not a part of the indictment. A conviction may be sustained on the basis of a statute or regulation other than that cited. *Williams v. United States*, 168 U.S. 382, 389, 18 S.Ct. 92, 42 L.Ed. 509; *United States v. Hutcheson*, 312 U.S. 219, 229, 61 S.Ct. 463, 85 L.Ed. 788. The provision of the rule, in view of the many statutes and regulations, is for the benefit of the defendant and is not intended to cause a dismissal of the indictment, but simply to provide a means by which he can be properly informed without danger to the prosecution.

Note to Subdivision (d). This rule introduces a means of protecting the defendant against immaterial or irrelevant allegations in an indictment or information, which may, however, be prejudicial. The authority of the court to strike such surplusage is to be limited to doing so on defendant's motion, in the light of the rule that the guaranty of indictment by a grand jury implies that an indictment may not be amended, *Ex parte Bain*, 121 U.S. 1, 7 S.Ct. 781, 30 L.Ed. 849. By making such a motion, the defendant would, however, waive his rights in this respect.

Note to Subdivision (e). This rule continues the existing law that, unlike an indictment, an information may be amended, *Muncy v. United States*, 4 Cir., 289 F. 780.

Note to Subdivision (f). This rule is substantially a restatement of existing law on bills of particulars.

1966 Amendments

The amendment to the first sentence eliminating the requirement of a showing of cause is designed to encourage a more liberal attitude by the courts toward bills of particulars without taking away the discretion which courts must have in dealing with such motions in individual cases. For an illustration of wise use of this discretion see the opinion by Justice Whittaker written when he was a district judge in *United States v. Smith*, 16 F.R.D. 372 (W.D.Mo.1954).

The amendment to the second sentence gives discretion to the court to permit late filing of motions for bills of particulars in meritorious cases. Use of late motions for the purpose of delaying trial should not, of course be permitted. The courts have not been agreed as to their power to accept late motions in the absence of a local rule or a previous order. See *United States v. Miller*, 217 F.Supp. 760 (E.D.Pa.1963); *United States v. Taylor*, 25 F.R.D. 225 (E.D.N.Y.1960); *United States v. Sterling*, 122 F.Supp. 81 (E.D.Pa.1954) (all taking a limited view of the power of the court). But cf. *United States v. Brown*, 179 F.Supp. 893 (E.D.N.Y.1959) (exercising discretion to permit an out of time motion).

1972 Amendments

Subdivision (c)(2) is new. It is intended to provide procedural implementation of the recently enacted criminal forfeiture provision of the Organized Crime Control Act of 1970, Title IX, § 1963, and the Comprehensive Drug Abuse Prevention and Control Act of 1970, Title II, § 408(a)(2).

The Congress viewed the provisions of the Organized Crime Control Act of 1970 as reestablishing a limited common law criminal forfeiture. S.Rep.No. 91–617, 91st Cong., 1st Sess., 79–80 (1969). The legislative history of the Comprehensive Drug Abuse Prevention and Control Act of 1970 indicates a congressional purpose to have similar procedures apply to the forfeiture of profits or interests under that act. H.Rep. No. 91–1444 (part I), 91st Cong., 2d Sess. 81–85 (1970).

Under the common law, in a criminal forfeiture proceeding the defendant was apparently entitled to notice, trial, and a special jury finding on the factual issues surrounding the declaration of forfeiture which followed his criminal conviction. Subdivision (c)(2) provides for notice. Changes in rules 31 and 32 provide for a special jury finding and for a judgment authorizing the Attorney General to seize the interest or property forfeited.

1979 Amendments

The amendment to rule 7(c) (2) is intended to clarify its meaning. Subdivision (c) (2) was added in 1972, and, as noted in the Advisory Committee Note thereto, was "intended to provide procedural implementation of the recently enacted criminal forfeiture provision of the Organized Crime Control Act of 1970, Title IX, § 1963, and the Comprehensive Drug Abuse Prevention and Control Act of 1970, Title II, § 408(a) (2)." These provisions reestablished a limited common law criminal forfeiture, necessitating the addition of subdivision (c) (2) and corresponding changes in rules 31 and 32, for at common law the defendant in a criminal forfeiture proceeding was entitled to notice, trial, and a special jury finding on the factual issues surrounding the declaration of forfeiture which followed his criminal conviction.

Although there is some doubt as to what forfeitures should be characterized as "punitive" rather than "remedial," see Note, 62 Cornell L.Rev. 768 (1977), subdivision (c) (2) is intended to apply to those forfeitures which are criminal in the sense that they result from a special verdict under rule 31(e) and a judgment under rule 32(b) (2), and not to those resulting from a separate in rem proceeding. Because some confusion in this regard has resulted from the present wording of subdivision (c) (2), United States v. Hall, 521 F.2d 406 (9th Cir. 1975), a clarifying amendment is in order.

1987 Amendments

The amendments are technical. No substantive change is intended.

2000 Amendments

The rule is amended to reflect new Rule 32.2, which now governs criminal forfeiture procedures.

GAP Report—Rule 7

The Committee initially made no changes to the published draft of the Rule 7 amendment. However, because of changes to Rule 32.2(a), discussed *infra*, the proposed language has been changed to reflect that the indictment must provide notice of an intent to seek forfeiture.

2002 Amendments

The language of Rule 7 has been amended as part of the general restyling of the Criminal Rules to make them more easily understood and to make style and terminology consistent throughout the rules. These changes are intended to be stylistic.

The Committee has deleted the references to "hard labor" in the rule. This punishment is not found in current federal statutes.

The Committee added an exception for criminal contempt to the requirement in Rule 7(a)(1) that a prosecution for felony must be initiated by indictment. This is consistent with case law, *e.g., United States v. Eichhorst*, 544 F.2d 1383 (7th Cir. 1976), which has sustained the use of the special procedures for instituting criminal contempt proceedings found in Rule 42. While indictment is not a required method of bringing felony criminal contempt charges, however, it is a permissible one. *See United States v. Williams*, 622 F.2d 830 (5th Cir. 1980). No change in practice is intended.

The title of Rule 7(c)(3) has been amended. The Committee believed that potential confusion could arise with the use of the term "harmless error." Rule 52, which deals with the issues of harmless error and plain error, is sufficient to address the topic. Potentially, the topic of harmless error could arise with regard to any of the other rules and there is insufficient need to highlight the term in Rule 7. Rule 7(c)(3), on the other hand, focuses specifically on the effect of an error in the citation of authority in the indictment. That material remains but without any reference to harmless error.

HISTORICAL NOTES

Guam

Applicability of requirement for indictment by grand jury in certain cases, to criminal prosecutions in the District Court of Guam, see section 1424 of Title 48, Territories and Insular Possessions.

Virgin Islands

Prosecutions in District Court of the Virgin Islands to be by information except such as may be required by local law to be by indictment by grand jury, see section 1615 of Title 48, Territories and Insular Possessions.

Rule 8. Joinder of Offenses or Defendants

(a) Joinder of Offenses. The indictment or information may charge a defendant in separate counts with 2 or more offenses if the offenses charged—whether felonies or misdemeanors or both—are of the same or similar character, or are based on the same act or transaction, or are connected with or constitute parts of a common scheme or plan.

(b) Joinder of Defendants. The indictment or information may charge 2 or more defendants if they are alleged to have participated in the same act or transaction, or in the same series of acts or transactions, constituting an offense or offenses. The defendants may be charged in one or more counts together or separately. All defendants need not be charged in each count.

(As amended Apr. 29, 2002, eff. Dec. 1, 2002.)

ADVISORY COMMITTEE NOTES

1944 Adoption

Note to Subdivision (a). This rule is substantially a restatement of existing law, 18 U.S.C. former § 557 (Indictments and presentments; joinder of charges).

Note to Subdivision (b). The first sentence of the rule is substantially a restatement of existing law, 9 Edmunds, Cyclopedia of Federal Procedure, 2d Ed., 4116. The second sentence formulates a practice now approved in some circuits, *Caringella v. United States*, 78 F.2d 563, 567, C.C.A.7th.

2002 Amendments

The language of Rule 8 has been amended as part of the general restyling of the Criminal Rules to make them more easily understood and to make style and terminology consistent throughout the rules. These changes are intended to be stylistic only.

Rule 9. Arrest Warrant or Summons on an Indictment or Information

(a) Issuance. The court must issue a warrant—or at the government's request, a summons—for each defendant named in an indictment or named in an information if one or more affidavits accompanying the information establish probable cause to believe that an offense has been committed and that the defendant committed it. The court may issue more than one warrant or summons for the same defendant. If a defendant fails to appear in response to a summons, the court may, and upon request of an attorney for the government must, issue a warrant. The court must issue the arrest warrant to an officer authorized to execute it or the summons to a person authorized to serve it.

(b) Form.

(1) Warrant. The warrant must conform to Rule 4(b)(1) except that it must be signed by the clerk and must describe the offense charged in the indictment or information.

(2) Summons. The summons must be in the same form as a warrant except that it must require the defendant to appear before the court at a stated time and place.

(c) Execution or Service; Return; Initial Appearance.

(1) Execution or Service.

(A) The warrant must be executed or the summons served as provided in Rule 4(c)(1), (2), and (3).

(B) The officer executing the warrant must proceed in accordance with Rule 5(a)(1).

(2) Return. A warrant or summons must be returned in accordance with Rule 4(c)(4).

(3) Initial Appearance. When an arrested or summoned defendant first appears before the court, the judge must proceed under Rule 5.

(As amended Apr. 24, 1972, eff. Oct. 1, 1972; Apr. 22, 1974, eff. Dec. 1, 1975; July 31, 1975, Pub.L. 94–64, § 3(4), 89 Stat. 370; Dec. 12, 1975, Pub.L. 94–149, § 5, 89 Stat. 806; Apr. 30, 1979, eff. Aug. 1, 1979; Apr. 28, 1982, eff. Aug. 1, 1982; Apr. 22, 1993, eff. Dec. 1, 1993; Apr. 29, 2002, eff. Dec. 1, 2002.)

ADVISORY COMMITTEE NOTES

1944 Adoption

1. See Note to Rule 4, supra.

2. The provision of rule 9(a) that a warrant may be issued on the basis of an information only if the latter is supported by oath is necessitated by the Fourth Amendment to the Constitution of the United States. See *Albrecht v. United States*, 47 S.Ct. 250, 273 U.S. 1, 5, 71 L.Ed. 505.

3. The provision of rule 9(b)(1) that the amount of bail may be fixed by the court and endorsed on the warrant states a practice now prevailing in many districts and is intended to facilitate the giving of bail by the defendant and eliminate delays between the arrest and the giving of bail, which might ensue if bail cannot be fixed until after arrest.

1972 Amendments

Subdivision (b) is amended to make clear that the person arrested shall be brought before a United States magistrate if the information or indictment charges a "minor offense" triable by the United States magistrate.

Subdivision (c) is amended to reflect the office of United States magistrate.

Subdivision (d) is new. It provides for a remand to the United States magistrate of cases in which the person is charged with a "minor offense." The magistrate can then proceed in accordance with rule 5 to try the case if the right to trial before a judge of the district court is waived.

1974 Amendments

Rule 9 is revised to give high priority to the issuance of a summons unless a "valid reason" is given for the issuance of an arrest warrant. See a comparable provision in rule 4.

Under the rule, a summons will issue by the clerk unless the attorney for the government presents a valid reason for the issuance of an arrest warrant. Under the old rule, it has been argued that the court must issue an arrest warrant if one is desired by the attorney for the government. See authorities listed in Frankel, Bench Warrants Upon the Prosecutor's Demand: A View From the Bench, 71 Colum.L.Rev. 403, 410 n. 25 (1971). For an expression of the view that this is undesirable policy, see Frankel, *supra*, pp. 410–415.

A summons may issue if there is an information supported by oath. The indictment itself is sufficient to establish the existence of probable cause. See C. Wright, Federal Practice and Procedure: Criminal § 151 (1969); 8 J. Moore, Federal Practice ¶ 9.02[2] at p. 9–4 (2d ed.) Cipes (1969); *Giordenello v. United States*, 357 U.S. 480, 78 S.Ct. 1245, 2 L.Ed.2d 1503 (1958). This is not necessarily true in the case of an information. See C. Wright, *supra*, § 151; 8 J. Moore, *supra*, ¶ 9.02. If the government requests a warrant rather than a summons, good practice would obviously require the judge to satisfy himself that there is probable cause. This may appear from the information or from an affidavit filed with the information. Also a defendant can, at a proper time, challenge an information issued without probable cause.

1975 Enactment

A. Amendments Proposed by the Supreme Court. Rule 9 of the Federal Rules of Criminal Procedure is closely related to Rule 4. Rule 9 deals with arrest procedures after an information has been filed or an indictment returned. The present rule gives the prosecutor the authority to decide whether a summons or a warrant shall issue.

The Supreme Court's amendments to Rule 9 parallel its amendments to Rule 4. The basic change made in Rule 4 is also made in Rule 9.

B. Committee Action. For the reasons set forth above in connection with Rule 4, the Committee endorses and accepts the basic change in Rule 9. The Committee made changes in Rule 9 similar to the changes it made in Rule 4. House Report No. 94–247.

1979 Amendments

Subdivision (a) is amended to make explicit the fact that a warrant may issue upon the basis of an information only if the information or an affidavit filed with the information shows probable cause for the arrest. This had generally been assumed to be the state of the law even though not specifically set out in rule 9; see C. Wright, Federal Practice and Procedure: Criminal § 151 (1969); 8 J. Moore, Federal Practice par. 9.02[2] (2d ed. 1976).

In *Gerstein v. Pugh*, 420 U.S. 103 (1975), the Supreme Court rejected the contention "that the prosecutor's decision to file an information is itself a determination of probable cause that furnishes sufficient reason to detain a defendant pending trial," commenting:

Although a conscientious decision that the evidence warrants prosecution affords a measure of protection against unfounded detention, we do not think prosecutorial judgment standing alone meets the requirements of the Fourth Amendment. Indeed, we think the Court's previous decisions compel disapproval of [such] procedure. In *Albrecht v. United States*, 273 U.S. 1, 5, 47 S.Ct. 250, 251, 71 L.Ed. 505 (1927), the Court held that an arrest warrant issued solely upon a United States Attorney's information was invalid because the accompanying affidavits were defective. Although the Court's opinion did not explicitly state that the prosecutor's official oath could not furnish probable cause, that conclusion was implicit in the judgment that the arrest was illegal under the Fourth Amendment.

No change is made in the rule with respect to warrants issuing upon indictments. In *Gerstein*, the Court indicated it was not disturbing the prior rule that "an indictment, 'fair upon its face,' and returned by a 'properly constituted grand jury' conclusively determines the existence of probable cause and requires issuance of an arrest warrant without further inquiry." See *Ex parte United States*, 287 U.S. 241, 250 (1932).

The provision to the effect that a summons shall issue "by direction of the court" has been eliminated because it conflicts with the first sentence of the rule, which states that a warrant "shall" issue when requested by the attorney for the government, if properly supported. However, an addition has been made providing that if the attorney for the government does not make a request for either a warrant or summons, then the court may in its discretion issue either one. Other stylistic changes ensure greater consistency with comparable provisions in rule 4.

1982 Amendments

Subdivision (a). The amendment of subdivision (a), by reference to Rule 5, clarifies what is to be done once the defendant is brought before the magistrate. This means, among other things, that no preliminary hearing is to be held in a Rule 9 case, as Rule 5(c) provides that no such hearing is to be had "if the defendant is indicted or if an information against the defendant is filed."

Subdivision (b). The amendment of subdivision (b) conforms Rule 9 to the comparable provisions in Rule 4(c) (1) and (2).

Subdivision (c). The amendment of subdivision (c) conforms Rule 9 to the comparable provisions in Rules 4(d) (4) and 5(a) concerning return of the warrant.

Subdivision (d). This subdivision, incorrect in its present form in light of the recent amendment of 18 U.S.C. § 3401(a), has been abrogated as unnecessary in light of the change to subdivision (a).

1993 Amendments

The Rule is amended to conform to the Judicial Improvements Act of 1990 [P.L. 101–650, Title III, Section 321] which provides that each United States magistrate appointed under section 631 of title 28, United States Code, shall be known as a United States magistrate judge.

2002 Amendments

The language of Rule 9 has been amended as part of the general restyling of the Criminal Rules to make them more easily understood and to make style and terminology consistent throughout the rules. These changes are intended to be stylistic only, except as noted below.

Rule 9 has been changed to reflect its relationship to Rule 4 procedures for obtaining an arrest warrant or summons. Thus, rather than simply repeating material that is already located in Rule 4, the Committee determined that where appropriate, Rule 9 should simply direct the reader to the procedures specified in Rule 4.

Rule 9(a) has been amended to permit a judge discretion whether to issue an arrest warrant when a defendant fails to respond to a summons on a complaint. Under the current language of the rule, if the defendant fails to appear, the judge must issue a warrant. Under the amended version, if the defendant fails to appear and the government requests that a warrant be issued, the judge must issue one. In the absence of such a request, the judge has the discretion to do so. This change mirrors language in amended Rule 4(a).

A second amendment has been made in Rule 9(b)(1). The rule has been amended to delete language permitting the court to set the amount of bail on the warrant. The Committee believes that this language is inconsistent with the 1984 Bail Reform Act. *See United States v. Thomas*, 992 F. Supp. 782 (D.V.I. 1998) (bail amount endorsed on warrant that has not been determined in proceedings conducted under Bail Reform Act has no bearing on decision by judge conducting Rule 40 hearing).

The language in current Rule 9(c)(1), concerning service of a summons on an organization, has been moved to Rule 4.

HISTORICAL NOTES

Change of Name

United States magistrate appointed under section 631 of Title 28, Judiciary and Judicial Procedure, to be known as United States magistrate judge after Dec. 1, 1990, with any reference to United States magistrate or magistrate in Title

28, in any other Federal statute, etc., deemed a reference to United States magistrate judge appointed under section 631 of Title 28, see section 321 of Pub.L. 101–650, set out as a note under section 631 of Title 28.

Effective and Applicability Provisions

1975 Acts. Amendments of this rule embraced in the order of the United States Supreme Court on Apr. 22, 1974, and the amendments of this rule made by section 3 of Pub.L. 94–64, effective Dec. 1, 1975, see section 2 of Pub.L. 94–64, set out as a note under rule 4 of these rules.

IV. ARRAIGNMENT AND PREPARATION FOR TRIAL

Rule 10. Arraignment

(a) In General. An arraignment must be conducted in open court and must consist of:

(1) ensuring that the defendant has a copy of the indictment or information;

(2) reading the indictment or information to the defendant or stating to the defendant the substance of the charge; and then

(3) asking the defendant to plead to the indictment or information.

(b) Waiving Appearance. A defendant need not be present for the arraignment if:

(1) the defendant has been charged by indictment or misdemeanor information;

(2) the defendant, in a written waiver signed by both the defendant and defense counsel, has waived appearance and has affirmed that the defendant received a copy of the indictment or information and that the plea is not guilty; and

(3) the court accepts the waiver.

(c) Video Teleconferencing. Video teleconferencing may be used to arraign a defendant if the defendant consents.

(As amended Mar. 9, 1987, eff. Aug. 1, 1987; Apr. 29, 2002, eff. Dec. 1, 2002.)

ADVISORY COMMITTEE NOTES

1944 Adoption

1. The first sentence states the prevailing practice.

2. The requirement that the defendant shall be given a copy of the indictment or information before he is called upon to plead, contained in the second sentence, is new.

3. Failure to comply with arraignment requirements has been held not to be jurisdictional, but a mere technical irregularity not warranting a reversal of a conviction, if not raised before trial. *Garland v. State of Washington*, 34 S.Ct. 456, 232 U.S. 642, 58 L.Ed. 772.

1987 Amendments

The amendments are technical. No substantive change is intended.

2002 Amendments

The language of Rule 10 has been amended as part of the general restyling of the Criminal Rules to make them more easily understood and to make style and terminology consistent throughout the rules. These changes are intended to be stylistic only, except as noted below.

Read together, Rules 10 and 43 require the defendant to be physically present in court for the arraignment. *See, e.g., Valenzuela-Gonzales v. United States*, 915 F.2d 1276, 1280 (9th Cir. 1990) (Rules 10 and 43 are broader in protection than the Constitution). The amendments to Rule 10 create two exceptions to that requirement. The first provides that the court may hold an arraignment in the defendant's absence when the defendant has waived the right to be present in writing and the court consents to that waiver. The second permits the court to hold arraignments by video teleconferencing when the defendant is at a different location. A conforming amendment has also been made to Rule 43.

In amending Rule 10 and Rule 43, the Committee was concerned that permitting a defendant to be absent from the arraignment could be viewed as an erosion of an important element of the judicial process. First, it may be important for a defendant to see and experience first-hand the formal impact of the reading of the charge. Second, it may be necessary for the court to personally see and speak with the defendant at the arraignment, especially when there is a real question whether the defendant actually understands the gravity of the proceedings. And third, there may be difficulties in providing the defendant with effective and confidential assistance of counsel if counsel, but not the defendant, appears at the arraignment.

The Committee nonetheless believed that in appropriate circumstances the court, and the defendant, should have the option of conducting the arraignment in the defendant's absence. The question of when it would be appropriate for a defendant to waive an appearance is not spelled out in the rule. That is left to the defendant and the court in each case.

A critical element to the amendment is that no matter how convenient or cost effective a defendant's absence might be, the defendant's right to be present in court stands unless he or she waives that right in writing. Under the amendment, both the defendant and the defendant's attorney must sign the waiver. Further, the amendment requires that the waiver specifically state that the defendant has received a copy of the charging instrument.

If the trial court has reason to believe that in a particular case the defendant should not be permitted to waive the right, the court may reject the waiver and require that the defendant actually appear in court. That might be particularly appropriate when the court wishes to discuss substantive or procedural matters in conjunction with the arraignment and the court believes that the defendant's presence is important in resolving those matters. It might also be appropriate to reject a requested waiver where an attorney for the government presents reasons for requiring the defendant to appear personally.

The amendment does not permit waiver of an appearance when the defendant is charged with a felony information. In that instance, the defendant is required by Rule 7(b) to be present in court to waive the indictment. Nor does the amendment permit a waiver of appearance when the defendant is standing mute (*see* Rule 11(a)(4)), or entering a conditional plea (*see* Rule 11(a)(2)), a nolo contendere plea (*see* Rule 11(a)(3)), or a guilty plea (*see* Rule 11(a)(1)). In each of those instances the Committee believed that it was more appropriate for the defendant to appear personally before the court.

It is important to note that the amendment does not permit the defendant to waive the arraignment itself, which may be a triggering mechanism for other rules.

Rule 10(c) addresses the second substantive change in the rule. That provision permits the court to conduct arraignments through video teleconferencing, if the defendant waives the right to be arraigned in court. Although the practice is now used in state courts and in some federal courts, Rules 10 and 43 have generally prevented federal courts from using that method for arraignments in criminal cases. *See, e.g., Valenzuela-Gonzales v. United States, supra* (Rules 10 and 43 mandate physical presence of defendant at arraignment and that arraignment take place in open court). A similar amendment was proposed by the Committee in 1993 and published for public comment. The amendment was later withdrawn from consideration in order to consider the results of several planned pilot programs. Upon further consideration, the Committee believed that the benefits of using video teleconferencing outweighed the costs of doing so. This amendment also parallels an amendment in Rule 5(f) that would permit initial appearances to be conducted by video teleconferencing.

In amending Rules 5, 10, and 43 (which generally requires the defendant's presence at all proceedings), the Committee carefully considered the argument that permitting a defendant to appear by video teleconferencing might be considered an erosion of an important element of the judicial process. Much can be lost when video teleconferencing occurs. First, the setting itself may not promote the public's confidence in the integrity and solemnity of a federal criminal proceeding; that is the view of some who have witnessed the use of such proceedings in some state jurisdictions. While it is difficult to quantify the intangible benefits and impact of requiring a defendant to be brought before a federal judicial officer in a federal courtroom, the Committee realizes that something is lost when a defendant is not required to make a personal appearance. A related consideration is that the defendant may be located in a room that bears no resemblance whatsoever to a judicial forum and the equipment may be inadequate for high-quality transmissions. Second, using video teleconferencing can interfere with counsel's ability to meet personally with his or her client at what, at least in that jurisdiction, might be an important appearance before a magistrate judge. Third, the defendant may miss an opportunity to meet with family or friends, and others who might be able to assist the defendant, especially in any attempts to obtain bail. Finally, the magistrate judge may miss an opportunity to accurately assess the physical, emotional, and mental condition of a defendant—a factor that may weigh on pretrial decisions, such as release from detention.

On the other hand, the Committee considered that in some jurisdictions, the courts face a high volume of criminal proceedings. The Committee was also persuaded to adopt the amendment because in some jurisdictions delays may occur in travel time from one location to another—in some cases requiring either the magistrate judge or the participants to travel long distances. In those instances, it is not unusual for a defense counsel to recognize the benefit of conducting a video teleconferenced proceeding, which will eliminate lengthy and sometimes expensive travel or permit the arraignment to be conducted much sooner. Finally, the Committee was aware that in some jurisdictions, courtrooms now contain high quality technology for conducting such procedures, and that some courts are already using video teleconferencing—with the consent of the parties.

The Committee believed that, on balance and in appropriate circumstances, the court and the defendant should have the option of using video teleconferencing for arraignments, as long as the defendant consents to that procedure. The question of when it would be appropriate for a defendant to consent is not spelled out in the rule. That is left to the defendant and the court in each case. Although the rule does not specify any particular technical requirements regarding the system to be used, if the equipment or technology is deficient, the public may lose confidence in the integrity and dignity of the proceedings.

The amendment does not require a court to adopt or use video teleconferencing. In deciding whether to use such procedures, a court may wish to consider establishing clearly articulated standards and procedures. For example, the court would normally want to insure that the location used for televising the video teleconferencing is conducive to the solemnity of a federal criminal proceeding. That might require additional coordination, for example, with the detention facility to insure that the room, furniture, and furnishings reflect the dignity associated with a federal courtroom. Provision should also be made to insure that the judge, or a surrogate, is in a position to carefully assess the condition of the defendant. And the court should also consider establishing procedures for insuring that counsel and the defendant (and even the defendant's immediate family) are provided an ample opportunity to confer in private.

Although the rule requires the defendant to waive a personal appearance for an arraignment, the rule does not require that the waiver for video teleconferencing be in writing. Nor does it require that the defendant waive that appearance in person, in open court. It would normally be sufficient for the defendant to waive an appearance while participating through a video teleconference.

The amendment leaves to the courts the decision first, whether to permit video arraignments, and second, the procedures to be used. The Committee was satisfied that the technology has progressed to the point that video teleconferencing can address the concerns raised in the past about the ability of the court and the defendant to see each other and for the defendant and counsel to be in contact with each other, either at the same location or by a secure remote connection.

Rule 11. Pleas

(a) Entering a Plea.

(1) In General. A defendant may plead not guilty, guilty, or (with the court's consent) nolo contendere.

(2) Conditional Plea. With the consent of the court and the government, a defendant may enter a conditional plea of guilty or nolo contendere, reserving in writing the right to have an appellate court review an adverse determination of a specified pretrial motion. A defendant who prevails on appeal may then withdraw the plea.

(3) Nolo Contendere Plea. Before accepting a plea of nolo contendere, the court must consider the parties' views and the public interest in the effective administration of justice.

(4) Failure to Enter a Plea. If a defendant refuses to enter a plea or if a defendant organization fails to appear, the court must enter a plea of not guilty.

(b) Considering and Accepting a Guilty or Nolo Contendere Plea.

(1) Advising and Questioning the Defendant. Before the court accepts a plea of guilty or nolo contendere, the defendant may be placed under oath, and the court must address the defendant personally in open court. During this address, the court must inform the defendant of, and determine that the defendant understands, the following:

(A) the government's right, in a prosecution for perjury or false statement, to use against the defendant any statement that the defendant gives under oath;

(B) the right to plead not guilty, or having already so pleaded, to persist in that plea;

(C) the right to a jury trial;

(D) the right to be represented by counsel—and if necessary have the court appoint counsel—at trial and at every other stage of the proceeding;

(E) the right at trial to confront and cross-examine adverse witnesses, to be protected from compelled self-incrimination, to testify and present evidence, and to compel the attendance of witnesses;

(F) the defendant's waiver of these trial rights if the court accepts a plea of guilty or nolo contendere;

(G) the nature of each charge to which the defendant is pleading;

(H) any maximum possible penalty, including imprisonment, fine, and term of supervised release;

(I) any mandatory minimum penalty;

(J) any applicable forfeiture;

(K) the court's authority to order restitution;

(L) the court's obligation to impose a special assessment;

(M) the court's obligation to apply the Sentencing Guidelines, and the court's discretion to depart from those guidelines under some circumstances; and

(N) the terms of any plea-agreement provision waiving the right to appeal or to collaterally attack the sentence.

(2) Ensuring That a Plea Is Voluntary. Before accepting a plea of guilty or nolo contendere, the court must address the defendant personally in open court and determine that the plea is voluntary and did not result from force, threats, or promises (other than promises in a plea agreement).

(3) Determining the Factual Basis for a Plea. Before entering judgment on a guilty plea, the court must determine that there is a factual basis for the plea.

(c) Plea Agreement Procedure.

(1) In General. An attorney for the government and the defendant's attorney, or the defendant when proceeding pro se, may discuss and reach a plea agreement. The court must not participate in these discussions. If the defendant pleads guilty or nolo contendere to either a charged offense or a lesser or related offense, the plea agreement may specify that an attorney for the government will:

(A) not bring, or will move to dismiss, other charges;

(B) recommend, or agree not to oppose the defendant's request, that a particular sentence or sentencing range is appropriate or that a particular provision of the Sentencing Guidelines, or policy statement, or sentencing factor does or does not apply (such a recommendation or request does not bind the court); or

(C) agree that a specific sentence or sentencing range is the appropriate disposition of the case, or that a particular provision of the Sentencing Guidelines, or policy statement, or sentencing factor does or does not apply (such a recommendation or request binds the court once the court accepts the plea agreement).

(2) Disclosing a Plea Agreement. The parties must disclose the plea agreement in open court when the plea is offered, unless the court for good cause allows the parties to disclose the plea agreement in camera.

(3) Judicial Consideration of a Plea Agreement.

(A) To the extent the plea agreement is of the type specified in Rule 11(c)(1)(A) or (C), the court may accept the agreement, reject it, or defer a decision until the court has reviewed the presentence report.

(B) To the extent the plea agreement is of the type specified in Rule 11(c)(1)(B), the court must advise the defendant that the defendant has no right to withdraw the plea if the court does not follow the recommendation or request.

(4) Accepting a Plea Agreement. If the court accepts the plea agreement, it must inform the defendant that to the extent the plea agreement is of the type specified in Rule 11(c)(1)(A) or (C), the agreed disposition will be included in the judgment.

(5) Rejecting a Plea Agreement. If the court rejects a plea agreement containing provisions of the type specified in Rule 11(c)(1)(A) or (C), the court must do the following on the record and in open court (or, for good cause, in camera):

(A) inform the parties that the court rejects the plea agreement;

(B) advise the defendant personally that the court is not required to follow the plea agreement and give the defendant an opportunity to withdraw the plea; and

(C) advise the defendant personally that if the plea is not withdrawn, the court may dispose of the case less favorably toward the defendant than the plea agreement contemplated.

(d) Withdrawing a Guilty or Nolo Contendere Plea. A defendant may withdraw a plea of guilty or nolo contendere:

(1) before the court accepts the plea, for any reason or no reason; or

(2) after the court accepts the plea, but before it imposes sentence if:

(A) the court rejects a plea agreement under Rule 11(c)(5); or

(B) the defendant can show a fair and just reason for requesting the withdrawal.

(e) Finality of a Guilty or Nolo Contendere Plea. After the court imposes sentence, the defendant may not withdraw a plea of guilty or nolo contendere, and the plea may be set aside only on direct appeal or collateral attack.

(f) Admissibility or Inadmissibility of a Plea, Plea Discussions, and Related Statements. The admissibility or inadmissibility of a plea, a plea discussion, and any related statement is governed by Federal Rule of Evidence 410.

(g) Recording the Proceedings. The proceedings during which the defendant enters a plea must be recorded by a court reporter or by a suitable recording device. If there is a guilty plea or a nolo contendere plea, the record must include the inquiries and advice to the defendant required under Rule 11(b) and (c).

(h) Harmless Error. A variance from the requirements of this rule is harmless error if it does not affect substantial rights.

(As amended Feb. 28, 1966, eff. July 1, 1966; Apr. 22, 1974, eff. Dec. 1, 1975; July 31, 1975, Pub.L. 94–64, § 3(5)–(10), 89 Stat. 371, 372; Apr. 30, 1979, eff. Aug. 1, 1979, and Dec. 1, 1980; Apr. 28, 1982, eff. Aug. 1, 1982; Apr. 28, 1983, eff. Aug. 1, 1983; Apr. 29, 1985, eff. Aug. 1, 1985; Mar. 9, 1987, eff. Aug. 1, 1987; Nov. 18, 1988, Pub.L. 100–690, Title VII, § 7076, 102 Stat. 4406; Apr. 25, 1989, eff. Dec. 1, 1989; Apr. 29, 1999, eff. Dec. 1, 1999; Apr. 29, 2002, eff. Dec. 1, 2002.)

ADVISORY COMMITTEE NOTES

1944 Adoption

1. This rule is substantially a restatement of existing law and practice, 18 U.S.C. § 564 (Standing mute); Fogus v. United States, 34 F.2d 97, C.C.A.4th, (duty of court to ascertain that plea of guilty is intelligently and voluntarily made).

2. The plea of nolo contendere has always existed in the Federal courts. *Hudson v. United States*, 47 S.Ct. 127, 272 U.S. 451, 71 L.Ed. 347; *United States v. Norris*, 50 S.Ct. 424, 281 U.S. 619, 74 L.Ed. 1076. The use of the plea is recognized by the Probation Act, 18 U.S.C. former (now § 3651) 724. While at times criticized as theoretically lacking in logical basis, experience has shown that it performs a useful function from a practical standpoint.

1966 Amendments

The great majority of all defendants against whom indictments or informations are filed in the federal courts plead guilty. Only a comparatively small number go to trial. See United States Attorneys Statistical Report, Fiscal Year 1964, p. 1. The fairness and adequacy of the procedures on acceptance of pleas of guilty are of vital importance in according equal justice to all in the federal courts.

Three changes are made in the second sentence. The first change makes it clear that before accepting either a plea of guilty or nolo contendere the court must determine that the plea is made voluntarily with understanding of the nature of the charge. The second change expressly requires the court to address the defendant personally in the course of determining that the plea is made voluntarily and with understanding of the nature of the charge. The reported cases reflect some confusion over this matter. Compare *United States v. Diggs*, 304 F.2d 929 (6th Cir.1962); *Domenica v. United States*, 292 F.2d 483 (1st Cir.1961); *Gundlach v. United States*, 262 F.2d 72 (4th Cir.1958), cert. den., 360 U.S. 904 (1959); and *Julian v. United States*, 236 F.2d 155 (6th Cir.1956), which contain the implication that personal interrogation of the defendant is the better practice even when he is represented by counsel, with *Meeks v. United States*, 298 F.2d 204 (5th Cir.1962); *Nunley v. United States*, 294 F.2d 579 (10th Cir.1961), cert. den., 368 U.S. 991 (1962); and *United States v. Von der Heide*, 169 F.Supp. 560 (D.D.C. 1959).

The third change in the second sentence adds the words "and the consequences of his plea" to state what clearly is the law. See, e.g., *Von Moltke v. Gillies*, 332 U.S. 708, 724 (1948); *Kerchevel v. United States*, 274 U.S. 220, 223 (1927); *Munich v. United States*, 337 F.2d 356 (9th Cir.1964); *Pilkington v. United States*, 315 F.2d 204 (4th Cir.1963); *Smith v. United States*, 324 F.2d 436 (D.C.Cir.1963); but cf. *Marvel v. United States*, 335 F.2d 101 (5th Cir.1964).

A new sentence is added at the end of the rule to impose a duty on the court in cases where the defendant pleads guilty to satisfy itself that there is a factual basis for the plea before entering judgment. The court should satisfy itself, by inquiry of the defendant or the attorney for the government, or by examining the presentence report, or otherwise, that the conduct which the defendant admits constitutes the offense charged in the indictment or information or an offense included therein to which the defendant has pleaded guilty. Such inquiry should, e.g., protect a defendant who is in the position of pleading voluntarily with an understanding of the nature of the charge but without realizing that his conduct does not actually fall within the charge. For a similar requirement see Mich.Stat.Ann. § 28.1058 (1954); Mich.Sup. Ct.Rule 35A; *In re Valle*, 364 Mich. 471, 110 N.W.2d 673 (1961); *People v. Barrows*, 358 Mich. 267, 99 N.W.2d 347 (1959); *People v. Bumpus*, 355 Mich. 374, 94 N.W.2d 854 (1959); *People v. Coates*, 337 Mich. 56, 59 N.W.2d 83 (1953). See also *Stinson v. United States*, 316 F.2d 554 (5th Cir. 1963). The normal consequence of a determination that there is not a factual basis for the plea would be for the court to set aside the plea and enter a plea of not guilty.

For a variety of reasons it is desirable in some cases to permit entry of judgment upon a plea of nolo contendere without inquiry into the factual basis for the plea. The new third sentence is not, therefore, made applicable to pleas of nolo contendere. It is not intended by this omission to reflect any view upon the effect of a plea nolo contendere in relation to a plea of guilty. That problem has been dealt with by the courts. See e.g. *Lott v. United States*, 367 U.S. 421, 426 (1961).

1974 Amendments

The amendments to rule 11 are designed to achieve two principal objectives:

(1) Subdivision (c) prescribes the advice which the court must give to insure that the defendant who pleads guilty has made an informed plea.

(2) Subdivision (e) provides a plea agreement procedure designed to give recognition to the propriety of plea discussions; to bring the existence of a plea agreement out into the open in court; and to provide methods for court acceptance or rejection of a plea agreement.

Other less basic changes are also made. The changes are discussed in the order in which they appear in the rule.

Subdivision (b) retains the requirement that the defendant obtain the consent of the court in order to plead nolo contendere. It adds that the court shall, in deciding whether to accept the plea, consider the view of the prosecution and of the defense and also the larger public interest in the administration of criminal justice.

Although the plea of nolo contendere has long existed in the federal courts, *Hudson v. United States*, 272 U.S. 451, 47 S.Ct. 127, 71 L.Ed. 347 (1926), the desirability of the plea has been a subject of disagreement. Compare Lane-Reticker, Nolo Contendere in North Carolina, 34 N.C.L.Rev. 280, 290–291 (1956), with Note, The Nature and Consequences of the Plea of Nolo Contendere, 33 Neb.L.Rev. 428, 434 (1954), favoring the plea. The American Bar Association Project on Standards for Criminal Justice takes the position that "the case for the nolo plea is not strong enough to justify a minimum standard supporting its use," but because "use of the plea contributes in some degree to the avoidance of unnecessary trials" it does not proscribe use of the plea. ABA, Standards Relating to Pleas of Guilty § 1.1(a) Commentary at 16 (Approved Draft, 1968).

A plea of nolo contendere is, for purposes of punishment, the same as the plea of guilty. See discussion of the history of the nolo plea in North *Carolina v. Alford*, 400 U.S. 25, 35–36 n. 8, 91 S.Ct. 160, 27 L.Ed.2d 162 (1970). Note, The Nature and Consequences of the Plea of Nolo Contendere, 33 Neb.L.Rev. 428, 430 (1954). A judgment upon the plea is a conviction and may be used to apply multiple offender statutes. Lenvin and Meyers, Nolo Contendere: Its Nature and Implications, 51 Yale L.J. 1255, 1265 (1942). Unlike a plea of guilty, however, it cannot be used against a defendant as an admission in a subsequent criminal or civil case. 4 Wigmore § 1066(4), at 58 (3d ed. 1940, Supp.1970); Rules of Evidence for United States Courts and Magistrates, rule 803(22) (Nov. 1971). See Lenvin and Meyers, Nolo Contendere: Its Nature and Implications, 51 Yale L.J. 1255 (1942); ABA Standards Relating to Pleas of Guilty §§ 1.1(a) and (b), Commentary at 15–18 (Approved Draft, 1968).

The factors considered relevant by particular courts in determining whether to permit the plea of nolo contendere vary. Compare *United States v. Bagliore*, 182 F.Supp. 714, 716 (E.D.N.Y.1960), where the view is taken that the plea should be rejected unless a compelling reason for acceptance is established, with *United States v. Jones*, 119 F.Supp. 288, 290 (S.D.Cal.1954), where the view is taken that the plea should be accepted in the absence of a compelling reason to the contrary.

A defendant who desires to plead nolo contendere will commonly want to avoid pleading guilty because the plea of guilty can be introduced as an admission in subsequent civil litigation. The prosecution may oppose the plea of nolo contendere because it wants a definite resolution of the defendant's guilty or innocence either for correctional purposes or for reasons of subsequent litigation. ABA Standards Relating to Pleas of Guilty § 1.1(b) Commentary at 16–18 (Approved Draft, 1968). Under subdivision (b) of the new rule the balancing of the interests is left to the trial judge, who is mandated to take into account the larger public interest in the effective administration of justice.

Subdivision (c) prescribes the advice which the court must give to the defendant as a prerequisite to the acceptance of a plea of guilty. The former rule required that the court determine that the plea was made with "understanding of the nature of the charge and the consequences of the plea." The amendment identifies more specifically what must be explained to the defendant and also codifies, in the rule, the requirements of *Boykin v. Alabama*, 395 U.S. 238, 89 S.Ct. 1709, 23 L.Ed.2d 274 (1969), which held that a defendant must be apprised of the fact that he relinquishes certain constitutional rights by pleading guilty.

Subdivision (c) retains the requirement that the court address the defendant personally. See *McCarthy v. United States*, 394 U.S. 459, 466, 89 S.Ct. 1166, 22 L.Ed.2d 418 (1969). There is also an amendment to rule 43 to make clear that a defendant must be in court at the time of the plea.

Subdivision (c)(1) retains the current requirement that the court determine that the defendant understands the nature of the charge. This is a common requirement. See ABA Standards Relating to Pleas of Guilty § 1.4(a) (Approved Draft, 1968); Illinois Supreme Court Rule 402(a)(1) (1970),

Ill.Rev.Stat.1973, ch. 110A, § 402(a)(1). The method by which the defendant's understanding of the nature of the charge is determined may vary from case to case, depending on the complexity of the circumstances and the particular defendant. In some cases, a judge may do this by reading the indictment and by explaining the elements of the offense to the defendants. Thompson, The Judge's Responsibility on a Plea of Guilty, 62 W.Va.L.Rev. 213, 220 (1960); Resolution of Judges of U.S. District Court for D.C., June 24, 1959.

Former rule 11 required the court to inform the defendant of the "consequences of the plea." Subdivision (c)(2) changes this and requires instead that the court inform the defendant of and determine that he understands "the mandatory minimum penalty provided by law, if any, and the maximum possible penalty provided by law for the offense to which the plea is offered." The objective is to insure that a defendant knows what minimum sentence the judge **must** impose and what maximum sentence the judge **may** impose. This information is usually readily ascertainable from the face of the statute defining the crime, and thus it is feasible for the judge to know specifically what to tell the defendant. Giving this advice tells a defendant the shortest mandatory sentence and also the longest possible sentence for the offense to which he is pleading guilty.

It has been suggested that it is desirable to inform a defendant of additional consequences which might follow from his plea of guilty. *Durant v. United States*, 410 F.2d 689 (1st Cir.1969), held that a defendant must be informed of his ineligibility for parole. *Trujillo v. United States*, 377 F.2d 266 (5th Cir.1967), cert. denied 389 U.S. 899, 88 S.Ct. 224, 19 L.Ed.2d 221 (1967), held that advice about eligibility for parole is not required. It has been suggested that a defendant be advised that a jury might find him guilty only of a lesser included offense. C. Wright, Federal Practice and Procedure: Criminal § 173 at 374 (1969). See contra *Dorrough v. United States*, 385 F.2d 887 (5th Cir.1967). The ABA Standards Relating to Pleas of Guilty § 1.4(c)(iii) (Approved Draft, 1968) recommend that the defendant be informed that he may be subject to additional punishment if the offense charged is one for which a different or additional punishment is authorized by reason of the defendant's previous conviction.

Under the rule the judge is not required to inform a defendant about these matters, though a judge is free to do so if he feels a consequence of a plea of guilty in a particular case is likely to be of real significance to the defendant. Currently, certain consequences of a plea of guilty, such as parole eligibility, may be so complicated that it is not feasible to expect a judge to clearly advise the defendant. For example, the judge may impose a sentence under 18 U.S.C. § 4202 making the defendant eligible for parole when he has served one third of the judicially imposed maximum; or, under 18 U.S.C. § 4208(a)(1), making parole eligibility after a specified period of time less than one third of the maximum; or, under 18 U.S.C. § 4208(a)(2), leaving eligibility to the discretion of the parole board. At the time the judge is required to advise the defendant of the consequences of his plea, the judge will usually not have seen the presentence report and thus will have no basis for giving a defendant any very realistic advice as to when he might be eligible for parole. Similar complications exist with regard to other, particularly collateral, consequences of a plea of guilty in a given case.

Subdivisions (c)(3) and (4) specify the constitutional rights that the defendant waives by a plea of guilty or nolo contendere. These subdivisions are designed to satisfy the requirements of understanding waiver set forth in *Boykin v. Alabama*, 395 U.S. 238, 89 S.Ct. 1709, 23 L.Ed.2d 274 (1969). Subdivision (c)(3) is intended to require that the judge inform the defendant and determine that he understands that he waives his fifth amendment rights. The rule takes the position that the defendant's right not to incriminate himself is best explained in terms of his right to plead not guilty and to persist in that plea if it has already been made. This is language identical to that adopted in Illinois for the same purpose. See Illinois Supreme Court Rule 402(a)(3) (1970), Ill.Rev.Stat.1973, ch. 110A, § 402(a)(3).

Subdivision (c)(4) assumes that a defendant's right to have his guilt proved beyond a reasonable doubt and the right to confront his accusers are best explained by indicating that the right to trial is waived. Specifying that there will be no future trial of any kind makes this fact clear to those defendants who, though knowing they have waived trial by jury, are under the mistaken impression that some kind of trial will follow. Illinois has recently adopted similar language. Illinois Supreme Court Rule 402(a)(4) (1970), Ill.Rev. Stat.1973, ch. 110A, § 402(a)(4). In explaining to a defendant that he waives his right to trial, the judge may want to explain some of the aspects of trial such as the right to confront witnesses, to subpoena witnesses, to testify in his own behalf, or, if he chooses, not to testify. What is required, in this respect, to conform to *Boykin* is left to future case-law development.

Subdivision (d) retains the requirement that the court determine that a plea of guilty or nolo contendere is voluntary before accepting it. It adds the requirement that the court also inquire whether the defendant's willingness to plead guilty or nolo contendere results from prior plea discussions between the attorney for the government and the defendant or his attorney. See *Santobello v. New York*, 404 U.S. 257, 261–262, 92 S.Ct. 495, 30 L.Ed.2d 427 (1971): "The plea must, of course, be voluntary and knowing and if it was induced by promises, the essence of those promises must in some way be made known." Subdivisions (d) and (e) afford the court adequate basis for rejecting an improper plea agreement induced by threats or inappropriate promises.

The new rule specifies that the court personally address the defendant in determining the voluntariness of the plea.

By personally interrogating the defendant, not only will the judge be better able to ascertain the plea's voluntariness, but he will also develop a more complete record to support his determination in a subsequent postconviction attack. * * * Both of these goals are undermined in proportion to the degree the district judge resorts to "assumptions" not based upon recorded responses to his inquiries. *McCarthy v. United States*, 394 U.S. 459, 466, 467, 89 S.Ct. 1166, 22 L.Ed.2d 418 (1969).

Subdivision (e) provides a plea agreement procedure. In doing so it gives recognition to the propriety of plea discussions and plea agreements provided that they are disclosed in open court and subject to acceptance or rejection by the trial judge.

Although reliable statistical information is limited, one recent estimate indicated that guilty pleas account for the disposition of as many as 95% of all criminal cases. ABA Standards Relating to Pleas of Guilty, pp. 1–2 (Approved

Draft, 1968). A substantial number of these are the result of plea discussions. The President's Commission on Law Enforcement and Administration of Justice, Task Force Report: The Courts 9 (1967); D. Newman, Conviction: The Determination of Guilt or Innocence Without Trial 3 (1966); L. Weinreb, Criminal Process 437 (1969); Note, Guilty Plea Bargaining: Compromises By Prosecutors To Secure Guilty Pleas, 112 U.Pa.L.Rev. 865 (1964).

There is increasing acknowledgment of both the inevitability and the propriety of plea agreements. See, e.g., ABA Standards Relating to Pleas of Guilty § 3.1 (Approved Draft, 1968); Illinois Supreme Court Rule 402 (1970), Ill.Rev.Stat. 1973, ch. 110A, § 402.

In *Brady v. United States*, 397 U.S. 742, 752–753, 90 S.Ct. 1463, 25 L.Ed.2d 747 (1970), the court said:

Of course, that the prevalence of guilty pleas is explainable does not necessarily validate those pleas or the system which produces them. But we cannot hold that it is unconstitutional for the State to extend a benefit to a defendant who in turn extends a substantial benefit to the State and who demonstrates by his plea that he is ready and willing to admit his crime and to enter the correctional system in a frame of mind that affords hope for success in rehabilitation over a shorter period of time than might otherwise be necessary.

In *Santobello v. New York*, 404 U.S. 257, 260, 92 S.Ct. 495, 498, 30 L.Ed.2d 427 (1971), the court said:

The disposition of criminal charges by agreement between the prosecutor and the accused, sometimes loosely called "plea bargaining," is an essential component of the administration of justice. Properly administered, it is to be encouraged.

Administratively, the criminal justice system has come to depend upon pleas of guilty and, hence, upon plea discussions. See, e.g., President's Commission on Law Enforcement and Administration of Justice, Task Force Report. The Courts 9 (1967); Note, Guilty Plea Bargaining: Compromises By Prosecutors To Secure Guilty Pleas, 112 U.Pa. L.Rev. 865 (1964). But expediency is not the basis for recognizing the propriety of a plea agreement practice. Properly implemented, a plea agreement procedure is consistent with both effective and just administration of the criminal law. *Santobello v. New York*, 404 U.S. 257, 92 S.Ct. 495, 30 L.Ed.2d 427. This is the conclusion reached in the ABA Standards Relating to Pleas of Guilty § 1.8 (Approved Draft, 1968); the ABA Standards Relating to The Prosecution Function and The Defense Function pp. 243–253 (Approved Draft, 1971); and the ABA Standards Relating to the Function of the Trial Judge, § 4.1 (App.Draft, 1972). The Supreme Court of California recently recognized the propriety of plea bargaining. See People v. West, 3 Cal.3d 595, 91 Cal.Rptr. 385, 477 P.2d 409 (1970). A plea agreement procedure has recently been decided in the District of Columbia Court of General Sessions upon the recommendation of the United States Attorney. See 51 F.R.D. 109 (1971).

Where the defendant by his plea aids in insuring prompt and certain application of correctional measures, the proper ends of the criminal justice system are furthered because swift and certain punishment serves the ends of both general deterrence and the rehabilitation of the individual defendant. Cf. Note, The Influence of the Defendant's Plea on Judicial Determination of Sentence, 66 Yale L.J. 204, 211 (1956). Where the defendant has acknowledged his guilt and shown a willingness to assume responsibility for his conduct, it has been thought proper to recognize this in sentencing. See also ALI, Model Penal Code § 7.01 (P.O.D.1962); NPPA Guides for Sentencing (1957). Granting a charge reduction in return for a plea of guilty may give the sentencing judge needed discretion, particularly where the facts of a case do not warrant the harsh consequences of a long mandatory sentence or collateral consequences which are unduly severe. A plea of guilty avoids the necessity of a public trial and may protect the innocent victim of a crime against the trauma of direct and cross-examination.

Finally, a plea agreement may also contribute to the successful prosecution of other more serious offenders. See D. Newman, Conviction: The Determination of Guilt or Innocence Without Trial, chs. 2 and 3 (1966); Note, Guilty Plea Bargaining: Compromises By Prosecutors To Secure Guilty Pleas, 112 U.Pa.L.Rev. 865, 881 (1964).

Where plea discussions and agreements are viewed as proper, it is generally agreed that it is preferable that the fact of the plea agreement be disclosed in open court and its propriety be reviewed by the trial judge.

We have previously recognized plea bargaining as an ineradicable fact. Failure to recognize it tends not to destroy it but to drive it underground. We reiterate what we have said before: that when plea bargaining occurs it ought to be spread on the record [The Bench Book prepared by the Federal Judicial Center for use by United States District Judges now suggests that the defendant be asked by the court "if he believes there is any understanding or if any predictions have been made to him concerning the sentence he will receive." Bench Book for United States District Judges, Federal Judicial Center (1969) at 1.05.3.] and publicly disclosed. *United States v. Williams*, 407 F.2d 940 (4th Cir.1969). * * * In the future we think that the district judges should not only make the general inquiry under Rule 11 as to whether the plea of guilty has been coerced or induced by promises, but should specifically inquire of counsel whether plea bargaining has occurred. Logically the general inquiry should elicit information about plea bargaining, but it seldom has in the past. Raines v. United, 423 F.2d 526, 530 (4th Cir.1970).

In the past, plea discussions and agreements have occurred in an informal and largely invisible manner. Enker, Perspectives on Plea Bargaining, in President's Commission on Law Enforcement and Administration of Justice, Task Force Report: The Courts 108, 115 (1967). There has often been a ritual of denial that any promises have been made, a ritual in which judges, prosecutors, and defense counsel have participated. ABA Standards Relating to Pleas of Guilty § 3.1, Commentary at 60–69 (Approved Draft 1968); Task Force Report: The Courts 9. Consequently, there has been a lack of effective judicial review of the propriety of the agreements, thus increasing the risk of real or apparent unfairness. See ABA Standards Relating to Pleas of Guilty § 3.1, Commentary at 60 et seq.; Task Force Report: The Courts 9–13.

The procedure described in subdivision (e) is designed to prevent abuse of plea discussions and agreements by providing appropriate and adequate safeguards.

Subdivision (e)(1) specifies that the "attorney for the government and the attorney for the defendant or the defendant when acting pro se may" participate in plea discussions. The inclusion of "the defendant when acting pro se" is intended to reflect the fact that there are situations in which a defendant insists upon representing himself. It may be desirable that an attorney for the government not enter plea discussions with a defendant personally. If necessary, counsel can be appointed for purposes of plea discussions. (Subdivision (d) makes it mandatory that the court inquire of the defendant whether his plea is the result of plea discussions between him and the attorney for the government. This is intended to enable the court to reject an agreement reached by an unrepresented defendant unless the court is satisfied that acceptance of the agreement adequately protects the rights of the defendant and the interests of justice.) This is substantially the position of the ABA Standards Relating to Pleas of Guilty § 3.1(a), Commentary at 65–66 (Approved Draft, 1968). Apparently, it is the practice of most prosecuting attorneys to enter plea discussions only with defendant's counsel. Note, Guilty Plea Bargaining: Compromises By Prosecutors To Secure Guilty Pleas, 112 U.Pa.L.Rev. 865, 904 (1964). Discussions without benefit of counsel increase the likelihood that such discussions may be unfair. Some courts have indicated that plea discussions in the absence of defendant's attorney may be constitutionally prohibited. See *Anderson v. North Carolina*, 221 F.Supp. 930, 935 (W.D.N.C. 1963); *Shape v. Sigler*, 230 F.Supp. 601, 606 (D.Neb.1964).

Subdivision (e)(1) is intended to make clear that there are four possible concessions that may be made in a plea agreement. First, the charge may be reduced to a lesser or related offense. Second, the attorney for the government may promise to move for dismissal of other charges. Third, the attorney for the government may agree to recommend or not oppose the imposition of a particular sentence. Fourth, the attorneys for the government and the defense may agree that a given sentence is an appropriate disposition of the case. This is made explicit in subdivision (e)(2) where reference is made to an agreement made "in the expectation that a specific sentence will be imposed." See Note, Guilty Plea Bargaining: Compromises By Prosecutors To Secure Guilty Pleas, 112 U.Pa.L.Rev. 865, 898 (1964).

Subdivision (e)(1) prohibits the court from participating in plea discussions. This is the position of the ABA Standards Relating to Pleas of Guilty § 3.3(a) (Approved Draft, 1968).

It has been stated that it is common practice for a judge to participate in plea discussions. See D. Newman, Conviction: The Determination of Guilt or Innocence Without Trial 32–52, 78–104 (1966); Note, Guilty Plea Bargaining: Compromises By Prosecutors To Secure Guilty Pleas, 112 U.Pa. L.Rev. 865, 891, 905 (1964).

There are valid reasons for a judge to avoid involvement in plea discussions. It might lead the defendant to believe that he would not receive a fair trial, were there a trial before the same judge. The risk of not going along with the disposition apparently desired by the judge might induce the defendant to plead guilty, even if innocent. Such involvement makes it difficult for a judge to objectively assess the voluntariness of the plea. See ABA Standards Relating to Pleas of Guilty § 3.3(a), Commentary at 72–74 (Approved Draft, 1968); Note, Guilty Plea Bargaining: Compromises By Prosecutors To Secure Guilty Pleas, 112 U.Pa.L.Rev. 865, 891–892 (1964); Comment, Official Inducements to Plead Guilty: Suggested Morals for a Marketplace, 32 U.Chi.L.Rev. 167, 180–183 (1964); Informal Opinion No. 779 ABA Professional Ethics Committee ("A judge should not be a party to advance arrangements for the determination of sentence, whether as a result of a guilty plea or a finding of guilt based on proof."), 51 A.B.A.J. 444 (1965). As has been recently pointed out:

> The unequal positions of the judge and the accused, one with the power to commit to prison and the other deeply concerned to avoid prison, at once raise a question of fundamental fairness. When a judge becomes a participant in plea bargaining he brings to bear the full force and majesty of his office. His awesome power to impose a substantially longer or even maximum sentence in excess of that proposed is present whether referred to or not. A defendant needs no reminder that if he rejects the proposal, stands upon his right to trial and is convicted, he faces a significantly longer sentence. *United States ex rel. Elksnis v. Gilligan*, 256 F.Supp. 244, 254 (S.D.N.Y.1966).

On the other hand, one commentator has taken the position that the judge may be involved in discussions either after the agreement is reached or to help elicit facts and an agreement. Enker, Perspectives on Plea Bargaining, in President's Commission on Law Enforcement and Administration of Justice, Task Force Report: The Courts 108, 117–118 (1967).

The amendment makes clear that the judge should not participate in plea discussions leading to a plea agreement. It is contemplated that the judge may participate in such discussions as may occur when the plea agreement is disclosed in open court. This is the position of the recently adopted Illinois Supreme Court Rule 402(d)(1) (1970), Ill.Rev. Stat.1973, ch. 110A, § 402(d)(1). As to what may constitute "participation," contrast People v. Earegood, 12 Mich.App. 256, 268–269, 162 N.W.2d 802, 809–810 (1968), with Kruse v. State, 47 Wis.2d 460, 177 N.W.2d 322 (1970).

Subdivision (e)(2) provides that the judge shall require the disclosure of any plea agreement in open court. In People v. West, 3 Cal.3d 595, 91 Cal.Rptr. 385, 477 P.2d 409 (1970), the court said:

> [T]he basis of the bargain should be disclosed to the court and incorporated in the record. * * *
>
> Without limiting that court to those we set forth, we note four possible methods of incorporation: (1) the bargain could be stated orally and recorded by the court reporter, whose notes then must be preserved or transcribed; (2) the bargain could be set forth by the clerk in the minutes of the court; (3) the parties could file a written stipulation stating the terms of the bargain; (4) finally, counsel or the court itself may find it useful to prepare and utilize forms for the recordation of plea bargains. 91 Cal.Rptr. 393, 394, 477 P.2d at 417, 418.

The District of Columbia Court of General Sessions is using a "Sentence-Recommendation Agreement" form.

Upon notice of the plea agreement, the court is given the option to accept or reject the agreement or defer its decision until receipt of the presentence report.

The judge may, and often should, defer his decision until he examines the presentence report. This is made possible by rule 32 which allows a judge, with the defendant's consent, to inspect a presentence report to determine whether a plea agreement should be accepted. For a discussion of the use of conditional plea acceptance, see ABA Standards Relating to Pleas of Guilty § 3.3(b), Commentary at 74–76, and Supplement, Proposed Revisions § 3.3(b) at 2–3 (Approved

Draft, 1968); Illinois Supreme Court Rule 402(d)(2) (1970), Ill.Rev.Stat.1973, ch. 110A, § 402(d)(2).

The plea agreement procedure does not attempt to define criteria for the acceptance or rejection of a plea agreement. Such a decision is left to the discretion of the individual trial judge.

Subdivision (e)(3) makes it mandatory, if the court decides to accept the plea agreement, that it inform the defendant that it will embody in the judgment and sentence the disposition provided in the plea agreement, or one more favorable to the defendant. This serves the purpose of informing the defendant immediately that the agreement will be implemented.

Subdivision (e)(4) requires the court, if it rejects the plea agreement, to inform the defendant of this fact and to advise the defendant personally, in open court, that the court is not bound by the plea agreement. The defendant must be afforded an opportunity to withdraw his plea and must be advised that if he persists in his guilty plea or plea of nolo contendere, the disposition of the case may be less favorable to him than that contemplated by the plea agreement. That the defendant should have the opportunity to withdraw his plea if the court rejects the plea agreement is the position taken in ABA Standards Relating to Pleas of Guilty, Supplement, Proposed Revisions § 2.1(a)(ii)(5) (Approved Draft, 1968). Such a rule has been adopted in Illinois. Illinois Supreme Court Rule 402(d)(2) (1970), Ill.Rev.Stat.1973, ch. 110A, § 402(d)(2).

If the court rejects the plea agreement and affords the defendant the opportunity to withdraw the plea, the court is not precluded from accepting a guilty plea from the same defendant at a later time, when such plea conforms to the requirements of rule 11.

Subdivision (e)(5) makes it mandatory that, except for good cause shown, the court be notified of the existence of a plea agreement at the arraignment or at another time prior to trial fixed by the court. Having a plea entered at this stage provides a reasonable time for the defendant to consult with counsel and for counsel to complete any plea discussions with the attorney for the government. ABA Standards Relating to Pleas of Guilty § 1.3 (Approved Draft, 1968). The objective of the provision is to make clear that the court has authority to require a plea agreement to be disclosed sufficiently in advance of trial so as not to interfere with the efficient scheduling of criminal cases.

Subdivision (e)(6) is taken from rule 410, Rules of Evidence for United States Courts and Magistrates (Nov.1971). See Advisory Committee Note thereto. See also the ABA Standards Relating to Pleas of Guilty § 2.2 (Approved Draft, 1968); Illinois Supreme Court Rule 402(f) (1970), Ill.Rev. Stat.1973, ch. 110A, § 402(f).

Subdivision (f) retains the requirement of old rule 11 that the court should not enter judgment upon a plea of guilty without making such an inquiry as will satisfy it that there is a factual basis for the plea. The draft does not specify that any particular type of inquiry be made. See *Santobello v. New York*, 404 U.S. 257, 261, 92 S.Ct. 495, 30 L.Ed.2d 427 (1971): "Fed.Rule Crim.Proc. 11, governing pleas in federal courts, now makes clear that the sentencing judge must develop, **on the record,** the factual basis for the plea, as, for example, by having the accused describe the conduct that gave rise to the charge." An inquiry might be made of the defendant, of the attorneys for the government and the defense, of the presentence report when one is available, or by whatever means is appropriate in a specific case. This is the position of the ABA Standards Relating to Pleas of Guilty § 1.6 (Approved Draft, 1968). Where inquiry is made of the defendant himself it may be desirable practice to place the defendant under oath. With regard to a determination that there is a factual basis for a plea of guilty to a "lesser or related offense," compare ABA Standards Relating to Pleas of Guilty § 3.1(b)(ii), Commentary at 67–68 (Approved Draft, 1968), with ALI, Model Penal Code § 1.07(5) (P.O.D.1962). The rule does not speak directly to the issue of whether a judge may accept a plea of guilty where there is a factual basis for the plea but the defendant asserts his innocence. *North Carolina v. Alford*, 400 U.S. 25, 91 S.Ct. 160, 27 L.Ed.2d 162 (1970). The procedure in such case would seem to be to deal with this as a plea of nolo contendere, the acceptance of which would depend upon the judge's decision as to whether acceptance of the plea is consistent with "the interest of the public in the effective administration of justice" [new rule 11(b)]. The defendant who asserts his innocence while pleading guilty or nolo contendere is often difficult to deal with in a correctional setting, and it may therefore be preferable to resolve the issue of guilt or innocence at the trial stage rather than leaving that issue unresolved, thus complicating subsequent correctional decisions. The rule is intended to make clear that a judge may reject a plea of nolo contendere and require the defendant either to plead not guilty or to plead guilty under circumstances in which the judge is able to determine that the defendant is in fact guilty of the crime to which he is pleading guilty.

Subdivision (g) requires that a verbatim record be kept of the proceedings. If there is a plea of guilty or nolo contendere, the record must include, without limitation, the court's advice to the defendant, the inquiry into the voluntariness of the plea and the plea agreement, and the inquiry into the accuracy of the plea. Such a record is important in the event of a postconviction attack. ABA Standards Relating to Pleas of Guilty § 1.7 (Approved Draft, 1968). A similar requirement was adopted in Illinois: Illinois Supreme Court Rule 402(e) (1970), Ill.Rev.Stat.1973, ch. 110A, § 402(e).

1975 Enactment

A. Amendments Proposed by the Supreme Court. Rule 11 of the Federal Rules of Criminal Procedure deals with pleas. The Supreme Court has proposed to amend this rule extensively.

Rule 11 provides that a defendant may plead guilty, not guilty, or nolo contendere. The Supreme Court's amendments to Rule 11(b) provide that a nolo contendere plea "shall be accepted by the court only after due consideration of the views of the parties and the interest of the public in the effective administration of justice."

The Supreme Court amendments to Rule 11(c) spell out the advice that the court must give to the defendant before accepting the defendant's plea of guilty or nolo contendere. The Supreme Court amendments to Rule 11(d) set forth the steps that the court must take to insure that a guilty or nolo contendere plea has been voluntarily made.

The Supreme Court amendments to Rule 11(e) establish a plea agreement procedure. This procedure permits the parties to discuss disposing of a case without a trial and sets forth the type of agreements that the parties can reach concerning the disposition of the case. The procedure is not mandatory; a court is free not to permit the parties to present plea agreements to it.

The Supreme Court amendments to Rule 11(f) require that the court, before entering judgment upon a plea of guilty, satisfy itself that "there is a factual basis for the plea." The Supreme Court amendments to Rule 11(g) require that a verbatim record be kept of the proceedings at which the defendant enters a plea.

B. Committee Action. The proposed amendments to Rule 11, particularly those relating to the plea negotiating procedure, have generated much comment and criticism. No observer is entirely happy that our criminal justice system must rely to the extent it does on negotiated dispositions of cases. However, crowded court dockets make plea negotiating a fact that the Federal Rules of Criminal Procedure should contend with. The Committee accepts the basic structure and provisions of Rule 11(e).

Rule 11(e) as proposed permits each federal court to decide for itself the extent to which it will permit plea negotiations to be carried on within its own jurisdiction. No court is compelled to permit any plea negotiations at all. Proposed Rule 11(e) regulates plea negotiations and agreements if, and to the extent that, the court permits such negotiations and agreements. [Proposed Rule 11(e) has been criticized by some federal judges who read it to mandate the court to permit plea negotiations and the reaching of plea agreements. The Advisory Committee stressed during its testimony that the rule does not mandate that a court permit any form of plea agreement to be presented to it. See, e.g., the remarks of United States Circuit Judge William H. Webster in Hearings II, at 196. See also the exchange of correspondence between Judge Webster and United States District Judge Frank A. Kaufman in Hearings II, at 289–90.]

Proposed Rule 11(e) contemplates 4 different types of plea agreements. First, the defendant can plead guilty or nolo contendere in return for the prosecutor's reducing the charge to a less serious offense. Second, the defendant can plead guilty or nolo contendere in return for the prosecutor dropping, or not bringing, a charge or charges relating to other offenses. Third, the defendant can plead guilty or nolo contendere in return for the prosecutor's recommending a sentence. Fourth, the defendant and prosecutor can agree that a particular sentence is the appropriate disposition of the case. [It is apparent, though not explicitly stated, that Rule 11(e) contemplates that the plea agreement may bind the defendant to do more than just plead guilty or nolo contendere. For example, the plea agreement may bind the defendant to cooperate with the prosecution in a different investigation. The Committee intends by its approval of Rule 11(e) to permit the parties to agree on such terms in a plea agreement.]

The Committee added language in subdivisions (e)(2) and (e)(4) to permit a plea agreement to be disclosed to the court, or rejected by it, in camera. There must be a showing of good cause before the court can conduct such proceedings in camera. The language does not address itself to whether the showing of good cause may be made in open court or in camera. That issue is left for the courts to resolve on a case-by-case basis. These changes in subdivisions (e)(2) and (e)(4) will permit a fair trial when there is substantial media interest in a case and the court is rejecting a plea agreement.

The Committee added an exception to subdivision (e)(6). That subdivision provides:

Evidence of a plea of guilty, later withdrawn, or a plea of nolo contendere, or of an offer to plead guilty or nolo contendere to the crime charged or any other crime, or of statements made in connection with any of the foregoing pleas or offers, is not admissible in any civil or criminal proceeding against the person who made the plea or offer.

The Committee's exception permits the use of such evidence in a perjury or false statement prosecution where the plea, offer, or related statement was made by the defendant on the record, under oath and in the presence of counsel. The Committee recognizes that even this limited exception may discourage defendants from being completely candid and open during plea negotiations and may even result in discouraging the reaching of plea agreements. However, the Committee believes that, on balance, it is more important to protect the integrity of the judicial process from willful deceit and untruthfulness. [The Committee does not intend its language to be construed as mandating or encouraging the swearing-in of the defendant during proceedings in connection with the disclosure and acceptance or rejection of a plea agreement.]

The Committee recast the language of Rule 11(c), which deals with the advice given to a defendant before the court can accept his plea of guilty or nolo contendere. The Committee acted in part because it believed that the warnings given to the defendant ought to include those that Boykin v. Alabama, 395 U.S. 238 (1969), said were constitutionally required. In addition, and as a result of its change in subdivision (e)(6), the Committee thought it only fair that the defendant be warned that his plea of guilty (later withdrawn) or nolo contendere, or his offer of either plea, or his statements made in connection with such pleas or offers, could later be used against him in a perjury trial if made under oath, on the record, and in the presence of counsel. House Report No. 94–247.

Note to subdivision (c). Rule 11(c) enumerates certain things that a judge must tell a defendant before the judge can accept that defendant's plea of guilty or nolo contendere. The House version expands upon the list originally proposed by the Supreme Court. The Senate version adopts the Supreme Court's proposal.

The Conference adopts the House provision.

Note to subdivision (e)(1). Rule 11(e)(1) outlines some general considerations concerning the plea agreement procedure. The Senate version makes nonsubstantive change in the House version.

The Conference adopts the Senate provision.

Note to subdivision (e)(6). Rule 11(e)(6) deals with the use of statements made in connection with plea agreements. The House version permits a limited use of pleas of guilty, later withdrawn, or nolo contendere, offers of such pleas, and statements made in connection with such pleas or offers. Such evidence can be used in a perjury or false statement prosecution if the plea, offer, or related statement was made under oath, on the record, and in the presence of counsel. The Senate version permits evidence of voluntary and reliable statements made in court on the record to be used for the purpose of impeaching the credibility of the declarant or in a perjury or false statement prosecution.

The Conference adopts the House version with changes. The Conference agrees that neither a plea nor the offer of a plea ought to be admissible for any purpose. The Conference-adopted provision, therefore, like the Senate provision, permits only the use of statements made in connection with a plea of guilty, later withdrawn, or a plea of nolo contendere, or in connection with an offer of a guilty or nolo contendere plea. House Report No. 94–414.

1979 Amendments

Note to Subdivision (e)(2). The amendment to rule 11(e)(2) is intended to clarify the circumstances in which the court may accept or reject a plea agreement, with the consequences specified in subdivision (e) (3) and (4). The present language has been the cause of some confusion and has led to results which are not entirely consistent. *Compare United States v. Sarubbi*, 416 F.Supp. 633 (D.N.J.1976); with *United States v. Hull*, 413 F.Supp. 145 (E.D.Tenn.1976).

Rule 11(e) (1) specifies three types of plea agreements, namely, those in which the attorney for the government might

(A) move for dismissal of other charges; or

(B) make a recommendation, or agree not to oppose the defendant's request, for a particular sentence, with the understanding that such recommendation or request shall not be binding upon the court; or

(C) agree that a specific sentence is the appropriate disposition of the case.

A (B) type of plea agreement is clearly of a different order than the other two, for an agreement to recommend or not to oppose is discharged when the prosecutor performs as he agreed to do. By comparison, critical to a type (A) or (C) agreement is that the defendant receive the contemplated charge dismissal or agreed-to sentence. Consequently, there must ultimately be an acceptance or rejection by the court of a type (A) or (C) agreement so that it may be determined whether the defendant shall receive the bargained-for concessions or shall instead be afforded an opportunity to withdraw his plea. But this is not so as to a type (B) agreement; there is no "disposition provided for" in such a plea agreement so as to make the acceptance provisions of subdivision (e)(3) applicable, nor is there a need for rejection with opportunity for withdrawal under subdivision (e)(4) in light of the fact that the defendant knew the nonbinding character of the recommendation or request. *United States v. Henderson*, 565 F.2d 1119 (9th Cir. 1977); *United States v. Savage*, 561 F.2d 554 (4th Cir. 1977).

Because a type (B) agreement is distinguishable from the others in that it involves only a recommendation or request not binding upon the court, it is important that the defendant be aware that this is the nature of the agreement into which he has entered. The procedure contemplated by the last sentence of amended subdivision (e) (2) will establish for the record that there is such awareness. This provision conforms to ABA Standards Relating to Pleas of Guilty § 1.5 (Approved Draft, 1968), which provides that "the court must advise the defendant personally that the recommendations of the prosecuting attorney are not binding on the court."

Sometimes a plea agreement will be partially but not entirely of the (B) type, as where a defendant, charged with counts 1, 2 and 3, enters into an agreement with the attorney for the government wherein it is agreed that if defendant pleads guilty to count 1, the prosecutor will recommend a certain sentence as to that count and will move for dismissal of counts 2 and 3. In such a case, the court must take particular care to ensure that the defendant understands which components of the agreement involve only a (B) type recommendation and which do not. In the above illustration, that part of the agreement which contemplates the dismissal of counts 2 and 3 is an (A) type agreement, and thus under rule 11(e) the court must either accept the agreement to dismiss these counts or else reject it and allow the defendant to withdraw his plea. If rejected, the defendant must be allowed to withdraw the plea on count 1 even if the type (B) promise to recommend a certain sentence on that count is kept, for a multi-faceted plea agreement is nonetheless a single agreement. On the other hand, if counts 2 and 3 are dismissed and the sentence recommendation is made, then the defendant is not entitled to withdraw his plea even if the sentence recommendation is not accepted by the court, for the defendant received all he was entitled to under the various components of the plea agreement.

Note to Subdivision (e)(6). The major objective of the amendment to rule 11(e)(6) is to describe more precisely, consistent with the original purpose of the provision, what evidence relating to pleas or plea discussions is inadmissible. The present language is susceptible to interpretation which would make it applicable to a wide variety of statements made under various circumstances other than within the context of those plea discussions authorized by rule 11(e) and intended to be protected by subdivision (e)(6) of the rule. See *United States v. Herman*, 544 F.2d 791 (5th Cir. 1977), discussed herein.

Fed.R.Ev. 410, as originally adopted by Pub.L. 93–595, provided in part that "evidence of a plea of guilty, later withdrawn, or a plea of nolo contendere, or of an offer to plead guilty or nolo contendere to the crime charged or any other crime, or of statements made in connection with any of the foregoing pleas or offers, is not admissible in any civil or criminal action, case, or proceeding against the person who made the plea or offer." (This rule was adopted with the proviso that it "shall be superseded by any amendment to the Federal Rules of Criminal Procedure which is inconsistent with this rule.") As the Advisory Committee Note explained: "Exclusion of offers to plead guilty or nolo has as its purpose the promotion of disposition of criminal cases by compromise." The amendment of Fed.R.Crim.P. 11, transmitted to Congress by the Supreme Court in April 1974, contained a subdivision (e) (6) essentially identical to the rule 410 language quoted above, as a part of a substantial revision of rule 11. The most significant feature of this revision was the express recognition given to the fact that the "attorney for the government and the attorney for the defendant or the defendant when acting pro se may engage in discussions with a view toward reaching" a plea agreement. Subdivision (e) (6) was intended to encourage such discussions. As noted in H.R.Rep. No. 94–247, 94th Cong., 1st Sess. 7 (1975), the purpose of subdivision (e) (6) is to not "discourage defendants from being completely candid and open during plea negotiations." Similarly, H.R.Rep. No. 94–414, 94th Cong., 1st Sess. 10 (1975), states that "Rule 11e(6) deals with the use of statements made in connection with plea agreements." (Rule 11(e) (6) was thereafter enacted, with the addition of the proviso allowing use of statements in a prosecution for perjury, and with the qualification that the inadmissible statements must also be "relevant to" the inadmissible pleas or offers. Pub.L. 94–64; Fed.R.Ev. 410 was then amended to conform. form. Pub.L. 94–149.)

While this history shows that the purpose of Fed.R.Ev. 410 and Fed.R.Crim.P. 11(e)(6) is to permit the unrestrained candor which produces effective plea discussions between the "attorney for the government and the attorney for the defendant or the defendant when acting pro se," given visibility and sanction in rule 11(e), a literal reading of the language of these two rules could reasonably lead to the conclusion that a broader rule of inadmissibility obtains. That is, because "statements" are generally inadmissible if "made in connection with, and relevant to" an "offer to plead guilty," it might be thought that an otherwise voluntary admission to law enforcement officials is rendered inadmissible merely because it was made in the hope of obtaining leniency by a plea. Some decisions interpreting rule 11(e)(6) point in this direction. See *United States v. Herman*, 544 F.2d 791 (5th Cir. 1977) (defendant in custody of two postal inspectors during continuance of removal hearing instigated conversation with them and at some point said he would plead guilty to armed robbery if the murder charge was dropped; one inspector stated they were not "in position" to make any deals in this regard; held, defendant's statement inadmissible under rule 11(e)(6) because the defendant "made the statements during the course of a conversation in which he sought concessions from the government in return for a guilty plea"); *United States v. Brooks*, 536 F.2d 1137 (6th Cir. 1976) (defendant telephoned postal inspector and offered to plead guilty if he got 2-year maximum; statement inadmissible).

The amendment makes inadmissible statements made "in the course of any proceedings under this rule regarding" either a plea of guilty later withdrawn or a plea of nolo contendere, and also statements "made in the course of plea discussions with an attorney for the government which do not result in a plea of guilty or which result in a plea of guilty later withdrawn." It is not limited to statements by the defendant himself, and thus would cover statements by defense counsel regarding defendant's incriminating admissions to him. It thus fully protects the plea discussion process authorized by rule 11 without attempting to deal with confrontations between suspects and law enforcement agents, which involve problems of quite different dimensions. See, e.g., ALI Model Code of Pre-Arraignment Procedure, art. 140 and § 150.2(8) (Proposed Official Draft, 1975) (latter section requires exclusion if "a law enforcement officer induces any person to make a statement by promising leniency"). This change, it must be emphasized, does not compel the conclusion that statements made to law enforcement agents, especially when the agents purport to have authority to bargain, are inevitably admissible. Rather, the point is that such cases are not covered by the per se rule of 11(e)(6) and thus must be resolved by that body of law dealing with police interrogations.

If there has been a plea of guilty later withdrawn or a plea of nolo contendere, subdivision (e)(6)(C) makes inadmissible statements made "in the course of any proceedings under this rule" regarding such pleas. This includes, for example, admissions by the defendant when he makes his plea in court pursuant to rule 11 and also admissions made to provide the factual basis pursuant to subdivision (f). However, subdivision (e)(6)(C) is not limited to statements made in court. If the court were to defer its decision on a plea agreement pending examination of the presentence report, as authorized by subdivision (e)(2), statements made to the probation officer in connection with the preparation of that report would come within this provision.

This amendment is fully consistent with all recent and major law reform efforts on this subject. ALI Model Code of Pre-Arraignment Procedure § 350.7 (Proposed Official Draft, 1975), and ABA Standards Relating to Pleas of Guilty § 3.4 (Approved Draft, 1968) both provide:

> Unless the defendant subsequently enters a plea of guilty or nolo contendere which is not withdrawn, the fact that the defendant or his counsel and the prosecuting attorney engaged in plea discussions or made a plea agreement should not be received in evidence against or in favor of the defendant in any criminal or civil action or administrative proceedings.

The Commentary to the latter states:

> The above standard is limited to discussions and agreements with the prosecuting attorney. Sometimes defendants will indicate to the police their willingness to bargain, and in such instances these statements are sometimes admitted in court against the defendant. *State v. Christian*, 245 S.W.2d 895 (Mo.1952). If the police initiate this kind of discussion, this may have some bearing on the admissibility of the defendant's statement. However, the policy considerations relevant to this issue are better dealt with in the context of standards governing in-custody interrogation by the police.

Similarly, Unif.R.Crim.P. 441(d) (Approved Draft, 1974), provides that except under limited circumstances "no discussion between the parties or statement by the defendant or his lawyer under this Rule," i.e., the rule providing "the parties may meet to discuss the possibility of pretrial diversion * * * or of a plea agreement," are admissible. The amendment is likewise consistent with the typical state provision on this subject; see, e.g., Ill.S.Ct. Rule 402(f).

The language of the amendment identifies with more precision than the present language the necessary relationship between the statements and the plea or discussion. See the dispute between the majority and concurring opinions in *United States v. Herman*, 544 F.2d 791 (5th Cir. 1977), concerning the meanings and effect of the phrases "connection to" and "relevant to" in the present rule. Moreover, by relating the statements to "plea discussions" rather than "an offer to plead," the amendment ensures "that even an attempt to open plea bargaining [is] covered under the same rule of inadmissibility." *United States v. Brooks*, 536 F.2d 1137 (6th Cir. 1976).

The last sentence of Rule 11(e)(6) is amended to provide a second exception to the general rule of nonadmissibility of the described statements. Under the amendment, such a statement is also admissible "in any proceeding wherein another statement made in the course of the same plea or plea discussions has been introduced and the statement ought in fairness be considered contemporaneously with it." This change is necessary so that, when evidence of statements made in the course of or as a consequence of a certain plea or plea discussions are introduced under circumstances not prohibited by this rule (e.g., not "against" the person who made the plea), other statements relating to the same plea or plea discussions may also be admitted when relevant to the matter at issue. For example, if a defendant upon a motion to dismiss a prosecution on some ground were able to admit certain statements made in aborted plea discussions in his favor, then other relevant statements made in the same plea discussions should be admissible against the defendant in the interest of determining the truth of the matter at issue. The language of the amendment follows closely that in Fed. R.Evid. 106, as the considerations involved are very similar.

The phrase "in any civil or criminal proceeding" has been moved from its present position, following the word "against," for purposes of clarity. An ambiguity presently exists because the word "against" may be read as referring either to the kind of proceeding in which the evidence is offered or the purpose for which it is offered. The change makes it clear that the latter construction is correct. No change is intended with respect to provisions making evidence rules inapplicable in certain situations. See, e.g., Fed.R.Evid. 104(a) and 1101(d).

Unlike ABA Standards Relating to Pleas of Guilty § 3.4 (Approved Draft, 1968), and ALI Model Code of Pre-Arraignment Procedure § 350.7 (Proposed Official Draft, 1975), rule 11(e)(6) does not also provide that the described evidence is inadmissible "in favor of" the defendant. This is not intended to suggest, however, that such evidence will inevitably be admissible in the defendant's favor. Specifically, no disapproval is intended of such decisions as *United States v. Verdoorn*, 528 F.2d 103 (8th Cir. 1976), holding that the trial judge properly refused to permit the defendants to put into evidence at their trial the fact the prosecution had attempted to plea bargain with them, as "meaningful dialogue between the parties would, as a practical matter, be impossible if either party had to assume the risk that plea offers would be admissible in evidence."

1982 Amendments

Subdivision (c)(1). Subdivision (c)(1) has been amended by specifying "the effect of any special parole term" as one of the matters about which a defendant who has tendered a plea of guilty or nolo contendere is to be advised by the court. This amendment does not make any change in the law, as the courts are in agreement that such advice is presently required by Rule 11. See, e.g., *Moore v. United States*, 592 F.2d 753 (4th Cir. 1979); *United States v. Eaton*, 579 F.2d 1181 (10th Cir. 1978); *Richardson v. United States*, 577 F.2d 447 (8th Cir. 1978); *United States v. Del Prete*, 567 F.2d 928 (9th Cir. 1978); *United States v. Watson*, 548 F.2d 1058 (D.C.Cir.1977); *United States v. Crusco*, 536 F.2d 21 (2d Cir.1976); *United States v. Yazbeck*, 524 F.2d 641 (1st Cir. 1975); *United States v. Wolak*, 510 F.2d 164 (6th Cir. 1975). In *United States v. Timmreck*, 441 U.S. 780 (1979), 99 S.Ct. 2085, 60 L.Ed.2d 634 (1979), the Supreme Court assumed that the judge's failure in that case to describe the mandatory special parole term constituted "a failure to comply with the formal requirements of the Rule."

The purpose of the amendment is to draw more specific attention to the fact that advice concerning special parole terms is a necessary part of Rule 11 procedure. As noted in *Moore v. United States*, supra:

> Special parole is a significant penalty. * * * Unlike ordinary parole, which does not involve supervision beyond the original prison term set by the court and the violation of which cannot lead to confinement beyond that sentence, special parole increases the possible period of confinement. It entails the possibility that a defendant may have to serve his original sentence plus a substantial additional period, without credit for time spent on parole. Explanation of special parole in open court is therefore essential to comply with the Rule's mandate that the defendant be informed of "the maximum possible penalty provided by law."

As the aforecited cases indicate, in the absence of specification of the requirement in the rule it has sometimes happened that such advice has been inadvertently omitted from Rule 11 warnings.

The amendment does not attempt to enumerate all of the characteristics of the special parole term which the judge ought to bring to the defendant's attention. Some flexibility in this respect must be preserved although it is well to note that the unique characteristics of this kind of parole are such that they may not be readily perceived by laymen. *Moore v. United States supra*, recommends that in an appropriate case the judge inform the defendant and determine that he understands the following:

(1) that a special parole term will be added to any prison sentence he receives;

(2) the minimum length of the special parole term that must be imposed and the absence of a statutory maximum;

(3) that special parole is entirely different from—and in addition to—ordinary parole; and

(4) that if the special parole is violated, the defendant can be returned to prison for the remainder of his sentence and the full length of his special parole term.

The amendment should not be read as meaning that a failure to comply with this particular requirement will inevitably entitle the defendant to relief. See *United States v. Timmreck, supra*. Likewise, the amendment makes no change in the existing law to the effect that many aspects of traditional parole need not be communicated to the defendant by the trial judge under the umbrella of Rule 11. For example, a defendant need not be advised of all conceivable consequences such as when he may be considered for parole or that, if he violates his parole, he will again be imprisoned. *Bunker v. Wise*, 550 F.2d 1155, 1158 (9th Cir. 1977).

Subdivision (c)(4). The amendment to subdivision (c)(4) is intended to overcome the present conflict between the introductory language of subdivision (c), which contemplates the advice being given "[b]efore accepting a plea of guilty or nolo contendere," and thus presumably after the plea has been tendered, and the "if he pleads" language of subdivision (c)(4) which suggests the plea has not been tendered.

As noted by Judge Doyle in *United States v. Sinagub*, 468 F.Supp. 353 (W.D.Wis.1979):

> Taken literally, this wording of subsection (4) of 11(c) suggests that before eliciting any plea at an arraignment, the court is required to insure that a defendant understands that if he or she pleads guilty or nolo contendere, the defendant will be waiving the right to trial. Under subsection (3) of 11(c), however, there is no requirement that at this pre-plea stage, the court must insure that the defendant understands that he or she enjoys the right to a trial and, at trial, the right to the assistance of counsel, the right to confront and cross-examine witnesses against him or her, and the right not to be compelled to incriminate himself or herself. It would be incongruous to require that at the pre-plea stage the court insure that the defendant understands that if he enters a plea of guilty or nolo contendere he will be waiving a right, the existence and nature of which need not be explained until after such a

plea has been entered. I conclude that the insertion of the words "that if he pleads guilty or nolo contendere," as they appear in subsection (4) of 11(c), was an accident of draftsmanship which occurred in the course of Congressional rewriting of 11(c) as it has been approved by the Supreme Court. Those words are to be construed consistently with the words "Before accepting a plea of guilty or nolo contendere," as they appear in the opening language of 11(c), and consistently with the omission of the words "that if he pleads" from subsections (1), (2), and (3) of 11(c). That is, as they appear in subsection (4) of 11(c), the words, "that if he pleads guilty or nolo contendere" should be construed to mean "that if his plea of guilty or nolo contendere is accepted by the court."

Although this is a very logical interpretation of the present language, the amendment will avoid the necessity to engage in such analysis in order to determine the true meaning of subdivision (c) (4).

Subdivision (c)(5). Subdivision (c)(5), in its present form, may easily be read as contemplating that in every case in which a plea of guilty or nolo contendere is tendered, warnings must be given about the possible use of defendant's statements, obtained under oath, on the record and in the presence of counsel, in a later prosecution for perjury or false statement. The language has prompted some courts to reach the remarkable result that a defendant who pleads guilty or nolo contendere without receiving those warnings must be allowed to overturn his plea on appeal even though he was never questioned under oath, on the record, in the presence of counsel about the offense to which he pleaded. *United States v. Artis, No. 78–5012* (4th Cir. March 12, 1979); *United States v. Boone*, 543 F.2d 1090 (4th Cir. 1976). Compare *United States v. Michaelson*, 552 F.2d 472 (2d Cir. 1977) (failure to give subdivision (c) (5) warnings not a basis for reversal, "at least when, as here, defendant was not put under oath before questioning about his guilty plea"). The present language of subdivision (c) (5) may also have contributed to the conclusion, not otherwise supported by the rule, that "Rule 11 requires that the defendant be under oath for the entirety of the proceedings" conducted pursuant to that rule and that failure to place the defendant under oath would itself make necessary overturning the plea on appeal. *United States v. Aldridge*, 553 F.2d 922 (5th Cir. 1977).

When questioning of the kind described in subdivision (c) (5) is not contemplated by the judge who is receiving the plea, no purpose is served by giving the (c) (5) warnings, which in such circumstances can only confuse the defendant and detract from the force of the other warnings required by Rule 11. As correctly noted in *United States v. Sinagub, supra*,

> subsection (5) of section (c) of Rule 11 is qualitatively distinct from the other sections of the Rule. It does not go to whether the plea is knowingly or voluntarily made, nor to whether the plea should be accepted and judgment entered. Rather, it does go to the possible consequences of an event which may or may not occur during the course of the arraignment hearing itself, namely, the administration of an oath to the defendant. Whether this event is to occur is wholly within the control of the presiding judge. If the event is not to occur it is pointless to inform the defendant of its consequences. If a presiding judge intends that an oath not be administered to a defendant during an arraignment hearing, but alters that intention at some point, only then would the need arise to inform the defendant of the possible consequences of the administration of the oath.

The amendment to subdivision (c) (5) is intended to make it clear that this is the case.

The amendment limits the circumstances in which the warnings must be given, but does not change the fact as noted in Sinagub that these warnings are "qualitatively distinct" from the other advice required by Rule 11(c). This being the case, a failure to give the subdivision (c) (5) warnings even when the defendant was questioned under oath, on the record and in the presence of counsel would in no way affect the validity of the defendant's plea. Rather, this failure bears upon the admissibility of defendant's answers pursuant to subdivision (e) (6) in a later prosecution for perjury or false statement.

1983 Amendments

Rule 11(a). There are many defenses, objections and requests which a defendant must ordinarily raise by pretrial motion. See, e.g., 18 U.S.C. § 3162(a)(2); Fed.R.Crim.P. 12(b). Should that motion be denied, interlocutory appeal of the ruling by the defendant is seldom permitted. See *United States v. MacDonald*, 435 U.S. 850 (1978) (defendant may not appeal denial of his motion to dismiss based upon Sixth Amendment speedy trial grounds); *DiBella v. United States*, 369 U.S. 121 (1962) (defendant may not appeal denial of pretrial motion to suppress evidence); compare *Abney v. United States*, 431 U.S. 651 (1977) (interlocutory appeal of denial of motion to dismiss on double jeopardy grounds permissible). Moreover, should the defendant thereafter plead guilty or nolo contendere, this will usually foreclose later appeal with respect to denial of the pretrial motion. "When a criminal defendant has solemnly admitted in open court that he is in fact guilty of the offense with which he is charged, he may not thereafter raise independent claims relating to the deprivation of constitutional rights that occurred prior to the entry of the guilty plea." *Tollett v. Henderson*, 411 U.S. 258, (1973). Though a nolo plea differs from a guilty plea in other respects, it is clear that it also constitutes a waiver of all nonjurisdictional defects in a manner equivalent to a guilty plea. *Lott v. United States*, 367 U.S. 421 (1961).

As a consequence, a defendant who has lost one or more pretrial motions will often go through an entire trial simply to preserve the pretrial issues for later appellate review. This results in a waste of prosecutorial and judicial resources, and causes delay in the trial of other cases, contrary to the objectives underlying the Speedy Trial Act of 1974, 18 U.S.C. § 3161 et seq. These unfortunate consequences may be avoided by the conditional plea device expressly authorized by new subdivision (a)(2).

The development of procedures to avoid the necessity for trials which are undertaken for the sole purpose of preserving pretrial objections has been consistently favored by the commentators. See ABA Standards Relating to the Administration of Criminal Justice, standard 21–1.3(c) (2d ed. 1978); Model Code of Pre–Arraignment Procedure § SS 290.1(4)(b) (1975); Uniform Rules of Criminal Procedure, rule 444(d) (Approved Draft, 1974); 1 C. Wright, Federal Practice and Procedure—Criminal § 175 (1969); 3 W. LaFave, Search and Seizure § 11.1 (1978). The Supreme Court has characterized the New York practice, whereby appeals from suppression motions may be appealed notwithstanding a guilty plea, as a "commendable effort to relieve the problem of congested trial calendars in a manner that does not diminish the opportunity for the assertion of rights guaranteed by the Constitution." *Lefkowitz v. Newsome*, 420 U.S. 283, 293 (1975). That Court has never discussed conditional pleas as such, but has permitted without comment a federal appeal on issues preserved by a conditional plea. *Jaben v. United States*, 381 U.S. 214 (1965).

In the absence of specific authorization by statute or rule for a conditional plea, the circuits have divided on the permissibility of the practice. Two circuits have actually approved the entry of conditional pleas, *United States v. Burke*, 517 F.2d 377 (2d Cir.1975); *United States v. Moskow*, 588 F.2d 882 (3d Cir.1978); and two others have praised the conditional plea concept, *United States v. Clark*, 459 F.2d 977 (8th Cir.1972); *United States v. Dorsey*, 449 F.2d 1104 (D.C.Cir.1971). Three circuits have expressed the view that a conditional plea is logically inconsistent and thus improper, *United States v. Brown*, 499 F.2d 829 (7th Cir.1974); *United States v. Sepe*, 472 F.2d 784, aff'd en banc, 486 F.2d 1044 (5th Cir.1973); *United States v. Cox*, 464 F.2d 937 (6th Cir.1972); three others have determined only that conditional pleas are not now authorized in the federal system, *United States v. Benson*, 579 F.2d 508 (9th Cir.1978); *United States v. Nooner*, 565 F.2d 633 (10th Cir.1977); *United States v. Matthews*, 472 F.2d 1173 (4th Cir.1973); while one circuit has reserved judgment on the issue, *United States v. Warwar*, 478 F.2d 1183 (1st Cir.1973). (At the state level, a few jurisdictions by statute allow appeal from denial of a motion to suppress notwithstanding a subsequent guilty plea, Cal.Penal Code § 1538.5(m); N.Y.Crim.Proc.Law § 710.20(1); Wis.Stat.Ann. § 971.31(10), but in the absence of such a provision the state courts are also in disagreement as to whether a conditional plea is permissible; see cases collected in Comment, 26 U.C.L.A.L.Rev. 360, 373 (1978).)

The conditional plea procedure provided for in subdivision (a)(2) will, as previously noted, serve to conserve prosecutorial and judicial resources and advance speedy trial objectives. It will also produce much needed uniformity in the federal system on this matter; see *United States v. Clark, supra*, noting the split of authority and urging resolution by statute or rule. Also, the availability of a conditional plea under specified circumstances will aid in clarifying the fact that traditional, unqualified pleas do constitute a waiver of nonjurisdictional defects. See *United States v. Nooner, supra* (defendant sought appellate review of denial of pretrial suppression motion, despite his prior unqualified guilty plea, claiming the Second Circuit conditional plea practice led him to believe a guilty plea did not bar appeal of pretrial issues).

The obvious advantages of the conditional plea procedure authorized by subdivision (a)(2) are not outweighed by any significant or compelling disadvantages. As noted in Comment, supra, at 375: "Four major arguments have been raised by courts disapproving of conditioned pleas. The objections are that the procedure encourages a flood of appellate litigation, militates against achieving finality in the criminal process, reduces effectiveness of appellate review due to the lack of a full trial record, and forces decision on constitutional questions that could otherwise be avoided by invoking the harmless error doctrine." But, as concluded therein, those "arguments do not withstand close analysis." Ibid.

As for the first of those arguments, experience in states which have permitted appeals of suppression motions notwithstanding a subsequent plea of guilty is most relevant, as conditional pleas are likely to be most common when the objective is to appeal that kind of pretrial ruling. That experience has shown that the number of appeals has not increased substantially. See Comment, 9 Hous.L.Rev. 305, 315–19 (1971). The minimal added burden at the appellate level is certainly a small price to pay for avoiding otherwise unnecessary trials.

As for the objection that conditional pleas conflict with the government's interest in achieving finality, it is likewise without force. While it is true that the conditional plea does not have the complete finality of the traditional plea of guilty or nolo contendere because "the essence of the agreement is that the legal guilt of the defendant exists only if the prosecution's case" survives on appeal, the plea

> continues to serve a partial state interest in finality, however, by establishing admission of the defendant's factual guilt. The defendant stands guilty and the proceedings come to an end if the reserved issue is ultimately decided in the government's favor.

Comment, 26 U.C.L.A.L.Rev. 360, 378 (1978).

The claim that the lack of a full trial record precludes effective appellate review may on occasion be relevant. Cf. *United States v. MacDonald*, supra (holding interlocutory appeal not available for denial of defendant's pretrial motion to dismiss on speedy trial grounds, and noting that "most speedy trial claims * * * are best considered only after the relevant facts have been developed at trial"). However, most of the objections which would likely be raised by pretrial motion and preserved for appellate review by a conditional plea are subject to appellate resolution without a trial record. Certainly this is true as to the very common motion to suppress evidence, as is indicated by the fact that appellate courts presently decide such issues upon interlocutory appeal by the government.

With respect to the objection that conditional pleas circumvent application of the harmless error doctrine, it must be acknowledged that "[a]bsent a full trial record, containing all the government's evidence against the defendant, invocation of the harmless error rule is arguably impossible." Comment, supra, at 380. But, the harmless error standard with respect to constitutional objections is sufficiently high, see *Chapman v. California*, 386 U.S. 18 (1967), that relatively few appellate decisions result in affirmance upon that basis. Thus it will only rarely be true that the conditional plea device will cause an appellate court to consider constitutional questions which could otherwise have been avoided by invocation of the doctrine of harmless error.

To the extent that these or related objections would otherwise have some substance, they are overcome by the provision in Rule 11(a)(2) that the defendant may enter a conditional plea only "with the approval of the court and the consent of the government." (In this respect, the rule adopts the practice now found in the Second Circuit.) The requirement of approval by the court is most appropriate, as it ensures, for example, that the defendant is not allowed to take an appeal on a matter which can only be fully developed by proceeding to trial; cf. *United States v. MacDonald*, supra. As for consent by the government, it will ensure that conditional pleas will be allowed only when the decision of the court of appeals will dispose of the case either by allowing the plea to stand or by such action as compelling dismissal of the indictment or suppressing essential evidence. Absent such circumstances, the conditional plea might only serve to postpone the trial and require the government to try the case after substantial delay, during which time witnesses may be lost, memories dimmed, and the offense grown so stale as to lose jury appeal. The government is in a unique position to determine whether the matter at issue would be case-dispositive, and, as a party to the litigation, should have an absolute right to refuse to consent to potentially prejudicial delay. Although it was suggested in *United States v. Moskow*, supra, that the government should have no right to prevent the entry of a conditional plea because a defendant has no comparable right to block government appeal of a pretrial ruling pursuant to 18 U.S.C. § 3731, that analogy is unconvincing. That statute requires the government to certify that the appeal is not taken for purposes of delay. Moreover, where the pretrial ruling is case-dispositive, § 3731 is the only mechanism by which the government can obtain appellate review, but a defendant may always obtain review by pleading not guilty.

Unlike the state statutes cited earlier, Rule 11(a)(2) is not limited to instances in which the pretrial ruling the defendant wishes to appeal was in response to defendant's motion to suppress evidence. Though it may be true that the conditional plea device will be most commonly employed as to such rulings, the objectives of the rule are well served by extending it to other pretrial rulings as well. See, e.g., ABA Standards, supra (declaring the New York provision "should be enlarged to include other pretrial defenses"); Uniform Rules of Criminal Procedure, rule 44(d) (Approved Draft, 1974) ("any pretrial motion which, if granted, would be dispositive of the case").

The requirement that the conditional plea be made by the defendant "reserving in writing the right to appeal from the adverse determination of any specified pretrial motion," though extending beyond the Second Circuit practice, will ensure careful attention to any conditional plea. It will document that a particular plea was in fact conditional, and will identify precisely what pretrial issues have been preserved for appellate review. By requiring this added step, it will be possible to avoid entry of a conditional plea without the considered acquiescence of the government (see *United States v. Burke*, supra, holding that failure of the government to object to entry of a conditional plea constituted consent) and post-plea claims by the defendant that his plea should be deemed conditional merely because it occurred after denial of his pretrial motions (see *United States v. Nooner*, supra).

It must be emphasized that the *only* avenue of review of the specified pretrial ruling permitted under a rule 11(a)(2) conditional plea is an appeal, which must be brought in compliance with Fed.R.App.P. 4(b). Relief via 28 U.S.C. § 2255 is not available for this purpose.

The Supreme Court has held that certain kinds of constitutional objections may be raised after a plea of guilty. *Menna v. New York*, 423 U.S. 61 (1975) (double jeopardy violation); *Blackledge v. Perry*, 417 U.S. 21 (1974) (due process violation by charge enhancement following defendant's exercise of right to trial de novo). Subdivision 11(a)(2) has no application to such situations, and should not be interpreted as either broadening or narrowing the Menna-Blackledge doctrine or as establishing procedures for its application.

Rule 11(h). Subdivision (h) makes clear that the harmless error rule of Rule 52(a) is applicable to Rule 11. The provision does not, however, attempt to define the meaning of "harmless error," which is left to the case law. Prior to the amendments which took effect on Dec. 1, 1975, Rule 11 was very brief; it consisted of but four sentences. The 1975 amendments increased significantly the procedures which must be undertaken when a defendant tenders a plea of guilty or nolo contendere, but this change was warranted by the "two principal objectives" then identified in the Advisory Committee Note: (1) ensuring that the defendant has made an informed plea; and (2) ensuring that plea agreements are brought out into the open in court. An inevitable consequence of the 1975 amendments was some increase in the risk that a trial judge, in a particular case, might inadvertently deviate to some degree from the procedure which a very literal reading of Rule 11 would appear to require.

This being so, it became more apparent than ever that Rule 11 should not be given such a crabbed interpretation that ceremony was exalted over substance. As stated in *United States v. Scarf*, 551 F.2d 1124 (8th Cir.1977), concerning amended Rule 11: "It is a salutary rule, and district courts are required to act in substantial compliance with it although * * * ritualistic compliance is not required." As similarly pointed out in *United States v. Saft*, 558 F.2d 1073 (2d Cir.1977),

> the Rule does not say that compliance can be achieved only by reading the specified items *in haec verba*. Congress meant to strip district judges of freedom to decide *what* they must explain to a defendant who wishes to plead guilty, not to tell them precisely *how* to perform this important task in the great variety of cases that would come before them. While a judge who contents himself with literal application of the Rule will hardly be reversed, it cannot be supposed that Congress preferred this to a more meaningful explanation, provided that all the specified elements were covered.

Two important points logically flow from these sound observations. One concerns the matter of construing Rule 11: it is not to be read as requiring a litany or other ritual which can be carried out only by word-for-word adherence to a set "script." The other, specifically addressed in new subdivision (h), is that even when it may be concluded Rule 11 has not been complied with in all respects, it does not inevitably follow that the defendant's plea of guilty or nolo contendere is invalid and subject to being overturned by any remedial device then available to the defendant.

Notwithstanding the declaration in Rule 52(a) that "[a]ny error, defect, irregularity or variance which does not affect substantial rights shall be disregarded," there has existed for some years considerable disagreement concerning the applicability of the harmless error doctrine to Rule 11 violations. In large part, this is attributable to uncertainty as to the continued vitality and the reach of *McCarthy v. United States*, 394 U.S. 459 (1969). In *McCarthy*, involving a direct appeal from a plea of guilty because of noncompliance with Rule 11, the Court concluded

> that prejudice inheres in a failure to comply with Rule 11, for noncompliance deprives the defendant of the Rule's procedural safeguards, which are designed to facilitate a more accurate determination of the voluntariness of his plea. Our holding [is] that a defendant whose plea has

been accepted in violation of Rule 11 should be afforded the opportunity to plead anew * * *.

McCarthy has been most frequently relied upon in cases where, as in that case, the defendant sought relief because of a Rule 11 violation by the avenue of direct appeal. It has been held that in such circumstances a defendant's conviction must be reversed whenever the "district court accepts his guilty plea without fully adhering to the procedure provided for in Rule 11," *United States v. Boone*, 543 F.2d 1090 (4th Cir.1976), and that in this context any reliance by the government on the Rule 52(a) harmless error concept "must be rejected." *United States v. Journet*, 544 F.2d 633 (2d Cir. 1976). On the other hand, decisions are to be found taking a harmless error approach on direct appeal where it appeared the nature and extent of the deviation from Rule 11 was such that it could not have had any impact on the defendant's decision to plead or the fairness in now holding him to his plea. *United States v. Peters*, No. 77–1700 (4th Cir., Dec. 22, 1978) (where judge failed to comply fully with Rule 11(c)(1), in that defendant not correctly advised of maximum years of special parole term but was told it is at least 3 years, and defendant thereafter sentenced to 15 years plus 3-year special parole term, government's motion for summary affirmance granted, as "the error was harmless"); *United States v. Coronado*, 554 F.2d 166 (5th Cir.1977) (court first holds that charge of conspiracy requires some explanation of what conspiracy means to comply with Rule 11(c)(1), but then finds no reversible error "because the rule 11 proceeding on its face discloses, despite the trial court's failure sufficiently to make the required explication of the charges, that Coronado understood them").

But this conflict has not been limited to cases involving nothing more than a direct appeal following defendant's plea. For example, another type of case is that in which the defendant has based a post-sentence motion to withdraw his plea on a Rule 11 violation. Rule 32(d) says that such a motion may be granted "to correct manifest injustice," and some courts have relied upon this latter provision in holding that post-sentence plea withdrawal need not be permitted merely because Rule 11 was not fully complied with and that instead the district court should hold an evidentiary hearing to determine "whether manifest injustice will result if the conviction based on the guilty plea is permitted to stand." *United States v. Scarf*, 551 F.2d 1124 (8th Cir.1977). Others, however, have held that *McCarthy* applies and prevails over the language of Rule 32(d), so that "a failure to scrupulously comply with Rule 11 will invalidate a plea without a showing of manifest injustice." *United States v. Cantor*, 469 F.2d 435 (3d Cir.1972).

Disagreement has also existed in the context of collateral attack upon pleas pursuant to 28 U.S.C. § 2255. On the one hand, it has been concluded that "[n]ot every violation of Rule 11 requires that the plea be set aside" in a § 2255 proceeding, and that "a guilty plea will be set aside on collateral attack only where to not do so would result in a miscarriage of justice, or where there exists exceptional circumstances justifying such relief." *Evers v. United States*, 579 F.2d 71 (10th Cir.1978). The contrary view was that McCarthy governed in § 2255 proceedings because "the Supreme Court hinted at no exceptions to its policy of strict enforcement of Rule 11." *Timmreck v. United States*, 577 F.2d 377 (6th Cir.1978). But a unanimous Supreme Court resolved this conflict in *United States v. Timmreck*, 441 U.S. 780 (1979), where the Court concluded that the reasoning of *Hill v. United States*, 368 U.S. 424 (1962) (ruling a collateral attack could not be predicated on a violation of Rule 32(a)) is equally applicable to a formal violation of Rule 11. * * *

Indeed, if anything, this case may be a stronger one for foreclosing collateral relief than the Hill case. For the concern with finality served by the limitation on collateral attack has special force with respect to convictions based on guilty pleas.

"Every inroad on the concept of finality undermines confidence in the integrity of our procedures; and, by increasing the volume of judicial work, inevitably delays and impairs the orderly administration of justice. The impact is greatest when new grounds for setting aside guilty pleas are approved because the vast majority of criminal convictions result from such pleas. Moreover, the concern that unfair procedures may have resulted in the conviction of an innocent defendant is only rarely raised by a petition to set aside a guilty plea."

This interest in finality is strongest in the collateral attack context the Court was dealing with in *Timmreck*, which explains why the Court there adopted the *Hill* requirement that in a § 2255 proceeding the rule violation must amount to "a fundamental defect which inherently results in a complete miscarriage of justice" or "an omission inconsistent with the rudimentary demands of fair procedure." The interest in finality of guilty pleas described in *Timmreck* is of somewhat lesser weight when a direct appeal is involved (so that the *Hill* standard is obviously inappropriate in that setting), but yet is sufficiently compelling to make unsound the proposition that reversal is required even where it is apparent that the Rule 11 violation was of the harmless error variety.

Though the *McCarthy* per se rule may have been justified at the time and in the circumstances which obtained when the plea in that case was taken, this is no longer the case. For one thing, it is important to recall that *McCarthy* dealt only with the much simpler pre–1975 version of Rule 11, which required only a brief procedure during which the chances of a minor, insignificant and inadvertent deviation were relatively slight. This means that the chances of a *truly* harmless error (which was not involved in *McCarthy* in any event, as the judge made *no* inquiry into the defendant's understanding of the nature of the charge, and the government had presented only the extreme argument that a court "could properly assume that petitioner was entering that plea with a complete understanding of the charge against him" merely from the fact he had stated he desired to plead guilty) are much greater under present Rule 11 than under the version before the Court in *McCarthy*. It also means that the more elaborate and lengthy procedures of present Rule 11, again as compared with the version applied in *McCarthy*, make it more apparent than ever that a guilty plea is not "a mere gesture, a temporary and meaningless formality reversible at the defendant's whim," but rather " 'a grave and solemn act,' which is 'accepted only with care and discernment.' " *United States v. Barker*, 514 F.2d 208 (D.C.Cir.1975), quoting from *Brady v. United States*, 397 U.S. 742 (1970). A plea of that character should not be overturned, even on direct appeal, when there has been a minor and technical violation of Rule 11 which amounts to harmless error.

Secondly, while *McCarthy* involved a situation in which the defendant's plea of guilty was before the court of appeals on direct appeal, the Supreme Court appears to have been primarily concerned with § 2255–type cases, for the Court referred exclusively to cases of that kind in the course of concluding that a per se rule was justified as to Rule 11 violations because of "the difficulty of achieving [rule 11's] purposes through a post–conviction voluntariness hearing." But that reasoning has now been substantially undercut by *United States v. Timmreck,* supra, for the Court there concluded § 2255 relief "is not available when all that is shown is a failure to comply with the formal requirements of the Rule," at least absent "other aggravating circumstances," which presumably could often only be developed in the course of a later evidentiary hearing.

Although all of the aforementioned considerations support the policy expressed in new subdivision (h), the Advisory Committee does wish to emphasize two important cautionary notes. The first is that subdivision (h) should *not* be read as supporting extreme or speculative harmless error claims or as, in effect, nullifying important Rule 11 safeguards. There would *not* be harmless error under subdivision (h) where, for example, as in *McCarthy,* there had been absolutely no inquiry by the judge into defendant's understanding of the nature of the charge and the harmless error claim of the government rests upon nothing more than the assertion that it may be "assumed" defendant possessed such understanding merely because he expressed a desire to plead guilty. Likewise, it would *not* be harmless error if the trial judge totally abdicated to the prosecutor the responsibility for giving to the defendant the various Rule 11 warnings, as this "results in the creation of an atmosphere of subtle coercion that clearly contravenes the policy behind Rule 11." *United States v. Crook,* 526 F.2d 708 (5th Cir.1976).

Indeed, it is fair to say that the kinds of Rule 11 violations which might be found to constitute harmless error upon direct appeal are fairly limited, as in such instances the matter "must be resolved solely on the basis of the Rule 11 transcript" and the other portions (e.g., sentencing hearing) of the limited record made in such cases. *United States v. Coronado,* supra. Illustrative are: where the judge's compliance with subdivision (c)(1) was not absolutely complete, in that some essential element of the crime was not mentioned, but the defendant's responses clearly indicate his awareness of that element, see *United States v. Coronado,* supra; where the judge's compliance with subdivision (c)(2) was erroneous in part in that the judge understated the maximum penalty somewhat, but the penalty actually imposed did not exceed that indicated in the warnings, see *United States v. Peters,* supra; and where the judge completely failed to comply with subdivision (c)(5), which of course has no bearing on the validity of the plea itself, cf. *United States v. Sinagub,* supra.

The second cautionary note is that subdivision (h) should *not* be read as an invitation to trial judges to take a more casual approach to Rule 11 proceedings. It is still true, as the Supreme Court pointed out in *McCarthy,* that thoughtful and careful compliance with Rule 11 best serves the cause of fair and efficient administration of criminal justice, as it

> will help reduce the great waste of judicial resources required to process the frivolous attacks on guilty plea convictions that are encouraged, and are more difficult to dispose of, when the original record is inadequate. It is, therefore, not too much to require that, before sentencing defendants to years of imprisonment, district judges take the few minutes necessary to inform them of their rights and to determine whether they understand the action they are taking.

Subdivision (h) makes *no change* in the responsibilities of the judge at Rule 11 proceedings, but instead merely rejects the extreme sanction of automatic reversal.

It must also be emphasized that a harmless error provision has been added to Rule 11 because some courts have read *McCarthy* as meaning that the general harmless error provision in Rule 52(a) cannot be utilized with respect to Rule 11 proceedings. Thus, the addition of subdivision (h) should *not* be read as suggesting that Rule 52(a) does not apply in other circumstances because of the absence of a provision comparable to subdivision (h) attached to other rules.

1985 Amendments

Subd. (c)(1). Section 5 of the Victim and Witness Protection Act of 1982, Pub.L. No. 97–291, 96 Stat. 1248 (1982), adds 18 U.S.C. § 3579, providing that when sentencing a defendant convicted of a Title 18 offense or of violating various subsections of the Federal Aviation Act of 1958, the court "may order, in addition to or in lieu of any other penalty authorized by law, that the defendant make restitution to any victim of the offense." Under this law restitution is favored; if the court "does not order restitution, or orders only partial restitution, . . . the court shall state on the record the reasons therefor." Because this restitution is deemed an aspect of the defendant's sentence, S.Rept. No. 97–532, 97th Cong., 2d Sess., 30–33 (1982), it is a matter about which a defendant tendering a plea of guilty or nolo contendere should be advised.

Because this new legislation contemplates that the amount of the restitution to be ordered will be ascertained later in the sentencing process, this amendment to Rule 11(c)(1) merely requires that the defendant be told of the court's power to order restitution. The exact amount or upper limit cannot and need not be stated at the time of the plea. Failure of a court to advise a defendant of the possibility of a restitution order would constitute harmless error under subdivision (h) if no restitution were thereafter ordered.

1987 Amendments

The amendments are technical. No substantive change is intended.

1989 Amendments

The Committee believes that a technical change, adding the words "or supervised release," is necessary to recognize that defendants sentenced under the guideline approach will be concerned about supervised release rather than special parole. See 18 U.S.C. 3583, and 3624(e). The words "special parole" are left in the rule, since the district courts continue to handle pre-guideline cases.

The amendment mandates that the district court inform a defendant that the court is required to consider any applicable guidelines but may depart from them under some circumstances. This requirement assures that the existence of guidelines will be known to a defendant before a plea of guilty or nolo contendere is accepted. Since it will be impracticable, if not impossible, to know which guidelines will be relevant prior to the formulation of a presentence report and resolution of disputed facts, the amendment does not require the court to specify which guidelines will be important or which grounds for departure might prove to be significant. The advice that the court is required to give cannot guarantee that a defendant who pleads guilty will not later claim a lack of understanding as to the importance of guidelines at the time of the plea. No advice is likely to serve as a complete protection against post-plea claims of ignorance or confusion. By giving the advice, the court places the defendant and defense counsel on notice of the importance that guidelines may play in sentencing and of the possibility of a departure from those guidelines. A defendant represented by competent counsel will be in a position to enter an intelligent plea.

The amended rule does not limit the district court's discretion to engage in a more extended colloquy with the defendant in order to impart additional information about sentencing guidelines or to inquire into the defendant's knowledge concerning guidelines. The amended rule sets forth only the minimum advice that must be provided to the defendant by the court.

1999 Amendments

Subdivision (a). The amendment deletes use of the term "corporation" and substitutes in its place the term "organization," with a reference to the definition of that term in 18 U.S.C. § 18.

Subdivision (c)(6). Rule 11(c) has been amended specifically to reflect the increasing practice of including provisions in plea agreements which require the defendant to waive certain appellate rights. The increased use of such provisions is due in part to the increasing number of direct appeals and collateral reviews challenging sentencing decisions. Given the increased use of such provisions, the Committee believed it was important to insure that first, a complete record exists regarding any waiver provisions, and second, that the waiver was voluntarily and knowingly made by the defendant. Although a number of federal courts have approved the ability of a defendant to enter into such waiver agreements, the Committee takes no position on the underlying validity of such waivers.

Subdivision (e). Amendments have been made to Rule 11(e)(1)(B) and (C) to reflect the impact of the Sentencing Guidelines on guilty pleas. Although Rule 11 is generally silent on the subject, it has become clear that the courts have struggled with the subject of guideline sentencing vis a vis plea agreements, entry and timing of guilty pleas, and the ability of the defendant to withdraw a plea of guilty. The amendments are intended to address two specific issues.

First, both subdivisions (e)(1)(B) and (e)(1)(C) have been amended to recognize that a plea agreement may specifically address not only what amounts to an appropriate sentence, but also a sentencing guideline, a sentencing factor, or a policy statement accompanying a sentencing guideline or factor. Under an (e)(1)(B) agreement, the government, as before, simply agrees to make a recommendation to the court, or agrees not to oppose a defense request concerning a particular sentence or consideration of a sentencing guideline, factor, or policy statement. The amendment makes it clear that this type of agreement is not binding on the court. Second, under an (e)(1)(C) agreement, the government and defense have actually agreed on what amounts to an appropriate sentence or have agreed to one of the specified components. The amendment also makes it clear that this agreement is binding on the court once the court accepts it. As is the situation under the current Rule, the court retains absolute discretion whether to accept a plea agreement.

GAP Report—Rule 11.

The Committee made no changes to the published draft amendments to Rule 11. But it did add language to the Committee Note which reflects the view that the amendment is not intended to signal its approval of the underlying practice of including waiver provisions in pretrial agreements.

2002 Amendments

The language of Rule 11 has been amended and reorganized as part of the general restyling of the Criminal Rules to make them more easily understood and to make style and terminology consistent throughout the rules. These changes are intended to be stylistic only, except as noted below.

Amended Rule 11(b)(1) requires the court to apprise the defendant of his or her rights before accepting a plea of guilty or nolo contendere. The Committee determined to expand upon the incomplete listing in the current rule of the elements of the "maximum possible penalty" and any "mandatory minimum" penalty to include advice as to the maximum or minimum term of imprisonment, forfeiture, fine, and special assessment, in addition to the two types of maximum and minimum penalties presently enumerated: restitution and supervised release. The outmoded reference to a term of "special parole" has been eliminated.

Amended Rule 11(b)(2), formerly Rule 11(d), covers the issue of determining that the plea is voluntary, and not the result of force, threats, or promises (other than those in a plea agreement). The reference to an inquiry in current Rule 11(d) whether the plea has resulted from plea discussions with the government has been deleted. That reference, which was often a source of confusion to defendants who were clearly pleading guilty as part of a plea agreement with the government, was considered unnecessary.

Rule 11(c)(1)(A) includes a change, which recognizes a common type of plea agreement—that the government will "not bring" other charges.

The Committee considered whether to address the practice in some courts of using judges to facilitate plea agreements. The current rule states that "the court shall not participate in any discussions between the parties concerning such plea agreement." Some courts apparently believe that that language acts as a limitation only upon the judge taking the defendant's plea and thus permits other judges to serve as facilitators for reaching a plea agreement between the government and the defendant. *See, e.g., United States v. Torres*, 999 F.2d 376, 378 (9th Cir. 1993) (noting practice and concluding that presiding judge had not participated in a plea agreement that had resulted from discussions involving another judge). The Committee decided to leave the Rule as it is with the understanding that doing so was in no way intended either to approve or disapprove the existing law interpreting that provision.

Amended Rules 11(c)(3) to (5) address the topics of consideration, acceptance, and rejection of a plea agreement. The amendments are not intended to make any change in practice. The topics are discussed separately because in the past there has been some question about the possible interplay between the court's consideration of the guilty plea in conjunction with a plea agreement and sentencing and the ability of the defendant to withdraw a plea. *See United States v. Hyde*, 520 U.S. 670 (1997) (holding that plea and plea agreement need not be accepted or rejected as a single unit; "guilty pleas can be accepted while plea agreements are deferred, and the acceptance of the two can be separated in time."). Similarly, the Committee decided to more clearly spell out in Rule 11(d) and 11(e) the ability of the defendant to withdraw a plea. *See United States v. Hyde, supra.*

Amended Rule 11(e) is a new provision, taken from current Rule 32(e), that addresses the finality of a guilty or nolo contendere plea after the court imposes sentence. The provision makes it clear that it is not possible for a defendant to withdraw a plea after sentence is imposed.

The reference to a "motion under 28 U.S.C. § 2255" has been changed to the broader term "collateral attack" to recognize that in some instances a court may grant collateral relief under provisions other than § 2255. *See United States v. Jeffers*, 234 F.3d 277 (5th Cir. 2000) (petition under § 2241 may be appropriate where remedy under § 2255 is ineffective or inadequate).

Currently, Rule 11(e)(5) requires that unless good cause is shown, the parties are to give pretrial notice to the court that a plea agreement exists. That provision has been deleted. First, the Committee believed that although the provision was originally drafted to assist judges, under current practice few counsel would risk the consequences in the ordinary case of not informing the court that an agreement exists. Secondly, the Committee was concerned that there might be rare cases where the parties might agree that informing the court of the existence of an agreement might endanger a defendant or compromise an ongoing investigation in a related case. In the end, the Committee believed that, on balance, it would be preferable to remove the provision and reduce the risk of pretrial disclosure.

Finally, revised Rule 11(f), which addresses the issue of admissibility or inadmissibility of pleas and statements made during the plea inquiry, cross references Federal Rule of Evidence 410.

HISTORICAL NOTES

References in Text

The Federal Rules of Evidence, referred to in subd. (f), are set out in the Appendix to Title 28, Fed.Rules Evid. Rule 101 et seq., 28 U.S.C.A.

Effective and Applicability Provisions

1979 Acts. Amendment of subd. (e)(6) of this rule by order of the United States Supreme Court of Apr. 30, 1979, effective Dec. 1, 1980, pursuant to section 1(1) of Pub.L. 96–42, July 31, 1979, 93 Stat. 326.

1975 Acts. Amendments of this rule embraced in the order of the United States Supreme Court on Apr. 22, 1974, and the amendments of this rule made by section 3 of Pub.L. 94–64, effective Dec. 1, 1975, except with respect to the amendment adding subd. (e)(6) of this rule, effective Aug. 1, 1975, pursuant to section 2 of Pub.L. 94–64.

Rule 12. Pleadings and Pretrial Motions

(a) Pleadings. The pleadings in a criminal proceeding are the indictment, the information, and the pleas of not guilty, guilty, and nolo contendere.

(b) Pretrial Motions.

(1) In General. Rule 47 applies to a pretrial motion.

(2) Motions That May Be Made Before Trial. A party may raise by pretrial motion any defense, objection, or request that the court can determine without a trial of the general issue.

(3) Motions That Must Be Made Before Trial. The following must be raised before trial:

(A) a motion alleging a defect in instituting the prosecution;

(B) a motion alleging a defect in the indictment or information—but at any time while the case is pending, the court may hear a claim that the indictment or information fails to invoke the court's jurisdiction or to state an offense;

(C) a motion to suppress evidence;

(D) a Rule 14 motion to sever charges or defendants; and

(E) a Rule 16 motion for discovery.

(4) Notice of the Government's Intent to Use Evidence.

(A) At the Government's Discretion. At the arraignment or as soon afterward as practicable, the government may notify the defendant of its intent to use specified evidence at trial in order to afford the defendant an opportunity to object before trial under Rule 12(b)(3)(C).

(B) At the Defendant's Request. At the arraignment or as soon afterward as practicable, the defendant may, in order to have an opportunity to move to suppress evidence under Rule 12(b)(3)(C), request notice of the government's intent to use (in its evidence-in-chief at trial) any evidence that the defendant may be entitled to discover under Rule 16.

(c) Motion Deadline. The court may, at the arraignment or as soon afterward as practicable, set a deadline for the parties to make pretrial motions and may also schedule a motion hearing.

(d) Ruling on a Motion. The court must decide every pretrial motion before trial unless it finds good cause to defer a ruling. The court must not defer ruling on a pretrial motion if the deferral will adversely affect a party's right to appeal. When factual issues are involved in deciding a motion, the court must state its essential findings on the record.

(e) Waiver of a Defense, Objection, or Request. A party waives any Rule 12(b)(3) defense, objection, or request not raised by the deadline the court sets under Rule 12(c) or by any extension the court provides. For good cause, the court may grant relief from the waiver.

(f) Recording the Proceedings. All proceedings at a motion hearing, including any findings of fact and conclusions of law made orally by the court, must be recorded by a court reporter or a suitable recording device.

(g) Defendant's Continued Custody or Release Status. If the court grants a motion to dismiss based on a defect in instituting the prosecution, in the indictment, or in the information, it may order the defendant to be released or detained under 18 U.S.C. § 3142 for a specified time until a new indictment or information is filed. This rule does not affect any federal statutory period of limitations.

(h) Producing Statements at a Suppression Hearing. Rule 26.2 applies at a suppression hearing under Rule 12(b)(3)(C). At a suppression hearing, a law enforcement officer is considered a government witness.

(As amended Apr. 22, 1974, eff. Dec. 1, 1975; July 31, 1975, Pub.L. 94–64, § 3(11), (12), 89 Stat. 372; Apr. 28, 1983, eff. Aug. 1, 1983; Mar. 9, 1987, eff. Aug. 1, 1987; Apr. 22, 1993, eff. Dec. 1, 1993; Apr. 29, 2002, eff. Dec. 1, 2002.)

ADVISORY COMMITTEE NOTES

1944 Adoption

Note to Subdivision (a). 1. This rule abolishes pleas to the jurisdiction, pleas in abatement, demurrers, special pleas in bar, and motions to quash. A motion to dismiss or for other appropriate relief is substituted for the purpose of raising all defenses and objections heretofore interposed in any of the foregoing modes. "This should result in a reduction of opportunities for dilatory tactics and, at the same time, relieve the defense of embarrassment. Many competent practitioners have been baffled and mystified by the distinctions between pleas in abatement, pleas in bar, demurrers, and motions to quash, and have, at times, found difficulty in determining which of these should be invoked." Homer Cummings, 29 A.B.A.Jour. 655. See also, Medalie, 4 Lawyers Guild R. (3) 1, 4.

2. A similar change was introduced by the Federal Rules of Civil Procedure (Rule 7(a)) which has proven successful. It is also proposed by the A.L.I. Code of Criminal Procedure (Sec. 209).

Note to Subdivision (b)(1) and (2). These two paragraphs classify into two groups all objections and defenses to be interposed by motion prescribed by Rule 12(a). In one group are defenses and objections which must be raised by motion, failure to do so constituting a waiver. In the other group are defenses and objections which at the defendant's option may be raised by motion, failure to do so, however, not constituting a waiver. (Cf. Rule 12 of Federal Rules of Civil Procedure, 28 U.S.C., Appendix.)

In the first of these groups are included all defenses and objections that are based on defects in the institution of the prosecution or in the indictment and information, other than lack of jurisdiction or failure to charge an offense. All such defenses and objections must be included in a single motion. (Cf. Rule 12(g) of Federal Rules of Civil Procedure, 28 U.S.C. Appendix.) Among the defenses and objections in this group are the following: Illegal selection or organization of the grand jury, disqualification of individual grand jurors, presence of unauthorized persons in the grand jury room, other irregularities in grand jury proceedings, defects in indictment or information other than lack of jurisdiction or failure to state an offense, etc. The provision that these defenses and objections are waived if not raised by motion substantially continues existing law, as they are waived at present unless raised before trial by plea in abatement, demurrer, motion to quash, etc.

In the other group of objections and defenses, which the defendant at his option may raise by motion before trial, are included all defenses and objections which are capable of determination without a trial of the general issue. They include such matters as former jeopardy, former conviction, former acquittal, statute of limitations, immunity, lack of jurisdiction, failure of indictment or information to state an offense, etc. Such matters have been heretofore raised by demurrers, special pleas in bar and motions to quash.

Note to Subdivision (b)(3). This rule, while requiring the motion to be made before pleading, vests discretionary authority in the court to permit the motion to be made within a reasonable time thereafter. The rule supersedes 18 U.S.C.A. § 566a [now 18 U.S.C.A. §§ 3288, 3289], fixing a definite limitation of time for pleas in abatement and motions to quash. The rule also eliminates the requirement for technical withdrawal of a plea if it is desired to interpose a preliminary objection or defense after the plea has been entered. Under this rule a plea will be permitted to stand in the meantime.

Note to Subdivision (b)(4). This rule substantially restates existing law. It leaves with the court discretion to determine in advance of trial defenses and objections raised by motion or to defer them for determination at the trial. It preserves the right to jury trial in those cases in which the right is given under the Constitution or by statute. In all other cases it vests in the court authority to determine issues of fact in such manner as the court deems appropriate.

Note to Subdivision (b)(5). 1. The first sentence substantially restates existing law, [former] 18 U.S.C. § 561 (Indictments and presentments; judgment on demurrer), which provides that in case a demurrer to an indictment or information is overruled, the judgment shall be respondeat ouster.

2. The last sentence of the rule that "Nothing in this rule shall be deemed to affect the provisions of any act of Congress relating to periods of limitations" is intended to preserve the provisions of statutes which permit a reindictment if the original indictment is found defective or is dismissed for other irregularities and the statute of limitations has run in the meantime, 18 U.S.C. § 587 [now 18 U.S.C. § 3288] (Defective indictment; defect found after period of limitations; reindictment); Id. 18 U.S.C. § 588 [now 18 U.S.C. § 3289] (Defective indictment; defect found before period of limitations; reindictment); Id. 18 U.S.C. § 589 [now 18 U.S.C. §§ 3288, 3289] (Defective indictment; defense of limitations to new indictment); Id. 18 U.S.C. § 556a [now 18 U.S.C. §§ 3288, 3289] (Indictments and presentments; objections to drawing or qualification of grand jury; time for filing; suspension of statute of limitations).

1974 Amendment

Subdivision (a) remains as it was in the old rule. It "speaks only of defenses and objections that prior to the rules could have been raised by a plea, demurrer, or motion to quash" (C. Wright, Federal Practice and Procedure: Criminal § 191 at p. 397 (1969)), and this might be interpreted as limiting the scope of the rule. However, some courts have assumed that old rule 12 does apply to pretrial motions generally, and the amendments to subsequent subdivisions of the rule should make clear that the rule is applicable to pretrial motion practice generally. (See e.g., rule 12(b)(3), (4), (5) and rule 41(e).)

Subdivision (b) is changed to provide for some additional motions and requests which **must** be made prior to trial. Subdivisions (b)(1) and (2) are restatements of the old rule.

Subdivision (b)(3) makes clear that objections to evidence on the ground that it was illegally obtained must be raised prior to trial. This is the current rule with regard to evidence obtained as a result of an illegal search. See rule 41(e); C. Wright, Federal Practice and Procedure: Criminal § 673 (1969, Supp.1971). It is also the practice with regard to other forms of illegality such as the use of unconstitutional means to obtain a confession. See C. Wright, Federal Practice and Procedure: Criminal § 673 at p. 108 (1969). It seems apparent that the same principle should apply whatever the claimed basis for the application of the exclusionary rule of evidence may be. This is consistent with the court's statement in *Jones v. United States*, 362 U.S. 257, 264, 80 S.Ct. 725, 4 L.Ed.2d 697 (1960):

This provision of Rule 41(e), requiring the motion to suppress to be made before trial, is a crystallization of decisions of this Court requiring that procedure, and is designed to eliminate from the trial disputes over police conduct not immediately relevant to the question of guilt. (Emphasis added.)

Subdivision (b)(4) provides for a pretrial request for discovery by either the defendant or the government to the extent to which such discovery is authorized by rule 16.

Subdivision (b)(5) provides for a pretrial request for a severance as authorized in rule 14.

Subdivision (c) provides that a time for the making of motions shall be fixed at the time of the arraignment or as soon thereafter as practicable by court rule or direction of a judge. The rule leaves to the individual judge whether the motions may be oral or written. This and other amendments to rule 12 are designed to make possible and to encourage the making of motions prior to trial, whenever possible, and in a single hearing rather than in a series of hearings. This is the recommendation of the American Bar Association's Committee on Standards Relating to Discovery and Procedure Before Trial (Approved Draft, 1970); see especially §§ 5.2 and 5.3. It also is the procedure followed in those jurisdictions which have used the so-called "omnibus hearing" originated by Judge James Carter in the Southern District of California. See 4 Defender Newsletter 44 (1967); Miller, The Omnibus Hearing—An Experiment in Federal Criminal Discovery, 5 San Diego L.Rev. 293 (1968); American Bar Association, Standards Relating to Discovery and Procedure Before Trial, Appendices B, C, and D (Approved Draft, 1970). The omnibus hearing is also being used, on an experimental basis, in several other district courts. Although the Advisory Committee is of the view that it would be premature to write the omnibus hearing procedure into the rules, it is of the view that the single pretrial hearing should be made possible and its use encouraged by the rules.

There is a similar trend in state practice. See, e.g., *State ex rel. Goodchild v. Burke*, 27 Wis.2d 244, 133 N.W.2d 753 (1965); *State ex rel. Rasmussen v. Tahash*, 272 Minn. 539, 141 N.W.2d 3 (1965).

The rule provides that the motion date be set at "the arraignment or as soon thereafter as practicable." This is the practice in some federal courts including those using the omnibus hearing. (In order to obtain the advantage of the omnibus hearing, counsel routinely plead not guilty at the initial arraignment on the information or indictment and then may indicate a desire to change the plea to guilty following the omnibus hearing. This practice builds a more adequate record in guilty plea cases.) The rule further provides that the date may be set before the arraignment if local rules of court so provide.

Subdivision (d) provides a mechanism for insuring that a defendant knows of the government's intention to use evidence to which the defendant may want to object. On some occasions the resolution of the admissibility issue prior to trial may be advantageous to the government. In these situations the attorney for the government can make effective defendant's obligation to make his motion to suppress prior to trial by giving defendant notice of the government's intention to use certain evidence. For example, in United States v. Desist, 384 F.2d 889, 897 (2d Cir.1967), the court said:

Early in the pre-trial proceedings, the Government commendably informed both the court and defense counsel that an electronic listening device had been used in investigating the case, and suggested a hearing be held as to its legality.

See also the "Omnibus Crime Control and Safe Streets Act of 1968," 18 U.S.C. § 2518(9):

The contents of any intercepted wire or oral communication or evidence derived therefrom shall not be received in evidence or otherwise disclosed in any trial, hearing, or other proceeding in a Federal or State court unless each party, not less than ten days before the trial, hearing, or proceeding, has been furnished with a copy of the court order, and accompanying application, under which the interception was authorized or approved.

In cases in which defendant wishes to know what types of evidence the government intends to use so that he can make his motion to suppress prior to trial, he can request the government to give notice of its intention to use specified evidence which the defendant is entitled to discover under rule 16. Although the defendant is already entitled to discovery of such evidence prior to trial under rule 16, rule 12 makes it possible for him to avoid the necessity of moving to suppress evidence which the government does not intend to use. No sanction is provided for the government's failure to comply with the court's order because the committee believes that attorneys for the government will in fact comply and that judges have ways of insuring compliance. An automatic exclusion of such evidence, particularly where the failure to give notice was not deliberate, seems to create too heavy a burden upon the exclusionary rule of evidence, especially when defendant has opportunity for broad discovery under rule 16. Compare ABA Project on Standards for Criminal Justice, Standards Relating to Electronic Surveillance (Approved Draft, 1971) at p. 116:

A failure to comply with the duty of giving notice could lead to the suppression of evidence. Nevertheless, the standards make it explicit that the rule is intended to be a matter of procedure which need not under appropriate circumstances automatically dictate that evidence otherwise admissible be suppressed.

Pretrial notice by the prosecution of its intention to use evidence which may be subject to a motion to suppress is increasingly being encouraged in state practice. See, e.g., *State ex rel. Goodchild v. Burke*, 27 Wis.2d 244, 264, 133 N.W.2d 753, 763 (1965):

In the interest of better administration of criminal justice we suggest that wherever practicable the prosecutor should within a reasonable time before trial notify the defense as to whether any alleged confession or admission will be offered in evidence at the trial. We also suggest, in cases where such notice is given by the prosecution, that the defense, if it intends to attack the confession or admission as involuntary, notify the prosecutor of a desire by the defense for a special determination on such issue.

See also *State ex rel. Rasmussen v. Tahash*, 272 Minn. 539, 553–556, 141 N.W.2d 3, 13–15 (1965):

At the time of arraignment when a defendant pleads not guilty, or as soon as possible thereafter, the state will advise the court as to whether its case against the defendant will include evidence obtained as the result of a search and seizure; evidence discovered because of a confession or statements in the nature of a confession obtained from the defendant; or confessions or statements in the nature of confessions.

Upon being so informed, the court will formally advise the attorney for the defendant (or the defendant himself if he refuses legal counsel) that he may, if he chooses, move the court to suppress the evidence so secured or the confession so obtained if his contention is that such evidence was secured or confession obtained in violation of defendant's constitutional rights. * * *

The procedure which we have outlined deals only with evidence obtained as the result of a search and seizure and evidence consisting of or produced by confession on the part of the defendant. However, the steps which have been suggested as a method of dealing with evidence of this type will indicate to counsel and to the trial courts that the pretrial consideration of other evidentiary problems, the resolution of which is needed to assure the integrity of the trial when conducted, will be most useful and that this court encourages the use of such procedures whenever practical.

Subdivision (e) provides that the court shall rule on a pretrial motion before trial unless the court orders that it be decided upon at the trial of the general issue or after verdict. This is the old rule. The reference to issues which must be tried by the jury is dropped as unnecessary, without any intention of changing current law or practice. The old rule begs the question of when a jury decision is required at the trial, providing only that a jury is necessary if "required by the Constitution or an act of Congress." It will be observed that subdivision (e) confers general authority to defer the determination of any pretrial motion until after verdict. However, in the case of a motion to suppress evidence the power should be exercised in the light of the possibility that if the motion is ultimately granted a retrial of the defendant may not be permissible.

Subdivision (f) provides that a failure to raise the objections or make the requests specified in subdivision (b) constitutes a waiver thereof, but the court is allowed to grant relief from the waiver if adequate cause is shown. See C. Wright, Federal Practice and Procedure: Criminal § 192 (1969), where it is pointed out that the old rule is unclear as to whether the waiver results only from a failure to raise the issue prior to trial or from the failure to do so at the time fixed by the judge for a hearing. The amendment makes clear that the defendant and, where appropriate, the government have an obligation to raise the issue at the motion date set by the judge pursuant to subdivision (c).

Subdivision (g) requires that a verbatim record be made of pretrial motion proceedings and requires the judge to make a record of his findings of fact and conclusions of law. This is desirable if pretrial rulings are to be subject to post-conviction review on the record. The judge may find and rule orally from the bench, so long as a verbatim record is taken. There is no necessity of a separate written memorandum containing the judge's findings and conclusions.

Subdivision (h) is essentially old rule 12(b)(5) except for the deletion of the provision that defendant may plead if the motion is determined adversely to him or, if he has already entered a plea, that that plea stands. This language seems unnecessary particularly in light of the experience in some district courts where a pro forma plea of not guilty is entered at the arraignment, pretrial motions are later made, and depending upon the outcome the defendant may then change his plea to guilty or persist in his plea of not guilty.

1975 Enactment

A. Amendments Proposed by the Supreme Court. Rule 12 of the Federal Rules of Criminal Procedure deals with pretrial motions and pleadings. The Supreme Court proposed several amendments to it. The more significant of these are set out below.

Subdivision (b) as proposed to be amended provides that the pretrial motions may be oral or written, at the court's discretion. It also provides that certain types of motions must be made before trial.

Subdivision (d) as proposed to be amended provides that the government, either on its own or in response to a request by the defendant, must notify the defendant of its intention to use certain evidence in order to give the defendant an opportunity before trial to move to suppress that evidence.

Subdivision (e) as proposed to be amended permits the court to defer ruling on a pretrial motion until the trial of the general issue or until after verdict.

Subdivision (f) as proposed to be amended provides that the failure before trial to file motions or requests or to raise defenses which must be filed or raised prior to trial, results in a waiver. However, it also provides that the court, for cause shown, may grant relief from the waiver.

Subdivision (g) as proposed to be amended requires that a verbatim record be made of the pretrial motion proceedings and that the judge make a record of his findings of fact and conclusions of law.

B. Committee Action. The Committee modified subdivision (e) to permit the court to defer its ruling on a pretrial motion until after the trial only for good cause. Moreover, the court cannot defer its ruling if to do so will adversely affect a party's right to appeal. The Committee believes that the rule proposed by the Supreme Court could deprive the government of its appeal rights under statutes like section

3731 of title 18 of the United States Code. Further, the Committee hopes to discourage the tendency to reserve rulings on pretrial motions until after verdict in the hope that the jury's verdict will make a ruling unnecessary.

The Committee also modified subdivision (h), which deals with what happens when the court grants a pretrial motion based upon a defect in the institution of the prosecution or in the indictment or information. The Committee's change provides that when such a motion is granted, the court may order that the defendant be continued in custody or that his bail be continued for a specified time. A defendant should not automatically be continued in custody when such a motion is granted. In order to continue the defendant in custody, the court must not only determine that there is probable cause, but it must also determine, in effect, that there is good cause to have the defendant arrested. House Report No. 94–247.

1983 Amendment

Rule 12(i). As noted in the recent decision of *United States v. Raddatz*, 447 U.S. 667 [100 S.Ct. 2406, 65 L.Ed.2d 424] (1980), hearings on pretrial suppression motions not infrequently necessitate a determination of the credibility of witnesses. In such a situation, it is particularly important, as also highlighted by *Raddatz*, that the record include some other evidence which tends to either verify or controvert the assertions of the witness. (This is especially true in light of the *Raddatz* holding that a district judge, in order to make an independent evaluation of credibility, is not required to rehear testimony on which a magistrate based his findings and recommendations following a suppression hearing before the magistrate.) One kind of evidence which can often fulfill this function is prior statements of the testifying witness, yet courts have consistently held that in light of the Jencks Act, 18 U.S.C. § 3500, such production of statements cannot be compelled at a pretrial suppression hearing. *United States v. Spagnuolo*, 515 F.2d 818 (9th Cir.1975); *United States v. Sebastian*, 497 F.2d 1267 (2nd Cir.1974); *United States v. Montos*, 421 F.2d 215 (5th Cir.1970). This result, which finds no express Congressional approval in the legislative history of the Jencks Act, see *United States v. Sebastian*, supra; *United States v. Covello*, 410 F.2d 536 (2d Cir.1969), would be obviated by new subdivision (i) of rule 12.

This change will enhance the accuracy of the factual determinations made in the context of pretrial suppression hearings. As noted in *United States v. Sebastian*, supra, it can be argued most persuasively that the case for pre-trial disclosure is strongest in the framework of a suppression hearing. Since findings at such a hearing as to admissibility of challenged evidence will often determine the result at trial and, at least in the case of fourth amendment suppression motions, cannot be relitigated later before the trier of fact, pre-trial production of the statements of witnesses would aid defense counsel's impeachment efforts at perhaps the most crucial point in the case. * * * [A] government witness at the suppression hearing may not appear at trial so that defendants could never test his credibility with the benefits of Jencks Act material.

The latter statement is certainly correct, for not infrequently a police officer who must testify on a motion to suppress as to the circumstances of an arrest or search will not be called at trial because he has no information necessary to the determination of defendant's guilt. See, e.g., *United States v. Spagnuolo*, supra (dissent notes that "under the prosecution's own admission, it did not intend to produce at trial the witnesses called at the pre-trial suppression hearing"). Moreover, even if that person did testify at the trial, if that testimony went to a different subject matter, then under rule 26.2(c) only portions of prior statements covering the same subject matter need be produced, and thus portions which might contradict the suppression hearing testimony would not be revealed. Thus, while it may be true, as declared in *United States v. Montos*, supra, that "due process does not require premature production at pre-trial hearings on motions to suppress of statements ultimately subject to discovery under the Jencks Act," the fact of the matter is that those statements—or, the essential portions thereof—are not necessarily subject to later discovery.

Moreover, it is not correct to assume that somehow the problem can be solved by leaving the suppression issue "open" in some fashion for resolution once the trial is under way, at which time the prior statements will be produced. In *United States v. Spagnuolo*, supra, the court responded to the defendant's dilemma of inaccessible prior statements by saying that the suppression motion could simply be deferred until trial. But, under the current version of rule 12 this is not possible; subdivision (b) declares that motions to suppress "must" be made before trial, and subdivision (e) says such motions cannot be deferred for determination at trial "if a party's right to appeal is adversely affected," which surely is the case as to suppression motions. As for the possibility of the trial judge reconsidering the motion to suppress on the basis of prior statements produced at trial and casting doubt on the credibility of a suppression hearing witness, it is not a desirable or adequate solution. For one thing, as already noted, there is no assurance that the prior statements will be forthcoming. Even if they are, it is not efficient to delay the continuation of the trial to undertake a reconsideration of matters which could have been resolved in advance of trial had the critical facts then been available. Furthermore, if such reconsideration is regularly to be expected of the trial judge, then this would give rise on appeal to unnecessary issues of the kind which confronted the court in *United States v. Montos*, supra—whether the trial judge was obligated either to conduct a new hearing or to make a new determination in light of the new evidence.

The second sentence of subdivision (i) provides that a law enforcement officer is to be deemed a witness called by the government. This means that when such a federal, state or local officer has testified at a suppression hearing, the defendant will be entitled to any statement of the officer in the possession of the government and relating to the subject matter concerning which the witness has testified, without regard to whether the officer was in fact called by the government or the defendant. There is considerable variation in local practice as to whether the arresting or searching officer is considered the witness of the defendant or of the government, but the need for the prior statement exists in either instance.

The second sentence of subdivision (i) also provides that upon a claim of privilege the court is to excise the privileged matter before turning over the statement. The situation most likely to arise is that in which the prior statement of the testifying officer identifies an informant who supplied some or all of the probable cause information to the police. Under *McCray v. Illinois*, 386 U.S. 300 [87 S.Ct. 1056, 18 L.Ed.2d

62] (1967), it is for the judge who hears the motion to decide whether disclosure of the informant's identity is necessary in the particular case. Of course, the government in any case may prevent disclosure of the informant's identity by terminating reliance upon information from that informant.

1987 Amendment

The amendment is technical. No substantive change is intended.

1993 Amendment

The amendment to subdivision (i) is one of a series of contemporaneous amendments to Rules 26.2, 32(f) [sic], 32.1, 46, and Rule 8 of the Rules Governing § 2255 Hearings, which extended Rule 26.2, Production of Witness Statements, to other proceedings or hearings conducted under the Rules of Criminal Procedure. Rule 26.2(c) now explicitly states that the trial court may excise privileged matter from the requested witness statements. That change rendered similar language in Rule 12(i) redundant.

2002 Amendments

The language of Rule 12 has been amended as part of the general restyling of the Criminal Rules to make them more easily understood and to make style and terminology consistent throughout the rules. These changes are intended to be stylistic only, except as noted below.

The last sentence of current Rule 12(a), referring to the elimination of "all other pleas, and demurrers and motions to quash" has been deleted as unnecessary.

Rule 12(b) is modified to more clearly indicate that Rule 47 governs any pretrial motions filed under Rule 12, including form and content. The new provision also more clearly delineates those motions that *must* be filed pretrial and those that *may* be filed pretrial. No change in practice is intended.

Rule 12(b)(4) is composed of what is currently Rule 12(d). The Committee believed that that provision, which addresses the government's requirement to disclose discoverable information for the purpose of facilitating timely defense objections and motions, was more appropriately associated with the pretrial motions specified in Rule 12(b)(3).

Rule 12(c) includes a non-stylistic change. The reference to the "local rule" exception has been deleted to make it clear that judges should be encouraged to set deadlines for motions. The Committee believed that doing so promotes more efficient case management, especially when there is a heavy docket of pending cases. Although the rule permits some discretion in setting a date for motion hearings, the Committee believed that doing so at an early point in the proceedings would also promote judicial economy.

Moving the language in current Rule 12(d) caused the relettering of the subdivisions following Rule 12(c).

Although amended Rule 12(e) is a revised version of current Rule 12(f), the Committee intends to make no change in the current law regarding waivers of motions or defenses.

HISTORICAL NOTES

Effective and Applicability Provisions

1975 Acts. Amendments of this rule embraced in the order of the United States Supreme Court on Apr. 22, 1974, and the amendments of this rule made by section 3 of Pub.L. 94–64, effective Dec. 1, 1975, pursuant to section 2 of Pub.L. 94–64.

Rule 12.1. Notice of an Alibi Defense

(a) Government's Request for Notice and Defendant's Response.

(1) Government's Request. An attorney for the government may request in writing that the defendant notify an attorney for the government of any intended alibi defense. The request must state the time, date, and place of the alleged offense.

(2) Defendant's Response. Within 10 days after the request, or at some other time the court sets, the defendant must serve written notice on an attorney for the government of any intended alibi defense. The defendant's notice must state:

(A) each specific place where the defendant claims to have been at the time of the alleged offense; and

(B) the name, address, and telephone number of each alibi witness on whom the defendant intends to rely.

(b) Disclosing Government Witnesses.

(1) Disclosure. If the defendant serves a Rule 12.1(a)(2) notice, an attorney for the government must disclose in writing to the defendant or the defendant's attorney:

(A) the name, address, and telephone number of each witness the government intends to rely on to establish the defendant's presence at the scene of the alleged offense; and

(B) each government rebuttal witness to the defendant's alibi defense.

(2) Time to Disclose. Unless the court directs otherwise, an attorney for the government must give its Rule 12.1(b)(1) disclosure within 10 days after the defendant serves notice of an intended alibi defense under Rule 12.1(a)(2), but no later than 10 days before trial.

(c) Continuing Duty to Disclose. Both an attorney for the government and the defendant must promptly disclose in writing to the other party the name, address, and telephone number of each additional witness if:

(1) the disclosing party learns of the witness before or during trial; and

(2) the witness should have been disclosed under Rule 12.1(a) or (b) if the disclosing party had known of the witness earlier.

(d) Exceptions. For good cause, the court may grant an exception to any requirement of Rule 12.1(a)—(c).

(e) Failure to Comply. If a party fails to comply with this rule, the court may exclude the testimony of any undisclosed witness regarding the defendant's alibi. This rule does not limit the defendant's right to testify.

(f) Inadmissibility of Withdrawn Intention. Evidence of an intention to rely on an alibi defense, later withdrawn, or of a statement made in connection with that intention, is not, in any civil or criminal proceeding, admissible against the person who gave notice of the intention.

(Added Apr. 22, 1974, eff. Dec. 1, 1975, and amended July 31, 1975, Pub.L. 94–64, § 3(13), 89 Stat. 372; Apr. 29, 1985, eff. Aug. 1, 1985; Mar. 9, 1987, eff. Aug. 1, 1987; Apr. 29, 2002, eff. Dec. 1, 2002.)

ADVISORY COMMITTEE NOTES

Rule 12.1 is new. See rule 87 of the United States District Court Rules for the District of Columbia for a somewhat comparable provision.

The Advisory Committee has dealt with the issue of notice of alibi on several occasions over the course of the past three decades. In the Preliminary Draft of the Federal Rules of Criminal Procedure, 1943, and the Second Preliminary Draft, 1944, an alibi-notice rule was proposed. But the Advisory Committee was closely divided upon whether there should be a rule at all and, if there were to be a rule, what the form of the rule should be. Orfield, The Preliminary Draft of the Federal Rules of Criminal Procedure, 22 Texas L.Rev. 37, 57–58 (1943). The principal disagreement was whether the prosecutor or the defendant should initiate the process. The Second Preliminary Draft published in 1944 required the defendant to initiate the process by a motion to require the government to state with greater particularity the time and place it would rely on. Upon receipt of this information, defendant was required to give his notice of alibi. This formulation was "vehemently objected" to by five members of the committee (out of a total of eighteen) and two alternative rule proposals were submitted to the Supreme Court. Both formulations—one requiring the prosecutor to initiate the process, the other requiring the defendant to initiate the process—were rejected by the Court. See Epstein, Advance Notice of Alibi, 55 J.Crim.L., C. & P.S. 29, 30 (1964) in which the view is expressed that the unresolved split over the rule "probably caused" the court to reject an alibi-notice rule.

Rule 12.1 embodies an intermediate position. The initial burden is upon the defendant to raise the defense of alibi, but he need not specify the details of his alibi defense until the government specifies the time, place, and date of alleged offense. Each party must, at the appropriate time, disclose the names and addresses of witnesses.

In 1962 the Advisory Committee drafted an alibi-notice rule and included it in the Preliminary Draft of December 1962, rule 12A at pp. 5–6. This time the Advisory Committee withdrew the rule without submitting it to the Standing Committee on Rules of Practice and Procedure. Wright, Proposed Changes in Federal, Civil, Criminal, and Appellate Procedure, 35 F.R.D. 317, 326 (1964). Criticism of the December 1962 alibi-notice rule centered on constitutional questions and questions of general fairness to the defendant. See Everett, Discovery in Criminal Cases—In Search of a Standard, 1964 Duke L.J. 477, 497–499.

Doubts about the constitutionality of a notice-of-alibi rule were to some extent resolved by *Williams v. Florida*, 399 U.S. 78, 90 S.Ct. 1893, 26 L.Ed.2d 446 (1970). In that case the court sustained the constitutionality of the Florida notice-of-alibi statute, but left unresolved two important questions.

(1) The court said that it was not holding that a notice-of-alibi requirement was valid under conditions where a defendant does not enjoy "reciprocal discovery against the State." 399 U.S. at 82 n. 11, 90 S.Ct. 1893. Under the revision of rule 16, the defendant is entitled to substantially enlarged discovery in federal cases, and it would seem appropriate to conclude that the rules will comply with the "reciprocal discovery" qualifications of the Williams decision. [*Wardius v. Oregon*, 412 U.S. 470, 93 S.Ct. 2208, 37 L.Ed.2d 82 (1973) was decided after the approval of proposed Rule 12.1 by the Judicial Conference of the United States. In that case the Court held the Oregon Notice-of-Alibi statute unconstitutional because of the failure to give the defendant adequate reciprocal discovery rights.]

(2) The court said that it did not consider the question of the "validity of the threatened sanction, had petitioner chosen not to comply with the notice-of-alibi rule." 399 U.S. at 83 n. 14, 90 S.Ct. 1893. This issue remains unresolved. [See *Wardius v. Oregon*, 412 U.S. at 472, Note 4, 93 S.Ct. 2208.] Rule 12.1(e) provides that the court may exclude the testimony of any witness whose name has not been disclosed pursuant to the requirements of the rule. The defendant may, however, testify himself. Prohibiting from testifying a witness whose name was not disclosed is a common provision in state statutes. See Epstein, *supra*, at 35. It is generally assumed that the sanction is essential if the notice-of-alibi rule is to have practical significance. See Epstein, *supra*, at 36. The use of the term "may" is intended to make clear that the judge may allow the alibi witness to testify if, under the particular circumstances, there is cause shown for the failure to conform to the requirements of the rules. This is further emphasized by subdivision (f) which provides for exceptions whenever "good cause" is shown for the exception.

The Supreme Court of Illinois recently upheld an Illinois statute which requires a defendant to give notice of his alibi witnesses although the prosecution is not required to disclose its alibi rebuttal witnesses. *People v. Holiday*, 47 Ill.2d 300, 265 N.E.2d 634 (1970). Because the defense complied with the requirement, the court did not have to consider the propriety of penalizing noncompliance.

The requirement of notice of alibi seems to be an increasingly common requirement of state criminal procedure. State statutes and court rules are cited in 399 U.S. at 82 n. 11, 90 S.Ct. 1893. See also Epstein, *supra*.

Rule 12.1 will serve a useful purpose even though rule 16 now requires disclosure of the names and addresses of government and defense witnesses. There are cases in which the identity of defense witnesses may be known, but it may come as a surprise to the government that they intend to testify as to an alibi and there may be no advance notice of the details of the claimed alibi. The result often is an unnecessary interruption and delay in the trial to enable the government to conduct an appropriate investigation. The objective of rule 12.1 is to prevent this by providing a mechanism which will enable the parties to have specific information in advance of trial to prepare to meet the issue of alibi during the trial.

1975 Enactment

A. Amendments Proposed by the Supreme Court. Rule 12.1 is a new rule that deals with the defense of alibi. It provides that a defendant must notify the government of his intention to rely upon the defense of alibi. Upon receipt of such notice, the government must advise the defendant of the specific time, date, and place at which the offense is alleged to have been committed. The defendant must then inform the government of the specific place at which he claims to have been when the offense is alleged to have been committed, and of the names and addresses of the witnesses on whom he intends to rely to establish his alibi. The government must then inform the defendant of the names and addresses of the witnesses on whom it will rely to establish the defendant's presence at the scene of the crime. If either party fails to comply with the provisions of the rule, the court may exclude the testimony of any witness whose identity is not disclosed. The rule does not attempt to limit the right of the defendant to testify in his own behalf.

B. Committee Action. The Committee disagrees with the defendant-triggered procedures of the rule proposed by the Supreme Court. The major purpose of a notice-of-alibi rule is to prevent unfair surprise to the prosecution. The Committee, therefore, believes that it should be up to the prosecution to trigger the alibi defense discovery procedures. If the prosecution is worried about being surprised by an alibi defense, it can trigger the alibi defense discovery procedures. If the government fails to trigger the procedures and if the defendant raises an alibi defense at trial, then the government cannot claim surprise and get a continuance of the trial.

The Committee has adopted a notice-of-alibi rule similar to the one now used in the District of Columbia. [See Rule 2–5(b) of the Rules of the United States District Court for the District of Columbia. See also Rule 16–1 of the Rules of Criminal Procedure for the Superior Court of the District of Columbia]. The rule is prosecution-triggered. If the prosecutor notifies the defendant of the time, place, and date of the alleged offense, then the defendant has 10 days in which to notify the prosecutor of his intention to rely upon an alibi defense, specify where he claims to have been at the time of the alleged offense, and provide a list of his alibi witnesses. The prosecutor, within 10 days but no later than 10 days before trial, must then provide the defendant with a list of witnesses who will place the defendant at the scene of the alleged crime and those witnesses who will be used to rebut the defendant's alibi witnesses.

The Committee's rule does not operate only to the benefit of the prosecution. In fact, its rule will provide the defendant with more information than the rule proposed by the Supreme Court. The rule proposed by the Supreme Court permits the defendant to obtain a list of only those witnesses who will place him at the scene of the crime. The defendant, however, would get the names of these witnesses anyway as part of his discovery under Rule 16(a)(1)(E). The Committee rule not only requires the prosecution to provide the names of witnesses who place the defendant at the scene of the crime, but it also requires the prosecution to turn over the names of those witnesses who will be called in rebuttal to the defendant's alibi witnesses. This is information that the defendant is not otherwise entitled to discover. House Report No. 94–247.

1985 Amendment

Rule 12.1(f). This clarifying amendment is intended to serve the same purpose as a comparable change made in 1979 to similar language in Rule 11(e)(6). The change makes it clear that evidence of a withdrawn intent or of statements made in connection therewith is thereafter inadmissible against the person who gave the notice in any civil or criminal proceeding, without regard to whether the proceeding is against that person.

1987 Amendment

The amendments are technical. No substantive change is intended.

2002 Amendments

The language of Rule 12.1 has been amended as part of the general restyling of the Criminal Rules to make them more easily understood and to make style and terminology consistent throughout the rules. These changes are intended to be stylistic only, except as noted below.

Current Rules 12.1(d) and 12.1(e) have been switched in the amended rule to improve the organization of the rule.

Finally, the amended rule includes a new requirement that in providing the names and addresses of alibi and any rebuttal witnesses, the parties must also provide the phone numbers of those witnesses. *See* Rule 12.1(a)(2), Rule 12.1(b)(1), and Rule 12.1(c). The Committee believed that requiring such information would facilitate locating and interviewing those witnesses.

HISTORICAL NOTES

Effective and Applicability Provisions

1975 Acts. This rule, and the amendments of this rule made by section 3 of Pub.L. 94–64, effective Dec. 1, 1975, pursuant to section 2 of Pub.L. 94–64.

Rule 12.2. Notice of an Insanity Defense; Mental Examination

(a) Notice of an Insanity Defense. A defendant who intends to assert a defense of insanity at the time of the alleged offense must so notify an attorney for the government in writing within the time provided for filing a pretrial motion, or at any later time the court sets, and file a copy of the notice with the clerk. A defendant who fails to do so cannot rely on an insanity defense. The court may, for good cause, allow the defendant to file the notice late, grant additional trial-preparation time, or make other appropriate orders.

(b) Notice of Expert Evidence of a Mental Condition. If a defendant intends to introduce expert evidence relating to a mental disease or defect or any other mental condition of the defendant bearing on either (1) the issue of guilt or (2) the issue of punishment in a capital case, the defendant must—within the time provided for filing a pretrial motion or at any later time the court sets—notify an attorney for the government in writing of this intention and file a copy of the notice with the clerk. The court may, for good cause, allow the defendant to file the notice late, grant the parties additional trial-preparation time, or make other appropriate orders.

(c) Mental Examination.

(1) Authority to Order an Examination; Procedures.

(A) The court may order the defendant to submit to a competency examination under 18 U.S.C. § 4241.

(B) If the defendant provides notice under Rule 12.2(a), the court must, upon the government's motion, order the defendant to be examined under 18 U.S.C. § 4242. If the defendant provides notice under Rule 12.2(b) the court may, upon the government's motion, order the defendant to be examined under procedures ordered by the court.

(2) Disclosing Results and Reports of Capital Sentencing Examination. The results and reports of any examination conducted solely under Rule 12.2(c)(1) after notice under Rule 12.2(b)(2) must be sealed and must not be disclosed to any attorney for the government or the defendant unless the defendant is found guilty of one or more capital crimes and the defendant confirms an intent to offer during sentencing proceedings expert evidence on mental condition.

(3) Disclosing Results and Reports of the Defendant's Expert Examination. After disclosure under Rule 12.2(c)(2) of the results and reports of the government's examination, the defendant must disclose to the government the results and reports of any examination on mental condition conducted by the defendant's expert about which the defendant intends to introduce expert evidence.

(4) Inadmissibility of a Defendant's Statements. No statement made by a defendant in the course of any examination conducted under this rule (whether conducted with or without the defendant's consent), no testimony by the expert based on the statement, and no other fruits of the statement may be admitted into evidence against the defendant in any criminal proceeding except on an issue regarding mental condition on which the defendant:

(A) has introduced evidence of incompetency or evidence requiring notice under Rule 12.2(a) or (b)(1), or

(B) has introduced expert evidence in a capital sentencing proceeding requiring notice under Rule 12.2(b)(2).

(d) Failure to Comply.

(1) Failure to Give Notice or to Submit to Examination. The court may exclude any expert evidence from the defendant on the issue of the defendant's mental disease, mental defect, or any other mental condition bearing on the defendant's guilt or the issue of punishment in a capital case if the defendant fails to:

(A) give notice under Rule 12.2(b); or

(B) submit to an examination when ordered under Rule 12.2(c).

(2) Failure to Disclose. The court may exclude any expert evidence for which the defendant has failed to comply with the disclosure requirement of Rule 12.2(c)(3).

(e) Inadmissibility of Withdrawn Intention. Evidence of an intention as to which notice was given under Rule 12.2(a) or (b), later withdrawn, is not, in any civil or criminal proceeding, admissible against the person who gave notice of the intention.

(Added Apr. 22, 1974, eff. Dec. 1, 1975, and amended July 31, 1975, Pub.L. 94–64, § 3(14), 89 Stat. 373; Apr. 28, 1983, eff. Aug. 1, 1983; Oct. 12, 1984, Pub.L. 98–473, Title II, § 404, 98 Stat. 2067; Oct. 30, 1984, Pub.L. 98–596, § 11(a), (b), 98 Stat. 3138; Apr. 29, 1985, eff. Aug. 1, 1985; Nov. 10, 1986, Pub.L. 99–646, § 24, 100 Stat. 3597; Mar. 9, 1987, eff. Aug. 1, 1987; Apr. 29, 2002, eff. Dec. 1, 2002; Apr. 25, 2005, eff. Dec. 1, 2005.)

ADVISORY COMMITTEE NOTES

Rule 12.2 is designed to require a defendant to give notice prior to trial of his intention (1) to rely upon the defense of insanity or (2) to introduce expert testimony of mental disease or defect on the theory that such mental condition is inconsistent with the mental state required for the offense charged. This rule does not deal with the issue of mental competency to stand trial.

The objective is to give the government time to prepare to meet the issue, which will usually require reliance upon expert testimony. Failure to give advance notice commonly results in the necessity for a continuance in the middle of a trial, thus unnecessarily delaying the administration of justice.

A requirement that the defendant give notice of his intention to rely upon the defense of insanity was proposed by the Advisory Committee in the Second Preliminary Draft of Proposed Amendments (March 1964), rule 12.1, p. 7. The objective of the 1964 proposal was explained in a brief Advisory Committee Note:

Under existing procedure although insanity is a defense, once it is raised the burden to prove sanity beyond a reasonable doubt rests with the government. *Davis v. United States*, 160 U.S. 469, 16 S.Ct. 353, 40 L.Ed. 499 (1895). This rule requires pretrial notice to the government of an insanity defense, thus permitting it to prepare to meet the issue. Furthermore, in *Lynch v. Overholser*, 369 U.S. 705, 82 S.Ct. 1063, 8 L.Ed.2d 211 (1962), the Supreme Court held that, at least in the face of a mandatory commitment statute, the defendant had a right to determine whether or not to raise the issue of insanity. The rule gives the defendant a method of raising the issue and precludes any problem of deciding whether or not the defendant relied on insanity.

The Standing Committee on Rules of Practice and Procedure decided not to recommend the proposed Notice of Insanity rule to the Supreme Court. Reasons were not given.

Requiring advance notice of the defense of insanity is commonly recommended as a desirable procedure. The Working Papers of the National Commission on Reform of Federal Criminal Laws, Vol. 1, p. 254 (1970), state in part:

It is recommended that procedural reform provide for advance notice that evidence of mental disease or defect will be relied upon in defense. . . .

Requiring advance notice is proposed also by the American Law Institute's Model Penal Code, § 4.03 (P.O.D.1962). The commentary in Tentative Draft No. 4 at 193–194 (1955) indicates that, as of that time, six states required pretrial notice and an additional eight states required that the defense of insanity be specially pleaded.

For recent state statutes see N.Y. CPL § 250.10 (McKinney's Consol.Laws, c. 11–A, 1971) enacted in 1970 which provides that no evidence by a defendant of a mental disease negativing criminal responsibility shall be allowed unless defendant has served notice on the prosecutor of his intention to rely upon such defense. See also New Jersey Penal Code (Final Report of the New Jersey Criminal Law Revision Commission, Oct. 1971) § 2c:4–3; New Jersey Court Rule 3:12; State v. Whitlow, 45 N.J. 3, 22 n. 3, 210 A.2d 763 (1965), holding the requirement of notice to be both appropriate and not in violation of the privilege against self-incrimination.

Subdivision (a) deals with notice of the "defense of insanity." In this context the term insanity has a well-understood meaning. See, e.g., Tydings, A Federal Verdict of Not Guilty by Reason of Insanity and a Subsequent Commitment Procedure, 27 Md.L.Rev. 131 (1967). Precisely how the defense of insanity is phrased does, however, differ somewhat from circuit to circuit. See Study Draft of a New Federal Criminal Code, § 503 Comment at 37 (USGPO 1970). For a more extensive discussion of present law, see Working Papers of the National Commission on Reform of Federal Criminal Laws, Vol. 1, pp. 229–247 (USGPO 1970). The National Commission recommends the adoption of a single test patterned after the proposal of the American Law Institute's Model Penal Code. The proposed definition provides in part:

In any prosecution for an offense lack of criminal responsibility by reason of mental disease or defect is a defense. [Study Draft of a New Federal Criminal Code § 503 at 36–37.]

Should the proposal of the National Commission be adopted by the Congress, the language of subdivision (a) probably ought to be changed to read "defense of lack of criminal responsibility by reason of mental disease or defect" rather than "defense of insanity."

Subdivision (b) is intended to deal with the issue of expert testimony bearing upon the issue of whether the defendant had the "mental state required for the offense charged."

There is some disagreement as to whether it is proper to introduce evidence of mental disease or defect bearing not upon the defense of insanity, but rather upon the existence of the mental state required by the offense charged. The American Law Institute's Model Penal Code takes the position that such evidence is admissible [§ 4.02(1) (P.O.D. 1962)]. See also *People v. Gorshen*, 51 Cal.2d 716, 336 P.2d 492 (1959).

The federal cases reach conflicting conclusions. See *Rhodes v. United States*, 282 F.2d 59, 62 (4th Cir.1960):

The proper way would have been to ask the witness to describe the defendant's mental condition and symptoms, his pathological beliefs and motivations, if he was thus afflicted, and to explain how these influenced or could have influenced his behavior, particularly his mental capacity knowingly to make the false statement charged, or knowingly to forge the signatures * * *.

Compare *Fisher v. United States*, 328 U.S. 463, 66 S.Ct. 1318, 90 L.Ed. 1382 (1946).

Subdivision (b) does not attempt to decide when expert testimony is admissible on the issue of the requisite mental state. It provides only that the defendant must give pretrial notice when he intends to introduce such evidence. The purpose is to prevent the need for a continuance when such evidence is offered without prior notice. The problem of unnecessary delay has arisen in jurisdictions which do not require prior notice of an intention to use expert testimony on the issue of mental state. Referring to this, the California Special Commission on Insanity and Criminal Offenders, First Report 30 (1962) said:

The abuses of the present system are great. Under a plea of "not guilty" without any notice to the people that the defense of insanity will be relied upon, defendant has been able to raise the defense upon the trial of the issue as to whether he committed the offense charged.

As an example of the delay occasioned by the failure to heretofore require a pretrial notice by the defendant, see *United States v. Albright*, 388 F.2d 719 (4th Cir.1968), where a jury trial was recessed for 23 days to permit a psychiatric examination by the prosecution when the defendant injected a surprise defense of lack of mental competency.

Subdivision (c) gives the court the authority to order the defendant to submit to a psychiatric examination by a psychiatrist designated by the court. A similar provision is found in ALI, Model Penal Code § 4.05(1) (P.O.D.1962). This is a common provision of state law, the constitutionality of which has been sustained. Authorities are collected in ALI, Model Penal Code, pp. 195–196 Tent. Draft No. 4, 1955). For a recent proposal, see the New Jersey Penal Code § 2c: 4–5 (Final Report of the New Jersey Criminal Law Revision Commission, Oct. 1971) authorizing appointment of "at least one qualified psychiatrist to examine and report upon the mental condition of the defendant." Any issue of self-incrimination which might arise can be dealt with by the court as, for example, by a bifurcated trial which deals separately with the issues of guilt and of mental responsibility. For statutory authority to appoint a psychiatrist with respect to competency to stand trial, see 18 U.S.C. § 4244.

Subdivision (d) confers authority on the court to exclude expert testimony in behalf of a defendant who has failed to give notice under subdivision (b) or who refuses to be examined by a court-appointed psychiatrist under subdivision (c). See *State v. Whitlow*, 45 N.J. 3, 23, 210 A.2d 763 (1965), which indicates that it is proper to limit or exclude testimony by a defense psychiatrist whenever defendant refuses to be examined.

1975 Enactment

A. Amendments Proposed by the Supreme Court. Rule 12.2 is a new rule that deals with defense based upon mental condition. It provides that: (1) The defendant must notify the prosecution in writing of his intention to rely upon the defense of insanity. If the defendant fails to comply, "insanity may not be raised as a defense." (2) If the defendant intends to introduce expert testimony relating to mental disease or defect on the issue whether he had the requisite mental state, he must notify the prosecution in writing. (3) The court, on motion of the prosecution, may order the defendant to submit to a psychiatric examination by a court-appointed psychiatrist. (4) If the defendant fails to undergo the court-ordered psychiatric examination, the court may exclude any expert witness the defendant offers on the issue of his mental state.

B. Committee Action. The Committee agrees with the proposed rule but has added language concerning the use of statements made to a psychiatrist during the course of a psychiatric examination provided for by Rule 12.2. The language provides:

> No statement made by the accused in the course of any examination provided for by this rule, whether the examination shall be with or without the consent of the accused, shall be admitted in evidence against the accused before the judge who or jury which determines the guilt of the accused, prior to the determination of guilt.

The purpose of this rule is to secure the defendant's fifth amendment right against self-incrimination. See *State v. Raskin*, 34 Wis.2d 607, 150 N.W.2d 318 (1967). The provision is flexible and does not totally preclude the use of such statements. For example, the defendant's statement can be used at a separate determination of the issue of sanity or for sentencing purposes once guilt has been determined. A limiting instruction to the jury in a single trial to consider statements made to the psychiatrist only on the issue of sanity would not satisfy the requirements of the rule as amended. The prejudicial effect on the determination of guilt would be inescapable.

The Committee notes that the rule does not attempt to resolve the issue whether the court can constitutionally compel a defendant to undergo a psychiatric examination when the defendant is unwilling to undergo one. The provisions of subdivision (c) are qualified by the phrase, "In an appropriate case." If the court cannot constitutionally compel an unwilling defendant to undergo a psychiatric examination, then the provisions of subdivision (c) are inapplicable in every instance where the defendant is unwilling to undergo a court-ordered psychiatric examination. The Committee, by its approval of subdivision (c), intends to take no stand whatever on the constitutional question. House Report No. 94–247.

Rule 12.2(c) deals with court-ordered psychiatric examinations. The House version provides that no statement made by a defendant during a court-ordered psychiatric examination could be admitted in evidence against the defendant before the trier of fact that determines the issue of guilt, prior to the determination of guilt. The Senate version deletes this provision.

The Conference adopts a modified House provision and restores to the bill the language of H.R. 6799 as it was originally introduced. The Conference-adopted language provides that no statement made by the defendant during a psychiatric examination provided for by the rule shall be admitted against him on the issue of guilt in any criminal proceeding.

The Conference believes that the provision in H.R. 6799 as originally introduced in the House adequately protects the defendant's fifth amendment right against self-incrimination. The rule does not preclude use of statements made by a defendant during a court-ordered psychiatric examination. The statements may be relevant to the issue of defendant's sanity and admissable on that issue. However, a limiting instruction would not satisfy the rule if a statement is so prejudicial that a limiting instruction would be ineffective. Cf. practice under 18 U.S.C. 4244. House Report No. 94–414.

1983 Amendment

Rule 12.2(b). Courts have recently experienced difficulty with the question of what kind of expert testimony offered for what purpose falls within the notice requirement of rule 12.2(b). See, e.g., *United States v. Hill*, 655 F.2d 512 (3d Cir.1980) (rule not applicable to tendered testimony of psychologist concerning defendant's susceptibility of inducement, offered to reinforce defendant's entrapment defense); *United States v. Webb*, 625 F.2d 709 (5th Cir.1980) (rule not applicable to expert testimony tendered to show that defendant lacked the "propensity to commit a violent act," as this testimony was offered "to prove that Webb did not commit the offense charged," shooting at a helicopter, "not that certain conduct was unaccompanied by criminal intent"); *United States v. Perl*, 584 F.2d 1316 (4th Cir.1978) (because entrapment defense properly withheld from jury, it was unnecessary to decide if the district court erred in holding rule applicable to tendered testimony of the doctor that defendant had increased susceptibility to suggestion as a result of medication he was taking); *United States v. Olson*, 576 F.2d 1267 (8th Cir.1978) (rule applicable to tendered testimony of an alcoholism and drug therapist that defendant was not responsible for his actions because of a problem with alcohol); *United States v. Staggs*, 553 F.2d 1073 (7th Cir. 1977) (rule applicable to tendered testimony of psychologist that defendant, charged with assaulting federal officer, was more likely to hurt himself than to direct his aggressions toward others, as this testimony bears upon whether defendant intended to put victim in apprehension when he picked up the gun).

What these cases illustrate is that expert testimony about defendant's mental condition may be tendered in a wide variety of circumstances well beyond the situation clearly within rule 12.2(b), i.e., where a psychiatrist testifies for the defendant regarding his diminished capacity. In all of these situations and others like them, there is good reason to make applicable the notice provisions of rule 12.2(b). This is because in all circumstances in which the defendant plans to offer expert testimony concerning his mental condition at the time of the crime charged, advance disclosure to the government will serve "to permit adequate pretrial preparation, to prevent surprise at trial, and to avoid the necessity of delays during trial." 2 A.B.A. Standards for Criminal Justice 11–55 (2d 1980). Thus, while the district court in *United States v. Hill*, 481 F.Supp. 558 (E.D.Pa.1979), incorrectly concluded that present rule 12.2(b) covers testimony by a psychologist bearing on the defense of entrapment, the court quite properly concluded that the government would be seriously disadvantaged by lack of notice. This would have meant that the government would not have been equipped to cross-examine the expert, that any expert called by the government would not have had an opportunity to hear the defense expert testify, and that the government would not have had an opportunity to conduct the kind of investigation needed to acquire rebuttal testimony on defendant's claim that he was especially susceptible to inducement. Consequently, rule 12.2(b) has been expanded to cover all of the aforementioned situations.

Rule 12.2(c). The amendment of the first sentence of subdivision (c), recognizing that the government may seek to have defendant subjected to a mental examination by an expert other than a psychiatrist, is prompted by the same considerations discussed above. Because it is possible that the defendant will submit to examination by an expert of his own other than a psychiatrist, it is necessary to recognize that it will sometimes be appropriate for defendant to be examined by a government expert other than a psychiatrist.

The last sentence of subdivision (c) has been amended to more accurately reflect the Fifth Amendment considerations at play in this context. See *Estelle v. Smith*, 451 U.S. 454 [, 101 S.Ct. 1866, 68 L.Ed.2d 359] (1981), holding that self-incrimination protections are not inevitably limited to the guilt phase of a trial and that the privilege, when applicable, protects against use of defendant's statement and also the fruits thereof, including expert testimony based upon defendant's statements to the expert. *Estelle* also intimates that "a defendant can be required to submit to a sanity examination," and presumably some other form of mental examination, when "his silence may deprive the State of the only effective means it has of controverting his proof on an issue that he interjected into the case."

Rule 12.2(d). The broader term "mental condition" is appropriate here in light of the above changes to subdivisions (b) and (c).

Rule 12.2(e). New subdivision (e), generally consistent with the protection afforded in rule 12.1(f) with respect to notice of alibi, ensures that the notice required under subdivision (b) will not deprive the defendant of an opportunity later to elect not to utilize any expert testimony. This provision is consistent with *Williams v. Florida*, 399 U.S. 78 [, 90 S.Ct. 1893, 26 L.Ed.2d 446] (1970), holding the privilege against self-incrimination is not violated by requiring the defendant to give notice of a defense where the defendant retains the "unfettered choice" of abandoning the defense.

Dissenting Statement of Justice O'Connor to 1983 Amendment. With one minor reservation, I join the Court in its adoption of the proposed amendments. They represent the product of considerable effort by the Advisory Committee, and they will institute desirable reforms. My sole disagreement with the Court's action today lies in its failure to recommend correction of an apparent error in the drafting of Proposed Rule 12.2(e).

As proposed, Rule 12.2(e) reads:

"Evidence of an intention as to which notice was given under subdivision (a) or (b), later withdrawn, is not admissible in any civil or criminal proceeding against the person who gave notice of the intention."

Identical language formerly appeared in Fed.Rules Crim. Proc. 11(e)(6) and Fed.Rules Evid. 410, each of which stated that

"[Certain material] is not admissible in any civil or criminal proceeding against the defendant."

Those rules were amended, Supreme Court Order April 30, 1979, 441 U.S. 970, 987, 1007, Pub.Law 96–42, approved July 31, 1979, 93 Stat. 326. After the amendments, the relevant language read,

"[Certain material] is not, in any civil or criminal proceeding, admissible against the defendant."

As the Advisory Committee explained, this minor change was necessary to eliminate an ambiguity. Before the amendment, the word "against" could be read as referring either to the kind of proceeding in which the evidence was offered or to the purpose for which it was offered. Thus, for instance, if a person was a witness in a suit but not a party, it was unclear whether the evidence could be used to impeach him. In such a case, the *use* would be against the person, but the *proceeding* would not be against him. Similarly, if the person wished to introduce the evidence in a proceeding in which he was the defendant, the use, but not the proceeding, would be against him. To eliminate the ambiguity, the Advisory Committee proposed the amendment clarifying that the evidence was inadmissible against the person, regardless of whether the particular proceeding was against the person. See Adv.Comm. Note to Fed.Rules Crim.Proc. 11(e)(6); Adv. Comm. Note to Fed.Rules Evid. 410.

The same ambiguity inheres in the proposed version of Rule 12.2(e). We should recommend that it be eliminated now. To that extent, I respectfully dissent.

1985 Amendment

Subd. (e). This clarifying amendment is intended to serve the same purpose as a comparable change made in 1979 to similar language in Rule 11(e)(6). The change makes it clear that evidence of a withdrawn intent is thereafter inadmissible against the person who gave the notice in any civil or criminal proceeding, without regard to whether the proceeding is against that person.

1987 Amendment

The amendments are technical. No substantive change is intended.

2002 Amendments

The language of Rule 12.2 has been amended as part of the general restyling of the Criminal Rules to make them more easily understood and to make style and terminology consistent throughout the rules. These changes are intended to be stylistic only, except as noted below.

The substantive changes to Rule 12.2 are designed to address five issues. First, the amendment clarifies that a court may order a mental examination for a defendant who has indicated an intention to raise a defense of mental condition bearing on the issue of guilt. Second, the defendant is required to give notice of an intent to present expert evidence of the defendant's mental condition during a capital sentencing proceeding. Third, the amendment addresses the ability of the trial court to order a mental examination for a defendant who has given notice of an intent to present evidence of mental condition during capital sentencing proceedings and when the results of that examination may be disclosed. Fourth, the amendment addresses the timing of disclosure of the results and reports of the defendant's expert examination. Finally, the amendment extends the sanctions for failure to comply with the rule's requirements to the punishment phase of a capital case.

Under current Rule 12.2(b), a defendant who intends to offer expert testimony on the issue of his or her mental condition on the question of guilt must provide a pretrial notice of that intent. The amendment extends that notice requirement to a defendant who intends to offer expert evidence, testimonial or otherwise, on his or her mental condition during a capital sentencing proceeding. As several courts have recognized, the better practice is to require pretrial notice of that intent so that any mental examinations can be conducted without unnecessarily delaying capital sentencing proceedings. *See, e.g., United States v. Beckford*, 962 F. Supp. 748, 754–64 (E.D. Va. 1997); *United States v. Haworth*, 942 F. Supp. 1406, 1409 (D.N.M. 1996). The amendment adopts that view.

Revised Rule 12.2(c)(1) addresses and clarifies the authority of the court to order mental examinations for a defendant—to determine competency of a defendant to stand trial under 18 U.S.C. § 4241; to determine the defendant's sanity at the time of the alleged offense under 18 U.S.C. § 4242; or in those cases where the defendant intends to present expert testimony on his or her mental condition. Rule 12.2(c)(1)(A) reflects the traditional authority of the court to order competency examinations. With regard to examinations to determine insanity at the time of the offense, current Rule 12.2(c) implies that the trial court *may* grant a government motion for a mental examination of a defendant who has indicated under Rule 12.2(a) an intent to raise the defense of insanity. But the corresponding statute, 18 U.S.C. § 4242, *requires* the court to order an examination if the defendant has provided notice of an intent to raise that defense and the government moves for the examination. Revised Rule 12.2(c)(1)(B) now conforms the rule to § 4242. Any examination conducted on the issue of the insanity defense would thus be conducted in accordance with the procedures set out in that statutory provision.

Revised Rule 12.2(c)(1)(B) also addresses those cases where the defendant is not relying on an insanity defense, but intends to offer expert testimony on the issue of mental condition. While the authority of a trial court to order a mental examination of a defendant who has registered an intent to raise the insanity defense seems clear, the authority under the rule to order an examination of a defendant who intends only to present expert testimony on his or her mental condition on the issue of guilt is not as clear. Some courts have concluded that a court may order such an examination. *See, e.g., United States v. Stackpole*, 811 F.2d 689, 697 (1st Cir. 1987); *United States v. Buchbinder*, 796 F.2d 910, 915 (1st Cir. 1986); and *United States v. Halbert*, 712 F.2d 388 (9th Cir. 1983). In *United States v. Davis*, 93 F.3d 1286 (6th Cir. 1996), however, the court in a detailed analysis of the issue concluded that the district court lacked the authority under the rule to order a mental examination of a defendant who had provided notice of an intent to offer evidence on a defense of diminished capacity. The court noted first that the defendant could not be ordered to undergo commitment and examination under 18 U.S.C. § 4242, because that provision relates to situations when the defendant intends to rely on the defense of insanity. The court also rejected the argument that the examination could be ordered under Rule 12.2(c) because this was, in the words of the rule, an "appropriate case." The court concluded, however, that the trial court had the inherent authority to order such an examination.

The amendment clarifies that the authority of a court to order a mental examination under Rule 12.2(c)(1)(B) extends to those cases when the defendant has provided notice, under Rule 12.2(b), of an intent to present expert testimony on the defendant's mental condition, either on the merits or at capital sentencing. *See, e.g., United States v. Hall*, 152 F.3d 381 (5th Cir. 1998), *cert. denied*, 119 S. Ct. 1767 (1999).

The amendment to Rule 12.2(c)(1) is not intended to affect any statutory or inherent authority a court may have to order other mental examinations.

The amendment leaves to the court the determination of what procedures should be used for a court-ordered examination on the defendant's mental condition (apart from insanity). As currently provided in the rule, if the examination is being ordered in connection with the defendant's stated intent to present an insanity defense, the procedures are dictated by 18 U.S.C. § 4242. On the other hand, if the examination is being ordered in conjunction with a stated intent to present expert testimony on the defendant's mental condition (not amounting to a defense of insanity) either at the guilt or sentencing phases, no specific statutory counterpart is available. Accordingly, the court is given the discretion to specify the procedures to be used. In so doing, the court may certainly be informed by other provisions, which address hearings on a defendant's mental condition. *See, e.g.*, 18 U.S.C. § 4241, et seq.

Additional changes address the question when the results of an examination ordered under Rule 12.2(b)(2) may, or must, be disclosed. The Supreme Court has recognized that use of a defendant's statements during a court-ordered examination may compromise the defendant's right against self-incrimination. *See Estelle v. Smith*, 451 U.S. 454 (1981) (defendant's privilege against self-incrimination violated when he was not advised of right to remain silent during court-ordered examination and prosecution introduced statements during capital sentencing hearing). But subsequent cases have indicated that the defendant waives the privilege if the defendant introduces expert testimony on his or her mental condition. *See, e.g., Powell v. Texas*, 492 U.S. 680, 683–84 (1989); *Buchanan v. Kentucky*, 483 U.S. 402, 421–24 (1987); *Presnell v. Zant*, 959 F.2d 1524, 1533 (11th Cir. 1992); *Williams v. Lynaugh*, 809 F.2d 1063, 1068 (5th Cir. 1987); *United States v. Madrid*, 673 F.2d 1114, 1119–21 (10th Cir. 1982). That view is reflected in Rule 12.2(c), which indicates that the statements of the defendant may be used against the defendant only after the defendant has introduced testimony on his or her mental condition. What the current rule does not address is if, and to what extent, the prosecution may see the results of the examination, which may include the defendant's statements, when evidence of the defendant's mental condition is being presented solely at a capital sentencing proceeding.

The proposed change in Rule 12.2(c)(2) adopts the procedure used by some courts to seal or otherwise insulate the results of the examination until it is clear that the defendant will introduce expert evidence about his or her mental condition at a capital sentencing hearing; i.e., after a verdict of guilty on one or more capital crimes, and a reaffirmation by the defendant of an intent to introduce expert mental-condition evidence in the sentencing phase. *See, e.g., United States v. Beckford*, 962 F. Supp. 748 (E.D. Va. 1997). Most courts that have addressed the issue have recognized that if the government obtains early access to the accused's statements, it will be required to show that it has not made any derivative use of that evidence. Doing so can consume time and resources. *See, e.g., United States v. Hall, supra*, 152 F.3d at 398 (noting that sealing of record, although not constitutionally required, "likely advances interests of judicial economy by avoiding litigation over [derivative use issue]").

Except as provided in Rule 12.2(c)(3), the rule does not address the time for disclosing results and reports of any expert examination conducted by the defendant. New Rule 12.2(c)(3) provides that upon disclosure under subdivision (c)(2) of the results and reports of the government's examination, disclosure of the results and reports of the defendant's expert examination is mandatory, if the defendant intends to introduce expert evidence relating to the examination.

Rule 12.2(c), as previously written, restricted admissibility of the defendant's statements during the course of an examination conducted under the rule to an issue respecting mental condition on which the defendant "has introduced testimony"—expert or otherwise. As amended, Rule 12.2(c)(4) provides that the admissibility of such evidence in a capital sentencing proceeding is triggered only by the defendant's introduction of expert evidence. The Committee believed that, in this context, it was appropriate to limit the government's ability to use the results of its expert mental examination to instances in which the defendant has first introduced expert evidence on the issue.

Rule 12.2(d) has been amended to extend sanctions for failure to comply with the rule to the penalty phase of a capital case. The selection of an appropriate remedy for the failure of a defendant to provide notice or submit to an examination under subdivisions (b) and (c) is entrusted to the discretion of the court. While subdivision (d) recognizes that the court may exclude the evidence of the defendant's own expert in such a situation, the court should also consider "the effectiveness of less severe sanctions, the impact of preclusion on the evidence at trial and the outcome of the case, the extent of prosecutorial surprise or prejudice, and whether the violation was willful." *Taylor v. Illinois*, 484 U.S. 400, 414 n.19 (1988) (citing *Fendler v. Goldsmith*, 728 F.2d 1181 (9th Cir. 1983)).

2005 Amendments

The amendment to Rule 12.2(d) fills a gap created in the 2002 amendments to the rule. The substantively amended rule that took effect December 1, 2002, permits a sanction of exclusion of "any expert evidence" for failure to give notice or failure to submit to an examination, but provides no sanction for failure to disclose reports. The proposed amendment is designed to address that specific issue.

Rule 12.2(d)(1) is a slightly restructured version of current Rule 12.2(d). Rule 12.2(d)(2) is new and permits the court to exclude any expert evidence for failure to comply with the disclosure requirement in Rule 12.2(c)(3). The sanction is intended to relate only to the evidence related to the matters addressed in the report, which the defense failed to disclose. Unlike the broader sanction for the two violations listed in Rule 12.2(d)(1)—which can substantially affect the entire hearing—the Committee believed that it would be overbroad to expressly authorize exclusion of "any" expert evidence, even evidence unrelated to the results and reports that were not disclosed, as required in Rule 12.2(c)(3).

The rule assumes that the sanction of exclusion will result only where there has been a complete failure to disclose the report. If the report is disclosed, albeit in an untimely fashion, other relief may be appropriate, for example, granting a continuance to the government to review the report.

HISTORICAL NOTES

Effective and Applicability Provisions

1984 Acts. Section 11(c) of Pub.L. 98–596 provided that: "The amendments and repeals made by subsections (a) and (b) of this section [amending this rule] shall apply on and after the enactment of the joint resolution entitled 'Joint resolution making continuing appropriations for the fiscal year 1985, and for other purposes'. H.J.Res. 648, Ninety-eighth Congress [Pub.L. 98–473, Oct. 12, 1984]."

1975 Acts. This rule, and the amendments of this rule made by section 3 of Pub.L. 94–64, effective Dec. 1, 1975, pursuant to section 2 of Pub.L. 94–64.

Rule 12.3. Notice of a Public–Authority Defense

(a) Notice of the Defense and Disclosure of Witnesses.

(1) Notice in General. If a defendant intends to assert a defense of actual or believed exercise of public authority on behalf of a law enforcement agency or federal intelligence agency at the time of the alleged offense, the defendant must so notify an attorney for the government in writing and must file a copy of the notice with the clerk within the time provided for filing a pretrial motion, or at any later time the court sets. The notice filed with the clerk must be under seal if the notice identifies a federal intelligence agency as the source of public authority.

(2) Contents of Notice. The notice must contain the following information:

(A) the law enforcement agency or federal intelligence agency involved;

(B) the agency member on whose behalf the defendant claims to have acted; and

(C) the time during which the defendant claims to have acted with public authority.

(3) Response to the Notice. An attorney for the government must serve a written response on the defendant or the defendant's attorney within 10 days after receiving the defendant's notice, but no later than 20 days before trial. The response must admit or deny that the defendant exercised the public authority identified in the defendant's notice.

(4) Disclosing Witnesses.

(A) Government's Request. An attorney for the government may request in writing that the defendant disclose the name, address, and telephone number of each witness the defendant intends to rely on to establish a public-authority defense. An attorney for the government may serve the request when the government serves its response to the defendant's notice under Rule 12.3(a)(3), or later, but must serve the request no later than 20 days before trial.

(B) Defendant's Response. Within 7 days after receiving the government's request, the defendant must serve on an attorney for the government a written statement of the name, address, and telephone number of each witness.

(C) Government's Reply. Within 7 days after receiving the defendant's statement, an attorney for the government must serve on the defendant or the defendant's attorney a written statement of the name, address, and telephone number of each witness the government intends to rely on to oppose the defendant's public-authority defense.

(5) Additional Time. The court may, for good cause, allow a party additional time to comply with this rule.

(b) Continuing Duty to Disclose. Both an attorney for the government and the defendant must promptly disclose in writing to the other party the name, address, and telephone number of any additional witness if:

(1) the disclosing party learns of the witness before or during trial; and

(2) the witness should have been disclosed under Rule 12.3(a)(4) if the disclosing party had known of the witness earlier.

(c) Failure to Comply. If a party fails to comply with this rule, the court may exclude the testimony of any undisclosed witness regarding the public-authority defense. This rule does not limit the defendant's right to testify.

(d) Protective Procedures Unaffected. This rule does not limit the court's authority to issue appropriate protective orders or to order that any filings be under seal.

(e) Inadmissibility of Withdrawn Intention. Evidence of an intention as to which notice was given under Rule 12.3(a), later withdrawn, is not, in any civil or criminal proceeding, admissible against the person who gave notice of the intention.

(Added Pub.L. 100–690, Title VI, § 6483, Nov. 18, 1988, 102 Stat. 4382; Apr. 29, 2002, eff. Dec. 1, 2002.)

ADVISORY COMMITTEE NOTES

2002 Amendments

The language of Rule 12.3 has been amended as part of the general restyling of the Criminal Rules to make them more easily understood and to make style and terminology consistent throughout the rules. These changes are intended to be stylistic only, except as noted below.

Substantive changes have been made in Rule 12.3(a)(4) and 12.3(b). As in Rule 12.1, the Committee decided to include in the restyled rule the requirement that the parties provide the telephone numbers of any witnesses disclosed under the rule.

Rule 12.4. Disclosure Statement

(a) Who Must File.

(1) Nongovernmental Corporate Party. Any nongovernmental corporate party to a proceeding in a district court must file a statement that identifies any parent corporation and any publicly held corporation that owns 10% or more of its stock or states that there is no such corporation.

(2) Organizational Victim. If an organization is a victim of the alleged criminal activity, the government must file a statement identifying the victim. If the organizational victim is a corporation, the statement must also disclose the information required by Rule 12.4(a)(1) to the extent it can be obtained through due diligence.

(b) Time for Filing; Supplemental Filing. A party must:

(1) file the Rule 12.4(a) statement upon the defendant's initial appearance; and

(2) promptly file a supplemental statement upon any change in the information that the statement requires.

(Added Apr. 29, 2002, eff. Dec. 1, 2002.)

ADVISORY COMMITTEE NOTES

2002 Adoption

Rule 12.4 is a new rule modeled after Federal Rule of Appellate Procedure 26.1 and parallels similar provisions being proposed in new Federal Rule of Civil Procedure 7.1. The purpose of the rule is to assist judges in determining whether they must recuse themselves because of a "financial interest in the subject matter in controversy." Code of Judicial Conduct, Canon 3C(1)(c) (1972). It does not, however, deal with other circumstances that might lead to disqualification for other reasons.

Under Rule 12.4(a)(1), any nongovernmental corporate party must file a statement that indicates whether it has any parent corporation that owns 10% or more of its stock or indicates that there is no such corporation. Although the term "nongovernmental corporate party" will almost always involve organizational defendants, it might also cover any third party that asserts an interest in property to be forfeited under new Rule 32.2.

Rule 12.4(a)(2) requires an attorney for the government to file a statement that lists any organizational victims of the alleged criminal activity; the purpose of this disclosure is to alert the court to the fact that a possible ground for disqualification might exist. Further, if the organizational victim is a corporation, the statement must include the same information required of any nongovernmental corporate party. The rule requires an attorney for the government to use due diligence in obtaining that information from a corporate organizational victim, recognizing that the timing requirements of Rule 12.4(b) might make it difficult to obtain the necessary information by the time the initial appearance is conducted.

Although the disclosures required by Rule 12.4 may seem limited, they are calculated to reach the majority of circumstances that are likely to call for disqualification on the basis of information that a judge may not know or recollect. Framing a rule that calls for more detailed disclosure is problematic and will inevitably require more information than is necessary for purposes of automatic recusal. Unnecessary disclosure of volumes of information may create the risk that a judge will overlook the one bit of information that might require disqualification, and may also create the risk that courts will experience unnecessary disqualifications rather than attempt to unravel a potentially difficult question.

The same concerns about overbreadth are potentially present in any local rules that might address this topic. Rule 12.4 does not address the promulgation of any local rules that might address the same issue, or supplement the requirements of the rule.

The rule does not cover disclosure of all financial information that could be relevant to a judge's decision whether to recuse himself or herself from a case. The Committee believes that with the various disclosure practices in the federal courts and with the development of technology, more comprehensive disclosure may be desirable and feasible.

Rule 12.4(b)(1) indicates that the time for filing the disclosure statement is at the point when the defendant enters an initial appearance under Rule 5. Although there may be other instances where an earlier appearance of a party in a civil proceeding would raise concerns about whether the presiding judicial officer should be notified of a possible grounds for recusal, the Committee believed that in criminal cases, the most likely time for that to occur is at the initial appearance and that it was important to set a uniform triggering event for disclosures under this rule.

Finally, Rule 12.4(b)(2) requires the parties to file supplemental statements with the court if there are any changes in the information required in the statement.

Rule 13. Joint Trial of Separate Cases

The court may order that separate cases be tried together as though brought in a single indictment or information if all offenses and all defendants could have been joined in a single indictment or information.

(As amended Apr. 29, 2002, eff. Dec. 1, 2002.)

ADVISORY COMMITTEE NOTES

1944 Adoption

This rule is substantially a restatement of existing law 18 U.S.C. § 557 (Indictments and presentments; joinder of charges); *Logan v. United States*, 144 U.S. 263, 296, 12 S.Ct. 617, 36 L.Ed. 429; *Showalter v. United States*, 4 Cir., 260 F. 719 certiorari denied, 250 U.S. 672, 40 S.Ct. 14, 63 L.Ed. 1200; *Hostetter v. United States*, 8 Cir., 16 F.2d 921; *Capone v. United States*, 7 Cir., 51 F.2d 609, 619, 620, C.C.A.7th.

2002 Amendments

The language of Rule 13 has been amended as part of the general restyling of the Criminal Rules to make them more easily understood and to make style and terminology consistent throughout the rules. These changes are intended to be stylistic only.

Rule 14. Relief from Prejudicial Joinder

(a) Relief. If the joinder of offenses or defendants in an indictment, an information, or a consolidation for trial appears to prejudice a defendant or the government, the court may order separate trials of counts, sever the defendants' trials, or provide any other relief that justice requires.

(b) Defendant's Statements. Before ruling on a defendant's motion to sever, the court may order an attorney for the government to deliver to the court for in camera inspection any defendant's statement that the government intends to use as evidence.

(As amended Feb. 28, 1966, eff. July 1, 1966; Apr. 29, 2002, eff. Dec. 1, 2002.)

ADVISORY COMMITTEE NOTES

1944 Adoption

This rule is a restatement of existing law under which severance and other similar relief is entirely in the discretion of the court, 18 U.S.C. former § 557 (Indictments and presentments; joinder of charges); *Pointer v. United States*, 151 U.S. 396, 14 S.Ct. 410, 38 L.Ed. 208; *Pierce v. United States*, 160 U.S. 355, 16 S.Ct. 321, 40 L.Ed. 454; *United States v. Ball*, 163 U.S. 662, 673, 16 S.Ct. 1192, 41 L.Ed. 300; *Stilson v. United States*, 250 U.S. 583, 40 S.Ct. 28, 63 L.Ed. 1154.

1966 Amendment

A defendant may be prejudiced by the admission in evidence against a co-defendant of a statement or confession made by that co-defendant. This prejudice cannot be dispelled by cross-examination if the co-defendant does not take the stand. Limiting instructions to the jury may not in fact erase the prejudice. While the question whether to grant a severance is generally left within the discretion of the trial court, recent Fifth Circuit cases have found sufficient prejudice involved to make denial of a motion for severance reversible error. See *Schaffer v. United States*, 221 F.2d 17 (5th Cir.1955); *Barton v. United States*, 263 F.2d 894 (5th Cir.1959). It has even been suggested that when the confession of the co-defendant comes as a surprise at the trial, it may be error to deny a motion or a mistrial. See *Belvin v. United States*, 273 F.2d 583 (5th Cir.1960).

The purpose of the amendment is to provide a procedure whereby the issue of possible prejudice can be resolved on the motion for severance. The judge may direct the disclosure of the confessions or statements of the defendants to him for in camera inspection as an aid to determining whether the possible prejudice justifies ordering separate trials. Cf. note, Joint and Single Trials Under Rules 8 and 14 of the Federal Rules of Criminal Procedure, 74 Yale L.J. 551, 565 (1965).

2002 Amendments

The language of Rule 14 has been amended as part of the general restyling of the Criminal Rules to make them more easily understood and to make style and terminology consistent throughout the rules. These changes are intended to be stylistic only.

The reference to a defendant's "confession" in the last sentence of the current rule has been deleted. The Committee believed that the reference to the "defendant's statements" in the amended rule would fairly embrace any confessions or admissions by a defendant.

Rule 15. Depositions

(a) When Taken.

(1) In General. A party may move that a prospective witness be deposed in order to preserve testimony for trial. The court may grant the motion because of exceptional circumstances and in the interest of justice. If the court orders the deposition to be taken, it may also require the deponent to produce at the deposition any designated material that is not privileged, including any book, paper, document, record, recording, or data.

(2) Detained Material Witness. A witness who is detained under 18 U.S.C. § 3144 may request to be deposed by filing a written motion and giving notice to the parties. The court may then order that the deposition be taken and may discharge the witness after the witness has signed under oath the deposition transcript.

(b) Notice.

(1) In General. A party seeking to take a deposition must give every other party reasonable written notice of the deposition's date and location. The notice must state the name and address of each deponent. If requested by a party receiving the notice, the court may, for good cause, change the deposition's date or location.

(2) To the Custodial Officer. A party seeking to take the deposition must also notify the officer who has custody of the defendant of the scheduled date and location.

(c) Defendant's Presence.

(1) Defendant in Custody. The officer who has custody of the defendant must produce the defendant at the deposition and keep the defendant in the witness's presence during the examination, unless the defendant:

(A) waives in writing the right to be present; or

(B) persists in disruptive conduct justifying exclusion after being warned by the court that disruptive conduct will result in the defendant's exclusion.

(2) Defendant Not in Custody. A defendant who is not in custody has the right upon request to be present at the deposition, subject to any conditions imposed by the court. If the government tenders the defendant's expenses as provided in Rule 15(d) but the defendant still fails to appear, the defendant—absent good cause—waives both the right to appear and any objection to the taking and use of the deposition based on that right.

(d) Expenses. If the deposition was requested by the government, the court may—or if the defendant is unable to bear the deposition expenses, the court must—order the government to pay:

(1) any reasonable travel and subsistence expenses of the defendant and the defendant's attorney to attend the deposition; and

(2) the costs of the deposition transcript.

(e) Manner of Taking. Unless these rules or a court order provides otherwise, a deposition must be taken and filed in the same manner as a deposition in a civil action, except that:

(1) A defendant may not be deposed without that defendant's consent.

(2) The scope and manner of the deposition examination and cross-examination must be the same as would be allowed during trial.

(3) The government must provide to the defendant or the defendant's attorney, for use at the deposition, any statement of the deponent in the government's possession to which the defendant would be entitled at trial.

(f) Use as Evidence. A party may use all or part of a deposition as provided by the Federal Rules of Evidence.

(g) Objections. A party objecting to deposition testimony or evidence must state the grounds for the objection during the deposition.

(h) Depositions by Agreement Permitted. The parties may by agreement take and use a deposition with the court's consent.

(As amended Apr. 22, 1974, eff. Dec. 1, 1975; July 31, 1975, Pub.L. 94–64, § 3(15)–(19), 89 Stat. 373, 374; Oct. 12, 1984, Pub.L. 98–473, Title II, § 209(b), 98 Stat. 1986; Mar. 9, 1987, eff. Aug. 1, 1987; Apr. 29, 2002, eff. Dec. 1, 2002.)

ADVISORY COMMITTEE NOTES

1944 Adoption

Note to Subdivision (a). 1. This rule continues the existing law permitting defendants to take depositions in certain limited classes of cases under *dedimus potestatem* and *in perpetuam rei memoriam*, 28 U.S.C. former § 644. This statute has been generally held applicable to criminal cases, *Clymer v. United States*, 38 F.2d 581, C.C.A.10th; *Wong Yim v. United States*, 118 F.2d 667, C.C.A.9th, certiorari denied, 313 U.S. 589, 61 S.Ct. 1112, 85 L.Ed. 1544; *United States v. Cameron*, C.C.E.D.Mo., 15 F. 794, C.C.E.D.Mo.; *United States v. Hoffmann*, 24 F.Supp. 847, S.D.N.Y. Contra, *Luxenberg v. United States*, 45 F.2d 497, C.C.A.4th, certiorari denied, 283 U.S. 820, 51 S.Ct. 345, 75 L.Ed. 1436. The rule continues the limitation of the statute that the taking of depositions is to be restricted to cases in which they are necessary "in order to prevent a failure of justice."

2. Unlike the practice in civil cases in which depositions may be taken as a matter of right by notice without permission of the court (Rules 26(a) and 30, Federal Rules of Civil Procedure, 28 U.S.C., Appendix), this rule permits depositions to be taken only by order of the court, made in the exercise of discretion and on notice to all parties. It was contemplated that in criminal cases depositions would be used only in exceptional situations, as has been the practice heretofore.

3. This rule introduces a new feature in authorizing the taking of the deposition of a witness committed for failure to give bail (see Rule 46(b)). This matter is, however, left to the discretion of the court. The purpose of the rule is to afford a method of relief for such a witness, if the court finds it proper to extend it.

Note to Subdivision (b). This subdivision, as well as subdivisions (d) and (f), sets forth the procedure to be followed in the event that the court grants an order for the taking of a deposition. The procedure prescribed is similar to that in civil cases, Rules 28–31, Federal Rules of Civil Procedure, 28 U.S.C., Appendix.

Note to Subdivision (c). This rule introduces a new feature for the purpose of protecting the rights of an indigent defendant.

Note to Subdivision (d). See Note to Subdivision (b), supra.

Note to Subdivision (e). In providing when and for what purpose a deposition may be used at the trial, this rule generally follows the corresponding provisions of the Federal Rules of Civil Procedure, Rule 26(d)(3). The only difference is that in civil cases a deposition may be introduced at the trial if the witness is at a greater distance than 100 miles from the place of trial, while this rule requires that the witness be out of the United States. The distinction results from the fact that a subpoena in a civil case runs only within the district where issued or 100 miles from the place of trial, (Rule 45(e)(1), Federal Rules of Civil Procedure), while a subpoena in a criminal case runs throughout the United States (see Rule 17(e)(1), infra).

Note to Subdivision (f). See Note to Subdivision (b), supra.

1974 Amendment

Rule 15 authorizes the taking of depositions by the government. Under former rule 15 only a defendant was authorized to take a deposition.

The revision is similar to Title VI of the Organized Crime Control Act of 1970. The principal difference is that Title VI (18 U.S.C. § 3503) limits the authority of the government to take depositions to cases in which the Attorney General certifies that the "proceeding is against a person who is believed to have participated in an organized criminal activity." This limitation is not contained in rule 15.

Dealing with the issue of government depositions so soon after the enactment of 18 U.S.C. § 3503 is not inconsistent with the congressional purpose. On the floor of the House Congressman Poff, a principal spokesman for the proposal, said that the House version was not designed to "limit the Judicial Conference of the United States in the exercise of its rulemaking authority . . . from addressing itself to other problems in this area or from adopting a broader approach." 116 Cong.Rec. 35293 (1970).

The recently enacted Title VI of the Organized Crime Control Act of 1970 (18 U.S.C. § 3503) is based upon earlier efforts of the Advisory Committee on Criminal Rules which has over the past twenty-five years submitted several proposals authorizing government depositions.

The earlier drafts of the Federal Rules of Criminal Procedure proposed that the government be allowed to take depositions. Orfield, The Federal Rules of Criminal Procedure, 33 Calif.L.Rev. 543, 559 (1945). The Fifth Draft of what became rule 15 (then rule 20) dated June 1942, was submitted to the Supreme Court for comment. The court had a number of unfavorable comments about allowing government depositions. These comments were not published. The only reference to the fact that the court made comments is in 2 Orfield, Criminal Procedure under the Federal Rules § 15:1 (1966); and Orfield, Depositions in Federal Criminal Procedure, 9 S.C.L.Q. 376, 380–381 (1957).

The Advisory Committee, in the 1940's, continued to recommend the adoption of a provision authorizing government depositions. The final draft submitted to the Supreme Court contained a section providing:

The following additional requirements shall apply if the deposition is taken at the instance of the government or of a witness. The officer having custody of a defendant shall be notified of the time and place set for examination, and shall produce him at the examination and keep him in the presence of the witness during the examination. A defendant not in custody shall be given notice and shall have the right to be present at the examination. The government shall pay in advance to the defendant's attorney and a defendant not in custody expenses of travel and subsistence for attendance at the examination.

See 2 Orfield, Criminal Procedure under the Federal Rules § 15:3, pp. 447–448 (1966); Orfield, Depositions in Federal Criminal Procedure, 9 S.C.L.Q. 376, 383 (1957).

The Supreme Court rejected this section in this entirety, thus eliminating the provision for depositions by the government. These changes were made without comment.

The proposal to allow government depositions was renewed in the amendments to the Federal Rules of Criminal Procedure in the early 1960's. The Preliminary Draft of Proposed Amendments to Rules of Criminal Procedure for the United States District Courts (December 1962) proposed to amend rule 15 by eliminating the words "of a defendant" from the first sentence of subdivision (a) and adding a subdivision (g) which was practically identical to the subdivision rejected by the Supreme Court in the original draft of the rules.

The Second Preliminary Draft of Proposed Amendments to Rules of Criminal Procedure for the United States District Courts (March 1964) continued to propose allowing governments depositions. Subdivision (g) was substantially modified, however.

The following additional requirements shall apply if the deposition is taken at the instance of the government or a witness. Both the defendant and his attorney shall be given reasonable advance notice of the time and place set for the examination. The officer having custody of a defendant shall be notified of the time and place set for the examination, and shall produce him at the examination and keep him in the presence of the witness during the examination. A defendant not in custody shall have the right to be present at the examination but his failure to appear after notice and tender of expenses shall constitute a waiver of that right. The government shall pay to the defendant's attorney and to a defendant not in custody expenses of travel and subsistence for attendance at the examination. The government shall make available to the defendant for his examination and use at the taking of the deposition any statement of the witness being deposed which is in the possession of the government and which the government would be required to make available to the defendant if the witness were testifying at the trial.

The proposal to authorize government depositions was rejected by the Standing Committee on Rules of Practice and Procedure, C. Wright, Federal Practice and Procedure § 241 at 477 (1969). 4 Barron, Federal Practice and Procedure (Supp.1967). The Report of the Judicial Conference, submitted to the Supreme Court for approval late in 1965, contained no proposal for an amendment to rule 15. See 39 F.R.D. 69, 168–211 (1966).

When the Organized Crime Control Act of 1970 was originally introduced in the Senate (S. 30) it contained a government deposition provision which was similar to the 1964 proposal of the Criminal Rules Advisory Committee, except that the original bill (S. 30) failed to provide standards to control the use of depositions at the trial. For an explanation and defense of the original proposal see McClellan, The Organized Crime Act (S. 30) or Its Critics: Which Threatens Civil Liberties?, 46 Notre Dame Lawyer 55, 100–108 (1970). This omission was remedied, prior to passage, with the addition of what is now 18 U.S.C. § 3503(f) which prescribes the circumstances in which a deposition can be used. The standards are the same as those in former rule 15(e) with the addition of language allowing the use of the deposition when "the witness refuses in the trial or hearing to testify concerning the subject of the deposition or the part offered."

Before the Organized Crime Control Act of 1970 was enacted an additional amendment was added providing that the right of the government to take a deposition is limited to cases in which the Attorney General certifies that the defendant is "believed to have participated in an organized criminal activity" [18 U.S.C. § 3503(a)]. The argument in favor of the amendment was that the whole purpose of the act was to deal with organized crime and therefore its provisions, including that providing for government depositions, should be limited to organized crime type cases.

There is another aspect of Advisory Committee history which is relevant. In January 1970, the Advisory Committee circulated proposed changes in rule 16, one of which gives the government, when it has disclosed the identity of its witnesses, the right to take a deposition and use it "in the event the witness has become unavailable without the fault of the government or if the witness has changed his testimony." [See Preliminary Draft of Proposed Amendments to the Federal Rules of Criminal Procedure for the United States District Courts, rule 16(a)(1)(vi) (January 1970).] This provision is now incorporated within rule 16(a)(1)(v).

Because neither the court nor the standing committee gave reasons for rejecting the government deposition proposal, it is not possible to know why they were not approved. To the extent that the rejection was based upon doubts as to the constitutionality of such a proposal, those doubts now seem resolved by *California v. Green*, 399 U.S. 149, 90 S.Ct. 1930, 26 L.Ed.2d 489 (1970).

On the merits, the proposal to allow the government to take depositions is consistent with the revision of rule 16 and with section 804(b)(1) of the Rules of Evidence for the United States Courts and Magistrates (November 1971) which provides that the following is not excluded by the hearsay rule if the declarant is unavailable:

(1) Former Testimony. Testimony given as a witness at another hearing of the same or a different proceeding, or in a deposition taken in compliance with law in the course of another proceeding, at the instance of or against a party with an opportunity to develop the testimony by direct, cross, or redirect examination, with motive and interest similar to those of the party against whom now offered.

Subdivision (a) is revised to provide that the government as well as the defendant is entitled to take a deposition. The phrase "whenever due to special circumstances of the case it is in the interest of justice," is intended to make clear that the decision by the court as to whether to order the taking of a deposition shall be made in the context of the circumstances of the particular case. The principal objective is the preservation of evidence for use at trial. It is not to provide a method of pretrial discovery nor primarily for the purpose of obtaining a basis for later cross-examination of an adverse witness. Discovery is a matter dealt with in rule 16. An obviously important factor is whether a deposition will expedite, rather than delay, the administration of criminal justice. Also important is the presence or absence of factors which determine the use of a deposition at the trial, such as the agreement of the parties to the use of the deposition; the possible unavailability of the witness; or the possibility that coercion may be used upon the witness to induce him to change his testimony or not to testify. See rule 16(a)(1)(v).

Subdivision (a) also makes explicit that only the "testimony of a prospective witness of a party" can be taken. This means the party's own witness and does not authorize a discovery deposition of an adverse witness. The language "for use at trial" is intended to give further emphasis to the importance of the criteria for use specified in subdivision (e).

In subdivision (b) reference is made to the defendant in custody. If he is in state custody, a writ of habeas corpus ad testificandum (to produce the prisoner for purposes of testimony) may be required to accomplish his presence.

In subdivision (d) the language "except as otherwise provided in these rules" is meant to make clear that the subpoena provisions of rule 17 control rather than the provisions of the civil rules.

The use of the phrase "and manner" in subdivision (d)(2) is intended to emphasize that the authorization is not to conduct an adverse examination of an opposing witness.

In subdivision (e) the phrase "as substantive evidence" is added to make clear that the deposition can be used as evidence in chief as well as for purposes of impeachment.

Subdivision (e) also makes clear that the deposition can be used as affirmative evidence whenever the witness is available but gives testimony inconsistent with that given in the deposition. A California statute which contained a similar provision was held constitutional in *California v. Green*, 399 U.S. 149, 90 S.Ct. 1930, 26 L.Ed.2d 489 (1970). This is also consistent with section 801(d)(1) of the Rules of Evidence for United States Courts and Magistrates (Nov.1971).

Subdivision (f) is intended to insure that a record of objections and the grounds for the objections is made at the time the deposition is taken when the witness is available so that the witness can be examined further, if necessary, on the point of the objection so that there will be an adequate record for the court's later ruling upon the objection.

Subdivision (g) uses the "unavailability" definition of the Rules of Evidence for the United States Courts and Magistrates, 804(a) (Nov. 1971).

Subdivision (h) is intended to make clear that the court always has authority to order the taking of a deposition, or to allow the use of a deposition, where there is an agreement of the parties to the taking or to the use.

1975 Enactment

A. Amendments Proposed by the Supreme Court. Rule 15 of the Federal Rules of Criminal Procedure provides for the taking of depositions. The present rule permits only the defendant to move that a deposition of a prospective witness be taken. The court may grant the motion if it appears that (a) the prospective witness will be unable to attend or be prevented from attending the trial, (b) the prospective witness' testimony is material, and (c) the prospective witness' testimony is necessary to prevent a failure of justice.

The Supreme Court promulgated several amendments to Rule 15. The more significant amendments are described below.

Subdivision (a) as proposed to be amended permits either party to move the court for the taking of a deposition of a witness. However, a party may only move to take the deposition of one of its own witnesses, not one of the adversary party's witnesses.

Subdivision (c) as proposed to be amended provides that whenever a deposition is taken at the instance of the government or of an indigent defendant, the expenses of the taking of the deposition must be paid by the government.

Subdivision (e) as proposed to be amended provides that part or all of the deposition may be used at trial as substantive evidence if the witness if "unavailable" or if the witness gives testimony inconsistent with his deposition.

Subdivision (b) * as proposed to be amended defines "unavailable." "Unavailable" as a witness includes situations in which the deponent:

(1) is exempted by ruling of the judge on the ground of privilege from testifying concerning the subject matter of his deposition; or

(2) persists in refusing to testify concerning the subject matter of his deposition despite an order of the judge to do so; or

(3) testifies to a lack of memory of the subject matter of his deposition; or

(4) is unable to be present or to testify at the hearing because of death or then existing physical or mental illness or infirmity; or

(5) is absent from the hearing and the proponent of his deposition has been unable to procure his attendance by process or other reasonable means. A deponent is not unavailable as a witness if his exemption, refusal, claim of lack of memory, inability, or absence is due to the procurement or wrongdoing of the proponent of his deposition for the purpose of preventing the witness from attending or testifying.

B. Committee Action. The Committee narrowed the definition of "unavailability" in subdivision (g). The Committee deleted language from that subdivision that provided that a witness was "unavailable" if the court exempts him from testifying at the trial on the ground of privilege. The Committee does not want to encourage the use of depositions at trial, especially in view of the importance of having live testimony from a witness on the witness stand.

The Committee added a provision to subdivision (b) to parallel the provision of Rule 43(b)(2). This is to make it clear that a disruptive defendant may be removed from the place where a deposition is being taken.

The Committee added language to subdivision (c) to make clear that the government must pay for the cost of the transcript of a deposition when the deposition is taken at the instance of an indigent defendant or of the government. In order to use a deposition at trial, it must be transcribed. The proposed rule did not explicitly provide for payment of the cost of transcribing, and the Committee change rectifies this.

The Committee notes that subdivision (e) permits the use of a deposition when the witness "gives testimony at the trial or hearing inconsistent with his deposition." Since subdivision (e) refers to the rules of evidence, the Committee understands that the Federal Rules of Evidence will govern the admissibility and use of the deposition. The Committee, by adopting subdivision (e) as proposed to be amended by the Supreme Court, intends the Federal Rules of Evidence to govern the admissibility and use of the deposition.

The Committee believes that Rule 15 will not encourage trials by deposition. A deposition may be taken only in "exceptional circumstances" when "it is in the interest of justice that the testimony of a prospective witness of a party be taken and preserved. . . ." A deposition, once it is taken, is not automatically admissible at trial, however. It may only be used at trial if the witness is unavailable, and the rule narrowly defines unavailability. The procedure established in Rule 15 is similar to the procedure established by the Organized Crime Control Act of 1970 for the taking and use of depositions in organized crime cases. See 18 U.S.C. 3503. House Report No. 94–247.

* So in original. Probably should be "(g)".

Rule 15 deals with the taking of depositions and the use of depositions at trial. Rule 15(e) permits a deposition to be used if the witness is unavailable. Rule 15(g) defines that term.

The Supreme Court's proposal defines five circumstances in which the witness will be considered unavailable. The House version of the bill deletes a provision that said a witness is unavailable if he is exempted at trial, on the ground of privilege, from testifying about the subject-matter of his deposition. The Senate version of the bill, by cross reference to the Federal Rules of Evidence, restores the Supreme Court proposal.

The Conference adopts the Senate provision. House Report No. 94–414.

1987 Amendment

The amendments are technical. No substantive change is intended.

2002 Amendments

The language of Rule 15 has been amended as part of the general restyling of the Criminal Rules to make them more easily understood and to make style and terminology consistent throughout the rules. These changes are intended to be stylistic only, except as noted below.

In Rule 15(a), the list of materials to be produced has been amended to include the expansive term "data" to reflect the fact that in an increasingly technological culture, the information may exist in a format not already covered by the more conventional list, such as a book or document.

The last portion of current Rule 15(b), dealing with the defendant's presence at a deposition, has been moved to amended Rule 15(c).

Revised Rule 15(d) addresses the payment of expenses incurred by the defendant and the defendant's attorney. Under the current rule, if the government requests the deposition, or if the defendant requests the deposition and is unable to pay for it, the court *may* direct the government to pay for travel and subsistence expenses for both the defendant and the defendant's attorney. In either case, the current rule requires the government to pay for the transcript. Under the amended rule, if the government requested the deposition, the court *must* [So in original; however, see subsec. (d) of this rule] require the government to pay reasonable subsistence and travel expenses and the cost of the deposition transcript. If the defendant is unable to pay the deposition expenses, the court *must* order the government to pay reasonable subsistence and travel expenses and the deposition transcript costs—regardless of who requested the deposition. Although the current rule places no apparent limits on the amount of funds that should be reimbursed, the Committee believed that insertion of the word "reasonable" was consistent with current practice.

Rule 15(f) is intended to more clearly reflect that the admissibility of any deposition taken under the rule is governed not by the rule itself, but instead by the Federal Rules of Evidence.

HISTORICAL NOTES

References in Text

The Federal Rules of Evidence, referred to in subd. (f), are set out in the Appendix to Title 28, Fed.Rules Evid. Rule 101 et seq., 28 U.S.C.A.

Effective and Applicability Provisions

1975 Acts. Amendments of this rule embraced in the order of the United States Supreme Court on Apr. 22, 1974, and the amendments of this rule made by section 3 of Pub.L. 94–64, effective Dec. 1, 1975, pursuant to section 2 of Pub.L. 94–64.

Rule 16. Discovery and Inspection

(a) Government's Disclosure.

(1) Information Subject to Disclosure.

(A) Defendant's Oral Statement. Upon a defendant's request, the government must disclose to the defendant the substance of any relevant oral statement made by the defendant, before or after arrest, in response to interrogation by a person the defendant knew was a government agent if the government intends to use the statement at trial.

(B) Defendant's Written or Recorded Statement. Upon a defendant's request, the government must disclose to the defendant, and make available for inspection, copying, or photographing, all of the following:

(i) any relevant written or recorded statement by the defendant if:

- the statement is within the government's possession, custody, or control; and
- the attorney for the government knows—or through due diligence could know—that the statement exists;

(ii) the portion of any written record containing the substance of any relevant oral statement made before or after arrest if the defendant made the statement in response to interrogation by a person the defendant knew was a government agent; and

(iii) the defendant's recorded testimony before a grand jury relating to the charged offense.

(C) Organizational Defendant. Upon a defendant's request, if the defendant is an organization, the government must disclose to the defendant any statement described in Rule 16(a)(1)(A) and (B) if the government contends that the person making the statement:

(i) was legally able to bind the defendant regarding the subject of the statement because of that person's position as the defendant's director, officer, employee, or agent; or

(ii) was personally involved in the alleged conduct constituting the offense and was legally able to bind the defendant regarding that conduct because of that person's position as the defendant's director, officer, employee, or agent.

(D) Defendant's Prior Record. Upon a defendant's request, the government must furnish the defendant with a copy of the defendant's prior criminal record that is within the government's possession, custody, or control if the attorney for the government knows—or through due diligence could know—that the record exists.

(E) Documents and Objects. Upon a defendant's request, the government must permit the defendant to inspect and to copy or photograph books, papers, documents, data, photographs, tangible objects, buildings or places, or copies or portions of any of these items, if the item is within the government's possession, custody, or control and:

(i) the item is material to preparing the defense;

(ii) the government intends to use the item in its case-in-chief at trial; or

(iii) the item was obtained from or belongs to the defendant.

(F) Reports of Examinations and Tests. Upon a defendant's request, the government must permit a defendant to inspect and to copy or photograph the results or reports of any physical or mental examination and of any scientific test or experiment if:

(i) the item is within the government's possession, custody, or control;

(ii) the attorney for the government knows—or through due diligence could know—that the item exists; and

(iii) the item is material to preparing the defense or the government intends to use the item in its case-in-chief at trial.

(G) Expert witnesses.—At the defendant's request, the government must give to the defendant a written summary of any testimony that the government intends to use under Rules 702, 703, or 705 of the Federal Rules of Evidence during its case-in-chief at trial. If the government requests discovery under subdivision (b)(1)(C)(ii) and the defendant complies, the government must, at the defendant's request, give to the defendant a written summary of testimony that the government intends to use under Rules 702, 703, or 705 of the Federal Rules of Evidence as evidence at trial on the issue of the defendant's mental condition. The summary provided under this subparagraph must describe the witness's opinions, the bases and reasons for those opinions, and the witness's qualifications.

(2) Information Not Subject to Disclosure. Except as Rule 16(a)(1) provides otherwise, this rule does not authorize the discovery or inspection of reports, memoranda, or other internal government documents made by an attorney for the government or other government agent in connection with investigating or prosecuting the case. Nor does this rule authorize the discovery or inspection of statements made by prospective government witnesses except as provided in 18 U.S.C. § 3500.

(3) Grand Jury Transcripts. This rule does not apply to the discovery or inspection of a grand jury's recorded proceedings, except as provided in Rules 6, 12(h), 16(a)(1), and 26.2.

(b) Defendant's Disclosure.

(1) Information Subject to Disclosure.

(A) Documents and Objects. If a defendant requests disclosure under Rule 16(a)(1)(E) and the government complies, then the defendant must permit the government, upon request, to inspect and to copy or photograph books, papers, documents, data, photographs, tangible objects, buildings or places, or copies or portions of any of these items if:

(i) the item is within the defendant's possession, custody, or control; and

(ii) the defendant intends to use the item in the defendant's case-in-chief at trial.

(B) Reports of Examinations and Tests. If a defendant requests disclosure under Rule 16(a)(1)(F) and the government complies, the defendant must permit the government, upon request, to inspect and to copy or photograph the results or reports of any physical or mental examination and of any scientific test or experiment if:

(i) the item is within the defendant's possession, custody, or control; and

(ii) the defendant intends to use the item in the defendant's case-in-chief at trial, or intends to call the witness who prepared the report and the report relates to the witness's testimony.

(C) Expert witnesses.—The defendant must, at the government's request, give to the government a written summary of any testimony that the defendant intends to use under Rules 702, 703, or 705 of the Federal Rules of Evidence as evidence at trial, if—

(i) the defendant requests disclosure under subdivision (a)(1)(G) and the government complies; or

(ii) the defendant has given notice under Rule 12.2(b) of an intent to present expert testimony on the defendant's mental condition.

This summary must describe the witness's opinions, the bases and reasons for those opinions, and the witness's qualifications.

(2) Information Not Subject to Disclosure. Except for scientific or medical reports, Rule 16(b)(1) does not authorize discovery or inspection of:

(A) reports, memoranda, or other documents made by the defendant, or the defendant's attorney or agent, during the case's investigation or defense; or

(B) a statement made to the defendant, or the defendant's attorney or agent, by:

(i) the defendant;

(ii) a government or defense witness; or

(iii) a prospective government or defense witness.

(c) Continuing Duty to Disclose. A party who discovers additional evidence or material before or during trial must promptly disclose its existence to the other party or the court if:

(1) the evidence or material is subject to discovery or inspection under this rule; and

(2) the other party previously requested, or the court ordered, its production.

(d) Regulating Discovery.

(1) Protective and Modifying Orders. At any time the court may, for good cause, deny, restrict, or defer discovery or inspection, or grant other appropriate relief. The court may permit a party to show good cause by a written statement that the court will inspect ex parte. If relief is granted, the court must preserve the entire text of the party's statement under seal.

(2) Failure to Comply. If a party fails to comply with this rule, the court may:

(A) order that party to permit the discovery or inspection; specify its time, place, and manner; and prescribe other just terms and conditions;

(B) grant a continuance;

(C) prohibit that party from introducing the undisclosed evidence; or

(D) enter any other order that is just under the circumstances.

(As amended Feb. 28, 1966, eff. July 1, 1966; Apr. 22, 1974, eff. Dec. 1, 1975; July 31, 1975, Pub.L. 94–64, § 3(20)–(28), 89 Stat. 374, 375; Dec. 12, 1975, Pub.L. 94–149, § 5, 89 Stat. 806; Apr. 28, 1983, eff. Aug. 1, 1983; Mar. 9, 1987, eff. Aug. 1, 1987; Apr. 30, 1991, eff. Dec. 1, 1991; Apr. 22, 1993, eff. Dec. 1, 1993; Apr. 29, 1994, eff. Dec. 1, 1994; Apr. 29, 2002, eff. Dec. 1, 2002; Nov. 2, 2002, eff. Dec. 1, 2002; Pub.L. 107–273, Div. C, Title I, § 11019(b), Nov. 2, 2002, 116 Stat. 1825.)

ADVISORY COMMITTEE NOTES

1944 Adoption

Whether under existing law discovery may be permitted in criminal cases is doubtful, *United States v. Rosenfeld*, 57 F.2d 74, C.C.A.2d certiorari denied 52 S.Ct. 642, 286 U.S. 556, 76 L.Ed. 1290. The courts have, however, made orders granting to the defendant an opportunity to inspect impounded documents belonging to him, *United States v. B. Goedde and Co.*, 40 F.Supp. 523, 534, E.D.Ill. The rule is a restatement of this procedure. In addition, it permits the procedure to be invoked in cases of objects and documents obtained from others by seizure or by process, on the theory that such evidential matter would probably have been accessible to the defendant if it had not previously been seized by the prosecution. The entire matter is left within the discretion of the court.

1966 Amendment

The extent to which pretrial discovery should be permitted in criminal cases is a complex and controversial issue. The problems have been explored in detail in recent legal literature, most of which has been in favor of increasing the range of permissible discovery. See, e.g., Brennan, The Criminal Prosecution: Sporting Event or Quest for Truth, 1963 Wash. U.L.Q. 279; Everett, Discovery in Criminal Cases—In Search of a Standard, 1964 Duke L.J. 477; Fletcher, Pretrial Discovery in State Criminal Cases, 12 Stan.L.Rev. 293 (1960); Goldstein, The State and the Accused: Balance of Advantage in Criminal Procedure, 69 Yale L.J. 1149, 1172–1198 (1960); Krantz, Pretrial Discovery in Criminal Cases: A Necessity for Fair and Impartial Justice, 42 Neb. L.Rev. 127 (1962); Louisell, Criminal Discovery: Dilemma Real or Apparent, 49 Calif.L.Rev. 56 (1961); Louisell, The Theory of Criminal Discovery and the Practice of Criminal Law, 14 Vand.L.Rev. 921 (1961); Moran, Federal Criminal Rules Changes: Aid or Illusion for the Indigent Defendant? 51 A.B.A.J. 64 (1965); Symposium, Discovery in Federal Criminal Cases, 33 F.R.D. 47–128 (1963); Traynor, Ground Lost and Found in Criminal Discovery, 39 N.Y.U.L.Rev. 228 (1964); Developments in the Law—Discovery, 74 Harv. L.Rev. 940, 1051–1063. Full judicial exploration of the conflicting policy considerations will be found in *State v. Tune*, 13 N.J. 203, 98 A.2d 881 (1953) and *State v. Johnson*, 28 N.J. 133, 145 A.2d 313 (1958); cf. *State v. Murphy*, 36 N.J. 172, 175 A.2d 622 (1961); *State v. Moffa*, 36 N.J. 219, 176 A.2d 1 (1961). The rule has been revised to expand the scope of pretrial discovery. At the same time provisions are made to guard against possible abuses.

Subdivision (a).—The court is authorized to order the attorney for the government to permit the defendant to inspect and copy or photograph three different types of material:

(1) Relevant written or recorded statements or confessions made by the defendant, or copies thereof. The defendant is not required to designate because he may not always be aware that his statements or confessions are being recorded. The government's obligation is limited to production of such statements as are within the possession, custody or control of the government, the existence of which is known, or by the exercise of due diligence may become known, to the attorney for the government. Discovery of statements and confessions is in line with what the Supreme Court has described as the "better practice" (*Cicenia v. LaGay*, 357 U.S. 504, 511 (1958)), and with the law in a number of states. See e.g. Del.Rules Crim.Proc., Rule 16; Ill.Stat. Ch. 38, § 729; Md.Rules Proc., Rule 728; *State v. McGee*, 91 Ariz. 101, 370 P.2d 261 (1962); *Cash v. Superior Court*, 53 Cal.2d 72, 346 P.2d 407 (1959); *State v. Bickham*, 239 La. 1094, 121 So.2d 207, cert. den. 364 U.S. 874 (1960); *People v. Johnson*, 356 Mich. 619, 97 N.W.2d 739 (1959); *State v. Johnson*, supra; *People v. Stokes*, 24 Miss.2d 755, 204 N.Y.Supp.2d 827 (Ct.Gen.Sess.1960). The amendment also makes it clear that discovery extends to recorded as well as written statements. For state cases upholding the discovery of recordings, see, e.g., *People v. Cartier*, 51 Cal.2d 590, 335 P.2d 114 (1959); *State v. Minor*, 177 A.2d 215 (Del.Super.Ct.1962).

(2) Relevant results or reports of physical or mental examinations, and of scientific tests or experiments (including fingerprint and handwriting comparisons) made in connection with the particular case, or copies thereof. Again the defendant is not required to designate but the government's obligation is limited to production of items within the possession, custody or control of the government, the existence of which is known, or by the exercise of due diligence may become known, to the attorney for the government. With respect to results or reports of scientific tests or experiments the range of materials which must be produced by the government is further limited to those made in connection

with the particular case. Cf. Fla.Stats. § 909.18; *State v. Superior Court*, 90 Ariz. 133, 367 P.2d 6 (1961); *People v. Cooper*, 53 Cal.2d 755, 770, 3 Cal.Rptr. 148, 157, 349 P.2d 964, 973 (1960); *People v. Stokes*, supra, at 762, 204 N.Y.Supp.2d at 835.

(3) Relevant recorded testimony of a defendant before a grand jury. The policy which favors pretrial disclosure to a defendant of his statements to government agents also supports, pretrial disclosure of his testimony before a grand jury. Courts, however, have tended to require a showing of special circumstances before ordering such disclosure. See, e.g., *United States v. Johnson*, 215 F.Supp. 300 (D.Md.1963). Disclosure is required only where the statement has been recorded and hence can be transcribed.

Subdivision (b).—This subdivision authorizes the court to order the attorney for the government to permit the defendant to inspect the copy or photograph all other books, papers, documents, tangible objects, buildings or places, or copies or portions thereof, which are within the possession, custody or control of the government. Because of the necessarily broad and general terms in which the items to be discovered are described, several limitations are imposed:

(1) While specific designation is not required of the defendant, the burden is placed on him to make a showing of materiality to the preparation of his defense and that his request is reasonable. The requirement of reasonableness will permit the court to define and limit the scope of the government's obligation to search its files while meeting the legitimate needs of the defendant. The court is also authorized to limit discovery to portions of items sought.

(2) Reports, memoranda, and other internal government documents made by government agents in connection with the investigation or prosecution of the case are exempt from discovery. Cf. *Palermo v. United States*, 360 U.S. 343 (1959); *Ogden v. United States*, 303 F.2d 724 (9th Cir.1962).

(3) Except as provided for reports of examinations and tests in subdivision (a)(2), statements made by government witnesses or prospective government witnesses to agents of the government are also exempt from discovery except as provided by 18 U.S.C. § 3500.

Subdivision (c).—This subdivision permits the court to condition a discovery order under subdivision (a)(2) and subdivision (b) by requiring the defendant to permit the government to discover similar items which the defendant intends to produce at the trial and which are within his possession, custody or control under restrictions similar to those placed in subdivision (b) upon discovery by the defendant. While the government normally has resources adequate to secure the information necessary for trial, there are some situations in which mutual disclosure would appear necessary to prevent the defendant from obtaining an unfair advantage. For example, in cases where both prosecution and defense have employed experts to make psychiatric examinations, it seems as important for the government to study the opinions of the experts to be called by the defendant in order to prepare for trial as it does for the defendant to study those of the government's witnesses. Or in cases (such as antitrust cases) in which the defendant is well represented and well financed, mutual disclosure so far as consistent with the privilege against self-incrimination would seem as appropriate as in civil cases. State cases have indicated that a requirement that the defendant disclose in advance of trial materials which he intends to use on his own behalf at the trial is not a violation of the privilege against self-incrimination. See *Jones v. Superior Court*, 58 Cal.2d 56, 22 Cal.Rptr. 879, 372 P.2d 919 (1962); *People v. Lopez*, 60 Cal.2d 223, 32 Cal.Rptr. 424, 384 P.2d 16 (1963); Traynor, Ground Lost and Found in Criminal Discovery, 39 N.Y.U.L.Rev. 228, 246 (1964); Comment, The Self-Incrimination Privilege: Barrier to Criminal Discovery, 51 Calif.L.Rev. 135 (1963); Note, 76 Harv.L.Rev. 838 (1963).

Subdivision (d).—This subdivision is substantially the same as the last sentence of the existing rule.

Subdivision (e).—This subdivision gives the court authority to deny, restrict or defer discovery upon a sufficient showing. Control of the abuses of discovery is necessary if it is to be expanded in the fashion proposed in subdivisions (a) and (b). Among the considerations to be taken into account by the court will be the safety of witnesses and others, a particular danger or perjury or witness intimidation, the protection of information vital to the national security, and the protection of business enterprises from economic reprisals.

For an example of a use of a protective order in state practice, see *People v. Lopez*, 60 Cal.2d 223, 32 Cal.Rptr. 424, 384 P.2d 16 (1963). See also Brennan, Remarks on Discovery, 33 F.R.D. 56, 65 (1963); Traynor, Ground Lost and Found in Criminal Discovery, 39 N.Y.U.L.Rev. 228, 244, 250.

In some cases it would defeat the purpose of the protective order if the government were required to make its showing in open court. The problem arises in its most extreme form where matters of national security are involved. Hence a procedure is set out where upon motion by the government the court may permit the government to make its showing, in whole or in part, in a written statement to be inspected by the court in camera. If the court grants relief based on such showing, the government's statement is to be sealed and preserved in the records of the court to be made available to the appellate court in the event of an appeal by the defendant. Cf. 18 U.S.C. § 3500.

Subdivision (f).—This subdivision is designed to encourage promptness in making discovery motions and to give the court sufficient control to prevent unnecessary delay and court time consequent upon a multiplication of discovery motions. Normally one motion should encompass all relief sought and a subsequent motion permitted only upon a showing of cause. Where pretrial hearings are used pursuant to Rule 17.1, discovery issues may be resolved at such hearings.

Subdivision (g).—The first sentence establishes a continuing obligation on a party subject to a discovery order with respect to material discovered after initial compliance. The duty provided is to notify the other party, his attorney or the court of the existence of the material. A motion can then be made by the other party for additional discovery and, where the existence of the material is disclosed shortly before or during the trial, for any necessary continuance.

The second sentence gives wide discretion to the court in dealing with the failure of either party to comply with a discovery order. Such discretion will permit the court to consider the reasons why disclosure was not made, the extent of the prejudice, if any, to the opposing party, the feasibility of rectifying that prejudice by a continuance, and any other relevant circumstances.

1974 Amendment

Rule 16 is revised to give greater discovery to both the prosecution and the defense. Subdivision (a) deals with disclosure of evidence by the government. Subdivision (b) deals with disclosure of evidence by the defendant. The majority of the Advisory Committee is of the view that the two—prosecution and defense discovery—are related and that the giving of a broader right of discovery to the defense is dependent upon giving also a broader right of discovery to the prosecution.

The draft provides for a right of prosecution discovery independent of any prior request for discovery by the defendant. The Advisory Committee is of the view that this is the most desirable approach to prosecution discovery. See American Bar Association, Standards Relating to Discovery and Procedure Before Trial, pp. 7, 43–46 (Approved Draft, 1970).

The language of the rule is recast from "the court may order" or "the court shall order" to "the government shall permit" or "the defendant shall permit." This is to make clear that discovery should be accomplished by the parties themselves, without the necessity of a court order unless there is dispute as to whether the matter is discoverable or a request for a protective order under subdivision (d)(1). The court, however, has the inherent right to enter an order under this rule.

The rule is intended to prescribe the minimum amount of discovery to which the parties are entitled. It is not intended to limit the judge's discretion to order broader discovery in appropriate cases. For example, subdivision (a)(3) is not intended to deny a judge's discretion to order disclosure of grand jury minutes where circumstances make it appropriate to do so.

Subdivision (a)(1)(A) amends the old rule to provide, upon request of the defendant, the government shall permit discovery if the conditions specified in subdivision (a)(1)(A) exist. Some courts have construed the current language as giving the court discretion as to whether to grant discovery of defendant's statements. See *United States v. Kaminsky*, 275 F.Supp. 365 (S.D.N.Y.1967), denying discovery because the defendant did not demonstrate that his request for discovery was warranted; *United States v. Diliberto*, 264 F.Supp. 181 (S.D.N.Y.1967), holding that there must be a showing of actual need before discovery would be granted; *United States v. Louis Carreau*, Inc., 42 F.R.D. 408 (S.D.N.Y.1967), holding that in the absence of a showing of good cause the government cannot be required to disclose defendant's prior statements in advance of trial. In *United States v. Louis Carreau*, Inc. at p. 412, the court stated that if rule 16 meant that production of the statements was mandatory, the word "shall" would have been used instead of "may." See also *United States v. Wallace*, 272 F.Supp. 838 (S.D.N.Y.1967); *United States v. Wood*, 270 F.Supp. 963 (S.D.N.Y.1967); *United States v. Leighton*, 265 F.Supp. 27 (S.D.N.Y.1967); *United States v. Longarzo*, 43 F.R.D. 395 (S.D.N.Y.1967); *Loux v. United States*, 389 F.2d 911 (9th Cir.1968); and the discussion of discovery in Discovery in Criminal Cases, 44 F.R.D. 481 (1968). Other courts have held that even though the current rules make discovery discretionary, the defendant need not show cause when he seeks to discover his own statements. See *United States v. Aadal*, 280 F.Supp. 859 (S.D.N.Y.1967); *United States v. Federman*, 41 F.R.D. 339 (S.D.N.Y.1967); and *United States v. Projansky*, 44 F.R.D. 550 (S.D.N.Y.1968).

The amendment making disclosure mandatory under the circumstances prescribed in subdivision (a)(1)(A) resolves such ambiguity as may currently exist, in the direction of more liberal discovery. See C. Wright, Federal Practice and Procedure: Criminal § 253 (1969, Supp.1971), Rezneck, The New Federal Rules of Criminal Procedure, 54 Geo.L.J. 1276 (1966); Fla.Stat.Ann. § 925.05 (Supp.1971–1972); N.J.Crim. Prac. Rule 35–11(a) (1967). This is done in the view that broad discovery contributes to the fair and efficient administration of criminal justice by providing the defendant with enough information to make an informed decision as to plea; by minimizing the undesirable effect of surprise at the trial; and by otherwise contributing to an accurate determination of the issue of guilt or innocence. This is the ground upon which the American Bar Association Standards Relating to Discovery and Procedure Before Trial (Approved Draft, 1970) has unanimously recommended broader discovery. The United States Supreme Court has said that the pretrial disclosure of a defendant's statements "may be the 'better practice.'" *Cicenia v. La Gay*, 357 U.S. 504, 511, 78 S.Ct. 1297, 2 L.Ed.2d 1523 (1958). See also *Leland v. Oregon*, 343 U.S. 790, 72 S.Ct. 1002, 96 L.Ed. 1302 (1952); *State v. Johnson*, 28 N.J. 133, 145 A.2d 313 (1958).

The requirement that the statement be disclosed prior to trial, rather than waiting until the trial, also contributes to efficiency of administration. It is during the pretrial stage that the defendant usually decides whether to plead guilty. See *United States v. Projansky*, supra. The pretrial stage is also the time during which many objections to the admissibility of types of evidence ought to be made. Pretrial disclosure ought, therefore, to contribute both to an informed guilty plea practice and to a pretrial resolution of admissibility questions. See ABA, Standards Relating to Discovery and Procedure Before Trial § 1.2 and Commentary pp. 40–43 (Approved Draft, 1970).

The American Bar Association Standards mandate the prosecutor to make the required disclosure even though not requested to do so by the defendant. The proposed draft requires the defendant to request discovery, although obviously the attorney for the government may disclose without waiting for a request, and there are situations in which due process will require the prosecution, on its own, to disclose evidence "helpful" to the defense. *Brady v. Maryland*, 373 U.S. 83, 83 S.Ct. 1194, 10 L.Ed.2d 215 (1963); *Giles v. Maryland*, 386 U.S. 66, 87 S.Ct. 793, 17 L.Ed.2d 737 (1967).

The requirement in subdivision (a)(1)(A) is that the government produce "statements" without further discussion of what "statement" includes. There has been some recent controversy over what "statements" are subject to discovery under the current rule. See Discovery in Criminal Cases, 44 F.R.D. 481 (1968); C. Wright, Federal Practice and Procedure: Criminal § 253, pp. 505–506 (1969, Supp.1971). The kinds of "statements" which have been held to be within the rule include "substantially verbatim and contemporaneous" statements, *United States v. Elife*, 43 F.R.D. 23 (S.D.N.Y. 1967); statements which reproduce the defendant's "exact words," *United States v. Armantrout*, 278 F.Supp. 517 (S.D.N.Y.1968); a memorandum which was not verbatim but included the substance of the defendant's testimony, *United States v. Scharf*, 267 F.Supp. 19 (S.D.N.Y.1967); Summaries of the defendant's statements, *United States v. Morrison*, 43

F.R.D. 516 (N.D.Ill.1967); and statements discovered by means of electronic surveillance, *United States v. Black*, 282 F.Supp. 35 (D.D.C.1968). The court in *United States v. Iovinelli*, 276 F.Supp. 629, 631 (N.D.Ill.1967), declared that "statements" as used in old rule 16 is not restricted to the "substantially verbatim recital of an oral statement" or to statements which are a "recital of past occurrences."

The Jencks Act, 18 U.S.C. § 3500, defines "statements" of government witnesses discoverable for purposes of cross-examination as: (1) a "written statement" signed or otherwise approved by a witness, (2) "a stenographic, mechanical, electrical, or other recording, or a transcription thereof, which is a substantially verbatim recital of an oral statement made by said witness to an agent of the government and recorded contemporaneously with the making of such oral statement." 18 U.S.C. § 3500(e). The language of the Jencks Act has most often led to a restrictive definition of "statements," confining "statements" to the defendant's "own words." See *Hanks v. United States*, 388 F.2d 171 (10th Cir.1968), and *Augenblick v. United States*, 377 F.2d 586, 180 Ct.Cl. 131 (1967).

The American Bar Association's Standards Relating to Discovery and Procedure Before Trial (Approved Draft, 1970) do not attempt to define "statements" because of a disagreement among members of the committee as to what the definition should be. The majority rejected the restrictive definition of "statements" contained in the Jencks Act, 18 U.S.C. § 3500(e), in the view that the defendant ought to be able to see his statement in whatever form it may have been preserved in fairness to the defendant and to discourage the practice, where it exists, of destroying original notes, after transforming them into secondary transcriptions, in order to avoid cross-examination based upon the original notes. See *Campbell v. United States*, 373 U.S. 487, 83 S.Ct. 1356, 10 L.Ed.2d 501 (1963). The minority favored a restrictive definition of "statements" in the view that the use of other than "verbatim" statements would subject witnesses to unfair cross-examination. See American Bar Association's Standards Relating to Discovery and Procedure Before Trial pp. 61–64 (Approved Draft, 1970). The draft of subdivision (a)(1)(A) leaves the matter of the meaning of the term unresolved and thus left for development on a case-by-case basis.

Subdivision (a)(1)(A) also provides for mandatory disclosure of a summary of any oral statement made by defendant to a government agent which the attorney for the government intends to use in evidence. The reasons for permitting the defendant to discover his own statements seem obviously to apply to the substance of any oral statement which the government intends to use in evidence at the trial. See American Bar Association Standards Relating to Discovery and Procedure Before Trial § 2.1(a)(ii) (Approved Draft, 1970). Certainly disclosure will facilitate the raising of objections to admissibility prior to trial. There have been several conflicting decisions under the current rules as to whether the government must disclose the substance of oral statements of the defendant which it has in its possession. Cf. *United States v. Baker*, 262 F.Supp. 657 (D.C.D.C.1966); *United States v. Curry*, 278 F.Supp. 508 (N.D.Ill.1967); *United States v. Morrison*, 43 F.R.D. 516 (N.D.Ill.1967); *United States v. Reid*, 43 F.R.D. 520 (N.D.Ill.1967); *United States v. Armantrout*, 278 F.Supp. 517 (S.D.N.Y.1968); and *United States v. Elife*, 43 F.R.D. 23 (S.D.N.Y.1967). There is, however, considerable support for the policy of disclosing the substance of the defendant's oral statement. Many courts have indicated that this is a "better practice" than denying such disclosure. E.g., *United States v. Curry*, supra; *Loux v. United States*, 389 F.2d 911 (9th Cir.1968); and *United States v. Baker*, supra.

Subdivision (a)(1)(A) also provides for mandatory disclosure of any "recorded testimony" which defendant gives before a grand jury if the testimony "relates to the offense charged." The present rule is discretionary and is applicable only to those of defendant's statements which are "relevant."

The traditional rationale behind grand jury secrecy—protection of witnesses—does not apply when the accused seeks discovery of his own testimony. Cf. *Dennis v. United States*, 384 U.S. 855, 86 S.Ct. 1840, 16 L.Ed.2d 973 (1966); and *Allen v. United States*, 129 U.S.App.D.C. 61, 390 F.2d 476 (1968). In interpreting the rule many judges have granted defendant discovery without a showing of need or relevance. *United States v. Gleason*, 259 F.Supp. 282 (S.D.N.Y.1966); *United States v. Longarzo*, 43 F.R.D. 395 (S.D.N.Y.1967); and *United States v. United Concrete Pipe Corp.*, 41 F.R.D. 538 (N.D.Tex.1966). Making disclosure mandatory without a showing of relevance conforms to the recommendation of the American Bar Association Standards Relating to Discovery and Procedure Before Trial § 2.1(a)(iii) and Commentary pp. 64–66 (Approved Draft, 1970). Also see Note, Discovery by a Criminal Defendant of His Own Grand-Jury Testimony, 68 Columbia L.Rev. 311 (1968).

In a situation involving a corporate defendant, statements made by present and former officers and employees relating to their employment have been held discoverable as statements of the defendant. *United States v. Hughes*, 413 F.2d 1244 (5th Cir.1969). The rule makes clear that such statements are discoverable if the officer or employee was "able legally to bind the defendant in respect to the activities involved in the charges."

Subdivision (a)(1)(B) allows discovery of the defendant's prior criminal record. A defendant may be uncertain of the precise nature of his prior record and it seems therefore in the interest of efficient and fair administration to make it possible to resolve prior to trial any disputes as to the correctness of the relevant criminal record of the defendant.

Subdivision (a)(1)(C) gives a right of discovery of certain tangible objects under the specified circumstances. Courts have construed the old rule as making disclosure discretionary with the judge. Cf. *United States v. Kaminsky*, 275 F.Supp. 365 (S.D.N.Y.1967); *Gevinson v. United States*, 358 F.2d 761 (5th Cir.1966), cert. denied, 385 U.S. 823, 87 S.Ct. 51, 17 L.Ed.2d 60 (1966); and *United States v. Tanner*, 279 F.Supp. 457 (N.D.Ill.1967). The old rule requires a "showing of materiality to the preparation of his defense and that the request is reasonable." The new rule requires disclosure if any one of three situations exists: (a) the defendant shows that disclosure of the document or tangible object is material to the defense, (b) the government intends to use the document or tangible object in its presentation of its case in chief, or (c) the document or tangible object was obtained from or belongs to the defendant.

Disclosure of documents and tangible objects which are "material" to the preparation of the defense may be required under the rule of *Brady v. Maryland*, 373 U.S. 83, 83 S.Ct. 1194, 10 L.Ed.2d 215 (1963), without an additional showing that the request is "reasonable." In *Brady* the court held that "due process" requires that the prosecution disclose evidence favorable to the accused. Although the Advisory Committee decided not to codify the Brady Rule, the requirement that the government disclose documents and tangible objects "material to the preparation of his defense" underscores the importance of disclosure of evidence favorable to the defendant.

Limiting the rule to situations in which the defendant can show that the evidence is material seems unwise. It may be difficult for a defendant to make this showing if he does not know what the evidence is. For this reason subdivision (a)(1)(C) also contains language to compel disclosure if the government intends to use the property as evidence at the trial or if the property was obtained from or belongs to the defendant. See ABA Standards Relating to Discovery and Procedure Before Trial § 2.1(a)(v) and Commentary pp. 68–69 (Approved Draft, 1970). This is probably the result under old rule 16 since the fact that the government intends to use the physical evidence at the trial is probably sufficient proof of "materiality." C. Wright, Federal Practice and Procedure: Criminal § 254 especially n. 70 at p. 513 (1969, Supp.1971). But it seems desirable to make this explicit in the rule itself.

Requiring disclosure of documents and tangible objects which "were obtained from or belong to the defendant" probably is also making explicit in the rule what would otherwise be the interpretation of "materiality." See C. Wright, Federal Practice and Procedure: Criminal § 254 at p. 510 especially n. 58 (1969, Supp.1971).

Subdivision (a)(1)(C) is also amended to add the word "photographs" to the objects previously listed. See ABA Standards Relating to Discovery and Procedure Before Trial § 2.1(a)(v) (Approved Draft, 1970).

Subdivision (a)(1)(D) makes disclosure of the reports of examinations and tests mandatory. This is the recommendation of the ABA Standards Relating to Discovery and Procedure Before Trial § 2.1(a)(iv) and Commentary pp. 66–68 (Approved Draft, 1970). The obligation of disclosure applies only to scientific tests or experiments "made in connection with the particular case." So limited, mandatory disclosure seems justified because: (1) it is difficult to test expert testimony at trial without advance notice and preparation; (2) it is not likely that such evidence will be distorted or misused if disclosed prior to trial; and (3) to the extent that a test may be favorable to the defense, its disclosure is mandated under the rule of *Brady v. Maryland*, supra.

Subdivision (a)(1)(E) is new. It provides for discovery of the names of witnesses to be called by the government and of the prior criminal record of these witnesses. Many states have statutes or rules which require that the accused be notified prior to trial of the witnesses to be called against him. See, e.g., Alaska R.Crim.Proc. 7(c); Ariz.R.Crim.Proc. 153, 17 A.R.S. (1956); Ark.Stat.Ann. § 43–1001 (1947); Cal. Pen.Code § 995n (West 1957); Colo.Rev.Stat.Ann. §§ 39–3–6, 39–4–2 (1963); Fla.Stat.Ann. § 906.29 (1944); Idaho Code Ann. § 19–1404 (1948); Ill.Rev.Stat. ch. 38, § 114–9 (1970); Ind.Ann.Stat. § 9–903 (1956), IC 1971, 35–1–16–3; Iowa Code Ann. § 772.3 (1950); Kan.Stat.Ann. § 62–931 (1964); Ky.R.Crim.Proc. 6.08 (1962); Mich.Stat. Ann. § 28.980, M.C.L.A. § 767.40 (Supp.1971); Minn.Stat. Ann. § 628.08 (1947); Mo.Ann.Stat. § 545.070 (1953); Mont. Rev.Codes Ann. § 95–1503 (Supp.1969); Neb.Rev.Stat. § 29–1602 (1964); Nev.Rev.Stat. § 173.045 (1967); Okl.Stat. tit. 22, § 384 (1951); Ore.Rev.Stat. § 132.580 (1969); Tenn. Code Ann. § 40–1708 (1955); Utah Code Ann. § 77–20–3 (1953). For examples of the ways in which these requirements are implemented, see *State v. Mitchell*, 181 Kan. 193, 310 P.2d 1063 (1957); *State v. Parr*, 129 Mont. 175, 283 P.2d 1086 (1955); *Phillips v. State*, 157 Neb. 419, 59 N.W.2d 598 (1953).

Witnesses' prior statements must be made available to defense counsel after the witness testifies on direct examination for possible impeachment purposes during trial; 18 U.S.C. § 3500.

The American Bar Association's Standards Relating to Discovery and Procedure Before Trial § 2.1(a)(i) (Approved Draft, 1970) require disclosure of both the names and the statements of prosecution witnesses. Subdivision (a)(1)(E) requires only disclosure, prior to trial, of names, addresses, and prior criminal record. It does not require disclosure of the witnesses' statements although the rule does not preclude the parties from agreeing to disclose statements prior to trial. This is done, for example, in courts using the so-called "omnibus hearing."

Disclosure of the prior criminal record of witnesses places the defense in the same position as the government, which normally has knowledge of the defendant's record and the record of anticipated defense witnesses. In addition, the defendant often lacks means of procuring this information on his own. See American Bar Association Standards Relating to Discovery and Procedure Before Trial § 2.1(a)(vi) (Approved Draft, 1970).

A principal argument against disclosure of the identity of witnesses prior to trial has been the danger to the witness, his being subjected either to physical harm or to threats designed to make the witness unavailable or to influence him to change his testimony. Discovery in Criminal cases, 44 F.R.D. 481, 499–500 (1968); Ratnoff, The New Criminal Deposition Statute in Ohio—Help or Hindrance to Justice?, 19 Case Western Reserve L.Rev. 279, 284 (1968). See, e.g., *United States v. Estep*, 151 F.Supp. 668, 672–673 (N.D.Tex. 1957):

> Ninety per cent of the convictions had in the trial court for sale and dissemination of narcotic drugs are linked to the work and the evidence obtained by an informer. If that informer is not to have his life protected there won't be many informers hereafter.

See also the dissenting opinion of Mr. Justice Clark in *Roviaro v. United States*, 353 U.S. 53, 66–67, 77 S.Ct. 623, 1 L.Ed.2d 639 (1957). Threats of market retaliation against witnesses in criminal antitrust cases are another illustration. *Bergen Drug Co. v. Parke, Davis & Company*, 307 F.2d 725 (3d Cir.1962); and *House of Materials, Inc. v. Simplicity Pattern Co.*, 298 F.2d 867 (2d Cir.1962). The government has two alternatives when it believes disclosure will create an undue risk of harm to the witness: It can ask for a protective order under subdivision (d)(1). See ABA Standards Relating to Discovery and Procedure Before Trial § 2.5(b) (Approved Draft, 1970). It can also move the court to allow the perpetuation of a particular witness's testimony for use at trial if the witness is unavailable or later changes his testimony. The purpose of the latter alternative is to make pretrial disclosure possible and at the same time to minimize any inducement to use improper means to force the witness either to not show up or to change his testimony before a jury. See rule 15.

Subdivision (a)(2) is substantially unchanged. It limits the discovery otherwise allowed by providing that the government need not disclose "reports, memoranda, or other internal government documents made by the attorney for the government or other government agents in connection with the investigation or prosecution of the case" or "statements made by government witnesses or prospective government witnesses." The only proposed change is that the "reports, memoranda, or other internal government documents made by the attorney for the government" are included to make clear that the work product of the government attorney is protected. See C. Wright, Federal Practice and Procedure: Criminal § 254 n. 92 (1969, Supp.1971); *United States v. Rothman*, 179 F.Supp. 935 (W.D.Pa.1959); Note, "Work Product" in Criminal Discovery, 1966 Wash.U.L.Q. 321; American Bar Association, Standards Relating to Discovery and Procedure Before Trial § 2.6(a) (Approved Draft, 1970); cf. *Hickman v. Taylor*, 329 U.S. 495, 67 S.Ct. 385, 91 L.Ed. 451 (1947). *Brady v. Maryland*, 373 U.S. 83, 83 S.Ct. 1194, 10 L.Ed.2d 215 (1963), requires the disclosure of evidence favorable to the defendant. This is, of course, not changed by this rule.

Subdivision (a)(3) is included to make clear that recorded proceedings of a grand jury are explicitly dealt with in rule 6 and subdivision (a)(1)(A) of rule 16 and thus are not covered by other provisions such as subdivision (a)(1)(C) which deals generally with discovery of documents in the possession, custody, or control of the government.

Subdivision (a)(4) is designed to insure that the government will not be penalized if it makes a full disclosure of all potential witnesses and then decides not to call one or more of the witnesses listed. This is not, however, intended to abrogate the defendant's right to comment generally upon the government's failure to call witnesses in an appropriate case.

Subdivision (b) deals with the government's right to discovery of defense evidence or, put in other terms, with the extent to which a defendant is required to disclose its evidence to the prosecution prior to trial. Subdivision (b) replaces old subdivision (c).

Subdivision (b) enlarges the right of government discovery in several ways: (1) it gives the government the right to discovery of lists of defense witnesses as well as physical evidence and the results of examinations and tests; (2) it requires disclosure if the defendant has the evidence under his control and intends to use it at trial in his case in chief, without the additional burden, required by the old rule, of having to show, in behalf of the government, that the evidence is material and the request reasonable; and (3) it gives the government the right to discovery without conditioning that right upon the existence of a prior request for discovery by the defendant.

Although the government normally has resources adequate to secure much of the evidence for trial, there are situations in which pretrial disclosure of evidence to the government is in the interest of effective and fair criminal justice administration. For example, the experimental "omnibus hearing" procedure (see discussion in Advisory Committee Note to rule 12) is based upon an assumption that the defendant, as well as the government, will be willing to disclose evidence prior to trial.

Having reached the conclusion that it is desirable to require broader disclosure by the defendant under certain circumstances, the Advisory Committee has taken the view that it is preferable to give the right of discovery to the government independently of a prior request for discovery by the defendant. This is the recommendation of the American Bar Association Standards Relating to Discovery and Procedure Before Trial, Commentary, pp. 43–46 (Approved Draft, 1970). It is sometimes asserted that making the government's right of discovery conditional will minimize the risk that government discovery will be viewed as an infringement of the defendant's constitutional rights. See discussion in C. Wright, Federal Practice and Procedure: Criminal § 256 (1969, Supp.1971); Moore, Criminal Discovery, 19 Hastings L.J. 865 (1968); Wilder, Prosecution Discovery and the Privilege Against Self-Incrimination, 6 Am.Cr.L.Q. 3 (1967). There are assertions that prosecution discovery, even if conditioned upon the defendant's being granted discovery, is a violation of the privilege. See statements of Mr. Justice Black and Mr. Justice Douglas, 39 F.R.D. 69, 272, 277–278 (1966); C. Wright, Federal Practice and Procedure: Criminal § 256 (1969, Supp.1971). Several states require defense disclosure of an intended defense of alibi and, in some cases, a list of witnesses in support of an alibi defense, without making the requirement conditional upon prior discovery being given to the defense. E.g., Ariz.R.Crim.P. 192(B), 17 A.R.S. (1956); Ind.Ann.Stat. § 9–1631 to 9–1633 (1956), IC 1971, 35–5–1–1 to 35–5–1–3; Mich.Comp.Laws Ann. §§ 768.20, 768.21 (1968); N.Y.CPL § 250.20 (McKinney's Consol.Laws, c. 11–A, 1971); and Ohio Rev.Code Ann. § 2945.58 (1954). State courts have refused to hold these statutes violative of the privilege against self-incrimination. See *State v. Thayer*, 124 Ohio St. 1, 176 N.E. 656 (1931), and *People v. Rakiec*, 260 App.Div. 452, 23 N.Y.S.2d 607, aff'd, 289 N.Y. 306, 45 N.E.2d 812 (1942). See also rule 12.1 and Advisory Committee Note thereto.

Some state courts have held that a defendant may be required to disclose, in advance of trial, evidence which he intends to use on his own behalf at trial without violating the privilege against self-incrimination. See *Jones v. Superior Court of Nevada County*, 58 Cal.2d 56, 22 Cal.Rptr. 879, 372 P.2d 919 (1962); *People v. Lopez*, 60 Cal.2d 223, 32 Cal.Rptr. 424, 384 P.2d 16 (1963); Comment, The Self-Incrimination Privilege: Barrier to Criminal Discovery?, 51 Calif.L.Rev. 135 (1963); Note, 76 Harv.L.Rev. 838 (1963). The court in *Jones v. Superior Court of Nevada County*, supra, suggests that if mandatory disclosure applies only to those items which the accused intends to introduce in evidence at trial, neither the incriminatory nor the involuntary aspects of the privilege against self-incrimination are present.

On balance the Advisory Committee is of the view that an independent right of discovery for both the defendant and the government is likely to contribute to both effective and fair administration. See Louisell, Criminal Discovery and Self-Incrimination: Roger Traynor Confronts the Dilemma, 53 Calif.L.Rev. 89 (1965), for an analysis of the difficulty of weighing the value of broad discovery against the value which inheres in not requiring the defendant to disclose anything which might work to his disadvantage.

Subdivision (b)(1)(A) provides that the defendant shall disclose any documents and tangible objects which he has in his possession, custody, or control and which he intends to introduce in evidence in his case in chief.

Subdivision (b)(1)(B) provides that the defendant shall disclose the results of physical or mental examinations and scientific tests or experiments if (a) they were made in connection with a particular case; (b) the defendant has them under his control; and (c) he intends to offer them in evidence in his case in chief or which were prepared by a defense witness and the results or reports relate to the witness's testimony. In cases where both prosecution and defense have employed experts to conduct tests such as psychiatric examinations, it seems as important for the government to be able to study the results reached by defense experts which are to be called by the defendant as it does for the defendant to study those of government experts. See Schultz, Criminal Discovery by the Prosecution: Frontier Developments and Some Proposals for the Future, 22 N.Y.U.Intra.L.Rev. 268 (1967); American Bar Association, Standards Relating to Discovery and Procedure Before Trial § 3.2 (Supp., Approved Draft, 1970).

Subdivision (b)(1)(C) provides for discovery of a list of witnesses the defendant intends to call in his case in chief. State cases have indicated that disclosure of a list of defense witnesses does not violate the defendant's privilege against self-incrimination. See *Jones v. Superior Court of Nevada County*, supra, and *People v. Lopez*, supra. The defendant has the same option as does the government if it is believed that disclosure of the identity of a witness may subject that witness to harm or a threat of harm. The defendant can ask for a protective order under subdivision (d)(1) or can take a deposition in accordance with the terms of rule 15.

Subdivision (b)(2) is unchanged, appearing as the last sentence of subdivision (c) of old rule 16.

Subdivision (b)(3) provides that the defendant's failure to introduce evidence or call witnesses shall not be admissible in evidence against him. In states which require pretrial disclosure of witnesses' identity, the prosecution is not allowed to comment upon the defendant's failure to call a listed witness. See *O'Connor v. State*, 31 Wis.2d 684, 143 N.W.2d 489 (1966); *People v. Mancini*, 6 N.Y.2d 853, 188 N.Y.S.2d 559, 160 N.E.2d 91 (1959); and *State v. Cocco*, 73 Ohio App. 182, 55 N.E.2d 430 (1943). This is not, however, intended to abrogate the government's right to comment generally upon the defendant's failure to call witnesses in an appropriate case, other than the defendant's failure to testify.

Subdivision (c) is a restatement of part of old rule 16(g).

Subdivision (d)(1) deals with the protective order. Although the rule does not attempt to indicate when a protective order should be entered, it is obvious that one would be appropriate where there is reason to believe that a witness would be subject to physical or economic harm if his identity is revealed. See *Will v. United States*, 389 U.S. 90, 88 S.Ct. 269, 19 L.Ed.2d 305 (1967). The language "by the judge alone" is not meant to be inconsistent with *Alderman v. United States*, 394 U.S. 165, 89 S.Ct. 961, 22 L.Ed.2d 176 (1969). In Alderman the court points out that there may be appropriate occasions for the trial judge to decide questions relating to pretrial disclosure. See *Alderman v. United States*, 394 U.S. at 182 n. 14, 89 S.Ct. 961.

Subdivision (d)(2) is a restatement of part of old rule 16(g) and (d).

Old subdivision (f) of rule 16 dealing with time of motions is dropped because rule 12(c) provides the judge with authority to set the time for the making of pretrial motions including requests for discovery. Rule 12 also prescribes the consequences which follow from a failure to make a pretrial motion at the time fixed by the court. See rule 12(f).

1975 Enactment

A. Amendments Proposed by the Supreme Court. Rule 16 of the Federal Rules of Criminal Procedure regulates discovery by the defendant of evidence in possession of the prosecution, and discovery by the prosecution of evidence in possession of the defendant. The present rule permits the defendant to move the court to discover certain material. The prosecutor's discovery is limited and is reciprocal—that is, if the defendant is granted discovery of certain items, then the prosecution may move for discovery of similar items under the defendant's control.

As proposed to be amended, the rule provides that the parties themselves will accomplish discovery—no motion need be filed and no court order is necessary. The court will intervene only to resolve a dispute as to whether something is discoverable or to issue a protective order.

The proposed rule enlarges the scope of the defendant's discovery to include a copy of his prior criminal record and a list of the names and addresses, plus record of prior felony convictions, of all witnesses the prosecution intends to call during its case-in-chief. It also permits the defendant to discover the substance of any oral statement of his which the prosecution intends to offer at trial, if the statement was given in response to interrogation by any person known by defendant to be a government agent.

Proposed subdivision (a)(2) provides that Rule 16 does not authorize the defendant to discover "reports, memoranda, or other internal government documents made by the attorney for the government or other government agents in connection with the investigation or prosecution of the case. . . ."

The proposed rule also enlarges the scope of the government's discovery of materials in the custody of the defendant. The government is entitled to a list of the names and addresses of the witnesses the defendant intends to call during his case-in-chief. Proposed subdivision (b)(2) protects the defendant from having to disclose "reports, memoranda, or other internal defense documents . . . made in connection with the investigation or defense of the case. . . ."

Subdivision (d)(1) of the proposed rule permits the court to deny, restrict, or defer discovery by either party, or to make such other order as is appropriate. Upon request, a party may make a showing that such an order is necessary. This showing shall be made to the judge alone if the party so requests. If the court enters an order after such a showing, it must seal the record of the showing and preserve it in the event there is an appeal.

B. Committee Action. The Committee agrees that the parties should, to the maximum possible extent, accomplish discovery themselves. The court should become involved only when it is necessary to resolve a dispute or to issue an order pursuant to subdivision (d).

Perhaps the most controversial amendments to this rule were those dealing with witness lists. Under present law, the government must turn over a witness list *only* in capital cases. [Section 3432 of title 18 of the United States Code provides: A person charged with treason or other capital offense shall at least three entire days before commencement of trial be furnished with a copy of the indictment and a list of the veniremen, and of the witnesses to be produced on the trial for proving the indictment, stating the place of abode of each venireman and witness.] The defendant never needs to turn over a list of his witnesses. The proposed rule requires both the government and the defendant to turn over witness lists in every case, capital or noncapital. Moreover, the lists must be furnished to the adversary party upon that party's request.

The proposed rule was sharply criticized by both prosecutors and defenders. The prosecutors feared that pretrial disclosure of prosecution witnesses would result in harm to witnesses. The defenders argued that a defendant cannot constitutionally be compelled to disclose his witnesses.

The Committee believes that it is desirable to promote greater pretrial discovery. As stated in the Advisory Committee Note,

> broader discovery by both the defense and the prosecution will contribute to the fair and efficient administration of criminal justice by aiding in informed plea negotiations, by minimizing the undesirable effect of surprise at trial, and by otherwise contributing to an accurate determination of the issue of guilt or innocence....

The Committee, therefore, endorses the principle that witness lists are discoverable. However, the Committee has attempted to strike a balance between the narrow provisions of existing law and the broad provisions of the proposed rule.

The Committee rule makes the procedures defendant-triggered. If the defendant asks for and receives a list of prosecution witnesses, then the prosecution may request a list of defense witnesses. The witness lists need not be turned over until 3 days before trial. The court can modify the terms of discovery upon a sufficient showing. Thus, the court can require disclosure of the witness lists earlier than 3 days before trial, or can permit a party not to disclose the identity of a witness before trial.

The Committee provision promotes broader discovery and its attendant values—informed disposition of cases without trial, minimizing the undesirable effect of surprise, and helping insure that the issue of guilt or innocence is accurately determined. At the same time, it avoids the problems suggested by both the prosecutors and the defenders.

The major argument advanced by prosecutors is the risk of danger to their witnesses if their identities are disclosed prior to trial. The Committee recognizes that there may be a risk but believes that the risk is not as great as some fear that it is. Numerous states require the prosecutor to provide the defendant with a list of prosecution witnesses prior to trial. [These States include Alaska, Arizona, Arkansas, California, Colorado, Florida, Idaho, Illinois, Indiana, Iowa, Kansas, Kentucky, Michigan, Minnesota, Missouri, Montana, Nebraska, Nevada, Oklahoma, Oregon, Tennessee,and Utah. See Advisory Committee Note, House Document 93–292, at 60.] The evidence before the Committee indicates that these states have not experienced unusual problems of witness intimidation. [See the comments of the Standing Committee on Criminal Law and Procedure of the State Bar of California in Hearings II, at 302.]

Some federal jurisdictions have adopted an omnibus pretrial discovery procedure that calls upon the prosecutor to give the defendant its witness lists. One such jurisdiction is the Southern District of California. The evidence before the Committee indicates that there has been no unusual problems with witness intimidation in that district. Charles Sevilla, Chief Trial Attorney for the Federal Defenders of San Diego, Inc., which operates in the Southern District of California, testified as follows:

> The Government in one of its statements to this committee indicated that providing the defense with witness lists will cause coerced witness perjury. This does not happen. We receive Government witness lists as a matter of course in the Southern District, and it's a rare occasion when there is any overture by a defense witness or by a defendant to a Government witness. It simply doesn't happen except on the rarest of occasion. When the Government has that fear it can resort to the protective order. [Hearings II, at 42.]

Mr. Sevilla's observations are corroborated by the views of the U.S. Attorney for the Southern District of California:

> Concerning the modifications to Rule 16, we have followed these procedures informally in this district for a number of years. We were one of the districts selected for the pilot projects of the Omnibus Hearing in 1967 or 1968. We have found that the courts in our district will not require us to disclose names of proposed witnesses when in our judgment to do so would not be advisable. Otherwise we routinely provide defense counsel with full discovery, including names and addresses of witnesses. We have not had any untowards results by following this program, having in mind that the courts will, and have, excused us from discovery where the circumstances warrant. [Hearings I, at 109.]

Much of the prosecutorial criticism of requiring the prosecution to give a list of its witnesses to the defendant reflects an unwillingness to trust judges to exercise sound judgment in the public interest. Prosecutors have stated that they frequently will open their files to defendants in order to induce pleas. [See testimony of Richard L. Thornburgh, United States Attorney for the Western District of Pennsylvania, in Hearings I, at 150.]

Prosecutors are willing to determine on their own when they can do this without jeopardizing the safety of witnesses. There is no reason why a judicial officer cannot exercise the same discretion in the public interest.

The Committee is convinced that in the usual case there is no serious risk of danger to prosecution witnesses from pretrial disclosure of their identities. In exceptional instances, there may be a risk of danger. The Committee rule, however, is capable of dealing with those exceptional instances while still providing for disclosure of witnesses in the usual case.

The Committee recognizes the force of the constitutional arguments advanced by defenders. Requiring a defendant, upon request, to give to the prosecution material which may be incriminating, certainly raises very serious constitutional problems. The Committee deals with these problems by having the defendant trigger the discovery procedures. Since the defendant has no constitutional right to discover any of the prosecution's evidence (unless it is exculpatory within the meaning of *Brady v. Maryland*, 373 U.S. 83 (1963), it is permissible to condition his access to nonexculpatory evidence upon his turning over a list of defense witnesses. Rule 16 currently operates in this manner.

The Committee also changed subdivisions (a)(2) and (b)(2), which set forth "work product" exceptions to the general discovery requirements. The subsections proposed by the

Supreme Court are cast in terms of the type of document involved (e.g., report), rather than in terms of the content (e.g., legal theory). The Committee recast these provisions by adopting language from Rule 26(b)(3) of the Federal Rules of Civil Procedure.

The Committee notes that subdivision (a)(1)(C) permits the defendant to discover certain items that "were obtained from or belong to the defendant." The Committee believes that, as indicated in the Advisory Committee Note [House Document 93–292, at 59], items that "were obtained from or belong to the defendant" are items that are material to the preparation of his defense.

The Committee added language to subdivision (a)(1)(B) to conform it to provisions in subdivision (a)(1)(A). The rule as changed by the Committee requires the prosecutor to give the defendant such copy of the defendant's prior criminal record as is within the prosecutor's "possession, custody, or control, the existence of which is known, or by the exercise of due diligence may become known" to the prosecutor. The Committee also made a similar conforming change in subdivision (a)(1)(E), dealing with the criminal records of government witnesses. The prosecutor can ordinarily discharge his obligation under these two subdivisions. (a)(1)(B) and (E), by obtaining a copy of the F.B.I. "rap sheet."

The Committee made an additional change in subdivision (a)(1)(E). The proposed rule required the prosecutor to provide the defendant with a record of the felony convictions of government witnesses. The major purpose for letting the defendant discover information about the record of government witnesses, is to provide him with information concerning the credibility of those witnesses. Rule 609(a) of the Federal Rules of Evidence permits a party to attack the credibility of a witness with convictions other than just felony convictions. The Committee, therefore, changed subdivision (a)(1)(E) to require the prosecutor to turn over a record of all criminal convictions, not just felony convictions.

The Committee changed subdivision (d)(1), which deals with protective orders. Proposed (d)(1) required the court to conduct an ex parte proceeding whenever a party so requested. The Committee changed the mandatory language to permissive language. A Court may, not must, conduct an ex parte proceeding if a party so requests. Thus, if a party requests a protective or modifying order and asks to make its showing ex parte, the court has two separate determinations to make. First, it must determine whether an ex parte proceeding is appropriate, bearing in mind that ex parte proceedings are disfavored and not to be encouraged. [An ex parte proceeding would seem to be appropriate if any adversary proceeding would defeat the purpose of the protective or modifying order. For example, the identity of a witness would be disclosed and the purpose of the protective order is to conceal that witness' identity.] Second, it must determine whether a protective or modifying order shall issue. House Report No. 94–247.

Rule 16 deals with pretrial discovery by the defendant and the government. The House and Senate versions of the bill differ on Rule 16 in several respects.

A. Reciprocal vs. Independent Discovery for the Government.—The House version of the bill provides that the government's discovery is reciprocal. If the defendant requires and receives certain items from the government, then the government is entitled to get similar items from the defendant. The Senate version of the bill gives the government an independent right to discover material in the possession of the defendant.

The Conference adopts the House provisions.

B. Rule 16(a)(1)(A).—The House version permits an organization to discover relevant recorded grand jury testimony of any witness who was, at the time of the acts charged or of the grand jury proceedings, so situated as an officer or employee as to have been able legally to bind it in respect to the activities involved in the charges. The Senate version limits discovery of this material to testimony of a witness who was, at the time of the grand jury proceeding, so situated as an officer or employee as to have been legally to bind the defendant in respect to the activities involved in the charges.

The Conferees share a concern that during investigations, ex-employees and ex-officers of potential corporate defendants are a critical source of information regarding activities of their former corporate employers. It is not unusual that, at the time of their testimony or interview, these persons may have interests which are substantially adverse to or divergent from the putative corporate defendant. It is also not unusual that such individuals, though no longer sharing a community of interest with the corporation, may nevertheless be subject to pressure from their former employers. Such pressure may derive from the fact that the ex-employees or ex-officers have remained in the same industry or related industry, are employed by competitors, suppliers, or customers of their former employers, or have pension or other deferred compensation arrangements with former employers.

The Conferees also recognize that considerations of fairness require that a defendant corporation or other legal entity be entitled to the grand jury testimony of a former officer or employee if that person was personally involved in the conduct constituting the offense and was able legally to bind the defendant in respect to the conduct in which he was involved.

The Conferees decided that, on balance, a defendant organization should not be entitled to the relevant grand jury testimony of a former officer or employee in every instance. However, a defendant organization should be entitled to it if the former officer or employee was personally involved in the alleged conduct constituting the offense and was so situated as to have been able legally to bind the defendant in respect to the alleged conduct. The Conferees note that, even in those situations where the rule provides for disclosure of the testimony, the Government may, upon a sufficient showing, obtain a protective or modifying order pursuant to Rule 16(d)(1).

The Conference adopts a provision that permits a defendant organization to discover relevant grand jury testimony of a witness who (1) was, at the time of his testimony, so situated as an officer or employee as to have been able legally to bind the defendant in respect to conduct constituting the offense, or (2) was, at the time of the offense, personally involved in the alleged conduct constituting the offense and so situated as an officer or employee as to have been able legally to bind the defendant in respect to that alleged conduct in which he was involved.

C. Rules 16(a)(1)(E) and (b)(1)(C) (witness lists).—The House version of the bill provides that each party, the government and the defendant, may discover the names and addresses of the other party's witnesses 3 days before trial.

The Senate version of the bill eliminates these provisions, thereby making the names and addresses of a party's witnesses nondiscoverable. The Senate version also makes a conforming change in Rule 16(d)(1). The Conference adopts the Senate version.

A majority of the Conferees believe it is not in the interest of the effective administration of criminal justice to require that the government or the defendant be forced to reveal the names and addresses of its witnesses before trial. Discouragement of witnesses and improper contact directed at influencing their testimony, were deemed paramount concerns in the formulation of this policy.

D. Rules 16(a)(2) and (b)(2).—Rules 16(a)(2) and (b)(2) define certain types of materials ("work product") not to be discoverable. The House version defines work product to be "the mental impressions, conclusions, opinions, or legal theories of the attorney for the government or other government agents." This is parallel to the definition in the Federal Rules of Civil Procedure. The Senate version returns to the Supreme Court's language and defines work product to be "reports, memoranda, or other internal government documents." This is the language of the present rule.

The Conference adopts the Senate provision.

The Conferees note that a party may not avoid a legitimate discovery request merely because something is labelled "report", "memorandum", or "internal document". For example if a document qualifies as a statement of the defendant within the meaning of the Rule 16(a)(1)(A), then the labelling of that document as "report", "memorandum", or "internal government document" will not shield that statement from discovery. Likewise, if the results of an experiment qualify as the results of a scientific test within the meaning of Rule 16(b)(1)(B), then the results of that experiment are not shielded from discovery even if they are labelled "report", "memorandum", or "internal defense document". House Report No. 94–414.

1983 Amendment

Rule 16(a)(3). The added language is made necessary by the addition of Rule 26.2 and new subdivision (i) of Rule 12, which contemplate the production of statements, including those made to a grand jury, under specified circumstances.

1987 Amendment

The amendments are technical. No substantive change is intended.

1991 Amendment

The amendment to Rule 16(a)(1)(A) expands slightly government disclosure to the defense of statements made by the defendant. The rule now requires the prosecution, upon request, to disclose any written record which contains reference to a relevant oral statement by the defendant which was in response to interrogation, without regard to whether the prosecution intends to use the statement at trial. The change recognizes that the defendant has some proprietary interest in statements made during interrogation regardless of the prosecution's intent to make any use of the statements.

The written record need not be a transcription or summary of the defendant's statement but must only be some written reference which would provide some means for the prosecution and defense to identify the statement. Otherwise, the prosecution would have the difficult task of locating and disclosing the myriad oral statements made by a defendant, even if it had no intention of using the statements at trial. In a lengthy and complicated investigation with multiple interrogations by different government agents, that task could become unduly burdensome.

The existing requirement to disclose oral statements which the prosecution intends to introduce at trial has also been changed slightly. Under the amendment, the prosecution must also disclose any relevant oral statement which it intends to use at trial, without regard to whether it intends to introduce the statement. Thus, an oral statement by the defendant which would only be used for impeachment purposes would be covered by the rule.

The introductory language to the rule has been modified to clarify that without regard to whether the defendant's statement is oral or written, it must at a minimum be disclosed. Although the rule does not specify the means for disclosing the defendant's statements, if they are in written or recorded form, the defendant is entitled to inspect, copy, or photograph them.

1993 Amendment

New subdivisions (a)(1)(E) and (b)(1)(C) expand federal criminal discovery by requiring disclosure of the intent to rely on expert opinion testimony, what the testimony will consist of, and the bases of the testimony. The amendment is intended to minimize surprise that often results from unexpected expert testimony, reduce the need for continuances, and to provide the opponent with a fair opportunity to test the merit of the expert's testimony through focused cross-examination. See Eads, Adjudication by Ambush: Federal Prosecutors' Use of Nonscientific Experts in a System of Limited Criminal Discovery, 67 N.C.L.Rev. 577, 622 (1989).

Like other provisions in Rule 16, subdivision (a)(1)(E) requires the government to disclose information regarding its expert witnesses if the defendant first requests the information. Once the requested information is provided, the government is entitled, under (b)(1)(C) to reciprocal discovery of the same information from the defendant. The disclosure is in the form of a written summary and only applies to expert witnesses that each side intends to call. Although no specific timing requirements are included, it is expected that the parties will make their requests and disclosures in a timely fashion.

With increased use of both scientific and nonscientific expert testimony, one of counsel's most basic discovery needs is to learn that an expert is expected to testify. See Gianelli, Criminal Discovery, Scientific Evidence, and DNA, 44 Vand. L.Rev. 793 (1991); Symposium on Science and the Rules of Legal Procedure, 101 F.R.D. 599 (1983). This is particularly important if the expert is expected to testify on matters which touch on new or controversial techniques or opinions. The amendment is intended to meet this need by first, requiring notice of the expert's qualifications which in turn will permit the requesting party to determine whether in fact the witness is an expert within the definition of Federal Rule of Evidence 702. Like Rule 702, which generally provides a broad definition of who qualifies as an "expert," the amendment is broad in that it includes both scientific and nonscientific experts. It does not distinguish between those cases where the expert will be presenting testimony on novel scientific evidence. The rule does not extend, however, to witnesses who may offer only lay opinion testimony under Federal Rule of Evidence 701. Nor does the amendment extend to summary witnesses who may testify under Federal Rule of Evidence 1006 unless the witness is called to offer expert opinions apart from, or in addition to, the summary evidence.

Second, the requesting party is entitled to a summary of the expected testimony. This provision is intended to permit more complete pretrial preparation by the requesting party. For example, this should inform the requesting party whether the expert will be providing only background information on a particular issue or whether the witness will actually offer an opinion. In some instances, a generic description of the likely witness and that witness's qualifications may be sufficient, e.g., where a DEA laboratory chemist will testify, but it is not clear which particular chemist will be available.

Third, and perhaps most important, the requesting party is to be provided with a summary of the bases of the expert's opinion. Rule 16(a)(1)(D) covers disclosure and access to any results or reports of mental or physical examinations and scientific testing. But the fact that no formal written reports have been made does not necessarily mean that an expert will not testify at trial. At least one federal court has concluded that that provision did not otherwise require the government to disclose the identity of its expert witnesses where no reports had been prepared. See, e.g., *United States v. Johnson*, 713 F.2d 654 (11th Cir.1983), cert. denied, 484 U.S. 956 (1984) (there is no right to witness list and Rule 16 was not implicated because no reports were made in the case). The amendment should remedy that problem. Without regard to whether a party would be entitled to the underlying bases for expert testimony under other provisions of Rule 16, the amendment requires a summary of the bases relied upon by the expert. That should cover not only written and oral reports, tests, reports, and investigations, but any information that might be recognized as a legitimate basis for an opinion under Federal Rule of Evidence 703, including opinions of other experts.

The amendments are not intended to create unreasonable procedural hurdles. As with other discovery requests under Rule 16, subdivision (d) is available to either side to seek ex parte a protective or modifying order concerning requests for information under (a)(1)(E) or (b)(1)(C).

1994 Amendments

The amendment is intended to clarify that the discovery and disclosure requirements of the rule apply equally to individual and organizational defendants. See *In re United States*, 918 F.2d 138 (11th Cir. 1990) (rejecting distinction between individual and organizational defendants). Because an organizational defendant may not know what its officers or agents have said or done in regard to a charged offense, it is important that it have access to statements made by persons whose statements or actions could be binding on the defendant. See also *United States v. Hughes*, 413 F.2d 1244, 1251–52 (5th Cir. 1969), vacated as moot, 397 U.S. 93 (1970) (prosecution of corporations "often resembles the most complex civil cases, necessitating a vigorous probing of the mass of detailed facts to seek out the truth").

The amendment defines defendant in a broad, nonexclusive fashion. *See also* 18 U.S.C. § 18 (the term "organization" includes a person other than an individual). And the amendment recognizes that an organizational defendant could be bound by an agent's statement, *see, e.g.*, Federal Rule of Evidence 801(d)(2), or be vicariously liable for an agent's actions. The amendment contemplates that, upon request of the defendant, the Government will disclose any statements within the purview of the rule and made by persons whom the Government contends to be among the classes of persons described in the rule. There is no requirement that the defense stipulate or admit that such persons were in a position to bind the defendant.

1997 Amendment

Subdivision (a)(1)(E). Under rule 16(a)(1)(E), as amended in 1993, the defense is entitled to disclosure of certain information about expert witnesses which the government intends to call during the trial. And if the government provides that information, it is entitled to reciprocal discovery under (b)(1)(C). This amendment is a parallel reciprocal disclosure provision which is triggered by a government request for information concerning defense expert witnesses as to the defendant's mental condition, which is provided for in an amendment to (b)(1)(C), *infra*.

Subdivision (b)(1)(C). Amendments in 1993 to Rule 16 included provisions for pretrial disclosure of information, including names and expected testimony of both defense and government expert witnesses. Those disclosures are triggered by defense requests for the information. If the defense makes such requests and the government complies, the government is entitled to similar, reciprocal discovery. The amendment to Rule 16(b((1)(C) provides that if the defendant has notified the government under Rule 12.2 of an intent to rely on expert testimony to show the defendant's mental condition, the government may request the defense to disclose information about its expert witnesses. Although Rule 12.2 insures that the government will not be surprised by the nature of the defense or that the defense intends t o call an expert witness, that rule makes no provision for discovery of the identity, the expected testimony, or the qualifications of the expert witness. The amendment provides the government with the limited right to respond to the notice provided under Rule 12.2 by requesting more specific information about the expert. If the government requests the specified information, and the defense complies., the defense is entitled to reciprocal discovery under an amendment to subdivision (a)(1)(E), *supra*.

2002 Amendments

The language of Rule 16 has been amended as part of the general restyling of the Criminal Rules to make them more easily understood and to make style and terminology consistent throughout the rules. These changes are intended to be stylistic only, except as noted below.

Current Rule 16(a)(1)(A) is now located in Rule 16(a)(1)(A), (B), and (C). Current Rule 16(a)(1)(B), (C), (D), and (E) have been relettered.

Amended Rule 16(b)(1)(B) includes a change that may be substantive in nature. Rule 16(a)(1)(E) and 16(a)(1)(F) require production of specified information if the government intends to "use" the information "in its case-in-chief at trial." The Committee believed that the language in revised Rule 16(b)(1)(B), which deals with a defendant's disclosure of information to the government, should track the similar language in revised Rule 16(a)(1). In Rule 16(b)(1)(B)(ii), the Committee changed the current provision which reads: "the defendant intends to *introduce* as evidence" to the "defendant intends to *use* the item . . . " The Committee recognized that this might constitute a substantive change in the rule but believed that it was a necessary conforming change with the provisions in Rule16(a)(1)(E) and (F), noted *supra*, regarding use of evidence by the government.

In amended Rule 16(d)(1), the last phrase in the current subdivision—which refers to a possible appeal of the court's discovery order—has been deleted. In the Committee's view, no substantive change results from that deletion. The language is unnecessary because the court, regardless of whether there is an appeal, will have maintained the record.

Finally, current Rule 16(e), which addresses the topic of notice of alibi witnesses, has been deleted as being unnecessarily duplicative of Rule 12.1.

HISTORICAL NOTES

References in Text

The Federal Rules of Evidence, referred to in subds. (a)(1)(G) and (b)(1)(C), are set out in the Appendix to Title 28, Fed.Rules Evid. Rule 101 et seq., 28 U.S.C.A.

Effective and Applicability Provisions

2002 Acts. Pub.L. 107–273, Div. C, Title I, § 11019(c), Nov. 2, 2002, 116 Stat. 1826, provided that: "The amendments made by subsection (b) [amending this rule] shall take effect on December 1, 2002."

1975 Acts. Amendments of this rule embraced in the order of the United States Supreme Court on Apr. 22, 1974, and the amendments of this rule made by section 3 of Pub.L. 94–64, effective Dec. 1, 1975, pursuant to section 2 of Pub.L. 94–64.

Rule 17. Subpoena

(a) Content. A subpoena must state the court's name and the title of the proceeding, include the seal of the court, and command the witness to attend and testify at the time and place the subpoena specifies. The clerk must issue a blank subpoena—signed and sealed—to the party requesting it, and that party must fill in the blanks before the subpoena is served.

(b) Defendant Unable to Pay. Upon a defendant's ex parte application, the court must order that a subpoena be issued for a named witness if the defendant shows an inability to pay the witness's fees and the necessity of the witness's presence for an adequate defense. If the court orders a subpoena to be issued, the process costs and witness fees will be paid in the same manner as those paid for witnesses the government subpoenas.

(c) Producing Documents and Objects.

(1) In General. A subpoena may order the witness to produce any books, papers, documents, data, or other objects the subpoena designates. The court may direct the witness to produce the designated items in court before trial or before they are to be offered in evidence. When the items arrive, the court may permit the parties and their attorneys to inspect all or part of them.

(2) Quashing or Modifying the Subpoena. On motion made promptly, the court may quash or modify the subpoena if compliance would be unreasonable or oppressive.

(d) Service. A marshal, a deputy marshal, or any nonparty who is at least 18 years old may serve a subpoena. The server must deliver a copy of the subpoena to the witness and must tender to the witness one day's witness-attendance fee and the legal mileage allowance. The server need not tender the attendance fee or mileage allowance when the United States, a federal officer, or a federal agency has requested the subpoena.

(e) Place of Service.

(1) In the United States. A subpoena requiring a witness to attend a hearing or trial may be served at any place within the United States.

(2) In a Foreign Country. If the witness is in a foreign country, 28 U.S.C. § 1783 governs the subpoena's service.

(f) Issuing a Deposition Subpoena.

(1) Issuance. A court order to take a deposition authorizes the clerk in the district where the deposition is to be taken to issue a subpoena for any witness named or described in the order.

(2) Place. After considering the convenience of the witness and the parties, the court may order—and the subpoena may require—the witness to appear anywhere the court designates.

(g) Contempt. The court (other than a magistrate judge) may hold in contempt a witness who, without adequate excuse, disobeys a subpoena issued by a federal court in that district. A magistrate judge may hold in contempt a witness who, without adequate excuse, disobeys a subpoena issued by that magistrate judge as provided in 28 U.S.C. § 636(e).

(h) Information Not Subject to a Subpoena. No party may subpoena a statement of a witness or of a prospective witness under this rule. Rule 26.2 governs the production of the statement.

(As amended Dec. 27, 1948, eff. Oct. 20, 1949; Feb. 28, 1966, eff. July 1, 1966; Apr. 24, 1972, eff. Oct. 1, 1972; Apr. 22, 1974, eff. Dec. 1, 1975; July 31, 1975, Pub.L. 94–64, § 3(29), 89 Stat. 375; Apr. 30, 1979, eff. Dec. 1, 1980; Mar. 9, 1987, eff. Aug. 1, 1987; Apr. 22, 1993, eff. Dec. 1, 1993; Apr. 29, 2002, eff. Dec. 1, 2002.)

ADVISORY COMMITTEE NOTES

1944 Adoption

Note to Subdivision (a) This rule is substantially the same as rule 45(a) of the Federal Rules of Civil Procedure., 28 U.S.C., Appendix

Note to Subdivision (b) This rule preserves the existing right of an indigent defendant to secure attendance of witnesses at the expense of the Government, former 28 U.S.C. § 656 (Witnesses for indigent defendants). Under existing law, however, the right is limited to witnesses who are within the district in which the court is held or within one hundred miles of the place of trial. No procedure now exists whereby an indigent defendant can procure at Government expense the attendance of witnesses found in another district and more than 100 miles of the place of trial. This limitation is abrogated by the rule so that an indigent defendant will be able to secure the attendance of witnesses at the expense of the Government no matter where they are located. The showing required by the rule to justify such relief is the same as that now exacted by 28 U.S.C. former § 656.

Note to Subdivision (c). This rule is substantially the same as rule 45(b) of the Federal Rules of Civil Procedure., 28 U.S.C., Appendix.

Note to Subdivision (d). This rule is substantially the same as rule 45(c) of the Federal Rules of Civil Procedure, 28 U.S.C., Appendix. The provision permitting persons other than the marshal to serve the subpoena, and requiring the payment of witness fees in Government cases is new matter.

Note to Subdivision (e)(1). This rule continues existing law, 28 U.S.C. § 654 (Witnesses; subpoenas; may run into another district). The rule is different in civil cases in that in such cases, unless a statute otherwise provides, a subpoena may be served only within the district or within 100 miles of the place of trial, 28 U.S.C. former § 654; Rule 45(e)(1) of the Federal Rules of Civil Procedure, 28 U.S.C., Appendix.

Note to Subdivision (e)(2). This rule is substantially the same as rule 45(e)(2) of the Federal Rules of Civil Procedure, 28 U.S.C., Appendix. See *Blackmer v. United States*, 284 U.S. 421, 52 S.Ct. 252, 76 L.Ed. 375, upholding the validity of the statute referred to in the rule.

Note to Subdivision (f). This rule is substantially the same as rule 45(d) of the Federal Rules of Civil Procedure, 28 U.S.C., Appendix.

Note to Subdivision (g). This rule is substantially the same as rule 45(f) of the Federal Rules of Civil Procedure, 28 U.S.C., Appendix.

1948 Amendment

The amendment is to substitute proper reference to Title 28 in place of the repealed act.

1966 Amendment

Subdivision (b). Criticism has been directed at the requirement that an indigent defendant disclose in advance the theory of his defense in order to obtain the issuance of a subpoena at government expense while the government and defendants able to pay may have subpoenas issued in blank without any disclosure. See Report of the Attorney General's Committee on Poverty and the Administration of Criminal Justice (1963) p. 27. The Attorney General's Committee also urged that the standard of financial inability to pay be substituted for that of indigency. Id. at 40–41. In one case it was held that the affidavit filed by an indigent defendant under this subdivision could be used by the government at his trial for purposes of impeachment. *Smith v. United States*, 312 F.2d 867 (D.C.Cir.1962). There has also been doubt as to whether the defendant need make a showing beyond the face of his affidavit in order to secure issuance of a subpoena. *Greenwell v. United States*, 317 F.2d 108 (D.C.Cir.1963).

The amendment makes several changes. The references to a judge are deleted since applications should be made to the court. An ex parte application followed by a satisfactory showing is substituted for the requirement of a request or motion supported by affidavit. The court is required to order the issuance of a subpoena upon finding that the defendant is unable to pay the witness fees and that the presence of the witness is necessary to an adequate defense.

Subdivision (d). The subdivision is revised to bring it into conformity with 28 U.S.C. § 1825.

1972 Amendment

Subdivisions (a) and (g) are amended to reflect the existence of the "United States magistrate," a phrase defined in rule 54.

1974 Amendment

Subdivision (f)(2) is amended to provide that the court has discretion over the place at which the deposition is to be taken. Similar authority is conferred by Civil Rule 45(d)(2). See C. Wright, Federal Practice and Procedure: Criminal § 278 (1969).

Ordinarily the deposition should be taken at the place most convenient for the witness but, under certain circumstances, the parties may prefer to arrange for the presence of the witness at a place more convenient to counsel.

1975 Enactment

A. Amendments Proposed by the Supreme Court. Rule 17 of the Federal Rules of Criminal Procedure deals with subpoenas. Subdivision (f)(2) as proposed by the Supreme Court provides:

The witness whose deposition is to be taken may be required by subpoena to attend at any place designated by the trial court.

B. Committee Action. The Committee added language to the proposed amendment that directs the court to consider the convenience of the witness and the parties when compelling a witness to attend where a deposition will be taken. House Report No. 94–247.

1979 Amendment

This addition to rule 17 is necessary in light of proposed rule 26.2, which deals with the obtaining of statements of government and defense witnesses.

1987 Amendment

The amendments are technical. No substantive change is intended.

1993 Amendment

The Rule is amended to conform to the Judicial Improvements Act of 1990 [P.L. 101–650, Title III, Section 321] which provides that each United States magistrate appointed under section 631 of title 28, United States Code, shall be known as a United States magistrate judge.

2002 Amendments

The language of Rule 17 has been amended as part of the general restyling of the Criminal Rules to make them more easily understood and to make style and terminology consistent throughout the rules. These changes are intended to be stylistic only, except as noted below.

A potential substantive change has been made in Rule 17(c)(1); the word "data" has been added to the list of matters that may be subpoenaed. The Committee believed that inserting that term will reflect the fact that in an increasingly technological culture, the information may exist in a format not already covered by the more conventional list, such as a book or document.

Rule 17(g) has been amended to recognize the contempt powers of a court (other than a magistrate judge) and a magistrate judge.

HISTORICAL NOTES

Change of Name

United States magistrate appointed under section 631 of Title 28, Judiciary and Judicial Procedure, to be known as United States magistrate judge after Dec. 1, 1990, with any reference to United States magistrate or magistrate in Title 28, in any other Federal statute, etc., deemed a reference to United States magistrate judge appointed under section 631 of Title 28, see section 321 of Pub.L. 101–650, set out as a note under section 631 of Title 28.

Effective and Applicability Provisions

1979 Acts. Amendment of this rule by addition of subd. (h) by order of the United States Supreme Court of Apr. 30, 1979, effective Dec. 1, 1980, pursuant to section 1(1) of Pub.L. 96–42, July 31, 1979, 93 Stat. 326.

Effective Date of Amendments Proposed Apr. 22, 1974; Effective Date of 1975 Amendments

Amendments of this rule embraced in the order of the United States Supreme Court on Apr. 22, 1974, and the amendments of this rule made by section 3 of Pub.L. 94–64, effective Dec. 1, 1975, pursuant to section 2 of Pub.L. 94–64.

Supersedure

Provision of subd. (d) of this rule that witness shall be tendered the fee for 1 day's attendance and mileage allowed by law as superseded by section 1825 of Title 28, Judiciary and Judicial Procedure, see such section and Reviser's Note thereunder.

Rule 17.1. Pretrial Conference

On its own, or on a party's motion, the court may hold one or more pretrial conferences to promote a fair and expeditious trial. When a conference ends, the court must prepare and file a memorandum of any matters agreed to during the conference. The government may not use any statement made during the conference by the defendant or the defendant's attorney unless it is in writing and is signed by the defendant and the defendant's attorney.

(Added Feb. 28, 1966, eff. July 1, 1966, and amended Mar. 9, 1987, eff. Aug. 1, 1987; Apr. 29, 2002, eff. Dec. 1, 2002.)

ADVISORY COMMITTEE NOTES

1966 Addition

This new rule establishes a basis for pretrial conferences with counsel for the parties in criminal cases within the discretion of the court. Pretrial conferences are now being utilized to some extent even in the absence of a rule. See, generally, Brewster, Criminal Pre-Trials—Useful Techniques, 29 F.R.D. 442 (1962); Estes, Pre-Trial Conferences in Criminal Cases, 23 F.R.D. 560 (1959); Kaufman, Pre-Trial in Criminal Cases, 23 F.R.D. 551 (1959); Kaufman, Pre-Trial in Criminal Cases, 42 J.Am.Jud.Soc. 150 (1959); Kaufman, The Appalachian Trial: Further Observations on Pre-Trial in Criminal Cases, 44 J.Am.Jud.Soc. 53 (1960); West, Criminal Pre-Trials—Useful Techniques, 29 F.R.D. 436 (1962); Handbook of Recommended Procedures for the Trial of Protracted Cases, 25 F.R.D. 399–403, 468–470 (1960). Cf. Mo.Sup.Ct. Rule 25.09; Rules Governing the N.J. Courts, § 3:5–3.

The rule is cast in broad language so as to accommodate all types of pretrial conferences. As the third sentence suggests, in some cases it may be desirable or necessary to have the defendant present. See Committee on Pretrial Procedure of the Judicial Conference of the United States, Recommended Procedures in Criminal Pretrials, 37 F.R.D. 95 (1965).

1987 Amendment

The amendments are technical. No substantive change is intended.

2002 Amendments

The language of Rule 17.1 has been amended as part of the general restyling of the Criminal Rules to make them more easily understood and to make style and terminology consistent throughout the rules. These changes are intended to be stylistic only, except as noted below.

Current Rule 17.1 prohibits the court from holding a pretrial conference where the defendant is not represented by counsel. It is unclear whether this would bar such a conference when the defendant invokes the constitutional right to self-representation. *See Faretta v. California*, 422 U.S. 806 (1975). The amended version makes clear that a pretrial conference may be held in these circumstances. Moreover, the Committee believed that pretrial conferences might be particularly useful in those cases where the defendant is proceeding pro se.

V. VENUE

Rule 18. Place of Prosecution and Trial

Unless a statute or these rules permit otherwise, the government must prosecute an offense in a district where the offense was committed. The court must set the place of trial within the district with due regard for the convenience of the defendant and the witnesses, and the prompt administration of justice.

(As amended Feb. 28, 1966, eff. July 1, 1966; Apr. 30, 1979, eff. Aug. 1, 1979; Apr. 29, 2002, eff. Dec. 1, 2002.)

ADVISORY COMMITTEE NOTES

1944 Adoption

1. The Constitution of the United States, Article III, Section 2, Paragraph 3, provides:

The Trial of all Crimes, except in Cases of Impeachment, shall be by Jury; and such Trial shall be held in the State where the said Crimes shall have been committed; but when not committed within any State, the Trial shall be at such Place or Places as the Congress may by Law have directed.

Amendment VI provides:

In all criminal prosecutions, the accused shall enjoy the right to a speedy and public trial, by an impartial jury of the State and district wherein the crime shall have been committed, which district shall have been previously ascertained by law * * *.

28 U.S.C. former § 114 (now §§ 1393, 1441) provides:

All prosecutions for crimes or offenses shall be had within the division of such districts where the same were committed, unless the court, or the judge thereof, upon the application of the defendant, shall order the cause to be transferred for prosecution to another division of the district.

The word "prosecutions", as used in this statute, does not include the finding and return of an indictment. The prevailing practice of impaneling a grand jury for the entire district at a session in some division and of distributing the indictments among the divisions in which the offenses were committed is deemed proper and legal, *Salinger v. Loisel*, 44 S.Ct. 519, 265 U.S. 224, 237, 44 S.Ct. 519, 68 L.Ed. 989. The court stated that this practice is "attended with real advantages". The rule is a restatement of existing law and is intended to sanction the continuance of this practice. For this reason, the rule requires that only the trial be held in the division in which the offense was committed and permits other proceedings to be had elsewhere in the same district.

2. Within the framework of the foregoing constitutional provisions and the provisions of the general statute, 28 U.S.C. former § 114 (now §§ 1393, 1441), supra, numerous statutes have been enacted to regulate the venue of criminal proceedings, particularly in respect to continuing offenses and offenses consisting of several transactions occurring in different districts. *Armour Packing Co. v. United States*, 28 S.Ct. 428, 209 U.S. 56, 73–77, 52 L.Ed. 681; *United States v. Johnson*, 65 S.Ct. 249, 323 U.S. 273, 89 L.Ed. 236. These special venue provisions are not affected by the rule. Among these statutes are the following:

U.S.C. Title 8 former:

§ 138 [now §§ 1326, 1328, 1329] (Importation of aliens for immoral purposes; attempt to reenter after deportation; penalty)

U.S.C. Title 15:

§ 78aa (Regulation of Securities Exchanges; jurisdiction of offenses and suits)

§ 79y (Control of Public Utility Holding Companies; jurisdiction of Offenses and suits)

§ 80a–43 (Investment Companies; jurisdiction of offenses and suits)

§ 80b–14 (Investment Advisers; jurisdiction of offenses and suits)

§ 298 (Falsely Stamped Gold or Silver, etc., violations of law; penalty; jurisdiction of prosecutions)

§ 715i (Interstate Transportation of Petroleum Products; restraining violations; civil and criminal proceedings; jurisdiction of District Courts; review)

§ 717u (Natural Gas Act; jurisdiction of offenses; enforcement of liabilities and duties)

U.S.C. Title 18 former:

§ 39 [now §§ 5, 3241] (Enforcement of neutrality; United States defined; jurisdiction of offenses; prior offenses; partial invalidity of provisions)

§ 336 [now § 1302] (Lottery, or gift enterprise circulars not mailable; place of trial)

§ 338a [now §§ 876, 3239] (Mailing threatening communications)

§ 338b [now §§ 877, 3239] (Same: mailing in foreign country for delivery in the United States)

§ 345 [now § 1717] (Using or attempting to use mails for transmission of matter declared nonmailable by title; jurisdiction of offense)

§ 396e [now § 1762] (Transportation or importation of convict made goods with intent to use in violation of local law; jurisdiction of violations)

§ 401 [now § 2421] (White slave traffic; jurisdiction of prosecutions)

§ 408 [now §§ 10, 2311 to 2313] (Motor vehicles; transportation, etc., of stolen vehicles)

§ 408d [now §§ 10, 2311 to 2313] (Threatening communications in interstate commerce)

§ 408e [now § 1073] (Moving in interstate or foreign commerce to avoid prosecution for felony or giving testimony)

§ 409 [now §§ 659, 660, 2117] (Larceny, etc., of goods in interstate or foreign commerce; penalty)

§ 412 [now § 660] (Embezzlement, etc., by officers of carrier; jurisdiction; double jeopardy)

§ 418 [now § 3237] (National Stolen Property Act; jurisdiction)

§ 419d [now § 3237] (Transportation of stolen cattle in interstate or foreign commerce; jurisdiction of offense)

§ 420d [now § 1951] (Interference with trade and commerce by violence, threats, etc., jurisdiction of offenses)

§ 494 [now § 1654] (Arming vessel to cruise against citizen; trials)

§ 553 [now § 3236] (Place of committal of murder or manslaughter determined)

U.S.C. Title 21:

§ 17 (Introduction into, or sale in, State or Territory or District of Columbia of dairy or food products falsely labeled or branded; penalty; jurisdiction of prosecutions)

§ 118 (Prevention of introduction and spread of contagion; duty of district attorneys)

U.S.C. Title 28 former:

§ 101 [now 18 U.S.C. § 3235] (Capital cases)

§ 102 [now 18 U.S.C. § 3238] (Offenses on the high seas)

§ 103 [now 18 U.S.C. § 3237] (Offenses begun in one district and completed in another)

§ 121 [now 18 U.S.C. § 3240] (Creation of new district or division)

U.S.C. Title 47:

§ 33 (Submarine Cables; jurisdiction and venue of actions and offenses)

§ 505 (Special Provisions Relating to Radio; venue of trials)

U.S.C. Title 49:

§ 41 (Legislation Supplementary to Interstate Commerce Act; liability of corporation carriers and agents; offenses and penalties—(1) Liability of corporation common carriers; offenses; penalties; jurisdiction)

former § 623 [now § 1473] (Civil Aeronautics Act; venue and prosecution of offenses)

1966 Amendments

The amendment eliminates the requirement that the prosecution shall be in a division in which the offense was committed and vests discretion in the court to fix the place of trial at any place within the district with due regard to the convenience of the defendant and his witnesses.

The Sixth Amendment provides that the defendant shall have the right to a trial "by an impartial jury of the State and district wherein the crime shall have been committed, which district shall have been previously ascertained by law. * * *" There is no constitutional right to trial within a division. See *United States v. Anderson*, 328 U.S. 699, 704, 705 (1946); *Barrett v. United States*, 169 U.S. 218 (1898); *Lafoon v. United States*, 250 F.2d 958 (5th Cir. 1958); *Carrillo v. Squier*, 137 F.2d 648 (9th Cir. 1943); *McNealy v. Johnston*, 100 F.2d 280, 282 (9th Cir. 1938). Cf. *Platt v. Minnesota Mining and Manufacturing Co.*, 376 U.S. 240 (1964).

The former requirement for venue within the division operated in an irrational fashion. Divisions have been created in only half of the districts, and the differentiation between those districts with and those without divisions often bears no relationship to comparative size or population. In many districts a single judge is required to sit in several divisions and only brief and infrequent terms may be held in particular divisions. As a consequence under the original rule there was often undue delay in the disposition of criminal cases—delay which was particularly serious with respect to defendants who had been unable to secure release on bail pending the holding of the next term of court.

If the court is satisfied that there exists in the place fixed for trial prejudice against the defendant so great as to render the trial unfair, the court may, of course, fix another place of trial within the district (if there be such) where such prejudice does not exist. Cf. Rule 21 dealing with transfers between districts.

1979 Amendments

This amendment is intended to eliminate an inconsistency between rule 18, which in its present form has been interpreted not to allow trial in a division other than that in which the offense was committed except as dictated by the convenience of the defendant and witnesses, *Dupoint v. United States*, 388 F.2d 39 (5th Cir. 1968), and the Speedy Trial Act of 1974. This Act provides:

In any case involving a defendant charged with an offense, the appropriate judicial officer, at the earliest practicable time, shall, after consultation with the counsel for the defendant and the attorney for the Government, set the case for trial on a day certain, or list it for trial on a weekly or other short-term trial calendar at a place within the judicial district, so as to assure a speedy trial. 18 U.S.C. § 3161(a).

This provision is intended to "permit the trial of a case at any place within the judicial district. This language was included in anticipation of problem which might occur in districts with statutory divisions, where it could be difficult to set trial outside the division." H.R.Rep. No. 93–1508, 93d Cong., 2d Sess. 29 (1974).

The change does not offend the venue or vicinage provisions of the Constitution. Article III, § 2, clause 3 places venue (the geographical location of the trial) "in the State where the said Crimes shall have been committed," while the Sixth Amendment defines the vicinage (the geographical location of the jurors) as "the State and district wherein the crime shall have been committed, which district shall have been previously ascertained by law." The latter provision makes "no reference to a division within a judicial district." *United States v. James*, 528 F.2d 999 (5th Cir. 1976). "It follows a fortiori that when a district is not separated into divisions, * * * trial at any place within the district is allowable under the Sixth Amendment * * *." *United States v. Fernandez*, 480 F.2d 726 (2d Cir. 1973). See also *Zicarelli v. Gray*, 543 F.2d 466 (3d Cir. 1976) and cases cited therein.

Nor is the change inconsistent with the Declaration of Policy in the Jury Selection and Service Act of 1968, which reads:

It is the policy of the United States that all litigants in Federal courts entitled to trial by jury shall have the right to grand and petit juries selected at random from a fair cross section of the community in the district or division wherein the court convenes.

28 U.S.C. § 1861. This language does *not* mean that the Act requires "the trial court to convene not only in the district but also in the division wherein the offense occurred," as:

The amendment to rule 18 does not eliminate either of the existing considerations which bear upon fixing the place of trial within a district, but simply adds yet another consideration in the interest of ensuring compliance with the requirements of the Speedy Trial Act of 1974. The amendment does not authorize the fixing of the place of trial for yet other reasons. Cf. United States v. Fernandez, 480 F.2d 726 (2d Cir. 1973) (court in the exercise of its supervisory power held improper the fixing of the place of trial "for no apparent reason other than the convenience of the judge").

There is no hint in the statutory history that the Jury Selection Act was intended to do more than provide improved judicial machinery so that grand and petit jurors would be selected at random by the use of objective qualification criteria to ensure a representative cross section of the district or division in which the grand or petit jury sits. *United States v. Cates*, 485 F.2d 26 (1st Cir. 1974).

2002 Amendments

The language of Rule 18 has been amended as part of the general restyling of the Criminal Rules to make them more easily understood and to make style and terminology consistent throughout the rules. These changes are intended to be stylistic only.

Rule 19. [Reserved]

Rule 20. Transfer for Plea and Sentence

(a) Consent to Transfer. A prosecution may be transferred from the district where the indictment or information is pending, or from which a warrant on a complaint has been issued, to the district where the defendant is arrested, held, or present if:

(1) the defendant states in writing a wish to plead guilty or nolo contendere and to waive trial in the district where the indictment, information, or complaint is pending, consents in writing to the court's disposing of the case in the transferee district, and files the statement in the transferee district; and

(2) the United States attorneys in both districts approve the transfer in writing.

(b) Clerk's Duties. After receiving the defendant's statement and the required approvals, the clerk where the indictment, information, or complaint is pending must send the file, or a certified copy, to the clerk in the transferee district.

(c) Effect of a Not Guilty Plea. If the defendant pleads not guilty after the case has been transferred under Rule 20(a), the clerk must return the papers to the court where the prosecution began, and that court must restore the proceeding to its docket. The defendant's statement that the defendant wished to plead guilty or nolo contendere is not, in any civil or criminal proceeding, admissible against the defendant.

(d) Juveniles.

(1) Consent to Transfer. A juvenile, as defined in 18 U.S.C. § 5031, may be proceeded against as a juvenile delinquent in the district where the juvenile is arrested, held, or present if:

(A) the alleged offense that occurred in the other district is not punishable by death or life imprisonment;

(B) an attorney has advised the juvenile;

(C) the court has informed the juvenile of the juvenile's rights—including the right to be returned to the district where the offense allegedly occurred—and the consequences of waiving those rights;

(D) the juvenile, after receiving the court's information about rights, consents in writing to be proceeded against in the transferee district, and files the consent in the transferee district;

(E) the United States attorneys for both districts approve the transfer in writing; and

(F) the transferee court approves the transfer.

(2) Clerk's Duties. After receiving the juvenile's written consent and the required approvals, the clerk where the indictment, information, or complaint is pending or where the alleged offense occurred must send the file, or a certified copy, to the clerk in the transferee district.

(As amended Feb. 28, 1966, eff. July 1, 1966; Apr. 22, 1974, eff. Dec. 1, 1975; July 31, 1975, Pub.L. 94–64, § 3(30), 89 Stat. 375; Apr. 28, 1982, eff. Aug. 1, 1982; Mar. 9, 1987, eff. Aug. 1, 1987; Apr. 29, 2002, eff. Dec. 1, 2002.)

ADVISORY COMMITTEE NOTES

1944 Adoption

This rule introduces a new procedure in the interest of defendants who intend to plead guilty and are arrested in a district other than that in which the prosecution has been instituted. This rule would accord to a defendant in such a situation an opportunity to secure a disposition of the case in the district where the arrest takes place, thereby relieving him of whatever hardship may be involved in a removal to the place where the prosecution is pending. In order to prevent possible interference with the administration of justice, however, the consent of the United States attorneys involved is required.

1966 Amendments

Rule 20 has proved to be most useful. In some districts, however, literal compliance with the procedures spelled out by the rule has resulted in unnecessary delay in the disposition of cases. This delay has been particularly troublesome where the defendant has been arrested prior to the filing of an indictment or information against him. See e.g., the procedure described in *Donovan v. United States*, 205 F.2d 557 (10th Cir. 1953). Furthermore, the benefit of the rule has not been available to juveniles electing to be proceeded against under 18 U.S.C. §§ 5031 to 5037. In an attempt to clarify and simplify the procedure the rule has been recast into four subdivisions.

Subdivision (a).—This subdivision is intended to apply to the situation in which an indictment or information is pending at the time at which the defendant indicates his desire to have the transfer made. Two amendments are made to the present language of the rule. In the first sentence the words "or held" and "or is held" are added to make it clear that a person already in state or federal custody within a district may request a transfer of federal charges pending against him in another district. See 4 Barron, Federal Practice and Procedure 146 (1951). The words "after receiving a copy of the indictment or information" are deleted.

The defendant should be permitted, if he wishes, to initiate transfer proceedings under the Rule without waiting for a copy of the indictment or information to be obtained. The defendant is protected against prejudice by the fact that under subdivision (c) he can, in effect, rescind his action by pleading not guilty after the transfer has been completed.

Subdivision (b).—This subdivision is intended to apply to the situation in which no indictment or information is pending but the defendant has been arrested on a warrant issued upon a complaint in another district. Under the procedure set out he may initiate the transfer proceedings without waiting for the filing of an indictment or information in the district where the complaint is pending. Also it is made clear that the defendant may validate an information previously filed by waiving indictment in open court when he is brought before the court to plead. See *United States v. East*, 5 F.R.D. 389 (N.D.Ind.1946); *Potter v. United States*, 36 F.R.D. 394 (W.D.Mo.1965). Here again the defendant is fully protected by the fact that at the time of pleading in the transferee court he may then refuse to waive indictment and rescind the transfer by pleading not guilty.

Subdivision (c).—The last two sentences of the original rule are included here. The last sentence is amended to forbid use against the defendant of his statement that he wishes to plead guilty or nolo contendere whether or not he was represented by counsel when it was made. Since under the amended rule the defendant may make his statement prior to receiving a copy of the indictment or information, it would be unfair to permit use of that statement against him.

Subdivision (d).—Under 18 U.S.C. § 5033 a juvenile who has committed an act in violation of the law of the United States in one district and is apprehended in another must be returned to the district "having cognizance of the alleged violation" before he can consent to being proceeded against as a juvenile delinquent. This subdivision will permit a juvenile after he has been advised by counsel and with the approval of the court and the United States attorney to consent to be proceeded against in the district in which he is arrested or held. Consent is required only of the United States attorney in the district of the arrest in order to permit expeditious handling of juvenile cases. If it is necessary to recognize special interests of particular districts where offenses are committed—e.g., the District of Columbia with its separate Juvenile Court (District of Columbia Code § 11–1551(a))—the Attorney General may do so through his administrative control over United States attorneys.

Subdivision (e).—This subdivision is added to make it clear that a defendant who appears in one district in response to a summons issued in the district where the offense was committed may initiate transfer proceedings under the rule.

1974 Amendments

Rule 20 is amended to provide that a person "present" in a district other than the district in which he is charged with a criminal offense may, subject to the other provisions of rule 20, plead guilty in the district in which he is "present." See rule 6(b), Rules of Procedure for the Trial of Minor Offenses Before Magistrates.

Under the former rule, practice was to have the district in which the offense occurred issue a bench warrant authorizing the arrest of the defendant in the district in which he was located. This is a procedural complication which serves no interest of either the government or the defense and therefore can properly be dispensed with.

Making the fact that a defendant is "present" in the district an adequate basis for allowing him to plead guilty there makes it unnecessary to retain subdivision (e) which makes appearance in response to a summons equivalent to an arrest. Dropping (e) will eliminate some minor ambiguity created by that subdivision. See C. Wright, Federal Practice and Procedure: Criminal § 322 n. 26, p. 612 (1969, Supp. 1971).

There are practical advantages which will follow from the change. In practice a person may turn himself in in a district other than that in which the prosecution is pending. It may be more convenient to have him plead in the district in which he is present rather than having him or the government incur the expense of his return to the district in which the charge is pending.

The danger of "forum shopping" can be controlled by the requirement that both United States Attorneys agree to the handling of the case under provisions of this rule.

1975 Enactment

A. Amendments Proposed by the Supreme Court Rule. 20 of the Federal Rules of Criminal Procedure deals with transferring a defendant from one district to another for the purpose of pleading and being sentenced. It deals with the situation where a defendant is located in one district (A) and is charged with a crime in another district (B). Under the present rule, if such a defendant desires to waive trial and plead guilty or nolo contendere, a judge in district B would issue a bench warrant for the defendant, authorizing his arrest in district A and his transport to district B for the purpose of pleading and being sentenced.

The Supreme Court amendments permit the defendant in the above example to plead guilty or nolo contendere in district A, if the United States Attorneys for districts A and B consent.

B. Committee Action. The Committee has added a conforming amendment to subdivision (d), which establishes procedures for dealing with defendants who are juveniles. House Report No. 94–247.

1982 Amendments

Subdivision (b). This amendment to subdivision (b) is intended to expedite transfer proceedings under Rule 20. At present, considerable delay—sometimes as long as three or four weeks—occurs in subdivision (b) cases, that is, where no indictment or information is pending. This time is spent on the transmittal of defendant's statement to the district where the complaint is pending, the filing of an information or return of an indictment there, and the transmittal of papers in the case from that district to the district where the defendant is present. Under the amendment, the defendant, by also waiving venue, would make it possible for charges to be filed in the district of his arrest or presence. This would advance the interests of both the prosecution and defendant in a timely entry of a plea of guilty. No change has been made in the requirement that the transfer occur with the consent of both United States attorneys.

1987 Amendments

The amendments are technical. No substantive change is intended.

2002 Amendments

The language of Rule 20 has been amended as part of the general restyling of the Criminal Rules to make them more easily understood and to make style and terminology consistent throughout the rules. These changes are intended to be stylistic only, except as noted below.

New Rule 20(d)(2) applies to juvenile cases and has been added to parallel a similar provision in new Rule 20(b). The new provision provides that after the court has determined that the provisions in Rule 20(d)(1) have been completed and the transfer is approved, the file (or certified copy) must be transmitted from the original court to the transferee court.

HISTORICAL NOTES

Effective and Applicability Provisions

1975 Acts. Amendments of this rule embraced in the order of the United States Supreme Court on Apr. 22, 1974, and the amendments of this rule made by § 3 of Pub.L. 94–64, effective Dec. 1, 1975, pursuant to § 2 of Pub.L. 94–64.

Rule 21. Transfer for Trial

(a) For Prejudice. Upon the defendant's motion, the court must transfer the proceeding against that defendant to another district if the court is satisfied that so great a prejudice against the defendant exists in the transferring district that the defendant cannot obtain a fair and impartial trial there.

(b) For Convenience. Upon the defendant's motion, the court may transfer the proceeding, or one or more counts, against that defendant to another district for the convenience of the parties and witnesses and in the interest of justice.

(c) Proceedings on Transfer. When the court orders a transfer, the clerk must send to the transferee district the file, or a certified copy, and any bail taken. The prosecution will then continue in the transferee district.

(d) Time to File a Motion to Transfer. A motion to transfer may be made at or before arraignment or at any other time the court or these rules prescribe.

(As amended Feb. 28, 1966, eff. July 1, 1966; Mar. 9, 1987, eff. Aug. 1, 1987; Apr. 29, 2002, eff. Dec. 1, 2002.)

ADVISORY COMMITTEE NOTES

1944 Adoption

Note to Subdivisions (a) and (b). 1. This rule introduces an addition to existing law. "Lawyers not thoroughly familiar with Federal practice are somewhat astounded to learn that they may not move for a change of venue, even if they are able to demonstrate that public feeling in the vicinity of the crime may render impossible a fair and impartial trial. This seems to be a defect in the federal law, which the proposed rules would cure." Homer Cummings, 29 A.B.A.Jour. 655; Medalie, 4 Lawyers Guild R. (3) 1, 5.

2. The rule provides for two kinds of motions that may be made by the defendant for a change of venue. The first is a motion on the ground that so great a prejudice exists against the defendant that he cannot obtain a fair and impartial trial in the district or division where the case is pending. Express provisions to a similar effect are found in many State statutes. See, e.g., Ala.Code (1940), Title 15, § 267; Cal.Pen. Code (Deering, 1941), § 1033; Conn.Gen.Stat. (1930), § 6445; Mass.Gen.Laws (1932) c. 277, § 51 (in capital cases); N.Y.Code of Criminal Procedure, § 344. The second is a motion for a change of venue in cases involving an offense alleged to have been committed in more than one district or division. In such cases the court, on defendant's motion, will be authorized to transfer the case to another district or division in which the commission of the offense is charged, if the court is satisfied that it is in the interest of justice to do so. The effect of this provision would be to modify the existing practice under which in such cases the Government had the final choice of the jurisdiction where the prosecution should be conducted. The matter will now be left in the discretion of the court.

3. The rule provides for a change of venue only on defendant's motion and does not extend the same right to the prosecution, since the defendant has a constitutional right to a trial in the district where the offense was committed, Constitution of the United States, Article III, § 2, Par. 3; Amendment VI. By making a motion for a change of venue, however, the defendant waives this constitutional right.

4. This rule is in addition to and does not supersede existing statutes enabling a party to secure a change of judge on the ground of personal bias or prejudice, 28 U.S.C. former § 25 [now § 144]; or enabling the defendant to secure a change of venue as of right in certain cases involving offenses committed in more than one district. 18 U.S.C. former § 338a(d) [now §§ 876, 3239] (Mailing threatening communications); Id. 18 U.S.C. former § 403d(d) [now §§ 875, 3239] (Threatening communications in interstate commerce).

Note to Subdivision (c). Cf. 28 U.S.C. former § 114 [now §§ 1393, 1441] and Rule 20, supra.

1966 Amendments

Subdivision (a).—All references to divisions are eliminated in accordance with the amendment to Rule 18 eliminating division venue. The defendant is given the right to a transfer only when he can show that he cannot obtain a fair and impartial trial at any place fixed by law for holding court in the district. Transfers within the district to avoid prejudice will be within the power of the judge to fix the place of trial as provided in the amendments to Rule 18. It is also made clear that on a motion to transfer under this subdivision the court may select the district to which the transfer may be made. Cf. *United States v. Parr*, 17 F.R.D. 512, 519 (S.D.Tex.1955); *Parr v. United States*, 351 U.S. 513 (1956).

Subdivision (b).—The original rule limited change of venue for reasons other than prejudice in the district to those cases where venue existed in more than one district. Upon occasion, however, convenience of the parties and witnesses and the interest of justice would best be served by trial in a district in which no part of the offense was committed. See, e.g., *Travis v. United States*, 364 U.S. 631 (1961), holding that the only venue of a charge of making or filing a false non-Communist affidavit required by § 9(h) of the National Labor Relations Act is in Washington, D.C. even though all the relevant witnesses may be located at the place where the affidavit was executed and mailed. See also Barber, Venue in Federal Criminal cases: A Plea for Return to Principle, 42 Tex.L.Rev. 39 (1963); Wright, Proposed Changes in Federal

Civil, Criminal and Appellate Procedure, 35 F.R.D. 317, 329 (1964). The amendment permits a transfer in any case on motion of the defendant on a showing that it would be for the convenience of parties and witnesses, and in the interest of justice. Cf. 28 U.S.C. § 1404(a), stating a similar standard for civil cases. See also *Platt v. Minnesota Min. & Mfg. Co.*, 376 U.S. 240 (1964). Here, as in subdivision (a), the court may select the district to which the transfer is to be made. The amendment also makes it clear that the court may transfer all or part of the offenses charged in a multi-count indictment or information. Cf. *United States v. Choate*, 276 F.2d 724 (5th Cir. 1960). References to divisions are eliminated in accordance with the amendment to Rule 18.

Subdivision (c).—The reference to division is eliminated in accordance with the amendment to Rule 18.

1987 Amendments

The amendments are technical. No substantive change is intended.

2002 Amendments

The language of Rule 21 has been amended as part of the general restyling of the Criminal Rules to make them more easily understood and to make style and terminology consistent throughout the rules. These changes are intended to be stylistic only.

Amended Rule 21(d) consists of what was formerly Rule 22. The Committee believed that the substance of Rule 22, which addressed the issue of the timing of motions to transfer, was more appropriate for inclusion in Rule 21.

Rule 22. [Transferred]

ADVISORY COMMITTEE NOTES

2002 Amendments

Rule 22 has been abrogated. The substance of the rule is now located in Rule 21(d).

VI. TRIAL

Rule 23. Jury or Nonjury Trial

(a) Jury Trial. If the defendant is entitled to a jury trial, the trial must be by jury unless:

(1) the defendant waives a jury trial in writing;

(2) the government consents; and

(3) the court approves.

(b) Jury Size.

(1) In General. A jury consists of 12 persons unless this rule provides otherwise.

(2) Stipulation for a Smaller Jury. At any time before the verdict, the parties may, with the court's approval, stipulate in writing that:

(A) the jury may consist of fewer than 12 persons; or

(B) a jury of fewer than 12 persons may return a verdict if the court finds it necessary to excuse a juror for good cause after the trial begins.

(3) Court Order for a Jury of 11. After the jury has retired to deliberate, the court may permit a jury of 11 persons to return a verdict, even without a stipulation by the parties, if the court finds good cause to excuse a juror.

(c) Nonjury Trial. In a case tried without a jury, the court must find the defendant guilty or not guilty. If a party requests before the finding of guilty or not guilty, the court must state its specific findings of fact in open court or in a written decision or opinion.

(As amended Feb. 28, 1966, eff. July 1, 1966; Apr. 26, 1976, eff. Oct. 1, 1977; Pub.L. 95–78, § 2(b), July 30, 1977, 91 Stat. 320; Apr. 28, 1983, eff. Aug. 1, 1983; Apr. 29, 2002, eff. Dec. 1, 2002.)

ADVISORY COMMITTEE NOTES

1944 Adoption

Note to Subdivision (a). 1. This rule is a formulation of the constitutional guaranty of trial by jury, Constitution of the United States, Article III, § 2, Par. 3: "The Trial of all Crimes, except in Cases of Impeachment, shall be by Jury * * *"; Amendment VI: "In all criminal prosecutions, the accused shall enjoy the right to a speedy and public trial, by an impartial jury * * *." The right to a jury trial, however, does not apply to petty offenses, *District of Columbia v. Clawans*, 57 S.Ct. 660, 300 U.S. 617, 81 L.Ed. 843; *Schick v. United States*, 24 S.Ct. 826, 195 U.S. 65, 49 L.Ed. 99, 1 Ann.Cas. 585; Frankfurter and Corcoran, 39 Harv.L.R. 917. Cf. Rules 38(a) of the Federal Rules of Civil Procedure.

2. The provision for a waiver of jury trial by the defendant embodies existing practice, the constitutionality of which has been upheld, *Patton v. United States*, 50 S.Ct. 253, 281 U.S. 276, 74 L.Ed. 854, 70 A.L.R. 263; *Adams v. United States ex rel. McCann*, 63 S.Ct. 236, 317 U.S. 269, 87 L.Ed. 268, 143 A.L.R. 435; Cf. Rules 38 and 39 of Federal Rules of Civil Procedure, 28 U.S.C., Appendix. Many States by express statutory provision permit waiver of jury trial in criminal cases. See A.L.I.Code of Criminal Procedure Commentaries, pp. 807 to 811.

Note to Subdivision (b). This rule would permit either a stipulation before the trial that the case be tried by a jury composed of less than 12 or a stipulation during the trial consenting that the case be submitted to less than 12 jurors. The second alternative is useful in case it becomes necessary during the trial to excuse a juror owing to illness or for some other cause and no alternate juror is available. The rule is a restatement of existing practice, the constitutionality of which was approved in *Patton v. United States*, 50 S.Ct. 253, 281 U.S. 276, 74 L.Ed. 854, 70 A.L.R. 263.

Note to Subdivision (c). This rule changes existing law in so far as it requires the court in a case tried without a jury to make special findings of fact if requested. Cf. Connecticut practice, under which a judge in a criminal case tried by the court without a jury makes findings of fact. *State v. Frost*, 105 Conn. 326, 135 A. 446.

1966 Amendments

This amendment adds to the rule a provision added to Civil Rule 52(a) in 1946.

1977 Enactment

Section 2(b) of Pub.L. 95–78 provided that: "The amendments proposed by the Supreme Court [in its order of Apr. 26, 1976] to subdivisions (b) and (c) of rule 23 of such Rules of Criminal Procedure [subd. (b) and (c) of this rule] are approved."

1977 Amendments

The amendment to subdivision (b) makes it clear that the parties, with the approval of the court, may enter into an agreement to have the case decided by less than twelve jurors if one or more jurors are unable or disqualified to continue. For many years the Eastern District of Virginia has used a form entitled, "Waiver of Alternate Jurors." In a substantial percentage of cases the form is signed by the defendant, his attorney, and the Assistant United States Attorney in advance of trial, generally on the morning of trial. It is handled automatically by the courtroom deputy clerk who, after completion, exhibits it to the judge.

This practice would seem to be authorized by existing rule 23(b), but there has been some doubt as to whether the pretrial stipulation is effective unless again agreed to by a defendant at the time a juror or jurors have to be excused. See 8 J. Moore, Federal Practice ¶23.04 (2d ed. Cipes, 1969); C. Wright, Federal Practice and Procedure: Criminal § 373 (1969). The proposed amendment is intended to make clear that the pretrial stipulation is an effective waiver, which need not be renewed at the time the incapacity or disqualification of the juror becomes known.

In view of the fact that a defendant can make an effective pretrial waiver of trial by jury or by a jury of twelve, it would seem to follow that he can also effectively waive trial by a jury of twelve in situations where a juror or jurors cannot continue to serve.

As has been the practice under rule 23(b), a stipulation addressed to the possibility that some jurors many later be excused need not be open-ended. That is, the stipulation may be conditioned upon the jury not being reduced below a certain size. See, e.g., *Williams v. United States*, 332 F.2d 36 (7th Cir. 1964) (agreement to proceed if no more than 2 jurors excused for illness); *Rogers v. United States*, 319 F.2d 5 (7th Cir. 1963) (same).

Subdivision (c) is changed to make clear the deadline for making a request for findings of fact and to provide that findings may be oral. The oral findings, of course, become a part of the record, as findings of fact are essential to proper appellate review on a conviction resulting from a nonjury trial. *United States v. Livingston*, 459 F.2d 797 (3d Cir. 1972).

The meaning of current subdivision (c) has been in some doubt because there is no time specified within which a defendant must make a "request" that the court "find the facts specially." See, e.g., *United States v. Rivera*, 444 F.2d 136 (2d Cir. 1971), where the request was not made until the sentence had been imposed. In the opinion the court said: This situation might have raised the interesting and apparently undecided question of when a request for findings under Fed.R.Crim.P. 23(c) is too late, since Rivera's request was not made until the day after sentence was imposed. See generally *Benchwick v. United States*, 297 F.2d 330, 335 (9th Cir. 1961); *United States v. Morris*, 263 F.2d 594 (7th Cir.1959).

Subsection (b) of section 2 of the bill simply approves the Supreme Court proposed changes in subdivisions (b) and (c) of rule 23 for the reasons given by the Advisory Committee on Rules of Practice and Procedure to the Judicial Conference.

1983 Amendments

Rule 23(b). The amendment to subdivision (b) addresses a situation which does not occur with great frequency but which, when it does occur, may present a most difficult issue concerning the fair and efficient administration of justice. This situation is that in which, after the jury has retired to consider its verdict and any alternate jurors have been discharged, one of the jurors is seriously incapacitated or otherwise found to be unable to continue service upon the jury. The problem is acute when the trial has been a lengthy one and consequently the remedy of mistrial would necessitate a second expenditure of substantial prosecution, defense and court resources. See, e.g., *United States v. Meinster*, 484 F.Supp. 442 (S.D.Fla.1980), aff'd sub nom. *United States v. Phillips*, 664 F.2d 971 (5th Cir.1981) (juror had heart attack during deliberations after "well over four months of trial"); *United States v. Barone*, 83 F.R.D. 565 (S.D.Fla.1979) (juror removed upon recommendation of psychiatrist during deliberations after "approximately six months of trial").

It is the judgment of the Committee that when a juror is lost during deliberations, especially in circumstances like those in Barone and Meinster, it is essential that there be available a course of action other than mistrial. Proceeding with the remaining 11 jurors, though heretofore impermissible under rule 23(b) absent stipulation by the parties and approval of the court, *United States v. Taylor*, 507 F.2d 166 (5th Cir.1975), is constitutionally permissible. In *Williams v. Florida*, 399 U.S. 78 (1970), the Court concluded

> the fact that the jury at common law was composed of precisely 12 is an historical accident, unnecessary to effect the purposes of the jury system and wholly without significance "except to mystics." * * * To read the Sixth Amendment as forever codifying a feature so incidental to the real purpose of the Amendment is to ascribe a blind formalism to the Framers which would require considerably more evidence than we have been able to discover in the history and language of the Constitution or in the reasoning of our past decisions. * * * Our holding does no more than leave these considerations to Congress and the States, unrestrained by an interpretation of the Sixth Amendment which would forever dictate the precise number which can constitute a jury.

Williams held that a six-person jury was constitutional because such a jury had the "essential feature of a jury," i.e., "the interposition between the accused and his accuser of the common-sense judgment of a group of laymen, and in the community participation and shared responsibility which results from that group's determination of guilt or innocence," necessitating only a group "large enough to promote group deliberation, free from outside attempts at intimidation, and to provide a fair possibility for obtaining a representative cross section of the community." This being the case, quite clearly the occasional use of a jury of slightly less than 12, as contemplated by the amendment to rule 23(b), is constitutional. Though the alignment of the Court and especially the separate opinion by Justice Powell in *Apodoca v. Oregon*, 406 U.S. 404 (1972), makes it at best uncertain whether less-than-unanimous verdicts would be constitutionally permissible in federal trials, it hardly follows that a requirement of unanimity of a group slightly less than 12 is similarly suspect.

The *Meinster* case clearly reflects the need for a solution other than mistrial. There twelve defendants were named in a 36-count, 100-page indictment for RICO offenses and related violations, and the trial lasted more than four months. Before the jury retired for deliberations, the trial judge inquired of defense counsel whether they would now agree to a jury of less than 12 should a juror later be unable to continue during the deliberations which were anticipated to be lengthy. All defense counsel rejected that proposal. When one juror was excused a day later after suffering a heart attack, all defense counsel again rejected the proposal that deliberations continue with the remaining 11 jurors. Thus, the solution now provided in rule 23(b), stipulation to a jury of less than 12, was not possible in that case, just as it will not be possible in any case in which defense counsel believe some tactical advantage will be gained by retrial. Yet, to declare a mistrial at that point would have meant that over four months of trial time would have gone for naught and that a comparable period of time would have to be expended on retrial. For a variety of reasons, not the least of which is the impact such a retrial would have upon that court's ability to comply with speedy trial limits in other cases, such a result is most undesirable.

That being the case, it is certainly understandable that the trial judge in *Meinster* (as in *Barone*) elected to substitute an alternate juror at that point. Given the rule 23(b) bar on a verdict of less than 12 absent stipulation, *United States v. Taylor*, supra, such substitution seemed the least objectionable course of action. But in terms of what change in the Federal Rules of Criminal Procedure is to be preferred in order to facilitate response to such situations in the future, the judgment of the Advisory Committee is that it is far better to permit the deliberations to continue with a jury of 11 than to make a substitution at that point.

In rejecting the substitution-of-juror alternative, the Committee's judgment is in accord with that of most commentators and many courts.

> There have been proposals that the rule should be amended to permit an alternate to be substituted if a regular juror becomes unable to perform his duties after the case has been submitted to the jury. An early draft of the original Criminal Rules had contained such a provision, but it was withdrawn when the Supreme Court itself indicated to the Advisory Committee on Criminal Rules doubts as to the desirability and constitutionality of such a procedure. These doubts are as forceful now as they were a quarter century ago. To permit substitution of an alternate after deliberations have begun would require either that the alternate participate though he has missed part of the jury discussion, or that he sit in with the jury in every cases on the chance he might be needed. Either course is subject to practical difficulty and to strong constitutional objection.

Wright, *Federal Practice and Procedure* § 388 (1969). See also Moore, *Federal Practice* par. 24.05 (2d ed. Cipes 1980) ("The inherent coercive effect upon an alternate who joins a jury leaning heavily toward a guilty verdict may result in the alternate reaching a premature guilty verdict"); 3 *ABA Standards for Criminal Justice* § 15–2.7, commentary (2d ed. 1980) ("it is not desirable to allow a juror who is unfamiliar with the prior deliberations to suddenly join the group and participate in the voting without the benefit of earlier group discussion"); United States v. Lamb, 529 F.2d 1153 (9th Cir.1975); *People v. Ryan*, 19 N.Y.2d 100, 224 N.E.2d 710 (1966). Compare *People v. Collins*, 17 Cal.3d 687, 131 Cal.Rptr. 782, 522 P.2d 742 (1976); *Johnson v. State*, 267 Ind. 256, 396 N.E.2d 623 (1977).

The central difficulty with substitution, whether viewed only as a practical problem or a question of constitutional dimensions (procedural due process under the Fifth Amendment or jury trial under the Sixth Amendment), is that there does not appear to be any way to nullify the impact of what has occurred without the participation of the new juror. Even were it required that the jury "review" with the new juror their prior deliberations or that the jury upon substitution start deliberations anew, it still seems likely that the continuing jurors would be influenced by the earlier deliberations and that the new juror would be somewhat intimidated by the others by virtue of being a newcomer to the deliberations. As for the possibility of sending in the alternates at the very beginning with instructions to listen but not to participate until substituted, this scheme is likewise attended by practical difficulties and offends "the cardinal principle that the deliberations of the jury shall remain private and secret in every case." *United States v. Virginia Erection Corp.*, 335 F.2d 868 (4th Cir.1964).

The amendment provides that if a juror is excused after the jury has retired to consider its verdict, it is within the discretion of the court whether to declare a mistrial or to permit deliberations to continue with 11 jurors. If the trial has been brief and not much would be lost by retrial, the court might well conclude that the unusual step of allowing a jury verdict by less than 12 jurors absent stipulation should not be taken. On the other hand, if the trial has been protracted the court is much more likely to opt for continuing with the remaining 11 jurors.

2002 Amendments

The language of Rule 23 has been amended as part of the general restyling of the Criminal Rules to make them more easily understood and to make style and terminology consistent throughout the rules. These changes are intended to be stylistic only.

In current Rule 23(b), the term "just cause" has been replaced with the more familiar term "good cause," that appears in other rules. No change in substance is intended.

HISTORICAL NOTES

Effective and Applicability Provisions

1977 Acts. Amendment of this rule by order of the United States Supreme Court on Apr. 26, 1976, approved by Pub.L. 95–78, effective Oct. 1, 1977, pursuant to section 4 of Pub.L. 95–78.

Complete Annotation Materials, see Title 18 U.S.C.A.

Rule 24. Trial Jurors

(a) Examination.

(1) In General. The court may examine prospective jurors or may permit the attorneys for the parties to do so.

(2) Court Examination. If the court examines the jurors, it must permit the attorneys for the parties to:

(A) ask further questions that the court considers proper; or

(B) submit further questions that the court may ask if it considers them proper.

(b) Peremptory Challenges. Each side is entitled to the number of peremptory challenges to prospective jurors specified below. The court may allow additional peremptory challenges to multiple defendants, and may allow the defendants to exercise those challenges separately or jointly.

(1) Capital Case. Each side has 20 peremptory challenges when the government seeks the death penalty.

(2) Other Felony Case. The government has 6 peremptory challenges and the defendant or defendants jointly have 10 peremptory challenges when the defendant is charged with a crime punishable by imprisonment of more than one year.

(3) Misdemeanor Case. Each side has 3 peremptory challenges when the defendant is charged with a crime punishable by fine, imprisonment of one year or less, or both.

(c) Alternate Jurors.

(1) In General. The court may impanel up to 6 alternate jurors to replace any jurors who are unable to perform or who are disqualified from performing their duties.

(2) Procedure.

(A) Alternate jurors must have the same qualifications and be selected and sworn in the same manner as any other juror.

(B) Alternate jurors replace jurors in the same sequence in which the alternates were selected. An alternate juror who replaces a juror has the same authority as the other jurors.

(3) Retaining Alternate Jurors. The court may retain alternate jurors after the jury retires to deliberate. The court must ensure that a retained alternate does not discuss the case with anyone until that alternate replaces a juror or is discharged. If an alternate replaces a juror after deliberations have begun, the court must instruct the jury to begin its deliberations anew.

(4) Peremptory Challenges. Each side is entitled to the number of additional peremptory challenges to prospective alternate jurors specified below. These additional challenges may be used only to remove alternate jurors.

(A) One or Two Alternates. One additional peremptory challenge is permitted when one or two alternates are impaneled.

(B) Three or Four Alternates. Two additional peremptory challenges are permitted when three or four alternates are impaneled.

(C) Five or Six Alternates. Three additional peremptory challenges are permitted when five or six alternates are impaneled.

(As amended Feb. 28, 1966, eff. July 1, 1966; Mar. 9, 1987, eff. Aug. 1, 1987; Apr. 29, 1999, eff. Dec. 1, 1999; Apr. 29, 2002, eff. Dec. 1, 2002.)

ADVISORY COMMITTEE NOTES

1944 Adoption

Note to Subdivision (a). This rule is similar to rule 47(a) of the Federal Rules of Civil Procedure, 28 U.S.C., Appendix, and also embodies the practice now followed by many Federal courts in criminal cases. Uniform procedure in civil and criminal cases on this point seems desirable.

Note to Subdivision (b). This rule embodies existing law, 28 U.S.C. former § 424 [now § 1870] (Challenges), with the following modifications. In capital cases the number of challenges is equalized as between the defendant and the United States so that both sides have 20 challenges, which only the defendant has at present. While continuing the existing rule that multiple defendants are deemed a single party for purposes of challenges, the rule vests in the court discretion to allow additional peremptory challenges to multiple defendants and to permit such changes to be exercised separately or jointly. Experience with cases involving numerous defendants indicates the desirability of this modification.

Note to Subdivision (c). This rule embodies existing law, 28 U.S.C. former § 417a (Alternate jurors), as well as the practice prescribed for civil cases by Rule 47(b) of the Federal Rules of Civil Procedure, 28 U.S.C., Appendix, except that the number of possible alternate jurors that may be empaneled is increased from two to four, with a corresponding adjustment of challenges.

1966 Amendments

Experience has demonstrated that four alternate jurors may not be enough for some lengthy criminal trials. See, e.g., *United States v. Bentvena*, 288 F.2d 442 (2d Cir.1961); Reports of the Proceedings of the Judicial Conference of the United States, 1961, p. 104. The amendment to the first sentence increases the number authorized from four to six. The fourth sentence is amended to provide an additional peremptory challenge where a fifth or sixth alternate juror is used.

The words "or are found to be" are added to the second sentence to make clear that an alternate juror may be called in the situation where it is first discovered during the trial that a juror was unable or disqualified to perform his duties at the time he was sworn. See *United States v. Goldberg*, 330 F.2d 30 (3rd Cir.1964), cert. den. 377 U.S. 953 (1964).

1977 Enactment

Pub.L. 95–78, § 2(c), July 30, 1977, 91 Stat. 320, effective Oct. 1, 1977, provided that: "The amendment proposed by the Supreme Court [in its order of Apr. 26, 1976] to rule 24 of such Rules of Criminal Procedure is disapproved and shall not take effect."

The proposed amendment read:

(b) Peremptory challenges.

(1) *Number of challenges.*

(A) Capital cases. If the offense charged is punishable by death, each side is entitled to 12 peremptory challenges.

(B) Felony cases. If the offense charged is punishable by imprisonment for not more than one year, each side is entitled to 5 peremptory challenges.

(C) Misdemeanor cases. If the offense charged is punishable by imprisonment for not more than one year or by fine or both, each side is entitled to 2 peremptory challenges.

(2) *Relief from limitations.*

(A) For cause. For good cause shown, the court may grant such additional challenges as it, in its discretion, believes necessary and proper.

(B) Multiple defendants. If there is more than one defendant the court may allow the parties additional challenges and permit them to be exercised separately or jointly.

(C) Time for making motion. A motion for relief under (b) (2) shall be filed at least 1 week in advance of the first scheduled trial date or within such other time as may be provided by the rules of the district court.

1987 Amendments

The amendments are technical. No substantive change is intended.

1999 Amendments

As currently written, Rule 24(c) explicitly requires the court to discharge all of the alternate jurors—who have not been selected to replace other jurors—when the jury retires to deliberate. That requirement is grounded on the concern that after the case has been submitted to the jury, its deliberations must be private and inviolate. *United States v. Houlihan*, 92 F.3d 1271, 1285 (1st Cir. 1996), citing *United States v. Virginia Election Corp.*, 335 F.2d 868, 872 (4th Cir. 1964).

Rule 23(b) provides that in some circumstances a verdict may be returned by eleven jurors. In addition, there may be cases where it is better to retain the alternates when the jury retires, insulate them from the deliberation process. And have them available should one or more vacancies occur in the jury. That might be especially appropriate in a long, costly, and complicated case. To that end the Committee believed that the court should have the discretion to decide whether to retain or discharge the alternates at the time the jury retires to deliberate and to use Rule 23(b) to proceed with eleven jurors or to substitute a juror or jurors with alternate jurors who have not been discharged.

In order to protect the sanctity of the deliberative process, the rule requires the court to take appropriate steps to insulate the alternate jurors. That may be done, for example, by separating the alternates from the deliberating jurors and instructing the alternate jurors not to discuss the case with any other person until they replace a regular juror. *See, e.g., United States v. Olano*, 507 U.S. 725 (1993) (not plain error to permit alternate jurors to sit in during deliberations); *United States v. Houlihan*, 92 F.3d 1271, 1286–88 (1st Cir. 1996) (harmless error to retain alternate jurors in violation of Rule 24(c); in finding harmless error the court cited the steps taken by the trial judge to insulate the alternates). If alternates are used, the jurors must be instructed that they must begin their deliberations anew.

Finally, subsection (c) has been reorganized and restyled.

GAP Report—Rule 24(c).

The final sentence of Rule 24(c) was moved from the committee note to the rule to emphasize that if an alternate replaces a juror during deliberations, the court shall instruct the jury to begin its deliberations anew.

2002 Amendments

The language of Rule 24 has been amended as part of the general restyling of the Criminal Rules to make them more easily understood and to make style and terminology consistent throughout the rules. These changes are intended to be stylistic only, except as noted below.

In restyling Rule 24(a), the Committee deleted the language that authorized the defendant to conduct voir dire of prospective jurors. The Committee believed that the current language was potentially ambiguous and could lead one incorrectly to conclude that a defendant, represented by counsel, could personally conduct voir dire or additional voir dire. The Committee believed that the intent of the current provision was to permit a defendant to participate personally in voir dire only if the defendant was acting pro se. Amended Rule 24(a) refers only to attorneys for the parties, i.e., the defense counsel and the attorney for the government, with the understanding that if the defendant is not represented by counsel, the court may still, in its discretion, permit the defendant to participate in voir dire. In summary, the Committee intends no change in practice.

Finally, the rule authorizes the court in multi-defendant cases to grant additional peremptory challenges to the defendants. If the court does so, the prosecution may request additional challenges in a multi-defendant case, not to exceed the total number available to the defendants jointly. The court, however, is not required to equalize the number of challenges where additional challenges are granted to the defendant.

Rule 25. Judge's Disability

(a) During Trial. Any judge regularly sitting in or assigned to the court may complete a jury trial if:

(1) the judge before whom the trial began cannot proceed because of death, sickness, or other disability; and

(2) the judge completing the trial certifies familiarity with the trial record.

(b) After a Verdict or Finding of Guilty.

(1) In General. After a verdict or finding of guilty, any judge regularly sitting in or assigned to a court may complete the court's duties if the judge who presided at trial cannot perform those duties because of absence, death, sickness, or other disability.

(2) Granting a New Trial. The successor judge may grant a new trial if satisfied that:

(A) a judge other than the one who presided at the trial cannot perform the post-trial duties; or

(B) a new trial is necessary for some other reason.

(As amended Feb. 28, 1966, eff. July 1, 1966; Mar. 9, 1987, eff. Aug. 1, 1987; Apr. 29, 2002, eff. Dec. 1, 2002.)

ADVISORY COMMITTEE NOTES

1944 Adoption

This rule is similar to rule 63 of the Federal Rules of Civil Procedure 28 U.S.C., Appendix. See, also, 28 U.S.C. former § 776 (Bill of exceptions; authentication; signing of by judge).

1966 Amendments

In September, 1963, the Judicial Conference of the United States approved a recommendation of its Committee on Court Administration that provision be made for substitution of a judge who becomes disabled during trial. The problem has become serious because of the increase in the number of long criminal trials. See 1963 Annual Report of the Director of the Administrative Office of the United States Courts, p. 114, reporting a 25% increase in criminal trials lasting more than one week in fiscal year 1963 over 1962.

Subdivision (a).—The amendment casts the rule into two subdivisions and in subdivision (a) provides for substitution of a judge during a jury trial upon his certification that he has familiarized himself with the record of the trial. For similar provisions see Alaska Rules of Crim.Proc., Rule 25; California Penal Code, § 1053.

Subdivision (b).—The words "from the district" are deleted to permit the local judge to act in those situations where a judge who has been assigned from within the district to try the case is, at the time for sentence, etc., back at his regular place of holding court which may be several hundred miles from the place of trial. It is not intended, of course, that substitutions shall be made where the judge who tried the case is available within a reasonable distance from the place of trial.

1987 Amendments

The amendments are technical. No substantive change is intended.

2002 Amendments

The language of Rule 25 has been amended as part of the general restyling of the Criminal Rules to make them more easily understood and to make style and terminology consistent throughout the rules. These changes are intended to be stylistic only.

Rule 25(b)(2) addresses the possibility of a new trial when a judge determines that no other judge could perform post-trial duties or when the judge determines that there is some other reason for doing so. The current rule indicates that those reasons must be "appropriate." The Committee, however, believed that a better term would be "necessary," because that term includes notions of manifest necessity. No change in meaning or practice is intended.

Rule 26. Taking Testimony

In every trial the testimony of witnesses must be taken in open court, unless otherwise provided by a statute or by rules adopted under 28 U.S.C. §§ 2072–2077.

(As amended Nov. 20, 1972; Apr. 29, 2002, eff. Dec. 1, 2002.)

ADVISORY COMMITTEE NOTES

1944 Adoption

1. This rule contemplates the development of a uniform body of rules of evidence to be applicable in trials of criminal cases in the Federal courts. It is based on *Funk v. United States*, 54 S.Ct. 212, 290 U.S. 371, 78 L.Ed. 369, 93 A.L.R. 1136, and *Wolfle v. United States*, 54 S.Ct. 279, 291 U.S. 7, 78 L.Ed. 617, which indicated that in the absence of statute the Federal courts in criminal cases are not bound by the State law of evidence, but are guided by common law principles as interpreted by the Federal courts "in the light of reason and experience". The rule does not fetter the applicable law of evidence to that originally existing at common law. It is contemplated that the law may be modified and adjusted from time to time by judicial decisions. See Homer Cummings, 29 A.B.A.Jour. 655; Vanderbilt, 29 A.B.A.Jour. 377; Holtzoff, 12 George Washington L.R. 119, 131–132; Holtzoff, 3 F.R.D. 445, 453; Howard, 51 Yale L.Jour. 763; Medalie, 4 Lawyers Guild R. (3) 1, 5–6.

2. This rule differs from the corresponding rule for civil cases (Federal Rules of Civil Procedure, rule 43(a), 28 U.S.C., Appendix), in that this rule contemplates a uniform body of rules of evidence to govern in criminal trials in the Federal courts, while the rule for civil cases prescribes partial conformity to State law and, therefore, results in a divergence as between various districts. Since in civil actions in which Federal jurisdiction is based on diversity of citizenship, the State substantive law governs the rights of the parties, uniformity of rules of evidence among different districts does not appear necessary. On the other hand, since all Federal crimes are statutory and all criminal prosecutions in the Federal courts are based on acts of Congress, uniform rules of evidence appear desirable if not essential in criminal cases, as otherwise the same facts under differing rules of evidence may lead to a conviction in one district and to an acquittal in another.

3. This rule expressly continues existing statutes governing the admissibility of evidence and the competency and privileges of witnesses. Among such statutes are the following:

8 U.S.C. former § 138 [now §§ 1326, 1328, 1329] (Importation of aliens for immoral purposes; attempt to reenter after deportation; penalty)

28 U.S.C. former § 632 [now 18 U.S.C. § 3481] (Competency of witnesses governed by State laws; defendants in criminal cases)

28 U.S.C. former § 633 (Competency of witnesses governed by State laws; husband or wife of defendant in prosecution for bigamy)

28 U.S.C. former § 634 [now 18 U.S.C. § 3486] (Testimony of witness before Congress)

28 U.S.C. former § 638 [now § 1731] (Comparison of handwriting to determine genuineness)

28 U.S.C. former § 695 [now § 1732] (Admissibility)

28 U.S.C. former § 695a [now 18 U.S.C. § 3491] (Foreign documents)

46 U.S.C. § 193 (Bills of lading to be issued; contents)

1972 Amendments

The first sentence is retained, with appropriate narrowing of the title, since its subject is not covered in the Rules of Evidence. The second sentence is deleted because the Rules of Evidence govern admissibility of evidence, competency of witnesses, and privilege. The language is broadened, however, to take account of the Rules of Evidence and any other rules adopted by the Supreme Court.

2002 Amendments

The language of Rule 26 has been amended as part of the general restyling of the Criminal Rules to make them more easily understood and to make style and terminology consistent throughout the rules. These changes are intended to be stylistic only, except as noted below.

Rule 26 is amended, by deleting the word "orally," to accommodate witnesses who are not able to present oral testimony in open court and may need, for example, a sign language interpreter. The change conforms the rule, in that respect, to Federal Rule of Civil Procedure 43.

HISTORICAL NOTES

Effective and Applicability Provisions

1975 Acts. Amendment of this rule embraced by the order entered by the Supreme Court of the United States on Nov. 20, 1972, effective on the 180th day beginning after Jan. 2, 1975, [effective July 1, 1975], see § 3 of Pub.L. 93–595, Jan. 2, 1975, 88 Stat.1959, set out as a note under § 3771 of this title.

Rule 26.1. Foreign Law Determination

A party intending to raise an issue of foreign law must provide the court and all parties with reasonable written notice. Issues of foreign law are questions of law, but in deciding such issues a court may consider any relevant material or source—including testimony—without regard to the Federal Rules of Evidence.

(Added Feb. 28, 1966, eff. July 1, 1966, and amended Nov. 20, 1972; Apr. 29, 2002, eff. Dec. 1, 2002.)

ADVISORY COMMITTEE NOTES

1944 Addition

The original Federal Rules of Criminal Procedure did not contain a provision explicitly regulating the determination of foreign law. The resolution of issues of foreign law, when relevant in federal criminal proceedings, falls within the general compass of Rule 26 which provides for application of "the [evidentiary] principles of the common law as they may be interpreted by the courts of the United States in the light of reason and experience." See Green, Preliminary Report on the Advisability and Feasibility of Developing Uniform Rules of Evidence for the United States District Courts 6–7, 17–18 (1962). Although traditional "common-law" methods for determining foreign-country law have proved inadequate, the courts have not developed more appropriate practices on the basis of this flexible rule. *Cf.* Green, op. cit. supra at 26–28. On the inadequacy of common-law procedures for determining foreign law, see, *e.g.*, Nussbaum, Proving the Law of Foreign Countries, 3 Am.J.Comp.L. 60 (1954).

Problems of foreign law that must be resolved in accordance with the Federal Rules of Criminal Procedure are most likely to arise in places such as Washington, D.C., the Canal Zone, Guam, and the Virgin Islands, where the federal courts have general criminal jurisdiction. However, issues of foreign law may also arise in criminal proceedings commenced in other federal districts. For example, in an extradition proceeding, reasonable ground to believe that the person sought to be extradited is charged with, or was convicted of, a crime under the laws of the demanding state must generally be shown. See *Factor v. Laubenheimer*, 290 U.S. 276 (1933); *Fernandez v. Phillips*, 268 U.S. 311 (1925); Bishop, International Law: Cases and Materials (2d ed. 1962). Further, foreign law may be invoked to justify non-compliance with a subpoena duces tecum, *Application of Chase Manhattan Bank*, 297 F.2d 611 (2d Cir. 1962), and under certain circumstances, as a defense to prosecution. *Cf. American Banana Co. v. United Fruit Co.*, 213 U.S. 347 (1909). The content of foreign law may also be relevant in proceedings arising under 18 U.S.C. §§ 1201, 2312 to 2317.

Rule 26.1 is substantially the same as Civil Rule 44.1. A full explanation of the merits and practicability of the rule appear in the Advisory Committee's Note to Civil Rule 44.1. It is necessary here to add only one comment to the explanations there made. The second sentence of the rule frees the court from the restraints of the ordinary rules of evidence in determining foreign law. This freedom, made necessary by the peculiar nature of the issue of foreign law, should not constitute an unconstitutional deprivation of the defendant's rights to confrontation of witnesses. The issue is essentially one of law rather than of fact. Furthermore, the cases have held that the Sixth Amendment does not serve as a rigid barrier against the development of reasonable and necessary exceptions to the hearsay rule. See *Kay v. United States*, 255 F.2d 476, 480 (4th Cir. 1958), cert. den., 358 U.S. 825 (1958); *Matthews v. United States*, 217 F.2d 409, 418 (5th Cir. 1954); *United States v. Leathers*, 135 F.2d 507 (2d Cir. 1943); and cf., *Painter v. Texas*, 85 S.Ct. 1065 (1965); *Douglas v. Alabama*, 85 S.Ct. 1074 (1965).

1972 Amendments

Since the purpose is to free the judge, in determining foreign law, from restrictive evidentiary rules, the reference is made to the Rules of Evidence generally.

2002 Amendments

The language of Rule 26.1 has been amended as part of the general restyling of the Criminal Rules to make them more easily understood and to make style and terminology consistent throughout the rules. These changes are intended to be stylistic only.

HISTORICAL NOTES

References in Text

The Federal Rules of Evidence, referred to in text, are set out in the Appendix to Title 28, Fed.Rules Evid. Rule 101 et seq., 28 U.S.C.A.

Effective and Applicability Provisions

1975 Acts. Amendment of this rule embraced by the order entered by the Supreme Court of the United States on Nov. 20, 1972, effective on the 180th day beginning after Jan. 2, 1975, [effective July 1, 1975], see § 3 of Pub.L. 93–595, Jan. 2, 1975, 88 Stat.1959, set out as a note under § 3771 of this title.

Rule 26.2. Producing a Witness's Statement

(a) Motion to Produce. After a witness other than the defendant has testified on direct examination, the court, on motion of a party who did not call the witness, must order an attorney for the government or the defendant and the defendant's attorney to produce, for the examination and use of the moving party, any statement of the witness that is in their possession and that relates to the subject matter of the witness's testimony.

(b) Producing the Entire Statement. If the entire statement relates to the subject matter of the witness's testimony, the court must order that the statement be delivered to the moving party.

(c) Producing a Redacted Statement. If the party who called the witness claims that the statement contains information that is privileged or does not relate to the subject matter of the witness's testimony, the court must inspect the statement in camera. After excising any privileged or unrelated portions, the court must order delivery of the redacted statement to the moving party. If the defendant objects to an excision, the court must preserve the entire statement with the excised portion indicated, under seal, as part of the record.

(d) Recess to Examine a Statement. The court may recess the proceedings to allow time for a party to examine the statement and prepare for its use.

(e) Sanction for Failure to Produce or Deliver a Statement. If the party who called the witness disobeys an order to produce or deliver a statement, the court must strike the witness's testimony from the record. If an attorney for the government disobeys the order, the court must declare a mistrial if justice so requires.

(f) "Statement" Defined. As used in this rule, a witness's "statement" means:

(1) a written statement that the witness makes and signs, or otherwise adopts or approves;

(2) a substantially verbatim, contemporaneously recorded recital of the witness's oral statement that is contained in any recording or any transcription of a recording; or

(3) the witness's statement to a grand jury, however taken or recorded, or a transcription of such a statement.

(g) Scope. This rule applies at trial, at a suppression hearing under Rule 12, and to the extent specified in the following rules:

(1) Rule 5.1(h) (preliminary hearing);

(2) Rule 32(i)(2) (sentencing);

(3) Rule 32.1(e) (hearing to revoke or modify probation or supervised release);

(4) Rule 46(j) (detention hearing); and

(5) Rule 8 of the Rules Governing Proceedings under 28 U.S.C. § 2255.

(Added Apr. 30, 1979, eff. Dec. 1, 1980, and amended Mar. 9, 1987, eff. Aug. 1, 1987; Apr. 22, 1993, eff. Dec. 1, 1993 Apr. 24, 1998, eff. Dec. 1, 1998; Apr. 29, 2002, eff. Dec. 1, 2002.)

ADVISORY COMMITTEE NOTES

1979 Addition

S. 1437, 95th Cong., 1st Sess. (1977), would place in the criminal rules the substance of what is now 18 U.S.C. § 3500 (the Jencks Act). Underlying this and certain other additions to the rules contemplated by S. 1437 is the notion that provisions which are purely procedural in nature should appear in the Federal Rules of Criminal Procedure rather than in Title 18. See Reform of the Federal Criminal Laws, Part VI: Hearings on S. 1, S. 716, and S. 1400, Subcomm. on Criminal Laws and Procedures, Senate Judiciary Comm., 93rd Cong., 1st Sess. (statement of Judge Albert B. Maris, at page 5503). Rule 26.2 is identical to the S. 1437 rule except as indicated by the marked additions and deletions. As those changes show, rule 26.2 provides for production of the statements of defense witnesses at trial in essentially the same manner as is now provided for with respect to the statements of government witnesses. Thus, the proposed rule reflects these two judgments: (i) that the subject matter—production of the statements of witnesses—is more appropriately dealt with in the criminal rules; and (ii) that in light of *United States v. Nobles*, 422 U.S. 225 (1975), it is important to establish procedures for the production of defense witnesses' statements as well. The rule is not intended to discourage the practice of voluntary disclosure at an earlier time so as to avoid delays at trial.

In *Nobles*, defense counsel sought to introduce the testimony of a defense investigator who prior to trial had interviewed prospective prosecution witnesses and had prepared a report embodying the essence of their conversation. When the defendant called the investigator to impeach eyewitness testimony identifying the defendant as the robber, the trial judge granted the prosecutor the right to inspect those portions of the investigator's report relating to the witnesses' statements, as a potential basis for cross-examination of the investigator. When the defense declined to produce the report, the trial judge refused to permit the investigator to testify. The Supreme Court unanimously upheld the trial court's actions, findings that neither the Fifth nor Sixth Amendments nor the attorney work product doctrine prevented disclosure of such a document at trial. Noting "the federal judiciary's inherent power to require the prosecution to produce the previously recorded statements of its witnesses so that the defense may get the full benefit of cross-examinations and the truth-finding process may be enhanced," the Court rejected the notion "that the Fifth Amendment renders criminal discovery 'basically a one-way street,'" and thus concluded that "in a proper case, the prosecution can call upon that same power for production of witness statements that facilitate 'full disclosure of all the [relevant] facts.'"

The rule, consistent with the reasoning in *Nobles*, is designed to place the disclosure of prior relevant statements of a defense witness in the possession of the defense on the same legal footing as is the disclosure of prior statements of prosecution witnesses in the hands of the government under the Jencks Act, 18 U.S.C. § 3500 (which S. 1437 would replace with the rule set out therein). See *United States v. Pulvirenti*, 408 F.Supp. 12 (E.D.Mich.1976), holding that under Nobles "[t]he obligation [of disclosure] placed on the defendant should be the reciprocal of that placed upon the government * * * [as] defined by the Jencks Act." Several state courts have likewise concluded that witness statements in the hands of the defense at trial should be disclosed on the same basis that prosecution witness statements are disclosed, in order to promote the concept of the trial as a search for truth. See, e.g., *People v. Sanders*, 110 Ill.App.2d 85, 249 N.E.2d 124 (1969); *State v. Montague*, 55 N.J. 371, 262 A.2d 398 (1970); *People v. Damon*, 24 N.Y.2d 256, 299 N.Y.S.2d 830, 247 N.E.2d 651 (1959).

The rule, with minor exceptions, makes the procedure identical for both prosecution and defense witnesses, including the provision directing the court, whenever a claim is made that disclosure would be improper because the statement contains irrelevant matter, to examine the statements in camera and excise such matter as should not be disclosed. This provision acts as a safeguard against abuse and will enable a defendant who believes that a demand is being improperly made to secure a swift and just resolution of the issue.

The treatment as to defense witnesses of necessity differs slightly from the treatment as to prosecution witnesses in terms of the sanction for a refusal to comply with the court's disclosure order. Under the Jencks Act and the rule proposed in S. 1437, if the prosecution refuses to abide by the court's order, the court is required to strike the witness's testimony unless in its discretion it determines that the more serious sanction of a mistrial in favor of the accused is warranted. Under this rule, if a defendant refuses to comply with the court's disclosure order, the court's only alternative is to enter an order striking or precluding the testimony of the witness, as was done in *Nobles*.

Under subdivision (a) of the rule, the motion for production may be made by "a party who did not call the witness." Thus, it also requires disclosure of statements in the possession of either party when the witness is called neither by the prosecution nor the defense but by the court pursuant to the Federal Rules of Evidence. Present law does not deal with this situation, which consistency requires be treated in an identical manner as the disclosure of statements of witnesses called by a party to the case.

1987 Amendments

The amendments are technical. No substantive change is intended.

1993 Amendments

New subdivision (g) recognizes other contemporaneous amendments in the Rules of Criminal Procedure which extend the application of Rule 26.2 to other proceedings. Those changes are thus consistent with the extension of Rule 26.2 in 1983 to suppression hearings conducted under Rule 12. See Rule 12(i).

In extending Rule 26.2 to suppression hearings in 1983, the Committee offered several reasons. First, production of witness statements enhances the ability of the court to assess the witnesses' credibility and thus assists the court in making accurate factual determinations at suppression hearings. Second, because witnesses testifying at a suppression hearing may not necessarily testify at the trial itself, waiting until after a witness testifies at trial before requiring production of that witness's statement would be futile. Third, the Committee believed that it would be feasible to leave the suppression issue open until trial, where Rule 26.2 would then be applicable. Finally, one of the central reasons for requiring production of statements at suppression hearings was the recognition that by its nature, the results of a suppression hearing have a profound and ultimate impact on the issues presented at trial.

The reasons given in 1983 for extending Rule 26.2 to a suppression hearing are equally compelling with regard to other adversary type hearings which ultimately depend on accurate and reliable information. That is, there is a continuing need for information affecting the credibility of witnesses who present testimony. And that need exists without regard to whether the witness is presenting testimony at a pretrial hearing, at a trial, or at a post-trial proceeding.

As noted in the 1983 Advisory Committee Note to Rule 12(i), the courts have generally declined to extend the Jencks Act, 18 U.S.C. § 3500, beyond the confines of actual trial testimony. That result will be obviated by the addition of Rule 26.2(g) and amendments to the Rules noted in that new subdivision.

Although amendments to Rules 32, 32.1, 46, and Rule 8 of the Rules Governing Proceedings under 28 U.S.C. § 2255 specifically address the requirement of producing a witness's statement, Rule 26.2 has become known as the central "rule" requiring production of statements. Thus, the references in the Rule itself will assist the bench and bar in locating other Rules which include similar provisions.

The amendment to Rule 26.2 and the other designated Rules is not intended to require production of a witness's statement before the witness actually testifies.

Minor conforming amendments have been made to subsection (d) to reflect that Rule 26.2 will be applicable to proceedings other than the trial itself. And language has been added to subsection (c) to recognize explicitly that privileged matter may be excised from the witness's prior statement.

1998 Amendments

The amendment to subdivision (g) mirrors similar amendments made in 1993 to this rule and to other Rules of Criminal Procedure which extended the application of Rule

26.2 to other proceedings, both pretrial and post-trial. This amendment extends the requirement of producing a witness' statement to preliminary examinations conducted under Rule 5.1.

Subdivision (g)(1) has been amended to reflect changes to Rule 32.

2002 Amendments

The language of Rule 26.2 has been amended as part of the general restyling of the Criminal Rules to make them more easily understood and to make style and terminology consistent throughout the rules. These changes are intended to be stylistic only, except as noted below.

Current Rule 26.2(c) states that if the court withholds a portion of a statement, over the defendant's objection, "the attorney for the government" must preserve the statement. The Committee believed that the better rule would be for the court to simply seal the entire statement as a part of the record, in the event that there is an appeal.

Also, the terminology in Rule 26.2(c) has been changed. The rule now speaks in terms of a "redacted" statement instead of an "excised" statement. No change in practice is intended.

Finally, the list of proceedings in Rule 26.2(g) has been placed in rule-number order.

HISTORICAL NOTES

References in Text

The Rules Governing Proceedings under 28 U.S.C.A. § 2255, referred to in subsec. (g)(5), are set out under 28 U.S.C.A. § 2255.

Rule 26.3. Mistrial

Before ordering a mistrial, the court must give each defendant and the government an opportunity to comment on the propriety of the order, to state whether that party consents or objects, and to suggest alternatives.

(Added Apr. 22, 1993, eff. Dec. 1, 1993, and amended Apr. 29, 2002, eff. Dec. 1, 2002.)

ADVISORY COMMITTEE NOTES

1993 Adoption

Rule 26.3 is a new rule designed to reduce the possibility of an erroneously ordered mistrial which could produce adverse and irretrievable consequences. The Rule is not designed to change the substantive law governing mistrials. Instead it is directed at providing both sides an opportunity to place on the record their views about the proposed mistrial order. In particular, the court must give each side an opportunity to state whether it objects or consents to the order.

Several cases have held that retrial of a defendant was barred by the Double Jeopardy Clause of the Constitution because the trial court had abused its discretion in declaring a mistrial. See *United States v. Dixon*, 913 F.2d 1305 (8th Cir.1990); *United States v. Bates*, 917 F.2d 388 (9th Cir. 1990). In both cases the appellate courts concluded that the trial court had acted precipitately and had failed to solicit the parties' views on the necessity of a mistrial and the feasibility of any alternative action. The new Rule is designed to remedy that situation.

The Committee regards the Rule as a balanced and modest procedural device that could benefit both the prosecution and the defense. While the *Dixon* and *Bates* decisions adversely affected the government's interest in prosecuting serious crimes, the new Rule could also benefit defendants. The Rule ensures that a defendant has the opportunity to dissuade a judge from declaring a mistrial in a case where granting one would not be an abuse of discretion, but the defendant believes that the prospects for a favorable outcome before that particular court, or jury, are greater than they might be upon retrial.

2002 Amendments

The language of Rule 26.3 has been amended as part of the general restyling of the Criminal Rules to make them more easily understood and to make style and terminology consistent throughout the rules. These changes are intended to be stylistic only.

Rule 27. Proving an Official Record

A party may prove an official record, an entry in such a record, or the lack of a record or entry in the same manner as in a civil action.

(As amended Apr. 29, 2002, eff. Dec. 1, 2002.)

ADVISORY COMMITTEE NOTES

1944 Adoption

This rule incorporates by reference rule 44 of the Federal Rules of Civil Procedure, 28 U.S.C., Appendix, which provided a simple and uniform method of proving public records and entry or lack of entry therein. The rule does not supersede statutes regulating modes of proof in respect to specific official records. In such cases parties have the option of following the general rule or the pertinent statute. Among the many statutes are:

28 U.S.C. former:

§ 661 [now § 1733] (Copies of department or corporation records and papers; admissibility; seal)

§ 662 [now § 1733] (Same; in office of General Counsel of the Treasury)

§ 663 [now § 1733] (Instruments and papers of Comptroller of Currency; admissibility)

§ 664 [now § 1733] (Organization certificates of national banks; admissibility)

§ 665 [now § 1733] (Transcripts from books of Treasury in suits against delinquents; admissibility)

§ 666 [now § 1733] (Same; certificate by Secretary or Assistant Secretary)

§ 668 [now 18 U.S.C. § 3497] (Same; indictments for embezzlement of public moneys)

§ 669 (Copies of returns in returns office admissible)

§ 670 [now § 1743] (Admissibility of copies of statements of demands by Post Office Department)

§ 671 [now § 1733] (Admissibility of copies of post office records and statement of accounts)

§ 672 [See § 1733] (Admissibility of copies of records in General Land Office)

§ 673 [now § 1744] (Admissibility of copies of records, and so forth, of Patent Office)

§ 674 [now § 1745] (Copies of foreign letters patent as prima facie evidence)

§ 675 (Copies of specifications and drawings of patents admissible)

§ 676 [now § 1736] (Extracts from Journals of Congress admissible when injunction of secrecy removed)

§ 677 [now § 1740] (Copies of records in offices of United States consuls admissible)

§ 678 (Books and papers in certain district courts)

§ 679 (Records in clerks' offices, western district of North Carolina)

§ 680 (Records in clerks' offices of former district of California)

§ 681 [now § 1734] (Original records lost or destroyed; certified copy admissible)

§ 682 [now § 1734] (Same; when certified copy not obtainable)

§ 685 [now § 1735] (Same; certified copy of official papers)

§ 687 [now § 1738] (Authentication of legislative acts; proof of judicial proceedings of State)

§ 688 [now § 1739] (Proofs of records in offices not pertaining to courts)

§ 689 [now § 1742] (Copies of foreign records relating to land titles)

§§ 695a to 695h [now 18 U.S.C. §§ 3491 to 3496; 22 U.S.C. § 1204; § 1741] (Foreign documents)

1 U.S.C. former:

§ 30 [now § 112] (Statutes at Large; contents; admissibility in evidence)

§ 30a [now § 113] ("Little and Brown's" edition of laws and treaties competent evidence of Acts of Congress)

§ 54 [now § 204] (Codes and Supplements as establishing prima facie the Laws of United States and District of Columbia, citation of Codes and Supplements)

§ 55 [now § 209] (Copies of Supplements to Code of Laws of United States and of District of Columbia Code and Supplements; conclusive evidence of original)

5 U.S.C. former:

§ 490 [now 28 U.S.C. § 1733] (Records of Department of Interior; authenticated copies as evidence)

8 U.S.C. former:

§ 717(b) [now §§ 1435, 1482] (Former citizens of United States excepted from certain requirements; citizenship lost by spouse's alienage or loss of United States citizenship, or by entering armed forces of foreign state or acquiring its nationality)

§ 727(g) [now § 1443] (Administration of naturalization laws; rules and regulations; instruction in citizenship; forms; oaths; depositions; documents in evidence; photographic studio)

15 U.S.C. former:

§ 127 [now § 1057(e)] (Trade-marks; copies of records as evidence)

20 U.S.C.:

§ 52 (Smithsonian Institution; evidence of title to site and buildings)

25 U.S.C.:

§ 6 (Bureau of Indian Affairs; seal; authenticated and certified documents; evidence)

31 U.S.C.:

§ 46 (Laws governing General Accounting Office; copies of books, records, etc., thereof as evidence)

38 U.S.C. former:

§ 11g [now § 202] (Seal of Veterans' Administration; authentication of copies of records)

43 U.S.C.:

§ 57 (Authenticated copies or extracts from records as evidence)

§ 58 (Transcripts from records of Louisiana)

§ 59 (Official papers in office of surveyor general in California; papers; copies)

§ 83 (Transcripts of records as evidence)

44 U.S.C. former:

§ 300h [now §§ 2105, 2112] (National Archives; seal; reproduction of archives; fee; admissibility in evidence of reproductions)

§ 307 [now § 1507] (Filing document as constructive notice; publication in Register as presumption of validity; judicial notice; citation)

47 U.S.C.:

§ 412 (Documents filed with Federal Communications Commission as public records; prima facie evidence; confidential records)

49 U.S.C.:

§ 16 (Orders of Commission and enforcement thereof; forfeitures—(13) copies of schedules, tariffs, contracts, etc., kept as public records; evidence)

2002 Amendments

The language of Rule 27 has been amended as part of the general restyling of the Criminal Rules to make them more easily understood and to make style and terminology consistent throughout the rules. These changes are intended to be stylistic only.

Rule 28. Interpreters

The court may select, appoint, and set the reasonable compensation for an interpreter. The compensation must be paid from funds provided by law or by the government, as the court may direct.

(As amended Feb. 28, 1966, eff. July 1, 1966; Nov. 20, 1972; Apr. 29, 2002, eff. Dec. 1, 2002.)

ADVISORY COMMITTEE NOTES

1944 Adoption

The power of the court to call its own witnesses, though rarely invoked, is recognized in the federal courts, *Young v. United States*, C.C.A.5th, 107 F.2d 490; *Litsinger v. United States*, C.C.A.7th, 44 F.2d 45. This rule provides a procedure whereby the court may, if it chooses, exercise this power in connection with expert witnesses. The rule is based, in part, on the Uniform Expert Testimony Act, drafted by the Commissioners on Uniform State Laws. Hand Book of the National Conference of Commissioners on Uniform State Laws (1937), 337; see, also, Wigmore—Evidence, 3d Ed., § 563; A.L.I.Code of Criminal Procedure, §§ 307–309; National Commission on Law of Observance and Enforcement—Report on Criminal Procedure, 37. Similar provisions are found in the statutes of a number of States: Wisconsin—Wis.Stat. (1941), § 357.12; Indiana—Ind.Stat. Ann. (Burns, 1933), § 9–1702; California—Cal.Pen.Code (Deering, 1941), § 1027.

1966 Amendments

Subdivision (a.)—The original rule is made a separate subdivision. The amendment permits the court to inform the witness of his duties in writing since it often constitutes an unnecessary inconvenience and expense to require the witness to appear in court for such purpose.

Subdivision (b).—This new subdivision authorizes the court to appoint and provide for the compensation of interpreters. General language is used to give discretion to the court to appoint interpreters in all appropriate situations. Interpreters may be needed to interpret the testimony of non-English speaking witnesses or to assist non-English speaking defendants in understanding the proceedings or in communicating with assigned counsel. Interpreters may also be needed where a witness or a defendant is deaf.

1972 Amendments

Subdivision (a).—This subdivision is stricken, since the subject of court-appointed expert witnesses is covered in Evidence Rule 706 in detail.

Subdivision (b).—The provisions of subdivision (b) are retained. Although Evidence Rule 703 specifies the qualifications of interpreters and the form of oath to be administered to them, it does not cover their appointment or compensation.

2002 Amendments

The language of Rule 28 has been amended as part of the general restyling of the Criminal Rules to make them more easily understood and to make style and terminology consistent throughout the rules. These changes are intended to be stylistic only.

HISTORICAL NOTES

Effective and Applicability Provisions

1975 Acts. Amendment of this rule embraced by the order entered by the Supreme Court of the United States on Nov. 20, 1972, effective on the 180th day beginning after Jan. 2, 1975, [effective July 1, 1975], see § 3 of Pub.L. 93–595, Jan. 2, 1975, 88 Stat.1959, set out as a note under § 3771 of this title.

Rule 29. Motion for a Judgment of Acquittal

(a) Before Submission to the Jury. After the government closes its evidence or after the close of all the evidence, the court on the defendant's motion must enter a judgment of acquittal of any offense for which the evidence is insufficient to sustain a conviction. The court may on its own consider whether the evidence is insufficient to sustain a conviction. If the court denies a motion for a judgment of acquittal at the close of the government's evidence, the defendant may offer evidence without having reserved the right to do so.

(b) Reserving Decision. The court may reserve decision on the motion, proceed with the trial (where the motion is made before the close of all the evidence), submit the case to the jury, and decide the motion either before the jury returns a verdict or after it returns a verdict of guilty or is discharged without having returned a verdict. If the court reserves decision, it must decide the motion on the basis of the evidence at the time the ruling was reserved.

(c) After Jury Verdict or Discharge.

(1) Time for a Motion. A defendant may move for a judgment of acquittal, or renew such a motion, within 7 days after a guilty verdict or after the court discharges the jury, whichever is later.

(2) Ruling on the Motion. If the jury has returned a guilty verdict, the court may set aside the verdict and enter an acquittal. If the jury has failed to return a verdict, the court may enter a judgment of acquittal.

(3) No Prior Motion Required. A defendant is not required to move for a judgment of acquittal before the court submits the case to the jury as a prerequisite for making such a motion after jury discharge.

(d) Conditional Ruling on a Motion for a New Trial.

(1) Motion for a New Trial. If the court enters a judgment of acquittal after a guilty verdict, the court must also conditionally determine whether any motion for a new trial should be granted if the judgment of acquittal is later vacated or reversed. The court must specify the reasons for that determination.

(2) Finality. The court's order conditionally granting a motion for a new trial does not affect the finality of the judgment of acquittal.

(3) Appeal.

(A) Grant of a Motion for a New Trial. If the court conditionally grants a motion for a new trial and an appellate court later reverses the judgment of acquittal, the trial court must proceed with the new trial unless the appellate court orders otherwise.

(B) Denial of a Motion for a New Trial. If the court conditionally denies a motion for a new trial, an appellee may assert that the denial was erroneous. If the appellate court later reverses the judgment of acquittal, the trial court must proceed as the appellate court directs.

(As amended Feb. 28, 1966, eff. July 1, 1966; Nov. 10, 1986, Pub.L. 99–646, § 54(a), 100 Stat. 3607; Apr. 29, 1994, eff. Dec. 1, 1994; Apr. 29, 2002, eff. Dec. 1, 2002; Apr. 25, 2005, eff. Dec. 1, 2005.)

ADVISORY COMMITTEE NOTES

1944 Adoption

Note to Subdivision (a). 1. The purpose of changing the name of a motion for a directed verdict to a motion for judgment of acquittal is to make the nomenclature accord with the realities. The change of nomenclature, however, does not modify the nature of the motion or enlarge the scope of matters that may be considered.

2. The second sentence is patterned on New York Code of Criminal Procedure, § 410.

3. The purpose of the third sentence is to remove the doubt existing in a few jurisdictions on the question whether the defendant is deemed to have rested his case if he moves for a directed verdict at the close of the prosecution's case. The purpose of the rule is expressly to preserve the right of the defendant to offer evidence in his own behalf, if such motion is denied. This is a restatement of the prevailing practice, and is also in accord with the practice prescribed for civil cases by rule 50(a) of the Federal Rules of Civil Procedure, 28 U.S.C., Appendix.

Note to Subdivision (b). This rule is in substance similar to rule 50(b) of the Federal Rules of Civil Procedure, 28 U.S.C., Appendix, and permits the court to render judgment for the defendant notwithstanding a verdict of guilty. Some Federal courts have recognized and approved the use of a judgment non obstante veredicto for the defendant in a criminal case. *Ex parte United States*, 101 F.2d 870, C.C.A.7th, affirmed by an equally divided court, *United States v. Stone*, 60 S.Ct. 177, 308 U.S. 519, 84 L.Ed. 441. The rule sanctions this practice.

1966 Amendments

Subdivision (a). A minor change has been made in the caption.

Subdivision (b). The last three sentences are deleted with the matters formerly covered by them transferred to the new subdivision (c).

Subdivision (c). The new subdivision makes several changes in the former procedure. A motion for judgment of acquittal may be made after discharge of the jury whether or not a motion was made before submission to the jury. No legitimate interest of the government is intended to be prejudiced by permitting the court to direct an acquittal on a post-verdict motion. The constitutional requirement of a jury trial in criminal cases is primarily a right accorded to the defendant. Cf. *Adams v. United States, ex rel. McCann*, 317 U.S. 269 (1942); *Singer v. United States*, 380 U.S. 24 (1965); Note, 65 Yale L.J. 1032 (1956).

The time in which the motion may be made has been changed to 7 days in accordance with the amendment to Rule 45(a) which by excluding Saturday from the days to be counted when the period of time is less than 7 days would make 7 days the normal time for a motion required to be made in 5 days. Also the court is authorized to extend the time as is provided for motions for new trial (Rule 33) and in arrest of judgment (Rule 34).

References in the original rule to the motion for a new trial as an alternate to the motion for judgment of acquittal and to the power of the court to order a new trial have been eliminated. Motions for new trial are adequately covered in Rule 33. Also the original wording is subject to the interpretation that a motion for judgment of acquittal gives the court power to order a new trial even though the defendant does not wish a new trial and has not asked for one.

1994 Amendments

The amendment permits the reservation of a motion for a judgment of acquittal made at the close of the government's case in the same manner as the rule now permits for motions made at the close of all of the evidence. Although the rule as written did not permit the court to reserve such motions made at the end of the government's case, trial courts on occasion have nonetheless reserved ruling. *See, e.g., United States v. Bruno*, 873 F.2d 555 (2d Cir.), cert. denied, 110 S.Ct. 125 (1989); *United States v. Reifsteck*, 841 F.2d 701 (6th Cir. 1988). While the amendment will not affect a large number of cases, it should remove the dilemma in those close cases in which the court would feel pressured into making an immediate, and possibly erroneous, decision or violating the rule as presently written by reserving its ruling on the motion.

The amendment also permits the trial court to balance the defendant's interest in an immediate resolution of the motion against the interest of the government in proceeding to a verdict thereby preserving its right to appeal in the event a verdict of guilty is returned but is then set aside by the granting of a judgment of acquittal. Under the double jeopardy clause the government may appeal the granting of a motion for judgment of acquittal only if there would be no necessity for another trial, i.e., only where the jury has returned a verdict of guilty. *United States v. Martin Linen Supply Co.*, 430 U.S. 564 (1977). Thus, the government's right to appeal a Rule 29 motion is only preserved where the ruling is reserved until after the verdict.

In addressing the issue of preserving the government's right to appeal and at the same time recognizing double jeopardy concerns, the Supreme Court observed:

We should point out that it is entirely possible for a trial court to reconcile the public interest in the Government's right to appeal from an erroneous conclusion of law with the defendant's interest in avoiding a second prosecution. In *United States v. Wilson*, 420 U.S. 332 (1975), the court permitted the case to go to the jury, which returned a verdict of guilty, but it subsequently dismissed the indictment for preindictment delay on the basis of evidence adduced at trial. Most recently in *United States v. Ceccolini*, 435 U.S. 268 (1978), we described similar action with approval: 'The District Court had sensibly made its finding on the factual question of guilt or innocence, and then ruled on the motion to suppress; a reversal of these rulings would require no further proceeding in the District Court, but merely a reinstatement of the finding of guilt.' Id. at 271.

United States v. Scott, 437 U.S. 82, 100 n. 13 (1978). By analogy, reserving a ruling on a motion for judgment of acquittal strikes the same balance as that reflected by the Supreme Court in *Scott*.

Reserving a ruling on a motion made at the end of the government's case does pose problems, however, where the defense decides to present evidence and run the risk that such evidence will support the government's case. To address that problem, the amendment provides that the trial court is to consider only the evidence submitted at the time of the motion in making its ruling, whenever made. And in reviewing a trial court's ruling, the appellate court would be similarly limited.

2002 Amendments

The language of Rule 29 has been amended as part of the general restyling of the Criminal Rules to make them more easily understood and to make style and terminology consistent throughout the rules. These changes are intended to be stylistic only, except as noted below.

In Rule 29(a), the first sentence abolishing "directed verdicts" has been deleted because it is unnecessary. The rule continues to recognize that a judge may sua sponte enter a judgment of acquittal.

Rule 29(c)(1) addresses the issue of the timing of a motion for judgment of acquittal. The amended rule now includes language that the motion must be made within 7 days after a guilty verdict or after the judge discharges the jury, whichever occurs later. That change reflects the fact that in a capital case or in a case involving criminal forfeiture, for example, the jury may not be discharged until it has completed its sentencing duties. The court may still set another time for the defendant to make or renew the motion, if it does so within the 7–day period.

2005 Amendments

Rule 29(c) has been amended to remove the requirement that the court must act within seven days after a guilty verdict or after the court discharges the jury, if it sets another time for filing a motion for a judgment of acquittal. This amendment parallels similar changes to Rules 33 and 34. Further, a conforming amendment has been made to Rule 45(b)(2).

Currently, Rule 29(c) requires the defendant to move for a judgment of acquittal within seven days of the guilty verdict, or after the court discharges the jury, whichever occurs later, or some other time set by the court in an order issued within that same seven-day period. Similar provisions exist in Rules 33 and 34. Courts have held that the seven-day rule is jurisdictional. Thus, if a defendant files a request for an extension of time to file a motion for a judgment of acquittal within the seven-day period, the court must rule on that motion or request within the same seven-day period. If for some reason the court does not rule on the request within the seven days, it loses jurisdiction to act on the underlying substantive motion. *See, e.g., United States v. Smith*, 331 U.S. 469, 473–474 (1947) (rejecting argument that trial court had power to grant new trial on its own motion after expiration of time in Rule 33); *United States v. Marquez*, 291 F.3d 23, 27–28 (D.C. Cir. 2002) (citing language of Rule 33, and holding that "district court forfeited the power to act when it failed to . . . fix a new time for filing a motion for a new trial within seven days of the verdict").

Assuming that the current rule was intended to promote finality, there is nothing to prevent the court from granting a significant extension of time, so long as it does so within the seven-day period. Thus, the Committee believed that the rule should be amended to be consistent with all of the other timing requirements in the rules, which do not force the court to act on a motion to extend the time for filing within a particular period of time or lose jurisdiction to do so.

Accordingly, the amendment deletes the language regarding the court's acting within seven days to set the time for filing. Read in conjunction with the conforming amendment to Rule 45(b), the defendant is still required to file a timely motion for a judgment of acquittal under Rule 29 within the seven-day period specified. The defendant may, under Rule 45, seek an extension of time to file the underlying motion as long as the defendant does so within the seven-day period. But the court itself is not required to act on that motion within any particular time. Further, under Rule 45(b)(1)(B), if for some reason the defendant fails to file the underlying motion within the specified time, the court may nonetheless consider that untimely motion if the court determines that the failure to file it on time was the result of excusable neglect.

HISTORICAL NOTES

Effective and Applicability Provisions

1986 Acts. Section 54(b) of Pub.L. 99–646 provided that: "The amendments made by this section [enacting subd. (d)] shall take effect 30 days after the date of the enactment of this Act [Nov. 10, 1986]."

Rule 29.1. Closing Argument

Closing arguments proceed in the following order:

(a) the government argues;

(b) the defense argues; and

(c) the government rebuts.

(Added Apr. 22, 1974, eff. Dec. 1, 1975, and amended Apr. 29, 2002, eff. Dec. 1, 2002.)

ADVISORY COMMITTEE NOTES

1974 Addition

This rule is designed to control the order of closing argument. It reflects the Advisory Committee's view that it is desirable to have a uniform federal practice. The rule is drafted in the view that fair and effective administration of justice is best served if the defendant knows the arguments actually made by the prosecution in behalf of conviction before the defendant is faced with the decision whether to reply and what to reply.

1975 Enactment

A. Amendments Proposed by the Supreme Court. Rule 29.1 is a new rule that was added to regulate closing arguments. It prescribes that the government shall make its closing argument and then the defendant shall make his. After the defendant has argued, the government is entitled to reply in rebuttal.

B. Committee Action. The Committee endorses and adopts this proposed rule in its entirety. The Committee believes that as the Advisory Committee Note has stated, fair and effective administration of justice is best served if the defendant knows the arguments actually made by the prosecution in behalf of conviction before the defendant is faced with the decision whether to reply and what to reply. Rule 29.1 does not specifically address itself to what happens if the prosecution waives its initial closing argument. The Committee is of the view that the prosecutor, when he waives his initial closing argument, also waives his rebuttal. [See the remarks of Senior United States Circuit Judge J. Edward Lumbard in Hearings II, at 207.] House Report No. 94–247.

2002 Amendments

The language of Rule 29.1 has been amended as part of the general restyling of the Criminal Rules to make them more easily understood and to make style and terminology consistent throughout the rules. These changes are intended to be stylistic only.

HISTORICAL NOTES

Effective and Applicability Provisions

1975 Acts. This rule effective Dec. 1, 1975, see § 2 of Pub.L. 94–64, set out as a note under rule 4 of these rules.

Rule 30. Jury Instructions

(a) In General. Any party may request in writing that the court instruct the jury on the law as specified in the request. The request must be made at the close of the evidence or at any earlier time that the court reasonably sets. When the request is made, the requesting party must furnish a copy to every other party.

(b) Ruling on a Request. The court must inform the parties before closing arguments how it intends to rule on the requested instructions.

(c) Time for Giving Instructions. The court may instruct the jury before or after the arguments are completed, or at both times.

(d) Objections to Instructions. A party who objects to any portion of the instructions or to a failure to give a requested instruction must inform the court of the specific objection and the grounds for the objection before the jury retires to deliberate. An opportunity must be given to object out of the jury's hearing and, on request, out of the jury's presence. Failure to object in accordance with this rule precludes appellate review, except as permitted under Rule 52(b).

(As amended Feb. 28, 1966, eff. July 1, 1966; Mar. 9, 1987, eff. Aug. 1, 1987; Apr. 25, 1988, eff. Aug. 1, 1988; Apr. 29, 2002, eff. Dec. 1, 2002.)

ADVISORY COMMITTEE NOTES

1944 Adoption

This rule corresponds to rule 51 of the Federal Rules of Civil Procedure, the second sentence alone being new. It seemed appropriate that on a point such as instructions to juries there should be no difference in procedure between civil and criminal cases.

1966 Amendments

The amendment requires the court, on request of any party, to require the jury to withdraw in order to permit full argument of objections to instructions.

1987 Amendments

In its current form, Rule 30 requires that the court instruct the jury after the arguments of counsel. In some districts, usually where the state practice is otherwise, the parties prefer to stipulate to instruction before closing arguments. The purpose of the amendment is to give the court discretion to instruct the jury before or after closing arguments, or at both times. The amendment will permit courts to continue instructing the jury after arguments as Rule 30 had previously required. It will also permit courts to instruct before arguments in order to give the parties an opportunity to argue to the jury in light of the exact language used by the court. See generally Raymond, *Merits and Demerits of the Missouri System in Instructing Juries*, 5 St. Louis U.L.J. 317 (1959). Finally, the amendment plainly indicates that the court may instruct both before and after arguments, which assures that the court retains power to remedy omissions in pre-argument instructions or to add instructions necessitated by the arguments.

1988 Amendments

The amendment is technical. No substantive change is intended.

2002 Amendments

The language of Rule 30 has been amended as part of the general restyling of the Criminal Rules to make them more easily understood and to make style and terminology consistent throughout the rules. These changes are intended to be stylistic only, except as noted below.

Rule 30(a) reflects a change in the timing of requests for instructions. As currently written, the trial court may not direct the parties to file such requests before trial without violating Rules 30 and 57. While the amendment falls short of requiring all requests to be made before trial in all cases, the amendment permits a court to do so in a particular case or as a matter of local practice under local rules promulgated under Rule 57. The rule does not preclude the practice of permitting the parties to supplement their requested instructions during the trial.

Rule 30(d) clarifies what, if anything, counsel must do to preserve a claim of error regarding an instruction or failure to instruct. The rule retains the requirement of a contemporaneous and specific objection (before the jury retires to deliberate). As the Supreme Court recognized in *Jones v. United States*, 527 U.S. 373 (1999), read literally, current Rule 30 could be construed to bar any appellate review absent a timely objection when in fact a court may conduct a limited review under a plain error standard. The amendment does not address the issue of whether objections to the instructions must be renewed after the instructions are given, in order to preserve a claim of error. No change in practice is intended by the amendment.

HISTORICAL NOTES

Effective and Applicability Provisions

1988 Acts. The Order of the Supreme Court dated April 25, 1988, provided in part: "That the foregoing amendments to the Federal Rules of Criminal Procedure [this rule and rule 56] shall take effect on August 1, 1988 and shall govern all proceedings in criminal cases thereafter commenced and, insofar as just and practicable, all proceedings in criminal cases then pending." See order preceding rule 1.

Rule 31. Jury Verdict

(a) Return. The jury must return its verdict to a judge in open court. The verdict must be unanimous.

(b) Partial Verdicts, Mistrial, and Retrial.

(1) Multiple Defendants. If there are multiple defendants, the jury may return a verdict at any time during its deliberations as to any defendant about whom it has agreed.

(2) Multiple Counts. If the jury cannot agree on all counts as to any defendant, the jury may return a verdict on those counts on which it has agreed.

(3) Mistrial and Retrial. If the jury cannot agree on a verdict on one or more counts, the court may declare a mistrial on those counts. The government may retry any defendant on any count on which the jury could not agree.

(c) Lesser Offense or Attempt. A defendant may be found guilty of any of the following:

(1) an offense necessarily included in the offense charged;

(2) an attempt to commit the offense charged; or

(3) an attempt to commit an offense necessarily included in the offense charged, if the attempt is an offense in its own right.

(d) Jury Poll. After a verdict is returned but before the jury is discharged, the court must on a party's request, or may on its own, poll the jurors individually. If the poll reveals a lack of unanimity, the court may direct the jury to deliberate further or may declare a mistrial and discharge the jury.

(As amended Apr. 24, 1972, eff. Oct. 1, 1972; Apr. 24, 1998, eff. Dec. 1, 1998; Apr. 17, 2000, eff. Dec. 1, 2000; Apr. 29, 2002, eff. Dec. 1, 2002.)

ADVISORY COMMITTEE NOTES

1944 Adoption

Note to Subdivision (a). This rule is a restatement of existing law and practice. It does not embody any regulation of sealed verdicts, it being contemplated that this matter would be governed by local practice in the various district courts. The rule does not affect the existing statutes relating to qualified verdicts in cases in which capital punishment may be imposed. 18 U.S.C. former § 408a [now § 1201] (Kidnapped persons); 18 U.S.C. former § 412a [now § 1992] (Wrecking trains); 18 U.S.C. former § 567 [now § 1111] (Verdicts; qualified verdicts).

Note to Subdivision (b). This rule is a restatement of existing law, 18 U.S.C. former § 566 (Verdicts; several joint defendants.

Note to Subdivision (c). This rule is a restatement of existing law, 18 U.S.C. former § 565 (Verdicts; less offense than charged).

Note to Subdivision (d). This rule is a restatement of existing law and practice, *Mackett v. United States*, 90 F.2d 462, 465, C.C.A.7th; *Bruce v. Chestnut Farms Chevy Chase Dairy*, 126 F.2d 224, App.D.C.

1972 Amendments

Subdivision (e) is new. It is intended to provide procedural implementation of the recently enacted criminal forfeiture provision of the Organized Crime Control Act of 1970, Title IX, § 1963, and the Comprehensive Drug Abuse Prevention and Control Act of 1970, Title II, § 408(a)(2).

The assumption of the draft is that the amount of the interest or property subject to criminal forfeiture is an element of the offense to be alleged and proved. See Advisory Committee Note to rule 7(c)(2).

Although special verdict provisions are rare in criminal cases, they are not unknown. See *United States v. Spock*, 416 F.2d 165 (1st Cir. 1969), especially footnote 41 where authorities are listed.

1998 Amendments

The right of a party to have the jury polled is an "undoubted right." *Humphries v. District of Columbia*, 174 U.S. 190, 194 (1899). Its purpose is to determine with certainty that "each of the jurors approves of the verdict as returned; that no one has been coerced or induced to sign a verdict to which he does not fully assent." *Id.*

Currently, Rule 31(d) is silent on the precise method of polling the jury. Thus, a court in its discretion may conduct the poll collectively or individually. As one court has noted, although the prevailing view is that the method used is a matter within the discretion of the trial court, *United States v. Miller*, 59 F.3d 417, 420 (3rd Cir. 1995)(citing cases), the preference, nonetheless of the appellate and trial courts, seems to favor individual polling. *Id.* (citing cases). That is the position taken in the American Bar Association Standards for Criminal Justice § 15–4.5. Those sources favoring individual polling observe that conducting a poll of the jurors collectively saves little time and does not always adequately insure that an individual juror who has been forced to join the majority during deliberations will voice dissent from a collective response. On the other hand, an advantage to individual polling is the "likelihood that it will discourage post–trial efforts to challenge the verdict on allegations of coercion on the part of some of the jurors." *Miller, Id.* at 420 (citing *Audette v. Isaksen Fishing Corp.*, 789 F.2d 956, 961, n. 6 (1st Cir. 1986)).

The Committee is persuaded by the authorities and practice that there are advantages of conducting an individual poll of the jurors. Thus, the rule requires that the jurors be polled individually when a polling is requested, or when polling is directed sua sponte by the court. The amendment, however, leaves to the court the discretion as to whether to conduct a separate poll for each defendant, each count of the indictment or complaint, or on other issues.

2000 Amendments

The rule is amended to reflect the creation of new Rule 32.2, which now governs criminal forfeiture procedures.

GAP Report—Rule 31

The Committee made no changes to the published draft amendment to Rule 31.

2002 Amendments

The language of Rule 31 has been amended as part of the general restyling of the Criminal Rules to make them more easily understood and to make style and terminology consistent throughout the rules. These changes are intended to be stylistic only.

Rule 31(b) has been amended to clarify that a jury may return partial verdicts, either as to multiple defendants or multiple counts, or both. *See, e.g., United States v. Cunningham*, 145 F.3d 1385, 1388–90 (D.C. Cir. 1998) (partial verdicts on multiple defendants and counts). No change in practice is intended.

VII. POST-CONVICTION PROCEDURES

Rule 32. Sentencing and Judgment

(a) Definitions. The following definitions apply under this rule:

(1) "Crime of violence or sexual abuse" means:

(A) a crime that involves the use, attempted use, or threatened use of physical force against another's person or property; or

(B) a crime under 18 U.S.C. §§ 2241–2248 or §§ 2251–2257.

(2) "Victim" means an individual against whom the defendant committed an offense for which the court will impose sentence.

(b) Time of Sentencing.

(1) In General. The court must impose sentence without unnecessary delay.

(2) Changing Time Limits. The court may, for good cause, change any time limits prescribed in this rule.

(c) Presentence Investigation.

(1) Required Investigation.

(A) In General. The probation officer must conduct a presentence investigation and submit a report to the court before it imposes sentence unless:

(i) 18 U.S.C. § 3593(c) or another statute requires otherwise; or

(ii) the court finds that the information in the record enables it to meaningfully exercise its sentencing authority under 18 U.S.C. § 3553, and the court explains its finding on the record.

(B) Restitution. If the law requires restitution, the probation officer must conduct an investigation and submit a report that contains sufficient information for the court to order restitution.

(2) Interviewing the Defendant. The probation officer who interviews a defendant as part of a presentence investigation must, on request, give the defendant's attorney notice and a reasonable opportunity to attend the interview.

(d) Presentence Report.

(1) Applying the Sentencing Guidelines. The presentence report must:

(A) identify all applicable guidelines and policy statements of the Sentencing Commission;

(B) calculate the defendant's offense level and criminal history category;

(C) state the resulting sentencing range and kinds of sentences available;

(D) identify any factor relevant to:

(i) the appropriate kind of sentence, or

(ii) the appropriate sentence within the applicable sentencing range; and

(E) identify any basis for departing from the applicable sentencing range.

(2) Additional Information. The presentence report must also contain the following information:

(A) the defendant's history and characteristics, including:

(i) any prior criminal record;

(ii) the defendant's financial condition; and

(iii) any circumstances affecting the defendant's behavior that may be helpful in imposing sentence or in correctional treatment;

(B) verified information, stated in a nonargumentative style, that assesses the financial, social, psychological, and medical impact on any individual against whom the offense has been committed;

(C) when appropriate, the nature and extent of nonprison programs and resources available to the defendant;

(D) when the law provides for restitution, information sufficient for a restitution order;

(E) if the court orders a study under 18 U.S.C. § 3552(b), any resulting report and recommendation; and

(F) any other information that the court requires.

(3) Exclusions. The presentence report must exclude the following:

(A) any diagnoses that, if disclosed, might seriously disrupt a rehabilitation program;

(B) any sources of information obtained upon a promise of confidentiality; and

(C) any other information that, if disclosed, might result in physical or other harm to the defendant or others.

(e) Disclosing the Report and Recommendation.

(1) Time to Disclose. Unless the defendant has consented in writing, the probation officer must not submit a presentence report to the court or disclose its contents to anyone until the defendant has pleaded guilty or nolo contendere, or has been found guilty.

(2) Minimum Required Notice. The probation officer must give the presentence report to the defendant, the defendant's attorney, and an attorney for the government at least 35 days before sentencing unless the defendant waives this minimum period.

(3) Sentence Recommendation. By local rule or by order in a case, the court may direct the probation officer not to disclose to anyone other than the court the officer's recommendation on the sentence.

(f) Objecting to the Report.

(1) Time to Object. Within 14 days after receiving the presentence report, the parties must state in writing any objections, including objections to material information, sentencing guideline ranges, and policy statements contained in or omitted from the report.

(2) Serving Objections. An objecting party must provide a copy of its objections to the opposing party and to the probation officer.

(3) Action on Objections. After receiving objections, the probation officer may meet with the parties to discuss the objections. The probation officer may then investigate further and revise the presentence report as appropriate.

(g) Submitting the Report. At least 7 days before sentencing, the probation officer must submit to the court and to the parties the presentence report and an addendum containing any unresolved objections, the grounds for those objections, and the probation officer's comments on them.

(h) Notice of Possible Departure from Sentencing Guidelines. Before the court may depart from the applicable sentencing range on a ground not identified for departure either in the presentence report or in a party's prehearing submission, the court must give the parties reasonable notice that it is contemplating such a departure. The notice must specify any ground on which the court is contemplating a departure.

(i) Sentencing.

(1) In General. At sentencing, the court:

(A) must verify that the defendant and the defendant's attorney have read and discussed the presentence report and any addendum to the report;

(B) must give to the defendant and an attorney for the government a written summary of—or summarize in camera—any information excluded from the presentence report under Rule 32(d)(3) on which the court will rely in sentencing, and give them a reasonable opportunity to comment on that information;

(C) must allow the parties' attorneys to comment on the probation officer's determinations and other matters relating to an appropriate sentence; and

(D) may, for good cause, allow a party to make a new objection at any time before sentence is imposed.

(2) Introducing Evidence; Producing a Statement. The court may permit the parties to introduce evidence on the objections. If a witness testifies at sentencing, Rule 26.2(a)–(d) and (f) applies. If a party fails to comply with a Rule 26.2 order to produce a witness's statement, the court must not consider that witness's testimony.

(3) Court Determinations. At sentencing, the court:

(A) may accept any undisputed portion of the presentence report as a finding of fact;

(B) must—for any disputed portion of the presentence report or other controverted matter—rule on the dispute or determine that a ruling is unnecessary either because the matter will not affect sentencing, or because the court will not consider the matter in sentencing; and

(C) must append a copy of the court's determinations under this rule to any copy of the presentence report made available to the Bureau of Prisons.

(4) Opportunity to Speak.

(A) By a Party. Before imposing sentence, the court must:

(i) provide the defendant's attorney an opportunity to speak on the defendant's behalf;

(ii) address the defendant personally in order to permit the defendant to speak or present any information to mitigate the sentence; and

(iii) provide an attorney for the government an opportunity to speak equivalent to that of the defendant's attorney.

(B) By a Victim. Before imposing sentence, the court must address any victim of a crime of violence or sexual abuse who is present at sentencing and must permit the victim to speak or submit any information about the sentence.

Whether or not the victim is present, a victim's right to address the court may be exercised by the following persons if present:

(i) a parent or legal guardian, if the victim is younger than 18 years or is incompetent; or

(ii) one or more family members or relatives the court designates, if the victim is deceased or incapacitated.

(C) In Camera Proceedings. Upon a party's motion and for good cause, the court may hear in camera any statement made under Rule 32(i)(4).

(j) Defendant's Right to Appeal.

(1) Advice of a Right to Appeal.

(A) Appealing a Conviction. If the defendant pleaded not guilty and was convicted, after sentencing the court must advise the defendant of the right to appeal the conviction.

(B) Appealing a Sentence. After sentencing—regardless of the defendant's plea—the court must advise the defendant of any right to appeal the sentence.

(C) Appeal Costs. The court must advise a defendant who is unable to pay appeal costs of the right to ask for permission to appeal in forma pauperis.

(2) Clerk's Filing of Notice. If the defendant so requests, the clerk must immediately prepare and file a notice of appeal on the defendant's behalf.

(k) Judgment.

(1) In General. In the judgment of conviction, the court must set forth the plea, the jury verdict or the court's findings, the adjudication, and the sentence. If the defendant is found not guilty or is otherwise entitled to be discharged, the court must so order. The judge must sign the judgment, and the clerk must enter it.

(2) Criminal Forfeiture. Forfeiture procedures are governed by Rule 32.2.

(As amended Feb. 28, 1966, eff. July 1, 1966; Apr. 24, 1972, eff. Oct. 1, 1972; Apr. 22, 1974, eff. Dec. 1, 1975; July 31, 1975, Pub.L. 94–64, § 3(31)–(34), 89 Stat. 376; Apr. 30, 1979, eff. Aug. 1, 1979, Dec. 1, 1980; Oct. 12, 1982, Pub.L. 97–291, § 3, 96 Stat. 1249; Apr. 28, 1983, eff. Aug. 1, 1983; Oct. 12, 1984, Pub.L. 98–473, Title II, § 215(a), 98 Stat. 2014; Nov. 10, 1986, Pub.L. 99–646, § 25(a), 100 Stat. 3597; Mar. 9, 1987, eff. Aug. 1, 1987; Apr. 25, 1989, eff. Dec. 1, 1989; Apr. 30, 1991, eff. Dec. 1, 1991; Apr. 22, 1993, eff. Dec. 1, 1993; Apr. 29, 1994, eff. Dec. 1, 1994; Sept. 13, 1994, Pub.L. 103–322, Title XXIII, § 230101(b), 108 Stat. 2078; Apr. 23, 1996, eff. Dec. 1, 1996; Apr. 24, 1996, Pub.L. 104–132, Title II, § 207(a), 110 Stat. 1236; Apr. 17, 2000, eff. Dec. 1, 2000; Apr. 29, 2002, eff. Dec. 1, 2002.)

Rule Applicable to Offenses Committed Prior to Nov. 1, 1987

This rule as in effect prior to amendment by Pub.L. 98–473 read as follows:

"Rule 32. Sentence and Judgment

"(a) Sentence.

"(1) Imposition of Sentence. Sentence shall be imposed without unreasonable delay. Before imposing sentence the court shall

"(A) determine that the defendant and the defendant's counsel have had the opportunity to read and discuss the presentence investigation report made available pursuant to subdivision (c)(3)(A) or summary thereof made available pursuant to subdivision (c)(3)(B);

"(B) afford counsel an opportunity to speak on behalf of the defendant; and

"(C) address the defendant personally and ask the defendant if the defendant wishes to make a statement in the defendant's own behalf and to present any information in mitigation of punishment.

The attorney for the government shall have an equivalent opportunity to speak to the court.

"(2) Notification of Right to Appeal. After imposing sentence in a case which has gone to trial on a plea of not guilty, the court shall advise the defendant of the defendant's right to appeal, and of the right of a person who is unable to pay the cost of an appeal to apply for leave to appeal in forma pauperis. There shall be no duty on the court to advise the defendant of any right of appeal after sentence is imposed following a plea of guilty or nolo contendere. If the defendant so requests, the clerk of the court shall prepare and file forthwith a notice of appeal on behalf of the defendant.

"(b) Judgment.

"(1) In General. A judgment of conviction shall set forth the plea, the verdict or findings, and the adjudication and sentence. If the defendant is found not guilty or for any other reason is entitled to be discharged, judgment shall be entered accordingly. The judgment shall be signed by the judge and entered by the clerk.

"(2) Criminal Forfeiture. When a verdict contains a finding of property subject to a criminal forfeiture, the judgment of criminal forfeiture shall authorize the Attorney General to seize the interest or property subject to forfeiture, fixing such terms and conditions as the court shall deem proper.

"(c) Presentence Investigation.

"(1) When Made. The probation service of the court shall make a presentence investigation and report to the court before the imposition of sentence or the granting of probation unless, with the permission of the court, the defendant waives a presentence investigation and report, or the court finds that there is in the record information sufficient to enable the meaningful exercise of sentencing discretion, and the court explains this finding on the record.

"The report shall not be submitted to the court or its contents disclosed to anyone unless the defendant has pleaded guilty or nolo contendere or has been found guilty, except that a judge may, with the written consent of the defendant, inspect a presentence report at any time.

"(2) Report. The presentence report shall contain—

"(A) any prior criminal record of the defendant;

"(B) a statement of the circumstances of the commission of the offense and circumstances affecting the defendant's behavior;

"(C) information concerning any harm, including financial, social, psychological, and physical harm, done to or loss suffered by any victim of the offense; and

"(D) any other information that may aid the court in sentencing, including the restitution needs of any victim of the offense.

"(3) Disclosure.

"(A) At a reasonable time before imposing sentence the court shall permit the defendant and the defendant's counsel to read the report of the presentence investigation exclusive of any recommendation as to sentence, but not to the extent that in the opinion of the court the report contains diagnostic opinions which, if disclosed, might seriously disrupt a program of rehabilitation; or sources of information obtained upon a promise of confidentiality; or any other information which, if disclosed, might result in harm, physical or otherwise, to the defendant or other persons. The court shall afford the defendant and the defendant's counsel an opportunity to comment on the report and, in the discretion of the court, to introduce testimony or other information relating to any alleged factual inaccuracy contained in it.

"(B) If the court is of the view that there is information in the presentence report which should not be disclosed under subdivision (c)(3)(A) of this rule, the court in lieu of making the report or part thereof available shall state orally or in writing a summary of the factual information contained therein to be relied on in determining sentence, and shall give the defendant and the defendant's counsel an opportunity to comment thereon. The statement may be made to the parties in camera.

"(C) Any material which may be disclosed to the defendant and the defendant's counsel shall be disclosed to the attorney for the government.

"(D) If the comments of the defendant and the defendant's counsel or testimony or other information introduced by them allege any factual inaccuracy in the presentence investigation report or the summary of the report or part thereof, the court shall, as to each matter controverted, make (i) a finding as to the allegation, or (ii) a determination that no such finding is necessary because the matter controverted will not be taken into account in sentencing. A written record of such findings and determinations shall be appended to and accompany any copy of the presentence investigation report thereafter made available to the Bureau of Prisons or the Parole Commission.

"(E) Any copies of the presentence investigation report made available to the defendant and the defendant's counsel and the attorney for the government shall be returned to the probation officer immediately following the imposition of sentence or the granting of probation, unless the court, in its discretion otherwise directs.

"(F) The reports of studies and recommendations contained therein made by the Director of the Bureau of Prisons or the Parole Commission pursuant to 18 U.S.C. §§ 4205(c), 4252, 5010(e), or 5037(c) shall be considered a presentence investigation within the meaning of subdivision (c)(3) of this rule.

"(d) Plea Withdrawal. If a motion for withdrawal of a plea of guilty or nolo contendere is made before sentence is imposed, imposition of sentence is suspended, or disposition is had under 18 U.S.C. § 4205(c), the court may permit withdrawal of the plea upon a showing by the defendant of any fair and just reason. At any later time, a plea may be set aside only on direct appeal or by motion under 28 U.S.C. § 2255.

"(e) Probation. After conviction of an offense not punishable by death or by life imprisonment, the defendant may be placed on probation if permitted by law.

"(f) [Revocation of Probation.] (Abrogated Apr. 30, 1979, eff. Dec. 1, 1980)."

For applicability of sentencing provisions to offenses, see Effective Date and Savings Provisions, etc., note, section 235 of Pub.L. 98–473, as amended, set out under section 3551 of Title 18, Crimes and Criminal Procedure.

ADVISORY COMMITTEE NOTES

1944 Adoption

Note to Subdivision (a). This rule is substantially a restatement of existing procedure. Rule I of the Criminal Appeals Rules of 1933, 292 U.S. 661 [18 U.S.C. formerly following § 688]. See Rule 43 relating to the presence of the defendant.

Note to Subdivision (b). This rule is substantially a restatement of existing procedure. Rule I of the Criminal Appeals Rules of 1933, 292 U.S. 661 [18 U.S.C. formerly following § 688].

Note to Subdivision (c). The purpose of this provision is to encourage and broaden the use of presentence investigations, which are nor being utilized to good advantage in many cases. See, "The Presentence Investigation" published by Administrative Office of the United States Courts, Division of Probation.

Note to Subdivision (d). This rule modifies existing practice by abrogating the ten-day limitation on a motion for leave to withdraw a plea of guilty. See rule II(4) of the Criminal Appeals Rules of 1933, 292 U.S. 661 [18 U.S.C. formerly following § 688].

Note to Subdivision (e). See 18 U.S.C. former § 724 et seq. [now § 3651 et seq.].

1966 Amendments

Subdivision (a)(1).—The amendment writes into the rule the holding of the Supreme Court that the court before imposing sentence must afford an opportunity to the defendant personally to speak in his own behalf. See *Green v. United States,* 365 U.S. 301 (1961); *Hill v. United States,* 368 U.S. 424 (1962). The amendment also provides an opportunity for counsel to speak on behalf of the defendant.

Subdivision (a)(2).—This amendment is a substantial revision and a relocation of the provision originally found in Rule 37(a)(2): "When a court after trial imposes sentence upon a defendant not represented by counsel, the defendant shall be advised of his right to appeal and if he so requests, the clerk shall prepare and file forthwith a notice of appeal on behalf of the defendant." The court is required to advise the defendant of his right to appeal in all cases which have gone to trial after plea of not guilty because situations arise in which a defendant represented by counsel at the trial is not adequately advised by such counsel of his right to appeal. Trial counsel may not regard his responsibility as extending beyond the time of imposition of sentence. The defendant may be removed from the courtroom immediately upon sentence and held in custody under circumstances which make it difficult for counsel to advise him. See, e.g., *Hodges v. United States,* 368 U.S. 139 (1961). Because indigent defendants are most likely to be without effective assistance of counsel at this point in the proceedings, it is also provided that defendants be notified of the right of a person without funds to apply for leave to appeal in forma pauperis. The provision is added here because this rule seems the most appropriate place to set forth a procedure to be followed by the court at the time of sentencing.

Subdivision (c)(2).—It is not a denial of due process of law for a court in sentencing to rely on a report of a presentence investigation without disclosing such report to the defendant or giving him an opportunity to rebut it. *Williams v. New York,* 337 U.S. 241 (1949); *Williams v. Oklahoma,* 358 U.S. 576 (1959). However, the question whether as a matter of policy the defendant should be accorded some opportunity to see and refute allegations made in such reports has been the subject of heated controversy. For arguments favoring disclosure, see Tappan, Crime, Justice, and Correction, 558 (1960); Model Penal Code, 54–55 (Tent. Draft No. 2, 1954); Thomsen, Confidentiality of the Presentence Report: A Middle Position, 28 Fed.Prob., March 1964, p. 8; Wyzanski, A. Trial Judge's Freedom and Responsibility, 65 Harv.L.Rev. 1281, 1291–2 (1952); Note, Employment of Social Investigation Reports in Criminal and Juvenile Proceedings, 58 Colum.L.Rev. 702 (1958); cf. Kadish, The Advocate and the Expert: Counsel in the Peno-Correctional Process, 45 Minn.L.Rev. 803, 806, (1961). For arguments opposing disclosure, see Barnett and Gronewold, Confidentiality of the Presentence Report, 26 Fed.Prob. March 1962, p. 26; Judicial Conference Committee on Administration of the Probation System, Judicial Opinion on Proposed Change in Rule 32(c) of the Federal Rules of Criminal Procedure—a Survey (1964); Keve, The Probation Officer Investigates, 6–15 (1960); Parsons, The Presentence Investigation Report Must be Preserved as a Confidential Document, 28 Fed.Prob. March 1964, p. 3; Sharp, The Confidential Nature of Presentence Reports, 5 Cath. U.L.Rev. 127 (1955); Wilson, A New Arena is Emerging to Test the Confidentiality of Presentence Reports, 25 Fed. Prob.Dec.1961, p. 6; Federal Judge's Views on Probation Practices, 24 Fed.Prob. March 1960, p. 10.

In a few jurisdictions the defendant is given a right of access to the presentence report. In England and California a copy of the report is given to the defendant in every case. English Criminal Justice Act of 1948, 11 & 12 Geo. 6, c. 58, § 43; Cal.Pen.C. § 1203. In Alabama the defendant has a right to inspect the report. Ala.Code, Title 42, § 23. In Ohio and Virginia the probation officer reports in open court and the defendant is given the right to examine him on his report. Ohio Rev.Code, § 2947.06; Va.Code, § 53–278.1. The Minnesota Criminal Code of 1963, § 609.115(4), provides that any presentence report "shall be open for inspection by the prosecuting attorney and the defendant's attorney prior to sentence and on the request of either of them a summary hearing in chambers shall be held on any matter brought in issue, but confidential sources of information shall not be disclosed unless the court otherwise directs." Cf. Model Penal Code § 7.07(5) (P.O.D. 1962): "Before imposing sentence, the Court shall advise the defendant or his counsel of the factual contents and the conclusions of any presentence investigation or psychiatric examination and afford fair opportunity, if the defendant so requests, to controvert them. The sources of confidential information need not, however, be disclosed."

Practice in the federal courts is mixed, with a substantial minority of judges permitting disclosure while most deny it. See the recent survey prepared for the Judicial Conference of the District of Columbia by the Junior Bar Section of the Bar Association of the District of Columbia, reported in Conference Papers on Discovery in Federal Criminal Cases, 33 F.R.D. 101, 125–127 (1963). See also Gronewold, Presentence Investigation Practices in the Federal Probation System, Fed.Prob. Sept.1958, pp. 27, 31. For divergent judicial opinions see *Smith v. United States,* 223 F.2d 750, 754 (5th Cir.1955) (supporting disclosure); *United States v. Durham,* 181 F.Supp. 503 (D.D.C.1960) (supporting secrecy).

Substantial objections to compelling disclosure in every case have been advanced by federal judges, including many who in practice often disclose all or parts of presentence reports. See Judicial Conference Committee on the Administration of the Probation System, Judicial Opinion on Proposed Change in Rule 32(c) of the Federal Rules of Criminal Procedure—A Survey (1964). Hence, the amendment goes no further than to make it clear that courts may disclose all or part of the presentence report to the defendant or to his counsel. It is hoped that courts will make increasing use of their discretion to disclose so that defendants generally may be given full opportunity to rebut or explain facts in presentence reports which will be material factors in determining sentences. For a description of such a practice in one district, see Thomsen, Confidentiality of the Presentence Report: A Middle Position, 28 Fed.Prob., March 1964, p. 8.

It is also provided that any material disclosed to the defendant or his counsel shall be disclosed to the attorney for the government. Such disclosure will permit the government to participate in the resolution of any factual questions raised by the defendant.

Subdivision (f).—This new subdivision writes into the rule the procedure which the cases have derived from the provision in 18 U.S.C. § 3653 that a person arrested for violation of probation "shall be taken before the court" and that thereupon the court may revoke the probation. See *Escoe v. Zerbst,* 295 U.S. 490 (1935); *Brown v. United States,* 236 F.2d 253 (9th Cir. 1956) certiorari denied 356 U.S. 922 (1958). Compare Model Penal Code § 301.4 (P.O.D.1962); Hink, The Application of Constitutional Standards of Protection to Probation, 29 U.Chi.L.Rev. 483 (1962).

1972 Amendments

Subdivision (b)(2) is new. It is intended to provide procedural implementation of the recently enacted criminal forfeiture provisions of the Organized Crime Control Act of 1970, Title IX, § 1963, and the Comprehensive Drug Abuse Prevention and Control Act of 1970, Title II, § 408(a)(2).

18 U.S.C. § 1963(c) provides for property seizure and disposition. In part it states:

(c) Upon conviction of a person under this section, the court shall authorize the Attorney General to seize all property or other interest declared forfeited under this section upon such terms and conditions as the court shall deem proper.

Although not specifically provided for in the Comprehensive Drug Abuse Prevention and Control Act of 1970, the provision of Title II, § 408(a)(2) forfeiting "profits" or "interest" will need to be implemented procedurally, and therefore new rule 32(b)(2) will be applicable also to that legislation.

For a brief discussion of the procedural implications of a criminal forfeiture, see Advisory Committee Note to rule 7(c)(2).

1974 Amendments

Subdivision (a)(1) is amended by deleting the reference to commitment or release pending sentencing. This issue is dealt with explicitly in the proposed revision of rule 46(c).

Subdivision (a)(2) is amended to make clear that there is no duty on the court to advise the defendant of the right to appeal after sentence is imposed following a plea of guilty or nolo contendere.

To require the court to advise the defendant of a right to appeal after a plea of guilty, accepted pursuant to the increasingly stringent requirements of rule 11, is likely to be confusing to the defendant. See American Bar Association, Standards Relating to Criminal Appeals § 2.1(b) (Approved Draft, 1970), limiting the court's duty to advise to "contested cases."

The Advisory Committee is of the opinion that such advice, following a sentence imposed after a plea of guilty, will merely tend to build false hopes and encourage frivolous appeals, with the attendant expense to the defendant or the taxpayers.

Former rule 32(a)(2) imposes a duty only upon conviction after "trial on a plea of not guilty." The few federal cases dealing with the question have interpreted rule 32(a)(2) to say that the court has no duty to advise defendant of his right to appeal after conviction following a guilty plea. Burton v. United States, 307 F.Supp. 448, 450 (D.Ariz.1970); Alaway v. United States, 280 F.Supp. 326, 336 (C.D.Calif.1968); Crow v. United States, 397 F.2d 284, 285 (10th Cir. 1968).

Prior to the 1966 amendment of rule 32, the court's duty was even more limited. At that time [rule 37(a)(2)] the court's duty to advise was limited to those situations in which sentence was imposed after trial upon a not guilty plea of a defendant not represented by counsel. 8A J. Moore, Federal Practice ¶32.01[3] (2d ed. Cipes 1969); C. Wright, Federal Practice and Procedure: Criminal § 528 (1969); 5 L. Orfield, Criminal Procedure Under the Federal Rules § 32:11 (1967).

With respect to appeals in forma pauperis, see appellate rule 24.

Subdivision (c)(1) makes clear that a presentence report is required except when the court otherwise directs for reasons stated of record. The requirement of reasons on the record for not having a presentence report is intended to make clear that such a report ought to be routinely required except in cases where there is a reason for not doing so. The presentence report is of great value for correctional purposes and will serve as a valuable aid in reviewing sentences to the extent that sentence review may be authorized by future rule change. For an analysis of the current rule as it relates to the situation in which a presentence investigation is required, see C. Wright, Federal Practice and Procedure: Criminal § 522 (1969); 8A J. Moore, Federal Practice ¶32.03[1] (2d ed. Cipes 1969).

Subdivision (c)(1) is also changed to permit the judge, after obtaining defendant's consent, to see the presentence report in order to decide whether to accept a plea agreement, and also to expedite the imposition of sentence in a case in which the defendant has indicated that he may plead guilty or nolo contendere.

Former subdivision (c)(1) provides that "The report shall not be submitted to the court * * * unless the defendant has pleaded guilty * * *." This precludes a judge from seeing a presentence report prior to the acceptance of the plea of guilty. L. Orfield, Criminal Procedure Under the Federal Rules § 32:35 (1967); 8A J. Moore, Federal Practice ¶32.03[2], p. 32–22 (2d ed. Cipes 1969); C. Wright, Federal Practice and Procedure: Criminal § 523, p. 392 (1969); Gregg v. United States, 394 U.S. 489, 89 S.Ct. 1134, 22 L.Ed.2d 442 (1969).

Because many plea agreements will deal with the sentence to be imposed, it will be important, under rule 11, for the judge to have access to sentencing information as a basis for deciding whether the plea agreement is an appropriate one.

It has been suggested that the problem be dealt with by allowing the judge to indicate approval of the plea agreement subject to the condition that the information in the presentence report is consistent with what he has been told about the case by counsel. See American Bar Association, Standards Relating to Pleas of Guilty § 3.3 (Approved Draft, 1963); President's Commission on Law Enforcement and Administration of Justice, The Challenge of Crime in a Free Society 136 (1967).

Allowing the judge to see the presentence report prior to his decision as to whether to accept the plea agreement is, in the view of the Advisory Committee, preferable to a conditional acceptance of the plea. See Enker, Perspectives on Plea Bargaining, Appendix A of President's Commission on Law Enforcement and Administration of Justice, Task Force Report: The Courts at 117 (1967). It enables the judge to have all of the information available to him at the time he is called upon to decide whether or not to accept the plea of guilty and thus avoids the necessity of a subsequent appearance whenever the information is such that the judge decides to reject the plea agreement.

There is presently authority to have a presentence report *prepared* prior to the acceptance of the plea of guilty. In *Gregg v. United States,* 394 U.S. 489, 491, 89 S.Ct. 1134, 22 L.Ed.2d 442 (1969), the court said that the "language [of rule 32] clearly permits the preparation of a presentence report before guilty plea or conviction 3 * * *." In footnote 3 the court said:

The history of the rule confirms this interpretation. The first Preliminary Draft of the rule would have required the consent of the defendant or his attorney to commence the investigation before the determination of guilt. Advisory Committee on Rules of Criminal Procedure, Fed.Rules Crim. Proc., Preliminary Draft 130, 133 (1943). The Second Preliminary Draft omitted this requirement and imposed no limitation on the time when the report could be made and submitted to the court. Advisory Committee on Rules of Criminal Procedure, Fed.Rules Crim.Proc., Second Preliminary Draft 126–128 (1944). The third and final draft, which was adopted as Rule 32, was evidently a compromise between those who opposed any time limitation, and those who preferred that the entire investigation be conducted after determination of guilt. See 5 L. Orfield, Criminal Procedure Under the Federal Rules § 32.2 (1967).

Where the judge rejects the plea agreement after seeing the presentence report, he should be free to recuse himself from later presiding over the trial of the case. This is left to the discretion of the judge. There are instances involving prior convictions where a judge may have seen a presentence report, yet can properly try a case on a plea of not guilty. *Webster v. United States*, 330 F.Supp. 1080 (E.D.Va.1971). Unlike the situation in *Gregg v. United States*, subdivision (e)(3) provides for disclosure of the presentence report to the defendant, and this will enable counsel to know whether the information thus made available to the judge is likely to be prejudicial. Presently trial judges who decide pretrial motions to suppress illegally obtained evidence are not, for that reason alone, precluded from presiding at a later trial.

Subdivision (c)(3)(A) requires disclosure of presentence information to the defense, exclusive of any recommendation of sentence. The court is required to disclose the report to defendant or his counsel unless the court is of the opinion that disclosure would seriously interfere with rehabilitation, compromise confidentiality, or create risk of harm to the defendant or others.

Any recommendation as to sentence should not be disclosed as it may impair the effectiveness of the probation officer if the defendant is under supervision on probation or parole.

The issue of disclosure of presentence information to the defense has been the subject of recommendations from the Advisory Committee in 1944, 1962, 1964, and 1966. The history is dealt with in considerable detail in C. Wright, Federal Practice and Procedure: Criminal § 524 (1969), and 8A J. Moore, Federal Practice ¶32.03[4] (2d ed. Cipes 1969).

In recent years, three prestigious organizations have recommended that the report be disclosed to the defense. See American Bar Association, Standards Relating to Sentencing Alternatives and Procedures § 4.4 (Approved Draft, 1968); American Law Institute, Model Penal Code § 7.07(5) (P.O.D. 1962); National Council on Crime and Delinquency, Model Sentencing Act § 4 (1963). This is also the recommendation of the President's Commission on Law Enforcement and Administration of Justice, The Challenge of Crime in a Free Society (1967) at p. 145:

In the absence of compelling reasons for nondisclosure of special information, the defendant and his counsel should be permitted to examine the entire presentence report.

The arguments for and against disclosure are well known and are effectively set forth in American Bar Association Standards Relating to Sentencing Alternatives and Procedures, § 4.4 Commentary at pp. 214 to 225 (Approved Draft, 1968). See also Lehrich, The Use and Disclosure of Presentence Reports in the United States, 47 F.R.D. 225 (1969).

A careful account of existing practices in Detroit, Michigan and Milwaukee, Wisconsin is found in R. Dawson, Sentencing (1969).

Most members of the federal judiciary have, in the past, opposed compulsory disclosure. See the view of District Judge Edwin M. Stanley, American Bar Association Standards Relating to Sentencing Alternatives and Procedures, Appendix A. (Appendix A also contains the results of a survey of all federal judges showing that the clear majority opposed disclosure.)

The Advisory Committee is of the view that accuracy of sentencing information is important not only to the defendant but also to effective correctional treatment of a convicted offender. The best way of insuring accuracy is disclosure with an opportunity for the defendant and counsel to point out to the court information thought by the defense to be inaccurate, incomplete, or otherwise misleading. Experience in jurisdictions which require disclosure does not lend support to the argument that disclosure will result in less complete presentence reports or the argument that sentencing procedures will become unnecessarily protracted. It is not intended that the probation officer would be subjected to any rigorous examination by defense counsel, or that he will even be sworn to testify. The proceedings may be very informal in nature unless the court orders a full hearing.

Subdivision (c)(3)(B) provides for situations in which the sentencing judge believes that disclosure should not be made under the criteria set forth in subdivision (c)(3)(A). He may disclose only a summary of that factual information "to be relied on in determining sentence." This is similar to the proposal of the American Bar Association Standards Relating to Sentencing Alternatives and Procedures § 4.4(b) and Commentary at pp. 216 to 224.

Subdivision (c)(3)(D) provides for the return of disclosed presentence reports to insure that they do not become available to unauthorized persons. See National Council on Crime and Delinquency, Model Sentencing Act § 4 (1963): "Such reports shall be part of the record but shall be sealed and opened only on order of the court."

Subdivision (c)(3)(E) makes clear that diagnostic studies under 18 U.S.C. §§ 4208(b), 5010(c), or 5034 are covered by this rule and also that 18 U.S.C. § 4252 is included within the disclosure provisions of subdivision (c). Section 4252 provides for the presentence examination of an "eligible offender" who is believed to be an addict to determine whether "he is an addict and is likely to be rehabilitated through treatment."

Both the Organized Crime Control Act of 1970 [§ 3775(b)] and the Comprehensive Drug Abuse Prevention and Control Act of 1970 [§ 409(b)] have special provisions for presentence investigation in the implementation of the dangerous special offender provision. It is, however, unnecessary to incorporate them by reference in rule 32 because each contains a specific provision requiring disclosure of the presentence report. The judge does have authority to withhold some information "in extraordinary cases" provided notice is given the parties and the court's reasons for withholding information are made part of the record.

Subdivision (e) is amended to clarify the meaning.

1975 Enactment

A. Amendments Proposed by the Supreme Court

Rule 32 of the Federal Rules of Criminal Procedure deals with sentencing matters.

Proposed subdivision (a)(2) provides that the court is not duty bound to advise the defendant of a right to appeal when the sentence is imposed following a plea of guilty or nolo contendere.

Proposed subdivision (e) provides that the probation service must make a presentence investigation and report unless the court orders otherwise "for reasons stated on the record." The presentence report will not be submitted to the court until after the defendant pleads nolo contendere or guilty, or is found guilty, unless the defendant consents in writing. Upon the defendant's request, the court must permit the defendant to read the presentence report, except for the recommendation as to sentence. However, the court may decline to let the defendant read the report if it contains (a) diagnostic opinion that might seriously disrupt a rehabilitation program, (b) sources of information obtained upon a promise of confidentiality, or (c) any other information that, if disclosed, might result in harm to the defendant or other persons. The court must give the defendant an opportunity to comment upon the presentence report. If the court decides that the defendant should not see the report, then it must provide the defendant, orally or in writing, a summary of the factual information in the report upon which it is relying in determining sentence. No party may keep the report or make copies of it.

B. Committee Action

The Committee added language to subdivision (a)(1) to provide that the attorney for the government may speak to the court at the time of sentencing. The language does not require that the attorney for the government speak but permits him to do so if he wishes.

The Committee recast the language of subdivision (c)(1), which defines when presentence reports must be obtained. The Committee's provision makes it more difficult to dispense with a presentence report. It requires that a presentence report be made unless (a) the defendant waives it, or (b) the court finds that the record contains sufficient information to enable the meaningful exercise of sentencing discretion and explains this finding on the record. The Committee believes that presentence reports are important aids to sentencing and should not be dispensed with easily.

The Committee added language to subdivision (c)(3)(A) that permits a defendant to offer testimony or information to rebut alleged factual inaccuracies in the presentence report. Since the presentence report is to be used by the court in imposing sentence and since the consequence of any significant inaccuracy can be very serious to the defendant, the Committee believes that it is essential that the presentence report be completely accurate in every material respect. The Committee's addition to subdivision (c)(3)(A) will help insure the accuracy of the presentence report.

The Committee added language to subdivision (c)(3)(D) that gives the court the discretion to permit either the prosecutor or the defense counsel to retain a copy of the presentence report. There may be situations when it would be appropriate for either or both of the parties to retain the presentence report. The Committee believes that the rule should give the court the discretion in such situations to permit the parties to retain their copies. House Report No. 94–247.

1979 Amendments

Rule 32 (c) (3) (E). The amendment to rule 32(c) (3) (E) is necessary in light of recent changes in the applicable statutes.

Rule 32 (f). This subdivision is abrogated. The subject matter is now dealt with in greater detail in proposed new rule 32.1.

1983 Amendments

Rule 32(a)(1). Subdivision (a)(1) has been amended so as to impose upon the sentencing court the additional obligation of determining that the defendant and his counsel have had an opportunity to read the presentence investigation report or summary thereof. This change is consistent with the amendment of subdivision (c)(3), discussed below, providing for disclosure of the report (or, in the circumstances indicated, a summary thereof) to *both* defendant *and* his counsel *without request.* This amendment is also consistent with the findings of a recent empirical study that under present rule 32 meaningful disclosure is often lacking and "that some form of judicial prodding is necessary to achieve full disclosure." Fennell & Hall, *Due Process at Sentencing: An Empirical and Legal Analysis of the Disclosure of Presentence Reports in Federal Courts,* 93 Harv.L.Rev. 1613, 1651 (1980):

> The defendant's interest in an accurate and reliable presentence report does not cease with the imposition of sentence. Rather, these interests are implicated at later stages in the correctional process by the continued use of the presentence report as a basic source of information in the handling of the defendant. If the defendant is incarcerated, the presentence report accompanies him to the correctional institution and provides background information for the Bureau of Prisons' classification summary, which, in turn, determines the defendant's classification within the facility, his ability to obtain furloughs, and the choice of treatment programs. The presentence report also plays a crucial role during parole determination. Section 4207 of the Parole Commission and Reorganization Act directs the parole hearing examiner to consider, if available, the presentence report as well as other records concerning the prisoner. In addition to its general use as background at the parole hearing, the presentence report serves as the primary source of information for calculating the inmate's parole guideline score.

Though it is thus important that the defendant be aware *now* of all these potential uses, the Advisory Committee has considered but not adopted a requirement that the trial judge specifically advise the defendant of these matters. The Committee believes that this additional burden should not be placed upon the trial judge, and that the problem is best dealt with by a form attached to the presentence report, to be signed by the defendant, advising of these potential uses of the report. This suggestion has been forwarded to the Probation Committee of the Judicial Conference.

Rule 32(c)(3)(A), (B) & (C). Three important changes are made in subdivision (c)(3): disclosure of the presentence report is no longer limited to those situations in which a request is made; disclosure is now provided to both defendant and his counsel; and disclosure is now required a reasonable time before sentencing. These changes have been prompted by findings in a recent empirical study that the extent and nature of disclosure of the presentence investigation report in federal courts under current rule 32 is insufficient to ensure accuracy of sentencing information. In 14 districts, disclosure is made only on request, and such requests are received in fewer than 50% of the cases. Forty–two of 92 probation offices do not provide automatic notice to defendant or counsel of the availability of the report; in 18 districts, a majority of the judges do not provide any notice of the availability of the report, and in 20 districts such notice is given only on the day of sentencing. In 28 districts, the report itself is not disclosed until the day of sentencing in a majority of cases. Thirty–one courts generally disclose the report only to counsel and not to the defendant, unless the defendant makes a specific request. Only 13 districts disclose the presentence report to both defendant and counsel prior to the day of sentencing in 90% or more of the cases. Fennell & Hall, supra, at 1640–49.

These findings make it clear that rule 32 in its present form is failing to fulfill its purpose. Unless disclosure is made sufficiently in advance of sentencing to permit the assertion and resolution of claims of inaccuracy prior to the sentencing hearing, the submission of additional information by the defendant when appropriate, and informed comment on the presentence report, the purpose of promoting accuracy by permitting the defendant to contest erroneous information is defeated. Similarly, if the report is not made available to the defendant and his counsel in a timely fashion, and if disclosure is only made on request, their opportunity to review the report may be inadequate. Finally, the failure to disclose the report to the defendant, or to require counsel to review the report with the defendant, significantly reduces the likelihood that false statements will be discovered, as much of the content of the presentence report will ordinarily be outside the knowledge of counsel.

The additional change to subdivision (c)(3)(C) is intended to make it clear that the government's right to disclosure does not depend upon whether the defendant elects to exercise his right to disclosure.

Rule 32(c)(3)(D). Subdivision (c)(3)(D) is entirely new. It requires the sentencing court, as to each matter controverted, either to make a finding as to the accuracy of the challenged factual proposition or to determine that no reliance will be placed on that proposition at the time of sentencing. This new provision also requires that a record of this action accompany any copy of the report later made available to the Bureau of Prisons or Parole Commission.

As noted above, the Bureau of Prisons and the Parole Commission make substantial use of the presentence investigation report. Under current practice, this can result in reliance upon assertions of fact in the report in the making of critical determinations relating to custody or parole. For example, it is possible that the Bureau or Commission, in the course of reaching a decision on such matters as institution assignment, eligibility for programs, or computation of salient factors, will place great reliance upon factual assertions in the report which are in fact untrue and which remained unchallenged at the time of sentencing because defendant or his counsel deemed the error unimportant in the sentencing context (e.g., where the sentence was expected to conform to an earlier plea agreement, or where the judge said he would disregard certain controverted matter in setting the sentence).

The first sentence of new subdivision (3)(c)(D) is intended to ensure that a record is made as to exactly what resolution occurred as to controverted matter. The second sentence is intended to ensure that this record comes to the attention of the Bureau or Commission when these agencies utilize the presentence investigation report. In current practice, "less than one–fourth of the district courts (twenty of ninety–two) communicate to the correctional agencies the defendant's challenges to information in the presentence report and the resolution of these challenges." Fennell & Hall, supra, at 1680.

New subdivision (c)(3)(D) does not impose an onerous burden. It does not even require the preparation of a transcript. As is now the practice in some courts, these findings and determinations can be simply entered onto a form which is then appended to the report.

Rule 32(c)(3)(E) & (F). Former subdivisions (c)(3)(D) and (E) have been renumbered as (c)(3)(E) and (F). The only change in the former, necessitated because disclosure is now to defendant and his counsel.

The issue of access to the presentence report at the institution was discussed by the Advisory Committee, but no action was taken on that matter because it was believed to be beyond the scope of the rule-making power. Rule 32 in its present form does not speak to this issue, and thus the Bureau of Prisons and the Parole Commission are free to make provision for disclosure to inmates and their counsel.

Rule 32(d). The amendment to Rule 32(d) is intended to clarify (i) the standard applicable to plea withdrawal under this rule, and (ii) the circumstances under which the appropriate avenue of relief is other than a withdrawal motion under this rule. Both of these matters have been the source of considerable confusion under the present rule. In its present form, the rule declares that a motion to withdraw a plea of guilty or nolo contendere may be made only before sentence is imposed, but then states the standard for permitting withdrawal after sentence. In fact, "there is no limitation upon the time within which relief thereunder may, after sentencing, be sought." *United States v. Watson,* 548 F.2d 1058 (D.C.Cir.1977). It has been critically stated that "the Rule offers little guidance as to the applicable standard for a pre-sentence withdrawal of plea," *United States v. Michaelson,* 552 F.2d 472 (2d Cir.1977), and that as a result "the contours of [the presentence] standard are not easily defined." *Bruce v. United States,* 379 F.2d 113 (D.C.Cir.1967).

By replacing the "manifest injustice" standard with a requirement that, in cases to which it applied, the defendant must (unless taking a direct appeal) proceed under 28 U.S.C. § 2255, the amendment avoids language which has been a cause of unnecessary confusion. Under the amendment, a defendant who proceeds too late to come under the more generous "fair and just reason" standard must seek relief under § 2255, meaning the applicable standard is that stated in *Hill v. United States,* 368 U.S. 424 (1962): "a fundamental defect which inherently results in a complete miscarriage of justice" or "an omission inconsistent with the rudimentary demands of fair procedure."

Some authority is to be found to the effect that the rule 32(d) "manifest injustice" standard is indistinguishable from the § 2255 standard. In *United States v. Hamilton,* 553 F.2d 63 (10th Cir.1977), for example, the court, after first concluding defendant was not entitled to relief under the § 2255 "miscarriage of justice" test, then held that "[n]othing is to be gained by the invocation of Rule 32(d)" and its "manifest injustice" standard. Some courts, however, have indicated that the rule 32(d) standard provides a somewhat broader basis for relief than § 2255. *United States v. Dabdoub-Diaz,* 599 F.2d 96 (5th Cir.1979); *United States v. Watson,* 548 F.2d 1058 (D.C.Cir.1977); *Meyer v. United*

States, 424 F.2d 1181 (8th Cir.1970); *United States v. Kent*, 397 F.2d 446 (7th Cir.1968). It is noteworthy, however, that in Dabdoub-Diaz, Meyer and Kent the defendant did not prevail under either § 2255 or Rule 32(d), and that in Watson, though the § 2255 case was remanded for consideration as a 32(d) motion, defendant's complaint (that he was not advised of the special parole term, though the sentence he received did not exceed that he was warned about by the court) was one as to which relief had been denied even upon direct appeal from the conviction. *United States v. Peters*, No. 77–1700 (4th Cir. Dec. 22, 1978).

Indeed, it may more generally be said that the results in § 2255 and 32(d) guilty plea cases have been for the most part the same. Relief has often been granted or recognized as available via either of these routes for essentially the same reasons: that there exists a complete constitutional bar to conviction on the offense charged, *Brooks v. United States*, 424 F.2d 425 (5th Cir.1970) (§ 2255), *United States v. Bluso*, 519 F.2d 473 (4th Cir.1975) (Rule 32); that the defendant was incompetent at the time of his plea. *United States v. Masthers*, 539 F.2d 721 (D.C.Cir.1976) (§ 2255), *Kienlen v. United States*, 379 F.2d 20 (10th Cir.1967) (Rule 32); and that the bargain the prosecutor made with defendant was not kept, *Walters v. Harris*, 460 F.2d 988 (4th Cir.1972) (§ 2255), *United States v. Hawthorne*, 502 F.2d 1183 (3rd Cir.1974) (Rule 32). Perhaps even more significant is the fact that relief has often been denied under like circumstances whichever of the two procedures was used: a mere technical violation of Rule 11, *United States v. Timmreck*, 441 U.S. 780 (1979) (§ 2255), *United States v. Saft*, 558 F.2d 1073 (2d Cir.1977) (Rule 32); the mere fact defendants expected a lower sentence, *United States v. White*, 572 F.2d 1007 (4th Cir.1978) (§ 2255), *Masciola v. United States*, 469 F.2d 1057 (3rd Cir.1972) (Rule 32); or mere familial coercion, *Wojtowicz v. United States*, 550 F.2d 786 (2d Cir.1977) (§ 2255), *United States v. Bartoli*, 572 F.2d 188 (8th Cir.1978) (Rule 32).

The one clear instance in which a Rule 32(d) attack might prevail when a § 2255 challenge would not is present in those circuits which have reached the questionable result that post-sentence relief under 32(d) is available not merely upon a showing of a "manifest injustice" but also for any deviation from literal compliance with Rule 11. *United States v. Cantor*, 469 F.2d 435 (3d Cir.1972). See Advisory Committee Note to Rule 11(h), noting the unsoundness of that position.

The change in Rule 32(d), therefore, is at best a minor one in terms of how post-sentence motions to withdraw pleas will be decided. It avoids the confusion which now obtains as to whether a § 2255 petition must be assumed to also be a 32(d) motion and, if so, whether this bears significantly upon how the matter should be decided. See, e.g., *United States v. Watson*, supra. It also avoids the present undesirable situation in which the mere selection of one of two highly similar avenues of relief, rule 32(d) or § 2255, may have significant procedural consequences, such as whether the government can take an appeal from the district court's adverse ruling (possible under § 2255 only). Moreover, because § 2255 and Rule 32(d) are properly characterized as the "two principal procedures for collateral attack of a federal plea conviction," Borman, The Hidden Right to Direct Appeal From a Federal Conviction, 64 Cornell L.Rev. 319, 327 (1979), this amendment is also in keeping with the proposition underlying the Supreme Court's decision in *United States v. Timmreck*, supra, namely, that "the concern with finality served by the limitation on collateral attack has special force with respect to convictions based on guilty pleas." The amendment is likewise consistent with ALI Code of Pre-Arraignment Procedure § 350.9 (1975) ("Allegations of noncompliance with the procedures provided in Article 350 shall not be a basis for review of a conviction after the appeal period for such conviction has expired, unless such review is required by the Constitution of the United States or of this State or otherwise by the law of this State other than Article 350"); ABA Standards Relating to the Administration of Criminal Justice § 14–2.1 (2d ed. 1978) (using "manifest injustice" standard, but listing six specific illustrations each of which would be basis for relief under § 2255); Unif.R.Crim.P. 444(e) (Approved Draft, 1974) (using "interest of justice" test, but listing five specific illustrations each of which would be basis for relief under § 2255).

The first sentence of the amended rule incorporates the "fair and just" standard which the federal courts, relying upon dictum in *Kercheval v. United States*, 274 U.S. 220 (1927), have consistently applied to presentence motions. See, e.g., *United States v. Strauss*, 563 F.2d 127 (4th Cir. 1977); *United States v. Bradin*, 535 F.2d 1039 (8th Cir.1976); *United States v. Barker*, 514 F.2d 208 (D.C.Cir.1975). Under the rule as amended, it is made clear that the defendant has the burden of showing a "fair and just" reason for withdrawal of the plea. This is consistent with the prevailing view, which is that "the defendant has the burden of satisfying the trial judge that there are valid grounds for withdrawal," see *United States v. Michaelson*, supra, and cases cited therein. (Illustrative of a reason which would meet this test but would likely fall short of the § 2255 test is where the defendant now wants to pursue a certain defense which he for good reason did not put forward earlier, *United States v. Barker*, supra.)

Although "the terms 'fair and just' lack any pretense of scientific exactness," *United States v. Barker*, supra, guidelines have emerged in the appellate cases for applying this standard. Whether the movant has asserted his legal innocence is an important factor to be weighed, *United States v. Joslin*, 434 F.2d 526 (D.C.Cir.1970), as is the reason why the defenses were not put forward at the time of original pleading. *United States v. Needles*, 472 F.2d 652 (2d Cir.1973). The amount of time which has passed between the plea and the motion must also be taken into account.

> A swift change of heart is itself strong indication that the plea was entered in haste and confusion * * *. By contrast, if the defendant has long delayed his withdrawal motion, and has had the full benefit of competent counsel at all times, the reasons given to support withdrawal must have considerably more force.

United States v. Barker, supra.

If the defendant establishes such a reason, it is then appropriate to consider whether the government would be prejudiced by withdrawal of the plea. Substantial prejudice may be present for a variety of reasons. See *United States v. Jerry*, 487 F.2d 600 (3d Cir.1973) (physical evidence had been discarded); *United States v. Vasquez-Velasco*, 471 F.2d 294 (9th Cir.1973) (death of chief government witness); *United States v. Lombardozzi*, 436 F.2d 878 (2d Cir.1971) (other defendants with whom defendant had been joined for trial had already been tried in a lengthy trial); *Farnsworth v.*

Sanford, 115 F.2d 375 (5th Cir.1940) (prosecution had dismissed 52 witnesses who had come from all over the country and from overseas bases).

There is currently some disparity in the manner in which presentence motions to withdraw a guilty plea are dealt with. Some courts proceed as if any desire to withdraw the plea before sentence is "fair and just" so long as the government fails to establish that it would be prejudiced by the withdrawal. Illustrative is *United States v. Savage,* 561 F.2d 554 (4th Cir.1977), where the defendant pleaded guilty pursuant to a plea agreement that the government would recommend a sentence of 5 years. At the sentencing hearing, the trial judge indicated his unwillingness to follow the government's recommendation, so the defendant moved to withdraw his plea. That motion was denied. On appeal, the court held that there had been no violation of Rule 11, in that refusal to accept the government's recommendation does not constitute a rejection of the plea agreement. But the court then proceeded to hold that absent any showing of prejudice by the government, "the defendant should be allowed to withdraw his plea"; only upon such a showing by the government must the court "weigh the defendant's reasons for seeking to withdraw his plea against the prejudice which the government will suffer." The other view is that there is no occasion to inquire into the matter of prejudice unless the defendant first shows a good reason for being allowed to withdraw his plea. As stated in *United States v. Saft,* 558 F.2d 1073 (2d Cir.1977): "The Government is not required to show prejudice when a defendant has shown no sufficient grounds for permitting withdrawal of a guilty plea, although such prejudice may be considered by the district court in exercising its discretion." The second sentence of the amended rule, by requiring that the defendant show a "fair and just" reason, adopts the *Saft* position and rejects that taken in Savage.

The *Savage* position, as later articulated in *United States v. Strauss,* supra, is that the "sounder view, supported by both the language of the rule and by the reasons for it, would be to allow withdrawal of the plea prior to sentencing unless the prosecution has been substantially prejudiced by reliance upon the defendant's plea." (Quoting 2 C. Wright, Federal Practice and Procedure § 538, at 474–75 (1969).) Although that position may once have been sound, this is no longer the case in light of the recent revisions of Rule 11. Rule 11 now provides for the placing of plea agreements on the record, for full inquiry into the voluntariness of the plea, for detailed advice to the defendant concerning his rights and the consequences of his plea and a determination that the defendant understands these matters, and for a determination of the accuracy of the plea. Given the great care with which pleas are taken under this revised Rule 11, there is no reason to view pleas so taken as merely "tentative," subject to withdrawal before sentence whenever the government cannot establish prejudice.

Were withdrawal automatic in every case where the defendant decided to alter his tactics and present his theory of the case to the jury, the guilty plea would become a mere gesture, a temporary and meaningless formality reversible at the defendant's whim. In fact, however, a guilty plea is no such trifle, but "a grave and solemn act," which is "accepted only with care and discernment."

United States v. Barker, supra, quoting from *Brady v. United States,* 397 U.S. 742 (1970).

The facts of the *Savage* case reflect the wisdom of this position. In *Savage,* the defendant had entered into a plea agreement whereby he agreed to plead guilty in exchange for the government's promise to recommend a sentence of 5 years, which the defendant knew was not binding on the court. Yet, under the approach taken in *Savage,* the defendant remains free to renege on his plea bargain, notwithstanding full compliance therewith by the attorney for the government, if it later appears to him from the presentence report or the comments of the trial judge or any other source that the court will not follow the government's recommendation. Having bargained for a recommendation pursuant to Rule 11(e)(1)(B), the defendant should not be entitled, in effect, to unilaterally convert the plea agreement into a Rule 11(e)(1)(C) type of agreement (i.e., one with a guarantee of a specific sentence which, if not given, permits withdrawal of the plea).

The first sentence of subdivision (d) provides that the motion, to be judged under the more liberal "fair and just reason" test, must have been made before sentence is imposed, imposition of sentence is suspended, or disposition is had under 18 U.S.C. § 4205(c). The latter of these has been added to the rule to make it clear that the lesser standard also governs prior to the second stage of sentencing when the judge, pursuant to that statute, has committed the defendant to the custody of the Attorney General for study pending final disposition. Several circuits have left this issue open, e.g., *United States v. McCoy,* 477 F.2d 550 (5th Cir. 1973); *Callaway v. United States,* 367 F.2d 140 (10th Cir. 1966); while some have held that a withdrawal motion filed between tentative and final sentencing should be judged against the presentence standard, *United States v. Barker,* 514 F.2d 208 (D.C.Cir.1975); *United States v. Thomas,* 415 F.2d 1216 (9th Cir.1969).

Inclusion of the § 4205(c) situation under the presentence standard is appropriate. As explained in *Barker*:

Two reasons of policy have been advanced to explain the near-presumption which Rule 32(d) erects against post-sentence withdrawal motions. The first is that post-sentence withdrawal subverts the "stability" of "final judgments." * * * The second reason is that the post-sentence withdrawal motion often constitutes a veiled attack on the judge's sentencing decision; to grant such motions in lenient fashion might undermine respect for the courts and fritter away the time and painstaking effort devoted to the sentence process.

* * * Concern for the "stability of final judgments" has little application to withdrawal motions filed between tentative and final sentencing under Section 4208(b) [now 4205(c)]. The point at which a defendant's judgment of conviction becomes "final" for purposes of appeal—whether at tentative or at final sentencing—is wholly within the defendant's discretion. * * * Concern for the integrity of the sentencing process is, however, another matter. The major point, in our view, is that tentative sentencing under Section 4208(b) [now 4205(c)] leaves the defendant ignorant of his final sentence. He will therefore be unlikely to use a withdrawal motion as an oblique attack on the judge's sentencing policy. The relative leniency of the "fair and just" standard is consequently not out of place.

1987 Amendments

The amendments are technical. No substantive change is intended.

1989 Amendments

The amendment to subdivision (a)(1) is intended to clarify that the court is expected to proceed without unnecessary delay, and that it may be necessary to delay sentencing when an applicable sentencing factor cannot be resolved at the time set for sentencing. Often, the factor will relate to a defendant's agreement to cooperate with the government. But, other factors may be capable of resolution if the court delays sentencing while additional information is generated. As currently written, the rule might imply that a delay requested by one party or suggested by the Court *sua sponte* might be unreasonable. The amendment rids the rule of any such implication and provides the sentencing court with desirable discretion to assure that relevant factors are considered and accurately resolved. In exercising this discretion, the court retains under the amendment the authority to refuse to delay sentencing when a delay is inappropriate under the circumstances.

In amending subdivision (c)(1), the Committee conformed the rule to the current practice in some courts: i.e., to permit the defendant and the prosecutor to see a presentence report prior to a plea of guilty if the court, with the written consent of the defendant, receives the report at that time. The amendment permits, but does not require, disclosure of the report with the written consent of the defendant.

The amendment to change the "reasonable time" language in subdivision (c)(3)(A) to at least 10 days prior to sentencing, unless the defendant waives the minimum period, conforms the rule to 18 U.S.C. 3552(d). Nothing in the statue [sic] or the rule prohibits a court from requiring disclosure at an earlier time before sentencing. The inclusion of a specific waiver provision is intended to conform the rule to the statute and is not intended to suggest that waiver of other rights is precluded when no specific waiver provision is set forth in a rule or portion thereof.

The language requiring the court to provide the defendant and defense counsel with a copy of the presentence report complements the abrogation of subdivision (E), which had required the defense to return the probation report. Because a defendant or the government may seek to appeal a sentence, an option that is permitted under some circumstances, there will be cases in which the defendant has a need for the presentence report during the preparation of, or the response to, an appeal. This is one reason why the Committee decided that the defendant should not be required to return the nonconfidential portions of the presentence report that have been disclosed. Another reason is that district courts may find it desirable to adopt portions of the presentence report when making findings of fact under the guidelines. They would be inhibited unnecessarily from relying on careful, accurate presentence reports if such reports could not be retained by defendants. A third reason why defendant should be able to retain the reports disclosed to them is that the Supreme Court's decision in *United States Department of Justice v. Julian*, 486 U.S. 1 (1988), 108 S.Ct. 1606 (1988), suggests that defendants will routinely be able to secure their reports through Freedom of Information Act suits. No public interest is served by continuing to require the return of reports, and unnecessary FOIA litigation should be avoided as a result of the amendment to Rule 32.

The amended rule does not direct whether the defendant or the defendant's lawyer should retain the presentence report. In exceptional cases where retention of a report in a local detention facility might pose a danger to persons housed there, the district judge may direct that the defendant not personally retain a copy of the report until the defendant has been transferred to the facility where the sentence will be served.

Because the parties need not return the presentence report to the probation officer, the Solicitor General should be able to review the report in deciding whether to permit the United States to appeal a sentence under the Sentencing Reform Act of 1984, 18. U.S.C. § 3551 et seq.

Although the Committee was concerned about the potential unfairness of having confidential or diagnostic material included in presentence reports but not disclosed to a defendant who might be adversely affected by such material, it decided not to recommend at this time a change in the rule which would require complete disclosure. Some diagnostic material might be particularly useful when a court imposes probation, and might well be harmful to the defendant if disclosed. Moreover, some of this material might assist correctional officials in prescribing treatment programs for an incarcerated defendant. Information provided by confidential sources and information posing a possible threat of harm to third parties was particularly troubling to the Committee, since this information is often extremely negative and thus potentially harmful to a defendant. The Committee concluded, however, that it was preferable to permit the probation officer to include this information in a report so that the sentencing court may determine whether is [it] ought to be disclosed to the defendant. If the court determines that it should not be disclosed, it will have to decide whether to summarize the contents of the information or to hold that no finding as to the undisclosed information will be made because such information will not be taken into account in sentencing. Substantial due process problems may arise if a court attempts to summarize information in a presentence report, the defendant challenges the information, and the court attempts to make a finding as to the accuracy of the information without disclosing to the defendant the source of the information or the details placed before the court. In deciding not to require disclosure of everything in a presentence report, the Committee made no judgment that findings could validly be made based upon nondisclosed information.

Finally, portions of the rule were gender-neutralized.

1991 Amendments

The amendments are technical. No substantive changes are intended.

1993 Amendments

The original subdivision (e) has been deleted due to statutory changes affecting the authority of a court to grant probation. See 18 U.S.C. 3561(a). Its replacement is one of a number of contemporaneous amendments extending Rule 26.2 to hearings and proceedings other than the trial itself. The amendment to Rule 32 specifically codifies the result in cases such as *United States v. Rosa*, 891 F.2d 1074 (3d Cir.1989). In that case the defendant pleaded guilty to a drug offense. During sentencing the defendant unsuccessfully attempted to obtain Jencks Act materials relating to a co-accused who testified as a government witness at sentencing. In concluding that the trial court erred in not ordering the government to produce its witness's statement, the court stated:

We believe the sentence imposed on a defendant is the most critical stage of criminal proceedings, and is, in effect, the "bottom-line" for the defendant, particularly where the defendant has pled guilty. This being so, we can perceive no purpose in denying the defendant the ability to effectively cross-examine a government witness where such testimony may, if accepted, add substantially to the defendant's sentence. In such a setting, we believe that the rationale of *Jencks v. United States* . . . and the purpose of the Jencks Act would be disserved if the government at such a grave stage of a criminal proceeding could deprive the accused of material valuable not only to the defense but to his very liberty. Id. at 1079.

The court added that the defendant had not been sentenced under the new Sentencing Guidelines and that its decision could take on greater importance under those rules. Under Guideline sentencing, said the court, the trial judge has less discretion to moderate a sentence and is required to impose a sentence based upon specific factual findings which need not be established beyond a reasonable doubt. Id. at n. 3.

Although the *Rosa* decision decided only the issue of access by the defendant to Jencks material, the amendment parallels Rules 26.2 (applying Jencks Act to trial) and 12(i) (applying Jencks Act to suppression hearing) in that both the defense and the prosecution are entitled to Jencks material.

Production of a statement is triggered by the witness's oral testimony. The sanction provision rests on the assumption that the proponent of the witness's testimony has deliberately elected to withhold relevant material.

1994 Amendments

The amendments to Rule 32 are intended to accomplish two primary objectives. First, the amendments incorporate elements of a "Model Local Rule for Guideline Sentencing" which was proposed by the Judicial Conference Committee on Probation Administration in 1987. That model rule and the accompanying report were prepared to assist trial judges in implementing guideline sentencing mandated by the Sentencing Reform Act of 1984. *See* Committee on the Admin. of the Probation Sys., Judicial Conference of the U.S., Recommended Procedures for Guideline Sentencing and Commentary: Model Local Rule for Guideline Sentencing, Reprinted in T. Hutchinson & D. Yellen, *Federal Sentencing Law and Practice,* app. 8, at 431 (1989). It was anticipated that sentencing hearings would become more complex due to the new fact finding requirements imposed by guideline sentencing methodology. *See* U.S.S.G. § 6A1.2. Accordingly, the model rule focused on preparation of the presentence report as a means of identifying and narrowing the issues to be decided at the sentencing hearing.

Second, in the process of effecting those amendments, the rule was reorganized. Over time, numerous amendments to the rule had created a sort of hodgepodge; the reorganization represents as attempt to reflect as appropriate sequential order in the sentencing procedures.

Subdivision (a). Subdivision (a) retains the general mandate that sentence be imposed without unnecessary delay thereby permitting the court to regulate the time to be allowed for the probation officer to complete the presentence investigation and submit the report. The only requirement is that sufficient time be allowed for completion of the process prescribed by subdivision (b) (6) unless the time periods established in the subdivision are shortened or lengthened by the court for good cause. Such limits are not intended to create any new substantive right for the defendant or the Government which would entitle either to relief if a time limit prescribed in the rule is not kept.

The remainder of subdivision (a), which addressed the sentencing hearing, is now located in subdivision (c).

Subdivision (b). Subdivision (b) (formerly subdivision (c)), which addresses the presentence investigation, has been modified in several respects.

First, subdivision (b)(2) is a new provision which provides that, on request, defense counsel is entitled to notice and a reasonable opportunity to be present at any interview of the defendant conducted by the probation officer. Although the courts have not held that presentence interviews are a critical stage of the trial for purposes of the Sixth Amendment right to counsel, the amendment reflects case law which has indicated that requests for counsel to be present should be honored. *See,* e.g., *United States v. Herrera-Figueroa,* 918 F.2d 1430, 1437 (9th Cir. 1990)(court relied on its supervisory power to hold that probation officers must honor request for counsel's presence); *United States v. Tisdale,* 952 F.2d 934, 940 (6th Cir. 1992)(court agreed with rule requiring probation officers to honor defendant's request for attorney or request from attorney not to interview defendant in absence of counsel). The Committee believes that permitting counsel to be present during such interviews may avoid unnecessary misunderstandings between the probation officer and the defendant. The rule does not further define the term "interview." The Committee intended for the provision to apply to any communication initiated by the probation officer where he or she is asking the defendant to provide information which will be used in preparation of the presentence investigation. Spontaneous or unplanned encounters between the defendant and the probation officer would normally not fall within the purview of the rule. The Committee also believed that the burden should rest on defense counsel, having received notice, to respond as promptly as possible to enable timely completion of the presentence report.

Subdivision (b)(6), formerly (c)(3), includes several changes which recognize the key role the presentence report is playing under guideline sentencing. The major thrust of these changes is to address the problem of resolving objections by the parties to the probation officer's presentence report. Subdivision (b)(6)(A) now provides that the probation officer must present the presentence report to the parties not later than 35 days before the sentencing hearing (rather than 10 days before imposition of the sentence) in order to provide some additional time to the parties and the probation officer to attempt to resolve objections to the report. There has been a slight change in the practice of deleting from the copy of the report given to the parties certain information specified in (b)(6)(A). Under that new provision (changing former subdivision (c)(3)(A)), the court has the discretion (in an individual case or in accordance with a local rule) to direct the probation officer to withhold any final recommendation concerning the sentence. Otherwise, the recommendation, if any, is subject to disclosure. The prior practice of not disclosing confidential information, or other information which might result in harm to the defendant or other persons, is retained in (b)(5).

New subdivisions (b)(6)(B), (C), and (D) now provide explicit deadlines and guidance on resolving disputes about the contents of the presentence report. The amendments are intended to provide early resolution of such disputes by (1) requiring the parties to provide the probation officer with a written list of objections to the report with in 14 days of receiving the report; (2) permitting the probation officer to meet with the defendant, the defendant's counsel, and the attorney for the Government to discuss objections to the report, conduct and additional investigation, and to make revisions to the report as deemed appropriate; (3) requiring the probation officer to submit the report to the court and the parties not later that 7 days before the sentencing hearing, noting any unresolved disputes; and (4) permitting the court to treat the report as its findings of fact, except for the parties' unresolved objections. Although the rule does not explicitly address the question of whether counsel's objections to the report are to be filed with the court, there is nothing in the rule which would prohibit a court from requiring the parties to file their original objections or have them included as an addendum to the presentence report.

This procedure, which generally mirrors the approach in the Model Local Rule for Guideline Sentencing, supra, is intended to maximize judicial economy by providing for more orderly sentencing hearings while also providing fair opportunity for both parties to review, object to, and comment upon, the probation officer's report in advance of the sentencing hearing. Under the amendment, the parties would still be free at the sentencing hearing to comment on the presentence report, and in the discretion of the court, to introduce evidence concerning their objections to the report.

Subdivision (c). Subdivision (c) addresses the imposition of sentence and makes no major changes in current practice. The provision consists largely of material formerly located in subdivision (a). Language formerly in (a)(1) referring to the court's disclosure to the parties of the probation officer's determination of the sentencing classifications and sentencing guideline range is now located in subdivisions (b)(4)(B) and (c)(1). Likewise, the brief reference in former (a)(1) to the ability of the parties to comment on the probation officer's determination of sentencing classifications and sentencing guideline range is now located in (c)(1) and (c)(3).

Subdivision (c)(1) is not intended to require that resolution of objections and imposition of the sentence occur at the same time or during the same hearing. It requires only that the court rule on any objections before sentence is imposed. In considering objections during the sentencing hearing, the court may in its discretion, permit the parties to introduce evidence. The rule speaks in terms of the court's discretion, but the Sentencing Guidelines specifically provide that the court must provide the parties with a reasonable opportunity to offer information concerning a sentencing factor reasonably in dispute. See U.S.S.G. § 6A1.3(a). Thus, it may be an issue of discretion not to permit the introduction of additional evidence. Although the rules of evidence do not apply to sentencing proceedings, *see* Fed. R. Evid. 1101(d)(3), the court clearly has discretion in determining the mode, timing, and extent of the evidence offered. *See, e.g., United States v. Zuleta-Alvarez,* 922 F.2d 33, 36 (1st Cir. 1990)(trial court did not err in denying defendant's late request to introduce rebuttal evidence by way of cross-examination).

Subdivision (c)(1) (formerly subdivision (c)(3)(D)) indicates that the court need not resolve controverted matters which will "not be taken into account in, or will not affect, sentencing." the words "will not affect" did not exist in the former provision but were added in the revision in recognition that there might be situations, due to overlaps in the sentencing ranges, where a controverted matter would not alter the sentence even if the sentencing range were changed.

The provision for disclosure of a witness' statements, which was recently proposed as an amendment to Rule 32 as new subdivision (e), is now located in subdivisions (c)(2).

Subdivision (c)(3) includes minor changes. First, if the court intends to rely on information otherwise excluded from the presentence report under subdivision (b)(5), that information is to be summarized in writing and submitted to the defendant and the defendant's counsel. Under the former provision in (c)(3)(A), such information could be summarized orally. Once the information is presented, the defendant and the defendant's counsel are to be given a reasonable opportunity to comment; in appropriate cases, that may require a continuance of the sentencing proceedings.

Subdivision (c)(5), concerning notification of the right to appeal, was formerly included in subdivision (a)(2). Although the provision has been rewritten, the Committee intends no substantive change in practice. That is, the court may , but is not required to , advise a defendant who has entered a guilty plea, nolo contendere plea or a conditional guilty plea of any right to appeal (such as an appeal challenging jurisdiction). However, the duty to advise the defendant in such cases extends only to advice on the right to appeal any sentence imposed.

Subdivision (d). Subdivision (d), dealing with entry of the court's judgement, is former subdivision (b).

Subdivision (e). Subdivision (e), which addresses the topic of withdrawing pleas, was formerly subdivision (d). Both provisions remain the same except for minor stylistic changes.

Under present practice, the court may permit, but is not required to hear, victim allocution before imposing sentence. The Committee considered, but rejected, a provision which would have required the court to hear victim allocution at sentencing.

1996 Amendments

Subdivision (d)(2). A provision for including a verdict of criminal forfeiture as a part of the sentence was added in 1972 to Rule 32. Since then, the rule has been interpreted to mean that any forfeiture order is a part of the judgment of conviction and cannot be entered before sentencing. *See, e.g., United States v. Alexander,* 772 F.Supp. 440 (D.Minn. 1990).

Delaying forfeiture proceedings, however, can pose real problems, especially in light of the implementation of the Sentencing Reform Act in 1987 and the resulting delays between verdict and sentencing in complex cases. First, the government's statutory right to discover the location of property subject to forfeiture is triggered by entry of an order of forfeiture. *See* 18 U.S.C. § 1963(k) and 21 U.S.C. § 853(m). If that order is delayed until sentencing, valuable time may be lost in locating assets which may have become unavailable or unusable. Second, third persons with an interest in the property subject to forfeiture must also wait to petition the court to begin ancillary proceedings until the forfeiture order has been entered. *See* 18 U.S.C. § 1963(*l*) and 21 U.S.C. § 853(m). And third, because the government cannot actually seize the property until an order of forfeiture is entered, it may be necessary for the court to enter restraining orders to maintain the status quo.

The amendment to Rule 32 is intended to address these concerns by specifically recognizing the authority of the court to enter a preliminary forfeiture order before sentencing. Entry of an order of forfeiture before sentencing rests within the discretion of the court, which may take into account anticipated delays in sentencing, the nature of the property, and the interests of the defendant, the government, and third persons.

The amendment permits the court to enter its order of forfeiture at any time before sentencing. Before entering the order of forfeiture, however, the court must provide notice to the defendant and a reasonable opportunity to be heard on the question of timing and form of any order of forfeiture.

The rule specifies that the order, which must ultimately be made a part of the sentence and included in the judgment, must contain authorization for the Attorney General to seize the property in question and to conduct appropriate discovery and to begin any necessary ancillary proceedings to protect third parties who have an interest in the property.

2000 Amendments

The rule is amended to reflect the creation of new Rule 32.2, which now governs criminal forfeiture procedures.

2002 Amendments

The language of Rule 32 has been amended as part of the general restyling of the Criminal Rules to make them more easily understood and to make style and terminology consistent throughout the rules. These changes are intended to be stylistic only, except as noted below.

The rule has been completely reorganized to make it easier to follow and apply. For example, the definitions in the rule have been moved to the first section and the sequencing of the sections generally follows the procedure for presentencing and sentencing procedures.

Revised Rule 32(a) contains definitions that currently appear in Rule 32(f). One substantive change was made in Rule 32(a)(2). The Committee expanded the definition of victims of crimes of violence or sexual abuse to include victims of child pornography under 18 U.S.C. §§ 2251–2257 (child pornography and related offenses). The Committee considered those victims to be similar to victims of sexual offenses under 18 U.S.C. §§ 2241–2248, who already possess that right.

Revised Rule 32(d) has been amended to more clearly set out the contents of the presentence report concerning the application of the Sentencing Guidelines.

Current Rule 32(e), which addresses the ability of a defendant to withdraw a guilty plea, has been moved to Rule 11(e).

Rule 32(h) is a new provision that reflects *Burns v. United States*, 501 U.S. 129, 138–39 (1991). In *Burns*, the Court held that, before a sentencing court could depart upward on a ground not previously identified in the presentence report as a ground for departure, Rule 32 requires the court to give the parties reasonable notice that it is contemplating such a ruling and to identify the specific ground for the departure. The Court also indicated that because the procedural entitlements in Rule 32 apply equally to both parties, it was equally appropriate to frame the issue as whether notice is required before the sentencing court departs either upward or downward. *Id.* at 135, n.4.

Revised Rule 32(i)(3) addresses changes to current Rule 32(c)(1). Under the current rule, the court is required to "rule on any unresolved objections to the presentence report." The rule does not specify, however, whether that provision should be read literally to mean every objection that might have been made to the report or only on those objections that might in some way actually affect the sentence. The Committee believed that a broad reading of the current rule might place an unreasonable burden on the court without providing any real benefit to the sentencing process. Revised Rule 32(i)(3) narrows the requirement for court findings to those instances when the objection addresses a "controverted matter." If the objection satisfies that criterion, the court must either make a finding on the objection or decide that a finding is not required because the matter will not affect sentencing or that the matter will not be considered at all in sentencing.

Revised Rule 32(i)(4)(B) provides for the right of certain victims to address the court during sentencing. As noted, *supra*, revised Rule 32(a)(2) expands the definition of victims to include victims of crimes under 18 U.S.C. §§ 2251–57 (child pornography and related offenses). Thus, they too will now be permitted to address the court.

Revised Rule 32(i)(1)(B) is intended to clarify language that currently exists in Rule 32(h)(3), that the court must inform both parties that the court will rely on information not in the presentence report and provide them with an opportunity to comment on the information.

Rule 32(i)(4)(C) includes a change concerning who may request an in camera proceeding. Under current Rule 32(c)(4), the parties must file a joint motion for an in camera proceeding to hear the statements by defense counsel, the defendant, the attorney for the government, or any victim. Under the revised rule, any party may move (for good cause) that the court hear in camera any statement—by a party or a victim—made under revised Rule 32(i)(4).

Finally, the Committee considered, but did not adopt, an amendment that would have required the court to rule on any "unresolved objection to a material matter" in the presentence report, whether or not the court will consider it in imposing an appropriate sentence. The amendment was considered because an unresolved objection that has no impact on determining a sentence under the Sentencing Guidelines may affect other important post-sentencing decisions. For example, the Bureau of Prisons consults the presentence report in deciding where a defendant will actually serve his or her sentence of confinement. *See A Judicial Guide to the Federal Bureau of Prisons*, 11 (United States Department of Justice, Federal Bureau of Prisons 1995) (noting that the "Bureau relies primarily on the Presentence Investigator Report . . ."). And as some courts have recognized, Rule 32 was intended to guard against adverse consequences of a statement in the presentence report that the court may have been found to be false. *United States v. Velasquez*, 748 F.2d 972, 974 (8th Cir. 1984) (rule designed to protect against evil that false allegation that defendant was notorious alien smuggler would affect defendant for years to come); *see also*

United States v. Brown, 715 F.2d 387, 389 n.2 (5th Cir. 1983) (sentencing report affects "place of incarceration, chances for parole, and relationships with social service and correctional agencies after release from prison").

To avoid unduly burdening the court, the Committee elected not to require resolution of objections that go only to service of sentence. However, because of the presentence report's critical role in post-sentence administration, counsel may wish to point out to the court those matters that are typically considered by the Bureau of Prisons in designating the place of confinement. For example, the Bureau considers:

> the type of offense, the length of sentence, the defendant's age, the defendant's release residence, the need for medical or other special treatment, and any placement recommendation made by the court.

A Judicial Guide to the Federal Bureau of Prisons, supra, at 11. Further, a question as to whether or not the defendant has a "drug problem" could have an impact on whether the defendant would be eligible for prison drug abuse treatment programs. 18 U.S.C. § 3621(e) (Substance abuse treatment).

If counsel objects to material in the presentence report that could affect the defendant's service of sentence, the court may resolve the objection, but is not required to do so.

HISTORICAL NOTES

Effective and Applicability Provisions

1996 Acts. Amendment by Pub.L. 104–132 to be effective, to the extent constitutionally permissible, for sentencing proceedings in cases in which the defendant is convicted on or after Apr. 24, 1996, see section 211 of Pub.L. 104–132, set out as a note under section 2248 of this title.

1994 Acts. Section 230101(c) of Pub.L. 103–322 provided that: "The amendments made by subsection (b) [amending this rule] shall become effective on December 1, 1994."

1986 Acts. Section 25(b) of Pub.L. 99–646 provided that: "The amendment made by subsection (a) shall take effect on the taking effect of the amendment made by section 215(a)(5) of the Comprehensive Crime Control Act of 1984 [§ 215(a)(5) of Pub.L. 98–473, effective Nov. 1, 1987]."

1984 Acts. Amendment by Pub.L. 98–473 effective on the first day of first calendar month beginning thirty six months after Oct. 12, 1984, applicable only to offenses committed after taking effect of sections 211 to 239 of Pub.L. 98–473, and except as otherwise provided for therein, see section 235 of Pub.L. 98–473, as amended, set out as a note under section 3551 of Title 18, Crimes and Criminal Procedure.

1982 Acts. Amendment by Pub.L. 97–291 effective Oct. 14, 1982, see section 9(a) of Pub.L. 97–291 set out as a note under section 1512 of Title 18, Crimes and Criminal Procedure.

1975 Acts. Amendments of this rule embraced in the order of the United States Supreme Court on Apr. 22, 1974, and the amendments of this rule made by section 3 of Pub.L. 94–64, effective Dec. 1, 1975, see section 2 of Pub.L. 94–64, set out as a note under rule 4 of these rules. The effective date of the amendments proposed on Apr. 22, 1974 was initially postponed until Aug. 1, 1975. See Pub.L. 93–361, July 30, 1974, 88 Stat. 397, set out as a note under section 3771 of Title 18, Crimes and Criminal Procedure.

Rule 32.1. Revoking or Modifying Probation or Supervised Release

(a) Initial Appearance.

(1) Person In Custody. A person held in custody for violating probation or supervised release must be taken without unnecessary delay before a magistrate judge.

(A) If the person is held in custody in the district where an alleged violation occurred, the initial appearance must be in that district.

(B) If the person is held in custody in a district other than where an alleged violation occurred, the initial appearance must be in that district, or in an adjacent district if the appearance can occur more promptly there.

(2) Upon a Summons. When a person appears in response to a summons for violating probation or supervised release, a magistrate judge must proceed under this rule.

(3) Advice. The judge must inform the person of the following:

(A) the alleged violation of probation or supervised release;

(B) the person's right to retain counsel or to request that counsel be appointed if the person cannot obtain counsel; and

(C) the person's right, if held in custody, to a preliminary hearing under Rule 32.1(b)(1).

(4) Appearance in the District With Jurisdiction. If the person is arrested or appears in the district that has jurisdiction to conduct a revocation hearing—either originally or by transfer of jurisdiction—the court must proceed under Rule 32.1(b)–(e).

(5) Appearance in a District Lacking Jurisdiction. If the person is arrested or appears in a district that does not have jurisdiction to conduct a revocation hearing, the magistrate judge must:

(A) if the alleged violation occurred in the district of arrest, conduct a preliminary hearing under Rule 32.1(b) and either:

(i) transfer the person to the district that has jurisdiction, if the judge finds probable cause to believe that a violation occurred; or

(ii) dismiss the proceedings and so notify the court that has jurisdiction, if the judge finds no probable cause to believe that a violation occurred; or

(B) if the alleged violation did not occur in the district of arrest, transfer the person to the district that has jurisdiction if:

(i) the government produces certified copies of the judgment, warrant, and warrant application, or produces copies of those certified documents by reliable electronic means; and

(ii) the judge finds that the person is the same person named in the warrant.

(6) Release or Detention. The magistrate judge may release or detain the person under 18 U.S.C. § 3143(a) pending further proceedings. The burden of establishing that the person will not flee or pose a danger to any other person or to the community rests with the person.

(b) Revocation.

(1) Preliminary Hearing.

(A) In General. If a person is in custody for violating a condition of probation or supervised release, a magistrate judge must promptly conduct a hearing to determine whether there is probable cause to believe that a violation occurred. The person may waive the hearing.

(B) Requirements. The hearing must be recorded by a court reporter or by a suitable recording device. The judge must give the person:

(i) notice of the hearing and its purpose, the alleged violation, and the person's right to retain counsel or to request that counsel be appointed if the person cannot obtain counsel;

(ii) an opportunity to appear at the hearing and present evidence; and

(iii) upon request, an opportunity to question any adverse witness, unless the judge determines that the interest of justice does not require the witness to appear.

(C) Referral. If the judge finds probable cause, the judge must conduct a revocation hearing. If the judge does not find probable cause, the judge must dismiss the proceeding.

(2) Revocation Hearing. Unless waived by the person, the court must hold the revocation hearing within a reasonable time in the district having jurisdiction. The person is entitled to:

(A) written notice of the alleged violation;

(B) disclosure of the evidence against the person;

(C) an opportunity to appear, present evidence, and question any adverse witness unless the court determines that the interest of justice does not require the witness to appear;

(D) notice of the person's right to retain counsel or to request that counsel be appointed if the person cannot obtain counsel; and

(E) an opportunity to make a statement and present any information in mitigation.

(c) Modification.

(1) In General. Before modifying the conditions of probation or supervised release, the court must hold a hearing, at which the person has the right to counsel and an opportunity to make a statement and present any information in mitigation.

(2) Exceptions. A hearing is not required if:

(A) the person waives the hearing; or

(B) the relief sought is favorable to the person and does not extend the term of probation or of supervised release; and

(C) an attorney for the government has received notice of the relief sought, has had a reasonable opportunity to object, and has not done so.

(d) Disposition of the Case. The court's disposition of the case is governed by 18 U.S.C. § 3563 and § 3565 (probation) and § 3583 (supervised release).

(e) Producing a Statement. Rule 26.2(a)–(d) and (f) applies at a hearing under this rule. If a party fails to comply with a Rule 26.2 order to produce a witness's statement, the court must not consider that witness's testimony.

(Added Apr. 30, 1979, eff. Dec. 1, 1980, and amended Nov. 10, 1986, Pub.L. 99–646, § 12(b), 100 Stat. 3594; Mar. 9, 1987, eff. Aug. 1, 1987; Apr. 25, 1989, eff. Dec. 1, 1989; Apr. 30, 1991, eff. Dec. 1, 1991; Apr. 22, 1993, eff. Dec. 1, 1993; Apr. 29, 2002, eff. Dec. 1, 2002; Apr. 25, 2005, eff. Dec. 1, 2005; Apr. 12, 2006, eff. Dec. 1, 2006.)

ADVISORY COMMITTEE NOTES

1979 Addition

Rule 32.1 (a) (1). Since *Morrissey v. Brewer,* 408 U.S. 471 (1972), and *Gagnon v. Scarpelli,* 411 U.S. 778 (1973), it is clear that a probationer can no longer be denied due process in reliance on the dictum in *Escoe v. Zerbst,* 295 U.S. 490, 492 (1935), that probation is an "act of grace." See Van Alstyne, The Demise of the Right-Privilege Distinction in Constitutional Law, 81 Harv.L.Rev. 1439 (1968); President's Commission on Law Enforcement and Administration of Justice, Task Force Report: Corrections 86 (1967).

Subdivision (a) (1) requires, consistent with the holding in *Scarpelli* that a prompt preliminary hearing must be held whenever "a probationer is held in custody on the ground that he has violated a condition of his probation." See 18 U.S.C. § 3653 regarding arrest of the probationer with or without a warrant. If there is to be a revocation hearing but there has not been a holding in custody for a probation violation, there need not be a preliminary hearing. It was the fact of such a holding in custody "which prompted the Court to determine that a preliminary as well as a final revocation hearing was required to afford the petitioner due process of law." *United States v. Tucker,* 524 F.2d 77 (5th Cir.1975). Consequently, a preliminary hearing need not be held if the probationer was at large and was not arrested but was allowed to appear voluntarily, *United States v. Strada,* 503 F.2d 1081 (8th Cir.1974), or in response to a show cause order which "merely requires his appearance in court," *United States v. Langford,* 369 F.Supp. 1107 (N.D.Ill.1973); if the probationer was in custody pursuant to a new charge, *Thomas v. United States,* 391 F.Supp. 202 (W.D.Pa.1975), or pursuant to a final conviction of a subsequent offense, *United States v. Tucker,* supra; or if he was arrested but obtained his release.

Subdivision (a) (1) (A), (B) and (C) list the requirements for the preliminary hearing, as developed in *Morrissey* and made applicable to probation revocation cases in *Scarpelli.*

Under (A), the probationer is to be given notice of the hearing and its purpose and of the alleged violation of probation. "Although the allegations in a motion to revoke probation need not be as specific as an indictment, they must be sufficient to apprise the probationer of the conditions of his probation which he is alleged to have violated, as well as the dates and events which support the charge." *Kartman v. Parratt,* 397 F.Supp. 531 (D.Neb.1975). Under (B), the probationer is permitted to appear and present evidence in his own behalf. And under (C), *upon request* by the probationer, adverse witnesses shall be made available for questioning unless the magistrate determines that the informant would be subjected to risk of harm if his identity were disclosed.

Subdivision (a) (1) (D) provides for notice to the probationer of his right to be represented by counsel at the preliminary hearing. Although Scarpelli did not impose as a constitutional requirement a right to counsel in all instances, under 18 U.S.C. § 3006A(b) a defendant is entitled to be represented by counsel whenever charged "with a violation of probation."

The federal magistrate (see definition in rule 54(c)) is to keep a record of what transpires at the hearing and, if he finds probable cause of a violation, hold the probationer for a revocation hearing. The probationer may be released pursuant to rule 46(c) pending the revocation hearing.

Rule 32.1 (a) (2). Subdivision (a) (2) mandates a final revocation hearing within a reasonable time to determine whether the probationer has, in fact, violated the conditions of his probation and whether his probation should be revoked. Ordinarily this time will be measured from the time of the probable cause finding (if a preliminary hearing was held) or of the issuance of an order to show cause. However, what constitutes a reasonable time must be determined on the facts of the particular case, such as whether the probationer is available or could readily be made available. If the probationer has been convicted of and is incarcerated for a new crime, and that conviction is the basis of the pending revocation proceedings, it would be relevant whether the probationer waived appearance at the revocation hearing.

The hearing required by rule 32.1(a) (2) is not a formal trial; the usual rules of evidence need not be applied. See *Morrissey v. Brewer,* supra ("the process should be flexible enough to consider evidence including letters, affidavits, and other material that would not be admissible in an adversary criminal trial"); Rule 1101(d) (e) of the Federal Rules of Evidence (rules not applicable to proceedings "granting or revoking probation"). Evidence that would establish guilt beyond a reasonable doubt is not required to support an order revoking probation. *United States v. Francischine,* 512 F.2d 827 (5th Cir.1975). This hearing may be waived by the probationer.

Subdivisions (a) (2) (A)–(E) list the rights to which a probationer is entitled at the final revocation hearing. The final hearing is less a summary one because the decision under consideration is the ultimate decision to revoke rather than a mere determination of probable cause. Thus, the probationer has certain rights not granted at the preliminary hearing; (i) the notice under (A) must be written; (ii) under (B) disclosure of all the evidence against the probationer is required; and (iii) under (D) the probationer does not have to specifically request the right to confront adverse witnesses, and the court may not limit the opportunity to question the witnesses against him.

Under subdivision (a) (2) (E) the probationer must be given notice of his right to be represented by counsel. Although *Scarpelli* holds that the Constitution does not compel counsel in all probation revocation hearings, under 18 U.S.C. § 3006A(b) a defendant is entitled to be represented by counsel whenever charged "with a violation of probation."

Revocation of probation is proper if the court finds a violation of the conditions of probation and that such violation warrants revocation. Revocation followed by imprisonment is an appropriate disposition if the court finds on the basis of the original offense and the intervening conduct of the probationer that:

(i) confinement is necessary to protect the public from further criminal activity by the offender; or

(ii) the offender is in need of correctional treatment which can most effectively be provided if he is confined; or

(iii) it would unduly depreciate the seriousness of the violation if probation were not revoked.

See American Bar Association, Standards Relating to Probation § 5.1 (Approved Draft, 1970)

If probation is revoked, the probationer may be required to serve the sentence originally imposed, or any lesser sentence, and if imposition of sentence was suspended he may receive any sentence which might have been imposed. 18 U.S.C. § 3653. When a split sentence is imposed under 18 U.S.C. § 3651 and probation is subsequently revoked, the probationer is entitled to credit for the time served in jail but not for the time he was on probation. *Thomas v. United States,* 327 F.2d 795 (10th Cir.), cert. denied 377 U.S. 1000 (1964); *Schley v. Peyton,* 280 F.Supp. 307 (W.D.Va.1968).

Rule 32.1 (b). Subdivision (b) concerns proceedings on modification of probation (as provided for in 18 U.S.C. § 3651). The probationer should have the right to apply to the sentencing court for a clarification or change of conditions. American Bar Association, Standards Relating to Probation § 3.1(c) (Approved Draft, 1970). This avenue is important for two reasons: (1) the probationer should be able to obtain resolution of a dispute over an ambiguous term or the meaning of a condition without first having to violate it; and (2) in cases of neglect, overwork, or simply unreasonableness on the part of the probation officer, the probationer should have recourse to the sentencing court when a condition needs clarification or modification.

Probation conditions should be subject to modification, for the sentencing court must be able to respond to changes in the probationer's circumstances as well as new ideas and methods of rehabilitation. See generally ABA Standards, supra, § 3.3. The sentencing court is given the authority to shorten the term or end probation early upon its own motion without a hearing. And while the modification of probation is a part of the sentencing procedure, so that the probationer is ordinarily entitled to a hearing and presence of counsel, a modification favorable to the probationer may be accomplished without a hearing in the presence of defendant and counsel. *United States v. Bailey,* 343 F.Supp. 76 (W.D.Mo. 1971).

1987 Amendments

The amendments are technical. No substantive change is intended.

1989 Amendments

The amendments recognize that convicted defendants may be on supervised release as well as on probation. See 18 U.S.C. §§ 3583, and 3624(e).

1991 Amendments

The amendment is technical. No substantive change is intended.

1993 Amendments

The addition of subdivision (c) is one of several amendments that extend Rule 26.2 to Rules 32(f), 32.1, 46, and Rule 8 of the Rules Governing Proceedings under 28 U.S.C. § 2255. As noted in the Committee Note to Rule 26.2, the primary reason for extending that Rule to other hearings and proceedings rests heavily upon the compelling need for accurate information affecting the witnesses' credibility. While that need is certainly clear in a trial on the merits, it is equally compelling, if not more so, in other pretrial and post-trial proceedings in which both the prosecution and defense have high interests at stake. In the case of revocation or modification of probation or supervised release proceedings, not only is the defendant's liberty interest at stake, the government has a stake in protecting the interests of the community.

Requiring production of witness statements at hearings conducted under Rule 32.1 will enhance the procedural due process which the rule now provides and which the Supreme Court required in *Morrissey v. Brewer,* 408 U.S. 471 (1972) and *Gagnon v. Scarpelli,* 411 U.S. 778 (1973). Access to prior statements of a witness will enhance the ability of both the defense and prosecution to test the credibility of the other side's witnesses under Rule 32.1(a)(1), (a)(2), and (b) and thus will assist the court in assessing credibility.

A witness's statement must be produced only if the witness testifies.

2002 Amendments

The language of Rule 32.1 has been amended as part of the general restyling of the Criminal Rules to make them more easily understood and to make style and terminology consistent throughout the rules. These changes are intended to be stylistic only, except as noted below.

Rule 32.1 has been completely revised and expanded. The Committee believed that it was important to spell out more completely in this rule the various procedural steps that must be met when dealing with a revocation or modification of probation or supervised release. To that end, some language formerly located in Rule 40 has been moved to revised Rule 32.1. Throughout the rule, the terms "magistrate judge," and "court" (*see* revised Rule 1(b)(Definitions)) are used to reflect that in revocation cases, initial proceedings in both felony and misdemeanor cases will normally be conducted before a magistrate judge, although a district judge may also conduct them. But a district judge must make the revocation decision if the offense of conviction was a felony. *See* 18 U.S.C. § 3401(i) (recognizing that district judge may designate a magistrate judge to conduct a hearing and submit proposed findings of fact and recommendations).

Revised Rule 32.1(a)(1)-(4) is new material. Presently, there is no provision in the rules for conducting initial appearances for defendants charged with violating probation or supervised release—although some districts apply such procedures. Although the rule labels these proceedings as initial appearances, the Committee believed that it was best to separate those proceedings from Rule 5 proceedings, because the procedures differ for persons who are charged with violating conditions of probation or supervised release.

The Committee is also aware that, in some districts, it is not the practice to have an initial appearance for a revocation of probation or supervised release proceeding. Although Rule 32.1(a) will require such an appearance, nothing in the rule prohibits a court from combining the initial appearance proceeding, if convened consistent with the "without unnecessary delay" time requirement of the rule, with the preliminary hearing under Rule 32.1(b).

Revised Rule 32.1(a)(5) is derived from current Rule 40(d).

Revised Rule 32.1(a)(6), which is derived from current Rule 46(c), provides that the defendant bears the burden of showing that he or she will not flee or pose a danger pending a hearing on the revocation of probation or supervised release. The Committee believes that the new language is not a substantive change because it makes no change in practice.

Rule 32.1(b)(1)(B)(iii) and Rule 32.1(b)(2)(C) address the ability of a releasee to question adverse witnesses at the preliminary and revocation hearings. Those provisions recognize that the court should apply a balancing test at the hearing itself when considering the releasee's asserted right to cross-examine adverse witnesses. The court is to balance the person's interest in the constitutionally guaranteed right to confrontation against the government's good cause for denying it. *See, e.g., Morrissey v. Brewer,* 408 U.S. 471, 489 (1972); *United States v. Comito,* 177 F.3d 1166 (9th Cir. 1999); *United States v. Walker,* 117 F.3d 417 (9th Cir. 1997); *United States v. Zentgraf,* 20 F.3d 906 (8th Cir. 1994).

Rule 32.1(c)(2)(A) permits the person to waive a hearing to modify the conditions of probation or supervised release. Although that language is new to the rule, the Committee believes that it reflects current practice.

The remainder of revised Rule 32.1 is derived from the current Rule 32.1.

2005 Amendments

The amendments to Rule 32.1(b) and (c) are intended to address a gap in the rule. As noted by the court in *United States v. Frazier,* 283 F.3d 1242 (11th Cir. 2002) (per curiam), there is no explicit provision in current Rule 32.1 for allocution rights for a person upon revocation of supervised release. In that case the court noted that several circuits had concluded that the right to allocution in Rule 32 extended to supervised release revocation hearings. *See United States v. Patterson,* 128 F.3d 1259, 1261 (8th Cir. 1997) (Rule 32 right to allocution applies); *United States v. Rodriguez,* 23 F.3d 919, 921 (5th Cir. 1997) (right of allocution, in Rule 32, applies at revocation proceeding). But the court agreed with the Sixth Circuit that the allocution right in Rule 32 was not incorporated into Rule 32.1. *See United States v. Waters,* 158 F.3d 933 (6th Cir. 1998) (allocution right in Rule 32 does not apply to revocation proceedings). The *Frazier* court observed that the problem with the incorporation approach is that it would require application of other provisions specifically applicable to sentencing proceedings under Rule 32, but not expressly addressed in Rule 32.1. 283 F.3d at 1245. The court, however, believed that it would be "better practice" for courts to provide for allocution at revocation proceedings and stated that "[t]he right of allocution seems both important and firmly embedded in our jurisprudence." *Id.*

The amended rule recognizes the importance of allocution and now explicitly recognizes that right at Rule 32.1(b)(2) revocation hearings, and extends it as well to Rule 32.1(c)(1) modification hearings where the court may decide to modify the terms or conditions of the defendant's probation. In each instance the court is required to give the defendant the opportunity to make a statement and present any mitigating information.

2006 Amendments

Subdivision (a)(5)(B)(i). Rule 32.1(a)(5)(B)(i) has been amended to permit the magistrate judge to accept a judgment, warrant, and warrant application by reliable electronic means. Currently, the rule requires the government to produce certified copies of those documents. This amendment parallels similar changes to Rules 5 and 41.

The amendment reflects a number of significant improvements in technology. First, receiving documents by facsimile has become very commonplace and many courts are now equipped to receive filings by electronic means, and indeed, some courts encourage or require that certain documents be filed by electronic means. Second, the technology has advanced to the state where such filings could be sent from, and received at, locations outside the courthouse. Third, electronic media can now provide improved quality of transmission and security measures. In short, in a particular case, using electronic media to transmit a document might be just as reliable and efficient as using a facsimile.

The term "electronic" is used to provide some flexibility to the rule and make allowance for further technological advances in transmitting data. The Committee envisions that the term "electronic" would include use of facsimile transmissions.

The rule requires that if electronic means are to be used to transmit a warrant to the magistrate judge, the means used be "reliable." While the rule does not further define that term, the Committee envisions that a court or magistrate judge would make that determination as a local matter. In deciding whether a particular electronic means, or media, would be reliable, the court might consider first, the expected quality and clarity of the transmission. For example, is it possible to read the contents of the warrant in its entirety, as though it were the original or a clean photocopy? Second, the court may wish to consider whether security measures are available to insure that the transmission is not compromised. In this regard, most courts are now equipped to require that certain documents contain a digital signature, or some other similar system for restricting access. Third, the court may consider whether there are reliable means of preserving the document for later use.

HISTORICAL NOTES

Effective and Applicability Provisions

1986 Acts. Section 12(c)(2) of Pub.L. 99–646 provided that: "The amendments made by subsection (b) [to subd. (b) of this rule] shall take effect 30 days after the date of enactment of this Act [Nov. 10, 1986]."

Change of Name

United States magistrate appointed under section 631 of Title 28, Judiciary and Judicial Procedure, to be known as United States magistrate judge after Dec. 1, 1990, with any reference to United States magistrate or magistrate in Title 28, in any other Federal statute, etc., deemed a reference to United States magistrate judge appointed under section 631 of Title 28, see section 321 of Pub.L. 101–650, set out as a note under section 631 of Title 28.

Rule 32.2. Criminal Forfeiture

(a) Notice to the Defendant. A court must not enter a judgment of forfeiture in a criminal proceeding unless the indictment or information contains notice to the defendant that the government will seek the forfeiture of property as part of any sentence in accordance with the applicable statute.

(b) Entering a Preliminary Order of Forfeiture.

(1) In General. As soon as practicable after a verdict or finding of guilty, or after a plea of guilty or nolo contendere is accepted, on any count in an indictment or information regarding which criminal forfeiture is sought, the court must determine what property is subject to forfeiture under the applicable statute. If the government seeks forfeiture of specific property, the court must determine whether the government has established the requisite nexus between the property and the offense. If the government seeks a personal money judgment, the court must determine the amount of money that the defendant will be ordered to pay. The court's determination may be based on evidence already in the record, including any written plea agreement or, if the forfeiture is contested, on evidence or information presented by the parties at a hearing after the verdict or finding of guilt.

(2) Preliminary Order. If the court finds that property is subject to forfeiture, it must promptly enter a preliminary order of forfeiture setting forth the amount of any money judgment or directing the forfeiture of specific property without regard to any third party's interest in all or part of it. Determining whether a third party has such an interest must be deferred until any third party files a claim in an ancillary proceeding under Rule 32.2(c).

(3) Seizing Property. The entry of a preliminary order of forfeiture authorizes the Attorney General (or a designee) to seize the specific property subject to forfeiture; to conduct any discovery the court considers proper in identifying, locating, or disposing of the property; and to commence proceedings that comply with any statutes governing third-party rights. At sentencing—or at any time before sentencing if the defendant consents—the order of forfeiture becomes final as to the defendant and must be made a part of the sentence and be included in the judgment. The court may include in the order of forfeiture conditions reasonably necessary to preserve the property's value pending any appeal.

(4) Jury Determination. Upon a party's request in a case in which a jury returns a verdict of guilty, the jury must determine whether the government has established the requisite nexus between the property and the offense committed by the defendant.

(c) Ancillary Proceeding; Entering a Final Order of Forfeiture.

(1) In General. If, as prescribed by statute, a third party files a petition asserting an interest in the property to be forfeited, the court must conduct an ancillary proceeding, but no ancillary proceeding is required to the extent that the forfeiture consists of a money judgment.

(A) In the ancillary proceeding, the court may, on motion, dismiss the petition for lack of standing, for failure to state a claim, or for any other lawful reason. For purposes of the motion, the facts set forth in the petition are assumed to be true.

(B) After disposing of any motion filed under Rule 32.2(c)(1)(A) and before conducting a hearing on the petition, the court may permit the parties to conduct discovery in accordance with the Federal Rules of Civil Procedure if the court determines that discovery is necessary or desirable to resolve factual issues. When discovery ends, a party may move for summary judgment under Federal Rule of Civil Procedure 56.

(2) Entering a Final Order. When the ancillary proceeding ends, the court must enter a final order of forfeiture by amending the preliminary order as necessary to account for any third-party rights. If no third party files a timely petition, the preliminary order becomes the final order of forfeiture if the court finds that the defendant (or any combination of defendants convicted in the case) had an interest in the property that is forfeitable under the applicable statute. The defendant may not object to the entry of the final order on the ground that the property belongs, in whole or in part, to a codefendant or third party; nor may a third party object to the final order on the ground that the third party had an interest in the property.

(3) Multiple Petitions. If multiple third-party petitions are filed in the same case, an order dismissing or granting one petition is not appealable until rulings are made on all the petitions, unless the court determines that there is no just reason for delay.

(4) Ancillary Proceeding Not Part of Sentencing. An ancillary proceeding is not part of sentencing.

(d) Stay Pending Appeal. If a defendant appeals from a conviction or an order of forfeiture, the court may stay the order of forfeiture on terms appropriate to ensure that the property remains available pending appellate review. A stay does not delay the ancillary proceeding or the determination of a third party's rights or interests. If the court rules in favor of any third party while an appeal is pending, the court may amend the order of forfeiture but must not transfer any property interest to a third party until the decision on appeal becomes final, unless the defendant consents in writing or on the record.

(e) Subsequently Located Property; Substitute Property.

(1) In General. On the government's motion, the court may at any time enter an order of forfeiture or amend an existing order of forfeiture to include property that:

(A) is subject to forfeiture under an existing order of forfeiture but was located and identified after that order was entered; or

(B) is substitute property that qualifies for forfeiture under an applicable statute.

(2) Procedure. If the government shows that the property is subject to forfeiture under Rule 32.2(e)(1), the court must:

(A) enter an order forfeiting that property, or amend an existing preliminary or final order to include it; and

(B) if a third party files a petition claiming an interest in the property, conduct an ancillary proceeding under Rule 32.2(c).

(3) Jury Trial Limited. There is no right to a jury trial under Rule 32.2(e).

(Added Apr. 17, 2000, eff. Dec. 1, 2000, and amended Apr. 29, 2002, eff. Dec. 1, 2002.)

ADVISORY COMMITTEE NOTES

2000 Adoption

Rule 32.2 consolidates a number of procedural rules governing the forfeiture of assets in a criminal case. Existing Rules 7(c)(2), 31(e) and 32(d)(2) are also amended to conform to the new rule. In addition, the forfeiture-related provisions of Rule 38(e) are stricken.

Subdivision (a). Subdivision (a) is derived from Rule 7(c)(2) which provides that notwithstanding statutory authority for the forfeiture of property following a criminal conviction, no forfeiture order may be entered unless the defendant was given notice of the forfeiture in the indictment or information. As courts have held, subdivision (a) is not intended to require that an itemized list of the property to be forfeited appear in the indictment or information itself. The subdivision reflects the trend in caselaw interpreting present Rule 7(c). Under the most recent cases, Rule 7(c) sets forth a requirement that the government give the defendant notice that it will be seeking forfeiture in accordance with the applicable statute . It does not require a substantive allegation in which the property subject to forfeiture, or the defendant's interest in the property, must be described in detail. *See United States v. DeFries*, 129 F.3d 1293 (D.C.Cir. 1997) (it is not necessary to specify in either the indictment or a bill of particulars that the government is seeking forfeiture of a particular asset, such as the defendant's salary; to comply with Rule 7(c), the government need only put the defendant on notice that it will seek to forfeit everything subject to forfeiture under the applicable statute, such as all property "acquired or maintained" as a result of a RICO violation). *See also United States v. Moffitt, Zwerling & Kemler, P.C.*, 83 F.3d 660, 665 (4th Cir. 1996), *aff'g* 846 F.Supp. 463 (E.D. Va. 1994) (*Moffitt* I) (indictment need not list each asset subject to forfeiture; under Rule 7(c), this can be done with bill of particulars); *United States v. Voigt*, 89 F.3d 1050 (3rd Cir. 1996) (court may amend order of forfeiture at any time to include substitute assets).

Subdivision (b). Subdivision (b) replaces Rule 31(e) which provides that the jury in a criminal case must return a special verdict "as to the extent of the interest or property subject to forfeiture." *See United States v. Saccoccia*, 58 F.3d 754 (1st Cir. 1995) (Rule 31(e) only applies to jury trials; no special verdict required when defendant waives right to jury on forfeiture issues).

One problem under Rule 31(e) concerns the scope of the determination that must be made prior to entering an order of forfeiture. This issue is the same whether the determination is made by the court or by the jury.

As mentioned, the current rule requires the jury to return a special verdict "as to the extent of the interest or property subject to forfeiture ." Some courts interpret this to mean only that the jury must answer "yes" or "no" when asked if the property named in the indictment is subject to forfeiture under the terms of the forfeiture statute—*e.g.* was the property used to facilitate a drug offense? Other courts also ask the jury if the defendant has a legal interest in the forfeited property. Still other courts, including the Fourth Circuit, require the jury to determine the *extent* of the defendant's interest in the property vis a vis third parties. *See United States v. Ham*, 58 F.3d 78 (4th Cir. 1995) (case remanded to the district court to impanel a jury to determine, in the first instance, the extent of the defendant's forfeitable interest in the subject property).

The notion that the "extent" of the defendant's interest must be established as part of the criminal trial is related to the fact that criminal forfeiture is an *in personam* action in which only the defendant's interest in the property may be forfeited. *United States v. Riley*, 78 F.3d 367 (8th Cir. 1996). When the criminal forfeiture statutes were first enacted in the 1970's, it was clear that a forfeiture of property other than the defendant's could not occur in a criminal case, but there was no mechanism designed to limit the forfeiture to the defendant's interest. Accordingly, Rule 31(e) was drafted to make a determination of the "extent" of the defendant's interest part of the verdict.

The problem is that third parties who might have an interest in the forfeited property are not parties to the criminal case. At the same time, a defendant who has no interest in property has no incentive, at trial, to dispute the government's forfeiture allegations. Thus, it was apparent by the 1980's that Rule 31(e) was an inadequate safeguard against the inadvertent forfeiture of property in which the defendant held no interest.

In 1984, Congress addressed this problem when it enacted a statutory scheme whereby third party interests in criminally forfeited property are litigated by the court in an ancillary proceeding following the conclusion of the criminal case and the entry of a preliminary order of forfeiture. *See* 21 U.S.C. § 853(n); 18 U. S. C. § 1963(1). Under this scheme, the court orders the forfeiture of the defendant's interest in the property—whatever that interest may be—in the criminal case. At that point, the court conducts a separate proceeding in which all potential third party claimants are given an opportunity to challenge the forfeiture by asserting a superior interest in the property. This proceeding does not involve relitigation of the forfeitability of the property; its only purpose is to determine whether any third party has a legal interest in the forfeited property.

The notice provisions regarding the ancillary proceeding are equivalent to the notice provisions that govern civil forfeitures. *Compare* 21 U.S.C . § 853(n)(1) *with* 19 U.S.C. § 1607(a); *see United States v. Bouler*, 927 F. Supp. 911 (W.D.N.C. 1996) (civil notice rules apply to ancillary criminal proceedings). Notice is published and sent to third parties that have a potential interest. *See United States v. BCCI Holdings (Luxembourg) S.A. (In re Petition of Indosuez Bank)*, 916 F. Supp. 1276 (D.D.C. 1996) (discussing steps taken by government to provide notice of criminal forfeiture to third parties). If no one files a claim, or if all claims are denied following a hearing, the forfeiture becomes final and the United States is deemed to have clear title to the property. 21 U.S.C. § 853(n)(7); *United States v. Hentz*, 1996 WL 355327 (E.D. Pa. June 20, 1996) (once third party fails to file a claim in the ancillary proceeding, government has clear title under § 853(n)(7) and can market the property notwithstanding third party's name on the deed).

Thus, the ancillary proceeding has become the forum for determining the extent of the defendant's forfeitable interest in the property. This allows the court to conduct a proceeding in which all third party claimants can participate and which ensures that the property forfeited actually belongs to the defendant.

Since the enactment of the ancillary proceeding statutes, the requirement in Rule 31(e) that the court (or jury) determine the extent of the defendant' s interest in the property as part of the criminal trial has become an unnecessary anachronism that leads more often than not to duplication and a waste of judicial resources. There is no longer any reason to delay the conclusion of the criminal trial with a lengthy hearing over the extent of the defendant's interest in property when the same issues will have to be litigated a second time in the ancillary proceeding if someone files a claim challenging the forfeiture. For example, in *United States v. Messino*, 917 F. Supp. 1307 (N.D. Ill. 1996), the court allowed the defendant to call witnesses to attempt to establish that they, not he, were the true owners of the property. After the jury rejected this evidence and the property was forfeited, the court conducted an ancillary proceeding in which the same witnesses litigated their claims to the same property.

A more sensible procedure would be for the court, once it (or a jury) determines that property was involved in the criminal offense for which the defendant has been convicted, to order the forfeiture of whatever interest a defendant may have in the property without having to determine exactly what that interest is. If third parties assert that they have an interest in all or part of the property, those interests can be adjudicated at one time in the ancillary proceeding.

This approach would also address confusion that occurs in multi-defendant cases where it is clear that each defendant should forfeit whatever interest he may have in the property used to commit the offense, but it is not at all clear which defendant is the actual owner of the property. For example, suppose A and B are co-defendants in a drug and money laundering case in which the government seeks to forfeit property involved in the scheme that is held in B's name but of which A may be the true owner. It makes no sense to invest the court's time in determining which of the two defendants holds the interest that should be forfeited. Both defendants should forfeit whatever interest they may have. Moreover, if under the current rule the court were to find that A is the true owner of the property, then B would have the right to file a claim in the ancillary proceeding where he may attempt to recover the property despite his criminal conviction. *United States v. Real Property in Waterboro*, 64 F.3d 752 (1st Cir. 1995) (co-defendant in drug/money laundering case who is not alleged to be the owner of the property is considered a third party for the purpose of challenging the forfeiture of the other co-defendant's interest).

The new rule resolves these difficulties by postponing the determination of the extent of the defendant's interest until the ancillary proceeding. As provided in (b)(1), the court, as soon as practicable after the verdict or finding of guilty in the criminal case, would determine if the property was subject to forfeiture in accordance with the applicable statute, *e.g.*, whether the property represented the proceeds of the offense, was used to facilitate the offense, or was involved in the offense in some other way. The determination could be made based on the evidence in the record from the criminal trial or the facts set forth in a written plea agreement submitted to the court at the time of the defendant's guilty plea, or the court could hold a hearing to determine if the requisite relationship existed between the property and the offense. Subdivision (b)(2) provides that it is not necessary to determine at this stage what interest any defendant might have in the property. Instead, the court would order the forfeiture of whatever interest each defendant might have in the property and conduct the ancillary proceeding.

Subdivision (b)(1) recognizes that there are different kinds of forfeiture judgments in criminal cases. One type is a personal judgment for a sum of money; another is a judgment forfeiting a specific asset. *See, e.g., United States v. Voigt*, 89 F.3d 1050 (3d Cir. 1996) (government is entitled to a personal money judgment equal to the amount involved in the money laundering offense, as well as order forfeiting specific assets involved in, or traceable to, the offense; in addition, if the statutory requirements are met, the government may be entitled to forfeit substitute assets); *United States v. Cleveland*, 1997 WL 537707 (E.D. La. Aug. 26, 1997), *modified*, 1997 WL 602186 (E.D.La. Sept. 29, 1997) (government entitled to a money judgment equal to the amount of money defendant laundered in money laundering case). The finding the court is required to make will depend on the nature of the forfeiture judgment. A number of cases have approved use of money judgment forfeitures. The Committee takes no position on the correctness of those rulings.

To the extent that the government is seeking forfeiture of a particular asset, such as the money on deposit in a particular bank account that is alleged to be the proceeds of a criminal offense, or a parcel of land that is traceable to that offense, the court must find that the government has established the requisite nexus between the property and the offense. To the extent that the government is seeking a money judgment, such as a judgment for the amount of money derived from a drug trafficking offense or the amount involved in a money laundering offense where the actual property subject to forfeiture has not been found or is unavailable, the court must determine the amount of money that the defendant should be ordered to forfeit.

The court may make the determination based on evidence in the record, or on additional evidence submitted by the defendant or evidence submitted by the government in support of the motion for the entry of a judgment of forfeiture. The defendant would have no standing to object to the forfeiture on the ground that the property belonged to someone else.

Under subdivision (b)(2), if the court finds that property is forfeitable, it must enter a preliminary order of forfeiture. It also recognizes that any determination of a third person's interest in the property is deferred until an ancillary proceeding, if any, is held under subdivision (c).

Subdivision (b)(3) replaces Rule 32(d)(2) (effective December 1996). It provides that once the court enters a preliminary order of forfeiture directing the forfeiture of whatever interest each defendant may have in the forfeited property, the government may seize the property and commence an ancillary proceeding to determine the interests of any third party. The subdivision also provides that the Attorney General may designate someone outside of the Department of Justice to seize forfeited property. This is necessary because in cases in which the lead investigative agency is in the Treasury Department, for example, the seizure of the forfeited property is typically handled by agencies other than the Department of Justice.

If no third party files a claim, the court, at the time of sentencing, will enter a final order forfeiting the property in accordance with subdivision (c)(2), discussed *infra*. If a third party files a claim, the order of forfeiture will become final as to the defendant at the time of sentencing but will be subject to amendment in favor of a third party pending the conclusion of the ancillary proceeding.

Because the order of forfeiture becomes final as to the defendant at the time of sentencing, his right to appeal from that order begins to run at that time. As courts have held, because the ancillary hearing has no bearing on the defendant's right to the property, the defendant has no right to appeal when a final order is, or is not, amended to recognize third party rights. *See, e.g., United States v. Christunas*, 126 F.3d 765 (6th Cir. 1997) (preliminary order of forfeiture is final as to the defendant and is immediately appealable).

Because it is not uncommon for sentencing to be postponed for an extended period to allow a defendant to cooperate with the government in an ongoing investigation, the rule would allow the order of forfeiture to become final as to the defendant before sentencing, if the defendant agrees to that procedure. Otherwise, the government would be unable to dispose of the property until the sentencing took place.

Subdivision (b)(4) addresses the right of either party to request that a jury make the determination of whether any property is subject to forfeiture. The provision gives the defendant, in all cases where a jury has returned a guilty verdict, the option of asking that the jury be retained to hear additional evidence regarding the forfeitability of the property. The only issue for the jury in such cases would be whether the government has established the requisite nexus between the property and the offense. For example, if the defendant disputes the government's allegation that a parcel of real property is traceable to the offense, the defendant would have the right to request that the jury hear evidence on that issue, and return a special verdict, in a bifurcated proceeding that would occur after the jury returns the guilty verdict. The government would have the same option of requesting a special jury verdict on this issue, as is the case under current law. *See* Rule 23(a) (trial by jury may be waived only with the consent of the government).

When Rule 31(e) was promulgated, it was assumed that criminal forfeiture was akin to a separate criminal offense on which evidence would be presented and the jury would have to return a verdict. In *Libretti v. United States*, 516 U.S. 29 (1995), however, the Supreme Court held that criminal forfeiture constitutes an aspect of the sentence imposed in a criminal case and that the defendant has no constitutional right to have the jury determine any part of the forfeiture. The special verdict requirement in Rule 31(e), the Court said, is in the nature of a statutory right that can be modified or repealed at any time.

Even before *Libretti*, lower courts had determined that criminal forfeiture is a sentencing matter and concluded that criminal trials therefore should be bifurcated so that the jury first returns a verdict on guilt or innocence and then returns to hear evidence regarding the forfeiture. In the second part of the bifurcated proceeding, the jury is instructed that the government must establish the forfeitability of the property by a preponderance of the evidence. *See United States v. Myers*, 21 F.3d 826 (8th Cir. 1994) (preponderance standard applies because criminal forfeiture is part of the sentence in money laundering cases); *United States v. Voigt*, 89 F.3d 1050 (3rd Cir. 1996) (following *Myers*); *United States v. Smith*, 966 F.2d 1045, 1050–53 (6th Cir. 1992) (same for drug cases); *United States v. Bieri*, 21 F.3d 819 (8th Cir. 1994) (same).

Although an argument could be made under *Libretti*, that a jury trial is no longer appropriate on any aspect of the forfeiture issue, which is a part of sentencing, the Committee decided to retain the right for the parties, in a trial held before a jury, to have the jury determine whether the government has established the requisite statutory nexus between the offense and the property to be forfeited. The jury, however, would not have any role in determining whether a defendant had an interest in the property to be forfeited. This is a matter for the ancillary proceeding which, by statute, is conducted "before the court alone, without a jury." *See* 21 U.S.C. § 853(n)(2).

Subdivision (c). Subdivision (c) sets forth a set of rules governing the conduct of the ancillary proceeding. When the ancillary hearing provisions were added to 18 U.S.C. § 1963 and 21 U.S.C. § 853 in 1984, Congress apparently assumed that the proceedings under the new provisions would involve simple questions of ownership that could, in the ordinary case, be resolved in 30 days. *See* 18 U.S.C. § 1963(1)(4). Presumably for that reason, the statute contains no procedures governing motions practice or discovery such as would be available in an ordinary civil case. Subdivision (c)(1) makes clear that no ancillary proceeding is required to the extent that the order of forfeiture consists of a money judgment. A money judgment is an *in personam* judgment against the defendant and not an order directed at specific assets in which any third party could have any interest.

Experience has shown that ancillary hearings can involve issues of enormous complexity that require years to resolve. *See United States v. BCCI Holdings (Luxembourg) S.A.*, 833 F.Supp. 9 (D.D.C. 1993) (ancillary proceeding involving over 100 claimants and $451 million); *United States v . Porcelli*, CR–85–00756 (CPS), 1992 U.S. Dist. LEXIS 17928 (E.D.N.Y Nov. 5, 1992) (litigation over third party claim continuing 6 years after RICO conviction). In such cases, procedures akin to those available under the Federal Rules of Civil Procedure should be available to the court and the parties to aid in the efficient resolution of the claims.

Because an ancillary hearing is connected to a criminal case, it would not be appropriate to make the Civil Rules applicable in all respects. The amendment, however, describes several fundamental areas in which procedures analogous to those in the Civil Rules may be followed. These include the filing of a motion to dismiss a claim, conducting discovery, disposing of a claim on a motion for summary judgment, and appealing a final disposition of a claim. Where applicable, the amendment follows the prevailing case law on the issue. *See, e.g., United States v. Lavin*, 942 F.2d 177 (3rd Cir. 1991) (ancillary proceeding treated as civil case for purposes of applying Rules of Appellate Procedure); *United States v. BCCI Holdings (Luxembourg) S.A. (In re Petitions of General Creditors)*, 919 F. Supp. 31 (D.D.C. 1996) ("If a third party fails to allege in its petition all elements necessary for recovery, including those relating to standing, the court may dismiss the petition without providing a hearing"); *United States v. BCCI (Holdings) Luxembourg S.A. (In re Petition of Department of Private Affairs)*, 1993 WL 760232 (D.D.C. Dec. 8, 1993) (applying court's inherent powers to permit third party to obtain discovery from defendant in accordance with civil rules). The provision governing appeals in cases where there are multiple claims is derived from Fed.R. Civ. P. 54(b). *See also United States v. BCCI Holdings (Luxembourg) S.A. (Petition of Banque Indosuez)*, 961 F.Supp. 282 (D.D.C. 1997) (in resolving motion to dismiss court assumes all facts pled by third party petitioner to be true, applying Rule 12(b)(6) and denying government's motion because whether claimant had superior title turned on factual dispute; government acted reasonably in not making any discovery requests in ancillary proceeding until court ruled on its motion to dismiss).

Subdivision (c)(2) provides for the entry of a final order of forfeiture at the conclusion of the ancillary proceeding. Under this provision, if no one files a claim in the ancillary proceeding, the preliminary order would become the final order of forfeiture, but the court would first have to make an independent finding that at least one of the defendants had an interest in the property such that it was proper to order the forfeiture of the property in a criminal case. In making that determination, the court may rely upon reasonable inferences. For example, the fact that the defendant used the property in committing the crime and no third party claimed an interest in the property may give rise to the inference that the defendant had a forfeitable interest in the property.

This subdivision combines and preserves two established tenets of current law. One is that criminal forfeitures are *in personam* actions that are limited to the property interests of the defendant. (This distinguishes criminal forfeiture, which is imposed as part of the defendant's sentence, from civil forfeiture which may be pursued as an action against the property *in rem* without regard to who the owner may be.) The other tenet of current law is that if a third party has notice of the forfeiture but fails to file a timely claim, his or her interests are extinguished, and may not be recognized when the court enters the final order of forfeiture. *See United States v. Hentz*, 1996 WL 355327 (E.D.Pa. June 20, 1996) (once third party fails to file a claim in the ancillary proceeding, government has clear title under 21 U.S.C. § 853(n)(7) and can market the property notwithstanding third party's name on the deed). In the rare event that a third party claims that he or she was not afforded adequate notice of a criminal forfeiture action, the person may file a motion under Rule 60(b) of the Federal Rules of Civil Procedure to reopen the ancillary proceeding. *See United States v. Bouler*, 927 F.Supp.911 (W.D.N.C. 1996) (Rule 60(b) is the proper means by which a third party may move to reopen an ancillary proceeding).

If no third parties assert their interests in the ancillary proceeding, the court must nonetheless determine that the defendant, or combination of defendants, had an interest in the property. Criminal defendants may be jointly and severally liable for the forfeiture of the entire proceeds of the criminal offense. *See United States v. Hurley*, 63 F.3d 1 (1st Cir. 1995) (government can collect the proceeds only once, but subject to that cap, it can collect from any defendant so much of the proceeds as was foreseeable to that defendant); *United States v. Cleveland*, 1997 WL 602186 (E.D. La. Sept. 29, 1997) (same); *United States v. McCarroll*, 1996 WL 355371 at *9 (N.D. Ill. June 25, 1996) (following *Hurley*), *aff'd sub nom. United States v. Jarrett*, 133 F.3d 519 (7th Cir. 1998); *United States v. DeFries*, 909 F.Supp. 13, 19–20 (D.D.C. 1995)(defendants are jointly and severally liable even where government is able to determine precisely how much each defendant benefitted from the scheme), *rev'd on other grounds*, 129 F.3d 1293 (D.C. Cir. 1997). Therefore, the conviction of any of the defendants is sufficient to support the forfeiture of the entire proceeds of the offense, even if the defendants have divided the money among themselves.

As noted in (c)(4), the ancillary proceeding is not considered a part of sentencing. Thus, the Federal Rules of Evidence would apply to the ancillary proceeding, as is the case currently.

Subdivision (d). Subdivision (d) replaces the forfeiture provisions of Rule 38(e) which provide that the court may stay an order of forfeiture pending appeal. The purpose of the provision is to ensure that the property remains intact and unencumbered so that it may be returned to the defendant in the event the appeal is successful. Subdivision (d) makes clear, however, that a district court is not divested of jurisdiction over an ancillary proceeding even if the defendant appeals his or her conviction. This allows the court to proceed with the resolution of third party claims even as the appellate court considers the appeal. Otherwise, third parties would have to await the conclusion of the appellate process even to *begin* to have their claims heard. *See United States v. Messino*, 907 F. Supp. 1231 (N.D . Ill. 1995) (the district court retains jurisdiction over forfeiture matters while an appeal is pending).

Finally, subdivision (d) provides a rule to govern what happens if the court determines that a third-party claim should be granted but the defendant's appeal is still pending. The defendant is barred from filing a claim in the ancillary proceeding. *See* 18 U.S.C. § 1963(1)(2); 21 U.S.C. § 853(n)(2). Thus, the court's determination, in the ancillary proceeding, that a third party has an interest in the property superior to that of the defendant cannot be binding on the defendant. So, in the event that the court finds in favor of the third party, that determination is final only with respect to the government's alleged interest. If the defendant prevails on appeal, he or she recovers the property as if no conviction or forfeiture ever took place. But if the order of forfeiture is affirmed, the amendment to the order of forfeiture in favor of the third party becomes effective.

Subdivision (e). Subdivision (e) makes clear, as courts have found, that the court retains jurisdiction to amend the order of forfeiture at any time to include subsequently located property which was originally included in the forfeiture order and any substitute property. *See United States v. Hurley*, 63 F.3d 1 (1st Cir. 1995) (court retains authority to order forfeiture of substitute assets after appeal is filed); *United States v. Voigt*, 89 F.3d 1050 (3rd Cir. 1996) (following *Hurley*). Third parties, of course, may contest the forfeiture of substitute assets in the ancillary proceeding. *See United States v. Lester*, 85 F.3d 1409 (9th Cir. 1996).

Subdivision (e)(1) makes clear that the right to a bifurcated jury trial to determine whether the government has established the requisite nexus between the property and the offense, *see* (b)(4), does not apply to the forfeiture of substitute assets or to the addition of newly-discovered property to an existing order of forfeiture. It is well established in the case law that the forfeiture of substitute assets is solely an issue for the court. *See United States v. Hurley*, 63 F.3d 1 (1st Cir. 1995) (court retains authority to order forfeiture of substitute assets after appeal is filed); *United States v. Voigt*, 89 F.3d 1050 (3d Cir. 1996) (following *Hurley*; court may amend order of forfeiture at any time to include substitute assets); *United States v. Thompson*, 837 F. Supp. 585 (S.D.N.Y. 1993) (court, not jury, orders forfeiture of substitute assets). As a practical matter, courts have also determined that they, not the jury, must determine the forfeitability of assets discovered after the trial is over and the jury has been dismissed. *See United States v. Saccoccia*, 898 F. Supp. 53 (D.R.I. 1995) (government may conduct post-trial discovery to determine location and identity of forfeitable assets; post-trial discovery resulted in discovery of gold bars buried in defendant's mother's backyard several years after the entry of an order directing the defendant to forfeit all property, up to $137 million, involved in his money laundering offense).

GAP Report—Rule 32.2

The Committee amended the rule to clarify several key points. First, subdivision (b) was redrafted to make it clear that if no third party files a petition to assert property rights, the trial court must determine whether the defendant has an interest in the property to be forfeited and the extent of that interest. As published, the rule would have permitted the trial judge to order the defendant to forfeit the property in its entirety if no third party filed a claim.

Second, Rule 32.2(c)(4) was added to make it clear that the ancillary proceeding is not a part of sentencing.

Third, the Committee clarified the procedures to be used if the government (1) discovers property subject to forfeiture after the court has entered an order of forfeiture and (2) seeks the forfeiture of "substitute" property under a statute authorizing such substitution.

2002 Amendments

The language of Rule 32.2 has been amended as part of the general restyling of the Criminal Rules to make them more easily understood and to make style and terminology consistent throughout the rules. These changes are intended to be stylistic only.

Rule 33. New Trial

(a) Defendant's Motion. Upon the defendant's motion, the court may vacate any judgment and grant a new trial if the interest of justice so requires. If the case was tried without a jury, the court may take additional testimony and enter a new judgment.

(b) Time to File.

(1) Newly Discovered Evidence. Any motion for a new trial grounded on newly discovered evidence must be filed within 3 years after the verdict or finding of guilty. If an appeal is pending, the court may not grant a motion for a new trial until the appellate court remands the case.

(2) Other Grounds. Any motion for a new trial grounded on any reason other than newly discovered evidence must be filed within 7 days after the verdict or finding of guilty.

(As amended Feb. 28, 1966, eff. July 1, 1966; Mar. 9, 1987, eff. Aug. 1, 1987; Apr. 24, 1998, eff. Dec. 1, 1998; Apr. 29, 2002, eff. Dec. 1, 2002; Apr. 25, 2005, eff. Dec. 1, 2005.)

ADVISORY COMMITTEE NOTES

1944 Adoption

This rule enlarges the time limit for motions for new trial on the ground of newly discovered evidence, from 60 days to two years; and for motions for new trial on other grounds from three to five days. Otherwise, it substantially continues existing practice. See former Rule II of the Criminal Appeals Rules of 1933, 292 U.S. 661 [18 U.S.C. formerly following § 688]. Cf. Rule 59(a) of the Federal Rules of Civil Procedure, 28 U.S.C., Appendix.

1966 Amendments

The amendments to the first two sentences make it clear that a judge has no power to order a new trial on his own motion, that he can act only in response to a motion timely made by a defendant. Problems of double jeopardy arise when the court acts on its own motion. See *United States v. Smith,* 331 U.S. 469 (1947). These amendments do not, of course, change the power which the court has in certain circumstances, prior to verdict or finding of guilty, to declare a mistrial and order a new trial on its own motion. See e.g., *Gori v. United States,* 367 U.S. 364 (1961); *Downum v. United States,* 372 U.S. 734 (1963); *United States v. Tateo,* 377 U.S. 463 (1964). The amendment to the last sentence changes the time in which the motion may be made to 7 days. See the Advisory Committee's Note to Rule 29.

1987 Amendments

The amendment is technical. No substantive change is intended.

1998 Amendments

As currently written, the time for filing a motion for new trial on the ground of newly discovered evidence runs from the "final judgment." The courts, in interpreting that language, have uniformly concluded that that language refers to the action of the Court of Appeals. *See, e.g., United States v. Reyes*, 49 F.3d 63, 66 (2nd Cir. 1995)(citing cases). It is less clear whether that action is the appellate court's judgment or the issuance of its mandate. In *Reyes*, the court concluded that it was the latter event. In either case, it is clear that the present approach of using the appellate court's final judgment as the triggering event can cause great disparity in the amount of time available to a defendant to file timely a motion for new trial. This would be especially true if, as noted by the Court in *Reyes, supra* at 67, an appellate court stayed its mandate pending review by the Supreme Court. *See also Herrera v. Collins*, 506 U.S. 390, 410–412 (1993) (noting divergent treatment by States of time for filing motions for new trial).

It is the intent of the Committee to remove that element of inconsistency by using the trial court's verdict or finding of guilty as the triggering event. The change also furthers internal consistency within the rule itself; the time for filing a motion for new trial on any other ground currently runs from that same event.

Finally, the time to file a motion for new trial based upon newly discovered evidence is increased to three years to compensate for what would have otherwise resulted in less time than that currently contemplated in the rule for filing such motions.

2002 Amendments

The language of Rule 33 has been amended as part of the general restyling of the Criminal Rules to make them more easily understood and to make style and terminology consistent throughout the rules. These changes are intended to be stylistic only.

2005 Amendments

Rule 33(b)(2) has been amended to remove the requirement that the court must act within seven days after a verdict or finding of guilty if it sets another time for filing a motion for a new trial. This amendment parallels similar changes to Rules 29 and 34. Further, a conforming amendment has been made to Rule 45(b)(2).

Currently, Rule 33(b)(2) requires the defendant to move for a new trial within seven days after the verdict or the finding of guilty verdict, or within some other time set by the court in an order issued during that same seven-day period. Similar provisions exist in Rules 29 and 34. Courts have held that the seven-day rule is jurisdictional. Thus, if a defendant files a request for an extension of time to file a motion for a new trial within the seven-day period, the court must rule on that motion or request within the same seven-day period. If for some reason the court does not rule on the request within the seven days, it loses jurisdiction to act on the underlying substantive motion. *See, e.g., United States v. Smith,* 331 U.S. 469, 473–474 (1947) (rejecting argument that trial court had power to grant new trial on its own motion after expiration of time in Rule 33); *United States v. Marquez,* 291 F.3d 23, 27–28 (D.C. Cir. 2002) (citing language of Rule 33, and holding that "district court forfeited the power to act when it failed to . . . fix a new time for a filing a motion for new trial within seven days of the verdict").

Assuming that the current rule was intended to promote finality, there is nothing to prevent the court from granting the defendant a significant extension of time, so long as it does so within the seven-day period. Thus, the Committee believed that the rule should be amended to be consistent with all of the other timing requirements in the rules, which do not force the court to act on a motion to extend the time for filing within a particular period of time or lose jurisdiction to do so.

Accordingly, the amendment deletes the language regarding the court's acting within seven days to set the time for filing. Read in conjunction with the conforming amendment to Rule 45(b), the defendant is still required to file a timely motion for a new trial under Rule 33(b)(2) within the seven-day period specified. The defendant may, under Rule 45, seek an extension of time to file the underlying motion as long as the defendant does so within the seven-day period. But the court itself is not required to act on that motion within any particular time. Further, under Rule 45(b)(1)(B), if for some reason the defendant fails to file the underlying motion for new trial within the specified time, the court may nonetheless consider that untimely underlying motion if the court determines that the failure to file it on time was the result of excusable neglect.

Rule 34. Arresting Judgment

(a) In General. Upon the defendant's motion or on its own, the court must arrest judgment if:

(1) the indictment or information does not charge an offense; or

(2) the court does not have jurisdiction of the charged offense.

(b) Time to File. The defendant must move to arrest judgment within 7 days after the court accepts a verdict or finding of guilty, or after a plea of guilty or nolo contendere.

(As amended Feb. 28, 1966, eff. July 1, 1966; Apr. 29, 2002, eff. Dec. 1, 2002; Apr. 25, 2005, eff. Dec. 1, 2005.)

ADVISORY COMMITTEE NOTES

1944 Adoption

This rule continues existing law except that it enlarges the time for making motions in arrest of judgment from 3 days to 5 days. See rule II(2) of Criminal Appeals Rules of 1933, 292 U.S. 661 [18 U.S.C. formerly following § 688].

1966 Amendments

The words "on motion of a defendant" are added to make clear here, as in Rule 33, that the court may act only pursuant to a timely motion by the defendant.

The amendment to the second sentence is designed to clarify an ambiguity in the rule as originally drafted. In *Lott v. United States,* 367 U.S. 421 (1961) the Supreme Court held that when a defendant pleaded nolo contendere the time in which a motion could be made under this rule did not begin to run until entry of the judgment. The Court held that such a plea was not a "determination of guilt." No reason of policy appears to justify having the time for making this motion commence with the verdict or finding of guilt but not with the acceptance of the plea of nolo contendere or the plea of guilty. The amendment changes the result in the *Lott* case and makes the periods uniform. The amendment also changes the time in which the motion may be made to 7 days. See the Advisory Committee's Note to Rule 29.

2002 Amendments

The language of Rule 34 has been amended as part of the general restyling of the Criminal Rules to make them more easily understood and to make style and terminology consistent throughout the rules. These changes are intended to be stylistic only.

2005 Amendments

Rule 34(b) has been amended to remove the requirement that the court must act within seven days after the court accepts a verdict or finding of guilty, or after a plea of guilty or nolo contendere if it sets another time for filing a motion to arrest a judgment. The amendment parallels similar amendments to Rules 29 and 33. Further, a conforming amendment has been made to Rule 45(b).

Currently, Rule 34(b) requires the defendant to move to arrest judgment within seven days after the court accepts a verdict or finding of guilty, or after a plea of guilty or nolo contendere, or within some other time set by the court in an order issued by the court within that same seven-day period. Similar provisions exist in Rules 29 and 33. Courts have held that the seven-day rule is jurisdictional. Thus, if a defendant files a request for an extension of time to file a motion to arrest judgment within the seven-day period, the judge must rule on that motion or request within the same seven-day period. If for some reason the court does not rule on the request within the seven days, the court loses jurisdiction to act on the underlying substantive motion, if it is not filed within the seven days. *See, e.g., United States v. Smith,* 331 U.S. 469, 473–474 (1947) (rejecting argument that trial court had power to grant new trial on its own motion after expiration of time in Rule 33); *United States v. Marquez,* 291 F.3d 23, 27–28 (D.C. Cir. 2002) (citing language of Rule 33, and holding that "district court forfeited the power to act when it failed to . . . fix a new time for filing a motion for a new trial within seven days of the verdict").

Assuming that the current rule was intended to promote finality, there is nothing to prevent the court from granting the defendant a significant extension of time, so long as it does so within the seven-day period. Thus, the Committee believed that the rule should be amended to be consistent with all of the other timing requirements in the rules, which do not force the court to rule on a motion to extend the time for filing within a particular period of time or lose jurisdiction to do so.

Accordingly, the amendment deletes the language regarding the court's acting within seven days to set the time for filing. Read in conjunction with the conforming amendment to Rule 45(b), the defendant is still required to file a timely motion to arrest judgment under Rule 34 within the seven-day period specified. The defendant may, under Rule 45, seek an extension of time to file the underlying motion as long as the defendant does so within the seven-day period. But the court itself is not required to act on that motion within any particular time. Further, under Rule 45(b)(1)(B), if for some reason the defendant fails to file the underlying motion within the specified time, the court may nonetheless consider that untimely motion if the court determines that the failure to file it on time was the result of excusable neglect.

Rule 35. Correcting or Reducing a Sentence

(a) Correcting Clear Error. Within 7 days after sentencing, the court may correct a sentence that resulted from arithmetical, technical, or other clear error.

(b) Reducing a Sentence for Substantial Assistance.

(1) In General. Upon the government's motion made within one year of sentencing, the court may reduce a sentence if:

(A) the defendant, after sentencing, provided substantial assistance in investigating or prosecuting another person; and

(B) reducing the sentence accords with the Sentencing Commission's guidelines and policy statements.

(2) Later Motion. Upon the government's motion made more than one year after sentencing, the court may reduce a sentence if the defendant's substantial assistance involved:

(A) information not known to the defendant until one year or more after sentencing;

(B) information provided by the defendant to the government within one year of sentencing, but which did not become useful to the government until more than one year after sentencing; or

(C) information the usefulness of which could not reasonably have been anticipated by the defendant until more than one year after sentencing and which was promptly provided to the government after its usefulness was reasonably apparent to the defendant.

(3) Evaluating Substantial Assistance. In evaluating whether the defendant has provided substantial assistance, the court may consider the defendant's presentence assistance.

(4) Below Statutory Minimum. When acting under Rule 35(b), the court may reduce the sentence to a level below the minimum sentence established by statute.

(c) "Sentencing" Defined. As used in this rule, "sentencing" means the oral announcement of the sentence.

(As amended Feb. 28, 1966, eff. July 1, 1966; Apr. 30, 1979, eff. Aug. 1, 1979; Apr. 28, 1983, eff. Aug. 1, 1983; Oct. 12, 1984, Pub.L. 98–473, Title II, § 215(b), 98 Stat. 2015; Apr. 29, 1985, eff. Aug. 1, 1985; Oct. 27, 1986, Pub.L. 99–570, Title X, § 1009, 100 Stat. 3207–8; Apr. 30, 1991, eff. Dec. 1, 1991; Apr. 24, 1998, eff. Dec. 1, 1998; Apr. 29, 2002, eff. Dec. 1, 2002; Apr. 26, 2004, eff. Dec. 1, 2004.)

Rule Applicable to Offenses Committed Prior to Nov. 1, 1987

This rule as in effect prior to amendment by Pub.L. 98–473 read as follows:

"Rule 35. Correction or Reduction of Sentence

"(a) Correction of Sentence. The court may correct an illegal sentence at any time and may correct a sentence imposed in an illegal manner within the time provided herein for the reduction of sentence.

"(b) Reduction of Sentence. A motion to reduce a sentence may be made, or the court may reduce a sentence without motion, within 120 days after the sentence is imposed or probation is revoked, or within 120 days after receipt by the court of a mandate issued upon affirmance of the judgment or dismissal of the appeal, or within 120 days after entry of any order or judgment of the Supreme Court denying review of, or having the effect of upholding, a judgment of conviction or probation revocation. The court shall determine the motion within a reasonable time. Changing a sentence from a sentence of incarceration to a grant of probation shall constitute a permissible reduction of sentence under this subdivision."

For applicability of sentencing provisions to offenses, see Effective Date and Savings Provisions, etc., note, section 235 of Pub.L. 98–473, as amended, set out under section 3551 of Title 18, Crimes and Criminal Procedure. See, also, Codification note below.

ADVISORY COMMITTEE NOTES

1944 Adoption

The first sentence of the rule continues existing law. The second sentence introduces a flexible time limitation on the power of the court of reduce a sentence, in lieu of the present limitation of the term of court. Rule 45(c) abolishes the expiration of a term of court as a time limitation, thereby necessitating the introduction of a specific time limitation as to all proceedings now governed by the term of court as a limitation. The Federal Rules of Civil Procedure (Rule 6(c)), 28 U.S.C. Appendix, abolishes the term of court as a time limitation in respect to civil actions. The two rules together thus do away with the significance of the expiration of a term of court which has largely become an anachronism.

1966 Amendments

The amendment to the first sentence gives the court power to correct a sentence imposed in an illegal manner within the same time limits as those provided for reducing a sentence. In *Hill v. United States,* 368 U.S. 424 (1962) the court held that a motion to correct an illegal sentence was not an appropriate way for a defendant to raise the question whether when he appeared for sentencing the court had afforded him an opportunity to make a statement in his own behalf as required by Rule 32(a). The amendment recognizes the distinction between an illegal sentence, which may be corrected at any time, and a sentence imposed in an illegal manner, and provides a limited time for correcting the latter.

The second sentence has been amended to increase the time within which the court may act from 60 days to 120 days. The 60-day period is frequently too short to enable the defendant to obtain and file the evidence, information and argument to support a reduction in sentence. Especially where a defendant has been committed to an institution at a distance from the sentencing court, the delays involved in institutional mail inspection procedures and the time required to contact relatives, friends and counsel may result in the 60-day period passing before the court is able to consider the case.

The other amendments to the second sentence clarify ambiguities in the timing provisions. In those cases in which the mandate of the court of appeals is issued prior to action by the Supreme Court on the defendant's petition for certiorari, the rule created problems in three situations: (1) If the writ were denied, the last phrase of the rule left obscure the point at which the period began to run because orders of the Supreme Court denying applications for writs are not sent to the district courts. See *Johnson v. United States,* 235 F.2d 459 (5th Cir. 1956). (2) If the writ were granted but later dismissed as improvidently granted, the rule did not provide any time period for reduction of sentence. (3) If the writ were granted and later the Court affirmed a judgment of the court of appeals which had affirmed the conviction, the rule did not provide any time period for reduction of sentence. The amendment makes it clear that in each of these three situations the 120-day period commences to run with the entry of the order or judgment of the Supreme Court.

The third sentence has been added to make it clear that the time limitation imposed by Rule 35 upon the reduction of a sentence does not apply to such reduction upon the revocation of probation as authorized by 18 U.S.C. § 3653.

1979 Amendments

Rule 35 is amended in order to make it clear that a judge may, in his discretion, reduce a sentence of incarceration to probation. To the extent that this permits the judge to grant probation to a defendant who has already commenced service of a term of imprisonment, it represents a change in the law. See *United States v. Murray,* 275 U.S. 347 (1928) (Probation Act construed not to give power to district court to grant probation to convict after beginning of service of sentence, even in the same term of court); *Affronti v. United States,* 350 U.S. 79 (1955) (Probation Act construed to mean that after a sentence of consecutive terms on multiple counts of an indictment has been imposed and service of sentence for the first such term has commenced, the district court may not suspend sentence and grant probation as to the remaining term or terms). In construing the statute in *Murray and Affronti,* the Court concluded Congress could not have intended to make the probation provisions applicable during the *entire* period of incarceration (the only other conceivable interpretation of the statute), for this would result in undue duplication of the three methods of mitigating a sentence—probation, pardon and parole—and would impose upon district judges the added burden of responding to probation applications from prisoners throughout the service of their terms of imprisonment. Those concerns do not apply to the instant provisions, for the reduction may occur only within the time specified in subdivision (b). This change gives "meaningful effect" to the motion-to-reduce remedy by allowing the court "to consider all alternatives that were available at the time of imposition of the original sentence." *United States v. Golphin,* 362 F.Supp. 698 (W.D.Pa.1973).

Should the reduction to a sentence of probation occur after the defendant has been incarcerated more than six months, this would put into issue the applicability of 18 U.S.C. § 3651, which provides that initially the court "may impose a sentence in excess of six months and provide that the defendant be confined in a jail-type institution for a period not exceeding six months and that the execution of the remainder of the sentence be suspended and the defendant placed on probation for such period and upon such terms and conditions as the court deems best."

1983 Amendments

Rule 35(b). There is currently a split of authority on the question of whether a court may reduce a sentence within 120 days after revocation of probation when the sentence was imposed earlier but execution of the sentence had in the interim been suspended in part or in its entirety. Compare *United States v. Colvin,* 644 F.2d 703 (8th Cir.1981) (yes); *United States v. Johnson,* 634 F.2d 94 (3d Cir.1980) (yes); with *United States v. Rice,* 671 F.2d 455 (11th Cir.1982) (no); *United States v. Kahane,* 527 F.2d 491 (2d Cir.1975) (no). The Advisory Committee believes that the rule should be clarified in light of this split, and has concluded that as a policy matter the result reached in *Johnson* is preferable.

The Supreme Court declared in *Korematsu v. United States,* 319 U.S. 432, 435 (1943), that "the difference to the probationer between imposition of sentence followed by probation .... and suspension of the imposition of sentence [followed by probation]" is not a meaningful one. When imposition of sentence is suspended entirely at the time a defendant is placed on probation, that defendant has 120 days after revocation of probation and imposition of sentence to petition for leniency. The amendment to subdivision (b) makes it clear that similar treatment is to be afforded probationers for whom execution, rather than imposition, of sentence was originally suspended.

The change facilitates the underlying objective of rule 35, which is to "give every convicted defendant a second round before the sentencing judge, and [afford] the judge an opportunity to reconsider the sentence in the light of any further information about the defendant or the case which may have been presented to him in the interim." *United States v. Ellenbogan,* 390 F.2d 537, 543 (2d Cir.1968). It is only technically correct that a reduction may be sought when a suspended sentence is imposed. As noted in *Johnson,* supra, at 96:

> It frequently will be unrealistic for a defendant whose sentence has just been suspended to petition the court for the further relief of a reduction of that suspended sentence.
>
> Just as significant, we doubt that sentencing judges would be very receptive to Rule 35 motions proffered at the time the execution of a term of imprisonment is suspended in whole or in part and the defendant given a term of probation. Moreover, the sentencing judge cannot know of events that

might occur later and that might bear on what would constitute an appropriate term of imprisonment should the defendant violate his probation .... In particular, it is only with the revocation hearing that the judge is in a position to consider whether a sentence originally suspended pending probation should be reduced. The revocation hearing is thus the first point at which an offender can be afforded a realistic opportunity to plead for a light sentence. If the offender is to be provided two chances with the sentencing judge, to be meaningful this second sentence must occur subsequent to the revocation hearing.

1985 Amendments

Subd. (b). This amendment to Rule 35(b) conforms its language to the nonliteral interpretation which most courts have already placed upon the rule, namely, that it suffices that the defendant's motion was made within the 120 days and that the court determines the motion within a reasonable time thereafter. *United States v. DeMier,* 671 F.2d 1200 (8th Cir.1982); *United States v. Smith,* 650 F.2d 206 (9th Cir.1981); *United States v. Johnson,* 634 F.2d 94 (3d Cir. 1980); *United States v. Mendoza,* 581 F.2d 89 (5th Cir.1978); *United States v. Stollings,* 516 F.2d 1287 (4th Cir.1975). Despite these decisions, a change in the language is deemed desirable to remove any doubt which might arise from dictum in some cases, e.g., *United States v. Addonizio,* 442 U.S. 178, 189 (1979), that Rule 35 only "authorizes District Courts to reduce a sentence within 120 days" and that this time period "is jurisdictional, and may not be extended." See *United States v. Kajevic,* 711 F.2d 767 (7th Cir.1983), following the *Addonizio* dictum.

As for the "reasonable time" limitation, reasonableness in this context "must be evaluated in light of the policies supporting the time limitations and the reasons for the delay in each case." *United States v. Smith, supra,* at 209. The time runs "at least for so long as the judge reasonably needs time to consider and act upon the motion." *United States v. Stollings, supra,* at 1288.

In some instances the court may decide to reduce a sentence even though no motion seeking such action is before the court. When that is the case, the amendment makes clear, the reduction must actually occur within the time specified.

This amendment does not preclude the filing of a motion by a defendant for further reduction of sentence after the court has reduced a sentence on its own motion, if filed within the 120 days specified in this rule.

1991 Amendments

Rule 35(b), as amended in 1987 as part of the Sentencing Reform Act of 1984, reflects a method by which the government may obtain valuable assistance from defendants in return for an agreement to file a motion to reduce the sentence, even if the reduction would reduce the sentence below the mandatory minimum sentence.

The title of subsection (b) has been amended to reflect that there is a difference between correcting an illegal or improper sentence, as in subsection (a), and reducing an otherwise legal sentence for special reasons under subsection (b).

Under the 1987 amendment, the trial court was required to rule on the government's motion to reduce a defendant's sentence within one year after imposition of the sentence. This caused problems, however, in situations where the defendant's assistance could not be fully assessed in time to make a timely motion which could be ruled upon before one year had elapsed. The amendment requires the government to make its motion to reduce the sentence before one year has elapsed but does not require the court to rule on the motion within the one year limit. This change should benefit both the government and the defendant and will permit completion of the defendant's anticipated cooperation with the government. Although no specific time limit is set on the court's ruling on the motion to reduce the sentence, the burden nonetheless rests on the government to request and justify a delay in the court's ruling.

The amendment also recognizes that there may be those cases where the defendant's assistance or cooperation may not occur until after one year has elapsed. For example, the defendant may not have obtained information useful to the government until after the time limit had passed. In those instances the trial court in its discretion may consider what would otherwise be an untimely motion if the government establishes that the cooperation could not have been furnished within the one-year time limit. In deciding whether to consider an untimely motion, the court may, for example, consider whether the assistance was provided as early as possible.

Subdivision (c) is intended to adopt, in part, a suggestion from the Federal Courts Study Committee 1990 that Rule 35 be amended to recognize explicitly the ability of the sentencing court to correct a sentence imposed as a result of an obvious arithmetical, technical or other clear error, if the error is discovered shortly after the sentence is imposed. At least two courts of appeals have held that the trial court has the inherent authority, notwithstanding the repeal of former Rule 35(a) by the Sentencing Reform Act of 1984, to correct a sentence within the time allowed for sentence appeal by any party under 18 U.S.C. 3742. *See United States v. Cook,* 890 F.2d 672 (4th Cir.1989) (error in applying sentencing guidelines); *United States v. Rico,* 902 F.2d 1065 (2nd Cir. 1990) (failure to impose prison sentence required by terms of plea agreement). The amendment in effect codifies the result in those two cases but provides a more stringent time requirement. The Committee believed that the time for correcting such errors should be narrowed within the time for appealing the sentence to reduce the likelihood of jurisdictional questions in the event of an appeal and to provide the parties with an opportunity to address the court's correction of the sentence, or lack thereof, in any appeal of the sentence. A shorter period of time would also reduce the likelihood of abuse of the rule by limiting its application to acknowledged and obvious errors in sentencing.

The authority to correct a sentence under this subdivision is intended to be very narrow and to extend only to those cases in which an obvious error or mistake has occurred in the sentence, that is, errors which would almost certainly result in a remand of the case to the trial court for further action under Rule 35(a). The subdivision is not intended to afford the court the opportunity to reconsider the application or interpretation of the sentencing guidelines or for the court simply to change its mind about the appropriateness of the sentence. Nor should it be used to reopen issues previously resolved at the sentencing hearing through the exercise of the court's discretion with regard to the application of the sentencing guidelines. Furthermore, the Committee did not intend that the rule relax any requirement that the parties state all objections to a sentence at or before the sentencing hearing. *See, e.g., United States v. Jones,* 899 F.2d 1097 (11th Cir.1990).

The subdivision does not provide for any formalized method of bringing the error to the attention of the court and recognizes that the court could *sua sponte* make the correction. Although the amendment does not expressly address the issue of advance notice to the parties or whether the defendant should be present in court for resentencing, the Committee contemplates that the court will act in accordance with Rules 32 and 43 with regard to any corrections in the sentence. *Compare United States v. Cook, supra* (court erred in correcting sentence *sua sponte* in absence of defendant) with *United States v. Rico, supra* (court heard arguments on request by government to correct sentence). The Committee contemplates that the court would enter an order correcting the sentence and that such order must be entered within the seven (7) day period so that the appellate process (if a timely appeal is taken) may proceed without delay and without jurisdictional confusion.

Rule 35(c) provides an efficient and prompt method for correcting obvious technical errors that are called to the court's attention immediately after sentencing. But the addition of this subdivision is not intended to preclude a defendant from obtaining statutory relief from a plainly illegal sentence. The Committee's assumption is that a defendant detained pursuant to such a sentence could seek relief under 28 U.S.C. § 2255 if the seven day period provided in Rule 35(c) has elapsed. Rule 35(c) and § 2255 should thus provide sufficient authority for a district court to correct obvious sentencing errors.

The Committee considered, but rejected, a proposal from the Federal Courts Study Committee to permit modification of a sentence, within 120 days of sentencing, based upon new factual information not known to the defendant at the time of sentencing. Unlike the proposed subdivision (c) which addresses obvious technical mistakes, the ability of the defendant (and perhaps the government) to come forward with new evidence would be a significant step toward returning Rule 35 to its former state. The Committee believed that such a change would inject into Rule 35 a degree of post-sentencing discretion which would raise doubts about the finality of determinate sentencing that Congress attempted to resolve by eliminating former Rule 35(a). It would also tend to confuse the jurisdiction of the courts of appeals in those cases in which a timely appeal is taken with respect to the sentence. Finally, the Committee was not persuaded by the available evidence that a problem of sufficient magnitude existed at this time which would warrant such an amendment.

1998 Amendments

The amendment to Rule 35(b) is intended to fill a gap in current practice. Under the Sentencing Reform Act and the applicable guidelines, a defendant who has provided "substantial" assistance to the Government before sentencing may receive a reduced sentence under United States Sentencing Guideline § 5K1.1. In addition, a defendant who provides substantial assistance after the sentence has been imposed may receive a reduction of the sentence if the government files a motion under Rule 35(b). In theory, a defendant who has provided substantial assistance both before and after sentencing could benefit from both § 5K1.1 and Rule 35(b). But a defendant who has provided, on the whole, substantial assistance may not be able to benefit from either provision because each provision requires "substantial assistance." As one court has noted, those two provisions contain distinct "temporal boundaries." *United States v. Drown,* 942 F.2d 55, 59 (1st Cir. 1991).

Although several decisions suggest that a court may aggregate the defendant's pre-sentencing and post-sentencing assistance in determining whether the "substantial assistance" requirement of Rule 35(b) has been met, *United States v. Speed,* 53 F.3d 643, 647–649 (4th Cir. 1995)(Ellis, J. concurring), there is no formal mechanism for doing so. The amendment to Rule 35(b) is designed to fill that need. Thus, the amendment permits the court to consider, in determining the substantiality of post-sentencing assistance, the defendant's pre-sentencing assistance, irrespective of whether that assistance, standing alone, was substantial.

The amendment, however, is not intended to provide a double benefit to the defendant. Thus, if the defendant has already received a reduction of sentence under U.S.S.G. § 5K1.1 for substantial pre-sentencing assistance, he or she may not have that assistance counted again in a post-sentence Rule 35(b) motion.

2002 Amendments

The language of Rule 35 has been amended as part of the general restyling of the Criminal Rules to make them more easily understood and to make style and terminology consistent throughout the rules. These changes are intended to be stylistic only, except as noted below.

The Committee deleted current Rule 35(a) (Correction on Remand). Congress added that rule, which currently addresses the issue of the district court's actions following a remand on the issue of sentencing, in the Sentencing Reform Act of 1984. Pub. L. No. 98–473. The rule cross-references 18 U.S.C. § 3742, also enacted in 1984, which provides detailed guidance on the various options available to the appellate courts in addressing sentencing errors. In reviewing both provisions, the Committee concluded that Rule 35(a) was no longer needed. First, the statute clearly covers the subject matter and second, it is not necessary to address an issue that would be very clear to a district court following a decision by a court of appeals.

Former Rule 35(c), which addressed the authority of the court to correct certain errors in the sentence, is now located in Rule 35(a). In the current version of Rule 35(c), the sentencing court is authorized to correct errors in the sentence if the correction is made within seven days of the imposition of the sentence. The revised rule uses the term "sentencing." No change in practice is intended by using that term.

A substantive change has been made in revised Rule 35(b). Under current Rule 35(b), if the government believes that a sentenced defendant has provided substantial assistance in investigating or prosecuting another person, it may move the court to reduce the original sentence; ordinarily, the motion must be filed within one year of sentencing. In 1991, the rule was amended to permit the government to file such motions after more than one year had elapsed if the government could show that the defendant's substantial assistance involved "information or evidence not known by the defendant" until more than one year had elapsed. The current rule, however, did not address the question whether a motion to reduce a sentence could be filed and granted in those instances when the defendant's substantial assistance involved information provided by the defendant within one year of sentence but that did not become useful to the government until more than one year after sentencing (e.g., when the government starts an investigation to which the information is pertinent). The courts were split on the issue. *Compare United States v. Morales*, 52 F.3d 7 (1st Cir. 1995) (permitting filing and granting of motion) *with United States v. Orozco*, 160 F.3d 1309 (11th Cir. 1998) (denying relief and citing cases). Although the court in *Orozco* felt constrained to deny relief under Rule 35(b), the court urged an amendment of the rule to:

> address the apparent unforeseen situation presented in this case where a convicted defendant provides information to the government prior to the expiration of the jurisdictional, one-year period from sentence imposition, but that information does not become useful to the government until more than one year after sentence imposition. *Id.* at 1316, n. 13.

Nor does the existing rule appear to allow a substantial assistance motion under equally deserving circumstances where a defendant, who fails to provide information within one year of sentencing because its usefulness could not reasonably have been anticipated, later provides the information to the government promptly upon its usefulness becoming apparent.

Revised Rule 35(b) is intended to address both of those situations. First, Rule 35(b)(2)(B) makes clear that a sentence reduction motion is permitted in those instances identified by the court in *Orozco*. Second, Rule 35(b)(2)(C) recognizes that a post-sentence motion is also appropriate in those instances where the defendant did not provide any information within one year of sentencing, because its usefulness was not reasonably apparent to the defendant during that period. But the rule requires that once the defendant realizes the importance of the information the defendant promptly provide the information to the government. What constitutes "prompt" notification will depend on the circumstances of the case.

The rule's one-year restriction generally serves the important interests of finality and of creating an incentive for defendants to provide promptly what useful information they might have. Thus, the proposed amendment would not eliminate the one-year requirement as a generally operative element. But where the usefulness of the information is not reasonably apparent until a year or more after sentencing, no sound purpose is served by the current rule's removal of any incentive to provide that information to the government one year or more after the sentence (or if previously provided, for the government to seek to reward the defendant) when its relevance and substantiality become evident.

By using the term "involves" in Rule 35(b)(2) in describing the sort of information that may result in substantial assistance, the Committee recognizes that a court does not lose jurisdiction to consider a Rule 35(b)(2) motion simply because other information, not covered by any of the three provisions in Rule 35(b)(2), is presented in the motion.

2004 Amendments

Rule 35(c) is a new provision, which defines sentencing for purposes of Rule 35 as the oral announcement of the sentence.

Originally, the language in Rule 35 had used the term "imposition of sentence." The term "imposition of sentence" was not defined in the rule and the courts addressing the meaning of the term were split. The majority view was that the term meant the oral announcement of the sentence and the minority view was that it meant the entry of the judgment. *See United States v. Aguirre*, 214 F.3d 1122, 1124–25 (9th Cir. 2000) (discussion of original Rule 35(c) and citing cases). During the restyling of all of the Criminal Rules in 2000 and 2001, the Committee determined that the uniform term " sentencing" throughout the entire rule was the more appropriate term. After further reflection, and with the recognition that some ambiguity may still be present in using the term "sentencing," the Committee believes that the better approach is to make clear in the rule itself that the term " sentencing" in Rule 35 means the oral announcement of the sentence. That is the meaning recognized in the majority of the cases addressing the issue.

Changes Made to Rule 35 After Publication and Comment. The Committee changed the definition of the triggering event for the timing requirements in Rule 35 to conform to the majority view in the circuit courts and adopted a special definitional section, Rule 35(c), to define sentencing as the "oral announcement of the sentence."

HISTORICAL NOTES

Codifications

Amendment of subsec. (b) by Supreme Court Order dated Apr. 29, 1985, eff. Aug. 1, 1985, which was executed to text, was to terminate Nov. 1, 1986, pursuant to section 2 of the Order, when section 215(b) of Pub.L. 98–473, Oct. 12, 1984, 98 Stat. 2015, became effective. Pub.L. 99–217, § 4, Dec. 26, 1985, 99 Stat. 1728, amended section 235(a)(1) of Pub.L. 98–473, which provided for effective date for section 215(b) of Pub.L. 98–473, to provide for effective date of Nov. 1, 1987. See section 22 of Pub.L. 100–182, set out as a note below.

Effective and Applicability Provisions

1986 Acts. Section 1009(b) of Pub.L. 99–570 provided that: "The amendment made by this section [amending subd. (a)] shall take effect on the date of the taking effect of rule 35(b) of the Federal Rules of Criminal Procedure, as amended by section 215(b) of the Comprehensive Crime Control Act of 1984 [Nov. 1, 1987]."

1985 Acts. Section 2 of the Order of the Supreme Court dated April 29, 1985, provided: "That the foregoing amendments to the Federal Rules of Criminal Procedure shall take effect on August 1, 1985 and shall govern all proceedings in criminal cases thereafter commenced and, insofar as just and practicable, all proceedings in criminal cases then pending. The amendment to Rule 35(b) shall be effective until November 1, 1986, when Section 215(b) of the Comprehensive Crime Control Act of 1984, Pub.L. 98–473, approved October 12, 1984, 98 Stat. 2015, goes into effect."

1984 Acts. Amendment by Pub.L. 98–473 effective Nov. 1, 1987, and applicable only to offenses committed after taking effect of such amendment, see section 235(a)(1) of Pub.L.

98–473, as amended, set out as a note under section 3551 of Title 18, Crimes and Criminal Procedure.

Application of Rule 35(b) to Conduct Occurring Before Effective Date of Sentencing Guidelines

Pub.L. 100–182, § 22, Dec. 7, 1987, 101 Stat. 1271, provided that: "The amendment to rule 35(b) of the Federal Rules of Criminal Procedure [subd. (b) of this rule] made by the order of the Supreme Court on April 29, 1985, shall apply with respect to all offenses committed before the taking effect of section 215(b) of the Comprehensive Crime Control Act of 1984 [section 215(b) of Pub.L. 98–473, effective Nov. 1, 1987]."

Authority to Lower Sentences Below Statutory Minimum for Old Offenses

Subd. (b) of this rule as amended by section 215(b) of Pub.L. 98–473 and subd. (b) of this rule as in effect before the taking effect of the initial set of guidelines promulgated by the United States Sentencing Commission pursuant to chapter 58 (§ 991 et seq.) of Title 28, Judiciary and Judicial Procedure, to apply in the case of an offense committed before the taking effect of such guidelines notwithstanding section 235 of Pub.L. 98–473, see section 24 of Pub.L. 100–182, set out as a note under section 3553 of Title 18, Crimes and Criminal Procedure.

Rule 36. Clerical Error

After giving any notice it considers appropriate, the court may at any time correct a clerical error in a judgment, order, or other part of the record, or correct an error in the record arising from oversight or omission.

(As amended Apr. 29, 2002, eff. Dec. 1, 2002.)

ADVISORY COMMITTEE NOTES

1944 Adoption

This rule continues existing law. *Rupinski v. United States,* 4 F.2d 17, C.C.A. 6th. The rule is similar to rule 60(a) of the Federal Rules of Civil Procedure, 28 U.S.C., Appendix.

2002 Amendments

The language of Rule 36 has been amended as part of the general restyling of the Criminal Rules to make them more easily understood and to make style and terminology consistent throughout the rules. These changes are intended to be stylistic only.

Rule 37. [Reserved]

Rule 38. Staying a Sentence or a Disability

(a) Death Sentence. The court must stay a death sentence if the defendant appeals the conviction or sentence.

(b) Imprisonment.

(1) Stay Granted. If the defendant is released pending appeal, the court must stay a sentence of imprisonment.

(2) Stay Denied; Place of Confinement. If the defendant is not released pending appeal, the court may recommend to the Attorney General that the defendant be confined near the place of the trial or appeal for a period reasonably necessary to permit the defendant to assist in preparing the appeal.

(c) Fine. If the defendant appeals, the district court, or the court of appeals under Federal Rule of Appellate Procedure 8, may stay a sentence to pay a fine or a fine and costs. The court may stay the sentence on any terms considered appropriate and may require the defendant to:

(1) deposit all or part of the fine and costs into the district court's registry pending appeal;

(2) post a bond to pay the fine and costs; or

(3) submit to an examination concerning the defendant's assets and, if appropriate, order the defendant to refrain from dissipating assets.

(d) Probation. If the defendant appeals, the court may stay a sentence of probation. The court must set the terms of any stay.

(e) Restitution and Notice to Victims.

(1) In General. If the defendant appeals, the district court, or the court of appeals under Federal Rule of Appellate Procedure 8, may stay—on any terms considered appropriate—any sentence providing for restitution under 18 U.S.C. § 3556 or notice under 18 U.S.C. § 3555.

(2) Ensuring Compliance. The court may issue any order reasonably necessary to ensure compliance with a restitution order or a notice order after disposition of an appeal, including:

(A) a restraining order;

(B) an injunction;

(C) an order requiring the defendant to deposit all or part of any monetary restitution into the district court's registry; or

(D) an order requiring the defendant to post a bond.

(f) Forfeiture. A stay of a forfeiture order is governed by Rule 32.2(d).

(g) Disability. If the defendant's conviction or sentence creates a civil or employment disability under federal law, the district court, or the court of appeals under Federal Rule of Appellate Procedure 8, may stay the disability pending appeal on any terms considered appropriate. The court may issue any order reasonably necessary to protect the interest represented by the disability pending appeal, including a restraining order or an injunction.

(As amended Dec. 27, 1948, eff. Jan. 1, 1949; Feb. 28, 1966, eff. July 1, 1966; Dec. 4, 1967, eff. July 1, 1968; Apr. 24, 1972, eff. Oct. 1, 1972; Oct. 12, 1984, Pub.L. 98–473, Title II, § 215(c), 98 Stat. 2016; Mar. 9, 1987, eff. Aug. 1, 1987; Apr. 17, 2000, eff. Dec. 1, 2000; Apr. 29, 2002, eff. Dec. 1, 2002.)

Rule Applicable to Offenses Committed Prior to Nov. 1, 1987

This rule as in effect prior to amendment by Pub.L. 98–473 read as follows:

Rule 38. Stay of Execution, and Relief Pending Review

(a) Stay of Execution.

(1) Death. A sentence of death shall be stayed if an appeal is taken.

(2) Imprisonment. A sentence of imprisonment shall be stayed if an appeal is taken and the defendant is released pending disposition of appeal pursuant to Rule 9(b) of the Federal Rules of Appellate Procedure. If not stayed, the court may recommend to the Attorney General that the defendant be retained at, or transferred to, a place of confinement near the place of trial or the place where an appeal is to be heard, for a period reasonably necessary to permit the defendant to assist in the preparation of an appeal to the court of appeals.

(3) Fine. A sentence to pay a fine or a fine and costs, if an appeal is taken, may be stayed by the district court or by the court of appeals upon such terms as the court deems proper. The court may require the defendant pending appeal to deposit the whole or any part of the fine and costs in the registry of the district court, or to give bond for the payment thereof, or to submit to an examination of assets, and it may make any appropriate order to restrain the defendant from dissipating such defendant's assets.

(4) Probation. An order placing the defendant on probation may be stayed if an appeal is taken. If not stayed, the court shall specify when the term of probation shall commence. If the order is stayed the court shall fix the terms of the stay.

[(b) Bail.] (Abrogated Dec. 4, 1967, eff. July 1, 1968)

[(c) Application for Relief Pending Review.] (Abrogated Dec. 4, 1967, eff. July 1, 1968)

For applicability of sentencing provisions to offenses, see Effective Date and Savings Provisions, etc., note, section 235 of Pub.L. 98–473, as amended, set out under section 3551 of Title 18, Crimes and Criminal Procedure.

ADVISORY COMMITTEE NOTES

1944 Adoption

This rule substantially continues existing law except that it provides that in case an appeal is taken from a judgment imposing a sentence of imprisonment, a stay shall be granted only if the defendant so elects, or is admitted to bail. Under the present rule the sentence is automatically stayed unless the defendant elects to commence service of the sentence pending appeal. The new rule merely changes the burden of making the election. See Rule V of the Criminal Appeals Rules, 1933, 292 U.S. 661 [18 U.S.C. formerly following § 688].

1966 Amendments

A defendant sentenced to a term of imprisonment is committed to the custody of the Attorney General who is empowered by statute to designate the place of his confinement. 18 U.S.C. § 4082. The sentencing court has no authority to designate the place of imprisonment. See, e.g., *Hogue v. United States,* 287 F.2d 99 (5th Cir. 1961), cert. den., 368 U.S. 932 (1961).

When the place of imprisonment has been designated, and notwithstanding the pendency of an appeal, the defendant is usually transferred from the place of his temporary detention within the district of his conviction unless he has elected "not to commence service of the sentence." This transfer can be avoided only if the defendant makes the election, a course sometimes advised by counsel who may deem it necessary to consult with the defendant from time to time before the appeal is finally perfected. However, the election deprives the defendant of a right to claim credit for the time spent in jail pending the disposition of the appeal because 18 U.S.C. § 3568 provides that the sentence of imprisonment commences, to run only from "the date on which such person is received at the penitentiary, reformatory, or jail for service of said sentence." See, e.g., *Shelton v. United States,* 234 F.2d 132 (5th Cir. 1956).

The amendment eliminates the procedure for election not to commence service of sentence. In lieu thereof it is provided that the court may recommend to the Attorney General that the defendant be retained at or transferred to a place of confinement near the place of trial or the place where the appeal is to be heard for the period reasonably necessary to permit the defendant to assist in the preparation of his appeal to the court of appeals. Under this procedure the defendant would no longer be required to serve dead time in a local jail in order to assist in preparation of his appeal.

1968 Amendments

Subdivisions (b) and (c) of this rule relate to appeals, the provisions of which are transferred to and covered by the Federal Rules of Appellate Procedure. See Advisory Committee Note under rule 37.

1972 Amendments

Rule 38(a)(2) is amended to reflect rule 9(b), Federal Rules of Appellate Procedure. The criteria for the stay of a sentence of imprisonment pending disposition of an appeal are those specified in rule 9(c) which incorporates 18 U.S.C. § 3148 by reference.

The last sentence of subdivision (a)(2) is retained although easy access to the defendant has become less important with the passage of the Criminal Justice Act which provides for compensation to the attorney to travel to the place at which the defendant is confined. Whether the court will recommend confinement near the place of trial or place where the appeal is to be heard will depend upon a balancing of convenience against the possible advantage of confinement at a more remote correctional institution where facilities and program may be more adequate.

The amendment to subdivision (a)(4) gives the court discretion in deciding whether to stay the order placing the defendant on probation. It also makes mandatory the fixing of conditions for the stay if a stay is granted. The court cannot release the defendant pending appeal without either placing him on probation or fixing the conditions for the stay under the Bail Reform Act, 18 U.S.C. § 3148.

Former rule 38(a)(4) makes mandatory a stay of an order placing the defendant on probation whenever an appeal is noted. The court may or may not impose conditions upon the stay. See rule 46, Federal Rules of Criminal Procedure; and the Bail Reform Act, 18 U.S.C. § 3148.

Having the defendant on probation during the period of appeal may serve the objectives of both community protection and defendant rehabilitation. In current practice, the order of probation is sometimes stayed for an appeal period as long as two years. In a situation where the appeal is unsuccessful, the defendant must start under probation supervision after so long a time that the conditions of probation imposed at the time of initial sentencing may no longer appropriately relate either to the defendant's need for rehabilitation or to the community's need for protection. The purposes of probation are more likely to be served if the judge can exercise discretion, in appropriate cases, to require the defendant to be under probation during the period of appeal. The American Bar Association Project on Standards for Criminal Justice takes the position that prompt imposition of sentence aids in the rehabilitation of defendants, ABA Standards Relating to Pleas of Guilty § 1.8(a)(i), Commentary p. 40 (Approved Draft, 1968). See also Sutherland and Cressey, Principles of Criminology 336 (1966).

Under 18 U.S.C. § 3148 the court now has discretion to impose conditions of release which are necessary to protect the community against danger from the defendant. This is in contrast to release prior to conviction, where the only appropriate criterion is insuring the appearance of the defendant. 18 U.S.C. § 3146. Because the court may impose conditions of release to insure community protection, it seems appropriate to enable the court to do so by ordering the defendant to submit to probation supervision during the period of appeal, thus giving the probation service responsibility for supervision.

A major difference between probation and release under 18 U.S.C. § 3148 exists if the defendant violates the conditions imposed upon his release. In the event that release is under 18 U.S.C. § 3148, the violation of the condition may result in his being placed in custody pending the decision on appeal. If the appeal were unsuccessful, the order placing him on probation presumably would become effective at that time, and he would then be released under probation supervision. If the defendant were placed on probation, his violation of a condition could result in the imposition of a jail or prison sentence. If the appeal were unsuccessful, the jail or prison sentence would continue to be served.

1987 Amendments

The amendments are technical. No substantive change is intended.

2000 Amendments

The rule is amended to reflect the creation of new Rule 32.2 which now governs criminal forfeiture procedures.

GAP Report—Rule 38

The Committee made no changes to the published draft.

2002 Amendments

The language of Rule 38 has been amended as part of the general restyling of the Criminal Rules to make them more easily understood and to make style and terminology consistent throughout the rules. These changes are intended to be stylistic only.

The reference to Appellate Rule 9(b) is deleted. The Committee believed that the reference was unnecessary and its deletion was not intended to be substantive in nature.

HISTORICAL NOTES

References in Text

The Federal Rules of Appellate Procedure, referred to in subds. (c), (e)(1), and (g), are set out in the Appendix to Title 28, Federal Rules of Appellate Procedure Rule 1 et seq., 28 U.S.C.A.

Effective and Applicability Provisions

1984 Acts. Amendment by Pub.L. 98–473 effective Nov. 1, 1987, and applicable only to offenses committed after taking effect of such amendment, see section 235(a)(1) of Pub.L. 98–473, as amended, set out as a note under section 3551 of Title 18, Crimes and Criminal Procedure.

Rule 39. [Reserved]

VIII. SUPPLEMENTARY AND SPECIAL PROCEEDINGS

Rule 40. Arrest for Failing to Appear in Another District or for Violating Conditions of Release Set in Another District

(a) In General. A person must be taken without unnecessary delay before a magistrate judge in the district of arrest if the person has been arrested under a warrant issued in another district for:

(i) failing to appear as required by the terms of that person's release under 18 U.S.C. §§ 3141–3156 or by a subpoena; or

(ii) violating conditions of release set in another district.

(b) Proceedings. The judge must proceed under Rule 5(c)(3) as applicable.

(c) Release or Detention Order. The judge may modify any previous release or detention order issued in another district, but must state in writing the reasons for doing so.

(As amended Feb. 28, 1966, eff. July 1, 1966; Apr. 24, 1972, eff. Oct. 1, 1972; Apr. 30, 1979, eff. Aug. 1, 1979; July 31, 1979, Pub.L. 96–42, § 1(2), 93 Stat. 326; Apr. 28, 1982, eff. Aug. 1, 1982; Oct. 12, 1984, Pub.L. 98–473, Title II, §§ 209(c), 215(d), 98 Stat. 1986, 2016; Mar. 9, 1987, eff. Aug. 1, 1987; Apr. 25, 1989, eff. Dec. 1, 1989; Apr. 22, 1993, eff. Dec. 1, 1993; Apr. 29, 1994, eff. Dec. 1, 1994; Apr. 27, 1995, eff. Dec. 1, 1995; Apr. 29, 2002, eff. Dec. 1, 2002; Apr. 12, 2006, eff. Dec. 1, 2006.)

Former Subd. (d) of this Rule Applicable to Offenses Committed Prior to Nov. 1, 1987

Subd. (d) of this rule [relocated to Rule 32.1(a)(5); see 2002 Advisory Committee Note under this section] as in effect prior to amendment by Pub.L. 98–473 read as follows:

(d) Arrest of Probationer. If a person is arrested for a violation of probation in a district other than the district having probation jurisdiction, such person shall be taken without unnecessary delay before the nearest available federal magistrate. The federal magistrate shall:

(1) Proceed under Rule 32.1 if jurisdiction over the probationer is transferred to that district pursuant to 18 U.S.C. § 3653;

(2) Hold a prompt preliminary hearing if the alleged violation occurred in that district, and either (i) hold the probationer to answer in the district court of the district having probation jurisdiction or (ii) dismiss the proceedings and so notify that court; or

(3) Otherwise order the probationer held to answer in the district court of the district having probation jurisdiction upon production of certified copies of the probation order, the warrant, and the application for the warrant, and upon a finding that the person before the magistrate is the person named in the warrant.

For applicability of sentencing provisions to offenses, see Effective Date and Savings Provisions, etc., note, section 235 of Pub.L. 98–473, as amended, set out under section 3551 of Title 18, Crimes and Criminal Procedure.

ADVISORY COMMITTEE NOTES

1944 Adoption

1. This rule modifies and revamps existing procedure. The present practice has developed as a result of a series of judicial decisions, the only statute dealing with the subject being exceedingly general, 18 U.S.C.A. former § 591 [now § 3041] (Arrest and removal for trial):

For any crime or offense against the United States, the offender may, by any justice or judge of the United States, or by any United States commissioner, or by any chancellor, judge of a supreme or superior court, chief or first judge of common pleas, mayor of a city, justice of the peace, or other magistrate, of any State where he may be found, and agreeably to the usual mode of process against offenders in such State, and at the expense of the United States, be arrested and imprisoned, or bailed, as the case may be, for trial before such court of the United States as by law has cognizance of the offense. * * * Where any offender or witness is committed in any district other than that where the offense is to be tried, it shall be the duty of the judge of the district where such offender or witness is imprisoned, seasonably to issue, and of the marshal to execute, a warrant for his removal to the district where the trial is to be had.

The scope of a removal hearing, the issues to be considered, and other similar matters are governed by judicial decisions, *Beavers v. Henkel,* 24 S.Ct. 605, 194 U.S. 73, 48 L.Ed. 882; *Tinsley v. Treat,* 27 S.Ct. 430, 205 U.S. 20, 51 L.Ed. 689; *Henry v. Henkel,* 235 U.S. 219; *Rodman v. Pothier,* 44 S.Ct. 360, 264 U.S. 399, 68 L.Ed. 759; *Morse v. United States,* 45 S.Ct. 209, 267 U.S. 80, 69 L.Ed. 522; *Fetters v. United States ex rel. Cunningham,* 51 S.Ct. 596, 283 U.S. 638, 75 L.Ed. 1321; *United States ex rel. Kassin v. Mulligan,* 55 S.Ct. 781, 295 U.S. 396, 79 L.Ed. 1501; see, also, 9 Edmunds, Cyclopedia of Federal Procedure 3905, et seq.

2. The purpose of removal proceedings is to accord safeguards to a defendant against an improvident removal to a distant point for trial. On the other hand, experience has shown that removal proceedings have at times been used by defendants for dilatory purposes and in attempting to frustrate prosecution by preventing or postponing transportation even as between adjoining districts and between places a few miles apart. The object of the rule is adequately to meet each of these two situations.

3. For the purposes of removal, all cases in which the accused is apprehended in a district other than that in which the prosecution is pending have been divided into two groups: first, those in which the place of arrest is either in another district of the same State, or if in another State, then less than 100 miles from the place where the prosecution is pending; and second, cases in which the arrest occurs in a State other than that in which the prosecution is pending and the place of arrest is 100 miles or more distant from the latter place.

In the first group of cases, removal proceedings are abolished. The defendant's right to the usual preliminary hearing is, of course, preserved, but the committing magistrate, if he holds defendant would bind him over to the district court in which the prosecution is pending. As ordinarily there are no removal proceedings in State prosecutions as between different parts of the same State, but the accused is transported by virtue of the process under which he was arrested, it seems reasonable that no removal proceedings should be required in the Federal courts as between districts in the same State. The provision as to arrest in another State but at a place less than 100 miles from the place where the prosecution is pending was added in order to preclude obstruction against bringing the defendant a short distance for trial.

In the second group of cases mentioned in the first paragraph, removal proceedings are continued. The practice to be followed in removal hearings will depend on whether the demand for removal is based upon an indictment or upon an information or complaint. In the latter case, proof of identity and proof of reasonable cause to believe the defendant guilty will have to be adduced in order to justify the issuance of a warrant of removal. In the former case, proof of identity coupled with a certified copy of the indictment will be sufficient, as the indictment will be conclusive proof of probable cause. The distinction is based on the fact that in case of an indictment, the grand jury, which is an arm of the court, has already found probable cause. Since the action of the grand jury is not subject to review by a district judge in the district in which the grand jury sits, it seems illogical to permit such review collaterally in a removal proceeding by a judge in another district.

4. For discussions of this rule see, Homer Cummings, 29 A.B.A.Jour. 654, 656; Holtzoff, 3 F.R.D. 445, 450–452; Holtzoff, 12 George Washington L.R. 119, 127–130; Holtzoff, The Federal Bar Journal, October 1944, 18–37; Berge, 42 Mich. L.R. 353, 374; Medalie, 4 Lawyers Guild R. (3) 1, 4.

Note to Subdivision (b). The rule provides that all removal hearings shall take place before a United States commissioner or a Federal judge. It does not confer such jurisdiction on State or local magistrates. While theoretically under existing law State and local magistrates have authority to conduct removal hearings, nevertheless as a matter of universal practice, such proceedings are always conducted before a United States commissioner or a Federal judge. 9 Edmunds, Cyclopedia of Federal Procedure 3919.

1966 Amendments

The amendment conforms to the change made in the corresponding procedure in Rule 5(b).

1972 Amendments

Subdivision (a) is amended to make clear that the person shall be taken before the federal magistrate "without unnecessary delay." Although the former rule was silent in this regard, it probably would have been interpreted to require prompt appearance, and there is therefore advantage in making this explicit in the rule itself. See C. Wright, Federal Practice and Procedure: Criminal § 652 (1969, Supp.1971). Subdivision (a) is amended to also make clear that the person is to be brought before a "federal magistrate" rather than a state or local magistrate authorized by 18 U.S.C. § 3041. The former rules were inconsistent in this regard. Although rule 40(a) provided that the person may be brought before a state or local officer authorized by former rule 5(a), such state or local officer lacks authority to conduct a preliminary examination under rule 5(c), and a principal purpose of the appearance is to hold a preliminary examination where no prior indictment or information has issued. The Federal Magistrates Act should make it possible to bring a person before a federal magistrate. See C. Wright, Federal Practice and Procedure: Criminal § 653, especially n. 35 (1969, Supp.1971).

Subdivision (b)(2) is amended to provide that the federal magistrate should inform the defendant of the fact that he may avail himself of the provisions of rule 20 if applicable in the particular case. However, the failure to so notify the defendant should not invalidate the removal procedure. Although the old rule is silent in this respect, it is current practice to so notify the defendant, and it seems desirable, therefore, to make this explicit in the rule itself.

The requirement than an order of removal under subdivision (b)(3) can be made only by a judge of the United States and cannot be made by a United States magistrate is retained. However, subdivision (b)(5) authorizes issuance of the warrant of removal by a United States magistrate if he is authorized to do so by a rule of district court adopted in accordance with 28 U.S.C. § 636(b):

Any district court * * * by the concurrence of a majority of all the judges * * * may establish rules pursuant to which any full-time United States magistrate * * * may be assigned * * * such additional duties as are not inconsistent with the Constitution and laws of the United States.

Although former rule 40(b)(3) required that the warrant of removal be issued by a judge of the United States, there appears no constitutional or statutory prohibition against conferring this authority upon a United States magistrate in accordance with 28 U.S.C. § 636(b). The background history is dealt with in detail in 8A J. Moore, Federal Practice ¶¶40.01 and 40.02 (2d ed. Cipes 1970, Supp. 1971).

Subdivision (b)(4) makes explicit reference to provisions of the Bail Reform Act of 1966 by incorporating a cross-reference to 18 U.S.C. § 3146 and § 3148.

1979 Amendments

This substantial revision of rule 40 abolishes the present distinction between arrest in a nearby district and arrest in a distant district, clarifies the authority of the magistrate with respect to the setting of bail where bail had previously been fixed in the other district, adds a provision dealing with arrest of a probationer in a district other than the district of supervision, and adds a provision dealing with arrest of a defendant or witness for failure to appear in another district.

Note to Subdivision (a). Under subdivision (a) of the present rule, if a person is arrested in a nearby district (another district in the same state, or a place less than 100 miles away), the usual rule 5 and 5.1 preliminary proceedings are conducted. But under subdivision (b) of the present rule, if a person is arrested in a distant district, then a hearing leading to a warrant of removal is held. New subdivision (a) would make no distinction between these two situations and would provide for rule 5 and 5.1 proceedings in all instances in which the arrest occurs outside the district where the warrant issues or where the offense is alleged to have been committed.

This abolition of the distinction between arrest in a nearby district and arrest in a distant district rests upon the conclusion that the procedures prescribed in rules 5 and 5.1 are adequate to protect the rights of an arrestee wherever he might be arrested. If the arrest is without a warrant, it is necessary under rule 5 that a complaint be filed forthwith complying with the requirements of rule 4(a) with respect to the showing of probable cause. If the arrest is with a warrant, that warrant will have been issued upon the basis of an indictment or of a complaint or information showing probable cause, pursuant to rules 4(a) and 9(a). Under rule 5.1, dealing with the preliminary examination, the defendant is to be held to answer only upon a showing of probable cause that an offense has been committed and that the defendant committed it.

Under subdivision (a), there are two situations in which no preliminary examination will be held. One is where "an indictment has been returned or an information filed," which pursuant to rule 5(c) obviates the need for a preliminary examination. The other is where "the defendant elects to have the preliminary examination conducted in the district in which the prosecution is pending." A defendant might wish to elect that alternative when, for example, the law in that district is that the complainant and other material witnesses may be required to appear at the preliminary examination and give testimony. See *Washington v. Clemmer*, 339 F.2d 715 (D.C.Cir.1964).

New subdivision (a) continues the present requirement that if the arrest was without a warrant a warrant must thereafter issue in the district in which the offense is alleged to have been committed. This will ensure that in the district of anticipated prosecution there will have been a probable cause determination by a magistrate or grand jury.

Note to Subdivision (b). New subdivision (b) follows existing subdivision (b) (2) in requiring the magistrate to inform the defendant of the provisions of rule 20 applicable in the particular case. Failure to so notify the defendant should not invalidate the proceedings.

Note to Subdivision (c). New subdivision (c) follows existing subdivision (b) (4) as to transmittal of papers.

Note to Subdivision (d). New subdivision (d) has no counterpart in the present rule. It provides a procedure for dealing with the situation in which a probationer is arrested in a district other than the district of supervision, consistent with 18 U.S.C. § 3653, which provides in part:

If the probationer shall be arrested in any district other than that in which he was last supervised, he shall be returned to the district in which the warrant was issued, unless jurisdiction over him is transferred as above provided to the district in which he is found, and in that case he shall be detained pending further proceedings in such district.

One possibility, provided for in subdivision (d) (1), is that of transferring jurisdiction over the probationer to the district in which he was arrested. This is permissible under the aforementioned statute, which provides in part:

Whenever during the period of his probation, a probationer heretofore or hereafter placed on probation, goes from the district in which he is being supervised to another district, jurisdiction over him may be transferred, in the discretion of the court, from the court for the district from which he goes to the court for the other district, with the concurrence of the latter court. Thereupon the court for the district to which jurisdiction is transferred shall have all power with respect to the probationer that was previously possessed by the court for the district from which the transfer is made, except that the period of probation shall not be changed without the consent of the sentencing court. This process under the same conditions may be repeated whenever during the period of his probation the probationer goes from the district in which he is being supervised to another district.

Such transfer may be particularly appropriate when it is found that the probationer has now taken up residence in the district where he was arrested or where the alleged occurrence deemed to constitute a violation of probation took place in the district of arrest. In current practice, probationers arrested in a district other than that of their present supervision are sometimes unnecessarily returned to the district of their supervision, at considerable expense and loss of time, when the more appropriate course of action would have been transfer of probation jurisdiction.

Subdivisions (d)(2) and (3) deal with the situation in which there is not a transfer of probation jurisdiction to the district of arrest. If the alleged probation violation occurred in the district of arrest, then, under subdivision (d)(2), the preliminary hearing provided for in rule 32.1(a)(1) is to be held in that district. This is consistent with the reasoning in *Morrissey v. Brewer,* 408 U.S. 471 (1972), made applicable to probation cases in *Gagnon v. Scarpelli,* 411 U.S. 778 (1973), where the Court stressed that often a parolee "is arrested at a place distant from the state institution, to which he may be returned before the final decision is made concerning revocation," and cited this as a factor contributing to the conclusion that due process requires "that some minimal inquiry be conducted at or reasonably near the place of this alleged parole violation or arrest and as promptly as convenient after arrest while information is fresh and sources are available." As later noted in *Gerstein v. Pugh,* 420 U.S. 103 (1975):

In *Morrissey v. Brewer* * * * and *Gagnon v. Scarpelli* * * * we held that a parolee or probationer arrested prior to revocation is entitled to an informal preliminary hearing at the place of arrest, with some provision for live testimony. * * * That preliminary hearing, more than the probable cause determination required by the Fourth Amendment, serves the purpose of gathering and preserving live testimony, since the final revocation hearing frequently is held at some distance from the place where the violation occurred.

However, if the alleged violation did not occur in that district, then first-hand testimony concerning the violation is unlikely to be available there, and thus the reasoning of *Morrissey and Gerstein* does not call for holding the preliminary hearing in that district. In such a case, as provided in subdivision (d) (3), the probationer should be held to answer in the district court of the district having probation jurisdiction. The purpose of the proceeding there provided for is to ascertain the identity of the probationer and provide him with copies of the warrant and the application for the warrant. A probationer is subject to the reporting condition at all times and is also subject to the continuing power of the court to modify such conditions. He therefore stands subject to return back to the jurisdiction district without the necessity of conducting a hearing in the district of arrest to determine whether there is probable cause to revoke his probation.

Note to Subdivision (e). New subdivision (e) has no counterpart in the present rule. It has been added because some confusion currently exists as to whether present rule 40(b) is applicable to the case in which a bench warrant has issued for the return of a defendant or witness who has absented himself and that person is apprehended in a distant district. In *Bandy v. United States,* 408 F.2d 518 (8th Cir.1969), a defendant, who had been released upon his personal recognizance after conviction and while petitioning for certiorari and who failed to appear as required after certiorari was denied, objected to his later arrest in New York and removal to Leavenworth without compliance with the rule 40 procedures. The court concluded:

The short answer to Bandy's first argument is found in Rush v. United States, 290 F.2d 709, 710 (5 Cir.1961): "The provisions of Rules 5 and 40, Federal Rules of Criminal Procedure, 18 U.S.C.A. may not be availed of by a prisoner in escape status * * *." As noted by Holtzoff, "Removal of Defendants in Federal Criminal Procedure", 4 F.R.D. 455, 458 (1946):

"Resort need not be had, however, to this [removal] procedure for the purpose of returning a prisoner who has been recaptured after an escape from custody. It has been pointed out that in such a case the court may summarily direct his return under its general power to issue writs not specifically provided for by statute, which may be necessary for the exercise of its jurisdiction and agreeable to the usages and principles of law. In fact, in such a situation no judicial process appears necessary. The prisoner may be retaken and administratively returned to the custody from which he escaped."

Bandy's arrest in New York was pursuant to a bench warrant issued by the United States District Court for the District of North Dakota on May 1, 1962, when Bandy failed to surrender himself to commence service of his sentence on the conviction for filing false income tax refunds. As a fugitive from justice, Bandy was not entitled upon apprehension to a removal hearing, and he was properly removed to the United States Penitentiary at Leavenworth, Kansas to commence service of sentence.

Consistent with *Bandy,* new subdivision (e) does not afford such a person all of the protections provided for in subdivision (a). However, subdivision (e) does ensure that a determination of identity will be made before that person is held to answer in the district of arrest.

Note to Subdivision (f). Although the matter of bail is dealt with in rule 46 and 18 U.S.C. §§ 3146 and 3148, new subdivision (f) has been added to clarify the situation in which a defendant makes his initial appearance before the United States magistrate and there is a warrant issued by a judge of a different district who has endorsed the amount of bail on the warrant. The present ambiguity of the rule is creating practical administrative problems. If the United States magistrate concludes that a lower bail is appropriate, the judge who fixed the original bail on the warrant has, on occasion, expressed the view that this is inappropriate conduct by the magistrate. If the magistrate, in such circumstances, does not reduce the bail to the amount supported by all of the facts, there may be caused unnecessary inconvenience to the defendant, and there would arguably be a violation of at least the spirit of the Bail Reform Act and the Eighth Amendment.

The Procedures Manual for United States Magistrates, issued under the authority of the Judicial Conference of the United States, provides in ch. 6, pp. 8–9:

Where the arrest occurs in a "distant" district, the rules do not expressly limit the discretion of the magistrate in the setting of conditions of release. However, whether or not the magistrate in the district of arrest has authority to set his own bail under Rule 40, considerations of propriety and comity would dictate that the magistrate should not attempt to set bail in a lower amount than that fixed by a judge in another district. If an unusual situation should arise where it appears from all the information available to the magistrate that the amount of bail endorsed on the warrant is excessive, he should consult with a judge of his own district or with the judge in the other district who fixed the bail in order to resolve any difficulties. (Where an amount of bail is merely recommended on the indictment by the United States attorney, the magistrate has complete discretion in setting conditions of release.)

Rule 40 as amended would encourage the above practice and hopefully would eliminate the present confusion and misunderstanding.

The last sentence of subdivision (f) requires that the magistrate set forth the reasons for his action in writing whenever he fixes bail in an amount different from that previously fixed. Setting forth the reasons for the amount of bail fixed, certainly a sound practice in all circumstances, is particularly appropriate when the bail differs from that previously fixed in another district. The requirement that reasons be set out will ensure that the "considerations of propriety and comity" referred to above will be specifically taken into account.

1982 Amendments

The amendment to 40(d) is intended to make it clear that the transfer provisions therein apply whenever the arrest occurs other than in the district of probation jurisdiction, and that if probable cause is found at a preliminary hearing held pursuant to Rule 40(d) (2) the probationer should be held to answer in the district having probation jurisdiction.

On occasion, the district of probation supervision and the district of probation jurisdiction will not be the same. See, *e.g.*, Cupp v. Byington, 179 F.Supp. 669 (S.D.Ind.1960) (supervision in Southern District of Indiana, but jurisdiction never transferred from District of Nevada). In such circumstances, it is the district having jurisdiction which may revoke the defendant's probation. *Cupp v. Byington, supra;* 18 U.S.C. § 3653 ("the court for the district having jurisdiction over him * * * may revoke the probation"; if probationer goes to another district, "jurisdiction over him may be transferred," and only then does "the court for the district to which jurisdiction is transferred * * * have all the power with respect to the probationer that was previously possessed by the court for the district from which the transfer was made"). That being the case, that is the jurisdiction to which the probationer should be transferred as provided in Rule 40(d).

Because Rule 32.1 has now taken effect, a cross-reference to those provisions has been made in subdivision (d) (1) so as to clarify how the magistrate is to proceed if jurisdiction is transferred.

1987 Amendments

The amendments are technical. No substantive change is intended.

1989 Amendments

The amendments recognize that convicted defendants may be on supervised release as well as on probation. See 18 U.S.C. §§ 3583, and 3624(e).

1993 Amendments

The amendment to subdivision (a) is intended to expedite determining where a defendant will be held to answer by permitting facsimile transmission of a warrant or a certified copy of the warrant. The amendment recognizes an increased reliance by the public in general, and the legal profession in particular, on accurate and efficient transmission of important legal documents by facsimile machines.

The Rule is also amended to conform to the Judicial Improvements Act of 1990 [P.L. 101–650, Title III, Section 321] which provides that each United States magistrate appointed under section 631 of title 28, United States Code, shall be known as a United States magistrate judge.

1994 Amendments

The amendment to subdivision (d) is intended to clarify the authority of a magistrate judge to set conditions of release in those cases where a probationer or supervised releasee is arrested in a district other than the district having jurisdiction. As written, there appeared to be a gap in Rule 40, especially under (d)(1) where the alleged violation occurs in a jurisdiction other than the district having jurisdiction.

A number of rules contain references to pretrial, trial, and post-trial release or detention of defendants, probationers and supervised releasees. Rule 46, for example, addresses the topic of release from custody. Although Rule 46(c) addresses custody pending sentencing and notice of appeal, the rule makes no explicit provision for detaining or releasing probationers or supervised releasees who are later arrested for violating terms of their probation or release. Rule 32.1 provides guidance on proceedings involving revocation of probation or supervised release. In particular, Rule 32.1 (a)(1) recognizes that when a person is held in custody on the ground that the person violated a condition of probation or supervised release, the judge or United States magistrate judge may release the person under Rule 46(c), pending the revocation proceeding. But no other explicit reference is made in Rule 32.1 to the authority of a judge or magistrate judge to determine conditions of release for a probationer or supervised releasee who is arrested in a district other than the district having jurisdiction.

The amendment recognizes that a judge or magistrate judge considering the case of a probationer or supervised releasee under Rule 40(d) has the same authority vis a vis decisions regarding custody as a judge or magistrate judge proceeding under Rule 32.1(a)(1). Thus, regardless of the ultimate disposition of an arrested probationer or supervised releasee under Rule 40(d), a judge or magistrate judge acting under that rule may rely upon Rule 46(c) in determining whether custody should be continued and if not, what conditions, if any, should be placed upon the person.

1995 Amendments

The amendment to Rule 40(a) is a technical, conforming change to reflect an amendment to Rule 5, which recognizes a limited exception to the general rule that all arrestees must be taken before a federal magistrate judge.

2002 Amendments

The language of Rule 40 has been amended as part of the general restyling of the Criminal Rules to make them more easily understood and to make style and terminology consistent throughout the rules. These changes are intended to be stylistic only.

Rule 40 has been completely revised. The Committee believed that it would be much clearer and more helpful to locate portions of Rule 40 in Rules 5 (initial appearances), 5.1 (preliminary hearings), and 32.1 (revocation or modification of probation or supervised release). Accordingly, current Rule 40(a) has been relocated in Rules 5 and 5.1. Current Rule 40(b) has been relocated in Rule 5(c)(2)(B) and current Rule 40(c) has been moved to Rule 5(c)(2)(F).

Current Rule 40(d) has been relocated in Rule 32.1(a)(5). The first sentence of current Rule 40(e) is now located in revised Rule 40(a). The second sentence of current Rule 40(e) is now in revised Rule 40(b) and current Rule 40(f) is revised Rule 40(c).

2006 Amendments

Subdivision (a). Rule 40 currently refers only to a person arrested for failing to appear in another district. The amendment is intended to fill a perceived gap in the rule that a magistrate judge in the district of arrest lacks authority to set release conditions for a person arrested only for violation of conditions of release. *See, e.g., United States v. Zhu*, 215 F.R.D. 21, 26 (D. Mass. 2003). The Committee believes that it would be inconsistent for the magistrate judge to be empowered to release an arrestee who had failed to appear altogether, but not to release one who only violated conditions of release in a minor way. Rule 40(a) is amended to expressly cover not only failure to appear, but also violation of any other condition of release.

HISTORICAL NOTES

Effective and Applicability Provisions

1984 Acts. Amendment by section 215(d) of Pub.L. 98–473 effective Nov. 1, 1987, and applicable only to offenses committed after taking effect of such amendment, see section 235(a)(1) of Pub.L. 98–473, as amended, set out as a note under section 3551 of Title 18, Crimes and Criminal Procedure.

Change of Name

United States magistrate appointed under section 631 of Title 28, Judiciary and Judicial Procedure, to be known as United States magistrate judge after Dec. 1, 1990, with any reference to United States magistrate or magistrate in Title 28, in any other Federal statute, etc., deemed a reference to United States magistrate judge appointed under section 631 of Title 28, see section 321 of Pub.L. 101–650, set out as a note under section 631 of Title 28.

Congressional Disapproval of Proposed Amendment of Rule 40.1

Pub.L. 95–78, § 2(d), July 30, 1977, 91 Stat. 320, effective Oct. 1, 1977, provided that: "The amendment proposed by the Supreme Court [in its order Apr. 26, 1977] to such Rules of Criminal Procedure adding a new rule designated as rule 40.1 [relating to a petition for removal of a criminal prosecution from a state court to a United States district court], is disapproved and shall not take effect."

Rule 41. Search and Seizure

(a) Scope and Definitions.

(1) Scope. This rule does not modify any statute regulating search or seizure, or the issuance and execution of a search warrant in special circumstances.

(2) Definitions. The following definitions apply under this rule:

(A) "Property" includes documents, books, papers, any other tangible objects, and information.

(B) "Daytime" means the hours between 6:00 a.m. and 10:00 p.m. according to local time.

(C) "Federal law enforcement officer" means a government agent (other than an attorney for the government) who is engaged in enforcing the criminal laws and is within any category of officers authorized by the Attorney General to request a search warrant.

(D) "Domestic terrorism" and "international terrorism" have the meanings set out in 18 U.S.C. § 2331.

(E) "Tracking device" has the meaning set out in 18 U.S.C. § 3117(b).

(b) Authority to Issue a Warrant. At the request of a federal law enforcement officer or an attorney for the government:

(1) a magistrate judge with authority in the district — or if none is reasonably available, a judge of a state court of record in the district — has authority to issue a warrant to search for and seize a person or property located within the district;

(2) a magistrate judge with authority in the district has authority to issue a warrant for a person or property outside the district if the person or property is located within the district when the warrant is issued but might move or be moved outside the district before the warrant is executed;

(3) a magistrate judge—in an investigation of domestic terrorism or international terrorism—with authority in any district in which activities related to the terrorism may have occurred has authority to issue a warrant for a person or property within or outside that district; and

(4) a magistrate judge with authority in the district has authority to issue a warrant to install within the district a tracking device; the warrant may authorize use of the device to track the movement of a person or property located within the district, outside the district, or both.

(c) Persons or Property Subject to Search or Seizure. A warrant may be issued for any of the following:

(1) evidence of a crime;

(2) contraband, fruits of crime, or other items illegally possessed;

(3) property designed for use, intended for use, or used in committing a crime; or

(4) a person to be arrested or a person who is unlawfully restrained.

(d) Obtaining a Warrant.

(1) In General. After receiving an affidavit or other information, a magistrate judge—or if authorized by Rule 41(b), a judge of a state court of record—must issue the warrant if there is probable cause to search for and seize a person or property or to install and use a tracking device.

(2) Requesting a Warrant in the Presence of a Judge.

(A) Warrant on an Affidavit. When a federal law enforcement officer or an attorney for the government presents an affidavit in support of a warrant, the judge may require the affiant to appear personally and may examine under oath the affiant and any witness the affiant produces.

(B) Warrant on Sworn Testimony. The judge may wholly or partially dispense with a written affidavit and base a warrant on sworn testimony if doing so is reasonable under the circumstances.

(C) Recording Testimony. Testimony taken in support of a warrant must be recorded by a court reporter or by a suitable recording device, and the judge must file the transcript or recording with the clerk, along with any affidavit.

(3) Requesting a Warrant by Telephonic or Other Means.

(A) In General. A magistrate judge may issue a warrant based on information communicated by telephone or other reliable electronic means.

(B) Recording Testimony. Upon learning that an applicant is requesting a warrant under Rule 41(d)(3)(A), a magistrate judge must:

(i) place under oath the applicant and any person on whose testimony the application is based; and

(ii) make a verbatim record of the conversation with a suitable recording device, if available, or by a court reporter, or in writing.

(C) Certifying Testimony. The magistrate judge must have any recording or court reporter's notes transcribed, certify the transcription's accuracy, and file a copy of the record and the transcription with the clerk. Any written verbatim record must be signed by the magistrate judge and filed with the clerk.

(D) Suppression Limited. Absent a finding of bad faith, evidence obtained from a warrant issued under Rule 41(d)(3)(A) is not subject to suppression on the ground that issuing the warrant in that manner was unreasonable under the circumstances.

(e) Issuing the Warrant.

(1) In General. The magistrate judge or a judge of a state court of record must issue the warrant to an officer authorized to execute it.

(2) Contents of the Warrant.

(A) Warrant to Search for and Seize a Person or Property. Except for a tracking-device warrant, the warrant must identify the person or property to be searched, identify any person or property to be seized, and designate the magistrate judge to whom it must be returned. The warrant must command the officer to:

(i) execute the warrant within a specified time no longer than 10 days;

(ii) execute the warrant during the daytime, unless the judge for good cause expressly authorizes execution at another time; and

(iii) return the warrant to the magistrate judge designated in the warrant.

(B) Warrant for a Tracking Device. A tracking-device warrant must identify the person or property to be tracked, designate the magistrate judge to whom it must be returned, and specify a reasonable length of time that the device may be used. The time must not exceed 45 days from the date the warrant was issued. The court may, for good cause, grant one or more extensions for a reasonable period not to exceed

45 days each. The warrant must command the officer to:

(i) complete any installation authorized by the warrant within a specified time no longer than 10 calendar days;

(ii) perform any installation authorized by the warrant during the daytime, unless the judge for good cause expressly authorizes installation at another time; and

(iii) return the warrant to the judge designated in the warrant.

(3) Warrant by Telephonic or Other Means. If a magistrate judge decides to proceed under Rule 41(d)(3)(A), the following additional procedures apply:

(A) Preparing a Proposed Duplicate Original Warrant. The applicant must prepare a "proposed duplicate original warrant" and must read or otherwise transmit the contents of that document verbatim to the magistrate judge.

(B) Preparing an Original Warrant. If the applicant reads the contents of the proposed duplicate original warrant, the magistrate judge must enter those contents into an original warrant. If the applicant transmits the contents by reliable electronic means, that transmission may serve as the original warrant.

(C) Modification. The magistrate judge may modify the original warrant. The judge must transmit any modified warrant to the applicant by reliable electronic means under Rule 41(e)(3)(D) or direct the applicant to modify the proposed duplicate original warrant accordingly.

(D) Signing the Warrant. Upon determining to issue the warrant, the magistrate judge must immediately sign the original warrant, enter on its face the exact date and time it is issued, and transmit it by reliable electronic means to the applicant or direct the applicant to sign the judge's name on the duplicate original warrant.

(f) Executing and Returning the Warrant.

(1) Warrant to Search for and Seize a Person or Property.

(A) Noting the Time. The officer executing the warrant must enter on it the exact date and time it was executed.

(B) Inventory. An officer present during the execution of the warrant must prepare and verify an inventory of any property seized. The officer must do so in the presence of another officer and the person from whom, or from whose premises, the property was taken. If either one is not present, the officer must prepare and verify the inventory in the presence of at least one other credible person.

(C) Receipt. The officer executing the warrant must give a copy of the warrant and a receipt for the property taken to the person from whom, or from whose premises, the property was taken or leave a copy of the warrant and receipt at the place where the officer took the property.

(D) Return. The officer executing the warrant must promptly return it—together with a copy of the inventory—to the magistrate judge designated on the warrant. The judge must, on request, give a copy of the inventory to the person from whom, or from whose premises, the property was taken and to the applicant for the warrant.

(2) Warrant for a Tracking Device.

(A) Noting the Time. The officer executing a tracking-device warrant must enter on it the exact date and time the device was installed and the period during which it was used.

(B) Return. Within 10 calendar days after the use of the tracking device has ended, the officer executing the warrant must return it to the judge designated in the warrant.

(C) Service. Within 10 calendar days after the use of the tracking device has ended, the officer executing a tracking-device warrant must serve a copy of the warrant on the person who was tracked or whose property was tracked. Service may be accomplished by delivering a copy to the person who, or whose property, was tracked; or by leaving a copy at the person's residence or usual place of abode with an individual of suitable age and discretion who resides at that location and by mailing a copy to the person's last known address. Upon request of the government, the judge may delay notice as provided in Rule 41(f)(3).

(3) Delayed Notice. Upon the government's request, a magistrate judge—or if authorized by Rule 41(b), a judge of a state court of record—may delay any notice required by this rule if the delay is authorized by statute.

(g) Motion to Return Property. A person aggrieved by an unlawful search and seizure of property or by the deprivation of property may move for the property's return. The motion must be filed in the district where the property was seized. The court must receive evidence on any factual issue necessary to decide the motion. If it grants the motion, the court must return the property to the movant, but may impose reasonable conditions to protect access to the property and its use in later proceedings.

(h) Motion to Suppress. A defendant may move to suppress evidence in the court where the trial will occur, as Rule 12 provides.

(i) Forwarding Papers to the Clerk. The magistrate judge to whom the warrant is returned must attach to the warrant a copy of the return, of the inventory, and of all other related papers and must deliver them to the clerk in the district where the property was seized.

(As amended Dec. 27, 1948, eff. Oct. 20, 1949; Apr. 9, 1956, eff. July 8, 1956; Apr. 24, 1972, eff. Oct. 1, 1972; Mar. 18, 1974, eff. July 1, 1974; Apr. 26, 1976, eff. Aug. 1, 1976; July 30, 1977, Pub.L. 95–78, § 2(e), 91 Stat. 320; Apr. 30, 1979, eff. Aug. 1, 1979; Mar. 9, 1987, eff. Aug. 1, 1987; Apr. 25, 1989, eff. Dec. 1, 1989; May 1, 1990, eff. Dec. 1, 1990; Apr. 22, 1993, eff. Dec. 1, 1993; Oct. 26, 2001, Pub.L. 107–56, Title II, § 219, 115 Stat. 291; Apr. 29, 2002, eff. Dec. 1, 2002; Apr. 12, 2006, eff. Dec. 1, 2006.)

ADVISORY COMMITTEE NOTES

1944 Adoption

This rule is a codification of existing law and practice.

Note to Subdivision (a). This rule is a restatement of existing law, 18 U.S.C. former § 611.

Note to Subdivision (b). This rule is a restatement of existing law, 18 U.S.C. former § 612; *Conyer v. United States,* 80 F.2d 292, C.C.A.6th. This provision does not supersede or repeal special statutory provisions permitting the issuance of search warrants in specific circumstances. See Subdivision (g) and Note thereto, infra.

Note to Subdivision (c). This rule is a restatement of existing law, 18 U.S.C. former §§ 613 to 616, 620; *Dumbra v. United States,* 45 S.Ct. 546, 268 U.S. 435, 69 L.Ed. 1032.

Note to Subdivision (d). This rule is a restatement of existing law, 18 U.S.C. former §§ 621 to 624.

Note to Subdivision (e). This rule is a restatement of existing law and practice, with the exception hereafter note, 18 U.S.C. former §§ 625, 626; *Weeks v. United States,* 34 S.Ct. 341, 232 U.S. 383, 58 L.Ed. 652; *Silverthorne Lumber Co. v. United States,* 40 S.Ct. 182, 251 U.S. 385, 64 L.Ed. 319; *Agello v. United States,* 46 S.Ct. 4, 269 U.S. 20, 70 L.Ed. 145; *Gouled v. United States,* 41 S.Ct. 261, 255 U.S. 298, 65 L.Ed. 647. While under existing law a motion to suppress evidence or to compel return of property obtained by an illegal search and seizure may be made either before a commissioner subject to review by the court on motion, or before the court, the rule provides that such motion may be made only before the court. The purpose is to prevent multiplication of proceedings and to bring the matter before the court in the first instance. While during the life of the Eighteenth Amendment when such motions were numerous it was a common practice in some districts for commissioners to hear such motions, the prevailing practice at the present time is to make such motions before the district court. This practice, which is deemed to be preferable, is embodied in the rule.

Note to Subdivision (f). This rule is a restatement of existing law, 18 U.S.C. former § 627; Cf. Rule 5(c) (last sentence).

Note to Subdivision (g). While Rule 41 supersedes the general provisions of 18 U.S.C. former §§ 611 to 626 [now 18 U.S.C. §§ 3105, 3109], relating to search warrants, it does not supersede, but preserves, all other statutory provisions permitting searches and seizures in specific situations. Among such statutes are the following:

U.S.C. Title 18 former:

§ 287 (Search warrant for suspected counterfeiture)

U.S.C. Title 19:

§ 1595 (Customs duties; searches and seizures)

U.S.C. Title 26 former:

§ 3117 [now § 5557] (Officers and agents authorized to investigate, issue search warrants, and prosecute for violations)

For statutes which incorporate by reference 18 U.S.C. former § 98, and therefore are now controlled by this rule, see, e.g.:

U.S.C. Title 18 former:

§ 12 (Subversive activities; undermining loyalty, discipline, or morale of armed forces; searches and seizures)

U.S.C. Title 26 former:

§ 3116 [now § 7302] (Forfeitures and seizures)

Statutory provision for a warrant for detention of war materials seized under certain circumstances is found in 22 U.S.C. former § 402 [now § 401] (Seizure of war materials intended for unlawful export.)

Other statutes providing for searches and seizures or entry without warrants are the following:

U.S.C. Title 19:

§ 482 (Search of vehicles and persons)

U.S.C. Title 25 former:

§ 246 [now 18 U.S.C. § 3113] (Searches and seizures)

U.S.C. Title 26 former:

§ 3601 [now § 7606] (Entry of premises for examination of taxable objects)

U.S.C. Title 29:

§ 211 (Investigations, inspections, and records)

U.S.C. Title 49:

§ 781 (Unlawful use of vessels, vehicles, and aircrafts; contraband article defined)

§ 782 (Seizure and forfeiture)

§ 784 (Application of related laws)

1948 Amendments

The amendment is to substitute proper reference to Title 18 in place of the repealed acts.

To eliminate reference to sections of the Act of June 15, 1917, c. 30, which have been repealed by the Act of June 25, 1948, c. 645, which enacted Title 18.

1972 Amendments

Subdivision (a) is amended to provide that a search warrant may be issued only upon the request of a federal law enforcement officer or an attorney for the government. The phrase "federal law enforcement officer" is defined in subdivision (h) in a way which will allow the Attorney General to designate the category of officers who are authorized to make application for a search warrant. The phrase "attorney for the government" is defined in rule 54.

The title to subdivision (b) is changed to make it conform more accurately to the content of the subdivision. Subdivision (b) is also changed to modernize the language used to describe the property which may be seized with a lawfully issued search warrant and to take account of a recent Supreme Court decision (*Warden v. Hayden,* 387 U.S. 294 (1967)) and recent congressional action (18 U.S.C. § 3103a) which authorize the issuance of a search warrant to search for items of solely evidential value. 18 U.S.C. § 3103a provides that "a warrant may be issued to search for and seize any property that constitutes evidence of a criminal offense . . . ."

Recent state legislation authorizes the issuance of a search warrant for evidence of crime. See, *e.g.*, Cal.Penal Code § 1524(4) (West Supp.1968); Ill.Rev.Stat. ch. 38, § 108–3 (1965); LSA C.Cr.P. art. 161 (1967); N.Y. CPL § 690.10(4) (McKinney, 1971); Ore.Rev.Stat. § 141.010 (1969); Wis.Stat. § 968.13(2) (1969).

The general weight of recent text and law review comment has been in favor of allowing a search for evidence. 8 Wigmore, Evidence § 2184a. (McNaughton rev.1961); Kamisar. The Wiretapping-Eavesdropping Problem: A Professor's View, 44 Minn.L.Rev. 891 (1960); Kaplan, Search and Seizure: A No-Man's Land in the Criminal Law, 49 Calif.L.Rev. 474 (1961); Comments: 66 Colum.L.Rev. 355 (1966), 45 N.C.L.Rev. 512 (1967), 20 U.Chi.L.Rev. 319 (1953).

There is no intention to limit the protection of the fifth amendment against compulsory self-incrimination, so items which are solely "testimonial" or "communicative" in nature might well be inadmissible on those grounds. *Schmerber v. California*, 384 U.S. 757 (1966). The court referred to the possible fifth amendment limitation in *Warden v. Hayden*, supra:

This case thus does not require that we consider whether there are items of evidential value whose very nature precludes them from being the object of a reasonable search and seizure. [387 U.S. at 303].

See ALI Model Code of Pre-Arraignment Procedure § 551.03(2) and commentary at pp. 3–5 (April 30, 1971).

It seems preferable to allow the fifth amendment limitation to develop as cases arise rather than attempt to articulate the constitutional doctrine as part of the rule itself.

The amendment to subdivision (c) is intended to make clear that a search warrant may properly be based upon a finding of probable cause based upon hearsay. That a search warrant may properly be issued on the basis of hearsay is current law. See, *e.g.*, *Jones v. United States*, 362 U.S. 257 (1960); *Spinelli v. United States*, 393 U.S. 410 (1969). See also *State v. Beal*, 40 Wis.2d 607, 162 N.W.2d 640 (1968), reversing prior Wisconsin cases which held that a search warrant could not properly issue on the basis of hearsay evidence.

The provision in subdivision (c) that the magistrate may examine the affiant or witnesses under oath is intended to assure him an opportunity to make a careful decision as to whether there is probable cause. It seems desirable to do this as an incident to the issuance of the warrant rather than having the issue raised only later on a motion to suppress the evidence. See L. Tiffany, D. McIntyre, and D. Rotenberg, Detection of Crime 118 (1967). If testimony is taken it must be recorded, transcribed, and made part of the affidavit or affidavits. This is to insure an adequate basis for determining the sufficiency of the evidentiary grounds for the issuance of the search warrant if that question should later arise.

The requirement that the warrant itself state the grounds for its issuance and the names of any affiants, is eliminated as unnecessary paper work. There is no comparable requirement for an arrest warrant in rule 4. A person who wishes to challenge the validity of a search warrant has access to the affidavits upon which the warrant was issued.

The former requirement that the warrant require that the search be conducted "forthwith" is changed to read "within a specified period of time not to exceed 10 days." The former rule contained an inconsistency between subdivision (c) requiring that the search be conducted "forthwith" and subdivision (d) requiring execution "within 10 days after its date." The amendment resolves this ambiguity and confers discretion upon the issuing magistrate to specify the time within which the search may be conducted to meet the needs of the particular case.

The rule is also changed to allow the magistrate to authorize a search at a time other than "daytime," where there is "reasonable cause shown" for doing so. To make clear what "daytime" means, the term is defined in subdivision (h).

Subdivision (d) is amended to conform its language to the Federal Magistrates Act. The language "The warrant may be executed and returned only within 10 days after its date" is omitted as unnecessary. The matter is now covered adequately in proposed subdivision (c) which gives the issuing officer authority to fix the time within which the warrant is to be executed.

The amendment to subdivision (e) and the addition of subdivision (f) are intended to require the motion to suppress evidence to be made in the trial court rather than in the district in which the evidence was seized as now allowed by the rule. In *DiBella v. United States*, 369 U.S. 121 (1962), the court, in effect, discouraged motions to suppress in the district in which the property was seized:

There is a decision in the Second Circuit, *United States v. Klapholz*, 230 F.2d 494 (1956), allowing the Government an appeal from an order granting a post-indictment motion to suppress, apparently for the single reason that the motion was filed in the district of seizure rather than of trial; but the case was soon thereafter taken by a District Court to have counseled declining jurisdiction of such motions for reasons persuasive against allowing the appeal: "This course will avoid a needless duplication of effort by two courts and provide a more expeditious resolution of the controversy besides avoiding the risk of determining prematurely and inadequately the admissibility of evidence at the trial. . . . A piecemeal adjudication such as that which would necessarily follow from a disposition of the motion here might conceivably result in prejudice either to the Government or the defendants, or both." *United States v. Lester*, 21 F.R.D. 30, 31 (D.C.S.D.N.Y.1957). Rule 41(e), of course, specifically provides for making of the motion in the district of seizure. On a summary hearing, however, the ruling there is likely always to be tentative. We think it accords most satisfactorily with sound administration of the Rules to treat such rulings as interlocutory. [369 U.S. at 132–133.]

As amended, subdivision (e) provides for a return of the property if (1) the person is entitled to lawful possession *and* (2) the seizure was illegal. This means that the judge in the district of seizure does not have to decide the legality of the seizure in cases involving contraband which, even if seized illegally, is not to be returned.

The five grounds for returning the property, presently listed in the rule, are dropped for two reasons—(1) substantive grounds for objecting to illegally obtained evidence (*e.g.*, *Miranda*) are not ordinarily codified in the rules and (2) the categories are not entirely accurate. See *United States v. Howard*, 138 F.Supp. 376, 380 (D.Md.1956).

A sentence is added to subdivision (e) to provide that a motion for return of property, made in the district of trial, shall be treated also as a motion to suppress under rule 12. This change is intended to further the objective of rule 12 which is to have all pretrial motions disposed of in a single court appearance rather than to have a series of pretrial motions made on different dates, causing undue delay in administration.

Subdivision (f) is new and reflects the position that it is best to have the motion to suppress made in the court of the district of trial rather than in the court of the district in which the seizure occurred. The motion to suppress in the district of trial should be made in accordance with the provisions of rule 12.

Subdivision (g) is changed to conform to subdivision (c) which requires the return to be made before a federal judicial officer even though the search warrant may have been issued by a nonfederal magistrate.

Subdivision (h) is former rule 41(g) with the addition of a definition of the term "daytime" and the phrase "federal law enforcement officer."

1977 Amendments

Rule 41(c) (2) is added to establish a procedure for the issuance of a search warrant when it is not reasonably practicable for the person obtaining the warrant to present a written affidavit to a magistrate or a state judge as required by subdivision (c) (1). At least two states have adopted a similar procedure, Ariz.Rev.Stat.Ann. §§ 13–1444(c)–1445(c) (Supp.1973); Cal.Pen. Code §§ 1526(b), 1528(b) (West Supp. 1974), and comparable amendments are under consideration in other jurisdictions. See Israel, Legislative Regulation of Searches and Seizures: The Michigan Proposals, 73 Mich. L.Rev. 221, 258–63 (1975); Nakell, Proposed Revisions of North Carolina's Search and Seizure Law, 52 N.Car.L.Rev. 277, 306–11 (1973). It has been strongly recommended that "every State enact legislation that provides for the issuance of search warrants pursuant to telephoned petitions and affidavits from police officers." National Advisory Commission on Criminal Justice Standards and Goals, Report on Police 95 (1973). Experience with the procedure has been most favorable. Miller, Telephonic Search Warrants: The San Diego Experience, 9 The Prosecutor 385 (1974).

The trend of recent Supreme Court decisions has been to give greater priority to the use of a search warrant as the proper way of making a lawful search: It is a cardinal rule that, in seizing goods and articles, law enforcement agents must secure and use search warrants whenever reasonably practicable. . . . This rule rests upon the desirability of having magistrates rather than police officers determine when searches and seizures are permissible and what limitations should be placed upon such activities. *Trupiano v. United States,* 334 U.S. 699, 705 (1948), quoted with approval in *Chimel v. California,* 395 U.S. 752, 758 (1969).

See also *Coolidge v. New Hampshire,* 403 U.S. 443 (1971); Note, *Chambers v. Maroney: New Dimensions in the Law of Search and Seizure,* 46 Indiana L.J. 257, 262 (1971).

Use of search warrants can best be encouraged by making it administratively feasible to obtain a warrant when one is needed. One reason for the nonuse of the warrant has been the administrative difficulties involved in getting a warrant, particularly at times of the day when a judicial officer is ordinarily unavailable. See L. Tiffany, D. McIntyre, and D. Rotenberg, Detection of Crime 105–116 (1967); LaFave, Improving Police Performance Through the Exclusionary Rule, 30 Mo.L.Rev. 391, 411 (1965). Federal law enforcement officers are not infrequently confronted with situations in which the circumstances are not sufficiently "exigent" to justify the serious step of conducting a warrantless search of private promises, but yet there exists a significant possibility that critical evidence would be lost in the time it would take to obtain a search warrant by traditional means. See, e.g., *United States v. Johnson,* —— F.2d —— (D.C.Cir. June 16, 1975).

Subdivision (c) (2) provides that a warrant may be issued on the basis of an oral statement of a person not in the physical presence of the federal magistrate. Telephone, radio, or other electronic methods of communication are contemplated. For the warrant to properly issue, four requirements must be met:

(1) The applicant—a federal law enforcement officer or an attorney for the government, as required by subdivision (a)—must persuade the magistrate that the circumstances of time and place make it reasonable to request the magistrate to issue a warrant on the basis of oral testimony. This restriction on the issuance of a warrant recognizes the inherent limitations of an oral warranted procedure, the lack of demeanor evidence, and the lack of a written record for the reviewing magistrate to consider before issuing the warrant. See Comment, Oral Search Warrants: A New Standard of Warrant Availability, 21 U.C.L.A. Law Review 691, 701 (1974). Circumstances making it reasonable to obtain a warrant on oral testimony exist if delay in obtaining the warrant might result in the destruction or disappearance of the property [see *Chimel v. California,* 395 U.S. 752, 773–774 (1969) (White, dissenting); Landynski, The Supreme Court's Search for Fourth Amendment Standards: The Warrantless Search, 45 Conn.B.J. 2, 25 (1971)]; or because of the time when the warrant is sought, the distance from the magistrate of the person seeking the warrant, or both.

(2) The applicant must orally state facts sufficient to satisfy the probable cause requirement for the issuance of the search warrant. (See subdivision (c) (1).) This information may come from either the applicant federal law enforcement officer or the attorney for the government or a witness willing to make an oral statement. The oral testimony must be recorded at this time so that the transcribed affidavit will provide an adequate basis for determining the sufficiency of the evidence if that issue should later arise. See Kipperman, Inaccurate Search Warrant Affidavits as a Ground for Suppressing Evidence, 84 Harv.L.Rev. 825 (1971). It is contemplated that the recording of the oral testimony will be made by a court reporter, by a mechanical recording device, or by a verbatim contemporaneous writing by the magistrate. Recording a telephone conversation is no longer difficult with many easily operated recorders available. See 86:2 L.A. Daily Journal 1 (1973); Miller, Telephonic Search Warrants: The San Diego Experience, 9 The Prosecutor 385, 386 (1974).

(3) The applicant must read the contents of the warrant to the federal magistrate in order to enable the magistrate to know whether the requirements of certainty in the warrant are satisfied. The magistrate may direct that changes be made in the warrant. If the magistrate approves the warrant as requested or as modified by the magistrate, he then issues the warrant by directing the applicant to sign the

magistrate's name to the duplicate original warrant. The magistrate then causes to be made a written copy of the approved warrant. This constitutes the original warrant. The magistrate enters the time of issuance of the duplicate original warrant on the face of the original warrant.

(4) Return of the duplicate original warrant and the original warrant must conform to subdivision (d). The transcript of the sworn oral testimony setting forth the grounds for issuance of the warrant must be signed by affiant in the presence of the magistrate and filed with the court.

Because federal magistrates are likely to be accessible through the use of the telephone or other electronic devices, it is unnecessary to authorize state judges to issue warrants under subdivision (c) (2).

Although the procedure set out in subdivision (c) (2) contemplates resort to technology which did not exist when the Fourth Amendment was adopted, the Advisory Committee is of the view that the procedure complies with all of the requirements of the Amendment. The telephonic search warrant process has been upheld as constitutional by the courts, e.g., *People v. Peck,* 38 Cal.App.3d 993, 113 Cal.Rptr. 806 (1974), and has consistently been so viewed by commentators. See Israel, Legislative Regulation of Searches and Seizures: The Michigan Proposals, 73 Mich.L.Rev. 221, 260 (1975); Nakell, Proposed Revisions of North Carolina's Search and Seizure Law, 52 N.Car.L.Rev. 277, 310 (1973); Comment, Oral Search Warrants: A New Standard of Warrant Availability, 21 U.C.L.A. Rev. 691, 697 (1973).

Reliance upon oral testimony as a basis for issuing a search warrant is permissible under the Fourth Amendment. *Campbell v. Minnesota,* 487 F.2d 1 (8th Cir.1973); *United States ex rel. Gaugler v. Brierley,* 477 F.2d 516 (3d Cir. 1973); *Tabasko v. Barton,* 472 F.2d 871 (6th Cir.1972); *Frazier v. Roberts,* 441 F.2d 1224 (8th Cir.1971). Thus, the procedure authorized under subdivision (c) (2) is not objectionable on the ground that the oral statement is not transcribed in advance of the issuance of the warrant. *People v. Peck,* 38 Cal.App.3d 993, 113 Cal.Rptr. 806 (1974). Although it has been questioned whether oral testimony will suffice under the Fourth Amendment if some kind of contemporaneous record is not made of that testimony, see dissent from denial of certiorari in *Christofferson v. Washington,* 393 U.S. 1090 (1969), this problem is not present under the procedure set out in subdivision (c) (2).

The Fourth Amendment requires that warrants issue "upon probable cause, supported by Oath or affirmation." The significance of the oath requirement is "that someone must take the responsibility for the facts alleged, giving rise to the probable cause for the issuance of a warrant." *United States ex rel. Pugh v. Pate,* 401 F.2d 6 (7th Cir. 1968); See also *Frazier v. Roberts,* 441 F.2d 1224 (8th Cir.1971). This is accomplished under the procedure required by subdivision (c) (2); the need for an oath under the Fourth Amendment does not "require a face to face confrontation between the magistrate and the affiant." *People v. Chavaz,* 27 Cal.App.3d 883, 104 Cal.Rptr. 247 (1972). See also *People v. Aguirre,* 26 Cal.App.3d 7, 103 Cal.Rptr. 153 (1972), noting it is unnecessary that "oral statements [be] taken in the physical presence of the magistrate."

The availability of the procedure authorized by subdivision (c) (2) will minimize the necessity of federal law enforcement officers engaging in other practices which, at least on occasion, might threaten to a greater extent those values protected by the Fourth Amendment. Although it is permissible for an officer in the field to relay his information by radio or telephone to another officer who has more ready access to a magistrate and who will thus act as the affiant, *Lopez v. United States,* 370 F.2d 8 (5th Cir.1966); *State v. Banks,* 250 N.C. 728, 110 S.E.2d 322 (1959), that procedure is less desirable than that permitted under subdivision (c) (2), for it deprives "the magistrate of the opportunity to examine the officer at the scene, who is in a much better position to answer questions relating to probable cause and the requisite scope of the search." Israel, Legislative Regulation of Searches and Seizures: The Michigan Proposals, 73 Mich. L.Rev. 221, 260 (1975). Or, in the absence of the subdivision (c) (2) procedure, officers might take "protective custody" of the premises and occupants for a significant period of time while a search warrant was sought by traditional means. The extent to which the "protective custody" procedure may be employed consistent with the Fourth Amendment is uncertain at best; see Griswold, Criminal Procedure, 1969—Is It a Means or an End?, 29 Md.L.Rev. 307, 317 (1969). The unavailability of the subdivision (c) (2) procedure also makes more tempting an immediate resort to a warrantless search in the hope that the circumstances will later be found to have been sufficiently "exigent" to justify such a step. See Miller, Telephonic Search Warrants: The San Diego Experience, 9 The Prosecutor 385, 386 (1974), noting a dramatic increase in police utilization of the warrant process following enactment of a telephonic warrant statute.

1977 Enactment

The committee agrees with the Supreme Court that it is desirable to encourage Federal law enforcement officers to seek search warrants in situations where they might otherwise conduct warrantless searches by providing for a telephone search warrant procedure with the basic characteristics suggested in the proposed Rule 41(c) (2). As the Supreme Court has observed, "It is a cardinal rule that, in seizing goods and articles, law enforcement agents must secure and use search warrants whenever reasonably practicable. After consideration of the Supreme Court version and a proposal set forth in H.R. 7888, the committee decided to use the language of the House bill as the vehicle, with certain modifications.

A new provision, as indicated in subparagraph (c) (2) (A), is added to establish a procedure for the issuance of a search warrant where the circumstances make it reasonable to dispense with a written affidavit to be presented in person to a magistrate. At least two States have adopted a similar procedure—Arizona and California—and comparable amendments are under consideration in other jurisdictions. Such a procedure has been strongly recommended by the National Advisory Commission on Criminal Justice Standards and Goals and State experience with the procedure has been favorable. The telephone search warrant process has been upheld as constitutional by the courts and has consistently been so viewed by commentators.

In recommending a telephone search warrant procedure, the Advisory Committee note on the Supreme Court proposal points out that the preferred method of conducting a search is with a search warrant. The note indicates that the rationale for the proposed change is to encourage Federal law enforcement officers to seek search warrants in situations when they might otherwise conduct warrantless searches. "Federal law enforcement officers are not infrequently confronted with situations in which the circumstances are not sufficiently 'exigent' to justify the serious step of conducting a warrantless search of private premises, but yet there exists a significant possibility that critical evidence would be lost in the time it would take to obtain a search warrant by traditional means."

Subparagraph (c) (2) (B) provides that the person requesting the warrant shall prepare a "duplicate original warrant" which will be read and recorded verbatim by the magistrate on an "original warrant." The magistrate may direct that the warrant be modified.

Subparagraph (c) (2) (C) provides that, if the magistrate is satisfied that the circumstances are such as to make it reasonable to dispense with a written affidavit and that grounds for the application exist or there is probable cause to believe that they exist, he shall order the issuance of the warrant by directing the requestor to sign the magistrate's name on the duplicate original warrant. The magistrate is required to sign the original warrant and enter the time of issuance thereon. The finding of probable cause may be based on the same type of evidence appropriate for a warrant upon affidavit.

Subparagraph (c) (2) (D) requires the magistrate to place the requestor and any witness under oath and, if a voice recording device is available, to record the proceeding. If a voice recording is not available, the proceeding must be recorded verbatim stenographically or in longhand. Verified copies must be filed with the court as specified.

Subparagraph (c) (2) (E) provides that the contents of the warrant upon oral testimony shall be the same as the contents of a warrant upon affidavit.

Subparagraph (c) (2) (F) provides that the person who executes the warrant shall enter the exact time of execution on the face of the duplicate original warrant. Unlike H.R. 7888, this subparagraph does not require the person who executes the warrant to have physical possession of the duplicate original warrant at the time of the execution of the warrant. The committee believes this would make an unwise and unnecessary distinction between execution of regular warrants issued on written affidavits and warrants issued by telephone that would limit the flexibility and utility of this procedure for no useful purpose.

Finally, subparagraph (c) (2) (G) makes it clear that, absent a finding of bad faith by the government, the magistrate's judgment that the circumstances made it reasonable to dispense with a written affidavit—a decision that does not go the core question of whether there was probable cause to issue a warrant—is not a ground for granting a motion to suppress evidence. Senate Report No. 95–354.

Congressional Modification of Proposed Amendment

Section 2(e) of Pub.L. 95–78 provided in part that the amendment by the Supreme Court [in its order of Apr. 26, 1976] to subdivision (c) of rule 41 of the Federal Rules of Criminal Procedure [subd. (c) of this rule] is approved in a modified form.

1979 Amendments

This amendment to Rule 41 is intended to make it possible for a search warrant to issue to search *for* a person under two circumstances: (i) when there is probable cause to arrest that person; or (ii) when that person is being unlawfully restrained. There may be instances in which a search warrant would be required to conduct a search in either of these circumstances. Even when a search warrant would not be required to enter a place to search for a person, a procedure for obtaining a warrant should be available so that law enforcement officers will be encouraged to resort to the preferred alternative of acquiring "an objective predetermination of probable cause," *Katz v. United States,* 389 U.S. 347, 88 S.Ct. 507, 19 L.Ed.2d 576 (1967), in this instance, that the person sought is at the place to be searched.

That part of the amendment which authorizes issuance of a search warrant to search for a person unlawfully restrained is consistent with ALI Model Code of Pre-Arraignment Procedure § SS 210.3(1) (d) (Proposed Official Draft, 1975), which specifies that a search warrant may issue to search for "an individual * * * who is unlawfully held in confinement or other restraint." As noted in the Commentary thereto, id. at p. 507:

> Ordinarily such persons will be held against their will and in that case the persons are, of course, not subject to "seizure." But they are, in a sense, "evidence" of crime, and the use of search warrants for these purposes presents no conceptual difficulties.

Some state search warrant provisions also provide for issuance of a warrant in these circumstances. See, e.g., Ill.Rev. Stat. ch. 38, § 108–3 ("Any person who has been kidnapped in violation of the laws of this State, or who has been kidnapped in another jurisdiction and is now concealed within this State").

It may be that very often exigent circumstances, especially the need to act very promptly to protect the life or well-being of the kidnap victim, would justify an immediate warrantless search for the person restrained. But this is not inevitably the case. Moreover, as noted above there should be available a process whereby law enforcement agents may acquire in advance a judicial determination that they have cause to intrude upon the privacy of those at the place where the victim is thought to be located.

That part of the amendment which authorizes issuance of a search warrant to search for a person to be arrested is also consistent with ALI Model Code of Pre-Arraignment Procedure § SS 210.3(1) (d) (Proposed Official Draft, 1975), which states that a search warrant may issue to search for "an individual for whose arrest there is reasonable cause." As noted in the Commentary thereto, id. at p. 507, it is desirable that there be "explicit statutory authority for such searches." Some state search warrant provisions also expressly provide for the issuance of a search warrant to search for a person to be arrested. See, e.g., Del. Code Ann. tit. 11, § 2305 ("Persons for whom a warrant of arrest has been issued"). This part of the amendment to Rule 41 covers a defendant or witness for whom an arrest warrant has theretofore issued, or a defendant for whom grounds to arrest exist even though no arrest warrant has theretofore issued. It also covers the arrest of a deportable alien under 8 U.S.C. § 1252, whose presence at a certain place might be important evidence of criminal conduct by another person, such as the harboring of undocumented aliens under 8 U.S.C. § 1324(a) (3).

In *United States v. Watson,* 423 U.S. 411, 96 S.Ct. 820, 46 L.Ed.2d 598 (1976), the Court once again alluded to "the still unsettled question" of whether, absent exigent circumstances, officers acting without a warrant may enter private premises to make an arrest. Some courts have indicated that probable cause alone ordinarily is sufficient to support an arrest entry, *United States v. Fernandez,* 480 F.2d 726 (2d Cir. 1973); *United States ex rel. Wright v. Woods,* 432 F.2d 1143 (7th Cir. 1970). There exists some authority, however, that except under exigent circumstances a warrant is required to enter the defendant's own premises, *United States v. Calhoun,* 542 F.2d 1094 (9th Cir. 1976); *United States v. Lindsay,* 506 F.2d 166 (D.C.Cir.1974); *Dorman v. United States,* 435 F.2d 385 (D.C.Cir.1970), or, at least, to enter the premises of a third party, *Virgin Islands v. Gereau,* 502 F.2d 914 (3d Cir. 1974); *Fisher v. Volz,* 496 F.2d 333 (3d Cir. 1974); *Huotari v. Vanderport,* 380 F.Supp. 645 (D.Minn.1974).

It is also unclear, assuming a need for a warrant, what kind of warrant is required, although it is sometimes assumed that an arrest warrant will suffice, e.g., *United States v. Calhoun,* supra; *United States v. James,* 528 F.2d 999 (5th Cir.1976). There is a growing body of authority however, that what is needed to justify entry of the premises of a third party to arrest is a search warrant, e.g., *Virgin Islands v. Gereau,* supra; *Fisher v. Volz,* supra. The theory is that if the privacy of this third party is to be protected adequately, what is needed is a probable cause determination by a magistrate that the wanted person is presently within that party's premises. "A warrant for the arrest of a suspect may indicate that the police officer has probable cause to believe the suspect committed the crime; it affords no basis to believe the suspect is in some stranger's home." *Fisher v. Volz,* supra.

It has sometimes been contended that a search warrant should be required for a nonexigent entry to arrest even when the premises to be entered are those of the person to be arrested. Rotenberg & Tanzer, Searching for the Person to be Seized, 35 Ohio St.L.J. 56, 69 (1974). Case authority in support is lacking, and it may be that the protections of a search warrant are less important in such a situation because ordinarily "rudimentary police procedure dictates that a suspect's residence be eliminated as a possible hiding place before a search is conducted elsewhere." *People v. Sprovieri,* 95 Ill.App.2d 10, 238 N.E.2d 115 (1968).

Despite these uncertainties, the fact remains that in some circuits under some circumstances a search warrant is required to enter private premises to arrest. Moreover, the law on this subject is in a sufficient state of uncertainty that this position may be taken by other courts. It is thus important that Rule 41 clearly express that a search warrant for this purpose may issue. And even if future decisions head the other direction, the need for the amendment would still exist. It is clear that law enforcement officers "may not constitutionally enter the home of a private individual to search for another person, though he be named in a valid arrest warrant in their possession, absent probable cause to believe that the named suspect is present within at the time." *Fisher v. Volz,* supra. The cautious officer is entitled to a procedure whereby he may have this probable cause determination made by a neutral and detached magistrate in advance of the entry.

1987 Amendments

The amendments are technical. No substantive change is intended.

1989 Amendments

The amendment to Rule 41(e) conforms the rule to the practice in most districts and eliminates language that is somewhat confusing. The Supreme Court has upheld warrants for the search and seizure of property in the possession of persons who are not suspected of criminal activity. *See, e.g., Zurcher v. Stanford Daily,* 436 U.S. 547 (1978). Before the amendment, Rule 41(e) permitted such persons to seek return of their property if they were aggrieved by an unlawful search and seizure. But, the rule failed to address the harm that may result from the interference with the lawful use of property by persons who are not suspected of wrongdoing. Courts have recognized that once the government no longer has a need to use evidence, it should be returned. *See e.g., United States v. Wilson,* 540 F.2d 1100 (D.C. Cir. 1976). Prior to the amendment, Rule 41(e) did not explicitly recognize a right of a property owner to obtain return of lawfully seized property even though the government might be able to protect its legitimate law enforcement interests in the property despite its return—*e.g.,* by copying documents or by conditioning the return on government access to the property at a future time. As amended, Rule 41(e) provides that an aggrieved person may seek return of property that has been unlawfully seized, and a person whose property has been lawfully seized may seek return of property when aggrieved by the government's continued possession of it.

No standard is set forth in the rule to govern the determination of whether property should be returned to a person aggrieved either by an unlawful seizure or by deprivation of the property. The fourth amendment protects people from unreasonable seizures as well as unreasonable searches, *United States v. Place,* 462 U.S. 696, 701 (1983), and reasonableness under all of the circumstances must be the test when a person seeks to obtain the return of property. If the United States has a need for the property in an investigation or prosecution, its retention of the property generally is reasonable. But, if the United States' legitimate interests can be satisfied even if the property is returned, continued retention of the property would become unreasonable.

The amendment deletes language dating from 1944 stating that evidence shall not be admissible at a hearing or at a trial if the court grants the motion to return property under Rule 41(e). This language has not kept pace with the development of exclusionary rule doctrine and is currently only confusing. The Supreme Court has now held that evidence seized in violation of the fourth amendment, but in good faith pursuant to a warrant, may be used even against a person aggrieved by the constitutional violation. *United States v. Leon,* 468 U.S. 897 (1984). The Court has also held that illegally seized evidence may be admissible against persons who are not personally aggrieved by an illegal search or seizure. *Rakas v. Illinois,* 439 U.S. 128 (1978). Property that is inadmissible for one purpose (*e.g.,* as part of the government's case-in-chief) may be admissible for another purpose (*e.g.,* impeachment, *United States v. Havens,* 446 U.S. 620 (1980)). Federal courts have relied upon these decision and permitted the government to retain and to use evidence as permitted by the fourth amendment.

Rule 41(e) is not intended to deny the United States the use of evidence permitted by the fourth amendment and federal statutes, even if the evidence might have been unlawfully seized. *See, e.g., United States v. Calandra,* 414 U.S. 338, 349 n.6 (1978) ("Rule 41(e) does not constitute a statutory expansion of the exclusionary rule."); *United States v. Roberts,* 852 F.2d 671 (2nd Cir.1988) (exceptions to exclusionary rule applicable to Rule 41(e)). Thus, the exclusionary provision is deleted, and the scope of the exclusionary rule is reserved for judicial decisions.

In opting for a reasonableness approach and in deleting the exclusionary language, the Committee rejects the analysis of *Sovereign News Co. v. United States,* 690 F.2d 569 (6th Cir. 1982), *cert. denied,* 464 U.S. 814 (1983), which held that the United States must return photocopies of lawfully seized business records unless it could demonstrate that the records were "necessary for a specific investigation." As long as the government has a law enforcement purpose in copying records, there is no reason why it should be saddled with a heavy burden of justifying the copying. Although some cases have held that the government must return copies of records where the originals were illegally seized—*See, e.g., United States v. Wallace & Tiernan Co.,* 336 U.S. 793, 801 (1948); *Goodman v. United States,* 369 F.2d 166 (9th Cir. 1966)—these holdings are questionable in situations in which the government is permitted under Supreme Court decisions to use illegally seized evidence, and their reasoning does not apply to legally seized evidence.

As amended, Rule 41(e) avoids an all or nothing approach whereby the government must either return records and make no copies or keep originals notwithstanding the hardship to their owner. The amended rule recognizes that reasonable accommodations might protect both the law enforcement interests of the United States and the property rights of property owners and holders. In many instances documents and records that are relevant to ongoing or contemplated investigations and prosecutions may be returned to their owner as long as the government preserves a copy for future use. In some circumstances, however, equitable considerations might justify an order requiring the government to return or destroy all copies of records that it has seized. *See, e.g., Paton v. LaPrade,* 524 F.2d 862, 867–69 (3rd Cir. 1975). The amended rule contemplates judicial action that will respect both possessory and law enforcement interests.

The word "judge" is changed to "court" in the second sentence of subdivision (e) to clarify that a magistrate may receive evidence in the course of making a finding or a proposed finding for consideration by the district judge.

1990 Amendments

Rule 41(a). The amendment to Rule 41(a) serves several purposes. First, it furthers the constitutional preference for warrants by providing a mechanism whereby a warrant may be issued in a district for a person or property that is moving into or through a district or might move outside the district while the warrant is sought or executed. Second, it clarifies the authority of federal magistrates to issue search warrants for property that is relevant to criminal investigation being conducted in a district and, although located outside the United States, that is in a place where the United States may lawfully conduct a search.

The amendment is not intended to expand the class of persons authorized to request a warrant and the language "upon request of a federal law enforcement officer," modifies all warrants covered by Rule 41. The amendment is intended to make clear that judges of state courts of record within a federal district may issue search warrants for persons or property located within that district. The amendment does not prescribe the circumstances in which a warrant is required and is not intended to change the law concerning warrant requirements. Rather the rule provides a mechanism for the issuance of a warrant when one is required, or when a law enforcement officer desires to seek a warrant even though warrantless activity is permissible.

Rule 41(a)(1) permits anticipatory warrants by omitting the words "is located," which in the past required that in all instances the object of the search had to be located within the district at the time the warrant was issued. Now a search for property or a person within the district, or expected to be within the district, is valid if it otherwise complies with the rule.

Rule 41(a)(2) authorizes execution of search warrants in another district under limited circumstances. Because these searches are unusual, the rule limits to federal magistrates the authority to issue such warrants. The rule permits a federal magistrate to issue a search warrant for property within the district which is moving or may move outside the district. The amendment recognizes that there are inevitable delays between the application for a warrant and its authorization, on the one hand, and the execution of the warrant, on the other hand. The amendment also recognizes that when property is in motion, there may be good reason to delay execution until the property comes to rest. The amendment provides a practical tool for federal law enforcement officers that avoids the necessity of their either seeking several warrants in different districts for the same property or their relying on an exception to the warrant requirement for search of property or a person that has moved outside a district.

The amendment affords a useful warrant procedure to cover familiar fact patterns, like the one typified by *United States v. Chadwick,* 433 U.S. 1 (1976). In *Chadwick,* agents in San Diego observed suspicious activities involving a footlocker carried onto a train. When the train arrived in Boston, the agents made an arrest and conducted a warrantless search of the footlocker (which the Supreme Court held was invalid). Under the amended rule, agents who have probable cause in San Diego would be able to obtain a warrant for a search of the footlocker even though it is moving outside the district. Agents, who will not be sure exactly where the footlocker will be unloaded from the train, may execute the warrant when the journey ends. *See also United States v. Karo,* 468 U.S. 705 (1984) (rejecting argument that obtaining warrant to monitor beeper would not comply with requirement of particularity because its final destination may not be known); *United States v. Knotts,* 460 U.S. 276 (1983) (agents followed beeper across state lines). The Supreme Court's holding in *Chadwick* permits law enforcement officers to seize and hold an object like a footlocker while seeking a warrant. Although the amended rule would not disturb this holding, it provides a mechanism for agents to seek a probable cause determination and a warrant before interfering with the property and seizing it. It encourages reliance on warrants.

The amendment is not intended to abrogate the requirements of probable cause and prompt execution. At some point, a warrant issued in one district might become stale when executed in another district. But staleness can be a problem even when a warrant is executed in the district in which it was issued. *See generally United States v. Harris,*

403 U.S. 573, 579, 589 (1971). And at some point, an intervening event might make execution of a warrant unreasonable. *Cf. Illinois v. Andreas,* 463 U.S. 765, 772 (1983). Evaluations of the execution of a warrant must, in the nature of things, be made after the warrant is issued.

Nor does the amendment abrogate the requirement of particularity. Thus, it does not authorize searches of premises other than a particular place. As recognized by the Supreme Court in *Karo, supra,* although agents may not know exactly where moving property will come to rest, they can still describe with particularity the object to be searched.

The amendment would authorize the search of a particular object or container provided that law enforcement officials were otherwise in a lawful position to execute the search without making an impermissible intrusion. For example, it would authorize the search of luggage moving aboard a plane.

[The Supreme Court has not adopted the addition of clause (3) to Rule 41(a), discussed below, which had been recommended by the Judicial Conference of the United States. The Court was of the view that this proposal required further consideration.]

Rule 41(a)(3) provides for warrants to search property outside the United States. No provision for search warrants for persons is made lest the rule be read as a substitute for extradition proceedings. As with the provision for searches outside a district, *supra,* this provision is limited to search warrants issued by federal magistrates. The phrase "relevant to criminal investigation" is intended to encompass all of the types of property that are covered by Rule 41(b), which is unchanged by the amendment. That phrase also is intended to include those investigations which begin with the request for the search warrant.

Some searches and seizures by federal officers outside the territory of the United States may be governed by the fourth amendment. *See generally* Saltzburg, the Reach of the Bill of Rights Beyond the Terra Firma of the United States, 20 Va.J.Int'l L. 741 (1980). Prior to the amendment of the rule, it was unclear how federal officers might obtain warrants authorizing searches outside the district of the issuing magistrate. Military Rule of Evidence 315 provided guidance for searches of military personnel and property and nonmilitary property in a foreign country. But it had no civilian counterpart. *See generally* S. Saltzburg, L. Schinasi, & D. Schlueter, *Military Rules of Evidence Manual* 274–95 (2d ed. 1986).

Although the amendment rests on the assumption that the Constitution applies to some extraterritorial searches, *cf. United States v. Verdugo–Urquidez,* 110 S.Ct. 1056, 494 U.S. 259 (1990) fourth amendment inapplicable to extraterritorial searches of property owned by nonresident aliens), it does not address the question of when the Constitution requires a warrant. Nor does it address the issue of whether international agreements or treaties or the law of a foreign nation might be applicable. *See United States v. Patterson,* 812 F.2d 486 (9th Cir.1987). Instead, the amendment is intended to provide necessary clarification as to how a warrant may be obtained when law enforcement officials are required, or find it desirable, to do so.

1993 Amendments

The amendment to Rule 41(c)(2)(A) is intended to expand the authority of magistrates and judges in considering oral requests for search warrants. It also recognizes the value of, and the public's increased dependence on facsimile machines to transmit written information efficiently and accurately. As amended, the Rule should thus encourage law enforcement officers to seek a warrant, especially when it is necessary, or desirable, to supplement oral telephonic communications by written materials which may now be transmitted electronically as well. The magistrate issuing the warrant may require that the original affidavit be ultimately filed. The Committee considered, but rejected, amendments to the Rule which would have permitted other means of electronic transmission, such as the use of computer modems. In its view, facsimile transmissions provide some method of assuring the authenticity of the writing transmitted by the affiant.

The Committee considered amendments to Rule 41(c)(2)(B), Application, Rule 41(c)(2)(C), Issuance, and Rule 41(g), Return of Papers to Clerk, but determined that allowing use of facsimile transmissions in those instances would not save time and would present problems and questions concerning the need to preserve facsimile copies.

The Rule is also amended to conform to the Judicial Improvements Act of 1990 [P.L. 101–650, Title III, Section 321] which provides that each United States magistrate appointed under section 631 of title 28, United States Code, shall be known as a United States magistrate judge.

2002 Amendments

The language of Rule 41 has been amended as part of the general restyling of the Criminal Rules to make them more easily understood and to make style and terminology consistent throughout the rules. These changes are intended to be stylistic only, except as otherwise noted below. Rule 41 has been completely reorganized to make it easier to read and apply its key provisions.

Rule 41(b)(3) is a new provision that incorporates a congressional amendment to Rule 41 as a part of the Uniting and Strengthening America by Providing Appropriate Tools Required to Intercept and Obstruct Terrorism (USA PATRIOT ACT) Act of 2001. The provision explicitly addresses the authority of a magistrate judge to issue a search warrant in an investigation of domestic or international terrorism. As long as the magistrate judge has authority in a district where activities related to terrorism may have occurred, the magistrate judge may issue a warrant for persons or property not only within the district, but outside the district as well.

Current Rule 41(c)(1), which refers to the fact that hearsay evidence may be used to support probable cause, has been deleted. That language was added to the rule in 1972, apparently to reflect emerging federal case law. *See* Advisory Committee Note to 1972 Amendments to Rule 41 (citing cases). Similar language was added to Rule 4 in 1974. In the intervening years, however, the case law has become perfectly clear on that proposition. Thus, the Committee believed that the reference to hearsay was no longer necessary. Furthermore, the limited reference to hearsay evidence was misleading to the extent that it might have suggested that other forms of inadmissible evidence could not be considered. For example, the rule made no reference to considering a defendant's prior criminal record, which clearly may be considered in deciding whether probable cause exists. *See, e.g., Brinegar v. United States,* 338 U.S. 160 (1949) (officer's knowledge of defendant's prior criminal activity). Rather than address that issue, or any other similar issues, the Committee believed that the matter was best addressed in Rule 1101(d)(3), Federal Rules of Evidence. That rule explicitly provides that the Federal Rules of Evidence do not apply to "preliminary examinations in criminal cases, . . . issuance of warrants for arrest, criminal summonses, and search warrants . . . ." The Advisory Committee Note accompanying that rule recognizes that: "The nature of the proceedings makes application of the formal rules of evidence inappropriate and impracticable." The Committee did not intend to make any substantive changes in practice by deleting the reference to hearsay evidence.

Current Rule 41(d) provides that the officer taking the property under the warrant must provide a receipt for the property and complete an inventory. The revised rule indicates that the inventory may be completed by an officer present during the execution of the warrant, and not necessarily the officer actually executing the warrant.

2006 Amendments

The amendments to Rule 41 address three issues: first, procedures for issuing tracking device warrants; second, a provision for delaying any notice required by the rule; and third, a provision permitting a magistrate judge to use reliable electronic means to issue warrants.

Subdivision (a). Amended Rule 41(a)(2) includes two new definitional provisions. The first, in Rule 41(a)(2)(D), addresses the definitions of "domestic terrorism" and "international terrorism," terms used in Rule 41(b)(2). The second, in Rule 41(a)(2)(E), addresses the definition of "tracking device."

Subdivision (b). Amended Rule 41(b)(4) is a new provision, designed to address the use of tracking devices. Such searches are recognized both by statute, *see* 18 U.S.C. § 3117(a) and by caselaw, *see, e.g., United States v. Karo*, 468 U.S. 705 (1984); *United States v. Knotts*, 460 U.S. 276 (1983). Warrants may be required to monitor tracking devices when they are used to monitor persons or property in areas where there is a reasonable expectation of privacy. *See, e.g., United States v. Karo, supra* (although no probable cause was required to install beeper, officers' monitoring of its location in defendant's home raised Fourth Amendment concerns). Nonetheless, there is no procedural guidance in current Rule 41 for those judicial officers who are asked to issue tracking device warrants. As with traditional search warrants for persons or property, tracking device warrants may implicate law enforcement interests in multiple districts.

The amendment provides that a magistrate judge may issue a warrant, if he or she has the authority to do so in the district, to install and use a tracking device, as that term is defined in 18 U.S.C. § 3117(b). The magistrate judge's authority under this rule includes the authority to permit entry into an area where there is a reasonable expectation of privacy, installation of the tracking device, and maintenance and removal of the device. The Committee did not intend by this amendment to expand or contract the definition of what might constitute a tracking device. The amendment is based on the understanding that the device will assist officers only in tracking the movements of a person or property. The warrant may authorize officers to track the person or property within the district of issuance, or outside the district.

Because the authorized tracking may involve more than one district or state, the Committee believes that only federal judicial officers should be authorized to issue this type of warrant. Even where officers have no reason to believe initially that a person or property will move outside the district of issuance, issuing a warrant to authorize tracking both inside and outside the district avoids the necessity of obtaining multiple warrants if the property or person later crosses district or state lines.

The amendment reflects the view that if the officers intend to install or use the device in a constitutionally protected area, they must obtain judicial approval to do so. If, on the other hand, the officers intend to install and use the device without implicating any Fourth Amendment rights, there is no need to obtain the warrant. *See, e.g., United States v. Knotts, supra*, where the officers' actions in installing and following tracking device did not amount to a search under the Fourth Amendment.

Subdivision (d). Amended Rule 41(d) includes new language on tracking devices. The tracking device statute, 18 U.S.C. § 3117, does not specify the standard an applicant must meet to install a tracking device. The Supreme Court has acknowledged that the standard for installation of a tracking device is unresolved, and has reserved ruling on the issue until it is squarely presented by the facts of a case. *See United States v. Karo*, 468 U.S. 705, 718 n. 5 (1984). The amendment to Rule 41 does not resolve this issue or hold that such warrants may issue only on a showing of probable cause. Instead, it simply provides that if probable cause is shown, the magistrate judge must issue the warrant. And the warrant is only needed if the device is installed (for example, in the trunk of the defendant's car) or monitored (for example, while the car is in the defendant's garage) in an area in which the person being monitored has a reasonable expectation of privacy.

Subdivision (e). Rule 41(e) has been amended to permit magistrate judges to use reliable electronic means to issue warrants. Currently, the rule makes no provision for using such media. The amendment parallels similar changes to Rules 5 and 32.1(a)(5)(B)(i).

The amendment recognizes the significant improvements in technology. First, more counsel, courts, and magistrate judges now routinely use facsimile transmissions of documents. And many courts and magistrate judges are now equipped to receive filings by electronic means. Indeed, some courts encourage or require that certain documents be filed by electronic means. Second, the technology has advanced to the state where such filings may be sent from, and received at, locations outside the courthouse. Third, electronic media can now provide improved quality of transmission and security measures. In short, in a particular case, using facsimiles and electronic media to transmit a warrant can be both reliable and efficient use of judicial resources.

The term "electronic" is used to provide some flexibility to the rule and make allowance for further technological advances in transmitting data. Although facsimile transmissions are not specifically identified, the Committee envisions that facsimile transmissions would fall within the meaning of "electronic means."

While the rule does not impose any special requirements on use of facsimile transmissions, neither does it presume that those transmissions are reliable. The rule treats all electronic transmissions in a similar fashion. Whatever the mode, the means used must be "reliable." While the rule does not further define that term, the Committee envisions that a court or magistrate judge would make that determination as a local matter. In deciding whether a particular electronic means, or media, would be reliable, the court might consider first, the expected quality and clarity of the transmission. For example, is it possible to read the contents of the warrant in its entirety, as though it were the original or a clean photocopy? Second, the court may consider whether security measures are available to insure that the transmission is not compromised. In this regard, most courts are now equipped to require that certain documents contain a digital signature, or some other similar system for restricting access. Third, the court may consider whether there are reliable means of preserving the document for later use.

Amended Rule 41(e)(2)(B) is a new provision intended to address the contents of tracking device warrants. To avoid open-ended monitoring of tracking devices, the revised rule requires the magistrate judge to specify in the warrant the length of time for using the device. Although the initial time stated in the warrant may not exceed 45 days, extensions of time may be granted for good cause. The rule further specifies that any installation of a tracking device authorized by the warrant must be made within ten calendar days and, unless otherwise provided, that any installation occur during daylight hours.

Subdivision (f). Current Rule 41(f) has been completely revised to accommodate new provisions dealing with tracking device warrants. First, current Rule 41(f)(1) has been revised to address execution and delivery of warrants to search for and seize a person or property; no substantive change has been made to that provision. New Rule 41(f)(2) addresses execution and delivery of tracking device warrants. That provision generally tracks the structure of revised Rule 41(f)(1), with appropriate adjustments for the particular requirements of tracking device warrants. Under Rule 41(f)(2)(A) the officer must note on the warrant the time the device was installed and the period during which the device was used. And under new Rule 41(f)(2)(B), the officer must return the tracking device warrant to the magistrate judge designated in the warrant, within 10 calendar days after use of the device has ended.

Amended Rule 41(f)(2)(C) addresses the particular problems of serving a copy of a tracking device warrant on the person who has been tracked, or whose property has been tracked. In the case of other warrants, current Rule 41 envisions that the subjects of the search typically know that they have been searched, usually within a short period of time after the search has taken place. Tracking device warrants, on the other hand, are by their nature covert intrusions and can be successfully used only when the person being investigated is unaware that a tracking device is being used. The amendment requires that the officer must serve a copy of the tracking device warrant on the person within 10 calendar days after the tracking has ended. That service may be accomplished by either personally serving the person, or both by leaving a copy at the person's residence or usual abode and by sending a copy by mail. The Rule also provides, however, that the officer may (for good cause) obtain the court's permission to delay further service of the warrant. That might be appropriate, for example, where the owner of the tracked property is undetermined, or where the officer establishes that the investigation is ongoing and that disclosure of the warrant will compromise that investigation.

Use of a tracking device is to be distinguished from other continuous monitoring or observations that are governed by statutory provisions or caselaw. *See* Title III, Omnibus Crime Control and Safe Streets Act of 1968, *as amended* by Title I of the 1986 Electronic Communications Privacy Act, 18 U.S.C. §§ 2510–2520; *United States v. Biasucci*, 786 F.2d 504 (2d Cir. 1986) (video camera); *United States v. Torres*, 751 F.2d 875 (7th Cir. 1984) (television surveillance).

Finally, amended Rule 41(f)(3) is a new provision that permits the government to request, and the magistrate judge to grant, a delay in any notice required in Rule 41. The amendment is co-extensive with 18 U.S.C. § 3103a(b). That new provision, added as part of the Uniting and Strengthening America by Providing Appropriate Tools Required to Intercept and Obstruct Terrorism (USA PATRIOT) Act of 2001, authorizes a court to delay any notice required in conjunction with the issuance of any search warrants.

HISTORICAL NOTES

Effective and Applicability Provisions

1977 Acts. Amendment of this rule by order of the United States Supreme Court on Apr. 26, 1976, modified and approved by Pub.L. 95–78, effective Oct. 1, 1977, pursuant to section 4 of Pub.L. 95–78.

1976 Acts. Amendment of subsec. (c) (1) of this rule effective Aug. 1, 1976, pursuant to Pub.L. 94–349, § 1, July 8, 1976, 90 Stat. 822.

1956 Acts. Amendment by Order of Apr. 9, 1956, became effective 90 days thereafter.

Rule 42. Criminal Contempt

(a) Disposition After Notice. Any person who commits criminal contempt may be punished for that contempt after prosecution on notice.

(1) Notice. The court must give the person notice in open court, in an order to show cause, or in an arrest order. The notice must:

(A) state the time and place of the trial;

(B) allow the defendant a reasonable time to prepare a defense; and

(C) state the essential facts constituting the charged criminal contempt and describe it as such.

(2) Appointing a Prosecutor. The court must request that the contempt be prosecuted by an attorney for the government, unless the interest of justice requires the appointment of another attorney. If the government declines the request, the court must appoint another attorney to prosecute the contempt.

(3) Trial and Disposition. A person being prosecuted for criminal contempt is entitled to a jury trial in any case in which federal law so provides and must be released or detained as Rule 46 provides. If the criminal contempt involves disrespect toward or criticism of a judge, that judge is disqualified from presiding at the contempt trial or hearing unless the defendant consents. Upon a finding or verdict of guilty, the court must impose the punishment.

(b) Summary Disposition. Notwithstanding any other provision of these rules, the court (other than a magistrate judge) may summarily punish a person who commits criminal contempt in its presence if the judge saw or heard the contemptuous conduct and so certifies; a magistrate judge may summarily punish a person as provided in 28 U.S.C. § 636(e). The contempt order must recite the facts, be signed by the judge, and be filed with the clerk.

(As amended Mar. 9, 1987, eff. Aug. 1, 1987; Apr. 29, 2002, eff. Dec. 1, 2002.)

ADVISORY COMMITTEE NOTES

1944 Adoption

The rule-making power of the Supreme Court with respect to criminal proceedings was extended to proceedings to punish for criminal contempt of court by the Act of November 21, 1941 (55 Stat. 779), 18 U.S.C. former § 689 [now §§ 3771, 3772].

Note to Subdivision (a). This rule is substantially a restatement of existing law, *Ex parte Terry,* 128 U.S. 289; *Cooke v. United States,* 45 S.Ct. 390, 267 U.S. 517, 534, 69 L.Ed. 767.

Note to Subdivision (b). 1. This rule is substantially a restatement of the procedure prescribed in 28 U.S.C. former §§ 386 to 390 [now 18 U.S.C. §§ 401, 402, 3285, 3691], and 29 U.S.C. former § 111 [now 18 U.S.C. § 3692].

2. The requirement in the second sentence that the notice shall describe the criminal contempt as such is intended to obviate the frequent confusion between criminal and civil contempt proceedings and follows the suggestion made in *McCann v. New York Stock Exchange,* 80 F.2d 211, C.C.A.2d. See, also, *Nye v. United States,* 61 S.Ct. 810, 313 U.S. 33, 42–43, 85 L.Ed. 1172.

3. The fourth sentence relating to trial by jury preserves the right to a trial by jury in those contempt cases in which it is granted by statute, but does not enlarge the right or extend it to additional cases. The respondent in a contempt proceeding may demand a trial by jury as of right if the proceeding is brought under the Act of March 23, 1932, c. 90, § 11, 47 Stat. 72, 29 U.S.C. former § 111 [now 18 U.S.C. § 3692] (Norris-La Guardia Act), or the Act of October 15, 1914, c. 323, § 22, 38 Stat. 738, 28 U.S.C. § 387 (Clayton Act).

4. The provision in the sixth sentence disqualifying the judge affected by the contempt if the charge involves disrespect to or criticism of him, is based, in part, on 29 U.S.C. former § 112 (Contempts; demand for retirement of judge sitting in proceeding) and the observations of Chief Justice Taft in *Cooke v. United States,* 45 S.Ct. 390, 267 U.S. 517, 539, 69 L.Ed. 767.

5. Among the statutory provisions defining criminal contempts are the following:

U.S.C. Title 7:

§ 499m (Perishable Agricultural Commodities Act; investigation of complaints; procedure; penalties; etc.—(c) Disobedience to subpoenas; remedy; contempt)

U.S.C. Title 9:

§ 7 (Witnesses before arbitrators; fees, compelling attendance)

U.S.C. Title 11:

§ 69 (Referees; contempts before)

U.S.C. Title 15:

§ 49 (Federal Trade Commission; documentary evidence; depositions; witnesses)

§ 78u (Regulation of Securities Exchanges; investigation; injunctions and prosecution of offenses)

§ 100 (Trade-marks; destruction of infringing labels; service of injunction, and proceedings for enforcement)

§ 155 (China Trade Act; authority of registrar in obtaining evidence)

U.S.C. Title 17 former:

§ 36 [now § 112] (Injunctions; service and enforcement)

U.S.C. Title 19:

§ 1333 (Tariff Commission; testimony and production of papers—(b) Witnesses and evidence)

U.S.C. Title 22 former:

§ 270f (International Bureaus; Congresses, etc.; perjury; contempts; penalties)

U.S.C. Title 28 former:

§ 385 [now § 459; 18 U.S.C. § 401] (Administration of oaths; contempts)

§ 386 [now 18 U.S.C. §§ 402, 3691] (Contempts; when constituting also criminal offense)

§ 387 [now 18 U.S.C. § 402] (Same; procedure; bail; attachment; trial; punishment) (Clayton Act; jury trial; section)

§ 388 (Same; review of conviction)

§ 389 [now 18 U.S.C. §§ 402, 3691] (Same; not specifically enumerated)

§ 390 [now 18 U.S.C. § 3825] (Same; limitations)

§ 390a [now 18 U.S.C. § 402] ("Person" or "persons" defined)

§ 648 [now 18 U.S.C., Appendix, R. 17(f); 28 U.S.C., Appendix, R. 45(d)] (Depositions under dedimus potestatem; witnesses; when required to attend)

§ 703 (Punishment of witness for contempt)

§ 714 [now § 1784] (Failure of witness to obey subpoena; order to show cause in contempt proceedings)

§ 715 [now § 1784] (Direction in order to show cause for seizure of property of witness in contempt)

§ 716 [now § 1784] (Service of order to show cause)

§ 717 [now § 1784] (Hearing on order to show cause; judgment; satisfaction)

§ 750 [now § 2405] (Garnishees in suits by United States against a corporation; garnishee failing to appear)

U.S.C. Title 29 former:

§ 111 [now 18 U.S.C. § 3692] (Contempts; speedy and public trial; jury) (Norris-La Guardia Act)

§ 112 [now 18 U.S.C., Appendix, R. 42] (Contempts; demands for retirement of judge sitting in proceeding)

§ 160 (Prevention of unfair labor practices—(h) Jurisdiction of courts unaffected by limitations prescribed in §§ 101 to 115 of Title 29)

§ 161 (Investigatory powers of Board—(2) Court aid in compelling production of evidence and attendance of witnesses)

§ 209 (Fair Labor Standards Act; attendance of witnesses)

U.S.C. Title 33:

§ 927 (Longshoremen's and Harbor Workers' Compensation Act; powers of deputy commissioner)

U.S.C. Title 35 former:

§ 56 [now § 24] (Failing to attend or testify)

U.S.C. Title 47:

§ 409 (Federal Communications Commission; hearing; subpoenas; oaths; witnesses; production of books and papers; contempts; depositions; penalties)

U.S.C. Title 48 former:

§ 1345a (Canal Zone; general jurisdiction of district court; issue of process at request of officials; witnesses; contempt)

U.S.C. Title 49:

§ 12 (Interstate Commerce Commission; authority and duties of commission; witnesses; depositions—(3) Compelling attendance and testimony of witnesses, etc.)

FEDERAL RULES OF CIVIL PROCEDURE

Rule 45 (Subpoena) subdivision (f) (Contempt)

1987 Amendments

The amendments are technical. No substantive change is intended.

2002 Amendments

The language of Rule 42 has been amended as part of the general restyling of the Criminal Rules to make them more easily understood and to make style and terminology consistent throughout the rules. These changes are intended to be stylistic only, except as noted below.

The revised rule is intended to more clearly set out the procedures for conducting a criminal contempt proceeding. The current rule implicitly recognizes that an attorney for the government may be involved in the prosecution of such cases. Revised Rule 42(a)(2) now explicitly addresses the appointment of a "prosecutor" and adopts language to reflect the holding in *Young v. United States ex rel. Vuitton*, 481 U.S. 787 (1987). In that case the Supreme Court indicated that ordinarily the court should request that an attorney for the government prosecute the contempt; only if that request is denied, should the court appoint a private prosecutor. The rule envisions that a disinterested counsel should be appointed to prosecute the contempt.

Rule 42(b) has been amended to make it clear that a court may summarily punish a person for committing contempt in the court's presence without regard to whether other rules, such as Rule 32 (sentencing procedures), might otherwise apply. *See, e.g., United States v. Martin–Trigona*, 759 F.2d 1017 (2d Cir. 1985). Further, Rule 42(b) has been amended to recognize the contempt powers of a court (other than a magistrate judge) and a magistrate judge.

HISTORICAL NOTES

Taft-Hartley Injunctions

Former § 112 of Title 29, Labor, upon which subd. (b) of this rule is in part based, as inapplicable to injunctions issued under the Taft-Hartley Act, see § 178 of Title 29.

IX. GENERAL PROVISIONS

Rule 43. Defendant's Presence

(a) When Required. Unless this rule, Rule 5, or Rule 10 provides otherwise, the defendant must be present at:

(1) the initial appearance, the initial arraignment, and the plea;

(2) every trial stage, including jury impanelment and the return of the verdict; and

(3) sentencing.

(b) When Not Required. A defendant need not be present under any of the following circumstances:

(1) Organizational Defendant. The defendant is an organization represented by counsel who is present.

(2) Misdemeanor Offense. The offense is punishable by fine or by imprisonment for not more than one year, or both, and with the defendant's written consent, the court permits arraignment, plea, trial, and sentencing to occur in the defendant's absence.

(3) Conference or Hearing on a Legal Question. The proceeding involves only a conference or hearing on a question of law.

(4) Sentence Correction. The proceeding involves the correction or reduction of sentence under Rule 35 or 18 U.S.C. § 3582(c).

(c) Waiving Continued Presence.

(1) In General. A defendant who was initially present at trial, or who had pleaded guilty or nolo contendere, waives the right to be present under the following circumstances:

(A) when the defendant is voluntarily absent after the trial has begun, regardless of whether the court informed the defendant of an obligation to remain during trial;

(B) in a noncapital case, when the defendant is voluntarily absent during sentencing; or

(C) when the court warns the defendant that it will remove the defendant from the courtroom for disruptive behavior, but the defendant persists in conduct that justifies removal from the courtroom.

(2) Waiver's Effect. If the defendant waives the right to be present, the trial may proceed to completion, including the verdict's return and sentencing, during the defendant's absence.

(As amended Apr. 22, 1974, eff. Dec. 1, 1975; July 31, 1975, Pub.L. 94–64, § 3(35), 89 Stat. 376; Mar. 9, 1987, eff. Aug. 1, 1987; Apr. 27, 1995, eff. Dec. 1, 1995; Apr. 24, 1998, eff. Dec. 1, 1998; Apr. 29, 2002, eff. Dec. 1, 2002.)

ADVISORY COMMITTEE NOTES

1944 Adoption

1. The first sentence of the rule setting forth the necessity of the defendant's presence at arraignment and trial is a restatement of existing law. *Lewis v. United States,* 13 S.Ct. 136, 146 U.S. 370, 36 L.Ed. 1011; *Diaz v. United States,* 32 S.Ct. 250, 223 U.S. 442, 455, 56 L.Ed. 500, Ann.Cas.1913C, 1138. This principle does not apply to hearings on motions made prior to or after trial. *United States v. Lynch,* C.C.A.3d, 132 F.2d 111.

2. The second sentence of the rule is a restatement of existing law that, except in capital cases, the defendant may not defeat the proceedings by voluntarily absenting himself after the trial has been commenced in his presence. *Diaz v. United States,* 32 S.Ct. 250, 223 U.S. 442, 455, 56 L.Ed. 500, Ann.Cas.1913C, 1138; *United States v. Noble,* 294 F. 689 (D. Mont.)—affirmed, 300 F. 689, C.C.A.9th; *United States v. Barracota,* 45 F.Supp. 38, S.D.N.Y.; *United States v. Vassalo,* 52 F.2d 699, E.D.Mich.

3. The fourth sentence of the rule, empowering the court in its discretion, with the defendant's written consent, to conduct proceedings in misdemeanor cases in defendant's absence adopts a practice prevailing in some districts comprising very large areas. In such districts appearance in court may require considerable travel, resulting in expense and hardship not commensurate with the gravity of the charge, if a minor infraction is involved and a small fine is eventually imposed. The rule, which is in the interest of defendants in such situations, leaves it discretionary with the court to permit defendants in misdemeanor cases to absent themselves and, if so, to determine in what types of misdemeanors and to what extent. Similar provisions are found in the statutes of a number of States. See A.L.I. Code of Criminal Procedure, pp. 881 to 882.

4. The purpose of the last sentence of the rule is to resolve a doubt that at times has arisen as to whether it is necessary to bring the defendant to court from an institution in which he is confined, possibly at a distant point, if the court determines to reduce the sentence previously imposed. It seems in the interest of both the Government and the defendant not to require such presence, because of the delay and expense that are involved.

1974 Amendment

The revision of rule 43 is designed to reflect *Illinois v. Allen,* 397 U.S. 337, 90 S.Ct. 1057, 25 L.Ed.2d 353 (1970). In *Allen,* the court held that "there are at least three constitutionally permissible ways for a trial judge to handle an obstreperous defendant like Allen: (1) bind and gag him, thereby keeping him present; (2) cite him for contempt; (3) take him out of the courtroom until he promises to conduct himself properly." 397 U.S. at 343–344, 90 S.Ct. 1057.

Since rule 43 formerly limited trial in absentia to situations in which there is a "voluntary absence after the trial has been commenced," it could be read as precluding a federal judge from exercising the third option held to be constitutionally permissible in *Allen.* The amendment is designed to make clear that the judge does have the power to exclude the defendant from the courtroom when the circumstances warrant such action.

The decision in *Allen,* makes no attempt to spell out standards to guide a judge in selecting the appropriate method to ensure decorum in the courtroom and there is no attempt to do so in the revision of the rule.

The concurring opinion of Mr. Justice Brennan stresses that the trial judge should make a reasonable effort to enable an excluded defendant "to communicate with his attorney and, if possible, to keep apprised of the progress of the trial." 397 U.S. at 351, 90 S.Ct. 1057. The Federal Judicial Center is presently engaged in experimenting with closed circuit television in courtrooms. The experience gained from these experiments may make closed circuit television readily available in federal courtrooms through which an excluded defendant would be able to hear and observe the trial.

The defendant's right to be present during the trial on a capital offense has been said to be so fundamental that it may not be waived. *Diaz v. United States,* 223 U.S. 442, 455, 32 S.Ct. 250, 56 L.Ed. 500 (1912) (dictum); *Near v. Cunningham,* 313 F.2d 929, 931 (4th Cir. 1963); C. Wright, Federal Practice and Procedure: Criminal § 723 at 199 (1969, Supp. 1971).

However, in *Illinois v. Allen, supra,* the court's opinion suggests that sanctions such as contempt may be least effective where the defendant is ultimately facing a far more serious sanction such as the death penalty. 397 U.S. at 345, 90 S.Ct. 1057. The ultimate determination of when a defendant can waive his right to be present in a capital case (assuming a death penalty provision is held constitutional, see *Furman v. Georgia,* 408 U.S. 238, 92 S.Ct. 2726, 33 L.Ed.2d 346 (1972)) is left for further clarification by the courts.

Subdivision (b)(1) makes clear that voluntary absence may constitute a waiver even if the defendant has not been informed by the court of his obligation to remain during the trial. Of course, proof of voluntary absence will require a showing that the defendant knew of the fact that the trial or other proceeding was going on. C. Wright, Federal Practice and Procedure: Criminal § 723 n. 35 (1969). But it is unnecessary to show that he was specifically warned of his obligation to be present; a warning seldom is thought necessary in current practice. [See *Taylor v. United States,* 414 U.S. 17, 94 S.Ct. 194, 38 L.Ed.2d 174 (1973).]

Subdivision (c)(3) makes clear that the defendant need not be present at a conference held by the court and counsel where the subject of the conference is an issue of law.

The other changes in the rule are editorial in nature. In the last phrase of the first sentence, "these rules" is changed to read "this rule," because there are no references in any of the other rules to situations where the defendant is not required to be present. The phrase "at the time of the plea," is added to subdivision (a) to make perfectly clear that defendant must be present at the time of the plea. See rule 11(c)(5) which provides that the judge may set a time, other than arraignment, for the holding of a plea agreement procedure.

1975 Enactment

A. Amendments Proposed by the Supreme Court

Rule 43 of the Federal Rules of Criminal Procedure deals with the presence of the defendant during the proceedings against him. It presently permits a defendant to be tried in absentia only in non-capital cases where the defendant has voluntarily absented himself after the trial has begun.

The Supreme Court amendments provide that a defendant has waived his right to be present at the trial of a capital or noncapital case in two circumstances: (1) when he voluntarily absents himself after the trial has begun; and (2) where he "engages in conduct which is such as to justify his being excluded from the courtroom."

B. Committee Action

The Committee added language to subdivision (b)(2), which deals with excluding a disruptive defendant from the courtroom. The Advisory Committee Note indicates that the rule proposed by the Supreme Court was drafted to reflect the decision in *Illinois v. Allen,* 397 U.S. 337 (1970). The Committee found that subdivision (b)(2) as proposed did not fully track the *Allen* decision. Consequently, language was added to that subsection to require the court to warn a disruptive defendant before excluding him from the courtroom. House Report No. 94–247.

1987 Amendment

The amendments are technical. No substantive change is intended.

1995 Amendments

The revisions to Rule 43 focus on two areas. First, the amendments make clear that a defendant who, initially present at trial or who has entered a plea of guilty or nolo contendere, but who voluntarily flees before sentencing, may nonetheless be sentenced in absentia. Second, the rule is amended to extend to organizational defendants. In addition, some stylistic changes have been made.

Subdivision (a). The changes to subdivision (a) are stylistic in nature and the Committee intends no substantive change in the operation of that provision.

Subdivision (b). The changes in subdivision (b) are intended to remedy the situation where a defendant voluntarily flees before sentence is imposed. Without the amendment, it is doubtful that a court could sentence a defendant who had been present during the entire trial but flees before sentencing. Delay in conducting the sentencing hearing under such circumstances may result in difficulty later in gathering and presenting the evidence necessary to formulate a guideline sentence.

The right to be present at court, although important, is not absolute. The caselaw, and practice in many jurisdictions, supports the proposition that the right to be present at trial may be waived through, inter alia, the act of fleeing. *See generally Crosby v. United States,* 113 S.Ct. 748, 506 U.S. 255 (1993). The amendment extends only to noncapital cases and applies only where the defendant is voluntarily absent after the trial has commenced or where the defendant has entered a plea of guilty or nolo contendere. The Committee envisions that defense counsel will continue to represent the interests of the defendant at sentencing.

The words "at trial, or having pleaded guilty or nolo contendere" have been added at the end of the first sentence to make clear that the trial of an absent defendant is possible only if the defendant was previously present at the trial or has entered a plea of guilty or nolo contendere. *See Crosby v. United States, supra.*

Subdivision (c). The change to subdivision (c) is technical in nature and replaces the word 'corporation' with a reference to 'organization,' as that term is defined in 18 U.S.C. § 18 to include entities other than corporations.

1998 Amendments

The amendment to Rule 43(c)(4) is intended to address two issues. First, the rule is rewritten to clarify whether a defendant is entitled to be present at resentencing proceedings conducted under Rule 35. As a result of amendments over the last several years to Rule 35, implementation of the Sentencing Reform Act, and caselaw interpretations of Rules 35 and 43, questions had been raised whether the defendant has to be present at those proceedings. Under the present version of the rule, it could be possible to require the defendant's presence at a "reduction" of sentence hearing conducted under Rule 35(b), but not a "correction" of sentence hearing conducted under Rule 35(a). That potential result seemed at odds with sound practice. As amended, Rule 43(c)(4) would permit a court to reduce or correct a sentence under Rule 35(b) or (c), respectively, without the defendant being present. But a sentencing proceeding being conducted on remand by an appellate court under Rule 35(a) would continue to require the defendant's presence. *See, e.g., United States v. Moree,* 928 F.2d 654, 655-656 (5th Cir. 1991)(noting distinction between presence of defendant at modification of sentencing proceedings and those hearings that impose new sentence after original sentence has been set aside).

The second issue addressed by the amendment is the applicability of Rule 43 to resentencing hearings conducted under 18 U.S.C. § 3582(c). Under that provision, a resentencing may be conducted as a result of retroactive changes to the Sentencing Guidelines by the United States Sentencing Commission or as a result of a motion by the Bureau of Prisons to reduce a sentence based on "extraordinary and compelling reasons." The amendment provides that a defendant's presence is not required at such proceedings. In the Committee's view, those proceedings are analogous to Rule 35(b) as it read before the Sentencing Reform Act of 1984, where the defendant's presence was not required. Further, the court may only reduce the original sentence under these proceedings.

2002 Amendments

The language of Rule 43 has been amended as part of the general restyling of the Criminal Rules to make them more easily understood and to make style and terminology consistent throughout the rules. These changes are intended to be stylistic only, except as noted below.

The first substantive change is reflected in Rule 43(a), which recognizes several exceptions to the requirement that a defendant must be present in court for all proceedings. In addition to referring to exceptions that might exist in Rule 43 itself, the amendment recognizes that a defendant need not be present when the court has permitted video teleconferencing procedures under Rules 5 and 10 or when the defendant has waived the right to be present for the arraignment under Rule 10. Second, by inserting the word "initial" before "arraignment," revised Rule 43(a)(1) reflects the view that a defendant need not be present for subsequent arraignments based upon a superseding indictment.

The Rule has been reorganized to make it easier to read and apply; revised Rule 43(b) is former Rule 43(c).

HISTORICAL NOTES

Effective and Applicability Provisions

1975 Acts. Amendments of this rule embraced in the order of the United States Supreme Court on Apr. 22, 1974, and the amendments of this rule made by § 3 of Pub.L. 94–64, effective Dec. 1, 1975, see § 2 of Pub.L. 94–64, set out as a note under rule 4 of these rules.

Rule 44. Right to and Appointment of Counsel

(a) Right to Appointed Counsel. A defendant who is unable to obtain counsel is entitled to have counsel appointed to represent the defendant at every stage of the proceeding from initial appearance through appeal, unless the defendant waives this right.

(b) Appointment Procedure. Federal law and local court rules govern the procedure for implementing the right to counsel.

(c) Inquiry Into Joint Representation.

(1) Joint Representation. Joint representation occurs when:

(A) two or more defendants have been charged jointly under Rule 8(b) or have been joined for trial under Rule 13; and

(B) the defendants are represented by the same counsel, or counsel who are associated in law practice.

(2) Court's Responsibilities in Cases of Joint Representation. The court must promptly inquire about the propriety of joint representation and must personally advise each defendant of the right to the effective assistance of counsel, including separate representation. Unless there is good cause to believe that no conflict of interest is likely to arise, the court must take appropriate measures to protect each defendant's right to counsel.

(As amended Feb. 28, 1966, eff. July 1, 1966; Apr. 24, 1972, eff. Oct. 1, 1972; Apr. 30, 1979, eff. Dec. 1, 1980; Mar. 9, 1987, eff. Aug. 1, 1987; Apr. 22, 1993, eff. Dec. 1, 1993; Apr. 29, 2002, eff. Dec. 1, 2002.)

ADVISORY COMMITTEE NOTES

1944 Adoption

1. This rule is a restatement of existing law in regard to the defendant's constitutional right of counsel as defined in recent judicial decisions. The Sixth Amendment provides:

"In all criminal prosecutions, the accused shall enjoy the right * * * to have the Assistance of Counsel for his defense."

28 U.S.C. former § 394 [now § 1654] provided:

"In all the courts of the United States the parties may plead and manage their own causes personally, or by the assistance of such counsel or attorneys at law as, by the rules of the said courts, respectively, are permitted to manage and conduct causes therein."

18 U.S.C. former § 563 [now § 3005], which is derived from the Act of April 30, 1790 (1 Stat. 118), provides:

"Every person who is indicted of treason or other capital crime, shall be allowed to make his full defense by counsel learned in the law; and the court before which he is tried, or some judge thereof, shall immediately, upon his request, assign to him such counsel, not exceeding two, as he may desire, and they shall have free access to him at all seasonable hours."

The present extent of the right of counsel has been defined recently in *Johnson v. Zerbst*, 58 S.Ct. 1919, 304 U.S. 458, 82 L.Ed. 1461; *Walker v. Johnston*, 61 S.Ct. 574, 312 U.S. 275, 85 L.Ed. 830; and *Glasser v. United States*, 62 S.Ct. 457, 315 U.S. 60, 86 L.Ed. 680, rehearing denied 62 S.Ct. 629, 637, two cases, 315 U.S. 827, 86 L.Ed. 1222. The rule is a restatement of the principles enunciated in these decisions. See, also, Holtzoff, 20 N.Y.U.L.Q.R. 1.

2. The rule is intended to indicate that the right of the defendant to have counsel assigned by the court relates only to proceedings in court and, therefore, does not include preliminary proceedings before a committing magistrate. Although the defendant is not entitled to have counsel assigned to him in connection with preliminary proceedings, he is entitled to be represented by counsel retained by him, if he so chooses, Rule 5(b) (Proceedings before the Commissioner; Statement by the Commissioner) and Rule 40(b)(2) (Commitment to Another District; Removal—Arrest in Distant District—Statement by Commissioner or Judge). As to defendant's right of counsel in connection with the taking of depositions, see Rule 15(c) (Depositions—Defendant's Counsel and Payment of Expenses).

1966 Amendment

A new rule is provided as a substitute for the old to provide for the assignment of counsel to defendants unable to obtain counsel during all stages of the proceeding. The Supreme Court has recently made clear the importance of providing counsel both at the earliest possible time after arrest and on appeal. See *Crooker v. California*, 357 U.S. 433 (1958); *Cicenia v. LaGay*, 357 U.S. 504 (1958); *White v. Maryland*, 373 U.S. 59 (1963); *Gideon v. Wainwright*, 372 U.S. 335 (1963); *Douglas v. California*, 372 U.S. 353 (1963). See also Association of the Bar of the City of New York, Special Committee to Study the Defender System, Equal Justice for the Accused (1959); Report of the Attorney General's Committee on Poverty and the Administration of Justice (1963); Beaney, Right to Counsel Before Arraignment, 45 Minn.L.Rev. 771 (1961); Boskey, The Right to Counsel in Appellate Proceedings, 45 Minn.L.Rev. 783 (1961); Douglas, The Right to Counsel—A Foreword, 45 Minn. L.Rev. 693 (1961); Kamisar, The Right to Counsel and the Fourteenth Amendment; A Dialogue on "The Most Pervasive Right" of an Accused, 30 U. Chi.L.Rev. 1 (1962); Kamisar, Betts v. Brady Twenty Years Later: The Right to Counsel and Due Process Values, 61 Mich.L.Rev. 219 (1962); Symposium, The Right to Counsel, 22 Legal Aid Briefcase 4–48 (1963). Provision has been made by law for a Legal Aid Agency in the District of Columbia which is charged with the duty of providing counsel and courts are admonished to assign such counsel "as early in the proceeding as practicable." D.C.Code § 2–2202. Congress has now made provision for assignment of counsel and their compensation in all of the districts. Criminal Justice Act of 1964 (78 Stat. 552).

Like the original rule the amended rule provides a right to counsel which is broader in two respects than that for which compensation is provided in the Criminal Justice Act of 1964: (1) the right extends to petty offenses to be tried in the district courts, and (2) the right extends to defendants unable to obtain counsel for reasons other than financial. These rules do not cover procedures other than those in the courts of the United States and before United States commissioners. See Rule 1. Hence, the problems relating to the providing of counsel prior to the initial appearance before a court or commissioner are not dealt with in this rule. Cf. *Escobedo v. United States,* 378 U.S. 478 (1964); Enker and Elsen, Counsel for the Suspect: *Massiah v. United States* and *Escobedo v. Illinois,* 49 Minn.L.Rev. 47 (1964).

Subdivision (a).—The subdivision expresses the right of the defendant unable to obtain counsel to have such counsel assigned at any stage of the proceedings from his initial appearance before the commissioner or court through the appeal, unless he waives such right. The phrase "from his initial appearance before the commissioner or court" is intended to require the assignment of counsel as promptly as possible after it appears that the defendant is unable to obtain counsel. The right to assignment of counsel is not limited to those financially unable to obtain counsel. If a defendant is able to compensate counsel but still cannot obtain counsel, he is entitled to the assignment of counsel even though not to free counsel.

Subdivision (b).—The new subdivision reflects the adoption of the Criminal Justice Act of 1964. See Report of the Judicial Conference of the United States on the Criminal Justice Act of 1964, 36 F.R.D. 277 (1964).

1972 Amendment

Subdivision (a) is amended to reflect the Federal Magistrates Act of 1968. The phrase "federal magistrate" is defined in rule 54.

1979 Amendment

Rule 44(c) establishes a procedure for avoiding the occurrence of events which might otherwise give rise to a plausible post-conviction claim that because of joint representation the defendants in a criminal case were deprived of their Sixth Amendment right to the effective assistance of counsel. Although "courts have differed with respect to the scope and nature of the affirmative duty of the trial judge to assure that criminal defendants are not deprived of their right to the effective assistance of counsel by joint representation of conflicting interests," *Holloway v. Arkansas,* 98 S.Ct. 1173 (1978) (where the Court found it unnecessary to reach this issue), this amendment is generally consistent with the current state of the law in several circuits. As held in *United States v. Carrigan,* 543 F.2d 1053 (2d Cir.1976):

> When a potential conflict of interest arises, either where a court has assigned the same counsel to represent several defendants or where the same counsel has been retained by co-defendants in a criminal case, the proper course of action for the trial judge is to conduct a hearing to determine whether a conflict exists to the degree that a defendant may be prevented from receiving advice and assistance sufficient to afford him the quality of representation guaranteed by the Sixth Amendment. The defendant should be fully advised by the trial court of the facts underlying the potential conflict and be given the opportunity to express his views.

See also *United States v. Lawriw,* 568 F.2d 98 (8th Cir.1977) (duty on trial judge to make inquiry where joint representation by appointed or retained counsel, and "without such an inquiry a finding of knowing and intelligent waiver will seldom, if ever, be sustained by this Court"); *Abraham v. United States,* 549 F.2d 236 (2d Cir.1977); *United States v. Mari,* 526 F.2d 117 (2d Cir.1975); *United States v. Truglio,* 493 F.2d 574 (4th Cir.1974) (joint representation should cause trial judge "to inquire whether the defenses to be presented in any way conflict"); *United States v. DeBerry,* 487 F.2d 488 (2d Cir.1973); *United States ex rel. Hart v. Davenport,* 478 F.2d 203 (3d Cir.1973) (noting there "is much to be said for the rule . . . which assumes prejudice and nonwaiver if there has been no on-the-record inquiry by the court as to the hazards to defendants from joint representation"); *United States v. Alberti,* 470 F.2d 878 (2d Cir.1973); *United States v. Foster,* 469 F.2d 1 (1st Cir.1972) (lack of sufficient inquiry shifts the burden of proof on the question of prejudice to the government); *Campbell v. United States,* 352 F.2d 359 (D.C.Cir.1965) (where joint representation, court "has a duty to ascertain whether each defendant has an awareness of the potential risks of that course and nevertheless has knowingly chosen it"). Some states have taken a like position; see, e.g., *State v. Olsen,* Minn. 1977, 258 N.W.2d 898.

This procedure is also consistent with that recommended in the ABA Standards Relating to the Function of the Trial Judge (Approved Draft, 1972), which provide in § 3.4(b):

> Whenever two or more defendants who have been jointly charged, or whose cases have been consolidated, are represented by the same attorney, the trial judge should inquire into potential conflicts which may jeopardize the right of each defendant to the fidelity of his counsel.

Avoiding a conflict-of-interest situation is in the first instance a responsibility of the attorney. If a lawyer represents "multiple clients having potentially differing interests, he must weigh carefully the possibility that his judgment may be impaired or his loyalty divided if he accepts or continues the employment," and he is to "resolve all doubts against the propriety of the representation." Code of Professional Responsibility, Ethical Consideration 5–15. See also ABA Standards Relating to the Defense Function § 3.5(b) (Approved Draft, 1971), concluding that the "potential for conflict of interest in representing multiple defendants is so grave that ordinarily a lawyer should decline to act for more than one of several co-defendants except in unusual situations when, after careful investigation, it is clear that no conflict is likely to develop and when the several defendants give an informed consent to such multiple representation."

It by no means follows that the inquiry provided for by rule 44(c) is unnecessary. For one thing, even the most diligent attorney may be unaware of facts giving rise to a potential conflict. Often "counsel must operate somewhat in the dark and feel their way uncertainly to an understanding of what their clients may be called upon to meet upon a trial" and consequently "are frequently unable to foresee developments which may require changes in strategy." *United States v. Carrigan,* supra (concurring opinion). "Because the conflicts are often subtle it is not enough to rely upon counsel, who may not be totally disinterested, to make sure that each of his joint clients has made an effective waiver." *United States v. Lawriw,* supra.

Moreover, it is important that the trial judge ascertain whether the effective and fair administration of justice would be adversely affected by continued joint representation, even when an actual conflict is not then apparent. As noted in *United States v. Mari,* supra (concurring opinion):

> Trial court insistence that, except in extraordinary circumstances, codefendants retain separate counsel will in the long run . . . prove salutary not only to the administration of justice and the appearance of justice but the cost of justice; habeas corpus petitions, petitions for new trials, appeals and occasionally retrials . . . can be avoided. Issues as to whether there is an actual conflict of interest, whether the conflict has resulted in prejudice, whether there has been a waiver, whether the waiver is intelligent and knowledgeable, for example, can all be avoided. Where a conflict that first did not appear subsequently arises in or before trial, . . . continuances or mistrials can be saved. Essentially by the time a case . . . gets to the appellate level the harm to the appearance of justice has already been done, whether or not reversal occurs; at the trial level it is a matter which is so easy to avoid.

A rule 44(c) inquiry is required whether counsel is assigned or retained. It "makes no difference whether counsel is appointed by the court or selected by the defendants; even where selected by the defendants the same dangers of potential conflict exist, and it is also possible that the rights of the public to the proper administration of justice may be affected adversely." *United States v. Mari,* supra (concurring opinion). See also *United States v. Lawriw,* supra. When there has been "no discussion as to possible conflict initiated by the court," it cannot be assumed that the choice of counsel by the defendants "was intelligently made with knowledge of any possible conflict." *United States v. Carrigan,* supra. As for assigned counsel, it is provided by statute that "the court shall appoint separate counsel for defendants having interests that cannot properly be represented by the same counsel, or when other good cause is shown." 18 U.S.C. § 3006(A) (b). Rule 44(c) is not intended to prohibit the automatic appointment of separate counsel in the first instance, see *Ford v. United States,* 379 F.2d 123 (D.C.Cir. 1967); *Lollar v. United States,* 376 F.2d 243 (D.C.Cir.1967), which would obviate the necessity for an inquiry.

Under rule 44(c), an inquiry is called for when the joined defendants are represented by the same attorney and also when they are represented by attorneys "associated in the practice of law." This is consistent with Code of Professional Responsibility, Disciplinary Rule 5–105(D) (providing that if "a lawyer is required to decline employment or to withdraw from employment" because of a potential conflict, "no partner or associate of his or his firm may accept or continue such employment"); and ABA Standards Relating to the Defense Function § 3.5(b) (Approved Draft, 1971) (applicable to "a lawyer or lawyers who are associated in practice"). Attorneys representing joined defendants should so advise the court if they are associated in the practice of law.

The rule 44(c) procedure is not limited to cases expected to go to trial. Although the more dramatic conflict situations, such as when the question arises as to whether the several defendants should take the stand, *Morgan v. United States,* 396 F.2d 110 (2d Cir.1968), tend to occur in a trial context, serious conflicts may also arise when one or more of the jointly represented defendants pleads guilty.

> The problem is that even where as here both codefendants pleaded guilty there are frequently potential conflicts of interest . . . [T]he prosecutor may be inclined to accept a guilty plea from one codefendant which may harm the interests of the other. The contrast in the dispositions of the cases may have a harmful impact on the codefendant who does not initially plead guilty; he may be pressured into pleading guilty himself rather than face his codefendant's bargained-for testimony at a trial. And it will be his own counsel's recommendation to the initially pleading codefendant which will have contributed to this harmful impact upon him . . . [I]n a given instance it would be at least conceivable that the prosecutor would be willing to accept pleas to lesser offenses from two defendants in preference to a plea of guilty by one defendant to a greater offense.

United States v. Mari, supra (concurring opinion). To the same effect is ABA Standards Relating to the Defense Function at 213–14.

It is contemplated that under rule 44(c) the court will make appropriate inquiry of the defendants and of counsel regarding the possibility of a conflict of interest developing. Whenever it is necessary to make a more particularized inquiry into the nature of the contemplated defense, the court should "pursue the inquiry with defendants and their counsel on the record but in chambers" so as "to avoid the possibility of prejudicial disclosures to the prosecution." *United States v. Foster,* supra. It is important that each defendant be "fully advised of the facts underlying the potential conflict and is given an opportunity to express his or her views." *United States v. Alberti,* supra. The rule specifically requires that the court personally advise each defendant of his right to effective assistance of counsel, including separate representation. See *United States v. Foster,* supra, requiring that the court make a determination that the court make a defendants "understand that they may retain separate counsel, or if qualified, may have such counsel appointed by the court and paid for by the government."

Under rule 44(c), the court is to take appropriate measures to protect each defendant's right to counsel unless it appears "there is good cause to believe no conflict of interest is likely to arise" as a consequence of the continuation of such joint representation. A less demanding standard would not adequately protect the Sixth Amendment right to effective assistance of counsel or the effective administration of criminal justice. Although joint representation "is not per se violative of constitutional guarantees of effective assistance of counsel, *Holloway v. Arkansas,* supra, it would not suffice to require the court to act only when a conflict of interest is then apparent, for it is not possible to "anticipate with complete accuracy the course that a criminal trial may take." *Fryar v.*

United States, 404 F.2d 1071 (10th Cir.1968). This is particularly so in light of the fact that if a conflict later arises and a defendant thereafter raises a Sixth Amendment objection, a court must grant relief without indulging "in nice calculations as to the amount of prejudice arising from its denial." *Glasser v. United States,* 315 U.S. 60 (1942). This is because, as the Supreme Court more recently noted in *Holloway v. Arkansas,* supra, "in a case of joint representation of conflicting interests the evil . . . is in what the advocate finds himself compelled to refrain from doing," and this makes it "virtually impossible" to assess the impact of the conflict.

Rule 44(c) does not specify what particular measures must be taken. It is appropriate to leave this within the court's discretion, for the measures which will best protect each defendant's right to counsel may well vary from case to case. One possible course of action is for the court to obtain a knowing, intelligent and voluntary waiver of the right to separate representation, for, as noted in *Holloway v. Arkansas,* supra, "a defendant may waive his right to the assistance of an attorney unhindered by a conflict of interests." See *United States v. DeBerry,* supra, holding that defendants should be jointly represented only if "the court has ascertained that . . . each understands clearly the possibilities of a conflict of interest and waives any rights in connection with it." It must be emphasized that a "waiver of the right to separate representation should not be accepted by the court unless the defendants have each been informed of the probable hazards; and the voluntary character of their waiver is apparent." ABA Standards Relating to the Function of the Trial Judge at 45. *United States v. Garcia,* supra, [517 F.2d 272] spells out in significant detail what should be done to assure an adequate waiver:

> As in Rule 11 procedures, the district court should address each defendant personally and forthrightly advise him of the potential dangers of representation by counsel with a conflict of interest. The defendant must be at liberty to question the district court as to the nature and consequences of his legal representation. Most significantly, the court should seek to elicit a narrative response from each defendant that he has been advised of his right to effective representation, that he understands the details of his attorney's possible conflict of interest and the potential perils of such a conflict, that he has discussed the matter with his attorney or if he wishes with outside counsel, and that he voluntarily waives his Sixth Amendment protections. It is, of course, vital that the waiver be established by "clear, unequivocal, and unambiguous language." . . . Mere assent in response to a series of questions from the bench may in some circumstances constitute an adequate waiver, but the court should nonetheless endeavor to have each defendant personally articulate in detail his intent to forego this significant constitutional protection. Recordation of the waiver colloquy between defendant and judge, will also serve the government's interest by assisting in shielding any potential conviction from collateral attack, either on Sixth Amendment grounds or on a Fifth or Fourteenth Amendment "fundamental fairness" basis.

See also Hyman, Joint Representation of Multiple Defendants in a Criminal Trial: The Court's Headache, 5 Hofstra L.Rev. 315, 334 (1977).

Another possibility is that the court will order that the defendants be separately represented in subsequent proceedings in the case.

> Though the court must remain alert to and take account of the fact that "certain advantages might accrue from joint representation," Holloway v. Arkansas, supra, it need not permit the joint representation to continue merely because the defendants express a willingness to so proceed. That is, there will be cases where the court should require separate counsel to represent certain defendants despite the expressed wishes of such defendants. Indeed, failure of the trial court to require separate representation may . . . require a new trial, even though the defendants have expressed a desire to continue with the same counsel. The right to effective representation by counsel whose loyalty is undivided is so paramount in the proper administration of criminal justice that it must in some cases take precedence over all other considerations, including the expressed preference of the defendants concerned and their attorney.

United States v. Carrigan, supra (concurring opinion). See also *United States v. Lawriw,* supra; *Abraham v. United States,* supra; ABA Standards Relating to the Defense Function at 213, concluding that in some circumstances "even full disclosure and consent of the client may not be an adequate protection." As noted in *United States v. Dolan,* 570 F.2d 1177 (3d Cir.1978), such an order may be necessary where the trial judge is

> not satisfied that the waiver is proper. For example, a defendant may be competent enough to stand trial, but not competent enough to understand the complex, subtle, and sometimes unforeseeable dangers inherent in multiple representation. More importantly, the judge may find that the waiver cannot be intelligently made simply because he is not in a position to inform the defendant of the foreseeable prejudices multiple representation might entail for him.

As concluded in *Dolan,* "exercise of the court's supervisory powers by disqualifying an attorney representing multiple criminal defendants in spite of the defendants' express desire to retain that attorney does not necessarily abrogate defendant's sixth amendment rights". It does not follow from the absolute right of self-representation recognized in *Faretta v. California,* 422 U.S. 806 (1975), that there is an absolute right to counsel of one's own choice. Thus,

> when a trial court finds an actual conflict of interest which impairs the ability of a criminal defendant's chosen counsel to conform with the ABA Code of Professional Responsibility, the court should not be required to tolerate an inadequate representation of a defendant. Such representation not only constitutes a breach of professional ethics and invites disrespect for the integrity of the court, but it is also detrimental to the independent interest of the trial judge to be free from future attacks over the adequacy of the waiver or the fairness of the proceedings in his own court and the subtle problems implicating the defendant's comprehension of the waiver. Under such circumstances, the court can elect to exercise its supervisory authority over members of the bar to enforce the ethical standard requiring an attorney to decline multiple representation.

United States v. Dolan, supra. See also Geer, Conflict of Interest and Multiple Defendants in a Criminal Case: Professional Responsibilities of the Defense Attorney, 62 Minn.

L.Rev. 119 (1978); Note, Conflict of Interests in Multiple Representation of Criminal Co-Defendants, 68 J.Crim.L. & C. 226 (1977).

The failure in a particular case to conduct a rule 44(c) inquiry would not, standing alone, necessitate the reversal of a conviction of a jointly represented defendant. However, as is currently the case, a reviewing court is more likely to assume a conflict resulted from the joint representation when no inquiry or an inadequate inquiry was conducted. *United States v. Carrigan,* supra; *United States v. DeBerry,* supra. On the other hand, the mere fact that a rule 44(c) inquiry was conducted in the early stages of the case does not relieve the court of all responsibility in this regard thereafter. The obligation placed upon the court by rule 44(c) is a continuing one, and thus in a particular case further inquiry may be necessary on a later occasion because of new developments suggesting a potential conflict of interest.

1987 Amendment

The amendments are technical. No substantive change is intended.

1993 Amendment

The Rule is amended to conform to the Judicial Improvements Act of 1990 [P.L. 101–650, Title III, Section 321] which provides that each United States magistrate appointed under section 631 of title 28, United States Code, shall be known as a United States magistrate judge.

2002 Amendments

The language of Rule 44 has been amended as part of the general restyling of the Criminal Rules to make them more easily understood and to make style and terminology consistent throughout the rules. These changes are intended to be stylistic only.

Revised Rule 44 now refers to the "appointment" of counsel, rather than the assignment of counsel; the Committee believed the former term was more appropriate. *See* 18 U.S.C. § 3006A. In Rule 44(c), the term "retained or assigned" has been deleted as being unnecessary, without changing the court's responsibility to conduct an inquiry where joint representation occurs.

Rule 45. Computing and Extending Time

(a) Computing Time. The following rules apply in computing any period of time specified in these rules, any local rule, or any court order:

(1) Day of the Event Excluded. Exclude the day of the act, event, or default that begins the period.

(2) Exclusion from Brief Periods. Exclude intermediate Saturdays, Sundays, and legal holidays when the period is less than 11 days.

(3) Last Day. Include the last day of the period unless it is a Saturday, Sunday, legal holiday, or day on which weather or other conditions make the clerk's office inaccessible. When the last day is excluded, the period runs until the end of the next day that is not a Saturday, Sunday, legal holiday, or day when the clerk's office is inaccessible.

(4) "Legal Holiday" Defined. As used in this rule, "legal holiday" means:

(A) the day set aside by statute for observing:

(i) New Year's Day;

(ii) Martin Luther King, Jr.'s Birthday;

(iii) Washington's Birthday;

(iv) Memorial Day;

(v) Independence Day;

(vi) Labor Day;

(vii) Columbus Day;

(viii) Veterans' Day;

(ix) Thanksgiving Day;

(x) Christmas Day; and

(B) any other day declared a holiday by the President, the Congress, or the state where the district court is held.

(b) Extending Time.

(1) In General. When an act must or may be done within a specified period, the court on its own may extend the time, or for good cause may do so on a party's motion made:

(A) before the originally prescribed or previously extended time expires; or

(B) after the time expires if the party failed to act because of excusable neglect.

(2) Exception. The court may not extend the time to take any action under Rule 35, except as stated in that rule.

(c) Additional Time After Service. When these rules permit or require a party to act within a specified period after a notice or a paper has been served on that party, 3 days are added to the period if service occurs in the manner provided under Federal Rule of Civil Procedure 5(b)(2)(B), (C), or (D).

(As amended Feb. 28, 1966, eff. July 1, 1966; Dec. 4, 1967, eff. July 1, 1968; Mar. 1, 1971, eff. July 1, 1971; Apr. 28, 1982, eff. Aug. 1, 1982; Apr. 29, 1985, eff. Aug. 1, 1985; Mar. 9, 1987, eff. Aug. 1, 1987; Apr. 29, 2002, eff. Dec. 1, 2002; Apr. 25, 2005, eff. Dec. 1, 2005.)

ADVISORY COMMITTEE NOTES

1944 Adoption

The rule is in substance the same as Rule 6 of the Federal Rules of Civil Procedure. It seems desirable that matters covered by this rule should be regulated in the same manner for civil and criminal cases, in order to preclude possibility of confusion.

Note to Subdivision (a). This rule supersedes the method of computing time prescribed by rule 13 of the Criminal Appeals Rules, promulgated on May 7, 1934, 292 U.S. 661.

Note to Subdivision (c). This rule abolishes the expiration of a term of court as a time limitation for the taking of any step in a criminal proceeding, as is done for civil cases by rule 6(c) of the Federal Rules of Civil Procedure, 28 U.S.C., Appendix. In view of the fact that the duration of terms of court varies among the several districts and the further fact that the length of time for the taking of any step limited by a term of court depends on the stage within the term when the time begins to run, specific time limitations have been substituted for the taking of any step which previously had to be taken within the term of court.

Note to Subdivision (d). Cf. Rule 47 (Motions) and rule 49 (Service and filing of papers).

1966 Amendment

Subdivision (a).—This amendment conforms the subdivision with the amendments made effective on July 1, 1963, to the comparable provision in Civil Rule 6(a). The only major change is to treat Saturdays as legal holidays for the purpose of computing time.

Subdivision (b).—The amendment conforms the subdivision to the amendments made effective in 1948 to the comparable provision in Civil Rule 6(b). One of these conforming changes, substituting the words "extend the time" for the words "enlarge the period" clarifies the ambiguity which gave rise to the decision in *United States v. Robinson*, 361 U.S. 220 (1960). The amendment also, in connection with the amendments to Rules 29 and 37, makes it clear that the only circumstances under which extensions can be granted under Rules 29, 33, 34, 35, 37(a)(2) and 39(c) are those stated in them.

Subdivision (c).—Subdivision (c) of Rule 45 is rescinded as unnecessary in view of the 1963 amendment to 28 U.S.C. § 138 eliminating terms of court.

1968 Amendment

The amendment eliminates inappropriate references to Rules 37 and 39 which are to be abrogated.

1971 Amendment

The amendment adds Columbus Day to the list of legal holidays to conform the subdivision to the Act of June 28, 1968, 82 Stat. 250, which constituted Columbus Day a legal holiday effective after January 1, 1971.

The Act, which amended Title 5, U.S.C., § 6103(a), changes the day on which certain holidays are to be observed. Washington's Birthday, Memorial Day and Veterans Day are to be observed on the third Monday in February, the Last Monday in May and the forth Monday in October, respectively, rather than, as heretofore, on February 22, May 30, and November 11, respectively. Columbus Day is to be observed on the second Monday in October. New Year's Day, Independence Day, Thanksgiving Day and Christmas continue to be observed on the traditional days.

1982 Amendment

Subdivision (a). The amendment to subdivision (a) takes account of the fact that on rare occasion severe weather conditions or other circumstances beyond control will make it impossible to meet a filing deadline under Rule 45(a). Illustrative is an incident which occurred in Columbus, Ohio during the "great blizzard of 1978," in which weather conditions deteriorated to the point where personnel in the clerk's office found it virtually impossible to reach the courthouse, and where the GSA Building Manager found it necessary to close and secure the entire building. The amendment covers that situation and also similar situations in which weather or other conditions made the clerk's office, though open, not readily accessible to the lawyer. Whether the clerk's office was in fact "inaccessible" on a given date is to be determined by the district court. Some state time computation statutes contain language somewhat similar to that in the amendment; see, e.g., Md. Code Ann. art. 94, § 2.

1985 Amendment

The rule is amended to extend the exclusion of intermediate Saturdays, Sundays, and legal holidays to the computation of time periods less than 11 days. Under the current version of the Rule, parties bringing motions under rules with 10-day periods could have as few as 5 working days to prepare their motions. This change corresponds to the change being made in the comparable provision in Fed. R.Civ.P. 6(a).

The Birthday of Martin Luther King, Jr., which becomes a legal holiday effective January 1986, has been added to the list of legal holidays enumerated in the Rule.

1987 Amendment

The amendments are technical. No substantive change is intended.

2002 Amendments

The language of Rule 45 has been amended as part of the general restyling of the Criminal Rules to make them more easily understood and to make style and terminology consistent throughout the rules. These changes are intended to be stylistic only.

The additional three days provided by Rule 45(c) is extended to the means of service authorized by the new paragraph (D) added to Rule 5(b) of the Federal Rules of Civil Procedure, including—with the consent of the person served—service by electronic means. The means of service authorized in civil actions apply to criminal cases under Rule 49 (b).

Rule 45(d), which governs the timing of written motions and affidavits, has been moved to Rule 47.

2005 Amendments

Rule 45(b) has been amended to conform to amendments to Rules 29, 33, and 34, which have been amended to remove the requirement that the court must act within the seven-day period specified in each of those rules if it sets another time for filing a motion under those rules.

Currently, Rules 29(c)(1), 33(b)(2), and 34(b) require the defendant to move for relief under those rules within the seven-day periods specified in those rules or within some other time set by the court in an order issued during that same seven-day period. Courts have held that the seven-day rule is jurisdictional. Thus, for example, if a defendant files a request for an extension of time to file a motion for a judgment of acquittal or a motion for new trial within the seven-day period, the court must rule on that motion or request within the same seven-day period. If for some reason the court does not rule on the request for an extension of time within the seven days, the court loses jurisdiction to act on the underlying substantive motion. *See, e.g., United States v. Smith*, 331 U.S. 469, 473–474 (1947) (rejecting argument that trial court had power to grant new trial on its own motion after expiration of time in Rule 33); *United States v. Marquez*, 291 F.3d 23, 27–28 (D.C. Cir. 2002) (citing language of Rule 33, and holding that "district court forfeited the power to act when it failed to . . . fix a new time for filing a motion for a new trial within seven days of the verdict").

Rule 45(b)(2) currently specifies that a court may not extend the time for taking action under Rules 29, 33, or 34, except as provided in those rules.

Assuming that the current provisions in Rules 29, 33, and 34 were intended to promote finality, there is nothing to prevent the court from granting the defendant a significant extension of time, under those rules, as long as it does so within the seven-day period. Thus, the Committee believed that those rules should be amended to be consistent with all of the other timing requirements in the rules, which do not force the court to rule on a motion to extend the time for filing, within a particular period of time or lose jurisdiction to do so. The change to Rule 45(b)(2) is thus a conforming amendment.

The defendant is still required to file motions under Rules 29, 33, and 34 within the seven-day period specified in those rules. The defendant, however, may consistently with Rule 45, seek an extension of time to file the underlying motion as long as the defendant does so within the seven-day period. But the court itself is not required to act on that motion within any particular time. Further, under Rule 45(b)(1)(B), if for some reason the defendant fails to file the underlying motion within the specified time, the court may nonetheless consider that untimely motion if the court determines that the failure to file it on time was the result of excusable neglect.

HISTORICAL AND STATUTORY NOTES

References in Text

Federal Rule of Civil Procedure 5, referred to in subd. (c), is set out in the Appendix to Title 28, Fed.Rules Civ.Proc. Rule 5, 28 U.S.C.A.

Rule 46. Release from Custody; Supervising Detention

(a) Before Trial. The provisions of 18 U.S.C. §§ 3142 and 3144 govern pretrial release.

(b) During Trial. A person released before trial continues on release during trial under the same terms and conditions. But the court may order different terms and conditions or terminate the release if necessary to ensure that the person will be present during trial or that the person's conduct will not obstruct the orderly and expeditious progress of the trial.

(c) Pending Sentencing or Appeal. The provisions of 18 U.S.C. § 3143 govern release pending sentencing or appeal. The burden of establishing that the defendant will not flee or pose a danger to any other person or to the community rests with the defendant.

(d) Pending Hearing on a Violation of Probation or Supervised Release. Rule 32.1(a)(6) governs release pending a hearing on a violation of probation or supervised release.

(e) Surety. The court must not approve a bond unless any surety appears to be qualified. Every surety, except a legally approved corporate surety, must demonstrate by affidavit that its assets are adequate. The court may require the affidavit to describe the following:

(1) the property that the surety proposes to use as security;

(2) any encumbrance on that property;

(3) the number and amount of any other undischarged bonds and bail undertakings the surety has issued; and

(4) any other liability of the surety.

(f) Bail Forfeiture.

(1) Declaration. The court must declare the bail forfeited if a condition of the bond is breached.

(2) Setting Aside. The court may set aside in whole or in part a bail forfeiture upon any condition the court may impose if:

(A) the surety later surrenders into custody the person released on the surety's appearance bond; or

(B) it appears that justice does not require bail forfeiture.

(3) Enforcement.

(A) Default Judgment and Execution. If it does not set aside a bail forfeiture, the court must, upon the government's motion, enter a default judgment.

(B) Jurisdiction and Service. By entering into a bond, each surety submits to the district court's jurisdiction and irrevocably appoints the district clerk as its agent to receive service of any filings affecting its liability.

(C) Motion to Enforce. The court may, upon the government's motion, enforce the surety's liability without an independent action. The government must serve any motion, and notice as the court prescribes, on the district clerk. If so served, the clerk must promptly mail a copy to the surety at its last known address.

(4) Remission. After entering a judgment under Rule 46(f)(3), the court may remit in whole or in part the judgment under the same conditions specified in Rule 46(f)(2).

(g) Exoneration. The court must exonerate the surety and release any bail when a bond condition has been satisfied or when the court has set aside or remitted the forfeiture. The court must exonerate a surety who deposits cash in the amount of the bond or timely surrenders the defendant into custody.

(h) Supervising Detention Pending Trial.

(1) In General. To eliminate unnecessary detention, the court must supervise the detention within the district of any defendants awaiting trial and of any persons held as material witnesses.

(2) Reports. An attorney for the government must report biweekly to the court, listing each material witness held in custody for more than 10 days pending indictment, arraignment, or trial. For each material witness listed in the report, an attorney for the government must state why the witness should not be released with or without a deposition being taken under Rule 15(a).

(i) Forfeiture of Property. The court may dispose of a charged offense by ordering the forfeiture of 18 U.S.C. § 3142(c)(1)(B)(xi) property under 18 U.S.C. § 3146(d), if a fine in the amount of the property's value would be an appropriate sentence for the charged offense.

(j) Producing a Statement.

(1) In General. Rule 26.2(a)–(d) and (f) applies at a detention hearing under 18 U.S.C. § 3142, unless the court for good cause rules otherwise.

(2) Sanctions for Not Producing a Statement. If a party disobeys a Rule 26.2 order to produce a witness's statement, the court must not consider that witness's testimony at the detention hearing.

(As amended Apr. 9, 1956, eff. July 8, 1956; Feb. 28, 1966, eff. July 1, 1966; Apr. 24, 1972, eff. Oct. 1, 1972; Oct. 12, 1984, Pub.L. 98–473, Title II, § 209(d), 98 Stat. 1987; Mar. 9, 1987, eff. Aug. 1, 1987; Apr. 30, 1991, eff. Dec. 1, 1991; Apr. 22, 1993, eff. Dec. 1, 1993; Sept. 13, 1994, Pub.L. 103–322, Title XXXIII, § 330003(h), 108 Stat. 2141; Apr. 29, 2002, eff. Dec. 1, 2002.)

ADVISORY COMMITTEE NOTES

1944 Adoption

Note to Subdivision (a)(1). This rule is substantially a restatement of 18 U.S.C. former §§ 596, 597 [now § 3141].

Note to Subdivision (a)(2). This rule is substantially a restatement of rule 6 of Criminal Appeals Rules, with the addition of a reference to bail pending certiorari. This rule does not supersede 18 U.S.C. former § 682 [now § 3731] (Appeals; on behalf of the United States; rules of practice and procedure), which provides for the admission of the defendant to bail on his own recognizance pending an appeal taken by the Government.

Note to Subdivision (b). This rule is substantially a restatement of 28 U.S.C. former § 657.

Note to Subdivision (e). This rule is a restatement of existing practice, and is based in part on 6 U.S.C. § 15 (Bonds or notes of United States in lieu of recognizance, stipulation, bond, guaranty, or undertaking; place of deposit; return to depositor; contractors' bonds).

Note to Subdivision (e). This rule is similar to § 79 of A.L.I. Code of Criminal Procedure introducing, however, an element of flexibility. Corporate sureties are regulated by 6 U.S.C. §§ 6 to 14.

Note to Subdivision (f). 1. With the exception hereafter noted, this rule is substantially a restatement of existing law in somewhat greater detail than contained in 18 U.S.C. former § 601 (Remission of penalty of recognizance).

2. Subdivision (f)(2) changes existing law in that it increases the discretion of the court to set aside a forfeiture. The power of the court under 18 U.S.C. former § 601 was limited to cases in which the defendant's default had not been willful.

3. The second sentence of paragraph (3) is similar to rule 73(f) of the Federal Rules of Civil Procedure, 28 U.S.C., Appendix. This paragraph also substitutes simple motion procedure for enforcing forfeited bail bonds for the procedure by scire facias, which was abolished by rule 81(b) of the Federal Rules of Civil Procedure, 28 U.S.C., Appendix.

Note to Subdivision (g). This rule is a restatement of existing law and practice. It is based in part on 18 U.S.C. former § 599 [now § 3142] (Surrender by bail).

1966 Amendment

Subdivision (c).—The more inclusive word "terms" is substituted for "amount" in view of the amendment to subdivision (d) authorizing releases without security on such conditions as are necessary to insure the appearance of the defendant. The phrase added at the end of this subdivision is designed to encourage commissioners and judges to set the terms of bail so as to eliminate unnecessary detention. See *Stack v. Boyle*, 342 U.S. 1 (1951); *Bandy v. United States*, 81 S.Ct. 197 (1960); *Bandy v. United States*, 82 S.Ct. 11 (1961); *Carbo v. United States*, 82 S.Ct. 662 (1962); review den. 369 U.S. 868 (1962).

Subdivision (d).—The amendments are designed to make possible (and to encourage) the release on bail of a greater percentage of indigent defendants than now are released. To the extent that other considerations make it reasonably likely that the defendant will appear it is both good practice and good economics to release him on bail even though he cannot arrange for cash or bonds in even small amounts. In fact it has been suggested that it may be a denial of constitutional rights to hold indigent prisoners in custody for no other reason than their inability to raise the money for a bond. *Bandy v. United States*, 81 S.Ct. 197 (1960).

The first change authorizes the acceptance as security of a deposit of cash or government securities in an amount less than the face amount of the bond. Since a defendant typically purchases a bail bond for a cash payment of a certain percentage of the face of the bond, a direct deposit with the court of that amount (returnable to the defendant upon his appearance) will often be equally adequate as a deterrent to flight. Cf. Ill.Code Crim.Proc. § 110–7 (1963).

The second change authorizes the release of the defendant without financial security on his written agreement to appear when other deterrents appear reasonably adequate. See the discussion of such deterrents in *Bandy v. United States*, 81 S.Ct. 197 (1960). It also permits the imposition of nonfinancial conditions as the price of dispensing with security for the bond. Such conditions are commonly used in England. Devlin, The Criminal Prosecution in England, 89 (1958). See the suggestion in Note, Bail: An Ancient Practice Reexamined, 70 Yale L.J. 966, 975 (1961) that such conditions "* * * might include release in custody of a third party, such as the accused's employer, minister, attorney, or a private organization; release subject to a duty to report periodically to the court or other public official; or even release subject to a duty to return to jail each night." Willful failure to appear after forfeiture of bail is a separate criminal offense and hence an added deterrent to flight. 18 U.S.C. § 3146.

For full discussion and general approval of the changes made here see Report of the Attorney General's Committee on Poverty and the Administration of Criminal Justice 58–89 (1963).

Subdivision (h).—The purpose of this new subdivision is to place upon the court in each district the responsibility for supervising the detention of defendants and witnesses and for eliminating all unnecessary detention. The device of the report by the attorney for the government is used because in many districts defendants will be held in custody in places where the court sits only at infrequent intervals and hence they cannot be brought personally before the court without substantial delay. The magnitude of the problem is suggested by the facts that during the fiscal year ending June 30, 1960, there were 23,811 instances in which persons were held in custody pending trial and that the average length of detention prior to disposition (i.e., dismissal, acquittal, probation, sentence to imprisonment, or any other method of removing the case from the court docket) was 25.3 days. Federal Prisons 1960, table 22, p. 60. Since 27,645 of the 38,855 defendants whose cases were terminated during the fiscal year ending June 30, 1960, pleaded guilty (United States Attorneys Statistical Report, October 1960, p. 1 and table 2), it would appear that the greater part of the detention reported occurs prior to the initial appearance of the defendant before the court.

1972 Amendment

The amendments are intended primarily to bring rule 46 into general conformity with the Bail Reform Act of 1966 and to deal in the rule with some issues not now included within the rule.

Subdivision (a) makes explicit that the Bail Reform Act of 1966 controls release on bail prior to trial. 18 U.S.C. § 3146 refers to release of a defendant. 18 U.S.C. § 3149 refers to release of a material witness.

Subdivision (b) deals with an issue not dealt with by the Bail Reform Act of 1966 or explicitly in former rule 46, that is, the issue of bail during trial. The rule gives the trial judge discretion to continue the prior conditions of release or to impose such additional conditions as are adequate to insure presence at trial or to insure that his conduct will not obstruct the orderly and expeditious progress of the trial.

Subdivision (c) provides for release during the period between a conviction and sentencing and for the giving of a notice of appeal or of the expiration of the time allowed for filing notice of appeal. There are situations in which defense counsel may informally indicate an intention to appeal but not actually give notice of appeal for several days. To deal with this situation the rule makes clear that the district court has authority to release under the terms of 18 U.S.C. § 3148 pending notice of appeal (*e.g.*, during the ten days after entry of judgement; see rule 4(b) of the Rules of Appellate Procedure). After the filing of notice of appeal, release by the district court shall be in accordance with the provisions of rule 9(b) of the Rules of Appellate Procedure. The burden of establishing that grounds for release exist is placed upon the defendant in the view that the fact of conviction justifies retention in custody in situations where doubt exists as to whether a defendant can be safely released pending either sentence or the giving of notice of appeal.

Subdivisions (d), (e), (f), and (g) remain unchanged. They were formerly lettered (e), (f), (g), and (h).

1987 Amendment

The amendments are technical. No substantive change is intended.

1991 Amendment

The amendment is technical. No substantive change is intended.

1993 Amendment

The addition of subdivision (i) is one of a series of similar amendments to Rules 26.2, 32, 32.1, and Rule 8 of the Rules Governing Proceedings Under 28 U.S.C. § 2255 which extend Rule 26.2 to other proceedings and hearings. As pointed out in the Committee Note to the amendment to Rule 26.2, there is continuing and compelling need to assess the credibility and reliability of information relied upon by the court, whether the witness's testimony is being considered at a pretrial proceeding, at trial, or a post-trial proceeding. Production of a witness's prior statements directly furthers that goal.

The need for reliable information is no less crucial in a proceeding to determine whether a defendant should be released from custody. The issues decided at pretrial detention hearings are important to both a defendant and the community. For example, a defendant charged with criminal acts may be incarcerated prior to an adjudication of guilt without bail on grounds of future dangerousness which is not subject to proof beyond a reasonable doubt. Although the defendant clearly has an interest in remaining free prior to trial, the community has an equally compelling interest in being protected from potential criminal activity committed by persons awaiting trial.

In upholding the constitutionality of pretrial detention based upon dangerousness, the Supreme Court in *United States v. Salerno*, 481 U.S. 739 (1986), stressed the existence of procedural safeguards in the Bail Reform Act. The Act provides for the right to counsel and the right to cross-examine adverse witnesses. See, e.g., 18 U.S.C. § 3142(f) (right of defendant to cross-examine adverse witness). Those safeguards, said the Court, are "specifically designed to further the accuracy of that determination." 481 U.S. at 751. The Committee believes that requiring the production of a witness's statement will further enhance the fact-finding process.

The Committee recognized that pretrial detention hearings are often held very early in a prosecution, and that a particular witness's statement may not yet be on file, or even known about. Thus, the amendment recognizes that in a particular case, the court may decide that good cause exists for not applying the rule.

2002 Amendments

The language of Rule 46 has been amended as part of the general restyling of the Criminal Rules to make them more easily understood and to make style and terminology consistent throughout the rules. These changes are intended to be stylistic only, except as noted below.

Although the general rule is that an appeal to a circuit court deprives the district court of jurisdiction, Rule 46(c) recognizes the apparent exception to that rule—that the district court retains jurisdiction to decide whether the defendant should be detained, even if a notice of appeal has been filed. *See, e.g., United States v. Meyers*, 95 F.3d 1475 (10th Cir. 1996), *cert. denied*, 522 U.S. 1006 (1997) (initial decision of whether to release defendant pending appeal is to be made by district court); *United States v. Affleck*, 765 F.2d 944 (10th Cir. 1985); *Jago v. United States District Court*, 570 F.2d 618 (6th Cir. 1978) (release of defendant pending appeal must first be sought in district court). *See also* Federal Rule of Appellate Procedure 9(b) and the accompanying Committee Note.

Revised Rule 46(h) deletes the requirement that the attorney for the government file bi-weekly reports with the court concerning the status of any defendants in pretrial detention. The Committee believed that the requirement was no longer necessary in light of the Speedy Trial Act provisions. 18 U.S.C. §§ 3161, et seq. On the other hand, the requirement that the attorney for the government file reports regarding detained material witnesses has been retained in the rule.

Rule 46(i) addresses the ability of a court to order forfeiture of property where a defendant has failed to appear as required by the court. The language in the current rule, Rule 46(h), was originally included by Congress. The new language has been restyled with no change in substance or practice intended. Under this provision, the court may only forfeit property as permitted under 18 U.S.C. §§ 3146(d) and 3142(c)(1)(B)(xi). The term "appropriate sentence" means a sentence that is consistent with the Sentencing Guidelines.

HISTORICAL NOTES

Effective and Applicability Provisions

1956 Acts. Amendment by Order of Apr. 9, 1956, became effective 90 days thereafter.

Rule 47. Motions and Supporting Affidavits

(a) In General. A party applying to the court for an order must do so by motion.

(b) Form and Content of a Motion. A motion—except when made during a trial or hearing—must be in writing, unless the court permits the party to make the motion by other means. A motion must state the grounds on which it is based and the relief or order sought. A motion may be supported by affidavit.

(c) Timing of a Motion. A party must serve a written motion—other than one that the court may hear ex parte—and any hearing notice at least 5 days before the hearing date, unless a rule or court order sets a different period. For good cause, the court may set a different period upon ex parte application.

(d) Affidavit Supporting a Motion. The moving party must serve any supporting affidavit with the motion. A responding party must serve any opposing affidavit at least one day before the hearing, unless the court permits later service.

(As amended Apr. 29, 2002, eff. Dec. 1, 2002.)

ADVISORY COMMITTEE NOTES

1944 Adoption

1. This rule is substantially the same as the corresponding civil rule (first sentence of rule 7(b)(1), Federal Rules of Civil Procedure, 28 U.S.C., Appendix), except that it authorizes the court to permit motions to be made orally and does not require that the grounds upon which a motion is made shall be stated "with particularity," as is the case with the civil rule.

2. This rule is intended to state general requirements for all motions. For particular provisions applying to specific motions, see rules 6(b)(2), 12, 14, 15, 16, 17(b) and (c), 21, 22, 29 and rule 41(e). See also rule 49.

3. The last sentence providing that a motion may be supported by affidavit is not intended to permit "speaking motions" (e.g. motion to dismiss an indictment for insufficiency supported by affidavits), but to authorize the use of affidavits when affidavits are appropriate to establish a fact (e.g. authority to take a deposition or former jeopardy).

2002 Amendments

The language of Rule 47 has been amended as part of the general restyling of the Criminal Rules to make them more easily understood and to make style and terminology consistent throughout the rules. These changes are intended to be stylistic only, except as noted below.

In Rule 47(b), the word "orally" has been deleted. The Committee believed, first, that the term should not act as a limitation on those who are not able to speak orally and, second, a court may wish to entertain motions through electronic or other reliable means. Deletion of the term also comports with a similar change in Rule 26, regarding the taking of testimony during trial. In place of that word, the Committee substituted the broader phrase "by other means."

Rule 48. Dismissal

(a) By the Government. The government may, with leave of court, dismiss an indictment, information, or complaint. The government may not dismiss the prosecution during trial without the defendant's consent.

(b) By the Court. The court may dismiss an indictment, information, or complaint if unnecessary delay occurs in:

(1) presenting a charge to a grand jury;

(2) filing an information against a defendant; or

(3) bringing a defendant to trial.

(As amended Apr. 29, 2002, eff. Dec. 1, 2002.)

ADVISORY COMMITTEE NOTES

1944 Adoption

Note to Subdivision (a). 1. The first sentence of this rule will change existing law. The common-law rule that the public prosecutor may enter a nolle prosequi in his discretion, without any action by the court, prevails in the Federal courts, *Confiscation Cases*, 7 Wall. 454, 457; *United States v.*

Woody, 2 F.2d 262 (D. Mont.). This provision will permit the filing of a nolle prosequi only by leave of court. This is similar to the rule now prevailing in many States. A.L.I.Code of Criminal Procedure, Commentaries, pp. 895 to 897.

2. The rule confers the power to file a dismissal by leave of court on the Attorney General, as well as on the United States attorney, since under existing law the Attorney General exercises "general superintendence and direction" over the United States attorneys "as to the manner of discharging their respective duties," 5 U.S.C. former § 317 [now 28 U.S.C. §§ 507, 547]. Moreover it is the administrative practice for the Attorney General to supervise the filing of a nolle prosequi by United States attorneys. Consequently it seemed appropriate that the Attorney General should have such power directly.

3. The rule permits the filing of a dismissal of an indictment, information or complaint. The word "complaint" was included in order to resolve a doubt prevailing in some districts as to whether the United States attorney may file a nolle prosequi between the time when the defendant is bound over by the United States commissioner and the finding of an indictment. It has been assumed in a few districts that the power does not exist and that the United States attorney must await action of the grand jury, even if he deems it proper to dismiss the prosecution. This situation is an unnecessary hardship to some defendants.

4. The second sentence is a restatement of existing law, *Confiscation Cases*, 7 Wall. 454–457; *United States v. Shoemaker*, 27 Fed.Cases No. 16,279, C.C.Ill. If the trial has commenced, the defendant has a right to insist on a disposition on the merits and may properly object to the entry of a nolle prosequi.

Note to Subdivision (b). This rule is a restatement of the inherent power of the court to dismiss a case for want of prosecution. *Ex parte Altman*, 34 F.Supp. 106, S.D.Cal.

2002 Amendments

The language of Rule 48 has been amended as part of the general restyling of the Criminal Rules to make them more easily understood and to make style and terminology consistent throughout the rules. These changes are intended to be stylistic only.

The Committee considered the relationship between Rule 48(b) and the Speedy Trial Act. *See* 18 U.S.C. §§ 3161, et seq. Rule 48(b), of course, operates independently from the Act. *See, e.g., United States v. Goodson*, 204 F.3d 508 (4th Cir. 2000) (noting purpose of Rule 48(b)); *United States v. Carlone*, 666 F.2d 1112, 1116 (7th Cir. 1981) (suggesting that Rule 48(b) could provide an alternate basis in an extreme case to dismiss an indictment, without reference to Speedy Trial Act); *United States v. Balochi*, 527 F.2d 562, 563–64 (4th Cir. 1976) (per curiam) (Rule 48(b) is broader in compass). In re-promulgating Rule 48(b), the Committee intends no change in the relationship between that rule and the Speedy Trial Act.

Rule 49. Serving and Filing Papers

(a) When Required. A party must serve on every other party any written motion (other than one to be heard ex parte), written notice, designation of the record on appeal, or similar paper.

(b) How Made. Service must be made in the manner provided for a civil action. When these rules or a court order requires or permits service on a party represented by an attorney, service must be made on the attorney instead of the party, unless the court orders otherwise.

(c) Notice of a Court Order. When the court issues an order on any post-arraignment motion, the clerk must provide notice in a manner provided for in a civil action. Except as Federal Rule of Appellate Procedure 4(b) provides otherwise, the clerk's failure to give notice does not affect the time to appeal, or relieve—or authorize the court to relieve—a party's failure to appeal within the allowed time.

(d) Filing. A party must file with the court a copy of any paper the party is required to serve. A paper must be filed in a manner provided for in a civil action.

(As amended Feb. 28, 1966, eff. July 1, 1966; Dec. 4, 1967, eff. July 1, 1968; Apr. 29, 1985, eff. Aug. 1, 1985; Mar. 9, 1987, eff. Aug. 1, 1987; Apr. 22, 1993, eff. Dec. 1, 1993; Apr. 27, 1995, eff. Dec. 1, 1995; Apr. 29, 2002, eff. Dec. 1, 2002.)

ADVISORY COMMITTEE NOTES

1944 Adoption

Note to Subdivision (a). This rule is substantially the same as rule 5(a) of the Federal Rules of Civil Procedure, 28 U.S.C., Appendix, with such adaptations as are necessary for criminal cases.

Note to Subdivision (b). The first sentence of this rule is in substance the same as the first sentence of rule 5(b) of the Federal Rules of Civil Procedure, 28 U.S.C., Appendix. The second sentence incorporates by reference the second and third sentences of rule 5(b) of the Federal Rules of Civil Procedure, 28 U.S.C., Appendix.

Note to Subdivision (c). This rule is an adaptation for criminal proceedings of rule 77(d) of the Federal Rules of Civil Procedure, 28 U.S.C., Appendix. No consequence attaches to the failure of the clerk to give the prescribed notice, but in a case in which the losing party in reliance on the clerk's obligation to send a notice failed to file a timely notice of appeal, it was held competent for the trial judge, in the exercise of sound discretion, to vacate the judgment because of clerk's failure to give notice and to enter a new judgment, the term of court not having expired. *Hill v. Hawes*, 64 S.Ct. 334, 320 U.S. 520, 88 L.Ed. 283, rehearing denied 64 S.Ct. 515, 321 U.S. 801, 88 L.Ed. 1088.

Note to Subdivision (d). This rule incorporates by reference rule 5(d) and (e) of the Federal Rules of Civil Procedure, 28 U.S.C., Appendix.

1966 Amendment

Subdivision (a).—The words "adverse parties" in the original rule introduced a question of interpretation. When, for example, is a co-defendant an adverse party. The amendment requires service on each of the parties thus avoiding the problem of interpretation and promoting full exchange of information among the parties. No restriction is intended, however, upon agreements among co-defendants or between the defendants and the government restricting exchange of papers in the interest of eliminating unnecessary expense. Cf. the amendment made effective July 1, 1963, to Civil Rule 5(a).

Subdivision (c).—The words "affected thereby" are deleted in order to require notice to all parties. Cf. the similar change made effective July, 1, 1963, to Civil Rule 77(d).

The sentence added at the end of the subdivision eliminates the possibility of extension of the time to appeal beyond the provision for a 30 day extension on a showing or "excusable neglect" provided in Rule 37(a)(2). Cf. the similar change made in Civil Rule 77(d) effective in 1948. The question has arisen in a number of cases whether failure or delay in giving notice on the part of the clerk results in an extension of the time for appeal. The "general rule" has been said to be that in the event of such failure or delay "the time for taking an appeal runs from the date of later actual notice or receipt of the clerk's notice rather than from the date of entry of the order." *Lohman v. United States*, 237 F.2d 645, 646 (6th Cir.1956). See also *Rosenbloom v. United States*, 355 U.S. 80 (1957) (permitting an extension). In two cases it has been held that no extension results from the failure to give notice of entry of judgments (as opposed to orders) since such notice is not required by Rule 49(d). *Wilkinson v. United States*, 278 F.2d 604 (10th Cir.1960), cert. den. 363 U.S. 829; *Hyche v. United States*, 278 F.2d 915 (5th Cir.1960), cert. den. 364 U.S. 881. The excusable neglect extension provision in Rule 37(a)(2) will cover most cases where failure of the clerk to give notice of judgments or orders has misled the defendant. No need appears for an indefinite extension without time limit beyond the 30 day period.

1968 Amendment

The amendment corrects the reference to Rule 37(a)(2), the pertinent provisions of which are contained in Rule 4(b) of the Federal Rules of Appellate Procedure.

1985 Amendment

18 U.S.C. § 3575(a) and 21 U.S.C. § 849(a), dealing respectively with dangerous special offender sentencing and dangerous special drug offender sentencing, provide for the prosecutor to file notice of such status "with the court" and for the court to "order the notice sealed" under specified circumstances, but also declare that disclosure of this notice shall not be made "to the presiding judge without the consent of the parties" before verdict or plea of guilty or nolo contendere. It has been noted that these provisions are "regrettably unclear as to where, in fact, such notice is to be filed" and that possibly filing with the chief judge is contemplated. *United States v. Tramunti*, 377 F.Supp. 6 (S.D.N.Y. 1974). But such practice has been a matter of dispute when the chief judge would otherwise have been the presiding judge in the case, *United States v. Gaylor*, No. 80–5016 (4th Cir.1981), and "it does not solve the problem in those districts where there is only one federal district judge appointed," *United States v. Tramunti, supra*.

The first sentence of subdivision (e) clarifies that the filing of such notice with the court is to be accomplished by filing with the clerk of the court, which is generally the procedure for filing with the court; see subdivision (d) of this rule. Except in a district having a single judge and no United States magistrate, the clerk will then, as provided in the second sentence, transmit the notice to the chief judge or to some other judge or a United States magistrate if the chief judge is scheduled to be the presiding judge in the case, so that the determination regarding sealing of the notice may be made without the disclosure prohibited by the aforementioned statutes. But in a district having a single judge and no United States magistrate this prohibition means the clerk may not disclose the notice to the court at all until the time specified by statute. The last sentence of subdivision (e) contemplates that in such instances the clerk will seal the notice if the case falls within the local rule describing when "a public record may prejudice fair consideration of a pending criminal matter," the determination called for by the aforementioned statutes. The local rule might provide, for example, that the notice is to be sealed upon motion by any party.

1987 Amendment

The amendment is technical. No substantive change is intended.

1993 Amendment

The Rule is amended to conform to the Judicial Improvements Act of 1990 [P.L. 101–650, Title III, Section 321] which provides that each United States magistrate appointed under section 631 of title 28, United States Code, shall be known as a United States magistrate judge.

1995 Amendments

Subdivision (e) has been deleted because both of the statutory provisions cited in the rule have been abrogated.

2002 Amendments

The language of Rule 49 has been amended as part of the general restyling of the Criminal Rules to make them more easily understood and to make style and terminology consistent throughout the rules.

Rule 49(c) has been amended to reflect proposed changes in the Federal Rules of Civil Procedure that permit (but do not require) a court to provide notice of its orders and judgments through electronic means. *See* Federal Rules of Civil Procedure 5(b) and 77(d). As amended, Rule 49(c) now parallels a similar extant provision in Rule 49(b), regarding service of papers.

HISTORICAL NOTES

Change of Name

United States magistrate appointed under section 631 of Title 28, Judiciary and Judicial Procedure, to be known as United States magistrate judge after Dec. 1, 1990, with any reference to United States magistrate or magistrate in Title 28, in any other Federal statute, etc., deemed a reference to United States magistrate judge appointed under section 631 of Title 28, see section 321 of Pub.L. 101–650, set out as a note under section 631 of Title 28.

Rule 50. Prompt Disposition

Scheduling preference must be given to criminal proceedings as far as practicable.

(As amended Apr. 24, 1972, eff. Oct. 1, 1972; Mar. 18, 1974, eff. July 1, 1974; Apr. 26, 1976, eff. Aug. 1, 1976; Apr. 22, 1993, eff. Dec. 1, 1993; Apr. 29, 2002, eff. Dec. 1, 2002.)

ADVISORY COMMITTEE NOTES

1944 Adoption

This rule is a restatement of the inherent residual power of the court over its own calendars, although as a matter of practice in most districts the assignment of criminal cases for trial is handled by the United States attorney. Cf. Federal Rules of Civil Procedure, Rules 40 and 78, 28 U.S.C., Appendix. The direction that preference shall be given to criminal proceedings as far as practicable is generally recognized as desirable in the orderly administration of justice.

1972 Amendment

The addition to the rule proposed by subdivision (b) is designed to achieve the more prompt disposition of criminal cases.

Preventing undue delay in the administration of criminal justice has become an object of increasing interest and concern. This is reflected in the Congress. See, e.g., 116 Cong.Rec. S7291–97 (daily ed. May 18, 1970) (remarks of Senator Ervin). Bills have been introduced fixing specific time limits. See S. 3936, H.R. 14822, H.R. 15888, 91st Cong., 2d Sess. (1970).

Proposals for dealing with the problem of delay have also been made by the President's Commission on Law Enforcement and Administration of Justice, Task Force Report: The Courts (1967) especially pp. 84 to 90, and by the American Bar Association Project on Standards for Criminal Justice, Standards Relating to Speedy Trial (Approved Draft, 1968). Both recommend specific time limits for each stage in the criminal process as the most effective way of achieving prompt disposition of criminal cases. See also Note, Nevada's 1967 Criminal Procedure Law from Arrest to Trial: One State's Response to a Widely Recognized Need, 1969 Utah L.Rev. 520, 542 n. 114.

Historically, the right to a speedy trial has been thought of as a protection for the defendant. Delay can cause a hardship to a defendant who is in custody awaiting trial. Even if afforded the opportunity for pretrial release, a defendant nonetheless is likely to suffer anxiety during a period of unwanted delay, and he runs the risk that his memory and those of his witnesses may suffer as time goes on.

Delay can also adversely affect the prosecution. Witnesses may lose interest or disappear or their memories may fade thus making them more vulnerable to cross-examination. See Note, The Right to a Speedy Criminal Trial, 57 Colum.L.Rev. 846 (1957).

There is also a larger public interest in the prompt disposition of criminal cases which may transcend the interest of the particular prosecutor, defense counsel, and defendant. Thus there is need to try to expedite criminal cases even when both prosecution and defense may be willing to agree to a continuance or continuances. It has long been said that it is the certain and prompt imposition of a criminal sanction rather than its severity that has a significant deterring effect upon potential criminal conduct. See Banfield and Anderson, Continuances in the Cook County Criminal Courts, 35 U.Chi. L.Rev. 259, 259–63 (1968).

Providing specific time limits for each stage of the criminal justice system is made difficult, particularly in federal courts, by the widely varying conditions which exist between the very busy urban districts on the one hand and the far less busy rural districts on the other hand. In the former, account must be taken of the extremely heavy caseload, and the prescription of relatively short time limits is realistic only if there is provided additional prosecutorial and judicial manpower. In some rural districts, the availability of a grand jury only twice a year makes unrealistic the provision of short time limits within which an indictment must be returned. This is not to say that prompt disposition of criminal cases cannot be achieved. It means only that the achieving of prompt disposition may require solutions which vary from district to district. Finding the best methods will require innovation and experimentation. To encourage this, the proposed draft mandates each district court to prepare a plan to achieve the prompt disposition of criminal cases in the district. The method prescribed for the development and approval of the district plans is comparable to that prescribed in the Jury Selection and Service Act of 1968, 28 U.S.C. § 1863(a).

Each plan shall include rules which specify time limits and a means for reporting the status of criminal cases. The appropriate length of the time limits is left to the discretion of the individual district courts. This permits each district court to establish time limits that are appropriate in light of its criminal caseload, frequency of grand jury meetings, and any other factors which affect the progress of criminal actions. Where local conditions exist which contribute to delay, it is contemplated that appropriate efforts will be made to eliminate those conditions. For example, experience in some rural districts demonstrates that grand juries can be kept on call thus eliminating the grand jury as a cause for prolonged delay. Where manpower shortage is a major cause for delay, adequate solutions will require congressional action. But the development and analysis of the district plans should disclose where manpower shortages exist; how large the shortages are; and what is needed, in the way of additional manpower, to achieve the prompt disposition of criminal cases.

The district court plans must contain special provision for prompt disposition of cases in which there is reason to believe that the pretrial liberty of a defendant poses danger to himself, to any other person, or to the community. Prompt disposition of criminal cases may provide an alternative to the pretrial detention of potentially dangerous defendants. See 116 Cong.Rec. S7291–97 (daily ed. May 18, 1970) (remarks of Senator Ervin). Prompt disposition of criminal cases in which the defendant is held in pretrial detention would ensure that the deprivation of liberty prior to conviction would be minimized.

Approval of the original plan and any subsequent modification must be obtained from a reviewing panel made up of one judge from the district submitting the plan (either the chief judge or another active judge appointed by him) and the members of the judicial council of the circuit. The makeup of this reviewing panel is the same as that provided by the Jury Selection and Service Act of 1968, 28 U.S.C. § 1863(a).

This reviewing panel is also empowered to direct the modification of a district court plan.

The Circuit Court of Appeals for the Second Circuit recently adopted a set of rules for the prompt disposition of criminal cases. See 8 Cr.L. 2251 (Jan. 13, 1971). These rules, effective July 5, 1971, provide time limits for the early trial of high risk defendants, for court control over the granting of continuances, for criteria to control continuance practice, and for sanction against the prosecution or defense in the event of noncompliance with prescribed time limits.

1976 Amendment

This amendment to rule 50(b) takes account of the enactment of The Speedy Trial Act of 1974, 18 U.S.C. §§ 3152–3156, 3161–3174. As the various provisions of the Act take effect, see 18 U.S.C. § 3163, they and the district plans adopted pursuant thereto will supplant the plans heretofore adopted under rule 50(b). The first such plan must be prepared and submitted by each district court before July 1, 1976. 18 U.S.C. § 3165(e) (1).

That part of rule 50(b) which sets out the necessary contents of district plans has been deleted, as the somewhat different contents of the plans required by the Act are enumerated in 18 U.S.C. § 3166. That part of rule 50(b) which describes the manner in which district plans are to be submitted, reviewed, modified and reported upon has also been deleted, for these provisions now appear in 18 U.S.C. § 3165(c) and (d).

1993 Amendment

The Rule is amended to conform to the Judicial Improvements Act of 1990 [P.L. 101–650, Title III, Section 321] which provides that each United States magistrate appointed under section 631 of title 28, United States Code, shall be known as a United States magistrate judge.

2002 Amendments

The language of Rule 50 has been amended as part of the general restyling of the Criminal Rules to make them more easily understood and to make style and terminology consistent throughout the rules. These changes are intended to be stylistic only, except as noted below.

The first sentence in current Rule 50(a), which says that a court may place criminal proceedings on a calendar, has been deleted. The Committee believed that the sentence simply stated a truism and was no longer necessary.

Current Rule 50(b), which simply mirrors 18 U.S.C. § 3165, has been deleted in its entirety. The rule was added in 1971 to meet congressional concerns in pending legislation about deadlines in criminal cases. Provisions governing deadlines were later enacted by Congress and protections were provided in the Speedy Trial Act. The Committee concluded that in light of those enactments, Rule 50(b) was no longer necessary.

HISTORICAL NOTES

Effective and Applicability Provisions

1976 Acts. Amendment effective Aug. 1, 1976, see Pub.L. 94–349, § 1, July 8, 1976, 90 Stat. 822, set out as a note under rule 6 of these rules.

Change of Name

United States magistrate appointed under section 631 of Title 28, Judiciary and Judicial Procedure, to be known as United States magistrate judge after Dec. 1, 1990, with any reference to United States magistrate or magistrate in Title 28, in any other Federal statute, etc., deemed a reference to United States magistrate judge appointed under section 631 of Title 28, see section 321 of Pub.L. 101–650, set out as a note under section 631 of Title 28.

Rule 51. Preserving Claimed Error

(a) Exceptions Unnecessary. Exceptions to rulings or orders of the court are unnecessary.

(b) Preserving a Claim of Error. A party may preserve a claim of error by informing the court—when the court ruling or order is made or sought—of the action the party wishes the court to take, or the party's objection to the court's action and the grounds for that objection. If a party does not have an opportunity to object to a ruling or order, the absence of an objection does not later prejudice that party. A ruling or order that admits or excludes evidence is governed by Federal Rule of Evidence 103.

(As amended Mar. 9, 1987, eff. Aug. 1, 1987; Apr. 29, 2002, eff. Dec. 1, 2002.)

ADVISORY COMMITTEE NOTES

1944 Adoption

1. This rule is practically identical with rule 46 of the Federal Rules of Civil Procedure, 28 U.S.C., Appendix. It relates to a matter of trial practice which should be the same in civil and criminal cases in the interest of avoiding confusion. The corresponding civil rule has been construed in *Ulm v. Moore-McCormack Lines, Inc.*, 115 F.2d 492, C.C.A.2d, and *Bucy v. Nevada Construction Company*, 125 F.2d 213, 218, C.C.A.9th. See, also, *Orfield*, 22 Texas L.R. 194, 221. As to the method of taking objections to instructions to the jury, see rule 30.

2. Many States have abolished the use of exceptions in criminal and civil cases. See, e.g., Cal.Pen.Code (Deering, 1941), § 1259; Mich.Stat.Ann. (Henderson, 1938), §§ 28.1046, 28.1053; Ohio Gen.Code Ann. (Page, 1938), §§ 11560, 13442–7; Oreg.Comp.Laws Ann. (1940), §§ 5–704, 26–1001.

1987 Amendment

The amendments are technical. No substantive change is intended.

2002 Amendments

The language of Rule 51 has been amended as part of the general restyling of the Criminal Rules to make them more easily understood and to make style and terminology consistent throughout the rules. These changes are intended to be stylistic only.

The Rule includes a new sentence that explicitly states that any rulings regarding evidence are governed by Federal Rule of Evidence 103. The sentence was added because of concerns about the Supersession Clause, 28 U.S.C. § 2072(b), of the Rules Enabling Act, and the possibility that an argument might have been made that Congressional approval of this rule would supersede that Rule of Evidence.

HISTORICAL AND STATUTORY NOTES

References in Text

Federal Rule of Evidence 103, referred to in subd. (b), is set out in the Appendix to Title 28, Fed.Rules Evid. Rule 103, 28 U.S.C.A.

Rule 52. Harmless and Plain Error

(a) Harmless Error. Any error, defect, irregularity, or variance that does not affect substantial rights must be disregarded.

(b) Plain Error. A plain error that affects substantial rights may be considered even though it was not brought to the court's attention.

(As amended Apr. 29, 2002, eff. Dec. 1, 2002.)

ADVISORY COMMITTEE NOTES

1944 Adoption

Note to Subdivision (a). This rule is a restatement of existing law, 28 U.S.C. former § 391 (second sentence): "On the hearing of any appeal, certiorari, writ of error, or motion for a new trial, in any case, civil or criminal, the court shall give judgment after an examination of the entire record before the court, without regard to technical errors, defects, or exceptions which do not affect the substantial rights of the parties"; 18 U.S.C. former § 556; "No indictment found and presented by a grand jury in any district or other court of the United States shall be deemed insufficient, nor shall the trial, judgment, or other proceeding thereon be affected by reason of any defect or imperfection in matter of form only, which shall not tend to the prejudice of the defendant, * * *." A similar provision is found in rule 61 of the Federal Rules of Civil Procedure, 28 U.S.C., Appendix.

Note to Subdivision (b). This rule is a restatement of existing law, *Wiborg v. United States*, 16 S.Ct. 1127, 1197, 2 cases, 163 U.S. 632, 658, 41 L.Ed. 289; *Hemphill v. United States*, 112 F.2d 505, C.C.A.9th, reversed 312 U.S. 657, 85 L.Ed. 1106, 61 S.Ct. 729, conformed to 120 F.2d 115, certiorari denied 62 S.Ct. 111, 314 U.S. 627, 86 L.Ed. 503. Rule 27 of the Rules of the Supreme Court, 28 U.S.C., formerly following § 354, provides that errors not specified will be disregarded, "save as the court, at its option, may notice a plain error not assigned or specified." Similar provisions are found in the rules of several circuit courts of appeals.

2002 Amendments

The language of Rule 52 has been amended as part of the general restyling of the Criminal Rules to make them more easily understood and to make style and terminology consistent throughout the rules. These changes are intended to be stylistic only.

Rule 52(b) has been amended by deleting the words "or defect" after the words "plain error." The change is intended to remove any ambiguity in the rule. As noted by the Supreme Court, the language "plain error or defect" was misleading to the extent that it might be read in the disjunctive. *See United States v. Olano*, 507 U.S. 725, 732 (1993) (incorrect to read Rule 52(b) in the disjunctive); *United States v. Young*, 470 U.S. 1, 15 n. 12 (1985) (use of disjunctive in Rule 52(b) is misleading).

Rule 53. Courtroom Photographing and Broadcasting Prohibited

Except as otherwise provided by a statute or these rules, the court must not permit the taking of photographs in the courtroom during judicial proceedings or the broadcasting of judicial proceedings from the courtroom.

(As amended Apr. 29, 2002, eff. Dec. 1, 2002.)

ADVISORY COMMITTEE NOTES

1944 Adoption

While the matter to which the rule refers has not been a problem in the Federal courts as it has been in some State tribunals, the rule was nevertheless included with a view to giving expression to a standard which should govern the conduct of judicial proceedings, Orfield, 22 Texas L.R. 194, 222–3; Robbins, 21 A.B.A.Jour. 301, 304. See, also, Report of the Special Committee on Cooperation between Press, Radio and Bar, as to Publicity Interfering with Fair Trial of Judicial and Quasi-Judicial Proceedings (1937), 62 A.B.A.Rep. 851, 862–865; 1932, 18 A.B.A.Jour. 762; (1926) 12 Id. 488; (1925) 11 Id. 64.

2002 Amendments

The language of Rule 53 has been amended as part of the general restyling of the Criminal Rules to make them more easily understood and to make style and terminology consistent throughout the rules. These changes are intended to be stylistic only, except as noted below.

Although the word "radio" has been deleted from the rule, the Committee does not believe that the amendment is a substantive change but rather one that accords with judicial interpretation applying the current rule to other forms of broadcasting and functionally equivalent means. *See, e.g., United States v. Hastings*, 695 F.2d 1278, 1279, n. 5 (11th Cir. 1983) (television proceedings prohibited); *United States v. McVeigh*, 931 F. Supp. 753 (D. Colo. 1996) (release of tape recordings of proceedings prohibited). Given modern technology capabilities, the Committee believed that a more generalized reference to "broadcasting" is appropriate.

Also, although the revised rule does not explicitly recognize exceptions within the rules themselves, the restyled rule recognizes that other rules might permit, for example, video teleconferencing, which clearly involves "broadcasting" of the proceedings, even if only for limited purposes.

Rule 54. [Transferred [1]]

[1] All of Rule 54 was moved to Rule 1.

HISTORICAL NOTES

Former Rule 54 relating to application and exception, which was derived from Dec. 27, 1948, eff. Oct. 20, 1949; April 9, 1956, eff. July 8, 1956; Feb. 28, 1966, eff. July 1, 1966; Apr. 24, 1972, eff. Oct. 1, 1972; Apr. 28, 1982, eff. Aug. 1, 1982; Oct. 12, 1984, Pub.L. 98–473, Title II, §§ 209(e), 215(e), 98 Stat. 1987, 2016; Nov. 18, 1988, Pub.L. 100–690, Title VII, § 7089(c), 102 Stat. 4409; May 1, 1990, eff. Dec. 1,

1990; Apr. 30, 1991, eff. Dec. 1, 1991; Apr. 22, 1993, eff. Dec. 1, 1993; Apr. 29, 1999, eff. Dec. 1, 1999, was transferred by court order dated Apr. 29, 2002, eff. Dec. 1, 2002.)

Prior to transfer to Rule 1, Rule 54 read:

"(a) Courts.

"These rules apply to all criminal proceedings in the United States District Courts; in the District Court of Guam; in the District Court for the Northern Mariana Islands, except as otherwise provided in articles IV and V of the covenant provided by the Act of March 24, 1976 (90 Stat. 263); and in the District Court of the Virgin Islands; in the United States Courts of Appeals; and in the Supreme Court of the United States; except that the prosecution of offenses in the District Court of the Virgin Islands shall be by indictment or information as otherwise provided by law.

"(b) Proceedings.

"(1) Removed Proceedings. These rules apply to criminal prosecutions removed to the United States district courts from state courts and govern all procedure after removal, except that dismissal by the attorney for the prosecution shall be governed by state law.

"(2) Offenses Outside a District or State. These rules apply to proceedings for offenses committed upon the high seas or elsewhere out of the jurisdiction of any particular state or district, except that such proceedings may be had in any district authorized by 18 U.S.C. § 3238.

"(3) Peace Bonds. These rules do not alter the power of judges of the United States or of United States magistrate judges to hold to security of the peace and for good behavior under Revised Statutes, § 4069, 50 U.S.C. § 23, but in such cases the procedure shall conform to these rules so far as they are applicable.

"(4) Proceedings Before United States Magistrate Judges. Proceedings involving misdemeanors and other petty offenses are governed by Rule 58.

"(5) Other Proceedings. These rules are not applicable to extradition and rendition of fugitives; civil forfeiture of property for violation of a statute of the United States; or the collection of fines and penalties. Except as provided in Rule 20(d) they do not apply to proceedings under 18 U.S.C. Chapter 403—Juvenile Delinquency—so far as they are inconsistent with that chapter. They do not apply to summary trials for offenses against the navigation laws under Revised Statutes §§ 4300–4305, 33 U.S.C. §§ 391–396, or to proceedings involving disputes between seamen under Revised Statutes, §§ 4079–4081, as amended, 22 U.S.C. §§ 256–258, or to proceedings for fishery offenses under the Act of June 28, 1937, c. 392, 50 Stat. 325–327, 16 U.S.C. §§ 772–772i, or to proceedings against a witness in a foreign country under 28 U.S.C. § 1784.

"(c) Application of Terms. As used in these rules the following terms have the designated meanings.

" 'Act of Congress' includes any act of Congress locally applicable to and in force in the District of Columbia, in Puerto Rico, in a territory or in an insular possession.

" 'Attorney for the government' means the Attorney General, an authorized assistant of the Attorney General, a United States Attorney, an authorized assistant of a United States Attorney, when applicable to cases arising under the laws of Guam the Attorney General of Guam or such other person or persons as may be authorized by the laws of Guam to act therein, and when applicable to cases arising under the laws of the Northern Mariana Islands the Attorney General of the Northern Mariana Islands or any other person or persons as may be authorized by the laws of the Northern Marianas to act therein.

" 'Civil action' refers to a civil action in a district court.

"The words 'demurrer,' 'motion to quash,' 'plea in abatement,' 'plea in bar' and 'special plea in bar,' or words to the same effect, in any act of Congress shall be construed to mean the motion raising a defense or objection provided in Rule 12.

" 'District court' includes all district courts named in subdivision (a) of this rule.

" 'Federal magistrate judge' means a United States magistrate judge as defined in 28 U.S.C. §§ 631–639, a judge of the United States or another judge or judicial officer specifically empowered by statute in force in any territory or possession, the Commonwealth of Puerto Rico, or the District of Columbia, to perform a function to which a particular rule relates.

" 'Judge of the United States' includes a judge of a district court, court of appeals, or the Supreme Court.

" 'Law' includes statutes and judicial decisions.

" 'Magistrate judge' includes a United States magistrate judge as defined in 28 U.S.C. §§ 631–639, a judge of the United States, another judge or judicial officer specifically empowered by statute in force in any territory or possession, the Commonwealth of Puerto Rico, or the District of Columbia, to perform a function to which a particular rule relates, and a state or local judicial officer, authorized by 18 U.S.C. § 3041 to perform the functions prescribed in Rules 3, 4, and 5.

" 'Oath' includes affirmations.

" 'Petty offense' is defined in 18 U.S.C. § 19.

" 'State' includes District of Columbia, Puerto Rico, territory and insular possession.

" 'United States magistrate judge' means the officer authorized by 28 U.S.C. §§ 631–639."

Subd. (c) of this rule as in effect prior to amendment by Pub.L. 98–473, § 215(e), read as follows:

"(c) Application of Terms. As used in these rules the following terms have the designated meanings.

" 'Act of Congress' includes any act of Congress locally applicable to and in force in the District of Columbia, in Puerto Rico, in a territory or in an insular possession.

" 'Attorney for the government' means the Attorney General, an authorized assistant of the Attorney General, a United States Attorney, an authorized assistant of a United States Attorney, when applicable to cases arising under the laws of Guam the Attorney General of Guam or such other person or persons as may be authorized by the laws of Guam to act therein, and when applicable to cases arising under the laws of the Northern Mariana Islands the Attorney General of the Northern Mariana Islands or any other person or persons as may be authorized by the laws of the Northern Marianas to act therein.

" 'Civil action' refers to a civil action in a district court.

"The words 'demurrer,' 'motion to quash,' 'plea in abatement,' 'plea in bar' and 'special plea in bar,' or words to the same effect, in any act of Congress shall be construed to mean the motion raising a defense or objection provided in Rule 12.

" 'District court' includes all district courts named in subdivision (a) of this rule.

" 'Federal magistrate' means a United States magistrate as defined in 28 U.S.C. §§ 631–639, a judge of the United States or another judge or judicial officer specifically empowered by statute in force in any territory or possession, the Commonwealth of Puerto Rico, or the District of Columbia, to perform a function to which a particular rule relates.

" 'Judge of the United States' includes a judge of a district court, court of appeals, or the Supreme Court.

" 'Law' includes statutes and judicial decisions.

" 'Magistrate' includes a United States magistrate as defined in 28 U.S.C. §§ 631–639, a judge of the United States, another judge or judicial officer specifically empowered by statute in force in any territory or possession, the Commonwealth of Puerto Rico, or the District of Columbia, to perform a function to which a particular rule relates, and a state or local judicial officer, authorized by 18 U.S.C. § 3041 to perform the functions prescribed in Rules 3, 4, and 5.

" 'Oath' includes affirmations.

" 'Petty offense' is defined in 18 U.S.C. § 1(3).

" 'State' includes District of Columbia, Puerto Rico, territory and insular possession.

" 'United States magistrate' means the officer authorized by 28 U.S.C. §§ 631–639.

"For applicability of sentencing provisions to offenses, see Effective Date and Savings Provisions, etc., note, section 235 of Pub.L. 98–473, as amended, set out under section 3551 of Title 18, Crimes and Criminal Procedure."

ADVISORY COMMITTEE NOTES

1944 Adoption

Note to Subdivision (a)(1). 1. The Act of June 28, 1940 (54 Stat. 688; 18 U.S.C. former § 687 [now § 3771]), authorizing the Supreme Court to prescribe rules of criminal procedure for the district courts of the United States in respect to proceedings prior to and including verdict or finding of guilty or not guilty or plea of guilty, is expressly applicable to the district courts of Alaska, Hawaii, Puerto Rico, Canal Zone, Virgin Islands, the Supreme Courts of Hawaii and Puerto Rico, and the United States Court for China. This is likewise true of the Act of February 24, 1933 (47 Stat. 904; 18 U.S.C. former § 688 [now § 3772]), authorizing the Supreme Court to prescribe rules in respect to proceedings after verdict or finding or after plea of guilty. In this respect these two statutes differ from the Act of June 19, 1934 (48 Stat. 1064; 28 U.S.C. former §§ 723b, 723c [now § 2072]), authorizing the Supreme Court to prescribe rules of civil procedure. The last-mentioned Act comprises only district courts of the United States and the courts of the District of Columbia. The phrase "district courts of the United States" was held not to include district courts in the territories and insular possessions, *Mookini v. United States*, 303 U.S. 201, 58 S.Ct. 543, 82 L.Ed. 748, conformed to 95 F.2d 960. By subsequent legislation the Federal Rules of Civil Procedure, 28 U.S.C., Appendix, were extended to the District Court of the United States for Hawaii and to appeals therefrom (Act of June 19, 1939; 53 Stat. 841; 48 U.S.C. former § 646) and to the District Court of the United States for Puerto Rico and to appeals therefrom (Act of February 12, 1940; 54 Stat. 22; 48 U.S.C. former § 873a).

2. While the specific reference in the rule to the District Court of the United States for the District of Columbia is probably superfluous, since that court has the same powers and exercises the same jurisdiction as other district courts of the United States in addition to such local powers and jurisdiction as have been conferred upon it by statute (D.C.Code, 1940, Title 11, § 305), nevertheless it was listed in the rule in view of the fact that the Federal Rules of Civil Procedure 28 U.S.C., Appendix, contain a somewhat similar provision (Rule 81(d), 28 U.S.C., Appendix).

3. The United States Court for China has been omitted from the rule in view of the fact that the court has recently been abolished with the abandonment by the United States of its extraterritorial jurisdiction in China.

4. Although, as indicated above, the rule-making power of the Supreme Court in respect to criminal cases extends to the Supreme Courts of Hawaii and Puerto Rico, the rules are not made applicable to those two courts, in view of the fact that they are purely local appellate courts having no appellate jurisdiction over the district courts of the United States in those territories. Alaska and Hawaii have dual systems of courts: local courts exercising purely local jurisdiction and United States district courts exercising Federal jurisdiction. The Supreme Court of each of the two territories hears appeals only from the local courts.

5. Alaska.—There is a district court for the Territory of Alaska consisting of four divisions, established on a territorial basis, 48 U.S.C. §§ 101, 101a. As the only court in the Territory, it acts in a dual capacity: it has jurisdiction over cases arising under the laws of the United States as well as those arising under local laws. Although a legislative rather than a constitutional court, it is, nevertheless, deemed a court of the United States and has the jurisdiction of district courts of the United States, 48 U.S.C. §§ 101, 101a; *Steamer Coquitlam v. United States*, 16 S.Ct. 1117, 163 U.S. 346, 41 L.Ed. 184; *McAllister v. United States*, 11 S.Ct. 949, 141 U.S. 174, 179, 35 L.Ed. 693; *Ex parte Krause*, 228 F. 547, 549, W.D.Wash. Criminal procedure is now regulated by Acts of Congress, by the Alaska Code of Criminal Procedure (Alaska Comp.Laws, 1933, pp. 959 to 1018), and by rules promulgated by the district court.

6. Hawaii.—Hawaii has a dual system of courts. The United States District Court for the Territory of Hawaii, a legislative court, has the jurisdiction of district courts of the United States and proceeds therein "in the same manner as a district court," 48 U.S.C. former §§ 641, 642. In addition, there are circuit courts having jurisdiction over cases arising under local laws. Appeals from the circuit courts run to the Supreme Court of the Territory, 48 U.S.C. § 631. These rules are made applicable to the district court, but not to the local courts. The Federal Rules of Civil Procedure 28 U.S.C., Appendix, have been made applicable to the district court and to appeals therefrom, 48 U.S.C. former § 646.

7. Puerto Rico.—Puerto Rico has a dual system of courts. The District Court of the United States for Puerto Rico, a legislative court, has jurisdiction of all cases cognizable in the district courts of the United States and proceeds "In the same manner," 48 U.S.C. § 863.

In addition, there are local courts for the trial of cases arising under local law, appeals therefrom running to the

Supreme Court of the Territory. These rules are made applicable to the district court, but not to the local courts. The Federal Rules of Civil Procedure, 28 U.S.C., Appendix, have been extended to the district court, 48 U.S.C. former § 873a.

8. Virgin Islands.—In the Virgin Islands there is a District Court of the Virgin Islands, a legislative court, consisting of two divisions and exercising both Federal and local jurisdiction, 48 U.S.C. §§ 1405z, 1406. Heretofore the rules of practice and procedure have been prescribed "by law or ordinance or by rules and regulations of the district judge not inconsistent with law or ordinance," 48 U.S.C. § 1405z.

9. Canal Zone.—In the Canal Zone there is a United States District Court for the District of the Canal Zone, a legislative court, exercising both Federal and local jurisdiction, 48 U.S.C. former §§ 1344, 1345. Criminal procedure is regulated by the Code of Criminal Procedure of the Canal Zone (Canal Zone Code, Title 6; 48 Stat. 1122), and by rules of practice and procedure prescribed by the district judge, 48 U.S.C. former § 1344. There are no grand juries in the district, all prosecutions being instituted by information. In the light of these circumstances and because of the peculiar status of the Canal Zone and its quasi-military nature, these rules have been made applicable to its district court, only with respect to proceedings after verdict or finding of guilty or plea of guilty.

10. By order dated March 31, 1941, effective July 1, 1941, the Supreme Court extended the rules of practice and procedure after plea of guilty, verdict or finding of guilty, in criminal cases, to the district courts of Alaska, Hawaii, Puerto Rico, Canal Zone, and Virgin Islands, and all subsequent proceedings in such cases in the United States circuit courts of appeals and in the Supreme Court of the United States, 312 U.S. 721.

Note to Subdivision (a)(2). 1. Rules 3, 4, and 5, supra, relate to proceedings before United States commissioners.

2. Justices and judges of the United States, as well as United States commissioners, may issue warrants and conduct proceedings as committing magistrates, 18 U.S.C. former § 591 [now § 3041] (Arrest and removal for trial); 9 Edmunds, Cyclopedia of Federal Procedure, 2d Ed., §§ 3800, 3819.

3. In the District of Columbia judges of the Municipal Court have authority to issue warrants and conduct proceedings as committing magistrates, D.C.Code, 1940, Title 11, §§ 602, 755. These proceedings are governed by these rules. The Municipal Court of the District of Columbia is also a local court for the trial of misdemeanors, but when so acting it is not a court of the United States. These rules, therefore, do not apply to such proceedings.

4. State and local judges and magistrates may issue warrants and act as committing magistrates in Federal cases, 18 U.S.C. former § 591 [now § 3041]. Only a very small proportion of cases are brought before them, however, and then ordinarily only in an emergency. Since these judicial officers may not be familiar with Federal procedure, these rules have not been made applicable to such proceedings.

Note to Subdivision (b)(1). 1. Certain types of State criminal prosecutions, principally those in which defendant is an officer appointed under or acting by authority of a revenue law of the United States and is prosecuted on account of an act done under color of his office, are removable to a Federal court on defendant's motion, 28 U.S.C. former § 74 [now §§ 1443, 1446, 1447] (Removal of suits from State courts; causes against persons denied civil rights); former § 76 [now §§ 1442, 1446, 1447] (Removal of suits from State courts; suits and prosecutions against revenue officers). In such cases the Federal court applies the substantive law of the State, but follows Federal procedure; *State of Tennessee v. Davis,* 100 U.S. 257, 25 L.Ed. 648; *Carter v. Tennessee,* 18 F.2d 850, C.C.A.6th; *Miller v. Kentucky,* 40 F.2d 820, C.C.A.6th. See, also, *State of Maryland v. Soper,* 46 S.Ct. 185, 270 U.S. 9, 70 L.Ed. 449. The rule is, therefore, a restatement of existing law, except that it does not affect whatever power the State prosecutor may have as to dismissal.

2. The rule does not affect the mode of removing a case from a State to a Federal court and leaves undisturbed the statutes governing this matter, 28 U.S.C. former §§ 74 to 76 [now §§ 1442, 1443, 1446, 1447].

Note to Subdivision (b)(2). This rule should be read in conjunction with Rule 18, which provides that "Except as otherwise permitted by statute or by these rules, the prosecution shall be held in a district in which the offense was committed * * *".

Note to Subdivision (b)(4). United States commissioners specially designated for that purpose by the court by which they are appointed have trial jurisdiction over petty offenses committed on Federal reservations if the defendant waives his right to be tried in the district court and consents to be tried before the commissioner. Act of October 9, 1940, 54 Stat. 1058, 18 U.S.C. former § 576 [now § 3041]. A petty offense is an offense the penalty for which does not exceed confinement in a common jail without hard labor for a period of six months or a fine of $500, or both, 18 U.S.C. former § 541 [now § 1]. Appeals from convictions by commissioners lie to the district court, 18 U.S.C. former § 576a [now § 3402]. These rules do not apply to trials before United States commissioners in such cases, since rules of procedure and practice in such matters were specially prescribed by the Supreme Court on January 6, 1941, 311 U.S. 733 et seq. The substantive law applicable in such cases with respect to offenses other than so-called Federal offenses is governed by 18 U.S.C. former § 468 [now § 13] (Laws of States adopted for punishing wrongful acts; effect of repeal). In addition, National Park commissioners have limited trial jurisdiction with respect to offenses committed in National Parks. Trials before commissioners in such cases are not governed by these rules, although when a National Park commissioner conducts a proceeding as a committing magistrate, these rules are applicable.

Among the statutes relating to jurisdiction of and proceedings before National Park commissioners are the following: U.S.C. Title 16:

§ 10 (Arrests by employees of park service for violation of laws and regulations)

§ 10a (Arrests by employees for violation of regulations made under § 9a)

§ 27 [now 28 U.S.C. §§ 131, 631, 632] (Yellowstone National Park; commissioner; jurisdiction and powers)

§ 66 [now 28 U.S.C. §§ 631, 632] (Yosemite and Sequoia National Parks; commissioners; appointment; jurisdiction)

§ 70 [now 18 U.S.C. §§ 3041, 3141; 18 U.S.C., App., Rules 4, 5(c), 9] (Same; arrests by commissioners for certain offenses; holding persons arrested for trial; bail)

§ 101 [now 18 U.S.C. §§ 3041, 3141; 18 U.S.C., App., Rule 4; 28 U.S.C., App., Rule 4] (Mount Rainier National Park; commissioner; arrest; bail)

§ 102 [now 18 U.S.C. § 3053; 18 U.S.C. App., Rule 4; 28 U.S.C., App., Rule 4] (Same; commissioner; direction of process of; arrests by other officers)

§ 117b [now 18 U.S.C. § 13] (Mesa Verde National Park; application of Colorado laws to offenses)

§ 117f [now 18 U.S.C. §§ 3041, 3141; 18 U.S.C., App., Rules 4, 5(c), 9] (Same; criminal offenses not covered by § 117c; jurisdiction of commissioner)

§ 117g [now 18 U.S.C. § 3053; 18 U.S.C., App., Rule 4; 28 U.S.C., App., Rule 4] (Same; process to whom issued; arrests without process)

§ 129 [now 28 U.S.C. §§ 631, 632] (Crater Lake National Park; commissioner; appointment; powers and duties)

§ 130 [now 18 U.S.C. §§ 3041, 3141; 18 U.S.C., App., Rules 4, 5(c), 9] (Same; commissioner; arrests by; bail)

§ 131 [now 18 U.S.C. § 3053; 18 U.S.C., App., Rule 4; 28 U.S.C., App., Rule 4] (Same; Commissioner; direction of process; arrest without process)

§ 172 [now 28 U.S.C. §§ 631, 632] (Glacier National Park; commissioner; jurisdiction; powers and duties)

§ 173 [now 18 U.S.C. §§ 3041, 3141; 18 U.S.C., App., Rules 4, 5(c), 9] (Same; commissioner; arrest of offenders, confinement, and bail)

§ 174 [now 18 U.S.C. § 3053; 28 U.S.C., App., Rule 4] (Same; commissioner; process directed to marshal; arrest without process)

§ 198b [now 18 U.S.C. § 13] (Rocky Mountain National Park; punishment of offenses; Colorado laws when followed)

§ 198e [now 28 U.S.C. §§ 631, 632] (Same; United States Commissioner; appointment; jurisdiction; issuing process; appeals; rules of procedure)

§ 198f [now 18 U.S.C. §§ 3041, 3141; 18 U.S.C., App., Rules 4, 5(c), 9] (Same; United States Commissioner; arrest of persons for offenses not covered by § 198c; bail)

§ 198g [now 18 U.S.C. § 3053; 18 U.S.C., App., Rule 4; 28 U.S.C., App., Rule 4] (Same; United States Commissioner; process to whom directed; arrest without process)

§ 204b [now 18 U.S.C. § 13] (Lassen Volcanic National Park; application of California laws to offenses)

§ 204e [now 28 U.S.C. §§ 631, 632] (Same; United States Commissioner; appointment; jurisdiction of offenses; appeals; rules of procedure)

§ 204f [now 18 U.S.C. §§ 3041, 3141; 18 U.S.C., App., Rules 4, 5(c), 9] (Same; criminal offenses not covered by § 204c; jurisdiction of commissioner)

§ 204g [now 18 U.S.C. § 3053; 18 U.S.C., App., Rule 4; 28 U.S.C., App., Rule 4] (Same; process to whom issued; arrests without process)

§ 376 [now 28 U.S.C. § 632] (Hot Springs National Park; prosecutions for violations of law or rules and regulations)

§ 377 [now 18 U.S.C. §§ 3041, 3141; 18 U.S.C., App., Rules 4, 5(c), 9] (Same; prosecutions for other offenses)

§ 378 [now 18 U.S.C. § 3053; 18 U.S.C., App., Rule 4; 28 U.S.C., App., Rule 4] (Same; process directed to marshal; arrests by others)

§ 381 [now 18 U.S.C. § 3041] (Same; execution of sentence on conviction)

§ 382 [now 18 U.S.C. § 3041] (Same; imprisonment for nonpayment of fines or costs)

§ 395b [now 18 U.S.C. § 13] (Hawaii National Park; application of Hawaiian laws to offenses)

§ 395e [now 28 U.S.C. §§ 631, 632] (Same; United States Commissioner; appointment; jurisdiction of offenses; appeals; rules of procedure; acting commissioners)

§ 395f [now 18 U.S.C. §§ 3041, 3141; 18 U.S.C., App., Rules 4, 5(c), 9] (Same; criminal offenses not covered by § 395c; jurisdiction of commissioner)

§ 395g [now 18 U.S.C. 3053; 18 U.S.C., App., Rule 4] (Same; process to whom issued; arrests without process)

§ 403c–1 (Shenandoah National Park and Great Smoky Mountains National Park; notice of assumption of police jurisdiction over Shenandoah Park by United States; exceptions)

§ 403c–5 [now 28 U.S.C. §§ 631, 632] (Same; United States Commissioner; appointment; jurisdiction of offenses; appeals; rules of procedure)

§ 403c–6 [now 28 U.S.C. § 632] (Same; jurisdiction of other commissioners)

§ 403c–7 [now 18 U.S.C. §§ 3041, 3141; 18 U.S.C., App., Rules 4, 5(c), 9] (Same; commissioner's jurisdiction of offenses not covered by § 403c–3)

§ 403c–8 [now 18 U.S.C. § 3053; 18 U.S.C., App., Rule 4; 28 U.S.C., App., Rule 4] (Same; process to whom directed; arrest without process)

§ 415 (National Military Parks; arrest and prosecution of offenders)

Note to Subdivision (b)(5). 1. Foreign extradition proceedings are governed by the following statutes:

U.S.C. Title 18 former:

§ 651 [now § 3184] (Fugitives from foreign country)

§ 652 [now § 3185] (Fugitives from country under control of United States)

§ 653 [now § 3186] (Surrender of fugitive)

§ 654 [now § 3188] (Time allowed for extradition)

§ 655 [now § 3190] (Evidence on hearing)

§ 656 [now § 3191] (Witnesses for indigent defendants)

§ 657 [now § 3189] (Place and character of hearing)

§ 658 [now § 3181] (Continuance of provisions limited)

§ 659 [now § 3192] (Protection of accused)

§ 660 [now § 3193] (Agent receiving offenders; powers)

Interstate rendition or extradition proceedings are governed by the following statutes:

U.S.C. Title 18 former:

§ 662 [now §§ 3182, 3195] (Fugitives from State or Territory)

§ 662c [now §§ 752, 3183, 3195] (Fugitives from State or Territory; arrest and removal)

§ 662d [now §§ 3187, 3195] (Fugitives from State or Territory; provisional arrest and detention)

2. Proceedings relating to forfeiture of property used in connection with a violation of a statute of the United States are governed by various statutes, among which are following:

U.S.C. Title 16:

§ 26 (Yellowstone Park; regulations for hunting and fishing in; punishment for violations; forfeitures)

§ 65 (Yosemite and Sequoia National Parks; seizure and forfeiture of guns, traps, teams, horses, and so forth)

§ 99 (Mount Rainier National Park; protection of game and fish; forfeitures of guns, traps, teams, and so forth)

§ 117d (Mesa Verde National Park; forfeiture of property used for unlawful purpose)

§ 128 (Crater Lake National Park; hunting and fishing; forfeitures or seizure of guns, traps, teams, etc., for violating regulations)

§ 171 (Glacier National Park; hunting and fishing; forfeitures and seizures of guns, traps, teams, and so forth)

§ 198d (Rocky Mountain National Park; forfeiture of property used in commission of offenses)

§ 204d (Lassen Volcanic National Park; forfeiture of property used for unlawful purposes)

§ 635 (Importing illegally taken skins; forfeiture)

§ 706 (Arrests; search warrants)

§ 727 (Upper Mississippi River Wild Life and Fish Refuge; powers of employees of Department of the Interior; searches and seizures)

§ 772e (Penalties and forfeitures)

U.S.C. Title 18 former:

§ 286 [now § 492] (Forfeiture of counterfeit obligations, etc.; failure to deliver)

§ 645 [now § 3611] (Confiscation of firearms possessed by convicted felons)

§ 646 [now § 3617] (Remission or mitigation of forfeitures under liquor laws; possession pending trial)

§ 647 [now § 3616] (Use of confiscated motor vehicles)

U.S.C. Title 19:

§ 483 [now § 1595a] (Forfeitures; penalty for aiding unlawful importation)

§ 1592 (Fraud; penalty against goods)

§ 1602 (Seizure; report to collector)

§ 1603 (Seizure; collector's reports)

§ 1604 (Seizure; prosecution)

§ 1605 (Seizure; custody)

§ 1606 (Seizure; appraisement)

§ 1607 (Seizure; value $1,000 or less)

§ 1608 (Seizure; claims; judicial condemnation)

§ 1609 (Seizure; summary of forfeiture and sale)

§ 1610 (Seizure; value more than $1,000)

§ 1611 (Seizure; sale unlawful)

§ 1612 (Seizure; summary sale)

§ 1613 (Disposition of proceeds of forfeited property)

§ 1614 (Release of seized property)

§ 1615 (Burden of proof in forfeiture proceedings)

§ 1703 (Seizure and forfeiture of vessels)

§ 1705 (Destruction of forfeited vessel)

U.S.C. Title 21:

§ 334 (Seizure)

§ 337 (Proceedings in name of United States; provision as to subpenas)

U.S.C. Title 22:

§ 401 (Seizure of war materials intended for unlawful export generally; forfeiture)

§ 402 (Seizure of war materials intended for unlawful export generally; warrant for detention of seized property)

§ 403 (Seizure of war materials intended for unlawful export generally; petition for restoration of seized property)

§ 404 (Seizure of war materials intended for unlawful export generally; libel and sale of seized property)

§ 405 (Seizure of war materials intended for unlawful export generally; method of trial; bond for redelivery)

§ 406 (Seizure of war materials intended for unlawful export generally; sections not to interfere with foreign trade)

U.S.C. Title 26:

§ 3116 [now § 7302] (Forfeitures and seizures)

3. Collection of fines and penalties is accomplished in the same manner as the collection of a civil judgment. See Rule 69(a) of the Federal Rules of Civil Procedure, 28 U.S.C., Appendix. For mode of discharging indigent convicts imprisoned for non-payment of fine, see 18 U.S.C. former § 641 [now § 3569].

4. The Federal Juvenile Delinquency Act, 18 U.S.C. former §§ 921 to 929 [now §§ 5031 to 5037], authorizes prosecution of a juvenile delinquent on the charge of juvenile delinquency, if the juvenile consents to this procedure. In such cases the court may be convened at any time and place, in chambers or otherwise, and the trial is without a jury. The purpose of excepting proceedings under the Act is to make inapplicable to them the requirement of an arraignment in open court (Rule 10) and other similar provisions.

5. As habeas corpus proceedings are regarded as civil proceedings, they are not governed by these rules. The procedure in such cases is prescribed by 28 U.S.C. former §§ 451 to 466 [now §§ 2241 to 2243, 2251 to 2253]. Appeals in habeas corpus proceedings are governed by the Federal Rules of Civil Procedure (Rule 81(a)(2) of the Federal Rules of Civil Procedure, 28 U.S.C., Appendix).

Note to Subdivision (c). 1. This rule is analogous to Rule 81(e) of the Federal Rules of Civil Procedure, 28 U.S.C., Appendix.

2. 1 U.S.C. §§ 1 to 6, containing general rules of construction, should be read in conjunction with this rule.

3. In connection with the definition of "attorney for the Government", see the following statutes:

U.S.C. Title 5:

§ 291 [now 28 U.S.C. §§ 501, 503] (Establishment of Department)

§ 293 [now 28 U.S.C. § 505] (Solicitor General)

§ 294 [now 28 U.S.C. § 504] (Assistant to Attorney General)

§ 295 [now 28 U.S.C. § 506] (Assistant Attorneys General)

§ 309 [now 28 U.S.C. § 518] (Conduct and argument of cases by Attorney General and Solicitor General)

§ 310 [now 28 U.S.C. § 515] (Conduct of legal proceedings)

§ 311 [now 28 U.S.C. § 510] (Performance of duty by officers of Department)

§ 312 [now 28 U.S.C. §§ 503, 507, 508] (Counsel to aid district attorneys)

§ 315 [now 28 U.S.C. § 515] (Appointment and oath of special attorneys or counsel)

U.S.C. Title 28 former:

§ 481 [now § 501] (District attorneys)

§ 483 [now § 502] (Assistant district attorneys)

§ 485 [now § 507] (District attorneys; duties)

4. The last sentence of this rule has particular reference to 18 U.S.C. former § 682 [now § 3731] (Appeals; on behalf of the United States; rules of practice and procedure), which authorizes the United States to appeal in criminal cases from a decision on a motion to quash, a demurrer or a special plea in bar, if the defendant has not been placed in jeopardy. It is intended that the right of the Government to appeal in such cases should not be affected as the result of the substitution of a motion under Rule 12 for a demurrer, motion to quash and a special plea in bar. The rule is equally applicable to any other statute employing the same terminology.

1948 Amendment

To conform to the nomenclature of revised Title 28 with respect to district courts and courts of appeals (28 U.S.C. §§ 132(a), 43(a); to eliminate special reference to the district courts for the District of Columbia, Hawaii and Puerto Rico which are now United States district courts for all purposes (28 U.S.C. §§ 88, 91, 119, 132, 133, 451), and to eliminate special reference to the court of appeals for the District of Columbia which is now a United States court of appeals for all purposes (28 U.S.C. §§ 41, 43).

The amendment to paragraph (1) is to incorporate nomenclature of Revised Title 28 and in paragraphs (2), (3), (4) and (5) to insert proper reference to Titles 18 and 28 in place of repealed acts.

Under revised Title 28 the justices of the United States Court of Appeals and District Court for the District of Columbia become circuit and district judges (see 28 U.S.C. §§ 44, 133) and the use of the descriptive phrase "senior circuit judge" is abandoned in favor of the title "chief judge" in all circuits including the District of Columbia.

1966 Amendment

Subdivision (a).—The first change reflects the granting of statehood to Alaska. The second change conforms to § 3501 of the Canal Zone Code.

Subdivision (b).—The change is made necessary by the new provision in Rule 20(d).

1972 Amendment

Subdivisions (a) and (b) are amended to delete the references to "commissioners" and to substitute, where appropriate, the phrase "United States magistrates."

Subdivision (a)(2) is deleted. In its old form it makes reference to "rules applicable to criminal proceedings before commissioners," which are now replaced by the Rules of Procedure for the Trial of Minor Offenses before United States Magistrates (1971). Rule 1 of the magistrates' rules provides that they are applicable to cases involving "minor offenses" as defined in 18 U.S.C. § 3401 "before United States magistrates." Cases involving "minor offenses" brought before a judge of the district court will be governed by the Rules of Criminal Procedure for the United States District Courts.

The last sentence of old subdivision (a)(2) is stricken for two reasons: (1) Whenever possible, cases should be brought before a United States magistrate rather than before a state or local judicial officer authorized by 18 U.S.C. § 3041. (2) When a state or local judicial officer is involved, he should conform to the federal rules.

Subdivision (b)(4) makes clear that minor offense cases before United States magistrates are governed by the Rules of Procedure for the Trial of Minor Offenses before United States Magistrates (1971). See rule 1 of the magistrates' rules.

In subdivision (b)(5) the word "civil" is added before the word "forfeiture" to make clear that the rules do apply to criminal forfeitures. This is clearly the intention of Congress. See Senate Report No. 91–617, 91st Cong., 1st Sess., Dec. 16, 1969, at 160:

Subsection (a) provides the remedy of criminal forfeiture. Forfeiture trials are to be governed by the Fed.R.Crim.P. But see Fed.R.Crim.P. 54(b)(5).

Subdivision (c) is amended to list the defined terms in alphabetical order to facilitate the use of the rule. There are added six new definitions.

"Federal magistrate" is a phrase to be used whenever the rule is intended to confer authority on any federal judicial officer including a United States magistrate.

"Judge of the United States" is a phrase defined to include district court, court of appeals, and supreme court judges. It is used in the rules to indicate that only a judge (not to include a United States magistrate) is authorized to act.

"Magistrate" is a term used when both federal and state judicial officers may be authorized to act. The scope of authority of state or local judicial officers is clarified by the enumeration of those rules (3, 4, and 5) under which they are authorized to act.

"United States magistrate" is a phrase which refers to the federal judicial officer created by the Federal Magistrates Act (28 U.S.C. §§ 631 to 639).

Also added are cross references to the statutory definitions of "minor offense" and "petty offense."

1982 Amendment

Subdivision (a). The amendment of subdivision (a) conforms to 48 U.S.C. § 1694(c), which provides that "the rules heretofore or hereafter promulgated and made effective by the Congress or the Supreme Court of the United States pursuant to Titles 11, 18, and 28 shall apply to the District Court for the Northern Mariana Islands and appeals therefrom where appropriate, except as otherwise provided in articles IV and V of the covenant provided by the Act of March 24, 1976 (90 Stat. 263)." The reference is to the "Covenant To Establish a Commonwealth of the Northern Mariana Islands in Political Union with the United States of America." Article IV of the covenant provides that except when exercising "the jurisdiction of a district court of the United States," the District Court will be considered a court of the Northern Mariana Islands for the purposes of determining the requirements of indictment by grand jury or trial by jury." Article V provides that "neither trial by jury nor indictment by grand jury shall be required in any civil action or criminal prosecution based on local law, except when required by local law."

Subdivision (b) (4). This change is necessitated by the recent amendment of 18 U.S.C. § 3401 of the Federal Magistrate Act of 1979.

Subdivision (c). The first amendment to subdivision (c) conforms to 48 U.S.C. § 1694(c), which states: "The terms 'attorney for the government' and 'United States Attorney' as used in the Federal Rules of Criminal Procedure (Rule 54(c)) shall, when applicable to cases arising under the laws of the Northern Mariana Islands, include the attorney general of the Northern Mariana Islands or any other person or persons as may be authorized by the laws of the Northern Marianas to act therein."

The second amendment to subdivision (c) eliminates any reference to minor offenses. By virtue of the recent amendment of 18 U.S.C. § 3401 by the Federal Magistrate Act of 1979, the term "minor offense" is no longer utilized in the statute. It is likewise no longer used in these rules. See amendments to Rules 5(b) and 9(d).

1991 Amendment

The amendment to 54(a) conforms the Rule to legislative changes affecting the prosecution of federal cases in Guam and the Virgin Islands by indictment or information. The "except" clause in Rule 54(a) addressing the availability of indictments by grand jury Guam has been effectively repealed by Public Law 98–454 (1984), 48 U.S.C. § 1424–4 which made the Federal Rules of Criminal Procedure (including Rule 7, relating to use of indictments) applicable in Guam notwithstanding Rule 54(a). That legislation apparently codified what had been the actual practice in Guam for a number of years. *See* 130 Cong.Rec., H25476 (daily ed. Sept. 14, 1984). With regard to the Virgin Islands, Public Law 98–454 (1984) also amended 48 U.S.C. §§ 1561 and 1614(b) to permit (but not require) use of indictments in the Virgin Islands.

1993 Amendment

The Rule is amended to conform to the Judicial Improvements Act of 1990 [P.L. 101–650, Title III, Section 321] which provides that each United States magistrate appointed under section 631 of title 28, United States Code, shall be known as a United States magistrate judge.

1999 Amendment

The amendment to Rule 54(a) is a technical amendment removing the reference to the court in the Canal Zone, which no longer exists.

GAP Report—Rule 54.

The Committee made no changes to the published draft.

2002 Amendments

Certain provisions in current Rule 54 have been moved to revised Rule 1 as part of a general restyling of the Criminal Rules to make them more easily understood and to make style and terminology consistent throughout the rules. Other provisions in Rule 54 have been deleted as being unnecessary.

Rule 55. Records

The clerk of the district court must keep records of criminal proceedings in the form prescribed by the Director of the Administrative Office of the United States courts. The clerk must enter in the records every court order or judgment and the date of entry.

(As amended Dec. 27, 1948, eff. Oct. 20, 1949; Feb. 28, 1966, eff. July 1, 1966; Apr. 24, 1972, eff. Oct. 1, 1972; Apr. 28, 1983, eff. Aug. 1, 1983; Apr. 22, 1993, eff. Dec. 1, 1993; Apr. 29, 2002, eff. Dec. 1, 2002.)

ADVISORY COMMITTEE NOTES

1944 Adoption

The Federal Rules of Civil Procedure Rule 79, 28 U.S.C., Appendix, prescribed in detail the books and records to be kept by the clerk in civil cases. Subsequently to the effective date of the civil rules, however, the Act establishing the Administrative Office of the United States Courts became law (Act of August 7, 1939; 53 Stat. 1223; 28 U.S.C. former §§ 444 to 450 [now §§ 332 to 333, 456, 601 to 610]). One of the duties of the Director of that Office is to have charge, under the supervision and direction of the Conference of Senior Circuit Judges, of all administrative matters relating to the offices of the clerks and other clerical and administrative personnel of the courts, 28 U.S.C. former § 446 [now §§ 604, 609]. In view of this circumstance it seemed best not to prescribe the records to be kept by the clerks of the district courts and by the United States commissioners, in criminal proceedings, but to vest the power to do so in the Director of the Administrative Office of the United States Courts with the approval of the Conference of Senior Circuit Judges.

1948 Amendment

To incorporate nomenclature provided for by Revised Title 28 U.S.C., § 331.

1966 Amendment

Rule 37(a)(2) provides that for the purpose of commencing the running of the time for appeal a judgment or order is entered "when it is entered in the criminal docket." The sentence added here requires that such a docket be kept and that it show the dates on which judgments or orders are entered therein. Cf. Civil Rule 79(a).

1983 Amendment

The Advisory Committee Note to original Rule 55 observes that, in light of the authority which the Director and Judicial Conference have over the activities of clerks, "it seems best not to prescribe the records to be kept by clerks." Because of current experimentation with automated record-keeping, this approach is more appropriate than ever before. The amendment will make it possible for the Director to permit use of more sophisticated record-keeping techniques, including those which may obviate the need for a "criminal docket" book. The reference to the Judicial Conference has been stricken as unnecessary. See 28 U.S.C. § 604.

1993 Amendment

The Rule is amended to conform to the Judicial Improvements Act of 1990 [P.L. 101–650, Title III, Section 321] which provides that each United States magistrate appointed under section 631 of title 28, United States Code, shall be known as a United States magistrate judge.

2002 Amendments

The language of Rule 55 has been amended as part of the general restyling of the Criminal Rules to make them more easily understood and to make style and terminology consistent throughout the rules. These changes are intended to be stylistic only.

HISTORICAL NOTES

Change of Name

United States magistrate appointed under section 631 of Title 28, Judiciary and Judicial Procedure, to be known as United States magistrate judge after Dec. 1, 1990, with any reference to United States magistrate or magistrate in Title 28, in any other Federal statute, etc., deemed a reference to United States magistrate judge appointed under section 631 of Title 28, see section 321 of Pub.L. 101–650, set out as a note under section 631 of Title 28.

Rule 56. When Court is Open

(a) In General. A district court is considered always open for any filing, and for issuing and returning process, making a motion, or entering an order.

(b) Office Hours. The clerk's office—with the clerk or a deputy in attendance—must be open during business hours on all days except Saturdays, Sundays, and legal holidays.

(c) Special Hours. A court may provide by local rule or order that its clerk's office will be open for specified hours on Saturdays or legal holidays other than those set aside by statute for observing New Year's Day, Martin Luther King, Jr.'s Birthday, Washington's Birthday, Memorial Day, Independence Day, Labor Day, Columbus Day, Veterans' Day, Thanksgiving Day, and Christmas Day.

(As amended Dec. 27, 1948, eff. Oct. 20, 1949; Feb. 28, 1966, eff. July 1, 1966; Dec. 4, 1967, eff. July 1, 1968; Mar. 1, 1971, eff. July 1, 1971; Apr. 25, 1988, eff. Aug. 1, 1988; Apr. 29, 2002, eff. Dec. 1, 2002.)

ADVISORY COMMITTEE NOTES

1944 Adoption

1. The first sentence of this rule is substantially the same as Rule 77(a) of the Federal Rules of Civil Procedure, 28 U.S.C., Appendix, except that it is applicable to courts of appeals as well as to district courts.

2. In connection with this rule, see 28 U.S.C. former § 14 (Monthly adjournments for trial of criminal causes) and 28 U.S.C. former § 15 [now § 141] (Special terms). These sections "indicate a policy of avoiding the hardships consequent upon a closing of the court during vacations," *Abbott v. Brown,* 241 U.S. 606, 611, 36 S.Ct. 689, 60 L.Ed. 1199.

3. The second sentence of the rule is identical with the first sentence of Rule 77(c) of the Federal Rules of Civil Procedure, 28 U.S.C., Appendix.

4. The term "legal holidays" includes Federal holidays as well as holidays prescribed by the laws of the State where the clerk's office is located.

1948 Amendment

To incorporate nomenclature provided for by Revised Title 28, U.S.C. § 43(a).

1966 Amendment

The change is in conformity with the changes made in Rule 45. See the similar changes in Civil Rule 77(c) made effective July 1, 1963.

1967 Amendment

The provisions relating to courts of appeals are included in Rule 47 of the Federal Rules of Appellate Procedure.

1968 Amendment

The provisions relating to courts of appeals are included in Rule 47 of the Federal Rules of Appellate Procedure.

1971 Amendment

The amendment adds Columbus Day to the list of legal holidays. See the Note accompanying the amendment of Rule 45(a).

1988 Amendment

The amendment is technical. No substantive change is intended.

2002 Amendments

The language of Rule 56 has been amended as part of the general restyling of the Criminal Rules to make them more easily understood and to make style and terminology consistent throughout the rules. These changes are intended to be stylistic only.

HISTORICAL NOTES

Effective and Applicability Provisions

1993 Acts. The Order of the Supreme Court dated April 25, 1988, provided in part: "That the foregoing amendments to the Federal Rules of Criminal Procedure [this rule and rule 30] shall take effect on August 1, 1988 and shall govern all proceedings in criminal cases thereafter commenced and, insofar as just and practicable, all proceedings in criminal cases then pending." See order preceding rule 1.

Rule 57. District Court Rules

(a) In General.

(1) Adopting Local Rules. Each district court acting by a majority of its district judges may, after giving appropriate public notice and an opportunity to comment, make and amend rules governing its practice. A local rule must be consistent with—but not duplicative of—federal statutes and rules adopted under 28 U.S.C. § 2072 and must conform to any uniform numbering system prescribed by the Judicial Conference of the United States.

(2) Limiting Enforcement. A local rule imposing a requirement of form must not be enforced in a manner that causes a party to lose rights because of an unintentional failure to comply with the requirement.

(b) Procedure When There Is No Controlling Law. A judge may regulate practice in any manner consistent with federal law, these rules, and the local rules of the district. No sanction or other disadvantage may be imposed for noncompliance with any requirement not in federal law, federal rules, or the local district rules unless the alleged violator was furnished with actual notice of the requirement before the noncompliance.

(c) Effective Date and Notice. A local rule adopted under this rule takes effect on the date specified by the district court and remains in effect unless amended by the district court or abrogated by the judicial council of the circuit in which the district is located. Copies of local rules and their amendments, when promulgated, must be furnished to the judicial council and the Administrative Office of the United States Courts and must be made available to the public.

(As amended Dec. 27, 1948, eff. Oct. 20, 1949; Dec. 4, 1967, eff. July 1, 1968; Apr. 29, 1985, eff. Aug. 1, 1985; Apr. 22, 1993, eff. Dec. 1, 1993; Apr. 27, 1995, eff. Dec. 1, 1995; Apr. 29, 2002, eff. Dec. 1, 2002.)

ADVISORY COMMITTEE NOTES

1944 Adoption

Note to Subdivision (a). This rule is substantially a restatement of 28 U.S.C. former § 731 [now § 2071] (Rules of practice in district courts). A similar provision is found in rule 83 of the Federal Rules of Civil Procedure, 28 U.S.C., Appendix.

Note to Subdivision (b). 1. One of the purposes of this rule is to abrogate any existing requirement of conformity to State procedure on any point whatsoever. The Federal Rules of Civil Procedure, 28 U.S.C., Appendix, have been held to repeal the Conformity Act, 28 U.S.C. former § 724, *Sibbach v. Wilson*, 61 S.Ct. 422, 312 U.S. 1, 10, 85 L.Ed. 479.

2. While the rules are intended to constitute a comprehensive procedural code for criminal cases in the Federal courts, nevertheless it seemed best not to endeavor to prescribe a uniform practice as to some matters of detail, but to leave the individual courts free to regulate them, either by local rules or by usage. Among such matters are the mode of impaneling a jury, the manner and order of interposing challenges to jurors, the manner of selecting the foreman of a trial jury, the matter of sealed verdicts, the order of counsel's arguments to the jury, and other similar details.

1948 Amendment

To incorporate nomenclature provided for by Revised Title 28, U.S.C. § 43(a).

1968 Amendment

The provisions relating to the court of appeals are included in Rule 47 of the Federal Rules of Appellate Procedure.

1985 Amendment

Rule 57 has been reformulated to correspond to Fed. R.Civ.P. 83, including the proposed amendments thereto. The purpose of the reformulation is to emphasize that the procedures for adoption of local rules by a district court are the same under both the civil and the criminal rules. In particular, the major purpose of the reformulation is to enhance the local rulemaking process by requiring appropriate public notice of proposed rules and an opportunity to comment on them. See Committee Note to Fed.R.Civ.P. 83.

1993 Amendment

The Rule is amended to conform to the Judicial Improvements Act of 1990 [P.L. 101–650, Title III, Section 321] which provides that each United States magistrate appointed under section 631 of title 28, United States Code, shall be known as a United States magistrate judge.

1995 Amendments

Subdivision (a). This rule is amended to reflect the requirement that local rules be consistent not only with the national rules but also with Acts of Congress. The amendment also states that local rules should not repeat national rules and Acts of Congress.

The amendment also requires that the numbering of local rules conform with any numbering system that may be prescribed by the Judicial Conference. Lack of uniform numbering might create unnecessary traps for counsel and litigants. A uniform numbering system would make it easier for an increasingly national bar to locate a local rule that applies to a particular procedural issue.

Paragraph (2) is new. Its aim is to protect against loss of rights in the enforcement of local rules relating to matters of form. The proscription of paragraph (2) is narrowly drawn—covering only nonwillful violations and only those involving local rules directed to matters of form. It does not limit the court's power to impose substantive penalties upon a party if it or its attorney stubbornly or repeatedly violates a local rule, even one involving merely a matter of form. Nor does it affect the court's power to enforce local rules that involve more than mere matters of form—for example, a local rule requiring that the defendant waive a jury trial within a specified time.

Subdivision (b). This rule provides flexibility to the court in regulating practice when there is no controlling law. Specifically, it permits the court to regulate practice in any manner consistent with Acts of Congress, with rules adopted under 28 U.S.C. § 2072, and with the district's local rules. This rule recognizes that courts rely on multiple directives to control practice. Some courts regulate practice through the published Federal Rules and the local rules of the court. Some courts also have used internal operating procedures, standing orders, and other internal directives. Although such directives continue to be authorized, they can lead to problems. Counsel or litigants may be unaware of the various directives. In addition, the sheer volume of directives may impose an unreasonable barrier. For example, it may be difficult to obtain copies of the directives. Finally, counsel or litigants may be unfairly sanctioned for failing to comply with a directive. For these reasons, the amendment disapproves imposing any sanction or other disadvantage on a person for noncompliance with such an internal directive, unless the alleged violator has been furnished in a particular case with actual notice of the requirement.

There should be no adverse consequence to a party or attorney for violating special requirements relating to practice before a particular judge unless the party or attorney has actual notice of those requirements. Furnishing litigants with a copy outlining the judge's practices—or attaching instructions to a notice setting a case for conference or trial—would suffice to give actual notice, as would an order in a case specifically adopting by reference a judge's standing order and indicating how copies can be obtained.

2002 Amendments

The language of Rule 57 has been amended as part of the general restyling of the Criminal Rules to make them more easily understood and to make style and terminology consistent throughout the rules. These changes are intended to be stylistic only.

Rule 58. Petty Offenses and Other Misdemeanors

(a) Scope.

(1) In General. These rules apply in petty offense and other misdemeanor cases and on appeal to a district judge in a case tried by a magistrate judge, unless this rule provides otherwise.

(2) Petty Offense Case Without Imprisonment. In a case involving a petty offense for which no sentence of imprisonment will be imposed, the court may follow any provision of these rules that is not inconsistent with this rule and that the court considers appropriate.

(3) Definition. As used in this rule, the term "petty offense for which no sentence of imprisonment will be imposed" means a petty offense for which the court determines that, in the event of conviction, no sentence of imprisonment will be imposed.

(b) Pretrial Procedure.

(1) Charging Document. The trial of a misdemeanor may proceed on an indictment, information, or complaint. The trial of a petty offense may also proceed on a citation or violation notice.

(2) Initial Appearance. At the defendant's initial appearance on a petty offense or other misdemeanor charge, the magistrate judge must inform the defendant of the following:

(A) the charge, and the minimum and maximum penalties, including imprisonment, fines, any special assessment under 18 U.S.C. § 3013, and restitution under 18 U.S.C. § 3556;

(B) the right to retain counsel;

(C) the right to request the appointment of counsel if the defendant is unable to retain counsel—unless the charge is a petty offense for which the appointment of counsel is not required;

(D) the defendant's right not to make a statement, and that any statement made may be used against the defendant;

(E) the right to trial, judgment, and sentencing before a district judge—unless:

(i) the charge is a petty offense; or

(ii) the defendant consents to trial, judgment, and sentencing before a magistrate judge;

(F) the right to a jury trial before either a magistrate judge or a district judge—unless the charge is a petty offense; and

(G) any right to a preliminary hearing under Rule 5.1, and the general circumstances, if any, under which the defendant may secure pretrial release.

(3) Arraignment.

(A) Plea Before a Magistrate Judge. A magistrate judge may take the defendant's plea in a petty offense case. In every other misdemeanor case, a magistrate judge may take the plea only if the defendant consents either in writing or on the record to be tried before a magistrate judge and specifically waives trial before a district judge. The defendant may plead not guilty, guilty, or (with the consent of the magistrate judge) nolo contendere.

(B) Failure to Consent. Except in a petty offense case, the magistrate judge must order a defendant who does not consent to trial before a magistrate judge to appear before a district judge for further proceedings.

(c) Additional Procedures in Certain Petty Offense Cases. The following procedures also apply in a case involving a petty offense for which no sentence of imprisonment will be imposed:

(1) Guilty or Nolo Contendere Plea. The court must not accept a guilty or nolo contendere plea unless satisfied that the defendant understands the nature of the charge and the maximum possible penalty.

(2) Waiving Venue.

(A) Conditions of Waiving Venue. If a defendant is arrested, held, or present in a district different from the one where the indictment, information, complaint, citation, or violation notice is pending, the defendant may state in writing a desire to plead guilty or nolo contendere; to waive venue and trial in the district where the proceeding is pending; and to consent to the court's disposing of the case in the district where the defendant was arrested, is held, or is present.

(B) Effect of Waiving Venue. Unless the defendant later pleads not guilty, the prosecution will proceed in the district where the defendant was arrested, is held, or is present. The district clerk must notify the clerk in the original district of the defendant's waiver of venue. The defendant's statement of a desire to plead guilty or nolo contendere is not admissible against the defendant.

(3) Sentencing. The court must give the defendant an opportunity to be heard in mitigation and then proceed immediately to sentencing. The court may, however, postpone sentencing to allow the probation service to investigate or to permit either party to submit additional information.

(4) Notice of a Right to Appeal. After imposing sentence in a case tried on a not-guilty plea, the court must advise the defendant of a right to appeal the conviction and of any right to appeal the sentence. If the defendant was convicted on a plea of guilty or nolo contendere, the court must advise the defendant of any right to appeal the sentence.

(d) Paying a Fixed Sum in Lieu of Appearance.

(1) In General. If the court has a local rule governing forfeiture of collateral, the court may accept a fixed-sum payment in lieu of the defendant's appearance and end the case, but the fixed sum may not exceed the maximum fine allowed by law.

(2) Notice to Appear. If the defendant fails to pay a fixed sum, request a hearing, or appear in response to a citation or violation notice, the district clerk or a magistrate judge may issue a notice for the defendant to appear before the court on a date certain. The notice may give the defendant an additional opportunity to pay a fixed sum in lieu of appearance. The district clerk must serve the notice on the defendant by mailing a copy to the defendant's last known address.

(3) Summons or Warrant. Upon an indictment, or upon a showing by one of the other charging documents specified in Rule 58(b)(1) of probable cause to believe that an offense has been committed and that the defendant has committed it, the court may issue an arrest warrant or, if no warrant is requested by an attorney for the government, a summons. The showing of probable cause must be made under oath or under penalty of perjury, but the affiant need not appear before the court. If the defendant fails to appear before the court in response to a summons, the court may summarily issue a warrant for the defendant's arrest.

(e) Recording the Proceedings. The court must record any proceedings under this rule by using a court reporter or a suitable recording device.

(f) New Trial. Rule 33 applies to a motion for a new trial.

(g) Appeal.

(1) From a District Judge's Order or Judgment. The Federal Rules of Appellate Procedure govern an appeal from a district judge's order or a judgment of conviction or sentence.

(2) From a Magistrate Judge's Order or Judgment.

(A) Interlocutory Appeal. Either party may appeal an order of a magistrate judge to a district judge within 10 days of its entry if a district judge's order could similarly be appealed. The party appealing must file a notice with the clerk specifying the order being appealed and must serve a copy on the adverse party.

(B) Appeal from a Conviction or Sentence. A defendant may appeal a magistrate judge's judgment of conviction or sentence to a district judge within 10 days of its entry. To appeal, the defendant must file a notice with the clerk specifying the judgment being appealed and must serve a copy on an attorney for the government.

(C) Record. The record consists of the original papers and exhibits in the case; any transcript, tape, or other recording of the proceedings; and a certified copy of the docket entries. For purposes of the appeal, a copy of the record of the proceedings must be made available to a defendant who establishes by affidavit an inability to pay or give security for the record. The Director of the Administrative Office of the United States Courts must pay for those copies.

(D) Scope of Appeal. The defendant is not entitled to a trial de novo by a district judge. The scope of the appeal is the same as in an appeal to the court of appeals from a judgment entered by a district judge.

(3) Stay of Execution and Release Pending Appeal. Rule 38 applies to a stay of a judgment of conviction or sentence. The court may release the defendant pending appeal under the law relating to release pending appeal from a district court to a court of appeals.

(Added May 1, 1990, eff. Dec. 1, 1990, and amended Apr. 30, 1991, eff. Dec. 1, 1991; Apr. 22, 1993, eff. Dec. 1, 1993; Apr. 29, 2002, eff. Dec. 1, 2002; Apr. 12, 2006, eff. Dec. 1, 2006.)

ADVISORY COMMITTEE NOTES

1990 Addition

This new rule is largely a restatement of the Rules of Procedure for the Trial of Misdemeanors before United

States Magistrates which were promulgated in 1980 to replace the Rules for the Trial of Minor Offenses before United States Magistrates (1970). The Committee believed that a new single rule should be incorporated into the Rules of Criminal Procedure where those charged with its execution could readily locate it and realize its relationship with the other Rules. A number of technical changes have been made throughout the rule and unless otherwise noted, no substantive changes were intended in those amendments. The Committee envisions no major changes in the way in which the trial of misdemeanors and petty offenses are currently handled.

The title of the rule has been changed by deleting the phrase "Before United States Magistrates" to indicate that this rule may be used by district judges as well as magistrates. The phrase "and Petty Offenses" has been added to the title and elsewhere throughout the rule because the term "misdemeanor" does not include an "infraction." See 18 U.S.C. § 3559(a). A petty offense, however, is defined in 18 U.S.C. § 19 as a Class B misdemeanor, a Class C misdemeanor, or an infraction, with limitations on fines of no more than $5,000 for an individual and $10,000 for an organization.

Subdivision (a) is an amended version of current Magistrates Rule 1. Deletion of the phrase "before United States Magistrates under 18 U.S.C. § 3401" in Rule 1(a) will enable district judges to use the abbreviated procedures of this rule. Consistent with that change, the term "magistrate" is amended to read "the court," wherever appropriate throughout the rule, to indicate that both judges and magistrates may use the rule. The last sentence in (a)(1) has been amended to reflect that the rule also governs an appeal from a magistrate's decision to a judge of the district court. An appeal from a district judge's decision would be governed by the Federal Rules of Appellate Procedure. Subdivision (a)(2) rephrases prior language in Magistrate Rule 1(b). Subdivision (a)(3) adds a statutory reference to 18 U.S.C. § 19, which defines a petty offense as a "Class B misdemeanor, a Class C misdemeanor, or an infraction" with the $5,000 and $10,000 fine limitations noted *supra*. The phrase "regardless of the penalty authorized by law" has been deleted.

Subdivision (b) is an amended version of current Magistrates Rule 2. The last sentence in current Rule 2(a) has been deleted because 18 U.S.C. § 3401(a), provides that a magistrate will have jurisdiction to try misdemeanor cases when specially designated to do so by the district court or courts served by the Magistrate.

Subdivision (b)(2) reflects the standard rights advisements currently included in Magistrates Rule 2 with several amendments. Subdivision (b)(2)(A) specifically requires that the defendant be advised of all penalties which may be imposed upon conviction, including specifically a special assessment and restitution. A number of technical, nonsubstantive, changes have been made in the contents of advisement of rights. A substantive change is reflected in subdivision (b)(2)(G), currently Magistrates Rule 2(b)(7), and (8). That rule currently provides that, unless the prosecution is on an indictment or information, a defendant who is charged with a misdemeanor other than a petty offense has a right to a preliminary hearing, if the defendant does not consent to be tried by the magistrate. As amended, only a defendant in custody has a right to a preliminary hearing.

Subdivision (b)(3)(A) is based upon Magistrates Rule 2(c) and has been amended by deleting the last sentence, which provides that trial may occur within 30 days "upon written consent of the defendant." The change is warranted because the Speedy Trial Act does not apply to petty offenses. *See* 18 U.S.C. § 3172(2). Subdivision (b)(3)(B), "Failure to Consent," currently appears in Magistrates Rule 3(a). The first sentence has been amended to make it applicable to all misdemeanor and petty offense defendants who fail to consent. The last sentence of Rule 3(a) has been deleted entirely. Because the clerk is responsible for all district court case files, including those for misdemeanor and petty offense cases tried by magistrates, it is not necessary to state that the file be transmitted to the clerk of court.

Subdivision (c) is an amended version of current Magistrates Rule 3 with the exception of Rule 3(a), which, as noted *supra* is now located in subdivision (b)(3)(B) of the new rule. The phrase "petty offense for which no sentence of imprisonment will be imposed" has been deleted because the heading for subdivision (c) limits its application to those petty offenses. The Committee recognizes that subdivision (c)(2) might result in attempted forum shopping. *See, e.g., United States v. Shaw,* 467 F.Supp. 86 (W.D.La.1979), *affm'd,* 615 F.2d 251 (5th Cir.1980). In order to maintain a streamlined and less formal procedure which is consistent with the remainder of the Rule, subdivision (c)(2) does not require the formal "consent" of the United States Attorneys involved before a waiver of venue may be accomplished. *Cf.* Rule 20 (Transfer From the District for Plea and Sentence). The Rule specifically envisions that there will be communication and coordination between the two districts involved. To that end, reasonable efforts should be made to contact the United States Attorney in the district in which the charges were instituted. Subdivision (c)(4), formerly Rule 3(d), now specifically provides that the defendant be advised of the right to appeal the sentence. This subdivision is also amended to provide for advising the defendant of the right to appeal a sentence under the Sentencing Reform Act when the defendant is sentenced following a plea of guilty. Both amendments track the language of Rule 32(a)(2), as amended by the Sentencing Reform Act.

Subdivision (d) is an amended version of Magistrates Rule 4. The amendments are technical in nature and no substantive change is intended.

Subdivision (e) consists of the first sentence of Magistrates Rule 5. The second sentence of that Rule was deleted as being inconsistent with 28 U.S.C. § 753(b) which gives the court discretion to decide how the proceedings will be recorded. The third sentence is deleted to preclude routine waivers of a verbatim record and to insure that all petty offenses are recorded.

Subdivision (f) replaces Magistrates Rule 6 and simply incorporates by reference Rule 33.

Subdivision (g) is an amended version of Magistrates Rule 7. Because the new rule may be used by both magistrates and judges, subdivision (g)(1) was added to make it clear that the Federal Rules of Appellate Procedure govern any appeal in a case tried by a district judge pursuant to the new rule. Subdivision (g)(2)(B), based upon Magistrates Rule 7(b), now provides for appeal of a sentence by a magistrate and is thus consistent with the provisions of 18 U.S.C. § 3742(f). Finally, subdivision (g)(3) is based upon Magistrates Rule 7(d) but has been amended to provide that a stay of execution is applicable, if an appeal is taken from a sentence as well as from a conviction. This change is consistent with the recent amendment of Rule 38 by the Sentencing Reform Act.

The new rule does not include Magistrates Rules 8 and 9. Rule 8 has been deleted because the subject of local rules is covered in Rule 57. Rule 9, which defined a petty offense, is now covered in 18 U.S.C. § 19.

1991 Amendment

The amendments are technical. No substantive changes are intended.

1993 Amendment

The Rule is amended to conform to the Judicial Improvements Act of 1990 [P.L. 101–650, Title III, Section 321] which provides that each United States magistrate appointed under section 631 of title 28, United States Code, shall be known as a United States magistrate judge.

1997 Amendment

The Federal Courts Improvement Act of 1996, Sec. 202, amended 18 U.S.C. § 3401(b) and 28 U.S.C. § 636(a) to remove the requirement that a defendant must consent to a trial before a magistrate judge in a petty offense that is a class B misdemeanor charging a motor vehicle offense, a class C misdemeanor, or an infraction. Section 202 also changed 18 U.S.C. § 3401(b) to provide that in all other misdemeanor cases, the defendant may consent to trial either orally on the record or in writing. The amendments to Rule 58(b)(2) and (3) conform the rule to the new statutory language and include minor stylistic changes.

2002 Amendments

The language of Rule 58 has been amended as part of the general restyling of the Criminal Rules to make them more easily understood and to make style and terminology consistent throughout the rules. These changes are intended to be stylistic only.

The title of the rule has been changed to "Petty Offenses and Other Misdemeanors." In Rule 58(c)(2)(B) (regarding waiver of venue), the Committee amended the rule to require that the "district clerk," instead of the magistrate judge, inform the original district clerk if the defendant waives venue and the prosecution proceeds in the district where the defendant was arrested. The Committee intends no change in practice.

In Rule 58(g)(1) and (g)(2)(A), the Committee deleted as unnecessary the word "decision" because its meaning is covered by existing references to an "order, judgment, or sentence" by a district judge or magistrate judge. In the Committee's view, deletion of that term does not amount to a substantive change.

2006 Amendments

Subdivision (b)(2)(G). Rule 58(b)(2)(G) sets out the advice to be given to defendants at an initial appearance on a misdemeanor charge, other than a petty offense. As currently written, the rule is restricted to those cases where the defendant is held in custody, thus creating a conflict and some confusion when compared to Rule 5.1(a) concerning the right to a preliminary hearing. Paragraph (G) is incomplete in its description of the circumstances requiring a preliminary hearing. In contrast, Rule 5.1(a) is a correct statement of the law concerning the defendant's entitlement to a preliminary hearing and is consistent with 18 U.S.C. § 3060 in this regard. Rather than attempting to define, or restate, in Rule 58 when a defendant may be entitled to a Rule 5.1 preliminary hearing, the rule is amended to direct the reader to Rule 5.1.

HISTORICAL NOTES

Change of Name

United States magistrate appointed under section 631 of Title 28, Judiciary and Judicial Procedure, to be known as United States magistrate judge after Dec. 1, 1990, with any reference to United States magistrate or magistrate in Title 28, in any other Federal statute, etc., deemed a reference to United States magistrate judge appointed under section 631 of Title 28, see section 321 of Pub.L. 101–650, set out as a note under section 631 of Title 28.

Rule 59. Matters Before a Magistrate Judge

(a) Nondispositive Matters. A district judge may refer to a magistrate judge for determination any matter that does not dispose of a charge or defense. The magistrate judge must promptly conduct the required proceedings and, when appropriate, enter on the record an oral or written order stating the determination. A party may serve and file objections to the order within 10 days after being served with a copy of a written order or after the oral order is stated on the record, or at some other time the court sets. The district judge must consider timely objections and modify or set aside any part of the order that is contrary to law or clearly erroneous. Failure to object in accordance with this rule waives a party's right to review.

(b) Dispositive Matters.

(1) Referral to Magistrate Judge. A district judge may refer to a magistrate judge for recommendation a defendant's motion to dismiss or quash an indictment or information, a motion to suppress evidence, or any matter that may dispose of a charge or defense. The magistrate judge must promptly conduct the required proceedings. A record must be made of any evidentiary proceeding and of any other proceeding if the magistrate judge considers it necessary. The magistrate judge must enter on the record a recommendation for disposing of the matter, including any proposed findings of fact. The clerk must immediately serve copies on all parties.

(2) Objections to Findings and Recommendations. Within 10 days after being served with a copy of the recommended disposition, or at some other time the court sets, a party may serve and file specific written objections to the proposed findings and recommendations. Unless the district judge directs otherwise, the objecting party must promptly arrange for transcribing the record, or whatever portions of it the parties agree to or the magistrate judge considers sufficient. Failure to object in accordance with this rule waives a party's right to review.

(3) De Novo Review of Recommendations. The district judge must consider de novo any objection to the magistrate judge's recommendation. The district judge may accept, reject, or modify the recommendation, receive further evidence, or resubmit the matter to the magistrate judge with instructions.

(Added Apr. 25, 2005, eff. Dec. 1, 2005.)

ADVISORY COMMITTEE NOTES

2002 Amendments

A former Rule 59, which dealt with the effective date of the Federal Rules of Criminal Procedure, was deleted.

2005 Adoption

Rule 59 is a new rule that creates a procedure for a district judge to review nondispositive and dispositive decisions by magistrate judges. The rule is derived in part from Federal Rule of Civil Procedure 72.

The Committee's consideration of a new rule on the subject of review of a magistrate judge's decisions resulted from *United States v. Abonce–Barrera,* 257 F.3d 959 (9th Cir. 2001). In that case the Ninth Circuit held that the Criminal Rules do not require appeals from nondispositive decisions by magistrate judges to district judges as a requirement for review by a court of appeals. The court suggested that Federal Rule of Civil Procedure 72 could serve as a suitable model for a criminal rule.

Rule 59(a) sets out procedures to be used in reviewing nondispositive matters, that is, those matters that do not dispose of the case. The rule requires that if the district judge has referred a matter to a magistrate judge, the magistrate judge must issue an oral or written order on the record. To preserve the issue for further review, a party must object to that order within 10 days after being served with a copy of the order or after the oral order is stated on the record or at some other time set by the court. If an objection is made, the district court is required to consider the objection. If the court determines that the magistrate judge's order, or a portion of the order, is contrary to law or is clearly erroneous, the court must set aside the order, or the affected part of the order. *See also* 28 U.S.C. § 636(b)(1)(A).

Rule 59(b) provides for assignment and review of recommendations made by magistrate judges on dispositive matters, including motions to suppress or quash an indictment or information. The rule directs the magistrate judge to consider the matter promptly, hold any necessary evidentiary hearings, and enter his or her recommendation on the record. After being served with a copy of the magistrate judge's recommendation, under Rule 59(b)(2), the parties have a period of 10 days to file any objections. If any objections are filed, the district court must consider the matter de novo and accept, reject, or modify the recommendation, or return the matter to the magistrate judge for further consideration.

Both Rule 59(a) and (b) contain a provision that explicitly states that failure to file an objection in accordance with the rule amounts to a waiver of the issue. This waiver provision is intended to establish the requirements for objecting in a district court in order to preserve appellate review of magistrate judges' decisions. In *Thomas v. Arn,* 474 U.S. 140, 155 (1985), the Supreme Court approved the adoption of waiver rules on matters for which a magistrate judge had made a decision or recommendation. The Committee believes that the waiver provisions will enhance the ability of a district court to review a magistrate judge's decision or recommendation by requiring a party to promptly file an objection to that part of the decision or recommendation at issue. Further, the Supreme Court has held that a de novo review of a magistrate judge's decision or recommendation is required to satisfy Article III concerns only where there is an objection. *Peretz v. United States,* 501 U.S. 293 (1991).

Despite the waiver provisions, the district judge retains the authority to review any magistrate judge's decision or recommendation whether or not objections are timely filed. This discretionary review is in accord with the Supreme Court's decision in *Thomas v. Arn, supra,* at 154. *See also Matthews v. Weber,* 423 U.S. 261, 270–271 (1976).

Although the rule distinguishes between "dispositive" and "nondispositive" matters, it does not attempt to define or otherwise catalog motions that may fall within either category. Instead, that task is left to the case law.

Rule 60. Title

These rules may be known and cited as the Federal Rules of Criminal Procedure.

(As amended Apr. 29, 2002, eff. Dec. 1, 2002.)

ADVISORY COMMITTEE NOTES

1944 Adoption

This rule is similar to Rule 85 of the Federal Rules of Civil Procedure, 28 U.S.C., Appendix, which reads as follows:

These rules may be known and cited as the Federal Rules of Civil Procedure.

2002 Amendments

No changes have been made to Rule 60, as a result of the general restyling of the Criminal Rules.

HISTORICAL NOTES

Short Title

1975 Amendments. Pub.L. 94–64, § 1, July 31, 1975, 89 Stat. 370, provided: "That this Act [amending rules 4, 9, 11, 12, 12.1, 12.2, 15, 16, 17, 20, 32 and 43 of these rules and enacting provisions set out as a note under rule 41 may be cited as the 'Federal Rules of Criminal Procedure Amendments Act of 1975'."

APPENDIX OF FORMS [ABROGATED]

HISTORICAL NOTES

Forms 1 to 25—Abrogated, Apr. 28, 1983, eff. Aug. 1, 1983. Forms 26 and 27—Abrogated, Dec. 4, 1967, eff. July 1, 1968.

Rule 58 and the Appendix of Forms are unnecessary and have been abrogated. Forms of indictment and information are made available to United States Attorneys' offices by the Department of Justice. Forms used by the courts are made available by the Director of the Administrative Office of the United States Courts.

RULES GOVERNING SECTION 2254 CASES IN THE UNITED STATES DISTRICT COURTS

Effective February 1, 1977
Amendments received to February 2, 2007

APPENDIX OF FORMS

ORDERS OF THE SUPREME COURT OF THE UNITED STATES ADOPTING AND AMENDING RULES GOVERNING SECTION 2254 PROCEEDINGS IN THE UNITED STATES DISTRICT COURTS

ORDER OF APRIL 26, 1976

1. That the rules and forms governing proceedings in the United States District Courts under Section 2254 and Section 2255 of Title 28, United States Code, as approved by the Judicial Conference of the United States be, and they hereby are, prescribed pursuant to Section 2072 of Title 28, United States Code and Sections 3771 and 3772 of Title 18, United States Code.

2. That the aforementioned rules and forms shall take effect August 1, 1976, and shall be applicable to all proceedings then pending except to the extent that in the opinion of the court their application in a particular proceeding would not be feasible or would work injustice.

3. That THE CHIEF JUSTICE be, and he hereby is, authorized to transmit the aforementioned rules and forms governing Section 2254 and Section 2255 proceedings to the Congress in accordance with the provisions of Section 2072 of Title 28 and Sections 3771 and 3772 of Title 18, United States Code.

CONGRESSIONAL ACTION ON PROPOSED RULES AND FORMS GOVERNING PROCEEDING UNDER 28 U.S.C. §§ 2254 AND 2255

Pub.L. 94–349, § 2, July 8, 1976, 90 Stat. 822, provided: "That, notwithstanding the provisions of section 2072 of title 28 of the United States Code, the rules and forms governing section 2254 cases in the United States district courts and the rules and forms governing section 2255 proceedings in the United States district courts which are embraced by the order entered by the United States Supreme Court on April 26, 1976, and which were transmitted to the Congress on or about April 26, 1976, shall not take effect until thirty days after the adjournment sine die of the 94th Congress, or until and to the extent approved by Act of Congress, whichever is earlier."

Pub.L. 94–426, § 1, Sept. 28, 1976, 90 Stat. 1334, provided: "That the rules governing section 2254 cases in the United States district courts and the rules governing section 2255 proceedings for the United States Supreme Court, which were delayed by the Act entitled 'An Act to delay the effective date of certain proposed amendments to the Federal Rules of Criminal Procedure and certain other rules promulgated by the United States Supreme Court' (Public Law 94–349), are approved with the amendments set forth in section 2 of this Act and shall take effect as so amended, with respect to petitions under section 2254 and motions under section 2255 of title 28 of the United States Code filed on or after February 1, 1977."

ORDER OF APRIL 30, 1979

1. That Rule 10 of the Rules Governing Proceedings in the United States District Courts on application under Section 2254 of Title 28, United States Code, be, and hereby is, amended to read as follows:

[See amendment made thereby under Rule 10, post.]

2. That Rules 10 and 11 of the Rules Governing Proceedings in the United States District Courts on a motion under Section 2255 of Title 28, United States Code, be, and they hereby are, amended to read as follows:

[See amendments made hereby under Rules 10 and 11 set out following section 2255.]

3. That the foregoing amendments to the Rules Governing Proceedings in the United States District Courts under Section 2254 and Section 2255 of Title 28, United States Code, shall take effect on August 1, 1979, and shall be applicable to all proceedings then pending except to the extent that in the opinion of the court their application in a particular proceeding would not be feasible or would work injustice.

4. That THE CHIEF JUSTICE be, and he hereby is, authorized to transmit the aforementioned amendments to the Rules Governing Section 2254 and Section 2255 Proceed-

ings to the Congress in accordance with the provisions of Section 2072 of Title 28, United States Code, and Sections 3771 and 3772 of Title 18, United States Code.

ORDER OF APRIL 28, 1982

1. That the rules and forms governing proceedings in the United States district courts under Section 2254 and Section 2255 of Title 28, United States Code, be, and they hereby are, amended by including therein an amendment to Rule 2(c) of the rules for Section 2254 cases, an amendment to Rule 2(b) of the rules for Section 2255 proceedings, and amendments to the model forms for use in applications under Section 2254 and motions under Section 2255, as hereinafter set forth:

[See amendments made thereby under respective rules and forms post and following section 2255.]

2. That the aforementioned amendments shall take effect August 1, 1982, and shall be applicable to all proceedings thereafter commenced and, insofar as just and practicable, all proceedings then pending.

3. That THE CHIEF JUSTICE be, and he hereby is, authorized to transmit the aforementioned amendments to the Congress in accordance with Section 2072 of Title 28 and Sections 3771 and 3772 of Title 18, United States Code.

ORDER OF APRIL 26, 2004

1. That the Federal Rules of Criminal Procedure be, and they hereby are, amended by including therein an amendment to Criminal Rule 35.

2. That the rules and forms governing cases in the United States District Courts under Section 2254 and Section 2255 of Title 28, United States Code, be, and they hereby are, amended by including therein amendments to Rules 1 through 11 of the Rules Governing Section 2254 Cases in the United States District Courts, Rules 1 through 12 of the Rules Governing Section 2255 Cases in the United States District Courts, and forms for use in applications under Section 2254 and motions under Section 2255.

[See amendments made thereby under respective rules, post.]

3. That the foregoing amendments to the Federal Rules of Criminal Procedure, the Rules Governing Section 2254 Cases in the United States District Courts, and the Rules Governing Section 2255 Cases in the United States District Courts shall take effect on December 1, 2004, and shall govern in all proceedings thereafter commenced and, insofar as just and practicable, all proceedings then pending.

4. That the CHIEF JUSTICE be, and hereby is, authorized to transmit to the Congress the foregoing amendments to the Federal Rules of Criminal Procedure, the Rules Governing Section 2254 Cases in the United States District Courts, and the Rules Governing Section 2255 Cases in the United States District Courts in accordance with the provisions of Section 2072 of Title 28, United States Code.

HISTORICAL NOTES

Effective Date of Rules; 1976 Act

Rules governing section 2254 cases, and the amendments thereto by Pub.L. 94–426, Sept. 28, 1976, 90 Stat. 1334, effective with respect to petitions under section 2254 of this title and motions under section 2255 of this title filed on or after Feb. 1, 1977, see section 1 of Pub.L. 94–426, set out as a note under section 2254 of this title.

Rule 1. Scope

(a) Cases Involving a Petition under 28 U.S.C. § 2254. These rules govern a petition for a writ of habeas corpus filed in a United States district court under 28 U.S.C. § 2254 by:

(1) a person in custody under a state-court judgment who seeks a determination that the custody violates the Constitution, laws, or treaties of the United States; and

(2) a person in custody under a state-court or federal-court judgment who seeks a determination that future custody under a state-court judgment would violate the Constitution, laws, or treaties of the United States.

(b) Other Cases. The district court may apply any or all of these rules to a habeas corpus petition not covered by Rule 1(a).

(As amended Apr. 26, 2004, eff. Dec. 1, 2004.)

ADVISORY COMMITTEE NOTES

1976 Adoption

Rule 1 provides that the habeas corpus rules are applicable to petitions by persons in custody pursuant to a judgment of a state court. See *Preiser v. Rodriguez,* 411 U.S. 475, 484 (1973). Whether the rules ought to apply to other situations (*e.g.,* person in active military service, *Glazier v. Hackel,* 440 F.2d 592 (9th Cir. 1971); or a reservist called to active duty but not reported, *Hammond v. Lenfest,* 398 F.2d 705 (2d Cir. 1968)) is left to the discretion of the court.

The basic scope of habeas corpus is prescribed by statute. 28 U.S.C. § 2241(c) provides that the "writ of habeas corpus shall not extend to a prisoner unless * * * (h)e is *in custody* in violation of the Constitution." 28 U.S.C. § 2254 deals specifically with state custody, providing that habeas corpus shall apply only "in behalf of a person in custody pursuant to a judgment of a state court * * *."

In *Preiser v. Rodriguez, supra,* the court said: "It is clear . . . that the essence of habeas corpus is an attack by a person in custody upon the legality of that custody, and that the traditional function of the writ is to secure release from illegal custody." 411 U.S. at 484.

Initially the Supreme Court held that habeas corpus was appropriate only in those situations in which petitioner's claim would, if upheld, result in an immediate release from a present custody. *McNally v. Hill,* 293 U.S. 131 (1934). This was changed in *Peyton v. Rowe,* 391 U.S. 54 (1968), in which the court held that habeas corpus was a proper way to attack a consecutive sentence to be served in the future, expressing the view that consecutive sentences resulted in present custody under both judgments, not merely the one imposing the first sentence. This view was expanded in *Carafas v. LaVallee,* 391 U.S. 234 (1968), to recognize the propriety of habeas corpus in a case in which petitioner was in custody when the petition had been originally filed but had since been unconditionally released from custody.

See also *Preiser v. Rodriguez,* 411 U.S. at 486 et seq.

Since *Carafas,* custody has been construed more liberally by the courts so as to make a § 2255 motion or habeas corpus petition proper in more situations. "In custody" now includes a person who is: on parole, *Jones v. Cunningham,* 371 U.S. 236 (1963); at large on his own recognizance but subject to several conditions pending execution of his sentence, *Hensley v. Municipal Court,* 411 U.S. 345 (1973); or released on bail after conviction pending final disposition of his case, *Lefkowitz v. Newsome,* 95 S.Ct. 886 (1975). See also *United States v. Re,* 372 F.2d 641 (2d Cir.), cert. denied, 388 U.S. 912 (1967) (on probation); *Walker v. North Carolina,* 262 F.Supp. 102 (W.D.N.C.1966), aff'd per curiam, 372 F.2d 129 (4th Cir.), cert. denied, 388 U.S. 917 (1967) (recipient of a conditionally suspended sentence); *Burris v. Ryan,* 397 F.2d 553 (7th Cir. 1968); *Marden v. Purdy,* 409 F.2d 784 (5th Cir. 1969) (free on bail); *United States ex rel. Smith v. Dibella,* 314 F.Supp. 446 (D.Conn.1970) (release on own recognizance); *Choung v. California,* 320 F.Supp. 625 (E.D.Cal.1970) (federal stay of state court sentence); *United States ex rel. Meadows v. New York,* 426 F.2d 1176 (2d Cir. 1970), cert. denied, 401 U.S. 941 (1971) (subject to parole detainer warrant); *Capler v. City of Greenville,* 422 F.2d 299 (5th Cir. 1970) (released on appeal bond); *Glover v. North Carolina,* 301 F.Supp. 364 (E.D.N.C.1969) (sentence served, but as convicted felon disqualified from engaging in several activities).

The courts are not unanimous in dealing with the above situations, and the boundaries of custody remain somewhat unclear. In *Morgan v. Thomas,* 321 F.Supp. 565 (S.D.Miss. 1970), the court noted:

> It is axiomatic that actual physical custody or restraint is not required to confer habeas jurisdiction. Rather, the term is synonymous with restraint of liberty. The real question is how much restraint of one's liberty is necessary before the right to apply for the writ comes into play. * * *
>
> It is clear however, that something more than moral restraint is necessary to make a case for habeas corpus.

321 F.Supp. at 573

Hammond v. Lenfest, 398 F.2d 705 (2d Cir. 1968), reviewed prior "custody" doctrine and reaffirmed a generalized flexible approach to the issue. In speaking about 28 U.S.C. § 2241, the first section in the habeas corpus statutes, the court said:

> While the language of the Act indicates that a writ of habeas corpus is appropriate only when a petitioner is "in custody" * * * the Act "does not attempt to mark the boundaries of 'custody' nor in any way other than by use of that word attempt to limit the situations in which the writ can be used." * * * And, recent Supreme Court decisions have made clear that "[i]t [habeas corpus] is not now and never has been a static, narrow, formalistic remedy; its scope has grown to achieve its grand purpose—the protection of individuals against erosion of their right to be free from wrongful restraints upon their liberty." * * * "[B]esides physical imprisonment, there are other restraints on a man's liberty, restraints not shared by the public generally, which have been thought sufficient in the English-speaking world to support the issuance of habeas corpus."

398 F.2d at 710–711

There is, as of now, no final list of the situations which are appropriate for habeas corpus relief. It is not the intent of these rules or notes to define or limit "custody."

It is, however, the view of the Advisory Committee that claims of improper conditions of custody or confinement (not related to the propriety of the custody itself), can better be handled by other means such as 42 U.S.C. § 1983 and other related statutes. In *Wilwording v. Swanson,* 404 U.S. 249 (1971), the court treated a habeas corpus petition by a state prisoner challenging the conditions of confinement as a claim for relief under 42 U.S.C. § 1983, the Civil Rights Act. Compare *Johnson v. Avery,* 393 U.S. 483 (1969).

The distinction between duration of confinement and conditions of confinement may be difficult to draw. Compare *Preiser v. Rodriguez,* 411 U.S. 475 (1973), with *Clutchette v. Procunier,* 497 F.2d 809 (9th Cir. 1974), modified, 510 F.2d 613 (1975).

2004 Amendments

The language of Rule 1 has been amended as part of general restyling of the rules to make them more easily understood and to make style and terminology consistent throughout the rules. These changes are intended to be stylistic and no substantive change is intended.

Rule 2. The Petition

(a) Current Custody; Naming the Respondent. If the petitioner is currently in custody under a state-court judgment, the petition must name as respondent the state officer who has custody.

(b) Future Custody; Naming the Respondents and Specifying the Judgment. If the petitioner is not yet in custody—but may be subject to future custody—under the state-court judgment being contested, the petition must name as respondents both the officer who has current custody and the attorney general of the state where the judgment was entered. The petition must ask for relief from the state-court judgment being contested.

(c) Form. The petition must:

(1) specify all the grounds for relief available to the petitioner;

(2) state the facts supporting each ground;

(3) state the relief requested;

(4) be printed, typewritten, or legibly handwritten; and

(5) be signed under penalty of perjury by the petitioner or by a person authorized to sign it for the petitioner under 28 U.S.C. § 2242.

(d) Standard Form. The petition must substantially follow either the form appended to these rules or a form prescribed by a local district-court rule. The clerk must make forms available to petitioners without charge.

(e) Separate Petitions for Judgments of Separate Courts. A petitioner who seeks relief from judgments of more than one state court must file a separate petition covering the judgment or judgments of each court.

(As amended Pub.L. 94–426, § 2(1), (2), Sept. 28, 1976, 90 Stat. 1334; Apr. 28, 1982, eff. Aug. 1, 1982; Apr. 26, 2004, eff. Dec. 1, 2004.)

ADVISORY COMMITTEE NOTES

1976 Adoption

Rule 2 describes the requirements of the actual petition, including matters relating to its form, contents, scope, and sufficiency. The rule provides more specific guidance for a petitioner and the court than 28 U.S.C. § 2242, after which it is patterned.

Subdivision (a) provides that an applicant challenging a state judgment, pursuant to which he is presently in custody, must make his application in the form of a petition for a writ of habeas corpus. It also requires that the state officer having custody of the applicant be named as respondent. This is consistent with 28 U.S.C. § 2242, which says in part, [Application for a writ of habeas corpus] shall allege * * * the name of the person who has custody over [the applicant] * * *." The proper person to be served in the usual case is either the warden of the institution in which the petitioner is incarcerated (*Sanders v. Bennett,* 148 F.2d 19 (D.C.Cir. 1945)) or the chief officer in charge of state penal institutions.

Subdivision (b) prescribes the procedure to be used for a petition challenging a judgment under which the petitioner will be subject to custody in the future. In this event the relief sought will usually not be released from present custody, but rather for a declaration that the judgment being attacked is invalid. Subdivision (b) thus provides for a prayer for "appropriate relief." It is also provided that the attorney general of the state of the judgment as well as the state officer having actual custody of the petitioner shall be named as respondents. This is appropriate because no one will have custody of the petitioner in the state of the judgment being attacked, and the habeas corpus action will usually be defended by the attorney general. The attorney general is in the best position to inform the court as to who the proper party respondent is. If it is not the attorney general, he can move for a substitution of party.

Since the concept of "custody" requisite to the consideration of a petition for habeas corpus has been enlarged significantly in recent years, it may be worthwhile to spell out the various situations which might arise and who should be named as respondent(s) for each situation.

(1) The applicant is in jail, prison, or other actual physical restraint due to the state action he is attacking. The named respondent shall be the state officer who has official custody of the petitioner (for example, the warden of the prison).

(2) The applicant is on probation or parole due to the state judgment he is attacking. The named respondents shall be the particular probation or parole officer responsible for supervising the applicant, and the official in charge of the parole or probation agency, or the state correctional agency, as appropriate.

(3) The applicant is in custody in any other manner differing from (1) and (2) above due to the effects of the state action he seeks relief from. The named respondent should be the attorney general of the state wherein such action was taken.

(4) The applicant is in jail, prison, or other actual physical restraint but is attacking a state action which will cause him to be kept in custody in the future rather than the government action under which he is presently confined. The named respondents shall be the state or federal officer who has official custody of him at the time the petition is filed and the attorney general of the state whose action subjects the petitioner to future custody.

(5) The applicant is in custody, although not physically restrained, and is attacking a state action which will result in his future custody rather than the government action out of which his present custody arises. The named respondent(s) shall be the attorney general of the state whose action subjects the petitioner to future custody, as well as the government officer who has present official custody of the petitioner if there is such an officer and his identity is ascertainable.

In any of the above situations the judge may require or allow the petitioner to join an additional or different party as a respondent if to do so would serve the ends of justice.

As seen in rule 1 and paragraphs (4) and (5) above, these rules contemplate that a petitioner currently in federal custody will be permitted to apply for habeas relief from a state restraint which is to go into effect in the future. There has been disagreement in the courts as to whether they have jurisdiction of the habeas application under these circumstances (compare *Piper v. United States,* 306 F.Supp. 1259 (D.Conn.1969), with *United States ex rel. Meadows v. New York,* 426 F.2d 1176 (2d Cir. 1970), cert. denied, 401 U.S. 941 (1971)). This rule seeks to make clear that they do have such jurisdiction.

Subdivision (c) provides that unless a district court requires otherwise by local rule, the petition must be in the form annexed to these rules. Having a standard prescribed form has several advantages. In the past, petitions have frequently contained mere conclusions of law, unsupported by any facts. Since it is the relationship of the facts to the claim asserted that is important, these petitions were obviously deficient. In addition, lengthy and often illegible petitions, arranged in no logical order, were submitted to judges who have had to spend hours deciphering them. For example, in *Passic v. Michigan,* 98 F.Supp. 1015, 1016 (E.D.Mich. 1951), the court dismissed a petition for habeas corpus, describing it as "two thousand pages of irrational, prolix and redundant pleadings * * *."

Administrative convenience, of benefit to both the court and the petitioner, results from the use of a prescribed form. Judge Hubert L. Will briefly described the experience with the use of a standard form in the Northern District of Illinois:

> Our own experience, though somewhat limited, has been quite satisfactory. * * *
>
> In addition, [petitions] almost always contain the necessary basic information * * *. Very rarely do we get the kind of hybrid federal-state habeas corpus petition with

civil rights allegations thrown in which were not uncommon in the past. * * * [W]hen a real constitutional issue is raised it is quickly apparent * * *.

33 F.R.D. 363, 384

Approximately 65 to 70% of all districts have adopted forms or local rules which require answers to essentially the same questions as contained in the standard form annexed to these rules. All courts using forms have indicated the petitions are time-saving and more legible. The form is particularly helpful in getting information about whether there has been an exhaustion of state remedies or, at least, where that information can be obtained.

The requirement of a standard form benefits the petitioner as well. His assertions are more readily apparent, and a meritorious claim is more likely to be properly raised and supported. The inclusion in the form of the ten most frequently raised grounds in habeas corpus petitions is intended to encourage the applicant to raise all his asserted grounds in one petition. It may better enable him to recognize if an issue he seeks to raise is cognizable under habeas corpus and hopefully inform him of those issues as to which he must first exhaust his state remedies.

Some commentators have suggested that the use of forms is of little help because the questions usually are too general, amounting to little more than a restatement of the statute. They contend the blanks permit a prisoner to fill in the same ambiguous answers he would have offered without the aid of a form. See Comment, Developments in the Law—Federal Habeas Corpus, 83 Harv.L.Rev. 1038, 1177–1178 (1970). Certainly, as long as the statute requires factual pleading, the adequacy of a petition will continue to be affected largely by the petitioner's intelligence and the legal advice available to him. On balance, however, the use of forms has contributed enough to warrant mandating their use.

Giving the petitioner a list of often—raised grounds may, it is said, encourage perjury. See Comment, Developments in the Law—Federal Habeas Corpus, 83 Harv.L.Rev. 1038, 1178 (1970). Most inmates are aware of, or have access to, some common constitutional grounds for relief. Thus, the risk of perjury is not likely to be substantially increased and the benefit of the list for some inmates seems sufficient to outweigh any slight risk that perjury will increase. There is a penalty for perjury, and this would seem the most appropriate way to try to discourage it.

Legal assistance is increasingly available to inmates either through paraprofessional programs involving law students or special programs staffed by members of the bar. See Jacob and Sharma, Justice After Trial: Prisoners' Need for Legal Services in the Criminal-Correctional Process, 18 Kan.L.Rev. 493 (1970). In these situations, the prescribed form can be filled out more competently, and it does serve to ensure a degree of uniformity in the manner in which habeas corpus claims are presented.

Subdivision (c) directs the clerk of the district court to make available to applicants upon request, without charge, blank petitions in the prescribed form.

Subdivision (c) also requires that all available grounds for relief be presented in the petition, including those grounds of which, by the exercise of reasonable diligence, the petitioner should be aware. This is reinforced by rule 9(b), which allows dismissal of a second petition which fails to allege new grounds or, if new grounds are alleged, the judge finds an inexcusable failure to assert the ground in the prior petition.

Both subdivision (c) and the annexed form require a legibly handwritten or typewritten petition. As required by 28 U.S.C. § 2242, the petition must be signed and sworn to by the petitioner (or someone acting in his behalf).

Subdivision (d) provides that a single petition may assert a claim only against the judgment or judgments of a single state court (*i.e.*, a court of the same county or judicial district or circuit). This permits, but does not require, an attack in a single petition on judgments based upon separate indictments or on separate counts even though sentences were imposed on separate days by the same court. A claim against a judgment of a court of a different political subdivision must be raised by means of a separate petition.

Subdivision (e) allows the clerk to return an insufficient petition to the petitioner, and it must be returned if the clerk is so directed by a judge of the court. Any failure to comply with the requirements of rule 2 or 3 is grounds for insufficiency. In situations where there may be arguable noncompliance with another rule, such as rule 9, the judge, not the clerk, must make the decision. If the petition is returned it must be accompanied by a statement of the reason for its return. No petitioner should be left to speculate as to why or in what manner his petition failed to conform to these rules.

Subdivision (e) also provides that the clerk shall retain one copy of the insufficient petition. If the prisoner files another petition, the clerk will be in a better position to determine the sufficiency of the new petition. If the new petition is insufficient, comparison with the prior petition may indicate whether the prisoner has failed to understand the clerk's prior explanation for its insufficiency, so that the clerk can make another, hopefully successful, attempt at transmitting this information to the petitioner. If the petitioner insists that the original petition was in compliance with the rules, a copy of the original petition is available for the consideration of the judge. It is probably better practice to make a photocopy of a petition which can be corrected by the petitioner, thus saving the petitioner the task of completing an additional copy.

1982 Amendment

Subdivision (c). The amendment takes into account 28 U.S.C. § 1746, enacted after adoption of the § 2254 rules. Section 1746 provides that in lieu of an affidavit an unsworn statement may be given under penalty of perjury in substantially the following form if executed within the United States, its territories, possessions or commonwealths: "I declare (or certify, verify, or state) under penalty of perjury that the foregoing is true and correct. Executed on (date). (Signature)." The statute is "intended to encompass prisoner litigation," and the statutory alternative is especially appropriate in such cases because a notary might not be readily available. *Carter v. Clark*, 616 F.2d 228 (5th Cir. 1980). The § 2254 forms have been revised accordingly.

2004 Amendments

The language of Rule 2 has been amended as part of general restyling of the rules to make them more easily understood and to make style and terminology consistent throughout the rules. These changes are intended to be stylistic and no substantive change is intended, except as described below.

Revised Rule 2(c)(5) has been amended by removing the requirement that the petition be signed personally by the petitioner. As reflected in 28 U.S.C. § 2242, an application for habeas corpus relief may be filed by the person who is seeking relief, or by someone acting on behalf of that person. *See, e.g., Whitmore v. Arkansas,* 495 U.S. 149 (1990) (discussion of requisites for "next friend" standing in petition for habeas corpus). Thus, under the, amended rule the petition may be signed by petitioner personally or by someone acting on behalf of the petitioner, assuming that the person is authorized to do so, for example, an attorney for the petitioner. The Committee envisions that the courts will apply third-party, or "next-friend," standing analysis in deciding whether the signer was actually authorized to sign the petition on behalf of the petitioner.

The language in new Rule 2(d) has been changed to reflect that a petitioner must substantially follow the standard form, which is appended to the rules, or a form provided by the court. The current rule, Rule 2(c), seems to indicate a preference for the standard "national" form. Under the amended rule, there is no stated preference. The Committee understood that current practice in some courts is that if the petitioner first files a petition using the national form, the courts may then ask the petitioner to supplement it with the local form.

Current Rule 2(e), which provided for returning an insufficient petition, has been deleted. The Committee believed that the approach in Federal Rule of Civil Procedure 5(e) was more appropriate for dealing with petitions that do not conform to the form requirements of the rule. That Rule provides that the clerk may not refuse to accept a filing solely for the reason that it fails to comply with these rules or local rules. Before the adoption of a one-year statute of limitations in the Antiterrorism and Effective Death Penalty Act of 1996, 110 Stat. 1214, the petitioner suffered no penalty, other than delay, if the petition was deemed insufficient. Now that a one-year statute of limitations applies to petitions filed under § 2254, *see* 28 U.S.C. § 2244(d)(1), the court's dismissal of a petition because it is not in proper form may pose a significant penalty for a petitioner, who may not be able to file another petition within the one-year limitations period. Now, under revised Rule 3(b), the clerk is required to file a petition, even though it may otherwise fail to comply with the provisions in revised Rule 2(c). The Committee believed that the better procedure was to accept the defective petition and require the petitioner to submit a corrected petition that conforms to Rule 2(c).

Rule 3. Filing the Petition; Inmate Filing

(a) Where to File; Copies; Filing Fee. An original and two copies of the petition must be filed with the clerk and must be accompanied by:

(1) the applicable filing fee, or

(2) a motion for leave to proceed in forma pauperis, the affidavit required by 28 U.S.C. § 1915, and a certificate from the warden or other appropriate officer of the place of confinement showing the amount of money or securities that the petitioner has in any account in the institution.

(b) Filing. The clerk must file the petition and enter it on the docket.

(c) Time to File. The time for filing a petition is governed by 28 U.S.C. § 2244(d).

(d) Inmate Filing. A paper filed by an inmate confined in an institution is timely if deposited in the institution's internal mailing system on or before the last day for filing. If an institution has a system designed for legal mail, the inmate must use that system to receive the benefit of this rule. Timely filing may be shown by a declaration in compliance with 28 U.S.C. § 1746 or by a notarized statement, either of which must set forth the date of deposit and state that first-class postage has been prepaid.

(As amended Apr. 26, 2004, eff. Dec. 1, 2004.)

ADVISORY COMMITTEE NOTES

1976 Adoption

Rule 3 sets out the procedures to be followed by the petitioner and the court in filing the petition. Some of its provisions are currently dealt with by local rule or practice, while others are innovations. Subdivision (a) specifies the petitioner's responsibilities. It requires that the petition, which must be accompanied by two conformed copies thereof, be filed in the office of the clerk of the district court. The petition must be accompanied by the filing fee prescribed by law (presently $5; see 28 U.S.C. § 1914(a)), unless leave to prosecute the petition in forma pauperis is applied for and granted. In the event the petitioner desires to prosecute the petition in forma pauperis, he must file the affidavit required by 28 U.S.C. § 1915, together with a certificate showing the amount of funds in his institutional account.

Requiring that the petition be filed in the office of the clerk of the district court provides an efficient and uniform system of filing habeas corpus petitions.

Subdivision (b) requires the clerk to file the petition. If the filing fee accompanies the petition, it may be filed immediately, and, if not, it is contemplated that prompt attention will be given to the request to proceed in forma pauperis. The court may delegate the issuance of the order to the clerk in those cases in which it is clear from the petition that there is full compliance with the requirements to proceed in forma pauperis.

Requiring the copies of the petition to be filed with the clerk will have an impact not only upon administrative matters, but upon more basic problems as well. In districts with more than one judge, a petitioner under present circumstances may send a petition to more than one judge. If no central filing system exists for each district, two judges may independently take different action on the same petition. Even if the action taken is consistent, there may be needless duplication of effort.

The requirement of an additional two copies of the form of the petition is a current practice in many courts. An efficient filing system requires one copy for use by the court (central file), one for the respondent (under 3(b), the respondent receives a copy of the petition whether an answer is required or not), and one for petitioner's counsel, if appointed. Since rule 2 provides that blank copies of the petition in the prescribed form are to be furnished to the applicant free of charge, there should be no undue burden created by this requirement.

Attached to copies of the petition supplied in accordance with rule 2 is an affidavit form for the use of petitioners desiring to proceed in forma pauperis. The form requires information concerning the petitioner's financial resources.

In forma pauperis cases, the petition must also be accompanied by a certificate indicating the amount of funds in the petitioner's institution account. Usually the certificate will be from the warden. If the petitioner is on probation or parole, the court might want to require a certificate from the supervising officer. Petitions by persons on probation or parole are not numerous enough, however, to justify making special provision for this situation in the text of the rule.

The certificate will verify the amount of funds credited to the petitioner in an institution account. The district court may by local rule require that any amount credited to the petitioner, in excess of a stated maximum, must be used for the payment of the filing fee. Since prosecuting an action in forma pauperis is a privilege (see *Smart v. Heinze,* 347 F.2d 114, 116 (9th Cir. 1965), it is not to be granted when the petitioner has sufficient resources.

Subdivision (b) details the clerk's duties with regard to filing the petition. If the petition does not appear on its face to comply with the requirements of rules 2 and 3, it may be returned in accordance with rule 2(e). If it appears to comply, it must be filed and entered on the docket in the clerk's office. However, under this subdivision the respondent is not required to answer or otherwise move with respect to the petition unless so ordered by the court.

2004 Amendments

The language of Rule 3 has been amended as part of general restyling of the rules to make them more easily understood and to make style and terminology consistent throughout the rules. These changes are intended to be stylistic and no substantive change is intended except as described below.

The last sentence of current Rule 3(b), dealing with an answer being filed by the respondent, has been moved to revised Rule 5(a).

Revised Rule 3(b) is new and is intended to parallel Federal Rule of Civil Procedure 5(e), which provides that the clerk may not refuse to accept a filing solely for the reason that it fails to comply with these rules or local rules. Before the adoption of a one-year statute of limitations in the Antiterrorism and Effective Death Penalty Act of 1996, 110 Stat. 1214, the petitioner suffered no penalty, other than delay, if the petition was deemed insufficient. That Act, however, added a one-year statute of limitations to petitions filed under § 2254, *see* 28 U.S.C. § 2244(d)(1). Thus, a court's dismissal of a defective petition may pose a significant penalty for a petitioner who may not be able to file a corrected petition within the one-year limitations period. The Committee believed that the better procedure was to accept the defective petition and require the petitioner to submit a corrected petition that conforms to Rule 2. Thus, revised Rule 3(b) requires the clerk to file a petition, even though it may otherwise fail to comply with Rule 2. The rule, however, is not limited to those instances where the petition is defective only in form; the clerk would also be required, for example, to file the petition even though it lacked the requisite filing fee or an *in forma pauperis* form.

Revised Rule 3(c), which sets out a specific reference to 28 U.S.C. § 2244(d), is new and has been added to put petitioners on notice that a one-year statute of limitations applies to petitions filed under these Rules. Although the rule does not address the issue, every circuit that has addressed the issue has taken the position that equitable tolling of the statute of limitations is available in appropriate circumstances. *See, e.g., Smith v. McGinnis,* 208 F.3d 13, 17–18 (2d Cir. 2000); *Miller v. New Jersey State Department of Corrections,* 145 F.3d 616, 618–19 (3d Cir. 1998); *Harris v. Hutchinson,* 209 F.3d 325, 330 (4th Cir. 2000). The Supreme Court has not addressed the question directly. *See Duncan v. Walker,* 533 U.S. 167, 181 (2001) ("We . . . have no occasion to address the question that Justice Stevens raises concerning the availability of equitable tolling.").

Rule 3(d) is new and provides guidance on determining whether a petition from an inmate is considered to have been filed in a timely fashion. The new provision parallels Federal Rule of Appellate Procedure 25(a)(2)(C).

Rule 4. Preliminary Review; Serving the Petition and Order

The clerk must promptly forward the petition to a judge under the court's assignment procedure, and the judge must promptly examine it. If it plainly appears from the petition and any attached exhibits that the petitioner is not entitled to relief in the district court, the judge must dismiss the petition and direct the clerk to notify the petitioner. If the petition is not dismissed, the judge must order the respondent to file an answer, motion, or other response within a fixed time, or to take other action the judge may order. In every case, the clerk must serve a copy of the petition and any order on the respondent and on the attorney general or other appropriate officer of the state involved.

(As amended Apr. 26, 2004, eff. Dec. 1, 2004.)

ADVISORY COMMITTEE NOTES

1976 Adoption

Rule 4 outlines the options available to the court after the petition is properly filed. The petition must be promptly presented to and examined by the judge to whom it is assigned. If it plainly appears from the face of the petition and any exhibits attached thereto that the petitioner is not entitled to relief in the district court, the judge must enter an order summarily dismissing the petition and cause the petitioner to be notified. If summary dismissal is not ordered, the judge must order the respondent to file an answer or to otherwise plead to the petition within a time period to be fixed in the order.

28 U.S.C. § 2243 requires that the writ shall be awarded, or an order to show cause issued, "unless it appears from the application that the applicant or person detained is not entitled thereto." Such consideration may properly encompass any exhibits attached to the petition, including, but not limited to, transcripts, sentencing records, and copies of state court opinions. The judge may order any of these items for

his consideration if they are not yet included with the petition. See 28 U.S.C. § 753(f) which authorizes payment for transcripts in habeas corpus cases.

It has been suggested that an answer should be required in every habeas proceeding, taking into account the usual petitioner's lack of legal expertise and the important functions served by the return. See Developments in the Law—Federal Habeas Corpus, 83 Harv.L.Rev. 1038, 1178 (1970). However, under § 2243 it is the duty of the court to screen out frivolous applications and eliminate the burden that would be placed on the respondent by ordering an unnecessary answer. *Allen v. Perini*, 424 F.2d 134, 141 (6th Cir. 1970). In addition, "notice" pleading is not sufficient, for the petition is expected to state facts that point to a "real possibility of constitutional error." See *Aubut v. State of Maine*, 431 F.2d 688, 689 (1st Cir. 1970).

In the event an answer is ordered under rule 4, the court is accorded greater flexibility than under § 2243 in determining within what time period an answer must be made. Under § 2243, the respondent must make a return within three days after being so ordered, with additional time of up to forty days allowed under the Federal Rules of Civil Procedure, Rule 81(a)(2), for good cause. In view of the widespread state of work overload in prosecutors' offices (see, *e.g., Allen*, 424 F.2d at 141), additional time is granted in some jurisdictions as a matter of course. Rule 4, which contains no fixed time requirement, gives the court the discretion to take into account various factors such as the respondent's workload and the availability of transcripts before determining a time within which an answer must be made.

Rule 4 authorizes the judge to "take such other action as the judge deems appropriate." This is designed to afford the judge flexibility in a case where either dismissal or an order to answer may be inappropriate. For example, the judge may want to authorize the respondent to make a motion to dismiss based upon information furnished by respondent, which may show that petitioner's claims have already been decided on the merits in a federal court; that petitioner has failed to exhaust state remedies; that the petitioner is not in custody within the meaning of 28 U.S.C. § 2254; or that a decision in the matter is pending in state court. In these situations, a dismissal may be called for on procedural grounds, which may avoid burdening the respondent with the necessity of filing an answer on the substantive merits of the petition. In other situations, the judge may want to consider a motion from respondent to make the petition more certain. Or the judge may want to dismiss some allegations in the petition, requiring the respondent to answer only those claims which appear to have some arguable merit.

Rule 4 requires that a copy of the petition and any order be served by certified mail on the respondent and the attorney general of the state involved. See 28 U.S.C. § 2252. Presently, the respondent often does not receive a copy of the petition unless the court directs an answer under 28 U.S.C. § 2243. Although the attorney general is served, he is not required to answer if it is more appropriate for some other agency to do so. Although the rule does not specifically so provide, it is assumed that copies of the court orders to respondent will be mailed to petitioner by the court.

2004 Amendments

The language of Rule 4 has been amended as part of general restyling of the rules to make them more easily understood and to make style and terminology consistent throughout the rules. These changes are intended to be stylistic and no substantive change is intended, except as described below.

The amended rule reflects that the response to a habeas petition may be a motion.

The requirement that in every case the clerk must serve a copy of the petition on the respondent by certified mail has been deleted. In addition, the current requirement that the petition be sent to the Attorney General of the state has been modified to reflect practice in some jurisdictions that the appropriate state official may be someone other than the Attorney General, for example, the officer in charge of a local confinement facility. This comports with a similar provision in 28 U.S.C. § 2252, which addresses notice of habeas corpus proceedings to the state's attorney general or other appropriate officer of the state.

Rule 5. The Answer and the Reply

(a) When Required. The respondent is not required to answer the petition unless a judge so orders.

(b) Contents: Addressing the Allegations; Stating a Bar. The answer must address the allegations in the petition. In addition, it must state whether any claim in the petition is barred by a failure to exhaust state remedies, a procedural bar, non-retroactivity, or a statute of limitations.

(c) Contents: Transcripts. The answer must also indicate what transcripts (of pretrial, trial, sentencing, or post-conviction proceedings) are available, when they can be furnished, and what proceedings have been recorded but not transcribed. The respondent must attach to the answer parts of the transcript that the respondent considers relevant. The judge may order that the respondent furnish other parts of existing transcripts or that parts of untranscribed recordings be transcribed and furnished. If a transcript cannot be obtained, the respondent may submit a narrative summary of the evidence.

(d) Contents: Briefs on Appeal and Opinions. The respondent must also file with the answer a copy of:

(1) any brief that the petitioner submitted in an appellate court contesting the conviction or sentence, or contesting an adverse judgment or order in a post-conviction proceeding;

(2) any brief that the prosecution submitted in an appellate court relating to the conviction or sentence; and

(3) the opinions and dispositive orders of the appellate court relating to the conviction or the sentence.

(e) Reply. The petitioner may submit a reply to the respondent's answer or other pleading within a time fixed by the judge.

(As amended Apr. 26, 2004, eff. Dec. 1, 2004.)

ADVISORY COMMITTEE NOTES

1976 Adoption

Rule 5 details the contents of the "answer". (This is a change in terminology from "return," which is still used below when referring to prior practice.) The answer plays an obviously important role in a habeas proceeding:

> The return serves several important functions: it permits the court and the parties to uncover quickly the disputed issues; it may reveal to the petitioner's attorney grounds for release that the petitioner did not know; and it may demonstrate that the petitioner's claim is wholly without merit.
>
> Developments in the Law—Federal Habeas Corpus, 83 Harv.L.Rev. 1083, 1178 (1970).

The answer must respond to the allegations of the petition. While some districts require this by local rule (see, *e.g.*, E.D.N.C.R. 17(B)), under 28 U.S.C. § 2243 little specificity is demanded. As a result, courts occasionally receive answers which contain only a statement certifying the true cause of detention, or a series of delaying motions such as motions to dismiss. The requirement of the proposed rule that the "answer shall respond to the allegations of the petition" is intended to ensure that a responsive pleading will be filed and thus the functions of the answer fully served.

The answer must also state whether the petitioner has exhausted his state remedies. This is a prerequisite to eligibility for the writ under 28 U.S.C. § 2254(b) and applies to every ground the petitioner raises. Most form petitions now in use contain questions requiring information relevant to whether the petitioner has exhausted his remedies. However, the exhaustion requirement is often not understood by the unrepresented petitioner. The attorney general has both the legal expertise and access to the record and thus is in a much better position to inform the court on the matter of exhaustion of state remedies. An alleged failure to exhaust state remedies as to any ground in the petition may be raised by a motion by the attorney general, thus avoiding the necessity of a formal answer as to that ground.

The rule requires the answer to indicate what transcripts are available, when they can be furnished, and also what proceedings have been recorded and not transcribed. This will serve to inform the court and petitioner as to what factual allegations can be checked against the actual transcripts. The transcripts include pretrial transcripts relating, for example, to pretrial motions to suppress; transcripts of the trial or guilty plea proceeding; and transcripts of any post-conviction proceedings which may have taken place. The respondent is required to furnish those portions of the transcripts which he believes relevant. The court may order the furnishing of additional portions of the transcripts upon the request of petitioner or upon the court's own motion.

Where transcripts are unavailable, the rule provides that a narrative summary of the evidence may be submitted.

Rule 5 (and the general procedure set up by this entire set of rules) does not contemplate a traverse to the answer, except under special circumstances. See advisory committee note to rule 9. Therefore, the old common law assumption of verity of the allegations of a return until impeached, as codified in 28 U.S.C. § 2248, is no longer applicable. The meaning of the section, with its exception to the assumption "to the extent that the judge finds from the evidence that they (the allegations) are not true," has given attorneys and courts a great deal of difficulty. It seems that when the petition and return pose an issue of fact, no traverse is required; *Stewart v. Overholser*, 186 F.2d 339 (D.C.Cir. 1950).

> We read § 2248 of the Judicial Code as not requiring a traverse when a factual issue has been clearly framed by the petition and the return or answer. This section provides that the allegations of a return or answer to an order to show cause shall be accepted as true if not traversed, except to the extent the judge finds from the evidence that they are not true. This contemplates that where the petition and return or answer do present an issue of fact material to the legality of detention, evidence is required to resolve that issue despite the absence of a traverse. This reference to evidence assumes a hearing on issues raised by the allegations of the petition and the return or answer to the order to show cause.
>
> **186 F.2d at 342, n. 5**

In actual practice, the traverse tends to be a mere pro forma refutation of the return, serving little if any expository function. In the interests of a more streamlined and manageable habeas corpus procedure, it is not required except in those instances where it will serve a truly useful purpose. Also, under rule 11 the court is given the discretion to incorporate Federal Rules of Civil Procedure when appropriate, so civil rule 15(a) may be used to allow the petitioner to amend his petition when the court feels this is called for by the contents of the answer.

Rule 5 does not indicate who the answer is to be served upon, but it necessarily implies that it will be mailed to the petitioner (or to his attorney if he has one). The number of copies of the answer required is left to the court's discretion. Although the rule requires only a copy of petitioner's brief on appeal, respondent is free also to file a copy of respondent's brief. In practice, courts have found it helpful to have a copy of respondent's brief.

2004 Amendments

The language of Rule 5 has been amended as part of general restyling of the rules to make them more easily understood and to make style and terminology consistent throughout the rules. These changes are intended to be stylistic and no substantive change is intended, except as described below.

Revised Rule 5(a), which provides that the respondent is not required to file an answer to the petition, unless a judge so orders, is taken from current Rule 3(b). The revised rule does not address the practice in some districts, where the respondent files a pre-answer motion to dismiss the petition. But revised Rule 4 permits that practice and reflects the view that if the court does not dismiss the petition, it may require (or permit) the respondent to file a motion.

Rule 5(b) has been amended to require that the answer address not only failure to exhaust state remedies, but also procedural bars, non-retroactivity, and any statute of limitations. Although the latter three matters are not addressed in the current rule, the Committee intends no substantive change with the additional new language. *See, e.g.,* 28 U.S.C. § 2254(b)(3). Instead, the Committee believes that the explicit mention of those issues in the rule conforms to current case law and statutory provisions. *See, e.g.,* 28 U.S.C. § 2244(d)(1).

Revised Rule 5(d) includes new material. First, Rule 5(d)(2), requires a respondent—assuming an answer is filed—to provide the court with a copy of any brief submitted by the prosecution to the appellate court. And Rule 5(d)(3) now provides that the respondent also file copies of any opinions and dispositive orders of the appellate court concerning the conviction or sentence. These provisions are intended to ensure that the court is provided with additional information that may assist it in resolving the issues raised, or not raised, in the petition.

Finally, revised Rule 5(e) adopts the practice in some jurisdictions of giving the petitioner an opportunity to file a reply to the respondent's answer. Rather than using terms such as "traverse," *see* 28 U.S.C. § 2248, to identify the petitioner's response to the answer, the rule uses the more general term "reply." The Rule prescribes that the court set the time for such responses and in lieu of setting specific time limits in each case, the court may decide to include such time limits in its local rules.

Rule 6. Discovery

(a) Leave of Court Required. A judge may, for good cause, authorize a party to conduct discovery under the Federal Rules of Civil Procedure and may limit the extent of discovery. If necessary for effective discovery, the judge must appoint an attorney for a petitioner who qualifies to have counsel appointed under 18 U.S.C. § 3006A.

(b) Requesting Discovery. A party requesting discovery must provide reasons for the request. The request must also include any proposed interrogatories and requests for admission, and must specify any requested documents.

(c) Deposition Expenses. If the respondent is granted leave to take a deposition, the judge may require the respondent to pay the travel expenses, subsistence expenses, and fees of the petitioner's attorney to attend the deposition.

(As amended Apr. 26, 2004, eff. Dec. 1, 2004.)

ADVISORY COMMITTEE NOTES

1976 Adoption

This rule prescribes the procedures governing discovery in habeas corpus cases. Subdivision (a) provides that any party may utilize the processes of discovery available under the Federal Rules of Civil Procedure (rules 26–37) if, and to the extent that, the judge allows. It also provides for the appointment of counsel for a petitioner who qualifies for this when counsel is necessary for effective utilization of discovery procedures permitted by the judge.

Subdivision (a) is consistent with *Harris v. Nelson,* 394 U.S. 286 (1969). In that case the court noted,

> [I]t is clear that there was no intention to extend to habeas corpus, as a matter of right, the broad discovery provisions * * * of the new [Federal Rules of Civil Procedure].

394 U.S. at 295

However, citing the lack of methods for securing information in habeas proceedings, the court pointed to an alternative.

> Clearly, in these circumstances * * * the courts may fashion appropriate modes of procedure, by analogy to existing rules or otherwise in conformity with judicial usage. * * * Their authority is expressly confirmed in the All Writs Act, 28 U.S.C. § 1651.

394 U.S. at 299

The court concluded that the issue of discovery in habeas corpus cases could best be dealt with as part of an effort to provide general rules of practice for habeas corpus cases:

> In fact, it is our view that the rulemaking machinery should be invoked to formulate rules of practice with respect to federal habeas corpus and § 2255 proceedings, on a comprehensive basis and not merely one confined to discovery. The problems presented by these proceedings are materially different from those dealt with in the Federal Rules of Civil Procedure and the Federal Rules of Criminal Procedure, and reliance upon usage and the opaque language of Civil Rule 81(a)(2) is transparently inadequate. In our view the results of a meticulous formulation and adoption of special rules for federal habeas corpus and § 2255 proceedings would promise much benefit.

394 U.S. at 301 n. 7

Discovery may, in appropriate cases, aid in developing facts necessary to decide whether to order an evidentiary hearing or to grant the writ following an evidentiary hearing:

> We are award that confinement sometimes induces fantasy which has its basis in the paranoia of prison rather than in fact. But where specific allegations before the court show reason to believe that the petitioner may, if the facts are fully developed, be able to demonstrate that he is confined illegally and is therefore entitled to relief, it is the duty of the court to provide the necessary facilities and procedures for an adequate inquiry. Obviously, in exercising this power, the court may utilize familiar procedures, as appropriate, whether these are found in the civil or criminal rules or elsewhere in the "usages and principles."

Granting discovery is left to the discretion of the court, discretion to be exercised where there is a showing of good cause why discovery should be allowed. Several commentators have suggested that at least some discovery should be permitted without leave of court. It is argued that the courts will be burdened with weighing the propriety of requests to which the discovered party has no objection. Additionally, the availability of protective orders under Fed. R.Civ.R., Rules 30(b) and 31(d) will provide the necessary safeguards. See Developments in the Law—Federal Habeas Corpus, 83 Harv.L.Rev. 1038, 1186–87 (1970); Civil Discovery in Habeas Corpus, 67 Colum.L.Rev. 1296, 1310 (1967).

Nonetheless, it is felt the requirement of prior court approval of all discovery is necessary to prevent abuse, so this requirement is specifically mandated in the rule.

While requests for discovery in habeas proceedings normally follow the granting of an evidentiary hearing, there may be instances in which discovery would be appropriate beforehand. Such an approach was advocated in *Wagner v. United States*, 418 F.2d 618, 621 (9th Cir.1969), where the opinion stated the trial court could permit interrogatories, provide for deposing witnesses, "and take such other prehearing steps as may be appropriate." While this was an action under § 2255, the reasoning would apply equally well to petitions by state prisoners. Such pre-hearing discovery may show an evidentiary hearing to be unnecessary, as when there are "no disputed issues of law or fact." 83 Harv.L.Rev. 1038, 1181 (1970). The court in Harris alluded to such a possibility when it said "the court may * * * authorize such proceedings with respect to development, *before or in conjunction with the hearing* of the facts * * *." [emphasis added] 394 U.S. at 300. Such pre-hearing discovery, like all discovery under rule 6, requires leave of court. In addition, the provisions in rule 7 for the use of an expanded record may eliminate much of the need for this type of discovery. While probably not as frequently sought or granted as discovery in conjunction with a hearing, it may nonetheless serve a valuable function.

In order to make pre-hearing discovery meaningful, subdivision (a) provides that the judge should appoint counsel for a petitioner who is without counsel and qualifies for appointment when this is necessary for the proper utilization of discovery procedures. Rule 8 provides for the appointment of counsel at the evidentiary hearing stage (see rule 8(b) and advisory committee note), but this would not assist the petitioner who seeks to utilize discovery to stave off dismissal of his petition (see rule 9 and advisory committee note) or to demonstrate that an evidentiary hearing is necessary. Thus, if the judge grants a petitioner's request for discovery prior to making a decision as to the necessity for an evidentiary hearing, he should determine whether counsel is necessary for the effective utilization of such discovery and, if so, appoint counsel for the petitioner if the petitioner qualifies for such appointment.

This rule contains very little specificity as to what types and methods of discovery should be made available to the parties in a habeas proceeding, or how, once made available, these discovery procedures should be administered. The purpose of this rule is to get some experience in how discovery would work in actual practice by letting district court judges fashion their own rules in the context of individual cases. When the results of such experience are available it would be desirable to consider whether further, more specific codification should take place.

Subdivision (b) provides for judicial consideration of all matters subject to discovery. A statement of the interrogatories, or requests for admission sought to be answered, and a list of any documents sought to be produced, must accompany a request for discovery. This is to advise the judge of the necessity for discovery and enable him to make certain that the inquiry is relevant and appropriately narrow.

Subdivision (c) refers to the situation where the respondent is granted leave to take the deposition of the petitioner or any other person. In such a case the judge may direct the respondent to pay the expenses and fees of counsel for the petitioner to attend the taking of the deposition, as a condition granting the respondent such leave. While the judge is not required to impose this condition subdivision (c) will give the court the means to do so. Such a provision affords some protection to the indigent petitioner who may be prejudiced by his inability to have counsel, often court-appointed, present at the taking of a deposition. It is recognized that under 18 U.S.C. § 3006A(g), court-appointed counsel in a § 2254 proceeding is entitled to receive up to $250 and reimbursement for expenses reasonably incurred. (Compare Fed.R.Crim.P. 15(c).) Typically, however, this does not adequately reimburse counsel if he must attend the taking of depositions or be involved in other pre-hearing proceedings. Subdivision (c) is intended to provide additional funds, if necessary, to be paid by the state government (respondent) to petitioner's counsel.

Although the rule does not specifically so provide, it is assumed that a petitioner who qualifies for the appointment of counsel under 18 U.S.C. § 3006A(g) and is granted leave to take a deposition will be allowed witness costs. This will include recording and transcription of the witness's statement. Such costs are payable pursuant to 28 U.S.C. § 1825. See Opinion of Comptroller General, February 28, 1974.

Subdivision (c) specifically recognizes the right of the respondent to take the deposition of the petitioner. Although the petitioner could not be called to testify against his will in a criminal trial, it is felt the nature of the habeas proceeding, along with the safeguards accorded by the Fifth Amendment and the presence of counsel, justify this provision. See 83 Harv.L.Rev. 1038, 1183–84 (1970).

2004 Amendments

The language of Rule 6 has been amended as part of general restyling of the rules to make them more easily understood and to make style and terminology consistent throughout the rules. These changes are intended to be stylistic and no substantive change is intended.

Although current Rule 6(b) contains no requirement that the parties provide reasons for the requested discovery, the revised rule does so and also includes a requirement that the request be accompanied by any proposed interrogatories and requests for admission, and must specify any requested documents. The Committee believes that the revised rule makes explicit what has been implicit in current practice.

Rule 7. Expanding the Record

(a) In General. If the petition is not dismissed, the judge may direct the parties to expand the record by submitting additional materials relating to the petition. The judge may require that these materials be authenticated.

(b) Types of Materials. The materials that may be required include letters predating the filing of the petition, documents, exhibits, and answers under oath to written interrogatories propounded by the judge. Affidavits may also be submitted and considered as part of the record.

(c) Review by the Opposing Party. The judge must give the party against whom the additional materials are offered an opportunity to admit or deny their correctness.

(As amended Apr. 26, 2004, eff. Dec. 1, 2004.)

ADVISORY COMMITTEE NOTES

1976 Adoption

This rule provides that the judge may direct that the record be expanded. The purpose is to enable the judge to dispose of some habeas petitions not dismissed on the pleadings, without the time and expense required for an evidentiary hearing. An expanded record may also be helpful when an evidentiary hearing is ordered.

The record may be expanded to include additional material relevant to the merits of the petition. While most petitions are dismissed either summarily or after a response has been made, of those that remain, by far the majority require an evidentiary hearing. In the fiscal year ending June 30, 1970, for example, of 8,423 § 2254 cases terminated, 8,231 required court action. Of these, 7,812 were dismissed before a prehearing conference and 469 merited further court action (*e.g.*, expansion of the record, prehearing conference, or an evidentiary hearing). Of the remaining 469 cases, 403 required an evidentiary hearing, often time-consuming, costly, and, at least occasionally, unnecessary. See Director of the Administrative Office of the United States Courts, Annual Report, 245a–245c (table C4) (1970). In some instances these hearings were necessitated by slight omissions in the state record which might have been cured by the use of an expanded record.

Authorizing expansion of the record will, hopefully, eliminate some unnecessary hearings. The value of this approach was articulated in *Raines v. United States*, 423 F.2d 526, 529–530 (4th Cir. 1970):

> Unless it is clear from the pleadings and the files and records that the prisoner is entitled to no relief, the statute makes a hearing mandatory. We think there is a permissible intermediate step that may avoid the necessity for an expensive and time consuming evidentiary hearing in every Section 2255 case. It may instead be perfectly appropriate, depending upon the nature of the allegations, for the district court to proceed by requiring that the record be expanded to include letters, documentary evidence, and, in an appropriate case, even affidavits. *United States v. Carlino,* 400 F.2d 56 (2nd Cir. 1968); *Mirra v. United States,* 379 F.2d 782 (2nd Cir. 1967); *Accardi v. United States,* 379 F.2d 312 (2nd Cir. 1967). When the issue is one of credibility, resolution on the basis of affidavits can rarely be conclusive, but that is not to say they may not be helpful.

In *Harris v. Nelson,* 394 U.S. 286, 300 (1969), the court said:

> At any time in the proceedings * * * *either on [the court's] own motion* or upon cause shown by the petitioner, it may issue such writs and take or authorize such proceedings * * * *before* or in conjunction with the hearing of the facts * * *. [emphasis added]

Subdivision (b) specifies the materials which may be added to the record. These include, without limitation, letters predating the filing of the petition in the district court, documents, exhibits, and answers under oath directed to written interrogatories propounded by the judge. Under this subdivision affidavits may be submitted and considered part of the record. Subdivision (b) is consistent with 28 U.S.C. §§ 2246 and 2247 and the decision in *Raines* with regard to types of material that may be considered upon application for a writ of habeas corpus. See *United States v. Carlino,* 400 F.2d 56, 58 (2d Cir. 1968), and *Machibroda v. United States,* 368 U.S. 487 (1962).

Under subdivision (c) all materials proposed to be included in the record must be submitted to the party against whom they are to be offered.

Under subdivision (d) the judge can require authentication if he believes it desirable to do so.

2004 Amendments

The language of Rule 7 has been amended as part of general restyling of the rules to make them more easily understood and to make style and terminology consistent throughout the rules. These changes are intended to be stylistic and no substantive change is intended, except as noted below.

Revised Rule 7(a) is not intended to restrict the court's authority to expand the record through means other than requiring the parties themselves to provide the information. Further, the rule has been changed to remove the reference to the "merits" of the petition in the recognition that a court may wish to expand the record in order to assist it in deciding an issue other than the merits of the petition.

The language in current Rule 7(d), which deals with authentication of materials in the expanded record, has been moved to revised Rule 7(a).

Rule 8. Evidentiary Hearing

(a) Determining Whether to Hold a Hearing. If the petition is not dismissed, the judge must review the answer, any transcripts and records of state-court proceedings, and any materials submitted under Rule 7 to determine whether an evidentiary hearing is warranted.

(b) Reference to a Magistrate Judge. A judge may, under 28 U.S.C. § 636(b), refer the petition to a magistrate judge to conduct hearings and to file proposed findings of fact and recommendations for disposition. When they are filed, the clerk must promptly serve copies of the proposed findings and recommendations on all parties. Within 10 days after being served, a party may file objections as provided by local court rule. The judge must determine *de novo* any proposed finding or recommendation to which objection is made. The judge may accept, reject, or modify any proposed finding or recommendation.

(c) Appointing Counsel; Time of Hearing. If an evidentiary hearing is warranted, the judge must appoint an attorney to represent a petitioner who qualifies to have counsel appointed under 18 U.S.C. § 3006A. The judge must conduct the hearing as soon as practicable after giving the attorneys adequate time to investigate and prepare. These rules do not limit the appointment of counsel under § 3006A at any stage of the proceeding.

(As amended Pub.L. 94–426, § 2(5), Sept. 28, 1976, 90 Stat. 1334; Pub.L. 94–577, § 2(a)(1), (b)(1), Oct. 21, 1976, 90 Stat. 2730, 2731; Apr. 26, 2004, eff. Dec. 1, 2004.)

ADVISORY COMMITTEE NOTES

1976 Adoption

This rule outlines the procedure to be followed by the court immediately prior to and after the determination of whether to hold an evidentiary hearing.

The provisions are applicable if the petition has not been dismissed at a previous stage in the proceeding [including a summary dismissal under Rule 4; a dismissal pursuant to a motion by the respondent; a dismissal after the answer and petition are considered; or a dismissal after consideration of the pleadings and an expanded record].

If dismissal has not been ordered, the court must determine whether an evidentiary hearing is required. This determination is to be made upon a review of the answer, the transcript and record of state court proceedings, and if there is one, the expanded record. As the United States Supreme Court noted in *Townsend v. Sam,* 372 U.S. 293, 319 (1963):

> Ordinarily [the complete state-court] record—including the transcript of testimony (or if unavailable some adequate substitute, such as a narrative record), the pleadings, court opinions, and other pertinent documents—is indispensable to determining whether the habeas applicant received a full and fair state-court evidentiary hearing resulting in reliable findings.

Subdivision (a) contemplates that all of these materials, if available, will be taken into account. This is especially important in view of the standard set down in *Townsend* for determining *when* a hearing in the federal habeas proceeding is mandatory.

> The appropriate standard * * * is this: Where the facts are in dispute, the federal court in habeas corpus must hold an evidentiary hearing if the habeas applicant did not receive a full and fair evidentiary hearing in a state court, either at the time of the trial or in a collateral proceeding.

372 U.S. at 312

The circumstances under with a federal hearing is mandatory are now specified in 28 U.S.C. § 2254(d). The 1966 amendment clearly places the burden on the petitioner, when there has already been a state hearing, to show that it was not a fair or adequate hearing for one or more of the specifically enumerated reasons, in order to force a federal evidentiary hearing. Since the function of an evidentiary hearing is to try issues of fact (372 U.S. at 309), such a hearing is unnecessary when only issues of law are raised. See, *e.g., Yeaman v. United States,* 326 F.2d 293 (9th Cir. 1963).

In situations in which an evidentiary hearing is not mandatory, the judge may nonetheless decide that an evidentiary hearing is desirable:

> The purpose of the test is to indicate the situations in which the holding of an evidentiary hearing is mandatory. In all other cases where the material facts are in dispute, the holding of such a hearing is in the discretion of the district judge.

372 U.S. at 318

If the judge decides that an evidentiary hearing is neither required nor desirable, he shall make such a disposition of the petition "as justice shall require." Most habeas petitions are dismissed before the prehearing conference stage (see Director of the Administrative Office of the United States Courts, Annual Report 245–245c (table C4) (1970)) and of those not dismissed, the majority raise factual issues that necessitate an evidentiary hearing. If no hearing is required, most petitions are dismissed, but in unusual cases the court may grant the relief sought without a hearing. This includes immediate release from custody or nullification of a judgment under which the sentence is to be served in the future.

Subdivision (b) provides that a magistrate, when so empowered by rule of the district court, may recommend to the district judge that an evidentiary hearing be held or that the petition be dismissed, provided he gives the district judge a sufficiently detailed description of the facts so that the judge may decide whether or not to hold an evidentiary hearing. This provision is not inconsistent with the holding in *Wingo v. Wedding,* 418 U.S. 461 (1974), that the Federal Magistrates Act did not change the requirement of the habeas corpus statute that federal judges personally conduct habeas evidentiary hearings, and that consequently a local district court rule was invalid insofar as it authorized a magistrate to hold such hearings. 28 U.S.C. § 636(b) provides that a district court may by rule authorize any magistrate to perform certain additional duties, including preliminary review of applications for posttrial relief made by individuals convicted of criminal offenses, and submission of a report and recommendations to facilitate the decision of the district judge having jurisdiction over the case as to whether there should be a hearing.

As noted in *Wingo,* review "by Magistrates of applications for post-trial relief is thus limited to review for the purpose of proposing, not holding, evidentiary hearings."

Utilization of the magistrate as specified in subdivision (b) will aid in the expeditious and fair handling of habeas petitions.

> A qualified, experienced magistrate will, it is hoped, acquire an expertise in examining these [postconviction review] applications and summarizing their important contents for the district judge, thereby facilitating his decisions. Law clerks are presently charged with this responsibility by many judges, but judges have noted that the normal 1-year clerkship does not afford law clerks the time or experience necessary to attain real efficiency in handling such applications.

S.Rep. No. 371, 90th Cong., 1st Sess., 26 (1967).

Under subdivision (c) there are two provisions that differ from the procedure set forth in 28 U.S.C. § 2243. These are the appointment of counsel and standard for determining how soon the hearing will be held.

If an evidentiary hearing is required the judge must appoint counsel for a petitioner who qualified [sic] for appointment under the Criminal Justice Act. Currently, the appointment of counsel is not recognized as a right at any stage of a habeas proceeding. See, *e.g., United States ex rel. Marshall v. Wilkins,* 338 F.2d 404 (2d Cir. 1964). Some district courts have, however, by local rule, required that counsel must be provided for indigent petitioners in cases requiring a hearing. See, *e.g., D.N.M.R. 21(f), E.D.N.Y.R. 26(d).* Appointment of counsel at this stage is mandatory under subdivision (c). This requirement will not limit the authority of the court to provide counsel at an earlier stage if it is thought desirable to do so as is done in some courts under current practice. At the evidentiary hearing stage, however, an indigent petitioner's access to counsel should not depend on local practice and, for this reason, the furnishing of counsel is made mandatory.

Counsel can perform a valuable function benefiting both the court and the petitioner. The issues raised can be more clearly identified if both sides have the benefit of trained legal personnel. The presence of counsel at the prehearing conference may help to expedite the evidentiary hearing or make it unnecessary, and counsel will be able to make better use of available prehearing discovery procedures. Compare ABA Project on Standards for Criminal Justice, Standards Relating to Post-Conviction Remedies § 4.4, p. 66 (Approved Draft 1968). At a hearing, the petitioner's claims are more likely to be effectively and properly presented by counsel.

Under 18 U.S.C. § 3006A(g), payment is allowed counsel up to $250, plus reimbursement for expenses reasonably incurred. The standards of indigency under this section are less strict than those regarding eligibility to prosecute a petition in forma pauperis, and thus many who cannot qualify to proceed under 28 U.S.C. § 1915 will be entitled to the benefits of counsel under 18 U.S.C. § 3006A(g). Under Rule 6(c), the court may order the respondent to reimburse counsel from state funds for fees and expenses incurred as the result of the utilization of discovery procedures by the respondent.

Subdivision (c) provides that the hearing shall be conducted as promptly as possible, taking into account "the need of counsel for both parties for adequate time for investigation and preparation." This differs from the language of 28 U.S.C. § 2243, which requires that the day for the hearing be set "not more than five days after the return unless for good cause additional time is allowed." This time limit fails to take into account the function that may be served by a prehearing conference and the time required to prepare adequately for an evidentiary hearing. Although "additional time" is often allowed under § 2243, subdivision (c) provides more flexibility to take account of the complexity of the case, the availability of important materials, the workload of the attorney general, and the time required by appointed counsel to prepare.

While the rule does not make specific provision for a prehearing conference, the omission is not intended to cast doubt upon the value of such a conference:

> The conference may limit the questions to be resolved, identify areas of agreement and dispute, and explore evidentiary problems that may be expected to arise. * * * [S]uch conferences may also disclose that a hearing is unnecessary * * *.
>
> ABA Project on Standards for Criminal Justice, Standards Relating to Post-Conviction Remedies § 4.6, commentary pp. 74–75. (Approved Draft, 1968.)

See also Developments in the Law—Federal Habeas Corpus, 83 Harv.L.Rev. 1038, 1188 (1970).

The rule does not contain a specific provision on the subpoenaing of witnesses. It is left to local practice to determine the method for doing this. The implementation of 28 U.S.C. § 1825 on the payment of witness fees is dealt with in an opinion of the Comptroller General, February 28, 1974.

2004 Amendments

The language of Rule 8 has been amended as part of general restyling of the rules to make them more easily understood and to make style and terminology consistent throughout the rules. These changes are intended to be stylistic and no substantive change is intended.

Rule 8(a) is not intended to supersede the restrictions on evidentiary hearings contained in 28 U.S.C. § 2254(e)(2).

The requirement in current Rule 8(b)(2) that a copy of the magistrate judge's findings must be promptly mailed to all parties has been changed in revised Rule 8(b) to require that copies of those findings be served on all parties. As used in this rule, "service" means service consistent with Federal Rule of Civil Procedure 5(b), which allows mailing the copies.

HISTORICAL NOTES

Effective and Applicability Provisions

1976 Acts. Section 2(c) of Pub.L. 94–577 provided that: "The amendments made by this section [amending subdivs. (b) and (c) of this rule and Rule 8(b), (c) of the Rules Governing Proceedings Under Section 2255 of this title] shall take effect with respect to petitions under section 2254 and motions under section 2255 of title 28 of the United States Code filed on or after February 1, 1977."

Rule 9. Second or Successive Petitions

Before presenting a second or successive petition, the petitioner must obtain an order from the appropriate court of appeals authorizing the district court to consider the petition as required by 28 U.S.C. § 2244(b)(3) and (4).

(As amended Pub.L. 94–426, § 2(7), (8), Sept. 28, 1976, 90 Stat. 1335; Apr. 26, 2004, eff. Dec. 1, 2004.)

ADVISORY COMMITTEE NOTES

1976 Adoption

This rule is intended to minimize abuse of the writ of habeas corpus by limiting the right to assert stale claims and to file multiple petitions. Subdivision (a) deals with the delayed petition. Subdivision (b) deals with the second or successive petition.

Subdivision (a) provides that a petition attacking the judgment of a state court may be dismissed on the grounds of delay if the petitioner knew or should have known of the existence of the grounds he is presently asserting in the petition and the delay has resulted in the state being prejudiced in its ability to respond to the petition. If the delay is more than five years after the judgment of conviction, prejudice is presumed, although this presumption is rebuttable by the petitioner. Otherwise, the state has the burden of showing such prejudice.

The assertion of stale claims is a problem which is not likely to decrease in frequency. Following the decisions in *Jones v. Cunningham*, 371 U.S. 236 (1963), and *Benson v. California*, 328 F.2d 159 (9th Cir. 1964), the concept of custody expanded greatly, lengthening the time period during which a habeas corpus petition may be filed. The petitioner who is not unconditionally discharged may be on parole or probation for many years. He may at some date, perhaps ten or fifteen years after conviction, decide to challenge the state court judgment. The grounds most often troublesome to the courts are ineffective counsel, denial of right of appeal, plea of guilty unlawfully induced, use of a coerced confession, and illegally constituted jury. The latter four grounds are often interlocked with the allegation of ineffective counsel. When they are asserted after the passage of many years, both the attorney for the defendant and the state have difficulty in ascertaining what the facts are. It often develops that the defense attorney has little or no recollection as to what took place and that many of the participants in the trial are dead or their whereabouts unknown. The court reporter's notes may have been lost or destroyed, thus eliminating any exact record of what transpired. If the case was decided on a guilty plea, even if the record is intact, it may not satisfactorily reveal the extent of the defense attorney's efforts in behalf of the petitioner. As a consequence, there is obvious difficulty in investigating petitioner's allegations.

The interest of both the petitioner and the government can best be served if claims are raised while the evidence is still fresh. The American Bar Association has recognized the interest of the state in protecting itself against stale claims by limiting the right to raise such claims after completion of service of a sentence imposed pursuant to a challenged judgment. See ABA Standards Relating to Post-Conviction Remedies § 2.4(c), p. 45 (Approved Draft, 1968). Subdivision (a) is not limited to those who have completed their sentence. Its reach is broader, extending to all instances where delay by the petitioner has prejudiced the state, subject to the qualifications and conditions contained in the subdivision.

In *McMann v. Richardson*, 397 U.S. 759 (1970), the court made reference to the issue of the stale claim:

> What is at stake in this phase of the case is not the integrity of the state convictions obtained on guilty pleas, *but whether, years later*, defendants must be permitted to withdraw their pleas, which were perfectly valid when made, and be given another choice between admitting their guilt and putting the State to its proof. [Emphasis added.]

397 U.S. at 773

The court refused to allow this, intimating its dislike of collateral attacks on sentences long since imposed which disrupt the state's interest in finality of convictions which were constitutionally valid when obtained.

Subdivision (a) is not a statute of limitations. Rather, the limitation is based on the equitable doctrine of laches. "Laches is such delay in enforcing one's rights as works disadvantage to another." 30A C.J.S. Equity § 112, p. 19. Also, the language of the subdivision, "a petition *may* be dismissed" [emphasis added], is permissive rather than mandatory. This clearly allows the court which is considering the petition to use discretion in assessing the equities of the particular situation.

The use of a flexible rule analogous to laches to bar the assertion of stale claims is suggested in ABA Standards Relating to Post-Conviction Remedies § 2.4, commentary at 48 (Approved Draft, 1968). Additionally, in *Fay v. Noia*, 372 U.S. 391 (1963), the Supreme Court noted:

> Furthermore, habeas corpus has traditionally been regarded as governed by equitable principles. *United States ex rel. Smith v. Baldi*, 344 U.S. 561, 573 (dissenting opinion). Among them is the principle that a suitor's conduct in relation to the matter at hand may disentitle him to the relief he seeks.

372 U.S. at 438

Finally, the doctrine of laches has been applied with reference to another postconviction remedy, the writ of coram nobis. See 24 C.J.S. Criminal Law § 1606(25), p. 779.

The standard used for determining if the petitioner shall be barred from asserting his claim is consistent with that used in laches provisions generally. The petitioner is held to a standard of reasonable diligence. Any inference or presumption arising by reason of the failure to attack collaterally a conviction may be disregarded where (1) there has been a change of law or fact (new evidence) or (2) where the court, in the interest of justice, feels that the collateral attack should be entertained and the prisoner makes a proper showing as to why he has not asserted a particular ground for relief.

Subdivision (a) establishes the presumption that the passage of more than five years from the time of the judgment of conviction to the time of filing a habeas petition is prejudicial to the state. "Presumption" has the meaning given it by Fed.R.Evid. 301. The prisoner has "the burden of going forward with evidence to rebut or meet the presumption" that the state has not been prejudiced by the passage of a substantial period of time. This does not impose too heavy a burden on the petitioner. He usually knows what persons are important to the issue of whether the state has been prejudiced. Rule 6 can be used by the court to allow petitioner liberal discovery to learn whether witnesses have died or whether other circumstances prejudicial to the state have occurred. Even if the petitioner should fail to overcome the presumption of prejudice to the state, he is not automatically barred from asserting his claim. As discussed previously, he may proceed if he neither knew nor, by the exercise of reasonable diligence, could have known of the grounds for relief.

The presumption of prejudice does not come into play if the time lag is not more than five years.

The time limitation should have a positive effect in encouraging petitioners who have knowledge of it to assert all their claims as soon after conviction as possible. The implementation of this rule can be substantially furthered by the development of greater legal resources for prisoners. See ABA Standards Relating to Post-Conviction Remedies § 3.1, pp. 49–50 (Approved Draft, 1968).

Subdivision (a) does not constitute an abridgement or modification of a substantive right under 28 U.S.C. § 2072. There are safeguards for the hardship case. The rule provides a flexible standard for determining when a petition will be barred.

Subdivision (b) deals with the problem of successive habeas petitions. It provides that the judge may dismiss a second or successive petition (1) if it fails to allege new or different grounds for relief or (2) if new or different grounds for relief are alleged and the judge finds the failure of the petitioner to assert those grounds in a prior petition is inexcusable.

In *Sanders v. United States*, 373 U.S. 1 (1963), the court, in dealing with the problem of successive applications, stated:

> Controlling weight *may* be given to denial of a prior application for federal habeas corpus or § 2255 relief only if (1) the same ground presented in the subsequent application was determined adversely to the applicant on the prior application, (2) the prior determination was on the

merits, and (3) the ends of justice would not be served by reaching the merits of the subsequent application. [Emphasis added.]

373 U.S. at 15

The requirement is that the prior determination of the same ground has been on the merits. This requirement is in 28 U.S.C. § 2244(b) and has been reiterated in many cases since *Sanders.* See *Gains v. Allgood,* 391 F.2d 692 (5th Cir. 1968); *Hutchinson v. Craven,* 415 F.2d 278 (9th Cir. 1969); *Brown v. Peyton,* 435 F.2d 1352 (4th Cir. 1970).

With reference to a successive application asserting a new ground or one not previously decided on the merits, the court in *Sanders* noted:

In either case, full consideration of the merits of the new application can be avoided only if there has been an abuse of the writ * * * and this the Government has the burden of pleading. * * *

Thus, for example, if a prisoner deliberately withholds one of two grounds for federal collateral relief at the time of filing his first application, * * * he may be deemed to have waived his right to a hearing on a second application presenting the withheld ground.

373 U.S. at 17–18

Subdivision (b) has incorporated this principle and requires that the judge find petitioner's failure to have asserted the new grounds in the prior petition to be inexcusable.

Sanders, 18 [sic] U.S.C. § 2244, and subdivision (b) make it clear that the court has discretion to entertain a successive application.

The burden is on the government to plead abuse of the writ. See *Sanders v. United States,* 373 U.S. 1, 10 (1963); *Dixon v. Jacobs,* 427 F.2d 589, 596 (D.C.Cir.1970); cf. *Johnson v. Copinger,* 420 F.2d 395 (4th Cir. 1969). Once the government has done this, the petitioner has the burden of proving that he has not abused the writ. In *Price v. Johnston,* 334 U.S. 266, 292 (1948), the court said:

[I]f the Government chooses * * * to claim that the prisoner has abused the writ of *habeas corpus,* it rests with the Government to make that claim with clarity and particularity in its return to the order to show cause. That is not an intolerable burden. The Government is usually well acquainted with the facts that are necessary to make such a claim. Once a particular abuse has been alleged, the prisoner has the burden of answering that allegation and of proving that he has not abused the writ.

Subdivision (b) is consistent with the important and well established purpose of habeas corpus. It does not eliminate a remedy to which the petitioner is rightfully entitled. However, in *Sanders,* the court pointed out:

Nothing in the traditions of habeas corpus requires the federal courts to tolerate needless piecemeal litigation, or to entertain collateral proceedings whose only purpose is to vex, harass, or delay.

373 U.S. at 18

There are instances in which petitioner's failure to assert a ground in a prior petition is excusable. A retroactive change in the law and newly discovered evidence are examples. In rare instances, the court may feel a need to entertain a petition alleging grounds that have already been decided on the merits. *Sanders,* 373 U.S. at 1, 16. However, abusive use of the writ should be discouraged, and instances of abuse are frequent enough to require a means of dealing with them. For example, a successive application, already decided on the merits, may be submitted in the hope of getting before a different judge in multijudge courts. A known ground may be deliberately withheld in the hope of getting two or more hearings or in the hope that delay will result in witnesses and records being lost. There are instances in which a petitioner will have three or four petitions pending at the same time in the same court. There are many hundreds of cases where the application is at least the second one by the petitioner. This subdivision is aimed at screening out the abusive petitions from this large volume, so that the more meritorious petitions can get quicker and fuller consideration.

The form petition, supplied in accordance with Rule 2(c), encourages the petitioner to raise all of his available grounds in one petition. It sets out the most common grounds asserted so that these may be brought to his attention.

Some commentators contend that the problem of abuse of the writ of habeas corpus is greatly overstated:

Most prisoners, of course, are interested in being released as soon as possible; only rarely will one inexcusably neglect to raise all available issues in his first federal application. The purpose of the "abuse" bar is apparently to deter repetitious applications from those few bored or vindictive prisoners * * *.

83 Harv.L.Rev. at 1153–1154

See also ABA Standards Relating to Post-Conviction Remedies § 6.2, commentary at 92 (Approved Draft, 1968), which states: "The occasional, highly litigious prisoner stands out as the rarest exception." While no recent systematic study of repetitious applications exists, there is no reason to believe that the problem has decreased in significance in relation to the total number of § 2254 petitions filed. That number has increased from 584 in 1949 to 12,088 in 1971. See Director of the Administrative Office of the United States Courts, Annual Report, table 16 (1971). It is appropriate that action be taken by rule to allow the courts to deal with this problem, whatever its specific magnitude. The bar set up by subdivision (b) is not one of rigid application, but rather is within the discretion of the courts on a case-by-case basis.

If it appears to the court after examining the petition and answer (where appropriate) that there is a high probability that the petition will be barred under either subdivision of Rule 9, the court ought to afford petitioner an opportunity to explain his apparent abuse. One way of doing this is by the use of the form annexed hereto. The use of a form will ensure a full airing of the issue so that the court is in a better position to decide whether the petition should be barred. This conforms with *Johnson v. Copinger,* 420 F.2d 395 (4th Cir. 1969), where the court stated:

[T]he petitioner is obligated to present facts demonstrating that his earlier failure to raise his claims is excusable and does not amount to an abuse of the writ. However, it is inherent in this obligation placed upon the petitioner that he must be given an opportunity to make his explanation, if he has one. If he is not afforded such an opportunity, the requirement that he satisfy the court that he has not abused the writ is meaningless. Nor do we think that a procedure which allows the imposition of a forfeiture for abuse of the writ, without allowing the petitioner an opportunity to be heard on the issue, comports with the minimum requirements of fairness.

420 F.2d at 399

Use of the recommended form will contribute to an orderly handling of habeas petitions and will contribute to the ability of the court to distinguish the excusable from the inexcusable delay or failure to assert a ground for relief in a prior petition.

2004 Amendments

The language of Rule 9 has been amended as part of general restyling of the rules to make them more easily understood and to make style and terminology consistent throughout the rules. These changes are intended to be stylistic and no substantive change is intended, except as noted below.

First, current Rule 9(a) has been deleted as unnecessary in light of the applicable one-year statute of limitations for § 2254 petitions, added as part of the Antiterrorism and Effective Death Penalty Act of 1996, 28 U.S.C. § 2244(d).

Second, current Rule 9(b), now Rule 9, has been changed to also reflect provisions in the Antiterrorism and Effective Death Penalty Act of 1996, 28 U.S.C. § 2244(b)(3) and (4), which now require a petitioner to obtain approval from the appropriate court of appeals before filing a second or successive petition.

Finally, the title of Rule 9 has been changed to reflect the fact that the only topic now addressed in the rules is that of second or successive petitions.

Rule 10. Powers of a Magistrate Judge

A magistrate judge may perform the duties of a district judge under these rules, as authorized under 28 U.S.C. § 636.

(As amended Pub.L. 94–426, § 2(11), Sept. 28, 1976, 90 Stat. 1335; Apr. 30, 1979, eff. Aug. 1, 1979; Apr. 26, 2004, eff. Dec. 1, 2004.)

ADVISORY COMMITTEE NOTES

1976 Adoption

Under this rule the duties imposed upon the judge of the district court by rules 2, 3, 4, 6, and 7 may be performed by a magistrate if and to the extent he is empowered to do so by a rule of the district court. However, when such duties involve the making of an order under rule 4 disposing of the petition, that order must be made by the court. The magistrate in such instances must submit to the court his report as to the facts and his recommendation with respect to the order.

The Federal Magistrates Act allows magistrates, when empowered by local rule, to perform certain functions in proceedings for post-trial relief. See 28 U.S.C. § 636(b)(3). The performance of such functions, when authorized, is intended to "afford some degree of relief to district judges and their law clerks, who are presently burdened with burgeoning numbers of habeas corpus petitions and applications under 28 U.S.C. § 2255." Committee on the Judiciary, The Federal Magistrates Act, S.Rep. No. 371, 90th Cong., 1st sess., 26 (1967).

> Under 28 U.S.C. § 636(b), any district court, by the concurrence of a majority of all the judges of such district court, may establish rules pursuant to which any full-time United States magistrate * * * may be assigned within the territorial jurisdiction of such court such additional duties as are not inconsistent with the Constitution and laws of the United States.

The proposed rule recognizes the limitations imposed by 28 U.S.C. § 636(b) upon the powers of magistrates to act in federal postconviction proceedings. These limitations are: (1) that the magistrate may act only pursuant to a rule passed by the majority of the judges in the district court in which the magistrate serves, and (2) that the duties performed by the magistrate pursuant to such rule be consistent with the Constitution and laws of the United States.

It has been suggested magistrates be empowered by law to hold hearings and make final decisions in habeas proceedings. See Proposed Reformation of Federal Habeas Corpus Procedure: Use of Federal Magistrates, 54 Iowa L.Rev. 1147, 1158 (1969). However, the Federal Magistrates Act does not authorize such use of magistrates. *Wingo v. Wedding,* 418 U.S. 461 (1974). See advisory committee note to Rule 8. While the use of magistrates can help alleviate the strain imposed on the district courts by the large number of unmeritorious habeas petitions, neither 28 U.S.C. § 636(b) nor this rule contemplate the abdication by the court of its decision-making responsibility. See also Developments in the Law—Federal Habeas Corpus, 83 Harv.L.Rev. 1038, 1188 (1970).

Where a full-time magistrate is not available, the duties contemplated by this rule may be assigned to a part-time magistrate.

2004 Amendments

The language of Rule 10 has been amended as part of general restyling of the rules to make them more easily understood and to make style and terminology consistent throughout the rules. These changes are intended to be stylistic and no substantive change is intended.

HISTORICAL NOTES

Change of Name

United States magistrate appointed under section 631 of Title 28, Judiciary and Judicial Procedure, to be known as United States magistrate judge after Dec. 1, 1990, with any reference to United States magistrate or magistrate in Title 28, in any other Federal statute, etc., deemed a reference to United States magistrate judge appointed under section 631 of Title 28, see section 321 of Pub.L. 101–650, set out as a note under section 631 of Title 28.

Rule 11. Applicability of the Federal Rules of Civil Procedure

The Federal Rules of Civil Procedure, to the extent that they are not inconsistent with any statutory provisions or these rules, may be applied to a proceeding under these rules.

(As amended Apr. 26, 2004, eff. Dec. 1, 2004.)

ADVISORY COMMITTEE NOTES

1976 Adoption

Habeas corpus proceedings are characterized as civil in nature. See, *e.g., Fisher v. Baker,* 203 U.S. 174, 181 (1906). However, under Fed.R.Civ.P. 81(a)(2), the applicability of the civil rules to habeas corpus actions has been limited, although the various courts which have considered this problem have had difficulty in setting out the boundaries of this limitation. See *Harris v. Nelson,* 394 U.S. 286 (1969) at 289, footnote 1. Rule 11 is intended to conform with the Supreme Court's approach in the *Harris* case. There the court was dealing with the petitioner's contention that Civil Rule 33 granting the right to discovery via written interrogatories is wholly applicable to habeas corpus proceedings. The court held:

> We agree with the Ninth Circuit that Rule 33 of the Federal Rules of Civil Procedure is not applicable to habeas corpus proceedings and that 28 U.S.C. § 2246 does not authorize interrogatories except in limited circumstances not applicable to this case; but we conclude that, in appropriate circumstances, a district court, confronted by a petition for habeas corpus which establishes a prima facie case for relief, may use or authorize the use of suitable discovery procedures, including interrogatories, reasonably fashioned to elicit facts necessary to help the court to "dispose of the matter as law and justice require" 28 U.S.C. § 2243.

394 U.S. at 290

The court then went on to consider the contention that the "conformity" provision of Rule 81(a)(2) should be rigidly applied so that the civil rules would be applicable only to the extent that habeas corpus practice had conformed to the practice in civil actions at the time of the adoption of the Federal Rules of Civil Procedure on September 16, 1938. The court said:

> Although there is little direct evidence, relevant to the present problem, of the purpose of the "conformity" provision of Rule 81(a)(2), the concern of the draftsmen, as a general matter, seems to have been to provide for the continuing applicability of the "civil" rules in their new form to those areas of practice in habeas corpus and other enumerated proceedings in which the "specified" proceedings had theretofore utilized the modes of civil practice. Otherwise, those proceedings were to be considered outside of the scope of the rules without prejudice, of course, to the use of particular rules by analogy or otherwise, where appropriate.

394 U.S. at 294

The court then reiterated its commitment to judicial discretion in formulating rules and procedures for habeas corpus proceedings by stating:

> [T]he habeas corpus jurisdiction and the duty to exercise it being present, the courts may fashion appropriate modes of procedure, by analogy to existing rules or otherwise in conformity with judicial usage.

Where their duties require it, this is the inescapable obligation of the courts. Their authority is expressly confirmed in the All Writs Act, 28 U.S.C. § 1651.

394 U.S. at 299

Rule 6 of these proposed rules deals specifically with the issue of discovery in habeas actions in a manner consistent with *Harris.* Rule 11 extends this approach to allow the court considering the petition to use any of the rules of civil procedure (unless inconsistent with these rules of habeas corpus) when in its discretion the court decides they are appropriate under the circumstances of the particular case. The court does not have to rigidly apply rules which would be inconsistent or inequitable in the overall framework of habeas corpus. Rule 11 merely recognizes and affirms their discretionary power to use their judgment in promoting the ends of justice.

Rule 11 permits application of the civil rules only when it would be appropriate to do so. Illustrative of an inappropriate application is that rejected by the Supreme Court in *Pitchess v. Davis,* 95 S.Ct. 1748 (1975), holding that Fed. R.Civ.P. 60(b) should not be applied in a habeas case when it would have the effect of altering the statutory exhaustion requirement of 28 U.S.C. § 2254.

2004 Amendments

The language of Rule 11 has been amended as part of general restyling of the rules to make them more easily understood and to make style and terminology consistent throughout the rules. These changes are intended to be stylistic and no substantive change is intended.

APPENDIX OF FORMS

Petition for Relief From a Conviction or Sentence By a Person in State Custody (Petition Under 28 U.S.C. § 2254 for a Writ of Habeas Corpus)

Instructions

1. To use this form, you must be a person who is currently serving a sentence under a judgment against you in a state court. You are asking for relief from the conviction or the sentence. This form is your petition for relief.

2. You may also use this form to challenge a state judgment that imposed a sentence to be served in the future, but you must fill in the name of the state where the judgment was entered. If you want to challenge a federal judgment that imposed a sentence to be served in the future, you should file a motion under 28 U.S.C. § 2255 in the federal court that entered the judgment.

3. Make sure the form is typed or neatly written.

4. You must tell the truth and sign the form. If you make a false statement of a material fact, you may be prosecuted for perjury.

5. Answer all the questions. You do not need to cite law. You may submit additional pages if necessary. If you do not fill out the form properly, you will be asked to submit additional or correct information. If you want to submit a brief or arguments, you must submit them in a separate memorandum.

6. You must pay a fee of $5. If the fee is paid, your petition will be filed. If you cannot pay the fee, you may ask to proceed *in forma pauperis* (as a poor person). To do that, you must fill out the last page of this form. Also, you must submit a certificate signed by an officer at the institution where you are confined showing the amount of money that the institution is holding for you. If your account exceeds $___, you must pay the filing fee.

7. In this petition, you may challenge the judgment entered by only one court. If you want to challenge a judgment entered by a different court (either in the same state or in different states), you must file a separate petition.

8. When you have completed the form, send the original and two copies to the Clerk of the United States District Court at this address:

   Clerk, United States District Court for _____
   Address
   City, State Zip Code

9. **CAUTION: You must include in this petition all the grounds for relief from the conviction or sentence that you challenge. And you must state the facts that support each ground. If you fail to set forth all the grounds in this petition, you may be barred from presenting additional grounds at a later date.**

10. **CAPITAL CASES: If you are under a sentence of death, you are entitled to the assistance of counsel and should request the appointment of counsel.**

PETITION UNDER 28 U.S.C. § 2254 FOR WRIT OF HABEAS CORPUS BY A PERSON IN STATE CUSTODY

United States District Court	District
Name (under which you were convicted):	Docket or Case No.:
Place of Confinement:	Prisoner No.:
Petitioner (include the name under which you were convicted)	Respondent (authorized person having custody of petitioner)

v.

The Attorney General of the State of

PETITION

1. (a) Name and location of court that entered the judgment of conviction you are challenging: ________
   (b) Criminal docket or case number (if you know): ____
2. (a) Date of the judgment of conviction (if you know): ________
   (b) Date of sentencing: ________
3. Length of sentence: ________
4. In this case, were you convicted on more than one count or of more than one crime? Yes ☐ No ☐
5. Identify all crimes of which you were convicted and sentenced in this case: ________
6. (a) What was your plea? (Check one)
   (1) Not guilty ☐ (3) Nolo contendere (no contest) ☐
   (2) Guilty ☐ (4) Insanity plea ☐
   (b) If you entered a guilty plea to one count or charge and a not guilty plea to another count or charge, what did you plead guilty to and what did you plead not guilty to? ________

(c) If you went to trial, what kind of trial did you have? (Check one)

Jury ☐ Judge only ☐

7. Did you testify at a pretrial hearing, trial, or a post-trial hearing?

Yes ☐ No ☐

8. Did you appeal from the judgment of conviction?

Yes ☐ No ☐

9. If you did appeal, answer the following:

(a) Name of court: ______

(b) Docket or case number (if you know): ______

(c) Result: ______

(d) Date of result (if you know): ______

(e) Citation to the case (if you know): ______

(f) Grounds raised: ______

(g) Did you seek further review by a higher state court? Yes ☐ No ☐

If yes, answer the following:

(1) Name of court: ______

(2) Docket or case number (if you know): ______

(3) Result: ______

(4) Date of result (if you know): ______

(5) Citation to the case (if you know): ______

(6) Grounds raised: ______

(h) Did you file a petition for certiorari in the United States Supreme Court?

Yes ☐ No ☐

If yes, answer the following:

(1) Docket or case number (if you know): ______

(2) Result: ______

(3) Date of result (if you know): ______

(4) Citation to the case (if you know): ______

10. Other than the direct appeals listed above, have you previously filed any other petitions, applications, or motions concerning this judgment of conviction in any state court?

Yes ☐ No ☐

11. If your answer to Question 10 was "Yes," give the following information:

(a) (1) Name of court: ______

(2) Docket or case number (if you know): ______

(3) Date of filing (if you know): ______

(4) Nature of the proceeding: ______

(5) Grounds raised: ______

(6) Did you receive a hearing where evidence was given on your petition, application, or motion?

Yes ☐ No ☐

(7) Result: ______

(8) Date of result (if you know): ______

(b) If you filed any second petition, application, or motion, give the same information:

(1) Name of court: ______

(2) Docket or case number (if you know): ______

(3) Date of filing (if you know): ______

(4) Nature of the proceeding: ______

(5) Grounds raised: ______

(6) Did you receive a hearing where evidence was given on your petition, application, or motion?

Yes ☐ No ☐

(7) Result: ______

(8) Date of result (if you know):

(c) If you filed any third petition, application, or motion, give the same information:

(1) Name of court: ______

(2) Docket or case number (if you know): ______

(3) Date of filing (if you know): ______

(4) Nature of the proceeding: ______

(5) Grounds raised: ______

(6) Did you receive a hearing where evidence was given on your petition, application, or motion?

Yes ☐ No ☐

(7) Result: ______

(8) Date of result (if you know):

(d) Did you appeal to the highest state court having jurisdiction over the action taken on your petition, application, or motion?

(1) First petition: Yes ☐ No ☐

(2) Second petition: Yes ☐ No ☐

(3) Third petition: Yes ☐ No ☐

(e) If you did not appeal to the highest state court having jurisdiction, explain why you did not: ______

12. For this petition, state every ground on which you claim that you are being held in violation of the Constitution, laws, or treaties of the United States. Attach additional pages if you have more than four grounds. State the facts supporting each ground.

CAUTION: To proceed in the federal court, you must ordinarily first exhaust (use up) your available state-court remedies on each ground on which you request action by the federal court. Also, if you fail to set forth all the grounds in this petition, you may be barred from presenting additional grounds at a later date.

GROUND ONE: ______

(a) Supporting facts (Do not argue or cite law. Just state the specific facts that support your claim.): ______

(b) If you did not exhaust your state remedies on Ground One, explain why: ______

(c) **Direct Appeal of Ground One:**

(1) If you appealed from the judgment of conviction, did you raise this issue?

Yes ☐ No ☐

(2) If you did not raise this issue in your direct appeal, explain why: ______

(d) **Post-Conviction Proceedings:**

(1) Did you raise this issue through a post-conviction motion or petition for habeas corpus in a state trial court?

Yes ☐ No ☐

(2) If your answer to Question (d)(1) is "Yes," state:

Type of motion or petition: ______

Name and location of the court where the motion or petition was filed: ______

Docket or case number (if you know): ______

Date of the court's decision: ______

Result (attach a copy of the court's opinion or order, if available): ______

(3) Did you receive a hearing on your motion or petition?

Yes ☐ No ☐

(4) Did you appeal from the denial of your motion or petition?

Yes ☐ No ☐

(5) If your answer to Question (d)(4) is "Yes," did you raise this issue in the appeal?

Yes ☐ No ☐

(6) If your answer to Question (d)(4) is "Yes," state:

Name and location of the court where the appeal was filed: ______

Docket or case number (if you know): ______

Date of the court's decision: ______

Result (attach a copy of the court's opinion or order, if available): ______

(7) If your answer to Question (d)(4) or Question (d)(5) is "No," explain why you did not raise this issue: ______

(e) **Other Remedies:** Describe any other procedures (such as habeas corpus, administrative remedies, etc.) that you have used to exhaust your state remedies on Ground One: ______

GROUND TWO: ______

(a) Supporting facts (Do not argue or cite law. Just state the specific facts that support your claim.): ______

(b) If you did not exhaust your state remedies on Ground Two, explain why: ______

(c) **Direct Appeal of Ground Two:**

(1) If you appealed from the judgment of conviction, did you raise this issue?

Yes ☐ No ☐

(2) If you did not raise this issue in your direct appeal, explain why: ______

(d) **Post-Conviction Proceedings:**

(1) Did you raise this issue through a post-conviction motion or petition for habeas corpus in a state trial court?

Yes ☐ No ☐

(2) If your answer to Question (d)(1) is "Yes," state:

Type of motion or petition: ______

Name and location of the court where the motion or petition was filed: ______

Docket or case number (if you know): ______

Date of the court's decision: ______

Result (attach a copy of the court's opinion or order, if available): ______

(3) Did you receive a hearing on your motion or petition?

Yes ☐ No ☐

(4) Did you appeal from the denial of your motion or petition?

Yes ☐ No ☐

(5) If your answer to Question (d)(4) is "Yes," did you raise this issue in the appeal?

Yes ☐ No ☐

(6) If your answer to Question (d)(4) is "Yes," state:

Name and location of the court where the appeal was filed: ______

Docket or case number (if you know): ______
Date of the court's decision: ______
Result (attach a copy of the court's opinion or order, if available): ______

(7) If your answer to Question (d)(4) or Question (d)(5) is "No," explain why you did not raise this issue: ______

(e) **Other Remedies:** Describe any other procedures (such as habeas corpus, administrative remedies, etc.) that you have used to exhaust your state remedies on Ground Two: ______

GROUND THREE: ______

(a) Supporting facts (Do not argue or cite law. Just state the specific facts that support your claim.): ______

(b) If you did not exhaust your state remedies on Ground Three, explain why: ______

(c) **Direct Appeal of Ground Three:**

(1) If you appealed from the judgment of conviction, did you raise this issue?
Yes ☐ No ☐

(2) If you did not raise this issue in your direct appeal, explain why: ______

(d) **Post-Conviction Proceedings:**

(1) Did you raise this issue through a post-conviction motion or petition for habeas corpus in a state trial court?
Yes ☐ No ☐

(2) If your answer to Question (d)(1) is "Yes," state:
Type of motion or petition: ______
Name and location of the court where the motion or petition was filed: ______

Docket or case number (if you know): ______
Date of the court's decision: ______
Result (attach a copy of the court's opinion or order, if available): ______

(3) Did you receive a hearing on your motion or petition?
Yes ☐ No ☐

(4) Did you appeal from the denial of your motion or petition?
Yes ☐ No ☐

(5) If your answer to Question (d)(4) is "Yes," did you raise this issue in the appeal?
Yes ☐ No ☐

(6) If your answer to Question (d)(4) is "Yes," state:
Name and location of the court where the appeal was filed: ______

Docket or case number (if you know): ______
Date of the court's decision: ______
Result (attach a copy of the court's opinion or order, if available): ______

(7) If your answer to Question (d)(4) or Question (d)(5) is "No," explain why you did not raise this issue: ______

(e) **Other Remedies:** Describe any other procedures (such as habeas corpus, administrative remedies, etc.) that you have used to exhaust your state remedies on Ground Three: ______

GROUND FOUR: ______

(a) Supporting facts (Do not argue or cite law. Just state the specific facts that support your claim.): ______

(b) If you did not exhaust your state remedies on Ground Four, explain why: ______

(c) **Direct Appeal of Ground Four:**

(1) If you appealed from the judgment of conviction, did you raise this issue?
Yes ☐ No ☐

(2) If you did not raise this issue in your direct appeal, explain why:

(d) **Post-Conviction Proceedings:**

(1) Did you raise this issue through a post-conviction motion or petition for habeas corpus in a state trial court?
Yes ☐ No ☐

(2) If your answer to Question (d)(1) is "Yes," state:
Type of motion or petition: ______
Name and location of the court where the motion or petition was filed: ______
Docket or case number (if you know): ______
Date of the court's decision: ______
Result (attach a copy of the court's opinion or order, if available): ______

(3) Did you receive a hearing on your motion or petition?
Yes ☐ No ☐
(4) Did you appeal from the denial of your motion or petition?
Yes ☐ No ☐
(5) If your answer to Question (d)(4) is "Yes," did you raise this issue in the appeal?
Yes ☐ No ☐
(6) If your answer to Question (d)(4) is "Yes," state:
Name and location of the court where the appeal was filed:
Docket or case number (if you know):
Date of the court's decision:
Result (attach a copy of the court's opinion or order, if available):

(7) If your answer to Question (d)(4) or Question (d)(5) is "No," explain why you did not raise this issue:

(e) **Other Remedies:** Describe any other procedures (such as habeas corpus, administrative remedies, etc.) that you have used to exhaust your state remedies on Ground Four:

13. Please answer these additional questions about the petition you are filing:
(a) Have all grounds for relief that you have raised in this petition been presented to the highest state court having jurisdiction? Yes ☐ No ☐
If your answer is "No," state which grounds have not been so presented and give your reason(s) for not presenting them:

(b) Is there any ground in this petition that has not been presented in some state or federal court? If so, which ground or grounds have not been presented, and state your reasons for not presenting them:

14. Have you previously filed any type of petition, application, or motion in a federal court regarding the conviction that you challenge in this petition? Yes ☐ No ☐
If "Yes," state the name and location of the court, the docket or case number, the type of proceeding, the issues raised, the date of the court's decision, and the result for each petition, application, or motion filed. Attach a copy of any court opinion or order, if available.

15. Do you have any petition or appeal now pending (filed and not decided yet) in any court, either state or federal, for the judgment you are challenging? Yes ☐ No ☐
If "Yes," state the name and location of the court, the docket or case number, the type of proceeding, and the issues raised.

16. Give the name and address, if you know, of each attorney who represented you in the following stages of the judgment you are challenging:
(a) At preliminary hearing:
(b) At arraignment and plea:
(c) At trial:
(d) At sentencing:
(e) On appeal:
(f) In any post-conviction proceeding:
(g) On appeal from any ruling against you in a post-conviction proceeding:

17. Do you have any future sentence to serve after you complete the sentence for the judgment that you are challenging? Yes ☐ No ☐
(a) If so, give name and location of court that imposed the other sentence you will serve in the future:
(b) Give the date the other sentence was imposed:
(c) Give the length of the other sentence:
(d) Have you filed, or do you plan to file, any petition that challenges the judgment or sentence to be served in the future? Yes ☐ No ☐

18. TIMELINESS OF PETITION: If your judgment of conviction became final over one year ago, you must explain why the one-year statute of limitations as contained in 28 U.S.C. § 2244(d) does not bar your petition.*

____
____
____
____

* The Antiterrorism and Effective Death Penalty Act of 1996 ("AEDPA") as contained in 28 U.S.C. § 2244(d) provides in part that:

(1) A one-year period of limitation shall apply to an application for a writ of habeas corpus by a person in custody pursuant to the judgment of a State court. The limitation period shall run from the latest of—

(A) the date on which the judgment became final by the conclusion of direct review or the expiration of the time for seeking such review;

(B) the date on which the impediment to filing an application created by State action in violation of the Constitution or laws of the United States is removed, if the applicant was prevented from filing by such state action;

(C) the date on which the constitutional right asserted was initially recognized by the Supreme Court, if the right has been newly recognized by the Supreme Court and made retroactively applicable to cases on collateral review; or

(D) the date on which the factual predicate of the claim or claims presented could have been discovered through the exercise of due diligence.

(2) The time during which a properly filed application for State post-conviction or other collateral review with respect to the pertinent judgment or claim is pending shall not be counted toward any period of limitation under this subsection.

Therefore, petitioner asks that the Court grant the following relief: ______________________________
____
____

or any other relief to which petitioner may be entitled.

____
Signature of Attorney (if any)

I declare (or certify, verify, or state) under penalty of perjury that the foregoing is true and correct and that this Petition for Writ of Habeas Corpus was placed in the prison mailing system on ______________ ______________(month, date, year).

____
Executed (signed) on (date).

____
Signature of Petitioner

If the person signing is not petitioner, state relationship to petitioner and explain why petitioner is not signing this petition. ______________________________
____
____

* * * * *

(As amended Apr. 28, 1982, eff. Aug. 1, 1982; Apr. 26, 2004, eff. Dec. 1, 2004.)

RULES GOVERNING SECTION 2255 PROCEEDINGS FOR THE UNITED STATES DISTRICT COURTS

Effective February 1, 1977
Amendments received to February 2, 2007

ORDERS OF THE SUPREME COURT OF THE UNITED STATES ADOPTING AND AMENDING RULES GOVERNING SECTION 2255 PROCEEDINGS

ORDER OF APRIL 26, 1976

1. That the rules and forms governing proceedings in the United States District Courts under Section 2254 and Section 2255 of Title 28, United States Code, as approved by the Judicial Conference of the United States be, and they hereby are, prescribed pursuant to Section 2072 of Title 28, United States Code and Sections 3771 and 3772 of Title 18, United States Code.

2. That the aforementioned rules and forms shall take effect August 1, 1976, and shall be applicable to all proceedings then pending except to the extent that in the opinion of the court their application in a particular proceeding would not be feasible or would work injustice.

3. That THE CHIEF JUSTICE be, and he hereby is, authorized to transmit the aforementioned rules and forms governing Section 2254 and Section 2255 proceedings to the Congress in accordance with the provisions of Section 2072 of Title 28 and Sections 3771 and 3772 of Title 18, United States Code.

CONGRESSIONAL ACTION ON PROPOSED RULES AND FORMS GOVERNING PROCEEDING UNDER 28 U.S.C. §§ 2254 AND 2255

Pub.L. 94–349, § 2, July 8, 1976, 90 Stat. 822, provided: "That, notwithstanding the provisions of section 2072 of title 28 of the United States Code, the rules and forms governing section 2254 cases in the United States district courts and the rules and forms governing section 2255 proceedings in the United States district courts which are embraced by the order entered by the United States Supreme Court on April 26, 1976, and which were transmitted to the Congress on or about April 26, 1976, shall not take effect until thirty days after the adjournment sine die of the 94th Congress, or until and to the extent approved by Act of Congress, whichever is earlier."

Pub.L. 94–426, § 1, Sept. 28, 1976, 90 Stat. 1334, provided: "That the rules governing section 2254 cases in the United States district courts and the rules governing section 2255 proceedings for the United States district courts, as proposed by the United States Supreme Court, which were delayed by the Act entitled 'An Act to delay the effective date of certain proposed amendments to the Federal Rules of Criminal Procedure and certain other rules promulgated by the United States Supreme Court' (Public Law 94–349), are approved with the amendments set forth in section 2 of this Act and shall take effect as so amended, with respect to petitions under section 2254 and motions under section 2255 of title 28 of the United States Code filed on or after February 1, 1977."

ORDER OF APRIL 30, 1979

1. That Rule 10 of the Rules Governing Proceedings in the United States District Courts on application under Section 2254 of Title 28, United States Code, be, and hereby is, amended to read as follows:

[See amendment made thereby under Rule 10 set out following section 2254.]

2. That Rules 10 and 11 of the Rules Governing Proceedings in the United States District Courts on a motion under Section 2255 of Title 28, United States Code, be, and they hereby are, amended to read as follows:

[See amendments made thereby under the respective rules, post.]

3. That the foregoing amendments to the Rules Governing Proceedings in the United States District Courts under Section 2254 and Section 2255 of Title 28, United States Code, shall take effect on August 1, 1979, and shall be applicable to all proceedings then pending except to the extent that in the opinion of the court their application in a particular proceeding would not be feasible or would work injustice.

4. That THE CHIEF JUSTICE be, and he hereby is, authorized to transmit the aforementioned amendments to the Rules Governing Section 2254 and Section 2255 Proceedings to the Congress in accordance with the provisions of

Section 2072 of Title 28, United States Code, and Sections 3771 and 3772 of Title 18, United States Code.

ORDER OF APRIL 28, 1982

1. That the rules and forms governing proceedings in the United States district courts under Section 2254 and Section 2255 of Title 28, United States Code, be, and they hereby are, amended by including therein an amendment to Rule 2(c) of the rules for Section 2254 cases, an amendment to Rule 2(b) of the rules for Section 2255 proceedings, and amendments to the model forms for use in applications under Section 2254 and motions under Section 2255, as hereinafter set forth:

[See amendments made thereby under respective rules and forms post and following section 2254.]

2. That the aforementioned amendments shall take effect August 1, 1982, and shall be applicable to all proceedings thereafter commenced and, insofar as just and practicable, all proceedings then pending.

3. That THE CHIEF JUSTICE be, and he hereby is, authorized to transmit the aforementioned amendments to the Congress in accordance with Section 2072 of Title 28 and Sections 3771 and 3772 of Title 18, United States Code.

ORDER OF APRIL 22, 1993

1. That the Federal Rules of Criminal Procedure for the United States District Courts be, and they hereby are, amended by including therein amendments to Criminal Rules 1, 3, 4, 5, 5.1, 6, 9, 12, 16, 17, 26.2, 32, 32.1, 40, 41, 44, 46, 49, 50, 54, 55, 57, and 58, and new Rule 26.3, and an amendment to Rule 8 of the Rules Governing Section 2255 Proceedings.

[See amendments made thereby under the respective rules set out in the Federal Criminal Code and Rules and under Rule 8, post.]

2. That the foregoing amendments to the Federal Rules of Criminal Procedure shall take effect on December 1, 1993, and shall govern all proceedings in criminal cases thereafter commenced and, insofar as just and practicable, all proceedings in criminal cases then pending.

3. That THE CHIEF JUSTICE be, and he hereby is, authorized to transmit to the Congress the foregoing amendments to the Federal Rules of Criminal Procedure in accordance with the provisions of Section 2072 of Title 28, United States Code.

ORDER OF APRIL 26, 2004

1. That the Federal Rules of Criminal Procedure be, and they hereby are, amended by including therein an amendment to Criminal Rule 35.

2. That the rules and forms governing cases in the United States District Courts under Section 2254 and Section 2255 of Title 28, United States Code, be, and they hereby are, amended by including therein amendments to Rules 1 through 11 of the Rules Governing Section 2254 Cases in the United States District Courts, Rules 1 through 12 of the Rules Governing Section 2255 Cases in the United States District Courts, and forms for use in applications under Section 2254 and motions under Section 2255.

[See amendments made thereby under respective rules, post.]

3. That the foregoing amendments to the Federal Rules of Criminal Procedure, the Rules Governing Section 2254 Cases in the United States District Courts, and the Rules Governing Section 2255 Cases in the United States District Courts shall take effect on December 1, 2004, and shall govern in all proceedings thereafter commenced and, insofar as just and practicable, all proceedings then pending.

4. That the CHIEF JUSTICE be, and hereby is, authorized to transmit to the Congress the foregoing amendments to the Federal Rules of Criminal Procedure, the Rules Governing Section 2254 Cases in the United States District Courts, and the Rules Governing Section 2255 Cases in the United States District Courts in accordance with the provisions of Section 2072 of Title 28, United States Code.

HISTORICAL NOTES

Effective Date of Rules; 1976 Act

Rules, and the amendments thereto by Pub.L. 94–426, Sept. 28, 1976, 90 Stat. 1334, effective with respect to petitions under section 2254 of this title and motions under section 2255 of this title filed on or after Feb. 1, 1977, see section 1 of Pub.L. 94–426, set out as a note under section 2255 of this title.

Rule 1. Scope

These rules govern a motion filed in a United States district court under 28 U.S.C. § 2255 by:

(a) a person in custody under a judgment of that court who seeks a determination that:

(1) the judgment violates the Constitution or laws of the United States;

(2) the court lacked jurisdiction to enter the judgment;

(3) the sentence exceeded the maximum allowed by law; or

(4) the judgment or sentence is otherwise subject to collateral review; and

(b) a person in custody under a judgment of a state court or another federal court, and subject to future custody under a judgment of the district court, who seeks a determination that:

(1) future custody under a judgment of the district court would violate the Constitution or laws of the United States;

(2) the district court lacked jurisdiction to enter the judgment;

(3) the district court's sentence exceeded the maximum allowed by law; or

(4) the district court's judgment or sentence is otherwise subject to collateral review.

(As amended Apr. 26, 2004, eff. Dec. 1, 2004.)

ADVISORY COMMITTEE NOTES

1976 Adoption

The basic scope of this postconviction remedy is prescribed by 28 U.S.C. § 2255. Under these rules the person seeking relief from federal custody files a motion to vacate, set aside, or correct sentence, rather than a petition for habeas corpus. This is consistent with the terminology used in section 2255 and indicates the difference between this remedy and federal habeas for a state prisoner. Also, habeas corpus is available to the person in federal custody if his "remedy by motion is inadequate or ineffective to test the legality of his detention."

Whereas sections 2241–2254 (dealing with federal habeas corpus for those in state custody) speak of the district court judge "issuing the writ" as the operative remedy, section 2255 provides that, if the judge finds the movant's assertions to be meritorious, he "shall discharge the prisoner or resentence him or grant a new trial or correct the sentence as may appear appropriate." This is possible because a motion under § 2255 is a further step in the movant's criminal case and not a separate civil action, as appears from the legislative history of section 2 of S. 20, 80th Congress, the provisions of which were incorporated by the same Congress in title 28 U.S.C. as § 2255. In reporting S. 20 favorably the Senate Judiciary Committee said (Sen.Rep. 1526, 80th Cong.2d Sess., p. 2):

The two main advantages of such motion remedy over the present habeas corpus are as follows:

First, habeas corpus is a separate civil action and not a further step in the criminal case in which petitioner is sentenced (Ex parte *Tom Tong,* 108 U.S. 556, 559 (1883)). It is not a determination of guilt or innocence of the charge upon which petitioner was sentenced. Where a prisoner sustains his right to discharge in habeas corpus, it is usually because some right—such as lack of counsel—has been denied which reflects no determination of his guilt or innocence but affects solely the fairness of his earlier criminal trial. Even under the broad power in the statute "to dispose of the party as law and justice require" (28 U.S.C.A., sec. 461), the court or judge is by no means in the same advantageous position in habeas corpus to do justice as would be so if the matter were determined in the criminal proceeding (see *Medley,* petitioner, 134 U.S. 160, 174 (1890)). For instance, the judge (by habeas corpus) cannot grant a new trial in the criminal case. Since the motion remedy is in the criminal proceeding, this section 2 affords the opportunity and expressly gives the broad powers to set aside the judgment and to "discharge the prisoner or resentence him or grant a new trial or correct the sentence as may appear appropriate."

The fact that a motion under § 2255 is a further step in the movant's criminal case rather than a separate civil action has significance at several points in these rules. See, *e.g.,* advisory committee note to Rule 3 (re no filing fee), advisory committee note to Rule 4 (re availability of files, etc., relating to the judgment), advisory committee note to Rule 6 (re availability of discovery under criminal procedure rules), advisory committee note to Rule 11 (re no extension of time for appeal), and advisory committee note to Rule 12 (re applicability of federal criminal rules). However, the fact that Congress has characterized the motion as a further step in the criminal proceedings does *not* mean that proceedings upon such a motion are of necessity governed by the legal principles which are applicable at a criminal trial regarding such matters as counsel, presence, confrontation, self-incrimination, and burden of proof.

The challenge of decisions such as the revocation of probation or parole are not appropriately dealt with under 28 U.S.C. § 2255, which is a continuation of the original criminal action. Other remedies, such as habeas corpus, are available in such situations.

Although Rule 1 indicates that these rules apply to a motion for a determination that the judgment was imposed "in violation of the . . . laws of the United States," the language of 28 U.S.C. § 2255, it is not the intent of these rules to define or limit what is encompassed within that phrase. See *Davis v. United States,* 417 U.S. 333 (1974), holding that it is not true "that every asserted error of law can be raised on a § 2255 motion," and that the appropriate inquiry is "whether the claimed error of law was 'a fundamental defect which inherently results in a complete miscarriage of justice,' and whether '[i]t . . . present[s] exceptional circumstances where the need for the remedy afforded by the writ of habeas corpus is apparent.' "

For a discussion of the "custody" requirement and the intended limited scope of this remedy, see advisory committee note to § 2254 Rule 1.

2004 Amendments

The language of Rule 1 has been amended as part of general restyling of the rules to make them more easily understood and to make style and terminology consistent throughout the rules. These changes are intended to be stylistic and no substantive change is intended.

Rule 2. The Motion

(a) Applying for Relief. The application must be in the form of a motion to vacate, set aside, or correct the sentence.

(b) Form. The motion must:

(1) specify all the grounds for relief available to the moving party;

(2) state the facts supporting each ground;

(3) state the relief requested;

(4) be printed, typewritten, or legibly handwritten; and

(5) be signed under penalty of perjury by the movant or by a person authorized to sign it for the movant.

(c) Standard Form. The motion must substantially follow either the form appended to these rules or a form prescribed by a local district-court rule. The clerk must make forms available to moving parties without charge.

(d) Separate Motions for Separate Judgments. A moving party who seeks relief from more than one judgment must file a separate motion covering each judgment.

(As amended Pub.L. 94–426, § 2(3), (4), Sept. 28, 1976, 90 Stat. 1334; Apr. 28, 1982, eff. Aug. 1, 1982; Apr. 26, 2004, eff. Dec. 1, 2004.)

ADVISORY COMMITTEE NOTES

1976 Adoption

Under these rules the application for relief is in the form of a motion rather than a petition (see Rule 1 and advisory committee note). Therefore, there is no requirement that the movant name a respondent. This is consistent with 28 U.S.C. § 2255. The United States Attorney for the district in which the judgment under attack was entered is the proper party to oppose the motion since the federal government is the movant's adversary of record.

If the movant is attacking a federal judgment which will subject him to future custody, he must be in present custody (see Rule 1 and advisory committee note) as the result of a state or federal governmental action. He need not alter the nature of the motion by trying to include the government officer who presently has official custody of him as a pseudo-respondent, or third-party plaintiff, or other fabrication. The court hearing his motion attacking the future custody can exercise jurisdiction over those having him in present custody without the use of artificial pleading devices.

There is presently a split among the courts as to whether a person currently in state custody may use a § 2255 motion to obtain relief from a federal judgment under which he will be subjected to custody in the future. Negative, see *Newton v. United States,* 329 F.Supp. 90 (S.D. Texas 1971); affirmative, see *Desmond v. The United States Board of Parole,* 397 F.2d 386 (1st Cir.1968), *cert. denied,* 393 U.S. 919 (1968); and *Paalino v. United States,* 314 F.Supp. 875 (C.D.Cal.1970). It is intended that these rules settle the matter in favor of the prisoner's being able to file a § 2255 motion for relief under those circumstances. The proper district in which to file such a motion is the one in which is situated the court which rendered the sentence under attack.

Under Rule 35, Federal Rules of Criminal Procedure, the court may correct an illegal sentence or a sentence imposed in an illegal manner, or may reduce the sentence. This remedy should be used, rather than a motion under these § 2255 rules, whenever applicable, but there is some overlap between the two proceedings which has caused the courts difficulty.

The movant should not be barred from an appropriate remedy because he has misstyled his motion. See *United States v. Morgan,* 346 U.S. 502, 505 (1954). The court should construe it as whichever one is proper under the circumstances and decide it on its merits. For a § 2255 motion construed as a Rule 35 motion, see *Heflin v. United States,* 358 U.S. 415 (1959); and *United States v. Coke,* 404 F.2d 836 (2d Cir.1968). For writ of error coram nobis treated as a Rule 35 motion, see *Hawkins v. United States,* 324 F.Supp. 223 (E.D. Texas, Tyler Division 1971). For a Rule 35 motion treated as a § 2255 motion, see *Moss v. United States,* 263 F.2d 615 (5th Cir.1959); *Jones v. United States,* 400 F.2d 892 (8th Cir.1968), cert. denied 394 U.S. 991 (1969); and *United States v. Brown,* 413 F.2d 878 (9th Cir.1969), cert. denied, 397 U.S. 947 (1970).

One area of difference between § 2255 and Rule 35 motions is that for the latter there is no requirement that the movant be "in custody." *Heflin v. United States,* 358 U.S. 415, 418, 422 (1959); *Duggins v. United States,* 240 F.2d 479, 483 (6th Cir.1957). Compare with Rule 1 and advisory committee note for § 2255 motions. The importance of this distinction has decreased since *Peyton v. Rowe,* 391 U.S. 54 (1968), but it might still make a difference in particular situations.

A Rule 35 motion is used to attack the sentence imposed, not the basis for the sentence. The court in *Gilinsky v. United States,* 335 F.2d 914, 916 (9th Cir.1964), stated, "a Rule 35 motion presupposes a valid conviction. * * * [C]ollateral attack on errors allegedly committed at trial is not permissible under Rule 35." By illustration the court noted at page 917: "a Rule 35 proceeding contemplates the correction of a sentence of a court having jurisdiction. * * * [J]urisdictional defects * * * involve a collateral attack, they must ordinarily be presented under 28 U.S.C. § 2255." In *United States v. Semet,* 295 F.Supp. 1084 (E.D.Okla.1968), the prisoner moved under Rule 35 and § 2255 to invalidate the sentence he was serving on the grounds of his failure to understand the charge to which he pleaded guilty. The court said:

> As regards Defendant's Motion under Rule 35, said Motion must be denied as its [sic] presupposes a valid conviction of the offense with which he was charged and may be used only to attack the sentence. It may not be used to examine errors occurring prior to the imposition of sentence.

295 F.Supp. at 1085

See also: *Moss v. United States,* 263 F.2d at 616; *Duggins v. United States,* 240 F.2d at 484; *Migdal v. United States,* 298 F.2d 513, 514 (9th Cir.1961); *Jones v. United States,* 400 F.2d at 894; *United States v. Coke,* 404 F.2d at 847; and *United States v. Brown,* 413 F.2d at 879.

A major difficulty in deciding whether Rule 35 or § 2255 is the proper remedy is the uncertainty as to what is meant by an "illegal sentence." The Supreme Court dealt with this issue in *Hill v. United States,* 368 U.S. 424 (1962). The prisoner brought a § 2255 motion to vacate sentence on the ground that he had not been given a Fed.R.Crim.P. 32(a) opportunity to make a statement in his own behalf at the time of sentencing. The majority held this was not an error subject to collateral attack under § 2255. The five-member majority considered the motion as one brought pursuant to Rule 35, but denied relief, stating:

> [T]he narrow function of Rule 35 is to permit correction at any time of an illegal *sentence,* not to re-examine errors occurring at the trial or other proceedings prior to the imposition of sentence. The sentence in this case was not illegal. The punishment meted out was not in excess of that prescribed by the relevant statutes, multiple terms were not imposed for the same offense, nor were the terms of the sentence itself legally or constitutionally invalid in any other respect.

368 U.S. at 430

The four dissenters felt the majority definition of "illegal" was too narrow.

> [Rule 35] provides for the correction of an "illegal sentence" without regard to the reasons why that sentence is illegal and contains not a single word to support the Court's conclusion that only a sentence illegal by reason of the punishment it imposes is "illegal" within the meaning of the Rule. I would have thought that a sentence imposed in an illegal manner—whether the amount or form of the punishment meted out constitutes an additional

violation of law or not—would be recognized as an "illegal sentence" under any normal reading of the English language.

368 U.S. at 431–432

The 1966 amendment of Rule 35 added language permitting correction of a sentence imposed in an "illegal manner." However, there is a 120-day time limit on a motion to do this, and the added language does not clarify the intent of the rule or its relation to § 2255.

The courts have been flexible in considering motions under circumstances in which relief might appear to be precluded by *Hill v. United States.* In *Peterson v. United States,* 432 F.2d 545 (8th Cir.1970), the court was confronted with a motion for reduction of sentence by a prisoner claiming to have received a harsher sentence than his codefendants because he stood trial rather than plead guilty. He alleged that this violated his constitutional right to a jury trial. The court ruled that, even though it was past the 120-day time period for a motion to reduce sentence, the claim was still cognizable under Rule 35 as a motion to correct an illegal sentence.

The courts have made even greater use of § 2255 in these types of situations. In *United States v. Lewis,* 392 F.2d 440 (4th Cir.1968), the prisoner moved under § 2255 and Rule 35 for relief from a sentence he claimed was the result of the judge's misunderstanding of the relevant sentencing law. The court held that he could not get relief under Rule 35 because it was past the 120 days for correction of a sentence imposed in an illegal manner and under *Hill v. United States* it was not an illegal sentence. However, § 2255 was applicable because of its "otherwise subject to collateral attack" language. The flaw was not a mere trial error relating to the finding of guilt, but a rare and unusual error which amounted to "exceptional circumstances" embraced in § 2255's words "collateral attack." See 368 U.S. at 444 for discussion of other cases allowing use of § 2255 to attack the sentence itself in similar circumstances, especially where the judge has sentenced out of a misapprehension of the law.

In *United States v. McCarthy,* 433 F.2d 591, 592 (1st Cir.1970), the court allowed a prisoner who was past the time limit for a proper Rule 35 motion to use § 2255 to attack the sentence which he received upon a plea of guilty on the ground that it was induced by an unfulfilled promise of the prosecutor to recommend leniency. The court specifically noted that under § 2255 this was a proper collateral attack on the sentence and there was no need to attack the conviction as well.

The court in *United States v. Malcolm,* 432 F.2d 809, 814, 818 (2d Cir.1970), allowed a prisoner to challenge his sentence under § 2255 without attacking the conviction. It held Rule 35 inapplicable because the sentence was not illegal on its face, but the manner in which the sentence was imposed raised a question of the denial of due process in the sentencing itself which was cognizable under § 2255.

The flexible approach taken by the courts in the above cases seems to be the reasonable way to handle these situations in which Rule 35 and § 2255 appear to overlap. For a further discussion of this problem, see C. Wright, Federal Practice and Procedure: Criminal §§ 581–587 (1969, Supp. 1975).

See the advisory committee note to Rule 2 of the § 2254 rules for further discussion of the purposes and intent of Rule 2 of these § 2255 rules.

1982 Amendment

Subdivision (b). The amendment takes into account 28 U.S.C. § 1746, enacted after adoption of the § 2255 rules. Section 1746 provides that in lieu of an affidavit an unsworn statement may be given under penalty of perjury in substantially the following form if executed within the United States, its territories, possessions or commonwealths: "I declare (or certify, verify, or state) under penalty of perjury that the foregoing is true and correct. Executed on (date). (Signature)." The statute is "intended to encompass prisoner litigation," and the statutory alternative is especially appropriate in such cases because a notary might not be readily available. *Carter v. Clark,* 616 F.2d 228 (5th Cir.1980). The § 2255 forms have been revised accordingly.

2004 Amendments

The language of Rule 2 has been amended as part of general restyling of the rules to make them more easily understood and to make style and terminology consistent throughout the rules. These changes are intended to be stylistic and no substantive change is intended, except as described below.

Revised Rule 2(b)(5) has been amended by removing the requirement that the motion be signed personally by the moving party. Thus, under the amended rule the motion may be signed by movant personally or by someone acting on behalf of the movant, assuming that the person is authorized to do so, for example, an attorney for the movant. The Committee envisions that the courts would apply third-party, or "next-friend," standing analysis in deciding whether the signer was actually authorized to sign the motion on behalf of the movant. *See generally Whitmore v. Arkansas,* 495 U.S. 149 (1990) (discussion of requisites for "next friend" standing in habeas petitions). *See also* 28 U.S.C. § 2242 (application for state habeas corpus relief may be filed by the person who is seeking relief, or by someone acting on behalf of that person).

The language in new Rule 2(c) has been changed to reflect that a moving party must substantially follow the standard form, which is appended to the rules, or a form provided by the court. The current rule, Rule 2(c), seems to indicate a preference for the standard "national" form. Under the amended rule, there is no stated preference. The Committee understood that the current practice in some courts is that if the moving party first files a motion using the national form, that courts may ask the moving party to supplement it with the local form.

Current Rule 2(d), which provided for returning an insufficient motion has been deleted. The Committee believed that the approach in Federal Rule of Civil Procedure 5(e) was more appropriate for dealing with motions that do not conform to the form requirements of the rule. That Rule provides that the clerk may not refuse to accept a filing solely for the reason that it fails to comply with these rules or local rules. Before the adoption of a one-year statute of limitations in the Antiterrorism and Effective Death Penalty Act of 1996, 110 Stat. 1214, the moving party suffered no penalty, other than delay, if the motion was deemed insufficient. Now that a one-year statute of limitations applies to motions filed under § 2255, *see* 28 U.S.C. § 2244(d) (1), the court's dismissal of a motion because it is not in proper form may pose a significant penalty for a moving party, who may not be able to file another motion within the one-year limitations period. Now, under revised Rule 3(b), the clerk is required to file a motion, even though it may otherwise fail to comply with the provisions in revised Rule 2(b). The Committee believed that the better procedure was to accept the defective motion and require the moving party to submit a corrected motion that conforms to Rule 2(b).

Rule 3. Filing the Motion; Inmate Filing

(a) Where to File; Copies. An original and two copies of the motion must be filed with the clerk.

(b) Filing and Service. The clerk must file the motion and enter it on the criminal docket of the case in which the challenged judgment was entered. The clerk must then deliver or serve a copy of the motion on the United States attorney in that district, together with a notice of its filing.

(c) Time to File. The time for filing a motion is governed by 28 U.S.C. § 2255 para. 6.

(d) Inmate Filing. A paper filed by an inmate confined in an institution is timely if deposited in the institution's internal mailing system on or before the last day for filing. If an institution has a system designed for legal mail, the inmate must use that system to receive the benefit of this rule. Timely filing may be shown by a declaration in compliance with 28 U.S.C. § 1746 or by a notarized statement, either of which must set forth the date of deposit and state that first-class postage has been prepaid.

(As amended Apr. 26, 2004, eff. Dec. 1, 2004.)

ADVISORY COMMITTEE NOTES

1976 Adoption

There is no filing fee required of a movant under these rules. This is a change from the practice of charging $15 and is done to recognize specifically the nature of a § 2255 motion as being a continuation of the criminal case whose judgment is under attack.

The long-standing practice of requiring a $15 filing fee has followed from 28 U.S.C. § 1914(a) whereby "parties instituting any civil action * * * pay a filing fee of $15, except that on an application for a writ of habeas corpus the filing fee shall be $5." This has been held to apply to a proceeding under § 2255 despite the rationale that such a proceeding is a motion and thus a continuation of the criminal action. (See note to Rule 1.)

> A motion under Section 2255 is a civil action and the clerk has no choice but to charge a $15.00 filing fee unless by leave of court it is filed in forma pauperis.

McCune v. United States, 406 F.2d 417, 419 (6th Cir.1969).

Although the motion has been considered to be a new civil action in the nature of habeas corpus for filing purposes, the reduced fee for habeas has been held not applicable. The Tenth Circuit considered the specific issue in *Martin v. United States,* 273 F.2d 775 (10th Cir.1960), cert. denied, 365 U.S. 853 (1961), holding that the reduced fee was exclusive to habeas petitions.

> Counsel for Martin insists that, if a docket fee must be paid, the amount is $5 rather than $15 and bases his contention on the exception contained in 28 U.S.C. § 1914 that in habeas corpus the fee is $5. This reads into § 1914 language which is not there. While an application under § 2255 may afford the same relief as that previously obtainable by habeas corpus, it is not a petition for a writ of habeas corpus. A change in § 1914 must come from Congress.

273 F.2d at 778

Although for most situations § 2255 is intended to provide to the federal prisoner a remedy equivalent to habeas corpus as used by state prisoners, there is a major distinction between the two. Calling a § 2255 request for relief a motion rather than a petition militates toward charging no new filing fee, not an increased one. In the absence of convincing evidence to the contrary, there is no reason to suppose that Congress did not mean what it said in making a § 2255 action a motion. Therefore, as in other motions filed in a criminal action, there is no requirement of a filing fee. It is appropriate that the present situation of docketing a § 2255 motion as a new action and charging a $15 filing fee be remedied by rule when the whole question of § 2255 motions is thoroughly thought through and organized.

Even though there is no need to have a forma pauperis affidavit to proceed with the action since there is no requirement of a fee for filing the motion the affidavit remains attached to the form to be supplied potential movants. Most such movants are indigent, and this is a convenient way of getting this into the official record so that the judge may appoint counsel, order the government to pay witness fees, allow docketing of an appeal, and grant any other rights to which an indigent is entitled in the course of a § 2255 motion, when appropriate to the particular situation, without the need for an indigency petition and adjudication at such later point in the proceeding. This should result in a streamlining of the process to allow quicker disposition of these motions.

For further discussion of this rule, see the advisory committee note to Rule 3 of the § 2254 rules.

2004 Amendments

The language of Rule 3 has been amended as part of general restyling of the rules to make them more easily understood and to make style and terminology consistent throughout the rules. These changes are intended to be stylistic and no substantive change is intended, except as indicated below.

Revised Rule 3(b) is new and is intended to parallel Federal Rule of Civil Procedure 5(e), which provides that the clerk may not refuse to accept a filing solely for the reason that it fails to comply with these rules or local rules. Before the adoption of a one-year statute of limitations in the Antiterrorism and Effective Death Penalty Act of 1996, 110 Stat. 1214, the moving party suffered no penalty, other than delay, if the petition was deemed insufficient. That Act, however, added a one-year statute of limitations to motions filed under § 2255, *see* 28 U.S.C. § 2244(d)(1). Thus, a court's dismissal of a defective motion may pose a significant penalty for a moving party who may not be able to file a corrected motion within the one-year limitation period. The Committee believed that the better procedure was to accept the defective motion and require the moving party to submit a corrected motion that conforms to Rule 2. Thus, revised Rule 3(b) requires the clerk to file a motion, even though it may otherwise fail to comply with Rule 2.

Revised Rule 3(c), which sets out a specific reference to 28 U.S.C. § 2255, paragraph 6, is new and has been added to put moving parties on notice that a one-year statute of limitations applies to motions filed under these Rules. Although the rule does not address the issue, every circuit that has addressed the issue has taken the position that equitable tolling of the statute of limitations is available in appropriate circumstances. *See, e.g., Dunlap v. United States,* 250 F.3d 1001, 1004–07 (6th Cir. 2001); *Moore v. United States,* 173 F.3d 1131, 1133–35 (8th Cir. 1999); *Sandvik v. United States,* 177 F.3d 1269, 1270–72 (11th Cir. 1999). The Supreme Court has not addressed the question directly. *See Duncan v. Walker,* 533 U.S. 167, 181 (2001) ("We . . . have no occasion to address the question that Justice Stevens raises concerning the availability of equitable tolling.").

Rule 3(d) is new and provides guidance on determining whether a motion from an inmate is considered to have been filed in a timely fashion. The new provision parallels Federal Rule of Appellate Procedure 25(a)(2)(C).

Rule 4. Preliminary Review

(a) Referral to a Judge. The clerk must promptly forward the motion to the judge who conducted the trial and imposed sentence or, if the judge who imposed sentence was not the trial judge, to the judge who conducted the proceedings being challenged. If the appropriate judge is not available, the clerk must forward the motion to a judge under the court's assignment procedure.

(b) Initial Consideration by the Judge. The judge who receives the motion must promptly examine it. If it plainly appears from the motion, any attached exhibits, and the record of prior proceedings that the moving party is not entitled to relief, the judge must dismiss the motion and direct the clerk to notify the moving party. If the motion is not dismissed, the judge must order the United States attorney to file an answer, motion, or other response within a fixed time, or to take other action the judge may order.

(As amended Apr. 26, 2004, eff. Dec. 1, 2004.)

ADVISORY COMMITTEE NOTES

1976 Adoption

Rule 4 outlines the procedure for assigning the motion to a specific judge of the district court and the options available to the judge and the government after the motion is properly filed.

The long-standing majority practice in assigning motions made pursuant to § 2255 has been for the trial judge to determine the merits of the motion. In cases where the § 2255 motion is directed against the sentence, the merits have traditionally been decided by the judge who imposed sentence. The reasoning for this was first noted in *Carvell v. United States,* 173 F.2d 348–349 (4th Cir.1949):

> Complaint is made that the judge who tried the case passed upon the motion. Not only was there no impropriety in this, but it is highly desirable in such cases that the motions be passed on by the judge who is familiar with the facts and circumstances surrounding the trial, and is consequently not likely to be misled by false allegations as to what occurred.

This case, and its reasoning, has been almost unanimously endorsed by other courts dealing with the issue.

Commentators have been critical of having the motion decided by the trial judge. See Developments in the Law—Federal Habeas Corpus, 83 Harv.L.Rev. 1038, 1206–1208 (1970).

> [T]he trial judge may have become so involved with the decision that it will be difficult for him to review it objectively. Nothing in the legislative history suggests that "court" refers to a specific judge, and the procedural advantages of section 2255 are available whether or not the trial judge presides at the hearing.
>
> The theory that Congress intended the trial judge to preside at a section 2255 hearing apparently originated in *Carvell v. United States,* 173 F.2d 348 (4th Cir.1949) (per curiam), where the panel of judges included Chief Judge Parker of the Fourth Circuit, chairman of the Judicial Conference committee which drafted section 2255. But the legislative history does not indicate that Congress wanted the trial judge to preside. Indeed the advantages of section 2255 can all be achieved if the case is heard in the sentencing district, regardless of which judge hears it. According to the Senate committee report the purpose of the bill was to make the proceeding a part of the criminal action so the court could resentence the applicant, or grant him a new trial. (A judge presiding over a habeas corpus action does not have these powers.) In addition, Congress did not want the cases heard in the district of confinement because that tended to concentrate the burden on a few districts, and made it difficult for witnesses and records to be produced.

83 Harv.L.Rev. at 1207–1208

The Court of Appeals for the First Circuit has held that a judge other than the trial judge should rule on the 2255 motion. See *Halliday v. United States,* 380 F.2d 270 (1st Cir.1967).

There is a procedure by which the movant can have a judge other than the trial judge decide his motion in courts adhering to the majority rule. He can file an affidavit alleging bias in order to disqualify the trial judge. And there are circumstances in which the trial judge will, on his own, disqualify himself. See, *e.g., Webster v. United States,* 330 F.Supp. 1080 (1972). However, there has been some questioning of the effectiveness of this procedure. See Developments in the Law—Federal Habeas Corpus, 83 Harv.L.Rev. 1038, 1200–1207 (1970).

Subdivision (a) adopts the majority rule and provides that the trial judge, or sentencing judge if different and appropriate for the particular motion, will decide the motion made pursuant to these rules, recognizing that, under some circumstances, he may want to disqualify himself. A movant is not without remedy if he feels this is unfair to him. He can file an affidavit of bias. And there is the right to appellate review if the trial judge refuses to grant his motion. Because the trial judge is thoroughly familiar with the case, there is obvious administrative advantage in giving him the first opportunity to decide whether there are grounds for granting the motion.

Since the motion is part of the criminal action in which was entered the judgment to which it is directed, the files, records, transcripts, and correspondence relating to that judgment are automatically available to the judge in his consideration of the motion. He no longer need order them incorporated for that purpose.

Rule 4 has its basis in § 2255 (rather than 28 U.S.C. § 2243 in the corresponding habeas corpus rule) which does not have a specific time limitation as to when the answer must be made. Also, under § 2255, the United States Attorney for the district is the party served with the notice and a copy of the motion and required to answer (when appropriate). Subdivision (b) continues this practice since there is no respondent involved in the motion (unlike habeas) and the United States Attorney, as prosecutor in the case in question, is the most appropriate one to defend the judgment and oppose the motion.

The judge has discretion to require an answer or other appropriate response from the United States Attorney. See advisory committee note to Rule 4 of the § 2254 rules.

2004 Amendments

The language of Rule 4 has been amended as part of general restyling of the rules to make them more easily understood and to make style and terminology consistent throughout the rules. These changes are intended to be stylistic and no substantive change is intended.

The amended rule reflects that the response to a Section 2255 motion may be a motion to dismiss or some other response.

Rule 5. The Answer and the Reply

(a) When Required. The respondent is not required to answer the motion unless a judge so orders.

(b) Contents. The answer must address the allegations in the motion. In addition, it must state whether the moving party has used any other federal remedies, including any prior post-conviction motions under these rules or any previous rules, and whether the moving party received an evidentiary hearing.

(c) Records of Prior Proceedings. If the answer refers to briefs or transcripts of the prior proceedings that are not available in the court's records, the judge must order the government to furnish them within a reasonable time that will not unduly delay the proceedings.

(d) Reply. The moving party may submit a reply to the respondent's answer or other pleading within a time fixed by the judge.

(As amended Apr. 26, 2004, eff. Dec. 1, 2004.)

ADVISORY COMMITTEE NOTES

1976 Adoption

Unlike the habeas corpus statutes (see 28 U.S.C. §§ 2243, 2248) § 2255 does not specifically call for a return or answer by the United States Attorney or set any time limits as to when one must be submitted. The general practice, however, if the motion is not summarily dismissed, is for the government to file an answer to the motion as well as counter-affidavits, when appropriate. Rule 4 provides for an answer to the motion by the United States Attorney, and Rule 5 indicates what its contents should be.

There is no requirement that the movant exhaust his remedies prior to seeking relief under § 2255. However, the courts have held that such a motion is inappropriate if the movant is simultaneously appealing the decision.

> We are of the view that there is no jurisdictional bar to the District Court's entertaining a Section 2255 motion during the pendency of a direct appeal but that the orderly administration of criminal law precludes considering such a motion absent extraordinary circumstances.

Womack v. United States, **395 F.2d 630, 631 (D.C.Cir.1968)**

Also see *Masters v. Eide,* 353 F.2d 517 (8th Cir.1965). The answer may thus cut short consideration of the motion if it discloses the taking of an appeal which was omitted from the form motion filed by the movant.

There is nothing in § 2255 which corresponds to the § 2248 requirement of a traverse to the answer. Numerous cases have held that the government's answer and affidavits are not conclusive against the movant, and if they raise disputed issues of fact a hearing must be held. *Machibroda v. United States,* 368 U.S. 487, 494, 495 (1962); *United States v. Salerno,* 290 F.2d 105, 106 (2d Cir.1961); *Romero v. United States,* 327 F.2d 711, 712 (5th Cir.1964); *Scott v. United States,* 349 F.2d 641, 642, 643 (6th Cir.1965); *Schiebelhut v. United States,* 357 F.2d 743, 745 (6th Cir.1966); and *Del Piano v. United States,* 362 F.2d 931, 932, 933 (3d Cir.1966). None of these cases make any mention of a traverse by the movant to the government's answer. As under Rule 5 of the § 2254 rules, there is no intention here that such a traverse be required, except under special circumstances. See advisory committee note to Rule 9.

Subdivision (b) provides for the government to supplement its answers with appropriate copies of transcripts or briefs if for some reason the judge does not already have them under his control. This is because the government will in all probability have easier access to such papers than the movant, and it will conserve the court's time to have the government produce them rather than the movant, who would in most instances have to apply in forma pauperis for the government to supply them for him anyway.

For further discussion, see the advisory committee note to Rule 5 of the § 2254 rules.

2004 Amendments

The language of Rule 5 has been amended as part of general restyling of the rules to make them more easily understood and to make style and terminology consistent throughout the rules. These changes are intended to be stylistic and no substantive change is intended.

Revised Rule 5(a), which provides that the respondent is not required to file an answer to the motion, unless a judge so orders, is taken from current Rule 3(b). The revised rule does not address the practice in some districts, where the respondent files a pre-answer motion to dismiss the motion. But revised Rule 4(b) contemplates that practice and has been changed to reflect the view that if the court does not dismiss the motion, it may require (or permit) the respondent to file a motion.

Finally, revised Rule 5(d) adopts the practice in some jurisdictions giving the movant an opportunity to file a reply to the respondent's answer. Rather than using terms such as "traverse," *see* 28 U.S.C. § 2248, to identify the movant's response to the answer, the rule uses the more general term " reply." The Rule prescribes that the court set the time for such responses, and in lieu of setting specific time limits in each case, the court may decide to include such time limits in its local rules.

Rule 6. Discovery

(a) Leave of Court Required. A judge may, for good cause, authorize a party to conduct discovery under the Federal Rules of Criminal Procedure or Civil Procedure, or in accordance with the practices and principles of law. If necessary for effective discovery, the judge must appoint an attorney for a moving party who qualifies to have counsel appointed under 18 U.S.C. § 3006A.

(b) Requesting Discovery. A party requesting discovery must provide reasons for the request. The request must also include any proposed interrogatories and requests for admission, and must specify any requested documents.

(c) Deposition Expenses. If the government is granted leave to take a deposition, the judge may require the government to pay the travel expenses, subsistence expenses, and fees of the moving party's attorney to attend the deposition.

(As amended Apr. 26, 2004, eff. Dec. 1, 2004.)

ADVISORY COMMITTEE NOTES

1976 Adoption

This rule differs from the corresponding discovery rule under the § 2254 rules in that it includes the processes of discovery available under the Federal Rules of Criminal Procedure as well as the civil. This is because of the nature of a § 2255 motion as a continuing part of the criminal proceeding (see advisory committee note to Rule 1) as well as a remedy analogous to habeas corpus by state prisoners.

See the advisory committee note to rule 6 of the § 2254 rules. The discussion there is fully applicable to discovery under these rules for § 2255 motions.

2004 Amendments

The language of Rule 6 has been amended as part of general restyling of the rules to make them more easily understood and to make style and terminology consistent throughout the rules. These changes are intended to be stylistic and no substantive change is intended, except as indicated below.

Although current Rule 6(b) contains no requirement that the parties provide reasons for the requested discovery, the revised rule does so and also includes a requirement that the request be accompanied by any proposed interrogatories and requests for admission, and must specify any requested documents. The Committee believes that the revised rule makes explicit what has been implicit in current practice.

Rule 7. Expanding the Record

(a) In General. If the motion is not dismissed, the judge may direct the parties to expand the record by submitting additional materials relating to the motion. The judge may require that these materials be authenticated.

(b) Types of Materials. The materials that may be required include letters predating the filing of the motion, documents, exhibits, and answers under oath to written interrogatories propounded by the judge. Affidavits also may be submitted and considered as part of the record.

(c) Review by the Opposing Party. The judge must give the party against whom the additional materials are offered an opportunity to admit or deny their correctness.

(As amended Apr. 26, 2004, eff. Dec. 1, 2004.)

ADVISORY COMMITTEE NOTES

1976 Adoption

It is less likely that the court will feel the need to expand the record in a § 2255 proceeding than in a habeas corpus proceeding, because the trial (or sentencing) judge is the one hearing the motion (see Rule 4) and should already have a complete file on the case in his possession. However, Rule 7 provides a convenient method for supplementing his file if the case warrants it.

See the advisory committee note to Rule 7 of the § 2254 rules for a full discussion of reasons and procedures for expanding the record.

2004 Amendments

The language of Rule 7 has been amended as part of general restyling of the rules to make them more easily understood and to make style and terminology consistent throughout the rules. These changes are intended to be stylistic and no substantive change is intended.

Revised Rule 7(a) is not intended to restrict the court's authority to expand the record through means other than requiring the parties themselves to provide the information.

The language in current Rule 7(d), which deals with authentication of materials in the expanded record, has been moved to revised Rule 7(a).

Rule 8. Evidentiary Hearing

(a) Determining Whether to Hold a Hearing. If the motion is not dismissed, the judge must review the answer, any transcripts and records of prior proceedings, and any materials submitted under Rule 7 to determine whether an evidentiary hearing is warranted.

(b) Reference to a Magistrate Judge. A judge may, under 28 U.S.C. § 636(b), refer the motion to a magistrate judge to conduct hearings and to file proposed findings of fact and recommendations for disposition. When they are filed, the clerk must promptly serve copies of the proposed findings and recommendations on all parties. Within 10 days after being served, a party may file objections as provided by local court rule. The judge must determine *de novo* any proposed finding or recommendation to which objection is made. The judge may accept, reject, or modify any proposed finding or recommendation.

(c) Appointing Counsel; Time of Hearing. If an evidentiary hearing is warranted, the judge must appoint an attorney to represent a moving party who qualifies to have counsel appointed under 18 U.S.C. § 3006A. The judge must conduct the hearing as soon as practicable after giving the attorneys adequate time to investigate and prepare. These rules do not limit the appointment of counsel under § 3006A at any stage of the proceeding.

(d) Producing a Statement. Federal Rule of Criminal Procedure 26.2(a)–(d) and (f) applies at a hearing under this rule. If a party does not comply with a Rule 26.2(a) order to produce a witness's statement, the court must not consider that witness's testimony.

(As amended Pub.L. 94–426, § 2(6), Sept. 28, 1976, 90 Stat. 1335; Pub.L. 94–577, § 2(a) (2), (b) (2), Oct. 21, 1976, 90 Stat. 2730, 2731; Apr. 22, 1993, eff. Dec. 1, 1993; Apr. 26, 2004, eff. Dec. 1, 2004.)

ADVISORY COMMITTEE NOTES

1976 Adoption

The standards for § 2255 hearings are essentially the same as for evidentiary hearings under a habeas petition, except that the previous federal fact-finding proceeding is in issue rather than the state's. Also § 2255 does not set specific time limits for holding the hearing, as does § 2243 for a habeas action. With these minor differences in mind, see the advisory committee note to Rule 8 of § 2254 rules, which is applicable to Rule 8 of these § 2255 rules.

1993 Amendment

The amendment to Rule 8 is one of a series of parallel amendments to Federal Rules of Criminal Procedure 32, 32.1, and 46 which extend the scope of Rule 26.2 (Production of Witness Statements) to proceedings other than the trial itself. The amendments are grounded on the compelling need for accurate and credible information in making decisions concerning the defendant's liberty. *See* the Advisory Committee Note to Rule 26.2(g). A few courts have recognized the authority of a judicial officer to order production of prior statements by a witness at a Section 2255 hearing, see, e.g., *United States v. White,* 342 F.2d 379, 382, n. 4 (4th Cir.1959). The amendment to Rule 8 grants explicit authority to do so. The amendment is not intended to require production of a witness's statement before the witness actually presents oral testimony.

2004 Amendments

The language of Rule 8 has been amended as part of general restyling of the rules to make them more easily understood and to make style and terminology consistent throughout the rules. These changes are intended to be stylistic and no substantive change is intended, except as described below.

The requirement in current Rule 8(b)(2) that a copy of the magistrate judge's findings must be promptly mailed to all parties has been changed in revised Rule 8(b) to require that copies of those findings be served on all parties. As used in this rule, "service" means service consistent with Federal Rule of Civil Procedure 5(b), which allows mailing the copies.

HISTORICAL NOTES

Effective and Applicability Provisions

1976 Acts. Amendments made by Pub.L. 94–577 effective with respect to motions under section 2255 of this title filed on or after Feb. 1, 1977, see section 2(c) of Pub.L. 94–577, set out as a note under Rule 8 of the Rules Governing Cases Under Section 2254 of this title.

Rule 9. Second or Successive Motions

Before presenting a second or successive motion, the moving party must obtain an order from the appropriate court of appeals authorizing the district court to consider the motion, as required by 28 U.S.C. § 2255, para. 8.

(As amended Pub.L. 94–426, § 2(9), (10), Sept. 28, 1976, 90 Stat. 1335; Apr. 26, 2004, eff. Dec. 1, 2004.)

ADVISORY COMMITTEE NOTES

1976 Adoption

Unlike the statutory provisions on habeas corpus (28 U.S.C. §§ 2241–2254), § 2255 specifically provides that "a motion for such relief may be made *at any time.*" [Emphasis added.] Subdivision (a) provides that delayed motions may be barred from consideration if the government has been prejudiced in its ability to respond to the motion by the delay and the movant's failure to seek relief earlier is not excusable within the terms of the rule. Case law, dealing with this issue, is in conflict.

Some courts have held that the literal language of § 2255 precludes any possible time bar to a motion brought under it. In *Heflin v. United States,* 358 U.S. 415 (1959), the concurring opinion noted:

> The statute [28 U.S.C. § 2255] further provides: "A motion * * * may be made at any time." This * * * simply means that, as in habeas corpus, there is no statute of limitations, no *res judicata,* and that the doctrine of laches is inapplicable.

358 U.S. at 420

McKinney v. United States, 208 F.2d 844 (D.C.Cir.1953) reversed the district court's dismissal of a § 2255 motion for being too late, the court stating:

McKinney's present application for relief comes late in the day: he has served some fifteen years in prison. But tardiness is irrelevant where a constitutional issue is raised and where the prisoner is still confined.

208 F.2d at 846, 847

In accord, see; *Juelich v. United States,* 300 F.2d 381, 383 (5th Cir.1962); *Conners v. United States,* 431 F.2d 1207, 1208 (9th Cir.1970); *Sturrup v. United States,* 218 F.Supp. 279, 281 (E.D.N.Car.1963); and *Banks v. United States,* 319 F.Supp. 649, 652 (S.D.N.Y.1970).

It has also been held that delay in filing a § 2255 motion does not bar the movant because of lack of reasonable diligence in pressing the claim.

The statute [28 U.S.C. § 2255], when it states that the motion may be made at any time, excludes the addition of a showing of diligence in delayed filings. A number of courts have considered contentions similar to those made here and have concluded that there are no time limitations. This result excludes the requirement of diligence which is in reality a time limitation.

***Haier v. United States,* 334 F.2d 441, 442 (10th Cir.1964)**

Other courts have recognized that delay may have a negative effect on the movant. In *Raines v. United States,* 423 F.2d 526 (4th Cir.1970), the court stated:

[B]oth petitioners' silence for extended periods, one for 28 months and the other for nine years, serves to render their allegations less believable. "Although a delay in filing a section 2255 motion is not a controlling element * * * it may merit some consideration * * *."

423 F.2d at 531

In *Aiken v. United States,* 191 F.Supp. 43, 50 (M.D.N.Car. 1961), aff'd 296 F.2d 604 (4th Cir.1961), the court said: "While motions under 28 U.S.C. § 2255 may be made at any time, the lapse of time affects the good faith and credibility of the moving party." For similar conclusions, see: *Parker v. United States,* 358 F.2d 50, 54 n. 4 (7th Cir.1965), cert. denied, 386 U.S. 916 (1967); *Le Clair v. United States,* 241 F.Supp. 819, 824 (N.D.Ind.1965); *Malone v. United States,* 299 F.2d 254, 256 (6th Cir.1962), cert. denied, 371 U.S. 863 (1962); *Howell v. United States,* 442 F.2d 265, 274 (7th Cir.1971); and *United States v. Wiggins,* 184 F.Supp. 673, 676 (D.C.Cir.1960).

There have been holdings by some courts that a delay in filing a § 2255 motion operates to increase the burden of proof which the movant must meet to obtain relief. The reasons for this, as expressed in *United States v. Bostic,* 206 F.Supp. 855 (D.C.Cir.1962), are equitable in nature.

Obviously, the burden of proof on a motion to vacate a sentence under 28 U.S.C. § 2255 is on the moving party. . . . The burden is particularly heavy if the issue is one of fact and a long time has elapsed since the trial of the case. While neither the statute of limitations nor laches can bar the assertion of a constitutional right, nevertheless, the passage of time may make it impracticable to retry a case if the motion is granted and a new trial is ordered. No doubt, at times such a motion is a product of an afterthought. Long delay may raise a question of good faith.

206 F.Supp. at 856–857

See also *United States v. Wiggins,* 184 F.Supp. at 676.

A requirement that the movant display reasonable diligence in filing a § 2255 motion has been adopted by some courts dealing with delayed motions. The court in *United States v. Moore,* 166 F.2d 102 (7th Cir.1948), cert. denied, 334 U.S. 849 (1948), did this, again for equitable reasons.

[W]e agree with the District Court that the petitioner has too long slept upon his rights. * * * [A]pparently there is no limitation of time within which * * * a motion to vacate may be filed, except that an applicant must show reasonable diligence in presenting his claim. * * *

The reasons which support the rule requiring diligence seem obvious. * * * Law enforcement officials change, witnesses die, memories grow dim. The prosecuting tribunal is put to a disadvantage if an unexpected retrial should be necessary after long passage of time.

166 F.2d at 105

In accord see *Desmond v. United States,* 333 F.2d 378, 381 (1st Cir.1964), on remand, 345 F.2d 225 (1st Cir.1965).

One of the major arguments advanced by the courts which would penalize a movant who waits an unduly long time before filing a § 2255 motion is that such delay is highly prejudicial to the prosecution. In *Desmond v. United States,* writing of a § 2255 motion alleging denial of effective appeal because of deception by movant's own counsel, the court said:

[A]pplications for relief such as this must be made promptly. It will not do for a prisoner to wait until government witnesses have become unavailable as by death, serious illness or absence from the country, or until the memory of available government witnesses has faded. It will not even do for a prisoner to wait any longer than is reasonably necessary to prepare appropriate moving papers, however inartistic, after discovery of the deception practiced upon him by his attorney.

333 F.2d at 381

In a similar vein are *United States v. Moore* and *United States v. Bostic,* supra, and *United States v. Wiggins,* 184 F.Supp. at 676.

Subdivision (a) provides a flexible, equitable time limitation based on laches to prevent movants from withholding their claims so as to prejudice the government both in meeting the allegations of the motion and in any possible retrial. It includes a reasonable diligence requirement for ascertaining possible grounds for relief. If the delay is found to be excusable, or nonprejudicial to the government, the time bar is inoperative.

Subdivision (b) is consistent with the language of § 2255 and relevant case law.

The annexed form is intended to serve the same purpose as the comparable one included in the § 2254 rules.

For further discussion applicable to this rule, see the advisory committee note to Rule 9 of the § 2254 rules.

2004 Amendments

The language of Rule 9 has been amended as part of general restyling of the rules to make them more easily understood and to make style and terminology consistent throughout the rules. These changes are intended to be stylistic and no substantive change is intended, except as indicated below.

First, current Rule 9(a) has been deleted as unnecessary in light of the applicable one-year statute of limitations for § 2255 motions, added as part of the Antiterrorism and Effective Death Penalty Act of 1996, 28 U.S.C. § 2255, para. 6.

Second, the remainder of revised Rule 9 reflects provisions in the Antiterrorism and Effective Death Penalty Act of 1996, 28 U.S.C. § 2255, para. 8, which now require a moving party to obtain approval from the appropriate court of appeals before filing a second or successive motion.

Finally, the title of the rule has been changed to reflect the fact that the revised version addresses only the topic of second or successive motions.

Rule 10. Powers of a Magistrate Judge

A magistrate judge may perform the duties of a district judge under these rules, as authorized by 28 U.S.C. § 636.

(As amended Pub.L. 94–426, § 2(12), Sept. 28, 1976, 90 Stat. 1335; Apr. 30, 1979, eff. Aug. 1, 1979; Apr. 26, 2004, eff. Dec. 1, 2004.)

ADVISORY COMMITTEE NOTES

1976 Adoption

See the advisory committee note to Rule 10 of the § 2254 rules for a discussion fully applicable here as well.

1979 Amendment

This amendment conforms the rule to 18 U.S.C. § 636. See Advisory Committee Note to Rule 10 of the Rules Governing Section 2254 Cases in the United States District Courts.

2004 Amendments

The language of Rule 10 has been amended as part of general restyling of the rules to make them more easily understood and to make style and terminology consistent throughout the rules. These changes are intended to be stylistic and no substantive change is intended.

HISTORICAL NOTES

Change of Name

United States magistrate appointed under section 631 of Title 28, Judiciary and Judicial Procedure, to be known as United States magistrate judge after Dec. 1, 1990, with any reference to United States magistrate or magistrate in Title 28, in any other Federal statute, etc., deemed a reference to United States magistrate judge appointed under section 631 of Title 28, see section 321 of Pub.L. 101–650, set out as a note under section 631 of Title 28.

Rule 11. Time to Appeal

Federal Rule of Appellate Procedure 4(a) governs the time to appeal an order entered under these rules. These rules do not extend the time to appeal the original judgment of conviction.

(As amended Apr. 30, 1979, eff. Aug. 1, 1979; Apr. 26, 2004, eff. Dec. 1, 2004.)

ADVISORY COMMITTEE NOTES

1976 Adoption

Rule 11 is intended to make clear that, although a § 2255 action is a continuation of the criminal case, the bringing of a § 2255 action does not extend the time.

1979 Amendment

Prior to the promulgation of the Rules Governing Section 2255 Proceedings, the courts consistently held that the time for appeal in a section 2255 case is as provided in Fed. R.App.P. 4(a), that is, 60 days when the government is a party, rather than as provided in appellate rule 4(b), which says that the time is 10 days in criminal cases. This result has often been explained on the ground that rule 4(a) has to do with civil cases and that "proceedings under section 2255 are civil in nature." E.g., *Rothman v. United States,* 508 F.2d 648 (3d Cir.1975). Because the new section 2255 rules are based upon the premise "that a motion under § 2255 is a further step in the movant's criminal case rather than a separate civil action," see Advisory Committee Note to Rule 1, the question has arisen whether the new rules have the effect of shortening the time for appeal to that provided in appellate rule 4(b). A sentence has been added to Rule 11 in order to make it clear that this is not the case.

Even though section 2255 proceedings are a further step in the criminal case, the added sentence correctly states current law. In *United States v. Hayman,* 342 U.S. 205 (1952), the Supreme Court noted that such appeals "are governed by the civil rules applicable to appeals from final judgments in habeas corpus actions." In support, the Court cited *Mercado v. United States,* 183 F.2d 486 (1st Cir.1950), a case rejecting the argument that because § 2255 proceedings are criminal in nature the time for appeal is only 10 days. The *Mercado* court concluded that the situation was governed by that part of 28 U.S.C. § 2255 which reads: "An appeal may be taken to the court of appeals from the order entered on the motion as from a final judgment on application for a writ of habeas corpus." Thus, because appellate rule 4(a) is applicable in habeas cases, it likewise governs in § 2255 cases even though they are criminal in nature.

2004 Amendments

The language of Rule 11 has been amended as part of general restyling of the rules to make them more easily understood and to make style and terminology consistent throughout the rules. These changes are intended to be stylistic and no substantive change is intended.

Rule 12. Applicability of the Federal Rules of Civil Procedure and the Federal Rules of Criminal Procedure

The Federal Rules of Civil Procedure and the Federal Rules of Criminal Procedure, to the extent that they are not inconsistent with any statutory provisions or these rules, may be applied to a proceeding under these rules.

(As amended Apr. 26, 2004, eff. Dec. 1, 2004.)

ADVISORY COMMITTEE NOTES

1976 Adoption

This rule differs from rule 11 of the § 2254 rules in that it includes the Federal Rules of Criminal Procedure as well as the civil. This is because of the nature of a § 2255 motion as a continuing part of the criminal proceeding (see advisory committee note to Rule 1) as well as a remedy analogous to habeas corpus by state prisoners.

Since § 2255 has been considered analogous to habeas as respects the restrictions in Fed.R.Civ.P. 81(a) (2) (see *Sullivan v. United States,* 198 F.Supp. 624 (S.D.N.Y.1961)), Rule 12 is needed. For discussion, see the advisory committee note to Rule 11 of the § 2254 rules.

2004 Amendments

The language of Rule 12 has been amended as part of general restyling of the rules to make them more easily understood and to make style and terminology consistent throughout the rules. These changes are intended to be stylistic and no substantive change is intended.

APPENDIX OF FORMS

Motion to Vacate, Set Aside, or Correct a Sentence By a Person in Federal Custody (Motion Under 28 U.S.C. § 2255)

Instructions

1. To use this form, you must be a person who is serving a sentence under a judgment against you in a federal court. You are asking for relief from the conviction or the sentence. This form is your motion for relief.

2. You must file the form in the United States district court that entered the judgment that you are challenging. If you want to challenge a federal judgment that imposed a sentence to be served in the future, you should file the motion in the federal court that entered that judgment.

3. Make sure the form is typed or neatly written.

4. You must tell the truth and sign the form. If you make a false statement of a material fact, you may be prosecuted for perjury.

5. Answer all the questions. You do not need to cite law. You may submit additional pages if necessary. If you do not fill out the form properly, you will be asked to submit additional or correct information. If you want to submit a brief or arguments, you must submit them in a separate memorandum.

6. If you cannot pay for the costs of this motion (such as costs for an attorney or transcripts), you may ask to proceed *in forma pauperis* (as a poor person). To do that, you must fill out the last page of this form. Also, you must submit a certificate signed by an officer at the institution where you are confined showing the amount of money that the institution is holding for you.

7. In this motion, you may challenge the judgment entered by only one court. If you want to challenge a judgment entered by a different judge or division (either in the same district or in a different district), you must file a separate motion.

8. When you have completed the form, send the original and two copies to the Clerk of the United States District Court at this address:

   Clerk, United States District Court for ______

   Address
   City, State Zip Code

9. **CAUTION: You must include in this motion all the grounds for relief from the conviction or sentence that you challenge. And you must state the facts that support each ground. If you fail to set forth all the grounds in this motion, you may be barred from presenting additional grounds at a later date.**

10. **CAPITAL CASES: If you are under a sentence of death, you are entitled to the assistance of counsel and should request the appointment of counsel.**

MOTION UNDER 28 U.S.C. § 2255 TO VACATE, SET ASIDE, OR CORRECT SENTENCE BY A PERSON IN FEDERAL CUSTODY

United States District Court District

Name (under which you were convicted): Docket or Case No.:

Place of Confinement: Prisoner No.:

UNITED STATES OF AMERICA Movant (include name under which convicted)

v.

MOTION

1. (a) Name and location of court that entered the judgment of conviction you are challenging:
   (b) Criminal docket or case number (if you know):
2. (a) Date of the judgment of conviction (if you know):
   (b) Date of sentencing:
3. Length of sentence:
4. Nature of crime (all counts):
5. (a) What was your plea? (Check one)
   (1) Not guilty ☐ (2) Guilty ☐ (3) Nolo contendere (no contest) ☐
   (b) If you entered a guilty plea to one count or indictment, and a not guilty plea to another count or indictment, what did you plead guilty to and what did you plead not guilty to?
6. If you went to trial, what kind of trial did you have? (Check one) Jury ☐ Judge only ☐
7. Did you testify at a pretrial hearing, trial, or post-trial hearing? Yes ☐ No ☐
8. Did you appeal from the judgment of conviction? Yes ☐ No ☐
9. If you did appeal, answer the following:
   (a) Name of court:
   (b) Docket or case number (if you know):
   (c) Result:
   (d) Date of result (if you know):
   (e) Citation to the case (if you know):
   (f) Grounds raised:
   (g) Did you file a petition for certiorari in the United States Supreme Court?
   Yes ☐ No ☐
   If "Yes," answer the following:
   (1) Docket or case number (if you know):
   (2) Result:
   (3) Date of result (if you know):
   (4) Citation to the case (if you know):
   (5) Grounds raised:
10. Other than the direct appeals listed above, have you previously filed any other motions, petitions, or applications concerning this judgment of conviction in any court?
    Yes ☐ No ☐
11. If your answer to Question 10 was "Yes," give the following information:
    (a) (1) Name of court:
    (2) Docket or case number (if you know):
    (3) Date of filing (if you know):
    (4) Nature of the proceeding:
    (5) Grounds raised:
    (6) Did you receive a hearing where evidence was given on your motion, petition, or application?
    Yes ☐ No ☐
    (7) Result:
    (8) Date of result (if you know):
    (b) If you filed any second motion, petition, or application, give the same information:
    (1) Name of court:
    (2) Docket or case number (if you know):
    (3) Date of filing (if you know):
    (4) Nature of the proceeding:
    (5) Grounds raised:
    (6) Did you receive a hearing where evidence was given on your motion, petition, or application?
    Yes ☐ No ☐
    (7) Result:
    (8) Date of result (if you know):
    (c) Did you appeal to a federal appellate court having jurisdiction over the action taken on your motion, petition, or application?
    (1) First petition: Yes ☐ No ☐
    (2) Second petition: Yes ☐ No ☐

(d) If you did not appeal from the action on any motion, petition, or application, explain briefly why you did not: ______

12. For this motion, state every ground on which you claim that you are being held in violation of the Constitution, laws, or treaties of the United States. Attach additional pages if you have more than four grounds. State the facts supporting each ground.

GROUND ONE: ______

(a) Supporting facts (Do not argue or cite law. Just state the specific facts that support your claim.): ______

(b) **Direct Appeal of Ground One:**
(1) If you appealed from the judgment of conviction, did you raise this issue?
Yes ☐ No ☐
(2) If you did not raise this issue in your direct appeal, explain why: ______

(c) **Post-Conviction Proceedings:**
(1) Did you raise this issue in any post-conviction motion, petition, or application?
Yes ☐ No ☐
(2) If your answer to Question (c)(1) is "Yes," state:
Type of motion or petition: ______
Name and location of the court where the motion or petition was filed: ______
Docket or case number (if you know): ______
Date of the court's decision: ______
Result (attach a copy of the court's opinion or order, if available): ______
(3) Did you receive a hearing on your motion, petition, or application?
Yes ☐ No ☐
(4) Did you appeal from the denial of your motion, petition, or application?
Yes ☐ No ☐
(5) If your answer to Question (c)(4) is "Yes," did you raise this issue in the appeal?
Yes ☐ No ☐
(6) If your answer to Question (c)(4) is "Yes," state:
Name and location of the court where the appeal was filed: ______
Docket or case number (if you know): ______
Date of the court's decision: ______
Result (attach a copy of the court's opinion or order, if available): ______
(7) If your answer to Question (c)(4) or Question (c)(5) is "No," explain why you did not appeal or raise this issue: ______

GROUND TWO: ______

(a) Supporting facts (Do not argue or cite law. Just state the specific facts that support your claim.): ______

(b) **Direct Appeal of Ground Two:**
(1) If you appealed from the judgment of conviction, did you raise this issue?
Yes ☐ No ☐
(2) If you did not raise this issue in your direct appeal, explain why: ______

(c) **Post-Conviction Proceedings:**
(1) Did you raise this issue in any post-conviction motion, petition, or application?
Yes ☐ No ☐
(2) If your answer to Question (c)(1) is "Yes," state:
Type of motion or petition: ______
Name and location of the court where the motion or petition was filed: ______
Docket or case number (if you know): ______
Date of the court's decision: ______
Result (attach a copy of the court's opinion or order, if available): ______
(3) Did you receive a hearing on your motion, petition, or application?
Yes ☐ No ☐
(4) Did you appeal from the denial of your motion, petition, or application?
Yes ☐ No ☐
(5) If your answer to Question (c)(4) is "Yes," did you raise this issue in the appeal?
Yes ☐ No ☐
(6) If your answer to Question (c)(4) is "Yes," state:
Name and location of the court where the appeal was filed: ______
Docket or case number (if you know): ______
Date of the court's decision: ______
Result (attach a copy of the court's opinion or order, if available): ______
(7) If your answer to Question (c)(4) or Question (c)(5) is "No," explain why you did not appeal or raise this

issue: ______

GROUND THREE: ______

(a) Supporting facts (Do not argue or cite law. Just state the specific facts that support your claim.): ______

(b) **Direct Appeal of Ground Three:**
(1) If you appealed from the judgment of conviction, did you raise this issue?
Yes ☐ No ☐
(2) If you did not raise this issue in your direct appeal, explain why: ______

(c) **Post-Conviction Proceedings:**
(1) Did you raise this issue in any post-conviction motion, petition, or application?
Yes ☐ No ☐
(2) If your answer to Question (c)(1) is "Yes," state:
Type of motion or petition: ______
Name and location of the court where the motion or petition was filed: ______
Docket or case number (if you know): ______
Date of the court's decision: ______
Result (attach a copy of the court's opinion or order, if available): ______
(3) Did you receive a hearing on your motion, petition, or application?
Yes ☐ No ☐
(4) Did you appeal from the denial of your motion, petition, or application?
Yes ☐ No ☐
(5) If your answer to Question (c)(4) is "Yes," did you raise this issue in the appeal?
Yes ☐ No ☐
(6) If your answer to Question (c)(4) is "Yes," state:
Name and location of the court where the appeal was filed: ______
Docket or case number (if you know): ______
Date of the court's decision: ______
Result (attach a copy of the court's opinion or order, if available): ______
(7) If your answer to Question (c)(4) or Question (c)(5) is "No," explain why you did not appeal or raise this issue: ______

GROUND FOUR: ______

(a) Supporting facts (Do not argue or cite law. Just state the specific facts that support your claim.):
(b) **Direct Appeal of Ground Four:**
(1) If you appealed from the judgment of conviction, did you raise this issue?
Yes ☐ No ☐
(2) If you did not raise this issue in your direct appeal, explain why: ______

(c) **Post-Conviction Proceedings:**
(1) Did you raise this issue in any post-conviction motion, petition, or application?
Yes ☐ No ☐
(2) If your answer to Question (c)(1) is "Yes," state:
Type of motion or petition: ______
Name and location of the court where the motion or petition was filed: ______
Docket or case number (if you know): ______
Date of the court's decision: ______
Result (attach a copy of the court's opinion or order, if available): ______
(3) Did you receive a hearing on your motion, petition, or application?
Yes ☐ No ☐
(4) Did you appeal from the denial of your motion, petition, or application?
Yes ☐ No ☐
(5) If your answer to Question (c)(4) is "Yes," did you raise this issue in the appeal?
Yes ☐ No ☐
(6) If your answer to Question (c)(4) is "Yes," state:
Name and location of the court where the appeal was filed: ______
Docket or case number (if you know): ______
Date of the court's decision: ______
Result (attach a copy of the court's opinion or order, if available): ______
(7) If your answer to Question (c)(4) or Question (c)(5) is "No," explain why you did not appeal or raise this issue: ______

13. Is there any ground in this motion that you have not previously presented in some federal court? If so, which ground or grounds have not been presented, and state your reasons for not presenting them: ______

14. Do you have any motion, petition, or appeal now pending (filed and not decided yet) in any court for the judgment you are challenging? Yes ☐ No ☐
If "Yes," state the name and location of the court, the docket or case number, the type of proceeding, and the issues raised. __________

15. Give the name and address, if known, of each attorney who represented you in the following stages of the judgment you are challenging:
(a) At preliminary hearing: __________
(b) At arraignment and plea: __________
(c) At trial: __________
(d) At sentencing: __________
(e) On appeal: __________
(f) In any post-conviction proceeding: __________
(g) On appeal from any ruling against you in a post-conviction proceeding: __________

16. Were you sentenced on more than one count of an indictment, or on more than one indictment, in the same court and at the same time? Yes ☐ No ☐

17. Do you have any future sentence to serve after you complete the sentence for the judgment that you are challenging? Yes ☐ No ☐
(a) If so, give name and location of court that imposed the other sentence you will serve in the future: __________
(b) Give the date the other sentence was imposed: ____
(c) Give the length of the other sentence:
(d) Have you filed, or do you plan to file, any motion, petition, or application that challenges the judgment or sentence to be served in the future? Yes ☐ No ☐

18. TIMELINESS OF MOTION: If your judgment of conviction became final over one year ago, you must explain why the one-year statute of limitations as contained in 28 U.S.C. § 2255 does not bar your motion.* __________

* The Antiterrorism and Effective Death Penalty Act of 1996 (" AEDPA") as contained in 28 U.S.C. § 2255, paragraph 6, provides in part that:

> A one-year period of limitation shall apply to a motion under this section. The limitation period shall run from the latest of—
> (1) the date on which the judgment of conviction became final;
> (2) the date on which the impediment to making a motion created by governmental action in violation of the Constitution or laws of the United States is removed, if the movant was prevented from making such a motion by such governmental action;
> (3) the date on which the right asserted was initially recognized by the Supreme Court, if that right has been newly recognized by the Supreme Court and made retroactively applicable to cases on collateral review; or
> (4) the date on which the facts supporting the claim or claims presented could have been discovered through the exercise of due diligence.

Therefore, movant asks that the Court grant the following relief: __________

or any other relief to which movant may be entitled.

____
Signature of Attorney (if any)

I declare (or certify, verify, or state) under penalty of perjury that the foregoing is true and correct and that this Motion Under 28 U.S.C. § 2255 was placed in the prison mailing system on __________ (month, date, year).

Executed (signed) on _____ (date).

____
Signature of Movant

If the person signing is not movant, state relationship to movant and explain why movant is not signing this motion. __________

* * * * *

(As amended Apr. 28, 1982, eff. Aug. 1, 1982; Apr. 26, 2004, eff. Dec. 1, 2004.)

RULES OF PROCEDURE
FOR THE
TRIAL OF MISDEMEANORS
BEFORE
UNITED STATES MAGISTRATES

Prior Federal Rules of Procedure for the Trial of Minor Offenses Before United States Magistrates were superseded by Rules of Procedure for the Trial of Misdemeanors before United States Magistrates, promulgated April 14, 1980, effective June 1, 1980, which were abrogated effective Dec. 1, 1990.

[Rules 1 to 9. Abrogated May 1, 1990, Effective Dec. 1, 1990]

HISTORICAL NOTES

Codification

See rule 58 of the Federal Rules of Criminal Procedure.

RULES FOR THE ALIEN TERRORIST REMOVAL COURT OF THE UNITED STATES

Amendments received to February 2, 2007

Rule 1. Name of Court

This Court, established pursuant to the Antiterrorism and Effective Death Penalty Act of 1996, Pub.L. No. 104–132, Title IV, 110 Stat. 1214, 1258, (Title V of the Immigration and Nationality Act), and as amended by the Omnibus Consolidated Appropriations Act for 1997, Public Law No. 104–208, Title I, § 354, 110 Stat. 3009, shall be known as the Alien Terrorist Removal Court of the United States (8 U.S.C. § 1531 et seq.).

Rule 2. Seal

The seal of the Court shall contain the words "Alien Terrorist Removal Court" in the upper sector of space included within the two outer concentric circles and the words "of the United States of America" in the lower sector, and shall contain the standardized eagle rampant in the center.

Rule 3. Situs

The situs of the Court shall be at the United States Courthouse, Washington, D.C., 20001.

Rule 4. Clerk

(a) The Clerk of the District Court for the District of Columbia shall be the Clerk of this Court.

(b) The Clerk shall supply a deputy clerk and other personnel as the business of this Court may require.

(c) Personnel responsible for filing and maintaining records of this Court containing classified information shall have appropriate levels of security clearance in compliance with Executive Branch procedures governing classified information.

Rule 5. Application for Removal

(a) The Attorney General, acting on behalf of the United States as applicant, shall file an original and two copies of an application seeking removal of an alleged alien, named as respondent.

(b) The application shall be submitted ex parte and in camera and shall be filed under seal with the Clerk of this Court.

(c) The application shall state, to the extent known, the level of classified information, if any, that the Attorney General will present in support of removal.

(d) The application shall state whether the respondent is a permanent resident alien.

Rule 6. Assignment of Cases

(a) The Clerk shall promptly advise the Chief Judge, by a secured means, of the filing of an application. The Chief Judge shall thereupon make an assignment of the case to a member of the Court for consideration and determination of that case.

(b) Cases shall be assigned to judges of the Court in such a manner that each judge, if available for an assignment, shall receive an assignment before any other judge receives a second or successive assignment.

Rule 7. Service of an Order Granting an Application and Notice of a Removal Hearing

(a) If an order is entered granting an ex parte application, an authorized representative of the Attorney General shall serve the respondent who is the subject of the application with a copy of the order, excluding any classified information in the order, together with a Notice pursuant to 8 U.S.C. § 1534(b). The Notice shall also set an expeditious date for the Removal Hearing.

(b) The Attorney General shall file with the Clerk a certificate of service of the order and Notice.

(c) Retained counsel for a respondent shall promptly file an appearance with the Clerk.

(d) If a respondent is financially unable to obtain adequate representation, the respondent may request appointment of counsel from the Criminal Justice Panel for United States District Court for the District of Columbia, as provided for in Section 3006A of Title 18 (Criminal Justice Act).

Rule 8. Interim Hearing

(a) For the convenience of the assigned judge and the parties, the judge may conduct an Interim Hearing or Hearings for the purpose of resolving issues relating to representation of the respondent, special issues relating to a permanent resident alien respondent, issues relating to classified information, or if required by statute. When appropriate, the Interim Hearing will be conducted ex parte and in camera.

(b) Any Interim Hearing shall be conducted in the United States Courthouse in Washington, D.C.

Rule 9. Place of Conducting Removal Hearing

The Removal Hearing shall be held in the United States Courthouse in Washington, D.C. The Removal Hearing shall be conducted publicly, except that any part of the argument that refers to evidence received in camera and ex parte, shall be heard in camera and ex parte.

Rule 10. Verbatim Record of Proceedings

All ex parte, in camera, and public hearings of the Court shall be recorded verbatim by a reporter retained pursuant to 28 U.S.C. § 753, by shorthand, mechanical means, electronic sound recording, or any other method, subject to regulations promulgated by the Judicial Conference of the United States.

Rule 11. Motions

(a) Any motion shall include or be accompanied by a statement of the specific points of law and authority that support the motion, including where appropriate a concise statement of facts. If a table of cases is provided, counsel shall place asterisks in the margin to the left of those cases or authorities on which counsel chiefly relies.

(b) Within 15 days of the date of service or at such other time as the assigned judge may direct, an opposing party shall serve and file a memorandum of points and authorities in opposition to the motion. If such a memorandum is not filed within the prescribed time, the judge may treat the motion as uncontested.

(c) Each motion shall be accompanied by a proposed order.

(d) Within 10 days after service of the memorandum in opposition, the moving party may serve and file a reply memorandum.

(e) A memorandum of points and authorities in support of or in opposition to a motion shall not exceed 15 pages and a reply memorandum shall not exceed 10 pages, without prior approval of the assigned judge.

(f) A party may in a motion or opposition request oral argument, but its allowance shall be within the discretion of the assigned judge.

Rule 12. Subpoenas

Except for good cause shown, requests for issuance of a subpoena pursuant to 8 U.S.C. § 1534(d) by either the respondent or applicant, shall be made at least 10 days prior to the date of the removal hearing.

Rule 13. Classified Information

(a) The ex parte and in camera examination of any classified information, pursuant to 8 U.S.C. § 1534(e)(3)(A)–(E), and of the proposed unclassified summary of specific information shall both be conducted on the day of the Interim Hearing unless the assigned judge otherwise directs.

(b) The unclassified summary, following approval by the judge, shall be delivered to the respondent without delay.

(c) When the respondent is a lawful permanent resident alien, who is denied an unclassified summary pursuant to 8 U.S.C. § 1534(e)(3)(F), the judge shall designate a special attorney to assist the respondent by reviewing the classified information.

(d) When the appointed special attorney moves to challenge the veracity of the evidence contained in the classified information pursuant to 8 U.S.C. § 1534(e)(3)(F)(i)(II), the assigned judge shall schedule an in camera proceeding prior to the Removal Hearing to consider the motion.

Rule 14. Removal Hearing Memorandum

Seven days prior to the Removal Hearing, counsel for the applicant and the respondent shall file with the Clerk and serve on each other a Hearing Memorandum setting forth any legal issues to be raised, a summary of the anticipated testimony (exclusive of classified information), and copies of exhibits (exclusive of classified information). The names of individuals involved in the investigation and prospective witnesses need not be included in the material filed with the Court.

RULES OF EVIDENCE FOR UNITED STATES COURTS AND MAGISTRATES

Pub.L. 93–595, § 1, January 2, 1975, 88 Stat. 1926
Amendments received to February 2, 2007

ORDERS OF THE SUPREME COURT OF THE UNITED STATES ADOPTING AND AMENDING RULES

ORDER OF NOVEMBER 20, 1972

1. That the rules hereinafter set forth, to be known as the Federal Rules of Evidence, be, and they hereby are, prescribed pursuant to Sections 3402, 3771, and 3772, Title 18, United States Code, and Sections 2072 and 2075, Title 28, United States Code, to govern procedure, in the proceedings and to the extent set forth therein, in the United States courts of appeals, the United States district courts, the District Court for the District of the Canal Zone and the district courts of Guam and the Virgin Islands, and before United States magistrates.

2. That the aforementioned Federal Rules of Evidence shall take effect on July 1, 1973, and shall be applicable to actions and proceedings brought thereafter and also to further procedure in actions and proceedings then pending, except to the extent that in the opinion of the court their application in a particular action or proceeding then pending would not be feasible or would work injustice in which event the former procedure applies.

3. That subdivision (c) of Rule 30 and Rules 43 and 44.1 of the Federal Rules of Civil Procedure be, and they hereby are, amended, effective July 1, 1973, to read as hereinafter set forth:

[See amendments made thereby under the respective Rules of Civil Procedure.]

4. That subdivision (c) of Rule 32 of the Federal Rules of Civil Procedure be, and it hereby is, abrogated, effective July 1, 1973.

5. That Rules 26, 26.1 and 28 of the Federal Rules of Criminal Procedure be, and they hereby are, amended effective July 1, 1973, to read as hereinafter set forth.

[See amendments made thereby under the respective Rules of Criminal Procedure.]

6. That the Chief Justice be, and he hereby is, authorized to transmit the foregoing new rules and amendments to and abrogation of existing rules to the Congress at the beginning of its next regular session, in accordance with the provisions of Title 18 U.S.C. § 3771 and Title 28 U.S.C. §§ 2072 and 2075.

CONGRESSIONAL ACTION ON PROPOSED RULES OF EVIDENCE AND 1972 AMENDMENTS TO FEDERAL RULES OF CIVIL PROCEDURE AND FEDERAL RULES OF CRIMINAL PROCEDURE

Pub.L. 93–12, Mar. 30, 1973, 87 Stat. 9, provided: "That notwithstanding any other provisions of law, the Rules of Evidence for United States Courts and Magistrates, the Amendments to the Federal Rules of Civil Procedure, and the Amendments to the Federal Rules of Criminal Procedure, which are embraced by the orders entered by the Supreme Court of the United States on Monday, November 20, 1972, and Monday, December 18, 1972, shall have no force or effect except to the extent, and with such amendments, as they may be expressly approved by Act of Congress."

Pub.L. 93–595, § 3, Jan. 2, 1975, 88 Stat. 1959, provided that: "The Congress expressly approves the amendments to the Federal Rules of Civil Procedure, and the amendments to the Federal Rules of Criminal Procedure, which are embraced by the orders entered by the Supreme Court of the United States on November 20, 1972, and December 18, 1972, and such amendments shall take effect on the one hundred and eightieth day beginning after the date of the enactment of this Act [Jan. 2, 1975]."

ORDER OF APRIL 30, 1979

1. That Rule 410 of the Federal Rules of Evidence be, and it hereby is, amended to read as follows:

[See amendment made thereby following Rule 410, post.]

2. That the foregoing amendment to the Federal Rules of Evidence shall take effect on November 1, 1979, and shall be applicable to all proceedings then pending except to the extent that in the opinion of the court the application of the amended rule in a particular proceeding would not be feasible or would work injustice.

3. That THE CHIEF JUSTICE be, and he hereby is, authorized to transmit to the Congress the foregoing amendment to the Federal Rules of Evidence in accordance with the provisions of 28 U.S.C. § 2076.

CONGRESSIONAL ACTION ON AMENDMENT PROPOSED APRIL 30, 1979

Pub.L. 96–42, July 31, 1979, 93 Stat. 326, provided that the amendment proposed and transmitted to the Federal Rules of Evidence affecting rule 410, shall not take effect until Dec. 1, 1980, or until and then only to the extent approved by Act of Congress, whichever is earlier.

ORDER OF MARCH 2, 1987

1. That the Federal Rules of Evidence be, and they hereby are, amended by including therein amendments to Rules 101, 104, 106, 404, 405, 411, 602, 603, 604, 606, 607, 608, 609, 610, 611, 612, 613, 615, 701, 703, 705, 706, 801, 803, 804, 806, 902, 1004, 1007 and 1101, as hereinafter set forth:

[See amendments made thereby under respective rules, post.]

2. That the foregoing changes in the Federal Rules of Evidence shall take effect on October 1, 1987.

3. That THE CHIEF JUSTICE be, and he hereby is, authorized to transmit to the Congress the foregoing changes in the rules of evidence in accordance with the provisions of Section 2076 of Title 28, United States Code.

ORDER OF APRIL 25, 1988

1. That the Federal Rules of Evidence be, and they hereby are, amended by including therein amendments to Rules 101, 602, 608, 613, 615, 902, and 1101, as hereinafter set forth:

[See amendments made thereby under respective rules, post.]

2. That the foregoing changes in the Federal Rules of Evidence shall take effect on November 1, 1988.

3. That THE CHIEF JUSTICE be, and he hereby is, authorized to transmit to the Congress the foregoing changes in the rules of evidence in accordance with the provisions of Section 2076 of Title 28, United States Code.

ORDER OF JANUARY 26, 1990

1. That the Federal Rules of Evidence be, and they hereby are, amended by including therein amendments to Rule 609(a)(1) and (2), as hereinafter set forth:

[See amendment made thereby, post].

2. That the foregoing changes in the Federal Rules of Evidence shall take effect on December 1, 1990.

3. That THE CHIEF JUSTICE be, and he hereby is, authorized to transmit to the Congress the foregoing changes in the rules of evidence in accordance with the provisions of Section 2074 of Title 28, United States Code.

ORDER OF APRIL 30, 1991

1. That the Federal Rules of Evidence for the United States District Courts be, and they hereby are, amended by including therein amendments to Evidence Rules 404(b) and 1102.

[See amendments made thereby under respective rules, post.]

2. That the foregoing amendments to the Federal Rules of Evidence shall take effect on December 1, 1991, and shall govern in all proceedings thereafter commenced and, insofar as just and practicable, all proceedings then pending.

3. That THE CHIEF JUSTICE be, and he hereby is, authorized to transmit to the Congress the foregoing amendments to the Federal Rules of Evidence in accordance with the provisions of Section 2072 of Title 28, United States Code.

ORDER OF APRIL 22, 1993

1. That the Federal Rules of Evidence for the United States District Courts be, and they hereby are, amended by including therein amendments to Evidence Rules 101, 705, and 1101.

[See amendments made thereby under respective rules, post.]

2. That the foregoing amendments to the Federal Rules of Evidence shall take effect on December 1, 1993, and shall govern in all proceedings thereafter commenced and, insofar as just and practicable, all proceedings then pending.

3. That THE CHIEF JUSTICE be, and he hereby is, authorized to transmit to the Congress the foregoing amendments to the Federal Rules of Evidence in accordance with the provisions of Section 2072 of Title 28, United States Code.

ORDER OF APRIL 29, 1994

ORDERED:

1. That the Federal Rules of Evidence for the United States District Courts be, and they hereby are, amended by including therein an amendment to Evidence Rule 412.

[See amendment made hereby under Rule 412, post.]

2. That the foregoing amendment to the Federal Rules of Evidence shall take effect on December 1, 1994, and shall govern in all proceedings thereafter commenced and, insofar as just and practicable, all proceedings then pending.

3. That THE CHIEF JUSTICE be, and he hereby is, authorized to transmit to the Congress the foregoing amendment to the Federal Rules of Evidence in accordance with the provisions of Section 2072 of Title 28, United States Code.

ORDER OF APRIL 11, 1997

ORDERED:

1. That the Federal Rules of Evidence be, and they hereby are, amended by including therein amendments to Evidence Rules 407, 801, 803(24), 804(b)(5), and 806, and new Rules 804(b)(6) and 807.

[See amendments made thereby under respective rules, post.]

2. That the foregoing amendments to the Federal Rules of Evidence shall take effect on December 1, 1997, and shall govern in all proceedings thereafter commenced and, insofar as just and practicable, all proceedings then pending.

3. That THE CHIEF JUSTICE be, and hereby is, authorized to transmit to the Congress the foregoing amendments to the Federal Rules of Evidence in accordance with the provisions of Section 2072 of Title 28, United States Code.

ORDER OF APRIL 24, 1998

ORDERED:

1. That the Federal Rules of Evidence be, and they hereby are, amended by including therein amendments to Evidence Rule 615.

[See amendments made thereby under respective rules, post.]

2. That the foregoing amendments to the Federal Rules of Evidence shall take effect on December 1, 1998, and shall govern in all proceedings thereafter commenced and, insofar as just and practicable, all proceedings then pending.

3. That THE CHIEF JUSTICE be, and hereby is, authorized to transmit to the Congress the foregoing amendments to the Federal Rules of Evidence in accordance with the provisions of Section 2072 of Title 28, United States Code.

ORDER OF APRIL 17, 2000

ORDERED:

1. That the Federal Rules of Evidence for the United States District Courts be, and they hereby are, amended by including therein amendments to Evidence Rules 103, 404, 701, 702, 703, 803(6), and 902.

[See amendments made thereby under respective rules, post.]

2. That the foregoing amendments to the Federal Rules of Evidence shall take effect on December 1, 2000, and shall govern all proceedings thereafter commenced and, insofar as just and practicable, all proceedings then pending .

3. That THE CHIEF JUSTICE be, and hereby is, authorized to transmit to the Congress the foregoing amendments to the Federal Rules of Evidence in accordance with the provisions of Section 2072 of Title 28, United States Code.

ORDER OF MARCH 27, 2003

ORDERED:

1. That the Federal Rules of Evidence be, and they hereby are, amended by including therein the amendments to Evidence Rule 608(b).

[See amendments made thereby under respective rules, post.]

2. That the foregoing amendments to the Federal Rules of Evidence shall take effect on December 1, 2003, and shall govern in all proceedings thereafter commenced and, insofar as just and practicable, all proceedings then pending.

3. That THE CHIEF JUSTICE be, and hereby is, authorized to transmit to the Congress the foregoing amendments to the Federal Rules of Evidence in accordance with the provisions of Section 2072 of Title 28, United States Code.

ORDER OF APRIL 12, 2006

1. That the Federal Rules of Evidence be, and they hereby are, amended by including therein the amendments to Evidence Rules 404, 408, 606, and 609.

[See amendments made thereby under respective rules, post.]

2. That the foregoing amendments to the Federal Rules of Evidence shall take effect on December 1, 2006, and shall govern in all proceedings thereafter commenced and, insofar as just and practicable, all proceedings then pending.

3. That THE CHIEF JUSTICE be, and hereby is, authorized to transmit to the Congress the foregoing amendments to the Federal Rules of Evidence in accordance with the provisions of Section 2072 of Title 28, United States Code.

HISTORICAL NOTES

1978 Amendments. Pub.L. 95–540, § 2(b), Oct. 28, 1978, 92 Stat. 2047, added item 412.

1975 Amendments. Pub.L. 94–149, § 1(1) to (8), Dec. 12, 1975, 89 Stat. 805, amended analysis as follows: Item 106, substituted "or" for "on"; Item 301 inserted "in" immediately following "General"; Item 405(a), inserted "or opinion" following "Reputation" and preceding the period; Item 410, substituted "Inadmissibility of Pleas, Offers of Pleas, and Related Statements" for "Offer to Plead Guilty; Nolo Contendere; Withdrawn Plea of Guilty"; Item 608(a), substituted "Opinion and reputation" for "Reputation"; Item 901(b)(8), substituted "compilation" for "compilations"; and Item 1101(c), substituted "Rule" for "Rules".

Effective Date and Application of Rules

The Federal Rules of Evidence were adopted by order of the Supreme Court on Nov. 20, 1972, transmitted to Congress by the Chief Justice on Feb. 5, 1973, and to have become effective on July 1, 1973. Pub.L. 93–12, Mar. 30, 1973, 87 Stat. 9, provided that the proposed rules "shall have no force or effect except to the extent, and with such amendments, as they may be expressly approved by Act of Congress". Pub.L. 93–595, Jan. 2, 1975, 88 Stat. 1926, enacted the Federal Rules of Evidence proposed by the Supreme Court, with amendments made by Congress, to take effect on July 1, 1975.

The Rules have been amended Oct. 16, 1975, Pub.L. 94–113, § 1, 89 Stat. 576, eff. Oct. 31, 1975; Dec. 12, 1975, Pub.L. 94–149, § 1, 89 Stat. 805; Oct. 28, 1978, Pub.L. 95–540, § 2, 92 Stat. 2046; Nov. 6, 1978, Pub.L. 95–598, Title II, § 251, 92 Stat. 2673, eff. Oct. 1, 1979; Apr. 30, 1979, eff. Dec. 1, 1980; Apr. 2, 1982, Pub.L. 97–164, Title I, § 142, Title IV, § 402, 96 Stat. 45, 57, eff. Oct. 1, 1982; Oct. 12, 1984, Pub.L. 98–473, Title IV, § 406, 98 Stat. 2067; Mar. 2, 1987, eff. Oct. 1, 1987; Apr. 25, 1988, eff. Nov. 1, 1988; Nov. 18, 1988, Pub.L. 100–690, Title VII, §§ 7046, 7075, 102 Stat. 4400, 4405; Jan. 26, 1990, eff. Dec. 1, 1990; Apr. 30, 1991, eff. Dec. 1, 1991; Apr. 22, 1993, eff. Dec. 1, 1993; Apr. 29, 1994, eff. Dec. 1, 1994; Apr. 11, 1997, eff. Dec. 1, 1997; Apr. 24, 1998, eff. Dec. 1, 1998; Apr. 17, 2000, eff. Dec. 1, 2000; Mar. 27, 2003, eff. Dec. 1, 2003; Apr. 12, 2006, eff. Dec. 1, 2006.

ARTICLE I. GENERAL PROVISIONS

HISTORICAL NOTES

Change of Name

United States magistrate appointed under section 631 of Title 28, Judiciary and Judicial Procedure, to be known as United States magistrate judge after Dec. 1, 1990, with any reference to United States magistrate or magistrate in Title 28, in any other Federal statute, etc., deemed a reference to United States magistrate judge appointed under section 631 of Title 28, see section 321 of Pub.L. 101–650, set out as a note under section 631 of Title 28.

Rule 101. Scope

These rules govern proceedings in the courts of the United States and before the United States bankruptcy judges and United States magistrate judges, to the extent and with the exceptions stated in rule 1101.

(Pub.L. 93–595, § 1, Jan. 2, 1975, 88 Stat. 1929; Mar. 2, 1987, eff. Oct. 1, 1987; Apr. 25, 1988, eff. Nov. 1, 1988; Apr. 22, 1993, eff. Dec. 1, 1993.)

ADVISORY COMMITTEE NOTES

1972 Proposed Rules

Rule 1101 specifies in detail the courts, proceedings, questions, and stages of proceedings to which the rules apply in whole or in part.

1987 Amendments

United States bankruptcy judges are added to conform this rule with Rule 1101(b) and Bankruptcy Rule 9017.

1988 Amendments

The amendment is technical. No substantive change is intended.

1993 Amendments

This revision is made to conform the rule to changes made by the Judicial Improvements Act of 1990.

HISTORICAL NOTES

Change of Name

United States magistrate appointed under section 631 of Title 28, Judiciary and Judicial Procedure, to be known as United States magistrate judge after Dec. 1, 1990, with any reference to United States magistrate or magistrate in Title 28, in any other Federal statute, etc., deemed a reference to United States magistrate judge appointed under section 631 of Title 28, see section 321 of Pub.L. 101–650, set out as a note under section 631 of Title 28.

Rule 102. Purpose and Construction

These rules shall be construed to secure fairness in administration, elimination of unjustifiable expense and delay, and promotion of growth and development of the law of evidence to the end that the truth may be ascertained and proceedings justly determined.

(Pub.L. 93–595, § 1, Jan. 2, 1975, 88 Stat.1929.)

ADVISORY COMMITTEE NOTES

1972 Proposed Rules

For similar provisions see Rule 2 of the Federal Rules of Criminal Procedure, Rule 1 of the Federal Rules of Civil Procedure, California Evidence Code § 2, and New Jersey Evidence Rule 5.

Rule 103. Rulings on Evidence

(a) Effect of Erroneous Ruling.—Error may not be predicated upon a ruling which admits or excludes evidence unless a substantial right of the party is affected, and

(1) Objection.—In case the ruling is one admitting evidence, a timely objection or motion to strike appears of record, stating the specific ground of objection, if the specific ground was not apparent from the context; or

(2) Offer of Proof.—In case the ruling is one excluding evidence, the substance of the evidence was made known to the court by offer or was apparent from the context within which questions were asked.

Once the court makes a definitive ruling on the record admitting or excluding evidence, either at or before trial, a party need not renew an objection or offer of proof to preserve a claim of error for appeal.

(b) Record of Offer and Ruling.—The court may add any other or further statement which shows the character of the evidence, the form in which it was offered, the objection made, and the ruling thereon. It may direct the making of an offer in question and answer form.

(c) Hearing of Jury.—In jury cases, proceedings shall be conducted, to the extent practicable, so as to prevent inadmissible evidence from being suggested to the jury by any means, such as making statements or offers of proof or asking questions in the hearing of the jury.

(d) Plain Error.—Nothing in this rule precludes taking notice of plain errors affecting substantial rights although they were not brought to the attention of the court.

(Pub.L. 93–595, § 1, Jan. 2, 1975, 88 Stat. 1929; Apr. 17, 2000, eff. Dec. 1, 2000.)

ADVISORY COMMITTEE NOTES

1972 Proposed Rules

Note to Subdivision (a). Subdivision (a) states the law as generally accepted today. Rulings on evidence cannot be assigned as error unless (1) a substantial right is affected, and (2) the nature of the error was called to the attention of the judge, so as to alert him to the proper course of action and enable opposing counsel to take proper corrective measures. The objection and the offer of proof are the techniques for accomplishing these objectives. For similar provisions see Uniform Rules 4 and 5; California Evidence Code §§ 353 and 354; Kansas Code of Civil Procedure §§ 60–404 and 60–405. The rule does not purport to change the law with respect to harmless error. See 28 USC § 2111, F.R.Civ.P. 61, F.R.Crim.P. 52, and decisions construing them. The status of constitutional error as harmless or not is treated in Chapman v. California, 386 U.S. 18, 87 S.Ct. 824, 17 L.Ed.2d 705 (1967), reh. denied id. 987, 87 S.Ct. 1283, 18 L.Ed.2d 241.

Note to Subdivision (b). The first sentence is the third sentence of Rule 43(c) of the Federal Rules of Civil Procedure virtually verbatim. Its purpose is to reproduce for an appellate court, insofar as possible, a true reflection of what occurred in the trial court. The second sentence is in part derived from the final sentence of Rule 43(c). It is designed to resolve doubts as to what testimony the witness would have in fact given, and, in nonjury cases, to provide the appellate court with material for a possible final disposition of the case in the event of reversal of a ruling which excluded evidence. See 5 Moore's Federal Practice § 43.11 (2d ed. 1968). Application is made discretionary in view of the practical impossibility of formulating a satisfactory rule in mandatory terms.

Note to Subdivision (c). This subdivision proceeds on the supposition that a ruling which excludes evidence in a jury case is likely to be a pointless procedure if the excluded evidence nevertheless comes to the attention of the jury. *Bruton v. United States,* 389 U.S. 818, 88 S.Ct. 126, 19 L.Ed.2d 70 (1968). Rule 43(c) of the Federal Rules of Civil Procedure provides: "The court may require the offer to be made out of the hearing of the jury." *In re McConnell,* 370 U.S. 230, 82 S.Ct. 1288, 8 L.Ed.2d 434 (1962), left some doubt whether questions on which an offer is based must first be asked in the presence of the jury. The subdivision answers in the negative. The judge can foreclose a particular line of testimony and counsel can protect his record without a series of questions before the jury, designed at best to waste time and at worst "to waft into the jury box" the very matter sought to be excluded.

Note to Subdivision (d). This wording of the plain error principle is from Rule 52(b) of the Federal Rules of Criminal Procedure. While judicial unwillingness to be constructed by mechanical breakdowns of the adversary system has been more pronounced in criminal cases, there is no scarcity of decisions to the same effect in civil cases. In general, see Campbell, Extent to Which Courts of Review Will Consider Questions Not Properly Raised and Preserved, 7 Wis.L.Rev. 91, 160 (1932); Vestal, Sua Sponte Consideration in Appellate Review, 27 Fordham L.Rev. 477 (1958–59); 64 Harv.L.Rev. 652 (1951). In the nature of things the application of the plain error rule will be more likely with respect to the admission of evidence than to exclusion, since failure to comply with normal requirements of offers of proof is likely to produce a record which simply does not disclose the error.

2000 Amendment

The amendment applies to all rulings on evidence whether they occur at or before trial, including so-called "*in limine*" rulings. One of the most difficult questions arising from *in limine* and other evidentiary rulings is whether a losing party must renew an objection or offer of proof when the evidence is or would be offered at trial, in order to preserve a claim of error on appeal. Courts have taken differing approaches to this question. Some courts have held that a renewal at the time the evidence is to be offered at trial is always required. *See, e.g., Collins v. Wayne Corp.,* 621 F.2d 777 (5th Cir. 1980). Some courts have taken a more flexible approach, holding that renewal is not required if the issue decided is one that (1) was fairly presented to the trial court for an initial ruling, (2) may be decided as a final matter before the evidence is actually offered, and (3) was ruled on definitively by the trial judge, *See, e.g., Rosenfeld v. Basquiat,* 78 F.3d 84 (2d Cir. 1996) (admissibility of former testimony under the Dead Man's Statute; renewal not required). Other courts have distinguished between objections to evidence, which must be renewed when evidence is offered, and offers of proof, which need not be renewed after a definitive determination is made that the evidence is inadmissible. *See, e.g., Fusco v. General Motors Corp.,* 11 F.3d 259 (1st Cir. 1993). Another court, aware of this Committee's proposed amendment, has adopted its approach. *Wilson v. Williams,* 182 F. 3d 562 (7th Cir.1999) (en banc). Differing views on this question create uncertainty for litigants and unnecessary work for the appellate courts.

The amendment provides that a claim of error with respect to a definitive ruling is preserved for review when the party has otherwise satisfied the objection or offer of proof requirements of Rule 103(a). When the ruling is definitive, a renewed objection or offer of proof at the time the evidence is to be offered is more a formalism than a necessity. *See* Fed.R.Civ.P. 46 (formal exceptions unnecessary); Fed. R.Cr.P. 51 (same); *United States v. Mejia–Alarcon,* 995 F.2d 982, 986 (10th Cir. 1993) ("Requiring a party to renew an objection when the district court has issued a definitive ruling on a matter that can be fairly decided before trial would be in the nature of a formal exception and therefore unnecessary."). On the other hand, when the trial court appears to have reserved its ruling or to have indicated that the ruling is provisional, it makes sense to require the party to bring the issue to the court's attention subsequently. *See, e.g., United States v. Vest,* 116 F.3d 1179, 1188 (7th Cir. 1997) (where the trial court ruled *n limine* that testimony from defense witnesses could not be admitted, but allowed the defendant to seek leave at trial to call the witnesses should their testimony turn out to be relevant, the defendant's failure to seek such leave at trial meant that it was "too late to reopen the issue now on appeal"); *United States v. Valenti,* 60 F.3d 941 (2d Cir. 1995) (failure to proffer evidence at trial waives any claim of error where the trial judge had stated that he would reserve judgment on the *in limine* motion until he had heard the trial evidence).

The amendment imposes the obligation on counsel to clarify whether an *in limine* or other evidentiary ruling is definitive when there is doubt on that point. *See, e.g., Walden v. Georgia–Pacific Corp.,* 126 F.3d 506, 520 (3d Cir. 1997) (although "the district court told plaintiffs' counsel not to reargue every ruling, it did not countermand its clear opening statement that all of its rulings were tentative, and counsel never requested clarification, as he might have done.").

Even where the court's ruling is definitive, nothing in the amendment prohibits the court from revisiting its decision when the evidence is to be offered. If the court changes its initial ruling, or if the opposing party violates the terms of the initial ruling, objection must be made when the evidence is offered to preserve the claim of error for appeal. The error, if any, in such a situation occurs only when the evidence is offered and admitted. *United States Aviation Underwriters, Inc. v. Olympia Wings, Inc.,* 896 F.2d 949, 956 (5th Cir. 1990) ("objection is required to preserve error when an opponent, or the court itself, violates a motion *in limine* that was granted"); *United States v. Roenigk,* 810 F.2d 809 (8th Cir. 1987) (claim of error was not preserved where the defendant failed to object at trial to secure the benefit of a favorable advance ruling).

A definitive advance ruling is reviewed in light of the facts and circumstances before the trial court at the time of the ruling. If the relevant facts and circumstances change materially after the advance ruling has been made, those facts and circumstances cannot be relied upon on appeal unless they have been brought to the attention of the trial court by way of a renewed, and timely, objection, offer of proof, or motion to strike. *See Old Chief v. United States,* 519 U.S. 172, 182, n.6 (1997) ("It is important that a reviewing court evaluate the trial court's decision from its perspective when it had to rule and not indulge in review by hindsight."). Similarly, if the court decides in an advance ruling that proffered evidence is admissible subject to the eventual introduction by the proponent of a foundation for the evidence, and that foundation is never provided, the opponent cannot claim error based on the failure to establish the foundation unless the opponent calls that failure to the court's attention by a timely motion to strike or other suitable motion. *See Huddleston v. United States*, 485 U.S. 681, 690, n.7 (1988) ("It is, of course, not the responsibility of the judge *sua sponte* to ensure that the foundation evidence is offered; the objector must move to strike the evidence if at the close of the trial the offeror has failed to satisfy the condition.").

Nothing in the amendment is intended to affect the provisions of Fed.R.Civ.P. 72(a) or 28 U.S.C. § 636(b)(1) pertaining to nondispositive pretrial rulings by magistrate judges in proceedings that are not before a magistrate judge by consent of the parties. Fed.R.Civ.P. 72(a) provides that a party who fails to file a written objection to a magistrate judge's nondispositive order within ten days of receiving a copy "may not thereafter assign as error a defect" in the order. 28 U.S.C. § 636(b)(1) provides that any party "may serve and file written objections to such proposed findings and recommendations as provided by rules of court" within ten days of receiving a copy of the order. Several courts have held that a party must comply with this statutory provision in order to preserve a claim of error. *See, e.g., Wells v. Shriners Hospital*, 109 F.3d 198, 200 (4th Cir. 1997)("[i]n this circuit, as in others, a party 'may' file objections within ten days or he may not, as he chooses, but he 'shall' do so if he wishes further consideration."). When Fed.R.Civ.P. 72(a) or 28 U.S.C. § 636(b)(1) is operative, its requirement must be satisfied in order for a party to preserve a claim of error on appeal, even where Evidence Rule 103(a) would not require a subsequent objection or offer of proof.

Nothing in the amendment is intended to affect the rule set forth in *Luce v. United States*, 469 U.S. 38 (1984), and its progeny. The amendment provides that an objection or offer of proof need not be renewed to preserve a claim of error with respect to a definitive pretrial ruling. *Luce* answers affirmatively a separate question: whether a criminal defendant must testify at trial in order to preserve a claim of error predicated upon a trial court's decision to admit the defendant's prior convictions for impeachment. The *Luce* principle has been extended by many lower courts to other situations. *See United States v. DiMatteo*, 759 F.2d 831 (11th Cir. 1985) (applying *Luce* where the defendant's witness would be impeached with evidence offered under Rule 608). *See also United States v. Goldman*, 41 F.3d 785, 788 (1st Cir. 1994) ("Although *Luce* involved impeachment by conviction under Rule 609, the reasons given by the Supreme Court for requiring the defendant to testify apply with full force to the kind of Rule 403 and 404 objections that are advanced by Goldman in this case."); *Palmieri v. DeFaria*, 88 F.3d 136 (2d Cir. 1996) (where the plaintiff decided to take an adverse judgment rather than challenge an advance ruling by putting on evidence at trial, the *in limine* ruling would not be reviewed on appeal); *United States v. Ortiz*, 857 F.2d 900 (2d Cir. 1988) (where uncharged misconduct is ruled admissible if the defendant pursues a certain defense, the defendant must actually pursue that defense at trial in order to preserve a claim of error on appeal); *United States v. Bond*, 87 F.3d 695 (5th Cir. 1996) (where the trial court rules *in limine* that the defendant would waive his fifth amendment privilege were he to testify, the defendant must take the stand and testify in order to challenge that ruling on appeal).

The amendment does not purport to answer whether a party who objects to evidence that the court finds admissible in a definitive ruling, and who then offers the evidence to "remove the sting" of its anticipated prejudicial effect, thereby waives the right to appeal the trial court's ruling. *See, e.g., United States v. Fisher*, 106 F.3d 622 (5th Cir. 1997) (where the trial judge ruled *in limine* that the government could use a prior conviction to impeach the defendant if he testified, the defendant did not waive his right to appeal by introducing the conviction on direct examination); *Judd v. Rodman*, 105 F.3d 1339 (11th Cir. 1997) (an objection made *in limine* is sufficient to preserve a claim of error when the movant, as a matter of trial strategy, presents the objectionable evidence herself on direct examination to minimize its prejudicial effect); *Gill v. Thomas*, 83 F.3d 537, 540 (1st Cir. 1996) ("by offering the misdemeanor evidence himself, Gill waived his opportunity to object and thus did not preserve the issue for appeal"); *United States v. Williams*, 939 F.2d 721 (9th Cir. 1991) (objection to impeachment evidence was waived where the defendant was impeached on direct examination).

GAP Report—Proposed Amendment to Rule 103(a)

The Committee made the following changes to the published draft of the proposed amendment to Evidence Rule 103(a):

1. A minor stylistic change was made in the text, in accordance with the suggestion of the Style Subcommittee of the Standing Committee on Rules of Practice and Procedure.

2. The second sentence of the amended portion of the published draft was deleted, and the Committee Note was amended to reflect the fact that nothing in the amendment is intended to affect the rule of *Luce v. United States*.

3. The Committee Note was updated to include cases decided after the proposed amendment was issued for public comment.

4. The Committee Note was amended to include a reference to a Civil Rule and a statute requiring objections to certain Magistrate Judge rulings to be made to the District Court.

5. The Committee Note was revised to clarify that an advance ruling does not encompass subsequent developments at trial that might be the subject of an appeal.

HISTORICAL NOTES

Conference Committee Notes, House Report No. 93–1597

The House bill contains the word "judge". The Senate amendment substitutes the word "court" in order to conform with usage elsewhere in the House bill.

The Conference adopts the Senate amendment.

Rule 104. Preliminary Questions

(a) Questions of admissibility generally. Preliminary questions concerning the qualification of a person to be a witness, the existence of a privilege, or the admissibility of evidence shall be determined by the court, subject to the provisions of subdivision (b). In making its determination it is not bound by the rules of evidence except those with respect to privileges.

(b) Relevancy conditioned on fact. When the relevancy of evidence depends upon the fulfillment of a condition of fact, the court shall admit it upon, or subject to, the introduction of evidence sufficient to support a finding of the fulfillment of the condition.

(c) Hearing of jury. Hearings on the admissibility of confessions shall in all cases be conducted out of the hearing of the jury. Hearings on other preliminary matters shall be so conducted when the interests of justice require, or when an accused is a witness and so requests.

(d) Testimony by accused. The accused does not, by testifying upon a preliminary matter, become subject to cross-examination as to other issues in the case.

(e) Weight and credibility. This rule does not limit the right of a party to introduce before the jury evidence relevant to weight or credibility.

(Pub.L. 93–595, § 1, Jan. 2, 1975, 88 Stat.1930; Mar. 2, 1987, eff. Oct. 1, 1987.)

ADVISORY COMMITTEE NOTES

1972 Proposed Rule

Note to Subdivision (a). The applicability of a particular rule of evidence often depends upon the existence of a condition. Is the alleged expert a qualified physician? Is a witness whose former testimony is offered unavailable? Was a stranger present during a conversation between attorney and client? In each instance the admissibility of evidence will turn upon the answer to the question of the existence of the condition. Accepted practice, incorporated in the rule, places on the judge the responsibility for these determinations. McCormick § 53; Morgan, Basic Problems of Evidence 45–50 (1962).

To the extent that these inquiries are factual, the judge acts as a trier of fact. Often, however, rulings on evidence call for an evaluation in terms of a legally set standard. Thus when a hearsay statement is offered as a declaration against interest, a decision must be made whether it possesses the required against-interest characteristics. These decisions, too, are made by the judge.

In view of these considerations, this subdivision refers to preliminary requirements generally by the broad term "questions," without attempt at specification.

This subdivision is of general application. It must, however, be read as subject to the special provisions for "conditional relevancy" in subdivision (b) and those for confessions in subdivision (d).

If the question is factual in nature, the judge will of necessity receive evidence pro and con on the issue. The rule provides that the rules of evidence in general do not apply to this process. McCormick § 53, p. 123, n. 8, points out that the authorities are "scattered and inconclusive," and observes:

"Should the exclusionary law of evidence, 'the child of the jury system' in Thayer's phrase, be applied to this hearing before the judge? Sound sense backs the view that it should not, and that the judge should be empowered to hear any relevant evidence, such as affidavits or other reliable hearsay."

This view is reinforced by practical necessity in certain situations. An item, offered and objected to, may itself be considered in ruling on admissibility, though not yet admitted in evidence. Thus, the content of an asserted declaration against interest must be considered in ruling whether it is against interest. Again, common practice calls for considering the testimony of a witness, particularly a child, in determining competency. Another example is the requirement of Rule 602 dealing with personal knowledge. In the case of hearsay, it is enough, if the declarant "so far as appears [has] had an opportunity to observe the fact declared." McCormick, § 10, p. 19.

If concern is felt over the use of affidavits by the judge in preliminary hearings on admissibility, attention is directed to the many important judicial determinations made on the basis of affidavits. Rule 47 of the Federal Rules of Criminal Procedure provides:

"An application to the court for an order shall be by motion. * * * It may be supported by affidavit."

The Rules of Civil Procedure are more detailed. Rule 43(e), dealing with motions generally, provides:

"When a motion is based on facts not appearing of record the court may hear the matter on affidavits presented by the respective parties, but the court may direct that the matter be heard wholly or partly on oral testimony or depositions."

Rule 4(g) provides for proof of service by affidavit. Rule 56 provides in detail for the entry of summary judgment based on affidavits. Affidavits may supply the foundation for temporary restraining orders under Rule 65(b).

The study made for the California Law Revision Commission recommended an amendment to Uniform Rule 2 as follows:

"In the determination of the issue aforesaid [preliminary determination], exclusionary rules shall not apply, subject, however, to Rule 45 and any valid claim of privilege." Tentative Recommendation and a Study Relating to the Uniform Rules of Evidence (Article VIII, Hearsay), Cal.Law Revision Comm'n, Rep., Rec. & Studies, 470 (1962). The proposal was not adopted in the California Evidence Code. The Uniform Rules are likewise silent on the subject. However, New Jersey Evidence Rule 8(1), dealing with preliminary inquiry by the judge, provides:

"In his determination the rules of evidence shall not apply except for Rule 4 [exclusion on grounds of confusion, etc.] or a valid claim of privilege."

Note to Subdivision (b). In some situations, the relevancy of an item of evidence, in the large sense, depends upon the existence of a particular preliminary fact. Thus when a spoken statement is relied upon to prove notice to X, it is without probative value unless X heard it. Or if a letter purporting to be from Y is relied upon to establish an admission by him, it has no probative value unless Y wrote or authorized it. Relevance in this sense has been labelled "conditional relevancy." Morgan, Basic Problems of Evidence 45–46 (1962). Problems arising in connection with it are to be distinguished from problems of logical relevancy, e.g., evidence in a murder case that accused on the day before purchased a weapon of the kind used in the killing, treated in Rule 401.

If preliminary questions of conditional relevancy were determined solely by the judge, as provided in subdivision (a), the functioning of the jury as a trier of fact would be greatly restricted and in some cases virtually destroyed. These are appropriate questions for juries. Accepted treatment, as provided in the rule, is consistent with that given fact questions generally. The judge makes a preliminary determination whether the foundation evidence is sufficient to support a finding of fulfillment of the condition. If so, the item is admitted. If after all the evidence on the issue is in, pro and con, the jury could reasonably conclude that fulfillment of the condition is not established, the issue is for them. If the evidence is not such as to allow a finding, the judge withdraws the matter from their consideration. Morgan, *supra;* California Evidence Code § 403; New Jersey Rule 8(2). See also Uniform Rules 19 and 67.

The order of proof here, as generally, is subject to the control of the judge.

Note to Subdivision (c). Preliminary hearings on the admissibility of confessions must be conducted outside the hearing of the jury. See *Jackson v. Denno,* 378 U.S. 368, 84 S.Ct. 1774, 12 L.Ed.2d 908 (1964). Otherwise, detailed treatment of when preliminary matters should be heard outside the hearing of the jury is not feasible. The procedure is time consuming. Not infrequently the same evidence which is relevant to the issue of establishment of fulfillment of a condition precedent to admissibility is also relevant to weight or credibility, and time is saved by taking foundation proof in the presence of the jury. Much evidence on preliminary questions, though not relevant to jury issues, may be heard by the jury with no adverse effect. A great deal must be left to the discretion of the judge who will act as the interests of justice require.

Note to Subdivision (d). The limitation upon cross-examination is designed to encourage participation by the accused in the determination of preliminary matters. He may testify concerning them without exposing himself to cross-examination generally. The provision is necessary because of the breadth of cross-examination under Rule 611(b).

The rule does not address itself to questions of the subsequent use of testimony given by an accused at a hearing on a preliminary matter. See *Walder v. United States,* 347 U.S. 62 (1954); *Simmons v. United States,* 390 U.S. 377 (1968); *Harris v. New York,* 401 U.S. 222 (1971).

Note to Subdivision (e). For similar provisions see Uniform Rule 8; California Evidence Code § 406; Kansas Code of Civil Procedure § 60–408; New Jersey Evidence Rule 8(1).

1974 Enactment

Rule 104(c) as submitted to the Congress provided that hearings on the admissibility of confessions shall be conducted outside the presence of the jury and hearings on all other preliminary matters should be so conducted when the interests of justice require. The Committee amended the Rule to provide that where an accused is a witness as to a preliminary matter, he has the right, upon his request, to be heard outside the jury's presence. Although recognizing that in some cases duplication of evidence would occur and that the procedure could be subject to abuse, the Committee believed that a proper regard for the right of an accused not to testify generally in the case dictates that he be given an option to testify out of the presence of the jury on preliminary matters.

The Committee construes the second sentence of subdivision (c) as applying to civil actions and proceedings as well as to criminal cases, and on this assumption has left the sentence unamended. House Report No. 93–650.

Under rule 104(c) the hearing on a preliminary matter may at times be conducted in front of the jury. Should an accused testify in such a hearing, waiving his privilege against self-incrimination as to the preliminary issue, rule 104(d) provides that he will not generally be subject to cross-examination as to any other issue. This rule is not, however, intended to immunize the accused from cross-examination where, in testifying about a preliminary issue, he injects other issues into the hearing. If he could not be cross-examined about any issues gratuitiously raised by him beyond the scope of the preliminary matters, injustice might result. Accordingly, in order to prevent any such unjust result, the committee intends the rule to be construed to provide that the accused may subject himself to cross-examination as to issues raised by his own testimony upon a preliminary matter before a jury. Senate Report No. 93–1277.

1987 Amendments

The amendments are technical. No substantive change is intended.

Rule 105. Limited Admissibility

When evidence which is admissible as to one party or for one purpose but not admissible as to another party or for another purpose is admitted, the court, upon request, shall restrict the evidence to its proper scope and instruct the jury accordingly.

(Pub.L. 93–595, § 1, Jan. 2, 1975, 88 Stat. 1930.)

ADVISORY COMMITTEE NOTES

1972 Proposed Rules

A close relationship exists between this rule and Rule 403 which requires exclusion when "probative value is substantially outweighed by the danger of unfair prejudice, confusion of the issues, or misleading the jury." The present rule recognizes the practice of admitting evidence for a limited purpose and instructing the jury accordingly. The availability and effectiveness of this practice must be taken into consideration in reaching a decision whether to exclude for unfair prejudice under Rule 403. In *Bruton v. United States,* 389 U.S. 818, 88 S.Ct. 126, 19 L.Ed.2d 70 (1968), the Court ruled that a limiting instruction did not effectively protect the accused against the prejudicial effect of admitting in evidence the confession of a codefendant which implicated him. The decision does not, however, bar the use of limited admissibility with an instruction where the risk of prejudice is less serious.

Similar provisions are found in Uniform Rule 6; California Evidence Code § 355; Kansas Code of Civil Procedure § 60–406; New Jersey Evidence Rule 6. The wording of the present rule differs, however, in repelling any implication that limiting or curative instructions are sufficient in all situations.

1974 Enactment

Rule 106 as submitted by the Supreme Court (now Rule 105 in the bill) dealt with the subject of evidence which is admissible as to one party or for one purpose but is not admissible against another party or for another purpose. The Committee adopted this Rule without change on the understanding that it does not affect the authority of a court to order a severance in a multi-defendant case. House Report No. 93–650.

Rule 106. Remainder of or Related Writings or Recorded Statements

When a writing or recorded statement or part thereof is introduced by a party, an adverse party may require the introduction at that time of any other part or any other writing or recorded statement which ought in fairness to be considered contemporaneously with it.

(Pub.L. 93–595, § 1, Jan. 2, 1975, 88 Stat. 1930; Mar. 2, 1987, eff. Oct. 1, 1987.)

ADVISORY COMMITTEE NOTES

1972 Proposed Rules

The rule is an expression of the rule of completeness. McCormick § 56. It is manifested as to depositions in Rule 32(a)(4) of the Federal Rules of Civil Procedure, of which the proposed rule is substantially a restatement.

The rule is based on two considerations. The first is the misleading impression created by taking matters out of context. The second is the inadequacy of repair work when delayed to a point later in the trial. See McCormick § 56; California Evidence Code § 356. The rule does not in any way circumscribe the right of the adversary to develop the matter on cross-examination or as part of his own case.

For practical reasons, the rule is limited to writings and recorded statements and does not apply to conversations.

1987 Amendments

The amendments are technical. No substantive change is intended.

ARTICLE II. JUDICIAL NOTICE

Rule 201. Judicial Notice of Adjudicative Facts

(a) Scope of rule. This rule governs only judicial notice of adjudicative facts.

(b) Kinds of facts. A judicially noticed fact must be one not subject to reasonable dispute in that it is either (1) generally known within the territorial jurisdiction of the trial court or (2) capable of accurate and ready determination by resort to sources whose accuracy cannot reasonably be questioned.

(c) When discretionary. A court may take judicial notice, whether requested or not.

(d) When mandatory. A court shall take judicial notice if requested by a party and supplied with the necessary information.

(e) Opportunity to be heard. A party is entitled upon timely request to an opportunity to be heard as to the propriety of taking judicial notice and the tenor of the matter noticed. In the absence of prior notification, the request may be made after judicial notice has been taken.

(f) Time of taking notice. Judicial notice may be taken at any stage of the proceeding.

(g) Instructing jury. In a civil action or proceeding, the court shall instruct the jury to accept as conclusive any fact judicially noticed. In a criminal case, the court shall instruct the jury that it may, but is not required to, accept as conclusive any fact judicially noticed.

(Pub.L. 93–595, § 1, Jan. 2, 1975, 88 Stat. 1930.)

ADVISORY COMMITTEE NOTES

1972 Proposed Rules

Note to Subdivision (a). This is the only evidence rule on the subject of judicial notice. It deals only with judicial notice of "adjudicative" facts. No rule deals with judicial notice of "legislative" facts. Judicial notice of matters of foreign law is treated in Rule 44.1 of the Federal Rules of Civil Procedure and Rule 26.1 of the Federal Rules of Criminal Procedure.

The omission of any treatment of legislative facts results from fundamental differences between adjudicative facts and legislative facts. Adjudicative facts are simply the facts of the particular case. Legislative facts, on the other hand, are those which have relevance to legal reasoning and the lawmaking process, whether in the formulation of a legal principle or ruling by a judge or court or in the enactment of a legislative body. The terminology was coined by Professor Kenneth Davis in his article An Approach to Problems of Evidence in the Administrative Process, 55 Harv.L.Rev. 364, 404–407 (1942). The following discussion draws extensively upon his writings. In addition, see the same author's Judicial Notice, 55 Colum.L.Rev. 945 (1955); Administrative Law Treatise, ch. 15 (1958); A System of Judicial Notice Based on Fairness and Convenience, in Perspectives of Law 69 (1964).

The usual method of establishing adjudicative facts is through the introduction of evidence, ordinarily consisting of the testimony of witnesses. If particular facts are outside the area of reasonable controversy, this process is dispensed with as unnecessary. A high degree of indisputability is the essential prerequisite.

Legislative facts are quite different. As Professor Davis says:

"My opinion is that judge-made law would stop growing if judges, in thinking about questions of law and policy, were forbidden to take into account the facts they believe, as distinguished from facts which are 'clearly * * * within the domain of the indisputable.' Facts most needed in thinking about difficult problems of law and policy have a way of being outside the domain of the clearly indisputable." A System of Judicial Notice Based on Fairness and Convenience, *supra*, at 82.

An illustration is *Hawkins v. United States*, 358 U.S. 74, 79 S.Ct. 136, 3 L.Ed.2d 125 (1958), in which the Court refused to discard the common law rule that one spouse could not testify against the other, saying, "Adverse testimony given in criminal proceedings would, we think, be likely to destroy almost any marriage." This conclusion has a large intermixture of fact, but the factual aspect is scarcely "indisputable." See Hutchins and Slesinger, Some Observations on the Law of Evidence—Family Relations, 13 Minn.L.Rev. 675 (1929). If the destructive effect of the giving of adverse testimony by a spouse is not indisputable, should the Court have refrained from considering it in the absence of supporting evidence?

"If the Model Code or the Uniform Rules had been applicable, the Court would have been barred from thinking about the essential factual ingredient of the problems before it, and such a result would be obviously intolerable. What the law needs at its growing points is more, not less, judicial thinking about the factual ingredients of problems of what the law ought to be, and the needed facts are seldom 'clearly' indisputable." Davis, *supra*, at 83.

Professor Morgan gave the following description of the methodology of determining domestic law:

"In determining the content or applicability of a rule of domestic law, the judge is unrestricted in his investigation and conclusion. He may reject the propositions of either party or of both parties. He may consult the sources of pertinent data to which they refer, or he may refuse to do so. He may make an independent search for persuasive data or rest content with what he has or what the parties present. * * * [T]he parties do no more than to assist; they control no part of the process." Morgan, Judicial Notice, 57 Harv. L.Rev. 269, 270–271 (1944).

This is the view which should govern judicial access to legislative facts. It renders inappropriate any limitation in the form of indisputability, any formal requirements of notice other than those already inherent in affording opportunity to hear and be heard and exchanging briefs, and any requirement of formal findings at any level. It should, however leave open the possibility of introducing evidence through regular channels in appropriate situations. See *Borden's Farm Products Co. v. Baldwin,* 293 U.S. 194, 55 S.Ct. 187, 79 L.Ed. 281 (1934), where the cause was remanded for the taking of evidence as to the economic conditions and trade practices underlying the New York Milk Control Law.

Similar considerations govern the judicial use of non-adjudicative facts in ways other than formulating laws and rules. Thayer described them as a part of the judicial reasoning process.

"In conducting a process of judicial reasoning, as of other reasoning, not a step can be taken without assuming something which has not been proved; and the capacity to do this with competent judgment and efficiency, is imputed to judges and juries as part of their necessary mental outfit." Thayer, Preliminary Treatise on Evidence 279–280 (1898).

As Professor Davis points out, A System of Judicial Notice Based on Fairness and Convenience, in Perspectives of Law 69, 73 (1964), every case involves the use of hundreds or thousands of non-evidence facts. When a witness in an automobile accident case says "car," everyone, judge and jury included, furnishes, from non-evidence sources within himself, the supplementing information that the "car" is an automobile, not a railroad car, that it is self-propelled, probably by an internal combustion engine, that it may be assumed to have four wheels with pneumatic rubber tires, and so on. The judicial process cannot construct every case from scratch, like Descartes creating a world based on the postulate *Cogito, ergo sum.* These items could not possibly be introduced into evidence, and no one suggests that they be. Nor are they appropriate subjects for any formalized treatment of judicial notice of facts. See Levin and Levy, Persuading the Jury with Facts Not in Evidence: The Fiction–Science Spectrum, 105 U.Pa.L.Rev. 139 (1956).

Another aspect of what Thayer had in mind is the use of non-evidence facts to appraise or assess the adjudicative facts of the case. Pairs of cases from two jurisdictions illustrate this use and also the difference between non-evidence facts thus used and adjudicative facts. In People v. Strook, 347 Ill. 460, 179 N.E. 821 (1932), venue in Cook County had been held not established by testimony that the crime was committed at 7956 South Chicago Avenue, since judicial notice would not be taken that the address was in Chicago. However, the same court subsequently ruled that venue in Cook County was established by testimony that a crime occurred at 8900 South Anthony Avenue, since notice would be taken of the common practice of omitting the name of the city when speaking of local addresses, and the witness was testifying in Chicago. *People v. Pride,* 16 Ill.2d 82, 156 N.E.2d 551 (1951). And in *Hughes v. Vestal,* 264 N.C. 500, 142 S.E.2d 361 (1965), the Supreme Court of North Carolina disapproved the trial judge's admission in evidence of a state-published table of automobile stopping distances on the basis of judicial notice, though the court itself had referred to the same table in an earlier case in a "rhetorical and illustrative" way in determining that the defendant could not have stopped her car in time to avoid striking a child who suddenly appeared in the highway and that a nonsuit was properly granted. *Ennis v. Dupree,* 262 N.C. 224, 136 S.E.2d 702 (1964). See also *Brown v. Hale,* 263 N.C. 176, 139 S.E.2d 210 (1964); *Clayton v. Rimmer,* 262 N.C. 302, 136 S.E.2d 562 (1964). It is apparent that this use of non-evidence facts in evaluating the adjudicative facts of the case is not an appropriate subject for a formalized judicial notice treatment.

In view of these considerations, the regulation of judicial notice of facts by the present rule extends only to adjudicative facts.

What, then, are "adjudicative" facts? Davis refers to them as those "which relate to the parties," or more fully:

"When a court or an agency finds facts concerning the immediate parties—who did what, where, when, how, and with what motive or intent—the court or agency is performing an adjudicative function, and the facts are conveniently called adjudicative facts. * * *

"Stated in other terms, the adjudicative facts are those to which the law is applied in the process of adjudication. They are the facts that normally go to the jury in a jury case. They relate to the parties, their activities, their properties, their businesses." 2 Administrative Law Treatise 353.

Note to Subdivision (b). With respect to judicial notice of adjudicative facts, the tradition has been one of caution in requiring that the matter be beyond reasonable controversy. This tradition of circumspection appears to be soundly based, and no reason to depart from it is apparent. As Professor Davis says:

"The reason we use trial-type procedure, I think, is that we make the practical judgment, on the basis of experience, that taking evidence, subject to cross-examination and rebuttal, is the best way to resolve controversies involving disputes of adjudicative facts, that is, facts pertaining to the parties. The reason we require a determination on the record is that we think fair procedure in resolving disputes of adjudicative facts calls for giving each party a chance to meet in the appropriate fashion the facts that come to the tribunal's attention, and the appropriate fashion for meeting disputed adjudicative facts includes rebuttal evidence, cross-examination, usually confrontation, and argument (either written or oral or both). The key to a fair trial is opportunity to use the appropriate weapons (rebuttal evidence, cross-examination, and argument) to meet adverse materials that come to the tribunal's attention." A System of Judicial Notice Based on Fairness and Convenience, in Perspectives of Law 69, 93 (1964).

The rule proceeds upon the theory that these considerations call for dispensing with traditional methods of proof only in clear cases. Compare Professor Davis' conclusion that judicial notice should be a matter of convenience, subject to requirements of procedural fairness. *Id.*, 94.

This rule is consistent with Uniform Rule 9(1) and (2) which limit judicial notice of facts to those "so universally known that they cannot reasonably be the subject of dispute," those "so generally known or of such common notoriety within the territorial jurisdiction of the court that they cannot reasonably be the subject of dispute," and those "capable of immediate and accurate determination by resort to easily accessible sources of indisputable accuracy." The traditional textbook treatment has included these general categories (matters of common knowledge, facts capable of verification), McCormick §§ 324, 325, and then has passed on into detailed treatment of such specific topics as facts relating to the personnel and records of the court, *Id.* § 327, and other governmental facts, *Id.* § 328. The California draftsmen, with a background of detailed statutory regulation of judicial notice, followed a somewhat similar pattern. California Evidence Code §§ 451, 452. The Uniform Rules, however, were drafted on the theory that these particular matters are included within the general categories and need no specific mention. This approach is followed in the present rule.

The phrase "propositions of generalized knowledge," found in Uniform Rule 9(1) and (2) is not included in the present rule. It was, it is believed, originally included in Model Code Rules 801 and 802 primarily in order to afford some minimum recognition to the right of the judge in his "legislative" capacity (not acting as the trier of fact) to take judicial notice of very limited categories of generalized knowledge. The limitations thus imposed have been discarded herein as undesirable, unworkable, and contrary to existing practice. What is left, then, to be considered, is the status of a "proposition of generalized knowledge" as an "adjudicative" fact to be noticed judicially and communicated by the judge to the jury. Thus viewed, it is considered to be lacking practical significance. While judges use judicial notice of "propositions of generalized knowledge" in a variety of situations: determining the validity and meaning of statutes, formulating common law rules, deciding whether evidence should be admitted, assessing the sufficiency and effect of evidence, all are essentially nonadjudicative in nature. When judicial notice is seen as a significant vehicle for progress in the law, these are the areas involved, particularly in developing fields of scientific knowledge. See McCormick 712. It is not believed that judges now instruct juries as to "propositions of generalized knowledge" derived from encyclopedias or other sources, or that they are likely to do so, or, indeed, that it is desirable that they do so. There is a vast difference between ruling on the basis of judicial notice that radar evidence of speed is admissible and explaining to the jury its principles and degree of accuracy, or between using a table of stopping distances of automobiles at various speeds in a judicial evaluation of testimony and telling the jury its precise application in the case. For cases raising doubt as to the propriety of the use of medical texts by lay triers of fact in passing on disability claims in administrative proceedings, see *Sayers v. Gardner*, 380 F.2d 940 (6th Cir.1967); *Ross v. Gardner*, 365 F.2d 554 (6th Cir.1966); *Sosna v. Celebrezze*, 234 F.Supp. 289 (E.D.Pa.1964); *Glendenning v. Ribicoff*, 213 F.Supp. 301 (W.D.Mo.1962).

Notes to Subdivisions (c) and (d). Under subdivision (c) the judge has a discretionary authority to take judicial notice, regardless of whether he is so requested by a party. The taking of judicial notice is mandatory, under subdivision (d), only when a party requests it and the necessary information is supplied. This scheme is believed to reflect existing practice. It is simple and workable. It avoids troublesome distinctions in the many situations in which the process of taking judicial notice is not recognized as such.

Compare Uniform Rule 9 making judicial notice of facts universally known mandatory without request, and making judicial notice of facts generally known in the jurisdiction or capable of determination by resort to accurate sources discretionary in the absence of request but mandatory if request is made and the information furnished. But see Uniform Rule 10(3), which directs the judge to decline to take judicial notice if available information fails to convince him that the matter falls clearly within Uniform Rule 9 or is insufficient to enable him to notice it judicially. Substantially the same approach is found in California Evidence Code §§ 451–453 and in New Jersey Evidence Rule 9. In contrast, the present rule treats alike all adjudicative facts which are subject to judicial notice.

Note to Subdivision (e). Basic considerations of procedural fairness demand an opportunity to be heard on the propriety of taking judicial notice and the tenor of the matter noticed. The rule requires the granting of that opportunity upon request. No formal scheme of giving notice is provided. An adversely affected party may learn in advance that judicial notice is in contemplation, either by virtue of being served with a copy of a request by another party under subdivision (d) that judicial notice be taken, or through an advance indication by the judge. Or he may have no advance notice at all. The likelihood of the latter is enhanced by the frequent failure to recognize judicial notice as such. And in the absence of advance notice, a request made after the fact could not in fairness be considered untimely. See the provision for hearing on timely request in the Administrative Procedure Act, 5 U.S.C. § 556(e). See also Revised Model State Administrative Procedure Act (1961), 9C U.L.A. § 10(4) (Supp.1967).

Note to Subdivision (f). In accord with the usual view, judicial notice may be taken at any stage of the proceedings, whether in the trial court or on appeal. Uniform Rule 12; California Evidence Code § 459; Kansas Rules of Evidence § 60–412; New Jersey Evidence Rule 12; McCormick § 330, p. 712.

Note to Subdivision (g). Much of the controversy about judicial notice has centered upon the question whether evidence should be admitted in disproof of facts of which judicial notice is taken.

The writers have been divided. Favoring admissibility are Thayer, Preliminary Treatise on Evidence 308 (1898); 9 Wigmore § 2567; Davis, A System of Judicial Notice Based on Fairness and Convenience, in Perspectives of Law, 69, 76–77 (1964). Opposing admissibility are Keeffe, Landis and Shaad, Sense and Nonsense about Judicial Notice, 2 Stan. L.Rev. 664, 668 (1950); McNaughton, Judicial Notice—Excerpts Relating to the Morgan–Whitmore Controversy, 14 Vand.L.Rev. 779 (1961); Morgan, Judicial Notice, 57 Harv. L.Rev. 269, 279 (1944); McCormick 710–711. The Model Code and the Uniform Rules are predicated upon indisputability of judicially noticed facts.

The proponents of admitting evidence in disproof have concentrated largely upon legislative facts. Since the present rule deals only with judicial notice of adjudicative facts, arguments directed to legislative facts lose their relevancy.

Within its relatively narrow area of adjudicative facts, the rule contemplates there is to be no evidence before the jury in disproof. The judge instructs the jury to take judicially noticed facts as established. This position is justified by the undesirable effects of the opposite rule in limiting the rebutting party, though not his opponent, to admissible evidence, in defeating the reasons for judicial notice, and in affecting the substantive law to an extent and in ways largely unforeseeable. Ample protection and flexibility are afforded by the broad provision for opportunity to be heard on request, set forth in subdivision (e).

Authority upon the propriety of taking judicial notice against an accused in a criminal case with respect to matters other than venue is relatively meager. Proceeding upon the theory that the right of jury trial does not extend to matters which are beyond reasonable dispute, the rule does not distinguish between criminal and civil cases. *People v. Mayes*, 113 Cal. 618, 45 P. 860 (1896); *Ross v. United States*, 374 F.2d 97 (8th Cir.1967). Cf. *State v. Main*, 94 R.I. 338, 180 A.2d 814 (1962); *State v. Lawrence*, 120 Utah 323, 234 P.2d 600 (1951).

Note on Judicial Notice of Law. By rules effective July 1, 1966, the method of invoking the law of a foreign country is covered elsewhere. Rule 44.1 of the Federal Rules of Civil Procedure; Rule 26.1 of the Federal Rules of Criminal Procedure. These two new admirably designed rules are founded upon the assumption that the manner in which law is fed into the judicial process is never a proper concern of the rules of evidence but rather of the rules of procedure. The Advisory Committee on Evidence, believing that this assumption is entirely correct, proposes no evidence rule with respect to judicial notice of law, and suggests that those matters of law which, in addition to foreign-country law, have traditionally been treated as requiring pleading and proof and more recently as the subject of judicial notice be left to the Rules of Civil and Criminal Procedure.

1974 Enactment

Rule 201(g) as received from the Supreme Court provided that when judicial notice of a fact is taken, the court shall instruct the jury to accept that fact as established. Being of the view that mandatory instruction to a jury in a criminal case to accept as conclusive any fact judicially noticed is inappropriate because contrary to the spirit of the Sixth Amendment right to a jury trial, the Committee adopted the 1969 Advisory Committee draft of this subsection, allowing a mandatory instruction in civil actions and proceedings and a discretionary instruction in criminal cases. House Report No. 93–650.

ARTICLE III. PRESUMPTIONS IN CIVIL ACTIONS AND PROCEEDINGS

Rule 301. Presumptions in General in Civil Actions and Proceedings

In all civil actions and proceedings not otherwise provided for by Act of Congress or by these rules, a presumption imposes on the party against whom it is directed the burden of going forward with evidence to rebut or meet the presumption, but does not shift to such party the burden of proof in the sense of the risk of nonpersuasion, which remains throughout the trial upon the party on whom it was originally cast.

(Pub.L. 93–595, § 1, Jan. 2, 1975, 88 Stat. 1931.)

ADVISORY COMMITTEE NOTES

1972 Proposed Rules

This rule governs presumptions generally. See Rule 302 for presumptions controlled by state law and Rule 303 [deleted] for those against an accused in a criminal case.

Presumptions governed by this rule are given the effect of placing upon the opposing party the burden of establishing the nonexistence of the presumed fact, once the party invoking the presumption establishes the basic facts giving rise to it. The same considerations of fairness, policy, and probability which dictate the allocation of the burden of the various elements of a case as between the prima facie case of a plaintiff and affirmative defenses also underlie the creation of presumptions. These considerations are not satisfied by giving a lesser effect to presumptions. Morgan and Maguire, Looking Backward and Forward at Evidence, 50 Harv. L.Rev. 909, 913 (1937); Morgan, Instructing the Jury upon Presumptions and Burden of Proof, 47 Harv.L.Rev. 59, 82 (1933); Cleary, Presuming and Pleading: An Essay on Juristic Immaturity, 12 Stan.L.Rev. 5 (1959).

The so-called "bursting bubble" theory, under which a presumption vanishes upon the introduction of evidence which would support a finding of the nonexistence of the presumed fact, even though not believed, is rejected as according presumptions too "slight and evanescent" an effect. Morgan and Maguire, *supra*, at p. 913.

In the opinion of the Advisory Committee, no constitutional infirmity attends this view of presumptions. In *Mobile, J. & K. C. R. Co. v. Turnipseed*, 219 U.S. 35, 31 S.Ct. 136, 55 L.Ed. 78 (1910), the Court upheld a Mississippi statute which provided that in actions against railroads proof of injury inflicted by the running of trains should be prima facie evidence of negligence by the railroad. The injury in the case had resulted from a derailment. The opinion made the points (1) that the only effect of the statute was to impose on the railroad the duty of producing some evidence to the contrary, (2) that an inference may be supplied by law if there is a rational connection between the fact proved and the fact presumed, as long as the opposite party is not precluded from presenting his evidence to the contrary, and (3) that considerations of public policy arising from the character of the business justified the application in question. Nineteen years later, in *Western & Atlantic R. Co. v. Henderson,* 279 U.S. 639, 49 S.Ct. 445, 73 L.Ed. 884 (1929), the Court overturned a Georgia statute making railroads liable for damages done by trains, unless the railroad made it appear that reasonable care had been used, the presumption being against the railroad. The declaration alleged the death of plaintiff's husband from a grade crossing collision, due to specified acts of negligence by defendant. The jury were instructed that proof of the injury raised a presumption of negligence; the burden shifted to the railroad to prove ordinary care; and unless it did so, they should find for plaintiff. The instruction was held erroneous in an opinion stating (1) that there was no rational connection between the mere fact of collision and negligence on the part of anyone, and (2) that the statute was different from that in *Turnipseed* in imposing a burden upon the railroad. The reader is left in a state of some confusion. Is the difference between a derailment and a grade crossing collision of no significance? Would the *Turnipseed* presumption have been bad if it had imposed a burden of persuasion on defendant, although that would in nowise have impaired its "rational connection"? If *Henderson* forbids imposing a burden of persuasion on defendants, what happens to affirmative defenses?

Two factors serve to explain *Henderson.* The first was that it was common ground that negligence was indispensable to liability. Plaintiff thought so, drafted her complaint accordingly, and relied upon the presumption. But how in logic could the same presumption establish her alternative grounds of negligence that the engineer was so blind he could not see decedent's truck and that he failed to stop after he saw it? Second, take away the basic assumption of no liability without fault, as *Turnipseed* intimated might be done ("considerations of public policy arising out of the character of the business"), and the structure of the decision in *Henderson* fails. No question of logic would have arisen if the statute had simply said: a prima facie case of liability is made by proof of injury by a train; lack of negligence is an affirmative defense, to be pleaded and proved as other affirmative defenses. The problem would be one of economic due process only. While it seems likely that the Supreme Court of 1929 would have voted that due process was denied, that result today would be unlikely. See, for example, the shift in the direction of absolute liability in the consumer cases. Prosser, The Assault upon the Citadel (Strict Liability to the Consumer), 69 Yale L.J. 1099 (1960).

Any doubt as to the constitutional permissibility of a presumption imposing a burden of persuasion of the nonexistence of the presumed fact in civil cases is laid at rest by *Dick v. New York Life Ins. Co.,* 359 U.S. 437, 79 S.Ct. 921, 3 L.Ed.2d 935 (1959). The Court unhesitatingly applied the North Dakota rule that the presumption against suicide imposed on defendant the burden of proving that the death of insured, under an accidental death clause, was due to suicide.

"Proof of coverage and of death by gunshot wound shifts the burden to the insurer to establish that the death of the insured was due to his suicide." 359 U.S. at 443, 79 S.Ct. at 925.

"In a case like this one, North Dakota presumes that death was accidental and places on the insurer the burden of proving that death resulted from suicide." *Id.* at 446, 79 S.Ct. at 927.

The rational connection requirement survives in criminal cases, *Tot v. United States,* 319 U.S. 463, 63 S.Ct. 1241, 87 L.Ed. 1519 (1943), because the Court has been unwilling to extend into that area the greater-includes-the-lesser theory of *Ferry v. Ramsey,* 277 U.S. 88, 48 S.Ct. 443, 72 L.Ed. 796 (1928). In that case the Court sustained a Kansas statute under which bank directors were personally liable for deposits made with their assent and with knowledge of insolvency, and the fact of insolvency was prima facie evidence of assent and knowledge of insolvency. Mr. Justice Holmes pointed out that the state legislature could have made the directors personally liable to depositors in every case. Since the statute imposed a less stringent liability, "the thing to be considered is the result reached, not the possibly inartificial or clumsy way of reaching it." *Id.* at 94, 48 S.Ct. at 444. Mr. Justice Sutherland dissented: though the state could have created an absolute liability, it did not purport to do so; a rational connection was necessary, but lacking, between the liability created and the prima facie evidence of it; the result might be different if the basis of the presumption were being open for business.

The Sutherland view has prevailed in criminal cases by virtue of the higher standard of notice there required. The fiction that everyone is presumed to know the law is applied to the substantive law of crimes as an alternative to complete unenforceability. But the need does not extend to criminal evidence and procedure, and the fiction does not encompass them. "Rational connection" is not fictional or artificial, and so it is reasonable to suppose that Gainey should have known that his presence at the site of an illicit still could convict him of being connected with (carrying on) the business, *United States v. Gainey,* 380 U.S. 63, 85 S.Ct. 754, 13 L.Ed.2d 658 (1965), but not that Romano should have known that his presence at a still could convict him of possessing it, *United States v. Romano,* 382 U.S. 136, 86 S.Ct. 279, 15 L.Ed.2d 210 (1965).

In his dissent in Gainey, Mr. Justice Black put it more artistically:

"It might be argued, although the Court does not so argue or hold, that Congress if it wished could make presence at a still a crime in itself, and so Congress should be free to create crimes which are called 'possession' and 'carrying on an illegal distillery business' but which are defined in such a way that unexplained presence is sufficient and indisputable evidence in all cases to support conviction for those offenses. See *Ferry v. Ramsey,* 277 U.S. 88, 48 S.Ct. 443, 72 L.Ed. 796. Assuming for the sake of argument that Congress could make unexplained presence a criminal act, and ignoring also the refusal of this Court in other cases to uphold a statutory presumption on such a theory, see *Heiner v. Donnan,* 285 U.S. 312, 52 S.Ct. 358, 76 L.Ed. 772, there is no indication here that Congress intended to adopt such a misleading method of draftsmanship, nor in my judgment could the statutory provisions if so construed escape condemnation for vagueness, under the principles applied in *Lanzetta v. New*

Jersey, 306 U.S. 451, 59 S.Ct. 618, 83 L.Ed. 888, and many other cases." 380 U.S. at 84, n. 12, 85 S.Ct. at 766.

And the majority opinion in *Romano* agreed with him:

"It may be, of course, that Congress has the power to make presence at an illegal still a punishable crime, but we find no clear indication that it intended to so exercise this power. The crime remains possession, not presence, and with all due deference to the judgment of Congress, the former may not constitutionally be inferred from the latter." 382 U.S. at 144, 86 S.Ct. at 284.

The rule does not spell out the procedural aspects of its application. Questions as to when the evidence warrants submission of a presumption and what instructions are proper under varying states of fact are believed to present no particular difficulties.

1974 Enactment

Rule 301 as submitted by the Supreme Court provided that in all cases a presumption imposes on the party against whom it is directed the burden of proving that the nonexistence of the presumed fact is more probable than its existence. The Committee limited the scope of Rule 301 to "civil actions and proceedings" to effectuate its decision not to deal with the question of presumptions in criminal cases. (See note on [proposed] Rule 303 in discussion of Rules deleted). With respect to the weight to be given a presumption in a civil case, the Committee agreed with the judgment implicit in the Court's version that the so-called "bursting bubble" theory of presumptions, whereby a presumption vanishes upon the appearance of any contradicting evidence by the other party, gives to presumptions too slight an effect. On the other hand, the Committee believed that the Rule proposed by the Court, whereby a presumption permanently alters the burden of persuasion, no matter how much contradicting evidence is introduced—a view shared by only a few courts—lends too great a force to presumptions. Accordingly, the Committee amended the Rule to adopt an intermediate position under which a presumption does not vanish upon the introduction of contradicting evidence, and does not change the burden of persuasion; instead it is merely deemed sufficient evidence of the fact presumed, to be considered by the jury or other finder of fact. House Report No. 93–650.

The rule governs presumptions in civil cases generally. Rule 302 provides for presumptions in cases controlled by State law.

As submitted by the Supreme Court, presumptions governed by this rule were given the effect of placing upon the opposing party the burden of establishing the nonexistence of the presumed fact, once the party invoking the presumption established the basic facts giving rise to it.

Instead of imposing a burden of persuasion on the party against whom the presumption is directed, the House adopted a provision which shifted the burden of going forward with the evidence. They further provided that "even though met with contradicting evidence, a presumption is sufficient evidence of the fact presumed, to be considered by the trier of fact." The effect of the amendment is that presumptions are to be treated as evidence.

The committee feels the House amendment is ill-advised. As the joint committees (the Standing Committee on Practice and Procedure of the Judicial Conference and the Advisory Committee on the Rules of Evidence) stated: "Presumptions are not evidence, but ways of dealing with evidence." This treatment requires juries to perform the task of considering "as evidence" facts upon which they have no direct evidence and which may confuse them in performance of their duties. California had a rule much like that contained in the House amendment. It was sharply criticized by Justice Traynor in *Speck v. Sarver* [20 Cal.2d 585, 128 P.2d 16, 21 (1942)] and was repealed after 93 troublesome years [Cal.Ev.Code 1965 § 600].

Professor McCormick gives a concise and compelling critique of the presumption as evidence rule:

> "Another solution, formerly more popular than now, is to instruct the jury that the presumption is 'evidence', to be weighed and considered with the testimony in the case. This avoids the danger that the jury may infer that the presumption is conclusive, but it probably means little to the jury, and certainly runs counter to accepted theories of the nature of evidence." [McCormick, Evidence, 669 (1954); *Id.* 825 (2d ed. 1972)].

For these reasons the committee has deleted that provision of the House-passed rule that treats presumptions as evidence. The effect of the rule as adopted by the committee is to make clear that while evidence of facts giving rise to a presumption shifts the burden of coming forward with evidence to rebut or meet the presumption, it does not shift the burden of persuasion on the existence of the presumed facts. The burden of persuasion remains on the party to whom it is allocated under the rules governing the allocation in the first instance.

The court may instruct the jury that they may infer the existence of the presumed fact from proof of the basic facts giving rise to the presumption. However, it would be inappropriate under this rule to instruct the jury that the inference they are to draw is conclusive. Senate Report 93–1277.

The House bill provides that a presumption in civil actions and proceedings shifts to the party against whom it is directed the burden of going forward with evidence to meet or rebut it. Even though evidence contradicting the presumption is offered, a presumption is considered sufficient evidence of the presumed fact to be considered by the jury. The Senate amendment provides that a presumption shifts to the party against whom it is directed the burden of going forward with evidence to meet or rebut the presumption, but it does not shift to that party the burden of persuasion on the existence of the presumed fact.

Under the Senate amendment, a presumption is sufficient to get a party past an adverse party's motion to dismiss made at the end of his case-in-chief. If the adverse party offers no evidence contradicting the presumed fact, the court will instruct the jury that if it finds the basic facts, it may presume the existence of the presumed fact. If the adverse party does offer evidence contradicting the presumed fact, the court cannot instruct the jury that it may *presume* the existence of the presumed fact from proof of the basic facts. The court may, however, instruct the jury that it may infer the existence of the presumed fact from proof of the basic facts.

The conference adopts the Senate amendment. House Conference Report No. 93–1597.

Rule 302. Applicability of State Law in Civil Actions and Proceedings

In civil actions and proceedings, the effect of a presumption respecting a fact which is an element of a claim or defense as to which State law supplies the rule of decision is determined in accordance with State law.

(Pub.L. 93–595, § 1, Jan. 2, 1975, 88 Stat. 1931.)

ADVISORY COMMITTEE NOTES

1972 Proposed Rules

A series of Supreme Court decisions in diversity cases leaves no doubt of the relevance of *Erie Railroad Co. v. Tompkins*, 304 U.S. 64, 58 S.Ct. 817, 82 L.Ed. 1188 (1938), to questions of burden of proof. These decisions are *Cities Service Oil Co. v. Dunlap*, 308 U.S. 208, 60 S.Ct. 201, 84 L.Ed. 196 (1939), *Palmer v. Hoffman*, 318 U.S. 109, 63 S.Ct. 477, 87 L.Ed. 645 (1943), and *Dick v. New York Life Ins. Co.*, 359 U.S. 437, 79 S.Ct. 921, 3 L.Ed.2d 935 (1959). They involved burden of proof, respectively, as to status as bona fide purchaser, contributory negligence, and nonaccidental death (suicide) of an insured. In each instance the state rule was held to be applicable. It does not follow, however, that all presumptions in diversity cases are governed by state law. In each case cited, the burden of proof question had to do with a substantive element of the claim or defense. Application of the state law is called for only when the presumption operates upon such an element. Accordingly the rule does not apply state law when the presumption operates upon a lesser aspect of the case, i.e. "tactical" presumptions.

The situations in which the state law is applied have been tagged for convenience in the preceding discussion as "diversity cases." The designation is not a completely accurate one since *Erie* applies to any claim or issue having its source in state law, regardless of the basis of federal jurisdiction, and does not apply to a federal claim or issue, even though jurisdiction is based on diversity. *Vestal, Erie R.R. v. Tompkins:* A Projection, 48 Iowa L.Rev. 248, 257 (1963); Hart and Wechsler, The Federal Courts and the Federal System, 697 (1953); 1A Moore, Federal Practice ¶ 0.305[3] (2d ed. 1965); Wright, Federal Courts, 217–218 (1963). Hence the rule employs, as appropriately descriptive, the phrase "as to which state law supplies the rule of decision." See A.L.I. Study of the Division of Jurisdiction Between State and Federal Courts, § 2344(c), p. 40, P.F.D. No. 1 (1965).

ARTICLE IV. RELEVANCY AND ITS LIMITS

1988 Amendments

Pub.L. 100–690, Title VII, § 7046(b), Nov. 18, 1988, 102 Stat. 4401, substituted in item relating to rule 412 "Sex Offense" for "Rape".

Rule 401. Definition of "Relevant Evidence"

"Relevant evidence" means evidence having any tendency to make the existence of any fact that is of consequence to the determination of the action more probable or less probable than it would be without the evidence.

(Pub.L. 93–595, § 1, Jan. 2, 1975, 88 Stat.1931.)

ADVISORY COMMITTEE NOTES

1972 Proposed Rules

Problems of relevancy call for an answer to the question whether an item of evidence, when tested by the processes of legal reasoning, possesses sufficient probative value to justify receiving it in evidence. Thus, assessment of the probative value of evidence that a person purchased a revolver shortly prior to a fatal shooting with which he is charged is a matter of analysis and reasoning.

The variety of relevancy problems is coextensive with the ingenuity of counsel in using circumstantial evidence as a means of proof. An enormous number of cases fall in no set pattern, and this rule is designed as a guide for handling them. On the other hand, some situations recur with sufficient frequency to create patterns susceptible of treatment by specific rules. Rule 404 and those following it are of that variety; they also serve as illustrations of the application of the present rule as limited by the exclusionary principles of Rule 403.

Passing mention should be made of so-called "conditional" relevancy. Morgan, Basic Problems of Evidence 45–46 (1962). In this situation, probative value depends not only upon satisfying the basic requirement of relevancy as described above but also upon the existence of some matter of fact. For example, if evidence of a spoken statement is relied upon to prove notice, probative value is lacking unless the person sought to be charged heard the statement. The problem is one of fact, and the only rules needed are for the purpose of determining the respective functions of judge and jury. See Rules 104(b) and 901. The discussion which follows in the present note is concerned with relevancy generally, not with any particular problem of conditional relevancy.

Relevancy is not an inherent characteristic of any item of evidence but exists only as a relation between an item of evidence and a matter properly provable in the case. Does the item of evidence tend to prove the matter sought to be proved? Whether the relationship exists depends upon principles evolved by experience or science, applied logically to the situation at hand. James, Relevancy, Probability and the Law, 29 Calif.L.Rev. 689, 696, n. 15 (1941), in Selected Writings on Evidence and Trial 610, 615, n. 15 (Fryer ed. 1957). The rule summarizes this relationship as a "tendency to make the existence" of the fact to be proved "more probable or less probable." Compare Uniform Rule 1(2) which states the crux of relevancy as "a tendency in reason," thus perhaps emphasizing unduly the logical process and ignoring the need to draw upon experience or science to validate the general principle upon which relevancy in a particular situation depends.

The standard of probability under the rule is "more * * * probable than it would be without the evidence." Any more stringent requirement is unworkable and unrealistic. As McCormick § 152, p. 317, says, "A brick is not a wall," or, as

Falknor, Extrinsic Policies Affecting Admissibility, 10 Rutgers L.Rev. 574, 576 (1956), quotes Professor McBaine, "* * * [I]t is not to be supposed that every witness can make a home run." Dealing with probability in the language of the rule has the added virtue of avoiding confusion between questions of admissibility and questions of the sufficiency of the evidence.

The rule uses the phrase "fact that is of consequence to the determination of the action" to describe the kind of fact to which proof may properly be directed. The language is that of California Evidence Code § 210; it has the advantage of avoiding the loosely used and ambiguous word "material." Tentative Recommendation and a Study Relating to the Uniform Rules of Evidence (Art. I. General Provisions), Cal.Law Revision Comm'n, Rep., Rec. & Studies, 10–11 (1964). The fact to be proved may be ultimate, intermediate, or evidentiary; it matters not, so long as it is of consequence in the determination of the action. Cf. Uniform Rule 1(2) which requires that the evidence relate to a "material" fact.

The fact to which the evidence is directed need not be in dispute. While situations will arise which call for the exclusion of evidence offered to prove a point conceded by the opponent, the ruling should be made on the basis of such considerations as waste of time and undue prejudice (see Rule 403), rather than under any general requirement that evidence is admissible only if directed to matters in dispute. Evidence which is essentially background in nature can scarcely be said to involve disputed matter, yet it is universally offered and admitted as an aid to understanding. Charts, photographs, views of real estate, murder weapons, and many other items of evidence fall in this category. A rule limiting admissibility to evidence directed to a controversial point would invite the exclusion of this helpful evidence, or at least the raising of endless questions over its admission. Cf. California Evidence Code § 210, defining relevant evidence in terms of tendency to prove a disputed fact.

Rule 402. Relevant Evidence Generally Admissible; Irrelevant Evidence Inadmissible

All relevant evidence is admissible, except as otherwise provided by the Constitution of the United States, by Act of Congress, by these rules, or by other rules prescribed by the Supreme Court pursuant to statutory authority. Evidence which is not relevant is not admissible.

(Pub.L. 93–595, § 1, Jan. 2, 1975, 88 Stat. 1931.)

ADVISORY COMMITTEE NOTES

1972 Proposed Rules

The provisions that all relevant evidence is admissible, with certain exceptions, and that evidence which is not relevant is not admissible are "a presupposition involved in the very conception of a rational system of evidence." Thayer, Preliminary Treatise on Evidence 264 (1898). They constitute the foundation upon which the structure of admission and exclusion rests. For similar provisions see California Evidence Code §§ 350, 351. Provisions that all relevant evidence is admissible are found in Uniform Rule 7(f); Kansas Code of Civil Procedure § 60–407(f); and New Jersey Evidence Rule 7(f); but the exclusion of evidence which is not relevant is left to implication.

Not all relevant evidence is admissible. The exclusion of relevant evidence occurs in a variety of situations and may be called for by these rules, by the Rules of Civil and Criminal Procedure, by Bankruptcy Rules, by Act of Congress, or by constitutional considerations.

Succeeding rules in the present article, in response to the demands of particular policies, require the exclusion of evidence despite its relevancy. In addition, Article V recognizes a number of privileges; Article VI imposes limitations upon witnesses and the manner of dealing with them; Article VII specifies requirements with respect to opinions and expert testimony; Article VIII excludes hearsay not falling within an exception; Article IX spells out the handling of authentication and identification; and Article X restricts the manner of proving the contents of writings and recordings.

The Rules of Civil and Criminal Procedure in some instances require the exclusion of relevant evidence. For example, Rules 30(b) and 32(a)(3) of the Rules of Civil Procedure, by imposing requirements of notice and unavailability of the deponent, place limits on the use of relevant depositions. Similarly, Rule 15 of the Rules of Criminal Procedure restricts the use of depositions in criminal cases, even though relevant. And the effective enforcement of the command, originally statutory and now found in Rule 5(a) of the Rules of Criminal Procedure, that an arrested person be taken without unnecessary delay before a commissioner or other similar officer is held to require the exclusion of statements elicited during detention in violation thereof. *Mallory v. United States,* 354 U.S. 449, 77 S.Ct. 1356, 1 L.Ed.2d 1479 (1957); 18 U.S.C. § 3501(c).

While congressional enactments in the field of evidence have generally tended to expand admissibility beyond the scope of the common law rules, in some particular situations they have restricted the admissibility of relevant evidence. Most of this legislation has consisted of the formulation of a privilege or of a prohibition against disclosure. 8 U.S.C. § 1202(f), records of refusal of visas or permits to enter United States confidential, subject to discretion of Secretary of State to make available to court upon certification of need; 10 U.S.C. § 3693, replacement certificate of honorable discharge from Army not admissible in evidence; 10 U.S.C. § 8693, same as to Air Force; 11 U.S.C. § 25(a)(10), testimony given by bankrupt on his examination not admissible in criminal proceedings against him, except that given in hearing upon objection to discharge; 11 U.S.C. § 205(a), railroad reorganization petition, if dismissed, not admissible in evidence; 11 U.S.C. § 403(a), list of creditors filed with municipal composition plan not an admission; 13 U.S.C. § 9(a), census information confidential, retained copies of reports privileged; 47 U.S.C. § 605, interception and divulgence of wire or radio communications prohibited unless authorized by sender. These statutory provisions would remain undisturbed by the rules.

The rule recognizes but makes no attempt to spell out the constitutional considerations which impose basic limitations upon the admissibility of relevant evidence. Examples are evidence obtained by unlawful search and seizure. *Weeks v. United States,* 232 U.S. 383, 34 S.Ct. 341, 58 L.Ed. 652 (1914); *Katz v. United States,* 389 U.S. 347, 88 S.Ct. 507, 19 L.Ed.2d 576 (1967); incriminating statement elicited from an accused in violation of right to counsel. *Massiah v. United States*, 377 U.S. 201, 84 S.Ct. 1199, 12 L.Ed.2d 246 (1964).

1974 Enactment

Rule 402 as submitted to the Congress contained the phrase "or by other rules adopted by the Supreme Court". To accommodate the view that the Congress should not appear to acquiesce in the Court's judgment that it has authority under the existing Rules Enabling Acts to promulgate Rules of Evidence, the Committee amended the above phrase to read "or by other rules prescribed by the Supreme Court pursuant to statutory authority" in this and other Rules where the reference appears. House Report No. 93–650.

Rule 403. Exclusion of Relevant Evidence on Grounds of Prejudice, Confusion, or Waste of Time

Although relevant, evidence may be excluded if its probative value is substantially outweighed by the danger of unfair prejudice, confusion of the issues, or misleading the jury, or by considerations of undue delay, waste of time, or needless presentation of cumulative evidence.

(Pub.L. 93–595, § 1, Jan. 2, 1975, 88 Stat. 1932.)

ADVISORY COMMITTEE NOTES

1972 Proposed Rules

The case law recognizes that certain circumstances call for the exclusion of evidence which is of unquestioned relevance. These circumstances entail risks which range all the way from inducing decision on a purely emotional basis, at one extreme, to nothing more harmful than merely wasting time, at the other extreme. Situations in this area call for balancing the probative value of and need for the evidence against the harm likely to result from its admission. Slough, Relevancy Unraveled, 5 Kan.L.Rev. 1, 12–15 (1956); Trautman, Logical or Legal Relevancy—A Conflict in Theory, 5 Van. L.Rev. 385, 392 (1952); McCormick § 152, pp. 319–321. The rules which follow in this Article are concrete applications evolved for particular situations. However, they reflect the policies underlying the present rule, which is designed as a guide for the handling of situations for which no specific rules have been formulated.

Exclusion for risk of unfair prejudice, confusion of issues, misleading the jury, or waste of time, all find ample support in the authorities. "Unfair prejudice" within its context means an undue tendency to suggest decision on an improper basis, commonly, though not necessarily, an emotional one.

The rule does not enumerate surprise as a ground for exclusion, in this respect following Wigmore's view of the common law. 6 Wigmore § 1849. Cf. McCormick § 152, p. 320, n. 29, listing unfair surprise as a ground for exclusion but stating that it is usually "coupled with the danger of prejudice and confusion of issues." While Uniform Rule 45 incorporates surprise as a ground and is followed in Kansas Code of Civil Procedure § 60–445, surprise is not included in California Evidence Code § 352 or New Jersey Rule 4, though both the latter otherwise substantially embody Uniform Rule 45. While it can scarcely be doubted that claims of unfair surprise may still be justified despite procedural requirements of notice and instrumentalities of discovery, the granting of a continuance is a more appropriate remedy than exclusion of the evidence. Tentative Recommendation and a Study Relating to the Uniform Rules of Evidence (Art. VI. Extrinsic Policies Affecting Admissibility), Cal.Law Revision Comm'n, Rep., Rec. & Studies, 612 (1964). Moreover, the impact of a rule excluding evidence on the ground of surprise would be difficult to estimate.

In reaching a decision whether to exclude on grounds of unfair prejudice, consideration should be given to the probable effectiveness or lack of effectiveness of a limiting instruction. See Rule 106 [now 105] and Advisory Committee's Note thereunder. The availability of other means of proof may also be an appropriate factor.

Rule 404. Character Evidence Not Admissible To Prove Conduct; Exceptions; Other Crimes

(a) Character evidence generally.—Evidence of a person's character or a trait of character is not admissible for the purpose of proving action in conformity therewith on a particular occasion, except:

(1) Character of accused.—In a criminal case, evidence of a pertinent trait of character offered by an accused, or by the prosecution to rebut the same, or if evidence of a trait of character of the alleged victim of the crime is offered by an accused and admitted under Rule 404(a)(2), evidence of the same trait of character of the accused offered by the prosecution;

(2) Character of alleged victim.—In a criminal case, and subject to the limitations imposed by Rule 412, evidence of a pertinent trait of character of the alleged victim of the crime offered by an accused, or by the prosecution to rebut the same, or evidence of a character trait of peacefulness of the alleged victim offered by the prosecution in a homicide case to rebut evidence that the alleged victim was the first aggressor;

(3) Character of witness.—Evidence of the character of a witness, as provided in Rules 607, 608, and 609.

(b) Other Crimes, Wrongs, or Acts.—Evidence of other crimes, wrongs, or acts is not admissible to prove the character of a person in order to show action in conformity therewith. It may, however, be admissible for other purposes, such as proof of motive, opportunity, intent, preparation, plan, knowledge, identity, or absence of mistake or accident, provided that upon request by the accused, the prosecution in a criminal case shall provide reasonable notice in advance of trial, or during trial if the court excuses pretrial notice on good cause shown, of the general nature of any such evidence it intends to introduce at trial.

(Pub.L. 93–595, § 1, Jan. 2, 1975, 88 Stat.1932; Mar. 2, 1987, eff. Oct. 1, 1987; Apr. 30, 1991, eff. Dec. 1, 1991; Apr. 17, 2000, eff. Dec. 1, 2000; Apr. 12, 2006, eff. Dec. 1, 2006.)

ADVISORY COMMITTEE NOTES

1972 Proposed Rules

Note to Subdivision (a). This subdivision deals with the basic question whether character evidence should be admitted. Once the admissibility of character evidence in some form is established under this rule, reference must then be made to Rule 405, which follows, in order to determine the appropriate method of proof. If the character is that of a witness, see Rules 608 and 610 for methods of proof.

Character questions arise in two fundamentally different ways. (1) Character may itself be an element of a crime, claim, or defense. A situation of this kind is commonly referred to as "character in issue." Illustrations are: the chastity of the victim under a statute specifying her chastity as an element of the crime of seduction, or the competency of the driver in an action for negligently entrusting a motor vehicle to an incompetent driver. No problem of the general relevancy of character evidence is involved, and the present rule therefore has no provision on the subject. The only question relates to allowable methods of proof, as to which see Rule 405, immediately following. (2) Character evidence is susceptible of being used for the purpose of suggesting an inference that the person acted on the occasion in question consistently with his character. This use of character is often described as "circumstantial." Illustrations are: evidence of a violent disposition to prove that the person was the aggressor in an affray, or evidence of honesty in disproof of a charge of theft. This circumstantial use of character evidence raises questions of relevancy as well as questions of allowable methods of proof.

In most jurisdictions today, the circumstantial use of character is rejected but with important exceptions: (1) an accused may introduce pertinent evidence of good character (often misleadingly described as "putting his character in issue"), in which event the prosecution may rebut with evidence of bad character; (2) an accused may introduce pertinent evidence of the character of the victim, as in support of a claim of self-defense to a charge of homicide or consent in a case of rape, and the prosecution may introduce similar evidence in rebuttal of the character evidence, or, in a homicide case, to rebut a claim that deceased was the first aggressor, however proved; and (3) the character of a witness may be gone into as bearing on his credibility. McCormick §§ 155–161. This pattern is incorporated in the rule. While its basis lies more in history and experience than in logic an underlying justification can fairly be found in terms of the relative presence and absence of prejudice in the various situations. Falknor, Extrinsic Policies Affecting Admissibility, 10 Rutgers L.Rev. 574, 584 (1956); McCormick § 157. In any event, the criminal rule is so deeply imbedded in our jurisprudence as to assume almost constitutional proportions and to override doubts of the basic relevancy of the evidence.

The limitation to pertinent traits of character, rather than character generally, in paragraphs (1) and (2) is in accordance with the prevailing view. McCormick § 158, p. 334. A similar provision in Rule 608, to which reference is made in paragraph (3), limits character evidence respecting witnesses to the trait of truthfulness or untruthfulness.

The argument is made that circumstantial use of character ought to be allowed in civil cases to the same extent as in criminal cases, i.e. evidence of good (nonprejudicial) character would be admissible in the first instance, subject to rebuttal by evidence of bad character. Falknor, Extrinsic Policies Affecting Admissibility, 10 Rutgers L.Rev. 574, 581–583 (1956); Tentative Recommendation and a Study Relating to the Uniform Rules of Evidence (Art. VI. Extrinsic Policies Affecting Admissibility), Cal.Law Revision Comm'n, Rep., Rec. & Studies, 657–658 (1964). Uniform Rule 47 goes farther, in that it assumes that character evidence in general satisfies the conditions of relevancy, except as provided in Uniform Rule 48. The difficulty with expanding the use of character evidence in civil cases is set forth by the California Law Revision Commission in its ultimate rejection of Uniform Rule 47, *id.*, 615:

"Character evidence is of slight probative value and may be very prejudicial. It tends to distract the trier of fact from the main question of what actually happened on the particular occasion. It subtly permits the trier of fact to reward the good man and to punish the bad man because of their respective characters despite what the evidence in the case shows actually happened."

Much of the force of the position of those favoring greater use of character evidence in civil cases is dissipated by their support of Uniform Rule 48 which excludes the evidence in negligence cases, where it could be expected to achieve its maximum usefulness. Moreover, expanding concepts of "character," which seem of necessity to extend into such areas as psychiatric evaluation and psychological testing, coupled with expanded admissibility, would open up such vistas of mental examinations as caused the Court concern in *Schlagenhauf v. Holder,* 379 U.S. 104, 85 S.Ct. 234, 13 L.Ed.2d 152 (1964). It is believed that those espousing change have not met the burden of persuasion.

Note to Subdivision (b). Subdivision (b) deals with a specialized but important application of the general rule excluding circumstantial use of character evidence. Consistently with that rule, evidence of other crimes, wrongs, or acts is not admissible to prove character as a basis for suggesting the inference that conduct on a particular occasion was in conformity with it. However, the evidence may be offered for another purpose, such as proof of motive, opportunity, and so on, which does not fall within the prohibition. In this situation the rule does not require that the evidence be excluded. No mechanical solution is offered. The determination must be made whether the danger of undue prejudice outweighs the probative value of the evidence in view of the availability of other means of proof and other facts appropriate for making decision of this kind under Rule 403. Slough and Knightly, Other Vices, Other Crimes, 41 Iowa L.Rev. 325 (1956).

1974 Enactment

Note to Subdivision (b). The second sentence of Rule 404(b) as submitted to the Congress began with the words "This subdivision does not exclude the evidence when offered". The Committee amended this language to read "It may, however, be admissible", the words used in the 1971 Advisory Committee draft, on the ground that this formulation properly placed greater emphasis on admissibility than did the final Court version. House Report No. 93–650.

Note to Subdivision (b). This rule provides that evidence of other crimes, wrongs, or acts is not admissible to prove character but may be admissible for other specified purposes such as proof of motive.

Although your committee sees no necessity in amending the rule itself, it anticipates that the use of the discretionary word "may" with respect to the admissibility of evidence of crimes, wrongs, or acts is not intended to confer any arbitrary discretion on the trial judge. Rather, it is anticipated that with respect to permissible uses for such evidence, the trial judge may exclude it only on the basis of those considerations set forth in Rule 403, i.e., prejudice, confusion or waste of time. Senate Report No. 93–1277.

1987 Amendments

The amendments are technical. No substantive change is intended.

1991 Amendments

Rule 404(b) has emerged as one of the most cited Rules in the Rules of Evidence. And in many criminal cases evidence of an accused's extrinsic acts is viewed as an important asset in the prosecution's case against an accused. Although there are a few reported decisions on use of such evidence by the defense, *see, e.g., United States v. McClure*, 546 F.2d 670 (5th Cir.1990) (acts of informant offered in entrapment defense), the overwhelming number of cases involve introduction of that evidence by the prosecution.

The amendment to Rule 404(b) adds a pretrial notice requirement in criminal cases and is intended to reduce surprise and promote early resolution on the issue of admissibility. The notice requirement thus places Rule 404(b) in the mainstream with notice and disclosure provisions in other rules of evidence. *See, e.g.,* Rule 412 (written motion of intent to offer evidence under rule), Rule 609 (written notice of intent to offer conviction older than 10 years), Rule 803(24) and 804(b)(5) (notice of intent to use residual hearsay exceptions).

The Rule expects that counsel for both the defense and the prosecution will submit the necessary request and information in a reasonable and timely fashion. Other than requiring pretrial notice, no specific time limits are stated in recognition that what constitutes a reasonable request or disclosure will depend largely on the circumstances of each case. *Compare* Fla.Stat.Ann. § 90.404(2)(b) (notice must be given at least 10 days before trial) *with* Tex.R.Evid. 404(b) (no time limit).

Likewise, no specific form of notice is required. The Committee considered and rejected a requirement that the notice satisfy the particularity requirements normally required of language used in a charging instrument. *Cf.* Fla.Stat.Ann. § 90.404(2)(b) (written disclosure must describe uncharged misconduct with particularity required of an indictment or information). Instead, the Committee opted for a generalized notice provision which requires the prosecution to apprise the defense of the general nature of the evidence of extrinsic acts. The Committee does not intend that the amendment will supercede other rules of admissibility or disclosure, such as the Jencks Act, 18 U.S.C. § 3500, et. seq. nor require the prosecution to disclose directly or indirectly the names and addresses of its witnesses, something it is currently not required to do under Federal Rule of Criminal Procedure 16.

The amendment requires the prosecution to provide notice, regardless of how it intends to use the extrinsic act evidence at trial, i.e., during its case-in-chief, for impeachment, or for possible rebuttal. The court in its discretion may, under the facts, decide that the particular request or notice was not reasonable, either because of the lack of timeliness or completeness. Because the notice requirement serves as condition precedent to admissibility of 404(b) evidence, the offered evidence is inadmissible if the court decides that the notice requirement has not been met.

Nothing in the amendment precludes the court from requiring the government to provide it with an opportunity to rule *in limine* on 404(b) evidence before it is offered or even mentioned during trial. When ruling *in limine,* the court may require the government to disclose to it the specifics of such evidence which the court must consider in determining admissibility.

The amendment does not extend to evidence of acts which are "intrinsic" to the charged offense, *see United States v. Williams,* 900 F.2d 823 (5th Cir.1990) (noting distinction between 404(b) evidence and intrinsic offense evidence). Nor is the amendment intended to redefine what evidence would otherwise be admissible under Rule 404(b). Finally, the Committee does not intend through the amendment to affect the role of the court and the jury in considering such evidence. *See United States v. Huddleston,* 485 U.S. 681, 108 S.Ct. 1496 (1988).

2000 Amendments

Rule 404(a)(1) has been amended to provide that when the accused attacks the character of an alleged victim under subdivision (a)(2) of this Rule, the door is opened to an attack on the same character trait of the accused. Current law does not allow the government to introduce negative character evidence as to the accused unless the accused introduces evidence of good character. *See, e.g., United States v. Fountain,* 768 F.2d 790 (7th Cir. 1985) (when the accused offers proof of self-defense, this permits proof of the alleged victim's character trait for peacefulness, but it does not permit proof of the accused's character trait for violence).

The amendment makes clear that the accused cannot attack the alleged victim's character and yet remain shielded from the disclosure of equally relevant evidence concerning the same character trait of the accused. For example, in a murder case with a claim of self-defense, the accused, to bolster this defense, might offer evidence of the alleged victim's violent disposition. If the government has evidence that the accused has a violent character, but is not allowed to offer this evidence as part of its rebuttal, the jury has only part of the information it needs for an informed assessment of the probabilities as to who was the initial aggressor. This may be the case even if evidence of the accused's prior violent acts is admitted under Rule 404(b), because such evidence can be admitted only for limited purposes and not to show action in conformity with the accused's character on a specific occasion. Thus, the amendment is designed to permit a more balanced presentation of character evidence when an accused chooses to attack the character of the alleged victim.

The amendment does not affect the admissibility of evidence of specific acts of uncharged misconduct offered for a purpose other than proving character under Rule 404(b). Nor does it affect the standards for proof of character by evidence of other sexual behavior or sexual offenses under Rules 412–415. By its placement in Rule 404(a)(1), the amendment covers only proof of character by way of reputation or opinion.

The amendment does not permit proof of the accused's character if the accused merely uses character evidence for a purpose other than to prove the alleged victim's propensity to act in a certain way. *See United States v. Burks*, 470 F.2d 432, 434–5 (D.C.Cir. 1972) (evidence of the alleged victim's violent character, when known by the accused, was admissible "on the issue of whether or not the defendant reasonably feared he was in danger of imminent great bodily harm"). Finally, the amendment does not permit proof of the accused's character when the accused attacks the alleged victim's character as a witness under Rule 608 or 609.

The term "alleged" is inserted before each reference to "victim" in the Rule, in order to provide consistency with Evidence Rule 412.

GAP Report—Proposed Amendment to Rule 404(a)

The Committee made the following changes to the published draft of the proposed amendment to Evidence Rule 404(a):

1. The term "a pertinent trait of character" was changed to "the same trait of character," in order to limit the scope of the government's rebuttal. The Committee Note was revised to accord with this change in the text.

2. The word "alleged" was added before each reference in the Rule to a "victim" in order to provide consistency with Evidence Rule 412. The Committee Note was amended to accord with this change in the text.

3. The Committee Note was amended to clarify that rebuttal is not permitted under this Rule if the accused proffers evidence of the alleged victim's character for a purpose other than to prove the alleged victim's propensity to act in a certain manner.

2006 Amendments

The Rule has been amended to clarify that in a civil case evidence of a person's character is never admissible to prove that the person acted in conformity with the character trait. The amendment resolves the dispute in the case law over whether the exceptions in subdivisions (a)(1) and (2) permit the circumstantial use of character evidence in civil cases. *Compare Carson v. Polley*, 689 F.2d 562, 576 (5th Cir. 1982) ("when a central issue in a case is close to one of a criminal nature, the exceptions to the Rule 404(a) ban on character evidence may be invoked"), *with SEC v. Towers Financial Corp.*, 966 F.Supp. 203 (S.D.N.Y. 1997) (relying on the terms "accused" and "prosecution" in Rule 404(a) to conclude that the exceptions in subdivisions (a)(1) and (2) are inapplicable in civil cases). The amendment is consistent with the original intent of the Rule, which was to prohibit the circumstantial use of character evidence in civil cases, even where closely related to criminal charges. *See Ginter v. Northwestern Mut. Life Ins. Co.*, 576 F.Supp. 627, 629–30 (D. Ky.1984) ("It seems beyond peradventure of doubt that the drafters of F.R.Evi. 404(a) explicitly intended that all character evidence, except where 'character is at issue' was to be excluded" in civil cases).

The circumstantial use of character evidence is generally discouraged because it carries serious risks of prejudice, confusion and delay. *See Michelson v. United States*, 335 U.S. 469, 476 (1948) ("The overriding policy of excluding such evidence, despite its admitted probative value, is the practical experience that its disallowance tends to prevent confusion of issues, unfair surprise and undue prejudice."). In criminal cases, the so-called "mercy rule" permits a criminal defendant to introduce evidence of pertinent character traits of the defendant and the victim. But that is because the accused, whose liberty is at stake, may need "a counterweight against the strong investigative and prosecutorial resources of the government." C. Mueller & L. Kirkpatrick, *Evidence: Practice Under the Rules*, pp. 264–5 (2d ed. 1999). See also Richard Uviller, *Evidence of Character to Prove Conduct: Illusion, Illogic, and Injustice in the Courtroom*, 130 U.Pa. L.Rev. 845, 855 (1982) (the rule prohibiting circumstantial use of character evidence "was relaxed to allow the criminal defendant with so much at stake and so little available in the way of conventional proof to have special dispensation to tell the factfinder just what sort of person he really is"). Those concerns do not apply to parties in civil cases.

The amendment also clarifies that evidence otherwise admissible under Rule 404(a)(2) may nonetheless be excluded in a criminal case involving sexual misconduct. In such a case, the admissibility of evidence of the victim's sexual behavior and predisposition is governed by the more stringent provisions of Rule 412.

Nothing in the amendment is intended to affect the scope of Rule 404(b). While Rule 404(b) refers to the "accused," the "prosecution," and a "criminal case," it does so only in the context of a notice requirement. The admissibility standards of Rule 404(b) remain fully applicable to both civil and criminal cases.

Rule 405. Methods of Proving Character

(a) Reputation or opinion. In all cases in which evidence of character or a trait of character of a person is admissible, proof may be made by testimony as to reputation or by testimony in the form of an opinion. On cross-examination, inquiry is allowable into relevant specific instances of conduct.

(b) Specific instances of conduct. In cases in which character or a trait of character of a person is an essential element of a charge, claim, or defense, proof may also be made of specific instances of that person's conduct.

(Pub.L. 93–595, § 1, Jan. 2, 1975, 88 Stat. 1932; Mar. 2, 1987, eff. Oct. 1, 1987.)

ADVISORY COMMITTEE NOTES

1972 Proposed Rules

The rule deals only with allowable methods of proving character, not with the admissibility of character evidence, which is covered in Rule 404.

Of the three methods of proving character provided by the rule, evidence of specific instances of conduct is the most convincing. At the same time it possesses the greatest capacity to arouse prejudice, to confuse, to surprise, and to consume time. Consequently the rule confines the use of evidence of this kind to cases in which character is, in the strict sense, in issue and hence deserving of a searching inquiry. When character is used circumstantially and hence occupies a lesser status in the case, proof may be only by reputation and opinion. These latter methods are also available when character is in issue. This treatment is, with respect to specific instances of conduct and reputation, conventional contemporary common law doctrine. McCormick § 153.

In recognizing opinion as a means of proving character, the rule departs from usual contemporary practice in favor of that of an earlier day. See 7 Wigmore § 1986, pointing out that the earlier practice permitted opinion and arguing strongly for evidence based on personal knowledge and belief as contrasted with "the secondhand, irresponsible product of multiplied guesses and gossip which we term 'reputation'." It seems likely that the persistence of reputation evidence is due to its largely being opinion in disguise. Traditionally character has been regarded primarily in moral overtones of good and bad: chaste, peaceable, truthful, honest. Nevertheless, on occasion nonmoral considerations crop up, as in the case of the incompetent driver, and this seems bound to happen increasingly. If character is defined as the kind of person one is, then account must be taken of varying ways of arriving at the estimate. These may range from the opinion of the employer who has found the man honest to the opinion of the psychiatrist based upon examination and testing. No effective dividing line exists between character and mental capacity, and the latter traditionally has been provable by opinion.

According to the great majority of cases, on cross-examination inquiry is allowable as to whether the reputation witness has heard of particular instances of conduct pertinent to the trait in question. *Michelson v. United States,* 335 U.S. 469, 69 S.Ct. 213, 93 L.Ed. 168 (1948); Annot., 47 A.L.R.2d 1258. The theory is that, since the reputation witness relates what he has heard, the inquiry tends to shed light on the accuracy of his hearing and reporting. Accordingly, the opinion witness would be asked whether he knew, as well as whether he had heard. The fact is, of course, that these distinctions are of slight if any practical significance, and the second sentence of subdivision (a) eliminates them as a factor in formulating questions. This recognition of the propriety of inquiring into specific instances of conduct does not circumscribe inquiry otherwise into the bases of opinion and reputation testimony.

The express allowance of inquiry into specific instances of conduct on cross-examination in subdivision (a) and the express allowance of it as part of a case in chief when character is actually in issue in subdivision (b) contemplate that testimony of specific instances is not generally permissible on the direct examination of an ordinary opinion witness to character. Similarly as to witnesses to the character of witnesses under Rule 608(b). Opinion testimony on direct in these situations ought in general to correspond to reputation testimony as now given, *i.e.,* be confined to the nature and extent of observation and acquaintance upon which the opinion is based. See Rule 701.

1974 Enactment

Note to Subdivision (a). Rule 405(a) as submitted proposed to change existing law by allowing evidence of character in the form of opinion as well as reputation testimony. Fearing, among other reasons, that wholesale allowance of opinion testimony might tend to turn a trial into a swearing contest between conflicting character witnesses, the Committee decided to delete from this Rule, as well as from Rule 608(a) which involves a related problem, reference to opinion testimony. House Report No. 93–650.

The Senate makes two language changes in the nature of conforming amendments. The Conference adopts the Senate amendments. House Report No. 93–1597.

1987 Amendments

The amendment is technical. No substantive change is intended.

Rule 406. Habit; Routine Practice

Evidence of the habit of a person or of the routine practice of an organization, whether corroborated or not and regardless of the presence of eyewitnesses, is relevant to prove that the conduct of the person or organization on a particular occasion was in conformity with the habit or routine practice.

(Pub.L. 93–595, § 1, Jan. 2, 1975, 88 Stat. 1932.)

ADVISORY COMMITTEE NOTES

1972 Proposed Rules

An oft-quoted paragraph, McCormick, § 162, p. 340, describes habit in terms effectively contrasting it with character:

"Character and habit are close akin. Character is a generalized description of one's disposition, or of one's disposition in respect to a general trait, such as honesty, temperance, or peacefulness. 'Habit,' in modern usage, both lay and psychological, is more specific. It describes one's regular response to a repeated specific situation. If we speak of character for care, we think of the person's tendency to act prudently in all the varying situations of life, in business, family life, in handling automobiles and in walking across the street. A habit, on the other hand, is the person's regular practice of meeting a particular kind of situation with a specific type of conduct, such as the habit of going down a particular stairway two stairs at a time, or of giving the hand-signal for a left turn, or of alighting from railway cars while they are moving. The doing of the habitual acts may become semi-automatic."

Equivalent behavior on the part of a group is designated "routine practice of an organization" in the rule.

Agreement is general that habit evidence is highly persuasive as proof of conduct on a particular occasion. Again quoting McCormick § 162, p. 341:

"Character may be thought of as the sum of one's habits though doubtless it is more than this. But unquestionably the uniformity of one's response to habit is far greater than the consistency with which one's conduct conforms to character or disposition. Even though character comes in only exceptionally as evidence of an act, surely any sensible man in investigating whether X did a particular act would be greatly helped in his inquiry by evidence as to whether he was in the habit of doing it."

When disagreement has appeared, its focus has been upon the question what constitutes habit, and the reason for this is readily apparent. The extent to which instances must be multiplied and consistency of behavior maintained in order to rise to the status of habit inevitably gives rise to differences of opinion. Lewan, Rationale of Habit Evidence, 16 Syracuse L.Rev. 39, 49 (1964). While adequacy of sampling and uniformity of response are key factors, precise standards for measuring their sufficiency for evidence purposes cannot be formulated.

The rule is consistent with prevailing views. Much evidence is excluded simply because of failure to achieve the status of habit. Thus, evidence of intemperate "habits" is generally excluded when offered as proof of drunkenness in accident cases, Annot., 46 A.L.R.2d 103, and evidence of other assaults is inadmissible to prove the instant one in a civil assault action, Annot., 66 A.L.R.2d 806. In *Levin v. United States,* 119 U.S.App.D.C. 156, 338 F.2d 265 (1964), testimony as to the religious "habits" of the accused, offered as tending to prove that he was at home observing the Sabbath rather than out obtaining money through larceny by trick, was held properly excluded:

"It seems apparent to us that an individual's religious practices would not be the type of activities which would lend themselves to the characterization of 'invariable regularity.' [1 Wigmore 520.] Certainly the very volitional basis of the activity raises serious questions as to its invariable nature, and hence its probative value." *Id.* at 272.

These rulings are not inconsistent with the trend towards admitting evidence of business transactions between one of the parties and a third person as tending to prove that he made the same bargain or proposal in the litigated situation. Slough, Relevancy Unraveled, 6 Kan.L.Rev. 38–41 (1957). Nor are they inconsistent with such cases as *Whittemore v. Lockheed Aircraft Corp.,* 65 Cal.App.2d 737, 151 P.2d 670 (1944), upholding the admission of evidence that plaintiff's intestate had on four other occasions flown planes from defendant's factory for delivery to his employer airline, offered to prove that he was piloting rather than a guest on a plane which crashed and killed all on board while en route for delivery.

A considerable body of authority has required that evidence of the routine practice of an organization be corroborated as a condition precedent to its admission in evidence. Slough, Relevancy Unraveled, 5 Kan.L.Rev. 404, 449 (1957). This requirement is specifically rejected by the rule on the ground that it relates to the sufficiency of the evidence rather than admissibility. A similar position is taken in New Jersey Rule 49. The rule also rejects the requirement of the absence of eyewitnesses, sometimes encountered with respect to admitting habit evidence to prove freedom from contributory negligence in wrongful death cases. For comment critical of the requirements see Frank, J., in *Cereste v. New York,* N.H. & H.R. Co., 231 F.2d 50 (2d Cir.1956), cert. denied 351 U.S. 951, 76 S.Ct. 848, 100 L.Ed. 1475, 10 Vand.L.Rev. 447 (1957); McCormick § 162, p. 342. The omission of the requirement from the California Evidence Code is said to have effected its elimination. Comment, Cal.Ev.Code § 1105.

Rule 407. Subsequent Remedial Measures

When, after an injury or harm allegedly caused by an event, measures are taken that, if taken previously, would have made the injury or harm less likely to occur, evidence of the subsequent measures is not admissible to prove negligence, culpable conduct, a defect in a product, a defect in a product's design, or a need for a warning or instruction. This rule does not require the exclusion of evidence of subsequent measures when offered for another purpose, such as proving ownership, control, or feasibility of precautionary measures, if controverted, or impeachment.

(Pub.L. 93–595, § 1, Jan. 2, 1975, 88 Stat. 1932; Apr. 11, 1997, eff. Dec. 1, 1997.)

ADVISORY COMMITTEE NOTES

1972 Proposed Rules

The rule incorporates conventional doctrine which excludes evidence of subsequent remedial measures as proof of an admission of fault. The rule rests on two grounds. (1) The conduct is not in fact an admission, since the conduct is equally consistent with injury by mere accident or through contributory negligence. Or, as Baron Bramwell put it, the rule rejects the notion that "because the world gets wiser as it gets older, therefore it was foolish before." *Hart v. Lancashire & Yorkshire Ry. Co.,* 21 L.T.R. N.S. 261, 263 (1869). Under a liberal theory of relevancy this ground alone would not support exclusion as the inference is still a possible one. (2) The other, and more impressive, ground for exclusion rests on a social policy of encouraging people to take, or at least not discouraging them from taking, steps in furtherance of added safety. The courts have applied this principle to exclude evidence of subsequent repairs, installation of safety devices, changes in company rules, and discharge of employees, and the language of the present rule is broad enough to encompass all of them. See Falknor, Extrinsic Policies Affecting Admissibility, 10 Rutgers L.Rev. 574, 590 (1956).

The second sentence of the rule directs attention to the limitations of the rule. Exclusion is called for only when the evidence of subsequent remedial measures is offered as proof of negligence or culpable conduct. In effect it rejects the suggested inference that fault is admitted. Other purposes are, however, allowable, including ownership or control, existence of duty, and feasibility of precautionary measures, if controverted, and impeachment. 2 Wigmore § 283; Annot., 64 A.L.R.2d 1296. Two recent federal cases are illustrative. *Boeing Airplane Co. v. Brown,* 291 F.2d 310 (9th Cir.1961), an action against an airplane manufacturer for using an allegedly defectively designed alternator shaft which caused a plane crash, upheld the admission of evidence of subsequent design modification for the purpose of showing that design changes and safeguards were feasible. And *Powers v. J.B. Michael & Co.,* 329 F.2d 674 (6th Cir.1964), an action against a road contractor for negligent failure to put out warning signs, sustained the admission of evidence that defendant subsequently put out signs to show that the portion of the road in question was under defendant's control. The requirement that the other purpose be controverted calls for automatic exclusion unless a genuine issue be present and allows the opposing party to lay the groundwork for exclusion by making an admission. Otherwise the factors of undue prejudice, confusion of issues, misleading the jury, and waste of time remain for consideration under Rule 403.

For comparable rules, see Uniform Rule 51; California Evidence Code § 1151; Kansas Code of Civil Procedure § 60–451; New Jersey Evidence Rule 51.

1997 Amendments

The amendment to Rule 407 makes two changes in the rule. First, the words "an injury or harm allegedly caused by" were added to clarify that the rule applies only to changes made after the occurrence that produced the damages giving rise to the action. Evidence of measures taken by the defendant prior to the "event" causing "injury or harm" do not fall within the exclusionary scope of Rule 407 even if they occurred after the manufacture or design of the product. See *Chase v. General Motors Corp.*, 856 F.2d 17, 21–22 (4th Cir. 1988).

Second, Rule 407 has been amended to provide that evidence of subsequent remedial measures may not be used to prove "a defect in a product or its design, or that a warning or instruction should have accompanied a product." This amendment adopts the view of a majority of the circuits that have interpreted Rule 407 to apply to products liability actions. See *Raymond v. Raymond Corp., 938 F.2d 1518, 1522 (1st Cir. 1991); In re Joint Eastern District and Southern District Asbestos Litigation v. Armstrong World industries, Inc.*, 995 F.2d 343 (2d Cir. 1993); *Cann v. Ford Motor Co.*, 658 F.2d 54, 60 (2d Cir. 1981), *cert. denied*, 456 U.S. 960 (1982); *Kelly v. Crown Equipment Co.*, 970 F.2d 1273, 1275 (3d Cir. 1992); *Werner v. Upjohn, Inc.*, 628 F.2d 848 (4th Cir. 1980); *cert. denied*, 449 U.S. 1080 (1981); *Grenada Steel Industries, Inc. v. Alabama Oxygen Co., Inc.*, 695 F.2d 883 (5th Cir. 1983); *Bauman v. Volkswagenwerk Aktiengesellschaft*, 621 F.2d 230, 232 (6th Cir. 1980); *Flaminio v. Honda Motor Company, Ltd.*, 733 F.2d 463, 469 (7th Cir. 1984); *Gauthier v. AMF, Inc.*, 788 F.2d 634, 636–37 (9th Cir. 1986).

Although this amendment adopts a uniform federal rule, it should be noted that evidence of subsequent remedial measures may be admissible pursuant to the second sentence of Rule 407. Evidence of subsequent measures that is not barred by Rule 407 may still be subject to exclusion on Rule 403 grounds when the dangers of prejudice or confusion substantially outweigh the probative value of the evidence.

Rule 408. Compromise and Offers to Compromise

(a) Prohibited uses.—Evidence of the following is not admissible on behalf of any party, when offered to prove liability for, invalidity of, or amount of a claim that was disputed as to validity or amount, or to impeach through a prior inconsistent statement or contradiction:

(1) furnishing or offering or promising to furnish—or accepting or offering or promising to accept—a valuable consideration in compromising or attempting to compromise the claim; and

(2) conduct or statements made in compromise negotiations regarding the claim, except when offered in a criminal case and the negotiations related to a claim by a public office or agency in the exercise of regulatory, investigative, or enforcement authority.

(b) Permitted uses.—This rule does not require exclusion if the evidence is offered for purposes not prohibited by subdivision (a). Examples of permissible purposes include proving a witness's bias or prejudice; negating a contention of undue delay; and proving an effort to obstruct a criminal investigation or prosecution.

(Pub.L. 93–595, § 1, Jan. 2, 1975, 88 Stat. 1933; Apr. 12, 2006, eff. Dec. 1, 2006.)

ADVISORY COMMITTEE NOTES

1972 Proposed Rules

As a matter of general agreement, evidence of an offer to compromise a claim is not receivable in evidence as an admission of, as the case may be, the validity or invalidity of the claim. As with evidence of subsequent remedial measures, dealt with in Rule 407, exclusion may be based on two grounds. (1) The evidence is irrelevant, since the offer may be motivated by a desire for peace rather than from any concession of weakness of position. The validity of this position will vary as the amount of the offer varies in relation to the size of the claim and may also be influenced by other circumstances. (2) A more consistently impressive ground is promotion of the public policy favoring the compromise and settlement of disputes. McCormick §§ 76, 251. While the rule is ordinarily phrased in terms of offers of compromise, it is apparent that a similar attitude must be taken with respect to completed compromises when offered against a party thereto. This latter situation will not, of course, ordinarily occur except when a party to the present litigation has compromised with a third person.

The same policy underlies the provision of Rule 68 of the Federal Rules of Civil Procedure that evidence of an unaccepted offer of judgment is not admissible except in a proceeding to determine costs.

The practical value of the common law rule has been greatly diminished by its inapplicability to admissions of fact, even though made in the course of compromise negotiations, unless hypothetical, stated to be "without prejudice," or so connected with the offer as to be inseparable from it. McCormick § 251, pp. 540–541. An inevitable effect is to inhibit freedom of communication with respect to compromise, even among lawyers. Another effect is the generation of controversy over whether a given statement falls within or without the protected area. These considerations account for the expansion of the rule herewith to include evidence of conduct or statements made in compromise negotiations, as well as the offer or completed compromise itself. For similar provisions see California Evidence Code §§ 1152, 1154.

The policy considerations which underlie the rule do not come into play when the effort is to induce a creditor to settle an admittedly due amount for a lesser sum. McCormick § 251, p. 540. Hence the rule requires that the claim be disputed as to either validity or amount.

The final sentence of the rule serves to point out some limitations upon its applicability. Since the rule excludes only when the purpose is proving the validity or invalidity of the claim or its amount, an offer for another purpose is not within the rule. The illustrative situations mentioned in the rule are supported by the authorities. As to proving bias or prejudice of a witness, see Annot., 161 A.L.R. 395, *contra, Fenberg v. Rosenthal,* 348 Ill.App. 510, 109 N.E.2d 402 (1952), and negativing a contention of lack of due diligence in presenting a claim, 4 Wigmore § 1061. An effort to "buy off" the prosecution or a prosecuting witness in a criminal case is not within the policy of the rule of exclusion. McCormick § 251, p. 542.

For other rules of similar import, see Uniform Rules 52 and 53; California Evidence Code §§ 1152, 1154; Kansas Code of Civil Procedure §§ 60–452, 60–453; New Jersey Evidence Rules 52 and 53.

1974 Enactment

Under existing federal law evidence of conduct and statements made in compromise negotiations is admissible in subsequent litigation between the parties. The second sentence of Rule 408 as submitted by the Supreme Court proposed to reverse that doctrine in the interest of further promoting non-judicial settlement of disputes. Some agencies of government expressed the view that the Court formulation was likely to impede rather than assist efforts to achieve settlement of disputes. For one thing, it is not always easy to tell when compromise negotiations begin, and informal dealings end. Also, parties dealing with government agencies would be reluctant to furnish factual information at preliminary meetings; they would wait until "compromise negotiations" began and thus hopefully effect an immunity for themselves with respect to the evidence supplied. In light of these considerations, the Committee recast the Rule so that admissions of liability or opinions given during compromise negotiations continue inadmissible, but evidence of unqualified factual assertions is admissible. The latter aspect of the Rule is drafted, however, so as to preserve other possible objections to the introduction of such evidence. The Committee intends no modification of current law whereby a party may protect himself from future use of his statements by couching them in hypothetical conditional form. House Report No. 93–650.

This rule as reported makes evidence of settlement or attempted settlement of a disputed claim inadmissible when offered as an admission of liability or the amount of liability. The purpose of this rule is to encourage settlements which would be discouraged if such evidence were admissible.

Under present law, in most jurisdictions, statements of fact made during settlement negotiations, however, are excepted from this ban and are admissible. The only escape from admissibility of statements of fact made in a settlement negotiation is if the declarant or his representative expressly states that the statement is hypothetical in nature or is made without prejudice. Rule 408 as submitted by the Court reversed the traditional rule. It would have brought statements of fact within the ban and made them, as well as an offer of settlement, inadmissible.

The House amended the rule and would continue to make evidence of facts disclosed during compromise negotiations admissible. It thus reverted to the traditional rule. The House committee report states that the committee intends to preserve current law under which a party may protect himself by couching his statements in hypothetical form [See House Report No. 93–650 above]. The real impact of this amendment, however, is to deprive the rule of much of its salutary effect. The exception for factual admissions was believed by the Advisory Committee to hamper free communication between parties and thus to constitute an unjustifiable restraint upon efforts to negotiate settlements—the encouragement of which is the purpose of the rule. Further, by protecting hypothetically phrased statements, it constituted a preference for the sophisticated, and a trap for the unwary.

Three States which had adopted rules of evidence patterned after the proposed rules prescribed by the Supreme Court opted for versions of rule 408 identical with the Supreme Court draft with respect to the inadmissibility of conduct or statements made in compromise negotiations [Nev.Rev.Stats. § 48.105; N.Mex.Stats.Anno. (1973 Supp.) § 20–4–408; West's Wis.Stats.Anno. (1973 Supp.) § 904.08].

For these reasons, the committee has deleted the House amendment and restored the rule to the version submitted by the Supreme Court with one additional amendment. This amendment adds a sentence to insure that evidence, such as documents, is not rendered inadmissible merely because it is presented in the course of compromise negotiations if the evidence is otherwise discoverable. A party should not be able to immunize from admissibility documents otherwise discoverable merely by offering them in a compromise negotiation. Senate Report No. 93–1277.

The House bill provides that evidence of admissions of liability or opinions given during compromise negotiations is not admissible, but that evidence of facts disclosed during compromise negotiations is not inadmissible by virtue of having been first disclosed in the compromise negotiations. The Senate amendment provides that evidence of conduct or statements made in compromise negotiations is not admissible. The Senate amendment also provides that the rule does not require the exclusion of any evidence otherwise discoverable merely because it is presented in the course of compromise negotiations.

The House bill was drafted to meet the objection of executive agencies that under the rule as proposed by the Supreme Court, a party could present a fact during compromise negotiations and thereby prevent an opposing party from offering evidence of that fact at trial even though such evidence was obtained from independent sources. The Senate amendment expressly precludes this result.

The Conference adopts the Senate amendment. House Report No. 93–1597.

2006 Amendment

Rule 408 has been amended to settle some questions in the courts about the scope of the Rule, and to make it easier to read. First, the amendment provides that Rule 408 does not prohibit the introduction in a criminal case of statements or conduct during compromise negotiations regarding a civil dispute by a government regulatory, investigative, or enforcement agency. *See, e.g., United States v. Prewitt,* 34 F.3d 436, 439 (7th Cir. 1994) (admissions of fault made in compromise of a civil securities enforcement action were admissible against the accused in a subsequent criminal action for mail fraud). Where an individual makes a statement in the presence of government agents, its subsequent admission in a criminal case should not be unexpected. The individual can seek to protect against subsequent disclosure through negotiation and agreement with the civil regulator or an attorney for the government.

Statements made in compromise negotiations of a claim by a government agency may be excluded in criminal cases where the circumstances so warrant under Rule 403. For example, if an individual was unrepresented at the time the statement was made in a civil enforcement proceeding, its probative value in a subsequent criminal case may be minimal. But there is no absolute exclusion imposed by Rule 408.

In contrast, statements made during compromise negotiations of other disputed claims are not admissible in subsequent criminal litigation, when offered to prove liability for, invalidity of, or amount of those claims. When private parties enter into compromise negotiations they cannot protect against the subsequent use of statements in criminal cases by way of private ordering. The inability to guarantee protection against subsequent use could lead to parties refusing to admit fault, even if by doing so they could favorably settle the private matter. Such a chill on settlement negotiations would be contrary to the policy of Rule 408.

The amendment distinguishes statements and conduct (such as a direct admission of fault) made in compromise negotiations of a civil claim by a government agency from an offer or acceptance of a compromise of such a claim. An offer or acceptance of a compromise of any civil claim is excluded under the Rule if offered against the defendant as an admission of fault. In that case, the predicate for the evidence would be that the defendant, by compromising with the government agency, has admitted the validity and amount of the civil claim, and that this admission has sufficient probative value to be considered as evidence of guilt. But unlike a direct statement of fault, an offer or acceptance of a compromise is not very probative of the defendant's guilt. Moreover, admitting such an offer or acceptance could deter a defendant from settling a civil regulatory action, for fear of evidentiary use in a subsequent criminal action. *See, e.g.*, Fishman, *Jones on Evidence, Civil and Criminal*, § 22:16 at 199, n.83 (7th ed. 2000) ("A target of a potential criminal investigation may be unwilling to settle civil claims against him if by doing so he increases the risk of prosecution and conviction.").

The amendment retains the language of the original rule that bars compromise evidence only when offered as evidence of the "validity," "invalidity," or "amount" of the disputed claim. The intent is to retain the extensive case law finding Rule 408 inapplicable when compromise evidence is offered for a purpose other than to prove the validity, invalidity, or amount of a disputed claim. *See, e.g., Athey v. Farmers Ins. Exchange*, 234 F.3d 357 (8th Cir. 2000) (evidence of settlement offer by insurer was properly admitted to prove insurer's bad faith); *Coakley & Williams v. Structural Concrete Equip.*, 973 F.2d 349 (4th Cir. 1992) (evidence of settlement is not precluded by Rule 408 where offered to prove a party's intent with respect to the scope of a release); *Cates v. Morgan Portable Bldg. Corp.*, 708 F.2d 683 (7th Cir. 1985) (Rule 408 does not bar evidence of a settlement when offered to prove a breach of the settlement agreement, as the purpose of the evidence is to prove the fact of settlement as opposed to the validity or amount of the underlying claim); *Uforma/Shelby Bus. Forms, Inc. v. NLRB*, 111 F.3d 1284 (6th Cir. 1997) (threats made in settlement negotiations were admissible; Rule 408 is inapplicable when the claim is based upon a wrong that is committed during the course of settlement negotiations). So for example, Rule 408 is inapplicable if offered to show that a party made fraudulent statements in order to settle a litigation.

The amendment does not affect the case law providing that Rule 408 is inapplicable when evidence of the compromise is offered to prove notice. *See, e.g., United States v. Austin*, 54 F.3d 394 (7th Cir. 1995) (no error to admit evidence of the defendant's settlement with the FTC, because it was offered to prove that the defendant was on notice that subsequent similar conduct was wrongful); *Spell v. McDaniel*, 824 F.2d 1380 (4th Cir. 1987) (in a civil rights action alleging that an officer used excessive force, a prior settlement by the City of another brutality claim was properly admitted to prove that the City was on notice of aggressive behavior by police officers).

The amendment prohibits the use of statements made in settlement negotiations when offered to impeach by prior inconsistent statement or through contradiction. Such broad impeachment would tend to swallow the exclusionary rule and would impair the public policy of promoting settlements. *See McCormick on Evidence* at 186 (5th ed. 1999) ("Use of statements made in compromise negotiations to impeach the testimony of a party, which is not specifically treated in Rule 408, is fraught with danger of misuse of the statements to prove liability, threatens frank interchange of information during negotiations, and generally should not be permitted."). *See also EEOC v. Gear Petroleum, Inc.*, 948 F.2d 1542 (10th Cir.1991) (letter sent as part of settlement negotiation cannot be used to impeach defense witnesses by way of contradiction or prior inconsistent statement; such broad impeachment would undermine the policy of encouraging uninhibited settlement negotiations).

The amendment makes clear that Rule 408 excludes compromise evidence even when a party seeks to admit its own settlement offer or statements made in settlement negotiations. If a party were to reveal its own statement or offer, this could itself reveal the fact that the adversary entered into settlement negotiations. The protections of Rule 408 cannot be waived unilaterally because the Rule, by definition, protects both parties from having the fact of negotiation disclosed to the jury. Moreover, proof of statements and offers made in settlement would often have to be made through the testimony of attorneys, leading to the risks and costs of disqualification. *See generally Pierce v. F.R. Tripler & Co.*, 955 F.2d 820, 828 (2d Cir. 1992) (settlement offers are excluded under Rule 408 even if it is the offeror who seeks to admit them; noting that the "widespread admissibility of the substance of settlement offers could bring with it a rash of motions for disqualification of a party's chosen counsel who would likely become a witness at trial").

The sentence of the Rule referring to evidence "otherwise discoverable" has been deleted as superfluous. *See, e.g.*, Advisory Committee Note to Maine Rule of Evidence 408 (refusing to include the sentence in the Maine version of Rule 408 and noting that the sentence "seems to state what the law would be if it were omitted"); Advisory Committee Note to Wyoming Rule of Evidence 408 (refusing to include the sentence in Wyoming Rule 408 on the ground that it was "superfluous"). The intent of the sentence was to prevent a party from trying to immunize admissible information, such as a pre-existing document, through the pretense of disclosing it during compromise negotiations. *See Ramada Devel-*

opment Co. v. Rauch, 644 F.2d 1097 (5th Cir. 1981). But even without the sentence, the Rule cannot be read to protect pre-existing information simply because it was presented to the adversary in compromise negotiations.

Rule 409. Payment of Medical and Similar Expenses

Evidence of furnishing or offering or promising to pay medical, hospital, or similar expenses occasioned by an injury is not admissible to prove liability for the injury.

(Pub.L. 93–595, § 1, Jan. 2, 1975, 88 Stat.1933.)

ADVISORY COMMITTEE NOTES

1972 Proposed Rules

The considerations underlying this rule parallel those underlying Rules 407 and 408, which deal respectively with subsequent remedial measures and offers of compromise. As stated in Annot., 20 A.L.R.2d 291, 293:

"[G]enerally, evidence of payment of medical, hospital, or similar expenses of an injured party by the opposing party, is not admissible, the reason often given being that such payment or offer is usually made from humane impulses and not from an admission of liability, and that to hold otherwise would tend to discourage assistance to the injured person."

Contrary to Rule 408, dealing with offers of compromise, the present rule does not extend to conduct or statements not a part of the act of furnishing or offering or promising to pay. This difference in treatment arises from fundamental differences in nature. Communication is essential if compromises are to be effected, and consequently broad protection of statements is needed. This is not so in cases of payments or offers or promises to pay medical expenses, where factual statements may be expected to be incidental in nature.

For rules on the same subject, but phrased in terms of "humanitarian motives," see Uniform Rule 52; California Evidence Code § 1152; Kansas Code of Civil Procedure § 60–452; New Jersey Evidence Rule 52.

Rule 410. Inadmissibility of Pleas, Plea Discussions, and Related Statements

Except as otherwise provided in this rule, evidence of the following is not, in any civil or criminal proceeding, admissible against the defendant who made the plea or was a participant in the plea discussions:

(1) a plea of guilty which was later withdrawn;

(2) a plea of nolo contendere;

(3) any statement made in the course of any proceedings under Rule 11 of the Federal Rules of Criminal Procedure or comparable state procedure regarding either of the foregoing pleas; or

(4) any statement made in the course of plea discussions with an attorney for the prosecuting authority which do not result in a plea of guilty or which result in a plea of guilty later withdrawn.

However, such a statement is admissible (i) in any proceeding wherein another statement made in the course of the same plea or plea discussions has been introduced and the statement ought in fairness be considered contemporaneously with it, or (ii) in a criminal proceeding for perjury or false statement if the statement was made by the defendant under oath, on the record and in the presence of counsel.

(Pub.L. 93–595, § 1, Jan. 2, 1975, 88 Stat. 1933; Pub.L. 94–149, § 1(9), Dec. 12, 1975, 89 Stat. 805; Apr. 30, 1979, eff. Dec. 1, 1980.)

ADVISORY COMMITTEE NOTES

1972 Proposed Rules

Withdrawn pleas of guilty were held inadmissible in federal prosecutions in *Kercheval v. United States*, 274 U.S. 220, 47 S.Ct. 582, 71 L.Ed. 1009 (1927). The Court pointed out that to admit the withdrawn plea would effectively set at naught the allowance of withdrawal and place the accused in a dilemma utterly inconsistent with the decision to award him a trial. The New York Court of Appeals, in *People v. Spitaleri*, 9 N.Y.2d 168, 212 N.Y.S.2d 53, 173 N.E.2d 35 (1961), reexamined and overturned its earlier decisions which had allowed admission. In addition to the reasons set forth in Kercheval, which was quoted at length, the court pointed out that the effect of admitting the plea was to compel defendant to take the stand by way of explanation and to open the way for the prosecution to call the lawyer who had represented him at the time of entering the plea. State court decisions for and against admissibility are collected in Annot., 86 A.L.R.2d 326.

Pleas of *nolo contendere* are recognized by Rule 11 of the Rules of Criminal Procedure, although the law of numerous States is to the contrary. The present rule gives effect to the principal traditional characteristic of the *nolo* plea, i.e. avoiding the admission of guilt which is inherent in pleas of guilty. This position is consistent with the construction of Section 5 of the Clayton Act, 15 U.S.C. § 16(a), recognizing the inconclusive and compromise nature of judgments based on *nolo* pleas. *General Electric Co. v. City of San Antonio*, 334 F.2d 480 (5th Cir.1964); *Commonwealth Edison Co. v. Allis–Chalmers Mfg. Co.*, 323 F.2d 412 (7th Cir.1963), cert. denied 376 U.S. 939, 84 S.Ct. 794, 11 L.Ed.2d 659; *Armco Steel Corp. v. North Dakota*, 376 F.2d 206 (8th Cir.1967); *City of Burbank v. General Electric Co.*, 329 F.2d 825 (9th Cir.1964). See also state court decisions in Annot., 18 A.L.R.2d 1287, 1314.

Exclusion of offers to plead guilty or *nolo* has as its purpose the promotion of disposition of criminal cases by compromise. As pointed out in McCormick § 251, p. 543. "Effective criminal law administration in many localities would hardly be possible if a large proportion of the charges were not disposed of by such compromises."

See also *People v. Hamilton*, 60 Cal.2d 105, 32 Cal.Rptr. 4, 383 P.2d 412 (1963), discussing legislation designed to achieve this result. As with compromise offers generally, Rule 408, free communication is needed, and security against having an offer of compromise or related statement admitted in evidence effectively encourages it.

Limiting the exclusionary rule to use against the accused is consistent with the purpose of the rule, since the possibility of use for or against other persons will not impair the effectiveness of withdrawing pleas or the freedom of discussion which the rule is designed to foster. See A.B.A. Standards Relating to Pleas of Guilty § 2.2 (1968). See also the narrower provisions of New Jersey Evidence Rule 52(2) and the unlimited exclusion provided in California Evidence Code § 1153.

1974 Enactment

The Committee added the phrase "Except as otherwise provided by Act of Congress" to Rule 410 as submitted by the Court in order to preserve particular congressional policy judgments as to the effect of a plea of guilty or of nolo contendere. See 15 U.S.C. 16(a). The Committee intends that its amendment refers to both present statutes and statutes subsequently enacted. House Report No. 93–650.

As adopted by the House, rule 410 would make inadmissible pleas of guilty or nolo contendere subsequently withdrawn as well as offers to make such pleas. Such a rule is clearly justified as a means of encouraging pleading. However, the House rule would then go on to render inadmissible for any purpose statements made in connection with these pleas or offers as well.

The committee finds this aspect of the House rule unjustified. Of course, in certain circumstances such statements should be excluded. If, for example, a plea is vitiated because of coercion, statements made in connection with the plea may also have been coerced and should be inadmissible on that basis. In other cases, however, voluntary statements of an accused made in court on the record, in connection with a plea, and determined by a court to be reliable should be admissible even though the plea is subsequently withdrawn. This is particularly true in those cases where, if the House rule were in effect, a defendant would be able to contradict his previous statements and thereby lie with impunity [See *Harris v. New York*, 401 U.S. 222 (1971)]. To prevent such an injustice, the rule has been modified to permit the use of such statements for the limited purposes of impeachment and in subsequent perjury or false statement prosecutions. Senate Report No. 93–1277.

The House bill provides that evidence of a guilty or nolo contendere plea, of an offer of either plea, or of statements made in connection with such pleas or offers of such pleas, is inadmissible in any civil or criminal action, case or proceeding against the person making such plea or offer. The Senate amendment makes the rule inapplicable to a voluntary and reliable statement made in court on the record where the statement is offered in a subsequent prosecution of the declarant for perjury or false statement.

The issues raised by Rule 410 are also raised by proposed Rule 11(e)(6) of the Federal Rules of Criminal Procedure presently pending before Congress. This proposed rule, which deals with the admissibility of pleas of guilty or nolo contendere, offers to make such pleas, and statements made in connection with such pleas, was promulgated by the Supreme Court on April 22, 1974, and in the absence of congressional action will become effective on August 1, 1975. The conferees intend to make no change in the presently-existing case law until that date, leaving the courts free to develop rules in this area on a case-by-case basis.

The Conferees further determined that the issues presented by the use of guilty and nolo contendere pleas, offers of such pleas, and statements made in connection with such pleas or offers, can be explored in greater detail during Congressional consideration of Rule 11(e)(6) of the Federal Rules of Criminal Procedure. The Conferees believe, therefore, that it is best to defer its effective date until August 1, 1975. The Conferees intend that Rule 410 would be superseded by any subsequent Federal Rule of Criminal Procedure or act of Congress with which it is inconsistent, if the Federal Rule of Criminal Procedure or Act of Congress takes effect or becomes law after the date of the enactment of the act establishing the rules of evidence.

The conference adopts the Senate amendment with an amendment that expresses the above intentions. House Report No. 93–1597.

1979 Amendments

Present rule 410 conforms to rule 11(e)(6) of the Federal Rules of Criminal Procedure. A proposed amendment to rule 11(e)(6) would clarify the circumstances in which pleas, plea discussions and related statements are inadmissible in evidence: see Advisory Committee Note thereto. The amendment proposed above would make comparable changes in rule 410.

HISTORICAL NOTES

References in Text

Rule 11 of the Federal Rules of Criminal Procedure, referred to in par. (3), is classified to Title 18, Federal Rules of Criminal Procedure.

Rule 411. Liability Insurance

Evidence that a person was or was not insured against liability is not admissible upon the issue whether the person acted negligently or otherwise wrongfully. This rule does not require the exclusion of evidence of insurance against liability when offered for another purpose, such as proof of agency, ownership, or control, or bias or prejudice of a witness.

(Pub.L. 93–595, § 1, Jan. 2, 1975, 88 Stat.1933; Mar. 2, 1987, eff. Oct. 1, 1987.)

ADVISORY COMMITTEE NOTES

1972 Proposed Rules

The courts have with substantial unanimity rejected evidence of liability insurance for the purpose of proving fault, and absence of liability insurance as proof of lack of fault. At best the inference of fault from the fact of insurance coverage is a tenuous one, as is its converse. More important, no doubt, has been the feeling that knowledge of the presence or absence of liability insurance would induce juries to decide cases on improper grounds. McCormick § 168; Annot., 4 A.L.R.2d 761. The rule is drafted in broad terms so as to include contributory negligence or other fault of a plaintiff as well as fault of a defendant.

The second sentence points out the limits of the rule, using well established illustrations. *Id.*

For similar rules see Uniform Rule 54; California Evidence Code § 1155; Kansas Code of Civil Procedure § 60–454; New Jersey Evidence Rule 54.

1987 Amendments

The amendment is technical. No substantive change is intended.

Rule 412. Sex Offense Cases; Relevance of Alleged Victim's Past Sexual Behavior or Alleged Sexual Predisposition

(a) Evidence generally inadmissible.—The following evidence is not admissible in any civil or criminal proceeding involving alleged sexual misconduct except as provided in subdivisions (b) and (c):

(1) Evidence offered to prove that any alleged victim engaged in other sexual behavior.

(2) Evidence offered to prove any alleged victim's sexual predisposition.

(b) Exceptions.—

(1) In a criminal case, the following evidence is admissible, if otherwise admissible under these rules:

(A) evidence of specific instances of sexual behavior by the alleged victim offered to prove that a person other than the accused was the source of semen, injury or other physical evidence;

(B) evidence of specific instances of sexual behavior by the alleged victim with respect to the person accused of the sexual misconduct offered by the accused to prove consent or by the prosecution; and

(C) evidence the exclusion of which would violate the constitutional rights of the defendant.

(2) In a civil case, evidence offered to prove the sexual behavior or sexual predisposition of any alleged victim is admissible if it is otherwise admissible under these rules and its probative value substantially outweighs the danger of harm to any victim and of unfair prejudice to any party. Evidence of an alleged victim's reputation is admissible only if it has been placed in controversy by the alleged victim.

(c) Procedure to determine admissibility.—

(1) A party intending to offer evidence under subdivision (b) must—

(A) file a written motion at least 14 days before trial specifically describing the evidence and stating the purpose for which it is offered unless the court, for good cause requires a different time for filing or permits filing during trial; and

(B) serve the motion on all parties and notify the alleged victim or, when appropriate, the alleged victim's guardian or representative.

(2) Before admitting evidence under this rule the court must conduct a hearing in camera and afford the victim and parties a right to attend and be heard. The motion, related papers, and the record of the hearing must be sealed and remain under seal unless the court orders otherwise.

(Added Pub.L. 95–540, § 2(a), Oct. 28, 1978, 92 Stat. 2046, and amended Pub.L. 100–690, Title VII, § 7046(a), Nov. 18, 1988, 102 Stat. 4400; Apr. 29, 1994, eff. Dec. 1, 1994; Pub.L. 103–322, Title IV, § 40141(b), Sept. 13, 1994, 108 Stat. 1919.)

ADVISORY COMMITTEE NOTES

1994 Amendments

Rule 412 has been revised to diminish some of the confusion engendered by the original rule and to expand the protection afforded alleged victims of sexual misconduct. Rule 412 applies to both civil and criminal proceedings. The rule aims to safeguard the alleged victim against the invasion of privacy, potential embarrassment and sexual stereotyping that is associated with public disclosure of intimate sexual details and the infusion of sexual innuendo into the factfinding process. By affording victims protection in most instances, the rule also encourages victims of sexual misconduct to institute and to participate in legal proceedings against alleged offenders

Rule 412 seeks to achieve these objectives by barring evidence relating to the alleged victim's sexual behavior or alleged sexual predisposition, whether offered as substantive evidence of for impeachment, except in designated circumstances in which the probative value of the evidence significantly outweighs possible harm to the victim.

The revised rule applies in all cases involving sexual misconduct without regard to whether the alleged victim or person accused is a party to the litigation. Rule 412 extends to "pattern" witnesses in both criminal and civil cases whose testimony about other instances of sexual misconduct by the person accused is otherwise admissible. When the case does not involve alleged sexual misconduct, evidence relating to a third-party witness' alleged sexual activities is not within the ambit of Rule 412. The witness will, however, be protected by other rules such as Rules 404 and 608, as well as Rule 403.

The terminology "alleged victim" is used because there will frequently be a factual dispute as to whether sexual misconduct occurred. It does not connote any requirement that the misconduct be alleged in the pleadings. Rule 412 does not, however, apply unless the person against whom the evidence is offered can reasonably be characterized as a "victim of alleged sexual misconduct." When this is not the case, as for instance in a defamation action involving statements concerning sexual misconduct in which the evidence is offered to show that the alleged defamatory statements were true or did not damage the plaintiff's reputation, neither Rule 404 nor this rule will operate to bar the evidence; Rule 401 and 403 will continue to control. Rule 412 will, however, apply in a Title VII action in which the plaintiff has alleged sexual harassment.

The reference to a person "accused" is also used in a non-technical sense. There is no requirement that there be a criminal charge pending against the person or even that the misconduct would constitute a criminal offense. Evidence offered to prove allegedly false prior claims by the victim is not barred by Rule 412. However, the evidence is subject to the requirements of Rule 404.

Subdivision (a). As amended, Rule 412 bars evidence offered to prove the victim's sexual behavior and alleged sexual predisposition. Evidence, which might otherwise be admissible under Rules 402, 404(b), 405, 607, 608, 609 of some other evidence rule, must be excluded if Rule 412 so requires. The word "other" is used to suggest some flexibility in admitting evidence "intrinsic" to the alleged sexual misconduct. *Cf.* Committee Note to 1991 amendment to Rule 404(b)

Past sexual behavior connotes all activities that involve actual physical conduct, i.e. sexual intercourse or sexual contact. *See, e.g., United States v. Galloway*, 937 F.2d 542 (10th Cir. 1991), *cert. denied*, 113 S.Ct. 418 (1992) (use of contraceptives inadmissible since use implies sexual activity); *United States v. One Feather*, 702 F.2d 736 (8th Cir. 1983) (birth of an illegitimate child inadmissible); *State v. Carmichael*, 727 P.2d 918, 925 (Kan. 1986) (evidence of venereal disease inadmissible). In addition, the word "behavior" should be construed to include activities of the mind, such as fantasies of dreams. *See* 23 C. Wright and K. Graham, Jr., *Federal Practice and Procedure*, § 5384 at p. 548 (1980) ("While there may be some doubt under statutes that require 'conduct,' it would seem that the language of Rule 412 is broad enough to encompass the behavior of the mind.").

The rule has been amended to also exclude all other evidence relating to an alleged victim of sexual misconduct that is offered to prove a sexual predisposition. This amendment is designed to exclude evidence that does not directly refer to sexual activities or thoughts but that the proponent believes may have a sexual connotation for the factfinder. Admission of such evidence would contravene Rule 412's objectives of shielding the alleged victim from potential embarrassment and safeguarding the victim against stereotypical thinking. Consequently, unless the (b)(2) exception is satisfied, evidence such as that relating to the alleged victim's mode of dress, speech, or life-style will not be admissible.

The introductory phrase in subdivision (a) was deleted because it lacked clarity and contained no explicit reference to the other provisions of the law that were intended to be overridden. The conditional clause, "except as provided in subdivisions (b) and (c)" is intended to make clear that evidence of the types described in subdivision (a) is admissible only under the strictures of those sections.

The reason for extending the rule to all criminal cases is obvious. The strong social policy of protecting a victim's privacy and encouraging victims to come forward to report criminal acts is not confined to cases that involve a charge of sexual assault. The need to protect the victim is equally great when a defendant is charged with kidnapping, and evidence is offered, either to prove motive or as background, that the defendant sexually assaulted the victim.

The reason for extending Rule 412 to civil cases is equally obvious. The need to protect alleged victims against invasions of privacy, potential embarrassment, and unwarranted sexual stereotyping, and the wish to encourage victims to come forward when they have been sexually molested do not disappear because the context has shifted from a criminal prosecution to a claim for damages or injunctive relief. There is a strong social policy in not only punishing those who engage in sexual misconduct, but in also providing relief to the victim. Thus, Rule 412 applies in any civil case in which a person claims to be the victim of sexual misconduct, such as actions for sexual battery or sexual harassment.

Subdivision (b). Subdivision (b) spells out the specific circumstances in which some evidence may be admissible that would otherwise be barred by the general rule expressed in subdivision (a). As amended, Rule 412 will be virtually unchanged in criminal cases, but will provide protection to any person alleged to be a victim of sexual misconduct regardless of the charge actually brought against an accused. A new exception has been added for civil cases.

In a criminal case, evidence may be admitted under subdivision (b)(1) pursuant to three possible exceptions, provided the evidence also satisfies other requirements for admissibility specified in the Federal Rules of Evidence, including Rule 403. Subdivisions (b)(1)(A) and (b)(1)(B) require proof in the form of specific instances of sexual behavior in recognition of the limited probative value and dubious reliability of evidence of reputation or evidence in the form of an opinion.

Under subdivision (b)(1)(A), evidence of specific instances of sexual behavior with persons other than the person whose sexual misconduct is alleged may be admissible if it is offered to prove that another person was the source of semen, injury or other physical evidence. Where the prosecution has directly or indirectly asserted that the physical evidence originated with the accused, the defendant must be afforded an opportunity to prove that another person was responsible. See *United States v. Begay*, 937 F.2d 515, 523 n. 10 (10th Cir. 1991). Evidence offered for the specific purpose identified in this subdivision may still be excluded if it does not satisfy Rules 401 or 403. *See, e.g., United States v. Azure*, 845 F.2d 1503, 1505-06 (8th Cir. 1988) (10 year old victim's injuries indicated recent use of force; court excluded evidence of consensual sexual activities with witness who testified at in camera hearing that he had never hurt victim and failed to establish recent activities).

Under the exception in subdivision (b)(1)(B), evidence of specific instances of sexual behavior with respect to the person whose sexual misconduct is alleged is admissible if offered to prove consent, or offered by the prosecution. Admissible pursuant to this exception might be evidence of prior instances of sexual activities between the alleged victim and the accused, as well as statements in which the alleged victim expresses an intent to engage in sexual intercourse with the accused, or voiced sexual fantasies involving that specific accused. In a prosecution for child sexual abuse, for example, evidence of uncharged sexual activity between the accused and the alleged victim offered by the prosecution may be admissible pursuant to Rule 404(b) to show a pattern of behavior. Evidence relating to the victim's alleged sexual predisposition is not admissible pursuant to this exception.

Under subdivision (b)(1)(C), evidence of specific instances of conduct may not be excluded if the result would be to deny a criminal defendant the protections afforded by the Constitution. For example, statements in which the victim has expressed an intent to have sex with the first person encountered on a particular occasion might not be excluded without violating the due process right of a rape defendant seeking to prove consent. Recognition of this basic principle was expressed on subdivision (b)(1) of the original rule. The United States Supreme Court has recognized that in various circumstances a defendant may have a right to introduce evidence otherwise precluded by an evidence rule under the Confrontation Clause. *See, e.g., Olden v. Kentucky*, 488 U.S. 227 (1988) (defendant in rape cases had right to inquire into alleged victim's cohabitation with another man to show bias).

Subdivision (b)(2) governs the admissibility of otherwise proscribed evidence in civil cases. It employs a balancing test rather than the specific exceptions stated in subdivision (b)(1) in recognition of the difficulty of foreseeing future developments in the law. Greater flexibility is needed to accommodate evolving causes of action such as claims for sexual harassment.

The balancing test requires the proponent of the evidence, whether plaintiff or defendant, to convince the court that the probative value of the proffered evidence "substantially outweighs the danger of harm to any victim and of unfair prejudice of any party." This test for admitting evidence offered to prove sexual behavior or sexual propensity in civil cases differs in three respects from the general rule governing admissibility set forth in Rule 403. First, it Reverses that usual procedure spelled out in Rule 403 by shifting the burden to the proponent to demonstrate admissibility rather than making the opponent justify exclusion of the evidence. Second, the standard expressed in subdivision (b)(2) is more stringent than in the original rule; it raises the threshold for admission by requiring that the probative value of the evidence *substantially* outweigh the specified dangers. Finally, the Rule 412 test puts "harm to the victim" on the scale in addition to prejudice to the parties.

Evidence of reputation may be received in a civil case only if the alleged victim has put his or her reputation into controversy. The victim may do so without making a specific allegation in a pleading. *Cf.* Fed.R.Civ.P. 35(a).

Subdivision (c). Amended subdivision (c) is more concise and understandable than the subdivision it replaces. The requirement of a motion before trial is continued in the amended rule, as is the provision that a late motion may be permitted for good cause shown. In deciding whether to permit late filing, the court may take into account the conditions previously included in the rule: namely whether the evidence is newly discovered and could not have been obtained earlier through the existence of due diligence, and whether the issue to which such evidence relates has newly arisen in the case. The rule recognizes that in some instances the circumstances that justify an application to introduce evidence otherwise barred by Rule 412 will not become apparent until trial.

The amended rule provides that before admitting evidence that falls within that prohibition of Rule 412(a), the court must hold a hearing in camera at which the alleged victim and any party must be afforded the right to be present and an opportunity to be heard. All papers connected with the motion must be kept and remain under seal during the course of trial and appellate proceedings unless otherwise ordered. This is to assure that the privacy of the alleged victim is preserved in all cases in which the court rules that proffered evidence is not admissible, and in which the hearing refers to matters that are not received, or are received in another form.

The procedures set forth in subdivision (c) do not apply to discovery of a victim's past sexual conduct or predisposition in civil cases, which will be continued to be governed by Fed. R. Civ. P. 26. In order not to undermine the rationale of Rule 412, however, courts should enter appropriate orders pursuant to Fed. R. Civ. P. 26 (c) to protect the victim against unwarranted inquiries and to ensure confidentiality. Courts should presumptively issue protective orders barring discovery unless the party seeking discovery makes a showing that the evidence sought to be discovered would be relevant under the facts and theories of the particular case, and cannot be obtained except through discovery. In an action for sexual harassment, for instance, while some evidence of the alleged victim's sexual behavior and/or predisposition in the workplace may perhaps be relevant, non-work place conduct will usually be irrelevant. *Cf. Burns v. McGregor Electronic Industries, Inc.*, 989 F.2d 959, 962-63 (8th Cir. 1993) (posing for a nude magazine outside work hours is irrelevant to issue of unwelcomeness of sexual advances at work). Confidentiality orders should be presumptively granted as well.

One substantive change made in subdivision (c) is the elimination of the following sentence: "Notwithstanding subdivision (b) of Rule 104, if the relevancy of the evidence which the accused seeks to offer in trial depends upon the fulfillment of a condition of fact, the court, at the hearing in chambers or at a subsequent hearing in chambers scheduled for such purpose, shall accept evidence on the issue of whether such condition of fact is fulfilled and shall determine such issue." On its face, this language would appear to authorize a trial judge to exclude evidence of past sexual conduct between alleged victim and an accused or a defendant in a civil case based upon the judge's belief that such past acts did not occur. Such an authorization raises questions of invasion of the right to a jury trial under the Sixth and Seventh Amendments. *See* 1 S. Saltzburg & M. Martin, *Federal Rules of Evidence Manual*, 396-97 (5th ed. 1990).

The Advisory Committee concluded that the amended rule provided adequate protection for all persons claiming to be the victims of sexual misconduct, and that it was inadvisable to continue to include a provision in the rule that has been confusing and that raises substantial constitutional issues. [Advisory Committee Note adopted by Congressional Conference Report accompanying Pub.L. 103–322. See H.R. Conf. Rep. No. 103–711, 103rd Cong., 2nd Sess., 383 (1994).]

Congressional Discussion

The following discussion in the House of Representatives of October 10, 1978, preceded passage of H.R. 4727, which enacted Rule 412. The discussion appears in 124 Cong.Record, at page H. 11944.

Mr. MANN. Mr. Speaker, I yield myself such time as I may consume.

Mr. Speaker, for many years in this country, evidentiary rules have permitted the introduction of evidence about a rape victim's prior sexual conduct. Defense lawyers were permitted great latitude in bringing out intimate details about a rape victim's life. Such evidence quite often serves no real purpose and only results in embarrassment to the rape victim and unwarranted public intrusion into her private life.

The evidentiary rules that permit such inquiry have in recent years come under question; and the States have taken the lead to change and modernize their evidentiary rules about evidence of a rape victim's prior sexual behavior. The bill before us similarly seeks to modernize the Federal Evidentiary rules.

The present Federal Rules of Evidence reflect the traditional approach. If a defendant in a rape case raises the defense of consent, that defendant may then offer evidence about the victim's prior sexual behavior. Such evidence may be in the form of opinion evidence, evidence of reputation, or evidence of specific instances of behavior. Rule 404(a)(2) of the Federal Rules of Evidence permits the introduction of evidence of a "pertinent character trait." The advisory committee note to that rule cites, as an example of what the rule covers, the character of a rape victim when the issue is consent. Rule 405 of the Federal Rules of Evidence permits the use of opinion or reputation evidence or the use of evidence of specific behavior to show a character trait.

Thus, Federal evidentiary rules permit a wide ranging inquiry into the private conduct of a rape victim, even though that conduct may have at best a tenuous connection to the offense for which the defendant is being tried.

H.R. 4727 amends the Federal Rules of Evidence to add a new rule, applicable only in criminal cases, to spell out when, and under what conditions, evidence of a rape victim's prior sexual behavior can be admitted. The new rule provides that reputation or opinion evidence about a rape victim's prior sexual behavior is not admissible. The new rule also provides that a court cannot admit evidence of specific instances of a rape victim's prior sexual conduct except in three circumstances.

The first circumstance is where the Constitution requires that the evidence be admitted. This exception is intended to cover those infrequent instances where, because of an unusual chain of circumstances, the general rule of inadmissibility, if followed, would result in denying the defendant a constitutional right.

The second circumstance in which the defendant can offer evidence of specific instances of a rape victim's prior sexual behavior is where the defendant raises the issue of consent and the evidence is of sexual behavior with the defendant. To admit such evidence, however, the court must find that the evidence is relevant and that its probative value outweighs the danger of unfair prejudice.

The third circumstance in which a court can admit evidence of specific instances of a rape victim's prior sexual behavior is where the evidence is of behavior with someone other than the defendant and is offered by the defendant on the issue of whether or not he was the source of semen or injury. Again, such evidence will be admitted only if the court finds that the evidence is relevant and that its probative value outweighs the danger of unfair prejudice.

The new rule further provides that before evidence is admitted under any of these exceptions, there must be an in camera hearing—that is, a proceeding that takes place in the judge's chambers out of the presence of the jury and the general public. At this hearing, the defendant will present the evidence he intends to offer and be able to argue why it should be admitted. The prosecution, of course, will be able to argue against that evidence being admitted.

The purpose of the in camera hearing is twofold. It gives the defendant an opportunity to demonstrate to the court why certain evidence is admissible and ought to be presented to the jury. At the same time, it protects the privacy of the rape victim in those instances when the court finds that evidence is inadmissible. Of course, if the court finds the evidence to be admissible, the evidence will be presented to the jury in open court.

The effect of this legislation, therefore, is to preclude the routine use of evidence of specific instances of a rape victim's prior sexual behavior. Such evidence will be admitted only in clearly and narrowly defined circumstances and only after an in camera hearing. In determining the admissibility of such evidence, the court will consider all of the facts and circumstances surrounding the evidence, such as the amount of time that lapsed between the alleged prior act and the rape charged in the prosecution. The greater the lapse of time, of course, the less likely it is that such evidence will be admitted.

Mr. Speaker, the principal purpose of this legislation is to protect rape victims from the degrading and embarrassing disclosure of intimate details about their private lives. It does so by narrowly circumscribing when such evidence may be admitted. It does not do so, however, by sacrificing any constitutional right possessed by the defendant. The bill before us fairly balances the interests involved—the rape victim's interest in protecting her private life from unwarranted public exposure; the defendant's interest in being able adequately to present a defense by offering relevant and probative evidence; and society's interest in a fair trial, one where unduly prejudicial evidence is not permitted to becloud the issues before the jury.

I urge support of the bill.

Mr. WIGGINS. Mr. Speaker, I yield myself such time as I may consume.

(Mr. WIGGINS asked and was given permission to revise and extend his remarks.)

Mr. WIGGINS. Mr. Speaker, this legislation addresses itself to a subject that is certainly a proper one for our consideration. Many of us have been troubled for years about the indiscriminate and prejudicial use of testimony with respect to a victim's prior sexual behavior in rape and similar cases. This bill deals with that problem. It is not, in my opinion, Mr. Speaker, a perfect bill in the manner in which it deals with the problem, but my objections are not so fundamental as would lead me to oppose the bill.

I think, Mr. Speaker, that it is unwise to adopt a per se rule absolutely excluding evidence of reputation and opinion with respect to the victim—and this bill does that—but it is difficult for me to foresee the specific case in which such evidence might be admissible. The trouble is this, Mr. Speaker: None of us can foresee perfectly all of the various circumstances under which the propriety of evidence might be before the court. If this bill has a defect, in my view it is because it adopts a per se rule with respect to opinion and reputation evidence.

Alternatively we might have permitted that evidence to be considered in camera as we do other evidence under the bill.

I should note, however, in fairness, having expressed minor reservations, that the bill before the House at this time does improve significantly upon the bill which was presented to our committee.

I will not detail all of those improvements but simply observe that the bill upon which we shall soon vote is a superior product to that which was initially considered by our subcommittee.

Mr. Speaker, I ask my colleagues to vote for this legislation as being, on balance, worthy of their support, and urge its adoption.

I reserve the balance of my time.

Mr. MANN. Mr. Speaker, this legislation has more than 100 cosponsors, but its principal sponsor, as well as its architect is the gentlewoman from New York (Ms. Holtzman). As the drafter of the legislation she will be able to provide additional information about the probable scope and effect of the legislation.

I yield such time as she may consume to the gentlewoman from New York (Ms. Holtzman).

(Ms. HOLTZMAN asked and was given permission to revise and extend her remarks.)

Ms. HOLTZMAN. Mr. Speaker, I would like to begin first by complimenting the distinguished gentleman from South Carolina (Mr. Mann), the chairman of the subcommittee, for his understanding of the need for corrective legislation in this area and for the fairness with which he has conducted the subcommittee hearings. I would like also to compliment the other members of the subcommittee, including the gentleman from California (Mr. Wiggins).

Too often in this country victims of rape are humiliated and harassed when they report and prosecute the rape. Bullied and cross-examined about their prior sexual experiences, many find the trial almost as degrading as the rape itself. Since rape trials become inquisitions into the victim's morality, not trials of the defendant's innocence or guilt, it is not surprising that it is the least reported crime. It is estimated that as few as one in ten rapes is ever reported.

Mr. Speaker, over 30 States have taken some action to limit the vulnerability of rape victims to such humiliating cross-examination of their past sexual experiences and intimate personal histories. In federal courts, however, it is permissible still to subject rape victims to brutal cross-examination about their past sexual histories. H.R. 4727 would rectify this problem in Federal courts and I hope, also serve as a model to suggest to the remaining states that reform of existing rape laws is important to the equity of our criminal justice system.

H.R. 4727 applies only to criminal rape cases in Federal courts. The bill provides that neither the prosecution nor the defense can introduce any reputation or opinion evidence about the victim's past sexual conduct. It does permit, however, the introduction of specific evidence about the victim's past sexual conduct in three very limited circumstances.

First, this evidence can be introduced if it deals with the victim's past sexual relations with the defendant and is relevant to the issue of whether she consented. Second, when the defendant claims he had no relations with the victim, he can use evidence of the victim's past sexual relations with others if the evidence rebuts the victim's claim that the rape caused certain physical consequences, such as semen or injury. Finally, the evidence can be introduced if it is constitutionally required. This last exception, added in subcommittee, will insure that the defendant's constitutional rights are protected.

Before any such evidence can be introduced, however, the court must determine at a hearing in chambers that the evidence falls within one of the exceptions.

Furthermore, unless constitutionally required, the evidence of specific instances of prior sexual conduct cannot be introduced at all it if would be more prejudicial and inflammatory that probative.

Mr. Speaker, I urge adoption of this bill. It will protect women from both injustice and indignity.

Mr. MANN. Mr. Speaker, I have no further requests for time, and I yield back the balance of my time.

Mr. WIGGINS. Mr. Speaker, I have no further requests for time, and yield back the balance of my time.

The SPEAKER pro tempore. The question is on the motion offered by the gentleman from South Carolina (Mr. Mann) that the House suspend the rules and pass the bill H.R. 4727, as amended.

The question was taken; and (two-thirds having voted in favor thereof) the rules were suspended and the bill, as amended, was passed.

A motion to reconsider was laid on the table.

HISTORICAL NOTES

Effective and Applicability Provisions

1978 Acts. Section 3 of Pub.L. 95–540 provided that: "The amendments made by this Act [enacting this rule] shall apply to trials which begin more than thirty days after the date of the enactment of this Act [Oct. 28, 1978]."

Rule 413. Evidence of Similar Crimes in Sexual Assault Cases

(a) In a criminal case in which the defendant is accused of an offense of sexual assault, evidence of the defendant's commission of another offense or offenses of sexual assault is admissible, and may be considered for its bearing on any matter to which it is relevant.

(b) In a case in which the Government intends to offer evidence under this rule, the attorney for the Government shall disclose the evidence to the defendant, including statements of witnesses or a summary of the substance of any testimony that is expected to be offered, at least fifteen days before the scheduled date of trial or at such later time as the court may allow for good cause.

(c) This rule shall not be construed to limit the admission or consideration of evidence under any other rule.

(d) For purposes of this rule and Rule 415, "offense of sexual assault" means a crime under Federal law or the law of a State (as defined in section 513 of title 18, United States Code) that involved—

(1) any conduct proscribed by chapter 109A of title 18, United States Code;

(2) contact, without consent, between any part of the defendant's body or an object and the genitals or anus of another person;

(3) contact, without consent, between the genitals or anus of the defendant and any part of another person's body;

(4) deriving sexual pleasure or gratification from the infliction of death, bodily injury, or physical pain on another person; or

(5) an attempt or conspiracy to engage in conduct described in paragraphs (1)–(4).

(Added Pub.L. 103–322, Title XXXII, § 320935(a), Sept. 13, 1994, 108 Stat. 2136.)

HISTORICAL NOTES

Effective and Applicability Provisions

Section 320935(b) to (e) of Pub.L. 103–322, as amended Pub.L. 104–208, Div. A, Title I, § 101(a), [Title I, § 120], Sept. 30, 1996, 110 Stat. 3009–25, provided that:

"(b) Implementation.—The amendments made by subsection (a) [enacting Federal Rules of Evidence 413, 414, and 415] shall become effective pursuant to subsection (d).

"(c) Recommendations by Judicial Conference.—Not later than 150 days after the date of enactment of this Act [Sept. 13, 1994], the Judicial Conference of the United States shall transmit to Congress a report containing recommendations for amending the Federal Rules of Evidence as they affect the admission of evidence of a defendant's prior sexual assault or child molestation crimes in cases involving sexual assault and child molestation. The Rules Enabling Act [28 U.S.C.A. § 2072] shall not apply to the recommendations made by the Judicial Conference pursuant to this section.

"(d) Congressional action.—

"(1) If the recommendations described in subsection (c) are the same as the amendment made by subsection (a) [enacting Federal Rules of Evidence 413, 414, and 415], then the amendments made by subsection (a) shall become effective 30 days after the transmittal of the recommendations.

"(2) If the recommendations described in subsection (c) are different than the amendments made by subsection (a) [enacting Federal Rules of Evidence 413, 414, and 415], the amendments made by subsection (a) shall become effective 150 days after the transmittal of the recommendations unless otherwise provided by law.

"(3) If the Judicial Conference fails to comply with subsection (c), the amendments made by subsection (a) [enacting Federal of Evidence 413, 414, and 415] shall become effective 150 days after the date the recommendations were due under subsection (c) unless otherwise provided by law.

"(e) Application.—The amendments made by subsection (a) [enacting Federal Rules of Evidence 413, 414, and 415] shall apply to proceedings commenced on or after the effective date of such amendments, including all trials commenced on or after the effective date of such amendments."

[The Judicial Conference transmitted a report to Congress on Feb. 9, 1995, containing recommendations described in subsec. (c) different than the amendments made by section 320935(a) of Pub.L. 103–322. Congress did not follow the recommendations submitted or provide otherwise by law. Accordingly, Rules 413, 414, and 415, as added by section 320935(a) of Pub.L. 103–322, became effective on July 9, 1995.]

Submitted to the Congress in accordance with section 320935 of the Violent Crime Control and Law Enforcement Act of 1994 (Pub.L. No. 103–322)

I. INTRODUCTION

This report is transmitted to Congress in accordance with the Violent Crime Control and Law Enforcement Act of 1994, Pub.L. No. 103–322 (September 13, 1994). Section 320935 of the Act invited the Judicial Conference of the United States within 150 days (February 10, 1995) to submit "a report containing recommendations for amending the Federal Rules of Evidence as they affect the admission of evidence of a defendant's prior sexual assault or child molestation crimes in cases involving sexual assault or child molestation."

Under the Act, new Rules 413, 414, and 415 would be added to the Federal Rules of Evidence. These Rules would admit evidence of a defendant's past similar acts in criminal and civil cases involving a sexual assault or child molestation offense for its bearing on any matter to which it is relevant. The effective date of new Rules 413–415 is contingent in part upon the nature of the recommendations submitted by the Judicial Conference.

After careful study, the Judicial Conference urges Congress to reconsider its decision on the policy questions underlying the new rules for reasons set out in Part III below.

If Congress does not reconsider its decision on the underlying policy questions, the Judicial Conference recommends incorporation of the provisions of new Rules 413–415 as amendments to Rules 404 and 405 of the Federal Rules of Evidence. The amendments would not change the substance of the congressional enactment but would clarify drafting ambiguities and eliminate possible constitutional infirmities.

II. BACKGROUND

Under the Act, the Judicial Conference was provided 150 days within which to make and submit to Congress alternative recommendations to new Evidence Rules 413–415. Consideration of Rules 413–415 by the Judicial Conference was specifically excepted from the exacting review procedures set forth in the Rules Enabling Act (codified at 28 U.S.C. §§ 2071–2077). Although the Conference acted on these new rules on an expedited basis to meet the Act's deadlines, the review process was thorough.

The new rules would apply to both civil and criminal cases. Accordingly, the Judicial Conference's Advisory Committee on Criminal Rules and the Advisory Committee on Civil Rules reviewed the rules at separate meetings in October 1994. At the same time and in preparation for its consideration of the new rules, the Advisory Committee on Evidence Rules sent out a notice soliciting comment on new Evidence Rules 413, 414, and 415. The notice was sent to the courts, including all federal judges, about 900 evidence law professors, 40 women's rights organizations, and 1,000 other individuals and interested organizations.

III. DISCUSSION

On October 17–18, 1994, the Advisory Committee on Evidence Rules met in Washington, D.C. It considered the public responses, which included 84 written comments, representing 112 individuals, 8 local and 8 national legal organizations. The overwhelming majority of judges, lawyers, law professors, and legal organizations who responded opposed new Evidence Rules 413, 414, and 415. The principal objections expressed were that the rules would permit the admission of unfairly prejudicial evidence and contained numerous drafting problems not intended by their authors.

The Advisory Committee on Evidence Rules submitted its report to the Judicial Conference Committee on Rules of Practice and Procedure (Standing Committee) for review at its January 11–13, 1995 meeting. The committee's report was unanimous except for a dissenting vote by the representative of the Department of Justice. The advisory committee believed that the concerns expressed by Congress and embodied in new Evidence Rules 413, 414, and 415 are already adequately addressed in the existing Federal Rules of Evidence. In particular, Evidence Rule 404(b) now allows the admission of evidence against a criminal defendant of the commission of prior crimes, wrongs, or acts for specified purposes, including to show intent, plan, motive, preparation, identity, knowledge, or absence of mistake or accident.

Furthermore, the new rules, which are not supported by empirical evidence, could diminish significantly the protections that have safeguarded persons accused in criminal cases and parties in civil cases against undue prejudice. These protections form a fundamental part of American jurisprudence and have evolved under long-standing rules and case law. A significant concern identified by the committee was the danger of convicting a criminal defendant for past, as opposed to charged, behavior or for being a bad person.

In addition, the advisory committee concluded that, because prior bad acts would be admissible even though not the subject of a conviction, mini-trials within trials concerning those acts would result when a defendant seeks to rebut such evidence. The committee also noticed that many of the comments received had concluded that the Rules, as drafted, were mandatory—that is, such evidence had to be admitted regardless of other rules of evidence such as the hearsay rule or the Rule 403 balancing test. The committee believed that this position was arguable because Rules 413–415 declare without qualification that such evidence "is admissible." In contrast, the new Rule 412, passed as part of the same legislation, provided that certain evidence "is admissible if it is otherwise admissible under these Rules." Fed.R.Evid. 412(b)(2). If the critics are right, Rules 413–415 free the prosecution from rules that apply to the defendant—including the hearsay rule and Rule 403. If so, serious constitutional questions would arise.

The Advisory Committees on Criminal and Civil Rules unanimously, except for representatives of the Department of Justice, also opposed the new rules. Those committees also concluded that the new rules would permit the introduction of unreliable but highly prejudicial evidence and would complicate trials by causing mini-trials of other alleged wrongs. After the advisory committees reported, the Standing Committee unanimously, again except for the representative of the Department of Justice, agreed with the view of the advisory committees.

It is important to note the highly unusual unanimity of the members of the Standing and Advisory Committees, composed of over 40 judges, practicing lawyers, and academicians, in taking the view that Rules 413–415 are undesirable. Indeed, the only supporters of the Rules were representatives of the Department of Justice.

For these reasons, the Standing Committee recommended that Congress reconsider its decision on the policy questions embodied in new Evidence Rules 413, 414, and 415.

However, if Congress will not reconsider its decision on the policy questions, the Standing Committee recommended that Congress consider an alternative draft recommended by the Advisory Committee on Evidence Rules. That Committee drafted proposed amendments to existing Evidence Rules 404 and 405 that would both correct ambiguities and possible constitutional infirmities identified in new Evidence Rules 413, 414, and 415 yet still effectuate Congressional intent. In particular, the proposed amendments:

(1) expressly apply the other rules of evidence to evidence offered under the new rules;

(2) expressly allow the party against whom such evidence is offered to use similar evidence in rebuttal;

(3) expressly enumerate the factors to be weighed by a court in making its Rule 403 determination;

(4) render the notice provisions consistent with the provisions in existing Rule 404 regarding criminal cases;

(5) eliminate the special notice provisions of Rules 413–415 in civil cases so that notice will be required as provided in the Federal Rules of Civil Procedure; and

(6) permit reputation or opinion evidence after such evidence is offered by the accused or defendant.

The Standing Committee reviewed the new rules and the alternative recommendations. It concurred with the views of the Evidence Rules Committee and recommended that the Judicial Conference adopt them.

IV. RECOMMENDATIONS

The Judicial Conference concurs with the views of the Standing Committee and urges that Congress reconsider its policy determinations underlying Evidence Rules 413–415. In the alternative, the attached amendments to Evidence Rules 404 and 405 are recommended, in lieu of new Evidence Rules 413, 414, and 415. The alternative amendments to Evidence Rules 404 and 405 are accompanied by the Advisory Committee Notes, which explain them in detail.

RULE 404. CHARACTER EVIDENCE NOT ADMISSIBLE TO PROVE CONDUCT; EXCEPTIONS; OTHER CRIMES

* * * * * * *

(4) **Character in sexual misconduct cases.** Evidence of another act of sexual assault or child molestation, or evidence to rebut such proof or an inference therefrom, if that evidence is otherwise admissible under these rules, in a criminal case in which the accused is charged with sexual assault or child molestation, or in a civil case in which a claim is predicated on a party's alleged commission of sexual assault or child molestation.

(A) In weighing the probative value of such evidence, the court may, as part of its rule 403 determination, consider:

(i) proximity in time to the charged or predicate misconduct;

(ii) similarity to the charged or predicate misconduct;

(iii) frequency of the other acts;

(iv) surrounding circumstances;

(v) relevant intervening events; and

(vi) other relevant similarities or differences.

(B) In a criminal case in which the prosecution intends to offer evidence under this subdivision, it must disclose the evidence, including statements of witnesses or a summary of the substance of any testimony, at a reasonable time in advance of trial, or during trial if the court excuses pretrial notice on good cause shown.

(C) For purposes of this subdivision.

(i) "sexual assault" means conduct—or an attempt or conspiracy to engage in conduct—of the type proscribed by chapter 109A of title 18, United States Code, or conduct that involved deriving sexual pleasure or gratification from inflicting death, bodily injury, or physical pain on another person irrespective of the age of the victim—regardless of whether that conduct would have subjected the actor to federal jurisdiction.

(ii) "child molestation" means conduct—or an attempt or conspiracy to engage in conduct—of the type proscribed by chapter 110 of title 18, United States Code, or conduct, committed in relation to a child below the age of 14 years, either of the type proscribed by chapter 109A of title 18, United States Code, or that involved deriving sexual pleasure or gratification from inflicting death, bodily injury, or physical pain on another person—regardless of whether that conduct would have subjected the actor to federal jurisdiction.

(b) Other crimes, wrongs, or acts. Evidence of other crimes, wrongs, or acts is not admissible to prove the character of a person in order to show action in conformity therewith except as provided in subdivision (a)....

Note to Rule 404(a)(4)

The Committee has redrafted Rules 413, 414 and 415 which the Violent Crime Control and Law Enforcement Act of 1994 conditionally added to the Federal Rules of Evidence.[1] These modifications do not change the substance of the congressional enactment. The changes were made in order to integrate the provisions both substantively and stylistically with the existing Rules of Evidence; to illuminate the intent expressed by the principal drafters of the measure; to clarify drafting ambiguities that might necessitate considerable judicial attention if they remained unresolved; and to eliminate possible constitutional infirmities.

The Committee placed the new provisions in Rule 404 because this rule governs the admissibility of character evidence. The congressional enactment constitutes a new exception to the general rule stated in subdivision (a). The Committee also combined the three separate rules proposed by Congress into one subdivision (a)(4) in accordance with the rules' customary practice of treating criminal and civil issues jointly. An amendment to Rule 405 has been added because the authorization of a new form of character evidence in this rule has an impact on methods of proving character that were not explicitly addressed by Congress. The stylistic changes are self-evident. They are particularly noticeable in the definition section in subdivision (a)(4)(C) in which the Committee eliminated, without any change in meaning, graphic details of sexual acts.

The Committee added language that explicitly provides that evidence under this subdivision must satisfy other rules of evidence such as the hearsay rules in Article VIII and the expert testimony rules in Article VII. Although principal sponsors of the legislation had stated that they intended other evidentiary rules to apply, the Committee believes that the opening phrase of the new subdivision 'if otherwise admissible under these rules' is needed to clarify the relationship between subdivision (a)(4) and other evidentiary provisions.

The Committee also expressly made subdivision (a)(4) subject to Rule 403 balancing in accordance with the repeatedly stated objectives of the legislation's sponsors with which representatives of the Justice Department expressed agreement. Many commentators on Rules 413–415 had objected that Rule 403's applicability was obscured by the actual language employed.

In addition to clarifying the drafters' intent, an explicit reference to Rule 403 may be essential to insulate the rule against constitutional challenge. Constitutional concerns also led the Committee to acknowledge specifically the opposing party's right to offer in rebuttal character evidence that the rules would otherwise bar, including evidence of a third person's prior acts of sexual misconduct offered to prove that the third person rather than the party committed the acts in issue.

In order to minimize the need for extensive and time-consuming judicial interpretation, the Committee listed factors that a court may consider in discharging Rule 403 balancing. Proximity in time is taken into account in a related rule. See Rule 609(b). Similarity, frequency and surrounding circumstances have long been considered by courts in handling other crimes evidence pursuant to Rule 404(b). Relevant intervening events, such as extensive medical treatment of the accused between the time of the prior proffered act and the charged act, may affect the strength of the propensity inference for which the evidence is offered. The final factor—'other relevant similarities or differences'—is added in recognition of the endless variety of circumstances that confront a trial court in rulings on admissibility. Although subdivision (4)(A) explicitly refers to factors that bear on probative value, this enumeration does not eliminate a judge's responsibility to take into account the other factors mentioned in Rule 403 itself—'the danger of unfair prejudice, confusion of the issues, ... misleading the jury, ... undue delay, waste of time, or needless presentation of cumulative evidence.' In addition, the Advisory Committee Note to Rule 403 reminds judges that 'The availability of other means of proof may also be an appropriate factor.'

The Committee altered slightly the notice provision in criminal cases. Providing the trial court with some discretion to excuse pretrial notice was thought preferable to the inflexible 15-day rule provided in Rules 414 and 415. Furthermore, the formulation is identical to that contained in the 1991 amendment to Rule 404(b) so that no confusion will result from having two somewhat different notice provisions in the same rule. The Committee eliminated the notice provision for civil cases stated in Rule 415 because it did not believe that Congress intended to alter the usual time table for disclosure and discovery provided by the Federal Rules of Civil Procedure.

The definition section was simplified with no change in meaning. The reference to 'the law of a State' was eliminated as unnecessarily confusing and restrictive. Conduct committed outside the United States ought equally to be eligible for admission. Evidence offered pursuant to subdivision (a)(4) must relate to a form of conduct proscribed by either chapter 109A or 110 of title 18, United States Code, regardless of whether the actor was subject to federal jurisdiction.

RULE 405. METHODS OF PROVING CHARACTER

(a) Reputation or opinion. In all cases in which evidence of character or a trait of character of a person is admissible, proof may be made by testimony as to reputation or by testimony in the form of an opinion except as provided in subdivision (c) of this rule. On cross-examination, inquiry is allowable into relevant specific instances of conduct.

* * * * * * *

(c) Proof in sexual misconduct cases. In a case in which evidence is offered under rule 404(a)(4), proof may be made by specific instances of conduct, testimony as to reputation, or testimony in the form of an opinion, except that the prosecution or claimant may offer reputation or opinion testimony only after the opposing party has offered such testimony.

Note to Rule 405(c)

The addition of a new subdivision (a)(4) to Rule 404 necessitates adding a new subdivision (c) to Rule 405 to govern methods of proof. Congress clearly intended no change in the preexisting law that precludes the prosecution or a claimant from offering reputation or opinion testimony in its case in chief to prove that the opposing party acted in conformity with character. When evidence is admissible pursuant to Rule 404(a)(4), the proponents proof must consist of specific instances of conduct. The opposing party, however, is free to respond with reputation or opinion testimony (including expert testimony if otherwise admissible) as well as evidence of specific instances. In a criminal case, the admissibility of reputation or opinion testimony would, in any event, be authorized by Rule 404(a)(1). The extension to civil cases is essential in order to provide the opponent with an adequate opportunity to refute allegations about a character for sexual misconduct. Once the opposing party offers reputation or opinion testimony, however, the prosecution or claimant may counter using such methods of proof.

[1] Congress provided that the rules would take effect unless within a specified time period the Judicial Conference made recommendations to amend the rules that Congress enacted.

Congressional Discussion

Floor Statement of the Principal House Sponsor, Representative Susan Molinari, Concerning the Prior Crimes Evidence Rules for Sexual Assault and Child Molestation Cases (Cong.Rec. H8991–92, Aug. 21, 1994):

Mr. Speaker, the revised conference bill contains a critical reform that I have long sought to protect the public from crimes of sexual violence—general rules of admissibility in sexual assault and child molestation cases for evidence that the defendant has committed offenses of the same type on other occasions. The enactment of this reform is first and foremost a triumph for the public—for the women who will not be raped and the children who will not be molested because we have strengthened the legal system's tools for bringing the perpetrators of these atrocious crimes to justice.

Senator Dole and I initially proposed this reform in February of 1991 in the Women's Equal Opportunity Act bill, and we later re-introduced it in the Sexual Assault Prevention Act bills of the 102d and 103d Congresses. The proposal also enjoyed the strong support of the Administration in the 102d Congress, and was included in President Bush's violent crime bill of that Congress, S. 635. The Senate passed the proposed rules on Nov. 5, 1993, by a vote of 75 to 19, in a crime bill amendment offered by Senate Dole. This Chamber endorsed the same rules on June 29, 1994, by a vote of 348 to 62, through a motion to instruct conferees that I offered.

The rules in the revised conference bill are substantially identical to our earlier proposals. We have agreed to a temporary deferral of the effective date of the new rules, pending a report by the Judicial Conference, in order to accommodate procedural objections raised by opponents of the reform. However, regardless of what the Judicial Conference may recommend, the new rules will take effect within at most 300 days of the enactment of this legislation, unless repealed or modified by subsequent legislation.

The need for these rules, their precedential support, their interpretation, and the issues and policy questions they raise have been analyzed at length in the legislative history of this proposal. I would direct the Members' attention particularly to two earlier statements:

The first is the portion of the section-by-section analysis accompanying these rules in section 801 of S. 635, which President Bush transmitted to Congress in 1991. That statement appears on pages S 3238 [to] S 3242 of the daily edition of the Congressional Record for March 13, 1991.

The second is the prepared text of an address—entitled "Evidence of Propensity and Probability in Sex Offense Cases and Other Cases"—by Senior Counsel David J. Karp of the Office of Policy Development of the U.S. Department of Justice. Mr. Karp, who is the author of the new evidence rules, presented this statement on behalf of the Justice Department to the Evidence Section of the Association of American Law Schools on January 9, 1993. The statement provided a detailed account of the views of the legislative sponsors and the Administration concerning the proposed reform, and should also be considered an authoritative part of its legislative history.

These earlier statements address the issues raised by this reform in considerable detail. In my present remarks, I will simply emphasize the following essential points:

The new rules will supersede in sex offense cases the restrictive aspects of Federal Rule of Evidence 404(b). In contrast to Rule 404(b)'s general prohibition of evidence of character or propensity, the new rules for sex offense cases authorize admission and consideration of evidence of an uncharged offense for its bearing "on any matter to which it is relevant." This includes the defendant's propensity to commit sexual assault or child molestation offenses, and assessment of the probability or improbability that the defendant has been falsely or mistakenly accused of such an offense.

In other respects, the general standards of the rules of evidence will continue to apply, including the restrictions on hearsay evidence and the court's authority under Evidence Rule 403 to exclude evidence whose probative value is substantially outweighed by its prejudicial effect. Also, the government (or the plaintiff in a civil case) will generally have to disclose to the defendant any evidence that is to be offered under the new rules at least 15 days before trial.

The proposed reform is critical to the protection of the public from rapists and child molesters, and is justified by the distinctive characteristics of the cases it will affect. In child molestation cases, for example, a history of similar acts tends to be exceptionally probative because it shows an unusual disposition of the defendant—a sexual or sadosexual interest in children—that simply does not exist in ordinary people. Moreover, such cases require reliance on child victims whose credibility can readily be attacked in the absence of substantial corroboration. In such cases, there is a compelling public interest in admitting all significant evidence that will illumine the credibility of the charge and any denial by the defense.

Similarly, adult-victim sexual assault cases are distinctive, and often turn on difficult credibility determinations. Alleged consent by the victim is rarely an issue in prosecutions for other violent crimes—the accused mugger does not claim that the victim freely handed over [his] wallet as a gift—but the defendant in a rape case often contends that the victim engaged in consensual sex and then falsely accused him. Knowledge that the defendant has committed rapes on other occasions is frequently critical in assessing the relative plausibility of these claims and accurately deciding cases that would otherwise become unresolvable swearing matches.

The practical effect of the new rules is to put evidence of uncharged offenses in sexual assault and child molestation cases on the same footing as other types of relevant evidence that are not subject to a special exclusionary rule. The presumption is in favor of admission. The underlying legislative judgment is that the evidence admissible pursuant to the proposed rules is typically relevant and probative, and that its probative value is normally not outweighed by any risk of prejudice or other adverse effects.

In line with this judgment, the rules do not impose arbitrary or artificial restrictions on the admissibility of evidence. Evidence of offenses for which the defendant has not previously been prosecuted or convicted will be admissible, as well as evidence of prior convictions. No time limit is imposed on the uncharged offenses for which evidence may be admitted; as a practical matter, evidence of other sex offenses by the defendant is often probative and properly admitted, notwithstanding very substantial lapses of time in relation to the charged offense or offenses. *See, e.g., United States v. Hadley*, 918 F.2d 848, 850–51 (9th Cir. 1990), *cert. dismissed*, 113 S.Ct. 486 (1992) (evidence of offenses occurring up to 15 years earlier admitted); *State v. Plymate*, 345 N.W.2d 327 (Neb.1984) (evidence of defendant's commission of other child molestations more than 20 years earlier admitted).

Finally, the practical efficacy of these rules will depend on faithful execution by judges of the will of Congress in adopting this critical reform. To implement the legislative intent, the courts must liberally construe these rules to provide the basis for a fully informed decision of sexual assault and child molestation cases, including assessment of the defendant's propensities and questions of probability in light of the defendant's past conduct.

Rule 414. Evidence of Similar Crimes in Child Molestation Cases

(a) In a criminal case in which the defendant is accused of an offense of child molestation, evidence of the defendant's commission of another offense or offenses of child molestation is admissible, and may be considered for its bearing on any matter to which it is relevant.

(b) In a case in which the Government intends to offer evidence under this rule, the attorney for the Government shall disclose the evidence to the defendant, including statements of witnesses or a summary of the substance of any testimony that is expected to be offered, at least fifteen days before the scheduled date of trial or at such later time as the court may allow for good cause.

(c) This rule shall not be construed to limit the admission or consideration of evidence under any other rule.

(d) For purposes of this rule and Rule 415, "child" means a person below the age of fourteen, and "offense of child molestation" means a crime under Federal law or the law of a State (as defined in section 513 of title 18, United States Code) that involved—

(1) any conduct proscribed by chapter 109A of title 18, United States Code, that was committed in relation to a child;

(2) any conduct proscribed by chapter 110 of title 18, United States Code;

(3) contact between any part of the defendant's body or an object and the genitals or anus of a child;

(4) contact between the genitals or anus of the defendant and any part of the body of a child;

(5) deriving sexual pleasure or gratification from the infliction of death, bodily injury, or physical pain on a child; or

(6) an attempt or conspiracy to engage in conduct described in paragraphs (1)–(5).

(Added Pub.L. 103–322, Title XXXII, § 320935(a), Sept. 13, 1994, 108 Stat. 2135.)

HISTORICAL NOTES

Effective and Applicability Provisions

1995 Acts. Rule effective July 9, 1995, see section 320935(b) to (e) of Pub.L. 103–322, set out as a note under rule 413 of these rules.

Congressional Discussion

See Floor Statement following Rule 413.

Rule 415. Evidence of Similar Acts in Civil Cases Concerning Sexual Assault or Child Molestation

(a) In a civil case in which a claim for damages or other relief is predicated on a party's alleged commission of conduct constituting an offense of sexual assault or child molestation, evidence of that party's commission of another offense or offenses of sexual assault or child molestation is admissible and may be considered as provided in Rule 413 and Rule 414 of these rules.

(b) A party who intends to offer evidence under this Rule shall disclose the evidence to the party against whom it will be offered, including statements of witnesses or a summary of the substance of any testimony that is expected to be offered, at least fifteen days before the scheduled date of trial or at such later time as the court may allow for good cause.

(c) This rule shall not be construed to limit the admission or consideration of evidence under any other rule.

(Added Pub.L. 103–322, Title XXXII, § 320935(a), Sept. 13, 1994, 108 Stat. 2137.)

HISTORICAL NOTES

Effective and Applicability Provisions

1995 Acts. Rule effective July 9, 1995, see section 320935(b) to (e) of Pub.L. 103–322, set out as a note under rule 413 of these rules.

Congressional Discussion

See Floor Statement following Rule 413.

ARTICLE V. PRIVILEGES

Rule 501. General Rule

Except as otherwise required by the Constitution of the United States or provided by Act of Congress or in rules prescribed by the Supreme Court pursuant to statutory authority, the privilege of a witness, person, government, State, or political subdivision thereof shall be governed by the principles of the common law as they may be interpreted by the courts of the United States in the light of reason and experience. However, in civil actions and proceedings, with respect to an element of a claim or defense as to which State law supplies the rule of decision, the privilege of a witness, person, government, State, or political subdivision thereof shall be determined in accordance with State law.

(Pub.L. 93–595, § 1, Jan. 2, 1975, 88 Stat. 1933.)

ADVISORY COMMITTEE NOTES

1974 Enactment

Article V as submitted to Congress contained thirteen Rules. Nine of those Rules defined specific non-constitutional privileges which the federal courts must recognize (i.e. required reports, lawyer-client, psychotherapist-patient, husband-wife, communications to clergymen, political vote, trade secrets, secrets of state and other official information, and identity of informer.) Another Rule provided that only those privileges set forth in Article V or in some other Act of Congress could be recognized by the federal courts. The three remaining Rules addressed collateral problems as to waiver of privilege by voluntary disclosure, privileged matter disclosed under compulsion or without opportunity to claim privilege, comment upon or inference from a claim of privilege, and jury instruction with regard thereto.

The Committee amended Article V to eliminate all of the Court's specific Rules on privileges. Instead, the Committee, through a single Rule, 501, left the law of privileges in its present state and further provided that privileges shall continue to be developed by the courts of the United States under a uniform standard applicable both in civil and criminal cases. That standard, derived from Rule 26 of the Federal Rules of Criminal Procedure, mandates the application of the principles of the common law as interpreted by the courts of the United States in the light of reason and experience. The words "person, government, State, or political subdivision thereof" were added by the Committee to the lone term "witnesses" used in Rule 26 to make clear that, as under present law, not only witnesses may have privileges.

The Committee also included in its amendment a proviso modeled after Rule 302 and similar to language added by the Committee to Rule 601 relating to the competency of witnesses. The proviso is designed to require the application of State privilege law in civil actions and proceedings governed by *Erie R. Co. v. Tompkins,* 304 U.S. 64 (1938), a result in accord with current federal court decisions. See *Republic Gear Co. v. Borg–Warner Corp.,* 381 F.2d 551, 555–556 n. 2 (2nd Cir.1967). The Committee deemed the proviso to be necessary in the light of the Advisory Committee's view (see its note to Court [proposed] Rule 501) that this result is not mandated under *Erie.*

The rationale underlying the proviso is that federal law should not supersede that of the States in substantive areas such as privilege absent a compelling reason. The Committee believes that in civil cases in the federal courts where an element of a claim or defense is not grounded upon a federal question, there is no federal interest strong enough to justify departure from State policy. In addition, the Committee considered that the Court's proposed Article V would have promoted forum shopping in some civil actions, depending upon differences in the privilege law applied as among the State and federal courts. The Committee's proviso, on the other hand, under which the federal courts are bound to apply the State's privilege law in actions founded upon a State-created right or defense, removes the incentive to "shop". House Report No. 93–650.

Article V as submitted to Congress contained 13 rules. Nine of those rules defined specific nonconstitutional privileges which the Federal courts must recognize (i.e., required reports, lawyer-client, psychotherapist-patient, husband-wife, communications to clergymen, political vote, trade secrets, secrets of state and other official information, and identity of informer). Many of these rules contained controversial modifications or restrictions upon common law privileges. As noted supra, the House amended article V to eliminate all of the Court's specific rules on privileges. Through a single rule, 501, the House provided that privileges shall be governed by the principles of the common law as interpreted by the courts of the United States in the light of reason and experience (a standard derived from rule 26 of the Federal Rules of Criminal Procedure) except in the case of an element of a civil claim or defense as to which State law supplies the rule of decision, in which event state privilege law was to govern.

The committee agrees with the main thrust of the House amendment: that a federally developed common law based on modern reason and experience shall apply except where the State nature of the issues renders deference to State privilege law the wiser course, as in the usual diversity case.

The committee understands that thrust of the House amendment to require that State privilege law be applied in "diversity" cases (actions on questions of State law between citizens of different States arising under 28 U.S.C. § 1332). The language of the House amendment, however, goes beyond this in some respects, and falls short of it in others: State privilege law applies even in nondiversity, Federal question civil cases, where an issue governed by State substantive law is the object of the evidence (such issues do sometimes arise in such cases); and, in all instances where State privilege law is to be applied, e.g., on proof of a State issue in a diversity case, a close reading reveals that State privilege law is not to be applied unless the matter to be proved is an element of that state claim or defense, as distinguished from a step along the way in the proof of it.

The committee is concerned that the language used in the House amendment could be difficult to apply. It provides that "in civil actions * * * with respect to an element of a claim or defense as to which State law supplies the rule of decision," State law on privilege applies. The question of what is an element of a claim or defense is likely to engender considerable litigation. If the matter in question constitutes an element of a claim, State law supplies the privilege rule; whereas if it is a mere item of proof with respect to a claim, then, even though State law might supply the rule of decision, Federal law on the privilege would apply. Further, disputes will arise as to how the rule should be applied in an antitrust action or in a tax case where the Federal statute is silent as to a particular aspect of the substantive law in question, but Federal cases had incorporated State law by reference to State law. [For a discussion of reference to State substantive law, see note on Federal Incorporation by Reference of State Law, Hart & Wechsler, The Federal Courts and the Federal System, pp. 491–494 (2d ed. 1973).] Is a claim (or defense) based on such a reference a claim or defense as to which federal or State law supplies the rule of decision?

Another problem not entirely avoidable is the complexity or difficulty the rule introduces into the trial of a Federal case containing a combination of Federal and State claims and defenses, e.g. an action involving Federal antitrust and State unfair competition claims. Two different bodies of privilege law would need to be consulted. It may even develop that the same witness-testimony might be relevant on both counts and privileged as to one but not the other. [The problems with the House formulation are discussed in Rothstein, The Proposed Amendments to the Federal Rules of Evidence, 62 Georgetown University Law Journal 125 (1973) at notes 25, 26 and 70–74 and accompanying text.]

The formulation adopted by the House is pregnant with litigious mischief. The committee has, therefore, adopted what we believe will be a clearer and more practical guideline for determining when courts should respect State rules of privilege. Basically, it provides that in criminal and Federal question civil cases, federally evolved rules on privilege should apply since it is Federal policy which is being enforced. [It is also intended that the Federal law of privileges should be applied with respect to pendent State law claims when they arise in a Federal question case.] Conversely, in diversity cases where the litigation in question turns on a substantive question of State law, and is brought in the Federal courts because the parties reside in different States, the committee believes it is clear that State rules of privilege should apply unless the proof is directed at a claim or defense for which Federal law supplies the rule of decision (a situation which would not commonly arise.) [While such a situation might require use of two bodies of privilege law, federal and state, in the same case, nevertheless the occasions on which this would be required are considerably reduced as compared with the House version, and confined to situations where the Federal and State interests are such as to justify application of neither privilege law to the case as a whole. If the rule proposed here results in two conflicting bodies of privilege law applying to the same piece of evidence in the same case, it is contemplated that the rule favoring reception of the evidence should be applied. This policy is based on the present rule 43(a) of the Federal Rules of Civil Procedure which provides: In any case, the statute or rule which favors the reception of the evidence governs and the evidence shall be presented according to the most convenient method prescribed in any of the statutes or rules to which reference is herein made.] It is intended that the State rules of privilege should apply equally in original diversity actions and diversity actions removed under 28 U.S.C. § 1441(b).

Two other comments on the privilege rule should be made. The committee has received a considerable volume of correspondence from psychiatric organizations and psychiatrists concerning the deletion of rule 504 of the rule submitted by the Supreme Court. It should be clearly understood that, in approving this general rule as to privileges, the action of Congress should not be understood as disapproving any recognition of a psychiatrist-patient, or husband-wife, or any other of the enumerated privileges contained in the Supreme Court rules. Rather, our action should be understood as reflecting the view that the recognition of a privilege based on a confidential relationship and other privileges should be determined on a case-by-case basis.

Further, we would understand that the prohibition against spouses testifying against each other is considered a rule of privilege and covered by this rule and not by rule 601 of the competency of witnesses. Senate Report No. 93–1277.

Rule 501 deals with the privilege of a witness not to testify. Both the House and Senate bills provide that federal privilege law applies in criminal cases. In civil actions and proceedings, the House bill provides that state privilege law applies "to an element of a claim or defense as to which State law supplies the rule of decision." The Senate bill provides that "in civil actions and proceedings arising under 28 U.S.C. § 1332 or 28 U.S.C. § 1335, or between citizens of different States and removed under 28 U.S.C. § 1441(b) the privilege of a witness, person, government, State or political subdivision thereof is determined in accordance with State law, unless with respect to the particular claim or defense, Federal law supplies the rule of decision."

The wording of the House and Senate bills differs in the treatment of civil actions and proceedings. The rule in the House bill applies to evidence that relates to "an element of a claim or defense." If an item of proof tends to support or defeat a claim or defense, or an element of a claim or defense, and if state law supplies the rule of decision for that claim or defense, then state privilege law applies to that item of proof.

Under the provision in the House bill, therefore, state privilege law will usually apply in diversity cases. There may be diversity cases, however, where a claim or defense is based upon federal law. In such instances, federal privilege law will apply to evidence relevant to the federal claim or defense. See *Sola Electric Co. v. Jefferson Electric Co.*, 317 U.S. 173 (1942).

In nondiversity jurisdiction civil cases, federal privilege law will generally apply. In those situations where a federal court adopts or incorporates state law to fill interstices or gaps in federal statutory phrases, the court generally will apply federal privilege law. As Justice Jackson has said:

> A federal court sitting in a non-diversity case such as this does not sit as a local tribunal. In some cases it may see fit for special reasons to give the law of a particular state highly persuasive or even controlling effect, but in the last analysis its decision turns upon the law of the United States, not that of any state.

D'Oench, Duhme & Co. v. Federal Deposit Insurance Corp., 315 U.S. 447, 471 (1942) (Jackson, J., concurring). When a federal court chooses to absorb state law, it is applying the state law as a matter of federal common law. Thus, state law does not supply the rule of decision (even though the federal court may apply a rule derived from state decisions), and state privilege law would not apply. See C.A. Wright, Federal Courts 251–252 (2d ed. 1970); *Holmberg v. Armbrecht*, 327 U.S. 392 (1946); *DeSylva v. Ballentine*, 351 U.S. 570, 581 (1956); 9 Wright & Miller, Federal Rules and Procedure § 2408.

In civil actions and proceedings, where the rule of decision as to a claim or defense or as to an element of a claim or defense is supplied by state law, the House provision requires that state privilege law apply.

The Conference adopts the House provision. House Report No. 93–1597.

ARTICLE VI. WITNESSES

Rule 601. General Rule of Competency

Every person is competent to be a witness except as otherwise provided in these rules. However, in civil actions and proceedings, with respect to an element of a claim or defense as to which State law supplies the rule of decision, the competency of a witness shall be determined in accordance with State law.

(Pub.L. 93–595, § 1, Jan. 2, 1975, 88 Stat.1934.)

ADVISORY COMMITTEE NOTES

1972 Proposed Rules

This general ground-clearing eliminates all grounds of incompetency not specifically recognized in the succeeding rules of this Article. Included among the grounds thus abolished are religious belief, conviction of crime, and connection with the litigation as a party or interested person or spouse of a party or interested person. With the exception of the so-called Dead Man's Acts, American jurisdictions generally have ceased to recognize these grounds.

The Dead Man's Acts are surviving traces of the common law disqualification of parties and interested persons. They exist in variety too great to convey conviction of their wisdom and effectiveness. These rules contain no provision of this kind. For the reasoning underlying the decision not to give effect to state statutes in diversity cases, see the Advisory Committee's Note to Rule 501.

No mental or moral qualifications for testifying as a witness are specified. Standards of mental capacity have proved elusive in actual application. A leading commentator observes that few witnesses are disqualified on that ground. Weihofen, Testimonial Competence and Credibility, 34 Geo. Wash.L.Rev. 53 (1965). Discretion is regularly exercised in favor of allowing the testimony. A witness wholly without capacity is difficult to imagine. The question is one particularly suited to the jury as one of weight and credibility, subject to judicial authority to review the sufficiency of the evidence. 2 Wigmore §§ 501, 509. Standards of moral qualification in practice consist essentially of evaluating a person's truthfulness in terms of his own answers about it. Their principal utility is in affording an opportunity on voir dire examination to impress upon the witness his moral duty. This result may, however, be accomplished more directly, and without haggling in terms of legal standards, by the manner of administering the oath or affirmation under Rule 603.

Admissibility of religious belief as a ground of impeachment is treated in Rule 610. Conviction of crime as a ground of impeachment is the subject of Rule 609. Marital relationship is the basis for privilege under Rule 505. Interest in the outcome of litigation and mental capacity are, of course, highly relevant to credibility and require no special treatment to render them admissible along with other matters bearing upon the perception, memory, and narration of witnesses.

1974 Enactment

Rule 601 as submitted to the Congress provided that "Every person is competent to be a witness except as otherwise provided in these rules." One effect of the Rule as proposed would have been to abolish age, mental capacity, and other grounds recognized in some State jurisdictions as making a person incompetent as a witness. The greatest controversy centered around the Rule's rendering inapplicable in the federal courts the so-called Dead Man's Statutes which exist in some States. Acknowledging that there is substantial disagreement as to the merit of Dead Man's Statutes, the Committee nevertheless believed that where such statutes have been enacted they represent State policy which should not be overturned in the absence of a compelling federal interest. The Committee therefore amended the Rule to make competency in civil actions determinable in accordance with State law with respect to elements of claims or defenses as to which State law supplies the rule of decision. Cf. *Courtland v. Walston & Co., Inc.*, 340 F.Supp. 1076, 1087–1092 (S.D.N.Y.1972). House Report No. 93–650.

The amendment to rule 601 parallels the treatment accorded Rule 501 discussed immediately above. Senate Report No. 93–1277.

Rule 601 deals with competency of witnesses. Both the House and Senate bills provide that federal competency law applies in criminal cases. In civil actions and proceedings, the House bill provides that state competency law applies "to an element of a claim or defense as to which State law supplies the rule of decision." The Senate bill provides that "in civil actions and proceedings arising under 28 U.S.C. § 1332 or 28 U.S.C. § 1335, or between citizens of different States and removed under 28 U.S.C. § 1441(b) the competency of a witness, person, government, State or political subdivision thereof is determined in accordance with State law, unless with respect to the particular claim or defense, Federal law supplies the rule of decision."

The wording of the House and Senate bills differs in the treatment of civil actions and proceedings. The rule in the House bill applies to evidence that relates to "an element of a claim or defense." If an item of proof tends to support or defeat a claim or defense, or an element of a claim or defense, and if state law supplies the rule of decision for that claim or defense, then state competency law applies to that item of proof.

For reasons similar to those underlying its action on Rule 501, the Conference adopts the House provision. House Report No. 93–1597.

Rule 602. Lack of Personal Knowledge

A witness may not testify to a matter unless evidence is introduced sufficient to support a finding that the witness has personal knowledge of the matter. Evidence to prove personal knowledge may, but need not, consist of the witness' own testimony. This rule is subject to the provisions of rule 703, relating to opinion testimony by expert witnesses.

(Pub.L. 93–595, § 1, Jan. 2, 1975, 88 Stat. 1934; Mar. 2, 1987, eff. Oct. 1, 1987; Apr. 25, 1988, eff. Nov. 1, 1988.)

ADVISORY COMMITTEE NOTES

1972 Proposed Rules

"* * * [T]he rule requiring that a witness who testifies to a fact which can be perceived by the senses must have had an opportunity to observe, and must have actually observed the fact" is a "most pervasive manifestation" of the common law insistence upon "the most reliable sources of information." McCormick § 10, p. 19. These foundation requirements may, of course, be furnished by the testimony of the witness himself; hence personal knowledge is not an absolute but may consist of what the witness thinks he knows from personal perception. 2 Wigmore § 650. It will be observed that the rule is in fact a specialized application of the provisions of Rule 104(b) on conditional relevancy.

This rule does not govern the situation of a witness who testifies to a hearsay statement as such, if he has personal knowledge of the making of the statement. Rules 801 and 805 would be applicable. This rule would, however, prevent him from testifying to the subject matter of the hearsay statement, as he has no personal knowledge of it.

The reference to Rule 703 is designed to avoid any question of conflict between the present rule and the provisions of that rule allowing an expert to express opinions based on facts of which he does not have personal knowledge.

1987 Amendments

The amendments are technical. No substantive change is intended.

1988 Amendments

The amendment is technical. No substantive change is intended.

Rule 603. Oath or Affirmation

Before testifying, every witness shall be required to declare that the witness will testify truthfully, by oath or affirmation administered in a form calculated to awaken the witness' conscience and impress the witness' mind with the duty to do so.

(Pub.L. 93–595, § 1, Jan. 2, 1975, 88 Stat. 1934; Mar. 2, 1987, eff. Oct. 1, 1987.)

ADVISORY COMMITTEE NOTES

1972 Proposed Rules

The rule is designed to afford the flexibility required in dealing with religious adults, atheists, conscientious objectors, mental defectives, and children. Affirmation is simply a solemn undertaking to tell the truth; no special verbal formula is required. As is true generally, affirmation is recognized by federal law. "Oath" includes affirmation, 1 U.S.C. § 1; judges and clerks may administer oaths and affirmations, 28 U.S.C. §§ 459, 953; and affirmations are acceptable in lieu of oaths under Rule 43(d) of the Federal Rules of Civil Procedure. Perjury by a witness is a crime, 18 U.S.C. § 1621.

1987 Amendments

The amendments are technical. No substantive change is intended.

Rule 604. Interpreters

An interpreter is subject to the provisions of these rules relating to qualification as an expert and the administration of an oath or affirmation to make a true translation.

(Pub.L. 93–595, § 1, Jan. 2, 1975, 88 Stat. 1934; Mar. 2, 1987, eff. Oct. 1, 1987.)

ADVISORY COMMITTEE NOTES

1972 Proposed Rules

The rule implements Rule 43(f) of the Federal Rules of Civil Procedure and Rule 28(b) of the Federal Rules of Criminal Procedure, both of which contain provisions for the appointment and compensation of interpreters.

1987 Amendments

The amendment is technical. No substantive change is intended.

Rule 605. Competency of Judge as Witness

The judge presiding at the trial may not testify in that trial as a witness. No objection need be made in order to preserve the point.

(Pub.L. 93–595, § 1, Jan. 2, 1975, 88 Stat. 1934.)

ADVISORY COMMITTEE NOTES

1972 Proposed Rules

In view of the mandate of 28 U.S.C. § 455 that a judge disqualify himself in "any case in which he * * * is or has been a material witness," the likelihood that the presiding judge in a federal court might be called to testify in the trial over which he is presiding is slight. Nevertheless the possibility is not totally eliminated.

The solution here presented is a broad rule of incompetency, rather than such alternatives as incompetency only as to material matters, leaving the matter to the discretion of the judge, or recognizing no incompetency. The choice is the result of inability to evolve satisfactory answers to questions which arise when the judge abandons the bench for the witness stand. Who rules on objections? Who compels him to answer? Can he rule impartially on the weight and admissibility of his own testimony? Can he be impeached or cross-examined effectively? Can he, in a jury trial, avoid conferring his seal of approval on one side in the eyes of the jury? Can he, in a bench trial, avoid an involvement destructive of impartiality? The rule of general incompetency has substantial support. See Report of the Special Committee on the Propriety of Judges Appearing as Witnesses, 36 A.B.A.J. 630 (1950); cases collected in Annot. 157 A.L.R. 311; McCormick § 68, p. 147; Uniform Rule 42; California Evidence Code § 703; Kansas Code of Civil Procedure § 60–442; New Jersey Evidence Rule 42. Cf. 6 Wigmore § 1909, which advocates leaving the matter to the discretion of the judge, and statutes to that effect collected in Annot. 157 A.L.R. 311.

The rule provides an "automatic" objection. To require an actual objection would confront the opponent with a choice between not objecting, with the result of allowing the testimony, and objecting, with the probable result of excluding the testimony but at the price of continuing the trial before a judge likely to feel that his integrity had been attacked by the objector.

Rule 606. Competency of Juror as Witness

(a) At the trial. A member of the jury may not testify as a witness before that jury in the trial of the case in which the juror is sitting. If the juror is called so to testify, the opposing party shall be afforded an opportunity to object out of the presence of the jury.

(b) Inquiry into validity of verdict or indictment. Upon an inquiry into the validity of a verdict or indictment, a juror may not testify as to any matter or statement occurring during the course of the jury's deliberations or to the effect of anything upon that or any other juror's mind or emotions as influencing the juror to assent to or dissent from the verdict or indictment or concerning the juror's mental processes in connection therewith. But a juror may testify about (1) whether extraneous prejudicial information was improperly brought to the jury's attention, (2) whether any outside influence was improperly brought to bear upon any juror, or (3) whether there was a mistake in entering the verdict onto the verdict form. A juror's affidavit or evidence of any statement by the juror may not be received on a matter about which the juror would be precluded from testifying.

(Pub.L. 93–595, § 1, Jan. 2, 1975, 88 Stat. 1934; Pub.L. 94–149, § 1(10), Dec. 12, 1975, 89 Stat. 805; Mar. 2, 1987, eff. Oct. 1, 1987; Apr. 12, 2006, eff. Dec. 1, 2006.)

ADVISORY COMMITTEE NOTES

1972 Proposed Rules

Note to Subdivision (a). The considerations which bear upon the permissibility of testimony by a juror in the trial in which he is sitting as juror bear an obvious similarity to those evoked when the judge is called as a witness. See Advisory Committee's Note to Rule 605. The judge is not, however in this instance so involved as to call for departure from usual principles requiring objection to be made; hence the only provision on objection is that opportunity be afforded for its making out of the presence of the jury. Compare Rule 605.

Note to Subdivision (b). Whether testimony, affidavits, or statements of jurors should be received for the purpose of invalidating or supporting a verdict or indictment, and if so, under what circumstances, has given rise to substantial differences of opinion. The familiar rubric that a juror may not impeach his own verdict, dating from Lord Mansfield's time, is a gross oversimplification. The values sought to be promoted by excluding the evidence include freedom of deliberation, stability and finality of verdicts, and protection of jurors against annoyance and embarrassment. *McDonald v. Pless,* 238 U.S. 264, 35 S.Ct. 783, 59 L.Ed. 1300 (1915). On the other hand, simply putting verdicts beyond effective reach can only promote irregularity and injustice. The rule offers an accommodation between these competing considerations.

The mental operations and emotional reactions of jurors in arriving at a given result would, if allowed as a subject of inquiry, place every verdict at the mercy of jurors and invite tampering and harassment. See *Grenz v. Werre,* 129 N.W.2d 681 (N.D.1964). The authorities are in virtually complete accord in excluding the evidence. Fryer, Note on Disqualification of Witnesses, Selected Writings on Evidence and Trial 345, 347 (Fryer ed. 1957); Maguire, Weinstein, et al., Cases on Evidence 887 (5th ed. 1965); 8 Wigmore § 2349 (McNaughton Rev.1961). As to matters other than mental operations and emotional reactions of jurors, substantial authority refuses to allow a juror to disclose irregularities which occur in the jury room, but allows his testimony as to irregularities occurring outside and allows outsiders to testify as to occurrences both inside and out. 8 Wigmore § 2354 (McNaughton Rev.1961). However, the door of the jury room is not necessarily a satisfactory dividing point, and the Supreme Court has refused to accept it for every situation. *Mattox v. United States,* 146 U.S. 140, 13 S.Ct. 50, 36 L.Ed. 917 (1892).

Under the federal decisions the central focus has been upon insulation of the manner in which the jury reached its verdict, and this protection extends to each of the components of deliberation, including arguments, statements, discussions, mental and emotional reactions, votes, and any other feature of the process. Thus testimony or affidavits of jurors have been held incompetent to show a compromise verdict. *Hyde v. United States,* 225 U.S. 347, 382 (1912); a quotient verdict, *McDonald v. Pless,* 238 U.S. 264 (1915);

speculation as to insurance coverage. *Holden v. Porter,* 405 F.2d 878 (10th Cir.1969); *Farmers Coop. Elev. Ass'n v. Strand,* 382 F.2d 224, 230 (8th Cir.1967), cert. denied 389 U.S. 1014; misinterpretation of instructions, *Farmers Coop. Elev. Ass'n v. Strand,* supra; mistake in returning verdict, *United States v. Chereton,* 309 F.2d 197 (6th Cir.1962); interpretation of guilty plea by one defendant as implicating others, *United States v. Crosby,* 294 F.2d 928, 949 (2d Cir.1961). The policy does not, however, foreclose testimony by jurors as to prejudicial extraneous information or influences injected into or brought to bear upon the deliberative process. Thus a juror is recognized as competent to testify to statements by the bailiff or the introduction of a prejudicial newspaper account into the jury room, *Mattox v. United States,* 146 U.S. 140 (1892). See also *Parker v. Gladden,* 385 U.S. 363 (1966).

This rule does not purport to specify the substantive grounds for setting aside verdicts for irregularity; it deals only with the competency of jurors to testify concerning those grounds. Allowing them to testify as to matters other than their own inner reactions involves no particular hazard to the values sought to be protected. The rule is based upon this conclusion. It makes no attempt to specify the substantive grounds for setting aside verdicts for irregularity.

See also Rule 6(e) of the Federal Rules of Criminal Procedure and 18 U.S.C. § 3500, governing the secrecy of grand jury proceedings. The present rule does not relate to secrecy and disclosure but to the competency of certain witnesses and evidence.

1974 Enactment

Note to Subdivision (b). As proposed by the Court, Rule 606(b) limited testimony by a juror in the course of an inquiry into the validity of a verdict or indictment. He could testify as to the influence of extraneous prejudicial information brought to the jury's attention (e.g. a radio newscast or a newspaper account) or an outside influence which improperly had been brought to bear upon a juror (e.g. a threat to the safety of a member of his family), but he could not testify as to other irregularities which occurred in the jury room. Under this formulation a quotient verdict could not be attacked through the testimony of a juror, nor could a juror testify to the drunken condition of a fellow juror which so disabled him that he could not participate in the jury's deliberations.

The 1969 and 1971 Advisory Committee drafts would have permitted a member of the jury to testify concerning these kinds of irregularities in the jury room. The Advisory Committee note in the 1971 draft stated that "* * * the door of the jury room is not a satisfactory dividing point, and the Supreme Court has refused to accept it." The Advisory Committee further commented that—

> The trend has been to draw the dividing line between testimony as to mental processes, on the one hand, and as to the existence of conditions or occurrences of events calculated improperly to influence the verdict on the other hand, without regard to whether the happening is within or without the jury room. * * * The jurors are the persons who know what really happened. Allowing them to testify as to matters other than their own reactions involves no particular hazard to the values sought to be protected. The rule is based upon this conclusion. It makes no attempt to specify the substantive grounds for setting aside verdicts for irregularity.

Objective jury misconduct may be testified to in California, Florida, Iowa, Kansas, Nebraska, New Jersey, North Dakota, Ohio, Oregon, Tennessee, Texas, and Washington.

Persuaded that the better practice is that provided for in the earlier drafts, the Committee amended subdivision (b) to read in the text of those drafts. House Report No. 93–650.

Note to Subdivision (b). As adopted by the House, this rule would permit the impeachment of verdicts by inquiry into, not the mental processes of the jurors, but what happened in terms of conduct in the jury room. This extension of the ability to impeach a verdict is felt to be unwarranted and ill-advised.

The rule passed by the House embodies a suggestion by the Advisory Committee of the Judicial Conference that is considerably broader than the final version adopted by the Supreme Court, which embodied long-accepted Federal law. Although forbidding the impeachment of verdicts by inquiry into the jurors' mental processes, it deletes from the Supreme Court version the proscription against testimony "as to any matter or statement occurring during the course of the jury's deliberations." This deletion would have the effect of opening verdicts up to challenge on the basis of what happened during the jury's internal deliberations, for example, where a juror alleged that the jury refused to follow the trial judge's instructions or that some of the jurors did not take part in deliberations.

Permitting an individual to attack a jury verdict based upon the jury's internal deliberations has long been recognized as unwise by the Supreme Court. In *McDonald v. Pless,* the Court stated:

* * * * * * *

> [L]et it once be established that verdicts solemnly made and publicly returned into court can be attacked and set aside on the testimony of those who took part in their publication and all verdicts could be, and many would be, followed by an inquiry in the hope of discovering something which might invalidate the finding. Jurors would be harassed and beset by the defeated party in an effort to secure from them evidence of facts which might establish misconduct sufficient to set aside a verdict. If evidence thus secured could be thus used, the result would be to make what was intended to be a private deliberation, the constant subject of public investigation—to the destruction of all frankness and freedom of discussion and conference [238 U.S. 264, at 267 (1914)].

* * * * * * *

As it stands then, the rule would permit the harassment of former jurors by losing parties as well as the possible exploitation of disgruntled or otherwise badly-motivated ex-jurors.

Public policy requires a finality to litigation. And common fairness requires that absolute privacy be preserved for jurors to engage in the full and free debate necessary to the attainment of just verdicts. Jurors will not be able to function effectively if their deliberations are to be scrutinized in post-trial litigation. In the interest of protecting the jury system and the citizens who make it work, rule 606 should not permit any inquiry into the internal deliberations of the jurors. Senate Report No. 93–1277.

Note to Subdivision (b). Rule 606(b) deals with juror testimony in an inquiry into the validity of a verdict or indictment. The House bill provides that a juror cannot testify about his mental processes or about the effect of anything upon his or another juror's mind as influencing him to assent to or dissent from a verdict or indictment. Thus, the House bill allows a juror to testify about objective matters occurring during the jury's deliberation, such as the misconduct of another juror or the reaching of a quotient verdict. The Senate bill does not permit juror testimony about any matter or statement occurring during the course of the jury's deliberations. The Senate bill does provide, however, that a juror may testify on the question whether extraneous prejudicial information was improperly brought to the jury's attention and on the question whether any outside influence was improperly brought to bear on any juror.

The Conference adopts the Senate amendment. The Conferees believe that jurors should be encouraged to be conscientious in promptly reporting to the court misconduct that occurs during jury deliberations. House Report No. 93–1597.

1987 Amendments

The amendments are technical. No substantive change is intended.

2006 Amendments

Rule 606(b) has been amended to provide that juror testimony may be used to prove that the verdict reported was the result of a mistake in entering the verdict on the verdict form. The amendment responds to a divergence between the text of the Rule and the case law that has established an exception for proof of clerical errors. *See, e.g., Plummer v. Springfield Term. Ry.*, 5 F.3d 1, 3 (1st Cir. 1993) ("A number of circuits hold, and we agree, that juror testimony regarding an alleged clerical error, such as announcing a verdict different than that agreed upon, does not challenge the validity of the verdict or the deliberation of mental processes, and therefore is not subject to Rule 606(b)."); *Teevee Toons, Inc., v. MP3.Com, Inc.*, 148 F.Supp.2d 276, 278 (S.D.N.Y. 2001) (noting that Rule 606(b) has been silent regarding inquiries designed to confirm the accuracy of a verdict).

In adopting the exception for proof of mistakes in entering the verdict on the verdict form, the amendment specifically rejects the broader exception, adopted by some courts, permitting the use of juror testimony to prove that the jurors were operating under a misunderstanding about the consequences of the result that they agreed upon. *See, e.g., Attridge v. Cencorp Div. of Dover Techs. Int'l, Inc.*, 836 F.2d 113, 116 (2d Cir. 1987); *Eastridge Development Co., v. Halpert Associates, Inc.*, 853 F.2d 772 (10th Cir. 1988). The broader exception is rejected because an inquiry into whether the jury misunderstood or misapplied an instruction goes to the jurors' mental processes underlying the verdict, rather than the verdict's accuracy in capturing what the jurors had agreed upon. *See, e.g.* , *Karl v. Burlington Northern R.R.*, 880 F.2d 68, 74 (8th Cir. 1989) (error to receive juror testimony on whether verdict was the result of jurors' misunderstanding of instructions: "The jurors did not state that the figure written by the foreman was different from that which they agreed upon, but indicated that the figure the foreman wrote down was intended to be a net figure, not a gross figure. Receiving such statements violates Rule 606(b) because the testimony relates to how the jury interpreted the court's instructions, and concerns the jurors' 'mental processes,' which is forbidden by the rule."); *Robles v. Exxon Corp.*, 862 F.2d 1201, 1208 (5th Cir. 1989) ("the alleged error here goes to the substance of what the jury was asked to decide, necessarily implicating the jury's mental processes insofar as it questions the jury's understanding of the court's instructions and application of those instructions to the facts of the case"). Thus, the exception established by the amendment is limited to cases such as "where the jury foreperson wrote down, in response to an interrogatory, a number different from that agreed upon by the jury, or mistakenly stated that the defendant was 'guilty' when the jury had actually agreed that the defendant was not guilty." *Id.*

It should be noted that the possibility of errors in the verdict form will be reduced substantially by polling the jury. Rule 606(b) does not, of course, prevent this precaution. *See* 8 C. Wigmore, *Evidence*, § 2350 at 691 (McNaughten ed. 1961) (noting that the reasons for the rule barring juror testimony, "namely, the dangers of uncertainty and of tampering with the jurors to procure testimony, disappear in large part if such investigation as may be desired is *made by the judge* and takes place *before the jurors' discharge* and separation") (emphasis in original). Errors that come to light after polling the jury "may be corrected on the spot, or the jury may be sent out to continue deliberations, or, if necessary, a new trial may be ordered." C. Mueller & L. Kirkpatrick, *Evidence Under the Rules* at 671 (2d ed. 1999) (citing *Sincox v. United States*, 571 F.2d 876, 878–79 (5th Cir. 1978)).

Rule 607. Who May Impeach

The credibility of a witness may be attacked by any party, including the party calling the witness.

(Pub.L. 93–595, § 1, Jan. 2, 1975, 88 Stat.1934; Mar. 2, 1987, eff. Oct. 1, 1987.)

ADVISORY COMMITTEE NOTES

1972 Proposed Rules

The traditional rule against impeaching one's own witness is abandoned as based on false premises. A party does not hold out his witnesses as worthy of belief, since he rarely has a free choice in selecting them. Denial of the right leaves the party at the mercy of the witness and the adversary. If the impeachment is by a prior statement, it is free from hearsay dangers and is excluded from the category of hearsay under Rule 801(d)(1). Ladd, Impeachment of One's Own Witness—New Developments, 4 U.Chi.L.Rev. 69 (1936); McCormick § 38; 3 Wigmore §§ 896–918. The substantial inroads into the old rule made over the years by decisions, rules, and statutes are evidence of doubts as to its basic soundness and workability. Cases are collected in 3 Wigmore § 905. Revised Rule 32(a)(1) of the Federal Rules of Civil Procedure allows any party to impeach a witness by means of his deposition, and Rule 43(b) has allowed the calling and impeachment of an adverse party or person identified with him. Illustrative statutes allowing a party to impeach his own witness under varying circumstances are

Ill.Rev.Stats.1967, c. 110, § 60; Mass.Laws Annot. 1959, c. 233, § 23; 20 N.M.Stats.Annot. 1953, § 20–2–4; N.Y. CPLR § 4514 (McKinney 1963); 12 Vt.Stats.Annot.1959, §§ 1641a, 1642. Complete judicial rejection of the old rule is found in *United States v. Freeman*, 302 F.2d 347 (2d Cir.1962). The same result is reached in Uniform Rule 20; California Evidence Code § 785; Kansas Code of Civil Procedure § 60–420. See also New Jersey Evidence Rule 20.

1987 Amendments

The amendment is technical. No substantive change is intended.

Rule 608. Evidence of Character and Conduct of Witness

(a) Opinion and reputation evidence of character. The credibility of a witness may be attacked or supported by evidence in the form of opinion or reputation, but subject to these limitations: (1) the evidence may refer only to character for truthfulness or untruthfulness, and (2) evidence of truthful character is admissible only after the character of the witness for truthfulness has been attacked by opinion or reputation evidence or otherwise.

(b) Specific instances of conduct. Specific instances of the conduct of a witness, for the purpose of attacking or supporting the witness' character for truthfulness, other than conviction of crime as provided in rule 609, may not be proved by extrinsic evidence. They may, however, in the discretion of the court, if probative of truthfulness or untruthfulness, be inquired into on cross-examination of the witness (1) concerning the witness' character for truthfulness or untruthfulness, or (2) concerning the character for truthfulness or untruthfulness of another witness as to which character the witness being cross-examined has testified.

The giving of testimony, whether by an accused or by any other witness, does not operate as a waiver of the accused's or the witness' privilege against self-incrimination when examined with respect to matters that relate only to character for truthfulness.

(Pub.L. 93–595, § 1, Jan. 2, 1975, 88 Stat.1935; Mar. 2, 1987, eff. Oct. 1, 1987; Apr. 25, 1988, eff. Nov. 1, 1988; Mar. 27, 2003, eff. Dec. 1, 2003.)

ADVISORY COMMITTEE NOTES

1972 Proposed Rules

Note to Subdivision (a). In Rule 404(a) the general position is taken that character evidence is not admissible for the purpose of proving that the person acted in conformity therewith, subject, however, to several exceptions, one of which is character evidence of a witness as bearing upon his credibility. The present rule develops that exception.

In accordance with the bulk of judicial authority, the inquiry is strictly limited to character for veracity, rather than allowing evidence as to character generally. The result is to sharpen relevancy, to reduce surprise, waste of time, and confusion, and to make the lot of the witness somewhat less unattractive. McCormick § 44.

The use of opinion and reputation evidence as means of proving the character of witnesses is consistent with Rule 405(a). While the modern practice has purported to exclude opinion, witnesses who testify to reputation seem in fact often to be giving their opinions, disguised somewhat misleadingly as reputation. See McCormick § 44. And even under the modern practice, a common relaxation has allowed inquiry as to whether the witnesses would believe the principal witness under oath. *United States v. Walker*, 313 F.2d 236 (6th Cir.1963), and cases cited therein; McCormick § 44, pp. 94–95, n. 3.

Character evidence in support of credibility is admissible under the rule only after the witness' character has first been attacked, as has been the case at common law. Maguire, Weinstein, et al., Cases on Evidence 295 (5th ed. 1965); McCormick § 49, p. 105; 4 Wigmore § 1104. The enormous needless consumption of time which a contrary practice would entail justifies the limitation. Opinion or reputation that the witness is untruthful specifically qualifies as an attack under the rule, and evidence of misconduct, including conviction of crime, and of corruption also fall within this category. Evidence of bias or interest does not. McCormick § 49; 4 Wigmore §§ 1106, 1107. Whether evidence in the form of contradiction is an attack upon the character of the witness must depend upon the circumstances. McCormick § 49. Cf. 4 Wigmore §§ 1108, 1109.

As to the use of specific instances on direct by an opinion witness, see the Advisory Committee's Note to Rule 405, *supra*.

Note to Subdivision (b). In conformity with Rule 405, which forecloses use of evidence of specific incidents as proof in chief of character unless character is an issue in the case, the present rule generally bars evidence of specific instances of conduct of a witness for the purpose of attacking or supporting his credibility. There are, however, two exceptions: (1) specific instances are provable when they have been the subject of criminal conviction, and (2) specific instances may be inquired into on cross-examination of the principal witness or of a witness giving an opinion of his character for truthfulness.

(1) Conviction of crime as a technique of impeachment is treated in detail in Rule 609, and here is merely recognized as an exception to the general rule excluding evidence of specific incidents for impeachment purposes.

(2) Particular instances of conduct, though not the subject of criminal conviction, may be inquired into on cross-examination of the principal witness himself or of a witness who testifies concerning his character for truthfulness. Effective cross-examination demands that some allowance be made for going into matters of this kind, but the possibilities of abuse are substantial. Consequently safeguards are erected in the form of specific requirements that the instances inquired into be probative of truthfulness or its opposite and not remote in time. Also, the overriding protection of Rule 403 requires that probative value not be outweighed by danger of unfair prejudice, confusion of issues, or misleading the jury, and that of Rule 611 bars harassment and undue embarrassment.

The final sentence constitutes a rejection of the doctrine of such cases as *People v. Sorge*, 301 N.Y. 198, 93 N.E.2d 637 (1950), that any past criminal act relevant to credibility may be inquired into on cross-examination, in apparent disregard of the privilege against self-incrimination. While it is clear that an ordinary witness cannot make a partial disclosure of incriminating matter and then invoke the privilege on cross-examination, no tenable contention can be made that merely by testifying he waives his right to foreclose inquiry on cross-examination into criminal activities for the purpose of attacking his credibility. So to hold would reduce the privilege to a nullity. While it is true that an accused, unlike an ordinary witness, has an option whether to testify, if the option can be exercised only at the price of opening up inquiry as to any and all criminal acts committed during his lifetime, the right to testify could scarcely be said to possess much vitality. In *Griffin v. California*, 380 U.S. 609, 85 S.Ct. 1229, 14 L.Ed.2d 106 (1965), the Court held that allowing comment on the election of an accused not to testify exacted a constitutionally impermissible price, and so here. While no specific provision in terms confers constitutional status on the right of an accused to take the stand in his own defense, the existence of the right is so completely recognized that a denial of it or substantial infringement upon it would surely be of due process dimensions. See *Ferguson v. Georgia*, 365 U.S. 570, 81 S.Ct. 756, 5 L.Ed.2d 783 (1961); McCormick § 131; 8 Wigmore § 2276 (McNaughton Rev.1961). In any event, wholly aside from constitutional considerations, the provision represents a sound policy.

1974 Enactment

Note to Subdivision (a). Rule 608(a) as submitted by the Court permitted attack to be made upon the character for truthfulness or untruthfulness of a witness either by reputation or opinion testimony. For the same reason underlying its decision to eliminate the admissibility of opinion testimony in Rule 405(a), the Committee amended Rule 608(a) to delete the reference to opinion testimony.

Note to Subdivision (b). The second sentence of Rule 608(b) as submitted by the Court permitted specific instances of misconduct of a witness to be inquired into on cross-examination for the purpose of attacking his credibility, if probative of truthfulness or untruthfulness, "and not remote in time". Such cross-examination could be of the witness himself or of another witness who testifies as to "his" character for truthfulness or untruthfulness.

The Committee amended the Rule to emphasize the discretionary power of the court in permitting such testimony and deleted the reference to remoteness in time as being unnecessary and confusing (remoteness from time of trial or remoteness from the incident involved?). As recast, the Committee amendment also makes clear the antecedent of "his" in the original Court proposal. House Report No. 93–650.

The Senate amendment adds the words "opinion or" to conform the first sentence of the rule with the remainder of the rule.

The Conference adopts the Senate amendment. House Report No. 93–1597.

1987 Amendments

The amendments are technical. No substantive change is intended.

1988 Amendments

The amendment is technical. No substantive change is intended.

2003 Amendments

The Rule has been amended to clarify that the absolute prohibition on extrinsic evidence applies only when the sole reason for proffering that evidence is to attack or support the witness' character for truthfulness. *See United States v. Abel*, 469 U.S. 45 (1984); *United States v. Fusco*, 748 F.2d 996 (5th Cir. 1984) (Rule 608(b) limits the use of evidence "designed to show that the witness has done things, unrelated to the suit being tried, that make him more or less believable per se"); Ohio R.Evid. 608(b). On occasion the Rule's use of the overbroad term "credibility" has been read "to bar extrinsic evidence for bias, competency and contradiction impeachment since they too deal with credibility." American Bar Association Section of Litigation, *Emerging Problems Under the Federal Rules of Evidence* at 161 (3d ed. 1998). The amendment conforms the language of the Rule to its original intent, which was to impose an absolute bar on extrinsic evidence only if the sole purpose for offering the evidence was to prove the witness' character for veracity. *See* Advisory Committee Note to Rule 608(b) (stating that the Rule is "[i]n conformity with Rule 405, which forecloses use of evidence of specific incidents as proof in chief of character unless character is in issue in the case . . . ").

By limiting the application of the Rule to proof of a witness' character for truthfulness, the amendment leaves the admissibility of extrinsic evidence offered for other grounds of impeachment (such as contradiction, prior inconsistent statement, bias and mental capacity) to Rules 402 and 403. *See, e.g., United States v. Winchenbach*, 197 F.3d 548 (1st Cir. 1999) (admissibility of a prior inconsistent statement offered for impeachment is governed by Rules 402 and 403, not Rule 608(b)); *United States v. Tarantino*, 846 F.2d 1384 (D.C. Cir. 1988) (admissibility of extrinsic evidence offered to contradict a witness is governed by Rules 402 and 403); *United States v. Lindemann*, 85 F.3d 1232 (7th Cir. 1996) (admissibility of extrinsic evidence of bias is governed by Rules 402 and 403).

It should be noted that the extrinsic evidence prohibition of Rule 608(b) bars any reference to the consequences that a witness might have suffered as a result of an alleged bad act. For example, Rule 608(b) prohibits counsel from mentioning that a witness was suspended or disciplined for the conduct that is the subject of impeachment, when that conduct is offered only to prove the character of the witness. *See United States v. Davis*, 183 F.3d 231, 257 n.12 (3d Cir. 1999) (emphasizing that in attacking the defendant's character for truthfulness "the government cannot make reference to Davis's forty-four day suspension or that Internal Affairs found that he lied about" an incident because "[s]uch evidence would not only be hearsay to the extent it contains assertion of fact, it would be inadmissible extrinsic evidence under Rule 608(b)"). *See also* Stephen A. Saltzburg, *Impeaching the Witness: Prior Bad Acts and Extrinsic Evidence*, 7 Crim. Just. 28, 31 (Winter 1993) ("counsel should not be permitted to circumvent the no-extrinsic-evidence provision by tucking a third person's opinion about prior acts into a question asked of the witness who has denied the act").

For purposes of consistency the term "credibility" has been replaced by the term "character for truthfulness" in the last sentence of subdivision (b). The term "credibility" is also used in subdivision (a). But the Committee found it unnecessary to substitute "character for truthfulness" for "credibility" in Rule 608(a), because subdivision (a)(1) already serves to limit impeachment to proof of such character.

Rules 609(a) and 610 also use the term "credibility" when the intent of those Rules is to regulate impeachment of a witness' character for truthfulness. No inference should be derived from the fact that the Committee proposed an amendment to Rule 608(b) but not to Rules 609 and 610.

Rule 609. Impeachment by Evidence of Conviction of Crime

(a) General rule.—For the purpose of attacking the character for truthfulness of a witness,

(1) evidence that a witness other than an accused has been convicted of a crime shall be admitted, subject to Rule 403, if the crime was punishable by death or imprisonment in excess of one year under the law under which the witness was convicted, and evidence that an accused has been convicted of such a crime shall be admitted if the court determines that the probative value of admitting this evidence outweighs its prejudicial effect to the accused; and

(2) evidence that any witness has been convicted of a crime shall be admitted regardless of the punishment, if it readily can be determined that establishing the elements of the crime required proof or admission of an act of dishonesty or false statement by the witness.

(b) Time limit. Evidence of a conviction under this rule is not admissible if a period of more than ten years has elapsed since the date of the conviction or of the release of the witness from the confinement imposed for that conviction, whichever is the later date, unless the court determines, in the interests of justice, that the probative value of the conviction supported by specific facts and circumstances substantially outweighs its prejudicial effect. However, evidence of a conviction more than 10 years old as calculated herein, is not admissible unless the proponent gives to the adverse party sufficient advance written notice of intent to use such evidence to provide the adverse party with a fair opportunity to contest the use of such evidence.

(c) Effect of pardon, annulment, or certificate of rehabilitation.—Evidence of a conviction is not admissible under this rule if (1) the conviction has been the subject of a pardon, annulment, certificate of rehabilitation, or other equivalent procedure based on a finding of the rehabilitation of the person convicted, and that person has not been convicted of a subsequent crime that was punishable by death or imprisonment in excess of one year, or (2) the conviction has been the subject of a pardon, annulment, or other equivalent procedure based on a finding of innocence.

(d) Juvenile adjudications. Evidence of juvenile adjudications is generally not admissible under this rule. The court may, however, in a criminal case allow evidence of a juvenile adjudication of a witness other than the accused if conviction of the offense would be admissible to attack the credibility of an adult and the court is satisfied that admission in evidence is necessary for a fair determination of the issue of guilt or innocence.

(e) Pendency of appeal. The pendency of an appeal therefrom does not render evidence of a conviction inadmissible. Evidence of the pendency of an appeal is admissible.

(Pub.L. 93–595, § 1, Jan. 2, 1975, 88 Stat.1935; Mar. 2, 1987, eff. Oct. 1, 1987; Jan. 26, 1990, eff. Dec. 1, 1990; Apr. 12, 2006, eff. Dec. 1, 2006.)

ADVISORY COMMITTEE NOTES

1972 Proposed Rules

As a means of impeachment, evidence of conviction of crime is significant only because it stands as proof of the commission of the underlying criminal act. There is little dissent from the general proposition that at least some crimes are relevant to credibility but much disagreement among the cases and commentators about which crimes are usable for this purpose. See McCormick § 43; 2 Wright, Federal Practice and Procedure: Criminal § 416 (1969). The weight of traditional authority has been to allow use of felonies generally, without regard to the nature of the particular offense, and of *crimen falsi* without regard to the grade of the offense. This is the view accepted by Congress in the 1970 amendment of § 14–305 of the District of Columbia Code, P.L. 91–358, 84 Stat. 473. Uniform Rule 21 and Model Code Rule 106 permit only crimes involving "dishonesty or false statement." Others have thought that the trial judge should have discretion to exclude convictions if the probative value of the evidence of the crime is substantially outweighed by the danger of unfair prejudice. *Luck v. United States*, 121 U.S.App.D.C. 151, 348 F.2d 763 (1965); McGowan, Impeachment of Criminal Defendants by Prior Convictions, 1970 Law & Soc.Order 1. Whatever may be the merits of those views, this rule is drafted to accord with the Congressional policy manifested in the 1970 legislation.

The proposed rule incorporates certain basic safeguards, in terms applicable to all witnesses but of particular significance to an accused who elects to testify. These protections include the imposition of definite time limitations, giving effect to demonstrated rehabilitation, and generally excluding juvenile adjudications.

Note to Subdivision (a). For purposes of impeachment, crimes are divided into two categories by the rule: (1) those of what is generally regarded as felony grade, without particular regard to the nature of the offense, and (2) those involving dishonesty or false statement, without regard to the grade of the offense. Probable convictions are not limited to violations of federal law. By reason of our constitutional structure, the federal catalog of crimes is far from being a complete one, and resort must be had to the laws of the states for the specification of many crimes. For example, simple theft as compared with theft from interstate commerce. Other instances of borrowing are the Assimilative Crimes Act, making the state law of crimes applicable to the special territorial and maritime jurisdiction of the United States, 18 U.S.C. § 13, and the provision of the Judicial Code disqualifying persons as jurors on the grounds of state as well as federal convictions, 28 U.S.C. § 1865. For evaluation of the crime in terms of seriousness, reference is made to the congressional measurement of felony (subject to imprisonment in excess of one year) rather than adopting state definitions which vary considerably. See 28 U.S.C. § 1865, *supra*, disqualifying jurors for conviction in state or federal court of crime punishable by imprisonment for more than one year.

Note to Subdivision (b). Few statutes recognize a time limit on impeachment by evidence of conviction. However, practical considerations of fairness and relevancy demand that some boundary be recognized. See Ladd, Credibility Tests—Current Trends, 89 U.Pa.L.Rev. 166, 176–177 (1940). This portion of the rule is derived from the proposal advanced in Recommendation Proposing in Evidence Code, § 788(5), p. 142, Cal.Law Rev.Comm'n (1965), though not adopted. See California Evidence Code § 788.

Note to Subdivision (c). A pardon or its equivalent granted solely for the purpose of restoring civil rights lost by virtue of a conviction has no relevance to an inquiry into character. If, however, the pardon or other proceeding is hinged upon a showing of rehabilitation the situation is otherwise. The result under the rule is to render the conviction inadmissible. The alternative of allowing in evidence both the conviction and the rehabilitation has not been adopted for reasons of policy, economy of time, and difficulties of evaluation.

A similar provision is contained in California Evidence Code § 788. Cf. A.L.I. Model Penal Code, Proposed Official Draft § 306.6(3)(e) (1962), and discussion in A.L.I. Proceedings 310 (1961).

Pardons based on innocence have the effect, of course, of nullifying the conviction *ab initio*.

Note to Subdivision (d). The prevailing view has been that a juvenile adjudication is not usable for impeachment. *Thomas v. United States*, 74 App.D.C. 167, 121 F.2d 905 (1941); *Cotton v. United States*, 355 F.2d 480 (10th Cir.1966). This conclusion was based upon a variety of circumstances. By virtue of its informality, frequently diminished quantum of required proof, and other departures from accepted standards for criminal trials under the theory of *parens patriae*, the juvenile adjudication was considered to lack the precision and general probative value of the criminal conviction. While *In re Gault*, 387 U.S. 1, 87 S.Ct. 1428, 18 L.Ed.2d 527 (1967), no doubt eliminates these characteristics insofar as objectionable, other obstacles remain. Practical problems of administration are raised by the common provisions in juvenile legislation that records be kept confidential and that they be destroyed after a short time. While *Gault* was skeptical as to the realities of confidentiality of juvenile records, it also saw no constitutional obstacles to improvement. 387 U.S. at 25, 87 S.Ct. 1428. See also Note, Rights and Rehabilitation in the Juvenile Courts, 67 Colum.L.Rev. 281, 289 (1967). In addition, policy considerations much akin to those which dictate exclusion of adult convictions after rehabilitation has been established strongly suggest a rule of excluding juvenile adjudications. Admittedly, however, the rehabilitative process may in a given case be a demonstrated failure, or the strategic importance of a given witness may be so great as to require the overriding of general policy in the interests of particular justice. See *Giles v. Maryland*, 386 U.S. 66, 87 S.Ct. 793, 17 L.Ed.2d 737 (1967). Wigmore was outspoken in his condemnation of the disallowance of juvenile adjudications to impeach, especially when the witness is the complainant in a case of molesting a minor. 1 Wigmore § 196; 3 *Id.* §§ 924a, 980. The rule recognizes discretion in the judge to effect an accommodation among these various factors by departing from the general principle of exclusion. In deference to the general pattern and policy of juvenile statutes, however, no discretion is accorded when the witness is the accused in a criminal case.

Note to Subdivision (e). The presumption of correctness which ought to attend judicial proceedings supports the position that pendency of an appeal does not preclude use of a conviction for impeachment. *United States v. Empire Packing Co.*, 174 F.2d 16 (7th Cir.1949), cert. denied 337 U.S. 959, 69 S.Ct. 1534, 93 L.Ed. 1758; *Bloch v. United States*, 226 F.2d 185 (9th Cir.1955), cert. denied 350 U.S. 948, 76 S.Ct. 323, 100 L.Ed. 826 and 353 U.S. 959, 77 S.Ct. 868, 1 L.Ed.2d 910; and see *Newman v. United States*, 331 F.2d 968 (8th Cir.1964). *Contra, Campbell v. United States*, 85 U.S.App.D.C. 133, 176 F.2d 45 (1949). The pendency of an appeal is, however, a qualifying circumstance properly considerable.

1974 Enactment

Note to Subdivision (a). Rule 609(a) as submitted by the Court was modeled after Section 133(a) of Public Law 91–358, 14 D.C.Code 305(b)(1), enacted in 1970. The Rule provided that:

> For the purpose of attacking the credibility of a witness, evidence that he has been convicted of a crime is admissible but only if the crime (1) was punishable by death or imprisonment in excess of one year under the law under which he was convicted or (2) involved dishonesty or false statement regardless of the punishment.

As reported to the Committee by the Subcommittee, Rule 609(a) was amended to read as follows:

> For the purpose of attacking the credibility of a witness, evidence that he has been convicted of a crime is admissible only if the crime (1) was punishable by death or imprisonment in excess of one year, unless the court determines that the danger of unfair prejudice outweighs the probative value of the evidence of the conviction, or (2) involved dishonesty or false statement.

In full committee, the provision was amended to permit attack upon the credibility of a witness by prior conviction only if the prior crime involved dishonesty or false statement. While recognizing that the prevailing doctrine in the federal courts and in most States allows a witness to be impeached by evidence of prior felony convictions without restriction as to type, the Committee was of the view that, because of the danger of unfair prejudice in such practice and the deterrent effect upon an accused who might wish to testify, and even upon a witness who was not the accused, cross-examination by evidence of prior conviction should be limited to those kinds of convictions bearing directly on credibility, *i.e.*, crimes involving dishonesty or false statement.

Note to Subdivision (b). Rule 609(b) as submitted by the Court was modeled after Section 133(a) of Public Law 91–358, 14 D.C.Code 305(b)(2)(B), enacted in 1970. The Rule provided:

> Evidence of a conviction under this rule is not admissible if a period of more than ten years has elapsed since the date of the release of the witness from confinement imposed for his most recent conviction, or the expiration of the period of his parole, probation, or sentence granted or imposed with respect to his most recent conviction, whichever is the later date.

Under this formulation, a witness' entire past record of criminal convictions could be used for impeachment (provided the conviction met the standard of subdivision (a)), if the witness had been most recently released from confinement, or the period of his parole or probation had expired, within ten years of the conviction.

The Committee amended the Rule to read in the text of the 1971 Advisory Committee version to provide that upon the expiration of ten years from the date of a conviction of a witness, or of his release from confinement for that offense, that conviction may no longer be used for impeachment. The Committee was of the view that after ten years following a person's release from confinement (or from the date of his conviction) the probative value of the conviction with respect to that person's credibility diminished to a point where it should no longer be admissible.

Note to Subdivision (c). Rule 609(c) as submitted by the Court provided in part that evidence of a witness' prior conviction is not admissible to attack his credibility if the conviction was the subject of a pardon, annulment, or other equivalent procedure, based on a showing of rehabilitation, and the witness has not been convicted of a subsequent crime. The Committee amended the Rule to provide that the "subsequent crime" must have been "punishable by death or imprisonment in excess of one year", on the ground that a subsequent conviction of an offense not a felony is insufficient to rebut the finding that the witness has been rehabilitated. The Committee also intends that the words "based on a finding of the rehabilitation of the person convicted" apply not only to "certificate of rehabilitation, or other equivalent procedure", but also to "pardon" and "annulment.". House Report No. 93–650.

Note to Subdivision (a). As proposed by the Supreme Court, the rule would allow the use of prior convictions to impeach if the crime was a felony or a misdemeanor if the misdemeanor involved dishonesty or false statement. As modified by the House, the rule would admit prior convictions for impeachment purposes only if the offense, whether felony or misdemeanor, involved dishonesty or false statement.

The committee has adopted a modified version of the House-passed rule. In your committee's view, the danger of unfair prejudice is far greater when the accused, as opposed to other witnesses, testifies, because the jury may be prejudiced not merely on the question of credibility but also on the ultimate question of guilt or innocence. Therefore, with respect to defendants, the committee agreed with the House limitation that only offenses involved false statement or dishonesty may be used. By that phrase, the committee means crimes such as perjury or subornation of perjury, false statement, criminal fraud, embezzlement or false pretense, or any other offense, in the nature of *crimen falsi* the commission of which involves some element of untruthfulness, deceit or falsification bearing on the accused's propensity to testify truthfully.

With respect to other witnesses, in addition to any prior conviction involving false statement or dishonesty, any other felony may be used to impeach if, and only if, the court finds that the probative value of such evidence outweighs its prejudicial effect against the party offering that witness.

Notwithstanding this provision, proof of any prior offense otherwise admissible under Rule 404 could still be offered for the purposes sanctioned by that rule. Furthermore, the committee intends that notwithstanding this rule, a defendant's misrepresentation regarding the existence or nature of prior convictions may be met by rebuttal evidence, including the record of such prior convictions. Similarly, such records may be offered to rebut representations made by the defendant regarding his attitude toward or willingness to commit a general category of offense, although denials or other representations by the defendant regarding the specific conduct which forms the basis of the charge against him shall not make prior convictions admissible to rebut such statement.

In regard to either type of representation, of course, prior convictions may be offered in rebuttal only if the defendant's statement is made in response to defense counsel's questions or is made gratuitously in the course of cross-examination. Prior convictions may not be offered as rebuttal evidence if the prosecution has sought to circumvent the purpose of this rule by asking questions which elicit such representations from the defendant.

One other clarifying amendment has been added to this subsection, that is, to provide that the admissibility of evidence of a prior conviction is permitted only upon cross-examination of a witness. It is not admissible if a person does not testify. It is to be understood, however, that a court record of a prior conviction is admissible to prove that conviction if the witness has forgotten or denies its existence.

Note to Subdivision (b). Although convictions over ten years old generally do not have much probative value, there may be exceptional circumstances under which the conviction substantially bears on the credibility of the witness. Rather than exclude all convictions over 10 years old, the committee adopted an amendment in the form of a final clause to the section granting the court discretion to admit convictions over 10 years old, but only upon a determination by the court that the probative value of the conviction supported by specific facts and circumstances, substantially outweighs its prejudicial effect.

It is intended that convictions over 10 years old will be admitted very rarely and only in exceptional circumstances. The rules provide that the decision be supported by specific facts and circumstances thus requiring the court to make specific findings on the record as to the particular facts and circumstances it has considered in determining that the probative value of the conviction substantially outweighs its prejudicial impact. It is expected that, in fairness, the court will give the party against whom the conviction is introduced a full and adequate opportunity to contest its admission. Senate Report No. 93–1277.

Rule 609 defines when a party may use evidence of a prior conviction in order to impeach a witness. The Senate amendments make changes in two subsections of Rule 609.

Note to Subdivision (a). The House bill provides that the credibility of a witness can be attacked by proof of prior conviction of a crime only if the crime involves dishonesty or false statement. The Senate amendment provides that a witness' credibility may be attacked if the crime (1) was punishable by death or imprisonment in excess of one year under the law under which he was convicted or (2) involves dishonesty or false statement, regardless of the punishment.

The Conference adopts the Senate amendment with an amendment. The Conference amendment provides that the credibility of a witness, whether a defendant or someone else, may be attacked by proof of a prior conviction but only if the crime: (1) was punishable by death or imprisonment in excess of one year under the law under which he was convicted and the court determines that the probative value of the conviction outweighs its prejudicial effect to the defendant; or (2) involved dishonesty or false statement regardless of the punishment.

By the phrase "dishonesty and false statement" the Conference means crimes such as perjury or subornation of perjury, false statement, criminal fraud, embezzlement, or false pretense, or any other offense in the nature of *crimen falsi,* the commission of which involves some element of deceit, untruthfulness, or falsification bearing on the accused's propensity to testify truthfully.

The admission of prior convictions involving dishonesty and false statement is not within the discretion of the Court. Such convictions are peculiarly probative of credibility and, under this rule, are always to be admitted. Thus, judicial discretion granted with respect to the admissibility of other prior convictions is not applicable to those involving dishonesty or false statement.

With regard to the discretionary standard established by paragraph (1) of Rule 609(a), the Conference determined that the prejudicial effect to be weighed against the probative value of the conviction is specifically the prejudicial effect *to the defendant.* The danger of prejudice to a witness other than the defendant (such as injury to the witness' reputation in his community) was considered and rejected by the Conference as an element to be weighed in determining admissibility. It was the judgment of the Conference that the danger of prejudice to a nondefendant witness is outweighed by the need for the trier of fact to have as much relevant evidence on the issue of credibility as possible. Such evidence should only be excluded where it presents a danger of improperly influencing the outcome of the trial by persuading the trier of fact to convict the defendant on the basis of his prior criminal record.

Note to Subdivision (b). The House bill provides in subsection (b) that evidence of conviction of a crime may not be used for impeachment purposes under subsection (a) if more than ten years have elapsed since the date of the conviction or the date the witness was released from confinement imposed for the conviction, whichever is later. The Senate amendment permits the use of convictions older than ten years, if the court determines, in the interests of justice, that the probative value of the conviction, supported by specific facts and circumstances, substantially outweighs its prejudicial effect.

The Conference adopts the Senate amendment with an amendment requiring notice by a party that he intends to request that the court allow him to use a conviction older than ten years. The Conferees anticipate that a written notice, in order to give the adversary a fair opportunity to contest the use of the evidence, will ordinarily include such information as the date of the conviction, the jurisdiction, and the offense or statute involved. In order to eliminate the possibility that the flexibility of this provision may impair the ability of a party-opponent to prepare for trial, the Conferees intend that the notice provision operate to avoid surprise. House Report No. 93–1597.

1987 Amendments

The amendments are technical. No substantive change is intended.

1990 Amendments

The amendment to Rule 609(a) makes two changes in the rule. The first change removes from the rule the limitation that the conviction may only be elicited during cross-examination, a limitation that virtually every circuit has found to be inapplicable. It is common for witnesses to reveal on direct examination their convictions to "remove the sting" of the impeachment. *See e.g., United States v. Bad Cob,* 560 F.2d 877 (8th Cir.1977). The amendment does not contemplate that a court will necessarily permit proof of prior convictions through testimony, which might be time-consuming and more prejudicial than proof through a written record. Rules 403 and 611(a) provide sufficient authority for the court to protect against unfair or disruptive methods of proof.

The second change effected by the amendment resolves an ambiguity as to the relationship of Rules 609 and 403 with respect to impeachment of witnesses other than the criminal defendant. *See, Green v. Bock Laundry Machine Co.,* 109 S.Ct. 1981, 490 U.S. 504 (1989). The amendment does not disturb the special balancing test for the criminal defendant who chooses to testify. Thus, the rule recognizes that, in virtually every case in which prior convictions are used to impeach the testifying defendant, the defendant faces a unique risk of prejudice—*i.e.,* the danger that convictions that would be excluded under Fed.R.Evid. 404 will be misused by a jury as propensity evidence despite their introduction solely for impeachment purposes. Although the rule does not forbid all use of convictions to impeach a defendant, it requires that the government show that the probative value of convictions as impeachment evidence outweighs their prejudicial effect.

Prior to the amendment, the rule appeared to give the defendant the benefit of the special balancing test when defense witnesses other than the defendant were called to testify. In practice, however, the concern about unfairness to the defendant is most acute when the defendant's own convictions are offered as evidence. Almost all of the decided cases concern this type of impeachment, and the amendment does not deprive the defendant of any meaningful protection, since Rule 403 now clearly protects against unfair impeachment of any defense witness other than the defendant. There are cases in which a defendant might be prejudiced when a defense witness is impeached. Such cases may arise, for example, when the witness bears a special relationship to the defendant such that the defendant is likely to suffer some spill-over effect from impeachment of the witness.

The amendment also protects other litigants from unfair impeachment of their witnesses. The danger of prejudice from the use of prior convictions is not confined to criminal defendants. Although the danger that prior convictions will be misused as character evidence is particularly acute when the defendant is impeached, the danger exists in other situations as well. The amendment reflects the view that it is desirable to protect all litigants from the unfair use of prior convictions, and that the ordinary balancing test of Rule 403, which provides that evidence shall not be excluded unless its prejudicial effect substantially outweighs its probative value, is appropriate for assessing the admissibility of prior convictions for impeachment of any witness other than a criminal defendant.

The amendment reflects a judgment that decisions interpreting Rule 609(a) as requiring a trial court to admit convictions in civil cases that have little, if anything, to do with credibility reach undesirable results. *See, e.g., Diggs v. Lyons,* 741 F.2d 577 (3d Cir.1984), *cert. denied,* 105 S.Ct. 2157 (1985). The amendment provides the same protection against unfair prejudice arising from prior convictions used for impeachment purposes as the rules provide for other evidence. The amendment finds support in decided cases. *See, e.g., Petty v. Ideco,* 761 F.2d 1146 (5th Cir.1985); *Czaka v. Hickman,* 703 F.2d 317 (8th Cir.1983).

Fewer decided cases address the question whether Rule 609(a) provides any protection against unduly prejudicial prior convictions used to impeach government witnesses. Some courts have read Rule 609(a) as giving the government no protection for its witnesses. *See, e.g., United States v. Thorne,* 547 F.2d 56 (8th Cir.1976); *United States v. Nevitt,* 563 F.2d 406 (9th Cir.1977), *cert. denied,* 444 U.S. 847 (1979). This approach also is rejected by the amendment. There are cases in which impeachment of government witnesses with prior convictions that have little, if anything, to do with credibility may result in unfair prejudice to the government's interest in a fair trial and unnecessary embarrassment to a witness. Fed.R.Evid. 412 already recognizes this and excluded certain evidence of past sexual behavior in the context of prosecutions for sexual assaults.

The amendment applies the general balancing test of Rule 403 to protect all litigants against unfair impeachment of witnesses. The balancing test protects civil litigants, the government in criminal cases, and the defendant in a criminal case who calls other witnesses. The amendment addresses prior convictions offered under Rule 609, not for other purposes, and does not run afoul, therefore, of *Davis v. Alaska,* 415 U.S. 308 (1974). *Davis* involved the use of a prior juvenile adjudication not to prove a past law violation, but to prove bias. The defendant in a criminal case has the right to demonstrate the bias of a witness and to be assured a fair trial, but not to unduly prejudice a trier of fact. *See generally* Rule 412. In any case in which the trial court believes that confrontation rights require admission of impeachment evidence, obviously the Constitution would take precedence over the rule.

The probability that prior convictions of an ordinary government witness will be unduly prejudicial is low in most criminal cases. Since the behavior of the witness is not the issue in dispute in most cases, there is little chance that the trier of fact will misuse the convictions offered as impeachment evidence as propensity evidence. Thus, trial courts will be skeptical when the government objects to impeachment of its witnesses with prior convictions. Only when the government is able to point to a real danger of prejudice that is sufficient to outweigh substantially the probative value of the conviction for impeachment purposes will the conviction be excluded.

The amendment continues to divide subdivision (a) into subsections (1) and (2) thus facilitating retrieval under current computerized research programs which distinguish the two provisions. The Committee recommended no substantive change in subdivision (a)(2), even though some cases raise a concern about the proper interpretation of the words "dishonesty or false statement." These words were used but not explained in the original Advisory Committee Note accompanying Rule 609. Congress extensively debated the rule, and the Report of the House and Senate Conference Committee states that "[b]y the phrase 'dishonesty and false statement,' the Conference means crimes such as perjury, subornation of perjury, false statement, criminal fraud, embezzlement, or false pretense, or any other offense in the nature of *crimen falsi,* commission of which involves some element of deceit, untruthfulness, or falsification bearing on the accused's propensity to testify truthfully." The Advisory Committee concluded that the Conference Report provides sufficient guidance to trial courts and that no amendment is necessary, notwithstanding some decisions that take an unduly broad view of "dishonesty," admitting convictions such as for bank robbery or bank larceny. Subsection (a)(2) continues to apply to any witness, including a criminal defendant.

Finally, the Committee determined that it was unnecessary to add to the rule language stating that, when a prior conviction is offered under Rule 609, the trial court is to consider the probative value of the prior conviction *for impeachment,* not for other purposes. The Committee concluded that the title of the rule, its first sentence, and its placement among the impeachment rules clearly establish that evidence offered under Rule 609 is offered only for purposes of impeachment.

2006 Amendments

The amendment provides that Rule 609(a)(2) mandates the admission of evidence of a conviction only when the conviction required the proof of (or in the case of a guilty plea, the admission of) an act of dishonesty or false statement. Evidence of all other convictions is inadmissible under this subsection, irrespective of whether the witness exhibited dishonesty or made a false statement in the process of the commission of the crime of conviction. Thus, evidence that a witness was convicted for a crime of violence, such as murder, is not admissible under Rule 609(a)(2), even if the witness acted deceitfully in the course of committing the crime.

The amendment is meant to give effect to the legislative intent to limit the convictions that are to be automatically admitted under subdivision (a)(2). The Conference Committee provided that by "dishonesty and false statement" it meant "crimes such as perjury, subornation of perjury, false statement, criminal fraud, embezzlement, or false pretense, or any other offense in the nature of *crimen falsi,* the commission of which involves some element of deceit, untruthfulness, or falsification bearing on the [witness's] propensity to testify truthfully." Historically, offenses classified as *crimina falsi* have included only those crimes in which the ultimate criminal act was itself an act of deceit. *See* Green, *Deceit and the Classification of Crimes: Federal Rule of Evidence 609(a)(2) and the Origins of* Crimen Falsi, 90 J. Crim. L. & Criminology 1087 (2000).

Evidence of crimes in the nature of *crimina falsi* must be admitted under Rule 609(a)(2), regardless of how such crimes are specifically charged. For example, evidence that a witness was convicted of making a false claim to a federal agent is admissible under this subdivision regardless of whether the crime was charged under a section that expressly references deceit (e.g., 18 U.S.C. § 1001, Material Misrepresentation to the Federal Government) or a section that does not (*e.g.*, 18 U.S.C. § 1503, Obstruction of Justice).

The amendment requires that the proponent have ready proof that the conviction required the factfinder to find, or the defendant to admit, an act of dishonesty or false statement. Ordinarily, the statutory elements of the crime will indicate whether it is one of dishonesty or false statement. Where the deceitful nature of the crime is not apparent from the statute and the face of the judgment — as, for example, where the conviction simply records a finding of guilt for a statutory offense that does not reference deceit expressly — a proponent may offer information such as an indictment, a statement of admitted facts, or jury instructions to show that the factfinder had to find, or the defendant had to admit, an act of dishonesty or false statement in order for the witness to have been convicted. *Cf. Taylor v. United States*, 495 U.S. 575, 602 (1990) (providing that a trial court may look to a charging instrument or jury instructions to ascertain the nature of a prior offense where the statute is insufficiently clear on its face); *Shepard v. United States*, 125 S.Ct. 1254 (2005) (the inquiry to determine whether a guilty plea to a crime defined by a nongeneric statute necessarily admitted elements of the generic offense was limited to the charging document's terms, the terms of a plea agreement or transcript of colloquy between judge and defendant in which the factual basis for the plea was confirmed by the defendant, or a comparable judicial record). But the amendment does not contemplate a "mini-trial" in which the court plumbs the record of the previous proceeding to determine whether the crime was in the nature of *crimen falsi*.

The amendment also substitutes the term "character for truthfulness" for the term "credibility" in the first sentence of the Rule. The limitations of Rule 609 are not applicable if a conviction is admitted for a purpose other than to prove the witness's character for untruthfulness. *See, e.g., United States v. Lopez*, 979 F.2d 1024 (5th Cir. 1992) (Rule 609 was not applicable where the conviction was offered for purposes of contradiction). The use of the term "credibility" in subdivision (d) is retained, however, as that subdivision is intended to govern the use of a juvenile adjudication for any type of impeachment.

Rule 610. Religious Beliefs or Opinions

Evidence of the beliefs or opinions of a witness on matters of religion is not admissible for the purpose of showing that by reason of their nature the witness' credibility is impaired or enhanced.

(Pub.L. 93–595, § 1, Jan. 2, 1975, 88 Stat.1936; Mar. 2, 1987, eff. Oct. 1, 1987.)

ADVISORY COMMITTEE NOTES

1972 Proposed Rules

While the rule forecloses inquiry into the religious beliefs or opinions of a witness for the purpose of showing that his character for truthfulness is affected by their nature, an inquiry for the purpose of showing interest or bias because of them is not within the prohibition. Thus disclosure of affiliation with a church which is a party to the litigation would be allowable under the rule. Cf. Tucker v. Reil, 51 Ariz. 357, 77 P.2d 203 (1938). To the same effect, though less specifically worded, is California Evidence Code § 789. See 3 Wigmore § 936.

1987 Amendments

The amendment is technical. No substantive change is intended.

Rule 611. Mode and Order of Interrogation and Presentation

(a) Control by court. The court shall exercise reasonable control over the mode and order of interrogating witnesses and presenting evidence so as to (1) make the interrogation and presentation effective for the ascertainment of the truth, (2) avoid needless consumption of time, and (3) protect witnesses from harassment or undue embarrassment.

(b) Scope of cross-examination. Cross-examination should be limited to the subject matter of the direct examination and matters affecting the credibility of the witness. The court may, in the exercise of discretion, permit inquiry into additional matters as if on direct examination.

(c) Leading questions. Leading questions should not be used on the direct examination of a witness except as may be necessary to develop the witness' testimony. Ordinarily leading questions should be permitted on cross-examination. When a party calls a hostile witness, an adverse party, or a witness identified with an adverse party, interrogation may be by leading questions.

(Pub.L. 93–595, § 1, Jan. 2, 1975, 88 Stat. 1936; Mar. 2, 1987, eff. Oct. 1, 1987.)

ADVISORY COMMITTEE NOTES

1972 Proposed Rules

Note to Subdivision (a). Spelling out detailed rules to govern the mode and order of interrogating witnesses and presenting evidence is neither desirable nor feasible. The ultimate responsibility for the effective working of the adversary system rests with the judge. The rule sets forth the objectives which he should seek to attain.

Item (1) restates in broad terms the power and obligation of the judge as developed under common law principles. It covers such concerns as whether testimony shall be in the form of a free narrative or responses to specific questions, McCormick § 5, the order of calling witnesses and presenting evidence, 6 Wigmore § 1867, the use of demonstrative evidence, McCormick § 179, and the many other questions arising during the course of a trial which can be solved only by the judge's common sense and fairness in view of the particular circumstances.

Item (2) is addressed to avoidance of needless consumption of time, a matter of daily concern in the disposition of cases. A companion piece is found in the discretion vested in the judge to exclude evidence as a waste of time in Rule 403(b).

Item (3) calls for a judgment under the particular circumstances whether interrogation tactics entail harassment or undue embarrassment. Pertinent circumstances include the importance of the testimony, the nature of the inquiry, its relevance to credibility, waste of time, and confusion. McCormick § 42. In *Alford v. United States,* 282 U.S. 687, 694, 51 S.Ct. 218, 75 L.Ed. 624 (1931), the Court pointed out that, while the trial judge should protect the witness from questions which "go beyond the bounds of proper cross-examination merely to harass, annoy or humiliate," this protection by no means forecloses efforts to discredit the witness. Reference to the transcript of the prosecutor's cross-examination in *Berger v. United States,* 295 U.S. 78, 55 S.Ct. 629, 79 L.Ed. 1314 (1935), serves to lay at rest any doubts as to the need for judicial control in this area.

The inquiry into specific instances of conduct of a witness allowed under Rule 608(b) is, of course, subject to this rule.

Note to Subdivision (b). The tradition in the federal courts and in numerous state courts has been to limit the scope of cross-examination to matters testified to on direct, plus matters bearing upon the credibility of the witness. Various reasons have been advanced to justify the rule of limited cross-examination. (1) A party vouches for his own witness but only to the extent of matters elicited on direct. *Resurrection Gold Mining Co. v. Fortune Gold Mining Co.,* 129 F. 668, 675 (8th Cir.1904), quoted in Maguire, Weinstein, et al., Cases on Evidence 277, n. 38 (5th ed. 1965). But the concept of vouching is discredited, and Rule 607 rejects it. (2) A party cannot ask his own witness leading questions. This is a problem properly solved in terms of what is necessary for a proper development of the testimony rather than by a mechanistic formula similar to the vouching concept. See discussion under subdivision (c). (3) A practice of limited cross-examination promotes orderly presentation of the case. *Finch v. Weiner,* 109 Conn. 616, 145 A. 31 (1929). While this latter reason has merit, the matter is essentially one of the order of presentation and not one in which involvement at the appellate level is likely to prove fruitful. See, for example, *Moyer v. Aetna Life Ins. Co.,* 126 F.2d 141 (3rd Cir.1942); *Butler v. New York Central R. Co.,* 253 F.2d 281 (7th Cir.1958); *United States v. Johnson,* 285 F.2d 35 (9th Cir.1960); *Union Automobile Indemnity Ass'n v. Capitol Indemnity Ins. Co.,* 310 F.2d 318 (7th Cir.1962). In evaluating these considerations, McCormick says:

"The foregoing considerations favoring the wide-open or restrictive rules may well be thought to be fairly evenly balanced. There is another factor, however, which seems to swing the balance overwhelmingly in favor of the wide-open rule. This is the consideration of economy of time and energy. Obviously, the wide-open rule presents little or no opportunity for dispute in its application. The restrictive practice in all its forms, on the other hand, is productive in many court rooms, of continual bickering over the choice of the numerous variations of the 'scope of the direct' criterion, and of their application to particular cross-questions. These controversies are often reventilated on appeal, and reversals for error in their determination are frequent. Observance of these vague and ambiguous restrictions is a matter of constant and hampering concern to the cross-examiner. If these efforts, delays and misprisions were the necessary incidents to the guarding of substantive rights or the fundamentals of fair trial, they might be worth the cost. As the price of the choice of an obviously debatable regulation of the order of evidence, the sacrifice seems misguided. The American Bar Association's Committee for the Improvement of the Law of Evidence for the year 1937–38 said this:

'The rule limiting cross-examination to the precise subject of the direct examination is probably the most frequent rule (except the Opinion rule) leading in the trial practice today to refined and technical quibbles which obstruct the progress of the trial, confuse the jury, and give rise to appeal on technical grounds only. Some of the instances in which Supreme Courts have ordered new trials for the mere transgression of this rule about the order of evidence have been astounding.

'We recommend that the rule allowing questions upon any part of the issue known to the witness * * * be adopted. * * * '" McCormick, § 27, p. 51. See also 5 Moore's Federal Practice ¶ 43.10 (2nd ed. 1964).

The provision of the second sentence, that the judge may in the interests of justice limit inquiry into new matters on cross-examination, is designed for those situations in which the result otherwise would be confusion, complication, or protraction of the case, not as a matter of rule but as demonstrable in the actual development of the particular case.

The rule does not purport to determine the extent to which an accused who elects to testify thereby waives his privilege against self-incrimination. The question is a constitutional one, rather than a mere matter of administering the trial. Under *Simmons v. United States,* 390 U.S. 377, 88 S.Ct. 967, 19 L.Ed.2d 1247 (1968), no general waiver occurs when the accused testifies on such preliminary matters as the validity of a search and seizure or the admissibility of a confession. Rule 104(d), *supra.* When he testifies on the merits, however, can he foreclose inquiry into an aspect or element of the crime by avoiding it on direct? The affirmative answer given in *Tucker v. United States,* 5 F.2d 818 (8th Cir.1925), is inconsistent with the description of the waiver as extending to "all other relevant facts" in *Johnson v. United States,* 318 U.S. 189, 195, 63 S.Ct. 549, 87 L.Ed. 704 (1943). See also *Brown v. United States,* 356 U.S. 148, 78 S.Ct. 622, 2 L.Ed.2d 589 (1958). The situation of an accused who desires to testify on some but not all counts of a multiple-count indictment is one to be approached, in the first instance at least, as a problem of severance under Rule 14 of the Federal Rules of Criminal Procedure. *Cross v. United States,* 118 U.S.App. D.C. 324, 335 F.2d 987 (1964). Cf. *United States v. Baker,* 262 F.Supp. 657, 686 (D.D.C.1966). In all events, the extent of the waiver of the privilege against self-incrimination ought not to be determined as a by-product of a rule on scope of cross-examination.

Note to Subdivision (c). The rule continues the traditional view that the suggestive powers of the leading question are as a general proposition undesirable. Within this tradition, however, numerous exceptions have achieved recognition: The witness who is hostile, unwilling, or biased; the child witness or the adult with communication problems; the witness whose recollection is exhausted; and undisputed preliminary matters. 3 Wigmore §§ 774–778. An almost total unwillingness to reverse for infractions has been manifested by appellate courts. See cases cited in 3 Wigmore § 770. The matter clearly falls within the area of control by the judge over the mode and order of interrogation and presentation and accordingly is phrased in words of suggestion rather than command.

The rule also conforms to tradition in making the use of leading questions on cross-examination a matter of right. The purpose of the qualification "ordinarily" is to furnish a basis for denying the use of leading questions when the cross-examination is cross-examination in form only and not in fact, as for example the "cross-examination" of a party by his own counsel after being called by the opponent (savoring more of re-direct) or of an insured defendant who proves to be friendly to the plaintiff.

The final sentence deals with categories of witnesses automatically regarded and treated as hostile. Rule 43(b) of the Federal Rules of Civil Procedure has included only "an adverse party or an officer, director, or managing agent of a public or private corporation or of a partnership or association which is an adverse party." This limitation virtually to persons whose statements would stand as admissions is believed to be an unduly narrow concept of those who may safely be regarded as hostile without further demonstration. See, for example, *Maryland Casualty Co. v. Kador,* 225 F.2d 120 (5th Cir.1955), and *Degelos v. Fidelity and Casualty Co.,* 313 F.2d 809 (5th Cir.1963), holding despite the language of Rule 43(b) that an insured fell within it, though not a party in an action under the Louisiana direct action statute. The phrase of the rule, "witness identified with" an adverse party, is designed to enlarge the category of persons thus callable.

1974 Enactment

Note to Subdivision (b). As submitted by the Court, Rule 611(b) provided:

> A witness may be cross-examined on any matter relevant to any issue in the case, including credibility. In the interests of justice, the judge may limit cross-examination with respect to matters not testified to on direct examination.

The Committee amended this provision to return to the rule which prevails in the federal courts and thirty-nine State jurisdictions. As amended, the Rule is in the text of the 1969 Advisory Committee draft. It limits cross-examination to credibility and to matters testified to on direct examination, unless the judge permits more, in which event the cross-examiner must proceed as if on direct examination. This traditional rule facilitates orderly presentation by each party at trial. Further, in light of existing discovery procedures, there appears to be no need to abandon the traditional rule.

Note to Subdivision (c). The third sentence of Rule 611(c) as submitted by the Court provided that:

> In civil cases, a party is entitled to call an adverse party or witness identified with him and interrogate by leading questions.

The Committee amended this Rule to permit leading questions to be used with respect to any hostile witness, not only an adverse party or person identified with such adverse party. The Committee also substituted the word "When" for the phrase "In civil cases" to reflect the possibility that in criminal cases a defendant may be entitled to call witnesses identified with the government, in which event the Committee believed the defendant should be permitted to inquire with leading questions. House Report No. 93–650.

Note to Subdivision (b). Rule 611(b) as submitted by the Supreme Court permitted a broad scope of cross-examination: "cross-examination on any matter relevant to any issue in the case" unless the judge, in the interests of justice, limited the scope of cross-examination.

The House narrowed the Rule to the more traditional practice of limiting cross-examination to the subject matter of direct examination (and credibility), but with discretion in the judge to permit inquiry into additional matters in situations where that would aid in the development of the evidence or otherwise facilitate the conduct of the trial.

The committee agrees with the House amendment. Although there are good arguments in support of broad cross-examination from perspectives of developing all relevant evidence, we believe the factors of insuring an orderly and predictable development of the evidence weigh in favor of the narrower rule, especially when discretion is given to the trial judge to permit inquiry into additional matters. The committee expressly approves this discretion and believes it will permit sufficient flexibility allowing a broader scope of cross-examination whenever appropriate.

The House amendment providing broader discretionary cross-examination permitted inquiry into additional matters only as if on direct examination. As a general rule, we concur with this limitation, however, we would understand that this limitation would not preclude the utilization of leading questions if the conditions of subsection (c) of this rule were met, bearing in mind the judge's discretion in any case to limit the scope of cross-examination [see McCormick on Evidence, §§ 24–26 (especially 24) (2d ed. 1972)].

Further, the committee has received correspondence from Federal judges commenting on the applicability of this rule to section 1407 of title 28. It is the committee's judgment that this rule as reported by the House is flexible enough to provide sufficiently broad cross-examination in appropriate situations in multidistrict litigation.

Note to Subdivision (c). As submitted by the Supreme Court, the rule provided: "In civil cases, a party is entitled to call an adverse party or witness identified with him and interrogate by leading questions."

The final sentence of subsection (c) was amended by the House for the purpose of clarifying the fact that a "hostile witness"—that is a witness who is hostile in fact—could be subject to interrogation by leading questions. The rule as submitted by the Supreme Court declared certain witnesses hostile as a matter of law and thus subject to interrogation by leading questions without any showing of hostility in fact. These were adverse parties or witnesses identified with adverse parties. However, the wording of the first sentence of subsection (c) while generally prohibiting the use of leading questions on direct examination, also provides "except as may be necessary to develop his testimony." Further, the first paragraph of the Advisory Committee note explaining the subsection makes clear that they intended that leading questions could be asked of a hostile witness or a witness who was unwilling or biased and even though that witness was not associated with an adverse party. Thus, we question whether the House amendment was necessary.

However, concluding that it was not intended to affect the meaning of the first sentence of the subsection and was intended solely to clarify the fact that leading questions are permissible in the interrogation of a witness, who is hostile in fact, the committee accepts that House amendment.

The final sentence of this subsection was also amended by the House to cover criminal as well as civil cases. The committee accepts this amendment, but notes that it may be difficult in criminal cases to determine when a witness is "identified with an adverse party," and thus the rule should be applied with caution. Senate Report No. 93–1277.

1987 Amendments

The amendment is technical. No substantive change is intended.

Rule 612. Writing Used to Refresh Memory

Except as otherwise provided in criminal proceedings by section 3500 of title 18, United States Code, if a witness uses a writing to refresh memory for the purpose of testifying, either—

(1) while testifying, or

(2) before testifying, if the court in its discretion determines it is necessary in the interests of justice,

an adverse party is entitled to have the writing produced at the hearing, to inspect it, to cross-examine the witness thereon, and to introduce in evidence those portions which relate to the testimony of the witness. If it is claimed that the writing contains matters not related to the subject matter of the testimony the court shall examine the writing in camera, excise any portions not so related, and order delivery of the remainder to the party entitled thereto. Any portion withheld over objections shall be preserved and made available to the appellate court in the event of an appeal. If a writing is not produced or delivered pursuant to order under this rule, the court shall make any order justice requires, except that in criminal cases when the prosecution elects not to comply, the order shall be one striking the testimony or, if the court in its discretion determines that the interests of justice so require, declaring a mistrial.

(Pub.L. 93–595, § 1, Jan. 2, 1975, 88 Stat. 1936; Mar. 2, 1987, eff. Oct. 1, 1987.)

ADVISORY COMMITTEE NOTES

1972 Proposed Rules

The treatment of writings used to refresh recollection while on the stand is in accord with settled doctrine. McCormick § 9, p. 15. The bulk of the case law has, however, denied the existence of any right to access by the opponent when the writing is used prior to taking the stand, though the judge may have discretion in the matter. *Goldman v. United States,* 316 U.S. 129, 62 S.Ct. 993, 86 L.Ed. 1322 (1942); *Needelman v. United States,* 261 F.2d 802 (5th Cir.1958), cert. dismissed 362 U.S. 600, 80 S.Ct. 960, 4 L.Ed.2d 980, rehearing denied 363 U.S. 858, 80 S.Ct. 1606, 4 L.Ed.2d 1739, Annot., 82 A.L.R.2d 473, 562 and 7 A.L.R.3d 181, 247. An increasing group of cases has repudiated the distinction. *People v. Scott,* 29 Ill.2d 97, 193 N.E.2d 814 (1963); *State v. Mucci,* 25 N.J. 423, 136 A.2d 761 (1957); *State v. Hunt,* 25 N.J. 514, 138 A.2d 1 (1958); *State v. Deslovers,* 40 R.I. 89, 100 A. 64 (1917), and this position is believed to be correct. As Wigmore put it, "the risk of imposition and the need of safeguard is just as great" in both situations. 3 Wigmore § 762, p. 111. To the same effect is McCormick, § 9, p. 17.

The purpose of the phrase "for the purpose of testifying" is to safeguard against using the rule as a pretext for wholesale exploration of an opposing party's files and to insure that access is limited only to those writings which may fairly be said in fact to have an impact upon the testimony of the witness.

The purpose of the rule is the same as that of the *Jencks* statute, 18 U.S.C. § 3500: to promote the search of credibility and memory. The same sensitivity to disclosure of government files may be involved; hence the rule is expressly made subject to the statute, subdivision (a) of which provides: "In any criminal prosecution brought by the United States, no statement or report in the possession of the United States which was made by a Government witness or prospective Government witness (other than the defendant) shall be the subject of subpena, discovery, or inspection until said witness has testified on direct examination in the trial of the case." Items falling within the purview of the statute are producible only as provided by its terms, *Palermo v. United States,* 360 U.S. 343, 351 (1959), and disclosure under the rule is limited similarly by the statutory conditions. With this limitation in mind, some differences of application may be noted. The *Jencks* statute applies only to statements of witnesses; the rule is not so limited. The statute applies only to criminal cases; the rule applies to all cases. The statute applies only to government witnesses; the rule applies to all witnesses. The statute contains no requirement that the statement be consulted for purposes of refreshment before or while testifying; the rule so requires. Since many writings would qualify under either statute or rule, a substantial overlap exists, but the identity of procedures makes this of no importance.

The consequences of nonproduction by the government in a criminal case are those of the *Jencks* statute, striking the testimony or in exceptional cases a mistrial. 18 U.S.C. § 3500(d). In other cases these alternatives are unduly limited, and such possibilities as contempt, dismissal, finding issues against the offender, and the like are available. See Rule 16(g) of the Federal Rules of Criminal Procedure and Rule 37(b) of the Federal Rules of Civil Procedure for appropriate sanctions.

1974 Enactment

As submitted to Congress, Rule 612 provided that except as set forth in 18 U.S.C. 3500, if a witness uses a writing to refresh his memory for the purpose of testifying, "either before or while testifying," an adverse party is entitled to have the writing produced at the hearing, to inspect it, to cross-examine the witness on it, and to introduce in evidence those portions relating to the witness' testimony. The Committee amended the Rule so as still to require the production of writings used by a witness while testifying, but to render the production of writings used by a witness to refresh his memory before testifying discretionary with the court in the interests of justice, as is the case under existing federal law. See Goldman v. United States, 316 U.S. 129 (1942). The Committee considered that permitting an adverse party to require the production of writings used before testifying could result in fishing expeditions among a multitude of papers which a witness may have used in preparing for trial.

The Committee intends that nothing in the Rule be construed as barring the assertion of a privilege with respect to writings used by a witness to refresh his memory. House Report No. 93–650.

1987 Amendments

The amendment is technical. No substantive change is intended.

Rule 613. Prior Statements of Witnesses

(a) Examining witness concerning prior statement. In examining a witness concerning a prior statement made by the witness, whether written or not, the statement need not be shown nor its contents disclosed to the witness at that time, but on request the same shall be shown or disclosed to opposing counsel.

(b) Extrinsic evidence of prior inconsistent statement of witness. Extrinsic evidence of a prior inconsistent statement by a witness is not admissible unless the witness is afforded an opportunity to explain or deny the same and the opposite party is afforded an opportunity to interrogate the witness thereon, or the interests of justice otherwise require. This provision does not apply to admissions of a party-opponent as defined in rule 801(d)(2).

(Pub.L. 93–595, § 1, Jan. 2, 1975, 88 Stat.1936; Mar. 2, 1987, eff. Oct. 1, 1987; Apr. 25, 1988, eff. Nov. 1, 1988.)

ADVISORY COMMITTEE NOTES

1972 Proposed Rules

Note to Subdivision (a). The Queen's Case, 2 Br. & B. 284, 129 Eng.Rep. 976 (1820), laid down the requirement that a cross-examiner, prior to questioning the witness about his own prior statement in writing, must first show it to the witness. Abolished by statute in the country of its origin, the requirement nevertheless gained currency in the United States. The rule abolishes this useless impediment, to cross-examination. Ladd, Some Observations on Credibility: Impeachment of Witnesses, 52 Cornell L.Q. 239, 246–247 (1967); McCormick § 28; 4 Wigmore §§ 1259–1260. Both oral and written statements are included.

The provision for disclosure to counsel is designed to protect against unwarranted insinuations that a statement has been made when the fact is to the contrary.

The rule does not defeat the application of Rule 1002 relating to production of the original when the contents of a writing are sought to be proved. Nor does it defeat the application of Rule 26(b)(3) of the Rules of Civil Procedure, as revised, entitling a person on request to a copy of his own statement, though the operation of the latter may be suspended temporarily.

Note to Subdivision (b). The familiar foundation requirement that an impeaching statement first be shown to the witness before it can be proved by extrinsic evidence is preserved but with some modifications. See Ladd, Some Observations on Credibility: Impeachment of Witnesses, 52 Cornell L.Q. 239, 247 (1967). The traditional insistence that the attendance of the witness be directed to the statement on cross-examination is relaxed in favor of simply providing the witness an opportunity to explain and the opposite party an opportunity to examine on the statement, with no specification of any particular time or sequence. Under this procedure, several collusive witnesses can be examined before disclosure of a joint prior inconsistent statement. See Comment to California Evidence Code § 770. Also, dangers of oversight are reduced. See McCormick § 37, p. 68.

In order to allow for such eventualities as the witness becoming unavailable by the time the statement is discovered, a measure of discretion is conferred upon the judge. Similar provisions are found in California Evidence Code § 770 and New Jersey Evidence Rule 22(b).

Under principles of *expression unius* the rule does not apply to impeachment by evidence of prior inconsistent conduct. The use of inconsistent statements to impeach a hearsay declaration is treated in Rule 806.

1987 Amendments

The amendments are technical. No substantive change is intended.

1988 Amendments

The amendment is technical. No substantive change is intended.

Rule 614. Calling and Interrogation of Witnesses by Court

(a) Calling by court. The court may, on its own motion or at the suggestion of a party, call witnesses, and all parties are entitled to cross-examine witnesses thus called.

(b) Interrogation by court. The court may interrogate witnesses, whether called by itself or by a party.

(c) Objections. Objections to the calling of witnesses by the court or to interrogation by it may be made at the time or at the next available opportunity when the jury is not present.

(Pub.L. 93–595, § 1, Jan. 2, 1975, 88 Stat.1937.)

ADVISORY COMMITTEE NOTES

1972 Proposed Rules

Note to Subdivision (a). While exercised more frequently in criminal than in civil cases, the authority of the judge to call witnesses is well established. McCormick § 8, p. 14; Maguire, Weinstein, et al., Cases on Evidence 303–304 (5th ed. 1965); 9 Wigmore § 2484. One reason for the practice, the old rule against impeaching one's own witness, no longer exists by virtue of Rule 607, *supra.* Other reasons remain, however, to justify the continuation of the practice of calling court's witnesses. The right to cross-examine, with all it implies, is assured. The tendency of juries to associate a witness with the party calling him, regardless of technical aspects of vouching, is avoided. And the judge is not imprisoned within the case as made by the parties.

Note to Subdivision (b). The authority of the judge to question witnesses is also well established. McCormick § 8, pp. 12–13; Maguire, Weinstein, et al., Cases on Evidence 737–739 (5th ed. 1965); 3 Wigmore § 784. The authority is, of course, abused when the judge abandons his proper role and assumes that of advocate, but the manner in which interrogation should be conducted and the proper extent of its exercise are not susceptible of formulation in a rule. The omission in no sense precludes courts of review from continuing to reverse for abuse.

Note to Subdivision (c). The provision relating to objections is designed to relieve counsel of the embarrassment attendant upon objecting to questions by the judge in the presence of the jury, while at the same time assuring that objections are made in apt time to afford the opportunity to take possible corrective measures. Compare the "automatic" objection feature of Rule 605 when the judge is called as a witness.

Rule 615. Exclusion of Witnesses

At the request of a party the court shall order witnesses excluded so that they cannot hear the testimony of other witnesses, and it may make the order of its own motion. This rule does not authorize exclusion of (1) a party who is a natural person, or (2) an officer or employee of a party which is not a natural person designated as its representative by its attorney, or (3) a person whose presence is shown by a party to be essential to the presentation of the party's cause, or (4) a person authorized by statute to be present.

(Pub.L. 93–595, § 1, Jan. 2, 1975, 88 Stat.1937; Mar. 2, 1987, eff. Oct. 1, 1987; Apr. 25, 1988, eff. Nov. 1, 1988; Pub.L. 100–690, Nov. 18, 1988, Title VII, § 7075(a), 102 Stat. 4405; Apr. 24, 1998, eff. Dec. 1, 1998.)

ADVISORY COMMITTEE NOTES

1972 Proposed Rules

The efficacy of excluding or sequestering witnesses has long been recognized as a means of discouraging and exposing fabrication, inaccuracy, and collusion. 6 Wigmore §§ 1837–1838. The authority of the judge is admitted, the only question being whether the matter is committed to his discretion or one of right. The rule takes the latter position. No time is specified for making the request.

Several categories of persons are excepted. (1) Exclusion of persons who are parties would raise serious problems of confrontation and due process. Under accepted practice they are not subject to exclusion. 6 Wigmore § 1841. (2) As the equivalent of the right of a natural-person party to be present, a party which is not a natural person is entitled to have a representative present. Most of the cases have involved allowing a police officer who has been in charge of an investigation to remain in court despite the fact that he will be a witness. United States v. Infanzon, 235 F.2d 318, (2d Cir.1956); *Portomene v. United States,* 221 F.2d 582 (5th Cir.1955); *Powell v. United States,* 208 F.2d 618 (6th Cir. 1953); *Jones v. United States,* 252 F.Supp. 781 (W.D.Okl. 1966). Designation of the representative by the attorney rather than by the client may at first glance appear to be an inversion of the attorney-client relationship, but it may be assumed that the attorney will follow the wishes of the client, and the solution is simple and workable. See California Evidence Code § 777. (3) The category contemplates such persons as an agent who handled the transaction being litigated or an expert needed to advise counsel in the management of the litigation. See 6 Wigmore § 1841, n. 4.

1974 Enactment

Many district courts permit government counsel to have an investigative agent at counsel table throughout the trial although the agent is or may be a witness. The practice is permitted as an exception to the rule of exclusion and compares with the situation defense counsel finds himself in—he always has the client with him to consult during the trial. The investigative agent's presence may be extremely important to government counsel, especially when the case is complex or involves some specialized subject matter. The agent, too, having lived with the case for a long time, may be able to assist in meeting trial surprises where the best-prepared counsel would otherwise have difficulty. Yet, it would not seem the Government could often meet the burden under rule 615 of showing that the agent's presence is essential. Furthermore, it could be dangerous to use the agent as a witness as early in the case as possible, so that he might then help counsel as a nonwitness, since the agent's testimony could be needed in rebuttal. Using another, non-witness agent from the same investigative agency would not generally meet government counsel's needs.

This problem is solved if it is clear that investigative agents are within the group specified under the second exception made in the rule, for "an officer or employee of a party which is not a natural person designated as its representative by its attorney." It is our understanding that this was the intention of the House committee. It is certainly this committee's construction of the rule. Senate Report No. 93–1277.

1987 Amendments

The amendment is technical. No substantive change is intended.

1988 Amendments

The amendment is technical. No substantive change is intended.

1998 Amendments

The amendment is in response to: (1) the Victim's Rights and Restitution Act of 1990, 42 U.S.C. § 10606, which guarantees, within certain limits, the right of a crime victim to attend the trial; and (2) the Victim Rights Clarification Act of 1997 (18 U.S.C. § 3510).

HISTORICAL NOTES

1988 Amendments

Pub.L. 100–690 inserted "a" before "party which is not a natural person".

Rules 616 to 700. Reserved for future legislation

ARTICLE VII. OPINIONS AND EXPERT TESTIMONY

Rule 701. Opinion Testimony by Lay Witnesses

If the witness is not testifying as an expert, the witness' testimony in the form of opinions or inferences is limited to those opinions or inferences which are (a) rationally based on the perception of the witness, (b) helpful to a clear understanding of the witness' testimony or the determination of a fact in issue, and (c) not based on scientific, technical, or other specialized knowledge within the scope of Rule 702.

(Pub.L. 93–595, § 1, Jan. 2, 1975, 88 Stat.1937; Mar. 2, 1987, eff. Oct. 1, 1987; Apr. 17, 2000, eff. Dec. 1, 2000.)

ADVISORY COMMITTEE NOTES

1972 Proposed Rules

The rule retains the traditional objective of putting the trier of fact in possession of an accurate reproduction of the event.

Limitation (a) is the familiar requirement of first-hand knowledge or observation.

Limitation (b) is phrased in terms of requiring testimony to be helpful in resolving issues. Witnesses often find difficulty in expressing themselves in language which is not that of an opinion or conclusion. While the courts have made concessions in certain recurring situations, necessity as a standard for permitting opinions and conclusions has proved too elusive and too unadaptable to particular situations for purposes of satisfactory judicial administration. McCormick § 11. Moreover, the practical impossibility of determining by rule what is a "fact," demonstrated by a century of litigation of the question of what is a fact for purposes of pleading under the Field Code, extends into evidence also. 7 Wigmore § 1919. The rule assumes that the natural characteristics of the adversary system will generally lead to an acceptable result, since the detailed account carries more conviction than the broad assertion, and a lawyer can be expected to display his witness to the best advantage. If he fails to do so, cross-examination and argument will point up the weakness. See Ladd, Expert Testimony, 5 Vand.L.Rev. 414, 415–417 (1952). If, despite these considerations, attempts are made to introduce meaningless assertions which amount to little more than choosing up sides, exclusion for lack of helpfulness is called for by the rule.

The language of the rule is substantially that of Uniform Rule 56(1). Similar provisions are California Evidence Code § 800; Kansas Code of Civil Procedure § 60–456(a); New Jersey Evidence Rule 56(1).

1987 Amendments

The amendments are technical. No substantive change is intended.

2000 Amendments

Rule 701 has been amended to eliminate the risk that the reliability requirements set forth in Rule 702 will be evaded through the simple expedient of proffering an expert in lay witness clothing. Under the amendment, a witness' testimony must be scrutinized under the rules regulating expert opinion to the extent that the witness is providing testimony based on scientific, technical, or other specialized knowledge within the scope of Rule 702. *See generally Asplundh Mfg. Div. v. Benton Harbor Eng'g*, 57 F.3d 1190 (3d Cir. 1995). By channeling testimony that is actually expert testimony to Rule 702, the amendment also ensures that a party will not evade the expert witness disclosure requirements set forth in Fed.R.Civ.P. 26 and Fed.R.Crim.P. 16 by simply calling an expert witness in the guise of a layperson. *See* Joseph, *Emerging Expert Issues Under the 1993 Disclosure Amendments to the Federal Rules of Civil Procedure*, 164 F.R.D. 97, 108 (1996) (noting that "there is no good reason to allow what is essentially surprise expert testimony." and that "the Court should be vigilant to preclude manipulative conduct designed to thwart the expert disclosure and discovery process") *See also United States v. Figueroa–Lopez*, 125 F.3d 1241, 1246 (9th Cir. 1997) (law enforcement agents testifying that the defendant's conduct was consistent with that of a drug trafficker could not testify as lay witnesses; to permit such testimony under Rule 701 "subverts the requirements of Federal Rule of Criminal Procedure 16(a)(1)(E)").

The amendment does not distinguish between expert and lay *witnesses*, but rather between expert and lay *testimony*. Certainly it is possible for the same witness to provide both lay and expert testimony in a single case. *See, e.g, United States v. Figueroa–Lopez*, 125 F.3d 1241, 1246 (9th Cir. 1997) (law enforcement agents could testify that the defendant was acting suspiciously, without being qualified as experts; however, the rules on experts were applicable where the agents testified on the basis of extensive experience that the defendant was using code words to refer to drug quantities and prices). The amendment makes clear that any part of a witness' testimony that is based upon scientific, technical, or other specialized knowledge within the scope of Rule 702 is governed by the standards of Rule 702 and the corresponding disclosure requirements of the Civil and Criminal Rules.

The amendment is not intended to affect the "prototypical example[s] of the type of evidence contemplated by the adoption of Rule 701 relat[ing] to the appearance of persons or things, identity, the manner of conduct, competency of a person, degrees of light or darkness, sound, size, weight, distance, and an endless number of items that cannot be described factually in words apart from inferences." *Asplundh Mfg. Div. v. Benton Harbor Eng' g*, 57 F.3d 1190, 1196 (3d Cir. 1995).

For example, most courts have permitted the owner or officer of a business to testify to the value or projected profits of the business, without the necessity of qualifying the witness as an accountant, appraiser, or similar expert. *See, e.g., Lightning Lube, Inc. v. Witco Corp.* 4 F.3d 1153 (3d Cir. 1993) (no abuse of discretion in permitting the plaintiff's owner to give lay opinion testimony as to damages, as it was based on his knowledge and participation in the day-to-day affairs of the business). Such opinion testimony is admitted not because of experience, training or specialized knowledge within the realm of an expert, but because of the particularized knowledge that the witness has by virtue of his or her position in the business. The amendment does not purport to change this analysis. Similarly, courts have permitted lay witnesses to testify that a substance appeared to be a narcotic, so long as a foundation of familiarity with the substance is established. *See, e.g., United States v. Westbrook*, 896 F.2d 330 (8th Cir. 1990) (two lay witnesses who were heavy amphetamine users were properly permitted to testify that a substance was amphetamine; but it was error to permit another witness to make such an identification where she had no experience with amphetamines). Such testimony is not based on specialized knowledge within the scope of Rule 702, but rather is based upon a layperson's personal knowledge. If, however, that witness were to describe how a narcotic was manufactured, or to describe the intricate workings of a narcotic distribution network, then the witness would have to qualify as an expert under Rule 702. *United States v . Figueroa–Lopez, supra.*

The amendment incorporates the distinctions set forth in *State v. Brown*, 836 S.W.2d 530, 549 (1992), a case involving former Tennessee Rule of Evidence 701, a rule that precluded lay witness testimony based on "special knowledge." In *Brown*, the court declared that the distinction between lay and expert witness testimony is that lay testimony "results from a process of reasoning familiar in everyday life," while expert testimony "results from a process of reasoning which can be mastered only by specialists in the field." The court in *Brown* noted that a lay witness with experience could testify that a substance appeared to be blood, but that a witness would have to qualify as an expert before he could testify that bruising around the eyes is indicative of skull trauma. That is the kind of distinction made by the amendment to this Rule.

GAP Report—Proposed Amendment to Rule 701

The Committee made the following changes to the published draft of the proposed amendment to Evidence Rule 701:

1. The words "within the scope of Rule 702" were added at the end of the proposed amendment, to emphasize that the Rule does not require witnesses to qualify as experts unless their testimony is of the type traditionally considered within the purview of Rule 702. The Committee Note was amended to accord with this textual change.

2. The Committee Note was revised to provide further examples of the kind of testimony that could and could not be proffered under the limitation imposed by the proposed amendment.

Rule 702. Testimony by Experts

If scientific, technical, or other specialized knowledge will assist the trier of fact to understand the evidence or to determine a fact in issue, a witness qualified as an expert by knowledge, skill, experience, training, or education, may testify thereto in the form of an opinion or otherwise, if (1) the testimony is based upon sufficient facts or data, (2) the testimony is the product of reliable principles and methods, and (3) the witness has applied the principles and methods reliably to the facts of the case.

(Pub.L. 93–595, § 1, Jan. 2, 1975, 88 Stat. 1937; Apr. 17, 2000, eff. Dec. 1, 2000.)

ADVISORY COMMITTEE NOTES

1972 Proposed Rules

An intelligent evaluation of facts is often difficult or impossible without the application of some scientific, technical, or other specialized knowledge. The most common source of this knowledge is the expert witness, although there are other techniques for supplying it.

Most of the literature assumes that experts testify only in the form of opinions. The assumption is logically unfounded. The rule accordingly recognizes that an expert on the stand may give a dissertation or exposition of scientific or other principles relevant to the case, leaving the trier of fact to apply them to the facts. Since much of the criticism of expert testimony has centered upon the hypothetical question, it seems wise to recognize that opinions are not indispensable and to encourage the use of expert testimony in non-opinion form when counsel believes the trier can itself draw the requisite inference. The use of opinions is not abolished by the rule, however. It will continue to be permissible for the experts to take the further step of suggesting the inference which should be drawn from applying the specialized knowledge to the facts. See Rules 703 to 705.

Whether the situation is a proper one for the use of expert testimony is to be determined on the basis of assisting the trier. "There is no more certain test for determining when experts may be used than the common sense inquiry whether the untrained layman would be qualified to determine intelligently and to the best possible degree the particular issue without enlightenment from those having a specialized understanding of the subject involved in the dispute." Ladd, Expert Testimony, 5 Vand.L.Rev. 414, 418 (1952). When opinions are excluded, it is because they are unhelpful and therefore superfluous and a waste of time. 7 Wigmore § 1918.

The rule is broadly phrased. The fields of knowledge which may be drawn upon are not limited merely to the "scientific" and "technical" but extend to all "specialized" knowledge. Similarly, the expert is viewed, not in a narrow sense, but as a person qualified by "knowledge, skill, experience, training or education." Thus within the scope of the rule are not only experts in the strictest sense of the word, e.g., physicians, physicists, and architects, but also the large group sometimes called "skilled" witnesses, such as bankers or landowners testifying to land values.

2000 Amendments

Rule 702 has been amended in response to *Daubert v. Merrell Dow Pharmaceuticals, Inc.*, 509 U.S. 579 (1993), and to the many cases applying *Daubert*, including *Kumho Tire Co. v. Carmichael*, 119 S.Ct. 1167 (1999). In *Daubert* the Court charged trial judges with the responsibility of acting as gatekeepers to exclude unreliable expert testimony, and the Court in *Kumho* clarified that this gatekeeper function applies to all expert testimony, not just testimony based in science. *See also Kumho*, 119 S.Ct. at 1178 (citing the Committee Note to the proposed amendment to Rule 702, which had been released for public comment before the date of the *Kumho* decision). The amendment affirms the trial court's role as gatekeeper and provides some general standards that the trial court must use to assess the reliability and helpfulness of proffered expert testimony. Consistently with *Kumho*, the Rule as amended provides that all types of expert testimony present questions of admissibility for the trial court in deciding whether the evidence is reliable and helpful. Consequently, the admissibility of all expert testimony is governed by the principles of Rule 104(a). Under that

Rule, the proponent has the burden of establishing that the pertinent admissibility requirements are met by a preponderance of the evidence. *See Bourjaily v. United States*, 483 U.S. 171 (1987).

Daubert set forth a non-exclusive checklist for trial courts to use in assessing the reliability of scientific expert testimony. The specific factors explicated by the *Daubert* Court are (1) whether the expert's technique or theory can be or has been tested—that is, whether the expert's theory can be challenged in some objective sense, or whether it is instead simply a subjective, conclusory approach that cannot reasonably be assessed for reliability; (2) whether the technique or theory has been subject to peer review and publication; (3) the known or potential rate of error of the technique or theory when applied; (4) the existence and maintenance of standards and controls; and (5) whether the technique or theory has been generally accepted in the scientific community. The Court in *Kumho* held that these factors might also be applicable in assessing the reliability of non-scientific expert testimony, depending upon "the particular circumstances of the particular case at issue." 119 S.Ct. at 1175.

No attempt has been made to "codify" these specific factors. *Daubert* itself emphasized that the factors were neither exclusive nor dispositive. Other cases have recognized that not all of the specific *Daubert* factors can apply to every type of expert testimony. In addition to *Kumho*, 119 S.Ct. at 1175, *see Tyus v. Urban Search Management*, 102 F.3d 256 (7th Cir. 1996) (noting that the factors mentioned by the Court in *Daubert* do not neatly apply to expert testimony from a sociologist). *See also Kannankeril v. Terminix Int'l, Inc.*, 128 F.3d 802, 809 (3d Cir. 1997) (holding that lack of peer review or publication was not dispositive where the expert's opinion was supported by "widely accepted scientific knowledge"). The standards set forth in the amendment are broad enough to require consideration of any or all of the specific *Daubert* factors where appropriate.

Courts both before and after *Daubert* have found other factors relevant in determining whether expert testimony is sufficiently reliable to be considered by the trier of fact. These factors include:

(1) Whether experts are "proposing to testify about matters growing naturally and directly out of research they have conducted independent of the litigation, or whether they have developed their opinions expressly for purposes of testifying." *Daubert v. Merrell Dow Pharmaceuticals, Inc.*, 43 F.3d 1311, 1317 (9th Cir. 1995).

(2) Whether the expert has unjustifiably extrapolated from an accepted premise to an unfounded conclusion. *See General Elec. Co. v. Joiner*, 522 U.S. 136, 146 (1997) (noting that in some cases a trial court "may conclude that there is simply too great an analytical gap between the data and the opinion proffered").

(3) Whether the expert has adequately accounted for obvious alternative explanations. *See Claar v. Burlington N.R.R.*, 29 F.3d 499 (9th Cir. 1994) (testimony excluded where the expert failed to consider other obvious causes for the plaintiff's condition). *Compare Ambrosini v. Labarraque*, 101 F.3d 129 (D.C. Cir. 1996) (the possibility of some uneliminated causes presents a question of weight, so long as the most obvious causes have been considered and reasonably ruled out by the expert).

(4) Whether the expert "is being as careful as he would be in his regular professional work outside his paid litigation consulting." *Sheehan v. Daily Racing Form, Inc.*, 104 F.3d 940, 942 (7th Cir. 1997). *See Kumho Tire Co. v. Carmichael*, 119 S.Ct. 1167, 1176 (1999) (*Daubert* requires the trial court to assure itself that the expert "employs in the courtroom the same level of intellectual rigor that characterizes the practice of an expert in the relevant field").

(5) Whether the field of expertise claimed by the expert is known to reach reliable results for the type of opinion the expert would give. *See Kumho Tire Co. v. Carmichael*, 119 S.Ct.1167, 1175 (1999) (*Daubert's* general acceptance factor does not "help show that an expert's testimony is reliable where the discipline itself lacks reliability, as for example, do theories grounded in any so-called generally accepted principles of astrology or necromancy."), *Moore v. Ashland Chemical, Inc.*, 151 F.3d 269 (5th Cir. 1998) (en banc) (clinical doctor was properly precluded from testifying to the toxicological cause of the plaintiff's respiratory problem, where the opinion was not sufficiently grounded in scientific methodology); *Sterling v. Velsicol Chem. Corp.*, 855 F.2d 1188 (6th Cir. 1988) (rejecting testimony based on "clinical ecology" as unfounded and unreliable).

All of these factors remain relevant to the determination of the reliability of expert testimony under the Rule as amended. Other factors may also be relevant. *See Kumho*, 119 S.Ct. 1167, 1176 ("[W]e conclude that the trial judge must have considerable leeway in deciding in a particular case how to go about determining whether particular expert testimony is reliable."). Yet no single factor is necessarily dispositive of the reliability of a particular expert's testimony. *See, e.g., Heller v. Shaw Industries, Inc.*, 167 F.3d 146, 155 (3d Cir. 1999) ("not only must each stage of the expert's testimony be reliable, but each stage must be evaluated practically and flexibly without bright-line exclusionary (or inclusionary) rules."); *Daubert v. Merrell Dow Pharmaceuticals, Inc.*, 43 F.3d 1311, 1317, n.5 (9th Cir. 1995) (noting that some expert disciplines "have the courtroom as a principal theatre of operations" and as to these disciplines "the fact that the expert has developed an expertise principally for purposes of litigation will obviously not be a substantial consideration.").

A review of the caselaw after *Daubert* shows that the rejection of expert testimony is the exception rather than the rule. *Daubert* did not work a "seachange over federal evidence law," and "the trial court's role as gatekeeper is not intended to serve as a replacement for the adversary system." *United States v. 14.38 Acres of Land Situated in Leflore County, Mississippi*, 80 F.3d 1074, 1078 (5th Cir. 1996). As the Court in *Daubert* stated: "Vigorous cross-examination, presentation of contrary evidence, and careful instruction on the burden of proof are the traditional and appropriate means of attacking shaky but admissible evidence." 509 U.S. at 595. Likewise, this amendment is not intended to provide an excuse for an automatic challenge to the testimony of every expert. *See Kumho Tire Co. v . Carmichael*, 119 S.Ct.1167, 1176 (1999) (noting that the trial judge has the discretion "both to avoid unnecessary 'reliability' proceedings in ordinary cases where the reliability of an expert's methods is properly taken for granted, and to require appropriate proceedings in the less usual or more complex cases where cause for questioning the expert's reliability arises.").

When a trial court, applying this amendment, rules that an expert's testimony is reliable, this does not necessarily mean that contradictory expert testimony is unreliable. The amendment is broad enough to permit testimony that is the product of competing principles or methods in the same field of expertise. *See, e.g., Heller v. Shaw Industries, Inc.*, 167 F.3d 146, 160 (3d Cir. 1999) (expert testimony cannot be excluded simply because the expert uses one test rather than another, when both tests are accepted in the field and both reach reliable results). As the court stated in *In re Paoli R.R. Yard PCB Litigation*, 35 F.3d 717, 744 (3d Cir. 1994), proponents "do not have to demonstrate to the judge by a preponderance of the evidence that the assessments of their experts are correct, they only have to demonstrate by a preponderance of evidence that their opinions are reliable.... The evidentiary requirement of reliability is lower than the merits standard of correctness." *See also Daubert v. Merrell Dow Pharmaceuticals, Inc.*, 43 F.3d 1311, 1318 (9th Cir. 1995) (scientific experts might be permitted to testify if they could show that the methods they used were also employed by "a recognized minority of scientists in their field."); *Ruiz-Troche v. Pepsi Cola*, 161 F.3d 77, 85 (1st Cir. 1998) ("*Daubert* neither requires nor empowers trial courts to determine which of several competing scientific theories has the best provenance.").

The Court in *Daubert* declared that the "focus, of course, must be solely on principles and methodology, not on the conclusions they generate." 509 U.S. at 595. Yet as the Court later recognized, "conclusions and methodology are not entirely distinct from one another." *General Elec. Co. v. Joiner*, 522 U.S. 136, 146 (1997). Under the amendment, as under *Daubert*, when an expert purports to apply principles and methods in accordance with professional standards, and yet reaches a conclusion that other experts in the field would not reach, the trial court may fairly suspect that the principles and methods have not been faithfully applied. *See Lust v. Merrell Dow Pharmaceuticals, Inc.*, 89 F.3d 594, 598 (9th Cir. 1996). The amendment specifically provides that the trial court must scrutinize not only the principles and methods used by the expert, but also whether those principles and methods have been properly applied to the facts of the case. As the court noted in *In re Paoli R.R. Yard PCB Litig.*, 35 F.3d 717, 745 (3d Cir. 1994), "*any* step that renders the analysis unreliable ... renders the expert's testimony inadmissible. *This is true whether the step completely changes a reliable methodology or merely misapplies that methodology.*"

If the expert purports to apply principles and methods to the facts of the case, it is important that this application be conducted reliably. Yet it might also be important in some cases for an expert to educate the factfinder about general principles, without ever attempting to apply these principles to the specific facts of the case. For example, experts might instruct the factfinder on the principles of thermodynamics, or bloodclotting, or on how financial markets respond to corporate reports, without ever knowing about or trying to tie their testimony into the facts of the case. The amendment does not alter the venerable practice of using expert testimony to educate the factfinder on general principles. For this kind of generalized testimony, Rule 702 simply requires that: (1) the expert be qualified; (2) the testimony address a subject matter on which the factfinder can be assisted by an expert; (3) the testimony be reliable; and (4) the testimony "fit" the facts of the case.

As stated earlier, the amendment does not distinguish between scientific and other forms of expert testimony. The trial court's gatekeeping function applies to testimony by any expert. *See Kumho Tire Co. v. Carmichael*, 119 S.Ct. 1167, 1171 (1999) ("We conclude that *Daubert's* general holding—setting forth the trial judge's general 'gatekeeping' obligation—applies not only to testimony based on 'scientific' knowledge, but also to testimony based on 'technical' and 'other specialized' knowledge."). While the relevant factors for determining reliability will vary from expertise to expertise, the amendment rejects the premise that an expert's testimony should be treated more permissively simply because it is outside the realm of science. An opinion from an expert who is not a scientist should receive the same degree of scrutiny for reliability as an opinion from an expert who purports to be a scientist. *See Watkins v. Telsmith, Inc.*, 121 F.3d 984, 991 (5th Cir. 1997) ("[I]t seems exactly backwards that experts who purport to rely on general engineering principles and practical experience might escape screening by the district court simply by stating that their conclusions were not reached by any particular method or technique."). Some types of expert testimony will be more objectively verifiable, and subject to the expectations of falsifiability, peer review, and publication, than others. Some types of expert testimony will not rely on anything like a scientific method, and so will have to be evaluated by reference to other standard principles attendant to the particular area of expertise. The trial judge in all cases of proffered expert testimony must find that it is properly grounded, well-reasoned, and not speculative before it can be admitted. The expert's testimony must be grounded in an accepted body of learning or experience in the expert's field, and the expert must explain how the conclusion is so grounded. *See, e.g.*, American College of Trial Lawyers, *Standards and Procedures for Determining the Admissibility of Expert Testimony after* Daubert, *157 F.R.D. 571, 579 (1994) ("[W]hether the testimony concerns economic principles, accounting standards, property valuation or other non-scientific subjects, it should be evaluated by reference to the 'knowledge and experience' of that particular field.")*.

The amendment requires that the testimony must be the product of reliable principles and methods that are reliably applied to the facts of the case. While the terms "principles" and "methods" may convey a certain impression when applied to scientific knowledge, they remain relevant when applied to testimony based on technical or other specialized knowledge. For example, when a law enforcement agent testifies regarding the use of code words in a drug transaction, the principle used by the agent is that participants in such transactions regularly use code words to conceal the nature of their activities. The method used by the agent is the application of extensive experience to analyze the meaning of the conversations. So long as the principles and methods are reliable and applied reliably to the facts of the case, this type of testimony should be admitted.

Nothing in this amendment is intended to suggest that experience alone—or experience in conjunction with other knowledge, skill, training or education—may not provide a sufficient foundation for expert testimony. To the contrary, the text of Rule 702 expressly contemplates that an expert may be qualified on the basis of experience. In certain fields, experience is the predominant, if not sole, basis for a great deal of reliable expert testimony. *See, e.g., United States v. Jones*, 107 F.3d 1147 (6th Cir. 1997) (no abuse of discretion in admitting the testimony of a handwriting examiner who had years of practical experience and extensive training, and who explained his methodology in detail); *Tassin v. Sears Roebuck*, 946 F.Supp. 1241, 1248 (M.D.La. 1996) (design engineer's testimony can be admissible when the expert's opinions "are based on facts, a reasonable investigation, and traditional technical/mechanical expertise, and he provides a reasonable link between the information and procedures he uses and the conclusions he reaches"). *See also Kumho Tire Co. v. Carmichael*, 119 S.Ct. 1167, 1178 (1999) (stating that "no one denies that an expert might draw a conclusion from a set of observations based on extensive and specialized experience.").

If the witness is relying solely or primarily on experience, then the witness must explain how that experience leads to the conclusion reached, why that experience is a sufficient basis for the opinion, and how that experience is reliably applied to the facts. The trial court's gatekeeping function requires more than simply "taking the expert's word for it." *See Daubert v. Merrell Dow Pharmaceuticals, Inc.*, 43 F.3d 1311, 1319 (9th Cir. 1995) ("We've been presented with only the experts' qualifications, their conclusions and their assurances of reliability. Under *Daubert*, that's not enough."). The more subjective and controversial the expert's inquiry, the more likely the testimony should be excluded as unreliable. *See O'Conner v. Commonwealth Edison Co.*, 13 F.3d 1090 (7th Cir. 1994) (expert testimony based on a completely subjective methodology held properly excluded). *See also Kumho Tire Co. v. Carmichael*, 119 S.Ct . 1167, 1176 (1999) ("[I]t will at times be useful to ask even of a witness whose expertise is based purely on experience, say, a perfume tester able to distinguish among 140 odors at a sniff, whether his preparation is of a kind that others in the field would recognize as acceptable.").

Subpart (1) of Rule 702 calls for a quantitative rather than qualitative analysis. The amendment requires that expert testimony be based on sufficient underlying "facts or data." The term "data" is intended to encompass the reliable opinions of other experts. See the original Advisory Committee Note to Rule 703. The language "facts or data" is broad enough to allow an expert to rely on hypothetical facts that are supported by the evidence. *Id.*

When facts are in dispute, experts sometimes reach different conclusions based on competing versions of the facts. The emphasis in the amendment on " sufficient facts or data" is not intended to authorize a trial court to exclude an expert's testimony on the ground that the court believes one version of the facts and not the other.

There has been some confusion over the relationship between Rules 702 and 703. The amendment makes clear that the sufficiency of the basis of an expert' s testimony is to be decided under Rule 702. Rule 702 sets forth the overarching requirement of reliability, and an analysis of the sufficiency of the expert's basis cannot be divorced from the ultimate reliability of the expert's opinion. In contrast, the "reasonable reliance" requirement of Rule 703 is a relatively narrow inquiry. When an expert relies on inadmissible information, Rule 703 requires the trial court to determine whether that information is of a type reasonably relied on by other experts in the field. If so, the expert can rely on the information in reaching an opinion. However, the question whether the expert is relying on a *sufficient* basis of information—whether admissible information or not—is governed by the requirements of Rule 702.

The amendment makes no attempt to set forth procedural requirements for exercising the trial court's gatekeeping function over expert testimony. *See* Daniel J. Capra, *The Daubert Puzzle*, 38 Ga.L.Rev. 699, 766 (1998) ("Trial courts should be allowed substantial discretion in dealing with *Daubert* questions; any attempt to codify procedures will likely give rise to unnecessary changes in practice and create difficult questions for appellate review."). Courts have shown considerable ingenuity and flexibility in considering challenges to expert testimony under *Daubert*, and it is contemplated that this will continue under the amended Rule. *See, e.g., Cortes-Irizarry v. Corporacion Insular*, 111 F.3d 184 (1st Cir. 1997) (discussing the application of *Daubert* in ruling on a motion for summary judgment); *In re Paoli R.R. Yard PCB Litig.*, 35 F.3d 717, 736, 739 (3d Cir. 1994) (discussing the use of *in limine* hearings); *Claar v. Burlington N.R.R.*, 29 F.3d 499, 502–05 (9th Cir. 1994) (discussing the trial court's technique of ordering experts to submit serial affidavits explaining the reasoning and methods underlying their conclusions).

The amendment continues the practice of the original Rule in referring to a qualified witness as an "expert." This was done to provide continuity and to minimize change. The use of the term "expert" in the Rule does not, however, mean that a jury should actually be informed that a qualified witness is testifying as an "expert." Indeed, there is much to be said for a practice that prohibits the use of the term "expert" by both the parties and the court at trial. Such a practice "ensures that trial courts do not inadvertently put their stamp of authority" on a witness's opinion, and protects against the jury's being "overwhelmed by the so-called 'experts'." Hon. Charles Richey, *Proposals to Eliminate the Prejudicial Effect of the Use of the Word "Expert" Under the Federal Rules of Evidence in Criminal and Civil Jury Trials*, 154 F.R.D. 537, 559 (1994) (setting forth limiting instructions and a standing order employed to prohibit the use of the term " expert" injury trials).

GAP Report—Proposed Amendment to Rule 702

The Committee made the following changes to the published draft of the proposed amendment to Evidence Rule 702:

1. The word "reliable" was deleted from Subpart (1) of the proposed amendment, in order to avoid an overlap with Evidence Rule 703, and to clarify that an expert opinion need not be excluded simply because it is based on hypothetical facts. The Committee Note was amended to accord with this textual change.

2. The Committee Note was amended throughout to include pertinent references to the Supreme Court's decision in *Kumho Tire Co. v. Carmichael*, which was rendered after the proposed amendment was released for public comment. Other citations were updated as well.

3. The Committee Note was revised to emphasize that the amendment is not intended to limit the right to jury trial, nor to permit a challenge to the testimony of every expert, nor to preclude the testimony of experience-based experts, nor to prohibit testimony based on competing methodologies within a field of expertise.

4. Language was added to the Committee Note to clarify that no single factor is necessarily dispositive of the reliability inquiry mandated by Evidence Rule 702.

Rule 703. Bases of Opinion Testimony by Experts

The facts or data in the particular case upon which an expert bases an opinion or inference may be those perceived by or made known to the expert at or before the hearing. If of a type reasonably relied upon by experts in the particular field in forming opinions or inferences upon the subject, the facts or data need not be admissible in evidence in order for the opinion or inference to be admitted. Facts or data that are otherwise inadmissible shall not be disclosed to the jury by the proponent of the opinion or inference unless the court determines that their probative value in assisting the jury to evaluate the expert's opinion substantially outweighs their prejudicial effect.

(Pub.L. 93–595, § 1, Jan. 2, 1975, 88 Stat.1937; Mar. 2, 1987, eff. Oct. 1, 1987; Apr. 17, 2000, eff. Dec. 1, 2000.)

ADVISORY COMMITTEE NOTES

1972 Proposed Rules

Facts or data upon which expert opinions are based may, under the rule, be derived from three possible sources. The first is the firsthand observation of the witness with opinions based thereon traditionally allowed. A treating physician affords an example. Rheingold, The Basis of Medical Testimony, 15 Vand.L.Rev. 473, 489 (1962). Whether he must first relate his observations is treated in Rule 705. The second source, presentation at the trial, also reflects existing practice. The technique may be the familiar hypothetical question or having the expert attend the trial and hear the testimony establishing the facts. Problems of determining what testimony the expert relied upon, when the latter technique is employed and the testimony is in conflict, may be resolved by resort to Rule 705. The third source contemplated by the rule consists of presentation of data to the expert outside of court and other than by his own perception. In this respect the rule is designed to broaden the basis for expert opinions beyond that current in many jurisdictions and to bring the judicial practice into line with the practice of the experts themselves when not in court. Thus a physician in his own practice bases his diagnosis on information from numerous sources and of considerable variety, including statements by patients and relatives, reports and opinions from nurses, technicians and other doctors, hospital records, and X rays. Most of them are admissible in evidence, but only with the expenditure of substantial time in producing and examining various authenticating witnesses. The physician makes life-and-death decisions in reliance upon them. His validation, expertly performed and subject to cross-examination, ought to suffice for judicial purposes. Rheingold, *supra*, at 531; McCormick § 15. A similar provision is California Evidence Code § 801(b).

The rule also offers a more satisfactory basis for ruling upon the admissibility of public opinion poll evidence. Attention is directed to the validity of the techniques employed rather than to relatively fruitless inquiries whether hearsay is involved. See Judge Feinberg's careful analysis in Zippo Mfg. Co. v. Rogers Imports, Inc., 216 F.Supp. 670 (S.D.N.Y. 1963). See also Blum et al., The Art of Opinion Research: A Lawyer's Appraisal of an Emerging Service, 24 U.Chi.L.Rev. 1 (1956); Bonynge Trademark Surveys and Techniques and Their Use in Litigation, 48 A.B.A.J. 329 (1962); Zeisel, The Uniqueness of Survey Evidence, 45 Cornell L.Q. 322 (1960); Annot., 76 A.L.R.2d 919.

If it be feared that enlargement of permissible data may tend to break down the rules of exclusion unduly, notice should be taken that the rule requires that the facts or data "be of a type reasonably relied upon by experts in the particular field." The language would not warrant admitting in evidence the opinion of an "accidentologist" as to the point of impact in an automobile collision based on statements of bystanders since this requirement is not satisfied. See Comment, Cal.Law Rev.Comm'n, Recommendation Proposing an Evidence Code 148–150 (1965).

1987 Amendments

The amendment is technical. No substantive change is intended.

2000 Amendments

Rule 703 has been amended to emphasize that when an expert reasonably relies on inadmissible information to form an opinion or inference, the underlying information is not admissible simply because the opinion or inference is admitted. Courts have reached different results on how to treat inadmissible information when it is reasonably relied upon by an expert in forming an opinion or drawing an inference. *Compare United States v. Rollins*, 862 F.2d 1282 (7th Cir. 1988) (admitting, as part of the basis of an FBI agent's expert opinion on the meaning of code language, the hearsay statements of an informant), *with United States v. 0.59 Acres of Land*, 109 F.3d 1493 (9th Cir. 1997) (error to admit hearsay offered as the basis of an expert opinion, without a limiting instruction). Commentators have also taken differing views. *See e.g.*, Ronald Carlson, *Policing the Bases of Modern Expert Testimony*, 39 Vand.L.Rev. 577 (1986) (advocating limits on the jury's consideration of otherwise inadmissible evidence used as the basis for an expert opinion); Paul Rice, *Inadmissible Evidence as a Basis for Expert Testimony: A Response to Professor Carlson*, 40 Vand.L.Rev. 583 (1987) (advocating unrestricted use of information reasonably relied upon by an expert).

When information is reasonably relied upon by an expert and yet is admissible only for the purpose of assisting the jury in evaluating an expert's opinion, a trial court applying this Rule must consider the information's probative value in assisting the jury to weigh the expert's opinion on the one hand, and the risk of prejudice resulting from the jury's potential misuse of the information for substantive purposes on the other. The information may be disclosed to the jury, upon objection, only if the trial court finds that the probative value of the information in assisting the jury to evaluate the expert's opinion substantially outweighs its prejudicial effect. If the otherwise inadmissible information is admitted under this balancing test, the trial judge must give a limiting instruction upon request, informing the jury that the underlying information must not be used for substantive purposes. *See* Rule 105. In determining the appropriate course, the trial court should consider the probable effectiveness or lack of effectiveness of a limiting instruction under the particular circumstances.

The amendment governs only the disclosure to the jury of information that is reasonably relied on by an expert, when that information is not admissible for substantive purposes. It is not intended to affect the admissibility of an expert's testimony. Nor does the amendment prevent an expert from relying on information that is inadmissible for substantive purposes.

Nothing in this Rule restricts the presentation of underlying expert facts or data when offered by an adverse party. *See* Rule 705. Of course, an adversary's attack on an expert's basis will often open the door to a proponent's rebuttal with information that was reasonably relied upon by the expert, even if that information would not have been discloseable initially under the balancing test provided by this amendment. Moreover, in some circumstances the proponent might wish to disclose information that is relied upon by the expert in order to "remove the sting" from the opponent's anticipated attack, and thereby prevent the jury from drawing an unfair negative inference. The trial court should take this consideration into account in applying the balancing test provided by this amendment.

This amendment covers facts or data that cannot be admitted for any purpose other than to assist the jury to evaluate the expert's opinion. The balancing test provided in this amendment is not applicable to facts or data that are admissible for any other purpose but have not yet been offered for such a purpose at the time the expert testifies.

The amendment provides a presumption against disclosure to the jury of information used as the basis of an expert's opinion and not admissible for any substantive purpose, when that information is offered by the proponent of the expert. In a multi-party case, where one party proffers an expert whose testimony is also beneficial to other parties, each such party should be deemed a "proponent" within the meaning of the amendment.

GAP Report—Proposed Amendment to Rule 703

The Committee made the following changes to the published draft of the proposed amendment to Evidence Rule 703:

1. A minor stylistic change was made in the text, in accordance with the suggestion of the Style Subcommittee of the Standing Committee on Rules of Practice and Procedure.

2. The words "in assisting the jury to evaluate the expert's opinion" were added to the text, to specify the proper purpose for offering the otherwise inadmissible information relied on by an expert. The Committee Note was revised to accord with this change in the text.

3. Stylistic changes were made to the Committee Note.

4. The Committee Note was revised to emphasize that the balancing test set forth in the proposal should be used to determine whether an expert's basis may be disclosed to the jury either (1) in rebuttal or (2) on direct examination to "remove the sting" of an opponent's anticipated attack on an expert's basis.

Rule 704. Opinion on Ultimate Issue

(a) Except as provided in subdivision (b), testimony in the form of an opinion or inference otherwise admissible is not objectionable because it embraces an ultimate issue to be decided by the trier of fact.

(b) No expert witness testifying with respect to the mental state or condition of a defendant in a criminal case may state an opinion or inference as to whether the defendant did or did not have the mental state or condition constituting an element of the crime charged or of a defense thereto. Such ultimate issues are matters for the trier of fact alone.

(Pub.L. 93–595, § 1, Jan. 2, 1975, 88 Stat. 1937; Pub.L. 98–473, Title IV, § 406, Oct. 12, 1984, 98 Stat. 2067.)

ADVISORY COMMITTEE NOTES

1972 Proposed Rules

The basic approach to opinions, lay and expert, in these rules is to admit them when helpful to the trier of fact. In order to render this approach fully effective and to allay any doubt on the subject, the so-called "ultimate issue" rule is specifically abolished by the instant rule.

The older cases often contained strictures against allowing witnesses to express opinions upon ultimate issues, as a particular aspect of the rule against opinions. The rule was unduly restrictive, difficult of application, and generally served only to deprive the trier of fact of useful information. 7 Wigmore §§ 1920, 1921; McCormick § 12. The basis usually assigned for the rule, to prevent the witness from "usurping the province of the jury," is aptly characterized as "empty rhetoric." 7 Wigmore § 1920, p. 17. Efforts to meet the felt needs of particular situations led to odd verbal circumlocutions which were said not to violate the rule. Thus a witness could express his estimate of the criminal responsibility of an accused in terms of sanity or insanity, but not in terms of ability to tell right from wrong or other more modern standard. And in cases of medical causation, witnesses were sometimes required to couch their opinions in cautious phrases of "might or could," rather than "did," though the result was to deprive many opinions of the positiveness to which they were entitled, accompanied by the hazard of a ruling of insufficiency to support a verdict. In other instances the rule was simply disregarded, and, as concessions to need, opinions were allowed upon such matters as intoxication, speed, handwriting, and value, although more precise coincidence with an ultimate issue would scarcely be possible.

Many modern decisions illustrate the trend to abandon the rule completely. People v. Wilson, 25 Cal.2d 341, 153 P.2d 720 (1944), whether abortion necessary to save life of patient; *Clifford–Jacobs Forging Co. v. Industrial Comm.*, 19 Ill.2d 236, 166 N.E.2d 582 (1960), medical causation; *Dowling v. L. H. Shattuck,* Inc., 91 N.H. 234, 17 A.2d 529 (1941), proper method of shoring ditch; *Schweiger v. Solbeck,* 191 Or. 454, 230 P.2d 195 (1951), cause of landslide. In each instance the opinion was allowed.

The abolition of the ultimate issue rule does not lower the bars so as to admit all opinions. Under Rules 701 and 702, opinions must be helpful to the trier of fact, and Rule 403 provides for exclusion of evidence which wastes time. These provisions afford ample assurances against the admission of opinions which would merely tell the jury what result to reach, somewhat in the manner of the oath-helpers of an earlier day. They also stand ready to exclude opinions phrased in terms of inadequately explored legal criteria. Thus the question, "Did T have capacity to make a will?" would be excluded, while the question, "Did T have sufficient mental capacity to know the nature and extent of his property and the natural objects of his bounty and to formulate a rational scheme of distribution?" would be allowed. McCormick § 12.

For similar provisions see Uniform Rule 56(4); California Evidence Code § 805; Kansas Code of Civil Procedure § 60–456(d); New Jersey Evidence Rule 56(3).

Rule 705. Disclosure of Facts or Data Underlying Expert Opinion

The expert may testify in terms of opinion or inference and give reasons therefor without first testifying to the underlying facts or data, unless the court requires otherwise. The expert may in any event be required to disclose the underlying facts or data on cross-examination.

(Pub.L. 93–595, § 1, Jan. 2, 1975, 88 Stat. 1938; Mar. 2, 1987, eff. Oct. 1, 1987; Apr. 22, 1993, eff. Dec. 1, 1993.)

ADVISORY COMMITTEE NOTES

1972 Proposed Rules

The hypothetical question has been the target of a great deal of criticism as encouraging partisan bias, affording an opportunity for summing up in the middle of the case, and as complex and time consuming. Ladd, Expert Testimony, 5 Vand.L.Rev. 414, 426–427 (1952). While the rule allows counsel to make disclosure of the underlying facts or data as a preliminary to the giving of an expert opinion, if he chooses, the instances in which he is required to do so are reduced. This is true whether the expert bases his opinion on data furnished him at secondhand or observed by him at firsthand.

The elimination of the requirement of preliminary disclosure at the trial of underlying facts or data has a long background of support. In 1937 the Commissioners on Uniform State Laws incorporated a provision to this effect in their Model Expert Testimony Act, which furnished the basis for Uniform Rules 57 and 58. Rule 4515, N.Y. CPLR (McKinney 1963), provides:

"Unless the court orders otherwise, questions calling for the opinion of an expert witness need not be hypothetical in form, and the witness may state his opinion and reasons without first specifying the data upon which it is based. Upon cross-examination, he may be required to specify the data * * *."

See also California Evidence Code § 802; Kansas Code of Civil Procedure §§ 60–456, 60–457; New Jersey Evidence Rules 57, 58.

If the objection is made that leaving it to the cross-examiner to bring out the supporting data is essentially unfair, the answer is that he is under no compulsion to bring out any facts or data except those unfavorable to the opinion. The answer assumes that the cross-examiner has the advance knowledge which is essential for effective cross-examination. This advance knowledge has been afforded, though imperfectly, by the traditional foundation requirement. Rule 26(b)(4) of the Rules of Civil Procedure, as revised, provides for substantial discovery in this area, obviating in large measure the obstacles which have been raised in some instances to discovery of findings, underlying data, and even the identity of the experts. Friedenthal Discovery and Use of an Adverse Party's Expert Information, 14 Stan.L.Rev. 455 (1962).

These safeguards are reinforced by the discretionary power of the judge to require preliminary disclosure in any event.

1987 Amendment

The amendment is technical. No substantive change is intended.

1993 Amendment

This rule, which relates to the manner of presenting testimony at trial, is revised to avoid an arguable conflict with revised Rules 26(a)(2)(B) and 26(e)(1) of the Federal Rules of Civil Procedure or with revised Rule 16 of the Federal Rules of Criminal Procedure, which require disclosure in advance of trial of the basis and reasons for an expert's opinions.

If a serious question is raised under Rule 702 or 703 as to the admissibility of expert testimony, disclosure of the underlying facts or data on which opinions are based may, of course, be needed by the court before deciding whether, and to what extent, the person should be allowed to testify. This rule does not preclude such an inquiry.

Rule 706. Court Appointed Experts

(a) Appointment. The court may on its own motion or on the motion of any party enter an order to show cause why expert witnesses should not be appointed, and may request the parties to submit nominations. The court may appoint any expert witnesses agreed upon by the parties, and may appoint expert witnesses of its own selection. An expert witness shall not be appointed by the court unless the witness consents to act. A witness so appointed shall be informed of the witness' duties by the court in writing, a copy of which shall be filed with the clerk, or at a conference in which the parties shall have opportunity to participate. A witness so appointed shall advise the parties of the witness' findings, if any; the witness' deposition may be taken by any party; and the witness may be called to testify by the court or any party. The witness shall be subject to cross-examination by each party, including a party calling the witness.

(b) Compensation. Expert witnesses so appointed are entitled to reasonable compensation in whatever sum the court may allow. The compensation thus fixed is payable from funds which may be provided by law in criminal cases and civil actions and proceedings involving just compensation under the fifth amendment. In other civil actions and proceedings the compensation shall be paid by the parties in such proportion and at such time as the court directs, and thereafter charged in like manner as other costs.

(c) Disclosure of appointment. In the exercise of its discretion, the court may authorize disclosure to the jury of the fact that the court appointed the expert witness.

(d) Parties' experts of own selection. Nothing in this rule limits the parties in calling expert witnesses of their own selection.

(Pub.L. 93–595, § 1, Jan. 2, 1975, 88 Stat.1938; Mar. 2, 1987, eff. Oct. 1, 1987.)

ADVISORY COMMITTEE NOTES

1972 Proposed Rules

The practice of shopping for experts, the venality of some experts, and the reluctance of many reputable experts to involve themselves in litigation, have been matters of deep concern. Though the contention is made that court appointed experts acquire an aura of infallibility to which they are not entitled, Levy, Impartial Medical Testimony—Revisited, 34 Temple L.Q. 416 (1961), the trend is increasingly to provide for their use. While experience indicates that actual appointment is a relatively infrequent occurrence, the assumption may be made that the availability of the procedure in itself decreases the need for resorting to it. The ever-present possibility that the judge may appoint an expert in a given case must inevitably exert a sobering effect on the expert witness of a party and upon the person utilizing his services.

The inherent power of a trial judge to appoint an expert of his own choosing is virtually unquestioned. *Scott v. Spanjer Bros., Inc.,* 298 F.2d 928 (2d Cir.1962); *Danville Tobacco Assn. v. Bryant–Buckner Associates,* Inc., 333 F.2d 202 (4th Cir.1964); Sink, The Unused Power of a Federal Judge to Call His Own Expert Witnesses, 29 S.Cal.L.Rev. 195 (1956); 2 Wigmore § 563, 9 *id.* § 2484; Annot., 95 A.L.R.2d 383. Hence the problem becomes largely one of detail.

The New York plan is well known and is described in Report by Special Committee of the Association of the Bar of the City of New York: Impartial Medical Testimony (1956). On recommendation of the Section of Judicial Administration, local adoption of an impartial medical plan was endorsed by the American Bar Association. 82 A.B.A.Rep. 184–185 (1957). Descriptions and analyses of plans in effect in various parts of the country are found in Van Dusen, A United States District Judge's View of the Impartial Medical Expert System, 32 F.R.D. 498 (1963); Wick and Kightlinger, Impartial Medical Testimony Under the Federal Civil Rules: A Tale of Three Doctors, 34 Ins. Counsel J. 115 (1967); and numerous articles collected in Klein, Judicial Administration and the Legal Profession 393 (1963). Statutes and rules include California Evidence Code §§ 730–733; Illinois Supreme Court Rule 215(d), Ill.Rev.Stat.1969, c. 110A, § 215(d); Burns Indiana Stats.1956, § 9–1702; Wisconsin Stats.Annot.1958, § 957.27.

In the federal practice, a comprehensive scheme for court appointed experts was initiated with the adoption of Rule 28 of the Federal Rules of Criminal Procedure in 1946. The Judicial Conference of the United States in 1953 considered court appointed experts in civil cases, but only with respect to whether they should be compensated from public funds, a proposal which was rejected. Report of the Judicial Conference of the United States 23 (1953). The present rule expands the practice to include civil cases.

Note to Subdivision (a). Subdivision (a) is based on Rule 28 of the Federal Rules of Criminal Procedure, with a few changes, mainly in the interest of clarity. Language has been added to provide specifically for the appointment either on motion of a party or on the judge's own motion. A provision subjecting the court appointed expert to deposition procedures has been incorporated. The rule has been revised to make definite the right of any party, including the party calling him, to cross-examine.

Note to Subdivision (b). Subdivision (b) combines the present provision for compensation in criminal cases with what seems to be a fair and feasible handling of civil cases, originally found in the Model Act and carried from there into Uniform Rule 60. See also California Evidence Code §§ 730–731. The special provision for Fifth Amendment compensation cases is designed to guard against reducing constitutionally guaranteed just compensation by requiring the recipient to pay costs. See Rule 71A(*l*) of the Rules of Civil Procedure.

Note to Subdivision (c). Subdivision (c) seems to be essential if the use of court appointed experts is to be fully effective. Uniform Rule 61 so provides.

Note to Subdivision (d). Subdivision (d) is in essence the last sentence of Rule 28(a) of the Federal Rules of Criminal Procedure.

1987 Amendment

The amendments are technical. No substantive change is intended.

ARTICLE VIII. HEARSAY

ADVISORY COMMITTEE NOTES

1972 Proposed Rules

Introductory Note; The Hearsay Problem. The factors to be considered in evaluating the testimony of a witness are perception, memory, and narration. Morgan, Hearsay Dangers and the Application of the Hearsay Concept, 62 Harv. L.Rev. 177 (1948), Selected Writings on Evidence and Trial 764, 765 (Fryer ed. 1957); Shientag, Cross-Examination—A Judge's Viewpoint, 3 Record 12 (1948); Strahorn, A Reconsideration of the Hearsay Rule and Admissions, 85 U.Pa. L.Rev. 484, 485 (1937), Selected Writings, *supra,* 756, 757; Weinstein, Probative Force of Hearsay, 46 Iowa L.Rev. 331 (1961). Sometimes a fourth is added, sincerity, but in fact it seems merely to be an aspect of the three already mentioned.

In order to encourage the witness to do his best with respect to each of these factors, and to expose any inaccuracies which may enter in, the Anglo–American tradition has evolved three conditions under which witnesses will ideally be required to testify: (1) under oath, (2) in the personal presence of the trier of fact, (3) subject to cross-examination.

(1) Standard procedure calls for the swearing of witnesses. While the practice is perhaps less effective than in an earlier time, no disposition to relax the requirement is apparent, other than to allow affirmation by persons with scruples against taking oaths.

(2) The demeanor of the witness traditionally has been believed to furnish trier and opponent with valuable clues. *Universal Camera Corp. v. N.L.R.B.*, 340 U.S. 474, 495–496, 71 S.Ct. 456, 95 L.Ed. 456 (1951); Sahm, Demeanor Evidence: Elusive and Intangible Imponderables, 47 A.B.A.J. 580 (1961), quoting numerous authorities. The witness himself will probably be impressed with the solemnity of the occasion and the possibility of public disgrace. Willingness to falsify may reasonably become more difficult in the presence of the person against whom directed. Rules 26 and 43(a) of the Federal Rules of Criminal and Civil Procedure, respectively, include the general requirement that testimony be taken orally in open court. The Sixth Amendment right of confrontation is a manifestation of these beliefs and attitudes.

(3) Emphasis on the basis of the hearsay rule today tends to center upon the condition of cross-examination. All may not agree with Wigmore that cross-examination is "beyond doubt the greatest legal engine ever invented for the discovery of truth," but all will agree with his statement that it has become a "vital feature" of the Anglo–American system. 5 Wigmore § 1367, p. 29. The belief, or perhaps hope, that cross-examination is effective in exposing imperfections of perception, memory, and narration is fundamental. Morgan, Foreword to Model Code of Evidence 37 (1942).

The logic of the preceding discussion might suggest that no testimony be received unless in full compliance with the three ideal conditions. No one advocates this position. Common sense tells that much evidence which is not given under the three conditions may be inherently superior to much that is. Moreover, when the choice is between evidence which is less than best and no evidence at all, only clear folly would dictate an across-the-board policy of doing without. The problem thus resolves itself into effecting a sensible accommodation between these considerations and the desirability of giving testimony under the ideal conditions.

The solution evolved by the common law has been a general rule excluding hearsay but subject to numerous exceptions under circumstances supposed to furnish guarantees of trustworthiness. Criticisms of this scheme are that it is bulky and complex, fails to screen good from bad hearsay realistically, and inhibits the growth of the law of evidence.

Since no one advocates excluding all hearsay, three possible solutions may be considered: (1) abolish the rule against hearsay and admit all hearsay; (2) admit hearsay possessing sufficient probative force, but with procedural safeguards; (3) revise the present system of class exceptions.

(1) Abolition of the hearsay rule would be the simplest solution. The effect would not be automatically to abolish the giving of testimony under ideal conditions. If the declarant were available, compliance with the ideal conditions would be optional with either party. Thus the proponent could call the declarant as a witness as a form of presentation more impressive than his hearsay statement. Or the opponent could call the declarant to be cross-examined upon his statement. This is the tenor of Uniform Rule 63(1), admitting the hearsay declaration of a person "who is present at the hearing and available for cross-examination." Compare the treatment of declarations of available declarants in Rule 801(d)(1) of the instant rules. If the declarant were unavailable, a rule of free admissibility would make no distinctions in terms of degrees of noncompliance with the ideal conditions and would exact no quid pro quo in the form of assurances of trustworthiness. Rule 503 of the Model Code did exactly that, providing for the admissibility of any hearsay declaration by an unavailable declarant, finding support in the Massachusetts act of 1898, enacted at the instance of Thayer, Mass.Gen.L.1932, c. 233, § 65, and in the English act of 1938, St.1938, c. 28, Evidence. Both are limited to civil cases. The draftsmen of the Uniform Rules chose a less advanced and more conventional position. Comment, Uniform Rule 63. The present Advisory Committee has been unconvinced of the wisdom of abandoning the traditional requirement of some particular assurance of credibility as a condition precedent to admitting the hearsay declaration of an unavailable declarant.

In criminal cases, the Sixth Amendment requirement of confrontation would no doubt move into a large part of the area presently occupied by the hearsay rule in the event of the abolition of the latter. The resultant split between civil and criminal evidence is regarded as an undesirable development.

(2) Abandonment of the system of class exceptions in favor of individual treatment in the setting of the particular case, accompanied by procedural safeguards, has been impressively advocated. Weinstein, The Probative Force of Hearsay, 46 Iowa L.Rev. 331 (1961). Admissibility would be determined by weighing the probative force of the evidence against the possibility of prejudice, waste of time, and the availability of more satisfactory evidence. The bases of the traditional hearsay exceptions would be helpful in assessing probative force. Ladd, The Relationship of the Principles of Exclusionary Rules of Evidence to the Problem of Proof, 18 Minn.L.Rev. 506 (1934). Procedural safeguards would consist of notice of intention to use hearsay, free comment by the judge on the weight of the evidence, and a greater measure of authority in both trial and appellate judges to deal with evidence on the basis of weight. The Advisory Committee has rejected this approach to hearsay as involving too great a measure of judicial discretion, minimizing the predictability of rulings, enhancing the difficulties of preparation for trial, adding a further element to the already overcomplicated congeries of pretrial procedures, and requiring substantially different rules for civil and criminal cases. The only way in which the probative force of hearsay differs from the probative force of other testimony is in the absence of oath, demeanor, and cross-examination as aids in determining credibility. For a judge to exclude evidence because he does not believe it has been described as "altogether atypical, extraordinary. * * * " Chadbourn, Bentham and the Hearsay Rule—A Benthamic View of Rule 63(4)(c) of the Uniform Rules of Evidence, 75 Harv.L.Rev. 932, 947 (1962).

(3) The approach to hearsay in these rules is that of the common law, i.e., a general rule excluding hearsay, with exceptions under which evidence is not required to be excluded even though hearsay. The traditional hearsay exceptions are drawn upon for the exceptions, collected under two rules, one dealing with situations where availability of the declarant is regarded as immaterial and the other with those where unavailability is made a condition to the admission of the hearsay statement. Each of the two rules concludes with a provision for hearsay statements not within one of the specified exceptions "but having comparable circumstantial guarantees of trustworthiness." Rules 803(24) and 804(b)(6). This plan is submitted as calculated to encourage growth and development in this area of the law, while conserving the values and experience of the past as a guide to the future.

Confrontation and Due Process. Until very recently, decisions invoking the confrontation clause of the Sixth Amendment were surprisingly few, a fact probably explainable by the former inapplicability of the clause to the states and by the hearsay rule's occupancy of much the same ground. The pattern which emerges from the earlier cases invoking the clause is substantially that of the hearsay rule, applied to criminal cases: an accused is entitled to have the witnesses against him testify under oath, in the presence of himself and trier, subject to cross-examination; yet considerations of public policy and necessity require the recognition of such exceptions as dying declarations and former testimony of unavailable witnesses. *Mattox v. United States,* 156 U.S. 237, 15 S.Ct. 337, 39 L.Ed. 409 (1895); *Motes v. United States,* 178 U.S. 458, 20 S.Ct. 993, 44 L.Ed. 1150 (1900); *Delaney v. United States,* 263 U.S. 586, 44 S.Ct. 206, 68 L.Ed. 462 (1924). Beginning with *Snyder v. Massachusetts,* 291 U.S. 97, 54 S.Ct. 330, 78 L.Ed. 674 (1934), the Court began to speak of confrontation as an aspect of procedural due process, thus extending its applicability to state cases and to federal cases other than criminal. The language of *Snyder* was that of an elastic concept of hearsay. The deportation case of *Bridges v. Wixon,* 326 U.S. 135, 65 S.Ct. 1443, 89 L.Ed. 2103 (1945), may be read broadly as imposing a strictly construed right of confrontation in all kinds of cases or narrowly as the product of a failure of the Immigration and Naturalization Service to follow its own rules. *In re Oliver,* 333 U.S. 257, 68 S.Ct. 499, 92 L.Ed. 682 (1948), ruled that cross-examination was essential to due process in a state contempt proceeding, but in *United States v. Nugent,* 346 U.S. 1, 73 S.Ct. 991, 97 L.Ed. 1417 (1953), the court held that it was not an essential aspect of a "hearing" for a conscientious objector under the Selective Service Act. *Stein v. New York,* 346 U.S. 156, 196, 73 S.Ct. 1077, 97 L.Ed. 1522 (1953), disclaimed any purpose to read the hearsay rule into the Fourteenth Amendment, but in *Greene v. McElroy,* 360 U.S. 474, 79 S.Ct. 1400, 3 L.Ed.2d 1377 (1959), revocation of security clearance without confrontation and cross-examination was held unauthorized, and a similar result was reached in *Willner v. Committee on Character,* 373 U.S. 96, 83 S.Ct. 1175, 10 L.Ed.2d 224 (1963). Ascertaining the constitutional dimensions of the confrontation-hearsay aggregate against the background of these cases is a matter of some difficulty, yet the general pattern is at least not inconsistent with that of the hearsay rule.

In 1965 the confrontation clause was held applicable to the states. *Pointer v. Texas,* 380 U.S. 400, 85 S.Ct. 1065, 13 L.Ed.2d 923 (1965). Prosecution use of former testimony given at a preliminary hearing where petitioner was not represented by counsel was a violation of the clause. The same result would have followed under conventional hearsay doctrine read in the light of a constitutional right to counsel, and nothing in the opinion suggests any difference in essential outline between the hearsay rule and the right of confrontation. In the companion case of *Douglas v. Alabama,* 380 U.S. 415, 85 S.Ct. 1074, 13 L.Ed.2d 934 (1965), however, the result reached by applying the confrontation clause is one reached less readily via the hearsay rule. A confession implicating petitioner was put before the jury by reading it to the witness in portions and asking if he made that statement. The witness refused to answer on grounds of self-incrimination. The result, said the Court, was to deny cross-examination, and hence confrontation. True, it could broadly be said that the confession was a hearsay statement which for all practical purposes was put in evidence. Yet a more easily accepted explanation of the opinion is that its real thrust was in the direction of curbing undesirable prosecutorial behavior, rather than merely applying rules of exclusion, and that the confrontation clause was the means selected to achieve this end. Comparable facts and a like result appeared in *Brookhart v. Janis,* 384 U.S. 1, 86 S.Ct. 1245, 16 L.Ed.2d 314 (1966).

The pattern suggested in *Douglas* was developed further and more distinctly in a pair of cases at the end of the 1966 term. *United States v. Wade,* 388 U.S. 218, 87 S.Ct. 1926, 18 L.Ed.2d 1149 (1967), and *Gilbert v. California,* 388 U.S. 263, 87 S.Ct. 1951, 18 L.Ed.2d 1178 (1967), hinged upon practices followed in identifying accused persons before trial. This pretrial identification was said to be so decisive an aspect of the case that accused was entitled to have counsel present; a pretrial identification made in the absence of counsel was not itself receivable in evidence and, in addition, might fatally infect a courtroom identification. The presence of counsel at the earlier identification was described as a necessary prerequisite for "a meaningful confrontation at trial." *United States v. Wade, supra,* 388 U.S. at p. 236, 87 S.Ct. at p. 1937. *Wade* involved no evidence of the fact of a prior identification and hence was not susceptible of being decided on hearsay grounds. In *Gilbert,* witnesses did testify to an earlier identification, readily classifiable as hearsay under a fairly strict view of what constitutes hearsay. The Court, however, carefully avoided basing the decision on the hearsay ground, choosing confrontation instead. 388 U.S. 263, 272, n. 3, 87 S.Ct. 1951. See also *Parker v. Gladden,* 385 U.S. 363, 87 S.Ct. 468, 17 L.Ed.2d 420 (1966), holding that the right of confrontation was violated when the bailiff made prejudicial statements to jurors, and Note, 75 Yale L.J. 1434 (1966).

Under the earlier cases, the confrontation clause may have been little more than a constitutional embodiment of the hearsay rule, even including traditional exceptions but with some room for expanding them along similar lines. But under the recent cases the impact of the clause clearly extends beyond the confines of the hearsay rule. These considerations have led the Advisory Committee to conclude that a hearsay rule can function usefully as an adjunct to the confrontation right in constitutional areas and independently in nonconstitutional areas. In recognition of the separateness of the confrontation clause and the hearsay rule, and to avoid inviting collisions between them or between the hearsay rule and other exclusionary principles, the exceptions set forth in Rules 803 and 804 are stated in terms of exemption from the general exclusionary mandate of the hearsay rule, rather than in positive terms of admissibility. See Uniform Rule 63(1) to (31) and California Evidence Code §§ 1200–1340.

Rule 801. Definitions

The following definitions apply under this article:

(a) Statement. A "statement" is (1) an oral or written assertion or (2) nonverbal conduct of a person, if it is intended by the person as an assertion.

(b) Declarant. A "declarant" is a person who makes a statement.

(c) Hearsay. "Hearsay" is a statement, other than one made by the declarant while testifying at the trial or hearing, offered in evidence to prove the truth of the matter asserted.

(d) Statements which are not hearsay. A statement is not hearsay if—

(1) Prior statement by witness. The declarant testifies at the trial or hearing and is subject to cross-examination concerning the statement, and the statement is (A) inconsistent with the declarant's testimony, and was given under oath subject to the penalty of perjury at a trial, hearing, or other proceeding, or in a deposition, or (B) consistent with the declarant's testimony and is offered to rebut an express or implied charge against the declarant of recent fabrication or improper influence or motive, or (C) one of identification of a person made after perceiving the person; or

(2) Admission by party-opponent. The statement is offered against a party and is (A) the party's own statement, in either an individual or a representative capacity or (B) a statement of which the party has manifested an adoption or belief in its truth, or (C) a statement by a person authorized by the party to make a statement concerning the subject, or (D) a statement by the party's agent or servant concerning a matter within the scope of the agency or employment, made during the existence of the relationship, or (E) a statement by a coconspirator of a party during the course and in furtherance of the conspiracy. The contents of the statement shall be considered but are not alone sufficient to establish the declarant's authority under subdivision (C), the agency or employment relationship and scope thereof under subdivision (D), or the existence of the conspiracy and the participation therein of the declarant and the party against whom the statement is offered under subdivision (E).

(Pub.L. 93–595, § 1, Jan. 2, 1975, 88 Stat.1938; Pub.L. 94–113, § 1, Oct. 16, 1975, 89 Stat. 576; Mar. 2, 1987, eff. Oct. 1, 1987; Apr. 11, 1997, eff. Dec. 1, 1997.)

ADVISORY COMMITTEE NOTES

1972 Proposed Rules

Note to Subdivision (a). The definition of "statement" assumes importance because the term is used in the definition of hearsay in subdivision (c). The effect of the definition of "statement" is to exclude from the operation of the hearsay rule all evidence of conduct, verbal or nonverbal, not intended as an assertion. The key to the definition is that nothing is an assertion unless intended to be one.

It can scarcely be doubted that an assertion made in words is intended by the declarant to be an assertion. Hence verbal assertions readily fall into the category of "statement." Whether nonverbal conduct should be regarded as a statement for purposes of defining hearsay requires further consideration. Some nonverbal conduct, such as the act of pointing to identify a suspect in a lineup, is clearly the equivalent of words, assertive in nature, and to be regarded as a statement. Other nonverbal conduct, however, may be offered as evidence that the person acted as he did because of his belief in the existence of the condition sought to be proved, from which belief the existence of the condition may be inferred. This sequence is, arguably, in effect an assertion of the existence of the condition and hence properly includable within the hearsay concept. See Morgan, Hearsay Dangers and the Application of the Hearsay Concept, 62 Harv.L.Rev. 177, 214, 217 (1948), and the elaboration in Finman, Implied Assertions as Hearsay: Some Criticisms of the Uniform Rules of Evidence, 14 Stan.L.Rev. 682 (1962). Admittedly evidence of this character is untested with respect to the perception, memory, and narration (or their equivalents) of the actor, but the Advisory Committee is of the view that these dangers are minimal in the absence of an intent to assert and do not justify the loss of the evidence on hearsay grounds. No class of evidence is free of the possibility of fabrication, but the likelihood is less with nonverbal than with assertive verbal conduct. The situations giving rise to the nonverbal conduct are such as virtually to eliminate questions of sincerity. Motivation, the nature of the conduct, and the presence or absence of reliance will bear heavily upon the weight to be given the evidence. Falknor, The "Hear–Say" Rule as a "See–Do" Rule: Evidence of Conduct, 33 Rocky Mt.L.Rev. 133 (1961). Similar considerations govern nonassertive verbal conduct and verbal conduct which is assertive but offered as a basis for inferring something other than the matter asserted, also excluded from the definition of hearsay by the language of subdivision (c).

When evidence of conduct is offered on the theory that it is not a statement, and hence not hearsay, a preliminary determination will be required to determine whether an assertion is intended. The rule is so worded as to place the burden upon the party claiming that the intention existed; ambiguous and doubtful cases will be resolved against him and in favor of admissibility. The determination involves no greater difficulty than many other preliminary questions of fact. Maguire, The Hearsay System: Around and Through the Thicket, 14 Vand.L.Rev. 741, 765–767 (1961).

For similar approaches, see Uniform Rule 62(1); California Evidence Code §§ 225, 1200; Kansas Code of Civil Procedure § 60–459(a); New Jersey Evidence Rule 62(1).

Note to Subdivision (c). The definition follows along familiar lines in including only statements offered to prove the truth of the matter asserted. McCormick § 225; 5 Wigmore § 1361, 6 *id.* § 1766. If the significance of an offered statement lies solely in the fact that it was made, no issue is raised as to the truth of anything asserted, and the statement is not hearsay. *Emich Motors Corp. v. General Motors Corp.*, 181 F.2d 70 (7th Cir.1950), rev'd on other grounds 340 U.S. 558, 71 S.Ct. 408, 95 L.Ed. 534, letters of complaint from customers offered as a reason for cancellation of dealer's franchise, to rebut contention that franchise was revoked for refusal to finance sales through affiliated finance company. The effect is to exclude from hearsay the entire category of "verbal acts" and "verbal parts of an act," in which the statement itself affects the legal rights of the parties or is a circumstance bearing on conduct affecting their rights.

The definition of hearsay must, of course, be read with reference to the definition of statement set forth in subdivision (a).

Testimony given by a witness in the course of court proceedings is excluded since there is compliance with all the ideal conditions for testifying.

Note to Subdivision (d). Several types of statements which would otherwise literally fall within the definition are expressly excluded from it:

(1) *Prior statement by witness.* Considerable controversy has attended the question whether a prior out-of-court statement by a person now available for cross-examination concerning it, under oath and in the presence of the trier of fact, should be classed as hearsay. If the witness admits on the stand that he made the statement and that it was true, he adopts the statement and there is no hearsay problem. The hearsay problem arises when the witness on the stand denies having made the statement or admits having made it but denies its truth. The argument in favor of treating these latter statements as hearsay is based upon the ground that the conditions of oath, cross-examination, and demeanor observation did not prevail at the time the statement was made and cannot adequately be supplied by the later examination. The logic of the situation is troublesome. So far as concerns the oath, its mere presence has never been regarded as sufficient to remove a statement from the hearsay category, and it receives much less emphasis than cross-examination as a truth-compelling device. While strong expressions are found to the effect that no conviction can be had or important right taken away on the basis of statements not made under fear of prosecution for perjury, *Bridges v. Wixon,* 326 U.S. 135, 65 S.Ct. 1443, 89 L.Ed. 2103 (1945), the fact is that, of the many common law exceptions to the hearsay rule, only that for reported testimony has required the statement to have been made under oath. Nor is it satisfactorily explained why cross-examination cannot be conducted subsequently with success. The decisions contending most vigorously for its inadequacy in fact demonstrate quite thorough exploration of the weaknesses and doubts attending the earlier statement. *State v. Saporen,* 205 Minn. 358, 285 N.W. 898 (1939); *Ruhala v. Roby,* 379 Mich. 102, 150 N.W.2d 146 (1967); *People v. Johnson,* 68 Cal.2d 646, 68 Cal.Rptr. 599, 441 P.2d 111 (1968). In respect to demeanor, as Judge Learned Hand observed in *Di Carlo v. United States,* 6 F.2d 364 (2d Cir.1925), when the jury decides that the truth is not what the witness says now, but what he said before, they are still deciding from what they see and hear in court. The bulk of the case law nevertheless has been against allowing prior statements of witnesses to be used generally as substantive evidence. Most of the writers and Uniform Rule 63(1) have taken the opposite position.

The position taken by the Advisory Committee in formulating this part of the rule is funded upon an unwillingness to countenance the general use of prior prepared statements as substantive evidence, but with a recognition that particular circumstances call for a contrary result. The judgment is one more of experience than of logic. The rule requires in each instance, as a general safeguard, that the declarant actually testify as a witness, and it then enumerates three situations in which the statement is excepted from the category of hearsay. Compare Uniform Rule 63(1) which allows any out-of-court statement of a declarant who is present at the trial and available for cross-examination.

(A) Prior inconsistent statements traditionally have been admissible to impeach but not as substantive evidence. Under the rule they are substantive evidence. As has been said by the California Law Revision Commission with respect to a similar provision:

"Section 1235 admits inconsistent statements of witnesses because the dangers against which the hearsay rule is designed to protect are largely nonexistent. The declarant is in court and may be examined and cross-examined in regard to his statements and their subject matter. In many cases, the inconsistent statement is more likely to be true than the testimony of the witness at the trial because it was made nearer in time to the matter to which it relates and is less likely to be influenced by the controversy that gave rise to the litigation. The trier of fact has the declarant before it and can observe his demeanor and the nature of his testimony as he denies or tries to explain away the inconsistency. Hence, it is in as good a position to determine the truth or falsity of the prior statement as it is to determine the truth or falsity of the inconsistent testimony given in court. Moreover, Section 1235 will provide a party with desirable protection against the 'turncoat' witness who changes his story on the stand and deprives the party calling him of evidence essential to his case." Comment, California Evidence Code § 1235. See also McCormick § 39. The Advisory Committee finds these views more convincing than those expressed in *People v. Johnson,* 68 Cal.2d 646, 68 Cal.Rptr. 599, 441 P.2d 111 (1968). The constitutionality of the Advisory Committee's view was upheld in *California v. Green,* 399 U.S. 149, 90 S.Ct. 1930, 26 L.Ed.2d 489 (1970). Moreover, the requirement that the statement be inconsistent with the testimony given assures a thorough exploration of both versions while the witness is on the stand and bars any general and indiscriminate use of previously prepared statements.

(B) Prior consistent statements traditionally have been admissible to rebut charges of recent fabrication or improper influence or motive but not as substantive evidence. Under the rule they are substantive evidence. The prior statement is consistent with the testimony given on the stand, and, if the opposite party wishes to open the door for its admission in evidence, no sound reason is apparent why it should not be received generally.

(C) The admission of evidence of identification finds substantial support, although it falls beyond a doubt in the category of prior out-of-court statements. Illustrative are *People v. Gould,* 54 Cal.2d 621, 7 Cal.Rptr. 273, 354 P.2d 865 (1960); *Judy v. State,* 218 Md. 168, 146 A.2d 29 (1958); *State v. Simmons,* 63 Wash.2d 17, 385 P.2d 389 (1963); California Evidence Code § 1238; New Jersey Evidence Rule 63(1)(c); N.Y.Code of Criminal Procedure § 393–b. Further cases are found in 4 Wigmore § 1130. The basis is the generally unsatisfactory and inconclusive nature of courtroom identifications as compared with those made at an earlier time under less suggestive conditions. The Supreme Court considered the admissibility of evidence of prior identification in *Gilbert v. California,* 388 U.S. 263, 87 S.Ct. 1951, 18 L.Ed.2d 1178 (1967). Exclusion of lineup identification was held to be required because the accused did not then have the assistance of counsel. Significantly, the Court carefully refrained from placing its decision on the ground that testimony as to the making of a prior out-of-court identification ("That's the man") violated either the hearsay rule or the right of confrontation because not made under oath, subject to immediate cross-examination, in the presence of the trier. Instead the Court observed:

"There is a split among the States concerning the admissibility of prior extra-judicial identifications, as independent evidence of identity, both by the witness and third parties present at the prior identification. See 71 ALR2d 449. It has been held that the prior identification is hearsay, and, when admitted through the testimony of the identifier, is merely a prior consistent statement. The recent trend, however, is to admit the prior identification under the exception that admits as substantive evidence a prior communication by a witness who is available for cross-examination at the trial. See 5 ALR2d Later Case Service 1225–1228. * * * " 388 U.S. at 272, n. 3, 87 S.Ct. at 1956.

(2) *Admissions.* Admissions by a party-opponent are excluded from the category of hearsay on the theory that their admissibility in evidence is the result of the adversary system rather than satisfaction of the conditions of the hearsay rule. Strahorn, A Reconsideration of the Hearsay Rule and Admissions, 85 U.Pa.L.Rev. 484, 564 (1937); Morgan, Basic Problems of Evidence 265 (1962); 4 Wigmore § 1048. No guarantee of trustworthiness is required in the case of an admission. The freedom which admissions have enjoyed from technical demands of searching for an assurance of truthworthiness in some against-interest circumstance, and from the restrictive influences of the opinion rule and the rule requiring firsthand knowledge, when taken with the apparently prevalent satisfaction with the results, calls for generous treatment of this avenue to admissibility.

The rule specifies five categories of statements for which the responsibility of a party is considered sufficient to justify reception in evidence against him:

(A) A party's own statement is the classic example of an admission. If he has a representative capacity and the statement is offered against him in that capacity, no inquiry whether he was acting in the representative capacity in making the statement is required; the statement need only be relevant to represent affairs. To the same effect in California Evidence Code § 1220. Compare Uniform Rule 63(7), requiring a statement to be made in a representative capacity to be admissible against a party in a representative capacity.

(B) Under established principles an admission may be made by adopting or acquiescing in the statement of another. While knowledge of contents would ordinarily be essential, this is not inevitably so: "X is a reliable person and knows what he is talking about." See McCormick § 246, p. 527, n. 15. Adoption or acquiescence may be manifested in any appropriate manner. When silence is relied upon, the theory is that the person would, under the circumstances, protest the statement made in his presence, if untrue. The decision in each case calls for an evaluation in terms of probable human behavior. In civil cases, the results have generally been satisfactory. In criminal cases, however, troublesome questions have been raised by decisions holding that failure to deny is an admission: the inference is a fairly weak one, to begin with; silence may be motivated by advice of counsel or realization that "anything you say may be used against you"; unusual opportunity is afforded to manufacture evidence; and encroachment upon the privilege against self-incrimination seems inescapably to be involved. However, recent decisions of the Supreme Court relating to custodial interrogation and the right to counsel appear to resolve these difficulties. Hence the rule contains no special provisions concerning failure to deny in criminal cases.

(C) No authority is required for the general proposition that a statement authorized by a party to be made should have the status of an admission by the party. However, the question arises whether only statements to third persons should be so regarded, to the exclusion of statements by the agent to the principal. The rule is phrased broadly so as to encompass both. While it may be argued that the agent authorized to make statements to his principal does not speak for him, Morgan, Basic Problems of Evidence 273 (1962), communication to an outsider has not generally been thought to be an essential characteristic of an admission. Thus a party's books or records are usable against him, without regard to any intent to disclose to third persons. 5 Wigmore § 1557. See also McCormick § 78, pp. 159–161. In accord is New Jersey Evidence Rule 63(8)(a). Cf. Uniform Rule 63(8)(a) and California Evidence Code § 1222 which limit status as an admission in this regard to statements authorized by the party to be made "for" him, which is perhaps an ambiguous limitation to statements to third persons. Falknor, Vicarious Admissions and the Uniform Rules, 14 Vand.L.Rev. 855, 860–861 (1961).

(D) The tradition has been to test the admissibility of statements by agents, as admissions, by applying the usual test of agency. Was the admission made by the agent acting in the scope of his employment? Since few principals employ agents for the purpose of making damaging statements, the usual result was exclusion of the statement. Dissatisfaction with this loss of valuable and helpful evidence has been increasing. A substantial trend favors admitting statements related to a matter within the scope of the agency or employment. *Grayson v. Williams,* 256 F.2d 61 (10th Cir. 1958); *Koninklijke Luchtvaart Maatschappij N.V. KLM Royal Dutch Airlines v. Tuller,* 110 U.S.App.D.C. 282, 292 F.2d 775, 784 (1961); *Martin v. Savage Truck Lines,* Inc., 121 F.Supp. 417 (D.D.C.1954), and numerous state court decisions collected in 4 Wigmore, 1964 Supp. pp. 66–73, with comments by the editor that the statements should have been excluded as not within scope of agency. For the traditional view see *Northern Oil Co. v. Socony Mobil Oil Co.,* 347 F.2d 81, 85 (2d Cir.1965) and cases cited therein. Similar provisions are found in Uniform Rule 63(9)(a), Kansas Code of Civil Procedure § 60–460(i)(1), and New Jersey Evidence Rule 63(9)(a).

(E) The limitation upon the admissibility of statements of co-conspirators to those made "during the course and in furtherance of the conspiracy" is in the accepted pattern. While the broadened view of agency taken in item (iv) might suggest wider admissibility of statements of co-conspirators, the agency theory of conspiracy is at best a fiction and ought not to serve as a basis for admissibility beyond that already established. See Levie, Hearsay and Conspiracy, 52 Mich. L.Rev. 1159 (1954); Comment, 25 U.Chi.L.Rev. 530 (1958). The rule is consistent with the position of the Supreme Court in denying admissibility to statements made after the objectives of the conspiracy have either failed or been achieved. *Krulewitch v. United States,* 336 U.S. 440, 69 S.Ct. 716, 93 L.Ed. 790 (1949); *Wong Sun v. United States,* 371 U.S. 471, 490, 83 S.Ct. 407, 9 L.Ed.2d 441 (1963). For similarly limited provisions see California Evidence Code § 1223 and New Jersey Rule 63(9)(b). Cf. Uniform Rule 63(9)(b).

1974 Enactment

Note to Subdivision (d)(1). Present federal law, except in the Second Circuit, permits the use of prior inconsistent statements of a witness for impeachment only. Rule 801(d)(1) as proposed by the Court would have permitted all such statements to be admissible as substantive evidence, an approach followed by a small but growing number of State jurisdictions and recently held constitutional in California v. Green, 399 U.S. 149 (1970). Although there was some support expressed for the Court Rule, based largely on the need to counteract the effect of witness intimidation in criminal cases, the Committee decided to adopt a compromise version of the Rule similar to the position of the Second Circuit. The Rule as amended draws a distinction between types of prior inconsistent statements (other than statements of identification of a person made after perceiving him which are currently admissible, see United States v. Anderson, 406 F.2d 719, 720 (4th Cir.), cert. denied, 395 U.S. 967 (1969)) and allows only those made while the declarant was subject to cross-examination at a trial or hearing or in a deposition, to be admissible for their truth. Compare United States v. DeSisto, 329 F.2d 929 (2nd Cir.), cert. denied, 377 U.S. 979 (1964); United States v. Cunningham, 446 F.2d 194 (2nd Cir.1971) (restricting the admissibility of prior inconsistent statements as substantive evidence to those made under oath in a formal proceeding, but not requiring that there have been an opportunity for cross-examination). The rationale for the Committee's decision is that (1) unlike in most other situations involving unsworn or oral statements, there can be no dispute as to whether the prior statement was made; and (2) the context of a formal proceeding, an oath, and the opportunity for cross-examination provide firm additional assurances of the reliability of the prior statement. House Report No. 93–650.

Note to Subdivision (d)(1)(A). Rule 801 defines what is and what is not hearsay for the purpose of admitting a prior statement as substantive evidence. A prior statement of a witness at a trial or hearing which is inconsistent with his testimony is, of course, always admissible for the purpose of impeaching the witness' credibility.

As submitted by the Supreme Court, subdivision (d)(1)(A) made admissible as substantive evidence the prior statement of a witness inconsistent with his present testimony.

The House severely limited the admissibility of prior inconsistent statements by adding a requirement that the prior statement must have been subject to cross-examination, thus precluding even the use of grand jury statements. The requirement that the prior statement must have been subject to cross-examination appears unnecessary since this rule comes into play only when the witness testifies in the present trial. At that time, he is on the stand and can explain an earlier position and be cross-examined as to both.

The requirement that the statement be under oath also appears unnecessary. Notwithstanding the absence of an oath contemporaneous with the statement, the witness, when on the stand, qualifying or denying the prior statement, is under oath. In any event, of all the many recognized exceptions to the hearsay rule, only one (former testimony) requires that the out-of-court statement have been made under oath. With respect to the lack of evidence of the demeanor of the witness at the time of the prior statement, it would be difficult to improve upon Judge Learned Hand's observation that when the jury decides that the truth is not what the witness says now but what he said before, they are still deciding from what they see and hear in court. [*Di Carlo v. U.S.*, 6 F.2d 364 (2d Cir.1925)].

The rule as submitted by the Court has positive advantages. The prior statement was made nearer in time to the events, when memory was fresher and intervening influences had not been brought into play. A realistic method is provided for dealing with the turncoat witness who changes his story on the stand [see Comment, California Evidence Code § 1235; McCormick, Evidence, § 38 (2nd ed. 1972)].

New Jersey, California, and Utah have adopted a rule similar to this one; and Nevada, New Mexico, and Wisconsin have adopted the identical Federal rule.

For all of these reasons, we think the House amendment should be rejected and the rule as submitted by the Supreme Court reinstated. [It would appear that some of the opposition to this Rule is based on a concern that a person could be convicted solely upon evidence admissible under this Rule. The Rule, however, is not addressed to the question of the sufficiency of evidence to send a case to the jury, but merely as to its admissibility. Factual circumstances could well arise where, if this were the sole evidence, dismissal would be appropriate.]

Note to Subdivision (d)(1)(C). As submitted by the Supreme Court and as passed by the House, subdivision (d)(1)(C) of rule 801 made admissible the prior statement identifying a person made after perceiving him. The committee decided to delete this provision because of the concern that a person could be convicted solely upon evidence admissible under this subdivision.

Note to Subdivision 801(d)(2)(E). The House approved the long-accepted rule that "a statement by a coconspirator of a party during the course and in furtherance of the conspiracy" is not hearsay as it was submitted by the Supreme Court. While the rule refers to a coconspirator, it is this committee's understanding that the rule is meant to carry forward the universally accepted doctrine that a joint venturer is considered as a coconspirator for the purposes of this rule even though no conspiracy has been charged. *United States v. Rinaldi*, 393 F.2d 97, 99 (2d Cir.), cert. denied 393 U.S. 913 (1968); *United States v. Spencer*, 415 F.2d 1301, 1304 (7th Cir., 1969). Senate Report No. 93–1277.

Rule 801 supplies some basic definitions for the rules of evidence that deal with hearsay. Rule 801(d)(1) defines certain statements as not hearsay. The Senate amendments make two changes in it.

Note to Subdivision (d)(1)(A). The House bill provides that a statement is not hearsay if the declarant testifies and is subject to cross-examination concerning the statement and if the statement is inconsistent with his testimony and was given under oath subject to cross-examination and subject to the penalty of perjury at a trial or hearing or in a deposition. The Senate amendment drops the requirement that the prior statement be given under oath subject to cross-examination and subject to the penalty of perjury at a trial or hearing or in a deposition.

The Conference adopts the Senate amendment with an amendment, so that the rule now requires that the prior inconsistent statement be given under oath subject to the penalty of perjury at a trial, hearing, or other proceeding, or in a deposition. The rule as adopted covers statements before a grand jury. Prior inconsistent statements may, of course, be used for impeaching the credibility of a witness. When the prior inconsistent statement is one made by a defendant in a criminal case, it is covered by Rule 801(d)(2).

Note to Subdivision (d)(1)(C). The House bill provides that a statement is not hearsay if the declarant testifies and is subject to cross-examination concerning the statement and the statement is one of identification of a person made after perceiving him. The Senate amendment eliminated this provision.

The Conference adopts the Senate amendment. House Report No. 93–1597.

1987 Amendment

The amendments are technical. No substantive change is intended.

1997 Amendment

Rule 801(d)(2) has been amended in order to respond to three issues raised by *Bourjaily v. United States*, 483 U.S. 171 (1987). First, the amendment codifies the holding in *Bourjaily* by stating expressly that a court shall consider the contents of a coconspirator's statement in determining "the existence of the conspiracy and the participation therein of the declarant and the party against whom the statement is offered." According to *Bourjaily*, Rule 104(a) requires these preliminary questions to be established by a preponderance of the evidence.

Second, the amendment resolves an issue on which the Court had reserved decision. It provides that the contents of the declarant's statement do not alone suffice to establish a conspiracy in which the declarant and the defendant participated. The court must consider in addition the circumstances surrounding the statement, such as the identity of the speaker, the context in which the statement was made, or evidence corroborating the contents of the statement in making its determination as to each preliminary question. This amendment is in accordance with existing practice. Every court of appeals that has resolved this issue requires some evidence in addition to the contents of the statement. *See, e.g., United States v. Beckham*, 968 F.2d 47, 51 (D.C.Cir. 1992); *United States v. Sepulveda*, 15 F.3d 1161, 1181–82 (1st Cir.1993), *cert. denied*, 114 S.Ct. 2714 (1994); *United States v. Daly*, 842 F.2d 1380, 1386 (2d Cir.), *cert. denied*, 488 U.S. 821 (1988); *United States v. Clark*, 18 F.3d 1337, 1341–42 (6th Cir.), *cert. denied*, 115 S.Ct. 152 (1994); *United States v. Zambrana*, 841 F.2d 1320, 1344–45 (7th Cir.1988); *United States v. Silverman*, 861 F.2d 571, 577 (9th Cir.1988); *United States v. Gordon*, 844 F.2d 1397, 1402 (9th Cir.1988); *United States v. Hernandez*, 829 F.2d 988, 993 (10th Cir. 1987), *cert. denied*, 485 U.S. 1013 (1988); *United States v. Byrom*, 910 F.2d 725, 736 (11th Cir.1990).

Third, the amendment extends the reasoning of Bourjaily to statements offered under subdivisions (C) and (D) of Rule 801(d)(2). In Bourjaily, the Court rejected treating foundational facts pursuant to the law of agency in favor of an evidentiary approach governed by Rule 104(a). The Advisory Committee believes it appropriate to treat analogously preliminary questions relating to the declarant's authority under subdivision (C), and the agency or employment relationship and scope thereof under subdivision (D).

GAP Report on Rule 801. The word "shall" was substituted for the word "may" in line 19. The second sentence of the committee note was changed accordingly.

HISTORICAL NOTES

For legislative history and purpose of Pub.L. 94–113, see 1975 U.S.Code Cong. and Adm.News, p. 1092.

Effective and Applicability Provisions

1975 Acts. Section 2 of Pub.L. 94–113 provided that: "This Act [enacting cl. (c) of subd. (d)] shall become effective on the fifteenth day after the date of the enactment of this Act [Oct. 16, 1975]."

Rule 802. Hearsay Rule

Hearsay is not admissible except as provided by these rules or by other rules prescribed by the Supreme Court pursuant to statutory authority or by Act of Congress.

(Pub.L. 93–595, § 1, Jan. 2, 1975, 88 Stat. 1939.)

ADVISORY COMMITTEE NOTES

1972 Proposed Rules

The provision excepting from the operation of the rule hearsay which is made admissible by other rules adopted by the Supreme Court or by Act of Congress continues the admissibility thereunder of hearsay which would not qualify under these Evidence Rules. The following examples illustrate the working of the exception:

Federal Rules of Civil Procedure

Rule 4(g): proof of service by affidavit.

Rule 32: admissibility of depositions.

Rule 43(e): affidavits when motion based on facts not appearing of record.

Rule 56: affidavits in summary judgment proceedings.

Rule 65(b): showing by affidavit for temporary restraining order.

Federal Rules of Criminal Procedure

Rule 4(a): affidavits to show grounds for issuing warrants.

Rule 12(b)(4): affidavits to determine issues of fact in connection with motions.

Acts of Congress

10 U.S.C. § 7730: affidavits of unavailable witnesses in actions for damages caused by vessel in naval service, or towage or salvage of same, when taking of testimony or bringing of action delayed or stayed on security grounds.

29 U.S.C. § 161(4): affidavit as proof of service in NLRB proceedings.

38 U.S.C. § 5206: affidavit as proof of posting notice of sale of unclaimed property by Veterans Administration.

Rule 803. Hearsay Exceptions; Availability of Declarant Immaterial

The following are not excluded by the hearsay rule, even though the declarant is available as a witness:

(1) Present sense impression. A statement describing or explaining an event or condition made while the declarant was perceiving the event or condition, or immediately thereafter.

(2) Excited utterance. A statement relating to a startling event or condition made while the declarant was under the stress of excitement caused by the event or condition.

(3) Then existing mental, emotional, or physical condition. A statement of the declarant's then existing state of mind, emotion, sensation, or physical condition (such as intent, plan, motive, design, mental feeling, pain, and bodily health), but not including a statement of memory or belief to prove the fact remembered or believed unless it relates to the execution, revocation, identification, or terms of declarant's will.

(4) Statements for purposes of medical diagnosis or treatment. Statements made for purposes of medical diagnosis or treatment and describing medical history, or past or present symptoms, pain, or sensations, or the inception or general character of the cause or external source thereof insofar as reasonably pertinent to diagnosis or treatment.

(5) Recorded recollection. A memorandum or record concerning a matter about which a witness once had knowledge but now has insufficient recollection to enable the witness to testify fully and accurately, shown to have been made or adopted by the witness when the matter was fresh in the witness' memory and to reflect that knowledge correctly. If admitted, the memorandum or record may be read into evidence but may not itself be received as an exhibit unless offered by an adverse party.

(6) Records of Regularly Conducted Activity.—A memorandum, report, record, or data compilation, in any form, of acts, events, conditions, opinions, or diagnoses, made at or near the time by, or from information transmitted by, a person with knowledge, if kept in the course of a regularly conducted business activity, and if it was the regular practice of that business activity to make the memorandum, report, record or data compilation, all as shown by the testimony of the custodian or other qualified witness, or by certification that complies with Rule 902(11), Rule 902(12), or a statute permitting certification, unless the source of information or the method or circumstances of preparation indicate lack of trustworthiness. The term "business" as used in this paragraph includes business, institution, association, profession, occupation, and calling of every kind, whether or not conducted for profit.

(7) Absence of entry in records kept in accordance with the provisions of paragraph (6). Evidence that a matter is not included in the memoranda reports, records, or data compilations, in any form, kept in accordance with the provisions of paragraph (6), to prove the nonoccurrence or nonexistence of the matter, if the matter was of a kind of which a memorandum, report, record, or data compilation was regularly made and preserved, unless the sources of information or other circumstances indicate lack of trustworthiness.

(8) Public records and reports. Records, reports, statements, or data compilations, in any form, of public offices or agencies, setting forth (A) the activities of the office or agency, or (B) matters observed pursuant to duty imposed by law as to which matters there was a duty to report, excluding, however, in criminal cases matters observed by police officers and other law enforcement personnel, or (C) in civil actions and proceedings and against the Government in criminal cases, factual findings resulting from an investigation made pursuant to authority granted by law, unless the sources of information or other circumstances indicate lack of trustworthiness.

(9) Records of vital statistics. Records or data compilations, in any form, of births, fetal deaths, deaths, or marriages, if the report thereof was made to a public office pursuant to requirements of law.

(10) Absence of public record or entry. To prove the absence of a record, report, statement, or data compilation, in any form, or the nonoccurrence or nonexistence of a matter of which a record, report, statement, or data compilation, in any form, was regularly made and preserved by a public office or agency, evidence in the form of a certification in accordance with rule 902, or testimony, that diligent search failed to disclose the record, report, statement, or data compilation, or entry.

(11) Records of religious organizations. Statements of births, marriages, divorces, deaths, legitimacy, ancestry, relationship by blood or marriage, or other similar facts of personal or family history, contained in a regularly kept record of a religious organization.

(12) Marriage, baptismal, and similar certificates. Statements of fact contained in a certificate that the maker performed a marriage or other ceremony or administered a sacrament, made by a clergyman, public official, or other person authorized by the rules or practices of a religious organization or by law to perform the act certified, and purporting to have been issued at the time of the act or within a reasonable time thereafter.

(13) Family records. Statements of fact concerning personal or family history contained in family Bibles, genealogies, charts, engravings on rings, inscriptions on family portraits, engravings on urns, crypts, or tombstones, or the like.

(14) Records of documents affecting an interest in property. The record of a document purporting to establish or affect an interest in property, as proof of the content of the original recorded document and its execution and delivery by each person by whom it purports to have been executed, if the record is a record of a public office and an applicable statute authorizes the recording of documents of that kind in that office.

(15) Statements in documents affecting an interest in property. A statement contained in a document purporting to establish or affect an interest in property if the matter stated was relevant to the purpose of the document, unless dealings with the property since the document was made have been inconsistent with the truth of the statement or the purport of the document.

(16) Statements in ancient documents. Statements in a document in existence twenty years or more the authenticity of which is established.

(17) Market reports, commercial publications. Market quotations, tabulations, lists, directories, or other published compilations, generally used and relied upon by the public or by persons in particular occupations.

(18) Learned treatises. To the extent called to the attention of an expert witness upon cross-examination or relied upon by the expert witness in direct examination, statements contained in published treatises, periodicals, or pamphlets on a subject of history, medicine, or other science or art, established as a reliable authority by the testimony or admission of the witness or by other expert testimony or by judicial notice. If admitted, the statements may be read into evidence but may not be received as exhibits.

(19) Reputation concerning personal or family history. Reputation among members of a person's family by blood, adoption, or marriage, or among a person's associates, or in the community, concerning a person's birth, adoption, marriage, divorce, death, legitimacy, relationship by blood, adoption, or marriage, ancestry, or other similar fact of personal or family history.

(20) Reputation concerning boundaries or general history. Reputation in a community, arising before the controversy, as to boundaries of or customs affecting lands in the community, and reputation as to events of general history important to the community or State or nation in which located.

(21) Reputation as to character. Reputation of a person's character among associates or in the community.

(22) Judgment of previous conviction. Evidence of a final judgment, entered after a trial or upon a plea of guilty (but not upon a plea of nolo contendere), adjudging a person guilty of a crime punishable by death or imprisonment in excess of one year, to prove any fact essential to sustain the judgment, but not including, when offered by the Government in a criminal prosecution for purposes other than impeachment, judgments against persons other than the accused. The pendency of an appeal may be shown but does not affect admissibility.

(23) Judgment as to personal, family, or general history, or boundaries. Judgments as proof of matters of personal, family or general history, or boundaries, essential to the judgment, if the same would be provable by evidence of reputation.

(24) [Transferred to Rule 807]

(Pub.L. 93–595, § 1, Jan. 2, 1975, 88 Stat. 1939; Pub.L. 94–149, § 1(11), Dec. 12, 1975, 89 Stat. 805; Mar. 2, 1987, eff. Oct. 1, 1987; Apr. 11, 1997, eff. Dec. 1, 1997; Apr. 17, 2000, eff. Dec. 1, 2000.)

ADVISORY COMMITTEE NOTES

1972 Proposed Rules

The exceptions are phrased in terms of nonapplication of the hearsay rule, rather than in positive terms of admissibility, in order to repel any implication that other possible grounds for exclusion are eliminated from consideration.

The present rule proceeds upon the theory that under appropriate circumstances a hearsay statement may possess circumstantial guarantees of trustworthiness sufficient to justify nonproduction of the declarant in person at the trial even though he may be available. The theory finds vast support in the many exceptions to the hearsay rule developed by the common law in which unavailability of the declarant is not a relevant factor. The present rule is a synthesis of them, with revision where modern developments and conditions are believed to make that course appropriate.

In a hearsay situation, the declarant is, of course, a witness, and neither this rule nor Rule 804 dispenses with the requirement of firsthand knowledge. It may appear from his statement or be inferable from circumstances. See Rule 602.

Note to Paragraphs (1) and (2). In considerable measure these two examples overlap, though based on somewhat different theories. The most significant practical difference will lie in the time lapse allowable between event and statement.

The underlying theory of Exception [paragraph] (1) is that substantial contemporaneity of event and statement negate the likelihood of deliberate or conscious misrepresentation. Moreover, if the witness is the declarant, he may be examined on the statement. If the witness is not the declarant, he may be examined as to the circumstances as an aid in evaluating the statement. Morgan, Basic Problems of Evidence 340–341 (1962).

The theory of Exception [paragraph] (2) is simply that circumstances may produce a condition of excitement which temporarily stills the capacity of reflection and produces utterances free of conscious fabrication. 6 Wigmore § 1747, p. 135. Spontaneity is the key factor in each instance, though arrived at by somewhat different routes. Both are needed in order to avoid needless niggling.

While the theory of Exception [paragraph] (2) has been criticized on the ground that excitement impairs accuracy of observation as well as eliminating conscious fabrication, Hutchins and Slesinger, Some Observations on the Law of Evidence: Spontaneous Exclamations, 28 Colum.L.Rev. 432 (1928), it finds support in cases without number. See cases in 6 Wigmore § 1750; Annot. 53 A.L.R.2d 1245 (statements as to cause of or responsibility for motor vehicle accident); Annot., 4 A.L.R.3d 149 (accusatory statements by homicide victims). Since unexciting events are less likely to evoke comment, decisions involving Exception [paragraph] (1) are far less numerous. Illustrative are *Tampa Elec. Co. v. Getrost,* 151 Fla. 558, 10 So.2d 83 (1942); *Houston Oxygen Co. v. Davis,* 139 Tex. 1, 161 S.W.2d 474 (1942); and cases cited in McCormick § 273, p. 585, n. 4.

With respect to the *time element,* Exception [paragraph] (1) recognizes that in many, if not most, instances precise contemporaneity is not possible and hence a slight lapse is allowable. Under Exception [paragraph] (2) the standard of measurement is the duration of the state of excitement. "How long can excitement prevail? Obviously there are no pat answers and the character of the transaction or event will largely determine the significance of the time factor." Slough, Spontaneous Statements and State of Mind, 46 Iowa L.Rev. 224, 243 (1961); McCormick § 272, p. 580.

Participation by the declarant is not required: a non-participant may be moved to describe what he perceives, and one may be startled by an event in which he is not an actor. Slough, *supra;* McCormick, *supra;* 6 Wigmore § 1755; Annot. 78 A.L.R.2d 300.

Whether *proof of the startling event* may be made by the statement itself is largely an academic question, since in most cases there is present at least circumstantial evidence that something of a startling nature must have occurred. For cases in which the evidence consists of the condition of the declarant (injuries, state of shock), see *Insurance Co. v. Mosely,* 75 U.S. (8 Wall.) 397, 19 L.Ed. 437 (1869); *Wheeler v. United States,* 93 U.S. App.D.C. 159, 211 F.2d 19 (1953), cert. denied 347 U.S. 1019, 74 S.Ct. 876, 98 L.Ed. 1140; *Wetherbee v. Safety Casualty Co.,* 219 F.2d 274 (5th Cir. 1955); *Lampe v. United States,* 97 U.S.App.D.C. 160, 229 F.2d 43 (1956). Nevertheless, on occasion the only evidence may be the content of the statement itself, and rulings that it may be sufficient are described as "increasing," Slough, *supra* at 246, and as the "prevailing practice," McCormick § 272, p. 579. Illustrative are *Armour & Co. v. Industrial Commission,* 78 Colo. 569, 243 P. 546 (1926); *Young v. Stewart,* 191 N.C. 297, 131 S.E. 735 (1926). Moreover, under Rule 104(a) the judge is not limited by the hearsay rule in passing upon preliminary questions of fact.

Proof of declarant's perception by his statement presents similar considerations when declarant is identified. *People v. Poland,* 22 Ill.2d 175, 174 N.E.2d 804 (1961). However, when declarant is an unidentified bystander, the cases indicate hesitancy in upholding the statement alone as sufficient, *Garrett v. Howden,* 73 N.M. 307, 387 P.2d 874 (1963); *Beck v. Dye,* 200 Wash. 1, 92 P.2d 1113 (1939), a result which would under appropriate circumstances be consistent with the rule.

Permissible *subject matter* of the statement is limited under Exception [paragraph] (1) to description or explanation of the event or condition, the assumption being that spontaneity, in the absence of a startling event, may extend no farther. In Exception [paragraph] (2), however, the statement need only "relate" to the startling event or condition, thus affording a broader scope of subject matter coverage. 6 Wigmore §§ 1750, 1754. See *Sanitary Grocery Co. v. Snead,* 67 App.D.C. 129, 90 F.2d 374 (1937), slip-and-fall case sustaining admissibility of clerk's statement. "That has been on the floor for a couple of hours," and *Murphy Auto Parts Co., Inc. v. Ball,* 101 U.S.App.D.C. 416, 249 F.2d 508 (1957), upholding admission, on issue of driver's agency, of his statement that he had to call on a customer and was in a hurry to get home. Quick, Hearsay, Excitement, Necessity and the Uniform Rules: A Reappraisal of Rule 63(4), 6 Wayne L.Rev. 204, 206–209 (1960).

Similar provisions are found in Uniform Rule 63(4)(a) and (b); California Evidence Code § 1240 (as to Exception (2) only); Kansas Code of Civil Procedure § 60–460(d)(1) and (2); New Jersey Evidence Rule 63(4).

Note to Paragraph (3). Exception [paragraph] (3) is essentially a specialized application of Exception [paragraph] (1), presented separately to enhance its usefulness and accessibility. See McCormick §§ 265, 268.

The exclusion of "statements of memory or belief to prove the fact remembered or believed" is necessary to avoid the virtual destruction of the hearsay rule which would otherwise result from allowing state of mind, provable by a hearsay statement, to serve as the basis for an inference of the happening of the event which produced the state of mind. *Shepard v. United States,* 290 U.S. 96, 54 S.Ct. 22, 78 L.Ed. 196 (1933); Maguire, The Hillmon Case—Thirty-three Years After, 38 Harv.L.Rev. 709, 719–731 (1925); Hinton, States of Mind and the Hearsay Rule, 1 U.Chi.L.Rev. 394, 421–423 (1934). The rule of *Mutual Life Ins. Co. v. Hillmon,* 145 U.S. 285, 12 S.Ct. 909, 36 L.Ed. 706 (1892), allowing evidence of intention as tending to prove the doing of the act intended, is, of course, left undisturbed.

The carving out, from the exclusion mentioned in the preceding paragraph, of declarations relating to the execution, revocation, identification, or terms of declarant's will represents and *ad hoc* judgment which finds ample reinforcement in the decisions, resting on practical grounds of necessity and expediency rather than logic. McCormick § 271, pp. 577–578; Annot. 34 A.L.R.2d 588, 62 A.L.R.2d 855. A similar recognition of the need for and practical value of this kind of evidence is found in California Evidence Code § 1260.

Note to Paragraph (4). Even those few jurisdictions which have shied away from generally admitting statements of present condition have allowed them if made to a physician for purposes of diagnosis and treatment in view of the patient's strong motivation to be truthful. McCormick § 266, p. 563. The same guarantee of trustworthiness extends to statements of past conditions and medical history, made for purposes of diagnosis or treatment. It also extends to statements as to causation, reasonably pertinent to the same purposes, in accord with the current trend. *Shell Oil Co. v. Industrial Commission,* 2 Ill.2d 590, 119 N.E.2d 224 (1954); McCormick § 266, p. 564; New Jersey Evidence Rule 63(12)(c). Statements as to fault would not ordinarily qualify under this latter language. Thus a patient's statement that he was struck by an automobile would qualify but not his statement that the car was driven through a red light. Under the exception the statement need not have been made to a physician. Statements to hospital attendants, ambulance drivers, or even members of the family might be included.

Conventional doctrine has excluded from the hearsay exception, as not within its guarantee of truthfulness, statements to a physician consulted only for the purpose of enabling him to testify. While these statements were not admissible as substantive evidence, the expert was allowed to state the basis of his opinion, including statements of this kind. The distinction thus called for was one most unlikely to be made by juries. The rule accordingly rejects the limitation. This position is consistent with the provision of Rule 703 that the facts on which expert testimony is based need not be admissible in evidence if of a kind ordinarily relied upon by experts in the field.

Note to Paragraph (5). A hearsay exception for recorded recollection is generally recognized and has been described as having "long been favored by the federal and practically all the state courts that have had occasion to decide the question." *United States v. Kelly,* 349 F.2d 720, 770 (2d Cir.1965), citing numerous cases and sustaining the exception against a claimed denial of the right of confrontation. Many additional cases are cited in Annot., 82 A.L.R.2d 473, 520. The guarantee of trustworthiness is found in the reliability inherent in a record made while events were still fresh in mind and accurately reflecting them. *Owens v. State,* 67 Md. 307, 316, 10 A. 210, 212 (1887).

The principal controversy attending the exception has centered, not upon the propriety of the exception itself, but upon the question whether a preliminary requirement of impaired memory on the part of the witness should be imposed. The authorities are divided. If regard be had only to the accuracy of the evidence, admittedly impairment of the memory of the witness adds nothing to it and should not be required. McCormick § 277, p. 593; 3 Wigmore § 738, p. 76; *Jordan v. People,* 151 Colo. 133, 376 P.2d 699 (1962), cert. denied 373 U.S. 944, 83 S.Ct. 1553, 10 L.Ed.2d 699; *Hall v. State,* 223 Md. 158, 162 A.2d 751 (1960); *State v. Bindhammer,* 44 N.J. 372, 209 A.2d 124 (1965). Nevertheless, the absence of the requirement, it is believed, would encourage the use of statements carefully prepared for purposes of litigation under the supervision of attorneys, investigators, or claim adjusters. Hence the example includes a requirement that the witness not have "sufficient recollection to enable him to testify fully and accurately." To the same effect are California Evidence Code § 1237 and New Jersey Rule 63(1)(b), and this has been the position of the federal courts. *Vicksburg & Meridian R.R. v. O'Brien,* 119 U.S. 99, 7 S.Ct. 118, 30 L.Ed. 299 (1886); Ahern v. Webb, 268 F.2d 45 (10th Cir.1959); and see *N.L.R.B. v. Hudson Pulp and Paper Corp.,* 273 F.2d 660, 665 (5th Cir.1960); *N.L.R.B. v. Federal Dairy Co.,* 297 F.2d 487 (1st Cir.1962). But cf. *United States v. Adams,* 385 F.2d 548 (2d Cir.1967).

No attempt is made in the exception to spell out the method of establishing the initial knowledge or the contemporaneity and accuracy of the record, leaving them to be dealt with as the circumstances of the particular case might indicate. Multiple person involvement in the process of observing and recording, as in *Rathbun v. Brancatella,* 93 N.J.L. 222, 107 A. 279 (1919), is entirely consistent with the exception.

Locating the exception at this place in the scheme of the rules is a matter of choice. There were two other possibilities. The first was to regard the statement as one of the group of prior statements of a testifying witness which are excluded entirely from the category of hearsay by Rule 801(d)(1). That category, however, requires that declarant be "subject to cross-examination," as to which the impaired memory aspect of the exception raises doubts. The other possibility was to include the exception among those covered by Rule 804. Since unavailability is required by that rule and lack of memory is listed as a species of unavailability by the definition of the term in Rule 804(a)(3), that treatment at first impression would seem appropriate. The fact is, however, that the unavailability requirement of the exception is of a limited and peculiar nature. Accordingly, the exception is located at this point rather than in the context of a rule where unavailability is conceived of more broadly.

Note to Paragraph (6). Exception [paragraph] (6) represents an area which has received much attention from those seeking to improve the law of evidence. The Commonwealth Fund Act was the result of a study completed in 1927 by a distinguished committee under the chairmanship of Professor Morgan. Morgan et al., The Law of Evidence: Some Proposals for its Reform 63 (1927). With changes too minor to mention, it was adopted by Congress in 1936 as the rule for federal courts. 28 U.S.C. § 1732. A number of states took similar action. The Commissioners on Uniform State Laws in 1936 promulgated the Uniform Business Records as Evidence Act, 9A U.L.A. 506, which has acquired a substantial following in the states. Model Code Rule 514 and Uniform Rule 63(13) also deal with the subject. Difference of varying degrees of importance exist among these various treatments.

These reform efforts were largely within the context of business and commercial records, as the kind usually encountered, and concentrated considerable attention upon relaxing the requirement of producing as witnesses, or accounting for the nonproduction of, all participants in the process of gathering, transmitting, and recording information which the common law had evolved as a burdensome and crippling aspect of using records of this type. In their areas of primary emphasis on witnesses to be called and the general admissibility of ordinary business and commercial records, the Commonwealth Fund Act and the Uniform Act appear to have worked well. The exception seeks to preserve their advantages.

On the subject of what witnesses must be called, the Commonwealth Fund Act eliminated the common law requirement of calling or accounting for all participants by failing to mention it. *United States v. Mortimer,* 118 F.2d 266 (2d Cir.1941); *La Porte v. United States,* 300 F.2d 878 (9th Cir.1962); McCormick § 290, p. 608. Model Code Rule 514 and Uniform Rule 63(13) did likewise. The Uniform Act, however, abolished the common law requirement in express terms, providing that the requisite foundation testimony might be furnished by "the custodian or other qualified witness." Uniform Business Records as Evidence Act, § 2; 9A U.L.A. 506. The exception follows the Uniform Act in this respect.

The element of unusual reliability of business records is said variously to be supplied by systematic checking, by regularity and continuity which produce habits of precision, by actual experience of business in relying upon them, or by a duty to make an accurate record as part of a continuing job or occupation. McCormick §§ 281, 286, 287; Laughlin, Business Entries and the Like, 46 Iowa L.Rev. 276 (1961). The model statutes and rules have sought to capture these factors and to extend their impact by employing the phrase "regular course of business," in conjunction with a definition of "business" far broader than its ordinarily accepted meaning. The result is a tendency unduly to emphasize a requirement of routineness and repetitiveness and an insistence that other types of records be squeezed into the fact patterns which give rise to traditional business records. The rule therefore adopts the phrase "the course of a regularly conducted activity" as capturing the essential basis of the hearsay exception as it has evolved and the essential element which can be abstracted from the various specifications of what is a "business."

Amplification of the kinds of activities producing admissible records has given rise to problems which conventional business records by their nature avoid. They are problems of the source of the recorded information, of entries in opinion form, of motivation, and of involvement as participant in the matters recorded.

Sources of information presented no substantial problem with ordinary business records. All participants, including the observer or participant furnishing the information to be recorded, were acting routinely, under a duty of accuracy, with employer reliance on the result, or in short "in the regular course of business." If, however, the supplier of the information does not act in the regular course, an essential link is broken; the assurance of accuracy does not extend to the information itself, and the fact that it may be recorded with scrupulous accuracy is of no avail. An illustration is the police report incorporating information obtained from a bystander: the officer qualifies as acting in the regular course but the informant does not. The leading case, *Johnson v. Lutz,* 253 N.Y. 124, 170 N.E. 517 (1930), held that a report thus prepared was inadmissible. Most of the authorities have agreed with the decision. Gencarella v. Fyfe, 171 F.2d 419 (1st Cir.1948); *Gordon v. Robinson,* 210 F.2d 192 (3d Cir.1954); *Standard Oil Co. of California v. Moore,* 251 F.2d 188, 214 (9th Cir.1957), cert. denied 356 U.S. 975, 78 S.Ct. 1139, 2 L.Ed.2d 1148; *Yates v. Bair Transport,* Inc., 249 F.Supp. 681 (S.D.N.Y.1965); Annot., 69 A.L.R.2d 1148. Cf. *Hawkins v. Gorea Motor Express, Inc.,* 360 F.2d 933 (2d Cir.1966); *Contra,* 5 Wigmore § 1530a, n. 1, pp. 391–392. The point is not dealt with specifically in the Commonwealth Fund Act, the Uniform Act, or Uniform Rule 63(13). However, Model Code Rule 514 contains the requirement "that it was the regular course of that business for one with personal knowledge * * * to make such a memorandum or record or to transmit information thereof to be included in such a memorandum or record * * *." The rule follows this lead in requiring an informant with knowledge acting in the course of the regularly conducted activity.

Entries in the form of opinions were not encountered in traditional business records in view of the purely factual nature of the items recorded, but they are now commonly encountered with respect to medical diagnoses, prognoses, and test results, as well as occasionally in other areas. The Commonwealth Fund Act provided only for records of an "act, transaction, occurrence, or event," while the Uniform Act, Model Code Rule 514, and Uniform Rule 63(13) merely added the ambiguous term "condition." The limited phrasing of the Commonwealth Fund Act, 28 U.S.C. § 1732, may account for the reluctance of some federal decisions to admit diagnostic entries. *New York Life Ins. Co. v. Taylor,* 79 U.S.App.D.C. 66, 147 F.2d 297 (1945); *Lyles v. United States,* 103 U.S.App.D.C. 22, 254 F.2d 725 (1957), cert. denied 356 U.S. 961, 78 S.Ct. 997, 2 L.Ed.2d 1067; *England v. United States,* 174 F.2d 466 (5th Cir.1949); *Skogen v. Dow Chemical Co.,* 375 F.2d 692 (8th Cir.1967). Other federal decisions, however, experienced no difficulty in freely admitting diagnostic entries. *Reed v. Order of United Commercial Travelers,* 123 F.2d 252 (2d Cir.1941); *Buckminster's Estate v. Commissioner of Internal Revenue,* 147 F.2d 331 (2d Cir.1944); *Medina v. Erickson,* 226 F.2d 475 (9th Cir. 1955); *Thomas v. Hogan,* 308 F.2d 355 (4th Cir.1962); *Glawe v. Rulon,* 284 F.2d 495 (8th Cir.1960). In the state courts, the trend favors admissibility. Borucki v. MacKenzie Bros. Co., 125 Conn. 92, 3 A.2d 224 (1938); *Allen v. St. Louis Public Service Co.,* 365 Mo. 677, 285 S.W.2d 663, 55 A.L.R.2d 1022 (1956); *People v. Kohlmeyer,* 284 N.Y. 366, 31 N.E.2d 490 (1940); *Weis v. Weis,* 147 Ohio St. 416, 72 N.E.2d 245 (1947). In order to make clear its adherence to the latter position, the rule specifically includes both diagnoses and opinions, in addition to acts, events, and conditions, as proper subjects of admissible entries.

Problems of the motivation of the informant have been a source of difficulty and disagreement. In *Palmer v. Hoffman,* 318 U.S. 109, 63 S.Ct. 477, 87 L.Ed. 645 (1943), exclusion of an accident report made by the since deceased engineer, offered by defendant railroad trustees in a grade crossing collision case, was upheld. The report was not "in the regular course of business," not a record of the systematic conduct of the business as a business, said the Court. The report was prepared for use in litigating, not railroading. While the opinion mentions the motivation of the engineer only obliquely, the emphasis on records of routine operations is significant only by virtue of impact on motivation to be accurate. Absence of routineness raises lack of motivation to be accurate. The opinion of the Court of Appeals had gone beyond mere lack of motive to be accurate: the engineer's statement was "dripping with motivations to misrepresent." *Hoffman v. Palmer,* 129 F.2d 976, 991 (2d Cir.1942). The direct introduction of motivation is a disturbing factor, since absence of motive to misrepresent has not traditionally been a requirement of the rule; that records might be self-serving has not been a ground for exclusion. Laughlin, Business Records and the Like, 46 Iowa L.Rev. 276, 285 (1961). As Judge Clark said in his dissent, "I submit that there is hardly a grocer's account book which could not be excluded on that basis." 129 F.2d at 1002. A physician's evaluation report of a personal injury litigant would appear to be in the routine of his business. If the report is offered by the party at whose instance it was made, however, it has been held inadmissible, *Yates v. Bair Transport, Inc.,* 249 F.Supp. 681 (S.D.N.Y.1965), otherwise if offered by the opposite party, *Korte v. New York, N.H. & H.R. Co.,* 191 F.2d 86 (2d Cir.1951), cert. denied 342 U.S. 868, 72 S.Ct. 108, 96 L.Ed. 652.

The decisions hinge on motivation and which party is entitled to be concerned about it. Professor McCormick believed that the doctor's report or the accident report were sufficiently routine to justify admissibility. McCormick § 287, p. 604. Yet hesitation must be experienced in admitting everything which is observed and recorded in the course of a regularly conducted activity. Efforts to set a limit are illustrated by *Hartzog v. United States,* 217 F.2d 706 (4th Cir.1954), error to admit worksheets made by since deceased deputy collector in preparation for the instant income tax evasion prosecution, and *United States v. Ware,* 247 F.2d 698

(7th Cir.1957), error to admit narcotics agents' records of purchases. See also Exception [paragraph] (8), *infra,* as to the public record aspects of records of this nature. Some decisions have been satisfied as to motivation of an accident report if made pursuant to statutory duty, United States v. New York Foreign Trade Zone Operators, 304 F.2d 792 (2d Cir.1962); Taylor v. Baltimore & O.R. Co., 344 F.2d 281 (2d Cir.1965), since the report was oriented in a direction other than the litigation which ensued. Cf. Matthews v. United States, 217 F.2d 409 (5th Cir.1954). The formulation of specific terms which would assure satisfactory results in all cases is not possible. Consequently the rule proceeds from the base that records made in the course of a regularly conducted activity will be taken as admissible but subject to authority to exclude if "the sources of information or other circumstances indicate lack of trustworthiness."

Occasional decisions have reached for enhanced accuracy by requiring involvement as a participant in matters reported. *Clainos v. United States,* 82 U.S.App.D.C. 278, 163 F.2d 593 (1947), error to admit police records of convictions; *Standard Oil Co. of California v. Moore,* 251 F.2d 188 (9th Cir.1957), cert. denied 356 U.S. 975, 78 S.Ct. 1139, 2 L.Ed.2d 1148, error to admit employees' records of observed business practices of others. The rule includes no requirement of this nature. Wholly acceptable records may involve matters merely observed, e.g. the weather.

The form which the "record" may assume under the rule is described broadly as a "memorandum, report, record, or data compilation, in any form." The expression "data compilation" is used as broadly descriptive of any means of storing information other than the conventional words and figures in written or documentary form. It includes, but is by no means limited to, electronic computer storage. The term is borrowed from revised Rule 34(a) of the Rules of Civil Procedure.

Note to Paragraph (7). Failure of a record to mention a matter which would ordinarily be mentioned is satisfactory evidence of its nonexistence. Uniform Rule 63(14), Comment. While probably not hearsay as defined in Rule 801, *supra,* decisions may be found which class the evidence not only as hearsay but also as not within any exception. In order to set the question at rest in favor of admissibility, it is specifically treated here. McCormick § 289, p. 609; Morgan, Basic Problems of Evidence 314 (1962); 5 Wigmore § 1531; Uniform Rule 63(14); California Evidence Code § 1272; Kansas Code of Civil Procedure § 60–460(n); New Jersey Evidence Rule 63(14).

Note to Paragraph (8). Public records are a recognized hearsay exception at common law and have been the subject of statutes without number. McCormick § 291. See, for example, 28 U.S.C. § 1733, the relative narrowness of which is illustrated by its nonapplicability to nonfederal public agencies, thus necessitating resort to the less appropriate business record exception to the hearsay rule. *Kay v. United States,* 255 F.2d 476 (4th Cir.1958). The rule makes no distinction between federal and nonfederal offices and agencies.

Justification for the exception is the assumption that a public official will perform his duty properly and the unlikelihood that he will remember details independently of the record. *Wong Wing Foo v. McGrath,* 196 F.2d 120 (9th Cir.1952), and see *Chesapeake & Delaware Canal Co. v. United States,* 250 U.S. 123, 39 S.Ct. 407, 63 L.Ed. 889 (1919). As to items (a) and (b), further support is found in the reliability factors underlying records of regularly conducted activities generally. See Exception [paragraph] (6), supra.

(a) Cases illustrating the admissibility of records of the office's or agency's own activities are numerous. *Chesapeake & Delaware Canal Co. v. United States,* 250 U.S. 123, 39 S.Ct. 407, 63 L.Ed. 889 (1919), Treasury records of miscellaneous receipts and disbursements; *Howard v. Perrin,* 200 U.S. 71, 26 S.Ct. 195, 50 L.Ed. 374 (1906), General Land Office records; *Ballew v. United States,* 160 U.S. 187, 16 S.Ct. 263, 40 L.Ed. 388 (1895). Pension Office records.

(b) Cases sustaining admissibility of records of matters observed are also numerous. *United States v. Van Hook,* 284 F.2d 489 (7th Cir.1960), remanded for resentencing 365 U.S. 609, 81 S.Ct. 823, 5 L.Ed.2d 821, letter from induction officer to District Attorney, pursuant to army regulations, stating fact and circumstances of refusal to be inducted; *T'Kach v. United States,* 242 F.2d 937 (5th Cir.1957), affidavit of White House personnel officer that search of records showed no employment of accused, charged with fraudulently representing himself as an envoy of the President; *Minnehaha County v. Kelley,* 150 F.2d 356 (8th Cir.1945); Weather Bureau records of rainfall; *United States v. Meyer,* 113 F.2d 387 (7th Cir.1940), cert. denied 311 U.S. 706, 61 S.Ct. 174, 85 L.Ed. 459, map prepared by government engineer from information furnished by men working under his supervision.

(c) The more controversial area of public records is that of the so-called "evaluative" report. The disagreement among the decisions has been due in part, no doubt, to the variety of situations encountered, as well as to differences in principle. Sustaining admissibility are such cases as *United States v. Dumas,* 149 U.S. 278, 13 S.Ct. 872, 37 L.Ed. 734 (1893), statement of account certified by Postmaster General in action against postmaster; *McCarty v. United States,* 185 F.2d 520 (5th Cir.1950), reh. denied 187 F.2d 234, Certificate of Settlement of General Accounting Office showing indebtedness and letter from Army official stating Government had performed, in action on contract to purchase and remove waste food from Army camp; *Moran v. Pittsburgh–Des Moines Steel Co.,* 183 F.2d 467 (3d Cir.1950), report of Bureau of Mines as to cause of gas tank explosion; Petition of W___, 164 F.Supp. 659 (E.D.Pa.1958), report by Immigration and Naturalization Service investigator that petitioner was known in community as wife of man to whom she was not married. To the opposite effect and denying admissibility are *Franklin v. Skelly Oil Co.,* 141 F.2d 568 (10th Cir. 1944), State Fire Marshal's report of cause of gas explosion; *Lomax Transp. Co. v. United States,* 183 F.2d 331 (9th Cir.1950), Certificate of Settlement from General Accounting Office in action for naval supplies lost in warehouse fire; *Yung Jin Teung v. Dulles,* 229 F.2d 244 (2d Cir.1956), "Status Reports" offered to justify delay in processing passport applications. Police reports have generally been excluded except to the extent to which they incorporate firsthand observations of the officer. Annot., 69 A.L.R.2d 1148. Various kinds of evaluative reports are admissible under federal statutes: 7 U.S.C. § 78, findings of Secretary of Agriculture prima facie evidence of true grade of grain; 7 U.S.C. § 210(f), findings of Secretary of Agriculture prima facie evidence in action for damages against stockyard owner; 7 U.S.C. § 292, order by Secretary of Agriculture prima facie evidence in judicial enforcement proceedings against producers association monopoly; 7 U.S.C. § 1622(h), Department of Agriculture inspection certificates of products shipped in interstate commerce prima facie evidence; 8 U.S.C. § 1440(c), separation of alien from military service on conditions other than honorable provable by certificate from department in proceedings to revoke citizenship; 18 U.S.C. § 4245, certificate of Director of Prisons that convicted person has been examined and found probably incompetent at time of trial prima facie evidence in court hearing on competency; 42 U.S.C. § 269(b), bill of health by appropriate official prima facie evidence of vessel's sanitary history and condition and compliance with regulations; 46 U.S.C. § 679, certificate of consul presumptive evidence of refusal of master to transport destitute seamen to United States. While these statutory exceptions to the hearsay rule are left undisturbed, Rule 802, the willingness of Congress to recognize a substantial measure of admissibility for evaluative reports is a helpful guide.

Factors which may be of assistance in passing upon the admissibility of evaluative reports include: (1) the timeliness of the investigation, McCormick, Can the Courts Make Wider Use of Reports of Official Investigations? 42 Iowa L.Rev. 363 (1957); (2) the special skill or experience of the official, *id.*, (3) whether a hearing was held and the level at which conducted, Franklin v. Skelly Oil Co., 141 F.2d 568 (10th Cir.1944); (4) possible motivation problems suggested by Palmer v. Hoffman, 318 U.S. 109, 63 S.Ct. 477, 87 L.Ed. 645 (1943). Others no doubt could be added.

The formulation of an approach which would give appropriate weight to all possible factors in every situation is an obvious impossibility. Hence the rule, as in Exception [paragraph] (6), assumes admissibility in the first instance but with ample provision for escape if sufficient negative factors are present. In one respect, however, the rule with respect to evaluative reports under item (c) is very specific: they are admissible only in civil cases and against the government in criminal cases in view of the almost certain collision with confrontation rights which would result from their use against the accused in a criminal case.

Note to Paragraph (9). Records of vital statistics are commonly the subject of particular statutes making them admissible in evidence, Uniform Vital Statistics Act, 9C U.L.A. 350 (1957). The rule is in principle narrower than Uniform Rule 63(16) which includes reports required of persons performing functions authorized by statute, yet in practical effect the two are substantially the same. Comment Uniform Rule 63(16). The exception as drafted is in the pattern of California Evidence Code § 1281.

Note to Paragraph (10). The principle of proving nonoccurrence of an event by evidence of the absence of a record which would regularly be made of its occurrence, developed in Exception [paragraph] (7) with respect to regularly conducted activities, is here extended to public records of the kind mentioned in Exceptions [paragraphs] (8) and (9). 5 Wigmore § 1633(6), p. 519. Some harmless duplication no doubt exists with Exception [paragraph] (7). For instances of federal statutes recognizing this method of proof, see 8 U.S.C. § 1284(b), proof of absence of alien crewman's name from outgoing manifest prima facie evidence of failure to detain or deport, and 42 U.S.C. § 405(c)(3), (4)(B), (4)(C), absence of HEW [Department of Health, Education, and Welfare] record prima facie evidence of no wages or self-employment income.

The rule includes situations in which absence of a record may itself be the ultimate focal point of inquiry, e.g. People v. Love, 310 Ill. 558, 142 N.E. 204 (1923), certificate of Secretary of State admitted to show failure to file documents required by Securities Law, as well as cases where the absence of a record is offered as proof of the nonoccurrence of an event ordinarily recorded.

The refusal of the common law to allow proof by certificate of the lack of a record or entry has no apparent justification, 5 Wigmore § 1678(7), p. 752. The rule takes the opposite position, as to Uniform Rule 63(17); California Evidence Code § 1284; Kansas Code of Civil Procedure § 60–460(c); New Jersey Evidence Rule 63(17). Congress has recognized certification as evidence of the lack of a record. 8 U.S.C. § 1360(d), certificate of Attorney General or other designated officer that no record of Immigration and Naturalization Service of specified nature or entry therein is found, admissible in alien cases.

Note to Paragraph (11). Records of activities of religious organizations are currently recognized as admissible at least to the extent of the business records exception to the hearsay rule, 5 Wigmore § 1523, p. 371, and Exception [paragraph] (6) would be applicable. However, both the business record doctrine and Exception [paragraph] (6) require that the person furnishing the information be one in the business or activity. The result is such decisions as Daily v. Grand Lodge, 311 Ill. 184, 142 N.E. 478 (1924), holding a church record admissible to prove fact, date, and place of baptism, but not age of child except that he had at least been born at the time. In view of the unlikelihood that false information would be furnished on occasions of this kind, the rule contains no requirement that the informant be in the course of the activity. See California Evidence Code § 1315 and Comment.

Note to Paragraph (12). The principle of proof by certification is recognized as to public officials in Exceptions [paragraphs] (8) and (10), and with respect to authentication in Rule 902. The present exception is a duplication to the extent that it deals with a certificate by a public official, as in the case of a judge who performs a marriage ceremony. The area covered by the rule is, however, substantially larger and extends the certification procedure to clergymen and the like who perform marriages and other ceremonies or administer sacraments. Thus certificates of such matters as baptism or confirmation, as well as marriage, are included. In principle they are as acceptable evidence as certificates of public officers. See 5 Wigmore § 1645, as to marriage certificates. When the person executing the certificate is not a public official, the self-authenticating character of documents purporting to emanate from public officials, see Rule 902, is lacking and proof is required that the person was authorized and did make the certificate. The time element, however, may safely be taken as supplied by the certificate, once authority and authenticity are established, particularly in view of the presumption that a document was executed on the date it bears.

For similar rules, some limited to certificates of marriage, with variations in foundation requirements, see Uniform Rule 63(18); California Evidence Code § 1316; Kansas Code of Civil Procedure § 60–460(p); New Jersey Evidence Rule 63(18).

Note to Paragraph (13). Records of family history kept in family Bibles have by long tradition been received in evidence. 5 Wigmore §§ 1495, 1496, citing numerous statutes and decisions. See also Regulations, Social Security Administration, 20 C.F.R. § 404.703(c), recognizing family Bible entries as proof of age in the absence of public or church records. Opinions in the area also include inscriptions on tombstones, publicly displayed pedigrees, and engravings on rings. Wigmore, *supra.* The rule is substantially identical in coverage with California Evidence Code § 1312.

Note to Paragraph (14). The recording of title documents is a purely statutory development. Under any theory of the admissibility of public records, the records would be receivable as evidence of the contents of the recorded document, else the recording process would be reduced to a nullity. When, however, the record is offered for the further purpose of proving execution and delivery, a problem of lack of firsthand knowledge by the recorder, not present as to contents, is presented. This problem is solved, seemingly in all jurisdictions, by qualifying for recording only those documents shown by a specified procedure, either acknowledgement or a form of probate, to have been executed and delivered. 5 Wigmore §§ 1647–1651. Thus what may appear in the rule, at first glance, as endowing the record with an effect independently of local law and inviting difficulties of an *Erie* nature under *Cities Service Oil Co. v. Dunlap,* 308 U.S. 208, 60 S.Ct. 201, 84 L.Ed. 196 (1939), is not present, since the local law in fact governs under the example.

Note to Paragraph (15). Dispositive documents often contain recitals of fact. Thus a deed purporting to have been executed by an attorney in fact may recite the existence of the power of attorney, or a deed may recite that the grantors are all the heirs of the last record owner. Under the rule, these recitals are exempted from the hearsay rule. The circumstances under which dispositive documents are executed and the requirement that the recital be germane to the purpose of the document are believed to be adequate guarantees of trustworthiness, particularly in view of the nonapplicability of the rule if dealings with the property have been inconsistent with the document. The age of the document is of no significance, though in practical application the document will most often be an ancient one. See Uniform Rule 63(29), Comment.

Similar provisions are contained in Uniform Rule 63(29); California Evidence Code § 1330; Kansas Code of Civil Procedure § 60–460(aa); New Jersey Evidence Rule 63(29).

Note to Paragraph (16). Authenticating a document as ancient, essentially in the pattern of the common law, as provided in Rule 901(b)(8), leaves open as a separate question the admissibility of assertive statements contained therein as against a hearsay objection. 7 Wigmore § 2145a. Wigmore further states that the ancient document technique of authentication is universally conceded to apply to all sorts of documents, including letters, records, contracts, maps, and certificates, in addition to title documents, citing numerous decisions. *Id.* § 2145. Since most of these items are significant evidentially only insofar as they are assertive, their admission in evidence must be as a hearsay exception. But see 5 *id.* § 1573, p. 429, referring to recitals in ancient deeds as a "limited" hearsay exception. The former position is believed to be the correct one in reason and authority. As pointed out in McCormick § 298, danger of mistake is minimized by authentication requirements, and age affords assurance that the writing antedates the present controversy. See *Dallas County v. Commercial Union Assurance Co.,* 286 F.2d 388 (5th Cir.1961), upholding admissibility of 58–year–old newspaper story. Cf. Morgan, Basic Problems of Evidence 364 (1962), but see *id.* 254.

For a similar provision, but with the added requirement that "the statement has since generally been acted upon as true by persons having an interest in the matter," see California Evidence Code § 1331.

Note to Paragraph (17). Ample authority at common law supported the admission in evidence of items falling in this category. While Wigmore's text is narrowly oriented to lists, etc., prepared for the use of a trade or profession, 6 Wigmore § 1702, authorities are cited which include other kinds of publications, for example, newspaper market reports, telephone directories, and city directories. *Id.* §§ 1702–1706. The basis of trustworthiness is general reliance by the public or by a particular segment of it, and the motivation of the compiler to foster reliance by being accurate.

For similar provisions, see Uniform Rule 63(30); California Evidence Code § 1340; Kansas Code of Civil Procedure § 60–460(bb); New Jersey Evidence Rule 63(30). Uniform Commercial Code § 2–724 provides for admissibility in evidence of "reports in official publications or trade journals or in newspapers or periodicals of general circulation published as the reports of such [established commodity] market."

Note to Paragraph (18). The writers have generally favored the admissibility of learned treatises, McCormick § 296, p. 621; Morgan, Basic Problems of Evidence 366 (1962); 6 Wigmore § 1692, with the support of occasional decisions and rules, *City of Dothan v. Hardy,* 237 Ala. 603, 188 So. 264 (1939); *Lewandowski v. Preferred Risk Mut. Ins. Co.,* 33 Wis.2d 69, 146 N.W.2d 505 (1966), 66 Mich.L.Rev. 183 (1967); Uniform Rule 63(31); Kansas Code of Civil Procedure § 60–460(cc), but the great weight of authority has been that learned treatises are not admissible as substantive evidence though usable in the cross-examination of experts. The foundation of the minority view is that the hearsay objection must be regarded as unimpressive when directed against treatises since a high standard of accuracy is engendered by various factors: the treatise is written primarily and impartially for professionals, subject to scrutiny and exposure for inaccuracy, with the reputation of the writer at stake. 6 Wigmore § 1692. Sound as this position may be with respect to trustworthiness, there is, nevertheless, an additional difficulty in the likelihood that the treatise will be misunderstood and misapplied without expert assistance and supervision. This difficulty is recognized in the cases demonstrating unwillingness to sustain findings relative to disability on the basis of judicially noticed medical texts. *Ross v. Gardner,* 365 F.2d 554 (6th Cir.1966); *Sayers v. Gardner,* 380 F.2d 940 (6th Cir.1967); *Colwell v. Gardner,* 386 F.2d 56 (6th Cir.1967); *Glendenning v. Ribicoff,* 213 F.Supp. 301 (W.D.Mo.1962); *Cook v. Celebrezze,* 217 F.Supp. 366 (W.D.Mo.1963); *Sosna v. Celebrezze,* 234 F.Supp. 289 (E.D.Pa.1964); and see *McDaniel v. Celebrezze,* 331 F.2d 426 (4th Cir.1964). The rule avoids the danger of misunderstanding and misapplication by limiting the use of treatises as substantive evidence to situations in which an expert is on the stand and available to explain and assist in the application of the treatise if desired. The limitation upon receiving the publication itself physically in evidence, contained in the last sentence, is designed, to further this policy.

The relevance of the use of treatises on cross-examination is evident. This use of treatises has been the subject of varied views. The most restrictive position is that the witness must have stated expressly on direct his reliance upon the treatise. A slightly more liberal approach still insists upon reliance but allows it to be developed on cross-examination. Further relaxation dispenses with reliance but requires recognition as an authority by the witness, developable on cross-examination. The greatest liberality is found in decisions allowing use of the treatise on cross-examination when its status as an authority is established by any means. Annot., 60 A.L.R.2d 77. The exception is hinged upon this last position, which is that of the Supreme Court, *Reilly v. Pinkus*, 338 U.S. 269, 70 S.Ct. 110, 94 L.Ed. 63 (1949), and of recent well considered state court decisions, *City of St. Petersburg v. Ferguson*, 193 So.2d 648 (Fla.App.1967), cert. denied Fla., 201 So.2d 556; *Darling v. Charleston Memorial Community Hospital*, 33 Ill.2d 326, 211 N.E.2d 253 (1965); *Dabroe v. Rhodes Co.*, 64 Wash.2d 431, 392 P.2d 317 (1964).

In Reilly v. Pinkus, *supra*, the Court pointed out that testing of professional knowledge was incomplete without exploration of the witness' knowledge of and attitude toward established treatises in the field. The process works equally well in reverse and furnishes the basis of the rule.

The rule does not require that the witness rely upon or recognize the treatise as authoritative, thus avoiding the possibility that the expert may at the outset block cross-examination by refusing to concede reliance or authoritativeness. Dabroe v. Rhodes Co., *supra*. Moreover, the rule avoids the unreality of admitting evidence for the purpose of impeachment only, with an instruction to the jury not to consider it otherwise. The parallel to the treatment of prior inconsistent statements will be apparent. See Rules 613(b) and 801(d)(1).

Note to Paragraphs (19), (20) and (21). Trustworthiness in reputation evidence is found "when the topic is such that the facts are likely to have been inquired about and that persons having personal knowledge have disclosed facts which have thus been discussed in the community; and thus the community's conclusion, if any has been formed, is likely to be a trustworthy one." 5 Wigmore § 1580, p. 444, and see also § 1583. On this common foundation, reputation as to land boundaries, customs, general history, character, and marriage have come to be regarded as admissible. The breadth of the underlying principle suggests the formulation of an equally broad exception, but tradition has in fact been much narrower and more particularized, and this is the pattern of these exceptions in the rule.

Exception [paragraph] (19) is concerned with matters of personal and family history. Marriage is universally conceded to be a proper subject of proof by evidence of reputation in the community. 5 Wigmore § 1602. As to such items as legitimacy, relationship, adoption, birth, and death, the decisions are divided. *Id.* § 1605. All seem to be susceptible to being the subject of well founded repute. The "world" in which the reputation may exist may be family, associates, or community. This world has proved capable of expanding with changing times from the single uncomplicated neighborhood, in which all activities take place, to the multiple and unrelated worlds of work, religious affiliation, and social activity, in each of which a reputation may be generated. *People v. Reeves*, 360 Ill. 55, 195 N.E. 443 (1935); *State v. Axilrod*, 248 Minn. 204, 79 N.W.2d 677 (1956); Mass.Stat. 1947, c. 410, M.G.L.A. c. 233 § 21A; 5 Wigmore § 1616. The family has often served as the point of beginning for allowing community reputation. 5 Wigmore § 1488. For comparable provisions see Uniform Rule 63(26), (27)(c); California Evidence Code §§ 1313, 1314; Kansas Code of Civil Procedure § 60–460(x), (y)(3); New Jersey Evidence Rule 63(26), (27)(c).

The first portion of Exception [paragraph] (20) is based upon the general admissibility of evidence of reputation as to land boundaries and land customs, expanded in this country to include private as well as public boundaries. McCormick § 299, p. 625. The reputation is required to antedate the controversy, though not to be ancient. The second portion is likewise supported by authority, *id.*, and is designed to facilitate proof of events when judicial notice is not available. The historical character of the subject matter dispenses with any need that the reputation antedate the controversy with respect to which it is offered. For similar provisions see Uniform Rule 63(27)(a), (b); California Evidence Code §§ 1320–1322; Kansas Code of Civil Procedure § 60–460(y), (1), (2); New Jersey Evidence Rule 63(27)(a), (b).

Exception [paragraph] (21) recognizes the traditional acceptance of reputation evidence as a means of proving human character. McCormick §§ 44, 158. The exception deals only with the hearsay aspect of this kind of evidence. Limitations upon admissibility based on other grounds will be found in Rules 404, relevancy of character evidence generally, and 608, character of witness. The exception is in effect a reiteration, in the context of hearsay, of Rule 405(a). Similar provisions are contained in Uniform Rule 63(28); California Evidence Code § 1324; Kansas Code of Civil Procedure § 60–460(z); New Jersey Evidence Rule 63(28).

Note to Paragraph (22). When the status of a former judgment is under consideration in subsequent litigation, three possibilities must be noted: (1) the former judgment is conclusive under the doctrine of res judicata, either as a bar or a collateral estoppel; or (2) it is admissible in evidence for what it is worth; or (3) it may be of no effect at all. The first situation does not involve any problem of evidence except in the way that principles of substantive law generally bear upon the relevancy and materiality of evidence. The rule does not deal with the substantive effect of the judgment as a bar or collateral estoppel. When, however, the doctrine of res judicata does not apply to make the judgment either a bar or a collateral estoppel, a choice is presented between the second and third alternatives. The rule adopts the second for judgments of criminal conviction of felony grade. This is the direction of the decisions, Annot., 18 A.L.R.2d 1287, 1299, which manifest an increasing reluctance to reject *in toto* the validity of the law's factfinding processes outside the confines of res judicata and collateral estoppel. While this may leave a jury with the evidence of conviction but without means to evaluate it, as suggested by Judge Hinton, Note 27 Ill.L.Rev. 195 (1932), it seems safe to assume that the jury will give it substantial effect unless defendant offers a satisfactory explanation, a possibility not foreclosed by the provision. But see *North River Ins. Co. v. Militello*, 104 Colo. 28, 88 P.2d 567 (1939), in which the jury found for plaintiff on a fire policy despite the introduction of his conviction for arson. For supporting federal decisions see Clark, J., in *New York & Cuba Mail S.S. Co. v. Continental Cas. Co.*, 117 F.2d 404, 411 (2d Cir.1941); *Connecticut Fire Ins. Co. v. Farrara*, 277 F.2d 388 (8th Cir.1960).

Practical considerations require exclusion of convictions of minor offenses, not because the administration of justice in its lower echelons must be inferior, but because motivation to defend at this level is often minimal or nonexistent. *Cope v. Goble,* 39 Cal.App.2d 448, 103 P.2d 598 (1940); *Jones v. Talbot,* 87 Idaho 498, 394 P.2d 316 (1964); *Warren v. Marsh,* 215 Minn. 615, 11 N.W.2d 528 (1943); Annot., 18 A.L.R.2d 1287, 1295–1297; 16 Brooklyn L.Rev. 286 (1950); 50 Colum.L.Rev. 529 (1950); 35 Cornell L.Q. 872 (1950). Hence the rule includes only convictions of felony grade, measured by federal standards.

Judgments of conviction based upon pleas of *nolo contendere* are not included. This position is consistent with the treatment of *nolo* pleas in Rule 410 and the authorities cited in the Advisory Committee's Note in support thereof.

While these rules do not in general purport to resolve constitutional issues, they have in general been drafted with a view to avoiding collision with constitutional principles. Consequently the exception does not include evidence of the conviction of a third person, offered against the accused in a criminal prosecution to prove any fact essential to sustain the judgment of conviction. A contrary position would seem clearly to violate the right of confrontation. *Kirby v. United States,* 174 U.S. 47, 19 S.Ct. 574, 43 L.Ed. 890 (1899), error to convict of possessing stolen postage stamps with the only evidence of theft being the record of conviction of the thieves. The situation is to be distinguished from cases in which conviction of another person is an element of the crime, e.g. 15 U.S.C. § 902(d), interstate shipment of firearms to a known convicted felon, and, as specifically provided, from impeachment.

For comparable provisions see Uniform Rule 63(20); California Evidence Code § 1300; Kansas Code of Civil Procedure § 60–460(r); New Jersey Evidence Rule 63(20).

Note to Paragraph (23). A hearsay exception in this area was originally justified on the ground that verdicts were evidence of reputation. As trial by jury graduated from the category of neighborhood inquests, this theory lost its validity. It was never valid as to chancery decrees. Nevertheless the rule persisted, though the judges and writers shifted ground and began saying that the judgment or decree was as good evidence as reputation. See *City of London v. Clerke,* Carth. 181, 90 Eng.Rep. 710 (K.B. 1691); *Neill v. Duke of Devonshire,* 8 App.Cas. 135 (1882). The shift appears to be correct, since the process of inquiry, sifting, and scrutiny which is relied upon to render reputation reliable is present in perhaps greater measure in the process of litigation. While this might suggest a broader area of application, the affinity to reputation is strong, and paragraph [paragraph] (23) goes no further, not even including character.

The leading case in the *United States, Patterson v. Gaines,* 47 U.S. (6 How.) 550, 599, 12 L.Ed. 553 (1847), follows in the pattern of the English decisions, mentioning as illustrative matters thus provable: manorial rights, public rights of way, immemorial custom, disputed boundary, and pedigree. More recent recognition of the principle is found in *Grant Bros. Construction Co. v. United States,* 232 U.S. 647, 34 S.Ct. 452, 58 L.Ed. 776 (1914), in action for penalties under Alien Contract Labor Law, decision of board of inquiry of Immigration Service admissible to prove alienage of laborers, as a matter of pedigree; *United States v. Mid–Continent Petroleum Corp.,* 67 F.2d 37 (10th Cir.1933), records of commission enrolling Indians admissible on pedigree; *Jung Yen Loy v. Cahill,* 81 F.2d 809 (9th Cir.1936), board decisions as to citizenship of plaintiff's father admissible in proceeding for declaration of citizenship. *Contra,* In re Estate of Cunha, 49 Haw. 273, 414 P.2d 925 (1966).

1974 Enactment

Note to Paragraph (3). Rule 803(3) was approved in the form submitted by the Court to Congress. However, the Committee intends that the Rule be construed to limit the doctrine of *Mutual Life Insurance Co. v. Hillmon,* 145 U.S. 285, 295–300 (1892), so as to render statements of intent by a declarant admissible only to prove his future conduct, not the future conduct of another person.

Note to Paragraph (4). After giving particular attention to the question of physical examination made solely to enable a physician to testify, the Committee approved Rule 803(4) as submitted to Congress, with the understanding that it is not intended in any way to adversely affect present privilege rules or those subsequently adopted.

Note to Paragraph (5). Rule 803(5) as submitted by the Court permitted the reading into evidence of a memorandum or record concerning a matter about which a witness once had knowledge but now has insufficient recollection to enable him to testify accurately and fully, "shown to have been made when the matter was fresh in his memory and to reflect that knowledge correctly." The Committee amended this Rule to add the words "or adopted by the witness" after the phrase "shown to have been made", a treatment consistent with the definition of "statement" in the Jencks Act, 18 U.S.C. 3500. Moreover, it is the Committee's understanding that a memorandum or report, although barred under this Rule, would nonetheless be admissible if it came within another hearsay exception. This last stated principle is deemed applicable to all the hearsay rules.

Note to Paragraph (6). Rule 803(6) as submitted by the Court permitted a record made "in the course of a regularly conducted activity" to be admissible in certain circumstances. The Committee believed there were insufficient guarantees of reliability in records made in the course of activities falling outside the scope of "business" activities as that term is broadly defined in 28 U.S.C. 1732. Moreover, the Committee concluded that the additional requirement of Section 1732 that it must have been the regular practice of a business to make the record is a necessary further assurance of its trustworthiness. The Committee accordingly amended the Rule to incorporate these limitations.

Note to Paragraph (7). Rule 803(7) as submitted by the Court concerned the *absence* of entry in the records of a "regularly conducted activity." The Committee amended this Rule to conform with its action with respect to Rule 803(6).

Note to Paragraph (8). The Committee approved Rule 803(8) without substantive change from the form in which it was submitted by the Court. The Committee intends that the phrase "factual findings" be strictly construed and that evaluations or opinions contained in public reports shall not be admissible under this Rule.

Note to Paragraph (13). The Committee approved this Rule in the form submitted by the Court, intending that the phrase "Statements of fact concerning personal or family history" be read to include the specific types of such statements enumerated in Rule 803(11). House Report No. 93–650.

Note to Paragraph (4). The House approved this rule as it was submitted by the Supreme Court "with the understanding that it is not intended in any way to adversely affect present privilege rules." We also approve this rule, and we would point out with respect to the question of its relation to privileges, it must be read in conjunction with rule 35 of the Federal Rules of Civil Procedure which provides that whenever the physical or mental condition of a party (plaintiff or defendant) is in controversy, the court may require him to submit to an examination by a physician. It is these examinations which will normally be admitted under this exception.

Note to Paragraph (5). Rule 803(5) as submitted by the Court permitted the reading into evidence of a memorandum or record concerning a matter about which a witness once had knowledge but now has insufficient recollection to enable him to testify accurately and fully, "shown to have been made when the matter was fresh in his memory and to reflect that knowledge correctly." The House amended the rule to add the words "or adopted by the witness" after the phrase "shown to have been made," language parallel to the Jencks Act [18 U.S.C. § 3500].

The committee accepts the House amendment with the understanding and belief that it was not intended to narrow the scope of applicability of the rule. In fact, we understand it to clarify the rule's applicability to a memorandum adopted by the witness as well as one made by him. While the rule as submitted by the Court was silent on the question of who made the memorandum, we view the House amendment as a helpful clarification, noting, however, that the Advisory Committee's note to this rule suggests that the important thing is the accuracy of the memorandum rather than who made it.

The committee does not view the House amendment as precluding admissibility in situations in which multiple participants were involved.

When the verifying witness has not prepared the report, but merely examined it and found it accurate, he has adopted the report, and it is therefore admissible. The rule should also be interpreted to cover other situations involving multiple participants, e.g., employer dictating to secretary, secretary making memorandum at direction of employer, or information being passed along a chain of persons, as in *Curtis v. Bradley* [65 Conn. 99, 31 Atl. 591 (1894); see, also, *Rathbun v. Brancatella*, 93 N.J.L. 222, 107 Atl. 279 (1919); see, also, McCormick on Evidence, § 303 (2d ed. 1972)].

The committee also accepts the understanding of the House that a memorandum or report, although barred under this rule, would nonetheless be admissible if it came within another hearsay exception. We consider this principle to be applicable to all the hearsay rules.

Note to Paragraph (6). Rule 803(6) as submitted by the Supreme Court permitted a record made in the course of a regularly conducted activity to be admissible in certain circumstances. This rule constituted a broadening of the traditional business records hearsay exception which has been long advocated by scholars and judges active in the law of evidence.

The House felt there were insufficient guarantees of reliability of records not within a broadly defined business records exception. We disagree. Even under the House definition of "business" including profession, occupation, and "calling of every kind," the records of many regularly conducted activities will, or may be, excluded from evidence. Under the principle of ejusdem generis, the intent of "calling of every kind" would seem to be related to work-related endeavors—e.g., butcher, baker, artist, etc.

Thus, it appears that the records of many institutions or groups might not be admissible under the House amendments. For example, schools, churches, and hospitals will not normally be considered businesses within the definition. Yet, these are groups which keep financial and other records on a regular basis in a manner similar to business enterprises. We believe these records are of equivalent trustworthiness and should be admitted into evidence.

Three states, which have recently codified their evidence rules, have adopted the Supreme Court version of rule 803(6), providing for admission of memoranda of a "regularly conducted activity." None adopted the words "business activity" used in the House amendment. [See Nev.Rev.Stats. § 15.135; N.Mex.Stats. (1973 Supp.) § 20–4–803(6); West's Wis.Stats.Anno. (1973 Supp.) § 908.03(6).]

Therefore, the committee deleted the word "business" as it appears before the word "activity". The last sentence then is unnecessary and was also deleted.

It is the understanding of the committee that the use of the phrase "person with knowledge" is not intended to imply that the party seeking to introduce the memorandum, report, record, or data compilation must be able to produce, or even identify, the specific individual upon whose first-hand knowledge the memorandum, report, record or data compilation was based. A sufficient foundation for the introduction of such evidence will be laid if the party seeking to introduce the evidence is able to show that it was the regular practice of the activity to base such memorandums, reports, records, or data compilations upon a transmission from a person with knowledge, e.g., in the case of the content of a shipment of goods, upon a report from the company's receiving agent or in the case of a computer printout, upon a report from the company's computer programmer or one who has knowledge of the particular record system. In short, the scope of the phrase "person with knowledge" is meant to be coterminous with the custodian of the evidence or other qualified witness. The committee believes this represents the desired rule in light of the complex nature of modern business organizations.

Note to Paragraph (8). The House approved rule 803(8), as submitted by the Supreme Court, with one substantive change. It excluded from the hearsay exception reports containing matters observed by police officers and other law enforcement personnel in criminal cases. Ostensibly, the reason for this exclusion is that observations by police officers at the scene of the crime or the apprehension of the defendant are not as reliable as observations by public officials in other cases because of the adversarial nature of the confrontation between the police and the defendant in criminal cases.

The committee accepts the House's decision to exclude such recorded observations where the police officer is available to testify in court about his observation. However, where he is unavailable as unavailability is defined in rule 804(a)(4) and (a)(5), the report should be admitted as the best available evidence. Accordingly, the committee has amended rule 803(8) to refer to the provision of [proposed] rule 804(b)(5) [deleted], which allows the admission of such reports, records or other statements where the police officer or other law enforcement officer is unavailable because of death, then existing physical or mental illness or infirmity, or not being successfully subject to legal process.

The House Judiciary Committee report contained a statement of intent that "the phrase 'factual findings' in subdivision (c) be strictly construed and that evaluations or opinions contained in public reports shall not be admissible under this rule." The committee takes strong exception to this limiting understanding of the application of the rule. We do not think it reflects an understanding of the intended operation of the rule as explained in the Advisory Committee notes to this subsection. The Advisory Committee notes on subsection (c) of this subdivision point out that various kinds of evaluative reports are now admissible under Federal statutes. 7 U.S.C. § 78, findings of Secretary of Agriculture prima facie evidence of true grade of grain; 42 U.S.C. § 269(b), bill of health by appropriate official prima facie evidence of vessel's sanitary history and condition and compliance with regulations. These statutory exceptions to the hearsay rule are preserved. Rule 802. The willingness of Congress to recognize these and other such evaluative reports provides a helpful guide in determining the kind of reports which are intended to be admissible under this rule. We think the restrictive interpretation of the House overlooks the fact that while the Advisory Committee assumes admissibility in the first instance of evaluative reports, they are not admissible if, as the rule states, "the sources of information or other circumstances indicate lack of trustworthiness."

The Advisory Committee explains the factors to be considered:

* * * * * * *

Factors which may be assistance in passing upon the admissibility of evaluative reports include: (1) the timeliness of the investigation, McCormick, Can the Courts Make Wider Use of Reports of Official Investigations? 42 Iowa L.Rev. 363 (1957); (2) the special skill or experience of the official, id.; (3) whether a hearing was held and the level at which conducted, *Franklin v. Skelly Oil Co.,* 141 F.2d 568 (19th Cir.1944); (4) possible motivation problems suggested by *Palmer v. Hoffman,* 318 U.S. 109, 63 S.Ct. 477, 87 L.Ed. 645 (1943). Others no doubt could be added.

* * * * * * *

The committee concludes that the language of the rule together with the explanation provided by the Advisory Committee furnish sufficient guidance on the admissibility of evaluative reports.

Note to Paragraph (24). The proposed Rules of Evidence submitted to Congress contained identical provisions in rules 803 and 804 (which set forth the various hearsay exceptions), admitting any hearsay statement not specifically covered by any of the stated exceptions, if the hearsay statement was found to have "comparable circumstantial guarantees of trustworthiness." The House deleted these provisions (proposed rules 803(24) and 804(b)(6)[(5)]) as injecting "too much uncertainty" into the law of evidence and impairing the ability of practitioners to prepare for trial. The House felt that rule 102, which directs the courts to construe the Rules of Evidence so as to promote growth and development, would permit sufficient flexibility to admit hearsay evidence in appropriate cases under various factual situations that might arise.

We disagree with the total rejection of a residual hearsay exception. While we view rule 102 as being intended to provide for a broader construction and interpretation of these rules, we feel that, without a separate residual provision, the specifically enumerated exceptions could become tortured beyond any reasonable circumstances which they were intended to include (even if broadly construed). Moreover, these exceptions, while they reflect the most typical and well recognized exceptions to the hearsay rule, may not encompass every situation in which the reliability and appropriateness of a particular piece of hearsay evidence make clear that it should be heard and considered by the trier of fact.

The committee believes that there are certain exceptional circumstances where evidence which is found by a court to have guarantees of trustworthiness equivalent to or exceeding the guarantees reflected by the presently listed exceptions, and to have a high degree of prolativeness [sic] and necessity could properly be admissible.

The case of *Dallas County v. Commercial Union Assoc. Co., Ltd.,* 286 F.2d 388 (5th Cir.1961) illustrates the point. The issue in that case was whether the tower of the county courthouse collapsed because it was struck by lightning (covered by insurance) or because of structural weakness and deterioration of the structure (not covered). Investigation of the structure revealed the presence of charcoal and charred timbers. In order to show that lightning may not have been the cause of the charring, the insurer offered a copy of a local newspaper published over 50 years earlier containing an unsigned article describing a fire in the courthouse while it was under construction. The court found that the newspaper did not qualify for admission as a business record or an ancient document and did not fit within any other recognized hearsay exception. The court concluded, however, that the article was trustworthy because it was inconceivable that a newspaper reporter in a small town would report a fire in the courthouse if none had occurred. See also *United States v. Barbati,* 284 F.Supp. 409 (E.D.N.Y.1968).

Because exceptional cases like the *Dallas County* case may arise in the future, the committee has decided to reinstate a residual exception for rules 803 and 804(b).

The committee, however, also agrees with those supporters of the House version who felt that an overly broad residual hearsay exception could emasculate the hearsay rule and the recognized exceptions or vitiate the rationale behind codification of the rules.

Therefore, the committee has adopted a residual exception for rules 803 and 804(b) of much narrower scope and applicability than the Supreme Court version. In order to qualify for admission, a hearsay statement not falling within one of the recognized exceptions would have to satisfy at least four conditions. First, it must have "equivalent circumstantial guarantees of trustworthiness." Second, it must be offered as evidence of a material fact. Third, the court must determine that the statement "is more probative on the point for which it is offered than any other evidence which the proponent can procure through reasonable efforts." This requirement is intended to insure that only statements which have high probative value and necessity may qualify for admission under the residual exceptions. Fourth, the court must determine that "the general purposes of these rules and the interests of justice will best be served by admission of the statement into evidence."

It is intended that the residual hearsay exceptions will be used very rarely, and only in exceptional circumstances. The committee does not intend to establish a broad license for trial judges to admit hearsay statements that do not fall within one of the other exceptions contained in rules 803 and 804(b). The residual exceptions are not meant to authorize major judicial revisions of the hearsay rule, including its present exceptions. Such major revisions are best accomplished by legislative action. It is intended that in any case in which evidence is sought to be admitted under these subsections, the trial judge will exercise no less care, reflection and caution than the courts did under the common law in establishing the now-recognized exceptions to the hearsay rule.

In order to establish a well-defined jurisprudence, the special facts and circumstances which, in the court's judgment, indicates that the statement has a sufficiently high degree of trustworthiness and necessity to justify its admission should be stated on the record. It is expected that the court will give the opposing party a full and adequate opportunity to contest the admission of any statement sought to be introduced under these subsections. Senate Report No. 93–1277.

Rule 803 defines when hearsay statements are admissible in evidence even though the declarant is available as a witness. The Senate amendments make three changes in this rule.

Note to Paragraph (6). The House bill provides in subsection (6) that records of a regularly conducted "business" activity qualify for admission into evidence as an exception to the hearsay rule. "Business" is defined as including "business, profession, occupation and calling of every kind." The Senate amendment drops the requirement that the records be those of a "business" activity and eliminates the definition of "business." The Senate amendment provides that records are admissible if they are records of a regularly conducted "activity."

The Conference adopts the House provision that the records must be those of a regularly conducted "business" activity. The Conferees changed the definition of "business" contained in the House provision in order to make it clear that the records of institutions and associations like schools, churches and hospitals are admissible under this provision. The records of public schools and hospitals are also covered by Rule 803(8), which deals with public records and reports.

Note to Paragraph (8). The Senate amendment adds language, not contained in the House bill, that refers to another rule that was added by the Senate in another amendment ([proposed] Rule 804(b)(5)—Criminal law enforcement records and reports [deleted]).

In view of its action on [proposed] Rule 804(b)(5) (Criminal law enforcement records and reports) [deleted], the Conference does not adopt the Senate amendment and restores the bill to the House version.

Note to Paragraph (24). The Senate amendment adds a new subsection, (24), which makes admissible a hearsay statement not specifically covered by any of the previous twenty-three subsections, if the statement has equivalent circumstantial guarantees of trustworthiness and if the court determines that (A) the statement is offered as evidence of a material fact; (B) the statement is more probative on the point for which it is offered than any other evidence the proponent can procure through reasonable efforts; and (C) the general purposes of these rules and the interests of justice will best be served by admission of the statement into evidence.

The House bill eliminated a similar, but broader, provision because of the conviction that such a provision injected too much uncertainty into the law of evidence regarding hearsay and impaired the ability of a litigant to prepare adequately for trial.

The Conference adopts the Senate amendment with an amendment that provides that a party intending to request the court to use a statement under this provision must notify any adverse party of this intention as well as of the particulars of the statement, including the name and address of the declarant. This notice must be given sufficiently in advance of the trial or hearing to provide any adverse party with a fair opportunity to prepare to contest the use of the statement. House Report No. 93–1597.

1987 Amendment

The amendments are technical. No substantive change is intended.

1997 Amendment

The contents of Rule 803(24) and Rule 804(b)(5) have been combined and transferred to a new Rule 807. This was done to facilitate additions to Rules 803 and 804. No change in meaning is intended.

GAP Report on Rule 803. The words "Transferred to Rule 807" were substituted for "Abrogated."

2000 Amendment

The amendment provides that the foundation requirements of Rule 803(6) can be satisfied under certain circumstances without the expense and inconvenience of producing time-consuming foundation witnesses. Under current law, courts have generally required foundation witnesses to testify. *See, e.g., Tongil Co., Ltd. v. Hyundai Merchant Marine Corp.*, 968 F.2d 999 (9th Cir. 1992) (reversing a judgment based on business records where a qualified person filed an affidavit but did not testify). Protections are provided by the authentication requirements of Rule 902(11) for domestic records, Rule 902(12) for foreign records in civil cases, and 18 U.S.C. § 3505 for foreign records in criminal cases.

GAP Report—Proposed Amendment to Rule 803(6)

The Committee made no changes to the published draft of the proposed amendment to Evidence Rule 803(6).

Rule 804. Hearsay Exceptions; Declarant Unavailable

(a) Definition of unavailability. "Unavailability as a witness" includes situations in which the declarant—

(1) is exempted by ruling of the court on the ground of privilege from testifying concerning the subject matter of the declarant's statement; or

(2) persists in refusing to testify concerning the subject matter of the declarant's statement despite an order of the court to do so; or

(3) testifies to a lack of memory of the subject matter of the declarant's statement; or

(4) is unable to be present or to testify at the hearing because of death or then existing physical or mental illness or infirmity; or

(5) is absent from the hearing and the proponent of a statement has been unable to procure the declarant's attendance (or in the case of a hearsay exception under subdivision (b)(2), (3), or (4), the declarant's attendance or testimony) by process or other reasonable means.

A declarant is not unavailable as a witness if exemption, refusal, claim of lack of memory, inability, or absence is due to the procurement or wrongdoing of the proponent of a statement for the purpose of preventing the witness from attending or testifying.

(b) Hearsay exceptions. The following are not excluded by the hearsay rule if the declarant is unavailable as a witness:

(1) Former testimony. Testimony given as a witness at another hearing of the same or a different proceeding, or in a deposition taken in compliance with law in the course of the same or another proceeding, if the party against whom the testimony is now offered, or, in a civil action or proceeding, a predecessor in interest, had an opportunity and similar motive to develop the testimony by direct, cross, or redirect examination.

(2) Statement under belief of impending death. In a prosecution for homicide or in a civil action or proceeding, a statement made by a declarant while believing that the declarant's death was imminent, concerning the cause or circumstances of what the declarant believed to be impending death.

(3) Statement against interest. A statement which was at the time of its making so far contrary to the declarant's pecuniary or proprietary interest, or so far tended to subject the declarant to civil or criminal liability, or to render invalid a claim by the declarant against another, that a reasonable person in the declarant's position would not have made the statement unless believing it to be true. A statement tending to expose the declarant to criminal liability and offered to exculpate the accused is not admissible unless corroborating circumstances clearly indicate the trustworthiness of the statement.

(4) Statement of personal or family history. (A) A statement concerning the declarant's own birth, adoption, marriage, divorce, legitimacy, relationship by blood, adoption, or marriage, ancestry, or other similar fact of personal or family history, even though declarant had no means of acquiring personal knowledge of the matter stated; or (B) a statement concerning the foregoing matters, and death also, of another person, if the declarant was related to the other by blood, adoption, or marriage or was so intimately associated with the other's family as to be likely to have accurate information concerning the matter declared.

(5) [Transferred to Rule 807]

(6) Forfeiture by wrongdoing. A statement offered against a party that has engaged or acquiesced in wrongdoing that was intended to, and did, procure the unavailability of the declarant as a witness.

(Pub.L. 93–595, § 1, Jan. 2, 1975, 88 Stat. 1942; Pub.L. 94–149, § 1(12), (13), Dec. 12, 1975, 89 Stat. 806; Mar. 2, 1987, eff. Oct. 1, 1987; Pub.L. 100–690, Title VII, § 7075(b), Nov. 18, 1988, 102 Stat. 4405; Apr. 11, 1997, eff. Dec. 1, 1997.)

ADVISORY COMMITTEE NOTES

1972 Proposed Rules

As to firsthand knowledge on the part of hearsay declarants, see the introductory portion of the Advisory Committee's Note to Rule 803.

Note to Subdivision (a). The definition of unavailability implements the division of hearsay exceptions into two categories by Rules 803 and 804(b).

At common law the unavailability requirement was evolved in connection with particular hearsay exceptions rather than along general lines. For example, see the separate explications of unavailability in relation to former testimony, declarations against interest, and statements of pedigree, separately developed in McCormick §§ 234, 257, and 297. However, no reason is apparent for making distinctions as to what satisfies unavailability for the different exceptions. The treatment in the rule is therefore uniform although differences in the range of process for witnesses between civil and criminal cases will lead to a less exacting requirement under item (5). See Rule 45(e) of the Federal Rules of Civil Procedure and Rule 17(e) of the Federal Rules of Criminal Procedure.

Five instances of unavailability are specified:

(1) Substantial authority supports the position that exercise of a claim of privilege by the declarant satisfies the requirement of unavailability (usually in connection with former testimony). *Wyatt v. State,* 35 Ala.App. 147, 46 So.2d 837 (1950); *State v. Stewart,* 85 Kan. 404, 116 P. 489 (1911); Annot., 45 A.L.R.2d 1354; Uniform Rule 62(7)(a); California Evidence Code § 240(a)(1); Kansas Code of Civil Procedure § 60–459(g)(1). A ruling by the judge is required, which clearly implies that an actual claim of privilege must be made.

(2) A witness is rendered unavailable if he simply refuses to testify concerning the subject matter of his statement despite judicial pressures to do so, a position supported by similar considerations of practicality. *Johnson v. People,* 152 Colo. 586, 384 P.2d 454 (1963); *People v. Pickett,* 339 Mich. 294, 63 N.W.2d 681, 45 A.L.R.2d 1341 (1954). *Contra, Pleau v. State,* 255 Wis. 362, 38 N.W.2d 496 (1949).

(3) The position that a claimed lack of memory by the witness of the subject matter of his statement constitutes unavailability likewise finds support in the cases, though not without dissent. McCormick § 234, p. 494. If the claim is successful, the practical effect is to put the testimony beyond reach, as in the other instances. In this instance, however, it will be noted that the lack of memory must be established by the testimony of the witness himself, which clearly contemplates his production and subjection to cross-examination.

(4) Death and infirmity find general recognition as grounds. McCormick §§ 234, 257, 297; Uniform Rule 62(7)(c); California Evidence Code § 240(a)(3); Kansas Code of Civil Procedure § 60–459(g)(3); New Jersey Evidence Rule 62(6)(c). See also the provisions on use of depositions in Rule 32(a)(3) of the Federal Rules of Civil Procedure and Rule 15(e) of the Federal Rules of Criminal Procedure.

(5) Absence from the hearing coupled with inability to compel attendance by process or other reasonable means also satisfies the requirement. McCormick § 234; Uniform Rule 62(7)(d) and (e); California Evidence Code § 240(a)(4) and (5); Kansas Code of Civil Procedure § 60–459(g)(4) and (5); New Jersey Rule 62(6)(b) and (d). See the discussion of procuring attendance of witnesses who are nonresidents or in custody in *Barber v. Page*, 390 U.S. 719, 88 S.Ct. 1318, 20 L.Ed.2d 255 (1968).

If the conditions otherwise constituting unavailability result from the procurement or wrongdoing of the proponent of the statement, the requirement is not satisfied. The rule contains no requirement that an attempt be made to take the deposition of a declarant.

Note to Subdivision (b). Rule 803, *supra*, is based upon the assumption that a hearsay statement falling within one of its exceptions possesses qualities which justify the conclusion that whether the declarant is available or unavailable is not a relevant factor in determining admissibility. The instant rule proceeds upon a different theory: hearsay which admittedly is not equal in quality to testimony of the declarant on the stand may nevertheless be admitted if the declarant is unavailable and if his statement meets a specified standard. The rule expresses preferences: testimony given on the stand in person is preferred over hearsay, and hearsay, if of the specified quality, is preferred over complete loss of the evidence of the declarant. The exceptions evolved at common law with respect to declarations of unavailable declarants furnish the basis for the exceptions enumerated in the proposal. The term "unavailable" is defined in subdivision (a).

Exception (1). Former testimony does not rely upon some set of circumstances to substitute for oath and cross-examination, since both oath and opportunity to cross-examine were present in fact. The only missing one of the ideal conditions for the giving of testimony is the presence of trier and opponent ("demeanor evidence"). This is lacking with all hearsay exceptions. Hence it may be argued that former testimony is the strongest hearsay and should be included under Rule 803, supra. However, opportunity to observe demeanor is what in a large measure confers depth and meaning upon oath and cross-examination. Thus in cases under Rule 803 demeanor lacks the significance which it possesses with respect to testimony. In any event, the tradition, founded in experience, uniformly favors production of the witness if he is available. The exception indicates continuation of the policy. This preference for the presence of the witness is apparent also in rules and statutes on the use of depositions, which deal with substantially the same problem.

Under the exception, the testimony may be offered (1) against the party *against* whom it was previously offered or (2) against the party *by* whom it was previously offered. In each instance the question resolves itself into whether fairness allows imposing, upon the party against whom now offered, the handling of the witness of the earlier occasion. (1) If the party against whom now offered is the one against whom the testimony was offered previously, no unfairness is apparent in requiring him to accept his own prior conduct of cross-examination or decision not to cross-examine. Only demeanor has been lost, and that is inherent in the situation. (2) If the party against whom now offered is the one *by* whom the testimony was offered previously, a satisfactory answer becomes somewhat more difficult. One possibility is to proceed somewhat along the line of an adoptive admission, i.e. by offering the testimony proponent in effect adopts it. However, this theory savors of discarded concepts of witnesses' belonging to a party, of litigants' ability to pick and choose witnesses, and of vouching for one's own witnesses. Cf. McCormick § 246, pp. 526–527; 4 Wigmore § 1075. A more direct and acceptable approach is simply to recognize direct and redirect examination of one's own witness as the equivalent of cross-examining an opponent's witness. Falknor, Former Testimony and the Uniform Rules: A Comment, 38 N.Y.U.L.Rev. 651, n. 1 (1963); McCormick § 231, p. 483. See also 5 Wigmore § 1389. Allowable techniques for dealing with hostile, double-crossing, forgetful, and mentally deficient witnesses leave no substance to a claim that one could not adequately develop his own witness at the former hearing. An even less appealing argument is presented when failure to develop fully was the result of a deliberate choice.

The common law did not limit the admissibility of former testimony to that given in an earlier trial of the same case, although it did require identity of issues as a means of insuring that the former handling of the witness was the equivalent of what would now be done if the opportunity were presented. Modern decisions reduce the requirement to "substantial" identity. McCormick § 233. Since identity of issues is significant only in that it bears on motive and interest in developing fully the testimony of the witness, expressing the matter in the latter terms is preferable. *Id.* Testimony given at a preliminary hearing was held in *California v. Green*, 399 U.S. 149, 90 S.Ct. 1930, 26 L.Ed.2d 489 (1970), to satisfy confrontation requirements in this respect.

As a further assurance of fairness in thrusting upon a party the prior handling of the witness, the common law also insisted upon identity of parties, deviating only to the extent of allowing substitution of successors in a narrowly construed privity. Mutuality as an aspect of identity is now generally discredited, and the requirement of identity of the offering party disappears except as it might affect motive to develop the testimony. Falknor, *supra*, at 652; McCormick § 232, pp. 487–488. The question remains whether strict identity, or privity, should continue as a requirement with respect to the party against whom offered. The rule departs to the extent of allowing substitution of one with the right and opportunity to develop the testimony with similar motive and interest. This position is supported by modern decisions. McCormick § 232, pp. 489–490; 5 Wigmore § 1388.

Provisions of the same tenor will be found in Uniform Rule 63(3)(b); California Evidence Code §§ 1290–1292; Kansas Code of Civil Procedure § 60–460(c)(2); New Jersey Evidence Rule 63(3). Unlike the rule, the latter three provide either that former testimony is not admissible if the right of confrontation is denied or that it is not admissible if the accused was not a party to the prior hearing. The genesis of these limitations is a caveat in Uniform Rule 63(3) Comment that use of former testimony against an accused may violate his right of confrontation. *Mattox v. United States,* 156 U.S. 237, 15 S.Ct. 337, 39 L.Ed. 409 (1895), held that the right was not violated by the Government's use, on a retrial of the same case, of testimony given at the first trial by two witnesses since deceased. The decision leaves open the questions (1) whether direct and redirect are equivalent to cross-examination for purposes of confrontation, (2) whether testimony given in a different proceeding is acceptable, and (3) whether the accused must himself have been a party to the earlier proceeding or whether a similarly situated person will serve the purpose. Professor Falknor concluded that, if a dying declaration untested by cross-examination is constitutionally admissible, former testimony tested by the cross-examination of one similarly situated does not offend against confrontation. Falknor, *supra,* at 659–660. The constitutional acceptability of dying declarations has often been conceded. *Mattox v. United States,* 156 U.S. 237, 243, 15 S.Ct. 337, 39 L.Ed. 409 (1895); *Kirby v. United States,* 174 U.S. 47, 61, 19 S.Ct. 574, 43 L.Ed. 890 (1899); *Pointer v. Texas,* 380 U.S. 400, 407, 85 S.Ct. 1065, 13 L.Ed.2d 923 (1965).

Exception (2). The exception is the familiar dying declaration of the common law, expanded somewhat beyond its traditionally narrow limits. While the original religious justification for the exception may have lost its conviction for some persons over the years, it can scarcely be doubted that powerful psychological pressures are present. See 5 Wigmore § 1443 and the classic statement of Chief Baron Eyre in Rex v. Woodcock, 1 Leach 500, 502, 168 Eng.Rep. 352, 353 (K.B.1789).

The common law required that the statement be that of the victim, offered in a prosecution for criminal homicide. Thus declarations by victims in prosecutions for other crimes, e.g. a declaration by a rape victim who dies in childbirth, and all declarations in civil cases were outside the scope of the exception. An occasional statute has removed these restrictions, as in Colo.R.S. § 52–1–20, or has expanded the area of offenses to include abortions, 5 Wigmore § 1432, p. 224, n. 4. Kansas by decision extended the exception to civil cases. *Thurston v. Fritz,* 91 Kan. 468, 138 P. 625 (1914). While the common law exception no doubt originated as a result of the exceptional need for the evidence in homicide cases, the theory of admissibility applies equally in civil cases and in prosecutions for crimes other than homicide. The same considerations suggest abandonment of the limitation to circumstances attending the event in question, yet when the statement deals with matters other than the supposed death, its influence is believed to be sufficiently attenuated to justify the limitation. Unavailability is not limited to death. See subdivision (a) of this rule. Any problem as to declarations phrased in terms of opinion is laid at rest by Rule 701, and continuation of a requirement of firsthand knowledge is assured by Rule 602.

Comparable provisions are found in Uniform Rule 63(5); California Evidence Code § 1242; Kansas Code of Civil Procedure § 60–460(e); New Jersey Evidence Rule 63(5).

Exception (3). The circumstantial guaranty of reliability for declarations against interest is the assumption that persons do not make statements which are damaging to themselves unless satisfied for good reason that they are true. *Hileman v. Northwest Engineering Co.,* 346 F.2d 668 (6th Cir.1965). If the statement is that of a party, offered by his opponent, it comes in as an admission, Rule 803(d)(2) [sic; probably should be "Rule 801(d)(2)"], and there is no occasion to inquire whether it is against interest, this not being a condition precedent to admissibility of admissions by opponents.

The common law required that the interest declared against be pecuniary or proprietary but within this limitation demonstrated striking ingenuity in discovering an against-interest aspect. Higham v. Ridgway, 10 East 109, 103 Eng.Rep. 717 (K.B.1808); Reg. v. Overseers of Birmingham, 1 B. & S. 763, 121 Eng.Rep. 897 (Q.B.1861); McCormick, § 256, p. 551, nn. 2 and 3.

The exception discards the common law limitation and expands to the full logical limit. One result is to remove doubt as to the admissibility of declarations tending to establish a tort liability against the declarant or to extinguish one which might be asserted by him, in accordance with the trend of the decisions in this country. McCormick § 254, pp. 548–549. Another is to allow statements tending to expose declarant to hatred, ridicule, or disgrace, the motivation here being considered to be as strong as when financial interests are at stake. McCormick § 255, p. 551. And finally, exposure to criminal liability satisfies the against-interest requirement. The refusal of the common law to concede the adequacy of a penal interest was no doubt indefensible in logic, see the dissent of Mr. Justice Holmes in *Donnelly v. United States,* 228 U.S. 243, 33 S.Ct. 449, 57 L.Ed. 820 (1913), but one senses in the decisions a distrust of evidence of confessions by third persons offered to exculpate the accused arising from suspicions of fabrication either of the fact of the making of the confession or in its contents, enhanced in either instance by the required unavailability of the declarant. Nevertheless, an increasing amount of decisional law recognizes exposure to punishment for crime as a sufficient stake. *People v. Spriggs,* 60 Cal.2d 868, 36 Cal.Rptr. 841, 389 P.2d 377 (1964); *Sutter v. Easterly,* 354 Mo. 282, 189 S.W.2d 284 (1945); Band's Refuse Removal, Inc. v. Fairlawn Borough, 62 N.J.Super. 522, 163 A.2d 465 (1960); *Newberry v. Commonwealth,* 191 Va. 445, 61 S.E.2d 318 (1950); Annot., 162 A.L.R. 446. The requirement of corroboration is included in the rule in order to effect an accommodation between these competing considerations. When the statement is offered by the accused by way of exculpation, the resulting situation is not adapted to control by rulings as to the weight of the evidence, and hence the provision is cast in terms of a requirement preliminary to admissibility. Cf. Rule 406(a). The requirement of corroboration should be construed in such a manner as to effectuate its purpose of circumventing fabrication.

Ordinarily the third-party confession is thought of in terms of exculpating the accused, but this is by no means always or necessarily the case: it may include statements implicating him, and under the general theory of declarations against interest they would be admissible as related statements.

Douglas v. Alabama, 380 U.S. 415, 85 S.Ct. 1074, 13 L.Ed.2d 934 (1965), and Bruton v. United States, 389 U.S. 818, 88 S.Ct. 126, 19 L.Ed.2d 70 (1968), both involved confessions by codefendants which implicated the accused. While the confession was not actually offered in evidence in *Douglas,* the procedure followed effectively put it before the jury, which the Court ruled to be error. Whether the confession might have been admissible as a declaration against penal interest was not considered or discussed. *Bruton* assumed the inadmissibility, as against the accused, of the implicating confession of his codefendant, and centered upon the question of the effectiveness of a limiting instruction. These decisions, however, by no means require that all statements implicating another person be excluded from the category of declarations against interest. Whether a statement is in fact against interest must be determined from the circumstances of each case. Thus a statement admitting guilt and implicating another person, made while in custody, may well be motivated by a desire to curry favor with the authorities and hence fail to qualify as against interest. See the dissenting opinion of Mr. Justice White in *Bruton.* On the other hand, the same words spoken under different circumstances, e.g., to an acquaintance, would have no difficulty in qualifying. The rule does not purport to deal with questions of the right of confrontation.

The balancing of self-serving against dissenting aspects of a declaration is discussed in McCormick § 256.

For comparable provisions, see Uniform Rule 63(10); California Evidence Code § 1230; Kansas Code of Civil Procedure § 60–460(j); New Jersey Evidence Rule 63(10).

Exception (4). The general common law requirement that a declaration in this area must have been made *ante litem motam* has been dropped, as bearing more appropriately on weight than admissibility. See 5 Wigmore § 1483. Item (i)[(A)] specifically disclaims any need of firsthand knowledge respecting declarant's own personal history. In some instances it is self-evident (marriage) and in others impossible and traditionally not required (date of birth). Item (ii)[(B)] deals with declarations concerning the history of another person. As at common law, declarant is qualified if related by blood or marriage. 5 Wigmore § 1489. In addition, and contrary to the common law, declarant qualifies by virtue of intimate association with the family. *Id.,* § 1487. The requirement sometimes encountered that when the subject of the statement is the relationship between two other persons the declarant must qualify as to both is omitted. Relationship is reciprocal. *Id.,* § 1491.

For comparable provisions, see Uniform Rule 63(23), (24), (25); California Evidence Code §§ 1310, 1311; Kansas Code of Civil Procedure § 60–460(u), (v), (w); New Jersey Evidence Rules 63–23), 63(24), 63(25).

1974 Enactment

Note to Subdivision (a)(3). Rule 804(a)(3) was approved in the form submitted by the Court. However, the Committee intends no change in existing federal law under which the court may choose to disbelieve the declarant's testimony as to his lack of memory. See *United States v. Insana,* 423 F.2d 1165, 1169–1170 (2nd Cir.), cert. denied, 400 U.S. 841 (1970).

Note to Subdivision (a)(5). Rule 804(a)(5) as submitted to the Congress provided, as one type of situation in which a declarant would be deemed "unavailable", that he be "absent from the hearing and the proponent of his statement has been unable to procure his attendance by process or other reasonable means." The Committee amended the Rule to insert after the word "attendance" the parenthetical expression "(or, in the case of a hearsay exception under subdivision (b)(2), (3), or (4), his attendance or testimony)". The amendment is designed primarily to require that an attempt be made to depose a witness (as well as to seek his attendance) as a precondition to the witness being deemed unavailable. The Committee, however, recognized the propriety of an exception to this additional requirement when it is the declarant's former testimony that is sought to be admitted under subdivision (b)(1).

Note to Subdivision (b)(1). Rule 804(b)(1) as submitted by the Court allowed prior testimony of an unavailable witness to be admissible if the party against whom it is offered or a person "with motive and interest similar" to his had an opportunity to examine the witness. The Committee considered that it is generally unfair to impose upon the party against whom the hearsay evidence is being offered responsibility for the manner in which the witness was previously handled by another party. The sole exception to this, in the Committee's view, is when a party's predecessor in interest in a civil action or proceeding had an opportunity and similar motive to examine the witness. The Committee amended the Rule to reflect these policy determinations.

Note to Subdivision (b)(2). Rule 804(b)(3) as submitted by the Court (now Rule 804(b)(2) in the bill) proposed to expand the traditional scope of the dying declaration exception (i.e. a statement of the victim in a homicide case as to the cause or circumstances of his believed imminent death) to allow such statements in all criminal and civil cases. The Committee did not consider dying declarations as among the most reliable forms of hearsay. Consequently, it amended the provision to limit their admissibility in criminal cases to homicide prosecutions, where exceptional need for the evidence is present. This is existing law. At the same time, the Committee approved the expansion to civil actions and proceedings where the stakes do not involve possible imprisonment, although noting that this could lead to forum shopping in some instances.

Note to Subdivision (b)(3). Rule 804(b)(4) as submitted by the Court (now Rule 804(b)(3) in the bill) provided as follows:

Statement against interest.—A statement which was at the time of its making so far contrary to the declarant's pecuniary or proprietary interest or so far tended to subject him to civil or criminal liability or to render invalid a claim by him against another or to make him an object of hatred, ridicule, or disgrace, that a reasonable man in his position would not have made the statement unless he believed it to be true. A statement tending to exculpate the accused is not admissible unless corroborated.

The Committee determined to retain the traditional hearsay exception for statements against pecuniary or proprietary interest. However, it deemed the Court's additional references to statements tending to subject a declarant to civil liability or to render invalid a claim by him against another to be redundant as included within the scope of the reference to statements against pecuniary or proprietary interest. See *Gichner v. Antonio Triano Tile and Marble*

Co., 410 F.2d 238 (D.C.Cir.1968). Those additional references were accordingly deleted.

The Court's Rule also proposed to expand the hearsay limitation from its present federal limitation to include statements subjecting the declarant to criminal liability and statements tending to make him an object of hatred, ridicule, or disgrace. The Committee eliminated the latter category from the subdivision as lacking sufficient guarantees of reliability. See *United States v. Dovico,* 380 F.2d 325, 327 nn. 2, 4 (2nd Cir.), cert. denied, 389 U.S. 944 (1967). As for statements against penal interest, the Committee shared the view of the Court that some such statements do possess adequate assurances of reliability and should be admissible. It believed, however, as did the Court, that statements of this type tending to exculpate the accused are more suspect and so should have their admissibility conditioned upon some further provision insuring trustworthiness. The proposal in the Court Rule to add a requirement of simple corroboration was, however, deemed ineffective to accomplish this purpose since the accused's own testimony might suffice while not necessarily increasing the reliability of the hearsay statement. The Committee settled upon the language "unless corroborating circumstances clearly indicate the trustworthiness of the statement" as affording a proper standard and degree of discretion. It was contemplated that the result in such cases as *Donnelly v. United States,* 228 U.S. 243 (1912), where the circumstances plainly indicated reliability, would be changed. The Committee also added to the Rule the final sentence from the 1971 Advisory Committee draft, designed to codify the doctrine of *Bruton v. United States,* 391 U.S. 123 (1968). The Committee does not intend to affect the existing exception to the *Bruton* principle where the codefendant takes the stand and is subject to cross-examination, but believed there was no need to make specific provision for this situation in the Rule, since in that event the declarant would not be "unavailable". House Report No. 93–650.

Note to Subdivision (a)(5). Subdivision (a) of rule 804 as submitted by the Supreme Court defined the conditions under which a witness was considered to be unavailable. It was amended in the House.

The purpose of the amendment, according to the report of the House Committee on the Judiciary, is "primarily to require that an attempt be made to depose a witness (as well as to seek his attendance) as a precondition to the witness being unavailable."

Under the House amendment, before a witness is declared unavailable, a party must try to depose a witness (declarant) with respect to dying declarations, declarations against interest, and declarations of pedigree. None of these situations would seem to warrant this needless, impractical and highly restrictive complication. A good case can be made for eliminating the unavailability requirement entirely for declarations against interest cases. [Uniform rule 63(10); Kan. Stat.Anno. 60–460(j); 2A N.J.Stats.Anno. 84–63(10).]

In dying declaration cases, the declarant will usually, though not necessarily, be deceased at the time of trial. Pedigree statements which are admittedly and necessarily based largely on word of mouth are not greatly fortified by a deposition requirement.

Depositions are expensive and time-consuming. In any event, deposition procedures are available to those who wish to resort to them. Moreover, the deposition procedures of the Civil Rules and Criminal Rules are only imperfectly adapted to implementing the amendment. No purpose is served unless the deposition, if taken, may be used in evidence. Under Civil Rule (a)(3) the Criminal Rule 15(e), a deposition, though taken, may not be admissible, and under Criminal Rule 15(a) substantial obstacles exist in the way of even taking a deposition.

For these reasons, the committee deleted the House amendment.

The committee understands that the rule as to unavailability, as explained by the Advisory Committee "contains no requirement that an attempt be made to take the deposition of a declarant." In reflecting the committee's judgment, the statement is accurate insofar as it goes. Where, however, the proponent of the statement, with knowledge of the existence of the statement, fails to confront the declarant with the statement at the taking of the deposition, then the proponent should not, in fairness, be permitted to treat the declarant as "unavailable" simply because the declarant was not amenable to process compelling his attendance at trial. The committee does not consider it necessary to amend the rule to this effect because such a situation abuses, not conforms to, the rule. Fairness would preclude a person from introducing a hearsay statement on a particular issue if the person taking the deposition was aware of the issue at the time of the deposition but failed to depose the unavailable witness on that issue.

Note to Subdivision (b)(1). Former testimony.—Rule 804(b)(1) as submitted by the Court allowed prior testimony of an unavailable witness to be admissible if the party against whom it is offered or a person "with motive and interest similar" to his had an opportunity to examine the witness.

The House amended the rule to apply only to a party's predecessor in interest. Although the committee recognizes considerable merit to the rule submitted by the Supreme Court, a position which has been advocated by many scholars and judges, we have concluded that the difference between the two versions is not great and we accept the House amendment.

Note to Subdivision (b)(3). The rule defines those statements which are considered to be against interest and thus of sufficient trustworthiness to be admissible even though hearsay. With regard to the type of interest declared against, the version submitted by the Supreme Court included inter alia, statements tending to subject a declarant to civil liability or to invalidate a claim by him against another. The House struck these provisions as redundant. In view of the conflicting case law construing pecuniary or proprietary interests narrowly so as to exclude, e.g., tort cases, this deletion could be misconstrued.

Three States which have recently codified their rules of evidence have followed the Supreme Court's version of this rule, i.e., that a statement is against interest if it tends to subject a declarant to civil liability. [Nev.Rev.Stats. § 51.345; N.Mex.Stats. (1973 Supp.) § 20–4–804(4); West's Wis.Stats.Anno. (1973 Supp.) § 908.045(4).]

The committee believes that the reference to statements tending to subject a person to civil liability constitutes a desirable clarification of the scope of the rule. Therefore, we have reinstated the Supreme Court language on this matter.

The Court rule also proposed to expand the hearsay limitation from its present federal limitation to include statements subjecting the declarant to statements tending to make him an object of hatred, ridicule, or disgrace. The House eliminated the latter category from the subdivision as lacking sufficient guarantees of reliability. Although there is considerable support for the admissibility of such statements (all three of the State rules referred to supra, would admit such statements), we accept the deletion by the House.

The House amended this exception to add a sentence making inadmissible a statement or confession offered against the accused in a criminal case, made by a codefendant or other person implicating both himself and the accused. The sentence was added to codify the constitutional principle announced in *Bruton v. United States,* 391 U.S. 123 (1968). Bruton held that the admission of the extrajudicial hearsay statement of one codefendant inculpating a second codefendant violated the confrontation clause of the sixth amendment.

The committee decided to delete this provision because the basic approach of the rules is to avoid codifying, or attempting to codify, constitutional evidentiary principles, such as the fifth amendment's right against self-incrimination and, here, the sixth amendment's right of confrontation. Codification of a constitutional principle is unnecessary and, where the principle is under development, often unwise. Furthermore, the House provision does not appear to recognize the exceptions to the *Bruton* rule, e.g. where the codefendant takes the stand and is subject to cross examination; where the accused confessed, see *United States v. Mancusi,* 404 F.2d 296 (2d Cir.1968), cert. denied 397 U.S. 942 (1907); where the accused was placed at the scene of the crime, see *United States v. Zelker,* 452 F.2d 1009 (2d Cir.1971). For these reasons, the committee decided to delete this provision.

Note to Subdivision (b)(5). See Note to Paragraph (24), Notes of Committee on the Judiciary, Senate Report No. 93–1277, set out as a note under rule 803 of these rules. Senate Report No. 93–1277.

Rule 804 defines what hearsay statements are admissible in evidence if the declarant is unavailable as a witness. The Senate amendments make four changes in the rule.

Note to Subdivision (a)(5). Subsection (a) defines the term "unavailability as a witness". The House bill provides in subsection (a)(5) that the party who desires to use the statement must be unable to procure the declarant's attendance by process or other reasonable means. In the case of dying declarations, statements against interest and statements of personal or family history, the House bill requires that the proponent must also be unable to procure the declarant's *testimony* (such as by deposition or interrogatories) by process or other reasonable means. The Senate amendment eliminates this latter provision.

The Conference adopts the provision contained in the House bill.

Note to Subdivision (b)(3). The Senate amendment to subsection (b)(3) provides that a statement is against interest and not excluded by the hearsay rule when the declarant is unavailable as a witness, if the statement tends to subject a person to civil or criminal liability or renders invalid a claim by him against another. The House bill did not refer specifically to civil liability and to rendering invalid a claim against another. The Senate amendment also deletes from the House bill the provision that subsection (b)(3) does not apply to a statement or confession, made by a codefendant or another, which implicates the accused and the person who made the statement, when that statement or confession is offered against the accused in a criminal case.

The Conference adopts the Senate amendment. The Conferees intend to include within the purview of this rule, statements subjecting a person to civil liability and statements rendering claims invalid. The Conferees agree to delete the provision regarding statements by a codefendant, thereby reflecting the general approach in the Rules of Evidence to avoid attempting to codify constitutional evidentiary principles.

Note to Subdivision (b)(5). The Senate amendment adds a new subsection, (b)(6) [now (b)(5)], which makes admissible a hearsay statement not specifically covered by any of the five previous subsections, if the statement has equivalent circumstantial guarantees of trustworthiness and if the court determines that (A) the statement is offered as evidence of a material fact; (B) the statement is more probative on the point for which it is offered than any other evidence the proponent can procure through reasonable efforts; and (C) the general purposes of these rules and the interests of justice will best be served by admission of the statement into evidence.

The House bill eliminated a similar, but broader, provision because of the conviction that such a provision injected too much uncertainty into the law of evidence regarding hearsay and impaired the ability of a litigant to prepare adequately for trial.

The Conference adopts the Senate amendment with an amendment that renumbers this subsection and provides that a party intending to request the court to use a statement under this provision must notify any adverse party of this intention as well as of the particulars of the statement, including the name and address of the declarant. This notice must be given sufficiently in advance of the trial or hearing to provide any adverse party with a fair opportunity to prepare to contest the use of the statement. House Report No. 93–1597.

1987 Amendments

The amendments are technical. No substantive change is intended.

1997 Amendments

Subdivision (b)(5). The contents of Rule 803(24) and Rule 804(b)(5) have been combined and transferred to a new Rule 807. This was done to facilitate additions to Rules 803 and 804. No change in meaning is intended.

Subdivision (b)(6). Rule 804(b)(6) has been added to provide that a party forfeits the right to object on hearsay grounds to the admission of a declarant's prior statement when the party's deliberate wrongdoing or acquiescence therein procured the unavailability of the declarant as a witness. This recognizes the need for a prophylactic rule to deal with abhorrent behavior "which strikes at the heart of the system of justice itself." *United States v. Mastrangelo,* 693 F.2d 269, 273 (2d Cir.1982), *cert. denied,* 467 U.S. 1204 (1984). The wrongdoing need not consist of a criminal act. The rule applies to all parties, including the government.

Every circuit that has resolved the question has recognized the principle of forfeiture by misconduct, although the tests for determining whether there is a forfeiture have varied. *See, e.g., United States v. Aguiar,* 975 F.2d 45, 47 (2d

Cir.1992); *United States v. Potamitis*, 739 F.2d 784, 789 (2d Cir.), *cert. denied*, 469 U.S. 918 (1984); *Steele v. Taylor*, 684 F.2d 1193, 1199 (6th Cir.1982), *cert. denied*, 460 U.S. 1053 (1983); United States v. Balano, 618 F.2d 624, 629 (10th Cir.1979), *cert. denied*, 449 U.S. 840 (1980); *United States v. Carlson*, 547 F.2d 1346, 1358–59 (8th Cir.), *cert. denied*, 431 U.S. 914 (1977). The foregoing cases apply a preponderance of the evidence standard. *Contra United States v. Thevis*, 665 F.2d 616, 631 (5th Cir.) (clear and convincing standard), *cert. denied*, 459 U.S. 825 (1982). The usual Rule 104(a) preponderance of the evidence standard has been adopted in light of the behavior the new Rule 804(b)(6) seeks to discourage.

GAP Report on Rule 804(b)(5). The words "Transferred to Rule 807" were substituted for "Abrogated".

GAP Report on Rule 804(b)(6). The title of the rule was changed to "Forfeiture by wrongdoing." The word "who" in line 24 was changed to "that" to indicate that the rule is potentially applicable against the government. Two sentences were added to the first paragraph of the committee note to clarify that the wrongdoing need not be criminal in nature, and to indicate the rule's potential applicability to the government. The word "forfeiture" was substituted for "waiver" in the note.

Rule 805. Hearsay Within Hearsay

Hearsay included within hearsay is not excluded under the hearsay rule if each part of the combined statements conforms with an exception to the hearsay rule provided in these rules.

(Pub.L. 93–595, § 1, Jan. 2, 1975, 88 Stat. 1943.)

ADVISORY COMMITTEE NOTES

1972 Proposed Rules

On principle it scarcely seems open to doubt that the hearsay rule should not call for exclusion of a hearsay statement which includes a further hearsay statement when both conform to the requirements of a hearsay exception. Thus a hospital record might contain an entry of the patient's age based on information furnished by his wife. The hospital record would qualify as a regular entry except that the person who furnished the information was not acting in the routine of the business. However, her statement independently qualifies as a statement of pedigree (if she is unavailable) or as a statement made for purposes of diagnosis or treatment, and hence each link in the chain falls under sufficient assurances. Or, further to illustrate, a dying declaration may incorporate a declaration against interest by another declarant. See McCormick § 290, p. 611.

Rule 806. Attacking and Supporting Credibility of Declarant

When a hearsay statement, or a statement defined in Rule 801(d)(2)(C), (D), or (E), has been admitted in evidence, the credibility of the declarant may be attacked, and if attacked may be supported, by any evidence which would be admissible for those purposes if declarant had testified as a witness. Evidence of a statement or conduct by the declarant at any time, inconsistent with the declarant's hearsay statement, is not subject to any requirement that the declarant may have been afforded an opportunity to deny or explain. If the party against whom a hearsay statement has been admitted calls the declarant as a witness, the party is entitled to examine the declarant on the statement as if under cross-examination.

(Pub.L. 93–595, § 1, Jan. 2, 1975, 88 Stat. 1943; Mar. 2, 1987, eff. Oct. 1, 1987; Apr. 11, 1997, eff. Dec. 1, 1997.)

ADVISORY COMMITTEE NOTES

1972 Proposed Rules

The declarant of a hearsay statement which is admitted in evidence is in effect a witness. His credibility should in fairness be subject to impeachment and support as though he had in fact testified. See Rules 608 and 609. There are however, some special aspects of the impeaching of a hearsay declarant which require consideration. These special aspects center upon impeachment by inconsistent statement, arise from factual differences which exist between the use of hearsay and an actual witness and also between various kinds of hearsay, and involve the question of applying to declarants the general rule disallowing evidence of an inconsistent statement to impeach a witness unless he is afforded an opportunity to deny or explain. See Rule 613(b).

The principal difference between using hearsay and an actual witness is that the inconsistent statement will in the case of the witness almost inevitably of necessity in the nature of things be a *prior* statement, which it is entirely possible and feasible to call to his attention, while in the case of hearsay the inconsistent statement may well be a *subsequent* one, which practically precludes calling it to the attention of the declarant. The result of insisting upon observation of this impossible requirement in the hearsay situation is to deny the opponent, already barred from cross-examination, any benefit of this important technique of impeachment. The writers favor allowing the subsequent statement. McCormick § 37, p. 69; 3 Wigmore § 1033. The cases, however, are divided. Cases allowing the impeachment include *People v. Collup,* 27 Cal.2d 829, 167 P.2d 714 (1946); *People v. Rosoto,* 58 Cal.2d 304, 23 Cal.Rptr. 779, 373 P.2d 867 (1962); *Carver v. United States,* 164 U.S. 694, 17 S.Ct. 228, 41 L.Ed. 602 (1897). *Contra, Mattox v. United States,* 156 U.S. 237, 15 S.Ct. 337, 39 L.Ed. 409 (1895); *People v. Hines,* 284 N.Y. 93, 29 N.E.2d 483 (1940). The force of *Mattox,* where the hearsay was the former testimony of a deceased witness and the denial of use of a subsequent inconsistent statement was upheld, is much diminished by *Carver,* where the hearsay was a dying declaration and denial of use of a subsequent inconsistent statement resulted in reversal. The difference in the particular brand of hearsay seems unimportant when the inconsistent statement is a *subsequent* one. True, the opponent is not totally deprived of cross-examination when the hearsay is former testimony or a deposition but he is deprived of cross-examining on the statement or along lines suggested by it. Mr. Justice Shiras, with two justices joining him, dissented vigorously in *Mattox.*

When the impeaching statement was made prior to the hearsay statement, differences in the kinds of hearsay appear which arguably may justify differences in treatment. If the hearsay consisted of a simple statement by the witness, e.g. a dying declaration or a declaration against interest, the feasibility of affording him an opportunity to deny or explain encounters the same practical impossibility as where the statement is a subsequent one, just discussed, although here the impossibility arises from the total absence of anything resembling a hearing at which the matter could be put to him. The courts by a large majority have ruled in favor of allowing the statement to be used under these circumstances. McCormick § 37, p. 69; 3 Wigmore § 1033. If, however, the hearsay consists of former testimony or a deposition, the possibility of calling the prior statement to the attention of the witness or deponent is not ruled out, since the opportunity to cross-examine was available. It might thus be concluded that with former testimony or depositions the conventional foundation should be insisted upon. Most of the cases involve depositions, and Wigmore describes them as divided. 3 Wigmore § 1031. Deposition procedures at best are cumbersome and expensive, and to require the laying of the foundation may impose an undue burden. Under the federal practice, there is no way of knowing with certainty at the time of taking a deposition whether it is merely for discovery or will ultimately end up in evidence. With respect to both former testimony and depositions the possibility exists that knowledge of the statement might not be acquired until after the time of the cross-examination. Moreover, the expanded admissibility of former testimony and depositions under Rule 804(b)(1) calls for a correspondingly expanded approach to impeachment. The rule dispenses with the requirement in all hearsay situations, which is readily administered and best calculated to lead to fair results.

Notice should be taken that Rule 26(f) of the Federal Rules of Civil Procedure, as originally submitted by the Advisory Committee, ended with the following:

"* * * and, without having first called them to the deponent's attention, may show statements contradictory thereto made at any time by the deponent."

This language did not appear in the rule as promulgated in December, 1937. See 4 Moore's Federal Practice ¶¶ 26.01[9], 26.35 (2d ed.1967). In 1951, Nebraska adopted a provision strongly resembling the one stricken from the federal rule:

"Any party may impeach any adverse deponent by self-contradiction without having laid foundation for such impeachment at the time such deposition was taken." R.S.Neb. § 25–1267.07.

For similar provisions, see Uniform Rule 65; California Evidence Code § 1202; Kansas Code of Civil Procedure § 60–462; New Jersey Evidence Rule 65.

The provision for cross-examination of a declarant upon his hearsay statement is a corollary of general principles of cross-examination. A similar provision is found in California Evidence Code § 1203.

1974 Enactment

Rule 906, as passed by the House and as proposed by the Supreme Court provides that whenever a hearsay statement is admitted, the credibility of the declarant of the statement may be attacked, and if attacked may be supported, by any evidence which would be admissible for those purposes if the declarant had testified as a witness. Rule 801 defines what is a hearsay statement. While statements by a person authorized by a party-opponent to make a statement concerning the subject, by the party-opponent's agent or by a coconspirator of a party—see rule 801(d)(2)(c), (d) and (e)—are traditionally defined as exceptions to the hearsay rule, rule 801 defines such admission by a party-opponent as statements which are not hearsay. Consequently, rule 806 by referring exclusively to the admission of hearsay statements, does not appear to allow the credibility of the declarant to be attacked when the declarant is a coconspirator, agent or authorized spokesman. The committee is of the view that such statements should open the declarant to attacks on his credibility. Indeed, the reason such statements are excluded from the operation of rule 806 is likely attributable to the drafting technique used to codify the hearsay rule, viz. some statements, instead of being referred to as exceptions to the hearsay rule, are defined as statements which are not hearsay. The phrase "or a statement defined in rule 801(d)(2)(c), (d) and (e)" is added to the rule in order to subject the declarant of such statements, like the declarant of hearsay statements, to attacks on his credibility. [The committee considered it unnecessary to include statements contained in rule 801(d)(2)(A) and (B)—the statement by the party-opponent himself or the statement of which he has manifested his adoption—because the credibility of the party-opponent is always subject to an attack on his credibility]. Senate Report No. 93–1277.

The Senate amendment permits an attack upon the credibility of the declarant of a statement if the statement is one by a person authorized by a party-opponent to make a statement concerning the subject, one by an agent of a party-opponent, or one by a coconspirator of the party-opponent, as these statements are defined in Rules 801(d)(2)(C), (D) and (E). The House bill has no such provision.

The Conference adopts the Senate amendment. The Senate amendment conforms the rule to present practice. House Report No. 93–1597.

1987 Amendments

The amendments are technical. No substantive change is intended.

1997 Amendments

The amendment is technical. No substantive change is intended.

GAP Report. Restylization changes in the rule were eliminated.

Rule 807. Residual Exception

A statement not specifically covered by Rule 803 or 804 but having equivalent circumstantial guarantees of trustworthiness, is not excluded by the hearsay rule, if the court determines that (A) the statement is offered as evidence of a material fact; (B) the statement is more probative on the point for which it is offered than any other evidence which the proponent can procure through reasonable efforts; and (C) the general purposes of these rules and the interests of justice will best be served by admission of the statement into evidence. However, a statement may not be admitted under this exception unless the proponent of it makes known to the adverse party sufficiently in advance of the trial or hearing to provide the adverse party with a fair opportunity to prepare to meet it, the proponent's intention to offer the statement and the particulars of it, including the name and address of the declarant.

(Added Apr. 11, 1997, eff. Dec. 1, 1997.)

ADVISORY COMMITTEE NOTES

1997 Amendments

The contents of Rule 803(24) and Rule 804(b)(5) have been combined and transferred to a new Rule 807. This was done to facilitate additions to Rules 803 and 804. No change in meaning is intended.

GAP Report on Rule 807. Restylization changes in the rule were eliminated.

ARTICLE IX. AUTHENTICATION AND IDENTIFICATION

Rule 901. Requirement of Authentication or Identification

(a) General provision. The requirement of authentication or identification as a condition precedent to admissibility is satisfied by evidence sufficient to support a finding that the matter in question is what its proponent claims.

(b) Illustrations. By way of illustration only, and not by way of limitation, the following are examples of authentication or identification conforming with the requirements of this rule:

(1) Testimony of witness with knowledge. Testimony that a matter is what it is claimed to be.

(2) Nonexpert opinion on handwriting. Nonexpert opinion as to the genuineness of handwriting, based upon familiarity not acquired for purposes of the litigation.

(3) Comparison by trier or expert witness. Comparison by the trier of fact or by expert witnesses with specimens which have been authenticated.

(4) Distinctive characteristics and the like. Appearance, contents, substance, internal patterns, or other distinctive characteristics, taken in conjunction with circumstances.

(5) Voice identification. Identification of a voice, whether heard firsthand or through mechanical or electronic transmission or recording, by opinion based upon hearing the voice at any time under circumstances connecting it with the alleged speaker.

(6) Telephone conversations. Telephone conversations, by evidence that a call was made to the number assigned at the time by the telephone company to a particular person or business, if (A) in the case of a person, circumstances, including self-identification, show the person answering to be the one called, or (B) in the case of a business, the call was made to a place of business and the conversation related to business reasonably transacted over the telephone.

(7) Public records or reports. Evidence that a writing authorized by law to be recorded or filed and in fact recorded or filed in a public office, or a purported public record, report, statement, or data compilation, in any form, is from the public office where items of this nature are kept.

(8) Ancient documents or data compilation. Evidence that a document or data compilation, in any form, (A) is in such condition as to create no suspicion concerning its authenticity, (B) was in a place where it, if authentic, would likely be, and (C) has been in existence 20 years or more at the time it is offered.

(9) Process or system. Evidence describing a process or system used to produce a result and showing that the process or system produces an accurate result.

(10) Methods provided by statute or rule. Any method of authentication or identification provided by Act of Congress or by other rules prescribed by the Supreme Court pursuant to statutory authority.

(Pub.L. 93–595, § 1, Jan. 2, 1975, 88 Stat.1943.)

ADVISORY COMMITTEE NOTES

1972 Proposed Rules

Note to Subdivision (a). Authentication and identification represent a special aspect of relevancy. Michael and Adler, Real Proof, 5 Vand.L.Rev. 344, 362 (1952); McCormick §§ 179, 185; Morgan, Basic Problems of Evidence 378 (1962). Thus a telephone conversation may be irrelevant because on an unrelated topic or because the speaker is not identified. The latter aspect is the one here involved. Wigmore describes the need for authentication as "an inherent logical necessity." 7 Wigmore § 2129, p. 564.

This requirement of showing authenticity or identity falls in the category of relevancy dependent upon fulfillment of a condition of fact and is governed by the procedure set forth in Rule 104(b).

The common law approach to authentication of documents has been criticized as an "attitude of agnosticism," McCormick, Cases on Evidence 388, n. 4 (3rd ed. 1956), as one which "departs sharply from men's customs in ordinary affairs," and as presenting only a slight obstacle to the introduction of forgeries in comparison to the time and expense devoted to proving genuine writings which correctly show their origin on their face, McCormick § 185, pp. 395, 396. Today, such available procedures as requests to admit and pretrial conference afford the means of eliminating much of the need for authentication or identification. Also, significant inroads upon the traditional insistence on authentication and identification have been made by accepting as at least prima facie genuine items of the kind treated in Rule 902, *infra.* However, the need for suitable methods of proof still remains, since criminal cases pose their own obstacles to the use of preliminary procedures, unforeseen contingencies may arise, and cases of genuine controversy will still occur.

Note to Subdivision (b). The treatment of authentication and identification draws largely upon the experience embodied in the common law and in statutes to furnish illustrative applications of the general principle set forth in subdivision (a). The examples are not intended as an exclusive enumeration of allowable methods but are meant to guide and suggest, leaving room for growth and development in this area of the law.

The examples relate for the most part to documents, with some attention given to voice communications and computer printouts. As Wigmore noted, no special rules have been developed for authenticating chattels. Wigmore, Code of Evidence § 2086 (3rd ed. 1942).

It should be observed that compliance with requirements of authentication or identification by no means assures admission of an item into evidence, as other bars, hearsay for example, may remain.

Example (1). Example (1) contemplates a broad spectrum ranging from testimony of a witness who was present at the signing of a document to testimony establishing narcotics as taken from an accused and accounting for custody through the period until trial, including laboratory analysis. See California Evidence Code § 1413, eyewitness to signing.

Example (2). Example (2) states conventional doctrine as to lay identification of handwriting, which recognizes that a sufficient familiarity with the handwriting of another person may be acquired by seeing him write, by exchanging correspondence, or by other means, to afford a basis for identifying it on subsequent occasions. McCormick § 189. See also California Evidence Code § 1416. Testimony based upon familiarity acquired for purposes of the litigation is reserved to the expert under the example which follows.

Example (3). The history of common law restrictions upon the technique of proving or disproving the genuineness of a disputed specimen of handwriting through comparison with a genuine specimen, by either the testimony of expert witnesses or direct viewing by the triers themselves, is detailed in 7 Wigmore §§ 1991–1994. In breaking away, the English Common Law Procedure Act of 1854, 17 and 18 Vict., c. 125, § 27, cautiously allowed expert or trier to use exemplars "proved to the satisfaction of the judge to be genuine" for purposes of comparison. The language found its way into numerous statutes in this country, e.g., California Evidence Code §§ 1417, 1418. While explainable as a measure of prudence in the process of breaking with precedent in the handwriting situation, the reservation to the judge of the question of the genuineness of exemplars and the imposition of an unusually high standard of persuasion are at variance with the general treatment of relevancy which depends upon fulfillment of a condition of fact. Rule 104(b). No similar attitude is found in other comparison situations, e.g., ballistics comparison by jury, as in *Evans v. Commonwealth,* 230 Ky. 411, 19 S.W.2d 1091 (1929), or by experts, Annot., 26 A.L.R.2d 892, and no reason appears for its continued existence in handwriting cases. Consequently Example (3) sets no higher standard for handwriting specimens and treats all comparison situations alike, to be governed by Rule 104(b). This approach is consistent with 28 U.S.C. § 1731: "The admitted or proved handwriting of any person shall be admissible, for purposes of comparison, to determine genuineness of other handwriting attributed to such person."

Precedent supports the acceptance of visual comparison as sufficiently satisfying preliminary authentication requirements for admission in evidence. *Brandon v. Collins,* 267 F.2d 731 (2d Cir.1959); *Wausau Sulphate Fibre Co. v. Commissioner of Internal Revenue,* 61 F.2d 879 (7th Cir. 1932); *Desimone v. United States,* 227 F.2d 864 (9th Cir. 1955).

Example (4). The characteristics of the offered item itself, considered in the light of circumstances, afford authentication techniques in great variety. Thus a document or telephone conversation may be shown to have emanated from a particular person by virtue of its disclosing knowledge of facts known peculiarly to him; *Globe Automatic Sprinkler Co. v. Braniff,* 89 Okl. 105, 214 P. 127 (1923); California Evidence Code § 1421; similarly, a letter may be authenticated by content and circumstances indicating it was in reply to a duly authenticated one. McCormick § 192; California Evidence Code § 1420. Language patterns may indicate authenticity or its opposite. *Magnuson v. State,* 187 Wis. 122, 203 N.W. 749 (1925); Arens and Meadow, Psycholinguistics and the Confession Dilemma, 56 Colum.L.Rev. 19 (1956).

Example (5). Since aural voice identification is not a subject of expert testimony, the requisite familiarity may be acquired either before or after the particular speaking which is the subject of the identification, in this respect resembling visual identification of a person rather than identification of handwriting. Cf. Example (2), *supra, People v. Nichols,* 378 Ill. 487, 38 N.E.2d 766 (1942); *McGuire v. State,* 200 Md. 601, 92 A.2d 582 (1952); *State v. McGee,* 336 Mo. 1082, 83 S.W.2d 98 (1935).

Example (6). The cases are in agreement that a mere assertion of his identity by a person talking on the telephone is not sufficient evidence of the authenticity of the conversation and that additional evidence of his identity is required. The additional evidence need not fall in any set pattern. Thus the content of his statements or the reply technique, under Example (4), *supra,* or voice identification under Example (5), may furnish the necessary foundation. Outgoing calls made by the witness involve additional factors bearing upon authenticity. The calling of a number assigned by the telephone company reasonably supports the assumption that the listing is correct and that the number is the one reached. If the number is that of a place of business, the mass of authority allows an ensuing conversation if it relates to business reasonably transacted over the telephone, on the theory that the maintenance of the telephone connection is an invitation to do business without further identification. *Matton v. Hoover Co.,* 350 Mo. 506, 166 S.W.2d 557 (1942); *City of Pawhuska v. Crutchfield,* 147 Okl. 4, 293 P. 1095 (1930); *Zurich General Acc. & Liability Ins. Co. v. Baum,* 159 Va. 404, 165 S.E. 518 (1932). Otherwise, some additional circumstance of identification of the speaker is required. The authorities divide on the question whether the self-identifying statement of the person answering suffices. Example (6) answers in the affirmative on the assumption that usual conduct respecting telephone calls furnish adequate assurances of regularity, bearing in mind that the entire matter is open to exploration before the trier of fact. In general, see McCormick § 193; 7 Wigmore § 2155; Annot., 71 A.L.R. 5, 105 id. 326.

Example (7). Public records are regularly authenticated by proof of custody, without more. McCormick § 191; 7 Wigmore §§ 2158, 2159. The example extends the principle to include data stored in computers and similar methods, of which increasing use in the public records area may be expected. See California Evidence Code §§ 1532, 1600.

Example (8). The familiar ancient document rule of the common law is extended to include data stored electronically or by other similar means. Since the importance of appearance diminishes in this situation, the importance of custody or place where found increases correspondingly. This expansion is necessary in view of the widespread use of methods of storing data in forms other than conventional written records.

Any time period selected is bound to be arbitrary. The common law period of 30 years is here reduced to 20 years, with some shift of emphasis from the probable unavailability of witnesses to the unlikeliness of a still viable fraud after the lapse of time. The shorter period is specified in the English Evidence Act of 1938, 1 & 2 Geo. 6, c. 28, and in Oregon R.S.1963, § 41.360(34). See also the numerous statutes prescribing periods of less than 30 years in the case of recorded documents. 7 Wigmore § 2143.

The application of Example (8) is not subject to any limitation to title documents or to any requirement that possession, in the case of a title document, has been consistent with the document. See McCormick § 190.

Example (9). Example (9) is designed for situations in which the accuracy of a result is dependent upon a process or system which produces it. X rays afford a familiar instance. Among more recent developments is the computer, as to which see Transport Indemnity Co. v. Seib, 178 Neb. 253, 132 N.W.2d 871 (1965); *State v. Veres,* 7 Ariz.App. 117, 436 P.2d 629 (1968); *Merrick v. United States Rubber Co.,* 7 Ariz.App. 433, 440 P.2d 314 (1968); Freed, Computer Print–Outs as Evidence, 16 Am.Jur.Proof of Facts 273; Symposium, Law and Computers in the Mid–Sixties, ALI–ABA (1966); 37 Albany L.Rev. 61 (1967). Example (9) does not, of course, foreclose taking judicial notice of the accuracy of the process or system.

Example (10). The example makes clear that methods of authentication provided by Act of Congress and by the Rules of Civil and Criminal Procedure or by Bankruptcy Rules are not intended to be superseded. Illustrative are the provisions for authentication of official records in Civil Procedure Rule 44 and Criminal Procedure Rule 27, for authentication of records of proceedings by court reporters in 28 U.S.C. § 753(b) and Civil Procedure Rule 80(c), and for authentication of depositions in Civil Procedure Rule 30(f).

Rule 902. Self-authentication

Extrinsic evidence of authenticity as a condition precedent to admissibility is not required with respect to the following:

(1) Domestic public documents under seal. A document bearing a seal purporting to be that of the United States, or of any State, district, Commonwealth, territory, or insular possession thereof, or the Panama Canal Zone, or the Trust Territory of the Pacific Islands, or of a political subdivision, department, officer, or agency thereof, and a signature purporting to be an attestation or execution.

(2) Domestic public documents not under seal. A document purporting to bear the signature in the official capacity of an officer or employee of any entity included in paragraph (1) hereof, having no seal, if a public officer having a seal and having official duties in the district or political subdivision of the officer or employee certifies under seal that the signer has the official capacity and that the signature is genuine.

(3) Foreign public documents. A document purporting to be executed or attested in an official capacity by a person authorized by the laws of a foreign country to make the execution or attestation, and accompanied by a final certification as to the genuineness of the signature and official position (A) of the executing or attesting person, or (B) of any foreign official whose certificate of genuineness of signature and official position relates to the execution or attestation or is in a chain of certificates of genuineness of signature and official position relating to the execution or attestation. A final certification may be made by a secretary of an embassy or legation, consul general, consul, vice consul, or consular agent of the United States, or a diplomatic or consular official of the foreign country assigned or accredited to the United States. If reasonable opportunity has been given to all parties to investigate the authenticity and accuracy of official documents, the court may, for good cause shown, order that they be treated as presumptively authentic without final certification or permit them to be evidenced by an attested summary with or without final certification.

(4) Certified copies of public records. A copy of an official record or report or entry therein, or of a document authorized by law to be recorded or filed and actually recorded or filed in a public office, including data compilations in any form, certified as correct by the custodian or other person authorized to make the certification, by certificate complying with paragraph (1), (2), or (3) of this rule or complying with any Act of Congress or rule prescribed by the Supreme Court pursuant to statutory authority.

(5) Official publications. Books, pamphlets, or other publications purporting to be issued by public authority.

(6) Newspapers and periodicals. Printed materials purporting to be newspapers or periodicals.

(7) Trade inscriptions and the like. Inscriptions, signs, tags, or labels purporting to have been affixed in the course of business and indicating ownership, control, or origin.

(8) Acknowledged documents. Documents accompanied by a certificate of acknowledgment executed in the manner provided by law by a notary public or other officer authorized by law to take acknowledgments.

(9) Commercial paper and related documents. Commercial paper, signatures thereon, and documents relating thereto to the extent provided by general commercial law.

(10) Presumptions under Acts of Congress. Any signature, document, or other matter declared by Act of Congress to be presumptively or prima facie genuine or authentic.

(11) Certified Domestic Records of Regularly Conducted Activity.—The original or a duplicate of a domestic record of regularly conducted activity that would be admissible under Rule 803(6) if accompanied by a written declaration of its custodian or other qualified person, in a manner complying with any Act of Congress or rule prescribed by the Supreme Court pursuant to statutory authority, certifying that the record—

(A) was made at or near the time of the occurrence of the matters set forth by, or from information transmitted by, a person with knowledge of those matters;

(B) was kept in the course of the regularly conducted activity; and

(C) was made by the regularly conducted activity as a regular practice.

A party intending to offer a record into evidence under this paragraph must provide written notice of that intention to all adverse parties, and must make the record and declaration available for inspection sufficiently in advance of their offer into evidence to provide an adverse party with a fair opportunity to challenge them.

(12) Certified Foreign Records of Regularly Conducted Activity.—In a civil case, the original or a duplicate of a foreign record of regularly conducted activity that would be admissible under Rule 803(6) if accompanied by a written declaration by its custodian or other qualified person certifying that the record—

(A) was made at or near the time of the occurrence of the matters set forth by, or from information transmitted by, a person with knowledge of those matters;

(B) was kept in the course of the regularly conducted activity; and

(C) was made by the regularly conducted activity as a regular practice.

The declaration must be signed in a manner that, if falsely made, would subject the maker to criminal penalty under the laws of the country where the declaration is signed. A party intending to offer a record into evidence under this paragraph must provide written notice of that intention to all adverse parties, and must make the record and declaration available for inspection sufficiently in advance of their offer into evidence to provide an adverse party with a fair opportunity to challenge them.

(Pub.L. 93–595, § 1, Jan. 2, 1975, 88 Stat. 1944; Mar. 2, 1987, eff. Oct. 1, 1987; Apr. 25, 1988, eff. Nov. 1, 1988; Apr. 17, 2000, eff. Dec. 1, 2000.)

ADVISORY COMMITTEE NOTES

1972 Proposed Rules

Case law and statutes have, over the years, developed a substantial body of instances in which authenticity is taken as sufficiently established for purposes of admissibility without extrinsic evidence to that effect, sometimes for reasons of policy but perhaps more often because practical considerations reduce the possibility of unauthenticity to a very small dimension. The present rule collects and incorporates these situations, in some instances expanding them to occupy a larger area which their underlying considerations justify. In no instance is the opposite party foreclosed from disputing authenticity.

Note to Paragraph (1). The acceptance of documents bearing a public seal and signature, most often encountered in practice in the form of acknowledgments or certificates authenticating copies of public records, is actually of broad application. Whether theoretically based in whole or in part upon judicial notice, the practical underlying considerations are that forgery is a crime and detection is fairly easy and certain. 7 Wigmore § 2161, p. 638; California Evidence Code § 1452. More than 50 provisions for judicial notice of official seals are contained in the United States Code.

Note to Paragraph (2). While statutes are found which raise a presumption of genuineness of purported official signatures in the absence of an official seal, 7 Wigmore § 2167; California Evidence Code § 1453, the greater ease of effecting a forgery under these circumstances is apparent. Hence this paragraph of the rule calls for authentication by an officer who has a seal. Notarial acts by members of the armed forces and other special situations are covered in paragraph (10).

Note to Paragraph (3). Paragraph (3) provides a method for extending the presumption of authenticity to foreign official documents by a procedure of certification. It is derived from Rule 44(a)(2) of the Rules of Civil Procedure but is broader in applying to public documents rather than being limited to public records.

Note to Paragraph (4). The common law and innumerable statutes have recognized the procedure of authenticating copies of public records by certificate. The certificate qualifies as a public document, receivable as authentic when in conformity with paragraph (1), (2), or (3). Rule 44(a) of the Rules of Civil Procedure and Rule 27 of the Rules of Criminal Procedure have provided authentication procedures of this nature for both domestic and foreign public records. It will be observed that the certification procedure here provided extends only to public records, reports, and recorded documents, all including data compilations, and does not apply to public documents generally. Hence documents provable when presented in original form under paragraphs (1), (2), or (3) may not be provable by certified copy under paragraph (4).

Note to Paragraph (5). Dispensing with preliminary proof of the genuineness of purportedly official publications, most commonly encountered in connection with statutes, court reports, rules, and regulations, has been greatly enlarged by statutes and decisions. 5 Wigmore § 1684. Paragraph (5), it will be noted, does not confer admissibility upon all official publications; it merely provides a means whereby their authenticity may be taken as established for purposes of admissibility. Rule 44(a) of the Rules of Civil Procedure has been to the same effect.

Note to Paragraph (6). The likelihood of forgery of newspapers or periodicals is slight indeed. Hence no danger is apparent in receiving them. Establishing the authenticity of the publication may, of course, leave still open questions of authority and responsibility for items therein contained. See 7 Wigmore § 2150. Cf. 39 U.S.C. § 4005(b), public advertisement prima facie evidence of agency of person named, in postal fraud order proceeding; Canadian Uniform Evidence Act, Draft of 1936, printed copy of newspaper prima facie evidence that notices or advertisements were authorized.

Note to Paragraph (7). Several factors justify dispensing with preliminary proof of genuineness of commercial and mercantile labels and the like. The risk of forgery is minimal. Trademark infringement involves serious penalties. Great efforts are devoted to inducing the public to buy in reliance on brand names, and substantial protection is given them. Hence the fairness of this treatment finds recognition in the cases. *Curtiss Candy Co. v. Johnson,* 163 Miss. 426, 141 So. 762 (1932), Baby Ruth candy bar; *Doyle v. Continental Baking Co.,* 262 Mass. 516, 160 N.E. 325 (1928), loaf of bread; *Weiner v. Mager & Throne, Inc.,* 167 Misc. 338, 3 N.Y.S.2d 918 (1938), same. And see W.Va.Code 1966, § 47–3–5, trademark on bottle prima facie evidence of ownership. *Contra, Keegan v. Green Giant Co.,* 150 Me. 283, 110 A.2d 599 (1954); *Murphy v. Campbell Soup Co.,* 62 F.2d 564 (1st Cir.1933). Cattle brands have received similar acceptance in the western states. Rev.Code Mont.1947, § 46–606, *State v. Wolfley,* 75 Kan. 406, 89 P. 1046 (1907); Annot., 11 L.R.A.(N.S.) 87. Inscriptions on trains and vehicles are held to be prima facie evidence of ownership or control. *Pittsburgh, Ft. W. & C. Ry. v. Callaghan,* 157 Ill. 406, 41 N.E. 909 (1895); 9 Wigmore § 2510a. See also the provision of 19 U.S.C. § 1615(2) that marks, labels, brands, or stamps indicating foreign origin are prima facie evidence of foreign origin of merchandise.

Note to Paragraph (8). In virtually every state, acknowledged title documents are receivable in evidence without further proof. Statutes are collected in 5 Wigmore § 1676. If this authentication suffices for documents of the importance of those affecting titles, logic scarcely permits denying this method when other kinds of documents are involved. Instances of broadly inclusive statutes are California Evidence Code § 1451 and N.Y.CPLR 4538, McKinney's Consol.Laws 1963.

Note to Paragraph (9). Issues of the authenticity of commercial paper in federal courts will usually arise in diversity cases, will involve an element of a cause of action or defense, and with respect to presumptions and burden of proof will be controlled by *Erie Railroad Co. v. Tompkins,* 304 U.S. 64, 58 S.Ct. 817, 82 L.Ed. 1188 (1938). Rule 302, *supra.* There may, however, be questions of authenticity involving lesser segments of a case or the case may be one governed by federal common law. *Clearfield Trust Co. v. United States,* 318 U.S. 363, 63 S.Ct. 573, 87 L.Ed. 838 (1943). Cf. *United States v. Yazell,* 382 U.S. 341, 86 S.Ct. 500, 15 L.Ed.2d 404 (1966). In these situations, resort to the useful authentication provisions of the Uniform Commercial Code is provided for. While the phrasing is in terms of "general commercial law," in order to avoid the potential complications inherent in borrowing local statutes, today one would have difficulty in determining the general commercial law without referring to the Code. See *Williams v. Walker–Thomas Furniture Co.,* 121 U.S.App.D.C. 315, 350 F.2d 445 (1965). Pertinent Code provisions are sections 1–202, 3–307, and 3–510, dealing with third-party documents, signatures on negotiable instruments, protests, and statements of dishonor.

Note to Paragraph (10). The paragraph continues in effect dispensations with preliminary proof of genuineness provided in various Acts of Congress. See, for example, 10 U.S.C. § 936, signature, without seal, together with title, prima facie evidence of authenticity of acts of certain military personnel who are given notarial powers; 15 U.S.C. § 77f(a), signature on SEC registration presumed genuine; 26 U.S.C. § 6064, signature to tax return prima facie genuine.

1974 Enactment

Note to Paragraph (8). Rule 902(8) as submitted by the Court referred to certificates of acknowledgment "under the hand and seal of" a notary public or other officer authorized by law to take acknowledgments. The Committee amended the Rule to eliminate the requirement, believed to be inconsistent with the law in some States, that a notary public must affix a seal to a document acknowledged before him. As amended the Rule merely requires that the document be executed in the manner prescribed by State law.

Note to Paragraph (9). The Committee approved Rule 902(9) as submitted by the Court. With respect to the meaning of the phrase "general commercial law", the Committee intends that the Uniform Commercial Code, which has been adopted in virtually every State, will be followed generally, but that federal commercial law will apply where federal commercial paper is involved. See Clearfield Trust Co. v. United States, 318 U.S. 363 (1943). Further, in those instances in which the issues are governed by Erie R. Co. v. Tompkins, 304 U.S. 64 (1938), State law will apply irrespective of whether it is the Uniform Commercial Code. House Report No. 93–650.

1987 Amendments

The amendments are technical. No substantive change is intended.

1988 Amendments

These two sentences were inadvertently eliminated from the 1987 amendments. The amendment is technical. No substantive change is intended.

2000 Amendments

The amendment adds two new paragraphs to the rule on self-authentication. It sets forth a procedure by which parties can authenticate certain records of regularly conducted activity, other than through the testimony of a foundation witness. See the amendment to Rule 803(6). 18 U.S.C. § 3505 currently provides a means for certifying foreign records of regularly conducted activity in criminal cases, and this amendment is intended to establish a similar procedure for domestic records, and for foreign records offered in civil cases.

A declaration that satisfies 28 U.S.C. § 1746 would satisfy the declaration requirement of Rule 902(11), as would any comparable certification under oath.

The notice requirement in Rules 902(11) and (12) is intended to give the opponent of the evidence a full opportunity to test the adequacy of the foundation set forth in the declaration.

GAP Report—Proposed Amendment to Rule 902

The Committee made the following changes to the published draft of the proposed amendment to Evidence Rule 902:

1. Minor stylistic changes were made in the text, in accordance with suggestions of the Style Subcommittee of the Standing Committee on Rules of Practice and Procedure.

2. The phrase "in a manner complying with any Act of Congress or rule prescribed by the Supreme Court pursuant to statutory authority" was added to proposed Rule 902(11), to provide consistency with Evidence Rule 902(4). The Committee Note was amended to accord with this textual change.

3. Minor stylistic changes were made in the text to provide a uniform construction of the terms "declaration" and "certifying."

4. The notice provisions in the text were revised to clarify that the proponent must make both the declaration and the underlying record available for inspection.

Rule 903. Subscribing Witness' Testimony Unnecessary

The testimony of a subscribing witness is not necessary to authenticate a writing unless required by the laws of the jurisdiction whose laws govern the validity of the writing.

(Pub.L. 93–595, § 1, Jan. 2, 1975, 88 Stat.1945.)

ADVISORY COMMITTEE NOTES

1972 Proposed Rules

The common law required that attesting witnesses be produced or accounted for. Today the requirement has generally been abolished except with respect to documents which must be attested to be valid, e.g. wills in some states. McCormick § 188. Uniform Rule 71; California Evidence Code § 1411; Kansas Code of Civil Procedure § 60–468; New Jersey Evidence Rule 71; New York CPLR Rule 4537.

ARTICLE X. CONTENTS OF WRITINGS, RECORDINGS AND PHOTOGRAPHS

Rule 1001. Definitions

For purposes of this article the following definitions are applicable:

(1) Writings and recordings. "Writings" and "recordings" consist of letters, words, or numbers, or their equivalent, set down by handwriting, typewriting, printing, photostating, photographing, magnetic impulse, mechanical or electronic recording, or other form of data compilation.

(2) Photographs. "Photographs" include still photographs, X-ray films, video tapes, and motion pictures.

(3) Original. An "original" of a writing or recording is the writing or recording itself or any counterpart intended to have the same effect by a person executing or issuing it. An "original" of a photograph includes the negative or any print therefrom. If data are stored in a computer or similar device, any printout or other output readable by sight, shown to reflect the data accurately, is an "original".

(4) Duplicate. A "duplicate" is a counterpart produced by the same impression as the original, or from the same matrix, or by means of photography, including enlargements and miniatures, or by mechanical or electronic re-recording, or by chemical reproduction, or by other equivalent techniques which accurately reproduces the original.

(Pub.L. 93–595, § 1, Jan. 2, 1975, 88 Stat. 1945.)

ADVISORY COMMITTEE NOTES

1972 Proposed Rules

In an earlier day, when discovery and other related procedures were strictly limited, the misleading named "best evidence rule" afforded substantial guarantees against inaccuracies and fraud by its insistence upon production or original documents. The great enlargement of the scope of discovery and related procedures in recent times has measurably reduced the need for the rule. Nevertheless important areas of usefulness persist: discovery of documents outside the jurisdiction may require substantial outlay of time and money; the unanticipated document may not practically be discoverable; criminal cases have built-in limitations on discovery. Cleary and Strong, The Best Evidence Rule: An Evaluation in Context, 51 Iowa L.Rev. 825 (1966).

Note to Paragraph (1). Traditionally the rule requiring the original centered upon accumulations of data and expressions affecting legal relations set forth in words and figures. this meant that the rule was one essentially related to writings. Present day techniques have expanded methods of storing data, yet the essential form which the information ultimately assumes for usable purposes is words and figures. Hence the considerations underlying the rule dictate its expansion to include computers, photographic systems, and other modern developments.

Note to Paragraph (3). In most instances, what is an original will be self-evident and further refinement will be unnecessary. However, in some instances particularized definition is required. A carbon copy of a contract executed in duplicate becomes an original, as does a sales ticket carbon copy given to a customer. While strictly speaking the original of a photograph might be thought to be only the negative, practicality and common usage require that any print from the negative be regarded as an original. Similarly, practicality and usage confer the status of original upon any computer printout. *Transport Indemnity Co. v. Seib,* 178 Neb. 253, 132 N.W.2d 871 (1965).

Note to Paragraph (4). The definition describes "copies" produced by methods possessing an accuracy which virtually eliminates the possibility of error. Copies thus produced are given the status of originals in large measure by Rule 1003, *infra.* Copies subsequently produced manually, whether handwritten or typed, are not within the definition. It should be noted that what is an original for some purposes may be a duplicate for others. Thus a bank's microfilm record of checks cleared is the original as a record. However, a print offered as a copy of a check whose contents are in controversy is a duplicate. This result is substantially consistent with 28 U.S.C. § 1732(b). Compare 26 U.S.C. § 7513(c), giving full status as originals to photographic reproductions of tax returns and other documents, made by authority of the Secretary of the Treasury, and 44 U.S.C. § 399(a), giving original status to photographic copies in the National Archives.

1974 Enactment

Note to Paragraph (2). The Committee amended this Rule expressly to include "video tapes" in the definition of "photographs." House Report No. 93–650.

Rule 1002. Requirement of Original

To prove the content of a writing, recording, or photograph, the original writing, recording, or photograph is required, except as otherwise provided in these rules or by Act of Congress.

(Pub.L. 93–595, § 1, Jan. 2, 1975, 88 Stat. 1946.)

ADVISORY COMMITTEE NOTES

1972 Proposed Rules

The rule is the familiar one requiring production of the original of a document to prove its contents, expanded to include writings, recordings, and photographs, as defined in Rule 1001(1) and (2), *supra.*

Application of the rule requires a resolution of the question whether contents are sought to be proved. Thus an event may be proved by nondocumentary evidence, even though a written record of it was made. If, however, the event is sought to be proved by the written record, the rule applies. For example, payment may be proved without producing the written receipt which was given. Earnings may be proved without producing books of account in which they are entered. McCormick § 198; 4 Wigmore § 1245. Nor does the rule apply to testimony that books or records have been examined and found not to contain any reference to a designated matter.

The assumption should not be made that the rule will come into operation on every occasion when use is made of a photograph in evidence. On the contrary, the rule will seldom apply to ordinary photographs. In most instances a party *wishes* to introduce the item and the question raised is the propriety of receiving it in evidence. Cases in which an offer is made of the testimony of a witness as to what he saw in a photograph or motion picture, without producing the same, are most unusual. The usual course is for a witness on the stand to identify the photograph or motion picture as a correct representation of events which he saw or of a scene with which he is familiar. In fact he adopts the picture as his testimony, or, in common parlance, uses the picture to illustrate his testimony. Under these circumstances, no effort is made to prove the contents of the picture, and the rule is inapplicable. Paradis, The Celluloid Witness, 37 U.Colo. L.Rev. 235, 249–251 (1965).

On occasion, however, situations arise in which contents are sought to be proved. Copyright, defamation, and invasion of privacy by photograph or motion picture falls in this category. Similarly as to situations in which the picture is offered as having independent probative value, e.g. automatic photograph of bank robber. See *People v. Doggett,* 83 Cal.App.2d 405, 188 P.2d 792 (1948), photograph of defendants engaged in indecent act; Mouser and Philbin, Photographic Evidence—Is There a Recognized Basis for Admissibility? 8 Hastings L.J. 310 (1957). the most commonly encountered of this latter group is of course, the X ray, with substantial authority calling for production of the original. *Daniels v. Iowa City,* 191 Iowa 811, 183 N.W. 415 (1921); *Cellamare v. Third Acc. Transit Corp.,* 273 App.Div. 260, 77 N.Y.S.2d 91 (1948); *Patrick & Tilman v. Matkin,* 154 Okl. 232, 7 P.2d 414 (1932); *Mendoza v. Rivera,* 78 P.R.R. 569 (1955).

It should be noted, however, that Rule 703, *supra,* allows an expert to give an opinion based on matters not in evidence, and the present rule must be read as being limited accordingly in its application. Hospital records which may be admitted as business records under Rule 803(6) commonly contain reports interpreting X-rays by the staff radiologist, who qualifies as an expert, and these reports need not be excluded from the records by the instant rule.

The reference to Acts of Congress is made in view of such statutory provisions as 26 U.S.C. § 7513, photographic reproductions of tax returns and documents, made by authority of the Secretary of the Treasury, treated as originals, and 44 U.S.C. § 399(a), photographic copies in National Archives treated as originals.

Rule 1003. Admissibility of Duplicates

A duplicate is admissible to the same extent as an original unless (1) a genuine question is raised as to the authenticity of the original or (2) in the circumstances it would be unfair to admit the duplicate in lieu of the original.

(Pub.L. 93–595, § 1, Jan. 2, 1975, 88 Stat. 1946.)

ADVISORY COMMITTEE NOTES

1972 Proposed Rules

When the only concern is with getting the words or other contents before the court with accuracy and precision, then a counterpart serves equally as well as the original, if the counterpart is the product of a method which insures accuracy and genuineness. By definition in Rule 1001(4), *supra,* a "duplicate" possesses this character.

Therefore, if no genuine issue exists as to authenticity and no other reason exists for requiring the original, a duplicate is admissible under the rule. This position finds support in the decisions, *Myrick v. United States,* 332 F.2d 279 (5th Cir.1964), no error in admitting photostatic copies of checks instead of original microfilm in absence of suggestion to trial judge that photostats were incorrect; *Johns v. United States*, 323 F.2d 421 (5th Cir.1963), not error to admit concededly accurate tape recording made from original wire recording; *Sauget v. Johnston*, 315 F.2d 816 (9th Cir.1963), not error to admit copy of agreement when opponent had original and did not on appeal claim any discrepancy. Other reasons for acquiring the original may be present when only a part of the original is reproduced and the remainder is needed for cross-examination or may disclose matters qualifying the part offered or otherwise useful to the opposing party. *United States v. Alexander*, 326 F.2d 736 (4th Cir. 1964). And see *Toho Bussan Kaisha, Ltd. v. American President Lines, Ltd.*, 265 F.2d 418, 76 A.L.R.2d 1344 (2d Cir.1959).

1974 Enactment

The Committee approved this Rule in the form submitted by the Court, with the expectation that the courts would be liberal in deciding that a "genuine question is raised as to the authenticity of the original." House Report No. 93–650.

Rule 1004. Admissibility of Other Evidence of Contents

The original is not required, and other evidence of the contents of a writing, recording, or photograph is admissible if—

(1) Originals lost or destroyed. All originals are lost or have been destroyed, unless the proponent lost or destroyed them in bad faith; or

(2) Original not obtainable. No original can be obtained by any available judicial process or procedure; or

(3) Original in possession of opponent. At a time when an original was under the control of the party against whom offered, that party was put on notice, by the pleadings or otherwise, that the contents would be a subject of proof at the hearing, and that party does not produce the original at the hearing; or

(4) Collateral matters. The writing, recording, or photograph is not closely related to a controlling issue.

(Pub.L. 93–595, § 1, Jan. 2, 1975, 88 Stat. 1946; Mar. 2, 1987, eff. Oct. 1, 1987.)

ADVISORY COMMITTEE NOTES

1972 Proposed Rules

Basically the rule requiring the production of the original as proof of contents has developed as a rule of preference: if failure to produce the original is satisfactorily explained, secondary evidence is admissible. The instant rule specifies the circumstances under which production of the original is excused.

The rule recognizes no "degrees" of secondary evidence. While strict logic might call for extending the principle of preference beyond simply preferring the original, the formulation of a hierarchy of preferences and a procedure for making it effective is believed to involve unwarranted complexities. Most, if not all, that would be accomplished by an extended scheme of preferences will, in any event, be achieved through the normal motivation of a party to present the most convincing evidence possible and the arguments and procedures available to his opponent if he does not. Compare McCormick § 207.

Note to Paragraph (1). Loss or destruction of the original, unless due to bad faith of the proponent, is a satisfactory explanation of nonproduction. McCormick § 201.

Note to Paragraph (2). When the original is in the possession of a third person, inability to procure it from him by resort to process or other judicial procedure is a sufficient explanation of nonproduction. Judicial procedure includes subpoena duces tecum as an incident to the taking of a deposition in another jurisdiction. No further showing is required. See McCormick § 202.

Note to Paragraph (3). A party who has an original in his control has no need for the protection of the rule if put on notice that proof of contents will be made. He can ward off secondary evidence by offering the original. The notice procedure here provided is not to be confused with orders to produce or other discovery procedures, as the purpose of the procedure under this rule is to afford the opposite party an opportunity to produce the original, not to compel him to do so. McCormick § 203.

Note to Paragraph (4). While difficult to define with precision, situations arise in which no good purpose is served by production of the original. Examples are the newspaper in an action for the price of publishing defendant's advertisement, *Foster–Holcomb Investment Co. v. Little Rock Publishing Co.*, 151 Ark. 449, 236 S.W. 597 (1922), and the streetcar transfer of plaintiff claiming status as a passenger, *Chicago City Ry. Co. v. Carroll*, 206 Ill. 318, 68 N.E. 1087 (1903). Numerous cases are collected in McCormick § 200, p. 412, n. 1.

1974 Enactment

Note to Paragraph (1). The Committee approved Rule 1004(1) in the form submitted to Congress. However, the Committee intends that loss or destruction of an original by another person at the instigation of the proponent should be considered as tantamount to loss or destruction in bad faith by the proponent himself. House Report No. 93–650.

1987 Amendments

The amendments are technical. No substantive change is intended.

Rule 1005. Public Records

The contents of an official record, or of a document authorized to be recorded or filed and actually recorded or filed, including data compilations in any form, if otherwise admissible, may be proved by copy, certified as correct in accordance with rule 902 or testified to be correct by a witness who has compared it with the original. If a copy which complies with the foregoing cannot be obtained by the exercise of reasonable diligence, then other evidence of the contents may be given.

(Pub.L. 93–595, § 1, Jan. 2, 1975, 88 Stat. 1946.)

ADVISORY COMMITTEE NOTES

1972 Proposed Rules

Public records call for somewhat different treatment. Removing them from their usual place of keeping would be attended by serious inconvenience to the public and to the custodian. As a consequence judicial decisions and statutes commonly hold that no explanation need be given for failure to produce the original of a public record. McCormick § 204; 4 Wigmore §§ 1215–1228. This blanket dispensation from producing or accounting for the original would open the door to the introduction of every kind of secondary evidence of contents of public records were it not for the preference given certified or compared copies. Recognition of degrees of secondary evidence in this situation is an appropriate *quid pro quo* for not applying the requirement of producing the original.

The provisions of 28 U.S.C. § 1733(b) apply only to departments or agencies of the United States. The rule, however, applies to public records generally and is comparable in scope in this respect to Rule 44(a) of the Rules of Civil Procedure.

Rule 1006. Summaries

The contents of voluminous writings, recordings, or photographs which cannot conveniently be examined in court may be presented in the form of a chart, summary, or calculation. The originals, or duplicates, shall be made available for examination or copying, or both, by other parties at reasonable time and place. The court may order that they be produced in court.

(Pub.L. 93–595, § 1, Jan. 2, 1975, 88 Stat. 1946.)

ADVISORY COMMITTEE NOTES

1972 Proposed Rules

The admission of summaries of voluminous books, records, or documents offers the only practicable means of making their contents available to judge and jury. The rule recognizes this practice, with appropriate safeguards. 4 Wigmore § 1230.

Rule 1007. Testimony or Written Admission of Party

Contents of writings, recordings, or photographs may be proved by the testimony or deposition of the party against whom offered or by that party's written admission, without accounting for the nonproduction of the original.

(Pub.L. 93–595, § 1, Jan. 2, 1975, 88 Stat. 1947; Mar. 2, 1987, eff. Oct. 1, 1987.)

ADVISORY COMMITTEE NOTES

1972 Proposed Rules

While the parent case, *Slatterie v. Pooley*, 6 M. & W. 664, 151 Eng.Rep. 579 (Exch.1840), allows proof of contents by evidence of an oral admission by the party against whom offered, without accounting for nonproduction of the original, the risk of inaccuracy is substantial and the decision is at odds with the purpose of the rule giving preference to the original. See 4 Wigmore § 1255. The instant rule follows Professor McCormick's suggestion of limiting this use of admissions to those made in the course of giving testimony or in writing. McCormick § 208, p. 424. The limitation, of course, does not call for excluding evidence of an oral admission when nonproduction of the original has been accounted for and secondary evidence generally has become admissible. Rule 1004, supra.

A similar provision is contained in New Jersey Evidence Rule 70(1)(h).

1987 Amendments

The amendment is technical. No substantive change is intended.

Rule 1008. Functions of Court and Jury

When the admissibility of other evidence of contents of writings, recordings, or photographs under these rules depends upon the fulfillment of a condition of fact, the question whether the condition has been fulfilled is ordinarily for the court to determine in accordance with the provisions of rule 104. However, when an issue is raised (a) whether the asserted writing ever existed, or (b) whether another writing, recording, or photograph produced at the trial is the original, or (c) whether other evidence of contents correctly reflects the contents, the issue is for the trier of fact to determine as in the case of other issues of fact.

(Pub.L. 93–595, § 1, Jan. 2, 1975, 88 Stat. 1947.)

ADVISORY COMMITTEE NOTES

1972 Proposed Rules

Most preliminary questions of fact in connection with applying the rule preferring the original as evidence of contents are for the judge, under the general principles announced in Rule 104, *supra*. Thus, the question whether the loss of the originals has been established, or of the fulfillment of other conditions specified in Rule 1004, supra, is for the judge. However, questions may arise which go beyond the mere administration of the rule preferring the original and into the merits of the controversy. For example, plaintiff offers secondary evidence of the contents of an alleged contract, after first introducing evidence of loss of the original, and defendant counters with evidence that no such contract was ever executed. If the judge decides that the contract was never executed and excludes the secondary evidence, the case is at an end without ever going to the jury on a central issue. Levin, Authentication and Content of Writings, 10 Rutgers L.Rev. 632, 644 (1956). The latter portion of the instant rule is designed to insure treatment of these situations as raising jury questions. The decision is not one for uncontrolled discretion of the jury but is subject to the control exercised generally by the judge over jury determinations. See Rule 104(b), *supra*.

For similar provisions, see Uniform Rule 70(2); Kansas Code of Civil Procedure § 60–467(b); New Jersey Evidence Rule 70(2), (3).

ARTICLE XI. MISCELLANEOUS RULES

Rule 1101. Applicability of Rules

(a) Courts and judges. These rules apply to the United States district courts, the District Court of Guam, the District Court of the Virgin Islands, the District Court for the Northern Mariana Islands, the United States courts of appeals, the United States Claims Court, and to United States bankruptcy judges and United States magistrate judges, in the actions, cases, and proceedings and to the extent hereinafter set forth. The terms "judge" and "court" in these rules include United States bankruptcy judges and United States magistrate judges.

(b) Proceedings generally. These rules apply generally to civil actions and proceedings, including admiralty and maritime cases, to criminal cases and proceedings, to contempt proceedings except those in which the court may act summarily, and to proceedings and cases under title 11, United States Code.

(c) Rule of privilege. The rule with respect to privileges applies at all stages of all actions, cases, and proceedings.

(d) Rules inapplicable. The rules (other than with respect to privileges) do not apply in the following situations:

(1) Preliminary questions of fact. The determination of questions of fact preliminary to admissibility of evidence when the issue is to be determined by the court under rule 104.

(2) Grand jury. Proceedings before grand juries.

(3) Miscellaneous proceedings. Proceedings for extradition or rendition; preliminary examinations in criminal cases; sentencing, or granting or revoking probation; issuance of warrants for arrest, criminal summonses, and search warrants; and proceedings with respect to release on bail or otherwise.

(e) Rules applicable in part. In the following proceedings these rules apply to the extent that matters of evidence are not provided for in the statutes which govern procedure therein or in other rules prescribed by the Supreme Court pursuant to statutory authority: the trial of misdemeanors and other petty offenses before United States magistrate judges; review of agency actions when the facts are subject to trial de novo under section 706(2)(F) of title 5, United States Code; review of orders of the Secretary of Agriculture under section 2 of the Act entitled "An Act to authorize association of producers of agricultural products" approved February 18, 1922 (7 U.S.C. 292), and under sections 6 and 7(c) of the Perishable Agricultural Commodities Act, 1930 (7 U.S.C. 499f, 499g(c)); naturalization and revocation of naturalization under sections 310–318 of the Immigration and Nationality Act (8 U.S.C. 1421–1429); prize proceedings in admiralty under sections 7651–7681 of title 10, United States Code; review of orders of the Secretary of the Interior under section 2 of the Act entitled "An Act authorizing associations of producers of aquatic products" approved June 25, 1934 (15 U.S.C. 522); review of orders of petroleum control boards under section 5 of the Act entitled "An Act to regulate interstate and foreign commerce in petroleum and its products by prohibiting the shipment in such commerce of petroleum and its products produced in violation of State law, and for other purposes", approved February 22, 1935 (15 U.S.C. 715d); actions for fines, penalties, or forfeitures under part V of title IV of the Tariff Act of 1930 (19 U.S.C. 1581–1624), or under the Anti–Smuggling Act (19 U.S.C. 1701–1711); criminal libel for condemnation, exclusion of imports, or other proceedings under the Federal Food, Drug, and Cosmetic Act (21 U.S.C. 301–392); disputes between seamen under sections 4079, 4080, and 4081 of the Revised Statutes (22 U.S.C. 256–258); habeas corpus under sections 2241–2254 of title 28, United States Code; motions to vacate, set aside or correct sentence under section 2255 of title 28, United States Code; actions for penalties for refusal to transport destitute seamen under section 4578 of the Revised Statutes (46 U.S.C. 679); actions against the United States under the Act entitled "An Act authorizing suits against the United States in admiralty for damage caused by and salvage service rendered to public vessels belonging to the United States, and for other purposes", approved March 3, 1925 (46 U.S.C. 781–790), as implemented by section 7730 of title 10, United States Code.

(Pub.L. 93–595, § 1, Jan. 2, 1975, 88 Stat. 1947; Pub.L. 94–149, § 1(14), Dec. 12, 1975, 89 Stat. 806; Pub.L. 95–598, Title II, § 251, Nov. 6, 1978, 92 Stat. 2673; Pub.L. 97–164, Title I, § 142, Apr. 2, 1982, 96 Stat. 45; Mar. 2, 1987, eff. Oct. 1, 1987; Apr. 25, 1988, eff. Nov. 1, 1988; Pub.L. 100–690, Title VII, § 7075(c), Nov. 18, 1988, 102 Stat. 4405; Apr. 22, 1993, eff. Dec. 1, 1993.)

ADVISORY COMMITTEE NOTES

1972 Proposed Rules

Note to Subdivision (a). The various enabling acts contain differences in phraseology in their descriptions of the courts over which the Supreme Court's power to make rules of practice and procedure extends. The act concerning civil actions, as amended in 1966, refers to "the district courts * * * of the United States in civil actions, including admiralty and maritime cases. * * *" 28 U.S.C. § 2072, Pub.L. 89–773, § 1, 80 Stat. 1323. The bankruptcy authorization is for rules of practice and procedure "under the Bankruptcy Act." 28 U.S.C. § 2075, Pub.L. 88–623, § 1, 78 Stat. 1001. The Bankruptcy Act in turn creates bankruptcy courts of "the United States district courts and the district courts of the Territories and possessions to which this title is or may hereafter be applicable." 11 U.S.C. §§ 1(10), 11(a). The provision as to criminal rules up to and including verdicts applies to "criminal cases and proceedings to punish for criminal contempt of court in the United States district courts, in the district courts for the districts of the Canal Zone and Virgin Islands, in the Supreme Court of Puerto Rico, and in proceedings before United States magistrates." 18 U.S.C. § 3771.

These various provisions do not in terms describe the same courts. In congressional usage the phrase "district courts of the United States," without further qualification, traditionally has included the district courts established by Congress in the states under Article III of the Constitution, which are "constitutional" courts, and has not included the territorial courts created under Article IV, Section 3, clause 2, which are "legislative" courts. *Hornbuckle v. Toombs,* 85 U.S. 648, 21 L.Ed. 966 (1873). However, any doubt as to the inclusion of the District Court for the District of Columbia in the phrase is laid at rest by the provisions of the Judicial Code constituting the judicial districts, 28 U.S.C. § 81 et seq., creating district courts therein, id. § 132, and specifically providing that the term "district court of the United States" means the court so constituted. *Id.* § 451. The District of Columbia is included. *Id.* § 88. Moreover, when these provisions were enacted, reference to the District of Columbia was deleted from the original civil rules enabling act. 28 U.S.C. § 2072. Likewise Puerto Rico is made a district, with a district court, and included in the term. *Id.* § 119. The question is simply one of the extent of the authority conferred by Congress. With respect to civil rules it seems clearly to include the district courts in the states, the District Court for the District of Columbia, and the District Court for the District of Puerto Rico.

The bankruptcy coverage is broader. The bankruptcy courts include "the United States district courts," which includes those enumerated above. Bankruptcy courts also include "the district courts of the Territories and possessions to which this title is or may hereafter be applicable." 11 U.S.C. §§ 1(10), 11(a). These courts include the district courts of Guam and the Virgin Islands. 48 U.S.C. §§ 1424(b), 1615. Professor Moore points out that whether the District Court for the District of the Canal Zone is a court of bankruptcy "is not free from doubt in view of the fact that no other statute expressly or inferentially provides for the applicability of the Bankruptcy Act in the Zone." He further observes that while there seems to be little doubt that the Zone is a territory or possession within the meaning of the Bankruptcy Act, 11 U.S.C. § 1(10), it must be noted that the appendix to the Canal Zone Code of 1934 did not list the Act among the laws of the United States applicable to the Zone. 1 Moore's Collier on Bankruptcy ¶ 1.10, pp. 67, 72, n. 25 (14th ed. 1967). The Code of 1962 confers on the district court jurisdiction of:

"(4) actions and proceedings involving laws of the United States applicable to the Canal Zone; and

"(5) other matters and proceedings wherein jurisdiction is conferred by this Code or any other law." Canal Zone Code, 1962, Title 3, § 141.

Admiralty jurisdiction is expressly conferred. *Id.* § 142. General powers are conferred on the district court, "if the course of proceeding is not specifically prescribed by this Code, by the statute, or by applicable rule of the Supreme Court of the United States * * *" *Id.* § 279. Neither these provisions nor § 1(10) of the Bankruptcy Act ("district courts of the Territories and possessions to which this title is or may hereafter be applicable") furnishes a satisfactory answer as to the status of the District Court for the District of the Canal Zone as a court of bankruptcy. However, the fact is that this court exercises no bankruptcy jurisdiction in practice.

The criminal rules enabling act specified United States district courts, district courts for the districts of the Canal Zone and the Virgin Islands, the Supreme Court of the Commonwealth of Puerto Rico, and proceedings before United States commissioners. Aside from the addition of commissioners, now magistrates, this scheme differs from the bankruptcy pattern in that it makes no mention of the District Court of Guam but by specific mention removes the Canal Zone from the doubtful list.

The further difference in including the Supreme Court of the Commonwealth of Puerto Rico seems not to be significant for present purposes, since the Supreme Court of the Commonwealth of Puerto Rico is an appellate court. The Rules of Criminal Procedure have not been made applicable to it, as being unneeded and inappropriate, Rule 54(a) of the Federal Rules of Criminal Procedure, and the same approach is indicated with respect to rules of evidence.

If one were to stop at this point and frame a rule governing the applicability of the proposed rules of evidence in terms of the authority conferred by the three enabling acts, an irregular pattern would emerge as follows:

Civil actions, including admiralty and maritime cases—district courts in the states, District of Columbia, and Puerto Rico.

Bankruptcy—same as civil actions, plus Guam and Virgin Islands.

Criminal cases—same as civil actions, plus Canal Zone and Virgin Islands (but not Guam).

This irregular pattern need not, however, be accepted. Originally the Advisory Committee on the Rules of Civil Procedure took the position that, although the phrase "district courts of the United States" did not include territorial courts, provisions in the organic laws of Puerto Rico and Hawaii would make the rules applicable to the district courts thereof, though this would not be so as to Alaska, the Virgin Islands, or the Canal Zone, whose organic acts contained no corresponding provisions. At the suggestion of the Court, however, the Advisory Committee struck from its notes a statement to the above effect. 2 Moore's Federal Practice ¶ 1.07 (2nd ed. 1967); 1 Barron and Holtzoff, Federal Practice and Procedure § 121 (Wright ed. 1960). Congress thereafter by various enactments provided that the rules and future amendments thereto should apply to the district courts of Hawaii, 53 Stat. 841 (1939), Puerto Rico, 54 Stat. 22 (1940), Alaska, 63 Stat. 445 (1949), Guam, 64 Stat. 384–390 (1950), and the Virgin Islands, 68 Stat. 497, 507 (1954). The original enabling act for rules of criminal procedure specifically mentioned the district courts of the Canal Zone and the Virgin Islands. The Commonwealth of Puerto Rico was blanketed in by creating its court a "district court of the United States" as previously described. Although Guam is not mentioned in either the enabling act or in the expanded definition of "district court of the United States," the Supreme Court in 1956 amended Rule 54(a) to state that the

Rules of Criminal Procedure are applicable in Guam. The Court took this step following the enactment of legislation by Congress in 1950 that rules theretofore or thereafter promulgated by the Court in civil cases, admiralty, criminal cases and bankruptcy should apply to the District Court of Guam, 48 U.S.C. § 1424(b), and two Ninth Circuit decisions upholding the applicability of the Rules of Criminal Procedure to Guam. *Pugh v. United States,* 212 F.2d 761 (9th Cir.1954); *Hatchett v. Guam,* 212 F.2d 767 (9th Cir.1954); Orfield, The Scope of the Federal Rules of Criminal Procedure, 38 U. of Det.L.J. 173, 187 (1960).

From this history, the reasonable conclusion is that Congressional enactment of a provision that rules and future amendments shall apply in the courts of a territory or possession is the equivalent of mention in an enabling act and that a rule on scope and applicability may properly be drafted accordingly. Therefore the pattern set by Rule 54 of the Federal Rules of Criminal Procedure is here followed.

The substitution of magistrates in lieu of commissioners is made in pursuance of the Federal Magistrates Act, P.L. 90–578, approved October 17, 1968, 82 Stat. 1107.

Note to Subdivision (b). Subdivision (b) is a combination of the language of the enabling acts, supra, with respect to the kinds of proceedings in which the making of rules is authorized. It is subject to the qualifications expressed in the subdivisions which follow.

Note to Subdivision (c). Subdivision (c) singling out the rules of privilege for special treatment, is made necessary by the limited applicability of the remaining rules.

Note to Subdivision (d). The rule is not intended as an expression as to when due process or other constitutional provisions may require an evidentiary hearing. Paragraph (1) restates, for convenience, the provisions of the second sentence of Rule 104(a), *supra.* See Advisory Committee's Note to that rule.

(2) While some states have statutory requirements that indictments be based on "legal evidence," and there is some case law to the effect that the rules of evidence apply to grand jury proceedings, 1 Wigmore § 4(5), the Supreme Court has not accepted this view. In *Costello v. United States,* 350 U.S. 359, 76 S.Ct. 406, 100 L.Ed. 397 (1965), the Court refused to allow an indictment to be attacked, for either constitutional or policy reasons, on the ground that only hearsay evidence was presented.

"It would run counter to the whole history of the grand jury institution, in which laymen conduct their inquiries unfettered by technical rules. Neither justice nor the concept of a fair trial requires such a change." *Id.* at 364. The rule as drafted does not deal with the evidence required to support an indictment.

(3) The rule exempts preliminary examinations in criminal cases. Authority as to the applicability of the rules of evidence to preliminary examinations has been meagre and conflicting. Goldstein, The State and the Accused: Balance of Advantage in Criminal Procedure, 69 Yale L.J. 1149, 1168, n. 53 (1960); Comment, Preliminary Hearings on Indictable Offenses in Philadelphia, 106 U. of Pa.L.Rev. 589, 592–593 (1958). Hearsay testimony is, however, customarily received in such examinations. Thus in a Dyer Act case, for example, an affidavit may properly be used in a preliminary examination to prove ownership of the stolen vehicle, thus saving the victim of the crime the hardship of having to travel twice to a distant district for the sole purpose of testifying as to ownership. It is believed that the extent of the applicability of the Rules of Evidence to preliminary examinations should be appropriately dealt with by the Federal Rules of Criminal Procedure which regulate those proceedings.

Extradition and rendition proceedings are governed in detail by statute. 18 U.S.C. §§ 3181–3195. They are essentially administrative in character. Traditionally the rules of evidence have not applied. 1 Wigmore § 4(6). Extradition proceedings are accepted from the operation of the Rules of Criminal Procedure. Rule 54(b)(5) of Federal Rules of Criminal Procedure.

The rules of evidence have not been regarded as applicable to sentencing or probation proceedings, where great reliance is placed upon the presentence investigation and report. Rule 32(c) of the Federal Rules of Criminal Procedure requires a presentence investigation and report in every case unless the court otherwise directs. In *Williams v. New York,* 337 U.S. 241, 69 S.Ct. 1079, 93 L.Ed. 1337 (1949), in which the judge overruled a jury recommendation of life imprisonment and imposed a death sentence, the Court said that due process does not require confrontation or cross-examination in sentencing or passing on probation, and that the judge has broad discretion as to the sources and types of information relied upon. Compare the recommendation that the substance of all derogatory information be disclosed to the defendant, in A.B.A. Project on Minimum Standards for Criminal Justice, Sentencing Alternatives and Procedures § 4.4, Tentative Draft (1967, Sobeloff, Chm.). Williams was adhered to in *Specht v. Patterson,* 386 U.S. 605, 87 S.Ct. 1209, 18 L.Ed.2d 326 (1967), but not extended to a proceeding under the Colorado Sex Offenders Act, which was said to be a new charge leading in effect to punishment, more like the recidivist statutes where opportunity must be given to be heard on the habitual criminal issue.

Warrants for arrest, criminal summonses, and search warrants are issued upon complaint or affidavit showing probable cause. Rules 4(a) and 41(c) of the Federal Rules of Criminal Procedure. The nature of the proceedings makes application of the formal rules of evidence inappropriate and impracticable.

Criminal contempts are punishable summarily if the judge certifies that he saw or heard the contempt and that it was committed in the presence of the court. Rule 42(a) of the Federal Rules of Criminal Procedure. The circumstances which preclude application of the rules of evidence in this situation are not present, however, in other cases of criminal contempt.

Proceedings with respect to release on bail or otherwise do not call for application of the rules of evidence. The governing statute specifically provides:

"Information stated in, or offered in connection with, any order entered pursuant to this section need not conform to the rules pertaining to the admissibility of evidence in a court of law." 18 U.S.C.A. § 3146(f). This provision is consistent with the type of inquiry contemplated in A.B.A. Project on Minimum Standards for Criminal Justice, Standards Relating to Pretrial Release, § 4.5(b), (c), p. 16 (1968). The references to the weight of the evidence against the accused, in Rule 46(a)(1), (c) of the Federal Rules of Criminal Procedure and in 18 U.S.C.A. § 3146(b), as a factor to be considered, clearly do not have in view evidence introduced at a hearing under the rules of evidence.

The rule does not exempt habeas corpus proceedings. The Supreme Court held in *Walker v. Johnston,* 312 U.S. 275, 61 S.Ct. 574, 85 L.Ed. 830 (1941), that the practice of disposing of matters of fact on affidavit, which prevailed in some circuits, did not "satisfy the command of the statute that the judge shall proceed 'to determine the facts of the case, by hearing the testimony and arguments.'" This view accords with the emphasis in *Townsend v. Sain,* 372 U.S. 293, 83 S.Ct. 745, 9 L.Ed.2d 770 (1963), upon trial-type proceedings, *id.* 311, 83 S.Ct. 745, with demeanor evidence as a significant factor, *id.* 322, 83 S.Ct. 745, in applications by state prisoners aggrieved by unconstitutional detentions. Hence subdivision (3) applies the rules to habeas corpus proceedings to the extent not inconsistent with the statute.

Note to Subdivision (e). In a substantial number of special proceedings, *ad hoc* evaluation has resulted in the promulgation of particularized evidentiary provisions, by Act of Congress or by rule adopted by the Supreme Court. Well adapted to the particular proceedings, though not apt candidates for inclusion in a set of general rules, they are left undisturbed. Otherwise, however, the rules of evidence are applicable to the proceedings enumerated in the subdivision.

1974 Enactment

Note to Subdivision (a). Subdivision (a) as submitted to the Congress, in stating the courts and judges to which the Rules of Evidence apply, omitted the Court of Claims and commissioners of that Court. At the request of the Court of Claims, the Committee amended the Rule to include the Court and its commissioners within the purview of the Rules.

Note to Subdivision (b). Subdivision (b) was amended merely to substitute positive law citations for those which were not. House Report No. 93–650.

1987 Amendments

Subdivision (a) is amended to delete the reference to the District Court for the District of the Canal Zone, which no longer exists, and to add the District Court for the Northern Mariana Islands. The United States bankruptcy judges are added to conform the subdivision with Rule 1101(b) and Bankruptcy Rule 9017.

1988 Amendments

The amendments are technical. No substantive change is intended.

1993 Amendments

This revision is made to conform the rule to changes in terminology made by Rule 58 of the Federal Rules of Criminal Procedure and to the changes in the title of United States magistrates made by the Judicial Improvements Act of 1990.

HISTORICAL NOTES

References in Text

The Tariff Act of 1930, referred to in subsec. (e), is Act June 17, 1930, c. 497, 46 Stat. 590, as amended, which is classified principally to chapter 4 (section 1202 et seq.) of Title 19, Customs Duties. Part V of Title IV of the Tariff Act of 1930 enacted part V (section 1581 et seq.) of subtitle III of chapter 4 of Title 19. For complete classification of this Act to the Code, see section 1654 of Title 19 and Tables.

The Anti–Smuggling Act (19 U.S.C. 1701–1711), referred to in subsec. (e), is Act Aug. 5, 1935, c. 438, 49 Stat. 517, as amended, which is classified principally to chapter 5 (section 1701 et seq.) of Title 19, Customs Duties. For complete classification of this Act to the Code, see section 1711 of Title 19 and Tables.

The Federal Food, Drug, and Cosmetic Act (21 U.S.C. 301–392), referred to in subsec. (e), is Act June 25, 1938, c. 675, 52 Stat. 1040, as amended, which is classified generally to chapter 9 (section 301 et seq.) of Title 21, Food and Drugs. For complete classification of this Act to the Code, see section 301 of Title 21 and Tables.

"An Act authorizing suits against the United States in admiralty for damage caused by and salvage service rendered to public vessels belonging to the United States, and for other purposes," approved Mar. 3, 1925 (46 U.S.C. 781–790), referred to in subsec. (e), is Act Mar. 3, 1925, c. 428, 43 Stat. 1112, as amended, known as the "Public Vessels Act", which is classified generally to chapter 22 (section 781 et seq.) of Title 46, Shipping. For complete classification of this Act to the Code, see Short Title note set out under section 781 of Title 46 and Tables.

1988 Amendments

Subd. (a). Pub.L. 100–690, § 7075(c)(1), (2), substituted "rules" and "courts of appeals" for "Rules" and "Courts of Appeals".

1982 Amendments

Subd. (a). Pub.L. 97–164 substituted "United States Claims Court" for "Court of Claims" and struck out "and commissioners of the Court of Claims" following "these rules include United States magistrates".

1978 Amendments

Subd. (a). Pub.L. 95–598, § 251(a), struck out ", referees in bankruptcy," following "United States magistrates".

1978 Amendments

Subd. (a). Pub.L. 95–598, § 252, directed the amendment of this subd. by adding "the United States bankruptcy courts," after "the United States district courts,", which amendment did not become effective pursuant to section 402(b) of Pub.L. 95–598, as amended, set out as an Effective Date note preceding section 101 of Title 11, Bankruptcy.

Subd. (b). Pub.L. 95–598, § 251(b), substituted "title 11, United States Code" for "the Bankruptcy Act".

1975 Amendments

Subd. (e). Pub.L. 94–149 substituted "admiralty" for "admirality".

Effective and Applicability Provisions

1982 Acts. Amendment by Pub.L. 97–164 effective Oct. 1, 1982, see section 402 of Pub.L. 97–164, set out as a note under section 171 of this title.

1978 Acts. Amendment of subds. (a) and (b) of this rule by section 251 of Pub.L. 95–598 effective Oct. 1, 1979, see section 402(c) of Pub.L. 95–598, set out as a note preceding section 101 of Title 11, Bankruptcy.

Change of Name

United States magistrate appointed under section 631 of Title 28, Judiciary and Judicial Procedure, to be known as

United States magistrate judge after Dec. 1, 1990, with any reference to United States magistrate or magistrate in Title 28, in any other Federal statute, etc., deemed a reference to United States magistrate judge appointed under section 631 of Title 28, see section 321 of Pub.L. 101–650, set out as a note under section 631 of Title 28.

Pending Actions

Amendments of Supreme Court to the Federal Rules of Evidence effective December 1, 1993, applicable, insofar as just and practicable, in all proceedings then pending, pursuant to the Order of April 22, 1993.

Rule 1102. Amendments

Amendments to the Federal Rules of Evidence may be made as provided in section 2072 of title 28 of the United States Code.

(Pub.L. 93–595, § 1, Jan. 2, 1975, 88 Stat.1948); Apr. 30, 1991, eff. Dec. 1, 1991.)

ADVISORY COMMITTEE NOTES

1991 Amendments

The amendment is technical. No substantive change is intended.

Rule 1103. Title

These rules may be known and cited as the Federal Rules of Evidence.

(Pub.L. 93–595, § 1, Jan. 2, 1975, 88 Stat.1948.)

HISTORICAL NOTES

Short Title

1978 Amendments. Pub.L. 95–540, § 1, Oct. 28, 1978, 92 Stat. 2046, provided: "That this Act [enacting rule 412 of these rules and a provision set out as a note under rule 412 of these rules] may be cited as the 'Privacy Protection for Rape Victims Act of 1978'."

FEDERAL RULES OF APPELLATE PROCEDURE

Amendments received to February 2, 2007

ORDERS OF THE SUPREME COURT OF THE UNITED STATES ADOPTING AND AMENDING RULES

ORDER OF DECEMBER 4, 1967

ORDERED:

1. That the following rules, to be known as the Federal Rules of Appellate Procedure, be, and they hereby are, prescribed, pursuant to sections 3771 and 3772 of Title 18, United States Code, and sections 2072 and 2075 of Title 28, United States Code, to govern the procedure in appeals to United States courts of appeals from the United States district courts, in the review by United States courts of appeals of decisions of the Tax Court of the United States, in proceedings in the United States courts of appeals for the review or enforcement of orders of administrative agencies, boards, commissions and officers, and in applications for writs or other relief which a United States court of appeals or judge thereof is competent to give:

[See text of Rules of Appellate Procedure, post]

2. That the foregoing rules shall take effect on July 1, 1968, and shall govern all proceedings in appeals and petitions for review or enforcement of orders thereafter brought and in all such proceedings then pending, except to the extent that in the opinion of the court of appeals their application in a particular proceeding then pending would not be feasible or would work injustice, in which case the former procedure may be followed.

3. That Rules 6, 9, 41, 77 and 81 of the Rules of Civil Procedure for the United States District Courts be, and they hereby are, amended, effective July 1, 1968, as hereinafter set forth:

[For text of amendments, see pamphlet containing Federal Rules of Civil Procedure]

4. That the chapter heading "IX. APPEALS", all of Rules 72, 73, 74, 75 and 76 of the Rules of Civil Procedure for the United States District Courts, and Form 27 annexed to the said rules, be, and they hereby are, abrogated, effective July 1, 1968.

5. That Rules 45, 49, 56 and 57 of the Rules of Criminal Procedure for the United States District Courts be, and they hereby are, amended, effective July 1, 1968, as hereinafter set forth:

[See amendments made thereby under the Rules of Criminal Procedure, ante]

6. That the chapter heading "VIII. APPEAL", all of Rules 37 and 39, and subdivisions (b) and (c) of Rule 38, of the Rules of Criminal Procedure for the United States District Courts, and Forms 26 and 27 annexed to the said rules, be, and they hereby are, abrogated, effective July 1, 1968.

7. That the Chief Justice be, and he hereby is, authorized to transmit to the Congress the foregoing new rules and amendments to and abrogation of existing rules, in accordance with the provisions of Title 18, U.S.C., § 3771, and Title 28, U.S.C., §§ 2072 and 2075.

ORDER OF MARCH 30, 1970

1. That subdivisions (a) and (c) of Rule 30 and subdivision (a) of Rule 31 of the Federal Rules of Appellate Procedure be, and they hereby are, amended as follows:

[See the amendments made thereby under the respective rules, post]

2. That the foregoing amendments to the Federal Rules of Appellate Procedure shall take effect on July 1, 1970, and shall govern all proceedings in actions brought thereafter and also in all further proceedings in actions then pending, except to the extent that in the opinion of the court their application in a particular action then pending would not be feasible or would work injustice, in which event the former procedure applies.

3. That the Chief Justice be, and he hereby is, authorized to transmit to the Congress the foregoing amendments to existing rules, in accordance with the provisions of Title 18, U.S.C., § 3772, and Title 28, U.S.C., §§ 2072 and 2075.

ORDER OF MARCH 1, 1971

1. That subdivision (a) of Rule 6, paragraph (4) of subdivision (a) of Rule 27, paragraph (6) of subdivision (b) of Rule 30, subdivision (c) of Rule 77, and paragraph (2) of subdivision (a) of Rule 81 of the Federal Rules of Civil Procedure be, and hereby are, amended, effective July 1, 1971, to read as follows:

[For text of amendments, see pamphlet containing Federal Rules of Civil Procedure]

2. That subdivision (a) of Rule 45 and all of Rule 56 of the Federal Rules of Criminal Procedure be, and they hereby are, amended, effective July 1, 1971, to read as follows:

[See amendments made thereby under the respective Rules of Criminal Procedure, ante]

3. That subdivision (a) of Rule 26 and subdivision (a) of Rule 45 of the Federal Rules of Appellate Procedure be, and they hereby are, amended, effective July 1, 1971, to read as follows:

[See amendments made thereby under the respective rules, post]

4. That THE CHIEF JUSTICE be, and he hereby is, authorized to transmit to the Congress the foregoing amendments to the Rules of Civil, Criminal and Appellate Procedure, in accordance with the provisions of Title 18, U.S.C., § 3771, and Title 28, U.S.C., §§ 2072 and 2075.

MR. JUSTICE BLACK and MR. JUSTICE DOUGLAS dissent.

ORDER OF APRIL 24, 1972

1. That Rules 1, 3, 4(b) & (c), 5, 5.1, 6(b), 7(c), 9(b), (c) & (d), 17(a) & (g), 31(e), 32(b), 38(a), 40, 41, 44, 46, 50, 54 and 55 of the Federal Rules of Criminal Procedure be, and they hereby are, amended effective October 1, 1972, to read as follows:

[See amendments made thereby under the respective Rules of Criminal Procedure, ante]

2. That Rule 9(c) of the Federal Rules of Appellate Procedure be, and hereby is amended, effective October 1, 1972, to read as follows:

[See amendments made thereby under the respective rules, post]

3. That THE CHIEF JUSTICE be, and he hereby is, authorized to transmit to the Congress the foregoing amendments to Rules of Criminal and Appellate Procedure, in accordance with the provisions of Title 18, U.S.Code, §§ 3771 and 3772.

MR. JUSTICE DOUGLAS dissented to adoption of Rule 50(b) of the Federal Rules of Criminal Procedure.

ORDER OF APRIL 30, 1979

1. That the Federal Rules of Appellate Procedure be, and they hereby are, amended by including therein amendments to Rules 1(a), 3(c), (d) and (e), 4(a), 5(d), 6(d), 7, 10(b), 11(a), (b), (c) and (d), 12, 13(a), 24(b), 27(b), 28(g) and (j), 34(a) and (b), 35(b) and (c), 39(c) and (d), and 40 as hereinafter set forth:

[See amendments made thereby under the respective rules, post]

2. That the foregoing amendments to the Federal Rules of Appellate Procedure shall take effect on August 1, 1979, and shall govern all appellate proceedings thereafter commenced and, insofar as just and practicable, all proceedings then pending.

3. That THE CHIEF JUSTICE be, and he hereby is, authorized to transmit to the Congress the foregoing amendments to the Federal Rules of Appellate Procedure in accordance with the provisions of Section 3772 of Title 18, United States Code, and Sections 2072 and 2075 of Title 28, United States Code.

ORDER OF MARCH 10, 1986

1. That the Federal Rules of Appellate Procedure be, and they hereby are, amended by including therein new Appellate Rules 3.1, 5.1 and 15.1 and amendments to Appellate Rules 3(d), 8(b), 10(b) and (c), 11(b), 12(a), 19, 23(b) and (c), 24(a), 25(a) and (b), 26(a) and (c), 28(c) and (j), 30(a), (b) and (c), 31(a) and (c), 34(a) and (e), 39(c) and (d), 43(a) and (c), 45(a), (b), and (d), and 46(a) and (b), as hereinafter set forth:

[See amendments made thereby under the respective rules, post]

2. That the foregoing additions to and changes in the Federal Rules of Appellate Procedure, shall take effect on July 1, 1986 and shall govern all proceedings in appellate actions thereafter commenced and, insofar as just and practicable, all proceedings in appellate actions then pending.

3. That THE CHIEF JUSTICE be, and he hereby is, authorized to transmit to the Congress the foregoing additions to and changes in the rules of appellate procedure in accordance with the provisions of Section 3772 of Title 18 and Section 2072 of Title 28, United States Code.

ORDER OF APRIL 25, 1989

1. That the Federal Rules of Appellate Procedure be, and they hereby are, amended by including therein amendments to Appellate Rules 1(a), 3(a), 26(a), 27(a), 28(g) and new Rules 6 and 26.1, and a new Form 5 as hereinafter set forth:

[See amendments made thereby under the respective rules, post]

2. That the foregoing additions to and changes in the Federal Rules of Appellate Procedure, shall take effect on December 1, 1989 and shall govern all proceedings in appellate actions thereafter commenced and, insofar as just and practicable, all proceedings in appellate actions then pending.

3. That THE CHIEF JUSTICE be, and he hereby is, authorized to transmit to the Congress the foregoing additions to and changes in the rules of appellate procedure in accordance with the provisions of Section 2072 of Title 28, United States Code.

ORDER OF APRIL 30, 1991

1. That the Federal Rules of Appellate Procedure be, and they hereby are, amended by including therein amendments to Appellate Rules 4(a), 6, 10(c), 25(a), 26(a), 26.1, 28(a), (b), and (h), 30(b), and 34(d).

[See amendments made thereby under the respective rules, post]

2. That the foregoing amendments to the Federal Rules of Appellate Procedure shall take effect on December 1, 1991, and shall govern all proceedings in appellate cases thereafter commenced and, insofar as just and practicable, all proceedings in appellate cases then pending.

3. That THE CHIEF JUSTICE be, and he hereby is, authorized to transmit to the Congress the foregoing amendments to the Federal Rules of Appellate Procedure in accordance with the provisions of Section 2072 of Title 28, United States Code.

ORDER OF APRIL 22, 1993

1. That the Federal Rules of Appellate Procedure be, and they hereby are, amended by including therein amendments to Appellate Rules 3, 3.1, 4, 5.1, 6, 10, 12, 15, 25, 28, and 34, and to Forms 1, 2, and 3.

[See amendments made thereby under the respective rules and forms, post.]

2. That the foregoing amendments to the Federal Rules of Appellate Procedure shall take effect on December 1, 1993, and shall govern all proceedings in appellate cases thereafter commenced and, insofar as just and practicable, all proceedings in appellate cases then pending.

3. That THE CHIEF JUSTICE be, and he hereby is, authorized to transmit to the Congress the foregoing amendments to the Federal Rules of Appellate Procedure in accordance with the provisions of Section 2072 of Title 28, United States Code.

ORDER OF APRIL 29, 1994

1. That the Federal Rules of Appellate Procedure be, and they hereby are, amended by including therein amendments to Appellate Rules 1, 3, 5, 5.1, 9, 13, 21, 25, 26.1, 27, 28, 30, 31, 33, 35, 38, 40, 41, and 48.

[See amendments made hereby under respective rules, post]

2. That the foregoing amendments to the Federal Rules of Appellate Procedure shall take effect on December 1, 1994, and shall govern all proceedings in appellate cases

thereafter commenced and, insofar as just and practicable, all proceedings in appellate cases then pending.

3. That THE CHIEF JUSTICE be, and he hereby is, authorized to transmit to the Congress the foregoing amendments to the Federal Rules of Appellate Procedure in accordance with the provisions of Section 2072 of Title 28, United States Code.

ORDER OF APRIL 27, 1995

1. That the Federal Rules of Appellate Procedure be, and they hereby are, amended by including therein amendments to Appellate Rules 4, 8, 10, and 47.

[See amendments made thereby under the respective rules, post.]

2. That the foregoing amendments to the Federal Rules of Appellate Procedure shall take effect on December 1, 1995, and shall govern all proceedings in appellate cases thereafter commenced and, insofar as just and practicable, all proceedings in appellate cases then pending.

3. That THE CHIEF JUSTICE be, and he hereby is, authorized to transmit to the Congress the foregoing amendments to the Federal Rules of Appellate Procedure in accordance with the provisions of Section 2072 of Title 28, United States Code.

ORDER OF APRIL 23, 1996

1. That the Federal Rules of Appellate Procedure be, and they hereby are, amended by including therein amendments to Appellate Rules 21, 25, and 26.

[See amendments made thereby under respective rules, post]

2. That the foregoing amendments to the Federal Rules of Appellate Procedure shall take effect on December 1, 1996, and shall govern all proceedings in appellate cases thereafter commenced and, insofar as just and practicable, all proceedings in appellate cases then pending.

3. That THE CHIEF JUSTICE be, and hereby is, authorized to transmit to the Congress the foregoing amendments to the Federal Rules of Appellate Procedure in accordance with the provisions of Section 2072 of Title 28, United States Code.

ORDER OF APRIL 24, 1998

1. That the Federal Rules of Appellate Procedure be, and they hereby are, amended by including therein amendments to Appellate Rules 1–48 and to Form 4.

[See amendments made thereby under respective rules, post]

2. That the foregoing amendments to the Federal Rules of Appellate Procedure shall take effect on December 1, 1998, and shall govern in all proceedings thereafter commenced and, insofar as just and practicable, all proceedings then pending.

3. That THE CHIEF JUSTICE be, and hereby is, authorized to transmit to the Congress the foregoing amendments to the Federal Rules of Appellate Procedure in accordance with the provisions of Section 2072 of Title 28, United States Code.

ORDER OF APRIL 29, 2002

1. That the Federal Rules of Appellate Procedure be, and they hereby are, amended by including therein amendments to Appellate Rules 1, 4, 5, 21, 24, 25, 26, 26.1, 27, 28, 31, 32, 36, 41, 44, and 45 and new Form 6.

[See amendments made thereby under respective rules and forms, post]

2. That the foregoing amendments to the Federal Rules of Appellate Procedure shall take effect on December 1, 2002, and shall govern in all proceedings in appellate cases thereafter commenced and, insofar as just and practicable, all proceedings then pending.

3. That THE CHIEF JUSTICE be, and hereby is, authorized to transmit to the Congress the foregoing amendments to the Federal Rules of Appellate Procedure in accordance with the provisions of Section 2072 of Title 28, United States Code.

ORDER OF MARCH 27, 2003

1. That Forms 1, 2, 3, and 5 in the Appendix to the Federal Rules of Appellate Procedure be, and they hereby are, amended by replacing all references to "19___" with references to "20___."

[See amendments made thereby under respective forms, post]

2. That the foregoing amendments to the forms in the Appendix to the Federal Rules of Appellate Procedure shall take effect on December 1, 2003, and shall govern in all proceedings in appellate cases thereafter commenced and, insofar as just and practicable, all proceedings then pending.

3. That THE CHIEF JUSTICE be, and hereby is, authorized to transmit to the Congress the foregoing amendments to the Federal Rules of Appellate Procedure in accordance with the provisions of Section 2072 of Title 28, United States Code.

ORDER OF APRIL 25, 2005

1. That the Federal Rules of Appellate Procedure be, and they hereby are, amended by including therein amendments to Appellate Rules 4, 26, 27, 28, 32, 34, 35, 45, and new Rule 28.1.

[See amendments made thereby under respective rules, post]

2. That the foregoing amendments to the Federal Rules of Appellate Procedure shall take effect on December 1, 2005, and shall govern in all proceedings thereafter commenced and, insofar as just and practicable, all proceedings then pending.

3. That THE CHIEF JUSTICE be, and hereby is, authorized to transmit to the Congress the foregoing amendments to the Federal Rules of Appellate Procedure in accordance with the provisions of Section 2072 of Title 28, United States Code.

ORDER OF APRIL 12, 2006

1. That the Federal Rules of Appellate Procedure be, and they hereby are, amended by including therein an amendment to Appellate Rule 25 and a new Rule 32.1.

[See amendments made thereby under respective rules, post]

2. That the foregoing amendment and new rule shall take effect on December 1, 2006, and shall govern in all proceedings thereafter commenced and, insofar as just and practicable, all proceedings then pending.

3. That the CHIEF JUSTICE be, and hereby is, authorized to transmit to the Congress the foregoing amendments to the Federal Rules of Appellate Procedure in accordance with the provisions of Section 2072 of Title 28, United States Code.

HISTORICAL NOTES

Effective and Applicability Provisions; Application; Transmission to Congress

The Federal Rules of Appellate Procedure were adopted by order of the Supreme Court on Dec. 4, 1967, transmitted to Congress by the Chief Justice on Jan. 15, 1968, and became effective on July 1, 1968.

The Rules have been amended Mar. 30, 1970, eff. July 1, 1970; Mar. 1, 1971, eff. July 1, 1971; Apr. 24, 1972, eff. Oct. 1, 1972; Apr. 30, 1979, eff. Aug. 1, 1979; Oct. 12, 1984, Pub.L. 98–473, Title II, § 210, 98 Stat. 1987; Mar. 10, 1986, eff. July 1, 1986; Nov. 18, 1988, Pub.L. 100–690, Title VII, § 7111, 102 Stat. 4419; Apr. 25, 1989, eff. Dec. 1, 1989; Apr. 30, 1991, eff. Dec. 1, 1991; Apr. 22, 1993, eff. Dec. 1, 1993; Apr. 29, 1994, eff. Dec. 1, 1994; Apr. 27, 1995, eff. Dec. 1, 1995; Apr. 23, 1996, eff. Dec. 1, 1996; Apr. 24, 1998, eff. Dec. 1, 1998; Apr. 29, 2002, eff. Dec. 1, 2002; Mar. 27, 2003, eff. Dec. 1, 2003; Apr. 25, 2005, eff. Dec. 1, 2005; Apr. 12, 2006, eff. Dec. 1, 2006.

TITLE I. APPLICABILITY OF RULES

Rule 1. Scope of Rules; Title

(a) Scope of Rules.

(1) These rules govern procedure in the United States courts of appeals.

(2) When these rules provide for filing a motion or other document in the district court, the procedure must comply with the practice of the district court.

(b) [Abrogated]

(c) Title. These rules are to be known as the Federal Rules of Appellate Procedure.

(As amended Apr. 30, 1979, eff. Aug. 1, 1979; Apr. 25, 1989, eff. Dec. 1, 1989; Apr. 29, 1994, eff. Dec. 1, 1994; Apr. 24, 1998, eff. Dec. 1, 1998; Apr. 29, 2002, eff. Dec. 1, 2002.)

ADVISORY COMMITTEE NOTES

1967 Adoption

These rules are drawn under the authority of 28 U.S.C. § 2072 as amended by the Act of November 6, 1966, 80 Stat. 1323 (1 U.S.Code Cong. & Ad.News, p. 1546 (1966)) (Rules of Civil Procedure); 28 U.S.C. § 2075 (Bankruptcy Rules); and 18 U.S.C. §§ 3771 [§ 3771 of Title 18, Crimes and Criminal Procedure] (Procedure to and including verdict) and 3772 [§ 3772 of Title 18] (Procedure after verdict). Those statutes combine to give to the Supreme Court power to make rules of practice and procedure for all cases within the jurisdiction of the courts of appeals. By the terms of the statutes, after the rules have taken effect all laws in conflict with them are of no further force or effect. Practice and procedure in the eleven courts of appeals are now regulated by rules promulgated by each court under the authority of 28 U.S.C. § 2071. Rule 47 expressly authorizes the courts of appeals to make rules of practice not inconsistent with these rules.

As indicated by the titles under which they are found, the following rules are of special application: Rules 3 through 12 apply to appeals from judgments and orders of the district courts; Rules 13 and 14 apply to appeals from decisions of the Tax Court (Rule 13 establishes an appeal as the mode of review of decisions of the Tax Court in place of the present petition for review); Rules 15 through 20 apply to proceedings for review or enforcement of orders of administrative agencies, boards, commissions and officers. Rules 22 through 24 regulate habeas corpus proceedings and appeals in forma pauperis. All other rules apply to all proceedings in the courts of appeals.

1979 Amendment

The Federal Rules of Appellate Procedure were designed as an integrated set of rules to be followed in appeals to the courts of appeals, covering all steps in the appellate process, whether they take place in the district court or in the court of appeals, and with their adoption Rules 72 to 76 of the F.R.C.P. [rules 72 to 76, Federal Rules of Civil Procedure] were abrogated. In some instances, however, the F.R.A.P. provide that a motion or application for relief may, or must, be made in the district court. See Rules 4(a), 10(b) and 24. The proposed amendment would make it clear that when this is so the motion or application is to be made in the form and manner prescribed by the F.R.C.P. or F.R.Cr.P. [Federal Rules Criminal Procedure] and local rules relating to the form and presentation of motions and is not governed by Rule 27 of the F.R.A.P. See Rule 7(b) of the F.R.C.P. [rule 7(b), Federal Rules of Civil Procedure] and Rule 47 of the F.R.Cr.P. [rule 47, Federal Rules of Criminal Procedure].

1989 Amendment

The amendment is technical. No substantive change is intended.

1994 Amendment

Subdivision (c). A new subdivision is added to the rule. The text of new subdivision (c) has been moved from Rule 48 to Rule 1 to allow the addition of new rules at the end of the existing set of appellate rules without burying the title provision among other rules. In a similar fashion the Bankruptcy Rules combine the provisions governing the scope of the rules and the title in the first rule.

1998 Amendments

The language and organization of the rule are amended to make the rule more easily understood. In addition to changes made to improve the understanding, the Advisory Committee has changed language to make style and terminology consistent throughout the appellate rules. These changes are intended to be stylistic only. The Advisory Committee recommends deleting the language in subdivision (a) that describes the different types of proceedings that may be brought in a court of appeals. The Advisory Committee believes that the language is unnecessary and that it s omission does not work any substantive change.

2002 Amendments

Subdivision (b). Two recent enactments make it likely that, in the future, one or more of the Federal Rules of Appellate Procedure ("FRAP") will extend or limit the jurisdiction of the courts of appeals. In 1990, Congress amended the Rules Enabling Act to give the Supreme Court authority to use the federal rules of practice and procedure to define when a ruling of a district court is final for purposes of 28 U.S.C. § 1291. *See* 28 U.S.C. § 2072(c). In 1992, Congress amended 28 U.S.C. § 1292 to give the Supreme Court authority to use the federal rules of practice and procedure to provide for appeals of interlocutory decisions that are not already authorized by 28 U.S.C. § 1292. *See* 28 U.S.C. § 1292(e). Both § 1291 and § 1292 are unquestionably jurisdictional statutes, and thus, as soon as FRAP is amended to define finality for purposes of the former or to authorize interlocutory appeals not provided for by the latter, FRAP will "extend or limit the jurisdiction of the courts of appeals," and subdivision (b) will become obsolete. For that reason, subdivision (b) has been abrogated.

Changes Made After Publication and Comments No changes were made to the text of the proposed amendment or to the Committee Note.

HISTORICAL NOTES

Pending Actions

Amendments of Supreme Court to Federal Rules of Appellate Procedure effective December 1, 1993, applicable, insofar as just and practicable, in all proceedings then pending, pursuant to the Order of April 22, 1993.

Rule 2. Suspension of Rules

On its own or a party's motion, a court of appeals may—to expedite its decision or for other good cause—suspend any provision of these rules in a particular case and order proceedings as it directs, except as otherwise provided in Rule 26(b).

(As amended Apr. 24, 1998, eff. Dec. 1, 1998.)

ADVISORY COMMITTEE NOTES

1967 Adoption

The primary purpose of this rule is to make clear the power of the courts of appeals to expedite the determination of cases of pressing concern to the public or to the litigants by prescribing a time schedule other than that provided by the rules. The rule also contains a general authorization to the courts to relieve litigants of the consequences of default where manifest injustice would otherwise result. Rule 26(b) prohibits a court of appeals from extending the time for taking appeal or seeking review.

1998 Amendments

The language of the rule is amended to make the rule more easily understood. In addition to changes made to improve the understanding, the Advisory Committee has changed the language to make style and terminology consistent throughout the appellate rules. These changes are intended to by stylistic only.

TITLE II. APPEAL FROM A JUDGMENT OR ORDER OF A DISTRICT COURT

Rule 3. Appeal as of Right—How Taken

(a) Filing the Notice of Appeal.

(1) An appeal permitted by law as of right from a district court to a court of appeals may be taken only by filing a notice of appeal with the district clerk within the time allowed by Rule 4. At the time of filing, the appellant must furnish the clerk with enough copies of the notice to enable the clerk to comply with Rule 3(d).

(2) An appellant's failure to take any step other than the timely filing of a notice of appeal does not affect the validity of the appeal, but is ground only for the court of appeals to act as it considers appropriate, including dismissing the appeal.

(3) An appeal from a judgment by a magistrate judge in a civil case is taken in the same way as an appeal from any other district court judgment.

(4) An appeal by permission under 28 U.S.C. § 1292(b) or an appeal in a bankruptcy case may be taken only in the manner prescribed by Rules 5 and 6, respectively.

(b) Joint or Consolidated Appeals.

(1) When two or more parties are entitled to appeal from a district-court judgment or order, and their interests make joinder practicable, they may file a joint notice of appeal. They may then proceed on appeal as a single appellant.

(2) When the parties have filed separate timely notices of appeal, the appeals may be joined or consolidated by the court of appeals.

(c) Contents of the Notice of Appeal.

(1) The notice of appeal must:

(A) specify the party or parties taking the appeal by naming each one in the caption or body of the notice, but an attorney representing more than one party may describe those parties with such terms as "all plaintiffs," "the defendants," "the plaintiffs A, B, et al.," or "all defendants except X";

(B) designate the judgment, order, or part thereof being appealed; and

(C) name the court to which the appeal is taken.

(2) A pro se notice of appeal is considered filed on behalf of the signer and the signer's spouse and minor children (if they are parties), unless the notice clearly indicates otherwise.

(3) In a class action, whether or not the class has been certified, the notice of appeal is sufficient if it names one person qualified to bring the appeal as representative of the class.

(4) An appeal must not be dismissed for informality of form or title of the notice of appeal, or for failure to name a party whose intent to appeal is otherwise clear from the notice.

(5) Form 1 in the Appendix of Forms is a suggested form of a notice of appeal.

(d) Serving the Notice of Appeal.

(1) The district clerk must serve notice of the filing of a notice of appeal by mailing a copy to each party's counsel of record—excluding the appellant's—or, if a party is proceeding pro se, to the party's last known address. When a defendant in a criminal case appeals, the clerk must also serve a copy of the notice of appeal on the defendant, either by personal service or by mail addressed to the defendant. The clerk must promptly send a copy of the notice of appeal and of the docket entries—and any later docket entries—to the clerk of the court of appeals named in the notice. The district clerk must note, on each copy, the date when the notice of appeal was filed.

(2) If an inmate confined in an institution files a notice of appeal in the manner provided by Rule 4(c), the district clerk must also note the date when the clerk docketed the notice.

(3) The district clerk's failure to serve notice does not affect the validity of the appeal. The clerk must note on the docket the names of the parties to whom the clerk mails copies, with the date of mailing. Service is sufficient despite the death of a party or the party's counsel.

(e) Payment of Fees. Upon filing a notice of appeal, the appellant must pay the district clerk all required fees. The district clerk receives the appellate docket fee on behalf of the court of appeals.

(As amended Apr. 30, 1979, eff. Aug. 1, 1979; Mar. 10, 1986, eff. July 1, 1986; Apr. 25, 1989, eff. Dec. 1, 1989; Apr. 22, 1993, eff. Dec. 1, 1993; Apr. 29, 1994, eff. Dec. 1, 1994; Apr. 24, 1998, eff. Dec. 1, 1998.)

ADVISORY COMMITTEE NOTES

1967 Adoption

General Note. Rule 3 and Rule 4 combine to require that a notice of appeal be filed with the clerk of the district court within the time prescribed for taking an appeal. Because the timely filing of a notice of appeal is "mandatory and jurisdictional," *United States v. Robinson*, 361 U.S. 220, 224, 80 S.Ct. 282, 4 L.Ed.2d 259 (1960), compliance with the provisions of those rules is of the utmost importance. But the proposed rules merely restate, in modified form, provisions now found in the civil and criminal rules (FRCP 5(e), 73 [Rules 5(e) and 73, Federal Rules of Civil Procedure]; FRCrP 37 [rule 37, Federal Rules of Criminal Procedure], and decisions under the present rules which dispense with literal compliance in cases in which it cannot fairly be exacted should control interpretation of these rules. Illustrative decisions are: *Fallen v. United States*, 378 U.S. 139, 84 S.Ct. 1689, 12 L.Ed.2d 760 (1964) (notice of appeal by a prisoner, in the form of a letter delivered, well within the time fixed for appeal, to prison authorities for mailing to the clerk of the district court held timely filed notwithstanding that it was received by the clerk after expiration of the time for appeal; the appellant "did all he could" to effect timely filing); *Richey v. Wilkins*, 335 F.2d 1 (2d Cir. 1964) (notice filed in the court of appeals by a prisoner without assistance of counsel held sufficient); *Halfen v. United States*, 324 F.2d 52 (10th Cir. 1963) (notice mailed to district judge in time to have been received by him in normal course held sufficient); *Riffle v. United States*, 299 F.2d 802 (5th Cir. 1962) (letter of prisoner to judge of court of appeals held sufficient). Earlier cases evidencing "a liberal view of papers filed by indigent and incarcerated defendants" are listed in *Coppedge v. United States*, 369 U.S. 438, 442, n. 5, 82 S.Ct. 917, 8 L.Ed.2d 21 (1962).

Subdivision (a). The substance of this subdivision is derived from FRCP 73(a) [rule 73(a), Federal Rules of Civil Procedure] and FRCrP 37(a)(1) [rule 37(a)(1), Federal Rules of Criminal Procedure]. The proposed rule follows those rules in requiring nothing other than the filing of a notice of appeal in the district court for the perfection of the appeal. The petition for allowance (except for appeals governed by Rules 5 and 6), citations, assignments of error, summons and severance—all specifically abolished by earlier modern rules—are assumed to be sufficiently obsolete as no longer to require pointed abolition.

Subdivision (b). The first sentence is derived from FRCP 74 [rule 74, Federal Rules of Civil Procedure]. The second sentence is added to encourage consolidation of appeals whenever feasible.

Subdivision (c). This subdivision is identical with corresponding provisions in FRCP 73(b) [rule 73(b), Federal Rules of Civil Procedure] and FRCrP 37(a)(1) [rule 37(a)(1), Federal Rules of Criminal Procedure].

Subdivision (d). This subdivision is derived from FRCP 73(b) [rule 73(b), Federal Rules of Civil Procedure] and FRCrP 37(a)(1) [rule 37(a)(1), Federal Rules of Criminal Procedure]. The duty of the clerk to forward a copy of the notice of appeal and of the docket entries to the court of appeals in a criminal case is extended to habeas corpus and 28 U.S.C. § 2255 proceedings.

1979 Amendments

Subdivision (c). The proposed amendment would add the last sentence. Because of the fact that the timely filing of the notice of appeal has been characterized as jurisdictional (see, e.g., Brainerd v. Real (C.A. 7th, 1974) 498 F.2d 901, in which the filing of a notice of appeal one day late was fatal), it is important that the right to appeal not be lost by mistakes of mere form. In a number of decided cases it has been held that so long as the function of notice is met by the filing of a paper indicating an intention to appeal, the substance of the rule has been complied with. See, e.g., Cobb v. Lewis (C.A. 5th, 1974), 488 F.2d 41; *Holley v. Capps* (C.A. 5th, 1972) 468 F.2d 1366. The proposed amendment would give recognition to this practice.

When a notice of appeal is filed, the clerk should ascertain whether any judgment designated therein has been entered in compliance with Rules 58 and 79(a) of the F.R.C.P. [rules 58 and 79(a), Federal Rules of Civil Procedure]. See Note to Rule 4(a)(6), *infra.*

Subdivision (d). The proposed amendment would extend to civil cases the present provision applicable to criminal cases, habeas corpus cases, and proceedings under 28 U.S.C. § 2255, requiring the clerk of the district court to transmit to the clerk of the court of appeals a copy of the notice of appeal and of the docket entries, which should include reference to compliance with the requirements for payment of fees. See Note to (e), *infra.*

This requirement is the initial step in proposed changes in the rules to place in the court of appeals an increased practical control over the early steps in the appeal.

Subdivision (e). Proposed new Rule 3(e) represents the second step in shifting to the court of appeals the control of the early stages of an appeal. See Note to Rule 3(d) above. Under the present rules the payment of the fee prescribed by 28 U.S.C. 1917 is not covered. Under the statute, however, this fee is paid to the clerk of the district court at the time the notice of appeal is filed. Under present Rule 12, the "docket fee" fixed by the Judicial Conference of the United States under 28 U.S.C. § 1913 must be paid to the clerk of the court of appeals within the time fixed for transmission of the record, ". . . and the clerk shall thereupon enter the appeal upon the docket."

Under the proposed new Rule 3(e) both fees would be paid to the clerk of the district court at the time the notice of appeal is filed, the clerk of the district court receiving the docket fee on behalf of the court of appeals.

In view of the provision in Rule 3(a) that "[f]ailure of an appellant to take any step other than the timely filing of a notice of appeal does not affect the validity of the appeal, but is ground only for such action as the court of appeals deems appropriate, which may include dismissal of the appeal," the case law indicates that the failure to prepay the statutory filing fee does not constitute a jurisdictional defect. See *Parissi v. Telechron*, 349 U.S. 46 (1955); *Gould v. Members of N.J. Division of Water Policy & Supply*, 555 F.2d 340 (3d Cir. 1977). Similarly, under present Rule 12, failure to pay the docket fee within the time prescribed may be excused by the court of appeals. See, e.g., *Walker v. Mathews*, 546 F.2d 814 (9th Cir. 1976). Proposed new Rule 3(e) adopts the view of these cases, requiring that both fees be paid at the time the notice of appeal is filed, but subject to the provisions of Rule 26(b) preserving the authority of the court of appeals to permit late payment.

1986 Amendments

The amendments to Rule 3(d) are technical. No substantive change is intended.

1989 Amendments

The amendment is technical. No substantive change is intended.

1993 Amendments

Note to subdivision (c). The amendment is intended to reduce the amount of satellite litigation spawned by the Supreme Court's decision in Torres v. Oakland Scavenger Co., 487 U.S. 312 (1988). In Torres the Supreme Court held that the language in Rule 3(c) requiring a notice of appeal to "specify the party or parties taking the appeal" is a jurisdictional requirement and that naming the first named party and adding "et al.," without any further specificity is insufficient to identify the appellants. Since the Torres decision, there has been a great deal of litigation regarding whether a notice of appeal that contains some indication of the appellants' identities but does not name the appellants is sufficiently specific.

The amendment states a general rule that specifying the parties should be done by naming them. Naming an appellant in an otherwise timely and proper notice of appeal ensures that the appellant has perfected an appeal. However, in order to prevent the loss of a right to appeal through inadvertent omission of a party's name or continued use of such terms as "et al.," which are sufficient in all district court filings after the complaint, the amendment allows an attorney representing more than one party the flexibility to indicate which parties are appealing without naming them individually. The test established by the rule for determining whether such designations are sufficient is whether it is objectively clear that a party intended to appeal. A notice of appeal filed by a party proceeding pro se is filed on behalf of the party signing the notice and the signer's spouse and minor children, if they are parties, unless the notice clearly indicates a contrary intent.

In class actions, naming each member of a class as an appellant may be extraordinarily burdensome or even impossible. In class actions if class certification has been denied, named plaintiffs may appeal the order denying the class certification on their own behalf and on behalf of putative class members, *United States Parole Comm'n v. Geraghty*, 445 U.S. 388 (1980); or if the named plaintiffs choose not to appeal the order denying the class certification, putative class members may appeal, *United Airlines, Inc. v. McDonald*, 432 U.S. 385 (1977). If no class has been certified, naming each of the putative class members as an appellant would often be impossible. Therefore the amendment provides that in class actions, whether or not the class has been certified, it is sufficient for the notice to name one person qualified to bring the appeal as a representative of the class.

Finally, the rule makes it clear that dismissal of an appeal should not occur when it is otherwise clear from the notice that the party intended to appeal. If a court determines it is objectively clear that a party intended to appeal, there are neither administrative concerns nor fairness concerns that should prevent the appeal from going forward.

Note to subdivision (d). The amendment requires the district court clerk to send to the clerk of the court of appeals a copy of every docket entry in a case after the filing of a notice of appeal. This amendment accompanies the amendment to Rule 4(a)(4), which provides that when one of the posttrial motions enumerated in Rule 4(a)(4) is filed, a notice of appeal filed before the disposition of the motion becomes effective upon disposition of the motion. The court of appeals needs to be advised that the filing of a posttrial motion has suspended a notice of appeal. The court of appeals also needs to know when the district court has ruled on the motion. Sending copies of all docket entries after the filing of a notice of appeal should provide the courts of appeals with the necessary information.

1994 Amendments

Subdivision (a). The amendment requires a party filing a notice of appeal to provide the court with sufficient copies of the notice for service on all other parties.

1998 Amendments

The language and organization of the rule are amended to make the rule more easily understood. In addition to changes made to improve the understanding, the Advisory Committee has changed language to make style and terminology consistent throughout the appellate rules. These changes are generally intended to by stylistic only; in this rule, however, substantive changes are made in subdivisions (a), (b), and (d).

Subdivision (a). The provision in paragraph (a)(3) is transferred from former Rule 3.1(b). The Federal Courts Improvement Act of 1996, Pub.L. No. 104–317, repealed paragraphs (4) and (5) of 28 U.S.C. § 636(c). That statutory change made the continued separate existence of Rule 3.1 unnecessary. New paragraph (a)(3) of this rule simply makes it clear that an appeal from a judgment by a magistrate judge is taken in identical fashion to any other appeal from a district-court judgment.

Subdivision (b). A joint appeal is authorized only when two or more persons may appeal from a single judgment or order. A joint appeal is treated as a single appeal and the joint appellants file a single brief. Under existing Rule 3(b) parties decide whether to join their appeals. They may do so by filing a joint notice of appeal or by joining their appeals after filing separate notices of appeal.

In consolidated appeals the separate appeals do not merge into one. The parties do not proceed as a single appellant. Under existing Rule 3(b) it is unclear whether appeals may be consolidated without court order if the parties stipulate to consolidation. The language resolves that ambiguity by requiring court action.

The language also requires court action to join appeals after separate notices of appeal have been filed.

Subdivision (d). Paragraph (d)(2) has been amended to require that when an inmate files a notice of appeal by depositing the notice in the institution's internal mail system, the clerk must note the docketing date—rather than the receipt date—on the notice of appeal before serving copies of it. This change conforms to a change in Rule 4(c). Rule 4(c) is amended to provide that when an inmate files the first notice of appeal in a civil case by depositing the notice in an institution's internal mail system, the time for filing a cross–appeal runs from the date the district court dockets the inmate's notice of appeal. Existing Rule 4(c) says that in such a case the time for filing a cross–appeal runs from the date the district court receives the inmate's notice of appeal. A court may "receive" a paper when its mail is delivered to it even if the mail is not processed for a day or two, making the date of receipt uncertain. "Docketing" is an easily identified event. The change is made to eliminate the uncertainty.

[Rule 3.1. Abrogated Apr. 24, 1998, eff. Dec. 1, 1998]

ADVISORY COMMITTEE NOTES

1998 Amendments

The Federal Courts Improvement Act of 1996, Pub.L. No. 104–317, repealed paragraphs (4) and (5) of 28 U.S.C. § 636(c). That statutory change means that when parties consent to trial before a magistrate judge, appeal lies directly, and as a matter of right, to the court of appeals under § 636(c)(3). The parties may not choose to appeal first to a district judge and thereafter seek discretionary review in the court of appeals.

As a result of the statutory amendments, subdivision (a) of Rule 3.1 is no longer necessary. Since Rule 3.1 existed primarily because of the provisions in subdivision (a), subdivision (b) has been moved to Rule 3(a)(3) and Rule 3.1 has been abrogated.

HISTORICAL NOTES

The abrogated rule provided that: "When the parties consent to a trial before a magistrate judge under 28 U.S.C. § 636(c)(1), any appeal from the judgment must be heard by the court of appeals in accordance with 28 U.S.C. § 636(c)(3), unless the parties consent to an appeal on the record to a district judge and thereafter, by petition only, to the court of appeals, in accordance with 28 U.S.C. § 636(c)(4). An appeal under 28 U.S.C. § 636(c)(3) must be taken in identical fashion as an appeal from any other judgment of the district court."

Rule 4. Appeal as of Right—When Taken

(a) Appeal in a Civil Case.

(1) Time for Filing a Notice of Appeal.

(A) In a civil case, except as provided in Rules 4(a)(1)(B), 4(a)(4), and 4(c), the notice of appeal required by Rule 3 must be filed with the district clerk within 30 days after the judgment or order appealed from is entered.

(B) When the United States or its officer or agency is a party, the notice of appeal may be filed by any party within 60 days after the judgment or order appealed from is entered.

(C) An appeal from an order granting or denying an application for a writ of error coram nobis is an appeal in a civil case for purposes of Rule 4(a).

(2) Filing Before Entry of Judgment. A notice of appeal filed after the court announces a decision or order—but before the entry of the judgment or order—is treated as filed on the date of and after the entry.

(3) Multiple Appeals. If one party timely files a notice of appeal, any other party may file a notice of appeal within 14 days after the date when the first notice was filed, or within the time otherwise prescribed by this Rule 4(a), whichever period ends later.

(4) Effect of a Motion on a Notice of Appeal.

(A) If a party timely files in the district court any of the following motions under the Federal Rules of Civil Procedure, the time to file an appeal runs for all parties from the entry of the order disposing of the last such remaining motion:

(i) for judgment under Rule 50(b);

(ii) to amend or make additional factual findings under Rule 52(b), whether or not granting the motion would alter the judgment;

(iii) for attorney's fees under Rule 54 if the district court extends the time to appeal under Rule 58;

(iv) to alter or amend the judgment under Rule 59;

(v) for a new trial under Rule 59; or

(vi) for relief under Rule 60 if the motion is filed no later than 10 days after the judgment is entered.

(B)(i) If a party files a notice of appeal after the court announces or enters a judgment—but before it disposes of any motion listed in Rule 4(a)(4)(A)—the notice becomes effective to appeal a judgment or order, in whole or in part, when the order disposing of the last such remaining motion is entered.

(ii) A party intending to challenge an order disposing of any motion listed in Rule 4(a)(4)(A), or a judgment altered or amended upon such a motion, must file a notice of appeal, or an amended notice of appeal—in compliance with Rule 3(c)—within the time prescribed by this Rule measured from the entry of the order disposing of the last such remaining motion.

(iii) No additional fee is required to file an amended notice.

(5) Motion for Extension of Time.

(A) The district court may extend the time to file a notice of appeal if:

(i) a party so moves no later than 30 days after the time prescribed by this Rule 4(a) expires; and

(ii) regardless of whether its motion is filed before or during the 30 days after the time prescribed by this Rule 4(a) expires, that party shows excusable neglect or good cause.

(B) A motion filed before the expiration of the time prescribed in Rule 4(a)(1) or (3) may be ex parte unless the court requires otherwise. If the motion is filed after the expiration of the prescribed time, notice must be given to the other parties in accordance with local rules.

(C) No extension under this Rule 4(a)(5) may exceed 30 days after the prescribed time or 10 days after the date when the order granting the motion is entered, whichever is later.

(6) Reopening the Time to File an Appeal. The district court may reopen the time to file an appeal for a period of 14 days after the date when its order to reopen is entered, but only if all the following conditions are satisfied:

(A) the court finds that the moving party did not receive notice under Federal Rule of Civil Procedure 77(d) of the entry of the judgment or order sought to be appealed within 21 days after entry;

(B) the motion is filed within 180 days after the judgment or order is entered or within 7 days after the moving party receives notice under Federal Rule of Civil Procedure 77(d) of the entry, whichever is earlier; and

(C) the court finds that no party would be prejudiced.

(7) Entry Defined.

(A) A judgment or order is entered for purposes of this Rule 4(a):

(i) if Federal Rule of Civil Procedure 58(a)(1) does not require a separate document, when the judgment or order is entered in the civil docket under Federal Rule of Civil Procedure 79(a); or

(ii) if Federal Rule of Civil Procedure 58(a)(1) requires a separate document, when the judgment or order is entered in the civil docket under Federal Rule of Civil Procedure 79(a) and when the earlier of these events occurs:

- the judgment or order is set forth on a separate document, or
- 150 days have run from entry of the judgment or order in the civil docket under Federal Rule of Civil Procedure 79(a).

(B) A failure to set forth a judgment or order on a separate document when required by Federal Rule of Civil Procedure 58(a)(1) does not affect the validity of an appeal from that judgment or order.

(b) Appeal in a Criminal Case.

(1) Time for Filing a Notice of Appeal.

(A) In a criminal case, a defendant's notice of appeal must be filed in the district court within 10 days after the later of:

(i) the entry of either the judgment or the order being appealed; or

(ii) the filing of the government's notice of appeal.

(B) When the government is entitled to appeal, its notice of appeal must be filed in the district court within 30 days after the later of:

(i) the entry of the judgment or order being appealed; or

(ii) the filing of a notice of appeal by any defendant.

(2) Filing Before Entry of Judgment. A notice of appeal filed after the court announces a decision, sentence, or order—but before the entry of the judgment or order—is treated as filed on the date of and after the entry.

(3) Effect of a Motion on a Notice of Appeal.

(A) If a defendant timely makes any of the following motions under the Federal Rules of Criminal Procedure, the notice of appeal from a judgment of conviction must be filed within 10 days after the entry of the order disposing of the last such remaining motion, or within 10 days after the entry of the judgment of conviction, whichever period ends later. This provision applies to a timely motion:

(i) for judgment of acquittal under Rule 29;

(ii) for a new trial under Rule 33, but if based on newly discovered evidence, only if the motion is made no later than 10 days after the entry of the judgment; or

(iii) for arrest of judgment under Rule 34.

(B) A notice of appeal filed after the court announces a decision, sentence, or order—but before it disposes of any of the motions referred to in Rule 4(b)(3)(A)—becomes effective upon the later of the following:

(i) the entry of the order disposing of the last such remaining motion; or

(ii) the entry of the judgment of conviction.

(C) A valid notice of appeal is effective—without amendment—to appeal from an order disposing of any of the motions referred to in Rule 4(b)(3)(A).

(4) Motion for Extension of Time. Upon a finding of excusable neglect or good cause, the district court may—before or after the time has expired, with or without motion and notice—extend the time to file a notice of appeal for a period not to exceed 30 days from the expiration of the time otherwise prescribed by this Rule 4(b).

(5) Jurisdiction. The filing of a notice of appeal under this Rule 4(b) does not divest a district court of jurisdiction to correct a sentence under Federal Rule of Criminal Procedure 35(a), nor does the filing of a motion under 35(a) affect the validity of a notice of appeal filed before entry of the order disposing of the motion. The filing of a motion under Federal Rule of Criminal Procedure 35(a) does not suspend the time for filing a notice of appeal from a judgment of conviction.

(6) Entry Defined. A judgment or order is entered for purposes of this Rule 4(b) when it is entered on the criminal docket.

(c) Appeal by an Inmate Confined in an Institution.

(1) If an inmate confined in an institution files a notice of appeal in either a civil or a criminal case, the notice is timely if it is deposited in the institution's internal mail system on or before the last day for filing. If an institution has a system designed for legal mail, the inmate must use that system to receive the benefit of this rule. Timely filing may be shown by a declaration in compliance with 28 U.S.C. § 1746 or by a notarized statement, either of which must set forth the date of deposit and state that first-class postage has been prepaid.

(2) If an inmate files the first notice of appeal in a civil case under this Rule 4(c), the 14–day period provided in Rule 4(a)(3) for another party to file a notice of appeal runs from the date when the district court dockets the first notice.

(3) When a defendant in a criminal case files a notice of appeal under this Rule 4(c), the 30–day period for the government to file its notice of appeal runs from the entry of the judgment or order appealed from or from the district court's docketing of the defendant's notice of appeal, whichever is later.

(d) Mistaken Filing in the Court of Appeals. If a notice of appeal in either a civil or a criminal case is mistakenly filed in the court of appeals, the clerk of that court must note on the notice the date when it was received and send it to the district clerk. The notice is then considered filed in the district court on the date so noted.

(As amended Apr. 30, 1979, eff. Aug. 1, 1979; Nov. 18, 1988, Pub.L. 100–690, Title VII, § 7111, 102 Stat. 4419; Apr. 30, 1991, eff. Dec. 1, 1991; Apr. 22, 1993, eff. Dec. 1, 1993; Apr. 27, 1995, eff. Dec. 1, 1995; Apr. 24, 1998, eff. Dec. 1, 1998; Apr. 29, 2002, eff. Dec. 1, 2002; Apr. 25, 2005, eff. Dec. 1, 2005.)

ADVISORY COMMITTEE NOTES

1967 Adoption

Subdivision (a). This subdivision is derived from FRCP 73(a) [rule 73(a), Federal Rules of Civil Procedure, this title] without any change of substance. The requirement that a request for an extension of time for filing the notice of appeal made after expiration of the time be made by motion and on notice codifies the result reached under the present provisions of FRCP 73(a) and 6(b) [rules 73(a) and 6(b), Federal Rules of Civil Procedure]. *North Umberland Mining Co. v. Standard Accident Ins. Co.*, 193 F.2d 951 (9th Cir., 1952);

Cohen v. Plateau Natural Gas Co., 303 F.2d 273 (10th Cir., 1962); *Plant Economy, Inc. v. Mirror Insulation Co.*, 308 F.2d 275 (3d Cir., 1962).

Since this subdivision governs appeals in all civil cases, it supersedes the provisions of § 25 of the Bankruptcy Act (11 U.S.C. § 48). Except in cases to which the United States or an officer or agency thereof is a party, the change is a minor one, since a successful litigant in a bankruptcy proceeding may, under § 25, oblige an aggrieved party to appeal within 30 days after entry of judgment—the time fixed by this subdivision in cases involving private parties only—by serving him with notice of entry on the day thereof, and by the terms of § 25 and aggrieved party must in any event appeal within 40 days after entry of judgment. No reason appears why the time for appeal in bankruptcy should not be the same as that in civil cases generally. Furthermore, § 25 is a potential trap for the uninitiated. The time for appeal which it provides is not applicable to all appeals which may fairly be termed appeals in bankruptcy. Section 25 governs only those cause referred to in § 24 as "proceedings in bankruptcy" and "controversies arising in proceedings in bankruptcy." *Lowenstein v. Reikes*, 54 F.2d 481 (2d Cir., 1931), cert. den., 285 U.S. 539, 52 S.Ct. 311, 76 L.Ed. 932 (1932). The distinction between such cases and other cases which arise out of bankruptcy is often difficult to determine. See 2 Moore's Collier on Bankruptcy ¶24.12 through ¶24.36 (1962). As a result it is not always clear whether an appeal is governed by § 25 or by FRCP 73(a) [rule 73(a), Federal Rules of Civil Procedure, this title], which is applicable to such appeals in bankruptcy as are not governed by § 25.

In view of the unification of the civil and admiralty procedure accomplished by the amendments of the Federal Rules of Civil Procedure effective July 1, 1966, this subdivision governs appeals in those civil actions which involve admiralty or maritime claims and which prior to that date were known as suits in admiralty.

The only other change possibly effected by this subdivision is in the time for appeal from a decision of a district court on a petition for impeachment of an award of a board of arbitration under the Act of May 20, 1926, c. 347, § 9 (44 Stat. 585), 45 U.S.C. § 159. The act provides that a notice of appeal from such a decision shall be filed within 10 days of the decision. This singular provision was apparently repealed by the enactment in 1948 of 28 U.S.C. § 2107, which fixed 30 days from the date of entry of judgment as the time for appeal in all actions a civil nature except actions in admiralty or bankruptcy matters or those in which the United States is a party. But it was not expressly repealed, and its status is in doubt. See 7 Moore's Federal Practice ¶73.09[2] (1966). The doubt should be resolved, and no reason appears why appeals in such cases should not be taken within the time provided for civil cases generally.

Subdivision (b). This subdivision is derived from FRCrP 37(a)(2) [rule 37(a)(2), Federal Rules of Criminal Procedure] without change of substance.

1979 Amendment

Subdivision (a)(1). The words "(including a civil action which involves an admiralty or maritime claim and a proceeding in bankruptcy or a controversy arising therein)," which appear in the present rule are struck out as unnecessary and perhaps misleading in suggesting that there may be other categories that are not either civil or criminal within the meaning of Rule 4(a) and (b).

The phrases "within 30 days of such entry" and "within 60 days of such entry" have been changed to read "after" instead of "or." The change is for clarity only, since the word "of" in the present rule appears to be used to mean "after." Since the proposed amended rule deals directly with the premature filing of a notice of appeal, it was thought useful to emphasize the fact that except as provided, the period during which a notice of appeal may be filed is the 30 days, or 60 days as the case may be, following the entry of the judgment or order appealed from. See Notes to Rule 4(a)(2) and (4), below.

Subdivision (a)(2). The proposed amendment to Rule 4(a)(2) would extend to civil cases the provisions of Rule 4(b), dealing with criminal cases, designed to avoid the loss of the right to appeal by filing the notice of appeal prematurely. Despite the absence of such a provision in Rule 4(a) the courts of appeals quite generally have held premature appeals effective. See, e.g., *Matter of Grand Jury Empanelled Jan. 21, 1975*, 541 F.2d 373 (3d Cir. 1976); *Hodge v. Hodge*, 507 F.2d 87 (3d Cir. 1976); *Song Jook Suh v. Rosenberg*, 437 F.2d 1098 (9th Cir. 1971); *Ruby v. Secretary of the Navy*, 365 F.2d 385 (9th Cir. 1966); *Firchau v. Diamond Nat'l Corp.*, 345 F.2d 269 (9th Cir. 1965).

The proposed amended rule would recognize this practice but make an exception in cases in which a post trial motion has destroyed the finality of the judgment. See Note to Rule 4(a)(4) below.

Subdivision (a)(4). The proposed amendment would make it clear that after the filing of the specified post trial motions, a notice of appeal should await disposition of the motion. Since the proposed amendments to Rules 3, 10, and 12 contemplate that immediately upon the filing of the notice of appeal the fees will be paid and the case docketed in the court of appeals, and the steps toward its disposition set in motion, it would be undesirable to proceed with the appeal while the district court has before it a motion the granting of which would vacate or alter the judgment appealed from. See, e.g., *Keith v. Newcourt*, 530 F.2d 826 (8th Cir. 1976). Under the present rule, since docketing may not take place until the record is transmitted, premature filing is much less likely to involve waste effort. See, e.g. *Stockes v. Peyton's Inc.*, 508 F.2d 1287 (5th Cir. 1975). Further, since a notice of appeal filed before the disposition of a post trial motion, even if it were treated as valid for purposes of jurisdiction, would not embrace objections to the denial of the motion, it is obviously preferable to postpone the notice of appeal until after the motion is disposed of.

The present rule, since it provides for the "termination" of the "running" of the appeal time, is ambiguous in its application to a notice of appeal filed prior to a post trial motion filed within the 10 day limit. The amendment would make it clear that in such circumstances the appellant should not proceed with the appeal during pendency of the motion but should file a new notice of appeal after the motion is disposed of.

Subdivision (a)(5). Under the present rule it is provided that upon a showing of excusable neglect the district court at any time may extend the time for the filing of a notice of appeal for a period not to exceed 30 days from the expiration of the time otherwise prescribed by the rule, but that if the application is made after the original time has run, the order may be made only on motion with such notice as the court deems appropriate.

A literal reading of this provision would require that the extension be ordered and the notice of appeal filed within the 30 day period, but despite the surface clarity of the rule, it has produced considerable confusion. See the discussion by Judge Friendly in In re Orbitek, 520 F.2d 358 (2d Cir. 1975). The proposed amendment would make it clear that a motion to extend the time must be filed no later than 30 days after the expiration of the original appeal time, and that if the motion is timely filed the district court may act upon the motion at a later date, and may extend the time not in excess of 10 days measured from the date on which the order granting the motion is entered.

Under the present rule there is a possible implication that prior to the time the initial appeal time has run, the district court may extend the time on the basis of an informal application. The amendment would require that the application must be made by motion, though the motion may be made *ex parte*. After the expiration of the initial time a motion for the extension of the time must be made in compliance with the F.R.C.P. [Federal Rules of Civil Procedure] and local rules of the district court. See Note to proposed amended Rule 1, *supra*. And see Rules 6(d), 7(b) of the F.R.C.P. [rules 6(d) and 7(b), Federal Rules of Civil Procedure].

The proposed amended rule expands to some extent the standard for the grant of an extension of time. The present rule requires a "showing of excusable neglect." While this was an appropriate standard in cases in which the motion is made after the time for filing the notice of appeal has run, and remains so, it has never fit exactly the situation in which the appellant seeks an extension before the expiration of the initial time. In such a case "good cause," which is the standard that is applied in the granting of other extensions of time under Rule 26(b) seems to be more appropriate.

Subdivision (a)(6). The proposed amendment would call attention to the requirement of Rule 58 of the F.R.C.P. [Federal Rules of Civil Procedure] that the judgment constitute a separate document. See *United States v. Indrelunas*, 411 U.S. 216 (1973). When a notice of appeal is filed, the clerk should ascertain whether any judgment designated therein has been entered in compliance with Rules 58 and 79(a) and if not, so advise all parties and the district judge. While the requirement of Rule 58 is not jurisdictional, (see *Bankers Trust Co. v. Mallis*, 431 U.S. 928 (1977)), compliance is important since the time for the filing of a notice of appeal by other parties is measured by the time at which the judgment is properly entered.

1991 Amendment

The amendment provides a limited opportunity for relief in circumstances where the notice of entry of a judgment or order, required to be mailed by the clerk of the district court pursuant to Rule 77(d) of the Federal Rules of Civil Procedure, is either not received by a party or is received so late as to impair the opportunity to file a timely notice of appeal. The amendment adds a new subdivision (6) allowing a district court to reopen for a brief period the time for appeal upon a finding that notice of entry of a judgment or order was not received from the clerk or a party within 21 days of its entry and that no party would be prejudiced. By "prejudice" the Committee means some adverse consequence other than the cost of having to oppose the appeal and encounter the risk of reversal, consequences that are present in every appeal. Prejudice might arise, for example, if the appellee had taken some action in reliance on the expiration of the normal time period for filing a notice of appeal.

Reopening may be ordered only upon a motion filed within 180 days of the entry of a judgment or order or within 7 days of receipt of notice of such entry, whichever is earlier. This provision establishes an outer time limit of 180 days for a party who fails to receive timely notice of entry of a judgment to seek additional time to appeal and enables any winning party to shorten the 180-day period by sending (and establishing proof of receipt of) its own notice of entry of a judgment, as authorized by Fed.R.Civ.P. 77(d). Winning parties are encouraged to send their own notice in order to lessen the chance that a judge will accept a claim of non-receipt in the face of evidence that notices were sent by both the clerk and the winning party. Receipt of a winning party's notice will shorten only the time for reopening the time for appeal under this subdivision, leaving the normal time periods for appeal unaffected.

If the motion is granted, the district court may reopen the time for filing a notice of appeal only for a period of 14 days from the date of entry of the order reopening the time for appeal.

Transmittal Note: Upon transmittal of this rule to Congress, the Advisory Committee recommends that the attention of Congress be called to the fact that language in the fourth paragraph of 28 U.S.C. § 2107 might appropriately be revised in light of this proposed rule.

1993 Amendment

Note to Paragraph (a)(1). The amendment is intended to alert readers to the fact that paragraph (a)(4) extends the time for filing an appeal when certain posttrial motions are filed. The Committee hopes that awareness of the provisions of paragraph (a)(4) will prevent the filing of a notice of appeal when a posttrial tolling motion is pending.

Note to Paragraph (a)(2). The amendment treats a notice of appeal filed after the announcement of a decision or order, but before its formal entry, as if the notice had been filed after entry. The amendment deletes the language that made paragraph (a)(2) inapplicable to a notice of appeal filed after announcement of the disposition of a posttrial motion enumerated in paragraph (a)(4) but before the entry of the order, see *Acosta v. Louisiana Dep't of Health & Human Resources*, 478 U.S. 251 (1986) (per curiam); *Alerte v. McGinnis*, 898 F.2d 69 (7th Cir.1990). Because the amendment of paragraph (a)(4) recognizes all notices of appeal filed after announcement or entry of judgment—even those that are filed while the posttrial motions enumerated in paragraph (a)(4) are pending—the amendment of this paragraph is consistent with the amendment of paragraph (a)(4).

Note to Paragraph (a)(3). The amendment is technical in nature; no substantive change is intended.

Note to Paragraph (a)(4). The 1979 amendment of this paragraph created a trap for an unsuspecting litigant who files a notice of appeal before a posttrial motion, or while a posttrial motion is pending. The 1979 amendment requires a party to file a new notice of appeal after the motion's disposition. Unless a new notice is filed, the court of appeals lacks jurisdiction to hear the appeal. *Griggs v. Provident Consumer Discount Co.*, 459 U.S. 56 (1982). Many litigants, especially pro se litigants, fail to file the second notice of appeal, and several courts have expressed dissatisfaction with the rule. See, e.g., *Averhart v. Arrendondo*, 773 F.2d 919 (7th Cir.1985); *Harcon Barge Co. v. D & G Boat Rentals, Inc.*, 746 F.2d 278 (5th Cir.1984), cert. denied, 479 U.S. 930 (1986).

The amendment provides that a notice of appeal filed before the disposition of a specified posttrial motion will become effective upon disposition of the motion. A notice filed before the filing of one of the specified motions or after the filing of a motion but before disposition of the motion is, in effect, suspended until the motion is disposed of, whereupon, the previously filed notice effectively places jurisdiction in the court of appeals.

Because a notice of appeal will ripen into an effective appeal upon disposition of a posttrial motion, in some instances there will be an appeal from a judgment that has been altered substantially because the motion was granted in whole or in part. Many such appeals will be dismissed for want of prosecution when the appellant fails to meet the briefing schedule. But, the appellee may also move to strike the appeal. When responding to such a motion, the appellant would have an opportunity to state that, even though some relief sought in a posttrial motion was granted, the appellant still plans to pursue the appeal. Because the appellant's response would provide the appellee with sufficient notice of the appellant's intentions, the Committee does not believe that an additional notice of appeal is needed.

The amendment provides that a notice of appeal filed before the disposition of a posttrial tolling motion is sufficient to bring the underlying case, as well as any orders specified in the original notice, to the court of appeals. If the judgment is altered upon disposition of a posttrial motion, however, and if a party wishes to appeal from the disposition of the motion, the party must amend the notice to so indicate. When a party files an amended notice, no additional fees are required because the notice is an amendment of the original and not a new notice of appeal.

Paragraph (a)(4) is also amended to include, among motions that extend the time for filing a notice of appeal, a Rule 60 motion that is served within 10 days after entry of judgment. This eliminates the difficulty of determining whether a posttrial motion made within 10 days after entry of a judgment is a Rule 59(e) motion, which tolls the time for filing an appeal, or a Rule 60 motion, which historically has not tolled the time. The amendment comports with the practice in several circuits of treating all motions to alter or amend judgments that are made within 10 days after entry of judgment as Rule 59(e) motions for purposes of Rule 4(a)(4). See, e.g., *Finch v. City of Vernon*, 845 F.2d 256 (11th Cir.1988); *Rados v. Celotex Corp.*, 809 F.2d 170 (2d Cir.1986); *Skagerberg v. Oklahoma*, 797 F.2d 881 (10th Cir. 1986). To conform to a recent Supreme Court decision, however—*Budinich v. Becton Dickinson and Co.*, 486 U.S. 196 (1988)—the amendment excludes motions for attorney's fees from the class of motions that extend the filing time unless a district court, acting under Rule 58, enters an order extending the time for appeal. This amendment is to be read in conjunction with the amendment of Fed.R.Civ.P. 58.

Note to subdivision (b). The amendment grammatically restructures the portion of this subdivision that lists the types of motions that toll the time for filing an appeal. This restructuring is intended to make the rule easier to read. No substantive change is intended other than to add a motion for judgment of acquittal under Criminal Rule 29 to the list of tolling motions. Such a motion is the equivalent of a Fed.R.Civ.P. 50(b) motion for judgment notwithstanding the verdict, which tolls the running of time for an appeal in a civil case.

The proposed amendment also eliminates an ambiguity from the third sentence of this subdivision. Prior to this amendment, the third sentence provided that if one of the specified motions was filed, the time for filing an appeal would run from the entry of an order denying the motion. That sentence, like the parallel provision in Rule 4(a)(4), was intended to toll the running of time for appeal if one of the posttrial motions is timely filed. In a criminal case, however, the time for filing the motions runs not from entry of judgment (as it does in civil cases), but from the verdict or finding of guilt. Thus, in a criminal case, a posttrial motion may be disposed of more than 10 days before sentence is imposed, i.e. before the entry of judgment. *United States v. Hashagen*, 816 F.2d 899, 902 n. 5 (3d Cir.1987). To make it clear that a notice of appeal need not be filed before entry of judgment, the amendment states that an appeal may be taken within 10 days after the entry of an order disposing of the motion, or within 10 days after the entry of judgment, whichever is later. The amendment also changes the language in the third sentence providing that an appeal may be taken within 10 days after the entry of an order *denying* the motion; the amendment says instead that an appeal may be taken within 10 days after the entry of an order *disposing* of the last such motion outstanding. (Emphasis added) The change recognizes that there may be multiple posttrial motions filed and that, although one or more motions may be granted in whole or in part, a defendant may still wish to pursue an appeal.

The amendment also states that a notice of appeal filed before the disposition of any of the posttrial tolling motions becomes effective upon disposition of the motions. In most circuits this language simply restates the current practice. See *United States v. Cortes*, 895 F.2d 1245 (9th Cir.), cert. denied, 495 U.S. 939 (1990). Two circuits, however, have questioned that practice in light of the language of the rule, see *United States v. Gargano*, 826 F.2d 610 (7th Cir.1987), and *United States v. Jones*, 669 F.2d 559 (8th Cir.1982), and the Committee wishes to clarify the rule. The amendment is consistent with the proposed amendment of Rule 4(a)(4).

Subdivision (b) is further amended in light of new Fed. R.Crim.P. 35(c), which authorizes a sentencing court to correct any arithmetical, technical, or other clear errors in sentencing within 7 days after imposing the sentence. The Committee believes that a sentencing court should be able to act under Criminal Rule 35(c) even if a notice of appeal has already been filed; and that a notice of appeal should not be affected by the filing of a Rule 35(c) motion or by correction of a sentence under Rule 35(c).

Note to subdivision (c). In *Houston v. Lack*, 487 U.S. 266 (1988), the Supreme Court held that a *pro se* prisoner's notice of appeal is "filed" at the moment of delivery to prison authorities for forwarding to the district court. The amendment reflects that decision. The language of the amendment is similar to that in Supreme Court Rule 29.2.

Permitting an inmate to file a notice of appeal by depositing it in an institutional mail system requires adjustment of the rules governing the filing of cross-appeals. In a civil case, the time for filing a cross-appeal ordinarily runs from the date when the first notice of appeal is filed. If an inmate's notice of appeal is filed by depositing it in an institution's mail system, it is possible that the notice of appeal will not arrive in the district court until several days after the "filing" date and perhaps even after the time for filing a cross-appeal has expired. To avoid that problem, subdivision (c) provides that in a civil case when an institutionalized person files a notice of appeal by depositing it in the institution's mail system, the time for filing a cross-appeal runs from the district court's receipt of the notice. The amendment makes a parallel change regarding the time for the government to appeal in a criminal case.

1995 Amendment

Subdivision (a). Fed.R.Civ.P. 50, 52, and 59 were previously inconsistent with respect to whether certain post-judgment motions had to be filed or merely served no later than 10 days after entry of judgment. As a consequence Rule 4(a)(4) spoke of making or serving such motions rather than filing them. Civil Rules 50, 52, and 59, are being revised to require filing before the end of the 10–day period. As a consequence, this rule is being amended to provide that 'filing' must occur within the 10 day period in order to affect the finality of the judgment and extend the period for filing a notice of appeal.

The Civil Rules require the filing of postjudgment motions 'no later than 10 days after entry of judgment'—rather than 'within' 10 days—to include postjudgment motions that are filed before actual entry of the judgment by the clerk. This rule is amended, therefore, to use the same terminology.

The rule is further amended to clarify the fact that a party who wants to obtain review of an alteration or amendment of a judgment must file a notice of appeal or amend a previously filed notice to indicate intent to appeal from the altered judgment.

1998 Amendments

The language and organization of the rule are amended to make the rule more easily understood. In addition to changes made to improve the understanding the Advisory Committee has changed language to make style and terminology consistent throughout the appellate rules. These changes are intended to be stylistic only; in this rule, however, substantive changes are made in paragraphs (a)(6) and (b)(4), and in subdivision (c).

Subdivision (a), paragraph (1). Although the Advisory Committee does not intend to make any substantive changes in this paragraph, cross-references to Rules 4(a)(1)(B) and (4)(c) have been added to subparagraph (a)(1)(A).

Subdivision (a), paragraph (4). Item (iv) in subparagraph (A) of Rule 4(a)(4) provides that filing a motion for relief under Fed.R.Civ.P. 60 will extend the time for filing a notice of appeal if the Rule 60 motion is filed no later than 10 days after judgment is entered. Again, the Advisory Committee does not intend to make any substantive change in this paragraph. But because Fed.R.Civ.P. 6(a) and Fed.R.App.P. 26(a) have different methods for computing time, one might be uncertain whether the 10–day period referred to in Rule 4(a)(4) is computed using Civil Rule 6(a) or Appellate Rule 26(a). Because the Rule 60 motion is filed in the district court, and because Fed.R.App.P. 1(a)(2) says that when the appellate rules provide for filing a motion in the district court, "the procedure must comply with the practice of the district court," the rule provides that the 10–day period is computed using Fed.R.Civ.P. 6(a)

Subdivision (a), paragraph (6). Paragraph (6) permits a district court to reopen the time for appeal if a party has not received notice of the entry of judgment and no party would be prejudiced by the reopening. Before reopening the time for appeal, the existing rule requires the district court to find that the moving party was entitled to notice of the entry of judgment and did not receive it "from the clerk or any party within 21 days of its entry." The Advisory Committee makes a substantive change. The finding must be that the movant did not receive notice "from the district court or any party within 21 days after entry." This change broadens the type of notice that can preclude reopening the time for appeal. The existing rule provides that only notice from a party or from the clerk bars reopening. The new language precludes reopening if the movant has received notice from "the court."

Subdivision (b). Two substantive changes are made in what will be paragraph (b)(4). The current rule permits an extension of time to file a notice of appeal if there is a "showing of excusable neglect." First, the rule is amended to permit a court to extend the time for "good cause" as well as for excusable neglect. Rule 4(a) permits extensions for both reasons in civil cases and the Advisory Committee believes that "good cause" should be sufficient in criminal cases as well. The amendment does not limit extensions for good cause to instances in which the motion for extension of time is filed before the original time has expired. The rule gives the district court discretion to grant extensions for good cause whenever the court believes it appropriate to do so provided that the extended period does not exceed 30 days after the expiration of the time otherwise prescribed by Rule 4(b). Second, paragraph (b)(4) is amended to require only a "finding" of excusable neglect or good cause and not a "showing" of them. Because the rule authorizes the court to provide an extension without a motion, a "showing" is obviously not required; a "finding" is sufficient.

Subdivision (c). Substantive amendments are made in this subdivision. The current rule provides that if an inmate confined in an institution files a notice of appeal by depositing it in the institution's internal mail system, the notice is timely filed if deposited on or before the last day for filing. Some institutions have special internal mail systems for handling legal mail; such systems often record the date of deposit of mail by an inmate, the date of delivery of mail to an inmate, etc. The Advisory Committee amends the rule to require an inmate to use the system designed for legal mail, if there is one, in order to receive the benefit of this subdivision.

When an inmate uses the filing method authorized by subdivision (c), the current rule provides that the time for other parties to appeal begins to run from the date the district court "receives" the inmate's notice of appeal. The rule is amended so that the time for other parties begins to run when the district court "dockets" the inmates appeal. A court may "receive" a paper when its mail is delivered to it even if the mail is not processed for a day or two, making the date of receipt uncertain. "Docketing" is an easily identified event. The change eliminates uncertainty. Paragraph (c)(3) is further amended to make it clear that the time for the government to file its appeal runs from the later of the entry of the judgment or order appealed from or the district court's docketing of a defendant's notice filed under this paragraph (c).

2002 Amendments

Subdivision (a)(1)(C). The federal courts of appeals have reached conflicting conclusions about whether an appeal from an order granting or denying an application for a writ of error *coram nobis* is governed by the time limitations of Rule 4(a) (which apply in civil cases) or by the time limitations of Rule 4(b) (which apply in criminal cases). *Compare United States v. Craig*, 907 F.2d 653, 655–57, *amended* 919 F.2d 57 (7th Cir. 1990); *United States v. Cooper*, 876 F.2d 1192, 1193–94 (5th Cir. 1989); and *United States v. Keogh*, 391 F.2d 138, 140 (2d Cir. 1968) (applying the time limitations of Rule 4(a)); *with Yasui v. United States*, 772 F.2d 1496, 1498–99 (9th Cir. 1985); and *United States v. Mills*, 430 F.2d 526, 527–28 (8th Cir. 1970) (applying the time limitations of Rule 4(b)). A new part (C) has been added to Rule 4(a)(1) to resolve this conflict by providing that the time limitations of Rule 4(a) will apply.

Subsequent to the enactment of Fed. R. Civ. P. 60(b) and 28 U.S.C. § 2255, the Supreme Court has recognized the continued availability of a writ of error *coram nobis* in at least one narrow circumstance. In 1954, the Court permitted a litigant who had been convicted of a crime, served his full sentence, and been released from prison, but who was continuing to suffer a legal disability on account of the conviction, to seek a writ of error *coram nobis* to set aside the conviction. *United States v. Morgan*, 346 U.S. 502 (1954). As the Court recognized, in the *Morgan* situation an application for a writ of error *coram nobis* "is of the same general character as [a motion] under 28 U.S.C. § 2255." *Id.* at 506 n.4. Thus, it seems appropriate that the time limitations of Rule 4(a), which apply when a district court grants or denies relief under 28 U.S.C. § 2255, should also apply when a district court grants or denies a writ of error *coram nobis*. In addition, the strong public interest in the speedy resolution of criminal appeals that is reflected in the shortened deadlines of Rule 4(b) is not present in the *Morgan* situation, as the party seeking the writ of error *coram nobis* has already served his or her full sentence.

Notwithstanding *Morgan*, it is not clear whether the Supreme Court continues to believe that the writ of error *coram nobis* is available in federal court. In civil cases, the writ has been expressly abolished by Fed. R. Civ. P. 60(b). In criminal cases, the Supreme Court has recently stated that it has become " 'difficult to conceive of a situation' " in which the writ " 'would be necessary or appropriate.' " *Carlisle v. United States*, 517 U.S. 416, 429 (1996) (quoting *United States v. Smith*, 331 U.S. 469, 475 n.4 (1947)). The amendment to Rule 4(a)(1) is not intended to express any view on this issue; rather, it is merely meant to specify time limitations for appeals.

Rule 4(a)(1)(C) applies only to motions that are in substance, and not merely in form, applications for writs of error *coram nobis*. Litigants may bring and label as applications for a writ of error *coram nobis* what are in reality motions for a new trial under Fed. R. Crim. P. 33 or motions for correction or reduction of a sentence under Fed. R. Crim. P. 35. In such cases, the time limitations of Rule 4(b), and not those of Rule 4(a), should be enforced.

Changes Made After Publication and Comments No changes were made to the text of the proposed amendment or to the Committee Note.

Subdivision (a)(4)(A)(vi). Rule 4(a)(4)(A)(vi) has been amended to remove a parenthetical that directed that the 10–day deadline be "computed using Federal Rule of Civil Procedure 6(a)." That parenthetical has become superfluous because Rule 26(a)(2) has been amended to require that all deadlines under 11 days be calculated as they are under Fed. R. Civ. P. 6(a).

Changes Made After Publication and Comments No changes were made to the text of the proposed amendment or to the Committee Note.

Subdivision (a)(5)(A)(ii). Rule 4(a)(5)(A) permits the district court to extend the time to file a notice of appeal if two conditions are met. First, the party seeking the extension must file its motion no later than 30 days after the expiration of the time originally prescribed by Rule 4(a). Second, the party seeking the extension must show either excusable neglect or good cause. The text of Rule 4(a)(5)(A) does not distinguish between motions filed prior to the expiration of the original deadline and those filed after the expiration of the original deadline. Regardless of whether the motion is filed before or during the 30 days after the original deadline expires, the district court may grant an extension if a party shows either excusable neglect or good cause.

Despite the text of Rule 4(a)(5)(A), most of the courts of appeals have held that the good cause standard applies only to motions brought prior to the expiration of the original deadline and that the excusable neglect standard applies only to motions brought during the 30 days following the expiration of the original deadline. *See Pontarelli v. Stone*, 930 F.2d 104, 109–10 (1st Cir. 1991) (collecting cases from the Second, Fifth, Sixth, Seventh, Eighth, Ninth, and Eleventh Circuits). These courts have relied heavily upon the Advisory Committee Note to the 1979 amendment to Rule 4(a)(5). But the Advisory Committee Note refers to a draft of the 1979 amendment that was ultimately rejected. The rejected draft directed that the good cause standard apply only to motions filed prior to the expiration of the original deadline. Rule 4(a)(5), as actually amended, did not. *See* 16A CHARLES ALAN WRIGHT, ET AL., FEDERAL PRACTICE AND PROCEDURE § 3950.3, at 148–49 (2d ed. 1996).

The failure of the courts of appeals to apply Rule 4(a)(5)(A) as written has also created tension between that rule and Rule 4(b)(4). As amended in 1998, Rule 4(b)(4) permits the district court to extend the time for filing a notice of appeal in a *criminal* case for an additional 30 days upon a finding of excusable neglect or good cause. Both Rule 4(b)(4) and the Advisory Committee Note to the 1998 amendment make it clear that an extension can be granted for either excusable neglect or good cause, regardless of whether a motion for an extension is filed before or during the 30 days following the expiration of the original deadline.

Rule 4(a)(5)(A)(ii) has been amended to correct this misunderstanding and to bring the rule in harmony in this respect with Rule 4(b)(4). A motion for an extension filed prior to the expiration of the original deadline may be granted if the movant shows either excusable neglect or good cause. Likewise, a motion for an extension filed during the 30 days following the expiration of the original deadline may be granted if the movant shows either excusable neglect or good cause.

The good cause and excusable neglect standards have "different domains." *Lorenzen v. Employees Retirement Plan*, 896 F.2d 228, 232 (7th Cir. 1990). They are not interchangeable, and one is not inclusive of the other. The excusable neglect standard applies in situations in which there is fault; in such situations, the need for an extension is usually occasioned by something within the control of the movant. The good cause standard applies in situations in which there is no fault—excusable or otherwise. In such situations, the need for an extension is usually occasioned by something that is not within the control of the movant.

Thus, the good cause standard can apply to motions brought during the 30 days following the expiration of the original deadline. If, for example, the Postal Service fails to deliver a notice of appeal, a movant might have good cause to seek a post-expiration extension. It may be unfair to make such a movant prove that its "neglect" was excusable, given that the movant may not have been neglectful at all. Similarly, the excusable neglect standard can apply to motions brought prior to the expiration of the original deadline. For example, a movant may bring a pre-expiration motion for an extension of time when an error committed by the movant makes it unlikely that the movant will be able to meet the original deadline.

Changes Made After Publication and Comments No changes were made to the text of the proposed amendment. The stylistic changes to the Committee Note suggested by Judge Newman were adopted. In addition, two paragraphs were added at the end of the Committee Note to clarify the difference between the good cause and excusable neglect standards.

Subdivision (a)(7). Several circuit splits have arisen out of uncertainties about how Rule 4(a)(7)'s definition of when a judgment or order is "entered" interacts with the requirement in Fed. R. Civ. P. 58 that, to be "effective," a judgment must be set forth on a separate document. Rule 4(a)(7) and Fed. R. Civ. P. 58 have been amended to resolve those splits.

1. The first circuit split addressed by the amendments to Rule 4(a)(7) and Fed. R. Civ. P. 58 concerns the extent to which orders that dispose of post-judgment motions must be set forth on separate documents. Under Rule 4(a)(4)(A), the filing of certain post-judgment motions tolls the time to appeal the underlying judgment until the "entry" of the order disposing of the last such remaining motion. Courts have disagreed about whether such an order must be set forth on a separate document before it is treated as "entered." This disagreement reflects a broader dispute among courts about whether Rule 4(a)(7) independently imposes a separate document requirement (a requirement that is distinct from the separate document requirement that is imposed by the Federal Rules of Civil Procedure ("FRCP")) or whether Rule 4(a)(7) instead incorporates the separate document requirement as it exists in the FRCP. Further complicating the matter, courts in the former "camp" disagree among themselves about the scope of the separate document requirement that they interpret Rule 4(a)(7) as imposing, and courts in the latter "camp" disagree among themselves about the scope of the separate document requirement imposed by the FRCP.

Rule 4(a)(7) has been amended to make clear that it simply incorporates the separate document requirement as it exists in Fed. R. Civ. P. 58. If Fed. R. Civ. P. 58 does not require that a judgment or order be set forth on a separate document, then neither does Rule 4(a)(7); the judgment or order will be deemed entered for purposes of Rule 4(a) when it is entered in the civil docket. If Fed. R. Civ. P. 58 requires that a judgment or order be set forth on a separate document, then so does Rule 4(a)(7); the judgment or order will not be deemed entered for purposes of Rule 4(a) until it is so set forth and entered in the civil docket (with one important exception, described below).

In conjunction with the amendment to Rule 4(a)(7), Fed. R. Civ. P. 58 has been amended to provide that orders disposing of the postjudgment motions listed in new Fed. R. Civ. P. 58(a)(1) (which postjudgment motions include, but are not limited to, the post-judgment motions that can toll the time to appeal under Rule 4(a)(4)(A)) do not have to be set forth on separate documents. *See* Fed. R. Civ. P. 58(a)(1). Thus, such orders are entered for purposes of Rule 4(a) when they are entered in the civil docket pursuant to Fed. R. Civ. P. 79(a). *See* Rule 4(a)(7)(A)(1).

2. The second circuit split addressed by the amendments to Rule 4(a)(7) and Fed. R. Civ. P. 58 concerns the following question: When a judgment or order is required to be set forth on a separate document under Fed. R. Civ. P. 58 but is not, does the time to appeal the judgment or order—or the time to bring post-judgment motions, such as a motion for a new trial under Fed. R. Civ. P. 59—ever begin to run? According to every circuit except the First Circuit, the answer is "no." The First Circuit alone holds that parties will be deemed to have waived their right to have a judgment or order entered on a separate document three months after the judgment or order is entered in the civil docket. *See Fiore v. Washington County Community Mental Health Ctr.*, 960 F.2d 229, 236 (1st Cir. 1992) (en banc). Other circuits have rejected this cap as contrary to the relevant rules. *See, e.g., United States v. Haynes*, 158 F.3d 1327, 1331 (D.C. Cir. 1998); *Hammack v. Baroid Corp.*, 142 F.3d 266, 269–70 (5th Cir. 1998); *Rubin v. Schottenstein, Zox & Dunn*, 110 F.3d 1247, 1253 n.4 (6th Cir. 1997), *vacated on other grounds*, 143 F.3d 263 (6th Cir. 1998) (en banc). However, no court has questioned the wisdom of imposing such a cap as a matter of policy.

Both Rule 4(a)(7)(A) and Fed. R. Civ. P. 58 have been amended to impose such a cap. Under the amendments, a judgment or order is generally treated as entered when it is entered in the civil docket pursuant to Fed. R. Civ. P. 79(a). There is one exception: When Fed. R. Civ. P. 58(a)(1) requires the judgment or order to be set forth on a separate document, that judgment or order is not treated as entered until it is set forth on a separate document (in addition to being entered in the civil docket) or until the expiration of 150 days after its entry in the civil docket, whichever occurs first. This cap will ensure that parties will not be given forever to appeal (or to bring a postjudgment motion) when a court fails to set forth a judgment or order on a separate document in violation of Fed. R. Civ. P. 58(a)(1).

3. The third circuit split—this split addressed only by the amendment to Rule 4(a)(7)—concerns whether the appellant may waive the separate document requirement over the objection of the appellee. In *Bankers Trust Co. v. Mallis*, 435 U.S. 381, 387 (1978) (per curiam), the Supreme Court held that the "parties to an appeal may waive the separate-judgment requirement of Rule 58." Specifically, the Supreme Court held that when a district court enters an order and "clearly evidence[s] its intent that the . . . order . . . represent[s] the final decision in the case," the order is a "final decision" for purposes of 28 U.S.C. § 1291, even if the order has not been set forth on a separate document for purposes of Fed. R. Civ. P. 58. *Id.* Thus, the parties can choose to appeal without waiting for the order to be set forth on a separate document.

Courts have disagreed about whether the consent of all parties is necessary to waive the separate document requirement. Some circuits permit appellees to object to attempted *Mallis* waivers and to force appellants to return to the trial court, request that judgment be set forth on a separate document, and appeal a second time. *See, e.g., Selletti v. Carey*, 173 F.3d 104, 109–10 (2d Cir. 1999); *Williams v. Borg*, 139 F.3d 737, 739–40 (9th Cir. 1998); *Silver Star Enters., Inc. v. M/V Saramacca*, 19 F.3d 1008, 1013 (5th Cir. 1994). Other courts disagree and permit *Mallis* waivers even if the appellee objects. *See, e.g., Haynes*, 158 F.3d at 1331; *Miller v. Artistic Cleaners*, 153 F.3d 781, 783–84 (7th Cir. 1998); *Alvord-Polk, Inc. v. F. Schumacher & Co.*, 37 F.3d 996, 1006 n.8 (3d Cir. 1994).

New Rule 4(a)(7)(B) is intended both to codify the Supreme Court's holding in *Mallis* and to make clear that the decision whether to waive the requirement that the judgment or order be set forth on a separate document is the appellant's alone. It is, after all, the appellant who needs a clear signal as to when the time to file a notice of appeal has begun to run. If the appellant chooses to bring an appeal without waiting for the judgment or order to be set forth on a separate document, then there is no reason why the appellee should be able to object. All that would result from honoring the appellee's objection would be delay.

4. The final circuit split addressed by the amendment to Rule 4(a)(7) concerns the question whether an appellant who chooses to waive the separate document requirement must appeal within 30 days (60 days if the government is a party) from the entry in the civil docket of the judgment or order that should have been set forth on a separate document but was not. In *Townsend v. Lucas*, 745 F.2d 933 (5th Cir. 1984), the district court dismissed a 28 U.S.C. § 2254 action on May 6, 1983, but failed to set forth the judgment on a separate document. The plaintiff appealed on January 10, 1984. The Fifth Circuit dismissed the appeal, reasoning that, if the plaintiff waived the separate document requirement, then his appeal would be from the May 6 order, and if his appeal was from the May 6 order, then it was untimely under Rule 4(a)(1). The Fifth Circuit stressed that the plaintiff could return to the district court, move that the judgment be set forth on a separate document, and appeal from that judgment within 30 days. *Id.* at 934. Several other cases have embraced the *Townsend* approach. *See, e.g., Armstrong v. Ahitow*, 36 F.3d 574, 575 (7th Cir. 1994) (per curiam); *Hughes v. Halifax County Sch. Bd.*, 823 F.2d 832, 835–36 (4th Cir. 1987); *Harris v. McCarthy*, 790 F.2d 753, 756 n.1 (9th Cir. 1986).

Those cases are in the distinct minority. There are numerous cases in which courts have heard appeals that were not filed within 30 days (60 days if the government was a party) from the judgment or order that should have been set forth on a separate document but was not. *See, e.g., Haynes*, 158 F.3d at 1330–31; *Clough v. Rush*, 959 F.2d 182, 186 (10th Cir. 1992); *McCalden v. California Library Ass'n*, 955 F.2d 1214, 1218–19 (9th Cir. 1990). In the view of these courts, the remand in *Townsend* was "precisely the purposeless spinning of wheels abjured by the Court in the [*Mallis*] case." 15B CHARLES ALAN WRIGHT ET AL., FEDERAL PRACTICE AND PROCEDURE § 3915, at 259 n.8 (3d ed. 1992).

The Committee agrees with the majority of courts that have rejected the *Townsend* approach. In drafting new Rule 4(a)(7)(B), the Committee has been careful to avoid phrases such as "otherwise timely appeal" that might imply an endorsement of *Townsend*.

Changes Made After Publication and Comments No changes were made to the text of proposed Rule 4(a)(7)(B) or to the third or fourth numbered sections of the Committee Note, except that, in several places, references to a judgment being "entered" on a separate document were changed to references to a judgment being "set forth" on a separate document. This was to maintain stylistic consistency. The appellate rules and the civil rules consistently refer to "entering" judgments on the civil docket and to "setting forth" judgments on separate documents.

Two major changes were made to the text of proposed Rule 4(a)(7)(A)—one substantive and one stylistic. The substantive change was to increase the "cap" from 60 days to 150 days. The Appellate Rules Committee and the Civil Rules Committee had to balance two concerns that are implicated whenever a court fails to enter its final decision on a separate document. On the one hand, potential appellants need a clear signal that the time to appeal has begun to run, so that they do not unknowingly forfeit their rights. On the other hand, the time to appeal cannot be allowed to run forever. A party who receives no notice whatsoever of a judgment has only 180 days to move to reopen the time to appeal from that judgment. *See* Rule 4(a)(6)(A). It hardly seems fair to give a party who *does* receive notice of a judgment an unlimited amount of time to appeal, merely because that judgment was not set forth on a separate piece of paper. Potential appellees and the judicial system need *some* limit on the time within which appeals can be brought.

The 150–day cap properly balances these two concerns. When an order is not set forth on a separate document, what signals litigants that the order is final and appealable is a lack of further activity from the court. A 60–day period of inactivity is not sufficiently rare to signal to litigants that the court has entered its last order. By contrast, 150 days of inactivity is much less common and thus more clearly signals to litigants that the court is done with their case.

The major stylistic change to Rule 4(a)(7) requires some explanation. In the published draft, proposed Rule 4(a)(7)(A) provided that "[a] judgment or order is entered for purposes of this Rule 4(a) when it is entered for purposes of Rule 58(b) of the Federal Rules of Civil Procedure." In other words, Rule 4(a)(7)(A) told readers to look to FRCP 58(b) to ascertain when a judgment is entered for purposes of starting the running of the time to appeal. Sending appellate lawyers to the civil rules to discover when time began to run for purposes of the appellate rules was itself somewhat awkward, but it was made more confusing by the fact that, when readers went to proposed FRCP 58(b), they found this introductory clause: "Judgment is entered for purposes of Rules 50, 52, 54(d)(2)(B), 59, 60, and 62 when. . . . "

This introductory clause was confusing for both appellate lawyers and trial lawyers. It was confusing for appellate lawyers because Rule 4(a)(7) informed them that FRCP 58(b) would tell them when the time begins to run for purposes of the *appellate* rules, but when they got to FRCP 58(b) they found a rule that, by its terms, dictated only when the time begins to run for purposes of certain *civil* rules. The introductory clause was confusing for trial lawyers because FRCP 58(b) described when judgment is entered for some purposes under the civil rules, but then was completely silent about when judgment is entered for other purposes.

To avoid this confusion, the Civil Rules Committee, on the recommendation of the Appellate Rules Committee, changed the introductory clause in FRCP 58(b) to read simply: "Judgment is entered for purposes of *these Rules* when.... " In addition, Rule 4(a)(7)(A) was redrafted [1] so that the triggering events for the running of the time to appeal (entry in the civil docket, and being set forth on a separate document or passage of 150 days) were incorporated directly into Rule 4(a)(7), rather than indirectly through a reference to FRCP 58(b). This eliminates the need for appellate lawyers to examine Rule 58(b) and any chance that Rule 58(b)'s introductory clause (even as modified) might confuse them.

We do not believe that republication of Rule 4(a)(7) or FRCP 58 is necessary. In *substance*, rewritten Rule 4(a)(7)(A) and FRCP 58(b) operate identically to the published versions, except that the 60–day cap has been replaced with a 150–day cap—a change that was suggested by some of the commentators and that makes the cap more forgiving.

1. A redraft of Rule 4(a)(7) was faxed to members of the Appellate Rules Committee two weeks after our meeting in New Orleans. The Committee consented to the redraft without objection.

Subdivision (b)(5). Federal Rule of Criminal Procedure 35(a) permits a district court, acting within 7 days after the imposition of sentence, to correct an erroneous sentence in a criminal case. Some courts have held that the filing of a motion for correction of a sentence suspends the time for filing a notice of appeal from the judgment of conviction. *See, e.g., United States v. Carmouche*, 138 F.3d 1014, 1016 (5th Cir. 1998) (per curiam); *United States v. Morillo*, 8 F.3d 864, 869 (1st Cir. 1993). Those courts establish conflicting timetables for appealing a judgment of conviction after the filing of a motion to correct a sentence. In the First Circuit, the time to appeal is suspended only for the period provided by Fed. R. Crim. P. 35(a) for the district court to correct a sentence; the time to appeal begins to run again once 7 days have passed after sentencing, even if the motion is still pending. By contrast, in the Fifth Circuit, the time to appeal does not begin to run again until the district court actually issues an order disposing of the motion.

Rule 4(b)(5) has been amended to eliminate the inconsistency concerning the effect of a motion to correct a sentence on the time for filing a notice of appeal. The amended rule makes clear that the time to appeal continues to run, even if a motion to correct a sentence is filed. The amendment is consistent with Rule 4(b)(3)(A), which lists the motions that toll the time to appeal, and notably omits any mention of a Fed. R. Crim. P. 35(a) motion. The amendment also should promote certainty and minimize the likelihood of confusion concerning the time to appeal a judgment of conviction.

If a district court corrects a sentence pursuant to Fed. R. Crim. P. 35(a), the time for filing a notice of appeal of the corrected sentence under Rule 4(b)(1) would begin to run when the court enters a new judgment reflecting the corrected sentence.

Changes Made After Publication and Comments The reference to Federal Rule of Criminal Procedure 35(c) was changed to Rule 35(a) to reflect the pending amendment of Rule 35. The proposed amendment to Criminal Rule 35, if approved, will take effect at the same time that the proposed amendment to Appellate Rule 4 will take effect, if approved.

2005 Amendments

Rule 4(a)(6) has permitted a district court to reopen the time to appeal a judgment or order upon finding that four conditions were satisfied. First, the district court had to find that the appellant did not receive notice of the entry of the judgment or order from the district court or any party within 21 days after the judgment or order was entered. Second, the district court had to find that the appellant moved to reopen the time to appeal within 7 days after the appellant received notice of the entry of the judgment or order. Third, the district court had to find that the appellant moved to reopen the time to appeal within 180 days after the judgment or order was entered. Finally, the district court had to find that no party would be prejudiced by the reopening of the time to appeal.

Rule 4(a)(6) has been amended to specify more clearly what type of "notice" of the entry of a judgment or order precludes a party from later moving to reopen the time to appeal. In addition, Rule 4(a)(6) has been amended to address confusion about what type of "notice" triggers the 7–day period to bring a motion to reopen. Finally, Rule 4(a)(6) has been reorganized to set forth more logically the conditions that must be met before a district court may reopen the time to appeal.

Subdivision (a)(6)(A). Former subdivision (a)(6)(B) has been redesignated as subdivision (a)(6)(A), and one substantive change has been made. As amended, the subdivision will preclude a party from moving to reopen the time to appeal a judgment or order only if the party receives (within 21 days) formal notice of the entry of that judgment or order under Civil Rule 77(d). No other type of notice will preclude a party.

The reasons for this change take some explanation. Prior to 1998, former subdivision (a)(6)(B) permitted a district court to reopen the time to appeal if it found "that a party entitled to notice of the entry of a judgment or order did not receive such notice from the clerk or any party within 21 days of its entry." The rule was clear that the "notice" to which it referred was the notice required under Civil Rule 77(d), which must be served by the clerk pursuant to Civil Rule 5(b) and may also be served by a party pursuant to that same rule. In other words, prior to 1998, former subdivision (a)(6)(B) was clear that, if a party did not receive formal notice of the entry of a judgment or order under Civil Rule 77(d), that party could later move to reopen the time to appeal (assuming that the other requirements of subdivision (a)(6) were met).

In 1998, former subdivision (a)(6)(B) was amended to change the description of the type of notice that would preclude a party from moving to reopen. As a result of the amendment, former subdivision (a)(6)(B) no longer referred to the failure of the moving party to receive "*such* notice"—that is, the notice required by Civil Rule 77(d)—but instead referred to the failure of the moving party to receive "*the* notice." And former subdivision (a)(6)(B) no longer referred to the failure of the moving party to receive notice from "the *clerk* or any party," both of whom are explicitly mentioned in Civil Rule 77(d). Rather, former subdivision (a)(6)(B) referred to the failure of the moving party to receive notice from "the *district court* or any party."

The 1998 amendment meant, then, that the type of notice that precluded a party from moving to reopen the time to appeal was no longer limited to Civil Rule 77(d) notice. Under the 1998 amendment, *some* type of notice, in addition to Civil Rule 77(d) notice, precluded a party. But the text of the amended rule did not make clear what type of notice qualified. This was an invitation for litigation, confusion, and possible circuit splits.

To avoid such problems, former subdivision (a)(6)(B)—new subdivision (a)(6)(A)—has been amended to restore its pre–1998 simplicity. Under new subdivision (a)(6)(A), if the court finds that the moving party was not notified under Civil Rule 77(d) of the entry of the judgment or order that the party seeks to appeal within 21 days after that judgment or order was entered, then the court is authorized to reopen the time to appeal (if all of the other requirements of subdivision (a)(6) are met). Because Civil Rule 77(d) requires that notice of the entry of a judgment or order be formally served under Civil Rule 5(b), any notice that is not so served will not operate to preclude the reopening of the time to appeal under new subdivision (a)(6)(A).

Subdivision (a)(6)(B). Former subdivision (a)(6)(A) required a party to move to reopen the time to appeal "within 7 days after the moving party receives notice of the entry [of the judgment or order sought to be appealed]." Former subdivision (a)(6)(A) has been redesignated as subdivision (a)(6)(B), and one important substantive change has been made: The subdivision now makes clear that only formal notice of the entry of a judgment or order under Civil Rule 77(d) will trigger the 7–day period to move to reopen the time to appeal.

The circuits have been split over what type of "notice" is sufficient to trigger the 7–day period. The majority of circuits that addressed the question held that only *written* notice was sufficient, although nothing in the text of the rule suggested such a limitation. *See, e.g., Bass v. United States Dep't of Agric.*, 211 F.3d 959, 963 (5th Cir. 2000). By contrast, the Ninth Circuit held that while former subdivision (a)(6)(A) did not require written notice, "the quality of the communication [had to] rise to the functional equivalent of written notice." *Nguyen v. Southwest Leasing & Rental, Inc.*, 282 F.3d 1061, 1066 (9th Cir. 2002). Other circuits suggested in dicta that former subdivision (a)(6)(A) required only "actual notice," which, presumably, could have included oral notice that was not "the functional equivalent of written notice." *See, e.g., Lowry v. McDonnell Douglas Corp.*, 211 F.3d 457, 464 (8th Cir. 2000). And still other circuits read into former subdivision (a)(6)(A) restrictions that appeared only in former subdivision (a)(6)(B) (such as the requirement that notice be received "from the district court or any party," *see Benavides v. Bureau of Prisons*, 79 F.3d 1211, 1214 (D.C. Cir. 1996)) or that appeared in neither former subdivision (a)(6)(A) nor former subdivision (a)(6)(B) (such as the requirement that notice be served in the manner prescribed by Civil Rule 5, *see Ryan v. First Unum Life Ins. Co.*, 174 F.3d 302, 304–05 (2d Cir. 1999)).

Former subdivision (a)(6)(A)—new subdivision (a)(6)(B)—has been amended to resolve this circuit split by providing that only formal notice of the entry of a judgment or order under Civil Rule 77(d) will trigger the 7–day period. Using Civil Rule 77(d) notice as the trigger has two advantages: First, because Civil Rule 77(d) is clear and familiar, circuit splits are unlikely to develop over its meaning. Second, because Civil Rule 77(d) notice must be served under Civil Rule 5(b), establishing whether and when such notice was provided should generally not be difficult.

Using Civil Rule 77(d) notice to trigger the 7–day period will not unduly delay appellate proceedings. Rule 4(a)(6) applies to only a small number of cases—cases in which a party was not notified of a judgment or order by either the clerk or another party within 21 days after entry. Even with respect to those cases, an appeal cannot be brought more than 180 days after entry, no matter what the circumstances. In addition, Civil Rule 77(d) permits parties to serve notice of the entry of a judgment or order. The winning party can prevent Rule 4(a)(6) from even coming into play simply by serving notice of entry within 21 days. Failing that, the winning party can always trigger the 7–day deadline to move to reopen by serving belated notice.

Rule 5. Appeal by Permission

(a) Petition for Permission to Appeal.

(1) To request permission to appeal when an appeal is within the court of appeals' discretion, a party must file a petition for permission to appeal. The petition must be filed with the circuit clerk with proof of service on all other parties to the district-court action.

(2) The petition must be filed within the time specified by the statute or rule authorizing the appeal or, if no such time is specified, within the time provided by Rule 4(a) for filing a notice of appeal.

(3) If a party cannot petition for appeal unless the district court first enters an order granting permission to do so or stating that the necessary conditions are met, the district court may amend its order, either on its own or in response to a party's motion, to include the required permission or statement. In that event, the time to petition runs from entry of the amended order.

(b) Contents of the Petition; Answer or Cross–Petition; Oral Argument.

(1) The petition must include the following:

(A) the facts necessary to understand the question presented;

(B) the question itself;

(C) the relief sought;

(D) the reasons why the appeal should be allowed and is authorized by a statute or rule; and

(E) an attached copy of:

(i) the order, decree, or judgment complained of and any related opinion or memorandum, and

(ii) any order stating the district court's permission to appeal or finding that the necessary conditions are met.

(2) A party may file an answer in opposition or a cross-petition within 7 days after the petition is served.

(3) The petition and answer will be submitted without oral argument unless the court of appeals orders otherwise.

(c) Form of Papers; Number of Copies. All papers must conform to Rule 32(c)(2). Except by the court's permission, a paper must not exceed 20 pages, exclusive of the disclosure statement, the proof of service, and the accompanying documents required by Rule 5(b)(1)(E). An original and 3 copies must be filed unless the court requires a different number by local rule or by order in a particular case.

(d) Grant of Permission; Fees; Cost Bond; Filing the Record.

(1) Within 10 days after the entry of the order granting permission to appeal, the appellant must:

(A) pay the district clerk all required fees; and

(B) file a cost bond if required under Rule 7.

(2) A notice of appeal need not be filed. The date when the order granting permission to appeal is entered serves as the date of the notice of appeal for calculating time under these rules.

(3) The district clerk must notify the circuit clerk once the petitioner has paid the fees. Upon receiving this notice, the circuit clerk must enter the appeal on the docket. The record must be forwarded and filed in accordance with Rules 11 and 12(c).

(As amended Apr. 30, 1979, eff. Aug. 1, 1979; Apr. 29, 1994, eff. Dec. 1, 1994; Apr. 24, 1998, eff. Dec. 1, 1998; Apr. 29, 2002, eff. Dec. 1, 2002.)

ADVISORY COMMITTEE NOTES

1967 Adoption

This rule is derived in the main from Third Circuit Rule 11(2), which is similar to the rule governing appeals under 28 U.S.C. § 1292(b) in a majority of the circuits. The second sentence of subdivision (a) resolves a conflict over the question of whether the district court can amend an order by supplying the statement required by § 1292(b) at any time after entry of the order, with the result that the time fixed by the statute commences to run on the date of entry of the order as amended. Compare *Milbert v. Bison Laboratories*, 260 F.2d 431 (3d Cir., 1958) with *Sperry Rand Corporation v. Bell Telephone Laboratories*, 272 F.2d 29 (2d Cir., 1959), *Hadjipateras v. Pacifica, S.A.*, 290 F.2d 697 (5th Cir., 1961) and *Houston Fearless Corporation v. Teter*, 313 F.2d 91 (10th Cir., 1962). The view taken by the Second, Fifth and Tenth Circuits seems theoretically and practically sound, and the rule adopts it. Although a majority of the circuits now require the filing of a notice of appeal following the grant of permission to appeal, filing of the notice serves no function other than to provide a time from which the time for transmitting the record and docketing the appeal begins to run.

1979 Amendment

The proposed amendment [to subdivision (d)] adapts to the practice in appeals from interlocutory orders under 28 U.S.C. § 1292(b) the provisions of proposed Rule 3(e) above, requiring payment of all fees in the district court upon the filing of the notice of appeal. See Note to proposed amended Rule 3(e), *supra*.

1994 Amendments

Subdivision (c). The amendment makes it clear that a court may require a different number of copies either by rule or by order in an individual case. The number of copies of any document that a court of appeals needs varies depending upon the way in which the court conducts business. The internal operation of the courts of appeals necessarily varies from circuit to circuit because of differences in the number of judges, the geographic area included within the circuit, and other such factors. Uniformity could be achieved only by setting the number of copies artificially high so that parties in all circuits file enough copies to satisfy the needs of the court requiring the greatest number. Rather than do that, the Committee decided to make it clear that local rules may require a greater or lesser number of copies and that, if the circumstances of a particular case indicate the need for a different number of copies in that case, the court may so order.

1998 Amendments

In 1992 Congress added subsection (e) to 28 U.S.C. § 1292. Subsection (e) says that the Supreme Court has power to prescribe rules that "provide for an appeal of an interlocutory decision to the courts of appeals that is not otherwise provided for" in section 1292. The amendment of Rule 5 was prompted by the possibility of new rules authorizing additional interlocutory appeals. Rather than add a separate rule governing each such appeal, the Committee believes it is preferable to amend Rule 5 so that it will govern all such appeals.

In addition the Federal Courts Improvement Act of 12996, Pub.L. 104–317, abolished appeals by permission under 28 U.S.C. § 636(c)(5), making Rule 5.1 obsolete.

This new Rule 5 is intended to govern all discretionary appeals from district-court orders, judgments, or decrees. At this time that includes interlocutory appeals under 28 U.S.C. § 1292(b), (c)(1), (d)(1) & (2). If additional interlocutory appeals are authorized under § 1292(e), the new Rule is intended to govern them if the appeals are discretionary.

Subdivision (a). Paragraph (a)(1) says that when granting an appeal is within a court of appeals' discretion, a party may file a petition for permission to appeal. The time for filing provision states only that the petition must be filed within the time provided in the statute or rule authorizing the appeal or, if no such time is specified, within the time provided by Rule 4(a) for filing a notice of appeal.

Section 1292(b), (c), and (d) provide that the petition must be filed within 10 days after entry of the order containing the statement prescribed in the statute. Existing Rule 5(a) provides that if a district court amends an order to contain the prescribed statement, the petition must be filed within 10 days after entry of the amended order. The new rule similarly says that if a party cannot petition without the district court's permission or statement that necessary circumstances are present, the district court may amend its order to include such a statement and the time to petition runs from entry of the amended order.

The provision that the Rule 4(a) time for filing a notice of appeal should apply if the statute or rule is silent about the filing time was drawn from existing Rule 5.1

Subdivision (b). The changes made in the provisions in paragraph (b)(1) are intended only to broaden them sufficiently to make them appropriate for all discretionary appeals.

In paragraph (b)(2) a uniform time—7 days—is established for filing an answer in opposition or cross-petition. Seven days is the time for responding under existing Rule 5 and is an appropriate length of time when dealing with an interlocutory appeal. Although existing Rule 5.1 provides 14 days for responding, the Committee does not believe that the longer response time is necessary.

Subdivision (c). Subdivision (c) is substantively unchanged.

Subdivision (d). Paragraph (d)(2) is amended to state that "the date when the order granting permission to appeal is entered serves as the date of the notice of appeal" for purposes of calculating time under the rules. That language simply clarifies existing practice.

2002 Amendments

Subdivision (c). A petition for permission to appeal, a cross-petition for permission to appeal, and an answer to a petition or cross-petition for permission to appeal are all "other papers" for purposes of Rule 32(c)(2), and all of the requirements of Rule 32(a) apply to those papers, except as provided in Rule 32(c)(2). During the 1998 restyling of the Federal Rules of Appellate Procedure, Rule 5(c) was inadvertently changed to suggest that only the requirements of Rule 32(a)(1) apply to such papers. Rule 5(c) has been amended to correct that error.

Rule 5(c) has been further amended to limit the length of papers filed under Rule 5.

Changes Made After Publication and Comments No changes were made to the text of the proposed amendment or to the Committee Note.

[Rule 5.1. Appeal by Leave Under 28 U.S.C. § 636(c)(5)] (Abrogated Apr. 24, 1998, eff. Dec. 1, 1998)

ADVISORY COMMITTEE NOTES

1998 Amendments

The Federal Courts Improvement Act of 1996, Pub.L. No. 104–317, abolished appeals by permission under 28 U.S.C. § 636(c)(5), making Rule 5.1 obsolete. Rule 5.1 is, therefore, abrogated.

HISTORICAL NOTES

The abrogated rule provided that:

"(a) Petition for Leave to Appeal; Answer or Cross Petition. An appeal from a district court judgment, entered after an appeal under 28 U.S.C. § 636(c)(4) to a district judge from a judgment entered upon direction of a magistrate judge in a civil case, may be sought by filing a petition for leave to appeal. An appeal on petition for leave to appeal is not a matter of right, but its allowance is a matter of sound judicial discretion. The petition shall be filed with the clerk of the court of appeals within the time provided by Rule 4(a) for filing a notice of appeal, with proof of service on all parties to the action in the district court. A notice of appeal need not be filed. Within 14 days after service of the petition, a party may file an answer in opposition or a cross petition.

"(b) Content of Petition; Answer. The petition for leave to appeal shall contain a statement of the facts necessary to an understanding of the questions to be presented by the appeal; a statement of those questions and of the relief sought; a statement of the reasons why in the opinion of the petitioner the appeal should be allowed; and a copy of the order, decree or judgment complained of and any opinion or memorandum relating thereto. The petition and answer shall be submitted to a panel of judges of the court of appeals without oral argument unless otherwise ordered.

"(c) Form of Papers; Number of Copies. All papers may be typewritten. An original and three copies must be filed unless the court requires the filing of a different number by local rule or by order in a particular case.

"(d) Allowance of the Appeal; Fees; Cost Bond; Filing of Record. Within 10 days after the entry of an order granting the appeal, the appellant shall (1) pay to the clerk of the district court the fees established by statute and the docket fee prescribed by the Judicial Conference of the United States and (2) file a bond for costs if required pursuant to Rule 7. The clerk of the district court shall notify the clerk of the court of appeals of the payment of the fees. Upon receipt of such notice, the clerk of the court of appeals shall enter the appeal upon the docket. The record shall be transmitted and filed in accordance with Rules 11 and 12(b)."

Rule 6. Appeal in a Bankruptcy Case From a Final Judgment, Order, or Decree of a District Court or Bankruptcy Appellate Panel

(a) Appeal From a Judgment, Order, or Decree of a District Court Exercising Original Jurisdiction in a Bankruptcy Case. An appeal to a court of appeals from a final judgment, order, or decree of a district court exercising jurisdiction under 28 U.S.C. § 1334 is taken as any other civil appeal under these rules.

(b) Appeal From a Judgment, Order, or Decree of a District Court or Bankruptcy Appellate Panel Exercising Appellate Jurisdiction in a Bankruptcy Case.

(1) Applicability of Other Rules. These rules apply to an appeal to a court of appeals under 28 U.S.C. § 158(d) from a final judgment, order, or decree of a district court or bankruptcy appellate panel exercising appellate jurisdiction under 28 U.S.C. § 158(a) or (b). But there are 3 exceptions:

(A) Rules 4(a)(4), 4(b), 9, 10, 11, 12(b), 13–20, 22–23, and 24(b) do not apply;

(B) the reference in Rule 3(c) to 'Form 1 in the Appendix of Forms' must be read as a reference to Form 5; and

(C) when the appeal is from a bankruptcy appellate panel, the term 'district court,' as used in any applicable rule, means 'appellate panel.'

(2) Additional Rules. In addition to the rules made applicable by Rule 6(b)(1), the following rules apply:

(A) Motion for rehearing.

(i) If a timely motion for rehearing under Bankruptcy Rule 8015 is filed, the time to appeal for all parties runs from the entry of the order disposing of the motion. A notice of appeal filed after the district court or bankruptcy appellate panel announces or enters a judgment, order, or decree—but before disposition of the motion for rehearing—becomes effective when the order disposing of the motion for rehearing is entered.

(ii) Appellate review of the order disposing of the motion requires the party, in compliance with Rules 3(c) and 6(b)(1)(B), to amend a previously filed notice of appeal. A party intending to challenge an altered or amended judgment, order, or decree must file a notice of appeal or amended notice of appeal within the time prescribed by Rule 4—excluding Rules 4(a)(4) and 4(b)—measured from the entry of the order disposing of the motion.

(iii) No additional fee is required to file an amended notice.

(B) The record on appeal.

(i) Within 10 days after filing the notice of appeal, the appellant must file with the clerk possessing the record assembled in accordance with Bankruptcy Rule 8006—and serve on the appellee—a statement of the issues to be presented on appeal and a designation of the record to be certified and sent to the circuit clerk.

(ii) An appellee who believes that other parts of the record are necessary must, within 10 days after being served with the appellant's designation, file with the clerk and serve on the appellant a designation of additional parts to be included.

(iii) The record on appeal consists of:

- the redesignated record as provided above;
- the proceedings in the district court or bankruptcy appellate panel; and
- a certified copy of the docket entries prepared by the clerk under Rule 3(d).

(C) Forwarding the record.

(i) When the record is complete, the district clerk or bankruptcy appellate panel clerk must number the documents constituting the record and send them promptly to the circuit clerk together with a list of the documents correspondingly numbered and reasonably identified. Unless directed to do so by a party or the circuit clerk, the clerk will not send to the court of appeals documents of unusual bulk or weight, physical exhibits other than documents, or other parts of the record designated for omission by local rule of the court of appeals. If the exhibits are unusually bulky or heavy, a party must arrange with the clerks in advance for their transportation and receipt.

(ii) All parties must do whatever else is necessary to enable the clerk to assemble and forward the record. The court of appeals may provide by rule or order that a certified copy of the docket entries be sent in place of the redesignated record, but any party may request at any time during the pendency of the appeal that the redesignated record be sent.

(D) Filing the record. Upon receiving the record—or a certified copy of the docket entries sent in place of the redesignated record—the circuit clerk must file it and immediately notify all parties of the filing date.

(Added Apr. 25, 1989, eff. Dec. 1, 1989, and amended Apr. 30, 1991, eff. Dec. 1, 1991; Apr. 22, 1993, eff. Dec. 1, 1993; Apr. 24, 1998, eff. Dec. 1, 1998.)

ADVISORY COMMITTEE NOTES

1989 Addition

A new Rule 6 is proposed. The Bankruptcy Reform Act of 1978, Pub.L. No. 95–598, 92 Stat. 2549, the Supreme Court decision in *Northern Pipeline Construction Co. v. Marathon Pipe Line Co.,* 458 U.S. 50 (1982), and the Bankruptcy Amendments and Federal Judgeship Act of 1984, Pub.L. No. 98–353, 98 Stat. 333, have made the existing Rule 6 obsolete.

Subdivision (a). Subdivision (a) provides that when a district court exercises original jurisdiction in a bankruptcy matter, rather than referring it to a bankruptcy judge for a final determination, the appeal should be taken in identical fashion as appeals from district court decisions in other civil actions. A district court exercises original jurisdiction and this subdivision applies when the district court enters a final order or judgment upon consideration of a bankruptcy judge's proposed findings of fact and conclusions of law in a non-core proceeding pursuant to 28 U.S.C. § 157(c)(1) or when a district court withdraws a proceeding pursuant to 28 U.S.C. § 157(d). This subdivision is included to avoid uncertainty arising from the question of whether a bankruptcy case is a civil case. The rules refer at various points to the procedure "in a civil case", *see,* e.g. Rule 4(a)(1). Subdivision (a) makes it clear that such rules apply to an appeal from a district court bankruptcy decision.

Subdivision (b). Subdivision (b) governs appeals that follow intermediate review of a bankruptcy judge's decision by a district court or a bankruptcy appellate panel.

Subdivision (b)(1). Subdivision (b)(1) provides for the general applicability of the Federal Rules of Appellate Procedure, with specified exceptions, to appeals covered by subdivision (b) and makes necessary word adjustments.

Subdivision (b)(2). Paragraph (i) provides that the time for filing a notice of appeal shall begin to run anew from the entry of an order denying a rehearing or from the entry of a subsequent judgment. The Committee deliberately omitted from the rule any provision governing the validity of a notice of appeal filed prior to the entry of an order denying a rehearing; the Committee intended to leave undisturbed the current state of the law on that issue. Paragraph (ii) calls for a redesignation of the appellate record assembled in the bankruptcy court pursuant to Rule 8006 of the Rules of Bankruptcy Procedure. After an intermediate appeal, a party may well narrow the focus of its efforts on the second appeal and a redesignation of the record may eliminate unnecessary material. The proceedings during the first appeal are included to cover the possibility that independent error in the intermediate appeal, for example failure to follow appropriate procedures, may be assigned in the court of appeals. Paragraph (iii) provides for the transmission of the record and tracks the appropriate subsections of Rule 11. Paragraph (iv) provides for the filing of the record and notices to the parties. Paragraph (ii) and Paragraph (iv) both refer to "a certified copy of the docket entries". The "docket entries" referred to are the docket entries in the district court or the bankruptcy appellate panel, not the entire docket in the bankruptcy court.

1993 Amendments

Note to Subparagraph (b)(2)(i). The amendment accompanies concurrent changes to Rule 4(a)(4). Although Rule 6 never included language such as that being changed in Rule 4(a)(4), language that made a notice of appeal void if it was filed before, or during the pendency of, certain posttrial motions, courts have found that a notice of appeal is premature if it is filed before the court disposes of a motion for rehearing. See, e.g., *In re X-Cel, Inc.*, 823 F.2d 192 (7th Cir.1987); *In re Shah*, 859 F.2d 1463 (10th Cir.1988). The Committee wants to achieve the same result here as in Rule 4, the elimination of a procedural trap.

1998 Amendments

The language and organization of the rule are amended to make the rule more easily understood. In addition to changes made to improve the understanding, the Advisory Committee has changed language to make style and terminology consistent throughout the appellate rules. These changes are intended to be stylistic only.

Subdivision (b). Language is added to Rule 6(b)(2)(A)(ii) to conform with the corresponding provision in Rule 4(a)(4). The new language is clarifying rather than substantive. The existing rule states that a party intending to challenge an alteration or amendment of a judgment must file an amended notice of appeal. Of course, if a party has not previously filed a notice of appeal, the party would simply file a notice of appeal not an amended one. The new language states that the party must file "a notice of appeal or amended notice of appeal."

Rule 7. Bond for Costs on Appeal in a Civil Case

In a civil case, the district court may require an appellant to file a bond or provide other security in any form and amount necessary to ensure payment of costs on appeal. Rule 8(b) applies to a surety on a bond given under this rule.

(As amended Apr. 30, 1979, eff. Aug. 1, 1979; Apr. 24, 1998, eff. Dec. 1, 1998.)

ADVISORY COMMITTEE NOTES

1967 Adoption

This rule is derived from FRCP 73(c) [rule 73(c), Federal Rules of Civil Procedure, this title] without change in substance.

1979 Amendment

The amendment would eliminate the provision of the present rule that requires the appellant to file a $250 bond for costs on appeal at the time of filing his notice of appeal. The $250 provision was carried forward in the F.R.App.P. [these rules] from former Rule 73(c) of the F.R.Civ.P. [rule 73(c), Federal Rules of Civil Procedure], and the $250 figure has remained unchanged since the adoption of that rule in 1937. Today it bears no relationship to actual costs. The amended rule would leave the question of the need for a bond for costs and its amount in the discretion of the court.

1998 Amendments

The language of the rule is amended to make the rule more easily understood. In addition to changes made to improve the understanding, the Advisory Committee has changed language to make style and terminology consistent throughout the appellate rules. These changes are intended to be stylistic only.

Rule 8. Stay or Injunction Pending Appeal

(a) Motion for Stay.

(1) Initial Motion in the District Court. A party must ordinarily move first in the district court for the following relief:

(A) a stay of the judgment or order of a district court pending appeal;

(B) approval of a supersedeas bond; or

(C) an order suspending, modifying, restoring, or granting an injunction while an appeal is pending.

(2) Motion in the Court of Appeals; Conditions on Relief. A motion for the relief mentioned in Rule 8(a)(1) may be made to the court of appeals or to one of its judges.

(A) The motion must:

(i) show that moving first in the district court would be impracticable; or

(ii) state that, a motion having been made, the district court denied the motion or failed to afford the relief requested and state any reasons given by the district court for its action.

(B) The motion must also include:

(i) the reasons for granting the relief requested and the facts relied on;

(ii) originals or copies of affidavits or other sworn statements supporting facts subject to dispute; and

(iii) relevant parts of the record.

(C) The moving party must give reasonable notice of the motion to all parties.

(D) A motion under this Rule 8(a)(2) must be filed with the circuit clerk and normally will be considered by a panel of the court. But in an exceptional case in which time requirements make that procedure impracticable, the motion may be made to and considered by a single judge.

(E) The court may condition relief on a party's filing a bond or other appropriate security in the district court.

(b) Proceeding Against a Surety. If a party gives security in the form of a bond or stipulation or other undertaking with one or more sureties, each surety submits to the jurisdiction of the district court and irrevocably appoints the district clerk as the surety's agent on whom any papers affecting the surety's liability on the bond or undertaking may be served. On motion, a surety's liability may be enforced in the district court without the necessity of an independent action. The motion and any notice that the district court prescribes may be served on the district clerk, who must promptly mail a copy to each surety whose address is known.

(c) Stay in a Criminal Case. Rule 38 of the Federal Rules of Criminal Procedure governs a stay in a criminal case.

(As amended Mar. 10, 1986, eff. July 1, 1986; Apr. 27, 1995, eff. Dec. 1, 1995; Apr. 24, 1998, eff. Dec. 1, 1998.)

ADVISORY COMMITTEE NOTES

1967 Adoption

Subdivision (a). While the power of a court of appeals to stay proceedings in the district court during the pendency of an appeal is not explicitly conferred by statute, it exists by virtue of the all writs statute, 28 U.S.C. § 1651. *Eastern Greyhound Lines v. Fusco*, 310 F.2d 632 (6th Cir., 1962); *United States v. Lynd*, 301 F.2d 818 (5th Cir., 1962); *Public Utilities Commission of Dist. of Col. v. Capital Transit Co.*, 94 U.S.App.D.C. 140, 214 F.2d 242 (1954). And the Supreme Court has termed the power "inherent" (*In re McKenzie*, 180 U.S. 536, 551, 21 S.Ct. 468, 45 L.Ed. 657 (1901)) and "part of its (the court of appeals') traditional equipment for the administration of justice." (*Scripps-Howard Radio v. F.C.C.*, 316 U.S. 4, 9–10, 62 S.Ct. 875, 86 L.Ed. 1229 (1942)). The power of a single judge of the court of appeals to grant a stay pending appeal was recognized in *In re McKenzie, supra*. *Alexander v. United States*, 173 F.2d 865 (9th Cir., 1949) held that a single judge could not stay the judgment of a district court, but it noted the absence of a rule of court authorizing the practice. FRCP 62(g) [rule 62(g), Federal Rules of Civil Procedure] adverts to the grant of a stay by a single judge of the appellate court. The requirement that application be first made to the district court is the case law rule. *Cumberland Tel. & Tel. Co. v. Louisiana Public Service Commission*, 260 U.S. 212, 219, 43 S.Ct. 75, 67 L.Ed. 217 (1922); *United States v. El-O-Pathic Pharmacy*, 192 F.2d 62 (9th Cir., 1951); *United States v. Hansell*, 109 F.2d 613 (2d Cir., 1940). The requirement is explicitly stated in FRCrP 38(c) [rule 38(c), Federal Rules of Criminal Procedure] and in the rules of the First, Third, Fourth and Tenth Circuits. See also Supreme Court Rules 18 and 27.

The statement of the requirement in the proposed rule would work a minor change in present practice. FRCP 73(e) [rule 73(e), Federal Rules of Civil Procedure] requires that if a bond for costs on appeal or a supersedeas bond is offered after the appeal is docketed, leave to file the bond must be obtained from the court of appeals. There appears to be no reason why matters relating to supersedeas and cost bonds should not be initially presented to the district court whenever they arise prior to the disposition of the appeal. The requirement of FRCP 73(e) appears to be a concession of the view that once an appeal is perfected, the district court loses all power over its judgment. See *In re Federal Facilities Realty Trust*, 227 F.2d 651 (7th Cir., 1955) and cases cited at 654–655. No reason appears why all questions related to supersedeas or the bond for costs on appeal should not be presented in the first instance to the district court in the ordinary case.

Subdivision (b). The provisions respecting a surety upon a bond or other undertaking are based upon FRCP 65.1 [rule 65.1, Federal Rules of Civil Procedure].

1986 Amendment

The amendments to Rule 8(b) are technical. No substantive change is intended.

1995 Amendment

Subdivision (c). The amendment conforms subdivision (c) to previous amendments to Fed.R.Crim.P. 38. This amendment strikes the reference to subdivision (a) of Fed. R.Crim.P. 38 so that Fed.R.App.P. 8(c) refers instead to all of Criminal Rule 38. When Rule 8(c) was adopted Fed. R.Crim.P. 38(a) included the procedures for obtaining a stay of execution when the sentence in question was death, imprisonment, a fine, or probation. Criminal Rule 38 was later amended and now addresses those topics in separate subdivisions. Subdivision 38(a) now addresses only stays of death sentences. The proper cross reference is to all of Criminal Rule 38.

1998 Amendments

The language and organization of the rule are amended to make the rule more easily understood. In addition to changes made to improve the understanding, the Advisory Committee has changed language to make style and terminology consistent throughout the appellate rules. These changes are intended to by stylistic only.

Rule 9. Release in a Criminal Case

(a) Release Before Judgment of Conviction.

(1) The district court must state in writing, or orally on the record, the reasons for an order regarding the release or detention of a defendant in a criminal case. A party appealing from the order must file with the court of appeals a copy of the district court's order and the court's statement of reasons as soon as practicable after filing the notice of appeal. An appellant who questions the factual basis for the district court's order must file a transcript of the release proceedings or an explanation of why a transcript was not obtained.

(2) After reasonable notice to the appellee, the court of appeals must promptly determine the appeal on the basis of the papers, affidavits, and parts of the record that the parties present or the court requires. Unless the court so orders, briefs need not be filed.

(3) The court of appeals or one of its judges may order the defendant's release pending the disposition of the appeal.

(b) Release After Judgment of Conviction. A party entitled to do so may obtain review of a district-court order regarding release after a judgment of conviction by filing a notice of appeal from that order in the district court, or by filing a motion in the court of appeals if the party has already filed a notice of appeal from the judgment of conviction. Both the order and the review are subject to Rule 9(a). The papers filed by the party seeking review must include a copy of the judgment of conviction.

(c) Criteria for Release. The court must make its decision regarding release in accordance with the applicable provisions of 18 U.S.C. §§ 3142, 3143, and 3145(c).

(As amended Apr. 24, 1972, eff. Oct. 1, 1972; Oct. 12, 1984, Pub.L. 98–473, Title II, § 210, 98 Stat. 1987; Apr. 29, 1994, eff. Dec. 1, 1994; Apr. 24, 1998, eff. Dec. 1, 1998.)

ADVISORY COMMITTEE NOTES

1967 Adoption

Subdivision (a). The appealability of release orders entered prior to a judgment of conviction is determined by the provisions of 18 U.S.C. § 3147, as qualified by 18 U.S.C. § 3148, and by the rule announced in *Stack v. Boyle*, 342 U.S. 1, 72 S.Ct. 1, 96 L.Ed. 3 (1951), holding certain orders respecting release appealable as final orders under 28 U.S.C. § 1291. The language of the rule, "(a)n appeal authorized by law from an order refusing or imposing conditions of release," is intentionally broader than that used in 18 U.S.C. § 3147 in describing orders made appealable by that section. The summary procedure ordained by the rule is intended to apply to all appeals from orders respecting release, and it would appear that at least some orders not made appealable by 18 U.S.C. § 3147 are nevertheless appealable under the *Stack v. Boyle* rationale. See, for example, *United States v. Foster*, 278 F.2d 567 (2d Cir., 1960), holding appealable an order refusing to extend bail limits. Note also the provisions of 18 U.S.C. § 3148, which after withdrawing from persons charged with an offense punishable by death and from those who have been convicted of an offense the right of appeal granted by 18 U.S.C. § 3147, expressly preserves "other rights to judicial review of conditions of release or orders of detention."

The purpose of the subdivision is to insure the expeditious determination of appeals respecting release orders, an expedition commanded by 18 U.S.C. § 3147 and by the Court in *Stack v. Boyle*, supra. It permits such appeals to be heard on an informal record without the necessity of briefs and on reasonable notice. Equally important to the just and speedy disposition of these appeals is the requirement that the district court state the reasons for its decision. See *Jones v. United States*, 358 F.2d 543 (D.C.Cir., 1966); *Rhodes v. United States*, 275 F.2d 78 (4th Cir., 1960); *United States v. Williams*, 253 F.2d 144 (7th Cir., 1958).

Subdivision (b). This subdivision regulates procedure for review of an order respecting release at a time when the jurisdiction of the court of appeals has already attached by virtue of an appeal from the judgment of conviction. Notwithstanding the fact that jurisdiction has passed to the court of appeals, both 18 U.S.C. § 3148 and FRCrP 38(c) [rule 38(c), Federal Rules of Criminal Procedure] contemplate that the initial determination of whether a convicted defendant is to be released pending the appeal is to be made by the district court. But at this point there is obviously no need for a separate appeal from the order of the district court respecting release. The court of appeals or a judge thereof has power to effect release on motion as an incident to the pending appeal. See FRCrP 38(c) and 46(a)(2) [rules 38(c) and 46(a)(2), Federal Rules of Criminal Procedure. But the motion is functionally identical with the appeal regulated by subdivision (a) and requires the same speedy determination if relief is to be effective. Hence the similarity of the procedure outlined in the two subdivisions.

1972 Amendment

Subdivision (c) is intended to bring the rule into conformity with 18 U.S.C. § 3148 and to allocate to the defendant the burden of establishing that he will not flee and that he poses no danger to pay other person or to the community. The burden is placed upon the defendant in the view that the fact of his conviction justifies retention in custody in situations where doubt exists as to whether he can be safely released pending disposition of his appeal. Release pending appeal may also be denied if "it appears that an appeal is frivolous or taken for delay." 18 U.S.C. § 3148. The burden of establishing the existence of these criteria remains with the government.

1994 Amendments

Rule 9 has been entirely rewritten. The basic structure of the rule has been retained. Subdivision (a) governs appeals from bail decisions made before the judgment of conviction is entered at the time of sentencing. Subdivision (b) governs review of bail decisions made after sentencing and pending appeal.

Subdivision (a). The subdivision applies to appeals from "an order regarding release or detention" of a criminal defendant before judgment of conviction, *i.e.,* before sentencing. *See* Fed. R. Crim. P. 32. The old rule applied only to a defendant's appeal from an order "refusing or imposing conditions of release." The new broader language is needed because the government is now permitted to appeal bail decisions in certain circumstances. 18 U.S.C. §§ 3145 and 3731. For the same reason, the rule now requires a district court to state reasons for its decision in all instances, not only when it refuses release or imposes conditions on release.

The rule requires a party appealing from a district court's decision to supply the court of appeals with a copy of the district court's order and its statement of reasons. In addition, an appellant who questions the factual basis for the district court's decision must file a transcript of the release proceedings, if possible. The rule also permits a court to require additional papers. A court must act promptly to decide these appeals; lack of pertinent information can cause delays. The old rule left the determination of what should be filed entirely within the party's, discretion; it stated that the court of appeals would hear the appeal "upon such papers, affidavits, and portions of the record as the parties shall present."

Subdivision (b). This subdivision applies to review of a district court's decision regarding release made after judgment of conviction. As in subdivision (a), the language has been changed to accommodate the government's ability to seek review.

The word "review" is used in this subdivision, rather than "appeal" because review may be obtained, in some instances, upon motion. Review may be obtained by motion if the party has already filed a notice of appeal from the judgment of conviction. If the party desiring review of the release decision has not filed such a notice of appeal, review may be obtained only by filing a notice of appeal from the order regarding release.

The requirements of subdivision (a) apply to both the order and the review. That is, the district court must state its reasons for the order. The party seeking review must supply the court of appeals with the same information required by subdivision (a). In addition, the party seeking review must also supply the court with information about the conviction and the sentence.

Subdivision (c). This subdivision has been amended to include references to the correct statutory provisions.

1998 Amendments

The language and organization of the rule are amended to make the rule more easily understood. In addition to changes made to improve the understanding, the Advisory Committee has changed language to make style and terminology consistent throughout the appellate rules. These changes are intended to by stylistic only.

Rule 10. The Record on Appeal

(a) Composition of the Record on Appeal. The following items constitute the record on appeal:

(1) the original papers and exhibits filed in the district court;

(2) the transcript of proceedings, if any; and

(3) a certified copy of the docket entries prepared by the district clerk.

(b) The Transcript of Proceedings.

(1) Appellant's Duty to Order. Within 10 days after filing the notice of appeal or entry of an order disposing of the last timely remaining motion of a type specified in Rule 4(a)(4)(A), whichever is later, the appellant must do either of the following:

(A) order from the reporter a transcript of such parts of the proceedings not already on file as the appellant considers necessary, subject to a local rule of the court of appeals and with the following qualifications:

(i) the order must be in writing;

(ii) if the cost of the transcript is to be paid by the United States under the Criminal Justice Act, the order must so state; and

(iii) the appellant must, within the same period, file a copy of the order with the district clerk; or

(B) file a certificate stating that no transcript will be ordered.

(2) Unsupported Finding or Conclusion. If the appellant intends to urge on appeal that a finding or conclusion is unsupported by the evidence or is contrary to the evidence, the appellant must include in the record a transcript of all evidence relevant to that finding or conclusion.

(3) Partial Transcript. Unless the entire transcript is ordered:

(A) the appellant must—within the 10 days provided in Rule 10(b)(1)—file a statement of the issues that the appellant intends to present on the appeal and must serve on the appellee a copy of both the order or certificate and the statement;

(B) if the appellee considers it necessary to have a transcript of other parts of the proceedings, the appellee must, within 10 days after the service of the order or certificate and the statement of the issues, file and serve on the appellant a designation of additional parts to be ordered; and

(C) unless within 10 days after service of that designation the appellant has ordered all such parts, and has so notified the appellee, the appellee may within the following 10 days either order the parts or move in the district court for an order requiring the appellant to do so.

(4) Payment. At the time of ordering, a party must make satisfactory arrangements with the reporter for paying the cost of the transcript.

(c) Statement of the Evidence When the Proceedings Were Not Recorded or When a Transcript Is Unavailable. If the transcript of a hearing or trial is unavailable, the appellant may prepare a statement of the evidence or proceedings from the best available means, including the appellant's recollection. The statement must be served on the appellee, who may serve objections or proposed amendments within 10 days after being served. The statement and any objections or proposed amendments must then be submitted to the district court for settlement and approval. As settled and approved, the statement must be included by the district clerk in the record on appeal.

(d) Agreed Statement as the Record on Appeal. In place of the record on appeal as defined in Rule 10(a), the parties may prepare, sign, and submit to the district court a statement of the case showing how the issues presented by the appeal arose and were decided in the district court. The statement must set forth only those facts averred and proved or sought to be proved that are essential to the court's resolution of the issues. If the statement is truthful, it—together with any additions that the district court may consider necessary to a full presentation of the issues on appeal—must be approved by the district court and must then be certified to the court of appeals as the record on appeal. The district clerk must then send it to the circuit clerk within the time provided by Rule 11. A copy of the agreed statement may be filed in place of the appendix required by Rule 30.

(e) Correction or Modification of the Record.

(1) If any difference arises about whether the record truly discloses what occurred in the district court, the difference must be submitted to and settled by that court and the record conformed accordingly.

(2) If anything material to either party is omitted from or misstated in the record by error or accident, the omission or misstatement may be corrected and a supplemental record may be certified and forwarded:

(A) on stipulation of the parties;

(B) by the district court before or after the record has been forwarded; or

(C) by the court of appeals.

(3) All other questions as to the form and content of the record must be presented to the court of appeals.

(As amended Apr. 30, 1979, eff. Aug. 1, 1979; Mar. 10, 1986, eff. July 1, 1986; Apr. 30, 1991, eff. Dec. 1, 1991; Apr. 22, 1993, eff. Dec. 1, 1993; Apr. 27, 1995, eff. Dec. 1, 1995; Apr. 24, 1998, eff. Dec. 1, 1998.)

ADVISORY COMMITTEE NOTES

1967 Adoption

This rule is derived from FRCP 75(a), (b), (c) and (d) and FRCP 76 [rule 75(a), (b), (c) and (d) and rule 76, Federal Rules of Civil Procedure], without change in substance.

1979 Amendment

The proposed amendments to Rule 10(b) would require the appellant to place with the reporter a written order for the transcript of proceedings and file a copy with the clerk, and to indicate on the order if the transcript is to be provided under the Criminal Justice Act. If the appellant does not plan to order a transcript of any of the proceedings, he must file a certificate to that effect. These requirements make the appellant's steps in readying the appeal a matter of record and give the district court notice of requests for transcripts at the expense of the United States under the Criminal Justice Act. They are also the third step in giving the court of appeals some control over the production and transmission of the record. See Note to Rules 3(d)(e) above and Rule 11 below.

In the event the appellant orders no transcript, or orders a transcript of less than all the proceedings, the procedure under the proposed amended rule remains substantially as before. The appellant must serve on the appellee a copy of his order or in the event no order is placed, of the certificate to that effect, and a statement of the issues he intends to present on appeal, and the appellee may thereupon designate additional parts of the transcript to be included, and upon appellant's refusal to order the additional parts, may either order them himself or seek an order requiring the appellant to order them. The only change proposed in this procedure is to place a 10 day time limit on motions to require the appellant to order the additional portions.

Rule 10(b) is made subject to local rules of the courts of appeals in recognition of the practice in some circuits in some classes of cases, e.g., appeals by indigents in criminal cases after a short trial, of ordering immediate preparation of a complete transcript, thus making compliance with the rule unnecessary.

1986 Amendment

The amendments to Rules 10(b) and (c) are technical. No substantive change is intended.

1993 Amendment

The amendment is technical and no substantive change is intended.

1995 Amendment

Subdivision (b)(1). The amendment conforms this rule to amendments made in Rule 4(a)(4) in 1993. The amendments to Rule 4(a)(4) provide that certain postjudgment motions have the effect of suspending a filed notice of appeal until the disposition of the last of such motions. The purpose of this amendment is to suspend the 10–day period for ordering a transcript if a timely postjudgment motion is made and a notice of appeal is suspended under Rule 4(a)(4). The 10–day period set forth in the first sentence of this rule begins to run when the order disposing of the last of such postjudgment motions outstanding is entered.

1998 Amendments

The language and organization of the rule are amended to make the rule more easily understood. In addition to changes made to improve the understanding, the Advisory Committee has changed language to make style and terminology consistent throughout the appellate rules. These changes are intended to by stylistic only.

HISTORICAL NOTES

References in Text

The Criminal Justice Act, referred to in subd. (b)(1), probably means the Criminal Justice Act of 1964, Pub.L. 88–455, Aug. 20, 1964, 78 Stat. 552, which is classified to § 3006A of Title 18, Crimes and Criminal Procedure.

Rule 11. Forwarding the Record

(a) Appellant's Duty. An appellant filing a notice of appeal must comply with Rule 10(b) and must do whatever else is necessary to enable the clerk to assemble and forward the record. If there are multiple appeals from a judgment or order, the clerk must forward a single record.

(b) Duties of Reporter and District Clerk.

(1) Reporter's Duty to Prepare and File a Transcript. The reporter must prepare and file a transcript as follows:

(A) Upon receiving an order for a transcript, the reporter must enter at the foot of the order the date of its receipt and the expected completion date and send a copy, so endorsed, to the circuit clerk.

(B) If the transcript cannot be completed within 30 days of the reporter's receipt of the order, the reporter may request the circuit clerk to grant additional time to complete it. The clerk must note on the docket the action taken and notify the parties.

(C) When a transcript is complete, the reporter must file it with the district clerk and notify the circuit clerk of the filing.

(D) If the reporter fails to file the transcript on time, the circuit clerk must notify the district judge and do whatever else the court of appeals directs.

(2) District Clerk's Duty to Forward. When the record is complete, the district clerk must number the documents constituting the record and send them promptly to the circuit clerk together with a list of the documents correspondingly numbered and reasonably identified. Unless directed to do so by a party or the circuit clerk, the district clerk will not send to the court of appeals documents of unusual bulk or weight, physical exhibits other than documents, or other parts of the record designated for omission by local rule of the court of appeals. If the exhibits are unusually bulky or heavy, a party must arrange with the clerks in advance for their transportation and receipt.

(c) Retaining the Record Temporarily in the District Court for Use in Preparing the Appeal. The parties may stipulate, or the district court on motion may order, that the district clerk retain the record temporarily for the parties to use in preparing the papers on appeal. In that event the district clerk must certify to the circuit clerk that the record on appeal is complete. Upon receipt of the appellee's brief, or earlier if the court orders or the parties agree, the appellant must request the district clerk to forward the record.

(d) [Abrogated.]

(e) Retaining the Record by Court Order.

(1) The court of appeals may, by order or local rule, provide that a certified copy of the docket entries be forwarded instead of the entire record. But a party may at any time during the appeal request that designated parts of the record be forwarded.

(2) The district court may order the record or some part of it retained if the court needs it while the appeal is pending, subject, however, to call by the court of appeals.

(3) If part or all of the record is ordered retained, the district clerk must send to the court of appeals a copy of the order and the docket entries together with the parts of the original record allowed by the district court and copies of any parts of the record designated by the parties.

(f) Retaining Parts of the Record in the District Court by Stipulation of the Parties. The parties may agree by written stipulation filed in the district court that designated parts of the record be retained in the district court subject to call by the court of appeals or request by a party. The parts of the record so designated remain a part of the record on appeal.

(g) Record for a Preliminary Motion in the Court of Appeals. If, before the record is forwarded, a party makes any of the following motions in the court of appeals:

- for dismissal;
- for release;
- for a stay pending appeal;
- for additional security on the bond on appeal or on a supersedeas bond; or
- for any other intermediate order—

the district clerk must send the court of appeals any parts of the record designated by any party.

(As amended Apr. 30, 1979, eff. Aug. 1, 1979; Mar. 10, 1986, eff. July 1, 1986; Apr. 24, 1998, eff. Dec. 1, 1998.)

ADVISORY COMMITTEE NOTES

1967 Adoption

Subdivisions (a) and (b). These subdivisions are derived from FRCP 73(g) and FRCP 75(e) [rules 73(g) and 75(e), Federal Rules of Civil Procedure]. FRCP 75(e) presently directs the clerk of the district court to transmit the record within the time allowed or fixed for its filing, which, under the provisions of FRCP 73(g) is within 40 days from the date of filing the notice of appeal, unless an extension is obtained from the district court. The precise time at which the record must be transmitted thus depends upon the time required for delivery of the record from the district court to the court of appeals, since, to permit its timely filing, it must reach the court of appeals before expiration of the 40-day period or an extension thereof. Subdivision (a) of this rule provides that the record is to be transmitted within the 40-day period, or any extension thereof; subdivision (b) provides that transmission is effected when the clerk of the district court mails or otherwise forwards the record to the clerk of the court of appeals; Rule 12(b) directs the clerk of the court of appeals to file the record upon its receipt following timely docketing and transmittal. It can thus be determined with certainty precisely when the clerk of the district court must forward the record to the clerk of the court of appeals in order to effect timely filing: the final day of the 40-day period or of any extension thereof.

Subdivision (c). This subdivision is derived from FRCP 75(e) [rule 75(e), Federal Rules of Civil Procedure] without change of substance.

Subdivision (d). This subdivision is derived from FRCP 73(g) [rule 73(g), Federal Rules of Civil Procedure] and FRCrP 39(c) [rule 39(c), Federal Rules of Criminal Procedure]. Under present rules the district court is empowered to extend the time for filing the record and docketing the appeal. Since under the proposed rule timely transmission now insures timely filing (see note to subdivisions (a) and (b) above) the power of the district court is expressed in terms of its power to extend the time for transmitting the record. Restriction of that power to a period of 90 days after the filing of the notice of appeal represents a change in the rule with respect to appeals in criminal cases. FRCrP 39(c) now permits the district court to extend the time for filing and docketing without restriction. No good reason appears for a difference between the civil and criminal rule in this regard, and subdivision (d) limits the power of the district court to extend the time for transmitting the record in all cases to 90 days from the date of filing the notice of appeal, just as its power is now limited with respect to docketing and filing in civil cases. Subdivision (d) makes explicit the power of the court of appeals to permit the record to be filed at any time. See *Pyramid Motor Freight Corporation v. Ispass*, 330 U.S. 695, 67 S.Ct. 954, 91 L.Ed. 1184 (1947).

Subdivisions (e), (f) and (g). These subdivisions are derived from FRCP 75(f) [rule 75(f), Federal Rules of Civil Procedure], (a) and (g), respectively, without change of substance.

1979 Amendment

Under present Rule 11(a) it is provided that the record shall be transmitted to the court of appeals within 40 days after the filing of the notice of appeal. Under present Rule 11(d) the district court, on request made during the initial time or any extension thereof, and cause shown, may extend the time for the transmission of the record to a point not more than 90 days after the filing of the first notice of appeal. If the district court is without authority to grant a request to extend the time, or denies a request for extension, the appellant may make a motion for extension of time in the court of appeals. Thus the duty to see that the record is transmitted is placed on the appellant. Aside from ordering the transcript within the time prescribed the appellant has no control over the time at which the record is transmitted, since all steps beyond this point are in the hands of the reporter and the clerk. The proposed amendments recognize this fact and place the duty directly on the reporter and the clerk. After receiving the written order for the transcript (See Note to Rule 10(b) above), the reporter must acknowledge its receipt, indicate when he expects to have it completed, and mail the order so endorsed to the clerk of the court of appeals. Requests for extensions of time must be made by the reporter to the clerk of the court of appeals and action on such requests is entered on the docket. Thus from the point at which the transcript is ordered the clerk of the court of appeals is made aware of any delays. If the transcript is not filed on time, the clerk of the court of appeals will notify the district judge.

Present Rule 11(b) provides that the record shall be transmitted when it is "complete for the purposes of the appeal." The proposed amended rule continues this requirement. The record is complete for the purposes of the appeal when it contains the original papers on file in the clerk's office, all necessary exhibits, and the transcript, if one is to be included. Cf. present Rule 11(c). The original papers will be in the custody of the clerk of the district court at the time the notice of appeal is filed. See Rule 5(e) of the F.R.C.P. [rule 5(e), Federal Rules of Civil Procedure]. The custody of exhibits is often the subject of local rules. Some of them require that documentary exhibits must be deposited with the clerk. See Local Rule 13 of the Eastern District of Virginia. Others leave exhibits with counsel, subject to order of the court. See Local Rule 33 of the Northern District of Illinois. If under local rules the custody of exhibits is left with counsel, the district court should make adequate provision for their preservation during the time during which an appeal may be taken, the prompt deposit with the clerk of such as under Rule 11(b) are to be transmitted to the court of appeals, and the availability of others in the event that the court of appeals should require their transmission. Cf. Local Rule 11 of the Second Circuit [rule 11, U.S.Ct. of App. 2d Cir.].

Usually the record will be complete with the filing of the transcript. While the proposed amendment requires transmission "forthwith" when the record is complete, it was not designed to preclude a local requirement by the court of appeals that the original papers and exhibits be transmitted when complete without awaiting the filing of the transcript.

The proposed amendments continue the provision in the present rule that documents of unusual bulk or weight and physical exhibits other than documents shall not be transmitted without direction by the parties or by the court of appeals, and the requirement that the parties make special arrangements for transmission and receipt of exhibits of unusual bulk or weight. In addition, they give recognition to local rules that make transmission of other record items subject to order of the court of appeals. See Local Rule 4 of the Seventh Circuit [rule 4, U.S.Ct. of App. 7th Cir., this title].

1986 Amendment

The amendments to Rule 11(b) are technical. No substantive change is intended.

1998 Amendments

The language and organization of the rule are amended to make the rule more easily understood. In addition to changes made to improve the understanding, the Advisory Committee has changed language to make style and terminology consistent throughout the appellate rules. These changes are intended to be stylistic only.

Rule 12. Docketing the Appeal; Filing a Representation Statement; Filing the Record

(a) Docketing the Appeal. Upon receiving the copy of the notice of appeal and the docket entries from the district clerk under Rule 3(d), the circuit clerk must docket the appeal under the title of the district-court action and must identify the appellant, adding the appellant's name if necessary.

(b) Filing a Representation Statement. Unless the court of appeals designates another time, the attorney who filed the notice of appeal must, within 10 days after filing the notice, file a statement with the circuit clerk naming the parties that the attorney represents on appeal.

(c) Filing the Record, Partial Record, or Certificate. Upon receiving the record, partial record, or district clerk's certificate as provided in Rule 11, the circuit clerk must file it and immediately notify all parties of the filing date.

(As amended Apr. 30, 1979, eff. Aug. 1, 1979; Mar. 10, 1986, eff. July 1, 1986; Apr. 22, 1993, eff. Dec. 1, 1993; Apr. 24, 1998, eff. Dec. 1, 1998.)

ADVISORY COMMITTEE NOTES

1967 Adoption

Subdivision (a). All that is involved in the docketing of an appeal is the payment of the docket fee. In practice, after the clerk of the court of appeals receives the record from the clerk of the district court he notifies the appellant of its receipt and requests payment of the fee. Upon receipt of the fee, the clerk enters the appeal upon the docket and files the record. The appellant is allowed to pay the fee at any time within the time allowed or fixed for transmission of the record and thereby to discharge his responsibility for docketing. The final sentence is added in the interest of facilitating future reference and citation and location of cases in indexes. Compare 3d Cir.Rule 10(2) [rule 10(2), U.S.Ct. of App. 3d Cir.]; 4th Cir.Rule 9(8) [rule 9(8), U.S.Ct. of App. 4th Cir.]; 6th Cir.Rule 14(1) [rule 14(1), U.S.Ct. of App. 6th Cir.].

Subdivision (c). The rules of the circuits generally permit the appellee to move for dismissal in the event the appellant fails to effect timely filing of the record. See 1st Cir.Rule 21(3) [rule 21(3), U.S.Ct. of App. 1st Cir.]; 3d Cir.Rule 21(4) [rule 21(4), U.S.Ct. of App. 3d Cir.]; 5th Cir.Rule 16(1) [rule 16(1), U.S.Ct. of App. 5th Cir.]; 8th Cir.Rule 7(d) [rule 7(d), U.S.Ct. of App. 8th Cir.].

1979 Amendments

Subdivision (a). Under present Rule 12(a) the appellant must pay the docket fee within the time fixed for the transmission of the record, and upon timely payment of the fee, the appeal is docketed. The proposed amendment takes the docketing out of the hands of the appellant. The fee is paid at the time the notice of appeal is filed and the appeal is entered on the docket upon receipt of a copy of the notice of appeal and of the docket entries, which are sent to the court of appeals under the provisions of Rule 3(d). This is designed to give the court of appeals control of its docket at the earliest possible time so that within the limits of its facilities and personnel it can screen cases for appropriately different treatment, expedite the proceedings through prehearing conferences or otherwise, and in general plan more effectively for the prompt disposition of cases.

Subdivision (b). The proposed amendment conforms the provision to the changes in Rule 11.

1986 Amendments

The amendment to Rule 12(a) is technical. No substantive change is intended.

1993 Amendments

Note to new subdivision (b). This amendment is a companion to the amendment of Rule 3(c). The Rule 3(c) amendment allows an attorney who represents more than one party on appeal to "specify" the appellants by general description rather than by naming them individually. The requirement added here is that whenever an attorney files a notice of appeal, the attorney must soon thereafter file a statement indicating all parties represented on the appeal by that attorney. Although the notice of appeal is the jurisdictional document and it must clearly indicate who is bringing the appeal, the representation statement will be helpful especially to the court of appeals in identifying the individual appellants.

The rule allows a court of appeals to require the filing of the representation statement at some time other than specified in the rule so that if a court of appeals requires a docketing statement or appearance form the representation statement may be combined with it.

1998 Amendments

The language of the rule are amended to make the rule more easily understood. In addition to changes made to improve the understanding, the Advisory Committee has changed language to make style and terminology consistent throughout the appellate rules. These changes are intended to by stylistic only.

TITLE III. REVIEW OF A DECISION OF THE UNITED STATES TAX COURT

Rule 13. Review of a Decision of the Tax Court

(a) How Obtained; Time for Filing Notice of Appeal.

(1) Review of a decision of the United States Tax Court is commenced by filing a notice of appeal with the Tax Court clerk within 90 days after the entry of the Tax Court's decision. At the time of filing, the appellant must furnish the clerk with enough copies of the notice to enable the clerk to comply with Rule 3(d). If one party files a timely notice of appeal, any other party may file a notice of appeal within 120 days after the Tax Court's decision is entered.

(2) If, under Tax Court rules, a party makes a timely motion to vacate or revise the Tax Court's decision, the time to file a notice of appeal runs from the entry of the order disposing of the motion or from the entry of a new decision, whichever is later.

(b) Notice of Appeal; How Filed. The notice of appeal may be filed either at the Tax Court clerk's office in the District of Columbia or by mail addressed to the clerk. If sent by mail the notice is considered filed on the postmark date, subject to § 7502 of the Internal Revenue Code, as amended, and the applicable regulations.

(c) Contents of the Notice of Appeal; Service; Effect of Filing and Service. Rule 3 prescribes the contents of a notice of appeal, the manner of service, and the effect of its filing and service. Form 2 in the Appendix of Forms is a suggested form of a notice of appeal.

(d) The Record on Appeal; Forwarding; Filing.

(1) An appeal from the Tax Court is governed by the parts of Rules 10, 11, and 12 regarding the record on appeal from a district court, the time and manner of forwarding and filing, and the docketing in the court of appeals. References in those rules and in Rule 3 to the district court and district clerk are to be read as referring to the Tax Court and its clerk.

(2) If an appeal from a Tax Court decision is taken to more than one court of appeals, the original record must be sent to the court named in the first notice of appeal filed. In an appeal to any other court of appeals, the appellant must apply to that other court to make provision for the record.

(As amended Apr. 30, 1979, eff. Aug. 1, 1979; Apr. 29, 1994, eff. Dec. 1, 1994; Apr. 24, 1998, eff. Dec. 1, 1998.)

ADVISORY COMMITTEE NOTES

1967 Adoption

Subdivision (a). This subdivision effects two changes in practice respecting review of Tax Court decisions: (1) § 7483 of the Internal Revenue Code, 68A Stat. 891, 26 U.S.C. § 7483, provides that review of a Tax Court decision may be obtained by filing a petition for review. The subdivision provides for review by the filing of the simple and familiar notice of appeal used to obtain review of district court judgments; (2) § 7483, supra, requires that a petition for review be filed within 3 months after a decision is rendered, and provides that if a petition is so filed by one party, any other party may file a petition for review within 4 months after the decision is rendered. In the interest of fixing the time for review with precision, the proposed rule substitutes "90 days" and "120 days" for the statutory "3 months" and "4 months", respectively. The power of the Court to regulate these details of practice is clear. Title 28 U.S.C. § 2072, as amended by the Act of November 6, 1966, 80 Stat. 1323 (1 U.S.Code Cong. & Ad. News, p. 1546 (1966)), authorizes the Court to regulate ". . . practice and procedure in proceedings for the review by the courts of appeals of decisions of the Tax Court of the United States. . . ."

The second paragraph states the settled teaching of the case law. See *Robert Louis Stevenson Apartments, Inc. v. C.I.R.*, 337 F.2d 681, 10 A.L.R.3d 112 (8th Cir., 1964); *Denholm & McKay Co. v. C.I.R.*, 132 F.2d 243 (1st Cir., 1942); *Helvering v. Continental Oil Co.*, 63 App.D.C. 5, 68 F.2d 750 (1934); *Burnet v. Lexington Ice & Coal Co.*, 62 F.2d 906 (4th Cir.1933); *Griffiths v. C.I.R.*, 50 F.2d 782 (7th Cir., 1931).

Subdivision (b). The subdivision incorporates the statutory provision (Title 26, U.S.C., § 7502) that timely mailing is to be treated as timely filing. The statute contains special provisions respecting other than ordinary mailing. If the notice of appeal is sent by registered mail, registration is deemed prima facie evidence that the notice was delivered to the clerk of the Tax Court, and the date of registration is deemed the postmark date. If the notice of appeal is sent by certified mail, the effect of certification with respect to prima facie evidence of delivery and the postmark date depends upon regulations of the Secretary of the Treasury. The effect of a postmark made other than by the United States Post Office likewise depends upon regulations of the Secretary. Current regulations are found in 26 CFR § 301.7502–1.

1979 Amendments

The proposed amendment reflects the change in the title of the Tax Court to "United States Tax Court." See 26 U.S.C. § 7441.

1994 Amendments

Subdivision (a). The amendment requires a party filing a notice of appeal to provide the court with sufficient copies of the notice for service on all other parties.

1998 Amendments

The language and organization of the rule are amended to make the rule more easily understood. In addition to changes made to improve the understanding, the Advisory Committee has changed language to make style and terminology consistent throughout the appellate rules. These changes are intended to by stylistic only.

Rule 14. Applicability of Other Rules to the Review of a Tax Court Decision

All provisions of these rules, except Rules 4–9, 15–20, and 22–23, apply to the review of a Tax Court decision.

(As amended Apr. 24, 1998, eff. Dec. 1, 1998.)

ADVISORY COMMITTEE NOTES

1967 Adoption

The proposed rule continues the present uniform practice of the circuits of regulating review of decisions of the Tax Court by the general rules applicable to appeals from judgments of the district courts.

1998 Amendments

The language of the rule are amended to make the rule more easily understood. In addition to changes made to improve the understanding, the Advisory Committee has changed language to make style and terminology consistent throughout the appellate rules. These changes are intended to by stylistic only.

TITLE IV. REVIEW OR ENFORCEMENT OF AN ORDER OF AN ADMINISTRATIVE AGENCY, BOARD, COMMISSION, OR OFFICER

Rule 15. Review or Enforcement of an Agency Order—How Obtained; Intervention

(a) Petition for Review; Joint Petition.

(1) Review of an agency order is commenced by filing, within the time prescribed by law, a petition for review with the clerk of a court of appeals authorized to review the agency order. If their interests make joinder practicable, two or more persons may join in a petition to the same court to review the same order.

(2) The petition must:

(A) name each party seeking review either in the caption or the body of the petition—using such terms as 'et al.,' 'petitioners,' or 'respondents' does not effectively name the parties;

(B) name the agency as a respondent (even though not named in the petition, the United States is a respondent if required by statute); and

(C) specify the order or part thereof to be reviewed.

(3) Form 3 in the Appendix of Forms is a suggested form of a petition for review.

(4) In this rule 'agency' includes an agency, board, commission, or officer; 'petition for review' includes a petition to enjoin, suspend, modify, or otherwise review, or a notice of appeal, whichever form is indicated by the applicable statute.

(b) Application or Cross-Application to Enforce an Order; Answer; Default.

(1) An application to enforce an agency order must be filed with the clerk of a court of appeals authorized to enforce the order. If a petition is filed to review an agency order that the court may enforce, a party opposing the petition may file a cross-application for enforcement.

(2) Within 20 days after the application for enforcement is filed, the respondent must serve on the applicant an answer to the application and file it with the clerk. If the respondent fails to answer in time, the court will enter judgment for the relief requested.

(3) The application must contain a concise statement of the proceedings in which the order was entered, the facts upon which venue is based, and the relief requested.

(c) Service of the Petition or Application. The circuit clerk must serve a copy of the petition for review, or an application or cross-application to enforce an agency order, on each respondent as prescribed by Rule 3(d), unless a different manner of service is prescribed by statute. At the time of filing, the petitioner must:

(1) serve, or have served, a copy on each party admitted to participate in the agency proceedings, except for the respondents;

(2) file with the clerk a list of those so served; and

(3) give the clerk enough copies of the petition or application to serve each respondent.

(d) Intervention. Unless a statute provides another method, a person who wants to intervene in a proceeding under this rule must file a motion for leave to intervene with the circuit clerk and serve a copy on all parties. The motion—or other notice of intervention authorized by statute—must be filed within 30 days after the petition for review is filed and must contain a concise statement of the interest of the moving party and the grounds for intervention.

(e) Payment of Fees. When filing any separate or joint petition for review in a court of appeals, the petitioner must pay the circuit clerk all required fees.

(As amended Apr. 22, 1993, eff. Dec. 1, 1993; Apr. 24, 1998, eff. Dec. 1, 1998.)

ADVISORY COMMITTEE NOTES

1967 Adoption

General Note. The power of the Supreme Court to prescribe rules of practice and procedure for the judicial review or enforcement of orders of administrative agencies, boards, commissions, and officers is conferred by 28 U.S.C. § 2072, as amended by the Act of November 6, 1966, § 1, 80 Stat. 1323 (1 U.S.Code Cong. & Ad. News, p. 1546 (1966). Section 11 of the Hobbs Administrative Orders Review Act of 1950, 64 Stat. 1132, reenacted as 28 U.S.C. § 2352 (28 U.S.C.A. § 2352 (Supp.1966)), repealed by the Act of November 6, 1966, § 4, supra, directed the courts of appeals to adopt and promulgate, subject to approval by the Judicial Conference rules governing practice and procedure in proceedings to review the orders of boards, commissions and officers whose orders were made reviewable in the courts of appeals by the Act. Thereafter, the Judicial Conference approved a uniform rule, and that rule, with minor variations, is now in effect in all circuits. Third Circuit Rule 18 [rule 18, U.S.Ct. of App. 3rd Cir.] is a typical circuit rule, and for convenience it is referred to as the uniform rule in the notes which accompany rules under this Title.

Subdivision (a). The uniform rule (see General Note above) requires that the petition for review contain "a concise statement, in barest outline, of the nature of the proceedings as to which relief is sought, the facts upon which venue is based, the grounds upon which relief is sought, and the relief prayed." That language is derived from § 4 of the Hobbs Administrative Orders Review Act of 1950, 64 Stat. 1130, reenacted as 28 U.S.C. § 2344 (28 U.S.C.A. § 2344 (Supp. 1966)). A few other statutes also prescribe the content of the petition, but the great majority are silent on the point. The proposed rule supersedes 28 U.S.C. § 2344 and other statutory provisions prescribing the form of the petition for review and permits review to be initiated by the filing of a simple petition similar in form to the notice of appeal used in appeals from judgments of district courts. The more elaborate form of petition for review now required is rarely useful either to the litigants or to the courts. There is no effective, reasonable way of obliging petitioners to come to the real issues before those issues are formulated in the briefs. Other provisions of this subdivision are derived from §§ 1 and 2 of the uniform rule.

Subdivision (b). This subdivision is derived from §§ 3, 4 and 5 of the uniform rule.

Subdivision (c). This subdivision is derived from § 1 of the uniform rule.

Subdivision (d). This subdivision is based upon § 6 of the uniform rule. Statutes occasionally permit intervention by the filing of a notice of intention to intervene. The uniform rule does not fix a time limit for intervention, and the only time limits fixed by statute are the 30–day periods found in the Communications Act Amendments, 1952, § 402(e), 66 Stat. 719, 47 U.S.C. § 402(e), and the Sugar Act of 1948, § 205(d), 61 Stat. 927, 7 U.S.C. § 1115(d).

1993 Amendments

Subdivision (a). The amendment is a companion to the amendment of Rule 3(c). Both Rule 3(c) and Rule 15(a) state that a notice of appeal or petition for review must name the parties seeking appellate review. Rule 3(c), however, provides an attorney who represents more than one party on appeal the flexibility to describe the parties in general terms rather than naming them individually. Rule 15(a) does not allow that flexibility; each petitioner must be named. A petition for review of an agency decision is the first filing in any court and, therefore, is analogous to a complaint in which all parties must be named.

Subdivision (e). The amendment adds subdivision (e). Subdivision (e) parallels Rule 3(e) that requires the payment of fees when filing a notice of appeal. The omission of such a requirement from Rule 15 is an apparent oversight. Five circuits have local rules requiring the payment of such fees, see, e.g., Fifth Cir.Loc.R. 15.1, and Fed.Cir.Loc.R. 15(a)(2).

1998 Amendments

The language and organization of the rule are amended to make the rule more easily understood. In addition to changes made to improve the understanding, the Advisory Committee has changed language to make style and terminology consistent throughout the appellate rules. These changes are intended to by stylistic only.

Rule 15.1. Briefs and Oral Argument in a National Labor Relations Board Proceeding

In either an enforcement or a review proceeding, a party adverse to the National Labor Relations Board proceeds first on briefing and at oral argument, unless the court orders otherwise.

(Added Mar. 10, 1986, eff. July 1, 1986, and amended Apr. 24, 1998, eff. Dec. 1, 1998.)

ADVISORY COMMITTEE NOTES

1986 Addition

This rule simply confirms the existing practice in most circuits.

1998 Amendments

The language of the rule are amended to make the rule more easily understood. In addition to changes made to improve the understanding, the Advisory Committee has changed language to make style and terminology consistent throughout the appellate rules. These changes are intended to by stylistic only.

Rule 16. The Record on Review or Enforcement

(a) Composition of the Record. The record on review or enforcement of an agency order consists of:

(1) the order involved;

(2) any findings or report on which it is based; and

(3) the pleadings, evidence, and other parts of the proceedings before the agency.

(b) Omissions From or Misstatements in the Record. The parties may at any time, by stipulation, supply any omission from the record or correct a misstatement, or the court may so direct. If necessary, the court may direct that a supplemental record be prepared and filed.

(As amended Apr. 24, 1998, eff. Dec. 1, 1998.)

ADVISORY COMMITTEE NOTES

1967 Adoption

Subdivision (a) is based upon 28 U.S.C § 2112(b). There is no distinction between the record compiled in the agency proceeding and the record on review; they are one and the same. The record in agency cases is thus the same as that in appeals from the district court—the original papers, transcripts and exhibits in the proceeding below. Subdivision (b) is based upon § 8 of the uniform rule (see General Note following Rule 15).

1998 Amendments

The language and organization of the rule are amended to make the rule more easily understood. In addition to changes made to improve the understanding, the Advisory Committee has changed language to make style and terminology consistent throughout the appellate rules. These changes are intended to by stylistic only.

Rule 17. Filing the Record

(a) Agency to File; Time for Filing; Notice of Filing. The agency must file the record with the circuit clerk within 40 days after being served with a petition for review, unless the statute authorizing review provides otherwise, or within 40 days after it files an application for enforcement unless the respondent fails to answer or the court orders otherwise. The court may shorten or extend the time to file the record. The clerk must notify all parties of the date when the record is filed.

(b) Filing—What Constitutes.

(1) The agency must file:

(A) the original or a certified copy of the entire record or parts designated by the parties; or

(B) a certified list adequately describing all documents, transcripts of testimony, exhibits, and other material constituting the record, or describing those parts designated by the parties.

(2) The parties may stipulate in writing that no record or certified list be filed. The date when the stipulation is filed with the circuit clerk is treated as the date when the record is filed.

(3) The agency must retain any portion of the record not filed with the clerk. All parts of the record retained by the agency are a part of the record on review for all purposes and, if the court or a party so requests, must be sent to the court regardless of any prior stipulation.

(As amended Apr. 24, 1998, eff. Dec. 1, 1998.)

ADVISORY COMMITTEE NOTES

1967 Adoption

Subdivision (a). This subdivision is based upon § 7 of the uniform rule (see General Note following Rule 15). That rule does not prescribe a time for filing the record in enforcement cases. Forty days are allowed in order to avoid useless preparation of the record or certified list in cases where the application for enforcement is not contested.

Subdivision (b). This subdivision is based upon 28 U.S.C. § 2112 and § 7 of the uniform rule. It permits the agency to file either the record itself or a certified list of its contents. It also permits the parties to stipulate against transmission of designated parts of the record without the fear that an inadvertent stipulation may "diminish" the record. Finally, the parties may, in cases where consultation of the record is unnecessary, stipulate that neither the record nor a certified list of its contents be filed.

1998 Amendments

The language and organization of the rule are amended to make the rule more easily understood. In addition to changes made to improve the understanding, the Advisory Committee has changed language to make style and terminology consistent throughout the appellate rules. These changes are intended to by stylistic only; a substantive change is made, however, in subdivision (b).

Subdivision (b). The current rule provides that when a court of appeals is asked to review or enforce an agency order, the agency must file either "the entire record or such parts thereof as the parties may designate by stipulation filed with the agency" or a certified list describing the documents, transcripts, exhibits, and other material constituting the record. If the agency is not filing a certified list, the current rule requires the agency to file the entire record unless the parties file a "stipulation" designating only parts of the record. Such a "stipulation" presumably requires agreement of the parties as to the parts to be filed. The amended language in subparagraph (b)(1)(A) permits the filing of less than the entire record even when the parties do not agree as to which parts should be filed. Each party can designate the parts that it wants filed; the agency can then forward the parts designated by each party. In contrast, paragraph (b)(2) continues to require stipulation, that is agreement of the parties, that the agency need not file either the record or a certified list.

Rule 18. Stay Pending Review

(a) Motion for a Stay.

(1) Initial Motion Before the Agency. A petitioner must ordinarily move first before the agency for a stay pending review of its decision or order.

(2) Motion in the Court of Appeals. A motion for a stay may be made to the court of appeals or one of its judges.

(A) The motion must:

(i) show that moving first before the agency would be impracticable; or

(ii) state that, a motion having been made, the agency denied the motion or failed to afford the relief requested and state any reasons given by the agency for its action.

(B) The motion must also include:

(i) the reasons for granting the relief requested and the facts relied on;

(ii) originals or copies of affidavits or other sworn statements supporting facts subject to dispute; and

(iii) relevant parts of the record.

(C) The moving party must give reasonable notice of the motion to all parties.

(D) The motion must be filed with the circuit clerk and normally will be considered by a panel of the court. But in an exceptional case in which time requirements make that procedure impracticable, the motion may be made to and considered by a single judge.

(b) Bond. The court may condition relief on the filing of a bond or other appropriate security.

(As amended Apr. 24, 1998, eff. Dec. 1, 1998.)

ADVISORY COMMITTEE NOTES

1967 Adoption

While this rule has no counterpart in present rules regulating review of agency proceedings, it merely assimilates the procedure for obtaining stays in agency proceedings with that for obtaining stays in appeals from the district courts. The same considerations which justify the requirement of an initial application to the district court for a stay pending appeal support the requirement of an initial application to the agency pending review. See Note accompanying Rule 8. Title 5, U.S.C. § 705 (5 U.S.C.A. § 705 (1966 Pamphlet)), confers general authority on both agencies and reviewing courts to stay agency action pending review. Many of the statutes authorizing review of agency action by the courts of appeals deal with the question of stays, and at least one, the Act of June 15, 1936, 49 Stat. 1499 (7 U.S.C. § 10a), prohibits a stay pending review. The proposed rule in nowise affects such statutory provisions respecting stays. By its terms, it simply indicates the procedure to be followed when a stay is sought.

1998 Amendments

The language and organization of the rule are amended to make the rule more easily understood. In addition to changes made to improve the understanding, the Advisory Committee has changed language to make style and terminology consistent throughout the appellate rules. These changes are intended to by stylistic only.

Rule 19. Settlement of a Judgment Enforcing an Agency Order in Part

When the court files an opinion directing entry of judgment enforcing the agency's order in part, the agency must within 14 days file with the clerk and serve on each other party a proposed judgment conforming to the opinion. A party who disagrees with the agency's proposed judgment must within 7 days file with the clerk and serve the agency with a proposed judgment that the party believes conforms to the opinion. The court will settle the judgment and direct entry without further hearing or argument.

(As amended Mar. 10, 1986, eff. July 1, 1986; Apr. 24, 1998, eff. Dec. 1, 1998.)

ADVISORY COMMITTEE NOTES

1967 Adoption

This is § 12 of the uniform rule (see General Note following Rule 15) with changes in phraseology.

1986 Amendment

The deletion of the words "in whole or" is designed to eliminate delay in the issuance of a judgment when the court of appeals has either enforced completely the order of an agency or denied completely such enforcement. In such a clear-cut situation, it serves no useful purpose to delay the issuance of the judgment until a proposed judgment is submitted by the agency and reviewed by the respondent. This change conforms the Rule to the existing practice in most circuits. Other amendments are technical and no substantive change is intended.

1998 Amendments

The language of the rule are amended to make the rule more easily understood. In addition to changes made to improve the understanding, the Advisory Committee has changed language to make style and terminology consistent throughout the appellate rules. These changes are intended to by stylistic only.

Rule 20. Applicability of Rules to the Review or Enforcement of an Agency Order

All provisions of these rules, except Rules 3–14 and 22–23, apply to the review or enforcement of an agency order. In these rules, 'appellant' includes a petitioner or applicant, and 'appellee' includes a respondent.

(As amended Apr. 24, 1998, eff. Dec. 1, 1998.)

ADVISORY COMMITTEE NOTES

1967 Adoption

The proposed rule continues the present uniform practice of the circuits of regulating agency review or enforcement proceedings by the general rules applicable to appeals from judgments of the district courts.

1998 Amendments

The language of the rule are amended to make the rule more easily understood. In addition to changes made to improve the understanding, the Advisory Committee has changed language to make style and terminology consistent throughout the appellate rules. These changes are intended to by stylistic only.

TITLE V. EXTRAORDINARY WRITS

Rule 21. Writs of Mandamus and Prohibition, and Other Extraordinary Writs

(a) Mandamus or Prohibition to a Court: Petition, Filing, Service, and Docketing.

(1) A party petitioning for a writ of mandamus or prohibition directed to a court must file a petition with the circuit clerk with proof of service on all parties to the proceeding in the trial court. The party must also provide a copy to the trial-court judge. All parties to the proceeding in the trial court other than the petitioner are respondents for all purposes.

(2)(A) The petition must be titled 'In re [name of petitioner].'

(B) The petition must state:

(i) the relief sought;

(ii) the issues presented;

(iii) the facts necessary to understand the issue presented by the petition; and

(iv) the reasons why the writ should issue.

(C) The petition must include a copy of any order or opinion or parts of the record that may be essential to understand the matters set forth in the petition.

(3) Upon receiving the prescribed docket fee, the clerk must docket the petition and submit it to the court.

(b) Denial; Order Directing Answer; Briefs; Precedence.

(1) The court may deny the petition without an answer. Otherwise, it must order the respondent, if any, to answer within a fixed time.

(2) The clerk must serve the order to respond on all persons directed to respond.

(3) Two or more respondents may answer jointly.

(4) The court of appeals may invite or order the trial-court judge to address the petition or may invite an amicus curiae to do so. The trial-court judge may request permission to address the petition but may not do so unless invited or ordered to do so by the court of appeals.

(5) If briefing or oral argument is required, the clerk must advise the parties, and when appropriate, the trial-court judge or amicus curiae.

(6) The proceeding must be given preference over ordinary civil cases.

(7) The circuit clerk must send a copy of the final disposition to the trial-court judge.

(c) Other Extraordinary Writs. An application for an extraordinary writ other than one provided for in Rule 21(a) must be made by filing a petition with the circuit clerk with proof of service on the respondents. Proceedings on the application must conform, so far as is practicable, to the procedures prescribed in Rule 21(a) and (b).

(d) Form of Papers; Number of Copies. All papers must conform to Rule 32(c)(2). Except by the court's permission, a paper must not exceed 30 pages, exclusive of the disclosure statement, the proof of service, and the accompanying documents required by Rule 21(a)(2)(C). An original and 3 copies must be filed unless the court requires the filing of a different number by local rule or by order in a particular case.

(As amended Apr. 29, 1994, eff. Dec. 1, 1994; Apr. 23, 1996, eff. Dec. 1, 1996; Apr. 24, 1998, eff. Dec. 1, 1998; Apr. 29, 2002, eff. Dec. 1, 2002.)

ADVISORY COMMITTEE NOTES

1967 Adoption

The authority of courts of appeals to issue extraordinary writs is derived from 28 U.S.C. § 1651. Subdivisions (a) and (b) regulate in detail the procedure surrounding the writs most commonly sought—mandamus or prohibition directed to a judge or judges. Those subdivisions are based upon Supreme Court Rule 31, with certain changes which reflect the uniform practice among the circuits (Seventh Circuit Rule 19 is a typical circuit rule). Subdivision (c) sets out a very general procedure to be followed in applications for the variety of other writs which may be issued under the authority of 28 U.S.C. § 1651.

1994 Amendments

Subdivision (d). The amendment makes it clear that a court may require a different number of copies either by rule or by order in an individual case. The number of copies of any document that a court of appeals needs varies depending upon the way in which the court conducts business. The internal operation of the courts of appeals necessarily varies from circuit to circuit because of differences in the number of judges, the geographic area included within the circuit, and other such factors. Uniformity could be achieved only by setting the number of copies artificially high so that parties in all circuits file enough copies to satisfy the needs of the courts requiring the greatest number. Rather than do that, the Committee decided to make it clear that local rules may require a greater or lesser number of copies and that, if the circumstances of a particular case indicate the need for a different number of copies in that case, the court may so order.

1996 Amendments

In most instances, a writ of mandamus or prohibition is not actually directed to a judge in any more personal way than is an order reversing a court's judgment. Most often a petition for a writ of mandamus seeks review of the intrinsic merits of a judge's action and is in reality an adversary proceeding between the parties. See, *e.g., Walker v. Columbia Broadcasting System, Inc.*, 443 F.2d 33 (7th Cir.1971). In order to change the tone of the rule and of mandamus proceedings generally, the rule is amended so that the judge is not treated as a respondent. The caption and subdivision (a) are amended by deleting the reference to the writs as being "directed to a judge or judges."

Subdivision (a). Subdivision (a) applies to writs of mandamus or prohibition directed to a court, but it is amended so that a petition for a writ of mandamus or prohibition does not bear the name of the judge. The amendments to subdivision (a) speak, however, about mandamus or prohibition "directed to a court." This language is inserted to distinguish subdivision (a) from subdivision (c). Subdivision (c) governs all other extraordinary writs, including a writ of mandamus or prohibition directed to an administrative agency rather than to a court and a writ of habeas corpus.

The amendments require the petitioner to provide a copy of the petition to the trial court judge. This will alert the judge to the filing of the petition. This is necessary because the trial court judge is not treated as a respondent and, as a result, is not served. A companion amendment is made in subdivision (b). It requires the circuit clerk to send a copy of the disposition of the petition to the trial court judge.

Subdivision (b). The amendment provides that even if relief is requested of a particular judge, although the judge may request permission to respond, the judge may not do so unless the court invites or orders a response.

The court of appeals ordinarily will be adequately informed not only by the opinions or statements made by the trial court judge contemporaneously with the entry of the challenged order but also by the arguments made on behalf of the party opposing the relief. The latter does not create an attorney-client relationship between the party's attorney and the judge whose action is challenged, nor does it give rise to any right to compensation from the judge.

If the court of appeals desires to hear from the trial court judge, however, the court may invite or order the judge to respond. In some instances, especially those involving court administration or the failure of a judge to act, it may be that no one other than the judge can provide a thorough explanation of the matters at issue. Because it is ordinarily undesirable to place the trial court judge, even temporarily, in an adversarial posture with a litigant, the rule permits a court of appeals to invite an *amicus curiae* to provide a response to the petition. In those instances in which the respondent does not oppose issuance of the writ or does not have sufficient perspective on the issue to provide an adequate response, participation of an *amicus* may avoid the need for the trial judge to participate.

Subdivision (c). The changes are stylistic only. No substantive changes are intended.

1998 Amendments

The language and organization of the rule are amended to make the rule more easily understood. In addition to changes made to improve the understanding, the Advisory Committee has changed language to make style and terminology consistent throughout the appellate rules. These changes are intended to by stylistic only.

2002 Amendments

Subdivision (d). A petition for a writ of mandamus or prohibition, an application for another extraordinary writ, and an answer to such a petition or application are all "other papers" for purposes of Rule 32(c)(2), and all of the requirements of Rule 32(a) apply to those papers, except as provided in Rule 32(c)(2). During the 1998 restyling of the Federal Rules of Appellate Procedure, Rule 21(d) was inadvertently changed to suggest that only the requirements of Rule 32(a)(1) apply to such papers. Rule 21(d) has been amended to correct that error.

Rule 21(d) has been further amended to limit the length of papers filed under Rule 21.

Changes Made After Publication and Comments No changes were made to the text of the proposed amendment or to the Committee Note, except that the page limit was increased from 20 pages to 30 pages. The Committee was persuaded by some commentators that petitions for extraordinary writs closely resemble principal briefs on the merits and should be allotted more than 20 pages.

TITLE VI. HABEAS CORPUS; PROCEEDINGS IN FORMA PAUPERIS

Rule 22. Habeas Corpus and Section 2255 Proceedings

(a) Application for the Original Writ. An application for a writ of habeas corpus must be made to the appropriate district court. If made to a circuit judge, the application must be transferred to the appropriate district court. If a district court denies an application made or transferred to it, renewal of the application before a circuit judge is not permitted. The applicant may, under 28 U.S.C. § 2253, appeal to the court of appeals from the district court's order denying the application.

(b) Certificate of Appealability.

(1) In a habeas corpus proceeding in which the detention complained of arises from process issued by a state court, or in a 28 U.S.C. § 2255 proceeding, the applicant cannot take an appeal unless a circuit justice or a circuit or district judge issues a certificate of appealability under 28 U.S.C. § 2253(c). If an applicant files a notice of appeal, the district judge who rendered the judgment must either issue a certificate of appealability or state why a certificate should not issue. The district clerk must send the certificate or statement to the

court of appeals with the notice of appeal and the file of the district-court proceedings. If the district judge has denied the certificate, the applicant may request a circuit judge to issue the certificate.

(2) A request addressed to the court of appeals may be considered by a circuit judge or judges, as the court prescribes. If no express request for a certificate is filed, the notice of appeal constitutes a request addressed to the judges of the court of appeals.

(3) A certificate of appealability is not required when a state or its representative or the United States or its representative appeals.

(As amended Pub.L. 104–132, Title I, § 103, Apr. 24, 1996, 110 Stat. 1218; Apr. 24, 1998, eff. Dec. 1, 1998.)

ADVISORY COMMITTEE NOTES

1967 Adoption

Subdivision (a). Title 28 U.S.C. § 2241(a) authorizes circuit judges to issue the writ of habeas corpus. Section 2241(b) [§ 2241(b) of this title], however, authorizes a circuit judge to decline to entertain an application and to transfer it to the appropriate district court, and this is the usual practice. The first two sentences merely make present practice explicit. Title 28 U.S.C. § 2253 seems clearly to contemplate that once an application is presented to a district judge and is denied by him, the remedy is an appeal from the order of denial. But the language of 28 U.S.C. § 2241 seems to authorize a second original application to a circuit judge following a denial by a district judge. *In re Gersing*, 79 U.S.App.D. 245, 145 F.2d 481 (D.C.Cir., 1944) and *Chapman v. Teets*, 241 F.2d 186 (9th Cir., 1957) acknowledge the availability of such a procedure. But the procedure is ordinarily a waste of time for all involved, and the final sentence attempts to discourage it.

A court of appeals has no jurisdiction as a court to grant an original writ of habeas corpus, and courts of appeals have dismissed applications addressed to them. *Loum v. Alvis*, 263 F.2d 836 (6th Cir., 1959); *In re Berry*, 221 F.2d 798 (9th Cir., 1955); *Posey v. Dowd*, 134 F.2d 613 (7th Cir., 1943). The fairer and more expeditious practice is for the court of appeals to regard an application addressed to it as being addressed to one of its members, and to transfer the application to the appropriate district court in accordance with the provisions of this rule. Perhaps such a disposition is required by the rationale of *In re Burwell*, 350 U.S. 521, 76 S.Ct. 539, 100 L.Ed. 666 (1956).

Subdivision (b). Title 28 U.S.C. § 2253 provides that an appeal may not be taken in a habeas corpus proceeding where confinement is under a judgment of a state court unless the judge who rendered the order in the habeas corpus proceeding, or a circuit justice or judge, issues a certificate of probable cause. In the interest of insuring that the matter of the certificate will not be overlooked and that, if the certificate is denied, the reasons for denial in the first instance will be available on any subsequent application, the proposed rule requires the district judge to issue the certificate or to state reasons for its denial.

While 28 U.S.C. § 2253 does not authorize the court of appeals as a court to grant a certificate of probable cause, *In re Burwell*, 350 U.S. 521, 76 S.Ct. 539, 100 L.Ed. 666 (1956) makes it clear that a court of appeals may not decline to consider a request for the certificate addressed to it as a court but must regard the request as made to the judges thereof. The fourth sentence incorporates the Burwell rule.

Although 28 U.S.C. § 2253 appears to require a certificate of probable cause even when an appeal is taken by a state or its representative, the legislative history strongly suggests that the intention of Congress was to require a certificate only in the case in which an appeal is taken by an applicant for the writ. See *United States ex rel. Tillery v. Cavell*, 294 F.2d 12 (3d Cir., 1960). Four of the five circuits which have ruled on the point have so interpreted § 2253. *United States ex rel. Tillery v. Cavell*, supra; *Buder v. Bell*, 306 F.2d 71 (6th Cir., 1962); *United States ex rel. Calhoun v. Pate*, 341 F.2d 885 (7th Cir., 1965); *State of Texas v. Graves*, 352 F.2d 514 (5th Cir., 1965). Cf. *United States ex rel. Carrol v. LaVallee*, 342 F.2d 641 (2d Cir., 1965). The final sentence makes it clear that a certificate of probable cause is not required of a state or its representative.

1998 Amendments

The language and organization of the rule are amended to make the rule more easily understood. In addition to changes made to improve the understanding, the Advisory Committee has changed language to make style and terminology consistent throughout the appellate rules. These changes are intended to by stylistic only; in this rule, however, substantive changes are made in paragraphs (b)(1) and (b)(3).

Subdivision (b), paragraph (1). Two substantive changes are made in this paragraph. First, the paragraph is made applicable to 28 U.S.C. § 2255 proceedings. This brings the rule into conformity with 28 U.S.C. § 2253 as amended by the Anti-Terrorism and Effective Death Penalty Act of 1996, Pub.L. No. 104–132. Second, the rule states that a certificate of appealability may be issued by a "circuit justice or a circuit or district judge." That language adds a reference to the circuit justice which also brings the rule into conformity with section 2253. The language continues to state that in addition to the circuit justice, both a circuit and a district judge may issue a certificate of appealability. The language of section 2253 is ambiguous; it states that a certificate of appealability may be issued by "a circuit justice or judge." Since the enactment of the Anti–Terrorism and Effective Death Penalty Act, three circuits have held that both district and circuit judges, as well as the circuit justice, may issue a certificate of appealability. *Else v. Johnson*, 104 F.3d 82 (5th Cir. 1997); *Lyons v. Ohio Adult Parole Authority*, 105 F.3d 1063 (6th Cir. 1997); and *Hunter v. United States*, 101 F.3d 1565 (11th Cir. 1996). The approach taken by the rule is consistent with those decisions.

Subdivision (b), paragraph (3). The Anti-Terrorism and Effective Death Penalty Act of 1996, Pub.L. No. 104–132, amended 28 U.S.C. § 2253 to make it applicable to § 2255 proceedings. Accordingly, paragraph (3) is amended to provide that when the United States or its representative appeals, a certificate of appealability is not required.

Rule 23. Custody or Release of a Prisoner in a Habeas Corpus Proceeding

(a) Transfer of Custody Pending Review. Pending review of a decision in a habeas corpus proceeding commenced before a court, justice, or judge of the United States for the release of a prisoner, the person having custody of the prisoner must not transfer custody to another unless a transfer is directed in accordance with this rule. When, upon application, a custodian shows the need for a transfer, the court, justice, or judge rendering the decision under review may authorize the transfer and substitute the successor custodian as a party.

(b) Detention or Release Pending Review of Decision Not to Release. While a decision not to release a prisoner is under review, the court or judge rendering the decision, or the court of appeals, or the Supreme Court, or a judge or justice of either court, may order that the prisoner be:

(1) detained in the custody from which release is sought;

(2) detained in other appropriate custody; or

(3) released on personal recognizance, with or without surety.

(c) Release Pending Review of Decision Ordering Release. While a decision ordering the release of a prisoner is under review, the prisoner must—unless the court or judge rendering the decision, or the court of appeals, or the Supreme Court, or a judge or justice of either court orders otherwise—be released on personal recognizance, with or without surety.

(d) Modification of the Initial Order on Custody. An initial order governing the prisoner's custody or release, including any recognizance or surety, continues in effect pending review unless for special reasons shown to the court of appeals or the Supreme Court, or to a judge or justice of either court, the order is modified or an independent order regarding custody, release, or surety is issued.

(As amended Mar. 10, 1986, eff. July 1, 1986; Apr. 24, 1998, eff. Dec. 1, 1998.)

ADVISORY COMMITTEE NOTES

1967 Adoption

The rule is the same as Supreme Court Rule 49 as amended on June 12, 1967, effective October 2, 1967.

1986 Amendment

The amendments to Rules 23(b) and (c) are technical. No substantive change is intended.

1998 Amendments

The language and organization of the rule are amended to make the rule more easily understood. In addition to changes made to improve the understanding, the Advisory Committee has changed language to make style and terminology consistent throughout the appellate rules. These changes are intended to by stylistic only.

Subdivision (d). The current rule states that the initial order governing custody or release "shall govern review" in the court of appeals. The amended language says that the initial order generally "continues in effect" pending review.

When Rule 23 was adopted it used the same language as Supreme Court Rule 49, which then governed custody of prisoners in habeas corpus proceedings. The "shall govern review" language was drawn from the Supreme Court Rule. The Supreme Court has since amended its rule, now Rule 36, to say that the initial order "shall continue in effect" unless for reasons shown it is modified or a new order is entered. Rule 23 is amended to similarly state that the initial order "continues in effect." The new language is clearer. It removes the possible implication that the initial order created law of the case, a strange notion to attach to an order regarding custody or release.

Rule 24. Proceeding in Forma Pauperis

(a) Leave to Proceed in Forma Pauperis.

(1) Motion in the District Court. Except as stated in Rule 24(a)(3), a party to a district-court action who desires to appeal in forma pauperis must file a motion in the district court. The party must attach an affidavit that:

(A) shows in the detail prescribed by Form 4 of the Appendix of Forms the party's inability to pay or to give security for fees and costs;

(B) claims an entitlement to redress; and

(C) states the issues that the party intends to present on appeal.

(2) Action on the Motion. If the district court grants the motion, the party may proceed on appeal without prepaying or giving security for fees and costs, unless a statute provides otherwise. If the district court denies the motion, it must state its reasons in writing.

(3) Prior Approval. A party who was permitted to proceed in forma pauperis in the district-court action, or who was determined to be financially unable to obtain an adequate defense in a criminal case, may proceed on appeal in forma pauperis without further authorization, unless:

(A) the district court—before or after the notice of appeal is filed—certifies that the appeal is not taken in good faith or finds that the party is not otherwise entitled to proceed in forma pauperis and states in writing its reasons for the certification or finding; or

(B) a statute provides otherwise.

(4) Notice of District Court's Denial. The district clerk must immediately notify the parties and the court of appeals when the district court does any of the following:

(A) denies a motion to proceed on appeal in forma pauperis;

(B) certifies that the appeal is not taken in good faith; or

(C) finds that the party is not otherwise entitled to proceed in forma pauperis.

(5) **Motion in the Court of Appeals.** A party may file a motion to proceed on appeal in forma pauperis in the court of appeals within 30 days after service of the notice prescribed in Rule 24(a)(4). The motion must include a copy of the affidavit filed in the district court and the district court's statement of reasons for its action. If no affidavit was filed in the district court, the party must include the affidavit prescribed by Rule 24(a)(1).

(b) Leave to Proceed in Forma Pauperis on Appeal or Review of an Administrative-Agency Proceeding. When an appeal or review of a proceeding before an administrative agency, board, commission, or officer (including for the purpose of this rule the United States Tax Court) proceeds directly in a court of appeals, a party may file in the court of appeals a motion for leave to proceed on appeal in forma pauperis with an affidavit prescribed by Rule 24(a)(1).

(c) Leave to Use Original Record. A party allowed to proceed on appeal in forma pauperis may request that the appeal be heard on the original record without reproducing any part.

(As amended Apr. 30, 1979, eff. Aug. 1, 1979; Mar. 10, 1986, eff. July 1, 1986; Apr. 24, 1998, eff. Dec. 1, 1998; Apr. 29, 2002, eff. Dec. 1, 2002.)

ADVISORY COMMITTEE NOTES

1967 Adoption

Subdivision (a). Authority to allow prosecution of an appeal in forma pauperis is vested in "[a]ny court of the United States" by 28 U.S.C. § 1915(a). The second paragraph of § 1915(a) seems to contemplate initial application to the district court for permission to proceed in forma pauperis, and although the circuit rules are generally silent on the question, the case law requires initial application to the district court. *Hayes v. United States*, 258 F.2d 400 (5th Cir., 1958), cert. den. 358 U.S. 856, 79 S.Ct. 87, 3 L.Ed.2d 89 (1958); *Elkins v. United States*, 250 F.2d 145 (9th Cir., 1957) see 364 U.S. 206, 80 S.Ct. 1437, 4 L.Ed.2d 1669 (1960); *United States v. Farley*, 238 F.2d 575 (2d Cir., 1956) see 354 U.S. 521, 77 S.Ct. 1371, 1 L.Ed.2d 1529 (1957). D.C.Cir. Rule 41(a) requires initial application to the district court. The content of the affidavit follows the language of the statute; the requirement of a statement of the issues comprehends the statutory requirement of a statement of "the nature of the . . . appeal. . . ." The second sentence is in accord with the decision in *McGann v. United States*, 362 U.S. 309, 80 S.Ct. 725, 4 L.Ed.2d 734 (1960). The requirement contained in the third sentence has no counterpart in present circuit rules, but it has been imposed by decision in at least two circuits. *Ragan v. Cox*, 305 F.2d 58 (10th Cir., 1962); *United States ex rel. Breedlove v. Dowd*, 269 F.2d 693 (7th Cir., 1959).

The second paragraph permits one whose indigency has been previously determined by the district court to proceed on appeal in forma pauperis without the necessity of a redetermination of indigency, while reserving to the district court its statutory authority to certify that the appeal is not taken in good faith, 28 U.S.C. § 1915(a), and permitting an inquiry into whether the circumstances of the party who was originally entitled to proceed in forma pauperis have changed during the course of the litigation. Cf. Sixth Circuit Rule 26 [rule 26, U.S.Ct. of App. 6th Cir.].

The final paragraph establishes a subsequent motion in the court of appeals, rather than an appeal from the order of denial or from the certification of lack of good faith, as the proper procedure for calling in question the correctness of the action of the district court. The simple and expeditious motion procedure seems clearly preferable to an appeal. This paragraph applies only to applications for leave to appeal in forma pauperis. The order of a district court refusing leave to initiate an action in the district court in forma pauperis is reviewable on appeal. See *Roberts v. United States District Court*, 339 U.S. 844, 70 S.Ct. 954, 94 L.Ed. 1326 (1950).

Subdivision (b). Authority to allow prosecution in forma pauperis is vested only in a "court of the United States" (see Note to subdivision (a), above). Thus in proceedings brought directly in a court of appeals to review decisions of agencies or of the Tax Court, authority to proceed in forma pauperis should be sought in the court of appeals. If initial review of agency action is had in a district court, an application to appeal to a court of appeals in forma pauperis from the judgment of the district court is governed by the provisions of subdivision (a).

1979 Amendment

The proposed amendment reflects the change in the title of the Tax Court to "United States Tax Court." See 26 U.S.C. § 7441.

1986 Amendment

The amendments to Rule 24(a) are technical. No substantive change is intended.

1998 Amendments

The language and organization of the rule are amended to make the rule more easily understood. In addition to changes made to improve the understanding, the Advisory Committee has changed language to make style and terminology consistent throughout the appellate rules. These changes are intended to by stylistic only. The Advisory Committee deletes the language in subdivision (c) authorizing a party proceeding in forma pauperis to file papers in typewritten form because the authorization is unnecessary. The rules permit all parties to file typewritten documents.

2002 Amendments

Subdivision (a)(2). Section 804 of the Prison Litigation Reform Act of 1995 ("PLRA") amended 28 U.S.C. § 1915 to require that prisoners who bring civil actions or appeals from civil actions must "pay the full amount of a filing fee." 28 U.S.C. § 1915(b)(1). Prisoners who are unable to pay the full amount of the filing fee at the time that their actions or appeals are filed are generally required to pay part of the fee and then to pay the remainder of the fee in installments. 28 U.S.C. § 1915(b). By contrast, Rule 24(a)(2) has provided that, after the district court grants a litigant's motion to proceed on appeal in forma pauperis, the litigant may proceed "without prepaying or giving security for fees and costs." Thus, the PLRA and Rule 24(a)(2) appear to be in conflict.

Rule 24(a)(2) has been amended to resolve this conflict. Recognizing that future legislation regarding prisoner litigation is likely, the Committee has not attempted to incorporate into Rule 24 all of the requirements of the current version of 28 U.S.C. § 1915. Rather, the Committee has amended Rule 24(a)(2) to clarify that the rule is not meant to conflict with anything required by the PLRA or any other statute.

Subdivision (a)(3). Rule 24(a)(3) has also been amended to eliminate an apparent conflict with the PLRA. Rule 24(a)(3) has provided that a party who was permitted to proceed in forma pauperis in the district court may continue to proceed in forma pauperis in the court of appeals without further authorization, subject to certain conditions. The PLRA, by contrast, provides that a prisoner who was permitted to proceed in forma pauperis in the district court and who wishes to continue to proceed in forma pauperis on appeal may not do so "automatically," but must seek permission. *See, e.g., Morgan v. Haro*, 112 F.3d 788, 789 (5th Cir. 1997) ("A prisoner who seeks to proceed IFP on appeal must obtain leave to so proceed despite proceeding IFP in the district court.").

Rule 24(a)(3) has been amended to resolve this conflict. Again, recognizing that future legislation regarding prisoner litigation is likely, the Committee has not attempted to incorporate into Rule 24 all of the requirements of the current version of 28 U.S.C. § 1915. Rather, the Committee has amended Rule 24(a)(3) to clarify that the rule is not meant to conflict with anything required by the PLRA or any other statute.

Changes Made After Publication and Comments No changes were made to the text of the proposed amendment or to the Committee Note, except that "a statute provides otherwise" was substituted in place of "the law requires otherwise" in the text of the rule and conforming changes (as well as a couple of minor stylistic changes) were made to the Committee Note.

TITLE VII. GENERAL PROVISIONS

Rule 25. Filing and Service

(a) Filing.

(1) Filing with the Clerk. A paper required or permitted to be filed in a court of appeals must be filed with the clerk.

(2) Filing: Method and Timeliness.

(A) In general. Filing may be accomplished by mail addressed to the clerk, but filing is not timely unless the clerk receives the papers within the time fixed for filing.

(B) A brief or appendix. A brief or appendix is timely filed, however, if on or before the last day for filing, it is:

(i) mailed to the clerk by First–Class Mail, or other class of mail that is at least as expeditious, postage prepaid; or

(ii) dispatched to a third-party commercial carrier for delivery to the clerk within 3 calendar days.

(C) Inmate filing. A paper filed by an inmate confined in an institution is timely if deposited in the institution's internal mailing system on or before the last day for filing. If an institution has a system designed for legal mail, the inmate must use that system to receive the benefit of this rule. Timely filing may be shown by a declaration in compliance with 28 U.S.C. § 1746 or by a notarized statement, either of which must set forth the date of deposit and state that first-class postage has been prepaid.

(D) Electronic filing. A court of appeals may by local rule permit or require papers to be filed, signed, or verified by electronic means that are consistent with technical standards, if any, that the Judicial Conference of the United States establishes. A local rule may require filing by electronic means only if reasonable exceptions are allowed. A paper filed by electronic means in compliance with a local rule constitutes a written paper for the purpose of applying these rules.

(3) Filing a Motion with a Judge. If a motion requests relief that may be granted by a single judge, the judge may permit the motion to be filed with the judge; the judge must note the filing date on the motion and give it to the clerk.

(4) Clerk's Refusal of Documents. The clerk must not refuse to accept for filing any paper presented for that purpose solely because it is not presented in proper form as required by these rules or by any local rule or practice.

(b) Service of All Papers Required. Unless a rule requires service by the clerk, a party must, at or before the time of filing a paper, serve a copy on the other parties to the appeal or review. Service on a party represented by counsel must be made on the party's counsel.

(c) Manner of Service.

(1) Service may be any of the following:

(A) personal, including delivery to a responsible person at the office of counsel;

(B) by mail;

(C) by third-party commercial carrier for delivery within 3 calendar days; or

(D) by electronic means, if the party being served consents in writing.

(2) If authorized by local rule, a party may use the court's transmission equipment to make electronic service under Rule 25(c)(1)(D).

(3) When reasonable considering such factors as the immediacy of the relief sought, distance, and cost, service on a party must be by a manner at least as expeditious as the manner used to file the paper with the court.

(4) Service by mail or by commercial carrier is complete on mailing or delivery to the carrier. Service by electronic means is complete on transmission, unless the party making service is notified that the paper was not received by the party served.

(d) Proof of Service.

(1) A paper presented for filing must contain either of the following:

(A) an acknowledgment of service by the person served; or

(B) proof of service consisting of a statement by the person who made service certifying:

(i) the date and manner of service;

(ii) the names of the persons served; and

(iii) their mail or electronic addresses, facsimile numbers, or the addresses of the places of delivery, as appropriate for the manner of service.

(2) When a brief or appendix is filed by mailing or dispatch in accordance with Rule 25(a)(2)(B), the proof of service must also state the date and manner by which the document was mailed or dispatched to the clerk.

(3) Proof of service may appear on or be affixed to the papers filed.

(e) Number of Copies. When these rules require the filing or furnishing of a number of copies, a court may require a different number by local rule or by order in a particular case.

(As amended Mar. 10, 1986, eff. July 1, 1986; Apr. 30, 1991, eff. Dec. 1, 1991; Apr. 22, 1993, eff. Dec. 1, 1993; Apr. 29, 1994, eff. Dec. 1, 1994; Apr. 23, 1996, eff. Dec. 1, 1996; Apr. 24, 1998, eff. Dec. 1, 1998; Apr. 29, 2002, eff. Dec. 1, 2002: Apr. 12, 2006, eff. Dec. 1, 2006.)

ADVISORY COMMITTEE NOTES

1967 Adoption

The rule that filing is not timely unless the papers filed are received within the time allowed is the familiar one. *Ward v. Atlantic Coast Line R.R. Co.*, 265 F.2d 75 (5th Cir., 1959), rev'd on other grounds 362 U.S. 396, 80 S.Ct. 789, 4 L.Ed.2d 820 (1960); *Kahler-Ellis Co. v. Ohio Turnpike Commission*, 225 F.2d 922 (6th Cir., 1955). An exception is made in the case of briefs and appendices in order to afford the parties the maximum time for their preparation. By the terms of the exception, air mail delivery must be used whenever it is the most expeditious manner of delivery.

A majority of the circuits now require service of all papers filed with the clerk. The usual provision in present rules is for service on "adverse" parties. In view of the extreme simplicity of service by mail, there seems to be no reason why a party who files a paper should not be required to serve all parties to the proceeding in the court of appeals, whether or not they may be deemed adverse. The common requirement of proof of service is retained, but the rule permits it to be made by simple certification, which may be endorsed on the copy which is filed.

1986 Amendment

The amendments to Rules 25(a) and (b) are technical. No substantive change is intended.

1991 Amendment

Subdivision (a). The amendment permits, but does not require, courts of appeals to adopt local rules that allow filing of papers by electronic means. However, courts of appeals cannot adopt such local rules until the Judicial Conference of the United States authorizes filing by facsimile or other electronic means.

1993 Amendment

The amendment accompanies new subdivision (c) of Rule 4 and extends the holding in *Houston v. Lack*, 487 U.S. 266 (1988), to all papers filed in the courts of appeals by persons confined in institutions.

1994 Amendment

Subdivision (a). Several circuits have local rules that authorize the office of the clerk to refuse to accept for filing papers that are not in the form required by these rules or by local rules. This is not a suitable role for the office of the clerk and the practice exposes litigants to the hazards of time bars; for these reasons, such rules are proscribed by this rule. This provision is similar to Fed.R.Civ.P. 5(e) and Fed.R.Bankr.P. 5005.

The Committee wishes to make it clear that the provision prohibiting a clerk from refusing a document does not mean that a clerk's office may no longer screen documents to determine whether they comply with the rules. A court may delegate to the clerk authority to inform a party about any noncompliance with the rules and, if the party is willing to correct the document, to determine a date by which the corrected document must be resubmitted. If a party refuses to take the steps recommended by the clerk or if in the clerk's judgment the party fails to correct the noncompliance, the clerk must refer the matter to the court for a ruling.

Subdivision (d). Two changes have been made in this subdivision. Subdivision (d) provides that a paper presented for filing must contain proof of service.

The last sentence of subdivision (d) has been deleted as unnecessary. That sentence stated that a clerk could permit papers to be filed without the acknowledgment or proof of service but must require that it be filed promptly thereafter. In light of the change made in subdivision (a) which states that a clerk may not refuse to accept for filing a document because it is not in the proper form, there is no further need for a provision stating that a clerk may accept a paper lacking a proof of service. The clerk must accept such a paper. That portion of the deleted sentence stating that the clerk must require that proof of service be filed promptly after the filing of the document if the proof is not filed concurrently with the document is also unnecessary.

The second amendment requires that the certificate of service must state the addresses to which the papers were mailed or at which they were delivered. The Federal Circuit has a similar local rule, Fed.Cir.R. 25.

Subdivision (e). Subdivision (e) is a new subdivision. It makes it clear that whenever these rules require a party to file or furnish a number of copies a court may require a different number of copies either by rule or by order in an individual case. The number of copies of any document that a court of appeals needs varies depending upon the way in which the court conducts business. The internal operation of the courts of appeals necessarily varies from circuit to circuit because of differences in the number of judges, the geographic area included within the circuit, and other such factors. Uniformity could be achieved only by setting the number of copies artificially high so that parties in all circuits file enough copies to satisfy the needs of the court requiring the greatest number. Rather than do that, the Committee decided to make it clear that local rules may require a greater or lesser number of copies and that, if the circumstances of a particular case indicate the need for a different number of copies in that case, the court may so order.

A party must consult local rules to determine whether the court requires a different number than that specified in these national rules. The Committee believes it would be helpful if each circuit either: 1) included a chart at the beginning of its local rules showing the number of copies of each document required to be filed with the court along with citation to the controlling rule; or 2) made available such a chart to each party upon commencement of an appeal; or both. If a party fails to file the required number of copies, the failure does not create a jurisdictional defect. Rule 3(a) states: "Failure of an appellant to take any step other than the timely filing of a notice of appeal does not affect the validity of the appeal, but is ground only for such action as the court of appeals deems appropriate...."

1996 Amendments

Subdivision (a). The amendment deletes the language requiring a party to use "the most expeditious form of delivery by mail, except special delivery" in order to file a brief using the mailbox rule. That language was adopted before the Postal Service offered Express Mail and other expedited delivery services. The amendment makes it clear that it is sufficient to use First–Class Mail. Other equally or more expeditious classes of mail service, such as Express Mail, also may be used. In addition, the amendment permits the use of commercial carriers. The use of private, overnight courier services has become commonplace in law practice. Expedited services offered by commercial carriers often provide faster delivery than First–Class Mail; therefore, there should be no objection to the use of commercial carriers as long as they are reliable. In order to make use of the mailbox rule when using a commercial carrier, the amendment requires that the filer employ a carrier who undertakes to deliver the document in no more than three calendar days. The three-calendar-day period coordinates with the three-day extension provided by Rule 26(c).

Subdivision (c). The amendment permits service by commercial carrier if the carrier is to deliver the paper to the party being served within three days of the carrier's receipt of the paper. The amendment also expresses a desire that when reasonable, service on a party be accomplished by a manner as expeditious as the manner used to file the paper with the court. When a brief or motion is filed with the court by hand delivering the paper to the clerk's office, or by overnight courier, the copies should be served on the other parties by an equally expeditious manner—meaning either by personal service, if distance permits, or by overnight courier, if mail delivery to the party is not ordinarily accomplished overnight. The reasonableness standard is included so that if a paper is hand delivered to the clerk's office for filing but the other parties must be served in a different city, state, or region, personal service on them ordinarily will not be expected. If use of an equally expeditious manner of service is not reasonable, use of the next most expeditious manner may be. For example, if the paper is filed by hand delivery to the clerk's office but the other parties reside in distant cities, service on them need not be personal but in most instances should be by overnight courier. Even that may not be required, however, if the number of parties that must be served would make the use of overnight service too costly. A factor that bears upon the reasonableness of serving parties expeditiously is the immediacy of the relief requested.

Subdivision (d). The amendment adds a requirement that when a brief or appendix is filed by mail or commercial carrier, the certificate of service state the date and manner by which the document was mailed or dispatched to the clerk. Including that information in the certificate of service avoids the necessity for a separate certificate concerning the date and manner of filing.

1998 Amendments

The language and organization of the rule are amended to make the rule more easily understood. In addition to changes made to improve the understanding, the Advisory Committee has changed language to make style and terminology consistent throughout the appellate rules. These changes are intended to by stylistic only; a substantive amendment is made, however, in subdivision (a).

Subdivision (a). The substantive amendment in this subdivision is in subparagraph (a)(2)(C) and is a companion to an amendment in Rule 4(c). Currently Rule 25(a)(2(C) provides that if an inmate confined in an institution files a document by depositing it in the institution's internal mail system, the document is timely filed if deposited on or before the last day for filing. Some institutions have special internal mail systems for handling legal mail; such systems often record the date of deposit of mail by an inmate, the date of delivery of mail to an inmate, etc. The Advisory Committee amends the rule to require an inmate to use the system designed for legal mail, if there is one, in order to receive the benefit of this subparagraph

2002 Amendments

Rule 25(a)(2)(D) presently authorizes the courts of appeals to permit papers to be *filed* by electronic means. Rule 25 has been amended in several respects to permit papers also to be *served* electronically. In addition, Rule 25(c) has been reorganized and subdivided to make it easier to understand.

Subdivision (c)(1)(D). New subdivision (c)(1)(D) has been added to permit service to be made electronically, such as by e-mail or fax. No party may be served electronically, either by the clerk or by another party, unless the party has consented in writing to such service.

A court of appeals may not, by local rule, forbid the use of electronic service on a party that has consented to its use. At the same time, courts have considerable discretion to use local rules to regulate electronic service. Difficult and presently unforeseeable questions are likely to arise as electronic service becomes more common. Courts have the flexibility to use their local rules to address those questions. For example, courts may use local rules to set forth specific procedures that a party must follow before the party will be deemed to have given written consent to electronic service.

Parties also have the flexibility to define the terms of their consent; a party's consent to electronic service does not have to be "all-or-nothing." For example, a party may consent to service by facsimile transmission, but not by electronic mail; or a party may consent to electronic service only if "courtesy" copies of all transmissions are mailed within 24 hours; or a party may consent to electronic service of only documents that were created with Corel WordPerfect.

Subdivision (c)(2). The courts of appeals are authorized under Rule 25(a)(2)(D) to permit papers to be filed electronically. Technological advances may someday make it possible for a court to forward an electronically filed paper to all parties automatically or semi-automatically. When such court-facilitated service becomes possible, courts may decide to permit parties to use the courts' transmission facilities to serve electronically filed papers on other parties who have consented to such service. Court personnel would use the court's computer system to forward the papers, but the papers would be considered served by the filing parties, just as papers that are carried from one address to another by the United States Postal Service are considered served by the sending parties. New subdivision (c)(2) has been added so that the courts of appeals may use local rules to authorize such use of their transmission facilities, as well as to address the many questions that court-facilitated electronic service is likely to raise.

Subdivision (c)(4). The second sentence of new subdivision (c)(4) has been added to provide that electronic service is complete upon transmission. Transmission occurs when the sender performs the last act that he or she must perform to transmit a paper electronically; typically, it occurs when the sender hits the "send" or "transmit" button on an electronic mail program. There is one exception to the rule that electronic service is complete upon transmission: If the sender is notified—by the sender's e-mail program or otherwise—that the paper was not received, service is not complete, and the sender must take additional steps to effect service. A paper has been "received" by the party on which it has been served as long as the party has the ability to retrieve it. A party cannot defeat service by choosing not to access electronic mail on its server.

Changes Made After Publication and Comments No changes were made to the text of the proposed amendment. A paragraph was added to the Committee Note to clarify that consent to electronic service is not an "all-or-nothing" matter.

Subdivision (d)(1)(B)(iii). Subdivision (d)(1)(B)(iii) has been amended to require that, when a paper is served electronically, the proof of service of that paper must include the electronic address or facsimile number to which the paper was transmitted.

Changes Made After Publication and Comments The text of the proposed amendment was changed to refer to "electronic" addresses (instead of to "e-mail" addresses), to include "facsimile numbers," and to add the concluding phrase "as appropriate for the manner of service." Conforming changes were made to the Committee Note.

2006 Amendment

Subdivision (a)(2)(D). Amended Rule 25(a)(2)(D) acknowledges that many courts have required electronic filing by means of a standing order, procedures manual, or local rule. These local practices reflect the advantages that courts and most litigants realize from electronic filing. Courts that mandate electronic filing recognize the need to make exceptions when requiring electronic filing imposes a hardship on a party. Under Rule 25(a)(2)(D), a local rule that requires electronic filing must include reasonable exceptions, but Rule 25(a)(2)(D) does not define the scope of those exceptions. Experience with the local rules that have been adopted and that will emerge will aid in drafting new local rules and will facilitate gradual convergence on uniform exceptions, whether in local rules or in an amended Rule 25(a)(2)(D).

A local rule may require that both electronic and "hard" copies of a paper be filed. Nothing in the last sentence of Rule 25(a)(2)(D) is meant to imply otherwise.

Rule 26. Computing and Extending Time

(a) Computing Time. The following rules apply in computing any period of time specified in these rules or in any local rule, court order, or applicable statute:

(1) Exclude the day of the act, event, or default that begins the period.

(2) Exclude intermediate Saturdays, Sundays, and legal holidays when the period is less than 11 days, unless stated in calendar days.

(3) Include the last day of the period unless it is a Saturday, Sunday, legal holiday, or—if the act to be done is filing a paper in court—a day on which the weather or other conditions make the clerk's office inaccessible.

(4) As used in this rule, "legal holiday" means New Year's Day, Martin Luther King, Jr.'s Birthday, Washington's Birthday, Memorial Day, Independence Day, Labor Day, Columbus Day, Veterans' Day, Thanksgiving Day, Christmas Day, and any other day declared a holiday by the President, Congress, or the state in which is located either the district court that rendered the challenged judgment or order, or the circuit clerk's principal office.

(b) Extending Time. For good cause, the court may extend the time prescribed by these rules or by its order to perform any act, or may permit an act to be done after that time expires. But the court may not extend the time to file:

(1) a notice of appeal (except as authorized in Rule 4) or a petition for permission to appeal; or

(2) a notice of appeal from or a petition to enjoin, set aside, suspend, modify, enforce, or otherwise review an order of an administrative agency, board, commission, or officer of the United States, unless specifically authorized by law.

(c) Additional Time after Service. When a party is required or permitted to act within a prescribed period after a paper is served on that party, 3 calendar days are added to the prescribed period unless the paper is delivered on the date of service stated in the proof of service. For purposes of this Rule 26(c), a paper that is served electronically is not treated as delivered on the date of service stated in the proof of service.

(As amended Mar. 1, 1971, eff. July 1, 1971; Mar. 10, 1986, eff. July 1, 1986; Apr. 25, 1989, eff. Dec. 1, 1989; Apr. 30, 1991, eff. Dec. 1, 1991; Apr. 23, 1996, eff. Dec. 1, 1996; Apr. 24, 1998, eff. Dec. 1, 1998; Apr. 29, 2002, eff. Dec. 1, 2002; Apr. 25, 2005, eff. Dec. 1, 2005.)

ADVISORY COMMITTEE NOTES

1967 Adoption

The provisions of this rule are based upon FRCP 6(a), (b) and (e) [rule 6(a), (b) and (e), Federal Rules of Civil Procedure]. See also Supreme Court Rule 34 and FRCrP 45 [rule 45, Federal Rules of Criminal Procedure]. Unlike FRCP 6(b), this rule, read with Rule 27, requires that every request for enlargement of time be made by motion, with proof of service on all parties. This is the simplest, most convenient way of keeping all parties advised of developments. By the terms of Rule 27(b) a motion for enlargement of time under Rule 26(b) may be entertained and acted upon immediately, subject to the right of any party to seek reconsideration. Thus the requirement of motion and notice will not delay the granting of relief of a kind which a court is inclined to grant as of course. Specifically, if a court is of the view that an extension of time sought before expiration of the period originally prescribed or as extended by a previous order ought to be granted in effect ex parte, as FRCP 6(b) permits, it may grant motions seeking such relief without delay.

1971 Amendments

The amendment adds Columbus Day to the list of legal holidays to conform the subdivision to the Act of June 28, 1968, 82 Stat. 250, which constituted Columbus Day a legal holiday effective after January 1, 1971.

The Act, which amended Title 5, U.S.C. § 6103(a), changes the day on which certain holidays are to be observed. Washington's Birthday, Memorial Day and Veterans Day are to be observed on the third Monday in February, the last Monday in May and the fourth Monday in October, respectively, rather than, as heretofore, on February 22, May 30, and November 11, respectively. Columbus Day is to be observed on the second Monday in October. New Year's Day, Independence Day, Thanksgiving Day and Christmas continue to be observed on the traditional days.

1986 Amendments

The Birthday of Martin Luther King, Jr. is added to the list of national holidays in Rule 26(a). The amendment to Rule 26(c) is technical. No substantive change is intended.

1989 Amendments

The proposed amendment brings Rule 26(a) into conformity with the provisions of Rule 6(a) of the Rules of Civil Procedure, Rule 45(a) of the Rules of Criminal Procedure, and Rule 9006(a) of the Rules of Bankruptcy Procedure which allow additional time for filing whenever a clerk's office is inaccessible on the last day for filing due to weather or other conditions.

1996 Amendments

The amendment is a companion to the proposed amendments to Rule 25 that permit service on a party by commercial carrier. The amendments to subdivision (c) of this rule make the three-day extension applicable not only when service is accomplished by mail, but whenever delivery to the party being served occurs later than the date of service stated in the proof of service. When service is by mail or commercial carrier, the proof of service recites the date of mailing or delivery to the commercial carrier. If the party being served receives the paper on a later date, the three-day extension applies. If the party being served receives the paper on the same date as the date of service recited in the proof of service, the three-day extension is not available.

The amendment also states that the three-day extension is three calendar days. Rule 26(a) states that when a period prescribed or allowed by the rules is less than seven days, intermediate Saturdays, Sundays, and legal holidays do not count. Whether the three-day extension in Rule 26(c) is such a period, meaning that three-days could actually be five or even six days, is unclear. The D.C. Circuit recently held that the parallel three-day extension provided in the Civil Rules is not such a period and that weekends and legal holidays do count. *CNPq v. Inter-Trade, 50 F.3d 56 (D.C.Cir.1995).* The Committee believes that is the right result and that the issue should be resolved. Providing that the extension is three calendar days means that if a period would otherwise end on Thursday but the three-day extension applies, the paper must be filed on Monday. Friday, Saturday, and Sunday are the extension days. Because the last day of the period as extended is Sunday, the paper must be filed the next day, Monday.

1998 Amendments

The language and organization of the rule are amended to make the rule more easily understood. In addition to changes made to improve the understanding, the Advisory Committee has changed language to make style and terminology consistent throughout the appellate rules. These changes are intended to by stylistic only; two substantive changes are made, however, in subdivision (a).

Subdivision (a). First, the amendments make the computation method prescribed in this rule applicable to any time period imposed by a local rule. This means that if a local rule establishing a time limit is permitted, the national rule will govern the computation of that period.

Second, paragraph (a)(2) includes language clarifying that whenever the rules establish a time period in "calendar days," weekends and legal holidays are counted.

2002 Amendments

Subdivision (a)(2). The Federal Rules of Civil Procedure and the Federal Rules of Criminal Procedure compute time differently than the Federal Rules of Appellate Procedure. Fed. R. Civ. P. 6(a) and Fed. R. Crim. P. 45(a) provide that, in computing any period of time, "[w]hen the period of time prescribed or allowed is less than 11 days, intermediate Saturdays, Sundays, and legal holidays shall be excluded in the computation." By contrast, Rule 26(a)(2) provides that, in computing any period of time, a litigant should "[e]xclude intermediate Saturdays, Sundays, and legal holidays when the period is less than 7 days, unless stated in calendar days." Thus, deadlines of 7, 8, 9, and 10 days are calculated differently under the rules of civil and criminal procedure than they are under the rules of appellate procedure. This creates a trap for unwary litigants. No good reason for this discrepancy is apparent, and thus Rule 26(a)(2) has been amended so that, under all three sets of rules, intermediate Saturdays, Sundays, and legal holidays will be excluded when computing deadlines under 11 days but will be counted when computing deadlines of 11 days and over.

Changes Made After Publication and Comments No changes were made to the text of the proposed amendment or to the Committee Note.

Subdivision (c). Rule 26(c) has been amended to provide that when a paper is served on a party by electronic means, and that party is required or permitted to respond to that paper within a prescribed period, 3 calendar days are added to the prescribed period. Electronic service is usually instantaneous, but sometimes it is not, because of technical problems. Also, if a paper is electronically transmitted to a party on a Friday evening, the party may not realize that he or she has been served until two or three days later. Finally, extending the "3–day rule" to electronic service will encourage parties to consent to such service under Rule 25(c).

Changes Made After Publication and Comments No changes were made to the text of the proposed amendment or to the Committee Note.

2005 Amendments

Subdivision (a)(4). Rule 26(a)(4) has been amended to refer to the third Monday in February as "Washington's Birthday." A federal statute officially designates the holiday as "Washington's Birthday," reflecting the desire of Congress specially to honor the first president of the United States. *See* 5 U.S.C. § 6103(a). During the 1998 restyling of the Federal Rules of Appellate Procedure, references to "Washington's Birthday" were mistakenly changed to "Presidents' Day." The amendment corrects that error.

Rule 26.1. Corporate Disclosure Statement

(a) Who Must File. Any nongovernmental corporate party to a proceeding in a court of appeals must file a statement that identifies any parent corporation and any publicly held corporation that owns 10% or more of its stock or states that there is no such corporation.

(b) Time for Filing; Supplemental Filing. A party must file the Rule 26.1(a) statement with the principal brief or upon filing a motion, response, petition, or answer in the court of appeals, whichever occurs first, unless a local rule requires earlier filing. Even if the statement has already been filed, the party's principal brief must include the statement before the table of contents. A party must supplement its statement whenever the information that must be disclosed under Rule 26.1(a) changes.

(c) Number of Copies. If the Rule 26.1(a) statement is filed before the principal brief, or if a supplemental statement is filed, the party must file an original and 3 copies unless the court requires a different number by local rule or by order in a particular case.

(Added Apr. 25, 1989, eff. Dec. 1, 1989, and amended Apr. 30, 1991, eff. Dec. 1, 1991; Apr. 29, 1994, eff. Dec. 1, 1994; Apr. 24, 1998, eff. Dec. 1, 1998; Apr. 29, 2002, eff. Dec. 1, 2002.)

ADVISORY COMMITTEE NOTES

1989 Addition

The purpose of this rule is to assist judges in making a determination of whether they have any interests in any of a party's related corporate entities that would disqualify the judges from hearing the appeal. The committee believes that this rule represents minimum disclosure requirements. If a Court of Appeals wishes to require additional information, a court is free to do so by local rule. However, the committee requests the courts to consider the desirability of uniformity and the burden that varying circuit rules creates on attorneys who practice in many circuits.

1994 Amendment

The amendment requires a party to file three copies of the disclosure statement whenever the statement is filed before the party's principle brief. Because the statement is included in each copy of the party's brief, there is no need to require the filing of additional copies at that time. A court of appeals may require the filing of a different number of copies by local rule or by order in a particular case.

1998 Amendments

The language and organization of the rule are amended to make the rule more easily understood. In addition to changes made to improve the understanding, the Advisory Committee has changed language to make style and terminology consistent throughout the appellate rules. These changes are intended to by stylistic only; a substantive change is made, however, in subdivision (a).

Subdivision (a). The amendment deletes the requirement that a corporate party identify subsidiaries and affiliates that have issued shares to the public. Although several circuit rules require identification of such entities, the Committee believes that such disclosure is unnecessary.

A disclosure statement assists a judge in ascertaining whether or not the judge has an interest that should cause the judge to recuse himself or herself from the case. Given that purpose, disclosure of entities that would not be adversely affected by a decision in the case is unnecessary.

Disclosure of a party's parent corporation is necessary because a judgment against a subsidiary can negatively impact the parent. A judge who owns stock in the parent corporation, therefore, has an interest in litigation involving the subsidiary. The rule requires disclosure of all of a party's parent corporations meaning grandparent and great grandparent corporations as well. For example, if a party is a closely held corporation, the majority shareholder of which is a corporation formed by a publicly traded corporation for the purpose of acquiring and holding the shares of the party, the publicly traded grandparent corporation should be disclosed. Conversely, disclosure of a party's subsidiaries or affiliated corporations is ordinarily unnecessary. For example, if a party is a part owner of a corporation in which a judge owns stock, the possibility is quite remote that the judge might be biased by the fact that the judge and the litigant are co-owners of a corporation.

The amendment, however, adds a requirement that the party lists all its stockholders that are publicly held companies owning 10% or more of the stock of the party. A judgment against a corporate party can adversely affect the value of the company's stock and, therefore, persons owning stock in the party have an interest in the outcome of the litigation. A judge owning stock in a corporate party ordinarily recuses himself or herself. The new requirement takes the analysis one step further and assumes that if a judge owns stock in a publicly held corporation which in turn owns 10% or more of the stock in the party, the judge may have sufficient interest in the litigation to require recusal. The 10% threshold ensures that the corporation in which the judge may own stock is itself sufficiently invested in the party that a judgment adverse to the party could have an adverse impact upon the investing corporation in which the judge may own stock. This requirement is modeled on the Seventh Circuit's disclosure requirement.

Subdivision (b). The language requiring inclusion of the disclosure statement in a party's principal brief is moved to this subdivision because it deals with the time for filing the statement.

2002 Amendments

Subdivision (a). Rule 26.1(a) requires nongovernmental corporate parties to file a "corporate disclosure statement." In that statement, a nongovernmental corporate party is required to identify all of its parent corporations and all publicly held corporations that own 10% or more of its stock. The corporate disclosure statement is intended to assist judges in determining whether they must recuse themselves by reason of "a financial interest in the subject matter in controversy." Code of Judicial Conduct, Canon 3C(1)(c) (1972).

Rule 26.1(a) has been amended to require that nongovernmental corporate parties who have not been required to file a corporate disclosure statement—that is, nongovernmental corporate parties who do not have any parent corporations and at least 10% of whose stock is not owned by any publicly held corporation—inform the court of that fact. At present, when a corporate disclosure statement is not filed, courts do not know whether it has not been filed because there was nothing to report or because of ignorance of Rule 26.1.

Subdivision (b). Rule 26.1(b) has been amended to require parties to file supplemental disclosure statements whenever there is a change in the information that Rule 26.1(a) requires the parties to disclose. For example, if a publicly held corporation acquires 10% or more of a party's stock after the party has filed its disclosure statement, the party should file a supplemental statement identifying that publicly held corporation.

Subdivision (c). Rule 26.1(c) has been amended to provide that a party who is required to file a supplemental disclosure statement must file an original and 3 copies, unless a local rule or an order entered in a particular case provides otherwise.

Changes Made After Publication and Comments The Committee is submitting two versions of proposed Rule 26.1 for the consideration of the Standing Committee.

The first version—"Alternative One"—is the same as the version that was published, except that the rule has been amended to refer to "any information that may be *publicly designated* by the Judicial Conference" instead of to "any information that may be *required* by the Judicial Conference." At its April meeting, the Committee gave unconditional approval to all of "Alternative One," except the Judicial Conference provisions. The Committee conditioned its approval of the Judicial Conference provisions on the Standing Committee's assuring itself that lawyers would have ready access to any standards promulgated by the Judicial Conference and that the Judicial Conference provisions were consistent with the Rules Enabling Act.

The second version—"Alternative Two"—is the same as the version that was published, except that the Judicial Conference provisions have been eliminated. The Civil Rules Committee met several days after the Appellate Rules Committee and joined the Bankruptcy Rules Committee in disapproving the Judicial Conference provisions. Given the decreasing likelihood that the Judicial Conference provisions will be approved by the Standing Committee, I asked Prof. Schiltz to draft, and the Appellate Rules Committee to approve, a version of Rule 26.1 that omitted those provisions. "Alternative Two" was circulated to and approved by the Committee in late April.

I should note that, at its April meeting, the Appellate Rules Committee discussed the financial disclosure provision that was approved by the Bankruptcy Rules Committee. That provision defines the scope of the financial disclosure obligation much differently than the provisions approved by the Appellate, Civil, and Criminal Rules Committees, which are based on existing Rule 26.1. For example, the bankruptcy provision requires disclosure when a party "directly or indirectly" owns 10 percent or more of "any class" of a publicly *or* privately held corporation's "equity interests." Members of the Appellate Rules Committee expressed several concerns about the provision approved by the Bankruptcy Rules Committee, objecting both to its substance and to its ambiguity.

Rule 27. Motions

(a) In General.

(1) Application for Relief. An application for an order or other relief is made by motion unless these rules prescribe another form. A motion must be in writing unless the court permits otherwise.

(2) Contents of a Motion.

(A) Grounds and relief sought. A motion must state with particularity the grounds for the motion, the relief sought, and the legal argument necessary to support it.

(B) Accompanying documents.

(i) Any affidavit or other paper necessary to support a motion must be served and filed with the motion.

(ii) An affidavit must contain only factual information, not legal argument.

(iii) A motion seeking substantive relief must include a copy of the trial court's opinion or agency's decision as a separate exhibit.

(C) Documents barred or not required.

(i) A separate brief supporting or responding to a motion must not be filed.

(ii) A notice of motion is not required.

(iii) A proposed order is not required.

(3) Response.

(A) Time to file. Any party may file a response to a motion; Rule 27(a)(2) governs its contents. The response must be filed within 8 days after service of the motion unless the court shortens or extends the time. A motion authorized by Rules 8, 9, 18, or 41 may be granted before the 8–day period runs only if the court gives reasonable notice to the parties that it intends to act sooner.

(B) Request for affirmative relief. A response may include a motion for affirmative relief. The time to respond to the new motion, and to reply to that response, are governed by Rule 27(a)(3)(A) and (a)(4). The title of the response must alert the court to the request for relief.

(4) Reply to Response. Any reply to a response must be filed within 5 days after service of the response. A reply must not present matters that do not relate to the response.

(b) Disposition of a Motion for a Procedural Order. The court may act on a motion for a procedural order—including a motion under Rule 26(b)—at any time without awaiting a response, and may, by rule or by order in a particular case, authorize its clerk to act on specified types of procedural motions. A party adversely affected by the court's, or the clerk's, action may file a motion to reconsider, vacate, or modify that action. Timely opposition filed after the motion is granted in whole or in part does not constitute a request to reconsider, vacate, or modify the disposition; a motion requesting that relief must be filed.

(c) Power of a Single Judge to Entertain a Motion. A circuit judge may act alone on any motion, but may not dismiss or otherwise determine an appeal or other proceeding. A court of appeals may provide by rule or by order in a particular case that only the court may act on any motion or class of motions. The court may review the action of a single judge.

(d) Form of Papers; Page Limits; and Number of Copies.

(1) Format.

(A) Reproduction. A motion, response, or reply may be reproduced by any process that yields a clear black image on light paper. The paper must be opaque and unglazed. Only one side of the paper may be used.

(B) Cover. A cover is not required, but there must be a caption that includes the case number, the name of the court, the title of the case, and a brief descriptive title indicating the purpose of the motion and identifying the party or parties for whom it is filed. If a cover is used, it must be white.

(C) Binding. The document must be bound in any manner that is secure, does not obscure the text, and permits the document to lie reasonably flat when open.

(D) Paper size, line spacing, and margins. The document must be on 8½ by 11 inch paper. The text must be double-spaced, but quotations more than two lines long may be indented and single-spaced. Headings and footnotes may be single-spaced. Margins must be at least one inch on all four sides. Page numbers may be placed in the margins, but no text may appear there.

(E) Typeface and type styles. The document must comply with the typeface requirements of Rule 32(a)(5) and the type-style requirements of Rule 32(a)(6).

(2) Page Limits. A motion or a response to a motion must not exceed 20 pages, exclusive of the corporate disclosure statement and accompanying documents authorized by Rule 27(a)(2)(B), unless the court permits or directs otherwise. A reply to a response must not exceed 10 pages.

(3) Number of Copies. An original and 3 copies must be filed unless the court requires a different number by local rule or by order in a particular case.

(e) Oral Argument. A motion will be decided without oral argument unless the court orders otherwise.

(As amended Apr. 30, 1979, eff. Aug. 1, 1979; Apr. 25, 1989, eff. Dec. 1, 1989; Apr. 29, 1994, eff. Dec. 1, 1994; Apr. 24, 1998, eff. Dec. 1, 1998; Apr. 29, 2002, eff. Dec. 1, 2002; Apr. 25, 2005, eff. Dec. 1, 2005.)

ADVISORY COMMITTEE NOTES

1967 Adoption

Subdivisions (a) and (b). Many motions seek relief of a sort which is ordinarily unopposed or which is granted as of course. The provision of subdivision (a) which permits any party to file a response in opposition to a motion within 7 days after its service upon him assumes that the motion is one of substance which ought not be acted upon without affording affected parties an opportunity to reply. A motion to dismiss or otherwise determine an appeal is clearly such a motion. Motions authorized by Rules 8, 9, 18 and 41 are likewise motions of substance; but in the nature of the relief sought, to afford an adversary an automatic delay of at least 7 days is undesirable, thus such motions may be acted upon after notice which is reasonable under the circumstances.

The term "motions for procedural orders" is used in subdivision (b) to describe motions which do not substantially affect the rights of the parties or the ultimate disposition of the appeal. To prevent delay in the disposition of such motions, subdivision (b) provides that they may be acted upon immediately without awaiting a response, subject to the right of any party who is adversely affected by the action to seek reconsideration.

Subdivision (c). Within the general consideration of procedure on motions is the problem of the power of a single circuit judge. Certain powers are granted to a single judge of a court of appeals by statute. Thus, under 28 U.S.C. § 2101(f) a single judge may stay execution and enforcement of a judgment to enable a party aggrieved to obtain certiorari; under 28 U.S.C. § 2251 a judge before whom a habeas corpus proceeding involving a person detained by state authority is pending may stay any proceeding against the person; under 28 U.S.C. § 2253 a single judge may issue a certificate of probably cause. In addition, certain of these rules expressly grant power to a single judge. See Rules 8, 9 and 18.

This subdivision empowers a single circuit judge to act upon virtually all requests for intermediate relief which may be made during the course of an appeal or other proceeding. By its terms he may entertain and act upon any motion other than a motion to dismiss or otherwise determine an appeal or other proceeding. But the relief sought must be "relief which under these rules may properly be sought by motion."

Examples of the power conferred on a single judge by this subdivision are: to extend the time for transmitting the record or docketing the appeal (Rules 11 and 12); to permit intervention in agency cases (Rule 15), or substitution in any case (Rule 43); to permit an appeal in forma pauperis (Rule 24); to enlarge any time period fixed by the rules other than that for initiating a proceeding in the court of appeals (Rule 26(b)); to permit the filing of a brief by amicus curiae (Rule 29); to authorize the filing of a deferred appendix (Rule 30(c)), or dispense with the requirement of an appendix in a specific case (Rule 30(f)), or permit carbon copies of briefs or appendices to be used (Rule 32(a)); to permit the filing of additional briefs (Rule 28(c)), or the filing of briefs of extraordinary length (Rule 28(g)); to postpone oral argument (Rule 34(a)), or grant additional time therefor (Rule 34(b)).

Certain rules require that application for the relief or orders which they authorize be made by petition. Since relief under those rules may not properly be sought by motion, a single judge may not entertain requests for such relief. Thus a single judge may not act upon requests for permission to appeal (see Rules 5 and 6); or for mandamus or other extraordinary writs (see Rule 21), other than for stays or injunctions *pendente lite*, authority to grant which is "expressly conferred by these rules" on a single judge under certain circumstances (see Rules 8 and 18); or upon petitions for rehearing (see Rule 40).

A court of appeals may by order or rule abridge the power of a single judge if it is of the view that a motion or a class of motions should be disposed of by a panel. Exercise of any power granted a single judge is discretionary with the judge. The final sentence in this subdivision makes the disposition of any matter by a single judge subject to review by the court.

1979 Amendment

The proposed amendment would give sanction to local rules in a number of circuits permitting the clerk to dispose of specified types of procedural motions.

1989 Amendment

The amendment is technical. No substantive change is intended.

1994 Amendments

Subdivision (d). The amendment makes it clear that a court may require a different number of copies either by rule or by order in an individual case. The number of copies of any document that a court of appeals needs varies depending upon the way in which the court conducts business. The internal operation of the courts of appeals necessarily varies from circuit to circuit because of differences in the number of judges, the geographic area included within the circuit, and other such factors. Uniformity could be achieved only by setting the number of copies artificially high so that parties in all circuits file enough copies to satisfy the needs of the court requiring the greatest number. Rather than do that, the Committee decided to make it clear that local rules may require a greater or lesser number of copies and that, if the circumstances of a particular case indicate the need for a different number of copies in that case, the court may so order.

1998 Amendments

In addition to amending Rule 27 to conform to uniform drafting standards, several substantive amendments are made. The Advisory Committee had been working on substantive amendments to Rule 27 just prior to completion of this larger project.

Subdivision (a). Paragraph (1) retains the language of the existing rule indicating that an application for an order or other relief is made by filing a motion unless another form is required by some other provision in the rules.

Paragraph (1) also states that a motion must be in writing unless the court permits otherwise. The writing requirement has been implicit in the rule; the Advisory Committee decided to make it explicit. There are, however, instances in which a court may permit oral motions. Perhaps the most common such instance would be a motion made during oral argument in the presence of opposing counsel; for example, a request for permission to submit a supplemental brief on an issue raised by the court for the first time at oral argument. Rather than limit oral motions to those made during oral argument or, conversely, assume the propriety of making even extremely complex motions orally during argument, the Advisory Committee decided that it is better to leave the determination of the propriety of an oral motion to the court's discretion. The provision does not disturb the practice in those circuits that permit certain procedural motions, such as a motion for extension of time for filing a brief, to be made by telephone and ruled upon by the clerk.

Paragraph (2) outlines the contents of a motion. It begins with the general requirement from the current rule that a motion must state with particularity the grounds supporting it and the relief requested. It adds a requirement that all legal arguments should be presented in the body of the motion; a separate brief or memorandum supporting or responding to a motion must not be filed. The Supreme Court uses this single document approach. Sup. Ct. R. 21.1. In furtherance of the requirement that all legal argument must be contained in the body of the motion, paragraph (2) also states that an affidavit that is attached to a motion should contain only factual information and not legal argument.

Paragraph (2) further states that whenever a motion requests substantive relief, a copy of the trial court's opinion or agency's decision must be attached.

Although it is common to present a district court with a proposed order along with the motion requesting relief, that is not the practice in the courts of appeals. A proposed order is not required and is not expected or desired. Nor is a notice of motion required.

Paragraph (3) retains the provisions of the current rule concerning the filing of a response to a motion except that the time for responding has been expanded to 10 days rather than 7 days. Because the time periods in the rule apply to a substantive motion as well as a procedural motion, the longer time period may help reduce the number of motions for extension of time, or at least provide a more realistic time frame within which to make and dispose of such a motion.

A party filing a response in opposition to a motion may also request affirmative relief. It is the Advisory Committee's judgment that it is permissible to combine the response and the new motion in the same document. Indeed, because there may be substantial overlap of arguments in the response and in the request for affirmative relief, a combined document may be preferable. If a request for relief is combined with a response, the caption of the document must alert the court to the request for relief. The time for a response to such a new request and for reply to that response are governed by the general rules regulating responses and replies.

Paragraph (4) is new. Two circuits currently have rules authorizing a reply. As a general matter, a reply should not reargue propositions presented in the motion or present matters that do not relate to the response. Sometimes matters relevant to the motion arise after the motion is filed; treatment of such matters in the reply is appropriate even though strictly speaking it may not relate to the response.

Subdivision (b). The material in this subdivision remains substantively unchanged except to clarify that one may file a motion for reconsideration, etc. of a disposition by either the court or the clerk. A new sentence is added indicating that if a motion is granted in whole or in part before the filing of timely opposition to the motion, the filing of the opposition is not treated as a request for reconsideration, etc., A party wishing to have the court reconsider, vacate, or modify the disposition must file a new motion that addresses the order granting the motion.

Although the rule does not require a court to do so, it would be helpful if, whenever a motion is disposed of before receipt of any response from the opposing party, the ruling indicates that it was issued without awaiting a response. Such a statement will aid the opposing party in deciding whether to request reconsideration. The opposing party may have mailed a response about the time of the ruling and be uncertain whether the court has considered it.

Subdivision (c). The changes in this subdivision are stylistic only. No substantive changes are intended.

Subdivision (d). This subdivision has been substantially revised.

The format requirements have been moved from Rule 32(b) to paragraph (1) of this subdivision. No cover is required, but a caption is needed as well as a descriptive title indicating the purpose of the motion and identifying the party or parties for whom it is filed. Spiral binding or secure stapling at the upper left-hand corner satisfies the binding requirement. But they are not intended to be the exclusive methods of binding.

Paragraph (2) establishes page limits; twenty pages for a motion or a response, and ten pages for a reply. Three circuits have established page limits by local rule. This rule does not establish special page limits for those instances in which a party combines a response to a motion with a new request for affirmative relief. Because a combined document most often will be used when there is substantial overlap in the argument in opposition to the motion and in the argument for the affirmative relief, twenty pages may be sufficient in most instances. If it is not, the party may request additional pages. If ten pages is insufficient for the original movant to both reply to the response, and respond to the new request for affirmative relief, two separate documents may be used or a request for additional pages may be made.

The changes in paragraph (4) are stylistic only. No substantive changes are intended.

Subdivision (e). This new provision makes it clear that there is no right to oral argument on a motion. Seven circuits have local rules stating that oral argument of motions will not be held unless the court orders it.

2002 Amendments

Subdivision (a)(3)(A). Subdivision (a)(3)(A) presently requires that a response to a motion be filed within 10 days after service of the motion. Intermediate Saturdays, Sundays, and legal holidays are counted in computing that 10–day deadline, which means that, except when the 10–day deadline ends on a weekend or legal holiday, parties generally must respond to motions within 10 actual days.

Fed. R. App. P. 26(a)(2) has been amended to provide that, in computing any period of time, a litigant should "[e]xclude intermediate Saturdays, Sundays, and legal holidays when the period is less than 11 days, unless stated in calendar days." This change in the method of computing deadlines means that 10–day deadlines (such as that in subdivision (a)(3)(A)) have been lengthened as a practical matter. Under the new computation method, parties would never have less than 14 actual days to respond to motions, and legal holidays could extend that period to as much as 18 days.

Permitting parties to take two weeks or more to respond to motions would introduce significant and unwarranted delay into appellate proceedings. For that reason, the 10–day deadline in subdivision (a)(3)(A) has been reduced to 8 days. This change will, as a practical matter, ensure that every party will have at least 10 actual days—but, in the absence of a legal holiday, no more than 12 actual days—to respond to motions. The court continues to have discretion to shorten or extend that time in appropriate cases.

Changes Made After Publication and Comments In response to the objections of commentators, the time to respond to a motion was increased from the proposed 7 days to 8 days. No other changes were made to the text of the proposed amendment or to the Committee Note.

Subdivision (a)(4). Subdivision (a)(4) presently requires that a reply to a response to a motion be filed within 7 days after service of the response. Intermediate Saturdays, Sundays, and legal holidays are counted in computing that 7–day deadline, which means that, except when the 7–day deadline ends on a weekend or legal holiday, parties generally must reply to responses to motions within one week.

Fed. R. App. P. 26(a)(2) has been amended to provide that, in computing any period of time, a litigant should "[e]xclude intermediate Saturdays, Sundays, and legal holidays when the period is less than 11 days, unless stated in calendar days." This change in the method of computing deadlines means that 7–day deadlines (such as that in subdivision (a)(4)) have been lengthened as a practical matter. Under the new computation method, parties would never have less than 9 actual days to reply to responses to motions, and legal holidays could extend that period to as much as 13 days.

Permitting parties to take 9 or more days to reply to a response to a motion would introduce significant and unwarranted delay into appellate proceedings. For that reason, the 7–day deadline in subdivision (a)(4) has been reduced to 5 days. This change will, as a practical matter, ensure that every party will have 7 actual days to file replies to responses to motions (in the absence of a legal holiday).

Changes Made After Publication and Comments No changes were made to the text of the proposed amendment or to the Committee Note.

Subdivision (d)(1)(B). A cover is not required on motions, responses to motions, or replies to responses to motions. However, Rule 27(d)(1)(B) has been amended to provide that if a cover is nevertheless used on such a paper, the cover must be white. The amendment is intended to promote uniformity in federal appellate practice.

Changes Made After Publication and Comments No changes were made to the text of the proposed amendment or to the Committee Note.

2005 Amendments

Subdivision (d)(1)(E). A new subdivision (E) has been added to Rule 27(d)(1) to provide that a motion, a response to a motion, and a reply to a response to a motion must comply with the typeface requirements of Rule 32(a)(5) and the type-style requirements of Rule 32(a)(6). The purpose of the amendment is to promote uniformity in federal appellate practice and to prevent the abuses that might occur if no restrictions were placed on the size of typeface used in motion papers.

Rule 28. Briefs

(a) Appellant's Brief. The appellant's brief must contain, under appropriate headings and in the order indicated:

(1) a corporate disclosure statement if required by Rule 26.1;

(2) a table of contents, with page references;

(3) a table of authorities—cases (alphabetically arranged), statutes, and other authorities—with references to the pages of the brief where they are cited;

(4) a jurisdictional statement, including:

(A) the basis for the district court's or agency's subject-matter jurisdiction, with citations to applicable statutory provisions and stating relevant facts establishing jurisdiction;

(B) the basis for the court of appeals' jurisdiction, with citations to applicable statutory provisions and stating relevant facts establishing jurisdiction;

(C) the filing dates establishing the timeliness of the appeal or petition for review; and

(D) an assertion that the appeal is from a final order or judgment that disposes of all parties' claims, or information establishing the court of appeals' jurisdiction on some other basis;

(5) a statement of the issues presented for review;

(6) a statement of the case briefly indicating the nature of the case, the course of proceedings, and the disposition below;

(7) a statement of facts relevant to the issues submitted for review with appropriate references to the record (see Rule 28(e));

(8) a summary of the argument, which must contain a succinct, clear, and accurate statement of the arguments made in the body of the brief, and which must not merely repeat the argument headings;

(9) the argument, which must contain:

(A) appellant's contentions and the reasons for them, with citations to the authorities and parts of the record on which the appellant relies; and

(B) for each issue, a concise statement of the applicable standard of review (which may appear in the discussion of the issue or under a separate heading placed before the discussion of the issues);

(10) a short conclusion stating the precise relief sought; and

(11) the certificate of compliance, if required by Rule 32(a)(7).

(b) Appellee's Brief. The appellee's brief must conform to the requirements of Rule 28(a)(1)–(9) and (11), except that none of the following need appear unless the appellee is dissatisfied with the appellant's statement:

(1) the jurisdictional statement;

(2) the statement of the issues;

(3) the statement of the case;

(4) the statement of the facts; and

(5) the statement of the standard of review.

(c) Reply Brief. The appellant may file a brief in reply to the appellee's brief. Unless the court permits, no further briefs may be filed. A reply brief must contain a table of contents, with page references, and a table of authorities—cases (alphabetically arranged), statutes, and other authorities—with references to the pages of the reply brief where they are cited.

(d) References to Parties. In briefs and at oral argument, counsel should minimize use of the terms "appellant" and "appellee." To make briefs clear, counsel should use the parties' actual names or the designations used in the lower court or agency proceeding, or such descriptive terms as "the employee," "the injured person," "the taxpayer," "the ship," "the stevedore."

(e) References to the Record. References to the parts of the record contained in the appendix filed with the appellant's brief must be to the pages of the appendix. If the appendix is prepared after the briefs are filed, a party referring to the record must follow one of the methods detailed in Rule 30(c). If the original record is used under Rule 30(f) and is not consecutively paginated, or if the brief refers to an unreproduced part of the record, any reference must be to the page of the original document. For example:

- Answer p. 7;
- Motion for Judgment p. 2;
- Transcript p. 231.

Only clear abbreviations may be used. A party referring to evidence whose admissibility is in controversy must cite the pages of the appendix or of the transcript at which the evidence was identified, offered, and received or rejected.

(f) Reproduction of Statutes, Rules, Regulations, etc. If the court's determination of the issues presented requires the study of statutes, rules, regulations, etc., the relevant parts must be set out in the brief or in an addendum at the end, or may be supplied to the court in pamphlet form.

(g) [Reserved]

(h) [Deleted]

(i) Briefs in a Case Involving Multiple Appellants or Appellees. In a case involving more than one appellant or appellee, including consolidated cases, any number of appellants or appellees may join in a brief, and any party may adopt by reference a part of another's brief. Parties may also join in reply briefs.

(j) Citation of Supplemental Authorities. If pertinent and significant authorities come to a party's attention after the party's brief has been filed—or after oral argument but before decision—a party may promptly advise the circuit clerk by letter, with a copy to all other parties, setting forth the citations. The letter must state the reasons for the supplemental citations, referring either to the page of the brief or to a point argued orally. The body of the letter must not exceed 350 words. Any response must be made promptly and must be similarly limited.

(As amended Apr. 30, 1979, eff. Aug. 1, 1979; Mar. 10, 1986, eff. July 1, 1986; Apr. 25, 1989, eff. Dec. 1, 1989; Apr. 30, 1991, eff. Dec. 1, 1991; Apr. 22, 1993, eff. Dec. 1, 1993; Apr. 29, 1994, eff. Dec. 1, 1994; Apr. 24, 1998, eff. Dec. 1, 1998; Apr. 29, 2002, eff. Dec. 1, 2002; Apr. 25, 2005, eff. Dec. 1, 2005.)

ADVISORY COMMITTEE NOTES

1967 Adoption

This rule is based upon Supreme Court Rule 40. For variations in present circuit rules on briefs see 2d Cir. Rule 17 [rule 17, U.S.Ct. of App. 2d Cir.], 3d Cir. Rule 24 [rule 24, U.S.Ct. of App. 3d Cir.], 5th Cir. Rule 24 [rule 24, U.S.Ct. of App. 5th Cir.], and 7th Cir. Rule 17 [rule 17, U.S.Ct. of App. 7th Cir.]. All circuits now limit the number of pages of briefs, a majority limiting the brief to 50 pages of standard typographic printing. Fifty pages of standard typographic printing is the approximate equivalent of 70 pages of typewritten text, given the page sizes required by Rule 32 and the requirement set out there that text produced by a method other than standard typographic must be double spaced.

1979 Amendments

Subdivision (g). The proposed amendment eliminates the distinction appearing in the present rule between the permissible length in pages of printed and typewritten briefs, investigation of the matter having disclosed that the number of words on the printed page is little if any larger than the number on a page typed in standard elite type.

The provision is made subject to local rule to permit the court of appeals to require that typewritten briefs be typed in larger type and permit a correspondingly larger number of pages.

Subdivision (j). Proposed new Rule 28(j) makes provision for calling the court's attention to authorities that come to the party's attention after the brief has been filed. It is patterned after the practice under local rule in some of the circuits.

1986 Amendments

While Rule 28(g) can be read as requiring that tables of authorities be included in a reply brief, such tables are often not included. Their absence impedes efficient use of the reply brief to ascertain the appellant's response to a particular argument of the appellee or to the appellee's use of a particular authority. The amendment to Rule 28(c) is intended to make it clear that such tables are required in reply briefs.

The amendment to Rule 28(j) is technical. No substantive change is intended.

1989 Amendments

The amendment provides that the corporate disclosure statement required by new Rule 26.1 shall be treated similarly to tables of contents and tables of citations and shall not be counted for purposes of the number of pages allowed in a brief.

1991 Amendments

Subdivision (a). The amendment adds a new subparagraph (2) that requires an appellant to include a specific jurisdictional statement in the appellant's brief to aid the court of appeals in determining whether it has both federal subject matter and appellate jurisdiction.

Subdivision (b). The amendment requires the appellee to include a jurisdictional statement in the appellee's brief except that the appellee need not include the statement if the appellee is satisfied with the appellant's jurisdictional statement.

Subdivision (h). The amendment provides that when more than one party appeals from a judgment or order, the party filing the first appeal is normally treated as the appellant for purposes of this rule and Rules 30 and 31. The party who first files an appeal usually is the principal appellant and should be treated as such. Parties who file a notice of appeal after the first notice often bring protective appeals and they should be treated as cross appellants. Local rules in the Fourth and Federal Circuits now take that approach. If notices of appeal are filed on the same day, the rule follows the old approach of treating the plaintiff below as the appellant. For purposes of this rule, in criminal cases "the plaintiff" means the United States. In those instances where the designations provided by the rule are inappropriate, they may be altered by agreement of the parties or by an order of the court.

1993 Amendments

Note to paragraph (a)(5). The amendment requires an appellant's brief to state the standard of review applicable to each issue on appeal. Five circuits currently require these statements. Experience in those circuits indicates that requiring a statement of the standard of review generally results in arguments that are properly shaped in light of the standard.

1994 Amendments

Subdivision (a). The amendment adds a requirement that an appellant's brief contain a summary of the argument. A number of circuits have local rules requiring a summary and the courts report that they find the summary useful. See, D.C. Cir.R. 11(a)(5); 5th Cir.R. 28.2.2; 8th Cir.R. 28A(i)(6); 11th Cir.R. 28–2(i); and Fed. Cir.R. 28.

Subdivision (b). The amendment adds a requirement that an appellee's brief contain a summary of the argument.

Subdivision (g). The amendment adds proof of service to the list of items in a brief that do not count for purposes of the page limitation. The concurrent amendment to Rule 25(d) requires a certificate of service to list the addresses to which a paper was mailed or at which it was delivered. When a number of parties must be served, the listing of addresses may run to several pages and those pages should not count for purposes of the page limitation.

1998 Amendments

The language and organization of the rule are amended to make the rule more easily understood. In addition to changes made to improve the understanding, the Advisory Committee has changed language to make style and terminology consistent throughout the appellate rules. These changes are intended to by stylistic only.

Several substantive changes are made in this rule, however. Most of them are necessary to confirm Rule 28 with changes recommended in Rule 32.

Subdivision (a). The current rule requires a brief to include a statement of the case which includes a description of the nature of the case, the course of proceedings, the disposition of the case—all of which might be described as the procedural history—as well as a statement of the facts. The amendments separate this into two statements; one procedural, called the statement of the case; and one factual, called the statement of the facts. The Advisory Committee believes that the separation will be helpful to the judges. The table of contents and table of authorities have also been separated into two distinct items.

An additional amendment of subdivision (a) is made to conform it with an amendment being made to Rule 32. Rule 32(a)(7) generally requires a brief to include a certificate of compliance with type-volume limitations contained in that rule. (No certificate is required if a brief does not exceed 30 pages, or 15 pages for a reply brief.) Rule 28(a) is amended to include that certificate in the list of items that must be included in a brief whenever it is required by Rule 32.

Subdivision (g). The amendments delete subdivision (g) that limited a principal brief to 50 pages and a reply brief to 25 pages. The length limitations have been moved to Rule 32. Rule 32 deals generally with the format for a brief or appendix.

Subdivision (h). The amendment requires an appellee's brief to comply with Rule 28(a)(1) through (11) with regard to a cross-appeal. The addition of separate paragraphs requiring a corporate disclosure statement, table of authorities, statement of facts, and certificate of compliance increased the relevant paragraphs of subdivision (a) from (7) to (11). The other changes are stylistic; no substantive changes are intended.

2002 Amendments

Subdivision (j). In the past, Rule 28(j) has required parties to describe supplemental authorities "without argument." Enforcement of this restriction has been lax, in part because of the difficulty of distinguishing "state[ment] . . . [of] the reasons for the supplemental citations," which is required, from "argument" about the supplemental citations, which is forbidden.

As amended, Rule 28(j) continues to require parties to state the reasons for supplemental citations, with reference to the part of a brief or oral argument to which the supplemental citations pertain. But Rule 28(j) no longer forbids "argument." Rather, Rule 28(j) permits parties to decide for themselves what they wish to say about supplemental authorities. The only restriction upon parties is that the body of a

Rule 28(j) letter—that is, the part of the letter that begins with the first word after the salutation and ends with the last word before the complimentary close—cannot exceed 350 words. All words found in footnotes will count toward the 350–word limit.

Changes Made After Publication and Comments No changes were made to the text of the proposed amendment or to the Committee Note, except that the word limit was increased from 250 to 350 in response to the complaint of some commentators that parties would have difficulty bringing multiple supplemental authorities to the attention of the court in one 250–word letter.

2005 Amendments

Subdivision (c). Subdivision (c) has been amended to delete a sentence that authorized an appellee who had cross-appealed to file a brief in reply to the appellant's response. All rules regarding briefing in cases involving cross-appeals have been consolidated into new Rule 28.1.

Subdivision (h). Subdivision (h)—regarding briefing in cases involving cross-appeals—has been deleted. All rules regarding such briefing have been consolidated into new Rule 28.1.

Rule 28.1. Cross–Appeals

(a) Applicability. This rule applies to a case in which a cross-appeal is filed. Rules 28(a)-(c), 31(a)(1), 32(a)(2), and 32(a)(7)(A)-(B) do not apply to such a case, except as otherwise provided in this rule.

(b) Designation of Appellant. The party who files a notice of appeal first is the appellant for the purposes of this rule and Rules 30 and 34. If notices are filed on the same day, the plaintiff in the proceeding below is the appellant. These designations may be modified by the parties' agreement or by court order.

(c) Briefs. In a case involving a cross-appeal:

(1) Appellant's Principal Brief. The appellant must file a principal brief in the appeal. That brief must comply with Rule 28(a).

(2) Appellee's Principal and Response Brief. The appellee must file a principal brief in the cross-appeal and must, in the same brief, respond to the principal brief in the appeal. That appellee's brief must comply with Rule 28(a), except that the brief need not include a statement of the case or a statement of the facts unless the appellee is dissatisfied with the appellant's statement.

(3) Appellant's Response and Reply Brief. The appellant must file a brief that responds to the principal brief in the cross-appeal and may, in the same brief, reply to the response in the appeal. That brief must comply with Rule 28(a)(2)–(9) and (11), except that none of the following need appear unless the appellant is dissatisfied with the appellee's statement in the cross-appeal:

(A) the jurisdictional statement;

(B) the statement of the issues;

(C) the statement of the case;

(D) the statement of the facts; and

(E) the statement of the standard of review.

(4) Appellee's Reply Brief. The appellee may file a brief in reply to the response in the cross-appeal. That brief must comply with Rule 28(a)(2)–(3) and (11) and must be limited to the issues presented by the cross-appeal.

(5) No Further Briefs. Unless the court permits, no further briefs may be filed in a case involving a cross-appeal.

(d) Cover. Except for filings by unrepresented parties, the cover of the appellant's principal brief must be blue; the appellee's principal and response brief, red; the appellant's response and reply brief, yellow; the appellee's reply brief, gray; an intervenor's or amicus curiae's brief, green; and any supplemental brief, tan. The front cover of a brief must contain the information required by Rule 32(a)(2).

(e) Length.

(1) Page Limitation. Unless it complies with Rule 28.1(e)(2) and (3), the appellant's principal brief must not exceed 30 pages; the appellee's principal and response brief, 35 pages; the appellant's response and reply brief, 30 pages; and the appellee's reply brief, 15 pages.

(2) Type-Volume Limitation.

(A) The appellant's principal brief or the appellant's response and reply brief is acceptable if:

(i) it contains no more than 14,000 words; or

(ii) it uses a monospaced face and contains no more than 1,300 lines of text.

(B) The appellee's principal and response brief is acceptable if:

(i) it contains no more than 16,500 words; or

(ii) it uses a monospaced face and contains no more than 1,500 lines of text.

(C) The appellee's reply brief is acceptable if it contains no more than half of the type volume specified in Rule 28.1(e)(2)(A).

(3) Certificate of Compliance. A brief submitted under Rule 28.1(e)(2) must comply with Rule 32(a)(7)(C).

(f) Time to Serve and File a Brief. Briefs must be served and filed as follows:

(1) the appellant's principal brief, within 40 days after the record is filed;

(2) the appellee's principal and response brief, within 30 days after the appellant's principal brief is served;

(3) the appellant's response and reply brief, within 30 days after the appellee's principal and response brief is served; and

(4) the appellee's reply brief, within 14 days after the appellant's response and reply brief is served, but at least 3 days before argument unless the court, for good cause, allows a later filing.

(As added April 25, 2005, eff. Dec. 1, 2005.)

ADVISORY COMMITTEE NOTES

2005 Adoption

The Federal Rules of Appellate Procedure have said very little about briefing in cases involving cross-appeals. This vacuum has frustrated judges, attorneys, and parties who have sought guidance in the rules. More importantly, this vacuum has been filled by conflicting local rules regarding such matters as the number and length of briefs, the colors of the covers of briefs, and the deadlines for serving and filing briefs. These local rules have created a hardship for attorneys who practice in more than one circuit.

New Rule 28.1 provides a comprehensive set of rules governing briefing in cases involving cross-appeals. The few existing provisions regarding briefing in such cases have been moved into new Rule 28.1, and several new provisions have been added to fill the gaps in the existing rules. The new provisions reflect the practices of the large majority of circuits and, to a significant extent, the new provisions have been patterned after the requirements imposed by Rules 28, 31, and 32 on briefs filed in cases that do not involve cross-appeals.

Subdivision (a). Subdivision (a) makes clear that, in a case involving a cross-appeal, briefing is governed by new Rule 28.1, and not by Rules 28(a), 28(b), 28(c), 31(a)(1), 32(a)(2), 32(a)(7)(A), and 32(a)(7)(B), except to the extent that Rule 28.1 specifically incorporates those rules by reference.

Subdivision (b). Subdivision (b) defines who is the "appellant" and who is the "appellee" in a case involving a cross-appeal. Subdivision (b) is taken directly from former Rule 28(h), except that subdivision (b) refers to a party being designated as an appellant "for the purposes of this rule and Rules 30 and 34," whereas former Rule 28(h) also referred to Rule 31. Because the matter addressed by Rule 31(a)(1)—the time to serve and file briefs—is now addressed directly in new Rule 28.1(f), the cross-reference to Rule 31 is no longer necessary. In Rule 31 and in all rules other than Rules 28.1, 30, and 34, references to an "appellant" refer both to the appellant in an appeal and to the cross-appellant in a cross-appeal, and references to an "appellee" refer both to the appellee in an appeal and to the cross-appellee in a cross-appeal. Cf. Rule 31(c).

Subdivision (c). Subdivision (c) provides for the filing of four briefs in a case involving a cross-appeal. This reflects the practice of every circuit except the Seventh. *See* 7th Cir. R. 28(d)(1)(a).

The first brief is the "appellant's principal brief." That brief—like the appellant's principal brief in a case that does not involve a cross-appeal—must comply with Rule 28(a).

The second brief is the "appellee's principal and response brief." Because this brief serves as the appellee's principal brief on the merits of the cross-appeal, as well as the appellee's response brief on the merits of the appeal, it must also comply with Rule 28(a), with the limited exceptions noted in the text of the rule.

The third brief is the "appellant's response and reply brief." Like a response brief in a case that does not involve a cross-appeal—that is, a response brief that does not also serve as a principal brief on the merits of a cross-appeal—the appellant's response and reply brief must comply with Rule 28(a)(2)-(9) and (11), with the exceptions noted in the text of the rule. *See* Rule 28(b). The one difference between the appellant's response and reply brief, on the one hand, and a response brief filed in a case that does not involve a cross-appeal, on the other, is that the latter must include a corporate disclosure statement. *See* Rule 28(a)(1) and (b). An appellant filing a response and reply brief in a case involving a cross-appeal has already filed a corporate disclosure statement with its principal brief on the merits of the appeal.

The fourth brief is the "appellee's reply brief." Like a reply brief in a case that does not involve a cross-appeal, it must comply with Rule 28(c), which essentially restates the requirements of Rule 28(a)(2)–(3) and (11). (Rather than restating the requirements of Rule 28(a)(2)-(3) and (11), as Rule 28(c) does, Rule 28.1(c)(4) includes a direct cross-reference.) The appellee's reply brief must also be limited to the issues presented by the cross-appeal.

Subdivision (d). Subdivision (d) specifies the colors of the covers on briefs filed in a case involving a cross-appeal. It is patterned after Rule 32(a)(2), which does not specifically refer to cross-appeals.

Subdivision (e). Subdivision (e) sets forth limits on the length of the briefs filed in a case involving a cross-appeal. It is patterned after Rule 32(a)(7), which does not specifically refer to cross-appeals. Subdivision (e) permits the appellee's principal and response brief to be longer than a typical principal brief on the merits because this brief serves not only as the principal brief on the merits of the cross-appeal, but also as the response brief on the merits of the appeal. Likewise, subdivision (e) permits the appellant's response and reply brief to be longer than a typical reply brief because this brief serves not only as the reply brief in the appeal, but also as the response brief in the cross-appeal. For purposes of determining the maximum length of an amicus curiae's brief filed in a case involving a cross-appeal, Rule 29(d)'s reference to "the maximum length authorized by these rules for a party's principal brief" should be understood to refer to subdivision (e)'s limitations on the length of an appellant's principal brief.

Subdivision (f). Subdivision (f) provides deadlines for serving and filing briefs in a cross-appeal. It is patterned after Rule 31(a)(1), which does not specifically refer to cross-appeals.

Rule 29. Brief of an Amicus Curiae

(a) When Permitted. The United States or its officer or agency, or a State, Territory, Commonwealth, or the District of Columbia may file an amicus-curiae brief without the consent of the parties or leave of court. Any other amicus curiae may file a brief only by leave of court or if the brief states that all parties have consented to its filing.

(b) Motion for Leave to File. The motion must be accompanied by the proposed brief and state:

(1) the movant's interest; and

(2) the reason why an amicus brief is desirable and why the matters asserted are relevant to the disposition of the case.

(c) Contents and Form. An amicus brief must comply with Rule 32. In addition to the requirements of Rule 32, the cover must identify the party or parties supported and indicate whether the brief supports affirmance or reversal. If an amicus curiae is a corporation, the brief must include a disclosure statement like that required of parties by Rule 26.1. An amicus brief need not comply with Rule 28, but must include the following:

(1) a table of contents, with page references;

(2) a table of authorities—cases (alphabetically arranged), statutes and other authorities—with references to the pages of the brief where they are cited;

(3) a concise statement of the identity of the amicus curiae, its interest in the case, and the source of its authority to file;

(4) an argument, which may be preceded by a summary and which need not include a statement of the applicable standard of review; and

(5) a certificate of compliance, if required by Rule 32(a)(7).

(d) Length. Except by the court's permission, an amicus brief may be no more than one-half the maximum length authorized by these rules for a party's principal brief. If the court grants a party permission to file a longer brief, that extension does not affect the length of an amicus brief.

(e) Time for Filing. An amicus curiae must file its brief, accompanied by a motion for filing when necessary, no later than 7 days after the principal brief of the party being supported is filed. An amicus curiae that does not support either party must file its brief no later than 7 days after the appellant's or petitioner's principal brief is filed. A court may grant leave for later filing, specifying the time within which an opposing party may answer.

(f) Reply Brief. Except by the court's permission, an amicus curiae may not file a reply brief.

(g) Oral Argument. An amicus curiae may participate in oral argument only with the court's permission.

(As amended Apr. 24, 1998, eff. Dec. 1, 1998.)

ADVISORY COMMITTEE NOTES

1967 Adoption

Only five circuits presently regulate the filing of the brief of an amicus curiae. See D.C.Cir. Rule 18(j) [rule 18(j), U.S.Ct. of App.Dist. of Col.Cir., this title]; 1st Cir. Rule 23(10) [rule 23(10), U.S.Ct. of App. 1st Cir.]; 6th Cir. Rule 17(4) [rule 17(4), U.S.Ct. of App. 6th Cir.]; 9th Cir. Rule 18(9) [rule 18(9), U.S.Ct. of App. 9th Cir.]; 10th Cir. Rule 20 [rule 20, U.S.Ct. of App. 10th Cir.]. This rule follows the practice of a majority of circuits in requiring leave of court to file an amicus brief except under the circumstances stated therein. Compare Supreme Court Rule 42.

1998 Amendments

The language and organization of the rule are amended to make the rule more easily understood. In addition to changes made to improve the understanding, the Advisory Committee has changed language to make style and terminology consistent through the appellate rules. These changes are intended to be stylistic only.

Several substantive changes are made in this rule, however.

Subdivision (a). The major change in this subpart is that when a brief is filed with the consent of all parties, it is no longer necessary to obtain the parties' written consent and to file the consents with the brief. It is sufficient to obtain the parties' oral consent and to state in the brief that all parties have consented. It is sometimes difficult to obtain all the written consents by the filing deadline and it is not unusual for counsel to represent that parties have consented; for example, in a motion for extension of time to file a brief it is not unusual for the movant to state that the other parties have been consulted and they do not object to the extension. If a party's consent has been misrepresented, the party will be able to take action before the court considers the amicus brief.

The District of Columbia is added to the list of entities allowed to file an amicus brief without consent of all parties. The other changes in this material are stylistic.

Subdivision (b). The provision in the former rule, granting permission to conditionally file the brief with the motion, is changed to one requiring that the brief accompany the motion. Sup. Ct. R. 37.4 requires that the proposed brief be presented with the motion.

The former rule only required the motion to identify the applicant's interest and to generally state the reasons why an amicus brief is desirable. The amended rule additionally requires that the motion state the relevance of the matters asserted to the disposition of the case. As Sup. Ct. R. 37.1 states:

> An *amicus curiae* brief which brings relevant matter to the attention of the Court that has not already been brought to its attention by the parties is of considerable help to the Court. An *amicus curiae* brief which does not serve this purpose simply burdens the staff and facilities of the Court and its filing is not favored.

Because the relevance of the matters asserted by an amicus is ordinarily the most compelling reason for granting leave to file, the Committee believes that it is helpful to explicitly require such a showing.

Subdivision (c). The provisions in this subdivision are entirely new. Previously there was confusion as to whether an amicus brief must include all of the items listed in Rule 28. Out of caution practitioners in some circuits included all those items. Ordinarily that is unnecessary.

The requirement that the cover identify the party supported and indicate whether the amicus supports affirmance or reversal is an administrative aid.

Paragraph (c)(3) requires an amicus to state the source of its authority to file. The amicus simply must identify which of the provisions in Rule 29(a) provides the basis for the amicus to file its brief.

Subdivision (d). This new provision imposes a shorter page limit for an amicus brief than for a party's brief. This is appropriate for two reasons. First, an amicus may omit certain items that must be included in a party's brief. Second, an amicus brief is supplemental. It need not address all issues or all facets of a case. It should treat only matter not adequately addressed by a party.

Subdivision (e). The time limit for filing is changed. An amicus brief must be filed no later than 7 days after the principal brief of the party being supported is filed. Occasionally, an amicus supports neither party; in such instances, the amendment provides that the amicus brief must be filed no later than 7 days after the appellant's or petitioner's principal brief is filed. Note that in both instances the 7–day period runs from when a brief is filed. The passive voice—"is filed"—is used deliberately. A party or amicus can send its brief to a court for filing and, under Rule 25, the brief is timely if mailed within the filing period. Although the brief is timely if mailed within the filing period, it is not "filed" until the court receives it and file stamps it. "Filing" is done by the court, not by the party. It may be necessary for an amicus to contact the court to ascertain the filing date.

The 7–day stagger was adopted because it is long enough to permit an amicus to review the completed brief of the party being supported and avoid repetitious argument. A 7–day period also is short enough that no adjustment need be made in the opposing party's briefing schedule. The opposing party will have sufficient time to review arguments made by the amicus and address them in the party's responsive pleading. The timetable for filing the parties' briefs is unaffected by this change.

A court may grant permission to file an amicus brief in a context in which the party does not file a "principal brief"; for example, an amicus may be permitted to file in support of a party's petition for rehearing. In such instances the court will establish the filing time for the amicus.

The former rule's statement that a court may, for cause shown, grant leave for later filing is unnecessary. Rule 26(b) grants general authority to enlarge the time prescribed in these rules for good cause shown. This new rule, however, states that when a court grants permission for later filing, the court must specify the period within which an opposing party may answer the arguments of the amicus.

Subdivision (f). This subdivision generally prohibits the filing of a reply brief by an amicus curiae. Sup. Ct. R. 37 and local rules of the D.C., Ninth, and Federal Circuits state that an amicus may not file a reply brief. The role of an amicus should not require the use of a reply brief.

Subdivision (g). The language of this subdivision stating that an amicus will be granted permission to participate in oral argument "only for extraordinary reasons" has been deleted. The change is made to reflect more accurately the current practice in which it is not unusual for a court to permit an amicus to argue when a party is willing to share its argument time with the amicus. The Committee does not intend, however, to suggest that in other instances an amicus will be permitted to argue absent extraordinary circumstances.

Rule 30. Appendix to the Briefs

(a) Appellant's Responsibility.

(1) Contents of the Appendix. The appellant must prepare and file an appendix to the briefs containing:

(A) the relevant docket entries in the proceeding below;

(B) the relevant portions of the pleadings, charge, findings, or opinion;

(C) the judgment, order, or decision in question; and

(D) other parts of the record to which the parties wish to direct the court's attention.

(2) Excluded Material. Memoranda of law in the district court should not be included in the appendix unless they have independent relevance. Parts of the record may be relied on by the court or the parties even though not included in the appendix.

(3) Time to File; Number of Copies. Unless filing is deferred under Rule 30(c), the appellant must file 10 copies of the appendix with the brief and must serve one copy on counsel for each party separately represented. An unrepresented party proceeding in forma pauperis must file 4 legible copies with the clerk, and one copy must be served on counsel for each separately represented party. The court may by local rule or by order in a particular case require the filing or service of a different number.

(b) All Parties' Responsibilities.

(1) Determining the Contents of the Appendix. The parties are encouraged to agree on the contents of the appendix. In the absence of an agreement, the appellant must, within 10 days after the record is filed, serve on the appellee a designation of the parts of the record the appellant intends to include in the appendix and a statement of the issues the appellant intends to present for review. The appellee may, within 10 days after receiving the designation, serve on the appellant a designation of additional parts to which it wishes to direct the court's attention. The appellant must include the designated parts in the appendix. The parties must not engage in unnecessary designation of parts of the record, because the entire record is available to the court. This paragraph applies also to a cross-appellant and a cross-appellee.

(2) Costs of Appendix. Unless the parties agree otherwise, the appellant must pay the cost of the appendix. If the appellant considers parts of the record designated by the appellee to be unnecessary, the appellant may advise the appellee, who must then advance the cost of including those parts. The cost of the appendix is a taxable cost. But if any party causes unnecessary parts of the record to be included in the appendix, the court may impose the cost of those parts on that party. Each circuit must, by local rule, provide for sanctions against attorneys who unreasonably and vexatiously increase litigation costs by including unnecessary material in the appendix.

(c) Deferred Appendix.

(1) Deferral Until After Briefs Are Filed. The court may provide by rule for classes of cases or by order in a particular case that preparation of the appendix may be deferred until after the briefs have been filed and that the appendix may be filed 21 days after the appellee's brief is served. Even though the filing of the appendix may be deferred, Rule 30(b) applies; except that a party must designate the parts of the record it wants included in the appendix when it serves its brief, and need not include a statement of the issues presented.

(2) References to the Record.

(A) If the deferred appendix is used, the parties may cite in their briefs the pertinent pages of the record. When the appendix is prepared, the record pages cited in the briefs must be indicated by inserting record page numbers, in brackets, at places in the appendix where those pages of the record appear.

(B) A party who wants to refer directly to pages of the appendix may serve and file copies of the brief within the time required by Rule 31(a), containing appropriate references to pertinent pages of the record. In that event, within 14 days after the appendix is filed, the party must serve and file copies of the brief, containing references to the pages of the appendix in place of or in addition to the references to the pertinent pages of the record. Except for the correction of typographical errors, no other changes may be made to the brief.

(d) Format of the Appendix. The appendix must begin with a table of contents identifying the page at which each part begins. The relevant docket entries must follow the table of contents. Other parts of the record must follow chronologically. When pages from the transcript of proceedings are placed in the appendix, the transcript page numbers must be shown in brackets immediately before the included pages. Omissions in the text of papers or of the transcript must be indicated by asterisks. Immaterial formal matters (captions, subscriptions, acknowledgments, etc.) should be omitted.

(e) Reproduction of Exhibits. Exhibits designated for inclusion in the appendix may be reproduced in a separate volume, or volumes, suitably indexed. Four copies must be filed with the appendix, and one copy must be served on counsel for each separately represented party. If a transcript of a proceeding before an administrative agency, board, commission, or officer was used in a district-court action and has been designated for inclusion in the appendix, the transcript must be placed in the appendix as an exhibit.

(f) Appeal on the Original Record Without an Appendix. The court may, either by rule for all cases or classes of cases or by order in a particular case, dispense with the appendix and permit an appeal to proceed on the original record with any copies of the record, or relevant parts, that the court may order the parties to file.

(As amended Mar. 30, 1970, eff. July 1, 1970; Mar. 10, 1986, eff. July 1, 1986; Apr. 30, 1991, eff. Dec. 1, 1991; Apr. 29, 1994, eff. Dec. 1, 1994; Apr. 24, 1998. eff. Dec. 1, 1998.)

ADVISORY COMMITTEE NOTES

1967 Adoption

Subdivision (a). Only two circuits presently require a printed record (5th Cir. Rule 23(a) [rule 23(a), U.S.Ct. of App. 5th Cir.]; 8th Cir. Rule 10 [rule 10, U.S.Ct. of App. 8th Cir.] (in civil appeals only)), and the rules and practice in those circuits combine to make the difference between a printed record and the appendix, which is now used in eight circuits and in the Supreme Court in lieu of the printed record, largely nominal. The essential characteristics of the appendix method are: (1) the entire record may not be reproduced; (2) instead, the parties are to set out in an appendix to the briefs those parts of the record which in their judgment the judges must consult in order to determine the issues presented by the appeal; (3) the appendix is not the record but merely a selection therefrom for the convenience of the judges of the court of appeals; the record is the actual trial court record, and the record itself is always available to supply inadvertent omissions from the appendix. These essentials are incorporated, either by rule or by practice, in the circuits that continue to require the printed record rather than the appendix. See 5th Cir. Rule 23(a)(9) [23(a)(9), U.S.Ct. of App. 5th Cir.] and 8th Cir. Rule 10(a)–(d) [rule 10(a)–(d), U.S.Ct. of App. 8th Cir.].

Subdivision (b). Under the practice in six of the eight circuits which now use the appendix method, unless the parties agree to use a single appendix, the appellant files with his brief an appendix containing the parts of the record which he deems it essential that the court read in order to determine the questions presented. If the appellee deems additional parts of the record necessary he must include such parts as an appendix to his brief. The proposed rule differs from that practice. By the new rule a single appendix is to be filed. It is to be prepared by the appellant, who must include therein those parts which he deems essential and those which the appellee designates as essential.

Under the practice by which each party files his own appendix the resulting reproduction of essential parts of the record is often fragmentary; it is not infrequently necessary to piece several appendices together to arrive at a usable reproduction. Too, there seems to be a tendency on the part of some appellants to reproduce less than what is necessary for a determination of the issues presented (see *Moran Towing Corp. v. M. A. Gammino Construction Co.*, 363 F.2d 108 (1st Cir. 1966); *Walters v. Shari Music Publishing*

Corp., 298 F.2d 206 (2d Cir. 1962) and cases cited therein; *Morrison v. Texas Co.*, 289 F.2d 382 (7th Cir. 1961) and cases cited therein), a tendency which is doubtless encouraged by the requirement in present rules that the appellee reproduce in his separately prepared appendix such necessary parts of the record as are not included by the appellant.

Under the proposed rule responsibility for the preparation of the appendix is placed on the appellant. If the appellee feels that the appellant has omitted essential portions of the record, he may require the appellant to include such portions in the appendix. The appellant is protected against a demand that he reproduce parts which he considers unnecessary by the provisions entitling him to require the appellee to advance the costs of reproducing such parts and authorizing denial of costs for matter unnecessarily reproduced.

Subdivision (c). This subdivision permits the appellant to elect to defer the production of the appendix to the briefs until the briefs of both sides are written, and authorizes a court of appeals to require such deferred filing by rule or order. The advantage of this method of preparing the appendix is that it permits the parties to determine what parts of the record need to be reproduced in the light of the issues actually presented by the briefs. Often neither side is in a position to say precisely what is needed until the briefs are completed. Once the argument on both sides is known, it should be possible to confine the matter reproduced in the appendix to that which is essential to a determination of the appeal or review. This method of preparing the appendix is presently in use in the Tenth Circuit (Rule 17) [rule 17, U.S.Ct. of App. 10th Cir.] and in other circuits in review of agency proceedings, and it has proven its value in reducing the volume required to be reproduced. When the record is long, use of this method is likely to result in substantial economy to the parties.

Subdivision (e). The purpose of this subdivision is to reduce the cost of reproducing exhibits. While subdivision (a) requires that 10 copies of the appendix be filed, unless the court requires a lesser number, subdivision (e) permits exhibits necessary for the determination of an appeal to be bound separately, and requires only 4 copies of such a separate volume or volumes to be filed and a single copy to be served on counsel.

Subdivision (f). The subdivision authorizes a court of appeals to dispense with the appendix method of reproducing parts of the record and to hear appeals on the original record and such copies of it as the court may require.

Since 1962 the Ninth Circuit has permitted all appeals to be heard on the original record and a very limited number of copies. Under the practice as adopted in 1962, any party to an appeal could elect to have the appeal heard on the original record and two copies thereof rather than on the printed record theretofore required. The resulting substantial saving of printing costs led to the election of the new practice in virtually all cases, and by 1967 the use of printed records had ceased. By a recent amendment, the Ninth Circuit has abolished the printed record altogether. Its rules now provide that all appeals are to be heard on the original record, and it has reduced the number of copies required to two sets of copies of the transmitted original papers (excluding copies of exhibits, which need not be filed unless specifically ordered). See 9 Cir. Rule 10 [rule 10 U.S.Ct. of App. 9th Cir.], as amended June 2, 1967, effective September 1, 1967. The Eighth Circuit permits appeals in criminal cases and in habeas corpus and 28 U.S.C. § 2255 proceedings to be heard on the original record and two copies thereof. See 8 Cir. Rule 8(i)–(j) [rule 8(i)–(j), U.S.Ct. of App. 8th Cir.]. The Tenth Circuit permits appeals in all cases to be heard on the original record and four copies thereof whenever the record consists of two hundred pages or less. See 10 Cir. Rule 17(a) [rule 17(a), U.S.Ct. of App. 10th Cir.]. This subdivision expressly authorizes the continuation of the practices in the Eighth, Ninth and Tenth Circuits.

The judges of the Court of Appeals for the Ninth Circuit have expressed complete satisfaction with the practice there in use and have suggested that attention be called to the advantages which it offers in terms of reducing cost.

1970 Amendments

Subdivision (a). The amendment of subdivision (a) is related to the amendment of Rule 31(a), which authorizes a court of appeals to shorten the time for filing briefs. By virtue of this amendment, if the time for filing the brief of the appellant is shortened the time for filing the appendix is likewise shortened.

Subdivision (c). As originally written, subdivision (c) permitted the appellant to elect to defer filing of the appendix until 21 days after service of the brief of the appellee. As amended, subdivision (c) requires that an order of court be obtained before filing of the appendix can be deferred, unless a court permits deferred filing by local rule. The amendment should not cause use of the deferred appendix to be viewed with disfavor. In cases involving lengthy records, permission to defer filing of the appendix should be freely granted as an inducement to the parties to include in the appendix only matter that the briefs show to be necessary for consideration by the judges. But the Committee is advised that appellants have elected to defer filing of the appendix in cases involving brief records merely to obtain the 21 day delay. The subdivision is amended to prevent that practice.

1986 Amendments

Subdivision (a). During its study of the separate appendix [see Report of the Advisory Committee on the Federal Appellate Rules on the Operation of Rule 30, FRD (1985)], the Advisory Committee found that this document was frequently encumbered with memoranda submitted to the trial court. *United States v. Noall,* 587 F.2d 123, 125 n. 1 (2nd Cir.1978). See generally *Drewett v. Aetna Cas. & Sur. Co.*, 539 F.2d 496, 500 (5th Cir.1976); *Volkswagenwerk Aktiengesellschaft v. Church,* 413 F.2d 1126, 1128 (9th Cir.1969). Inclusion of such material makes the appendix more bulky and therefore less useful to the appellate panel. It also can increase significantly the costs of litigation.

There are occasions when such trial court memoranda have independent relevance in the appellate litigation. For instance, there may be a dispute as to whether a particular point was raised or whether a concession was made in the district court. In such circumstances, it is appropriate to include pertinent sections of such memoranda in the appendix.

Subdivision (b). The amendment to subdivision (b) is designed to require the circuits, by local rule, to establish a procedural mechanism for the imposition of sanctions against those attorneys who conduct appellate litigation in bad faith.

Both 28 U.S.C. § 1927 and the inherent power of the court authorize such sanctions. See *Brennan v. Local 357, International Brotherhood of Teamsters*, 709 F.2d 611 (9th Cir. 1983). See generally *Roadway Express, Inc. v. Piper*, 447 U.S. 752 (1980). While considerations of uniformity are important and doubtless will be taken into account by the judges of the respective circuits, the Advisory Committee believes that, at this time, the circuits need the flexibility to tailor their approach to the conditions of local practice. The local rule shall provide for notice and opportunity to respond before the imposition of any sanction.

Technical amendments also are made to subdivisions (a), (b) and (c) which are not intended to be substantive changes.

1991 Amendments

Subdivision (b). The amendment requires a cross appellant to serve the appellant with a statement of the issues that the cross appellant intends to pursue on appeal. No later than ten days after the record is filed, the appellant and cross appellant must serve each other with a statement of the issues each intends to present for review and with a designation of the parts of the record that each wants included in the appendix. Within the next ten days, both the appellee and the cross appellee may designate additional materials for inclusion in the appendix. The appellant must then include in the appendix the parts thus designated for both the appeal and any cross appeals. The Committee expects that simultaneous compliance with this subdivision by an appellant and a cross appellant will be feasible in most cases. If a cross appellant cannot fairly be expected to comply until receipt of the appellant's statement of issues, relief may be sought by motion in the court of appeals.

1994 Amendments

Subdivision (a). The only substantive change is to allow a court to require the filing of a greater number of copies of an appendix as well as a lesser number.

1998 Amendments

The language and organization of the new rule are amended to make the rule more easily understood. In addition to changes made to improve the understanding, the Advisory Committee has changed language to make style and terminology consistent throughout the appellate Rules. These changes are intended to be stylistic only.

Subdivision (a). Paragraph (a)(3) is amended so that it is consistent with Rule 31(b). An unrepresented party proceeding in forma pauperis is only required to file 4 copies of the appendix rather than 10.

Subdivision (c). When a deferred appendix is used, a brief must make reference to the original record rather than to the appendix because it does not exist when the briefs are prepared. Unless a party later files an amended brief with direct references to the pages of the appendix (as provided in subparagraph (c)(2)(B)), the material in the appendix must indicate the pages of the original record from which it was drawn so that a reader of the brief can make meaningful use of the appendix. The instructions in the current rule for cross-referencing the appendix materials to the original record are unclear. The language in paragraph (c)(2) has been amended to try to clarify the procedure.

Subdivision (d). In recognition of the fact that use of a typeset appendix is exceedingly rare in the courts of appeals, the last sentence—permitting a question and answer (as from a transcript) to be in a single paragraph—has been omitted.

HISTORICAL NOTES

Taxation of Fees in Appeals in Which Requirement of Appendix is Dispensed With

See item (6) in the Judicial Conference Schedule of Fees note under 28 U.S.C.A. § 1913.

Rule 31. Serving and Filing Briefs

(a) Time to Serve and File a Brief.

(1) The appellant must serve and file a brief within 40 days after the record is filed. The appellee must serve and file a brief within 30 days after the appellant's brief is served. The appellant may serve and file a reply brief within 14 days after service of the appellee's brief but a reply brief must be filed at least 3 days before argument, unless the court, for good cause, allows a later filing.

(2) A court of appeals that routinely considers cases on the merits promptly after the briefs are filed may shorten the time to serve and file briefs, either by local rule or by order in a particular case.

(b) Number of Copies. Twenty-five copies of each brief must be filed with the clerk and 2 copies must be served on each unrepresented party and on counsel for each separately represented party. An unrepresented party proceeding in forma pauperis must file 4 legible copies with the clerk, and one copy must be served on each unrepresented party and on counsel for each separately represented party. The court may by local rule or by order in a particular case require the filing or service of a different number.

(c) Consequence of Failure to File. If an appellant fails to file a brief within the time provided by this rule, or within an extended time, an appellee may move to dismiss the appeal. An appellee who fails to file a brief will not be heard at oral argument unless the court grants permission.

(As amended Mar. 30, 1970, eff. July 1, 1970; Mar. 10, 1986, eff. July 1, 1986; Apr. 29, 1994, eff. Dec. 1, 1994; Apr. 24, 1998, eff. Dec. 1, 1998; Apr. 29, 2002, eff. Dec. 1, 2002.)

ADVISORY COMMITTEE NOTES

1967 Adoption

A majority of the circuits now require the brief of the appellant to be filed within 30 days from the date on which the record is filed. But in those circuits an exchange of designations is unnecessary in the preparation of the appendix. The appellant files with his brief an appendix containing the parts of the record which he deems essential. If the appellee considers other parts essential, he includes those parts in his own appendix. Since the proposed rule requires the appellant to file with his brief an appendix containing necessary parts of the record as designated by both parties, the rule allows the appellant 40 days in order to provide time for the exchange of designations respecting the content of the appendix (see Rule 30(b)).

1970 Amendment

The time prescribed by Rule 31(a) for preparing briefs—40 days to the appellant, 30 days to the appellee—is well within the time that must ordinarily elapse in most circuits before an appeal can be reached for consideration. In those circuits, the time prescribed by the Rule should not be disturbed. But if a court of appeals maintains a current calendar, that is, if an appeal can be heard as soon as the briefs have been filed, or if the practice of the court permits the submission of appeals for preliminary consideration as soon as the briefs have been filed, the court should be free to prescribe shorter periods in the interest of expediting decision.

1986 Amendment

The amendments to Rules 31(a) and (c) are technical. No substantive change is intended.

1994 Amendments

Subdivision (b). The amendment allows a court of appeals to require the filing of a greater, as well as a lesser, number of copies of briefs. The amendment also allows the required number to be prescribed by local rule as well as by order in a particular case.

1998 Amendments

The language and organization of the rule are amended to make the rule more easily understood. In addition to changes made to improve the understanding, the advisory committee has changed language to make style and terminology consistent throughout the appellate rules. These changes are intended to by stylistic only; a substantive change is made, however, in subdivision (b).

Subdivision (a). Paragraph (a)(2) explicitly authorizes a court of appeals to shorten a briefing schedule if the court routinely considers cases on the merits promptly after the briefs are filed. Extensions of the briefing schedule, by order, are permitted under the general provisions of Rule 26(b).

Subdivision (b). The current rules says that a party who is permitted to file "typewritten ribbon and carbon copies of the brief" need only file and original and three copies of the brief. The quoted language, in conjunction with current rule 24(c), means that a party allowed to proceed in forma pauperis need not file 25 copies of the brief. Two changes are made in this subdivision. First, it is anachronistic to refer to a party who is allowed to file a typewritten brief as if that would distinguish the party from all other parties; any party is permitted to file a typewritten brief. The amended rule states directly that it applies to a party to proceed in forma pauperis. Second, the amended rule does not generally permit parties who are represented by counsel to file the lesser number of brief. Inexpensive methods of copying are generally available. Unless it would impose hardship, in which case a motion to file a lesser number should be filed, a represented party must file the usual number of briefs.

2002 Amendments

Subdivision (b). In requiring that two copies of each brief "must be served on counsel for each separately represented party," Rule 31(b) may be read to imply that copies of briefs need not be served on unrepresented parties. The Rule has been amended to clarify that briefs must be served on all parties, including those who are not represented by counsel.

Changes Made After Publication and Comments No changes were made to the text of the proposed amendment or to the Committee Note.

Rule 32. Form of Briefs, Appendices, and Other Papers

(a) Form of a Brief.

(1) Reproduction.

(A) A brief may be reproduced by any process that yields a clear black image on light paper. The paper must be opaque and unglazed. Only one side of the paper may be used.

(B) Text must be reproduced with a clarity that equals or exceeds the output of a laser printer.

(C) Photographs, illustrations, and tables may be reproduced by any method that results in a good copy of the original; a glossy finish is acceptable if the original is glossy.

(2) Cover. Except for filings by unrepresented parties, the cover of the appellant's brief must be blue; the appellee's, red; an intervenor's or amicus curiae's, green; any reply brief, gray; and any supplemental brief, tan. The front cover of a brief must contain:

(A) the number of the case centered at the top;

(B) the name of the court;

(C) the title of the case (see Rule 12(a));

(D) the nature of the proceeding (e.g., Appeal, Petition for Review) and the name of the court, agency, or board below;

(E) the title of the brief, identifying the party or parties for whom the brief is filed; and

(F) the name, office address, and telephone number of counsel representing the party for whom the brief is filed.

(3) Binding. The brief must be bound in any manner that is secure, does not obscure the text, and permits the brief to lie reasonably flat when open.

(4) Paper Size, Line Spacing, and Margins. The brief must be on 8½ by 11 inch paper. The text must be double-spaced, but quotations more than two lines long may be indented and single-spaced. Headings and footnotes may be single-spaced. Margins must be at least one inch on all four sides. Page numbers may be placed in the margins, but no text may appear there.

(5) Typeface. Either a proportionally spaced or a monospaced face may be used.

(A) A proportionally spaced face must include serifs, but sans-serif type may be used in headings and captions. A proportionally spaced face must be 14–point or larger.

(B) A monospaced face may not contain more than 10½ characters per inch.

(6) Type Styles. A brief must be set in a plain, roman style, although italics or boldface may be used for emphasis. Case names must be italicized or underlined.

(7) Length.

(A) Page limitation. A principal brief may not exceed 30 pages, or a reply brief 15 pages, unless it complies with Rule 32(a)(7)(B) and (C).

(B) Type-volume limitation.

(i) A principal brief is acceptable if:

- it contains no more than 14,000 words; or
- it uses a monospaced face and contains no more than 1,300 lines of text.

(ii) A reply brief is acceptable if it contains no more than half of the type volume specified in Rule 32(a)(7)(B)(i).

(iii) Headings, footnotes, and quotations count toward the word and line limitations. The corporate disclosure statement, table of contents, table of citations, statement with respect to oral argument, any addendum containing statutes, rules or regulations, and any certificates of counsel do not count toward the limitation.

(C) Certificate of compliance.

(i) A brief submitted under Rules 28.1(e)(2) or 32(a)(7)(B) must include a certificate by the attorney, or an unrepresented party, that the brief complies with the type-volume limitation. The person preparing the certificate may rely on the word or line count of the word-processing system used to prepare the brief. The certificate must state either:

- the number of words in the brief; or
- the number of lines of monospaced type in the brief.

(ii) Form 6 in the Appendix of Forms is a suggested form of a certificate of compliance. Use of Form 6 must be regarded as sufficient to meet the requirements of Rules 28.1(e)(3) and 32(a)(7)(C)(i).

(b) Form of an Appendix. An appendix must comply with Rule 32(a)(1), (2), (3), and (4), with the following exceptions:

(1) The cover of a separately bound appendix must be white.

(2) An appendix may include a legible photocopy of any document found in the record or of a printed judicial or agency decision.

(3) When necessary to facilitate inclusion of odd-sized documents such as technical drawings, an appendix may be a size other than 8½ by 11 inches, and need not lie reasonably flat when opened.

(c) Form of Other Papers.

(1) Motion. The form of a motion is governed by Rule 27(d).

(2) Other Papers. Any other paper, including a petition for panel rehearing and a petition for hearing or rehearing en banc, and any response to such a petition, must be reproduced in the manner prescribed by Rule 32(a), with the following exceptions:

(A) A cover is not necessary if the caption and signature page of the paper together contain the information required by Rule 32(a)(2). If a cover is used, it must be white.

(B) Rule 32(a)(7) does not apply.

(d) Signature. Every brief, motion, or other paper filed with the court must be signed by the party filing the paper or, if the party is represented, by one of the party's attorneys.

(e) Local Variation. Every court of appeals must accept documents that comply with the form requirements of this rule. By local rule or order in a particular case a court of appeals may accept documents that do not meet all of the form requirements of this rule.

(As amended Apr. 24, 1998, eff. Dec. 1, 1998; Apr. 29, 2002, eff. Dec. 1, 2002; Apr. 25, 2005, eff. Dec. 1, 2005.)

ADVISORY COMMITTEE NOTES

1967 Adoption

Only two methods of printing are now generally recognized by the circuits—standard typographic printing and the offset duplicating process (multilith). A third, mimeographing, is permitted in the Fifth Circuit. The District of Columbia, Ninth, and Tenth Circuits permit records to be reproduced by copying processes. The Committee feels that recent and impending advances in the arts of duplicating and copying warrant experimentation with less costly forms of reproduction than those now generally authorized. The proposed rule permits, in effect, the use of any process other than the carbon copy process which produces a clean, readable page. What constitutes such is left in first instance to the parties and ultimately to the court to determine. The final sentence of the first paragraph of subdivision (a) is added to allow the use of multilith, mimeograph, or other forms of copies of the reporter's original transcript whenever such are available.

1998 Amendments

In addition to amending Rule 32 to conform to uniform drafting standards, several substantive amendments are made. The Advisory Committee had been working on substantive amendments to Rule 32 for some time prior to completion of this larger project.

Subdivision (a). Form of a Brief.

Paragraph (a)(1). Reproduction.

The rule permits the use of "light" paper, not just "white" paper. Cream and buff colored paper, including recycled paper, are acceptable. The rule permits printing on only one side of the paper. Although some argue that paper could be saved by allowing double-sided printing, others argue that in order to preserve legibility a heavier weight paper would be needed, resulting in little, if any, paper saving. In addition, the blank sides of a brief are commonly used by judges and their clerks for making notes about the case.

Because photocopying is inexpensive and widely available and because use of carbon paper is now very rare, all references to the use of carbon copies have been deleted.

The rule requires that the text be reproduced with a clarity that equals or exceeds the output of a laser printer. That means that the method used must have a print resolution of 300 dots per inch (dpi) or more. This will ensure the legibility of the brief. A brief produced by a typewriter or a daisy wheel printer, as well as one produced by a laser printer, has a print resolution of 300 dpi or more. But a brief produced by a dot-matrix printer, fax machine, or portable printer that uses head or dye to transfer methods does not. Some ink jet printers are 300 dpi or more, but some are 216 dpi and would not be sufficient.

Photographs, illustrations, and tables may be reproduced by any method that results in a good copy.

Paragraph (a)(2). Cover.

The rule requires that the number of the case be centered at the top of the front cover of a brief. This will aid in identification of the brief. The idea was drawn from a local rule. The rule also requires that the title of the brief identify the party or parties on whose behalf the brief is filed. When there are multiple appellants or appellees, the information is necessary to the court. If, however, the brief is filed on behalf of all appellants or appellees, it may so indicate. Further, it may be possible to identify the class of parties on whose behalf the brief is filed. Otherwise, it may be necessary to name each party. The rule also requires that attorneys' telephone numbers appear on the front cover of a brief or appendix.

Paragraph (a)(3). Binding.

The rule requires a brief to be bound in any manner that is secure, does not obscure the text, and that permits the brief to lie reasonable flat when open. Many judges and most court employees do much of their work at computer keyboards and a brief that lies flat when open is significantly more convenient. One circuit already has such a requirement and another states a preference for it. While a spiral binding would comply with this requirement, it is not intended to be the exclusive method of binding. Stapling a brief at the upper left-hand corner also satisfies this requirement as long as it is sufficiently secure.

Paragraph (a)(4). Paper Size, Line Spacing, and Margins.

The provisions for pamphlet-size briefs are deleted because their use is so rare. If a circuit wishes to authorize their use, it has authority to do so under subdivision (d) of this rule.

Paragraph (a)(5). Typeface.

This paragraph and the next one, governing type style, are new. The existing rule simply states that a brief produced by the standard typographic process must be printed in at least 11 point type, or if produced in any other manner, the lines of text must be double spaced. Today few briefs are produced by commercial printers or by typewriters; most are produced on and printed by computer. The availability of computer fonts in a variety of sizes and styles has given rise to local rules limiting type styles. The Advisory Committee believes that some standards are needed both to ensure that all litigants have an equal opportunity to present their material and to ensure that the briefs are easily legible.

With regard to typeface there are two options; proportionally-spaced typeface or monospaced typeface.

A proportionally-spaced typeface gives a different amount of horizontal space to characters depending upon the width of the character. A capital "M" is given more horizontal space than a lower case "i". The rule requires that a proportionally-spaced typeface have serifs. Serifs are small horizontal or vertical strokes at the ends of the lines that make up the letters and numbers. Studies have shown that long passages of serif type are easier to read and comprehend than long passages of sans-serif type. The rule accordingly limits the principal sections of submissions to serif type although sans-serif type may be used in headings and captions. This is the same approach magazines, newspapers, and commercial printers take. Look at a professionally printed brief; you will find sans–serif type confined to captions, if it is used at all. The next line shows two characters enlarged for detail. The first has serifs, the second does not.

Y Y *

[* For original representation of characters, see House Document 105–269 of the 105th Congress, 2d Session dated May 11, 1998 entitled "Amendments to the Federal Rules of Appellate Procedure .... (Executive Communication No. 9072)."]

So that the type is easily legible, the rule requires a minimum type size of 14 points for proportionally-spaced typeface.

A monospaced typeface is one in which all characters have the same advance width. That means that each character is given the same horizontal space on the line. A wide letter such as a capital "M" and a narrow letter such as a lower case "i" are given the same space. Most typewriters produce mono-spaced type, and most computers also can do so using fonts with names such as "Courier."

This sentence is in a proportionally spaced font; as you can see, the m and i have different widths. *

[* For original representation of characters, see House Document 105–269 of the 105th Congress, 2d Session dated May 11, 1998 entitled "Amendments to the Federal Rules of Appellate Procedure .... (Executive Communication No. 9072)."]

This sentence is in a monospaced font; as you can see, the m and i have the same width. *

[* For original representation of characters, see House Document 105–269 of the 105th Congress, 2d Session dated May 11, 1998 entitled "Amendments to the Federal Rules of Appellate Procedure .... (Executive Communication No. 9072)."]

The rule requires use of a monospaced typeface that produces no more than 10 ½ characters per inch. A standard typewriter with pica type produces a monospaced typeface with 10 characters per inch (cpi). That is the ideal monospaced typeface. The rule permits up to 10 ½ cpi because some computer software programs contain monospaced fonts that purport to produce 10 cpi but that in fact produce slightly more than 10 cpi. In order to avoid the need to reprint a brief produced in good faith reliance upon such a program, the rule permits a bit of leeway. A monospaced typeface with no more than 10 cpi is preferred.

Paragraph (a)(6). Type Styles.

The rule requires use of plain roman, that is not italic or script, type. Italics and boldface may be used for emphasis. Italicizing case names is preferred but underlining may be used.

Paragraph (a)(7). Type-Volume Limitation.

Subparagraph (a)(7)(A) contains a safe-harbor provision. A principal brief that does not exceed 30 pages complies with the type-volume limitation without further question or certification. A reply brief that does not exceed 15 pages is similarly treated. The current limit is 50 pages but that limit was established when most briefs were produced on typewriters. The widespread use of personal computers has made a multitude of printing options available to practitioners. Use of a proportional typeface alone can greatly increase the amount of material per page as compared with use of a monospaced typeface. Even though the rule requires use of 14–point proportional type, there is great variation in the x-height of different 14–point typefaces. Selection of a typeface with a small x-height increases the amount of text per page. Computers also make possible fine gradations in spacing between lines and tight tracking between letters and words. All of this, and more, have made the 50–page limit virtually meaningless. Establishing a safe-harbor of 50 pages would permit a person who makes use of the multitude of printing "tricks" available with most personal computers to file a brief far longer than the "old" 50–page brief. Therefore, as to those briefs not subject to any other volume control than a page limit, a 30–page limit is imposed.

The limits in subparagraph (B) approximate the current 50–page limit and compliance with them is easy even for a person without a personal computer. The aim of these provisions is to create a level playing field. The rule gives every party an equal opportunity to make arguments, without permitting those with the best in-house typesetting an opportunity to expand their submissions.

The length can be determined either by counting words or lines. That is, the length of a brief is determined not by the number of pages but by the number or words or lines in the brief. This gives every party the same opportunity to present an argument without regard to the typeface used and eliminates any incentive to use footnotes or typographical "tricks" to squeeze more material onto a page.

The word counting method can be used with any typeface.

A monospaced brief can meet the volume limitation by using the word or a line count. If the line counting method is used, the number of lines may not exceed 1,300—26 lines per page in a 50–page brief. The number of lines is easily counted manually. Line counting is not sufficient if a proportionally spaced typeface is used, because the amount of material per line can vary widely.

A brief using the type-volume limitations in subparagraph (B) must include a certificate by the attorney, or party proceeding pro se, that the brief complies with the limitation. The rule permits the person preparing the certification to rely upon the word or line count of the word-processing system used to prepare the brief.

Currently, Rule 28(g) governs the length of a brief. Rule 28(g) begins with the words "[e]xcept by permission of the court," signaling that a party may file a motion to exceed the limits established in the rule. The absence of similar language in Rule 32 does not mean that the Advisory Committee intends to prohibit motions to deviate from the requirements of the rule. The Advisory Committee does not believe that any such language is needed to authorize such a motion.

Subdivision (b). Form of an Appendix.

The provisions governing the form of a brief generally apply to an appendix. The rule recognizes, however, that an appendix is usually produced by photocopying existing documents. The rule requires that the photocopies be legible.

The rule permits inclusion not only of documents from the record but also copies of a printed judicial or agency decision. If a decision that is part of the record in the case has been published, it is helpful to provide a copy of the published decision in place of a copy of the decision from the record.

Subdivision (c). Form of Other Papers.

The old rule required a petition for rehearing to be produced in the same manner as a brief or appendix. The new rule also requires that a petition for rehearing en banc and a response to either a petition for panel rehearing or a petition for rehearing en banc be prepared in the same manner. But the length limitations of paragraph (a)(7) do not apply to those documents and a cover is not required if all the formation needed by the court to properly identify the document and the parties is included in the caption or signature page.

Existing subdivision (b) states that other papers may be produced in like manner, or "they may be typewritten upon opaque, unglazed paper 8 ½ by 11 inches in size." The quoted language is deleted but that method of preparing documents is not eliminated because (a)(5)(b) permits use of standard pica type. The only change is that the new rule now specifies margins for typewritten documents.

Subdivision (d). Local Variation.

A brief that complies with the national rule should be acceptable in every court. Local rules may move in one direction only; they may authorize noncompliance with certain of the national norms. For example, a court that wishes to do so may authorize printing of briefs on both sides of the paper, or the use of smaller type size or sans-serif proportional type. A local rules may not, however, impose requirements that are not in the national rule.

2002 Amendments

Subdivision (a)(2). On occasion, a court may permit or order the parties to file supplemental briefs addressing an issue that was not addressed—or adequately addressed—in the principal briefs. Rule 32(a)(2) has been amended to require that tan covers be used on such supplemental briefs. The amendment is intended to promote uniformity in federal appellate practice. At present, the local rules of the circuit courts conflict. *See, e.g.*, D.C. Cir. R. 28(g) (requiring yellow covers on supplemental briefs); 11th Cir. R. 32, I.O.P. 1 (requiring white covers on supplemental briefs).

Changes Made After Publication and Comments No changes were made to the text of the proposed amendment or to the Committee Note.

Subdivision (a)(7)(C). If the principal brief of a party exceeds 30 pages, or if the reply brief of a party exceeds 15 pages, Rule 32(a)(7)(C) provides that the party or the party's attorney must certify that the brief complies with the type-volume limitation of Rule 32(a)(7)(B). Rule 32(a)(7)(C) has been amended to refer to Form 6 (which has been added to the Appendix of Forms) and to provide that a party or attorney who uses Form 6 has complied with Rule 32(a)(7)(C). No court may provide to the contrary, in its local rules or otherwise.

Form 6 requests not only the information mandated by Rule 32(a)(7)(C), but also information that will assist courts in enforcing the typeface requirements of Rule 32(a)(5) and the type style requirements of Rule 32(a)(6). Parties and attorneys are not required to use Form 6, but they are encouraged to do so.

Subdivision (c)(2)(A). Under Rule 32(c)(2)(A), a cover is not required on a petition for panel rehearing, petition for hearing or rehearing en banc, answer to a petition for panel rehearing, response to a petition for hearing or rehearing en banc, or any other paper. Rule 32(d) makes it clear that no court can require that a cover be used on any of these papers. However, nothing prohibits a court from providing in its local rules that if a cover on one of these papers is "voluntarily" used, it must be a particular color. Several circuits have adopted such local rules. *See, e.g.*, Fed. Cir. R. 35(c) (requiring yellow covers on petitions for hearing or rehearing en banc and brown covers on responses to such petitions); Fed. Cir. R. 40(a) (requiring yellow covers on petitions for panel rehearing and brown covers on answers to such petitions); 7th Cir. R. 28 (requiring blue covers on petitions for rehearing filed by appellants or answers to such petitions, and requiring red covers on petitions for rehearing filed by appellees or answers to such petitions); 9th Cir. R. 40–1 (requiring blue covers on petitions for panel rehearing filed by appellants and red covers on answers to such petitions, and requiring red covers on petitions for panel rehearing filed by appellees and blue covers on answers to such petitions); 11th Cir. R. 35–6 (requiring white covers on petitions for hearing or rehearing en banc).

These conflicting local rules create a hardship for counsel who practice in more than one circuit. For that reason, Rule 32(c)(2)(A) has been amended to provide that if a party chooses to use a cover on a paper that is not required to have one, that cover must be white. The amendment is intended to preempt all local rulemaking on the subject of cover colors and thereby promote uniformity in federal appellate practice.

Changes Made After Publication and Comments No changes were made to the text of the proposed amendment or to the Committee Note.

Subdivisions (d) and (e). Former subdivision (d) has been redesignated as subdivision (e), and a new subdivision (d) has been added. The new subdivision (d) requires that every brief, motion, or other paper filed with the court be signed by the attorney or unrepresented party who files it, much as Fed. R. Civ. P. 11(a) imposes a signature requirement on papers filed in district court. Only the original copy of every paper must be signed. An appendix filed with the court does not have to be signed at all.

By requiring a signature, subdivision (d) ensures that a readily identifiable attorney or party takes responsibility for every paper. The courts of appeals already have authority to sanction attorneys and parties who file papers that contain misleading or frivolous assertions, *see, e.g.*, 28 U.S.C. § 1912, Fed. R. App. P. 38 & 46(b)(1)(B), and thus subdivision (d) has not been amended to incorporate provisions similar to those found in Fed. R. Civ. P. 11(b) and 11(c).

Changes Made After Publication and Comments No changes were made to the text of the proposed amendment. A line was added to the Committee Note to clarify that only the original copy of a paper needs to be signed.

2005 Amendments

Subdivision (a)(7)(C). Rule 32(a)(7)(C) has been amended to add cross-references to new Rule 28.1, which governs briefs filed in cases involving cross-appeals. Rule 28.1(e)(2) prescribes type-volume limitations that apply to such briefs, and Rule 28.1(e)(3) requires parties to certify compliance with those type-volume limitations under Rule 32(a)(7)(C).

Rule 32.1. Citing Judicial Dispositions

(a) Citation Permitted. A court may not prohibit or restrict the citation of federal judicial opinions, orders, judgments, or other written dispositions that have been:

(i) designated as "unpublished," "not for publication," "non-precedential," "not precedent," or the like; and

(ii) issued on or after January 1, 2007.

(b) Copies Required. If a party cites a federal judicial opinion, order, judgment, or other written disposition that is not available in a publicly accessible electronic database, the party must file and serve a copy of that opinion, order, judgment, or disposition with the brief or other paper in which it is cited.

(Added Apr. 12, 2006, eff. Dec. 1, 2006.)

ADVISORY COMMITTEE NOTES

2006 Adoption

Rule 32.1 is a new rule addressing the citation of judicial opinions, orders, judgments, or other written dispositions that have been designated by a federal court as "unpublished," "not for publication," "non-precedential," "not precedent," or the like. This Committee Note will refer to these dispositions collectively as "unpublished" opinions.

Rule 32.1 is extremely limited. It does not require any court to issue an unpublished opinion or forbid any court from doing so. It does not dictate the circumstances under which a court may choose to designate an opinion as "unpublished" or specify the procedure that a court must follow in making that determination. It says nothing about what effect a court must give to one of its unpublished opinions or to the unpublished opinions of another court. Rule 32.1 addresses only the *citation* of federal judicial dispositions that have been *designated* as "unpublished" or "non-precedential" — whether or not those dispositions have been published in some way or are precedential in some sense.

Subdivision (a). Every court of appeals has allowed unpublished opinions to be cited in some circumstances, such as to support a contention of issue preclusion or claim preclusion. But the circuits have differed dramatically with respect to the restrictions that they have placed on the citation of unpublished opinions for their persuasive value. Some circuits have freely permitted such citation, others have discouraged it but permitted it in limited circumstances, and still others have forbidden it altogether.

Rule 32.1(a) is intended to replace these inconsistent standards with one uniform rule. Under Rule 32.1(a), a court of appeals may not prohibit a party from citing an unpublished opinion of a federal court for its persuasive value or for any other reason. In addition, under Rule 32.1(a), a court may not place any restriction on the citation of such opinions. For example, a court may not instruct parties that the citation of unpublished opinions is discouraged, nor may a court forbid parties to cite unpublished opinions when a published opinion addresses the same issue.

Rule 32.1(a) applies only to unpublished opinions issued on or after January 1, 2007. The citation of unpublished opinions issued before January 1, 2007, will continue to be governed by the local rules of the circuits.

Subdivision (b). Under Rule 32.1(b), a party who cites an opinion of a federal court must provide a copy of that opinion to the court of appeals and to the other parties, unless that opinion is available in a publicly accessible electronic database — such as a commercial database maintained by a legal research service or a database maintained by a court. A party who is required under Rule 32.1(b) to provide a copy of an opinion must file and serve the copy with the brief or other paper in which the opinion is cited. Rule 32.1(b) applies to all unpublished opinions, regardless of when they were issued.

Rule 33. Appeal Conferences

The court may direct the attorneys—and, when appropriate, the parties—to participate in one or more conferences to address any matter that may aid in disposing of the proceedings, including simplifying the issues and discussing settlement. A judge or other person designated by the court may preside over the conference, which may be conducted in person or by telephone. Before a settlement conference, the attorneys must consult with their clients and obtain as much authority as feasible to settle the case. The court may, as a result of the conference, enter an order controlling the course of the proceedings or implementing any settlement agreement.

(As amended Apr. 29, 1994, eff. Dec. 1, 1994; Apr. 24, 1998, eff. Dec. 1, 1998.)

ADVISORY COMMITTEE NOTES

1967 Adoption

The uniform rule for review or enforcement of orders of administrative agencies, boards, commissions or officers (see the general note following Rule 15) authorizes a prehearing conference in agency review proceedings. The same considerations which make a prehearing conference desirable in such proceedings may be present in certain cases on appeal from the district courts. The proposed rule is based upon subdivision 11 of the present uniform rule for review of agency orders.

1994 Amendment

Rule 33 has been entirely rewritten. The new rule makes several changes.

The caption of the rule has been changed from "Prehearing Conference" to "Appeal Conferences" to reflect the fact that occasionally a conference is held after oral argument.

The rule permits the court to require the parties to attend the conference in appropriate cases. The Committee does not contemplate that attendance of the parties will become routine, but in certain instances the parties' presence can be useful. The language of the rule is broad enough to allow a court to determine that an executive or an employee (other than the general counsel) of a corporation or government agency with authority regarding the matter at issue, constitutes "the party."

The rule includes the possibility of settlement among the possible conference topics.

The rule recognizes that conferences are often held by telephone.

The rule allows a judge or other person designated by the court to preside over a conference. A number of local rules permit persons other than judges to preside over conferences. 1st Cir. R. 47.5; 6th Cir. R. 18; 8th Cir. R. 33A; 9th Cir. R. 33–1; and 10th Cir. R. 33.

The rule requires an attorney to consult with his or her client before a settlement conference and obtain as much authority as feasible to settle the case. An attorney can never settle a case without his or her client's consent. Certain entities, especially government entities, have particular difficulty obtaining authority to settle a case. The rule requires counsel to obtain only as much authority "as feasible."

1998 Amendments

The language of the rule is amended to make the rule more easily understood. In addition to changes made to improve the understanding, the Advisory Committee has changed language to make style and terminology consistent throughout the appellate rules. These changes are intended to be stylistic only.

Rule 34. Oral Argument

(a) In General.

(1) Party's Statement. Any party may file, or a court may require by local rule, a statement explaining why oral argument should, or need not, be permitted.

(2) Standards. Oral argument must be allowed in every case unless a panel of three judges who have examined the briefs and record unanimously agrees that oral argument is unnecessary for any of the following reasons:

(A) the appeal is frivolous;

(B) the dispositive issue or issues have been authoritatively decided; or

(C) the facts and legal arguments are adequately presented in the briefs and record, and the decisional process would not be significantly aided by oral argument.

(b) Notice of Argument; Postponement. The clerk must advise all parties whether oral argument will be scheduled, and, if so, the date, time, and place for it, and the time allowed for each side. A motion to postpone the argument or to allow longer argument must be filed reasonably in advance of the hearing date.

(c) Order and Contents of Argument. The appellant opens and concludes the argument. Counsel must not read at length from briefs, records, or authorities.

(d) Cross-Appeals and Separate Appeals. If there is a cross-appeal, Rule 28.1(b) determines which party is the appellant and which is the appellee for purposes of oral argument. Unless the court directs otherwise, a cross-appeal or separate appeal must be argued when the initial appeal is argued. Separate parties should avoid duplicative argument.

(e) Nonappearance of a Party. If the appellee fails to appear for argument, the court must hear appellant's argument. If the appellant fails to appear for argument, the court may hear the appellee's argument. If neither party appears, the case will be decided on the briefs, unless the court orders otherwise.

(f) Submission on Briefs. The parties may agree to submit a case for decision on the briefs, but the court may direct that the case be argued.

(g) Use of Physical Exhibits at Argument; Removal. Counsel intending to use physical exhibits other than documents at the argument must arrange to place them in the courtroom on the day of the argument before the court convenes. After the argument, counsel must remove the exhibits from the courtroom, unless the court directs otherwise. The clerk may destroy or dispose of the exhibits if counsel does not reclaim them within a reasonable time after the clerk gives notice to remove them.

(As amended Apr. 30, 1979, eff. Aug. 1, 1979; Mar. 10, 1986, eff. July 1, 1986; Apr. 30, 1991, eff. Dec. 1, 1991; Apr. 22, 1993, eff. Dec. 1, 1993; Apr. 24, 1998, eff. Dec. 1, 1998; Apr. 25, 2005, eff. Dec. 1, 2005.)

ADVISORY COMMITTEE NOTES

1967 Adoption

A majority of circuits now limit oral argument to thirty minutes for each side, with the provision that additional time may be made available upon request. The Committee is of the view that thirty minutes to each side is sufficient in most cases, but that where additional time is necessary it should be freely granted on a proper showing of cause therefor. It further feels that the matter of time should be left ultimately to each court of appeals, subject to the spirit of the rule that a reasonable time should be allowed for argument. The term "side" is used to indicate that the time allowed by the rule is afforded to opposing interests rather than to individual parties. Thus if multiple appellants or appellees have a common interest, they constitute only a single side. If counsel for multiple parties who constitute a single side feel that additional time is necessary, they may request it. In other particulars this rule follows the usual practice among the circuits. See 3d Cir. Rule 31 [rule 31, U.S.Ct. of App.3rd Cir.]; 6th Cir. Rule 20 [rule 20, U.S.Ct. of App.6th Cir.]; 10th Cir. Rule 23 [rule 23, U.S.Ct. of App.10th Cir.].

1979 Amendment

The proposed amendment, patterned after the recommendations in the Report of the Commission on Revision of the Federal Court Appellate System, *Structure and Internal Procedures: Recommendations for Change,* 1975, created by Public Law 489 of the 92nd Cong.2nd Sess., 86 Stat. 807, sets forth general principles and minimum standards to be observed in formulating any local rule.

1986 Amendment

The amendments to Rules 34(a) and (e) are technical. No substantive change is intended.

1991 Amendment

Subdivision (d). The amendment of subdivision (d) conforms this rule with the amendment of Rule 28(h).

1993 Amendment

Subdivision (c). The amendment deletes the requirement that the opening argument must include a fair statement of the case. The Committee proposed the change because in some circuits the court does not want appellants to give such statements. In those circuits, the rule is not followed and is misleading. Nevertheless, the Committee does not want the deletion of the requirement to indicate disapproval of the practice. Those circuits that desire a statement of the case may continue the practice.

1998 Amendments

The language of the rule is amended to make the rule more easily understood. In addition to changes made to improve the understanding, the Advisory Committee has changed language to make style and terminology consistent throughout the appellate rules. These changes are intended to be stylistic only. Substantive changes are made in subdivision (a).

Subdivision (a). Currently subdivision (a) says that oral argument must be permitted unless, applying a local rule, a panel of three judges unanimously agrees that oral argument is not necessary. Rule 34 then outlines the criteria to be used to determine whether oral argument is needed and requires any local rule to "conform substantially" to the "minimum standard[s]" established in the national rule. The amendments omit the local rule requirement and make the criteria applicable by force of the national rule. The local rule is an unnecessary instrument.

Paragraph (a)(2) states that one reason for deciding that oral argument is unnecessary is that the dispositive issue has been authoritatively decided. the amended language no longer states that the issue must have been "recently" decided. The Advisory Committee does not intend any substantive change, but thinks that the use of "recently" may be misleading.

Subdivision (d). A cross–reference to Rule 28(h) has been substituted for a reiteration of the provisions of Rule 28(h).

2005 Amendments

Subdivision (d). A cross-reference in subdivision (d) has been changed to reflect the fact that, as part of an effort to collect within one rule all provisions regarding briefing in cases involving cross-appeals, former Rule 28(h) has been abrogated and its contents moved to new Rule 28.1(b).

Rule 35. En Banc Determination

(a) When Hearing or Rehearing En Banc May Be Ordered. A majority of the circuit judges who are in regular active service and who are not disqualified may order that an appeal or other proceeding be heard or reheard by the court of appeals en banc. An en banc hearing or rehearing is not favored and ordinarily will not be ordered unless:

(1) en banc consideration is necessary to secure or maintain uniformity of the court's decisions; or

(2) the proceeding involves a question of exceptional importance.

(b) Petition for Hearing or Rehearing En Banc. A party may petition for a hearing or rehearing en banc.

(1) The petition must begin with a statement that either:

(A) the panel decision conflicts with a decision of the United States Supreme Court or of the court to which the petition is addressed (with citation to the conflicting case or cases) and consideration by the full court is therefore necessary to secure and maintain uniformity of the court's decisions; or

(B) the proceeding involves one or more questions of exceptional importance, each of which must be concisely stated; for example, a petition may assert that a proceeding presents a question of exceptional importance if it involves an issue on which the panel decision conflicts with the authoritative decisions of other United States Courts of Appeals that have addressed the issue.

(2) Except by the court's permission, a petition for an en banc hearing or rehearing must not exceed 15 pages, excluding material not counted under Rule 32.

(3) For purposes of the page limit in Rule 35(b)(2), if a party files both a petition for panel rehearing and a petition for rehearing en banc, they are considered a single document even if they are filed separately, unless separate filing is required by local rule.

(c) Time for Petition for Hearing or Rehearing En Banc. A petition that an appeal be heard initially en banc must be filed by the date when the appellee's brief is due. A petition for a rehearing en banc must be filed within the time prescribed by Rule 40 for filing a petition for rehearing.

(d) Number of Copies. The number of copies to be filed must be prescribed by local rule and may be altered by order in a particular case.

(e) Response. No response may be filed to a petition for an en banc consideration unless the court orders a response.

(f) Call for a Vote. A vote need not be taken to determine whether the case will be heard or reheard en banc unless a judge calls for a vote.

(As amended Apr. 30, 1979, eff. Aug. 1, 1979; Apr. 29, 1994, eff. Dec. 1, 1994; Apr. 24, 1998, eff. Dec. 1, 1998; Apr. 25, 2005, eff. Dec. 1, 2005.)

ADVISORY COMMITTEE NOTES

1967 Adoption

Statutory authority for in banc hearings is found in 28 U.S.C. § 46(c). The proposed rule is responsive to the Supreme Court's view in *Western Pacific Ry. Corp. v. Western Pacific Ry. Co.*, 345 U.S. 247, 73 S.Ct. 656, 97 L.Ed. 986 (1953), that litigants should be free to suggest that a particular case is appropriate for consideration by all the judges of a court of appeals. The rule is addressed to the procedure whereby a party may suggest the appropriateness of convening the court in banc. It does not affect the power of a court of appeals to initiate in banc hearings *sua sponte*.

The provision that a vote will not be taken as a result of the suggestion of the party unless requested by a judge of the court in regular active service or by a judge who was a member of the panel that rendered a decision sought to be reheard is intended to make it clear that a suggestion of a party as such does not require any action by the court. See *Western Pacific Ry. Corp. v. Western Pacific Ry. Co.*, supra, 345 U.S. at 262, 73 S.Ct. 656. The rule merely authorizes a suggestion, imposes a time limit on suggestions for rehearings in banc, and provides that suggestions will be directed to the judges of the court in regular active service.

In practice, the suggestion of a party that a case be reheard in banc is frequently contained in a petition for rehearing, commonly styled "petition for rehearing in banc." Such a petition is in fact merely a petition for a rehearing, with a suggestion that the case be reheard in banc. Since no response to the suggestion, as distinguished from the petition for rehearing, is required, the panel which heard the case may quite properly dispose of the petition without reference to the suggestion. In such a case the fact that no response has been made to the suggestion does not affect the finality of the judgment or the issuance of the mandate, and the final sentence of the rule expressly so provides.

1979 Amendment

Under the present rule there is no specific provision for a response to a suggestion that an appeal be heard in banc. This has led to some uncertainty as to whether such a response may be filed. The proposed amendment would resolve this uncertainty.

While the present rule provides a time limit for suggestions for rehearing in banc, it does not deal with the timing of a request that the appeal be heard in banc initially. The proposed amendment fills this gap as well, providing that the suggestion must be made by the date of which the appellee's brief is filed.

Provision is made for circulating the suggestions to members of the panel despite the fact that senior judges on the panel would not be entitled to vote on whether a suggestion will be granted.

1994 Amendment

Subdivision (d). Subdivision (d) is added; it authorizes the courts of appeals to prescribe the number of copies of suggestions for hearing or rehearing in banc that must be filed. Because the number of copies needed depends directly upon the number of judges in the circuit, local rules are the best vehicle for setting the required number of copies.

1998 Amendments

The language and organization of the rule are amended to make the rule more easily understood. In addition to changes made to improve the understanding, the Advisory Committee has changed language to make style and terminology consistent throughout the appellate rules. These changes are intended to be stylistic only.

Several substantive changes are made to this rule, however.

One of the purposes of the substantive amendments is to treat a request for a rehearing en banc like a petition for panel rehearing so that a request for a rehearing en banc will suspend the finality of the court of appeals' judgment and delay the running of the period for filing a petition for writ of certiorari. Companion amendments are made to Rule 41.

Subdivision (a). The title of this subdivision is changed from "When hearing or rehearing in banc *will* be ordered" to "When Hearing or Rehearing En Banc *May* Be Ordered." The change emphasizes the discretion a court has with regard to granting en banc review.

Subdivision (b). The term "petition" for rehearing en banc is substituted for the term "suggestion" for rehearing en banc. The terminology change reflects the Committee's intent to treat similarly a petition for panel rehearing and a request for a rehearing en banc. The terminology change also delays the running of the time for filing a petition for a writ of certiorari because Sur. Ct. R. 13.3 says:

> if a petition for rehearing is timely filed in the lower court by any party, the time to file the petition for a writ of certiorari for all parties...runs from the date of the denial of the petition for rehearing or, if the petition for rehearing is granted, the subsequent entry of judgment.

The amendments also require each petition for en banc consideration to begin with a statement concisely demonstrating that the case meets the usual criteria for en banc consideration. It is the Committee's hope that requiring such a statement will cause the drafter of a petition to focus on the narrow grounds that support en banc consideration and to realize that a petition should not be filed unless the case meets those rigid standards.

Intercircuit conflict is cited as one reason for asserting that a proceeding involves a question of "exceptional importance." Intercircuit conflicts create problems. When the circuits construe the same federal law differently, parties' rights and duties depend upon where a case is litigated. Given the increase in the number of cases decided by the federal courts and the limitation on the number of cases the Supreme Court can hear, conflicts between the circuits may remain unresolved by the Supreme Court for an extended period of time. The existence of an intercircuit conflict often generates additional litigation in the other circuits as well as in the circuits that are already in conflict. Although an en banc proceeding will not necessarily prevent intercircuit conflicts, an en banc proceeding provides a safeguard against unnecessary intercircuit conflicts.

Some circuits have had rules or internal operating procedures that recognize a conflict with another circuit as a legitimate basis for granting a rehearing en banc. An intercircuit conflict may present a question of "exceptional importance" because of the costs that intercircuit conflicts impose on the system as a whole, in addition to the significance of the issues involved. It is not, however, the Committee's intent to make the granting of a hearing or rehearing en banc mandatory whenever there is an intercircuit conflict.

The amendment states that "a petition may assert that a proceeding presents a question of exceptional importance if it involves an issue on which the panel decision conflicts with the authoritative decisions of every other United States Court of Appeals that has addressed the issue." That language contemplates two situations in which a rehearing en banc may be appropriate. The first is when a panel decision creates a conflict. A panel decision creates a conflict when it conflicts with the decisions of all other circuits that have considered the issue. If a panel decision simply joins one side of an already existing conflict, a rehearing en banc may not be as important because it cannot avoid the conflict. The Second situation that may be a strong candidate for a rehearing en banc is one in which the circuit persists in a conflict created by a pre-existing decision of the same circuit and no other circuits have joined on that side of the conflict. The amendment states that the conflict must be with an "authoritative" decision of another circuit. "Authoritative" is used rather than "published" because in some circuits unpublished opinions may be treated as authoritative.

Counsel are reminded that their duty is fully discharged without filing a petition for rehearing en banc unless the case meets the rigid standards of subdivision (a) of this rule and even then the granting of a petition is entirely within the court's discretion.

Paragraph (2) of this subdivision establishes a maximum length for a petition. Fifteen pages is the length currently used in several circuits. Each request for en banc consideration must be studied by every active judge of the court and is a serious call on limited judicial resources. The extraordinary nature of the issue or the threat to uniformity of the court's decision can be established in most cases in less than fifteen pages. A court may shorten the maximum length on a case by case basis but the rule does not permit a circuit to shorten the length by local rule. The Committee has retained page limits rather than using word or line counts similar to those in amended Rule 32 because there has not been a serious enough problem to justify importing the word and line–count and typeface requirement that are applicable to briefs into other contexts.

Paragraph (3), although similar to (2), is separate because it deals with those instances in which a party files both a petition for rehearing en banc under this rule and a petition for panel rehearing under Rule 40.

To improve the clarity of the rule, the material dealing with filing a response to a petition and with voting on a petition have been moved to new subdivisions (e) and (f).

Subdivision (c). Two changes are made in this subdivision. First, the sentence stating that a request for a rehearing en banc does not affect the finality of the judgment or stay the issuance of the mandate is deleted. Second, the language permitting a party to include a request for rehearing en banc in a petition for panel rehearing is deleted. The Committee believes that those circuits that want to require two separate documents should have the option to do so.

Subdivision (e). This is a new subdivision. The substance of the subdivision, however, was drawn from former subdivision (b). The only changes are stylistic; no substantive changes are intended.

Subdivision (f). This is a new subdivision. The substance of the subdivision, however, was drawn from former subdivision (b).

Because of the discretionary nature of the en banc procedure, the filing of a suggestion for rehearing en banc has not required a vote; a vote is taken only when requested by a judge. It is not the Committee's intent to change the discretionary nature of the procedure or to require a vote on a petition for rehearing en banc. The rule continues, therefore, to provide that a court is not obligated to vote on such petitions. It is necessary, however, that each court develop a procedure for disposing of such petitions because they will suspend the finality of the court's judgment and toll the time for filing a petition for certiorari.

Former subdivision (b) contained language directing the clerk to distribute a "suggestion" to certain judges and indicating which judges may call for a vote. New subdivision (f) does not address those issues because they deal with internal court procedures.

2005 Amendments

Subdivision (a). Two national standards—28 U.S.C. § 46(c) and Rule 35(a)—provide that a hearing or rehearing en banc may be ordered by "a majority of the circuit judges who are in regular active service." Although these standards apply to all of the courts of appeals, the circuits are deeply divided over the interpretation of this language when one or more active judges are disqualified.

The Supreme Court has never addressed this issue. In *Shenker v. Baltimore & Ohio R.R. Co.*, 374 U.S. 1 (1963), the Court rejected a petitioner's claim that his rights under § 46(c) had been violated when the Third Circuit refused to rehear his case en banc. The Third Circuit had 8 active judges at the time; 4 voted in favor of rehearing the case, 2 against, and 2 abstained. No judge was disqualified. The Supreme Court ruled against the petitioner, holding, in essence, that § 46(c) did not provide a cause of action, but instead simply gave litigants "the right to know the administrative machinery that will be followed and the right to suggest that the *en banc* procedure be set in motion in his case." *Id.* at 5. *Shenker* did stress that a court of appeals has broad discretion in establishing internal procedures to handle requests for rehearings—or, as *Shenker* put it, " 'to devise its own administrative machinery to provide the *means* whereby a majority may order such a hearing.' " *Id.* (quoting *Western Pac. R.R. Corp. v. Western Pac. R.R. Co.*, 345 U.S. 247, 250 (1953) (emphasis added)). But *Shenker* did not address what is meant by "a majority" in § 46(c) (or Rule 35(a), which did not yet exist)—and *Shenker* certainly did not suggest that the phrase should have different meanings in different circuits.

In interpreting that phrase, 7 of the courts of appeals follow the "absolute majority" approach. *See* Marie Leary, Defining the "Majority" Vote Requirement in Federal Rule of Appellate Procedure 35(a) for Rehearings En Banc in the United States Courts of Appeals 8 tbl.1 (Federal Judicial Center 2002). Under this approach, disqualified judges are counted in the base in calculating whether a majority of judges have voted to hear a case en banc. Thus, in a circuit with 12 active judges, 7 must vote to hear a case en banc. If 5 of the 12 active judges are disqualified, all 7 non-disqualified judges must vote to hear the case en banc. The votes of 6 of the 7 non-disqualified judges are not enough, as 6 is not a majority of 12.

Six of the courts of appeals follow the "case majority" approach. *Id.* Under this approach, disqualified judges are not counted in the base in calculating whether a majority of judges have voted to hear a case en banc. Thus, in a case in which 5 of a circuit's 12 active judges are disqualified, only 4 judges (a majority of the 7 non-disqualified judges) must vote to hear a case en banc. (The First and Third Circuits explicitly qualify the case majority approach by providing that a case cannot be heard en banc unless a majority of all active judges—disqualified and non-disqualified—are eligible to participate.)

Rule 35(a) has been amended to adopt the case majority approach as a uniform national interpretation of § 46(c). The federal rules of practice and procedure exist to "maintain consistency," which Congress has equated with "promot[ing] the interest of justice." 28 U.S.C. § 2073(b). The courts of appeals should not follow two inconsistent approaches in deciding whether sufficient votes exist to hear a case en banc, especially when there is a governing statute and governing rule that apply to all circuits and that use identical terms, and especially when there is nothing about the local conditions of each circuit that justifies conflicting approaches.

The case majority approach represents the better interpretation of the phrase "the circuit judges . . . in regular active service" in the first sentence of § 46(c). The second sentence of § 46(c)—which defines which judges are eligible to participate in a case being heard or reheard en banc—uses the similar expression "all circuit judges in regular active service." It is clear that "all circuit judges in regular active service" in the second sentence does not include disqualified judges, as disqualified judges clearly cannot participate in a case being heard or reheard en banc. Therefore, assuming that two nearly identical phrases appearing in adjacent sentences in a statute should be interpreted in the same way, the best reading of "the circuit judges . . . in regular active service" in the first sentence of § 46(c) is that it, too, does not include disqualified judges.

Complete Annotation Materials, see Title 28 U.S.C.A.

This interpretation of § 46(c) is bolstered by the fact that the case majority approach has at least two major advantages over the absolute majority approach:

First, under the absolute majority approach, a disqualified judge is, as a practical matter, counted as voting against hearing a case en banc. This defeats the purpose of recusal. To the extent possible, the disqualification of a judge should not result in the equivalent of a vote for or against hearing a case en banc.

Second, the absolute majority approach can leave the en banc court helpless to overturn a panel decision with which almost all of the circuit's active judges disagree. For example, in a case in which 5 of a circuit's 12 active judges are disqualified, the case cannot be heard en banc even if 6 of the 7 non-disqualified judges strongly disagree with the panel opinion. This permits one active judge—perhaps sitting on a panel with a visiting judge—effectively to control circuit precedent, even over the objection of all of his or her colleagues. *See Gulf Power Co. v. FCC*, 226 F.3d 1220, 1222–23 (11th Cir. 2000) (Carnes, J., concerning the denial of reh'g en banc), *rev'd sub nom. National Cable & Telecomm. Ass'n, Inc. v. Gulf Power Co.*, 534 U.S. 327 (2002). Even though the en banc court may, in a future case, be able to correct an erroneous legal interpretation, the en banc court will never be able to correct the injustice inflicted by the panel on the parties to the case. Moreover, it may take many years before sufficient non-disqualified judges can be mustered to overturn the panel's erroneous legal interpretation. In the meantime, the lower courts of the circuit must apply—and the citizens of the circuit must conform their behavior to—an interpretation of the law that almost all of the circuit's active judges believe is incorrect.

The amendment to Rule 35(a) is not meant to alter or affect the quorum requirement of 28 U.S.C. § 46(d). In particular, the amendment is not intended to foreclose the possibility that § 46(d) might be read to require that more than half of all circuit judges in regular active service be eligible to participate in order for the court to hear or rehear a case en banc.

Rule 36. Entry of Judgment; Notice

(a) Entry. A judgment is entered when it is noted on the docket. The clerk must prepare, sign, and enter the judgment:

(1) after receiving the court's opinion—but if settlement of the judgment's form is required, after final settlement; or

(2) if a judgment is rendered without an opinion, as the court instructs.

(b) Notice. On the date when judgment is entered, the clerk must serve on all parties a copy of the opinion—or the judgment, if no opinion was written—and a notice of the date when the judgment was entered.

(As amended Apr. 24, 1998, eff. Dec. 1, 1998; Apr. 29, 2002, eff. Dec. 1, 2002.)

ADVISORY COMMITTEE NOTES

1967 Adoption

This is the typical rule. See 1st Cir. Rule 29 [rule 29, U.S.Ct. of App. 1st Cir.]; 3d Cir. Rule 32 [rule 32, U.S.Ct. of App. 3rd Cir.]; 6th Cir. Rule 21 [rule 21, U.S.Ct. of App. 6th Cir.]. At present, uncertainty exists as to the date of entry of judgment when the opinion directs subsequent settlement of the precise terms of the judgment, a common practice in cases involving enforcement of agency orders. See Stern and Gressman, Supreme Court Practice, p. 203 (3d Ed., 1962). The principle of finality suggests that in such cases entry of judgment should be delayed until approval of the judgment in final form.

1998 Amendments

The language and organization of the rule are amended to make the rule more easily understood. In addition to changes made to improve the understanding, the Advisory Committee has changed language to make style and terminology consistent throughout the appellate rules. These changes are intended to be stylistic only.

2002 Amendments

Subdivision (b). Subdivision (b) has been amended so that the clerk may use electronic means to serve a copy of the opinion or judgment or to serve notice of the date when judgment was entered upon parties who have consented to such service.

Changes Made After Publication and Comments No changes were made to the text of the proposed amendment or to the Committee Note.

Rule 37. Interest on Judgment

(a) When the Court Affirms. Unless the law provides otherwise, if a money judgment in a civil case is affirmed, whatever interest is allowed by law is payable from the date when the district court's judgment was entered.

(b) When the Court Reverses. If the court modifies or reverses a judgment with a direction that a money judgment be entered in the district court, the mandate must contain instructions about the allowance of interest.

(As amended Apr. 24, 1998, eff. Dec. 1, 1998.)

ADVISORY COMMITTEE NOTES

1967 Adoption

The first sentence makes it clear that if a money judgment is affirmed in the court of appeals, the interest which attaches to money judgments by force of law (see 28 U.S.C. § 1961 and § 2411) upon their initial entry is payable as if no appeal had been taken, whether or not the mandate makes mention of interest. There has been some confusion on this point. *See Blair v. Durham*, 139 F.2d 260 (6th Cir., 1943) and cases cited therein.

In reversing or modifying the judgment of the district court, the court of appeals may direct the entry of a money judgment, as, for example, when the court of appeals reverses a judgment notwithstanding the verdict and directs entry of judgment on the verdict. In such a case the question may arise as to whether interest is to run from the date of entry of the judgment directed by the court of appeals or from the date on which the judgment would have been entered in the district court except for the erroneous ruling corrected on appeal. In *Briggs v. Pennsylvania R. Co.*, 334 U.S. 304, 68 S.Ct. 1039, 92 L.Ed. 1403 (1948), the Court held that where the mandate of the court of appeals directed entry of judgment upon a verdict but made no mention of interest from the date of the verdict to the date of the entry of the judgment directed by the mandate, the district court was powerless to add such interest. The second sentence of the proposed rule is a reminder to the court, the clerk and counsel of the *Briggs* rule. Since the rule directs that the matter of interest be disposed of by the mandate, in cases where interest is simply overlooked, a party who conceives himself entitled to interest from a date other than the date of entry of judgment in accordance with the mandate should be entitled to seek recall of the mandate for determination of the question.

1998 Amendments

The language and organization of the rule are amended to make the rule more easily understood. In addition to changes made to improve the understanding, the Advisory Committee has changed language to make style and terminology consistent throughout the appellate rules. These changes are intended to be stylistic only.

Rule 38. Frivolous Appeal—Damages and Costs

If a court of appeals determines that an appeal is frivolous, it may, after a separately filed motion or notice from the court and reasonable opportunity to respond, award just damages and single or double costs to the appellee.

(As amended Apr. 29, 1994, eff. Dec. 1, 1994; Apr. 24, 1998, eff. Dec. 1, 1998.)

ADVISORY COMMITTEE NOTES

1967 Adoption

Compare 28 U.S.C. § 1912. While both the statute and the usual rule on the subject by courts of appeals (Fourth Circuit Rule 20 [rule 20, U.S.Ct. of App. 4th Cir.] is a typical rule) speak of "damages for delay," the courts of appeals quite properly allow damages, attorney's fees and other expenses incurred by an appellee if the appeal is frivolous without requiring a showing that the appeal resulted in delay. See *Dunscombe v. Sayle*, 340 F.2d 311 (5th Cir., 1965), cert. den., 382 U.S. 814, 86 S.Ct. 32, 15 L.Ed.2d 62 (1965); *Lowe v. Willacy*, 239 F.2d 179 (9th Cir., 1956); *Griffin Wellpoint Corp. v. Munro-Langstroth, Inc.*, 269 F.2d 64 (1st Cir., 1959); *Ginsburg v. Stern*, 295 F.2d 698 (3d Cir., 1961). The subjects of interest and damages are separately regulated, contrary to the present practice of combining the two (see Fourth Circuit Rule 20) to make it clear that the awards are distinct and independent. Interest is provided for by law; damages are awarded by the court in its discretion in the case of a frivolous appeal as a matter of justice to the appellee and as a penalty against the appellant.

1994 Amendments

The amendment requires that before a court of appeals may impose sanctions, the person to be sanctioned must have notice and an opportunity to respond. The amendment reflects the basic principle enunciated in the Supreme Court's opinion in *Roadway Express, Inc. v. Piper*, 447 U.S. 752, 767 (1980), that notice and opportunity to respond must precede the imposition of sanctions. A separately filed motion requesting sanctions constitutes notice. A statement inserted in a party's brief that the party moves for sanctions is not sufficient notice. Requests in briefs for sanctions have become so commonplace that it is unrealistic to expect careful responses to such requests without any indication that the court is actually contemplating such measures. Only a motion, the purpose of which is to request sanctions, is sufficient. If there is no such motion filed, notice must come from the court. The form of notice from the court and of the opportunity for comment purposely are left to the court's discretion.

1998 Amendments

Only the caption of this rule has been amended. The changes are intended to be stylistic only.

Rule 39. Costs

(a) Against Whom Assessed. The following rules apply unless the law provides or the court orders otherwise:

(1) if an appeal is dismissed, costs are taxed against the appellant, unless the parties agree otherwise;

(2) if a judgment is affirmed, costs are taxed against the appellant;

(3) if a judgment is reversed, costs are taxed against the appellee;

(4) if a judgment is affirmed in part, reversed in part, modified, or vacated, costs are taxed only as the court orders.

(b) Costs For and Against the United States. Costs for or against the United States, its agency, or officer will be assessed under Rule 39(a) only if authorized by law.

(c) Costs of Copies. Each court of appeals must, by local rule, fix the maximum rate for taxing the cost of producing necessary copies of a brief or appendix, or copies of records authorized by Rule 30(f). The rate must not exceed that generally charged for such work in the area where the clerk's office is located and should encourage economical methods of copying.

(d) Bill of Costs: Objections; Insertion in Mandate.

(1) A party who wants costs taxed must—within 14 days after entry of judgment—file with the circuit clerk, with proof of service, an itemized and verified bill of costs.

(2) Objections must be filed within 10 days after service of the bill of costs, unless the court extends the time.

(3) The clerk must prepare and certify an itemized statement of costs for insertion in the mandate, but issuance of the mandate must not be delayed for taxing costs. If the mandate issues before costs are finally determined, the district clerk must—upon the circuit clerk's request—add the statement of costs, or any amendment of it, to the mandate.

(e) Costs on Appeal Taxable in the District Court. The following costs on appeal are taxable in the district court for the benefit of the party entitled to costs under this rule:

(1) the preparation and transmission of the record;

(2) the reporter's transcript, if needed to determine the appeal;

(3) premiums paid for a supersedeas bond or other bond to preserve rights pending appeal; and

(4) the fee for filing the notice of appeal.

(As amended Apr. 30, 1979, eff. Aug. 1, 1979; Mar. 10, 1986, eff. July 1, 1986; Apr. 24, 1998, eff. Dec. 1, 1998.)

ADVISORY COMMITTEE NOTES

1967 Adoption

Subdivision (a). Statutory authorization for taxation of costs is found in 28 U.S.C. § 1920. The provisions of this subdivision follow the usual practice in the circuits. A few statutes contain specific provisions in derogation of these general provisions. (See 28 U.S.C. § 1928, which forbids the award of costs to a successful plaintiff in a patent infringement action under the circumstances described by the statute). These statutes are controlling in cases to which they apply.

Subdivision (b). The rules of the courts of appeals at present commonly deny costs to the United States except as allowance may be directed by statute. Those rules were promulgated at a time when the United States was generally invulnerable to an award of costs against it, and they appear to be based on the view that if the United States is not subject to costs if it loses, it ought not be entitled to recover costs if it wins.

The number of cases affected by such rules has been greatly reduced by the Act of July 18, 1966, 80 Stat. 308 (1 U.S.Code Cong. & Ad.News, p. 349 (1966), 89th Cong., 2d Sess., which amended 28 U.S.C. § 2412, the former general bar to the award of costs against the United States. Section 2412 as amended generally places the United States on the same footing as private parties with respect to the award of costs in civil cases. But the United States continues to enjoy immunity from costs in certain cases. By its terms amended § 2412 authorizes an award of costs against the United States only in civil actions, and it excepts from its general authorization of an award of costs against the United States cases which are "otherwise specifically provided (for) by statute." Furthermore, the Act of July 18, 1966, *supra*, provides that the amendments of § 2412 which it effects shall apply only to actions filed subsequent to the date of its enactment. The second clause continues in effect, for these and all other cases in which the United States enjoys immunity from costs, the presently prevailing rule that the United States may recover costs as the prevailing party only if it would have suffered them as the losing party.

Subdivision (c). While only five circuits (D.C.Cir. Rule 20(d) [rule 20(d), U.S.Ct. of App. Dist. of Col.]; 1st Cir. Rule 31(4) [rule 31(4), U.S.Ct. of App. 1st Cir.]; 3d Cir. Rule 35(4) [rule 35(4), U.S.Ct. of App. 3rd Cir.]; 4th Cir. Rule 21(4) [rule 21(4) U.S.Ct. of App. 4th Cir.]; 9th Cir. Rule 25 [rule 25, U.S.Ct. of App.9th Cir.], as amended June 2, 1967) presently tax the cost of printing briefs, the proposed rule makes the cost taxable in keeping with the principle of this rule that all cost items expended in the prosecution of a proceeding should be borne by the unsuccessful party.

Subdivision (e). The costs described in this subdivision are costs of the appeal and, as such, are within the undertaking of the appeal bond. They are made taxable in the district court for general convenience. Taxation of the cost of the reporter's transcript is specifically authorized by 28 U.S.C. § 1920, but in the absence of a rule some district courts have held themselves without authority to tax the cost (*Perlman v. Feldmann*, 116 F.Supp. 102 (D. Conn., 1953); *Firtag v. Gendleman*, 152 F.Supp. 226 (D.D.C., 1957); *Todd Atlantic Shipyards Corp. v. The Southport*, 100 F.Supp. 763 (E.D.S.C., 1951). Provision for taxation of the cost of premiums paid for supersedeas bonds is common in the local rules of district courts and the practice is established in the Second, Seventh, and Ninth Circuits. *Berner v. British Commonwealth Pacific Air Lines, Ltd.*, 362 F.2d 799 (2d Cir. 1966); *Land Oberoesterreich v. Gude*, 93 F.2d 292 (2d Cir., 1937); *In re Northern Ind. Oil Co.*, 192 F.2d 139 (7th Cir., 1951); *Lunn v. F. W. Woolworth*, 210 F.2d 159 (9th Cir., 1954).

1979 Amendment

Subdivision (c). The proposed amendment would permit variations among the circuits in regulating the maximum rates taxable as costs for printing or otherwise reproducing briefs, appendices, and copies of records authorized by Rule 30(f). The present rule has had a different effect in different circuits depending upon the size of the circuit, the location of the clerk's office, and the location of other cities. As a consequence there was a growing sense that strict adherence to the rule produces some unfairness in some of the circuits and the matter should be made subject to local rule.

Subdivision (d). The present rule makes no provision for objections to a bill of costs. The proposed amendment would allow 10 days for such objections. Cf. Rule 54(d) of the F.R.C.P. [rule 54(d), Federal Rules of Civil Procedure]. It provides further that the mandate shall not be delayed for taxation of costs.

1986 Amendment

The amendment to subdivision (c) is intended to increase the degree of control exercised by the courts of appeals over rates for printing and copying recoverable as costs. It further requires the courts of appeals to encourage cost-consciousness by requiring that, in fixing the rate, the court consider the most economical methods of printing and copying.

The amendment to subdivision (d) is technical. No substantive change is intended.

1998 Amendments

The language and organization of the rule are amended to make the rule more easily understood. In addition to changes made to improve the understanding, the Advisory Committee has changed language to make style and terminology consistent throughout the appellate rules. These changes are intended to be stylistic only. All references to the cost of "printing" have been deleted from subdivision (c) because commercial printing is so rarely used for preparation of documents filed with a court of appeals.

Rule 40. Petition for Panel Rehearing

(a) Time to File; Contents; Answer; Action by the Court if Granted.

(1) Time. Unless the time is shortened or extended by order or local rule, a petition for panel rehearing may be filed within 14 days after entry of judgment. But in a civil case, if the United States or its officer or agency is a party, the time within which any party may seek rehearing is 45 days after entry of judgment, unless an order shortens or extends the time.

(2) Contents. The petition must state with particularity each point of law or fact that the petitioner believes the court has overlooked or misapprehended and must argue in support of the petition. Oral argument is not permitted.

(3) Answer. Unless the court requests, no answer to a petition for panel rehearing is permitted. But ordinarily rehearing will not be granted in the absence of such a request.

(4) Action by the Court. If a petition for panel rehearing is granted, the court may do any of the following:

(A) make a final disposition of the case without reargument;

(B) restore the case to the calendar for reargument or resubmission; or

(C) issue any other appropriate order.

(b) Form of Petition; Length. The petition must comply in form with Rule 32. Copies must be served and filed as Rule 31 prescribes. Unless the court permits or a local rule provides otherwise, a petition for panel rehearing must not exceed 15 pages.

(As amended Apr. 30, 1979, eff. Aug. 1, 1979; Apr. 29, 1994, eff. Dec. 1, 1994; Apr. 24, 1998, eff. Dec. 1, 1998.)

ADVISORY COMMITTEE NOTES

1967 Adoption

This is the usual rule among the circuits, except that the express prohibition against filing a reply to the petition is found only in the rules of the Fourth, Sixth and Eighth Circuits (it is also contained in Supreme Court Rule 58(3) [rule 58(3), U.S.Sup.Ct.Rules). It is included to save time and expense to the party victorious on appeal. In the very rare instances in which a reply is useful, the court will ask for it.

1979 Amendment

Subdivision (a). The Standing Committee added to the first sentence of Rule 40(a) the words "or by local rule," to conform to current practice in the circuits. The Standing Committee believes the change noncontroversial.

Subdivision (b). The proposed amendment would eliminate the distinction drawn in the present rule between printed briefs and those duplicated from typewritten pages in fixing their maximum length. See Note to Rule 28. Since petitions for rehearing must be prepared in a short time, making typographic printing less likely, the maximum number of pages is fixed at 15, the figure used in the present rule for petitions duplicated by means other than typographic printing.

1994 Amendment

Subdivision (a). The amendment lengthens the time for filing a petition for rehearing from 14 to 45 days in civil cases involving the United States or its agencies or officers. It has no effect upon the time for filing in criminal cases. The amendment makes nation-wide the current practice in the District of Columbia and the Tenth Circuits, *see* D.C. Cir. R. 15 (a), 10th Cir. R. 40.3. This amendment, analogous to the provision in Rule 4(a) extending the time for filing a notice of appeal in cases involving the United States, recognizes that the Solicitor General needs time to conduct a thorough review of the merits of a case before requesting a rehearing. In a case in which a court of appeals believes it necessary to restrict the time for filing a rehearing petition, the amendment provides that the court may do so by order. Although the first sentence of Rule 40 permits a court of appeals to shorten or lengthen the usual 14 day filing period by order or by local rule, the sentence governing appeals in civil cases involving the United States purposely limits a court's power to alter the 45 day period to orders in specific cases. If a court of appeals could adopt a local rule shortening the time for filing a petition for rehearing in all cases involving the United States, the purpose of the amendment would be defeated.

1998 Amendments

The language and organization of the rule are amended to make the rule more easily understood. In addition to changes made to improve the understanding, the Advisory Committee has changed language to make style and terminology consistent throughout the appellate rules. These changes are intended to be stylistic only.

Rule 41. Mandate: Contents; Issuance and Effective Date; Stay

(a) Contents. Unless the court directs that a formal mandate issue, the mandate consists of a certified copy of the judgment, a copy of the court's opinion, if any, and any direction about costs.

(b) When Issued. The court's mandate must issue 7 calendar days after the time to file a petition for rehearing expires, or 7 calendar days after entry of an order denying a timely petition for panel rehearing, petition for rehearing en banc, or motion for stay of mandate, whichever is later. The court may shorten or extend the time.

(c) Effective Date. The mandate is effective when issued.

(d) Staying the Mandate.

(1) On Petition for Rehearing or Motion. The timely filing of a petition for panel rehearing, petition for rehearing en banc, or motion for stay of mandate, stays the mandate until disposition of the petition or motion, unless the court orders otherwise.

(2) Pending Petition for Certiorari.

(A) A party may move to stay the mandate pending the filing of a petition for a writ of certiorari in the Supreme Court. The motion must be served on all parties and must show that the certiorari petition would present a substantial question and that there is good cause for a stay.

(B) The stay must not exceed 90 days, unless the period is extended for good cause or unless the party who obtained the stay files a petition for the writ and so notifies the circuit clerk in writing within the period of the stay. In that case, the stay continues until the Supreme Court's final disposition.

(C) The court may require a bond or other security as a condition to granting or continuing a stay of the mandate.

(D) The court of appeals must issue the mandate immediately when a copy of a Supreme Court order denying the petition for writ of certiorari is filed.

(As amended Apr. 29, 1994, eff. Dec. 1, 1994; Apr. 24, 1998, eff. Dec. 1, 1998; Apr. 29, 2002, eff. Dec. 1, 2002.)

ADVISORY COMMITTEE NOTES

1967 Adoption

The proposed rule follows the rule or practice in a majority of circuits by which copies of the opinion and the judgment serve in lieu of a formal mandate in the ordinary case. Compare Supreme Court Rule 59. Although 28 U.S.C. § 2101(c) permits a writ of certiorari to be filed within 90 days after entry of judgment, seven of the eight circuits which now regulate the matter of stays pending application for certiorari limit the initial stay of the mandate to the 30-day period provided in the proposed rule. Compare D.C.Cir. Rule 27(e) [rule 27(e), U.S.Ct. of App. Dist. of Col.].

1994 Amendment

Subdivision (a). The amendment conforms Rule 41(a) to the amendment made to Rule 40(a). The amendment keys the time for issuance of the mandate to the expiration of the time for filing a petition for rehearing, unless such a petition is filed in which case the mandate issues 7 days after the entry of the order denying the petition. Because the amendment to Rule 40(a) lengthens the time for filing a petition for rehearing in civil cases involving the United States from 14 to 45 days, the rule requiring the mandate to issue 21 days after the entry of judgment would cause the mandate to issue while the government is still considering requesting a rehearing. Therefore, the amendment generally requires the mandate to issue 7 days after the expiration of the time for filing a petition for rehearing.

Subdivision (b). The amendment requires a party who files a motion requesting a stay of mandate to file, at the same time, proof of service on all other parties. The old rule required the party to give notice to the other parties; the amendment merely requires the party to provide the court with evidence of having done so.

The amendment also states that the motion must show that a petition for certiorari would present a substantial question and that there is good cause for a stay. The amendment is intended to alert the parties to the fact that a stay of mandate is not granted automatically and to the type of showing that needs to be made. The Supreme Court has established conditions that must be met before it will stay a mandate. *See* Robert L. Stern et al., Supreme Court Practice § 17.19 (6th ed. 1986).

1998 Amendments

The language and organization of the rule are amended to make the rule more easily understood. In addition to changes made to improve the understanding, the Advisory Committee has changed language to make style and terminology consistent throughout the appellate rules. These changes are intended to be stylistic only.

Several substantive changes are made in this rule, however.

Subdivision (b). The existing rule provides that the mandate issues 7 days after the time to file a petition for panel rehearing expires unless such a petition for rehearing en banc or motion for stay of mandate is filed, the mandate does not issue until 7 days after entry of an order denying the last of all such requests. If a petition for rehearing or a petition for rehearing en banc is granted, the court enters a new judgment after the rehearing and the mandate issues within the normal time after entry of that judgment.

Subdivision (c). Subdivision (c) is new. It provides that the mandate is effective when the court issues it. A court of appeals' judgment or order is not final until issuance of the mandate; at that time the parties' obligations become fixed. This amendment is intended to make it clear that the mandate is effective upon issuance and that its effectiveness is not delayed until receipt of the mandate by the trial court or agency, or until the trial court or agency acts upon it. This amendment is consistent with the current understanding. Unless the court orders that the mandate issue earlier than provided in the rule, the parties can easily calculate the anticipated date of issuance and verify issuance of the mandate, the entry of the order on the docket alerts the parties to that fact.

Subdivision (d). Amended paragraph (1) provides that the filing of a petition for panel rehearing, a petition for rehearing en banc or a motion for a stay of mandate pending petition to the Supreme Court for a writ of certiorari stays the issuance of the mandate until the court disposes of the petition or motion. The provision that a petition for rehearing en banc stays the mandate is a companion to the amendment of Rule 35 that deletes the language stating that a request for a rehearing en banc does not affect the finality of the judgment or stay the issuance of the mandate. The Committee's objective is to treat a request for a rehearing en banc like a petition for panel rehearing so that a request for a rehearing en banc will suspend the finality of the court of appeals' judgment and delay the running of the period for filing a petition for writ of certiorari. Because the filing of a petition for rehearing en banc will stay the mandate, a court of appeals will need to take final action on the petition but the procedure for doing so is left to local practice.

Paragraph (1) also provides that the filing of a motion for a stay of mandate pending petition to the Supreme Court for a writ of certiorari stays the mandate until the court disposes of the motion. If the court denies the motion, the court must issue the mandate 7 days after entering the order denying the motion. If the court grants the motion, the mandate is stayed according to the terms of the order granting the stay. Delaying issuance of the mandate eliminates the need to recall the mandate if the motion for a stay is granted. If, however, the court believes that it would be inappropriate to delay issuance of the mandate until disposition of the motion for a stay, the court may order that the mandate issue immediately.

Paragraph (2). The amendment changes the maximum period for a stay of mandate, absent the court of appeals granting an extension for cause, to 90 days. The presumptive 30–day period was adopted when a party had to file a petition for a writ of certiorari in criminal cases within 30 days after entry of judgment. Supreme Court Rule 13.1 now provides that a party has 90 days after entry of judgment by a court of appeals to file a petition for a writ of certiorari whether the case is civil or criminal.

The amendment does not require a court of appeals to grant a stay of mandate that is coextensive with the period granted for filing a petition for a writ of certiorari. The granting of a stay and the length of the stay remain within the discretion of the court of appeals. The amendment means only that a 90–day stay may be granted without a need to show cause for a stay longer than 30 days.

Subparagraph (C) is not new; it has been moved from the end of the rule to this position.

2002 Amendments

Subdivision (b). Subdivision (b) directs that the mandate of a court must issue 7 days after the time to file a petition for rehearing expires or 7 days after the court denies a timely petition for panel rehearing, petition for rehearing en banc, or motion for stay of mandate, whichever is later. Intermediate Saturdays, Sundays, and legal holidays are counted in computing that 7–day deadline, which means that, except when the 7–day deadline ends on a weekend or legal holiday, the mandate issues exactly one week after the triggering event.

Fed. R. App. P. 26(a)(2) has been amended to provide that, in computing any period of time, one should "[e]xclude intermediate Saturdays, Sundays, and legal holidays when the period is less than 11 days, unless stated in calendar days." This change in the method of computing deadlines means that 7–day deadlines (such as that in subdivision (b)) have been lengthened as a practical matter. Under the new computation method, a mandate would never issue sooner than 9 actual days after a triggering event, and legal holidays could extend that period to as much as 13 days.

Delaying mandates for 9 or more days would introduce significant and unwarranted delay into appellate proceedings. For that reason, subdivision (b) has been amended to require that mandates issue 7 *calendar* days after a triggering event.

Changes Made After Publication and Comments No changes were made to the text of the proposed amendment or to the Committee Note.

Rule 42. Voluntary Dismissal

(a) Dismissal in the District Court. Before an appeal has been docketed by the circuit clerk, the district court may dismiss the appeal on the filing of a stipulation signed by all parties or on the appellant's motion with notice to all parties.

(b) Dismissal in the Court of Appeals. The circuit clerk may dismiss a docketed appeal if the parties file a signed dismissal agreement specifying how costs are to be paid and pay any fees that are due. But no mandate or other process may issue without a court order. An appeal may be dismissed on the appellant's motion on terms agreed to by the parties or fixed by the court.

(As amended Apr. 24, 1998, eff. Dec. 1, 1998.)

ADVISORY COMMITTEE NOTES

1967 Adoption

Subdivision (a). This subdivision is derived from FRCP 73(a) [rule 73(a), Federal Rules of Civil Procedure] without change of substance.

Subdivision (b). The first sentence is a common provision in present circuit rules. The second sentence is added. Compare Supreme Court Rule 60.

1998 Amendments

The language of the rule is amended to make the rule more easily understood. In addition to changes made to improve the understanding, the Advisory Committee has changed language to make style and terminology consistent throughout the appellate rules. These changes are intended to be stylistic only.

Rule 43. Substitution of Parties

(a) Death of a Party.

(1) After Notice of Appeal Is Filed. If a party dies after a notice of appeal has been filed or while a proceeding is pending in the court of appeals, the decedent's personal representative may be substituted as a party on motion filed with the circuit clerk by the representative or by any party. A party's motion must be served on the representative in accordance with Rule 25. If the decedent has no representative, any party may suggest the death on the record, and the court of appeals may then direct appropriate proceedings.

(2) Before Notice of Appeal Is Filed—Potential Appellant. If a party entitled to appeal dies before filing a notice of appeal, the decedent's personal representative—or, if there is no personal representative, the decedent's attorney of record—may file a notice of appeal within the time prescribed by these rules. After the notice of appeal is filed, substitution must be in accordance with Rule 43(a)(1).

(3) Before Notice of Appeal Is Filed—Potential Appellee. If a party against whom an appeal may be taken dies after entry of a judgment or order in the district court, but before a notice of appeal is filed, an appellant may proceed as if the death had not occurred. After the notice of appeal is filed, substitution must be in accordance with Rule 43(a)(1).

(b) Substitution for a Reason Other Than Death. If a party needs to be substituted for any reason other than death, the procedure prescribed in Rule 43(a) applies.

(c) Public Officer: Identification; Substitution.

(1) Identification of Party. A public officer who is a party to an appeal or other proceeding in an official capacity may be described as a party by the public officer's official title rather than by name. But the court may require the public officer's name to be added.

(2) Automatic Substitution of Officeholder. When a public officer who is a party to an appeal or other proceeding in an official capacity dies, resigns, or otherwise ceases to hold office, the action does not abate. The public officer's successor is automatically substituted as a party. Proceedings following the substitution are to be in the name of the substituted party, but any misnomer that does not affect the substantial rights of the parties may be disregarded. An order of substitution may be entered at any time, but failure to enter an order does not affect the substitution.

(As amended Mar. 10, 1986, eff. July 1, 1986; Apr. 24, 1998, eff. Dec. 1, 1998.)

ADVISORY COMMITTEE NOTES

1967 Adoption

Subdivision (a). The first three sentences describe a procedure similar to the rule on substitution in civil actions in the district court. See FRCP 25(a) [rule 25(a), Federal Rules of Civil Procedure]. The fourth sentence expressly authorizes an appeal to be taken against one who has died after the entry of judgment. Compare FRCP 73(b) [rule 73(b), Federal Rules of Civil Procedure], which impliedly authorizes such an appeal.

The sixth sentence authorizes an attorney of record for the deceased to take an appeal on behalf of successors in interest if the deceased has no representative. At present, if a party entitled to appeal dies before the notice of appeal is filed, the appeal can presumably be taken only by his legal representative and must be taken within the time ordinarily prescribed. 13 Cyclopedia of Federal Procedure (3d Ed.) § 63.21. The states commonly make special provision for the even of the death of a party entitled to appeal, usually by extending the time otherwise prescribed. Rules of Civil Procedure for Superior Courts of Arizona, Rule 73(t), 16 A.R.S.; New Jersey Rev.Rules 1:3–3; New York Civil Practice Law and Rules, § 1022; Wisconsin Statutes Ann. 274.01(2). The Provision in the proposed rule is derived from California Code of Civil Procedure, § 941.

Subdivision (c). This subdivision is derived from FRCP 25(d) [rule 25(d), Federal Rules of Civil Procedure] and Supreme Court Rule 48, with appropriate changes.

1986 Amendment

The amendments to Rules 43(a) and (c) are technical. No substantive change is intended.

1998 Amendments

The language and organization of the rule are amended to make the rule more easily understood. In addition to changes made to improve the understanding, the Advisory Committee has changed language to make style and terminology consistent throughout the appellate rules. These changes are intended to be stylistic only.

Rule 44. Case Involving a Constitutional Question When the United States or the Relevant State is Not a Party

(a) Constitutional Challenge to Federal Statute. If a party questions the constitutionality of an Act of Congress in a proceeding in which the United States or its agency, officer, or employee is not a party in an official capacity, the questioning party must give written notice to the circuit clerk immediately upon the filing of the record or as soon as the question is raised in the court of appeals. The clerk must then certify that fact to the Attorney General.

(b) Constitutional Challenge to State Statute. If a party questions the constitutionality of a statute of a State in a proceeding in which that State or its agency, officer, or employee is not a party in an official capacity, the questioning party must give written notice to the circuit clerk immediately upon the filing of the record or as soon as the question is raised in the court of appeals. The clerk must then certify that fact to the attorney general of the State.

(As amended Apr. 24, 1998, eff. Dec. 1, 1998; Apr. 29, 2002, eff. Dec. 1, 2002.)

ADVISORY COMMITTEE NOTES

1967 Adoption

This rule is now found in the rules of a majority of the circuits. It is in response to the Act of August 24, 1937 (28

U.S.C. § 2403), which requires all courts of the United States to advise the Attorney General of the existence of an action or proceeding of the kind described in the rule.

1998 Amendments

The language of the rule is amended to make the rule more easily understood. In addition to changes made to improve the understanding, the Advisory Committee has changed language to make style and terminology consistent throughout the appellate rules. These changes are intended to be stylistic only.

2002 Amendments

Rule 44 requires that a party who "questions the constitutionality of an Act of Congress" in a proceeding in which the United States is not a party must provide written notice of that challenge to the clerk. Rule 44 is designed to implement 28 U.S.C. § 2403(a), which states that:

> In any action, suit or proceeding in a court of the United States to which the United States or any agency, officer or employee thereof is not a party, wherein the constitutionality of any Act of Congress affecting the public interest is drawn in question, the court shall certify such fact to the Attorney General, and shall permit the United States to intervene . . . for argument on the question of constitutionality.

The subsequent section of the statute—§ 2403(*b*)—contains virtually identical language imposing upon the courts the duty to notify the attorney general of a *state* of a constitutional challenge to any statute of that state. But § 2403(b), unlike § 2403(a), was not implemented in Rule 44.

Rule 44 has been amended to correct this omission. The text of former Rule 44 regarding constitutional challenges to federal statutes now appears as Rule 44(a), while new language regarding constitutional challenges to state statutes now appears as Rule 44(b).

Changes Made After Publication and Comments No changes were made to the text of the proposed amendment or to the Committee Note.

Rule 45. Clerk's Duties

(a) General Provisions.

(1) Qualifications. The circuit clerk must take the oath and post any bond required by law. Neither the clerk nor any deputy clerk may practice as an attorney or counselor in any court while in office.

(2) When Court Is Open. The court of appeals is always open for filing any paper, issuing and returning process, making a motion, and entering an order. The clerk's office with the clerk or a deputy in attendance must be open during business hours on all days except Saturdays, Sundays, and legal holidays. A court may provide by local rule or by order that the clerk's office be open for specified hours on Saturdays or on legal holidays other than New Year's Day, Martin Luther King, Jr.'s Birthday, Washington's Birthday, Memorial Day, Independence Day, Labor Day, Columbus Day, Veterans' Day, Thanksgiving Day, and Christmas Day.

(b) Records.

(1) The Docket. The circuit clerk must maintain a docket and an index of all docketed cases in the manner prescribed by the Director of the Administrative Office of the United States Courts. The clerk must record all papers filed with the clerk and all process, orders, and judgments.

(2) Calendar. Under the court's direction, the clerk must prepare a calendar of cases awaiting argument. In placing cases on the calendar for argument, the clerk must give preference to appeals in criminal cases and to other proceedings and appeals entitled to preference by law.

(3) Other Records. The clerk must keep other books and records required by the Director of the Administrative Office of the United States Courts, with the approval of the Judicial Conference of the United States, or by the court.

(c) Notice of an Order or Judgment. Upon the entry of an order or judgment, the circuit clerk must immediately serve a notice of entry on each party, with a copy of any opinion, and must note the date of service on the docket. Service on a party represented by counsel must be made on counsel.

(d) Custody of Records and Papers. The circuit clerk has custody of the court's records and papers. Unless the court orders or instructs otherwise, the clerk must not permit an original record or paper to be taken from the clerk's office. Upon disposition of the case, original papers constituting the record on appeal or review must be returned to the court or agency from which they were received. The clerk must preserve a copy of any brief, appendix, or other paper that has been filed.

(As amended Mar. 1, 1971, eff. July 1, 1971; Mar. 10, 1986, eff. July 1, 1986; Apr. 24, 1998, eff. Dec. 1, 1998; Apr. 29, 2002, eff. Dec. 1, 2002; Apr. 25, 2005, eff. Dec. 1, 2005.)

ADVISORY COMMITTEE NOTES

1967 Adoption

The duties imposed upon clerks of the courts of appeals by this rule are those imposed by rule or practice in a majority of the circuits. The second sentence of subdivision (a) authorizing the closing of the clerk's office on Saturday and non-national legal holidays follows a similar provision respecting the district court clerk's office found in FRCP 77(c) [rule 77(c), Federal Rules of Civil Procedure] and in FRCrP 56 [rule 56, Federal Rules of Criminal Procedure].

1971 Amendment

The amendment adds Columbus Day to the list of legal holidays. See the Note accompanying the amendment of Rule 26(a).

1986 Amendment

The amendment to Rule 45(b) permits the courts of appeals to maintain computerized dockets. The Committee believes that the Administrative Office of the United States Courts ought to have maximum flexibility in prescribing the format of this docket in order to ensure a smooth transition from manual to automated systems and subsequent adaptation to technological improvements.

The amendments to Rules 45(a) and (d) are technical. No substantive change is intended. The Birthday of Martin Luther King, Jr. has been added to the list of national holidays.

1998 Amendments

The language and organization of the rule are amended to make the rule more easily understood. In addition to changes made to improve the understanding, the Advisory Committee has changed language to make style and terminology consistent throughout the appellate rules. These changes are intended to be stylistic only.

2002 Amendments

Subdivision (c). Subdivision (c) has been amended so that the clerk may use electronic means to serve notice of entry of an order or judgment upon parties who have consented to such service.

Changes Made After Publication and Comments No changes were made to the text of the proposed amendment or to the Committee Note.

2005 Amendments

Subdivision (a)(2). Rule 45(a)(2) has been amended to refer to the third Monday in February as "Washington's Birthday." A federal statute officially designates the holiday as "Washington's Birthday," reflecting the desire of Congress specially to honor the first president of the United States. *See* 5 U.S.C. § 6103(a). During the 1998 restyling of the Federal Rules of Appellate Procedure, references to "Washington's Birthday" were mistakenly changed to "Presidents' Day." The amendment corrects that error.

Rule 46. Attorneys

(a) Admission to the Bar.

(1) Eligibility. An attorney is eligible for admission to the bar of a court of appeals if that attorney is of good moral and professional character and is admitted to practice before the Supreme Court of the United States, the highest court of a state, another United States court of appeals, or a United States district court (including the district courts for Guam, the Northern Mariana Islands, and the Virgin Islands).

(2) Application. An applicant must file an application for admission, on a form approved by the court that contains the applicant's personal statement showing eligibility for membership. The applicant must subscribe to the following oath or affirmation:

"I, ______________, do solemnly swear [or affirm] that I will conduct myself as an attorney and counselor of this court, uprightly and according to law; and that I will support the Constitution of the United States."

(3) Admission Procedures. On written or oral motion of a member of the court's bar, the court will act on the application. An applicant may be admitted by oral motion in open court. But, unless the court orders otherwise, an applicant need not appear before the court to be admitted. Upon admission, an applicant must pay the clerk the fee prescribed by local rule or court order.

(b) Suspension or Disbarment.

(1) Standard. A member of the court's bar is subject to suspension or disbarment by the court if the member:

(A) has been suspended or disbarred from practice in any other court; or

(B) is guilty of conduct unbecoming a member of the court's bar.

(2) Procedure. The member must be given an opportunity to show good cause, within the time prescribed by the court, why the member should not be suspended or disbarred.

(3) Order. The court must enter an appropriate order after the member responds and a hearing is held, if requested, or after the time prescribed for a response expires, if no response is made.

(c) Discipline. A court of appeals may discipline an attorney who practices before it for conduct unbecoming a member of the bar or for failure to comply with any court rule. First, however, the court must afford the attorney reasonable notice, an opportunity to show cause to the contrary, and, if requested, a hearing.

(As amended Mar. 10, 1986, eff. July 1, 1986; Apr. 24, 1998, eff. Dec. 1, 1998.)

ADVISORY COMMITTEE NOTES

1967 Adoption

Subdivision (a). The basic requirement of membership in the bar of the Supreme Court, or of the highest court of a state, or in another court of appeals or a district court is found, with minor variations, in the rules of ten circuits. The only other requirement in those circuits is that the applicant be of good moral and professional character. In the District of Columbia Circuit applicants other than members of the District of Columbia District bar or the Supreme Court bar must claim membership in the bar of the highest court of a state, territory or possession for three years prior to application for admission (D.C.Cir. Rule 7 [rule 7, U.S.Ct. of App. Dist. of Col.]). Members of the District of Columbia District bar and the Supreme Court bar again excepted, applicants for admission to the District of Columbia Circuit bar must meet precisely defined prelaw and law school study requirements (D.C.Cir. Rule 7½ [rule 7½, U.S.Ct. of App.Dist. of Col.]).

A few circuits now require that application for admission be made by oral motion by a sponsor member in open court.

The proposed rule permits both the application and the motion by the sponsor member to be in writing, and permits action on the motion without the appearance of the applicant or the sponsor, unless the court otherwise orders.

Subdivision (b). The provision respecting suspension or disbarment is uniform. Third Circuit Rule 8(3) [rule 8(3), U.S.Ct. of App. 3rd Cir.] is typical.

Subdivision (c). At present only Fourth Circuit Rule 36 [rule 36, U.S.Ct. of App. 4th Cir.] contains an equivalent provision. The purpose of this provision is to make explicit the power of a court of appeals to impose sanctions less serious than suspension or disbarment for the breach of rules. It also affords some measure of control over attorneys who are not members of the bar of the court. Several circuits permit a non-member attorney to file briefs and motions, membership being required only at the time of oral argument. And several circuits permit argument pro hac vice by non-member attorneys.

1986 Amendments

The amendments to Rules 46(a) and (b) are technical. No substantive change is intended.

1998 Amendments

The language and organization of the rule are amended to make the rule more easily understood. In addition to changes made to improve the understanding, the Advisory Committee has changed language to make style and terminology consistent throughout the appellate rules. These changes are intended to be stylistic only.

HISTORICAL NOTES

Termination of United States District Court for the District of the Canal Zone

For termination of the United States District Court for the District of the Canal Zone at end of the "transition period", being the 30–month period beginning Oct. 1, 1979, and ending midnight Mar. 31, 1982, see Paragraph 5 of Article XI of the Panama Canal Treaty of 1977 and sections 3831 and 3841 to 3843 of Title 22, Foreign Relations and Intercourse.

Rule 47. Local Rules by Courts of Appeals

(a) Local Rules.

(1) Each court of appeals acting by a majority of its judges in regular active service may, after giving appropriate public notice and opportunity for comment, make and amend rules governing its practice. A generally applicable direction to parties or lawyers regarding practice before a court must be in a local rule rather than an internal operating procedure or standing order. A local rule must be consistent with—but not duplicative of—Acts of Congress and rules adopted under 28 U.S.C. § 2072 and must conform to any uniform numbering system prescribed by the Judicial Conference of the United States. Each circuit clerk must send the Administrative Office of the United States Courts a copy of each local rule and internal operating procedure when it is promulgated or amended.

(2) A local rule imposing a requirement of form must not be enforced in a manner that causes a party to lose rights because of a nonwillful failure to comply with the requirement.

(b) Procedure When There Is No Controlling Law. A court of appeals may regulate practice in a particular case in any manner consistent with federal law, these rules, and local rules of the circuit. No sanction or other disadvantage may be imposed for noncompliance with any requirement not in federal law, federal rules, or the local circuit rules unless the alleged violator has been furnished in the particular case with actual notice of the requirement.

(As amended Apr. 27, 1995, eff. Dec. 1, 1995; Apr. 24, 1998, eff. Dec. 1, 1998.)

ADVISORY COMMITTEE NOTES

1967 Adoption

This rule continues the authority now vested in individual courts of appeals by 28 U.S.C. § 2071 to make rules consistent with rules of practice and procedure promulgated by the Supreme Court.

1995 Amendments

Subdivision (a). This rule is amended to require that a generally applicable direction regarding practice before a court of appeals must be in a local rule rather than an internal operating procedure or some other general directive. It is the intent of this rule that a local rule may not bar any practice that these rules explicitly or implicitly permit. Subdivision (b) allows a court of appeals to regulate practice in an individual case by entry of an order in the case. The amendment also reflects the requirement that local rules be consistent not only with the national rules but also with Acts of Congress. The amendment also states that local rules should not repeat national rules and Acts of Congress.

The amendment also requires that the numbering of local rules conform with any uniform numbering system that may be prescribed by the Judicial Conference. Lack of uniform numbering might create unnecessary traps for counsel and litigants. A uniform numbering system would make it easier for an increasingly national bar and for litigants to locate a local rule that applies to a particular procedural issue.

Paragraph (2) is new. Its aim is to protect against loss of rights in the enforcement of local rules relating to matters of form. The proscription of paragraph (2) is narrowly drawn—covering only violations that are not willful and only those involving local rules directed to matters of form. It does not limit the court's power to impose substantive penalties upon a party if it or its attorney stubbornly or repeatedly violates a local rule, even one involving merely a matter of form. Nor does it affect the court's power to enforce local rules that involve more than mere matters of form.

Subdivision (b). This rule provides flexibility to the court in regulating practice in a particular case when there is no controlling law. Specifically, it permits the court to regulate practice in any manner consistent with Acts of Congress, with rules adopted under 28 U.S.C. § 2072, and with the circuit's local rules.

The amendment to this rule disapproves imposing any sanction or other disadvantage on a person for noncompliance with such a directive, unless the alleged violator has been furnished in a particular case with actual notice of the requirement. There should be no adverse consequence to a party or attorney for violating special requirements relating to practice before a particular court unless the party or attorney has actual notice of those requirements.

1998 Amendments

The language of the rule is amended to make the rule more easily understood. In addition to changes made to improve the understanding, the Advisory Committee has changed language to make style and terminology consistent throughout the appellate rules. These changes are intended to be stylistic only.

Rule 48. Masters

(a) Appointment; Powers. A court of appeals may appoint a special master to hold hearings, if necessary, and to recommend factual findings and disposition in matters ancillary to proceedings in the court. Unless the order referring a matter to a master specifies or limits the master's powers, those powers include, but are not limited to, the following:

(1) regulating all aspects of a hearing;

(2) taking all appropriate action for the efficient performance of the master's duties under the order;

(3) requiring the production of evidence on all matters embraced in the reference; and

(4) administering oaths and examining witnesses and parties.

(b) Compensation. If the master is not a judge or court employee, the court must determine the master's compensation and whether the cost is to be charged to any party.

(As amended Apr. 29, 1994, eff. Dec. 1, 1994; Apr. 24, 1998, eff. Dec. 1, 1998.)

ADVISORY COMMITTEE NOTES

1994 Amendments

The text of the existing Rule 48 concerning the title was moved to Rule 1.

This new Rule 48 authorizes a court of appeals to appoint a special master to make recommendations concerning ancillary matters. The courts of appeals have long used masters in contempt proceedings where the issue is compliance with an enforcement order. See *Polish National Alliance v. NLRB*, 159 F.2d 38 (7th Cir. 1946); *NLRB v. Arcade-Sunshine Co.*, 132 F.2d 8 (D.C. Cir. 1942); *NLRB v. Remington Rand, Inc.*, 130 F.2d 919 (2d Cir. 1942). There are other instances when the question before a court of appeals requires a factual determination. An application for fees or eligibility for Criminal Justice Act status on appeal are examples.

Ordinarily when a factual issue is unresolved, a court of appeals remands the case to the district court or agency that originally heard the case. It is not the Committee's intent to alter that practice. However, when factual issues arise in the first instance in the court of appeals, such as fees for representation on appeal, it would be useful to have authority to refer such determinations to a master for a recommendation.

1998 Amendments

The language and organization of the rule are amended to make the rule more easily understood. In addition to changes made to improve the understanding, the Advisory Committee has changed language to make style and terminology consistent throughout the appellate rules. These changes are intended to be stylistic only.

APPENDIX OF FORMS

Form 1. Notice of Appeal to a Court of Appeals From a Judgment or Order of a District Court

United States District Court for the ______
District of ________
File Number ________

A.B., Plaintiff)
)
v.) *Notice of Appeal*
)
C.D., Defendant)

Notice is hereby given that [(here name all parties taking the appeal) , (plaintiffs) (defendants) in the above named case,[1]] hereby appeal to the United States Court of Appeals for the _____ Circuit (from the final judgment) (from an order (describing it)) entered in this action on the _____ day of ______, 20___.

(s)________________
Attorney for [__________]
[Address:______________]

(As amended Apr. 22, 1993, eff. Dec. 1, 1993; Mar. 27, 2003, eff. Dec. 1, 2003.)

[1] See Rule 3(c) for permissible ways of identifying appellants.

Form 2. Notice of Appeal to a Court of Appeals From a Decision of the United States Tax Court

UNITED STATES TAX COURT
Washington, D.C.

A.B., Petitioner)
)
v.) Docket No. _______
)
Commissioner of Internal)
Revenue, Respondent)

Notice of Appeal

Notice is hereby given that [here name all parties taking the appeal [1]], hereby appeals to the United States Court of Appeals for the ______ Circuit from (that part of) the decision of this court entered in the above captioned proceeding on the _______ day of _______, 20___ (relating to _______).

(s) ________________
Counsel for [__________]
[Address:______________]

(As amended Apr. 22, 1993, eff. Dec. 1, 1993; Mar. 27, 2003, eff. Dec. 1, 2003.)

[1] See Rule 3(c) for permissible ways of identifying appellants.

Form 3. Petition for Review of Order of an Agency, Board, Commission or Officer

United States Court of Appeals
for the _______ Circuit

A.B., Petitioner)
)
v.) Petition for Review
XYZ Commission, Respondent)

[(here name all parties bringing the petition[1]) ____] hereby petitions the court for review of the Order of the XYZ Commission (describe the order) entered on ______, 20____.

[(s)] ________________
Attorney for Petitioners
Address:______________

(As amended Apr. 22, 1993, eff. Dec. 1, 1993; Mar. 27, 2003, eff. Dec. 1, 2003.)

[1] See Rule 15.

Form 4. Affidavit Accompanying Motion for Permission to Appeal In Forma Pauperis

United States District Court
for the
_____ District of ______

A.B., Plaintiff
v. Case No. __________
C.D., Defendant

Affidavit in Support of Motion	**Instructions**
I swear or affirm under penalty of perjury that, because of my poverty, I cannot prepay the docket fees of my appeal or post a bond for them. I believe I am entitled to redress. I swear or affirm under penalty of perjury under United States laws that my answers on this form are true and correct. (28 U.S.C. § 1746; 18 U.S.C. § 1621.)	Complete all questions in this application and then sign it. Do not leave any blanks: if the answer to a question is "0," "none," or "not applicable (N/A)," write in that response. If you need more space to answer a question or to explain your answer, attach a separate sheet of paper identified with your name, your case's docket number, and the question number.

Signed: ________________ Date: ________________

My issues on appeal are:

1. For both you and your spouse estimate the average amount of money received from each of the following sources during the past 12 months. Adjust any amount that was received weekly, biweekly, quarterly, semiannually, or annually to show the monthly rate. Use gross amounts, that is, amounts before any deductions for taxes or otherwise.

Income source	**Average monthly amount during the past 12 months**		**Amount expected next month**	
	You	**Spouse**	**You**	**Spouse**
Employment	$_____	$_____	$_____	$_____
Self-employment	$_____	$_____	$_____	$_____
Income from real property (such as rental income)	$_____	$_____	$_____	$_____
Interest and dividends	$_____	$_____	$_____	$_____
Gifts	$_____	$_____	$_____	$_____
Alimony	$_____	$_____	$_____	$_____
Child support	$_____	$_____	$_____	$_____
Retirement (such as social security, pensions, annuities, insurance)	$_____	$_____	$_____	$_____
Disability (such as social security, insurance payments)	$_____	$_____	$_____	$_____
Unemployment payments	$_____	$_____	$_____	$_____
Public-assistance (such as welfare)	$_____	$_____	$_____	$_____
Other (specify): _	$_____	$_____	$_____	$_____
Total monthly income:	$_____	$_____	$_____	$_____

2. List your employment history, most recent employer first. (Gross monthly pay is before taxes or other deductions.)

Employer	**Address**	**Dates of employment**	**Gross monthly pay**

3. List your spouse's employment history, most recent employer first. (Gross monthly pay is before taxes or other deductions.)

Employer	**Address**	**Dates of employment**	**Gross monthly pay**

4. How much cash do you and your spouse have? $________

Below, state any money you or your spouse have in bank accounts or in any other financial institution.

Financial institution	**Type of account**	**Amount you have**	**Amount your spouse has**
		$	$
		$	$
		$	$

If you are a prisoner, you must attach a statement certified by the appropriate institutional officer showing all receipts, expenditures, and balances during the last six months in your institutional accounts. If you have multiple accounts, perhaps because you have been in multiple institutions, attach one certified statement of each account.

5. List the assets, and their values, which you own or your spouse owns. Do not list clothing and ordinary household furnishings.

Home	(Value)	**Other real estate**	(Value)	**Motor vehicle #1**	(Value)
				Make & year:	
				Model:	
				Registration #:	

	Motor vehicle #2 (Value)	**Other assets** (Value)	**Other assets** (Value)
Make & year:			
Model:			
Registration #:			

6. State every person, business, or organization owing you or your spouse money, and the amount owed.

Person owing you or your spouse money	**Amount owed to you**	**Amount owed to your spouse**

7. State the persons who rely on you or your spouse for support.

Name	**Relationship**	**Age**

8. Estimate the average monthly expenses of you and your family. Show separately the amounts paid by your spouse. Adjust any payments that are made weekly, biweekly, quarterly, semiannually, or annually to show the monthly rate.

	You	**Your Spouse**
Rent or home-mortgage payment (include lot rented for mobile home)	$_____	$_____
Are real-estate taxes included? ☐ Yes ☐ No		
Is property insurance included? ☐ Yes ☐ No		
Utilities (electricity, heating fuel, water, sewer, and Telephone)	$_____	$_____

Home maintenance (repairs and upkeep)	$______	$______
Food	$______	$______
Clothing	$______	$______
Laundry and dry-cleaning	$______	$______
Medical and dental expenses	$______	$______
Transportation (not including motor vehicle payments)	$______	$______
Recreation, entertainment, newspapers, magazines, etc.	$______	$______
Insurance (not deducted from wages or included in Mortgage payments)	$______	$______
Homeowner's or renter's	$______	$______
Life	$______	$______
Health	$______	$______
Motor Vehicle	$______	$______
Other: ______	$______	$______
Taxes (not deducted from wages or included in Mortgage payments) (specify):	$______	$______
Installment payments	$______	$______
Motor Vehicle	$______	$______
Credit card (name): ______	$______	$______
Department store (name): ___	$______	$______
Other: ______	$______	$______
Alimony, maintenance, and support paid to others	$______	$______
Regular expenses for operation of business, profession, or farm (attach detailed statement)	$______	$______
Other (specify): ____	$______	$______
Total monthly expenses:	$______	$______

9. Do you expect any major changes to your monthly income or expenses or in your assets or liabilities during the next 12 months?

☐ Yes ☐ No If yes, describe on an attached sheet.

10. Have you paid—or will you be paying—an attorney any money for services in connection with this case, including the completion of this form? Yes No

If yes, how much? $______

If yes, state the attorney's name, address, and telephone number:

____

____

____

11. Have you paid—or will you be paying—anyone other than an attorney (such as a paralegal or a typist) any money for services in connection with this case, including the completion of this form?

☐ Yes ☐ No

If yes, how much? $______

If yes, state the person's name, address, and telephone number:

____

____

____

12. Provide any other information that will help explain why you cannot pay the docket fees for your appeal.

13. State the address of your legal residence.

____

____

Your daytime phone number: ___ __________

Your age: ______ Your years of schooling: ______

Your social-security number: ____________

(As amended Apr. 24, 1998, eff. Dec. 1, 1998.)

Form 5. Notice of Appeal to a Court of Appeals from a Judgment or Order of a District Court or a Bankruptcy Appellate Panel

United States District Court for the ....
District of ....

In re)
)
...........................,)
Debtor)
) File No..........
.......................,)
Plaintiff)
)
v.)
)
.......................,)
Defendant)

Notice of Appeal to
United States Court of Appeals
for the .... Circuit

.........................., the plaintiff [or defendant or other party] appeals to the United States Court of Appeals for the .... Circuit from the final judgment [or order or decree] of the district court for the district of .... [or bankruptcy appellate panel of the .... circuit], entered in this case on ...., 20... [here describe the judgment, order, or decree] ....

The parties to the judgment [or order or decree] appealed from and the names and addresses of their respective attorneys are as follows:

Dated ....
Signed ....
Attorney for Appellant

Address: ....
....

(Added Apr. 25, 1989, eff. Dec. 1, 1989; Mar. 27, 2003, eff. Dec. 1, 2003.)

Form 6. Certificate of Compliance with Rule 32(a)

Certificate of Compliance With Type-Volume Limitation, Typeface Requirements, and Type Style Requirements

1. This brief complies with the type-volume limitation of Fed. R. App. P. 32(a)(7)(B) because:

☐ this brief contains [*state the number of*] words, excluding the parts of the brief exempted by Fed. R. App. P. 32(a)(7)(B)(iii), *or*

☐ this brief uses a monospaced typeface and contains [*state the number of*] lines of text, excluding the parts of the brief exempted by Fed. R. App. P. 32(a)(7)(B)(iii).

2. This brief complies with the typeface requirements of Fed. R. App. P. 32(a)(5) and the type style requirements of Fed. R. App. P. 32(a)(6) because:

☐ this brief has been prepared in a proportionally spaced typeface using [*state name and version of word processing program*] in [*state font size and name of type style*], *or*

☐ this brief has been prepared in a monospaced typeface using [*state name and version of word processing program*] with [*state number of characters per inch and name of type style*].

(s)____________________

Attorney for ____________________

Dated: ____________________

(Added Apr. 29, 2002, eff. Dec. 1, 2002.)

ADVISORY COMMITTEE NOTES

2002 Adoption

Changes Made After Publication and Comments No changes were made to the text of the proposed amendment or to the Committee Note.

RULES OF THE SUPREME COURT OF THE UNITED STATES

Adopted January 11, 1999
Effective May 3, 1999

Amendments received to February 2, 2007

PART I. THE COURT

Rule 1. Clerk

1. The Clerk receives documents for filing with the Court and has authority to reject any submitted filing that does not comply with these Rules.

2. The Clerk maintains the Court's records and will not permit any of them to be removed from the Court building except as authorized by the Court. Any document filed with the Clerk and made a part of the Court's records may not thereafter be withdrawn from the official Court files. After the conclusion of proceedings in this Court, original records and documents transmitted to this Court by any other court will be returned to the court from which they were received.

3. Unless the Court or the Chief Justice orders otherwise, the Clerk's office is open from 9 a.m. to 5 p.m., Monday through Friday, except on federal legal holidays listed in 5 U.S.C. § 6103.

Rule 2. Library

1. The Court's library is available for use by appropriate personnel of this Court, members of the Bar of this Court, Members of Congress and their legal staffs, and attorneys for the United States and for federal departments and agencies.

2. The library's hours are governed by regulations made by the Librarian with the approval of the Chief Justice or the Court.

3. Library books may not be removed from the Court building, except by a Justice or a member of a Justice's staff.

Rule 3. Term

The Court holds a continuous annual Term commencing on the first Monday in October and ending on the day before the first Monday in October of the following year. See 28 U.S.C. § 2. At the end of each Term, all cases pending on the docket are continued to the next Term.

Rule 4. Sessions and Quorum

1. Open sessions of the Court are held beginning at 10 a.m. on the first Monday in October of each year, and thereafter as announced by the Court. Unless it orders otherwise, the Court sits to hear arguments from 10 a.m. until noon and from 1 p.m. until 3 p.m.

2. Six Members of the Court constitute a quorum. See 28 U.S.C. § 1. In the absence of a quorum on any day appointed for holding a session of the Court, the Justices attending—or if no Justice is present, the Clerk or a Deputy Clerk—may announce that the Court will not meet until there is a quorum.

3. When appropriate, the Court will direct the Clerk or the Marshal to announce recesses.

PART II. ATTORNEYS AND COUNSELORS

Rule 5. Admission to the Bar

1. To qualify for admission to the Bar of this Court, an applicant must have been admitted to practice in the highest court of a State, Commonwealth, Territory or Possession, or the District of Columbia for a period of at least three years immediately before the date of application; must not have been the subject of any adverse disciplinary action pronounced or in effect during that 3–year period; and must appear to the Court to be of good moral and professional character.

2. Each applicant shall file with the Clerk (1) a certificate from the presiding judge, clerk, or other authorized official of that court evidencing the applicant's admission to practice there and the applicant's current good standing, and (2) a completely executed copy of the form approved by this Court and furnished by the Clerk containing (a) the applicant's personal statement, and (b) the statement of two sponsors endorsing the correctness of the applicant's statement, stating that the applicant possesses all the qualifications required for admission, and affirming that the applicant is of good moral and professional character. Both sponsors must be members of the Bar of this Court who personally know, but are not related to, the applicant.

3. If the documents submitted demonstrate that the applicant possesses the necessary qualifications, and if the applicant has signed the oath or affirmation and paid the required fee, the Clerk will notify the applicant of acceptance by the Court as a member of the Bar and issue a certificate of admission. An applicant who so wishes may be admitted in open court on oral motion by a member of the Bar of this Court, provided that all other requirements for admission have been satisfied.

4. Each applicant shall sign the following oath or affirmation: I, ..., do solemnly swear (or affirm) that as an attorney and as a counselor of this Court, I will conduct myself uprightly and according to law, and that I will support the Constitution of the United States.

5. The fee for admission to the Bar and a certificate bearing the seal of the Court is $100, payable to the United States Supreme Court. The Marshal will deposit such fees in a separate fund to be disbursed by the Marshal at the direction of the Chief Justice for the costs of admissions, for the benefit of the Court and its Bar, and for related purposes.

6. The fee for a duplicate certificate of admission to the Bar bearing the seal of the Court is $15, and the fee for a certificate of good standing is $10, payable to the United States Supreme Court. The proceeds will be maintained by the Marshal as provided in paragraph 5 of this Rule.

(As amended Jan. 11, 1999, eff. May 3, 1999.)

Rule 6. Argument *Pro Hac Vice*

1. An attorney not admitted to practice in the highest court of a State, Commonwealth, Territory or Possession, or the District of Columbia for the requisite three years, but otherwise eligible for admission to practice in this Court under Rule 5.1, may be permitted to argue *pro hac vice.*

2. An attorney qualified to practice in the courts of a foreign state may be permitted to argue *pro hac vice.*

3. Oral argument *pro hac vice* is allowed only on motion of the counsel of record for the party on whose behalf leave is requested. The motion shall state concisely the qualifications of the attorney who is to argue *pro hac vice.* It shall be filed with the Clerk, in the form required by Rule 21, no later than the date on which the respondent's or appellee's brief on the merits is due to be filed, and it shall be accompanied by proof of service as required by Rule 29.

Rule 7. Prohibition Against Practice

No employee of this Court shall practice as an attorney or counselor in any court or before any agency of government while employed by the Court; nor shall any person after leaving such employment participate in any professional capacity in any case pending before this Court or in any case being considered for filing in this Court, until two years have elapsed after separation; nor shall a former employee ever participate in any professional capacity in any case that was pending in this Court during the employee's tenure.

Rule 8. Disbarment and Disciplinary Action

1. Whenever a member of the Bar of this Court has been disbarred or suspended from practice in any court of record, or has engaged in conduct unbecoming a member of the Bar of this Court, the Court will enter an order suspending that member from practice before this Court and affording the member an opportunity to show cause, within 40 days, why a disbarment order should not be entered. Upon response, or if no response is timely filed, the Court will enter an appropriate order.

2. After reasonable notice and an opportunity to show cause why disciplinary action should not be taken, and after a hearing if material facts are in dispute, the Court may take any appropriate disciplinary action against any attorney who is admitted to practice before it for conduct unbecoming a member of the Bar or for failure to comply with these Rules or any Rule or order of the Court.

Rule 9. Appearance of Counsel

1. An attorney seeking to file a document in this Court in a representative capacity must first be admitted to practice before this Court as provided in Rule 5, except that admission to the Bar of this Court is not required for an attorney appointed under the Criminal Justice Act of 1964, see 18 U.S.C. § 3006A(d)(6), or under any other applicable federal statute. The attorney whose name, address, and telephone number appear on the cover of a document presented for filing is considered counsel of record, and a separate notice of appearance need not be filed. If the name of more than one attorney is shown on the cover of the document, the attorney who is counsel of record shall be clearly identified.

2. An attorney representing a party who will not be filing a document shall enter a separate notice of appearance as counsel of record indicating the name of the party represented. A separate notice of appearance shall also be entered whenever an attorney is substituted as counsel of record in a particular case.

PART III. JURISDICTION ON WRIT OF CERTIORARI

Rule 10. Considerations Governing Review on Certiorari

Review on a writ of certiorari is not a matter of right, but of judicial discretion. A petition for a writ of certiorari will be granted only for compelling reasons. The following, although neither controlling nor fully measuring the Court's discretion, indicate the character of the reasons the Court considers:

(a) a United States court of appeals has entered a decision in conflict with the decision of another United States court of appeals on the same important matter; has decided an important federal question in a way that conflicts with a decision by a state court of last resort; or has so far departed from the accepted and usual course of judicial proceedings, or sanctioned such a departure by a lower court, as to call for an exercise of this Court's supervisory power;

(b) a state court of last resort has decided an important federal question in a way that conflicts with the decision of another state court of last resort or of a United States court of appeals;

(c) a state court or a United States court of appeals has decided an important question of federal law that has not been, but should be, settled by this Court, or has decided an important federal question in a way that conflicts with relevant decisions of this Court.

A petition for a writ of certiorari is rarely granted when the asserted error consists of erroneous factual findings or the misapplication of a properly stated rule of law.

Rule 11. Certiorari to a United States Court of Appeals Before Judgment

A petition for a writ of certiorari to review a case pending in a United States court of appeals, before judgment is entered in that court, will be granted only upon a showing that the case is of such imperative public importance as to justify deviation from normal appellate practice and to require immediate determination in this Court. See 28 U.S.C. § 2101(e).

Rule 12. Review on Certiorari: How Sought; Parties

1. Except as provided in paragraph 2 of this Rule, the petitioner shall file 40 copies of a petition for a writ of certiorari, prepared as required by Rule 33.1, and shall pay the Rule 38(a) docket fee.

2. A petitioner proceeding *in forma pauperis* under Rule 39 shall file an original and 10 copies of a petition for a writ of certiorari prepared as required by Rule 33.2, together with an original and 10 copies of the motion for leave to proceed *in forma pauperis.* A copy of the motion shall precede and be attached to each copy of the petition. An inmate confined in an institution, if proceeding *in forma pauperis* and not represented by counsel, need file only an original petition and motion.

3. Whether prepared under Rule 33.1 or Rule 33.2, the petition shall comply in all respects with Rule 14 and shall be submitted with proof of service as required by Rule 29. The case then will be placed on the docket. It is the petitioner's duty to notify all respondents promptly, on a form supplied by the Clerk, of the date of filing, the date the case was placed on the docket, and the docket number of the case. The notice shall be served as required by Rule 29.

4. Parties interested jointly, severally, or otherwise in a judgment may petition separately for a writ of certiorari; or any two or more may join in a petition. A party not shown on the petition as joined therein at the time the petition is filed may not later join in that petition. When two or more judgments are sought to be reviewed on a writ of certiorari to the same court and involve identical or closely related questions, a single petition for a writ of certiorari covering all the judgments suffices. A petition for a writ of certiorari may not be joined with any other pleading, except that any motion for leave to proceed *in forma pauperis* shall be attached.

5. No more than 30 days after a case has been placed on the docket, a respondent seeking to file a conditional cross-petition (*i.e.,* a cross-petition that otherwise would be untimely) shall file, with proof of service as required by Rule 29, 40 copies of the cross-petition prepared as required by Rule 33.1, except that a cross-petitioner proceeding *in forma pauperis* under Rule 39 shall comply with Rule 12.2. The cross-petition shall comply in all respects with this Rule and Rule 14, except that material already reproduced in the appendix to the opening petition need not be reproduced again. A cross-petitioning respondent shall pay the Rule 38(a) docket fee or submit a motion for leave to proceed *in forma pauperis.* The cover of the cross-petition shall indicate clearly that it is a conditional cross-petition. The cross-petition then will be placed on the docket, subject to the provisions of Rule 13.4. It is the cross-petitioner's duty to notify all cross-respondents promptly, on a form supplied by the Clerk, of the date of filing, the date the cross-petition was placed on the docket, and the docket number of the cross-petition. The notice shall be served as required by Rule 29. A cross-petition for a writ of certiorari may not be joined with any other pleading, except that any motion for leave to proceed *in forma pauperis* shall be attached. The time to file a conditional cross-petition will not be extended.

6. All parties to the proceeding in the court whose judgment is sought to be reviewed are deemed parties entitled to file documents in this Court, unless the petitioner notifies the Clerk of this Court in writing of the petitioner's belief that one or more of the parties below have no interest in the outcome of the petition. A copy of such notice shall be served as required by Rule 29 on all parties to the proceeding below. A party noted as no longer interested may remain a party by notifying the Clerk promptly, with service on the other parties, of an intention to remain a party. All parties other than the petitioner are considered respondents, but any respondent who supports the position of a petitioner shall meet the petitioner's time schedule for filing documents, except that a response supporting the petition shall be filed within 20 days after the case is placed on the docket, and that time will not be extended. Parties who file no document will not qualify for any relief from this Court.

7. The clerk of the court having possession of the record shall keep it until notified by the Clerk of this Court to certify and transmit it. In any document filed with this Court, a party may cite or quote from the record, even if it has not been transmitted to this Court. When requested by the Clerk of this Court to certify and transmit the record, or any part of it, the clerk of the court having possession of the record shall number the documents to be certified and shall transmit therewith a numbered list specifically identifying each document transmitted. If the record, or stipulated portions, have been printed for the use of the court below, that printed record, plus the proceedings in the court below, may be certified as the record unless one of the parties or the Clerk of this Court requests otherwise. The record may consist of certified copies, but if the lower court is of the view that original documents of any kind should be seen by this Court, that court may provide by order for the transport, safekeeping, and return of such originals.

Rule 13. Review on Certiorari: Time for Petitioning

1. Unless otherwise provided by law, a petition for a writ of certiorari to review a judgment in any case, civil or criminal, entered by a state court of last resort or a United States court of appeals (including the United States Court of Appeals for the Armed Forces) is timely when it is filed with the Clerk of this Court within 90 days after entry of the judgment. A petition for a writ of certiorari seeking review of a judgment of a lower state court that is subject to discretionary review by the state court of last resort is timely when it is filed with the Clerk within 90 days after entry of the order denying discretionary review.

2. The Clerk will not file any petition for a writ of certiorari that is jurisdictionally out of time. See, *e.g.*, 28 U.S.C. § 2101(c).

3. The time to file a petition for a writ of certiorari runs from the date of entry of the judgment or order sought to be reviewed, and not from the issuance date of the mandate (or its equivalent under local practice). But if a petition for rehearing is timely filed in the lower court by any party, or if the lower court appropriately entertains an untimely petition for rehearing or *sua sponte* considers rehearing, the time to file the petition for a writ of certiorari for all parties (whether or not they requested rehearing or joined in the petition for rehearing) runs from the date of the denial of rehearing or, if rehearing is granted, the subsequent entry of judgment.

4. A cross-petition for a writ of certiorari is timely when it is filed with the Clerk as provided in paragraphs 1, 3, and 5 of this Rule, or in Rule 12.5. However, a conditional cross-petition (which except for Rule 12.5 would be untimely) will not be granted unless another party's timely petition for a writ of certiorari is granted.

5. For good cause, a Justice may extend the time to file a petition for a writ of certiorari for a period not exceeding 60 days. An application to extend the time to file shall set out the basis for jurisdiction in this Court, identify the judgment sought to be reviewed, include a copy of the opinion and any order respecting rehearing, and set out specific reasons why an extension of time is justified. The application must be filed with the Clerk at least 10 days before the date the petition is due, except in extraordinary circumstances. For the time and manner of presenting the application, see Rules 21, 22, 30, and 33.2. An application to extend the time to file a petition for a writ of certiorari is not favored.

(As amended Jan. 11, 1999, eff. May 3, 1999; Jan. 27, 2003, eff. May 1, 2003; Mar. 14, 2005, eff. May 2, 2005.)

Rule 14. Content of a Petition for a Writ of Certiorari

1. A petition for a writ of certiorari shall contain, in the order indicated:

(a) The questions presented for review, expressed concisely in relation to the circumstances of the case, without unnecessary detail. The questions should be short and should not be argumentative or repetitive. If the petitioner or respondent is under a death sentence that may be affected by the disposition of the petition, the notation "capital case" shall precede the questions presented. The questions shall be set out on the first page following the cover, and no other information may appear on that page. The statement of any question presented is deemed to comprise every subsidiary question fairly included therein. Only the questions set out in the petition, or fairly included therein, will be considered by the Court.

(b) A list of all parties to the proceeding in the court whose judgment is sought to be reviewed (unless the caption of the case contains the names of all the parties), and a corporate disclosure statement as required by Rule 29.6.

(c) If the petition exceeds five pages, a table of contents and a table of cited authorities.

(d) Citations of the official and unofficial reports of the opinions and orders entered in the case by courts or administrative agencies.

(e) A concise statement of the basis for jurisdiction in this Court, showing:

(i) the date the judgment or order sought to be reviewed was entered (and, if applicable, a statement that the petition is filed under this Court's Rule 11);

(ii) the date of any order respecting rehearing, and the date and terms of any order granting an extension of time to file the petition for a writ of certiorari;

(iii) express reliance on Rule 12.5, when a cross-petition for a writ of certiorari is filed under that Rule, and the date of docketing of the petition for a writ of certiorari in connection with which the cross-petition is filed;

(iv) the statutory provision believed to confer on this Court jurisdiction to review on a writ of certiorari the judgment or order in question; and

(v) if applicable, a statement that the notifications required by Rule 29.4(b) or (c) have been made.

(f) The constitutional provisions, treaties, statutes, ordinances, and regulations involved in the case, set out verbatim with appropriate citation. If the provisions involved are lengthy, their citation alone suffices at this point, and their pertinent text shall be set out in the appendix referred to in subparagraph 1(i).

(g) A concise statement of the case setting out the facts material to consideration of the questions presented, and also containing the following:

(i) If review of a state-court judgment is sought, specification of the stage in the proceedings, both in the court of first instance and in the appellate courts, when the federal questions sought to be reviewed were raised; the method or manner of raising them and the way in which they were passed on by those courts; and pertinent quotations of specific portions of the record or summary thereof, with specific reference to the places in the record where the matter appears (*e.g.*, court opinion, ruling on exception, portion of court's charge and exception thereto, assignment of error), so as to show that the federal question was timely and properly raised and that this Court has jurisdiction to review the judgment on a writ of certiorari. When the portions of the record relied on under this subparagraph are voluminous, they shall be included in the appendix referred to in subparagraph 1(i).

(ii) If review of a judgment of a United States court of appeals is sought, the basis for federal jurisdiction in the court of first instance.

(h) A direct and concise argument amplifying the reasons relied on for allowance of the writ. See Rule 10.

(i) An appendix containing, in the order indicated:

(i) the opinions, orders, findings of fact, and conclusions of law, whether written or orally given and transcribed, entered in conjunction with the judgment sought to be reviewed;

(ii) any other relevant opinions, orders, findings of fact, and conclusions of law entered in the case by courts or administrative agencies, and, if reference thereto is necessary to ascertain the grounds of the judgment, of those in companion cases (each document shall include the caption showing the name of the issuing court or agency, the title and number of the case, and the date of entry);

(iii) any order on rehearing, including the caption showing the name of the issuing court, the title and number of the case, and the date of entry;

(iv) the judgment sought to be reviewed if the date of its entry is different from the date of the opinion or order required in sub-subparagraph (i) of this subparagraph;

(v) material required by subparagraphs 1(f) or 1(g)(i); and

(vi) any other material the petitioner believes essential to understand the petition.

If the material required by this subparagraph is voluminous, it may be presented in a separate volume or volumes with appropriate covers.

2. All contentions in support of a petition for a writ of certiorari shall be set out in the body of the petition, as provided in subparagraph 1(h) of this Rule. No separate brief in support of a petition for a writ of certiorari may be filed, and the Clerk will not file any petition for a writ of certiorari to which any supporting brief is annexed or appended.

3. A petition for a writ of certiorari should be stated briefly and in plain terms and may not exceed the page limitations specified in Rule 33.

4. The failure of a petitioner to present with accuracy, brevity, and clarity whatever is essential to ready and adequate understanding of the points requiring consideration is sufficient reason for the Court to deny a petition.

5. If the Clerk determines that a petition submitted timely and in good faith is in a form that does not comply with this Rule or with Rule 33 or Rule 34, the Clerk will return it with a letter indicating the deficiency. A corrected petition received no more than 60 days after the date of the Clerk's letter will be deemed timely.

Rule 15. Briefs in Opposition; Reply Briefs; Supplemental Briefs

1. A brief in opposition to a petition for a writ of certiorari may be filed by the respondent in any case, but is not mandatory except in a capital case, see Rule 14.1(a), or when ordered by the Court.

2. A brief in opposition should be stated briefly and in plain terms and may not exceed the page limitations specified in Rule 33. In addition to presenting other arguments for denying the petition, the brief in opposition should address any perceived misstatement of fact or law in the petition that bears on what issues properly would be before the Court if certiorari were granted. Counsel are admonished that they have an obligation to the Court to point out in the brief in opposition, and not later, any perceived misstatement made in the petition. Any objection to consideration of a question presented based on what occurred in the proceedings below, if the objection does not go to jurisdiction, may be deemed waived unless called to the Court's attention in the brief in opposition.

3. Any brief in opposition shall be filed within 30 days after the case is placed on the docket, unless the time is extended by the Court or a Justice, or by the Clerk under Rule 30.4. Forty copies shall be filed, except that a respondent proceeding *in forma pauperis* under Rule 39, including an inmate of an institution, shall file the number of copies required for a petition by such a person under Rule 12.2, together with a motion for leave to proceed *in forma pauperis*, a copy of which shall precede and be attached to each copy of the brief in opposition. If the petitioner is proceeding *in forma pauperis*, the respondent may file an original and 10 copies of a brief in opposition prepared as required by Rule 33.2. Whether prepared under Rule 33.1 or Rule 33.2, the brief in opposition shall comply with the requirements of Rule 24 governing a respondent's brief, except that no summary of the argument is required. A brief in opposition may not be joined with any other pleading, except that any motion for leave to proceed *in forma pauperis* shall be attached. The brief in opposition shall be served as required by Rule 29.

4. No motion by a respondent to dismiss a petition for a writ of certiorari may be filed. Any objections to the jurisdiction of the Court to grant a petition for a writ of certiorari shall be included in the brief in opposition.

5. The Clerk will distribute the petition to the Court for its consideration upon receiving an express waiver of the right to file a brief in opposition, or, if no waiver or brief in opposition is filed, upon the expiration of the time allowed for filing. If a brief in opposition is timely filed, the Clerk will distribute the petition, brief in opposition, and any reply brief to the Court for its consideration no less than 10 days after the brief in opposition is filed.

6. Any petitioner may file a reply brief addressed to new points raised in the brief in opposition, but distribution and consideration by the Court under paragraph 5 of this Rule will not be deferred pending its receipt. Forty copies shall be filed, except that a petitioner proceeding *in forma pauperis* under Rule 39, including an inmate of an institution, shall file the number of copies required for a petition by such a person under Rule 12.2. The reply brief shall be served as required by Rule 29.

7. If a cross-petition for a writ of certiorari has been docketed, distribution of both petitions will be deferred until the cross-petition is due for distribution under this Rule.

8. Any party may file a supplemental brief at any time while a petition for a writ of certiorari is pending, calling attention to new cases, new legislation, or other intervening matter not available at the time of the party's last filing. A supplemental brief shall be restricted to new matter and shall follow, insofar as applicable, the form for a brief in opposition prescribed by this Rule. Forty copies shall be filed, except that a party proceeding *in forma pauperis* under Rule 39, including an inmate of an institution, shall file the number of copies required for a petition by such a person under Rule 12.2. The supplemental brief shall be served as required by Rule 29.

Rule 16. Disposition of a Petition for a Writ of Certiorari

1. After considering the documents distributed under Rule 15, the Court will enter an appropriate order. The order may be a summary disposition on the merits.

2. Whenever the Court grants a petition for a writ of certiorari, the Clerk will prepare, sign, and enter an order to that effect and will notify forthwith counsel of record and the court whose judgment is to be reviewed. The case then will be scheduled for briefing and oral argument. If the record has not previously been filed in this Court, the Clerk will request the clerk of the court having possession of the record to certify and transmit it. A formal writ will not issue unless specially directed.

3. Whenever the Court denies a petition for a writ of certiorari, the Clerk will prepare, sign, and enter an order to that effect and will notify forthwith counsel of record and the court whose judgment was sought to be reviewed. The order of denial will not be suspended pending disposition of a petition for rehearing except by order of the Court or a Justice.

PART IV. OTHER JURISDICTION

Rule 17. Procedure in an Original Action

1. This Rule applies only to an action invoking the Court's original jurisdiction under Article III of the Constitution of the United States. See also 28 U.S.C. § 1251 and U.S. Const., Amdt. 11. A petition for an extraordinary writ in aid of the Court's appellate jurisdiction shall be filed as provided in Rule 20.

2. The form of pleadings and motions prescribed by the Federal Rules of Civil Procedure is followed. In other respects, those Rules and the Federal Rules of Evidence may be taken as guides.

3. The initial pleading shall be preceded by a motion for leave to file, and may be accompanied by a brief in support of the motion. Forty copies of each document shall be filed, with proof of service. Service shall be as required by Rule 29, except that when an adverse party is a State, service shall be made on both the Governor and the Attorney General of that State.

4. The case will be placed on the docket when the motion for leave to file and the initial pleading are filed with the Clerk. The Rule 38(a) docket fee shall be paid at that time.

5. No more than 60 days after receiving the motion for leave to file and the initial pleading, an adverse party shall file 40 copies of any brief in opposition to the motion, with proof of service as required by Rule 29. The Clerk will distribute the filed documents to the Court for its consideration upon receiving an express waiver of the right to file a brief in opposition, or, if no waiver or brief is filed, upon the expiration of the time allowed for filing. If a brief in opposition is timely filed, the Clerk will distribute the filed documents to the Court for its consideration no less than 10 days after the brief in opposition is filed. A reply brief may be filed, but consideration of the case will not be deferred pending its receipt. The Court thereafter may grant or deny the motion, set it for oral argument, direct that additional documents be filed, or require that other proceedings be conducted.

6. A summons issued out of this Court shall be served on the defendant 60 days before the return day specified therein. If the defendant does not respond by the return day, the plaintiff may proceed *ex parte.*

7. Process against a State issued out of this Court shall be served on both the Governor and the Attorney General of that State.

Rule 18. Appeal from a United States District Court

1. When a direct appeal from a decision of a United States district court is authorized by law, the appeal is commenced by filing a notice of appeal with the clerk of the district court within the time provided by law after entry of the judgment sought to be reviewed. The time to file may not be extended. The notice of appeal shall specify the parties taking the appeal, designate the judgment, or part thereof, appealed from and the date of its entry, and specify the statute or statutes under which the appeal is taken. A copy of the notice of appeal shall be served on all parties to the proceeding as required by Rule 29, and proof of service shall be filed in the district court together with the notice of appeal.

2. All parties to the proceeding in the district court are deemed parties entitled to file documents in this Court, but a party having no interest in the outcome of the appeal may so notify the Clerk of this Court and shall serve a copy of the notice on all other parties. Parties interested jointly, severally, or otherwise in the judgment may appeal separately, or any two or more may join in an appeal. When two or more judgments involving identical or closely related questions are sought to be reviewed on appeal from the same court, a notice of appeal for each judgment shall be filed with the clerk of the district court, but a single jurisdictional statement covering all the judgments suffices. Parties who file no document will not qualify for any relief from this Court.

3. No more than 60 days after filing the notice of appeal in the district court, the appellant shall file 40 copies of a jurisdictional statement and shall pay the Rule 38 docket fee, except that an appellant proceeding *in forma pauperis* under Rule 39, including an inmate of an institution, shall file the number of copies required for a petition by such a person under Rule 12.2, together with a motion for leave to proceed *in forma pauperis,* a copy of which shall precede and be attached to each copy of the jurisdictional statement. The jurisdictional statement shall follow, insofar as applicable, the form for a petition for a writ of certiorari prescribed by Rule 14, and shall be served as required by Rule 29. The case will then be placed on the docket. It is the appellant's duty to notify all appellees promptly, on a form supplied by the Clerk, of the date of filing, the date the case was placed on the docket, and the docket number of the case. The notice shall be served as required by Rule 29. The appendix shall include a copy of the notice of appeal showing the date it was filed in the district court. For good cause, a Justice may extend the time to file a jurisdictional statement for a period not exceeding 60 days. An application to extend the time to file a jurisdictional statement shall set out the basis for jurisdiction in this Court; identify the judgment sought to be reviewed; include a copy of the opinion, any order respecting rehearing, and the notice of appeal; and set out specific reasons why an extension of time is justified. For the time and manner of presenting the application, see Rules 21, 22, and 30. An application to extend the time to file a jurisdictional statement is not favored.

4. No more than 30 days after a case has been placed on the docket, an appellee seeking to file a conditional cross-appeal (*i.e.*, a cross-appeal that otherwise would be untimely) shall file, with proof of service as required by Rule 29, a jurisdictional statement that complies in all respects (including number of copies filed) with paragraph 3 of this Rule, except that material already reproduced in the appendix to the opening jurisdictional statement need not be reproduced again. A cross-appealing appellee shall pay the Rule 38 docket fee or submit a motion for leave to proceed *in forma pauperis.* The cover of the cross-appeal shall indicate clearly that it is a conditional cross-appeal. The cross-appeal then will be placed on the docket. It is the cross-appellant's duty to notify all cross-appellees promptly, on a form supplied by the Clerk, of the date of filing, the date the cross-appeal was placed on the docket, and the docket number of the cross-appeal. The notice shall be served as required by Rule 29. A cross-appeal may not be joined with any other pleading, except that any motion for leave to proceed *in forma pauperis* shall be attached. The time to file a cross-appeal will not be extended.

5. After a notice of appeal has been filed in the district court, but before the case is placed on this Court's docket, the parties may dismiss the appeal by stipulation filed in the district court, or the district court may dismiss the appeal on the appellant's motion, with notice to all parties. If a notice of appeal has been filed, but the case has not been placed on this Court's docket within the time prescribed for docketing, the district court may dismiss the appeal on the appellee's motion, with notice to all parties, and may make any just order with respect to costs. If the district court has denied the appellee's motion to dismiss the appeal, the appellee may move this Court to docket and dismiss the appeal by filing an original and 10 copies of a motion presented in conformity with Rules 21 and 33.2. The motion shall be accompanied by proof of service as required by Rule 29, and by a certificate from the clerk of the district court, certifying that a notice of appeal was filed and that the appellee's motion to dismiss was denied. The appellant may not thereafter file a jurisdictional statement without special leave of the Court, and the Court may allow costs against the appellant.

6. Within 30 days after the case is placed on this Court's docket, the appellee may file a motion to dismiss, to affirm, or in the alternative to affirm or dismiss. Forty copies of the motion shall be filed, except that an appellee proceeding *in forma pauperis* under Rule 39, including an inmate of an institution, shall file the number of copies required for a petition by such a person under Rule 12.2, together with a motion for leave to proceed *in forma pauperis,* a copy of which shall precede and be attached to each copy of the motion to dismiss, to affirm, or in the alternative to affirm or dismiss. The motion shall follow, insofar as applicable, the form for a brief in opposition prescribed by Rule 15, and shall comply in all respects with Rule 21.

7. The Clerk will distribute the jurisdictional statement to the Court for its consideration upon receiving an express waiver of the right to file a motion to dismiss or to affirm or, if no waiver or motion is filed, upon the expiration of the time allowed for filing. If a motion to dismiss or to affirm is timely filed, the Clerk will distribute the jurisdictional statement, motion, and any brief opposing the motion to the Court for its consideration no less than 10 days after the motion is filed.

8. Any appellant may file a brief opposing a motion to dismiss or to affirm, but distribution and consideration by the Court under paragraph 7 of this Rule will not be deferred pending its receipt. Forty copies shall be filed, except that an appellant proceeding *in forma pauperis* under Rule 39, including an inmate of an institution, shall file the number of copies required for a petition by such a person under Rule 12.2. The brief shall be served as required by Rule 29.

9. If a cross-appeal has been docketed, distribution of both jurisdictional statements will be deferred until the cross-appeal is due for distribution under this Rule.

10. Any party may file a supplemental brief at any time while a jurisdictional statement is pending, calling attention to new cases, new legislation, or other intervening matter not available at the time of the party's last filing. A supplemental brief shall be restricted to new matter and shall follow, insofar as applicable, the form for a brief in opposition prescribed by Rule 15. Forty copies shall be filed, except that a party proceeding *in forma pauperis* under Rule 39, including an inmate of an institution, shall file the number of copies required for a petition by such a person under Rule 12.2. The supplemental brief shall be served as required by Rule 29.

11. The clerk of the district court shall retain possession of the record until notified by the Clerk of this Court to certify and transmit it. See Rule 12.7.

12. After considering the documents distributed under this Rule, the Court may dispose summarily of the appeal on the merits, note probable jurisdiction, or postpone consideration of jurisdiction until a hearing of the case on the merits. If not disposed of summarily, the case stands for briefing and oral argument on the merits. If consideration of jurisdiction is postponed, counsel, at the outset of their briefs and at oral argument, shall address the question of jurisdiction. If the record has not previously been filed in this Court, the Clerk of this Court will request the clerk of the court in possession of the record to certify and transmit it.

13. If the Clerk determines that a jurisdictional statement submitted timely and in good faith is in a form that does not comply with this Rule or with Rule 33 or Rule 34, the Clerk will return it with a letter indicating the deficiency. If a corrected jurisdictional statement is received no more than 60 days after the date of the Clerk's letter, its filing will be deemed timely.

Rule 19. Procedure on a Certified Question

1. A United States court of appeals may certify to this Court a question or proposition of law on which it seeks instruction for the proper decision of a case. The certificate shall contain a statement of the nature of the case and the facts on which the question or proposition of law arises. Only questions or propositions of law may be certified, and they shall be stated separately and with precision. The certificate shall be prepared as required by Rule 33.2 and shall be signed by the clerk of the court of appeals.

2. When a question is certified by a United States court of appeals, this Court, on its own motion or that of a party, may consider and decide the entire matter in controversy. See 28 U.S.C. § 1254(2).

3. When a question is certified, the Clerk will notify the parties and docket the case. Counsel shall then enter their appearances. After docketing, the Clerk will submit the certificate to the Court for a preliminary examination to determine whether the case should be briefed, set for argument, or dismissed. No brief may be filed until the preliminary examination of the certificate is completed.

4. If the Court orders the case briefed or set for argument, the parties will be notified and permitted to file briefs. The Clerk of this Court then will request the clerk of the court in possession of the record to certify and transmit it. Any portion of the record to which the parties wish to direct the Court's particular attention should be printed in a joint appendix, prepared in conformity with Rule 26 by the appellant or petitioner in the court of appeals, but the fact that any part of the record has not been printed does not prevent the parties or the Court from relying on it.

5. A brief on the merits in a case involving a certified question shall comply with Rules 24, 25, and 33.1, except that the brief for the party who is the appellant or petitioner below shall be filed within 45 days of the order requiring briefs or setting the case for argument.

Rule 20. Procedure on a Petition for an Extraordinary Writ

1. Issuance by the Court of an extraordinary writ authorized by 28 U.S.C. § 1651(a) is not a matter of right, but of discretion sparingly exercised. To justify the granting of any such writ, the petition must show that the writ will be in aid of the Court's appellate jurisdiction, that exceptional circumstances warrant the exercise of the Court's discretionary powers, and that adequate relief cannot be obtained in any other form or from any other court.

2. A petition seeking a writ authorized by 28 U.S.C. § 1651(a), § 2241, or § 2254(a) shall be prepared in all respects as required by Rules 33 and 34. The petition shall be captioned "*In re* [name of petitioner]" and shall follow, insofar as applicable, the form of a petition for a writ of certiorari prescribed by Rule 14. All contentions in support of the petition shall be included in the petition. The case will be placed on the docket when 40 copies of the petition are filed with the Clerk and the docket fee is paid, except that a petitioner proceeding *in forma pauperis* under Rule 39, including an inmate of an institution, shall file the number of copies required for a petition by such a person under Rule 12.2, together with a motion for leave to proceed *in forma pauperis,* a copy of which shall precede and be attached to each copy of the petition. The petition shall be served as required by Rule 29 (subject to subparagraph 4(b) of this Rule).

3. (a) A petition seeking a writ of prohibition, a writ of mandamus, or both in the alternative shall state the name and office or function of every person against whom relief is sought and shall set out with particularity why the relief sought is not available in any other court. A copy of the judgment with respect to which the writ is sought, including any related opinion, shall be appended to the petition together with any other document essential to understanding the petition.

(b) The petition shall be served on every party to the proceeding with respect to which relief is sought. Within 30 days after the petition is placed on the docket, a party shall file 40 copies of any brief or briefs in opposition thereto, which shall comply fully with Rule 15. If a party named as a respondent does not wish to respond to the petition, that party may so advise the Clerk and all other parties by letter. All persons served are deemed respondents for all purposes in the proceedings in this Court.

4. (a) A petition seeking a writ of habeas corpus shall comply with the requirements of 28 U.S.C. §§ 2241 and 2242, and in particular with the provision in the last paragraph of § 2242, which requires a statement of the "reasons for not making application to the district court of the district in which the applicant is held." If the relief sought is from the judgment of a state court, the petition shall set out specifically how and where the petitioner has exhausted available remedies in the state courts or otherwise comes within the provisions of 28 U.S.C. § 2254(b). To justify the granting of a writ of habeas corpus, the petitioner must show that exceptional circumstances warrant the exercise of the Court's discretionary powers, and that adequate relief cannot be obtained in any other form or from any other court. This writ is rarely granted.

(b) Habeas corpus proceedings, except in capital cases, are *ex parte,* unless the Court requires the respondent to show cause why the petition for a writ of habeas corpus should not be granted. A response, if ordered, or in a capital case, shall comply fully with Rule 15. Neither the denial of the petition, without more, nor an order of transfer to a district court under the authority of 28 U.S.C. § 2241(b), is an adjudication on the merits, and therefore does not preclude further application to another court for the relief sought.

5. The Clerk will distribute the documents to the Court for its consideration when a brief in opposition under subparagraph 3(b) of this Rule has been filed, when a response under subparagraph 4(b) has been ordered and filed, when the time to file has expired, or when the right to file has been expressly waived.

6. If the Court orders the case set for argument, the Clerk will notify the parties whether additional briefs are required, when they shall be filed, and, if the case involves a petition for a common-law writ of certiorari, that the parties shall prepare a joint appendix in accordance with Rule 26.

PART V. MOTIONS AND APPLICATIONS

Rule 21. Motions to the Court

1. Every motion to the Court shall clearly state its purpose and the facts on which it is based and may present legal argument in support thereof. No separate brief may be filed. A motion should be concise and shall comply with any applicable page limits. Rule 22 governs an application addressed to a single Justice.

2. (a) A motion in any action within the Court's original jurisdiction shall comply with Rule 17.3.

(b) A motion to dismiss as moot (or a suggestion of mootness), a motion for leave to file a brief as *amicus curiae,* and any motion the granting of which would dispose of the entire case or would affect the final judgment to be entered (other than a motion to docket and dismiss under Rule 18.5 or a motion for voluntary dismissal under Rule 46) shall be prepared as required by Rule 33.1, and 40 copies shall be filed, except that a movant proceeding *in forma pauperis* under Rule 39, including an inmate of an institution, shall file a motion prepared as required by Rule 33.2, and shall file the number of copies required for a petition by such a person under Rule 12.2. The motion shall be served as required by Rule 29.

(c) Any other motion to the Court shall be prepared as required by Rule 33.2; the moving party shall file an original and 10 copies. The Court subsequently may order the moving party to prepare the motion as required by Rule 33.1; in that event, the party shall file 40 copies.

3. A motion to the Court shall be filed with the Clerk and shall be accompanied by proof of service as required by Rule 29. No motion may be presented in open Court, other than a motion for admission to the Bar, except when the proceeding to which it refers is being argued. Oral argument on a motion will not be permitted unless the Court so directs.

4. Any response to a motion shall be filed as promptly as possible considering the nature of the relief sought and any asserted need for emergency action, and, in any event, within 10 days of receipt, unless the Court or a Justice, or the Clerk under Rule 30.4, orders otherwise. A response to a motion prepared as required by Rule 33.1, except a response to a motion for leave to file an *amicus curiae* brief (see Rule 37.5), shall be prepared in the same manner if time permits. In an appropriate case, the Court may act on a motion without waiting for a response.

Rule 22. Applications to Individual Justices

1. An application addressed to an individual Justice shall be filed with the Clerk, who will transmit it promptly to the Justice concerned if an individual Justice has authority to grant the sought relief.

2. The original and two copies of any application addressed to an individual Justice shall be prepared as required by Rule 33.2, and shall be accompanied by proof of service as required by Rule 29.

3. An application shall be addressed to the Justice allotted to the Circuit from which the case arises. When the Circuit Justice is unavailable for any reason, the application addressed to that Justice will be distributed to the Justice then available who is next junior to the Circuit Justice; the turn of the Chief Justice follows that of the most junior Justice.

4. A Justice denying an application will note the denial thereon. Thereafter, unless action thereon is restricted by law to the Circuit Justice or is untimely under Rule 30.2, the party making an application, except in the case of an application for an extension of time, may renew it to any other Justice, subject to the provisions of this Rule. Except when the denial is without prejudice, a renewed application is not favored. Renewed application is made by a letter to the Clerk, designating the Justice to whom the application is to be directed, and accompanied by 10 copies of the original application and proof of service as required by Rule 29.

5. A Justice to whom an application for a stay or for bail is submitted may refer it to the Court for determination.

6. The Clerk will advise all parties concerned, by appropriately speedy means, of the disposition made of an application.

Rule 23. Stays

1. A stay may be granted by a Justice as permitted by law.

2. A party to a judgment sought to be reviewed may present to a Justice an application to stay the enforcement of that judgment. See 28 U.S.C. § 2101(f).

3. An application for a stay shall set out with particularity why the relief sought is not available from any other court or judge. Except in the most extraordinary circumstances, an application for a stay will not be entertained unless the relief requested was first sought in the appropriate court or courts below or from a judge or judges thereof. An application for a stay shall identify the judgment sought to be reviewed and have appended thereto a copy of the order and opinion, if any, and a copy of the order, if any, of the court or judge below denying the relief sought, and shall set out specific reasons why a stay is justified. The form and content of an application for a stay are governed by Rules 22 and 33.2.

4. A judge, court, or Justice granting an application for a stay pending review by this Court may condition the stay on the filing of a supersedeas bond having an approved surety or sureties. The bond will be conditioned on the satisfaction of the judgment in full, together with any costs, interest, and damages for delay that may be awarded. If a part of the judgment sought to be reviewed has already been satisfied, or is otherwise secured, the bond may be conditioned on the satisfaction of the part of the judgment not otherwise secured or satisfied, together with costs, interest, and damages.

PART VI. BRIEFS ON THE MERITS AND ORAL ARGUMENT

Rule 24. Briefs on the Merits: In General

1. A brief on the merits for a petitioner or an appellant shall comply in all respects with Rules 33.1 and 34 and shall contain in the order here indicated:

(a) The questions presented for review under Rule 14.1(a). The questions shall be set out on the first page following the cover, and no other information may appear on that page. The phrasing of the questions presented need not be identical with that in the petition for a writ of certiorari or the jurisdictional statement, but the brief may not raise additional questions or change the substance of the questions already presented in those documents. At its option, however, the Court may consider a plain error not among the questions presented but evident from the record and otherwise within its jurisdiction to decide.

(b) A list of all parties to the proceeding in the court whose judgment is under review (unless the caption of the case in this Court contains the names of all parties). Any amended corporate disclosure statement as required by Rule 29.6 shall be placed here.

(c) If the brief exceeds five pages, a table of contents and a table of cited authorities.

(d) Citations of the official and unofficial reports of the opinions and orders entered in the case by courts and administrative agencies.

(e) A concise statement of the basis for jurisdiction in this Court, including the statutory provisions and time factors on which jurisdiction rests.

(f) The constitutional provisions, treaties, statutes, ordinances, and regulations involved in the case, set out verbatim with appropriate citation. If the provisions involved are lengthy, their citation alone suffices at this point, and their pertinent text, if not already set out in the petition for a writ of certiorari, jurisdictional statement, or an appendix to either document, shall be set out in an appendix to the brief.

(g) A concise statement of the case, setting out the facts material to the consideration of the questions presented, with appropriate references to the joint appendix, *e.g.*, App. 12, or to the record, *e.g.*, Record 12.

(h) A summary of the argument, suitably paragraphed. The summary should be a clear and concise condensation of the argument made in the body of the brief; mere repetition of the headings under which the argument is arranged is not sufficient.

(i) The argument, exhibiting clearly the points of fact and of law presented and citing the authorities and statutes relied on.

(j) A conclusion specifying with particularity the relief the party seeks.

2. A brief on the merits for a respondent or an appellee shall conform to the foregoing requirements, except that items required by subparagraphs 1(a), (b), (d), (e), (f), and (g) of this Rule need not be included unless the respondent or appellee is dissatisfied with their presentation by the opposing party.

3. A brief on the merits may not exceed the page limitations specified in Rule 33.1(g). An appendix to a brief may include only relevant material, and counsel are cautioned not to include in an appendix arguments or citations that properly belong in the body of the brief.

4. A reply brief shall conform to those portions of this Rule applicable to the brief for a respondent or an appellee, but, if appropriately divided by topical headings, need not contain a summary of the argument.

5. A reference to the joint appendix or to the record set out in any brief shall indicate the appropriate page number. If the reference is to an exhibit, the page numbers at which the exhibit appears, at which it was offered in evidence, and at which it was ruled on by the judge shall be indicated, *e.g.,* Pl.Exh. 14, Record 199, 2134.

6. A brief shall be concise, logically arranged with proper headings, and free of irrelevant, immaterial, or scandalous matter. The Court may disregard or strike a brief that does not comply with this paragraph.

Rule 25. Briefs on the Merits: Number of Copies and Time to File

1. The petitioner or appellant shall file 40 copies of the brief on the merits within 45 days of the order granting the writ of certiorari, noting probable jurisdiction, or postponing consideration of jurisdiction. Any respondent or appellee who supports the petitioner or appellant shall meet the petitioner's or appellant's time schedule for filing documents.

2. The respondent or appellee shall file 40 copies of the brief on the merits within 35 days after the brief for the petitioner or appellant is filed.

3. The petitioner or appellant shall file 40 copies of the reply brief, if any, within 35 days after the brief for the respondent or appellee is filed, but any reply brief must actually be received by the Clerk not later than one week before the date of oral argument. Any respondent or appellee supporting the petitioner or appellant may file a reply brief.

4. The time periods stated in paragraphs 1 and 2 of this Rule may be extended as provided in Rule 30. An application to extend the time to file a brief on the merits is not favored. If a case is advanced for hearing, the time to file briefs on the merits may be abridged as circumstances require pursuant to an order of the Court on its own motion or that of a party.

5. A party wishing to present late authorities, newly enacted legislation, or other intervening matter that was not available in time to be included in a brief may file 40 copies of a supplemental brief, restricted to such new matter and otherwise presented in conformity with these Rules, up to the time the case is called for oral argument or by leave of the Court thereafter.

6. After a case has been argued or submitted, the Clerk will not file any brief, except that of a party filed by leave of the Court.

7. The Clerk will not file any brief that is not accompanied by proof of service as required by Rule 29.

(As amended Jan. 11, 1999, eff. May 3, 1999; Jan. 27, 2003, eff. May 1, 2003.)

Rule 26. Joint Appendix

1. Unless the Clerk has allowed the parties to use the deferred method described in paragraph 4 of this Rule, the petitioner or appellant, within 45 days after entry of the order granting the writ of certiorari, noting probable jurisdiction, or postponing consideration of jurisdiction, shall file 40 copies of a joint appendix, prepared as required by Rule 33.1. The joint appendix shall contain: (1) the relevant docket entries in all the courts below; (2) any relevant pleadings, jury instructions, findings, conclusions, or opinions; (3) the judgment, order, or decision under review; and (4) any other parts of the record that the parties particularly wish to bring to the Court's attention. Any of the foregoing items already reproduced in a petition for a writ of certiorari, jurisdictional statement, brief in opposition to a petition for a writ of certiorari, motion to dismiss or affirm, or any appendix to the foregoing, that was prepared as required by Rule 33.1, need not be reproduced again in the joint appendix. The petitioner or appellant shall serve three copies of the joint appendix on each of the other parties to the proceeding as required by Rule 29.

2. The parties are encouraged to agree on the contents of the joint appendix. In the absence of agreement, the petitioner or appellant, within 10 days after entry of the order granting the writ of certiorari, noting probable jurisdiction, or postponing consideration of jurisdiction, shall serve on the respondent or appellee a designation of parts of the record to be included in the joint appendix. Within 10 days after receiving the designation, a respondent or appellee who considers the parts of the record so designated insufficient shall serve on the petitioner or appellant a designation of additional parts to be included in the joint appendix, and the petitioner or appellant shall include the parts so designated. If the Court has permitted the respondent or appellee to proceed *in forma pauperis,* the petitioner or appellant may seek by motion to be excused from printing portions of the record the petitioner or appellant considers unnecessary. In making these designations, counsel should include only those materials the Court should examine; unnecessary designations should be avoided. The record is on file with the Clerk and available to the Justices, and counsel may refer in briefs and in oral argument to relevant portions of the record not included in the joint appendix.

3. When the joint appendix is filed, the petitioner or appellant immediately shall file with the Clerk a statement of the cost of printing 50 copies and shall serve a copy of the statement on each of the other parties as required by Rule 29. Unless the parties agree otherwise, the cost of producing the joint appendix shall be paid initially by the petitioner or appellant; but a petitioner or appellant who considers that parts of the record designated by the respondent or appellee are unnecessary for the determination of the issues presented may so advise the respondent or appellee, who then shall advance the cost of printing the additional parts, unless the Court or a Justice otherwise fixes the initial allocation of the costs. The cost of printing the joint appendix is taxed as a cost in the case, but if a party unnecessarily causes matter to be included in the joint appendix or prints excessive copies, the Court may impose these costs on that party.

4. (a) On the parties' request, the Clerk may allow preparation of the joint appendix to be deferred until after the briefs have been filed. In that event, the petitioner or appellant shall file the joint appendix no more than 14 days after receiving the brief for the respondent or appellee. The provisions of paragraphs 1, 2, and 3 of this Rule shall be followed, except that the designations referred to therein shall be made by each party when that party's brief is served. Deferral of the joint appendix is not favored.

(b) If the deferred method is used, the briefs on the merits may refer to the pages of the record. In that event, the joint appendix shall include in brackets on each page thereof the page number of the record where that material may be found. A party wishing to refer directly to the pages of the joint appendix may serve and file copies of its brief prepared as required by Rule 33.2 within the time provided by Rule 25, with appropriate references to the pages of the record. In that event, within 10 days after the joint appendix is filed, copies of the brief prepared as required by Rule 33.1 containing references to the pages of the joint appendix in place of, or in addition to, the initial references to the pages of the record, shall be served and filed. No other change may be made in the brief as initially served and filed, except that typographical errors may be corrected.

5. The joint appendix shall be prefaced by a table of contents showing the parts of the record that it contains, in the order in which the parts are set out, with references to the pages of the joint appendix at which each part begins. The relevant docket entries shall be set out after the table of contents, followed by the other parts of the record in chronological order. When testimony contained in the reporter's transcript of proceedings is set out in the joint appendix, the page of the transcript at which the testimony appears shall be indicated in brackets immediately before the statement that is set out. Omissions in the transcript or in any other document printed in the joint appendix shall be indicated by asterisks. Immaterial formal matters (*e.g.,* captions, subscriptions, acknowledgments) shall be omitted. A question and its answer may be contained in a single paragraph.

6. Exhibits designated for inclusion in the joint appendix may be contained in a separate volume or volumes suitably indexed. The transcript of a proceeding before an administrative agency, board, commission, or officer used in an action in a district court or court of appeals is regarded as an exhibit for the purposes of this paragraph.

7. The Court, on its own motion or that of a party, may dispense with the requirement of a joint appendix and may permit a case to be heard on the original record (with such copies of the record, or relevant parts thereof, as the Court may require) or on the appendix used in the court below, if it conforms to the requirements of this Rule.

8. For good cause, the time limits specified in this Rule may be shortened or extended by the Court or a Justice, or by the Clerk under Rule 30.4.

Rule 27. Calendar

1. From time to time, the Clerk will prepare a calendar of cases ready for argument. A case ordinarily will not be called for argument less than two weeks after the brief on the merits for the respondent or appellee is due.

2. The Clerk will advise counsel when they are required to appear for oral argument and will publish a hearing list in advance of each argument session for the convenience of counsel and the information of the public.

3. The Court, on its own motion or that of a party, may order that two or more cases involving the same or related questions be argued together as one case or on such other terms as the Court may prescribe.

Rule 28. Oral Argument

1. Oral argument should emphasize and clarify the written arguments in the briefs on the merits. Counsel should assume that all Justices have read the briefs before oral argument. Oral argument read from a prepared text is not favored.

2. The petitioner or appellant shall open and may conclude the argument. A cross-writ of certiorari or cross-appeal will be argued with the initial writ of certiorari or appeal as one case in the time allowed for that one case, and the Court will advise the parties who shall open and close.

3. Unless the Court directs otherwise, each side is allowed one-half hour for argument. Counsel is not required to use all the allotted time. Any request for additional time to argue shall be presented by motion under Rule 21 no more than 15 days after the petitioner's or appellant's brief on the merits is filed, and shall set out specifically and concisely why the case cannot be presented within the half-hour limitation. Additional time is rarely accorded.

4. Only one attorney will be heard for each side, except by leave of the Court on motion filed no more than 15 days after the respondent's or appellee's brief on the merits is filed. Any request for divided argument shall be presented by motion under Rule 21 and shall set out specifically and concisely why more than one attorney should be allowed to argue. Divided argument is not favored.

5. Regardless of the number of counsel participating in oral argument, counsel making the opening argument shall present the case fairly and completely and not reserve points of substance for rebuttal.

6. Oral argument will not be allowed on behalf of any party for whom a brief has not been filed.

7. By leave of the Court, and subject to paragraph 4 of this Rule, counsel for an *amicus curiae* whose brief has been filed as provided in Rule 37 may argue orally on the side of a party, with the consent of that party. In the absence of consent, counsel for an *amicus curiae* may seek leave of the Court to argue orally by a motion setting out specifically and concisely why oral argument would provide assistance to the Court not otherwise available. Such a motion will be granted only in the most extraordinary circumstances.

PART VII. PRACTICE AND PROCEDURE

Rule 29. Filing and Service of Documents; Special Notifications; Corporate Listing

1. Any document required or permitted to be presented to the Court or to a Justice shall be filed with the Clerk.

2. A document is timely filed if it is received by the Clerk within the time specified for filing; or if it is sent to the Clerk through the United States Postal Service by first-class mail (including express or priority mail), postage prepaid, and bears a postmark, other than a commercial postage meter label, showing that the document was mailed on or before the last day for filing; or if it is delivered on or before the last day for filing to a third-party commercial carrier for delivery to the Clerk within 3 calendar days. If submitted by an inmate confined in an institution, a document is timely filed if it is deposited in the institution's internal mail system on or before the last day for filing and is accompanied by a notarized statement or declaration in compliance with 28 U.S.C. § 1746 setting out the date of deposit and stating that first-class postage has been prepaid. If the postmark is missing or not legible, or if the third-party commercial carrier does not provide the date the document was received by the carrier, the Clerk will require the person who sent the document to submit a notarized statement or declaration in compliance with 28 U.S.C. § 1746 setting out the details of the filing and stating that the filing took place on a particular date within the permitted time.

3. Any document required by these Rules to be served may be served personally, by mail, or by third-party commercial carrier for delivery within 3 calendar days on each party to the proceeding at or before the time of filing. If the document has been prepared as required by Rule 33.1, three copies shall be served on each other party separately represented in the proceeding. If the document has been prepared as required by Rule 33.2, service of a single copy on each other separately represented party suffices. If personal service is made, it shall consist of delivery at the office of the counsel of record, either to counsel or to an employee therein. If service is by mail or third-party commercial carrier, it shall consist of depositing the document with the United States Postal Service, with no less than first-class postage prepaid, or delivery to the carrier for delivery within 3 calendar days, addressed to counsel of record at the proper address. When a party is not represented by counsel, service shall be made on the party, personally, by mail, or by commercial carrier. Ordinarily, service on a party must be by a manner at least as expeditious as the manner used to file the document with the Court.

4. **(a)** If the United States or any federal department, office, agency, officer, or employee is a party to be served, service shall be made on the Solicitor General of the United States, Room 5614, Department of Justice, 950 Pennsylvania Ave., N.W., Washington, DC 20530-0001. When an agency of the United States that is a party is authorized by law to appear before this Court on its own behalf, or when an officer or employee of the United States is a party, the agency, officer, or employee shall be served in addition to the Solicitor General.

(b) In any proceeding in this Court in which the constitutionality of an Act of Congress is drawn into question, and neither the United States nor any federal department, office, agency, officer, or employee is a party, the initial document filed in this Court shall recite that 28 U.S.C. § 2403(a) may apply and shall be served on the Solicitor General of the United States, Room 5614, Department of Justice, 950 Pennsylvania Ave., N.W., Washington, DC 20530-0001. In such a proceeding from any court of the United States, as defined by 28 U.S.C. § 451, the initial document also shall state whether that court, pursuant to 28 U.S.C. § 2403(a), certified to the Attorney General the fact that the constitutionality of an Act of Congress was drawn into question. See Rule 14.1(e)(v).

(c) In any proceeding in this Court in which the constitutionality of any statute of a State is drawn into question, and neither the State nor any agency, officer, or employee thereof is a party, the initial document filed in this Court shall recite that 28 U.S.C. § 2403(b) may apply and shall be served on the Attorney General of that State. In such a proceeding from any court of the United States, as defined by 28 U.S.C. § 451, the initial document also shall state whether that court, pursuant to 28 U.S.C. § 2403(b), certified to the State Attorney General the fact that the constitutionality of a statute of that State was drawn into question. See Rule 14.1(e)(v).

5. Proof of service, when required by these Rules, shall accompany the document when it is presented to the Clerk for filing and shall be separate from it. Proof of service shall contain, or be accompanied by, a statement that all parties required to be served have been served, together with a list of the names, addresses, and telephone numbers of counsel indicating the name of the party or parties each counsel represents. It is not necessary that service on each party required to be served be made in the same manner or evidenced by the same proof. Proof of service may consist of any one of the following:

(a) an acknowledgment of service, signed by counsel of record for the party served, and bearing the address and telephone number of such counsel;

(b) a certificate of service, reciting the facts and circumstances of service in compliance with the appropriate paragraph or paragraphs of this Rule, and signed by a member of the Bar of this Court representing the party on whose behalf service is made or by an attorney appointed to represent that party under the Criminal Justice Act of 1964, see 18 U.S.C. § 3006A(d)(6), or under any other applicable federal statute; or

(c) a notarized affidavit or declaration in compliance with 28 U.S.C. § 1746, reciting the facts and circumstances of service in accordance with the appropriate paragraph or paragraphs of this Rule, whenever service is made by any person not a member of the Bar of this Court and not an attorney appointed to represent a party under the Criminal Justice Act of 1964, see 18 U.S.C. § 3006A(d)(6), or under any other applicable federal statute.

6. Every document, except a joint appendix or *amicus curiae* brief, filed by or on behalf of a nongovernmental corporation shall contain a corporate disclosure statement identifying the parent corporations and listing any publicly held company that owns 10% or more of the corporation's stock. If there is no parent or publicly held company owning 10% or more of the corporation's stock, a notation to this effect shall be included in the document. If a statement has been included in a document filed earlier in the case, reference may be made to the earlier document (except when the earlier statement appeared in a document prepared under Rule 33.2), and only amendments to the statement to make it current need be included in the document being filed.

(As amended Jan. 11, 1999, eff. May 3, 1999; Jan. 27, 2003, eff. May 1, 2003.)

Rule 30. Computation and Extension of Time

1. In the computation of any period of time prescribed or allowed by these Rules, by order of the Court, or by an applicable statute, the day of the act, event, or default from which the designated period begins to run is not included. The last day of the period shall be included, unless it is a Saturday, Sunday, federal legal holiday listed in 5 U.S.C. § 6103, or day on which the Court building is closed by order of the Court or the Chief Justice, in which event the period shall extend until the end of the next day that is not a Saturday, Sunday, federal legal holiday, or day on which the Court building is closed.

2. Whenever a Justice or the Clerk is empowered by law or these Rules to extend the time to file any document, an application seeking an extension shall be filed within the period sought to be extended. An application to extend the time to file a petition for a writ of certiorari or to file a jurisdictional statement must be filed at least 10 days before the specified final filing date as computed under these Rules; if filed less than 10 days before the final filing date, such application will not be granted except in the most extraordinary circumstances.

3. An application to extend the time to file a petition for a writ of certiorari, to file a jurisdictional statement, to file a reply brief on the merits, or to file a petition for rehearing shall be made to an individual Justice and presented and served on all other parties as provided by Rule 22. Once denied, such an application may not be renewed.

4. An application to extend the time to file any document or paper other than those specified in paragraph 3 of this Rule may be presented in the form of a letter to the Clerk setting out specific reasons why an extension of time is justified. The letter shall be served on all other parties as required by Rule 29. The application may be acted on by the Clerk in the first instance, and any party aggrieved by the Clerk's action may request that the application be submitted to a Justice or to the Court. The Clerk will report action under this paragraph to the Court as instructed.

(As amended Jan. 27, 2003, eff. May 1, 2003.)

Rule 31. Translations

Whenever any record to be transmitted to this Court contains material written in a foreign language without a translation made under the authority of the lower court, or admitted to be correct, the clerk of the court transmitting the record shall advise the Clerk of this Court immediately so that this Court may order that a translation be supplied and, if necessary, printed as part of the joint appendix.

Rule 32. Models, Diagrams, Exhibits, and Lodgings

1. Models, diagrams, and exhibits of material forming part of the evidence taken in a case and brought to this Court for its inspection shall be placed in the custody of the Clerk at least two weeks before the case is to be heard or submitted.

2. All models, diagrams, exhibits, and other items placed in the custody of the Clerk shall be removed by the parties no more than 40 days after the case is decided. If this is not done, the Clerk will notify counsel to remove the articles forthwith. If they are not removed within a reasonable time thereafter, the Clerk will destroy them or dispose of them in any other appropriate way.

3. Any party or *amicus curiae* desiring to lodge non-record material with the Clerk must set out in a letter, served on all parties, a description of the material proposed for lodging and the reasons why the non-record material may properly be considered by the Court. The material proposed for lodging may not be submitted until and unless requested by the Clerk.

(As amended Jan. 11, 1999, eff. May 3, 1999; Jan. 27, 2003, eff. May 1, 2003.)

Rule 33. Document Preparation: Booklet Format; 8½– by 11–inch Paper Format

1. Booklet Format: (a) Except for a document expressly permitted by these Rules to be submitted on 8½– by 11–inch paper, see, e.g., Rules 21, 22, and 39, every document filed with the Court shall be prepared in a 6⅛– by 9¼–inch booklet format using a standard typesetting process (e.g., hot metal, photocomposition, or computer typesetting) to produce text printed in typographic (as opposed to typewriter) characters. The process used must produce a clear, black image on white paper. The text must be reproduced with a clarity that equals or exceeds the output of a laser printer.

(b) The text of every booklet-format document, including any appendix thereto, shall be typeset in Roman 11–point or larger type with 2–point or more leading between lines. The typeface should be similar to that used in current volumes of the United States Reports. Increasing the amount of text by using condensed or thinner typefaces, or by reducing the space between letters, is strictly prohibited. Type size and face shall be consistent throughout. Quotations in excess of 50 words shall be indented. The typeface of footnotes shall be 9–point or larger with 2–point or more leading between lines. The text of the document must appear on both sides of the page.

(c) Every booklet-format document shall be produced on paper that is opaque, unglazed, and not less than 60 pounds in weight, and shall have margins of at least three-fourths of an inch on all sides. The text field, including footnotes, may not exceed 4⅛ by 7⅛ inches. The document shall be bound firmly in at least two places along the left margin (saddle stitch or perfect binding preferred) so as to permit easy opening, and no part of the text should be obscured by the binding. Spiral, plastic, metal, or string bindings may not be used. Copies of patent documents, except opinions, may be duplicated in such size as is necessary in a separate appendix.

(d) Every booklet-format document shall comply with the page limits shown on the chart in subparagraph 1(g) of this Rule. The page limits do not include the questions presented, the list of parties and the corporate disclosure statement, the table of contents, the table of cited authorities, or any appendix. Verbatim quotations required under Rule 14.1(f), if set out in the text of a brief rather than in the appendix, are also excluded. For good cause, the Court or a Justice may grant leave to file a document in excess of the page limits, but application for such leave is not favored. An application to exceed page limits shall comply with Rule 22 and must be received by the Clerk at least 15 days before the filing date of the document in question, except in the most extraordinary circumstances.

(e) Every booklet-format document shall have a suitable cover consisting of 65–pound weight paper in the color indicated on the chart in subparagraph 1(g) of this Rule. If a separate appendix to any document is filed, the color of its cover shall be the same as that of the cover of the document it supports. The Clerk will furnish a color chart upon request. Counsel shall ensure that there is adequate contrast between the printing and the color of the cover. A document filed by the United States, or by any other federal party represented by the Solicitor General, shall have a gray cover. A joint appendix, answer to a bill of complaint, motion for leave to intervene, and any other document not listed in subparagraph 1(g) of this Rule shall have a tan cover.

(f) Forty copies of a booklet-format document shall be filed.

(g) Page limits and cover colors for booklet-format documents are as follows:

	Type of Document	Page Limits	Color of Cover
(i)	Petition for a Writ of Certiorari (Rule 14); Motion for Leave to File a Bill of Complaint and Brief in Support (Rule 17.3); Jurisdictional Statement (Rule 18.3); Petition for an Extraordinary Writ (Rule 20.2)	30	white
(ii)	Brief in Opposition (Rule 15.3); Brief in Opposition to Motion for Leave to File an Original Action (Rule 17.5); Motion to Dismiss or Affirm (Rule 18.6); Brief in Opposition to Mandamus or Prohibition (Rule 20.3(b)); Response to a Petition for Habeas Corpus (Rule 20.4)	30	orange
(iii)	Reply to Brief in Opposition (Rules 15.6 and 17.5); Brief Opposing a Motion to Dismiss or Affirm (Rule 18.8)	10	tan
(iv)	Supplemental Brief (Rules 15.8, 17, 18.10, and 25.5)	10	tan
(v)	Brief on the Merits for Petitioner or Appellant (Rule 24); Exceptions by Plaintiff to Report of Special Master (Rule 17)	50	light blue
(vi)	Brief on the Merits for Respondent or Appellee (Rule 24.2); Brief on the Merits for Respondent or Appellee Supporting Petitioner or Appellant (Rule 12.6); Exceptions by Party Other Than Plaintiff to Report of Special Master (Rule 17)	50	light red
(vii)	Reply Brief on the Merits (Rule 24.4)	20	yellow
(viii)	Reply to Plaintiff's Exceptions to Report of Special Master (Rule 17)	50	orange
(ix)	Reply to Exceptions by Party Other Than Plaintiff to Report of Special Master (Rule 17)	50	yellow
(x)	Brief for an Amicus Curiae at the Petition Stage (Rule 37.2)	20	cream
(xi)	Brief for an Amicus Curiae in Support of the Plaintiff, Petitioner, or Appellant, or in Support of Neither Party, on the Merits or in an Original Action at the Exceptions Stage (Rule 37.3)	30	light green
(xii)	Brief for an Amicus Curiae in Support of the Defendant, Respondent, or Appellee, on the Merits or in an Original Action at the Exceptions Stage (Rule 37.3)	30	dark green
(xiii)	Petition for Rehearing (Rule 44)	10	tan

2. 8½– by 11–Inch Paper Format: (a) The text of every document, including any appendix thereto, expressly permitted by these Rules to be presented to the Court on 8½– by 11–inch paper shall appear double spaced, except for indented quotations, which shall be single spaced, on opaque, unglazed, white paper. The document shall be stapled or bound at the upper left-hand corner. Copies, if required, shall be produced on the same type of paper and shall be legible. The original of any such document (except a motion to dismiss or affirm under Rule 18.6) shall be signed by the party proceeding pro se or by counsel of record who must be a member of the Bar of this Court or an attorney appointed under the Criminal Justice Act of 1964, see 18 U.S.C. § 3006A(d)(6), or under any other applicable federal statute. Subparagraph 1(g) of this Rule does not apply to documents prepared under this paragraph.

(b) Page limits for documents presented on 8½– by 11–inch paper are: 40 pages for a petition for a writ of certiorari, jurisdictional statement, petition for an extraordinary writ, brief in opposition, or motion to dismiss or affirm; and 15 pages for a reply to a brief in opposition, brief opposing a motion to dismiss or affirm, supplemental brief, or petition for rehearing. The page exclusions specified in subparagraph 1(d) of this Rule apply.

(As amended Jan. 11, 1999, eff. May 3, 1999.)

Rule 34. Document Preparation: General Requirements

Every document, whether prepared under Rule 33.1 or Rule 33.2, shall comply with the following provisions:

1. Each document shall bear on its cover, in the order indicated, from the top of the page:

(a) the docket number of the case or, if there is none, a space for one;

(b) the name of this Court;

(c) the caption of the case as appropriate in this Court;

(d) the nature of the proceeding and the name of the court from which the action is brought (*e.g.*, "On Petition for Writ of Certiorari to the United States Court of Appeals for the Fifth Circuit"; or, for a merits brief, "On Writ of Certiorari to the United States Court of Appeals for the Fifth Circuit");

(e) the title of the document (*e.g.*, "Petition for Writ of Certiorari," "Brief for Respondent," "Joint Appendix");

(f) the name of the attorney who is counsel of record for the party concerned (who must be a member of the Bar of this Court except as provided in Rule 33.2), and on whom service is to be made, with a notation directly thereunder identifying the attorney as counsel of record and setting out counsel's office address and telephone number. Only one counsel of record may be noted on a single document. The names of other members of the Bar of this Court or of the bar of the highest court of a State acting as counsel, and, if desired, their addresses, may be added, but counsel of record shall be clearly identified. Names of persons other than attorneys admitted to a state bar may not be listed, unless the party is appearing *pro se*, in which case the party's name, address, and telephone number shall appear. The foregoing shall be displayed in an appropriate typographic manner and, except for the identification of counsel, may not be set in type smaller than standard 11–point, if the document is prepared as required by Rule 33.1.

2. Every document exceeding five pages (other than a joint appendix), whether prepared under Rule 33.1 or Rule 33.2, shall contain a table of contents and a table of cited authorities (*i.e.*, cases alphabetically arranged, constitutional provisions, statutes, treatises, and other materials) with references to the pages in the document where such authorities are cited.

3. The body of every document shall bear at its close the name of counsel of record and such other counsel, identified on the cover of the document in conformity with subparagraph 1(g) of this Rule, as may be desired.

(As amended Jan. 11, 1999, eff. May 3, 1999.)

Rule 35. Death, Substitution, and Revivor; Public Officers

1. If a party dies after the filing of a petition for a writ of certiorari to this Court, or after the filing of a notice of appeal, the authorized representative of the deceased party may appear and, on motion, be substituted as a party. If the representative does not voluntarily become a party, any other party may suggest the death on the record and, on motion, seek an order requiring the representative to become a party within a designated time. If the representative then fails to become a party, the party so moving, if a respondent or appellee, is entitled to have the petition for a writ of certiorari or the appeal dismissed, and if a petitioner or appellant, is entitled to proceed as in any other case of nonappearance by a respondent or appellee. If the substitution of a representative of the deceased is not made within six months after the death of the party, the case shall abate.

2. Whenever a case cannot be revived in the court whose judgment is sought to be reviewed, because the deceased party's authorized representative is not subject to that court's jurisdiction, proceedings will be conducted as this Court may direct.

3. When a public officer who is a party to a proceeding in this Court in an official capacity dies, resigns, or otherwise ceases to hold office, the action does not abate and any successor in office is automatically substituted as a party. The parties shall notify the Clerk in writing of any such successions. Proceedings following the substitution shall be in the name of the substituted party, but any misnomer not affecting substantial rights of the parties will be disregarded.

4. A public officer who is a party to a proceeding in this Court in an official capacity may be described as a party by the officer's official title rather than by name, but the Court may require the name to be added.

(As amended Jan. 11, 1999, eff. May 3, 1999.)

Rule 36. Custody of Prisoners in Habeas Corpus Proceedings

1. Pending review in this Court of a decision in a habeas corpus proceeding commenced before a court, Justice, or judge of the United States, the person having custody of the prisoner may not transfer custody to another person unless the transfer is authorized under this Rule.

2. Upon application by a custodian, the court, Justice, or judge who entered the decision under review may authorize transfer and the substitution of a successor custodian as a party.

3. (a) Pending review of a decision failing or refusing to release a prisoner, the prisoner may be detained in the custody from which release is sought or in other appropriate custody or may be enlarged on personal recognizance or bail, as may appear appropriate to the court, Justice, or judge who entered the

decision, or to the court of appeals, this Court, or a judge or Justice of either court.

(b) Pending review of a decision ordering release, the prisoner shall be enlarged on personal recognizance or bail, unless the court, Justice, or judge who entered the decision, or the court of appeals, this Court, or a judge or Justice of either court, orders otherwise.

4. An initial order respecting the custody or enlargement of the prisoner, and any recognizance or surety taken, shall continue in effect pending review in the court of appeals and in this Court unless for reasons shown to the court of appeals, this Court, or a judge or Justice of either court, the order is modified or an independent order respecting custody, enlargement, or surety is entered.

Rule 37. Brief for an Amicus Curiae

1. An *amicus curiae* brief that brings to the attention of the Court relevant matter not already brought to its attention by the parties may be of considerable help to the Court. An *amicus curiae* brief that does not serve this purpose burdens the Court, and its filing is not favored.

2. (a) An *amicus curiae* brief submitted before the Court's consideration of a petition for a writ of certiorari, motion for leave to file a bill of complaint, jurisdictional statement, or petition for an extraordinary writ, may be filed if accompanied by the written consent of all parties, or if the Court grants leave to file under subparagraph 2(b) of this Rule. The brief shall be submitted within the time allowed for filing a brief in opposition or for filing a motion to dismiss or affirm. The *amicus curiae* brief shall specify whether consent was granted, and its cover shall identify the party supported.

(b) When a party to the case has withheld consent, a motion for leave to file an *amicus curiae* brief before the Court's consideration of a petition for a writ of certiorari, motion for leave to file a bill of complaint, jurisdictional statement, or petition for an extraordinary writ may be presented to the Court. The motion, prepared as required by Rule 33.1 and as one document with the brief sought to be filed, shall be submitted within the time allowed for filing an *amicus curiae* brief, and shall indicate the party or parties who have withheld consent and state the nature of the movant's interest. Such a motion is not favored.

3. (a) An *amicus curiae* brief in a case before the Court for oral argument may be filed if accompanied by the written consent of all parties, or if the Court grants leave to file under subparagraph 3(b) of this Rule. The brief shall be submitted within the time allowed for filing the brief for the party supported, or if in support of neither party, within the time allowed for filing the petitioner's or appellant's brief. The *amicus curiae* brief shall specify whether consent was granted, and its cover shall identify the party supported or indicate whether it suggests affirmance or reversal. The Clerk will not file a reply brief for an *amicus curiae,* or a brief for an *amicus curiae* in support of, or in opposition to, a petition for rehearing.

(b) When a party to a case before the Court for oral argument has withheld consent, a motion for leave to file an *amicus curiae* brief may be presented to the Court. The motion, prepared as required by Rule 33.1 and as one document with the brief sought to be filed, shall be submitted within the time allowed for filing an *amicus curiae* brief, and shall indicate the party or parties who have withheld consent and state the nature of the movant's interest.

4. No motion for leave to file an *amicus curiae* brief is necessary if the brief is presented on behalf of the United States by the Solicitor General; on behalf of any agency of the United States allowed by law to appear before this Court when submitted by the agency's authorized legal representative; on behalf of a State, Commonwealth, Territory, or Possession when submitted by its Attorney General; or on behalf of a city, county, town, or similar entity when submitted by its authorized law officer.

5. A brief or motion filed under this Rule shall be accompanied by proof of service as required by Rule 29, and shall comply with the applicable provisions of Rules 21, 24, and 33.1 (except that it suffices to set out in the brief the interest of the *amicus curiae,* the summary of the argument, the argument, and the conclusion). A motion for leave to file may not exceed five pages. A party served with the motion may file an objection thereto, stating concisely the reasons for withholding consent; the objection shall be prepared as required by Rule 33.2.

6. Except for briefs presented on behalf of *amicus curiae* listed in Rule 37.4, a brief filed under this Rule shall indicate whether counsel for a party authored the brief in whole or in part and shall identify every person or entity, other than the *amicus curiae,* its members, or its counsel, who made a monetary contribution to the preparation or submission of the brief. The disclosure shall be made in the first footnote on the first page of text.

Rule 38. Fees

Under 28 U.S.C. § 1911, the fees charged by the Clerk are:

(a) for docketing a case on a petition for a writ of certiorari or on appeal or for docketing any other proceeding, except a certified question or a motion to docket and dismiss an appeal under Rule 18.5, $300;

(b) for filing a petition for rehearing or a motion for leave to file a petition for rehearing, $200;

(c) for reproducing and certifying any record or paper, $1 per page; and for comparing with the original thereof any photographic reproduction of any record or paper, when furnished by the person requesting its certification, $.50 per page;

(d) for a certificate bearing the seal of the Court, $10; and

(e) for a check paid to the Court, Clerk, or Marshal that is returned for lack of funds, $35.

Rule 39. Proceedings *In Forma Pauperis*

1. A party seeking to proceed *in forma pauperis* shall file a motion for leave to do so, together with the party's notarized affidavit or declaration (in compliance with 28 U.S.C. § 1746) in the form prescribed by the Federal Rules of Appellate Procedure, Form 4. The motion shall state whether leave to proceed *in forma pauperis* was sought in any other court and, if so, whether leave was granted. If the United States district court or the United States court of appeals has appointed counsel under the Criminal Justice Act of 1964, 18 U.S.C. § 3006A, or under any other applicable federal statute, no affidavit or declaration is required, but the motion shall cite the statute under which counsel was appointed.

2. If leave to proceed *in forma pauperis* is sought for the purpose of filing a document, the motion, and an affidavit or declaration if required, shall be filed together with that document and shall comply in every respect with Rule 21. As provided in that Rule, it suffices to file an original and 10 copies, unless the party is an inmate confined in an institution and is not represented by counsel, in which case the original, alone, suffices. A copy of the motion, and affidavit or declaration if required, shall precede and be attached to each copy of the accompanying document.

3. Except when these Rules expressly provide that a document shall be prepared as required by Rule 33.1, every document presented by a party proceeding under this Rule shall be prepared as required by Rule 33.2 (unless such preparation is impossible). Every document shall be legible. While making due allowance for any case presented under this Rule by a person appearing *pro se,* the Clerk will not file any document if it does not comply with the substance of these Rules or is jurisdictionally out of time.

4. When the documents required by paragraphs 1 and 2 of this Rule are presented to the Clerk, accompanied by proof of service as required by Rule 29, they will be placed on the docket without the payment of a docket fee or any other fee.

5. The respondent or appellee in a case filed *in forma pauperis* shall respond in the same manner and within the same time as in any other case of the same nature, except that the filing of an original and 10 copies of a response prepared as required by Rule 33.2, with proof of service as required by Rule 29, suffices. The respondent or appellee may challenge the grounds for the motion for leave to proceed *in forma pauperis* in a separate document or in the response itself.

6. Whenever the Court appoints counsel for an indigent party in a case set for oral argument, the briefs on the merits submitted by that counsel, unless otherwise requested, shall be prepared under the Clerk's supervision. The Clerk also will reimburse appointed counsel for any necessary travel expenses to Washington, D.C., and return in connection with the argument.

7. In a case in which certiorari has been granted, probable jurisdiction noted, or consideration of jurisdiction postponed, this Court may appoint counsel to represent a party financially unable to afford an attorney to the extent authorized by the Criminal Justice Act of 1964, 18 U.S.C. § 3006A, or by any other applicable federal statute.

8. If satisfied that a petition for a writ of certiorari, jurisdictional statement, or petition for an extraordinary writ is frivolous or malicious, the Court may deny leave to proceed *in forma pauperis.*

(As amended Jan. 27, 2003, eff. May 1, 2003.)

Rule 40. Veterans, Seamen, and Military Cases

1. A veteran suing to establish reemployment rights under any provision of law exempting veterans from the payment of fees or court costs, may file a motion for leave to proceed on papers prepared as required by Rule 33.2. The motion shall ask leave to proceed as a veteran and be accompanied by an affidavit or declaration setting out the moving party's veteran status. A copy of the motion shall precede and be attached to each copy of the petition for a writ of certiorari or other substantive document filed by the veteran.

2. A seaman suing under 28 U.S.C. § 1916 may proceed without prepayment of fees or costs or furnishing security therefor, but is not entitled to proceed under Rule 33.2, except as authorized by the Court on separate motion under Rule 39.

3. An accused person petitioning for a writ of certiorari to review a decision of the United States Court of Appeals for the Armed Forces under 28 U.S.C. § 1259 may proceed without prepayment of fees or costs or furnishing security therefor and without filing an affidavit of indigency, but is not entitled to proceed on papers prepared as required by Rule 33.2, except as authorized by the Court on separate motion under Rule 39.

PART VIII. DISPOSITION OF CASES

Rule 41. Opinions of the Court

Opinions of the Court will be released by the Clerk immediately upon their announcement from the bench, or as the Court otherwise directs. Thereafter, the Clerk will cause the opinions to be issued in slip form, and the Reporter of Decisions will prepare them for publication in the preliminary prints and bound volumes of the United States Reports.

Rule 42. Interest and Damages

1. If a judgment for money in a civil case is affirmed, any interest allowed by law is payable from the date the judgment under review was entered. If a judgment is modified or reversed with a direction that a judgment for money be entered below, the mandate will contain instructions with respect to the allowance of interest. Interest in cases arising in a state court is allowed at the same rate that similar judgments bear interest in the courts of the State in which judgment is directed to be entered. Interest in cases arising in a court of the United States is allowed at the interest rate authorized by law.

2. When a petition for a writ of certiorari, an appeal, or an application for other relief is frivolous, the Court may award the respondent or appellee just damages, and single or double costs under Rule 43. Damages or costs may be awarded against the petitioner, appellant, or applicant, against the party's counsel, or against both party and counsel.

Rule 43. Costs

1. If the Court affirms a judgment, the petitioner or appellant shall pay costs unless the Court otherwise orders.

2. If the Court reverses or vacates a judgment, the respondent or appellee shall pay costs unless the Court otherwise orders.

3. The Clerk's fees and the cost of printing the joint appendix are the only taxable items in this Court. The cost of the transcript of the record from the court below is also a taxable item, but shall be taxable in that court as costs in the case. The expenses of printing briefs, motions, petitions, or jurisdictional statements are not taxable.

4. In a case involving a certified question, costs are equally divided unless the Court otherwise orders, except that if the Court decides the whole matter in controversy, as permitted by Rule 19.2, costs are allowed as provided in paragraphs 1 and 2 of this Rule.

5. To the extent permitted by 28 U.S.C. § 2412, costs under this Rule are allowed for or against the United States or an officer or agent thereof, unless expressly waived or unless the Court otherwise orders.

6. When costs are allowed in this Court, the Clerk will insert an itemization of the costs in the body of the mandate or judgment sent to the court below. The prevailing side may not submit a bill of costs.

7. In extraordinary circumstances the Court may adjudge double costs.

Rule 44. Rehearing

1. Any petition for the rehearing of any judgment or decision of the Court on the merits shall be filed within 25 days after entry of the judgment or decision, unless the Court or a Justice shortens or extends the time. The petitioner shall file 40 copies of the rehearing petition and shall pay the filing fee prescribed by Rule 38(b), except that a petitioner proceeding *in forma pauperis* under Rule 39, including an inmate of an institution, shall file the number of copies required for a petition by such a person under Rule 12.2. The petition shall state its grounds briefly and distinctly and shall be served as required by Rule 29. The petition shall be presented together with certification of counsel (or of a party unrepresented by counsel) that it is presented in good faith and not for delay; one copy of the certificate shall bear the signature of counsel (or of a party unrepresented by counsel). A copy of the certificate shall follow and be attached to each copy of the petition. A petition for rehearing is not subject to oral argument and will not be granted except by a majority of the Court, at the instance of a Justice who concurred in the judgment or decision.

2. Any petition for the rehearing of an order denying a petition for a writ of certiorari or extraordinary writ shall be filed within 25 days after the date of the order of denial and shall comply with all the form and filing requirements of paragraph 1 of this Rule, including the payment of the filing fee if required, but its grounds shall be limited to intervening circumstances of a substantial or controlling effect or to other substantial grounds not previously presented. The petition shall be presented together with certification of counsel (or of a party unrepresented by counsel) that it is restricted to the grounds specified in this paragraph and that it is presented in good faith and not for delay; one copy of the certificate shall bear the signature of counsel (or of a party unrepresented by counsel). The certificate shall be bound with each copy of the petition. The Clerk will not file a petition without a certificate. The petition is not subject to oral argument.

3. The Clerk will not file any response to a petition for rehearing unless the Court requests a response. In the absence of extraordinary circumstances, the

Court will not grant a petition for rehearing without first requesting a response.

4. The Clerk will not file consecutive petitions and petitions that are out of time under this Rule.

5. The Clerk will not file any brief for an *amicus curiae* in support of, or in opposition to, a petition for rehearing.

6. If the Clerk determines that a petition for rehearing submitted timely and in good faith is in a form that does not comply with this Rule or with Rule 33 or Rule 34, the Clerk will return it with a letter indicating the deficiency. A corrected petition for rehearing received no more than 15 days after the date of the Clerk's letter will be deemed timely.

(As amended Jan. 11, 1999, eff. May 3, 1999; Jan. 27, 2003, eff. May 1, 2003.)

Rule 45. Process; Mandates

1. All process of this Court issues in the name of the President of the United States.

2. In a case on review from a state court, the mandate issues 25 days after entry of the judgment, unless the Court or a Justice shortens or extends the time, or unless the parties stipulate that it issue sooner. The filing of a petition for rehearing stays the mandate until disposition of the petition, unless the Court orders otherwise. If the petition is denied, the mandate issues forthwith.

3. In a case on review from any court of the United States, as defined by 28 U.S.C. § 451, a formal mandate does not issue unless specially directed; instead, the Clerk of this Court will send the clerk of the lower court a copy of the opinion or order of this Court and a certified copy of the judgment. The certified copy of the judgment, prepared and signed by this Court's Clerk, will provide for costs if any are awarded. In all other respects, the provisions of paragraph 2 of this Rule apply.

Rule 46. Dismissing Cases

1. At any stage of the proceedings, whenever all parties file with the Clerk an agreement in writing that a case be dismissed, specifying the terms for payment of costs, and pay to the Clerk any fees then due, the Clerk, without further reference to the Court, will enter an order of dismissal.

2. (a) A petitioner or appellant may file a motion to dismiss the case, with proof of service as required by Rule 29, tendering to the Clerk any fees due and costs payable. No more than 15 days after service thereof, an adverse party may file an objection, limited to the amount of damages and costs in this Court alleged to be payable or to showing that the moving party does not represent all petitioners or appellants. The Clerk will not file any objection not so limited.

(b) When the objection asserts that the moving party does not represent all the petitioners or appellants, the party moving for dismissal may file a reply within 10 days, after which time the matter will be submitted to the Court for its determination.

(c) If no objection is filed—or if upon objection going only to the amount of damages and costs in this Court, the party moving for dismissal tenders the additional damages and costs in full within 10 days of the demand therefor—the Clerk, without further reference to the Court, will enter an order of dismissal. If, after objection as to the amount of damages and costs in this Court, the moving party does not respond by a tender within 10 days, the Clerk will report the matter to the Court for its determination.

3. No mandate or other process will issue on a dismissal under this Rule without an order of the Court.

PART IX. DEFINITIONS AND EFFECTIVE DATE

Rule 47. Reference to "State Court" and "State Law"

The term "state court," when used in these Rules, includes the District of Columbia Court of Appeals, the Supreme Court of the Commonwealth of Puerto Rico, the courts of the Northern Mariana Islands, and the local courts of Guam. References in these Rules to the statutes of a State include the statutes of the District of Columbia, the Commonwealth of Puerto Rico, the Commonwealth of the Northern Mariana Islands, and the Territory of Guam.

(As amended Mar. 14, 2005, eff. May 2, 2005.)

Rule 48. Effective Date of Rules

1. These Rules, adopted January 27, 2003, will be effective May 1, 2003.

2. The Rules govern all proceedings after their effective date except to the extent that, in the opinion of the Court, their application to a pending matter would not be feasible or would work an injustice, in which event the former procedure applies.

TITLE 18

CRIMES AND CRIMINAL PROCEDURE

Act June 25, 1948, c. 645, § 1, 62 Stat. 683

Enactment of Title 18

Section 1 of Act June 25, 1948, c. 645, 62 Stat. 683, provided in part that: "Title 18 of the United States Code, entitled 'Crimes and Criminal Procedure', is hereby revised, codified and enacted into positive law, and may be cited as 'Title 18, U.S.C. § ___.' "

Sections 2 to 17, inclusive, of Act June 25, 1948, made enumerated conforming amendments to sections in other Titles of the United States Code.

Sections 18 to 20 of Act June 25, 1948, provided as follows:

"Sec. 18. If any part of Title 18, Crimes and Criminal Procedure as set out in section 1 of this Act, shall be held invalid the remainder shall not be affected thereby.

"Sec. 19. No inference of a legislative construction is to be drawn by reason of the chapter in Title 18, Crimes and Criminal Procedure, as set out in section 1 of this Act, in which any particular section is placed, nor by reason of the catchlines used in such title.

"Sec. 20. This Act shall take effect September 1, 1948".

Section 21 of Act June 25, 1948, repealed enumerated provisions of the Revised Statutes or Statutes at Large, and provided that any rights or liabilities now existing under such repealed provisions shall not be affected by this repeal.

[1] Appendix analysis editorially added.

HISTORICAL AND STATUTORY NOTES

1970 Amendments. Pub.L. 91–452, Title II, § 201(b), Oct. 15, 1970, 84 Stat. 928, added Part V.

PART I—CRIMES

[1] So in original. "Weapons" probably should not be capitalized.

[2] Heading of chapter 39 amended without amending Part I analysis to reflect the change.

[3] Editorially supplied. Chapter 119 added without corresponding amendment to Part I analysis.

HISTORICAL AND STATUTORY NOTES

Codifications

Pub.L. 104–294, Title VI, § 601(j)(2)(A), Oct. 11, 1996, 110 Stat. 3501, which directed that item for chapter relating to torture be redesignated from 113B to 113C, was incapable of execution due to prior identical amendment by section 303(c)(2) of Pub.L. 104–132.

Amendment by section 40221(b) of Pub.L. 103–322, adding item for chapter 110A, was executed to chapter analysis despite directory language referring to "part analysis", as the probable intent of Congress.

Section 506(b) of Pub.L. 103–236, directing that the item relating to chapter 113B, Torture, be inserted after the item relating to chapter 113A, was executed instead by inserting the item relating to chapter 113B, Torture, after the item relating to chapter 113B, Terrorism, as the probable intent of Congress.

CHAPTER 1—GENERAL PROVISIONS

HISTORICAL AND STATUTORY NOTES

Codifications

Amendment by section 241(b) of Pub.L. 104–191, Title II, Aug. 21, 1996, 110 Stat. 2016, which directed that item 24 be inserted into the table of sections at the beginning of chapter 2 of this title, was executed by inserting such item into the table of sections at the beginning of this chapter, as the probable intent of Congress.

Senate Revision Amendment

In the analysis of sections under this chapter heading, a new item, "14. Applicability to Canal Zone.", was inserted by Senate amendment, to follow underneath item 13, inasmuch as a new § 14, with such a catchline, was inserted, by Senate amendment, in this chapter. 80th Congress Senate Report No. 1620, Amendments 1 and 3.

Commission on the Advancement of Federal Law Enforcement

Pub.L. 104–132, Title VIII, § 806, Apr. 24, 1996, 110 Stat. 1305, provided that:

"**(a) Establishment.**—There is established a commission to be known as the 'Commission on the Advancement of Federal Law Enforcement' (hereinafter in this section [this note] referred to as the 'Commission').

"**(b) Duties.**—The Commission shall review, ascertain, evaluate, report, and recommend action to the Congress on the following matters:

"(1) The Federal law enforcement priorities for the 21st century, including Federal law enforcement capability to investigate and deter adequately the threat of terrorism facing the United States.

"(2) In general, the manner in which significant Federal criminal law enforcement operations are conceived, planned, coordinated, and executed.

"(3) The standards and procedures used by Federal law enforcement to carry out significant Federal criminal law enforcement operations, and their uniformity and compatibility on an interagency basis, including standards related to the use of deadly force.

"(4) The investigation and handling of specific Federal criminal law enforcement cases by the United States Government and the Federal law enforcement agencies therewith, selected at the Commission's discretion.

"(5) The necessity for the present number of Federal law enforcement agencies and units.

"(6) The location and efficacy of the office or entity directly responsible, aside from the President of the United States, for the coordination on an interagency basis of the operations, programs, and activities of all of the Federal law enforcement agencies.

"(7) The degree of assistance, training, education, and other human resource management assets devoted to increasing professionalism for Federal law enforcement officers.

"(8) The independent accountability mechanisms that exist, if any, and their efficacy to investigate, address, and to correct Federal law enforcement abuses.

"(9) The degree of coordination among law enforcement agencies in the area of international crime and the extent to which deployment of resources overseas diminishes domestic law enforcement.

"(10) The extent to which Federal law enforcement agencies coordinate with State and local law enforcement agencies on Federal criminal enforcement operations and programs that directly affect a State or local law enforcement agency's geographical jurisdiction.

"(11) Such other related matters as the Commission deems appropriate.

"**(c) Membership and administrative provisions.**—

"(1) Number and appointment.—The Commission shall be composed of 5 members appointed as follows:

"(A) 1 member appointed by the President pro tempore of the Senate.

"(B) 1 member appointed by the minority leader of the Senate.

"(C) 1 member appointed by the Speaker of the House of Representatives.

"(D) 1 member appointed by the minority leader of the House of Representatives.

"(E) 1 member (who shall chair the Commission) appointed by the Chief Justice of the Supreme Court.

"(2) **Disqualification.**—A person who is an officer or employee of the United States shall not be appointed a member of the Commission.

"(3) **Terms.**—Each member shall be appointed for the life of the Commission.

"(4) **Quorum.**—3 members of the Commission shall constitute a quorum but a lesser number may hold hearings.

"(5) **Meetings.**—The Commission shall meet at the call of the Chair of the Commission.

"(6) **Compensation.**—Each member of the Commission who is not an officer or employee of the Federal Government shall be compensated at a rate equal to the daily equivalent of the annual rate of basic pay prescribed for level IV of the Executive Schedule under section 5315 of title 5, United States Code [5 U.S.C.A. § 5315], for each day, including travel time, during which the member is engaged in the performance of the duties of the Commission.

"**(d) Staffing and support functions.**—

"(1) **Director.**—The Commission shall have a director who shall be appointed by the Chair of the Commission.

"(2) **Staff.**—Subject to rules prescribed by the Commission, the Director may appoint additional personnel as the Commission considers appropriate.

"(3) **Applicability of certain civil service laws.**—The Director and staff of the Commission shall be appointed subject to the provisions of title 5, United States Code, governing appointments in the competitive service, and shall be paid in accordance with the provisions of chapter 51 and subchapter III of chapter 53 of that title [5 U.S.C.A. §§ 5101 et seq. and 5331 et seq., respectively] relating to classification and General Schedule pay rates.

"(e) **Powers.**—

"(1) **Hearings and sessions.**—The Commission may, for the purposes of carrying out this Act [Pub.L. 104–132, Apr. 24, 1996, 110 Stat. 1214, for classification of which, see Short Title note under 18 U.S.C.A. § 1 and Tables], hold hearings, sit and act at times and places, take testimony, and receive evidence as the Commission considers appropriate. The Commission may administer oaths or affirmations to witnesses appearing before it. The Commission may establish rules for its proceedings.

"(2) **Powers of members and agents.**—Any member or agent of the Commission may, if authorized by the Commission, take any action which the Commission is authorized to take by this section.

"(3) **Obtaining official data.**—The Commission may secure directly from any department or agency of the United States information necessary to enable it to carry out this section [this note]. Upon request of the Chair of the Commission, the head of that department or agency shall furnish that information to the Commission, unless doing so would threaten the national security, the health or safety of any individual, or the integrity of an ongoing investigation.

"(4) **Administrative support services.**—Upon the request of the Commission, the Administrator of General Services shall provide to the Commission, on a reimbursable basis, the administrative support services necessary for the Commission to carry out its responsibilities under this title [Pub.L. 104–132, §§ 801 to 823, which enacted 18 U.S.C.A. § 3059B and former 40 U.S.C.A. § 137, amended 18 U.S.C.A. § 2703 and 42 U.S.C.A. § 3751, and enacted provisions set out as notes under 18 U.S.C.A. § 470, 15 U.S.C.A. § 2201, 28 U.S.C.A. §§ 509, 531, 533, 534, and 994, and 42 U.S.C.A. § 3721].

"(f) **Report.**—The Commission shall transmit a report to the Congress and the public not later than 2 years after a quorum of the Commission has been appointed. The report shall contain a detailed statement of the findings and conclusions of the Commission, together with the Commission's recommendations for such actions as the Commission considers appropriate.

"(g) **Termination.**—The Commission shall terminate 30 days after submitting the report required by this section [this note]."

National Commission on Reform of Federal Criminal Laws

Pub.L. 89–801, Nov. 8, 1966, 80 Stat. 1516, as amended Pub.L. 91–39, July 8, 1969, 83 Stat. 44, provided for the establishment of the National Commission on Reform of Federal Criminal Laws, its membership, duties, compensation of the members, the Director, and the staff of the Commission, established the Advisory Committee on Reform of Federal Criminal Laws, required the Commission to submit interim reports to the President and the Congress and to submit a final report within four years from Nov. 8, 1966, and further provided that the Commission shall cease to exist sixty days after the submission of the final report.

EXECUTIVE ORDERS

EXECUTIVE ORDER NO. 11396

Feb. 7, 1968, 33 F.R. 2689

COORDINATION BY ATTORNEY GENERAL OF FEDERAL LAW ENFORCEMENT AND CRIME PREVENTION PROGRAMS

WHEREAS the problem of crime in America today presents the Nation with a major challenge calling for maximum law enforcement efforts at every level of government;

WHEREAS coordination of all Federal criminal law enforcement activities and crime prevention programs is desirable in order to achieve more effective results;

WHEREAS the Federal Government has acknowledged the need to provide assistance to State and local law enforcement agencies in the development and administration of programs directed to the prevention and control of crime;

WHEREAS to provide such assistance the Congress has authorized various departments and agencies of the Federal Government to develop programs which may benefit State and local efforts directed at the prevention and control of crime, and the coordination of such programs is desirable to develop and administer them most effectively; and

WHEREAS the Attorney General, as the chief law officer of the Federal Government, is charged with the responsibility for all prosecutions for violations of the Federal criminal statutes and is authorized under the Law Enforcement Assistance Act of 1965 (79 Stat. 828) [formerly set out as a note preceding § 3001 of this title] to cooperate with and assist State, local, or other public or private agencies in matters relating to law enforcement organization, techniques and practices, and the prevention and control of crime:

NOW, THEREFORE, by virtue of the authority vested in the President by the Constitution and laws of the United States, it is ordered as follows:

Section 1. The Attorney General is hereby designated to facilitate and coordinate (1) the criminal law enforcement activities and crime prevention programs of all Federal departments and agencies, and (2) the activities of such departments and agencies relating to the development and implementation of Federal programs which are designed, in whole or in substantial part, to assist State and local law enforcement agencies and crime prevention activities. The Attorney General may promulgate such rules and regulations and take such actions as he shall deem necessary or appropriate to carry out his functions under this Order.

Sec. 2. Each Federal department and agency is directed to cooperate with the Attorney General in the performance of his functions under this Order and shall, to the extent permitted by law and within the limits of available funds, furnish him such reports, information, and assistance as he may request.

LYNDON B. JOHNSON

EXECUTIVE ORDER NO. 11534

Ex. Ord. No. 11534, June 4, 1970, 35 F.R. 8865, formerly set out as a note preceding section 1 at this title, which related to the National Council on Organized Crime, was revoked by Ex. Ord. No. 12110, Dec. 28, 1978, 44 F.R. 1069, set out as a note under section 14 of Appendix 2 to Title 5, Government Organization and Employees.

[§ 1. Repealed. Pub.L. 98–473, Title II, § 218(a)(1), Oct. 12, 1984, 98 Stat. 2027]

HISTORICAL AND STATUTORY NOTES

This section as in effect prior to repeal by Pub.L. 98–473 read as follows:

"§ 1. Offenses classified

"Notwithstanding any Act of Congress to the contrary:

"(1) Any offense punishable by death or imprisonment for a term exceeding one year is a felony.

"(2) Any other offense is a misdemeanor.

"(3) Any misdemeanor, the penalty for which, as set forth in the provision defining the offense, does not exceed imprisonment for a period of six months or a fine of not more than $5,000 for an individual and $10,000 for a person other than an individual, or both, is a petty offense.

"(June 25, 1948, c. 645, 62 Stat. 684; Oct. 30, 1984, Pub.L. 98–596, § 8, 98 Stat. 3138.)"

For applicability of sentencing provisions to offenses, see Effective Date and Savings Provisions, etc., note, section 235 of Pub.L. 98–473, as amended, set out under section 3551 of this title.

Effective and Applicability Provisions

1984 Amendments. Pub.L. 98–596, § 10, Oct. 30, 1984, 98 Stat. 3138, provided that: "The amendments made by sections 2 through 9 of this Act [enacting sections 3621, 3622, and 3623 of this title and amending this section and sections 3565, 3569, 3579, 3651, 3655, and 4209 of this title] shall apply with respect to offenses committed after December 31, 1984."

Effective Date of Repeal; Savings Provisions

Repeal by Pub.L. 98–473 effective on the first day of first calendar month beginning thirty six months after Oct. 12, 1984, applicable only to offenses committed after taking effect of sections 211 to 239 of Pub.L. 98–473, and except as otherwise provided for therein, see section 235 of Pub.L. 98–473, as amended, set out as a note under section 3551 of this title.

Severability of Provisions

Pub.L. 108–21, § 2, Apr. 30, 2003, 117 Stat. 651, provided that: "If any provision of this Act [the Prosecutorial Remedies and Other Tools to end the Exploitation of Children Today Act of 2003, or PROTECT Act; for classification of which, see Short Title note set out under this section and Tables], or the application of such provision to any person or circumstance, is held invalid, the remainder of this Act, and the application of such provision to other persons not similarly situated or to other circumstances, shall not be affected by such invalidation."

Pub.L. 107–56, § 2, Oct. 26, 2001, 115 Stat. 275, provided that: "Any provision of this Act [the Uniting and Strengthening America by Providing Appropriate Tools Required to Intercept and Obstruct Terrorism (USA PATRIOT ACT) Act of 2001, Pub.L. 107–56, Oct. 26, 2001, 115 Stat. 272; see Tables for complete classification] held to be invalid or unenforceable by its terms, or as applied to any person or circumstance, shall be construed so as to give it the maximum effect permitted by law, unless such holding shall be one of utter invalidity or unenforceability, in which event such provision shall be deemed severable from this Act and shall not affect the remainder thereof or the application of such provision to other persons not similarly situated or to other, dissimilar circumstances."

Pub.L. 104–132, Title IX, § 904, Apr. 24, 1996, 110 Stat. 1319, provided that: "If any provision of this Act [Pub.L. 104–132, Apr. 24, 1996, 110 Stat. 1214, for classification of which, see Short Title note under this section and Tables], an amendment made by this Act, or the application of such provision or amendment to any person or circumstance is held to be unconstitutional, the remainder of this Act, the amendments made by this Act, and the application of the provisions of such to any person or circumstance shall not be affected thereby."

Short Title

2007 Amendments. Pub. L. 109–476, § 1, Jan. 12, 2007, 120 Stat. 3568, provided that: "This Act [enacting 18 U.S.C.A. § 1039 and enacting provisions set out as a notes under 18 U.S.C.A. § 1039 and 28 U.S.C.A. § 994] may be cited as the 'Telephone Records and Privacy Protection Act of 2006'."

Pub.L. 109–481, § 1, Jan. 12, 2007, 120 Stat. 3673, provided that: "This Act [enacting 18 U.S.C.A. § 706a] may be cited as the 'Geneva Distinctive Emblems Protection Act of 2006'."

2006 Amendments. Pub.L. 109–437, § 1, Dec. 20, 2006, 120 Stat. 3266, provided that: "This Act [amending 18 U.S.C.A. § 704 and enacting provisions set out as a note under 18 U.S.C.A. § 704] may be cited as the 'Stolen Valor Act of 2005'."

Pub.L. 109–374, § 1, Nov. 27, 2006, 120 Stat. 2652, provided that: "This Act [amending 18 U.S.C.A. § 43] may be cited as the 'Animal Enterprise Terrorism Act'."

Pub.L. 109–181, § 1(a)(1), Mar. 16, 2006, 120 Stat. 285, provided that: "This section [amending 18 U.S.C.A. § 2320, enacting provisions set out as a note under 18 U.S.C.A. § 2320, and amending provisions set out in a note under 28 U.S.C.A. § 994] may be cited as the 'Stop Counterfeiting in Manufactured Goods Act'."

Pub.L. 109–181, § 2(a), Mar. 16, 2006, 120 Stat. 288, provided that: "This section [amending 17 U.S.C.A. § 1101, 18 U.S.C.A. §§ 2318, 2319, and 2320] may be cited as the 'Protecting American Goods and Services Act of 2005'."

Pub.L. 109–178, § 1, Mar. 9, 2006, 120 Stat. 278, provided that: "This Act [amending 12 U.S.C.A. § 3414, 15 U.S.C.A. §§ 1681u, 1681v, 18 U.S.C.A. § 2709, 50 U.S.C.A. §§ 436, 1861, and enacting provisions set out as a note under 12 U.S.C.A. § 3414] may be cited as the 'USA PATRIOT Act Additional Reauthorizing Amendments Act of 2006'."

Pub.L. 109–177, § 1(a), Mar. 9, 2006, 120 Stat. 192, provided that: "This Act [enacting 8 U.S.C.A. § 1107, 15 U.S.C.A. § 2233, 18 U.S.C.A. §§ 26, 226, 554, 987, 1992, 2237, 2282A, 2282B, 2283, 2284, 2290, 2291, 2292, 2293, 3056A, 3511, and 3599, 21 U.S.C.A. §§ 860a, 865, 871a, and 960a, 28 U.S.C.A. §§ 509A and 2265, 31 U.S.C.A. § 507A, and 42 U.S.C.A. §§ 3797cc, 3797cc–1, 3797cc–2, and 3797cc–3, amending 3 U.S.C.A. § 19, 5 U.S.C.A. §§ 5315 and 7323, 5 U.S.C.A. App. 3 §§ 8D and 8I, 12 U.S.C.A. § 3414, 15 U.S.C.A. §§ 1681u and 1681v, 18 U.S.C.A. §§ 32, 33, 545, 549, 659, 981, 1028,

1036, 1366, 1510, 1752, 1956, 1957, 1961, 2199, 2311, 2312, 2313, 2332b, 2339A, 2339C, 2341, 2342, 2343, 2344, 2345, 2346, 2516, 2702, 2709, 2711, 3056, 3103a, 3521, and 3583, 18 U.S.C.A. App. 3 § 9A, 19 U.S.C.A. § 1595a, 21 U.S.C.A. §§ 802, 814, 823, 826, 830, 841, 842, 844, 848, 853, 952, 960, and 971, 22 U.S.C.A. §§ 2291h, 2291j, 2291j–1, 2709, 4304, and 4314, 28 U.S.C.A. §§ 506, 545, 546, 561, 599A, 994, 2251, 2261, 2266, 2461, and 2466, 31 U.S.C.A. §§ 1537 and 5318, 42 U.S.C.A. §§ 3793, 3797u, 6921, and 10502, 49 U.S.C.A. § 5103, 50 U.S.C.A. §§ 403–6, 436, 1705, 1801, 1803, 1804, 1805, 1808, 1824, 1826, 1842, 1846, 1861, and 1862, repealing 3 U.S.C.A. §§ 202, 203, 204, 206, 207, 208, and 209, 18 U.S.C.A. §§ 1992 and 1993, and 28 U.S.C.A. § 2265, enacting provisions set out as notes under this section, 18 U.S.C.A. §§ 659, 2339C, 3056A, and 3511, 21 U.S.C.A. §§ 801, 802, 826, 830, 844, and 853, 22 U.S.C.A. §§ 2291 and 2291h, 28 U.S.C.A. §§ 545 and 2251, 49 U.S.C.A. § 46502, and 50 U.S.C.A. § 1805, amending provisions set out as notes under this section, 18 U.S.C.A. §§ 1801 and 3056, 28 U.S.C.A. §§ 519 and 533, and 50 U.S.C.A. § 1801, and repealing provisions set out as a notes under 18 U.S.C.A. §§ 983, 2332b, and 2510, and 21 U.S.C.A. § 802] may be cited as the 'USA PATRIOT Improvement and Reauthorization Act of 2005'."

Pub.L. 109–177, Title II, § 201, Mar. 9, 2006, 120 Stat. 230, provided that: "This title [enacting 18 U.S.C.A. § 3599, amending 18 U.S.C.A. § 3583 and 21 U.S.C.A. § 848, and enacting provisions set out as notes under 49 U.S.C.A. § 46502] may be cited as the 'Terrorist Death Penalty Enhancement Act of 2005'."

Pub.L. 109–177, Title III, § 301, Mar. 9, 2006, 120 Stat. 233, provided that: "This title [enacting 18 U.S.C.A. §§ 26, 226, 554, 2237, 2282A, 2282B, 2283, 2284, and 2290 to 2293, amending 18 U.S.C.A. §§ 545, 549, 659, 1036, 1956, 2199, 2311, 2312, and 2313, and 19 U.S.C.A. § 1595a, enacting provisions set out as a note under 18 U.S.C.A. § 659, and amending provisions set out as a note under 28 U.S.C.A. § 994] may be cited as the 'Reducing Crime and Terrorism at America's Seaports Act of 2005'."

Pub.L. 109–177, Title IV, § 401, Mar. 9, 2006, 120 Stat. 243, provided that: "This title [enacting 18 U.S.C.A. § 987, amending 18 U.S.C.A. §§ 33, 981, 1366, 1956, 1957, 1961, and 2339C, 28 U.S.C.A. §§ 2461 and 2466, 31 U.S.C.A. § 5318, and 50 U.S.C.A. § 1705, enacting provisions set out as a note under 18 U.S.C.A. § 2339C, and repealing provisions set out as a note under 18 U.S.C.A. § 983] may be cited as the 'Combating Terrorism Financing Act of 2005'."

Pub.L. 109–177, Title VI, § 601, Mar. 9, 2006, 120 Stat. 251, provided that: "This title [enacting 18 U.S.C.A. § 3056A, amending 5 U.S.C.A. App. 3 §§ 8D, 8I, 12 U.S.C.A. § 3414, 18 U.S.C.A. §§ 1028, 1752, and 3056, 22 U.S.C.A. §§ 2709, 4304, and 4314, and 31 U.S.C.A. § 1537, repealing Chapter 3 of Title 3 (3 U.S.C.A. § 201 et seq.), enacting provisions set out as a note under 18 U.S.C.A. § 3056A, and amending provisions set out as a note under 18 U.S.C.A. § 3056] may be cited as the 'Secret Service Authorization and Technical Modification Act of 2005'."

2004 Amendments. Pub.L. 108–458, Title VI, § 6701, Dec. 17, 2004, 118 Stat. 3764, provided that: "This subtitle [Pub.L. 108–458, Title VI, Subtitle H, §§ 6701 to 6704, Dec. 17, 2004, 118 Stat. 3764, which enacted 18 U.S.C.A. § 1038, amended 18 U.S.C.A. §§ 1001, 1505, and 1958, and enacted provisions set out in a note under 28 U.S.C.A. § 994] may be cited as the 'Stop Terrorist and Military Hoaxes Act of 2004'."

Pub.L. 108–458, Title VI, § 6801, Dec. 17, 2004, 118 Stat. 3766, provided that: "This subtitle [Pub.L. 108–458, Title VI, Subtitle I, §§ 6801 to 6803, Dec. 17, 2004, 118 Stat. 3766, which enacted 18 U.S.C.A. § 832, amended 18 U.S.C.A. §§ 175b, 1961, 2332a, and 2332b, and 42 U.S.C.A. §§ 2077 and 2122, and enacted provisions set out as a note under 18 U.S.C.A. § 175b] may be cited as the 'Weapons of Mass Destruction Prohibition Improvement Act of 2004'."

Pub.L. 108–458, Title VI, § 6901, Dec. 17, 2004, 118 Stat. 3769, provided that: "This subtitle [Pub.L. 108–458, Title VI, Subtitle J, §§ 6901 to 6911, Dec. 17, 2004, 118 Stat. 3769, enacting 18 U.S.C.A. §§ 175c, 2332g, and 2332h, amending 18 U.S.C.A. §§ 1956, 2332b, and 2516, 22 U.S.C.A. § 2778, and 42 U.S.C.A. §§ 2122 and 2272, and enacted provisions set out as a note under 18 U.S.C.A. § 175c] may be cited as the 'Prevention of Terrorist Access to Destructive Weapons Act of 2004'."

2003 Amendments. Pub.L. 108–21, § 1(a), Apr. 30, 2003, 117 Stat. 650, provided that: "This Act [enacting 18 U.S.C.A. §§ 25, 1466A, 2252B, and 3283, and 42 U.S.C.A. §§ 5791, 5791a, 5791b, 5791c, 5791d, and 13004, amending 18 U.S.C.A. §§ 1028, 1111, 1993, 1201, 1204, 1591, 2247, 2251, 2252, 2252A, 2256, 2257, 2422, 2423, 2426, 2516, 2702,3056, 3142, 3282, 3486, 3553, 3559, 3583, 3742, and Fed.Rules Cr.Proc. Rule 7, 18 U.S.C.A., 21 U.S.C.A. §§ 843 and 856, 28 U.S.C.A. §§ 991 and 994, 42 U.S.C.A. §§ 3796dd, 5773, 5777, 5779, 5792, 5792a, 13001b, 13032, 13975, and 14071, and 47 U.S.C.A. § 223, and enacting provisions set out as notes under 18 U.S.C.A. §§ 1001, 1466A, 2251, and 3553, 21 U.S.C.A. § 801, 28 U.S.C.A. §§ 991 and 994, and 42 U.S.C.A. §§ 5119a, 5601, and 14071] may be cited as the 'Prosecutorial Remedies and Other Tools to end the Exploitation of Children Today Act of 2003' or 'PROTECT Act'."

2002 Amendments. Pub.L. 107–273, Div. B, Title IV, § 4001, Nov. 2, 2002, 116 Stat. 1806, provided that: "This title [amending 18 U.S.C.A. §§ 115, 175b, 205, 247, 281, 372, 492, 510, 521, 665, 709, 752, 922, 924, 929, 981, 982, 1005, 1029, 1030, 1032, 1071, 1091, 1114, 1261, 1345, 1368, 1425 to 1427, 1513, 1541 to 1544, 1546, 1716, 1821, 1836, 1920, 1924, 1956, 1961, 1992, 2075, 2113, 2236, 2252A, 2254, 2311, 2332d, 2339, 2339A, 2339C, 2423, 2441, 2510, 2516, 2703, 2707, 3183, 3241, 3286, 3553, 3563, 3592, 3593, 3612, 3664 and 4104, 21 U.S.C.A. §§ 802, 841 to 843 and 881, 28 U.S.C.A. §§ 504, 509, 526, 529 and 534, and 50 U.S.C.A. § 1805, repealing 18 U.S.C.A. §§ 14 and 3503, enacting provisions set out as a notes under 18 U.S.C.A. §§ 247, 1091, 1956, 1961, 2339, 2441, 2707 and 3563, and 50 U.S.C.A. § 1805, and repealing provisions set out as a note under 28 U.S.C.A. § 504] may be cited as the 'Criminal Law Technical Amendments Act of 2002'."

2001 Amendments. Pub.L. 107–56, § 1(a), Oct. 26, 2001, 115 Stat. 272, as amended Pub.L. 109–177, Title I, § 101(b), Mar. 9, 2006, 120 Stat. 194, provided that: "This Act [see Tables for complete classification] may be cited as the 'Uniting and Strengthening America by Providing Appropriate Tools Required to Intercept and Obstruct Terrorism Act of 2001' or the 'USA PATRIOT Act'." [This Act is also known as the Antiterrorism Act.]

1998 Amendments. Pub.L. 105–314, § 1(a), Oct. 30, 1998, 112 Stat. 2974, provided that: "This Act [amending 18 U.S.C.A. §§ 1201, 2241, 2243, 2246, 2251, 2252, 2252A, 2253, 2254, 2255, 2421, 2422, 2423, 2702, 3156, 3486, 3559, and 42 U.S.C.A. § 14071, enacting 18 U.S.C.A. §§ 1470, 2425, 2426, 2427, 3486A, 28 U.S.C.A. § 540B, and 42 U.S.C.A. § 13032, and enacting provisions set out as notes under this section, 18 U.S.C.A. §§ 1470 and 4042, 28 U.S.C.A. §§ 531 and 994, and 42 U.S.C.A. § 14071] may be cited as the 'Protection of Children From Sexual Predators Act of 1998'.".

Pub.L. 105–184, § 1, June 23, 1998, 112 Stat. 520, provided that: "This Act [amending 18 U.S.C.A. §§ 709, 982, 2326, 2327, and 2703 and enacting provisions set out as a note under 28 U.S.C.A. § 994] may be cited as the 'Telemarketing Fraud Prevention Act of 1998'."

1996 Amendments. Pub.L. 104–294, § 1, Oct. 11, 1996, 110 Stat. 3488, provided that: "This Act [for classification of which to the Code, see Tables] may be cited as the 'Economic Espionage Act of 1996'."

Pub.L. 104–132, § 1, Apr. 24, 1996, 110 Stat. 1214, provided that: "This Act [see Tables for classification] may be cited as the 'Antiterrorism and Effective Death Penalty Act of 1996'."

1994 Amendments. Pub.L. 103–322, Title X, § 100001, Sept. 13, 1994, 108 Stat. 1996, provided that: "This title [amending section 13 of this title and section 3751 of Title 42, The Public Health and Welfare] may be cited as the 'Drunk Driving Child Protection Act of 1994'."

1990 Amendments. Pub.L. 101–647, § 1, Nov. 29, 1990, 104 Stat. 4789, provided that: "This Act [enacting section 2693 of Title 10, Armed Forces, sections 4201 to 4213, 4221 to 4230, and 4241 to 4221 of Title 12, Banks and Banking, section 2057b of Title 15, Commerce and Trade, sections 403, 1032, 1517, 2258, 3059A, 3509 and 4046 of this title, sections 3201 to 3203, and 3233 of Title 20, Education, sections 859 to 862, 888 and 889 of Title 21, Food and Drugs, sections 2844, 3001 to 3015, 3101 to 3105, 3201 to 3205, 3301 to 3308 of Title 28, Judiciary and Judicial Procedure, sections 3759, 3762a, 3762b, 3796aa to 3796aa–8, 3796bb to 3796bb–1, 5779, 5780, 10606, 10607, 13001 to 13004, 13011 to 13014, 13021 to 13024, 13031, 13041, 13051 to 13055 of Title 42, The Public Health and Welfare and section 446 of Title 45, Railroads, and amending sections 12, 14, 20, 114, 115, 209, 212, 213, 215, 219, 232, 245, 402, 510, 513, 648, 655 to 657, 666, 842, 844, 921 to 925, 930, 981, 982, 1004 to 1006, 1014, 1028 to 1030, 1084, 1113, 1114, 1168, 1201, 1262, 1341 to 1345, 1365, 1460, 1466, 1467, 1657, 1716A, 1717, 1730, 1761, 1864, 1906, 1952, 1956, 1963, 2113, 2114, 2248, 2251 to 2254, 2257, 2313 to 2316, 2318, 3013, 3077, 3124, 3142, 3154, 3165, 3166, 3184, 3551, 3572, 3582, 3583, 3611 to 3613, 3621, 3624, 3663, 3742, 4013, 4106A, 4109, 4124, 4246, 4285 4352 and 5032 of this title, sections 101, 328, 365, 502, 522 and 523 of Title 11, Bankruptcy, sections 1441a, 1786, 1787, 1818, 1828, 1829, 1831, 1833, 1921 and 4301 of Title 12, sections 1087ee, 3181, 3182, 3192, 3194 to 3196, 3212, 3216, 3217, 3224a and 3424b of Title 20, sections 333, 509, 802, 812, 841, 844, 859, 860, 861, 881 and 960 of Title 21, and sections 290aa–6, 2271, 3742, 3751, 3756, 3760, 3761, 3763 to 3766, 3782, 3783, 3789, 3793, 3796, 3796a, 3796b and 10601 of Title 42, and section 1903 of the Appendix to Title 46, Shipping, redesignating section 3117 of this title, repealing sections 45, 969, 1714, 1718, 2198 and 3286 of this title and sections 333a and 857 of Title 21, and enacting provisions set out as notes under this section and sections 921, 924, 930, 1001, 2251, 2257, 3141, 3624, 4042, 4046 and 4121 of this title and section 523 of Title 11, sections 1818 and 4201 of Title 12, section 1087ee of Title 20, sections 801, 802 and 829 of Title 21, sections 6103, 7203 and 7608 of Title 26, Internal Revenue Code, sections 1, 509, 522, 534, 994 and 3001 of Title 28, section 5311 of Title 31, Money and Finance, and sections 3721, 3796, 10601 and 10606 of Title 42, and repealing provisions set out as notes under sections 801 and 857 of Title 21] may be cited as the 'Crime Control Act of 1990'."

1988 Amendments. Pub.L. 100–690, Title VII, § 7011, Nov. 18, 1988, 102 Stat. 4395, provided that: "This subtitle [Subtitle B of Title VII, §§ 7011 to 7096, of Pub.L. 100–690, for classification see Tables volume] may be cited as the 'Minor and Technical Criminal Law Amendments Act of 1988'."

1987 Amendments. Pub.L. 100–185, § 1, Dec. 11, 1987, 101 Stat. 1279, provided that: "This Act [enacting section 19 of this title, amending sections 18, 3013, 3559, 3571, 3572, 3573, 3611, 3612, and 3663 of this title and section 604 of Title 28, Judiciary and Judicial Procedure, and enacting provisions set out as notes under section 3611 of this title] may be cited as the 'Criminal Fine Improvements Act of 1987'."

1986 Amendments. Pub.L. 99–646, § 1, Nov. 10, 1986, 100 Stat. 3592, provided that: "This Act [enacting sections 18, 1793, 2241 to 2245 (chapter 109A), 4044, and 4045 of this title; redesignating as chapter 232A former chapter 232 and as present sections the bracketed sections: 17 [20], 513 [511],1366 [1365], 2321 [2320], 3681 [3671], and 3682 [3672] of this title; amended sections 3, 113, 115, 201, 203, 209, 219, 351, 373, 546, 666, 875, 1028, 1029, 1111, 1153, 1201, 1512, 1515, 1791, 1792, 1961, 1963, 2113, 2232, 2315, 3050, 3076, 3141 to 3144, 3146 to 3148, former section 3150a, sections 3156, 3185, 3522, 3552, 3553, 3556, 3561, 3563, 3564, 3579, 3583, 3603, 3624, 3671 to 3673, 3731, 3742, 4082, 4203, 4214, 4208 to 4210, 4214, 4255, 5003, and 5037 of this title; enacting Rule 29(d) of Fed. Rules of Cr. Proc., amending Rules 12.2(c), 32(c)(2)(B), and 32.1(b) of such Rules and enacting note provisions under Rules 29, 32, and 32.1; amending sections 802, 812, 845, 873, 878, and 881 of Title 21, Food and Drugs; amending sections 524, 992 to 994, and 1921 of Title 28, Judiciary and Judicial Procedure; amending sections 257, 300w–3, 300w–4, 9511, 10601, 10603, and 10604 of Title 42, The Public Health and Welfare; and amending section 1472 of Title 49, Transportation; repealing chapter 99 (sections 2031, 2032) and sections 4216 and 4217 of this title; enacting note provisions under sections 201, 203, 1791, 1792, 2241, 3141, 3143, 3552, 3553, 3556, 3561, 3563, 3564, 3579, 3583, 3603, 3624, 3672, 3673, and 5037 of this title, section 1921 of Title 28, and section 257 of Title 42; amending note provision under section 3551 of this title; and repealing note provision under section 3143 of this title] may be cited as the 'Criminal Law and Procedure Technical Amendments Act of 1986'."

1984 Acts. Pub.L. 98–473, Title II, § 200, Oct. 12, 1984, 98 Stat. 1976, provided that: "This title [Pub.L. 98–473, Title II, §§ 201–2304, Oct. 12, 1984, 98 Stat. 1976–2194] may be cited as the 'Comprehensive Crime Control Act of 1984'." See Tables volume for classifications.

§ 2. Principals

(a) Whoever commits an offense against the United States or aids, abets, counsels, commands, induces or procures its commission, is punishable as a principal.

(b) Whoever willfully causes an act to be done which if directly performed by him or another would be an offense against the United States, is punishable as a principal.

(June 25, 1948, c. 645, 62 Stat. 684; Oct. 31, 1951, c. 655, § 17b, 65 Stat. 717.)

§ 3. Accessory after the fact

Whoever, knowing that an offense against the United States has been committed, receives, relieves, comforts or assists the offender in order to hinder or prevent his apprehension, trial or punishment, is an accessory after the fact.

Except as otherwise expressly provided by any Act of Congress, an accessory after the fact shall be imprisoned not more than one-half the maximum term of imprisonment or (notwithstanding section 3571) fined not more than one-half the maximum fine prescribed for the punishment of the principal, or both; or if the principal is punishable by life imprisonment or death, the accessory shall be imprisoned not more than 15 years.

(June 25, 1948, c. 645, 62 Stat. 684; Nov. 10, 1986, Pub.L. 99–646, § 43, 100 Stat. 3601; Nov. 29, 1990, Pub.L. 101–647, Title XXXV, § 3502, 104 Stat. 4921; Sept. 13, 1994, Pub.L. 103–322, Title XXXIII, §§ 330011(h), 330016(2)(A), 108 Stat. 2145, 2148.)

HISTORICAL AND STATUTORY NOTES

Effective and Applicability Provisions

1994 Amendments. Section 330011(h) of Pub.L. 103–322 provided in part that the amendment made by such section, amending section 3502 of Pub.L. 101–647 (which amended this section), was to take effect on the date section 3502 of Pub.L. 101–647 took effect; section 3502 of Pub.L. 101–647 took effect on the date of enactment of Pub.L. 101–647, which was approved Nov. 29, 1990.

§ 4. Misprision of felony

Whoever, having knowledge of the actual commission of a felony cognizable by a court of the United States, conceals and does not as soon as possible make known the same to some judge or other person in civil or military authority under the United States, shall be fined under this title or imprisoned not more than three years, or both.

(June 25, 1948, c. 645, 62 Stat. 684; Sept. 13, 1994, Pub.L. 103–322, Title XXXIII, § 330016(1)(G), 108 Stat. 2147.)

§ 5. United States defined

The term "United States", as used in this title in a territorial sense, includes all places and waters, continental or insular, subject to the jurisdiction of the United States, except the Canal Zone.

(June 25, 1948, c. 645, 62 Stat. 685.)

HISTORICAL AND STATUTORY NOTES

Senate Revision Amendment

Words, "except the Canal Zone.", were inserted in this section by Senate amendment. 80th Congress, Senate Report No. 1620, Amendment 2.

§ 6. Department and agency defined

As used in this title:

The term "department" means one of the executive departments enumerated in section 1 of Title 5, unless the context shows that such term was intended to describe the executive, legislative, or judicial branches of the government.

The term "agency" includes any department, independent establishment, commission, administration, authority, board or bureau of the United States or any corporation in which the United States has a proprietary interest, unless the context shows that such term was intended to be used in a more limited sense.

(June 25, 1948, c. 645, 62 Stat. 685.)

HISTORICAL AND STATUTORY NOTES

References in Text

Section 1 of Title 5, referred to in text, is now covered by § 101 of Title 5, Government Organization and Employees.

Canal Zone

Applicability of section to Canal Zone, see § 14 of this title.

§ 7. Special maritime and territorial jurisdiction of the United States defined

The term "special maritime and territorial jurisdiction of the United States", as used in this title, includes:

(1) The high seas, any other waters within the admiralty and maritime jurisdiction of the United States and out of the jurisdiction of any particular State, and any vessel belonging in whole or in part to the United States or any citizen thereof, or to any corporation created by or under the laws of the United States, or of any State, Territory, District, or possession thereof, when such vessel is within the admiralty and maritime jurisdiction of the United States and out of the jurisdiction of any particular State.

(2) Any vessel registered, licensed, or enrolled under the laws of the United States, and being on a voyage upon the waters of any of the Great Lakes, or any of the waters connecting them, or upon the Saint Lawrence River where the same constitutes the International Boundary Line.

(3) Any lands reserved or acquired for the use of the United States, and under the exclusive or concurrent jurisdiction thereof, or any place purchased or otherwise acquired by the United States by consent of the legislature of the State in which the same shall be, for the erection of a fort, magazine, arsenal, dockyard, or other needful building.

(4) Any island, rock, or key containing deposits of guano, which may, at the discretion of the President, be considered as appertaining to the United States.

(5) Any aircraft belonging in whole or in part to the United States, or any citizen thereof, or to any corporation created by or under the laws of the United States, or any State, Territory, District, or possession thereof, while such aircraft is in flight over the high seas, or over any other waters within the admiralty and maritime jurisdiction of the United States and out of the jurisdiction of any particular State.

(6) Any vehicle used or designed for flight or navigation in space and on the registry of the United States pursuant to the Treaty on Principles Governing the Activities of States in the Exploration and Use of Outer Space, Including the Moon and Other Celestial Bodies and the Convention on Registration of Objects Launched into Outer Space, while that vehicle is in flight, which is from the moment when all external doors are closed on Earth following embarkation until the moment when one such door is opened on Earth for disembarkation or in the case of a forced landing, until the competent authorities take over the responsibility for the vehicle and for persons and property aboard.

(7) Any place outside the jurisdiction of any nation with respect to an offense by or against a national of the United States.

(8) To the extent permitted by international law, any foreign vessel during a voyage having a scheduled departure from or arrival in the United States with respect to an offense committed by or against a national of the United States.

(9) With respect to offenses committed by or against a national of the United States as that term is used in section 101 of the Immigration and Nationality Act—

(A) the premises of United States diplomatic, consular, military or other United States Government missions or entities in foreign States, including the buildings, parts of buildings, and land appurtenant or ancillary thereto or used for purposes of those missions or entities, irrespective of ownership; and

(B) residences in foreign States and the land appurtenant or ancillary thereto, irrespective of ownership, used for purposes of those missions or entities or used by United States personnel assigned to those missions or entities.

Nothing in this paragraph shall be deemed to supersede any treaty or international agreement with which this paragraph conflicts. This paragraph does not apply with respect to an offense committed by a person described in section 3261(a) of this title.

(June 25, 1948, c. 645, 62 Stat. 685; July 12, 1952, c. 695, 66 Stat. 589; Dec. 21, 1981, Pub.L. 97–96, § 6, 95 Stat. 1210; Oct. 12, 1984, Pub.L. 98–473, Title II, § 1210, 98 Stat. 2164; Sept. 13, 1994, Pub.L. 103–322, Title XII, § 120002, 108 Stat. 2021; Oct. 26, 2001, Pub.L. 107–56, Title VIII, § 804, 115 Stat. 377.)

HISTORICAL AND STATUTORY NOTES

References in Text

Section 101 of the Immigration and Nationality Act, referred to in par. (9), is Act June 27, 1952, c. 477, Title I, § 101, 66 Stat. 166, as amended, which is classified to 8 U.S.C.A. § 1101. The term "national of the United States" is defined in par. (22) of that section.

Territorial Sea Extending to Twelve Miles Included in Special Maritime and Territorial Jurisdiction

Pub.L. 104–132, TItle IX, § 901(a), Apr. 24, 1996, 110 Stat. 1317, provided that: "The Congress declares that all the territorial sea of the United States, as defined by Presidential Proclamation 5928 of December 27, 1988 [set out as a note under section 1331 of Title 43, Public Lands], for purposes of Federal criminal jurisdiction is part of the United States, subject to its sovereignty, and is within the special maritime and territorial jurisdiction of the United States for the purposes of title 18, United States Code [this title]."

§ 8. Obligation or other security of the United States defined

The term "obligation or other security of the United States" includes all bonds, certificates of indebtedness, national bank currency, Federal Reserve notes, Federal Reserve bank notes, coupons, United States notes, Treasury notes, gold certificates, silver certificates, fractional notes, certificates of deposit, bills, checks, or drafts for money, drawn by or upon authorized officers of the United States, stamps and other representatives of value, of whatever denomination, issued under any Act of Congress, and canceled United States stamps.

(June 25, 1948, c. 645, 62 Stat. 685.)

HISTORICAL AND STATUTORY NOTES

Canal Zone

Applicability of section to Canal Zone, see § 14 of this title.

§ 9. Vessel of the United States defined

The term "vessel of the United States", as used in this title, means a vessel belonging in whole or in part to the United States, or any citizen thereof, or any corporation created by or under the laws of the United States, or of any State, Territory, District, or possession thereof.

(June 25, 1948, c. 645, 62 Stat. 685.)

§ 10. Interstate commerce and foreign commerce defined

The term "interstate commerce", as used in this title, includes commerce between one State, Territory, Possession, or the District of Columbia and another State, Territory, Possession, or the District of Columbia.

The term "foreign commerce", as used in this title, includes commerce with a foreign country.

(June 25, 1948, c. 645, 62 Stat. 686.)

§ 11. Foreign government defined

The term "foreign government", as used in this title except in sections 112, 878, 970, 1116, and 1201, includes any government, faction, or body of insurgents within a country with which the United States is at peace, irrespective of recognition by the United States.

(June 25, 1948, c. 645, 62 Stat. 686; Oct. 8, 1976, Pub.L. 94–467, § 11, 90 Stat. 2001.)

HISTORICAL AND STATUTORY NOTES

Canal Zone

Applicability of section to Canal Zone, see § 14 of this title.

§ 12. United States Postal Service defined

As used in this title, the term "Postal Service" means the United States Postal Service established under title 39, and every officer and employee of that Service, whether or not such officer or employee has taken the oath of office.

(June 25, 1948, c. 645, 62 Stat. 686; Aug. 12, 1970, Pub.L. 91–375, § 6(j) (2), 84 Stat. 777; Nov. 29, 1990, Pub.L. 101–647, Title XXXV, § 3505, 104 Stat. 4921.)

HISTORICAL AND STATUTORY NOTES

Effective and Applicability Provisions

1970 Amendments. Amendment by Pub.L. 91–375 effective within 1 year after Aug. 12, 1970, on date established therefor by the Board of Governors of the United States Postal Service and published by it in the Federal Register, see section 15(a) of Pub.L. 91–375, set out as a note preceding section 101 of Title 39, Postal Service.

§ 13. Laws of States adopted for areas within Federal jurisdiction

(a) Whoever within or upon any of the places now existing or hereafter reserved or acquired as provided in section 7 of this title, or on, above, or below any portion of the territorial sea of the United States not within the jurisdiction of any State, Commonwealth, territory, possession, or district is guilty of any act or omission which, although not made punishable by any enactment of Congress, would be punishable if committed or omitted within the jurisdiction of the State, Territory, Possession, or District in which such place is situated, by the laws thereof in force at the time of such act or omission, shall be guilty of a like offense and subject to a like punishment.

(b)(1) Subject to paragraph (2) and for purposes of subsection (a) of this section, that which may or shall be imposed through judicial or administrative action under the law of a State, territory, possession, or district, for a conviction for operating a motor vehicle under the influence of a drug or alcohol, shall be considered to be a punishment provided by that law. Any limitation on the right or privilege to operate a motor vehicle imposed under this subsection shall apply only to the special maritime and territorial jurisdiction of the United States.

(2)(A) In addition to any term of imprisonment provided for operating a motor vehicle under the influence of a drug or alcohol imposed under the law of a State, territory, possession, or district, the punishment for such an offense under this section shall include an additional term of imprisonment of not more than 1 year, or if serious bodily injury of a minor is caused, not more than 5 years, or if death of a minor is caused, not more than 10 years, and an additional fine under this title, or both, if—

(i) a minor (other than the offender) was present in the motor vehicle when the offense was committed; and

(ii) the law of the State, territory, possession, or district in which the offense occurred does not provide an additional term of imprisonment under the circumstances described in clause (i).

(B) For the purposes of subparagraph (A), the term "minor" means a person less than 18 years of age.

(c) Whenever any waters of the territorial sea of the United States lie outside the territory of any State, Commonwealth, territory, possession, or district, such waters (including the airspace above and the seabed and subsoil below, and artificial islands and fixed structures erected thereon) shall be deemed, for purposes of subsection (a), to lie within the area of the State, Commonwealth, territory, possession, or district that it would lie within if the boundaries of such State, Commonwealth, territory, possession, or district were extended seaward to the outer limit of the territorial sea of the United States.

(June 25, 1948, c. 645, 62 Stat. 686; Nov. 18, 1988, Pub.L. 100–690, Title VI, § 6477(a), 102 Stat. 4381; Sept. 13, 1994, Pub.L. 103–322, Title X, § 100002, 108 Stat. 1996; Apr. 24, 1996, Pub.L. 104–132, Title IX, § 901(b), 110 Stat. 1317; Oct. 11, 1996, Pub.L. 104–294, Title VI, § 604(b)(32), 110 Stat. 3508.)

HISTORICAL AND STATUTORY NOTES

Effective and Applicability Provisions

1996 Amendments. Section 604(d) of Pub.L. 104–294 provided that: "The amendments made by this section [see Tables for classification] shall take effect on the date of enactment of Public Law 103–322 [Pub.L. 103–322, 108 Stat. 1796, which was approved Sept. 13, 1994]."

[§ 14. Repealed. Pub.L. 107–273, Div. B, Title IV, § 4004(a), Nov. 2, 2002, 116 Stat. 1812]

HISTORICAL AND STATUTORY NOTES

Section, Acts June 25, 1948, c. 645, 62 Stat. 686; Aug. 5, 1953, c. 325, 67 Stat. 366; Oct. 18, 1962, Pub.L. 87–845,

§ 3(a), 76A Stat. 698; June 22, 1968, Pub.L. 90–357, § 59, 82 Stat. 248; Nov. 29, 1990, Pub.L. 101–647, Title XXXV, § 3519(c), 104 Stat. 4923; Sept. 13, 1994, Pub.L. 103–322, Title XXXIII, § 330010(9), 108 Stat. 2143, related to definitions and the applicability of certain sections of this title to the Canal Zone.

§ 15. Obligation or other security of foreign government defined

The term "obligation or other security of any foreign government" includes, but is not limited to, uncanceled stamps, whether or not demonetized.

(Added Pub.L. 85–921, § 3, Sept. 2, 1958, 72 Stat. 1771.)

§ 16. Crime of violence defined

The term "crime of violence" means—

(a) an offense that has as an element the use, attempted use, or threatened use of physical force against the person or property of another, or

(b) any other offense that is a felony and that, by its nature, involves a substantial risk that physical force against the person or property of another may be used in the course of committing the offense.

(Added Pub.L. 98–473, Title II, § 1001(a), Oct. 12, 1984, 98 Stat. 2136.)

§ 17. Insanity defense

(a) Affirmative defense.—It is an affirmative defense to a prosecution under any Federal statute that, at the time of the commission of the acts constituting the offense, the defendant, as a result of a severe mental disease or defect, was unable to appreciate the nature and quality or the wrongfulness of his acts. Mental disease or defect does not otherwise constitute a defense.

(b) Burden of proof.—The defendant has the burden of proving the defense of insanity by clear and convincing evidence.

(Added Pub.L. 98–473, Title II, § 402(a), Oct. 12, 1984, 98 Stat. 2057, § 20, and renumbered Pub.L. 99–646, § 34(a), Nov. 10, 1986, 100 Stat. 3599.)

§ 18. Organization defined

As used in this title, the term "organization" means a person other than an individual.

(Added Pub.L. 99–646, § 38(a), Nov. 10, 1986, 100 Stat. 3599, and amended Pub.L. 100–690, Title VII, § 7012, Nov. 18, 1988, 102 Stat. 4395.)

HISTORICAL AND STATUTORY NOTES

Codifications

Section 7012 of Pub.L. 100–690 amended the directory language of section 38 of Pub.L. 99–646 by substituting "section 34" for "section 23", which had previously been amended by section 4(c) of Pub.L. 100–185. See note under this section.

Section 4(c) of Pub.L. 100–185 amended the directory language of section 38(a) of Pub.L. 99–646 by substituting "34(a)" for "23" so that section 38(a) of Pub.L. 99–646 would provide that this section be added after the section redesignated by section 34(a) of Pub.L. 99–646, which is section 17 of this title.

§ 19. Petty offense defined

As used in this title, the term "petty offense" means a Class B misdemeanor, a Class C misdemeanor, or an infraction, for which the maximum fine is no greater than the amount set forth for such an offense in section 3571(b)(6) or (7) in the case of an individual or section 3571(c)(6) or (7) in the case of an organization.

(Added Pub.L. 100–185, § 4(a), Dec. 11, 1987, 101 Stat. 1279, and amended Pub.L. 100–690, Title VII, § 7089(a), Nov. 18, 1988, 102 Stat. 4409.)

§ 20. Financial institution defined

As used in this title, the term "financial institution" means—

(1) an insured depository institution (as defined in section 3(c)(2) of the Federal Deposit Insurance Act);

(2) a credit union with accounts insured by the National Credit Union Share Insurance Fund;

(3) a Federal home loan bank or a member, as defined in section 2 of the Federal Home Loan Bank Act (12 U.S.C. 1422), of the Federal home loan bank system;

(4) a System institution of the Farm Credit System, as defined in section 5.35(3) of the Farm Credit Act of 1971;

(5) a small business investment company, as defined in section 103 of the Small Business Investment Act of 1958 (15 U.S.C. 662);

(6) a depository institution holding company (as defined in section 3(w)(1) of the Federal Deposit Insurance Act;

(7) a Federal Reserve bank or a member bank of the Federal Reserve System;

(8) an organization operating under section 25 or section 25(a) of the Federal Reserve Act; or

(9) a branch or agency of a foreign bank (as such terms are defined in paragraphs (1) and (3) of section 1(b) of the International Banking Act of 1978).

(Added Oct. 12, 1984, Pub.L. 98–473, Title II, § 1107(a), 98 Stat. 2145, § 215(c); renumbered § 215(b) and amended Aug. 4, 1986, Pub.L. 99–370, § 2, 100 Stat. 779; renumbered § 20 and amended Aug. 9, 1989, Pub.L. 101–73, Title IX, § 962(e)(1), (2), 103 Stat. 503; Nov. 29, 1990, Pub.L. 101–647, Title XXV, § 2597(a), 104 Stat. 4908.)

HISTORICAL AND STATUTORY NOTES

References in Text

Section 3 of the Federal Deposit Insurance Act, referred to in pars. (1) and (6), is classified to section 1813 of Title 12, Banks and Banking.

Section 5.35(3), of the Farm Credit Act of 1971, referred to in par. (4), is classified to section 2271(3) of Title 12.

The Federal Reserve Act, referred to in par. (8), is Act Dec. 23, 1913, c. 6, 38 Stat. 251, as amended, which is classified principally to chapter 3 of Title 12, 12 U.S.C.A. § 221 et seq. Section 25 of the Federal Reserve Act is classified to subchapter I of chapter 6 of Title 12, 12 U.S.C.A. § 601 et seq. Section 25(a) of the Federal Reserve Act, which is classified to subchapter II of chapter 6 of Title 12, 12 U.S.C.A. § 611 et seq., was renumbered section 25A by Pub.L. 102–242, Title I, § 142(e)(2), Dec. 10, 1991, 105 Stat. 2281. See Tables and 12 U.S.C.A. § 226 for complete classification.

Section 1(b) of the International Banking Act of 1978, referred to in par. (9), is classified to section 3101 of Title 12.

Separability of Provisions

If any provision of Pub.L. 101–73 or the application thereof to any person or circumstance is held invalid, the remainder of Pub.L. 101–73 and the application of the provision to other persons not similarly situated or to other circumstances not to be affected thereby, see section 1221 of Pub.L. 101–73, set out as a note under section 1811 of Title 12, Banks and Banking.

§ 21. Stolen or counterfeit nature of property for certain crimes defined

(a) Wherever in this title it is an element of an offense that—

(1) any property was embezzled, robbed, stolen, converted, taken, altered, counterfeited, falsely made, forged, or obliterated; and

(2) the defendant knew that the property was of such character;

such element may be established by proof that the defendant, after or as a result of an official representation as to the nature of the property, believed the property to be embezzled, robbed, stolen, converted, taken, altered, counterfeited, falsely made, forged, or obliterated.

(b) For purposes of this section, the term "official representation" means any representation made by a Federal law enforcement officer (as defined in section 115) or by another person at the direction or with the approval of such an officer.

(Added Pub.L. 103–322, Title XXXII, § 320910(a), Sept. 13, 1994, 108 Stat. 2127.)

§ 23.[1] Court of the United States defined

As used in this title, except where otherwise expressly provided[2] the term "court of the United States" includes the District Court of Guam, the District Court for the Northern Mariana Islands, and the District Court of the Virgin Islands.

(Added Pub.L. 103–322, Title XXXII, § 320914(a), Sept. 13, 1994, 108 Stat. 2128.)

1 So in original. No section 22 has been enacted.

2 So in original. Probably should be followed by a comma.

§ 24. Definitions relating to Federal health care offense

(a) As used in this title, the term "Federal health care offense" means a violation of, or a criminal conspiracy to violate—

(1) section 669, 1035, 1347, or 1518 of this title;

(2) section 287, 371, 664, 666, 1001, 1027, 1341, 1343, or 1954 of this title, if the violation or conspiracy relates to a health care benefit program.

(b) As used in this title, the term "health care benefit program" means any public or private plan or contract, affecting commerce, under which any medical benefit, item, or service is provided to any individual, and includes any individual or entity who is providing a medical benefit, item, or service for which payment may be made under the plan or contract.

(Added Pub.L. 104–191, Title II, § 241(a), Aug. 21, 1996, 110 Stat. 2016.)

§ 25. Use of minors in crimes of violence

(a) **Definitions.**—In this section, the following definitions shall apply:

(1) **Crime of violence.**—The term "crime of violence" has the meaning set forth in section 16.

(2) **Minor.**—The term "minor" means a person who has not reached 18 years of age.

(3) **Uses.**—The term "uses" means employs, hires, persuades, induces, entices, or coerces.

(b) **Penalties.**—Any person who is 18 years of age or older, who intentionally uses a minor to commit a crime of violence for which such person may be prosecuted in a court of the United States, or to assist in avoiding detection or apprehension for such an offense, shall—

(1) for the first conviction, be subject to twice the maximum term of imprisonment and twice the maximum fine that would otherwise be authorized for the offense; and

(2) for each subsequent conviction, be subject to 3 times the maximum term of imprisonment and 3 times the maximum fine that would otherwise be authorized for the offense.

(Added Pub.L. 108–21, Title VI, § 601, Apr. 30, 2003, 117 Stat. 687.)

§ 26. Definition of seaport

As used in this title, the term "seaport" means all piers, wharves, docks, and similar structures, adjacent to any waters subject to the jurisdiction of the United States, to which a vessel may be secured, including areas of land, water, or land and water under and in immediate proximity to such structures, buildings on or contiguous to such structures, and the equipment and materials on such structures or in such buildings.

(Added Pub.L. 109–177, Title III, § 302(c), Mar. 9, 2006, 120 Stat. 233.)

CHAPTER 2—AIRCRAFT AND MOTOR VEHICLES

[1] So in original. Two sections 39 have been added.

§ 31. Definitions

(a) Definitions.—In this chapter, the following definitions apply:

(1) Aircraft.—The term "aircraft" means a civil, military, or public contrivance invented, used, or designed to navigate, fly, or travel in the air.

(2) Aviation quality.—The term "aviation quality", with respect to a part of an aircraft or space vehicle, means the quality of having been manufactured, constructed, produced, maintained, repaired, overhauled, rebuilt, reconditioned, or restored in conformity with applicable standards specified by law (including applicable regulations).

(3) Destructive substance.—The term "destructive substance" means an explosive substance, flammable material, infernal machine, or other chemical, mechanical, or radioactive device or matter of a combustible, contaminative, corrosive, or explosive nature.

(4) In flight.—The term "in flight" means—

(A) any time from the moment at which all the external doors of an aircraft are closed following embarkation until the moment when any such door is opened for disembarkation; and

(B) in the case of a forced landing, until competent authorities take over the responsibility for the aircraft and the persons and property on board.

(5) In service.—The term "in service" means—

(A) any time from the beginning of preflight preparation of an aircraft by ground personnel or by the crew for a specific flight until 24 hours after any landing; and

(B) in any event includes the entire period during which the aircraft is in flight.

(6) Motor vehicle.—The term "motor vehicle" means every description of carriage or other contrivance propelled or drawn by mechanical power and used for commercial purposes on the highways in the transportation of passengers, passengers and property, or property or cargo.

(7) Part.—The term "part" means a frame, assembly, component, appliance, engine, propeller, material, part, spare part, piece, section, or related integral or auxiliary equipment.

(8) Space vehicle.—The term "space vehicle" means a man-made device, either manned or unmanned, designed for operation beyond the Earth's atmosphere.

(9) State.—The term "State" means a State of the United States, the District of Columbia, and any commonwealth, territory, or possession of the United States.

(10) Used for commercial purposes.—The term "used for commercial purposes" means the carriage of persons or property for any fare, fee, rate, charge or other consideration, or directly or indirectly in connection with any business, or other undertaking intended for profit.

(b) Terms defined in other law.—In this chapter, the terms "aircraft engine", "air navigation facility", "appliance", "civil aircraft", "foreign air commerce", "interstate air commerce", "landing area", "overseas air commerce", "propeller", "spare part", and "special aircraft jurisdiction of the United States" have the meanings given those terms in sections 40102(a) and 46501 of title 49.

(Added July 14, 1956, c. 595, § 1, 70 Stat. 538, and amended Oct. 12, 1984, Pub.L. 98–473, Title II, §§ 1010, 2013(a), 98 Stat. 2141, 2187; Nov. 18, 1988, Pub.L. 100–690, Title VII, § 7015, 102 Stat. 4395; July 5, 1994, Pub.L. 103–272, § 5(e)(1), 108 Stat. 1373; Apr. 5, 2000, Pub.L. 106–181, Title V, § 506(b), 114 Stat. 136.)

HISTORICAL AND STATUTORY NOTES

Effective and Applicability Provisions

2000 Acts. Amendment by Pub.L. 106–181 applicable only to fiscal years beginning after September 30, 1999, see section 3 of Pub.L. 106–181, set out as a note under section 106 of Title 49.

1984 Acts. Section 2015 of Pub.L. 98–473 provided that: "This part [amending this section and section 32 of this title and sections 1301, 1471, and 1472 of Title 49, Transportation] shall become effective on the date of the enactment of this joint resolution [Oct. 12, 1984]."

Short Title

2000 Amendments. Pub.L. 106–181, Title V, § 506(a), Apr. 5, 2000, 114 Stat. 136, provided that: "This section [enacting section 38 of this title and amending sections 31 and 2516 of this title] may be cited as the 'Aircraft Safety Act of 2000'."

1984 Amendments. Section 2011 of Pub.L. 98–473 provided that: "This part [amending this section and section 32 of this title and sections 1301, 1471, and 1472 of Title 49, Transportation] may be cited as the 'Aircraft Sabotage Act'."

Congressional Statement and Declaration of Purpose

Section 2012 of Pub.L. 98–473 provided that: "The Congress hereby finds that—

"(1) the Convention for the Suppression of Unlawful Acts Against the Safety of Civil Aviation (ratified by the United States on November 1, 1972) requires each contracting State to establish its jurisdiction over certain offenses affecting the safety of civil aviation;

"(2) such offenses place innocent lives in jeopardy, endanger national security, affect domestic tranquility, gravely affect interstate and foreign commerce, and are offenses against the law of nations; and

"(3) the purpose of this subtitle is to implement fully the Convention for the Suppression of Unlawful Acts Against the Safety of Civil Aviation and to expand the protection accorded to aircraft and related facilities."

§ 32. Destruction of aircraft or aircraft facilities

(a) Whoever willfully—

(1) sets fire to, damages, destroys, disables, or wrecks any aircraft in the special aircraft jurisdiction of the United States or any civil aircraft used, operated, or employed in interstate, overseas, or foreign air commerce;

(2) places or causes to be placed a destructive device or substance in, upon, or in proximity to, or otherwise makes or causes to be made unworkable or unusable or hazardous to work or use, any such aircraft, or any part or other materials used or intended to be used in connection with the operation of such aircraft, if such placing or causing to be placed or such making or causing to be made is likely to endanger the safety of any such aircraft;

(3) sets fire to, damages, destroys, or disables any air navigation facility, or interferes by force or violence with the operation of such facility, if such fire, damaging, destroying, disabling, or interfering is likely to endanger the safety of any such aircraft in flight;

(4) with the intent to damage, destroy, or disable any such aircraft, sets fire to, damages, destroys, or disables or places a destructive device or substance in, upon, or in proximity to, any appliance or structure, ramp, landing area, property, machine, or apparatus, or any facility or other material used, or intended to be used, in connection with the operation, maintenance, loading, unloading or storage of any such aircraft or any cargo carried or intended to be carried on any such aircraft;

(5) interferes with or disables, with intent to endanger the safety of any person or with a reckless disregard for the safety of human life, anyone engaged in the authorized operation of such aircraft or any air navigation facility aiding in the navigation of any such aircraft;

(6) performs an act of violence against or incapacitates any individual on any such aircraft, if such act of violence or incapacitation is likely to endanger the safety of such aircraft;

(7) communicates information, knowing the information to be false and under circumstances in which such information may reasonably be believed, thereby endangering the safety of any such aircraft in flight; or

(8) attempts or conspires to do anything prohibited under paragraphs (1) through (7) of this subsection;

shall be fined under this title or imprisoned not more than twenty years or both.

(b) Whoever willfully—

(1) performs an act of violence against any individual on board any civil aircraft registered in a country other than the United States while such aircraft is in flight, if such act is likely to endanger the safety of that aircraft;

(2) destroys a civil aircraft registered in a country other than the United States while such aircraft is in service or causes damage to such an aircraft which renders that aircraft incapable of flight or which is likely to endanger that aircraft's safety in flight;

(3) places or causes to be placed on a civil aircraft registered in a country other than the United States while such aircraft is in service, a device or substance which is likely to destroy that aircraft, or to cause damage to that aircraft which renders that aircraft incapable of flight or which is likely to endanger that aircraft's safety in flight; or

(4) attempts or conspires to commit an offense described in paragraphs (1) through (3) of this subsection;

shall be fined under this title or imprisoned not more than twenty years, or both. There is jurisdiction over an offense under this subsection if a national of the United States was on board, or would have been on board, the aircraft; an offender is a national of the

United States; or an offender is afterwards found in the United States. For purposes of this subsection, the term "national of the United States" has the meaning prescribed in section 101(a)(22) of the Immigration and Nationality Act.

(c) Whoever willfully imparts or conveys any threat to do an act which would violate any of paragraphs (1) through (6) of subsection (a) or any of paragraphs (1) through (3) of subsection (b) of this section, with an apparent determination and will to carry the threat into execution shall be fined under this title or imprisoned not more than five years, or both.

(Added July 14, 1956, c. 595, § 1, 70 Stat. 539, and amended Oct. 12, 1984, Pub.L. 98–473, Title II, § 2013(b), 98 Stat. 2178; Nov. 18, 1988, Pub.L. 100–690, Title VII, § 7016, 102 Stat. 4395; Sept. 13, 1994, Pub.L. 103–322, Title XXXIII, § 330016(1)(O), (S), 108 Stat. 2148; Apr. 24, 1996, Pub.L. 104–132, Title VII, §§ 721(b), 723(a)(1), 110 Stat. 1298, 1300; Mar. 9, 2006, Pub.L. 109–177, Title I, § 123, 120 Stat. 226.)

HISTORICAL AND STATUTORY NOTES

References in Text

The Immigration and Nationality Act, referred to in subsec. (b), is Act June 27, 1952, c. 477, 66 Stat. 163, as amended, which is classified principally to chapter 12 (section 1101 et seq.) of Title 8, Aliens and Nationality. Section 101(a)(22) of such Act is classified to section 1101(a)(22) of Title 8. For complete classification of this Act to the Code, see Short Title note set out under section 1101 of Title 8 and Tables.

Effective and Applicability Provisions

1984 Acts. Amendment by Pub.L. 98–473, Title II, c. XX, § 2013(b), effective Oct. 12, 1984, see section 2015 of Pub.L. 98–473 set out as a note under section 31 of this title.

§ 33. Destruction of motor vehicles or motor vehicle facilities

(a) Whoever willfully, with intent to endanger the safety of any person on board or anyone who he believes will board the same, or with a reckless disregard for the safety of human life, damages, disables, destroys, tampers with, or places or causes to be placed any explosive or other destructive substance in, upon, or in proximity to, any motor vehicle which is used, operated, or employed in interstate or foreign commerce, or its cargo or material used or intended to be used in connection with its operation; or

Whoever willfully, with like intent, damages, disables, destroys, sets fire to, tampers with, or places or causes to be placed any explosive or other destructive substance in, upon, or in proximity to any garage, terminal, structure, supply, or facility used in the operation of, or in support of the operation of, motor vehicles engaged in interstate or foreign commerce or otherwise makes or causes such property to be made unworkable, unusable, or hazardous to work or use; or

Whoever, with like intent, willfully disables or incapacitates any driver or person employed in connection with the operation or maintenance of the motor vehicle, or in any way lessens the ability of such person to perform his duties as such; or

Whoever willfully attempts or conspires to do any of the aforesaid acts—

shall be fined under this title or imprisoned not more than twenty years, or both.

(b) Whoever is convicted of a violation of subsection (a) involving a motor vehicle that, at the time the violation occurred, carried high-level radioactive waste (as that term is defined in section 2(12) of the Nuclear Waste Policy Act of 1982 (42 U.S.C. 10101(12))) or spent nuclear fuel (as that term is defined in section 2(23) of the Nuclear Waste Policy Act of 1982 (42 U.S.C. 10101(23))), shall be fined under this title and imprisoned for any term of years not less than 30, or for life.

(Added July 14, 1956, c. 595, § 1, 70 Stat. 540, and amended Sept. 13, 1994, Pub.L. 103–322, Title XXXIII, § 330016(1)(L), 108 Stat. 2147; Dec. 29, 1995, Pub.L. 104–88, Title IV, § 402(a), 109 Stat. 955; Mar. 9, 2006, Pub.L. 109–177, Title IV, § 406(c)(1), 120 Stat. 245.)

HISTORICAL AND STATUTORY NOTES

Effective and Applicability Provisions

1995 Acts. Except as otherwise provided, amendment by section 402(a) of Pub.L. 104–88 effective Jan. 1, 1996, see section 2 of Pub.L. 104–88, set out as a note under section 701 of Title 49, Transportation.

§ 34. Penalty when death results

Whoever is convicted of any crime prohibited by this chapter, which has resulted in the death of any person, shall be subject also to the death penalty or to imprisonment for life.

(Added July 14, 1956, c. 595, § 1, 70 Stat. 540, and amended Sept. 13, 1994, Pub.L. 103–322, Title VI, § 60003(a)(1), 108 Stat. 1968.)

§ 35. Imparting or conveying false information

(a) Whoever imparts or conveys or causes to be imparted or conveyed false information, knowing the information to be false, concerning an attempt or alleged attempt being made or to be made, to do any act which would be a crime prohibited by this chapter or chapter 97 or chapter 111 of this title shall be subject to a civil penalty of not more than $1,000 which shall be recoverable in a civil action brought in the name of the United States.

(b) Whoever willfully and maliciously, or with reckless disregard for the safety of human life, imparts or conveys or causes to be imparted or conveyed false information, knowing the information to be false, concerning an attempt or alleged attempt being made or to be made, to do any act which would be a crime prohibited by this chapter or chapter 97 or chapter 111 of this title—shall be fined under this title, or imprisoned not more than five years, or both.

(Added July 14, 1956, c. 595, § 1, 70 Stat. 540, and amended Oct. 3, 1961, Pub.L. 87–338, 75 Stat. 751; July 7, 1965, Pub.L. 89–64, 79 Stat. 210; Sept. 13, 1994, Pub.L. 103–322, Title XXXIII, § 330016(1)(K), 108 Stat. 2147.)

§ 36. Drive-by shooting

(a) Definition.—In this section, "major drug offense" means—

(1) a continuing criminal enterprise punishable under section 408(c) of the Controlled Substances Act (21 U.S.C. 848(c));

(2) a conspiracy to distribute controlled substances punishable under section 406 of the Controlled Substances Act (21 U.S.C. 846) section[1] 1013 of the Controlled Substances Import and Export Act (21 U.S.C. 963); or

(3) an offense involving major quantities of drugs and punishable under section 401(b)(1)(A) of the Controlled Substances Act (21 U.S.C. 841(b)(1)(A)) or section 1010(b)(1) of the Controlled Substances Import and Export Act (21 U.S.C. 960(b)(1)).

(b) Offense and penalties.—(1) A person who, in furtherance or to escape detection of a major drug offense and with the intent to intimidate, harass, injure, or maim, fires a weapon into a group of two or more persons and who, in the course of such conduct, causes grave risk to any human life shall be punished by a term of no more than 25 years, by fine under this title, or both.

(2) A person who, in furtherance or to escape detection of a major drug offense and with the intent to intimidate, harass, injure, or maim, fires a weapon into a group of 2 or more persons and who, in the course of such conduct, kills any person shall, if the killing—

(A) is a first degree murder (as defined in section 1111(a)), be punished by death or imprisonment for any term of years or for life, fined under this title, or both; or

(B) is a murder other than a first degree murder (as defined in section 1111(a)), be fined under this title, imprisoned for any term of years or for life, or both.

(Added Pub.L. 103–322, Title VI, § 60008(b), Sept. 13, 1994, 108 Stat. 1971, and amended Pub.L. 104–294, Title VI, § 604(b)(30), Oct. 11, 1996, 110 Stat. 3508.)

1 So in original. Probably should be preceded by "or".

HISTORICAL AND STATUTORY NOTES

Effective and Applicability Provisions

1996 Acts. Amendment by section 604 of Pub.L. 104–294 effective Sept. 13, 1994, see section 604(d) of Pub.L. 104–294, set out as a note under section 13 of this title.

Short Title

1994 Amendments. Section 60008(a) of Pub.L. 103–322 provided that: "This section [enacting this section] may be cited as the 'Drive-By Shooting Prevention Act of 1994'."

§ 37. Violence at international airports

(a) Offense.—A person who unlawfully and intentionally, using any device, substance, or weapon—

(1) performs an act of violence against a person at an airport serving international civil aviation that causes or is likely to cause serious bodily injury (as defined in section 1365 of this title) or death; or

(2) destroys or seriously damages the facilities of an airport serving international civil aviation or a civil aircraft not in service located thereon or disrupts the services of the airport,

if such an act endangers or is likely to endanger safety at that airport, or attempts or conspires to do such an act, shall be fined under this title, imprisoned not more than 20 years, or both; and if the death of any person results from conduct prohibited by this subsection, shall be punished by death or imprisoned for any term of years or for life.

(b) Jurisdiction.—There is jurisdiction over the prohibited activity in subsection (a) if—

(1) the prohibited activity takes place in the United States; or

(2) the prohibited activity takes place outside the United States and (A) the offender is later found in the United States; or (B) an offender or a victim is a national of the United States (as defined in section 101(a)(22) of the Immigration and Nationality Act (8 U.S.C. 1101(a)(22))).

(c) Bar to prosecution.—It is a bar to Federal prosecution under subsection (a) for conduct that occurred within the United States that the conduct involved was during or in relation to a labor dispute, and such conduct is prohibited as a felony under the law of the State in which it was committed. For purposes of this section, the term "labor dispute" has the meaning set forth in section 2(c)[1] of the Norris-LaGuardia Act, as amended (29 U.S.C. 113(c)), and the term "State" means a State of the United States, the District of Columbia, and any commonwealth, territory, or possession of the United States.

(Added Pub.L. 103–322, Title VI, § 60021(a), Sept. 13, 1994, 108 Stat. 1979, and amended Pub.L. 104–132, Title VII, §§ 721(g), 723(a)(1), Apr. 24, 1996, 110 Stat. 1299, 1300; Pub.L. 104–294, Title VI, §§ 601(q), 607(*o*), Oct. 11, 1996, 110 Stat. 3502, 3512.)

1 So in original. Probably should be "section 13(c)".

HISTORICAL AND STATUTORY NOTES

References in Text

The Immigration and Nationality Act, referred to in subsec. (b)(2)(B), is Act June 27, 1952, c. 477, 66 Stat. 163, as amended, which is classified principally to chapter 12 (section 1101 et seq.) of Title 8, Aliens and Nationality. Section 101(a)(22) of such Act is classified to section 1101(a)(22) of Title 8. For complete classification of this Act to the Code, see Short Title note set out under section 1101 of Title 8 and Tables.

Effective and Applicability Provisions

1994 Acts. Section 60021(c) of Pub.L. 103–322 provided that: "The amendment made by subsection (a) [enacting this section] shall take effect on the later of—

"(1) the date of enactment of this Act [Sept. 13, 1994]; or

"(2) the date on which the Protocol for the Suppression of Unlawful Acts of Violence at Airports Serving International Civil Aviation, Supplementary to the Convention for the Suppression of Unlawful Acts Against the Safety of Civil Aviation, done at Montreal on 23 September 1971, has come into force and the United States has become a party to the Protocol."

[The date on which the Protocol for the Suppression of Unlawful Acts of Violence at Airports Serving International Civil Aviation, Supplementary to the Convention for the Suppression of Unlawful Acts Against the Safety of Civil Aviation, done at Montreal on 23 September 1971, came into force and the United States became a party to the Protocol, is November 18, 1994.]

§ 38. Fraud involving aircraft or space vehicle parts in interstate or foreign commerce

(a) Offenses.—Whoever, in or affecting interstate or foreign commerce, knowingly and with the intent to defraud—

(1)(A) falsifies or conceals a material fact concerning any aircraft or space vehicle part;

(B) makes any materially fraudulent representation concerning any aircraft or space vehicle part; or

(C) makes or uses any materially false writing, entry, certification, document, record, data plate, label, or electronic communication concerning any aircraft or space vehicle part;

(2) exports from or imports or introduces into the United States, sells, trades, installs on or in any aircraft or space vehicle any aircraft or space vehicle part using or by means of a fraudulent representation, document, record, certification, depiction, data plate, label, or electronic communication; or

(3) attempts or conspires to commit an offense described in paragraph (1) or (2),

shall be punished as provided in subsection (b).

(b) Penalties.—The punishment for an offense under subsection (a) is as follows:

(1) Aviation quality.—If the offense relates to the aviation quality of a part and the part is installed in an aircraft or space vehicle, a fine of not more than $500,000, imprisonment for not more than 15 years, or both.

(2) Failure to operate as represented.—If, by reason of the failure of the part to operate as represented, the part to which the offense is related is the proximate cause of a malfunction or failure that results in serious bodily injury (as defined in section 1365), a fine of not more than $1,000,000, imprisonment for not more than 20 years, or both.

(3) Failure resulting in death.—If, by reason of the failure of the part to operate as represented, the part to which the offense is related is the proximate cause of a malfunction or failure that results in the death of any person, a fine of not more than $1,000,000, imprisonment for any term of years or life, or both.

(4) Other circumstances.—In the case of an offense under subsection (a) not described in paragraph (1), (2), or (3) of this subsection, a fine under this title, imprisonment for not more than 10 years, or both.

(5) Organizations.—If the offense is committed by an organization, a fine of not more than—

(A) $10,000,000 in the case of an offense described in paragraph (1) or (4); and

(B) $20,000,000 in the case of an offense described in paragraph (2) or (3).

(c) Civil remedies.—

(1) In general.—The district courts of the United States shall have jurisdiction to prevent and restrain violations of this section by issuing appropriate orders, including—

(A) ordering a person (convicted of an offense under this section) to divest any interest, direct or indirect, in any enterprise used to commit or facilitate the commission of the offense, or to destroy, or to mutilate and sell as scrap, aircraft material or part inventories or stocks;

(B) imposing reasonable restrictions on the future activities or investments of any such person, including prohibiting engagement in the same type of endeavor as used to commit the offense; and

(C) ordering the dissolution or reorganization of any enterprise knowingly used to commit or facilitate the commission of an offense under this section making due provisions for the rights and interests of innocent persons.

(2) Restraining orders and prohibition.—Pending final determination of a proceeding brought under this section, the court may enter such restraining orders or prohibitions, or take such other actions (including the acceptance of satisfactory performance bonds) as the court deems proper.

(3) Estoppel.—A final judgment rendered in favor of the United States in any criminal proceeding brought under this section shall stop the defendant from denying the essential allegations of the criminal offense in any subsequent civil proceeding brought by the United States.

(d) Criminal forfeiture.—

(1) In general.—The court, in imposing sentence on any person convicted of an offense under this section, shall order, in addition to any other sentence and irrespective of any provision of State law, that the person forfeit to the United States—

(A) any property constituting, or derived from, any proceeds that the person obtained, directly or indirectly, as a result of the offense; and

(B) any property used, or intended to be used in any manner, to commit or facilitate the commission of the offense, if the court in its discretion so determines, taking into consideration the nature, scope, and proportionality of the use of the property on the offense.

(2) Application of other law.—The forfeiture of property under this section, including any seizure and disposition of the property, and any proceedings relating to the property, shall be governed by section 413 of the Comprehensive Drug Abuse and Prevention Act of 1970 (21 U.S.C. 853) (not including subsection (d) of that section).

(e) Construction with other law.—This section does not preempt or displace any other remedy, civil or criminal, provided by Federal or State law for the fraudulent importation, sale, trade, installation, or introduction into commerce of an aircraft or space vehicle part.

(f) Territorial scope.—This section also applies to conduct occurring outside the United States if—

(1) the offender is a natural person who is a citizen or permanent resident alien of the United States, or an organization organized under the laws of the United States or political subdivision thereof;

(2) the aircraft or spacecraft part as to which the violation relates was installed in an aircraft or space vehicle owned or operated at the time of the offense by a citizen or permanent resident alien of the United States, or by an organization thereof; or

(3) an act in furtherance of the offense was committed in the United States.

(Added Pub.L. 106–181, Title V, § 506(c)(1), Apr. 5, 2000, 114 Stat. 137.)

HISTORICAL AND STATUTORY NOTES

Effective and Applicability Provisions

2000 Acts. Section applicable only to fiscal years beginning after September 30, 1999, see section 3 of Pub.L. 106–181, set out as a note under section 106 of Title 49.

§ 39. [1]Traffic signal preemption transmitters

(a) Offenses.—

(1) Sale.—Whoever, in or affecting interstate or foreign commerce, knowingly sells a traffic signal preemption transmitter to a nonqualifying user shall be fined under this title, or imprisoned not more than 1 year, or both.

(2) Use.—Whoever, in or affecting interstate or foreign commerce, being a nonqualifying user makes unauthorized use of a traffic signal preemption transmitter shall be fined under this title, or imprisoned not more than 6 months, or both.

(b) Definitions.—In this section, the following definitions apply:

(1) Traffic signal preemption transmitter.—The term "traffic signal preemption transmitter" means any mechanism that can change or alter a traffic signal's phase time or sequence.

(2) Nonqualifying user.—The term "nonqualifying user" means a person who uses a traffic signal preemption transmitter and is not acting on behalf of a public agency or private corporation authorized by law to provide fire protection, law enforcement, emergency medical services, transit services, maintenance, or other services for a Federal, State, or local government entity, but does not include a person using a traffic signal preemption transmitter for classroom or instructional purposes.

(Added Pub.L. 109–59, Title II, § 2018(a), Aug. 10, 2005, 119 Stat. 1542.)

[1] So in original. Two sections 39 have been added.

§ 39. [1]Commercial motor vehicles required to stop for inspections

(a) A driver of a commercial motor vehicle (as defined in section 31132 of title 49) shall stop and submit to inspection of the vehicle, driver, cargo, and required records when directed to do so by an authorized employee of the Federal Motor Carrier Safety Administration of the Department of Transportation, at or in the vicinity of an inspection site. The driver shall not leave the inspection site until authorized to do so by an authorized employee.

(b) A driver of a commercial motor vehicle, as defined in subsection (a), who knowingly fails to stop for inspection when directed to do so by an authorized employee of the Administration at or in the vicinity of an inspection site, or leaves the inspection site without authorization, shall be fined under this title or imprisoned not more than 1 year, or both.

(Added Pub.L. 109–59, Title IV, § 4143(a), Aug. 10, 2005, 119 Stat. 1747.)

[1] So in original. Two sections 39 have been added.

CHAPTER 3—ANIMALS, BIRDS, FISH, AND PLANTS

§ 41. Hunting, fishing, trapping; disturbance or injury on wildlife refuges

Whoever, except in compliance with rules and regulations promulgated by authority of law, hunts, traps, captures, willfully disturbs or kills any bird, fish, or wild animal of any kind whatever, or takes or destroys the eggs or nest of any such bird or fish, on any lands or waters which are set apart or reserved as sanctuaries, refuges or breeding grounds for such birds, fish, or animals under any law of the United States or willfully injures, molests, or destroys any property of the United States on any such lands or waters, shall be fined under this title or imprisoned not more than six months, or both.

(June 25, 1948, c. 645, 62 Stat. 686; Sept. 13, 1994, Pub.L. 103–322, Title XXXIII, § 330016(1)(G), 108 Stat. 2147.)

§ 42. Importation or shipment of injurious mammals, birds, fish (including mollusks and crustacea), amphibia, and reptiles; permits, specimens for museums; regulations

(a)(1) The importation into the United States, any territory of the United States, the District of Columbia, the Commonwealth of Puerto Rico, or any possession of the United States, or any shipment between the continental United States, the District of Columbia, Hawaii, the Commonwealth of Puerto Rico, or any possession of the United States, of the mongoose of the species Herpestes auropunctatus; of the species of so-called "flying foxes" or fruit bats of the genus Pteropus; of the zebra mussel of the species Dreissena polymorpha; and such other species of wild mammals, wild birds, fish (including mollusks and crustacea), amphibians, reptiles, brown tree snakes, or the offspring or eggs of any of the foregoing which the Secretary of the Interior may prescribe by regulation to be injurious to human beings, to the interests of agriculture, horticulture, forestry, or to wildlife or the wildlife resources of the United States, is hereby prohibited. All such prohibited mammals, birds, fish (including mollusks and crustacea), amphibians, and reptiles, and the eggs or offspring therefrom, shall be promptly exported or destroyed at the expense of the importer or consignee. Nothing in this section shall be construed to repeal or modify any provision of the Public Health Service Act or Federal Food, Drug, and Cosmetic Act. Also, this section shall not authorize any action with respect to the importation of any plant pest as defined in the Federal Plant Pest Act, insofar as such importation is subject to regulation under that Act.

(2) As used in this subsection, the term "wild" relates to any creatures that, whether or not raised in captivity, normally are found in a wild state; and the terms "wildlife" and "wildlife resources" include those resources that comprise wild mammals, wild birds, fish (including mollusks and crustacea), and all other classes of wild creatures whatsoever, and all types of aquatic and land vegetation upon which such wildlife resources are dependent.

(3) Notwithstanding the foregoing, the Secretary of the Interior, when he finds that there has been a proper showing of responsibility and continued protection of the public interest and health, shall permit the importation for zoological, educational, medical, and scientific purposes of any mammals, birds, fish (including mollusks and crustacea), amphibia, and reptiles, or the offspring or eggs thereof, where such importation would be prohibited otherwise by or pursuant to this Act, and this Act shall not restrict importations by Federal agencies for their own use.

(4) Nothing in this subsection shall restrict the importation of dead natural-history specimens for museums or for scientific collections, or the importation of domesticated canaries, parrots (including all other species of psittacine birds), or such other cage birds as the Secretary of the Interior may designate.

(5) The Secretary of the Treasury and the Secretary of the Interior shall enforce the provisions of this subsection, including any regulations issued hereunder, and, if requested by the Secretary of the Interior, the Secretary of the Treasury may require the furnishing of an appropriate bond when desirable to insure compliance with such provisions.

(b) Whoever violates this section, or any regulation issued pursuant thereto, shall be fined under this title or imprisoned not more than six months, or both.

(c) The Secretary of the Interior within one hundred and eighty days of the enactment of the Lacey Act Amendments of 1981 shall prescribe such requirements and issue such permits as he may deem necessary for the transportation of wild animals and birds under humane and healthful conditions, and it shall be unlawful for any person, including any importer, knowingly to cause or permit any wild animal or bird to be transported to the United States, or any Territory or district thereof, under inhumane or unhealthful conditions or in violation of such requirements. In any criminal prosecution for violation of this subsection and in any administrative proceeding for the suspension of the issuance of further permits—

(1) the condition of any vessel or conveyance, or the enclosures in which wild animals or birds are confined therein, upon its arrival in the United States, or any Territory or district thereof, shall constitute relevant evidence in determining whether the provisions of this subsection have been violated; and

(2) the presence in such vessel or conveyance at such time of a substantial ratio of dead, crippled, diseased, or starving wild animals or birds shall be deemed prima facie evidence of the violation of the provisions of this subsection.

(June 25, 1948, c. 645, 62 Stat. 687; May 24, 1949, c. 139, § 2, 63 Stat. 89; Sept. 2, 1960, Pub.L. 86–702, § 1, 74 Stat. 753; Nov. 16, 1981, Pub.L. 97–79, § 9(d), 95 Stat. 1079; Nov. 29, 1990, Pub.L. 101–646, § 1208, 104 Stat. 4772; Dec. 13, 1991, Pub.L. 102–237, Title X, § 1013(e), 105 Stat. 1901; Sept. 13, 1994, Pub.L. 103–322, Title XXXIII, § 330016(1)(G), 108 Stat. 2147; Oct. 26, 1996, Pub.L. 104–332, § 2(h)(1), 110 Stat. 4091.)

HISTORICAL AND STATUTORY NOTES

References in Text

Public Health Service Act, referred to in subsection (a)(1), is classified to chapter 6A of Title 42, The Public Health and Welfare.

Federal Food, Drug and Cosmetic Act, referred to in subsection (a)(1), is classified to chapter 9 of Title 21, Food and Drugs.

The Federal Plant Pest Act, referred to in subsection (a)(1), is Pub.L. 85–36, Title I, May 23, 1957, 71 Stat. 31, as amended, which was classified generally to chapter 7B of Title 7, 7 U.S.C.A. § 150aa et seq., prior to repeal by Pub.L. 106–224, Title IV, § 438(a)(2), June 20, 2000, 114 Stat. 454. See Tables for complete classification,

This Act, referred to in subsection (a)(3), probably refers to Pub.L. 86–702, which amended this section and § 43 of this title.

The enactment of the Lacey Act Amendments of 1981, referred to in subsec. (c), is Pub.L. 97–79, which was approved on Nov. 16, 1981.

Effective and Applicability Provisions

1991 Acts. Amendment by Pub.L. 102–237 effective Dec. 13, 1991, see section 1101(a) of Pub.L. 102–237, set out as a note under section 1421 of Title 7, Agriculture.

Exotic Organisms

For provisions relating to restrictions on the introduction of exotic organisms into natural ecosystems of the United States, see Ex. Ord. No. 11987, May 24, 1977, 42 F.R. 26949, set out as a note under section 4321 of Title 42, The Public Health and Welfare.

§ 43. Force, violence, and threats involving animal enterprises

(a) Offense.—Whoever travels in interstate or foreign commerce, or uses or causes to be used the mail or any facility of interstate or foreign commerce—

(1) for the purpose of damaging or interfering with the operations of an animal enterprise; and

(2) in connection with such purpose—

(A) intentionally damages or causes the loss of any real or personal property (including animals or records) used by an animal enterprise, or any real or personal property of a person or entity having a connection to, relationship with, or transactions with an animal enterprise;

(B) intentionally places a person in reasonable fear of the death of, or serious bodily injury to that person, a member of the immediate family (as defined in section 115) of that person, or a spouse or intimate partner of that person by a course of conduct involving threats, acts of vandalism, property damage, criminal trespass, harassment, or intimidation; or

(C) conspires or attempts to do so;

shall be punished as provided for in subsection (b).

(b) Penalties.—The punishment for a violation of section[1] (a) or an attempt or conspiracy to violate subsection (a) shall be—

(1) a fine under this title or imprisonment not more than 1 year, or both, if the offense does not instill in another the reasonable fear of serious bodily injury or death and—

(A) the offense results in no economic damage or bodily injury; or

(B) the offense results in economic damage that does not exceed $10,000;

(2) a fine under this title or imprisonment for not more than 5 years, or both, if no bodily injury occurs and—

(A) the offense results in economic damage exceeding $10,000 but not exceeding $100,000; or

(B) the offense instills in another the reasonable fear of serious bodily injury or death;

(3) a fine under this title or imprisonment for not more than 10 years, or both, if—

(A) the offense results in economic damage exceeding $100,000; or

(B) the offense results in substantial bodily injury to another individual;

(4) a fine under this title or imprisonment for not more than 20 years, or both, if—

(A) the offense results in serious bodily injury to another individual; or

(B) the offense results in economic damage exceeding $1,000,000; and

(5) imprisonment for life or for any terms of years, a fine under this title, or both, if the offense results in death of another individual.

(c) Restitution.—An order of restitution under section 3663 or 3663A of this title with respect to a violation of this section may also include restitution—

(1) for the reasonable cost of repeating any experimentation that was interrupted or invalidated as a result of the offense;

(2) for the loss of food production or farm income reasonably attributable to the offense; and

(3) for any other economic damage, including any losses or costs caused by economic disruption, resulting from the offense.

(d) Definitions.—As used in this section—

(1) the term "animal enterprise" means—

(A) a commercial or academic enterprise that uses or sells animals or animal products for profit, food or fiber production, agriculture, education, research, or testing;

(B) a zoo, aquarium, animal shelter, pet store, breeder, furrier, circus, or rodeo, or other lawful competitive animal event; or

(C) any fair or similar event intended to advance agricultural arts and sciences;

(2) the term "course of conduct" means a pattern of conduct composed of 2 or more acts, evidencing a continuity of purpose;

(3) the term "economic damage'—

(A) means the replacement costs of lost or damaged property or records, the costs of repeating an interrupted or invalidated experiment, the loss of profits, or increased costs, including losses and increased costs resulting from threats, acts or vandalism, property damage, trespass, harassment, or intimidation taken against a person or entity on account of that person's or entity's connection to, relationship with, or transactions with the animal enterprise; but

(B) does not include any lawful economic disruption (including a lawful boycott) that results from lawful public, governmental, or business reaction to the disclosure of information about an animal enterprise;

(4) the term "serious bodily injury" means—

(A) injury posing a substantial risk of death;

(B) extreme physical pain;

(C) protracted and obvious disfigurement; or

(D) protracted loss or impairment of the function of a bodily member, organ, or mental faculty; and

(5) the term "substantial bodily injury" means—

(A) deep cuts and serious burns or abrasions;

(B) short–term or nonobvious disfigurement;

(C) fractured or dislocated bones, or torn members of the body;

(D) significant physical pain;

(E) illness;

(F) short-term loss or impairment of the function of a bodily member, organ, or mental faculty; or

(G) any other significant injury to the body.

(e) Rules of construction.—Nothing in this section shall be construed—

(1) to prohibit any expressive conduct (including peaceful picketing or other peaceful demonstration) protected from legal prohibition by the First Amendment to the Constitution;

(2) to create new remedies for interference with activities protected by the free speech or free exercise clauses of the First Amendment to the Constitution, regardless of the point of view expressed, or to limit any existing legal remedies for such interference; or

(3) to provide exclusive criminal penalties or civil remedies with respect to the conduct prohibited by this action, or to preempt State or local laws that may provide such penalties or remedies.

(Added Pub.L. 102–346, § 2(a), Aug. 26, 1992, 106 Stat. 928, and amended Pub.L. 104–294, Title VI, § 601(r)(3), Oct. 11, 1996, 110 Stat. 3502; Pub.L. 107–188, Title III, § 336, June 12, 2002, 116 Stat. 681; Pub.L. 109–374, § 2(a), Nov. 27, 2006, 120 Stat. 2652.)

1 So in original. Probably should be "subsection".

HISTORICAL AND STATUTORY NOTES

Prior Provisions

A prior section 43, Acts June 25, 1948, c. 645, 62 Stat. 687; Sept. 2, 1960, Pub.L. 86–702, § 2, 74 Stat. 754; Dec. 5, 1969, Pub.L. 91–135, § 7(a), 83 Stat. 279, related to the transportation of wildlife taken in violation of State, National, or foreign law, the receipt of such wildlife, and the making of false records in relation thereto, and was repealed by Pub.L. 97–79, § 9(b)(2), Nov. 16, 1981, 95 Stat. 1079. See section 3372(a) of Title 16, Conservation.

Short Title

1992 Amendments. Section 1 of Pub.L. 102–346 provided that: "This Act [enacting this section and provisions set out as notes under this section] may be cited as the 'Animal Enterprise Protection Act of 1992'."

Rule of Construction

Provisions of Title III, Pub.L. 107–188 not to be construed to alter the jurisdiction between the Secretary of Agriculture and the Secretary of Health and Human Services, see Pub.L. 107–188, Title III, § 315, June 12, 2002, 116 Stat. 675, set out as a note under 21 U.S.C.A. § 331.

Study of Effect of Terrorism on Certain Animal Enterprises

Section 3 of Pub.L. 102–346 provided that:

"(a) **Study.**—The Attorney General and the Secretary of Agriculture shall jointly conduct a study on the extent and effects of domestic and international terrorism on enterprises using animals for food or fiber production, agriculture, research, or testing.

"(b) **Submission of study.**—Not later than 1 year after the date of enactment of this Act [Aug. 26, 1992], the Attorney General and the Secretary of Agriculture shall submit a report that describes the results of the study conducted under subsection (a) together with any appropriate recommendations and legislation to the Congress."

[§ 44. Repealed. Pub.L. 97–79, § 9(b)(2), Nov. 16, 1981, 95 Stat. 1079]

HISTORICAL AND STATUTORY NOTES

Section, Acts June 25, 1948, c. 645, 62 Stat. 687; Dec. 5, 1969, Pub.L. 91–135, § 8, 83 Stat. 281, related to the marking of packages or containers used in the shipment of fish and wildlife. See section 3372(b) of Title 16, Conservation.

[§ 45. Repealed. Pub.L. 101–647, Title XII, § 1206(a), Nov. 29, 1990, 104 Stat. 4832]

HISTORICAL AND STATUTORY NOTES

Section, Act June 25, 1948, c. 645, 62 Stat. 688, related to penalties for capturing or killing carrier pigeons.

Canal Zone

Applicability of section to Canal Zone, see § 14 of this title.

§ 46. Transportation of water hyacinths

(a) Whoever knowingly delivers or receives for transportation, or transports, in interstate commerce, alligator grass (alternanthera philoxeroides), or water chestnut plants (trapa natans) or water hyacinth plants (eichhornia crassipes) or the seeds of such grass or plants; or

(b) Whoever knowingly sells, purchases, barters, exchanges, gives, or receives any grass, plant, or seed which has been transported in violation of subsection (a); or

(c) Whoever knowingly delivers or receives for transportation, or transports, in interstate commerce, an advertisement, to sell, purchase, barter, exchange, give, or receive alligator grass or water chestnut plants or water hyacinth plants or the seeds of such grass or plants—

shall be fined under this title, or imprisoned not more than six months, or both.

(Added Aug. 1, 1956, c. 825, § 1, 70 Stat. 797, and amended Sept. 13, 1994, Pub.L. 103–322, Title XXXIII, § 330016(1)(G), 108 Stat. 2147.)

§ 47. Use of aircraft or motor vehicles to hunt certain wild horses or burros; pollution of watering holes

(a) Whoever uses an aircraft or a motor vehicle to hunt, for the purpose of capturing or killing, any wild unbranded horse, mare, colt, or burro running at large on any of the public land or ranges shall be fined under this title, or imprisoned not more than six months, or both.

(b) Whoever pollutes or causes the pollution of any watering hole on any of the public land or ranges for the purpose of trapping, killing, wounding, or maiming any of the animals referred to in subsection (a) of this section shall be fined under this title, or imprisoned not more than six months, or both.

(c) As used in subsection (a) of this section—

(1) The term "aircraft" means any contrivance used for flight in the air; and

(2) The term "motor vehicle" includes an automobile, automobile truck, automobile wagon, motorcycle, or any other self-propelled vehicle designed for running on land.

(Added Pub.L. 86–234, § 1(a), Sept. 8, 1959, 73 Stat. 470, and amended Pub.L. 103–322, Title XXXIII, § 330016(1)(G), Sept. 13, 1994, 108 Stat. 2147.)

HISTORICAL AND STATUTORY NOTES

Short Tile

1959 Acts. This section is commonly known as the Wild Horse Annie Act.

§ 48. Depiction of animal cruelty

(a) **Creation, sale, or possession.**—Whoever knowingly creates, sells, or possesses a depiction of animal cruelty with the intention of placing that depiction in interstate or foreign commerce for commercial gain, shall be fined under this title or imprisoned not more than 5 years, or both.

(b) **Exception.**—Subsection (a) does not apply to any depiction that has serious religious, political, scientific, educational, journalistic, historical, or artistic value.

(c) **Definitions.**—In this section—

(1) the term "depiction of animal cruelty" means any visual or auditory depiction, including any photograph, motion-picture film, video recording, electronic image, or sound recording of conduct in which a living animal is intentionally maimed, mutilated, tortured, wounded, or killed, if such conduct is illegal under Federal law or the law of the State in which the creation, sale, or possession takes place, regardless of whether the maiming, mutilation, torture, wounding, or killing took place in the State; and

(2) the term "State" means each of the several States, the District of Columbia, the Commonwealth of Puerto Rico, the Virgin Islands, Guam, American Samoa, the Commonwealth of the Northern Mariana Islands, and any other commonwealth, territory, or possession of the United States.

(Added Pub.L. 106–152, § 1(a), Dec. 9, 1999, 113 Stat. 1732.)

CHAPTER 5—ARSON

§ 81. Arson within special maritime and territorial jurisdiction

Whoever, within the special maritime and territorial jurisdiction of the United States, willfully and maliciously sets fire to or burns any building, structure or vessel, any machinery or building materials or supplies, military or naval stores, munitions of war, or any structural aids or appliances for navigation or shipping, or attempts or conspires to do such an act, shall be imprisoned for not more than 25 years, fined the greater of the fine under this title or the cost of repairing or replacing any property that is damaged or destroyed, or both.

If the building be a dwelling or if the life of any person be placed in jeopardy, he shall be fined under this title or imprisoned for any term of years or for life, or both.

(June 25, 1948, c. 645, 62 Stat. 688; Sept. 13, 1994, Pub.L. 103–322, Title XXXIII, § 330016(1)(H), (K), 108 Stat. 2147; Apr. 24, 1996, Pub.L. 104–132, Title VII, § 708(b), 110 Stat. 1296; Oct. 26, 2001, Pub.L. 107–56, Title VIII, §§ 810(a), 811(a), 115 Stat. 380, 381.)

CHAPTER 7—ASSAULT

[1] Editorially supplied. Section was enacted without corresponding amendment to analysis.

§ 111. Assaulting, resisting, or impeding certain officers or employees

(a) In general.—Whoever—

(1) forcibly assaults, resists, opposes, impedes, intimidates, or interferes with any person designated in section 1114 of this title while engaged in or on account of the performance of official duties; or

(2) forcibly assaults or intimidates any person who formerly served as a person designated in section 1114 on account of the performance of official duties during such person's term of service,

shall, where the acts in violation of this section constitute only simple assault, be fined under this title or imprisoned not more than one year, or both, and in all other cases, be fined under this title or imprisoned not more than 8 years, or both.

(b) Enhanced penalty.—Whoever, in the commission of any acts described in subsection (a), uses a deadly or dangerous weapon (including a weapon intended to cause death or danger but that fails to do so by reason of a defective component) or inflicts bodily injury, shall be fined under this title or imprisoned not more than 20 years, or both.

(June 25, 1948, c. 645, 62 Stat. 688; Nov. 18, 1988, Pub.L. 100–690, Title VI, § 6487(a), 102 Stat. 4386; Sept. 13, 1994, Pub.L. 103–322, Title XXXII, § 320101(a), 108 Stat. 2108; Apr. 24, 1996, Pub.L. 104–132, Title VII, § 727(c), 110 Stat. 1302; Nov. 2, 2002, Pub.L. 107–273, Div. C, Title I, § 11008(b), 116 Stat. 1818.)

HISTORICAL AND STATUTORY NOTES

Short Title

2002 Amendments. Pub.L. 107–273, Div. C, Title I, § 11008(a), Nov. 2, 2002, 116 Stat. 1818, provided that: "This section [amending this section and 18 U.S.C.A. §§ 115 and 876, and amending provisions set out as a note under 28 U.S.C.A. 994] may be cited as the 'Federal Judiciary Protection Act of 2002'."

§ 112. Protection of foreign officials, official guests, and internationally protected persons

(a) Whoever assaults, strikes, wounds, imprisons, or offers violence to a foreign official, official guest, or internationally protected person or makes any other violent attack upon the person or liberty of such person, or, if likely to endanger his person or liberty, makes a violent attack upon his official premises, private accommodation, or means of transport or attempts to commit any of the foregoing shall be fined under this title or imprisoned not more than three years, or both. Whoever in the commission of any such act uses a deadly or dangerous weapon, or inflicts bodily injury, shall be fined under this title or imprisoned not more than ten years, or both.

(b) Whoever willfully—

(1) intimidates, coerces, threatens, or harasses a foreign official or an official guest or obstructs a foreign official in the performance of his duties;

(2) attempts to intimidate, coerce, threaten, or harass a foreign official or an official guest or obstruct a foreign official in the performance of his duties; or

(3) within the United States and within one hundred feet of any building or premises in whole or in part owned, used, or occupied for official business or for diplomatic, consular, or residential purposes by—

(A) a foreign government, including such use as a mission to an international organization;

(B) an international organization;

(C) a foreign official; or

(D) an official guest;

congregates with two or more other persons with intent to violate any other provision of this section;

shall be fined under this title or imprisoned not more than six months, or both.

(c) For the purpose of this section "foreign government", "foreign official", "internationally protected person", "international organization", "national of the United States", and "official guest" shall have the same meanings as those provided in section 1116(b) of this title.

(d) Nothing contained in this section shall be construed or applied so as to abridge the exercise of rights guaranteed under the first amendment to the Constitution of the United States.

(e) If the victim of an offense under subsection (a) is an internationally protected person outside the United States, the United States may exercise jurisdiction over the offense if (1) the victim is a representative, officer, employee, or agent of the United States, (2) an offender is a national of the United States, or (3) an offender is afterwards found in the United States. As used in this subsection, the United States includes all areas under the jurisdiction of the United States including any of the places within the provisions of sections 5 and 7 of this title and section 46501(2) of title 49.

(f) In the course of enforcement of subsection (a) and any other sections prohibiting a conspiracy or attempt to violate subsection (a), the Attorney General may request assistance from any Federal, State, or local agency, including the Army, Navy, and Air Force, any statute, rule, or regulation to the contrary, notwithstanding.

(June 25, 1948, c. 645, 62 Stat. 688; Aug. 27, 1964, Pub.L. 88–493, § 1, 78 Stat. 610; Oct. 24, 1972, Pub.L. 92–539, Title III, § 301, 86 Stat. 1072; Oct. 8, 1976, Pub.L. 94–467, § 5, 90 Stat. 1999; Nov. 9, 1977, Pub.L. 95–163, § 17(b)(1), 91 Stat. 1286; Oct. 24, 1978, Pub.L. 95–504, § 2(b), 92 Stat. 1705; Nov. 18, 1988, Pub.L. 100–690, Title VI, § 6478, 102 Stat. 4381; July 5, 1994, Pub.L. 103–272, § 5(e)(2), 108 Stat. 1373; Sept. 13, 1994, Pub.L. 103–322, Title XXXII, § 320101(b), Title XXXIII, § 330016(1)(G), (K), 108 Stat. 2108, 2147; Apr. 24, 1996, Pub.L. 104–132, Title VII, § 721(d), 110 Stat. 1298; Oct. 11, 1996, Pub.L. 104–294, Title VI, § 604(b)(12)(A), 110 Stat. 3507.)

HISTORICAL AND STATUTORY NOTES

Effective and Applicability Provisions

1996 Acts. Amendment by section 604 of Pub.L. 104–294 effective Sept. 13, 1994, see section 604(d) of Pub.L. 104–294, set out as a note under section 13 of this title.

Short Title

Section 1 of Pub.L. 94–467 provided: "That this Act [enacting section 878 of this title, amending this section and sections 11, 970, 1116, and 1201 of this title, and enacting provisions set out as notes under this section] may be cited as the 'Act for the Prevention and Punishment of Crimes Against Internationally Protected Persons'."

Section 1 of Pub.L. 92–539 provided: "That this Act [enacting sections 970, 1116 and 1117 of this title, amending this section and section 1201 of this title, and enacting provisions set out as notes under this section] may be cited as the 'Act for the Protection of Foreign Officials and Official Guests of the United States'."

Repeals

Pub.L. 103–322, Title XXXII, § 320101(b)(1), Sept. 13, 1994, 108 Stat. 2108, appearing in the credit of this section, was repealed by Pub.L. 104–294, Title VI, § 604(b)(12)(A), Oct. 11, 1996, 110 Stat. 3507.

Congressional Findings and Declaration of Policy

Section 2 of Pub.L. 92–539 provided that:

"The Congress recognizes that from the beginning of our history as a nation, the police power to investigate, prosecute, and punish common crimes such as murder, kidnaping, and assault has resided in the several States, and that such power should remain with the States.

"The Congress finds, however, that harassment, intimidation, obstruction, coercion, and acts of violence committed against foreign officials or their family members in the United States or against official guests of the United States adversely affect the foreign relations of the United States.

"Accordingly, this legislation is intended to afford the United States jurisdiction concurrent with that of the several States to proceed against those who by such acts interfere with its conduct of foreign affairs."

Federal Preemption

Section 3 of Pub.L. 92–539 provided that: "Nothing contained in this Act [enacting sections 970, 1116 and 1117 of this title, amending this section and section 1201 of this title, and enacting provisions set out as notes under this section] shall be construed to indicate an intent on the part of Congress to occupy the field in which its provisions operate to the exclusion of the laws of any State, Commonwealth, territory, possession, or the District of Columbia on the same subject matter, nor to relieve any person of any obligation imposed by any law of any State, Commonwealth, territory, possession, or the District of Columbia."

State and Local Laws Not Superseded

Section 10 of Pub.L. 94–467 provided that: "Nothing contained in this Act [see Short Title note under this section] shall be construed to indicate an intent on the part of Congress to occupy the field in which its provisions operate to the exclusion of the laws of any State, Commonwealth, territory, possession, or the District of Columbia, on the same subject matter, nor to relieve any person of any obligation imposed by any law of any State, Commonwealth, territory, possession, or the District of Columbia, including the obligation of all persons having official law enforcement powers to take appropriate action, such as effecting arrests, for Federal as well as non-Federal violations."

Immunity from Criminal Prosecution

Section 5 of Pub.L. 88–493 provided that: "Nothing contained in this Act [amending this section, and section 1114 of this title, and enacting former section 170e–1 of Title 5, Executive Departments and Government Officers and Employees] shall create immunity from criminal prosecution under any laws in any State, Commonwealth of Puerto Rico, territory, possession, or the District of Columbia.

§ 113. Assaults within maritime and territorial jurisdiction

(a) Whoever, within the special maritime and territorial jurisdiction of the United States, is guilty of an assault shall be punished as follows:

(1) Assault with intent to commit murder, by imprisonment for not more than twenty years.

(2) Assault with intent to commit any felony, except murder or a felony under chapter 109A, by a fine under this title or imprisonment for not more than ten years, or both.

(3) Assault with a dangerous weapon, with intent to do bodily harm, and without just cause or excuse, by a fine under this title or imprisonment for not more than ten years, or both.

(4) Assault by striking, beating, or wounding, by a fine under this title or imprisonment for not more than six months, or both.

(5) Simple assault, by a fine under this title or imprisonment for not more than six months, or both, or if the victim of the assault is an individual who has not attained the age of 16 years, by fine under this title or imprisonment for not more than 1 year, or both.

(6) Assault resulting in serious bodily injury, by a fine under this title or imprisonment for not more than ten years, or both.

(7) Assault resulting in substantial bodily injury to an individual who has not attained the age of 16 years, by fine under this title or imprisonment for not more than 5 years, or both.

(b) As used in this subsection—

(1) the term "substantial bodily injury" means bodily injury which involves—

(A) a temporary but substantial disfigurement; or

(B) a temporary but substantial loss or impairment of the function of any bodily member, organ, or mental faculty; and

(2) the term "serious bodily injury" has the meaning given that term in section 1365 of this title.

(June 25, 1948, c. 645, 62 Stat. 689; May 29, 1976, Pub.L. 94–297, § 3, 90 Stat. 585; Nov. 10, 1986, Pub.L. 99–646, § 87(c)(2), (3), 100 Stat. 3623; Nov. 14, 1986, Pub.L. 99–654, § 3(a)(2), (3), 100 Stat. 3663; Sept. 13, 1994, Pub.L. 103–322, Title XVII, § 170201(a)–(d), Title XXXII, § 320101(c), Title XXXIII, § 330016(2)(B), 108 Stat. 2042, 2043, 2108, 2148; Oct. 11, 1996, Pub.L. 104–294, Title VI, § 604(b)(7), (12)(B), 110 Stat. 3507.)

HISTORICAL AND STATUTORY NOTES

Effective and Applicability Provisions

1996 Acts. Amendment by section 604 of Pub.L. 104–294 effective Sept. 13, 1994, see section 604(d) of Pub.L. 104–294, set out as a note under section 13 of this title.

1986 Acts. Amendment by Pub.L. 99–654, effective 30 days after Nov. 14, 1986, see section 4 of Pub.L. 99–654, set out as a note under section 2241 of this title.

Amendment by section 87 of Pub.L. 99–646, effective 30 days after Nov. 10, 1986, see section 87(e) of Pub.L. 99–646, set out as a note under section 2241 of this title.

Repeals

Pub.L. 103–322, Title XVII, § 170201(c)(1) to (3), Sept. 13, 1994, 108 Stat. 2042, appearing in the credit of this section, was repealed by Pub.L. 104–294, Title VI, § 604(b)(7), Oct. 11, 1996, 110 Stat. 3507.

Pub.L. 103–322, Title XXXII, § 320101(c)(1)(A), (2)(A), Sept. 13, 1994, 108 Stat. 2108, appearing in the credit of this section, was repealed by Pub.L. 104–294, Title VI, § 604(b)(12)(B), Oct. 11, 1996, 110 Stat. 3507.

§ 114. Maiming within maritime and territorial jurisdiction

Whoever, within the special maritime and territorial jurisdiction of the United States, and with intent to torture (as defined in section 2340), maim, or disfigure, cuts, bites, or slits the nose, ear, or lip, or cuts out or disables the tongue, or puts out or destroys an eye, or cuts off or disables a limb or any member of another person; or

Whoever, within the special maritime and territorial jurisdiction of the United States, and with like intent, throws or pours upon another person, any scalding water, corrosive acid, or caustic substance—

Shall be fined under this title or imprisoned not more than twenty years, or both.

(June 25, 1948, c. 645, 62 Stat. 689; May 24, 1949, c. 139, § 3, 63 Stat. 90; Oct. 12, 1984, Pub.L. 98–473, Title II, § 1009A, 98 Stat. 2141; Nov. 29, 1990, Pub.L. 101–647, Title XXXV, § 3507, 104 Stat. 4922; Sept. 13, 1994, Pub.L. 103–322, Title XXXIII, § 330016(1)(O), 108 Stat. 2148; Apr. 24, 1996, Pub.L. 104–132, Title VII, § 705(a)(1), 110 Stat. 1295.)

§ 115. Influencing, impeding, or retaliating against a Federal official by threatening or injuring a family member

(a)(1) Whoever—

(A) assaults, kidnaps, or murders, or attempts or conspires to kidnap or murder, or threatens to assault, kidnap or murder a member of the immediate family of a United States official, a United States judge, a Federal law enforcement officer, or an official whose killing would be a crime under section 1114 of this title; or

(B) threatens to assault, kidnap, or murder, a United States official, a United States judge, a Federal law enforcement officer, or an official whose killing would be a crime under such section,

with intent to impede, intimidate, or interfere with such official, judge, or law enforcement officer while engaged in the performance of official duties, or with intent to retaliate against such official, judge, or law enforcement officer on account of the performance of official duties, shall be punished as provided in subsection (b).

(2) Whoever assaults, kidnaps, or murders, or attempts or conspires to kidnap or murder, or threatens to assault, kidnap, or murder, any person who formerly served as a person designated in paragraph (1), or a member of the immediate family of any person who formerly served as a person designated in paragraph (1), with intent to retaliate against such person on account of the performance of official duties during the term of service of such person, shall be punished as provided in subsection (b).

(b)(1) An assault in violation of this section shall be punished as provided in section 111 of this title.

(2) A kidnapping, attempted kidnapping, or conspiracy to kidnap in violation of this section shall be punished as provided in section 1201 of this title for the kidnapping or attempted kidnapping of, or a conspiracy to kidnap, a person described in section 1201(a)(5) of this title.

(3) A murder, attempted murder, or conspiracy to murder in violation of this section shall be punished as provided in sections 1111, 1113, and 1117 of this title.

(4) A threat made in violation of this section shall be punished by a fine under this title or imprisonment for a term of not more than 10 years, or both, except that imprisonment for a threatened assault shall not exceed 6 years.

(c) As used in this section, the term—

(1) "Federal law enforcement officer" means any officer, agent, or employee of the United States authorized by law or by a Government agency to engage in or supervise the prevention, detection, investigation, or prosecution of any violation of Federal criminal law;

(2) "immediate family member" of an individual means—

(A) his spouse, parent, brother or sister, child or person to whom he stands in loco parentis; or

(B) any other person living in his household and related to him by blood or marriage;

(3) "United States judge" means any judicial officer of the United States, and includes a justice of the Supreme Court and a United States magistrate judge; and

(4) "United States official" means the President, President-elect, Vice President, Vice President-elect, a Member of Congress, a member-elect of Congress, a member of the executive branch who is the head of a department listed in 5 U.S.C. 101, or the Director of the Central Intelligence Agency.

(d) This section shall not interfere with the investigative authority of the United States Secret Service, as provided under sections 3056, 871, and 879 of this title.

(Added Pub.L. 98–473, Title II, § 1008(a), Oct. 12, 1984, 98 Stat. 2140, and amended Pub.L. 99–646, §§ 37(a), 60, Nov. 10, 1986, 100 Stat. 3599, 3613; Pub.L. 100–690, Title VI, § 6487(f), Nov. 18, 1988, 102 Stat. 4386; Pub.L. 101–647, Title XXXV, § 3508, Nov. 29, 1990, 104 Stat. 4922; Pub.L. 101–650, Title III, § 321, Dec. 1, 1990, 104 Stat. 5117; Pub.L. 103–322, Title XXXIII, §§ 330016(2)(C), 330021(1), Sept. 13, 1994, 108 Stat. 2148, 2150; Pub.L. 104–132, Title VII, §§ 723(a), 727(b), Apr. 24, 1996, 110 Stat. 1300, 1302; Pub.L. 107–273, Div. B, Title IV, § 4002(b)(9), Div. C, Title I, § 11008(c), Nov. 2, 2002, 116 Stat. 1808, 1818.)

HISTORICAL AND STATUTORY NOTES

Codifications

Amendment by Pub.L. 104–132, § 727(b)(1), which directed the insertion of a new provision after "assaults, kidnaps, or murders, or attempts to kidnap or murder" in subsec. (a)(2) was executed by inserting the new provision after "assaults, kidnaps, or murders, or attempts or conspires to kidnap or murder" as the probable intent of Congress.

Change of Name

Reference to the Director of Central Intelligence or the Director of the Central Intelligence Agency in the Director's capacity as the head of the intelligence community deemed to be a reference to the Director of National Intelligence. Reference to the Director of Central Intelligence or the Director of the Central Intelligence Agency in the Director's capacity as the head of the Central Intelligence Agency deemed to be a reference to the Director of the Central Intelligence Agency. See Pub.L. 108–458, § 1081(a) and (b), set out as a note under 50 U.S.C.A. § 401.

"United States magistrate judge" substituted for "United States magistrate" in subsec. (c)(3) pursuant to section 321 of Pub.L. 101–650, set out as a note under 28 U.S.C.A. § 631.

Transfer of Functions

For transfer of the functions, personnel, assets, and obligations of the United States Secret Service, including the functions of the Secretary of the Treasury relating thereto, to the Secretary of Homeland Security, and for treatment of related references, see 6 U.S.C.A. §§ 381, 551(d), 552(d), and 557, and the Department of Homeland Security Reorganization Plan of November 25, 2002, as modified, set out as a note under 6 U.S.C.A. § 542.

§ 116. Female genital mutilation

(a) Except as provided in subsection (b), whoever knowingly circumcises, excises, or infibulates the whole or any part of the labia majora or labia minora or clitoris of another person who has not attained the age of 18 years shall be fined under this title or imprisoned not more than 5 years, or both.

(b) A surgical operation is not a violation of this section if the operation is—

(1) necessary to the health of the person on whom it is performed, and is performed by a person licensed in the place of its performance as a medical practitioner; or

(2) performed on a person in labor or who has just given birth and is performed for medical purposes connected with that labor or birth by a person licensed in the place it is performed as a medical practitioner, midwife, or person in training to become such a practitioner or midwife.

(c) In applying subsection (b)(1), no account shall be taken of the effect on the person on whom the operation is to be performed of any belief on the part of that person, or any other person, that the operation is required as a matter of custom or ritual.

(Added Pub.L. 104–208, Div. C, Title VI, § 645(b)(1), Sept. 30, 1996, 110 Stat. 3009–709.)

HISTORICAL AND STATUTORY NOTES

Effective and Applicability Provisions

1996 Acts. Section 645(c) of Div. C of Pub.L. 104–208 provided that: "The amendments made by subsection (b) [enacting this section] shall take effect on the date that is 180 days after the date of the enactment of this Act [Sept. 30, 1996]."

Severability of Provisions

If any provision of Division C of Pub.L. 104–208 or the application of such provision to any person or circumstances is held to be unconstitutional, the remainder of Division C of Pub.L. 104–208 and the application of the provisions of Division C of Pub.L. 104–208 to any person or circumstance not to be affected thereby, see section 1(e) of Pub.L. 104–208, set out as a note under section 1101 of Title 8, Aliens and Nationality.

Congressional Findings

Section 645(a) of Div. C of Pub.L. 104–208 provided that: "The Congress finds that—

"(1) the practice of female genital mutilation is carried out by members of certain cultural and religious groups within the United States;

"(2) the practice of female genital mutilation often results in the occurrence of physical and psychological health effects that harm the women involved;

"(3) such mutilation infringes upon the guarantees of rights secured by Federal and State law, both statutory and constitutional;

"(4) the unique circumstances surrounding the practice of female genital mutilation place it beyond the ability of any single State or local jurisdiction to control;

"(5) the practice of female genital mutilation can be prohibited without abridging the exercise of any rights guaranteed under the first amendment to the Constitution or under any other law; and

"(6) Congress has the affirmative power under section 8 of article I, the necessary and proper clause, section 5 of the fourteenth Amendment, as well as under the treaty clause, to the Constitution to enact such legislation."

§ 117. Domestic assault by an habitual offender[1]

(a) In general.—Any person who commits a domestic assault within the special maritime and territorial jurisdiction of the United States or Indian country and who has a final conviction on at least 2 separate prior occasions in Federal, State, or Indian tribal court proceedings for offenses that would be, if subject to Federal jurisdiction—

(1) any assault, sexual abuse, or serious violent felony against a spouse or intimate partner; or

(2) an offense under chapter 110A,

shall be fined under this title, imprisoned for a term of not more than 5 years, or both, except that if substantial bodily injury results from violation under this section, the offender shall be imprisoned for a term of not more than 10 years.

(b) Domestic assault defined.—In this section, the term "domestic assault" means an assault committed by a current or former spouse, parent, child, or guardian of the victim, by a person with whom the victim shares a child in common, by a person who is cohabitating with or has cohabitated with the victim as a spouse, parent, child, or guardian, or by a person similarly situated to a spouse, parent, child, or guardian of the victim.

(Added Pub.L. 109–162, Title IX, § 909, Jan. 5, 2006, 119 Stat. 3084.)

[1] Section was enacted without corresponding amendment to analysis.

HISTORICAL AND STATUTORY NOTES

References in Text

Chapter 110A, referred to in subsec. (a)(2), is Domestic Violence and Stalking, 18 U.S.C.A. § 2261 et seq.

§ 118. Interference with certain protective functions

Any person who knowingly and willfully obstructs, resists, or interferes with a Federal law enforcement agent engaged, within the United States or the special maritime territorial jurisdiction of the United States, in the performance of the protective functions authorized under section 37 of the State Department Basic Authorities Act of 1956 (22 U.S.C. 2709) or section 103 of the Diplomatic Security Act (22 U.S.C. 4802) shall be fined under this title, imprisoned not more than 1 year, or both.

(Pub.L. 109–472, § 4(a), Jan. 11, 2007, 120 Stat. 3555.)

CHAPTER 9—BANKRUPTCY

§ 151. Definition

As used in this chapter, the term "debtor" means a debtor concerning whom a petition has been filed under Title 11.

(June 25, 1948, c. 645, 62 Stat. 689; Nov. 6, 1978, Pub.L. 95–598, Title III, § 314(b)(1), 92 Stat. 2676; Sept. 13, 1994, Pub.L. 103–322, Title XXXIII, § 330008(5), 108 Stat. 2143.)

HISTORICAL AND STATUTORY NOTES

Effective and Applicability Provisions

1978 Acts. Amendment by Pub.L. 95–598 effective Oct. 1, 1979, see section 402(a) of Pub.L. 95–598, set out as a note preceding section 101 of Title 11, Bankruptcy.

Savings Provisions

Amendment by section 314 of Pub. L. 95–598 not to affect the application of this chapter to any act of any person (1) committed before Oct. 1, 1979, or (2) committed after Oct. 1, 1979, in connection with a case commenced before such date, see section 403(d) of Pub. L. 95–598, set out preceding section 101 of Title 11, Bankruptcy.

§ 152. Concealment of assets; false oaths and claims; bribery

A person who—

(1) knowingly and fraudulently conceals from a custodian, trustee, marshal, or other officer of the court charged with the control or custody of property, or, in connection with a case under title 11, from creditors or the United States Trustee, any property belonging to the estate of a debtor;

(2) knowingly and fraudulently makes a false oath or account in or in relation to any case under title 11;

(3) knowingly and fraudulently makes a false declaration, certificate, verification, or statement under penalty of perjury as permitted under section 1746 of title 28, in or in relation to any case under title 11;

(4) knowingly and fraudulently presents any false claim for proof against the estate of a debtor, or uses any such claim in any case under title 11, in a personal capacity or as or through an agent, proxy, or attorney;

(5) knowingly and fraudulently receives any material amount of property from a debtor after the filing of a case under title 11, with intent to defeat the provisions of title 11;

(6) knowingly and fraudulently gives, offers, receives, or attempts to obtain any money or property, remuneration, compensation, reward, advantage, or promise thereof for acting or forbearing to act in any case under title 11;

(7) in a personal capacity or as an agent or officer of any person or corporation, in contemplation of a case under title 11 by or against the person or any other person or corporation, or with intent to defeat the provisions of title 11, knowingly and fraudulently transfers or conceals any of his property or the property of such other person or corporation;

(8) after the filing of a case under title 11 or in contemplation thereof, knowingly and fraudulently conceals, destroys, mutilates, falsifies, or makes a false entry in any recorded information (including books, documents, records, and papers) relating to the property or financial affairs of a debtor; or

(9) after the filing of a case under title 11, knowingly and fraudulently withholds from a custodian, trustee, marshal, or other officer of the court or a United States Trustee entitled to its possession, any recorded information (including books, documents, records, and papers) relating to the property or financial affairs of a debtor,

shall be fined under this title, imprisoned not more than 5 years, or both.

(June 25, 1948, c. 645, 62 Stat. 689; June 12, 1960, Pub.L. 86–519, § 2, 74 Stat. 217; Sept. 2, 1960, Pub.L. 86–701, 74 Stat. 753; Oct. 18, 1976, Pub.L. 94–550, § 4, 90 Stat. 2535; Nov. 6, 1978, Pub.L. 95–598, Title III, § 314(a), (c), 92 Stat. 2676, 2677; Nov. 18, 1988, Pub.L. 100–690, Title VII, § 7017, 102 Stat. 4395; Sept. 13, 1994, Pub.L. 103–322, Title XXXIII, § 330016(1)(K), 108 Stat. 2147; Oct. 22, 1994, Pub.L. 103–394, Title III, § 312(a)(1)(A), 108 Stat. 4138; Oct. 11, 1996, Pub.L. 104–294, Title VI, § 601(a)(1), 110 Stat. 3498.)

HISTORICAL AND STATUTORY NOTES

Effective and Applicability Provisions

1994 Acts. Amendment by Pub.L. 103–394 effective on Oct. 22, 1994, and not to apply with respect to cases commenced under Title 11 of the United States Code before Oct. 22, 1994, see section 702 of Pub.L. 103–394, set out as a note under section 101 of Title 11, Bankruptcy.

1978 Acts. Amendment by Pub.L. 95–598 effective Oct. 1, 1979, see section 402(a) of Pub.L. 95–598, set out as a note preceding section 101 of Title 11, Bankruptcy.

Separability of Provisions

If any provision of or amendment made by Pub.L. 103–394 or the application of such provision or amendment to any person or circumstance is held to be unconstitutional, the remaining provisions of and amendments made by Pub.L. 103–394 and the application of such provisions and amendments to any person or circumstance shall not be affected thereby, see section 701 of Pub.L. 103–394, set out as a note under section 101 of Title 11, Bankruptcy.

Savings Provisions

Amendment by section 314 of Pub. L. 95–598 not to affect the application of this chapter to any act of any person (1) committed before Oct. 1, 1979, or (2) committed after Oct. 1, 1979, in connection with a case commenced before such date, see section 403(d) of Pub. L. 95–598, set out preceding section 101 of Title 11, Bankruptcy.

§ 153. Embezzlement against estate

(a) Offense.—A person described in subsection (b) who knowingly and fraudulently appropriates to the person's own use, embezzles, spends, or transfers any property or secretes or destroys any document belonging to the estate of a debtor shall be fined under this title, imprisoned not more than 5 years, or both.

(b) Person to whom section applies.—A person described in this subsection is one who has access to property or documents belonging to an estate by virtue of the person's participation in the administration of the estate as a trustee, custodian, marshal, attorney, or other officer of the court or as an agent, employee, or other person engaged by such an officer to perform a service with respect to the estate.

(June 25, 1948, c. 645, 62 Stat. 690; Nov. 6, 1978, Pub.L. 95–598, Title III, § 314(a)(1), (d)(1), (2), 92 Stat. 2676, 2677; Sept. 13, 1994, Pub.L. 103–322, Title XXXIII, § 330016(1)(K), 108 Stat. 2147; Oct. 22, 1994, Pub.L. 103–394, Title III, § 312(a)(1)(A), 108 Stat. 4139; Oct. 11, 1996, Pub.L. 104–294, Title VI, § 601(a)(1), 110 Stat. 3498.)

HISTORICAL AND STATUTORY NOTES

Effective and Applicability Provisions

1994 Acts. Amendment by Pub.L. 103–394 effective on Oct. 22, 1994, and not to apply with respect to cases commenced under Title 11 of the United States Code before Oct. 22, 1994, see section 702 of Pub.L. 103–394, set out as a note under section 101 of Title 11, Bankruptcy.

1978 Acts. Amendment by Pub.L. 95–598 effective Oct. 1, 1979, see section 402(a) of Pub.L. 95–598, set out as a note preceding section 101 of Title 11, Bankruptcy.

Savings Provisions

Amendment by section 314 of Pub. L. 95–598 not to affect the application of this chapter to any act of any person (1) committed before Oct. 1, 1979, or (2) committed after Oct. 1, 1979, in connection with a case commenced before such date, see section 403(d) of Pub. L. 95–598, set out preceding section 101 of Title 11, Bankruptcy.

Separability of Provisions

If any provision of or amendment made by Pub.L. 103–394 or the application of such provision or amendment to any person or circumstance is held to be unconstitutional, the remaining provisions of and amendments made by Pub.L. 103–394 and the application of such provisions and amendments to any person or circumstance shall not be affected thereby, see section 701 of Pub.L. 103–394, set out as a note under section 101 of Title 11, Bankruptcy.

§ 154. Adverse interest and conduct of officers

A person who, being a custodian, trustee, marshal, or other officer of the court—

(1) knowingly purchases, directly or indirectly, any property of the estate of which the person is such an officer in a case under title 11;

(2) knowingly refuses to permit a reasonable opportunity for the inspection by parties in interest of the documents and accounts relating to the affairs of estates in the person's charge by parties when directed by the court to do so; or

(3) knowingly refuses to permit a reasonable opportunity for the inspection by the United States Trustee of the documents and accounts relating to the affairs of an estate in the person's charge,

shall be fined under this title and shall forfeit the person's office, which shall thereupon become vacant.

(June 25, 1948, c. 645, 62 Stat. 690; Nov. 6, 1978, Pub.L. 95–598, Title III, § 314(a)(2), (e)(1), (2), 92 Stat. 2676, 2677; Sept. 13, 1994, Pub.L. 103–322, Title XXXIII, § 330016(1)(G), 108 Stat. 2147; Oct. 22, 1994, Pub.L. 103–394, Title III, § 312(a)(1)(A), 108 Stat. 4139; Oct. 11, 1996, Pub.L. 104–294, Title VI, § 601(a)(1), 110 Stat. 3498.)

HISTORICAL AND STATUTORY NOTES

Effective and Applicability Provisions

1994 Acts. Amendment by Pub.L. 103–394 effective on Oct. 22, 1994, and not to apply with respect to cases commenced under Title 11 of the United States Code before Oct. 22, 1994, see section 702 of Pub.L. 103–394, set out as a note under section 101 of Title 11, Bankruptcy.

1978 Acts. Amendment by Pub.L. 95–598 effective Oct. 1, 1979, see section 402(a) of Pub.L. 95–598, set out as a note preceding section 101 of Title 11, Bankruptcy.

Savings Provisions

Amendment by section 314 of Pub. L. 95–598 not to affect the application of this chapter to any act of any person (1) committed before Oct. 1, 1979, or (2) committed after Oct. 1, 1979, in connection with a case commenced before such date, see section 403(d) of Pub. L. 95–598, set out preceding section 101 of Title 11, Bankruptcy.

Separability of Provisions

If any provision of or amendment made by Pub.L. 103–394 or the application of such provision or amendment to any person or circumstance is held to be unconstitutional, the remaining provisions of and amendments made by Pub.L. 103–394 and the application of such provisions and amendments to any person or circumstance shall not be affected thereby, see section 701 of Pub.L. 103–394, set out as a note under section 101 of Title 11, Bankruptcy.

§ 155. Fee agreements in cases under title 11 and receiverships

Whoever, being a party in interest, whether as a debtor, creditor, receiver, trustee or representative of any of them, or attorney for any such party in interest, in any receivership or case under title 11 in any United States court or under its supervision, knowingly and fraudulently enters into any agreement, express or implied, with another such party in interest or attorney for another such party in interest, for the purpose of fixing the fees or other compensation to be paid to any party in interest or to any attorney for any party in interest for services rendered in connection therewith, from the assets of the estate, shall be fined under this title or imprisoned not more than one year, or both.

(June 25, 1948, c. 645, 62 Stat. 690; May 24, 1949, c. 139, § 4, 63 Stat. 90; Nov. 6, 1978, Pub.L. 95–598, Title III, § 314(f)(1), (2) 92 Stat. 2677; Sept. 13, 1994, Pub.L. 103–322, Title XXXIII, § 330016(1)(K), 108 Stat. 2147.)

HISTORICAL AND STATUTORY NOTES

Effective and Applicability Provisions

1978 Acts. Amendment by Pub.L. 95–598 effective Oct. 1, 1979, see section 402(a) of Pub.L. 95–598, set out as a note preceding section 101 of Title 11, Bankruptcy.

Savings Provisions

Amendment by section 314 of Pub. L. 95–598 not to affect the application of this chapter to any act of any person (1) committed before Oct. 1, 1979, or (2) committed after Oct. 1, 1979, in connection with a case commenced before such date, see section 403(d) of Pub. L. 95–598, set out preceding section 101 of Title 11, Bankruptcy.

§ 156. Knowing disregard of bankruptcy law or rule

(a) Definitions.—In this section—

(1) the term "bankruptcy petition preparer" means a person, other than the debtor's attorney or an employee of such an attorney, who prepares for compensation a document for filing; and

(2) the term "document for filing" means a petition or any other document prepared for filing by a debtor in a United States bankruptcy court or a United States district court in connection with a case under title 11.

(b) Offense.—If a bankruptcy case or related proceeding is dismissed because of a knowing attempt by a bankruptcy petition preparer in any manner to disregard the requirements of title 11, United States Code, or the Federal Rules of Bankruptcy Procedure, the bankruptcy petition preparer shall be fined under this title, imprisoned not more than 1 year, or both.

(Added Pub.L. 103–394, Title III, § 312(a)(1)(B), Oct. 22, 1994, 108 Stat. 4140, and amended Pub.L. 109–8, Title XII, § 1220, Apr. 20, 2005, 119 Stat. 195.)

HISTORICAL AND STATUTORY NOTES

References in Text

The Federal Rules of Bankruptcy Procedure, referred to in subsec. (b), are set out in Title 11, Bankruptcy.

Effective and Applicability Provisions

2005 Acts. Except as otherwise provided, amendments by Pub.L. 109–8 effective 180 days after April 20, 2005, and inapplicable with respect to cases commenced under Title 11 before the effective date, see Pub.L. 109–8, § 1501, set out as a note under 11 U.S.C.A. § 101.

1994 Acts. Section effective on Oct. 22, 1994, and not to apply with respect to cases commenced under Title 11 of the United States Code before Oct. 22, 1994, see section 702 of Pub.L. 103–394, set out as a note under section 101 of Title 11, Bankruptcy.

Separability of Provisions

If any provision of or amendment made by Pub.L. 103–394 or the application of such provision or amendment to any person or circumstance is held to be unconstitutional, the remaining provisions of and amendments made by Pub.L. 103–394 and the application of such provisions and amendments to any person or circumstance shall not be affected thereby, see section 701 of Pub.L. 103–394, set out as a note under section 101 of Title 11, Bankruptcy.

§ 157. Bankruptcy fraud

A person who, having devised or intending to devise a scheme or artifice to defraud and for the purpose of executing or concealing such a scheme or artifice or attempting to do so—

(1) files a petition under title 11, including a fraudulent involuntary bankruptcy petition under section 303 of such title;

(2) files a document in a proceeding under title 11; or

(3) makes a false or fraudulent representation, claim, or promise concerning or in relation to a proceeding under title 11, at any time before or after the filing of the petition, or in relation to a proceeding falsely asserted to be pending under such title,

shall be fined under this title, imprisoned not more than 5 years, or both.

(Added Pub.L. 103–394, Title III, § 312(a)(1)(B), Oct. 22, 1994, 108 Stat. 4140, and amended Pub.L. 109–8, Title III, § 332(c), Apr. 20, 2005, 119 Stat. 103.)

HISTORICAL AND STATUTORY NOTES

Codifications

Amendment by Pub.L. 109–8, § 332(c), which directed that ", including a fraudulent involuntary bankruptcy petition under section 303 of such title" be inserted after "title 11", was executed only to par. (1), as the probable intent of Congress.

Effective and Applicability Provisions

2005 Acts. Except as otherwise provided, amendments by Pub.L. 109–8 effective 180 days after April 20, 2005, and inapplicable with respect to cases commenced under Title 11 before the effective date, see Pub.L. 109–8, § 1501, set out as a note under 11 U.S.C.A. § 101.

1994 Acts. Section effective on Oct. 22, 1994, and not to apply with respect to cases commenced under Title 11 of the United States Code before Oct. 22, 1994, see section 702 of Pub.L. 103–394, set out as a note under section 101 of Title 11, Bankruptcy.

Separability of Provisions

If any provision of or amendment made by Pub.L. 103–394 or the application of such provision or amendment to any person or circumstance is held to be unconstitutional, the remaining provisions of and amendments made by Pub.L. 103–394 and the application of such provisions and amendments to any person or circumstance shall not be affected thereby, see section 701 of Pub.L. 103–394, set out as a note under section 101 of Title 11, Bankruptcy.

§ 158. Designation of United States attorneys and agents of the Federal Bureau of Investigation to address abusive reaffirmations of debt and materially fraudulent statements in bankruptcy schedules

(a) In general.—The Attorney General of the United States shall designate the individuals described in subsection (b) to have primary responsibility in carrying out enforcement activities in addressing violations of section 152 or 157 relating to abusive reaffirmations of debt. In addition to addressing the violations referred to in the preceding sentence, the individuals described under subsection (b) shall address violations of section 152 or 157 relating to materially fraudulent statements in bankruptcy schedules that are intentionally false or intentionally misleading.

(b) United States attorneys and agents of the Federal Bureau of Investigation.—The individuals referred to in subsection (a) are—

(1) the United States attorney for each judicial district of the United States; and

(2) an agent of the Federal Bureau of Investigation for each field office of the Federal Bureau of Investigation.

(c) Bankruptcy investigations.—Each United States attorney designated under this section shall, in addition to any other responsibilities, have primary responsibility for carrying out the duties of a United States attorney under section 3057.

(d) Bankruptcy procedures.—The bankruptcy courts shall establish procedures for referring any case that may contain a materially fraudulent statement in a bankruptcy schedule to the individuals designated under this section.

(Added Pub.L. 109–8, Title II, § 203(b)(1), Apr. 20, 2005, 119 Stat. 49.)

HISTORICAL AND STATUTORY NOTES

Effective and Applicability Provisions

2005 Acts. Except as otherwise provided, amendments by Pub.L. 109–8 effective 180 days after April 20, 2005, and inapplicable with respect to cases commenced under Title 11 before the effective date, see Pub.L. 109–8, § 1501, set out as a note under 11 U.S.C.A. § 101.

CHAPTER 10—BIOLOGICAL WEAPONS

Sec.

[1] So in original. Does not conform to section catchline.

§ 175. Prohibitions with respect to biological weapons

(a) In general.—Whoever knowingly develops, produces, stockpiles, transfers, acquires, retains, or possesses any biological agent, toxin, or delivery system for use as a weapon, or knowingly assists a foreign state or any organization to do so, or attempts, threatens, or conspires to do the same, shall be fined under this title or imprisoned for life or any term of years, or both. There is extraterritorial Federal jurisdiction over an offense under this section committed by or against a national of the United States.

(b) Additional offense.—Whoever knowingly possesses any biological agent, toxin, or delivery system of a type or in a quantity that, under the circumstances, is not reasonably justified by a prophylactic, protective, bona fide research, or other peaceful purpose, shall be fined under this title, imprisoned not more than 10 years, or both. In this subsection, the terms "biological agent" and "toxin" do not encompass any biological agent or toxin that is in its naturally occurring environment, if the biological agent or toxin has not been cultivated, collected, or otherwise extracted from its natural source.

(c) Definition.—For purposes of this section, the term "for use as a weapon" includes the development, production, transfer, acquisition, retention, or possession of any biological agent, toxin, or delivery system for other than prophylactic, protective, bona fide research, or other peaceful purposes.

(Added Pub.L. 101–298, § 3(a), May 22, 1990, 104 Stat. 201, and amended Pub.L. 104–132, Title V, § 511(b)(1), Apr. 24, 1996, 110 Stat. 1284; Pub.L. 107–56, Title VIII, § 817(1), Oct. 26, 2001, 115 Stat. 385; Pub.L. 107–188, Title II, § 231(c)(1), June 12, 2002, 116 Stat. 661.)

HISTORICAL AND STATUTORY NOTES

Short Title

Section 1 of Pub.L. 101–298 provided that: "This Act [enacting this chapter, amending section 2516 of this title, and enacting provisions set out as notes under this section] may be cited as the 'Biological Weapons Anti-Terrorism Act of 1989'."

Declaration of Purpose and Intent

Section 2 of Pub.L. 101–298 provided that:

"**(a) Purpose.**—The purpose of this Act [see Short Title note under this section] is to—

"(1) implement the Biological Weapons Convention, an international agreement unanimously ratified by the United States Senate in 1974 and signed by more than 100 other nations, including the Soviet Union; and

"(2) protect the United States against the threat of biological terrorism.

"**(b) Intent of Act.**—Nothing in this Act is intended to restrain or restrict peaceful scientific research or development."

§ 175a. Requests for military assistance to enforce prohibition in certain emergencies

The Attorney General may request the Secretary of Defense to provide assistance under section 382 of title 10 in support of Department of Justice activities relating to the enforcement of section 175 of this title in an emergency situation involving a biological weapon of mass destruction. The authority to make such a request may be exercised by another official of the Department of Justice in accordance with section 382(f)(2) of title 10.

(Added Pub.L. 104–201, Div. A, Title XIV, § 1416(c)(1)(A), Sept. 23, 1996, 110 Stat. 2723.)

§ 175b. Possession by restricted persons

(a)(1) No restricted person shall ship or transport in or affecting interstate or foreign commerce, or possess in or affecting interstate or foreign commerce, any biological agent or toxin, or receive any biological agent or toxin that has been shipped or transported in interstate or foreign commerce, if the biological agent or toxin is listed as a select agent in Appendix A of part 72 of title 42, Code of Federal Regulations, pursuant to section 351A of the Public Health Service Act, and is not exempted under subsection (h) of section 72.6, or Appendix A of part 72, of title 42, Code of Federal Regulations.

(2) Whoever knowingly violates this section shall be fined as provided in this title, imprisoned not more than 10 years, or both, but the prohibition contained in this section shall not apply with respect to any duly authorized United States governmental activity.

(b) Transfer to unregistered person.—

(1) Select agents.—Whoever transfers a select agent to a person who the transferor knows or has reasonable cause to believe is not registered as required by regulations under subsection (b) or (c) of section 351A of the Public Health Service Act shall be fined under this title, or imprisoned for not more than 5 years, or both.

(2) Certain other biological agents and toxins.—Whoever transfers a biological agent or toxin listed pursuant to section 212(a)(1) of the Agricultural Bioterrorism Protection Act of 2002 to a person who the transferor knows or has reasonable cause to believe is not registered as required by regulations under subsection (b) or (c) of section 212 of such Act shall be fined under this title, or imprisoned for not more than 5 years, or both.

(c) Unregistered for possession.—

(1) Select agents.—Whoever knowingly possesses a biological agent or toxin where such agent or toxin is a select agent for which such person has not obtained a registration required by regulations under section 351A(c) of the Public Health Service Act shall be fined under this title, or imprisoned for not more than 5 years, or both.

(2) Certain other biological agents and toxins.—Whoever knowingly possesses a biological agent or toxin where such agent or toxin is a biological agent or toxin listed pursuant to section 212(a)(1) of the Agricultural Bioterrorism Protection Act of 2002 for which such person has not obtained a registration required by regulations under section

212(c) of such Act shall be fined under this title, or imprisoned for not more than 5 years, or both.

(d) In this section:

(1) The term "select agent" means a biological agent or toxin to which subsection (a) applies. Such term (including for purposes of subsection (a)) does not include any such biological agent or toxin that is in its naturally-occurring environment, if the biological agent or toxin has not been cultivated, collected, or otherwise extracted from its natural source.

(2) The term "restricted person" means an individual who—

(A) is under indictment for a crime punishable by imprisonment for a term exceeding 1 year;

(B) has been convicted in any court of a crime punishable by imprisonment for a term exceeding 1 year;

(C) is a fugitive from justice;

(D) is an unlawful user of any controlled substance (as defined in section 102 of the Controlled Substances Act (21 U.S.C. 802));

(E) is an alien illegally or unlawfully in the United States;

(F) has been adjudicated as a mental defective or has been committed to any mental institution;

(G)(i) is an alien (other than an alien lawfully admitted for permanent residence) who is a national of a country as to which the Secretary of State, pursuant to section 6(j) of the Export Administration Act of 1979 (50 U.S.C. App. 2405(j)), section 620A of chapter 1 of part M of the Foreign Assistance Act of 1961 (22 U.S.C. 2371), or section 40(d) of chapter 3 of the Arms Export Control Act (22 U.S.C. 2780(d)), has made a determination (that remains in effect) that such country has repeatedly provided support for acts of international terrorism, or (ii) acts for or on behalf of, or operates subject to the direction or control of, a government or official of a country described in this subparagraph;

(H) has been discharged from the Armed Services of the United States under dishonorable conditions; or

(I) is a member of, acts for or on behalf of, or operates subject to the direction or control of, a terrorist organization as defined in section 212(a)(3)(B)(vi) of the Immigration and Nationality Act (8 U.S.C. 1182(a)(3)(B)(vi)).

(3) The term "alien" has the same meaning as in section section 101(a)(3) of the Immigration and Nationality Act (8 U.S.C. 1101(a)(3)).

(4) The term "lawfully admitted for permanent residence" has the same meaning as in section 101(a)(20) of the Immigration and Nationality Act (8 U.S.C. 1101(a)(20)).

(Added Pub.L. 107–56, Title VIII, § 817(2), Oct. 26, 2001, 115 Stat. 386, and amended Pub.L. 107–188, Title II, § 231(a), (b)(1), (c)(2), June 12, 2002, 116 Stat. 660, 661; Pub.L. 107–273, Div. B, Title IV, § 4005(g), Nov. 2, 2002, 116 Stat. 1813; Pub.L. 108–458, Title VI, § 6802(c), Dec. 17, 2004, 118 Stat. 3767.)

Amendment of Subsection (a)(1)

Pub.L. 108–458, Title VI, § 6802(d), Dec. 17, 2004, 118 Stat. 3767, provided that, effective at the same time that sections 73.4, 73.5, and 73.6 of Title 42, Code of Federal Regulations, become effective, subsec. (a)(1) of this section is amended by striking "as a select agent in Appendix A" and all that follows and inserting the following: "as a non-overlap or overlap select biological agent or toxin in sections 73.4 and 73.5 of title 42, Code of Federal Regulations, pursuant to section 351A of the Public Health Service Act, and is not excluded under sections 73.4 and 73.5 or exempted under section 73.6 of title 42, Code of Federal Regulations." See Effective and Applicability Provisions note set out under this section.

HISTORICAL AND STATUTORY NOTES

References in Text

Section 351A of the Public Health Service Act, referred to in text, is section 351A of Act July 1, 1944, c. 373, as added Pub.L. 107–188, Title II, § 201, June 12, 2002, 116 Stat. 637, which is classified to 42 U.S.C.A. § 262a.

Section 212 of the Agricultural Bioterrorism Protection Act of 2002, referred to in text, is Pub.L. 107–188, Title II, § 212, June 12, 2002, 116 Stat. 647, which is classified to 7 U.S.C.A. § 8401.

Section 102 of the Controlled Substances Act, referred to in subsec. (d)(2)(D), is Pub.L. 91–513, Title II, § 102, Oct. 27, 1970, 84 Stat. 1242, as amended, which is classified to 21 U.S.C.A. § 802. The term "controlled substance" is defined in par. (6) of that section.

Section 6(j) of the Export Administration Act of 1979, referred to in subsec. (d)(2)(G), is Pub.L. 96–72, § 6(j), Sept. 29, 1979, 93 Stat. 513, as amended, which is classified to 50 App. U.S.C.A. § 2405(j).

Section 620A of chapter 1 of part M of the Foreign Assistance Act of 1961, referred to in subsec. (d)(2)(G), is Pub. L. 87–195, Pt. III, § 620A, as added Pub. L. 94–329, Title III, § 303, June 30, 1976, 90 Stat. 753, as amended, which is classified to 22 U.S.C.A. § 2371

Section 40(d) of chapter 3 of the Arms Export Control Act, referred to in subsec. (d)(2)(G), is Pub.L. 90–629, c. 3, § 40, as added Pub.L. 99–399, Title V, § 509(a), Aug. 27, 1986, 100 Stat. 874, as amended, which is classified to 22 U.S.C.A. § 2780(d).

Section 212(a)(3)(B)(iii) of the Immigration and Nationality Act, referred to in subsec. (d)(2)(I), is Act June 27, 1952, c. 477, Title II, ch. 2, § 212(a)(3)(B)(vi), 66 Stat. 182, as amended, which is classified to 8 U.S.C.A. § 1182(a)(3)(B)(vi).

Section 101(a)(3) of the Immigration and Nationality Act, referred to in subsec. (d)(3), is Act June 27, 1952, c. 477, Title I, 101(a)(3), 66 Stat. 166, as amended, which is classified to 8 U.S.C.A. 1101(a)(3).

Section 101(a)(2) of the Immigration and Nationality Act, referred to in subsec. (d)(4), is Act June 27, 1952, c. 477, Title I, § 101(a)(2), 66 Stat. 166, as amended, which is classified to 8 U.S.C.A. § 1101(a)(2).

Effective and Applicability Provisions

2004 Acts. Pub.L. 108–458, Title VI, § 6802(d)(2), Dec. 17, 2004, 118 Stat. 3767, provided that: "The amendment made by paragraph (1) [amending subsec. (a)(1) of this section] shall take effect at the same time that sections 73.4, 73.5, and 73.6 of title 42, Code of Federal Regulations, become effective [probably means the effective date of the final rule revising sections 73.4, 73.5, and 73.6 of Title 42, C.F.R., which was Apr. 18, 2005, see 70 F.R. 13294]."

§ 175c. Variola virus

(a) Unlawful conduct.—

(1) In general.—Except as provided in paragraph (2), it shall be unlawful for any person to knowingly produce, engineer, synthesize, acquire, transfer directly or indirectly, receive, possess, import, export, or use, or possess and threaten to use, variola virus.

(2) Exception.—This subsection does not apply to conduct by, or under the authority of, the Secretary of Health and Human Services.

(b) Jurisdiction.—Conduct prohibited by subsection (a) is within the jurisdiction of the United States if—

(1) the offense occurs in or affects interstate or foreign commerce;

(2) the offense occurs outside of the United States and is committed by a national of the United States;

(3) the offense is committed against a national of the United States while the national is outside the United States;

(4) the offense is committed against any property that is owned, leased, or used by the United States or by any department or agency of the United States, whether the property is within or outside the United States; or

(5) an offender aids or abets any person over whom jurisdiction exists under this subsection in committing an offense under this section or conspires with any person over whom jurisdiction exists under this subsection to commit an offense under this section.

(c) Criminal penalties.—

(1) In general.—Any person who violates, or attempts or conspires to violate, subsection (a) shall be fined not more than $2,000,000 and shall be sentenced to a term of imprisonment not less than 25 years or to imprisonment for life.

(2) Other circumstances.—Any person who, in the course of a violation of subsection (a), uses, attempts or conspires to use, or possesses and threatens to use, any item or items described in subsection (a), shall be fined not more than $2,000,000 and imprisoned for not less than 30 years or imprisoned for life.

(3) Special circumstances.—If the death of another results from a person's violation of subsection (a), the person shall be fined not more than $2,000,000 and punished by imprisonment for life.

(d) Definition.—As used in this section, the term "variola virus" means a virus that can cause human smallpox or any derivative of the variola major virus that contains more than 85 percent of the gene sequence of the variola major virus or the variola minor virus.

(Added Pub.L. 108–458, Title VI, § 6906, Dec. 17, 2004, 118 Stat. 3773.)

HISTORICAL AND STATUTORY NOTES

Findings and Purpose

Pub.L. 108–458, Title VI, § 6902, Dec. 17, 2004, 118 Stat. 3769, provided that:

"**(a) Findings.**—Congress makes the following findings:

"(1) The criminal use of man-portable air defense systems (referred to in this section [this note] as 'MANPADS') presents a serious threat to civil aviation worldwide, especially in the hands of terrorists or foreign states that harbor them.

"(2) Atomic weapons or weapons designed to release radiation (commonly known as 'dirty bombs') could be used by terrorists to inflict enormous loss of life and damage to property and the environment.

"(3) Variola virus is the causative agent of smallpox, an extremely serious, contagious, and sometimes fatal disease. Variola virus is classified as a Category A agent by the Centers for Disease Control and Prevention, meaning that it is believed to pose the greatest potential threat for adverse public health impact and has a moderate to high potential for large-scale dissemination. The last case of smallpox in the United States was in 1949. The last naturally occurring case in the world was in Somalia in 1977. Although smallpox has been officially eradicated after a successful worldwide vaccination program, there remain two official repositories of the variola virus for research purposes. Because it is so dangerous, the variola virus may appeal to terrorists.

"(4) The use, or even the threatened use, of MANPADS, atomic or radiological weapons, or the variola virus, against the United States, its allies, or its people, poses a grave risk to the security, foreign policy, economy, and environment of the United States. Accordingly, the United States has a compelling national security interest in preventing unlawful activities that lead to the proliferation or spread of such items, including their unauthorized production, construction, acquisition, transfer, possession, import, or export. All of these activities markedly increase the chances that such items will be obtained by terrorist organizations or rogue states, which could use them to attack the United States, its allies, or United States nationals or corporations.

"(5) There is no legitimate reason for a private individual or company, absent explicit government authorization, to produce, construct, otherwise acquire, transfer, receive, possess, import, export, or use MANPADS, atomic or radiological weapons, or the variola virus.

"**(b) Purpose.**—The purpose of this subtitle [Pub.L. 108–458, Title VI, Subtitle J, §§ 6901 to 6911, Dec. 17, 2004, 118 Stat. 3769, which enacted this section and this note and enacted 18 U.S.C.A. §§ 2332g and 2332h, and amended 18 U.S.C.A. §§ 1956, 2332b, and 2516, 22 U.S.C.A. § 2778, and 42 U.S.C.A. §§ 2122 and 2272] is to combat the potential use of weapons that have the ability to cause widespread harm to United States persons and the United States economy (and that have no legitimate private use) and to threaten or harm the national security or foreign relations of the United States."

§ 176. Seizure, forfeiture, and destruction

(a) In general.—**(1)** Except as provided in paragraph (2), the Attorney General may request the issuance, in the same manner as provided for a search warrant, of a warrant authorizing the seizure of any biological agent, toxin, or delivery system that—

(A) pertains to conduct prohibited under section 175 of this title; or

(B) is of a type or in a quantity that under the circumstances has no apparent justification for prophylactic, protective, or other peaceful purposes.

(2) In exigent circumstances, seizure and destruction of any biological agent, toxin, or delivery system described in subparagraphs (A) and (B) of paragraph (1) may be made upon probable cause without the necessity for a warrant.

(b) Procedure.—Property seized pursuant to subsection (a) shall be forfeited to the United States after notice to potential claimants and an opportunity for a hearing. At such hearing, the Government shall bear the burden of persuasion by a preponderance of the evidence. Except as inconsistent herewith, the same procedures and provisions of law relating to a forfeiture under the customs laws shall extend to a seizure or forfeiture under this section. The Attorney General may provide for the destruction or other appropriate disposition of any biological agent, toxin, or delivery system seized and forfeited pursuant to this section.

(c) Affirmative defense.—It is an affirmative defense against a forfeiture under subsection (a)(1)(B) of this section that—

(1) such biological agent, toxin, or delivery system is for a prophylactic, protective, or other peaceful purpose; and

(2) such biological agent, toxin, or delivery system, is of a type and quantity reasonable for that purpose.

(Added Pub.L. 101–298, § 3(a), May 22, 1990, 104 Stat. 202, and amended Pub.L. 103–322, Title XXXIII, § 330010(16), Sept. 13, 1994, 108 Stat. 2144; Pub.L. 107–188, Title II, § 231(c)(3), June 12, 2002, 116 Stat. 661.)

§ 177. Injunctions

(a) In general.—The United States may obtain in a civil action an injunction against—

(1) the conduct prohibited under section 175 of this title;

(2) the preparation, solicitation, attempt, threat, or conspiracy to engage in conduct prohibited under section 175 of this title; or

(3) the development, production, stockpiling, transferring, acquisition, retention, or possession, or the attempted development, production, stockpiling, transferring, acquisition, retention, or possession of any biological agent, toxin, or delivery system of a type or in a quantity that under the circumstances has no apparent justification for prophylactic, protective, or other peaceful purposes.

(b) Affirmative defense.—It is an affirmative defense against an injunction under subsection (a)(3) of this section that—

(1) the conduct sought to be enjoined is for a prophylactic, protective, or other peaceful purpose; and

(2) such biological agent, toxin, or delivery system is of a type and quantity reasonable for that purpose.

(Added Pub.L. 101–298, § 3(a), May 22, 1990, 104 Stat. 202, and amended Pub.L. 104–132, Title V, § 511(b)(2), Apr. 24, 1996, 110 Stat. 1284.)

§ 178. Definitions

As used in this chapter—

(1) the term "biological agent" means any microorganism (including, but not limited to, bacteria, viruses, fungi, rickettsiae or protozoa), or infectious substance, or any naturally occurring, bioengineered or synthesized component of any such microorganism or infectious substance, capable of causing—

(A) death, disease, or other biological malfunction in a human, an animal, a plant, or another living organism;

(B) deterioration of food, water, equipment, supplies, or material of any kind; or

(C) deleterious alteration of the environment;

(2) the term "toxin" means the toxic material or product of plants, animals, microorganisms (including, but not limited to, bacteria, viruses, fungi, rickettsiae or protozoa), or infectious substances, or a recombinant or synthesized molecule, whatever their origin and method of production, and includes—

(A) any poisonous substance or biological product that may be engineered as a result of biotechnology produced by a living organism; or

(B) any poisonous isomer or biological product, homolog, or derivative of such a substance;

(3) the term "delivery system" means—

(A) any apparatus, equipment, device, or means of delivery specifically designed to deliver or disseminate a biological agent, toxin, or vector; or

(B) any vector;

(4) the term "vector" means a living organism, or molecule, including a recombinant or synthesized molecule, capable of carrying a biological agent or toxin to a host; and

(5) the term "national of the United States" has the meaning prescribed in section 101(a)(22) of the Immigration and Nationality Act (8 U.S.C. 1101(a)(22)).

(Added Pub.L. 101–298, § 3(a), May 22, 1990, 104 Stat. 202, and amended Pub.L. 104–132, Title V, § 511(b)(3), Title VII, § 721(h), Apr. 24, 1996, 110 Stat. 1284, 1299; Pub.L. 107–188, Title II, § 231(c)(4), June 12, 2002, 116 Stat. 661.)

HISTORICAL AND STATUTORY NOTES

References in Text

The Immigration and Nationality Act, referred to in par. (5), is Act June 27, 1952, c. 477, 66 Stat. 163, as amended, which is classified principally to chapter 12 (section 1101 et seq.) of Title 8, Aliens and Nationality. Section 101(a)(22) of such Act is classified to section 1101(a)(22) of Title 8. For complete classification of this Act to the Code, see Short Title note set out under section 1101 of Title 8 and Tables.

CHAPTER 11—BRIBERY, GRAFT, AND CONFLICTS OF INTEREST

HISTORICAL AND STATUTORY NOTES

Codifications

Section 501(b) of Pub.L. 95–521, which amended the item relating to section 207 in the analysis of this chapter, was completely revised by Pub.L. 101–194, Title VI, § 601(a), Nov. 30, 1989, 103 Stats. 1760, and is now set out in section 501(b) of Appendix 7 of Title 5, Government Organization and Employees. See Codification Note set out under section 207 of this title.

Change of Name

References to United States Claims Court deemed to refer to United States Court of Federal Claims and references to Claims Court deemed to refer to Court of Federal Claims, see section 902(b) of Pub.L. 102–572, set out as a note under section 171 of Title 28, Judiciary and Judicial Procedure.

§ 201. Bribery of public officials and witnesses

(a) For the purpose of this section—

(1) the term "public official" means Member of Congress, Delegate, or Resident Commissioner, either before or after such official has qualified, or an officer or employee or person acting for or on behalf of the United States, or any department, agency or branch of Government thereof, including the District of Columbia, in any official function, under or by authority of any such department, agency, or branch of Government, or a juror;

(2) the term "person who has been selected to be a public official" means any person who has been nominated or appointed to be a public official, or has been officially informed that such person will be so nominated or appointed; and

(3) the term "official act" means any decision or action on any question, matter, cause, suit, proceeding or controversy, which may at any time be pending, or which may by law be brought before

any public official, in such official's official capacity, or in such official's place of trust or profit.

(b) Whoever—

(1) directly or indirectly, corruptly gives, offers or promises anything of value to any public official or person who has been selected to be a public official, or offers or promises any public official or any person who has been selected to be a public official to give anything of value to any other person or entity, with intent—

(A) to influence any official act; or

(B) to influence such public official or person who has been selected to be a public official to commit or aid in committing, or collude in, or allow, any fraud, or make opportunity for the commission of any fraud, on the United States; or

(C) to induce such public official or such person who has been selected to be a public official to do or omit to do any act in violation of the lawful duty of such official or person;

(2) being a public official or person selected to be a public official, directly or indirectly, corruptly demands, seeks, receives, accepts, or agrees to receive or accept anything of value personally or for any other person or entity, in return for:

(A) being influenced in the performance of any official act;

(B) being influenced to commit or aid in committing, or to collude in, or allow, any fraud, or make opportunity for the commission of any fraud, on the United States; or

(C) being induced to do or omit to do any act in violation of the official duty of such official or person;

(3) directly or indirectly, corruptly gives, offers, or promises anything of value to any person, or offers or promises such person to give anything of value to any other person or entity, with intent to influence the testimony under oath or affirmation of such first-mentioned person as a witness upon a trial, hearing, or other proceeding, before any court, any committee of either House or both Houses of Congress, or any agency, commission, or officer authorized by the laws of the United States to hear evidence or take testimony, or with intent to influence such person to absent himself therefrom;

(4) directly or indirectly, corruptly demands, seeks, receives, accepts, or agrees to receive or accept anything of value personally or for any other person or entity in return for being influenced in testimony under oath or affirmation as a witness upon any such trial, hearing, or other proceeding, or in return for absenting himself therefrom;

shall be fined under this title or not more than three times the monetary equivalent of the thing of value, whichever is greater, or imprisoned for not more than fifteen years, or both, and may be disqualified from holding any office of honor, trust, or profit under the United States.

(c) Whoever—

(1) otherwise than as provided by law for the proper discharge of official duty—

(A) directly or indirectly gives, offers, or promises anything of value to any public official, former public official, or person selected to be a public official, for or because of any official act performed or to be performed by such public official, former public official, or person selected to be a public official; or

(B) being a public official, former public official, or person selected to be a public official, otherwise than as provided by law for the proper discharge of official duty, directly or indirectly demands, seeks, receives, accepts, or agrees to receive or accept anything of value personally for or because of any official act performed or to be performed by such official or person;

(2) directly or indirectly, gives, offers, or promises anything of value to any person, for or because of the testimony under oath or affirmation given or to be given by such person as a witness upon a trial, hearing, or other proceeding, before any court, any committee of either House or both Houses of Congress, or any agency, commission, or officer authorized by the laws of the United States to hear evidence or take testimony, or for or because of such person's absence therefrom;

(3) directly or indirectly, demands, seeks, receives, accepts, or agrees to receive or accept anything of value personally for or because of the testimony under oath or affirmation given or to be given by such person as a witness upon any such trial, hearing, or other proceeding, or for or because of such person's absence therefrom;

shall be fined under this title or imprisoned for not more than two years, or both.

(d) Paragraphs (3) and (4) of subsection (b) and paragraphs (2) and (3) of subsection (c) shall not be construed to prohibit the payment or receipt of witness fees provided by law, or the payment, by the party upon whose behalf a witness is called and receipt by a witness, of the reasonable cost of travel and subsistence incurred and the reasonable value of time lost in attendance at any such trial, hearing, or proceeding, or in the case of expert witnesses, a reasonable fee for time spent in the preparation of such opinion, and in appearing and testifying.

(e) The offenses and penalties prescribed in this section are separate from and in addition to those prescribed in sections 1503, 1504, and 1505 of this title.

(Added Pub.L. 87–849, § 1(a), Oct. 23, 1962, 76 Stat. 1119, and amended Pub.L. 91–405, Title II, § 204(d) (1), Sept. 22, 1970, 84 Stat. 853; Pub.L. 99–646, § 46(a)–(*l*), Nov. 10, 1986, 100 Stat. 3601–3604; Pub.L. 103–322, Title XXXIII, §§ 330011(b), 330016(2)(D), Sept. 13, 1994, 108 Stat. 2144, 2148.)

MEMORANDUM OF ATTORNEY GENERAL REGARDING CONFLICT OF INTEREST PROVISIONS OF PUBLIC LAW 87–849

Feb. 1, 1963, 28 F.R. 985

January 28, 1963

Public Law 87–849, "To strengthen the criminal laws relating to bribery, graft, and conflicts of interest, and for other purposes," came into force January 21, 1963. A number of departments and agencies of the Government have suggested that the Department of Justice prepare and distribute a memorandum analyzing the conflict of interest provisions contained in the new act. I am therefore distributing the attached memorandum.

One of the main purposes of the new legislation merits specific mention. That purpose is to help the Government obtain the temporary or intermittent services of persons with special knowledge and skills whose principal employment is outside the Government. For the most part the conflict of interest statutes superseded by Public Law 87–849 imposed the same restraints on a person serving the Government temporarily or intermittently as on a full-time employee, and those statutes often had an unnecessarily severe impact on the former. As a result, they impeded the departments and agencies in the recruitment of experts for important work. Public Law 87–849 meets this difficulty by imposing a lesser array of prohibitions on temporary and intermittent employees than on regular employees. I believe that a widespread appreciation of this aspect of the new law will lead to a significant expansion of the poll of talent on which the departments and agencies can draw for their special needs.

ROBERT F. KENNEDY,
Attorney General.

Memorandum re the Conflict of Interest Provisions of Public Law 87–849, 76 Stat. 1119, Approved October 23, 1962

INTRODUCTION

Public Law 87–849, which came into force January 21, 1963, affected seven statutes which applied to officers and employees of the Government and were generally spoken of as the "conflict of interest" laws. These included six sections of the criminal code, 18 U.S.C. 216, 281, 283, 284, 434 and 1914 [§§ 216, 281, 283, 284, 434 and 1914 of this title], and a statute containing no penalties, § 190 of the Revised Statutes (5 U.S.C. 99) [former § 99 of Title 5, now covered by § 207 of this title]. Public Law 87–849 (sometimes referred to hereinafter as "the Act") repealed § 190 and one of the criminal statutes, 18 U.S.C. 216, without replacing them.[1] In addition it repealed and supplanted the other five criminal statutes. It is the purpose of this memorandum to summarize the new law and to describe the principal differences between it and the legislation it has replaced.

The Act accomplished its revisions by enacting new §§ 203, 205, 207, 208 and 209 of title 18 of the United States Code [§§ 203, 205, 207, 208 and 209 of this title] and providing that they supplant the above-mentioned §§ 281, 283, 284, 434 and 1914 of title 18 [§§ 281, 283, 284, 434 and 1914 of this title] respectively.[2] It will be convenient, therefore, after summarizing the principal provisions of the new sections, to examine each section separately, comparing it with its precursor before passing to the next. First of all, however, it is necessary to describe the background and provisions of the new 18 U.S.C. 202(a) [§ 202(a) of this title], which has no counterpart among the statutes formerly in effect.

SPECIAL GOVERNMENT EMPLOYEES—NEW 18 U.S.C. 202(a)

In the main the prior conflict of interest laws imposed the same restrictions on individuals who serve the Government intermittently or for a short period of time as on those who serve full-time. The consequences of this generalized treatment were pointed out in the following paragraph of the Senate Judiciary Committee report on the bill which became Public Law 87–849:[3]

In considering the application of present law in relation to the Government's utilization of temporary or intermittent consultants and advisers, it must be emphasized that most of the existing conflict-of-interest statutes were enacted in the 19th century—that is, at a time when persons outside the Government rarely served it in this way. The laws were therefore directed at activities of regular Government employees, and their present impact on the occasionally needed experts—those whose main work is performed outside the Government—is unduly severe. This harsh impact constitutes an appreciable deterrent to the Government's obtaining needed part-time services.

The recruiting problem noted by the Committee generated a major part of the impetus for the enactment of Public Law 87–849. The Act dealt with the problem by creating a category of Government employees termed "special Government employees" and by excepting persons in this category from certain of the prohibitions imposed on ordinary employees. The new 18 U.S.C. 202(a) [§ 202(a) of this title] defines the term "special Government employee" to include, among others, officers and employees of the departments and agencies who are appointed or employed to serve, with or without compensation, for not more than 130 days during any period of 365 consecutive days either on a full-time or intermittent basis.

SUMMARY OF THE MAIN CONFLICT OF INTEREST PROVISIONS OF PUBLIC LAW 87–849

A regular officer or employee of the Government—that is, one appointed or employed to serve more than 130 days in any period of 365 days—is in general subject to the following major prohibitions (the citations are to the new sections of title 18):

1. He may not, except in the discharge of his official duties, represent anyone else before a court or Government agency in a matter in which the United States is a party or has an interest. This prohibition applies both to paid and unpaid representation of another (18 U.S.C. 203 and 205) [§§ 203 and 205 of this title].

2. He may not participate in his governmental capacity in any matter in which he, his spouse, minor child, outside business associate or person with whom he is negotiating for

employment has a financial interest (18 U.S.C. 208) [§ 208 of this title].

3. He may not, after his Government employment has ended, represent anyone other than the United States in connection with a matter in which the United States is a party or has an interest and in which he participated personally and substantially for the Government (18 U.S.C. 207(a)) [§ 207(a) of this title].

4. He may not, for 1 year after his Government employment has ended, represent anyone other than the United States in connection with a matter in which the United States is a party or has an interest and which was within the boundaries of his official responsibility [4] during the last year of his Government service (18 U.S.C. 207(b)) [§ 207(b) of this title]. This temporary restraint of course gives way to the permanent restraint described in paragraph 3 if the matter is one in which he participated personally and substantially.

5. He may not receive any salary, or supplementation of his Government salary, from a private source as compensation for his services to the Government (18 U.S.C. 209) [§ 209 of this title].

A special Government employee is in general subject only to the following major prohibitions:

1. (a) He may not, except in the discharge of his official duties, represent anyone else before a court or Government agency in a matter in which the United States is a party or has an interest and in which he has at any time participated personally and substantially for the Government (18 U.S.C. 203 and 205) [§§ 203 and 205 of this title].

(b) He may not, except in the discharge of his official duties, represent anyone else in a matter pending before the agency he serves unless he has served there no more than 60 days during the past 365 (18 U.S.C. 203 and 205) [§§ 203 and 205 of this title]. He is bound by this restraint despite the fact that the matter is not one in which he has ever participated personally and substantially.

The restrictions described in subparagraphs (a) and (b) apply to both paid and unpaid representation of another. These restrictions in combination are, of course, less extensive than the one described in the corresponding paragraph 1 in the list set forth above with regard to regular employees.

2. He may not participate in his governmental capacity in any matter in which he, his spouse, minor child, outside business associate or person with whom he is negotiating for employment has a financial interest (18 U.S.C. 208) [§ 208 of this title].

3. He may not, after his Government employment has ended, represent anyone other than the United States in connection with a matter in which the United States is a party or has an interest and in which he participated personally and substantially for the Government (18 U.S.C. 207(a)) [§ 207(a) of this title].

4. He may not, for 1 year after his Government employment has ended, represent anyone other than the United States in connection with a matter in which the United States is a party or has an interest and which was within the boundaries of his official responsibility during the last year of his Government service (18 U.S.C. 207(b)) [§ 207(b) of this title]. This temporary restraint of course gives way to the permanent restriction described in paragraph 3 if the matter is one in which he participated personally and substantially.

It will be seen that paragraphs 2, 3 and 4 for special Government employees are the same as the corresponding paragraphs for regular employees. Paragraph 5 for the latter, describing the bar against the receipt of salary for Government work from a private source, does not apply to special Government employees.

As appears below, there are a number of exceptions to the prohibitions summarized in the two lists.

Comparison of Old and New Conflict of Interest Sections of Title 18, United States Code

New 18 U.S.C. 203 [§ 203 of this title]. Subsection (a) of this section in general prohibits a Member of Congress and an officer or employee of the United States in any branch or agency of the Government from soliciting or receiving compensation for services rendered on behalf of another person before a Government department or agency in relation to any particular matter in which the United States is a party or has a direct and substantial interest. The subsection does not preclude compensation for services rendered on behalf of another in court.

Subsection (a) is essentially a rewrite of the repealed portion of 18 U.S.C. 281 [former § 281 of this title]. However, subsections (b) and (c) have no counterparts in the previous statutes.

Subsection (b) makes it unlawful for anyone to offer or pay compensation the solicitation or receipt of which is barred by subsection (a).

Subsection (c) narrows the application of subsection (a) in the case of a person serving as a special Government employee to two, and only two, situations. First, subsection (c) bars him from rendering services before the Government on behalf of others, for compensation, in relation to a matter involving a specific party or parties in which he has participated personally and substantially in the course of his Government duties. And second, it bars him from such activities in relation to a matter involving a specific party or parties, even though he has not participated in the matter personally and substantially, if it is pending in his department or agency and he has served therein more than 60 days in the immediately preceding period of a year.

New 18 U.S.C. 205 [§ 205 of this title]. This section contains two major prohibitions. The first prevents an officer or employee of the United States in any branch or agency of the Government from acting as agent or attorney for prosecuting any claim against the United States, including a claim in court, whether for compensation or not. It also prevents him from receiving a gratuity, or a share or interest in any such claim, for assistance in the prosecution thereof. This portion of § 205 is similar to the repealed portion of 18 U.S.C. 283 [former § 283 of this title], which dealt only with claims against the United States, but it omits a bar contained in the latter—i.e., a bar against rendering uncompensated aid or assistance in the prosecution or support of a claim against the United States.

The second main prohibition of § 205 is concerned with more than claims. It precludes an officer or employee of the Government from acting as agent or attorney for anyone else before a department, agency or court in connection with any particular matter in which the United States is a party or has a direct and substantial interest.

Section 205 provides for the same limited application to a special Government employee as § 203. In short, it precludes him from acting as agent or attorney only (1) in a matter involving a specific party or parties in which he has participated personally and substantially in his governmental capacity, and (2) in a matter involving a specific party or parties which is before his department or agency, if he has served therein more than 60 days in the year past.

Since new §§ 203 and 205 extend to activities in the same range of matters, they overlap to a greater extent than did their predecessor §§ 281 and 283. The following are the few important differences between §§ 203 and 205:

1. Section 203 applies to Members of Congress as well as officers and employees of the Government; § 205 applies only to the latter.

2. Section 203 bars services rendered for compensation solicited or received, but not those rendered without such compensation; § 205 bars both kinds of services.

3. Section 203 bars services rendered before the departments and agencies but not services rendered in court; § 205 bars both.

It will be seen that while § 203 is controlling as to Members of Congress, for all practical purposes § 205 completely overshadows § 203 in respect of officers and employees of the Government.

Section 205 permits a Government officer or employee to represent another person, without compensation, in a disciplinary, loyalty or other personnel matter. Another provision declares that the section does not prevent an officer or employee from giving testimony under oath or making statements required to be made under penalty for perjury or contempt.[5]

Section 205 also authorizes a limited waiver of its restrictions and those of § 203 for the benefit of an officer or employee, including a special Government employee, who represents his own parents, spouse or child, or a person or estate he serves as a fiduciary. The waiver is available to the officer or employee, whether acting for any such person with or without compensation, but only if approved by the official making appointments to his position. And in no event does the waiver extend to his representation of any such person in matters in which he has participated personally and substantially or which, even in the absence of such participation, are the subject of his official responsibility.

Finally, § 205 gives the head of a department or agency the power, notwithstanding any applicable restrictions in its provisions or those of § 203, to allow a special Government employee to represent his regular employer or other outside organization in the performance of work under a Government grant or contract. However, this action is open to the department or agency head only upon his certification, published in the FEDERAL REGISTER, that the national interest requires it.

New 18 U.S.C. 207 [§ 207 of this title]. Subsections (a) and (b) of this section contain post-employment prohibitions applicable to persons who have ended service as officers or employees of the executive branch, the independent agencies or the District of Columbia.[6] The prohibitions for persons who have served as special Government employees are the same as for persons who have performed regular duties.

The restraint of subsection (a) is against a former officer or employee's acting as agent or attorney for anyone other than the United States in connection with certain matters, whether pending in the courts or elsewhere. The matters are those involving a specific party or parties in which the United States is one of the parties or has a direct and substantial interest and in which the former officer or employee participated personally and substantially while holding a Government position.

Subsection (b) sets forth a 1-year postemployment prohibition in respect of those matters which were within the area of official responsibility of a former officer or employee at any time during the last year of his service but which do not come within subsection (a) because he did not participate in them personally and substantially. More particularly, the prohibition of subsection (b) prevents his personal appearance in such matters before a court or a department or agency of the Government as agent or attorney for anyone other than the United States.[7] Where, in the year prior to the end of his service, a former officer or employee has changed areas of responsibility by transferring from one agency to another, the period of his postemployment ineligibility as to matters in a particular area ends 1 year after his responsibility for that area ends. For example, if an individual transfers from a supervisory position in the Internal Revenue Service to a supervisory position in the Post Office Department and leaves that department for private employment 9 months later, he will be free of the restriction of subsection (b) in 3 months insofar as Internal Revenue matters are concerned. He will of course be bound by it for a year in respect of Post Office Department matters.

The proviso following subsections (a) and (b) authorizes an agency head, notwithstanding anything to the contrary in their provisions, to permit a former officer or employee with outstanding scientific qualifications to act as attorney or agent or appear personally before the agency for another in a matter in a scientific field. This authority may be exercised by the agency head upon a "national interest" certification published in the FEDERAL REGISTER.

Subsections (a) and (b) describe the activities they forbid as being in connection with "particular matter[s] involving a specific party or parties" in which the former officer or employee had participated. The quoted language does not include general rulemaking, the formulation of general policy or standards, or other similar matters. Thus, past participation in or official responsibility for a matter of this kind on behalf of the Government does not disqualify a former employee from representing another person in a proceeding which is governed by the rule or other result of such matter.

Subsection (a) bars permanently a greater variety of action than subsection (b) bars temporarily. The conduct made unlawful by the former is any action as agent or attorney, while that made unlawful by the latter is a personal appearance as agent or attorney. However, neither subsection precludes postemployment activities which may fairly be characterized as no more than aiding or assisting another.[8] An individual who has left an agency to accept private employment may, for example, immediately perform technical work in his company's plant in relation to a contract for which he had official responsibility—or, for that matter, in relation to one he helped the agency negotiate. On the other hand, he is forbidden for a year, in the first case, to appear personally before the agency as the agent or attorney of his company in connection with a dispute over the terms of the contract. And he may at no time appear personally before the agency or otherwise act as agent or attorney for his company in such dispute if he helped negotiate the contract.

Comparing subsection (a) with the antecedent 18 U.S.C. 284 [former § 284 of this title] discloses that it follows the latter in limiting disqualification to cases where a former officer or employee actually participated in a matter for the Government. However, subsection (a) covers all matters in which the United States is a party or has a direct and substantial interest and not merely the "claims against the United States" covered by 18 U.S.C. 284 [former § 284 of this title]. Subsection (a) also goes further than the latter in imposing a lifetime instead of a 2-year bar. Subsection (b) has no parallel in 18 U.S.C. 284 [former § 284 of this title] or any other provision of the former conflict of interest statutes.

It will be seen that subsections (a) and (b) in combination are less restrictive in some respects, and more restrictive in others, than the combination of the prior 18 U.S.C. 284 [former § 284 of this title] and 5 U.S.C. 99 [former § 99 of Title 5]. Thus, former officers or employees who were outside the Government when the Act came into force on January 21, 1963, will in certain situations be enabled to carry on activities before the Government which were previously barred. For example, the repeal of 5 U.S.C. 99 [former § 99 of Title 5] permits an attorney who left an executive department for private practice a year before to take certain cases against the Government immediately which would be subject to the bar of 5 U.S.C. 99 [former § 99 of Title 5] for another year. On the other hand, former officers or employees became precluded on and after January 21, 1963 from engaging or continuing to engage in certain activities which were permissible until that This result follows from the replacement of the 2-year bar of 18 U.S.C. 284 [former § 284 of this title] with the lifetime bar of subsection (a) in comparable situations, from the increase in the variety of matters covered by subsection (a) as compared with 18 U.S.C. 284 [former § 284 of this title] and from the introduction of the 1-year bar of subsection (b).

Subsection (c) of § 207 pertains to an individual outside the Government who is in a business or professional partnership with someone serving in the executive branch, an independent agency or the District of Columbia. The subsection prevents such individual from acting as attorney or agent for anyone other than the United States in any matters, including those in court, in which his partner in the Government is participating or has participated or which are the subject of his partner's official responsibility. Although included in a section dealing largely with postemployment activities, this provision is not directed to the postemployment situation.

The paragraph at the end of § 207 also pertains to individuals in a partnership but sets forth no prohibition. This paragraph, which is of importance mainly to lawyers in private practice, rules out the possibility that an individual will be deemed subject to § 203, 205, 207(a) or 207(b) solely because he has a partner who serves or has served in the Government either as a regular or a special Government employee.

New 18 U.S.C. 208 [§ 208 of this title]. This section forbids certain actions by an officer or employee of the Government in his role as a servant or representative of the Government. Its thrust is therefore to be distinguished from that of §§ 203 and 205 which forbid certain actions in his capacity as a representative of persons outside the Government.

Subsection (a) in substance requires an officer or employee of the executive branch, an independent agency or the District of Columbia, including a special Government employee, to refrain from participating as such in any matter in which, to his knowledge, he, his spouse, minor child or partner has a financial interest. He must also remove himself from a matter in which a business or nonprofit organization with which he is connected or is seeking employment has a financial interest.

Subsection (b) permits the agency of an officer or employee to grant him an *ad hoc* exemption from subsection (a) if the outside financial interest in a matter is deemed not substantial enough to have an effect on the integrity of his services. Financial interests of this kind may also be made nondisqualifying by a general regulation published in the FEDERAL REGISTER.

Section 208 is similar in purpose to the former 18 U.S.C. 434 [former § 434 of this title] but prohibits a greater variety of conduct than the "transaction of business with * * * [a] business entity" to which the prohibition of § 434 was limited. In addition, the provision in § 208 including the interests of a spouse and others is new, as is the provision authorizing exemptions for insignificant interests.

New 18 U.S.C. 209 [§ 209 of this title]. Subsection (a) prevents an officer or employee of the executive branch, an independent agency or the District of Columbia from receiving, and anyone from paying him, any salary or supplementation of salary from a private source as compensation for his services to the Government. This provision uses much of the language of the former 18 U.S.C. 1914 [former § 1914 of this title] and does not vary from that statute in substance. The remainder of § 209 is new.

Subsection (b) specifically authorizes an officer or employee covered by subsection (a) to continue his participation in a bona fide pension plan or other employee welfare or benefit plan maintained by a former employer.

Subsection (c) provides that § 209 does not apply to a special Government employee or to anyone serving the Government without compensation, whether or not he is a special Government employee.

Subsection (d) provides that the section does not prohibit the payment or acceptance of contributions, awards or other expenses under the terms of the Government Employees Training Act (72 Stat. 327, 5 U.S.C. 2301 to 2319 [§§ 2301 to 2319 to Title 5]).

Statutory Exemptions From Conflict of Interest Laws

Congress has in the past enacted statutes exempting persons in certain positions—usually advisory in nature—from the provisions of some or all of the former conflict of interest laws. Section 2 of the Act grants corresponding exemptions from the new laws with respect to legislative and judicial positions carrying such past exemptions. However, § 2 excludes positions in the executive branch, an independent agency and the District of Columbia from this grant. As a consequence, all statutory exemptions for persons serving in these sectors of the Government ended on January 21, 1963.

Retired Officers of the Armed Forces

Public Law 87–849 enacted a new 18 U.S.C. 206 [§ 206 of this title] which provides in general that the new §§ 203 and 205, replacing 18 U.S.C. 281 and 283 [former §§ 281 and 283 of this title], do not apply to retired officers of the armed forces and other uniformed services. However, 18 U.S.C. 281 and 283 [former §§ 281 and 283 of this title] contain special restrictions applicable to retired officers of the armed forces which are left in force by the partial repealer of those statutes set forth in § 2 of the Act.

The former 18 U.S.C. 284 [former § 284 of this title], which contained a 2-year disqualification against postemployment activities in connection with claims against the United States, applied by its terms to persons who had served as commissioned officers and whose active service had ceased either by reason of retirement or complete separation. Its replacement, the broader 18 U.S.C. 207 [§ 207 of this title], also applies to persons in those circumstances. Section 207, therefore applies to retired officers of the armed forces and overlaps the continuing provisions of 18 U.S.C. 281 and 283 [§§ 281 and 283 of this title] applicable to such officers although to a different extent than did 18 U.S.C. 284 [§ 284 of this title].

Voiding Transactions in Violation of the Conflict of Interest or Bribery Laws

Public Law 87–849 enacted a new section, 18 U.S.C. 218 [§ 218 of this title], which did not supplant a pre-existing section of the criminal code. However, it was modeled on the last sentence of the former 18 U.S.C. 216 [former § 216 of this title] authorizing the President to declare a Government contract void which was entered into in violation of that section. It will be recalled that § 216 was one of the two statutes repealed without replacement.

The new 18 U.S.C. 218 [§ 218 of this title] grants the President and, under presidential regulations, an agency head the power to void and rescind any transaction or matter in relation to which there has been a "final conviction" for a violation of the conflict of interest or bribery laws. The section also authorizes the Government's recovery, in addition to any penalty prescribed by law or in a contract, of the amount expended or thing transferred on behalf of the Government.

Section 218 specifically provides that the powers it grants are "in addition to any other remedies provided by law." Accordingly, it would not seem to override the decision in United States v. Mississippi Valley Generating Co., 364 U.S. 520 (1961), a case in which there was no "final conviction."

Bibliography

Set forth below are the citations to the legislative history of Public Law 87–849 and a list of recent material which is pertinent to a study of the Act. The listed 1960 report of the Association of the Bar of the City of New York is particularly valuable. For a comprehensive bibliography of earlier material relating to the conflict of interest laws, see 13 Record of the Association of the Bar of the City of New York 323 (May 1958).

Legislative History of Public Law 87–849 (H.R. 8140, 87th Cong.)

1. Hearings of June 1 and 2, 1961 before the Antitrust Subcommittee (Subcommittee No. 5) of the House Judiciary Committee, 87th Cong., 1st sess., ser. 3, on Federal Conflict of Interest Legislation.
2. H.Rept. 748, 87th Cong., 1st sess.
3. 107 Cong.Rec. 14774.
4. Hearing of June 21, 1962 before the Senate Judiciary Committee, 87th Cong., 2d sess., on Conflicts of Interest.
5. S.Rept. 2213, 87th Cong., 2d sess.
6. 108 Cong.Rec. 20805 and 21130 (daily ed., October 3 and 4, 1962).

Other Material

1. President's special message to Congress, April 27, 1961, and attached draft bill, 107 Cong.Rec. 6835.
2. President's Memorandum of February 9, 1962 to the heads of executive departments and agencies entitled Preventing Conflicts of Interest on the Part of Advisers and Consultants to the Government, 27 F.R. 1341.
3. 42 Op.A.G. No. 6, January 31, 1962.
4. Memorandum of December 10, 1956 for the Attorney General from the Office of Legal Counsel re conflict of interest statutes, Hearings before the Antitrust Subcommittee (Subcommittee No. 5) of House Judiciary Committee, 86th Cong., 2d sess., ser. 17, pt. 2, p. 619.
5. Staff report of Antitrust Subcommittee (Subcommittee No. 5) of House Judiciary Committee, 85th Cong., 2d sess., Federal Conflict of Interest Legislation (Comm. Print 1958).
6. Report of the Association of the Bar of the City of New York, Conflict of Interest and Federal Service (Harvard Univ.Press 1960).

Footnotes

[1] Section 190 of the Revised Statutes (5 U.S.C. 99), which was repealed by section 3 of Public Law 87–849, applied to a former officer or employee of the Government who had served in a department of the executive branch. It prohibited him, for a period of two years after his employment had ceased, from representing anyone in the prosecution of a claim against the United States which was pending in that or any other executive department during his period of employment. The subject of postemployment activities of former Government officers and employees was also dealt with in another statute which was repealed. 18 U.S.C. 284. Public Law 87–849 covers the subject in a single section enacted as the new 18 U.S.C. 207.

18 U.S.C. 216, which was repealed by section 1(c) of Public Law 87–849, prohibited the payment to or acceptance by a Member of Congress or officer or employee of the Government of any money or thing of value for giving or procuring a Government contract. Since this offense is within the scope of the newly enacted 18 U.S.C. 201 and 18 U.S.C. 203, relating to bribery and conflicts of interest, respectively, section 216 is no longer necessary.

[2] See section 2 of Public Law 87–849. 18 U.S.C. 281 and 18 U.S.C. 283 were not completely set aside by section 2 but remain in effect to the extent that they apply to retired officers of the Armed Forces (see "Retired Officers of the Armed Forces," infra).

[3] S.Rept. 2213, 87th Cong., 2d sess., p. 6.

[4] The term "official responsibility" is defined by the new 18 U.S.C. 202(b) to mean "the direct administrative or operating authority, whether intermediate or final, and either exercisable alone or with others, and either personally or through subordinates, approve, disapprove, or otherwise direct Government action."

[5] These two provisions of section 205 refer to an "officer or employee" and not, as do certain of the other provisions of the Act, to an "officer or employee, including a special Government employee." However, it is plain from the definition in section 202(a) that a special Government employee is embraced within the comprehensive term "officer or employee." There would seem to be little doubt, therefore,

that the instant provisions of section 205 apply to special Government employees even in the absence of an explicit reference to them.

6 The prohibitions of the two subsections apply to persons ending service in these areas whether they leave the Government entirely or move to the legislative or judicial branch. As a practical matter, however, the prohibitions would rarely be significant in the latter situation because officers and employees of the legislative and judicial branches are covered by sections 203 and 205.

7 Neither section 203 nor section 205 prevents a special Government employee, during his period of affiliation with the Government, from representing another person before the Government in a particular matter only because it is within his official responsibility. Therefore the inclusion of a former special Government employee within the 1-year postemployment ban of subsection (b) may subject him to a temporary restraint from which he was free prior to the end of his Government service. However, since special Government employees usually do not have "official responsibility," as that term is defined in section 202(b), their inclusion within the 1-year ban will not have a widespread effect.

8 Subsection (a), as it first appeared in H.R. 8140, the bill which became Public Law 87–849, made it unlawful for a former officer or employee to act as agent or attorney for, or aid or assist, anyone in a matter in which he had participated. The House Judiciary Committee struck the underlined words, and the bill became law without them. It should be noted also that the repealed provisions of 18 U.S.C. 283 made the distinction between one's acting as agent or attorney for another and his aiding or assisting another.

HISTORICAL AND STATUTORY NOTES

Codifications

Section 330016(2)(D) of Pub.L. 103–322, directing that this section be amended by inserting "under this title or" after "be fined" and by inserting "whichever is greater," before "or imprisoned", was executed to subsec. (b) of this section, rather than subsec. (c) of this section, as the probable intent of Congress.

A prior § 201, Act June 25, 1948, c. 645, 62 Stat. 691, which prescribed penalties for anyone who offered or gave anything of value to an officer or other person to influence his decisions, was eliminated in the general amendment of this chapter by Pub.L. 87–849, and is substantially covered by revised § 201.

Effective and Applicability Provisions

1994 Acts. Section 330011(b) of Pub.L. 103–322 provided in part that the amendment made by such section, amending directory language of section 46(b) of Pub.L. 99–646 (which amended subsec. (b) of this section), was to take effect as of the date on which section 46(b) of Pub.L. 99–646 took effect; for such effective date, see section 46(m) of Pub.L. 99–646, set out as a note under this section.

1986 Acts. Section 46(m) of Pub.L. 99–646 provided that: "The amendments made by this section [to this section] shall take effect 30 days after the date of enactment of this Act [Nov. 10, 1986]."

1970 Acts. Amendment by Pub.L. 91–405 effective on Sept. 22, 1970, see section 206(b) of Pub.L. 91–405, summarized in a note set out under section 25a of Title 2, The Congress.

1962 Acts. Section 4 of Pub.L. 87–849 provided that: "This Act [adding sections 201 to 209, and 218 of this title, redesignating sections 214, 215, 217 to 222 as 210, 211, 212 to 217 of this title respectively, repealing sections 223, 281 to 284, 434, and 1914 of this title, and section 99 of Title 5, and enacting provisions set out as notes under sections 281 and 282 of this title] shall take effect ninety days after the date of its enactment [Oct. 23, 1962]."

Prior Provisions

Provisions similar to those comprising this section were contained in former §§ 201 to 213 of this title, prior to the general amendment of this chapter by Pub.L. 87–849.

Short Title

2003 Amendments. Pub.L. 108–198, § 1, Dec. 19, 2003, 117 Stat. 2899, provided that: "This Act [enacting 18 U.S.C.A. §§ 212 and 213, and repealing former 18 U.S.C.A. §§ 212 and 213] may be cited as the 'Preserving Independence of Financial Institution Examinations Act of 2003'."

1996 Amendments. Pub.L. 104–177, § 1, Aug. 6, 1996, 110 Stat. 1563, provided that: "This Act [amending section 205 of this title] may be cited as the 'Federal Employee Representation Improvement Act of 1996'."

1986 Amendments. Pub.L. 99–370, § 1, Aug. 4, 1986, 100 Stat. 779, provided that: "This Act [amending section 215 of this title and enacting a provision set out as a note under section 215 of this title] may be cited as the 'Bank Bribery Amendments Act of 1985'."

Canal Zone

Applicability of section to Canal Zone, see § 14 of this title.

EXECUTIVE ORDERS

EXECUTIVE ORDER NO. 11222

Ex. Ord. No. 11222, May 8, 1965, 30 F.R. 6469, as amended Ex. Ord. No. 11590, Apr. 23, 1971, 36 F.R. 7831; Ex. Ord. 12107, Dec. 28, 1978, 44 F.R. 1055; Ex. Ord. No. 12565, Sept. 25, 1986, 51 F.R. 34437, which related to standards of ethical conduct for government officers and employees, was revoked by Ex. Ord. No. 12674, Apr. 12, 1989, 54 F.R. 15159, as amended set out as a note under section 7301 of Title 5, Government Organization and Employees. Ex. Ord. No. 12565, which amended Ex. Ord. No. 11222, was also revoked by Ex. Ord. No. 12674.

§ 202. Definitions

(a) For the purpose of sections 203, 205, 207, 208, and 209 of this title the term "special Government employee" shall mean an officer or employee of the executive or legislative branch of the United States Government, of any independent agency of the United States or of the District of Columbia, who is retained, designated, appointed, or employed to perform, with or without compensation, for not to exceed one hundred and thirty days during any period of three hundred and sixty-five consecutive days, temporary duties either on a full-time or intermittent basis, a part-time United States commissioner, a part-time United States magistrate judge, or, regardless of the number of days of appointment, an independent counsel appointed under chapter 40 of title 28 and any person appointed by that independent counsel under section 594(c) of title 28. Notwithstanding the next preceding sentence, every person serving as a part-time local representative of a Member of Congress in the Member's home district or State shall be classified as a special Government employee. Notwithstanding section 29(c) and (d) of the Act of August 10, 1956 (70A Stat. 632; 5 U.S.C. 30r(c) and (d)), a Reserve officer of the Armed Forces, or an officer of the National Guard of the United States, unless otherwise an officer or employee of the United States, shall be classified as a special Government employee while on active duty solely for training. A Reserve officer of the Armed Forces or an officer of the National Guard of the United States who is voluntarily serving a period of extended active duty in excess of one hundred and thirty days shall be classified as an officer of the United States within the meaning of section 203 and sections 205 through 209 and 218. A Reserve officer of the Armed Forces or an officer of the National Guard of the United States who is serving involuntarily shall be classified as a special Government employee. The terms "officer or employee" and "special Government employee" as used in sections 203, 205, 207 through 209, and 218, shall not include enlisted members of the Armed Forces.

(b) For the purposes of sections 205 and 207 of this title, the term "official responsibility" means the direct administrative or operating authority, whether intermediate or final, and either exercisable alone or with others, and either personally or through subordinates, to approve, disapprove, or otherwise direct Government action.

(c) Except as otherwise provided in such sections, the terms "officer" and "employee" in sections 203, 205, 207 through 209, and 218 of this title shall not include the President, the Vice President, a Member of Congress, or a Federal judge.

(d) The term "Member of Congress" in sections 204 and 207 means—

(1) a United States Senator; and

(2) a Representative in, or a Delegate or Resident Commissioner to, the House of Representatives.

(e) As used in this chapter, the term—

(1) "executive branch" includes each executive agency as defined in title 5, and any other entity or administrative unit in the executive branch;

(2) "judicial branch" means the Supreme Court of the United States; the United States courts of appeals; the United States district courts; the Court of International Trade; the United States bankruptcy courts; any court created pursuant to article I of the United States Constitution, including the Court of Appeals for the Armed Forces, the United States Court of Federal Claims, and the United States Tax Court, but not including a court of a territory or possession of the United States; the Federal Judicial Center; and any other agency, office, or entity in the judicial branch; and

(3) "legislative branch" means—

(A) the Congress; and

(B) the Office of the Architect of the Capitol, the United States Botanic Garden, the Government Accountability Office, the Government Printing Office, the Library of Congress, the Office of Technology Assessment, the Congressional Budget Office, the United States Capitol Police, and any other agency, entity, office, or commission established in the legislative branch.

(Added Pub.L. 87–849, § 1(a), Oct. 23, 1962, 76 Stat. 1121, and amended Pub.L. 90–578, Title III, § 301(b), Oct. 17, 1968, 82 Stat. 1115; Pub.L. 100–191, § 3(a), Dec. 15, 1987, 101 Stat. 1306; Pub.L. 101–194, Title IV, § 401, Nov. 30, 1989, 103 Stat. 1747; Pub.L. 101–280, § 5(a), May 4, 1990, 104 Stat. 158; Pub.L. 101–650, Title III, § 321, Dec. 1, 1990, 104 Stat. 5117; Pub.L. 102–572, Title IX, § 902(b)(1), Oct. 29, 1992, 106 Stat. 4516; Pub.L. 103–337, Div. A, Title IX, § 924(d)(1)(B), Oct. 5, 1994, 108 Stat. 2832; Pub.L. 108–271, § 8(b), July 7, 2004, 118 Stat. 814.)

HISTORICAL AND STATUTORY NOTES

References in Text

Section 29(c) and (d) of the Act of August 10, 1956, referred to in subsec. (a), was classified to former § 30r(c) and (d) of Title 5, and is now covered by 5 U.S.C.A. §§ 502, 2105 and 5534.

Effective and Applicability Provisions

1990 Acts. Amendment by Pub.L. 101–280 effective on May 4, 1990, see section 11 of Pub.L. 101–280, set out as a note under section 101 of Appendix 6 to Title 5, Government Organization and Employees.

1987 Acts. Amendment by Pub.L. 100–191 effective Dec. 15, 1987, applicable both to independent counsel proceedings initiated prior to, and still pending on, that date as well as to independent counsel proceedings initiated and independent counsels appointed on and after that date, see section 591 of Title 28, Judiciary and Judicial Procedure.

1968 Acts. Amendment by Pub.L. 90–578 effective Oct. 17, 1968, except when a later effective date is applicable, which is the earlier of date when implementation of amendment by appointment of magistrates and assumption of office takes place on third anniversary of enactment of Pub.L. 90–578 on Oct. 17, 1968, see § 403 of Pub.L. 90–578, set out as a note under § 631 of Title 28, Judiciary and Judicial Procedure.

1962 Acts. Section effective 90 days after Oct. 23, 1962, see § 4 of Pub.L. 87–849, set out as a note under § 201 of this title.

Change of Name

"United States magistrate judge" substituted for "United States magistrate" in subsec. (a) pursuant to section 321 of Pub.L. 101–650, set out as a note under 28 U.S.C.A. § 631.

United States magistrate appointed under section 631 of Title 28, Judiciary and Judicial Procedure, to be known as United States magistrate judge after Dec. 1, 1990, with any reference to United States magistrate or magistrate in Title 28, in any other Federal statute, etc., deemed a reference to

United States magistrate judge appointed under section 631 of Title 28, see section 321 of Pub.L. 101–650, set out as a note under section 631 of Title 28.

Prior Provisions

A prior § 202, Act June 25, 1948, c. 645, 62 Stat. 691, which prescribed penalties for any officer or other person who accepted or solicited anything of value to influence his decision, was eliminated in the general amendment of this chapter by Pub.L. 87–849, and is substantially covered by revised § 201.

Standards of Ethical Conduct for Special Government Employees

Standards of ethical conduct for special government employees, see Part III of Ex. Ord. No. 11222, May 8, 1965, 30 F.R. 6469, set out as a note under § 201 of this title.

Canal Zone

Applicability of section to Canal Zone, see § 14 of this title.

§ 203. Compensation to Members of Congress, officers, and others in matters affecting the Government

(a) Whoever, otherwise than as provided by law for the proper discharge of official duties, directly or indirectly—

(1) demands, seeks, receives, accepts, or agrees to receive or accept any compensation for any representational services, as agent or attorney or otherwise, rendered or to be rendered either personally or by another—

(A) at a time when such person is a Member of Congress, Member of Congress Elect, Delegate, Delegate Elect, Resident Commissioner, or Resident Commissioner Elect; or

(B) at a time when such person is an officer or employee or Federal judge of the United States in the executive, legislative, or judicial branch of the Government, or in any agency of the United States,

in relation to any proceeding, application, request for a ruling or other determination, contract, claim, controversy, charge, accusation, arrest, or other particular matter in which the United States is a party or has a direct and substantial interest, before any department, agency, court, court-martial, officer, or any civil, military, or naval commission; or

(2) knowingly gives, promises, or offers any compensation for any such representational services rendered or to be rendered at a time when the person to whom the compensation is given, promised, or offered, is or was such a Member, Member Elect, Delegate, Delegate Elect, Commissioner, Commissioner Elect, Federal judge, officer, or employee;

shall be subject to the penalties set forth in section 216 of this title.

(b) Whoever, otherwise than as provided by law for the proper discharge of official duties, directly or indirectly—

(1) demands, seeks, receives, accepts, or agrees to receive or accept any compensation for any representational services, as agent or attorney or otherwise, rendered or to be rendered either personally or by another, at a time when such person is an officer or employee of the District of Columbia, in relation to any proceeding, application, request for a ruling or other determination, contract, claim, controversy, charge, accusation, arrest, or other particular matter in which the District of Columbia is a party or has a direct and substantial interest, before any department, agency, court, officer, or commission; or

(2) knowingly gives, promises, or offers any compensation for any such representational services rendered or to be rendered at a time when the person to whom the compensation is given, promised, or offered, is or was an officer or employee of the District of Columbia;

shall be subject to the penalties set forth in section 216 of this title.

(c) A special Government employee shall be subject to subsections (a) and (b) only in relation to a particular matter involving a specific party or parties—

(1) in which such employee has at any time participated personally and substantially as a Government employee or as a special Government employee through decision, approval, disapproval, recommendation, the rendering of advice, investigation or otherwise; or

(2) which is pending in the department or agency of the Government in which such employee is serving except that paragraph (2) of this subsection shall not apply in the case of a special Government employee who has served in such department or agency no more than sixty days during the immediately preceding period of three hundred and sixty-five consecutive days.

(d) Nothing in this section prevents an officer or employee, including a special Government employee, from acting, with or without compensation, as agent or attorney for or otherwise representing his parents, spouse, child, or any person for whom, or for any estate for which, he is serving as guardian, executor, administrator, trustee, or other personal fiduciary except—

(1) in those matters in which he has participated personally and substantially as a Government employee or as a special Government employee through decision, approval, disapproval, recommendation, the rendering of advice, investigation, or otherwise; or

(2) in those matters that are the subject of his official responsibility,

subject to approval by the Government official responsible for appointment to his position.

(e) Nothing in this section prevents a special Government employee from acting as agent or attorney for another person in the performance of work under a grant by, or a contract with or for the benefit of, the United States if the head of the department or agency concerned with the grant or contract certifies in writing that the national interest so requires and publishes such certification in the Federal Register.

(f) Nothing in this section prevents an individual from giving testimony under oath or from making statements required to be made under penalty of perjury.

(Added Pub.L. 87–849, § 1(a), Oct. 23, 1962, 76 Stat. 1121, and amended Pub.L. 91–405, Title II, § 204(d) (2), (3), Sept. 22, 1970, 84 Stat. 853; Pub.L. 99–646, § 47(a), Nov. 10, 1986, 100 Stat. 3604; Pub.L. 101–194, Title IV, § 402, Nov. 30, 1989, 103 Stat. 1748; Pub.L. 101–280, § 5(b), May 4, 1990, 104 Stat. 159.)

HISTORICAL AND STATUTORY NOTES

Effective and Applicability Provisions

1990 Acts. Amendment by Pub.L. 101–280 effective on May 4, 1990, see section 11 of Pub.L. 101–280, set out as a note under section 101 of Appendix 6 to Title 5, Government Organization and Employees.

1986 Acts. Section 47(b) of Pub.L. 99–646 provided that: "The amendments made by this section [amending this section] shall take effect 30 days after the date of enactment of this Act [Nov. 10, 1986]."

1970 Acts. Amendment by Pub.L. 91–405 effective on Sept. 22, 1970, see section 206(b) of Pub.L. 91–405, summarized in a note set out under section 25a of Title 2, The Congress.

1962 Acts. Section effective 90 days after Oct. 23, 1962, see § 4 of Pub.L. 87–849, set out as a note under § 201 of this title.

Prior Provisions

A prior § 203, Act June 25, 1948, c. 645, 62 Stat. 692, which related to the acceptance or demand by district attorneys, or marshals and their assistants of any fee other than provided by law, was eliminated in the general amendment of this chapter by Pub.L. 87–849 and is substantially covered by revised § 201.

Provisions similar to those comprising this section were contained in former § 281 of this title prior to the repeal of such section and the general amendment of this chapter by Pub.L. 87–849.

Private Sector Representatives on United States Delegations to International Telecommunications Meetings and Conferences

Pub.L. 97–241, Title I, § 120, Aug. 24, 1982, 96 Stat. 280, provided that:

"**(a)** Sections 203, 205, 207, and 208 of title 18, United States Code [sections 203, 205, 207, and 208 of this title], shall not apply to a private sector representative on the United States delegation to an international telecommunications meeting or conference who is specifically designated to speak on behalf of or otherwise represent the interests of the United States at such meeting or conference with respect to a particular matter, if the Secretary of State (or the Secretary's designee) certifies that no Government employee on the delegation is as well qualified to represent United States interests with respect to such matter and that such designation serves the national interest. All such representatives shall have on file with the Department of State the financial disclosure report required for special Government employees.

"**(b)** As used in this section, the term 'international telecommunications meeting or conference' means the conferences of the International Telecommunications Union, meetings of its International Consultative Committees for Radio and for Telephone and Telegraph, and such other international telecommunications meetings or conferences as the Secretary of State may designate."

Canal Zone

Applicability of section to Canal Zone, see § 14 of this title.

§ 204. Practice in United States Court of Federal Claims or the United States Court of Appeals for the Federal Circuit by Members of Congress

Whoever, being a Member of Congress or Member of Congress Elect, practices in the United States Court of Federal Claims or the United States Court of Appeals for the Federal Circuit shall be subject to the penalties set forth in section 216 of this title.

(Added Pub.L. 87–849, § 1(a), Oct. 23, 1962, 76 Stat. 1122, and amended Pub.L. 91–405, Title II, § 204(d) (2), Sept. 22, 1970, 84 Stat. 853; Pub.L. 97–164, Title I, § 147, Apr. 2, 1982, 96 Stat. 45; Pub.L. 101–194, Title IV, § 403, Nov. 30, 1989, 103 Stat. 1749; Pub.L. 102–572, Title IX, § 902(b)(1), Oct. 29, 1992, 106 Stat. 4516.)

HISTORICAL AND STATUTORY NOTES

Effective and Applicability Provisions

1982 Acts. Amendment by Pub.L. 97–164 effective Oct. 1, 1982, see section 402 of Pub.L. 97–164, set out as a note under section 171 of Title 28, Judiciary and Judicial Procedure.

1970 Acts. Amendment by Pub.L. 91–405 effective on Sept. 22, 1970, see section 206(b) of Pub.L. 91–405, summarized in a note set out under section 25a of Title 2, The Congress.

1962 Acts. Section effective 90 days after Oct. 23, 1962, see § 4 of Pub.L. 87–849, set out as a note under § 201 of this title.

Change of Name

References to United States Claims Court deemed to refer to United States Court of Federal Claims and references to Claims Court deemed to refer to Court of Federal Claims, see section 902(b) of Pub.L. 102–572, set out as a note under section 171 of Title 28, Judiciary and Judicial Procedure.

Prior Provisions

A prior § 204, Act June 25, 1948, c. 645, 62 Stat. 692, which related to an offer to influence a Member of Congress, was eliminated in the general amendment of this chapter by Pub.L. 87–849 and is substantially covered by revised § 201.

Provisions similar to those comprising this section were contained in former § 282 of this title prior to the repeal of such section and the general amendment of this chapter by Pub.L. 87–849.

§ 205. Activities of officers and employees in claims against and other matters affecting the Government

(a) Whoever, being an officer or employee of the United States in the executive, legislative, or judicial branch of the Government or in any agency of the United States, other than in the proper discharge of his official duties—

(1) acts as agent or attorney for prosecuting any claim against the United States, or receives any gratuity, or any share of or interest in any such claim, in consideration of assistance in the prosecution of such claim; or

(2) acts as agent or attorney for anyone before any department, agency, court, court-martial, officer, or civil, military, or naval commission in connection with any covered matter in which the United States is a party or has a direct and substantial interest;

shall be subject to the penalties set forth in section 216 of this title.

(b) Whoever, being an officer or employee of the District of Columbia or an officer or employee of the Office of the United States Attorney for the District of Columbia, otherwise than in the proper discharge of official duties—

(1) acts as agent or attorney for prosecuting any claim against the District of Columbia, or receives any gratuity, or any share of or interest in any such claim in consideration of assistance in the prosecution of such claim; or

(2) acts as agent or attorney for anyone before any department, agency, court, officer, or commission in connection with any covered matter in which the District of Columbia is a party or has a direct and substantial interest;

shall be subject to the penalties set forth in section 216 of this title.

(c) A special Government employee shall be subject to subsections (a) and (b) only in relation to a covered matter involving a specific party or parties—

(1) in which he has at any time participated personally and substantially as a Government employee or special Government employee through decision, approval, disapproval, recommendation, the rendering of advice, investigation, or otherwise; or

(2) which is pending in the department or agency of the Government in which he is serving.

Paragraph (2) shall not apply in the case of a special Government employee who has served in such department or agency no more than sixty days during the immediately preceding period of three hundred and sixty-five consecutive days.

(d)(1) Nothing in subsection (a) or (b) prevents an officer or employee, if not inconsistent with the faithful performance of that officer's or employee's duties, from acting without compensation as agent or attorney for, or otherwise representing—

(A) any person who is the subject of disciplinary, loyalty, or other personnel administration proceedings in connection with those proceedings; or

(B) except as provided in paragraph (2), any cooperative, voluntary, professional, recreational, or similar organization or group not established or operated for profit, if a majority of the organization's or group's members are current officers or employees of the United States or of the District of Columbia, or their spouses or dependent children.

(2) Paragraph (1)(B) does not apply with respect to a covered matter that—

(A) is a claim under subsection (a)(1) or (b)(1);

(B) is a judicial or administrative proceeding where the organization or group is a party; or

(C) involves a grant, contract, or other agreement (including a request for any such grant, contract, or agreement) providing for the disbursement of Federal funds to the organization or group.

(e) Nothing in subsection (a) or (b) prevents an officer or employee, including a special Government employee, from acting, with or without compensation, as agent or attorney for, or otherwise representing, his parents, spouse, child, or any person for whom, or for any estate for which, he is serving as guardian, executor, administrator, trustee, or other personal fiduciary except—

(1) in those matters in which he has participated personally and substantially as a Government employee or special Government employee through decision, approval, disapproval, recommendation, the rendering of advice, investigation, or otherwise, or

(2) in those matters which are the subject of his official responsibility,

subject to approval by the Government official responsible for appointment to his position.

(f) Nothing in subsection (a) or (b) prevents a special Government employee from acting as agent or attorney for another person in the performance of work under a grant by, or a contract with or for the benefit of, the United States if the head of the department or agency concerned with the grant or contract certifies in writing that the national interest so requires and publishes such certification in the Federal Register.

(g) Nothing in this section prevents an officer or employee from giving testimony under oath or from making statements required to be made under penalty for perjury or contempt.

(h) For the purpose of this section, the term "covered matter" means any judicial or other proceeding, application, request for a ruling or other determination, contract, claim, controversy, investigation, charge, accusation, arrest, or other particular matter.

(i) Nothing in this section prevents an employee from acting pursuant to—

(1) chapter 71 of title 5;

(2) section 1004 or chapter 12 of title 39;

(3) section 3 of the Tennessee Valley Authority Act of 1933 (16 U.S.C. 831b);

(4) chapter 10 of title I of the Foreign Service Act of 1980 (22 U.S.C. 4104 et seq.); or

(5) any provision of any other Federal or District of Columbia law that authorizes labor-management relations between an agency or instrumentality of the United States or the District of Columbia and any labor organization that represents its employees.

(Added Pub.L. 87–849, § 1(a), Oct. 23, 1962, 76 Stat. 1122, and amended Pub.L. 101–194, Title IV, § 404, Nov. 30, 1989, 103 Stat. 1750; Pub.L. 101–280, § 5(c), May 4, 1990, 104 Stat. 159; Pub.L. 104–177, § 2, Aug. 6, 1996, 110 Stat. 1563; Pub.L. 107–273, Div. B, Title IV, § 4002(a)(9), Nov. 2, 2002, 116 Stat. 1807.)

HISTORICAL AND STATUTORY NOTES

References in Text

Section 3 of the Tennessee Valley Authority Act of 1933, referred to in subsec. (i)(3), is classified to section 831b of Title 16, Conservation.

Chapter 10 of title I of the Foreign Service Act of 1980, referred to in subsec. (i)(4), is classified to section 4101 et seq. of Title 22, Foreign Relations and Intercourse.

Effective and Applicability Provisions

1990 Acts. Amendment by Pub.L. 101–280 effective on May 4, 1990, see section 11 of Pub.L. 101–280, set out as a note under section 101 of Appendix 6 to Title 5, Government Organization and Employees.

1962 Acts. Section effective 90 days after Oct. 23, 1962, see § 4 of Pub.L. 87–849, set out as a note under § 201 of this title.

Delegation of Authority

Authority of the President under this section delegated to department or agency heads, see Part V of Ex. Ord. No. 11222, May 8, 1965, 30 F.R. 6469, set out as a note under § 201 of this title.

Prior Provisions

A prior § 205, Act June 25, 1948, c. 645, 62 Stat. 692, which related to the acceptance by a Member of Congress of anything of value to influence him, was eliminated in the general amendment of this chapter by Pub.L. 87–849 and is substantially covered by revised § 201.

Provisions similar to those comprising this section were contained in former § 283 of this title prior to the repeal of such section and the general amendment of this chapter by Pub.L. 87–849.

Canal Zone

Applicability of section to Canal Zone, see § 14 of this title.

§ 206. Exemption of retired officers of the uniformed services

Sections 203 and 205 of this title shall not apply to a retired officer of the uniformed services of the United States while not on active duty and not otherwise an officer or employee of the United States, or to any person specially excepted by Act of Congress.

(Added Pub.L. 87–849, § 1(a), Oct. 23, 1962, 76 Stat. 1123.)

HISTORICAL AND STATUTORY NOTES

Effective and Applicability Provisions

1962 Acts. Section effective 90 days after Oct. 23, 1962, see § 4 of Pub.L. 87–849, set out as a note under § 201 of this title.

Prior Provisions

A prior § 206, Act June 25, 1948, c. 645, 62 Stat. 692, which related to an offer to a judge of judicial officer to influence him, was eliminated in the general amendment of this chapter by Pub.L. 87–849 and is substantially covered by revised § 201.

§ 207. Restrictions on former officers, employees, and elected officials of the executive and legislative branches

(a) Restrictions on all officers and employees of the executive branch and certain other agencies.—

(1) Permanent restrictions on representation on particular matters.—Any person who is an officer or employee (including any special Government employee) of the executive branch of the United States (including any independent agency of the United States), or of the District of Columbia, and who, after the termination of his or her service or employment with the United States or the District of Columbia, knowingly makes, with the intent to influence, any communication to or appearance before any officer or employee of any department, agency, court, or court-martial of the United States or the District of Columbia, on behalf of any other person (except the United States or the District of Columbia) in connection with a particular matter—

(A) in which the United States or the District of Columbia is a party or has a direct and substantial interest,

(B) in which the person participated personally and substantially as such officer or employee, and

(C) which involved a specific party or specific parties at the time of such participation,

shall be punished as provided in section 216 of this title.

(2) Two-year restrictions concerning particular matters under official responsibility.—Any person subject to the restrictions contained in paragraph (1) who, within 2 years after the termination of his or her service or employment with the United States or the District of Columbia, knowingly makes, with the intent to influence, any communication to or appearance before any officer or employee of any department, agency, court, or court-martial of the United States or the District of Columbia, on behalf of any other person (except the United States or the District of Columbia), in connection with a particular matter—

(A) in which the United States or the District of Columbia is a party or has a direct and substantial interest,

(B) which such person knows or reasonably should know was actually pending under his or her official responsibility as such officer or employee within a period of 1 year before the termination of his or her service or employment with the United States or the District of Columbia, and

(C) which involved a specific party or specific parties at the time it was so pending,

shall be punished as provided in section 216 of this title.

(3) Clarification of restrictions.—The restrictions contained in paragraphs (1) and (2) shall apply—

(A) in the case of an officer or employee of the executive branch of the United States (including any independent agency), only with respect to communications to or appearances before any officer or employee of any department, agency, court, or court-martial of the United States on behalf of any other person (except the United States), and only with respect to a matter in which the United States is a party or has a direct and substantial interest; and

(B) in the case of an officer or employee of the District of Columbia, only with respect to communications to or appearances before any officer or employee of any department, agency, or court of the District of Columbia on behalf of any other person (except the District of Columbia), and only with respect to a matter in which the District of Columbia is a party or has a direct and substantial interest.

(b) One-year restrictions on aiding or advising.—

(1) In general.—Any person who is a former officer or employee of the executive branch of the United States (including any independent agency) and is subject to the restrictions contained in subsection (a)(1), or any person who is a former officer or employee of the legislative branch or a former Member of Congress, who personally and substantially participated in any ongoing trade or treaty negotiation on behalf of the United States within the 1-year period preceding the date on which his or her service or employment with the United States terminated, and who had access to information concerning such trade or treaty negotiation which is exempt from disclosure under section 552 of title 5, which is so designated by the appropriate department or agency, and which the person knew or should have known was so designated, shall not, on the basis of that information, knowingly represent, aid, or advise any other person (except the United States) concerning such ongoing trade or treaty negotiation for a period of 1 year after his or her service or employment with the United States terminates. Any person who violates this subsection shall be punished as provided in section 216 of this title.

(2) Definition.—For purposes of this paragraph—

(A) the term "trade negotiation" means negotiations which the President determines to undertake to enter into a trade agreement pursuant to section 1102 of the Omnibus Trade and Competitiveness Act of 1988, and does not include any action taken before that determination is made; and

(B) the term "treaty" means an international agreement made by the President that requires the advice and consent of the Senate.

(c) One-year restrictions on certain senior personnel of the executive branch and independent agencies.—

(1) Restrictions.—In addition to the restrictions set forth in subsections (a) and (b), any person who is an officer or employee (including any special Government employee) of the executive branch of the United States (including an independent agency), who is referred to in paragraph (2), and who, within 1 year after the termination of his or her service or employment as such officer or employee, knowingly makes, with the intent to influence, any communication to or appearance before any officer or employee of the department or agency in which such person served within 1 year before such termination, on behalf of any other person (except the

United States), in connection with any matter on which such person seeks official action by any officer or employee of such department or agency, shall be punished as provided in section 216 of this title.

(2) Persons to whom restrictions apply.—(A) Paragraph (1) shall apply to a person (other than a person subject to the restrictions of subsection (d))—

(i) employed at a rate of pay specified in or fixed according to subchapter II of chapter 53 of title 5,

(ii) employed in a position which is not referred to in clause (i) and for which that person is paid at a rate of basic pay which is equal to or greater than 86.5 percent of the rate of basic pay for level II of the Executive Schedule, or, for a period of 2 years following the enactment of the National Defense Authorization Act for Fiscal Year 2004, a person who, on the day prior to the enactment of that Act, was employed in a position which is not referred to in clause (i) and for which the rate of basic pay, exclusive of any locality-based pay adjustment under section 5304 or section 5304a of title 5, was equal to or greater than the rate of basic pay payable for level 5 of the Senior Executive Service on the day prior to the enactment of that Act,

(iii) appointed by the President to a position under section 105(a)(2)(B) of title 3 or by the Vice President to a position under section 106(a)(1)(B) of title 3,

(iv) employed in a position which is held by an active duty commissioned officer of the uniformed services who is serving in a grade or rank for which the pay grade (as specified in section 201 of title 37) is pay grade O–7 or above; or

(v) assigned from a private sector organization to an agency under chapter 37 of title 5.

(B) Paragraph (1) shall not apply to a special Government employee who serves less than 60 days in the 1-year period before his or her service or employment as such employee terminates.

(C) At the request of a department or agency, the Director of the Office of Government Ethics may waive the restrictions contained in paragraph (1) with respect to any position, or category of positions, referred to in clause (ii) or (iv) of subparagraph (A), in such department or agency if the Director determines that—

(i) the imposition of the restrictions with respect to such position or positions would create an undue hardship on the department or agency in obtaining qualified personnel to fill such position or positions, and

(ii) granting the waiver would not create the potential for use of undue influence or unfair advantage.

(d) Restrictions on very senior personnel of the executive branch and independent agencies.—

(1) Restrictions.—In addition to the restrictions set forth in subsections (a) and (b), any person who—

(A) serves in the position of Vice President of the United States,

(B) is employed in a position in the executive branch of the United States (including any independent agency) at a rate of pay payable for level I of the Executive Schedule or employed in a position in the Executive Office of the President at a rate of pay payable for level II of the Executive Schedule, or

(C) is appointed by the President to a position under section 105(a)(2)(A) of title 3 or by the Vice President to a position under section 106(a)(1)(A) of title 3,

and who, within 1 year after the termination of that person's service in that position, knowingly makes, with the intent to influence, any communication to or appearance before any person described in paragraph (2), on behalf of any other person (except the United States), in connection with any matter on which such person seeks official action by any officer or employee of the executive branch of the United States, shall be punished as provided in section 216 of this title.

(2) Persons who may not be contacted.—The persons referred to in paragraph (1) with respect to appearances or communications by a person in a position described in subparagraph (A), (B), or (C) of paragraph (1) are—

(A) any officer or employee of any department or agency in which such person served in such position within a period of 1 year before such person's service or employment with the United States Government terminated, and

(B) any person appointed to a position in the executive branch which is listed in section 5312, 5313, 5314, 5315, or 5316 of title 5.

(e) Restrictions on Members of Congress and officers and employees of the legislative branch.—

(1) Members of Congress and elected officers.—(A) Any person who is a Member of Congress or an elected officer of either House of Congress and who, within 1 year after that person leaves office, knowingly makes, with the intent to influence, any communication to or appearance before any of the persons described in subparagraph (B) or (C), on behalf of any other person (except the United States) in connection with any matter on which such former Member of Congress or elected officer seeks action by a Member, officer, or employee of either House of Congress, in his or her official capacity, shall be punished as provided in section 216 of this title.

(B) The persons referred to in subparagraph (A) with respect to appearances or communications by a former Member of Congress are any Member, officer, or employee of either House of Congress, and any employee of any other legislative office of the Congress.

(C) The persons referred to in subparagraph (A) with respect to appearances or communications by a former elected officer are any Member, officer, or employee of the House of Congress in which the elected officer served.

(2) Personal staff.—(A) Any person who is an employee of a Senator or an employee of a Member of the House of Representatives and who, within 1 year after the termination of that employment, knowingly makes, with the intent to influence, any communication to or appearance before any of the persons described in subparagraph (B), on behalf of any other person (except the United States) in connection with any matter on which such former employee seeks action by a Member, officer, or employee of either House of Congress, in his or her official capacity, shall be punished as provided in section 216 of this title.

(B) The persons referred to in subparagraph (A) with respect to appearances or communications by a person who is a former employee are the following:

(i) the Senator or Member of the House of Representatives for whom that person was an employee; and

(ii) any employee of that Senator or Member of the House of Representatives.

(3) Committee staff.—Any person who is an employee of a committee of Congress and who, within 1 year after the termination of that person's employment on such committee, knowingly makes, with the intent to influence, any communication to or appearance before any person who is a Member or an employee of that committee or who was a Member of the committee in the year immediately prior to the termination of such person's employment by the committee, on behalf of any other person (except the United States) in connection with any matter on which such former employee seeks action by a Member, officer, or employee of either House of Congress, in his or her official capacity, shall be punished as provided in section 216 of this title.

(4) Leadership staff.—(A) Any person who is an employee on the leadership staff of the House of Representatives or an employee on the leadership staff of the Senate and who, within 1 year after the termination of that person's employment on such staff, knowingly makes, with the intent to influence, any communication to or appearance before any of the persons described in subparagraph (B), on behalf of any other person (except the United States) in connection with any matter on which such former employee seeks action by a Member, officer, or employee of either House of Congress, in his or her official capacity, shall be punished as provided in section 216 of this title.

(B) The persons referred to in subparagraph (A) with respect to appearances or communications by a former employee are the following:

(i) in the case of a former employee on the leadership staff of the House of Representatives, those persons are any Member of the leadership of the House of Representatives and any employee on the leadership staff of the House of Representatives; and

(ii) in the case of a former employee on the leadership staff of the Senate, those persons are any Member of the leadership of the Senate and any employee on the leadership staff of the Senate.

(5) Other legislative offices.—(A) Any person who is an employee of any other legislative office of the Congress and who, within 1 year after the termination of that person's employment in such office, knowingly makes, with the intent to influence, any communication to or appearance before any of the persons described in subparagraph (B), on behalf of any other person (except the United States) in connection with any matter on which such former employee seeks action by any officer or employee of such office, in his or her official capacity, shall be punished as provided in section 216 of this title.

(B) The persons referred to in subparagraph (A) with respect to appearances or communications by a former employee are the employees and officers of the former legislative office of the Congress of the former employee.

(6) Limitation on restrictions.—(A) The restrictions contained in paragraphs (2), (3), and (4) apply only to acts by a former employee who, for at least 60 days, in the aggregate, during the 1–year period before that former employee's service as such employee terminated, was paid a rate of basic pay equal to or greater than an amount which is 75 percent of the basic rate of pay payable for a Member of the House of Congress in which such employee was employed.

(B) The restrictions contained in paragraph (5) apply only to acts by a former employee who, for at least 60 days, in the aggregate, during the 1–year period before that former employee's service as such employee terminated, was employed in a position for which the rate of basic pay, exclusive of any locality-based pay adjustment under section 5302 of title 5 (or any comparable adjustment pursuant to interim authority of the President), is equal to or greater than the basic rate of pay payable for level 5 of the Senior Executive Service.

(7) Definitions.—As used in this subsection—

(A) the term "committee of Congress" includes standing committees, joint committees, and select committees;

(B) a person is an employee of a House of Congress if that person is an employee of the Senate or an employee of the House of Representatives;

(C) the term "employee of the House of Representatives" means an employee of a Member of the House of Representatives, an employee of a committee of the House of Representatives, an employee of a joint committee of the Congress whose pay is disbursed by the Clerk of the House of Representatives, and an employee on the leadership staff of the House of Representatives;

(D) the term "employee of the Senate" means an employee of a Senator, an employee of a committee of the Senate, an employee of a joint committee of the Congress whose pay is disbursed by the Secretary of the Senate, and an employee on the leadership staff of the Senate;

(E) a person is an employee of a Member of the House of Representatives if that person is an employee of a Member of the House of Representatives under the clerk hire allowance;

(F) a person is an employee of a Senator if that person is an employee in a position in the office of a Senator;

(G) the term "employee of any other legislative office of the Congress" means an officer or employee of the Architect of the Capitol, the United States Botanic Garden, the Government Accountability Office, the Government Printing Office, the Library of Congress, the Office of Technology Assessment, the Congressional Budget Office, the Copyright Royalty Tribunal, the United States Capitol Police, and any other agency, entity, or office in the legislative branch not covered by paragraph (1), (2), (3), or (4) of this subsection;

(H) the term "employee on the leadership staff of the House of Representatives" means an employee of the office of a Member of the leadership of the House of Representatives described in subparagraph (L), and any elected minority employee of the House of Representatives;

(I) the term "employee on the leadership staff of the Senate" means an employee of the office of a Member of the leadership of the Senate described in subparagraph (M);

(J) the term "Member of Congress" means a Senator or a Member of the House of Representatives;

(K) the term "Member of the House of Representatives" means a Representative in, or a Delegate or Resident Commissioner to, the Congress;

(L) the term "Member of the leadership of the House of Representatives" means the Speaker, majority leader, minority leader, majority whip, minority whip, chief deputy majority whip, chief deputy minority whip, chairman of the Democratic Steering Committee, chairman and vice chairman of the Democratic Caucus, chairman, vice chairman, and secretary of the Republican Conference, chairman of the Republican Research Committee, and chairman of the Republican Policy Committee, of the House of Representatives (or any similar position created on or after the effective date set forth in section 102(a) of the Ethics Reform Act of 1989);

(M) the term "Member of the leadership of the Senate" means the Vice President, and the President pro tempore, Deputy President pro tempore, majority leader, minority leader, majority whip, minority whip, chairman and secretary of the Conference of the Majority, chairman and secretary of the Conference of the Minority, chairman and co-chairman of the Majority Policy Committee, and chairman of the Minority Policy Committee, of the Senate (or any similar position created on or after the effective date set forth in section 102(a) of the Ethics Reform Act of 1989).

(f) Restrictions relating to foreign entities.—

(1) Restrictions.—Any person who is subject to the restrictions contained in subsection (c), (d), or (e) and who knowingly, within 1 year after leaving the position, office, or employment referred to in such subsection—

(A) represents a foreign entity before any officer or employee of any department or agency of the United States with the intent to influence a decision of such officer or employee in carrying out his or her official duties, or

(B) aids or advises a foreign entity with the intent to influence a decision of any officer or employee of any department or agency of the United States, in carrying out his or her official duties,

shall be punished as provided in section 216 of this title.

(2) Special rule for Trade Representative.—With respect to a person who is the United States Trade Representative or Deputy United States Trade Representative, the restrictions described in paragraph (1) shall apply to representing, aiding, or advising foreign entities at any time after the termination of that person's service as the United States Trade Representative.

(3) Definition.—For purposes of this subsection, the term "foreign entity" means the government of a foreign country as defined in section 1(e) of the Foreign Agents Registration Act of 1938, as amended, or a foreign political party as defined in section 1(f) of that Act.

(g) Special rules for detailees.—For purposes of this section, a person who is detailed from one department, agency, or other entity to another department, agency, or other entity shall, during the period such person is detailed, be deemed to be an officer or employee of both departments, agencies, or such entities.

(h) Designations of separate statutory agencies and bureaus.—

(1) Designations.—For purposes of subsection (c) and except as provided in paragraph (2), whenever the Director of the Office of Government Ethics determines that an agency or bureau within a department or agency in the executive branch exercises functions which are distinct and separate from the remaining functions of the department or agency and that there exists no potential for use of undue influence or unfair advantage based on past Government service, the Director shall by rule designate such agency or bureau as a separate department or agency. On an annual basis the Director of the Office of Government Ethics shall review the designations and determinations made under this subparagraph and, in consultation with the department or agency concerned, make such additions and deletions as are necessary. Departments and agencies shall cooperate to the fullest extent with the Director of the Office of Government Ethics in the exercise of his or her responsibilities under this paragraph.

(2) Inapplicability of designations.—No agency or bureau within the Executive Office of the President may be designated under paragraph (1) as a separate department or agency. No designation under paragraph (1) shall apply to persons referred to in subsection (c)(2)(A)(i) or (iii).

(i) Definitions.—For purposes of this section—

(1) the term "officer or employee", when used to describe the person to whom a communication is made or before whom an appearance is made, with the intent to influence, shall include—

(A) in subsections (a), (c), and (d), the President and the Vice President; and

(B) in subsection (f), the President, the Vice President, and Members of Congress;

(2) the term "participated" means an action taken as an officer or employee through decision, approval, disapproval, recommendation, the rendering of advice, investigation, or other such action; and

(3) the term "particular matter" includes any investigation, application, request for a ruling or determination, rulemaking, contract, controversy, claim, charge, accusation, arrest, or judicial or other proceeding.

(j) Exceptions.—

(1) Official government duties.—The restrictions contained in this section shall not apply to acts done in carrying out official duties on behalf of the United States or the District of Columbia or as an elected official of a State or local government.

(2) State and local governments and institutions, hospitals, and organizations.—The restrictions contained in subsections (c), (d), and (e) shall not apply to acts done in carrying out official duties as an employee of—

(A) an agency or instrumentality of a State or local government if the appearance, communication, or representation is on behalf of such government, or

(B) an accredited, degree-granting institution of higher education, as defined in section 101 of the Higher Education Act of 1965, or a hospital or medical research organization, exempted and defined under section 501(c)(3) of the Internal Revenue Code of 1986, if the appearance, communication, or representation is on behalf of such institution, hospital, or organization.

(3) International organizations.—The restrictions contained in this section shall not apply to an appearance or communication on behalf of, or advice or aid to, an international organization in which the United States participates, if the Secretary of State certifies in advance that such activity is in the interests of the United States.

(4) Special knowledge.—The restrictions contained in subsections (c), (d), and (e) shall not prevent an individual from making or providing a statement, which is based on the individual's own special knowledge in the particular area that is the subject of the statement, if no compensation is thereby received.

(5) Exception for scientific or technological information.—The restrictions contained in subsections (a), (c), and (d) shall not apply with respect to the making of communications solely for the purpose of furnishing scientific or technological information, if such communications are made under procedures acceptable to the department or agency concerned or if the head of the department or agency concerned with the particular matter, in consultation with the Director of the Office of Government Ethics, makes a certification, published in the Federal Register, that the former officer or employee has outstanding qualifications in a scientific, technological, or other technical discipline, and is acting with respect to a particular matter which requires such qualifications, and that the national interest would be served by the participation of the former officer or employee. For purposes of this paragraph, the term "officer or employee" includes the Vice President.

(6) Exception for testimony.—Nothing in this section shall prevent an individual from giving testimony under oath, or from making statements required to be made under penalty of perjury. Notwithstanding the preceding sentence—

(A) a former officer or employee of the executive branch of the United States (including any independent agency) who is subject to the restrictions contained in subsection (a)(1) with respect to a particular matter may not, except pursuant to court order, serve as an expert witness for any other person (except the United States) in that matter; and

(B) a former officer or employee of the District of Columbia who is subject to the restrictions contained in subsection (a)(1) with respect to a particular matter may not, except pursuant to court order, serve as an expert witness for any other person (except the District of Columbia) in that matter.

(7) Political parties and campaign committees.—(A) Except as provided in subparagraph (B), the restrictions contained in subsections (c), (d), and (e) shall not apply to a communication or appearance made solely on behalf of a candidate in his or her capacity as a candidate, an authorized committee, a national committee, a national Federal campaign committee, a State committee, or a political party.

(B) Subparagraph (A) shall not apply to—

(i) any communication to, or appearance before, the Federal Election Commission by a former officer or employee of the Federal Election Commission; or

(ii) a communication or appearance made by a person who is subject to the restrictions contained in subsections [1] (c), (d), or (e) if, at the time of the communication or appearance, the person is employed by a person or entity other than—

(I) a candidate, an authorized committee, a national committee, a national Federal campaign committee, a State committee, or a political party; or

(II) a person or entity who represents, aids, or advises only persons or entities described in subclause (I).

(C) For purposes of this paragraph—

(i) the term "candidate" means any person who seeks nomination for election, or election, to Federal or State office or who has authorized others to explore on his or her behalf the possibility of seeking nomination for election, or election, to Federal or State office;

(ii) the term "authorized committee" means any political committee designated in writing by a candidate as authorized to receive contributions or make expenditures to promote the nomination for election, or the election, of such candidate, or to explore the possibility of seeking nomination for election, or the election, of such candidate, except that a political committee that receives contributions or makes expenditures to promote more than 1 candidate may not be designated as an authorized committee for purposes of subparagraph (A);

(iii) the term "national committee" means the organization which, by virtue of the bylaws of a political party, is responsible for the day-to-day operation of such political party at the national level;

(iv) the term "national Federal campaign committee" means an organization that, by virtue of the bylaws of a political party, is established primarily for the purpose of providing assistance, at the national level, to candidates nominated by that party for election to the office of Senator or Representative in, or Delegate or Resident Commissioner to, the Congress;

(v) the term "State committee" means the organization which, by virtue of the bylaws of a political party, is responsible for the day-to-day operation of such political party at the State level;

(vi) the term "political party" means an association, committee, or organization that nominates a candidate for election to any Federal or State elected office whose name appears on the election ballot as the candidate of such association, committee, or organization; and

(vii) the term "State" means a State of the United States, the District of Columbia, the Commonwealth of Puerto Rico, and any territory or possession of the United States.

(k)(1)(A) The President may grant a waiver of a restriction imposed by this section to any officer or employee described in paragraph (2) if the President determines and certifies in writing that it is in the public interest to grant the waiver and that the services of the officer or employee are critically needed for the benefit of the Federal Government. Not more than 25 officers and employees currently employed by the Federal Government at any one time may have been granted waivers under this paragraph.

(B)(i) A waiver granted under this paragraph to any person shall apply only with respect to activities engaged in by that person after that person's Federal Government employment is terminated and only to that person's employment at a Government-owned, contractor operated entity with which the person served as an officer or employee immediately before the person's Federal Government employment began.

(ii) Notwithstanding clause (i), a waiver granted under this paragraph to any person who was an officer or employee of Lawrence Livermore National Laboratory, Los Alamos National Laboratory, or Sandia National Laboratory immediately before the person's Federal Government employment began shall apply to that person's employment by any such national laboratory after the person's employment by the Federal Government is terminated.

(2) Waivers under paragraph (1) may be granted only to civilian officers and employees of the executive branch, other than officers and employees in the Executive Office of the President.

(3) A certification under paragraph (1) shall take effect upon its publication in the Federal Register and shall identify—

(A) the officer or employee covered by the waiver by name and by position, and

(B) the reasons for granting the waiver.

A copy of the certification shall also be provided to the Director of the Office of Government Ethics.

(4) The President may not delegate the authority provided by this subsection.

(5)(A) Each person granted a waiver under this subsection shall prepare reports, in accordance with subparagraph (B), stating whether the person has engaged in activities otherwise prohibited by this section for each six-month period described in subparagraph (B), and if so, what those activities were.

(B) A report under subparagraph (A) shall cover each six-month period beginning on the date of the termination of the person's Federal Government employment (with respect to which the waiver under this subsection was granted) and ending two years after that date. Such report shall be filed with the President and the Director of the Office of Government Ethics not later than 60 days after the end of the six-month period covered by the report. All reports filed with the Director under this paragraph shall be made available for public inspection and copying.

(C) If a person fails to file any report in accordance with subparagraphs (A) and (B), the President shall revoke the waiver and shall notify the person of the revocation. The revocation shall take effect upon the person's receipt of the notification and shall remain in effect until the report is filed.

(D) Any person who is granted a waiver under this subsection shall be ineligible for appointment in the civil service unless all reports required of such person by subparagraphs (A) and (B) have been filed.

(E) As used in this subsection, the term "civil service" has the meaning given that term in section 2101 of title 5.

(*l*) Contract advice by former details.—Whoever, being an employee of a private sector organization assigned to an agency under chapter 37 of title 5, within one year after the end of that assignment, knowingly represents or aids, counsels, or assists in representing any other person (except the United States) in connection with any contract with that agency shall be punished as provided in section 216 of this title.

(Added Pub.L. 87–849, § 1(a), Oct. 23, 1962, 76 Stat. 1123, and amended Pub.L. 95–521, Title V, § 501(a), Oct. 26, 1978, 92 Stat. 1864; Pub.L. 96–28, §§ 1, 2, June 22, 1979, 93 Stat. 76; Pub.L. 101–189, Div. A, Title VIII, § 814(d)(2), Nov. 29, 1989, 103 Stat. 1499; Pub.L. 101–194, Title I, § 101(a), Nov. 30, 1989, 103 Stat. 1716; Pub.L. 101–280, §§ 2(a), 5(d), May 4, 1990, 104 Stat. 149, 159; Pub.L. 101–509,Title V, § 529 [Title I, § 101 (b)(8)(A)], Nov. 5, 1990, 104 Stat.440; Pub.L. 102–25, Title VII, § 705(a), Apr. 6, 1991, 105 Stat. 120; Pub.L. 102–190, Div. B, Title XXXI, § 3138(a), Dec. 5, 1991, 105 Stat. 1579; Pub.L. 102–395, Title VI, § 609(a), Oct. 6, 1992, 106 Stat. 1873; Pub.L. 103–322, Title XXXIII, §§ 330002(i), 330010(15), Sept. 13, 1994, 108 Stat. 2140, 2144; Pub.L. 104–65, § 21(a), Dec. 19, 1995, 109 Stat. 704; Pub.L. 104–179, §§ 5, 6, Aug. 6, 1996, 110 Stat. 1567, 1568; Pub.L. 104–208, Div. A, Title I, § 101(f) [Title VI, § 635], Sept. 30, 1996, 110 Stat. 3009–363; Pub.L. 105–244, Title I, § 102(a)(5), Oct. 7, 1998, 112 Stat. 1618; Pub.L. 107–347, Title II, § 209(d)(1), (3), Dec. 17, 2002, 116 Stat. 2930; Pub.L. 108–136, Div. A, Title XI, § 1125(b)(1), Nov. 24, 2003, 117 Stat. 1639; Pub.L. 108–271, § 8(b), July 7, 2004, 118 Stat. 814.)

1 So in original. Probably should be "subsection".

HISTORICAL AND STATUTORY NOTES

References in Text

Section 1102 of the Omnibus Trade and Competitiveness Act of 1988, referred to in subsec. (b)(2)(A), is classified to section 2902 of Title 19, Customs Duties.

The National Defense Authorization Act for Fiscal Year 2004, referred to in subsec. (c)(2)(A)(ii), is Pub.L. 108–136, Nov. 24, 2003, 117 Stat. 1392, which was signed by the President on Nov. 24, 2003. For complete classification, see Tables.

Levels I and II of the Executive Schedule, referred to in subsecs. (c)(2)(A)(ii) and (d)(1)(B), are set out in 5 U.S.C.A. §§ 5312 and 5313, respectively.

Senior Executive Service, referred to in subsecs. (c)(2)(A)(ii) and (e)(6)(B), see section 5382 of Title 5.

Chapter 37 of title 5, referred to in subsec. (c)(2)(A)(v) and (*l*), is 5 U.S.C.A. § 3701 et seq.

The effective date set forth in section 102(a) of the Ethics Reform Act of 1989, referred to in subsec. (e)(7)(L), (M), is the effective date of the amendment to this section by section 101(a) of Pub.L. 101–194. See section 102 of Pub.L. 101–194, set out as an Effective Date of 1989 Amendment note under this section.

Section 1(e), (f) of the Foreign Agents Registration Act of 1938, as amended, referred to in subsec. (f)(3), is classified to section 611(e), (f) of Title 22, Foreign Relations and Intercourse.

Section 101 of the Higher Education Act of 1965, referred to in subsec. (j)(2)(B), is classified to section 1001 of Title 20, Education.

Section 501(c)(3) of the Internal Revenue Code of 1986, referred to in subsec. (j)(2)(B), is section 501(c)(3) of Title 26, Internal Revenue Code.

Codifications

Section 501(a) of Pub.L. 95–521, which amended this section, was completely revised by Pub.L. 101–194, Title VI, § 601(a), Nov. 30, 1989, 103 Stat. 1760, which reenacted such provisions as section 501(a) of Appendix 7 to Title 5, Government Organization and Employees. Such revision and reenactment is effective Jan. 1, 1991, except that under certain conditions provisions of section 601(a) of Pub.L. 101–194 shall cease to be effective insofar as they enact section 501(a) of Appendix 7, and provisions of section 501(a) of Pub.L. 95–521 as they amended this section shall be deemed to be reenacted, see section 603 of Pub.L. 101–194, set out as a note under section 7701 of Title 26, Internal Revenue Code.

Effective and Applicability Provisions

2003 Acts.. Except as otherwise provided, amendments by section 1125 of Pub.L. 108–136 shall take effect on the first day of the first pay period beginning on or after the first January 1 following the date of enactment of said section [Nov. 24, 2003], see Pub.L. 108–136, Div. A, Title XI, § 1125(c), Nov. 24, 2003, 117 Stat. 1640, set out as a note under 5 U.S.C.A. § 5304.

2002 Acts. Except as otherwise provided by section 402(a)(2) of Pub.L. 107–347, amendments made by Pub.L. 107–347, Titles I and II, §§ 101 to 216, effective 120 days after December 17, 2002, see section 402(a) of Pub.L. 107–347, set out as a note under 44 U.S.C.A. § 3601.

1998 Acts. Amendment by Pub.L. 105–244 effective Oct. 1, 1998, except as otherwise provided, see section 3 of Pub.L. 105–244, set out as a note under section 1001 of Title 20.

1995 Acts. Section 21(c) of Pub.L. 104–65 provided that: "The amendments made by this section [amending subsec. (f)(2) of this section and section 2171 of Title 19, Customs Duties] shall apply with respect to an individual appointed as United States Trade Representative or as a Deputy United States Trade Representative on or after the date of enactment of this Act [Dec. 19, 1995]."

1992 Acts. Section 609(b) of Pub.L. 102–395 provided that: "This section [amending this section] shall not apply to the person serving as the United States Trade Representative at the date of enactment of this Act [Oct. 6, 1992]."

1991 Acts. Section 3138(b) of Pub.L. 102–190 provided that: "The amendments made by subsection (a) [amending subsec. (k)(1)(B) of this section] shall take effect on the date of the enactment of this Act [Dec. 5, 1991] and shall apply to persons granted waivers under section 207(k)(1) of title 18, United States Code [subsec. (k) of this section], on or after that date."

Section 705(a) of Pub.L. 102–25 provided in part that subsec. (k) [reinstatement of subsec. (k) added by Pub.L. 101–189, § 814(d)(2) and omitted in revision of section by Pub.L. 101–194, § 101(a)] be effective Jan. 1, 1991.

1990 Acts. Section 529 [Title I, § 101(b)(8)(B)] of Pub.L. 101–509 provided that: "The amendments made by subparagraph (A) [amending subsecs. (c)(2)(A)(ii) and (e)(6) of this section] take effect on January 1, 1991."

Amendment to this section (and enactment or amendment of any note hereunder) by the Federal Employees Pay Comparability Act of 1990, as incorporated in section 529 of Pub.L. 101–509, to take effect on May 4, 1991, except that the Office of Personnel Management may establish an earlier effective date, but not earlier than Feb. 3, 1991, for any such provisions with respect to which the Office determines an earlier effective date to be appropriate, see Ex. Ord. No. 12748, Feb. 1, 1991, 56 F.R. 4521, set out as a note under section 5301 of Title 5, Government Organization and Employees.

Amendment by section 2(a) of Pub.L. 101–280 effective May 4, 1990, but to be executed to this section as this section had been amended in 1989 by section 101 of Pub.L. 101–194. Since the 1989 amendment by section 101 of Pub.L. 101–194 is effective Jan. 1, 1991, pursuant to section 102 of Pub.L. 101–194, the amendments under section 2(a) of Pub.L. 101–280 will be effective Jan. 1, 1991.

Amendment by section 5(d) of Pub.L. 101–280 effective May 4, 1990, see section 11 of Pub.L. 101–280, set out as a note under section 101 of Appendix 6 to Title 5, Government Organization and Employees.

1989 Acts. Section 102 of Pub.L. 101–194, as amended Pub.L. 101–280, § 2(b), May 4, 1990, 104 Stat. 152, provided that:

"**(a) In general.**—(1) Subject to paragraph (2) and to subsection (b), the amendments made by section 101 [amending this section] take effect on January 1, 1991.

"(2) Subject to subsection (b), the amendments made by section 101 [amending this section] take effect at noon on January 3, 1991, with respect to Members of Congress (within the meaning of section 207 of title 18, United States Code).

"**(b) Effect on Employment.**—(1) The amendments made by section 101 [amending this section] apply only to persons whose service as a Member of Congress, the Vice President, or an officer or employee to which such amendments apply terminates on or after the effective date of such amendments.

"(2) With respect to service as an officer or employee which terminates before the effective date set forth in subsection (a), section 207 of title 18, United States Code [this section] as in effect at the time of the termination of such service, shall continue to apply, on and after such effective date, with respect to such service."

1978 Acts. Section 503 of Pub.L. 95–521, which formerly provided that the amendments made by section 501 [amending this section] would become effective on July 1, 1979, was completely revised by Pub.L. 101–194, Title VI, § 601(a), Nov. 30, 1989, 103 Stat. 1760, and is now set out as section 502 of Appendix 7 of title 5, Government Organization and Employees. See Codification note under this section.

Section 502 of Pub.L. 95–521, which provided that the amendments made by section 501 [amending this section] shall not apply to those individuals who left Government service prior to the effective date of such amendments [July

1, 1979] or, in the case of individuals who occupied positions designated pursuant to section 207(d) of title 18, United States Code [subsec. (d) of this section] prior to the effective date of such designation; except that any such individual who returns to Government service on or after the effective date of such amendments or designation shall be thereafter covered by such amendments or designation, was completely revised by Pub.L. 101–194, title VI, § 601(a), Nov. 30, 1989, 103 Stat. 1760, and is now set out as Section 502 or Appendix 7 to Title 5, Government Organization and Employees. See Codification note under this section.

1962 Acts. Section effective 90 days after Oct. 23, 1962, see § 4 of Pub.L. 87–849, set out as a note under § 201 of this title.

Transfer of Functions

Any reference in any provision of law enacted before Jan. 4, 1995, to a function, duty, or authority of the Clerk of the House of Representatives treated as referring, with respect to that function, duty, or authority, to the officer of the House of Representatives exercising that function, duty, or authority, as determined by the Committee on House Oversight of the House of Representatives, see section 2(1) of Pub.L. 104–14, set out as a note preceding section 21 of Title 2, The Congress.

Certain functions of Clerk of House of Representatives transferred to Director of Non-legislative and Financial Services by section 7 of House Resolution No. 423, One Hundred Second Congress, Apr. 9, 1992. Any reference in any provision of law enacted before Jan. 4, 1995, to a function, duty, or authority of the Director of Non-legislative and Financial Services treated as referring, with respect to that function, duty, or authority, to the officer of the House of Representatives exercising that function, duty, or authority, as determined by the Committee on House Oversight of the House of Representatives, see section 2(4) of Pub.L. 104–14, set out as a note preceding section 21 of Title 2, The Congress.

Prior Provisions

A prior § 207, Act June 25, 1948, c. 645, 62 Stat. 692, which related to the acceptance of a bribe by a judge, was eliminated by the general amendment of this chapter by Pub.L. 87–849 and is substantially covered by revised § 201.

Provisions similar to those comprising this section were contained in § 284 of this title prior to the repeal of such section and the general amendment of this chapter by Pub.L. 87–849.

Canal Zone

Applicability of section to Canal Zone, see § 14 of this title.

§ 208. Acts affecting a personal financial interest

(a) Except as permitted by subsection (b) hereof, whoever, being an officer or employee of the executive branch of the United States Government, or of any independent agency of the United States, a Federal Reserve bank director, officer, or employee, or an officer or employee of the District of Columbia, including a special Government employee, participates personally and substantially as a Government officer or employee, through decision, approval, disapproval, recommendation, the rendering of advice, investigation, or otherwise, in a judicial or other proceeding, application, request for a ruling or other determination, contract, claim, controversy, charge, accusation, arrest, or other particular matter in which, to his knowledge, he, his spouse, minor child, general partner, organization in which he is serving as officer, director, trustee, general partner or employee, or any person or organization with whom he is negotiating or has any arrangement concerning prospective employment, has a financial interest—

Shall be subject to the penalties set forth in section 216 of this title.

(b) Subsection (a) shall not apply—

(1) if the officer or employee first advises the Government official responsible for appointment to his or her position of the nature and circumstances of the judicial or other proceeding, application, request for a ruling or other determination, contract, claim, controversy, charge, accusation, arrest, or other particular matter and makes full disclosure of the financial interest and receives in advance a written determination made by such official that the interest is not so substantial as to be deemed likely to affect the integrity of the services which the Government may expect from such officer or employee;

(2) if, by regulation issued by the Director of the Office of Government Ethics, applicable to all or a portion of all officers and employees covered by this section, and published in the Federal Register, the financial interest has been exempted from the requirements of subsection (a) as being too remote or too inconsequential to affect the integrity of the services of the Government officers or employees to which such regulation applies;

(3) in the case of a special Government employee serving on an advisory committee within the meaning of the Federal Advisory Committee Act (including an individual being considered for an appointment to such a position), the official responsible for the employee's appointment, after review of the financial disclosure report filed by the individual pursuant to the Ethics in Government Act of 1978, certifies in writing that the need for the individual's services outweighs the potential for a conflict of interest created by the financial interest involved; or

(4) if the financial interest that would be affected by the particular matter involved is that resulting solely from the interest of the officer or employee, or his or her spouse or minor child, in birthrights—

(A) in an Indian tribe, band, nation, or other organized group or community, including any Alaska Native village corporation as defined in or established pursuant to the Alaska Native Claims

Settlement Act, which is recognized as eligible for the special programs and services provided by the United States to Indians because of their status as Indians,

(B) in an Indian allotment the title to which is held in trust by the United States or which is inalienable by the allottee without the consent of the United States, or

(C) in an Indian claims fund held in trust or administered by the United States,

if the particular matter does not involve the Indian allotment or claims fund or the Indian tribe, band, nation, organized group or community, or Alaska Native village corporation as a specific party or parties.

(c)(1) For the purpose of paragraph (1) of subsection (b), in the case of class A and B directors of Federal Reserve banks, the Board of Governors of the Federal Reserve System shall be deemed to be the Government official responsible for appointment.

(2) The potential availability of an exemption under any particular paragraph of subsection (b) does not preclude an exemption being granted pursuant to another paragraph of subsection (b).

(d)(1) Upon request, a copy of any determination granting an exemption under subsection (b)(1) or (b)(3) shall be made available to the public by the agency granting the exemption pursuant to the procedures set forth in section 105 of the Ethics in Government Act of 1978. In making such determination available, the agency may withhold from disclosure any information contained in the determination that would be exempt from disclosure under section 552 of title 5. For purposes of determinations under subsection (b)(3), the information describing each financial interest shall be no more extensive than that required of the individual in his or her financial disclosure report under the Ethics in Government Act of 1978.

(2) The Office of Government Ethics, after consultation with the Attorney General, shall issue uniform regulations for the issuance of waivers and exemptions under subsection (b) which shall—

(A) list and describe exemptions; and

(B) provide guidance with respect to the types of interests that are not so substantial as to be deemed likely to affect the integrity of the services the Government may expect from the employee.

(Added Pub.L. 87–849, § 1(a), Oct. 23, 1962, 76 Stat. 1124, and amended Pub.L. 95–188, Title II, § 205, Nov. 16, 1977, 91 Stat. 1388; Pub.L. 101–194, Title IV, § 405, Nov. 30, 1989, 103 Stat. 1751; Pub.L. 101–280, § 5(e), May 4, 1990, 104 Stat. 159; Pub.L. 103–322, Title XXXIII, §§ 330002(b), 330008(6), Sept. 13, 1994, 108 Stat. 2140, 2143.)

HISTORICAL AND STATUTORY NOTES

References in Text

The Federal Advisory Committee Act, referred to in subsec. (b)(3), is Pub.L. 92–463, Oct. 6, 1972, 86 Stat. 770, as amended, which is set out in Appendix 2 to Title 5, Government Organization and Employees.

The Ethics in Government Act of 1978, referred to in subsecs. (b)(3) and (d)(1), is Pub.L. 95–521, Oct. 26, 1978, 92 Stat. 1824, as amended. For complete classification of this Act to the Code, see Short Title note set out under section 101 of Pub.L. 95–521 in Appendix 4 to Title 5, Government Organization and Employees, and Tables.

The Alaska Native Claims Settlement Act, referred to in subsec. (b)(4)(A), is Pub.L. 92–203, Dec. 18, 1971, 85 Stat. 688, as amended, which is classified generally to chapter 33 (section 1601 et seq.) of Title 43, Public Lands. For complete classification of this Act to the Code, see Short Title note set out under section 1601 of Title 43, and Tables.

Effective and Applicability Provisions

1990 Acts. Amendment by Pub.L. 101–280 effective on May 4, 1990, see section 11 of Pub.L. 101–280, set out as a note under section 101 of Appendix 4 to Title 5, Government Organization and Employees.

1962 Acts. Section effective 90 days after Oct. 23, 1962, see § 4 of Pub.L. 87–849, set out as a note under § 201 of this title.

Prior Provisions

A prior § 208, Act June 25, 1948, c. 645, 62 Stat. 693, which related to the acceptance of solicitation of a bribe by a judicial officer, was eliminated in the general amendment of this chapter by Pub.L. 87–849 and is substantially covered by revised § 201.

Provisions similar to those comprising this section were contained in § 434 of this title prior to the repeal of such section and the general amendment of this chapter by Pub.L. 87–849.

"Particular Matter" Defined

Pub.L. 100–446, Title III, § 319, Sept. 27, 1988, 102 Stat. 1826, which provided that notwithstanding any other provision of law, for the purposes of this section the term "particular matter", as applied to employees of the Department of the Interior and the Indian Health Service, would mean "particular matter involving specific parties", was repealed by Pub.L. 101–194, Title V, § 505(b), Nov. 30, 1989, 103 Stat. 1756, as amended Pub.L. 101–280, § 6(c), May 4, 1990, 104 Stat. 160. Similar provisions had previously appeared in Pub.L. 100–202, § 101(g) [Title III, § 318], Dec. 22, 1987, 101 Stat. 1329–255.

Canal Zone

Applicability of section to Canal Zone, see § 14 of this title.

§ 209. Salary of Government officials and employees payable only by United States

(a) Whoever receives any salary, or any contribution to or supplementation of salary, as compensation for his services as an officer or employee of the executive branch of the United States Government, of any independent agency of the United States, or of the District of Columbia, from any source other than the Government of the United States, except as may be contributed out of the treasury of any State, county, or municipality; or

Whoever, whether an individual, partnership, association, corporation, or other organization pays, makes any contribution to, or in any way supplements, the salary of any such officer or employee under circumstances which would make its receipt a violation of this subsection—

Shall be subject to the penalties set forth in section 216 of this title.

(b) Nothing herein prevents an officer or employee of the executive branch of the United States Government, or of any independent agency of the United States, or of the District of Columbia, from continuing to participate in a bona fide pension, retirement, group life, health or accident insurance, profit-sharing, stock bonus, or other employee welfare or benefit plan maintained by a former employer.

(c) This section does not apply to a special Government employee or to an officer or employee of the Government serving without compensation, whether or not he is a special Government employee, or to any person paying, contributing to, or supplementing his salary as such.

(d) This section does not prohibit payment or acceptance of contributions, awards, or other expenses under the terms of chapter 41 of title 5.

(e) This section does not prohibit the payment of actual relocation expenses incident to participation, or the acceptance of same by a participant in an executive exchange or fellowship program in an executive agency: *Provided,* That such program has been established by statute or Executive order of the President, offers appointments not to exceed three hundred and sixty-five days, and permits no extensions in excess of ninety additional days or, in the case of participants in overseas assignments, in excess of three hundred and sixty-five days.

(f) This section does not prohibit acceptance or receipt, by any officer or employee injured during the commission of an offense described in section 351 or 1751 of this title, of contributions or payments from an organization which is described in section 501(c) (3) of the Internal Revenue Code of 1986 and which is exempt from taxation under section 501(a) of such Code.

(g)(1) This section does not prohibit an employee of a private sector organization, while assigned to an agency under chapter 37 of title 5, from continuing to receive pay and benefits from such organization in accordance with such chapter.

(2) For purposes of this subsection, the term "agency" means an agency (as defined by section 3701 of title 5) and the Office of the Chief Technology Officer of the District of Columbia.

(h) This section does not prohibit a member of the reserve components of the armed forces on active duty pursuant to a call or order to active duty under a provision of law referred to in section 101(a)(13) of title 10 from receiving from any person that employed such member before the call or order to active duty any payment of any part of the salary or wages that such person would have paid the member if the member's employment had not been interrupted by such call or order to active duty.

(Added Pub.L. 87–849, § 1(a), Oct. 23, 1962, 76 Stat. 1125, and amended Pub.L. 96–174, Dec. 29, 1979, 93 Stat. 1288; Pub.L. 97–171, § 1, Apr. 13, 1982, 96 Stat. 67; Pub.L. 99–646, § 70, Nov. 10, 1986, 100 Stat. 3617; Pub.L. 101–194, Title IV, § 406, Nov. 30, 1989, 103 Stat. 1753; Pub.L. 101–647, Nov. 29, 1990, Title XXXV, § 3510, 104 Stat. 4922; Pub.L. 103–322, Title XXXIII, § 330008(7), Sept. 13, 1994, 108 Stat. 2143; Pub.L. 107–273, Div. A, Title III, § 302(3), Nov. 2, 2002, 116 Stat. 1781; Pub.L. 107–347, Title II, § 209(g)(2), Dec. 17, 2002, 116 Stat. 2932; Pub.L. 108–375, Div. A, Title VI, § 663, Oct. 28, 2004, 118 Stat. 1974.)

HISTORICAL AND STATUTORY NOTES

References in Text

Section 501(c)(3) and (a) of the Internal Revenue Code of 1954, referred to in subsec. (f), is section 501(c) (3) and (a) of Title 26, Internal Revenue Code.

Chapter 37 of title 5, referred to in subsec. (g)(1), is 5 U.S.C.A. § 3701 et seq.

Effective and Applicability Provisions

2002 Acts. Except as otherwise provided by section 402(a)(2) of Pub.L. 107–347, amendments made by Pub.L. 107–347, Titles I and II, §§ 101 to 216, effective 120 days after December 17, 2002, see section 402(a) of Pub.L. 107–347, set out as a note under 44 U.S.C.A. § 3601.

1962 Acts. Section effective 90 days after Oct. 23, 1962, see § 4 of Pub.L. 87–849, set out as a note under § 201 of this title.

Prior Provisions

A prior § 209, Act June 25, 1948, c. 645, 62 Stat. 693, which related to an offer of a bribe to a witness, was eliminated in the general amendment of this chapter by Pub.L. 87–849 and is substantially covered by § 201.

Provisions similar to those comprising this section were contained in § 1914 of this title prior to the repeal of such section and the general amendment of this chapter by Pub.L. 87–849.

Canal Zone

Applicability of section to Canal Zone, see § 14 of this title.

§ 210. Offer to procure appointive public office

Whoever pays or offers or promises any money or thing of value, to any person, firm, or corporation in consideration of the use or promise to use any influence to procure any appointive office or place under the United States for any person, shall be fined under this title or imprisoned not more than one year, or both.

(June 25, 1948, c. 645, 62 Stat. 694, § 210, formerly § 214, renumbered Oct. 23, 1962, Pub.L. 87–849, § 1(b), 76 Stat. 1125; Sept. 13, 1994, Pub.L. 103–322, Title XXXIII, § 330016(1)(H), 108 Stat. 2147.)

HISTORICAL AND STATUTORY NOTES

Prior Provisions

A prior § 210, Act June 25, 1948, c. 645, 62 Stat. 693, which related to acceptance of a bribe by a witness, was eliminated in the general amendment of this chapter by Pub.L. 87–849 and is substantially covered in revised § 201.

Canal Zone

Applicability of section to Canal Zone, see § 14 of this title.

§ 211. Acceptance or solicitation to obtain appointive public office

Whoever solicits or receives, either as a political contribution, or for personal emolument, any money or thing of value, in consideration of the promise of support or use of influence in obtaining for any person any appointive office or place under the United States, shall be fined under this title or imprisoned not more than one year, or both.

Whoever solicits or receives any thing of value in consideration of aiding a person to obtain employment under the United States either by referring his name to an executive department or agency of the United States or by requiring the payment of a fee because such person has secured such employment shall be fined under this title, or imprisoned not more than one year, or both. This section shall not apply to such services rendered by an employment agency pursuant to the written request of an executive department or agency of the United States.

(June 25, 1948, c. 645, 62 Stat. 694, § 211, formerly § 215, amended Sept. 13, 1951, c. 380, 65 Stat. 320, and renumbered Oct. 23, 1962, Pub.L. 87–849, § 1(b), 76 Stat. 1125; Sept. 13, 1994, Pub.L. 103–322, Title XXXIII, § 330016(1)(H), 108 Stat. 2147.)

HISTORICAL AND STATUTORY NOTES

Prior Provisions

A prior § 211, Act June 25, 1948, c. 645, 62 Stat. 693, which related to an offer of a gratuity to a revenue officer, was eliminated in the general amendment of this chapter by Pub.L. 87–849 and is substantially covered in revised § 201.

Canal Zone

Applicability of section to Canal Zone, see § 14 of this title.

§ 212. Offer of loan or gratuity to financial institution examiner

(a) In general.—Except as provided in subsection (b), whoever, being an officer, director, or employee of a financial institution, makes or grants any loan or gratuity, to any examiner or assistant examiner who examines or has authority to examine such bank, branch, agency, organization, corporation, association, or institution—

(1) shall be fined under this title, imprisoned not more than 1 year, or both; and

(2) may be fined a further sum equal to the money so loaned or gratuity given.

(b) Regulations.—A Federal financial institution regulatory agency may prescribe regulations establishing additional limitations on the application for and receipt of credit under this section and on the application and receipt of residential mortgage loans under this section, after consulting with each other Federal financial institution regulatory agency.

(c) Definitions.—In this section:

(1) Examiner.—The term "examiner" means any person—

(A) appointed by a Federal financial institution regulatory agency or pursuant to the laws of any State to examine a financial institution; or

(B) elected under the law of any State to conduct examinations of any financial institutions.

(2) Federal financial institution regulatory agency.—The term "Federal financial institution regulatory agency" means—

(A) the Office of the Comptroller of the Currency;

(B) the Board of Governors of the Federal Reserve System;

(C) the Office of Thrift Supervision;

(D) the Federal Deposit Insurance Corporation;

(E) the Federal Housing Finance Board;

(F) the Farm Credit Administration;

(G) the Farm Credit System Insurance Corporation; and

(H) the Small Business Administration.

(3) Financial institution.—The term "financial institution" does not include a credit union, a Federal Reserve Bank, a Federal home loan bank, or a depository institution holding company.

(4) Loan.—The term "loan" does not include any credit card account established under an open end consumer credit plan or a loan secured by residential real property that is the principal residence of the examiner, if—

(A) the applicant satisfies any financial requirements for the credit card account or residential real property loan that are generally applicable to all applicants for the same type of credit card account or residential real property loan;

(B) the terms and conditions applicable with respect to such account or residential real property loan, and any credit extended to the examiner under such account or residential real property loan, are no more favorable generally to the examiner than the terms and conditions that are generally applicable to credit card accounts or residential real property loans offered by the same financial institution to other borrowers cardholders [1] in comparable circumstances under open end consumer credit plans or for residential real property loans; and

(C) with respect to residential real property loans, the loan is with respect to the primary residence of the applicant.

(Pub.L. 108–198, § 2(a), Dec. 19, 2003, 117 Stat. 2899.)

[1] So in original.

HISTORICAL AND STATUTORY NOTES

Prior Provisions

A prior section 212 of this title, Act June 25, 1948, c. 645, 62 Stat. 694, § 212, formerly § 217, amended Aug. 21, 1958, Pub.L. 85–699, Title VII, § 701(a), 72 Stat. 698; Aug. 18, 1959, Pub.L. 86–168, Title I, § 104(h), 73 Stat. 387, and renumbered Oct. 23, 1962, Pub.L. 87–849, § 1(d), 76 Stat. 1125; Aug. 9, 1989, Pub.L. 101–73, Title IX, § 962(a)(1), 103 Stat. 501; Nov. 29, 1990, Pub.L. 101–647, Title XXV, § 2597(b), 104 Stat. 4908 Sept. 13, 1994, Pub.L. 103–322, Title XXXIII, §§ 330004(1), 330010(1), 330016(1)(K), 108 Stat. 2141, 2143, 2147, relating to an offer of loan or gratuity to bank examiner, was repealed by Pub.L. 108–198, § 2(a), Dec. 19, 2003, 117 Stat. 2899.

Another prior § 212, Act June 25, 1948, c. 645, 62 Stat. 693, which related to an offer or threat to a customs officer or employee, was eliminated in the general amendment to this chapter by Pub.L. 87–849 and is substantially covered by revised § 201.

§ 213. Acceptance of loan or gratuity by financial institution examiner

(a) In general.—Whoever, being an examiner or assistant examiner, accepts a loan or gratuity from any bank, branch, agency, organization, corporation, association, or institution examined by the examiner or from any person connected with it, shall—

(1) be fined under this title, imprisoned not more than 1 year, or both;

(2) may be fined a further sum equal to the money so loaned or gratuity given; and

(3) shall be disqualified from holding office as an examiner.

(b) Definitions.—In this section, the terms "examiner", "Federal financial institution regulatory agency", "financial institution", and "loan" have the same meanings as in section 212.

(Pub.L. 108–198, § 2(a), Dec. 19, 2003, 117 Stat. 2899.)

HISTORICAL AND STATUTORY NOTES

Prior Provisions

A prior section 213 of this title, Act June 25, 1948, c. 645, 62 Stat. 695, § 213, formerly § 218, amended Aug. 21, 1958, Pub.L. 85–699, Title VII, § 701(b), 72 Stat. 698, and renumbered Oct. 23, 1962, Pub.L. 87–849, § 1(d), 76 Stat. 1125; Aug. 9, 1989, Pub.L. 101–73, Title IX, § 962(a)(2), 103 Stat. 502; Nov. 29, 1990, Pub.L. 101–647, Title XXV, § 2597(c), 104 Stat. 4909; Sept. 13, 1994, Pub.L. 103–322, Title XXXIII, §§ 330004(2), 330016(1)(K), 108 Stat. 2141, 2147, relating to an acceptance of loan or gratuity by bank examiner, was repealed by Pub.L. 108–198, § 2(a), Dec. 19, 2003, 117 Stat. 2899.

Another prior § 213, Act June 25, 1948, c. 645, 62 Stat. 693, which related to the acceptance or demand of a bribe by a customs officer or employee, was eliminated in the general amendment to this chapter by Pub.L. 87–849 and is substantially covered by revised § 201.

§ 214. Offer for procurement of Federal Reserve bank loan and discount of commercial paper

Whoever stipulates for or gives or receives, or consents or agrees to give or receive, any fee, commission, bonus, or thing of value for procuring or endeavoring to procure from any Federal Reserve bank any advance, loan, or extension of credit or discount or purchase of any obligation or commitment with respect thereto, either directly from such Federal Reserve bank or indirectly through any financing institution, unless such fee, commission, bonus, or thing of value and all material facts with respect to the arrangement or understanding therefor shall be disclosed in writing in the application or request for such advance, loan, extension of credit, discount, purchase, or commitment, shall be fined under this title or imprisoned not more than one year, or both.

(June 25, 1948, c. 645, 62 Stat. 695, § 214, formerly § 219, renumbered Oct. 23, 1962, Pub.L. 87–849, § 1(d), 76 Stat. 1125; Sept. 13, 1994, Pub.L. 103–322, Title XXXIII, § 330016(1)(K), 108 Stat. 2147.)

HISTORICAL AND STATUTORY NOTES

Prior Provisions

A prior § 214 of this title was redesignated § 210.

§ 215. Receipt of commissions or gifts for procuring loans

(a) Whoever—

(1) corruptly gives, offers, or promises anything of value to any person, with intent to influence or reward an officer, director, employee, agent, or attorney of a financial institution in connection with any business or transaction of such institution; or

(2) as an officer, director, employee, agent, or attorney of a financial institution, corruptly solicits or demands for the benefit of any person, or corruptly accepts or agrees to accept, anything of value from any person, intending to be influenced or rewarded in connection with any business or transaction of such institution;

shall be fined not more than $1,000,000 or three times the value of the thing given, offered, promised, solicited, demanded, accepted, or agreed to be accepted, whichever is greater, or imprisoned not more than 30 years, or both, but if the value of the thing given, offered, promised, solicited, demanded, accepted, or agreed to be accepted does not exceed $1,000, shall be fined under this title or imprisoned not more than one year, or both.

[(b) Transferred § 20]

(c) This section shall not apply to bona fide salary, wages, fees, or other compensation paid, or expenses paid or reimbursed, in the usual course of business.

(d) Federal agencies with responsibility for regulating a financial institution shall jointly establish such guidelines as are appropriate to assist an officer, director, employee, agent, or attorney of a financial institution to comply with this section. Such agencies shall make such guidelines available to the public.

(June 25, 1948, c. 645, 62 Stat. 695, § 215, formerly § 220, amended Sept. 21, 1950, c. 967, § 4, 64 Stat. 894, and renumbered Oct. 23, 1962, Pub.L. 87–849, § 1(d), 76 Stat. 1125; Oct. 12, 1984, Pub.L. 98–473, Title II, § 1107(a), 98 Stat. 2145; Aug. 4, 1986, Pub.L. 99–370, § 2, 100 Stat. 779; Aug. 9, 1989, Pub.L. 101–73, Title IX, §§ 961(a), 962(e)(1), 103 Stat. 499, 503; Nov. 29, 1990, Pub.L. 101–647, Title XXV, § 2504(a), 104 Stat. 4861; Sept. 13, 1994, Pub.L. 103–322, Title XXXIII, § 330016(1)(H), 108 Stat. 2147; Oct. 11, 1996, Pub.L. 104–294, Title VI, § 606(a), 110 Stat. 3511.)

HISTORICAL AND STATUTORY NOTES

Effective and Applicability Provisions

1986 Acts. Section 3 of Pub.L. 99–370 provided that: "This Act and the amendments made by this Act [amending this section and enacting a provision set out as a note under section 201 of this title] shall take effect 30 days after the date of the enactment of this Act [Aug. 4, 1986]."

Prior Provisions

A prior § 215 of this title was redesignated § 211.

§ 216. Penalties and injunctions

(a) The punishment for an offense under section 203, 204, 205, 207, 208, or 209 of this title is the following:

(1) Whoever engages in the conduct constituting the offense shall be imprisoned for not more than one year or fined in the amount set forth in this title, or both.

(2) Whoever willfully engages in the conduct constituting the offense shall be imprisoned for not more than five years or fined in the amount set forth in this title, or both.

(b) The Attorney General may bring a civil action in the appropriate United States district court against any person who engages in conduct constituting an offense under section 203, 204, 205, 207, 208, or 209 of this title and, upon proof of such conduct by a preponderance of the evidence, such person shall be subject to a civil penalty of not more than $50,000 for each violation or the amount of compensation which the person received or offered for the prohibited conduct, whichever amount is greater. The imposition of a civil penalty under this subsection does not preclude any other criminal or civil statutory, common law, or administrative remedy, which is available by law to the United States or any other person.

(c) If the Attorney General has reason to believe that a person is engaging in conduct constituting an offense under section 203, 204, 205, 207, 208, or 209 of this title, the Attorney General may petition an appropriate United States district court for an order prohibiting that person from engaging in such conduct. The court may issue an order prohibiting that person from engaging in such conduct if the court finds that the conduct constitutes such an offense. The filing of a petition under this section does not preclude any other remedy which is available by law to the United States or any other person.

(Added Pub.L. 101–194, Title IV, § 407(a), Nov. 30, 1989, 103 Stat. 1753, and amended Pub.L. 101–280, § 5(f), May 4, 1990, 104 Stat. 159.)

HISTORICAL AND STATUTORY NOTES

Effective and Applicability Provisions

1990 Acts. Amendment by Pub.L. 101–280 effective on May 4, 1990, see section 11 of Pub.L. 101–280, set out as a note under section 101 of Appendix 6 to Title 5, Government Organization and Employees.

Prior Provisions

A prior section 216, Acts June 25, 1948, c. 645, 62 Stat. 695, § 216, formerly § 221, amended Aug. 21, 1958, Pub.L. 85–699, Title VII, § 702(a)–(c), 72 Stat. 698; Aug. 18, 1959, Pub.L. 86–168, Title I, § 104(h), 73 Stat. 387, and renumbered Oct. 23, 1962, Pub.L. 87–849, § 1(d), 76 Stat. 1125, which related to receipt or charge of commissions or gifts for farm loan, land bank, or small business transaction, was repealed by Pub.L. 98–473, Title II, § 1107(b), Oct. 12, 1984, 98 Stat. 2146. See section 215 of this title.

Another prior section 216, Act June 25, 1948, c. 645, 62 Stat. 694, which related to procurement of a contract by an officer or Member of Congress, was repealed by section 1(c) of Pub.L. 87–849.

§ 217. Acceptance of consideration for adjustment of farm indebtedness

Whoever, being an officer or employee of, or person acting for the United States or any agency thereof, accepts any fee, commission, gift, or other consideration in connection with the compromise, adjustment, or cancellation of any farm indebtedness as provided by sections 1150, 1150a, and 1150b of Title 12, shall be fined under this title or imprisoned not more than one year, or both.

(June 25, 1948, c. 645, 62 Stat. 696, § 217, formerly § 222, renumbered Oct. 23, 1962, Pub.L. 87–849, § 1(d), 76 Stat. 1125; Sept. 13, 1994, Pub.L. 103–322, Title XXXIII, § 330016(1)(H), 108 Stat. 2147.)

HISTORICAL AND STATUTORY NOTES

Prior Provisions

A prior § 217 of this title was redesignated § 212 of this title and subsequently repealed.

§ 218. Voiding transactions in violation of chapter; recovery by the United States

In addition to any other remedies provided by law the President or, under regulations prescribed by him, the head of any department or agency involved, may declare void and rescind any contract, loan, grant, subsidy, license, right, permit, franchise, use, authority, privilege, benefit, certificate, ruling, decision, opinion, or rate schedule awarded, granted, paid, furnished, or published, or the performance of any service or transfer or delivery of any thing to, by or for any agency of the United States or officer or employee of the United States or person acting on behalf thereof, in relation to which there has been a final conviction for any violation of this chapter, and the United States shall be entitled to recover in addition to any penalty prescribed by law or in a contract the amount expended or the thing transferred or delivered on its behalf, or the reasonable value thereof.

(Added Pub.L. 87–849, § 1(e), Oct. 23, 1962, 76 Stat. 1125.)

HISTORICAL AND STATUTORY NOTES

Effective and Applicability Provisions

1962 Acts. Section effective 90 days after Oct. 23, 1962, see § 4 of Pub.L. 87–849, set out as a note under § 201 of this title.

Prior Provisions

A prior § 218 of this title was redesignated § 213 of this title and subsequently repealed.

Canal Zone

Applicability of section to Canal Zone, see § 14 of this title.

EXECUTIVE ORDERS

EXECUTIVE ORDER NO. 12448

Nov. 4, 1983, 48 F.R. 51281

EXERCISE OF AUTHORITY

By the authority vested in me as President by the Constitution and statutes of the United States of America, including section 218 of title 18 of the United States Code [this section], and in order to provide federal agencies with the authority to promulgate regulations for voiding or rescinding contracts or other benefits obtained through bribery, graft or conflict of interest, it is hereby ordered as follows:

Section 1. The head of each Executive department, Military department and Executive agency is hereby delegated the authority vested in the President to declare void and rescind the transactions set forth in section 218 of title 18 of the United States Code [this section] in relation to which there has been a final conviction for any violation of chapter 11 of title 18 [section 201 et seq. of this title].

Sec. 2. The head of each Executive department and agency described in section 1 may exercise the authority hereby delegated by promulgating implementing regulations; provided that the Secretary of Defense, the Administrator of General Services and the Administrator of the National Aeronautics and Space Administration jointly shall issue government-wide implementing regulations related to voiding or rescission of contracts.

Sec. 3. Implementing regulations adopted pursuant to this Order shall, at a minimum, provide the following procedural protections:

(a) Written notice of the proposed action shall be given in each case to the person or entity affected;

(b) The person or entity affected shall be afforded an opportunity to submit pertinent information on its behalf before a final decision is made;

(c) Upon the request of the person or entity affected, a hearing shall be held at which it shall have the opportunity to call witnesses on its behalf and confront any witness the agency may present; and

(d) The head of the agency or his designee shall issue a final written decision specifying the amount of restitution or any other remedy authorized by section 218 [this section], provided that such remedy shall take into consideration the fair value of any tangible benefits received and retained by the agency.

§ 219. Officers and employees acting as agents of foreign principals

(a) Whoever, being a public official, is or acts as an agent of a foreign principal required to register under the Foreign Agents Registration Act of 1938 or a lobbyist required to register under the Lobbying Disclosure Act of 1995 in connection with the representation of a foreign entity, as defined in section 3(6) of that Act shall be fined under this title or imprisoned for not more than two years, or both.

(b) Nothing in this section shall apply to the employment of any agent of a foreign principal as a special Government employee in any case in which the head of the employing agency certifies that such employment is required in the national interest. A copy of any certification under this paragraph shall be forwarded by the head of such agency to the Attorney General who shall cause the same to be filed with the registration statement and other documents filed by such agent, and made available for public inspection in accordance with section 6 of the Foreign Agents Registration Act of 1938, as amended.

(c) For the purpose of this section "public official" means Member of Congress, Delegate, or Resident Commissioner, either before or after he has qualified, or an officer or employee or person acting for or on behalf of the United States, or any department, agency, or branch of Government thereof, including the District of Columbia, in any official function, under or by authority of any such department, agency, or branch of Government.

(Added Pub.L. 89–486, § 8(b), July 4, 1966, 80 Stat. 249, and amended Pub.L. 98–473, Title II, § 1116, Oct. 12, 1984, 98 Stat. 2149; Pub.L. 99–646, § 30, Nov. 10, 1986, 100 Stat. 3598; Pub.L. 101–647, Title XXXV, § 3511, Nov. 29, 1990, 104 Stat. 4922; Pub.L. 104–65, § 12(b), Dec. 19, 1995, 109 Stat. 701.)

HISTORICAL AND STATUTORY NOTES

References in Text

The Foreign Agents Registration Act of 1938, referred to in subsec. (a), is classified to section 611 et seq. of Title 22, Foreign Relations and Intercourse.

The Lobbying Disclosure Act of 1995, referred to in subsec. (a), is Pub.L. 104–65, Dec. 19, 1995, 109 Stat. 691, which is classified principally to chapter 26 (section 1601 et seq.) of Title 2, The Congress. Section 3(6) of such Act is classified to section 1602(6) of Title 2. For complete classification of this Act to the Code, see Short Title note set out under section 1601 of Title 2 and Tables.

Section 6 of the Foreign Agents Registration Act of 1938, as amended, referred to in subsec. (b), is classified to section 616 of Title 22.

Effective and Applicability Provisions

1995 Acts. Amendment by section 12(b) of Pub.L. 104–65 effective Jan. 1, 1996, except as otherwise provided, see section 24 of Pub.L. 104–65, set out as a note under section 1601 of Title 2, The Congress.

1966 Acts. Section effective ninety days after July 4, 1966, see § 9 of Pub.L. 89–486, set out as a note under § 611 of Title 22, Foreign Relations and Intercourse.

Prior Provisions

A prior § 219 was redesignated § 214 by Pub.L. 87–849, § 1(d), Oct. 23, 1962, 76 Stat. 1125.

[§§ 220 to 222. Redesignated]

HISTORICAL AND STATUTORY NOTES

Sections 220 to 222, Act June 25, 1948, c. 645, 62 Stat. 695, 696, were redesignated as sections 215 to 217 by Pub.L. 87–849, § 1(d), Oct. 23, 1962, 76 Stat. 1125.

[§ 223. Repealed. Pub.L. 87–849, § 1(c), Oct. 23, 1962, 76 Stat. 1125]

HISTORICAL AND STATUTORY NOTES

Section, Act June 25, 1948, c. 645, 62 Stat. 696, related to transactions of the Home Owners' Loan Corporation.

Effective Date of Repeal

Repeal of section effective 90 days after Oct. 23, 1962, see § 4 of Pub.L. 87–849, set out as a note under § 201 of this title.

§ 224. Bribery in sporting contests

(a) Whoever carries into effect, attempts to carry into effect, or conspires with any other person to carry into effect any scheme in commerce to influence, in any way, by bribery any sporting contest, with knowledge that the purpose of such scheme is to influence by bribery that contest, shall be fined under this title, or imprisoned not more than 5 years, or both.

(b) This section shall not be construed as indicating an intent on the part of Congress to occupy the field in which this section operates to the exclusion of a law of any State, territory, Commonwealth, or possession of the United States, and no law of any State, territory, Commonwealth, or possession of the United States, which would be valid in the absence of the section shall be declared invalid, and no local authorities shall be deprived of any jurisdiction over any offense over which they would have jurisdiction in the absence of this section.

(c) As used in this section—

(1) The term "scheme in commerce" means any scheme effectuated in whole or in part through the use in interstate or foreign commerce of any facility for transportation or communication;

(2) The term "sporting contest" means any contest in any sport, between individual contestants or teams of contestants (without regard to the amateur or professional status of the contestants therein), the occurrence of which is publicly announced before its occurrence;

(3) The term "person" means any individual and any partnership, corporation, association, or other entity.

(Added Pub.L. 88–316, § 1(a), June 6, 1964, 78 Stat. 203, and amended Pub.L. 103–322, Title XXXIII, § 330016(1)(L), Sept. 13, 1994, 108 Stat. 2147.)

§ 225. Continuing financial crimes enterprise

(a) Whoever—

(1) organizes, manages, or supervises a continuing financial crimes enterprise; and

(2) receives $5,000,000 or more in gross receipts from such enterprise during any 24–month period,

shall be fined not more than $10,000,000 if an individual, or $20,000,000 if an organization, and imprisoned for a term of not less than 10 years and which may be life.

(b) For purposes of subsection (a), the term "continuing financial crimes enterprise" means a series of violations under section 215, 656, 657, 1005, 1006, 1007, 1014, 1032, or 1344 of this title, or section 1341 or 1343 affecting a financial institution, committed by at least 4 persons acting in concert.

(Added Pub.L. 101–647, Nov. 29, 1990, Title XXV, § 2510(a), 104 Stat. 4863.)

§ 226. Bribery affecting port security

(a) In general.—Whoever knowingly—

(1) directly or indirectly, corruptly gives, offers, or promises anything of value to any public or private person, with intent to commit international terrorism or domestic terrorism (as those terms are defined under section 2331), to—

(A) influence any action or any person to commit or aid in committing, or collude in, or allow, any fraud, or make opportunity for the commission of any fraud affecting any secure or restricted area or seaport; or

(B) induce any official or person to do or omit to do any act in violation of the lawful duty of such official or person that affects any secure or restricted area or seaport; or

(2) directly or indirectly, corruptly demands, seeks, receives, accepts, or agrees to receive or accept anything of value personally or for any other person or entity in return for—

(A) being influenced in the performance of any official act affecting any secure or restricted area or seaport; and

(B) knowing that such influence will be used to commit, or plan to commit, international or domestic terrorism,

shall be fined under this title or imprisoned not more than 15 years, or both.

(b) Definition.—In this section, the term "secure or restricted area" means an area of a vessel or facility designated as secure in an approved security plan, as required under section 70103 of title 46, United States Code, and the rules and regulations promulgated under that section.

(Added Pub.L. 109–177, Title III, § 309(a), Mar. 9, 2006, 120 Stat. 241.)

CHAPTER 11A—CHILD SUPPORT

§ 228. Failure to pay legal child support obligations

(a) Offense.—Any person who—

(1) willfully fails to pay a support obligation with respect to a child who resides in another State, if such obligation has remained unpaid for a period longer than 1 year, or is greater than $5,000;

(2) travels in interstate or foreign commerce with the intent to evade a support obligation, if such obligation has remained unpaid for a period longer than 1 year, or is greater than $5,000; or

(3) willfully fails to pay a support obligation with respect to a child who resides in another State, if such obligation has remained unpaid for a period longer than 2 years, or is greater than $10,000;

shall be punished as provided in subsection (c).

(b) Presumption.—The existence of a support obligation that was in effect for the time period charged in the indictment or information creates a rebuttable presumption that the obligor has the ability to pay the support obligation for that time period.

(c) Punishment.—The punishment for an offense under this section is—

(1) in the case of a first offense under subsection (a)(1), a fine under this title, imprisonment for not more than 6 months, or both; and

(2) in the case of an offense under paragraph (2) or (3) of subsection (a), or a second or subsequent offense under subsection (a)(1), a fine under this title, imprisonment for not more than 2 years, or both.

(d) Mandatory restitution.—Upon a conviction under this section, the court shall order restitution under section 3663A in an amount equal to the total unpaid support obligation as it exists at the time of sentencing.

(e) Venue.—With respect to an offense under this section, an action may be inquired of and prosecuted in a district court of the United States for—

(1) the district in which the child who is the subject of the support obligation involved resided during a period during which a person described in subsection (a) (referred to in this subsection as an "obliger") failed to meet that support obligation;

(2) the district in which the obliger resided during a period described in paragraph (1); or

(3) any other district with jurisdiction otherwise provided for by law.

(f) Definitions.—As used in this section—

(1) the term "Indian tribe" has the meaning given that term in section 102 of the Federally Recognized Indian Tribe List Act of 1994 (25 U.S.C. 479a);

(2) the term "State" includes any State of the United States, the District of Columbia, and any commonwealth, territory, or possession of the United States; and

(3) the term "support obligation" means any amount determined under a court order or an order of an administrative process pursuant to the law of a State or of an Indian tribe to be due from a person for the support and maintenance of a child or of a child and the parent with whom the child is living.

(Added Pub.L. 102–521, § 2(a), Oct. 25, 1992, 106 Stat. 340, and amended Pub.L. 104–294, Title VI, § 607(*l*), Oct. 11,

1996, 110 Stat. 3512; Pub.L. 105–187, § 2, June 24, 1998, 112 Stat. 618.)

HISTORICAL AND STATUTORY NOTES

Short Title

1998 Amendments. Pub.L. 105–187, § 1, June 24, 1998, 112 Stat. 618, provided that: "This Act [which amended this section] may be cited as the 'Deadbeat Parents Punishment Act of 1998'."

1992 Acts. Section 1 of Pub.L. 102–521, provided that: "This Act [enacting this section and sections 3796cc to 3796cc–6 of Title 42, The Public Health and Welfare, amending section 3563 of this title and sections 3793 and 3797 of Title 42, and enacting a provision set out as a note under section 12301 of Title 42] may be cited as the 'Child Support Recovery Act of 1992'."

CHAPTER 11B—CHEMICAL WEAPONS

§ 229. Prohibited activities

(a) Unlawful conduct.—Except as provided in subsection (b), it shall be unlawful for any person knowingly—

(1) to develop, produce, otherwise acquire, transfer directly or indirectly, receive, stockpile, retain, own, possess, or use, or threaten to use, any chemical weapon; or

(2) to assist or induce, in any way, any person to violate paragraph (1), or to attempt or conspire to violate paragraph (1).

(b) Exempted agencies and persons.—

(1) In general.—Subsection (a) does not apply to the retention, ownership, possession, transfer, or receipt of a chemical weapon by a department, agency, or other entity of the United States, or by a person described in paragraph (2), pending destruction of the weapon.

(2) Exempted persons.—A person referred to in paragraph (1) is—

(A) any person, including a member of the Armed Forces of the United States, who is authorized by law or by an appropriate officer of the United States to retain, own, possess, transfer, or receive the chemical weapon; or

(B) in an emergency situation, any otherwise nonculpable person if the person is attempting to destroy or seize the weapon.

(c) Jurisdiction.—Conduct prohibited by subsection (a) is within the jurisdiction of the United States if the prohibited conduct—

(1) takes place in the United States;

(2) takes place outside of the United States and is committed by a national of the United States;

(3) is committed against a national of the United States while the national is outside the United States; or

(4) is committed against any property that is owned, leased, or used by the United States or by any department or agency of the United States, whether the property is within or outside the United States.

(Added Pub.L. 105–277, Div. I, Title II, § 201(a), Oct. 21, 1998, 112 Stat. 2681–866.)

HISTORICAL AND STATUTORY NOTES

FBI to Investigate Violations

Any investigation emanating from a possible violation of Ex. Ord. No. 13128, June 25, 1999, 64 F.R. 34703, or of any license, order, or regulation issued pursuant to this order, involving or revealing a possible violation of this section, shall be referred to the Federal Bureau of Investigation (FBI), which shall coordinate with the referring agency and other appropriate agencies, and the FBI shall timely notify the referring agency and other appropriate agencies of any action it takes on such referrals, see Ex. Ord. No. 13128, set out as a note under section 6711 of Title 22.

Revocations of Export Privileges

Pub.L. 105–277, Div. I, Title II, § 211, Oct. 21, 1998, 112 Stat. 2681–866, provided that: "If the President determines, after notice and an opportunity for a hearing in accordance with section 554 of title 5, United States Code, that any person within the United States, or any national of the United States located outside the United States, has committed any violation of section 229 of title 18, United States Code, the President may issue an order for the suspension or revocation of the authority of the person to export from the United States any goods or technology (as such terms are defined in section 16 of the Export Administration Act of 1979 (50 U.S.C. App. 2415))."

[For provisions authorizing the Secretary of Commerce to suspend or revoke export privileges pursuant to this note, see Ex. Ord. No. 13128, June 25, 1999, 64 F.R. 34703, set out as a note under section 6711 of this title.]

§ 229A. Penalties

(a) Criminal penalties.—

(1) In general.—Any person who violates section 229 of this title shall be fined under this title, or imprisoned for any term of years, or both.

(2) **Death penalty.**—Any person who violates section 229 of this title and by whose action the death of another person is the result shall be punished by death or imprisoned for life.

(b) **Civil penalties.**—

(1) **In general.**—The Attorney General may bring a civil action in the appropriate United States district court against any person who violates section 229 of this title and, upon proof of such violation by a preponderance of the evidence, such person shall be subject to pay a civil penalty in an amount not to exceed $100,000 for each such violation.

(2) **Relation to other proceedings.**—The imposition of a civil penalty under this subsection does not preclude any other criminal or civil statutory, common law, or administrative remedy, which is available by law to the United States or any other person.

(c) **Reimbursement of costs.**—The court shall order any person convicted of an offense under subsection (a) to reimburse the United States for any expenses incurred by the United States incident to the seizure, storage, handling, transportation, and destruction or other disposition of any property that was seized in connection with an investigation of the commission of the offense by that person. A person ordered to reimburse the United States for expenses under this subsection shall be jointly and severally liable for such expenses with each other person, if any, who is ordered under this subsection to reimburse the United States for the same expenses.

(Added Pub.L. 105–277, Div. I, Title II, § 201(a), Oct. 21, 1998, 112 Stat. 2681–867.)

§ 229B. Criminal forfeitures; destruction of weapons

(a) **Property subject to criminal forfeiture.**—Any person convicted under section 229A(a) shall forfeit to the United States irrespective of any provision of State law—

(1) any property, real or personal, owned, possessed, or used by a person involved in the offense;

(2) any property constituting, or derived from, and proceeds the person obtained, directly or indirectly, as the result of such violation; and

(3) any of the property used in any manner or part, to commit, or to facilitate the commission of, such violation.

The court, in imposing sentence on such person, shall order, in addition to any other sentence imposed pursuant to section 229A(a), that the person forfeit to the United States all property described in this subsection. In lieu of a fine otherwise authorized by section 229A(a), a defendant who derived profits or other proceeds from an offense may be fined not more than twice the gross profits or other proceeds

(b) **Procedures.**—

(1) **General.**—Property subject to forfeiture under this section, any seizure and disposition thereof, and any administrative or judicial proceeding in relation thereto, shall be governed by subsections (b) through (p) of section 413 of the Comprehensive Drug Abuse Prevention and Control Act of 1970 (21 U.S.C. 853), except that any reference under those subsections to—

(A) "this subchapter or subchapter II" shall be deemed to be a reference to section 229A(a); and

(B) "subsection (a)" shall be deemed to be a reference to subsection (a) of this section.

(2) **Temporary restraining orders.**—

(A) **In general.**—For the purposes of forfeiture proceedings under this section, a temporary restraining order may be entered upon application of the United States without notice or opportunity for a hearing when an information or indictment has not yet been filed with respect to the property, if, in addition to the circumstances described in section 413(e)(2) of the Comprehensive Drug Abuse Prevention and Control Act of 1970 (21 U.S.C. 853(e)(2)), the United States demonstrates that there is probable cause to believe that the property with respect to which the order is sought would, in the event of conviction, be subject to forfeiture under this section and exigent circumstances exist that place the life or health of any person in danger.

(B) **Warrant of seizure.**—If the court enters a temporary restraining order under this paragraph, it shall also issue a warrant authorizing the seizure of such property.

(C) **Applicable procedures.**—The procedures and time limits applicable to temporary restraining orders under section 413(e) (2) and (3) of the Comprehensive Drug Abuse Prevention and Control Act of 1970 (21 U.S.C. 853(e) (2) and (3)) shall apply to temporary restraining orders under this paragraph.

(c) **Affirmative defense.**—It is an affirmative defense against a forfeiture under subsection (b) that the property—

(1) is for a purpose not prohibited under the Chemical Weapons Convention; and

(2) is of a type and quantity that under the circumstances is consistent with that purpose.

(d) **Destruction or other disposition.**—The Attorney General shall provide for the destruction or other appropriate disposition of any chemical weapon seized and forfeited pursuant to this section.

(e) Assistance.—The Attorney General may request the head of any agency of the United States to assist in the handling, storage, transportation, or destruction of property seized under this section.

(f) Owner liability.—The owner or possessor of any property seized under this section shall be liable to the United States for any expenses incurred incident to the seizure, including any expenses relating to the handling, storage, transportation, and destruction or other disposition of the seized property.

(Added Pub.L. 105–277, Div. I, Title II, § 201(a), Oct. 21, 1998, 112 Stat. 2681–868.)

§ 229C. Individual self-defense devices

Nothing in this chapter shall be construed to prohibit any individual self-defense device, including those using a pepper spray or chemical mace.

(Added Pub.L. 105–277, Div. I, Title II, § 201(a), Oct. 21, 1998, 112 Stat. 2681–869.)

§ 229D. Injunctions

The United States may obtain in a civil action an injunction against—

(1) the conduct prohibited under section 229 or 229C of this title; or

(2) the preparation or solicitation to engage in conduct prohibited under section 229 or 229D[1] of this title.

(Added Pub.L. 105–277, Div. I, Title II, § 201(a), Oct. 21, 1998, 112 Stat. 2681–869.)

[1] So in original.

§ 229E. Requests for military assistance to enforce prohibition in certain emergencies

The Attorney General may request the Secretary of Defense to provide assistance under section 382 of title 10 in support of Department of Justice activities relating to the enforcement of section 229 of this title in an emergency situation involving a chemical weapon. The authority to make such a request may be exercised by another official of the Department of Justice in accordance with section 382(f)(2) of title 10.

(Added Pub.L. 105–277, Div. I, Title II, § 201(a), Oct. 21, 1998, 112 Stat. 2681–869.)

§ 229F. Definitions

In this chapter:

(1) Chemical weapon.—The term "chemical weapon" means the following, together or separately:

(A) A toxic chemical and its precursors, except where intended for a purpose not prohibited under this chapter as long as the type and quantity is consistent with such a purpose.

(B) A munition or device, specifically designed to cause death or other harm through toxic properties of those toxic chemicals specified in subparagraph (A), which would be released as a result of the employment of such munition or device.

(C) Any equipment specifically designed for use directly in connection with the employment of munitions or devices specified in subparagraph (B).

(2) Chemical weapons convention; convention.—The terms "Chemical Weapons Convention" and "Convention" mean the Convention on the Prohibition of the Development, Production, Stockpiling and Use of Chemical Weapons and on Their Destruction, opened for signature on January 13, 1993.

(3) Key component of a binary or multicomponent chemical system.—The term "key component of a binary or multicomponent chemical system" means the precursor which plays the most important role in determining the toxic properties of the final product and reacts rapidly with other chemicals in the binary or multicomponent system.

(4) National of the United States.—The term "national of the United States" has the same meaning given such term in section 101(a)(22) of the Immigration and Nationality Act (8 U.S.C. 1101(a)(22)).

(5) Person.—The term "person", except as otherwise provided, means any individual, corporation, partnership, firm, association, trust, estate, public or private institution, any State or any political subdivision thereof, or any political entity within a State, any foreign government or nation or any agency, instrumentality or political subdivision of any such government or nation, or other entity located in the United States.

(6) Precursor.—

(A) In general.—The term "precursor" means any chemical reactant which takes part at any stage in the production by whatever method of a toxic chemical. The term includes any key component of a binary or multicomponent chemical system.

(B) List of precursors.—Precursors which have been identified for the application of verification measures under Article VI of the Convention are listed in schedules contained in the Annex on Chemicals of the Chemical Weapons Convention.

(7) Purposes not prohibited by this chapter.—The term "purposes not prohibited by this chapter" means the following:

(A) Peaceful purposes.—Any peaceful purpose related to an industrial, agricultural, research, medical, or pharmaceutical activity or other activity.

(B) **Protective purposes.**—Any purpose directly related to protection against toxic chemicals and to protection against chemical weapons.

(C) **Unrelated military purposes.**—Any military purpose of the United States that is not connected with the use of a chemical weapon or that is not dependent on the use of the toxic or poisonous properties of the chemical weapon to cause death or other harm.

(D) **Law enforcement purposes.**—Any law enforcement purpose, including any domestic riot control purpose and including imposition of capital punishment.

(8) **Toxic chemical.**—

(A) **In general.**—The term "toxic chemical" means any chemical which through its chemical action on life processes can cause death, temporary incapacitation or permanent harm to humans or animals. The term includes all such chemicals, regardless of their origin or of their method of production, and regardless of whether they are produced in facilities, in munitions or elsewhere.

(B) **List of toxic chemicals.**—Toxic chemicals which have been identified for the application of verification measures under Article VI of the Convention are listed in schedules contained in the Annex on Chemicals of the Chemical Weapons Convention.

(9) **United States.**—The term "United States" means the several States of the United States, the District of Columbia, and the commonwealths, territories, and possessions of the United States and includes all places under the jurisdiction or control of the United States, including—

(A) any of the places within the provisions of paragraph (41) of section 40102 of Title 49, United States Code;

(B) any civil aircraft of the United States or public aircraft, as such terms are defined in paragraphs (17) and (37), respectively, of section 40102 of title 49, United States Code; and

(C) any vessel of the United States, as such term is defined in section 70502(b) of title 46, United States Code.

(Added Pub.L. 105–277, Div. I, Title II, § 201(a), Oct. 21, 1998, 112 Stat. 2681–869, and amended Pub.L. 109–304, § 17(d)(1), Oct. 6, 2006, 120 Stat. 1707.)

HISTORICAL AND STATUTORY NOTES

References in Text

Paragraphs (17), (37), and (41) of section 40102 of title 49, referred to in par. (9)(A), (B), probably means paragraphs (17), (37), and (41) of subsection (a) of section 40102 of title 49. Paragraphs (37) and (41) were subsequently redesignated as (41) and (46), respectively, by Pub.L. 108–176, Title II, § 225(a)(1), (3), Dec. 12, 2003, 117 Stat. 2528.

CHAPTER 12—CIVIL DISORDERS

§ 231. Civil disorders

(a)(1) Whoever teaches or demonstrates to any other person the use, application, or making of any firearm or explosive or incendiary device, or technique capable of causing injury or death to persons, knowing or having reason to know or intending that the same will be unlawfully employed for use in, or in furtherance of, a civil disorder which may in any way or degree obstruct, delay, or adversely affect commerce or the movement of any article or commodity in commerce or the conduct or performance of any federally protected function; or

(2) Whoever transports or manufactures for transportation in commerce any firearm, or explosive or incendiary device, knowing or having reason to know or intending that the same will be used unlawfully in furtherance of a civil disorder; or

(3) Whoever commits or attempts to commit any act to obstruct, impede, or interfere with any fireman or law enforcement officer lawfully engaged in the lawful performance of his official duties incident to and during the commission of a civil disorder which in any way or degree obstructs, delays, or adversely affects commerce or the movement of any article or commodity in commerce or the conduct or performance of any federally protected function—

Shall be fined under this title or imprisoned not more than five years, or both.

(b) Nothing contained in this section shall make unlawful any act of any law enforcement officer which is performed in the lawful performance of his official duties.

(Added Pub.L. 90–284, Title X, § 1002(a), Apr. 11, 1968, 82 Stat. 90, and amended Pub.L. 103–322, Title XXXIII, § 330016(1)(L), Sept. 13, 1994, 108 Stat. 2147.)

HISTORICAL AND STATUTORY NOTES

Short Title

Section 1001 of Pub.L. 90–284 provided that: "This title [which enacted this chapter] may be cited as the 'Civil Obedience Act of 1968'."

§ 232. Definitions

For purposes of this chapter:

(1) The term "civil disorder" means any public disturbance involving acts of violence by assemblages of three or more persons, which causes an immediate danger of or results in damage or injury to the property or person of any other individual.

(2) The term "commerce" means commerce (A) between any State or the District of Columbia and any place outside thereof; (B) between points within any State or the District of Columbia, but through any place outside thereof; or (C) wholly within the District of Columbia.

(3) The term "federally protected function" means any function, operation, or action carried out, under the laws of the United States, by any department, agency, or instrumentality of the United States or by an officer or employee thereof; and such term shall specifically include, but not be limited to, the collection and distribution of the United States mails.

(4) The term "firearm" means any weapon which is designed to or may readily be converted to expel any projectile by the action of an explosive; or the frame or receiver of any such weapon.

(5) The term "explosive or incendiary device" means (A) dynamite and all other forms of high explosives, (B) any explosive bomb, grenade, missile, or similar device, and (C) any incendiary bomb or grenade, fire bomb, or similar device, including any device which (i) consists of or includes a breakable container including a flammable liquid or compound, and a wick composed of any material which, when ignited, is capable of igniting such flammable liquid or compound, and (ii) can be carried or thrown by one individual acting alone.

(6) The term "fireman" means any member of a fire department (including a volunteer fire department) of any State, any political subdivision of a State, or the District of Columbia.

(7) The term "law enforcement officer" means any officer or employee of the United States, any State, any political subdivision of a State, or the District of Columbia, while engaged in the enforcement or prosecution of any of the criminal laws of the United States, a State, any political subdivision of a State, or the District of Columbia; and such term shall specifically include members of the National Guard (as defined in section 101 of title 10), members of the organized militia of any State, or territory of the United States, the Commonwealth of Puerto Rico, or the District of Columbia not included within the National Guard (as defined in section 101 of title 10), and members of the Armed Forces of the United States, while engaged in suppressing acts of violence or restoring law and order during a civil disorder.

(8) The term "State" includes a State of the United States, and any commonwealth, territory, or possession of the United States.

(Added Pub.L. 90–284, Title X, § 1002(a), Apr. 11, 1968, 82 Stat. 91, and amended Pub.L. 101–647, Title XII, § 1205(a), Nov. 29, 1990, 104 Stat. 4830; Pub.L. 102–484, Div. A, Title X, § 1051(b)(1), Oct. 23, 1992, 106 Stat. 2498.)

§ 233. Preemption

Nothing contained in this chapter shall be construed as indicating an intent on the part of Congress to occupy the field in which any provisions of the chapter operate to the exclusion of State or local laws on the same subject matter, nor shall any provision of this chapter be construed to invalidate any provision of State law unless such provision is inconsistent with any of the purposes of this chapter or any provision thereof.

(Added Pub.L. 90–284, Title X, § 1002(a), Apr. 11, 1968, 82 Stat. 91.)

CHAPTER 13—CIVIL RIGHTS

Sec.

§ 241. Conspiracy against rights

If two or more persons conspire to injure, oppress, threaten, or intimidate any person in any State, Territory, Commonwealth, Possession, or District in the free exercise or enjoyment of any right or privilege secured to him by the Constitution or laws of the United States, or because of his having so exercised the same; or

If two or more persons go in disguise on the highway, or on the premises of another, with intent to prevent or hinder his free exercise or enjoyment of any right or privilege so secured—

They shall be fined under this title or imprisoned not more than ten years, or both; and if death results from the acts committed in violation of this section or if such acts include kidnapping or an attempt to kidnap, aggravated sexual abuse or an attempt to commit aggravated sexual abuse, or an attempt to kill, they shall be fined under this title or imprisoned for any term of years or for life, or both, or may be sentenced to death.

(June 25, 1948, c. 645, 62 Stat. 696; Apr. 11, 1968, Pub.L. 90–284, Title I, § 103(a), 82 Stat. 75; Nov. 18, 1988, Pub.L. 100–690, Title VII, § 7018(a), (b)(1), 102 Stat. 4396; Sept. 13, 1994, Pub.L. 103–322, Title VI, § 60006(a), Title XXXII, §§ 320103(a), 320201(a), Title XXXIII, § 330016(1)(L), 108 Stat. 1970, 2109, 2113, 2147; Oct. 11, 1996, Pub.L. 104–294, Title VI, §§ 604(b)(14)(A), 607(a), 110 Stat. 3507, 3511.)

HISTORICAL AND STATUTORY NOTES

Effective and Applicability Provisions

1996 Acts. Amendment by section 604 of Pub.L. 104–294 effective Sept. 13, 1994, see section 604(d) of Pub.L. 104–294, set out as a note under section 13 of this title.

Short Title

1996 Amendments. Pub.L. 104–155, § 1, July 3, 1996, 110 Stat. 1392, provided that: "This Act [amending section 247 of this title and section 10602 of Title 42, The Public Health and Welfare, enacting provisions set out as a note under section 247 of this title, and amending provisions set out as a note under section 534 of Title 28, Judiciary and Judicial Procedure] may be cited as the 'Church Arson Prevention Act of 1996'."

Repeals

Pub.L. 103–322, Title XXXII, § 320103(a)(1), Sept. 13, 1994, 108 Stat. 2109, appearing in the credit of this section, was repealed by Pub.L. 104–294, Title VI, § 604(b)(14)(A), Oct. 11, 1996, 110 Stat. 3507.

§ 242. Deprivation of rights under color of law

Whoever, under color of any law, statute, ordinance, regulation, or custom, willfully subjects any person in any State, Territory, Commonwealth, Possession, or District to the deprivation of any rights, privileges, or immunities secured or protected by the Constitution or laws of the United States, or to different punishments, pains, or penalties, on account of such person being an alien, or by reason of his color, or race, than are prescribed for the punishment of citizens, shall be fined under this title or imprisoned not more than one year, or both; and if bodily injury results from the acts committed in violation of this section or if such acts include the use, attempted use, or threatened use of a dangerous weapon, explosives, or fire, shall be fined under this title or imprisoned not more than ten years, or both; and if death results from the acts committed in violation of this section or if such acts include kidnapping or an attempt to kidnap, aggravated sexual abuse, or an attempt to commit aggravated sexual abuse, or an attempt to kill, shall be fined under this title, or imprisoned for any term of years or for life, or both, or may be sentenced to death.

(June 25, 1948, c. 645, 62 Stat. 696; Apr. 11, 1968, Pub.L. 90–284, Title I, § 103(b), 82 Stat. 75; Nov. 18, 1988, Pub.L. 100–690, Title VII, § 7019, 102 Stat. 4396; Sept. 13, 1994, Pub.L. 103–322, Title VI, § 60006(b), Title XXXII, §§ 320103(b), 320201(b), Title XXXIII, § 330016(1)(H), 108 Stat. 1970, 2109, 2113, 2147; Oct. 11, 1996, Pub.L. 104–294, Title VI, §§ 604(b)(14)(B), 607(a), 110 Stat. 3507, 3511.)

HISTORICAL AND STATUTORY NOTES

Effective and Applicability Provisions

1996 Acts. Amendment by section 604 of Pub.L. 104–294 effective Sept. 13, 1994, see section 604(d) of Pub.L. 104–294, set out as a note under section 13 of this title.

Repeals

Pub.L. 103–322, Title XXXII, § 320103(b)(1), Sept. 13, 1994, 108 Stat. 2109, appearing in the credit of this section, was repealed by Pub.L. 104–294, Title VI, § 604(b)(14)(B), Oct. 11, 1996, 110 Stat. 3507.

§ 243. Exclusion of jurors on account of race or color

No citizen possessing all other qualifications which are or may be prescribed by law shall be disqualified for service as grand or petit juror in any court of the United States, or of any State on account of race, color, or previous condition of servitude; and whoever, being an officer or other person charged with any duty in the selection or summoning of jurors, excludes or fails to summon any citizen for such cause, shall be fined not more than $5,000.

(June 25, 1948, c. 645, 62 Stat. 696.)

§ 244. Discrimination against person wearing uniform of armed forces

Whoever, being a proprietor, manager, or employee of a theater or other public place of entertainment or amusement in the District of Columbia, or in any Territory, or Possession of the United States, causes any person wearing the uniform of any of the armed forces of the United States to be discriminated against because of that uniform, shall be fined under this title.

(June 25, 1948, c. 645, 62 Stat. 697; May 24, 1949, c. 139, § 5, 63 Stat. 90; Sept. 13, 1994, Pub.L. 103–322, Title XXXIII, § 330016(1)(G), 108 Stat. 2147.)

§ 245. Federally protected activities

(a)(1) Nothing in this section shall be construed as indicating an intent on the part of Congress to prevent any State, any possession or Commonwealth of the United States, or the District of Columbia, from exercising jurisdiction over any offense over which it would have jurisdiction in the absence of this section, nor shall anything in this section be construed as depriving State and local law enforcement authorities of responsibility for prosecuting acts that may be violations of this section and that are violations of State and local law. No prosecution of any offense described in this section shall be undertaken by the United States except upon the certification in writing of the Attorney General, the Deputy Attorney General, the Associate Attorney General, or any Assistant Attorney General specially designated by the Attorney General that in his judgment a prosecution by the

United States is in the public interest and necessary to secure substantial justice, which function of certification may not be delegated.

(2) Nothing in this subsection shall be construed to limit the authority of Federal officers, or a Federal grand jury, to investigate possible violations of this section.

(b) Whoever, whether or not acting under color of law, by force or threat of force willfully injures, intimidates or interferes with, or attempts to injure, intimidate or interfere with—

(1) any person because he is or has been, or in order to intimidate such person or any other person or any class of persons from—

(A) voting or qualifying to vote, qualifying or campaigning as a candidate for elective office, or qualifying or acting as a poll watcher, or any legally authorized election official, in any primary, special, or general election;

(B) participating in or enjoying any benefit, service, privilege, program, facility, or activity provided or administered by the United States;

(C) applying for or enjoying employment, or any perquisite thereof, by any agency of the United States;

(D) serving, or attending upon any court in connection with possible service, as a grand or petit juror in any court of the United States;

(E) participating in or enjoying the benefits of any program or activity receiving Federal financial assistance; or

(2) any person because of his race, color, religion or national origin and because he is or has been—

(A) enrolling in or attending any public school or public college;

(B) participating in or enjoying any benefit, service, privilege, program, facility or activity provided or administered by any State or subdivision thereof;

(C) applying for or enjoying employment, or any perquisite thereof, by any private employer or any agency of any State or subdivision thereof, or joining or using the services or advantages of any labor organization, hiring hall, or employment agency;

(D) serving, or attending upon any court of any State in connection with possible service, as a grand or petit juror,

(E) traveling in or using any facility of interstate commerce, or using any vehicle, terminal, or facility of any common carrier by motor, rail, water, or air;

(F) enjoying the goods, services, facilities, privileges, advantages, or accommodations of any inn, hotel, motel, or other establishment which provides lodging to transient guests, or of any restaurant, cafeteria, lunchroom, lunch counter, soda fountain, or other facility which serves the public and which is principally engaged in selling food or beverages for consumption on the premises, or of any gasoline station, or of any motion picture house, theater, concert hall, sports arena, stadium, or any other place of exhibition or entertainment which serves the public, or of any other establishment which serves the public and (i) which is located within the premises of any of the aforesaid establishments or within the premises of which is physically located any of the aforesaid establishments, and (ii) which holds itself out as serving patrons of such establishments; or

(3) during or incident to a riot or civil disorder, any person engaged in a business in commerce or affecting commerce, including, but not limited to, any person engaged in a business which sells or offers for sale to interstate travelers a substantial portion of the articles, commodities, or services which it sells or where a substantial portion of the articles or commodities which it sells or offers for sale have moved in commerce; or

(4) any person because he is or has been, or in order to intimidate such person or any other person or any class of persons from—

(A) participating, without discrimination on account of race, color, religion or national origin, in any of the benefits or activities described in subparagraphs (1)(A) through (1)(E) or subparagraphs (2)(A) through (2)(F); or

(B) affording another person or class of persons opportunity or protection to so participate; or

(5) any citizen because he is or has been, or in order to intimidate such citizen or any other citizen from lawfully aiding or encouraging other persons to participate, without discrimination on account of race, color, religion or national origin, in any of the benefits or activities described in subparagraphs (1)(A) through (1)(E) or subparagraphs (2)(A) through (2)(F), or participating lawfully in speech or peaceful assembly opposing any denial of the opportunity to so participate—

shall be fined under this title, or imprisoned not more than one year, or both; and if bodily injury results from the acts committed in violation of this section or if such acts include the use, attempted use, or threatened use of a dangerous weapon, explosives, or fire shall be fined under this title, or imprisoned not more than ten years, or both; and if death results from the acts committed in violation of this section or if such acts include kidnapping or an attempt to kidnap, aggravated sexual abuse or an attempt to commit aggravated sexual abuse, or an attempt to kill, shall be fined under this title or imprisoned for any term of years or for life, or both, or may be sentenced to death. As used in this section, the term "participating lawfully in speech or peaceful assembly" shall not mean the aiding, abetting, or inciting of other persons to riot or to commit any act of physical violence upon any individual or against any real or personal property in furtherance of a riot. Nothing in subparagraph (2)(F) or (4)(A) of this subsection shall apply to the proprietor of any establishment which provides lodging to transient guests, or to any employee acting on behalf of such proprietor, with respect to the enjoyment of the goods, services, facilities, privileges, advantages, or accommodations of such establishment if such establishment is located within a building which contains not more than five rooms for rent or hire and which is actually occupied by the proprietor as his residence.

(c) Nothing in this section shall be construed so as to deter any law enforcement officer from lawfully carrying out the duties of his office; and no law enforcement officer shall be considered to be in violation of this section for lawfully carrying out the duties of his office or lawfully enforcing ordinances and laws of the United States, the District of Columbia, any of the several States, or any political subdivision of a State. For purposes of the preceding sentence, the term "law enforcement officer" means any officer of the United States, the District of Columbia, a State, or political subdivision of a State, who is empowered by law to conduct investigations of, or make arrests because of, offenses against the United States, the District of Columbia, a State, or a political subdivision of a State.

(d) For purposes of this section, the term "State" includes a State of the United States, the District of Columbia, and any commonwealth, territory, or possession of the United States.

(Added Pub.L. 90–284, Title I, § 101(a), Apr. 11, 1968, 82 Stat. 73, and amended Pub.L. 100–690, Title VII, § 7020(a), Nov. 18, 1988, 102 Stat. 4396; Pub.L. 101–647, Title XII, § 1205(b), Nov. 29, 1990, 104 Stat. 4830; Pub.L. 103–322, Title VI, § 60006(c), Title XXXII, § 320103(c), Title XXXIII, § 330016(1)(H), (L), Sept. 13, 1994, 108 Stat. 1971, 2109, 2147; Pub.L. 104–294, Title VI, § 604(b)(14)(C), (37), Oct. 11, 1996, 110 Stat. 3507, 3509.)

HISTORICAL AND STATUTORY NOTES

Effective and Applicability Provisions

1996 Acts. Amendment by section 604 of Pub.L. 104–294 effective Sept. 13, 1994, see section 604(d) of Pub.L. 104–294, set out as a note under section 13 of this title.

Repeals

Pub.L. 103–322, Title XXXII, § 320103(c)(1), (3), Sept. 13, 1994, 108 Stat. 2109, appearing in the credit of this section, was repealed by Pub.L. 104–294, Title VI, § 604(b)(14)(C), Oct. 11, 1996, 110 Stat. 3507.

Fair Housing

Section 101(b) of Pub.L. 90–284 provided that: "Nothing contained in this section [enacting this section] shall apply to or affect activities under title VIII of this Act [sections 3601–3619 of Title 42, The Public Health and Welfare]."

Riots or Civil Disturbances, Suppression and Restoration of Law and Order; Acts or Omissions of Enforcement Officers and Members of Military Service Not Subject to This Section

Section 101(c) of Pub.L. 90–284 provided that: "The provisions of this section [enacting this section] shall not apply to acts or omissions on the part of law enforcement officers, members of the National Guard, as defined in section 101(9) of title 10, United States Code [section 101(9) of Title 10], members of the organized militia of any State or the District of Columbia, not covered by such section 101(9), or members of the Armed Forces of the United States, who are engaged in suppressing a riot or civil disturbance or restoring law and order during a riot or civil disturbance."

§ 246. Deprivation of relief benefits

Whoever directly or indirectly deprives, attempts to deprive, or threatens to deprive any person of any employment, position, work, compensation, or other benefit provided for or made possible in whole or in part by any Act of Congress appropriating funds for work relief or relief purposes, on account of political affiliation, race, color, sex, religion, or national origin, shall be fined under this title, or imprisoned not more than one year, or both.

(Added Pub.L. 94–453, § 4(a), Oct. 2, 1976, 90 Stat. 1517, and amended Pub.L. 103–322, Title XXXIII, § 330016(1)(L), Sept. 13, 1994, 108 Stat. 2147.)

§ 247. Damage to religious property; obstruction of persons in the free exercise of religious beliefs

(a) Whoever, in any of the circumstances referred to in subsection (b) of this section—

(1) intentionally defaces, damages, or destroys any religious real property, because of the religious character of that property, or attempts to do so; or

(2) intentionally obstructs, by force or threat of force, any person in the enjoyment of that person's free exercise of religious beliefs, or attempts to do so;

shall be punished as provided in subsection (d).

(b) The circumstances referred to in subsection (a) are that the offense is in or affects interstate or foreign commerce.

(c) Whoever intentionally defaces, damages, or destroys any religious real property because of the race, color, or ethnic characteristics of any individual associated with that religious property, or attempts to do so, shall be punished as provided in subsection (d).

(d) The punishment for a violation of subsection (a) of this section shall be—

(1) if death results from acts committed in violation of this section or if such acts include kidnapping or an attempt to kidnap, aggravated sexual abuse or an attempt to commit aggravated sexual abuse, or an attempt to kill, a fine in accordance with this title and imprisonment for any term of years or for life, or both, or may be sentenced to death;

(2) if bodily injury results to any person, including any public safety officer performing duties as a direct or proximate result of conduct prohibited by this section, and the violation is by means of fire or an explosive, a fine under this title or imprisonment for not more that 40 years, or both;

(3) if bodily injury to any person, including any public safety officer performing duties as a direct or proximate result of conduct prohibited by this section, results from the acts committed in violation of this section or if such acts include the use, attempted use, or threatened use of a dangerous weapon, explosives, or fire, a fine in accordance with this title and imprisonment for not more than 20 years, or both; and

(4) in any other case, a fine in accordance with this title and imprisonment for not more than one year, or both.

(e) No prosecution of any offense described in this section shall be undertaken by the United States except upon the certification in writing of the Attorney General or his designee that in his judgment a prosecution by the United States is in the public interest and necessary to secure substantial justice.

(f) As used in this section, the term "religious real property" means any church, synagogue, mosque, religious cemetery, or other religious real property, including fixtures or religious objects contained within a place of religious worship.

(g) No person shall be prosecuted, tried, or punished for any noncapital offense under this section unless the indictment is found or the information is instituted not later than 7 years after the date on which the offense was committed.

(Added Pub.L. 100–346, § 1, June 24, 1988, 102 Stat. 644, and amended Pub.L. 103–322, Title VI, § 60006(d), Title XXXII, § 320103(d), Sept. 13, 1994, 108 Stat. 1971, 2110; Pub.L. 104–155, § 3, July 3, 1996, 110 Stat. 1392; Pub.L. 104–294, Title VI, §§ 601(c)(3), 605(r), Oct. 11, 1996, 110 Stat. 3499, 3511; Pub.L. 107–273, Div. B, Title IV, § 4002(c)(1), (e)(4), Nov. 2, 2002, 116 Stat. 1808, 1810.)

HISTORICAL AND STATUTORY NOTES

Codifications

Due to prior amendment by Pub.L. 104–155, which redesignated former subsec. (d) as (e), subsequent amendments by sections 601(c)(3) and 605(r) of Pub.L. 104–294, both directing that "certification" be substituted for "notification" in subsec. (d), were executed to subsec. (e), as the probable intent of Congress.

Effective and Applicability Provisions

2002 Acts. Amendments by section 4002(c)(1) and (e)(4) of Pub.L. 107–273, as therein provided, effective Oct. 11, 1996, which is the date of enactment of Pub.L. 104–294, to which such amendments relate.

Repeals

Section 605(r) of Pub.L. 104–294, cited in the credit of this section, was repealed by Pub.L. 107–273, Div. B, Title IV, § 4002(c)(1), Nov. 2, 2002, 116 Stat. 1808, effective Oct. 11, 1996.

Congressional Findings

Section 2 of Pub.L. 104–155 provided that: "The Congress finds the following:

"(1) The incidence of arson or other destruction or vandalism of places of religious worship, and the incidence of violent interference with an individual's lawful exercise or attempted exercise of the right of religious freedom at a place of religious worship pose a serious national problem.

"(2) The incidence of arson of places of religious worship has recently increased, especially in the context of places of religious worship that serve predominantly African–American congregations.

"(3) Changes in Federal law are necessary to deal properly with this problem.

"(4) Although local jurisdictions have attempted to respond to the challenges posed by such acts of destruction or damage to religious property, the problem is sufficiently serious, widespread, and interstate in scope to warrant Federal intervention to assist State and local jurisdictions.

"(5) Congress has authority, pursuant to the Commerce Clause of the Constitution, to make acts of destruction or damage to religious property a violation of Federal law.

"(6) Congress has authority, pursuant to section 2 of the 13th amendment to the Constitution, to make actions of private citizens motivated by race, color, or ethnicity that interfere with the ability of citizens to hold or use religious property without fear of attack, violations of Federal criminal law."

§ 248. Freedom of access to clinic entrances

(a) Prohibited activities.—Whoever—

(1) by force or threat of force or by physical obstruction, intentionally injures, intimidates or interferes with or attempts to injure, intimidate or interfere with any person because that person is or has been, or in order to intimidate such person or any other person or any class of persons from, obtaining or providing reproductive health services;

(2) by force or threat of force or by physical obstruction, intentionally injures, intimidates or interferes with or attempts to injure, intimidate or interfere with any person lawfully exercising or seeking to exercise the First Amendment right of religious freedom at a place of religious worship; or

(3) intentionally damages or destroys the property of a facility, or attempts to do so, because such facility provides reproductive health services, or intentionally damages or destroys the property of a place of religious worship,

shall be subject to the penalties provided in subsection (b) and the civil remedies provided in subsection (c), except that a parent or legal guardian of a minor shall not be subject to any penalties or civil remedies under this section for such activities insofar as they are directed exclusively at that minor.

(b) Penalties.—Whoever violates this section shall—

(1) in the case of a first offense, be fined in accordance with this title, or imprisoned not more than one year, or both; and

(2) in the case of a second or subsequent offense after a prior conviction under this section, be fined in accordance with this title, or imprisoned not more than 3 years, or both;

except that for an offense involving exclusively a nonviolent physical obstruction, the fine shall be not more than $10,000 and the length of imprisonment shall be not more than six months, or both, for the first offense; and the fine shall, notwithstanding section 3571, be not more than $25,000 and the length of imprisonment shall be not more than 18 months, or both, for a subsequent offense; and except that if bodily injury results, the length of imprisonment shall be not more than 10 years, and if death results, it shall be for any term of years or for life.

(c) Civil remedies.—

(1) Right of action.—

(A) In general.—Any person aggrieved by reason of the conduct prohibited by subsection (a) may commence a civil action for the relief set forth in subparagraph (B), except that such an action may be brought under subsection (a)(1) only by a person involved in providing or seeking to provide, or obtaining or seeking to obtain, services in a facility that provides reproductive health services, and such an action may be brought under subsection (a)(2) only by a person lawfully exercising or seeking to exercise the First Amendment right of religious freedom at a place of religious worship or by the entity that owns or operates such place of religious worship.

(B) Relief.—In any action under subparagraph (A), the court may award appropriate relief, including temporary, preliminary or permanent injunctive relief and compensatory and punitive damages, as well as the costs of suit and reasonable fees for attorneys and expert witnesses. With respect to compensatory damages, the plaintiff may elect, at any time prior to the rendering of final judgment, to recover, in lieu of actual damages, an award of statutory damages in the amount of $5,000 per violation.

(2) Action by Attorney General of the United States.—

(A) In general.—If the Attorney General of the United States has reasonable cause to believe that any person or group of persons is being, has been, or may be injured by conduct constituting a violation of this section, the Attorney General may commence a civil action in any appropriate United States District Court.

(B) Relief.—In any action under subparagraph (A), the court may award appropriate relief, including temporary, preliminary or permanent injunctive relief, and compensatory damages to persons aggrieved as described in paragraph (1)(B). The court, to vindicate the public interest, may also assess a civil penalty against each respondent—

(i) in an amount not exceeding $10,000 for a nonviolent physical obstruction and $15,000 for other first violations; and

(ii) in an amount not exceeding $15,000 for a nonviolent physical obstruction and $25,000 for any other subsequent violation.

(3) Actions by State Attorneys General.—

(A) In general.—If the Attorney General of a State has reasonable cause to believe that any person or group of persons is being, has been, or may be injured by conduct constituting a violation of this section, such Attorney General may commence a civil action in the name of such State, as parens patriae on behalf of natural persons residing in such State, in any appropriate United States District Court.

(B) Relief.—In any action under subparagraph (A), the court may award appropriate relief, including temporary, preliminary or permanent injunctive relief, compensatory damages, and civil penalties as described in paragraph (2)(B).

(d) Rules of construction.—Nothing in this section shall be construed—

(1) to prohibit any expressive conduct (including peaceful picketing or other peaceful demonstration) protected from legal prohibition by the First Amendment to the Constitution;

(2) to create new remedies for interference with activities protected by the free speech or free exercise clauses of the First Amendment to the Constitution, occurring outside a facility, regardless of the point of view expressed, or to limit any existing legal remedies for such interference;

(3) to provide exclusive criminal penalties or civil remedies with respect to the conduct prohibited by this section, or to preempt State or local laws that may provide such penalties or remedies; or

(4) to interfere with the enforcement of State or local laws regulating the performance of abortions or other reproductive health services.

(e) **Definitions.**—As used in this section:

(1) **Facility.**—The term "facility" includes a hospital, clinic, physician's office, or other facility that provides reproductive health services, and includes the building or structure in which the facility is located.

(2) **Interfere with.**—The term "interfere with" means to restrict a person's freedom of movement.

(3) **Intimidate.**—The term "intimidate" means to place a person in reasonable apprehension of bodily harm to him- or herself or to another.

(4) **Physical obstruction.**—The term "physical obstruction" means rendering impassable ingress to or egress from a facility that provides reproductive health services or to or from a place of religious worship, or rendering passage to or from such a facility or place of religious worship unreasonably difficult or hazardous.

(5) **Reproductive health services.**—The term "reproductive health services" means reproductive health services provided in a hospital, clinic, physician's office, or other facility, and includes medical, surgical, counselling or referral services relating to the human reproductive system, including services relating to pregnancy or the termination of a pregnancy.

(6) **State.**—The term "State" includes a State of the United States, the District of Columbia, and any commonwealth, territory, or possession of the United States.

(Added Pub.L. 103–259, § 3, May 26, 1994, 108 Stat. 694, and amended Pub.L. 103–322, Title XXXIII, § 330023(a)(2), (3), Sept. 13, 1994, 108 Stat. 2150.)

HISTORICAL AND STATUTORY NOTES

Effective and Applicability Provisions

1994 Acts. Section 330023(b) of Pub.L. 103–322 provided that: "The amendments made by this subsection (a) [amending this section] shall take effect on the date of enactment of the Freedom of Access to Clinic Entrances Act of 1994 [May 26, 1994]."

Section 6 of Pub.L. 103–259 provided that: "This Act [enacting this section and provisions set out as notes under this section] takes effect on the date of enactment of this Act [May 26, 1994], and shall apply only with respect to conduct occurring on or after such date."

Severability of Provisions

Section 5 of Pub.L. 103–259 provided that: "If any provision of this Act [enacting this section and provisions set out as notes under this section], an amendment made by this Act, or the application of such provision or amendment to any person or circumstance is held to be unconstitutional, the remainder of this Act, the amendments made by this Act, and the application of the provisions of such to any other person or circumstance shall not be affected thereby."

Short Title

1996 Acts. Section 1 of Pub.L. 103–259 provided that: "This Act [enacting this section and provisions set out as notes under this section] may be cited as the 'Freedom of Access to Clinic Entrances Act of 1994'."

Congressional Statement of Purpose

Section 2 of Pub.L. 103–259 provided that: "Pursuant to the affirmative power of Congress to enact this legislation under section 8 of article I of the Constitution, as well as under section 5 of the fourteenth amendment to the Constitution, it is the purpose of this Act [enacting this section and provisions set out as notes under this section] to protect and promote the public safety and health and activities affecting interstate commerce by establishing Federal criminal penalties and civil remedies for certain violent, threatening, obstructive and destructive conduct that is intended to injure, intimidate or interfere with persons seeking to obtain or provide reproductive health services."

CHAPTER 15—CLAIMS AND SERVICES IN MATTERS AFFECTING GOVERNMENT

Effective and Applicability Provisions

2002 Acts. Amendment by section 4002(c)(1) of Pub.L. 107–273, as therein provided, effective Oct. 11, 1996, which is the date of enactment of Pub.L. 104–294 to which such amendment relates.

1989 Acts. Amendment by Pub.L. 101–123 deemed to be effective on Nov. 19, 1988, the date of enactment of Pub.L. 100–700, see section 3(b) of Pub.L. 101–123, set out as a note under section 293 of this title.

[§ 281. Repealed. Pub.L. 104–106, Div. D, Title XLIII, § 4304(b)(3), Feb. 10, 1996, 110 Stat. 664; Pub.L. 104–294, Title VI, § 602(d), Oct. 11, 1996, 110 Stat. 3503]

HISTORICAL AND STATUTORY NOTES

Section, added Pub.L. 100–180, Div. A, Title VIII, § 822(b)(1), Dec. 4, 1987, 101 Stat. 1132, related to restrictions on retired military officers regarding compensation for representing persons who sell to the United States through military departments. Section was suspended by Pub.L. 103–355, Title VI, § 6001(b), Title X, § 10001, Oct. 13, 1994, 108 Stat. 3362, 3404, which provided that effective Oct. 13, 1994, except as otherwise provided, this section had no effect during the period beginning on October 13, 1994 and ending at the end of December 31, 1996, and no applicability after that date to any relationship otherwise punishable under this section that existed during such period. Pub.L. 101–510, Div. A, Title VIII, § 815(a)(3), Nov. 1990, 104 Stat. 1597, provided that this section had no force or effect during the period beginning on Dec. 1, 1990, and ending on May 31, 1991. Pub.L. 101–194, Title V, § 507(3), Nov. 30, 1989, 103 Stat. 1760, provided that this section had no force or effect during the period beginning on Dec. 1, 1989, and ending one year after such date. Pub.L. 104–294, Title VI, § 602(d), Oct. 11, 1996, 110 Stat. 3503, purporting to repeal this section, was repealed by Pub.L. 107–273, Div. B, Title IV, § 4002(c)(1), Nov. 2, 2002, 116 Stat. 1808, effective Oct. 11, 1996, which is the date of enactment of Pub.L. 104–294.

Prior Provisions

A prior section 281, Acts June 25, 1948, c. 645, 62 Stat. 697; May 24, 1949, c. 139, § 6, 63 Stat. 90, related to compensation to Members of Congress, officers and others in matters affecting Government, and was repealed by Pub.L. 87–849, § 2, Oct. 23, 1962, 76 Stat. 1119, which continued limited applicability to retired officers of the Armed Forces of the United States. Pub.L. 100–180, Div. A, Title VIII, § 822(a), Dec. 4, 1987, 101 Stat. 1132, provided for repeal of such limited applicability.

Effective Date of Repeal

Repeal by Pub.L. 104–106 effective Feb. 10, 1996, except as otherwise provided, see section 4401 of Pub.L. 104–106, set out as a note under section 251 of Title 41, Public Contracts.

[§ 282. Repealed. Pub.L. 87–849, § 2, Oct. 23, 1962, 76 Stat. 1126]

HISTORICAL AND STATUTORY NOTES

Section, Act June 25, 1948, c. 645, 62 Stat. 697, related to practice in Court of Claims by Members of Congress. Section was supplanted by section 204 of this title.

Effective Date of Repeal

Repeal of section effective 90 days after Oct. 23, 1962, see section 4 of Pub.L. 87–849, set out as an Effective Date note under section 201 of this title.

[§ 283. Repealed. Pub.L. 87–849, § 2, Oct. 23, 1962, 76 Stat. 1126; Pub.L. 100–180, Div. A, Title VIII, § 822(a), Dec. 4, 1987, 101 Stat. 1132]

HISTORICAL AND STATUTORY NOTES

Section, Acts June 25, 1948, c. 645, 62 Stat. 697; June 28, 1949, c. 268, § 2(b), 63 Stat. 280, related to officers or employees interested in claims against the government. Pub.L. 87–849 continued limited applicability to retired officers of the Armed Forces of the United States. Pub.L. 100–180 repealed section to the extent that it had not been repealed by section 2 of Pub.L. 87–849. Section was supplanted by section 205 of this title.

Effective Date of Repeal

Repeal of section effective 90 days after Oct. 23, 1962, see section 4 of Pub.L. 87–849, set out as an Effective Date note under section 201 of this title.

[§ 284. Repealed. Pub.L. 87–849, § 2, Oct. 23, 1962, 76 Stat. 1126]

HISTORICAL AND STATUTORY NOTES

Section, Acts June 25, 1948, c. 645, 62 Stat. 698; May 24, 1949, c. 139, § 7, 63 Stat. 90, related to disqualifications of former officers and employees in matters connected with former duties. Section was supplanted by section 207 of this title.

Effective Date of Repeal

Repeal of section effective 90 days after Oct. 23, 1962, see section 4 of Pub.L. 87–849, set out as an Effective Date note under section 201 of this title.

§ 285. Taking or using papers relating to claims

Whoever, without authority, takes and carries away from the place where it was filed, deposited, or kept by authority of the United States, any certificate, affidavit, deposition, statement of facts, power of attorney, receipt, voucher, assignment, or other document, record, file, or paper prepared, fitted, or intended to be used or presented to procure the payment of money from or by the United States or any officer, employee, or agent thereof, or the allowance or payment of the whole or any part of any claim, account, or demand against the United States, whether the same has or has not already been so used or presented, and whether such claim, account, or demand, or any part thereof has or has not already been allowed or paid; or

Whoever presents, uses, or attempts to use any such document, record, file, or paper so taken and carried away, to procure the payment of any money from or by the United States, or any officer, employee, or agent thereof, or the allowance or payment of the whole or any part of any claim, account, or demand against the United States—

Shall be fined under this title or imprisoned not more than five years, or both.

(June 25, 1948, c. 645, 62 Stat. 698; Sept. 13, 1994, Pub.L. 103–322, Title XXXIII, § 330016(1)(K), 108 Stat. 2147.)

§ 286. Conspiracy to defraud the Government with respect to claims

Whoever enters into any agreement, combination, or conspiracy to defraud the United States, or any department or agency thereof, by obtaining or aiding to obtain the payment or allowance of any false, fictitious or fraudulent claim, shall be fined under this title or imprisoned not more than ten years, or both.

(June 25, 1948, c. 645, 62 Stat. 698; Sept. 13, 1994, Pub.L. 103–322, Title XXXIII, § 330016(1)(L), 108 Stat. 2147.)

§ 287. False, fictitious or fraudulent claims

Whoever makes or presents to any person or officer in the civil, military, or naval service of the United States, or to any department or agency thereof, any claim upon or against the United States, or any department or agency thereof, knowing such claim to be false, fictitious, or fraudulent, shall be imprisoned not more than five years and shall be subject to a fine in the amount provided in this title.

(June 25, 1948, c. 645, 62 Stat. 698; Oct. 27, 1986, Pub.L. 99–562, § 7, 100 Stat. 3169.)

HISTORICAL AND STATUTORY NOTES

Increased Penalties for False Claims in Defense Procurement

Pub.L. 99–145, Title IX, § 931, Nov. 8, 1985, 99 Stat. 699, provided that:

"(a) **Criminal Fines.**—Notwithstanding sections 287 and 3623 of title 18, United States Code [this section and section 3623 of this title], the maximum fine that may be imposed under such section for making or presenting any claim upon or against the United States related to a contract with the Department of Defense, knowing such claim to be false, fictitious, or fraudulent, is $1,000,000.

"(b) **Civil Penalties.**—[See Civil Penalties note under section 3729 of Title 31, Money and Finance.]

"(c) **Effective Date.**—Subsections (a) [set out above] and (b) [set out under section 3729 of Title 31] shall be applicable to claims made or presented on or after the date of the enactment of this Act [Nov. 8, 1985]."

Canal Zone

Applicability of section to Canal Zone, see § 14 of this title.

§ 288. False claims for postal losses

Whoever makes, alleges, or presents any claim or application for indemnity for the loss of any registered or insured letter, parcel, package, or other article or matter, or the contents thereof, knowing such claim or application to be false, fictitious, or fraudulent; or

Whoever for the purpose of obtaining or aiding to obtain the payment or approval of any such claim or application, makes or uses any false statement, certificate, affidavit, or deposition; or

Whoever knowingly and willfully misrepresents, or misstates, or, for the purpose aforesaid, knowingly and willfully conceals any material fact or circumstance in respect of any such claim or application for indemnity—

Shall be fined under this title or imprisoned not more than one year, or both.

Where the amount of such claim or application for indemnity is less than $1,000 only a fine shall be imposed.

(June 25, 1948, c. 645, 62 Stat. 699; Sept. 13, 1994, Pub.L. 103–322, Title XXXIII, § 330016(1)(G), 108 Stat. 2147; Oct. 11, 1996, Pub.L. 104–294, Title VI, § 606(a), 110 Stat. 3511.)

§ 289. False claims for pensions

Whoever knowingly and willfully makes, or presents any false, fictitious or fraudulent affidavit, declaration, certificate, voucher, endorsement, or paper or writing purporting to be such, concerning any claim for pension or payment thereof, or pertaining to any other matter within the jurisdiction of the Secretary of Veterans Affairs, or knowingly or willfully makes or presents any paper required as a voucher in drawing a pension, which paper bears a date subsequent to that upon which it was actually signed or acknowledged by the pensioner; or

Whoever knowingly and falsely certifies that the declarant, affiant, or witness named in such declaration, affidavit, voucher, endorsement, or other paper or writing personally appeared before him and was sworn thereto, or acknowledged the execution thereof—

Shall be fined under this title or imprisoned not more than five years, or both.

(June 25, 1948, c. 645, 62 Stat. 699; June 13, 1991, Pub.L. 102–54, § 13(f)(1), 105 Stat. 275; Sept. 13, 1994, Pub.L. 103–322, Title XXXIII, § 330016(1)(L), 108 Stat. 2147.)

§ 290. Discharge papers withheld by claim agent

Whoever, being a claim agent, attorney, or other person engaged in the collection of claims for pay, pension, or other allowances for any soldier, sailor, or marine, or for any commissioned officer of the military or naval forces, or for any person who may have been a soldier, sailor, marine, or officer of the regular or volunteer forces of the United States, or for his dependents or beneficiaries, retains, without the consent of the owner or owners thereof, or refuses to deliver or account for the same upon demand duly made by the owner or owners thereof, or by their agent or attorney, the discharge papers of any such soldier, sailor, or marine, or commissioned officer, which may have been placed in his hands for the purpose of collecting said claims, shall be fined under this title or imprisoned not more than six months, or both; and shall be debarred from prosecuting any such claim in any department or agency of the United States.

(June 25, 1948, c. 645, 62 Stat. 699; Sept. 13, 1994, Pub.L. 103–322, Title XXXIII, § 330016(1)(G), 108 Stat. 2147.)

§ 291. Purchase of claims for fees by court officials

Whoever, being a judge, clerk, or deputy clerk of any court of the United States or a Territory or

Possession thereof, or a United States district attorney, assistant attorney, marshal, deputy marshal, magistrate judge, or other person holding any office or employment, or position of trust or profit under the United States, directly or indirectly purchases at less than the full face value thereof, any claim against the United States for the fee, mileage, or expenses of any witness, juror, deputy marshal, or any other officer of such court, shall be fined under this title.

(June 25, 1948, c. 645, 62 Stat. 699; Dec. 1, 1990, Pub.L. 101–650, Title III, § 321, 104 Stat. 5117; Sept. 13, 1994, Pub.L. 103–322, Title XXXIII, § 330016(1)(H), 108 Stat. 2147.)

HISTORICAL AND STATUTORY NOTES

Change of Name

"United States magistrate judge" substituted for "United States magistrate" in text pursuant to section 321 of Pub.L. 101–650, set out as a note under 28 U.S.C.A. § 631. Previously, United States commissioners, referred to in text, were replaced by United States magistrates pursuant to Pub.L. 90–578, Oct. 17, 1968, 82 Stat. 1118. See chapter 43 of Title 28, 28 U.S.C.A. § 631 et seq.

§ 292. Solicitation of employment and receipt of unapproved fees concerning Federal employees' compensation

Whoever solicits employment for himself or another in respect to a case, claim, or award for compensation under, or to be brought under, subchapter I of chapter 81 of title 5; or

Whoever receives a fee, other consideration, or gratuity on account of legal or other services furnished in respect to a case, claim, or award for compensation under subchapter I of chapter 81 of title 5, unless the fee, consideration, or gratuity is approved by the Secretary of Labor—

Shall, for each offense, be fined under this title or imprisoned not more than one year, or both.

(Added Pub.L. 89–554, § 3(b), Sept. 6, 1966, 80 Stat. 608, and amended Pub.L. 103–322, Title XXXIII, § 330016(1)(H), Sept. 13, 1994, 108 Stat. 2147.)

[§ 293. Repealed. Pub.L. 101–123, § 3(a), Oct. 23, 1989, 103 Stat. 760]

HISTORICAL AND STATUTORY NOTES

Section, added Pub.L. 100–700, § 3(a), Nov. 19, 1988, 102 Stat. 4632, related to limitation on Government contract costs.

Effective Date of Repeal

Section 3(b) of Pub.L. 101–123 provided that: "The repeal made by this section [repealing this section and a provision set out as a note under this section] shall be deemed to be effective on the date of enactment of Public Law 100–700 [Nov. 19, 1988]."

Effective Date

Section 3(c) of Pub.L. 100–700, which provided that this section was to apply to contracts entered into after Nov. 19, 1988, was repealed by Pub.L. 101–123, § 3(a), Oct. 23, 1989, 103 Stat. 760.

§§ 294 to 330. Reserved for future legislation

CHAPTER 17—COINS AND CURRENCY

Sec.

§ 331. Mutilation, diminution, and falsification of coins

Whoever fraudulently alters, defaces, mutilates, impairs, diminishes, falsifies, scales, or lightens any of the coins coined at the mints of the United States, or any foreign coins which are by law made current or are in actual use or circulation as money within the United States; or

Whoever fraudulently possesses, passes, utters, publishes, or sells, or attempts to pass, utter, publish, or sell, or brings into the United States, any such coin, knowing the same to be altered, defaced, mutilated, impaired, diminished, falsified, scaled, or lightened—

Shall be fined under this title or imprisoned not more than five years, or both.

(June 25, 1948, c. 645, 62 Stat. 700; July 16, 1951, c. 226, § 1, 65 Stat. 121; Sept. 13, 1994, Pub.L. 103–322, Title XXXIII, § 330016(1)(I), 108 Stat. 2147.)

HISTORICAL AND STATUTORY NOTES

Canal Zone

Applicability of section to Canal Zone, see § 14 of this title.

§ 332. Debasement of coins; alteration of official scales, or embezzlement of metals

If any of the gold or silver coins struck or coined at any of the mints of the United States shall be debased, or made worse as to the proportion of fine gold or fine silver therein contained, or shall be of less weight or value than the same ought to be, pursuant to law, or if any of the scales or weights used at any of the mints or assay offices of the United States shall be defaced, altered, increased, or diminished through the fault or connivance of any officer or person employed at the said mints or assay offices, with a fraudulent intent; or if any such officer or person shall embezzle any of the metals at any time committed to his charge for the purpose of being coined, or any of the coins struck or coined at the said mints, or any medals, coins, or other moneys of said mints or assay offices at any time committed to his charge, or of which he may have assumed the charge, every such officer or person who commits any of the said offenses shall be fined under this title or imprisoned not more than ten years, or both.

(June 25, 1948, c. 645, 62 Stat. 700; Sept. 13, 1994, Pub.L. 103–322, Title XXXIII, § 330016(1)(L), 108 Stat. 2147.)

§ 333. Mutilation of national bank obligations

Whoever mutilates, cuts, defaces, disfigures, or perforates, or unites or cements together, or does any other thing to any bank bill, draft, note, or other evidence of debt issued by any national banking association, or Federal Reserve bank, or the Federal Reserve System, with intent to render such bank bill, draft, note, or other evidence of debt unfit to be reissued, shall be fined under this title or imprisoned not more than six months, or both.

(June 25, 1948, c. 645, 62 Stat. 700; Sept. 13, 1994, Pub.L. 103–322, Title XXXIII, § 330016(1)(B), 108 Stat. 2146.)

§ 334. Issuance of Federal Reserve or national bank notes

Whoever, being a Federal Reserve Agent, or an agent or employee of such Federal Reserve Agent, or of the Board of Governors of the Federal Reserve System, issues or puts in circulation any Federal Reserve notes, without complying with or in violation of the provisions of law regulating the issuance and circulation of such Federal Reserve notes; or

Whoever, being an officer acting under the provisions of chapter 2 of Title 12, countersigns or delivers to any national banking association, or to any other company or person, any circulating notes contemplated by that chapter except in strict accordance with its provisions—

Shall be fined under this title or imprisoned not more than five years, or both.

(June 25, 1948, c. 645, 62 Stat. 700; Sept. 13, 1994, Pub.L. 103–322, Title XXXIII, § 330016(1)(K), 108 Stat. 2147.)

§ 335. Circulation of obligations of expired corporations

Whoever, being a director, officer, or agent of a corporation created by Act of Congress, the charter of which has expired, or trustee thereof, or an agent of such trustee, or a person having in his possession or under his control the property of such corporation for the purpose of paying or redeeming its notes and obligations, knowingly issues, reissues, or utters as money, or in any other way knowingly puts in circulation any bill, note, check, draft, or other security purporting to have been made by any such corporation, or by any officer thereof, or purporting to have been made under authority derived therefrom, shall be fined under this title or imprisoned not more than five years, or both.

(June 25, 1948, c. 645, 62 Stat. 700; Sept. 13, 1994, Pub.L. 103–322, Title XXXIII, § 330016(1)(L), 108 Stat. 2147.)

§ 336. Issuance of circulating obligations of less than $1

Whoever makes, issues, circulates, or pays out any note, check, memorandum, token, or other obligation for a less sum than $1, intended to circulate as money or to be received or used in lieu of lawful money of the United States, shall be fined under this title or imprisoned not more than six months, or both.

(June 25, 1948, c. 645, 62 Stat. 701; Sept. 13, 1994, Pub.L. 103–322, Title XXXIII, § 330016(1)(G), 108 Stat. 2147.)

§ 337. Coins as security for loans

Whoever lends or borrows money or credit upon the security of such coins of the United States as the Secretary of the Treasury may from time to time designate by proclamation published in the Federal Register, during any period designated in such a proclamation, shall be fined under this title or imprisoned not more than one year, or both.

(Added Pub.L. 89–81, Title II, § 212(a), July 23, 1965, 79 Stat. 257, and amended Pub.L. 103–322, Title XXXIII, § 330016(1)(L), Sept. 13, 1994, 108 Stat. 2147.)

HISTORICAL AND STATUTORY NOTES

Effective and Applicability Provisions

1965 Acts. Section 212(c) of Pub.L. 89–81 provided that: "The amendments made by this section [adding this section] shall apply only with respect to loans made, renewed, or increased on or after the 31st day after the date of enactment of this Act [July 23, 1965]."

CHAPTER 17A—COMMON CARRIER OPERATION UNDER THE INFLUENCE OF ALCOHOL OR DRUGS

§ 341. Definitions

As used in this chapter, the term "common carrier" means a locomotive, a rail carrier, a sleeping car carrier, a bus transporting passengers in interstate commerce, a water common carrier, and an air common carrier.

(Added Pub.L. 99–570, Title I, § 1971(a), Oct. 27, 1986, 100 Stat. 3207–59, and amended Pub.L. 100–690, Title VI, § 6482(a), Nov. 18, 1988, 102 Stat. 4382.)

§ 342. Operation of a common carrier under the influence of alcohol or drugs

Whoever operates or directs the operation of a common carrier while under the influence of alcohol or any controlled substance (as defined in section 102 of the Controlled Substances Act (21 U.S.C. 802)), shall be imprisoned not more than fifteen years or fined under this title, or both.

(Added Pub.L. 99–570, Title I, § 1971(a), Oct. 27, 1986, 100 Stat. 3207–59, and amended Pub.L. 100–690, Title VI, §§ 6473(a), (b), 6482(b), Nov. 18, 1988, 102 Stat. 4379, 4382.)

HISTORICAL AND STATUTORY NOTES

References in Text

Section 102 of the Controlled Substances Act, referred to in text, is section 102 of Pub.L. 91–513, Title II, Oct. 27, 1970, 84 Stat. 1242, which is classified to section 802 of Title 21, Food and Drugs.

§ 343. Presumptions

For purposes of this chapter—

(1) an individual with a blood alcohol content of .10 percent or more shall be presumed to be under the influence of alcohol; and

(2) an individual shall be presumed to be under the influence of drugs if the quantity of the drug in the system of the individual would be sufficient to impair the perception, mental processes, or motor functions of the average individual.

(Added Pub.L. 99–570, Title I, § 1971(a), Oct. 27, 1986, 100 Stat. 3207–59, and amended Pub.L. 100–690, Title VI, § 6473(c), Nov. 18, 1988, 102 Stat. 4379.)

CHAPTER 18—CONGRESSIONAL, CABINET, AND SUPREME COURT ASSASSINATION, KIDNAPPING, AND ASSAULT

§ 351. Congressional, Cabinet, and Supreme Court assassination, kidnapping, and assault; penalties

(a) Whoever kills any individual who is a Member of Congress or a Member-of-Congress-elect, a member of the executive branch of the Government who is the head, or a person nominated to be head during the pendency of such nomination, of a department listed in section 101 of title 5 or the second ranking official in such department, the Director (or a person nominated to be Director during the pendency of such nomination) or Deputy Director of Central Intelligence, a major Presidential or Vice Presidential candidate (as defined in section 3056 of this title), or a Justice of the United States, as defined in section 451 of title 28, or a person nominated to be a Justice of the United States, during the pendency of such nomination, shall be punished as provided by sections 1111 and 1112 of this title.

(b) Whoever kidnaps any individual designated in subsection (a) of this section shall be punished (1) by imprisonment for any term of years or for life, or (2) by death or imprisonment for any term of years or for life, if death results to such individual.

(c) Whoever attempts to kill or kidnap any individual designated in subsection (a) of this section shall be punished by imprisonment for any term of years or for life.

(d) If two or more persons conspire to kill or kidnap any individual designated in subsection (a) of this section and one or more of such persons do any act to effect the object of the conspiracy, each shall be punished (1) by imprisonment for any term of years or for life, or (2) by death or imprisonment for any term of years or for life, if death results to such individual.

(e) Whoever assaults any person designated in subsection (a) of this section shall be fined under this title, or imprisoned not more than one year, or both; and if the assault involved the use of a dangerous weapon, or personal injury results, shall be fined under this title, or imprisoned not more than ten years, or both.

(f) If Federal investigative or prosecutive jurisdiction is asserted for a violation of this section, such assertion shall suspend the exercise of jurisdiction by a State or local authority, under any applicable State or local law, until Federal action is terminated.

(g) Violations of this section shall be investigated by the Federal Bureau of Investigation. Assistance may be requested from any Federal, State, or local agency, including the Army, Navy, and Air Force, any statute, rule, or regulation to the contrary notwithstanding.

(h) In a prosecution for an offense under this section the Government need not prove that the defendant knew that the victim of the offense was an individual protected by this section.

(i) There is extraterritorial jurisdiction over the conduct prohibited by this section.

(Added Pub.L. 91–644, Title IV, § 15, Jan. 2, 1971, 84 Stat. 1891, and amended Pub.L. 97–285, §§ 1, 2(a), Oct. 6, 1982, 96 Stat. 1219; Pub.L. 99–646, § 62, Nov. 10, 1986, 100 Stat. 3614; Pub.L. 100–690, Title VII, § 7074, Nov. 18, 1988, 102 Stat. 4405; Pub.L. 103–322, Title XXXII, § 320101(d), Title XXXIII, §§ 330016(1)(K), (L), 330021(1), Sept. 13, 1994, 108 Stat. 2108, 2147, 2150; Pub.L. 104–294, Title VI, § 604(b)(12)(C), (c)(2), Oct. 11, 1996, 110 Stat. 3507, 3509.)

HISTORICAL AND STATUTORY NOTES

Effective and Applicability Provisions

1996 Acts. Amendment by section 604 of Pub.L. 104–294 effective Sept. 13, 1994, see section 604(d) of Pub.L. 104–294, set out as a note under section 13 of this title.

Change of Name

Reference to the Director of Central Intelligence or the Director of the Central Intelligence Agency in the Director's capacity as the head of the intelligence community deemed to be a reference to the Director of National Intelligence. Reference to the Director of Central Intelligence or the Director of the Central Intelligence Agency in the Director's capacity as the head of the Central Intelligence Agency deemed to be a reference to the Director of the Central Intelligence Agency. See Pub.L. 108–458, § 1081(a) and (b), set out as a note under 50 U.S.C.A. § 401.

Repeals

Pub.L. 103–322, Title XXXII, § 320101(d)(3), Sept. 13, 1994, 108 Stat. 2108, appearing in the credit of this section, was repealed by Pub.L. 104–294, Title VI, § 604(b)(12)(C), Oct. 11, 1996, 110 Stat. 3507.

Report to Member of Congress on Investigation Conducted Subsequent to Threat on Member's Life

Pub.L. 95–624, § 19, Nov. 9, 1978, 92 Stat. 3466, provided that: "The Federal Bureau of Investigation shall provide a written report to a Member of Congress on any investigation conducted based on a threat on the Member's life under section 351 of title 18 of the United States Code [this section]."

CHAPTER 19—CONSPIRACY

Sec.

§ 371. Conspiracy to commit offense or to defraud United States

If two or more persons conspire either to commit any offense against the United States, or to defraud the United States, or any agency thereof in any manner or for any purpose, and one or more of such persons do any act to effect the object of the conspiracy, each shall be fined under this title or imprisoned not more than five years, or both.

If, however, the offense, the commission of which is the object of the conspiracy, is a misdemeanor only, the punishment for such conspiracy shall not exceed the maximum punishment provided for such misdemeanor.

(June 25, 1948, c. 645, 62 Stat. 701; Sept. 13, 1994, Pub.L. 103–322, Title XXXIII, § 330016(1)(L), 108 Stat. 2147.)

HISTORICAL AND STATUTORY NOTES

Canal Zone

Applicability of section to Canal Zone, see § 14 of this title.

§ 372. Conspiracy to impede or injure officer

If two or more persons in any State, Territory, Possession, or District conspire to prevent, by force, intimidation, or threat, any person from accepting or holding any office, trust, or place of confidence under the United States, or from discharging any duties thereof, or to induce by like means any officer of the United States to leave the place, where his duties as an officer are required to be performed, or to injure him in his person or property on account of his lawful discharge of the duties of his office, or while engaged in the lawful discharge thereof, or to injure his property so as to molest, interrupt, hinder, or impede him in the discharge of his official duties, each of such persons shall be fined under this title or imprisoned not more than six years, or both.

(June 25, 1948, c. 645, 62 Stat. 701; Nov. 2, 2002, Pub.L. 107–273, Div. B, Title IV, § 4002(d)(1)(D), 116 Stat. 1809.)

§ 373. Solicitation to commit a crime of violence

(a) Whoever, with intent that another person engage in conduct constituting a felony that has as an element the use, attempted use, or threatened use of physical force against property or against the person of another in violation of the laws of the United States, and under circumstances strongly corroborative of that intent, solicits, commands, induces, or otherwise endeavors to persuade such other person to engage in such conduct, shall be imprisoned not more than one-half the maximum term of imprisonment or (notwithstanding section 3571) fined not more than one-half of the maximum fine prescribed for the punishment of the crime solicited, or both; or if the crime solicited is punishable by life imprisonment or death, shall be imprisoned for not more than twenty years.

(b) It is an affirmative defense to a prosecution under this section that, under circumstances manifesting a voluntary and complete renunciation of his criminal intent, the defendant prevented the commission of the crime solicited. A renunciation is not "voluntary and complete" if it is motivated in whole or in part by a decision to postpone the commission of the crime until another time or to substitute another victim or another but similar objective. If the defendant raises the affirmative defense at trial, the defendant has the burden of proving the defense by a preponderance of the evidence.

(c) It is not a defense to a prosecution under this section that the person solicited could not be convicted of the crime because he lacked the state of mind required for its commission, because he was incompetent or irresponsible, or because he is immune from prosecution or is not subject to prosecution.

(Added Pub.L. 98–473, Title II, § 1003(a), Oct. 12, 1984, 98 Stat. 2138, and amended Pub.L. 99–646, § 26, Nov. 10, 1986, 100 Stat. 3597; Pub.L. 103–322, Title XXXIII, § 330016(2)(A), Sept. 13, 1994, 108 Stat. 2148.)

§§ 374 to 400. Reserved for future legislation

CHAPTER 21—CONTEMPTS

§ 401. Power of court

A court of the United States shall have power to punish by fine or imprisonment, or both, at its discretion, such contempt of its authority, and none other, as—

(1) Misbehavior of any person in its presence or so near thereto as to obstruct the administration of justice;

(2) Misbehavior of any of its officers in their official transactions;

(3) Disobedience or resistance to its lawful writ, process, order, rule, decree, or command.

(June 25, 1948, c. 645, 62 Stat. 701; Nov. 2, 2002, Pub.L. 107–273, Div. B, Title III, § 3002(a)(1), 116 Stat. 1805.)

§ 402. Contempts constituting crimes

Any person, corporation or association willfully disobeying any lawful writ, process, order, rule, decree, or command of any district court of the United States or any court of the District of Columbia, by doing any act or thing therein, or thereby forbidden, if the act or thing so done be of such character as to constitute also a criminal offense under any statute of the United States or under the laws of any State in which the act was committed, shall be prosecuted for such contempt as provided in section 3691 of this title and shall be punished by a fine under this title or imprisonment, or both.

Such fine shall be paid to the United States or to the complainant or other party injured by the act constituting the contempt, or may, where more than one is so damaged, be divided or apportioned among them as the court may direct, but in no case shall the fine to be paid to the United States exceed, in case the accused is a natural person, the sum of $1,000, nor shall such imprisonment exceed the term of six months.

This section shall not be construed to relate to contempts committed in the presence of the court, or so near thereto as to obstruct the administration of justice, nor to contempts committed in disobedience of any lawful writ, process, order, rule, decree, or command entered in any suit or action brought or prosecuted in the name of, or on behalf of, the United States, but the same, and all other cases of contempt not specifically embraced in this section may be punished in conformity to the prevailing usages at law.

For purposes of this section, the term "State" includes a State of the United States, the District of Columbia, and any commonwealth, territory, or possession of the United States.

(June 25, 1948, c. 645, 62 Stat. 701; May 24, 1949, c. 139, § 8(c), 63 Stat. 90; Pub.L. 101–647, Title XII, § 1205(c), Nov. 29, 1990, 104 Stat. 4830; Pub.L. 103–322, Title XXXIII, §§ 330011(f), 330016(2)(E), Sept. 13, 1994, 108 Stat. 2145, 2148.)

HISTORICAL AND STATUTORY NOTES

Effective and Applicability Provisions

1994 Acts. Section 330011(f) of Pub.L. 103–322 provided in part that the amendment made by that such section, amending directory language of section 1205(c) of Pub.L. 101–647 (which amended this section), was to take effect on the date section 1205(c) of Pub.L. 101–647 took effect; section 1205(c) of Pub.L. 101–647 took effect on the date of enactment of Pub.L. 101–647, which was approved Nov. 29, 1990.

§ 403. Protection of the privacy of child victims and child witnesses

A knowing or intentional violation of the privacy protection accorded by section 3509 of this title is a criminal contempt punishable by not more than one year's imprisonment, or a fine under this title, or both.

(Added Pub.L. 101–647, Title II, § 225(b)(1), Nov. 29, 1990, 104 Stat. 4805.)

CHAPTER 23—CONTRACTS

[1] Section repealed by Pub.L. 106–568 without corresponding amendment of chapter analysis.

§ 431. Contracts by Member of Congress

Whoever, being a Member of or Delegate to Congress, or a Resident Commissioner, either before or after he has qualified, directly or indirectly, himself, or by any other person in trust for him, or for his use or benefit, or on his account, undertakes, executes, holds, or enjoys, in whole or in part, any contract or agreement, made or entered into in behalf of the United States or any agency thereof, by any officer or person authorized to make contracts on its behalf, shall be fined under this title.

All contracts or agreements made in violation of this section shall be void; and whenever any sum of money is advanced by the United States or any agency thereof, in consideration of any such contract or agreement, it shall forthwith be repaid; and in case of failure or refusal to repay the same when demanded by the proper officer of the department or agency under whose authority such contract or agreement shall have been made or entered into, suit shall at once be brought against the person so failing or refusing and his sureties for the recovery of the money so advanced.

(June 25, 1948, c. 645, 62 Stat. 702; Oct. 31, 1951, c. 655, § 19, 65 Stat. 717; Sept. 13, 1994, Pub.L. 103–322, Title XXXIII, § 330016(1)(J), 108 Stat. 2147.)

§ 432. Officer or employee contracting with Member of Congress

Whoever, being an officer or employee of the United States, on behalf of the United States or any agency thereof, directly or indirectly makes or enters into any contract, bargain, or agreement, with any Member of or Delegate to Congress, or any Resident Commissioner, either before or after he has qualified, shall be fined under this title.

(June 25, 1948, c. 645, 62 Stat. 702; Sept. 13, 1994, Pub.L. 103–322, Title XXXIII, § 330016(1)(J), 108 Stat. 2147.)

§ 433. Exemptions with respect to certain contracts

Sections 431 and 432 of this title shall not extend to any contract or agreement made or entered into, or accepted by any incorporated company for the general benefit of such corporation; nor to the purchase or sale of bills of exchange or other property where the same are ready for delivery and payment therefor is made at the time of making or entering into the contract or agreement. Nor shall the provisions of such sections apply to advances, loans, discounts, purchase or repurchase agreements, extensions, or renewals thereof, or acceptances, releases or substitutions of security therefor or other contracts or agreements made or entered into under the Reconstruction Finance Corporation Act, the Agricultural Adjustment Act, the Federal Farm Loan Act, the Emergency Farm Mortgage Act of 1933, the Farm Credit Act of 1933, or the Home Owners Loan Act of 1933, the Farmers' Home Administration Act of 1946, the Bankhead-Jones Farm Tenant Act, or to crop insurance agreements or contracts or agreements of a kind which the Secretary of Agriculture may enter into with farmers.

Any exemption permitted by this section shall be made a matter of public record.

(June 25, 1948, c. 645, 62 Stat. 703; Oct. 4, 1961, Pub.L. 87–353, § 3(*o*), 75 Stat. 774.)

HISTORICAL AND STATUTORY NOTES

References in Text

The Reconstruction Finance Corporation Act, referred to in text, is Act Jan. 22, 1932, c. 8, 47 Stat. 5, as amended, which was classified to chapter 14 (§ 601 et seq.) of Title 15, Commerce and Trade, and has been eliminated from the Code.

The Agricultural Adjustment Act, referred to in text, is title I of Act May 12, 1933, c. 25, 48 Stat. 31, as amended, which is classified generally to chapter 26 (§ 601 et seq.) of Title 7, Agriculture.

The Federal Farm Loan Act, referred to in text, is Act July 17, 1916, c. 245, 39 Stat. 360, as amended, which was classified principally to sections 641 et seq. of Title 12, Banks and Banking. The Federal Farm Loan Act, as amended, was repealed by section 5.26(a) of the Farm Credit Act of 1971, Pub.L. 92–181, Dec. 10, 1971, 85 Stat. 624. Section 5.26(a) of the Farm Credit Act of 1971 also provided that all references in other legislation to the Acts repealed thereby "shall be deemed to refer to comparable provisions of this Act".

The Emergency Farm Mortgage Act of 1933, referred to in text, is title II of Act May 12, 1933, c. 25, 48 Stat. 31, as amended. Such title II was substantially repealed by Act June 30, 1947, c. 166, Title II, § 206(c), 61 Stat. 208; Act Aug. 6, 1953, c. 335, § 19, 67 Stat. 400: Act Oct. 4, 1961, Pub.L. 87–353, § 3(a), (b), (w), 75 Stat. 773, 774; Act Dec. 10, 1971, Pub.L. 92–181, Title V, § 5.26(a), 85 Stat. 624.

The Farm Credit Act of 1933, referred to in text, is Act June 16, 1933, c. 98, 48 Stat. 2, as amended, which was classified principally to subchapter IV (§ 1131 et seq.) of chapter 7 of Title 12, Banks and Banking. The Farm Credit Act of 1933, as amended, was repealed by section 5.26(a) of the Farm Credit Act of 1971, Pub.L. 92–181, Dec. 10, 1971, 85 Stat. 624. Section 5.26(a) of the Farm Credit Act of 1971 also provided that all references in other legislation to the Acts repealed thereby "shall be deemed to refer to comparable provisions of this Act".

The Home Owners Loan Act of 1933, referred to in text, is Act June 13, 1933, c. 64, 48 Stat. 128, as amended, now known as the Home Owner's Loan Act, which is classified generally to chapter 12 (§ 1461 et seq.) of Title 12.

The Farmers' Home Administration Act of 1946, referred to in text, is Act Aug. 14, 1946, c. 964, 60 Stat. 1062, as amended. Such Act was substantially repealed by Act June 25, 1948, c. 645, § 21, 62 Stat. 862, and Act Aug. 8, 1961, Pub.L. 87–128, Title III, § 341(a), 75 Stat. 318.

The Bankhead-Jones Farm Tenant Act, referred to in text, is Act July 22, 1937, c. 517, 50 Stat. 522, as amended, which is classified generally to chapter 33 (§ 1000 et seq.) of Title 7, Agriculture.

Transfer of Functions

All functions of all officers, agencies and employees of the Department of Agriculture were transferred, with certain exceptions, to the Secretary of Agriculture by 1953 Reorg. Plan No. 2, § 1, eff. June 4, 1953, 18 F.R. 3219, 67 Stat. 633, set out as a note under § 511 of this title.

Abolition of Home Owners' Loan Corporation

The Home Owners' Loan Corporation, which was created by the Home Owners' Loan Act of 1933, referred to in this section, was dissolved and abolished by Act June 30, 1953, c. 170, § 21, 67 Stat. 126, set out in note under § 1463 of Title 12, Banks and Banking.

Abolition of Reconstruction Finance Corporation

The Reconstruction Finance Corporation, which was created by the Reconstruction Finance Corporation Act, referred to in this section, was abolished by § 6(a) of 1957 Reorg. Plan No. 1, eff. June 30, 1957, 22 F.R. 4633, 71 Stat. 647, set out as a note under § 601 of Title 15, Commerce and Trade.

[§ 434. Repealed. Pub.L. 87–849, § 2, Oct. 23, 1962, 76 Stat. 1126]

HISTORICAL AND STATUTORY NOTES

Section, Act June 25, 1948, c. 645, 62 Stat. 703, related to interested persons acting as Government agents, and is now covered by § 208 of this title.

Effective Date of Repeal

Repeal of section effective 90 days after Oct. 23, 1962, see § 4 of Pub.L. 87–849, set out as a note under § 201 of this title.

Exemptions

Section 2 of Pub. L. 87–849 provided that all exemptions from the provisions of this section heretofore created or authorized by statute which are in force on the effective date of the repeal of this section deemed to be exemptions from § 208 of this title except to the extent that they affect officers or employees of the executive branch of the United States Government, of any independent agency of the United States, or of the District of Columbia, as to whom they are no longer applicable.

§ 435. Contracts in excess of specific appropriation

Whoever, being an officer or employee of the United States, knowingly contracts for the erection, repair, or furnishing of any public building, or for any public improvement, to pay a larger amount than the specific sum appropriated for such purpose, shall be fined under this title or imprisoned not more than one year, or both.

(June 25, 1948, c. 645, 62 Stat. 703; Sept. 13, 1994, Pub.L. 103–322, Title XXXIII, § 330016(1)(K), 108 Stat. 2147.)

Codification

Amendment by § 330016(1)(K) of Pub.L. 103–322, which directed that "under this title" be substituted for "not more than $5,000", was executed by substituting "under this title" for "not more than $1,000", as the probable intent of Congress.

§ 436. Convict labor contracts

Whoever, being an officer, employee, or agent of the United States or any department or agency thereof, contracts with any person or corporation, or permits any warden, agent, or official of any penal or correctional institution, to hire out the labor of any prisoners confined for violation of any laws of the United States, shall be fined under this title or imprisoned not more than three years, or both.

(June 25, 1948, c. 645, 62 Stat. 703; Sept. 13, 1994, Pub.L. 103–322, Title XXXIII, § 330016(1)(K), 108 Stat. 2147.)

Codification

Amendment by section 330016(1)(K) of Pub.L. 103–322, which directed that "under this title" be substituted for "not more than $5,000", was executed by substituting "under this title" for "not more than $1,000", as the probable intent of Congress.

[§ 437. Repealed. Pub.L. 104–178, § 1(a), Aug. 6, 1996, 110 Stat. 1565]

HISTORICAL AND STATUTORY NOTES

Section, Act June 25, 1948, c. 645, 62 Stat. 703; June 17, 1980, Pub.L. 96–277, § 1, 94 Stat. 544; Sept. 13, 1994, Pub.L. 103–322, Title XXXIII, § 330016(1)(L), 108 Stat. 2147, related to Federal employees contracting or trading with Indians.

Effective Date of Repeal

Section 1(c) of Pub.L. 104–178 provided that: "The repeal made by subsection (a) [repealing this section] shall—

"(1) take effect on the date of enactment of this Act [Aug. 6, 1996]; and

"(2) apply with respect to any contract obtained, and any purchase or sale occurring, on or after the date of enactment of this Act [Aug. 6, 1996]."

[§§ 438, 439. Repealed. Pub.L. 106–568, Title VIII, § 812(c)(2), Dec. 27, 2000, 114 Stat. 2917]

HISTORICAL AND STATUTORY NOTES

Section 438, Act June 25, 1948, c. 645, 62 Stat. 703; Sept. 13, 1994, Pub.L. 103–322, Title XXXIII, § 330016(1)(K), 108 Stat. 2147, related to Indian contracts for services generally.

Section 439, Act June 25, 1948, c. 645, 62 Stat. 704; Sept. 13, 1994, Pub.L. 103–322, Title XXXIII, § 330016(1)(H), 108 Stat. 2147, related to Indian enrollment contracts.

§ 440. Mail contracts

Whoever, being a person employed in the Postal Service, becomes interested in any contract for carrying the mail, or acts as agent, with or without compensation, for any contractor or person offering to become a contractor in any business before the Postal Service, shall be fined under this title or imprisoned not more than one year, or both.

(June 25, 1948, c. 645, 62 Stat. 704; Aug. 12, 1970, Pub.L. 91–375, § 6(j) (3), 84 Stat. 777; Sept. 13, 1994, Pub.L. 103–322, Title XXXIII, § 330016(1)(L), 108 Stat. 2147.)

HISTORICAL AND STATUTORY NOTES

Codifications

Amendment by section 330016(1)(L) of Pub.L. 103–322, which directed that "under this title" be substituted for "not more than $10,000", was executed by substituting "under this title" for "not more than $5,000", as the probable intent of Congress.

Effective and Applicability Provisions

1970 Acts. Amendment by Pub.L. 91–375 effective within 1 year after Aug. 12, 1970, on date established therefor by the Board of Governors of the United States Postal Service and published by it in the Federal Register, see section 15(a) of Pub.L. 91–375, set out as a note preceding section 101 of Title 39, Postal Service.

§ 441. Postal supply contracts

No contract for furnishing supplies to the Postal Service shall be made with any person who has entered, or proposed to enter, into any combination to prevent the making of any bid for furnishing such supplies, or to fix a price or prices therefor, or who has made any agreement, or given or performed, or promised to give or perform, any consideration whatever to induce any other person not to bid for any such contract, or to bid at a specified price or prices thereon.

Whoever violates this section shall be fined under this title or imprisoned not more than one year, or both; and if the offender is a contractor for furnishing such supplies his contract may be annulled.

(June 25, 1948, c. 645, 62 Stat. 704; Aug. 12, 1970, Pub.L. 91–375, § 6(j) (4), 84 Stat. 777; Sept. 13, 1994, Pub.L. 103–322, Title XXXIII, § 330016(1)(L), 108 Stat. 2147.)

HISTORICAL AND STATUTORY NOTES

Codifications

Amendment by section 330016(1)(L) of Pub.L. 103–322, which directed that "under this title" be substituted for "not more than $10,000", was executed by substituting "under this title" for "not more than $5,000", as the probable intent of Congress.

1994 Amendments. Pub.L. 103–322, which directed the amendment of this section by substituting "fined under this title" for "fined not more than $10,000", was executed by making the substitution for "fined not more than $5,000" in the second par., to reflect the probable intent of Congress.

1970 Amendments. Pub.L. 91–375 struck out "Post Office Department or the" preceding "Postal Service".

Effective and Applicability Provisions

1970 Acts. Amendment by Pub.L. 91–375 effective within 1 year after Aug. 12, 1970, on date established therefor by the Board of Governors of the United States Postal Service and published by it in the Federal Register and published by it in the Federal Register, out as a note preceding section 101 of Title 39, Postal Service.

§ 442. Printing contracts

Neither the Public Printer, superintendent of printing, superintendent of binding, nor any of their assistants shall, during their continuance in office, have any interest, direct or indirect, in the publication of any newspaper or periodical, or in any printing, binding, engraving, or lithographing of any kind, or in any contract for furnishing paper or other material connected with the public printing, binding, lithographing, or engraving.

Whoever violates this section shall be fined under this title or imprisoned not more than one year, or both.

(June 25, 1948, c. 645, 62 Stat. 704; Sept. 13, 1994, Pub.L. 103–322, Title XXXIII, § 330016(1)(H), 108 Stat. 2147.)

§ 443. War contracts

Whoever willfully secretes, mutilates, obliterates, or destroys—

(a) any records of a war contractor relating to the negotiation, award, performance, payment, interim financing, cancellation or other termination, or settlement of a war contract of $25,000 or more; or

(b) any records of a war contractor or purchaser relating to any disposition of termination inventory in which the consideration received by any war contractor or any government agency is $5,000 or more,

before the lapse of (1) five years after such disposition of termination inventory by such war contractor or government agency, or (2) five years after the final settlement of such war contract, whichever applicable period is longer, shall be fined under this title or imprisoned not more than five years, or both.

The Administrator of General Services, by regulation, may authorize the destruction of such records upon such terms and conditions as he deems appropriate, including the requirement for the making and retaining of photographs or microphotographs, which shall have the same force and effect as the originals thereof.

The definitions of terms in section 103 of Title 41 shall apply to similar terms used in this section.

(June 25, 1948, c. 645, 62 Stat. 705; Oct. 31, 1951, c. 655, § 20(a), 65 Stat. 717; Sept. 13, 1994, Pub.L. 103–322, Title XXXIII, §§ 330004(17), 330016(2)(F), 108 Stat. 2142, 2148.)

CHAPTER 25—COUNTERFEITING AND FORGERY

4-Year Congressional Review; Expedited Consideration

Effective on and after the first day of fiscal year 2005, amendments by Title III (§§ 301 to 377) of Pub.L. 107–56 shall terminate if Congress enacts a joint resolution to that effect; such resolution shall be given expedited consideration, see Pub.L. 107–56, Title III, § 303, Oct. 26, 2001, 115 Stat. 298, set out as a note under 31 U.S.C.A. § 5311.

§ 470. Counterfeit acts committed outside the United States

A person who, outside the United States, engages in the act of—

(1) making, dealing, or possessing any counterfeit obligation or other security of the United States; or

(2) making, dealing, or possessing any plate, stone, analog, digital, or electronic image, or other thing, or any part thereof, used to counterfeit such obligation or security,

if such act would constitute a violation of section 471, 473, or 474 if committed within the United States, shall be punished as is provided for the like offense within the United States.

(Added Pub.L. 103–322, Title XII, § 120003(a), Sept. 13, 1994, 108 Stat. 2021, and amended Pub.L. 107–56, Title III, § 374(a), Oct. 26, 2001, 115 Stat. 340.)

HISTORICAL AND STATUTORY NOTES

Termination Date of 2001 Amendment

Effective on and after the first day of fiscal year 2005, amendments by Title III (§§ 301 to 377) of Pub.L. 107–56 shall terminate if Congress enacts a joint resolution to that effect; such resolution shall be given expedited consideration, see Pub.L. 107–56, Title III, § 303, Oct. 26, 2001, 115 Stat. 298, set out as a note under 31 U.S.C.A. § 5311.

Combatting International Counterfeiting of United States Currency

Pub.L. 104–132, Title VIII, § 807, Apr. 24, 1996, 110 Stat. 1308, provided that:

"**(a) In general.**—The Secretary of the Treasury (hereafter in this section referred to as the 'Secretary'), in consultation with the advanced counterfeit deterrence steering committee, shall—

"(1) study the use and holding of United States currency in foreign countries; and

"(2) develop useful estimates of the amount of counterfeit United States currency that circulates outside the United States each year.

"**(b) Evaluation audit plan.**—

"**(1) In general.**—The Secretary shall develop an effective international evaluation audit plan that is designed to enable the Secretary to carry out the duties described in subsection (a) on a regular and thorough basis.

"**(2) Submission of detailed written summary.**—The Secretary shall submit a detailed written summary of the evaluation audit plan developed pursuant to paragraph (1) to the Congress before the end of the 6–month period beginning on the date of the enactment of this Act [Apr. 24, 1996].

"**(3) First evaluation audit under plan.**—The Secretary shall begin the first evaluation audit pursuant to the evaluation audit plan no later than the end of the 1–year period beginning on the date of the enactment of this Act [Apr. 24, 1996].

"**(4) Subsequent evaluation audits.**—At least 1 evaluation audit shall be performed pursuant to the evaluation audit plan during each 3–year period beginning after the date of the commencement of the evaluation audit referred to in paragraph (3).

"**(c) Reports.**—

"**(1) In general.**—The Secretary shall submit a written report to the Committee on Banking and Financial Services of the House of Representatives and the Committee on Banking, Housing, and Urban Affairs of the Senate on the results of each evaluation audit conducted pursuant to subsection (b) within 90 days after the completion of the evaluation audit.

"**(2) Contents.**—In addition to such other information as the Secretary may determine to be appropriate, each report submitted to the Congress pursuant to paragraph (1) shall include the following information:

"(A) A detailed description of the evaluation audit process and the methods used to develop estimates of the amount of counterfeit United States currency in circulation outside the United States.

"(B) The method used to determine the currency sample examined in connection with the evaluation audit and a statistical analysis of the sample examined.

"(C) A list of the regions of the world, types of financial institutions, and other entities included.

"(D) An estimate of the total amount of United States currency found in each region of the world.

"(E) The total amount of counterfeit United States currency and the total quantity of each counterfeit denomination found in each region of the world.

"**(3) Classification of information.**—

"**(A) In general.**—To the greatest extent possible, each report submitted to the Congress under this subsection shall be submitted in an unclassified form.

"**(B) Classified and unclassified forms.**—If, in the interest of submitting a complete report under this subsection, the Secretary determines that it is necessary to include classified information in the report, the report shall be submitted in a classified and an unclassified form.

"**(d) Sunset provision.**—This section [this note] shall cease to be effective as of the end of the 10–year period beginning on the date of the enactment of this Act [Apr. 24, 1996].

"**(e) Rule of construction.**—No provision of this section [this note] shall be construed as authorizing any entity to conduct investigations of counterfeit United States currency.

"**(f) Findings.**—The Congress hereby finds the following:

"(1) United States currency is being counterfeited outside the United States.

"(2) The One Hundred Third Congress enacted, with the approval of the President on September 13, 1994, section 470 of title 18, United States Code [this section], making such activity a crime under the laws of the United States.

"(3) The expeditious posting of agents of the United States Secret Service to overseas posts, which is necessary for the effective enforcement of section 470 [this section] and related criminal provisions, has been delayed.

"(4) While section 470 of title 18, United States Code [this section], provides for a maximum term of imprisonment of 20 years as opposed to a maximum term of 15 years for domestic counterfeiting, the United States Sentencing Commission has failed to provide, in its sentencing guidelines, for an appropriate enhancement of punishment for defendants convicted of counterfeiting United States currency outside the United States.

"**(g) Timely consideration of requests for concurrence in creation of overseas posts.**—

"**(1) In general.**—The Secretary of State shall—

"(A) consider in a timely manner the request by the Secretary of the Treasury for the placement of such number of agents of the United States Secret Service as the Secretary of the Treasury considers appropriate in posts in overseas embassies; and

"(B) reach an agreement with the Secretary of the Treasury on such posts as soon as possible and, in any event, not later than December 31, 1996.

"**(2) Cooperation of Treasury required.**—The Secretary of the Treasury shall promptly provide any information requested by the Secretary of State in connection with such requests.

"**(3) Reports required.**—The Secretary of the Treasury and the Secretary of State shall each submit, by February 1, 1997, a written report to the Committee on Banking and Financial Services of the House of Representatives and the Committee on Banking, Housing, and Urban Affairs of the Senate explaining the reasons for the rejection, if any, of any proposed post and the reasons for the failure, if any, to fill any approved post by such date.

"(h) Enhanced penalties for international counterfeiting of United States currency.—Pursuant to the authority of the United States Sentencing Commission under section 994 of title 28, United States Code [section 994 of Title 28, Judiciary and Judicial Procedure], the Commission shall amend the sentencing guidelines prescribed by the Commission to provide an appropriate enhancement of the punishment for a defendant convicted under section 470 of title 18 of such Code [this section]."

[For transfer of the functions, personnel, assets, and obligations of the United States Secret Service, including the functions of the Secretary of the Treasury relating thereto, to the Secretary of Homeland Security, and for treatment of related references, see 6 U.S.C.A. §§ 381, 551(d), 552(d) and 557, and the Department of Homeland Security Reorganization Plan of November 25, 2002, as modified, set out as a note under 6 U.S.C.A. § 542.]

§ 471. Obligations or securities of United States

Whoever, with intent to defraud, falsely makes, forges, counterfeits, or alters any obligation or other security of the United States, shall be fined under this title or imprisoned not more than 20 years, or both.

(June 25, 1948, c. 645, 62 Stat. 705; Sept. 13, 1994, Pub.L. 103–322, Title XXXIII, § 330016(1)(K), 108 Stat. 2147; Oct. 26, 2001, Pub.L. 107–56, Title III, § 374(b), 115 Stat. 340.)

HISTORICAL AND STATUTORY NOTES

Short Title

1992 Amendments. Pub.L. 102–550, Title XV, § 1551, Oct. 28, 1992, 106 Stat. 4070, provided that: "This subtitle [enacting 18 U.S.C.A. § 474A and amending 18 U.S.C.A. §§ 474 and 504] may be cited as the 'Counterfeit Deterrence Act of 1992'."

Termination Date of 2001 Amendment

Effective on and after the first day of fiscal year 2005, amendments by Title III (§§ 301 to 377) of Pub.L. 107–56 shall terminate if Congress enacts a joint resolution to that effect; such resolution shall be given expedited consideration, see Pub.L. 107–56, Title III, § 303, Oct. 26, 2001, 115 Stat. 298, set out as a note under 31 U.S.C.A. § 5311.

Canal Zone

Applicability of section to Canal Zone, see § 14 of this title.

§ 472. Uttering counterfeit obligations or securities

Whoever, with intent to defraud, passes, utters, publishes, or sells, or attempts to pass, utter, publish, or sell, or with like intent brings into the United States or keeps in possession or conceals any falsely made, forged, counterfeited, or altered obligation or other security of the United States, shall be fined under this title or imprisoned not more than 20 years, or both.

(June 25, 1948, c. 645, 62 Stat. 705; Sept. 13, 1994, Pub.L. 103–322, Title XXXIII, § 330016(1)(K), 108 Stat. 2147; Oct. 26, 2001, Pub.L. 107–56, Title III, § 374(c), 115 Stat. 340.)

HISTORICAL AND STATUTORY NOTES

Termination Date of 2001 Amendment

Effective on and after the first day of fiscal year 2005, amendments by Title III (§§ 301 to 377) of Pub.L. 107–56 shall terminate if Congress enacts a joint resolution to that effect; such resolution shall be given expedited consideration, see Pub.L. 107–56, Title III, § 303, Oct. 26, 2001, 115 Stat. 298, set out as a note under 31 U.S.C.A. § 5311.

Canal Zone

Applicability of section to Canal Zone, see § 14 of this title.

§ 473. Dealing in counterfeit obligations or securities

Whoever buys, sells, exchanges, transfers, receives, or delivers any false, forged, counterfeited, or altered obligation or other security of the United States, with the intent that the same be passed, published, or used as true and genuine, shall be fined under this title or imprisoned not more than 20 years, or both.

(June 25, 1948, c. 645, 62 Stat. 705; Sept. 13, 1994, Pub.L. 103–322, Title XXXIII, § 330016(1)(K), 108 Stat. 2147; Oct. 26, 2001, Pub.L. 107–56, Title III, § 374(d), 115 Stat. 340.)

HISTORICAL AND STATUTORY NOTES

Termination Date of 2001 Amendment

Effective on and after the first day of fiscal year 2005, amendments by Title III (§§ 301 to 377) of Pub.L. 107–56 shall terminate if Congress enacts a joint resolution to that effect; such resolution shall be given expedited consideration, see Pub.L. 107–56, Title III, § 303, Oct. 26, 2001, 115 Stat. 298, set out as a note under 31 U.S.C.A. § 5311.

Canal Zone

Applicability of section to Canal Zone, see § 14 of this title.

§ 474. Plates, stones, or analog, digital, or electronic images for counterfeiting obligations or securities

(a) Whoever, having control, custody, or possession of any plate, stone, or other thing, or any part thereof, from which has been printed, or which may be prepared by direction of the Secretary of the Treasury for the purpose of printing, any obligation or other security of the United States, uses such plate, stone, or other thing, or any part thereof, or knowingly suffers the same to be used for the purpose of printing any such or similar obligation or other security, or any part thereof, except as may be printed for the use of the United States by order of the proper officer thereof; or

Whoever makes or executes any plate, stone, or other thing in the likeness of any plate designated for the printing of such obligation or other security; or

Whoever, with intent to defraud, makes, executes, acquires, scans, captures, records, receives, transmits, reproduces, sells, or has in such person's control, custody, or possession, an analog, digital, or electronic image of any obligation or other security of the United States; or

Whoever sells any such plate, stone, or other thing, or brings into the United States any such plate, stone, or other thing, except under the direction of the Secretary of the Treasury or other proper officer, or with any other intent, in either case, than that such plate, stone, or other thing be used for the printing of the obligations or other securities of the United States; or

Whoever has in his control, custody, or possession any plate, stone, or other thing in any manner made after or in the similitude of any plate, stone, or other thing, from which any such obligation or other security has been printed, with intent to use such plate, stone, or other thing, or to suffer the same to be used in forging or counterfeiting any such obligation or other security, or any part thereof; or

Whoever has in his possession or custody, except under authority from the Secretary of the Treasury or other proper officer, any obligation or other security made or executed, in whole or in part, after the similitude of any obligation or other security issued under the authority of the United States, with intent to sell or otherwise use the same; or

Whoever prints, photographs, or in any other manner makes or executes any engraving, photograph, print, or impression in the likeness of any such obligation or other security, or any part thereof, or sells any such engraving, photograph, print, or impression, except to the United States, or brings into the United States, any such engraving, photograph, print, or impression, except by direction of some proper officer of the United States—

Is guilty of a class B felony.

(b) For purposes of this section, the term "analog, digital, or electronic image" includes any analog, digital, or electronic method used for the making, execution, acquisition, scanning, capturing, recording, retrieval, transmission, or reproduction of any obligation or security, unless such use is authorized by the Secretary of the Treasury. The Secretary shall establish a system (pursuant to section 504) to ensure that the legitimate use of such electronic methods and retention of such reproductions by businesses, hobbyists, press and others shall not be unduly restricted.

(June 25, 1948, c. 645, 62 Stat. 706; Oct. 28, 1992, Pub.L. 102–550, Title XV, § 1552, 106 Stat. 4070; Sept. 30, 1996, Pub.L. 104–208, Div. A, Title I, § 101(f) [Title VI, § 648(a)], Title II, § 2603(a), 110 Stat. 3009–367, 3009–470; Oct. 26, 2001, Pub.L. 107–56, Title III, § 374(e)(1) to (3), 115 Stat. 340.)

HISTORICAL AND STATUTORY NOTES

Codifications

In subsec. (a), Pub.L. 104–208, Div. A, Title I, § 101(f) [Title VI, § 648(a)] substituted "class B felony" for "class C felony". An identical amendment by Pub.L. 104–208, Div. A, Title II, § 2603(a), was not executed to text.

Effective and Applicability Provisions

1996 Acts. Section 101(f) [Title VI, § 648(c)] of Pub.L. 104–208 provided that: "This section and the amendments made by this section [enacting section 514 of this title and amending this section and section 474A of this title] shall become effective on the date of enactment of this Act [Sept. 30, 1996] and shall remain in effect during each fiscal year following that date of enactment."

1992 Acts. Except as otherwise provided, amendment by Pub.L. 102–550 effective Oct. 28, 1992, see section 2 of Pub.L. 102–550, set out as a note under section 5301 of Title 42, The Public Health and Welfare.

Termination Date of 2001 Amendment

Effective on and after the first day of fiscal year 2005, amendments by Title III (§§ 301 to 377) of Pub.L. 107–56 shall terminate if Congress enacts a joint resolution to that effect; such resolution shall be given expedited consideration, see Pub.L. 107–56, Title III, § 303, Oct. 26, 2001, 115 Stat. 298, set out as a note under 31 U.S.C.A. § 5311.

Canal Zone

Applicability of section to Canal Zone, see § 14 of this title.

§ 474A. Deterrents to counterfeiting of obligations and securities

(a) Whoever has in his control or possession, after a distinctive paper has been adopted by the Secretary of the Treasury for the obligations and other securities of the United States, any similar paper adapted to the making of any such obligation or other security, except under the authority of the Secretary of the Treasury, is guilty of a class B felony.

(b) Whoever has in his control or possession, after a distinctive counterfeit deterrent has been adopted by the Secretary of the Treasury for the obligations and other securities of the United States by publication in the Federal Register, any essentially identical feature or device adapted to the making of any such obligation or security, except under the authority of the Secretary of the Treasury, is guilty of a class B felony.

(c) As used in this section—

(1) the term "distinctive paper" includes any distinctive medium of which currency is made, whether of wood pulp, rag, plastic substrate, or other natural or artificial fibers or materials; and

(2) the term "distinctive counterfeit deterrent" includes any ink, watermark, seal, security thread, optically variable device, or other feature or device;

(A) in which the United States has an exclusive property interest; or

(B) which is not otherwise in commercial use or in the public domain and which the Secretary designates as being necessary in preventing the counterfeiting of obligations or other securities of the United States.

(Added Pub.L. 102–550, Title XV, § 1553(a), Oct. 28, 1992, 106 Stat. 4070, and amended Pub.L. 104–208, Div. A, Title I, § 101(f) [Title VI, § 648(a)], Title II, § 2603(a), Sept. 30, 1996, 110 Stat. 3009–367, 3009–470.)

HISTORICAL AND STATUTORY NOTES

Codifications

In subsecs. (a) and (b), Pub.L. 104–208, Div. A, Title I, § 101(f) [Title VI, § 648(a)], substituted "class B felony" for "class C felony" wherever appearing. An identical amendment by Pub.L. 104–208, Div. A, Title II, § 2603(a) was not executed to text.

Effective and Applicability Provisions

1996 Acts. Amendment by Pub.L. 104–208 effective Sept. 30, 1996, see section 101(f) [Title VI, § 648(c)] of Pub.L. 104–208, set out as a note under section 474 of this title.

§ 475. Imitating obligations or securities; advertisements

Whoever designs, engraves, prints, makes, or executes, or utters, issues, distributes, circulates, or uses any business or professional card, notice, placard, circular, handbill, or advertisement in the likeness or similitude of any obligation or security of the United States issued under or authorized by any Act of Congress or writes, prints, or otherwise impresses upon or attaches to any such instrument, obligation, or security, or any coin of the United States, any business or professional card, notice, or advertisement, or any notice or advertisement whatever, shall be fined under this title. Nothing in this section applies to evidence of postage payment approved by the United States Postal Service.

(June 25, 1948, c. 645, 62 Stat. 706; July 16, 1951, c. 226, § 2, 65 Stat. 122; Sept. 13, 1994, Pub.L. 103–322, Title XXXIII, § 330016(1)(G), 108 Stat. 2147; Jan. 5, 2006, Pub.L. 109–162, Title XI, § 1192, 119 Stat. 3129.)

HISTORICAL AND STATUTORY NOTES

Canal Zone

Applicability of section to Canal Zone, see § 14 of this title.

§ 476. Taking impressions of tools used for obligations or securities

Whoever, without authority from the United States, takes, procures, or makes an impression, stamp, analog, digital, or electronic image, or imprint of, from or by the use of any tool, implement, instrument, or thing used or fitted or intended to be used in printing, stamping, or impressing, or in making other tools, implements, instruments, or things to be used or fitted or intended to be used in printing, stamping, or impressing any obligation or other security of the United States, shall be fined under this title or imprisoned not more than 25 years, or both.

(June 25, 1948, c. 645, 62 Stat. 707; Sept. 13, 1994, Pub.L. 103–322, Title XXXIII, § 330016(1)(K), 108 Stat. 2147; Oct. 26, 2001, Pub.L. 107–56, Title III, § 374(f), 115 Stat. 341.)

HISTORICAL AND STATUTORY NOTES

1994 Amendments. Pub.L. 103–322, § 330016(1)(K), substituted "under this title" for "not more than $5,000" wherever appearing.

Termination Date of 2001 Amendment

Effective on and after the first day of fiscal year 2005, amendments by Title III (§§ 301 to 377) of Pub.L. 107–56 shall terminate if Congress enacts a joint resolution to that effect; such resolution shall be given expedited consideration, see Pub.L. 107–56, Title III, § 303, Oct. 26, 2001, 115 Stat. 298, set out as a note under 31 U.S.C.A. § 5311.

Canal Zone

Applicability of section to Canal Zone, see § 14 of this title.

§ 477. Possessing or selling impressions of tools used for obligations or securities

Whoever, with intent to defraud, possesses, keeps, safeguards, or controls, without authority from the United States, any imprint, stamp, analog, digital, or electronic image, or impression, taken or made upon any substance or material whatsoever, of any tool, implement, instrument or thing, used, fitted or intended to be used, for any of the purposes mentioned in section 476 of this title; or

Whoever, with intent to defraud, sells, gives, or delivers any such imprint, stamp, analog, digital, or electronic image, or impression to any other person—

Shall be fined under this title or imprisoned not more than 25 years, or both.

(June 25, 1948, c. 645, 62 Stat. 707; Sept. 13, 1994, Pub.L. 103–322, Title XXXIII, § 330016(1)(K), 108 Stat. 2147; Oct. 26, 2001, Pub.L. 107–56, Title III, § 374(g), 115 Stat. 341.)

HISTORICAL AND STATUTORY NOTES

Termination Date of 2001 Amendment

Effective on and after the first day of fiscal year 2005, amendments by Title III (§§ 301 to 377) of Pub.L. 107–56 shall terminate if Congress enacts a joint resolution to that effect; such resolution shall be given expedited consideration, see Pub.L. 107–56, Title III, § 303, Oct. 26, 2001, 115 Stat. 298, set out as a note under 31 U.S.C.A. § 5311.

Canal Zone

Applicability of section to Canal Zone, see § 14 of this title.

§ 478. Foreign obligations or securities

Whoever, within the United States, with intent to defraud, falsely makes, alters, forges, or counterfeits any bond, certificate, obligation, or other security of any foreign government, purporting to be or in imitation of any such security issued under the authority of such foreign government, or any treasury note, bill, or promise to pay, lawfully issued by such foreign government and intended to circulate as money, shall be fined under this title or imprisoned not more than 20 years, or both.

(June 25, 1948, c. 645, 62 Stat. 707; Sept. 13, 1994, Pub.L. 103–322, Title XXXIII, § 330016(1)(K), 108 Stat. 2147; Oct. 26, 2001, Pub.L. 107–56, Title III, § 375(a), 115 Stat. 341.)

HISTORICAL AND STATUTORY NOTES

Termination Date of 2001 Amendment

Effective on and after the first day of fiscal year 2005, amendments by Title III (§§ 301 to 377) of Pub.L. 107–56 shall terminate if Congress enacts a joint resolution to that effect; such resolution shall be given expedited consideration, see Pub.L. 107–56, Title III, § 303, Oct. 26, 2001, 115 Stat. 298, set out as a note under 31 U.S.C.A. § 5311.

Canal Zone

Applicability of section to Canal Zone, see § 14 of this title.

§ 479. Uttering counterfeit foreign obligations or securities

Whoever, within the United States, knowingly and with intent to defraud, utters, passes, or puts off, in payment or negotiation, any false, forged, or counterfeited bond, certificate, obligation, security, treasury note, bill, or promise to pay, mentioned in section 478 of this title, whether or not the same was made, altered, forged, or counterfeited within the United States, shall be fined under this title or imprisoned not more than 20 years, or both.

(June 25, 1948, c. 645, 62 Stat. 707; Sept. 13, 1994, Pub.L. 103–322, Title XXXIII, § 330016(1)(J), 108 Stat. 2147; Oct. 26, 2001, Pub.L. 107–56, Title III, § 375(b), 115 Stat. 341.)

HISTORICAL AND STATUTORY NOTES

Termination Date of 2001 Amendment

Effective on and after the first day of fiscal year 2005, amendments by Title III (§§ 301 to 377) of Pub.L. 107–56 shall terminate if Congress enacts a joint resolution to that effect; such resolution shall be given expedited consideration, see Pub.L. 107–56, Title III, § 303, Oct. 26, 2001, 115 Stat. 298, set out as a note under 31 U.S.C.A. § 5311.

Canal Zone

Applicability of section to Canal Zone, see § 14 of this title.

§ 480. Possessing counterfeit foreign obligations or securities

Whoever, within the United States, knowingly and with intent to defraud, possesses or delivers any false, forged, or counterfeit bond, certificate, obligation, security, treasury note, bill, promise to pay, bank note, or bill issued by a bank or corporation of any foreign country, shall be fined under this title or imprisoned not more than 20 years, or both.

(June 25, 1948, c. 645, 62 Stat. 707; Sept. 13, 1994, Pub.L. 103–322, Title XXXIII, § 330016(1)(H), 108 Stat. 2147; Oct. 26, 2001, Pub.L. 107–56, Title III, § 375(c), 115 Stat. 341.)

HISTORICAL AND STATUTORY NOTES

Termination Date of 2001 Amendment

Effective on and after the first day of fiscal year 2005, amendments by Title III (§§ 301 to 377) of Pub.L. 107–56 shall terminate if Congress enacts a joint resolution to that effect; such resolution shall be given expedited consideration, see Pub.L. 107–56, Title III, § 303, Oct. 26, 2001, 115 Stat. 298, set out as a note under 31 U.S.C.A. § 5311.

Canal Zone

Applicability of section to Canal Zone, see § 14 of this title.

§ 481. Plates, stones, or analog, digital, or electronic images for counterfeiting foreign obligations or securities

Whoever, within the United States except by lawful authority, controls, holds, or possesses any plate, stone, or other thing, or any part thereof, from which has been printed or may be printed any counterfeit note, bond, obligation, or other security, in whole or in part, of any foreign government, bank, or corporation, or uses such plate, stone, or other thing, or knowingly permits or suffers the same to be used in counterfeiting such foreign obligations, or any part thereof; or

Whoever, except by lawful authority, makes or engraves any plate, stone, or other thing in the likeness or similitude of any plate, stone, or other thing designated for the printing of the genuine issues of the obligations of any foreign government, bank, or corporation; or

Whoever, with intent to defraud, makes, executes, acquires, scans, captures, records, receives, transmits, reproduces, sells, or has in such person's control, custody, or possession, an analog, digital, or electronic image of any bond, certificate, obligation, or other security of any foreign government, or of any treasury note, bill, or promise to pay, lawfully issued by such foreign government and intended to circulate as money; or

Whoever, except by lawful authority, prints, photographs, or makes, executes, or sells any engraving, photograph, print, or impression in the likeness of any genuine note, bond, obligation, or other security, or any part thereof, of any foreign government, bank, or corporation; or

Whoever brings into the United States any counterfeit plate, stone, or other thing, engraving, photograph, print, or other impressions of the notes, bonds, obligations, or other securities of any foreign government, bank, or corporation—

Shall be fined under this title or imprisoned not more than 25 years, or both.

(June 25, 1948, c. 645, 62 Stat. 708; Sept. 13, 1994, Pub.L. 103–322, Title XXXIII, § 330016(1)(K), 108 Stat. 2147; Oct. 26, 2001, Pub.L. 107–56, Title III, §§ 375(d)(1) to (3), 115 Stat. 341.)

HISTORICAL AND STATUTORY NOTES

Termination Date of 2001 Amendment

Effective on and after the first day of fiscal year 2005, amendments by Title III (§§ 301 to 377) of Pub.L. 107–56 shall terminate if Congress enacts a joint resolution to that effect; such resolution shall be given expedited consideration, see Pub.L. 107–56, Title III, § 303, Oct. 26, 2001, 115 Stat. 298, set out as a note under 31 U.S.C.A. § 5311.

Canal Zone

Applicability of section to Canal Zone, see § 14 of this title.

§ 482. Foreign bank notes

Whoever, within the United States, with intent to defraud, falsely makes, alters, forges, or counterfeits any bank note or bill issued by a bank or corporation of any foreign country, and intended by the law or usage of such foreign country to circulate as money, such bank or corporation being authorized by the laws of such country, shall be fined under this title or imprisoned not more than 20 years, or both.

(June 25, 1948, c. 645, 62 Stat. 708; Sept. 13, 1994, Pub.L. 103–322, Title XXXIII, § 330016(1)(I), 108 Stat. 2147; Oct. 26, 2001, Pub.L. 107–56, Title III, § 375(e), 115 Stat. 342.)

HISTORICAL AND STATUTORY NOTES

Termination Date of 2001 Amendment

Effective on and after the first day of fiscal year 2005, amendments by Title III (§§ 301 to 377) of Pub.L. 107–56 shall terminate if Congress enacts a joint resolution to that effect; such resolution shall be given expedited consideration, see Pub.L. 107–56, Title III, § 303, Oct. 26, 2001, 115 Stat. 298, set out as a note under 31 U.S.C.A. § 5311.

Canal Zone

Applicability of section to Canal Zone, see § 14 of this title.

§ 483. Uttering counterfeit foreign bank notes

Whoever, within the United States, utters, passes, puts off, or tenders in payment, with intent to defraud, any such false, forged, altered, or counterfeited bank note or bill, mentioned in section 482 of this title, knowing the same to be so false, forged, altered, and counterfeited, whether or not the same was made, forged, altered, or counterfeited within the United States, shall be fined under this title or imprisoned not more than 20 years, or both.

(June 25, 1948, c. 645, 62 Stat. 708; Sept. 13, 1994, Pub.L. 103–322, Title XXXIII, § 330016(1)(H), 108 Stat. 2147; Oct. 26, 2001, Pub.L. 107–56, Title III, § 375(f), 115 Stat. 342.)

HISTORICAL AND STATUTORY NOTES

Termination Date of 2001 Amendment

Effective on and after the first day of fiscal year 2005, amendments by Title III (§§ 301 to 377) of Pub.L. 107–56 shall terminate if Congress enacts a joint resolution to that effect; such resolution shall be given expedited consideration, see Pub.L. 107–56, Title III, § 303, Oct. 26, 2001, 115 Stat. 298, set out as a note under 31 U.S.C.A. § 5311.

Canal Zone

Applicability of section to Canal Zone, see § 14 of this title.

§ 484. Connecting parts of different notes

Whoever so places or connects together different parts of two or more notes, bills, or other genuine instruments issued under the authority of the United States, or by any foreign government, or corporation, as to produce one instrument, with intent to defraud, shall be guilty of forgery in the same manner as if the parts so put together were falsely made or forged, and shall be fined under this title or imprisoned not more than 10 years, or both.

(June 25, 1948, c. 645, 62 Stat. 708; Sept. 13, 1994, Pub.L. 103–322, Title XXXIII, § 330016(1)(H), 108 Stat. 2147; Oct. 26, 2001, Pub.L. 107–56, Title III, § 374(h), 115 Stat. 341.)

HISTORICAL AND STATUTORY NOTES

Termination Date of 2001 Amendment

Effective on and after the first day of fiscal year 2005, amendments by Title III (§§ 301 to 377) of Pub.L. 107–56 shall terminate if Congress enacts a joint resolution to that effect; such resolution shall be given expedited consideration, see Pub.L. 107–56, Title III, § 303, Oct. 26, 2001, 115 Stat. 298, set out as a note under 31 U.S.C.A. § 5311.

Canal Zone

Applicability of section to Canal Zone, see § 14 of this title.

§ 485. Coins or bars

Whoever falsely makes, forges, or counterfeits any coin or bar in resemblance or similitude of any coin of a denomination higher than 5 cents or any gold or silver bar coined or stamped at any mint or assay office of the United States, or in resemblance or similitude of any foreign gold or silver coin current in the United States or in actual use and circulation as money within the United States; or

Whoever passes, utters, publishes, sells, possesses, or brings into the United States any false, forged, or counterfeit coin or bar, knowing the same to be false, forged, or counterfeit, with intent to defraud any body politic or corporate, or any person, or attempts the commission of any offense described in this paragraph—

Shall be fined under this title or imprisoned not more than fifteen years, or both.

(June 25, 1948, c. 645, 62 Stat. 708; July 23, 1965, Pub.L. 89–81, Title II, § 211(a), 79 Stat. 257; Sept. 13, 1994, Pub.L. 103–322, Title XXXIII, § 330016(1)(K), 108 Stat. 2147.)

HISTORICAL AND STATUTORY NOTES

Canal Zone

Applicability of section to Canal Zone, see § 14 of this title.

§ 486. Uttering coins of gold, silver or other metal

Whoever, except as authorized by law, makes or utters or passes, or attempts to utter or pass, any coins of gold or silver or other metal, or alloys of metals, intended for use as current money, whether in the resemblance of coins of the United States or of foreign countries, or of original design, shall be fined under this title or imprisoned not more than five years, or both.

(June 25, 1948, c. 645, 62 Stat. 709; Sept. 13, 1994, Pub.L. 103–322, Title XXXIII, § 330016(1)(I), 108 Stat. 2147.)

HISTORICAL AND STATUTORY NOTES

Canal Zone

Applicability of section to Canal Zone, see § 14 of this title.

§ 487. Making or possessing counterfeit dies for coins

Whoever, without lawful authority, makes any die, hub, or mold, or any part thereof, either of steel or plaster, or any other substance, in likeness or similitude, as to the design or the inscription thereon, of any die, hub, or mold designated for the coining or making of any of the genuine gold, silver, nickel, bronze, copper, or other coins coined at the mints of the United States; or

Whoever, without lawful authority, possesses any such die, hub, or mold, or any part thereof, or permits the same to be used for or in aid of the counterfeiting of any such coins of the United States—

Shall be fined under this title or imprisoned not more than fifteen years, or both.

(June 25, 1948, c. 645, 62 Stat. 709; Sept. 13, 1994, Pub.L. 103–322, Title XXXIII, § 330016(1)(K), 108 Stat. 2147.)

HISTORICAL AND STATUTORY NOTES

Canal Zone

Applicability of section to Canal Zone, see § 14 of this title.

§ 488. Making or possessing counterfeit dies for foreign coins

Whoever, within the United States, without lawful authority, makes any die, hub, or mold, or any part thereof, either of steel or of plaster, or of any other substance, in the likeness or similitude, as to the design or the inscription thereon, of any die, hub, or mold designated for the coining of the genuine coin of any foreign government; or

Whoever, without lawful authority, possesses any such die, hub, or mold, or any part thereof, or conceals, or knowingly suffers the same to be used for the counterfeiting of any foreign coin—

Shall be fined under this title or imprisoned not more than five years, or both.

(June 25, 1948, c. 645, 62 Stat. 709; Sept. 13, 1994, Pub.L. 103–322, Title XXXIII, § 330016(1)(K), 108 Stat. 2147.)

HISTORICAL AND STATUTORY NOTES

Canal Zone

Applicability of section to Canal Zone, see § 14 of this title.

§ 489. Making or possessing likeness of coins

Whoever, within the United States, makes or brings therein from any foreign country, or possesses with intent to sell, give away, or in any other manner uses the same, except under authority of the Secretary of the Treasury or other proper officer of the United States, any token, disk, or device in the likeness or similitude as to design, color, or the inscription thereon of any of the coins of the United States or of any foreign country issued as money, either under the authority of the United States or under the authority of any foreign government shall be fined under this title.

(June 25, 1948, c. 645, 62 Stat. 709; July 16, 1951, c. 226, § 3, 65 Stat. 122; Sept. 13, 1994, Pub.L. 103–322, Title XXXIII, § 330016(1)(B), 108 Stat. 2146.)

HISTORICAL AND STATUTORY NOTES

Canal Zone

Applicability of section to Canal Zone, see § 14 of this title.

§ 490. Minor coins

Whoever falsely makes, forges, or counterfeits any coin in the resemblance or similitude of any of the one-cent and 5-cent coins minted at the mints of the United States; or

Whoever passes, utters, publishes, or sells, or brings into the United States, or possesses any such false, forged, or counterfeited coin, with intent to defraud any person, shall be fined under this title or imprisoned not more than three years, or both.

(June 25, 1948, c. 645, 62 Stat. 709; Feb. 14, 1984, Pub.L. 98–216, § 3(b)(1), 98 Stat. 6; Sept. 13, 1994, Pub.L. 103–322, Title XXXIII, § 330016(1)(H), 108 Stat. 2147.)

HISTORICAL AND STATUTORY NOTES

Effective and Applicability Provisions

1984 Acts. Section 4(c) of Pub.L. 98–216 provided that: "The amendments made by sections 1(3), (4), and (7) and 3(b)(1) of this Act [amending this section and sections 3322, 3528, and 5132 of Title 31, Money and Finance] are effective as of September 13, 1982."

Canal Zone

Applicability of section to Canal Zone, see § 14 of this title.

§ 491. Tokens or paper used as money

(a) Whoever, being 18 years of age or over, not lawfully authorized, makes, issues, or passes any coin, card, token, or device in metal, or its compounds, intended to be used as money, or whoever, being 18 years of age or over, with intent to defraud, makes, utters, inserts, or uses any card, token, slug, disk, device, paper, or other thing similar in size and shape to any of the lawful coins or other currency of the United States or any coin or other currency not legal tender in the United States, to procure anything of value, or the use or enjoyment of any property or service from any automatic merchandise vending machine, postage-stamp machine, turnstile, fare box, coinbox telephone, parking meter or other lawful receptacle, depository, or contrivance designed to receive or to be operated by lawful coins or other currency of the United States, shall be fined under this title, or imprisoned not more than one year, or both.

(b) Whoever manufactures, sells, offers, or advertises for sale, or exposes or keeps with intent to furnish or sell any token, slug, disk, device, paper, or other thing similar in size and shape to any of the lawful coins or other currency of the United States, or any token, disk, paper, or other device issued or authorized in connection with rationing or food and fiber distribution by any agency of the United States, with knowledge or reason to believe that such tokens, slugs, disks, devices, papers, or other things are intended to be used unlawfully or fraudulently to procure anything of value, or the use or enjoyment of any property or service from any automatic merchandise vending machine, postage-stamp machine, turnstile, fare box, coinbox telephone, parking meter, or other lawful receptacle, depository, or contrivance designed to receive or to be operated by lawful coins or other currency of the United States shall be fined under this title or imprisoned not more than one year, or both.

Nothing contained in this section shall create immunity from criminal prosecution under the laws of any State, Commonwealth of Puerto Rico, territory, possession, or the District of Columbia.

(c) "Knowledge or reason to believe", within the meaning of paragraph (b) of this section, may be shown by proof that any law-enforcement officer has, prior to the commission of the offense with which the defendant is charged, informed the defendant that tokens, slugs, disks, or other devices of the kind manufactured, sold, offered, or advertised for sale by him or exposed or kept with intent to furnish or sell, are being used unlawfully or fraudulently to operate certain specified automatic merchandise vending machines, postage-stamp machines, turnstiles, fare boxes, coin-box telephones, parking meters, or other receptacles, depositories, or contrivances, designed to receive or to be operated by lawful coins of the United States.

(June 25, 1948, c. 645, 62 Stat. 709; Sept. 19, 1962, Pub.L. 87–667, 76 Stat. 555; Sept. 13, 1994, Pub.L. 103–322, Title XXXIII, § 330016(1)(H), 108 Stat. 2147.)

HISTORICAL AND STATUTORY NOTES

Canal Zone

Applicability of section to Canal Zone, see § 14 of this title.

§ 492. Forfeiture of counterfeit paraphernalia

All counterfeits of any coins or obligations or other securities of the United States or of any foreign government, or any articles, devices, and other things made, possessed, or used in violation of this chapter or of sections 331–333, 335, 336, 642 or 1720, of this title, or any material or apparatus used or fitted or intended to be used, in the making of such counterfeits, articles, devices or things, found in the possession of any person without authority from the Secretary of the Treasury or other proper officer, shall be forfeited to the United States.

Whoever, having the custody or control of any such counterfeits, material, apparatus, articles, devices, or other things, fails or refuses to surrender possession thereof upon request by any authorized agent of the Treasury Department, or other proper officer, shall be fined under this title or imprisoned not more than one year, or both.

Whenever, except as hereinafter in this section provided, any person interested in any article, device, or other thing, or material or apparatus seized under this section files with the Secretary of the Treasury, before the disposition thereof, a petition for the remission or mitigation of such forfeiture, the Secretary of the Treasury, if he finds that such forfeiture was incurred without willful negligence or without any intention on the part of the petitioner to violate the law, or finds the existence of such mitigating circumstances as to justify the remission or the mitigation of such forfeiture, may remit or mitigate the same upon such terms and conditions as he deems reasonable and just.

If the seizure involves offenses other than offenses against the coinage, currency, obligations or securities of the United States or any foreign government, the petition for the remission or mitigation of forfeiture shall be referred to the Attorney General, who may remit or mitigate the forfeiture upon such terms as he deems reasonable and just.

(June 25, 1948, c. 645, 62 Stat. 710; Nov. 2, 2002, Pub.L. 107–273, Div. B, Title IV, § 4002(d)(1)(A), 116 Stat. 1809.)

HISTORICAL AND STATUTORY NOTES

Canal Zone

Applicability of section to Canal Zone, see § 14 of this title.

§ 493. Bonds and obligations of certain lending agencies

Whoever falsely makes, forges, counterfeits or alters any note, bond, debenture, coupon, obligation, instrument, or writing in imitation or purporting to be in imitation of, a note, bond, debenture, coupon, obligation, instrument or writing, issued by the Reconstruction Finance Corporation, Federal Deposit Insurance Corporation, National Credit Union Administration, Home Owners' Loan Corporation, Farm Credit Administration, Department of Housing and Urban Development, or any land bank, intermediate credit bank, insured credit union, bank for cooperatives or any lending, mortgage, insurance, credit or savings and loan corporation or association authorized or acting under the laws of the United States, shall be fined under this title or imprisoned not more than 10 years, or both.

Whoever passes, utters, or publishes, or attempts to pass, utter or publish any note, bond, debenture, coupon, obligation, instrument or document knowing the same to have been falsely made, forged, counterfeited or altered, contrary to the provisions of this section, shall be fined under this title or imprisoned not more than 10 years, or both.

(June 25, 1948, c. 645, 62 Stat. 711; Oct. 4, 1961, Pub.L. 87–353, § 3(p), 75 Stat. 774; May 25, 1967, Pub.L. 90–19, § 24(a), 81 Stat. 27; Oct. 19, 1970, Pub.L. 91–468, § 3, 84 Stat. 1016; Sept. 13, 1994, Pub.L. 103–322, Title XXXIII, § 330016(1)(L), 108 Stat. 2147; Oct. 26, 2001, Pub.L. 107–56, Title III, § 374(i), 115 Stat. 341.)

HISTORICAL AND STATUTORY NOTES

Termination Date of 2001 Amendment

Effective on and after the first day of fiscal year 2005, amendments by Title III (§§ 301 to 377) of Pub.L. 107–56 shall terminate if Congress enacts a joint resolution, and such resolution shall be given expedited consideration, see Pub.L. 107–56, Title III, § 303, Oct. 26, 2001, 115 Stat. 298, set out as a note under 31 U.S.C.A. § 5311.

Exceptions from Transfer of Functions

Functions of the Corporations of the Department of Agriculture, the boards of directors and officers of such Corporations; the Advisory Board of the Commodity Credit Corporation; and the Farm Credit Administration or any agency, officer or entity of, under, or subject to the supervision of the said Administration were excepted from the functions of officers, agencies and employees transferred to the Secretary of Agriculture by 1953 Reorg. Plan No. 2, § 1, eff. June 4, 1953, 18 F.R. 3219, 67 Stat. 633, set out in the Appendix to Title 5, Government Organization and Employees.

Abolition of Home Owners' Loan Corporation

For dissolution and abolition of Home Owners' Loan Corporation, referred to in this section, by Act June 30, 1953, c. 170, § 21, 67 Stat. 126, see note under former § 1463 of Title 12, Banks and Banking.

Farm Credit Administration

Organization of Farm Credit Administration, see § 2241 et seq. of Title 12, Banks and Banking.

Abolition of Reconstruction Finance Corporation

Section 6(a) of 1957 Reorg. Plan No. 1, eff. June 30, 1957, 22 F.R. 4633, 71 Stat. 647, set out in the Appendix to Title 5, Government Organization and Employees, abolished the Reconstruction Finance Corporation.

Canal Zone

Applicability of section to Canal Zone, see § 14 of this title.

§ 494. Contractors' bonds, bids, and public records

Whoever falsely makes, alters, forges, or counterfeits any bond, bid, proposal, contract, guarantee, security, official bond, public record, affidavit, or other writing for the purpose of defrauding the United States; or

Whoever utters or publishes as true or possesses with intent to utter or publish as true, any such false, forged, altered, or counterfeited writing, knowing the same to be false, forged, altered, or counterfeited; or

Whoever transmits to, or presents at any office or to any officer of the United States, any such false, forged, altered, or counterfeited writing, knowing the same to be false, forged, altered, or counterfeited—

Shall be fined under this title or imprisoned not more than ten years, or both.

(June 25, 1948, c. 645, 62 Stat. 711; Sept. 13, 1994, Pub.L. 103–322, Title XXXIII, § 330016(1)(H), 108 Stat. 2147.)

HISTORICAL AND STATUTORY NOTES

Canal Zone

Applicability of section to Canal Zone, see § 14 of this title.

§ 495. Contracts, deeds, and powers of attorney

Whoever falsely makes, alters, forges, or counterfeits any deed, power of attorney, order, certificate, receipt, contract, or other writing, for the purpose of obtaining or receiving, or of enabling any other person, either directly or indirectly, to obtain or receive from the United States or any officers or agents thereof, any sum of money; or

Whoever utters or publishes as true any such false, forged, altered, or counterfeited writing, with intent to defraud the United States, knowing the same to be false, altered, forged, or counterfeited; or

Whoever transmits to, or presents at any office or officer of the United States, any such writing in support of, or in relation to, any account or claim, with intent to defraud the United States, knowing the same to be false, altered, forged, or counterfeited—

Shall be fined under this title or imprisoned not more than ten years, or both.

(June 25, 1948, c. 645, 62 Stat. 711; Sept. 13, 1994, Pub.L. 103–322, Title XXXIII, § 330016(1)(H), 108 Stat. 2147.)

HISTORICAL AND STATUTORY NOTES

Canal Zone

Applicability of section to Canal Zone, see § 14 of this title.

§ 496. Customs matters

Whoever forges, counterfeits or falsely alters any writing made or required to be made in connection with the entry or withdrawal of imports or collection of customs duties, or uses any such writing knowing the same to be forged, counterfeited or falsely altered, shall be fined under this title or imprisoned not more than three years, or both.

(June 25, 1948, c. 645, 62 Stat. 711; Sept. 13, 1994, Pub.L. 103–322, Title XXXIII, § 330016(1)(L), 108 Stat. 2147.)

HISTORICAL AND STATUTORY NOTES

Canal Zone

Applicability of section to Canal Zone, see § 14 of this title.

§ 497. Letters patent

Whoever falsely makes, forges, counterfeits, or alters any letters patent granted or purporting to have been granted by the President of the United States; or

Whoever passes, utters, or publishes, or attempts to pass, utter, or publish as genuine, any such letters patent, knowing the same to be forged, counterfeited or falsely altered—

Shall be fined under this title or imprisoned not more than ten years, or both.

(June 25, 1948, c. 645, 62 Stat. 712; Sept. 13, 1994, Pub.L. 103–322, Title XXXIII, § 330016(1)(K), 108 Stat. 2147.)

HISTORICAL AND STATUTORY NOTES

Canal Zone

Applicability of section to Canal Zone, see § 14 of this title.

§ 498. Military or naval discharge certificates

Whoever forges, counterfeits, or falsely alters any certificate of discharge from the military or naval service of the United States, or uses, unlawfully possesses or exhibits any such certificate, knowing the same to be forged, counterfeited, or falsely altered, shall be fined under this title or imprisoned not more than one year, or both.

(June 25, 1948, c. 645, 62 Stat. 712; Sept. 13, 1994, Pub.L. 103–322, Title XXXIII, § 330016(1)(K), 108 Stat. 2147.)

HISTORICAL AND STATUTORY NOTES

Canal Zone

Applicability of section to Canal Zone, see § 14 of this title.

§ 499. Military, naval, or official passes

Whoever falsely makes, forges, counterfeits, alters, or tampers with any naval, military, or official pass or permit, issued by or under the authority of the United States, or with intent to defraud uses or possesses any such pass or permit, or personates or falsely represents himself to be or not to be a person to whom such pass or permit has been duly issued, or willfully allows any other person to have or use any such pass or permit, issued for his use alone, shall be fined under this title or imprisoned not more than five years, or both.

(June 25, 1948, c. 645, 62 Stat. 712; Sept. 13, 1994, Pub.L. 103–322, Title XXXIII, § 330016(1)(I), 108 Stat. 2147.)

HISTORICAL AND STATUTORY NOTES

Canal Zone

Applicability of section to Canal Zone, see § 14 of this title.

§ 500. Money orders

Whoever, with intent to defraud, falsely makes, forges, counterfeits, engraves, or prints any order in imitation of or purporting to be a blank money order or a money order issued by or under the direction of the Post Office Department or Postal Service; or

Whoever forges or counterfeits the signature or initials of any person authorized to issue money orders upon or to any money order, postal note, or blank therefor provided or issued by or under the direction of the Post Office Department or Postal Service, or post office department or corporation of any foreign country, and payable in the United States, or any material signature or indorsement thereon, or any material signature to any receipt or certificate of identification thereof; or

Whoever falsely alters, in any material respect, any such money order or postal note; or

Whoever, with intent to defraud, passes, utters or publishes or attempts to pass, utter or publish any such forged or altered money order or postal note, knowing any material initials, signature, stamp impression or indorsement thereon to be false, forged, or counterfeited, or any material alteration therein to have been falsely made; or

Whoever issues any money order or postal note without having previously received or paid the full amount of money payable therefor, with the purpose of fraudulently obtaining or receiving, or fraudulently enabling any other person, either directly or indirectly, to obtain or receive from the United States or Postal Service, or any officer, employee, or agent thereof, any sum of money whatever; or

Whoever embezzles, steals, or knowingly converts to his own use or to the use of another, or without authority converts or disposes of any blank money order form provided by or under the authority of the Post Office Department or Postal Service; or

Whoever receives or possesses any such money order form with the intent to convert it to his own use or gain or use or gain of another knowing it to have been embezzled, stolen or converted; or

Whoever, with intent to defraud the United States, the Postal Service, or any person, transmits, presents, or causes to be transmitted or presented, any money order or postal note knowing the same—

(1) to contain any forged or counterfeited signature, initials, or any stamped impression, or

(2) to contain any material alteration therein unlawfully made, or

(3) to have been unlawfully issued without previous payment of the amount required to be paid upon such issue, or

(4) to have been stamped without lawful authority; or

Whoever steals, or with intent to defraud or without being lawfully authorized by the Post Office Department or Postal Service, receives, possesses, disposes of or attempts to dispose of any postal money order machine or any stamp, tool, or instrument specifically designed to be used in preparing or filling out the blanks on postal money order forms—

Shall be fined under this title or imprisoned not more than five years, or both.

(June 25, 1948, c. 645, 62 Stat. 712; Aug. 12, 1970, Pub.L. 91–375, § 6(j)(5), 84 Stat. 777; Sept. 23, 1972, Pub.L. 92–430, 86 Stat. 722; Sept. 13, 1994, Pub.L. 103–322, Title XXXIII, § 330016(1)(L), 108 Stat. 2147.)

HISTORICAL AND STATUTORY NOTES

Change of Name

The Post Office Department has been redesignated the United States Postal Service.

Effective and Applicability Provisions

1970 Acts. Amendment by Pub.L. 91–375 effective within 1 year after Aug. 12, 1970, on date established therefor by the Board of Governors of the United States Postal Service and published by it in the Federal Register, see § 15(a) of Pub.L. 91–375, set out as a note preceding § 101 of Title 39, Postal Service.

§ 501. Postage stamps, postage meter stamps, and postal cards

Whoever forges or counterfeits any postage stamp, postage meter stamp, or any stamp printed upon any stamped envelope, or postal card, or any die, plate, or engraving thereof; or

Whoever makes or prints, or knowingly uses or sells, or possesses with intent to use or sell, any such forged or counterfeited postage stamp, postage meter stamp, stamped envelope, postal card, die, plate, or engraving; or

Whoever makes, or knowingly uses or sells, or possesses with intent to use or sell, any paper bearing the watermark of any stamped envelope, or postal card, or any fraudulent imitation thereof; or

Whoever makes or prints, or authorizes to be made or printed, any postage stamp, postage meter stamp, stamped envelope, or postal card, of the kind authorized and provided by the Post Office Department or by the Postal Service, without the special authority and direction of the Department or Postal Service; or

Whoever after such postage stamp, postage meter stamp, stamped envelope, or postal card has been printed, with intent to defraud, delivers the same to any person not authorized by an instrument in writing, duly executed under the hand of the Postmaster General and the seal of the Post Office Department or the Postal Service, to receive it—

Shall be fined under this title or imprisoned not more than five years, or both.

(June 25, 1948, c. 645, 62 Stat. 713; Aug. 12, 1970, Pub.L. 91–375, § 6(j)(6), 84 Stat. 777; Oct. 14, 1970, Pub.L. 91–448, § 1(a), 84 Stat. 920; Sept. 13, 1994, Pub.L. 103–322, Title XXXIII, § 330016(1)(G), 108 Stat. 2147.)

HISTORICAL AND STATUTORY NOTES

Effective and Applicability Provisions

1970 Acts. Amendment by Pub.L. 91–375 effective within 1 year after Aug. 12, 1970, on date established therefor by the Board of Governors of the United States Postal Service and published by it in the Federal Register, see § 15(a) of Pub.L. 91–375, set out as a note preceding § 101 of Title 39, Postal Service.

Change of Name

The Post Office Department has been redesignated the United States Postal Service.

§ 502. Postage and revenue stamps of foreign governments

Whoever forges, or counterfeits, or knowingly utters or uses any forged or counterfeit postage stamp or revenue stamp of any foreign government, shall be fined under this title or imprisoned not more than five years, or both.

(June 25, 1948, c. 645, 62 Stat. 713; Sept. 13, 1994, Pub.L. 103–322, Title XXXIII, § 330016(1)(G), 108 Stat. 2147.)

§ 503. Postmarking stamps

Whoever forges or counterfeits any postmarking stamp, or impression thereof with intent to make it appear that such impression is a genuine postmark, or makes or knowingly uses or sells, or possesses with intent to use or sell, any forged or counterfeited postmarking stamp, die, plate, or engraving, or such impression thereof, shall be fined under this title or imprisoned not more than five years, or both.

(June 25, 1948, c. 645, 62 Stat. 713; Sept. 13, 1994, Pub.L. 103–322, Title XXXIII, § 330016(1)(H), 108 Stat. 2147.)

§ 504. Printing and filming of United States and foreign obligations and securities

Notwithstanding any other provision of this chapter, the following are permitted:

(1) The printing, publishing, or importation, or the making or importation of the necessary plates for such printing or publishing, of illustrations of—

(A) postage stamps of the United States,

(B) revenue stamps of the United States,

(C) any other obligation or other security of the United States, and

(D) postage stamps, revenue stamps, notes, bonds, and any other obligation or other security of any foreign government, bank, or corporation.

Illustrations permitted by the foregoing provisions of this section shall be made in accordance with the following conditions—

(i) all illustrations shall be in black and white, except that illustrations of postage stamps issued by the United States or by any foreign government and stamps issued under the Migratory Bird Hunting Stamp Act of 1934 may be in color;

(ii) all illustrations (including illustrations of uncanceled postage stamps in color and illustrations of stamps issued under the Migratory Bird Hunting Stamp Act of 1934 in color) shall be of a size less than three-fourths or more than one and one-half, in linear dimension, of each part of any matter so illustrated which is covered by subparagraph (A), (B), (C), or (D) of this paragraph, except that black and white illustrations of postage and revenue stamps issued by the United States or by any foreign government and colored illustrations of canceled postage stamps issued by the United States may be in the exact linear dimension in which the stamps were issued; and

(iii) the negatives and plates used in making the illustrations shall be destroyed after their final use in accordance with this section.

The Secretary of the Treasury shall prescribe regulations to permit color illustrations of such currency of the United States as the Secretary determines may be appropriate for such purposes.

(2) The provisions of this section shall not permit the reproduction of illustrations of obligations or other securities, by or through electronic methods used for the acquisition, recording, retrieval, transmission, or reproduction of any obligation or other security, unless such use is authorized by the Secretary of the Treasury. The Secretary shall establish a system to ensure that the legitimate use of such electronic methods and retention of such reproductions by businesses, hobbyists, press or others shall not be unduly restricted.

(3) The making or importation of motion-picture films, microfilms, or slides, for projection upon a screen or for use in telecasting, of postage and revenue stamps and other obligations and securities of the United States, and postage and revenue stamps, notes, bonds, and other obligations or securities of any foreign government, bank, or corporation. No prints or other reproductions shall be made from such films or slides, except for the purposes of paragraph (1), without the permission of the Secretary of the Treasury.

For the purposes of this section the term "postage stamp" includes postage meter stamps.

(June 25, 1948, c. 645, 62 Stat. 713; Sept. 2, 1958, Pub.L. 85–921, § 1, 72 Stat. 1771; June 20, 1968, Pub.L. 90–353, § 1, 82 Stat. 240; Oct. 14, 1970, Pub.L. 91–448, § 2, 84 Stat. 921; July 18, 1984, Pub.L. 98–369, Title X, § 1077(b)(1), (2), 98 Stat. 1054; Oct. 28, 1992, Pub.L. 102–550, Title XV, § 1554, 106 Stat. 4071; Oct. 11, 1996, Pub.L. 104–294, Title VI, § 601(e), (f)(3), 110 Stat. 3499.)

HISTORICAL AND STATUTORY NOTES

References in Text

The Migratory Bird Hunting Stamp Act of 1934, referred to in Par. (1)(D)(i), (ii), is Act Mar. 16, 1934, c. 71, 48 Stat. 452, as amended, which is classified generally to subchapter IV (§ 718 et seq.) of chapter 7 of Title 16, Conservation.

Effective and Applicability Provisions

1992 Acts. Except as otherwise provided, amendment by Pub.L. 102–550 effective Oct. 28, 1992, pursuant to section 2 of Pub.L. 102–550.

1984 Acts. Amendment by Pub.L. 98–369 effective July 18, 1984, see section 1077(c) of Pub.L. 98–369, set out as a note under section 718e of Title 16, Conservation.

§ 505. Seals of courts; signatures of judges or court officers

Whoever forges the signature of any judge, register, or other officer of any court of the United States, or of any Territory thereof, or forges or counterfeits the seal of any such court, or knowingly concurs in using any such forged or counterfeit signature or seal, for the purpose of authenticating any proceeding or document, or tenders in evidence any such proceeding or document with a false or counterfeit signature of any such judge, register, or other officer, or a false or counterfeit seal of the court, subscribed or attached thereto, knowing such signature or seal to be false or counterfeit, shall be fined under this title or imprisoned not more than five years, or both.

(June 25, 1948, c. 645, 62 Stat. 714; Sept. 13, 1994, Pub.L. 103–322, Title XXXIII, § 330016(1)(K), 108 Stat. 2147.)

HISTORICAL AND STATUTORY NOTES

Canal Zone

Applicability of section to Canal Zone, see § 14 of this title.

§ 506. Seals of departments or agencies

(a) Whoever—

(1) falsely makes, forges, counterfeits, mutilates, or alters the seal of any department or agency of the United States, or any facsimile thereof;

(2) knowingly uses, affixes, or impresses any such fraudulently made, forged, counterfeited, mutilated, or altered seal or facsimile thereof to or upon any certificate, instrument, commission, document, or paper of any description; or

(3) with fraudulent intent, possesses, sells, offers for sale, furnishes, offers to furnish, gives away, offers to give away, transports, offers to transport, imports, or offers to import any such seal or facsimile thereof, knowing the same to have been so falsely made, forged, counterfeited, mutilated, or altered,

shall be fined under this title, or imprisoned not more than 5 years, or both.

(b) Notwithstanding subsection (a) or any other provision of law, if a forged, counterfeited, mutilated, or altered seal of a department or agency of the United States, or any facsimile thereof, is—

(1) so forged, counterfeited, mutilated, or altered;

(2) used, affixed, or impressed to or upon any certificate, instrument, commission, document, or paper of any description; or

(3) with fraudulent intent, possessed, sold, offered for sale, furnished, offered to furnish, given away, offered to give away, transported, offered to transport, imported, or offered to import,

with the intent or effect of facilitating an alien's application for, or receipt of, a Federal benefit to which the alien is not entitled, the penalties which may be imposed for each offense under subsection (a) shall be two times the maximum fine, and 3 times the maximum term of imprisonment, or both, that would otherwise be imposed for an offense under subsection (a).

(c) For purposes of this section—

(1) the term "Federal benefit" means—

(A) the issuance of any grant, contract, loan, professional license, or commercial license provided by any agency of the United States or by appropriated funds of the United States; and

(B) any retirement, welfare, Social Security, health (including treatment of an emergency medical condition in accordance with section 1903(v) of the Social Security Act (19[1] U.S.C. 1396b(v))), disability, veterans, public housing, education, food stamps, or unemployment benefit, or any similar benefit for which payments or assistance are provided by an agency of the United States or by appropriated funds of the United States; and

(2) each instance of forgery, counterfeiting, mutilation, or alteration shall constitute a separate offense under this section.

(June 25, 1948, c. 645, 62 Stat. 714; Sept. 13, 1994, Pub.L. 103–322, Title XXXIII, § 330016(1)(K), 108 Stat. 2147; Sept. 30, 1996, Pub.L. 104–208, Div. C, Title V, § 561, 110 Stat. 3009–681.)

[1] So in original. Probably should be "42".

HISTORICAL AND STATUTORY NOTES

Effective and Applicability Provisions

1996 Acts. Title V of Div. C of Pub.L. 104–208 effective on Sept. 30, 1996, see section 591 of Pub.L. 104–208, set out as a note under section 1101 of Title 8, Aliens and Nationality.

Severability of Provisions

If any provision of Division C of Pub.L. 104–208 or the application of such provision to any person or circumstances is held to be unconstitutional, the remainder of Division C of Pub.L. 104–208 and the application of the provisions of Division C of Pub.L. 104–208 to any person or circumstance not to be affected thereby, see section 1(e) of Pub.L. 104–208, set out as a note under section 1101 of Title 8, Aliens and Nationality.

Canal Zone

Applicability of section to Canal Zone, see § 14 of this title.

§ 507. Ship's papers

Whoever falsely makes, forges, counterfeits, or alters any instrument in imitation of or purporting to be, an abstract or official copy or certificate of the documentation of any vessel, or a certificate of ownership, pass, or clearance, granted for any vessel, under the authority of the United States, or a permit, debenture, or other official document granted by any officer of the customs by virtue of his office; or

Whoever utters, publishes, or passes, or attempts to utter, publish, or pass, as true, any such false, forged, counterfeited, or falsely altered instrument, abstract, official copy, certificate, pass, clearance, permit, debenture, or other official document herein specified, knowing the same to be false, forged, counterfeited, or falsely altered, with an intent to defraud—

Shall be fined under this title or imprisoned not more than three years, or both.

(June 25, 1948, c. 645, 62 Stat. 714; Sept. 13, 1994, Pub.L. 103–322, Title XXXIII, § 330016(1)(H), 108 Stat. 2147; Oct. 6, 2006, Pub.L. 109–304, § 17(d)(2), 120 Stat. 1707.)

HISTORICAL AND STATUTORY NOTES

Transfer of Functions

All offices of collector of customs, comptroller of customs, surveyor of customs, and appraiser of merchandise in the Bureau of Customs of the Department of the Treasury to which appointments were required to be made by the President with the advice and consent of the Senate were ordered abolished, to be terminated not later than Dec. 31, 1966. All functions of the offices so eliminated were already vested in the Secretary of the Treasury.

Canal Zone

Applicability of section to Canal Zone, see § 14 of this title.

§ 508. Transportation requests of Government

Whoever falsely makes, forges, or counterfeits in whole or in part, any form or request in similitude of the form or request provided by the Government for requesting a common carrier to furnish transportation on account of the United States or any department or agency thereof, or knowingly alters any form or request provided by the Government for requesting a common carrier to furnish transportation on account of the United States or any department or agency thereof; or

Whoever knowingly passes, utters, publishes, or sells, or attempts to pass, utter, publish, or sell, any such false, forged, counterfeited, or altered form or request—

Shall be fined under this title or imprisoned not more than ten years, or both.

(June 25, 1948, c. 645, 62 Stat. 715; Sept. 13, 1994, Pub.L. 103–322, Title XXXIII, § 330016(1)(K), 108 Stat. 2147.)

HISTORICAL AND STATUTORY NOTES

Canal Zone

Applicability of section to Canal Zone, see § 14 of this title.

§ 509. Possessing and making plates or stones for Government transportation requests

Whoever, except by lawful authority, controls, holds or possesses any plate, stone, or other thing, or any part thereof, from which has been printed or may be printed any form or request for Government transportation, or uses such plate, stone, or other thing, or knowingly permits or suffers the same to be used in making any such form or request or any part of such a form or request; or

Whoever makes or engraves any plate, stone, or thing, in the likeness of any plate, stone, or thing designated for the printing of the genuine issues of the form or request for Government transportation; or

Whoever prints, photographs, or in any other manner makes, executes, or sells any engraving, photograph, print, or impression in the likeness of any genuine form or request for Government transportation, or any part thereof; or

Whoever brings into the United States or any place subject to the jurisdiction thereof, any plate, stone, or other thing, or engraving, photograph, print, or other impression of the form or request for Government transportation—

Shall be fined under this title or imprisoned not more than ten years, or both.

(June 25, 1948, c. 645, 62 Stat. 715; Sept. 13, 1994, Pub.L. 103–322, Title XXXIII, § 330016(1)(K), 108 Stat. 2147.)

HISTORICAL AND STATUTORY NOTES

Canal Zone

Applicability of section to Canal Zone, see § 14 of this title.

§ 510. Forging endorsements on Treasury checks or bonds or securities of the United States

(a) Whoever, with intent to defraud—

(1) falsely makes or forges any endorsement or signature on a Treasury check or bond or security of the United States; or

(2) passes, utters, or publishes, or attempts to pass, utter, or publish, any Treasury check or bond or security of the United States bearing a falsely made or forged endorsement or signature;

shall be fined under this title or imprisoned not more than ten years, or both.

(b) Whoever, with knowledge that such Treasury check or bond or security of the United States is stolen or bears a falsely made or forged endorsement or signature buys, sells, exchanges, receives, delivers, retains, or conceals any such Treasury check or bond or security of the United States shall be fined under this title or imprisoned not more than ten years, or both.

(c) If the face value of the Treasury check or bond or security of the United States or the aggregate face value, if more than one Treasury check or bond or security of the United States, does not exceed $1,000, in any of the above-mentioned offenses, the penalty shall be a fine under this title or imprisonment for not more than one year, or both.

(Added Pub.L. 98–151, § 115(a), Nov. 14, 1983, 97 Stat. 976, and amended Pub.L. 101–647, Title XXXV, § 3514, Nov. 29, 1990, 104 Stat. 4923; Pub.L. 103–322, Title XXXIII, § 330016(1)(H), (L), Sept. 13, 1994, 108 Stat. 2147; Pub.L. 104–294, Title VI, §§ 602(e), 606(b), Oct. 11, 1996, 110 Stat. 3503, 3511; Pub.L. 107–273, Div. B, Title IV, § 4002(a)(1), Nov. 2, 2002, 116 Stat. 1806.)

§ 511. Altering or removing motor vehicle identification numbers

(a) A person who—

(1) knowingly removes, obliterates, tampers with, or alters an identification number for a motor vehicle or motor vehicle part; or

(2) with intent to further the theft of a motor vehicle, knowingly removes, obliterates, tampers with, or alters a decal or device affixed to a motor vehicle pursuant to the Motor Vehicle Theft Prevention Act,

shall be fined under this title, imprisoned not more than 5 years, or both.

(b)(1) Subsection (a) of this section does not apply to a removal, obliteration, tampering, or alteration by a person specified in paragraph (2) of this subsection (unless such person knows that the vehicle or part involved is stolen).

(2) The persons referred to in paragraph (1) of this subsection are—

(A) a motor vehicle scrap processor or a motor vehicle demolisher who complies with applicable State law with respect to such vehicle or part;

(B) a person who repairs such vehicle or part, if the removal, obliteration, tampering, or alteration is reasonably necessary for the repair;

(C) a person who restores or replaces an identification number for such vehicle or part in accordance with applicable State law; and

(D) a person who removes, obliterates, tampers with, or alters a decal or device affixed to a motor vehicle pursuant to the Motor Vehicle Theft Prevention Act, if that person is the owner of the motor vehicle, or is authorized to remove, obliterate, tamper with or alter the decal or device by—

(i) the owner or his authorized agent;

(ii) applicable State or local law; or

(iii) regulations promulgated by the Attorney General to implement the Motor Vehicle Theft Prevention Act.

(c) As used in this section, the term—

(1) "identification number" means a number or symbol that is inscribed or affixed for purposes of identification under chapter 301 and part C of subtitle VI of title 49;

(2) "motor vehicle" has the meaning given that term in section 32101 of title 49;

(3) "motor vehicle demolisher" means a person, including any motor vehicle dismantler or motor vehicle recycler, who is engaged in the business of reducing motor vehicles or motor vehicle parts to metallic scrap that is unsuitable for use as either a motor vehicle or a motor vehicle part;

(4) "motor vehicle scrap processor" means a person—

(A) who is engaged in the business of purchasing motor vehicles or motor vehicle parts for reduction to metallic scrap for recycling;

(B) who, from a fixed location, uses machinery to process metallic scrap into prepared grades; and

(C) whose principal product is metallic scrap for recycling;

but such term does not include any activity of any such person relating to the recycling of a motor vehicle or a motor vehicle part as a used motor vehicle or a used motor vehicle part.

(d) For purposes of subsection (a) of this section, the term "tampers with" includes covering a program decal or device affixed to a motor vehicle pursuant to the Motor Vehicle Theft Prevention Act for the purpose of obstructing its visibility.

(Added Pub.L. 98–547, Title II, § 201(a), Oct. 25, 1984, 98 Stat. 2768, and amended Pub.L. 103–272, § 5(e)(3), July 5, 1994, 108 Stat. 1373; Pub.L. 103–322, Title XXII, § 220003(a) to (c), Sept. 13, 1994, 108 Stat. 2076; Pub.L. 104–294, Title VI, § 604(b)(8), Oct. 11, 1996, 110 Stat. 3507.)

HISTORICAL AND STATUTORY NOTES

References in Text

The Motor Vehicle Theft Prevention Act, referred to in subsecs. (a)(2), (b)(2)(D), and (d), is Pub.L. 103–322, Title XXII, Sept. 13, 1994, 108 Stat. 2074, which enacted section 511A of this title and section 14171 of Title 42, The Public Health and Welfare, amended this section, and enacted provisions set out as a note under section 13701 of Title 42. For complete classification of this Act to the Code, see Short Title note set out under section 13701 of Title 42 and Tables.

Effective and Applicability Provisions

1996 Acts. Amendment by section 604 of Pub.L. 104–294 effective Sept. 13, 1994, see section 604(d) of Pub.L. 104–294, set out as a note under section 13 of this title.

§ 511A. Unauthorized application of theft prevention decal or device

(a) Whoever affixes to a motor vehicle a theft prevention decal or other device, or a replica thereof, unless authorized to do so pursuant to the Motor Vehicle Theft Prevention Act, shall be punished by a fine not to exceed $1,000.

(b) For purposes of this section, the term "theft prevention decal or device" means a decal or other device designed in accordance with a uniform design for such devices developed pursuant to the Motor Vehicle Theft Prevention Act.

(Added Pub.L. 103–322, Title XXII, § 220003(d)(1), Sept. 13, 1994, 108 Stat. 2077.)

HISTORICAL AND STATUTORY NOTES

References in Text

The Motor Vehicle Theft Prevention Act, referred to in text, is Pub.L. 103–322, Title XXII, Sept. 13, 1994, 108 Stat. 2074, which enacted this section and section 14171 of Title 42, The Public Health and Welfare, amended section 511 of this title, and enacted provisions set out as a note under section 13701 of Title 42. For complete classification of this Act the Code, see Short Title note set out under section 13701 of Title 42 and Tables.

§ 512. Forfeiture of certain motor vehicles and motor vehicle parts

(a) If an identification number for a motor vehicle or motor vehicle part is removed, obliterated, tampered with, or altered, such vehicle or part shall be subject to seizure and forfeiture to the United States unless—

(1) in the case of a motor vehicle part, such part is attached to a motor vehicle and the owner of such motor vehicle does not know that the identification number has been removed, obliterated, tampered with, or altered;

(2) such motor vehicle or part has a replacement identification number that—

(A) is authorized by the Secretary of Transportation under chapter 301 of title 49; or

(B) conforms to applicable State law;

(3) such removal, obliteration, tampering, or alteration is caused by collision or fire or is carried out as described in section 511(b) of this title; or

(4) such motor vehicle or part is in the possession or control of a motor vehicle scrap processor who does not know that such identification number was removed, obliterated, tampered with, or altered in any manner other than by collision or fire or as described in section 511(b) of this title.

(b) All provisions of law relating to—

(1) the seizure and condemnation of vessels, vehicles, merchandise, and baggage for violation of customs laws, and procedures for summary and judicial forfeiture applicable to such violations;

(2) the disposition of such vessels, vehicles, merchandise, and baggage or the proceeds from such disposition;

(3) the remission or mitigation of such forfeiture; and

(4) the compromise of claims and the award of compensation to informers with respect to such forfeiture;

shall apply to seizures and forfeitures under this section, to the extent that such provisions are not inconsistent with this section. The duties of the collector of customs or any other person with respect to seizure and forfeiture under such provisions shall be performed under this section by such persons as may be designated by the Attorney General.

(c) As used in this section, the terms "identification number", "motor vehicle", and "motor vehicle scrap processor" have the meanings given those terms in section 511 of this title.

(Added Pub.L. 98–547, Title II, § 201(a), Oct. 25, 1984, 98 Stat. 2769, and amended Pub.L. 103–272, § 5(e)(4), July 5, 1994, 108 Stat. 1373.)

§ 513. Securities of the States and private entities

(a) Whoever makes, utters or possesses a counterfeited security of a State or a political subdivision thereof or of an organization, or whoever makes, utters or possesses a forged security of a State or political subdivision thereof or of an organization, with intent to deceive another person, organization, or government shall be fined under this title or imprisoned for not more than ten years, or both.

(b) Whoever makes, receives, possesses, sells or otherwise transfers an implement designed for or particularly suited for making a counterfeit or forged security with the intent that it be so used shall be punished by a fine under this title or by imprisonment for not more than ten years, or both.

(c) For purposes of this section—

(1) the term "counterfeited" means a document that purports to be genuine but is not, because it has been falsely made or manufactured in its entirety;

(2) the term "forged" means a document that purports to be genuine but is not because it has been falsely altered, completed, signed, or endorsed, or contains a false addition thereto or insertion therein, or is a combination of parts of two or more genuine documents;

(3) the term "security" means—

(A) a note, stock certificate, treasury stock certificate, bond, treasury bond, debenture, certificate of deposit, interest coupon, bill, check, draft, warrant, debit instrument as defined in section 916(c) of the Electronic Fund Transfer Act, money order, traveler's check, letter of credit, warehouse receipt, negotiable bill of lading, evidence of indebtedness, certificate of interest in or participation in any profit-sharing agreement, collateral-trust certificate, pre-reorganization certificate of subscription, transferable share, investment contract, voting trust certificate, or certificate of interest in tangible or intangible property;

(B) an instrument evidencing ownership of goods, wares, or merchandise;

(C) any other written instrument commonly known as a security;

(D) a certificate of interest in, certificate of participation in, certificate for, receipt for, or warrant or option or other right to subscribe to or purchase, any of the foregoing; or

(E) a blank form of any of the foregoing;

(4) the term "organization" means a legal entity, other than a government, established or organized for any purpose, and includes a corporation, company, association, firm, partnership, joint stock company, foundation, institution, society, union, or any other association of persons which operates in or the activities of which affect interstate or foreign commerce; and

(5) the term "State" includes a State of the United States, the District of Columbia, Puerto Rico, Guam, the Virgin Islands, and any other territory or possession of the United States.

(Added Pub.L. 98–473, Title II, § 1105(a), Oct. 12, 1984, 98 Stat. 2144; § 511; renumbered § 513, Pub.L. 99–646, § 31(a), Nov. 10, 1986, 100 Stat. 3598, and amended Pub.L. 101–647, Title XXXV, § 3515, Nov. 29, 1990, 104 Stat. 4923; Pub.L. 103–322, Title XXXIII, §§ 330008(1), 330016(2)(C), Sept. 13, 1994, 108 Stat. 2142, 2148.)

HISTORICAL AND STATUTORY NOTES

References in Text

Section 916(c) of the Electronic Fund Transfer Act, referred to in subsec. (c)(3)(A), is classified to section 1693(c) of Title 15, Commerce and Trade.

§ 514. Fictitious obligations

(a) Whoever, with the intent to defraud—

(1) draws, prints, processes, produces, publishes, or otherwise makes, or attempts or causes the same, within the United States;

(2) passes, utters, presents, offers, brokers, issues, sells, or attempts or causes the same, or with like intent possesses, within the United States; or

(3) utilizes interstate or foreign commerce, including the use of the mails or wire, radio, or other electronic communication, to transmit, transport, ship, move, transfer, or attempts or causes the same, to, from, or through the United States,

any false or fictitious instrument, document, or other item appearing, representing, purporting, or contriving through scheme or artifice, to be an actual security or other financial instrument issued under the authority of the United States, a foreign government, a State or other political subdivision of the United States, or an organization, shall be guilty of a class B felony.

(b) For purposes of this section, any term used in this section that is defined in section 513(c) has the same meaning given such term in section 513(c).

(c) The United States Secret Service, in addition to any other agency having such authority, shall have authority to investigate offenses under this section.

(Added Pub.L. 104–208, Div. A, Title I, § 101(f) [Title VI, § 648(b)(1)], Title II, § 2603(b)(1), Sept. 30, 1996, 110 Stat. 3009–367, 3009–470.)

HISTORICAL AND STATUTORY NOTES

Effective and Applicability Provisions

1996 Acts. Section effective Sept. 30, 1996, see section 101(f) [Title VI, § 648(c)] of Pub.L. 104–208, set out as a note under section 474 of this title.

Transfer of Functions

For transfer of the functions, personnel, assets, and obligations of the United States Secret Service, including the functions of the Secretary of the Treasury relating thereto, to the Secretary of Homeland Security, and for treatment of related references, see 6 U.S.C.A. §§ 381, 551(d), 552(d) and 557, and the Department of Homeland Security Reorganization Plan of November 25, 2002, as modified, set out as a note under 6 U.S.C.A. § 542.

CHAPTER 26—CRIMINAL STREET GANGS

§ 521. Criminal street gangs

(a) Definitions.—

"Conviction" includes a finding, under State or Federal law, that a person has committed an act of juvenile delinquency involving a violent or controlled substances felony.

"Criminal street gang" means an ongoing group, club, organization, or association of 5 or more persons—

(A) that has as 1 of its primary purposes the commission of 1 or more of the criminal offenses described in subsection (c);

(B) the members of which engage, or have engaged within the past 5 years, in a continuing series of offenses described in subsection (c); and

(C) the activities of which affect interstate or foreign commerce.

"State" means a State of the United States, the District of Columbia, and any commonwealth, territory, or possession of the United States.

(b) Penalty.—The sentence of a person convicted of an offense described in subsection (c) shall be increased by up to 10 years if the offense is committed under the circumstances described in subsection (d).

(c) Offenses.—The offenses described in this section are—

(1) a Federal felony involving a controlled substance (as defined in section 102 of the Controlled Substances Act (21 U.S.C. 802)) for which the maximum penalty is not less than 5 years;

(2) a Federal felony crime of violence that has as an element the use or attempted use of physical force against the person of another; and

(3) a conspiracy to commit an offense described in paragraph (1) or (2).

(d) Circumstances.—The circumstances described in this section are that the offense described in subsection (c) was committed by a person who—

(1) participates in a criminal street gang with knowledge that its members engage in or have engaged in a continuing series of offenses described in subsection (c);

(2) intends to promote or further the felonious activities of the criminal street gang or maintain or increase his or her position in the gang; and

(3) has been convicted within the past 5 years for—

(A) an offense described in subsection (c);

(B) a State offense—

(i) involving a controlled substance (as defined in section 102 of the Controlled Substances Act (21 U.S.C. 802)) for which the maximum penalty is not less than 5 years' imprisonment; or

(ii) that is a felony crime of violence that has as an element the use or attempted use of physical force against the person of another;

(C) any Federal or State felony offense that by its nature involves a substantial risk that physical force against the person of another may be used in the course of committing the offense; or

(D) a conspiracy to commit an offense described in subparagraph (A), (B), or (C).

(Added Pub.L. 103–322, Title XV, § 150001(a), Sept. 13, 1994, 108 Stat. 2034, and amended Pub.L. 104–294, Title VI, § 607(q), Oct. 11, 1996, 110 Stat. 3513; Pub.L. 107–273, Div. B, Title IV, § 4002(b)(3), Nov. 2, 2002, 116 Stat. 1807.)

HISTORICAL AND STATUTORY NOTES

References in Text

Section 102 of the Controlled Substances Act (21 U.S.C. 802), referred to in subsecs. (c)(1) and (d)(3)(B)(i), is Pub.L. 91–513, Title II, § 102, Oct. 27, 1970, 84 Stat. 1242, as amended, which is classified to section 802 of Title 21, Food and Drugs.

CHAPTER 27—CUSTOMS

[1] So in original. Two sections 554 have been enacted.

§ 541. Entry of goods falsely classified

Whoever knowingly effects any entry of goods, wares, or merchandise, at less than the true weight or measure thereof, or upon a false classification as to quality or value, or by the payment of less than the amount of duty legally due, shall be fined under this title or imprisoned not more than two years, or both.

(June 25, 1948, c. 645, 62 Stat. 715; Sept. 13, 1994, Pub.L. 103–322, Title XXXIII, § 330016(1)(K), 108 Stat. 2147.)

§ 542. Entry of goods by means of false statements

Whoever enters or introduces, or attempts to enter or introduce, into the commerce of the United States any imported merchandise by means of any fraudulent or false invoice, declaration, affidavit, letter, paper, or by means of any false statement, written or verbal, or by means of any false or fraudulent practice or appliance, or makes any false statement in any declaration without reasonable cause to believe the truth of such statement, or procures the making of any such false statement as to any matter material thereto without reasonable cause to believe the truth of such statement, whether or not the United States shall or may be deprived of any lawful duties; or

Whoever is guilty of any willful act or omission whereby the United States shall or may be deprived of any lawful duties accruing upon merchandise embraced or referred to in such invoice, declaration, affidavit, letter, paper, or statement, or affected by such act or omission—

Shall be fined for each offense under this title or imprisoned not more than two years, or both.

Nothing in this section shall be construed to relieve imported merchandise from forfeiture under other provisions of law.

The term "commerce of the United States", as used in this section, shall not include commerce with the Virgin Islands, American Samoa, Wake Island, Midway Islands, Kingman Reef, Johnston Island, or Guam.

(June 25, 1948, c. 645, 62 Stat. 715; June 30, 1955, c. 258, § 2(c), 69 Stat. 242; Sept. 13, 1994, Pub.L. 103–322, Title XXXIII, §§ 330004(18), 330016(1)(K), 108 Stat. 2142, 2147; Oct. 11, 1996, Pub.L. 104–294, Title VI, § 604(b)(23), 110 Stat. 3508.)

HISTORICAL AND STATUTORY NOTES

Effective and Applicability Provisions

1996 Acts. Amendment by section 604 of Pub.L. 104–294 effective Sept. 13, 1994, see section 604(d) of Pub.L. 104–294, set out as a note under section 13 of this title.

§ 543. Entry of goods for less than legal duty

Whoever, being an officer of the revenue, knowingly admits to entry, any goods, wares, or merchandise, upon payment of less than the amount of duty legally due, shall be fined under this title or imprisoned not more than two years, or both, and removed from office.

(June 25, 1948, c. 645, 62 Stat. 716; Sept. 13, 1994, Pub.L. 103–322, Title XXXIII, § 330016(1)(K), 108 Stat. 2147.)

§ 544. Relanding of goods

If any merchandise entered or withdrawn for exportation without payment of the duties thereon, or with intent to obtain a drawback of the duties paid, or of any other allowances given by law on the exportation thereof, is relanded at any place in the United States without entry having been made, such merchandise shall be considered as having been imported into the United States contrary to law, and each person concerned shall be fined under this title or imprisoned not more than two years, or both; and such merchandise shall be forfeited.

The term "any place in the United States", as used in this section, shall not include the Virgin Islands, American Samoa, Wake Island, Midway Islands, Kingman Reef, Johnston Island, or Guam.

(June 25, 1948, c. 645, 62 Stat. 716; June 30, 1955, c. 258, § 2(c), 69 Stat. 242; Sept. 13, 1994, Pub.L. 103–322, Title XXXIII, §§ 330004(18), 330016(1)(K), 108 Stat. 2142, 2147; Oct. 11, 1996, Pub.L. 104–294, Title VI, § 604(b)(23), 110 Stat. 3508.)

HISTORICAL AND STATUTORY NOTES

Effective and Applicability Provisions

1996 Acts. Amendment by section 604 of Pub.L. 104–294 effective Sept. 13, 1994, see section 604(d) of Pub.L. 104–294, set out as a note under section 13 of this title.

§ 545. Smuggling goods into the United States

Whoever knowingly and willfully, with intent to defraud the United States, smuggles, or clandestinely introduces or attempts to smuggle or clandestinely introduce into the United States any merchandise which should have been invoiced, or makes out or passes, or attempts to pass, through the customhouse any false, forged, or fraudulent invoice, or other document or paper; or

Whoever fraudulently or knowingly imports or brings into the United States, any merchandise contrary to law, or receives, conceals, buys, sells, or in any manner facilitates the transportation, concealment, or sale of such merchandise after importation, knowing the same to have been imported or brought into the United States contrary to law—

Shall be fined under this title or imprisoned not more than 20 years, or both.

Proof of defendant's possession of such goods, unless explained to the satisfaction of the jury, shall be deemed evidence sufficient to authorize conviction for violation of this section.

Merchandise introduced into the United States in violation of this section, or the value thereof, to be recovered from any person described in the first or second paragraph of this section, shall be forfeited to the United States.

The term "United States", as used in this section, shall not include the Virgin Islands, American Samoa, Wake Island, Midway Islands, Kingman Reef, Johnston Island, or Guam.

(June 25, 1948, c. 645, 62 Stat. 716; Aug. 24, 1954, c. 890, § 1, 68 Stat. 782; Sept. 1, 1954, c. 1213, Title V, § 507, 68 Stat. 1141; June 30, 1955, c. 258, § 2(c), 69 Stat. 242; Sept. 13, 1994, Pub.L. 103–322, Title XXXII, § 320903(c), Title XXXIII, §§ 330004(18), 330016(1)(L), 108 Stat. 2125, 2142, 2147; Oct. 11, 1996, Pub.L. 104–294, Title VI, § 604(b)(23), 110 Stat. 3508; Mar. 9, 2006, Pub.L. 109–177, Title III, § 310, 120 Stat. 242.)

HISTORICAL AND STATUTORY NOTES

Codifications

Amendment by Pub.L. 109–177, § 310, directing that the third undesignated paragraph of this section be amended by striking "5 years" and inserting "20 years", was executed by striking "five years" and inserting "20 years", as the probable intent of Congress.

Effective and Applicability Provisions

1996 Acts. Amendment by section 604 of Pub.L. 104–294 effective Sept. 13, 1994, see section 604(d) of Pub.L. 104–294, set out as a note under section 13 of this title.

§ 546. Smuggling goods into foreign countries

Any person owning in whole or in part any vessel of the United States who employs, or participates in, or allows the employment of, such vessel for the purpose of smuggling, or attempting to smuggle, or assisting in smuggling, any merchandise into the territory of any foreign government in violation of the laws there in force, if under the laws of such foreign government any penalty or forfeiture is provided for violation of the laws of the United States respecting the customs revenue, and any citizen of, or person domiciled in, or any corporation incorporated in, the United States, controlling or substantially participating in the control of any such vessel, directly or indirectly, whether through ownership of corporate shares or otherwise, and allowing the employment of said vessel for any such purpose, and any person found, or discovered to have been, on board of any such vessel so employed and participating or assisting in any such purpose, shall be fined under this title or imprisoned not more than two years, or both.

It shall constitute an offense under this section to hire out or charter a vessel if the lessor or charterer has knowledge or reasonable grounds for belief that the lessee or person chartering the vessel intends to employ such vessel for any of the purposes described in this section and if such vessel is, during the time such lease or charter is in effect, employed for any such purpose.

(June 25, 1948, c. 645, 62 Stat. 717; Sept. 13, 1994, Pub.L. 103–322, Title XXXIII, § 330016(1)(K), 108 Stat. 2147.)

§ 547. Depositing goods in buildings on boundaries

Whoever receives or deposits any merchandise in any building upon the boundary line between the United States and any foreign country, or carries any merchandise through the same, in violation of law, shall be fined under this title or imprisoned not more than two years, or both.

(June 25, 1948, c. 645, 62 Stat. 717; Sept. 13, 1994, Pub.L. 103–322, Title XXXIII, § 330016(1)(K), 108 Stat. 2147.)

§ 548. Removing or repacking goods in warehouses

Whoever fraudulently conceals, removes, or repacks merchandise in any bonded warehouse or fraudulently alters, defaces or obliterates any marks or numbers placed upon packages deposited in such warehouse, shall be fined under this title or imprisoned not more than two years, or both.

Merchandise so concealed, removed, or repacked, or packages upon which any marks or numbers have been so altered, defaced, or obliterated, shall be forfeited to the United States.

(June 25, 1948, c. 645, 62 Stat. 717; Sept. 13, 1994, Pub.L. 103–322, Title XXXIII, § 330016(1)(K), 108 Stat. 2147.)

§ 549. Removing goods from customs custody; breaking seals

Whoever, without authority, affixes or attaches a customs seal, fastening, or mark, or any seal, fastening, or mark purporting to be a customs seal, fastening, or mark to any vessel, vehicle, warehouse, or package; or

Whoever, without authority, willfully removes, breaks, injures, or defaces any customs seal or other fastening or mark placed upon any vessel, vehicle, warehouse, or package containing merchandise or baggage in bond or in customs custody; or

Whoever maliciously enters any bonded warehouse or any vessel or vehicle laden with or containing bonded merchandise with intent unlawfully to remove therefrom any merchandise or baggage therein, or unlawfully removes any merchandise or baggage in such vessel, vehicle, or bonded warehouse or otherwise in customs custody or control; or

Whoever receives or transports any merchandise or baggage unlawfully removed from any such vessel, vehicle, or warehouse, knowing the same to have been unlawfully removed—

Shall be fined under this title or imprisoned not more than 10 years, or both.

(June 25, 1948, c. 645, 62 Stat. 717; Sept. 13, 1994, Pub.L. 103–322, Title XXXIII, § 330016(1)(K), 108 Stat. 2147; Mar. 9, 2006, Pub.L. 109–177, Title III, § 311(e), 120 Stat. 242.)

§ 550. False claim for refund of duties

Whoever knowingly and willfully files any false or fraudulent entry or claim for the payment of drawback, allowance, or refund of duties upon the exportation of merchandise, or knowingly or willfully makes or files any false affidavit, abstract, record, certificate, or other document, with a view to securing the payment to himself or others of any drawback, allowance, or refund of duties, on the exportation of merchandise, greater than that legally due thereon, shall be fined under this title or imprisoned not more than two years, or both, and such merchandise or the value thereof shall be forfeited.

(June 25, 1948, c. 645, 62 Stat. 718; Sept. 13, 1994, Pub.L. 103–322, Title XXXIII, § 330016(1)(K), 108 Stat. 2147.)

§ 551. Concealing or destroying invoices or other papers

Whoever willfully conceals or destroys any invoice, book, or paper relating to any merchandise imported into the United States, after an inspection thereof has been demanded by the collector of any collection district; or

Whoever conceals or destroys at any time any such invoice, book, or paper for the purpose of suppressing any evidence of fraud therein contained—

Shall be fined under this title or imprisoned not more than two years, or both.

(June 25, 1948, c. 645, 62 Stat. 718; Sept. 13, 1994, Pub.L. 103–322, Title XXXIII, § 330016(1)(K), 108 Stat. 2147.)

HISTORICAL AND STATUTORY NOTES

Transfer of Functions

All offices of collector of customs, comptroller of customs, surveyor of customs, and appraiser of merchandise in the Bureau of Customs of the Department of the Treasury to which appointments were required to be made by the President with the advice and consent of the Senate were ordered abolished, to be terminated not later than Dec. 31, 1966. All functions of the offices so eliminated were already vested in the Secretary of the Treasury.

§ 552. Officers aiding importation of obscene or treasonous books and articles

Whoever, being an officer, agent, or employee of the United States, knowingly aids or abets any person engaged in any violation of any of the provisions of law prohibiting importing, advertising, dealing in, exhibiting, or sending or receiving by mail obscene or indecent publications or representations, or books, pamphlets, papers, writings, advertisements, circulars, prints, pictures, or drawings containing any matter advocating or urging treason or insurrection against the United States or forcible resistance to any law of the United States, or containing any threat to take the life of or inflict bodily harm upon any person in the United States, or means for procuring abortion, or other articles of indecent or immoral use or tendency, shall be fined under this title or imprisoned not more than ten years, or both.

(June 25, 1948, c. 645, 62 Stat. 718; Jan. 8, 1971, Pub.L. 91–662, § 2, 84 Stat. 1973; Sept. 13, 1994, Pub.L. 103–322, Title XXXIII, § 330016(1)(K), 108 Stat. 2147.)

HISTORICAL AND STATUTORY NOTES

Effective and Applicability Provisions

1971 Acts. Section 7 of Pub.L. 91–662 provided that: "The amendments made by this Act (other than by section 6) [amending this section, sections 1461 and 1462 of this title, and section 1305 of Title 19] shall take effect on the day after the date of the enactment of this Act [Jan. 8, 1971]".

§ 553. Importation or exportation of stolen motor vehicles, off-highway mobile equipment, vessels, or aircraft

(a) Whoever knowingly imports, exports, or attempts to import or export—

(1) any motor vehicle, off-highway mobile equipment, vessel, aircraft, or part of any motor vehicle, off-highway mobile equipment, vessel, or aircraft, knowing the same to have been stolen; or

(2) any motor vehicle or off-highway mobile equipment or part of any motor vehicle or off-highway mobile equipment, knowing that the identification number of such motor vehicle, equipment, or part has been removed, obliterated, tampered with, or altered;

shall be fined under this title or imprisoned not more than 10 years, or both.

(b) Subsection (a)(2) shall not apply if the removal, obliteration, tampering, or alteration—

(1) is caused by collision or fire; or

(2)(A) in the case of a motor vehicle, is not a violation of section 511 of this title (relating to altering or removing motor vehicle identification numbers); or

(B) in the case of off-highway mobile equipment, would not be a violation of section 511 of this title if such equipment were a motor vehicle.

(c) As used in this section, the term—

(1) "motor vehicle" has the meaning given that term in section 32101 of title 49;

(2) "off-highway mobile equipment" means any self-propelled agricultural equipment, self-propelled construction equipment, and self-propelled special use equipment, used or designed for running on land but not on rail or highway;

(3) "vessel" has the meaning given that term in section 401 of the Tariff Act of 1930 (19 U.S.C. 1401);

(4) "aircraft" has the meaning given that term in section 40102(a) of title 49; and

(5) "identification number"—

(A) in the case of a motor vehicle, has the meaning given that term in section 511 of this title; and

(B) in the case of any other vehicle or equipment covered by this section, means a number or symbol assigned to the vehicle or equipment, or part thereof, by the manufacturer primarily for the purpose of identifying such vehicle, equipment, or part.

(Added Pub.L. 98–547, Title III, § 301(a), Oct. 25, 1984, 98 Stat. 2771, and amended Pub.L. 100–690, Title VII, § 7021, Nov. 18, 1988, 102 Stat. 4397; Pub.L. 102–519, Title I, § 102, Oct. 25, 1992, 106 Stat. 3385; Pub.L. 103–272, § 5(e)(5), July 5, 1994, 108 Stat. 1374.)

§ 554. Smuggling goods from the United States [1]

(a) In general.—Whoever fraudulently or knowingly exports or sends from the United States, or attempts to export or send from the United States, any merchandise, article, or object contrary to any law or regulation of the United States, or receives, conceals, buys, sells, or in any manner facilitates the transportation, concealment, or sale of such merchandise, article or object, prior to exportation, knowing the same to be intended for exportation contrary to any law or regulation of the United States, shall be fined under this title, imprisoned not more than 10 years, or both.

(b) Definition.—In this section, the term "United States" has the meaning given that term in section 545.

(Added Pub.L. 109–177, Title III, § 311(a), Mar. 9, 2006, 120 Stat. 242.)

[1] Another section 554 is set out post.

§ 554. Border tunnels and passages [1]

(a) Any person who knowingly constructs or finances the construction of a tunnel or subterranean passage that crosses the international border between the United States and another country, other than a lawfully authorized tunnel or passage known to the Secretary of Homeland Security and subject to inspection by Immigration and Customs Enforcement, shall be fined under this title and imprisoned for not more than 20 years.

(b) Any person who knows or recklessly disregards the construction or use of a tunnel or passage described in subsection (a) on land that the person owns or controls shall be fined under this title and imprisoned for not more than 10 years.

(c) Any person who uses a tunnel or passage described in subsection (a) to unlawfully smuggle an alien, goods (in violation of section 545), controlled substances, weapons of mass destruction (including biological weapons), or a member of a terrorist organization (as defined in section 2339B(g)(6)) shall be subject to a maximum term of imprisonment that is twice the maximum term of imprisonment that would have otherwise been applicable had the unlawful activity not made use of such a tunnel or passage.

(Added Pub.L. 109–295, Title V, § 551(a), Oct. 4, 2006, 120 Stat. 1389.)

1 Another section 554 is set out ante.

HISTORICAL AND STATUTORY NOTES

Codifications

Another section 554 of this title, relating to smuggling goods from the United States, was enacted by Pub.L. 109–177, Title III, § 311(a), Mar. 9, 2006, 120 Stat. 242.

CHAPTER 29—ELECTIONS AND POLITICAL ACTIVITIES

HISTORICAL AND STATUTORY NOTES

Senate Revision Amendment

By Senate amendment, item 610 was changed to read, "610. Contributions or expenditures by national banks, corporations, or labor organizations". See Senate Report No. 1620, amendment Nos. 4 and 5, 80th Cong.

[§ 591. Repealed. Pub.L. 96–187, Title II, § 201(a) (1), Jan. 8, 1980, 93 Stat. 1367]

HISTORICAL AND STATUTORY NOTES

Section, Acts June 25, 1948, c. 645, 62 Stat. 719; May 24, 1949, c. 139, § 9, 63 Stat. 90; Sept. 22, 1970, Pub.L. 91–405, Title II, § 204(d) (4), 84 Stat. 853; Feb. 7, 1972, Pub.L. 92–225, Title II, § 201, 86 Stat. 8; Oct. 15, 1974, Pub.L. 93–443, Title I, §§ 101(f) (2), 102, 88 Stat. 1268, 1269; May 11, 1976, Pub.L. 94–283, Title I, § 115(g), Title II, § 202, 90 Stat. 496, 497, defined terms applicable to prohibitions respecting elections and political activities.

Effective Date of Repeal

Section repealed effective Jan. 8, 1980, see section 301(a) of Pub.L. 96–187, set out as a note under section 431 of Title 2, The Congress.

State Laws Affected; Definitions

Section 104 of Pub.L. 93–443 provided that:

"(a) The provisions of chapter 29 of title 18, United States Code [this chapter], relating to elections and political activities, supersede and preempt any provision of State law with respect to election to Federal office.

"(b) For purposes of this section, the terms 'election', 'Federal office', and 'State' have the meanings given them by section 591 of title 18, United States Code [this section]."

§ 592. Troops at polls

Whoever, being an officer of the Army or Navy, or other person in the civil, military, or naval service of the United States, orders, brings, keeps, or has under his authority or control any troops or armed men at any place where a general or special election is held, unless such force be necessary to repel armed enemies of the United States, shall be fined under this title or imprisoned not more than five years, or both; and be disqualified from holding any office of honor, profit, or trust under the United States.

This section shall not prevent any officer or member of the armed forces of the United States from exercising the right of suffrage in any election district to which he may belong, if otherwise qualified according to the laws of the State in which he offers to vote.

(June 25, 1948, c. 645, 62 Stat. 719; Sept. 13, 1994, Pub.L. 103–322, Title XXXIII, § 330016(1)(K), 108 Stat. 2147.)

§ 593. Interference by armed forces

Whoever, being an officer or member of the Armed Forces of the United States, prescribes or fixes or attempts to prescribe or fix, whether by proclamation, order or otherwise, the qualifications of voters at any election in any State; or

Whoever, being such officer or member, prevents or attempts to prevent by force, threat, intimidation, advice or otherwise any qualified voter of any State from fully exercising the right of suffrage at any general or special election; or

Whoever, being such officer or member, orders or compels or attempts to compel any election officer in any State to receive a vote from a person not legally qualified to vote; or

Whoever, being such officer or member, imposes or attempts to impose any regulations for conducting any general or special election in a State, different from those prescribed by law; or

Whoever, being such officer or member, interferes in any manner with an election officer's discharge of his duties—

Shall be fined under this title or imprisoned not more than five years, or both; and disqualified from holding any office of honor, profit or trust under the United States.

This section shall not prevent any officer or member of the Armed Forces from exercising the right of suffrage in any district to which he may belong, if otherwise qualified according to the laws of the State of such district.

(June 25, 1948, c. 645, 62 Stat. 719; Sept. 13, 1994, Pub.L. 103–322, Title XXXIII, § 330016(1)(K), 108 Stat. 2147.)

§ 594. Intimidation of voters

Whoever intimidates, threatens, coerces, or attempts to intimidate, threaten, or coerce, any other person for the purpose of interfering with the right of such other person to vote or to vote as he may choose, or of causing such other person to vote for, or not to vote for, any candidate for the office of President, Vice President, Presidential elector, Member of the Senate, Member of the House of Representatives, Delegate from the District of Columbia, or Resident Commissioner, at any election held solely or in part for the purpose of electing such candidate, shall be fined under this title or imprisoned not more than one year, or both.

(June 25, 1948, c. 645, 62 Stat. 720; Sept. 22, 1970, Pub.L. 91–405, Title II, § 204(d)(5), 84 Stat. 853; Sept. 13, 1994, Pub.L. 103–322, Title XXXIII, § 330016(1)(H), 108 Stat. 2147.)

HISTORICAL AND STATUTORY NOTES

Effective and Applicability Provisions

1970 Acts. Amendment by Pub.L. 91–405 effective Sept. 22, 1970, see § 206(b) of Pub.L. 91–405, summarized in a note set out under § 25 of Title 2, The Congress.

Canal Zone

Applicability of section to Canal Zone, see § 14 of this title.

§ 595. Interference by administrative employees of Federal, State, or Territorial Governments

Whoever, being a person employed in any administrative position by the United States, or by any department or agency thereof, or by the District of Columbia or any agency or instrumentality thereof, or by any State, Territory, or Possession of the United States, or any political subdivision, municipality, or agency thereof, or agency of such political subdivision or municipality (including any corporation owned or controlled by any State, Territory, or Possession of the United States or by any such political subdivision, municipality, or agency), in connection with any activity which is financed in whole or in part by loans or grants made by the United States, or any department or agency thereof, uses his official authority for the purpose of interfering with, or affecting, the nomination or the election of any candidate for the office of President, Vice President, Presidential elector, Member of the Senate, Member of the House of Representatives, Delegate from the District of Columbia, or Resident Commissioner, shall be fined under this title or imprisoned not more than one year, or both.

This section shall not prohibit or make unlawful any act by any officer or employee of any educational or research institution, establishment, agency, or system which is supported in whole or in part by any state or political subdivision thereof, or by the District of Columbia or by any Territory or Possession of the United States; or by any recognized religious, philanthropic or cultural organization.

(June 25, 1948, c. 645, 62 Stat. 720; Sept. 22, 1970, Pub.L. 91–405, Title II, § 204(d)(6), 84 Stat. 853; Sept. 13, 1994, Pub.L. 103–322, Title XXXIII, § 330016(1)(H), (L), 108 Stat. 2147.)

HISTORICAL AND STATUTORY NOTES

Effective and Applicability Provisions

1970 Acts. Amendment by Pub.L. 91–405 effective Sept. 22, 1970, see § 206(b) of Pub.L. 91–405, summarized in a note set out under § 25 of Title 2, The Congress.

Canal Zone

Applicability of section to Canal Zone, see § 14 of this title.

§ 596. Polling armed forces

Whoever, within or without the Armed Forces of the United States, polls any member of such forces, either within or without the United States, either before or after he executes any ballot under any Federal or State law, with reference to his choice of or his vote for any candidate, or states, publishes, or releases any result of any purported poll taken from or among the members of the Armed Forces of the United States or including within it the statement of choice for such candidate or of such votes cast by any member of the Armed Forces of the United States, shall be fined under this title or imprisoned for not more than one year, or both.

The word "poll" means any request for information, verbal or written, which by its language or form of expression requires or implies the necessity of an answer, where the request is made with the intent of compiling the result of the answers obtained, either for the personal use of the person making the request, or for the purpose of reporting the same to any other person, persons, political party, unincorporated association or corporation, or for the purpose of publishing the same orally, by radio, or in written or printed form.

(June 25, 1948, c. 645, 62 Stat. 720; Sept. 13, 1994, Pub.L. 103–322, Title XXXIII, § 330016(1)(H), 108 Stat. 2147.)

§ 597. Expenditures to influence voting

Whoever makes or offers to make an expenditure to any person, either to vote or withhold his vote, or to vote for or against any candidate; and

Whoever solicits, accepts, or receives any such expenditure in consideration of his vote or the withholding of his vote—

Shall be fined under this title or imprisoned not more than one year, or both; and if the violation was willful, shall be fined under this title or imprisoned not more than two years, or both.

(June 25, 1948, c. 645, 62 Stat. 721; Sept. 13, 1994, Pub.L. 103–322, Title XXXIII, § 330016(1)(H), 108 Stat. 2147; Oct. 11, 1996, Pub.L. 104–294, Title VI, § 601(a)(12), 110 Stat. 3498.)

§ 598. Coercion by means of relief appropriations

Whoever uses any part of any appropriation made by Congress for work relief, relief, or for increasing employment by providing loans and grants for public-works projects, or exercises or administers any authority conferred by any Appropriation Act for the purpose of interfering with, restraining, or coercing any individual in the exercise of his right to vote at any election, shall be fined under this title or imprisoned not more than one year, or both.

(June 25, 1948, c. 645, 62 Stat. 721; Sept. 13, 1994, Pub.L. 103–322, Title XXXIII, § 330016(1)(H), 108 Stat. 2147.)

HISTORICAL AND STATUTORY NOTES

Canal Zone

Applicability of section to Canal Zone, see § 14 of this title.

§ 599. Promise of appointment by candidate

Whoever, being a candidate, directly or indirectly promises or pledges the appointment, or the use of his influence or support for the appointment of any person to any public or private position or employment, for the purpose of procuring support in his candidacy shall be fined under this title or imprisoned not more than one year, or both; and if the violation was willful, shall be fined under this title or imprisoned not more than two years, or both.

(June 25, 1948, c. 645, 62 Stat. 721; Sept. 13, 1994, Pub.L. 103–322, Title XXXIII, § 330016(1)(H), (L), 108 Stat. 2147.)

§ 600. Promise of employment or other benefit for political activity

Whoever, directly or indirectly, promises any employment, position, compensation, contract, appointment, or other benefit, provided for or made possible in whole or in part by any Act of Congress, or any special consideration in obtaining any such benefit, to any person as consideration, favor, or reward for any political activity or for the support of or opposition to any candidate or any political party in connection with any general or special election to any political office, or in connection with any primary election or political convention or caucus held to select candidates for any political office, shall be fined under this title or imprisoned not more than one year, or both.

(June 25, 1948, c. 645, 62 Stat. 721; Feb. 7, 1972, Pub.L. 92–225, Title II, § 202, 86 Stat. 9; Oct. 2, 1976, Pub.L. 94–453, § 3, 90 Stat. 1517; Sept. 13, 1994, Pub.L. 103–322, Title XXXIII, § 330016(1)(L), 108 Stat. 2147.)

HISTORICAL AND STATUTORY NOTES

Effective and Applicability Provisions

1972 Acts. Amendment by Pub.L. 92–225 effective Dec. 31, 1971, or sixty days after Feb. 7, 1972, whichever is later, see § 408, formerly 406, of Pub.L. 92–225, set out as a note under § 431 of Title 2, The Congress.

Canal Zone

Applicability of section to Canal Zone, see § 14 of this title.

§ 601. Deprivation of employment or other benefit for political contribution

(a) Whoever, directly or indirectly, knowingly causes or attempts to cause any person to make a contribution of a thing of value (including services) for the benefit of any candidate or any political party, by means of the denial or deprivation, or the threat of the denial or deprivation, of—

(1) any employment, position, or work in or for any agency or other entity of the Government of the United States, a State, or a political subdivision of a State, or any compensation or benefit of such employment, position, or work; or

(2) any payment or benefit of a program of the United States, a State, or a political subdivision of a State;

if such employment, position, work, compensation, payment, or benefit is provided for or made possible in whole or in part by an Act of Congress, shall be fined under this title, or imprisoned not more than one year, or both.

(b) As used in this section—

(1) the term "candidate" means an individual who seeks nomination for election, or election, to Federal, State, or local office, whether or not such individual is elected, and, for purposes of this paragraph, an individual shall be deemed to seek nomination for election, or election, to Federal, State, or local office, if he has (A) taken the action necessary under the law of a State to qualify himself for nomination for election, or election, or (B) received contributions or made expenditures, or has given his consent for any other person to receive contributions or make expenditures, with a view to bringing about his nomination for election, or election, to such office;

(2) the term "election" means (A) a general, special primary, or runoff election, (B) a convention or caucus of a political party held to nominate a candidate, (C) a primary election held for the selection of delegates to a nominating convention of a political party, (D) a primary election held for the expression of a preference for the nomination of persons for election to the office of President, and (E) the election of delegates to a constitutional convention for proposing amendments to the Constitution of the United States or of any State; and

(3) the term "State" means a State of the United States, the District of Columbia, the Commonwealth of Puerto Rico, or any territory or possession of the United States.

(June 25, 1948, c. 645, 62 Stat. 721; Oct. 2, 1976, Pub.L. 94–453, § 1, 90 Stat. 1516; Sept. 13, 1994, Pub.L. 103–322, Title XXXIII, § 330016(1)(L), 108 Stat. 2147.)

HISTORICAL AND STATUTORY NOTES

Canal Zone

Applicability of section to Canal Zone, see § 14 of this title.

§ 602. Solicitation of political contributions

(a) It shall be unlawful for—

(1) a candidate for the Congress;

(2) an individual elected to or serving in the office of Senator or Representative in, or Delegate or Resident Commissioner to, the Congress;

(3) an officer or employee of the United States or any department or agency thereof; or

(4) a person receiving any salary or compensation for services from money derived from the Treasury of the United States; to knowingly solicit any contribution within the meaning of section 301(8) of the Federal Election Campaign Act of 1971 [2 U.S.C.A. § 431(8)] from any other such officer, employee, or person. Any person who violates this section shall be fined under this title or imprisoned not more than 3 years, or both.

(b) The prohibition in subsection (a) shall not apply to any activity of an employee (as defined in section 7322(1) of title 5) or any individual employed in or under the United States Postal Service or the Postal Regulatory Commission, unless that activity is prohibited by section 7323 or 7324 of such title.

(June 25, 1948, c. 645, 62 Stat. 722; Jan. 8, 1980, Pub.L. 96–187, Title II, § 201(a) (3), 93 Stat. 1367; Oct. 6, 1993, Pub.L. 103–94, § 4(a), 107 Stat. 1004; Sept. 13, 1994, Pub.L. 103–322, Title XXXIII, § 330016(1)(K), 108 Stat. 2147; Dec. 20, 2006, Pub.L. 109–435, Title VI, § 604(f), 120 Stat. 3242.)

HISTORICAL AND STATUTORY NOTES

References in Text

Section 301(8) of the Federal Election Campaign Act of 1971, referred to in subsec. (a)(4), is classified to section 431(8) of Title 2, The Congress.

Effective and Applicability Provisions

1993 Acts. Amendment by section 4(a) of Pub.L. 103–94 effective 120 days after Oct. 6, 1993, except as otherwise provided, see section 12 of Pub.L. 103–94, set out as a note under section 7321 of Title 5, Government Organization and Employees.

1980 Acts. Amendment by Pub.L. 96–187 effective on Jan. 8, 1980, see section 301(a) of Pub.L. 96–187, set out as a note under section 431 of Title 2, The Congress.

Retroactive Effect of 1993 Amendments

No provision of Pub.L. 103–94 to affect proceedings with respect to charges filed on or before effective date of amendments made by Pub.L. 103–94, and orders to be issued in such proceedings and appeals to be taken therefrom as if Pub.L. 103–94 had not been enacted, see section 12(c) of Pub.L. 103–94, set out as a note under section 7321 of Title 5, Government Organization and Employees.

Savings Provisions

Amendment or repeal of any provision of law made by Pub.L. 103–94 not to release or extinguish penalty, forfeiture or liability incurred under such provision, and such provision to be treated as remaining in force for purpose of proceeding or action for enforcement of such penalty, forfeiture or liability, see section 12(b) of Pub.L. 103–94, set out as a note under section 7321 of Title 5, Government Organization and Employees.

Delegate from District of Columbia; Effective Date

Provisions of Federal Corrupt Practices Act applicable, effective Sept. 22, 1970, with respect to Delegate to House of Representatives from District of Columbia in same manner and to same extent as applicable with respect to a Representative, see §§ 204(a), 206(b) of Pub.L. 91–405, Title II, Sept. 22, 1970, 84 Stat. 852, set out as notes under § 25 of Title 2, The Congress.

§ 603. Making political contributions

(a) It shall be unlawful for an officer or employee of the United States or any department or agency thereof, or a person receiving any salary or compensation for services from money derived from the Treasury of the United States, to make any contribution within the meaning of section 301(8) of the Federal Election Campaign Act of 1971 to any other such officer, employee or person or to any Senator or Representative in, or Delegate or Resident Commissioner to, the Congress, if the person receiving such contribution is the employer or employing authority of the person making the contribution. Any person who violates this section shall be fined under this title or imprisoned not more than three years, or both.

(b) For purposes of this section, a contribution to an authorized committee as defined in section 302(e)(1) of the Federal Election Campaign Act of 1971 shall be considered a contribution to the individual who has authorized such committee.

(c) The prohibition in subsection (a) shall not apply to any activity of an employee (as defined in section 7322(1) of title 5) or any individual employed in or under the United States Postal Service or the Postal Regulatory Commission, unless that activity is prohibited by section 7323 or 7324 of such title.

(June 25, 1948, c. 645, 62 Stat. 722; Oct. 31, 1951, c. 655, § 20(b), 65 Stat. 718; Jan. 8, 1980, Pub.L. 96–187, Title II, § 201(a)(4), 93 Stat. 1367; Oct. 6, 1993, Pub.L. 103–94, § 4(b), 107 Stat. 1005; Sept. 13, 1994, Pub.L. 103–322, Title XXXIII, § 330016(1)(K), 108 Stat. 2147; Dec. 20, 2006, Pub.L. 109–435, Title VI, § 604(f), 120 Stat. 3242.)

HISTORICAL AND STATUTORY NOTES

References in Text

Sections 301(8) and 302(e)(1) of the Federal Election Campaign Act of 1971, referred to in text, are classified to sections 431(8) and 432(e)(1), respectively, of Title 2, The Congress.

Effective and Applicability Provisions

1993 Acts. Amendment by section 4(b) of Pub.L. 103–94 effective 120 days after Oct. 6, 1993, except as otherwise provided, see section 12 of Pub.L. 103–94, set out as a note under section 7321 of Title 5, Government Organization and Employees.

1980 Acts. Amendment by Pub.L. 96–187 effective on Jan. 8, 1980, see section 301(a) of Pub.L. 96–187, set out as a note under section 431 of Title 2, The Congress.

Retroactive Effect of 1993 Amendments

No provision of Pub.L. 103–94 to affect proceedings with respect to charges filed on or before effective date of amendments made by Pub.L. 103–94, and orders to be issued in such proceedings and appeals to be taken therefrom as if Pub.L. 103–94 had not been enacted, see section 12(c) of Pub.L. 103–94, set out as a note under section 7321 of Title 5, Government Organization and Employees.

Savings Provisions

Amendment or repeal of any provision of law made by Pub.L. 103–94 not to release or extinguish penalty, forfeiture or liability incurred under such provision, and such provision to be treated as remaining in force for purpose of proceeding or action for enforcement of such penalty, forfeiture or liability, see section 12(b) of Pub.L. 103–94, set out as a note under section 7321 of Title 5, Government Organization and Employees.

§ 604. Solicitation from persons on relief

Whoever solicits or receives or is in any manner concerned in soliciting or receiving any assessment, subscription, or contribution for any political purpose from any person known by him to be entitled to, or receiving compensation, employment, or other benefit provided for or made possible by any Act of Congress appropriating funds for work relief or relief purposes, shall be fined under this title or imprisoned not more than one year, or both.

(June 25, 1948, c. 645, 62 Stat. 722; Sept. 13, 1994, Pub.L. 103–322, Title XXXIII, § 330016(1)(H), 108 Stat. 2147.)

HISTORICAL AND STATUTORY NOTES

Canal Zone

Applicability of section to Canal Zone, see § 14 of this title.

§ 605. Disclosure of names of persons on relief

Whoever, for political purposes, furnishes or discloses any list or names of persons receiving compensation, employment or benefits provided for or made possible by any Act of Congress appropriating, or authorizing the appropriation of funds for work relief or relief purposes, to a political candidate, committee, campaign manager, or to any person for delivery to a political candidate, committee, or campaign manager; and

Whoever receives any such list or names for political purposes—

Shall be fined under this title or imprisoned not more than one year, or both.

(June 25, 1948, c. 645, 62 Stat. 722; Sept. 13, 1994, Pub.L. 103–322, Title XXXIII, § 330016(1)(H), 108 Stat. 2147.)

HISTORICAL AND STATUTORY NOTES

Canal Zone

Applicability of section to Canal Zone, see § 14 of this title.

§ 606. Intimidation to secure political contributions

Whoever, being one of the officers or employees of the United States mentioned in section 602 of this title, discharges, or promotes, or degrades, or in any manner changes the official rank or compensation of any other officer or employee, or promises or threatens so to do, for giving or withholding or neglecting to make any contribution of money or other valuable thing for any political purpose, shall be fined under this title or imprisoned not more than three years, or both.

(June 25, 1948, c. 645, 62 Stat. 722; Sept. 13, 1994, Pub.L. 103–322, Title XXXIII, § 330016(1)(K), 108 Stat. 2147.)

§ 607. Place of solicitation

(a) Prohibition.—

(1) In general.—It shall be unlawful for any person to solicit or receive a donation of money or other thing of value in connection with a Federal, State, or local election from a person who is located in a room or building occupied in the discharge of official duties by an officer or employee of the United States. It shall be unlawful for an individual who is an officer or employee of the Federal Government, including the President, Vice President, and Members of Congress, to solicit or receive a donation of money or other thing of value in connection with a Federal, State, or local election, while in any room or building occupied in the discharge of official duties by an officer or employee of the United States, from any person.

(2) Penalty.—A person who violates this section shall be fined not more than $5,000, imprisoned not more than 3 years, or both.

(b) The prohibition in subsection (a) shall not apply to the receipt of contributions by persons on the staff of a Senator or Representative in, or Delegate or Resident Commissioner to, the Congress or Executive Office of the President, provided, that such contributions have not been solicited in any manner which directs the contributor to mail or deliver a contribution to any room, building, or other facility referred to in subsection (a), and provided that such contributions are transferred within seven days of receipt to a political committee within the meaning of section 302(e) of the Federal Election Campaign Act of 1971.

(June 25, 1948, c. 645, 62 Stat. 722; Jan. 8, 1980, Pub.L. 96–187, Title II, § 201(a)(5), 93 Stat. 1367; Sept. 13, 1994, Pub.L. 103–322, Title XXXIII, § 330016(1)(K), 108 Stat. 2147; Mar. 27, 2002, Pub.L. 107–155, Title III, § 302, 116 Stat. 96.)

HISTORICAL AND STATUTORY NOTES

References in Text

Section 302(e) of the Federal Election Campaign Act of 1971, referred to subsec. (b), is Pub.L. 92-225, Title III, 302(e), Feb. 7, 1972, 86 Stat. 12, as amended, which is classified to 2 U.S.C.A. § 432(e).

Effective and Applicability Provisions

2002 Acts. Except as otherwise provided, amendments by Pub.L. 107–155 generally effective Nov. 6, 2002, see Pub.L. 107–155, § 402, set out as a note under 2 U.S.C.A. § 431.

1980 Acts. Amendment by Pub.L. 96–187 effective on Jan. 8, 1980, see section 301(a) of Pub.L. 96–187, set out as a note under section 431 of Title 2, The Congress.

§ 608. Absent uniformed services voters and overseas voters

(a) Whoever knowingly deprives or attempts to deprive any person of a right under the Uniformed and Overseas Citizens Absentee Voting Act shall be fined in accordance with this title or imprisoned not more than five years, or both.

(b) Whoever knowingly gives false information for the purpose of establishing the eligibility of any person to register or vote under the Uniformed and Overseas Citizens Absentee Voting Act, or pays or offers to pay, or accepts payment for registering or voting under such Act shall be fined in accordance with this title or imprisoned not more than five years, or both.

(Added Pub.L. 99–410, Title II, § 202(a), Aug. 28, 1986, 100 Stat. 929.)

HISTORICAL AND STATUTORY NOTES

References in Text

The Uniformed and Overseas Citizens Absentee Voting Act, referred to in text, is Pub.L. 99–410, Aug. 28, 1986, 100 Stat. 924, which is classified principally to subchapter I–G (§ 1973ff et seq.) of chapter 20 of Title 42. For complete classification, see Short Title note under 42 U.S.C.A. § 1971 and Tables.

Effective and Applicability Provisions

1986 Acts. Section applicable with respect to elections taking place after Dec. 31, 1987, see section 204 of Pub.L. 99–410, set out as a note under section 1973ff of Title 42, The Public Health and Welfare.

Prior Provisions

A prior section 608, Acts June 25, 1948, c. 645, 62 Stat. 723; Feb. 7, 1972, Pub.L. 92–225, Title II, § 203, 86 Stat. 9; Oct. 15, 1974, Pub.L. 93–443, Title I, § 101(a), (b), 88 Stat. 1263, 1266, which set limitations on campaign contributions and expenditures, was repealed by Pub.L. 94–283, Title II, § 201(a), May 11, 1976, 90 Stat. 496.

§ 609. Use of military authority to influence vote of member of Armed Forces

Whoever, being a commissioned, noncommissioned, warrant, or petty officer of an Armed Force, uses military authority to influence the vote of a member of the Armed Forces or to require a member of the Armed Forces to march to a polling place, or attempts to do so, shall be fined in accordance with this title or imprisoned not more than five years, or both. Nothing in this section shall prohibit free discussion of political issues or candidates for public office.

(Added Pub.L. 99–410, Title II, § 202(a), Aug. 28, 1986, 100 Stat. 929.)

HISTORICAL AND STATUTORY NOTES

Effective and Applicability Provisions

1986 Acts. Section applicable with respect to elections taking place after Dec. 31, 1987, see section 204 of Pub.L. 99–410, set out as a note under section 1973ff of Title 42, The Public Health and Welfare.

Prior Provisions

A prior section 609, Act June 25, 1948, c. 645, 62 Stat. 723, which prescribed maximum contributions and expenditures limitation of $3,000,000 for any calendar year, was repealed by Pub.L. 92–225, Title II, § 204, Feb. 7, 1972, 86 Stat. 10.

§ 610. Coercion of political activity

It shall be unlawful for any person to intimidate, threaten, command, or coerce, or attempt to intimidate, threaten, command, or coerce, any employee of the Federal Government as defined in section 7322(1) of title 5, United States Code, to engage in, or not to engage in, any political activity, including, but not limited to, voting or refusing to vote for any candidate or measure in any election, making or refusing to make any political contribution, or working or refusing to work on behalf of any candidate. Any person who violates this section shall be fined under this title or imprisoned not more than three years, or both.

(Added Pub.L. 103–94, § 4(c)(1), Oct. 6, 1993, 107 Stat. 1005, and amended Pub.L. 104–294, Title VI, § 601(a)(1), Oct. 11, 1996, 110 Stat. 3498.)

HISTORICAL AND STATUTORY NOTES

Effective and Applicability Provisions

1993 Acts. Section effective 120 days after Oct. 6, 1993, except as otherwise provided, see section 12 of Pub.L. 103–94, set out as a note under section 7321 of Title 5, Government Organization and Employees.

Savings Provisions

Amendment or repeal of any provision of law made by Pub.L. 103–94 not to release or extinguish penalty, forfeiture or liability incurred under such provision, and such provision to be treated as remaining in force for purpose of proceeding or action for enforcement of such penalty, forfeiture or liability, see section 12(b) of Pub.L. 103–94, set out as a note under section 7321 of Title 5, Government Organization and Employees.

1993 Acts. No provision of Pub.L. 103–94 to affect proceedings with respect to charges filed on or before effective date of amendments made by Pub.L. 103–94, and orders to be issued in such proceedings and appeals to be taken therefrom as if Pub.L. 103–94 had not been enacted, see section 12(c) of Pub.L. 103–94, set out as a note under section 7321 of Title 5, Government Organization and Employees.

Prior Provisions

A prior section 610, Acts June 25, 1948, c. 645, 62 Stat. 723; May 24, 1949, c. 139, § 10, 63 Stat. 90; Oct. 31, 1951, c. 655, § 20(c), 65 Stat. 718; Feb. 7, 1972, Pub.L. 92–225, Title II, § 205, 86 Stat. 10; Oct. 15, 1974, Pub.L. 93–443, Title I, § 101(e)(1), 88 Stat. 1267, prohibited campaign contributions or expenditures by national banks, corporations, and labor organizations, prior to repeal by Pub.L. 94–283, Title II, § 201(a), May 11, 1976, 90 Stat. 496. See section 441b of Title 2, The Congress.

§ 611. Voting by aliens

(a) It shall be unlawful for any alien to vote in any election held solely or in part for the purpose of electing a candidate for the office of President, Vice President, Presidential elector, Member of the Senate, Member of the House of Representatives, Delegate from the District of Columbia, or Resident Commissioner, unless—

(1) the election is held partly for some other purpose;

(2) aliens are authorized to vote for such other purpose under a State constitution or statute or a local ordinance; and

(3) voting for such other purpose is conducted independently of voting for a candidate for such Federal offices, in such a manner that an alien has the opportunity to vote for such other purpose, but not an opportunity to vote for a candidate for any one or more of such Federal offices.

(b) Any person who violates this section shall be fined under this title, imprisoned not more than one year, or both.

(c) Subsection (a) does not apply to an alien if—

(1) each natural parent of the alien (or, in the case of an adopted alien, each adoptive parent of the alien) is or was a citizen (whether by birth or naturalization);

(2) the alien permanently resided in the United States prior to attaining the age of 16; and

(3) the alien reasonably believed at the time of voting in violation of such subsection that he or she was a citizen of the United States.

(Added Pub.L. 104–208, Div. C, Title II, § 216(a), Sept. 30, 1996, 110 Stat. 3009–572, and amended Pub.L. 106–395, Title II, § 201(d)(1), Oct. 30, 2000, 114 Stat. 1635.)

HISTORICAL AND STATUTORY NOTES

Effective and Applicability Provisions

2000 Acts. Pub.L. 106–395, Title II, § 201(d)(3), Oct. 30, 2000, 114 Stat. 1636, provided that: "The amendment made by paragraph (1) [adding subsec. (c) to this section] shall be effective as if included in the enactment of section 216 of the Illegal Immigration Reform and Immigrant Responsibility Act of 1996 (Public Law 104–208; 110 Stat. 3009–572) [Pub.L. 104–208, Div. C, § 216, Sept. 30, 1996, 110 Stat. 3009–572, which enacted this section]. The amendment made by paragraph (2)[amending section 1015 of this title] shall be effective as if included in the enactment of section 215 of the Illegal Immigration Reform and Immigrant Responsibility Act of 1996 (Public Law 104–208; 110 Stat. 3009–572) [Pub.L. 104–208, Div. C, § 215, Sept. 30, 1996, 110 Stat. 572, which enacted section 1015 of this title]. The amendments made by paragraphs (1) and (2) shall apply to an alien prosecuted on or after September 30, 1996, except in the case of an alien whose criminal proceeding (including judicial review thereof) has been finally concluded before the date of the enactment of this Act [Oct. 30, 2000]."

Severability of Provisions

If any provision of Division C of Pub.L. 104–208 or the application of such provision to any person or circumstances is held to be unconstitutional, the remainder of Division C of Pub.L. 104–208 and the application of the provisions of Division C of Pub.L. 104–208 to any person or circumstance not to be affected thereby, see section 1(e) of Pub.L. 104–208, set out as a note under section 1101 of Title 8, Aliens and Nationality.

Prior Provisions

A prior section 611, Acts June 25, 1948, c. 645, 62 Stat. 724; Feb. 7, 1972, Pub.L. 92–225, Title II, § 206, 86 Stat. 10; Oct. 15, 1974, Pub.L. 93–443, Title I, §§ 101(e)(2), 103, 88 Stat. 1267, 1272, which prohibited campaign contributions by government contractors, was repealed by Pub.L. 94–283, Title II, § 201(a), May 11, 1976, 90 Stat. 496. See § 441c of Title 2, The Congress.

[§§ 612 to 617. Repealed. Pub.L. 94–283, Title II, § 201(a), May 11, 1976, 90 Stat. 496]

HISTORICAL AND STATUTORY NOTES

Savings Provisions

Repeal of sections by Pub.L. 94–283 not to release or extinguish any penalty, forfeiture, or liability incurred under sections or penalties, with each section or penalty to be treated as remaining in force for the purpose of sustaining any proper action or prosecution for the enforcement of any penalty, forfeiture, or liability, see § 114 of Pub.L. 94–283.

CHAPTER 31—EMBEZZLEMENT AND THEFT

[1] So in original. Does not conform to section catchline.

§ 641. Public money, property or records

Whoever embezzles, steals, purloins, or knowingly converts to his use or the use of another, or without authority, sells, conveys or disposes of any record, voucher, money, or thing of value of the United States or of any department or agency thereof, or any property made or being made under contract for the United States or any department or agency thereof; or

Whoever receives, conceals, or retains the same with intent to convert it to his use or gain, knowing it to have been embezzled, stolen, purloined or converted—

Shall be fined under this title or imprisoned not more than ten years, or both; but if the value of such property in the aggregate, combining amounts from all the counts for which the defendant is convicted in a single case, does not exceed the sum of $1,000, he shall be fined under this title or imprisoned not more than one year, or both.

The word "value" means face, par, or market value, or cost price, either wholesale or retail, whichever is greater.

(June 25, 1948, c. 645, 62 Stat. 725; Sept. 13, 1994, Pub.L. 103–322, Title XXXIII, § 330016(1)(H), (L), 108 Stat. 2147; Oct. 11, 1996, Pub.L. 104–294, Title VI, § 606(a), 110 Stat. 3511; July 15, 2004, Pub.L. 108–275, § 4, 118 Stat. 833.)

HISTORICAL AND STATUTORY NOTES

Short Title

1984 Amendments. Pub.L. 98–473, Title II, § 1110, Oct. 12, 1984, 98 Stat. 2148, provided that: "This Part [enacting section 667 of this title and amended sections 2316 and 2317 of this title] may be cited as the 'Livestock Fraud Protection Act'."

§ 642. Tools and materials for counterfeiting purposes

Whoever, without authority from the United States, secretes within, or embezzles, or takes and carries away from any building, room, office, apartment, vault, safe, or other place where the same is kept, used, employed, placed, lodged, or deposited by authority of the United States, any tool, implement, or thing used or fitted to be used in stamping or printing, or in making some other tool or implement used or fitted to be used in stamping or printing any kind or description of bond, bill, note, certificate, coupon, postage stamp, revenue stamp, fractional currency note, or other paper, instrument, obligation, device, or document, authorized by law to be printed, stamped, sealed, prepared, issued, uttered, or put in circulation on behalf of the United States; or

Whoever, without such authority, so secretes, embezzles, or takes and carries away any paper, parchment, or other material prepared and intended to be used in the making of any such papers, instruments, obligations, devices, or documents; or

Whoever, without such authority, so secretes, embezzles, or takes and carries away any paper, parchment, or other material printed or stamped, in whole or part, and intended to be prepared, issued, or put in circulation on behalf of the United States as one of such papers, instruments, or obligations, or printed or stamped, in whole or part, in the similitude of any such paper, instrument, or obligation, whether intended to issue or put the same in circulation or not—

Shall be fined under this title or imprisoned not more than ten years, or both.

(June 25, 1948, c. 645, 62 Stat. 725; Sept. 13, 1994, Pub.L. 103–322, Title XXXIII, § 330016(1)(K), 108 Stat. 2147.)

§ 643. Accounting generally for public money

Whoever, being an officer, employee or agent of the United States or of any department or agency thereof, having received public money which he is not authorized to retain as salary, pay, or emolument, fails to render his accounts for the same as provided by law is guilty of embezzlement, and shall be fined under this title or in a sum equal to the amount of the money embezzled, whichever is greater, or imprisoned not more than ten years, or both; but if the amount embezzled does not exceed $1,000, he shall be fined under this title or imprisoned not more than one year, or both.

(June 25, 1948, c. 645, 62 Stat. 726; Sept. 13, 1994, Pub.L. 103–322, Title XXXIII, § 330016(1)(H), (2)(G), 108 Stat. 2147, 2148; Oct. 11, 1996, Pub.L. 104–294, Title VI, § 606(a), 110 Stat. 3511.)

§ 644. Banker receiving unauthorized deposit of public money

Whoever, not being an authorized depositary of public moneys, knowingly receives from any disbursing officer, or collector of internal revenue, or other agent of the United States, any public money on deposit, or by way of loan or accommodation, with or without interest, or otherwise than in payment of a debt against the United States, or uses, transfers, converts, appropriates, or applies any portion of the public money for any purpose not prescribed by law is guilty of embezzlement and shall be fined under this title or not more than the amount so embezzled, whichever is greater, or imprisoned not more than ten years, or both; but if the amount embezzled does not exceed $1,000, he shall be fined not more than $1,000 or imprisoned not more than one year, or both.

(June 25, 1948, c. 645, 62 Stat. 726; Sept. 13, 1994, Pub.L. 103–322, Title XXXIII, § 330016(2)(G), 108 Stat. 2148; Oct. 11, 1996, Pub.L. 104–294, Title VI, § 606(a), 110 Stat. 3511.)

§ 645. Court officers generally

Whoever, being a United States marshal, clerk, receiver, referee, trustee, or other officer of a United States court, or any deputy, assistant, or employee of any such officer, retains or converts to his own use or to the use of another or after demand by the party entitled thereto, unlawfully retains any money coming into his hands by virtue of his official relation, position or employment, is guilty of embezzlement and shall, where the offense is not otherwise punishable by enactment of Congress, be fined under this title or not more than double the value of the money so embezzled, whichever is greater, or imprisoned not more than ten years, or both; but if the amount embezzled does not exceed $1,000, he shall be fined under this title or imprisoned not more than one year, or both.

It shall not be a defense that the accused person had any interest in such moneys or fund.

(June 25, 1948, c. 645, 62 Stat. 726; Sept. 13, 1994, Pub.L. 103–322, Title XXXIII, § 330016(1)(H), (2)(G), 108 Stat. 2147, 2148; Oct. 11, 1996, Pub.L. 104–294, Title VI, § 606(a), 110 Stat. 3511.)

§ 646. Court officers depositing registry moneys

Whoever, being a clerk or other officer of a court of the United States, fails to deposit promptly any money belonging in the registry of the court, or paid into court or received by the officers thereof, with the Treasurer or a designated depositary of the United States, in the name and to the credit of such court, or retains or converts to his own use or to the use of another any such money, is guilty of embezzlement and shall be fined under this title or not more than the amount embezzled, whichever is greater, or imprisoned not more than ten years, or both; but if the amount embezzled does not exceed $1,000, he shall be fined under this title or imprisoned not more than one year, or both.

This section shall not prevent the delivery of any such money upon security, according to agreement of parties, under the direction of the court.

(June 25, 1948, c. 645, 62 Stat. 726; Sept. 13, 1994, Pub.L. 103–322, Title XXXIII, § 330016(1)(H), (2)(H), 108 Stat. 2147, 2148; Oct. 11, 1996, Pub.L. 104–294, Title VI, § 606(a), 110 Stat. 3511.)

§ 647. Receiving loan from court officer

Whoever knowingly receives, from a clerk or other officer of a court of the United States, as a deposit, loan, or otherwise, any money belonging in the registry of such court, is guilty of embezzlement, and shall be fined under this title or not more than the amount embezzled, whichever is greater, or imprisoned not more than ten years, or both; but if the amount embezzled does not exceed $1,000, he shall be fined under this title or imprisoned not more than one year, or both.

(June 25, 1948, c. 645, 62 Stat. 727; Sept. 13, 1994, Pub.L. 103–322, Title XXXIII, § 330016(1)(H), (2)(G), 108 Stat. 2147, 2148; Oct. 11, 1996, Pub.L. 104–294, Title VI, § 606(a), 110 Stat. 3511.)

§ 648. Custodians, generally, misusing public funds

Whoever, being an officer or other person charged by any Act of Congress with the safe-keeping of the public moneys, loans, uses, or converts to his own use, or deposits in any bank, including any branch or agency of a foreign bank (as such terms are defined in paragraphs (1) and (3) of section 1(b) of the International Banking Act of 1978, or exchanges for other funds, except as specially allowed by law, any portion of the public moneys intrusted to him for safe-keeping, is guilty of embezzlement of the money so loaned, used, converted, deposited, or exchanged, and shall be fined under this title or in a sum equal to the amount of money so embezzled, whichever is greater, or imprisoned not more than ten years, or both; but if the amount embezzled does not exceed $1,000, he shall be fined under this title or imprisoned not more than one year, or both.

(June 25, 1948, c. 645, 62 Stat. 727; Nov. 29, 1990, Pub.L. 101–647, Title XXV, § 2597(d), 104 Stat. 4909; Sept. 13, 1994, Pub.L. 103–322, Title XXXIII, § 330016(1)(H), (2)(G), 108 Stat. 2147, 2148; Oct. 11, 1996, Pub.L. 104–294, Title VI, § 606(a), 110 Stat. 3511.)

HISTORICAL AND STATUTORY NOTES

References in Text

Section 1(b) of the International Banking Act of 1978, referred to in text, is classified to section 3101 of Title 12, Banks and Banking.

§ 649. Custodians failing to deposit moneys; persons affected

(a) Whoever, having money of the United States in his possession or under his control, fails to deposit it with the Treasurer or some public depositary of the United States, when required so to do by the Secretary of the Treasury or the head of any other proper department or agency or by the Government Accountability Office, is guilty of embezzlement, and shall be fined under this title or in a sum equal to the amount of money embezzled, whichever is greater, or imprisoned not more than ten years, or both; but if the amount embezzled is $1,000 or less, he shall be fined under this title or imprisoned not more than one year, or both.

(b) This section and sections 643, 648, 650 and 653 of this title shall apply to all persons charged with the safe-keeping, transfer, or disbursement of the public money, whether such persons be charged as receivers or depositaries of the same.

(June 25, 1948, c. 645, 62 Stat. 727; Sept. 13, 1994, Pub.L. 103–322, Title XXXIII, § 330016(1)(H), (2)(G), 108 Stat. 2147, 2148; Oct. 11, 1996, Pub.L. 104–294, Title VI, § 606(a), 110 Stat. 3511; July 7, 2004, Pub.L. 108–271, § 8(b), 118 Stat. 814.)

HISTORICAL AND STATUTORY NOTES

Transfer of Functions

All functions of all officers of the Department of the Treasury, and all functions of all agencies and employees of such Department, were transferred, with certain exceptions, to the Secretary of the Treasury, with power vested in him to authorize their performance or the performance of any of his functions, by any of such officers, agencies, and employees, by 1950 Reorg. Plan No. 26, §§ 1, 2, eff. July 31, 1950, 15 F.R. 4935, 64 Stat. 1280, set out in the Appendix to Title 5, Government Organization and Employees. The Treasurer of the United States, referred to in this section, is an officer of the Treasury Department.

§ 650. Depositaries failing to safeguard deposits

If the Treasurer of the United States or any public depositary fails to keep safely all moneys deposited by any disbursing officer or disbursing agent, as well as all moneys deposited by any receiver, collector, or other person having money of the United States, he is guilty of embezzlement, and shall be fined under this title or in a sum equal to the amount of money so embezzled, whichever is greater, or imprisoned not more than ten years, or both; but if the amount embezzled does not exceed $1,000, he shall be fined under this title or imprisoned not more than one year, or both.

(June 25, 1948, c. 645, 62 Stat. 727; Sept. 13, 1994, Pub.L. 103–322, Title XXXIII, § 330016(1)(H), (2)(G), 108 Stat. 2147, 2148; Oct. 11, 1996, Pub.L. 104–294, Title VI, § 606(a), 110 Stat. 3511.)

HISTORICAL AND STATUTORY NOTES

Transfer of Functions

All functions of all officers of the Department of the Treasury, and all functions of all agencies and employees of such Department, were transferred, with certain exceptions, to the Secretary of the Treasury, with power vested in him to authorize their performance or the performance of any of his functions, by any of such officers, agencies, and employees, by 1950 Reorg. Plan No. 26, §§ 1, 2, eff. July 31, 1950, 15 F.R. 4935, 64 Stat. 1280, set out in the Appendix to Title 5, Government Organization and Employees. The Treasurer of the United States, referred to in this section, is an officer of the Treasury Department.

§ 651. Disbursing officer falsely certifying full payment

Whoever, being an officer charged with the disbursement of the public moneys, accepts, receives, or transmits to the Government Accountability Office to be allowed in his favor any receipt or voucher from a creditor of the United States without having paid the full amount specified therein to such creditor in such funds as the officer received for disbursement, or in such funds as he may be authorized by law to take in exchange, shall be fined under this title or in double the amount so withheld, whichever is greater, or imprisoned not more than two years, or both; but if the amount withheld does not exceed $1,000, he shall be fined under this title or imprisoned not more than one year, or both.

(June 25, 1948, c. 645, 62 Stat. 727; Sept. 13, 1994, Pub.L. 103–322, Title XXXIII, § 330016(1)(H), (2)(G), 108 Stat. 2147, 2148; Oct. 11, 1996, Pub.L. 104–294, Title VI, § 606(a), 110 Stat. 3511; July 7, 2004, Pub.L. 108–271, § 8(b), 118 Stat. 814.)

§ 652. Disbursing officer paying lesser in lieu of lawful amount

Whoever, being an officer, clerk, agent, employee, or other person charged with the payment of any appropriation made by Congress, pays to any clerk or other employee of the United States, or of any department or agency thereof, a sum less than that provided by law, and requires such employee to receipt or give a voucher for an amount greater than that actually paid to and received by him, is guilty of embezzlement, and shall be fined under this title or in double the amount so withheld, whichever is greater, or imprisoned not more than two years, or both; but if the amount embezzled is $1,000 or less, he shall be fined under this title or imprisoned not more than one year, or both.

(June 25, 1948, c. 645, 62 Stat. 727; Sept. 13, 1994, Pub.L. 103–322, Title XXXIII, § 330016(1)(H), (2)(G), 108 Stat. 2147, 2148; Oct. 11, 1996, Pub.L. 104–294, Title VI, § 606(a), 110 Stat. 3511.)

§ 653. Disbursing officer misusing public funds

Whoever, being a disbursing officer of the United States, or any department or agency thereof, or a person acting as such, in any manner converts to his own use, or loans with or without interest, or deposits in any place or in any manner, except as authorized by law, any public money intrusted to him; or, for any purpose not prescribed by law, withdraws from the Treasury or any authorized depositary, or transfers, or applies, any portion of the public money intrusted to him, is guilty of embezzlement of the money so converted, loaned, deposited, withdrawn, transferred, or applied, and shall be fined under this title or not more than the amount embezzled, whichever is greater, or imprisoned not more than ten years, or both; but if the amount embezzled is $1,000 or less, he shall be fined under this title or imprisoned not more than one year, or both.

(June 25, 1948, c. 645, 62 Stat. 728; Sept. 13, 1994, Pub.L. 103–322, Title XXXIII, § 330016(1)(H), (2)(G), 108 Stat. 2147, 2148; Oct. 11, 1996, Pub.L. 104–294, Title VI, § 606(a), 110 Stat. 3511.)

§ 654. Officer or employee of United States converting property of another

Whoever, being an officer or employee of the United States or of any department or agency thereof, embezzles or wrongfully converts to his own use the money or property of another which comes into his possession or under his control in the execution of such office or employment, or under color or claim of authority as such officer or employee, shall be fined under this title or not more than the value of the money and property thus embezzled or converted, whichever is greater, or imprisoned not more than ten years, or both; but if the sum embezzled is $1,000 or less, he shall be fined under this title or imprisoned not more than one year, or both.

(June 25, 1948, c. 645, 62 Stat. 728; Sept. 13, 1994, Pub.L. 103–322, Title XXXIII, § 330016(1)(H), (2)(H), 108 Stat. 2147, 2148; Oct. 11, 1996, Pub.L. 104–294, Title VI, § 606(a), 110 Stat. 3511.)

§ 655. Theft by bank examiner

Whoever, being a bank examiner or assistant examiner, steals, or unlawfully takes, or unlawfully conceals any money, note, draft, bond, or security or any other property of value in the possession of any bank or banking institution which is a member of the Federal Reserve System, which is insured by the Federal Deposit Insurance Corporation, which is a branch or agency of a foreign bank (as such terms are defined in paragraphs (1) and (3) of section 1(b) of the International Banking Act of 1978, or which is an organization operating under section 25 or section 25(a) of the Federal Reserve Act, or from any safe deposit box in or adjacent to the premises of such bank, branch, agency, or organization, shall be fined under this title or imprisoned not more than five years, or both; but if the amount taken or concealed does not exceed $1,000, he shall be fined under this title or imprisoned not more than one year, or both; and shall be disqualified from holding office as a national bank examiner or Federal Deposit Insurance Corporation examiner.

This section shall apply to all public examiners and assistant examiners who examine member banks of the Federal Reserve System, banks the deposits of which are insured by the Federal Deposit Insurance Corporation, branches or agencies of foreign banks (as such terms are defined in paragraphs (1) and (3) of section 1(b) of the International Banking Act of 1978, or organizations operating under section 25 or section 25(a) of the Federal Reserve Act, whether appointed by the Comptroller of the Currency, by the Board of Governors of the Federal Reserve System, by a Federal Reserve Agent, by a Federal Reserve bank, or by the Federal Deposit Insurance Corporation, or appointed or elected under the laws of any State; but shall not apply to private examiners or assistant examiners employed only by a clearing-house association or by the directors of a bank.

(June 25, 1948, c. 645, 62 Stat. 728; Nov. 29, 1990, Pub.L. 101–647, Title XXV, § 2597(e), 104 Stat. 4909; Sept. 13, 1994, Pub.L. 103–322, Title XXXIII, § 330016(1)(H), (K), 108 Stat. 2147; Oct. 11, 1996, Pub.L. 104–294, Title VI, § 606(a), 110 Stat. 3511.)

HISTORICAL AND STATUTORY NOTES

References in Text

Section 1(b) of the International Banking Act of 1978, referred to in text, is classified to section 3101 of Title 12, Banks and Banking.

The Federal Reserve Act, referred to in text, is Act Dec. 23, 1913, c. 6, 38 Stat. 251, as amended, which is classified principally to chapter 3 of Title 12, 12 U.S.C.A. § 221 et seq. Section 25 of the Federal Reserve Act is classified to subchapter I of chapter 6 of Title 12, 12 U.S.C.A. § 601 et seq. Section 25(a) of the Federal Reserve Act, which is classified to subchapter II of chapter 6 of Title 12, 12 U.S.C.A. § 611 et seq., was renumbered section 25A by of that Act Pub.L. 102–242, Title I, § 142(e)(2), Dec. 10, 1991, 105 Stat. 2281. See Tables and 12 U.S.C.A. § 226 for complete classification.

§ 656. Theft, embezzlement, or misapplication by bank officer or employee

Whoever, being an officer, director, agent or employee of, or connected in any capacity with any Federal Reserve bank, member bank, depository institution holding company, national bank, insured bank, branch or agency of a foreign bank, or organization operating under section 25 or section 25(a) of the Federal Reserve Act, or a receiver of a national bank, insured bank, branch, agency, or organization or any agent or employee of the receiver, or a Federal Reserve Agent, or an agent or employee of a Federal Reserve Agent or of the Board of Governors of the Federal Reserve System, embezzles, abstracts, purloins or willfully misapplies any of the moneys, funds or credits of such bank, branch, agency, or organization or holding company or any moneys, funds, assets or securities intrusted to the custody or care of such bank, branch, agency, or organization, or holding company or to the custody or care of any such agent, officer, director, employee or receiver, shall be fined not more than $1,000,000 or imprisoned not more than 30 years, or both; but if the amount embezzled, abstracted, purloined or misapplied does not exceed $1,000, he shall be fined under this title or imprisoned not more than one year, or both.

As used in this section, the term "national bank" is synonymous with "national banking association"; "member bank" means and includes any national bank, state bank, or bank and trust company which has become a member of one of the Federal Reserve banks; "insured bank" includes any bank, banking association, trust company, savings bank, or other banking institution, the deposits of which are insured by the Federal Deposit Insurance Corporation; and the term "branch or agency of a foreign bank" means a branch or agency described in section 20(9) of this title. For purposes of this section, the term "depository institution holding company" has the meaning given such term in section 3 of the Federal Deposit Insurance Act.

(June 25, 1948, c. 645, 62 Stat. 729; Aug. 9, 1989, Pub.L. 101–73, Title IX, § 961(b), 103 Stat. 499; Nov. 29, 1990, Pub.L. 101–647, Title XXV, §§ 2504(b), 2595(a)(1), 2597(f), 104 Stat. 4861, 4906, 4909; Sept. 13, 1994, Pub.L. 103–322, Title XXXIII, § 330016(1)(H), 108 Stat. 2147; Oct. 11, 1996, Pub.L. 104–294, Title VI, §§ 601(f)(1), 606(a), 110 Stat. 3499, 3511.)

HISTORICAL AND STATUTORY NOTES

Senate Revision Amendment

The text of this section was changed by Senate amendment. See Senate Report No. 1620, Amendment No. 6, 80th Congress.

References in Text

Section 3 of the Federal Deposit Insurance Act, referred to in text, is classified to section 1813 of Title 12, Banks and Banking.

The Federal Reserve Act, referred to in text, is Act Dec. 23, 1913, c. 6, 38 Stat. 251, as amended, which is classified principally to chapter 3 of Title 12, 12 U.S.C.A. § 221 et seq. Section 25 of the Federal Reserve Act is classified to subchapter I of chapter 6 of Title 12, 12 U.S.C.A. § 601 et seq. Section 25(a) of the Federal Reserve Act, which is classified to subchapter II of chapter 6 of Title 12, 12 U.S.C.A. § 611 et seq., was renumbered section 25A of that Act by Pub.L. 102–242, Title I, § 142(e)(2), Dec. 10, 1991, 105 Stat. 2281. See Tables and 12 U.S.C.A. § 226 for complete classification.

Separability of Provisions

If any provision of Pub.L. 101–73 or the application thereof to any person or circumstance is held invalid, the remainder of Pub.L. 101–73 and the application of the provision to other persons not similarly situated or to other circumstances not to be affected thereby, see section 1221 of Pub.L. 101–73, set out as a note under section 1811 of Title 12, Banks and Banking.

§ 657. Lending, credit and insurance institutions

Whoever, being an officer, agent or employee of or connected in any capacity with the Federal Deposit Insurance Corporation, National Credit Union Administration, Office of Thrift Supervision, the Resolution Trust Corporation, any Federal home loan bank, the Federal Housing Finance Board, Farm Credit Administration, Department of Housing and Urban Development, Federal Crop Insurance Corporation, the Secretary of Agriculture acting through the Farmers Home Administration or successor agency, the Rural Development Administration or successor agency, or the Farm Credit System Insurance Corporation, a Farm Credit Bank, a bank for cooperatives or any lending, mortgage, insurance, credit or savings and loan corporation or association authorized or acting under the laws of the United States or any institution, other than an insured bank (as defined in section 656), the accounts of which are insured by the Federal Deposit Insurance Corporation, or by the National Credit Union Administration Board or any small business investment company, or any community development financial institution receiving financial assistance under the Riegle Community Development and Regulatory Improvement Act of 1994, and whoever, being a receiver of any such institution, or agent or employee of the receiver, embezzles, abstracts, purloins or willfully misapplies any moneys, funds, credits, securities or other things of value belonging to such institution, or pledged or otherwise intrusted to its care, shall be fined not more than $1,000,000 or imprisoned not more than 30 years, or both; but if the amount or value embezzled, abstracted, purloined or misapplied does not exceed $1,000, he shall be fined under this title or imprisoned not more than one year, or both.

(June 25, 1948, c. 645, 62 Stat. 729; May 24, 1949, c. 139, § 11, 63 Stat. 90; July 28, 1956, c. 773, § 1, 70 Stat. 714; Aug. 21, 1958, Pub.L. 85–699, Title VII, § 703, 72 Stat. 698; Oct. 4, 1961, Pub.L. 87–353, § 3(q), 75 Stat. 774; May 25, 1967, Pub.L. 90–19, § 24(a), 81 Stat. 27; Oct. 19, 1970, Pub.L. 91–468, § 4, 84 Stat. 1016; Aug. 9, 1989, Pub.L. 101–73, Title IX, §§ 961(c), 962(a)(7), (8)(A), 103 Stat. 499, 502; Nov. 28, 1990, Pub.L. 101–624, Title XXIII, § 2303(e), 104 Stat. 3981; Nov. 29, 1990, Pub.L. 101–647, Title XVI, § 1603, Title XXV, §§ 2504(c), 2595(a)(2), 104 Stat. 4843, 4861, 4907; Sept. 13, 1994, Pub.L. 103–322, Title XXXIII, §§ 330004(6), 330016(1)(H), 108 Stat. 2141, 2147; Sept. 23, 1994, Pub.L. 103–325, Title I, § 119(c), 108 Stat. 2188; Oct. 11, 1996, Pub.L. 104–294, Title VI, § 606(a), 110 Stat. 3511; Oct. 22, 1999, Pub.L. 106–78, Title VII, § 767, 113 Stat. 1174.)

HISTORICAL AND STATUTORY NOTES

Senate Revision Amendment

Certain words were stricken from the section as being unnecessary and inconsistent with other sections of this revision defining embezzlement and without changing existing law. See Senate Report No. 1620, amendment No. 7, 80th Cong.

References in Text

The Riegle Community Development and Regulatory Improvement Act of 1994, referred to in text, is Pub.L. 103–325, Sept. 23, 1994, 108 Stat. 2160. For complete classification of this Act to the Code, see Short Title note set out under section 4701 of Title 12, Banks and Banking, and Tables.

Abolition of Home Owners' Loan Corporation

For dissolution and abolishment of Home Owners' Loan Corporation, referred to in this section, by Act June 30, 1953, c. 170, § 21, 67 Stat. 126, see note under former § 1463 of Title 12, Banks and Banking.

Farm Credit Administration

Organization of Farm Credit Administration, see 12 U.S.C.A. § 2241 et seq.

§ 658. Property mortgaged or pledged to farm credit agencies

Whoever, with intent to defraud, knowingly conceals, removes, disposes of, or converts to his own use or to that of another, any property mortgaged or pledged to, or held by, the Farm Credit Administration, any Federal intermediate credit bank, or the Federal Crop Insurance Corporation, the Secretary of Agriculture acting through the Farmers Home Administration or successor agency, the Rural Development Administration or successor agency, any production credit association organized under sections 1131–1134m of Title 12, any regional agricultural credit corporation, or any bank for cooperatives, shall be fined under this title or imprisoned not more than five years, or both; but if the value of such property does not exceed $1,000, he shall be fined under this title or imprisoned not more than one year, or both.

(June 25, 1948, c. 645, 62 Stat. 729; May 24, 1949, c. 139, § 12, 63 Stat. 91; Oct. 31, 1951, c. 655, § 21, 65 Stat. 718; July 26, 1956, c. 741, Title I, § 109, 70 Stat. 667; Oct. 4, 1961, Pub.L. 87–353, § 3(r), 75 Stat. 774; Nov. 28, 1990, Pub.L. 101–624, Title XXIII, § 2303(e), 104 Stat. 3981; Sept. 13, 1994, Pub.L. 103–322, Title XXXIII, §§ 330004(7), 330016(1)(H), (K), 108 Stat. 2141, 2147; Oct. 11, 1996, Pub.L. 104–294, Title VI, § 606(a), 110 Stat. 3511; Oct. 22, 1999, Pub.L. 106–78, Title VII, § 767, 113 Stat. 1174.)

HISTORICAL AND STATUTORY NOTES

References in Text

Sections 1131 to 1134m of Title 12, referred to in text, were either repealed or omitted from the Code.

Effective and Applicability Provisions

1956 Acts. Amendment of this section by Act July 26, 1956 effective Jan. 1, 1957, see § 202(a) of Act July 26, 1956.

Separability of Provisions

If any provision of Pub.L. 101–624 or the application thereof to any person or circumstance is held invalid, such invalidity not to affect other provisions or applications of Pub.L. 101–624 which can be given effect without regard to the invalid provision or application, see section 2519 of Pub.L. 101–624, set out as a note under section 1421 of Title 7, Agriculture.

Exceptions from Transfer of Functions

Functions of the Corporations of the Department of Agriculture, the boards of directors and officers of such corporations; the Advisory Board of the Commodity Credit Corporation; and the Farm Credit Administration or any agency, officer or entity of, under, or subject to the supervision of the said Administration were excepted from the functions of officers, agencies and employees transferred to the Secretary of Agriculture by 1953 Reorg. Plan No. 2, § 1, eff. June 4, 1953, 18 F.R. 3219, 67 Stat. 633, set out in the Appendix to Title 5, Government Organization and Employees.

Farm Credit Administration

Organization of Farm Credit Administration, see 12 U.S.C.A. § 2241 et seq.

National Agricultural Credit Corporation

Title II of the Agricultural Credits Act, Act Mar. 4, 1923, c. 252, Title II, §§ 201 to 217, 42 Stat. 1461, which authorized the creation of national agricultural credit corporations, was repealed by Pub.L. 86–230, Sept. 8, 1959, § 24, 73 Stat. 466. Prior to such repeal, Act June 16, 1933, c. 101, § 77, 48 Stat. 292, had prohibited the creation, after June 16, 1933, of national agricultural credit corporations authorized to be formed under the Agricultural Credits Act.

§ 659. Interstate or foreign shipments by carrier; State prosecutions

Whoever embezzles, steals, or unlawfully takes, carries away, or conceals, or by fraud or deception obtains from any pipeline system, railroad car, wagon, motortruck, trailer, or other vehicle, or from any tank or storage facility, station, station house, platform or depot or from any steamboat, vessel, or wharf, or from any aircraft, air cargo container, air terminal, airport, aircraft terminal or air navigation facility, or from any intermodal container, trailer, container freight station, warehouse, or freight consolidation facility, with intent to convert to his own use any goods or chattels moving as or which are a part of or which constitute an interstate or foreign shipment of freight, express, or other property; or

Whoever buys or receives or has in his possession any such goods or chattels, knowing the same to have been embezzled or stolen; or

Whoever embezzles, steals, or unlawfully takes, carries away, or by fraud or deception obtains with intent to convert to his own use any baggage which shall have come into the possession of any common carrier for transportation in interstate or foreign commerce or breaks into, steals, takes, carries away, or conceals any of the contents of such baggage, or buys, receives, or has in his possession any such baggage or any article therefrom of whatever nature, knowing the same to have been embezzled or stolen; or

Whoever embezzles, steals, or unlawfully takes by any fraudulent device, scheme, or game, from any railroad car, bus, vehicle, steamboat, vessel, or aircraft operated by any common carrier moving in interstate or foreign commerce or from any passenger thereon any money, baggage, goods, or chattels, or whoever buys, receives, or has in his possession any such money, baggage, goods, or chattels, knowing the same to have been embezzled or stolen—

Shall be fined under this title or imprisoned not more than 10 years, or both, but if the amount or value of such money, baggage, goods, or chattels is less than $1,000, shall be fined under this title or imprisoned for not more than 3 years, or both.

The offense shall be deemed to have been committed not only in the district where the violation first occurred, but also in any district in which the defendant may have taken or been in possession of the said money, baggage, goods, or chattels.

The carrying or transporting of any such money, freight, express, baggage, goods, or chattels in interstate or foreign commerce, knowing the same to have been stolen, shall constitute a separate offense and subject the offender to the penalties under this section for unlawful taking, and the offense shall be deemed to have been committed in any district into which such money, freight, express, baggage, goods, or chattels shall have been removed or into which the same shall have been brought by such offender.

To establish the interstate or foreign commerce character of any shipment in any prosecution under this section the waybill or other shipping document of such shipment shall be prima facie evidence of the place from which and to which such shipment was made. For purposes of this section, goods and chattel shall be construed to be moving as an interstate or foreign shipment at all points between the point of origin and the final destination (as evidenced by the waybill or other shipping document of the shipment), regardless of any temporary stop while awaiting transshipment or otherwise. The removal of property from a pipeline system which extends interstate shall be prima facie evidence of the interstate character of the shipment of the property.

A judgment of conviction or acquittal on the merits under the laws of any State shall be a bar to any prosecution under this section for the same act or acts. Nothing contained in this section shall be construed as indicating an intent on the part of Congress to occupy the field in which provisions of this section operate to the exclusion of State laws on the same subject matter, nor shall any provision of this section be construed as invalidating any provision of State law unless such provision is inconsistent with any of the purposes of this section or any provision thereof. (June 25, 1948, c. 645, 62 Stat. 729; May 24, 1949, c. 139, § 13, 63 Stat. 91; Oct. 14, 1966, Pub.L. 89–654, § 1(a) to (d), 80 Stat. 904; Sept. 13, 1994, Pub.L. 103–322, Title XXXIII, § 330016(1)(H), (K), 108 Stat. 2147; Oct. 11, 1996, Pub.L. 104–294, Title VI, § 606(a), 110 Stat. 3511; Mar. 9, 2006, Pub.L. 109–177, Title III, § 307(a), 120 Stat. 240.)

HISTORICAL AND STATUTORY NOTES

Senate Revision Amendment

The "corrective legislation", referred to in this paragraph, became Act Apr. 16, 1947, c. 39, 61 Stat. 52, and, as it amended § 411 of Title 18, U.S.C., such Act was an additional source of this section.

2006 Acts. House Conference Report No. 109–333, see 2006 U.S. Code Cong. and Adm. News, p. 184.

Statement by President, see 2006 U.S. Code Cong. and Adm. News, p. S7.

Annual Report of Law Enforcement Activities

Pub.L. 109–177, Title III, § 307(d), Mar. 9, 2006, 120 Stat. 240, provided that: "The Attorney General shall annually submit to Congress a report, which shall include an evaluation of law enforcement activities relating to the investigation and prosecution of offenses under section 659 of title 18, United States Code [this section], as amended by this title."

§ 660. Carrier's funds derived from commerce; State prosecutions

Whoever, being a president, director, officer, or manager of any firm, association, or corporation engaged in commerce as a common carrier, or whoever, being an employee of such common carrier riding in or upon any railroad car, motortruck, steamboat, vessel, aircraft or other vehicle of such carrier moving in interstate commerce, embezzles, steals, abstracts, or willfully misapplies, or willfully permits to be misapplied, any of the moneys, funds, credits, securities, property, or assets of such firm, association, or corporation arising or accruing from, or used in, such commerce, in whole or in part, or willfully or knowingly converts the same to his own use or to the use of another, shall be fined under this title or imprisoned not more than ten years, or both.

The offense shall be deemed to have been committed not only in the district where the violation first occurred but also in any district in which the defendant may have taken or had possession of such moneys, funds, credits, securities, property or assets.

A judgment of conviction or acquittal on the merits under the laws of any State shall be a bar to any prosecution hereunder for the same act or acts.

(June 25, 1948, c. 645, 62 Stat. 730; Sept. 13, 1994, Pub.L. 103–322, Title XXXIII, § 330016(1)(K), 108 Stat. 2147.)

§ 661. Within special maritime and territorial jurisdiction

Whoever, within the special maritime and territorial jurisdiction of the United States, takes and carries away, with intent to steal or purloin, any personal property of another shall be punished as follows:

If the property taken is of a value exceeding $1,000, or is taken from the person of another, by a fine under this title, or imprisonment for not more than five years, or both; in all other cases, by a fine under this title or by imprisonment not more than one year, or both.

If the property stolen consists of any evidence of debt, or other written instrument, the amount of money due thereon, or secured to be paid thereby and remaining unsatisfied, or which in any contingency might be collected thereon, or the value of the property the title to which is shown thereby, or the sum which might be recovered in the absence thereof, shall be the value of the property stolen.

(June 25, 1948, c. 645, 62 Stat. 731; Sept. 13, 1994, Pub.L. 103–322, Title XXXIII, § 330016(1)(H), (K), 108 Stat. 2147; Oct. 11, 1996, Pub.L. 104–294, Title VI, §§ 601(a)(3), 606(a), 110 Stat. 3498, 3511.)

§ 662. Receiving stolen property within special maritime and territorial jurisdiction

Whoever, within the special maritime and territorial jurisdiction of the United States, buys, receives, or conceals any money, goods, bank notes, or other thing which may be the subject of larceny, which has been feloniously taken, stolen, or embezzled, from any other person, knowing the same to have been so taken, stolen, or embezzled, shall be fined under this title or imprisoned not more than three years, or both; but if the amount or value of thing so taken, stolen or embezzled does not exceed $1,000, he shall be fined under this title or imprisoned not more than one year, or both.

(June 25, 1948, c. 645, 62 Stat. 731; Sept. 13, 1994, Pub.L. 103–322, Title XXXIII, § 330016(1)(H), 108 Stat. 2147; Oct. 11, 1996, Pub.L. 104–294, Title VI, § 606(a), 110 Stat. 3511.)

§ 663. Solicitation or use of gifts

Whoever solicits any gift of money or other property, and represents that such gift is being solicited for the use of the United States, with the intention of embezzling, stealing, or purloining such gift, or converting the same to any other use or purpose, or whoever, having come into possession of any money or property which has been donated by the owner thereof for the use of the United States, embezzles, steals or purloins such money or property, or converts the same to any other use or purpose, shall be fined under this title or imprisoned not more than five years, or both.

(June 25, 1948, c. 645, 62 Stat. 731; Sept. 13, 1994, Pub.L. 103–322, Title XXXIII, § 330016(1)(K), 108 Stat. 2147.)

§ 664. Theft or embezzlement from employee benefit plan

Any person who embezzles, steals, or unlawfully and willfully abstracts or converts to his own use or to the use of another, any of the moneys, funds, securities, premiums, credits, property, or other assets of any employee welfare benefit plan or employee pension benefit plan, or of any fund connected therewith, shall be fined under this title, or imprisoned not more than five years, or both.

As used in this section, the term "any employee welfare benefit plan or employee pension benefit plan" means any employee benefit plan subject to any provision of title I of the Employee Retirement Income Security Act of 1974.

(Added Pub.L. 87–420, § 17(a), Mar. 20, 1962, 76 Stat. 41, and amended Pub.L. 93–406, Title I, § 111(a)(2)(A), Sept. 2, 1974, 88 Stat. 851; Pub.L. 103–322, Title XXXIII, § 330016(1)(L), Sept. 13, 1994, 108 Stat. 2147.)

HISTORICAL AND STATUTORY NOTES

References in Text

Title I of the Employee Retirement Income Security Act of 1974, referred to in text, is classified generally to § 1001 et seq. of Title 29, Labor.

Effective and Applicability Provisions

1974 Acts. Amendment by Pub.L. 93–406 effective Jan. 1, 1975, except as provided in § 1031(b)(2) of Title 29, Labor, see § 1031(b)(1) of Title 29.

1962 Acts. Section 19 of Pub.L. 87–420 provided that: "The amendments made by this Act [adding sections 664, 1027, and 1954 of this title and sections 308a to 308f of Title 29, Labor, amending sections 302 to 308 and 309 of Title 29, and renumbering sections 10 to 12 of Pub.L. 85–536, classified to section 309 of Title 29 and as notes under section 301 of Title 29] shall take effect ninety days after the enactment of this Act [Mar. 20, 1962], except that section 13 of the Welfare and Pension Plans Disclosure Act [section 308d of Title 29] shall take effect one hundred eighty days after such date of enactment [Mar. 20, 1962]."

Short Title

1962 Acts. Pub.L. 87–420, § 1, Mar. 20, 1962, 76 Stat. 35, provided: "That this Act [enacting this section, 18 U.S.C.A. §§ 1027 and 1954 and 29 U.S.C.A. §§ 308a to 308f, amending 29 U.S.C.A. §§ 302 to 308 and 309 and renumbering sections 10 to 12 of Pub.L. 85–536, classified to 29 U.S.C.A. § 309 and as notes under 29 U.S.C.A. § 301] may be cited as the 'Welfare and Pension Plans Disclosure Act Amendments of 1962'."

§ 665. Theft or embezzlement from employment and training funds; improper inducement; obstruction of investigations

(a) Whoever, being an officer, director, agent, or employee of, or connected in any capacity with any agency or organization receiving financial assistance or any funds under the Job Training Partnership Act or title I of the Workforce Investment Act of 1998 knowingly enrolls an ineligible participant, embezzles, willfully misapplies, steals, or obtains by fraud any of the moneys, funds, assets, or property which are the subject of a financial assistance agreement or contract pursuant to such Act shall be fined under this title or imprisoned for not more than 2 years, or both; but if the amount so embezzled, misapplied, stolen, or obtained by fraud does not exceed $1,000, such person shall be fined under this title or imprisoned not more than 1 year, or both.

(b) Whoever, by threat or procuring dismissal of any person from employment or of refusal to employ or refusal to renew a contract of employment in connection with a financial assistance agreement or contract under the Job Training Partnership Act or title I of the Workforce Investment Act of 1998 induces any person to give up any money or thing of any value to any person (including such organization or agency receiving funds) shall be fined under this title, or imprisoned not more than 1 year, or both.

(c) Whoever willfully obstructs or impedes or willfully endeavors to obstruct or impede, an investigation or inquiry under the Job Training Partnership Act or title I of the Workforce Investment Act of 1998, or the regulations thereunder, shall be punished by a fine under this title, or by imprisonment for not more than 1 year, or by both such fine and imprisonment.

(Added Pub.L. 93–203, Title VII, § 711(a), formerly Title VI, § 611(a), Dec. 28, 1973, 87 Stat. 881; renumbered Title VII, § 711(a), Pub.L. 93–567, Title I, § 101, Dec. 31, 1974, 88 Stat. 1845, and amended Pub.L. 95–524, § 3(a), Oct. 27, 1978, 92 Stat. 2017; Pub.L. 97–300, Title I, § 182, Oct. 13, 1982, 96 Stat. 1357; Pub.L. 101–647, Title XXXV, § 3517, Nov. 29, 1990, 104 Stat. 4923; Pub.L. 103–322, Title XXXIII, § 330016(1)(H), (L), Sept. 13, 1994, 108 Stat. 2147; Pub.L. 104–294, Title VI, § 606(a), Oct. 11, 1996, 110 Stat. 3511; Pub.L. 105–277, Div. A, § 101(f) [Title VIII, § 405(d)(13)], Oct. 21, 1998, 112 Stat. 2681–420; Pub.L. 107–273, Div. B, Title IV, § 4002(d)(1)(B), Nov. 2, 2002, 116 Stat. 1809.)

HISTORICAL AND STATUTORY NOTES

References in Text

The Job Training Partnership Act, referred to in the text, is Pub.L. 197–300, Oct. 13, 1982, 96 Stat. 1324, as amended, which is classified generally to chapter 19 of Title 29 (29 U.S.C.A. § 1501 et seq.) and is repealed effective July 1, 2000, Pub.L. 105–205, Title I, § 199(b)(2), (c)(2)(B), Aug. 7, 1998, 112 Stat. 1059. For complete classification, see Short Title note set out under section 1501 of Title 29 and Tables. See, also, Change of Name notes set out under section 2940 of Title 29.

Effective and Applicability Provisions

1998 Acts. Amendment by section 101(f) [Title IV, § 405(d)] of Pub.L. 105–277, effective Oct. 21, 1998, see section 101(f) [Title IV, § 405(g)(1)] of Pub.L. 105–277, set out as a note under section 3502 of Title 5.

Change of Name

Effective August 7, 1998, all references in any provision of law (other than 18 U.S.C.A. § 665) to the Comprehensive Employment and Training Act, or the Job Training Partnership Act, deemed to refer to the Workforce Investment Act of 1998 (Pub.L. 105–220, Aug. 7, 1998, 112 Stat. 936), see section 2940 of Title 29.

All references in any other provision of law to a provision of the Comprehensive Employment and Training Act, or of the Job Training Partnership Act, deemed to refer to the corresponding provision of Title I of the Workforce Investment Act of 1998 (Pub.L. 105–220, Title I, §§ 101 to 199A, Aug. 7, 1998, 112 Stat. 936 [29 U.S.C.A. § 2801 et seq.]), see section 199A(c) of Pub.L. 105–220, set out as a note under section 2940 of Title 29.

§ 666. Theft or bribery concerning programs receiving Federal funds

(a) Whoever, if the circumstance described in subsection (b) of this section exists—

(1) being an agent of an organization, or of a State, local, or Indian tribal government, or any agency thereof—

(A) embezzles, steals, obtains by fraud, or otherwise without authority knowingly converts to the use of any person other than the rightful owner or intentionally misapplies, property that—

(i) is valued at $5,000 or more, and

(ii) is owned by, or is under the care, custody, or control of such organization, government, or agency; or

(B) corruptly solicits or demands for the benefit of any person, or accepts or agrees to accept, anything of value from any person, intending to be influenced or rewarded in connection with any business, transaction, or series of transactions of such organization, government, or agency involving any thing of value of $5,000 or more; or

(2) corruptly gives, offers, or agrees to give anything of value to any person, with intent to influence or reward an agent of an organization or of a State, local or Indian tribal government, or any agency thereof, in connection with any business, transaction, or series of transactions of such organization, government, or agency involving anything of value of $5,000 or more;

shall be fined under this title, imprisoned not more than 10 years, or both.

(b) The circumstance referred to in subsection (a) of this section is that the organization, government, or agency receives, in any one year period, benefits in excess of $10,000 under a Federal program involving a grant, contract, subsidy, loan, guarantee, insurance, or other form of Federal assistance.

(c) This section does not apply to bona fide salary, wages, fees, or other compensation paid, or expenses paid or reimbursed, in the usual course of business.

(d) As used in this section—

(1) the term "agent" means a person authorized to act on behalf of another person or a government and, in the case of an organization or government, includes a servant or employee, and a partner, director, officer, manager, and representative;

(2) the term "government agency" means a subdivision of the executive, legislative, judicial, or other branch of government, including a department, independent establishment, commission, administration, authority, board, and bureau, and a corporation or other legal entity established, and subject to control, by a government or governments for the execution of a governmental or intergovernmental program;

(3) the term "local" means of or pertaining to a political subdivision within a State;

(4) the term "State" includes a State of the United States, the District of Columbia, and any commonwealth, territory, or possession of the United States; and

(5) the term "in any one-year period" means a continuous period that commences no earlier than twelve months before the commission of the offense or that ends no later than twelve months after the commission of the offense. Such period may include time both before and after the commission of the offense.

(Added Pub.L. 98–473, Title II, § 1104(a), Oct. 12, 1984, 98 Stat. 2143, and amended Pub.L. 99–646, § 59(a), Nov. 10, 1986, 100 Stat. 3612; Pub.L. 101–647, Title XII, §§ 1205(d), 1209, Nov. 29, 1990, 104 Stat. 4831, 4832; Pub.L. 103–322, Title XXXIII, § 330003(c), Sept. 13, 1994, 108 Stat. 2140.)

§ 667. Theft of livestock

Whoever obtains or uses the property of another which has a value of $10,000 or more in connection with the marketing of livestock in interstate or foreign commerce with intent to deprive the other of a right to the property or a benefit of the property or to appropriate the property to his own use or the use of another shall be fined under this title or imprisoned not more than five years, or both. The term "livestock" has the meaning set forth in section 2311 of this title.

(Added Pub.L. 98–473, Title II, § 1111, Oct. 12, 1984, 98 Stat. 2149, and amended Pub.L. 103–322, Title XXXIII, §§ 330009(b), 330016(1)(L), Sept. 13, 1994, 108 Stat. 2143, 2147.)

§ 668. Theft of major artwork

(a) Definitions

In this section—

(1) "museum" means an organized and permanent institution, the activities of which affect interstate or foreign commerce, that—

(A) is situated in the United States;

(B) is established for an essentially educational or aesthetic purpose;

(C) has a professional staff; and

(D) owns, utilizes, and cares for tangible objects that are exhibited to the public on a regular schedule.

(2) "object of cultural heritage" means an object that is—

(A) over 100 years old and worth in excess of $5,000; or

(B) worth at least $100,000.

(b) Offenses

A person who—

(1) steals or obtains by fraud from the care, custody, or control of a museum any object of cultural heritage; or

(2) knowing that an object of cultural heritage has been stolen or obtained by fraud, if in fact the object was stolen or obtained from the care, custody, or control of a museum (whether or not that fact is known to the person), receives, conceals, exhibits, or disposes of the object,

shall be fined under this title, imprisoned not more than 10 years, or both.

(Added Pub.L. 103–322, Title XXXII, § 320902(a), Sept. 13, 1994, 108 Stat. 2123, and amended Pub.L. 104–294, Title VI, § 604(b)(18), Oct. 11, 1996, 110 Stat. 3507.)

HISTORICAL AND STATUTORY NOTES

Effective and Applicability Provisions

1996 Acts. Amendment by section 604 of Pub.L. 104–294 effective Sept. 13, 1994, see section 604(d) of Pub.L. 104–294, set out as a note under section 13 of this title.

§ 669. Theft or embezzlement in connection with health care

(a) Whoever knowingly and willfully embezzles, steals, or otherwise without authority converts to the use of any person other than the rightful owner, or intentionally misapplies any of the moneys, funds, securities, premiums, credits, property, or other assets of a health care benefit program, shall be fined under this title or imprisoned not more than 10 years, or both; but if the value of such property does not exceed the sum of $100 the defendant shall be fined under this title or imprisoned not more than one year, or both.

(b) As used in this section, the term "health care benefit program" has the meaning given such term in section 24(b) of this title.

(Added Pub.L. 104–191, Title II, § 243(a), Aug. 21, 1996, 110 Stat. 2017.)

CHAPTER 33—EMBLEMS, INSIGNIA, AND NAMES

[1] So in original. Does not conform to section catchline.

§ 700. Desecration of the flag of the United States; penalties

(a)(1) Whoever knowingly mutilates, defaces, physically defiles, burns, maintains on the floor or ground, or tramples upon any flag of the United States shall be fined under this title or imprisoned for not more than one year, or both.

(2) This subsection does not prohibit any conduct consisting of the disposal of a flag when it has become worn or soiled.

(b) As used in this section, the term "flag of the United States" means any flag of the United States, or any part thereof, made of any substance, of any size, in a form that is commonly displayed.

(c) Nothing in this section shall be construed as indicating an intent on the part of Congress to deprive any State, territory, possession, or the Commonwealth of Puerto Rico of jurisdiction over any offense over which it would have jurisdiction in the absence of this section.

(d)(1) An appeal may be taken directly to the Supreme Court of the United States from any interlocutory or final judgment, decree, or order issued by a United States district court ruling upon the constitutionality of subsection (a).

(2) The Supreme Court shall, if it has not previously ruled on the question, accept jurisdiction over the appeal and advance on the docket and expedite to the greatest extent possible.

(Added Pub.L. 90–381, § 1, July 5, 1968, 82 Stat. 291, and amended Pub.L. 101–131, §§ 2, 3, Oct. 28, 1989, 103 Stat. 777.)

HISTORICAL AND STATUTORY NOTES

Short Title

2000 Amendments. Pub.L. 106–547, § 1, Dec. 19, 2000, 114 Stat. 2738, provided that: "This Act [enacting sections 716 and 1036 of this title] may be cited as the 'Enhanced Federal Security Act of 2000'."

1989 Amendments. Section 1 of Pub.L. 101–131 provided that: "This Act [amending this section] may be cited as the 'Flag Protection Act of 1989'."

§ 701. Official badges, identification cards, other insignia

Whoever manufactures, sells, or possesses any badge, identification card, or other insignia, of the design prescribed by the head of any department or agency of the United States for use by any officer or employee thereof, or any colorable imitation thereof, or photographs, prints, or in any other manner makes or executes any engraving, photograph, print, or impression in the likeness of any such badge, identification card, or other insignia, or any colorable imitation thereof, except as authorized under regulations made pursuant to law, shall be fined under this title or imprisoned not more than six months, or both.

(June 25, 1948, c. 645, 62 Stat. 731; Sept. 13, 1994, Pub.L. 103–322, Title XXXIII, § 330016(1)(E), 108 Stat. 2146.)

§ 702. Uniform of armed forces and Public Health Service

Whoever, in any place within the jurisdiction of the United States or in the Canal Zone, without authority, wears the uniform or a distinctive part thereof or anything similar to a distinctive part of the uniform of any of the armed forces of the United States, Public Health Service or any auxiliary of such, shall be fined under this title or imprisoned not more than six months, or both.

(June 25, 1948, c. 645, 62 Stat. 732; May 24, 1949, c. 139, § 15(a), 63 Stat. 91; Sept. 13, 1994, Pub.L. 103–322, Title XXXIII, § 330016(1)(E), 108 Stat. 2146.)

HISTORICAL AND STATUTORY NOTES

Transfer of Functions

All functions of Public Health Service, of the Surgeon General of the Public Health Service, and of all other officers and employees of the Public Health Service, and all functions of all agencies of or in the Public Health Service transferred to Secretary of Health, Education, and Welfare by 1966 Reorg. Plan No. 3, 31 F.R. 8855, 80 Stat. 1610, eff. June 25, 1966, set out in the Appendix to Title 5, Government Organization and Employees.

The Department of Health, Education, and Welfare was redesignated the Department of Health and Human Services and the Secretary, or any other official, of Health, Education, and Welfare was redesignated the Secretary or official, as appropriate, of Health and Human Services by Pub.L. 96–88, Title V, § 509, Oct. 17, 1979, 93 Stat. 695.

§ 703. Uniform of friendly nation

Whoever, within the jurisdiction of the United States, with intent to deceive or mislead, wears any naval, military, police, or other official uniform, decoration, or regalia of any foreign state, nation, or government with which the United States is at peace, or anything so nearly resembling the same as to be calculated to deceive, shall be fined under this title or imprisoned not more than six months, or both.

(June 25, 1948, c. 645, 62 Stat. 732; Sept. 13, 1994, Pub.L. 103–322, Title XXXIII, § 330016(1)(E), 108 Stat. 2146.)

HISTORICAL AND STATUTORY NOTES

Canal Zone

Applicability of section to Canal Zone, see § 14 of this title.

§ 704. Military medals or decorations

(a) In general.—Whoever knowingly wears, purchases, attempts to purchase, solicits for purchase, mails, ships, imports, exports, produces blank certificates of receipt for, manufactures, sells, attempts to sell, advertises for sale, trades, barters, or exchanges for anything of value any decoration or medal authorized by Congress for the armed forces of the United States, or any of the service medals or badges awarded to the members of such forces, or the ribbon, button, or rosette of any such badge, decoration or medal, or any colorable imitation thereof, except when authorized under regulations made pursuant to law, shall be fined under this title or imprisoned not more than six months, or both.

(b) False claims about receipt of military decorations or medals.—Whoever falsely represents himself or herself, verbally or in writing, to have been awarded any decoration or medal authorized by Congress for the Armed Forces of the United States, any of the service medals or badges awarded to the members of such forces, the ribbon, button, or rosette of any such badge, decoration, or medal, or any colorable imitation of such item shall be fined under this title, imprisoned not more than six months, or both.

(c) Enhanced penalty for offenses involving Congressional Medal of Honor.—

(1) In general.—If a decoration or medal involved in an offense under subsection (a) or (b) is a Congressional Medal of Honor, in lieu of the punishment provided in that subsection, the offender shall be fined under this title, imprisoned not more than 1 year, or both.

(2) Congressional Medal of Honor defined.—In this subsection, the term "Congressional Medal of Honor" means—

(A) a medal of honor awarded under section 3741, 6241, or 8741 of title 10 or section 491 of title 14;

(B) a duplicate medal of honor issued under section 3754, 6256, or 8754 of title 10 or section 504 of title 14; or

(C) a replacement of a medal of honor provided under section 3747, 6253, or 8747 of title 10 or section 501 of title 14.

(d) Enhanced penalty for offenses involving certain other medals.—If a decoration or medal involved in an offense described in subsection (a) or (b) is a distinguished-service cross awarded under section 3742 of title 10, a Navy cross awarded under section 6242 of title 10, an Air Force cross awarded under section 8742 of section 10, a silver star awarded under section 3746, 6244, or 8746 of title 10, a Purple Heart awarded under section 1129 of title 10, or any replacement or duplicate medal for such medal as authorized by law, in lieu of the punishment provided in the applicable subsection, the offender shall be fined under this title, imprisoned not more than 1 year, or both.

(June 25, 1948, c. 645, 62 Stat. 732; May 24, 1949, c. 139, § 16, 63 Stat. 92; Sept. 13, 1994, Pub.L. 103–322, Title XXXII, § 320109, Title XXXIII, § 330016(1)(E), 108 Stat. 2113, 2146; Nov. 2, 1994, Pub.L. 103–442, 108 Stat. 4630; Oct. 11, 1996, Pub.L. 104–294, Title VI, § 604(b)(16), 110 Stat. 3507; December 28, 2001, Pub.L. 107–107, Div. A, Title V, § 553(e), 115 Stat. 1117; Dec. 20, 2006, Pub.L. 109–437, § 3, 120 Stat. 3266.)

HISTORICAL AND STATUTORY NOTES

Effective and Applicability Provisions

1996 Acts. Amendment by section 604 of Pub.L. 104–294 effective Sept. 13, 1994, see section 604(d) of Pub.L. 104–294, set out as a note under section 13 of this title.

Findings

Pub.L. 109–437, § 2, Dec. 20, 2006, 120 Stat. 3266, provided that:

"Congress makes the following findings:

"(1) Fraudulent claims surrounding the receipt of the Medal of Honor, the distinguished-service cross, the Navy cross, the Air Force cross, the Purple Heart, and other decorations and medals awarded by the President or the Armed Forces of the United States damage the reputation and meaning of such decorations and medals.

"(2) Federal law enforcement officers have limited ability to prosecute fraudulent claims of receipt of military decorations and medals.

"(3) Legislative action is necessary to permit law enforcement officers to protect the reputation and meaning of military decorations and medals."

§ 705. Badge or medal of veterans' organizations

Whoever knowingly manufactures, reproduces, sells or purchases for resale, either separately or on or appended to, any article of merchandise manufactured or sold, any badge, medal, emblem, or other insignia or any colorable imitation thereof, of any veterans' organization incorporated by enactment of Congress, or of any organization formally recognized by any such veterans' organization as an auxiliary of such veterans' organization, or knowingly prints, lithographs, engraves or otherwise reproduces on any poster, circular, periodical, magazine, newspaper, or other publication, or circulates or distributes any such printed matter bearing a reproduction of such badge, medal, emblem, or other insignia or any colorable imitation thereof, except when authorized under rules and regulations prescribed by any such organization, shall be fined under this title or imprisoned not more than six months, or both.

(June 25, 1948, c. 645, 62 Stat. 732; Aug. 4, 1950, c. 578, 64 Stat. 413; Sept. 13, 1994, Pub.L. 103–322, Title XXXIII, § 330016(1)(E), 108 Stat. 2146.)

§ 706. Red Cross

Whoever wears or displays the sign of the Red Cross or any insignia colored in imitation thereof for the fraudulent purpose of inducing the belief that he is a member of or an agent for the American National Red Cross; or

Whoever, whether a corporation, association or person, other than the American National Red Cross and its duly authorized employees and agents and the sanitary and hospital authorities of the armed forces of the United States, uses the emblem of the Greek red cross on a white ground, or any sign or insignia made or colored in imitation thereof or the words "Red Cross" or "Geneva Cross" or any combination of these words—

Shall be fined under this title or imprisoned not more than six months, or both.

This section shall not make unlawful the use of any such emblem, sign, insignia or words which was lawful on the date of enactment of this title.

(June 25, 1948, c. 645, 62 Stat. 732; May 24, 1949, c. 139, § 17, 63 Stat. 92; Sept. 13, 1994, Pub.L. 103–322, Title XXXIII, § 330016(1)(E), 108 Stat. 2146.)

§ 706a. Geneva distinctive emblems

(a) Whoever wears or displays the sign of the Red Crescent or the Third Protocol Emblem (the Red Crystal), or any insignia colored in imitation thereof for the fraudulent purpose of inducing the belief that he is a member of or an agent for an authorized national society using the Red Crescent or the Third Protocol Emblem, the International Committee of the Red Cross, or the International Federation of Red Cross and Red Crescent Societies shall be fined under this title or imprisoned not more than 6 months, or both.

(b) Except as set forth in section (c) and (d), whoever, whether a corporation, association, or person, uses the emblem of the Red Crescent or the Third Protocol Emblem on a white ground or any sign or insignia made or colored in imitation thereof or the designations "Red Crescent" or "Third Protocol Emblem" shall be fined under this title or imprisoned not more than 6 months, or both.

(c) The following may use such emblems and designations consistent with the Geneva Conventions of August 12, 1949, and, if applicable, the Additional Protocols:

(1) Authorized national societies that are members of the International Federation of Red Cross and Red Crescent Societies and their duly authorized employees and agents.

(2) The International Committee of the Red Cross and its duly authorized employees and agents.

(3) The International Federation of Red Cross and Red Crescent Societies and its duly authorized employees and agents.

(4) The sanitary and hospital authorities of the armed forces of State Parties to the Geneva Conventions of August 12, 1949.

(d) This section does not make unlawful the use of any such emblem, sign, insignia, or words which was lawful on or before December 8, 2005, if such use would not appear in time of armed conflict to confer the protections of the Geneva Conventions of August 12, 1949, and, if applicable, the Additional Protocols.

(e) A violation of this section or section 706 may be enjoined at the civil suit of the Attorney General.

(Pub.L. 109–481, § 2(a), Jan. 12, 2007, 120 Stat. 3673.)

§ 707. 4–H club emblem fraudulently used

Whoever, with intent to defraud, wears or displays the sign or emblem of the 4–H clubs, consisting of a green four-leaf clover with stem, and the letter H in white or gold on each leaflet, or any insignia in colorable imitation thereof, for the purpose of inducing the belief that he is a member of, associated with, or an agent or representative for the 4–H clubs; or

Whoever, whether an individual, partnership, corporation or association, other than the 4–H clubs and those duly authorized by them, the representatives of the United States Department of Agriculture, the land grant colleges, and persons authorized by the Secretary of Agriculture, uses, within the United States, such emblem or any sign, insignia, or symbol in colorable imitation thereof, or the words "4–H Club" or "4–H Clubs" or any combination of these or other words or characters in colorable imitation thereof—

Shall be fined under this title or imprisoned not more than six months, or both.

This section shall not make unlawful the use of any such emblem, sign, insignia or words which was lawful on the date of enactment of this title.

(June 25, 1948, c. 645, 62 Stat. 733; Sept. 13, 1994, Pub.L. 103–322, Title XXXIII, § 330016(1)(E), 108 Stat. 2146.)

§ 708. Swiss Confederation coat of arms

Whoever, whether a corporation, partnership, unincorporated company, association, or person within the United States, willfully uses as a trade mark, commercial label, or portion thereof, or as an advertisement or insignia for any business or organization or for any trade or commercial purpose, the coat of arms of the Swiss Confederation, consisting of an upright white cross with equal arms and lines on a red ground, or any simulation thereof, shall be fined under this title or imprisoned not more than six months, or both.

This section shall not make unlawful the use of any such design or insignia which was lawful on August 31, 1948.

(June 25, 1948, c. 645, 62 Stat. 733; Oct. 31, 1951, c. 655, § 21a, 65 Stat. 719; Sept. 13, 1994, Pub.L. 103–322, Title XXXIII, § 330016(1)(E), 108 Stat. 2146.)

§ 709. False advertising or misuse of names to indicate Federal agency

Whoever, except as permitted by the laws of the United States, uses the words "national", "Federal", "United States", "reserve", or "Deposit Insurance" as part of the business or firm name of a person, corporation, partnership, business trust, association or other business entity engaged in the banking, loan, building and loan, brokerage, factorage, insurance, indemnity, savings or trust business; or

Whoever falsely advertises or represents, or publishes or displays any sign, symbol or advertisement reasonably calculated to convey the impression that a nonmember bank, banking association, firm or partnership is a member of the Federal reserve system; or

Whoever, except as expressly authorized by Federal law, uses the words "Federal Deposit", "Federal Deposit Insurance", or "Federal Deposit Insurance Corporation" or a combination of any three of these words, as the name or a part thereof under which he or it does business, or advertises or otherwise represents falsely by any device whatsoever that his or its deposit liabilities, obligations, certificates, or shares are insured or guaranteed by the Federal Deposit Insurance Corporation, or by the United States or by any instrumentality thereof, or whoever advertises that his or its deposits, shares, or accounts are federally insured, or falsely advertises or otherwise represents by any device whatsoever the extent to which or the manner in which the deposit liabilities of an insured bank or banks are insured by the Federal Deposit Insurance Corporation; or

Whoever, other than a bona fide organization or association of Federal or State credit unions or except as permitted by the laws of the United States, uses as a firm or business name or transacts business using the words "National Credit Union", "National Credit Union Administration", "National Credit Union Board", "National Credit Union Share Insurance Fund", "Share Insurance", or "Central Liquidity Facility", or the letters "NCUA", "NCUSIF", or "CLF", or any other combination or variation of those words or letters alone or with other words or letters, or any device or symbol or other means, reasonably calculated to convey the false impression that such name or business has some connection with, or authorization from, the National Credit Union Administration, the Government of the United States, or any agency thereof, which does not in fact exist, or falsely advertises or otherwise represents by any device whatsoever that his or its business, product, or service has been in any way endorsed, authorized, or approved by the National Credit Union Administration, the Government of the United States, or any agency thereof, or falsely advertises or otherwise represents by any device whatsoever that his or its deposit liabilities, obligations, certificates, shares, or accounts are insured under the Federal Credit Union Act or by the United States or any instrumentality thereof, or being an insured credit union as defined in that Act falsely advertises or otherwise represents by any device whatsoever the extent to which or the manner in which share holdings in such credit union are insured under such Act; or

Whoever, not being organized under chapter 7 of Title 12, advertises or represents that it makes Federal Farm loans or advertises or offers for sale as Federal Farm loan bonds any bond not issued under chapter 7 of Title 12, or uses the word "Federal" or the words "United States" or any other words implying Government ownership, obligation or supervision in advertising or offering for sale any bond, note, mortgage or other security not issued by the Government of the United States under the provisions of said chapter 7 or some other Act of Congress; or

Whoever uses the words "Federal Home Loan Bank" or any combination or variation of these words alone or with other words as a business name or part of a business name, or falsely publishes, advertises or represents by any device or symbol or other means reasonably calculated to convey the impression that he or it is a Federal Home Loan Bank or member of or subscriber for the stock of a Federal Home Loan Bank; or

Whoever uses the words "Federal intermediate credit bank" as part of the business or firm name for any person, corporation, partnership, business trust, association or other business entity not organized as an intermediate credit bank under the laws of the United States; or

Whoever uses as a firm or business name the words "Department of Housing and Urban Development", "Housing and Home Finance Agency", "Federal Housing Administration", "Government National Mortgage Association", "United States Housing Authority", or "Public Housing Administration" or the letters "HUD", "FHA", "PHA", or "USHA", or any combination or variation of those words or the letters "HUD", "FHA", "PHA", or "USHA" alone or with other words or letters reasonably calculated to convey the false impression that such name or business has some connection with, or authorization from, the Department of Housing and Urban Development, the Housing and Home Finance Agency, the Federal Housing Administration, the Government National Mortgage Association, the United States Housing Authority, the Public Housing Administration, the Government of the United States, or any agency thereof, which does not in fact exist, or falsely claims that any repair, improvement, or alteration of any existing structure is required or recommended by the Department of Housing and Urban Development, the Housing and Home Finance Agency, the Federal Housing Administration, the Government National Mortgage Association, the United States Housing Authority, the Public Housing Administration, the Government of the United States, or any agency thereof, for the purpose of inducing any person to enter into a contract for the making of such repairs, alterations, or improvements, or falsely advertises or falsely represents by any device whatsoever that any housing unit, project, business, or product has been in any way endorsed, authorized, inspected, appraised, or approved by the Department of Housing and Urban Development, the Housing and Home Finance Agency, the Federal Housing Administration, the Government National Mortgage Association, the United States Housing Authority, the Public Housing Administration, the Government of the United States, or any agency thereof; or

Whoever, except with the written permission of the Director of the Federal Bureau of Investigation, knowingly uses the words "Federal Bureau of Investigation" or the initials "F.B.I.", or any colorable imitation of such words or initials, in connection with any advertisement, circular, book, pamphlet or other publication, play, motion picture, broadcast, telecast, or other production, in a manner reasonably calculated to convey the impression that such advertisement, circular, book, pamphlet or other publication, play, motion picture, broadcast, telecast, or other production, is approved, endorsed, or authorized by the Federal Bureau of Investigation; or

Whoever, except with written permission of the Director of the United States Secret Service, knowingly uses the words "Secret Service", "Secret Service Uniformed Division", the initials "U.S.S.S.", "U.D.", or any colorable imitation of such words or initials, in connection with, or as a part of any advertisement, circular, book, pamphlet or other publication, play, motion picture, broadcast, telecast, other production, product, or item, in a manner reasonably calculated to convey the impression that such advertisement, circular, book, pamphlet or other publication, product, or item, is approved, endorsed, or authorized by or associated in any manner with, the United States Secret

Service, or the United States Secret Service Uniformed Division; or

Whoever, except with the written permission of the Director of the United States Mint, knowingly uses the words "United States Mint" or "U.S. Mint" or any colorable imitation of such words, in connection with any advertisement, circular, book, pamphlet, or other publication, play, motion picture, broadcast, telecast, or other production, in a manner reasonably calculated to convey the impression that such advertisement, circular, book, pamphlet, or other publication, play, motion picture, broadcast, telecast, or other production, is approved, endorsed, or authorized by or associated in any manner with, the United States Mint; or

Whoever uses the words "Overseas Private Investment", "Overseas Private Investment Corporation", or "OPIC", as part of the business or firm name of a person, corporation, partnership, business trust, association, or business entity; or

Whoever, except with the written permission of the Administrator of the Drug Enforcement Administration, knowingly uses the words "Drug Enforcement Administration" or the initials "DEA" or any colorable imitation of such words or initials, in connection with any advertisement, circular, book, pamphlet, software or other publication, play, motion picture, broadcast, telecast, or other production, in a manner reasonably calculated to convey the impression that such advertisement, circular, book, pamphlet, software or other publication, play, motion picture, broadcast, telecast, or other production is approved, endorsed, or authorized by the Drug Enforcement Administration; or

Whoever, except with the written permission of the Director of the United States Marshals Service, knowingly uses the words "United States Marshals Service", "U.S. Marshals Service", "United States Marshal", "U.S. Marshal", "U.S.M.S.", or any colorable imitation of any such words, or the likeness of a United States Marshals Service badge, logo, or insignia on any item of apparel, in connection with any advertisement, circular, book, pamphlet, software, or other publication, or any play, motion picture, broadcast, telecast, or other production, in a manner that is reasonably calculated to convey the impression that the wearer of the item of apparel is acting pursuant to the legal authority of the United States Marshals Service, or to convey the impression that such advertisement, circular, book, pamphlet, software, or other publication, or such play, motion picture, broadcast, telecast, or other production, is approved, endorsed, or authorized by the United States Marshals Service;

Shall be punished as follows: a corporation, partnership, business trust, association, or other business entity, by a fine under this title; an officer or member thereof participating or knowingly acquiescing in such violation or any individual violating this section, by a fine under this title or imprisonment for not more than one year, or both.

This section shall not make unlawful the use of any name or title which was lawful on the date of enactment of this title.

This section shall not make unlawful the use of the word "national" as part of the name of any business or firm engaged in the insurance or indemnity business, whether such firm was engaged in the insurance or indemnity business prior or subsequent to the date of enactment of this paragraph.

A violation of this section may be enjoined at the suit of the United States Attorney, upon complaint by any duly authorized representative of any department or agency of the United States.

(June 25, 1948, c. 645, 62 Stat. 733; Sept. 21, 1950, c. 967, § 3(a), 64 Stat. 894; Oct. 31, 1951, c. 655, § 22, 65 Stat. 719; July 3, 1952, c. 547, 66 Stat. 321; Aug. 2, 1954, c. 649, Title I, § 131, 68 Stat. 609; Aug. 27, 1954, c. 1008, 68 Stat. 867; May 25, 1967, Pub.L. 90–19, § 24(b), 81 Stat. 27; Aug. 1, 1968, Pub.L. 90–448, Title VIII, § 807(i), 82 Stat. 545; Oct. 19, 1970, Pub.L. 91–468, § 5, 84 Stat. 1016; Nov. 10, 1978, Pub.L. 95–630, Title XVIII, § 1804, 92 Stat. 3723; Dec. 23, 1985, Pub.L. 99–204, § 16, 99 Stat. 1676; Nov. 18, 1988, Pub.L. 100–690, Title VII, § 7079(a), 102 Stat. 4406; Oct. 6, 1992, Pub.L. 102–390, Title II, § 223, 106 Stat. 1629; Sept. 13, 1994, Pub.L. 103–322, Title XXXII, § 320911(a), Title XXXIII, §§ 330004(3), 330016(2)(C), 108 Stat. 2127, 2141, 2148; Oct. 11, 1996, Pub.L. 104–294, Title VI, §§ 602(a), 604(b)(19), (41), 110 Stat. 3503, 3507, 3509; June 23, 1998, Pub.L. 105–184, § 7, 112 Stat. 522; Nov. 2, 2002, Pub.L. 107–273, Div. B, Title IV, § 4002(a)(10), 116 Stat. 1807.)

HISTORICAL AND STATUTORY NOTES

References in Text

The Federal Credit Union Act, referred to in text, is Act June 26, 1934, c. 750, 48 Stat. 1216, as amended, which is classified generally to chapter 14 (section 1751 et seq.) of Title 12, Banks and Banking. For complete classification of this Act to the Code, see section 1751 of Title 12 and Tables.

The date of enactment of this title, referred to in the sixteenth paragraph, means June 25, 1948.

The date of enactment of this paragraph, referred to in next to last paragraph, refers to July 3, 1952.

Codifications

Section 602(a) of Pub.L. 104–294, which directed that this section be amended by striking "Whoever uses as a firm or business name the words 'Reconstruction Finance Corporation' or any combination or variation of these words—", was incapable of execution due to prior amendment by section 330004(3) of Pub.L. 103–322, see 1994 Amendments notes set out under this section.

Effective and Applicability Provisions

1996 Acts. Amendment by section 604 of Pub.L. 104–294 effective Sept. 13, 1994, see section 604(d) of Pub.L. 104–294, set out as a note under section 13 of this title.

1994 Acts. Section 320911(b) of Pub.L. 103–322 provided that: "The amendment made by subsection (a) [amending this section] shall become effective on the date that is 90 days after the date of enactment of this Act [Sept. 13, 1994]."

1988 Acts. Section 7079(b) of Pub.L. 100–690 provided that: "This section [amending this section] shall take effect 90 days after the date of enactment of this Act [Nov. 18, 1988]."

Transfer of Functions

All the functions, powers, and duties of the Housing and Home Finance Agency, the Federal Housing Administration, and the Public Housing Authority were transferred to the Secretary of Housing and Urban Development.

The United States Housing Authority was consolidated with other agencies into the Housing and Home Finance Agency and the name of the authority was changed to the Public Housing Administration.

For transfer of the functions, personnel, assets, and obligations of the United States Secret Service, including the functions of the Secretary of the Treasury relating thereto, to the Secretary of Homeland Security, and for treatment of related references, see 6 U.S.C.A. §§ 381, 551(d), 552(d) and 557, and the Department of Homeland Security Reorganization Plan of November 25, 2002, as modified, set out as a note under 6 U.S.C.A. § 542.

§ 710. Cremation urns for military use

Whoever knowingly uses, manufactures, or sells any cremation urn of a design approved by the Secretary of Defense for use to retain the cremated remains of deceased members of the armed forces or an urn which is a colorable imitation of the approved design, except when authorized under regulation made pursuant to law, shall be fined under this title or imprisoned for not more than six months, or both.

(Added Sept. 28, 1950, c. 1092, § 1(b), 64 Stat. 1077, and amended Sept. 13, 1994, Pub.L. 103–322, Title XXXIII, § 330016(1)(E), 108 Stat. 2146.)

§ 711. "Smokey Bear" character or name

Whoever, except as authorized under rules and regulations issued by the Secretary of Agriculture after consultation with the Association of State Foresters and the Advertising Council, knowingly and for profit manufactures, reproduces, or uses the character "Smokey Bear", originated by the Forest Service, United States Department of Agriculture, in cooperation with the Association of State Foresters and the Advertising Council for use in public information concerning the prevention of forest fires, or any facsimile thereof, or the name "Smokey Bear" shall be fined under this title or imprisoned not more than six months, or both.

(Added May 23, 1952, c. 327, § 1, 66 Stat. 92, and amended June 22, 1974, Pub.L. 93–318, § 5, 88 Stat. 245; Sept. 13, 1994, Pub.L. 103–322, Title XXXIII, §§ 330004(4), 330016(1)(E), 108 Stat. 2141, 2146.)

HISTORICAL AND STATUTORY NOTES

Deposit of Fees; Availability

Deposit of fees collected under regulations governing "Smokey Bear" and availability for use, see § 488a of Title 31, Money and Finance.

§ 711a. "Woodsy Owl" character, name, or slogan

Whoever, except as authorized under rules and regulations issued by the Secretary, knowingly and for profit manufactures, reproduces, or uses the character "Woodsy Owl", the name "Woodsy Owl", or the associated slogan, "Give a Hoot, Don't Pollute" shall be fined under this title or imprisoned not more than six months, or both.

(Added Pub.L. 93–318, § 6, June 22, 1974, 88 Stat. 245, and amended Pub.L. 103–322, Title XXXIII, § 330016(1)(E), Sept. 13, 1994, 108 Stat. 2146.)

HISTORICAL AND STATUTORY NOTES

Description of "Woodsy Owl" Character

For description of character of "Woodsy Owl" as referred to in this section, see § 488b–3 of Title 31, Money and Finance.

§ 712. Misuse of names, words, emblems, or insignia

Whoever, in the course of collecting or aiding in the collection of private debts or obligations, or being engaged in furnishing private police, investigation, or other private detective services, uses or employs in any communication, correspondence, notice, advertisement, or circular the words "national", "Federal", or "United States", the initials "U.S.", or any emblem, insignia, or name, for the purpose of conveying and in a manner reasonably calculated to convey the false impression that such communication is from a department, agency, bureau, or instrumentality of the United States or in any manner represents the United States, shall be fined under this title or imprisoned not more than one year, or both.

(Added Pub.L. 86–291, § 1, Sept. 21, 1959, 73 Stat. 570, and amended Pub.L. 93–147, § 1(a), Nov. 3, 1973, 87 Stat. 554; Pub.L. 103–322, Title XXXIII, § 330016(1)(H), Sept. 13, 1994, 108 Stat. 2147.)

HISTORICAL AND STATUTORY NOTES

Effective and Applicability Provisions

1959 Acts. Section 2 of Pub.L. 86–291 provided that: "The provisions of this section shall become effective sixty days from the enactment thereof. [Sept. 21, 1959]".

§ 713. Use of likenesses of the great seal of the United States, the seals of the President and Vice President, the seal of the United States Senate, the seal of the United States House of Representatives, and the seal of the United States Congress

(a) Whoever knowingly displays any printed or other likeness of the great seal of the United States, or of the seals of the President or the Vice President of the United States, or the seal of the United States Senate, or the seal of the United States House of Representatives, or the seal of the United States Congress, or any facsimile thereof, in, or in connection with, any advertisement, poster, circular, book, pamphlet, or other publication, public meeting, play, motion picture, telecast, or other production, or on any building, monument, or stationery, for the purpose of conveying, or in a manner reasonably calculated to convey, a false impression of sponsorship or approval by the Government of the United States or by any department, agency, or instrumentality thereof, shall be fined under this title or imprisoned not more than six months, or both.

(b) Whoever, except as authorized under regulations promulgated by the President and published in the Federal Register, knowingly manufactures, reproduces, sells, or purchases for resale, either separately or appended to any article manufactured or sold, any likeness of the seals of the President or Vice President, or any substantial part thereof, except for manufacture or sale of the article for the official use of the Government of the United States, shall be fined under this title or imprisoned not more than six months, or both.

(c) Whoever, except as directed by the United States Senate, or the Secretary of the Senate on its behalf, knowingly uses, manufactures, reproduces, sells or purchases for resale, either separately or appended to any article manufactured or sold, any likeness of the seal of the United States Senate, or any substantial part thereof, except for manufacture or sale of the article for the official use of the Government of the United States, shall be fined under this title or imprisoned not more than six months, or both.

(d) Whoever, except as directed by the United States House of Representatives, or the Clerk of the House of Representatives on its behalf, knowingly uses, manufactures, reproduces, sells or purchases for resale, either separately or appended to any article manufactured or sold, any likeness of the seal of the United States House of Representatives, or any substantial part thereof, except for manufacture or sale of the article for the official use of the Government of the United States, shall be fined under this title or imprisoned not more than six months, or both.

(e) Whoever, except as directed by the United States Congress, or the Secretary of the Senate and the Clerk of the House of Representatives, acting jointly on its behalf, knowingly uses, manufactures, reproduces, sells or purchases for resale, either separately or appended to any article manufactured or sold, any likeness of the seal of the United States Congress, or any substantial part thereof, except for manufacture or sale of the article for the official use of the Government of the United States, shall be fined under this title or imprisoned not more than six months, or both.

(f) A violation of the provisions of this section may be enjoined at the suit of the Attorney General,

(1) in the case of the great seal of the United States and the seals of the President and Vice President, upon complaint by any authorized representative of any department or agency of the United States;

(2) in the case of the seal of the United States Senate, upon complaint by the Secretary of the Senate;

(3) in the case of the seal of the United States House of Representatives, upon complaint by the Clerk of the House of Representatives; and

(4) in the case of the seal of the United States Congress, upon complaint by the Secretary of the Senate and the Clerk of the House of Representatives, acting jointly.

(Added Pub.L. 89–807, § 1(a), Nov. 11, 1966, 80 Stat. 1525, and amended Pub.L. 91–651, § 1, Jan. 5, 1971, 84 Stat. 1940; Pub.L. 102–229, Title II, § 210(a)-(d), Dec. 12, 1991, 105 Stat. 1717; Pub.L. 103–322, Title XXXIII, § 330016(1)(E), Sept. 13, 1994, 108 Stat. 2146; Pub.L. 105–55, Title III, § 308(a)-(d), Oct. 7, 1997, 111 Stat. 1198.)

HISTORICAL AND STATUTORY NOTES

Codifications

"(3) redesignated as subsection (d)." set out in the language of Pub.L. 102–229, §210(c) has been editorially determined to be directory language and not part of the text changes for such section and has been executed as the probable intent of Congress.

Effective and Applicability Provisions

1971 Acts. Section 3 of Pub.L. 91–651 provided that: "The amendments made by this Act [amending this section] shall not make unlawful any preexisting use of the design of the great seal of the United States or of the seals of the President or Vice President of the United States that was lawful on the date of enactment of this Act [Jan. 5, 1971], until one year after the date of such enactment."

EXECUTIVE ORDERS

EXECUTIVE ORDER NO. 11649

Feb. 16, 1972, 37 F.R. 3625, as amended by Ex.Ord.No. 11916, May 28, 1976, 41 F.R. 22031

REGULATIONS GOVERNING SEALS OF PRESIDENT AND VICE PRESIDENT OF UNITED STATES

By virtue of the authority vested in me by § 713(b) of title 18, United States Code [subsec. (b) of this section], I hereby prescribe the following regulations governing the use of the Seals of the President and the Vice President of the United States:

Section 1. Except as otherwise provided by law, the knowing manufacture, reproduction, sale, or purchase for resale of the Seals or Coats of Arms of the President or the Vice President of the United States, or any likeness or substantial part thereof, shall be permitted only for the following uses:

(a) Use by the President or Vice President of the United States;

(b) Use in encyclopedias, dictionaries, books, journals, pamphlets, periodicals, or magazines incident to a description or history of seals, coats of arms, heraldry, or the Presidency or Vice Presidency;

(c) Use in libraries, museums, or educational facilities incident to descriptions or exhibits relating to seals, coats of arms, heraldry, or the Presidency or Vice Presidency;

(d) Use as an architectural embellishment in libraries, museums, or archives established to house the papers or effects of former Presidents or Vice Presidents;

(e) Use on a monument to a former President or Vice President;

(f) Use by way of photographic or electronic visual reproduction in pictures, moving pictures, or telecasts of bona fide news content;

(g) Such other uses for exceptional historical, educational, or newsworthy purposes as may be authorized in writing by the Counsel to the President.

Sec. 2. The manufacture, reproduction, sale, or purchase for resale, either separately or appended to any article manufactured or sold, of the Seals of the President or Vice President, or any likeness or substantial part thereof, except as provided in this Order or as otherwise provided by law, is prohibited.

RICHARD NIXON

[§ 714. Repealed. Pub.L. 97–258, § 2(d) (1) (B), Sept. 13, 1982, 96 Stat. 1058]

HISTORICAL AND STATUTORY NOTES

Section, added Pub.L. 91–419, § 3, Sept. 25, 1970, 84 Stat. 870, related to a definition of "Johnny Horizon" for the purposes of this Act.

§ 715. "The Golden Eagle Insignia"

As used in this section, "The Golden Eagle Insignia" means the words "The Golden Eagle" and the representation of an American Golden Eagle (colored gold) and a family group (colored midnight blue) enclosed within a circle (colored white with a midnight blue border) framed by a rounded triangle (colored gold with a midnight blue border) which was originated by the Department of the Interior as the official symbol for Federal recreation fee areas.

Whoever, except as authorized under rules and regulations issued by the Secretary of the Interior, knowingly manufactures, reproduces, or uses "The Golden Eagle Insignia", or any facsimile thereof, in such a manner as is likely to cause confusion, or to cause mistake, or to deceive, shall be fined under this title or imprisoned not more than six months, or both.

The use of any such emblem, sign, insignia, or words which was lawful on the date of enactment of this Act shall not be a violation of this section.

A violation of this section may be enjoined at the suit of the Attorney General, upon complaint by the Secretary of the Interior.

(Added Pub.L. 92–347, § 3(b), July 11, 1972, 86 Stat. 461, and amended Pub.L. 103–322, Title XXXIII, § 330016(1)(E), Sept. 13, 1994, 108 Stat. 2146.)

HISTORICAL AND STATUTORY NOTES

References in Text

The date of enactment of this Act, referred to in text, means the date of enactment of Pub.L. 92–347, which was approved July 11, 1972.

§ 716. Public employee insignia and uniform

(a) Whoever—

(1) knowingly transfers, transports, or receives, in interstate or foreign commerce, a counterfeit official insignia or uniform;

(2) knowingly transfers, in interstate or foreign commerce, a genuine official insignia or uniform to an individual, knowing that such individual is not authorized to possess it under the law of the place in which the badge is the official official [1] insignia or uniform;

(3) knowingly receives a genuine official insignia or uniform in a transfer prohibited by paragraph (2); or

(4) being a person not authorized to possess a genuine official insignia or uniform under the law of the place in which the badge is the official official [1] insignia or uniform, knowingly transports that badge in interstate or foreign commerce,

shall be fined under this title or imprisoned not more than 6 months, or both.

(b) It is a defense to a prosecution under this section that the insignia or uniform is other than a counterfeit insignia or uniform and is not used to mislead or deceive, or is used or is intended to be used exclusively—

(1) as a memento, or in a collection or exhibit;

(2) for decorative purposes;

(3) for a dramatic presentation, such as a theatrical, film, or television production; or

(4) for any other recreational purpose.

(c) As used in this section—

(1) the term "genuine police badge" means an official badge issued by public authority to identify an individual as a law enforcement officer having police powers;

(2) the term "counterfeit police badge" means an item that so resembles a police badge that it would

deceive an ordinary individual into believing it was a genuine police badge; and [2]

(3) the term "official insignia or uniform" means an article of distinctive clothing or insignia, including a badge, emblem or identification card, that is an indicium of the authority of a public employee;

(4) the term "public employee" means any officer or employee of the Federal Government or of a State or local government; and

(5) the term "uniform" means distinctive clothing or other items of dress, whether real or counterfeit, worn during the performance of official duties and which identifies the wearer as a public agency employee.

(d) It is a defense to a prosecution under this section that the official insignia or uniform is not used or intended to be used to mislead or deceive, or is a counterfeit insignia or uniform and is used or is intended to be used exclusively—

(1) for a dramatic presentation, such as a theatrical, film, or television production; or

(2) for legitimate law enforcement purposes.

(Added Pub.L. 106–547, § 3(a), Dec. 19, 2000, 114 Stat. 2739, and amended Pub.L. 109–162, Title XI, § 1191(a), Jan. 5, 2006, 119 Stat. 3128.)

[1] So in original. The second "official" probably should not appear.

[2] So in original. The word "and" probably should not appear.

HISTORICAL AND STATUTORY NOTES

Codifications

Amendment by Pub.L. 109–162, § 1191(a)(1), to strike "police badge" each place it appeared in subsec. (b) of this section and insert "official insignia or uniform" was incapable of execution. The term "police badge" does not appear in subsec. (b) of this section.

Amendment to subsec. (b) of this section by Pub.L. 109–162, § 1191(a)(3)(C), to insert "is not used to mislead or deceive, or" before "is used or intended", was executed by inserting that phrase before the phrase "is used or is intended to be used", as added by Pub.L. 109–162, § 1191(a)(3)(B), as the probable intent of Congress.

CHAPTER 35—ESCAPE AND RESCUE

§ 751. Prisoners in custody of institution or officer

(a) Whoever escapes or attempts to escape from the custody of the Attorney General or his authorized representative, or from any institution or facility in which he is confined by direction of the Attorney General, or from any custody under or by virtue of any process issued under the laws of the United States by any court, judge, or magistrate judge, or from the custody of an officer or employee of the United States pursuant to lawful arrest, shall, if the custody or confinement is by virtue of an arrest on a charge of felony, or conviction of any offense, be fined under this title or imprisoned not more than five years, or both; or if the custody or confinement is for extradition, or for exclusion or expulsion proceedings under the immigration laws, or by virtue of an arrest or charge of or for a misdemeanor, and prior to conviction, be fined under this title or imprisoned not more than one year, or both.

(b) Whoever escapes or attempts to escape from the custody of the Attorney General or his authorized representative, or from any institution or facility in which he is confined by direction of the Attorney General, or from any custody under or by virtue of any process issued under the laws of the United States by any court, judge, or magistrate judge, or from the custody of an officer or employee of the United States pursuant to lawful arrest, shall, if the custody or confinement is by virtue of a lawful arrest for a violation of any law of the United States not punishable by death or life imprisonment and committed before such person's eighteenth birthday, and as to whom the Attorney General has not specifically directed the institution of criminal proceedings, or by virtue of a commitment as a juvenile delinquent under section 5034 of this title, be fined under this title or imprisoned not more than one year, or both. Nothing herein contained shall be construed to affect the discretionary authority vested in the Attorney General pursuant to section 5032 of this title.

(June 25, 1948, c. 645, 62 Stat. 734; Dec. 30, 1963, Pub.L. 88–251, § 1, 77 Stat. 834; Sept. 10, 1965, Pub.L. 89–176, § 3, 79 Stat. 675; Nov. 18, 1988, Pub.L. 100–690, Title VII, § 7055, 102 Stat. 4402; Dec. 1, 1990, Pub.L. 101–650, Title III, § 321, 104 Stat. 5117; Sept. 13, 1994, Pub.L. 103–322, Title XXXIII, § 330016(1)(H), (K), 108 Stat. 2147.)

HISTORICAL AND STATUTORY NOTES

Change of Name

Words "magistrate judge" substituted for "magistrate" in text pursuant to section 321 of Pub.L. 101–650, set out as a note under 28 U.S.C.A. § 631. Previously, United States commissioners, referred to in text, were replaced by United States magistrates pursuant to Pub.L. 90–578, Oct. 17, 1968,

82 Stat. 1118. See chapter 43 of Title 28, 28 U.S.C.A. § 631 et seq.

§ 752. Instigating or assisting escape

(a) Whoever rescues or attempts to rescue or instigates, aids or assists the escape, or attempt to escape, of any person arrested upon a warrant or other process issued under any law of the United States, or committed to the custody of the Attorney General or to any institution or facility by his direction, shall, if the custody or confinement is by virtue of an arrest on a charge of felony, or conviction of any offense, be fined under this title or imprisoned not more than five years, or both; or, if the custody or confinement is for extradition, or for exclusion or expulsion proceedings under the immigration laws, or by virtue of an arrest or charge of or for a misdemeanor, and prior to conviction, be fined under this title or imprisoned not more than one year, or both.

(b) Whoever rescues or attempts to rescue or instigates, aids, or assists the escape or attempted escape of any person in the custody of the Attorney General or his authorized representative, or of any person arrested upon a warrant or other process issued under any law of the United States or from any institution or facility in which he is confined by direction of the Attorney General, shall, if the custody or confinement is by virtue of a lawful arrest for a violation of any law of the United States not punishable by death or life imprisonment and committed before such person's eighteenth birthday, and as to whom the Attorney General has not specifically directed the institution of criminal proceedings, or by virtue of a commitment as a juvenile delinquent under section 5034 of this title, be fined under this title or imprisoned not more than one year, or both.

(June 25, 1948, c. 645, 62 Stat. 735; May 28, 1956, c. 331, 70 Stat. 216; Dec. 30, 1963, Pub.L. 88–251, § 2, 77 Stat. 834; Sept. 10, 1965, Pub.L. 89–176, § 3, 79 Stat. 675; Nov. 18, 1988, Pub.L. 100–690, Title VII, § 7055, 102 Stat. 4402; Sept. 13, 1994, Pub.L. 103–322, Title XXXIII, § 330016(1)(H), 108 Stat. 2147; Nov. 2, 2002, Pub.L. 107–273, Div. B, Title IV, § 4002(d)(1)(D), 116 Stat. 1809.)

HISTORICAL AND STATUTORY NOTES

Canal Zone

Applicability of section to Canal Zone, see § 14 of this title.

§ 753. Rescue to prevent execution

Whoever, by force, sets at liberty or rescues any person found guilty in any court of the United States of any capital crime, while going to execution or during execution, shall be fined under this title or imprisoned not more than twenty-five years, or both.

(June 25, 1948, c. 645, 62 Stat. 735; Sept. 13, 1994, Pub.L. 103–322, Title XXXIII, § 330016(1)(O), 108 Stat. 2148.)

[§ 754. Repealed. Pub.L. 103–322, Title XXXIII, § 330004(5), Sept. 13, 1994, 108 Stat. 2141]

HISTORICAL AND STATUTORY NOTES

Section, Act June 25, 1948, c. 645, 62 Stat. 735; Sept. 13, 1994, Pub.L. 103–322, Title XXXIII, § 330016(1)(B), 108 Stat. 2146, related to rescue of bodies of executed offenders.

§ 755. Officer permitting escape

Whoever, having in his custody any prisoner by virtue of process issued under the laws of the United States by any court, judge, or magistrate judge, voluntarily suffers such prisoner to escape, shall be fined under this title or imprisoned not more than 5 years, or both; or if he negligently suffers such person to escape, he shall be fined under this title or imprisoned not more than one year, or both.

(June 25, 1948, c. 645, 62 Stat. 735; Dec. 1, 1990, Pub.L. 101–650, Title III, § 321, 104 Stat. 5117; Sept. 13, 1994, Pub.L. 103–322, Title XXXIII, § 330016(1)(G), (I), 108 Stat. 2147; Apr. 24, 1996, Pub.L. 104–132, Title VII, § 705(a)(2), 110 Stat. 1295.)

HISTORICAL AND STATUTORY NOTES

Senate Revision Amendment

The text of this section was changed by Senate amendment in view of the Act of June 21, 1947, c. 111, 61 Stat. 134, which, by amending § 244 of Title 18, U.S.C., became an additional source of this section. See Senate Report No. 1620, Amendment No. 8, 80th Cong.

Change of Name

Words "magistrate judge" substituted for "magistrate" in text pursuant to section 321 of Pub.L. 101–650, set out as a note under 28 U.S.C.A. § 631. Previously, United States commissioners, referred to in text, were replaced by United States magistrates pursuant to Pub.L. 90–578, Oct. 17, 1968, 82 Stat. 1118. See chapter 43 of Title 28, 28 U.S.C.A. § 631 et seq.

Canal Zone

Applicability of section to Canal Zone, see § 14 of this title.

§ 756. Internee of belligerent nation

Whoever, within the jurisdiction of the United States, aids or entices any person belonging to the armed forces of a belligerent nation or faction who is interned in the United States in accordance with the law of nations, to escape or attempt to escape from the jurisdiction of the United States or from the limits of internment prescribed, shall be fined under this title or imprisoned not more than five years, or both.

(June 25, 1948, c. 645, 62 Stat. 735; Sept. 13, 1994, Pub.L. 103–322, Title XXXIII, § 330016(1)(H), 108 Stat. 2147; Apr. 24, 1996, Pub.L. 104–132, Title VII, § 705(a)(3), 110 Stat. 1295.)

HISTORICAL AND STATUTORY NOTES

Canal Zone

Applicability of section to Canal Zone, see § 14 of this title.

§ 757. Prisoners of war or enemy aliens

Whoever procures the escape of any prisoner of war held by the United States or any of its allies, or the escape of any person apprehended or interned as an enemy alien by the United States or any of its allies, or advises, connives at, aids, or assists in such escape, or aids, relieves, transports, harbors, conceals, shelters, protects, holds correspondence with, gives intelligence to, or otherwise assists any such prisoner of war or enemy alien, after his escape from custody, knowing him to be such prisoner of war or enemy alien, or attempts to commit or conspires to commit any of the above acts, shall be fined under this title or imprisoned not more than ten years, or both.

The provisions of this section shall be in addition to and not in substitution for any other provision of law.

(June 25, 1948, c. 645, 62 Stat. 735; Sept. 13, 1994, Pub.L. 103–322, Title XXXIII, § 330016(1)(L), 108 Stat. 2147.)

§ 758. High speed flight from immigration checkpoint

Whoever flees or evades a checkpoint operated by the Immigration and Naturalization Service, or any other Federal law enforcement agency, in a motor vehicle and flees Federal, State, or local law enforcement agents in excess of the legal speed limit shall be fined under this title, imprisoned not more than five years, or both.

(Added Pub.L. 104–208, Div. C, Title I, § 108(b)(1), Sept. 30, 1996, 110 Stat. 3009–557.)

HISTORICAL AND STATUTORY NOTES

Abolition of Immigration and Naturalization Service and Transfer of Functions

For abolition of Immigration and Naturalization Service, transfer of functions, and treatment of related references, see note set out under 8 U.S.C.A. § 1551.

Severability of Provisions

If any provision of Division C of Pub.L. 104–208 or the application of such provision to any person or circumstances is held to be unconstitutional, the remainder of Division C of Pub.L. 104–208 and the application of the provisions of Division C of Pub.L. 104–208 to any person or circumstance not to be affected thereby, see section 1(e) of Pub.L. 104–208, set out as a note under section 1101 of Title 8, Aliens and Nationality.

Criminal Penalties For High Speed Flights From Immigration Checkpoints; Congressional Statement of Findings

Section 108(a) of Div. C of Pub.L. 104–208 provided that: "The Congress finds as follows:

"(1) Immigration checkpoints are an important component of the national strategy to prevent illegal immigration.

"(2) Individuals fleeing immigration checkpoints and leading law enforcement officials on high speed vehicle chases endanger law enforcement officers, innocent bystanders, and the fleeing individuals themselves.

"(3) The pursuit of suspects fleeing immigration checkpoints is complicated by overlapping jurisdiction among Federal, State, and local law enforcement officers."

CHAPTER 37—ESPIONAGE AND CENSORSHIP

1951 Amendments

Act Oct. 31, 1951, c. 655, § 23, 65 Stat. 719, added first item 798.

[§ 791. Repealed. Pub.L. 87–369, § 1, Oct. 4, 1961, 75 Stat. 795]

HISTORICAL AND STATUTORY NOTES

Section, Act June 25, 1948, c. 645, 62 Stat. 736, related to the application of the chapter within the admiralty and maritime jurisdiction of the United States, on the high seas, and within the United States.

§ 792. Harboring or concealing persons

Whoever harbors or conceals any person who he knows, or has reasonable grounds to believe or suspect, has committed, or is about to commit, an offense under sections 793 or 794 of this title, shall be fined under this title or imprisoned not more than ten years, or both.

(June 25, 1948, c. 645, 62 Stat. 736; Sept. 13, 1994, Pub.L. 103–322, Title XXXIII, § 330016(1)(L), 108 Stat. 2147.)

HISTORICAL AND STATUTORY NOTES

Indictment for Violating This Section and Sections 793, 794; Limitation Period

Act Sept. 23, 1950, c. 1024, § 19, 64 Stat. 1005, provided that an indictment for any violation of this section and sections 793 and 794 of this title, other than a violation constituting a capital offense, may be found at any time within ten years next after such violation shall have been committed, but that such section 19 shall not authorize prosecution, trial, or punishment for any offense "now" barred by the provisions of existing law.

1994 Acts. House Report Nos. 103–324 and 103–489, and House Conference Report No. 103–711, see 1994 U.S. Code Cong. and Adm. News, p. 1801.

Canal Zone

Applicability of section to Canal Zone, see § 14 of this title.

§ 793. Gathering, transmitting or losing defense information

(a) Whoever, for the purpose of obtaining information respecting the national defense with intent or reason to believe that the information is to be used to the injury of the United States, or to the advantage of any foreign nation, goes upon, enters, flies over, or otherwise obtains information concerning any vessel, aircraft, work of defense, navy yard, naval station, submarine base, fueling station, fort, battery, torpedo station, dockyard, canal, railroad, arsenal, camp, factory, mine, telegraph, telephone, wireless, or signal station, building, office, research laboratory or station or other place connected with the national defense owned or constructed, or in progress of construction by the United States or under the control of the United States, or of any of its officers, departments, or agencies, or within the exclusive jurisdiction of the United States, or any place in which any vessel, aircraft, arms, munitions, or other materials or instruments for use in time of war are being made, prepared, repaired, stored, or are the subject of research or development, under any contract or agreement with the United States, or any department or agency thereof, or with any person on behalf of the United States, or otherwise on behalf of the United States, or any prohibited place so designated by the President by proclamation in time of war or in case of national emergency in which anything for the use of the Army, Navy, or Air Force is being prepared or constructed or stored, information as to which prohibited place the President has determined would be prejudicial to the national defense; or

(b) Whoever, for the purpose aforesaid, and with like intent or reason to believe, copies, takes, makes, or obtains, or attempts to copy, take, make, or obtain, any sketch, photograph, photographic negative, blueprint, plan, map, model, instrument, appliance, document, writing, or note of anything connected with the national defense; or

(c) Whoever, for the purpose aforesaid, receives or obtains or agrees or attempts to receive or obtain from any person, or from any source whatever, any document, writing, code book, signal book, sketch, photograph, photographic negative, blueprint, plan, map, model, instrument, appliance, or note, of anything connected with the national defense, knowing or having reason to believe, at the time he receives or obtains, or agrees or attempts to receive or obtain it, that it has been or will be obtained, taken, made, or disposed of by any person contrary to the provisions of this chapter; or

(d) Whoever, lawfully having possession of, access to, control over, or being entrusted with any document, writing, code book, signal book, sketch, photograph, photographic negative, blueprint, plan, map, model, instrument, appliance, or note relating to the national defense, or information relating to the national defense which information the possessor has reason to believe could be used to the injury of the United States or to the advantage of any foreign nation, willfully communicates, delivers, transmits or causes to be communicated, delivered, or transmitted or attempts to communicate, deliver, transmit or cause to be communicated, delivered or transmitted the same to any person not entitled to receive it, or willfully retains the same and fails to deliver it on demand to the officer or employee of the United States entitled to receive it; or

(e) Whoever having unauthorized possession of, access to, or control over any document, writing, code book, signal book, sketch, photograph, photographic negative, blueprint, plan, map, model, instrument, appliance, or note relating to the national defense, or information relating to the national defense which information the possessor has reason to believe could be used to the injury of the United States or to the advantage of any foreign nation, willfully communicates, delivers, transmits or causes to be communicated, delivered, or transmitted, or attempts to communicate, deliver, transmit or cause to be communicated, delivered, or transmitted the same to any person not entitled to receive it, or willfully retains the same and fails to deliver it to the officer or employee of the United States entitled to receive it; or

(f) Whoever, being entrusted with or having lawful possession or control of any document, writing, code book, signal book, sketch, photograph, photographic negative, blueprint, plan, map, model, instrument, appliance, note, or information, relating to the national defense, (1) through gross negligence permits the same to be removed from its proper place of custody or delivered to anyone in violation of his trust, or to be lost, stolen, abstracted, or destroyed, or (2) having knowledge that the same has been illegally removed from its proper place of custody or delivered to anyone in violation of its trust, or lost, or stolen, abstracted, or destroyed, and fails to make prompt report of such loss, theft, abstraction, or destruction to his superior officer—

Shall be fined under this title or imprisoned not more than ten years, or both.

(g) If two or more persons conspire to violate any of the foregoing provisions of this section, and one or more of such persons do any act to effect the object of the conspiracy, each of the parties to such conspiracy shall be subject to the punishment provided for the offense which is the object of such conspiracy.

(h)(1) Any person convicted of a violation of this section shall forfeit to the United States, irrespective of any provision of State law, any property constituting, or derived from, any proceeds the person obtained, directly or indirectly, from any foreign government, or any faction or party or military or naval force within a foreign country, whether recognized or unrecognized by the United States, as the result of such violation. For the purposes of this subsection, the term "State" includes a State of the United States, the District of Columbia, and any commonwealth, territory, or possession of the United States.

(2) The court, in imposing sentence on a defendant for a conviction of a violation of this section, shall order that the defendant forfeit to the United States all property described in paragraph (1) of this subsection.

(3) The provisions of subsections (b), (c), and (e) through (p) of section 413 of the Comprehensive Drug Abuse Prevention and Control Act of 1970 (21 U.S.C. 853(b), (c), and (e)–(p)) shall apply to—

(A) property subject to forfeiture under this subsection;

(B) any seizure or disposition of such property; and

(C) any administrative or judicial proceeding in relation to such property,

if not inconsistent with this subsection.

(4) Notwithstanding section 524(c) of title 28, there shall be deposited in the Crime Victims Fund in the Treasury all amounts from the forfeiture of property under this subsection remaining after the payment of expenses for forfeiture and sale authorized by law. (June 25, 1948, c. 645, 62 Stat. 736; Sept. 23, 1950, c. 1024, Title I, § 18, 64 Stat. 1003; Aug. 27, 1986, Pub.L. 99–399, Title XIII, § 1306(a), 100 Stat. 898; Sept. 13, 1994, Pub.L. 103–322, Title XXXIII, § 330016(1)(L), 108 Stat. 2147; Oct. 14, 1994, Pub.L. 103–359, Title VIII, § 804(b)(1), 108 Stat. 3440; Oct. 11, 1996, Pub.L 104–294, Title VI, § 607(b), 110 Stat. 3511.)

HISTORICAL AND STATUTORY NOTES

References in Text

Subsections (b), (c), and (e) through (p) of section 413 of the Comprehensive Drug Abuse Prevention and Control Act of 1970, referred to in subsec. (h)(3), are classified to section 853(b), (c), and (e) through (p) of Title 21, Food and Drugs.

Indictment for Violating This Section; Limitation Period

Limitation period in connection with indictments for violating this section, see note under section 792 of this title.

Canal Zone

Applicability of section to Canal Zone, see § 14 of this title.

§ 794. Gathering or delivering defense information to aid foreign government

(a) Whoever, with intent or reason to believe that it is to be used to the injury of the United States or to the advantage of a foreign nation, communicates, delivers, or transmits, or attempts to communicate, deliver, or transmit, to any foreign government, or to any faction or party or military or naval force within a foreign country, whether recognized or unrecognized by the United States, or to any representative, officer, agent, employee, subject, or citizen thereof, either directly or indirectly, any document, writing, code book, signal book, sketch, photograph, photographic negative, blueprint, plan, map, model, note, instrument, appliance, or information relating to the national defense, shall be punished by death or by imprisonment for any term of years or for life, except that the sentence of death shall not be imposed unless the jury or, if there is no jury, the court, further finds that the offense resulted in the identification by a foreign power (as defined in section 101(a) of the Foreign Intelligence Surveillance Act of 1978) of an individual acting as an agent of the United States and consequently in the death of that individual, or directly concerned nuclear weaponry, military spacecraft or satellites, early warning systems, or other means of defense or retaliation against large-scale attack; war plans; communications intelligence or cryptographic information; or any other major weapons system or major element of defense strategy.

(b) Whoever, in time of war, with intent that the same shall be communicated to the enemy, collects, records, publishes, or communicates, or attempts to elicit any information with respect to the movement, numbers, description, condition, or disposition of any of the Armed Forces, ships, aircraft, or war materials of the United States, or with respect to the plans or conduct, or supposed plans or conduct of any naval or military operations, or with respect to any works or measures undertaken for or connected with, or intended for the fortification or defense of any place, or any other information relating to the public defense, which might be useful to the enemy, shall be punished by death or by imprisonment for any term of years or for life.

(c) If two or more persons conspire to violate this section, and one or more of such persons do any act to effect the object of the conspiracy, each of the parties to such conspiracy shall be subject to the punishment provided for the offense which is the object of such conspiracy.

(d)(1) Any person convicted of a violation of this section shall forfeit to the United States irrespective of any provision of State law—

(A) any property constituting, or derived from, any proceeds the person obtained, directly or indirectly, as the result of such violation, and

(B) any of the person's property used, or intended to be used, in any manner or part, to commit, or to facilitate the commission of, such violation.

For the purposes of this subsection, the term "State" includes a State of the United States, the District of Columbia, and any commonwealth, territory, or possession of the United States.

(2) The court, in imposing sentence on a defendant for a conviction of a violation of this section, shall order that the defendant forfeit to the United States all property described in paragraph (1) of this subsection.

(3) The provisions of subsections (b), (c) and (e) through (p) of section 413 of the Comprehensive Drug Abuse Prevention and Control Act of 1970 (21 U.S.C. 853(b), (c), and (e)-(p)) shall apply to—

(A) property subject to forfeiture under this subsection;

(B) any seizure or disposition of such property; and

(C) any administrative or judicial proceeding in relation to such property,

if not inconsistent with this subsection.

(4) Notwithstanding section 524(c) of title 28, there shall be deposited in the Crime Victims Fund in the Treasury all amounts from the forfeiture of property under this subsection remaining after the payment of expenses for forfeiture and sale authorized by law.

(June 25, 1948, c. 645, 62 Stat. 737; Sept. 3, 1954, c. 1261, Title II, § 201, 68 Stat. 1219; Aug. 27, 1986, Pub.L. 99–399, Title XIII, § 1306(b), 100 Stat. 898; Nov. 18, 1988, Pub.L. 100–690, Title VII, § 7064, 102 Stat. 4404; Sept. 13, 1994, Pub.L. 103–322, Title VI, § 60003(a)(2), 108 Stat. 1968; Oct. 14, 1994, Pub.L. 103–359, Title VIII, § 804(b)(2), 108 Stat. 3440; Oct. 11, 1996, Pub.L. 104–294, Title VI, §§ 604(b)(2), 607(b), 110 Stat. 3506, 3511.)

HISTORICAL AND STATUTORY NOTES

References in Text

Section 101(a) of the Foreign Intelligence Surveillance Act of 1978, referred to in subsec. (a), is classified to section 1801(a) of Title 50, War and National Defense.

Subsections (b), (c), and (e) through (p) of section 413 of the Comprehensive Drug Abuse Prevention and Control Act of 1970, referred to subsec. (d)(3), are classified to section 853(b), (c), and (e) through (p) of Title 21, Food and Drugs.

Effective and Applicability Provisions

1996 Acts. Amendment by section 604 of Pub.L. 104–294 effective Sept. 13, 1994, see section 604(d) of Pub.L. 104–294, set out as a note under section 13 of this title.

Indictment for Violating This Section; Limitation Period

Limitation period in connection with indictments for violating this section, see note under section 792 of this title.

Canal Zone

Applicability of section to Canal Zone, see § 14 of this title.

§ 795. Photographing and sketching defense installations

(a) Whenever, in the interests of national defense, the President defines certain vital military and naval installations or equipment as requiring protection against the general dissemination of information relative thereto, it shall be unlawful to make any photograph, sketch, picture, drawing, map, or graphical representation of such vital military and naval installations or equipment without first obtaining permission of the commanding officer of the military or naval post, camp, or station, or naval vessels, military and naval aircraft, and any separate military or naval command concerned, or higher authority, and promptly submitting the product obtained to such commanding officer or higher authority for censorship or such other action as he may deem necessary.

(b) Whoever violates this section shall be fined under this title or imprisoned not more than one year, or both.

(June 25, 1948, c. 645, 62 Stat. 737; Sept. 13, 1994, Pub.L. 103–322, Title XXXIII, § 330016(1)(H), 108 Stat. 2147.)

HISTORICAL AND STATUTORY NOTES

Canal Zone

Applicability of section to Canal Zone, see § 14 of this title.

EXECUTIVE ORDERS

EXECUTIVE ORDER NO. 10104

Feb. 1, 1950, 15 F.R. 597

DEFINITIONS OF VITAL MILITARY AND NAVAL INSTALLATIONS AND EQUIPMENT

Now, therefore, by virtue of the authority vested in me by the foregoing statutory provisions, and in the interests of national defense, I hereby define the following as vital military and naval installations or equipment requiring protection against the general dissemination of information relative thereto:

1. All military, naval, or air-force installations and equipment which are now classified, designated, or marked under the authority or at the direction of the President, the Secretary of Defense, the Secretary of the Army, the Secretary of the Navy, or the Secretary of the Air Force as "top secret", "secret", "confidential", or "restricted" and all military, naval, or air-force installations and equipment which may hereafter

be so classified, designated, or marked with the approval or at the direction of the President, and located within:

(a) Any military, naval, or air-force reservation, post, arsenal, proving ground, range, mine field, camp, base, airfield, fort, yard, station, district, or area.

(b) Any defensive sea area heretofore established by Executive order and not subsequently discontinued by Executive order, and any defensive sea area hereafter established under authority of § 2152 of Title 18 of the United States Code.

(c) Any airspace reservation heretofore or hereafter established under authority of section 4 of the Air Commerce Act of 1926 (44 Stat. 570: 49 U.S.C. 174) except the airspace reservation established by Executive Order No. 10092 of December 17, 1949.

(d) Any naval harbor closed to foreign vessels.

(e) Any area required for fleet purposes.

(f) Any commercial establishment engaged in the development or manufacture of classified military or naval arms, munitions, equipment, designs, ships, aircraft, or vessels for the United States Army, Navy, or Air Force.

2. All military, naval, or air-force aircraft, weapons, ammunition, vehicles, ships, vessels, instruments, engines, manufacturing machinery, tools, devices, or any other equipment whatsoever, in the possession of the Army, Navy, or Air Force or in the course of experimentation, development, manufacture, or delivery for the Army, Navy, or Air Force which are now classified, designated, or marked under the authority or at the direction of the President, the Secretary of Defense, the Secretary of the Army, the Secretary of the Navy, or the Secretary of the Air Force as "top secret", "secret", "confidential", or "restricted", and all such articles, materials, or equipment which may hereafter be so classified, designated, or marked with the approval or at the direction of the President.

3. All official military, naval, or air-force books, pamphlets, documents, reports, maps, charts, plans, designs, models, drawings, photographs, contracts, or specifications which are now marked under the authority or at the direction of the President, the Secretary of Defense, the Secretary of the Army, the Secretary of the Navy, or the Secretary of the Air Force as "top secret", "secret", "confidential" or "restricted" and all such articles or equipment which may hereafter be so marked with the approval or at the direction of the President.

This order supersedes Executive Order No. 8381 of March 22, 1940, entitled "Defining Certain Vital Military and Naval Installations and Equipment."

§ 796. Use of aircraft for photographing defense installations

Whoever uses or permits the use of an aircraft or any contrivance used, or designed for navigation or flight in the air, for the purpose of making a photograph, sketch, picture, drawing, map, or graphical representation of vital military or naval installations or equipment, in violation of section 795 of this title, shall be fined under this title or imprisoned not more than one year, or both.

(June 25, 1948, c. 645, 62 Stat. 738; Sept. 13, 1994, Pub.L. 103–322, Title XXXIII, § 330016(1)(H), 108 Stat. 2147.)

HISTORICAL AND STATUTORY NOTES

Canal Zone

Applicability of section to Canal Zone, see § 14 of this title.

§ 797. Publication and sale of photographs of defense installations

On and after thirty days from the date upon which the President defines any vital military or naval installation or equipment as being within the category contemplated under section 795 of this title, whoever reproduces, publishes, sells, or gives away any photograph, sketch, picture, drawing, map, or graphical representation of the vital military or naval installations or equipment so defined, without first obtaining permission of the commanding officer of the military or naval post, camp, or station concerned, or higher authority, unless such photograph, sketch, picture, drawing, map, or graphical representation has clearly indicated thereon that it has been censored by the proper military or naval authority, shall be fined under this title or imprisoned not more than one year, or both.

(June 25, 1948, c. 645, 62 Stat. 738; Sept. 13, 1994, Pub.L. 103–322, Title XXXIII, § 330016(1)(H), 108 Stat. 2147.)

HISTORICAL AND STATUTORY NOTES

Canal Zone

Applicability of section to Canal Zone, see § 14 of this title.

§ 798. Disclosure of classified information

(a) Whoever knowingly and willfully communicates, furnishes, transmits, or otherwise makes available to an unauthorized person, or publishes, or uses in any manner prejudicial to the safety or interest of the United States or for the benefit of any foreign government to the detriment of the United States any classified information—

(1) concerning the nature, preparation, or use of any code, cipher, or cryptographic system of the United States or any foreign government; or

(2) concerning the design, construction, use, maintenance, or repair of any device, apparatus, or appliance used or prepared or planned for use by the United States or any foreign government for cryptographic or communication intelligence purposes; or

(3) concerning the communication intelligence activities of the United States or any foreign government; or

(4) obtained by the processes of communication intelligence from the communications of any foreign government, knowing the same to have been obtained by such processes—

Shall be fined under this title or imprisoned not more than ten years, or both.

(b) As used in subsection (a) of this section—

The term "classified information" means information which, at the time of a violation of this section, is, for reasons of national security, specifically designated by a United States Government Agency for limited or restricted dissemination or distribution;

The terms "code," "cipher," and "cryptographic system" include in their meanings, in addition to their usual meanings, any method of secret writing and any mechanical or electrical device or method used for the purpose of disguising or concealing the contents, significance, or meanings of communications;

The term "foreign government" includes in its meaning any person or persons acting or purporting to act for or on behalf of any faction, party, department, agency, bureau, or military force of or within a foreign country, or for or on behalf of any government or any person or persons purporting to act as a government within a foreign country, whether or not such government is recognized by the United States;

The term "communication intelligence" means all procedures and methods used in the interception of communications and the obtaining of information from such communications by other than the intended recipients;

The term "unauthorized person" means any person who, or agency which, is not authorized to receive information of the categories set forth in subsection (a) of this section, by the President, or by the head of a department or agency of the United States Government which is expressly designated by the President to engage in communication intelligence activities for the United States.

(c) Nothing in this section shall prohibit the furnishing, upon lawful demand, of information to any regularly constituted committee of the Senate or House of Representatives of the United States of America, or joint committee thereof.

(d)(1) Any person convicted of a violation of this section shall forfeit to the United States irrespective of any provision of State law—

(A) any property constituting, or derived from, any proceeds the person obtained, directly or indirectly, as the result of such violation; and

(B) any of the person's property used, or intended to be used, in any manner or part, to commit, or to facilitate the commission of, such violation.

(2) The court, in imposing sentence on a defendant for a conviction of a violation of this section, shall order that the defendant forfeit to the United States all property described in paragraph (1).

(3) Except as provided in paragraph (4), the provisions of subsections (b), (c), and (e) through (p) of section 413 of the Comprehensive Drug Abuse Prevention and Control Act of 1970 (21 U.S.C. 853(b), (c), and (e)-(p)), shall apply to—

(A) property subject to forfeiture under this subsection;

(B) any seizure or disposition of such property; and

(C) any administrative or judicial proceeding in relation to such property,

if not inconsistent with this subsection.

(4) Notwithstanding section 524(c) of title 28, there shall be deposited in the Crime Victims Fund established under section 1402 of the Victims of Crime Act of 1984 (42 U.S.C. 10601) all amounts from the forfeiture of property under this subsection remaining after the payment of expenses for forfeiture and sale authorized by law.

(5) As used in this subsection, the term "State" means any State of the United States, the District of Columbia, the Commonwealth of Puerto Rico, and any territory or possession of the United States.

(Added Oct. 31, 1951, c. 655, § 24(a), 65 Stat. 719, and amended Sept. 13, 1994, Pub.L. 103–322, Title XXXIII, § 330016(1)(L), 108 Stat. 2147; Oct. 14, 1994, Pub.L. 103–359, Title VIII, § 804(a), 108 Stat. 3439; Oct. 11, 1996, Pub.L. 104–294, Title VI, § 602(c), 110 Stat. 3503.)

HISTORICAL AND STATUTORY NOTES

References in Text

Subsection (b), (c), and (e) through (p) of section 413 of the Comprehensive Drug Abuse Prevention and Control Act of 1970, referred to in subsec. (d)(3), are classified to section 853(b), (c), and (e) through (p) of Title 21, Food and Drugs.

Codifications

Another section 798 of this title, as added June 30, 1953, § 4, was renumbered section 798A of this title.

Canal Zone

Applicability of section to Canal Zone, see § 14 of this title.

§ 798A. Temporary extension of section 794

The provisions of section 794 of this title, as amended and extended by section 1(a)(29) of the Emergency Powers Continuation Act (66 Stat. 333), as further amended by Public Law 12, Eighty-third Congress, in addition to coming into full force and effect in time of war shall remain in full force and effect until six months after the termination of the national emergency proclaimed by the President on December 16, 1950 (Proc. 2912, 3 C.F.R., 1950 Supp., p. 71), or such earlier date as may be prescribed by concurrent resolution of the Congress, and acts which would give rise to legal consequences and penalties under section 794 when performed during a state of war shall give rise to the same legal consequences and penalties when they are performed during the period above provided for.

(Added June 30, 1953, c. 175, § 4, 67 Stat. 133, § 798, renumbered 798A, Pub.L. 101–647, Title XXXV, § 3519(a), Nov. 29, 1990, 104 Stat. 4923.)

HISTORICAL AND STATUTORY NOTES

References in Text

Section 1(a)(29) of the Emergency Powers Continuation Act (66 Stat. 333) as further amended by Public Law 12, Eighty-third Congress, referred to in text, was formerly set out as a note under § 791 of this title and was repealed by Act June 30, 1953, c. 175, § 7, 67 Stat. 134.

Proc. 2912, 3 C.F.R., 1950 Supp., p. 71, referred to in text, is an erroneous citation. It should refer to Proc. 2914 which is set out as a note preceding § 1 of Appendix to Title 50, War and National Defense.

§ 799. Violation of regulations of National Aeronautics and Space Administration

Whoever willfully shall violate, attempt to violate, or conspire to violate any regulation or order promulgated by the Administrator of the National Aeronautics and Space Administration for the protection or security of any laboratory, station, base or other facility, or part thereof, or any aircraft, missile, spacecraft, or similar vehicle, or part thereof, or other property or equipment in the custody of the Administration, or any real or personal property or equipment in the custody of any contractor under any contract with the Administration or any subcontractor of any such contractor, shall be fined under this title, or imprisoned not more than one year, or both.

(Added Pub.L. 85–568, Title III, § 304(c)(1), July 29, 1958, 72 Stat. 434, and amended Pub.L. 103–322, Title XXXIII, § 330016(1)(K), Sept. 13, 1994, 108 Stat. 2147.)

HISTORICAL AND STATUTORY NOTES

Codifications

Section was added by subsec. (c) of § 304 of Pub.L. 85–568. Subsecs. (a) and (b) of § 304 are classified to § 2455 of Title 42, The Public Health and Welfare. Subsec. (d) of § 304 is classified to § 1114 of this title. Subsec. (e) of § 304 is classified to § 2456 of Title 42.

Canal Zone

Applicability of section to Canal Zone, see § 14 of this title.

CHAPTER 39—EXPLOSIVES AND OTHER DANGEROUS ARTICLES

Sec.

§ 831. Prohibited transactions involving nuclear materials

(a) Whoever, if one of the circumstances described in subsection (c) of this section occurs—

(1) without lawful authority, intentionally receives, possesses, uses, transfers, alters, disposes of, or disperses any nuclear material or nuclear byproduct material and—

(A) thereby knowingly causes the death of or serious bodily injury to any person or substantial damage to property or to the environment; or

(B) circumstances exist, or have been represented to the defendant to exist, that are likely to cause the death or serious bodily injury to any person, or substantial damage to property or to the environment;

(2) with intent to deprive another of nuclear material or nuclear byproduct material, knowingly—

(A) takes and carries away nuclear material or nuclear byproduct material of another without authority;

(B) makes an unauthorized use, disposition, or transfer, of nuclear material or nuclear byproduct material belonging to another; or

(C) uses fraud and thereby obtains nuclear material or nuclear byproduct material belonging to another;

(3) knowingly—

(A) uses force; or

(B) threatens or places another in fear that any person other than the actor will imminently be subject to bodily injury;

and thereby takes nuclear material or nuclear byproduct material belonging to another from the person or presence of any other;

(4) intentionally intimidates any person and thereby obtains nuclear material or nuclear byproduct material belonging to another;

(5) with intent to compel any person, international organization, or governmental entity to do or refrain from doing any act, knowingly threatens to engage in conduct described in paragraph (2) (A) or (3) of this subsection;

(6) knowingly threatens to use nuclear material or nuclear byproduct material to cause death or serious bodily injury to any person or substantial damage to property or to the environment under circumstances in which the threat may reasonably be understood as an expression of serious purposes;

(7) attempts to commit an offense under paragraph (1), (2), (3), or (4) of this subsection; or

(8) is a party to a conspiracy of two or more persons to commit an offense under paragraph (1), (2), (3), or (4) of this subsection, if any of the parties intentionally engages in any conduct in furtherance of such offense;

shall be punished as provided in subsection (b) of this section.

(b) The punishment for an offense under—

(1) paragraphs (1) through (7) of subsection (a) of this section is—

(A) a fine under this title; and

(B) imprisonment—

(i) for any term of years or for life (I) if, while committing the offense, the offender knowingly causes the death of any person; or (II) if, while committing an offense under paragraph (1) or (3) of subsection (a) of this section, the offender, under circumstances manifesting extreme indifference to the life of an individual, knowingly engages in any conduct and thereby recklessly causes the death of or serious bodily injury to any person; and

(ii) for not more than 20 years in any other case; and

(2) paragraph (8) of subsection (a) of this section is—

(A) a fine under this title; and

(B) imprisonment—

(i) for not more than 20 years if the offense which is the object of the conspiracy is punishable under paragraph (1) (B) (i); and

(ii) for not more than 10 years in any other case.

(c) The circumstances referred to in subsection (a) of this section are that—

(1) the offense is committed in the United States or the special maritime and territorial jurisdiction of the United States, or the special aircraft jurisdiction of the United States (as defined in section 46501 of title 49);

(2) an offender or a victim is—

(A) a national of the United States; or

(B) a United States corporation or other legal entity;

(3) after the conduct required for the offense occurs the defendant is found in the United States, even if the conduct required for the offense occurs outside the United States;

(4) the conduct required for the offense occurs with respect to the carriage of a consignment of nuclear material or nuclear byproduct material by any means of transportation intended to go beyond the territory of the state where the shipment originates beginning with the departure from a facility of the shipper in that state and ending with the arrival at a facility of the receiver within the state of ultimate destination and either of such states is the United States; or

(5) either—

(A) the governmental entity under subsection (a)(5) is the United States; or

(B) the threat under subsection (a)(6) is directed at the United States.

(d) The Attorney General may request assistance from the Secretary of Defense under chapter 18 of title 10 in the enforcement of this section and the Secretary of Defense may provide such assistance in accordance with chapter 18 of title 10, except that the Secretary of Defense may provide such assistance through any Department of Defense personnel.

(e) **(1)** The Attorney General may also request assistance from the Secretary of Defense under this subsection in the enforcement of this section. Notwithstanding section 1385 of this title, the Secretary of Defense may, in accordance with other applicable law, provide such assistance to the Attorney General if—

(A) an emergency situation exists (as jointly determined by the Attorney General and the Secretary of Defense in their discretion); and

(B) the provision of such assistance will not adversely affect the military preparedness of the United States (as determined by the Secretary of Defense in such Secretary's discretion).

(2) As used in this subsection, the term "emergency situation" means a circumstance—

(A) that poses a serious threat to the interests of the United States; and

(B) in which—

(i) enforcement of the law would be seriously impaired if the assistance were not provided; and

(ii) civilian law enforcement personnel are not capable of enforcing the law.

(3) Assistance under this section may include—

(A) use of personnel of the Department of Defense to arrest persons and conduct searches and seizures with respect to violations of this section; and

(B) such other activity as is incidental to the enforcement of this section, or to the protection of persons or property from conduct that violates this section.

(4) The Secretary of Defense may require reimbursement as a condition of assistance under this section.

(5) The Attorney General may delegate the Attorney General's function under this subsection only to a Deputy, Associate, or Assistant Attorney General.

(f) As used in this section—

(1) the term "nuclear material" means material containing any—

(A) plutonium;

(B) uranium not in the form of ore or ore residue that contains the mixture of isotopes as occurring in nature;

(C) enriched uranium, defined as uranium that contains the isotope 233 or 235 or both in such amount that the abundance ratio of the sum of those isotopes to the isotope 238 is greater than the ratio of the isotope 235 to the isotope 238 occurring in nature; or

(D) uranium 233;

(2) the term "nuclear byproduct material" means any material containing any radioactive isotope created through an irradiation process in the operation of a nuclear reactor or accelerator;

(3) the term "international organization" means a public international organization designated as such pursuant to section 1 of the International Organizations Immunities Act (22 U.S.C. 288) or a public organization created pursuant to treaty or other agreement under international law as an instrument through or by which two or more foreign governments engage in some aspect of their conduct of international affairs;

(4) the term "serious bodily injury" means bodily injury which involves—

(A) a substantial risk of death;

(B) extreme physical pain;

(C) protracted and obvious disfigurement; or

(D) protracted loss or impairment of the function of a bodily member, organ, or mental faculty;

(5) the term "bodily injury" means—

(A) a cut, abrasion, bruise, burn, or disfigurement;

(B) physical pain;

(C) illness;

(D) impairment of a function of a bodily member, organ, or mental faculty; or

(E) any other injury to the body, no matter how temporary;

(6) the term "national of the United States" has the same meaning as in section 101(a)(22) of the Immigration and Nationality Act (8 U.S.C. 1101(a)(22)); and

(7) the term "United States corporation or other legal entity" means any corporation or other entity organized under the laws of the United States or any State, Commonwealth, territory, possession, or district of the United States.

(Added Pub.L. 97–351, § 2(a), Oct. 15, 1982, 96 Stat. 1663, and amended Pub.L. 100–690, Title VII, § 7022, Nov. 18, 1988, 102 Stat. 4397; Pub.L. 103–272, § 5(e)(6), July 5, 1994, 108 Stat. 1374; Pub.L. 103–322, Title XXXIII, § 330016(2)(C), Sept. 13, 1994, 108 Stat. 2148; Pub.L. 104–132, Title V, § 502, Apr. 24, 1996, 110 Stat. 1282.)

HISTORICAL AND STATUTORY NOTES

References in Text

Section 1 of the International Organizations Immunities Act, referred to in subsec. (f)(3), is classified to section 288 of Title 22, Foreign Relations and Intercourse.

Section 101(a)(22) of the Immigration and Nationality Act, referred to in subsec. (f)(6), is classified to section 1101(a)(22) of Title 8, Aliens and Nationality.

Short Title

1982 Amendments. Pub.L. 97–351, § 1, Oct. 15, 1982, 96 Stat. 1663, provided that: "This Act [enacting this section and amending 18 U.S.C.A. § 1116] may be cited as the 'Convention on the Physical Protection of Nuclear Material Implementation Act of 1982'."

Prior Provisions

A prior section 831 Acts June 25, 1948, c. 645, 62 Stat. 738; Sept. 6, 1960, Pub.L. 86–710, 74 Stat. 808; July 27, 1965, Pub.L. 89–95, 79 Stat. 285; Oct. 17, 1978, Pub.L. 95–473, § 2(a)(1)(A), 92 Stat. 1464, which defined terms used in this chapter, was repealed by Pub.L. 96–129, Title II, § 216(b), Nov. 30, 1979, 93 Stat. 1015. For savings provisions regarding former section 831, see section 218 of Pub.L. 96–129 set out as a note under former sections 832 to 835 of this title.

Findings and Purpose of Pub.L. 104–132, Title V

Section 501 of Pub.L. 104–132 provided that:

"(a) **Findings.**—The Congress finds that—

"(1) nuclear materials, including byproduct materials, can be used to create radioactive dispersal devices that are capable of causing serious bodily injury as well as substantial damage to property and to the environment;

"(2) the potential use of nuclear materials, including byproduct materials, enhances the threat posed by terrorist activities and thereby has a greater effect on the security interests of the United States;

"(3) due to the widespread hazards presented by the threat of nuclear contamination, as well as nuclear bombs, the United States has a strong interest in ensuring that persons who are engaged in the illegal acquisition and use of nuclear materials, including byproduct materials, are prosecuted for their offenses;

"(4) the threat that nuclear materials will be obtained and used by terrorist and other criminal organizations has increased substantially since the enactment in 1982 of the legislation that implemented the Convention on the Physical Protection of Nuclear Material, codified at section 831 of title 18, United States Code [this section];

"(5) the successful efforts to obtain agreements from other countries to dismantle nuclear weapons have resulted in increased packaging and transportation of nuclear materials, thereby decreasing the security of such materials by increasing the opportunity for unlawful diversion and theft;

"(6) the trafficking in the relatively more common, commercially available, and usable nuclear and byproduct materials creates the potential for significant loss of life and environmental damage;

"(7) report trafficking incidents in the early 1990's suggest that the individuals involved in trafficking in these materials from Eurasia and Eastern Europe frequently conducted their black market sales of these materials within the Federal Republic of Germany, the Baltic States, the former Soviet Union, Central Europe, and to a lesser extent in the Middle European countries;

"(8) the international community has become increasingly concerned over the illegal possession of nuclear and nuclear byproduct materials;

"(9) the potentially disastrous ramifications of increased access to nuclear and nuclear byproduct materials pose such a significant threat that the United States must use all lawful methods available to combat the illegal use of such materials;

"(10) the United States has an interest in encouraging United States corporations to do business in the countries that comprised the former Soviet Union, and in other developing democracies;

"(11) protection of such United States corporations from threats created by the unlawful use of nuclear materials is important to the success of the effort to encourage business ventures in these countries, and to further the foreign relations and commerce of the United States;

"(12) the nature of nuclear contamination is such that it may affect the health, environment, and property of United States nationals even if the acts that constitute the illegal activity occur outside the territory of the United States, and are primarily directed toward foreign nationals; and

"(13) there is presently no Federal criminal statute that provides adequate protection to United States interests from nonweapons grade, yet hazardous radioactive material, and from the illegal diversion of nuclear materials that are held for other than peaceful purposes.

"**(b) Purpose.**—The purpose of this title [Title V of Pub.L. 104–132 which enacted section 2332c of this title, amended this section and sections 175, 177, 178 and 2332a of this title and enacted provisions set out as notes under this section and section 262 of Title 42, The Public Health and Welfare, and section 1522 of Title 50, War and National Defense] is to provide Federal law enforcement agencies with the necessary means and the maximum authority permissible under the Constitution to combat the threat of nuclear contamination and proliferation that may result from the illegal possession and use of radioactive materials."

§ 832. Participation in nuclear and weapons of mass destruction threats to the United States

(a) Whoever, within the United States or subject to the jurisdiction of the United States, willfully participates in or knowingly provides material support or resources (as defined in section 2339A) to a nuclear weapons program or other weapons of mass destruction program of a foreign terrorist power, or attempts or conspires to do so, shall be imprisoned for not more than 20 years.

(b) There is extraterritorial Federal jurisdiction over an offense under this section.

(c) Whoever without lawful authority develops, possesses, or attempts or conspires to develop or possess a radiological weapon, or threatens to use or uses a radiological weapon against any person within the United States, or a national of the United States while such national is outside of the United States or against any property that is owned, leased, funded, or used by the United States, whether that property is within or outside of the United States, shall be imprisoned for any term of years or for life.

(d) As used in this section—

(1) "nuclear weapons program" means a program or plan for the development, acquisition, or production of any nuclear weapon or weapons;

(2) "weapons of mass destruction program" means a program or plan for the development, acquisition, or production of any weapon or weapons of mass destruction (as defined in section 2332a(c));

(3) "foreign terrorist power" means a terrorist organization designated under section 219 of the Immigration and Nationality Act, or a state sponsor of terrorism designated under section 6(j) of the Export Administration Act of 1979 or section 620A of the Foreign Assistance Act of 1961; and

(4) "nuclear weapon" means any weapon that contains or uses nuclear material as defined in section 831(f)(1).

(Added Pub.L. 108–458, Title VI, § 6803(c)(2), Dec. 17, 2004, 118 Stat. 3768.)

HISTORICAL AND STATUTORY NOTES

References in Text

Section 219 of the Immigration and Nationality Act, referred to in subsec. (d)(3), is Act June 27, 1952, c. 477, Title II, ch. 2, 219, as added Apr. 24, 1996, Pub.L. 104–132, Title III, § 302(a), 110 Stat. 1248, as amended, which is classified to 8 U.S.C.A. § 1189.

Section 6(j) of the Export Administration Act of 1979, referred to in subsec. (d)(3), is Pub.L. 96–72, § 6(j), Sept. 29, 1979, 93 Stat. 513, as amended, which is classified to 50 App. U.S.C.A. § 2405.

Section 620A of the Foreign Assistance Act of 1961, referred to in subsec. (d)(3), Pub.L. 87–195, Pt. III, § 620A, added Pub.L. 94–329, Title III, § 303, June 30, 1976, 90 Stat. 753, as amended, which is classified to 22 U.S.C.A. § 2371.

Prior Provisions

Section 832, Acts June 25, 1948, c. 645, 62 Stat. 738; Sept. 6, 1960, Pub.L. 86–710, 74 Stat. 809, related to the transportation of explosives, radioactive materials, etiologic agents, and other dangerous articles, was repealed by Pub.L. 96–129, Title II, § 216(b), Nov. 30, 1979, 93 Stat. 1015.

[§§ 833 to 835. Repealed. Pub.L. 96–129, Title II, § 216(b), Nov. 30, 1979, 93 Stat. 1015]

HISTORICAL AND STATUTORY NOTES

Section 833, Acts June 25, 1948, c. 645, 62 Stat. 739; Sept. 6, 1960, Pub.L. 86–710, 74 Stat. 810, related to the marking of packages containing explosives and other dangerous articles.

Section 834, Acts June 25, 1948, c. 645, 62 Stat. 739; Sept. 6, 1960, Pub.L. 86–710, 74 Stat. 810, related to the formulation of regulations by the Interstate Commerce Commission regarding transportation of explosives and other dangerous articles within the United States.

Section 835, Acts June 25, 1948, c. 645, 62 Stat. 739; Sept. 6, 1960, Pub.L. 86–710, 74 Stat. 811; Oct. 15, 1970, Pub.L. 91–452, Title II, § 222, 84 Stat. 929; Oct. 17, 1978, Pub.L. 95–473, § 2(a) (1) (B), 92 Stat. 1464, authorized the Interstate Commerce Commission to administer, execute and enforce all provisions of sections 831 to 835 of this title.

Savings Provisions

Pub.L. 96–129, Title II, § 218, Nov. 30, 1979, 93 Stat. 1015, which provided a savings provision for orders, determinations, rules, regulations, permits, contracts, certificates, licenses, and privileges issued, made, granted, or allowed to become effective under former sections 831 to 835 of this title, was repealed by Pub.L. 103–272, § 7(b), July 5, 1994, 108 Stat. 1379.

§ 836. Transportation of fireworks into State prohibiting sale or use

Whoever, otherwise than in the course of continuous interstate transportation through any State, transports fireworks into any State, or delivers them for transportation into any State, or attempts so to do, knowing that such fireworks are to be delivered, possessed, stored, transshipped, distributed, sold, or otherwise dealt with in a manner or for a use prohibited by the laws of such State specifically prohibiting or regulating the use of fireworks, shall be fined under this title or imprisoned not more than one year, or both.

This section shall not apply to a common or contract carrier or to international or domestic water carriers engaged in interstate commerce or to the transportation of fireworks into a State for the use of Federal agencies in the carrying out or the furtherance of their operations.

In the enforcement of this section, the definitions of fireworks contained in the laws of the respective States shall be applied.

As used in this section, the term "State" includes the several States, Territories, and possessions of the United States, and the District of Columbia.

This section shall be effective from and after July 1, 1954.

(Added June 4, 1954, c. 261, § 1, 68 Stat. 170, and amended Sept. 13, 1994, Pub.L. 103–322, Title XXXIII, § 330016(1)(H), 108 Stat. 2147.)

HISTORICAL AND STATUTORY NOTES

Fireworks for Agricultural Purposes

Section 3 of Act June 4, 1954 provided that this section should not be effective with respect to—

"(1) the transportation of fireworks into any State or Territory for use solely for agricultural purposes,

"(2) the delivery of fireworks for transportation into any State or Territory for use solely for agricultural purposes, or

"(3) any attempt to engage in any such transportation or delivery for use solely for agricultural purposes, until sixty days have elapsed after the commencement of the next regular session of the legislature of such State or Territory which begins after the date of enactment of this Act [June 4, 1954]."

[§ 837. Repealed. Pub.L. 91–452, Title XI, § 1106(b)(1), Oct. 15, 1970, 84 Stat. 960]

HISTORICAL AND STATUTORY NOTES

Section, Pub.L. 86–449, Title II, § 203, May 6, 1960, 74 Stat. 87, related to the illegal use or possession of explosives, and threats or false information concerning attempts to damage or destroy real or personal property by fire or explosives. See § 844 of this title.

CHAPTER 40—IMPORTATION, MANUFACTURE, DISTRIBUTION AND STORAGE OF EXPLOSIVE MATERIALS

Sec.

§ 841. Definitions

As used in this chapter—

(a) "Person" means any individual, corporation, company, association, firm, partnership, society, or joint stock company.

(b) "Interstate" or foreign commerce means commerce between any place in a State and any place outside of that State, or within any possession of the United States (not including the Canal Zone) or the District of Columbia, and commerce between places within the same State but through any place outside of that State. "State" includes the District of Columbia, the Commonwealth of Puerto Rico, and the possessions of the United States (not including the Canal Zone).

(c) "Explosive materials" means explosives, blasting agents, and detonators.

(d) Except for the purposes of subsections (d), (e), (f), (g), (h), (i), and (j) of section 844 of this title, "explosives" means any chemical compound mixture, or device, the primary or common purpose of which is to function by explosion; the term includes, but is not limited to, dynamite and other high explosives, black powder, pellet powder, initiating explosives, detonators, safety fuses, squibs, detonating cord, igniter cord, and igniters. The Attorney General shall publish and revise at least annually in the Federal Register a list of these and any additional explosives which he determines to be within the coverage of this chapter. For the purposes of subsections (d), (e), (f), (g), (h), and (i) of section 844 of this title, the term "explosive" is defined in subsection (j) of such section 844.

(e) "Blasting agent" means any material or mixture, consisting of fuel and oxidizer, intended for blasting, not otherwise defined as an explosive: *Provided,* That the finished product, as mixed for use or shipment, cannot be detonated by means of a numbered 8 test blasting cap when unconfined.

(f) "Detonator" means any device containing a detonating charge that is used for initiating detonation in an explosive; the term includes, but is not limited to, electric blasting caps of instantaneous and delay types, blasting caps for use with safety fuses and detonating-cord delay connectors.

(g) "Importer" means any person engaged in the business of importing or bringing explosive materials into the United States for purposes of sale or distribution.

(h) "Manufacturer" means any person engaged in the business of manufacturing explosive materials for purposes of sale or distribution or for his own use.

(i) "Dealer" means any person engaged in the business of distributing explosive materials at wholesale or retail.

(j) "Permittee" means any user of explosives for a lawful purpose, who has obtained either a user permit or a limited permit under the provisions of this chapter.

(k) "Attorney General" means the Attorney General of the United States.

(*l*) "Crime punishable by imprisonment for a term exceeding one year" shall not mean (1) any Federal or State offenses pertaining to antitrust violations, unfair trade practices, restraints of trade, or other similar offenses relating to the regulation of business practices as the Attorney General may by regulation designate, or (2) any State offense (other than one involving a firearm or explosive) classified by the laws of the State as a misdemeanor and punishable by a term of imprisonment of two years or less.

(m) "Licensee" means any importer, manufacturer, or dealer licensed under the provisions of this chapter.

(n) "Distribute" means sell, issue, give, transfer, or otherwise dispose of.

(*o*) "Convention on the Marking of Plastic Explosives" means the Convention on the Marking of Plastic Explosives for the Purpose of Detection, Done at Montreal on 1 March 1991.

(p) "Detection agent" means any one of the substances specified in this subsection when introduced into a plastic explosive or formulated in such explosive as a part of the manufacturing process in such a manner as to achieve homogeneous distribution in the finished explosive, including—

(1) Ethylene glycol dinitrate (EGDN), $C_2H_4(NO_3)_2$, molecular weight 152, when the minimum concentration in the finished explosive is 0.2 percent by mass;

(2) 2,3–Dimethyl–2,3–dinitrobutane (DMNB), $C_6H_{12}(NO_2)_2$, molecular weight 176, when the minimum concentration in the finished explosive is 0.1 percent by mass;

(3) Para-Mononitrotoluene (p–MNT), $C_7H_7NO_2$, molecular weight 137, when the minimum concentration in the finished explosive is 0.5 percent by mass;

(4) Ortho-Mononitrotoluene (*o*–MNT), $C_7H_7NO_2$, molecular weight 137, when the minimum concentration in the finished explosive is 0.5 percent by mass; and

(5) any other substance in the concentration specified by the Attorney General, after consultation with the Secretary of State and the Secretary of Defense, that has been added to the table in part 2 of the Technical Annex to the Convention on the Marking of Plastic Explosives.

(q) "Plastic explosive" means an explosive material in flexible or elastic sheet form formulated with one or more high explosives which in their pure form has a vapor pressure less than 10^{-4} Pa at a temperature of 25°C., is formulated with a binder material, and is as a mixture malleable or flexible at normal room temperature.

(r) "Alien" means any person who is not a citizen or national of the United States.

(s) "Responsible person" means an individual who has the power to direct the management and policies of the applicant pertaining to explosive materials.

(Added Pub.L. 91–452, Title XI, § 1102(a), Oct. 15, 1970, 84 Stat. 952, and amended Pub.L. 104–132, Title VI, § 602, Apr. 24, 1996, 110 Stat. 1288; Pub.L. 107–296, Title XI, §§ 1112(e)(1), (3), 1122(a), Nov. 25, 2002, 116 Stat. 2276, 2280.)

HISTORICAL AND STATUTORY NOTES

Effective and Applicability Provisions

2002 Acts. Amendment to this section by Pub.L. 107–296 effective 60 days after Nov. 25, 2002, see Pub.L. 107–296, § 4, set out as a note under 6 U.S.C.A. § 101.

Amendments to this section by Pub.L. 107–296, § 1122, effective 180 days after Nov. 25, 2002, see Pub.L. 107–296, § 1122(i), set out as an Effective and Applicability Provisions note under 18 U.S.C.A. § 843.

1996 Acts. Section 607 of Pub.L. 104–132 provided that: "Except as otherwise provided in this title [Title VI of Pub.L. 104–132, which amended this section and sections 842, 844, and 845 of this title and section 1595a of Title 19, Customs Duties], this title and the amendments made by this title shall take effect 1 year after the date of enactment of this Act [Apr. 24, 1996]."

Short Title

2002 Amendments. Pub.L. 107–296, Title XI, Subtitle C (§§ 1121 to 1128), § 1121, Nov. 25, 2002, 116 Stat. 2280, provided that: "This subtitle [amending this section and 18 U.S.C.A. §§ 843 to 845 and enacting provisions set out as a note under 18 U.S.C.A. § 843] may be referred to as the 'Safe Explosives Act'."

1982 Amendments. Pub.L. 97–298, § 1, Oct. 12, 1982, 96 Stat. 1319, provided: "That this Act [amending 18 U.S.C.A. § 844] may be cited as the 'Anti-Arson Act of 1982'."

1975 Amendments. Pub.L. 93–639, § 1, Jan. 4, 1975, 88 Stat. 2217, provided: "That this Act [amending 18 U.S.C.A. §§ 845 and 921] may be cited as 'Amendments of 1973 to Federal Law Relating to Explosives'."

Findings and Purposes of Pub.L. 104–132, Title VI

Pub.L. 104–132, Title VI, § 601, Apr. 24, 1996, 110 Stat. 1287, provided that:

"**(a) Findings.**—The Congress finds that—

"**(1)** plastic explosives were used by terrorists in the bombings of Pan American Airlines flight number 103 in December 1988 and UTA flight number 722 in September 1989;

"**(2)** plastic explosives can be used with little likelihood of detection for acts of unlawful interference with civil aviation, maritime navigation, and other modes of transportation;

"**(3)** the criminal use of plastic explosives places innocent lives in jeopardy, endangers national security, affects domestic tranquility, and gravely affects interstate and foreign commerce;

"**(4)** the marking of plastic explosives for the purpose of detection would contribute significantly to the prevention and punishment of such unlawful acts; and

"**(5)** for the purpose of deterring and detecting such unlawful acts, the Convention on the Marking of Plastic Explosives for the Purpose of Detection, Done at Montreal on 1 March 1991, requires each contracting State to adopt appropriate measures to ensure that plastic explosives are duly marked and controlled.

"**(b) Purpose.**—The purpose of this title [Title VI of Pub.L. 104–132, which amended this section and sections 842, 844, and 845 of this title and section 1595a of Title 19, Customs Duties, and enacted provisions set out as notes under this section] is to fully implement the Convention on the Marking of Plastic Explosives for the Purpose of Detection, Done at Montreal on 1 March 1991."

Marking, Rendering Inert, and Licensing of Explosive Materials Study

Pub.L. 104–132, Title VII, § 732, Apr. 24, 1996, 110 Stat. 1303, as amended Pub.L. 104–208, Div. A, Title I, § 101(a) [Title I, § 113], Sept. 30, 1996, 110 Stat. 3009–21, Pub.L. 105–61, Title I, Oct. 10, 1997, 111 Stat. 1272, provided that:

"**(a) Study.**—

"**(1) In general.**—Not later than 12 months after the date of enactment of this Act [Apr. 24, 1996], the Secretary of the Treasury (referred to in this section as the 'Secretary') shall conduct a study of—

"**(A)** the tagging of explosive materials for purposes of detection and identification;

"**(B)** the feasibility and practicability of rendering common chemicals used to manufacture explosive materials inert;

"**(C)** the feasibility and practicability of imposing controls on certain precursor chemicals used to manufacture explosive materials; and

"**(D)** State licensing requirements for the purchase and use of commercial high explosives, including—

"**(i)** detonators;

"**(ii)** detonating cords;

"**(iii)** dynamite;

"**(iv)** water gel;

"**(v)** emulsion;

"**(vi)** blasting agents; and

"**(vii)** boosters.

"**(2) Exclusion.**—No study conducted under this subsection or regulation proposed under subsection (e) shall include black or smokeless powder among the explosive materials considered.

"**(3) New prevention technologies.**—In addition to the study of taggants as provided herein, the Secretary, in consultation with the Attorney General, shall concurrently report to the Congress on the possible use, and exploitation of technologies such as vapor detection devices, computed tomography, nuclear quadropole resonance, thermal neutron analysis, pulsed fast-neutron analysis, and other technologies upon which recommendations to the Congress may be made for further study, funding, and use of the same in preventing and solving acts of terrorism involving explosive devices.

"**(b) Consultation.**—

"**(1) In general.**—In conducting the study under subsection (a), the Secretary shall consult with—

"**(A)** Federal, State, and local officials with expertise in the area of chemicals used to manufacture explosive materials; and

"**(B)** such other individuals as the Secretary determines are necessary.

"**(2) Fertilizer research centers.**—In conducting any portion of the study under subsection (a) relating to the regulation and use of fertilizer as a pre-explosive material, the Secretary of the Treasury shall consult with and receive input from non-profit fertilizer research centers.

"(c) **Report.**—Not later than 30 days after the completion of the study conducted under subsection (a), the Secretary shall submit a report to the Congress, which shall be made public, that contains—

"(1) the results of the study;

"(2) any recommendations for legislation; and

"(3) any opinions and findings of the fertilizer research centers.

"(d) **Hearings.**—Congress shall have not less than 90 days after the submission of the report under subsection (c) to—

"(1) review the results of the study; and

"(2) hold hearings and receive testimony regarding the recommendations of the Secretary.

"(e) **Regulations.**—

"(1) **In general.**—Not later than 6 months after the submission of the report required by subsection (c), the Secretary may submit to Congress and publish in the Federal Register draft regulations for the addition of tracer elements to explosive materials manufactured in or imported into the United States, of such character and in such quantity as the Secretary may authorize or require, if the results of the study conducted under subsection (a) indicate that the tracer elements—

"(A) will not pose a risk to human life or safety;

"(B) will substantially assist law enforcement officers in their investigative efforts;

"(C) will not substantially impair the quality of the explosive materials for their intended lawful use;

"(D) will not have a substantially adverse effect on the environment; and

"(E) the costs associated with the addition of the tracers will not outweigh benefits of their inclusion.

"(2) **Effective date.**—The regulations under paragraph (1) shall take effect 270 days after the Secretary submits proposed regulations to Congress pursuant to paragraph (1), except to the extent that the effective date is revised or the regulation is otherwise modified or disapproved by an Act of Congress.

"(f) **Special study.**—

"(1) **In general.**—Notwithstanding subsection (a), the Secretary of the Treasury shall enter into a contract with the National Academy of Sciences (referred to in this section as the 'Academy') to conduct a study of the tagging of smokeless and black powder by any viable technology for purposes of detection and identification. The study shall be conducted by an independent panel of 5 experts appointed by the Academy.

"(2) **Study elements.**—The study conducted under this subsection shall—

"(A) indicate whether the tracer elements, when added to smokeless and black powder—

"(i) will pose a risk to human life or safety;

"(ii) will substantially assist law enforcement officers in their investigative efforts;

"(iii) will impair the quality and performance of the powders (which shall include a broad and comprehensive sampling of all available powders) for their intended lawful use, including, but not limited to the sporting, defense, and handloading uses of the powders, as well as their use in display and lawful consumer pyrotechnics;

"(iv) will have a substantially adverse effect on the environment;

"(v) will incur costs which outweigh the benefits of their inclusion, including an evaluation of the probable production and regulatory cost of compliance to the industry, and the costs and effects on consumers, including the effect on the demand for ammunition; and

"(vi) can be evaded, and with what degree of difficulty, by terrorists or terrorist organizations, including evading tracer elements by the use of precursor chemicals to make black or other powders; and

"(B) provide for consultation on the study with Federal, State, and local officials, non-governmental organizations, including all national police organizations, national sporting organizations, and national industry associations with expertise in this area and such other individuals as shall be deemed necessary.

"(3) **Report and costs.**—The study conducted under this subsection shall be presented to Congress 2 years after the enactment of this subsection [Sept. 30, 1996] and be made available to the public, including any data tapes or data used to form such recommendations. There are authorized to be appropriated such sums as may be necessary to carry out the study."

Congressional Declaration of Purpose

Section 1101 of Pub.L. 91–452 provided that: "The Congress hereby declares that the purpose of this title [Title XI of Pub.L. 91–452] is to protect interstate and foreign commerce against interference and interruption by reducing the hazard to persons and property arising from misuse and unsafe or insecure storage of explosive materials. It is not the purpose of this title to place any undue or unnecessary Federal restrictions or burdens on law abiding citizens with respect to the acquisition, possession, storage, or use of explosive materials for industrial, mining, agricultural, or other lawful purposes, or to provide for the imposition by Federal regulations of any procedures or requirements other than those reasonably necessary to implement and effectuate the provisions of this title."

Modification of Other Provisions

Section 1104 of Pub.L. 91–452 provided that: "Nothing in this title [enacting this chapter, amending section 2516 of this title, repealing section 837 of this title and sections 121 to 144 of Title 50, U.S.C.A., War and National Defense, and enacting provisions set out as notes under this section] shall be construed as modifying or affecting any provision of—

"(a) The National Firearms Act (chapter 53 of the Internal Revenue Code of 1954) [chapter 53 of Title 26, Internal Revenue Code];

"(b) Section 414 of the Mutual Security Act of 1954 (22 U.S.C. 1934), as amended, relating to munitions control;

"(c) Section 1716 of title 18, United States Code [section 1716 of this title], relating to nonmailable materials;

"(d) Sections 831 through 836 of title 18, United States Code; or

"(e) Chapter 44 of title 18, United States Code."

Continuation in Business or Operation of Any Person Engaged in Business or Operation on October 15, 1970

Section 1105(c) of Pub.L. 91–452 provided that: "Any person (as defined in section 841(a) of title 18, United States Code) engaging in a business or operation requiring a license or permit under the provisions of chapter 40 of such title 18 who was engaged in such business or operation on the date of enactment of this Act [Oct. 15, 1970] and who has filed an application for a license or permit under the provisions of section 843 of such chapter 40 prior to the effective date of such section 843 [see section 1105(a), (b) of Pub.L. 91–452] may continue such business or operation pending final action on his application. All provisions of such chapter 40 shall apply to such applicant in the same manner and to the same extent as if he were a holder of a license or permit under such chapter 40."

Authorization of Appropriations

Section 1107 of Pub.L. 91–452 provided that: "There are hereby authorized to be appropriated such sums as are necessary to carry out the purposes of this title [enacting this chapter, amending section 2516 of this title, repealing section 837 of this title and sections 121 to 144 of Title 50, U.S.C.A., War and National Defense and enacting provisions set as notes under this section]."

§ 842. Unlawful acts

(a) It shall be unlawful for any person—

(1) to engage in the business of importing, manufacturing, or dealing in explosive materials without a license issued under this chapter;

(2) knowingly to withhold information or to make any false or fictitious oral or written statement or to furnish or exhibit any false, fictitious, or misrepresented identification, intended or likely to deceive for the purpose of obtaining explosive materials, or a license, permit, exemption, or relief from disability under the provisions of this chapter;

(3) other than a licensee or permittee knowingly—

(A) to transport, ship, cause to be transported, or receive any explosive materials; or

(B) to distribute explosive materials to any person other than a licensee or permittee; or

(4) who is a holder of a limited permit—

(A) to transport, ship, cause to be transported, or receive in interstate or foreign commerce any explosive materials; or

(B) to receive explosive materials from a licensee or permittee, whose premises are located outside the State of residence of the limited permit holder, or on more than 6 separate occasions, during the period of the permit, to receive explosive materials from 1 or more licensees or permittees whose premises are located within the State of residence of the limited permit holder.

(b) It shall be unlawful for any licensee or permittee to knowingly distribute any explosive materials to any person other than—

(1) a licensee;

(2) a holder of a user permit; or

(3) a holder of a limited permit who is a resident of the State where distribution is made and in which the premises of the transferor are located.

(c) It shall be unlawful for any licensee to distribute explosive materials to any person who the licensee has reason to believe intends to transport such explosive materials into a State where the purchase, possession, or use of explosive materials is prohibited or which does not permit its residents to transport or ship explosive materials into it or to receive explosive materials in it.

(d) It shall be unlawful for any person knowingly to distribute explosive materials to any individual who:

(1) is under twenty-one years of age;

(2) has been convicted in any court of a crime punishable by imprisonment for a term exceeding one year;

(3) is under indictment for a crime punishable by imprisonment for a term exceeding one year;

(4) is a fugitive from justice;

(5) is an unlawful user of or addicted to any controlled substance (as defined in section 102 of the Controlled Substances Act (21 U.S.C. 802));

(6) has been adjudicated a mental defective or who has been committed to a mental institution;

(7) is an alien, other than an alien who—

(A) is lawfully admitted for permanent residence (as defined in section 101 (a)(20) of the Immigration and Nationality Act);

(B) is in lawful nonimmigrant status, is a refugee admitted under section 207 of the Immigration and Nationality Act (8 U.S.C. 1157), or is in asylum status under section 208 of the Immigration and Nationality Act (8 U.S.C. 1158), and—

(i) is a foreign law enforcement officer of a friendly foreign government, as determined by the Secretary [1] in consultation with the Secretary of State, entering the United States on official law enforcement business, and the shipping, transporting, possession, or receipt of explosive materials is in furtherance of this official law enforcement business; or

(ii) is a person having the power to direct or cause the direction of the management and policies of a corporation, partnership, or association licensed pursuant to section 843(a), and the shipping, transporting, possession, or receipt of explosive materials is in furtherance of such power;

[(iii), (iv). Repealed. Pub.L. 108–177, Title III, § 372(a)(2)(B), Dec. 13, 2003, 117 Stat. 2627]

(C) is a member of a North Atlantic Treaty Organization (NATO) or other friendly foreign military force, as determined by the Attorney General in consultation with the Secretary of Defense, who is present in the United States under military orders for training or other military purpose authorized by the United States and the shipping, transporting, possession, or receipt of explosive materials is in furtherance of the authorized military purpose; or

(D) is lawfully present in the United States in cooperation with the Director of Central Intelligence, and the shipment, transportation, receipt, or possession of the explosive materials is in furtherance of such cooperation;

(8) has been discharged from the armed forces under dishonorable conditions;[2]

(9) having been a citizen of the United States, has renounced the citizenship of that person.

(e) It shall be unlawful for any licensee knowingly to distribute any explosive materials to any person in any State where the purchase, possession, or use by such person of such explosive materials would be in violation of any State law or any published ordinance applicable at the place of distribution.

(f) It shall be unlawful for any licensee or permittee willfully to manufacture, import, purchase, distribute, or receive explosive materials without making such records as the Attorney General may by regulation require, including, but not limited to, a statement of intended use, the name, date, place of birth, social security number or taxpayer identification number, and place of residence of any natural person to whom explosive materials are distributed. If explosive materials are distributed to a corporation or other business entity, such records shall include the identity and principal and local places of business and the name, date, place of birth, and place of residence of the natural person acting as agent of the corporation or other business entity in arranging the distribution.

(g) It shall be unlawful for any licensee or permittee knowingly to make any false entry in any record which he is required to keep pursuant to this section or regulations promulgated under section 847 of this title.

(h) It shall be unlawful for any person to receive, possess, transport, ship, conceal, store, barter, sell, dispose of, or pledge or accept as security for a loan, any stolen explosive materials which are moving as, which are part of, which constitute, or which have been shipped or transported in, interstate or foreign commerce, either before or after such materials were stolen, knowing or having reasonable cause to believe that the explosive materials were stolen.

(i) It shall be unlawful for any person—

(1) who is under indictment for, or who has been convicted in any court of, a crime punishable by imprisonment for a term exceeding one year;

(2) who is a fugitive from justice;

(3) who is an unlawful user of or addicted to any controlled substance (as defined in section 102 of the Controlled Substances Act (21 U.S.C. 802));

(4) who has been adjudicated as a mental defective or who has been committed to a mental institution;

(5) who is an alien, other than an alien who—

(A) is lawfully admitted for permanent residence (as that term is defined in section 101(a)(20) of the Immigration and Nationality Act);

(B) is in lawful nonimmigrant status, is a refugee admitted under section 207 of the Immigration and Nationality Act (8 U.S.C. 1157), or is in asylum status under section 208 of the Immigration and Nationality Act (8 U.S.C. 1158), and—

(i) is a foreign law enforcement officer of a friendly foreign government, as determined by the Secretary [1] in consultation with the Secretary of State, entering the United States on official law enforcement business, and the shipping, transporting, possession, or receipt of explosive materials is in furtherance of this official law enforcement business; or

(ii) is a person having the power to direct or cause the direction of the management and policies of a corporation, partnership, or association licensed pursuant to section 843(a), and the shipping, transporting, possession, or receipt of explosive materials is in furtherance of such power;

[(iii), (iv). Repealed. Pub.L. 108–177, Title III, § 372(b)(2)(B), Dec. 13, 2003, 117 Stat. 2627]

(C) is a member of a North Atlantic Treaty Organization (NATO) or other friendly foreign military force, as determined by the Attorney General in consultation with the Secretary of Defense, who is present in the United States under military orders for training or other military purpose authorized by the United States and the shipping, transporting, possession, or receipt of explosive materials is in furtherance of the authorized military purpose; or

(D) is lawfully present in the United States in cooperation with the Director of Central Intelligence, and the shipment, transportation, receipt, or possession of the explosive materials is in furtherance of such cooperation;

(6) who has been discharged from the armed forces under dishonorable conditions;[2]

(7) who, having been a citizen of the United States, has renounced the citizenship of that person[3]

to ship or transport any explosive in or affecting interstate or foreign commerce or to receive or possess any explosive which has been shipped or transported in or affecting interstate or foreign commerce.

(j) It shall be unlawful for any person to store any explosive material in a manner not in conformity with regulations promulgated by the Attorney General. In promulgating such regulations, the Attorney General shall take into consideration the class, type, and quantity of explosive materials to be stored, as well as the standards of safety and security recognized in the explosives industry.

(k) It shall be unlawful for any person who has knowledge of the theft or loss of any explosive materials from his stock, to fail to report such theft or loss within twenty-four hours of discovery thereof, to the Attorney General and to appropriate local authorities.

(*l*) It shall be unlawful for any person to manufacture any plastic explosive that does not contain a detection agent.

(m)(1) It shall be unlawful for any person to import or bring into the United States, or export from the United States, any plastic explosive that does not contain a detection agent.

(2) This subsection does not apply to the importation or bringing into the United States, or the exportation from the United States, of any plastic explosive that was imported or brought into, or manufactured in the United States prior to the date of enactment of this subsection by or on behalf of any agency of the United States performing military or police functions (including any military reserve component) or by or on behalf of the National Guard of any State, not later than 15 years after the date of entry into force of the Convention on the Marking of Plastic Explosives, with respect to the United States.

(n)(1) It shall be unlawful for any person to ship, transport, transfer, receive, or possess any plastic explosive that does not contain a detection agent.

(2) This subsection does not apply to—

(A) the shipment, transportation, transfer, receipt, or possession of any plastic explosive that was imported or brought into, or manufactured in the United States prior to the date of enactment of this subsection by any person during the period beginning on that date and ending 3 years after that date of enactment; or

(B) the shipment, transportation, transfer, receipt, or possession of any plastic explosive that was imported or brought into, or manufactured in the United States prior to the date of enactment of this subsection by or on behalf of any agency of the United States performing a military or police function (including any military reserve component) or by or on behalf of the National Guard of any State, not later than 15 years after the date of entry into force of the Convention on the Marking of Plastic Explosives, with respect to the United States.

(*o*) It shall be unlawful for any person, other than an agency of the United States (including any military reserve component) or the National Guard of any State, possessing any plastic explosive on the date of enactment of this subsection, to fail to report to the Attorney General within 120 days after such date of enactment the quantity of such explosives possessed, the manufacturer or importer, any marks of identification on such explosives, and such other information as the Attorney General may prescribe by regulation.

(p) Distribution of information relating to explosives, destructive devices, and weapons of mass destruction.—

(1) Definitions.—In this subsection—

(A) the term "destructive device" has the same meaning as in section 921(a)(4);

(B) the term "explosive" has the same meaning as in section 844(j); and

(C) the term "weapon of mass destruction" has the same meaning as in section 2332a(c)(2).

(2) Prohibition.—It shall be unlawful for any person—

(A) to teach or demonstrate the making or use of an explosive, a destructive device, or a weapon of mass destruction, or to distribute by any means information pertaining to, in whole or in part, the manufacture or use of an explosive, destructive device, or weapon of mass destruction, with the intent that the teaching, demonstration, or information be used for, or in furtherance of, an activity that constitutes a Federal crime of violence; or

(B) to teach or demonstrate to any person the making or use of an explosive, a destructive device, or a weapon of mass destruction, or to distribute to any person, by any means, information pertaining to, in whole or in part, the manufacture or use of an explosive, destructive device, or weapon of mass destruction, knowing that such person intends to use the teaching, demonstration, or information for, or in furtherance of, an activity that constitutes a Federal crime of violence.

(Added Pub.L. 91–452, Title XI, § 1102(a), Oct. 15, 1970, 84 Stat. 953, and amended Pub.L. 100–690, Title VI, § 6474(c),(d), Nov. 18, 1988, 102 Stat. 4380; Pub.L. 101–647, Title XXXV, § 3521, Nov. 29, 1990, 104 Stat. 4923; Pub.L. 103–322, Title XI, §§ 110508, 110516, Sept. 13, 1994, 108 Stat. 2018, 2020; Pub.L. 104–132, Title VI, § 603, Title VII, § 707, Apr. 24, 1996, 110 Stat. 1289, 1296; Pub.L. 106–54, § 2(a), Aug. 17, 1999, 113 Stat. 398; Pub.L. 107–296, Title XI,

§§ 1112(e)(3), 1122(b), 1123, Nov. 25, 2002, 116 Stat. 2276, 2280, 2283; Pub.L. 108–177, Title III, § 372, Dec. 13, 2003, 117 Stat. 2627.)

[1] So in original. Probably should be "Attorney General".

[2] So in original. Probably should be followed by "or".

[3] So in original. Probably should be followed by a semicolon.

HISTORICAL AND STATUTORY NOTES

References in Text

Section 102 of the Controlled Substances Act, referred to in subsecs. (d)(5) and (i)(3), is section 102 of Pub.L. 91–513, Title II, Oct. 27, 1970, 84 Stat. 1242, which is classified to section 802 of Title 21, Food and Drugs.

The Immigration and Nationality Act, referred to in subsec. (d)(7), is Act June 27, 1952, c. 477, 66 Stat. 163, as amended, which is classified principally to chapter 12 of Title 8, 8 U.S.C.A. § 1101 et seq. For complete classification, see Short Title note set out under 8 U.S.C.A. § 1101 and Tables.

Section 101(a)(20) of the Act, referred to in subsecs. (d)(7)(A) and (i)(5)(A), is classified to 8 U.S.C.A. § 1101(a)(20).

Section 207 of the Act, referred to in subsecs. (d)(7)(B) and (i)(5)(B), is classified to 8 U.S.C.A. § 1157.

Section 208 of the Act, referred to in subsecs. (d)(7)(B) and (i)(5)(B), is classified to 8 U.S.C.A. § 1158.

Effective and Applicability Provisions

2002 Acts. Amendment to this section by Pub.L. 107–296 effective 60 days after Nov. 25, 2002, see Pub.L. 107–296, § 4, set out as a note under 6 U.S.C.A. § 101.

Amendments to this section by Pub.L. 107–296, § 1122, effective 180 days after Nov. 25, 2002, see Pub.L. 107–296, § 1122(i), set out as an Effective and Applicability Provisions note under 18 U.S.C.A. § 843.

1996 Acts. Enactment of subsecs. (*l*), (m), (n), and (*o*) by section 603 of Pub.L. 104–132 effective Apr. 24, 1997, see section 607 of Pub.L. 104–132, set out as a note under section 841 of this title.

Change of Name

Reference to the Director of Central Intelligence or the Director of the Central Intelligence Agency in the Director's capacity as the head of the intelligence community deemed to be a reference to the Director of National Intelligence. Reference to the Director of Central Intelligence or the Director of the Central Intelligence Agency in the Director's capacity as the head of the Central Intelligence Agency deemed to be a reference to the Director of the Central Intelligence Agency. See Pub.L. 108–458, § 1081(a) and (b), set out as a note under 50 U.S.C.A. § 401.

§ 843. Licenses and user permits

(a) An application for a user permit or limited permit or a license to import, manufacture, or deal in explosive materials shall be in such form and contain such information as the Attorney General shall by regulation prescribe, including the names of and appropriate identifying information regarding all employees who will be authorized by the applicant to possess explosive materials, as well as fingerprints and a photograph of each responsible person. Each applicant for a license or permit shall pay a fee to be charged as set by the Attorney General, said fee not to exceed $50 for a limited permit and $200 for any other license or permit. Each license or user permit shall be valid for not longer than 3 years from the date of issuance and each limited permit shall be valid for not longer than 1 year from the date of issuance. Each license or permit shall be renewable upon the same conditions and subject to the same restrictions as the original license or permit, and upon payment of a renewal fee not to exceed one-half of the original fee.

(b) Upon the filing of a proper application and payment of the prescribed fee, and subject to the provisions of this chapter and other applicable laws, the Attorney General shall issue to such applicant the appropriate license or permit if—

(1) the applicant (or, if the applicant is a corporation, partnership, or association, each responsible person with respect to the applicant) is not a person described in section 842(i);

(2) the applicant has not willfully violated any of the provisions of this chapter or regulations issued hereunder;

(3) the applicant has in a State premises from which he conducts or intends to conduct business;

(4)(A) the Secretary [1] verifies by inspection or, if the application is for an original limited permit or the first or second renewal of such a permit, by such other means as the Secretary [1] determines appropriate, that the applicant has a place of storage for explosive materials which meets such standards of public safety and security against theft as the Attorney General by regulations shall prescribe; and

(B) subparagraph (A) shall not apply to an applicant for the renewal of a limited permit if the Secretary [1] has verified, by inspection within the preceding 3 years, the matters described in subparagraph (A) with respect to the applicant; and

(5) the applicant has demonstrated and certified in writing that he is familiar with all published State laws and local ordinances relating to explosive materials for the location in which he intends to do business;

(6) none of the employees of the applicant who will be authorized by the applicant to possess explosive materials is any person described in section 842(i); and

(7) in the case of a limited permit, the applicant has certified in writing that the applicant will not receive explosive materials on more than 6 separate occasions during the 12-month period for which the limited permit is valid.

(c) The Attorney General shall approve or deny an application within a period of 90 days for licenses and permits, beginning on the date such application is received by the Attorney General.

(d) The Attorney General may revoke any license or permit issued under this section if in the opinion of the Attorney General the holder thereof has violated any provision of this chapter or any rule or regulation prescribed by the Attorney General under this chapter, or has become ineligible to acquire explosive materials under section 842(d). The Secretary's [2] action under this subsection may be reviewed only as provided in subsection (e)(2) of this section.

(e)(1) Any person whose application is denied or whose license or permit is revoked shall receive a written notice from the Attorney General stating the specific grounds upon which such denial or revocation is based. Any notice of a revocation of a license or permit shall be given to the holder of such license or permit prior to or concurrently with the effective date of the revocation.

(2) If the Attorney General denies an application for, or revokes a license, or permit, he shall, upon request by the aggrieved party, promptly hold a hearing to review his denial or revocation. In the case of a revocation, the Attorney General may upon a request of the holder stay the effective date of the revocation. A hearing under this section shall be at a location convenient to the aggrieved party. The Attorney General shall give written notice of his decision to the aggrieved party within a reasonable time after the hearing. The aggrieved party may, within sixty days after receipt of the Secretary's written decision, file a petition with the United States court of appeals for the district in which he resides or has his principal place of business for a judicial review of such denial or revocation, pursuant to sections 701–706 of title 5, United States Code.

(f) Licensees and holders of user permits shall make available for inspection at all reasonable times their records kept pursuant to this chapter or the regulations issued hereunder, and licensees and permittees shall submit to the Attorney General such reports and information with respect to such records and the contents thereof as he shall by regulations prescribe. The Attorney General may enter during business hours the premises (including places of storage) of any licensee or holder of a user permit, for the purpose of inspecting or examining (1) any records or documents required to be kept by such licensee or permittee, under the provisions of this chapter or regulations issued hereunder, and (2) any explosive materials kept or stored by such licensee or permittee at such premises. Upon the request of any State or any political subdivision thereof, the Attorney General may make available to such State or any political subdivision thereof, any information which he may obtain by reason of the provisions of this chapter with respect to the identification of persons within such State or political subdivision thereof, who have purchased or received explosive materials, together with a description of such explosive materials. The Secretary [1] may inspect the places of storage for explosive materials of an applicant for a limited permit or, at the time of renewal of such permit, a holder of a limited permit, only as provided in subsection (b)(4).

(g) Licenses and user permits issued under the provisions of subsection (b) of this section shall be kept posted and kept available for inspection on the premises covered by the license and permit.

(h)(1) If the Secretary [1] receives, from an employer, the name and other identifying information of a responsible person or an employee who will be authorized by the employer to possess explosive materials in the course of employment with the employer, the Secretary [1] shall determine whether the responsible person or employee is one of the persons described in any paragraph of section 842(i). In making the determination, the Secretary [1] may take into account a letter or document issued under paragraph (2).

(2)(A) If the Secretary [1] determines that the responsible person or the employee is not one of the persons described in any paragraph of section 842(i), the Secretary [1] shall notify the employer in writing or electronically of the determination and issue, to the responsible person or employee, a letter of clearance, which confirms the determination.

(B) If the Secretary [1] determines that the responsible person or employee is one of the persons described in any paragraph of section 842(i), the Secretary [1] shall notify the employer in writing or electronically of the determination and issue to the responsible person or the employee, as the case may be, a document that—

(i) confirms the determination;

(ii) explains the grounds for the determination;

(iii) provides information on how the disability may be relieved; and

(iv) explains how the determination may be appealed.

(i) Furnishing of samples.—

(1) In general.—Licensed manufacturers and licensed importers and persons who manufacture or import explosive materials or ammonium nitrate shall, when required by letter issued by the Secretary [1], furnish—

(A) samples of such explosive materials or ammonium nitrate;

(B) information on chemical composition of those products; and

(C) any other information that the Secretary [1] determines is relevant to the identification of the explosive materials or to identification of the ammonium nitrate.

(2) **Reimbursement.**—The Secretary[1] shall, by regulation, authorize reimbursement of the fair market value of samples furnished pursuant to this subsection, as well as the reasonable costs of shipment.

(Added Pub.L. 91–452, Title XI, § 1102(a), Oct. 15, 1970, 84 Stat. 955, and amended Pub.L. 107–296, Title XI, §§ 1112(e)(3), 1122(c) to (h), 1124, Nov. 25, 2002, 116 Stat. 2276, 2280 to 2283, 2285.)

1 So in original. Probably should be "Attorney General".

2 So in original. Probably should be "Attorney General's".

HISTORICAL AND STATUTORY NOTES

References in Text

Sections 701 to 706 of title 5, United States Code, referred to in subsec. (e)(2), are §§ 701 to 706 of Title 5, Government Organization and Employees.

Effective and Applicability Provisions

2002 Acts. Amendment to this section by Pub.L. 107–296 effective 60 days after Nov. 25, 2002, see Pub.L. 107–296, § 4, set out as a note under 6 U.S.C.A. § 101.

Pub.L. 107–296, Title XI, § 1122(i), Nov. 25, 2002, 116 Stat. 2283, provided that:

"(1) **In general.**—The amendments made by this section [amending this section and 18 U.S.C.A. §§ 841 and 842] shall take effect 180 days after the date of enactment of this Act [Nov. 25, 2002].

"(2) **Exception.**—Notwithstanding any provision of this Act [the Homeland Security Act, Pub.L. 107–296, Nov. 25, 2002, 116 Stat. 2135; see Short Title note set out under 6 U.S.C.A. § 101 and Tables for complete classification], a license or permit issued under section 843 of title 18, United States Code [this section], before the date of enactment of this Act [Nov. 25, 2002], shall remain valid until that license or permit is revoked under section 843(d) [subsec. (d) of this section] or expires, or until a timely application for renewal is acted upon."

1970 Acts. Section effective 120 days after Oct. 15, 1970, see § 1105(a) of Pub.L. 91–452, set out as a note under § 841 of this tile.

Continuation in Business or Operation of Any Person Engaged in Business or Operation on October 15, 1970

Filing of application for a license or permit prior to the effective date of this section as authorizing any person engaged in a business or operation requiring a license or a permit on Oct. 15, 1970 to continue such business or operation pending final action on such application, see § 1195(c) of Pub.L. 91–452, set out as a note under § 841 of this title.

§ 844. Penalties

(a) Any person who—

(1) violates any of subsections (a) through (i) or (*l*) through (*o*) of section 842 shall be fined under this title, imprisoned for not more than 10 years, or both; and

(2) violates subsection (p)(2) of section 842, shall be fined under this title, imprisoned not more than 20 years, or both.

(b) Any person who violates any other provision of section 842 of this chapter shall be fined under this title or imprisoned not more than one year, or both.

(c)(1) Any explosive materials involved or used or intended to be used in any violation of the provisions of this chapter or any other rule or regulation promulgated thereunder or any violation of any criminal law of the United States shall be subject to seizure and forfeiture, and all provisions of the Internal Revenue Code of 1986 relating to the seizure, forfeiture, and disposition of firearms, as defined in section 5845(a) of that Code, shall, so far as applicable, extend to seizures and forfeitures under the provisions of this chapter.

(2) Notwithstanding paragraph (1), in the case of the seizure of any explosive materials for any offense for which the materials would be subject to forfeiture in which it would be impracticable or unsafe to remove the materials to a place of storage or would be unsafe to store them, the seizing officer may destroy the explosive materials forthwith. Any destruction under this paragraph shall be in the presence of at least 1 credible witness. The seizing officer shall make a report of the seizure and take samples as the Attorney General may by regulation prescribe.

(3) Within 60 days after any destruction made pursuant to paragraph (2), the owner of (including any person having an interest in) the property so destroyed may make application to the Attorney General for reimbursement of the value of the property. If the claimant establishes to the satisfaction of the Attorney General that—

(A) the property has not been used or involved in a violation of law; or

(B) any unlawful involvement or use of the property was without the claimant's knowledge, consent, or willful blindness,

the Attorney General shall make an allowance to the claimant not exceeding the value of the property destroyed.

(d) Whoever transports or receives, or attempts to transport or receive, in interstate or foreign commerce any explosive with the knowledge or intent that it will be used to kill, injure, or intimidate any individual or unlawfully to damage or destroy any building, vehicle, or other real or personal property, shall be imprisoned for not more than ten years, or fined under this title, or both; and if personal injury results to any person, including any public safety officer performing duties as a direct or proximate result of conduct prohibited by this subsection, shall be imprisoned for not more than twenty years or fined under this title, or both;

and if death results to any person, including any public safety officer performing duties as a direct or proximate result of conduct prohibited by this subsection, shall be subject to imprisonment for any term of years, or to the death penalty or to life imprisonment.

(e) Whoever, through the use of the mail, telephone, telegraph, or other instrument of interstate or foreign commerce, or in or affecting interstate or foreign commerce, willfully makes any threat, or maliciously conveys false information knowing the same to be false, concerning an attempt or alleged attempt being made, or to be made, to kill, injure, or intimidate any individual or unlawfully to damage or destroy any building, vehicle, or other real or personal property by means of fire or an explosive shall be imprisoned for not more than 10 years or fined under this title, or both.

(f)(1) Whoever maliciously damages or destroys, or attempts to damage or destroy, by means of fire or an explosive, any building, vehicle, or other personal or real property in whole or in part owned or possessed by, or leased to, the United States, or any department or agency thereof, or any institution or organization receiving Federal financial assistance, shall be imprisoned for not less than 5 years and not more than 20 years, fined under this title, or both.

(2) Whoever engages in conduct prohibited by this subsection, and as a result of such conduct, directly or proximately causes personal injury or creates a substantial risk of injury to any person, including any public safety officer performing duties, shall be imprisoned for not less than 7 years and not more than 40 years, fined under this title, or both.

(3) Whoever engages in conduct prohibited by this subsection, and as a result of such conduct directly or proximately causes the death of any person, including any public safety officer performing duties, shall be subject to the death penalty, or imprisoned for not less than 20 years or for life, fined under this title, or both.

(g)(1) Except as provided in paragraph (2), whoever possesses an explosive in an airport that is subject to the regulatory authority of the Federal Aviation Administration, or in any building in whole or in part owned, possessed, or used by, or leased to, the United States or any department or agency thereof, except with the written consent of the agency, department, or other person responsible for the management of such building or airport, shall be imprisoned for not more than five years, or fined under this title, or both.

(2) The provisions of this subsection shall not be applicable to—

(A) the possession of ammunition (as that term is defined in regulations issued pursuant to this chapter) in an airport that is subject to the regulatory authority of the Federal Aviation Administration if such ammunition is either in checked baggage or in a closed container; or

(B) the possession of an explosive in an airport if the packaging and transportation of such explosive is exempt from, or subject to and in accordance with, regulations of the Pipeline and Hazardous Materials Safety Administration for the handling of hazardous materials pursuant to chapter 51 of title 49.

(h) Whoever—

(1) uses fire or an explosive to commit any felony which may be prosecuted in a court of the United States, or

(2) carries an explosive during the commission of any felony which may be prosecuted in a court of the United States,

including a felony which provides for an enhanced punishment if committed by the use of a deadly or dangerous weapon or device shall, in addition to the punishment provided for such felony, be sentenced to imprisonment for 10 years. In the case of a second or subsequent conviction under this subsection, such person shall be sentenced to imprisonment for 20 years. Notwithstanding any other provision of law, the court shall not place on probation or suspend the sentence of any person convicted of a violation of this subsection, nor shall the term of imprisonment imposed under this subsection run concurrently with any other term of imprisonment including that imposed for the felony in which the explosive was used or carried.

(i) Whoever maliciously damages or destroys, or attempts to damage or destroy, by means of fire or an explosive, any building, vehicle, or other real or personal property used in interstate or foreign commerce or in any activity affecting interstate or foreign commerce shall be imprisoned for not less than 5 years and not more than 20 years, fined under this title, or both; and if personal injury results to any person, including any public safety officer performing duties as a direct or proximate result of conduct prohibited by this subsection, shall be imprisoned for not less than 7 years and not more than 40 years, fined under this title, or both; and if death results to any person, including any public safety officer performing duties as a direct or proximate result of conduct prohibited by this subsection, shall also be subject to imprisonment for any term of years, or to the death penalty or to life imprisonment.

(j) For the purposes of subsections (d), (e), (f), (g), (h), and (i) of this section and section 842(p), the term "explosive" means gunpowders, powders used for blasting, all forms of high explosives, blasting materials, fuzes (other than electric circuit breakers), detonators, and other detonating agents, smokeless powders, other explosive or incendiary devices within the meaning of paragraph (5) of section 232 of this title, and any chemical compounds, mechanical mixture, or device that contains any oxidizing and combustible units, or other ingredients, in such proportions, quantities, or packing that ignition by fire, by friction, by concussion, by percussion, or by detonation of the compound, mixture, or device or any part thereof may cause an explosion.

(k) A person who steals any explosives materials which are moving as, or are a part of, or which have moved in, interstate or foreign commerce shall be imprisoned for not more than 10 years, fined under this title, or both.

(*l*) A person who steals any explosive material from a licensed importer, licensed manufacturer, or licensed dealer, or from any permittee shall be fined under this title, imprisoned not more than 10 years, or both.

(m) A person who conspires to commit an offense under subsection (h) shall be imprisoned for any term of years not exceeding 20, fined under this title, or both.

(n) Except as otherwise provided in this section, a person who conspires to commit any offense defined in this chapter shall be subject to the same penalties (other than the penalty of death) as the penalties prescribed for the offense the commission of which was the object of the conspiracy.

(*o*) Whoever knowingly transfers any explosive materials, knowing or having reasonable cause to believe that such explosive materials will be used to commit a crime of violence (as defined in section 924(c)(3)) or drug trafficking crime (as defined in section 924(c)(2)) shall be subject to the same penalties as may be imposed under subsection (h) for a first conviction for the use or carrying of an explosive material.

(p) Theft reporting requirement.—

(1) In general.—A holder of a license or permit who knows that explosive materials have been stolen from that licensee or permittee, shall report the theft to the Secretary [1] not later than 24 hours after the discovery of the theft.

(2) Penalty.—A holder of a license or permit who does not report a theft in accordance with paragraph (1), shall be fined not more than $10,000, imprisoned not more than 5 years, or both.

(Added Pub.L. 91–452, Title XI, § 1102(a), Oct. 15, 1970, 84 Stat. 956, and amended Pub.L. 97–298, § 2, Oct. 12, 1982, 96 Stat. 1319; Pub.L. 98–473, Title II, § 1014, Oct. 12, 1984, 98 Stat. 2142; Pub.L. 100–690, Title VI, § 6474(a), (b), Nov. 18, 1988, 102 Stat. 4379, 4380; Pub.L. 101–647, Title XXXV, § 3522, Nov. 29, 1990, 104 Stat. 4924; Pub.L. 103–272, § 5(e)(7), July 5, 1994, 108 Stat. 1374; Pub.L. 103–322, Title VI, § 60003(a)(3), Title XI, §§ 110504(b), 110509, 110515(b), 110518(b), Title XXXII, §§ 320106, 320917(a), Title XXXIII, §§ 330016(1)(H), (K), (L), (N), Sept. 13, 1994, 108 Stat. 1969, 2016, 2018, 2020, 2111, 2129, 2147, 2148; Pub.L. 104–132, Title VI, § 604, Title VII, §§ 701, 706, 708(a), (c)(3), 724, Apr. 24, 1996, 110 Stat. 1289, 1291, 1295, 1296, 1297, 1300; Pub.L. 104–294, Title VI, § 603(a), Oct. 11, 1996, 110 Stat. 3503; Pub.L. 106–54, § 2(b), Aug. 17, 1999, 113 Stat. 399; Pub.L. 107–296, Title XI, §§ 1112(e)(3), 1125, 1127, Nov. 25, 2002, 116 Stat. 2276, 2285; Pub.L. 108–426, § 2(c)(6), Nov. 30, 2004, 118 Stat. 2424.)

[1] So in original. Probably should be "Attorney General".

HISTORICAL AND STATUTORY NOTES

Codifications

Section 603(a) of Pub.L. 104–294, which directed that subsec. (i) of this section be amended by striking out ",," each place it appeared and inserting a comma, was incapable of execution due to prior amendment of subsec. (i) by section 708(a)(4) of Pub.L. 104–132, see 1996 Amendments notes set out under this section.

Amendment to subsec. (i) by Pub.L. 104–132, § 708(a)(4)(B), which directed in part that "fined the greater of a fine" be struck out was executed by striking out "fined the greater of the fine", as the probable intent of Congress.

Effective and Applicability Provisions

2002 Acts. Amendment to this section by Pub.L. 107–296 effective 60 days after Nov. 25, 2002, see Pub.L. 107–296, § 4, set out as a note under 6 U.S.C.A. § 101.

1996 Acts. Amendment of subsec. (a) by section 604 of Pub.L. 104–132 effective Apr. 24, 1997, see section 607 of Pub.L. 104–132, set out as a note under section 841 of this title.

1994 Acts. Section 320917(b) of Pub.L. 103–322 provided that: "The amendment made by subsection (a) [amending subsec. (i) of this section] shall not apply to any offense described in the amendment that was committed more than 5 years prior to the date of enactment of this Act [Sept. 13, 1994]."

§ 845. Exceptions; relief from disabilities

(a) Except in the case of subsections [1] (*l*), (m), (n), or (*o*) of section 842 and subsections (d), (e), (f), (g), (h), and (i) of section 844 of this title, this chapter shall not apply to:

(1) aspects of the transportation of explosive materials via railroad, water, highway, or air that pertain to safety, including security, and are regulated by the Department of Transportation or the Department of Homeland Security;

(2) the use of explosive materials in medicines and medicinal agents in the forms prescribed by the official United States Pharmacopeia, or the National Formulary;

(3) the transportation, shipment, receipt, or importation of explosive materials for delivery to any agency of the United States or to any State or political subdivision thereof;

(4) small arms ammunition and components thereof;

(5) commercially manufactured black powder in quantities not to exceed fifty pounds, percussion caps, safety and pyrotechnic fuses, quills, quick and slow matches, and friction primers, intended to be used solely for sporting, recreational, or cultural purposes in antique firearms as defined in section 921(a)(16) of title 18 of the United States Code, or in antique devices as exempted from the term "destructive device" in section 921(a)(4) of title 18 of the United States Code; and

(6) the manufacture under the regulation of the military department of the United States of explosive materials for, or their distribution to or storage or possession by the military or naval services or other agencies of the United States; or to arsenals, navy yards, depots, or other establishments owned by, or operated by or on behalf of, the United States.

(b)(1) A person who is prohibited from shipping, transporting, receiving, or possessing any explosive under section 842(i) may apply to the Secretary [2] for relief from such prohibition.

(2) The Secretary [2] may grant the relief requested under paragraph (1) if the Secretary [2] determines that the circumstances regarding the applicability of section 842(i), and the applicant's record and reputation, are such that the applicant will not be likely to act in a manner dangerous to public safety and that the granting of such relief is not contrary to the public interest.

(3) A licensee or permittee who applies for relief, under this subsection, from the disabilities incurred under this chapter as a result of an indictment for or conviction of a crime punishable by imprisonment for a term exceeding 1 year shall not be barred by such disability from further operations under the license or permit pending final action on an application for relief filed pursuant to this section.

(c) It is an affirmative defense against any proceeding involving subsections (*l*) through (*o*) of section 842 if the proponent proves by a preponderance of the evidence that the plastic explosive—

(1) consisted of a small amount of plastic explosive intended for and utilized solely in lawful—

(A) research, development, or testing of new or modified explosive materials;

(B) training in explosives detection or development or testing of explosives detection equipment; or

(C) forensic science purposes; or

(2) was plastic explosive that, within 3 years after the date of enactment of the Antiterrorism and Effective Death Penalty Act of 1996, will be or is incorporated in a military device within the territory of the United States and remains an integral part of such military device, or is intended to be, or is incorporated in, and remains an integral part of a military device that is intended to become, or has become, the property of any agency of the United States performing military or police functions (including any military reserve component) or the National Guard of any State, wherever such device is located.

(3) For purposes of this subsection, the term "military device" includes, but is not restricted to, shells, bombs, projectiles, mines, missiles, rockets, shaped charges, grenades, perforators, and similar devices lawfully manufactured exclusively for military or police purposes.

(Added Pub.L. 91–452, Title XI, § 1102(a), Oct. 15, 1970, 84 Stat. 958, and amended Pub.L. 93–639, § 101, Jan. 4, 1975, 88 Stat. 2217; Pub.L. 104–132, Title VI, § 605, Apr. 24, 1996, 110 Stat. 1289; Pub.L. 107–296, Title XI, §§ 1112(e)(3), 1126, Nov. 25, 2002, 116 Stat. 2276, 2285; Pub.L. 109–59, Title VII, § 7127, Aug. 10, 2005, 119 Stat. 1909.)

[1] So in original. Probably should read "subsection".

[2] So in original. Probably should read "Attorney General".

HISTORICAL AND STATUTORY NOTES

Effective and Applicability Provisions

2002 Acts. Amendment to this section by Pub.L. 107–296 effective 60 days after Nov. 25, 2002, see Pub.L. 107–296, § 4, set out as a note under 6 U.S.C.A. § 101.

1996 Acts. Amendments of subsec. (a) and (a)(1) and enactment of subsec. (c) by Pub.L. 104–132 effective Apr. 24, 1997, see section 607 of Pub.L. 104–132, set out as a note under section 841 of this title.

§ 846. Additional powers of the Attorney General

(a) The Attorney General is authorized to inspect the site of any accident, or fire, in which there is reason to believe that explosive materials were involved, in order that if any such incident has been brought about by accidental means, precautions may be taken to prevent similar accidents from occurring. In order to carry out the purpose of this subsection, the Attorney General is authorized to enter into or upon any property where explosive materials have been used, are suspected of having been used, or have been found in an otherwise unauthorized location. Nothing in this chapter shall be construed as modifying or otherwise affecting in any way the investigative authority of any other Federal agency. In addition to any other investigatory authority they have with respect to violations of provisions of this chapter, the Federal Bureau of Investigation, together with the Bureau of Alcohol, Tobacco, Firearms, and Explosives, shall have authority to conduct investigations with respect to violations of subsection (d), (e), (f), (g), (h), or (i) of section 844 of this title.

(b) The Attorney General is authorized to establish a national repository of information on incidents involving arson and the suspected criminal misuse of explosives. All Federal agencies having information concerning such incidents shall report the information to the Attorney General pursuant to such regulations as deemed necessary to carry out the provisions of this subsection. The repository shall also contain information on incidents voluntarily reported to the Attorney General by State and local authorities.

(Added Pub.L. 91–452, Title XI, § 1102(a), Oct. 15, 1970, 84 Stat. 959, and amended Pub.L. 104–208, Div. A, Title I, § 101(f) [Title I, § 654(a)], Sept. 30, 1996, 110 Stat. 3009–369; Pub.L. 107–296, Title XI, § 1112(e)(2), (3), Nov. 25, 2002, 116 Stat. 2276.)

HISTORICAL AND STATUTORY NOTES

Effective and Applicability Provisions

2002 Acts. Amendment to this section by Pub.L. 107–296 effective 60 days after Nov. 25, 2002, see Pub.L. 107–296, § 4, set out as a note under 6 U.S.C.A. § 101.

1970 Acts. Section effective on Oct. 15, 1970, see section 1105(b) of Pub.L. 91–452, set out as a note under section 841 of this title.

Authorization of Appropriations For National Repository on Criminal Misuse of Explosives

Pub.L. 104–208, Div. A, Title I, § 101(f) [Title VI, § 654(b)], Sept. 30, 1996, 110 Stat. 3009–369, provided that: "There is authorized to be appropriated such sums as may be necessary to carry out the provisions of this subsection [amending this section]."

Certification of Explosives Detection Canines

Pub.L. 106–554, § 1(a)(3) [Title VI, § 626], Dec. 21, 2000, 114 Stat. 2763, 2763A–162, provided that: "Hereafter, the Secretary of the Treasury is authorized to establish scientific certification standards for explosives detection canines, and shall provide, on a reimbursable basis, for the certification of explosives detection canines employed by Federal agencies, or other agencies providing explosives detection services at airports in the United States."

Similar provisions were contained in the following prior appropriations Acts:

Pub.L. 106–58, Title VI, § 630, Sept. 29, 1999, 113 Stat. 473.

Pub.L. 105–277, Div. A, § 101(h) [Title VI, § 640], Oct. 21, 1998, 112 Stat. 2681–526

Pub.L. 105–61, Title VI, § 627, Oct. 10, 1997, 111 Stat. 1315.

Pub.L. 104–208, Div. A, Title I, § 101(f) [Title VI, § 653], Sept. 30, 1996, 110 Stat. 3009–369.

§ 847. Rules and regulations

The administration of this chapter shall be vested in the Attorney General. The Attorney General may prescribe such rules and regulations as he deems reasonably necessary to carry out the provisions of this chapter. The Attorney General shall give reasonable public notice, and afford to interested parties opportunity for hearing, prior to prescribing such rules and regulations.

(Added Pub.L. 91–452, Title XI, § 1102(a), Oct. 15, 1970, 84 Stat. 959, and amended Pub.L. 107–296, Title XI, § 1112(e)(3), Nov. 25, 2002, 116 Stat. 2276.)

HISTORICAL AND STATUTORY NOTES

Effective and Applicability Provisions

2002 Acts. Amendment to this section by Pub.L. 107–296 effective 60 days after Nov. 25, 2002, see Pub.L. 107–296, § 4, set out as a note under 6 U.S.C.A. § 101.

1970 Acts. Section effective on Oct. 15, 1970, see § 1105(b) of Pub.L. 91–452, set out as a note under § 841 of this title.

§ 848. Effect on State law

No provision of this chapter shall be construed as indicating an intent on the part of the Congress to occupy the field in which such provision operates to the exclusion of the law of any State on the same subject matter, unless there is a direct and positive conflict between such provision and the law of the State so that the two cannot be reconciled or consistently stand together.

(Added Pub.L. 91–452, Title XI, § 1102(a), Oct. 15, 1970, 84 Stat. 959.)

HISTORICAL AND STATUTORY NOTES

Effective and Applicability Provisions

1970 Acts. Section effective on Oct. 15, 1970, see § 1105(b) of Pub.L. 91–452, set out as a note under § 841 of this title.

§§ 849 to 870. Reserved for future legislation

CHAPTER 41—EXTORTION AND THREATS

Sec.

§ 871. Threats against President and successors to the Presidency

(a) Whoever knowingly and willfully deposits for conveyance in the mail or for a delivery from any post office or by any letter carrier any letter, paper, writing, print, missive, or document containing any threat to take the life of, to kidnap, or to inflict bodily harm upon the President of the United States, the President-elect, the Vice President or other officer next in the order of succession to the office of President of the United States, or the Vice President-elect, or knowingly and willfully otherwise makes any such threat against the President, President-elect, Vice President or other officer next in the order of succession to the office of President, or Vice President-elect, shall be fined under this title or imprisoned not more than five years, or both.

(b) The terms "President-elect" and "Vice President-elect" as used in this section shall mean such persons as are the apparent successful candidates for the offices of President and Vice President, respectively, as ascertained from the results of the general elections held to determine the electors of President and Vice President in accordance with title 3, United States Code, sections 1 and 2. The phrase "other officer next in the order of succession to the office of President" as used in this section shall mean the person next in the order of succession to act as President in accordance with title 3, United States Code, sections 19 and 20.

(June 25, 1948, c. 645, 62 Stat. 740; June 1, 1955, c. 115, § 1, 69 Stat. 80; Oct. 15, 1962, Pub.L. 87–829, § 1, 76 Stat. 956; Oct. 12, 1982, Pub.L. 97–297, § 2, 96 Stat. 1318; Sept. 13, 1994, Pub.L. 103–322, Title XXXIII, § 330016(1)(H), 108 Stat. 2147.)

HISTORICAL AND STATUTORY NOTES

Short Title

Pub.L. 106–544, § 1, Dec. 19, 2000, 114 Stat. 2715, provided that: "This Act [amending sections 879, 3056, and 3486 of this title, repealing section 3486A of this title, and enacting provisions set out as notes under section 3056 of this title, section 551 of Title 5, and section 566 of Title 28] may be cited as the 'Presidential Threat Protection Act of 2000'."

§ 872. Extortion by officers or employees of the United States

Whoever, being an officer, or employee of the United States or any department or agency thereof, or representing himself to be or assuming to act as such, under color or pretense of office or employment commits or attempts an act of extortion, shall be fined under this title or imprisoned not more than three years, or both; but if the amount so extorted or demanded does not exceed $1,000, he shall be fined under this title or imprisoned not more than one year, or both.

(June 25, 1948, c. 645, 62 Stat. 740; Oct. 31, 1951, c. 655, § 24(b), 65 Stat. 720; Sept. 13, 1994, Pub.L. 103–322, Title XXXIII, § 330016(1)(G), (K), 108 Stat. 2147; Oct. 11, 1996, Pub.L. 104–294, Title VI, § 606(a), 110 Stat. 3511.)

§ 873. Blackmail

Whoever, under a threat of informing, or as a consideration for not informing, against any violation of any law of the United States, demands or receives any money or other valuable thing, shall be fined under this title or imprisoned not more than one year, or both.

(June 25, 1948, c. 645, 62 Stat. 740; Sept. 13, 1994, Pub.L. 103–322, Title XXXIII, § 330016(1)(I), 108 Stat. 2147.)

§ 874. Kickbacks from public works employees

Whoever, by force, intimidation, or threat of procuring dismissal from employment, or by any other manner whatsoever induces any person employed in the construction, prosecution, completion or repair of any public building, public work, or building or work financed in whole or in part by loans or grants from the United States, to give up any part of the compensation to which he is entitled under his contract of employment, shall be fined under this title or imprisoned not more than five years, or both.

(June 25, 1948, c. 645, 62 Stat. 740; Sept. 13, 1994, Pub.L. 103–322, Title XXXIII, § 330016(1)(K), 108 Stat. 2147.)

§ 875. Interstate communications

(a) Whoever transmits in interstate or foreign commerce any communication containing any demand or request for a ransom or reward for the release of any kidnapped person, shall be fined under this title or imprisoned not more than twenty years, or both.

(b) Whoever, with intent to extort from any person, firm, association, or corporation, any money or other thing of value, transmits in interstate or foreign commerce any communication containing any threat to kidnap any person or any threat to injure the person of another, shall be fined under this title or imprisoned not more than twenty years, or both.

(c) Whoever transmits in interstate or foreign commerce any communication containing any threat to kidnap any person or any threat to injure the person of another, shall be fined under this title or imprisoned not more than five years, or both.

(d) Whoever, with intent to extort from any person, firm, association, or corporation, any money or other thing of value, transmits in interstate or foreign commerce any communication containing any threat to injure the property or reputation of the addressee or of another or the reputation of a deceased person or any threat to accuse the addressee or any other person of a crime, shall be fined under this title or imprisoned not more than two years, or both.

(June 25, 1948, c. 645, 62 Stat. 741; Nov. 10, 1986, Pub.L. 99–646, § 63, 100 Stat. 3614; Sept. 13, 1994, Pub.L. 103–322, Title XXXIII, § 330016(1)(G), (H), (K), 108 Stat. 2147.)

§ 876. Mailing threatening communications

(a) Whoever knowingly deposits in any post office or authorized depository for mail matter, to be sent or delivered by the Postal Service or knowingly causes to be delivered by the Postal Service according to the direction thereon, any communication, with or without a name or designating mark subscribed thereto, addressed to any other person, and containing any demand or request for ransom or reward for the release of any kidnapped person, shall be fined under this title or imprisoned not more than twenty years, or both.

(b) Whoever, with intent to extort from any person any money or other thing of value, so deposits, or causes to be delivered, as aforesaid, any communication containing any threat to kidnap any person or any threat to injure the person of the addressee or of another, shall be fined under this title or imprisoned not more than twenty years, or both.

(c) Whoever knowingly so deposits or causes to be delivered as aforesaid, any communication with or without a name or designating mark subscribed thereto, addressed to any other person and containing any threat to kidnap any person or any threat to injure the person of the addressee or of another, shall be fined under this title or imprisoned not more than five years, or both. If such a communication is addressed to a United States judge, a Federal law enforcement officer, or an official who is covered by section 1114, the individual shall be fined under this title, imprisoned not more than 10 years, or both.

(d) Whoever, with intent to extort from any person any money or other thing of value, knowingly so deposits or causes to be delivered, as aforesaid, any communication, with or without a name or designating mark subscribed thereto, addressed to any other person and containing any threat to injure the property or reputation of the addressee or of another, or the reputation of a deceased person, or any threat to accuse the addressee or any other person of a crime, shall be fined under this title or imprisoned not more than two years, or both. If such a communication is addressed to a United States judge, a Federal law enforcement officer, or an official who is covered by section 1114, the individual shall be fined under this title, imprisoned not more than 10 years, or both.

(June 25, 1948, c. 645, 62 Stat. 741; Aug. 12, 1970, Pub.L. 91–375, § 6(j)(7), 84 Stat. 777; Sept. 13, 1994, Pub.L. 103–322, Title XXXIII, §§ 330016(1)(G), (H), (K), 330021(2), 108 Stat. 2147, 2150; Nov. 2, 2002, Pub.L. 107–273, Div. C, Title I, § 11008(d), 116 Stat. 1818.)

HISTORICAL AND STATUTORY NOTES

Effective and Applicability Provisions

1970 Acts. Amendment by Pub.L. 91–375 effective within 1 year after Aug. 12, 1970, on date established therefor by the Board of Governors of the United States Postal Service and published by it in the Federal Register, see § 15(a) of Pub.L. 91–375, set out as a note preceding § 101 of Title 39, Postal Service.

§ 877. Mailing threatening communications from foreign country

Whoever knowingly deposits in any post office or authorized depository for mail matter of any foreign country any communication addressed to any person within the United States, for the purpose of having such communication delivered by the post office establishment of such foreign country to the Postal Service and by it delivered to such addressee in the United States, and as a result thereof such communication is delivered by the post office establishment of such foreign country to the Postal Service and by it delivered to the address to which it is directed in the United States, and containing any demand or request for ransom or reward for the release of any kidnapped person, shall be fined under this title or imprisoned not more than twenty years, or both.

Whoever, with intent to extort from any person any money or other thing of value, so deposits as aforesaid, any communication for the purpose aforesaid, containing any threat to kidnap any person or any threat to injure the person of the addressee or of another, shall be fined under this title or imprisoned not more than twenty years, or both.

Whoever knowingly so deposits as aforesaid, any communication, for the purpose aforesaid, containing any threat to kidnap any person or any threat to injure the person of the addressee or of another, shall be fined under this title or imprisoned not more than five years, or both.

Whoever, with intent to extort from any person any money or other thing of value, knowingly so deposits as aforesaid, any communication, for the purpose aforesaid, containing any threat to injure the property or reputation of the addressee or of another, or the reputation of a deceased person, or any threat to accuse the addressee or any other person of a crime, shall be fined under this title or imprisoned not more than two years, or both.

(June 25, 1948, c. 645, 62 Stat. 741; Aug. 12, 1970, Pub.L. 91–375, § 6(j)(8), 84 Stat. 777; Sept. 13, 1994, Pub.L. 103–322, Title XXXIII, §§ 330016(1)(G), (H), (K), 330021(2), 108 Stat. 2147, 2150.)

HISTORICAL AND STATUTORY NOTES

Effective and Applicability Provisions

1970 Acts. Amendment by Pub.L. 91–375 effective within 1 year after Aug. 12, 1970, on date established therefor by the Board of Governors of the United States Postal Service and published by it in the Federal Register, see § 15(a) of Pub.L. 91–375, set out as a note preceding § 101 of Title 39, Postal Service.

§ 878. Threats and extortion against foreign officials, official guests, or internationally protected persons

(a) Whoever knowingly and willfully threatens to violate section 112, 1116, or 1201 shall be fined under this title or imprisoned not more than five years, or both, except that imprisonment for a threatened assault shall not exceed three years.

(b) Whoever in connection with any violation of subsection (a) or actual violation of section 112, 1116, or 1201 makes any extortionate demand shall be fined under this title or imprisoned not more than twenty years, or both.

(c) For the purpose of this section "foreign official", "internationally protected person", "national of the United States", and "official guest" shall have the same meanings as those provided in section 1116(a) of this title.

(d) If the victim of an offense under subsection (a) is an internationally protected person outside the United States, the United States may exercise jurisdiction over the offense if (1) the victim is a representative, officer, employee, or agent of the United States, (2) an offender is a national of the United States, or (3) an offender is afterwards found in the United States. As used in this subsection, the United States includes all areas under the jurisdiction of the United States including any of the places within the provisions of sections 5 and 7 of this title and section 46501(2) of title 49.

(Added Pub.L. 94–467, § 8, Oct. 8, 1976, 90 Stat. 2000, and amended Pub.L. 95–163, § 17(b)(1), Nov. 9, 1977, 91 Stat. 1286; Pub.L. 95–504, § 2(b), Oct. 24, 1978, 92 Stat. 1705; Pub.L. 103–272, § 5(e)(2), July 5, 1994, 108 Stat. 1373; Pub.L. 103–322, Title XXXIII, § 330016(1)(K), (N), Sept. 13, 1994, 108 Stat. 2147, 2148; Pub.L. 104–132, Title VII, §§ 705(a)(4), 721(e), Apr. 24, 1996, 110 Stat. 1295, 1299.)

§ 879. Threats against former Presidents and certain other persons

(a) Whoever knowingly and willfully threatens to kill, kidnap, or inflict bodily harm upon—

(1) a former President or a member of the immediate family of a former President;

(2) a member of the immediate family of the President, the President-elect, the Vice President, or the Vice President-elect;

(3) a major candidate for the office of President or Vice President, or a member of the immediate family of such candidate; or

(4) a person protected by the Secret Service under section 3056(a)(6);

shall be fined under this title or imprisoned not more than 5 years, or both.

(b) As used in this section—

(1) the term "immediate family" means—

(A) with respect to subsection (a)(1) of this section, the wife of a former President during his lifetime, the widow of a former President until her death or remarriage, and minor children of a former President until they reach sixteen years of age; and

(B) with respect to subsection (a)(2) and (a)(3) of this section, a person to whom the President, President-elect, Vice President, Vice President-elect, or major candidate for the office of President or Vice President—

(i) is related by blood, marriage, or adoption; or

(ii) stands in loco parentis;

(2) the term "major candidate for the office of President or Vice President" means a candidate referred to in subsection (a)(7) of section 3056 of this title; and

(3) the terms "President-elect" and "Vice President-elect" have the meanings given those terms in section 871(b) of this title.

(Added Pub.L. 97–297, § 1(a), Oct. 12, 1982, 96 Stat. 1317, and amended Pub.L. 98–587, § 3(a), Oct. 30, 1984, 98 Stat. 3111; Pub.L. 103–322, Title XXXIII, § 330016(1)(H), Sept. 13, 1994, 108 Stat. 2147; Pub.L. 106–544, § 2(a), (b)(1), Dec. 19, 2000, 114 Stat. 2715.)

HISTORICAL AND STATUTORY NOTES

Transfer of Functions

For transfer of the functions, personnel, assets, and obligations of the United States Secret Service, including the functions of the Secretary of the Treasury relating thereto, to the Secretary of Homeland Security, and for treatment of related references, see 6 U.S.C.A. §§ 381, 551(d), 552(d) and 557, and the Department of Homeland Security Reorganization Plan of November 25, 2002, as modified, set out as a note under 6 U.S.C.A. § 542.

§ 880. Receiving the proceeds of extortion

A person who receives, possesses, conceals, or disposes of any money or other property which was obtained from the commission of any offense under this chapter that is punishable by imprisonment for more than 1 year, knowing the same to have been unlawfully obtained, shall be imprisoned not more than 3 years, fined under this title, or both.

(Added Pub.L. 103–322, Title XXXII, § 320601(a)(1), Sept. 13, 1994, 108 Stat. 2115.)

CHAPTER 42—EXTORTIONATE CREDIT TRANSACTIONS

Sec.

§ 891. Definitions and rules of construction

For the purposes of this chapter:

(1) To extend credit means to make or renew any loan, or to enter into any agreement, tacit or express, whereby the repayment or satisfaction of any debt or claim, whether acknowledged or disputed, valid or invalid, and however arising, may or will be deferred.

(2) The term "creditor", with reference to any given extension of credit, refers to any person making that extension of credit, or to any person claiming by, under, or through any person making that extension of credit.

(3) The term "debtor", with reference to any given extension of credit, refers to any person to whom that extension of credit is made, or to any person who guarantees the repayment of that extension of credit, or in any manner undertakes to indemnify the creditor against loss resulting from the failure of any person to whom that extension of credit is made to repay the same.

(4) The repayment of any extension of credit includes the repayment, satisfaction, or discharge in whole or in part of any debt or claim, acknowledged or disputed, valid or invalid, resulting from or in connection with that extension of credit.

(5) To collect an extension of credit means to induce in any way any person to make repayment thereof.

(6) An extortionate extension of credit is any extension of credit with respect to which it is the understanding of the creditor and the debtor at the time it is made that delay in making repayment or failure to make repayment could result in the use of violence or other criminal means to cause harm to the person, reputation, or property of any person.

(7) An extortionate means is any means which involves the use, or an express or implicit threat of use, of violence or other criminal means to cause harm to the person, reputation, or property of any person.

(8) The term "State" includes the District of Columbia, the Commonwealth of Puerto Rico, and territories and possessions of the United States.

(9) State law, including conflict of laws rules, governing the enforceability through civil judicial processes of repayment of any extension of credit or the performance of any promise given in consideration thereof shall be judicially noticed. This paragraph does not impair any authority which any court would otherwise have to take judicial notice of any matter of State law.

(Added Pub.L. 90–321, Title II, § 202(a), May 29, 1968, 82 Stat. 160.)

HISTORICAL AND STATUTORY NOTES

Effective and Applicability Provisions

1970 Acts. Section effective May 29, 1968, see § 504(a) of Pub.L. 90–321, set out as a note under § 1601 of Title 15, Commerce and Trade.

Congressional Findings and Declaration of Purpose

Section 201 of Pub.L. 90–321 provided that:

"**(a)** The Congress makes the following findings:

"(1) Organized crime is interstate and international in character. Its activities involve many billions of dollars each year. It is directly responsible for murders, willful injuries to person and property, corruption of officials, and terrorization of countless citizens. A substantial part of the income of organized crime is generated by extortionate credit transactions.

"(2) Extortionate credit transactions are characterized by the use, or the express or implicit threat of the use, of violence or other criminal means to cause harm to person, reputation, or property as a means of enforcing repayment. Among the factors which have rendered past efforts at prosecution almost wholly ineffective has been the existence of exclusionary rules of evidence stricter than necessary for the protection of constitutional rights.

"(3) Extortionate credit transactions are carried on to a substantial extent in interstate and foreign commerce and through the means and instrumentalities of such commerce. Even where extortionate credit transactions are purely intrastate in character, they nevertheless directly affect interstate and foreign commerce.

"(4) Extortionate credit transactions directly impair the effectiveness and frustrate the purposes of the laws enacted by the Congress on the subject of bankruptcies.

"**(b)** On the basis of the findings stated in subsection (a) of this section, the Congress determines that the provisions of chapter 42 of title 18 of the United States Code [this chapter] are necessary and proper for the purpose of carrying into execution the powers of Congress to regulate commerce and to establish uniform and effective laws on the subject of bankruptcy."

Annual Report to Congress by Attorney General

Section 203 of Pub.L. 90–321, which had directed the Attorney General to make an annual report to Congress of the activities of the Department of Justice in the enforcement of this chapter, was repealed by Pub.L. 97–375, Title I, § 109(b), Dec. 21, 1982, 96 Stat. 1820.

§ 892. Making extortionate extensions of credit

(a) Whoever makes any extortionate extension of credit, or conspires to do so, shall be fined under this title or imprisoned not more than 20 years, or both.

(b) In any prosecution under this section, if it is shown that all of the following factors were present in connection with the extension of credit in question, there is prima facie evidence that the extension of credit was extortionate, but this subsection is nonexclusive and in no way limits the effect or applicability of subsection (a):

(1) The repayment of the extension of credit, or the performance of any promise given in consideration thereof, would be unenforceable, through civil judicial processes against the debtor

(A) in the jurisdiction within which the debtor, if a natural person, resided or

(B) in every jurisdiction within which the debtor, if other than a natural person, was incorporated or qualified to do business

at the time the extension of credit was made.

(2) The extension of credit was made at a rate of interest in excess of an annual rate of 45 per centum calculated according to the actuarial method of allocating payments made on a debt between principal and interest, pursuant to which a payment is applied first to the accumulated interest and the balance is applied to the unpaid principal.

(3) At the time the extension of credit was made, the debtor reasonably believed that either

(A) one or more extensions of credit by the creditor had been collected or attempted to be collected by extortionate means, or the nonrepayment thereof had been punished by extortionate means; or

(B) the creditor had a reputation for the use of extortionate means to collect extensions of credit or to punish the nonrepayment thereof.

(4) Upon the making of the extension of credit, the total of the extensions of credit by the creditor to the debtor then outstanding, including any unpaid interest or similar charges, exceeded $100.

(c) In any prosecution under this section, if evidence has been introduced tending to show the existence of any of the circumstances described in subsection (b)(1) or (b)(2), and direct evidence of the actual belief of the debtor as to the creditor's collection practices is not available, then for the purpose of showing the understanding of the debtor and the creditor at the time the extension of credit was made, the court may in its discretion allow evidence to be introduced tending to show the reputation as to collection practices of the creditor in any community of which the debtor was a member at the time of the extension.

(Added Pub.L. 90–321, Title II, § 202(a), May 29, 1968, 82 Stat. 160, and amended Pub.L. 103–322, Title XXXIII, § 330016(1)(L), Sept. 13, 1994, 108 Stat. 2147.)

HISTORICAL AND STATUTORY NOTES

Effective and Applicability Provisions

1968 Acts. Section effective May 29, 1968, see § 504(a) of Pub.L. 90–321, set out as a note under § 1601 of Title 15, Commerce and Trade.

§ 893. Financing extortionate extensions of credit

Whoever willfully advances money or property, whether as a gift, as a loan, as an investment, pursuant to a partnership or profit-sharing agreement, or otherwise, to any person, with reasonable grounds to believe that it is the intention of that person to use the money or property so advanced directly or indirectly for the purpose of making extortionate extensions of credit, shall be fined under this title or an amount not exceeding twice the value of the money or property so advanced, whichever is greater, or shall be imprisoned not more than 20 years, or both.

(Added Pub.L. 90–321, Title II, § 202(a), May 29, 1968, 82 Stat. 161, and amended Pub.L. 103–322, Title XXXIII, § 330016(1)(L), Sept. 13, 1994, 108 Stat. 2147.)

HISTORICAL AND STATUTORY NOTES

Effective and Applicability Provisions

1968 Acts. Section effective May 29, 1968, see § 504(a) of Pub.L. 90–321, set out as a note under § 1601 of Title 15, Commerce and Trade.

§ 894. Collection of extensions of credit by extortionate means

(a) Whoever knowingly participates in any way, or conspires to do so, in the use of any extortionate means

(1) to collect or attempt to collect any extension of credit, or

(2) to punish any person for the nonrepayment thereof,

shall be fined under this title or imprisoned not more than 20 years, or both.

(b) In any prosecution under this section, for the purpose of showing an implicit threat as a means of collection, evidence may be introduced tending to show that one or more extensions of credit by the creditor were, to the knowledge of the person against whom the implicit threat was alleged to have been made, collected or attempted to be collected by extortionate means or that the nonrepayment thereof was punished by extortionate means.

(c) In any prosecution under this section, if evidence has been introduced tending to show the existence, at the time the extension of credit in question was made, of the circumstances described in section 892(b)(1) or the circumstances described in section 892(b)(2), and direct evidence of the actual belief of the debtor as to the creditor's collection practices is not available, then for the purpose of showing that words or other means of communication, shown to have been employed as a means of collection, in fact carried an express or implicit threat, the court may in its discretion allow evidence to be introduced tending to show the reputation of the defendant in any community of which the person against whom the alleged threat was made was a member at the time of the collection or attempt at collection.

(Added Pub.L. 90–321, Title II, § 202(a), May 29, 1968, 82 Stat. 161, and amended Pub.L. 103–322, Title XXXIII, § 330016(1)(L), Sept. 13, 1994, 108 Stat. 2147.)

HISTORICAL AND STATUTORY NOTES

Effective and Applicability Provisions

1968 Acts. Section effective May 29, 1968, see § 504(a) of Pub.L. 90–321, set out as a note under § 1601 of Title 15, Commerce and Trade.

[§ 895. Repealed. Pub.L. 91–452, Title II, § 223(a), Oct. 15, 1970, 84 Stat. 929]

HISTORICAL AND STATUTORY NOTES

Section, Pub.L. 90–321, Title II, § 202(a), May 29, 1968, 82 Stat. 162, related to the immunity from prosecution of any witness compelled to testify or produce evidence after claiming his privilege against self-incrimination. See § 6001 et seq. of this title.

Effective Date of Repeal

Repeal of section effective on the sixtieth day following Oct. 15, 1970, see § 260 of Pub.L. 91–452, set out as a note under § 6001 of this title.

Savings Provisions

Repeal of this section by Pub.L. 91–452 not to affect any immunity to which any individual was entitled under this section by reason of any testimony given before the sixtieth day following Oct. 15, 1970, see § 260 of Pub.L. 91–452, set out as a note under § 6001 of this title.

§ 896. Effect on State laws

This chapter does not preempt any field of law with respect to which State legislation would be permissible in the absence of this chapter. No law of any State which would be valid in the absence of this chapter may be held invalid or inapplicable by virtue of the existence of this chapter, and no officer, agency, or instrumentality of any State may be deprived by virtue of this chapter of any jurisdiction over any offense over which it would have jurisdiction in the absence of this chapter.

(Added Pub.L. 90–321, Title II, § 202(a), May 29, 1968, 82 Stat. 162.)

HISTORICAL AND STATUTORY NOTES

Effective and Applicability Provisions

1968 Acts. Section effective May 29, 1968, see § 504(a) of Pub.L. 90–321, set out as a note under § 1601 of Title 15, Commerce and Trade.

CHAPTER 43—FALSE PERSONATION

§ 911. Citizen of the United States

Whoever falsely and willfully represents himself to be a citizen of the United States shall be fined under this title or imprisoned not more than three years, or both.

(June 25, 1948, c. 645, 62 Stat. 742; Sept. 13, 1994, Pub.L. 103–322, Title XXXIII, § 330016(1)(H), 108 Stat. 2147.)

§ 912. Officer or employee of the United States

Whoever falsely assumes or pretends to be an officer or employee acting under the authority of the United States or any department, agency or officer thereof, and acts as such, or in such pretended character demands or obtains any money, paper, document, or thing of value, shall be fined under this title or imprisoned not more than three years, or both.

(June 25, 1948, c. 645, 62 Stat. 742; Sept. 13, 1994, Pub.L. 103–322, Title XXXIII, § 330016(1)(H), 108 Stat. 2147.)

§ 913. Impersonator making arrest or search

Whoever falsely represents himself to be an officer, agent, or employee of the United States, and in such assumed character arrests or detains any person or in any manner searches the person, buildings, or other property of any person, shall be fined under this title or imprisoned not more than three years, or both.

(June 25, 1948, c. 645, 62 Stat. 742; Sept. 13, 1994, Pub.L. 103–322, Title XXXIII, § 330016(1)(H), 108 Stat. 2147.)

§ 914. Creditors of the United States

Whoever falsely personates any true and lawful holder of any share or sum in the public stocks or debt of the United States, or any person entitled to any annuity, dividend, pension, wages, or other debt due from the United States, and, under color of such false personation, transfers or endeavors to transfer such public stock or any part thereof, or receives or endeavors to receive the money of such true and lawful holder thereof, or the money of any person really entitled to receive such annuity, dividend, pension, wages, or other debt, shall be fined under this title or imprisoned not more than five years, or both.

(June 25, 1948, c. 645, 62 Stat. 742; Sept. 13, 1994, Pub.L. 103–322, Title XXXIII, § 330016(1)(K), 108 Stat. 2147.)

§ 915. Foreign diplomats, consuls or officers

Whoever, with intent to defraud within the United States, falsely assumes or pretends to be a diplomatic, consular or other official of a foreign government duly accredited as such to the United States and acts as such, or in such pretended character, demands or obtains or attempts to obtain any money, paper, document, or other thing of value, shall be fined under this title or imprisoned not more than ten years, or both.

(June 25, 1948, c. 645, 62 Stat. 743; Sept. 13, 1994, Pub.L. 103–322, Title XXXIII, § 330016(1)(K), 108 Stat. 2147.)

HISTORICAL AND STATUTORY NOTES

Canal Zone

Applicability of section to Canal Zone, see § 14 of this title.

§ 916. 4–H Club members or agents

Whoever, falsely and with intent to defraud, holds himself out as or represents or pretends himself to be a member of, associated with, or an agent or representative for the 4–H clubs, an organization established by the Extension Service of the United States Department of Agriculture and the land grant colleges, shall be fined under this title or imprisoned not more than six months, or both.

(June 25, 1948, c. 645, 62 Stat. 743; Sept. 13, 1994, Pub.L. 103–322, Title XXXIII, § 330016(1)(F), 108 Stat. 2147.)

§ 917. Red Cross members or agents

Whoever, within the United States, falsely or fraudulently holds himself out as or represents or pretends himself to be a member of or an agent for the American National Red Cross for the purpose of soliciting, collecting, or receiving money or material, shall be fined under this title or imprisoned not more than 5 years, or both.

(June 25, 1948, c. 645, 62 Stat. 743; Sept. 13, 1994, Pub.L. 103–322, Title XXXIII, § 330016(1)(G), 108 Stat. 2147; Oct. 26, 2001, Pub.L. 107–56, Title X, § 1011(c), 115 Stat. 396.)

HISTORICAL AND STATUTORY NOTES

Canal Zone

Applicability of section to Canal Zone, see § 14 of this title.

CHAPTER 44—FIREARMS

HISTORICAL AND STATUTORY NOTES

Savings Provisions of Pub.L. 98–473, Title II, c. II

See section 235 of Pub.L. 98–473, Title II, c. II, Oct. 12, 1984, 98 Stat. 2031, as amended, set out as a note under section 3551 of this title.

§ 921. Definitions

(a) As used in this chapter—

(1) The term "person" and the term "whoever" include any individual, corporation, company, association, firm, partnership, society, or joint stock company.

(2) The term "interstate or foreign commerce" includes commerce between any place in a State and any place outside of that State, or within any possession of the United States (not including the Canal Zone) or the District of Columbia, but such term does not include commerce between places within the same State but through any place outside of that State. The term "State" includes the District of Columbia, the Commonwealth of Puerto Rico, and the possessions of the United States (not including the Canal Zone).

(3) The term "firearm" means (A) any weapon (including a starter gun) which will or is designed to or may readily be converted to expel a projectile by the action of an explosive; (B) the frame or receiver of any such weapon; (C) any firearm muffler or firearm silencer; or (D) any destructive device. Such term does not include an antique firearm.

(4) The term "destructive device" means—

(A) any explosive, incendiary, or poison gas—

(i) bomb,

(ii) grenade,

(iii) rocket having a propellant charge of more than four ounces,

(iv) missile having an explosive or incendiary charge of more than one-quarter ounce,

(v) mine, or

(vi) device similar to any of the devices described in the preceding clauses;

(B) any type of weapon (other than a shotgun or a shotgun shell which the Attorney General finds is generally recognized as particularly suitable for sporting purposes) by whatever name known which will, or which may be readily converted to, expel a projectile by the action of an explosive or other propellant, and which has any barrel with a bore of more than one-half inch in diameter; and

(C) any combination of parts either designed or intended for use in converting any device into any destructive device described in subparagraph (A) or

(B) and from which a destructive device may be readily assembled.

The term "destructive device" shall not include any device which is neither designed nor redesigned for use as a weapon; any device, although originally designed for use as a weapon, which is redesigned for use as a signaling, pyrotechnic, line throwing, safety, or similar device; surplus ordnance sold, loaned, or given by the Secretary of the Army pursuant to the provisions of section 4684(2), 4685, or 4686 of title 10; or any other device which the Attorney General finds is not likely to be used as a weapon, is an antique, or is a rifle which the owner intends to use solely for sporting, recreational or cultural purposes.

(5) The term "shotgun" means a weapon designed or redesigned, made or remade, and intended to be fired from the shoulder and designed or redesigned and made or remade to use the energy of an explosive to fire through a smooth bore either a number of ball shot or a single projectile for each single pull of the trigger.

(6) The term "short-barreled shotgun" means a shotgun having one or more barrels less than eighteen inches in length and any weapon made from a shotgun (whether by alteration, modification or otherwise) if such a weapon as modified has an overall length of less than twenty-six inches.

(7) The term "rifle" means a weapon designed or redesigned, made or remade, and intended to be fired from the shoulder and designed or redesigned and made or remade to use the energy of an explosive to fire only a single projectile through a rifled bore for each single pull of the trigger.

(8) The term "short-barreled rifle" means a rifle having one or more barrels less than sixteen inches in length and any weapon made from a rifle (whether by alteration, modification, or otherwise) if such weapon, as modified, has an overall length of less than twenty-six inches.

(9) The term "importer" means any person engaged in the business of importing or bringing firearms or ammunition into the United States for purposes of sale or distribution; and the term "licensed importer" means any such person licensed under the provisions of this chapter.

(10) The term "manufacturer" means any person engaged in the business of manufacturing firearms or ammunition for purposes of sale or distribution; and the term "licensed manufacturer" means any such person licensed under the provisions of this chapter.

(11) The term "dealer" means (A) any person engaged in the business of selling firearms at wholesale or retail, (B) any person engaged in the business of repairing firearms or of making or fitting special barrels, stocks, or trigger mechanisms to firearms, or (C) any person who is a pawnbroker. The term "licensed dealer" means any dealer who is licensed under the provisions of this chapter.

(12) The term "pawnbroker" means any person whose business or occupation includes the taking or receiving, by way of pledge or pawn, of any firearm as security for the payment or repayment of money.

(13) The term "collector" means any person who acquires, holds, or disposes of firearms as curios or relics, as the Attorney General shall by regulation define, and the term "licensed collector" means any such person licensed under the provisions of this chapter.

(14) The term "indictment" includes an indictment or information in any court under which a crime punishable by imprisonment for a term exceeding one year may be prosecuted.

(15) The term "fugitive from justice" means any person who has fled from any State to avoid prosecution for a crime or to avoid giving testimony in any criminal proceeding.

(16) The term "antique firearm" means—

(A) any firearm (including any firearm with a matchlock, flintlock, percussion cap, or similar type of ignition system) manufactured in or before 1898; or

(B) any replica of any firearm described in subparagraph (A) if such replica—

(i) is not designed or redesigned for using rimfire or conventional centerfire fixed ammunition, or

(ii) uses rimfire or conventional centerfire fixed ammunition which is no longer manufactured in the United States and which is not readily available in the ordinary channels of commercial trade; or

(C) any muzzle loading rifle, muzzle loading shotgun, or muzzle loading pistol, which is designed to use black powder, or a black powder substitute, and which cannot use fixed ammunition. For purposes of this subparagraph, the term "antique firearm" shall not include any weapon which incorporates a firearm frame or receiver, any firearm which is converted into a muzzle loading weapon, or any muzzle loading weapon which can be readily converted to fire fixed ammunition by replacing the barrel, bolt, breechblock, or any combination thereof.

(17)(A) The term "ammunition" means ammunition or cartridge cases, primers, bullets, or propellent powder designed for use in any firearm.

(B) The term "armor piercing ammunition" means—

(i) a projectile or projectile core which may be used in a handgun and which is constructed entirely (excluding the presence of traces of other substances) from one or a combination of tungsten alloys, steel, iron, brass, bronze, beryllium copper, or depleted uranium; or

(ii) a full jacketed projectile larger than .22 caliber designed and intended for use in a handgun and whose jacket has a weight of more than 25 percent of the total weight of the projectile.

(C) The term "armor piercing ammunition" does not include shotgun shot required by Federal or State environmental or game regulations for hunting purposes, a frangible projectile designed for target shooting, a projectile which the Attorney General finds is primarily intended to be used for sporting purposes, or any other projectile or projectile core which the Attorney General finds is intended to be used for industrial purposes, including a charge used in an oil and gas well perforating device.

(18) The term "Attorney General" means the Attorney General of the United States"[1]

(19) The term "published ordinance" means a published law of any political subdivision of a State which the Attorney General determines to be relevant to the enforcement of this chapter and which is contained on a list compiled by the Attorney General, which list shall be published in the Federal Register, revised annually, and furnished to each licensee under this chapter.

(20) The term "crime punishable by imprisonment for a term exceeding one year" does not include—

(A) any Federal or State offenses pertaining to antitrust violations, unfair trade practices, restraints of trade, or other similar offenses relating to the regulation of business practices, or

(B) any State offense classified by the laws of the State as a misdemeanor and punishable by a term of imprisonment of two years or less.

What constitutes a conviction of such a crime shall be determined in accordance with the law of the jurisdiction in which the proceedings were held. Any conviction which has been expunged, or set aside or for which a person has been pardoned or has had civil rights restored shall not be considered a conviction for purposes of this chapter, unless such pardon, expungement, or restoration of civil rights expressly provides that the person may not ship, transport, possess, or receive firearms.

(21) The term "engaged in the business" means—

(A) as applied to a manufacturer of firearms, a person who devotes time, attention, and labor to manufacturing firearms as a regular course of trade or business with the principal objective of livelihood and profit through the sale or distribution of the firearms manufactured;

(B) as applied to a manufacturer of ammunition, a person who devotes time, attention, and labor to manufacturing ammunition as a regular course of trade or business with the principal objective of livelihood and profit through the sale or distribution of the ammunition manufactured;

(C) as applied to a dealer in firearms, as defined in section 921(a)(11)(A), a person who devotes time, attention, and labor to dealing in firearms as a regular course of trade or business with the principal objective of livelihood and profit through the repetitive purchase and resale of firearms, but such term shall not include a person who makes occasional sales, exchanges, or purchases of firearms for the enhancement of a personal collection or for a hobby, or who sells all or part of his personal collection of firearms;

(D) as applied to a dealer in firearms, as defined in section 921(a)(11)(B), a person who devotes time, attention, and labor to engaging in such activity as a regular course of trade or business with the principal objective of livelihood and profit, but such term shall not include a person who makes occasional repairs of firearms, or who occasionally fits special barrels, stocks, or trigger mechanisms to firearms;

(E) as applied to an importer of firearms, a person who devotes time, attention, and labor to importing firearms as a regular course of trade or business with the principal objective of livelihood and profit through the sale or distribution of the firearms imported; and

(F) as applied to an importer of ammunition, a person who devotes time, attention, and labor to importing ammunition as a regular course of trade or business with the principal objective of livelihood and profit through the sale or distribution of the ammunition imported.

(22) The term "with the principal objective of livelihood and profit" means that the intent underlying the sale or disposition of firearms is predominantly one of obtaining livelihood and pecuniary gain, as opposed to other intents, such as improving or liquidating a personal firearms collection: *Provided,* That proof of profit shall not be required as to a person who engages in the regular and repetitive purchase and disposition of firearms for criminal purposes or terrorism. For purposes of this paragraph, the term "terrorism" means activity, directed against United States persons, which—

(A) is committed by an individual who is not a national or permanent resident alien of the United States;

(B) involves violent acts or acts dangerous to human life which would be a criminal violation if committed within the jurisdiction of the United States; and

(C) is intended—

(i) to intimidate or coerce a civilian population;

(ii) to influence the policy of a government by intimidation or coercion; or

(iii) to affect the conduct of a government by assassination or kidnapping.

(23) The term "machinegun" has the meaning given such term in section 5845(b) of the National Firearms Act (26 U.S.C. 5845(b)).

(24) The terms "firearm silencer" and "firearm muffler" mean any device for silencing, muffling, or diminishing the report of a portable firearm, including any combination of parts, designed or redesigned, and intended for use in assembling or fabricating a firearm silencer or firearm muffler, and any part intended only for use in such assembly or fabrication.

(25) The term "school zone" means—

(A) in, or on the grounds of, a public, parochial or private school; or

(B) within a distance of 1,000 feet from the grounds of a public, parochial or private school.

(26) The term "school" means a school which provides elementary or secondary education, as determined under State law.

(27) The term "motor vehicle" has the meaning given such term in section 13102 of title 49, United States Code.

(28) The term "semiautomatic rifle" means any repeating rifle which utilizes a portion of the energy of a firing cartridge to extract the fired cartridge case and chamber the next round, and which requires a separate pull of the trigger to fire each cartridge.

(29) The term "handgun" means—

(A) a firearm which has a short stock and is designed to be held and fired by the use of a single hand; and

(B) any combination of parts from which a firearm described in subparagraph (A) can be assembled.

[(30), (31) Repealed. Pub.L. 103–322, Title XI, § 110105(2), Sept. 13, 1994, 108 Stat. 2000]

(32) The term "intimate partner" means, with respect to a person, the spouse of the person, a former spouse of the person, an individual who is a parent of a child of the person, and an individual who cohabitates or has cohabited with the person.

(33)(A) Except as provided in subparagraph (C),[2] the term "misdemeanor crime of domestic violence" means an offense that—

(i) is a misdemeanor under Federal, State, or Tribal law; and

(ii) has, as an element, the use or attempted use of physical force, or the threatened use of a deadly weapon, committed by a current or former spouse, parent, or guardian of the victim, by a person with whom the victim shares a child in common, by a person who is cohabiting with or has cohabited with the victim as a spouse, parent, or guardian, or by a person similarly situated to a spouse, parent, or guardian of the victim

(B)(i) A person shall not be considered to have been convicted of such an offense for purposes of this chapter, unless—

(I) the person was represented by counsel in the case, or knowingly and intelligently waived the right to counsel in the case; and

(II) in the case of a prosecution for an offense described in this paragraph for which a person was entitled to a jury trial in the jurisdiction in which the case was tried, either

(aa) the case was tried by a jury, or

(bb) the person knowingly and intelligently waived the right to have the case tried by a jury, by guilty plea or otherwise.

(ii) A person shall not be considered to have been convicted of such an offense for purposes of this chapter if the conviction has been expunged or set aside, or is an offense for which the person has been pardoned or has had civil rights restored (if the law of the applicable jurisdiction provides for the loss of civil rights under such an offense) unless the pardon, expungement, or restoration of civil rights expressly provides that the person may not ship, transport, possess, or receive firearms.

(34) The term "secure gun storage or safety device" means—

(A) a device that, when installed on a firearm, is designed to prevent the firearm from being operated without first deactivating the device;

(B) a device incorporated into the design of the firearm that is designed to prevent the operation of the firearm by anyone not having access to the device; or

(C) a safe, gun safe, gun case, lock box, or other device that is designed to be or can be used to store a firearm and that is designed to be unlocked only by means of a key, a combination, or other similar means.

(35) The term "body armor" means any product sold or offered for sale, in interstate or foreign commerce, as personal protective body covering intended to protect against gunfire, regardless of whether the product is to be worn alone or is sold as a complement to another product or garment.

(b) For the purposes of this chapter, a member of the Armed Forces on active duty is a resident of the State in which his permanent duty station is located.

(Added Pub.L. 90–351, Title IV, § 902, June 19, 1968, 82 Stat. 226, and amended Pub.L. 90–618, Title I, § 102, Oct. 22, 1968, 82 Stat. 1214; Pub.L. 93–639, § 102, Jan. 4, 1975, 88 Stat. 2217; Pub.L. 99–308, § 101, May 19, 1986, 100 Stat. 449; Pub.L. 99–360, § 1(b), July 8, 1986, 100 Stat. 766; Pub.L. 99–408, § 1, Aug. 28, 1986, 100 Stat. 920; Pub.L. 101–647, Title XVII, § 1702(b)(2), Title XXII, § 2204(a), Nov. 29, 1990, 104 Stat. 4845, 4857; Pub.L. 103–159, Title I, § 102(a)(2), Nov. 30, 1993, 107 Stat. 1539; Pub.L. 103–322, Title XI, §§ 110102(b), 110103(b), 110105(2), 110401(a), 110519, Title XXXIII, § 330021(1), Sept. 13, 1994, 108 Stat. 1997, 1999, 2000, 2014, 2020, 2150; Pub.L. 104–88, Title III, § 303(1), Dec. 29, 1995, 109 Stat. 943; Pub.L. 104–208, Div. A, Title I, § 101(f) [Title VI, § 658(a)], Sept. 30, 1996, 110 Stat. 3009–371; Pub.L. 105–277, Div. A, § 101(b) [Title I, § 119(a)], § 101(h) [Title I, § 115], Oct. 21, 1998, 112 Stat. 2681–69, 2681–490; Pub.L. 107–273, Div. C, Title I, § 11009(e)(1), Nov. 2, 2002, 116 Stat. 1821; Pub.L. 107–296, Title XI, § 1112(f)(1) to (3), (6), Nov. 25, 2002, 116 Stat. 2276; Pub.L. 109–162, Title IX, § 908(a), Jan. 5, 2006, 119 Stat. 3083.)

[1] So in original. Probably should be followed by a period.

[2] So in original. No subparagraph (C) was enacted in subsec. (a)(33).

HISTORICAL AND STATUTORY NOTES

References in Text

Section 5845(b) of the National Firearms Act, referred to in subsec. (a)(23), is section 5845(b) of Title 26, Internal Revenue Code.

Codifications

Amendment by Pub.L. 109–162, § 908(a), to "[s]ection 921(33)(A)(i) of title 18" was executed to subsec. (a)(33)(A)(i) of this section as the probable intent of Congress.

Effective and Applicability Provisions

2002 Acts. Amendment to this section by Pub.L. 107–296 effective 60 days after Nov. 25, 2002, see Pub.L. 107–296, § 4, set out as a note under 6 U.S.C.A. § 101.

1998 Acts. Pub.L. 105–277, Div. A, § 101(b) [Title I, § 119(e)], Oct. 21, 1998, 112 Stat. 2681–70, provided that: "The amendments made by this section [amending this section and section 923 of this title and enacting provisions set out as a note under section 923 of this title] shall take effect 180 days after the date of enactment of this Act [Oct. 21, 1998]."

1995 Acts. Amendment by Pub.L. 104–88 effective Jan. 1, 1996, see section 2 of Pub.L. 104–88, set out as a note under 49 U.S.C.A. § 701.

1994 Acts. Section 110105 of Subtitle A, §§ 110101 to 110106, of Title XI of Pub.L. 103–322 provided that: "This subtitle [amending this section and sections 922, 923, and 924 of this title, and enacting provisions set out as notes under this section] and the amendments made by this subtitle—

"(1) shall take effect on the date of the enactment of this Act [Sept. 13, 1994]; and

"(2) are repealed effective as of the date that is 10 years after that date [Sept. 13, 2004]."

1990 Acts. Section 1702(b)(4) of Pub.L. 101–647 provided that: "The amendments made by this section [enacting subsec. (a)(25)–(27) of this section and sections 922(q) and 924(a)(4) of this title and note provisions set out under this section and section 922 of this title] shall apply to conduct engaged in after the end of the 60–day period beginning on the date of the enactment of this Act [Nov. 29, 1990]."

1986 Acts. Section 9 of Pub.L. 99–408 provided that: "The amendments made by this Act [amending this section and sections 922, 923(e) and (k), and 929 of this title and enacting provisions set out as notes under this section] shall take effect on the date of enactment of this Act [Aug. 28, 1986], except that sections 3 [amending section 923(a)(1)(A) of this title] 4 [amending section 923(a)(1)(C) of this title], and 5 [amending section 923(a)(2)(A) and (B) of this title] shall take effect on the first day of the first calendar month which begins more than ninety days after the date of the enactment of this Act [Aug. 28, 1986]."

Section 2 of Pub.L. 99–360 provided that: "This Act and the amendments made by this Act [enacting section 926A of this title, amending this section and section 923 of this title, and repealing former section 926A of this title], intended to amend the Firearms Owners' Protection Act [Pub.L. 99–308, May 19, 1986, 100 Stat. 449], shall become effective on the date on which the section they are intended to amend in such Firearms Owners' Protection Act becomes effective [see section 110 of Pub.L. 99–308, set out as a note under this section] and shall apply to the amendments to title 18, United States Code [this Title], made by such Act [see Short Title of 1986 Amendment note set out under this section]."

Short Title

2005 Amendments. Pub.L. 109–92, § 5(a), Oct. 26, 2005, 119 Stat. 2099, provided that: "This section [amending 18 U.S.C.A. §§ 922 and 924 and enacting provisions set out as notes under 18 U.S.C.A. § 922] may be cited as the 'Child Safety Lock Act of 2005'."

2004 Amendments. Pub.L. 108–277, § 1, July 22, 2004, 118 Stat. 865, provided that: "This Act [enacting 18 U.S.C.A §§ 926B and 926C] may be cited as the 'Law Enforcement Officers Safety Act of 2004'."

1994 Amendments. Section 110101 of Subtitle A, §§ 110101 to 110106, of Title XI of Pub.L. 103–322 provided that: "This subtitle [amending this section and sections 922, 923, and 924 of this title, and enacting provisions set out as notes under this section] may be cited as the 'Public Safety and Recreational Firearms Use Protection Act'."

[Amendments by sections 110101 to 110106 of Pub.L. 103–322, effective Sept. 13, 1994, are repealed effective 10 years after Sept. 13, 1994, see section 110105 of Pub.L. 103–322, set out as a note under this section.]

1993 Amendments. Section 101 of Pub.L. 103–159 provided that: "This title [enacting section 925A of this title, amending this section, sections 922 and 924 of this title, and section 3759 of Title 42, The Public Health and Welfare, and enacting provisions set out as notes under this section and section 922 of this title] may be cited as the 'Brady Handgun Violence Prevention Act'."

Section 301 of Pub.L. 103–159 provided that: "This title [amending sections 922, 923, and 924 of this title] may be cited as the 'Federal Firearms License Reform Act of 1993'."

1990 Amendments. Section 1702(a) of Pub.L. 101–647 provided that: "This section [enacting sections 921(a)(25) to (27), 922(q), and 924(a)(4) of this title and note provisions under this section and section 922 of this title] may be cited as the 'Gun-Free School Zones Act of 1990'."

1988 Amendments. Pub.L. 100–649, § 1, Nov. 10, 1988, 102 Stat. 3816, provided that: "This Act [amending sections 922, 924 and 925 of this title and enacting provisions set out as notes under section 922 of this title and section 1356 of Title 49 App., Transportation] may be cited as the 'Undetectable Firearms Act of 1988'."

1986 Amendments. Section 1401 of Pub.L. 99–570 provided that: "This subtitle [amending section 924 of this title] may be cited as the 'Career Criminals Amendment Act of 1986'."

Section 1(a) of Pub.L. 99–308 provided that: "This Act [enacting section 926A of this title, amending sections 921, 922, 923, 924, 925, 926, and 929 of this title and section 5845 of Title 26, Internal Revenue Code, repealing Title VII of the Omnibus Crime Control and Safe Streets Act of 1968, sections 1201 to 1203 of Pub.L. 90–351, set out in the Appendix to this title, and enacting provisions set out as notes under this section] may be cited as the 'Firearms Owners' Protection Act'."

1968 Acts. Section 1 of Pub.L. 90–618 provided: "That this Act [which enacted sections 5822, 5871 and 5872 of Title 26, amended this section and sections 922 to 928 of this title, and Appendix to this title, and sections 5801, 5802, 5811, 5812, 5821, 5841 to 5849, 5851 to 5854, 5861, 6806, and 7273 of Title 26, repealed sections 5692 and 6107 of Title 26, omitted sections 5803, 5813, 5814, 5831, 5855, and 5862 of Title 26, and enacted material set out as notes under this section and Appendix to this title, and section 5801 of Title 26] may be cited as the 'Gun Control Act of 1968'."

Study By Attorney General

Pub.L. 103–322, Title XI, § 110104, Sept. 13, 1994, 108 Stat. 2000, which required the Attorney General to study and investigate the effect of Subtitle A (§§ 110101 to 110106) of Title XI of Pub.L. 103–322, determine their impact on violent and drug trafficking crime, and submit a report to Congress, was repealed by section 110105(2) of Pub.L. of Pub.L. 103–322, effective 10 years after Sept. 13, 1994. See section 110105 of Pub.L. 103–322, set out as a note under this section.

Construction of Brady Handgun Violence Prevention Act with Computer Matching and Privacy Protection Acts

Section 105 of Pub.L. 103–159 provided that: "This Act and the amendments made by this Act [enacting section 925A of this title, amending sections 921, 922, 923, and 924 of this title and section 3759 of Title 42, The Public Health and Welfare, and enacting provisions set out as notes under this section and section 922 of this title] shall not be construed to alter or impair any right or remedy under section 552a of Title 5, United States Code [section 552a of Title 5, Government Organization and Employees]."

Definition of "Handgun" for Purposes of Subsec. (a)(17)(B)

Section 10 of Pub.L. 99–408 provided that: "For purposes of section 921(a)(17)(B) of title 18, United States Code, as added by the first section of this Act [Subsec. (a)(17)(B) of this section], 'handgun' means any firearm including a pistol or revolver designed to be fired by the use of a single hand. The term also includes any combination of parts from which a handgun can be assembled."

Publication of Compilation of State Laws and Published Ordinances of Which Licensees Are Presumed To Have Knowledge

Section 110 of Pub.L. 99–308 provided that:

"**(a) In general.**—The amendments made by this Act [enacting section 926A of this title, amending this section and sections 922 to 926, and 929 of this title and section 5845 of Title 26, Internal Revenue Code, repealing Title VII of the Omnibus Crime Control and Safe Streets Act of 1968, sections 1201 to 1203 of Pub.L. 90–351, set out in the Appendix to this title, and enacting provisions set out as notes under this section] shall become effective one hundred and eighty days after the date of the enactment of this Act [May 19, 1986]. Upon their becoming effective, the Secretary shall publish and provide to all licensees a compilation of the State laws and published ordinances of which licensees are presumed to have knowledge pursuant to chapter 44 of title 18, United States Code [this chapter], as amended by this Act. All amendments to such State laws and published ordinances as contained in the aforementioned compilation shall be published in the Federal Register, revised annually, and furnished to each person licensed under chapter 44 of title 18, United States Code, as amended by this Act.

"**(b) Pending actions, petitions, and appellate proceedings.**—The amendments made by sections 103(6)(B) [enacting section 923(f)(4) of this title], 105 [amending section 925 of this title], and 107 [enacting section 926A of this title] of this Act shall be applicable to any action, petition, or appellate proceeding pending on the date of the enactment of this Act [May 19, 1986].

"**(c) Machinegun prohibition.**—Section 102(9) [enacting section 922(*o*) of this title] shall take effect on the date of the enactment of this Act [May 19, 1986]."

Congressional Findings and Declaration

Section 1(b) of Pub.L. 99–308 provided that: "The Congress finds that—

"(1) the rights of citizens—

"(A) to keep and bear arms under the second amendment to the United States Constitution;

"(B) to security against illegal and unreasonable searches and seizures under the fourth amendment;

"(C) against uncompensated taking of property, double jeopardy, and assurance of due process of law under the fifth amendment; and

"(D) against unconstitutional exercise of authority under the ninth and tenth amendments;

require additional legislation to correct existing firearms statutes and enforcement policies; and

"(2) additional legislation is required to reaffirm the intent of the Congress, as expressed in section 101 of the Gun Control Act of 1968 [section 101 of Pub.L. 90–618, set out as a note under this section], that 'it is not the purpose of this title to place any undue or unnecessary Federal restrictions or burdens on law-abiding citizens with respect to the acquisition, possession, or use of firearms appropriate to the purpose of hunting, trap-shooting, target shooting, personal protection, or any other lawful activity, and that this title is not intended to discourage or eliminate the private ownership or use of firearms by law-abiding citizens for lawful purposes'."

Section 101 of Pub.L. 90–618 provided that: "The Congress hereby declares that the purpose of this title [which amended this chapter] is to provide support to Federal, State, and local law enforcement officials in their fight against crime and violence, and it is not the purpose of this title to place any undue or unnecessary Federal restrictions or burdens on law-abiding citizens with respect to the acquisition, possession, or use of firearms appropriate to the purpose of hunting, trapshooting, target shooting, personal protection, or any other lawful activity, and that this title is not intended to discourage or eliminate the private ownership or use of firearms by law-abiding citizens for lawful purposes, or provide for the imposition by Federal regulations of any procedures or requirements other than those reasonably necessary to implement and effectuate the provisions of this title."

Section 901 of Pub.L. 90–351 provided that:

"**(a)** The Congress hereby finds and declares—

"**(1)** that there is a widespread traffic in firearms moving in or otherwise affecting interstate or foreign commerce, and that the existing Federal controls over such traffic do not adequately enable the States to control this traffic within their own borders through the exercise of their police power;

"**(2)** that the ease with which any person can acquire firearms other than a rifle or shotgun (including criminals, juveniles without the knowledge or consent of their parents or guardians, narcotics addicts, mental defectives, armed groups who would supplant the functions of duly constituted public authorities, and others whose possession of such weapon is similarly contrary to the public interest) is a significant factor in the prevalence of lawlessness and violent crime in the United States;

"**(3)** that only through adequate Federal control over interstate and foreign commerce in these weapons, and over all persons engaging in the businesses of importing, manufacturing, or dealing in them, can this grave problem be properly dealt with, and effective State and local regulation of this traffic be made possible;

"**(4)** that the acquisition on a mail-order basis of firearms other than a rifle or shotgun by nonlicensed individuals, from a place other than their State of residence, has materially tended to thwart the effectiveness of State laws and regulations, and local ordinances;

"**(5)** that the sale or other disposition of concealable weapons by importers, manufacturers, and dealers holding Federal licenses, to nonresidents of the State in which the licensees' places of business are located, has tended to make ineffective the laws, regulations, and ordinances in the several States and local jurisdictions regarding such firearms;

"**(6)** that there is a causal relationship between the easy availability of firearms other than a rifle or shotgun and juvenile and youthful criminal behavior, and that such firearms have been widely sold by federally licensed importers and dealers to emotionally immature, or thrill-bent juveniles and minors prone to criminal behavior;

"**(7)** that the United States has become the dumping ground of the castoff surplus military weapons of other nations, and that such weapons, and the large volume of relatively inexpensive pistols and revolvers (largely worthless for sporting purposes), imported into the United States in recent years, has contributed greatly to lawlessness and to the Nation's law enforcement problems;

"**(8)** that the lack of adequate Federal control over interstate and foreign commerce in highly destructive weapons (such as bazookas, mortars, antitank guns, and so forth, and destructive devices such as explosive or incendiary grenades, bombs, missiles, and so forth) has allowed such weapons and devices to fall into the hands of lawless persons, including armed groups who would supplant lawful authority, thus creating a problem of national concern;

"**(9)** that the existing licensing system under the Federal Firearms Act [former sections 901 to 910 of Title 15] does not provide adequate license fees or proper standards for the granting or denial of licenses, and that this has led to licenses being issued to persons not reasonably entitled thereto, thus distorting the purposes of the licensing system.

"**(b)** The Congress further hereby declares that the purpose of this title [enacting this chapter and repealing sections 901 to 910 of Title 15] is to cope with the conditions referred to in the foregoing subsection, and that it is not the purpose of this title [enacting this chapter and repealing sections 901 to 910 of Title 15] to place any undue or unnecessary Federal restrictions or burdens on law-abiding citizens with respect to the acquisition, possession, or use of firearms appropriate to the purpose of hunting, trap shooting, target shooting, personal protection, or any other lawful activity, and that this title [enacting this chapter and repealing sections 901 to 910 of Title 15] is not intended to discourage or eliminate the private ownership or use of firearms by law-abiding citizens for lawful purposes, or provide for the imposition by Federal regulations of any procedures or requirements other than those reasonably necessary to implement and effectuate the provisions of this title [enacting this chapter and repealing sections 901 to 910 of Title 15]."

Administration and Enforcement by Attorney General

Pub.L. 90–618,Title I, § 103, Oct. 22, 1968, 82 Stat. 1226, as amended Pub.L. 107–296, Title XI, § 1112(s), Nov. 25, 2002, 116 Stat. 2279, provided that: "The administration and enforcement of the amendment made by this title [amending this chapter] shall be vested in the Attorney General."

Section 903 of Pub.L. 90–351 provided that: "The administration and enforcement of the amendment made by this title [enacting this chapter and provisions set out as notes under this section] shall be vested in the Secretary of the Treasury."

Modification of Other Laws

Section 104 of Pub.L. 90–618 provided that: "Nothing in this title or the amendment made thereby [amending this chapter] shall be construed as modifying or affecting any provision of—

"**(a)** the National Firearms Act (chapter 53 of the Internal Revenue Code of 1954) [section 5801 et seq. of Title 26];

"**(b)** section 414 of the Mutual Security Act of 1954 (22 U.S.C. 1934), as amended, relating to munitions control; or

"**(c)** section 1715 of title 18, United States Code, relating to nonmailable firearms."

Section 904 of Pub.L. 90–351 provided that: "Nothing in this title or amendment made thereby [enacting this chapter and provisions set out as notes under this section] shall be construed as modifying or affecting any provision of—

"(a) the National Firearms Act (chapter 53 of the Internal Revenue Code of 1954); or

"(b) section 414 of the Mutual Security Act of 1954 (22 U.S.C. 1934), as amended, relating to munitions control; or

"(c) section 1715 of title 18, United States Code, relating to nonmailable firearms."

§ 922. Unlawful acts

(a) It shall be unlawful—

(1) for any person—

(A) except a licensed importer, licensed manufacturer, or licensed dealer, to engage in the business of importing, manufacturing, or dealing in firearms, or in the course of such business to ship, transport, or receive any firearm in interstate or foreign commerce; or

(B) except a licensed importer or licensed manufacturer, to engage in the business of importing or manufacturing ammunition, or in the course of such business, to ship, transport, or receive any ammunition in interstate or foreign commerce;

(2) for any importer, manufacturer, dealer, or collector licensed under the provisions of this chapter to ship or transport in interstate or foreign commerce any firearm to any person other than a licensed importer, licensed manufacturer, licensed dealer, or licensed collector, except that—

(A) this paragraph and subsection (b)(3) shall not be held to preclude a licensed importer, licensed manufacturer, licensed dealer, or licensed collector from returning a firearm or replacement firearm of the same kind and type to a person from whom it was received; and this paragraph shall not be held to preclude an individual from mailing a firearm owned in compliance with Federal, State, and local law to a licensed importer, licensed manufacturer, licensed dealer, or licensed collector;

(B) this paragraph shall not be held to preclude a licensed importer, licensed manufacturer, or licensed dealer from depositing a firearm for conveyance in the mails to any officer, employee, agent, or watchman who, pursuant to the provisions of section 1715 of this title, is eligible to receive through the mails pistols, revolvers, and other firearms capable of being concealed on the person, for use in connection with his official duty; and

(C) nothing in this paragraph shall be construed as applying in any manner in the District of Columbia, the Commonwealth of Puerto Rico, or any possession of the United States differently than it would apply if the District of Columbia, the Commonwealth of Puerto Rico, or the possession were in fact a State of the United States;

(3) for any person, other than a licensed importer, licensed manufacturer, licensed dealer, or licensed collector to transport into or receive in the State where he resides (or if the person is a corporation or other business entity, the State where it maintains a place of business) any firearm purchased or otherwise obtained by such person outside that State, except that this paragraph (A) shall not preclude any person who lawfully acquires a firearm by bequest or intestate succession in a State other than his State of residence from transporting the firearm into or receiving it in that State, if it is lawful for such person to purchase or possess such firearm in that State, (B) shall not apply to the transportation or receipt of a firearm obtained in conformity with subsection (b)(3) of this section, and (C) shall not apply to the transportation of any firearm acquired in any State prior to the effective date of this chapter;

(4) for any person, other than a licensed importer, licensed manufacturer, licensed dealer, or licensed collector, to transport in interstate or foreign commerce any destructive device, machinegun (as defined in section 5845 of the Internal Revenue Code of 1986), short-barreled shotgun, or short-barreled rifle, except as specifically authorized by the Attorney General consistent with public safety and necessity;

(5) for any person (other than a licensed importer, licensed manufacturer, licensed dealer, or licensed collector) to transfer, sell, trade, give, transport, or deliver any firearm to any person (other than a licensed importer, licensed manufacturer, licensed dealer, or licensed collector) who the transferor knows or has reasonable cause to believe does not reside in (or if the person is a corporation or other business entity, does not maintain a place of business in) the State in which the transferor resides; except that this paragraph shall not apply to (A) the transfer, transportation, or delivery of a firearm made to carry out a bequest of a firearm to, or an acquisition by intestate succession of a firearm by, a person who is permitted to acquire or possess a firearm under the laws of the State of his residence, and (B) the loan or rental of a firearm to any person for temporary use for lawful sporting purposes;

(6) for any person in connection with the acquisition or attempted acquisition of any firearm or ammunition from a licensed importer, licensed manufacturer, licensed dealer, or licensed collector, knowingly to make any false or fictitious oral or written statement or to furnish or exhibit any false, fictitious, or misrepresented identification, intended

or likely to deceive such importer, manufacturer, dealer, or collector with respect to any fact material to the lawfulness of the sale or other disposition of such firearm or ammunition under the provisions of this chapter;

(7) for any person to manufacture or import armor piercing ammunition, unless—

(A) the manufacture of such ammunition is for the use of the United States, any department or agency of the United States, any State, or any department, agency, or political subdivision of a State;

(B) the manufacture of such ammunition is for the purpose of exportation; or

(C) the manufacture or importation of such ammunition is for the purpose of testing or experimentation and has been authorized by the Attorney General;

(8) for any manufacturer or importer to sell or deliver armor piercing ammunition, unless such sale or delivery—

(A) is for the use of the United States, any department or agency of the United States, any State, or any department, agency, or political subdivision of a State;

(B) is for the purpose of exportation; or

(C) is for the purpose of testing or experimentation and has been authorized by the Attorney General;

(9) for any person, other than a licensed importer, licensed manufacturer, licensed dealer, or licensed collector, who does not reside in any State to receive any firearms unless such receipt is for lawful sporting purposes.

(b) It shall be unlawful for any licensed importer, licensed manufacturer, licensed dealer, or licensed collector to sell or deliver—

(1) any firearm or ammunition to any individual who the licensee knows or has reasonable cause to believe is less than eighteen years of age, and, if the firearm, or ammunition is other than a shotgun or rifle, or ammunition for a shotgun or rifle, to any individual who the licensee knows or has reasonable cause to believe is less than twenty-one years of age;

(2) any firearm to any person in any State where the purchase or possession by such person of such firearm would be in violation of any State law or any published ordinance applicable at the place of sale, delivery or other disposition, unless the licensee knows or has reasonable cause to believe that the purchase or possession would not be in violation of such State law or such published ordinance;

(3) any firearm to any person who the licensee knows or has reasonable cause to believe does not reside in (or if the person is a corporation or other business entity, does not maintain a place of business in) the State in which the licensee's place of business is located, except that this paragraph (A) shall not apply to the sale or delivery of any rifle or shotgun to a resident of a State other than a State in which the licensee's place of business is located if the transferee meets in person with the transferor to accomplish the transfer, and the sale, delivery, and receipt fully comply with the legal conditions of sale in both such States (and any licensed manufacturer, importer or dealer shall be presumed, for purposes of this subparagraph, in the absence of evidence to the contrary, to have had actual knowledge of the State laws and published ordinances of both States), and (B) shall not apply to the loan or rental of a firearm to any person for temporary use for lawful sporting purposes;

(4) to any person any destructive device, machinegun (as defined in section 5845 of the Internal Revenue Code of 1986), short-barreled shotgun, or short-barreled rifle, except as specifically authorized by the Attorney General consistent with public safety and necessity; and

(5) any firearm or armor-piercing ammunition to any person unless the licensee notes in his records, required to be kept pursuant to section 923 of this chapter, the name, age, and place of residence of such person if the person is an individual, or the identity and principal and local places of business of such person if the person is a corporation or other business entity.

Paragraphs (1), (2), (3), and (4) of this subsection shall not apply to transactions between licensed importers, licensed manufacturers, licensed dealers, and licensed collectors. Paragraph (4) of this subsection shall not apply to a sale or delivery to any research organization designated by the Attorney General.

(c) In any case not otherwise prohibited by this chapter, a licensed importer, licensed manufacturer, or licensed dealer may sell a firearm to a person who does not appear in person at the licensee's business premises (other than another licensed importer, manufacturer, or dealer) only if—

(1) the transferee submits to the transferor a sworn statement in the following form:

"Subject to penalties provided by law, I swear that, in the case of any firearm other than a shotgun or a rifle, I am twenty-one years or more of age, or that, in the case of a shotgun or a rifle, I am eighteen years or more of age; that I am not prohibited by the provisions of chapter 44 of title 18, United States Code, from receiving a firearm in interstate or foreign commerce; and that my receipt of this firearm will not be in violation of any statute of the State and published ordinance applicable to the locality in which I reside. Further, the true title, name, and address of the principal law enforcement officer of the locality to which the firearm will be delivered are ....

Signature .... Date ...."

and containing blank spaces for the attachment of a true copy of any permit or other information required pursuant to such statute or published ordinance;

(2) the transferor has, prior to the shipment or delivery of the firearm, forwarded by registered or certified mail (return receipt requested) a copy of the sworn statement, together with a description of the firearm, in a form prescribed by the Attorney General, to the chief law enforcement officer of the transferee's place of residence, and has received a return receipt evidencing delivery of the statement or has had the statement returned due to the refusal of the named addressee to accept such letter in accordance with United States Post Office Department regulations; and

(3) the transferor has delayed shipment or delivery for a period of at least seven days following receipt of the notification of the acceptance or refusal of delivery of the statement.

A copy of the sworn statement and a copy of the notification to the local law enforcement officer, together with evidence of receipt or rejection of that notification shall be retained by the licensee as a part of the records required to be kept under section 923(g).

(d) It shall be unlawful for any person to sell or otherwise dispose of any firearm or ammunition to any person knowing or having reasonable cause to believe that such person—

(1) is under indictment for, or has been convicted in any court of, a crime punishable by imprisonment for a term exceeding one year;

(2) is a fugitive from justice;

(3) is an unlawful user of or addicted to any controlled substance (as defined in section 102 of the Controlled Substances Act (21 U.S.C. 802));

(4) has been adjudicated as a mental defective or has been committed to any mental institution;

(5) who, being an alien—

(A) is illegally or unlawfully in the United States; or

(B) except as provided in subsection (y)(2), has been admitted to the United States under a nonimmigrant visa (as that term is defined in section 101(a)(26) of the Immigration and Nationality Act (8 U.S.C. 1101(a)(26)));

(6) who [1] has been discharged from the Armed Forces under dishonorable conditions;

(7) who, having been a citizen of the United States, has renounced his citizenship;

(8) is subject to a court order that restrains such person from harassing, stalking, or threatening an intimate partner of such person or child of such intimate partner or person, or engaging in other conduct that would place an intimate partner in reasonable fear of bodily injury to the partner or child, except that this paragraph shall only apply to a court order that—

(A) was issued after a hearing of which such person received actual notice, and at which such person had the opportunity to participate; and

(B)(i) includes a finding that such person represents a credible threat to the physical safety of such intimate partner or child; or

(ii) by its terms explicitly prohibits the use, attempted use, or threatened use of physical force against such intimate partner or child that would reasonably be expected to cause bodily injury; or

(9) has been convicted in any court of a misdemeanor crime of domestic violence.

This subsection shall not apply with respect to the sale or disposition of a firearm or ammunition to a licensed importer, licensed manufacturer, licensed dealer, or licensed collector who pursuant to subsection (b) of section 925 of this chapter is not precluded from dealing in firearms or ammunition, or to a person who has been granted relief from disabilities pursuant to subsection (c) of section 925 of this chapter.

(e) It shall be unlawful for any person knowingly to deliver or cause to be delivered to any common or contract carrier for transportation or shipment in interstate or foreign commerce, to persons other than licensed importers, licensed manufacturers, licensed dealers, or licensed collectors, any package or other container in which there is any firearm or ammunition without written notice to the carrier that such firearm or ammunition is being transported or shipped; except that any passenger who owns or legally possesses a firearm or ammunition being transported aboard any common or contract carrier for movement with the passenger in interstate or foreign commerce may deliver said firearm or ammunition into the custody of the pilot, captain, conductor or operator of such common or contract carrier for the duration of the trip without violating any of the provisions of this chapter. No common or contract carrier shall require or cause any label, tag, or other written notice to be placed on the outside of any package, luggage, or other container that such package, luggage, or other container contains a firearm.

(f)(1) It shall be unlawful for any common or contract carrier to transport or deliver in interstate or foreign commerce any firearm or ammunition with knowledge or reasonable cause to believe that the shipment, transportation, or receipt thereof would be in violation of the provisions of this chapter.

(2) It shall be unlawful for any common or contract carrier to deliver in interstate or foreign commerce any firearm without obtaining written acknowledgement of receipt from the recipient of the package or other container in which there is a firearm.

(g) It shall be unlawful for any person—

(1) who has been convicted in any court of, a crime punishable by imprisonment for a term exceeding one year;

(2) who is a fugitive from justice;

(3) who is an unlawful user of or addicted to any controlled substance (as defined in section 102 of the Controlled Substances Act (21 U.S.C. 802));

(4) who has been adjudicated as a mental defective or who has been committed to a mental institution;

(5) who, being an alien—

(A) is illegally or unlawfully in the United States; or

(B) except as provided in subsection (y)(2), has been admitted to the United States under a nonimmigrant visa (as that term is defined in section 101(a)(26) of the Immigration and Nationality Act (8 U.S.C. 1101(a)(26)));

(6) who has been discharged from the Armed Forces under dishonorable conditions;

(7) who, having been a citizen of the United States, has renounced his citizenship;

(8) who is subject to a court order that—

(A) was issued after a hearing of which such person received actual notice, and at which such person had an opportunity to participate;

(B) restrains such person from harassing, stalking, or threatening an intimate partner of such person or child of such intimate partner or person, or engaging in other conduct that would place an intimate partner in reasonable fear of bodily injury to the partner or child; and

(C)(i) includes a finding that such person represents a credible threat to the physical safety of such intimate partner or child; or

(ii) by its terms explicitly prohibits the use, attempted use, or threatened use of physical force against such intimate partner or child that would reasonably be expected to cause bodily injury; or

(9) who has been convicted in any court of a misdemeanor crime of domestic violence,

to ship or transport in interstate or foreign commerce, or possess in or affecting commerce, any firearm or ammunition; or to receive any firearm or ammunition which has been shipped or transported in interstate or foreign commerce.

(h) It shall be unlawful for any individual, who to that individual's knowledge and while being employed for any person described in any paragraph of subsection (g) of this section, in the course of such employment—

(1) to receive, possess, or transport any firearm or ammunition in or affecting interstate or foreign commerce; or

(2) to receive any firearm or ammunition which has been shipped or transported in interstate or foreign commerce.

(i) It shall be unlawful for any person to transport or ship in interstate or foreign commerce, any stolen firearm or stolen ammunition, knowing or having reasonable cause to believe that the firearm or ammunition was stolen.

(j) It shall be unlawful for any person to receive, possess, conceal, store, barter, sell, or dispose of any stolen firearm or stolen ammunition, or pledge or accept as security for a loan any stolen firearm or stolen ammunition, which is moving as, which is a part of, which constitutes, or which has been shipped or transported in, interstate or foreign commerce, either before or after it was stolen, knowing or having reasonable cause to believe that the firearm or ammunition was stolen.

(k) It shall be unlawful for any person knowingly to transport, ship, or receive, in interstate or foreign commerce, any firearm which has had the importer's or manufacturer's serial number removed, obliterated, or altered or to possess or receive any firearm which has had the importer's or manufacturer's serial number removed, obliterated, or altered and has, at any time, been shipped or transported in interstate or foreign commerce.

(*l*) Except as provided in section 925(d) of this chapter, it shall be unlawful for any person knowingly to import or bring into the United States or any possession thereof any firearm or ammunition; and it shall be unlawful for any person knowingly to receive any firearm or ammunition which has been imported or brought into the United States or any possession thereof in violation of the provisions of this chapter.

(m) It shall be unlawful for any licensed importer, licensed manufacturer, licensed dealer, or licensed collector knowingly to make any false entry in, to fail to make appropriate entry in, or to fail to properly maintain, any record which he is required to keep pursuant to section 923 of this chapter or regulations promulgated thereunder.

(n) It shall be unlawful for any person who is under indictment for a crime punishable by imprisonment for a term exceeding one year to ship or transport in interstate or foreign commerce any firearm or ammunition or receive any firearm or ammunition which has been shipped or transported in interstate or foreign commerce.

(*o*)(1) Except as provided in paragraph (2), it shall be unlawful for any person to transfer or possess a machinegun.

(2) This subsection does not apply with respect to—

(A) a transfer to or by, or possession by or under the authority of, the United States or any department or agency thereof or a State, or a department, agency, or political subdivision thereof; or

(B) any lawful transfer or lawful possession of a machinegun that was lawfully possessed before the date this subsection takes effect.

(p)(1) It shall be unlawful for any person to manufacture, import, sell, ship, deliver, possess, transfer, or receive any firearm—

(A) that, after removal of grips, stocks, and magazines, is not as detectable as the Security Exemplar, by walk-through metal detectors calibrated and operated to detect the Security Exemplar; or

(B) any major component of which, when subjected to inspection by the types of x-ray machines commonly used at airports, does not generate an image that accurately depicts the shape of the component. Barium sulfate or other compounds may be used in the fabrication of the component.

(2) For purposes of this subsection—

(A) the term "firearm" does not include the frame or receiver of any such weapon;

(B) the term "major component" means, with respect to a firearm, the barrel, the slide or cylinder, or the frame or receiver of the firearm; and

(C) the term "Security Exemplar" means an object, to be fabricated at the direction of the Attorney General, that is—

(i) constructed of, during the 12–month period beginning on the date of the enactment of this subsection, 3.7 ounces of material type 17–4 PH stainless steel in a shape resembling a handgun; and

(ii) suitable for testing and calibrating metal detectors:

Provided, however, That at the close of such 12–month period, and at appropriate times thereafter the Attorney General shall promulgate regulations to permit the manufacture, importation, sale, shipment, delivery, possession, transfer, or receipt of firearms previously prohibited under this subparagraph that are as detectable as a "Security Exemplar" which contains 3.7 ounces of material type 17–4 PH stainless steel, in a shape resembling a handgun, or such lesser amount as is detectable in view of advances in state-of-the-art developments in weapons detection technology.

(3) Under such rules and regulations as the Attorney General shall prescribe, this subsection shall not apply to the manufacture, possession, transfer, receipt, shipment, or delivery of a firearm by a licensed manufacturer or any person acting pursuant to a contract with a licensed manufacturer, for the purpose of examining and testing such firearm to determine whether paragraph (1) applies to such firearm. The Attorney General shall ensure that rules and regulations adopted pursuant to this paragraph do not impair the manufacture of prototype firearms or the development of new technology.

(4) The Attorney General shall permit the conditional importation of a firearm by a licensed importer or licensed manufacturer, for examination and testing to determine whether or not the unconditional importation of such firearm would violate this subsection.

(5) This subsection shall not apply to any firearm which—

(A) has been certified by the Secretary of Defense or the Director of Central Intelligence, after consultation with the Attorney General and the Administrator of the Federal Aviation Administration, as necessary for military or intelligence applications; and

(B) is manufactured for and sold exclusively to military or intelligence agencies of the United States.

(6) This subsection shall not apply with respect to any firearm manufactured in, imported into, or possessed in the United States before the date of the enactment of the Undetectable Firearms Act of 1988.

(q)(1) The Congress finds and declares that—

(A) crime, particularly crime involving drugs and guns, is a pervasive, nationwide problem;

(B) crime at the local level is exacerbated by the interstate movement of drugs, guns, and criminal gangs;

(C) firearms and ammunition move easily in interstate commerce and have been found in increasing numbers in and around schools, as documented in numerous hearings in both the Committee on the Judiciary the [2] House of Representatives and the Committee on the Judiciary of the Senate;

(D) in fact, even before the sale of a firearm, the gun, its component parts, ammunition, and the raw materials from which they are made have considerably moved in interstate commerce;

(E) while criminals freely move from State to State, ordinary citizens and foreign visitors may fear to travel to or through certain parts of the country due to concern about violent crime and gun violence, and parents may decline to send their children to school for the same reason;

(F) the occurrence of violent crime in school zones has resulted in a decline in the quality of education in our country;

(G) this decline in the quality of education has an adverse impact on interstate commerce and the foreign commerce of the United States;

(H) States, localities, and school systems find it almost impossible to handle gun-related crime by themselves—even States, localities, and school systems that have made strong efforts to prevent, detect, and punish gun-related crime find their efforts unavailing due in part to the failure or inability of other States or localities to take strong measures; and

(I) the Congress has the power, under the interstate commerce clause and other provisions of the Constitution, to enact measures to ensure the integrity and safety of the Nation's schools by enactment of this subsection.

(2)(A) It shall be unlawful for any individual knowingly to possess a firearm that has moved in or that otherwise affects interstate or foreign commerce at a place that the individual knows, or has reasonable cause to believe, is a school zone.

(B) Subparagraph (A) does not apply to the possession of a firearm—

(i) on private property not part of school grounds;

(ii) if the individual possessing the firearm is licensed to do so by the State in which the school zone is located or a political subdivision of the State, and the law of the State or political subdivision requires that, before an individual obtains such a license, the law enforcement authorities of the State or political subdivision verify that the individual is qualified under law to receive the license;

(iii) that is—

(I) not loaded; and

(II) in a locked container, or a locked firearms rack that is on a motor vehicle;

(iv) by an individual for use in a program approved by a school in the school zone;

(v) by an individual in accordance with a contract entered into between a school in the school zone and the individual or an employer of the individual;

(vi) by a law enforcement officer acting in his or her official capacity; or

(vii) that is unloaded and is possessed by an individual while traversing school premises for the purpose of gaining access to public or private lands open to hunting, if the entry on school premises is authorized by school authorities.

(3)(A) Except as provided in subparagraph (B), it shall be unlawful for any person, knowingly or with reckless disregard for the safety of another, to discharge or attempt to discharge a firearm that has moved in or that otherwise affects interstate or foreign commerce at a place that the person knows is a school zone.

(B) Subparagraph (A) does not apply to the discharge of a firearm—

(i) on private property not part of school grounds;

(ii) as part of a program approved by a school in the school zone, by an individual who is participating in the program;

(iii) by an individual in accordance with a contract entered into between a school in a school zone and the individual or an employer of the individual; or

(iv) by a law enforcement officer acting in his or her official capacity.

(4) Nothing in this subsection shall be construed as preempting or preventing a State or local government from enacting a statute establishing gun free school zones as provided in this subsection.

(r) It shall be unlawful for any person to assemble from imported parts any semiautomatic rifle or any shotgun which is identical to any rifle or shotgun prohibited from importation under section 925(d)(3) of this chapter as not being particularly suitable for or readily adaptable to sporting purposes except that this subsection shall not apply to—

(1) the assembly of any such rifle or shotgun for sale or distribution by a licensed manufacturer to the United States or any department or agency thereof or to any State or any department, agency, or political subdivision thereof; or

(2) the assembly of any such rifle or shotgun for the purposes of testing or experimentation authorized by the Attorney General.

(s)(1) Beginning on the date that is 90 days after the date of enactment of this subsection and ending on the day before the date that is 60 months after such date of enactment, it shall be unlawful for any licensed importer, licensed manufacturer, or licensed dealer to sell, deliver, or transfer a handgun (other than the return of a handgun to the person from whom it was received) to an individual who is not licensed under section 923, unless—

(A) after the most recent proposal of such transfer by the transferee—

(i) the transferor has—

(I) received from the transferee a statement of the transferee containing the information described in paragraph (3);

(II) verified the identity of the transferee by examining the identification document presented;

(III) within 1 day after the transferee furnishes the statement, provided notice of the contents of the statement to the chief law enforcement officer of the place of residence of the transferee; and

(IV) within 1 day after the transferee furnishes the statement, transmitted a copy of the statement to the chief law enforcement officer of the place of residence of the transferee; and

(ii)(I) 5 business days (meaning days on which State offices are open) have elapsed from the date the transferor furnished notice of the contents of the statement to the chief law enforcement officer, during which period the transferor has not received information from the chief law enforcement officer that receipt or possession of the handgun by the transferee would be in violation of Federal, State, or local law; or

(II) the transferor has received notice from the chief law enforcement officer that the officer has no information indicating that receipt or possession of the handgun by the transferee would violate Federal, State, or local law;

(B) the transferee has presented to the transferor a written statement, issued by the chief law enforcement officer of the place of residence of the transferee during the 10-day period ending on the date of the most recent proposal of such transfer by the transferee, stating that the transferee requires access to a handgun because of a threat to the life of the transferee or of any member of the household of the transferee;

(C)(i) the transferee has presented to the transferor a permit that—

(I) allows the transferee to possess or acquire a handgun; and

(II) was issued not more than 5 years earlier by the State in which the transfer is to take place; and

(ii) the law of the State provides that such a permit is to be issued only after an authorized government official has verified that the information available to such official does not indicate that possession of a handgun by the transferee would be in violation of the law;

(D) the law of the State requires that, before any licensed importer, licensed manufacturer, or licensed dealer completes the transfer of a handgun to an individual who is not licensed under section 923, an authorized government official verify that the information available to such official does not indicate that possession of a handgun by the transferee would be in violation of law;

(E) the Attorney General has approved the transfer under section 5812 of the Internal Revenue Code of 1986; or

(F) on application of the transferor, the Attorney General has certified that compliance with subparagraph (A)(i)(III) is impracticable because—

(i) the ratio of the number of law enforcement officers of the State in which the transfer is to occur to the number of square miles of land area of the State does not exceed 0.0025;

(ii) the business premises of the transferor at which the transfer is to occur are extremely remote in relation to the chief law enforcement officer; and

(iii) there is an absence of telecommunications facilities in the geographical area in which the business premises are located.

(2) A chief law enforcement officer to whom a transferor has provided notice pursuant to paragraph (1)(A)(i)(III) shall make a reasonable effort to ascertain within 5 business days whether receipt or possession would be in violation of the law, including research in whatever State and local recordkeeping systems are available and in a national system designated by the Attorney General.

(3) The statement referred to in paragraph (1)(A)(i)(I) shall contain only—

(A) the name, address, and date of birth appearing on a valid identification document (as defined in section 1028(d)(1)) of the transferee containing a photograph of the transferee and a description of the identification used;

(B) a statement that the transferee—

(i) is not under indictment for, and has not been convicted in any court of, a crime punishable by imprisonment for a term exceeding 1 year, and has not been convicted in any court of a misdemeanor crime of domestic violence;

(ii) is not a fugitive from justice;

(iii) is not an unlawful user of or addicted to any controlled substance (as defined in section 102 of the Controlled Substances Act);

(iv) has not been adjudicated as a mental defective or been committed to a mental institution;

(v) is not an alien who—

(I) is illegally or unlawfully in the United States; or

(II) subject to subsection (y)(2), has been admitted to the United States under a nonimmigrant visa (as that term is defined in section 101(a)(26) of the Immigration and Nationality Act (8 U.S.C. 1101(a)(26)));

(vi) has not been discharged from the Armed Forces under dishonorable conditions; and

(vii) is not a person who, having been a citizen of the United States, has renounced such citizenship;

(C) the date the statement is made; and

(D) notice that the transferee intends to obtain a handgun from the transferor.

(4) Any transferor of a handgun who, after such transfer, receives a report from a chief law enforcement officer containing information that receipt or possession of the handgun by the transferee violates Federal, State, or local law shall, within 1 business day after receipt of such request, communicate any information related to the transfer that the transferor has about the transfer and the transferee to—

(A) the chief law enforcement officer of the place of business of the transferor; and

(B) the chief law enforcement officer of the place of residence of the transferee.

(5) Any transferor who receives information, not otherwise available to the public, in a report under this subsection shall not disclose such information except to the transferee, to law enforcement authorities, or pursuant to the direction of a court of law.

(6)(A) Any transferor who sells, delivers, or otherwise transfers a handgun to a transferee shall retain the copy of the statement of the transferee with respect to the handgun transaction, and shall retain evidence that the transferor has complied with subclauses (III) and (IV) of paragraph (1)(A)(i) with respect to the statement.

(B) Unless the chief law enforcement officer to whom a statement is transmitted under paragraph (1)(A)(i)(IV) determines that a transaction would violate Federal, State, or local law—

(i) the officer shall, within 20 business days after the date the transferee made the statement on the basis of which the notice was provided, destroy the statement, any record containing information derived from the statement, and any record created as a result of the notice required by paragraph (1)(A)(i)(III);

(ii) the information contained in the statement shall not be conveyed to any person except a person who has a need to know in order to carry out this subsection; and

(iii) the information contained in the statement shall not be used for any purpose other than to carry out this subsection.

(C) If a chief law enforcement officer determines that an individual is ineligible to receive a handgun and the individual requests the officer to provide the reason for such determination, the officer shall provide such reasons to the individual in writing within 20 business days after receipt of the request.

(7) A chief law enforcement officer or other person responsible for providing criminal history background information pursuant to this subsection shall not be liable in an action at law for damages—

(A) for failure to prevent the sale or transfer of a handgun to a person whose receipt or possession of the handgun is unlawful under this section; or

(B) for preventing such a sale or transfer to a person who may lawfully receive or possess a handgun.

(8) For purposes of this subsection, the term "chief law enforcement officer" means the chief of police, the sheriff, or an equivalent officer or the designee of any such individual.

(9) The Attorney General shall take necessary actions to ensure that the provisions of this subsection are published and disseminated to licensed dealers, law enforcement officials, and the public.

(t)(1) Beginning on the date that is 30 days after the Attorney General notifies licensees under section 103(d) of the Brady Handgun Violence Prevention Act that the national instant criminal background check system is established, a licensed importer, licensed manufacturer, or licensed dealer shall not transfer a firearm to any other person who is not licensed under this chapter, unless—

(A) before the completion of the transfer, the licensee contacts the national instant criminal background check system established under section 103 of that Act;

(B)(i) the system provides the licensee with a unique identification number; or

(ii) 3 business days (meaning a day on which State offices are open) have elapsed since the licensee contacted the system, and the system has not notified the licensee that the receipt of a firearm by such other person would violate subsection (g) or (n) of this section; and

(C) the transferor has verified the identity of the transferee by examining a valid identification document (as defined in section 1028(d) of this title) of the transferee containing a photograph of the transferee.

(2) If receipt of a firearm would not violate subsection (g) or (n) or State law, the system shall—

(A) assign a unique identification number to the transfer;

(B) provide the licensee with the number; and

(C) destroy all records of the system with respect to the call (other than the identifying number and the date the number was assigned) and all records of the system relating to the person or the transfer.

(3) Paragraph (1) shall not apply to a firearm transfer between a licensee and another person if—

(A)(i) such other person has presented to the licensee a permit that—

(I) allows such other person to possess or acquire a firearm; and

(II) was issued not more than 5 years earlier by the State in which the transfer is to take place; and

(ii) the law of the State provides that such a permit is to be issued only after an authorized government official has verified that the information available to such official does not indicate that possession of a firearm by such other person would be in violation of law;

(B) the Attorney General has approved the transfer under section 5812 of the Internal Revenue Code of 1986; or

(C) on application of the transferor, the Attorney General has certified that compliance with paragraph (1)(A) is impracticable because—

(i) the ratio of the number of law enforcement officers of the State in which the transfer is to occur to the number of square miles of land area of the State does not exceed 0.0025;

(ii) the business premises of the licensee at which the transfer is to occur are extremely remote in relation to the chief law enforcement officer (as defined in subsection (s)(8)); and

(iii) there is an absence of telecommunications facilities in the geographical area in which the business premises are located.

(4) If the national instant criminal background check system notifies the licensee that the information available to the system does not demonstrate that the receipt of a firearm by such other person would violate subsection (g) or (n) or State law, and the licensee transfers a firearm to such other person, the licensee shall include in the record of the transfer the unique identification number provided by the system with respect to the transfer.

(5) If the licensee knowingly transfers a firearm to such other person and knowingly fails to comply with paragraph (1) of this subsection with respect to the transfer and, at the time such other person most recently proposed the transfer, the national instant criminal background check system was operating and information was available to the system demonstrating that receipt of a firearm by such other person would violate subsection (g) or (n) of this section or State law, the Attorney General may, after notice and opportunity for a hearing, suspend for not more than 6 months or revoke any license issued to the licensee under section 923, and may impose on the licensee a civil fine of not more than $5,000.

(6) Neither a local government nor an employee of the Federal Government or of any State or local government, responsible for providing information to the national instant criminal background check system shall be liable in an action at law for damages—

(A) for failure to prevent the sale or transfer of a firearm to a person whose receipt or possession of the firearm is unlawful under this section; or

(B) for preventing such a sale or transfer to a person who may lawfully receive or possess a firearm.

(u) It shall be unlawful for a person to steal or unlawfully take or carry away from the person or the premises of a person who is licensed to engage in the business of importing, manufacturing, or dealing in firearms, any firearm in the licensee's business inventory that has been shipped or transported in interstate or foreign commerce.

[(v), (w) Repealed. Pub.L. 103–322, Title XI, § 110105(2), Sept. 13, 1994, 108 Stat. 2000]

(x)(1) It shall be unlawful for a person to sell, deliver, or otherwise transfer to a person who the transferor knows or has reasonable cause to believe is a juvenile—

(A) a handgun; or

(B) ammunition that is suitable for use only in a handgun.

(2) It shall be unlawful for any person who is a juvenile to knowingly possess—

(A) a handgun; or

(B) ammunition that is suitable for use only in a handgun.

(3) This subsection does not apply to—

(A) a temporary transfer of a handgun or ammunition to a juvenile or to the possession or use of a handgun or ammunition by a juvenile if the handgun and ammunition are possessed and used by the juvenile—

(i) in the course of employment, in the course of ranching or farming related to activities at the residence of the juvenile (or on property used for ranching or farming at which the juvenile, with the permission of the property owner or lessee, is performing activities related to the operation of the farm or ranch), target practice, hunting, or a course of instruction in the safe and lawful use of a handgun;

(ii) with the prior written consent of the juvenile's parent or guardian who is not prohibited by Federal, State, or local law from possessing a firearm, except—

(I) during transportation by the juvenile of an unloaded handgun in a locked container directly from the place of transfer to a place at which an activity described in clause (i) is to take place and transportation by the juvenile of that handgun, unloaded and in a locked container, directly from the place at which such an activity took place to the transferor; or

(II) with respect to ranching or farming activities as described in clause (i), a juvenile may possess and use a handgun or ammunition with the prior written approval of the juvenile's parent or legal guardian and at the direction of an adult who is not prohibited by Federal, State or local law from possessing a firearm;

(iii) the juvenile has the prior written consent in the juvenile's possession at all times when a handgun is in the possession of the juvenile; and

(iv) in accordance with State and local law;

(B) a juvenile who is a member of the Armed Forces of the United States or the National Guard who possesses or is armed with a handgun in the line of duty;

(C) a transfer by inheritance of title (but not possession) of a handgun or ammunition to a juvenile; or

(D) the possession of a handgun or ammunition by a juvenile taken in defense of the juvenile or other persons against an intruder into the residence of the juvenile or a residence in which the juvenile is an invited guest.

(4) A handgun or ammunition, the possession of which is transferred to a juvenile in circumstances in which the transferor is not in violation of this subsection shall not be subject to permanent confiscation by the Government if its possession by the juvenile subsequently becomes unlawful because of the conduct of the juvenile, but shall be returned to the lawful owner when such handgun or ammunition is no longer required by the Government for the purposes of investigation or prosecution.

(5) For purposes of this subsection, the term "juvenile" means a person who is less than 18 years of age.

(6)(A) In a prosecution of a violation of this subsection, the court shall require the presence of a juvenile defendant's parent or legal guardian at all proceedings.

(B) The court may use the contempt power to enforce subparagraph (A).

(C) The court may excuse attendance of a parent or legal guardian of a juvenile defendant at a proceeding in a prosecution of a violation of this subsection for good cause shown.

(y) Provisions relating to aliens admitted under nonimmigrant visas—

(1) Definitions.—In this subsection—

(A) the term "alien" has the same meaning as in section 101(a)(3) of the Immigration and Nationality Act (8 U.S.C. 1101(a)(3)); and

(B) the term "nonimmigrant visa" has the same meaning as in section 101(a)(26) of the Immigration and Nationality Act (8 U.S.C. 1101(a)(26)).

(2) Exceptions.—Subsections (d)(5)(B), (g)(5)(B), and (s)(3)(B)(v)(II) do not apply to any alien who has been lawfully admitted to the United States under a nonimmigrant visa, if that alien is—

(A) admitted to the United States for lawful hunting or sporting purposes or is in possession of a hunting license or permit lawfully issued in the United States;

(B) an official representative of a foreign government who is—

(i) accredited to the United States Government or the Government's mission to an international organization having its headquarters in the United States; or

(ii) en route to or from another country to which that alien is accredited;

(C) an official of a foreign government or a distinguished foreign visitor who has been so designated by the Department of State; or

(D) a foreign law enforcement officer of a friendly foreign government entering the United States on official law enforcement business.

(3) Waiver—

(A) Conditions for waiver.—Any individual who has been admitted to the United States under a nonimmigrant visa may receive a waiver from the requirements of subsection (g)(5), if—

(i) the individual submits to the Attorney General a petition that meets the requirements of subparagraph (C); and

(ii) the Attorney General approves the petition.

(B) Petition.—Each petition under subparagraph (B) shall—

(i) demonstrate that the petitioner has resided in the United States for a continuous period of not less than 180 days before the date on which the petition is submitted under this paragraph; and

(ii) include a written statement from the embassy or consulate of the petitioner, authorizing the petitioner to acquire a firearm or ammunition and certifying that the alien would not, absent the application of subsection (g)(5)(B), otherwise be prohibited from such acquisition under subsection (g).

(C) Approval of petition.—The Attorney General shall approve a petition submitted in accordance with this paragraph, if the Attorney General determines that waiving the requirements of subsection (g)(5)(B) with respect to the petitioner—

(i) would be in the interests of justice; and

(ii) would not jeopardize the public safety.

(z) Secure gun storage or safety device.—

(1) In general.—Except as provided under paragraph (2), it shall be unlawful for any licensed importer, licensed manufacturer, or licensed dealer to sell, deliver, or transfer any handgun to any person other than any person licensed under this chapter, unless the transferee is provided with a secure gun storage or safety device (as defined in section 921(a)(34)) for that handgun.

(2) Exceptions.—Paragraph (1) shall not apply to—

(A)(i) the manufacture for, transfer to, or possession by, the United States, a department or agency of the United States, a State, or a department, agency, or political subdivision of a State, of a handgun; or

(ii) the transfer to, or possession by, a law enforcement officer employed by an entity referred to in clause (i) of a handgun for law enforcement purposes (whether on or off duty); or

(B) the transfer to, or possession by, a rail police officer employed by a rail carrier and certified or commissioned as a police officer under the laws of a State of a handgun for purposes of law enforcement (whether on or off duty);

(C) the transfer to any person of a handgun listed as a curio or relic by the Secretary pursuant to section 921(a)(13); or

(D) the transfer to any person of a handgun for which a secure gun storage or safety device is temporarily unavailable for the reasons described in the exceptions stated in section 923(e), if the licensed manufacturer, licensed importer, or licensed dealer delivers to the transferee within 10 calendar days from the date of the delivery of the handgun to the transferee a secure gun storage or safety device for the handgun.

(3) Liability for use.—

(A) In general.—Notwithstanding any other provision of law, a person who has lawful possession and control of a handgun, and who uses a secure gun storage or safety device with the handgun, shall be entitled to immunity from a qualified civil liability action.

(B) Prospective actions.—A qualified civil liability action may not be brought in any Federal or State court.

(C) Defined term.—As used in this paragraph, the term "qualified civil liability action"—

(i) means a civil action brought by any person against a person described in subparagraph (A) for damages resulting from the criminal or unlawful misuse of the handgun by a third party, if—

(I) the handgun was accessed by another person who did not have the permission or authorization of the person having lawful possession and control of the handgun to have access to it; and

(II) at the time access was gained by the person not so authorized, the handgun had been made inoperable by use of a secure gun storage or safety device; and

(ii) shall not include an action brought against the person having lawful possession and control of the handgun for negligent entrustment or negligence per se.

[APPENDIX A Repealed. Pub.L. 103–322, Title XI, § 110105(2), Sept. 13, 1994, 108 Stat. 2000]

(Added Pub.L. 90–351, Title IV, § 902, June 19, 1968, 82 Stat. 228, and amended Pub.L. 90–618, Title I, § 102, Oct. 22, 1968, 82 Stat. 1216; Pub.L. 97–377, Title I, § 165(a), Dec. 21, 1982, 96 Stat. 1923; Pub.L. 99–308, § 102, May 19, 1986, 100 Stat. 451; Pub.L. 99–408, § 2, Aug. 28, 1986, 100 Stat. 920; Pub.L. 100–649, § 2(a), (f)(2)(A), Nov. 10, 1988, 102 Stat. 3816, 3818; Pub.L. 100–690, Title VII, § 7060(c), Nov. 18, 1988, 102 Stat. 4404; Pub.L. 101–647, Title XVII, § 1702(b)(1), Title XXII, §§ 2201, 2202, 2204(b), Title XXXV, § 3524, Nov. 29, 1990, 104 Stat. 4844, 4856, 4857, 4924; Pub.L. 103–159, Title I, § 102(a)(1), (b), Title III, § 302(a) to (c), Nov. 30, 1993, 107 Stat. 1536, 1539, 1545; Pub.L. 103–322, Title XI, §§ 110102(a), 110103(a), 110105(2), 110106, 110201(a), 110401(b), (c), 110511, 110514, Title XXXII, §§ 320904, 320927, Title XXXIII, § 330011(i), Sept. 13, 1994, 108 Stat. 1996, 1998, 2000, 2010, 2014, 2019, 2125, 2131, 2145; Pub.L. 104–208, Div. A, Title I, § 101(f) [Title VI, §§ 657, 658(b)], Sept. 30, 1996, 110 Stat. 3009–369, 3009–372; Pub.L. 104–294, Title VI, § 603(b), (c)(1), (d) to (f)(1), (g), Oct. 11, 1996, 110 Stat. 3503, 3504; Pub.L. 105–277, Div. A, § 101(b) [Title I, § 121], Oct. 21, 1998, 112 Stat. 2681–71; Pub.L. 107–273, Div. B, Title IV, § 4003(a)(1), Nov. 2, 2002, 116 Stat. 1811; Pub.L. 107–296, Title XI, § 1112(f)(4), (6), Nov. 25, 2002, 116 Stat. 2276; Pub.L. 109–92, §§ 5(c)(1), 6(a), Oct. 26, 2005, 119 Stat. 2099, 2101.)

1 So in original. The word "who" probably should not appear.

2 So in original. Probably should be "of the".

Repeal of Subsec. (p)

Pub.L. 100–649, § 2(f)(2)(A), Nov. 10, 1988, 102 Stat. 3818, as amended Pub.L. 105–277, Div. A, § 101(h) [Title VI, § 649], Oct. 21, 1998, 112 Stat. 2681–528; Pub.L. 108–174, § 1(1), Dec. 9, 2003, 117 Stat. 2481, provided that, effective 25 years after the 30th day beginning after Nov. 10, 1988 [see section 2(f)(1) of Pub.L. 100–649, set out as a note under this section], subsec. (p) of this section is repealed.

HISTORICAL AND STATUTORY NOTES

References in Text

The effective date of this chapter, referred to in subsec. (a)(3) of this section, is Dec. 16, 1968.

Section 5845 of the Internal Revenue Code of 1954, referred to in subsecs. (a)(4) and (b)(4) of this section, is classified to § 5845 of Title 26, Internal Revenue Code.

Section 102 of the Controlled Substances Act, referred to in subsecs. (d)(3), (g)(3), and (s)(3)(B)(iii), is section 102 of Pub.L. 91–513, which is classified to section 802 of Title 21, Food and Drugs.

Date this subsection takes effect, referred to in subsec. (*o*), is May 19, 1986. See section 110(c) of Pub.L. 99–308, set out as a note under section 921 of this title.

The date of the enactment of the Undetectable Firearms Act of 1988, referred to in subsec. (p)(6), is the date of the enactment of Pub.L. 100–649, which added subsec. (p) of this section and which was approved Nov. 10, 1988.

The date of enactment of this subsection, referred to in subsec. (s)(1), is the date of enactment of Pub.L. 103–159, which was approved Nov. 30, 1993.

Section 5812 of the Internal Revenue Code of 1986, referred to in subsecs. (s)(1)(E) and (t)(3)(B), is set out as section 5812 of Title 26, Internal Revenue Code.

Section 1028 of this title, referred to in subsecs. (s)(3)(A) and (t)(1)(C), was subsequently amended so that the definition of the term "identification document" now appears at 18 U.S.C.A. § 1028(d)(2).

Section 103 of the Brady Handgun Violence Prevention Act, referred to in subsec. (t)(1), is section 103 of Pub.L. 103–159, which is set out as a note under this section.

Codifications

Section 603(b) of Pub.L. 104–294, which directed that subsec. (g)(8)(C)(ii) be amended by striking the comma at the end and inserting a semicolon, was incapable of execution due to prior amendment of subsec. (g)(8)(C)(ii) by section 101(f) [Title VI, § 658(b)] of Pub.L. 104–208, see 1996 Amendments notes set out under this section.

2005 Acts. Pub.L. 109–92, § 5(d), Oct. 26, 2005, 119 Stat. 2101, provided that: "This section and the amendments made by this section [enacting subsec. (z) of this section and amending 18 U.S.C.A. § 924 and enacting provisions set out as notes under this section and 18 U.S.C.A. § 921] shall take effect 180 days after the date of enactment of this Act [Oct. 26, 2005]."

1968 Acts. Amendment by Pub.L. 90–618 effective Dec. 16, 1968, except subsec. (*l*) effective Oct. 22, 1968, see § 105 of Pub.L. 90–618, set out as a note under § 921 of this title.

Sunset Provision

Pub.L. 100–649, § 2(f), Nov. 10, 1988, 102 Stat. 3818, as amended Pub.L. 101–647, Title XXXV, § 3526(b), Nov. 29, 1990, 104 Stat. 4924; Pub.L. 105–277, Div. A, § 101(h) [Title VI, § 649], Oct. 21, 1998, 112 Stat. 2681–528; Pub.L. 108–174, § 1, Dec. 9, 2003, 117 Stat. 2481, provided that:

"**(1) Effective date.**—This Act [amending this section and 18 U.S.C.A. §§ 924 and 925, and enacting provisions set out as notes under this section, 18 U.S.C.A. § 921, and section 1356 of Title 49 App., Transportation] and the amendments made by this Act shall take effect on the 30th day beginning after the date of the enactment of this Act [Nov. 10, 1988].

"**(2) Sunset.**—Effective 25 years after the effective date of this Act—

"**(A)** subsection (p) of section 922 of title 18, United States Code, is hereby repealed;

"**(B)** subsection (f) of section 924 of such title is hereby repealed and subsections (g) through (*o*) of such section are hereby redesignated as subsections (f) through (n), respectively;

"**(C)** subsection (f) of section 925 of such title is hereby repealed;

"**(D)** section 924(a)(1) of such title is amended by striking 'this subsection, subsection (b), (c), or (f) of this section, or in section 929' and inserting 'this chapter'; and

"**(E)** section 925(a) of such title is amended—

"**(i)** in paragraph (1), by striking 'and provisions relating to firearms subject to the prohibitions of section 922(p)'; and

"**(ii)** in paragraph (2), by striking ', except for provisions relating to firearms subject to the prohibitions of section 922(p),'; and

"**(iii)** in each of paragraphs (3) and (4), by striking 'except for provisions relating to firearms subject to the prohibitions of section 922(p),'."

Change of Name

Reference to the Director of Central Intelligence or the Director of the Central Intelligence Agency in the Director's capacity as the head of the intelligence community deemed to be a reference to the Director of National Intelligence. Reference to the Director of Central Intelligence or the Director of the Central Intelligence Agency in the Director's capacity as the head of the Central Intelligence Agency deemed to be a reference to the Director of the Central Intelligence Agency. See Pub.L. 108–458, § 1081(a) and (b), set out as a note under 50 U.S.C.A. § 401.

Purposes

Pub.L. 109–92, § 5(b), Oct. 26, 2005, 119 Stat. 2099, provided that:

"The purposes of this section [the Child Safety Lock Act of 2005, which amended this section and 18 U.S.C.A. § 924 and enacted provisions set out as notes under this section and 18 U.S.C.A. § 921] are—

"(1) to promote the safe storage and use of handguns by consumers;

"(2) to prevent unauthorized persons from gaining access to or use of a handgun, including children who may not be in possession of a handgun; and

"(3) to avoid hindering industry from supplying firearms to law abiding citizens for all lawful purposes, including hunting, self-defense, collecting, and competitive or recreational shooting."

[This note effective 180 days after Oct. 26, 2005, see Pub.L. 109–92, § 5(d), set out as a note under this section.]

Liability; evidence

Pub.L. 109–92, § 5(c)(3), Oct. 26, 2005, 119 Stat. 2101, provided that:

"**(A) Liability.**—Nothing in this section [the Child Safety Lock Act of 2005, which amended this section and 18

U.S.C.A. § 924 and enacted provisions set out as notes under this section and 18 U.S.C.A. § 921] shall be construed to—

"(i) create a cause of action against any Federal firearms licensee or any other person for any civil liability; or

"(ii) establish any standard of care.

"(B) **Evidence.**—Notwithstanding any other provision of law, evidence regarding compliance or noncompliance with the amendments made by this section [amending this section and 18 U.S.C.A. § 924 and enacting provisions set out as notes under this section and 18 U.S.C.A. § 921] shall not be admissible as evidence in any proceeding of any court, agency, board, or other entity, except with respect to an action relating to section 922(z) of title 18, United States Code [subsec. (z) of this section], as added by this subsection.

"(C) **Rule of construction.**—Nothing in this paragraph shall be construed to bar a governmental action to impose a penalty under section 924(p) of title 18, United States Code, for a failure to comply with section 922(z) of that title."

[This note effective 180 days after Oct. 26, 2005, see Pub.L. 109–92, § 5(d), set out as a note under this section.]

Criminal Background Checks for Persons Offering a Firearm as Collateral for a Loan

Pub.L. 106–58, Title VI, § 634, Sept. 29, 1999, 113 Stat. 473, provided that: "None of the funds made available in this [the Treasury and General Government Appropriations Act, 2000; for complete classification, see Tables] or any other Act with respect to any fiscal year may be used for any system to implement section 922(t) of title 18, United States Code, unless the system allows, in connection with a person's delivery of a firearm to a Federal firearms licensee as collateral for a loan, the background check to be performed at the time the collateral is offered for delivery to such licensee: *Provided*, That the licensee notifies local law enforcement within 48 hours of the licensee receiving a denial on the person offering the collateral: *Provided further*, That the provisions of section 922(t) shall apply at the time of the redemption of the firearm."

Similar provisions were contained in the following prior Appropriations Acts:

Pub.L. 105–277, § 101(h) [Title VI, § 655], Oct. 21, 1998, 112 Stat. 2681–530.

Availability of Violent Crime Reduction Trust Fund to Fund Activities Authorized by the Brady Handgun Violence Prevention Act and the National Child Protection Act of 1993

Pub.L. 103–322, Title XXI, § 210603(a), Sept. 13, 1994, 108 Stat. 2074, which provided for availability of the Violent Crime Reduction Trust Fund to fund activities authorized by the Brady Handgun Violence Prevention Act and the National Child Protection Act of 1993, was repealed by Pub.L. 109–162, Title XI, § 1154(b)(4), Jan. 5, 2006, 119 Stat. 3113.

National Instant Criminal Background Check System

Section 103 of Pub.L. 103–159, as amended Pub.L. 103–322, Title XXI, § 210603(b), Sept. 13, 1994, 103 Stat. 2074; Pub.L. 104–294, Title VI, § 603(h), (i)(1), Oct. 11, 1996, 110 Stat. 3504; Pub.L. 109–162, Title XI, § 1154(b)(4), Jan. 5, 2006, 119 Stat. 3113, provided that:

"(a) **Determination of Timetables.** Not later than 6 months after the date of enactment of this Act [Nov. 30, 1993], the Attorney General shall—

"(1) determine the type of computer hardware and software that will be used to operate the national instant criminal background check system and the means by which State criminal records systems and the telephone or electronic device of licensees will communicate with the national system;

"(2) investigate the criminal records system of each State and determine for each State a timetable by which the State should be able to provide criminal records on an on-line capacity basis to the national system; and

"(3) notify each State of the determinations made pursuant to paragraphs (1) and (2).

"(b) **Establishment of System.** Not later than 60 months after the date of the enactment of this Act [Nov. 30, 1993], the Attorney General shall establish a national instant criminal background check system that any licensee may contact, by telephone or by other electronic means in addition to the telephone, for information, to be supplied immediately, on whether receipt of a firearm by a prospective transferee would violate section 922 of title 18, United States Code [this section], or State law.

"(c) **Expedited action by the Attorney General.** The Attorney General shall expedite—

"(1) the upgrading and indexing of State criminal history records in the Federal criminal records system maintained by the Federal Bureau of Investigation;

"(2) the development of hardware and software systems to link State criminal history check systems into the national instant criminal background check system established by the Attorney General pursuant to this section; and

"(3) the current revitalization initiatives by the Federal Bureau of Investigation for technologically advanced fingerprint and criminal records identification.

"(d) **Notification of Licensees.** On establishment of the system under this section, the Attorney General shall notify each licensee and the chief law enforcement officer of each State of the existence and purpose of the system and the means to be used to contact the system.

"(e) **Administrative Provisions.**

"(1) **Authority to obtain official information.** Notwithstanding any other law, the Attorney General may secure directly from any department or agency of the United States such information on persons for whom receipt of a firearm would violate subsection (g) or (n) of section 922 of title 18, United States Code [subsec. (g) or (n) of this section], or State law, as is necessary to enable the system to operate in accordance with this section. On request of the Attorney General, the head of such department or agency shall furnish such information to the system.

"(2) **Other authority.** The Attorney General shall develop such computer software, design and obtain such telecommunications and computer hardware, and employ such personnel, as are necessary to establish and operate the system in accordance with this section.

"(f) **Written Reasons Provided on Request.** If the national instant criminal background check system determines that an individual is ineligible to receive a firearm and the individual requests the system to provide the reasons for the determination, the system shall provide such reasons to the individual, in writing, within 5 business days after the date of the request.

"(g) Correction of Erroneous System Information. If the system established under this section informs an individual contacting the system that receipt of a firearm by a prospective transferee would violate subsection (g) or (n) of section 922 of title 18, United States Code [subsec. (g) or (n) of this section], or State law, the prospective transferee may request the Attorney General to provide the prospective transferee with the reasons therefor. Upon receipt of such a request, the Attorney General shall immediately comply with the request. The prospective transferee may submit to the Attorney General information to correct, clarify, or supplement records of the system with respect to the prospective transferee. After receipt of such information, the Attorney General shall immediately consider the information, investigate the matter further, and correct all erroneous Federal records relating to the prospective transferee and give notice of the error to any Federal department or agency or any State that was the source of such erroneous records.

"(h) Regulations. After 90 days' notice to the public and an opportunity for hearing by interested parties, the Attorney General shall prescribe regulations to ensure the privacy and security of the information of the system established under this section.

"(i) Prohibition Relating to Establishment of Registration Systems With Respect to Firearms. No department, agency, officer, or employee of the United States may—

"(1) require that any record or portion thereof generated by the system established under this section be recorded at or transferred to a facility owned, managed, or controlled by the United States or any State or political subdivision thereof; or

"(2) use the system established under this section to establish any system for the registration of firearms, firearm owners, or firearm transactions or dispositions, except with respect to persons, prohibited by section 922(g) or (n) of title 18, United States Code [subsec. (g) or (n) of this section], or State law, from receiving a firearm.

"(j) Definitions. As used in this section:

"(1) Licensee. The term 'licensee' means a licensed importer (as defined in section 921(a)(9) of title 18, United States Code [section 921(a)(9) of this title]), a licensed manufacturer (as defined in section 921(a)(10) of that title [section 921(a)(10) of this title]), or a licensed dealer (as defined in section 921(a)(11) of that title [section 921(a)(11) of this title]).

"(2) Other terms. The terms 'firearm', 'handgun', 'licensed importer', 'licensed manufacturer', and 'licensed dealer' have the meanings stated in section 921(a) of title 18, United States Code, as amended by subsection (a)(2) [probably means section 102(a)(2) of Pub.L. 103–159, which amended section 921(a) of this title].

"(k) Authorization of Appropriations. There are authorized to be appropriated such sums as are necessary to enable the Attorney General to carry out this section."

[Pub.L. 104–294, Title VI, § 603(i)(2), Oct. 11, 1996, 110 Stat. 3504, provided that: "The amendment made by paragraph (1) [amending section 210603(b) of Pub.L. 103–322, which amended sections 103(k) and 106(b)(2) of Pub.L. 103–159, both set out as notes under this section] shall take effect as if the amendment had been included in section 210603(b) of the Act referred to in paragraph (1) [section 210603(b) of Pub.L. 103–322] on the date of the enactment of such Act [Sept. 13, 1994]."]

Funding for Improvement of Criminal Records

Section 106(b) of Pub.L. 103–159, as amended Pub.L. 103–322, Title XXI, § 210603(b), Sept. 13, 1994, 108 Stat. 2074; Pub.L. 104–294, Title VI, § 603(i)(1), Oct. 11, 1996, 110 Stat. 3504; Pub.L. 109–162, Title XI, § 1154(b)(4), Jan. 5, 2006, 119 Stat. 3113, provided that:

"(1) Grants for the Improvement of Criminal Records. The Attorney General, through the Bureau of Justice Statistics, shall, subject to appropriations and with preference to States that as of the date of enactment of this Act [Nov. 30, 1993] have the lowest percent currency of case dispositions in computerized criminal history files, make a grant to each State to be used—

"(A) for the creation of a computerized criminal history record system or improvement of an existing system;

"(B) to improve accessibility to the national instant criminal background system; and

"(C) upon establishment of the national system, to assist the State in the transmittal of criminal records to the national system.

"(2) Authorization of Appropriations. There are authorized to be appropriated for grants under paragraph (1) a total of $200,000,000 for fiscal year 1994 and all fiscal years thereafter."

[Amendment by section 603(i)(1) of Pub.L. 104–294 to section 210603(b) of Pub.L. 103–322, which, in part, amended section 106(b)(2) of Pub.L. 103–159, effective as if included in section 210603(b) of Pub.L. 103–322 on the date of enactment of Pub.L. 103–322, which was approved Sept. 13, 1994, see Pub.L. 104–294, Title VI, § 603(i)(2), Oct. 11, 1996, 110 Stat. 3504, set out as a note following section 103 of Pub.L. 103–159, which is set out as a note under this section.]

Gun-Free Zone Signs

Pub.L. 101–647, Title XVII, § 1702(b)(5), Nov. 29, 1990, 104 Stat. 4845, provided that: "Federal, State, and local authorities are encouraged to cause signs to be posted around school zones giving warning of prohibition of the possession of firearms in a school zone."

Identification of Felons and Other Persons Ineligible to Purchase Handguns

Section 6213 of Pub.L. 100–690 provided that:

"(a) Identification of Felons Ineligible To Purchase Handguns. The Attorney General shall develop a system for immediate and accurate identification of felons who attempt to purchase 1 or more firearms but are ineligible to purchase firearms by reason of section 922(g)(1) of title 18, United States Code [subsec. (g)(1) of this section]. The system shall be accessible to dealers but only for the purpose of determining whether a potential purchaser is a convicted felon. The Attorney General shall establish a plan (including a cost analysis of the proposed system) for implementation of the system. In developing the system, the Attorney General shall consult with the Secretary of the Treasury, other Federal, State, and local law enforcement officials with expertise in the area, and other experts. The Attorney General shall begin implementation of the system 30 days after the report to the Congress as provided in subsection (b).

"**(b) Report To Congress.** Not later than 1 year after the date of the enactment of this Act [Nov. 18, 1988], the Attorney General shall report to the Congress a description of the system referred to in subsection (a) and a plan (including a cost analysis of the proposed system) for implementation of the system. Such report may include, if appropriate, recommendations for modifications of the system and legislation necessary in order to fully implement such system.

"**(c) Additional Study of Other Persons Ineligible To Purchase Firearms.** The Attorney General in consultation with the Secretary of the Treasury shall conduct a study to determine if an effective method for immediate and accurate identification of other persons who attempt to purchase 1 or more firearms but are ineligible to purchase firearms by reason of section 922(g) of title 18, United States Code [subsec. (g) of this section]. In conducting the study, the Attorney General shall consult with the Secretary of the Treasury, other Federal, State, and local law enforcement officials with expertise in the area, and other experts. Such study shall be completed within 18 months after the date of the enactment of this Act [Nov. 18, 1988] and shall be submitted to the Congress and made available to the public. Such study may include, if appropriate, recommendations for legislation.

"**(d) Definitions** As used in this section, the terms 'firearm' and 'dealer' shall have the meanings given such terms in section 921(a) of title 18, United States Code [section 921(a) of this title]."

Studies to Identify Equipment Capable of Distinguishing Security Exemplar From Other Metal Objects Likely to be Carried on One's Person

Section 2(e) of Pub.L. 100–649 provided that: "The Attorney General, the Secretary of the Treasury, and the Secretary of Transportation shall each conduct studies to identify available state-of-the-art equipment capable of detecting the Security Exemplar (as defined in section 922(p)(2)(C) of title 18, United States Code) [subsec. (p)(2)(C) of this section] and distinguishing the Security Exemplar from innocuous metal objects likely to be carried on one's person. Such studies shall be completed within 6 months after the date of the enactment of this Act and shall include a schedule providing for the installation of such equipment at the earliest practicable time at security checkpoints maintained or regulated by the agency conducting the study. Such equipment shall be installed in accordance with each schedule. In addition, such studies may include recommendations, where appropriate, concerning the use of secondary security equipment and procedures to enhance detection capability at security checkpoints."

Publication of Compilation of State Laws and Published Ordinances of Which Licensees Are Presumed To Have Knowledge

For provision requiring the Secretary to publish and provide to all licensees a compilation of the State laws and published ordinances of which licensees are presumed to have knowledge under this chapter and for amendments to and annual revision of such compilation, see section 110(a) of Pub.L. 99–308, set out as a note under section 921 of this title.

§ 923. Licensing

(a) No person shall engage in the business of importing, manufacturing, or dealing in firearms, or importing or manufacturing ammunition, until he has filed an application with and received a license to do so from the Attorney General. The application shall be in such form and contain only that information necessary to determine eligibility for licensing as the Attorney General shall by regulation prescribe and shall include a photograph and fingerprints of the applicant. Each applicant shall pay a fee for obtaining such a license, a separate fee being required for each place in which the applicant is to do business, as follows:

(1) If the applicant is a manufacturer—

(A) of destructive devices, ammunition for destructive devices or armor piercing ammunition, a fee of $1,000 per year;

(B) of firearms other than destructive devices, a fee of $50 per year; or

(C) of ammunition for firearms, other than ammunition for destructive devices or armor piercing ammunition, a fee of $10 per year.

(2) If the applicant is an importer—

(A) of destructive devices, ammunition for destructive devices or armor piercing ammunition, a fee of $1,000 per year; or

(B) of firearms other than destructive devices or ammunition for firearms other than destructive devices, or ammunition other than armor piercing ammunition, a fee of $50 per year.

(3) If the applicant is a dealer—

(A) in destructive devices or ammunition for destructive devices, a fee of $1,000 per year; or

(B) who is not a dealer in destructive devices, a fee of $200 for 3 years, except that the fee for renewal of a valid license shall be $90 for 3 years.

[**(C)** Repealed. Pub.L. 103–159, Title III, § 303(4), Nov. 30, 1993, 107 Stat. 1546]

(b) Any person desiring to be licensed as a collector shall file an application for such license with the Attorney General. The application shall be in such form and contain only that information necessary to determine eligibility as the Attorney General shall by regulation prescribe. The fee for such license shall be $10 per year. Any license granted under this subsection shall only apply to transactions in curios and relics.

(c) Upon the filing of a proper application and payment of the prescribed fee, the Attorney General shall issue to a qualified applicant the appropriate license which, subject to the provisions of this chapter and other applicable provisions of law, shall entitle the licensee to transport, ship, and receive firearms and ammunition covered by such license in interstate or foreign commerce during the period stated in the license. Nothing in this chapter shall be construed to prohibit a licensed manufacturer, importer, or dealer from maintaining and disposing of a personal collection of firearms, subject only to such restrictions as apply in this chapter to dispositions by a person other than a licensed manufacturer, importer, or dealer. If any firearm is so disposed of by a licensee within one year after its transfer from his business inventory into such licensee's personal collection or if such disposition or any other acquisition is made for the purpose of willfully evading the restrictions placed upon licensees by this chapter, then such firearm shall be deemed part of such licensee's business inventory, except that any licensed manufacturer, importer, or dealer who has maintained a firearm as part of a personal collection for one year and who sells or otherwise disposes of such firearm shall record the description of the firearm in a bound volume, containing the name and place of residence and date of birth of the transferee if the transferee is an individual, or the identity and principal and local places of business of the transferee if the transferee is a corporation or other business entity: *Provided,* That no other recordkeeping shall be required.

(d)(1) Any application submitted under subsection (a) or (b) of this section shall be approved if—

(A) the applicant is twenty-one years of age or over;

(B) the applicant (including, in the case of a corporation, partnership, or association, any individual possessing, directly or indirectly, the power to direct or cause the direction of the management and policies of the corporation, partnership, or association) is not prohibited from transporting, shipping, or receiving firearms or ammunition in interstate or foreign commerce under section 922(g) and (n) of this chapter;

(C) the applicant has not willfully violated any of the provisions of this chapter or regulations issued thereunder;

(D) the applicant has not willfully failed to disclose any material information required, or has not made any false statement as to any material fact, in connection with his application;

(E) the applicant has in a State (i) premises from which he conducts business subject to license under this chapter or from which he intends to conduct such business within a reasonable period of time, or (ii) in the case of a collector, premises from which he conducts his collecting subject to license under this chapter or from which he intends to conduct such collecting within a reasonable period of time;

(F) the applicant certifies that—

(i) the business to be conducted under the license is not prohibited by State or local law in the place where the licensed premise is located;

(ii)(I) within 30 days after the application is approved the business will comply with the requirements of State and local law applicable to the conduct of the business; and

(II) the business will not be conducted under the license until the requirements of State and local law applicable to the business have been met; and

(iii) that the applicant has sent or delivered a form to be prescribed by the Attorney General, to the chief law enforcement officer of the locality in which the premises are located, which indicates that the applicant intends to apply for a Federal firearms license; and

(G) in the case of an application to be licensed as a dealer, the applicant certifies that secure gun storage or safety devices will be available at any place in which firearms are sold under the license to persons who are not licensees (subject to the exception that in any case in which a secure gun storage or safety device is temporarily unavailable because of theft, casualty loss, consumer sales, backorders from a manufacturer, or any other similar reason beyond the control of the licensee, the dealer shall not be considered to be in violation of the requirement under this subparagraph to make available such a device).

(2) The Attorney General must approve or deny an application for a license within the 60-day period beginning on the date it is received. If the Attorney General fails to act within such period, the applicant may file an action under section 1361 of title 28 to compel the Attorney General to act. If the Attorney General approves an applicant's application, such applicant shall be issued a license upon the payment of the prescribed fee.

(e) The Attorney General may, after notice and opportunity for hearing, revoke any license issued under this section if the holder of such license has willfully violated any provision of this chapter or any rule or regulation prescribed by the Attorney General under this chapter or fails to have secure gun storage or safety devices available at any place in which firearms are sold under the license to persons who are not licensees (except that in any case in which a secure gun storage or safety device is temporarily unavailable because of theft, casualty loss, consumer sales, backorders from a manufacturer, or any other similar reason beyond the control of the licensee, the dealer shall not be considered to be in violation of the requirement to make available such a device). The Attorney General may, after notice and opportunity for hearing, revoke the license of a dealer who willfully transfers armor piercing ammunition. The Attorney General's action under this subsection may be reviewed only as provided in subsection (f) of this section.

(f)(1) Any person whose application for a license is denied and any holder of a license which is revoked shall receive a written notice from the Attorney General stating specifically the grounds upon which the application was denied or upon which the license was revoked. Any notice of a revocation of a license shall be given to the holder of such license before the effective date of the revocation.

(2) If the Attorney General denies an application for, or revokes, a license, he shall, upon request by the aggrieved party, promptly hold a hearing to review his denial or revocation. In the case of a revocation of a license, the Attorney General shall upon the request of the holder of the license stay the effective date of the revocation. A hearing held under this paragraph shall be held at a location convenient to the aggrieved party.

(3) If after a hearing held under paragraph (2) the Attorney General decides not to reverse his decision to deny an application or revoke a license, the Attorney General shall give notice of his decision to the aggrieved party. The aggrieved party may at any time within sixty days after the date notice was given under this paragraph file a petition with the United States district court for the district in which he resides or has his principal place of business for a de novo judicial review of such denial or revocation. In a proceeding conducted under this subsection, the court may consider any evidence submitted by the parties to the proceeding whether or not such evidence was considered at the hearing held under paragraph (2). If the court decides that the Attorney General was not authorized to deny the application or to revoke the license, the court shall order the Attorney General to take such action as may be necessary to comply with the judgment of the court.

(4) If criminal proceedings are instituted against a licensee alleging any violation of this chapter or of rules or regulations prescribed under this chapter, and the licensee is acquitted of such charges, or such proceedings are terminated, other than upon motion of the Government before trial upon such charges, the Attorney General shall be absolutely barred from denying or revoking any license granted under this chapter where such denial or revocation is based in whole or in part on the facts which form the basis of such criminal charges. No proceedings for the revocation of a license shall be instituted by the Attorney General more than one year after the filing of the indictment or information.

(g)(1)(A) Each licensed importer, licensed manufacturer, and licensed dealer shall maintain such records of importation, production, shipment, receipt, sale, or other disposition of firearms at his place of business for such period, and in such form, as the Attorney General may by regulations prescribe. Such importers, manufacturers, and dealers shall not be required to submit to the Attorney General reports and information with respect to such records and the contents thereof, except as expressly required by this section. The Attorney General, when he has reasonable cause to believe a violation of this chapter has occurred and that evidence thereof may be found on such premises, may, upon demonstrating such cause before a Federal magistrate judge and securing from such magistrate judge a warrant authorizing entry, enter during business hours the premises (including places of storage) of any licensed firearms importer, licensed manufacturer, licensed dealer, licensed collector, or any licensed importer or manufacturer of ammunition, for the purpose of inspecting or examining—

(i) any records or documents required to be kept by such licensed importer, licensed manufacturer, licensed dealer, or licensed collector under this chapter or rules or regulations under this chapter, and

(ii) any firearms or ammunition kept or stored by such licensed importer, licensed manufacturer, licensed dealer, or licensed collector, at such premises.

(B) The Attorney General may inspect or examine the inventory and records of a licensed importer, licensed manufacturer, or licensed dealer without such reasonable cause or warrant—

(i) in the course of a reasonable inquiry during the course of a criminal investigation of a person or persons other than the licensee;

(ii) for ensuring compliance with the record keeping requirements of this chapter—

(I) not more than once during any 12–month period; or

(II) at any time with respect to records relating to a firearm involved in a criminal investigation that is traced to the licensee; or

(iii) when such inspection or examination may be required for determining the disposition of one or more particular firearms in the course of a bona fide criminal investigation.

(C) The Attorney General may inspect the inventory and records of a licensed collector without such reasonable cause or warrant—

(i) for ensuring compliance with the record keeping requirements of this chapter not more than once during any twelve-month period; or

(ii) when such inspection or examination may be required for determining the disposition of one or more particular firearms in the course of a bona fide criminal investigation.

(D) At the election of a licensed collector, the annual inspection of records and inventory permitted under this paragraph shall be performed at the office of the Attorney General designated for such inspections which is located in closest proximity to the premises where the inventory and records of such licensed collector are maintained. The inspection and examination authorized by this paragraph shall not be construed as authorizing the Attorney General to seize any records or other documents other than those records or documents constituting material evidence of a violation of law. If the Attorney General seizes such records or documents, copies shall be provided the licensee within a reasonable time. The Attorney General may make available to any Federal, State, or local law enforcement agency any information which he may obtain by reason of this chapter with respect to the identification of persons prohibited from purchasing or receiving firearms or ammunition who have purchased or received firearms or ammunition, together with a description of such firearms or ammunition, and he may provide information to the extent such information may be contained in the records required to be maintained by this chapter, when so requested by any Federal, State, or local law enforcement agency.

(2) Each licensed collector shall maintain in a bound volume the nature of which the Attorney General may by regulations prescribe, records of the receipt, sale, or other disposition of firearms. Such records shall include the name and address of any person to whom the collector sells or otherwise disposes of a firearm. Such collector shall not be required to submit to the Attorney General reports and information with respect to such records and the contents thereof, except as expressly required by this section.

(3)(A) Each licensee shall prepare a report of multiple sales or other dispositions whenever the licensee sells or otherwise disposes of, at one time or during any five consecutive business days, two or more pistols, or revolvers, or any combination of pistols and revolvers totalling two or more, to an unlicensed person. The report shall be prepared on a form specified by the Attorney General and forwarded to the office specified thereon and to the department of State police or State law enforcement agency of the State or local law enforcement agency of the local jurisdiction in which the sale or other disposition took place, not later than the close of business on the day that the multiple sale or other disposition occurs.

(B) Except in the case of forms and contents thereof regarding a purchaser who is prohibited by subsection (g) or (n) of section 922 of this title from receipt of a firearm, the department of State police or State law enforcement agency or local law enforcement agency of the local jurisdiction shall not disclose any such form or the contents thereof to any person or entity, and shall destroy each such form and any record of the contents thereof no more than 20 days from the date such form is received. No later than the date that is 6 months after the effective date of this subparagraph, and at the end of each 6–month period thereafter, the department of State police or State law enforcement agency or local law enforcement agency of the local jurisdiction shall certify to the Attorney General of the United States that no disclosure contrary to this subparagraph has been made and that all forms and any record of the contents thereof have been destroyed as provided in this subparagraph.

(4) Where a firearms or ammunition business is discontinued and succeeded by a new licensee, the records required to be kept by this chapter shall appropriately reflect such facts and shall be delivered to the successor. Where discontinuance of the business is absolute, such records shall be delivered within thirty days after the business discontinuance to the Attorney General. However, where State law or local ordinance requires the delivery of records to other responsible authority, the Attorney General may arrange for the delivery of such records to such other responsible authority.

(5)(A) Each licensee shall, when required by letter issued by the Attorney General, and until notified to the contrary in writing by the Attorney General, submit on a form specified by the Attorney General, for periods and at the times specified in such letter, all record information required to be kept by this chapter or such lesser record information as the Attorney General in such letter may specify.

(B) The Attorney General may authorize such record information to be submitted in a manner other than that prescribed in subparagraph (A) of this paragraph when it is shown by a licensee that an alternate method of reporting is reasonably necessary and will not unduly hinder the effective administration of this chapter. A licensee may use an alternate method of reporting if the licensee describes the proposed alternate method of reporting and the need therefor in a letter application submitted to the Attorney General, and the Attorney General approves such alternate method of reporting.

(6) Each licensee shall report the theft or loss of a firearm from the licensee's inventory or collection, within 48 hours after the theft or loss is discovered, to the Attorney General and to the appropriate local authorities.

(7) Each licensee shall respond immediately to, and in no event later than 24 hours after the receipt of, a request by the Attorney General for information contained in the records required to be kept by this chapter as may be required for determining the disposition of 1 or more firearms in the course of a bona fide criminal investigation. The requested information shall be provided orally or in writing, as the Attorney General may require. The Attorney General shall implement a system whereby the licensee can positively identify and establish that an individual requesting information via telephone is employed by and authorized by the agency to request such information.

(h) Licenses issued under the provisions of subsection (c) of this section shall be kept posted and kept available for inspection on the premises covered by the license.

(i) Licensed importers and licensed manufacturers shall identify by means of a serial number engraved or cast on the receiver or frame of the weapon, in such manner as the Attorney General shall by regulations prescribe, each firearm imported or manufactured by such importer or manufacturer.

(j) A licensed importer, licensed manufacturer, or licensed dealer may, under rules or regulations prescribed by the Attorney General, conduct business temporarily at a location other than the location specified on the license if such temporary location is the location for a gun show or event sponsored by any national, State, or local organization, or any affiliate of any such organization devoted to the collection, competitive use, or other sporting use of firearms in the community, and such location is in the State which is specified on the license. Records of receipt and disposition of firearms transactions conducted at such temporary location shall include the location of the sale or other disposition and shall be entered in the permanent records of the licensee and retained on the location specified on the license. Nothing in this subsection shall authorize any licensee to conduct business in or from any motorized or towed vehicle. Notwithstanding the provisions of subsection (a) of this section, a separate fee shall not be required of a licensee with respect to business conducted under this subsection. Any inspection or examination of inventory or records under this chapter by the Attorney General at such temporary location shall be limited to inventory consisting of, or records relating to, firearms held or disposed at such temporary location. Nothing in this subsection shall be construed to authorize the Attorney General to inspect or examine the inventory or records of a licensed importer, licensed manufacturer, or licensed dealer at any location other than the location specified on the license. Nothing in this subsection shall be construed to diminish in any manner any right to display, sell, or otherwise dispose of firearms or ammunition, which is in effect before the date of the enactment of the Firearms Owners' Protection Act, including the right of a licensee to conduct "curios or relics" firearms transfers and business away from their business premises with another licensee without regard as to whether the location of where the business is conducted is located in the State specified on the license of either licensee.

(k) Licensed importers and licensed manufacturers shall mark all armor piercing projectiles and packages containing such projectiles for distribution in the manner prescribed by the Attorney General by regulation. The Attorney General shall furnish information to each dealer licensed under this chapter defining which projectiles are considered armor piercing ammunition as defined in section 921(a)(17)(B).

(*l*) The Attorney General shall notify the chief law enforcement officer in the appropriate State and local jurisdictions of the names and addresses of all persons in the State to whom a firearms license is issued.

(Added Pub.L. 90–351, Title IV, § 902, June 19, 1968, 82 Stat. 231, and amended Pub.L. 90–618, Title I, § 102, Oct. 22, 1968, 82 Stat. 1221; Pub.L. 97–377, Title I, § 165(b), Dec. 21, 1982, 96 Stat. 1923; Pub.L. 99–308, § 103, May 19, 1986, 100 Stat. 453; Pub.L. 99–360, § 1(c), July 8, 1986, 100 Stat. 766; Pub.L. 99–408, §§ 3 to 7, Aug. 28, 1986, 100 Stat. 921; Pub.L. 100–690, Title VII, § 7060(d), Nov. 18, 1988, 102 Stat. 4404; Pub.L. 101–647, Title XXII, § 2203(a), Title XXXV, § 3525, Nov. 29, 1990, 104 Stat. 4857, 4924; Pub.L. 101–650, Title III, § 321, Dec. 1, 1990, 104 Stat. 5117; Pub.L. 103–159, Title II, § 201, Title III, § 303, Nov. 30, 1993, 107 Stat. 1544, 1545; Pub.L. 103–322, Title XI, §§ 110102(d), 110103(d), 110105(2), 110301(a), 110302 to 110307, Title XXXIII, § 330011(i), Sept. 13, 1994, 108 Stat. 1998, 1999, 2000, 2012, 2013, 2014, 2145; Pub.L. 104–208, Div. A, Title I, § 101(f) [Title I, § 118], Sept. 30, 1996, 110 Stat. 3009–326; Pub.L. 104–294, Title VI, § 603(j)(1), (k), (*l*), Oct. 11, 1996, 110 Stat. 3504, 3405; Pub.L. 105–277, Div A, § 101(b) [Title I, § 119(b), (c)], Oct. 21, 1998, 112 Stat. 2681–69; Pub.L. 107–296, Title XI, § 1112(f)(5), (6), Nov. 25, 2002, 116 Stat. 2276.)

HISTORICAL AND STATUTORY NOTES

References in Text

The effective date of this subparagraph, referred to in subsec. (g)(3)(B), is the effective date of Pub.L. 103–159, which was approved Nov. 30, 1993.

The date of the enactment of the Firearms Owners' Protection Act, referred to in subsec. (j), is the date of enactment of Pub.L. 99–308, which was approved May 19, 1986.

Effective and Applicability Provisions

2002 Acts. Amendment by Pub.L. 107–296 effective 60 days after Nov. 25, 2002, see Pub.L. 107–296, § 4, set out as a note under 6 U.S.C.A. § 101.

1998 Acts. Amendment by Pub.L. 105–277, Div. A, § 101(b) [Title I, § 119(d)], effective 180 days after Oct. 21, 1998, see Div. A, § 101(b) [Title I, § 119(e)] of Pub.L. 105–277, set out as a note under 18 U.S.C.A. § 921.

1996 Acts. Section 603(j)(2) of Pub.L. 104–294 provided that: "The amendment made by paragraph (1) [amending section 201(1) of Pub.L. 103–159, which amended subsec.

(g)(3) of this section] shall take effect as if the amendment had been included in the Act referred to in paragraph (1) [Pub.L. 103–159, 107 Stat. 1536, for classification of which to the Code, see Tables] on the date of the enactment of such Act [Nov. 30, 1993]."

1994 Acts. Amendments by sections 110101 to 110106 of Pub.L. 103–322, effective Sept. 13, 1994, are repealed effective 10 years after Sept. 13, 1994, see section 110105 of Pub.L. 103–322, set out as a note under 18 U.S.C.A. § 921.

Section 330011(i) of Pub.L. 103–322 provided in part that the amendment made by such section, amending directory language of section 3525 of Pub.L. 101–647 (which amended this section), was to take effect on the date section 3525 of Pub.L. 101–647 took effect; section 3525 of Pub.L. 101–647 took effect on the date of enactment of Pub.L. 101–647, which was approved Nov. 29, 1990.

1986 Acts. Amendment of subsec. (a)(1)(A), (C), (2)(A), and (B), by Pub.L. 99–408 effective on the first day of the first calendar month which begins more than ninety days after Aug. 28, 1986, see section 9 of Pub.L. 99–408, set out as a note under 18 U.S.C.A. § 921.

Amendment of subsecs. (e) and (k) by Pub.L. 99–408 effective Aug. 28, 1986, see section 9 of Pub.L. 99–408, set out as a note under section 921 of this title. Amendment by Pub.L. 99–360 effective on the date on which the Firearms Owners' Protection Act, Pub.L. 99–308, becomes effective, see section 2 of Pub.L. 99–360, set out as a note under 18 U.S.C.A. § 921.

Amendment by section 103(1) to (6)(A), (7), and (8) of Pub.L. 99–308 effective 180 days after May 19, 1986, see section 110(a) of Pub.L. 99–308, set out as a note under 18 U.S.C.A. § 921.

Amendment by section 103(6)(B) of Pub.L. 99–308, enacting subsec. (f)(4), applicable to any action, petition, or appellate proceeding pending on May 19, 1986, see section 110(b) of Pub.L. 99–308, set out as a note under 18 U.S.C.A. § 921.

Change of Name

Words "magistrate judge" substituted for "magistrate" in subsec. (g)(1)(A) pursuant to section 321 of Pub.L. 101–650, set out as a note under 28 U.S.C.A. § 631.

Funding for Bureau of Alcohol, Tobacco, Firearms and Explosives Not Authorized for Disclosure of Databases

Pub.L. 109–108, Title I, Nov. 22, 2005, 119 Stat. 2295, provided in part: "That no funds appropriated under this or any other Act [the Science, State, Justice, Commerce, and Related Agencies Appropriations Act, 2006, Pub.L. 109–108, Nov. 22, 2005, 119 Stat. 2290; see Tables for classification] with respect to any fiscal year may be used to disclose part or all of the contents of the Firearms Trace System database maintained by the National Trace Center of the Bureau of Alcohol, Tobacco, Firearms and Explosives or any information required to be kept by licensees pursuant to section 923(g) of title 18, United States Code [subsec. (g) of this section], or required to be reported pursuant to paragraphs (3) and (7) of such section 923(g) [subsec. (g)(3) and (7) of this section], to anyone other than a Federal, State, or local law enforcement agency or a prosecutor solely in connection with and for use in a bona fide criminal investigation or prosecution and then only such information as pertains to the geographic jurisdiction of the law enforcement agency requesting the disclosure and not for use in any civil action or proceeding other than an action or proceeding commenced by the Bureau of Alcohol, Tobacco, Firearms and Explosives, or a review of such an action or proceeding, to enforce the provisions of chapter 44 of such title [this chapter], and all such data shall be immune from legal process and shall not be subject to subpoena or other discovery, shall be inadmissible in evidence, and shall not be used, relied on, or disclosed in any manner, nor shall testimony or other evidence be permitted based upon such data, in any civil action pending on or filed after the effective date of this Act in any State (including the District of Columbia) or Federal court or in any administrative proceeding other than a proceeding commenced by the Bureau of Alcohol, Tobacco, Firearms and Explosives to enforce the provisions of that chapter [this chapter], or a review of such an action or proceeding; except that this proviso shall not be construed to prevent the disclosure of statistical information concerning total production, importation, and exportation by each licensed importer (as defined in section 921(a)(9) of such title [18 U.S.C.A. § 921(a)(9)]) and licensed manufacturer (as defined in section 921(a)(10) of such title [18 U.S.C.A. § 921(a)(10)])."

Similar provisions were contained in the following prior Appropriations Act:

Pub.L. 108–447, Div. B, Title I, Dec. 8, 2004, 118 Stat. 2859.

Statutory Construction; Evidence

Pub.L. 105–277, Div. A, § 101(b) [Title I, § 119(d)], Oct. 21, 1998, 112 Stat. 2681–70, provided that:

"**(1) Statutory construction.**—Nothing in the amendments made by this section [amending this section and section 921 of this title and enacting provisions set out as a note under this section] shall be construed—

"**(A)** as creating a cause of action against any firearms dealer or any other person for any civil liability; or

"**(B)** as establishing any standard of care.

"**(2) Evidence.**—Notwithstanding any other provision of law, evidence regarding compliance or noncompliance with the amendments made by this section shall not be admissible as evidence in any proceeding of any court, agency, board, or other entity."

[Amendment by Pub.L. 105–277, Div. A, § 101(b) [Title I, § 119(d)], effective 180 days after Oct. 21, 1998, see Div. A, § 101(b) [Title I, § 119(e)] of Pub.L. 105–277, set out as a note under 18 U.S.C.A. § 921.]

§ 924. Penalties

(a)(1) Except as otherwise provided in this subsection, subsection (b), (c), (f), or (p) of this section, or in section 929, whoever—

(A) knowingly makes any false statement or representation with respect to the information required by this chapter to be kept in the records of a person licensed under this chapter or in applying for any license or exemption or relief from disability under the provisions of this chapter;

(B) knowingly violates subsection (a)(4), (f), (k), or (q) of section 922;

(C) knowingly imports or brings into the United States or any possession thereof any firearm or ammunition in violation of section 922(*l*); or

(D) willfully violates any other provision of this chapter,

shall be fined under this title, imprisoned not more than five years, or both.

(2) Whoever knowingly violates subsection (a)(6), (d), (g), (h), (i), (j), or (*o*) of section 922 shall be fined as provided in this title, imprisoned not more than 10 years, or both.

(3) Any licensed dealer, licensed importer, licensed manufacturer, or licensed collector who knowingly—

(A) makes any false statement or representation with respect to the information required by the provisions of this chapter to be kept in the records of a person licensed under this chapter, or

(B) violates subsection (m) of section 922,

shall be fined under this title, imprisoned not more than one year, or both.

(4) Whoever violates section 922(q) shall be fined under this title, imprisoned for not more than 5 years, or both. Notwithstanding any other provision of law, the term of imprisonment imposed under this paragraph shall not run concurrently with any other term of imprisonment imposed under any other provision of law. Except for the authorization of a term of imprisonment of not more than 5 years made in this paragraph, for the purpose of any other law a violation of section 922(q) shall be deemed to be a misdemeanor.

(5) Whoever knowingly violates subsection (s) or (t) of section 922 shall be fined under this title, imprisoned for not more than 1 year, or both.

(6)(A)(i) A juvenile who violates section 922(x) shall be fined under this title, imprisoned not more than 1 year, or both, except that a juvenile described in clause (ii) shall be sentenced to probation on appropriate conditions and shall not be incarcerated unless the juvenile fails to comply with a condition of probation.

(ii) A juvenile is described in this clause if—

(I) the offense of which the juvenile is charged is possession of a handgun or ammunition in violation of section 922(x)(2); and

(II) the juvenile has not been convicted in any court of an offense (including an offense under section 922(x) or a similar State law, but not including any other offense consisting of conduct that if engaged in by an adult would not constitute an offense) or adjudicated as a juvenile delinquent for conduct that if engaged in by an adult would constitute an offense.

(B) A person other than a juvenile who knowingly violates section 922(x)—

(i) shall be fined under this title, imprisoned not more than 1 year, or both; and

(ii) if the person sold, delivered, or otherwise transferred a handgun or ammunition to a juvenile knowing or having reasonable cause to know that the juvenile intended to carry or otherwise possess or discharge or otherwise use the handgun or ammunition in the commission of a crime of violence, shall be fined under this title, imprisoned not more than 10 years, or both.

(7) Whoever knowingly violates section 931 shall be fined under this title, imprisoned not more than 3 years, or both.

(b) Whoever, with intent to commit therewith an offense punishable by imprisonment for a term exceeding one year, or with knowledge or reasonable cause to believe that an offense punishable by imprisonment for a term exceeding one year is to be committed therewith, ships, transports, or receives a firearm or any ammunition in interstate or foreign commerce shall be fined under this title, or imprisoned not more than ten years, or both.

(c)(1)(A) Except to the extent that a greater minimum sentence is otherwise provided by this subsection or by any other provision of law, any person who, during and in relation to any crime of violence or drug trafficking crime (including a crime of violence or drug trafficking crime that provides for an enhanced punishment if committed by the use of a deadly or dangerous weapon or device) for which the person may be prosecuted in a court of the United States, uses or carries a firearm, or who, in furtherance of any such crime, possesses a firearm, shall, in addition to the punishment provided for such crime of violence or drug trafficking crime—

(i) be sentenced to a term of imprisonment of not less than 5 years;

(ii) if the firearm is brandished, be sentenced to a term of imprisonment of not less than 7 years; and

(iii) if the firearm is discharged, be sentenced to a term of imprisonment of not less than 10 years.

(B) If the firearm possessed by a person convicted of a violation of this subsection—

(i) is a short-barreled rifle, short-barreled shotgun, the person shall be sentenced to a term of imprisonment of not less than 10 years; or

(ii) is a machinegun or a destructive device, or is equipped with a firearm silencer or firearm muffler, the person shall be sentenced to a term of imprisonment of not less than 30 years.

(C) In the case of a second or subsequent conviction under this subsection, the person shall—

(i) be sentenced to a term of imprisonment of not less than 25 years; and

(ii) if the firearm involved is a machinegun or a destructive device, or is equipped with a firearm silencer or firearm muffler, be sentenced to imprisonment for life.

(D) Notwithstanding any other provision of law—

(i) a court shall not place on probation any person convicted of a violation of this subsection; and

(ii) no term of imprisonment imposed on a person under this subsection shall run concurrently with any other term of imprisonment imposed on the person, including any term of imprisonment imposed for the crime of violence or drug trafficking crime during which the firearm was used, carried, or possessed.

(2) For purposes of this subsection, the term "drug trafficking crime" means any felony punishable under the Controlled Substances Act (21 U.S.C. 801 et seq.), the Controlled Substances Import and Export Act (21 U.S.C. 951 et seq.), or chapter 705 of title 46.

(3) For purposes of this subsection the term "crime of violence" means an offense that is a felony and—

(A) has as an element the use, attempted use, or threatened use of physical force against the person or property of another, or

(B) that by its nature, involves a substantial risk that physical force against the person or property of another may be used in the course of committing the offense.

(4) For purposes of this subsection, the term "brandish" means, with respect to a firearm, to display all or part of the firearm, or otherwise make the presence of the firearm known to another person, in order to intimidate that person, regardless of whether the firearm is directly visible to that person.

(5) Except to the extent that a greater minimum sentence is otherwise provided under this subsection, or by any other provision of law, any person who, during and in relation to any crime of violence or drug trafficking crime (including a crime of violence or drug trafficking crime that provides for an enhanced punishment if committed by the use of a deadly or dangerous weapon or device) for which the person may be prosecuted in a court of the United States, uses or carries armor piercing ammunition, or who, in furtherance of any such crime, possesses armor piercing ammunition, shall, in addition to the punishment provided for such crime of violence or drug trafficking crime or conviction under this section—

(A) be sentenced to a term of imprisonment of not less than 15 years; and

(B) if death results from the use of such ammunition—

(i) if the killing is murder (as defined in section 1111), be punished by death or sentenced to a term of imprisonment for any term of years or for life; and

(ii) if the killing is manslaughter (as defined in section 1112), be punished as provided in section 1112.

(d)(1) Any firearm or ammunition involved in or used in any knowing violation of subsection (a)(4), (a)(6), (f), (g), (h), (i), (j), or (k) of section 922, or knowing importation or bringing into the United States or any possession thereof any firearm or ammunition in violation of section 922(*l*), or knowing violation of section 924, or willful violation of any other provision of this chapter or any rule or regulation promulgated thereunder, or any violation of any other criminal law of the United States, or any firearm or ammunition intended to be used in any offense referred to in paragraph (3) of this subsection, where such intent is demonstrated by clear and convincing evidence, shall be subject to seizure and forfeiture, and all provisions of the Internal Revenue Code of 1986 relating to the seizure, forfeiture, and disposition of firearms, as defined in section 5845(a) of that Code, shall, so far as applicable, extend to seizures and forfeitures under the provisions of this chapter: *Provided,* That upon acquittal of the owner or possessor, or dismissal of the charges against him other than upon motion of the Government prior to trial, or lapse of or court termination of the restraining order to which he is subject, the seized or relinquished firearms or ammunition shall be returned forthwith to the owner or possessor or to a person delegated by the owner or possessor unless the return of the firearms or ammunition would place the owner or possessor or his delegate in violation of law. Any action or proceeding for the forfeiture of firearms or ammunition shall be commenced within one hundred and twenty days of such seizure.

(2)(A) In any action or proceeding for the return of firearms or ammunition seized under the provisions of this chapter, the court shall allow the prevailing party, other than the United States, a reasonable attorney's fee, and the United States shall be liable therefor.

(B) In any other action or proceeding under the provisions of this chapter, the court, when it finds that such action was without foundation, or was initiated vexatiously, frivolously, or in bad faith, shall allow the prevailing party, other than the United States, a reasonable attorney's fee, and the United States shall be liable therefor.

(C) Only those firearms or quantities of ammunition particularly named and individually identified as involved in or used in any violation of the provisions of this chapter or any rule or regulation issued thereunder, or any other criminal law of the United States or as intended to be used in any offense referred to in paragraph (3) of this subsection, where such intent is demonstrated by clear and convincing evidence, shall be subject to seizure, forfeiture, and disposition.

(D) The United States shall be liable for attorneys' fees under this paragraph only to the extent provided in advance by appropriation Acts.

(3) The offenses referred to in paragraphs (1) and (2)(C) of this subsection are—

(A) any crime of violence, as that term is defined in section 924(c)(3) of this title;

(B) any offense punishable under the Controlled Substances Act (21 U.S.C. 801 et seq.) or the Controlled Substances Import and Export Act (21 U.S.C. 951 et seq.);

(C) any offense described in section 922(a)(1), 922(a)(3), 922(a)(5), or 922(b)(3) of this title, where the firearm or ammunition intended to be used in any such offense is involved in a pattern of activities which includes a violation of any offense described in section 922(a)(1), 922(a)(3), 922(a)(5), or 922(b)(3) of this title;

(D) any offense described in section 922(d) of this title where the firearm or ammunition is intended to be used in such offense by the transferor of such firearm or ammunition;

(E) any offense described in section 922(i), 922(j), 922(*l*), 922(n), or 924(b) of this title; and

(F) any offense which may be prosecuted in a court of the United States which involves the exportation of firearms or ammunition.

(e)(1) In the case of a person who violates section 922(g) of this title and has three previous convictions by any court referred to in section 922(g)(1) of this title for a violent felony or a serious drug offense, or both, committed on occasions different from one another, such person shall be fined under this title and imprisoned not less than fifteen years, and, notwithstanding any other provision of law, the court shall not suspend the sentence of, or grant a probationary sentence to, such person with respect to the conviction under section 922(g).

(2) As used in this subsection—

(A) the term "serious drug offense" means—

(i) an offense under the Controlled Substances Act (21 U.S.C. 801 et seq.), the Controlled Substances Import and Export Act (21 U.S.C. 951 et seq.), or chapter 705 of title 46, for which a maximum term of imprisonment of ten years or more is prescribed by law; or

(ii) an offense under State law, involving manufacturing, distributing, or possessing with intent to manufacture or distribute, a controlled substance (as defined in section 102 of the Controlled Substances Act (21 U.S.C. 802)), for which a maximum term of imprisonment of ten years or more is prescribed by law;

(B) the term "violent felony" means any crime punishable by imprisonment for a term exceeding one year, or any act of juvenile delinquency involving the use or carrying of a firearm, knife, or destructive device that would be punishable by imprisonment for such term if committed by an adult, that—

(i) has as an element the use, attempted use, or threatened use of physical force against the person of another; or

(ii) is burglary, arson, or extortion, involves use of explosives, or otherwise involves conduct that presents a serious potential risk of physical injury to another; and

(C) the term "conviction" includes a finding that a person has committed an act of juvenile delinquency involving a violent felony.

(f) In the case of a person who knowingly violates section 922(p), such person shall be fined under this title, or imprisoned not more than 5 years, or both.

(g) Whoever, with the intent to engage in conduct which—

(1) constitutes an offense listed in section 1961(1),

(2) is punishable under the Controlled Substances Act (21 U.S.C. 801 et seq.), the Controlled Substances Import and Export Act (21 U.S.C. 951 et seq.), or chapter 705 of title 46,

(3) violates any State law relating to any controlled substance (as defined in section 102(6) of the Controlled Substances Act (21 U.S.C. 802(6))), or

(4) constitutes a crime of violence (as defined in subsection (c)(3)),

travels from any State or foreign country into any other State and acquires, transfers, or attempts to acquire or transfer, a firearm in such other State in furtherance of such purpose, shall be imprisoned not more than 10 years, fined in accordance with this title, or both.

(h) Whoever knowingly transfers a firearm, knowing that such firearm will be used to commit a crime of violence (as defined in subsection (c)(3)) or drug trafficking crime (as defined in subsection (c)(2)) shall be imprisoned not more than 10 years, fined in accordance with this title, or both.

(i)(1) A person who knowingly violates section 922(u) shall be fined under this title, imprisoned not more than 10 years, or both.

(2) Nothing contained in this subsection shall be construed as indicating an intent on the part of Congress to occupy the field in which provisions of this subsection operate to the exclusion of State laws on the same subject matter, nor shall any provision of this subsection be construed as invalidating any provision of State law unless such provision is inconsistent with any of the purposes of this subsection.

(j) A person who, in the course of a violation of subsection (c), causes the death of a person through the use of a firearm, shall—

(1) if the killing is a murder (as defined in section 1111), be punished by death or by imprisonment for any term of years or for life; and

(2) if the killing is manslaughter (as defined in section 1112), be punished as provided in that section.

(k) A person who, with intent to engage in or to promote conduct that—

(1) is punishable under the Controlled Substances Act (21 U.S.C. 801 et seq.), the Controlled Substances Import and Export Act (21 U.S.C. 951 et seq.), or chapter 705 of title 46;

(2) violates any law of a State relating to any controlled substance (as defined in section 102 of the Controlled Substances Act, 21 U.S.C. 802); or

(3) constitutes a crime of violence (as defined in subsection (c)(3)),

smuggles or knowingly brings into the United States a firearm, or attempts to do so, shall be imprisoned not more than 10 years, fined under this title, or both.

(*l*) A person who steals any firearm which is moving as, or is a part of, or which has moved in, interstate or foreign commerce shall be imprisoned for not more than 10 years, fined under this title, or both.

(m) A person who steals any firearm from a licensed importer, licensed manufacturer, licensed dealer, or licensed collector shall be fined under this title, imprisoned not more than 10 years, or both.

(n) A person who, with the intent to engage in conduct that constitutes a violation of section 922(a)(1)(A), travels from any State or foreign country into any other State and acquires, or attempts to acquire, a firearm in such other State in furtherance of such purpose shall be imprisoned for not more than 10 years.

(*o*) A person who conspires to commit an offense under subsection (c) shall be imprisoned for not more than 20 years, fined under this title, or both; and if the firearm is a machinegun or destructive device, or is equipped with a firearm silencer or muffler, shall be imprisoned for any term of years or life.

(p) Penalties relating to secure gun storage or safety device.—

(1) In general.—

(A) Suspension or revocation of license; civil penalties.—With respect to each violation of section 922(z)(1) by a licensed manufacturer, licensed importer, or licensed dealer, the Secretary may, after notice and opportunity for hearing—

(i) suspend for not more than 6 months, or revoke, the license issued to the licensee under this chapter that was used to conduct the firearms transfer; or

(ii) subject the licensee to a civil penalty in an amount equal to not more than $2,500.

(B) Review.—An action of the Secretary under this paragraph may be reviewed only as provided under section 923(f).

(2) Administrative remedies.—The suspension or revocation of a license or the imposition of a civil penalty under paragraph (1) shall not preclude any administrative remedy that is otherwise available to the Secretary.

(Added Pub.L. 90–351, Title IV, § 902, June 19, 1968, 82 Stat. 233, and amended Pub.L. 90–618, Title I, § 102, Oct. 22, 1968, 82 Stat. 1223; Pub.L. 91–644, Title II, § 13, Jan. 2, 1971, 84 Stat. 1889; Pub.L. 98–473, Title II, §§ 223(a), 1005(a), Oct. 12, 1984, 98 Stat. 2028, 2138; Pub.L. 99–308, § 104(a), May 19, 1986, 100 Stat. 456; Pub.L. 99–570, Title I, § 1402, Oct. 27, 1986, 100 Stat. 3207–39; Pub.L. 100–649, § 2(b), (f)(2)(B), (D), Nov. 10, 1988, 102 Stat. 3817, 3818; Pub.L. 100–690, Title VI, §§ 6211, 6212, 6451, 6460, 6462, Title VII, §§ 7056, 7060(a), Nov. 18, 1988, 102 Stat. 4359, 4360, 4371, 4373, 4374, 4402, 4403; Pub.L. 101–647, Title XI, § 1101, Title XVII, § 1702(b)(3), Title XXII, §§ 2203(d), 2204(c), Title XXXV, §§ 3526, 3527, 3528, 3529, Nov. 29, 1990, 104 Stat. 4829, 4845, 4857, 4924; Pub.L. 103–159, Title I, § 102(c), Title III, § 302(d), Nov. 30, 1993, 107 Stat. 1541, 1545; Pub.L. 103–322, Title VI, § 60013, Title XI, §§ 110102(c), 110103(c), 110105(2), 110201(b), 110401(e), 110503, 110504(a), 110507, 110510, 110515(a), 110517, 110518(a), Title XXXIII, §§ 330002(h), 330003(f)(2), 330011(i), (j), 330016(1)(H), (K), (L), Sept. 13, 1994, 108 Stat. 1973, 1998, 1999, 2000, 2011, 2015, 2016, 2018, 2019, 2020, 2140, 2141, 2145, 2147; Pub.L. 104–294, Title VI, § 603(m)(1), (n) to (p)(1), (q) to (s), Oct. 11, 1996, 110 Stat. 3505; Pub.L. 105–386, § 1(a), Nov. 13, 1998, 112 Stat. 3469; Pub.L. 107–273, Div. B, Title IV, § 4002(d)(1)(E), Div. C, Title I, § 11009(e)(3), Nov. 2, 2002, 116 Stat. 1809, 1821; Pub.L. 109–92, §§ 5(c)(2), 6(b), Oct. 26, 2005, 119 Stat. 2100, 2102; Pub.L. 109–304, § 17(d)(3), Oct. 6, 2006, 120 Stat. 1707.)

Amendment of Section

Pub.L. 100–649, § 2(f)(2)(B), (D), Nov. 10, 1988, 102 Stat. 3818, as amended Pub.L. 101–647, Title XXXV, § 3526(b), Nov. 29, 1990, 104 Stat. 4924; Pub.L. 105–277, Div. A, § 101(h) [Title VI, § 649], Oct. 21, 1998, 112 Stat. 2681–528; Pub.L. 108–174, § 1, Dec. 9, 2003, 117 Stat. 2481, provided that, effective 25 years after the 30th day beginning after Nov. 10, 1988 [see section 2(f)(1) of Pub.L. 100–649, set out as a note under 18 U.S.C.A. § 922], subsec. (a)(1) of this section is amended by striking "this subsection, subsection (b), (c), or (f) of this section, or in section 929" and inserting "this chapter"; subsec. (f) of this section is repealed; and subsecs. (g) through (o) of this section are redesignated as subsecs. (f) through (n), respectively.

HISTORICAL AND STATUTORY NOTES

References in Text

The Controlled Substances Act, referred to in text, is Title II of Pub.L. 91–513, Oct. 27, 1970, 84 Stat. 1242, as amended, which is classified principally to subchapter I of chapter 13 of Title 21, Food and Drugs (21 U.S.C.A. § 801 et seq.). For complete classification of this Act to the Code, see Short Title note set out under section 801 of Title 21 and Tables.

The Controlled Substances Import and Export Act, referred to in text, is Title III of Pub.L. 91–513, Oct. 27, 1970, 84 Stat. 1285, as amended, which is classified principally to subchapter II of chapter 13 of Title 21 (21 U.S.C.A. § 951 et seq.). For complete classification of this Act to the Code, see Short Title note set out under section 951 of Title 21 and Tables.

Chapter 705 of title 46, referred to in text, is Maritime Drug Law Enforcement, 46 U.S.C.A. § 70501 et seq.

The Internal Revenue Code of 1986, referred to in subsec. (d)(1), is set out in Title 26, Internal Revenue Code.

Section 5845(a) of that Code, referred to in subsec. (d)(1) is classified to section 5845(a) of Title 26.

Section 102 of the Controlled Substances Act, referred to in subsec. (g)(3), is section 102 of Pub.L. 91–513, Title II, Oct. 27, 1970, 84 Stat. 1242, which is classified to section 802 of Title 21, Food and Drugs.

Codifications

Amendment by Pub.L. 103–322, § 110201(b)(1), which directed that "paragraph (2) or (3) of" be struck out of subsec. (a)(1), could not be executed to text as a prior identical amendment by section 102(c)(1) of Pub.L. 103–159 was executed on Nov. 30, 1993.

Amendment to subsec. (c)(1) by Pub.L. 103–322, § 110510(b), which directed striking "No person sentenced under this subsection shall be eligible for parole during the term of imprisonment imposed under this subsection.", was executed by striking "No person sentenced under this subsection shall be eligible for parole during the term of imprisonment imposed herein." as the probable intent of Congress.

Pub.L. 101–647, § 1101, directed that subsec. (c)(1) be amended by inserting "or a destructive device," following "a machinegun", wherever the term "machine gun" appeared. The amendment was executed by making the insertion wherever the term "machinegun" appeared, as the probable intent of Congress.

Amendment by section 6460(2)(B) of Pub.L. 100–690, which directed that "life imprisonment without release" be substituted for "20 years", was executed by making such substitution for "twenty years" as the probable intent of Congress.

Section 223(a) of Pub.L. 98–473, Title II, Oct. 12, 1984, 98 Stat. 2028, which amended subsec. (a) of this section by striking ", and shall become eligible for parole as the Board of Parole shall determine" effective Nov. 1, 1987, pursuant to section 235 of Pub.L. 98–473, as amended by Pub.L. 99–217, § 4, Dec. 26, 1985, 99 Stat. 1728, was incapable of execution in view of amendment by Pub.L. 99–308.

Effective and Applicability Provisions

2005 Acts. Amendments to this section by Pub.L. 109–92, § 5, effective 180 days after Oct. 26, 2005, see Pub.L. 109–92, § 5(d), set out as a note under 18 U.S.C.A. § 922.

1996 Acts. Section 603(m)(2) of Pub.L. 104–294 provided that: "The amendments made by paragraph (1) [amending section 110507 of Pub.L. 103–322, which amended subsec. (a)(1)(B), (2) of this section] shall take effect as if the amendments had been included in section 110507 of the Act referred to in paragraph (1) [section 110507 of Pub.L. 103–322] on the date of the enactment of such Act [Sept. 13, 1994]."

Section 603(p)(2) of Pub.L. 104–294 provided that: "The amendment made by paragraph (1) [amending section 110102(c)(2) of Pub.L. 103–322, which amended subsec. (c)(1) of this section] shall take effect as if the amendment had been included in section 110102(c)(2) of the Act referred to in paragraph (1) [section 110102(c)(2) of Pub.L. 103–322] on the date of the enactment of such Act [Sept. 13, 1994]."

1994 Acts. Amendments by sections 110101 to 110106 of Pub.L. 103–322, effective Sept. 13, 1994, are repealed effective 10 years after Sept. 13, 1994, see section 110105 of Pub.L. 103–322, set out as a note under 18 U.S.C.A. § 921.

Section 330011(i) of Pub.L. 103–322 provided in part that the amendment made by such section, amending the directory language of section 3528 of Pub.L. 101–647 (which amended this section), was to take effect on the date section 3528 of Pub.L. 101–647 took effect; section 3528 of Pub.L. 101–647 took effect on the date of enactment of Pub.L. 101–647, which was approved Nov. 29, 1990.

Section 330011(j) of Pub.L. 103–322 provided in part that the amendment made by such section, amending the directory language of section 3527 of Pub.L. 101–647 (which amended this section), was to take effect on the date section 3527 of Pub.L. 101–647 took effect; section 3527 of Pub.L. 101–647 took effect on the date of enactment of Pub.L. 101–647, which was approved Nov. 29, 1990.

1990 Acts. Section 2203(d) of Pub.L. 101–647 provided that amendment of subsec. (a) by section 2203(d) shall be effective with respect to any offense committed after Nov. 1, 1987.

Amendment by Pub.L. 101–647, § 1702(b)(3), applicable to conduct engaged in after the end of the 60–day period beginning on Nov. 29, 1990, see section 1702(b)(4) of Pub.L. 101–647, set out as a note under 18 U.S.C.A. § 921.

1988 Acts. Amendments by section 2(b) of Pub.L. 100–649 effective after the 30th day beginning after Nov. 10, 1988, see section 2(f)(1) of Pub.L. 100–649, as amended, set out as a note under 18 U.S.C.A. § 922.

Amendments by section 2(f)(2) of Pub.L. 100–649 effective 25 years after the effective date of Pub.L. 100–649, see section 2(f) of Pub.L. 100–649, as amended, set out as a note under 18 U.S.C.A. § 922.

1986 Acts. Amendment by Pub.L. 99–308 effective 180 days after May 19, 1986, see section 110(a) of Pub.L. 99–308, set out as a note under 18 U.S.C.A. § 921.

1984 Acts. Amendment by Pub.L. 98–473 effective on the first day of first calendar month beginning thirty six months after Oct. 12, 1984, applicable only to offenses committed after taking effect of sections 211 to 239 of Pub.L. 98–473, and except as otherwise provided for therein, see section 235 of Pub.L. 98–473, as amended, set out as a note under 18 U.S.C.A. § 3551.

Sunset Provision

Amendments by section 2(f)(2) of Pub.L. 100–649 effective 25 years after the 30th day beginning after Nov. 10, 1988, see section 2(f) of Pub.L. 100–649, as amended, set out as a note under 18 U.S.C.A. § 922.

Repeals

Pub.L. 103–322, Title XXXIII, § 330002(h), Sept. 13, 1994, 108 Stat. 2140, appearing in the credit of this section, was repealed by Pub.L. 104–294, Title VI, § 603(n), Oct. 11, 1996, 110 Stat. 3505, and thus deemed to have never been enacted.

§ 925. Exceptions: Relief from disabilities

(a)(1) The provisions of this chapter, except for sections 922(d)(9) and 922(g)(9) and provisions relating to firearms subject to the prohibitions of section 922(p), shall not apply with respect to the transportation, shipment, receipt, possession, or importation of any firearm or ammunition imported for, sold or shipped to, or issued for the use of, the United States or any department or agency thereof or any State or any department, agency, or political subdivision thereof.

(2) The provisions of this chapter, except for provisions relating to firearms subject to the prohibitions of section 922(p), shall not apply with respect to (A) the shipment or receipt of firearms or ammunition when sold or issued by the Secretary of the Army pursuant to section 4308 of title 10 before the repeal of such section by section 1624(a) of the Corporation for the Promotion of Rifle Practice and Firearms Safety Act, and (B) the transportation of any such firearm or ammunition carried out to enable a person, who lawfully received such firearm or ammunition from the Secretary of the Army, to engage in military training or in competitions.

(3) Unless otherwise prohibited by this chapter, except for provisions relating to firearms subject to the prohibitions of section 922(p), or any other Federal law, a licensed importer, licensed manufacturer, or licensed dealer may ship to a member of the United States Armed Forces on active duty outside the United States or to clubs, recognized by the Department of Defense, whose entire membership is composed of such members, and such members or clubs may receive a firearm or ammunition determined by the Secretary of the Treasury to be generally recognized as particularly suitable for sporting purposes and intended for the personal use of such member or club.

(4) When established to the satisfaction of the Attorney General to be consistent with the provisions of this chapter, except for provisions relating to firearms subject to the prohibitions of section 922(p), and other applicable Federal and State laws and published ordinances, the Attorney General may authorize the transportation, shipment, receipt, or importation into the United States to the place of residence of any member of the United States Armed Forces who is on active duty outside the United States (or who has been on active duty outside the United States within the sixty day period immediately preceding the transportation, shipment, receipt, or importation), of any firearm or ammunition which is (A) determined by the Attorney General to be generally recognized as particularly suitable for sporting purposes, or determined by the Department of Defense to be a type of firearm normally classified as a war souvenir, and (B) intended for the personal use of such member.

(5) For the purpose of paragraph (3) of this subsection, the term "United States" means each of the several States and the District of Columbia.

(b) A licensed importer, licensed manufacturer, licensed dealer, or licensed collector who is indicted for a crime punishable by imprisonment for a term exceeding one year, may, notwithstanding any other provision of this chapter, continue operation pursuant to his existing license (if prior to the expiration of the term of the existing license timely application is made for a new license) during the term of such indictment and until any conviction pursuant to the indictment becomes final.

(c) A person who is prohibited from possessing, shipping, transporting, or receiving firearms or ammunition may make application to the Attorney General for relief from the disabilities imposed by Federal laws with respect to the acquisition, receipt, transfer, shipment, transportation, or possession of firearms, and the Attorney General may grant such relief if it is established to his satisfaction that the circumstances regarding the disability, and the applicant's record and reputation, are such that the applicant will not be likely to act in a manner dangerous to public safety and that the granting of the relief would not be contrary to the public interest. Any person whose application for relief from disabilities is denied by the Attorney General may file a petition with the United States district court for the district in which he resides for a judicial review of such denial. The court may in its discretion admit additional evidence where failure to do so would result in a miscarriage of justice. A licensed importer, licensed manufacturer, licensed dealer, or licensed collector conducting operations under this chapter, who makes application for relief from the disabilities incurred under this chapter, shall not be barred by such disability from further operations under his license pending final action on an application for relief filed pursuant to this section. Whenever the Attorney General grants relief to any person pursuant to this section he shall promptly publish in the Federal Register notice of such action, together with the reasons therefor.

(d) The Attorney General shall authorize a firearm or ammunition to be imported or brought into the United States or any possession thereof if the firearm or ammunition—

(1) is being imported or brought in for scientific or research purposes, or is for use in connection with competition or training pursuant to chapter 401 of title 10;

(2) is an unserviceable firearm, other than a machinegun as defined in section 5845(b) of the Internal Revenue Code of 1986 (not readily restorable to firing condition), imported or brought in as a curio or museum piece;

(3) is of a type that does not fall within the definition of a firearm as defined in section 5845(a) of the Internal Revenue Code of 1986 and is generally recognized as particularly suitable for or readily adaptable to sporting purposes, excluding surplus military firearms, except in any case where the Attorney General has not authorized the importation of the firearm pursuant to this paragraph, it shall be unlawful to import any frame, receiver, or barrel of such firearm which would be prohibited if assembled; or

(4) was previously taken out of the United States or a possession by the person who is bringing in the firearm or ammunition.

The Attorney General shall permit the conditional importation or bringing in of a firearm or ammunition for examination and testing in connection with the making of a determination as to whether the importation or bringing in of such firearm or ammunition will be allowed under this subsection.

(e) Notwithstanding any other provision of this title, the Attorney General shall authorize the importation of, by any licensed importer, the following:

(1) All rifles and shotguns listed as curios or relics by the Attorney General pursuant to section 921(a)(13), and

(2) All handguns, listed as curios or relics by the Attorney General pursuant to section 921(a)(13), provided that such handguns are generally recognized as particularly suitable for or readily adaptable to sporting purposes.

(f) The Attorney General shall not authorize, under subsection (d), the importation of any firearm the importation of which is prohibited by section 922(p).

(Added Pub.L. 90–351, Title IV, § 902, June 19, 1968, 82 Stat. 233, and amended Pub.L. 90–618, Title I, § 102, Oct. 22, 1968, 82 Stat. 1224; Pub.L. 98–573, Title II, § 233, Oct. 30, 1984, 98 Stat. 2991; Pub.L. 99–308, § 105, May 19, 1986, 100 Stat. 459; Pub.L. 100–649, § 2(c), (f)(2)(C), (E), Nov. 10, 1988, 102 Stat. 3817; Pub.L. 101–647, Title XXII, § 2203(b), (c), Nov. 29, 1990, 104 Stat. 4857; Pub.L. 104–106, Div. A, Title XVI, § 1624(b)(3), Feb. 10, 1996, 110 Stat. 522; Pub.L. 104–208, Div. A, Title I, § 101(f) [Title VI, § 658(c)], Sept. 30, 1996, 110 Stat. 3009–372; Pub.L. 104–294, Title VI, § 607(c), Oct. 11, 1996, 110 Stat. 3511; Pub.L. 107–296, Title XI, § 1112(f)(6), Nov. 25, 2002, 116 Stat. 2276.)

Amendment of Subsecs. (a) and (f)

Pub.L. 100–649, § 2(f)(2)(C), (E), Nov. 10, 1988, 102 Stat. 3818, as amended Pub.L. 105–277, Div. A, § 101(h) [Title VI, § 649], Oct. 21, 1998, 112 Stat. 2681–528; Pub.L. 108–174, § 1(1), (3), Dec. 9, 2003, 117 Stat. 2481, provided that, effective 25 years after the 30th day beginning after Nov. 10, 1998 [see section 2(f)(1) of Pub.L. 100–649, as amended, set out as a note under 18 U.S.C.A. § 922], subsec. (f) of this section is repealed and subsec. (a) of this section is amended: in par. (1), by striking "and provisions relating to firearms subject to the prohibitions of section 922(p)"; in par. (2), by striking ", except for provisions relating to firearms subject to the prohibitions of section 922(p),"; and in each of pars. (3) and (4), by striking "except for provisions relating to firearms subject to the prohibitions of section 922(p),".

HISTORICAL AND STATUTORY NOTES

References in Text

Section 4308 of title 10 before the repeal of such section by section 1624(a) of the Corporation for the Promotion of Rifle Practice and Firearms Safety Act, referred to in subsec. (a)(2)(A), means section 4308 of Title 10, Armed Forces, prior to repeal by section 1624(a) of Pub.L. 104–106, Div. A, Title XVI, Feb. 10, 1996, 110 Stat. 522, which also repealed sections 4307, 4310, and 4311 of Title 10. For complete classification of this Act to the Code, see Short Title note set out under section 5501 of Title 36, Patriotic Societies and Observances, and Tables.

Codifications

Amendment by Pub.L. 107–296, § 1112(f)(6), to strike out "Secretary" and insert "Attorney General" each place it appeared was executed by striking out "Secretary" and inserting "Attorney General" each place it appeared except before "of the Army" in two places in subsec. (a)(2), and before "of the Treasury" in subsec. (a)(3), as the probable intent of Congress.

Effective and Applicability Provisions

2002 Acts. Amendment to this section by Pub.L. 107–296 effective 60 days after Nov. 25, 2002, see Pub.L. 107–296, § 4, set out as a note under 6 U.S.C.A. § 101.

1996 Acts. Amendments by Pub.L. 104–106 to take effect on the earlier of the date on which the Secretary of the Army submits certification in accordance with section 5523 of Title 36 or October 1, 1996, see section 1624(c) of Pub.L. 104–106, set out as a note under 10 U.S.C.A. § 4313.

1988 Acts. Amendment of subsecs. (a) and (f) by section 2(c) of Pub.L. 100–649 effective after the 30th day beginning after Nov. 10, 1988, see section 2(f)(1) of Pub.L. 100–649, as amended, set out as a note under 18 U.S.C.A. § 922.

Amendment of subsecs. (a) and (f) by section 2(f)(2)(C) and (E) of Pub.L. 100–649 effective 25 years after the effective date of Pub.L. 100–649, see section 2(f) of Pub.L. 100–649, as amended, set out as a note under 18 U.S.C.A. § 922.

1986 Acts. Amendment by Pub.L. 99–308 applicable to any action, petition, or appellate proceeding pending on May 19, 1986, see section 110(b) of Pub.L. 99–308, set out as a note under 18 U.S.C.A. § 921.

Sunset Provision

Amendments by section 2(f)(2) of Pub.L. 100–649 effective 25 years after the 30th day beginning after Nov. 10, 1988, see section 2(f) of Pub.L. 100–649, as amended, set out as a note under 18 U.S.C.A. § 922.

§ 925A. Remedy for erroneous denial of firearm

Any person denied a firearm pursuant to subsection (s) or (t) of section 922—

(1) due to the provision of erroneous information relating to the person by any State or political subdivision thereof, or by the national instant criminal background check system established under section 103 of the Brady Handgun Violence Prevention Act; or

(2) who was not prohibited from receipt of a firearm pursuant to subsection (g) or (n) of section 922,

may bring an action against the State or political subdivision responsible for providing the erroneous information, or responsible for denying the transfer, or against the United States, as the case may be, for an order directing that the erroneous information be corrected or that the transfer be approved, as the case may be. In any action under this section, the court, in its discretion, may allow the prevailing party a reasonable attorney's fee as part of the costs.

(Added Pub.L. 103–159, Title I, § 104(a), Nov. 30, 1993, 107 Stat. 1543.)

HISTORICAL AND STATUTORY NOTES

References in Text

Section 103 of the Brady Handgun Violence Prevention Act, referred to in par. (1), is section 103 of Pub.L. 103–159, which is set out as a note under section 922 of this title.

§ 926. Rules and regulations

(a) The Attorney General may prescribe only such rules and regulations as are necessary to carry out the provisions of this chapter, including—

(1) regulations providing that a person licensed under this chapter, when dealing with another person so licensed, shall provide such other licensed person a certified copy of this license;

(2) regulations providing for the issuance, at a reasonable cost, to a person licensed under this chapter, of certified copies of his license for use as provided under regulations issued under paragraph (1) of this subsection; and

(3) regulations providing for effective receipt and secure storage of firearms relinquished by or seized from persons described in subsection (d)(8) or (g)(8) of section 922.

No such rule or regulation prescribed after the date of the enactment of the Firearms Owners' Protection Act may require that records required to be maintained under this chapter or any portion of the contents of such records, be recorded at or transferred to a facility owned, managed, or controlled by the United States or any State or any political subdivision thereof, nor that any system of registration of firearms, firearms owners, or firearms transactions or dispositions be established. Nothing in this section expands or restricts the Attorney General's authority to inquire into the disposition of any firearm in the course of a criminal investigation.

(b) The Attorney General shall give not less than ninety days public notice, and shall afford interested parties opportunity for hearing, before prescribing such rules and regulations.

(c) The Attorney General shall not prescribe rules or regulations that require purchasers of black powder under the exemption provided in section 845(a)(5) of this title to complete affidavits or forms attesting to that exemption.

(Added Pub.L. 90–351, Title IV, § 902, June 19, 1968, 82 Stat. 234, and amended Pub.L. 90–618, Title I, § 102, Oct. 22, 1968, 82 Stat. 1226; Pub.L. 99–308, § 106, May 19, 1986, 100 Stat. 459; Pub.L. 103–322, Title XI, § 110401(d), Sept. 13, 1994, 108 Stat. 2015; Pub.L. 107–296, Title XI, § 1112(f)(6), Nov. 25, 2002, 116 Stat. 2276.)

HISTORICAL AND STATUTORY NOTES

References in Text

The date of enactment of the Firearms Owners' Protection Act, referred to in subsec. (a), is the date of enactment of Pub.L. 99–308, which was approved May 19, 1986.

Effective and Applicability Provisions

2002 Acts. Amendment to this section by Pub.L. 107–296 effective 60 days after Nov. 25, 2002, see Pub.L. 107–296, § 4, set out as a note under 6 U.S.C.A. § 101.

1986 Acts. Amendment by Pub.L. 99–308 effective 180 days after May 19, 1986, see section 110(a) of Pub.L. 99–308, set out as a note under section 921 of this title.

§ 926A. Interstate transportation of firearms

Notwithstanding any other provision of any law or any rule or regulation of a State or any political subdivision thereof, any person who is not otherwise prohibited by this chapter from transporting, shipping, or receiving a firearm shall be entitled to transport a firearm for any lawful purpose from any place where he may lawfully possess and carry such firearm to any other place where he may lawfully possess and carry such firearm if, during such transportation the firearm is unloaded, and neither the firearm nor any ammunition being transported is readily accessible or is directly accessible from the passenger compartment of such transporting vehicle: *Provided*, That in the case of a vehicle without a compartment separate from the driver's compartment the firearm or ammunition shall be contained in a locked container other than the glove compartment or console.

(Added Pub.L. 99–360, § 1(a), July 8, 1986, 100 Stat. 766.)

HISTORICAL AND STATUTORY NOTES

Effective and Applicability Provisions

1986 Acts. Section effective on the date on which the Firearms Owners' Protection Act, Pub.L. 99–308, becomes effective, see section 2 of Pub.L. 99–308, set out as a note under section 921 of this title.

Prior Provisions

A prior section 926A, added Pub.L. 99–308, § 107(a), May 19, 1986, 100 Stat. 460, which provided that any person not prohibited by this chapter from transporting, shipping, or receiving a firearm be entitled to transport an unloaded, not readily accessible firearm in interstate commerce notwithstanding any provision of any legislation enacted, or rule or regulation prescribed by any State or political subdivision thereof, was repealed by Pub.L. 99–360, § 1(a), July 8, 1986, 100 Stat. 766.

§ 926B. Carrying of concealed firearms by qualified law enforcement officers

(a) Notwithstanding any other provision of the law of any State or any political subdivision thereof, an individual who is a qualified law enforcement officer and who is carrying the identification required by subsection (d) may carry a concealed firearm that has been shipped or transported in interstate or foreign commerce, subject to subsection (b).

(b) This section shall not be construed to supersede or limit the laws of any State that—

(1) permit private persons or entities to prohibit or restrict the possession of concealed firearms on their property; or

(2) prohibit or restrict the possession of firearms on any State or local government property, installation, building, base, or park.

(c) As used in this section, the term "qualified law enforcement officer" means an employee of a governmental agency who—

(1) is authorized by law to engage in or supervise the prevention, detection, investigation, or prosecution of, or the incarceration of any person for, any violation of law, and has statutory powers of arrest;

(2) is authorized by the agency to carry a firearm;

(3) is not the subject of any disciplinary action by the agency;

(4) meets standards, if any, established by the agency which require the employee to regularly qualify in the use of a firearm;

(5) is not under the influence of alcohol or another intoxicating or hallucinatory drug or substance; and

(6) is not prohibited by Federal law from receiving a firearm.

(d) The identification required by this subsection is the photographic identification issued by the governmental agency for which the individual is employed as a law enforcement officer.

(e) As used in this section, the term "firearm" does not include—

(1) any machinegun (as defined in section 5845 of the National Firearms Act);

(2) any firearm silencer (as defined in section 921 of this title); and

(3) any destructive device (as defined in section 921 of this title).

(Added Pub.L. 108–277, § 2(a), July 22, 2004, 118 Stat. 865.)

HISTORICAL AND STATUTORY NOTES

References in Text

Section 5845 of the National Firearms Act, referred to in subsec. (e)(1), is 26 U.S.C.A. § 5845.

§ 926C. Carrying of concealed firearms by qualified retired law enforcement officers

(a) Notwithstanding any other provision of the law of any State or any political subdivision thereof, an individual who is a qualified retired law enforcement officer and who is carrying the identification required by subsection (d) may carry a concealed firearm that has been shipped or transported in interstate or foreign commerce, subject to subsection (b).

(b) This section shall not be construed to supersede or limit the laws of any State that—

(1) permit private persons or entities to prohibit or restrict the possession of concealed firearms on their property; or

(2) prohibit or restrict the possession of firearms on any State or local government property, installation, building, base, or park.

(c) As used in this section, the term "qualified retired law enforcement officer" means an individual who—

(1) retired in good standing from service with a public agency as a law enforcement officer, other than for reasons of mental instability;

(2) before such retirement, was authorized by law to engage in or supervise the prevention, detection, investigation, or prosecution of, or the incarceration of any person for, any violation of law, and had statutory powers of arrest;

(3)(A) before such retirement, was regularly employed as a law enforcement officer for an aggregate of 15 years or more; or

(B) retired from service with such agency, after completing any applicable probationary period of such service, due to a service-connected disability, as determined by such agency;

(4) has a nonforfeitable right to benefits under the retirement plan of the agency;

(5) during the most recent 12–month period, has met, at the expense of the individual, the State's standards for training and qualification for active law enforcement officers to carry firearms;

(6) is not under the influence of alcohol or another intoxicating or hallucinatory drug or substance; and

(7) is not prohibited by Federal law from receiving a firearm.

(d) The identification required by this subsection is—

(1) a photographic identification issued by the agency from which the individual retired from service as a law enforcement officer that indicates that the individual has, not less recently than one year before the date the individual is carrying the concealed firearm, been tested or otherwise found by the agency to meet the standards established by the agency for training and qualification for active law enforcement officers to carry a firearm of the same type as the concealed firearm; or

(2)(A) a photographic identification issued by the agency from which the individual retired from service as a law enforcement officer; and

(B) a certification issued by the State in which the individual resides that indicates that the individual has, not less recently than one year before the date the individual is carrying the concealed firearm, been tested or otherwise found by the State to meet the standards established by the State for training and qualification for active law enforcement officers to carry a firearm of the same type as the concealed firearm.

(e) As used in this section, the term "firearm" does not include—

(1) any machinegun (as defined in section 5845 of the National Firearms Act);

(2) any firearm silencer (as defined in section 921 of this title); and

(3) a destructive device (as defined in section 921 of this title).

(Added Pub.L. 108–277, § 3(a), July 22, 2004, 118 Stat. 866.)

HISTORICAL AND STATUTORY NOTES

References in Text

Section 5845 of the National Firearms Act, referred to in subsec. (e)(1), is 26 U.S.C.A. § 5845.

§ 927. Effect on State law

No provision of this chapter shall be construed as indicating an intent on the part of the Congress to occupy the field in which such provision operates to the exclusion of the law of any State on the same subject matter, unless there is a direct and positive conflict between such provision and the law of the State so that the two cannot be reconciled or consistently stand together.

(Added Pub.L. 90–351, Title IV, § 902, June 19, 1968, 82 Stat. 234, and amended Pub.L. 90–618, Title I, § 102, Oct. 22, 1968, 82 Stat. 1226.)

HISTORICAL AND STATUTORY NOTES

Effective and Applicability Provisions

1968 Acts. Amendment by Pub.L. 90–618 effective Dec. 16, 1968, see § 105 of Pub.L. 90–618, set out as a note under § 921 of this title.

§ 928. Separability

If any provision of this chapter or the application thereof to any person or circumstance is held invalid, the remainder of the chapter and the application of such provision to other persons not similarly situated or to other circumstances shall not be affected thereby.

(Added Pub.L. 90–351, Title IV, § 902, June 19, 1968, 82 Stat. 234, and amended Pub.L. 90–618, Title I, § 102, Oct. 22, 1968, 82 Stat. 1226.)

HISTORICAL AND STATUTORY NOTES

Effective and Applicability Provisions

1968 Acts. Amendment by Pub.L. 90–618 effective Dec. 16, 1968, see § 105 of Pub.L. 90–618, set out as a note under § 921 of this title.

§ 929. Use of restricted ammunition

(a)(1) Whoever, during and in relation to the commission of a crime of violence or drug trafficking crime (including a crime of violence or drug trafficking crime which provides for an enhanced punishment if committed by the use of a deadly or dangerous weapon or device) for which he may be prosecuted in a court of the United States, uses or carries a firearm and is in possession of armor piercing ammunition capable of being fired in that firearm, shall, in addition to the punishment provided for the commission of such crime of violence or drug trafficking crime be sentenced to a term of imprisonment for not less than five years.

(2) For purposes of this subsection, the term "drug trafficking crime" means any felony punishable under the Controlled Substances Act (21 U.S.C. 801 et seq.),

the Controlled Substances Import and Export Act (21 U.S.C. 951 et seq.), or chapter 705 of title 46.

(b) Notwithstanding any other provision of law, the court shall not suspend the sentence of any person convicted of a violation of this section, nor place the person on probation, nor shall the terms of imprisonment run concurrently with any other terms of imprisonment, including that imposed for the crime in which the armor piercing ammunition was used or possessed.

(Added Pub.L. 98–473, Title II, § 1006(a), Oct. 12, 1984, 98 Stat. 2139, and amended Pub.L. 99–308, § 108, May 19, 1986, 100 Stat. 460; Pub.L. 99–408, § 8, Aug. 28, 1986, 100 Stat. 921; Pub.L. 100–690, Title VI, § 6212, Title VII, § 7060(b), Nov. 18, 1988, 102 Stat. 4360, 4404; Pub.L. 107–273, Div. B, Title IV, § 4002(c)(4), Nov. 2, 2002, 116 Stat. 1809; Pub.L. 109–304, § 17(d)(4), Oct. 6, 2006, 120 Stat. 1707.)

HISTORICAL AND STATUTORY NOTES

References in Text

The Controlled Substances Act, referred to in subsec. (a)(2), is Title II of Pub.L. 91–513, Oct. 27, 1970, 84 Stat. 1242, as amended, which is classified principally to subchapter I (section 801 et seq.) of chapter 13 of Title 21, Food and Drugs. For complete classification of this Act to the Code, see Short Title note set out under section 801 of Title 21 and Tables.

The Controlled Substances Import and Export Act, referred to in subsec. (a)(2), is Title III of Pub.L. 91–513, § 1001 et seq., Oct. 27, 1970, 84 Stat. 1285, as amended, which is classified principally to subchapter II (section 951 et seq.) of chapter 13 of Title 21. For complete classification of this Act to the Code, see Short Title note set out under section 951 of Title 21 and Tables.

Chapter 705 of title 46, referred to in subsec. (a)(2), is Maritime Drug Law Enforcement, 46 U.S.C.A. § 70501 et seq.

Effective and Applicability Provisions

1986 Acts. Amendment by Pub.L. 99–408 effective Aug. 28, 1986, see section 9 of Pub.L. 99–408, set out as a note under section 921 of this title.

Amendment by Pub.L. 99–308 effective 180 days after May 19, 1986, see section 110(a) of Pub.L. 99–308, set out as a note under section 921 of this title.

§ 930. Possession of firearms and dangerous weapons in Federal facilities

(a) Except as provided in subsection (d), whoever knowingly possesses or causes to be present a firearm or other dangerous weapon in a Federal facility (other than a Federal court facility), or attempts to do so, shall be fined under this title or imprisoned not more than 1 year, or both.

(b) Whoever, with intent that a firearm or other dangerous weapon be used in the commission of a crime, knowingly possesses or causes to be present such firearm or dangerous weapon in a Federal facility, or attempts to do so, shall be fined under this title or imprisoned not more than 5 years, or both.

(c) A person who kills any person in the course of a violation of subsection (a) or (b), or in the course of an attack on a Federal facility involving the use of a firearm or other dangerous weapon, or attempts or conspires to do such an act, shall be punished as provided in sections 1111, 1112, 1113, and 1117.

(d) Subsection (a) shall not apply to—

(1) the lawful performance of official duties by an officer, agent, or employee of the United States, a State, or a political subdivision thereof, who is authorized by law to engage in or supervise the prevention, detection, investigation, or prosecution of any violation of law;

(2) the possession of a firearm or other dangerous weapon by a Federal official or a member of the Armed Forces if such possession is authorized by law; or

(3) the lawful carrying of firearms or other dangerous weapons in a Federal facility incident to hunting or other lawful purposes.

(e)(1) Except as provided in paragraph (2), whoever knowingly possesses or causes to be present a firearm in a Federal court facility, or attempts to do so, shall be fined under this title, imprisoned not more than 2 years, or both.

(2) Paragraph (1) shall not apply to conduct which is described in paragraph (1) or (2) of subsection (d).

(f) Nothing in this section limits the power of a court of the United States to punish for contempt or to promulgate rules or orders regulating, restricting, or prohibiting the possession of weapons within any building housing such court or any of its proceedings, or upon any grounds appurtenant to such building.

(g) As used in this section:

(1) The term "Federal facility" means a building or part thereof owned or leased by the Federal Government, where Federal employees are regularly present for the purpose of performing their official duties.

(2) The term "dangerous weapon" means a weapon, device, instrument, material, or substance, animate or inanimate, that is used for, or is readily capable of, causing death or serious bodily injury, except that such term does not include a pocket knife with a blade of less than 2½ inches in length.

(3) The term "Federal court facility" means the courtroom, judges' chambers, witness rooms, jury deliberation rooms, attorney conference rooms, prisoner holding cells, offices of the court clerks, the United States attorney, and the United States marshal, probation and parole offices, and adjoining corridors of any court of the United States.

(h) Notice of the provisions of subsections (a) and (b) shall be posted conspicuously at each public entrance to each Federal facility, and notice of subsection (e) shall be posted conspicuously at each public entrance to each Federal court facility, and no person shall be convicted of an offense under subsection (a) or (e) with respect to a Federal facility if such notice is not so posted at such facility, unless such person had actual notice of subsection (a) or (e), as the case may be.

(Added Pub.L. 100–690, Title VI, § 6215(a), Nov. 18, 1988, 102 Stat. 4361, and amended Pub.L. 101–647, Title XXII, § 2205(a), Nov. 29, 1990, 104 Stat. 4857; Pub.L. 103–322, Title VI, § 60014, Sept. 13, 1994, 108 Stat. 1973; Pub.L. 104–294, Title VI, § 603(t), (u), Oct. 11, 1996, 110 Stat. 3506; Pub.L. 107–56, Title VIII, § 811(b), Oct. 26, 2001, 115 Stat. 381.)

HISTORICAL AND STATUTORY NOTES

Effective and Applicability Provisions

1990 Acts. Section 2205(b) of Pub.L. 101–647 provided that: "The amendments made by subsection (a) [amending subsec. (a), enacting subsec. (d), redesignating as subsec. (e) former subsec. (d), redesignating as subsec. (f) former subsec. (e) and enacting subsec. (f)(3), and redesignating as subsec. (g) former subsec. (f) and amending subsec. (g) of this section] shall apply to conduct engaged in after the date of the enactment of this Act [Nov. 29, 1990]."

§ 931. Prohibition on purchase, ownership, or possession of body armor by violent felons

(a) In general.—Except as provided in subsection (b), it shall be unlawful for a person to purchase, own, or possess body armor, if that person has been convicted of a felony that is—

(1) a crime of violence (as defined in section 16); or

(2) an offense under State law that would constitute a crime of violence under paragraph (1) if it occurred within the special maritime and territorial jurisdiction of the United States.

(b) Affirmative defense.—

(1) In general.—It shall be an affirmative defense under this section that—

(A) the defendant obtained prior written certification from his or her employer that the defendant's purchase, use, or possession of body armor was necessary for the safe performance of lawful business activity; and

(B) the use and possession by the defendant were limited to the course of such performance.

(2) Employer.—In this subsection, the term "employer" means any other individual employed by the defendant's business that supervises defendant's activity. If that defendant has no supervisor, prior written certification is acceptable from any other employee of the business.

(Added Pub.L. 107–273, Div. C, Title I, § 11009(e)(2)(A), Nov. 2, 2002, 116 Stat. 1821.)

CHAPTER 45—FOREIGN RELATIONS

Sec.

§ 951. Agents of foreign governments

(a) Whoever, other than a diplomatic or consular officer or attaché, acts in the United States as an agent of a foreign government without prior notification to the Attorney General if required in subsection (b), shall be fined under this title or imprisoned not more than ten years, or both.

(b) The Attorney General shall promulgate rules and regulations establishing requirements for notification.

(c) The Attorney General shall, upon receipt, promptly transmit one copy of each notification statement filed under this section to the Secretary of State for such comment and use as the Secretary of State may determine to be appropriate from the point of view of the foreign relations of the United States. Failure of the Attorney General to do so shall not be a bar to prosecution under this section.

(d) For purposes of this section, the term "agent of a foreign government" means an individual who agrees to operate within the United States subject to the direction or control of a foreign government or official, except that such term does not include—

(1) a duly accredited diplomatic or consular officer of a foreign government, who is so recognized by the Department of State;

(2) any officially and publicly acknowledged and sponsored official or representative of a foreign government;

(3) any officially and publicly acknowledged and sponsored member of the staff of, or employee of, an officer, official, or representative described in paragraph (1) or (2), who is not a United States citizen; or

(4) any person engaged in a legal commercial transaction.

(e) Notwithstanding paragraph (d)(4), any person engaged in a legal commercial transaction shall be considered to be an agent of a foreign government for purposes of this section if—

(1) such person agrees to operate within the United States subject to the direction or control of a foreign government or official; and

(2) such person—

(A) is an agent of Cuba or any other country that the President determines (and so reports to the Congress) poses a threat to the national security interest of the United States for purposes of this section, unless the Attorney General, after consultation with the Secretary of State, determines and so reports to the Congress that the national security or foreign policy interests of the United States require that the provisions of this section do not apply in specific circumstances to agents of such country; or

(B) has been convicted of, or has entered a plea of nolo contendere with respect to, any offense under section 792 through 799, 831, or 2381 of this title or under section 11 of the Export Administration Act of 1979, except that the provisions of this subsection shall not apply to a person described in this clause for a period of more than five years beginning on the date of the conviction or the date of entry of the plea of nolo contendere, as the case may be.

(June 25, 1948, c. 645, 62 Stat. 743; Jan. 12, 1983, Pub.L. 97–462, § 6, 96 Stat. 2530; Oct. 12, 1984, Pub.L. 98–473, Title II, § 1209, 98 Stat. 2164; Oct. 27, 1986, Pub.L. 99–569, Title VII, § 703, 100 Stat. 3205; Dec. 17, 1993, Pub.L. 103–199, Title II, § 202, 107 Stat. 2321; Sept. 13, 1994, Pub.L. 103–322, Title XXXIII, § 330016(1)(R), 108 Stat. 2148.)

HISTORICAL AND STATUTORY NOTES

References in Text

Section 11 of the Export Administration Act of 1979, referred to in subsec. (e)(2)(B), is classified to section 2410 of Title 50, Appendix, War and National Defense.

Effective and Applicability Provisions

1983 Acts. Amendment by Pub.L. 97–462, increasing fines to $75,000 from $5,000, 45 days after Jan. 12, 1983, pursuant to section 4 of Pub.L. 97–462.

Canal Zone

Applicability of section to Canal Zone, see § 14 of this title.

§ 952. Diplomatic codes and correspondence

Whoever, by virtue of his employment by the United States, obtains from another or has or has had custody of or access to, any official diplomatic code or any matter prepared in any such code, or which purports to have been prepared in any such code, and without authorization or competent authority, willfully publishes or furnishes to another any such code or matter, or any matter which was obtained while in the process of transmission between any foreign government and its diplomatic mission in the United States, shall be fined under this title or imprisoned not more than ten years, or both.

(June 25, 1948, c. 645, 62 Stat. 743; Sept. 13, 1994, Pub.L. 103–322, Title XXXIII, § 330016(1)(L), 108 Stat. 2147.)

§ 953. Private correspondence with foreign governments

Any citizen of the United States, wherever he may be, who, without authority of the United States, directly or indirectly commences or carries on any correspondence or intercourse with any foreign government or any officer or agent thereof, with intent to influence the measures or conduct of any foreign government or of any officer or agent thereof, in relation to any disputes or controversies with the United States, or to defeat the measures of the United States, shall be fined under this title or imprisoned not more than three years, or both.

This section shall not abridge the right of a citizen to apply, himself or his agent, to any foreign government or the agents thereof for redress of any injury which he may have sustained from such government or any of its agents or subjects.

(June 25, 1948, c. 645, 62 Stat. 744; Sept. 13, 1994, Pub.L. 103–322, Title XXXIII, § 330016(1)(K), 108 Stat. 2147.)

HISTORICAL AND STATUTORY NOTES

Canal Zone

Applicability of section to Canal Zone, see § 14 of this title.

§ 954. False statements influencing foreign government

Whoever, in relation to any dispute or controversy between a foreign government and the United States, willfully and knowingly makes any untrue statement, either orally or in writing, under oath before any person authorized and empowered to administer oaths, which the affiant has knowledge or reason to believe will, or may be used to influence the measures or conduct of any foreign government, or of any officer or agent of any foreign government, to the injury of the United States, or with a view or intent to influence any measure of or action by the United States or any department or agency thereof, to the

injury of the United States, shall be fined under this title or imprisoned not more than ten years, or both.
(June 25, 1948, c. 645, 62 Stat. 744; Sept. 13, 1994, Pub.L. 103–322, Title XXXIII, § 330016(1)(K), 108 Stat. 2147.)

HISTORICAL AND STATUTORY NOTES

Canal Zone

Applicability of section to Canal Zone, see § 14 of this title.

§ 955. Financial transactions with foreign governments

Whoever, within the United States, purchases or sells the bonds, securities, or other obligations of any foreign government or political subdivision thereof or any organization or association acting for or on behalf of a foreign government or political subdivision thereof, issued after April 13, 1934, or makes any loan to such foreign government, political subdivision, organization or association, except a renewal or adjustment of existing indebtedness, while such government, political subdivision, organization or association, is in default in the payment of its obligations, or any part thereof, to the United States, shall be fined under this title or imprisoned for not more than five years, or both.

This section is applicable to individuals, partnerships, corporations, or associations other than public corporations created by or pursuant to special authorizations of Congress, or corporations in which the United States has or exercises a controlling interest through stock ownership or otherwise. While any foreign government is a member both of the International Monetary Fund and of the International Bank for Reconstruction and Development, this section shall not apply to the sale or purchase of bonds, securities, or other obligations of such government or any political subdivision thereof or of any organization or association acting for or on behalf of such government or political subdivision, or to making of any loan to such government, political subdivision, organization, or association.
(June 25, 1948, c. 645, 62 Stat. 744; Sept. 13, 1994, Pub.L. 103–322, Title XXXIII, § 330016(1)(L), 108 Stat. 2147.)

HISTORICAL AND STATUTORY NOTES

Applicability of Section

Pub.L. 102–511, Title IX, § 902, Oct. 24, 1992, 106 Stat. 3355, provided that: "Section 955 of title 18, United States Code [this section], shall not apply with respect to any obligations of the former Soviet Union, or any of the independent states of the former Soviet Union, or any political subdivision, organization, or association thereof."

§ 956. Conspiracy to kill, kidnap, maim, or injure persons or damage property in a foreign country

(a)(1) Whoever, within the jurisdiction of the United States, conspires with one or more other persons, regardless of where such other person or persons are located, to commit at any place outside the United States an act that would constitute the offense of murder, kidnapping, or maiming if committed in the special maritime and territorial jurisdiction of the United States shall, if any of the conspirators commits an act within the jurisdiction of the United States to effect any object of the conspiracy, be punished as provided in subsection (a)(2).

(2) The punishment for an offense under subsection (a)(1) of this section is—

(A) imprisonment for any term of years or for life if the offense is conspiracy to murder or kidnap; and

(B) imprisonment for not more than 35 years if the offense is conspiracy to maim.

(b) Whoever, within the jurisdiction of the United States, conspires with one or more persons, regardless of where such other person or persons are located, to damage or destroy specific property situated within a foreign country and belonging to a foreign government or to any political subdivision thereof with which the United States is at peace, or any railroad, canal, bridge, airport, airfield, or other public utility, public conveyance, or public structure, or any religious, educational, or cultural property so situated, shall, if any of the conspirators commits an act within the jurisdiction of the United States to effect any object of the conspiracy, be imprisoned not more than 25 years.
(June 25, 1948, c. 645, 62 Stat. 744; Sept. 13, 1994, Pub.L. 103–322, Title XXXIII, § 330016(1)(K), 108 Stat. 2147; Apr. 24, 1996, Pub.L. 104–132, Title VII, § 704(a), 110 Stat. 1294.)

HISTORICAL AND STATUTORY NOTES

Canal Zone

Applicability of section to Canal Zone, see § 14 of this title.

§ 957. Possession of property in aid of foreign government

Whoever, in aid of any foreign government, knowingly and willfully possesses or controls any property or papers used or designed or intended for use in violating any penal statute, or any of the rights or obligations of the United States under any treaty or the law of nations, shall be fined under this title or imprisoned not more than ten years, or both.
(June 25, 1948, c. 645, 62 Stat. 745; Sept. 13, 1994, Pub.L. 103–322, Title XXXIII, § 330016(1)(H), 108 Stat. 2147.)

HISTORICAL AND STATUTORY NOTES

Canal Zone

Applicability of section to Canal Zone, see § 14 of this title.

§ 958. Commission to serve against friendly nation

Any citizen of the United States who, within the jurisdiction thereof, accepts and exercises a commission to serve a foreign prince, state, colony, district, or people, in war, against any prince, state, colony, district, or people, with whom the United States is at peace, shall be fined under this title or imprisoned not more than three years, or both.

(June 25, 1948, c. 645, 62 Stat. 745; Sept. 13, 1994, Pub.L. 103–322, Title XXXIII, § 330016(1)(I), 108 Stat. 2147.)

HISTORICAL AND STATUTORY NOTES

Canal Zone

Applicability of section to Canal Zone, see § 14 of this title.

§ 959. Enlistment in foreign service

(a) Whoever, within the United States, enlists or enters himself, or hires or retains another to enlist or enter himself, or to go beyond the jurisdiction of the United States with intent to be enlisted or entered in the service of any foreign prince, state, colony, district, or people as a soldier or as a marine or seaman on board any vessel of war, letter of marque, or privateer, shall be fined under this title or imprisoned not more than three years, or both.

(b) This section shall not apply to citizens or subjects of any country engaged in war with a country with which the United States is at war, unless such citizen or subject of such foreign country shall hire or solicit a citizen of the United States to enlist or go beyond the jurisdiction of the United States with intent to enlist or enter the service of a foreign country. Enlistments under this subsection shall be under regulations prescribed by the Secretary of the Army.

(c) This section and sections 960 and 961 of this title shall not apply to any subject or citizen of any foreign prince, state, colony, district, or people who is transiently within the United States and enlists or enters himself on board any vessel of war, letter of marque, or privateer, which at the time of its arrival within the United States was fitted and equipped as such, or hires or retains another subject or citizen of the same foreign prince, state, colony, district, or people who is transiently within the United States to enlist or enter himself to serve such foreign prince, state, colony, district, or people on board such vessel of war, letter of marque, or privateer, if the United States shall then be at peace with such foreign prince, state, colony, district, or people.

(June 25, 1948, c. 645, 62 Stat. 745; Sept. 13, 1994, Pub.L. 103–322, Title XXXIII, § 330016(1)(H), 108 Stat. 2147.)

HISTORICAL AND STATUTORY NOTES

Canal Zone

Applicability of section to Canal Zone, see § 14 of this title.

§ 960. Expedition against friendly nation

Whoever, within the United States, knowingly begins or sets on foot or provides or prepares a means for or furnishes the money for, or takes part in, any military or naval expedition or enterprise to be carried on from thence against the territory or dominion of any foreign prince or state, or of any colony, district, or people with whom the United States is at peace, shall be fined under this title or imprisoned not more than three years, or both.

(June 25, 1948, c. 645, 62 Stat. 745; Sept. 13, 1994, Pub.L. 103–322, Title XXXIII, § 330016(1)(J), 108 Stat. 2147.)

HISTORICAL AND STATUTORY NOTES

Canal Zone

Applicability of section to Canal Zone, see § 14 of this title.

§ 961. Strengthening armed vessel of foreign nation

Whoever, within the United States, increases or augments the force of any ship of war, cruiser, or other armed vessel which, at the time of her arrival within the United States, was a ship of war, or cruiser, or armed vessel, in the service of any foreign prince or state, or of any colony, district, or people, or belonging to the subjects or citizens of any such prince or state, colony, district, or people, the same being at war with any foreign prince or state, or of any colony, district, or people, with whom the United States is at peace, by adding to the number of the guns of such vessel, or by changing those on board of her for guns of a larger caliber, or by adding thereto any equipment solely applicable to war, shall be fined under this title or imprisoned not more than one year, or both.

(June 25, 1948, c. 645, 62 Stat. 746; Sept. 13, 1994, Pub.L. 103–322, Title XXXIII, § 330016(1)(H), 108 Stat. 2147.)

HISTORICAL AND STATUTORY NOTES

Canal Zone

Applicability of section to Canal Zone, see § 14 of this title.

§ 962. Arming vessel against friendly nation

Whoever, within the United States, furnishes, fits out, arms, or attempts to furnish, fit out or arm, any vessel, with intent that such vessel shall be employed in the service of any foreign prince, or state, or of any colony, district, or people, to cruise, or commit hostilities against the subjects, citizens, or property of any foreign prince or state, or of any colony, district, or people with whom the United States is at peace; or

Whoever issues or delivers a commission within the United States for any vessel, to the intent that she may be so employed—

Shall be fined under this title or imprisoned not more than three years, or both.

Every such vessel, her tackle, apparel, and furniture, together with all materials, arms, ammunition, and stores which may have been procured for the building and equipment thereof, shall be forfeited, one half to the use of the informer and the other half to the use of the United States.

(June 25, 1948, c. 645, 62 Stat. 746; Sept. 13, 1994, Pub.L. 103–322, Title XXXIII, § 330016(1)(L), 108 Stat. 2147.)

HISTORICAL AND STATUTORY NOTES

Canal Zone

Applicability of section to Canal Zone, see § 14 of this title.

§ 963. Detention of armed vessel

(a) During a war in which the United States is a neutral nation, the President, or any person authorized by him, may detain any armed vessel owned wholly or in part by citizens of the United States, or any vessel, domestic or foreign (other than one which has entered the ports of the United States as a public vessel), which is manifestly built for warlike purposes or has been converted or adapted from a private vessel to one suitable for warlike use, until the owner or master, or person having charge of such vessel, shall furnish proof satisfactory to the President, or to the person duly authorized by him, that the vessel will not be employed to cruise against or commit or attempt to commit hostilities upon the subjects, citizens, or property of any foreign prince or state, or of any colony, district, or people with which the United States is at peace, and that the said vessel will not be sold or delivered to any belligerent nation, or to an agent, officer, or citizen of such nation, by them or any of them, within the jurisdiction of the United States, or upon the high seas.

(b) Whoever, in violation of this section takes, or attempts to take, or authorizes the taking of any such vessel, out of port or from the United States, shall be fined under this title or imprisoned not more than ten years, or both.

In addition, such vessel, her tackle, apparel, furniture, equipment, and her cargo shall be forfeited to the United States.

(June 25, 1948, c. 645, 62 Stat. 746; Sept. 13, 1994, Pub.L. 103–322, Title XXXIII, § 330016(1)(L), 108 Stat. 2147.)

HISTORICAL AND STATUTORY NOTES

Delegation of Functions

For delegation to Secretary of Homeland Security of authority vested in President by this section, see section 1(*l*) of Ex. Ord. No. 10637, Sept. 16, 1955, 20 F.R. 7025, as amended, set out as a note under 3 U.S.C.A. § 301.

Canal Zone. Applicability of section to Canal Zone, see § 14 of this title.

§ 964. Delivering armed vessel to belligerent nation

(a) During a war in which the United States is a neutral nation, it shall be unlawful to send out of the United States any vessel built, armed, or equipped as a vessel of war, or converted from a private vessel into a vessel of war, with any intent or under any agreement or contract that such vessel will be delivered to a belligerent nation, or to an agent, officer, or citizen of such nation, or with reasonable cause to believe that the said vessel will be employed in the service of any such belligerent nation after its departure from the jurisdiction of the United States.

(b) Whoever, in violation of this section, takes or attempts to take, or authorizes the taking of any such vessel, out of port or from the United States, shall be fined under this title or imprisoned not more than ten years, or both.

In addition, such vessel, her tackle, apparel, furniture, equipment, and her cargo shall be forfeited to the United States.

(June 25, 1948, c. 645, 62 Stat. 747; Sept. 13, 1994, Pub.L. 103–322, Title XXXIII, § 330016(1)(L), 108 Stat. 2147.)

HISTORICAL AND STATUTORY NOTES

Canal Zone

Applicability of section to Canal Zone, see § 14 of this title.

§ 965. Verified statements as prerequisite to vessel's departure

(a) During a war in which the United States is a neutral nation, every master or person having charge or command of any vessel, domestic or foreign, whether requiring clearance or not, before departure of such vessel from port shall, in addition to the facts required by section 431 of the Tariff Act of 1930 (19 U.S.C. 1431) and section 60105 of title 46, to be set out in the masters' and shippers' manifests before clearance will be issued to vessels bound to foreign ports, deliver to the Customs Service a statement, duly verified by oath, that the cargo or any part of the cargo is or is not to be delivered to other vessels in port or to be transshipped on the high seas, and, if it is to be so delivered or transshipped, stating the kind and quantities and the value of the total quantity of each kind of article so to be delivered or transshipped, and the name of the person, corporation, vessel, or government to whom the delivery or transshipment is to be made; and the owners, shippers, or consignors of the cargo of such vessel shall in the same manner and under the same conditions deliver to the Customs Service like statements under oath as to the cargo or the parts thereof laden or shipped by them, respectively.

(b) Whoever, in violation of this section, takes or attempts to take, or authorizes the taking of any such vessel, out of port or from the United States, shall be fined under this title or imprisoned not more than ten years, or both.

In addition, such vessel, her tackle, apparel, furniture, equipment, and her cargo shall be forfeited to the United States.

The Secretary of the Treasury is authorized to promulgate regulations upon compliance with which vessels engaged in the coastwise trade or fisheries or used solely for pleasure may be relieved from complying with this section.

(June 25, 1948, c. 645, 62 Stat. 747; Dec. 8, 1993, Pub.L. 103–182, Title VI, § 687, 107 Stat. 2221; Sept. 13, 1994, Pub.L. 103–322, Title XXXIII, § 330016(1)(L), 108 Stat. 2147; Oct. 6, 2006, Pub.L. 109–304, § 17(d)(5), 120 Stat. 1707.)

HISTORICAL AND STATUTORY NOTES

Effective and Applicability Provisions

1993 Acts. Amendment by section 687 of Pub.L. 103–182 effective Dec. 8, 1993, see section 692 of Pub.L. 103–182, set out as a note under section 58c of Title 19, Customs Duties.

Transfer of Functions

All offices of collector of customs, comptroller of customs, surveyor of customs, and appraiser of merchandise in the Bureau of Customs of the Department of the Treasury to which appointments were required to be made by the President with the advice and consent of the Senate were ordered abolished, to be terminated not later than Dec. 31, 1966. All functions of the offices so eliminated were already vested in the Secretary of the Treasury.

For transfer of functions, personnel, assets, and liabilities of the United States Customs Service of the Department of the Treasury, including functions of the Secretary of the Treasury relating thereto, to the Secretary of Homeland Security, and for treatment of related references, see 6 U.S.C.A. §§ 203(1), 551(d), 552(d), and 557, and the Department of Homeland Security Reorganization Plan of November 25, 2002, as modified, set out as a note under 6 U.S.C.A. § 542. All offices of collector of customs, comptroller of customs, surveyor of customs, and appraiser of merchandise in Bureau of Customs of Department of the Treasury to which appointments were required to be made by President with advice and consent of Senate ordered abolished, with such offices to be terminated not later than Dec. 31, 1966, by Reorg. Plan No. 1 of 1965, eff. May 25, 1965, 30 F.R. 7035, 79 Stat. 1317, set out in Appendix I of Title 5. All functions of offices eliminated were already vested in Secretary of the Treasury by Reorg. Plan No. 26 of 1950, eff. July 31, 1950, 15 F.R. 4935, 64 Stat. 1280, set out in Appendix I of Title 5.

Canal Zone

Applicability of section to Canal Zone, see § 14 of this title.

§ 966. Departure of vessel forbidden for false statements

(a) Whenever it appears that the vessel is not entitled to clearance or whenever there is reasonable cause to believe that the additional statements under oath required in section 965 of this title are false, the collector of customs for the district in which the vessel is located may, subject to review by the head of the department or agency charged with the administration of laws relating to clearance of vessels, refuse clearance to any vessel, domestic or foreign, and by formal notice served upon the owners, master, or person or persons in command or charge of any domestic vessel for which clearance is not required by law, forbid the departure of the vessel from the port or from the United States. It shall thereupon be unlawful for the vessel to depart.

(b) Whoever, in violation of this section, takes or attempts to take, or authorizes the taking of any such vessel, out of port or from the United States, shall be fined under this title or imprisoned not more than ten years, or both.

In addition, such vessel, her tackle, apparel, furniture, equipment, and her cargo shall be forfeited to the United States.

(June 25, 1948, c. 645, 62 Stat. 747; Sept. 13, 1994, Pub.L. 103–322, Title XXXIII, § 330016(1)(L), 108 Stat. 2147.)

HISTORICAL AND STATUTORY NOTES

Transfer of Functions

All offices of collector of customs, comptroller of customs, surveyor of customs, and appraiser of merchandise in the Bureau of Customs of the Department of the Treasury to which appointments were required to be made by the President with the advice and consent of the Senate were ordered abolished, to be terminated not later than Dec. 31, 1966. All functions of the offices so eliminated were already vested in the Secretary of the Treasury.

Canal Zone

Applicability of section to Canal Zone, see § 14 of this title.

§ 967. Departure of vessel forbidden in aid of neutrality

(a) During a war in which the United States is a neutral nation, the President, or any person authorized by him, may withhold clearance from or to any vessel, domestic or foreign, or, by service of formal notice upon the owner, master, or person in command or in charge of any domestic vessel not required to secure clearances, may forbid its departure from port or from the United States, whenever there is reasonable cause to believe that such vessel is about to carry fuel, arms, ammunition, men, supplies, dispatches, or information to any warship, tender, or supply ship of a foreign belligerent nation in violation of the laws, treaties, or obligations of the United States under the law of nations. It shall thereupon be unlawful for such vessel to depart.

(b) Whoever, in violation of this section, takes or attempts to take, or authorizes the taking of any such vessel, out of port or from the United States, shall be fined under this title or imprisoned not more than ten years, or both. In addition, such vessel, her tackle, apparel, furniture, equipment, and her cargo shall be forfeited to the United States.

(June 25, 1948, c. 645, 62 Stat. 748; Sept. 13, 1994, Pub.L. 103–322, Title XXXIII, § 330016(1)(L), 108 Stat. 2147.)

HISTORICAL AND STATUTORY NOTES

Delegation of Functions

For delegation to Secretary of Homeland Security of authority vested in President by this section, see section 1(*l*) of Ex. Ord. No. 10637, Sept. 16, 1955, 20 F.R. 7025, as amended, set out as a note under 3 U.S.C.A. § 301.

Canal Zone

Applicability of section to Canal Zone, see § 14 of this title.

[§ 968. Repealed. Aug. 26, 1954, c. 937, Title V, § 542(a)(14), 68 Stat. 861]

HISTORICAL AND STATUTORY NOTES

Section, Act June 25, 1948, c. 645, § 1, 62 Stat. 748, related exportation of war materials to certain countries, and is now covered by § 1934 of Title 22, Foreign Relations and Intercourse.

[§ 969. Repealed. Pub.L. 101–647, Title XII, § 1207(a), Nov. 29, 1990, 104 Stat. 4832]

HISTORICAL AND STATUTORY NOTES

Section, June 25, 1948, c. 645, 62 Stat. 748, related to penalties for exporting arms, liquor and narcotics to Pacific Islands.

§ 970. Protection of property occupied by foreign governments

(a) Whoever willfully injures, damages, or destroys, or attempts to injure, damage, or destroy, any property, real or personal, located within the United States and belonging to or utilized or occupied by any foreign government or international organization, by a foreign official or official guest, shall be fined under this title, or imprisoned not more than five years, or both.

(b) Whoever, willfully with intent to intimidate, coerce, threaten, or harass—

(1) forcibly thrusts any part of himself or any object within or upon that portion of any building or premises located within the United States, which portion is used or occupied for official business or for diplomatic, consular, or residential purposes by—

(A) a foreign government, including such use as a mission to an international organization;

(B) an international organization;

(C) a foreign official; or

(D) an official guest; or

(2) refuses to depart from such portion of such building or premises after a request—

(A) by an employee of a foreign government or of an international organization, if such employee is authorized to make such request by the senior official of the unit of such government or organization which occupies such portion of such building or premises;

(B) by a foreign official or any member of the foreign official's staff who is authorized by the foreign official to make such request;

(C) by an official guest or any member of the official guest's staff who is authorized by the official guest to make such request; or

(D) by any person present having law enforcement powers;

shall be fined under this title or imprisoned not more than six months, or both.

(c) For the purpose of this section "foreign government", "foreign official", "international organization", and "official guest" shall have the same meanings as those provided in section 1116(b) of this title.

(Added Pub.L. 92–539, Title IV, § 401, Oct. 24, 1972, 86 Stat. 1073, and amended Pub.L. 94–467, § 7, Oct. 8, 1976, 90 Stat. 2000; Pub.L. 103–322, Title XXXIII, § 330016(1)(L), Sept. 13, 1994, 108 Stat. 2147; Pub.L. 104–294, Title VI, § 601(a)(2), Oct. 11, 1996, 110 Stat. 3498.)

CHAPTER 46—FORFEITURE

Sec.

§ 981. Civil forfeiture

(a)(1) The following property is subject to forfeiture to the United States:

(A) Any property, real or personal, involved in a transaction or attempted transaction in violation of section 1956, 1957 or 1960 of this title, or any property traceable to such property.

(B) Any property, real or personal, within the jurisdiction of the United States, constituting, derived from, or traceable to, any proceeds obtained directly or indirectly from an offense against a foreign nation, or any property used to facilitate such an offense, if the offense—

(i) involves trafficking in nuclear, chemical, biological, or radiological weapons technology or material, or the manufacture, importation, sale, or distribution of a controlled substance (as that term is defined for purposes of the Controlled

Substances Act), or any other conduct described in section 1956(c)(7)(B);

(ii) would be punishable within the jurisdiction of the foreign nation by death or imprisonment for a term exceeding 1 year; and

(iii) would be punishable under the laws of the United States by imprisonment for a term exceeding 1 year, if the act or activity constituting the offense had occurred within the jurisdiction of the United States.

(C) Any property, real or personal, which constitutes or is derived from proceeds traceable to a violation of section 215, 471, 472, 473, 474, 476, 477, 478, 479, 480, 481, 485, 486, 487, 488, 501, 502, 510, 542, 545, 656, 657, 842, 844, 1005, 1006, 1007, 1014, 1028, 1029, 1030, 1032, or 1344 of this title or any offense constituting "specified unlawful activity" (as defined in section 1956(c)(7) of this title), or a conspiracy to commit such offense.

(D) Any property, real or personal, which represents or is traceable to the gross receipts obtained, directly or indirectly, from a violation of—

(i) section 666(a)(1) (relating to Federal program fraud);

(ii) section 1001 (relating to fraud and false statements);

(iii) section 1031 (relating to major fraud against the United States);

(iv) section 1032 (relating to concealment of assets from conservator or receiver of insured financial institution);

(v) section 1341 (relating to mail fraud); or

(vi) section 1343 (relating to wire fraud),

if such violation relates to the sale of assets acquired or held by the Resolution Trust Corporation, the Federal Deposit Insurance Corporation, as conservator or receiver for a financial institution, or any other conservator for a financial institution appointed by the Office of the Comptroller of the Currency or the Office of Thrift Supervision or the National Credit Union Administration, as conservator or liquidating agent for a financial institution.

(E) With respect to an offense listed in subsection (a)(1)(D) committed for the purpose of executing or attempting to execute any scheme or artifice to defraud, or for obtaining money or property by means of false or fraudulent statements, pretenses, representations or promises, the gross receipts of such an offense shall include all property, real or personal, tangible or intangible, which thereby is obtained, directly or indirectly.

(F) Any property, real or personal, which represents or is traceable to the gross proceeds obtained, directly or indirectly, from a violation of—

(i) section 511 (altering or removing motor vehicle identification numbers);

(ii) section 553 (importing or exporting stolen motor vehicles);

(iii) section 2119 (armed robbery of automobiles);

(iv) section 2312 (transporting stolen motor vehicles in interstate commerce); or

(v) section 2313 (possessing or selling a stolen motor vehicle that has moved in interstate commerce).

(G) All assets, foreign or domestic—

(i) of any individual, entity, or organization engaged in planning or perpetrating any any[1] Federal crime of terrorism (as defined in section 2332b(g)(5)) against the United States, citizens or residents of the United States, or their property, and all assets, foreign or domestic, affording any person a source of influence over any such entity or organization;

(ii) acquired or maintained by any person with the intent and for the purpose of supporting, planning, conducting, or concealing any Federal crime of terrorism (as defined in section 2332b(g)(5)[2] against the United States, citizens or residents of the United States, or their property;

(iii) derived from, involved in, or used or intended to be used to commit any Federal crime of terrorism (as defined in section 2332b(g)(5)) against the United States, citizens or residents of the United States, or their property; or

(iv) of any individual, entity, or organization engaged in planning or perpetrating any act of international terrorism (as defined in section 2331) against any international organization (as defined in section 209 of the State Department Basic Authorities Act of 1956 (22 U.S.C. 4309(b)) or against any foreign Government. Where the property sought for forfeiture is located beyond the territorial boundaries of the United States, an act in furtherance of such planning or perpetration must have occurred within the jurisdiction of the United States.

(H) Any property, real or personal, involved in a violation or attempted violation, or which constitutes or is derived from proceeds traceable to a violation, of section 2339C of this title.

(2) For purposes of paragraph (1), the term "proceeds" is defined as follows:

(A) In cases involving illegal goods, illegal services, unlawful activities, and telemarketing and health care fraud schemes, the term "proceeds" means property of any kind obtained directly or indirectly, as the result of the commission of the offense giving rise to forfeiture, and any property traceable thereto, and is not limited to the net gain or profit realized from the offense.

(B) In cases involving lawful goods or lawful services that are sold or provided in an illegal manner, the term "proceeds" means the amount of money acquired through the illegal transactions resulting in the forfeiture, less the direct costs incurred in providing the goods or services. The claimant shall have the burden of proof with respect to the issue of direct costs. The direct costs shall not include any part of the overhead expenses of the entity providing the goods or services, or any part of the income taxes paid by the entity.

(C) In cases involving fraud in the process of obtaining a loan or extension of credit, the court shall allow the claimant a deduction from the forfeiture to the extent that the loan was repaid, or the debt was satisfied, without any financial loss to the victim.

(b)(1) Except as provided in section 985, any property subject to forfeiture to the United States under subsection (a) may be seized by the Attorney General and, in the case of property involved in a violation investigated by the Secretary of the Treasury or the United States Postal Service, the property may also be seized by the Secretary of the Treasury or the Postal Service, respectively.

(2) Seizures pursuant to this section shall be made pursuant to a warrant obtained in the same manner as provided for a search warrant under the Federal Rules of Criminal Procedure, except that a seizure may be made without a warrant if—

(A) a complaint for forfeiture has been filed in the United States district court and the court issued an arrest warrant in rem pursuant to the Supplemental Rules for Certain Admiralty and Maritime Claims;

(B) there is probable cause to believe that the property is subject to forfeiture and—

(i) the seizure is made pursuant to a lawful arrest or search; or

(ii) another exception to the Fourth Amendment warrant requirement would apply; or

(C) the property was lawfully seized by a State or local law enforcement agency and transferred to a Federal agency.

(3) Notwithstanding the provisions of rule 41(a) of the Federal Rules of Criminal Procedure, a seizure warrant may be issued pursuant to this subsection by a judicial officer in any district in which a forfeiture action against the property may be filed under section 1355(b) of title 28, and may be executed in any district in which the property is found, or transmitted to the central authority of any foreign state for service in accordance with any treaty or other international agreement. Any motion for the return of property seized under this section shall be filed in the district court in which the seizure warrant was issued or in the district court for the district in which the property was seized.

(4)(A) If any person is arrested or charged in a foreign country in connection with an offense that would give rise to the forfeiture of property in the United States under this section or under the Controlled Substances Act, the Attorney General may apply to any Federal judge or magistrate judge in the district in which the property is located for an ex parte order restraining the property subject to forfeiture for not more than 30 days, except that the time may be extended for good cause shown at a hearing conducted in the manner provided in rule 43(e) of the Federal Rules of Civil Procedure.

(B) The application for the restraining order shall set forth the nature and circumstances of the foreign charges and the basis for belief that the person arrested or charged has property in the United States that would be subject to forfeiture, and shall contain a statement that the restraining order is needed to preserve the availability of property for such time as is necessary to receive evidence from the foreign country or elsewhere in support of probable cause for the seizure of the property under this subsection.

(c) Property taken or detained under this section shall not be repleviable, but shall be deemed to be in the custody of the Attorney General, the Secretary of the Treasury, or the Postal Service, as the case may be, subject only to the orders and decrees of the court or the official having jurisdiction thereof. Whenever property is seized under this subsection, the Attorney General, the Secretary of the Treasury, or the Postal Service, as the case may be, may—

(1) place the property under seal;

(2) remove the property to a place designated by him; or

(3) require that the General Services Administration take custody of the property and remove it, if practicable, to an appropriate location for disposition in accordance with law.

(d) For purposes of this section, the provisions of the customs laws relating to the seizure, summary and judicial forfeiture, condemnation of property for violation of the customs laws, the disposition of such property or the proceeds from the sale of such property under this section, the remission or mitigation of such forfeitures, and the compromise of claims (19 U.S.C. 1602 et seq.), insofar as they are applicable and not inconsistent with the provisions of this section, shall apply to seizures and forfeitures incurred, or alleged to have been incurred, under this section, except that such duties as are imposed upon the customs officer or any other person with respect to the seizure and forfeiture of property under the customs laws shall be performed with respect to seizures and forfeitures of property under this section by such officers, agents, or other persons as may be authorized or designated for that purpose by the Attorney General, the Secretary of the Treasury, or the Postal Service, as the case may be. The Attorney General shall have sole responsibility for disposing of petitions for remission or mitigation with respect to property involved in a judicial forfeiture proceeding.

(e) Notwithstanding any other provision of the law, except section 3 of the Anti Drug Abuse Act of 1986, the Attorney General, the Secretary of the Treasury, or the Postal Service, as the case may be, is authorized to retain property forfeited pursuant to this section, or to transfer such property on such terms and conditions as he may determine—

(1) to any other Federal agency;

(2) to any State or local law enforcement agency which participated directly in any of the acts which led to the seizure or forfeiture of the property;

(3) in the case of property referred to in subsection (a)(1)(C), to any Federal financial institution regulatory agency—

(A) to reimburse the agency for payments to claimants or creditors of the institution; and

(B) to reimburse the insurance fund of the agency for losses suffered by the fund as a result of the receivership or liquidation;

(4) in the case of property referred to in subsection (a)(1)(C), upon the order of the appropriate Federal financial institution regulatory agency, to the financial institution as restitution, with the value of the property so transferred to be set off against any amount later recovered by the financial institution as compensatory damages in any State or Federal proceeding;

(5) in the case of property referred to in subsection (a)(1)(C), to any Federal financial institution regulatory agency, to the extent of the agency's contribution of resources to, or expenses involved in, the seizure and forfeiture, and the investigation leading directly to the seizure and forfeiture, of such property;

(6) as restoration to any victim of the offense giving rise to the forfeiture, including, in the case of a money laundering offense, any offense constituting the underlying specified unlawful activity; or

(7) In [3] the case of property referred to in subsection (a)(1)(D), to the Resolution Trust Corporation, the Federal Deposit Insurance Corporation, or any other Federal financial institution regulatory agency (as defined in section 8(e)(7)(D) of the Federal Deposit Insurance Act).

The Attorney General, the Secretary of the Treasury, or the Postal Service, as the case may be, shall ensure the equitable transfer pursuant to paragraph (2) of any forfeited property to the appropriate State or local law enforcement agency so as to reflect generally the contribution of any such agency participating directly in any of the acts which led to the seizure or forfeiture of such property. A decision by the Attorney General, the Secretary of the Treasury, or the Postal Service pursuant to paragraph (2) shall not be subject to review. The United States shall not be liable in any action arising out of the use of any property the custody of which was transferred pursuant to this section to any non–Federal agency. The Attorney General, the Secretary of the Treasury, or the Postal Service may order the discontinuance of any forfeiture proceedings under this section in favor of the institution of forfeiture proceedings by State or local authorities under an appropriate State or local statute. After the filing of a complaint for forfeiture under this section, the Attorney General may seek dismissal of the complaint in favor of forfeiture proceedings under State or local law. Whenever forfeiture proceedings are discontinued by the United States in favor of State or local proceedings, the United States may transfer custody and possession of the seized property to the appropriate State or local official immediately upon the initiation of the proper actions by such officials. Whenever forfeiture proceedings are discontinued by the United States in favor of State or local proceedings, notice shall be sent to all known interested parties advising them of the discontinuance or dismissal. The United States shall not be liable in any action arising out of the seizure, detention, and transfer of seized property to State or local officials. The United States shall not be liable in any action arising out of a transfer under paragraph (3), (4), or (5) of this subsection.

(f) All right, title, and interest in property described in subsection (a) of this section shall vest in the United States upon commission of the act giving rise to forfeiture under this section.

(g)(1) Upon the motion of the United States, the court shall stay the civil forfeiture proceeding if the court determines that civil discovery will adversely affect the ability of the Government to conduct a related criminal investigation or the prosecution of a related criminal case.

(2) Upon the motion of a claimant, the court shall stay the civil forfeiture proceeding with respect to that claimant if the court determines that—

(A) the claimant is the subject of a related criminal investigation or case;

(B) the claimant has standing to assert a claim in the civil forfeiture proceeding; and

(C) continuation of the forfeiture proceeding will burden the right of the claimant against self-incrimination in the related investigation or case .

(3) With respect to the impact of civil discovery described in paragraphs (1) and (2), the court may determine that a stay is unnecessary if a protective order limiting discovery would protect the interest of one party without unfairly limiting the ability of the opposing party to pursue the civil case. In no case, however, shall the court impose a protective order as an alternative to a stay if the effect of such protective order would be to allow one party to pursue discovery while the other party is substantially unable to do so.

(4) In this subsection, the terms "related criminal case" and "related criminal investigation" mean an actual prosecution or investigation in progress at the time at which the request for the stay, or any subsequent motion to lift the stay is made. In determining whether a criminal case or investigation is "related" to a civil forfeiture proceeding, the court shall consider the degree of similarity between the parties, witnesses, facts, and circumstances involved in the two proceedings, without requiring an identity with respect to any one or more factors.

(5) In requesting a stay under paragraph (1), the Government may, in appropriate cases, submit evidence ex parte in order to avoid disclosing any matter that may adversely affect an ongoing criminal investigation or pending criminal trial.

(6) Whenever a civil forfeiture proceeding is stayed pursuant to this subsection, the court shall enter any order necessary to preserve the value of the property or to protect the rights of lienholders or other persons with an interest in the property while the stay is in effect.

(7) A determination by the court that the claimant has standing to request a stay pursuant to paragraph (2) shall apply only to this subsection and shall not preclude the Government from objecting to the standing of the claimant by dispositive motion or at the time of trial.

(h) In addition to the venue provided for in section 1395 of title 28 or any other provision of law, in the case of property of a defendant charged with a violation that is the basis for forfeiture of the property under this section, a proceeding for forfeiture under this section may be brought in the judicial district in which the defendant owning such property is found or in the judicial district in which the criminal prosecution is brought.

(i)(1) Whenever property is civilly or criminally forfeited under this chapter, the Attorney General or the Secretary of the Treasury, as the case may be, may transfer the forfeited personal property or the proceeds of the sale of any forfeited personal or real property to any foreign country which participated directly or indirectly in the seizure or forfeiture of the property, if such a transfer—

(A) has been agreed to by the Secretary of State;

(B) is authorized in an international agreement between the United States and the foreign country; and

(C) is made to a country which, if applicable, has been certified under section 481(h) of the Foreign Assistance Act of 1961.

A decision by the Attorney General or the Secretary of the Treasury pursuant to this paragraph shall not be subject to review. The foreign country shall, in the event of a transfer of property or proceeds of sale of property under this subsection, bear all expenses incurred by the United States in the seizure, maintenance, inventory, storage, forfeiture, and disposition of the property, and all transfer costs. The payment of all such expenses, and the transfer of assets pursuant to this paragraph, shall be upon such terms and conditions as the Attorney General or the Secretary of the Treasury may, in his discretion, set.

(2) The provisions of this section shall not be construed as limiting or superseding any other authority of the United States to provide assistance to a foreign country in obtaining property related to a crime committed in the foreign country, including property which is sought as evidence of a crime committed in the foreign country.

(3) A certified order or judgment of forfeiture by a court of competent jurisdiction of a foreign country concerning property which is the subject of forfeiture under this section and was determined by such court to be the type of property described in subsection (a)(1)(B) of this section, and any certified recordings or transcripts of testimony taken in a foreign judicial proceeding concerning such order or judgment of forfeiture, shall be admissible in evidence in a proceeding brought pursuant to this section. Such certified order or judgment of forfeiture, when admitted into evidence, shall constitute probable cause that the property forfeited by such order or judgment of forfeiture is subject to forfeiture under this section and creates a rebuttable presumption of the forfeitability of such property under this section.

(4) A certified order or judgment of conviction by a court of competent jurisdiction of a foreign country concerning an unlawful drug activity which gives rise to forfeiture under this section and any certified recordings or transcripts of testimony taken in a foreign judicial proceeding concerning such order or judgment of conviction shall be admissible in evidence in a proceeding brought pursuant to this section. Such certified order or judgment of conviction, when admitted into evidence, creates a rebuttable presumption that the unlawful drug activity giving rise to forfeiture under this section has occurred.

(5) The provisions of paragraphs (3) and (4) of this subsection shall not be construed as limiting the admissibility of any evidence otherwise admissible, nor shall they limit the ability of the United States to establish probable cause that property is subject to forfeiture by any evidence otherwise admissible.

(j) For purposes of this section—

(1) the term "Attorney General" means the Attorney General or his delegate; and

(2) the term "Secretary of the Treasury" means the Secretary of the Treasury or his delegate.

(k) Interbank accounts.—

(1) In general.—

(A) In general.—For the purpose of a forfeiture under this section or under the Controlled Substances Act (21 U.S.C. 801 et seq.), if funds are deposited into an account at a foreign financial institution (as defined in section 984(c)(2)(A) of this title), and that foreign financial institution (as defined in section 984(c)(2)(A) of this title) has an interbank account in the United States with a covered financial institution (as defined in section 5318(j)(1) of title 31), the funds shall be deemed to have been deposited into the interbank account in the United States, and any restraining order, seizure warrant, or arrest warrant in rem regarding the funds may be served on the covered financial institution, and funds in the interbank account, up to the value of the funds deposited into the account at the foreign financial institution (as defined in section 984(c)(2)(A) of this title), may be restrained, seized, or arrested.

(B) Authority to suspend.—The Attorney General, in consultation with the Secretary of the Treasury, may suspend or terminate a forfeiture under this section if the Attorney General determines that a conflict of law exists between the laws of the jurisdiction in which the foreign financial institution (as defined in section 984(c)(2)(A) of this title) is located and the laws of the United States with respect to liabilities arising from the restraint, seizure, or arrest of such funds, and that such suspension or termination would be in the interest of justice and would not harm the national interests of the United States.

(2) No requirement for Government to trace funds.—If a forfeiture action is brought against funds that are restrained, seized, or arrested under paragraph (1), it shall not be necessary for the Government to establish that the funds are directly traceable to the funds that were deposited into the foreign financial institution (as defined in section 984(c)(2)(A) of this title), nor shall it be necessary for the Government to rely on the application of section 984.

(3) Claims brought by owner of the funds.—If a forfeiture action is instituted against funds restrained, seized, or arrested under paragraph (1), the owner of the funds deposited into the account at the foreign financial institution (as defined in section 984(c)(2)(A) of this title) may contest the forfeiture by filing a claim under section 983.

(4) Definitions.—For purposes of this subsection, the following definitions shall apply:

(A) Interbank account.—The term "interbank account" has the same meaning as in section 984(c)(2)(B).

(B) Owner.—

(i) In general.—Except as provided in clause (ii), the term "owner"—

(I) means the person who was the owner, as that term is defined in section 983(d)(6), of the funds that were deposited into the foreign financial institution (as defined in section 984(c)(2)(A) of this title) at the time such funds were deposited; and

(II) does not include either the foreign financial institution (as defined in section 984(c)(2)(A) of this title) or any financial institution acting as an intermediary in the transfer of the funds into the interbank account.

(ii) Exception.—The foreign financial institution (as defined in section 984(c)(2)(A) of this title) may be considered the "owner" of the funds (and no other person shall qualify as the owner of such funds) only if—

(I) the basis for the forfeiture action is wrongdoing committed by the foreign financial institution (as defined in section 984(c)(2)(A) of this title); or

(II) the foreign financial institution (as defined in section 984(c)(2)(A) of this title) establishes, by a preponderance of the evidence, that prior to the restraint, seizure, or arrest of the funds, the foreign financial institution (as defined in section 984(c)(2)(A) of this title) had discharged all or part of its obligation to the prior owner of the funds, in which case the foreign financial institution (as defined in section 984(c)(2)(A) of this title) shall be deemed the owner of the funds to the extent of such discharged obligation.

(Added Pub.L. 99–570, Title I, § 1366(a), Oct. 27, 1986, 100 Stat. 3207–35, and amended Pub.L. 100–690, Title VI, §§ 6463(a), (b), 6469(b), 6470(b), (e), (f), 6471(c), Nov. 18, 1988, 102 Stat. 4374, 4377, 4378; Pub.L. 101–73, Title IX, § 963(a), (b), Aug. 9, 1989, 103 Stat. 504; Pub.L. 101–647, Title I, § 103, Title XXV, §§ 2508, 2524, 2525(a), Title XXXV, § 3531, Nov. 29, 1990, 104 Stat. 4791, 4862, 4873, 4874, 4924; Pub.L. 102–393, Title VI, § 638(d), Oct. 6, 1992, 106 Stat. 1788; Pub.L. 102–519, Title I, § 104(a), Oct. 25, 1992, 106 Stat. 3385; Pub.L. 102–550, Title XV, §§ 1525(c)(1), 1533, Oct. 28, 1992, 106 Stat. 4065, 4066; Pub.L. 103–322, Title XXXIII, § 330011(s)(2), Sept. 13, 1994, 108 Stat. 2146; Pub.L. 103–447, Title I, § 102(b), Nov. 2, 1994, 108 Stat.

4693; Pub.L. 106–185, §§ 2(c)(1), 5(a), 6, 8(a), 20, Apr. 25, 2000, 114 Stat. 210, 213 to 215, 224; Pub.L. 107–56, Title III, §§ 319(a), 320, 372(b)(1), 373(b), Title VIII, § 806, Oct. 26, 2001, 115 Stat. 311, 315, 339, 340, 378; Pub.L. 107–197, Title III, § 301(d), June 25, 2002, 116 Stat. 728; Pub.L. 107–273, Div. B, Title IV, § 4002(a)(2), Nov. 2, 2002, 116 Stat. 1806; Pub.L. 109–177, Title I, §§ 111, 120, Title IV, §§ 404, 406(a)(3), Mar. 9, 2006, 120 Stat. 209, 221, 244.)

[1] So in original. The second "any" probably should not appear.

[2] So in original. A closing parenthesis probably should appear.

[3] So in original. Probably should not be capitalized.

HISTORICAL AND STATUTORY NOTES

References in Text

The Controlled Substances Act, referred to in subsecs. (a)(1)(B)(i), (b)(4)(A), and (k)(1), is Pub.L. 91–513, Title II, Oct. 27, 1970, 84 Stat. 1242, as amended, which is classified principally to subchapter I of chapter 13 of Title 21, 21 U.S.C.A. § 801 et seq. For complete classification, see Short Title note set out under 21 U.S.C.A. § 801 and Tables.

Section 209 of the State Department Basic Authorities Act of 1956, referred to in subsec. (a)(1)(G)(iv), is section 209 of Act Aug. 1, 1956, c. 841, Title II, as added Aug. 24, 1982, Pub.L. 97–241, Title II, § 202(b) 96 Stat. 289, which is classified to 22 U.S.C.A. § 4309(b).

The Federal Rules of Criminal Procedure, referred to in subsec. (b), are set out under this title.

The Supplemental Rules for certain Admiralty and Maritime Claims, referred to in subsec. (b)(2), are set out under Title 28, Federal Rules of Civil Procedure.

Section 3 of the Anti Drug Abuse Act of 1986, referred to in subsec. (e), is section 3 of Pub.L. 99–570, which is set out as a note under section 801 of Title 21.

Section 481(h) of the Foreign Assistance Act of 1961, referred to in subsec. (i)(1)(C), was classified to section 2291(h) of Title 22, Foreign Relations and Intercourse, prior to repeal of subsec. (h) by Pub.L. 102–583, § 6(b)(2), Nov. 2, 108 Stat. 4932. Reference to section 481(h) of the Foreign Assistance Act of 1961 probably should be to section 490(a)(1) of the Act, which is classified to section 2291j(a)(1) of Title 22.

Codifications

Amendment by Pub.L. 109–177, § 120(1), which directed that subsec. (a)(1)(G)(i) of this section be amended by striking "act of international or domestic terrorism (as defined in section 2331)" and inserting "any Federal crime of terrorism (as defined in section 2332b(g)(5))", was executed by striking "act of domestic or international terrorism (as defined in section 2331)" and inserting "any Federal crime of terrorism (as defined in section 2332b(g)(5))", as the probable intent of Congress.

Amendment by Pub.L. 109–177, § 120(2), which directed that subsec. (a)(1)(G)(ii) of this section be amended "by striking 'an act of international or domestic terrorism (as defined in section 2331)' with 'any Federal crime of terrorism (as defined in section 2332b(g)(5)' ", was executed by striking "an act of domestic or international terrorism (as defined in section 2331)" and inserting "any Federal crime of terrorism (as defined in section 2332b(g)(5))", as the probable intent of Congress.

Amendment by Pub.L. 109–177, § 120(3), which directed that subsec. (a)(1)(G)(iii) of this section be amended by striking "act of international or domestic terrorism (as defined in section 2331)" and inserting "Federal crime of terrorism (as defined in section 2332b(g)(5))", was executed by striking "act of domestic or international terrorism (as defined in section 2331)" and inserting "Federal crime of terrorism (as defined in section 2332b(g)(5))", as the probable intent of Congress.

Effective and Applicability Provisions

2000 Acts. Amendments by Pub.L. 106–185, applicable to any forfeiture proceeding commenced on or after the date that is 120 days after April 25, 2000, see section 21 of Pub.L. 106–185, set out as a note under section 1324 of Title 8.

1994 Acts. Section 330011(s)(2) of Pub.L. 103–322 provided in part that the amendment made by such section, amending directory language of section 2525(a)(2) of Pub.L. 101–647 (which amended this section), was to take effect on the date section 2525(a)(2) of Pub.L. 101–647 took effect; section 2525(a)(2) of Pub.L. 101–647 took effect on the date of enactment of Pub.L. 101–647, which was approved Nov. 29, 1990.

1992 Acts. Substitution of "section 490 of the Foreign Assistance Act of 1961" for "section 481(h) of the Foreign Assistance Act of 1961" by section 6(a) of Pub.L. 102–583 effective Oct. 1, 1992, see section 6(a) of Pub.L. 102–583, set out as a note under section 2291h of Title 22, Foreign Relations and Intercourse.

Except as otherwise provided, amendment by Pub.L. 102–550 effective Oct. 28, 1992, see section 2 of Pub.L. 102–550, set out as a note under section 5301 of Title 42, The Public Health and Welfare.

Severability of Provisions

If any provision of Pub.L. 101–73 or the application thereof to any person or circumstance is held invalid, the remainder of Pub.L. 101–73 and the application of the provision to other persons not similarly situated or to other circumstances not to be affected thereby, see section 1221 of Pub.L. 101–73, set out as a note under section 1811 of Title 12, Banks and Banking.

Section 1367 of Pub.L. 99–570 provided that: "If any provision of this subtitle [Pub.L. 99–570, Title I, Subtitle H] or any amendment made by this Act [Pub.L. 99–570, Oct. 27, 1986, 100 Stat. 3207–39], or the application thereof to any person or circumstances is held invalid, the provisions of every other part, and their application, shall not be affected thereby."

Short Title

2000 Amendments. Pub.L. 106–185, § 1(a), Apr. 25, 2000, 114 Stat. 202, provided that: "This Act [enacting sections 983 and 985 of this title and sections 2466 and 2467 of Title 28, amending sections 1324 of Title 8, sections 981, 982, 984, 986, 2232, 2254, and 3322 of this title, section 1621 of Title 19, section 881 of Title 21, sections 524, 2461, 2465, and 2680 of Title 28, and section 2996f of Title 42, repealing section 888 of Title 21, and enacting provisions set out as notes under section 1324 of Title 8 and section 3724 of Title 31] may be cited as the 'Civil Asset Forfeiture Reform Act of 2000'."

Termination Date of 2001 Amendment

Effective on and after the first day of fiscal year 2005, amendments by Title III (§§ 301 to 377) of Pub.L. 107–56 shall terminate if Congress enacts a joint resolution to that effect; such resolution shall be given expedited consideration, see Pub.L. 107–56, Title III, § 303, Oct. 26, 2001, 115 Stat. 298, set out as a note under 31 U.S.C.A. § 5311.

§ 982. Criminal forfeiture

(a)(1) The court, in imposing sentence on a person convicted of an offense in violation of section 1956, 1957, or 1960 of this title, shall order that the person forfeit to the United States any property, real or personal, involved in such offense, or any property traceable to such property.

(2) The court, in imposing sentence on a person convicted of a violation of, or a conspiracy to violate—

(A) section 215, 656, 657, 1005, 1006, 1007, 1014, 1341, 1343, or 1344 of this title, affecting a financial institution, or

(B) section 471, 472, 473, 474, 476, 477, 478, 479, 480, 481, 485, 486, 487, 488, 501, 502, 510, 542, 545, 842, 844, 1028, 1029, or 1030 of this title,

shall order that the person forfeit to the United States any property constituting, or derived from, proceeds the person obtained directly or indirectly, as the result of such violation.

(3) The court, in imposing a sentence on a person convicted of an offense under—

(A) section 666(a)(1) (relating to Federal program fraud);

(B) section 1001 (relating to fraud and false statements);

(C) section 1031 (relating to major fraud against the United States);

(D) section 1032 (relating to concealment of assets from conservator, receiver, or liquidating agent of insured financial institution);

(E) section 1341 (relating to mail fraud); or

(F) section 1343 (relating to wire fraud),

involving the sale of assets acquired or held by the Resolution Trust Corporation, the Federal Deposit Insurance Corporation, as conservator or receiver for a financial institution or any other conservator for a financial institution appointed by the Office of the Comptroller of the Currency or the Office of Thrift Supervision, or the National Credit Union Administration, as conservator or liquidating agent for a financial institution, shall order that the person forfeit to the United States any property, real or personal, which represents or is traceable to the gross receipts obtained, directly or indirectly, as a result of such violation.

(4) With respect to an offense listed in subsection (a)(3) committed for the purpose of executing or attempting to execute any scheme or artifice to defraud, or for obtaining money or property by means of false or fraudulent statements, pretenses, representations, or promises, the gross receipts of such an offense shall include any property, real or personal, tangible or intangible, which is obtained, directly or indirectly, as a result of such offense.

(5) The court, in imposing sentence on a person convicted of a violation or conspiracy to violate—

(A) section 511 (altering or removing motor vehicle identification numbers);

(B) section 553 (importing or exporting stolen motor vehicles);

(C) section 2119 (armed robbery of automobiles);

(D) section 2312 (transporting stolen motor vehicles in interstate commerce); or

(E) section 2313 (possessing or selling a stolen motor vehicle that has moved in interstate commerce);

shall order that the person forfeit to the United States any property, real or personal, which represents or is traceable to the gross proceeds obtained, directly or indirectly, as a result of such violation.

(6)(A) The court, in imposing sentence on a person convicted of a violation of, or conspiracy to violate, section 274(a), 274A(a)(1), or 274A(a)(2) of the Immigration and Nationality Act or section 554, 1425, 1426, 1427, 1541, 1542, 1543, 1544, or 1546 of this title, or a violation of, or conspiracy to violate, section 1028 of this title if committed in connection with passport or visa issuance or use, shall order that the person forfeit to the United States, regardless of any provision of State law—

(i) any conveyance, including any vessel, vehicle, or aircraft used in the commission of the offense of which the person is convicted; and

(ii) any property real or personal—

(I) that constitutes, or is derived from or is traceable to the proceeds obtained directly or indirectly from the commission of the offense of which the person is convicted; or

(II) that is used to facilitate, or is intended to be used to facilitate, the commission of the offense of which the person is convicted.

(B) The court, in imposing sentence on a person described in subparagraph (A), shall order that the person forfeit to the United States all property described in that subparagraph.

(7) The court, in imposing sentence on a person convicted of a Federal health care offense, shall order the person to forfeit property, real or personal, that constitutes or is derived, directly or indirectly, from gross proceeds traceable to the commission of the offense.

(8) The court, in sentencing a defendant convicted of an offense under section 1028, 1029, 1341, 1342, 1343, or 1344, or of a conspiracy to commit such an offense, if the offense involves telemarketing (as that term is defined in section 2325), shall order that the defendant forfeit to the United States any real or personal property—

(A) used or intended to be used to commit, to facilitate, or to promote the commission of such offense; and

(B) constituting, derived from, or traceable to the gross proceeds that the defendant obtained directly or indirectly as a result of the offense.

(b)(1) The forfeiture of property under this section, including any seizure and disposition of the property and any related judicial or administrative proceeding, shall be governed by the provisions of section 413 (other than subsection (d) of that section) of the Comprehensive Drug Abuse Prevention and Control Act of 1970 (21 U.S.C. 853).

(2) The substitution of assets provisions of subsection 413(p) shall not be used to order a defendant to forfeit assets in place of the actual property laundered where such defendant acted merely as an intermediary who handled but did not retain the property in the course of the money laundering offense unless the defendant, in committing the offense or offenses giving rise to the forfeiture, conducted three or more separate transactions involving a total of $100,000 or more in any twelve month period.

(Added Pub.L. 99–570, Title I, § 1366(a), Oct. 27, 1986, 100 Stat. 3707–39, and amended Pub.L. 100–690, Title VI, §§ 6463(c), 6464, Nov. 18, 1988, 102 Stat. 4374, 4375; Pub.L. 101–73, Title IX, § 963(c), Aug. 9, 1989, 103 Stat. 504; Pub.L. 101–647, Title XIV, §§ 1401, 1403, Title XXV, § 2525(b), Nov. 29, 1990, 104 Stat. 4835, 4874; Pub.L. 102–393, Title VI, § 638(e), Oct. 6, 1992, 106 Stat. 1788; Pub.L. 102–519, Title I, § 104(b), Oct. 25, 1992, 106 Stat. 3385; Pub.L. 102–550, Title XV, § 1512(c), Oct. 28, 1992, 106 Stat. 4058; Pub.L. 103–322, Title XXXIII, § 330011(s)(1), Sept. 13, 1994, 108 Stat. 2145; Pub.L. 104–191, Title II, § 249(a), (b), Aug. 21, 1996, 110 Stat. 2020; Pub.L. 104–208, Div. C, Title II, § 217, Sept. 30, 1996, 110 Stat. 3009–573; Pub.L. 105–184, § 2, June 23, 1998, 112 Stat. 520; Pub.L. 105–318, § 6(a), Oct. 30, 1998, 112 Stat. 3010; Pub.L. 106–185, § 18(b), Apr. 25, 2000, 114 Stat. 223; Pub.L. 107–56, Title III, § 372(b)(2), Oct. 26, 2001, 115 Stat. 339; Pub.L. 107–273, Div. B, Title IV, § 4002(b)(10), Nov. 2, 2002, 116 Stat. 1808; Pub.L. 109–295, Title V, § 551(c), Oct. 4, 2006, 120 Stat. 1390.)

HISTORICAL AND STATUTORY NOTES

References in Text

Sections 274(a), 274A(a)(1), and 274A(a)(2) of the Immigration and Nationality Act, referred to in subsec. (a)(6), are classified to 8 U.S.C.A. §§ 1324(a), 1324a(a)(1), and 1324a(a)(2), respectively.

Effective and Applicability Provisions

2000 Acts. Amendments by Pub.L. 106–185 applicable to any forfeiture proceeding commenced on or after the date that is 120 days after April 25, 2000, see section 21 of Pub.L. 106–185, set out as a note under section 1324 of Title 8.

1994 Acts. Section 330011(s)(1) of Pub.L. 103–322 provided in part that the amendment made by such section, amending section 1401 of Pub.L. 101–647 (which amended this section), was to take effect on the date section 1401 of Pub.L. 101–647 took effect; section 1401 of Pub.L. 101–647 took effect on the date of enactment of Pub.L. 101–647, which was approved Nov. 29, 1990.

Severability of Provisions

If any provision of Division C of Pub.L. 104–208 or the application of such provision to any person or circumstances is held to be unconstitutional, the remainder of Division C of Pub.L. 104–208 and the application of the provisions of Division C of Pub.L. 104–208 to any person or circumstance not to be affected thereby, see section 1(e) of Pub.L. 104–208, set out as a note under section 1101 of Title 8, Aliens and Nationality.

If any provision of Pub.L. 101–73 or the application thereof to any person or circumstance is held invalid, the remainder of Pub.L. 101–73 and the application of the provision to other persons not similarly situated or to other circumstances not to be affected thereby, see section 1221 of Pub.L. 101–73, set out as a note under section 1811 of Title 12, Banks and Banking.

Termination Date of 2001 Amendment

Effective on and after the first day of fiscal year 2005, amendments by Title III (§§ 301 to 377) of Pub.L. 107–56 shall terminate if Congress enacts a joint resolution to that effect; such resolution shall be given expedited consideration, see Pub.L. 107–56, Title III, § 303, Oct. 26, 2001, 115 Stat. 298, set out as a note under 31 U.S.C.A. § 5311.

§ 983. General rules for civil forfeiture proceedings

(a) Notice; claim; complaint.—

(1)(A)(i) Except as provided in clauses (ii) through (v), in any nonjudicial civil forfeiture proceeding under a civil forfeiture statute, with respect to which the Government is required to send written notice to interested parties, such notice shall be sent in a manner to achieve proper notice as soon as practicable, and in no case more than 60 days after the date of the seizure.

(ii) No notice is required if, before the 60–day period expires, the Government files a civil judicial forfeiture action against the property and provides notice of that action as required by law.

(iii) If, before the 60–day period expires, the Government does not file a civil judicial forfeiture action, but does obtain a criminal indictment containing an allegation that the property is subject to forfeiture, the Government shall either—

(I) send notice within the 60 days and continue the nonjudicial civil forfeiture proceeding under this section; or

(II) terminate the nonjudicial civil forfeiture proceeding, and take the steps necessary to preserve its right to maintain custody of the property as provided in the applicable criminal forfeiture statute.

(iv) In a case in which the property is seized by a State or local law enforcement agency and turned over to a Federal law enforcement agency for the purpose of forfeiture under Federal law, notice shall be sent not more than 90 days after the date of seizure by the State or local law enforcement agency.

(v) If the identity or interest of a party is not determined until after the seizure or turnover but is determined before a declaration of forfeiture is entered, notice shall be sent to such interested party not later than 60 days after the determination by the Government of the identity of the party or the party's interest.

(B) A supervisory official in the headquarters office of the seizing agency may extend the period for sending notice under subparagraph (A) for a period not to exceed 30 days (which period may not be further extended except by a court), if the official determines that the conditions in subparagraph (D) are present.

(C) Upon motion by the Government, a court may extend the period for sending notice under subparagraph (A) for a period not to exceed 60 days, which period may be further extended by the court for 60-day periods, as necessary, if the court determines, based on a written certification of a supervisory official in the headquarters office of the seizing agency, that the conditions in subparagraph (D) are present.

(D) The period for sending notice under this paragraph may be extended only if there is reason to believe that notice may have an adverse result, including—

(i) endangering the life or physical safety of an individual;

(ii) flight from prosecution;

(iii) destruction of or tampering with evidence;

(iv) intimidation of potential witnesses; or

(v) otherwise seriously jeopardizing an investigation or unduly delaying a trial.

(E) Each of the Federal seizing agencies conducting nonjudicial forfeitures under this section shall report periodically to the Committees on the Judiciary of the House of Representatives and the Senate the number of occasions when an extension of time is granted under subparagraph (B).

(F) If the Government does not send notice of a seizure of property in accordance with subparagraph (A) to the person from whom the property was seized, and no extension of time is granted, the Government shall return the property to that person without prejudice to the right of the Government to commence a forfeiture proceeding at a later time. The Government shall not be required to return contraband or other property that the person from whom the property was seized may not legally possess.

(2)(A) Any person claiming property seized in a nonjudicial civil forfeiture proceeding under a civil forfeiture statute may file a claim with the appropriate official after the seizure.

(B) A claim under subparagraph (A) may be filed not later than the deadline set forth in a personal notice letter (which deadline may be not earlier than 35 days after the date the letter is mailed), except that if that letter is not received, then a claim may be filed not later than 30 days after the date of final publication of notice of seizure.

(C) A claim shall—

(i) identify the specific property being claimed;

(ii) state the claimant's interest in such property; and

(iii) be made under oath, subject to penalty of perjury.

(D) A claim need not be made in any particular form. Each Federal agency conducting nonjudicial forfeitures under this section shall make claim forms generally available on request, which forms shall be written in easily understandable language.

(E) Any person may make a claim under subparagraph (A) without posting bond with respect to the property which is the subject of the claim.

(3)(A) Not later than 90 days after a claim has been filed, the Government shall file a complaint for forfeiture in the manner set forth in the Supplemental Rules for Certain Admiralty and Maritime Claims or return the property pending the filing of a complaint, except that a court in the district in which the complaint will be filed may extend the period for filing a complaint for good cause shown or upon agreement of the parties.

(B) If the Government does not—

(i) file a complaint for forfeiture or return the property, in accordance with subparagraph (A); or

(ii) before the time for filing a complaint has expired—

(I) obtain a criminal indictment containing an allegation that the property is subject to forfeiture; and

(II) take the steps necessary to preserve its right to maintain custody of the property as provided in the applicable criminal forfeiture statute,

the Government shall promptly release the property pursuant to regulations promulgated by the Attorney General, and may not take any further action to effect the civil forfeiture of such property in connection with the underlying offense.

(C) In lieu of, or in addition to, filing a civil forfeiture complaint, the Government may include a forfeiture allegation in a criminal indictment. If criminal forfeiture is the only forfeiture proceeding commenced by the Government, the Government's right to continued possession of the property shall be governed by the applicable criminal forfeiture statute.

(D) No complaint may be dismissed on the ground that the Government did not have adequate evidence at the time the complaint was filed to establish the forfeitability of the property.

(4)(A) In any case in which the Government files in the appropriate United States district court a complaint for forfeiture of property, any person claiming an interest in the seized property may file a claim asserting such person's interest in the property in the manner set forth in the Supplemental Rules for Certain Admiralty and Maritime Claims, except that such claim may be filed not later than 30 days after the date of service of the Government's complaint or, as applicable, not later than 30 days after the date of final publication of notice of the filing of the complaint.

(B) A person asserting an interest in seized property, in accordance with subparagraph (A), shall file an answer to the Government's complaint for forfeiture not later than 20 days after the date of the filing of the claim.

(b) Representation.—

(1)(A) If a person with standing to contest the forfeiture of property in a judicial civil forfeiture proceeding under a civil forfeiture statute is financially unable to obtain representation by counsel, and the person is represented by counsel appointed under section 3006A of this title in connection with a related criminal case, the court may authorize counsel to represent that person with respect to the claim.

(B) In determining whether to authorize counsel to represent a person under subparagraph (A), the court shall take into account such factors as—

(i) the person's standing to contest the forfeiture; and

(ii) whether the claim appears to be made in good faith.

(2)(A) If a person with standing to contest the forfeiture of property in a judicial civil forfeiture proceeding under a civil forfeiture statute is financially unable to obtain representation by counsel, and the property subject to forfeiture is real property that is being used by the person as a primary residence, the court, at the request of the person, shall insure that the person is represented by an attorney for the Legal Services Corporation with respect to the claim.

(B)(i) At appropriate times during a representation under subparagraph (A), the Legal Services Corporation shall submit a statement of reasonable attorney fees and costs to the court.

(ii) The court shall enter a judgment in favor of the Legal Services Corporation for reasonable attorney fees and costs submitted pursuant to clause (i) and treat such judgment as payable under section 2465 of title 28, United States Code, regardless of the outcome of the case.

(3) The court shall set the compensation for representation under this subsection, which shall be equivalent to that provided for court-appointed representation under section 3006A of this title.

(c) Burden of proof.—In a suit or action brought under any civil forfeiture statute for the civil forfeiture of any property—

(1) the burden of proof is on the Government to establish, by a preponderance of the evidence, that the property is subject to forfeiture;

(2) the Government may use evidence gathered after the filing of a complaint for forfeiture to establish, by a preponderance of the evidence, that property is subject to forfeiture; and

(3) if the Government's theory of forfeiture is that the property was used to commit or facilitate the commission of a criminal offense, or was involved in the commission of a criminal offense, the Government shall establish that there was a substantial connection between the property and the offense.

(d) Innocent owner defense.—

(1) An innocent owner's interest in property shall not be forfeited under any civil forfeiture statute. The claimant shall have the burden of proving that the claimant is an innocent owner by a preponderance of the evidence.

(2)(A) With respect to a property interest in existence at the time the illegal conduct giving rise to forfeiture took place, the term "innocent owner" means an owner who—

(i) did not know of the conduct giving rise to forfeiture; or

(ii) upon learning of the conduct giving rise to the forfeiture, did all that reasonably could be expected under the circumstances to terminate such use of the property.

(B)(i) For the purposes of this paragraph, ways in which a person may show that such person did all that reasonably could be expected may include demonstrating that such person, to the extent permitted by law—

(I) gave timely notice to an appropriate law enforcement agency of information that led the person to know the conduct giving rise to a forfeiture would occur or has occurred; and

(II) in a timely fashion revoked or made a good faith attempt to revoke permission for those engaging in such conduct to use the property or took reasonable actions in consultation with a law enforcement agency to discourage or prevent the illegal use of the property.

(ii) A person is not required by this subparagraph to take steps that the person reasonably believes would be likely to subject any person (other than the person whose conduct gave rise to the forfeiture) to physical danger.

(3)(A) With respect to a property interest acquired after the conduct giving rise to the forfeiture has taken place, the term "innocent owner" means a person who, at the time that person acquired the interest in the property—

(i) was a bona fide purchaser or seller for value (including a purchaser or seller of goods or services for value); and

(ii) did not know and was reasonably without cause to believe that the property was subject to forfeiture.

(B) An otherwise valid claim under subparagraph (A) shall not be denied on the ground that the claimant gave nothing of value in exchange for the property if—

(i) the property is the primary residence of the claimant;

(ii) depriving the claimant of the property would deprive the claimant of the means to maintain reasonable shelter in the community for the claimant and all dependents residing with the claimant;

(iii) the property is not, and is not traceable to, the proceeds of any criminal offense; and

(iv) the claimant acquired his or her interest in the property through marriage, divorce, or legal separation, or the claimant was the spouse or legal dependent of a person whose death resulted in the transfer of the property to the claimant through inheritance or probate,

except that the court shall limit the value of any real property interest for which innocent ownership is recognized under this subparagraph to the value necessary to maintain reasonable shelter in the community for such claimant and all dependents residing with the claimant.

(4) Notwithstanding any provision of this subsection, no person may assert an ownership interest under this subsection in contraband or other property that it is illegal to possess.

(5) If the court determines, in accordance with this section, that an innocent owner has a partial interest in property otherwise subject to forfeiture, or a joint tenancy or tenancy by the entirety in such property, the court may enter an appropriate order—

(A) severing the property;

(B) transferring the property to the Government with a provision that the Government compensate the innocent owner to the extent of his or her ownership interest once a final order of forfeiture has been entered and the property has been reduced to liquid assets; or

(C) permitting the innocent owner to retain the property subject to a lien in favor of the Government to the extent of the forfeitable interest in the property.

(6) In this subsection, the term "owner"—

(A) means a person with an ownership interest in the specific property sought to be forfeited, including a leasehold, lien, mortgage, recorded security interest, or valid assignment of an ownership interest; and

(B) does not include—

(i) a person with only a general unsecured interest in, or claim against, the property or estate of another;

(ii) a bailee unless the bailor is identified and the bailee shows a colorable legitimate interest in the property seized; or

(iii) a nominee who exercises no dominion or control over the property.

(e) Motion to set aside forfeiture.—

(1) Any person entitled to written notice in any nonjudicial civil forfeiture proceeding under a civil forfeiture statute who does not receive such notice may file a motion to set aside a declaration of forfeiture with respect to that person's interest in the property, which motion shall be granted if—

(A) the Government knew, or reasonably should have known, of the moving party's interest and failed to take reasonable steps to provide such party with notice; and

(B) the moving party did not know or have reason to know of the seizure within sufficient time to file a timely claim.

(2)(A) Notwithstanding the expiration of any applicable statute of limitations, if the court grants a motion under paragraph (1), the court shall set aside the declaration of forfeiture as to the interest of the moving party without prejudice to the right of the Government to commence a subsequent forfeiture proceeding as to the interest of the moving party.

(B) Any proceeding described in subparagraph (A) shall be commenced—

(i) if nonjudicial, within 60 days of the entry of the order granting the motion; or

(ii) if judicial, within 6 months of the entry of the order granting the motion.

(3) A motion under paragraph (1) may be filed not later than 5 years after the date of final publication of notice of seizure of the property.

(4) If, at the time a motion made under paragraph (1) is granted, the forfeited property has been disposed of by the Government in accordance with law, the Government may institute proceedings against a substitute sum of money equal to the value of the moving party's interest in the property at the time the property was disposed of.

(5) A motion filed under this subsection shall be the exclusive remedy for seeking to set aside a declaration of forfeiture under a civil forfeiture statute.

(f) Release of seized property.—

(1) A claimant under subsection (a) is entitled to immediate release of seized property if—

(A) the claimant has a possessory interest in the property;

(B) the claimant has sufficient ties to the community to provide assurance that the property will be available at the time of the trial;

(C) the continued possession by the Government pending the final disposition of forfeiture proceedings will cause substantial hardship to the claimant, such as preventing the functioning of a business, preventing an individual from working, or leaving an individual homeless;

(D) the claimant's likely hardship from the continued possession by the Government of the seized property outweighs the risk that the property will be destroyed, damaged, lost, concealed, or transferred if it is returned to the claimant during the pendency of the proceeding; and

(E) none of the conditions set forth in paragraph (8) applies.

(2) A claimant seeking release of property under this subsection must request possession of the property from the appropriate official, and the request must set forth the basis on which the requirements of paragraph (1) are met.

(3)(A) If not later than 15 days after the date of a request under paragraph (2) the property has not been released, the claimant may file a petition in the district court in which the complaint has been filed or, if no complaint has been filed, in the district court in which the seizure warrant was issued or in the district court for the district in which the property was seized.

(B) The petition described in subparagraph (A) shall set forth—

(i) the basis on which the requirements of paragraph (1) are met; and

(ii) the steps the claimant has taken to secure release of the property from the appropriate official.

(4) If the Government establishes that the claimant's claim is frivolous, the court shall deny the petition. In responding to a petition under this subsection on other grounds, the Government may in appropriate cases submit evidence ex parte in order to avoid disclosing any matter that may adversely affect an ongoing criminal investigation or pending criminal trial.

(5) The court shall render a decision on a petition filed under paragraph (3) not later than 30 days after the date of the filing, unless such 30–day limitation is extended by consent of the parties or by the court for good cause shown.

(6) If—

(A) a petition is filed under paragraph (3); and

(B) the claimant demonstrates that the requirements of paragraph (1) have been met,

the district court shall order that the property be returned to the claimant, pending completion of proceedings by the Government to obtain forfeiture of the property.

(7) If the court grants a petition under paragraph (3)—

(A) the court may enter any order necessary to ensure that the value of the property is maintained while the forfeiture action is pending, including—

(i) permitting the inspection, photographing, and inventory of the property;

(ii) fixing a bond in accordance with rule E(5) of the Supplemental Rules for Certain Admiralty and Maritime Claims; and

(iii) requiring the claimant to obtain or maintain insurance on the subject property; and

(B) the Government may place a lien against the property or file a lis pendens to ensure that the property is not transferred to another person.

(8) This subsection shall not apply if the seized property—

(A) is contraband, currency, or other monetary instrument, or electronic funds unless such currency or other monetary instrument or electronic funds constitutes the assets of a legitimate business which has been seized;

(B) is to be used as evidence of a violation of the law;

(C) by reason of design or other characteristic, is particularly suited for use in illegal activities; or

(D) is likely to be used to commit additional criminal acts if returned to the claimant.

(g) Proportionality.—

(1) The claimant under subsection (a)(4) may petition the court to determine whether the forfeiture was constitutionally excessive.

(2) In making this determination, the court shall compare the forfeiture to the gravity of the offense giving rise to the forfeiture.

(3) The claimant shall have the burden of establishing that the forfeiture is grossly disproportional by a preponderance of the evidence at a hearing conducted by the court without a jury.

(4) If the court finds that the forfeiture is grossly disproportional to the offense it shall reduce or eliminate the forfeiture as necessary to avoid a violation of the Excessive Fines Clause of the Eighth Amendment of the Constitution.

(h) Civil fine.—

(1) In any civil forfeiture proceeding under a civil forfeiture statute in which the Government prevails, if the court finds that the claimant's assertion of an interest in the property was frivolous, the court may impose a civil fine on the claimant of an amount equal to 10 percent of the value of the forfeited property, but in no event shall the fine be less than $250 or greater than $5,000.

(2) Any civil fine imposed under this subsection shall not preclude the court from imposing sanctions under rule 11 of the Federal Rules of Civil Procedure.

(3) In addition to the limitations of section 1915 of title 28, United States Code, in no event shall a prisoner file a claim under a civil forfeiture statute or appeal a judgment in a civil action or proceeding based on a civil forfeiture statute if the prisoner has, on three or more prior occasions, while incarcerated or detained in any facility, brought an action or appeal in a court of the United States that was dismissed on the grounds that it is frivolous or malicious, unless the prisoner shows extraordinary and exceptional circumstances.

(i) Civil forfeiture statute defined.—In this section, the term "civil forfeiture statute"—

(1) means any provision of Federal law providing for the forfeiture of property other than as a sentence imposed upon conviction of a criminal offense; and

(2) does not include—

(A) the Tariff Act of 1930 or any other provision of law codified in title 19;

(B) the Internal Revenue Code of 1986;

(C) the Federal Food, Drug, and Cosmetic Act (21 U.S.C. 301 et seq.);

(D) the Trading with the Enemy Act (50 U.S.C. App. 1 et seq.) or the International Emergency Economic Powers Act (IEEPA) (50 U.S.C. 1701 et seq.); or

(E) section 1 of title VI of the Act of June 15, 1917 (40 Stat. 233; 22 U.S.C. 401).

(j) Restraining orders; protective orders.—

(1) Upon application of the United States, the court may enter a restraining order or injunction, require the execution of satisfactory performance bonds, create receiverships, appoint conservators, custodians, appraisers, accountants, or trustees, or take any other action to seize, secure, maintain, or preserve the availability of property subject to civil forfeiture—

(A) upon the filing of a civil forfeiture complaint alleging that the property with respect to which the order is sought is subject to civil forfeiture; or

(B) prior to the filing of such a complaint, if, after notice to persons appearing to have an interest in the property and opportunity for a hearing, the court determines that—

(i) there is a substantial probability that the United States will prevail on the issue of forfeiture and that failure to enter the order will result in the property being destroyed, removed from the jurisdiction of the court, or otherwise made unavailable for forfeiture; and

(ii) the need to preserve the availability of the property through the entry of the requested order outweighs the hardship on any party against whom the order is to be entered.

(2) An order entered pursuant to paragraph (1)(B) shall be effective for not more than 90 days, unless extended by the court for good cause shown, or unless a complaint described in paragraph (1)(A) has been filed.

(3) A temporary restraining order under this subsection may be entered upon application of the United States without notice or opportunity for a hearing when a complaint has not yet been filed with respect to the property, if the United States demonstrates that there is probable cause to believe that the property with respect to which the order is sought is subject to civil forfeiture and that provision of notice will jeopardize the availability of the property for forfeiture. Such a temporary order shall expire not more than 10 days after the date on which it is entered, unless extended for good cause shown or unless the party against whom it is entered consents to an extension for a longer period. A hearing requested concerning an order entered under this paragraph shall be held at the earliest

possible time and prior to the expiration of the temporary order.

(4) The court may receive and consider, at a hearing held pursuant to this subsection, evidence and information that would be inadmissible under the Federal Rules of Evidence.

(Added Pub.L. 106–185, § 2(a), Apr. 25, 2000, 114 Stat. 202, and amended Pub.L. 106–185, § 9, Apr. 25, 2000, 114 Stat. 216; Pub.L. 106–561, § 3(a), Dec. 21, 2000, 114 Stat. 2791; Pub.L. 107–56, Title III, § 316(d), Oct. 26, 2001, 115 Stat. 310.)

HISTORICAL AND STATUTORY NOTES

References in Text

The International Emergency Economic Powers Act, referred to in subsec. (i)(2)(D), is Pub.L. 95–223, Title II, Dec. 28, 1977, 91 Stat. 1626, as amended, which is classified generally to chapter 35 [§ 1701 et seq.] of Title 50. See Short Title note set out under 50 U.S.C.A. § 1701 and Tables for complete classification.

Rule E of the Supplemental Rules for Certain Admiralty and Maritime Claims, referred to in subsec. (f)(7)(A)(ii), is set out in Title 28.

The Tariff Act of 1930, referred to in subsec. (i)(2)(A), is codified generally as chapter 4 of Title 19 (19 U.S.C.A. § 1202 et seq.). See Tables for complete classification.

Title 19, referred to in subsec. (i)(2)(A), deals with Customs Duties. See 19 U.S.C.A. § 1 et seq.

The Internal Revenue Code of 1986, referred to in subsec. (i)(2)(B), is classified principally to Title 26. See 26 U.S.C.A. § 1 et seq.

The Act of June 15, 1917, referred to in subsec. (i)(2)(E), is one of the Embargo Acts. See Tables for complete classification.

Effective and Applicability Provisions

2000 Acts. Pub.L. 106–561, § 3(b), Dec. 21, 2000, 114 Stat. 2791, provided that: "The amendment made by this section [amending subsec. (a)(2)(C)(ii) of this section] shall take effect as if included in the amendment made by section 2(a) of Public Law 106–185."

Amendments by Pub.L. 106–185, applicable to any forfeiture proceeding commenced on or after the date that is 120 days after April 25, 2000, see section 21 of Pub.L. 106–185, set out as a note under section 1324 of Title 8.

Termination Date of 2001 Amendment

Effective on and after the first day of fiscal year 2005, amendments by Title III (§§ 301 to 377) of Pub.L. 107–56 shall terminate if Congress enacts a joint resolution to that effect; such resolution shall be given expedited consideration, see Pub.L. 107–56 Title III, § 303, Oct. 26, 2001, 115 Stat. 298, set out as a note under 31 U.S.C.A. § 5311.

Anti-Terrorist Forfeiture Protection

Pub.L. 107–56, Title III, § 316(a) to (c), Oct. 26, 2001, 115 Stat. 309, which provided that an owner of property that is confiscated under any law relating to the confiscation of assets of suspected international terrorists, may contest that confiscation by filing a claim in the manner set forth in the Federal Rules of Civil Procedure (Supplemental Rules for Certain Admiralty and Maritime Claims) by asserting an affirmative defense that the property is not subject to confiscation under such law or that the innocent owner provisions of subsec. (d) of this section apply to the case; provided that a court may admit evidence that is otherwise inadmissible under the Federal Rules of Evidence, if the court determines that the evidence is reliable, and that compliance with the Federal Rules of Evidence may jeopardize the national security interests of the United States; excluded certain provisions of Federal law from the definition of the term "civil forfeiture statute"; and provided other protections to the innocent property owner, was repealed by Pub.L. 109–177, Title IV, § 406(b)(2), Mar. 9, 2006, 120 Stat. 245.

§ 984. Civil forfeiture of fungible property

(a)(1) In any forfeiture action in rem in which the subject property is cash, monetary instruments in bearer form, funds deposited in an account in a financial institution (as defined in section 20 of this title), or precious metals—

(A) it shall not be necessary for the Government to identify the specific property involved in the offense that is the basis for the forfeiture; and

(B) it shall not be a defense that the property involved in such an offense has been removed and replaced by identical property.

(2) Except as provided in subsection (b), any identical property found in the same place or account as the property involved in the offense that is the basis for the forfeiture shall be subject to forfeiture under this section.

(b) No action pursuant to this section to forfeit property not traceable directly to the offense that is the basis for the forfeiture may be commenced more than 1 year from the date of the offense.

(c)(1) Subsection (a) does not apply to an action against funds held by a financial institution in an interbank account unless the account holder knowingly engaged in the offense that is the basis for the forfeiture.

(2) In this subsection—

(A) the term "financial institution" includes a foreign bank (as defined in section 1(b)(7) of the International Banking Act of 1978 (12 U.S.C. 3101(b)(7)) [1]; and

(B) the term "interbank account" means an account held by one financial institution at another financial institution primarily for the purpose of facilitating customer transactions.

(d) Nothing in this section may be construed to limit the ability of the Government to forfeit property under any provision of law if the property involved in the offense giving rise to the forfeiture or property traceable thereto is available for forfeiture.

(Added Pub.L. 102–550, Title XV, § 1522(a), Oct. 28, 1992, 106 Stat. 4063, and amended Pub.L. 103–325, Title IV,

§ 411(c)(2)(E), Sept. 23, 1994, 108 Stat. 2253; Pub.L. 106–185, § 13(a), Apr. 25, 2000, 114 Stat. 218.)

1 So in original. Probably should be "(12 U.S.C. 3101(7))".

HISTORICAL AND STATUTORY NOTES

Codifications

Section 13(a) of Pub.L. 106–185, Apr. 25, 2000, 114 Stat. 218, amended this section. There is no section 13(b) of Pub.L. 106–185.

Effective and Applicability Provisions

2000 Acts. Amendments by Pub.L. 106–185, applicable to any forfeiture proceeding commenced on or after the date that is 120 days after April 25, 2000, see section 21 of Pub.L. 106–185, set out as a note under section 1324 of Title 8.

1992 Acts. Section effective Oct. 28, 1992, see section 2 of Pub.L. 102–550, set out as a note under section 5301 of Title 42, The Public Health and Welfare.

§ 985. Civil forfeiture of real property

(a) Notwithstanding any other provision of law, all civil forfeitures of real property and interests in real property shall proceed as judicial forfeitures.

(b)(1) Except as provided in this section—

(A) real property that is the subject of a civil forfeiture action shall not be seized before entry of an order of forfeiture; and

(B) the owners or occupants of the real property shall not be evicted from, or otherwise deprived of the use and enjoyment of, real property that is the subject of a pending forfeiture action.

(2) The filing of a lis pendens and the execution of a writ of entry for the purpose of conducting an inspection and inventory of the property shall not be considered a seizure under this subsection.

(c)(1) The Government shall initiate a civil forfeiture action against real property by—

(A) filing a complaint for forfeiture;

(B) posting a notice of the complaint on the property; and

(C) serving notice on the property owner, along with a copy of the complaint.

(2) If the property owner cannot be served with the notice under paragraph (1) because the owner—

(A) is a fugitive;

(B) resides outside the United States and efforts at service pursuant to rule 4 of the Federal Rules of Civil Procedure are unavailing; or

(C) cannot be located despite the exercise of due diligence, constructive service may be made in accordance with the laws of the State in which the property is located.

(3) If real property has been posted in accordance with this subsection, it shall not be necessary for the court to issue an arrest warrant in rem, or to take any other action to establish in rem jurisdiction over the property.

(d)(1) Real property may be seized prior to the entry of an order of forfeiture if—

(A) the Government notifies the court that it intends to seize the property before trial; and

(B) the court—

(i) issues a notice of application for warrant, causes the notice to be served on the property owner and posted on the property, and conducts a hearing in which the property owner has a meaningful opportunity to be heard; or

(ii) makes an ex parte determination that there is probable cause for the forfeiture and that there are exigent circumstances that permit the Government to seize the property without prior notice and an opportunity for the property owner to be heard.

(2) For purposes of paragraph (1)(B)(ii), to establish exigent circumstances, the Government shall show that less restrictive measures such as a lis pendens, restraining order, or bond would not suffice to protect the Government's interests in preventing the sale, destruction, or continued unlawful use of the real property.

(e) If the court authorizes a seizure of real property under subsection (d)(1)(B)(ii), it shall conduct a prompt post-seizure hearing during which the property owner shall have an opportunity to contest the basis for the seizure.

(f) This section—

(1) applies only to civil forfeitures of real property and interests in real property;

(2) does not apply to forfeitures of the proceeds of the sale of such property or interests, or of money or other assets intended to be used to acquire such property or interests; and

(3) shall not affect the authority of the court to enter a restraining order relating to real property.

(Added Pub.L. 106–185, § 7(a), Apr. 25, 2000, 114 Stat. 214.)

HISTORICAL AND STATUTORY NOTES

References in Text

Rule 4 of the Federal Rules of Civil Procedure, referred to in subsec. (c)(2)(B), is set out in Title 28.

Effective and Applicability Provisions

2000 Acts. Enactment of this section by Pub.L. 106–185, applicable to any forfeiture proceeding commenced on or after the date that is 120 days after April 25, 2000, see section 21 of Pub.L. 106–185, set out as a note under section 1324 of Title 8.

§ 986. Subpoenas for bank records

(a) At any time after the commencement of any action for forfeiture in rem brought by the United

States under section 1956, 1957, or 1960 of this title, section 5322 or 5324 of title 31, United States Code, or the Controlled Substances Act, any party may request the Clerk of the Court in the district in which the proceeding is pending to issue a subpoena duces tecum to any financial institution, as defined in section 5312(a) of title 31, United States Code, to produce books, records and any other documents at any place designated by the requesting party. All parties to the proceeding shall be notified of the issuance of any such subpoena. The procedures and limitations set forth in section 985 of this title shall apply to subpoenas issued under this section.

(b) Service of a subpoena issued pursuant to this section shall be by certified mail. Records produced in response to such a subpoena may be produced in person or by mail, common carrier, or such other method as may be agreed upon by the party requesting the subpoena and the custodian of records. The party requesting the subpoena may require the custodian of records to submit an affidavit certifying the authenticity and completeness of the records and explaining the omission of any record called for in the subpoena.

(c) Nothing in this section shall preclude any party from pursuing any form of discovery pursuant to the Federal Rules of Civil Procedure.

(d) Access to records in bank secrecy jurisdictions.—

(1) In general.—In any civil forfeiture case, or in any ancillary proceeding in any criminal forfeiture case governed by section 413(n) of the Controlled Substances Act (21 U.S.C. 853(n)), in which—

(A) financial records located in a foreign country may be material—

(i) to any claim or to the ability of the Government to respond to such claim; or

(ii) in a civil forfeiture case, to the ability of the Government to establish the forfeitability of the property; and

(B) it is within the capacity of the claimant to waive the claimant's rights under applicable financial secrecy laws, or to obtain the records so that such records can be made available notwithstanding such secrecy laws,

the refusal of the claimant to provide the records in response to a discovery request or to take the action necessary otherwise to make the records available shall be grounds for judicial sanctions, up to and including dismissal of the claim with prejudice.

(2) Privilege.—This subsection shall not affect the right of the claimant to refuse production on the basis of any privilege guaranteed by the Constitution of the United States or any other provision of Federal law.

(Added Pub.L. 102–550, Title XV, § 1523(a), Oct. 28, 1992, 106 Stat. 4063, and amended Pub.L. 103–325, Title IV, § 411(c)(2)(E), Sept. 23, 1994, 108 Stat. 2253; Pub.L. 106–185, § 17, Apr. 25, 2000, 114 Stat. 221.)

HISTORICAL AND STATUTORY NOTES

References in Text

The Controlled Substances Act, referred to in subsec. (a), is Title II of Pub.L. 91–513, Oct. 27, 1970, 84 Stat. 1242, as amended, which is classified principally to subchapter I (section 801 et seq.) of chapter 13 of Title 21, Food and Drugs. For complete classification of this Act to the Code, see Short Title note set out under section 801 of Title 21 and Tables.

Section 985 of this title, referred to in subsec. (a), was enacted by Pub.L. 106–185 and relates to civil forfeiture of real property and not to procedures and limitations for subpoenas. The reference to section 985 was included in this section when it was enacted by Pub.L. 102–550, but at that time, there was no section 985 of this title.

The Federal Rules of Civil Procedure, referred to in subsec. (c), are set out in Title 28, U.S.C.A., Judiciary and Judicial Procedure.

Effective and Applicability Provisions

2000 Acts. Amendments by Pub.L. 106–185, applicable to any forfeiture proceeding commenced on or after the date that is 120 days after April 25, 2000, see section 21 of Pub.L. 106–185, set out as a note under section 1324 of Title 8.

1992 Acts. Section effective Oct. 28, 1992, see section 2 of Pub.L. 102–550, set out as a note under section 5301 of Title 42, The Public Health and Welfare.

§ 987. Anti-terrorist forfeiture protection

(a) Right to contest.—An owner of property that is confiscated under any provision of law relating to the confiscation of assets of suspected international terrorists, may contest that confiscation by filing a claim in the manner set forth in the Federal Rules of Civil Procedure (Supplemental Rules for Certain Admiralty and Maritime Claims), and asserting as an affirmative defense that—

(1) the property is not subject to confiscation under such provision of law; or

(2) the innocent owner provisions of section 983(d) of title 18, United States Code, apply to the case.

(b) Evidence.—In considering a claim filed under this section, a court may admit evidence that is otherwise inadmissible under the Federal Rules of Evidence, if the court determines that the evidence is reliable, and that compliance with the Federal Rules of Evidence may jeopardize the national security interests of the United States.

(c) Clarifications.—

(1) Protection of rights.—The exclusion of certain provisions of Federal law from the definition of the term "civil forfeiture statute" in section 983(i) of title 18, United States Code, shall not be construed to deny an owner of property the right to contest the confiscation of assets of suspected international terrorists under—

(A) subsection (a) of this section;

(B) the Constitution; or

(C) subchapter II of chapter 5 of title 5, United States Code (commonly known as the "Administrative Procedure Act").

(2) Savings clause.—Nothing in this section shall limit or otherwise affect any other remedies that may be available to an owner of property under section 983 of title 18, United States Code, or any other provision of law.

(Added Pub.L. 109–177, Title IV, § 406(b)(1)(B), Mar. 9, 2006, 120 Stat. 244.)

HISTORICAL AND STATUTORY NOTES

References in Text

The Federal Rules of Civil Procedure (Supplemental Rules for Certain Admiralty and Maritime Claims), referred to in subsec. (a), are set out under Title 28, Federal Rules of Civil Procedure, Fed.Rules Civ.Proc.Rule 1 et seq., 28 U.S.C.A.

The Federal Rules of Evidence, referred to in subsec. (b), are set out in Title 28, Judiciary and Judicial Procedure, Fed.Rules Evid.Rule 101 et seq., 28 U.S.C.A.

Subchapter II of chapter 5 of title 5, referred to in subsec. (c)(1)(C), is Administrative Procedure, 5 U.S.C.A. § 551 et seq.

CHAPTER 47—FRAUD AND FALSE STATEMENTS

[1] Section catchline amended by Pub.L. 108–21 without corresponding amendment of chapter analysis.

§ 1001. Statements or entries generally

(a) Except as otherwise provided in this section, whoever, in any matter within the jurisdiction of the executive, legislative, or judicial branch of the Government of the United States, knowingly and willfully—

(1) falsifies, conceals, or covers up by any trick, scheme, or device a material fact;

(2) makes any materially false, fictitious, or fraudulent statement or representation; or

(3) makes or uses any false writing or document knowing the same to contain any materially false, fictitious, or fraudulent statement or entry;

shall be fined under this title, imprisoned not more than 5 years or, if the offense involves international or domestic terrorism (as defined in section 2331), imprisoned not more than 8 years, or both. If the matter relates to an offense under chapter 109A, 109B, 110, or 117, or section 1591, then the term of imprisonment imposed under this section shall be not more than 8 years.

(b) Subsection (a) does not apply to a party to a judicial proceeding, or that party's counsel, for statements, representations, writings or documents submitted by such party or counsel to a judge or magistrate in that proceeding.

(c) With respect to any matter within the jurisdiction of the legislative branch, subsection (a) shall apply only to—

(1) administrative matters, including a claim for payment, a matter related to the procurement of property or services, personnel or employment practices, or support services, or a document required by law, rule, or regulation to be submitted to the Congress or any office or officer within the legislative branch; or

(2) any investigation or review, conducted pursuant to the authority of any committee, subcommittee, commission or office of the Congress, consistent with applicable rules of the House or Senate.

(June 25, 1948, c. 645, 62 Stat. 749; Sept. 13, 1994, Pub.L. 103–322, Title XXXIII, § 330016(1)(L), 108 Stat. 2147; Oct. 11, 1996, Pub.L. 104–292, § 2, 110 Stat. 3459; Dec. 17, 2004, Pub.L. 108–458, Title VI, § 6703(a), 118 Stat. 3766; July 27, 2006, Pub.L. 109–248, Title I, § 141(c), 120 Stat. 603.)

HISTORICAL AND STATUTORY NOTES

References in Text

Chapter 109A, referred to in subsec. (a), is chapter 109A of this title, entitled Sexual Abuse, 18 U.S.C.A. § 2241 et seq.

Chapter 109B, referred to in subsec. (a), is chapter 109B of this title, entitled Sex Offender and Crimes Against Children Registry, 18 U.S.C.A. § 2250 et seq.

Chapter 110, referred to in subsec. (a), is chapter 110 of this title, entitled Sexual Exploitation and Other Abuse of Children, 18 U.S.C.A. § 2251 et seq.

Chapter 117, referred to in subsec. (a), is chapter 117 of this title, entitled Transportation for Illegal Sexual Activity and Related Crimes, 18 U.S.C.A. § 2421 et seq.

Short Title

2004 Amendments. Pub.L. 108–275, § 1, July 15, 2004, 118 Stat. 831, provided that: "This Act [enacting 18 U.S.C.A. § 1028A; amending 18 U.S.C.A. §§ 641, 1028; and amending provisions set out as a note under 28 U.S.C.A. § 994] may be cited as the 'Identity Theft Penalty Enhancement Act'."

2003 Amendments. Pub.L. 108–21, Title VI, § 607(a), Apr. 30, 2003, 117 Stat. 689, provided that: "This section [amending 18 U.S.C.A. § 1028] may be cited as the 'Secure Authentication Feature and Enhanced Identification Defense Act of 2003' or 'SAFE ID Act'."

2000 Amendments. Pub.L. 106–578, § 1, Dec. 28, 2000, 114 Stat. 3075, provided that: "This Act [amending section 1028 of this title, repealing section 1738 of this title, and enacting provisions set out as notes under section 1028 of this title] may be cited as the 'Internet False Identification Prevention Act of 2000'."

1998 Amendments. Pub.L. 105–318, § 1, Oct. 30, 1998, 112 Stat. 3007, provided that: "This Act [Pub.L. 105–318, Oct. 30, 1998, 112 Stat. 3007, for complete classification of which, see Tables] may be cited as the 'Identity Theft and Assumption Deterrence Act of 1998'."

Pub.L. 105–172, § 1, Apr. 24, 1998, 112 Stat. 53, provided that: "This Act [which amended section 1029 of this title and enacted provisions set out as a note under section 994 of Title 28] may be cited as the 'Wireless Telephone Protection Act'."

1996 Amendments. Section 1 of Pub.L. 104–292 provided that: "This Act [amending this section and sections 1515 and 6005 of this title and section 1365 of Title 28, Judiciary and Judicial Procedure] may be cited as the 'False Statements Accountability Act of 1996'."

1994 Amendments. Section 290001(a) of Pub.L. 103–322, as amended Pub.L. 104–294, Title VI, § 604(b)(34), Oct. 11, 1996, 110 Stat. 3508, provided that: "This section [which amended section 1030 of this title] may be cited as the 'Computer Abuse Amendments Act of 1994'."

[Amendment by section 604 of Pub.L. 104–294 effective Sept. 13, 1994, see section 604(d) of Pub.L. 104–294, set out as a note under section 13 of this title.]

1990 Amendments. Pub.L. 101–647, Title XXV, § 2500, Nov. 29, 1990, 104 Stat. 4859, provided that: "This title [enacting sections 225, 1032, 1517, and 3059A of this title and sections 4201 to 4213, 4221 to 4230, and 4241 to 4247 of Title 12, Banks and Banking, amending sections 20, 212, 213, 215, 648, 655, 656, 657, 981, 982, 1004, 1005, 1006, 1007, 1014, 1030, 1341, 1343, 1344, 1345, 1906, 1956, 2113, 2516, 3289, 3293, and 3663 of this title, sections 101, 365, 507, 522, and 523 of Title 11, Bankruptcy, sections 1441a, 1786, 1787, 1818, 1821, 1828, 1829, 1831k, 1833a, and 3401 of Title 12, and sections 604 of Title 28, Judiciary and Judicial Procedure, and enacting provisions set out as notes under section 3293 of this title, section 4201 of Title 12, and sections 509, 522, and 994 of Title 28] may be cited as the 'Comprehensive Thrift and Bank Fraud Prosecution and Taxpayer Recovery Act of 1990'."

1989 Amendments. Pub.L. 101–123, § 1, Oct. 23, 1989, 103 Stat. 759, provided that: "This Act [amending section 1031 of this title, enacting provisions set out as notes under sections 293 and 1031 of this title, and repealing a provision set out as a note under section 293 of this title] may be cited as the 'Major Fraud Act Amendments of 1989'."

§ 1002. Possession of false papers to defraud United States

Whoever, knowingly and with intent to defraud the United States, or any agency thereof, possesses any false, altered, forged, or counterfeited writing or document for the purpose of enabling another to obtain from the United States, or from any agency, officer or agent thereof, any sum of money, shall be fined under this title or imprisoned not more than five years, or both.

(June 25, 1948, c. 645, 62 Stat. 749; Sept. 13, 1994, Pub.L. 103–322, Title XXXIII, § 330016(1)(L), 108 Stat. 2147.)

§ 1003. Demands against the United States

Whoever knowingly and fraudulently demands or endeavors to obtain any share or sum in the public stocks of the United States, or to have any part thereof transferred, assigned, sold, or conveyed, or to have any annuity, dividend, pension, wages, gratuity, or other debt due from the United States, or any part thereof, received, or paid by virtue of any false, forged, or counterfeited power of attorney, authority, or instrument, shall be fined under this title or imprisoned not more than five years, or both; but if the sum or value so obtained or attempted to be obtained does not exceed $1,000, he shall be fined under this title or imprisoned not more than one year, or both.

(June 25, 1948, c. 645, 62 Stat. 749; Sept. 13, 1994, Pub.L. 103–322, Title XXXIII, § 330016(1)(H), (L), 108 Stat. 2147; Oct. 11, 1996, Pub.L. 104–294, Title VI, § 606(a), 110 Stat. 3511.)

§ 1004. Certification of checks

Whoever, being an officer, director, agent, or employee of any Federal Reserve bank, member bank of the Federal Reserve System, insured bank (as defined in section 3(h) of the Federal Deposit Insurance Act), branch or agency of a foreign bank (as such terms are defined in paragraphs (1) and (3) of section 1(b) of the International Banking Act of 1978), or organization operating under section 25 or section 25(a) of the Federal Reserve Act, certifies a check before the amount thereof has been regularly deposited in the bank, branch, agency, or organization, by the drawer thereof, or resorts to any device, or receives any fictitious obligation, directly or collaterally, in order to evade any of the provisions of law relating to certification of checks, shall be fined under this title or imprisoned not more than five years, or both.

(June 25, 1948, c. 645, 62 Stat. 749; Nov. 29, 1990, Pub.L. 101–647, Title XXV, § 2597(g), 104 Stat. 4910; Sept. 13, 1994, Pub.L. 103–322, Title XXXIII, § 330016(1)(K), 108 Stat. 2147.)

HISTORICAL AND STATUTORY NOTES

References in Text

Section 3(h) of the Federal Deposit Insurance Act, referred to in text, is classified to section 1813(h) of Title 12, Banks and Banking.

Section 1(b) of the International Banking Act of 1978, referred to in text, is classified to section 3101 of Title 12.

The Federal Reserve Act, referred to in text, is Act Dec. 23, 1913, c. 6, 38 Stat. 251, as amended, which is classified principally to chapter 3 of Title 12, 12 U.S.C.A. § 221 et seq. Section 25 of the Federal Reserve Act is classified to subchapter I of chapter 6 of Title 12, 12 U.S.C.A. § 601 et seq. Section 25(a) of the Federal Reserve Act, which is classified to subchapter II of chapter 6 of Title 12, 12 U.S.C.A. § 611 et seq., was renumbered section 25A by Pub.L. 102–242, Title I, § 142(e)(2), Dec. 10, 1991, 105 Stat. 2281. See Tables and 12 U.S.C.A. § 226 for complete classification.

§ 1005. Bank entries, reports and transactions

Whoever, being an officer, director, agent or employee of any Federal Reserve bank, member bank, depository institution holding company, national bank, insured bank, branch or agency of a foreign bank, or organization operating under section 25 or section 25(a) of the Federal Reserve Act, without authority from the directors of such bank, branch, agency, or organization or company, issues or puts in circulation any notes of such bank, branch, agency, or organization or company; or

Whoever, without such authority, makes, draws, issues, puts forth, or assigns any certificate of deposit, draft, order, bill of exchange, acceptance, note, debenture, bond, or other obligation, or mortgage, judgment or decree; or

Whoever makes any false entry in any book, report, or statement of such bank, company, branch, agency, or organization with intent to injure or defraud such bank, company, branch, agency, or organization, or any other company, body politic or corporate, or any individual person, or to deceive any officer of such bank, company, branch, agency, or organization, or the Comptroller of the Currency, or the Federal Deposit Insurance Corporation, or any agent or examiner appointed to examine the affairs of such bank, company, branch, agency, or organization, or the Board of Governors of the Federal Reserve System; or

Whoever with intent to defraud the United States or any agency thereof, or any financial institution referred to in this section, participates or shares in or receives (directly or indirectly) any money, profit, property, or benefits through any transaction, loan, commission, contract, or any other act of any such financial institution—

Shall be fined not more than $1,000,000 or imprisoned not more than 30 years, or both.

As used in this section, the term "national bank" is synonymous with "national banking association"; "member bank" means and includes any national bank, state bank, or bank or trust company, which has become a member of one of the Federal Reserve banks; "insured bank" includes any state bank, banking association, trust company, savings bank, or other banking institution, the deposits of which are insured by the Federal Deposit Insurance Corporation; and the term "branch or agency of a foreign bank" means a branch or agency described in section 20(9) of this title. For purposes of this section, the term "depository institution holding company" has the meaning given such term in section 3(w)(1) of the Federal Deposit Insurance Act.

(June 25, 1948, c. 645, 62 Stat. 750; Aug. 9, 1989, Pub.L. 101–73, Title IX, § 961(d), 103 Stat. 499; Nov. 29, 1990, Pub.L. 101–647, Title XXV, §§ 2504(d), 2595(a)(3), 2597(h),

104 Stat. 4861, 4907, 4910; Pub.L. 107–273, Div. B, Title IV, § 4003(a)(2), Nov. 2, 2002, 116 Stat. 1811.)

HISTORICAL AND STATUTORY NOTES

References in Text

The Federal Reserve Act, referred to in text, is Act Dec. 23, 1913, c. 6, 38 Stat. 251, as amended, which is classified principally to chapter 3 of Title 12, 12 U.S.C.A. § 221 et seq. Section 25 of the Federal Reserve Act is classified to subchapter I of chapter 6 of Title 12, 12 U.S.C.A. § 601 et seq. Section 25(a) of the Federal Reserve Act, which is classified to subchapter II of chapter 6 of Title 12, 12 U.S.C.A. § 611 et seq., was renumbered section 25A by Pub.L. 102–242, Title I, § 142(e)(2), Dec. 10, 1991, 105 Stat. 2281. See Tables and 12 U.S.C.A. § 226 for complete classification.

Section 3(w)(1) of the Federal Deposit Insurance Act, referred to in text, is classified to section 1813(w)(1) of Title 12, Banks and Banking.

Severability of Provisions

If any provision of Pub.L. 101–73 or the application thereof to any person or circumstance is held invalid, the remainder of Pub.L. 101–73 and the application of the provision to other persons not similarly situated or to other circumstances not to be affected thereby, see section 1221 of Pub.L. 101–73, set out as a note under section 1811 of Title 12, Banks and Banking.

Exceptions as to Transfer of Functions

Functions vested by any provision of law in the Comptroller of the Currency, referred to in this section, were not included in the transfer of functions of officers, agencies and employees of the Department of the Treasury to the Secretary of the Treasury, made by 1950 Reorg. Plan No. 26, § 1, eff. July 31, 1950, 15 F.R. 4935, 64 Stat. 1280, set out in the Appendix to Title 5, Government Organization and Employees.

§ 1006. Federal credit institution entries, reports and transactions

Whoever, being an officer, agent or employee of or connected in any capacity with the Federal Deposit Insurance Corporation, National Credit Union Administration, Office of Thrift Supervision, any Federal home loan bank, the Federal Housing Finance Board, the Resolution Trust Corporation, Farm Credit Administration, Department of Housing and Urban Development, Federal Crop Insurance Corporation, the Secretary of Agriculture acting through the Farmers Home Administration or successor agency, the Rural Development Administration or successor agency, or the Farm Credit System Insurance Corporation, a Farm Credit Bank, a bank for cooperatives or any lending, mortgage, insurance, credit or savings and loan corporation or association authorized or acting under the laws of the United States or any institution, other than an insured bank (as defined in section 656), the accounts of which are insured by the Federal Deposit Insurance Corporation, or by the National Credit Union Administration Board or any small business investment company, with intent to defraud any such institution or any other company, body politic or corporate, or any individual, or to deceive any officer, auditor, examiner or agent of any such institution or of department or agency of the United States, makes any false entry in any book, report or statement of or to any such institution, or without being duly authorized, draws any order or bill of exchange, makes any acceptance, or issues, puts forth or assigns any note, debenture, bond or other obligation, or draft, bill of exchange, mortgage, judgment, or decree, or, with intent to defraud the United States or any agency thereof, or any corporation, institution, or association referred to in this section, participates or shares in or receives directly or indirectly any money, profit, property, or benefits through any transaction, loan, commission, contract, or any other act of any such corporation, institution, or association, shall be fined not more than $1,000,000 or imprisoned not more than 30 years, or both.

(June 25, 1948, c. 645, 62 Stat. 750; May 24, 1949, c. 139, § 20, 63 Stat. 92; July 28, 1956, c. 773, § 2, 70 Stat. 714; Aug. 21, 1958, Pub.L. 85–699, Title VII, § 704, 72 Stat. 698; Oct. 4, 1961, Pub.L. 87–353, § 3(s), 75 Stat. 774; May 25, 1967, Pub.L. 90–19, § 24(a), 81 Stat. 27; Oct. 19, 1970, Pub.L. 91–468, § 6, 84 Stat. 1016; Aug. 9, 1989, Pub.L. 101–73, Title IX, §§ 961(e), 962(a)(7), (8)(A), 103 Stat. 500, 502; Nov. 28, 1990, Pub.L. 101–624, Title XXIII, § 2303(e), 104 Stat. 3981; Nov. 29, 1990, Pub.L. 101–647, Title XVI, § 1603, Title XXV, §§ 2504(e), 2595(a)(4), 104 Stat. 4843, 4861, 4907; Sept. 13, 1994, Pub.L. 103–322, Title XXXIII, § 330004(6), 108 Stat. 2141; Oct. 22, 1999, Pub.L. 106–78, Title VII, § 767, 113 Stat. 1174.)

HISTORICAL AND STATUTORY NOTES

Severability of Provisions

If any provision of Pub.L. 101–624 or the application thereof to any person or circumstance is held invalid, such invalidity not to affect other provisions or applications of Pub.L. 101–624 which can be given effect without regard to the invalid provision or application, see section 2519 of Pub.L. 101–624, set out as a note under section 1421 of Title 7, Agriculture.

If any provision of Pub.L. 101–73 or the application thereof to any person or circumstance is held invalid, the remainder of Pub.L. 101–73 and the application of the provision to other persons not similarly situated or to other circumstances not to be affected thereby, see section 1221 of Pub.L. 101–73, set out as a note under section 1811 of Title 12, Banks and Banking.

Exceptions From Transfer of Functions

Functions of the corporations of the Department of Agriculture, the boards of directors and officers of such corporations; the Advisory Board of the Commodity Credit Corporation; and the Farm Credit Administration or any agency, officer or entity of, under, or subject to the supervision of the Administration were excepted from the functions of officers, agencies and employees transferred to the Secretary of Agriculture by 1953 Reorg. Plan No. 2, § 1, eff. June 4, 1953, 18 F.R. 3219, 67 Stat. 633, set out in the Appendix to Title 5, Government Organization and Employees.

Abolition of Home Owners' Loan Corporation

For dissolution and abolishment of Home Owners' Loan Corporation, referred to in this section, by Act June 30, 1953, c. 170, § 21, 67 Stat. 126, see note under former § 1463 of Title 12, Banks and Banking.

Farm Credit Administration

Organization of Farm Credit Administration, see § 2241 et seq. of Title 12, Banks and Banking.

National Agriculture Credit Corporation

Title II of the Agricultural Credits Act, Act Mar. 4, 1923, c. 252, Title II, §§ 201 to 217, 42 Stat. 1461, which authorized the creation of national agricultural credit corporations, was repealed by Pub.L. 86–230, Sept. 8, 1959, § 24, 73 Stat. 466. Prior to such repeal, Act June 16, 1933, c. 101, § 77, 48 Stat. 292, had prohibited the creation, after June 16, 1933, of national agricultural credit corporations authorized to be formed under the Agricultural Credits Act.

Abolition of Reconstruction Finance Corporation

Section 6(a) of 1957 Reorg. Plan No. 1, eff. June 30, 1957, 22 F.R. 4633, 71 Stat. 647, set out in the Appendix to Title 5, Government Organization and Employees, abolished the Reconstruction Finance Corporation. See notes preceding former §§ 601 to 616 of Title 15, Commerce and Trade.

§ 1007. Federal Deposit Insurance Corporation transactions

Whoever, for the purpose of influencing in any way the action of the Federal Deposit Insurance Corporation, knowingly makes or invites reliance on a false, forged, or counterfeit statement, document, or thing shall be fined not more than $1,000,000 or imprisoned not more than 30 years, or both.

(June 25, 1948, c. 645, 62 Stat. 750; Aug. 9, 1989, Pub.L. 101–73, Title IX, § 961(f), 103 Stat. 500; Nov. 29, 1990, Pub.L. 101–647, Title XXV, § 2504(f), 104 Stat. 4861; Sept. 13, 1994, Pub.L. 103–322, Title XXXIII, § 330002(c), 108 Stat. 2140.)

HISTORICAL AND STATUTORY NOTES

Severability of Provisions

If any provision of Pub.L. 101–73 or the application thereof to any person or circumstance is held invalid, the remainder of Pub.L. 101–73 and the application of the provision to other persons not similarly situated or to other circumstances not to be affected thereby, see section 1221 of Pub.L. 101–73, set out as a note under section 1811 of Title 12, Banks and Banking.

[§ 1008. Repealed. Pub.L. 101–73, Title IX, § 961(g)(1), Aug. 9, 1989, 103 Stat. 500]

HISTORICAL AND STATUTORY NOTES

Section, Act June 25, 1948, c. 645, 62 Stat. 751, provided that whoever, for the purpose of inducing the insurance of the accounts of any institution by the Federal Savings and Loan Insurance Corporation or for the purpose of obtaining any extension or renewal of such insurance by such Corporation or for the purpose of influencing in any way the action of such Corporation, made, passed, uttered, or published any statement, knowing the same to be false; or whoever, for the purpose of influencing in any way the action of such Corporation, uttered, forged, or counterfeited any instrument, paper, or document, or uttered, published, or passed as true any instrument, paper, or document, knowing it to have been uttered, forged, or counterfeited, or willfully overvalued any security, asset, or income, of any institution insured or applying for insurance by said Corporation would be fined not more than $5,000 or imprisoned not more than two years, or both.

[§ 1009. Repealed. Pub.L. 101–73, Title IX, § 962(a)(3), Aug. 9, 1989, 103 Stat. 502]

HISTORICAL AND STATUTORY NOTES

Section, Act June 25, 1948, c. 645, 62 Stat. 751, provided that whoever willfully and knowingly made, circulated, or transmitted to another or others any statement or rumor, written, printed or by word of mouth, which was untrue in fact and was directly or by inference derogatory to the financial condition or affects the solvency or financial standing of the Federal Savings and Loan Insurance Corporation, would be fined not more than $1,000 or imprisoned not more than one year, or both.

§ 1010. Department of Housing and Urban Development and Federal Housing Administration transactions

Whoever, for the purpose of obtaining any loan or advance of credit from any person, partnership, association, or corporation with the intent that such loan or advance of credit shall be offered to or accepted by the Department of Housing and Urban Development for insurance, or for the purpose of obtaining any extension or renewal of any loan, advance of credit, or mortgage insured by such Department, or the acceptance, release, or substitution of any security on such a loan, advance of credit, or for the purpose of influencing in any way the action of such Department, makes, passes, utters, or publishes any statement, knowing the same to be false, or alters, forges, or counterfeits any instrument, paper, or document, or utters, publishes, or passes as true any instrument, paper, or document, knowing it to have been altered, forged, or counterfeited, or willfully overvalues any security, asset, or income, shall be fined under this title or imprisoned not more than two years, or both.

(June 25, 1948, c. 645, 62 Stat. 751; May 25, 1967, Pub.L. 90–19, § 24(c), 81 Stat. 28; Sept. 13, 1994, Pub.L. 103–322, Title XXXIII, § 330016(1)(K), 108 Stat. 2147.)

§ 1011. Federal land bank mortgage transactions

Whoever, being a mortgagee, knowingly makes any false statement in any paper, proposal, or letter, relating to the sale of any mortgage, to any Federal land bank; or

Whoever, being an appraiser, willfully over-values any land securing such mortgage—

Shall be fined under this title or imprisoned not more than one year, or both.

(June 25, 1948, c. 645, 62 Stat. 751; Sept. 13, 1994, Pub.L. 103-322, Title XXXIII, § 330016(1)(K), 108 Stat. 2147.)

§ 1012. Department of Housing and Urban Development transactions

Whoever, with intent to defraud, makes any false entry in any book of the Department of Housing and Urban Development or makes any false report or statement to or for such Department; or

Whoever receives any compensation, rebate, or reward, with intent to defraud such Department or with intent unlawfully to defeat its purposes; or

Whoever induces or influences such Department to purchase or acquire any property or to enter into any contract and willfully fails to disclose any interest which he has in such property or in the property to which such contract relates, or any special benefit which he expects to receive as a result of such contract—

Shall be fined under this title or imprisoned not more than one year, or both.

(June 25, 1948, c. 645, 62 Stat. 752; Oct. 31, 1951, c. 655, § 26, 65 Stat. 720; May 25, 1967, Pub.L. 90-19, § 24(d), 81 Stat. 28; Sept. 13, 1994, Pub.L. 103-322, Title XXXIII, § 330016(1)(H), 108 Stat. 2147.)

§ 1013. Farm loan bonds and credit bank debentures

Whoever deceives, defrauds, or imposes upon, or attempts to deceive, defraud, or impose upon any person, partnership, corporation, or association by making any false pretense or representation concerning the character, issue, security, contents, conditions, or terms of any farm loan bond, or coupon, issued by any Federal land bank or banks; or of any debenture, coupon, or other obligation, issued by any Federal intermediate credit bank or banks; or by falsely pretending or representing that any farm loan bond, or coupon, is anything other than, or different from, what it purports to be on the face of said bond or coupon, shall be fined under this title or imprisoned not more than one year, or both.

(June 25, 1948, c. 645, 62 Stat. 752; Oct. 12, 1982, Pub.L. 97-297, § 4(a), 96 Stat. 1318; Sept. 13, 1994, Pub.L. 103-322, Title XXXIII, §§ 330004(8), 330016(1)(G), 108 Stat. 2141, 2147.)

HISTORICAL AND STATUTORY NOTES

National Agricultural Credit Corporation

Title II of the Agricultural Credits Act, Act Mar. 4, 1923, c. 252, Title II, §§ 201 to 217, 42 Stat. 1461, which authorized the creation of national agricultural credit corporations, was repealed by Pub.L. 86-230, Sept. 8, 1959, § 24, 73 Stat. 466. Prior to such repeal, Act June 16, 1933, c. 101, § 77, 48 Stat. 292, had prohibited the creation, after June 16, 1933, of national agricultural credit corporations authorized to be formed under the Agricultural Credits Act.

§ 1014. Loan and credit applications generally; renewals and discounts; crop insurance

Whoever knowingly makes any false statement or report, or willfully overvalues any land, property or security, for the purpose of influencing in any way the action of the Farm Credit Administration, Federal Crop Insurance Corporation or a company the Corporation reinsures, the Secretary of Agriculture acting through the Farmers Home Administration or successor agency, the Rural Development Administration or successor agency, any Farm Credit Bank, production credit association, agricultural credit association, bank for cooperatives, or any division, officer, or employee thereof, or of any regional agricultural credit corporation established pursuant to law, or a Federal land bank, a Federal land bank association, a Federal Reserve bank, a small business investment company, as defined in section 103 of the Small Business Investment Act of 1958 (15 U.S.C. 662), or the Small Business Administration in connection with any provision of that Act, a Federal credit union, an insured State-chartered credit union, any institution the accounts of which are insured by the Federal Deposit Insurance Corporation, the Office of Thrift Supervision, any Federal home loan bank, the Federal Housing Finance Board, the Federal Deposit Insurance Corporation, the Resolution Trust Corporation, the Farm Credit System Insurance Corporation, or the National Credit Union Administration Board, a branch or agency of a foreign bank (as such terms are defined in paragraphs (1) and (3) of section 1(b) of the International Banking Act of 1978), or an organization operating under section 25 or section 25(a) of the Federal Reserve Act, upon any application, advance, discount, purchase, purchase agreement, repurchase agreement, commitment, or loan, or any change or extension of any of the same, by renewal, deferment of action or otherwise, or the acceptance, release, or substitution of security therefor, shall be fined not more than $1,000,000 or imprisoned not more than 30 years, or both. The term "State-chartered credit union" includes a credit union chartered under the laws of a State of the United States, the District of Columbia, or any commonwealth, territory, or possession of the United States.

(June 25, 1948, c. 645, 62 Stat. 752; May 24, 1949, c. 139, § 21, 63 Stat. 92; July 26, 1956, c. 741, Title I, § 109, 70 Stat. 667; Aug. 21, 1958, Pub.L. 85-699, Title VII, § 705, 72 Stat. 699; Aug. 18, 1959, Pub.L. 86-168, Title I, § 104(h), 73 Stat. 387; Oct. 4, 1961, Pub.L. 87-353, § 3(t), 75 Stat. 774; July 2, 1964, Pub.L. 88-353, § 5, 78 Stat. 269; Oct. 19, 1970, Pub.L. 91-468, § 7, 84 Stat. 1017; Dec. 31, 1970, Pub.L. 91-609, Title IX, § 915, 84 Stat. 1815; Oct. 12, 1982, Pub.L. 97-297,

§ 4(b), 96 Stat. 1318; Aug. 9, 1989, Pub.L. 101–73, Title IX, §§ 961(h), 962(a)(7), (8)(B), 103 Stat. 500, 502; Nov. 28, 1990, Pub.L. 101–624, Title XXIII, § 2303(e), 104 Stat. 3981; Nov. 29, 1990, Pub.L. 101–647, Title XXV, §§ 2504(g), 2595(a)(5), 2597(i), 104 Stat. 4861, 4907, 4910; Sept. 13, 1994, Pub.L. 103–322, Title XXXIII, §§ 330002(d), 330008(8), 108 Stat. 2140, 2143; Oct. 13, 1994, Pub.L. 103–354, Title I, § 119(e), 108 Stat. 3208; Oct. 11, 1996, Pub.L. 104–294, Title VI, §§ 602(b), 604(b)(22), 605(b), 607(d), 110 Stat. 3503, 3508, 3509, 3511; Oct. 22, 1999, Pub.L. 106–78, Title VII, § 767, 113 Stat. 1174; Dec. 21, 2001, Pub.L. 107–100, § 4(a), 115 Stat. 966.)

HISTORICAL AND STATUTORY NOTES

References in Text

The Small Business Investment Act of 1958, referred to in text, is Pub.L. 85–699, Aug. 21, 1958, 72 Stat. 689, as amended, which is classified principally to chapter 14B of Title 15 (15 U.S.C.A. § 661 et seq.). See Short Title note set out under 15 U.S.C.A. § 661 and Tables for complete classification.

Section 1(b) of the International Banking Act of 1978, referred to in text, is classified to section 3101 of Title 12, Banks and Banking.

The Federal Reserve Act, referred to in text, is Act Dec. 23, 1913, c. 6, 38 Stat. 251, as amended, which is classified principally to chapter 3 of Title 12, 12 U.S.C.A. § 221 et seq. Section 25 of the Federal Reserve Act is classified to subchapter I of chapter 6 of Title 12, 12 U.S.C.A. § 601 et seq. Section 25(a) of the Federal Reserve Act, which is classified to subchapter II of chapter 6 of Title 12, 12 U.S.C.A. § 611 et seq., was renumbered section 25A by Pub.L. 102–242, Title I, § 142(e)(2), Dec. 10, 1991, 105 Stat. 2281. See Tables and 12 U.S.C.A. § 226 for complete classification.

Effective and Applicability Provisions

1996 Acts. Amendment by section 604 of Pub.L. 104–294 effective Sept. 13, 1994, see section 604(d) of Pub.L. 104–294, set out as a note under section 13 of this title.

Section 605(b) of Pub.L. 104–294 provided in part that amendment by such section 605(b) to section 961(h) of Pub.L. 101–73, which amended this section, was effective on the date of enactment of Pub.L. 101–73, which was approved Aug. 9, 1989.

1994 Acts. Amendment by section 119(e) of Pub.L. 103–354 effective Oct. 13, 1994, and applicable to provisions of crop insurance under the Federal Crop Insurance Act (section 1501 et seq. of Title 7, Agriculture) beginning with the 1995 crop year. With respect to the 1994 crop year, the Federal Crop Insurance Act (section 1501 et seq. of Title 7) as in effect on the day before Oct. 13, 1994, shall continue to apply. See section 120 of Pub.L. 103–354, set out as an Effective Date note under section 1502 of Title 7.

1959 Acts. Amendment by Pub.L. 86–168 effective Dec. 1, 1959 pursuant to section 104(k) of Pub.L. 86–168.

1956 Acts. Amendment by Act July 26, 1956 effective Jan. 1, 1957, see § 202(a) of Act July 26, 1956, set out as a note under § 1027 of Title 12, Banks and Banking.

Severability of Provisions

If any provision of Pub.L. 101–624 or the application thereof to any person or circumstance is held invalid, such invalidity not to affect other provisions or applications of Pub.L. 101–624 which can be given effect without regard to the invalid provision or application, see section 2519 of Pub.L. 101–624, set out as a note under section 1421 of Title 7, Agriculture.

If any provision of Pub.L. 101–73 or the application thereof to any person or circumstance is held invalid, the remainder of Pub.L. 101–73 and the application of the provision to other persons not similarly situated or to other circumstances not to be affected thereby, see section 1221 of Pub.L. 101–73, set out as a note under section 1811 of Title 12, Banks and Banking.

Abolition of Home Owners' Loan Corporation

For dissolution and abolishment of Home Owners' Loan Corporation, referred to in this section, by Act June 30, 1953, c. 170, § 21, 67 Stat. 126, see note under former § 1463 of Title 12, Banks and Banking.

Farm Credit Administration

Organization of Farm Credit Administration, see § 2241 et seq. of Title 12, Banks and Banking.

National Agricultural Credit Corporation

Title II of the Agricultural Credits Act, Act Mar. 4, 1923, c. 252, Title II, §§ 201 to 217, 42 Stat. 1461, which authorized the creation of national agricultural credit corporations, was repealed by Pub.L. 86–230, Sept. 8, 1959, § 24, 73 Stat. 466. Prior to such repeal, Act June 16, 1933, c. 101, § 77, 48 Stat. 292, had prohibited the creation, after June 16, 1933, of national agricultural credit corporations authorized to be formed under the Agricultural Credits Act.

Abolition of Reconstruction Finance Corporation

Section 6(a) of 1957 Reorg. Plan No. 1, eff. June 30, 1957, 22 F.R. 4633, 71 Stat. 647, set out in the Appendix to Title 5, Government Organization and Employees, abolished the Reconstruction Finance Corporation. See notes preceding former §§ 601 to 616 of Title 15, Commerce and Trade.

§ 1015. Naturalization, citizenship or alien registry

(a) Whoever knowingly makes any false statement under oath, in any case, proceeding, or matter relating to, or under, or by virtue of any law of the United States relating to naturalization, citizenship, or registry of aliens; or

(b) Whoever knowingly, with intent to avoid any duty or liability imposed or required by law, denies that he has been naturalized or admitted to be a citizen, after having been so naturalized or admitted; or

(c) Whoever uses or attempts to use any certificate of arrival, declaration of intention, certificate of naturalization, certificate of citizenship or other documentary evidence of naturalization or of citizenship, or any duplicate or copy thereof, knowing the same to have been procured by fraud or false evidence or without required appearance or hearing of the applicant in court or otherwise unlawfully obtained; or

(d) Whoever knowingly makes any false certificate, acknowledgment or statement concerning the appearance before him or the taking of an oath or affirmation or the signature, attestation or execution by any person with respect to any application, declaration, petition, affidavit, deposition, certificate of naturalization, certificate of citizenship or other paper or writing required or authorized by the laws relating to immigration, naturalization, citizenship, or registry of aliens; or

(e) Whoever knowingly makes any false statement or claim that he is, or at any time has been, a citizen or national of the United States, with the intent to obtain on behalf of himself, or any other person, any Federal or State benefit or service, or to engage unlawfully in employment in the United States; or

(f) Whoever knowingly makes any false statement or claim that he is a citizen of the United States in order to register to vote or to vote in any Federal, State, or local election (including an initiative, recall, or referendum)—

Shall be fined under this title or imprisoned not more than five years, or both. Subsection (f) does not apply to an alien if each natural parent of the alien (or, in the case of an adopted alien, each adoptive parent of the alien) is or was a citizen (whether by birth or naturalization), the alien permanently resided in the United States prior to attaining the age of 16, and the alien reasonably believed at the time of making the false statement or claim that he or she was a citizen of the United States.

(June 25, 1948, c. 645, 62 Stat. 752; Sept. 13, 1994, Pub.L. 103–322, Title XXXIII, § 330016(1)(K), 108 Stat. 2147; Sept. 30, 1996, Pub.L. 104–208, Div. C, Title II, § 215, 110 Stat. 3009–572; Oct. 30, 2000, Pub.L. 106–395, Title II, § 201(d)(2), 114 Stat. 1635.)

HISTORICAL AND STATUTORY NOTES

Effective and Applicability Provisions

2000 Acts. Amendments by Pub.L. 106–395 effective as if included in the enactment of section 215 of the Illegal Immigration Reform and Immigrant Responsibility Act of 1996 and applicable to an alien prosecuted on or after September 30, 1996, except in the case of an alien whose criminal proceeding (including judicial review thereof) has been finally concluded before the date of the enactment of this Act, see section 201(d)(3) of Pub.L. 106–395, set out as a note under 18 U.S.C.A. § 611.

Severability of Provisions

If any provision of Division C of Pub.L. 104–208 or the application of such provision to any person or circumstances is held to be unconstitutional, the remainder of Division C of Pub.L. 104–208 and the application of the provisions of Division C of Pub.L. 104–208 to any person or circumstance not to be affected thereby, see section 1(e) of Pub.L. 104–208, set out as a note under section 1101 of Title 8, Aliens and Nationality.

§ 1016. Acknowledgment of appearance or oath

Whoever, being an officer authorized to administer oaths or to take and certify acknowledgments, knowingly makes any false acknowledgment, certificate, or statement concerning the appearance before him or the taking of an oath or affirmation by any person with respect to any proposal, contract, bond, undertaking, or other matter submitted to, made with, or taken on behalf of the United States or any department or agency thereof, concerning which an oath or affirmation is required by law or lawful regulation, or with respect to the financial standing of any principal, surety, or other party to any such proposal, contract, bond, undertaking, or other instrument, shall be fined under this title or imprisoned not more than two years, or both.

(June 25, 1948, c. 645, 62 Stat. 753; Sept. 13, 1994, Pub.L. 103–322, Title XXXIII, § 330016(1)(I), 108 Stat. 2147.)

§ 1017. Government seals wrongfully used and instruments wrongfully sealed

Whoever fraudulently or wrongfully affixes or impresses the seal of any department or agency of the United States, to or upon any certificate, instrument, commission, document, or paper or with knowledge of its fraudulent character, with wrongful or fraudulent intent, uses, buys, procures, sells, or transfers to another any such certificate, instrument, commission, document, or paper, to which or upon which said seal has been so fraudulently affixed or impressed, shall be fined under this title or imprisoned not more than five years, or both.

(June 25, 1948, c. 645, 62 Stat. 753; Sept. 13, 1994, Pub.L. 103–322, Title XXXIII, § 330016(1)(K), 108 Stat. 2147.)

HISTORICAL AND STATUTORY NOTES

Canal Zone

Applicability of section to Canal Zone, see § 14 of this title.

§ 1018. Official certificates or writings

Whoever, being a public officer or other person authorized by any law of the United States to make or give a certificate or other writing, knowingly makes and delivers as true such a certificate or writing, containing any statement which he knows to be false, in a case where the punishment thereof is not elsewhere expressly provided by law, shall be fined under this title or imprisoned not more than one year, or both.

(June 25, 1948, c. 645, 62 Stat. 753; Sept. 13, 1994, Pub.L. 103–322, Title XXXIII, § 330016(1)(G), 108 Stat. 2147.)

§ 1019. Certificates by consular officers

Whoever, being a consul, or vice consul, or other person employed in the consular service of the United States, knowingly certifies falsely to any invoice, or other paper, to which his certificate is authorized or required by law, shall be fined under this title or imprisoned not more than three years, or both.

(June 25, 1948, c. 645, 62 Stat. 753; Sept. 13, 1994, Pub.L. 103–322, Title XXXIII, § 330016(1)(L), 108 Stat. 2147.)

§ 1020. Highway projects

Whoever, being an officer, agent, or employee of the United States, or of any State or Territory, or whoever, whether a person, association, firm, or corporation, knowingly makes any false statement, false representation, or false report as to the character, quality, quantity, or cost of the material used or to be used, or the quantity or quality of the work performed or to be performed, or the costs thereof in connection with the submission of plans, maps, specifications, contracts, or costs of construction of any highway or related project submitted for approval to the Secretary of Transportation; or

Whoever knowingly makes any false statement, false representation, false report, or false claim with respect to the character, quality, quantity, or cost of any work performed or to be performed, or materials furnished or to be furnished, in connection with the construction of any highway or related project approved by the Secretary of Transportation; or

Whoever knowingly makes any false statement or false representation as to a material fact in any statement, certificate, or report submitted pursuant to the provisions of the Federal-Aid Road Act approved July 11, 1916 (39 Stat. 355), as amended and supplemented,

Shall be fined under this title or imprisoned not more than five years, or both.

(June 25, 1948, c. 645, 62 Stat. 753; Oct. 31, 1951, c. 655, § 27, 65 Stat. 721; May 6, 1954, c. 181, § 18, 68 Stat. 76; Oct. 15, 1966, Pub.L. 89–670, § 10(f), 80 Stat. 948; Sept. 13, 1994, Pub.L. 103–322, Title XXXIII, § 330016(1)(L), 108 Stat. 2147; Oct. 11, 1996, Pub.L. 104–287, § 7(5), 110 Stat. 3400.)

HISTORICAL AND STATUTORY NOTES

References in Text

The Federal-Aid Road Act approved July 11, 1916 (39 Stat. 355), referred to in text, is Act July 11, 1916, c. 241, 39 Stat. 355, which was repealed by Pub.L. 85–767, § 2(1), Aug. 27, 1958, 72 Stat. 919. See Title 23, Highways.

Effective and Applicability Provisions

1966 Acts. Amendment by Pub.L. 89–670 effective Apr. 1, 1967 as prescribed by the President and published in the Federal Register, see § 15(a) of Pub.L. 89–670 and Ex. Ord. No. 11340, Mar. 30, 1967, 32 F.R. 5453, set out as notes under § 1651 of Title 49, Transportation.

Transfer of Functions

The Bureau of Public Roads, which is the principal road building agency of the Federal Government, and which was formerly under the Department of Agriculture, was redesignated the Public Roads Administration and, with its functions, transferred to the Federal Works Agency, and the functions of the Secretary of Agriculture, with respect thereto, were transferred to the Federal Works Administrator, by 1939 Reorg. Plan No. I, §§ 301, 302, eff. July 1, 1939, 4 F.R. 2727, 53 Stat. 1426, set out in the Appendix to Title 5. The Federal Property and Administrative Services Act of 1949, June 30, 1949, c. 288, Title I, § 103, 63 Stat. 380 (see now 40 U.S.C.A. § 303(b)), abolished the Federal Works Agency, transferred its functions, the functions of all agencies thereof, the functions of the Federal Works Administrator, and the functions of the Commissioner of Public Roads, to the Administrator of General Services, and transferred the Public Roads Administration, which it redesignated the Bureau of Public Roads, to the General Services Administration. 1949 Reorg. Plan No. 7, eff. Aug. 19, 1949, 14 F.R. 5228, 63 Stat. 1070, set out in the Appendix to Title 5, transferred such bureau and its functions and personnel to the Department of Commerce, and transferred the functions of the Administrator of General Services, with respect thereto, to the Secretary of Commerce, to be performed by him or, subject to his direction and control, by such officers, employees and agencies of the Department of Commerce as he should designate. 1950 Reorg. Plan No. 5, eff. May 24, 1950, 15 F.R. 3174, 64 Stat. 1263, set out in the Appendix to Title 5, transferred, with certain exceptions not applicable to this section, all functions of all other officers of the Department of Commerce, and all functions of all agencies and employees of such Department, to the Secretary of Commerce, with power vested in him to authorize their performance, or the performance of any of his functions, by any of such other officers, or by any agency or employee of the Department of Commerce.

Repeals

Pub.L. 89–670, § 10(f), Oct. 15, 1966, 80 Stat. 948, appearing in the credit of this section, was repealed by Pub.L. 104–287, § 7(5), Oct. 11, 1996, 110 Stat. 3400.

§ 1021. Title records

Whoever, being an officer or other person authorized by any law of the United States to record a conveyance of real property or any other instrument which by such law may be recorded, knowingly certifies falsely that such conveyance or instrument has or has not been recorded, shall be fined under this title or imprisoned not more than five years, or both.

(June 25, 1948, c. 645, 62 Stat. 754; Sept. 13, 1994, Pub.L. 103–322, Title XXXIII, § 330016(1)(H), 108 Stat. 2147.)

§ 1022. Delivery of certificate, voucher, receipt for military or naval property

Whoever, being authorized to make or deliver any certificate, voucher, receipt, or other paper certifying the receipt of arms, ammunition, provisions, clothing, or other property used or to be used in the military or naval service, makes or delivers the same to any other person without a full knowledge of the truth of the facts stated therein and with intent to defraud the United States, or any agency thereof, shall be fined under this title or imprisoned not more than ten years, or both.

(June 25, 1948, c. 645, 62 Stat. 754; Sept. 13, 1994, Pub.L. 103–322, Title XXXIII, § 330016(1)(L), 108 Stat. 2147.)

§ 1023. Insufficient delivery of money or property for military or naval service

Whoever, having charge, possession, custody, or control of any money or other public property used or to be used in the military or naval service, with intent to defraud the United States, or any agency thereof, or any corporation in which the United States has a proprietary interest, or intending to conceal such money or other property, delivers to any person having authority to receive the same any amount of such money or other property less than that for which he received a certificate or took a receipt, shall be fined under this title or imprisoned not more than ten years, or both.

(June 25, 1948, c. 645, 62 Stat. 754; Sept. 13, 1994, Pub.L. 103–322, Title XXXIII, § 330016(1)(L), 108 Stat. 2147.)

§ 1024. Purchase or receipt of military, naval, or veteran's facilities property

Whoever purchases, or receives in pledge from any person any arms, equipment, ammunition, clothing, military stores, or other property furnished by the United States under a clothing allowance or otherwise, to any member of the Armed Forces of the United States or of the National Guard or Naval Militia, or to any person accompanying, serving, or retained with the land or naval forces and subject to military or naval law, or to any former member of such Armed Forces at or by any hospital, home, or facility maintained by the United States, having knowledge or reason to believe that the property has been taken from the possession of or furnished by the United States under such allowance, or otherwise, shall be fined under this title or imprisoned not more than two years, or both.

(June 25, 1948, c. 645, 62 Stat. 754; Sept. 13, 1994, Pub.L. 103–322, Title XXXIII, § 330016(1)(G), 108 Stat. 2147.)

HISTORICAL AND STATUTORY NOTES

Canal Zone

Applicability of section to Canal Zone, see § 14 of this title.

§ 1025. False pretenses on high seas and other waters

Whoever, upon any waters or vessel within the special maritime and territorial jurisdiction of the United States, by any fraud, or false pretense, obtains from any person anything of value, or procures the execution and delivery of any instrument of writing or conveyance of real or personal property, or the signature of any person, as maker, endorser, or guarantor, to or upon any bond, bill, receipt, promissory note, draft, or check, or any other evidence of indebtedness, or fraudulently sells, barters, or disposes of any bond, bill, receipt, promissory note, draft, or check, or other evidence of indebtedness, for value, knowing the same to be worthless, or knowing the signature of the maker, endorser, or guarantor thereof to have been obtained by any false pretenses, shall be fined under this title or imprisoned not more than five years, or both; but if the amount, value or the face value of anything so obtained does not exceed $1,000, he shall be fined under this title or imprisoned not more than one year, or both.

(June 25, 1948, c. 645, 62 Stat. 755; May 24, 1949, c. 139, § 22, 63 Stat. 92; Sept. 13, 1994, Pub.L. 103–322, Title XXXIII, § 330016(1)(H), (K), 108 Stat. 2147; Oct. 11, 1996, Pub.L. 104–294, Title VI, § 606(a), 110 Stat. 3511.)

§ 1026. Compromise, adjustment, or cancellation of farm indebtedness

Whoever knowingly makes any false statement for the purpose of influencing in any way the action of the Secretary of Agriculture, or of any person acting under his authority, in connection with any compromise, adjustment, or cancellation of any farm indebtedness as provided by sections 1150, 1150a, and 1150b of Title 12, shall be fined under this title or imprisoned not more than one year, or both.

(June 25, 1948, c. 645, 62 Stat. 755; Sept. 13, 1994, Pub.L. 103–322, Title XXXIII, § 330016(1)(H), 108 Stat. 2147.)

§ 1027. False statements and concealment of facts in relation to documents required by the Employee Retirement Income Security Act of 1974

Whoever, in any document required by title I of the Employee Retirement Income Security Act of 1974 (as amended from time to time) to be published, or kept as part of the records of any employee welfare benefit plan or employee pension benefit plan, or certified to the administrator of any such plan, makes any false statement or representation of fact, knowing it to be false, or knowingly conceals, covers up, or fails to disclose any fact the disclosure of which is required by such title or is necessary to verify, explain, clarify or check for accuracy and completeness any report required by such title to be published or any information required by such title to be certified, shall be fined under this title, or imprisoned not more than five years, or both.

(Added Pub.L. 87–420, § 17(c), Mar. 20, 1962, 76 Stat. 42, and amended Pub.L. 93–406, Title I, § 111(a)(2)(B)(i), (ii), Sept. 2, 1974, 88 Stat. 851; Pub.L. 103–322, Title XXXIII, § 330016(1)(L), Sept. 13, 1994, 108 Stat. 2147.)

HISTORICAL AND STATUTORY NOTES

References in Text

Title I of the Employee Retirement Income Security Act of 1974, referred to in text, is classified to § 1001 et seq. of Title 29, Labor.

Effective and Applicability Provisions

1974 Acts. Amendment by Pub.L. 93–406 effective Jan. 1, 1975, except as provided in § 1031(b)(2) of Title 29, Labor, see § 1031(b)(1) of Title 29.

1962 Acts. Section effective 90 days after Mar. 20, 1962, see § 19 of Pub.L. 87–420, set out as a note under § 302 of Title 29, Labor.

§ 1028. Fraud and related activity in connection with identification documents, authentication features, and information [1]

(a) Whoever, in a circumstance described in subsection (c) of this section—

(1) knowingly and without lawful authority produces an identification document, authentication feature, or a false identification document;

(2) knowingly transfers an identification document, authentication feature, or a false identification document knowing that such document or feature was stolen or produced without lawful authority;

(3) knowingly possesses with intent to use unlawfully or transfer unlawfully five or more identification documents (other than those issued lawfully for the use of the possessor), authentication features, or false identification documents;

(4) knowingly possesses an identification document (other than one issued lawfully for the use of the possessor), authentication feature, or a false identification document, with the intent such document or feature be used to defraud the United States;

(5) knowingly produces, transfers, or possesses a document-making implement or authentication feature with the intent such document-making implement or authentication feature will be used in the production of a false identification document or another document-making implement or authentication feature which will be so used;

(6) knowingly possesses an identification document or authentication feature that is or appears to be an identification document or authentication feature of the United States or a sponsoring entity of an event designated as a special event of national significance which is stolen or produced without lawful authority knowing that such document or feature was stolen or produced without such authority;

(7) knowingly transfers, possesses, or uses, without lawful authority, a means of identification of another person with the intent to commit, or to aid or abet, or in connection with, any unlawful activity that constitutes a violation of Federal law, or that constitutes a felony under any applicable State or local law; or

(8) knowingly traffics in false or actual authentication features for use in false identification documents, document-making implements, or means of identification;

shall be punished as provided in subsection (b) of this section.

(b) The punishment for an offense under subsection (a) of this section is—

(1) except as provided in paragraphs (3) and (4), a fine under this title or imprisonment for not more than 15 years, or both, if the offense is—

(A) the production or transfer of an identification document, authentication feature, or false identification document that is or appears to be—

(i) an identification document or authentication feature issued by or under the authority of the United States; or

(ii) a birth certificate, or a driver's license or personal identification card;

(B) the production or transfer of more than five identification documents, authentication features, or false identification documents;

(C) an offense under paragraph (5) of such subsection; or

(D) an offense under paragraph (7) of such subsection that involves the transfer, possession, or use of 1 or more means of identification if, as a result of the offense, any individual committing the offense obtains anything of value aggregating $1,000 or more during any 1-year period;

(2) except as provided in paragraphs (3) and (4), a fine under this title or imprisonment for not more than 5 years, or both, if the offense is—

(A) any other production, transfer, or use of a means of identification, an identification document,,[2] authentication feature, or a false identification document; or

(B) an offense under paragraph (3) or (7) of such subsection;

(3) a fine under this title or imprisonment for not more than 20 years, or both, if the offense is committed—

(A) to facilitate a drug trafficking crime (as defined in section 929(a)(2));

(B) in connection with a crime of violence (as defined in section 924(c)(3)); or

(C) after a prior conviction under this section becomes final;

(4) a fine under this title or imprisonment for not more than 30 years, or both, if the offense is committed to facilitate an act of domestic terrorism (as defined under section 2331(5) of this title) or an act of international terrorism (as defined in section 2331(1) of this title);

(5) in the case of any offense under subsection (a), forfeiture to the United States of any personal property used or intended to be used to commit the offense; and

(6) a fine under this title or imprisonment for not more than one year, or both, in any other case.

(c) The circumstance referred to in subsection (a) of this section is that—

(1) the identification document, authentication feature, or false identification document is or appears to be issued by or under the authority of the United States or a sponsoring entity of an event designated as a special event of national significance or the document-making implement is designed or suited for making such an identification document, authentication feature, or false identification document;

(2) the offense is an offense under subsection (a)(4) of this section; or

(3) either—

(A) the production, transfer, possession, or use prohibited by this section is in or affects interstate or foreign commerce, including the transfer of a document by electronic means; or

(B) the means of identification, identification document, false identification document, or document-making implement is transported in the mail in the course of the production, transfer, possession, or use prohibited by this section.

(d) In this section and section 1028A—

(1) the term "authentication feature" means any hologram, watermark, certification, symbol, code, image, sequence of numbers or letters, or other feature that either individually or in combination with another feature is used by the issuing authority on an identification document, document-making implement, or means of identification to determine if the document is counterfeit, altered, or otherwise falsified;

(2) the term "document-making implement" means any implement, impression, template, computer file, computer disc, electronic device, or computer hardware or software, that is specifically configured or primarily used for making an identification document, a false identification document, or another document-making implement;

(3) the term "identification document" means a document made or issued by or under the authority of the United States Government, a State, political subdivision of a State, a sponsoring entity of an event designated as a special event of national significance, a foreign government, political subdivision of a foreign government, an international governmental or an international quasi-governmental organization which, when completed with information concerning a particular individual, is of a type intended or commonly accepted for the purpose of identification of individuals;

(4) the term "false identification document" means a document of a type intended or commonly accepted for the purposes of identification of individuals that—

(A) is not issued by or under the authority of a governmental entity or was issued under the authority of a governmental entity but was subsequently altered for purposes of deceit; and

(B) appears to be issued by or under the authority of the United States Government, a State, a political subdivision of a State, a sponsoring entity of an event designated by the President as a special event of national significance, a foreign government, a political subdivision of a foreign government, or an international governmental or quasi-governmental organization;

(5) the term "false authentication feature" means an authentication feature that—

(A) is genuine in origin, but, without the authorization of the issuing authority, has been tampered with or altered for purposes of deceit;

(B) is genuine, but has been distributed, or is intended for distribution, without the authorization of the issuing authority and not in connection with a lawfully made identification document, document-making implement, or means of identification to which such authentication feature is intended to be affixed or embedded by the respective issuing authority; or

(C) appears to be genuine, but is not;

(6) the term "issuing authority"—

(A) means any governmental entity or agency that is authorized to issue identification documents, means of identification, or authentication features; and

(B) includes the United States Government, a State, a political subdivision of a State, a sponsoring entity of an event designated by the President as a special event of national significance, a foreign government, a political subdivision of a foreign government, or an international government or quasi-governmental organization;

(7) the term "means of identification" means any name or number that may be used, alone or in conjunction with any other information, to identify a specific individual, including any—

(A) name, social security number, date of birth, official State or government issued driver's license or identification number, alien registration number, government passport number, employer or taxpayer identification number;

(B) unique biometric data, such as fingerprint, voice print, retina or iris image, or other unique physical representation;

(C) unique electronic identification number, address, or routing code; or

(D) telecommunication identifying information or access device (as defined in section 1029(e));

(8) the term "personal identification card" means an identification document issued by a State or local government solely for the purpose of identification;

(9) the term "produce" includes alter, authenticate, or assemble;

(10) the term "transfer" includes selecting an identification document, false identification document, or document-making implement and placing or directing the placement of such identification document, false identification document, or document-making implement on an online location where it is available to others;

(11) the term "State" includes any State of the United States, the District of Columbia, the Commonwealth of Puerto Rico, and any other commonwealth, possession, or territory of the United States; and

(12) the term "traffic" means—

(A) to transport, transfer, or otherwise dispose of, to another, as consideration for anything of value; or

(B) to make or obtain control of with intent to so transport, transfer, or otherwise dispose of.

(e) This section does not prohibit any lawfully authorized investigative, protective, or intelligence activity of a law enforcement agency of the United States, a State, or a political subdivision of a State, or of an intelligence agency of the United States, or any activity authorized under chapter 224 of this title.

(f) Attempt and conspiracy.—Any person who attempts or conspires to commit any offense under this section shall be subject to the same penalties as those prescribed for the offense, the commission of which was the object of the attempt or conspiracy.

(g) Forfeiture procedures.—The forfeiture of property under this section, including any seizure and disposition of the property and any related judicial or administrative proceeding, shall be governed by the provisions of section 413 (other than subsection (d) of that section) of the Comprehensive Drug Abuse Prevention and Control Act of 1970 (21 U.S.C. 853).

(h) Forfeiture; disposition.—In the circumstance in which any person is convicted of a violation of subsection (a), the court shall order, in addition to the penalty prescribed, the forfeiture and destruction or other disposition of all illicit authentication features, identification documents, document-making implements, or means of identification.

(i) Rule of construction.—For purpose of subsection (a)(7), a single identification document or false identification document that contains 1 or more means of identification shall be construed to be 1 means of identification.

(Added Pub.L. 97–398, § 2, Dec. 31, 1982, 96 Stat. 2009, and amended Pub.L. 99–646, § 44(a), Nov. 10, 1986, 100 Stat. 3601; Pub.L. 100–690, Title VII, § 7023, Nov. 18, 1988, 102 Stat. 4397; Pub.L. 101–647, Title XII, § 1205(e), Nov. 29, 1990, 104 Stat. 4831; Pub.L. 103–322, Title XXXIII, § 330016(1)(K), (M), (O), Sept. 13, 1994, 108 Stat. 2147, 2148; Pub.L. 104–208, Div. C, Title II, § 211(a)(1), Sept. 30, 1996, 110 Stat. 3009–569; Pub.L. 104–294, Title VI, § 601(a)(3), (p), Oct. 11, 1996, 110 Stat. 3498, 3502; Pub.L. 105–318, § 3(a) to (g), (h)(1), Oct. 30, 1998, 112 Stat. 3007 to 3009; Pub.L. 106–578, § 3, Title VI, Dec. 28, 2000, 114 Stat. 3076; Pub.L. 108–21, Title VI, § 607(b), Apr. 30, 2003, 117 Stat. 689; Pub.L. 108–275, §§ 2(c), 3, July 15, 2004, 118 Stat. 832; Pub.L. 108–458, Title VII, § 7216, Dec. 17, 2004, 118 Stat. 3833; Pub.L. 109–13, Div. B, Title II, § 203(a), May 11, 2005, 119 Stat. 315; Pub.L. 109–177, Title VI, § 603, Mar. 9, 2006, 120 Stat. 253.)

1 Section catchline amended by Pub.L. 108–21 without corresponding amendment to analysis.

2 So in original.

HISTORICAL AND STATUTORY NOTES

Effective and Applicability Provisions

2004 Acts. Notwithstanding any other provision of Pub.L. 108–458, Pub.L. 108–458, Title VII, Subtitle B (§§ 7201 to 7220), to take effect on Dec. 17, 2004, see Pub.L. 108–458, § 7219, which is set out as a note under 8 U.S.C.A. § 1202.

2000 Acts. Pub.L. 106–578, § 5, Dec. 28, 2000, 114 Stat. 3077, provided that: "This Act and the amendments made by this Act [amending this section, repealing section 1738 of this title, and enacting provisions set out as notes under this section] shall take effect 90 days after the date of enactment of this Act [Dec. 28, 2000]."

1996 Acts. Section 211(c) of Div. C of Pub.L. 104–208 provided that: "This section and the amendments made by this section [amending subsec. (b) of this section and sections 1425, 1426, 1427, 1541, 1542, 1543, 1544, and 1546 of this title and enacting a provision set out as a note under section 994 of Title 28, Judiciary and Judicial Procedure] shall apply with respect to offenses occurring on or after the date of the enactment of this Act [Sept. 30, 1996]."

Severability of Provisions

If any provision of Division C of Pub.L. 104–208 or the application of such provision to any person or circumstances is held to be unconstitutional, the remainder of Division C of Pub.L. 104–208 and the application of the provisions of Division C of Pub.L. 104–208 to any person or circumstance not to be affected thereby, see section 1(e) of Pub.L. 104–208, set out as a note under section 1101 of Title 8, Aliens and Nationality.

Coordinating Committee on False Identification

Pub.L. 106–578, § 2, Dec. 28, 2000, 114 Stat. 3075, provided that:

"(a) In general.—The Attorney General and the Secretary of the Treasury shall establish a coordinating committee to ensure, through existing interagency task forces or other means, that the creation and distribution of false identification documents (as defined in section 1028(d)(3) of title 18, United States Code, as added by section 3(2) of this Act [Pub.L. 106–578, § 3(2), Dec. 28, 2000, 114 Stat. 3075]) is vigorously investigated and prosecuted.

"(b) Membership.—The coordinating committee shall consist of the Director of the United States Secret Service, the Director of the Federal Bureau of Investigation, the Attorney General, the Commissioner of Social Security, and the Commissioner of Immigration and Naturalization, or their respective designees.

"(c) Term.—The coordinating committee shall terminate 2 years after the effective date of this Act [For effective date provisions see Pub.L. 106–578, § 5, Dec. 28, 2000, 114 Stat. 1077, set out as a note under this section.].

"(d) Report.—

"(1) In general.—The Attorney General and the Secretary of the Treasury, at the end of each year of the existence of the committee, shall report to the Committee on the Judiciary of the Senate and the Committee on the Judiciary of the House of Representatives on the activities of the committee.

"(2) Contents.—The report referred to in paragraph (1) shall include—

"(A) the total number of indictments and informations, guilty pleas, convictions, and acquittals resulting from the investigation and prosecution of the creation and distribution of false identification documents during the preceding year;

"(B) identification of the Federal judicial districts in which the indictments and informations were filed, and in which the subsequent guilty pleas, convictions, and acquittals occurred;

"(C) specification of the Federal statutes utilized for prosecution;

"(D) a brief factual description of significant investigations and prosecutions;

"(E) specification of the sentence imposed as a result of each guilty plea and conviction; and

"(F) recommendations, if any, for legislative changes that could facilitate more effective investigation and prosecution of the creation and distribution of false identification documents."

[Amendment by Pub.L. 106–578, § 2, effective 90 days after December 28, 2000, see Pub.L. 106–578, § 5, set out as a note under this section.]

[For transfer of the functions, personnel, assets, and obligations of the United States Secret Service, including the functions of the Secretary of the Treasury relating thereto, to the Secretary of Homeland Security, and for treatment of related references, see 6 U.S.C.A. §§ 381, 551(d), 552(d) and 557, and the Department of Homeland Security Reorganization Plan of November 25, 2002, as modified, set out as a note under 6 U.S.C.A. § 542.]

[For abolition of Immigration and Naturalization Service, transfer of functions, and treatment of related references, see note set out under 8 U.S.C.A. § 1551].

Constitutional Authority to Enact Identity Theft and Assumption Deterrence Act of 1998

Pub.L. 105–318, § 2, Oct. 30, 1998, 112 Stat. 3007, provided that: "The constitutional authority upon which this Act [Identity Theft and Assumption Deterrence Act of 1998, Pub.L. 105–318, Oct. 30, 1998, 112 Stat. 3007, for complete classification of which, see Tables] rests is the power of Congress to regulate commerce with foreign nations and among the several States, and the authority to make all laws which shall be necessary and proper for carrying into execution the powers vested by the Constitution in the Government of the United States or in any department or officer thereof, as set forth in article I, section 8 of the United States Constitution."

Centralized Complaint and Consumer Education Service for Victims of Identity Theft

Pub.L. 105–318, § 5, Oct. 30, 1998, 112 Stat. 3010, provided that:

"(a) In general.—Not later than 1 year after the date of enactment of this Act [Oct. 30, 1998], the Federal Trade Commission shall establish procedures to—

"(1) log and acknowledge the receipt of complaints by individuals who certify that they have a reasonable belief that 1 or more of their means of identification (as defined in section 1028 of title 18, United States Code, as amended by this Act [Identity Theft and Assumption Deterrence Act of 1998, Pub.L. 105–318, Oct. 30, 1998, 112 Stat. 3007, for complete classification of which, see Tables]) have been assumed, stolen, or otherwise unlawfully acquired in violation of section 1028 of title 18, United States Code, as amended by this Act;

"(2) provide informational materials to individuals described in paragraph (1); and

"(3) refer complaints described in paragraph (1) to appropriate entities, which may include referral to—

"(A) the 3 major national consumer reporting agencies; and

"(B) appropriate law enforcement agencies for potential law enforcement action.

"(b) Authorization of appropriations.—There are authorized to be appropriated such sums as may be necessary to carry out this section."

Fraud and Related Activity in Connection With Identification Documents

Pub.L. 98–473, Title II, § 609L, Oct. 12, 1984, 98 Stat. 2103, provided that:

"(a) For purposes of section 1028 of title 18, United States Code, [this section], to the maximum extent feasible, personal descriptors or identifiers utilized in identification documents, as defined in such section, shall utilize common descriptive terms and formats designed to—

"(1) reduce the redundancy and duplication of identification systems by providing information which can be utilized by the maximum number of authorities, and

"(2) facilitate positive identification of bona fide holders of identification documents.

"(b) The President shall, no later than 3 years after the date of enactment of this Act [Oct. 12, 1984], and after consultation with Federal, State, local, and international issuing authorities, and concerned groups make recommendations [sic] to the Congress for the enactment of comprehensive legislation on Federal identification systems. Such legislation shall—

"(1) give due consideration to protecting the privacy of persons who are the subject of any identification system,

"(2) recommend appropriate civil and criminal sanctions for the misuse or unauthorized disclosure of personal identification information, and

"(3) make recommendations providing for the exchange of personal identification information as authorized by

Federal or State law or Executive order of the President or the chief executive officer of any of the several States."

§ 1028A. Aggravated identity theft

(a) Offenses.—

(1) In general.—Whoever, during and in relation to any felony violation enumerated in subsection (c), knowingly transfers, possesses, or uses, without lawful authority, a means of identification of another person shall, in addition to the punishment provided for such felony, be sentenced to a term of imprisonment of 2 years.

(2) Terrorism offense.—Whoever, during and in relation to any felony violation enumerated in section 2332b(g)(5)(B), knowingly transfers, possesses, or uses, without lawful authority, a means of identification of another person or a false identification document shall, in addition to the punishment provided for such felony, be sentenced to a term of imprisonment of 5 years.

(b) Consecutive sentence.—Notwithstanding any other provision of law—

(1) a court shall not place on probation any person convicted of a violation of this section;

(2) except as provided in paragraph (4), no term of imprisonment imposed on a person under this section shall run concurrently with any other term of imprisonment imposed on the person under any other provision of law, including any term of imprisonment imposed for the felony during which the means of identification was transferred, possessed, or used;

(3) in determining any term of imprisonment to be imposed for the felony during which the means of identification was transferred, possessed, or used, a court shall not in any way reduce the term to be imposed for such crime so as to compensate for, or otherwise take into account, any separate term of imprisonment imposed or to be imposed for a violation of this section; and

(4) a term of imprisonment imposed on a person for a violation of this section may, in the discretion of the court, run concurrently, in whole or in part, only with another term of imprisonment that is imposed by the court at the same time on that person for an additional violation of this section, provided that such discretion shall be exercised in accordance with any applicable guidelines and policy statements issued by the Sentencing Commission pursuant to section 994 of title 28.

(c) Definition.—For purposes of this section, the term "felony violation enumerated in subsection (c)" means any offense that is a felony violation of—

(1) section 641 (relating to theft of public money, property, or rewards), section 656 (relating to theft, embezzlement, or misapplication by bank officer or employee), or section 664 (relating to theft from employee benefit plans);

(2) section 911 (relating to false personation of citizenship);

(3) section 922(a)(6) (relating to false statements in connection with the acquisition of a firearm);

(4) any provision contained in this chapter (relating to fraud and false statements), other than this section or section 1028(a)(7);

(5) any provision contained in chapter 63 (relating to mail, bank, and wire fraud);

(6) any provision contained in chapter 69 (relating to nationality and citizenship);

(7) any provision contained in chapter 75 (relating to passports and visas);

(8) section 523 of the Gramm–Leach–Bliley Act (15 U.S.C. 6823) (relating to obtaining customer information by false pretenses);

(9) section 243 or 266 of the Immigration and Nationality Act (8 U.S.C. 1253 and 1306) (relating to willfully failing to leave the United States after deportation and creating a counterfeit alien registration card);

(10) any provision contained in chapter 8 of title II of the Immigration and Nationality Act (8 U.S.C. 1321 et seq.) (relating to various immigration offenses); or

(11) section 208, 811, 1107(b), 1128B(a), or 1632 of the Social Security Act (42 U.S.C. 408, 1011, 1307(b), 1320a–7b(a), and 1383a) (relating to false statements relating to programs under the Act).

(Added Pub.L. 108–275, § 2(a), July 15, 2004, 118 Stat. 831.)

HISTORICAL AND STATUTORY NOTES

References in Text

Chapter 63 of Title 18, referred to in subsec. (c)(5), is classified to 18 U.S.C.A. § 1341 et seq.

Chapter 69, referred to in subsec. (c)(6), is classified to 18 U.S.C.A. § 1421 et seq.

Chapter 75, referred to in subsec. (c)(7), is classified to 18 U.S.C.A. § 1541 et seq.

Section 523 of the Gramm–Leach–Bliley Act, referred to in subsec. (c)(8), is Pub.L. 106–102, Title V, § 523, Nov. 12, 1999, 113 Stat. 1448, which is classified to 15 U.S.C.A. § 6823.

Section 243 or 266 of the Immigration and Nationality Act, referred to in subsec. (c)(9), is Act June 27, 1952, c. 477, Title II, § 243 or 266, 66 Stat. 212, 225, as amended, which is classified to 8 U.S.C.A. § 1253 or 1306.

Chapter 8 of title II of the Immigration and Nationality Act, referred to in subsec. (c)(10), is Act June 27, 1952, c. 477, Title II, ch. 8 [§ 271 et seq.], 66 Stat. 226, as amended, which is classified to part VIII of subchapter II of chapter 12 of Title 8, 8 U.S.C.A. § 1321 et seq.

Section 208 of the Social Security Act, referred to in subsec. (c)(11), is Act Aug. 14, 1935, c. 531, Title II, § 208, 49 Stat. 625, as amended, which is classified to 42 U.S.C.A. § 408.

Section 811 of the Social Security Act, referred to in subsec. (c)(11), is Act Aug. 14, 1935, c. 531, Title VIII, § 811, as added Dec. 14, 1999, Pub.L. 106–169, Title II, § 251(a), 113 Stat. 1852, and amended, which is classified to 42 U.S.C.A. § 1011.

Section 1107(b) of the Social Security Act, referred to in subsec. (c)(11), is Act Aug. 14, 1935, c. 531, Title XI, § 1107, as added Aug. 10, 1939, c. 666, Title VIII, § 802, 53 Stat. 1398, and amended, which is classified to 42 U.S.C.A. § 1307(b).

Section 1128B(A) of the Social Security Act, referred to in subsec. (c)(11), is Act Aug. 14, 1935, c. 531, Title XI, § 1128B, formerly Title XVIII, § 1877(d), and Title XIX, § 1909, as added and amended Oct. 30, 1972, Pub.L. 92–603, Title II, §§ 242(c), 278(b)(9), 86 Stat. 1419, 1454, which is classified to 42 U.S.C.A. § 1320a-7b(a).

Section 1632 of the Social Security Act, referred to in subsec. (c)(11), is Act Aug. 14, 1935, c. 531, Title XVI, 1632, as added Oct. 30, 1972, Pub.L. 92–603, Title III, 301, 86 Stat. 1478, and amended, which is classified to 42 U.S.C.A. § 1383a.

§ 1029. Fraud and related activity in connection with access devices

(a) Whoever—

(1) knowingly and with intent to defraud produces, uses, or traffics in one or more counterfeit access devices;

(2) knowingly and with intent to defraud traffics in or uses one or more unauthorized access devices during any one-year period, and by such conduct obtains anything of value aggregating $1,000 or more during that period;

(3) knowingly and with intent to defraud possesses fifteen or more devices which are counterfeit or unauthorized access devices;

(4) knowingly, and with intent to defraud, produces, traffics in, has control or custody of, or possesses device-making equipment;

(5) knowingly and with intent to defraud effects transactions, with 1 or more access devices issued to another person or persons, to receive payment or any other thing of value during any 1-year period the aggregate value of which is equal to or greater than $1,000;

(6) without the authorization of the issuer of the access device, knowingly and with intent to defraud solicits a person for the purpose of—

(A) offering an access device; or

(B) selling information regarding or an application to obtain an access device;

(7) knowingly and with intent to defraud uses, produces, traffics in, has control or custody of, or possesses a telecommunications instrument that has been modified or altered to obtain unauthorized use of telecommunications services;

(8) knowingly and with intent to defraud uses, produces, traffics in, has control or custody of, or possesses a scanning receiver;

(9) knowingly uses, produces, traffics in, has control or custody of, or possesses hardware or software, knowing it has been configured to insert or modify telecommunication identifying information associated with or contained in a telecommunications instrument so that such instrument may be used to obtain telecommunications service without authorization; or

(10) without the authorization of the credit card system member or its agent, knowingly and with intent to defraud causes or arranges for another person to present to the member or its agent, for payment, 1 or more evidences or records of transactions made by an access device;

shall, if the offense affects interstate or foreign commerce, be punished as provided in subsection (c) of this section.

(b)(1) Whoever attempts to commit an offense under subsection (a) of this section shall be subject to the same penalties as those prescribed for the offense attempted.

(2) Whoever is a party to a conspiracy of two or more persons to commit an offense under subsection (a) of this section, if any of the parties engages in any conduct in furtherance of such offense, shall be fined an amount not greater than the amount provided as the maximum fine for such offense under subsection (c) of this section or imprisoned not longer than one-half the period provided as the maximum imprisonment for such offense under subsection (c) of this section, or both.

(c) Penalties.—

(1) Generally.—The punishment for an offense under subsection (a) of this section is—

(A) in the case of an offense that does not occur after a conviction for another offense under this section—

(i) if the offense is under paragraph (1), (2), (3), (6), (7), or (10) of subsection (a), a fine under this title or imprisonment for not more than 10 years, or both; and

(ii) if the offense is under paragraph (4), (5), (8), or (9) of subsection (a), a fine under this title or imprisonment for not more than 15 years, or both;

(B) in the case of an offense that occurs after a conviction for another offense under this section, a fine under this title or imprisonment for not more than 20 years, or both; and

(C) in either case, forfeiture to the United States of any personal property used or intended to be used to commit the offense.

(2) Forfeiture procedure.—The forfeiture of property under this section, including any seizure and disposition of the property and any related administrative and judicial proceeding, shall be governed by section 413 of the Controlled Substances Act, except for subsection (d) of that section.

(d) The United States Secret Service shall, in addition to any other agency having such authority, have the authority to investigate offenses under this section. Such authority of the United States Secret Service shall be exercised in accordance with an agreement which shall be entered into by the Secretary of the Treasury and the Attorney General.

(e) As used in this section—

(1) the term "access device" means any card, plate, code, account number, electronic serial number, mobile identification number, personal identification number, or other telecommunications service, equipment, or instrument identifier, or other means of account access that can be used, alone or in conjunction with another access device, to obtain money, goods, services, or any other thing of value, or that can be used to initiate a transfer of funds (other than a transfer originated solely by paper instrument);

(2) the term "counterfeit access device" means any access device that is counterfeit, fictitious, altered, or forged, or an identifiable component of an access device or a counterfeit access device;

(3) the term "unauthorized access device" means any access device that is lost, stolen, expired, revoked, canceled, or obtained with intent to defraud;

(4) the term "produce" includes design, alter, authenticate, duplicate, or assemble;

(5) the term "traffic" means transfer, or otherwise dispose of, to another, or obtain control of with intent to transfer or dispose of;

(6) the term "device-making equipment" means any equipment, mechanism, or impression designed or primarily used for making an access device or a counterfeit access device;

(7) The term "credit card system member" means a financial institution or other entity that is a member of a credit card system, including an entity, whether affiliated with or identical to the credit card issuer, that is the sole member of a credit card system;

(8) the term "scanning receiver" means a device or apparatus that can be used to intercept a wire or electronic communication in violation of chapter 119 or to intercept an electronic serial number, mobile identification number, or other identifier of any telecommunications service, equipment, or instrument;

(9) the term "telecommunications service" has the meaning given such term in section 3 of title I of the Communications Act of 1934 (47 U.S.C. 153);

(10) the term "facilities-based carrier" means an entity that owns communications transmission facilities, is responsible for the operation and maintenance of those facilities, and holds an operating license issued by the Federal Communications Commission under the authority of title III of the Communications Act of 1934; and

(11) the term "telecommunication identifying information" means electronic serial number or any other number or signal that identifies a specific telecommunications instrument or account, or a specific communication transmitted from a telecommunications instrument.

(f) This section does not prohibit any lawfully authorized investigative, protective, or intelligence activity of a law enforcement agency of the United States, a State, or a political subdivision of a State, or of an intelligence agency of the United States, or any activity authorized under chapter 224 of this title. For purposes of this subsection, the term "State" includes a State of the United States, the District of Columbia, and any commonwealth, territory, or possession of the United States.

(g)(1) It is not a violation of subsection (a)(9) for an officer, employee, or agent of, or a person engaged in business with, a facilities-based carrier, to engage in conduct (other than trafficking) otherwise prohibited by that subsection for the purpose of protecting the property or legal rights of that carrier, unless such conduct is for the purpose of obtaining telecommunications service provided by another facilities-based carrier without the authorization of such carrier.

(2) In a prosecution for a violation of subsection (a)(9), (other than a violation consisting of producing or trafficking) it is an affirmative defense (which the defendant must establish by a preponderance of the evidence) that the conduct charged was engaged in for research or development in connection with a lawful purpose.

(h) Any person who, outside the jurisdiction of the United States, engages in any act that, if committed within the jurisdiction of the United States, would constitute an offense under subsection (a) or (b) of this section, shall be subject to the fines, penalties, imprisonment, and forfeiture provided in this title if—

(1) the offense involves an access device issued, owned, managed, or controlled by a financial institution, account issuer, credit card system member, or other entity within the jurisdiction of the United States; and

(2) the person transports, delivers, conveys, transfers to or through, or otherwise stores, secrets, or holds within the jurisdiction of the United States, any article used to assist in the commission of the offense or the proceeds of such offense or property derived therefrom.

(Added Pub.L. 98–473, Title II, § 1602(a), Oct. 12, 1984, 98 Stat. 2183, and amended Pub.L. 99–646, § 44(b), Nov. 10, 1986, 100 Stat. 3601; Pub.L. 101–647, Title XII, § 1205(f), Nov. 29, 1990, 104 Stat. 4831; Pub.L. 103–322, Title XXV, § 250007, Title XXXIII, § 330016(2)(I), Sept. 13, 1994, 108 Stat. 2087, 2148; Pub.L. 103–414, Title II, § 206, Oct. 25, 1994, 108 Stat. 4291; Pub.L. 104–294, Title VI, § 601(*l*), Oct. 11, 1996, 110 Stat. 3501; Pub.L. 105–172, § 2(a) – (d), Apr. 24, 1998, 112 Stat. 53; Pub.L. 107–56, Title III, § 377, Oct. 26, 2001, 115 Stat. 342; Pub.L. 107–273, Div. B, Title IV, § 4002(b)(11), Nov. 2, 2002, 116 Stat. 1808.)

HISTORICAL AND STATUTORY NOTES

References in Text

Section 413 of the Controlled Substance Act, referred to in subsec. (c)(2), is Pub.L. 98–473, Title II, § 303, Oct. 12, 1984, 98 Stat. 2044, as amended, which was classified to 21 USCA 853.

Section 3 of title I of the Communications Act of 1934, referred to in subsec. (e)(9), is Act June 19, 1934, c. 652, 48 Stat. 1065.

Title III of the Communications Act of 1934, referred to in subsec. (e)(10), is Act June 19, 1934, c. 652 Title III, 48 Stat. 1081, classified to 47 USCA § 301 et seq..

Termination Date of 2001 Amendment

Effective on and after the first day of fiscal year 2005, amendments by Title III (§§ 301 to 377) of Pub.L. 107–56 shall terminate if Congress enacts a joint resolution to that effect; such resolution shall be given expedited consideration, see Pub.L. 107–56, Title III, § 303, Oct. 26, 2001, 115 Stat. 298, set out as a note under 31 U.S.C.A. § 5311.

Transfer of Functions

For transfer of the functions, personnel, assets, and obligations of the United States Secret Service, including the functions of the Secretary of the Treasury relating thereto, to the Secretary of Homeland Security, and for treatment of related references, see 6 U.S.C.A. §§ 381, 551(d), 552(d) and 557, and the Department of Homeland Security Reorganization Plan of November 25, 2002, as modified, set out as a note under 6 U.S.C.A. § 542.

Report to Congress

Section 1603 of Pub.L. 98–473, provided that: "The Attorney General shall report to the Congress annually, during the first three years following the date of the enactment of this joint resolution [Oct. 12, 1984], concerning prosecutions under the section of title 18 of the United States Code [this section] added by this chapter."

§ 1030. Fraud and related activity in connection with computers

(a) Whoever—

(1) having knowingly accessed a computer without authorization or exceeding authorized access, and by means of such conduct having obtained information that has been determined by the United States Government pursuant to an Executive order or statute to require protection against unauthorized disclosure for reasons of national defense or foreign relations, or any restricted data, as defined in paragraph y. of section 11 of the Atomic Energy Act of 1954, with reason to believe that such information so obtained could be used to the injury of the United States, or to the advantage of any foreign nation willfully communicates, delivers, transmits, or causes to be communicated, delivered, or transmitted, or attempts to communicate, deliver, transmit or cause to be communicated, delivered, or transmitted the same to any person not entitled to receive it, or willfully retains the same and fails to deliver it to the officer or employee of the United States entitled to receive it;

(2) intentionally accesses a computer without authorization or exceeds authorized access, and thereby obtains—

(A) information contained in a financial record of a financial institution, or of a card issuer as defined in section 1602(n) of title 15, or contained in a file of a consumer reporting agency on a consumer, as such terms are defined in the Fair Credit Reporting Act (15 U.S.C. 1681 et seq.);

(B) information from any department or agency of the United States; or

(C) information from any protected computer if the conduct involved an interstate or foreign communication;

(3) intentionally, without authorization to access any nonpublic computer of a department or agency of the United States, accesses such a computer of that department or agency that is exclusively for the use of the Government of the United States or, in the case of a computer not exclusively for such use, is used by or for the Government of the United States and such conduct affects that use by or for the Government of the United States;

(4) knowingly and with intent to defraud, accesses a protected computer without authorization, or exceeds authorized access, and by means of such conduct furthers the intended fraud and obtains anything of value, unless the object of the fraud and the thing obtained consists only of the use of the computer and the value of such use is not more than $5,000 in any 1–year period;

(5)(A)(i) knowingly causes the transmission of a program, information, code, or command, and as a result of such conduct, intentionally causes damage without authorization, to a protected computer;

(ii) intentionally accesses a protected computer without authorization, and as a result of such conduct, recklessly causes damage; or

(iii) intentionally accesses a protected computer without authorization, and as a result of such conduct, causes damage; and

(B) by conduct described in clause (i), (ii), or (iii) of subparagraph (A), caused (or, in the case of an attempted offense, would, if completed, have caused)—

(i) loss to 1 or more persons during any 1-year period (and, for purposes of an investigation, prosecution, or other proceeding brought by the United States only, loss resulting from a related course of conduct affecting 1 or more other protected computers) aggregating at least $5,000 in value;

(ii) the modification or impairment, or potential modification or impairment, of the medical examination, diagnosis, treatment, or care of 1 or more individuals;

(iii) physical injury to any person;

(iv) a threat to public health or safety; or

(v) damage affecting a computer system used by or for a government entity in furtherance of the administration of justice, national defense, or national security;

(6) knowingly and with intent to defraud traffics (as defined in section 1029) in any password or similar information through which a computer may be accessed without authorization, if—

(A) such trafficking affects interstate or foreign commerce; or

(B) such computer is used by or for the Government of the United States; [1]

(7) with intent to extort from any person any money or other thing of value, transmits in interstate or foreign commerce any communication containing any threat to cause damage to a protected computer;

shall be punished as provided in subsection (c) of this section.

(b) Whoever attempts to commit an offense under subsection (a) of this section shall be punished as provided in subsection (c) of this section.

(c) The punishment for an offense under subsection (a) or (b) of this section is—

(1)(A) a fine under this title or imprisonment for not more than ten years, or both, in the case of an offense under subsection (a)(1) of this section which does not occur after a conviction for another offense under this section, or an attempt to commit an offense punishable under this subparagraph; and

(B) a fine under this title or imprisonment for not more than twenty years, or both, in the case of an offense under subsection (a)(1) of this section which occurs after a conviction for another offense under this section, or an attempt to commit an offense punishable under this subparagraph;

(2)(A) except as provided in subparagraph (B), a fine under this title or imprisonment for not more than one year, or both, in the case of an offense under subsection (a)(2), (a)(3), (a)(5)(A)(iii), or (a)(6) of this section which does not occur after a conviction for another offense under this section, or an attempt to commit an offense punishable under this subparagraph;

(B) a fine under this title or imprisonment for not more than 5 years, or both, in the case of an offense under subsection (a)(2), or an attempt to commit an offense punishable under this subparagraph, if—

(i) the offense was committed for purposes of commercial advantage or private financial gain;

(ii) the offense was committed in furtherance of any criminal or tortious act in violation of the Constitution or laws of the United States or of any State; or

(iii) the value of the information obtained exceeds $5,000; and

(C) a fine under this title or imprisonment for not more than ten years, or both, in the case of an offense under subsection (a)(2), (a)(3) or (a)(6) of this section which occurs after a conviction for another offense under this section, or an attempt to commit an offense punishable under this subparagraph;

(3)(A) a fine under this title or imprisonment for not more than five years, or both, in the case of an offense under subsection (a)(4) or (a)(7) of this section which does not occur after a conviction for another offense under this section, or an attempt to commit an offense punishable under this subparagraph; and

(B) a fine under this title or imprisonment for not more than ten years, or both, in the case of an offense under subsection (a)(4)[2] (a)(5)(A)(iii), or (a)(7) of this section which occurs after a conviction for another offense under this section, or an attempt to commit an offense punishable under this subparagraph;

(4)(A) except as provided in paragraph (5), a fine under this title, imprisonment for not more than 10 years, or both, in the case of an offense under subsection (a)(5)(A)(i), or an attempt to commit an offense punishable under that subsection;

(B) a fine under this title, imprisonment for not more than 5 years, or both, in the case of an offense under subsection (a)(5)(A)(ii), or an attempt to commit an offense punishable under that subsection;

(C) except as provided in paragraph (5), a fine under this title, imprisonment for not more than 20

years, or both, in the case of an offense under subsection (a)(5)(A)(i) or (a)(5)(A)(ii), or an attempt to commit an offense punishable under either subsection, that occurs after a conviction for another offense under this section; and

(5)(A) if the offender knowingly or recklessly causes or attempts to cause serious bodily injury from conduct in violation of subsection (a)(5)(A)(i), a fine under this title or imprisonment for not more than 20 years, or both; and

(B) if the offender knowingly or recklessly causes or attempts to cause death from conduct in violation of subsection (a)(5)(A)(i), a fine under this title or imprisonment for any term of years or for life, or both.

(d)(1) The United States Secret Service shall, in addition to any other agency having such authority, have the authority to investigate offenses under this section.

(2) The Federal Bureau of Investigation shall have primary authority to investigate offenses under subsection (a)(1) for any cases involving espionage, foreign counterintelligence, information protected against unauthorized disclosure for reasons of national defense or foreign relations, or Restricted Data (as that term is defined in section 11y of the Atomic Energy Act of 1954 (42 U.S.C. 2014(y)), except for offenses affecting the duties of the United States Secret Service pursuant to section 3056(a) of this title.

(3) Such authority shall be exercised in accordance with an agreement which shall be entered into by the Secretary of the Treasury and the Attorney General.

(e) As used in this section—

(1) the term "computer" means an electronic, magnetic, optical, electrochemical, or other high speed data processing device performing logical, arithmetic, or storage functions, and includes any data storage facility or communications facility directly related to or operating in conjunction with such device, but such term does not include an automated typewriter or typesetter, a portable hand held calculator, or other similar device;

(2) the term "protected computer" means a computer—

(A) exclusively for the use of a financial institution or the United States Government, or, in the case of a computer not exclusively for such use, used by or for a financial institution or the United States Government and the conduct constituting the offense affects that use by or for the financial institution or the Government; or

(B) which is used in interstate or foreign commerce or communication, including a computer located outside the United States that is used in a manner that affects interstate or foreign commerce or communication of the United States;

(3) the term "State" includes the District of Columbia, the Commonwealth of Puerto Rico, and any other commonwealth, possession or territory of the United States;

(4) the term "financial institution" means—

(A) an institution,[3] with deposits insured by the Federal Deposit Insurance Corporation;

(B) the Federal Reserve or a member of the Federal Reserve including any Federal Reserve Bank;

(C) a credit union with accounts insured by the National Credit Union Administration;

(D) a member of the Federal home loan bank system and any home loan bank;

(E) any institution of the Farm Credit System under the Farm Credit Act of 1971;

(F) a broker-dealer registered with the Securities and Exchange Commission pursuant to section 15 of the Securities Exchange Act of 1934;

(G) the Securities Investor Protection Corporation;

(H) a branch or agency of a foreign bank (as such terms are defined in paragraphs (1) and (3) of section 1(b) of the International Banking Act of 1978); and

(I) an organization operating under section 25 or section 25(a) of the Federal Reserve Act;

(5) the term "financial record" means information derived from any record held by a financial institution pertaining to a customer's relationship with the financial institution;

(6) the term "exceeds authorized access" means to access a computer with authorization and to use such access to obtain or alter information in the computer that the accesser is not entitled so to obtain or alter;

(7) the term "department of the United States" means the legislative or judicial branch of the Government or one of the executive departments enumerated in section 101 of title 5;

(8) the term "damage" means any impairment to the integrity or availability of data, a program, a system, or information;

(9) the term "government entity" includes the Government of the United States, any State or political subdivision of the United States, any foreign country, and any state, province, municipality, or other political subdivision of a foreign country;

(10) the term "conviction" shall include a conviction under the law of any State for a crime punishable by imprisonment for more than 1 year, an element of which is unauthorized access, or exceeding authorized access, to a computer;

(11) the term "loss" means any reasonable cost to any victim, including the cost of responding to an offense, conducting a damage assessment, and restoring the data, program, system, or information to its condition prior to the offense, and any revenue lost, cost incurred, or other consequential damages incurred because of interruption of service; and

(12) the term "person" means any individual, firm, corporation, educational institution, financial institution, governmental entity, or legal or other entity.

(f) This section does not prohibit any lawfully authorized investigative, protective, or intelligence activity of a law enforcement agency of the United States, a State, or a political subdivision of a State, or of an intelligence agency of the United States.

(g) Any person who suffers damage or loss by reason of a violation of this section may maintain a civil action against the violator to obtain compensatory damages and injunctive relief or other equitable relief. A civil action for a violation of this section may be brought only if the conduct involves 1 of the factors set forth in clause (i), (ii), (iii), (iv), or (v) of subsection (a)(5)(B). Damages for a violation involving only conduct described in subsection (a)(5)(B)(i) are limited to economic damages. No action may be brought under this subsection unless such action is begun within 2 years of the date of the act complained of or the date of the discovery of the damage. No action may be brought under this subsection for the negligent design or manufacture of computer hardware, computer software, or firmware.

(h) The Attorney General and the Secretary of the Treasury shall report to the Congress annually, during the first 3 years following the date of the enactment of this subsection, concerning investigations and prosecutions under subsection (a)(5).

(Added Pub.L. 98–473, Title II, § 2102(a), Oct. 12, 1984, 98 Stat. 2190, and amended Pub.L. 99–474, § 2, Oct. 16, 1986, 100 Stat. 1213; Pub.L. 100–690, Title VII, § 7065, Nov. 18, 1988, 102 Stat. 4404; Pub.L. 101–73, Title IX, § 962(a)(5), Aug. 9, 1989, 103 Stat. 502; Pub.L. 101–647, Title XII, § 1205(e), Title XXV, § 2597(j), Title XXXV, § 3533, Nov. 29, 1990, 104 Stat. 4831, 4910, 4925; Pub.L. 103–322, Title XXIX, § 290001(b) to (f), Sept. 13, 1994, 108 Stat. 2097–2099; Pub.L. 104–294, Title II, § 201, Title VI, § 604(b)(36), Oct. 11, 1996, 110 Stat. 3491, 3508; Pub.L. 107–56, Title V, § 506(a), Title VIII, § 814, Oct. 26, 2001, 115 Stat. 366, 382; Pub.L. 107–273, Title IV, §§ 4002(b)(1), (12), 4005(a)(3), (d)(3), Nov. 2, 2002, 116 Stat. 1807, 1808, 1812, 1813; Pub.L. 107–296, Title II, § 225(g), Nov. 25, 2002, 116 Stat. 2158.)

[1] So in original. Probably should be followed by "or".

[2] So in original. Probably should be followed by a comma.

[3] So in original. The comma probably should not appear.

HISTORICAL AND STATUTORY NOTES

References in Text

Reference to "paragraph y of section 11 of the Atomic Energy Act of 1954", referred to in subsec. (a)(1) is classified to section 2014(y) of Title 42, Public Health and Welfare.

The Fair Credit Reporting Act, referred to in subsec. (a)(2)(A), is Title VI of Pub.L. 90–321 as added by Pub.L. 91–508, Title VI, Oct. 26, 1970, 84 Stat. 1127, which is classified to subchapter III (section 1681 et seq.) of chapter 41 of Title 15, Commerce and Trade.

Section 11y of the Atomic Energy Act of 1954, referred to in subsec. (d)(2), is Aug. 1, 1946, c. 724, Title I, § 11(y), as added Aug. 30, 1954, c. 1073, § 1, 68 Stat. 922, as amended, which is classified to 42 U.S.C.A. § 2014(y).

The Farm Credit Act of 1971, referred to in subsec. (e)(4)(E), is Pub.L. 92–181, Dec. 10, 1971, 85 Stat. 585, as amended, which is classified generally to chapter 23 (section 2001 et seq.) of Title 12, Banks and Banking. For complete classification of this Act to the Code, see Short Title note set out under section 2001 of Title 12 and Tables.

Section 15 of the Securities Exchange Act of 1934, referred to in subsec. (e)(4)(F), is classified to section 78o of Title 15, Commerce and Trade.

Section 1(b) of the International Banking Act of 1978, referred to in subsec. (e)(4)(H), is classified to section 3101 of Title 12, Banks and Banking.

The Federal Reserve Act, referred to in text, is Act Dec. 23, 1913, c. 6, 38 Stat. 251, as amended, which is classified principally to chapter 3 of Title 12, 12 U.S.C.A. § 221 et seq. Section 25 of the Federal Reserve Act, referred to in subsec. (e)(4)(I), is classified to subchapter I of chapter 6 of Title 12, 12 U.S.C.A. § 601 et seq. Section 25(a) of the Federal Reserve Act, which is classified to subchapter II of chapter 6 of Title 12, 12 U.S.C.A. § 611 et seq., was renumbered section 25A by Pub.L. 102–242, Title I, § 142(e)(2), Dec. 10, 1991, 105 Stat. 2281. See Tables and 12 U.S.C.A. § 226 for complete classification.

The date of the enactment of this subsection, referred to in subsec. (h), means the date of the enactment of Pub.L. 103-322, 108 Stat. 1796, which enacted subsec. (h) and was approved Sept. 13, 1994.

Effective and Applicability Provisions

2002 Acts. Amendment to this section by Pub.L. 107–296 effective 60 days after Nov. 25, 2002, see Pub.L. 107–296, § 4, set out as a note under 6 U.S.C.A. § 101.

1996 Acts. Amendment by section 604 of Pub.L. 104–294 effective Sept. 13, 1994, see section 604(d) of Pub.L. 104–294, set out as a note under section 13 of this title.

Transfer of Functions

For transfer of the functions, personnel, assets, and obligations of the United States Secret Service, including the functions of the Secretary of the Treasury relating thereto, to the Secretary of Homeland Security, and for treatment of related references, see 6 U.S.C.A. §§ 381, 551(d), 552(d) and 557, and the Department of Homeland Security Reorganization Plan of November 25, 2002, as modified, set out as a note under 6 U.S.C.A. § 542.

Severability of Provisions

If any provision of Pub.L. 101–73 or the application thereof to any person or circumstance is held invalid, the remainder of Pub.L. 101–73 and the application of the provision to other persons not similarly situated or to other circumstances not to be affected thereby, see section 1221 of Pub.L. 101–73, set out as a note under section 1811 of Title 12, Banks and Banking.

Report to Congress

Section 2103 of Pub.L. 98–473 provided that: "The Attorney General shall report to the Congress annually, during the first three years following the date of the enactment of this joint resolution [Oct. 12, 1984], concerning prosecutions under the sections of title 18 of the United States Code added by this chapter [this section]."

§ 1031. Major fraud against the United States

(a) Whoever knowingly executes, or attempts to execute, any scheme or artifice with the intent—

(1) to defraud the United States; or

(2) to obtain money or property by means of false or fraudulent pretenses, representations, or promises,

in any procurement of property or services as a prime contractor with the United States or as a subcontractor or supplier on a contract in which there is a prime contract with the United States, if the value of the contract, subcontract, or any constituent part thereof, for such property or services is $1,000,000 or more shall, subject to the applicability of subsection (c) of this section, be fined not more than $1,000,000, or imprisoned not more than 10 years, or both.

(b) The fine imposed for an offense under this section may exceed the maximum otherwise provided by law, if such fine does not exceed $5,000,000 and—

(1) the gross loss to the Government or the gross gain to a defendant is $500,000 or greater; or

(2) the offense involves a conscious or reckless risk of serious personal injury.

(c) The maximum fine imposed upon a defendant for a prosecution including a prosecution with multiple counts under this section shall not exceed $10,000,000.

(d) Nothing in this section shall preclude a court from imposing any other sentences available under this title, including without limitation a fine up to twice the amount of the gross loss or gross gain involved in the offense pursuant to 18 U.S.C. section 3571(d).

(e) In determining the amount of the fine, the court shall consider the factors set forth in 18 U.S.C. sections 3553 and 3572, and the factors set forth in the guidelines and policy statements of the United States Sentencing Commission, including—

(1) the need to reflect the seriousness of the offense, including the harm or loss to the victim and the gain to the defendant;

(2) whether the defendant previously has been fined for a similar offense; and

(3) any other pertinent equitable considerations.

(f) A prosecution of an offense under this section may be commenced any time not later than 7 years after the offense is committed, plus any additional time otherwise allowed by law.

(g)(1) In special circumstances and in his or her sole discretion, the Attorney General is authorized to make payments from funds appropriated to the Department of Justice to persons who furnish information relating to a possible prosecution under this section. The amount of such payment shall not exceed $250,000. Upon application by the Attorney General, the court may order that the Department shall be reimbursed for a payment from a criminal fine imposed under this section.

(2) An individual is not eligible for such a payment if—

(A) that individual is an officer or employee of a Government agency who furnishes information or renders service in the performance of official duties;

(B) that individual failed to furnish the information to the individual's employer prior to furnishing it to law enforcement authorities, unless the court determines the individual has justifiable reasons for that failure;

(C) the furnished information is based upon public disclosure of allegations or transactions in a criminal, civil, or administrative hearing, in a congressional, administrative, or GAO report, hearing, audit or investigation, or from the news media unless the person is the original source of the information. For the purposes of this subsection, "original source" means an individual who has direct and independent knowledge of the information on which the allegations are based and has voluntarily provided the information to the Government; or

(D) that individual participated in the violation of this section with respect to which such payment would be made.

(3) The failure of the Attorney General to authorize a payment shall not be subject to judicial review.

(h) Any individual who—

(1) is discharged, demoted, suspended, threatened, harassed, or in any other manner discriminated against in the terms and conditions of employment by an employer because of lawful acts done by the employee on behalf of the employee or others in furtherance of a prosecution under this section (including investigation for, initiation of, testimony for, or assistance in such prosecution), and

(2) was not a participant in the unlawful activity that is the subject of said prosecution, may, in a civil action, obtain all relief necessary to make such individual whole. Such relief shall include reinstatement with the same seniority status such individual would have had but for the discrimination, 2 times the amount of back pay, interest on the back pay, and compensation for any special damages sustained as a result of the discrimination, including litigation costs and reasonable attorney's fees.

(Added Pub.L. 100–700, § 2(a), Nov. 19, 1988, 102 Stat. 4631, and amended Pub.L. 101–123, § 2(a), Oct. 23, 1989, 103 Stat. 759; Pub.L. 103–322, Title XXXIII, § 330002(a), (f), Sept. 13, 1994, 108 Stat. 2140.)

HISTORICAL AND STATUTORY NOTES

Effective and Applicability Provisions

1989 Acts. Section 2(b) of Pub.L. 101–123 provided that:"The amendment made by this section [enacting subsec. (g) of this section, relating to payments by the Attorney General] shall apply to contracts entered into on or after the date of the enactment of this Act [Oct. 23, 1989]."

Sentencing Guidelines

Section 2(b) of Pub.L. 100–700 provided that: "Pursuant to its authority under section 994(p) of title 28, United States Code [section 994(p) of Title 28, Judiciary and Judicial Procedure] and section 21 of the Sentencing Act of 1987 [set out as a note under section 994 of Title 28], the United States Sentencing Commission shall promulgate guidelines, or shall amend existing guidelines, to provide for appropriate penalty enhancements, where conscious or reckless risk of serious personal injury resulting from the fraud has occurred. The Commission shall consider the appropriateness of assigning to such a defendant an offense level under Chapter Two of the sentencing guidelines that is at least two levels greater than the level that would have been assigned had conscious or reckless risk of serious personal injury not resulted from the fraud."

§ 1032. Concealment of assets from conservator, receiver, or liquidating agent of financial institution

Whoever—

(1) knowingly conceals or endeavors to conceal an asset or property from the Federal Deposit Insurance Corporation, acting as conservator or receiver or in the Corporation's corporate capacity with respect to any asset acquired or liability assumed by the Corporation under section 11, 12, or 13 of the Federal Deposit Insurance Act, the Resolution Trust Corporation, any conservator appointed by the Comptroller of the Currency or the Director of the Office of Thrift Supervision, or the National Credit Union Administration Board, acting as conservator or liquidating agent;

(2) corruptly impedes or endeavors to impede the functions of such Corporation, Board, or conservator; or

(3) corruptly places or endeavors to place an asset or property beyond the reach of such Corporation, Board, or conservator,

shall be fined under this title or imprisoned not more than 5 years, or both.

(Added Pub.L. 101–647, Title XXV, § 2501(a), Nov. 29, 1990, 104 Stat. 4859, and amended Pub.L. 107–273, Div. B, Title IV, § 4002(b)(13), Nov. 2, 2002, 116 Stat. 1808.)

HISTORICAL AND STATUTORY NOTES

References in Text

Sections 11, 12, and 13 of the Federal Deposit Insurance Act, referred to in par. (1), are classified to 12 U.S.C.A. §§ 1821, 1822, 1823, respectively.

§ 1033. Crimes by or affecting persons engaged in the business of insurance whose activities affect interstate commerce

(a)(1) Whoever is engaged in the business of insurance whose activities affect interstate commerce and knowingly, with the intent to deceive, makes any false material statement or report or willfully and materially overvalues any land, property or security—

(A) in connection with any financial reports or documents presented to any insurance regulatory official or agency or an agent or examiner appointed by such official or agency to examine the affairs of such person, and

(B) for the purpose of influencing the actions of such official or agency or such an appointed agent or examiner,

shall be punished as provided in paragraph (2).

(2) The punishment for an offense under paragraph (1) is a fine as established under this title or imprisonment for not more than 10 years, or both, except that the term of imprisonment shall be not more than 15 years if the statement or report or overvaluing of land, property, or security jeopardized the safety and soundness of an insurer and was a significant cause of such insurer being placed in conservation, rehabilitation, or liquidation by an appropriate court.

(b)(1) Whoever—

(A) acting as, or being an officer, director, agent, or employee of, any person engaged in the business of insurance whose activities affect interstate commerce, or

(B) is engaged in the business of insurance whose activities affect interstate commerce or is involved (other than as an insured or beneficiary under a policy of insurance) in a transaction relating to the conduct of affairs of such a business,

willfully embezzles, abstracts, purloins, or misappropriates any of the moneys, funds, premiums, credits, or other property of such person so engaged shall be punished as provided in paragraph (2).

(2) The punishment for an offense under paragraph (1) is a fine as provided under this title or imprisonment for not more than 10 years, or both, except that if such embezzlement, abstraction, purloining, or misappropriation described in paragraph (1) jeopardized the safety and soundness of an insurer and was a significant cause of such insurer being placed in conservation, rehabilitation, or liquidation by an appropriate court, such imprisonment shall be not more than

15 years. If the amount or value so embezzled, abstracted, purloined, or misappropriated does not exceed $5,000, whoever violates paragraph (1) shall be fined as provided in this title or imprisoned not more than one year, or both.

(c)(1) Whoever is engaged in the business of insurance and whose activities affect interstate commerce or is involved (other than as an insured or beneficiary under a policy of insurance) in a transaction relating to the conduct of affairs of such a business, knowingly makes any false entry of material fact in any book, report, or statement of such person engaged in the business of insurance with intent to deceive any person, including any officer, employee, or agent of such person engaged in the business of insurance, any insurance regulatory official or agency, or any agent or examiner appointed by such official or agency to examine the affairs of such person, about the financial condition or solvency of such business shall be punished as provided in paragraph (2).

(2) The punishment for an offense under paragraph (1) is a fine as provided under this title or imprisonment for not more than 10 years, or both, except that if the false entry in any book, report, or statement of such person jeopardized the safety and soundness of an insurer and was a significant cause of such insurer being placed in conservation, rehabilitation, or liquidation by an appropriate court, such imprisonment shall be not more than 15 years.

(d) Whoever, by threats or force or by any threatening letter or communication, corruptly influences, obstructs, or impedes or endeavors corruptly to influence, obstruct, or impede the due and proper administration of the law under which any proceeding involving the business of insurance whose activities affect interstate commerce is pending before any insurance regulatory official or agency or any agent or examiner appointed by such official or agency to examine the affairs of a person engaged in the business of insurance whose activities affect interstate commerce, shall be fined as provided in this title or imprisoned not more than 10 years, or both.

(e)(1)(A) Any individual who has been convicted of any criminal felony involving dishonesty or a breach of trust, or who has been convicted of an offense under this section, and who willfully engages in the business of insurance whose activities affect interstate commerce or participates in such business, shall be fined as provided in this title or imprisoned not more than 5 years, or both.

(B) Any individual who is engaged in the business of insurance whose activities affect interstate commerce and who willfully permits the participation described in subparagraph (A) shall be fined as provided in this title or imprisoned not more than 5 years, or both.

(2) A person described in paragraph (1)(A) may engage in the business of insurance or participate in such business if such person has the written consent of any insurance regulatory official authorized to regulate the insurer, which consent specifically refers to this subsection.

(f) As used in this section—

(1) the term "business of insurance" means—

(A) the writing of insurance, or

(B) the reinsuring of risks,

by an insurer, including all acts necessary or incidental to such writing or reinsuring and the activities of persons who act as, or are, officers, directors, agents, or employees of insurers or who are other persons authorized to act on behalf of such persons;

(2) the term "insurer" means any entity the business activity of which is the writing of insurance or the reinsuring of risks, and includes any person who acts as, or is, an officer, director, agent, or employee of that business;

(3) the term "interstate commerce" means—

(A) commerce within the District of Columbia, or any territory or possession of the United States;

(B) all commerce between any point in the State, territory, possession, or the District of Columbia and any point outside thereof;

(C) all commerce between points within the same State through any place outside such State; or

(D) all other commerce over which the United States has jurisdiction; and

(4) the term "State" includes any State, the District of Columbia, the Commonwealth of Puerto Rico, the Northern Mariana Islands, the Virgin Islands, American Samoa, and the Trust Territory of the Pacific Islands.

(Added Pub.L. 103–322, Title XXXII, § 320603(a), Sept. 13, 1994, 108 Stat. 2115.)

§ 1034. Civil penalties and injunctions for violations of section 1033

(a) The Attorney General may bring a civil action in the appropriate United States district court against any person who engages in conduct constituting an offense under section 1033 and, upon proof of such conduct by a preponderance of the evidence, such person shall be subject to a civil penalty of not more than $50,000 for each violation or the amount of compensation which the person received or offered for the prohibited conduct, whichever amount is greater. If the offense has contributed to the decision of a court of appropriate jurisdiction to issue an order directing the conservation, rehabilitation, or liquidation of an insurer, such penalty shall be remitted to the appropriate regulatory official for the benefit of the policyholders, claimants, and creditors of such insurer. The imposition of a civil penalty under this subsection does not preclude any other criminal or civil statutory, common law, or administrative remedy, which is available by law to the United States or any other person.

(b) If the Attorney General has reason to believe that a person is engaged in conduct constituting an offense under section 1033, the Attorney General may petition an appropriate United States district court for an order prohibiting that person from engaging in such conduct. The court may issue an order prohibiting that person from engaging in such conduct if the court finds that the conduct constitutes such an offense. The filing of a petition under this section does not preclude any other remedy which is available by law to the United States or any other person.

(Added Pub.L. 103–322, Title XXXII, § 320603(a), Sept. 13, 1994, 108 Stat. 2118.)

§ 1035. False statements relating to health care matters

(a) Whoever, in any matter involving a health care benefit program, knowingly and willfully—

(1) falsifies, conceals, or covers up by any trick, scheme, or device a material fact; or

(2) makes any materially false, fictitious, or fraudulent statements or representations, or makes or uses any materially false writing or document knowing the same to contain any materially false, fictitious, or fraudulent statement or entry, in connection with the delivery of or payment for health care benefits, items, or services, shall be fined under this title or imprisoned not more than 5 years, or both.

(b) As used in this section, the term "health care benefit program" has the meaning given such term in section 24(b) of this title.

(Added Pub.L. 104–191, Title II, § 244(a), Aug. 21, 1996, 110 Stat. 2017.)

§ 1036. Entry by false pretenses to any real property, vessel, or aircraft of the United States or secure area of any airport or seaport

(a) Whoever, by any fraud or false pretense, enters or attempts to enter—

(1) any real property belonging in whole or in part to, or leased by, the United States;

(2) any vessel or aircraft belonging in whole or in part to, or leased by, the United States;

(3) any secure or restricted area of any seaport, designated as secure in an approved security plan, as required under section 70103 of title 46, United States Code, and the rules and regulations promulgated under that section; or

(4) any secure area of any airport,

shall be punished as provided in subsection (b) of this section.

(b) The punishment for an offense under subsection (a) of this section is—

(1) a fine under this title or imprisonment for not more than 10 years, or both, if the offense is committed with the intent to commit a felony; or

(2) a fine under this title or imprisonment for not more than 6 months, or both, in any other case.

(c) As used in this section—

(1) the term "secure area" means an area access to which is restricted by the airport authority, captain of the seaport, or a public agency; and

(2) the term "airport" has the meaning given such term in section 47102 of title 49.

(Added Pub.L. 106–547, § 2(a), Dec. 19, 2000, 114 Stat. 2738, and amended Pub.L. 109–177, Title III, § 302(a), Mar. 9, 2006, 120 Stat. 233.)

§ 1037. Fraud and related activity in connection with electronic mail

(a) In general.—Whoever, in or affecting interstate or foreign commerce, knowingly—

(1) accesses a protected computer without authorization, and intentionally initiates the transmission of multiple commercial electronic mail messages from or through such computer,

(2) uses a protected computer to relay or retransmit multiple commercial electronic mail messages, with the intent to deceive or mislead recipients, or any Internet access service, as to the origin of such messages,

(3) materially falsifies header information in multiple commercial electronic mail messages and intentionally initiates the transmission of such messages,

(4) registers, using information that materially falsifies the identity of the actual registrant, for five or more electronic mail accounts or online user accounts or two or more domain names, and intentionally initiates the transmission of multiple commercial electronic mail messages from any combination of such accounts or domain names, or

(5) falsely represents oneself to be the registrant or the legitimate successor in interest to the registrant of 5 or more Internet Protocol addresses, and intentionally initiates the transmission of multiple commercial electronic mail messages from such addresses, or conspires to do so, shall be punished as provided in subsection (b).

(b) Penalties.—The punishment for an offense under subsection (a) is—

(1) a fine under this title, imprisonment for not more than 5 years, or both, if—

(A) the offense is committed in furtherance of any felony under the laws of the United States or of any State; or

(B) the defendant has previously been convicted under this section or section 1030, or under the law of any State for conduct involving the transmission of multiple commercial electronic mail messages or unauthorized access to a computer system;

(2) a fine under this title, imprisonment for not more than 3 years, or both, if—

(A) the offense is an offense under subsection (a)(1);

(B) the offense is an offense under subsection (a)(4) and involved 20 or more falsified electronic mail or online user account registrations, or 10 or more falsified domain name registrations;

(C) the volume of electronic mail messages transmitted in furtherance of the offense exceeded 2,500 during any 24–hour period, 25,000 during any 30–day period, or 250,000 during any 1–year period;

(D) the offense caused loss to one or more persons aggregating $5,000 or more in value during any 1–year period;

(E) as a result of the offense any individual committing the offense obtained anything of value aggregating $5,000 or more during any 1–year period; or

(F) the offense was undertaken by the defendant in concert with three or more other persons with respect to whom the defendant occupied a position of organizer or leader; and

(3) a fine under this title or imprisonment for not more than 1 year, or both, in any other case.

(c) Forfeiture.—

(1) In general.—The court, in imposing sentence on a person who is convicted of an offense under this section, shall order that the defendant forfeit to the United States—

(A) any property, real or personal, constituting or traceable to gross proceeds obtained from such offense; and

(B) any equipment, software, or other technology used or intended to be used to commit or to facilitate the commission of such offense.

(2) Procedures.—The procedures set forth in section 413 of the Controlled Substances Act (21 U.S.C. 853), other than subsection (d) of that section, and in Rule 32.2 of the Federal Rules of Criminal Procedure, shall apply to all stages of a criminal forfeiture proceeding under this section.

(d) Definitions.—In this section:

(1) Loss.—The term "loss" has the meaning given that term in section 1030(e) of this title.

(2) Materially.—For purposes of paragraphs (3) and (4) of subsection (a), header information or registration information is materially falsified if it is altered or concealed in a manner that would impair the ability of a recipient of the message, an Internet access service processing the message on behalf of a recipient, a person alleging a violation of this section, or a law enforcement agency to identify, locate, or respond to a person who initiated the electronic mail message or to investigate the alleged violation.

(3) Multiple.—The term "multiple" means more than 100 electronic mail messages during a 24–hour period, more than 1,000 electronic mail messages during a 30–day period, or more than 10,000 electronic mail messages during a 1–year period.

(4) Other terms.—Any other term has the meaning given that term by section 3 of the CAN–SPAM Act of 2003.

(Added Pub.L. 108–187, § 4(a)(1), Dec. 16, 2003, 117 Stat. 2703.)

HISTORICAL AND STATUTORY NOTES

References in Text

Section 413 of the Controlled Substances Act, referred to in subsec. (c)(2), is section 413 of Pub.L. 91–513, Title II, § 413, as added Pub.L. 98–473, Title II, § 303, Oct. 12, 1984, 98 Stat. 2044, and amended, which is classified to 21 U.S.C.A. § 853.

Rule 32.2 of the Federal Rules of Criminal Procedure, referred to in subsec. (c)(2), is set out in the appendix to this title.

Section 3 of the CAN–SPAM Act of 2003, referred to in subsec. (d)(4), is Pub.L. 108–187, § 3, Dec. 16, 2003, 117 Stat. 2700, which is classified to 15 U.S.C.A. § 7702.

Effective and Applicability Provisions

2003 Acts. Section effective Jan. 1, 2004, see section 16 of Pub.L. 108–187, set out as a note under 15 U.S.C.A. § 7701.

§ 1038. False information and hoaxes

(a) Criminal violation.—

(1) In general.—Whoever engages in any conduct with intent to convey false or misleading information under circumstances where such information may reasonably be believed and where such information indicates that an activity has taken, is taking, or will take place that would constitute a violation of chapter 2, 10, 11B, 39, 40, 44, 111, or 113B of this title, section 236 of the Atomic Energy Act of 1954 (42 U.S.C. 2284), or section 46502, the second sentence of section 46504, section 46505(b)(3) or (c), section 46506 if homicide or attempted homicide is involved, or section 60123(b) of title 49, shall—

(A) be fined under this title or imprisoned not more than 5 years, or both;

(B) if serious bodily injury results, be fined under this title or imprisoned not more than 20 years, or both; and

(C) if death results, be fined under this title or imprisoned for any number of years up to life, or both.

(2) Armed forces.—Any person who makes a false statement, with intent to convey false or misleading information, about the death, injury, capture, or disappearance of a member of the Armed Forces of the United States during a war or armed conflict in which the United States is engaged—

(A) shall be fined under this title, imprisoned not more than 5 years, or both;

(B) if serious bodily injury results, shall be fined under this title, imprisoned not more than 20 years, or both; and

(C) if death results, shall be fined under this title, imprisoned for any number of years or for life, or both.

(b) Civil action.—Whoever engages in any conduct with intent to convey false or misleading information under circumstances where such information may reasonably be believed and where such information indicates that an activity has taken, is taking, or will take place that would constitute a violation of chapter 2, 10, 11B, 39, 40, 44, 111, or 113B of this title, section 236 of the Atomic Energy Act of 1954 (42 U.S.C. 2284), or section 46502, the second sentence of section 46504, section 46505 (b)(3) or (c), section 46506 if homicide or attempted homicide is involved, or section 60123(b) of title 49 is liable in a civil action to any party incurring expenses incident to any emergency or investigative response to that conduct, for those expenses.

(c) Reimbursement.—

(1) In general.—The court, in imposing a sentence on a defendant who has been convicted of an offense under subsection (a), shall order the defendant to reimburse any state or local government, or private not-for-profit organization that provides fire or rescue service incurring expenses incident to any emergency or investigative response to that conduct, for those expenses.

(2) Liability.—A person ordered to make reimbursement under this subsection shall be jointly and severally liable for such expenses with each other person, if any, who is ordered to make reimbursement under this subsection for the same expenses.

(3) Civil judgment.—An order of reimbursement under this subsection shall, for the purposes of enforcement, be treated as a civil judgment.

(d) Activities of law enforcement.—This section does not prohibit any lawfully authorized investigative, protective, or intelligence activity of a law enforcement agency of the United States, a State, or political subdivision of a State, or of an intelligence agency of the United States.

(Added Pub.L. 108–458, Title VI, § 6702(a), Dec. 17, 2004, 118 Stat. 3764.)

HISTORICAL AND STATUTORY NOTES

References in Text

Chapter 2, 10, 11B, 39, 40, 44, 111, or 113B of this title, referred to in subsecs. (a)(1) and (b)(1), are, respectively, 18 U.S.C.A. § 31 et seq. (Aircraft and motor vehicles), 18 U.S.C.A. § 175 et seq. (Biological weapons), 18 U.S.C.A. § 229 et seq. (Chemical weapons), 18 U.S.C.A. § 831 et seq. (Explosives and combustibles), 18 U.S.C.A. § 841 et seq. (Importation, manufacture, distribution and storage of explosive materials), 18 U.S.C.A. § 921 et seq. (Firearms), 18 U.S.C.A. § 2271 et seq. (Shipping), or 18 U.S.C.A. § 2331 et seq. (Terrorism).

Section 236 of the Atomic Energy Act of 1954, referred to in subsecs. (a)(1) and (b)(1), is Aug. 1, 1946, c. 724, Title I, § 236, added June 30, 1980, Pub.L. 96–295, Title II, § 204(a), 94 Stat. 787, as amended, which is classified to 42 U.S.C.A. § 2284.

§ 1039. Fraud and related activity in connection with obtaining confidential phone records information of a covered entity

(a) Criminal violation.—Whoever, in interstate or foreign commerce, knowingly and intentionally obtains, or attempts to obtain, confidential phone records information of a covered entity, by—

(1) making false or fraudulent statements or representations to an employee of a covered entity;

(2) making such false or fraudulent statements or representations to a customer of a covered entity;

(3) providing a document to a covered entity knowing that such document is false or fraudulent; or

(4) accessing customer accounts of a covered entity via the Internet, or by means of conduct that violates section 1030 of this title, without prior authorization from the customer to whom such confidential phone records information relates; shall be fined under this title, imprisoned for not more than 10 years, or both.

(b) Prohibition on sale or transfer of confidential phone records information.—

(1) Except as otherwise permitted by applicable law, whoever, in interstate or foreign commerce, knowingly and intentionally sells or transfers, or attempts to sell or transfer, confidential phone records information of a covered entity, without prior authorization from the customer to whom such confidential phone records information relates, or knowing or having reason to know such information was obtained fraudulently, shall be fined under this title, imprisoned not more than 10 years, or both.

(2) For purposes of this subsection, the exceptions specified in section 222(d) of the Communications Act of 1934 shall apply for the use of confidential phone records information by any covered entity, as defined in subsection (h).

(c) Prohibition on purchase or receipt of confidential phone records information.—

(1) Except as otherwise permitted by applicable law, whoever, in interstate or foreign commerce, knowingly and intentionally purchases or receives, or attempts to purchase or receive, confidential phone records information of a covered entity, without prior authorization from the customer to whom such confidential phone records information relates, or knowing or having reason to know such information was obtained fraudulently, shall be fined under this title, imprisoned not more than 10 years, or both.

(2) For purposes of this subsection, the exceptions specified in section 222(d) of the Communications Act of 1934 shall apply for the use of confidential phone records information by any covered entity, as defined in subsection (h).

(d) Enhanced penalties for aggravated cases.—Whoever violates, or attempts to violate, subsection (a), (b), or (c) while violating another law of the United States or as part of a pattern of any illegal activity involving more than $100,000, or more than 50 customers of a covered entity, in a 12-month period shall, in addition to the penalties provided for in such subsection, be fined twice the amount provided in subsection (b)(3) or (c)(3) (as the case may be) of section 3571 of this title, imprisoned for not more than 5 years, or both.

(e) Enhanced penalties for use of information in furtherance of certain criminal offenses.—

(1) Whoever, violates, or attempts to violate, subsection (a), (b), or (c) knowing that such information may be used in furtherance of, or with the intent to commit, an offense described in section 2261, 2261A, 2262, or any other crime of violence shall, in addition to the penalties provided for in such subsection, be fined under this title and imprisoned not more than 5 years.

(2) Whoever, violates, or attempts to violate, subsection (a), (b), or (c) knowing that such information may be used in furtherance of, or with the intent to commit, an offense under section 111, 115, 1114, 1503, 1512, 1513, or to intimidate, threaten, harass, injure, or kill any Federal, State, or local law enforcement officer shall, in addition to the penalties provided for in such subsection, be fined under this title and imprisoned not more than 5 years.

(f) Extraterritorial jurisdiction.—There is extraterritorial jurisdiction over an offense under this section.

(g) Nonapplicability to law enforcement agencies.—This section does not prohibit any lawfully authorized investigative, protective, or intelligence activity of a law enforcement agency of the United States, a State, or political subdivision of a State, or of an intelligence agency of the United States.

(h) Definitions.—In this section:

(1) Confidential phone records information.—The term "confidential phone records information" means information that—

(A) relates to the quantity, technical configuration, type, destination, location, or amount of use of a service offered by a covered entity, subscribed to by any customer of that covered entity, and kept by or on behalf of that covered entity solely by virtue of the relationship between that covered entity and the customer;

(B) is made available to a covered entity by a customer solely by virtue of the relationship between that covered entity and the customer; or

(C) is contained in any bill, itemization, or account statement provided to a customer by or on behalf of a covered entity solely by virtue of the relationship between that covered entity and the customer.

(2) Covered entity.—The term "covered entity"—

(A) has the same meaning given the term "telecommunications carrier" in section 3 of the Communications Act of 1934 (47 U.S.C. 153); and

(B) includes any provider of IP-enabled voice service.

(3) Customer.—The term "customer" means, with respect to a covered entity, any individual, partnership, association, joint stock company, trust, or corporation, or authorized representative of such customer, to whom the covered entity provides a product or service.

(4) IP-enabled voice service.—The term "IP-enabled voice service" means the provision of real-time voice communications offered to the public, or such class of users as to be effectively available to the public, transmitted through customer premises equipment using TCP/IP protocol, or a successor protocol, (whether part of a bundle of services or separately) with interconnection capability such that the service can originate traffic to, or terminate traffic from, the public switched telephone network, or a successor network.

(Added Pub.L. 109–476, § 3(a), Jan. 12, 2007, 120 Stat. 3569.)

HISTORICAL AND STATUTORY NOTES

References in Text

Section 222(d) of the Communications Act of 1934, referred to in subsecs. (b)(2) and (c)(2), is Act June 19, 1934, c. 652, Title II, 222(d), as added Feb. 8, 1996, Pub.L. 104–104, Title VII, § 702, 110 Stat. 148, as amended, which is classified to 47 U.S.C.A. § 222.

Section 3 of the Communications Act of 1934, referred to in subsec. (h)(2)(A), is Act June 19, 1934, c. 652, Title I, § 3, 48 Stat. 1065, as amended, which is classified to 47 U.S.C.A. § 153. The term "telecommunications carrier" is defined in par. (44) of 47 U.S.C.A. § 153.

Findings; Telephone Records and Privacy Protection

Pub.L. 109–476, § 2, Jan. 12, 2007, 120 Stat. 3568, provided that:

"Congress finds that—

"(1) telephone records can be of great use to criminals because the information contained in call logs may include a wealth of personal data;

"(2) call logs may reveal the names of telephone users' doctors, public and private relationships, business associates, and more;

"(3) call logs are typically maintained for the exclusive use of phone companies, their authorized agents, and authorized consumers;

"(4) Telephone records have been obtained without the knowledge or consent of consumers through the use of a number of fraudulent methods and devices that include—

"(A) telephone company employees selling data to unauthorized data brokers;

"(B) 'pretexting', whereby a data broker or other person represents that they are an authorized consumer and convinces an agent of the telephone company to release the data; or

"(C) gaining unauthorized Internet access to account data by improperly activating a consumer's account management features on a phone company's webpage or contracting with an Internet-based data broker who trafficks in such records; and

"(5) the unauthorized disclosure of telephone records not only assaults individual privacy but, in some instances, may further acts of domestic violence or stalking, compromise the personal safety of law enforcement officers, their families, victims of crime, witnesses, or confidential informants, and undermine the integrity of law enforcement investigations."

CHAPTER 49—FUGITIVES FROM JUSTICE

§ 1071. Concealing person from arrest

Whoever harbors or conceals any person for whose arrest a warrant or process has been issued under the provisions of any law of the United States, so as to prevent his discovery and arrest, after notice or knowledge of the fact that a warrant or process has been issued for the apprehension of such person, shall be fined under this title or imprisoned not more than one year, or both; except that if the warrant or process issued on a charge of felony, or after conviction of such person of any offense, the punishment shall be a fine under this title, or imprisonment for not more than five years, or both.

(June 25, 1948, c. 645, 62 Stat. 755; Aug. 20, 1954, c. 771, 68 Stat. 747; Sept. 13, 1994, Pub.L. 103–322, Title XXXIII, § 330016(1)(H), (K), 108 Stat. 2147; Nov. 2, 2002, Pub.L. 107–273, Div. B, Title IV, § 4003(a)(3), 116 Stat. 1811.)

§ 1072. Concealing escaped prisoner

Whoever willfully harbors or conceals any prisoner after his escape from the custody of the Attorney General or from a Federal penal or correctional institution, shall be imprisoned not more than three years.

(June 25, 1948, c. 645, 62 Stat. 755.)

§ 1073. Flight to avoid prosecution or giving testimony

Whoever moves or travels in interstate or foreign commerce with intent either (1) to avoid prosecution, or custody or confinement after conviction, under the laws of the place from which he flees, for a crime, or an attempt to commit a crime, punishable by death or which is a felony under the laws of the place from which the fugitive flees, or (2) to avoid giving testimony in any criminal proceedings in such place in which the commission of an offense punishable by death or which is a felony under the laws of such place, is charged, or (3) to avoid service of, or contempt proceedings for alleged disobedience of, lawful process requiring attendance and the giving of testimony or the production of documentary evidence before an agency of a State empowered by the law of such State to conduct investigations of alleged criminal activities, shall be fined under this title or imprisoned not more than five years, or both. For the purposes of clause (3) of this paragraph, the term "State" includes a State of the United States, the District of Columbia, and any commonwealth, territory, or possession of the United States.

Violations of this section may be prosecuted only in the Federal judicial district in which the original crime was alleged to have been committed, or in which the person was held in custody or confinement, or in which an avoidance of service of process or a contempt referred to in clause (3) of the first paragraph of this section is alleged to have been committed, and only upon formal approval in writing by the Attorney General, the Deputy Attorney General, the Associate Attorney General, or an Assistant Attorney General of the United States, which function of approving prosecutions may not be delegated.

(June 25, 1948, c. 645, 62 Stat. 755; Apr. 6, 1956, c. 177, § 1, 70 Stat. 100; Oct. 4, 1961, Pub.L. 87–368, 75 Stat. 795; Oct. 15, 1970, Pub.L. 91–452, Title III, § 302, 84 Stat. 932; Nov. 18, 1988, Pub.L. 100–690, Title VII, § 7020(b), 102 Stat. 4396; Sept. 13, 1994, Pub.L. 103–322, Title XXXIII, §§ 330004(19), 330016(1)(K), 108 Stat. 2142, 2147; Oct. 11, 1996, Pub.L. 104–294, Title VI, § 607(e), 110 Stat. 3511.)

HISTORICAL AND STATUTORY NOTES

Effective and Applicability Provisions

1956 Acts. Section 2 of Act Apr. 6, 1956, provided that: "The amendment made by the first-section of this Act [to this section] shall take effect on the thirtieth day after the date of enactment of this Act [April 6, 1956]."

Parental Kidnaping and Interstate or International Flight to Avoid Prosecution Under Applicable State Felony Statutes

Pub.L. 96–611, § 10, Dec. 28, 1980, 94 Stat. 3573, provided that:

"**(a)** In view of the findings of the Congress and the purposes of sections 6 to 10 of this Act set forth in section 302 [probably means section 7 of Pub.L. 96–611, set out as a note under section 1738A of Title 28, Judiciary and Judicial Procedure], the Congress hereby expressly declares its intent that section 1073 of title 18, United States Code [this section], apply to cases involving parental kidnaping and interstate or international flight to avoid prosecution under applicable State felony statutes.

"**(b)** The Attorney General of the United States, not later than 120 days after the date of the enactment of this section [Dec. 28, 1980] (and once every 6 months during the 3-year period following such 120-day period), shall submit a report to the Congress with respect to steps taken to comply with the intent of the Congress set forth in subsection (a). Each such report shall include—

"(1) data relating to the number of applications for complaints under section 1073 of title 18, United States Code [this section], in cases involving parental kidnaping;

"(2) data relating to the number of complaints issued in such cases; and

"(3) such other information as may assist in describing the activities of the Department of Justice in conformance with such intent."

Canal Zone

Applicability of section to Canal Zone, see § 14 of this title.

§ 1074. Flight to avoid prosecution for damaging or destroying any building or other real or personal property

(a) Whoever moves or travels in interstate or foreign commerce with intent either (1) to avoid prosecution, or custody, or confinement after conviction, under the laws of the place from which he flees, for willfully attempting to or damaging or destroying by fire or explosive any building, structure, facility, vehicle, dwelling house, synagogue, church, religious center or educational institution, public or private, or (2) to avoid giving testimony in any criminal proceeding relating to any such offense shall be fined under this title or imprisoned not more than five years, or both.

(b) Violations of this section may be prosecuted in the Federal judicial district in which the original crime was alleged to have been committed or in which the person was held in custody or confinement: *Provided, however*, That this section shall not be construed as indicating an intent on the part of Congress to prevent any State, Territory, Commonwealth, or possession of the United States of any jurisdiction over any offense over which they would have jurisdiction in the absence of such section.

(Added Pub.L. 86–449, Title II, § 201, May 6, 1960, 74 Stat. 86, and amended Pub.L. 103–322, Title XXXIII, § 330016(1)(K), Sept. 13, 1994, 108 Stat. 2147.)

CHAPTER 50—GAMBLING

Sec.

§ 1081. Definitions

As used in this chapter:

The term "gambling ship" means a vessel used principally for the operation of one or more gambling establishments. Such term does not include a vessel with respect to gambling aboard such vessel beyond the territorial waters of the United States during a covered voyage (as defined in section 4472 of the Internal Revenue Code of 1986 as in effect on January 1, 1994).

The term "gambling establishment" means any common gaming or gambling establishment operated for the purpose of gaming or gambling, including accepting, recording, or registering bets, or carrying on a policy game or any other lottery, or playing any game of chance, for money or other thing of value.

The term "vessel" includes every kind of water and air craft or other contrivance used or capable of being used as a means of transportation on water, or on water and in the air, as well as any ship, boat, barge, or other water craft or any structure capable of floating on the water.

The term "American vessel" means any vessel documented or numbered under the laws of the United States; and includes any vessel which is neither documented or numbered under the laws of the United States nor documented under the laws of any foreign country, if such vessel is owned by, chartered to, or otherwise controlled by one or more citizens or residents of the United States or corporations organized under the laws of the United States or of any State.

The term "wire communication facility" means any and all instrumentalities, personnel, and services (among other things, the receipt, forwarding, or delivery of communications) used or useful in the transmission of writings, signs, pictures, and sounds of all kinds by aid of wire, cable, or other like connection between the points of origin and reception of such transmission.

(Added May 24, 1949, c. 139, § 23, 63 Stat. 92, and amended Sept. 13, 1961, Pub.L. 87–216, § 1, 75 Stat. 491; Sept. 13, 1994, Pub.L. 103–322, Title XXXII, § 320501, 108 Stat. 2114.)

HISTORICAL AND STATUTORY NOTES

References in Text

Section 4472 of the Internal Revenue Code of 1986, referred to in text, is section 4472 of Title 26, Internal Revenue Code.

§ 1082. Gambling ships

(a) It shall be unlawful for any citizen or resident of the United States, or any other person who is on an American vessel or is otherwise under or within the jurisdiction of the United States, directly or indirectly—

(1) to set up, operate, or own or hold any interest in any gambling ship or any gambling establishment on any gambling ship; or

(2) in pursuance of the operation of any gambling establishment on any gambling ship, to conduct or deal any gambling game, or to conduct or operate any gambling device, or to induce, entice, solicit, or permit any person to bet or play at any such establishment,

if such gambling ship is on the high seas, or is an American vessel or otherwise under or within the jurisdiction of the United States, and is not within the jurisdiction of any State.

(b) Whoever violates the provisions of subsection (a) of this section shall be fined under this title or imprisoned not more than two years, or both.

(c) Whoever, being (1) the owner of an American vessel, or (2) the owner of any vessel under or within the jurisdiction of the United States, or (3) the owner of any vessel and being an American citizen, shall use, or knowingly permit the use of, such vessel in violation of any provision of this section shall, in addition to any other penalties provided by this chapter, forfeit such vessel, together with her tackle, apparel, and furniture, to the United States.

(Added May 24, 1949, c. 139, § 23, 63 Stat. 92, and amended Sept. 13, 1994, Pub.L. 103–322, Title XXXIII, § 330016(1)(L), 108 Stat. 2147.)

§ 1083. Transportation between shore and ship; penalties

(a) It shall be unlawful to operate or use, or to permit the operation or use of, a vessel for the carriage or transportation, or for any part of the carriage or transportation, either directly or indirectly, of any passengers, for hire or otherwise, between a point or place within the United States and a gambling ship which is not within the jurisdiction of any State. This section does not apply to any carriage or transportation to or from a vessel in case of emergency involving the safety or protection of life or property.

(b) The Secretary of the Treasury shall prescribe necessary and reasonable rules and regulations to enforce this section and to prevent violations of its provisions.

For the operation or use of any vessel in violation of this section or of any rule or regulation issued hereunder, the owner or charterer of such vessel shall be subject to a civil penalty of $200 for each passenger carried or transported in violation of such provisions, and the master or other person in charge of such vessel shall be subject to a civil penalty of $300. Such penalty shall constitute a lien on such vessel, and proceedings to enforce such lien may be brought summarily by way of libel in any court of the United States having jurisdiction thereof. The Secretary of the Treasury may mitigate or remit any of the penalties provided by this section on such terms as he deems proper.

(Added May 24, 1949, c. 139, § 23, 63 Stat. 92.)

§ 1084. Transmission of wagering information; penalties

(a) Whoever being engaged in the business of betting or wagering knowingly uses a wire communication facility for the transmission in interstate or foreign commerce of bets or wagers or information assisting in the placing of bets or wagers on any sporting event or contest, or for the transmission of a wire communication which entitles the recipient to receive money or credit as a result of bets or wagers, or for information assisting in the placing of bets or wagers, shall be fined under this title or imprisoned not more than two years, or both.

(b) Nothing in this section shall be construed to prevent the transmission in interstate or foreign commerce of information for use in news reporting of sporting events or contests, or for the transmission of information assisting in the placing of bets or wagers on a sporting event or contest from a State or foreign country where betting on that sporting event or contest is legal into a State or foreign country in which such betting is legal.

(c) Nothing contained in this section shall create immunity from criminal prosecution under any laws of any State.

(d) When any common carrier, subject to the jurisdiction of the Federal Communications Commission, is notified in writing by a Federal, State, or local law enforcement agency, acting within its jurisdiction, that any facility furnished by it is being used or will be used for the purpose of transmitting or receiving gambling information in interstate or foreign commerce in violation of Federal, State or local law, it shall discontinue or refuse, the leasing, furnishing, or maintaining of such facility, after reasonable notice to the subscriber, but no damages, penalty or forfeiture, civil or criminal, shall be found against any common carrier for any act done in compliance with any notice received from a law enforcement agency. Nothing in this section shall be deemed to prejudice the right of any person affected thereby to secure an appropriate determination, as otherwise provided by law, in a Federal court or in a State or local tribunal or agency, that such facility should not be discontinued or removed, or should be restored.

(e) As used in this section, the term "State" means a State of the United States, the District of Columbia, the Commonwealth of Puerto Rico, or a commonwealth, territory or possession of the United States.

(Added Pub.L. 87–216, § 2, Sept. 13, 1961, 75 Stat. 491, and amended Pub.L. 100–690, Title VII, § 7024, Nov. 18, 1988, 102 Stat. 4397; Pub.L. 101–647, Title XII, § 1205(g), Nov. 29, 1990, 104 Stat. 4831; Pub.L. 103–322, Title XXXIII, § 330016(1)(L), Sept. 13, 1994, 108 Stat. 2147.)

CHAPTER 50A—GENOCIDE

Sec.

§ 1091. Genocide

(a) Basic offense.—Whoever, whether in time of peace or in time of war, in a circumstance described in subsection (d) and with the specific intent to destroy, in whole or in substantial part, a national, ethnic, racial, or religious group as such—

(1) kills members of that group;

(2) causes serious bodily injury to members of that group;

(3) causes the permanent impairment of the mental faculties of members of the group through drugs, torture, or similar techniques;

(4) subjects the group to conditions of life that are intended to cause the physical destruction of the group in whole or in part;

(5) imposes measures intended to prevent births within the group; or

(6) transfers by force children of the group to another group;

or attempts to do so, shall be punished as provided in subsection (b).

(b) Punishment for basic offense.—The punishment for an offense under subsection (a) is—

(1) in the case of an offense under subsection (a)(1) where death results, by death or imprisonment for life and a fine of not more than $1,000,000, or both; and

(2) a fine of not more than $1,000,000 or imprisonment for not more than twenty years, or both, in any other case.

(c) Incitement offense.—Whoever in a circumstance described in subsection (d) directly and publicly incites another to violate subsection (a) shall be fined not more than $500,000 or imprisoned not more than five years, or both.

(d) Required circumstance for offenses.—The circumstance referred to in subsections (a) and (c) is that—

(1) the offense is committed within the United States; or

(2) the alleged offender is a national of the United States (as defined in section 101 of the Immigration and Nationality Act (8 U.S.C. 1101)).

(e) Nonapplicability of certain limitations.—Notwithstanding section 3282 of this title, in the case of an offense under subsection (a)(1), an indictment may be found, or information instituted, at any time without limitation.

(Added Pub.L. 100–606, § 2(a), Nov. 4, 1988, 102 Stat. 3045, and amended Pub.L. 103–322, Title VI, § 60003(a)(13), Sept. 13, 1994, 108 Stat. 1970; Pub.L. 107–273, Div. B, Title IV, § 4002(a)(4), (b)(7), Nov. 2, 2002, 116 Stat. 1806, 1808.)

HISTORICAL AND STATUTORY NOTES

References in Text

Section 101 of the Immigration and Nationality Act (8 U.S.C. 1101), referred to in subsec. (d)(2), is section 101 of Act June 27, 1952, c. 477, Title I, 66 Stat. 166, as amended, which is classified to section 1101 of Title 8, Aliens and Nationality.

Effective and Applicability Provisions

2002 Acts. Amendment by section 4002(a)(4) of Pub.L. 107–273, as therein provided, effective Sept. 13, 1994, which is the date of enactment of Pub.L. 103–322, to which such amendment relates.

Short Title

1988 Acts. Section 1 of Pub.L. 100–606 provided that: "This Act [enacting this chapter] may be cited as the 'Genocide Convention Implementation Act of 1987 (the Proxmire Act)'."

§ 1092. Exclusive remedies

Nothing in this chapter shall be construed as precluding the application of State or local laws to the conduct proscribed by this chapter, nor shall anything in this chapter be construed as creating any substantive or procedural right enforceable by law by any party in any proceeding.

(Added Pub.L. 100–606, § 2(a), Nov. 4, 1988, 102 Stat. 3046.)

§ 1093. Definitions

As used in this chapter—

(1) the term "children" means the plural and means individuals who have not attained the age of eighteen years;

(2) the term "ethnic group" means a set of individuals whose identity as such is distinctive in terms of common cultural traditions or heritage;

(3) the term "incites" means urges another to engage imminently in conduct in circumstances under which there is a substantial likelihood of imminently causing such conduct;

(4) the term "members" means the plural;

(5) the term "national group" means a set of individuals whose identity as such is distinctive in terms of nationality or national origins;

(6) the term "racial group" means a set of individuals whose identity as such is distinctive in terms of physical characteristics or biological descent;

(7) the term "religious group" means a set of individuals whose identity as such is distinctive in terms of common religious creed, beliefs, doctrines, practices, or rituals; and

(8) the term "substantial part" means a part of a group of such numerical significance that the destruction or loss of that part would cause the destruction of the group as a viable entity within the nation of which such group is a part.

(Added Pub.L. 100–606, § 2(a), Nov. 4, 1988, 102 Stat. 3046.)

CHAPTER 51—HOMICIDE

§ 1111. Murder

(a) Murder is the unlawful killing of a human being with malice aforethought. Every murder perpetrated by poison, lying in wait, or any other kind of willful, deliberate, malicious, and premeditated killing; or committed in the perpetration of, or attempt to perpetrate, any arson, escape, murder, kidnapping, treason, espionage, sabotage, aggravated sexual abuse or sexual abuse, child abuse, burglary, or robbery; or perpetrated as part of a pattern or practice of assault or torture against a child or children; or perpetrated from a premeditated design unlawfully and maliciously to effect the death of any human being other than him who is killed, is murder in the first degree.

Any other murder is murder in the second degree.

(b) Within the special maritime and territorial jurisdiction of the United States,

Whoever is guilty of murder in the first degree shall be punished by death or by imprisonment for life;

Whoever is guilty of murder in the second degree, shall be imprisoned for any term of years or for life.

(c) For purposes of this section—

(1) the term "assault" has the same meaning as given that term in section 113;

(2) the term "child" means a person who has not attained the age of 18 years and is—

(A) under the perpetrator's care or control; or

(B) at least six years younger than the perpetrator;

(3) the term "child abuse" means intentionally or knowingly causing death or serious bodily injury to a child;

(4) the term "pattern or practice of assault or torture" means assault or torture engaged in on at least two occasions;

(5) the term "serious bodily injury" has the meaning set forth in section 1365; and

(6) the term "torture" means conduct, whether or not committed under the color of law, that otherwise satisfies the definition set forth in section 2340(1).

(June 25, 1948, c. 645, 62 Stat. 756; Oct. 12, 1984, Pub.L. 98–473, Title II, § 1004, 98 Stat. 2138; Nov. 10, 1986, Pub.L. 99–646, § 87(c)(4), 100 Stat. 3623; Nov. 14, 1986, Pub.L. 99–654, § 3(a)(4), 100 Stat. 3663; Nov. 18, 1988, Pub.L. 100–690, Title VII, § 7025, 102 Stat. 4397; Sept. 13, 1994, Pub.L. 103–322, Title VI, § 60003(a)(4), 108 Stat. 1969; Apr. 30, 2003, Pub.L. 108–21, Title I, § 102, 117 Stat. 652.)

HISTORICAL AND STATUTORY NOTES

Effective and Applicability Provisions

1986 Acts. Amendment by section 87 of Pub.L. 99–646 effective 30 days after Nov. 10, 1986, see section 87(e) of Pub.L. 99–646, set out as a note under section 2241 of this title.

§ 1112. Manslaughter

(a) Manslaughter is the unlawful killing of a human being without malice. It is of two kinds:

Voluntary—Upon a sudden quarrel or heat of passion.

Involuntary—In the commission of an unlawful act not amounting to a felony, or in the commission in an unlawful manner, or without due caution and circumspection, of a lawful act which might produce death.

(b) Within the special maritime and territorial jurisdiction of the United States,

Whoever is guilty of voluntary manslaughter, shall be fined under this title or imprisoned not more than ten years, or both;

Whoever is guilty of involuntary manslaughter, shall be fined under this title or imprisoned not more than six years, or both.

(June 25, 1948, c. 645, 62 Stat. 756; Sept. 13, 1994, Pub.L. 103–322, Title XXXII, § 320102, Title XXXIII, § 330016(1)(H), 108 Stat. 2109, 2147; Oct. 11, 1996, Pub.L. 104–294, Title VI, § 604(b)(13), 110 Stat. 3507.)

HISTORICAL AND STATUTORY NOTES

Effective and Applicability Provisions

1996 Acts. Amendment by section 604 of Pub.L. 104–294 effective Sept. 13, 1994, see section 604(d) of Pub.L. 104–294, set out as a note under section 13 of this title.

Repeals

Pub.L. 103–322, Title XXXII, § 320102(2), Sept. 13, 1994, 108 Stat. 2109, appearing in the credit of this section, was repealed by Pub.L. 104–294, Title VI, § 604(b)(13), Oct. 11, 1996, 110 Stat. 3507.

§ 1113. Attempt to commit murder or manslaughter

Except as provided in section 113 of this title, whoever, within the special maritime and territorial jurisdiction of the United States, attempts to commit murder or manslaughter, shall, for an attempt to commit murder be imprisoned not more than twenty years or fined under this title, or both, and for an attempt to commit manslaughter be imprisoned not more than seven years or fined under this title, or both.

(June 25, 1948, c. 645, 62 Stat. 756; Nov. 18, 1988, Pub.L. 100–690, Title VII, § 7058(c), 102 Stat. 4403; Nov. 29, 1990, Pub.L. 101–647, Title XXXV, § 3534, 104 Stat. 4925; Apr. 24, 1996, Pub.L. 104–132, Title VII, § 705(a)(5), 110 Stat. 1295.)

HISTORICAL AND STATUTORY NOTES

Codifications

Amendment by Pub.L. 101–647 directed the deletion of the final period from this section. Such deletion had already been editorially executed, and therefore, no further change in text was required.

§ 1114. Protection of officers and employees of the United States

Whoever kills or attempts to kill any officer or employee of the United States or of any agency in any branch of the United States Government (including any member of the uniformed services) while such officer or employee is engaged in or on account of the performance of official duties, or any person assisting such an officer or employee in the performance of such duties or on account of that assistance, shall be punished—

(1) in the case of murder, as provided under section 1111;

(2) in the case of manslaughter, as provided under section 1112; or

(3) in the case of attempted murder or manslaughter, as provided in section 1113.

(June 25, 1948, c. 645, 62 Stat. 756; May 24, 1949, c. 139, § 24, 63 Stat. 93; Oct. 31, 1951, c. 655, § 28, 65 Stat. 721; June 27, 1952, c. 477, Title IV, § 402(c), 66 Stat. 276; July 29, 1958, Pub.L. 85–568, Title III, § 304(d), 72 Stat. 434; July 2, 1962, Pub.L. 87–518, § 10, 76 Stat. 132; Aug. 27, 1964, Pub.L. 88–493, § 3, 78 Stat. 610; July 15, 1965, Pub.L. 89–74, § 8(b), 79 Stat. 234; Aug. 2, 1968, Pub.L. 90–449, § 2, 82 Stat. 611; Aug. 12, 1970, Pub.L. 91–375, § 6(j) (9), 84 Stat. 777; Oct. 27, 1970, Pub.L. 91–513, Title II, § 701(i) (1), 84 Stat. 1282; Dec. 29, 1970, Pub.L. 91–596, § 17(h) (1), 84 Stat. 1607; Oct. 26, 1974, Pub.L. 93–481, § 5, 88 Stat. 1456; May 11, 1976, Pub.L. 94–284, § 18, 90 Stat. 514; Oct. 21, 1976, Pub.L. 94–582, § 16, 90 Stat. 2883; Aug. 3, 1977, Pub.L. 95–87, Title VII, § 704, 91 Stat. 520; Nov. 8, 1978, Pub.L. 95–616, § 3(j) (2), 92 Stat. 3112; Nov. 10, 1978, Pub.L. 95–630, Title III, § 307, 92 Stat. 3677; July 1, 1980, Pub.L. 96–296, § 26(c), 94 Stat. 819; Oct. 17, 1980, Pub.L. 96–466, Title VII, § 704, 94 Stat. 2216; Dec. 29, 1981, Pub.L. 97–143, § 1(b), 95 Stat. 1724; Sept. 13, 1982, Pub.L. 97–259, Title I,

§ 128, 96 Stat. 1099; Oct. 25, 1982, Pub.L. 97–365, § 6, 96 Stat. 1752; Jan. 12, 1983, Pub.L. 97–452, § 2(b), 96 Stat. 2478; July 30, 1983, Pub.L. 98–63, Title I, § 101, 97 Stat. 313; Oct. 12, 1984, Pub.L. 98–473, Title II, § 1012, 98 Stat. 2142; Oct. 30, 1984, Pub.L. 98–557, § 17(c), 98 Stat. 2868; Nov. 18, 1988, Pub.L. 100–690, Title VII, § 7026, 102 Stat. 4397; Aug. 9, 1989, Pub.L. 101–73, Title IX, § 962(a)(6), 103 Stat. 502; Nov. 29, 1990, Pub.L. 101–647, Title XII, § 1205(h), Title XVI, § 1606, Title XXXV, § 3535, 104 Stat. 4831, 4843, 4925; June 13, 1991, Pub.L. 102–54, § 13(f)(2), 105 Stat. 275; Sept. 3, 1992, Pub.L. 102–365, § 6, 106 Stat. 975; Sept. 13, 1994, Pub.L. 103–322, Title VI, § 60007, Title XXXIII, §§ 330009(c), 330011(g), 108 Stat. 1971, 2143, 2145; Apr. 24, 1996, Pub.L. 104–132, Title VII, § 727(a), 110 Stat. 1302; Oct. 11, 1996, Pub.L. 104–294, Title VI, § 601(f)(2), 110 Stat. 3499; Nov. 2, 2002, Pub.L. 107–273, Div. B, Title IV, § 4002(c)(1), 116 Stat. 1808.)

HISTORICAL AND STATUTORY NOTES

Codifications

Section 601(f)(2) of Pub.L. 104–294, which directed that this section be amended by substituting "1112," for "1112.", could not be executed to text due to prior amendment by section 727(a) of Pub.L. 104–132, which revised this section generally. See 2002 and 1996 Amendments notes under this section.

Section 704 of Pub.L. 95–87, in addition to amending this section, enacted section 1294 of Title 30, Mineral Lands and Mining.

Effective and Applicability Provisions

2002 Acts. Amendment by section 4002(c)(1) of Pub.L. 107–273, as therein provided, effective Oct. 11, 1996, which is the date of enactment of Pub.L. 104–294, to which such amendment relates.

1994 Acts. Section 330011(g) of Pub.L. 103–322 provided in part that the amendment made by such section, repealing section 1606 of Pub.L. 101–647 (which amended this section), was to take effect on the date of enactment of section 1606 of Pub.L. 101–647, which was approved Nov. 29, 1990.

1980 Acts. Section 802(g)(3) of Pub.L. 96–466 provided in part that the amendment by section 704 of Pub.L. 96–466 shall take effect on Oct. 17, 1980.

1978 Acts. Amendment by Pub.L. 95–630 effective upon expiration of 120 days after Nov. 10, 1978, see section 2101 of Pub.L. 95–630, set out as an Effective Date note under section 375b of Title 12, Banks and Banking.

1970 Acts. Amendment by Pub.L. 91–513 effective on the first day of the seventh calendar month that begins after Oct. 26, 1970, see section 704 of Pub.L. 91–513, set out as an Effective Date note under section 801 of Title 21, Food and Drugs.

Amendment by Pub.L. 91–375 effective within 1 year after Aug. 12, 1970, on date established therefor by the Board of Governors of the United States Postal Service and published by it in the Federal Register, see section 15(a) of Pub.L. 91–375, set out as an Effective Date note preceding section 101 of Title 39, Postal Service.

1965 Acts. Amendment by Pub.L. 89–74 effective July 15, 1965, see section 11 of Pub.L. 89–74.

Change of Name

The Department of Health, Education, and Welfare was redesignated the Department of Health and Human Services by Pub.L. 96–88, Title V, § 509(b), Oct. 17, 1979, 93 Stat. 695, which is classified to section 3508(b) of Title 20, Education.

Transfer of Functions

Interstate Commerce Commission abolished and functions of Commission transferred, except as otherwise provided in Pub.L. 104–88, to Surface Transportation Board effective Jan. 1, 1996, by sections 702 of Title 49, Transportation, and section 101 of Pub.L. 104–88, set out as a note under section 701 of Title 49. References to Interstate Commerce Commission deemed to refer to Surface Transportation Board, a member or employee of the Board, or Secretary of Transportation, as appropriate, see section 205 of Pub.L. 104–88, set out as a note under section 701 of Title 49.

The Bureau of Narcotics and Dangerous Drugs, including the office of Director thereof, in the Department of Justice was abolished by Reorg. Plan No. 2 of 1973, eff. July 1, 1973, 38 F.R. 15932, 87 Stat. 1091, set out in Appendix 1 to Title 5, Government Organization and Employees. Reorg. Plan No. 2 of 1973 also created in the Department of Justice a single, comprehensive agency for the enforcement of drug laws to be known as the Drug Enforcement Administration, empowered the Attorney General to authorize the performance by officers, employees, and agencies of the Department of functions transferred to him, and directed the Attorney General to coordinate all drug law enforcement functions to assure maximum cooperation between the Drug Enforcement Administration, the Federal Bureau of Investigation, and the other units of the Department of Justice involved in drug law enforcement.

The Coast Guard was transferred to the Department of Transportation and all functions, powers, and duties, relating to the Coast Guard, of the Secretary of the Treasury and of other offices and officers of the Department of the Treasury were transferred to the Secretary of Transportation by Pub.L. 89–670, Oct. 15, 1966, 80 Stat. 931, which created the Department of Transportation. See section 108 of Title 49, Transportation.

All functions of all officers of the Department of the Treasury, and all functions of all agencies and employees of such Department, were transferred, with certain exceptions, to the Secretary of the Treasury, with power vested in him to authorize their performance or the performance of any of his functions, by any of such officers, agencies, and employees, by Reorg. Plan No. 26 of 1950, §§ 1, 2, eff. July 31,1950, 15 F.R. 4935, 64 Stat. 1280, set out in Appendix 1 to Title 5, Government Organization and Employees. The Secret Service is an agency in the Treasury Department, the customs and internal revenue officials, referred to in this section, are officials in such Department.

All functions of all other officers of the Department of the Interior, and all functions of all agencies and employees of such Department, were, with two exceptions, transferred to the Secretary of the Interior, with power vested in him to authorize their performance or the performance of any of his functions by any of such officers, agencies, and employees, by Reorg. Plan No. 3 of 1950, §§ 1, 2, eff. May 24, 1950, 15 F.R. 3174, 64 Stat. 1262, set out in Appendix 1 to Title 5, Government Organization and Employees. Officers and employees of the National Park Service, and of the Indian field service, referred to in this section, are officers and employees of the Department of the Interior.

All functions of all other officers of the Department of Justice, and all functions of all agencies and employees of such Department, were, with a few exceptions, transferred to the Attorney General, with power vested in him to authorize their performance or the performance of any of his functions by any of such officers, agencies, and employees, by Reorg. Plan No. 2 of 1950, §§ 1, 2, eff. May 24, 1950, 15 F.R. 3173, 64 Stat. 1261, set out in Appendix 1 to Title 5, Government Organization and Employees. United States Attorneys, Assistant United States Attorneys, United States marshals, and deputy marshals, referred to in this section, are officers within the Department of Justice, the Federal Bureau of Investigation, also referred to in this section, is a bureau of such Department, and officers and employees of United States penal or correctional institutions and immigration officials, also referred to in this section, are officers and employees within such Department.

Repeals

Section 601(f)(2) of Pub.L. 104–294, cited in the credit of this section, was repealed by Pub.L. 107–273, Div. B, Title IV, § 4002(c)(1), Nov. 2, 2002, 116 Stat. 1808, effective Oct. 11, 1996.

Section 1606 of Pub.L. 101–647, cited in the credit of this section, was repealed by section 330011(g) of Pub.L. 103–322.

Savings Provisions

Amendment by Pub.L. 91–513 not to affect or abate any prosecutions for violation of law or any civil seizures or forfeitures and injunctive proceedings commenced prior to the effective date of such amendment and all administrative proceedings pending before the Bureau of Narcotics and Dangerous Drugs on Oct. 27, 1970, to be continued and brought to final determination in accord with laws and regulations in effect prior to Oct. 27, 1970, see section 702 of Pub.L. 91–513, set out as a Savings Provision note under section 321 of Title 21, Food and Drugs.

Severability of Provisions

If any provision of Pub.L. 101–73 or the application thereof to any person or circumstance is held invalid, the remainder of Pub.L. 101–73 and the application of the provision to other persons not similarly situated or to other circumstances not to be affected thereby, see section 1221 of Pub.L. 101–73, set out as a note under section 1811 of Title 12, Banks and Banking.

Life Imprisonment or Lesser Term for Killing Person in Performance of Investigative, Inspection, or Law Enforcement Functions

Section 17(h)(2) of Pub.L. 91–596 provided that: "Notwithstanding the provisions of sections 1111 and 1114 of title 18, United States Code, whoever, in violation of the provisions of section 1114 of such title, kills a person while engaged in or on account of the performance of investigative, inspection, or law enforcement functions added to such section 1114 by paragraph (1) of this subsection, and who would otherwise be subject to the penalty provisions of such section 1111, shall be punished by imprisonment for any term of years or for life."

Immunity from Criminal Prosecution

Section 5 of Pub.L. 88–493 which provided that nothing in Pub.L. 88–493, which amended this section and section 112 of this title, and enacted former section 170e–1 of Title 5, Government Organization and Employees, shall create immunity from criminal prosecution under the laws of any State, territory, possession, Puerto Rico, or the District of Columbia, is set out as a note under section 112 of this title.

§ 1115. Misconduct or neglect of ship officers

Every captain, engineer, pilot, or other person employed on any steamboat or vessel, by whose misconduct, negligence, or inattention to his duties on such vessel the life of any person is destroyed, and every owner, charterer, inspector, or other public officer, through whose fraud, neglect, connivance, misconduct, or violation of law the life of any person is destroyed, shall be fined under this title or imprisoned not more than ten years, or both.

When the owner or charterer of any steamboat or vessel is a corporation, any executive officer of such corporation, for the time being actually charged with the control and management of the operation, equipment, or navigation of such steamboat or vessel, who has knowingly and willfully caused or allowed such fraud, neglect, connivance, misconduct, or violation of law, by which the life of any person is destroyed, shall be fined under this title or imprisoned not more than ten years, or both.

(June 25, 1948, c. 645, 62 Stat. 757; Sept. 13, 1994, Pub.L. 103–322, Title XXXIII, § 330016(1)(L), 108 Stat. 2147.)

§ 1116. Murder or manslaughter of foreign officials, official guests, or internationally protected persons

(a) Whoever kills or attempts to kill a foreign official, official guest, or internationally protected person shall be punished as provided under sections 1111, 1112, and 1113 of this title.

(b) For the purposes of this section:

(1) "Family" includes (a) a spouse, parent, brother or sister, child, or person to whom the foreign official or internationally protected person stands in loco parentis, or (b) any other person living in his household and related to the foreign official or internationally protected person by blood or marriage.

(2) "Foreign government" means the government of a foreign country, irrespective of recognition by the United States.

(3) "Foreign official" means—

(A) a Chief of State or the political equivalent, President, Vice President, Prime Minister, Ambassador, Foreign Minister, or other officer of Cabinet rank or above of a foreign government or the chief executive officer of an international organization, or any person who has previously served in such capacity, and any member of his family, while in the United States; and

(B) any person of a foreign nationality who is duly notified to the United States as an officer or employee of a foreign government or international organization, and who is in the United States on official business, and any member of his family whose presence in the United States is in connection with the presence of such officer or employee.

(4) "Internationally protected person" means—

(A) a Chief of State or the political equivalent, head of government, or Foreign Minister whenever such person is in a country other than his own and any member of his family accompanying him; or

(B) any other representative, officer, employee, or agent of the United States Government, a foreign government, or international organization who at the time and place concerned is entitled pursuant to international law to special protection against attack upon his person, freedom, or dignity, and any member of his family then forming part of his household.

(5) "International organization" means a public international organization designated as such pursuant to section 1 of the International Organizations Immunities Act (22 U.S.C. 288) or a public organization created pursuant to treaty or other agreement under international law as an instrument through or by which two or more foreign governments engage in some aspect of their conduct of international affairs.

(6) "Official guest" means a citizen or national of a foreign country present in the United States as an official guest of the Government of the United States pursuant to designation as such by the Secretary of State.

(7) "National of the United States" has the meaning prescribed in section 101(a)(22) of the Immigration and Nationality Act (8 U.S.C. 1101(a)(22)).

(c) If the victim of an offense under subsection (a) is an internationally protected person outside the United States, the United States may exercise jurisdiction over the offense if (1) the victim is a representative, officer, employee, or agent of the United States, (2) an offender is a national of the United States, or (3) an offender is afterwards found in the United States. As used in this subsection, the United States includes all areas under the jurisdiction of the United States including any of the places within the provisions of sections 5 and 7 of this title and section 46501(2) of title 49.

(d) In the course of enforcement of this section and any other sections prohibiting a conspiracy or attempt to violate this section, the Attorney General may request assistance from any Federal, State, or local agency, including the Army, Navy, and Air Force, any statute, rule, or regulation to the contrary notwithstanding.

(Added Pub.L. 92–539, Title I, § 101, Oct. 24, 1972, 86 Stat. 1071, and amended Pub.L. 94–467, § 2, Oct. 8, 1976, 90 Stat. 1997; Pub.L. 95–163, § 17(b) (1), Nov. 9, 1977, 91 Stat. 1286; Pub.L. 95–504, § 2(b), Oct. 24, 1978, 92 Stat. 1705; Pub.L. 97–351, § 3, Oct. 15, 1982, 96 Stat. 1666; Pub.L. 103–272, § 5(e)(2), July 5, 1994, 108 Stat. 1373; Pub.L. 103–322, Title VI, § 60003(a)(5), Title XXXIII, § 330006, Sept. 13, 1994, 108 Stat. 1969, 2142; Pub.L. 104–132, Title VII, § 721(c), Apr. 24, 1996, 110 Stat. 1298; Pub.L. 104–294, Title VI, § 601(g)(2), Oct. 11, 1996, 110 Stat. 3500.)

HISTORICAL AND STATUTORY NOTES

References in Text

Section 1 of the International Organizations Immunities Act, referred to in subsec. (b)(5), is classified to section 288 of Title 22, Foreign Relations and Intercourse.

Codifications

Amendment of subsec. (a) by sections 60003(a)(5) and 330006 of Pub.L. 103–322 struck out exceptions to punishment as provided under sections 1111, 1112, and 1113 of this title, without striking out ", except that" at the end, and deleted the term ", and" twice. The term ", except that" was left unaltered as no Congressional intent as to its deletion was expressed, while the term ", and" was deleted once as the probable intent of Congress.

§ 1117. Conspiracy to murder

If two or more persons conspire to violate section 1111, 1114, 1116, or 1119 of this title, and one or more of such persons do any overt act to effect the object of the conspiracy, each shall be punished by imprisonment for any term of years or for life.

(Added Pub.L. 92–539, Title I, § 101, Oct. 24, 1972, 86 Stat. 1071, and amended Pub.L. 103–322, Title VI, § 60009(b)(1), Sept. 13, 1994, 108 Stat. 1972.)

§ 1118. Murder by a Federal prisoner

(a) Offense.—A person who, while confined in a Federal correctional institution under a sentence for a term of life imprisonment, commits the murder of another shall be punished by death or by life imprisonment.

(b) Definitions.—In this section—

"Federal correctional institution" means any Federal prison, Federal correctional facility, Federal community program center, or Federal halfway house.

"murder" means a first degree or second degree murder (as defined in section 1111).

"term of life imprisonment" means a sentence for the term of natural life, a sentence commuted to natural life, an indeterminate term of a minimum of at least fifteen years and a maximum of life, or an unexecuted sentence of death.

(Added Pub.L. 103–322, Title VI, § 60005(a), Sept. 13, 1994, 108 Stat. 1970.)

HISTORICAL AND STATUTORY NOTES

Prior Provisions

Another section 1118, relating to protection against HIV and added by Pub.L. 103–333, Title V, § 514, was renumbered section 1122 of this title.

§ 1119. Foreign murder of United States nationals

(a) Definition.—In this section, "national of the United States" has the meaning stated in section 101(a)(22) of the Immigration and Nationality Act (8 U.S.C. 1101(a)(22)).

(b) Offense.—A person who, being a national of the United States, kills or attempts to kill a national of the United States while such national is outside the United States but within the jurisdiction of another country shall be punished as provided under sections 1111, 1112, and 1113.

(c) Limitations on prosecution.—(1) No prosecution may be instituted against any person under this section except upon the written approval of the Attorney General, the Deputy Attorney General, or an Assistant Attorney General, which function of approving prosecutions may not be delegated. No prosecution shall be approved if prosecution has been previously undertaken by a foreign country for the same conduct.

(2) No prosecution shall be approved under this section unless the Attorney General, in consultation with the Secretary of State, determines that the conduct took place in a country in which the person is no longer present, and the country lacks the ability to lawfully secure the person's return. A determination by the Attorney General under this paragraph is not subject to judicial review.

(Added Pub.L. 103–322, Title VI, § 60009(a), Sept. 13, 1994, 108 Stat. 1972.)

§ 1120. Murder by escaped prisoners

(a) Definition.—In this section, "Federal correctional institution" and "term of life imprisonment" have the meanings stated in section 1118.

(b) Offense and penalty.—A person, having escaped from a Federal correctional institution where the person was confined under a sentence for a term of life imprisonment, kills another shall be punished as provided in sections 1111 and 1112.

(Added Pub.L. 103–322, Title VI, § 60012(a), Sept. 13, 1994, 108 Stat. 1973, and amended Pub.L. 104–294, Title VI, § 601(c)(2), Oct. 11, 1996, 110 Stat. 3499.)

§ 1121. Killing persons aiding Federal investigations or State correctional officers

(a) Whoever intentionally kills—

(1) a State or local official, law enforcement officer, or other officer or employee while working with Federal law enforcement officials in furtherance of a Federal criminal investigation—

(A) while the victim is engaged in the performance of official duties;

(B) because of the performance of the victim's official duties; or

(C) because of the victim's status as a public servant; or

(2) any person assisting a Federal criminal investigation, while that assistance is being rendered and because of it,

shall be sentenced according to the terms of section 1111, including by sentence of death or by imprisonment for life.

(b)(1) Whoever, in a circumstance described in paragraph (3) of this subsection, while incarcerated, intentionally kills any State correctional officer engaged in, or on account of the performance of such officer's official duties, shall be sentenced to a term of imprisonment which shall not be less than 20 years, and may be sentenced to life imprisonment or death.

(2) As used in this section, the term, "State correctional officer" includes any officer or employee of any prison, jail, or other detention facility, operated by, or under contract to, either a State or local governmental agency, whose job responsibilities include providing for the custody of incarcerated individuals.

(3) The circumstance referred to in paragraph (1) is that—

(A) the correctional officer is engaged in transporting the incarcerated person interstate; or

(B) the incarcerated person is incarcerated pursuant to a conviction for an offense against the United States.

(c) For the purposes of this section, the term "State" means a State of the United States, the District of Columbia, and any commonwealth, territory, or possession of the United States.

(Added Pub.L. 103–322, Title VI, § 60015(a), Sept. 13, 1994, 108 Stat. 1974, and amended Pub.L. 104–294, Title VI, § 607(k), Oct. 11, 1996, 110 Stat. 3512.)

§ 1122. Protection against the human immunodeficiency virus

(a) In general.—Whoever, after testing positive for the Human Immunodeficiency Virus (HIV) and receiving actual notice of that fact, knowingly donates or sells, or knowingly attempts to donate or sell, blood, semen, tissues, organs, or other bodily fluids for use by another, except as determined necessary for medical research or testing, shall be fined or imprisoned in accordance with subsection (c).

(b) Transmission not required.—Transmission of the Human Immunodeficiency Virus does not have to occur for a person to be convicted of a violation of this section.

(c) Penalty.—Any person convicted of violating the provisions of subsection (a) shall be subject to a fine under this title of not less than $10,000, imprisoned for not less than 1 year nor more than 10 years, or both.

(Added Pub.L. 103–333, Title V, § 514, Sept. 30, 1994, 108 Stat. 2574, § 1118, renumbered § 1122 and amended Pub.L. 104–294, Title VI, § 601(a)(5), Oct. 11, 1996, 110 Stat. 3498.)

CHAPTER 53—INDIANS

HISTORICAL AND STATUTORY NOTES

Savings Provisions of Pub.L. 98–473, Title II, c. II

See section 235 of Pub.L. 98–473, Title II, c. II, Oct. 12, 1984, 98 Stat. 2031, as amended, set out as a note under section 3551 of this title.

§ 1151. Indian country defined

Except as otherwise provided in sections 1154 and 1156 of this title, the term "Indian country", as used in this chapter, means (a) all land within the limits of any Indian reservation under the jurisdiction of the United States Government, notwithstanding the issuance of any patent, and, including rights-of-way running through the reservation, (b) all dependent Indian communities within the borders of the United States whether within the original or subsequently acquired territory thereof, and whether within or without the limits of a state, and (c) all Indian allotments, the Indian titles to which have not been extinguished, including rights-of-way running through the same.

(June 25, 1948, c. 645, 62 Stat. 757; May 24, 1949, c. 139, § 25, 63 Stat. 94.)

HISTORICAL AND STATUTORY NOTES

Short Title

1976 Amendments. Pub.L. 94–297, § 1, May 29, 1976, 90 Stat. 585, provided: "That this Act [amending sections 113, 1153, and 3242 of this title] may be cited as the 'Indian Crimes Act of 1976'."

§ 1152. Laws governing

Except as otherwise expressly provided by law, the general laws of the United States as to the punishment of offenses committed in any place within the sole and exclusive jurisdiction of the United States, except the District of Columbia, shall extend to the Indian country.

This section shall not extend to offenses committed by one Indian against the person or property of another Indian, nor to any Indian committing any offense in the Indian country who has been punished by the local law of the tribe, or to any case where, by treaty stipulations, the exclusive jurisdiction over such offenses is or may be secured to the Indian tribes respectively.

(June 25, 1948, c. 645, 62 Stat. 757.)

§ 1153. Offenses committed within Indian country

(a) Any Indian who commits against the person or property of another Indian or other person any of the following offenses, namely, murder, manslaughter, kidnapping, maiming, a felony under chapter 109A, incest, assault with intent to commit murder, assault with a dangerous weapon, assault resulting in serious bodily injury (as defined in section 1365 of this title), an assault against an individual who has not attained the age of 16 years, felony child abuse or neglect, arson, burglary, robbery, and a felony under section 661 of this title within the Indian country, shall be subject to the same law and penalties as all other persons committing any of the above offenses, within the exclusive jurisdiction of the United States.

(b) Any offense referred to in subsection (a) of this section that is not defined and punished by Federal law in force within the exclusive jurisdiction of the United States shall be defined and punished in accordance with the laws of the State in which such offense was committed as are in force at the time of such offense.

(June 25, 1948, c. 645, 62 Stat. 758; May 24, 1949, c. 139, § 26, 63 Stat. 94; Nov. 2, 1966, Pub.L. 89–707, § 1, 80 Stat. 1100; Apr. 11, 1968, Pub.L. 90–284, Title V, § 501, 82 Stat. 80; May 29, 1976, Pub.L. 94–297, § 2, 90 Stat. 585; Oct. 12, 1984, Pub.L. 98–473, Title II, § 1009, 98 Stat. 2141; May 15, 1986, Pub.L. 99–303, 100 Stat. 438; Nov. 10, 1986, Pub.L. 99–646, § 87(c)(5), 100 Stat. 3623; Nov. 10, 1986, Pub.L. 99–654, § 3(a)(5), 100 Stat. 3663; Nov. 18, 1988, Pub.L. 100–690, Title VII, § 7027, 102 Stat. 4397; Sept. 13, 1994, Pub.L. 103–322, Title XVII, § 170201(e), Title XXXIII, § 330021(1), 108 Stat. 2043, 2150; July 27, 2006, Pub.L. 109–248, Title II, § 215, 120 Stat. 617.)

HISTORICAL AND STATUTORY NOTES

Codifications

Amendment by section 7027 of Pub.L. 100–690 was executed to subsec. (a) as the probable intent of Congress despite section 7027 of Pub.L. 100–690 not specifying subsec. (a) as the subsection to be amended.

Pub.L. 99–646 and Pub.L. 99–654, which directed that this section be amended identically by substituting in the first paragraph "a felony under chapter 109A," for "rape, involuntary sodomy, carnal knowledge of any female, not his wife, who has attained the age of sixteen years, assault with intent to commit rape," and by striking out in the second and third paragraphs ", involuntary sodomy," was executed by making the substitution in subsec. (a) for "rape, involuntary sodomy, felonious sexual molestation of a minor, carnal knowledge of any female, not his wife, who has not attained the age of sixteen years, assault with intent to commit rape," as the probable intent of Congress in view of the prior amendment of this section by Pub.L. 99–303, but amendment of the second and third paragraphs could not be executed because such paragraphs were struck out by Pub.L. 99–303.

Effective and Applicability Provisions

1986 Acts. Amendment by Pub.L. 99–654 effective 30 days after Nov. 14, 1986, see section 4 of Pub.L. 99–654, set out as a note under section 2241 of this title.

Amendment by Pub.L. 99–646 effective 30 days after Nov. 10, 1986, see section 87(e) of Pub.L. 99–646, set out as a note under section 2241 of this title.

§ 1154. Intoxicants dispensed in Indian Country

(a) Whoever sells, gives away, disposes of, exchanges, or barters any malt, spirituous, or vinous liquor, including beer, ale, and wine, or any ardent or other intoxicating liquor of any kind whatsoever, except for scientific, sacramental, medicinal or mechanical purposes, or any essence, extract, bitters, preparation, compound, composition, or any article whatsoever, under any name, label, or brand, which produces intoxication, to any Indian to whom an allotment of land has been made while the title to the same shall be held in trust by the Government, or to any Indian who is a ward of the Government under charge of any Indian superintendent, or to any Indian, including mixed bloods, over whom the Government, through its departments, exercises guardianship, and whoever introduces or attempts to introduce any malt, spirituous, or vinous liquor, including beer, ale, and wine, or any ardent or intoxicating liquor of any kind whatsoever into the Indian country, shall, for the first offense, be fined under this title or imprisoned not more than one year, or both; and, for each subsequent offense, be fined under this title or imprisoned not more than five years, or both.

(b) It shall be a sufficient defense to any charge of introducing or attempting to introduce ardent spirits, ale, beer, wine, or intoxicating liquors into the Indian country that the acts charged were done under authority, in writing, from the Department of the Army or any officer duly authorized thereunto by the Department of the Army, but this subsection shall not bar the prosecution of any officer, soldier, sutler or storekeeper, attaché, or employee of the Army of the United States who barters, donates, or furnishes in any manner whatsoever liquors, beer, or any intoxicating beverage whatsoever to any Indian.

(c) The term "Indian country" as used in this section does not include fee-patented lands in non-Indian communities or rights-of-way through Indian reservations, and this section does not apply to such lands or rights-of-way in the absence of a treaty or statute extending the Indian liquor laws thereto.

(June 25, 1948, c. 645, 62 Stat. 758; May 24, 1949, c. 139, § 27, 63 Stat. 94; Sept. 13, 1994, Pub.L. 103–322, Title XXXIII, § 330016(1)(G), (I), 108 Stat. 2147.)

HISTORICAL AND STATUTORY NOTES

Transfer of Functions

All functions of all other officers of the Department of the Interior and all functions of all agencies and employees of such Department were, with two exceptions, transferred to the Secretary of the Interior, with power vested in him to authorize their performance or the performance of any of his functions by any of such officers, agencies, and employees, by Reorg. Plan No. 3 of 1950, §§ 1, 2, eff. May 24, 1950, 15 F.R. 3174, 64 Stat. 1262, set out in the Appendix to Title 5, Government Organization and Employees.

§ 1155. Intoxicants dispensed on school site

Whoever, on any tract of land in the former Indian country upon which is located any Indian school maintained by or under the supervision of the United States, manufactures, sells, gives away, or in any manner, or by any means furnishes to anyone, either for himself or another, any vinous, malt, or fermented liquors, or any other intoxicating drinks of any kind whatsoever, except for scientific, sacramental, medicinal or mechanical purposes, whether medicated or not, or who carries, or in any manner has carried, into such area any such liquors or drinks, or who shall be interested in such manufacture, sale, giving away, furnishing to anyone, or carrying into such area any of such liquors or drinks, shall be fined under this title or imprisoned not more than five years, or both.

(June 25, 1948, c. 645, 62 Stat. 758; Sept. 13, 1994, Pub.L. 103–322, Title XXXIII, § 330016(1)(G), 108 Stat. 2147.)

§ 1156. Intoxicants possessed unlawfully

Whoever, except for scientific, sacramental, medicinal or mechanical purposes, possesses intoxicating liquors in the Indian country or where the introduction is prohibited by treaty or an Act of Congress, shall, for the first offense, be fined under this title or imprisoned not more than one year, or both; and, for each subsequent offense, be fined under this title or imprisoned not more than five years, or both.

The term "Indian country" as used in this section does not include fee-patented lands in non-Indian communities or rights-of-way through Indian reservations, and this section does not apply to such lands or rights-of-way in the absence of a treaty or statute extending the Indian liquor laws thereto.

(June 25, 1948, c. 645, 62 Stat. 759; May 24, 1949, c. 139, § 28, 63 Stat. 94; Sept. 13, 1994, Pub.L. 103–322, Title XXXIII, § 330016(1)(G), (I), 108 Stat. 2147.)

[§ 1157. Repealed. Pub.L. 85–86, July 10, 1957, 71 Stat. 277]

HISTORICAL AND STATUTORY NOTES

Section, Acts June 25, 1948, c. 645, 62 Stat. 759; May 24, 1949, c. 139, § 29, 63 Stat. 94; Aug. 15, 1953, c. 506, § 2(a), 67 Stat. 590, prohibited purchase of Indian-owned livestock subject to unpaid loans from Federal revolving fund or from tribal loan funds.

§ 1158. Counterfeiting Indian Arts and Crafts Board trade mark

Whoever counterfeits or colorably imitates any Government trade mark used or devised by the Indian Arts and Crafts Board in the Department of the Interior as provided in section 305a of Title 25, or, except as authorized by the Board, affixes any such Government trade mark, or knowingly, willfully, and corruptly affixes any reproduction, counterfeit, copy, or colorable imitation thereof upon any products, or to any labels, signs, prints, packages, wrappers, or receptacles intended to be used upon or in connection with the sale of such products; or

Whoever knowingly makes any false statement for the purpose of obtaining the use of any such Government trade mark—

Shall (1) in the case of a first violation, if an individual, be fined under this title or imprisoned not more than five years, or both, and, if a person other than an individual, be fined not more than $1,000,000; and (2) in the case of subsequent violations, if an individual, be fined not more than $1,000,000 or imprisoned not more than fifteen years, or both, and, if a person other than an individual, be fined not more than $5,000,000; and (3) shall be enjoined from further carrying on the act or acts complained of.

(June 25, 1948, c. 645, 62 Stat. 759; Nov. 29, 1990, Pub.L. 101–644, Title I, § 106, 104 Stat. 4665; Sept. 13, 1994, Pub.L. 103–322, Title XXXIII, § 330016(1)(U), 108 Stat. 2148.)

HISTORICAL AND STATUTORY NOTES

Transfer of Functions

All functions of all other officers of the Department of the Interior and all functions of all agencies and employees of such Department were, with two exceptions, transferred to the Secretary of the Interior, with power vested in him to authorize their performance or the performance of any of his functions by any of such officers, agencies, and employees, by Reorg. Plan No. 3 of 1950, §§ 1, 2, eff. May 24, 1950, 15 F.R. 3174, 64 Stat. 1262, set out in the Appendix to Title 5, Government Organization and Employees.

§ 1159. Misrepresentation of Indian produced goods and products

(a) It is unlawful to offer or display for sale or sell any good, with or without a Government trademark, in a manner that falsely suggests it is Indian produced, an Indian product, or the product of a particular Indian or Indian tribe or Indian arts and crafts organization, resident within the United States.

(b) Whoever knowingly violates subsection (a) shall—

(1) in the case of a first violation, if an individual, be fined not more than $250,000 or imprisoned not more than five years, or both, and, if a person other than an individual, be fined not more than $1,000,000; and

(2) in the case of subsequent violations, if an individual, be fined not more than $1,000,000 or imprisoned not more than fifteen years, or both, and, if a person other than an individual, be fined not more than $5,000,000.

(c) As used in this section—

(1) the term "Indian" means any individual who is a member of an Indian tribe, or for the purposes of this section is certified as an Indian artisan by an Indian tribe;

(2) the terms "Indian product" and "product of a particular Indian tribe or Indian arts and crafts organization" has the meaning given such term in regulations which may be promulgated by the Secretary of the Interior;

(3) the term "Indian tribe" means—

(A) any Indian tribe, band, nation, Alaska Native village, or other organized group or community which is recognized as eligible for the special programs and services provided by the United

States to Indians because of their status as Indians; or

(B) any Indian group that has been formally recognized as an Indian tribe by a State legislature or by a State commission or similar organization legislatively vested with State tribal recognition authority; and

(4) the term "Indian arts and crafts organization" means any legally established arts and crafts marketing organization composed of members of Indian tribes.

(d) In the event that any provision of this section is held invalid, it is the intent of Congress that the remaining provisions of this section shall continue in full force and effect.

(June 25, 1948, c. 645, 62 Stat. 759; Pub.L. 101–644, Title I, § 104(a), Nov. 29, 1990, 104 Stat. 4663.)

HISTORICAL AND STATUTORY NOTES

Admission of Alaska as State

Admission of Alaska into the Union was accomplished Jan. 3, 1959, upon issuance of Proc. No. 3269, Jan. 3, 1959, 24 F.R. 81, 73 Stat. c. 16, as required by sections 1 and 8(c) of Pub.L. 85–508, July 7, 1958, 72 Stat. 339, set out as notes preceding section 21 of title 48, Territories and Insular Possessions.

§ 1160. Property damaged in committing offense

Whenever a non-Indian, in the commission of an offense within the Indian country takes, injures or destroys the property of any friendly Indian the judgment of conviction shall include a sentence that the defendant pay to the Indian owner a sum equal to twice the just value of the property so taken, injured, or destroyed.

If such offender shall be unable to pay a sum at least equal to the just value or amount, whatever such payment shall fall short of the same shall be paid out of the Treasury of the United States. If such offender cannot be apprehended and brought to trial, the amount of such property shall be paid out of the Treasury. But no Indian shall be entitled to any payment out of the Treasury of the United States, for any such property, if he, or any of the nation to which he belongs, have sought private revenge, or have attempted to obtain satisfaction by any force or violence.

(June 25, 1948, c. 645, 62 Stat. 759; Sept. 13, 1994, Pub.L. 103–322, Title XXXIII, § 330004(9), 108 Stat. 2141.)

§ 1161. Application of Indian liquor laws

The provisions of sections 1154, 1156, 3113, 3488, and 3669, of this title, shall not apply within any area that is not Indian country, nor to any act or transaction within any area of Indian country provided such act or transaction is in conformity both with the laws of the State in which such act or transaction occurs and with an ordinance duly adopted by the tribe having jurisdiction over such area of Indian country, certified by the Secretary of the Interior, and published in the Federal Register.

(Added Aug. 15, 1953, c. 502, § 2, 67 Stat. 586, and amended Oct. 12, 1984, Pub.L. 98–473, Title II, § 223(b), 98 Stat. 2028.)

HISTORICAL AND STATUTORY NOTES

Effective and Applicability Provisions

1984 Acts. Amendment by Pub.L. 98–473 effective on the first day of first calendar month beginning thirty six months after Oct. 12, 1984, applicable only to offenses committed after taking effect of sections 211 to 239 of Pub.L. 98–473, and except as otherwise provided for therein, see section 235 of Pub.L. 98–473, as amended, set out as a note under section 3551 of this title.

§ 1162. State jurisdiction over offenses committed by or against Indians in the Indian country

(a) Each of the States or Territories listed in the following table shall have jurisdiction over offenses committed by or against Indians in the areas of Indian country listed opposite the name of the State or Territory to the same extent that such State or Territory has jurisdiction over offenses committed elsewhere within the State or Territory, and the criminal laws of such State or Territory shall have the same force and effect within such Indian country as they have elsewhere within the State or Territory:

State or Territory of	Indian country affected
Alaska	All Indian country within the State, except that on Annette Islands, the Metlakatla Indian community may exercise jurisdiction over offenses committed by Indians in the same manner in which such jurisdiction may be exercised by Indian tribes in Indian country over which State jurisdiction has not been extended
California	All Indian country within the State
Minnesota	All Indian country within the State, except the Red Lake Reservation
Nebraska	All Indian country within the State
Oregon	All Indian country within the State, except the Warm Springs Reservation
Wisconsin	All Indian country within the State

(b) Nothing in this section shall authorize the alienation, encumbrance, or taxation of any real or personal property, including water rights, belonging to any Indian or any Indian tribe, band, or community that is held in trust by the United States or is subject to a restriction against alienation imposed by the United States; or shall authorize regulation of the use of such property in a manner inconsistent with any Federal treaty, agreement, or statute or with any regulation made pursuant thereto; or shall deprive any Indian or any Indian tribe, band, or community of any right, privilege, or immunity afforded under Federal treaty, agreement, or statute with respect to hunting, trapping, or fishing or the control, licensing, or regulation thereof.

(c) The provisions of sections 1152 and 1153 of this chapter shall not be applicable within the areas of Indian country listed in subsection (a) of this section as areas over which the several States have exclusive jurisdiction.

(Added Aug. 15, 1953, c. 505, § 2, 67 Stat. 588, and amended Aug. 24, 1954, c. 910, § 1, 68 Stat. 795; Aug. 8, 1958, Pub.L. 85–615, § 1, 72 Stat. 545; Nov. 25, 1970, Pub.L. 91–523, §§ 1, 2, 84 Stat. 1358.)

HISTORICAL AND STATUTORY NOTES

Admission of Alaska as State

Admission of Alaska into the Union was accomplished Jan. 3, 1959 upon issuance of Proc.No. 3269, Jan. 3, 1959, 24 F.R. 81, 73 Stat. c. 16, as required by sections 1 and 8(c) of Pub.L. 85-508, July 7, 1958, 72 Stat. 339, set out as notes preceding section 21 of Title 48, Territories and Insular Possessions.

Amendment of State Constitutions to Remove Legal Impediment; Effective Date

For amendments of State Constitutions to remove legal impediments and effective date thereof, see section 6 of Act Aug. 15, 1953, set out as a note under section 1360 of Title 28, Judiciary and Judicial Procedure.

Consent of United States to Other States to Assume Jurisdiction

Act Aug. 15, 1953, c. 505, § 7, 67 Stat. 590, which gave consent of the United States to any other State not having jurisdiction with respect to criminal offenses or civil causes of action, or with respect to both, as provided for in this section and section 1360 of Title 28, to assume jurisdiction at such time and in such manner as the people of the State shall, by legislative action, obligate and bind the State to assumption thereof, was repealed by section 403(b) of Pub.L. 90–284, Title IV, Apr. 11, 1968, 82 Stat. 79, such repeal not to affect any cession of jurisdiction made pursuant to such section prior to its repeal.

§ 1163. Embezzlement and theft from Indian tribal organizations

Whoever embezzles, steals, knowingly converts to his use or the use of another, willfully misapplies, or willfully permits to be misapplied, any of the moneys, funds, credits, goods, assets, or other property belonging to any Indian tribal organization or intrusted to the custody or care of any officer, employee, or agent of an Indian tribal organization; or

Whoever, knowing any such moneys, funds, credits, goods, assets, or other property to have been so embezzled, stolen, converted, misapplied or permitted to be misapplied, receives, conceals, or retains the same with intent to convert it to his use or the use of another—

Shall be fined under this title, or imprisoned not more than five years, or both; but if the value of such property does not exceed the sum of $1,000, he shall be fined under this title, or imprisoned not more than one year, or both.

As used in this section, the term "Indian tribal organization" means any tribe, band, or community of Indians which is subject to the laws of the United States relating to Indian affairs or any corporation, association, or group which is organized under any of such laws.

(Added Aug. 1, 1956, c. 822, § 2, 70 Stat. 792, and amended Sept. 13, 1994, Pub.L. 103–322, Title XXXIII, § 330016(1)(H), (K), 108 Stat. 2147; Oct. 11, 1996, Pub.L. 104–294, Title VI, § 606(a), 110 Stat. 3511.)

§ 1164. Destroying boundary and warning signs

Whoever willfully destroys, defaces, or removes any sign erected by an Indian tribe, or a Government agency (1) to indicate the boundary of an Indian reservation or of any Indian country as defined in section 1151 of this title or (2) to give notice that hunting, trapping, or fishing is not permitted thereon without lawful authority or permission, shall be fined under this title or imprisoned not more than six months, or both.

(Added Pub.L. 86–634, § 1, July 12, 1960, 74 Stat. 469, and amended Pub.L. 103–322, Title XXXIII, § 330016(1)(E), Sept. 13, 1994, 108 Stat. 2146.)

§ 1165. Hunting, trapping, or fishing on Indian land

Whoever, without lawful authority or permission, willfully and knowingly goes upon any land that belongs to any Indian or Indian tribe, band, or group and either are held by the United States in trust or are subject to a restriction against alienation imposed by the United States, or upon any lands of the United States that are reserved for Indian use, for the purpose of hunting, trapping, or fishing thereon, or for the removal of game, peltries, or fish therefrom, shall be fined under this title or imprisoned not more than ninety days, or both, and all game, fish, and peltries in his possession shall be forfeited.

(Added Pub.L. 86–634, § 2, July 12, 1960, 74 Stat. 469, and amended Pub.L. 103–322, Title XXXIII, § 330016(1)(D), Sept. 13, 1994, 108 Stat. 2146.)

§ 1166. Gambling in Indian country

(a) Subject to subsection (c), for purposes of Federal law, all State laws pertaining to the licensing, regulation, or prohibition of gambling, including but not limited to criminal sanctions applicable thereto, shall apply in Indian country in the same manner and to the same extent as such laws apply elsewhere in the State.

(b) Whoever in Indian country is guilty of any act or omission involving gambling, whether or not conducted or sanctioned by an Indian tribe, which, although not made punishable by any enactment of Congress, would be punishable if committed or omitted within the jurisdiction of the State in which the act or omission occurred, under the laws governing the licensing, regulation, or prohibition of gambling in force at the time of such act or omission, shall be guilty of a like offense and subject to a like punishment.

(c) For the purpose of this section, the term "gambling" does not include—

(1) class I gaming or class II gaming regulated by the Indian Gaming Regulatory Act, or

(2) class III gaming conducted under a Tribal-State compact approved by the Secretary of the Interior under section 11(d)(8) of the Indian Gaming Regulatory Act that is in effect.

(d) The United States shall have exclusive jurisdiction over criminal prosecutions of violations of State gambling laws that are made applicable under this section to Indian country, unless an Indian tribe pursuant to a Tribal-State compact approved by the Secretary of the Interior under section 11(d)(8) of the Indian Gaming Regulatory Act, or under any other provision of Federal law, has consented to the transfer to the State of criminal jurisdiction with respect to gambling on the lands of the Indian tribe.

(Added Pub.L. 100–497, § 23, Oct. 17, 1988, 102 Stat. 2487.)

HISTORICAL AND STATUTORY NOTES

References in Text

The Indian Gaming Regulatory Act, referred to in text, is Pub.L. 100–497, Oct. 17, 1988, 102 Stat. 2467. Section 11(d)(8) of such Act is classified to section 2710(d)(8) of Title 25, Indians. For complete classification of this Act to the Code, see Short Title note under section 2701 of Title 25 and Tables.

Tribes Engaged in Negotiating Tribal–State Compacts

For provisions relating to the term "class II gaming" as it applies to Indian tribes engaged in negotiating Tribal–State compacts, see section 6 of Pub.L. 101–301, set out as a note under section 2703 of Title 25, Indians.

§ 1167. Theft from gaming establishments on Indian lands

(a) Whoever abstracts, purloins, willfully misapplies, or takes and carries away with intent to steal, any money, funds, or other property of a value of $1,000 or less belonging to an establishment operated by or for or licensed by an Indian tribe pursuant to an ordinance or resolution approved by the National Indian Gaming Commission shall be fined under this title or be imprisoned for not more than one year, or both.

(b) Whoever abstracts, purloins, willfully misapplies, or takes and carries away with intent to steal, any money, funds, or other property of a value in excess of $1,000 belonging to a gaming establishment operated by or for or licensed by an Indian tribe pursuant to an ordinance or resolution approved by the National Indian Gaming Commission shall be fined under this title, or imprisoned for not more than ten years, or both.

(Added Pub.L. 100–497, § 23, Oct. 17, 1988, 102 Stat. 2487, and amended Pub.L. 103–322, Title XXXIII, § 330016(1)(S), (U), Sept. 13, 1994, 108 Stat. 2148.)

HISTORICAL AND STATUTORY NOTES

Tribes Engaged in Negotiating Tribal–State Compacts

For provisions relating to the term "class II gaming" as it applies to Indian tribes engaged in negotiating Tribal–State compacts, see section 6 of Pub.L. 101–301, set out as a note under section 2703 of Title 25, Indians.

§ 1168. Theft by officers or employees of gaming establishments on Indian lands

(a) Whoever, being an officer, employee, or individual licensee of a gaming establishment operated by or for or licensed by an Indian tribe pursuant to an ordinance or resolution approved by the National Indian Gaming Commission, embezzles, abstracts, purloins, willfully misapplies, or takes and carries away with intent to steal, any moneys, funds, assets, or other property of such establishment of a value of $1,000 or less shall be fined not more than $250,000 or imprisoned not more than five years, or both;

(b) Whoever, being an officer, employee, or individual licensee of a gaming establishment operated by or for or licensed by an Indian tribe pursuant to an ordinance or resolution approved by the National Indian Gaming Commission, embezzles, abstracts, purloins, willfully misapplies, or takes and carries away with intent to steal, any moneys, funds, assets, or other property of such establishment of a value in excess of $1,000 shall be fined not more than $1,000,000 or imprisoned for not more than twenty years, or both.

(Added Pub.L. 100–497, § 23, Oct. 17, 1988, 102 Stat. 2487, and amended Pub.L. 101–647, Title XXXV, § 3537, Nov. 29, 1990, 104 Stat. 4925.)

HISTORICAL AND STATUTORY NOTES

Tribes Engaged in Negotiating Tribal–State Compacts

For provisions relating to the term "class II gaming" as it applies to Indian tribes engaged in negotiating Tribal–State compacts, see section 6 of Pub.L. 101–301, set out as a note under section 2703 of Title 25, Indians.

§ 1169. Reporting of child abuse

(a) Any person who—

(1) is a—

(A) physician, surgeon, dentist, podiatrist, chiropractor, nurse, dental hygienist, optometrist, medical examiner, emergency medical technician, paramedic, or health care provider,

(B) teacher, school counselor, instructional aide, teacher's aide, teacher's assistant, or bus driver employed by any tribal, Federal, public or private school,

(C) administrative officer, supervisor of child welfare and attendance, or truancy officer of any tribal, Federal, public or private school,

(D) child day care worker, headstart teacher, public assistance worker, worker in a group home or residential or day care facility, or social worker,

(E) psychiatrist, psychologist, or psychological assistant,

(F) licensed or unlicensed marriage, family, or child counselor,

(G) person employed in the mental health profession, or

(H) law enforcement officer, probation officer, worker in a juvenile rehabilitation or detention facility, or person employed in a public agency who is responsible for enforcing statutes and judicial orders;

(2) knows, or has reasonable suspicion, that—

(A) a child was abused in Indian country, or

(B) actions are being taken, or are going to be taken, that would reasonably be expected to result in abuse of a child in Indian country; and

(3) fails to immediately report such abuse or actions described in paragraph (2) to the local child protective services agency or local law enforcement agency,

shall be fined under this title or imprisoned for not more than 6 months or both.

(b) Any person who—

(1) supervises, or has authority over, a person described in subsection (a)(1), and

(2) inhibits or prevents that person from making the report described in subsection (a),

shall be fined under this title or imprisoned for not more than 6 months or both.

(c) For purposes of this section, the term—

(1) "abuse" includes—

(A) any case in which—

(i) a child is dead or exhibits evidence of skin bruising, bleeding, malnutrition, failure to thrive, burns, fracture of any bone, subdural hematoma, soft tissue swelling, and

(ii) such condition is not justifiably explained or may not be the product of an accidental occurrence; and

(B) any case in which a child is subjected to sexual assault, sexual molestation, sexual exploitation, sexual contact, or prostitution;

(2) "child" means an individual who—

(A) is not married, and

(B) has not attained 18 years of age;

(3) "local child protective services agency" means that agency of the Federal Government, of a State, or of an Indian tribe that has the primary responsibility for child protection on any Indian reservation or within any community in Indian country; and

(4) "local law enforcement agency" means that Federal, tribal, or State law enforcement agency that has the primary responsibility for the investigation of an instance of alleged child abuse within the portion of Indian country involved.

(d) Any person making a report described in subsection (a) which is based upon their reasonable belief and which is made in good faith shall be immune from civil or criminal liability for making that report.

(Added Pub.L. 101–630, Title IV, § 404(a)(1), Nov. 28, 1990, 104 Stat. 4547, and amended Pub.L. 103–322, Title XXXIII, §§ 330011(d), 330016(1)(K), Sept. 13, 1994, 108 Stat. 2144, 2147; Pub.L. 104–294, Title VI, § 604(b)(25), Oct. 11, 1996, 110 Stat. 3508.)

HISTORICAL AND STATUTORY NOTES

Effective and Applicability Provisions

1996 Acts. Amendment by section 604 of Pub.L. 104–294 effective Sept. 13, 1994, see section 604(d) of Pub.L. 104–294, set out as a note under section 13 of this title.

1994 Acts. Section 330011(d) of Pub.L. 103–322 provided in part that the amendment made by such section, amending directory language of section 404(a)(1) of Pub.L. 101–630 (which enacted this section), was to take effect on the date section 404(a)(1) of Pub.L. 101–630 took effect; section 404(a)(1) of Pub.L. 101–630 took effect on the date of enactment of Pub.L. 101–630, which was approved Nov. 28, 1990.

§ 1170. Illegal trafficking in Native American human remains and cultural items

(a) Whoever knowingly sells, purchases, uses for profit, or transports for sale or profit, the human remains of a Native American without the right of possession to those remains as provided in the Native American Graves Protection and Repatriation Act shall be fined in accordance with this title, or imprisoned not more than 12 months, or both, and in the case of a second or subsequent violation, be fined in accordance with this title, or imprisoned not more than 5 years, or both.

(b) Whoever knowingly sells, purchases, uses for profit, or transports for sale or profit any Native American cultural items obtained in violation of the Native American Grave Protection and Repatriation Act shall be fined in accordance with this title, imprisoned not more than one year, or both, and in the case of a second or subsequent violation, be fined in accordance with this title, imprisoned not more than 5 years, or both.

(Added Pub.L. 101–601, § 4(a), Nov. 16, 1990, 104 Stat. 3052, and amended Pub.L. 103–322, Title XXXIII, § 330010(4), Sept. 13, 1994, 108 Stat. 2143.)

HISTORICAL AND STATUTORY NOTES

References in Text

The Native American Graves Protection and Repatriation Act, referred to in text, is Pub.L. 101–601, Nov. 16, 1990, 104 Stat. 3048, which is classified principally to chapter 32 (§ 3001 et seq.) of Title 25, Indians.

CHAPTER 55—KIDNAPPING

Sec.

Title 18 Appendix §§ 1201–1203

Sections 1201 to 1203 of Pub.L. 90–351, 82 Stat. 236, as amended, relating to Unlawful Possession or Receipt of Firearms, are set out in the Appendix to this title.

§ 1201. Kidnapping

(a) Whoever unlawfully seizes, confines, inveigles, decoys, kidnaps, abducts, or carries away and holds for ransom or reward or otherwise any person, except in the case of a minor by the parent thereof, when—

(1) the person is willfully transported in interstate or foreign commerce, regardless of whether the person was alive when transported across a State boundary, or the offender travels in interstate or foreign commerce or uses the mail or any means, facility, or instrumentality of interstate or foreign commerce in committing or in furtherance of the commission of the offense;

(2) any such act against the person is done within the special maritime and territorial jurisdiction of the United States;

(3) any such act against the person is done within the special aircraft jurisdiction of the United States as defined in section 46501 of title 49;

(4) the person is a foreign official, an internationally protected person, or an official guest as those terms are defined in section 1116(b) of this title; or

(5) the person is among those officers and employees described in section 1114 of this title and any such act against the person is done while the person is engaged in, or on account of, the performance of official duties,

shall be punished by imprisonment for any term of years or for life and, if the death of any person results, shall be punished by death or life imprisonment.

(b) With respect to subsection (a)(1), above, the failure to release the victim within twenty-four hours after he shall have been unlawfully seized, confined, inveigled, decoyed, kidnapped, abducted, or carried away shall create a rebuttable presumption that such person has been transported in interstate or foreign commerce. Notwithstanding the preceding sentence, the fact that the presumption under this section has not yet taken effect does not preclude a Federal investigation of a possible violation of this section before the 24–hour period has ended.

(c) If two or more persons conspire to violate this section and one or more of such persons do any overt act to effect the object of the conspiracy, each shall be punished by imprisonment for any term of years or for life.

(d) Whoever attempts to violate subsection (a) shall be punished by imprisonment for not more than twenty years.

(e) If the victim of an offense under subsection (a) is an internationally protected person outside the United States, the United States may exercise jurisdiction over the offense if (1) the victim is a representative, officer, employee, or agent of the United States, (2) an offender is a national of the United States, or (3) an offender is afterwards found in the United States. As used in this subsection, the United States includes all areas under the jurisdiction of the United States including any of the places within the provisions of sections 5 and 7 of this title and section 46501(2) of title 49. For purposes of this subsection, the term "national of the United States" has the meaning prescribed in section 101(a)(22) of the Immigration and Nationality Act (8 U.S.C. 1101(a)(22)).

(f) In the course of enforcement of subsection (a)(4) and any other sections prohibiting a conspiracy or attempt to violate subsection (a)(4), the Attorney General may request assistance from any Federal, State, or local agency, including the Army, Navy, and Air Force, any statute, rule, or regulation to the contrary notwithstanding.

(g) Special rule for certain offenses involving children.—

(1) To whom applicable.—If—

(A) the victim of an offense under this section has not attained the age of eighteen years; and

(B) the offender—

(i) has attained such age; and

(ii) is not—

(I) a parent;

(II) a grandparent;

(III) a brother;

(IV) a sister;

(V) an aunt;

(VI) an uncle; or

(VII) an individual having legal custody of the victim;

the sentence under this section for such offense shall include imprisonment for not less than 20 years.

[(2) **Repealed.** Pub.L. 108–21, Title I, § 104(b), Apr. 30, 2003, 117 Stat. 653]

(h) As used in this section, the term "parent" does not include a person whose parental rights with respect to the victim of an offense under this section have been terminated by a final court order.

(June 25, 1948, c. 645, 62 Stat. 760; Aug. 6, 1956, c. 971, 70 Stat. 1043; Oct. 24, 1972, Pub.L. 92–539, Title II, § 201, 86 Stat. 1072; Oct. 8, 1976, Pub.L. 94–467, § 4, 90 Stat. 1998; Nov. 9, 1977, Pub.L. 95–163, § 17(b)(1), 91 Stat. 1286; Oct. 24, 1978, Pub.L. 95–504, § 2(b), 92 Stat. 1705; Oct. 12, 1984, Pub.L. 98–473, Title II, § 1007, 98 Stat. 2139; Nov. 10, 1986, Pub.L. 99–646, §§ 36, 37(b), 100 Stat. 3599; Nov. 29, 1990, Pub.L. 101–647, Title IV, § 401, Title XXXV, § 3538, 104 Stat. 4819, 4925; July 5, 1994, Pub.L. 103–272, § 5(e)(2), (8), 108 Stat. 1373, 1374; Sept. 13, 1994, Pub.L. 103–322, Title VI, § 60003(a)(6), Title XXXII, §§ 320903(b), 320924, Title XXXIII, § 330021, 108 Stat. 1969, 2124, 2131, 2150; Apr. 24, 1996, Pub.L. 104–132, Title VII, § 721(f), 110 Stat. 1299; Oct. 30, 1998, Pub.L. 105–314, Title VII, § 702, 112 Stat. 2987; Apr. 30, 2003, Pub.L. 108–21, Title I, § 104(b), 117 Stat. 653; July 27, 2006, Pub.L. 109–248, Title II, § 213, July 27, 2006, 120 Stat. 616.)

HISTORICAL AND STATUTORY NOTES

Short Title

1993 Amendments. Pub.L. 103–173, § 1, Dec. 2, 1993, 107 Stat. 1998, provided that: "This Act [enacting section 1204 of this title and enacting provisions set out as a note under section 1204 of this title] may be cited as the 'International Parental Kidnapping Crime Act of 1993'."

1984 Amendments. Pub.L. 98–473, Title II, § 2001, Oct. 12, 1984, 98 Stat. 2186, provided that: "This part [enacting section 1203 of this title and enacting provisions set out as a note under section 1203 of this title] may be cited as the 'Act for the Prevention and Punishment of the Crime of Hostage-Taking'."

§ 1202. Ransom money

(a) Whoever receives, possesses, or disposes of any money or other property, or any portion thereof, which has at any time been delivered as ransom or reward in connection with a violation of section 1201 of this title, knowing the same to be money or property which has been at any time delivered as such ransom or reward, shall be fined under this title or imprisoned not more than ten years, or both.

(b) A person who transports, transmits, or transfers in interstate or foreign commerce any proceeds of a kidnapping punishable under State law by imprisonment for more than 1 year, or receives, possesses, conceals, or disposes of any such proceeds after they have crossed a State or United States boundary, knowing the proceeds to have been unlawfully obtained, shall be imprisoned not more than 10 years, fined under this title, or both.

(c) For purposes of this section, the term "State" has the meaning set forth in section 245(d) of this title.

(June 25, 1948, c. 645, 62 Stat. 760; Sept. 13, 1994, Pub.L. 103–322, Title XXXII, § 320601(b), Title XXXIII, § 330016(1)(L), 108 Stat. 2115, 2147.)

§ 1203. Hostage taking

(a) Except as provided in subsection (b) of this section, whoever, whether inside or outside the United States, seizes or detains and threatens to kill, to injure, or to continue to detain another person in order to compel a third person or a governmental organization to do or abstain from doing any act as an explicit or implicit condition for the release of the person detained, or attempts or conspires to do so, shall be punished by imprisonment for any term of years or for life and, if the death of any person results, shall be punished by death or life imprisonment.

(b)(1) It is not an offense under this section if the conduct required for the offense occurred outside the United States unless—

(A) the offender or the person seized or detained is a national of the United States;

(B) the offender is found in the United States; or

(C) the governmental organization sought to be compelled is the Government of the United States.

(2) It is not an offense under this section if the conduct required for the offense occurred inside the United States, each alleged offender and each person seized or detained are nationals of the United States, and each alleged offender is found in the United States, unless the governmental organization sought to be compelled is the Government of the United States.

(c) As used in this section, the term "national of the United States" has the meaning given such term in section 101(a)(22) of the Immigration and Nationality Act (8 U.S.C. 1101(a)(22)).

(Added Pub.L. 98–473, Title II, § 2002(a), Oct. 12, 1984, 98 Stat. 2186, and amended Pub.L. 100–690, Title VII, § 7028, Nov. 18, 1988, 102 Stat. 4397; Pub.L. 103–322, Title VI, § 60003(a)(10), Sept. 13, 1994, 108 Stat. 1969; Pub.L. 104–132, Title VII, § 723(a)(1), Apr. 24, 1996, 110 Stat. 1300.)

HISTORICAL AND STATUTORY NOTES

References in Text

The Immigration and Nationality Act, referred to in subsec. (c) is classified to section 1101 et seq. of Title 8, Aliens and Nationality. Section 101(a)(22) of such Act is classified to section 1101(a)(22) of Title 8.

Effective and Applicability Provisions

1984 Acts. Section 2003 of Pub.L. 98–473 provided that: "This part and the amendments made by this part [enacting this section] shall take effect on the later of—

"(1) the date of the enactment of this joint resolution [Oct. 12, 1984]; or

"(2) the date the International Convention Against the Taking of Hostages has come into force and the United States has become a party to that convention." [The convention entered into force June 6, 1983, and entered into force for the United States Jan. 6, 1985.]

§ 1204. International parental kidnapping

(a) Whoever removes a child from the United States, or attempts to do so, or retains a child (who has been in the United States) outside the United States with intent to obstruct the lawful exercise of parental rights shall be fined under this title or imprisoned not more than 3 years, or both.

(b) As used in this section—

(1) the term "child" means a person who has not attained the age of 16 years; and

(2) the term "parental rights", with respect to a child, means the right to physical custody of the child—

(A) whether joint or sole (and includes visiting rights); and

(B) whether arising by operation of law, court order, or legally binding agreement of the parties.

(c) It shall be an affirmative defense under this section that—

(1) the defendant acted within the provisions of a valid court order granting the defendant legal custody or visitation rights and that order was obtained pursuant to the Uniform Child Custody Jurisdiction Act or the Uniform Child Custody Jurisdiction and Enforcement Act and was in effect at the time of the offense;

(2) the defendant was fleeing an incidence or pattern of domestic violence; or

(3) the defendant had physical custody of the child pursuant to a court order granting legal custody or visitation rights and failed to return the child as a result of circumstances beyond the defendant's control, and the defendant notified or made reasonable attempts to notify the other parent or lawful custodian of the child of such circumstances within 24 hours after the visitation period had expired and returned the child as soon as possible.

(d) This section does not detract from The Hague Convention on the Civil Aspects of International Parental Child Abduction, done at The Hague on October 25, 1980.

(Added Pub.L. 103–173, § 2(a), Dec. 2, 1993, 107 Stat. 1998, and amended Pub.L. 108–21, Title I, § 107, Apr. 30, 2003, 117 Stat. 655.)

HISTORICAL AND STATUTORY NOTES

References in Text

The official text of the Uniform Child Custody Jurisdiction Act, as approved in 1968 by the National Conference of Commissioners on Uniform State Laws and the American Bar Association, is set out in Uniform Laws Annotated (U.L.A.), Matrimonial, Family and Health Laws, Volume 9, Part I.

The Uniform Child Custody Jurisdiction and Enforcement Act, referred to in subsec. (c)(1), as approved in 1997 by the National Conference of Commissioners on Uniform State Laws, is set out in Uniform Laws Annotated (U.L.A.).

Sense of the Congress Regarding Use of Procedures Under the Hague Convention on the Civil Aspects of International Parental Child Abduction

Section 2(b) of Pub.L. 103–173 provided that: "It is the sense of the Congress that, inasmuch as use of the procedures under the Hague Convention on the Civil Aspects of International Parental Child Abduction has resulted in the return of many children, those procedures, in circumstances in which they are applicable, should be the option of first choice for a parent who seeks the return of a child who has been removed from the parent."

CHAPTER 57—LABOR

§ 1231. Transportation of strikebreakers

Whoever willfully transports in interstate or foreign commerce any person who is employed or is to be employed for the purpose of obstructing or interfering by force or threats with (1) peaceful picketing by employees during any labor controversy affecting wages, hours, or conditions of labor, or (2) the exercise by employees of any of the rights of self-organization or collective bargaining; or

Whoever is knowingly transported or travels in interstate or foreign commerce for any of the purposes enumerated in this section—

Shall be fined under this title or imprisoned not more than two years, or both.

This section shall not apply to common carriers.

(June 25, 1948, c. 645, 62 Stat. 760; May 24, 1949, c. 139, § 30, 63 Stat. 94; Sept. 13, 1994, Pub.L. 103–322, Title XXXIII, § 330016(1)(K), 108 Stat. 2147.)

[§ 1232. Repealed. Aug. 10, 1956, c. 1041, § 53, 70A Stat. 641]

HISTORICAL AND STATUTORY NOTES

Section, Act June 25, 1948, c. 645, 62 Stat. 761, prohibited enticement of workman from armory or arsenal.

CHAPTER 59—LIQUOR TRAFFIC

§ 1261. Enforcement, regulations, and scope

(a) [1] The Attorney General —

(1) shall enforce the provisions of this chapter; and

(2) has the authority to issue regulations to carry out the provisions of this chapter.

(June 25, 1948, c. 645, 62 Stat. 761; May 24, 1949, c. 139, § 31, 63 Stat. 94; Nov. 2, 2002, Pub.L. 107–273, Div. B, Title IV, § 4004(b), 116 Stat. 1812; Nov. 25, 2002, Pub.L. 107–296, Title XI, § 1112(g), 116 Stat. 2276.)

[1] So in original. There is no subsec. (b).

HISTORICAL AND STATUTORY NOTES

Effective and Applicability Provisions

2002 Acts. Amendment to this section by Pub.L. 107–296 effective 60 days after Nov. 25, 2002, see Pub.L. 107–296, § 4, set out as a note under 6 U.S.C.A. § 101.

Transfer of Functions

All functions of all officers of the Department of the Treasury, and all functions of all agencies and employees of such Department, were transferred, with certain exceptions, to the Secretary of the Treasury, with power vested in him to authorize their performance or the performance of any of his functions, by any of such officers, agencies, and employees, by Reorg. Plan No. 26 of 1950, §§ 1, 2, eff. July 31, 1950, 15 F.R. 4935, 64 Stat. 1280, 1281, set out in the Appendix to Title 5, Government Organization and Employees. The Commissioner of Internal Revenue, referred to in this section, is an officer of the Treasury Department.

§ 1262. Transportation into State prohibiting sale

Whoever imports, brings, or transports any intoxicating liquor into any State, Territory, District, or Possession in which all sales, except for scientific, sacramental, medicinal, or mechanical purposes, of intoxicating liquor containing more than 4 per centum of alcohol by volume or 3.2 per centum of alcohol by weight are prohibited, otherwise than in the course of continuous interstate transportation through such State, Territory, District, or Possession or attempts so to do, or assists in so doing,

Shall (1) If such liquor is not accompanied by such permits, or licenses therefor as may be required by the laws of such State, Territory, District, or Possession or (2) if all importation, bringing, or transportation of intoxicating liquor into such State, Territory, District, or Possession is prohibited by the laws thereof, be fined under this title or imprisoned not more than one year, or both.

In the enforcement of this section, the definition of intoxicating liquor contained in the laws of the respective States, Territories, Districts, or Possessions shall be applied, but only to the extent that sales of such intoxicating liquor (except for scientific, sacramental, medicinal, and mechanical purposes) are prohibited therein.

(June 25, 1948, c. 645, 62 Stat. 761; May 24, 1949, c. 139, § 32, 63 Stat. 94; Nov. 29, 1990, Pub.L. 101–647, Title XXXV, § 3540, 104 Stat. 4925; Sept. 13, 1994, Pub.L. 103–322, Title XXXIII, § 330016(1)(H), 108 Stat. 2147.)

§ 1263. Marks and labels on packages

Whoever knowingly ships into any place within the United States any package containing any spirituous, vinous, malted, or other fermented liquor, or any compound containing any spirituous, vinous, malted, or other fermented liquor fit for use for beverage purposes, unless such shipment is accompanied by copy of a bill of lading, or other document showing the name of the consignee, the nature of its contents, and the quantity contained therein, shall be fined under this title or imprisoned not more than one year, or both.

(June 25, 1948, c. 645, 62 Stat. 761; Sept. 26, 1968, Pub.L. 90–518, § 1, 82 Stat. 872; Sept. 13, 1994, Pub.L. 103–322, Title XXXIII, § 330016(1)(H), 108 Stat. 2147.)

HISTORICAL AND STATUTORY NOTES

Effective and Applicability Provisions

1968 Acts. Section 3 of Pub.L. 90–518 provided that: "This Act [amending this section] shall become effective ninety days after the date of its enactment [Sept. 26, 1968]."

Congressional Disclaimer of Intent to Preempt State Regulation of Shipments of Intoxicating Liquor

Section 2 of Pub.L. 90–518 provided that: "Nothing contained in this Act [amending this section] shall be construed as indicating an intent on the part of Congress to deprive any

State of the power to enact additional prohibitions with respect to the shipment of intoxicating liquors."

§ 1264. Delivery to consignee

Whoever, being an officer, agent, or employee of any railroad company, express company, or other common carrier, knowingly delivers to any person other than the person to whom it has been consigned, unless upon the written order in each instance of the bona fide consignee, or to any fictitious person, or to any person under a fictitious name, any spirituous, vinous, malted, or other fermented liquor or any compound containing any spirituous, vinous, malted, or other fermented liquor fit for use for beverage purposes, which has been shipped into any place within the United States, shall be fined under this title or imprisoned not more than one year, or both.

(June 25, 1948, c. 645, 62 Stat. 761; Sept. 13, 1994, Pub.L. 103–322, Title XXXIII, § 330016(1)(H), 108 Stat. 2147.)

§ 1265. C.O.D. shipments prohibited

Any railroad or express company, or other common carrier which, or any person who, in connection with the transportation of any spirituous, vinous, malted, or other fermented liquor, or any compound containing any spirituous, vinous, malted, or other fermented liquor fit for use for beverage purposes, into any State, Territory, District or Possession of the United States, which prohibits the delivery or sale therein of such liquor, collects the purchase price or any part thereof, before, on, or after delivery, from the consignee, or from any other person, or in any manner acts as the agent of the buyer or seller of any such liquor, for the purpose of buying or selling or completing the sale thereof, saving only in the actual transportation and delivery of the same, shall be fined under this title or imprisoned not more than one year, or both.

(June 25, 1948, c. 645, 62 Stat. 762; Sept. 13, 1994, Pub.L. 103–322, Title XXXIII, § 330016(1)(K), 108 Stat. 2147.)

CHAPTER 61—LOTTERIES

Sec.

§ 1301. Importing or transporting lottery tickets

Whoever brings into the United States for the purpose of disposing of the same, or knowingly deposits with any express company or other common carrier for carriage, or carries in interstate or foreign commerce any paper, certificate, or instrument purporting to be or to represent a ticket, chance, share, or interest in or dependent upon the event of a lottery, gift enterprise, or similar scheme, offering prizes dependent in whole or in part upon lot or chance, or any advertisement of, or list of the prizes drawn or awarded by means of, any such lottery, gift, enterprise, or similar scheme; or, being engaged in the business of procuring for a person in 1 State such a ticket, chance, share, or interest in a lottery, gift, [1] enterprise or similar scheme conducted by another State (unless that business is permitted under an agreement between the States in question or appropriate authorities of those States), knowingly transmits in interstate or foreign commerce information to be used for the purpose of procuring such a ticket, chance, share, or interest; or knowingly takes or receives any such paper, certificate, instrument, advertisement, or list so brought, deposited, or transported, shall be fined under this title or imprisoned not more than two years, or both.

(June 25, 1948, c. 645, 62 Stat. 762; Sept. 13, 1994, Pub.L. 103–322, Title XXXII, § 320905, Title XXXIII, § 330016(1)(H), 108 Stat. 2126, 2147.)

[1] So in original. The comma probably should not appear.

HISTORICAL AND STATUTORY NOTES

Short Title

1988 Amendments. Pub.L. 100–625, § 1, Nov. 7, 1988, 102 Stat. 3205, provided that: "This Act [amending sections 1304 and 1307 of this title and section 3005 of Title 39, Postal Service, and enacting provisions set out as notes under sections 1304 and 1307 of this title] may be cited as the 'Charity Games Advertising Clarification Act of 1988'."

§ 1302. Mailing lottery tickets or related matter

Whoever knowingly deposits in the mail, or sends or delivers by mail:

Any letter, package, postal card, or circular concerning any lottery, gift enterprise, or similar scheme offering prizes dependent in whole or in part upon lot or chance;

Any lottery ticket or part thereof, or paper, certificate, or instrument purporting to be or to represent a ticket, chance, share, or interest in or dependent upon the event of a lottery, gift enterprise, or similar scheme offering prizes dependent in whole or in part upon lot or chance;

Any check, draft, bill, money, postal note, or money order, for the purchase of any ticket or part thereof, or of any share or chance in any such lottery, gift enterprise, or scheme;

Any newspaper, circular, pamphlet, or publication of any kind containing any advertisement of any lottery, gift enterprise, or scheme of any kind offering prizes dependent in whole or in part upon lot or chance, or containing any list of the prizes drawn or awarded by means of any such lottery, gift enterprise, or scheme, whether said list contains any part or all of such prizes;

Any article described in section 1953 of this title—

Shall be fined under this title or imprisoned not more than two years, or both; and for any subsequent offense shall be imprisoned not more than five years.

(June 25, 1948, c. 645, 62 Stat. 762; Oct. 31, 1951, c. 655, § 29, 65 Stat. 721; Sept. 13, 1961, Pub.L. 87–218, § 2, 75 Stat. 492; Sept. 13, 1994, Pub.L. 103–322, Title XXXIII, § 330016(1)(H), 108 Stat. 2147.)

§ 1303. Postmaster or employee as lottery agent [1]

Whoever, being an officer or employee of the Postal Service, acts as agent for any lottery office, or under color of purchase or otherwise, vends lottery tickets, or knowingly sends by mail or delivers any letter, package, postal card, circular, or pamphlet advertising any lottery, gift enterprise, or similar scheme, offering prizes dependent in whole or in part upon lot or chance, or any ticket, certificate, or instrument representing any chance, share, or interest in or dependent upon the event of any lottery, gift enterprise, or similar scheme offering prizes dependent in whole or in part upon lot or chance, or any list of the prizes awarded by means of any such scheme, shall be fined under this title or imprisoned not more than one year, or both.

(June 25, 1948, c. 645, 62 Stat. 763; Aug. 12, 1970, Pub.L. 91–375, § 6(j)(10), 84 Stat. 778; Sept. 13, 1994, Pub.L. 103–322, Title XXXIII, § 330016(1)(B), 108 Stat. 2146.)

[1] Section catchline was not amended to conform to change made in the text by Pub.L. 91–375.

HISTORICAL AND STATUTORY NOTES

Effective and Applicability Provisions

1970 Acts. Amendment Pub.L. 91–375 effective within 1 year after Aug. 12, 1970, on date established therefor by the Board of Governors of the United States Postal Service and published by it in the Federal Register, see section 15(a) of Pub.L. 91–375, set out as an Effective Date note preceding section 101 of Title 39, Postal Service.

§ 1304. Broadcasting lottery information

Whoever broadcasts by means of any radio or television station for which a license is required by any law of the United States, or whoever, operating any such station, knowingly permits the broadcasting of, any advertisement of or information concerning any lottery, gift enterprise, or similar scheme, offering prizes dependent in whole or in part upon lot or chance, or any list of the prizes drawn or awarded by means of any such lottery, gift enterprise, or scheme, whether said list contains any part or all of such prizes, shall be fined under this title or imprisoned not more than one year, or both.

Each day's broadcasting shall constitute a separate offense.

(June 25, 1948, c. 645, 62 Stat. 763; Nov. 7, 1988, Pub.L. 100–625, § 3(a)(4), 102 Stat. 3206; Sept. 13, 1994, Pub.L. 103–322, Title XXXIII, § 330016(1)(H), 108 Stat. 2147.)

HISTORICAL AND STATUTORY NOTES

Effective and Applicability Provisions

1988 Acts. Section 5 of Pub.L. 100–625 provided that: "The amendments made by this Act [amending this section and section 1307 of this title and section 3005 of Title 39, Postal Service and enacting provisions set out as a note under section 1307 of this title] shall take effect 18 months after the date of the enactment of this Act [Nov. 7, 1988]."

§ 1305. Fishing contests

The provisions of this chapter shall not apply with respect to any fishing contest not conducted for profit wherein prizes are awarded for the specie, size, weight, or quality of fish caught by contestants in any bona fide fishing or recreational event.

(Added Aug. 16, 1950, c. 722, § 1, 64 Stat. 451.)

§ 1306. Participation by financial institutions

Whoever knowingly violates section 5136A of the Revised Statutes of the United States, section 9A of the Federal Reserve Act, or section 20 of the Federal Deposit Insurance Act shall be fined under this title or imprisoned not more than one year, or both.

(Added Pub.L. 90–203, § 5(a), Dec. 15, 1967, 81 Stat. 611, and amended Pub.L. 101–73, Title IX, § 962(b), Aug. 9, 1989, 103 Stat. 502; Pub.L. 103–322, Title XXXIII, § 330016(1)(H), Sept. 13, 1994, 108 Stat. 2147.)

HISTORICAL AND STATUTORY NOTES

References in Text

Section 5136A of the Revised Statutes of the United States, referred to in text, is classified to section 25a of Title 12, Banks and Banking.

Section 9A of the Federal Reserve Act, referred to in text, is classified to section 339 of Title 12.

Section 20 of the Federal Deposit Insurance Act, referred to in text, is classified to section 1829a of Title 12.

Effective and Applicability Provisions

1968 Acts. Section effective Apr. 1, 1968, see section 6 of Pub.L. 90–203, set out as an Effective Date note under section 25a of Title 12, Banks and Banking.

Severability of Provisions

If any provision of Pub.L. 101–73 or the application thereof to any person or circumstance is held invalid, the remainder of Pub.L. 101–73 and the application of the provision to other persons not similarly situated or to other circumstances not to be affected thereby, see section 1221 of Pub.L. 101–73, set out as a note under section 1811 of Title 12, Banks and Banking.

§ 1307. Exceptions relating to certain advertisements and other information and to State-conducted lotteries

(a) The provisions of sections 1301, 1302, 1303, and 1304 shall not apply to—

(1) an advertisement, list of prizes, or other information concerning a lottery conducted by a State acting under the authority of State law which is—

(A) contained in a publication published in that State or in a State which conducts such a lottery; or

(B) broadcast by a radio or television station licensed to a location in that State or a State which conducts such a lottery; or

(2) an advertisement, list of prizes, or other information concerning a lottery, gift enterprise, or similar scheme, other than one described in paragraph (1), that is authorized or not otherwise prohibited by the State in which it is conducted and which is—

(A) conducted by a not-for-profit organization or a governmental organization; or

(B) conducted as a promotional activity by a commercial organization and is clearly occasional and ancillary to the primary business of that organization.

(b) The provisions of sections 1301, 1302, and 1303 shall not apply to the transportation or mailing—

(1) to addresses within a State of equipment, tickets, or material concerning a lottery which is conducted by that State acting under the authority of State law; or

(2) to an addressee within a foreign country of equipment, tickets, or material designed to be used within that foreign country in a lottery which is authorized by the law of that foreign country.

(c) For the purposes of this section (1) "State" means a State of the United States, the District of Columbia, the Commonwealth of Puerto Rico, or any territory or possession of the United States; and (2) "foreign country" means any empire, country, dominion, colony, or protectorate, or any subdivision thereof (other than the United States, its territories or possessions).

(d) For the purposes of subsection (b) of this section "lottery" means the pooling of proceeds derived from the sale of tickets or chances and allotting those proceeds or parts thereof by chance to one or more chance takers or ticket purchasers. "Lottery" does not include the placing or accepting of bets or wagers on sporting events or contests. For purposes of this section, the term a "not-for-profit organization" means any organization that would qualify as tax exempt under section 501 of the Internal Revenue Code of 1986.

(Added Pub.L. 93–583, § 1, Jan. 2, 1975, 88 Stat. 1916, and amended Pub.L. 94–525, § 1, Oct. 17, 1976, 90 Stat. 2478; Pub.L. 96–90, § 1, Oct. 23, 1979, 93 Stat. 698; Pub.L. 100–625, §§ 2(a), (b), 3(a)(1), (3), Nov. 7, 1988, 102 Stat. 3205, 3206.)

HISTORICAL AND STATUTORY NOTES

References in Text

Section 501 of the Internal Revenue Code of 1986, referred to in subsec. (d) is section 501 of Title 26, Internal Revenue Code.

Effective and Applicability Provisions

1988 Acts. Amendment by Pub.L. 100–625 effective 18 months after Nov. 7, 1988, see section 5 of Pub.L. 100–625, set out as note under section 1304 of this title.

Severability of Provisions

Section 4 of Pub.L. 100–625 provided that: "If any provision of this Act [amending this section and section 1304 of this title and section 3005 of Title 39, Postal Service, and enacting provisions set out as notes under this section and section 1304 of this title] or the amendments made by this Act, or the application of such provision to any person or circumstance, is held invalid, the remainder of this Act and the amendments made by this Act, and the application of such provision to other persons not similarly situated or to other circumstances, shall not be affected by such invalidation."

CHAPTER 63—MAIL FRAUD

Sec.

§ 1341. Frauds and swindles

Whoever, having devised or intending to devise any scheme or artifice to defraud, or for obtaining money or property by means of false or fraudulent pretenses, representations, or promises, or to sell, dispose of, loan, exchange, alter, give away, distribute, supply, or furnish or procure for unlawful use any counterfeit or spurious coin, obligation, security, or other article, or anything represented to be or intimated or held out to be such counterfeit or spurious article, for the purpose of executing such scheme or artifice or attempting so to do, places in any post office or authorized depository for mail matter, any matter or thing whatever to be sent or delivered by the Postal Service, or deposits or causes to be deposited any matter or thing whatever to be sent or delivered by any private or commercial interstate carrier, or takes or receives therefrom, any such matter or thing, or knowingly causes to be delivered by mail or such carrier according to the direction thereon, or at the place at which it is directed to be delivered by the person to whom it is addressed, any such matter or thing, shall be fined under this title or imprisoned not more than 20 years, or both. If the violation affects a financial institution, such person shall be fined not more than $1,000,000 or imprisoned not more than 30 years, or both.

(June 25, 1948, c. 645, 62 Stat. 763; May 24, 1949, c. 139, § 34, 63 Stat. 94; Aug. 12, 1970, Pub.L. 91–375, § 6(j)(11), 84 Stat. 778; Aug. 9, 1989, Pub.L. 101–73, Title IX, § 961(i), 103 Stat. 500; Nov. 29, 1990, Pub.L. 101–647, Title XXV, § 2504(h), 104 Stat. 4861; Sept. 13, 1994, Pub.L. 103–322, Title XXV, § 250006, Title XXXIII, 330016(1)(H), 108 Stat. 2087, 2147; July 30, 2002, Pub.L. 107–204, Title IX, § 903(a), 116 Stat. 805.)

HISTORICAL AND STATUTORY NOTES

Effective and Applicability Provisions

1970 Acts. Amendment by Pub.L. 91–375 effective within 1 year after Aug. 12, 1970, on date established therefor by the Board of Governors of the United States Postal Service and published by it in the Federal Register, see section 15(a) of Pub.L. 91–375, set out as an Effective Date note preceding section 101 of Title 39, Postal Service.

Severability of Provisions

If any provision of Pub.L. 101–73 or the application thereof to any person or circumstance is held invalid, the remainder of Pub.L. 101–73 and the application of the provision to other persons not similarly situated or to other circumstances not to be affected thereby, see section 1221 of Pub.L. 101–73, set out as a note under section 1811 of Title 12, Banks and Banking.

Short Title

2002 Amendments. Pub.L. 107–204, Title IX, § 901, July 30, 2002, 116 Stat. 804, provided that: "This title [enacting 18 U.S.C.A. §§ 1349 and 1350, amending this section, 18 U.S.C.A. § 1343, and 29 U.S.C.A. §1131, and amending provisions set out as a note under 28 U.S.C.A. § 994] may be cited as the 'White-Collar Crime Penalty Enhancement Act of 2002'."

§ 1342. Fictitious name or address

Whoever, for the purpose of conducting, promoting, or carrying on by means of the Postal Service, any scheme or device mentioned in section 1341 of this title or any other unlawful business, uses or assumes, or requests to be addressed by, any fictitious, false, or assumed title, name, or address or name other than his own proper name, or takes or receives from any post office or authorized depository of mail matter, any letter, postal card, package, or other mail matter addressed to any such fictitious, false, or assumed title, name, or address, or name other than his own proper name, shall be fined under this title or imprisoned not more than five years, or both.

(June 25, 1948, c. 645, 62 Stat. 763, Aug. 12, 1970, Pub.L. 91–375, § 6(j) (12), 84 Stat. 778; Sept. 13, 1994, Pub.L. 103–322, Title XXXIII, § 330016(1)(H), 108 Stat. 2147.)

HISTORICAL AND STATUTORY NOTES

Effective and Applicability Provisions

1970 Acts. Amendment by Pub.L. 91–375 effective within 1 year after Aug. 12, 1970, on date established therefor by the Board of Governors of the United States Postal Service and published by it in the Federal Register, see section 15(a) of Pub.L. 91–375, set out as an Effective Date note preceding section 101 of Title 39, Postal Service.

§ 1343. Fraud by wire, radio, or television

Whoever, having devised or intending to devise any scheme or artifice to defraud, or for obtaining money or property by means of false or fraudulent pretenses, representations, or promises, transmits or causes to be transmitted by means of wire, radio, or television communication in interstate or foreign commerce, any writings, signs, signals, pictures, or sounds for the purpose of executing such scheme or artifice, shall be fined under this title or imprisoned not more than 20 years, or both. If the violation affects a financial institution, such person shall be fined not more than $1,000,000 or imprisoned not more than 30 years, or both.

(Added July 16, 1952, c. 879, § 18(a), 66 Stat. 722, and amended July 11, 1956, c. 561, 70 Stat. 523; Aug. 9, 1989, Pub.L. 101–73, Title IX, § 961(j), 103 Stat. 500; Nov. 29, 1990, Pub.L. 101–647, Title XXV, § 2504(i), 104 Stat. 4861; Sept. 13, 1994, Pub.L. 103–322, Title XXXIII, § 330016(1)(H), 108 Stat. 2147; July 30, 2002, Pub.L. 107–204, Title IX, § 903(b), 116 Stat. 805.)

HISTORICAL AND STATUTORY NOTES

Severability of Provisions

If any provision of Pub.L. 101–73 or the application thereof to any person or circumstance is held invalid, the remainder of Pub.L. 101–73 and the application of the provision to other persons not similarly situated or to other circumstances not to be affected thereby, see section 1221 of Pub.L. 101–73, set out as a note under section 1811 of Title 12, Banks and Banking.

§ 1344. Bank fraud

Whoever knowingly executes, or attempts to execute, a scheme or artifice—

(1) to defraud a financial institution; or

(2) to obtain any of the moneys, funds, credits, assets, securities, or other property owned by, or

under the custody or control of, a financial institution, by means of false or fraudulent pretenses, representations, or promises;

shall be fined not more than $1,000,000 or imprisoned not more than 30 years, or both.

(Added Pub.L. 98–473, Title II, § 1108(a), Oct. 12, 1984, 98 Stat. 2147, and amended Pub.L. 101–73, Title IX, § 961(k), Aug. 9, 1989, 103 Stat. 500; Pub.L. 101–647, Title XXV, § 2504(j), Nov. 29, 1990, 104 Stat. 4861.)

HISTORICAL AND STATUTORY NOTES

Severability of Provisions

If any provision of Pub.L. 101–73 or the application thereof to any person or circumstance is held invalid, the remainder of Pub.L. 101–73 and the application of the provision to other persons not similarly situated or to other circumstances not to be affected thereby, see section 1221 of Pub.L. 101–73, set out as a note under section 1811 of Title 12, Banks and Banking.

§ 1345. Injunctions against fraud

(a)(1) If a person is—

(A) violating or about to violate this chapter or section 287, 371 (insofar as such violation involves a conspiracy to defraud the United States or any agency thereof), or 1001 of this title;

(B) committing or about to commit a banking law violation (as defined in section 3322(d) of this title); or

(C) committing or about to commit a Federal health care offense;

the Attorney General may commence a civil action in any Federal court to enjoin such violation.

(2) If a person is alienating or disposing of property, or intends to alienate or dispose of property, obtained as a result of a banking law violation (as defined in section 3322(d) of this title) or a Federal health care offense or property which is traceable to such violation, the Attorney General may commence a civil action in any Federal court—

(A) to enjoin such alienation or disposition of property; or

(B) for a restraining order to—

(i) prohibit any person from withdrawing, transferring, removing, dissipating, or disposing of any such property or property of equivalent value; and

(ii) appoint a temporary receiver to administer such restraining order.

(3) A permanent or temporary injunction or restraining order shall be granted without bond.

(b) The court shall proceed as soon as practicable to the hearing and determination of such an action, and may, at any time before final determination, enter such a restraining order or prohibition, or take such other action, as is warranted to prevent a continuing and substantial injury to the United States or to any person or class of persons for whose protection the action is brought. A proceeding under this section is governed by the Federal Rules of Civil Procedure, except that, if an indictment has been returned against the respondent, discovery is governed by the Federal Rules of Criminal Procedure.

(Added Pub.L. 98–473, Title II, § 1205(a), Oct. 12, 1984, 98 Stat. 2152, and amended Pub.L. 100–690, Title VII, § 7077, Nov. 18, 1988, 102 Stat. 4406; Pub.L. 101–647, Title XXV, § 2521(b)(2), Title XXXV, § 3542, Nov. 29, 1990, 104 Stat. 4865, 4925; Pub.L. 103–322, Title XXXIII, § 330011(k), Sept. 13, 1994, 108 Stat. 2145; Pub.L. 104–191, Title II, § 247, Aug. 21, 1996, 110 Stat. 2018; Pub.L. 107–273, Title IV, § 4002(b)(14), Nov. 2, 2002, 116 Stat. 1808.)

HISTORICAL AND STATUTORY NOTES

References in Text

The Federal Rules of Civil Procedure, referred to in text, are set out in Title 28, Judiciary and Judicial Procedure.

The Federal Rules of Criminal Procedure, referred to in text, are set out in this title.

Effective and Applicability Provisions

1994 Acts. Section 330011(k) of Pub.L. 103–322 provided in part that the amendment made by such section, repealing section 3542 of Pub.L. 101–647 (which amended this section), was to take effect on the date of enactment of section 3542 of Pub.L. 101–647, which was approved Nov. 29, 1990.

Repeals

Section 3542 of Pub.L. 101–647, amending this section, was repealed by section 330011(k) of Pub.L. 103–322.

§ 1346. Definition of "scheme or artifice to defraud"

For the purposes of this chapter, the term "scheme or artifice to defraud" includes a scheme or artifice to deprive another of the intangible right of honest services.

(Added Pub.L. 100–690, Title VII, § 7603(a), Nov. 18, 1988, 102 Stat. 4508.)

§ 1347. Health care fraud

Whoever knowingly and willfully executes, or attempts to execute, a scheme or artifice—

(1) to defraud any health care benefit program; or

(2) to obtain, by means of false or fraudulent pretenses, representations, or promises, any of the money or property owned by, or under the custody or control of, any health care benefit program,

in connection with the delivery of or payment for health care benefits, items, or services, shall be fined under this title or imprisoned not more than 10 years, or both. If the violation results in serious bodily injury (as defined in section 1365 of this title), such person shall be fined under this title or imprisoned not more than 20 years, or both; and if the violation results in death, such person shall be fined under this title, or imprisoned for any term of years or for life, or both.

(Added Pub.L. 104–191, Title II, § 242(a)(1), Aug. 21, 1996, 110 Stat. 2016.)

§ 1348. Securities fraud

Whoever knowingly executes, or attempts to execute, a scheme or artifice—

(1) to defraud any person in connection with any security of an issuer with a class of securities registered under section 12 of the Securities Exchange Act of 1934 (15 U.S.C. 78*l*) or that is required to file reports under section 15(d) of the Securities Exchange Act of 1934 (15 U.S.C. 78*o*(d)); or

(2) to obtain, by means of false or fraudulent pretenses, representations, or promises, any money or property in connection with the purchase or sale of any security of an issuer with a class of securities registered under section 12 of the Securities Exchange Act of 1934 (15 U.S.C. 78*l*) or that is required to file reports under section 15(d) of the Securities Exchange Act of 1934 (15 U.S.C. 78*o*(d));

shall be fined under this title, or imprisoned not more than 25 years, or both.

(Added Pub.L. 107–204, Title VIII, § 807(a), July 30, 2002, 116 Stat. 804.)

§ 1349. Attempt and conspiracy

Any person who attempts or conspires to commit any offense under this chapter shall be subject to the same penalties as those prescribed for the offense, the commission of which was the object of the attempt or conspiracy.

(Added Pub.L. 107–204, Title IX, § 902(a), July 30, 2002, 116 Stat. 805.)

§ 1350. Failure of corporate officers to certify financial reports

(a) Certification of periodic financial reports.—Each periodic report containing financial statements filed by an issuer with the Securities Exchange Commission pursuant to section 13(a) or 15(d) of the Securities Exchange Act of 1934 (15 U.S.C. 78m(a) or 78*o*(d)) shall be accompanied by a written statement by the chief executive officer and chief financial officer (or equivalent thereof) of the issuer.

(b) Content.—The statement required under subsection (a) shall certify that the periodic report containing the financial statements fully complies with the requirements of section 13(a) or 15(d) of the Securities Exchange Act pf[1] 1934 (15 U.S.C. 78m or 78*o*(d)) and that information contained in the periodic report fairly presents, in all material respects, the financial condition and results of operations of the issuer.

(c) Criminal penalties.—Whoever—

(1) certifies any statement as set forth in subsections (a) and (b) of this section knowing that the periodic report accompanying the statement does not comport with all the requirements set forth in this section shall be fined not more than $1,000,000 or imprisoned not more than 10 years, or both; or

(2) willfully certifies any statement as set forth in subsections (a) and (b) of this section knowing that the periodic report accompanying the statement does not comport with all the requirements set forth in this section shall be fined not more than $5,000,000, or imprisoned not more than 20 years, or both.

(Added Pub.L. 107–204, Title IX, § 906(a), July 30, 2002, 116 Stat. 806.)

[1] So in original. Probably should be "of".

CHAPTER 65—MALICIOUS MISCHIEF

HISTORICAL AND STATUTORY NOTES

Codifications

Amendment by section 3543 of Pub.L. 101–647 directed the placement of a period after item 1366. A period had already been editorially placed after such item, therefore, no further change was required.

§ 1361. Government property or contracts

Whoever willfully injures or commits any depredation against any property of the United States, or of any department or agency thereof, or any property which has been or is being manufactured or constructed for the United States, or any department or agency thereof, or attempts to commit any of the foregoing offenses, shall be punished as follows:

If the damage or attempted damage to such property exceeds the sum of $1,000, by a fine under this title or imprisonment for not more than ten years, or both; if the damage or attempted damage to such property does not exceed the sum of $1,000, by a fine under this title or by imprisonment for not more than one year, or both.

(June 25, 1948, c. 645, 62 Stat. 764; Sept. 13, 1994, Pub.L. 103–322, Title XXXII, § 320903(d)(1), Title XXXIII, § 330016(1)(H), (L), 108 Stat. 2125, 2147; Oct. 11, 1996, Pub.L. 104–294, Title VI, §§ 601(a)(3), 605(e), 606(a), 110 Stat. 3498, 3510, 3511.)

§ 1362. Communication lines, stations or systems

Whoever willfully or maliciously injures or destroys any of the works, property, or material of any radio, telegraph, telephone or cable, line, station, or system, or other means of communication, operated or controlled by the United States, or used or intended to be used for military or civil defense functions of the United States, whether constructed or in process of construction, or willfully or maliciously interferes in any way with the working or use of any such line, or system, or willfully or maliciously obstructs, hinders, or delays the transmission of any communication over any such line, or system, or attempts or conspires to do such an act, shall be fined under this title or imprisoned not more than ten years, or both.

In the case of any works, property, or material, not operated or controlled by the United States, this section shall not apply to any lawful strike activity, or other lawful concerted activities for the purposes of collective bargaining or other mutual aid and protection which do not injure or destroy any line or system used or intended to be used for the military or civil defense functions of the United States.

(June 25, 1948, c. 645, 62 Stat. 764; Sept. 26, 1961, Pub.L. 87–306, 75 Stat. 669; Sept. 13, 1994, Pub.L. 103–322, Title XXXII, § 320903(d)(2), Title XXXIII, § 330016(1)(L), 108 Stat. 2125, 2147; Oct. 26, 2001, Pub.L. 107–56, Title VIII, § 811(c), 115 Stat. 381.)

§ 1363. Buildings or property within special maritime and territorial jurisdiction

Whoever, within the special maritime and territorial jurisdiction of the United States, willfully and maliciously destroys or injures any structure, conveyance, or other real or personal property, or attempts or conspires to do such an act, shall be fined under this title or imprisoned not more than five years, or both, and if the building be a dwelling, or the life of any person be placed in jeopardy, shall be fined under this title or imprisoned not more than twenty years, or both.

(June 25, 1948, c. 645, 62 Stat. 764; Sept. 13, 1994, Pub.L. 103–322, Title XXXIII, § 330016(1)(H), (K), 108 Stat. 2147; Apr. 24, 1996, Pub.L. 104–132, Title VII, § 703, 110 Stat. 1294; Oct. 26, 2001, Pub.L. 107–56, Title VIII, § 811(d), 115 Stat. 381.)

§ 1364. Interference with foreign commerce by violence

Whoever, with intent to prevent, interfere with, or obstruct or attempt to prevent, interfere with, or obstruct the exportation to foreign countries of articles from the United States, injures or destroys, by fire or explosives, such articles or the places where they may be while in such foreign commerce, shall be fined under this title or imprisoned not more than twenty years, or both.

(June 25, 1948, c. 645, 62 Stat. 764; Sept. 13, 1994, Pub.L. 103–322, Title XXXIII, § 330016(1)(L), 108 Stat. 2147.)

§ 1365. Tampering with consumer products

(a) Whoever, with reckless disregard for the risk that another person will be placed in danger of death or bodily injury and under circumstances manifesting extreme indifference to such risk, tampers with any consumer product that affects interstate or foreign commerce, or the labeling of, or container for, any such product, or attempts to do so, shall—

(1) in the case of an attempt, be fined under this title or imprisoned not more than ten years, or both;

(2) if death of an individual results, be fined under this title or imprisoned for any term of years or for life, or both;

(3) if serious bodily injury to any individual results, be fined under this title or imprisoned not more than twenty years, or both; and

(4) in any other case, be fined under this title or imprisoned not more than ten years, or both.

(b) Whoever, with intent to cause serious injury to the business of any person, taints any consumer product or renders materially false or misleading the labeling of, or container for, a consumer product, if such consumer product affects interstate or foreign commerce, shall be fined under this title or imprisoned not more than three years, or both.

(c)(1) Whoever knowingly communicates false information that a consumer product has been tainted, if such product or the results of such communication affect interstate or foreign commerce, and if such tainting, had it occurred, would create a risk of death or bodily injury to another person, shall be fined under this title or imprisoned not more than five years, or both.

(2) As used in paragraph (1) of this subsection, the term "communicates false information" means communicates information that is false and that the communicator knows is false, under circumstances in which the information may reasonably be expected to be believed.

(d) Whoever knowingly threatens, under circumstances in which the threat may reasonably be expected to be believed, that conduct that, if it occurred, would violate subsection (a) of this section will occur, shall be fined under this title or imprisoned not more than five years, or both.

(e) Whoever is a party to a conspiracy of two or more persons to commit an offense under subsection (a) of this section, if any of the parties intentionally engages in any conduct in furtherance of such offense, shall be fined under this title or imprisoned not more than ten years, or both.

(f)(1) Whoever, without the consent of the manufacturer, retailer, or distributor, intentionally tampers with a consumer product that is sold in interstate or foreign commerce by knowingly placing or inserting any writing in the consumer product, or in the container for the consumer product, before the sale of the consumer product to any consumer shall be fined under this title, imprisoned not more than 1 year, or both.

(2) Notwithstanding the provisions of paragraph (1), if any person commits a violation of this subsection after a prior conviction under this section becomes final, such person shall be fined under this title, imprisoned for not more than 3 years, or both.

(3) In this subsection, the term "writing" means any form of representation or communication, including hand-bills, notices, or advertising, that contain letters, words, or pictorial representations.

(g) In addition to any other agency which has authority to investigate violations of this section, the Food and Drug Administration and the Department of Agriculture, respectively, have authority to investigate violations of this section involving a consumer product that is regulated by a provision of law such Administration or Department, as the case may be, administers.

(h) As used in this section—

(1) the term "consumer product" means—

(A) any "food", "drug", "device", or "cosmetic", as those terms are respectively defined in section 201 of the Federal Food, Drug, and Cosmetic Act (21 U.S.C. 321); or

(B) any article, product, or commodity which is customarily produced or distributed for consumption by individuals, or use by individuals for purposes of personal care or in the performance of services ordinarily rendered within the household, and which is designed to be consumed or expended in the course of such consumption or use;

(2) the term "labeling" has the meaning given such term in section 201(m) of the Federal Food, Drug, and Cosmetic Act (21 U.S.C. 321(m));

(3) the term "serious bodily injury" means bodily injury which involves—

(A) a substantial risk of death;

(B) extreme physical pain;

(C) protracted and obvious disfigurement; or

(D) protracted loss or impairment of the function of a bodily member, organ, or mental faculty; and

(4) the term "bodily injury" means—

(A) a cut, abrasion, bruise, burn, or disfigurement;

(B) physical pain;

(C) illness;

(D) impairment of the function of a bodily member, organ, or mental faculty; or

(E) any other injury to the body, no matter how temporary.

(Added Pub.L. 98–127, § 2, Oct. 13, 1983, 97 Stat. 831, and amended Pub.L. 101–647, Title XXXV, § 3544, Nov. 29, 1990, 104 Stat. 4926; Pub.L. 103–322, Title XXXIII, § 330016(1)(L), (O), (Q), (S), Sept. 13, 1994, 108 Stat. 2147, 2148, Pub.L. 107–307, § 2, Dec. 2, 2002, 116 Stat. 2445.)

HISTORICAL AND STATUTORY NOTES

References in Text

Section 201 of the Federal Food, Drug, and Cosmetic Act, referred to in subsec. (g), is classified to section 321 of Title 21, Food and Drugs.

Codifications

Section 3544 of Pub.L. 101–647 directed the placement of an open quotation mark before "device" in subsec. (g)(1)(A) of this section. Such quotation had already been editorially supplied, therefore, no further change was required.

Short Title

2002 Amendments. Pub.L. 107–307, § 1, Dec. 2, 2002, 116 Stat. 2445, provided that: "This Act [amending this section] may be cited as the 'Product Packaging Protection Act of 2002'."

1983 Amendments. Section 1 of Pub.L. 98–127 provided: "That this Act [enacting this section and section 155A of Title 35, Patents] may be cited as the 'Federal Anti-Tampering Act'."

§ 1366. Destruction of an energy facility

(a) Whoever knowingly and willfully damages or attempts or conspires to damage the property of an energy facility in an amount that in fact exceeds or would if the attempted offense had been completed, or if the object of the conspiracy had been achieved, have exceeded $100,000, or damages or attempts or conspires to damage the property of an energy facility in any amount and causes or attempts or conspires to cause a significant interruption or impairment of a function of an energy facility, shall be punishable by a fine under this title or imprisonment for not more than 20 years, or both.

(b) Whoever knowingly and willfully damages or attempts to damage the property of an energy facility in an amount that in fact exceeds or would if the attempted offense had been completed have exceeded $5,000 shall be punishable by a fine under this title, or imprisonment for not more than five years, or both.

(c) For purposes of this section, the term "energy facility" means a facility that is involved in the production, storage, transmission, or distribution of electricity, fuel, or another form or source of energy, or research, development, or demonstration facilities relating thereto, regardless of whether such facility is still under construction or is otherwise not functioning, except a facility subject to the jurisdiction, administration, or in the custody of the Nuclear Regulatory Commission or an interstate gas pipeline facility as defined in section 60101 of title 49.

(d) Whoever is convicted of a violation of subsection (a) or (b) that has resulted in the death of any person shall be subject to imprisonment for any term of years or life.

(Added Pub.L. 98–473, Title II, § 1011(a), Oct. 12, 1984, 98 Stat. 2141, § 1365; renumbered Pub.L. 99–646, § 29(a), Nov. 10, 1986, 100 Stat. 3598, and amended Pub.L. 101–647, Title XXXV, §§ 3545, 3546, Nov. 29, 1990, 104 Stat. 4926; Pub.L. 103–272, § 5(e)(9), July 5, 1994, 108 Stat. 1374; Pub.L. 103–322, Title XXXII, § 320903(d)(3), Title XXXIII, § 330016(2)(C), Sept. 13, 1994, 108 Stat. 2125, 2148; Pub.L. 107–56, Title VIII, § 810(b), Oct. 26, 2001, 115 Stat. 380; Pub.L. 109–177, Title IV, § 406(c)(2), Mar. 9, 2006, 120 Stat. 245.)

§ 1367. Interference with the operation of a satellite

(a) Whoever, without the authority of the satellite operator, intentionally or maliciously interferes with the authorized operation of a communications or weather satellite or obstructs or hinders any satellite transmission shall be fined in accordance with this title or imprisoned not more than ten years or both.

(b) This section does not prohibit any lawfully authorized investigative, protective, or intelligence activity of a law enforcement agency or of an intelligence agency of the United States.

(Added Pub.L. 99–508, Title III, § 303(a), Oct. 21, 1986, 100 Stat. 1872.)

HISTORICAL AND STATUTORY NOTES

Effective and Applicability Provisions

1986 Acts. Section effective 90 days after Oct. 21, 1986 except as otherwise provided in section 302 of Pub.L. 99–508 with respect to conduct pursuant to court order or extension, see section 302 of Pub.L. 99–508, set out as a note under section 3121 of this title.

§ 1368. Harming animals used in law enforcement

(a) Whoever willfully and maliciously harms any police animal, or attempts or conspires to do so, shall be fined under this title and imprisoned not more than 1 year. If the offense permanently disables or disfigures the animal, or causes serious bodily injury to or the death of the animal, the maximum term of imprisonment shall be 10 years.

(b) In this section, the term "police animal" means a dog or horse employed by a Federal agency (whether in the executive, legislative, or judicial branch) for the principal purpose of aiding in the detection of criminal activity, enforcement of laws, or apprehension of criminal offenders.

(Added Pub.L. 106–254, § 2(a), Aug. 2, 2000, 114 Stat. 638, and amended Pub.L. 107–273, Div. B, Title IV, § 4003(a)(4), Nov. 2, 2002, 116 Stat. 1811.)

HISTORICAL AND STATUTORY NOTES

Short Title

2000 Acts. Pub.L. 106–254, § 1, Aug. 2, 2000, 114 Stat. 638, provided that: "This Act [enacting this section] may be cited as the 'Federal Law Enforcement Animal Protection Act of 2000'."

§ 1369. Destruction of veterans' memorials

(a) Whoever, in a circumstance described in subsection (b), willfully injures or destroys, or attempts to injure or destroy, any structure, plaque, statue, or other monument on public property commemorating the service of any person or persons in the armed forces of the United States shall be fined under this title, imprisoned not more than 10 years, or both.

(b) A circumstance described in this subsection is that—

(1) in committing the offense described in subsection (a), the defendant travels or causes another to travel in interstate or foreign commerce, or uses the mail or an instrumentality of interstate or foreign commerce; or

(2) the structure, plaque, statue, or other monument described in subsection (a) is located on property owned by, or under the jurisdiction of, the Federal Government.

(Added Pub.L. 108–29, § 2(a), May 29, 2003, 117 Stat. 772.)

HISTORICAL AND STATUTORY NOTES

Short Title

2003 Acts. Pub.L. 108–29, § 1, May 29, 2003, 117 Stat. 772, provided that: "This Act [enacting this section and provisions set out as a note under 23 U.S.C.A. § 109] may be cited as the 'Veterans' Memorial Preservation and Recognition Act of 2003'."

CHAPTER 67—MILITARY AND NAVY

§ 1381. Enticing desertion and harboring deserters

Whoever entices or procures, or attempts or endeavors to entice or procure any person in the Armed Forces of the United States, or who has been recruited for service therein, to desert therefrom, or aids any such person in deserting or in attempting to desert from such service; or

Whoever harbors, conceals, protects, or assists any such person who may have deserted from such service, knowing him to have deserted therefrom, or refuses to give up and deliver such person on the demand of any officer authorized to receive him—

Shall be fined under this title or imprisoned not more than three years, or both.

(June 25, 1948, c. 645, 62 Stat. 764; Sept. 13, 1994, Pub.L. 103–322, Title XXXIII, § 330016(1)(I), 108 Stat. 2147.)

§ 1382. Entering military, naval, or Coast Guard property

Whoever, within the jurisdiction of the United States, goes upon any military, naval, or Coast Guard reservation, post, fort, arsenal, yard, station, or installation, for any purpose prohibited by law or lawful regulation; or

Whoever reenters or is found within any such reservation, post, fort, arsenal, yard, station, or installation, after having been removed therefrom or ordered not to reenter by any officer or person in command or charge thereof—

Shall be fined under this title or imprisoned not more than six months, or both.

(June 25, 1948, c. 645, 62 Stat. 765; Sept. 13, 1994, Pub.L. 103–322, Title XXXIII, § 330016(1)(G), 108 Stat. 2147.)

HISTORICAL AND STATUTORY NOTES

Transfer of Functions

For transfer of authorities, functions, personnel, and assets of the Coast Guard, including the authorities and functions of the Secretary of Transportation relating thereto to the Department of Homeland Security, see 6 U.S.C.A. §§ 468(b), 551(d), 552(d) and 557, and the Department of Homeland Security Reorganization Plan of November 25, 2002, as modified, set out as a note under 6 U.S.C.A. § 542.

All functions of all officers of the Department of the Treasury, and all functions of all agencies and employees of such Department were transferred, with certain exceptions, to the Secretary of the Treasury, with power vested in him to authorize their performance or the performance of any of his functions, by any of such officers, agencies, and employees, by Reorg. Plan No. 26 of 1950, §§ 1, 2, eff. July 31, 1950, 15 F.R. 4935, 64 Stat. 1280, 1281, set out in the Appendix to Title 5, Government Organization and Employees. The Coast Guard, referred to in this section, was generally a service in the Treasury Department, but such Plan excepted, from the transfer, the functions of the Coast Guard, and of the Commandant thereof, when the Coast Guard was operating as a part of the Navy under sections 1 and 3 of Title 14, Coast Guard.

The Coast Guard was transferred to the Department of Transportation and all functions, powers, and duties, relating to the Coast Guard, of the Secretary of the Treasury and of other offices and officers of the Department of the Treasury were transferred to the Secretary of Transportation by Pub.L. 89–670, Oct. 15, 1966, 80 Stat. 931, which created the Department of Transportation. See section 108 of Title 49, Transportation.

[§ 1383. Repealed. Pub.L. 94–412, Title V, § 501(e), Sept. 14, 1976, 90 Stat. 1258]

HISTORICAL AND STATUTORY NOTES

Section, Act June 25, 1948, c. 645, 62 Stat. 765, dealt with criminal penalties for persons entering, remaining in, leaving, or committing any act in a military area or zone contrary to restrictions imposed by Executive Order or Secretary of the Army.

Savings Provision

Repeal of this section by Pub.L. 94–412 not to affect any action taken or proceeding pending at the time of repeal, see section 501(h) of Pub.L. 94–412, set out as a Savings Provision note under section 1601 of Title 50, War and National Defense.

§ 1384. Prostitution near military and naval establishments

Within such reasonable distance of any military or naval camp, station, fort, post, yard, base, cantonment, training or mobilization place as the Secretary of the Army, the Secretary of the Navy, the Secretary of the Air Force, or any two or all of them shall determine to be needful to the efficiency, health, and welfare of the Army, the Navy, or the Air Force, and shall designate and publish in general orders or bulletins, whoever engages in prostitution or aids or abets prostitution or procures or solicits for purposes of prostitution, or keeps or sets up a house of ill fame, brothel, or bawdy house, or receives any person for purposes of lewdness, assignation, or prostitution into any vehicle, conveyance, place, structure, or building, or permits any person to remain for the purpose of lewdness, assignation, or prostitution in any vehicle, conveyance, place, structure, or building or leases or rents or contracts to lease or rent any vehicle, conveyance, place, structure or building, or part thereof, knowing or with good reason to know that it is intended to be used for any of the purposes herein prohibited shall be fined under this title or imprisoned not more than one year, or both.

The Secretaries of the Army, Navy, and Air Force and the Federal Security Administrator shall take such steps as they deem necessary to suppress and prevent such violations thereof, and shall accept the cooperation of the authorities of States and their counties, districts, and other political subdivisions in carrying out the purpose of this section.

This section shall not be construed as conferring on the personnel of the Departments of the Army, Navy, or Air Force or the Federal Security Agency any authority to make criminal investigations, searches, seizures, or arrests of civilians charged with violations of this section.

(June 25, 1948, c. 645, 62 Stat. 765; May 24, 1949, c. 139, § 35, 63 Stat. 94; Sept. 13, 1994, Pub.L. 103–322, Title XXXIII, § 330016(1)(H), 108 Stat. 2147.)

HISTORICAL AND STATUTORY NOTES

Transfer of Functions

The Secretary and Department of Health, Education, and Welfare was redesignated the Secretary and Department of Health and Human Services by section 3508(b) of Title 20, Education.

All functions of the Federal Security Administrator were transferred to the Secretary of Health, Education, and Welfare and all agencies of the Federal Security Agency were transferred to the Department of Health, Education, and Welfare by section 5 of Reorg. Plan No. 1 of 1953, eff. Apr. 11, 1953, 18 F.R. 2053, 67 Stat. 631, set out in the Appendix to Title 5, Government Organization and Employees. The Federal Security Agency and the office of Administrator were abolished by section 8 of Reorg. Plan No. 1 of 1953.

§ 1385. Use of Army and Air Force as posse comitatus

Whoever, except in cases and under circumstances expressly authorized by the Constitution or Act of Congress, willfully uses any part of the Army or the Air Force as a posse comitatus or otherwise to execute the laws shall be fined under this title or imprisoned not more than two years, or both.

(Added Aug. 10, 1956, c. 1041, § 18(a), 70A Stat. 626, and amended June 25, 1959, Pub.L. 86–70, § 17(d), 73 Stat. 144; Sept. 13, 1994, Pub.L. 103–322, Title XXXIII, § 330016(1)(L), 108 Stat. 2147.)

§ 1386. Keys and keyways used in security applications by the Department of Defense

(a)(1) Whoever steals, purloins, embezzles, or obtains by false pretense any lock or key to any lock, knowing that such lock or key has been adopted by any part of the Department of Defense, including all Department of Defense agencies, military departments, and agencies thereof, for use in protecting conventional arms, ammunition or explosives, special weapons, and classified information or classified equipment shall be punished as provided in subsection (b).

(2) Whoever—

(A) knowingly and unlawfully makes, forges, or counterfeits any key, knowing that such key has been adopted by any part of the Department of Defense, including all Department of Defense agencies, military departments, and agencies thereof, for use in protecting conventional arms, ammunition or explosives, special weapons, and classified information or classified equipment; or

(B) knowing that any lock or key has been adopted by any part of the Department of Defense, including all Department of Defense agencies, military departments, and agencies thereof, for use in protecting conventional arms, ammunition or explosives, special weapons, and classified information or classified equipment, possesses any such lock or key with the intent to unlawfully or improperly use, sell, or otherwise dispose of such lock or key or cause the same to be unlawfully or improperly used, sold, or otherwise disposed of,

shall be punished as provided in subsection (b).

(3) Whoever, being engaged as a contractor or otherwise in the manufacture of any lock or key knowing that such lock or key has been adopted by any part of the Department of Defense, including all Department of Defense agencies, military departments, and agencies thereof, for use in protecting conventional arms, ammunition or explosives, special weapons, and classified information or classified equipment, delivers any such finished or unfinished lock or any such key to any person not duly authorized by the Secretary of Defense or his designated representative to receive the same, unless the person receiving it is the contractor for furnishing the same or engaged in the manufacture thereof in the manner authorized by the contract, or the agent of such manufacturer, shall be punished as provided in subsection (b).

(b) Whoever commits an offense under subsection (a) shall be fined under this title or imprisoned not more than 10 years, or both.

(c) As used in this section, the term "key" means any key, keyblank, or keyway adopted by any part of the Department of Defense, including all Department of Defense agencies, military departments, and agencies thereof, for use in protecting conventional arms, ammunition or explosives, special weapons, and classified information or classified equipment.

(Added Pub.L. 102–190, Div. A, Title X, § 1090(a), Dec. 5, 1991, 105 Stat. 1485.)

§ 1387. Demonstrations at cemeteries under the control of the National Cemetery Administration and at Arlington National Cemetery

Whoever violates section 2413 of title 38 shall be fined under this title, imprisoned for not more than one year, or both.

(Added Pub.L. 109–228, § 3(a), May 29, 2006, 120 Stat. 388.)

Sec. 1388. Prohibition on disruptions of funerals of members or former members of the Armed Forces

(a) Prohibition.—For any funeral of a member or former member of the Armed Forces that is not located at a cemetery under the control of the National Cemetery Administration or part of Arlington National Cemetery, it shall be unlawful for any person to engage in an activity during the period beginning 60 minutes before and ending 60 minutes after such funeral, any part of which activity—

(1)(A) takes place within the boundaries of the location of such funeral or takes place within 150 feet of the point of the intersection between—

(i) the boundary of the location of such funeral; and

(ii) a road, pathway, or other route of ingress to or egress from the location of such funeral; and

(B) includes any individual willfully making or assisting in the making of any noise or diversion that is not part of such funeral and that disturbs or tends to disturb the peace or good order of such funeral with the intent of disturbing the peace or good order of that funeral; or

(2)(A) is within 300 feet of the boundary of the location of such funeral; and

(B) includes any individual willfully and without proper authorization impeding the access to or egress from such location with the intent to impede the access to or egress from such location.

(b) Penalty.—Any person who violates subsection (a) shall be fined under this title, imprisoned for not more than 1 year, or both.

(c) Definitions.—In this section:

(1) The term "Armed Forces" has the meaning given the term in section 101 of title 10.

(2) The term "funeral of a member or former member of the Armed Forces" means any ceremony or memorial service held in connection with the burial or cremation of a member or former member of the Armed Forces.

(3) The term "boundary of the location", with respect to a funeral of a member or former member of the Armed Forces, means—

(A) in the case of a funeral of a member or former member of the Armed Forces that is held at a cemetery, the property line of the cemetery;

(B) in the case of a funeral of a member or former member of the Armed Forces that is held at a mortuary, the property line of the mortuary;

(C) in the case of a funeral of a member or former member of the Armed Forces that is held at a house of worship, the property line of the house of worship; and

(D) in the case of a funeral of a member or former member of the Armed Forces that is held at any other kind of location, the reasonable property line of that location.

(Added Pub.L. 109–464, § 1(a), Dec. 22, 2006, 120 Stat. 3480.)

[CHAPTER 68—REPEALED]

[§§ 1401 to 1407. Repealed. Pub.L. 91–513, Title III, § 1101(b) (1) (A), Oct. 27, 1970, 84 Stat. 1292]

HISTORICAL AND STATUTORY NOTES

Section 1401, Acts July 18, 1956, c. 629, Title II, § 201, 70 Stat. 572; July 12, 1960, Pub.L. 86–624, § 13(a), 74 Stat. 413, defined the terms "heroin" and "United States".

Section 1402, Act July 18, 1956, c. 629, Title II, § 201, 70 Stat. 572, provided for the surrender to the Secretary of the Treasury of all legally possessed heroin within 120 days of July 19, 1956.

Section 1403, Act July 18, 1956, c. 629, Title II, § 201, 70 Stat. 573, set penalties for the unlawful use of communications facilities in the commission of offenses involving the importation of exportation of narcotics.

Section 1404, Act July 18, 1956, c. 629, Title II, § 201, 70 Stat. 573, granted the United States the right to appeal from the grant of a motion to suppress in prosecutions involving the unlawful exportation or importation of narcotics.

Section 1405, Acts July 18, 1956, c. 629, Title III, § 201, 70 Stat. 573; Oct. 17, 1968, Pub.L. 90–578, Title III, § 301(a) (1), 82 Stat. 1115, set out the procedure for the issuance of search warrants.

Section 1406, Act July 18, 1956, c. 629, Title II, § 201, 70 Stat. 574, provided for the authority to grant immunity from prosecution of any witnesses compelled to testify or produce evidence after claiming his privilege against self-incrimination. See section 6001 et seq. of this title. Section was repealed earlier by Pub.L. 91–452, Title II, § 224(a), Oct. 15, 1970, 84 Stat. 929, with such repeal to be effective on the sixtieth day following Oct. 15, 1970, but with such repeal not to affect any immunity to which any individual was entitled under this section by reason of any testimony given before the sixtieth day following Oct. 15, 1970.

Section 1407, Act July 18, 1956, c. 629, Title II, § 201, 70 Stat. 574, prohibited border crossings by any person addicted to or using drugs or any person convicted of any violation of narcotic or marihuana laws of the United States or of any State, the penalty for which is imprisonment for more than one year.

Effective Date of Repeal

Repeal of sections by Pub.L. 91–513 effective the first day of the seventh calendar month that begins after Oct. 26, 1970, see section 1105(a) of Pub.L. 91–513, set out as an Effective Date note under section 951 of Title 21, Food and Drugs.

Savings Provision

Prosecutions for any violation of law occurring, and civil seizures or forfeitures and injunctive proceedings commenced, prior to the effective date of repeal of these sections by section 1101 of Pub.L. 91–513 not to be affected or abated by reason thereof, see section 1103 of Pub.L. 91–513, set out as a Savings Provision note under section 171 of Title 21, Food and Drugs.

CHAPTER 69—NATIONALITY AND CITIZENSHIP

§ 1421. Accounts of court officers

Whoever, being a clerk or assistant clerk of a court, or other person charged by law with a duty to render true accounts of moneys received in any proceeding relating to citizenship, naturalization, or registration of aliens or to pay over any balance of such moneys due to the United States, willfully neglects to do so within thirty days after said payment shall become due and demand therefor has been made, shall be fined under this title or imprisoned not more than five years, or both.

(June 25, 1948, c. 645, 62 Stat. 766; Sept. 13, 1994, Pub.L. 103–322, Title XXXIII, § 330016(1)(K), 108 Stat. 2147.)

§ 1422. Fees in naturalization proceedings

Whoever knowingly demands, charges, solicits, collects, or receives, or agrees to charge, solicit, collect, or receive any other or additional fees or moneys in proceedings relating to naturalization or citizenship or the registry of aliens beyond the fees and moneys authorized by law, shall be fined under this title or imprisoned not more than five years, or both.

(June 25, 1948, c. 645, 62 Stat. 766; Sept. 13, 1994, Pub.L. 103–322, Title XXXIII, § 330016(1)(K), 108 Stat. 2147.)

§ 1423. Misuse of evidence of citizenship or naturalization

Whoever knowingly uses for any purpose any order, certificate, certificate of naturalization, certificate of citizenship, judgment, decree, or exemplification, unlawfully issued or made, or copies or duplicates thereof, showing any person to be naturalized or admitted to be a citizen, shall be fined under this title or imprisoned not more than five years, or both.

(June 25, 1948, c. 645, 62 Stat. 766; Sept. 13, 1994, Pub.L. 103–322, Title XXXIII, § 330016(1)(K), 108 Stat. 2147.)

§ 1424. Personation or misuse of papers in naturalization proceedings

Whoever, whether as applicant, declarant, petitioner, witness or otherwise, in any naturalization or citizenship proceeding, knowingly personates another or appears falsely in the name of a deceased person or in an assumed or fictitious name; or

Whoever knowingly and unlawfully uses or attempts to use, as showing naturalization or citizenship of any person, any order, certificate, certificate of naturalization, certificate of citizenship, judgment, decree, or exemplification, or copies or duplicates thereof, issued to another person, or in a fictitious name or in the name of a deceased person—

Shall be fined under this title or imprisoned not more than five years, or both.

(June 25, 1948, c. 645, 62 Stat. 766; Sept. 13, 1994, Pub.L. 103–322, Title XXXIII, § 330016(1)(K), 108 Stat. 2147.)

§ 1425. Procurement of citizenship or naturalization unlawfully

(a) Whoever knowingly procures or attempts to procure, contrary to law, the naturalization of any person, or documentary or other evidence of naturalization or of citizenship; or

(b) Whoever, whether for himself or another person not entitled thereto, knowingly issues, procures or obtains or applies for or otherwise attempts to procure or obtain naturalization, or citizenship, or a declaration of intention to become a citizen, or a certificate of arrival or any certificate or evidence of nationalization or citizenship, documentary or otherwise, or duplicates or copies of any of the foregoing—

Shall be fined under this title or imprisoned not more than 25 years (if the offense was committed to facilitate an act of international terrorism (as defined in section 2331 of this title)), 20 years (if the offense was committed to facilitate a drug trafficking crime (as defined in section 929(a) of this title)), 10 years (in the case of the first or second such offense, if the offense was not committed to facilitate such an act of international terrorism or a drug trafficking crime), or 15 years (in the case of any other offense), or both.

(June 25, 1948, c. 645, 62 Stat. 766; Sept. 13, 1994, Pub.L. 103–322, Title XXXIII, § 330016(1)(K), 108 Stat. 2147; Sept. 30, 1996, Pub.L. 104–208, Div. C, Title II, § 211(a)(2), 110 Stat. 3009–569; Nov. 2, 2002, Pub.L. 107–273, Div. B, Title IV, § 4002(a)(3), 116 Stat. 1806.)

HISTORICAL AND STATUTORY NOTES

Effective and Applicability Provisions

1996 Acts. Amendment by section 211(a)(2) of Pub.L. 104–208 applicable with respect to offenses occurring on or after Sept. 30, 1996, see section 211(c) of Pub.L. 104–208, set out as a note under section 1028 of this title.

Severability of Provisions

If any provision of Division C of Pub.L. 104–208 or the application of such provision to any person or circumstances is held to be unconstitutional, the remainder of Division C of Pub.L. 104–208 and the application of the provisions of Division C of Pub.L. 104–208 to any person or circumstance not to be affected thereby, see section 1(e) of Pub.L. 104–208, set out as a note under section 1101 of Title 8, Aliens and Nationality.

§ 1426. Reproduction of naturalization or citizenship papers

(a) Whoever falsely makes, forges, alters or counterfeits any oath, notice, affidavit, certificate of arrival, declaration of intention, certificate or documentary evidence of naturalization or citizenship or any order, record, signature, paper or proceeding or any copy thereof, required or authorized by any law relating to naturalization or citizenship or registry of aliens; or

(b) Whoever utters, sells, disposes of or uses as true or genuine, any false, forged, altered, antedated or counterfeited oath, notice, affidavit, certificate of arrival, declaration of intention to become a citizen, certificate or documentary evidence of naturalization or citizenship, or any order, record, signature or other instrument, paper or proceeding required or authorized by any law relating to naturalization or citizenship or registry of aliens, or any copy thereof, knowing the same to be false, forged, altered, antedated or counterfeited; or

(c) Whoever, with intent unlawfully to use the same, possesses any false, forged, altered, antedated or counterfeited certificate of arrival, declaration of intention to become a citizen, certificate or documentary evidence of naturalization or citizenship purporting to have been issued under any law of the United States, or copy thereof, knowing the same to be false, forged, altered, antedated or counterfeited; or

(d) Whoever, without lawful authority, engraves or possesses, sells or brings into the United States any plate in the likeness or similitude of any plate designed, for the printing of a declaration of intention, or certificate or documentary evidence of naturalization or citizenship; or

(e) Whoever, without lawful authority, brings into the United States any document printed therefrom; or

(f) Whoever, without lawful authority, possesses any blank certificate of arrival, blank declaration of intention or blank certificate of naturalization or citizenship provided by the Immigration and Naturalization Service, with intent unlawfully to use the same; or

(g) Whoever, with intent unlawfully to use the same, possesses a distinctive paper adopted by the proper officer or agency of the United States for the printing or engraving of a declaration of intention to become a citizen, or certificate of naturalization or certificate of citizenship; or

(h) Whoever, without lawful authority, prints, photographs, makes or executes any print or impression in the likeness of a certificate of arrival, declaration of intention to become a citizen, or certificate of naturalization or citizenship, or any part thereof—

Shall be fined under this title or imprisoned not more than 25 years (if the offense was committed to facilitate an act of international terrorism (as defined in section 2331 of this title)), 20 years (if the offense was committed to facilitate a drug trafficking crime (as defined in section 929(a) of this title)), 10 years (in the case of the first or second such offense, if the offense was not committed to facilitate such an act of international terrorism or a drug trafficking crime), or 15 years (in the case of any other offense), or both.

(June 25, 1948, c. 645, 62 Stat. 767; Sept. 13, 1994, Pub.L. 103–322, Title XXXIII, § 330016(1)(K), 108 Stat. 2147; Sept. 30, 1996, Pub.L. 104–208, Div. C, Title II, § 211(a)(2), 110 Stat. 3009–569; Nov. 2, 2002, Pub.L. 107–273, Div. B, Title IV, § 4002(a)(3), 116 Stat. 1806.)

HISTORICAL AND STATUTORY NOTES

Effective and Applicability Provisions

1996 Acts. Amendment by section 211(a)(2) of Pub.L. 104–208 applicable with respect to offenses occurring on or after Sept. 30, 1996, see section 211(c) of Pub.L. 104–208, set out as a note under section 1028 of this title.

Transfer of Functions

All functions of all other officers of the Department of Justice and all functions of all agencies and employees of such Department were, with a few exceptions, transferred to the Attorney General, with power vested in him to authorize their performance or the performance of any of his functions by any of such officers, agencies, and employees, by Reorg. Plan No. 2 of 1950, §§ 1, 2, eff. May 24, 1950, 15 F.R. 3173, 64 Stat. 1261, set out in the Appendix to Title 5, Government Organization and Employees.

Abolition of Immigration and Naturalization Service and Transfer of Functions

For abolition of Immigration and Naturalization Service, transfer of functions, and treatment of related references, see note set out under 8 U.S.C.A. § 1551.

Severability of Provisions

If any provision of Division C of Pub.L. 104–208 or the application of such provision to any person or circumstances is held to be unconstitutional, the remainder of Division C of Pub.L. 104–208 and the application of the provisions of Division C of Pub.L. 104–208 to any person or circumstance not to be affected thereby, see section 1(e) of Pub.L. 104–208, set out as a note under section 1101 of Title 8, Aliens and Nationality.

§ 1427. Sale of naturalization or citizenship papers

Whoever unlawfully sells or disposes of a declaration of intention to become a citizen, certificate of naturalization, certificate of citizenship or copies or duplicates or other documentary evidence of naturalization or citizenship, shall be fined under this title or imprisoned not more than 25 years (if the offense was committed to facilitate an act of international terrorism (as defined in section 2331 of this title)), 20 years (if the offense was committed to facilitate a drug trafficking crime (as defined in section 929(a) of this title)), 10 years (in the case of the first or second such offense, if the offense was not committed to facilitate such an act of international terrorism or a drug trafficking crime), or 15 years (in the case of any other offense), or both.

(June 25, 1948, c. 645, 62 Stat. 767; Sept. 13, 1994, Pub.L. 103–322, Title XXXIII, § 330016(1)(K), 108 Stat. 2147; Sept. 30, 1996, Pub.L. 104–208, Div. C, Title II, § 211(a)(2), 110 Stat. 3009–569; Nov. 2, 2002, Pub.L. 107–273, Div. B, Title IV, § 4002(a)(3), 116 Stat. 1806.)

HISTORICAL AND STATUTORY NOTES

Effective and Applicability Provisions

1996 Acts. Amendment by section 211(a)(2) of Pub.L. 104–208 applicable with respect to offenses occurring on or after Sept. 30, 1996, see section 211(c) of Pub.L. 104–208, set out as a note under section 1028 of this title.

Severability of Provisions

If any provision of Division C of Pub.L. 104–208 or the application of such provision to any person or circumstances is held to be unconstitutional, the remainder of Division C of Pub.L. 104–208 and the application of the provisions of Division C of Pub.L. 104–208 to any person or circumstance not to be affected thereby, see section 1(e) of Pub.L. 104–208, set out as a note under section 1101 of Title 8, Aliens and Nationality.

§ 1428. Surrender of canceled naturalization certificate

Whoever, having in his possession or control a certificate of naturalization or citizenship or a copy thereof which has been canceled as provided by law, fails to surrender the same after at least sixty days' notice by the appropriate court or the Commissioner or Deputy Commissioner of Immigration, shall be fined under this title or imprisoned not more than five years, or both.

(June 25, 1948, c. 645, 62 Stat. 767; Sept. 13, 1994, Pub.L. 103–322, Title XXXIII, § 330016(1)(K), 108 Stat. 2147.)

HISTORICAL AND STATUTORY NOTES

Transfer of Functions

All functions of all other officers of the Department of Justice and all functions of all agencies and employees of such Department were, with a few exceptions, transferred to the Attorney General, with power vested in him to authorize their performance or the performance of any of his functions by any of such officers, agencies, and employees, by Reorg. Plan No. 2 of 1950, §§ 1, 2, eff. May 24, 1950, 15 F.R. 3173, 64 Stat. 1261, set out in the Appendix to Title 5, Government Organization and Employees.

Abolition of Immigration and Naturalization Service and Transfer of Functions

For abolition of Immigration and Naturalization Service, transfer of functions, and treatment of related references, see note set out under 8 U.S.C.A. § 1551.

§ 1429. Penalties for neglect or refusal to answer subpena

Any person who has been subpenaed under the provisions of subsection (d) of section 336 of the Immigration and Nationality Act to appear at the final hearing of an application for naturalization, and who shall neglect or refuse to so appear and to testify, if in the power of such person to do so, shall be fined under this title or imprisoned not more than five years, or both.

(Added June 27, 1952, c. 477, Title IV, § 402(b), 66 Stat. 276, and amended Dec. 29, 1981, Pub.L. 97–116, § 18(u)(1), 95 Stat. 1621; Nov. 29, 1990, Pub.L. 101–649, Title IV, § 407(c)(21), 104 Stat. 5041; Sept. 13, 1994, Pub.L. 103–322, Title XXXIII, § 330016(1)(K), 108 Stat. 2147.)

HISTORICAL AND STATUTORY NOTES

References in Text

Subsection (d) of section 336 of the Immigration and Nationality Act, referred to in the text, is classified to section 1447(d) of Title 8, Aliens and Nationality.

Effective and Applicability Provisions

1990 Acts. Amendment by Title IV of Pub.L. 101–649 effective Nov. 29, 1990, with general savings provisions, see section 408(a)(3) and (d) of Pub.L. 101–649, set out as a note under section 1421 of Title 8, Aliens and Nationality.

1981 Acts. Amendment by Pub.L. 97–116 effective Dec. 29, 1981, see section 21(a) of Pub.L. 97–116, set out as a note under section 1101 of Title 8, Aliens and Nationality.

CHAPTER 71—OBSCENITY

[1]So in original. Section heading amended without corresponding amendment of analysis.

§ 1460. Possession with intent to sell, and sale, of obscene matter on Federal property

(a) Whoever, either—

(1) in the special maritime and territorial jurisdiction of the United States, or on any land or building owned by, leased to, or otherwise used by or under the control of the Government of the United States; or

(2) in the Indian country as defined in section 1151 of this title,

knowingly sells or possesses with intent to sell an obscene visual depiction shall be punished by a fine in accordance with the provisions of this title or imprisoned for not more than 2 years, or both.

(b) For the purposes of this section, the term "visual depiction" includes undeveloped film and videotape but does not include mere words.

(Added Pub.L. 100–690, Title VII, § 7526(a), Nov. 18, 1988, 102 Stat. 4503, and amended Pub.L. 101–647, Title III, § 323(c), Nov. 29, 1990, 104 Stat. 4819.)

§ 1461. Mailing obscene or crime-inciting matter

Every obscene, lewd, lascivious, indecent, filthy or vile article, matter, thing, device, or substance; and—

Every article or thing designed, adapted, or intended for producing abortion, or for any indecent or immoral use; and

Every article, instrument, substance, drug, medicine, or thing which is advertised or described in a manner calculated to lead another to use or apply it for producing abortion, or for any indecent or immoral purpose; and

Every written or printed card, letter, circular, book, pamphlet, advertisement, or notice of any kind giving information, directly or indirectly, where, or how, or from whom, or by what means any of such mentioned matters, articles, or things may be obtained or made, or where or by whom any act or operation of any kind for the procuring or producing of abortion will be done or performed, or how or by what means abortion may be produced, whether sealed or unsealed; and

Every paper, writing, advertisement, or representation that any article, instrument, substance, drug, medicine, or thing may, or can, be used or applied for producing abortion, or for any indecent or immoral purpose; and

Every description calculated to induce or incite a person to so use or apply any such article, instrument, substance, drug, medicine, or thing—

Is declared to be nonmailable matter and shall not be conveyed in the mails or delivered from any post office or by any letter carrier.

Whoever knowingly uses the mails for the mailing, carriage in the mails, or delivery of anything declared by this section or section 3001(e) of title 39 to be nonmailable, or knowingly causes to be delivered by mail according to the direction thereon, or at the place at which it is directed to be delivered by the person to whom it is addressed, or knowingly takes any such thing from the mails for the purpose of circulating or disposing thereof, or of aiding in the circulation or disposition thereof, shall be fined under this title or imprisoned not more than five years, or both, for the first such offense, and shall be fined under this title or imprisoned not more than ten years, or both, for each such offense thereafter.

The term "indecent", as used in this section includes matter of a character tending to incite arson, murder, or assassination.

(June 25, 1948, c. 645, 62 Stat. 768; June 28, 1955, c. 190, §§ 1, 2, 69 Stat. 183; Aug. 28, 1958, Pub.L. 85–796, § 1, 72 Stat. 962; Jan. 8, 1971, Pub.L. 91–662, §§ 3, 5(b), 6(3), 84 Stat. 1973, 1974; Sept. 13, 1994, Pub.L. 103–322, Title XXXII, § 330016(1)(K), (L), 108 Stat. 2147.)

HISTORICAL AND STATUTORY NOTES

Effective and Applicability Provisions

1971 Acts. Amendment by sections 3 and 5(b) of Pub.L. 91–662 effective Jan. 9, 1971, see section 7 of Pub.L. 91–662, set out as an Effective Date of 1971 Amendment note under section 552 of this title.

Section 6 of Pub.L. 91–662 provided in part that the amendment by section 6(3) of Pub.L. 91–662 shall be effective on the date that the Board of Governors of the United States Postal Service establishes as the effective date for section 3001 of title 39 of the United States Code, as enacted by the Postal Reorganization Act.

Commission on Obscenity and Pornography

Pub.L. 90–100, Oct. 3, 1967, 81 Stat. 253, as amended by Pub.L. 90–350, Title V, § 502, June 19, 1968, 82 Stat. 197; Pub.L. 91–74, Title V, § 503, Sept. 29, 1969, 83 Stat. 123, provided for the establishment of the Commission on Obscenity and Pornography, its membership, compensation of the members, powers, functions, and duties of the Commission, required the Commission to report to the President and to the Congress its findings and recommendations no later than Sept. 30, 1970, and provided for its termination ten days following the submission of the report.

§ 1462. Importation or transportation of obscene matters

Whoever brings into the United States, or any place subject to the jurisdiction thereof, or knowingly uses any express company or other common carrier or interactive computer service (as defined in section 230(e)(2) of the Communications Act of 1934), for carriage in interstate or foreign commerce—

(a) any obscene, lewd, lascivious, or filthy book, pamphlet, picture, motion-picture film, paper, letter, writing, print, or other matter of indecent character; or

(b) any obscene, lewd, lascivious, or filthy phonograph recording, electrical transcription, or other article or thing capable of producing sound; or

(c) any drug, medicine, article, or thing designed, adapted, or intended for producing abortion, or for any indecent or immoral use; or any written or printed card, letter, circular, book, pamphlet, advertisement, or notice of any kind giving information, directly or indirectly, where, how, or of whom, or by what means any of such mentioned articles, matters, or things may be obtained or made; or

Whoever knowingly takes or receives, from such express company or other common carrier or interactive computer service (as defined in section 230(e)(2) of the Communications Act of 1934) any matter or thing the carriage or importation of which is herein made unlawful—

Shall be fined under this title or imprisoned not more than five years, or both, for the first such offense and shall be fined under this title or imprisoned not more than ten years, or both, for each such offense thereafter.

(June 25, 1948, c. 645, 62 Stat. 768; May 27, 1950, c. 214, § 1, 64 Stat. 194; Aug. 28, 1958, Pub.L. 85–796, § 2, 72 Stat. 962; Jan. 8, 1971, Pub.L. 91–662, § 4, 84 Stat. 1973; Sept. 13, 1994, Pub.L. 103–322, Title XXXIII, § 330016(1)(K), (L), 108 Stat. 2147; Feb. 8, 1996, Pub.L. 104–104, Title V, § 507(a), 110 Stat. 137.)

HISTORICAL AND STATUTORY NOTES

References in Text

The Communications Act of 1934, referred to in text, is Act June 19, 1934, c. 652, 48 Stat. 1064, as amended, which is classified principally to chapter 5 of Title 47, 47 U.S.C.A. § 151 et seq. Section 230(e)(2), referred to in text, was redesignated 230(f)(2) of the Communications Act of 1934 by Pub.L. 105–277, Div. C, Title XIV, § 1404(a)(2), Oct. 21, 1998, 112 Stat. 2681–739, and is classified to 47 U.S.C.A. § 230(f)(2). For complete classification, see 47 U.S.C.A. § 609 and Tables.

Effective and Applicability Provisions

1971 Acts. Amendment by Pub.L. 91–662 effective Jan. 9, 1971, see section 7 of Pub.L. 91–662, set out as an Effective Date of 1971 Amendment note under section 552 of this title.

Construction of 1996 Amendment

Section 507(c) of Pub.L. 104–104 provided that: "The amendments made by this section [amending sections 1462 and 1465 of this title] are clarifying and shall not be interpreted to limit or repeal any prohibition contained in sections 1462 and 1465 of title 18, United States Code [18 U.S.C.A. §§ 1462, 1465], before such amendment, under the rule established in United States v. Alpers, 338 U.S. 680 (1950)."

§ 1463. Mailing indecent matter on wrappers or envelopes

All matter otherwise mailable by law, upon the envelope or outside cover or wrapper of which, and all postal cards upon which, any delineations, epithets, terms, or language of an indecent, lewd, lascivious, or obscene character are written or printed or otherwise impressed or apparent, are nonmailable matter, and shall not be conveyed in the mails nor delivered from any post office nor by any letter carrier, and shall be withdrawn from the mails under such regulations as the Postal Service shall prescribe.

Whoever knowingly deposits for mailing or delivery, anything declared by this section to be nonmailable matter, or knowingly takes the same from the mails for the purpose of circulating or disposing of or aiding in the circulation or disposition of the same, shall be fined under this title or imprisoned not more than five years, or both.

(June 25, 1948, c. 645, 62 Stat. 769; Aug. 12, 1970, Pub.L. 91–375, § 6(j)(13), 84 Stat. 778; Sept. 13, 1994, Pub.L. 103–322, Title XXXIII, § 330016(1)(K), 108 Stat. 2147.)

HISTORICAL AND STATUTORY NOTES

Effective and Applicability Provisions

1970 Acts. Amendment by Pub.L. 91–375 effective within 1 year after Aug. 12, 1970, on date established therefor by the Board of Governors of the United States Postal Service and published by it in the Federal Register, see section 15(a) of Pub.L. 91–375, set out as an effective Date note preceding section 101 of Title 39, Postal Service.

§ 1464. Broadcasting obscene language

Whoever utters any obscene, indecent, or profane language by means of radio communication shall be fined under this title or imprisoned not more than two years, or both.

(June 25, 1948, c. 645, 62 Stat. 769; Sept. 13, 1994, Pub.L. 103–322, Title XXXIII, § 330016(1)(L), 108 Stat. 2147.)

HISTORICAL AND STATUTORY NOTES

Promulgation of Regulations

For provisions requiring the Federal Communications Commission, in accordance with this section, to promulgate regulations for the enforcement of this section on a 24 hour per day basis by Jan. 31, 1989, see section 608 of Pub.L. 100–459, set out as a note under section 303 of Title 47, Telegraphs, Telephones, and Radiotelegraphs.

§ 1465. Production and transportation of obscene matters for sale or distribution [1]

Whoever knowingly produces with the intent to transport, distribute, or transmit in interstate or foreign commerce, or whoever knowingly transports or travels in, or uses a facility or means of, interstate or foreign commerce or an interactive computer service (as defined in section 230(e)(2) of the Communications Act of 1934) in or affecting such commerce, for the purpose of sale or distribution of any obscene, lewd, lascivious, or filthy book, pamphlet, picture, film, paper, letter, writing, print, silhouette, drawing, figure, image, cast, phonograph recording, electrical transcription or other article capable of producing sound or any other matter of indecent or immoral character, shall be fined under this title or imprisoned not more than five years, or both.

The transportation as aforesaid of two or more copies of any publication or two or more of any article of the character described above, or a combined total of five such publications and articles, shall create a presumption that such publications or articles are intended for sale or distribution, but such presumption shall be rebuttable.

(Added June 28, 1955, c. 190, § 3, 69 Stat. 183, and amended Nov. 18, 1988, Pub.L. 100–690, Title VII, §§ 7521(c), 7522(b), 102 Stat. 4489, 4494; Sept. 13, 1994, Pub.L. 103–322, Title XXXIII, § 330016(1)(K), 108 Stat. 2147; Feb. 8, 1996, Pub.L. 104–104, Title V, § 507(b), 110 Stat. 137; July 27, 2006, Pub.L. 109–248, Title V, § 506(a), 120 Stat. 630.)

[1] Section heading amended without corresponding amendment to analysis.

HISTORICAL AND STATUTORY NOTES

References in Text

The Communications Act of 1934, referred to in text, is Act June 19, 1934, c. 652, 48 Stat. 1064, as amended, and is classified generally to chapter 5 (section 151 et seq.) of Title 47, Telegraphs, Telephones, and Radiotelegraphs. Section 230(e)(2) is classified to section 230(e)(2) of Title 47. For complete classification of this Act to the Code, see section 609 of Title 47 and Tables.

Codifications

Pub.L. 109–248, § 506(a)(2), which directed the insertion of specified language after "whoever knowingly" and before "transports or travels in", was executed by inserting the language after "Whoever knowingly" and before "transports or travels in", as the probable intent of Congress. See 2006 Amendments note under this section.

Interpretation

Amendment of this section by Pub.L. 104–104 as clarifying and not be interpreted as limiting or repealing prohibition contained in sections 1462 and 1465 of this title, before such amendment, under the rule established in United States v. Alpers, 338 U.S. 680 (1950), see section 507(c) of Pub.L. 104–104, set out as a note under section 1462 of this title.

§ 1466. Engaging in the business of selling or transferring obscene matter

(a) Whoever is engaged in the business of producing with intent to distribute or sell, or selling or transferring obscene matter, who knowingly receives or possesses with intent to distribute any obscene book, magazine, picture, paper, film, videotape, or phonograph or other audio recording, which has been shipped or transported in interstate or foreign commerce, shall be punished by imprisonment for not more than 5 years or by a fine under this title, or both.

(b) As used in this section, the term "engaged in the business" means that the person who produces [1] sells or transfers or offers to sell or transfer obscene matter devotes time, attention, or labor to such activities, as a regular course of trade or business, with the objective of earning a profit, although it is not necessary that the person make a profit or that the production, selling or transferring or offering to sell or transfer such material be the person's sole or principal business or source of income. The offering for sale of or to transfer, at one time, two or more copies of any obscene publication, or two or more of any obscene article, or a combined total of five or more such publications and articles, shall create a rebuttable presumption that the person so offering them is "engaged in the business" as defined in this subsection.

(Added Pub.L. 100–690, Title VII, § 7521(a), Nov. 18, 1988, 102 Stat. 4489, and amended Pub.L. 101–647, Title XXXV, § 3548, Nov. 29, 1990, 104 Stat. 4926; Pub.L. 109–248, Title V, § 506(b), July 27, 2006, 120 Stat. 630.)

[1] So in original. A comma probably should appear after "produces".

§ 1466A. Obscene visual representations of the sexual abuse of children

(a) In general.—Any person who, in a circumstance described in subsection (d), knowingly produces, distributes, receives, or possesses with intent to distribute, a visual depiction of any kind, including a drawing, cartoon, sculpture, or painting, that—

(1)(A) depicts a minor engaging in sexually explicit conduct; and

(B) is obscene; or

(2)(A) depicts an image that is, or appears to be, of a minor engaging in graphic bestiality, sadistic or masochistic abuse, or sexual intercourse, including genital-genital, oral-genital, anal-genital, or oral-anal, whether between persons of the same or opposite sex; and

(B) lacks serious literary, artistic, political, or scientific value;

or attempts or conspires to do so, shall be subject to the penalties provided in section 2252A(b)(1), including the penalties provided for cases involving a prior conviction.

(b) Additional offenses.—Any person who, in a circumstance described in subsection (d), knowingly possesses a visual depiction of any kind, including a drawing, cartoon, sculpture, or painting, that—

(1)(A) depicts a minor engaging in sexually explicit conduct; and

(B) is obscene; or

(2)(A) depicts an image that is, or appears to be, of a minor engaging in graphic bestiality, sadistic or masochistic abuse, or sexual intercourse, including genital-genital, oral-genital, anal-genital, or oral-anal, whether between persons of the same or opposite sex; and

(B) lacks serious literary, artistic, political, or scientific value;

or attempts or conspires to do so, shall be subject to the penalties provided in section 2252A(b)(2), including the penalties provided for cases involving a prior conviction.

(c) Nonrequired element of offense.—It is not a required element of any offense under this section that the minor depicted actually exist.

(d) Circumstances.—The circumstance referred to in subsections (a) and (b) is that—

(1) any communication involved in or made in furtherance of the offense is communicated or transported by the mail, or in interstate or foreign commerce by any means, including by computer, or any means or instrumentality of interstate or foreign commerce is otherwise used in committing or in furtherance of the commission of the offense;

(2) any communication involved in or made in furtherance of the offense contemplates the transmission or transportation of a visual depiction by the mail, or in interstate or foreign commerce by any means, including by computer;

(3) any person travels or is transported in interstate or foreign commerce in the course of the commission or in furtherance of the commission of the offense;

(4) any visual depiction involved in the offense has been mailed, or has been shipped or transported in interstate or foreign commerce by any means, including by computer, or was produced using materials that have been mailed, or that have been shipped or transported in interstate or foreign commerce by any means, including by computer; or

(5) the offense is committed in the special maritime and territorial jurisdiction of the United States or in any territory or possession of the United States.

(e) Affirmative defense.—It shall be an affirmative defense to a charge of violating subsection (b) that the defendant—

(1) possessed less than 3 such visual depictions; and

(2) promptly and in good faith, and without retaining or allowing any person, other than a law enforcement agency, to access any such visual depiction—

(A) took reasonable steps to destroy each such visual depiction; or

(B) reported the matter to a law enforcement agency and afforded that agency access to each such visual depiction.

(f) Definitions.—For purposes of this section—

(1) the term "visual depiction" includes undeveloped film and videotape, and data stored on a computer disk or by electronic means which is capable of conversion into a visual image, and also includes any photograph, film, video, picture, digital image or picture, computer image or picture, or computer generated image or picture, whether made or produced by electronic, mechanical, or other means;

(2) the term "sexually explicit conduct" has the meaning given the term in section 2256(2)(A) or 2256(2)(B); and

(3) the term "graphic", when used with respect to a depiction of sexually explicit conduct, means that a viewer can observe any part of the genitals or pubic area of any depicted person or animal during any part of the time that the sexually explicit conduct is being depicted.

(Added Pub.L. 108–21, Title V, § 504(a), Apr. 30, 2003, 117 Stat. 681.)

HISTORICAL AND STATUTORY NOTES

Sentencing Guidelines

Pub.L. 108–21, Title V, § 504(c), Apr. 30, 2003, 117 Stat. 682, provided that:

"(1) **Category.**—Except as provided in paragraph (2), the applicable category of offense to be used in determining the sentencing range referred to in section 3553(a)(4) of title 18, United States Code, with respect to any person convicted under section 1466A of such title [this section], shall be the category of offenses described in section 2G2.2 of the Sentencing Guidelines [set out in this title].

"(2) **Ranges.**—The Sentencing Commission may promulgate guidelines specifically governing offenses under section 1466A of title 18, United States Code [this section], if such guidelines do not result in sentencing ranges that are lower than those that would have applied under paragraph (1)."

Report to Congressional Committees

Pub.L. 108–21, Title V, § 513(b), Apr. 30, 2003, 117 Stat. 685, provided that:

"(1) **In general.**—Not later than 9 months after the date of enactment of this Act [Apr. 30, 2003], and every 2 years thereafter, the Attorney General shall report to the Chairpersons and Ranking Members of the Committees on the Judiciary of the Senate and the House of Representatives on the Federal enforcement actions under chapter 110 [18 U.S.C.A. § 2251 et seq.] or section 1466A of title 18, United States Code [this section].

"(2) **Contents.**—The report required under paragraph (1) shall include—

"(A) an evaluation of the prosecutions brought under chapter 110 [18 U.S.C.A. § 2251 et seq.] or section 1466A of title 18, United States Code [this section];

"(B) an outcome-based measurement of performance; and

"(C) an analysis of the technology being used by the child pornography industry."

§ 1467. Criminal forfeiture

(a) Property subject to criminal forfeiture.—A person who is convicted of an offense involving obscene material under this chapter shall forfeit to the United States such person's interest in—

(1) any obscene material produced, transported, mailed, shipped, or received in violation of this chapter;

(2) any property, real or personal, constituting or traceable to gross profits or other proceeds obtained from such offense; and

(3) any property, real or personal, used or intended to be used to commit or to promote the commission of such offense.

(b) The provisions of section 413 of the Controlled Substances Act (21 U.S.C. 853), with the exception of subsections (a) and (d), shall apply to the criminal forfeiture of property pursuant to subsection (a).

(c) Any property subject to forfeiture pursuant to subsection (a) may be forfeited to the United States in a civil case in accordance with the procedures set forth in chapter 46 of this title.

[(d) to (n) Repealed. Pub.L. 109–248, Title V, § 505(a)(2), July 27, 2006, 120 Stat. 630]

(Added Pub.L. 100–690, Title VII, § 7522(a), Nov. 18, 1988, 102 Stat. 4490, and amended Pub.L. 101–647, Title XXXV, § 3549, Nov. 29, 1990, 104 Stat. 4926; Pub.L. 109–248, Title V, § 505(a), July 27, 2006, 120 Stat. 629.)

HISTORICAL AND STATUTORY NOTES

References in Text

Section 413 of the Controlled Substances Act, referred to in subsec. (b), is Pub.L. 91–513, Title II, § 413, as added Pub.L. 98–473, Title II, § 303, Oct. 12, 1984, 98 Stat. 2044, and amended, which is classified to 21 U.S.C.A. § 853.

Chapter 46 of this title, referred to in subsec. (c), is chapter 46 of this title, Forfeiture, 18 U.S.C.A. § 981 et seq.

§ 1468. Distributing obscene material by cable or subscription television

(a) Whoever knowingly utters any obscene language or distributes any obscene matter by means of cable television or subscription services on television, shall be punished by imprisonment for not more than 2 years or by a fine in accordance with this title, or both.

(b) As used in this section, the term "distribute" means to send, transmit, retransmit, telecast, broadcast, or cablecast, including by wire, microwave, or satellite, or to produce or provide material for such distribution.

(c) Nothing in this chapter, or the Cable Communications Policy Act of 1984, or any other provision of Federal law, is intended to interfere with or preempt the power of the States, including political subdivisions thereof, to regulate the uttering of language that is obscene or otherwise unprotected by the Constitution or the distribution of matter that is obscene or otherwise unprotected by the Constitution, of any sort, by means of cable television or subscription services on television.

(Added Pub.L. 100–690, Title VII, § 7523(a), Nov. 18, 1988, 102 Stat. 4502.)

HISTORICAL AND STATUTORY NOTES

References in Text

The Cable Communications Policy Act of 1984, referred to in subsec. (c), is Pub.L. 98–549, Oct. 30, 1984, 98 Stat. 2779, as amended, which is classified principally to subchapter V–A (section 521 et seq.) of chapter 5 of Title 47, Telegraphs, Telephones, and Radiotelegraphs. For complete classification of this Act to the code see Short Title of 1984 Amendment note set out under section 609 of Title 47 and Tables.

§ 1469. Presumptions

(a) In any prosecution under this chapter in which an element of the offense is that the matter in question was transported, shipped, or carried in interstate commerce, proof, by either circumstantial or direct evidence, that such matter was produced or manufactured in one State and is subsequently located in another State shall raise a rebuttable presumption that such matter was transported, shipped, or carried in interstate commerce.

(b) In any prosecution under this chapter in which an element of the offense is that the matter in question was transported, shipped, or carried in foreign commerce, proof, by either circumstantial or direct evidence, that such matter was produced or manufactured outside of the United States and is subsequently located in the United States shall raise a rebuttable presumption that such matter was transported, shipped, or carried in foreign commerce.

(Added Pub.L. 100–690, Title VII, § 7521(d), Nov. 18, 1988, 102 Stat. 4489.)

§ 1470. Transfer of obscene material to minors

Whoever, using the mail or any facility or means of interstate or foreign commerce, knowingly transfers obscene matter to another individual who has not attained the age of 16 years, knowing that such other individual has not attained the age of 16 years, or attempts to do so, shall be fined under this title, imprisoned not more than 10 years, or both.

(Added Pub.L. 105–314, Title IV, § 401(a), Oct. 30, 1998., 112 Stat. 2979.)

HISTORICAL AND STATUTORY NOTES

Study on Limiting the Availability of Pornography on the Internet

Pub.L. 105–314, Title IX, § 901, Oct. 30, 1998, 112 Stat. 2991, provided that:

"**(a) In general.**—Not later than 90 days after the date of enactment of this Act [Oct. 30, 1998], the Attorney General shall request that the National Academy of Sciences, acting through its National Research Council, enter into a contract to conduct a study of computer-based technologies and other approaches to the problem of the availability of pornographic material to children on the Internet, in order to develop possible amendments to Federal criminal law and other law enforcement techniques to respond to the problem.

"**(b) Contents of study.**—The study under this section shall address each of the following:

"(1) The capabilities of present-day computer-based control technologies for controlling electronic transmission of pornographic images.

"(2) Research needed to develop computer-based control technologies to the point of practical utility for controlling the electronic transmission of pornographic images.

"(3) Any inherent limitations of computer-based control technologies for controlling electronic transmission of pornographic images.

"(4) Operational policies or management techniques needed to ensure the effectiveness of these control technologies for controlling electronic transmission of pornographic images.

"**(c) Final report.**—Not later than 2 years after the date of enactment of this Act [Oct. 30, 1998], the Attorney General shall submit to the Committees on the Judiciary of the House of Representatives and the Senate a final report of the study under this section, which report shall—

"(1) set forth the findings, conclusions, and recommendations of the Council; and

"(2) be submitted by the Committees on the Judiciary of the House of Representatives and the Senate to relevant Government agencies and committees of Congress."

CHAPTER 73—OBSTRUCTION OF JUSTICE

§ 1501. Assault on process server

Whoever knowingly and willfully obstructs, resists, or opposes any officer of the United States, or other person duly authorized, in serving, or attempting to serve or execute, any legal or judicial writ or process of any court of the United States, or United States magistrate judge; or

Whoever assaults, beats, or wounds any officer or other person duly authorized, knowing him to be such officer, or other person so duly authorized, in serving or executing any such writ, rule, order, process, warrant, or other legal or judicial writ or process—

Shall, except as otherwise provided by law, be fined under this title or imprisoned not more than one year, or both.

(June 25, 1948, c. 645, 62 Stat. 769; Dec. 1, 1990, Pub.L. 101–650, Title III, § 321, 104 Stat. 5117; Sept. 13, 1994, Pub.L. 103–322, Title XXXIII, § 330016(1)(F), 108 Stat. 2147.)

HISTORICAL AND STATUTORY NOTES

Change of Name

"United States magistrate judge" substituted for "United States magistrate" in text pursuant to section 321 of Pub.L. 101–650, set out as a note under 28 U.S.C.A. § 631. Previously, United States commissioners, referred to in text, were replaced by United States magistrates pursuant to Pub.L. 90–578, Oct. 17, 1968, 82 Stat. 1118. See chapter 43 of Title 28, 28 U.S.C.A. § 631 et seq.

Short Title

2002 Amendments. Pub.L. 107–204, Title VIII, § 801, July 30, 2002, 116 Stat. 800, provided that: "This title [enacting 18 U.S.C.A. §§ 1348, 1514A, 1519, and 1520, amending 11 U.S.C.A. § 523 and 28 U.S.C.A. § 1658, enacting provisions set out as a note under 28 U.S.C.A. § 1658, and amending provisions set out as a note under 28 U.S.C.A. § 994] may be cited as the 'Corporate and Criminal Fraud Accountability Act of 2002'."

1982 Amendments. Pub.L. 97–291, § 1, Oct. 12, 1982, 96 Stat. 1248, provided: "That this Act [enacting sections 1512 to 1515, 3579, and 3580 of this title, amending sections 1503, 1505, 1510, and 3146 of this title and Rule 32 of the Federal Rules of Civil Procedure, and enacting provisions set out as notes under sections 1512 and 3579 of this title] may be cited as the 'Victim and Witness Protection Act of 1982'."

§ 1502. Resistance to extradition agent

Whoever knowingly and willfully obstructs, resists, or opposes an extradition agent of the United States in the execution of his duties, shall be fined under this title or imprisoned not more than one year, or both.

(June 25, 1948, c. 645, 62 Stat. 769; Sept. 13, 1994, Pub.L. 103–322, Title XXXIII, § 330016(1)(F), 108 Stat. 2147.)

§ 1503. Influencing or injuring officer or juror generally

(a) Whoever corruptly, or by threats or force, or by any threatening letter or communication, endeavors to influence, intimidate, or impede any grand or petit juror, or officer in or of any court of the United States, or officer who may be serving at any examination or other proceeding before any United States magistrate judge or other committing magistrate, in the discharge of his duty, or injures any such grand or petit juror in his person or property on account of any verdict or indictment assented to by him, or on account of his being or having been such juror, or injures any such officer, magistrate judge, or other committing magistrate in his person or property on account of the performance of his official duties, or corruptly or by threats or force, or by any threatening letter or communication, influences, obstructs, or impedes, or endeavors to influence, obstruct, or impede, the due administration of justice, shall be punished as provided in subsection (b). If the offense under this section occurs in connection with a trial of a criminal case, and the act in violation of this section involves the threat of physical force or physical force, the maximum term of imprisonment which may be imposed for the offense shall be the higher of that otherwise provided by law or the maximum term that could have been imposed for any offense charged in such case.

(b) The punishment for an offense under this section is—

(1) in the case of a killing, the punishment provided in sections 1111 and 1112;

(2) in the case of an attempted killing, or a case in which the offense was committed against a petit juror and in which a class A or B felony was charged, imprisonment for not more than 20 years, a fine under this title, or both; and

(3) in any other case, imprisonment for not more than 10 years, a fine under this title, or both.

(June 25, 1948, c. 645, 62 Stat. 769; Oct. 12, 1982, Pub.L. 97–291, § 4(c), 96 Stat. 1253; Sept. 13, 1994, Pub.L. 103–322, Title VI, § 60016, Title XXXIII, § 330016(1)(K), 108 Stat. 1974, 2147; Oct. 1, 1996, Pub.L. 104–214, § 1(3), 110 Stat. 3017.)

HISTORICAL AND STATUTORY NOTES

Change of Name

United States magistrate appointed under section 631 of this title to be known as United States magistrate judge after Dec. 1, 1990, with any reference to United States magistrate or magistrate in Title 28, in any other Federal statute, etc., deemed a reference to United States magistrate judge appointed under section 631 of Title 28, see section 321 of Pub.L. 101–650, set out as a note under section 631 of Title 28.

United States commissioners, referred to in text, were replaced by United States magistrates pursuant to Pub.L. 90–578, Oct. 17, 1968, 82 Stat. 1118. See chapter 43 (section 631 et seq.) of Title 28, Judiciary and Judicial Procedure.

Effective and Applicability Provisions

1982 Acts. Amendment by Pub.L. 92–291 effective Oct. 14, 1982, see section 9(a) of Pub.L. 97–291 set out as an Effective Date note under section 1512 of this title.

§ 1504. Influencing juror by writing

Whoever attempts to influence the action or decision of any grand or petit juror of any court of the United States upon any issue or matter pending before such juror, or before the jury of which he is a member, or pertaining to his duties, by writing or sending to him any written communication, in relation to such issue or matter, shall be fined under this title or imprisoned not more than six months, or both.

Nothing in this section shall be construed to prohibit the communication of a request to appear before the grand jury.

(June 25, 1948, c. 645, 62 Stat. 770; Sept. 13, 1994, Pub.L. 103–322, Title XXXIII, § 330016(1)(H), 108 Stat. 2147.)

§ 1505. Obstruction of proceedings before departments, agencies, and committees

Whoever, with intent to avoid, evade, prevent, or obstruct compliance, in whole or in part, with any civil investigative demand duly and properly made under the Antitrust Civil Process Act, willfully withholds, misrepresents, removes from any place, conceals, covers up, destroys, mutilates, alters, or by other means falsifies any documentary material, answers to written interrogatories, or oral testimony, which is the subject of such demand; or attempts to do so or solicits another to do so; or

Whoever corruptly, or by threats or force, or by any threatening letter or communication influences, obstructs, or impedes or endeavors to influence, obstruct, or impede the due and proper administration of the law under which any pending proceeding is being had before any department or agency of the United States, or the due and proper exercise of the power of inquiry under which any inquiry or investigation is being had by either House, or any committee of either House or any joint committee of the Congress—

Shall be fined under this title, imprisoned not more than 5 years or, if the offense involves international or domestic terrorism (as defined in section 2331), imprisoned not more than 8 years, or both.

(June 25, 1948, c. 645, 62 Stat. 770; Sept. 19, 1962, Pub.L. 87–664, § 6(a), 76 Stat. 551; Oct. 15, 1970, Pub.L. 91–452, Title IX, § 903, 84 Stat. 947; Sept. 30, 1976, Pub.L. 94–435, Title I, § 105, 90 Stat. 1389; Oct. 12, 1982, Pub.L. 97–291, § 4(d), 96 Stat. 1253; Sept. 13, 1994, Pub.L. 103–322, Title XXXIII, § 330016(1)(K), 108 Stat. 2147; Dec. 17, 2004, Pub.L. 108–458, Title VI, § 6703(a), 118 Stat. 3766.)

HISTORICAL AND STATUTORY NOTES

References in Text

The Antitrust Civil Process Act, referred to in text, is Pub.L. 87–664, Sept. 19, 1962, 76 Stat. 548, as amended, which is classified generally to chapter 34 (section 1311 et seq.) of Title 15, Commerce and Trade. For complete classification of this Act to the Code, see Short Title note set out under section 1311 of Title 15 and Tables.

Effective and Applicability Provisions

1982 Acts. Amendment by Pub.L. 97–291 effective Oct. 12, 1982, see section 9(a) of Pub.L. 97–291 set out as an Effective Date note under section 1512 of this title.

1976 Acts. Amendment by Pub.L. 94–435 as effective on Sept. 30, 1976, see section 106 of Pub.L. 94–435, set out as an Effective Date of 1976 Amendment note under section 1311 of Title 15, Commerce and Trade.

§ 1506. Theft or alteration of record or process; false bail

Whoever feloniously steals, takes away, alters, falsifies, or otherwise avoids any record, writ, process, or other proceeding, in any court of the United States, whereby any judgment is reversed, made void, or does not take effect; or

Whoever acknowledges, or procures to be acknowledged in any such court, any recognizance, bail, or judgment, in the name of any other person not privy or consenting to the same—

Shall be fined under this title or imprisoned not more than five years, or both.

(June 25, 1948, c. 645, 62 Stat. 770; Sept. 13, 1994, Pub.L. 103–322, Title XXXIII, § 330016(1)(K), 108 Stat. 2147.)

§ 1507. Picketing or parading

Whoever, with the intent of interfering with, obstructing, or impeding the administration of justice, or with the intent of influencing any judge, juror, witness, or court officer, in the discharge of his duty, pickets or parades in or near a building housing a court of the United States, or in or near a building or residence occupied or used by such judge, juror, witness, or court officer, or with such intent uses any sound-truck or similar device or resorts to any other demonstration in or near any such building or residence, shall be fined under this title or imprisoned not more than one year, or both.

Nothing in this section shall interfere with or prevent the exercise by any court of the United States of its power to punish for contempt.

(Added Sept. 23, 1950, c. 1024, Title I, § 31(a), 64 Stat. 1018, and amended Sept. 13, 1994, Pub.L. 103–322, Title XXXIII, § 330016(1)(K), 108 Stat. 2147.)

§ 1508. Recording, listening to, or observing proceedings of grand or petit juries while deliberating or voting

Whoever knowingly and willfully, by any means or device whatsoever—

(a) records, or attempts to record, the proceedings of any grand or petit jury in any court of the United States while such jury is deliberating or voting; or

(b) listens to or observes, or attempts to listen to or observe, the proceedings of any grand or petit jury of which he is not a member in any court of the

United States while such jury is deliberating or voting—

shall be fined under this title or imprisoned not more than one year, or both.

Nothing in paragraph (a) of this section shall be construed to prohibit the taking of notes by a grand or petit juror in any court of the United States in connection with and solely for the purpose of assisting him in the performance of his duties as such juror.

(Added Aug. 2, 1956, c. 879, § 1, 70 Stat. 935, and amended Sept. 13, 1994, Pub.L. 103–322, Title XXXIII, § 330016(1)(H), 108 Stat. 2147; Oct. 11, 1996, Pub.L. 104–294, Title VI, § 601(f)(13), 110 Stat. 3500.)

§ 1509. Obstruction of court orders

Whoever, by threats or force, willfully prevents, obstructs, impedes, or interferes with, or willfully attempts to prevent, obstruct, impede, or interfere with, the due exercise of rights or the performance of duties under any order, judgment, or decree of a court of the United States, shall be fined under this title or imprisoned not more than one year, or both.

No injunctive or other civil relief against the conduct made criminal by this section shall be denied on the ground that such conduct is a crime.

(Added Pub.L. 86–449, Title I, § 101, May 6, 1960, 74 Stat. 86, and amended Sept. 13, 1994, Pub.L. 103–322, Title XXXIII, § 330016(1)(H), 108 Stat. 2147.)

§ 1510. Obstruction of criminal investigations

(a) Whoever willfully endeavors by means of bribery to obstruct, delay, or prevent the communication of information relating to a violation of any criminal statute of the United States by any person to a criminal investigator shall be fined under this title, or imprisoned not more than five years, or both.

(b)(1) Whoever, being an officer of a financial institution, with the intent to obstruct a judicial proceeding, directly or indirectly notifies any other person about the existence or contents of a subpoena for records of that financial institution, or information that has been furnished to the grand jury in response to that subpoena, shall be fined under this title or imprisoned not more than 5 years, or both.

(2) Whoever, being an officer of a financial institution, directly or indirectly notifies—

(A) a customer of that financial institution whose records are sought by a grand jury subpoena; or

(B) any other person named in that subpoena;

about the existence or contents of that subpoena or information that has been furnished to the grand jury in response to that subpoena, shall be fined under this title or imprisoned not more than one year, or both.

(3) As used in this subsection—

(A) the term "an officer of a financial institution" means an officer, director, partner, employee, agent, or attorney of or for a financial institution; and

(B) the term "subpoena for records" means a Federal grand jury subpoena or a Department of Justice subpoena (issued under section 3486 of title 18), for customer records that has been served relating to a violation of, or a conspiracy to violate—

(i) section 215, 656, 657, 1005, 1006, 1007, 1014, 1344, 1956, 1957, or chapter 53 of title 31; or

(ii) section 1341 or 1343 affecting a financial institution.

(c) As used in this section, the term "criminal investigator" means any individual duly authorized by a department, agency, or armed force of the United States to conduct or engage in investigations of or prosecutions for violations of the criminal laws of the United States.

(d)(1) Whoever—

(A) acting as, or being, an officer, director, agent or employee of a person engaged in the business of insurance whose activities affect interstate commerce, or

(B) is engaged in the business of insurance whose activities affect interstate commerce or is involved (other than as an insured or beneficiary under a policy of insurance) in a transaction relating to the conduct of affairs of such a business,

with intent to obstruct a judicial proceeding, directly or indirectly notifies any other person about the existence or contents of a subpoena for records of that person engaged in such business or information that has been furnished to a Federal grand jury in response to that subpoena, shall be fined as provided by this title or imprisoned not more than 5 years, or both.

(2) As used in paragraph (1), the term "subpoena for records" means a Federal grand jury subpoena for records that has been served relating to a violation of, or a conspiracy to violate, section 1033 of this title.

(e) Whoever, having been notified of the applicable disclosure prohibitions or confidentiality requirements of section 2709(c)(1) of this title, section 626(d)(1) or 627(c)(1) of the Fair Credit Reporting Act (15 U.S.C. 1681u(d)(1) or 1681v(c)(1)), section 1114(a)(3)(A) or 1114(a)(5)(D)(i) of the Right to Financial Privacy Act (12 U.S.C. 3414(a)(3)(A) or 3414(a)(5)(D)(i)), or section 802(b)(1) of the National Security Act of 1947 (50 U.S.C. 436(b)(1)), knowingly and with the intent to obstruct an investigation or judicial proceeding violates such prohibitions or requirements applicable by law to such person shall be imprisoned for not more than five years, fined under this title, or both.

(Added Pub.L. 90–123, § 1(a), Nov. 3, 1967, 81 Stat. 362, and amended Pub.L. 97–291, § 4(e), Oct. 12, 1982, 96 Stat. 1253; Pub.L. 101–73, Title IX, § 962(c), Aug. 9, 1989, 103 Stat. 502;

Pub.L. 102–550, Title XV, § 1528, Oct. 28, 1992, 106 Stat. 4065; Pub.L. 103–322, Title XXXII, § 320604(c), Title XXXIII, § 330016(1)(K), Sept. 13, 1994, 108 Stat. 2119, 2147; Pub.L. 104–191, Title II, § 248(c), Aug. 21, 1996, 110 Stat. 2020; Pub.L. 109–177, Title I, § 117, Mar. 9, 2006, 120 Stat. 217.)

HISTORICAL AND STATUTORY NOTES

References in Text

The Fair Credit Reporting Act, referred to in subsec. (e), is Pub.L. 90–321, Title VI, as added by Pub.L. 91–508, Title VI, § 601, Oct. 26, 1970, 84 Stat. 1127, as amended, which is classified principally to subchapter III of chapter 41 of Title 15, 15 U.S.C.A. § 1681 et seq. Sections 626 and 627 of the Fair Credit Reporting Act are classified to 15 U.S.C.A. §§ 1681u and 1681v, respectively. For complete classification, see Short Title note set out under 15 U.S.C.A. § 1601 and Tables.

Section 1114 of the Right to Financial Privacy Act, referred to in subsec. (e), is Pub.L. 95–630, Title XI, § 1114, Nov. 10, 1978, 92 Stat. 3707, which is classified to 12 U.S.C.A. § 3414.

Section 802 of the National Security Act of 1947, referred to in subsec. (e), is July 26, 1947, c. 343, Title VIII, § 802, as added Oct. 14, 1994, Pub.L. 103–359, Title VIII, § 802(a), 108 Stat. 3436, which is classified to 50 U.S.C.A. § 436.

Effective and Applicability Provisions

1982 Acts. Amendment by Pub.L. 97–291 effective Oct. 12, 1982, see section 9(a) of Pub.L. 97–291 set out as an Effective Date note under section 1512 of this title.

Severability of Provisions

If any provision of Pub.L. 101–73 or the application thereof to any person or circumstance is held invalid, the remainder of Pub.L. 101–73 and the application of the provision to other persons not similarly situated or to other circumstances not to be affected thereby, see section 1221 of Pub.L. 101–73, set out as a note under section 1811 of Title 12, Banks and Banking.

§ 1511. Obstruction of State or local law enforcement

(a) It shall be unlawful for two or more persons to conspire to obstruct the enforcement of the criminal laws of a State or political subdivision thereof, with the intent to facilitate an illegal gambling business if—

(1) one or more of such persons does any act to effect the object of such a conspiracy;

(2) one or more of such persons is an official or employee, elected, appointed, or otherwise, of such State or political subdivision; and

(3) one or more of such persons conducts, finances, manages, supervises, directs, or owns all or part of an illegal gambling business.

(b) As used in this section—

(1) "illegal gambling business" means a gambling business which—

(i) is a violation of the law of a State or political subdivision in which it is conducted;

(ii) involves five or more persons who conduct, finance, manage, supervise, direct, or own all or part of such business; and

(iii) has been or remains in substantially continuous operation for a period in excess of thirty days or has a gross revenue of $2,000 in any single day.

(2) "gambling" includes but is not limited to pool-selling, bookmaking, maintaining slot machines, roulette wheels, or dice tables, and conducting lotteries, policy, bolita or numbers games, or selling chances therein.

(3) "State" means any State of the United States, the District of Columbia, the Commonwealth of Puerto Rico, and any territory or possession of the United States.

(c) This section shall not apply to any bingo game, lottery, or similar game of chance conducted by an organization exempt from tax under paragraph (3) of subsection (c) of section 501 of the Internal Revenue Code of 1986, as amended, if no part of the gross receipts derived from such activity inures to the benefit of any private shareholder, member, or employee of such organization, except as compensation for actual expenses incurred by him in the conduct of such activity.

(d) Whoever violates this section shall be punished by a fine under this title or imprisonment for not more than five years, or both.

(Added Pub.L. 91–452, Title VIII, § 802(a), Oct. 15, 1970, 84 Stat. 936, and amended Pub.L. 99–514, § 2, Oct. 22, 1986, 100 Stat. 2095; Pub.L. 103–322, Title XXXIII, § 330016(2)(C), Sept. 13, 1994, 108 Stat. 2148.)

HISTORICAL AND STATUTORY NOTES

References in Text

Paragraph (3) of subsection (c) of section 501 of the Internal Revenue Code of 1954, referred to in subsec. (c), is classified to section 501(c)(3) of Title 26, Internal Revenue Code of 1954.

Congressional Statement of Findings

Section 801 of Pub.L. 91–452 provided that: "The Congress finds that illegal gambling involves widespread use of, and has an effect upon, interstate commerce and the facilities thereof."

Priority of State Laws

Section 811 of Pub.L. 91–452 provided that: "No provision of this title [enacting this section and section 1955 of this title, amending section 2516 of this title and enacting provisions set out as notes under this section and section 1955 of this title] indicates an intent on the part of the Congress to occupy the field in which such provision operates to the exclusion of the law of a State or possession, or a political subdivision of a State or possession, on the same subject matter, or to relieve any person of any obligation imposed by any law of any State or possession, or political subdivision of a State or possession."

§ 1512. Tampering with a witness, victim, or an informant

(a)(1) Whoever kills or attempts to kill another person, with intent to—

(A) prevent the attendance or testimony of any person in an official proceeding;

(B) prevent the production of a record, document, or other object, in an official proceeding; or

(C) prevent the communication by any person to a law enforcement officer or judge of the United States of information relating to the commission or possible commission of a Federal offense or a violation of conditions of probation, parole, or release pending judicial proceedings;

shall be punished as provided in paragraph (3).

(2) Whoever uses physical force or the threat of physical force against any person, or attempts to do so, with intent to—

(A) influence, delay, or prevent the testimony of any person in an official proceeding;

(B) cause or induce any person to—

(i) withhold testimony, or withhold a record, document, or other object, from an official proceeding;

(ii) alter, destroy, mutilate, or conceal an object with intent to impair the integrity or availability of the object for use in an official proceeding;

(iii) evade legal process summoning that person to appear as a witness, or to produce a record, document, or other object, in an official proceeding; or

(iv) be absent from an official proceeding to which that person has been summoned by legal process; or

(C) hinder, delay, or prevent the communication to a law enforcement officer or judge of the United States of information relating to the commission or possible commission of a Federal offense or a violation of conditions of probation, supervised release, parole, or release pending judicial proceedings;

shall be punished as provided in paragraph (3).

(3) The punishment for an offense under this subsection is—

(A) in the case of murder (as defined in section 1111), the death penalty or imprisonment for life, and in the case of any other killing, the punishment provided in section 1112;

(B) in the case of—

(i) an attempt to murder; or

(ii) the use or attempted use of physical force against any person; imprisonment for not more than 20 years; and

(C) in the case of the threat of use of physical force against any person, imprisonment for not more than 10 years.

(b) Whoever knowingly uses intimidation, threatens, or corruptly persuades another person, or attempts to do so, or engages in misleading conduct toward another person, with intent to—

(1) influence, delay, or prevent the testimony of any person in an official proceeding;

(2) cause or induce any person to—

(A) withhold testimony, or withhold a record, document, or other object, from an official proceeding;

(B) alter, destroy, mutilate, or conceal an object with intent to impair the object's integrity or availability for use in an official proceeding;

(C) evade legal process summoning that person to appear as a witness, or to produce a record, document, or other object, in an official proceeding; or

(D) be absent from an official proceeding to which such person has been summoned by legal process; or

(3) hinder, delay, or prevent the communication to a law enforcement officer or judge of the United States of information relating to the commission or possible commission of a Federal offense or a violation of conditions of probation [1] supervised release,, [2] parole, or release pending judicial proceedings;

shall be fined under this title or imprisoned not more than ten years, or both.

(c) Whoever corruptly—

(1) alters, destroys, mutilates, or conceals a record, document, or other object, or attempts to do so, with the intent to impair the object's integrity or availability for use in an official proceeding; or

(2) otherwise obstructs, influences, or impedes any official proceeding, or attempts to do so,

shall be fined under this title or imprisoned not more than 20 years, or both.

(d) Whoever intentionally harasses another person and thereby hinders, delays, prevents, or dissuades any person from—

(1) attending or testifying in an official proceeding;

(2) reporting to a law enforcement officer or judge of the United States the commission or possible commission of a Federal offense or a violation of conditions of probation [1] supervised release,, [2] parole, or release pending judicial proceedings;

(3) arresting or seeking the arrest of another person in connection with a Federal offense; or

(4) causing a criminal prosecution, or a parole or probation revocation proceeding, to be sought or instituted, or assisting in such prosecution or proceeding;

or attempts to do so, shall be fined under this title or imprisoned not more than one year, or both.

(e) In a prosecution for an offense under this section, it is an affirmative defense, as to which the defendant has the burden of proof by a preponderance of the evidence, that the conduct consisted solely of lawful conduct and that the defendant's sole intention was to encourage, induce, or cause the other person to testify truthfully.

(f) For the purposes of this section—

(1) an official proceeding need not be pending or about to be instituted at the time of the offense; and

(2) the testimony, or the record, document, or other object need not be admissible in evidence or free of a claim of privilege.

(g) In a prosecution for an offense under this section, no state of mind need be proved with respect to the circumstance—

(1) that the official proceeding before a judge, court, magistrate judge, grand jury, or government agency is before a judge or court of the United States, a United States magistrate judge, a bankruptcy judge, a Federal grand jury, or a Federal Government agency; or

(2) that the judge is a judge of the United States or that the law enforcement officer is an officer or employee of the Federal Government or a person authorized to act for or on behalf of the Federal Government or serving the Federal Government as an adviser or consultant.

(h) There is extraterritorial Federal jurisdiction over an offense under this section.

(i) A prosecution under this section or section 1503 may be brought in the district in which the official proceeding (whether or not pending or about to be instituted) was intended to be affected or in the district in which the conduct constituting the alleged offense occurred.

(j) If the offense under this section occurs in connection with a trial of a criminal case, the maximum term of imprisonment which may be imposed for the offense shall be the higher of that otherwise provided by law or the maximum term that could have been imposed for any offense charged in such case.

(k) Whoever conspires to commit any offense under this section shall be subject to the same penalties as those prescribed for the offense the commission of which was the object of the conspiracy.

(Added Pub.L. 97–291, § 4(a), Oct. 12, 1982, 96 Stat. 1249, and amended Pub.L. 99–646, § 61, Nov. 10, 1986, 100 Stat. 3614; Pub.L. 100–690, Title VII, § 7029(a), (c), Nov. 18, 1988, 102 Stat. 4397, 4398; Pub.L. 101–650, Title III, § 321, Dec. 1, 1990, 104 Stat. 5117; Pub.L. 103–322, Title VI, § 60018, Title XXXIII, § 330016(1)(O), (U), Sept. 13, 1994, 108 Stat. 1975, 2148; Pub.L. 104–214, § 1(2), Oct. 1, 1996, 110 Stat. 3017; Pub.L. 104–294, Title VI, § 604(b)(31), Oct. 11, 1996, 110 Stat. 3508; Pub.L. 107–204, Title XI, § 1102, July 30, 2002, 116 Stat. 807; Pub.L. 107–273, Div. B, Title III, § 3001(a), (c)(1), Nov. 2, 2002, 116 Stat. 1803, 1804.)

[1] So in original. A comma probably should appear.

[2] So in original. The second comma probably should not appear.

HISTORICAL AND STATUTORY NOTES

Effective and Applicability Provisions

1996 Acts. Amendment by section 604 of Pub.L. 104–294 effective Sept. 13, 1994, see section 604(d) of Pub.L. 104–294, set out as a note under section 13 of this title.

1982 Acts. Section 9 of Pub.L. 97–291 provided that:

"**(a)** Except as provided in subsection (b), this Act and the amendments made by this Act [enacting sections 1512 to 1515, 3579, and 3580 of this title, amending sections 1503, 1505, 1510, and 3146 of this title and Rule 32 of the Federal Rules of Criminal Procedure, and enacting provisions set out as notes under sections 1501, 1512, and 3579 of this title] shall take effect on the date of the enactment of this Act [Oct. 12, 1982].

"**(b)(1)** The amendment made by section 2 of this Act [enacting provisions set out as a note under this section] shall apply to presentence reports ordered to be made on or after March 1, 1983.

"(2) The amendments made by section 5 of this Act [enacting sections 3579 and 3580 of this title] shall apply with respect to offenses occurring on or after January 1, 1983."

Change of Name

Words "magistrate judge" and "United States magistrate judge" substituted for "magistrate" and "United States magistrate", respectively, in subsec. (f)(1) pursuant to section 321 of Pub.L. 101–650, set out as a note under 28 U.S.C.A. § 631.

United States magistrate appointed under section 631 of this title to be known as United States magistrate judge after Dec. 1, 1990, with any reference to United States magistrate or magistrate in Title 28, in any other Federal statute, etc., deemed a reference to United States magistrate judge appointed under section 631 of Title 28, see section 321 of Pub.L. 101–650, set out as a note under section 631 of Title 28.

Congressional Findings and Declaration of Purposes

Section 2 of Pub.L. 97–291 provided that:

"**(a)** The Congress finds and declares that:

"(1) Without the cooperation of victims and witnesses, the criminal justice system would cease to function; yet with few exceptions these individuals are either ignored by the criminal justice system or simply used as tools to identify and punish offenders.

"(2) All too often the victim of a serious crime is forced to suffer physical, psychological, or financial hardship first as a result of the criminal act and then as a result of contact with a criminal justice system unresponsive to the real needs of such victim.

"(3) Although the majority of serious crimes falls under the jurisdiction of State and local law enforcement agencies, the Federal Government, and in particular the Attorney General, has an important leadership role to assume in ensuring that victims of crime, whether at the Federal, State, or local level, are given proper treatment by agencies administering the criminal justice system.

"(4) Under current law, law enforcement agencies must have cooperation from a victim of crime and yet neither the agencies nor the legal system can offer adequate protection or assistance when the victim, as a result of such cooperation, is threatened or intimidated.

"(5) While the defendant is provided with counsel who can explain both the criminal justice process and the rights of the defendant, the victim or witness has no counterpart and is usually not even notified when the defendant is released on bail, the case is dismissed, a plea to a lesser charge is accepted, or a court date is changed.

"(6) The victim and witness who cooperate with the prosecutor often find that the transportation, parking facilities, and child care services at the court are unsatisfactory and they must often share the pretrial waiting room with the defendant or his family and friends.

"(7) The victim may lose valuable property to a criminal only to lose it again for long periods of time to Federal law enforcement officials, until the trial and sometimes and [sic] appeals are over; many times that property is damaged or lost, which is particularly stressful for the elderly or poor.

"(b) The Congress declares that the purposes of this Act [see Short Title of 1982 Amendment note set out under section 1501 of this title] are—

"(1) to enhance and protect the necessary role of crime victims and witnesses in the criminal justice process;

"(2) to ensure that the Federal Government does all that is possible within limits of available resources to assist victims and witnesses of crime without infringing on the constitutional rights of the defendant; and

"(3) to provide a model for legislation for State and local governments."

Federal Guidelines for Treatment of Crime Victims and Witnesses in the Criminal Justice System

Section 6 of Pub.L. 97–291, as amended Pub.L. 98–473, Title II, § 1408(b), Oct. 12, 1984, 98 Stat. 2177, provided that:

"(a) Within two hundred and seventy days after the date of enactment of this Act [Oct. 12, 1982], the Attorney General shall develop and implement guidelines for the Department of Justice consistent with the purposes of this Act [see Short Title of 1982 Amendment note set out under section 1501 of this title]. In preparing the guidelines the Attorney General shall consider the following objectives:

"(1) **Services to victims of crime.**—Law enforcement personnel should ensure that victims routinely receive emergency social and medical services as soon as possible and are given information on the following—

"(A) availability of crime victim compensation (where applicable);

"(B) community-based victim treatment programs;

"(C) the role of the victim in the criminal justice process, including what they can expect from the system as well as what the system expects from them; and

"(D) stages in the criminal justice process of significance to a crime victim, and the manner in which information about such stages can be obtained.

"(2) **Notification of availability of protection.**—A victim or witness should routinely receive information on steps that law enforcement officers and attorneys for the Government can take to protect victims and witnesses from intimidation.

"(3) **Scheduling changes.**—All victims and witnesses who have been scheduled to attend criminal justice proceedings should either be notified as soon as possible of any scheduling changes which will affect their appearances or have available a system for alerting witnesses promptly by telephone or otherwise.

"(4) **Prompt notification to victims of serious crimes.**—Victims, witnesses, relatives of those victims and witnesses who are minors, and relatives of homicide victims should, if such persons provide the appropriate official with a current address and telephone number, receive prompt advance notification, if possible, of—

"(A) the arrest of an accused;

"(B) the initial appearance of an accused before a judicial officer;

"(C) the release of the accused pending judicial proceedings; and

"(D) proceedings in the prosecution and punishment of the accused (including entry of a plea of guilty, trial, sentencing, and, where a term of imprisonment is imposed, a hearing to determine a parole release date and the release of the accused from such imprisonment).

"(5) **Consultation with victim.**—The victim of a serious crime, or in the case of a minor child or a homicide, the family of the victim, should be consulted by the attorney for the Government in order to obtain the views of the victim or family about the disposition of any Federal criminal case brought as a result of such crime, including the views of the victim or family about—

"(A) dismissal;

"(B) release of the accused pending judicial proceedings;

"(C) plea negotiations; and

"(D) pretrial diversion program.

"(6) **Separate waiting area.**—Victims and other prosecution witnesses should be provided prior to court appearance a waiting area that is separate from all other witnesses.

"(7) **Property return.**—Law enforcement agencies and prosecutor should promptly return victim's property held for evidentiary purposes unless there is a compelling law enforcement reason for retaining it.

"(8) **Notification to employer.**—A victim or witness who so requests should be assisted by law enforcement agencies and attorneys for the Government in informing employers that the need for victim and witness cooperation in the prosecution of the case may necessitate absence of that victim or witness from work. A victim or witness who, as a direct result of a crime or of cooperation with law enforcement agencies or attorneys for the Government, is subjected to serious financial strain, should be assisted by such agencies and attorneys in explaining to creditors the reason for such serious financial strain.

"(9) Training by federal law enforcement training facilities.—Victim assistance education and training should be offered to persons taking courses at Federal law enforcement training facilities and attorneys for the Government so that victims may be promptly, properly, and completely assisted.

"(10) General victim assistance.—The guidelines should also ensure that any other important assistance to victims and witnesses, such as the adoption of transportation, parking, and translator services for victims in court be provided.

"**(b)** Nothing in this title shall be construed as creating a cause of action against the United States.

"**(c)** The Attorney General shall assure that all Federal law enforcement agencies outside of the Department of Justice adopt guidelines consistent with subsection (a) of this section."

§ 1513. Retaliating against a witness, victim, or an informant

(a)(1) Whoever kills or attempts to kill another person with intent to retaliate against any person for—

(A) the attendance of a witness or party at an official proceeding, or any testimony given or any record, document, or other object produced by a witness in an official proceeding; or

(B) providing to a law enforcement officer any information relating to the commission or possible commission of a Federal offense or a violation of conditions of probation [1] supervised release,,[2] parole, or release pending judicial proceedings,

shall be punished as provided in paragraph (2).

(2) The punishment for an offense under this subsection is—

(A) in the case of a killing, the punishment provided in sections 1111 and 1112; and

(B) in the case of an attempt, imprisonment for not more than 20 years.

(b) Whoever knowingly engages in any conduct and thereby causes bodily injury to another person or damages the tangible property of another person, or threatens to do so, with intent to retaliate against any person for—

(1) the attendance of a witness or party at an official proceeding, or any testimony given or any record, document, or other object produced by a witness in an official proceeding; or

(2) any information relating to the commission or possible commission of a Federal offense or a violation of conditions of probation [1] supervised release,,[2] parole, or release pending judicial proceedings given by a person to a law enforcement officer;

or attempts to do so, shall be fined under this title or imprisoned not more than ten years, or both.

(c) If the retaliation occurred because of attendance at or testimony in a criminal case, the maximum term of imprisonment which may be imposed for the offense under this section shall be the higher of that otherwise provided by law or the maximum term that could have been imposed for any offense charged in such case.

(d) There is extraterritorial Federal jurisdiction over an offense under this section.

(e) [3] Whoever knowingly, with the intent to retaliate, takes any action harmful to any person, including interference with the lawful employment or livelihood of any person, for providing to a law enforcement officer any truthful information relating to the commission or possible commission of any Federal offense, shall be fined under this title or imprisoned not more than 10 years, or both.

(e) [3] Whoever conspires to commit any offense under this section shall be subject to the same penalties as those prescribed for the offense the commission of which was the object of the conspiracy.

(Added Pub.L. 97–291, § 4(a), Oct. 12, 1982, 96 Stat. 1250, and amended Pub.L. 103–322, Title VI, § 60017, Title XXXIII, § 330016(1)(U), Sept. 13, 1994, 108 Stat. 1975, 2148; Pub.L. 104–214, § 1(1), Oct. 1, 1996, 110 Stat. 3017; Pub.L. 107–204, Title XI, § 1107(a), July 30, 2002, 116 Stat. 810; Pub.L. 107–273, Div. B, Title III, § 3001(b), (c)(2), Title IV, § 4002(b)(4), Nov. 2, 2002, 116 Stat. 1804, 1807.)

[1] So in original. A comma probably should appear.

[2] So in original. The second comma probably should not appear.

[3] So in original. Two subsecs. (e) have been enacted.

HISTORICAL AND STATUTORY NOTES

Effective and Applicability Provisions

1982 Acts. Section effective Oct. 12, 1982, see section 9(a) of Pub.L.97–291 set out as an Effective Date note under section 1512 of this title.

§ 1514. Civil action to restrain harassment of a victim or witness

(a)(1) A United States district court, upon application of the attorney for the Government, shall issue a temporary restraining order prohibiting harassment of a victim or witness in a Federal criminal case if the court finds, from specific facts shown by affidavit or by verified complaint, that there are reasonable grounds to believe that harassment of an identified victim or witness in a Federal criminal case exists or that such order is necessary to prevent and restrain an offense under section 1512 of this title, other than an offense consisting of misleading conduct, or under section 1513 of this title.

(2)(A) A temporary restraining order may be issued under this section without written or oral notice to the adverse party or such party's attorney in a civil action under this section if the court finds, upon written certification of facts by the attorney for the Government, that such notice should not be required and that there is a reasonable probability that the Government will prevail on the merits.

(B) A temporary restraining order issued without notice under this section shall be endorsed with the date and hour of issuance and be filed forthwith in the office of the clerk of the court issuing the order.

(C) A temporary restraining order issued under this section shall expire at such time, not to exceed 10 days from issuance, as the court directs; the court, for good cause shown before expiration of such order, may extend the expiration date of the order for up to 10 days or for such longer period agreed to by the adverse party.

(D) When a temporary restraining order is issued without notice, the motion for a protective order shall be set down for hearing at the earliest possible time and takes precedence over all matters except older matters of the same character, and when such motion comes on for hearing, if the attorney for the Government does not proceed with the application for a protective order, the court shall dissolve the temporary restraining order.

(E) If on two days notice to the attorney for the Government or on such shorter notice as the court may prescribe, the adverse party appears and moves to dissolve or modify the temporary restraining order, the court shall proceed to hear and determine such motion as expeditiously as the ends of justice require.

(F) A temporary restraining order shall set forth the reasons for the issuance of such order, be specific in terms, and describe in reasonable detail (and not by reference to the complaint or other document) the act or acts being restrained.

(b)(1) A United States district court, upon motion of the attorney for the Government, shall issue a protective order prohibiting harassment of a victim or witness in a Federal criminal case if the court, after a hearing, finds by a preponderance of the evidence that harassment of an identified victim or witness in a Federal criminal case exists or that such order is necessary to prevent and restrain an offense under section 1512 of this title, other than an offense consisting of misleading conduct, or under section 1513 of this title.

(2) At the hearing referred to in paragraph (1) of this subsection, any adverse party named in the complaint shall have the right to present evidence and cross-examine witnesses.

(3) A protective order shall set forth the reasons for the issuance of such order, be specific in terms, describe in reasonable detail (and not by reference to the complaint or other document) the act or acts being restrained.

(4) The court shall set the duration of effect of the protective order for such period as the court determines necessary to prevent harassment of the victim or witness but in no case for a period in excess of three years from the date of such order's issuance. The attorney for the Government may, at any time within ninety days before the expiration of such order, apply for a new protective order under this section.

(c) As used in this section—

(1) the term "harassment" means a course of conduct directed at a specific person that—

(A) causes substantial emotional distress in such person; and

(B) serves no legitimate purpose; and

(2) the term "course of conduct" means a series of acts over a period of time, however short, indicating a continuity of purpose.

(Added Pub.L. 97–291, § 4(a), Oct. 12, 1982, 96 Stat. 1250.)

HISTORICAL AND STATUTORY NOTES

Effective and Applicability Provisions

1982 Acts. Section effective Oct. 12, 1982, see section 9(a) of Pub.L. 97–291 set out as an Effective Date note under section 1512 of this title.

§ 1514A. Civil action to protect against retaliation in fraud cases

(a) Whistleblower protection for employees of publicly traded companies.—No company with a class of securities registered under section 12 of the Securities Exchange Act of 1934 (15 U.S.C. 78*l*), or that is required to file reports under section 15(d) of the Securities Exchange Act of 1934 (15 U.S.C. 78*o*(d)), or any officer, employee, contractor, subcontractor, or agent of such company, may discharge, demote, suspend, threaten, harass, or in any other manner discriminate against an employee in the terms and conditions of employment because of any lawful act done by the employee—

(1) to provide information, cause information to be provided, or otherwise assist in an investigation regarding any conduct which the employee reasonably believes constitutes a violation of section 1341, 1343, 1344, or 1348, any rule or regulation of the Securities and Exchange Commission, or any provision of Federal law relating to fraud against shareholders, when the information or assistance is provided to or the investigation is conducted by—

(A) a Federal regulatory or law enforcement agency;

(B) any Member of Congress or any committee of Congress; or

(C) a person with supervisory authority over the employee (or such other person working for the employer who has the authority to investigate, discover, or terminate misconduct); or

(2) to file, cause to be filed, testify, participate in, or otherwise assist in a proceeding filed or about to be filed (with any knowledge of the employer) relating to an alleged violation of section 1341, 1343, 1344, or 1348, any rule or regulation of the Securities and Exchange Commission, or any provision of Federal law relating to fraud against shareholders.

(b) Enforcement action.—

(1) In general.—A person who alleges discharge or other discrimination by any person in violation of subsection (a) may seek relief under subsection (c), by—

(A) filing a complaint with the Secretary of Labor; or

(B) if the Secretary has not issued a final decision within 180 days of the filing of the complaint and there is no showing that such delay is due to the bad faith of the claimant, bringing an action at law or equity for de novo review in the appropriate district court of the United States, which shall have jurisdiction over such an action without regard to the amount in controversy.

(2) Procedure.—

(A) In general.—An action under paragraph (1)(A) shall be governed under the rules and procedures set forth in section 42121(b) of title 49, United States Code.

(B) Exception.—Notification made under section 42121(b)(1) of title 49, United States Code, shall be made to the person named in the complaint and to the employer.

(C) Burdens of proof.—An action brought under paragraph (1)(B) shall be governed by the legal burdens of proof set forth in section 42121(b) of title 49, United States Code.

(D) Statute of limitations.—An action under paragraph (1) shall be commenced not later than 90 days after the date on which the violation occurs.

(c) Remedies.—

(1) In general.—An employee prevailing in any action under subsection (b)(1) shall be entitled to all relief necessary to make the employee whole.

(2) Compensatory damages.—Relief for any action under paragraph (1) shall include—

(A) reinstatement with the same seniority status that the employee would have had, but for the discrimination;

(B) the amount of back pay, with interest; and

(C) compensation for any special damages sustained as a result of the discrimination, including litigation costs, expert witness fees, and reasonable attorney fees.

(d) Rights retained by employee.—Nothing in this section shall be deemed to diminish the rights, privileges, or remedies of any employee under any Federal or State law, or under any collective bargaining agreement.

(Added Pub.L. 107–204, Title VIII, § 806(a), July 30, 2002, 116 Stat. 802.)

§ 1515. Definitions for certain provisions; general provision

(a) As used in sections 1512 and 1513 of this title and in this section—

(1) the term "official proceeding" means—

(A) a proceeding before a judge or court of the United States, a United States magistrate judge, a bankruptcy judge, a judge of the United States Tax Court, a special trial judge of the Tax Court, a judge of the United States Court of Federal Claims, or a Federal grand jury;

(B) a proceeding before the Congress;

(C) a proceeding before a Federal Government agency which is authorized by law; or

(D) a proceeding involving the business of insurance whose activities affect interstate commerce before any insurance regulatory official or agency or any agent or examiner appointed by such official or agency to examine the affairs of any person engaged in the business of insurance whose activities affect interstate commerce;

(2) the term "physical force" means physical action against another, and includes confinement;

(3) the term "misleading conduct" means—

(A) knowingly making a false statement;

(B) intentionally omitting information from a statement and thereby causing a portion of such statement to be misleading, or intentionally concealing a material fact, and thereby creating a false impression by such statement;

(C) with intent to mislead, knowingly submitting or inviting reliance on a writing or recording that is false, forged, altered, or otherwise lacking in authenticity;

(D) with intent to mislead, knowingly submitting or inviting reliance on a sample, specimen, map, photograph, boundary mark, or other object that is misleading in a material respect; or

(E) knowingly using a trick, scheme, or device with intent to mislead;

(4) the term "law enforcement officer" means an officer or employee of the Federal Government, or a person authorized to act for or on behalf of the Federal Government or serving the Federal Government as an adviser or consultant—

(A) authorized under law to engage in or supervise the prevention, detection, investigation, or prosecution of an offense; or

(B) serving as a probation or pretrial services officer under this title;

(5) the term "bodily injury" means—

(A) a cut, abrasion, bruise, burn, or disfigurement;

(B) physical pain;

(C) illness;

(D) impairment of the function of a bodily member, organ, or mental faculty; or

(E) any other injury to the body, no matter how temporary; and

(6) the term "corruptly persuades" does not include conduct which would be misleading conduct but for a lack of a state of mind.

(b) As used in section 1505, the term "corruptly" means acting with an improper purpose, personally or by influencing another, including making a false or misleading statement, or withholding, concealing, altering, or destroying a document or other information.

(c) This chapter does not prohibit or punish the providing of lawful, bona fide, legal representation services in connection with or anticipation of an official proceeding.

(Added Pub.L. 97–291, § 4(a), Oct. 12, 1982, 96 Stat. 1252, and amended Pub.L. 99–646, § 50(b), Nov. 10, 1986, 100 Stat. 3605; Pub.L. 100–690, Title VII, § 7029(b), (d), Nov. 18, 1988, 102 Stat. 4398; Pub.L. 101–650, Title III, § 321, Dec. 1, 1990, 104 Stat. 5117; Pub.L. 103–322, Title XXXII, § 320604(a), Sept. 13, 1994, 108 Stat. 2118; Pub.L. 104–292, § 3, Oct. 11, 1996, 110 Stat. 3460; Pub.L. 104–294, Title VI, § 604(b)(39), Oct. 11, 1996, 110 Stat. 3509.)

HISTORICAL AND STATUTORY NOTES

Effective and Applicability Provisions

1996 Acts. Amendment by section 604 of Pub.L. 104–294 effective Sept. 13, 1994, see section 604(d) of Pub.L. 104–294, set out as a note under section 13 of this title.

1982 Acts. Section effective Oct. 12, 1982, see section 9(a) of Pub.L. 97–291 set out as an Effective Date note under section 1512 of this title.

Change of Name

"United States magistrate judge" substituted for "United States magistrate" in subsec. (a)(1)(A) pursuant to section 321 of Pub.L. 101–650, set out as a note under 28 U.S.C.A. § 631.

§ 1516. Obstruction of Federal audit

(a) Whoever, with intent to deceive or defraud the United States, endeavors to influence, obstruct, or impede a Federal auditor in the performance of official duties relating to a person, entity, or program receiving in excess of $100,000, directly or indirectly, from the United States in any 1 year period under a contract or subcontract, grant, or cooperative agreement, or relating to any property that is security for a mortgage note that is insured, guaranteed, acquired, or held by the Secretary of Housing and Urban Development pursuant to any Act administered by the Secretary, or relating to any property that is security for a loan that is made or guaranteed under title V of the Housing Act of 1949, shall be fined under this title, or imprisoned not more than 5 years, or both.

(b) For purposes of this section—

(1) the term "Federal auditor" means any person employed on a full- or part-time or contractual basis to perform an audit or a quality assurance inspection for or on behalf of the United States; and

(2) the term "in any 1 year period" has the meaning given to the term "in any one-year period" in section 666.

(Added Pub.L. 100–690, Title VII, § 7078(a), Nov. 18, 1988, 102 Stat. 4406, and amended Pub.L. 103–322, Title XXXII, § 320609, Sept. 13, 1994, 108 Stat. 2120; Pub.L. 104–294, Title VI, § 604(b)(43), Oct. 11, 1996, 110 Stat. 3509; Pub.L. 105–65, Title V, § 564, Oct. 27, 1997, 111 Stat. 1420; Pub.L. 106–569, Title VII, § 709(b), Dec. 27, 2000, 114 Stat. 3018; Pub.L. 107–273, Div. A, Title II, § 205(c), Nov. 2, 2002, 116 Stat. 1778.)

HISTORICAL AND STATUTORY NOTES

References in Text

Title V of the Housing Act of 1949, referred to in subsec. (a), is Title V of Act July 15, 1949, c. 338, 63 Stat. 432, as amended, which is classified principally to subchapter III (§ 1471 et seq.) of chapter 8A of Title 42. For complete classification of this Act to the Code, see Short Title note set out under section 1441 of Title 42 and Tables.

Effective and Applicability Provisions

1996 Acts. Amendment by section 604 of Pub.L. 104–294 effective Sept. 13, 1994, see section 604(d) of Pub.L. 104–294, set out as a note under section 13 of this title.

Implementation of Regulations

For requirement that the Secretary of Housing and Urban Development issue regulations necessary to implement amendments made by Subtitle C (§§ 541 to 564) of Title V of Pub.L. 105–65 [amending this section], see section 541 of Pub.L. 105–65, set out as a note under section 1735f–14 of Title 12.

§ 1517. Obstructing examination of financial institution

Whoever corruptly obstructs or attempts to obstruct any examination of a financial institution by an agency of the United States with jurisdiction to conduct an examination of such financial institution shall be fined under this title, imprisoned not more than 5 years, or both.

(Added Pub.L. 101–647, Title XXV, § 2503(a), Nov. 29, 1990, 104 Stat. 4861.)

§ 1518. Obstruction of criminal investigations of health care offenses

(a) Whoever willfully prevents, obstructs, misleads, delays or attempts to prevent, obstruct, mislead, or delay the communication of information or records relating to a violation of a Federal health care offense to a criminal investigator shall be fined under this title or imprisoned not more than 5 years, or both.

(b) As used in this section the term "criminal investigator" means any individual duly authorized by a department, agency, or armed force of the United States to conduct or engage in investigations for prosecutions for violations of health care offenses.

(Added Pub.L. 104–191, Title II, § 245(a), Aug. 21, 1996, 110 Stat. 2017.)

§ 1519. Destruction, alteration, or falsification of records in Federal investigations and bankruptcy

Whoever knowingly alters, destroys, mutilates, conceals, covers up, falsifies, or makes a false entry in any record, document, or tangible object with the intent to impede, obstruct, or influence the investigation or proper administration of any matter within the jurisdiction of any department or agency of the United States or any case filed under title 11, or in relation to or contemplation of any such matter or case, shall be fined under this title, imprisoned not more than 20 years, or both.

(Added Pub.L. 107–204, Title VIII, § 802(a), July 30, 2002, 116 Stat. 800.)

§ 1520. Destruction of corporate audit records

(a)(1) Any accountant who conducts an audit of an issuer of securities to which section 10A(a) of the Securities Exchange Act of 1934 (15 U.S.C. 78j–1(a)) applies, shall maintain all audit or review workpapers for a period of 5 years from the end of the fiscal period in which the audit or review was concluded.

(2) The Securities and Exchange Commission shall promulgate, within 180 days, after adequate notice and an opportunity for comment, such rules and regulations, as are reasonably necessary, relating to the retention of relevant records such as workpapers, documents that form the basis of an audit or review, memoranda, correspondence, communications, other documents, and records (including electronic records) which are created, sent, or received in connection with an audit or review and contain conclusions, opinions, analyses, or financial data relating to such an audit or review, which is conducted by any accountant who conducts an audit of an issuer of securities to which section 10A(a) of the Securities Exchange Act of 1934 (15 U.S.C. 78j–1(a)) applies. The Commission may, from time to time, amend or supplement the rules and regulations that it is required to promulgate under this section, after adequate notice and an opportunity for comment, in order to ensure that such rules and regulations adequately comport with the purposes of this section.

(b) Whoever knowingly and willfully violates subsection (a)(1), or any rule or regulation promulgated by the Securities and Exchange Commission under subsection (a)(2), shall be fined under this title, imprisoned not more than 10 years, or both.

(c) Nothing in this section shall be deemed to diminish or relieve any person of any other duty or obligation imposed by Federal or State law or regulation to maintain, or refrain from destroying, any document.

(Added Pub.L. 107–204, Title VIII, § 802(a), July 30, 2002, 116 Stat. 800.)

CHAPTER 74—PARTIAL-BIRTH ABORTIONS

Sec.

§ 1531. Partial-birth abortions prohibited

(a) Any physician who, in or affecting interstate or foreign commerce, knowingly performs a partial-birth abortion and thereby kills a human fetus shall be fined under this title or imprisoned not more than 2 years, or both. This subsection does not apply to a partial-birth abortion that is necessary to save the life of a mother whose life is endangered by a physical disorder, physical illness, or physical injury, including a life-endangering physical condition caused by or arising from the pregnancy itself. This subsection takes effect 1 day after the enactment.

(b) As used in this section—

(1) the term "partial-birth abortion" means an abortion in which the person performing the abortion—

(A) deliberately and intentionally vaginally delivers a living fetus until, in the case of a head-first presentation, the entire fetal head is outside the body of the mother, or, in the case of breech presentation, any part of the fetal trunk past the navel is outside the body of the mother, for the purpose of performing an overt act that the person knows will kill the partially delivered living fetus; and

(B) performs the overt act, other than completion of delivery, that kills the partially delivered living fetus; and

(2) the term "physician" means a doctor of medicine or osteopathy legally authorized to practice medicine and surgery by the State in which the doctor performs such activity, or any other individual legally authorized by the State to perform abortions: *Provided, however*, That any individual who is not a physician or not otherwise legally authorized by the State to perform abortions, but who nevertheless directly performs a partial-birth abortion, shall be subject to the provisions of this section.

(c)(1) The father, if married to the mother at the time she receives a partial-birth abortion procedure, and if the mother has not attained the age of 18 years at the time of the abortion, the maternal grandparents of the fetus, may in a civil action obtain appropriate relief, unless the pregnancy resulted from the plaintiff's criminal conduct or the plaintiff consented to the abortion.

(2) Such relief shall include—

(A) money damages for all injuries, psychological and physical, occasioned by the violation of this section; and

(B) statutory damages equal to three times the cost of the partial-birth abortion.

(d)(1) A defendant accused of an offense under this section may seek a hearing before the State Medical Board on whether the physician's conduct was necessary to save the life of the mother whose life was endangered by a physical disorder, physical illness, or physical injury, including a life-endangering physical condition caused by or arising from the pregnancy itself.

(2) The findings on that issue are admissible on that issue at the trial of the defendant. Upon a motion of the defendant, the court shall delay the beginning of the trial for not more than 30 days to permit such a hearing to take place.

(e) A woman upon whom a partial-birth abortion is performed may not be prosecuted under this section, for a conspiracy to violate this section, or for an offense under section 2, 3, or 4 of this title based on a violation of this section.

(Added Pub.L. 108–105, § 3(a), Nov. 5, 2003, 117 Stat. 1206.)

HISTORICAL AND STATUTORY NOTES

References in Text

1 day after the enactment, referred to in subsec. (a), probably means 1 day after the enactment of Pub.L. 108–105, 117 Stat. 1201, which was approved Nov. 5, 2003.

Short Title

2003 Acts. Pub.L. 108–105, § 1, Nov. 5, 2003, 117 Stat. 1201, provided that: "This Act [enacting this chapter and provisions set out as a note under this section] may be cited as the 'Partial–Birth Abortion Ban Act of 2003'."

Congressional Findings

Pub.L. 108–105, § 2, Nov. 5, 2003, 117 Stat. 1201, provided that:

"The Congress finds and declares the following:

"(1) A moral, medical, and ethical consensus exists that the practice of performing a partial-birth abortion—an abortion in which a physician deliberately and intentionally vaginally delivers a living, unborn child's body until either the entire baby's head is outside the body of the mother, or any part of the baby's trunk past the navel is outside the body of the mother and only the head remains inside the womb, for the purpose of performing an overt act (usually the puncturing of the back of the child's skull and removing the baby's brains) that the person knows will kill the partially delivered infant, performs this act, and then completes delivery of the dead infant—is a gruesome and inhumane procedure that is never medically necessary and should be prohibited.

"(2) Rather than being an abortion procedure that is embraced by the medical community, particularly among physicians who routinely perform other abortion procedures, partial-birth abortion remains a disfavored procedure that is not only unnecessary to preserve the health of the mother, but in fact poses serious risks to the long-term health of women and in some circumstances, their lives. As a result, at least 27 States banned the procedure as did the United States Congress which voted to ban the procedure during the 104th, 105th, and 106th Congresses.

"(3) In Stenberg v. Carhart, 530 U.S. 914, 932 (2000), the United States Supreme Court opined 'that significant medical authority supports the proposition that in some circumstances, [partial birth abortion] would be the safest procedure' for pregnant women who wish to undergo an abortion. Thus, the Court struck down the State of Nebraska's ban on partial-birth abortion procedures, concluding that it placed an 'undue burden' on women seeking abortions because it failed to include an exception for partial-birth abortions deemed necessary to preserve the 'health' of the mother.

"(4) In reaching this conclusion, the Court deferred to the Federal district court's factual findings that the partial-birth abortion procedure was statistically and medically as safe as, and in many circumstances safer than, alternative abortion procedures.

"(5) However, substantial evidence presented at the Stenberg trial and overwhelming evidence presented and compiled at extensive congressional hearings, much of which was compiled after the district court hearing in Stenberg, and thus not included in the Stenberg trial record, demonstrates that a partial-birth abortion is never necessary to preserve the health of a woman, poses significant health risks to a woman upon whom the procedure is performed and is outside the standard of medical care.

"(6) Despite the dearth of evidence in the Stenberg trial court record supporting the district court's findings, the United States Court of Appeals for the Eighth Circuit and the Supreme Court refused to set aside the district court's factual findings because, under the applicable standard of appellate review, they were not 'clearly erroneous'. A finding of fact is clearly erroneous 'when although there is evidence to support it, the reviewing court on the entire evidence is left with the definite and firm conviction that a mistake has been committed'. Anderson v. City of Bessemer City, North Carolina, 470 U.S. 564, 573 (1985). Under this standard, 'if the district court's account of the evidence is plausible in light of the record viewed in its entirety, the court of appeals may not reverse it even though convinced that had it been sitting as the trier of fact, it would have weighed the evidence differently'. Id. at 574.

"(7) Thus, in Stenberg, the United States Supreme Court was required to accept the very questionable findings issued by the district court judge—the effect of which was to render null and void the reasoned factual findings and policy determinations of the United States Congress and at least 27 State legislatures.

"(8) However, under well-settled Supreme Court jurisprudence, the United States Congress is not bound to accept the same factual findings that the Supreme Court was bound to accept in Stenberg under the 'clearly erroneous' standard. Rather, the United States Congress is entitled to reach its own factual findings—findings that the Supreme Court accords great deference—and to enact legislation based upon these findings so long as it seeks to pursue a legitimate interest that is within the scope of the Constitution, and draws reasonable inferences based upon substantial evidence.

"(9) In Katzenbach v. Morgan, 384 U.S. 641 (1966), the Supreme Court articulated its highly deferential review of congressional factual findings when it addressed the constitutionality of section 4(e) of the Voting Rights Act of 1965 [42 U.S.C.A. § 1973b(e)]. Regarding Congress' factual determination that section 4(e) [42 U.S.C.A. § 1973b(e)] would assist the Puerto Rican community in 'gaining nondiscriminatory treatment in public services,' the Court stated that '[i]t was for Congress, as the branch that made this judgment, to assess and weigh the various conflicting considerations * * *. It is not for us to review the congressional resolution of these factors. It is enough that we be able to perceive a basis upon which the Congress might resolve the conflict as it did. There plainly was such a basis to support section 4(e) [42 U.S.C.A. § 1973b(e)] in the application in question in this case.'. Id. at 653.

"(10) Katzenbach's highly deferential review of Congress' factual conclusions was relied upon by the United States District Court for the District of Columbia when it upheld the 'bail-out' provisions of the Voting Rights Act of 1965 (42 U.S.C. 1973c), stating that 'congressional fact finding, to which we are inclined to pay great deference, strengthens the inference that, in those jurisdictions covered by the Act, state actions discriminatory in effect are discriminatory in purpose'. City of Rome, Georgia v. U.S., 472 F. Supp. 221 (D.D.C. 1979) aff'd City of Rome, Georgia v. U.S., 446 U.S. 156 (1980).

"(11) The Court continued its practice of deferring to congressional factual findings in reviewing the constitutionality of the must-carry provisions of the Cable Television Consumer Protection and Competition Act of 1992 [Pub.L. 102–385, Oct. 5, 1992, 106 Stat. 1460; see Tables for complete classification]. See Turner Broadcasting System, Inc. v. Federal Communications Commission, 512 U.S. 622 (1994) (Turner I) and Turner Broadcasting System, Inc. v. Federal Communications Commission, 520 U.S. 180 (1997) (Turner II). At issue in the Turner cases was Congress' legislative finding that, absent mandatory carriage rules, the continued viability of local broadcast television would be 'seriously jeopardized'. The Turner I Court recognized that as an institution, 'Congress is far better equipped than the judiciary to 'amass and evaluate the vast amounts of data' bearing upon an issue as complex and dynamic as that presented here', 512 U.S. at 665–66. Although the Court recognized that 'the deference afforded to legislative findings does 'not foreclose our independent judgment of the facts bearing on an issue of constitutional law,'' its 'obligation to exercise independent judgment when First Amendment rights are implicated is not a license to reweigh the evidence de novo, or to replace Congress' factual predictions with our own. Rather, it is to assure that, in formulating its judgments, Congress has drawn reasonable inferences based on substantial evidence.'. Id. at 666.

"(12) Three years later in Turner II, the Court upheld the 'must-carry' provisions based upon Congress' findings, stating the Court's 'sole obligation is 'to assure that, in formulating its judgments, Congress has drawn reasonable inferences based on substantial evidence.'' 520 U.S. at 195. Citing its ruling in Turner I, the Court reiterated that '[w]e owe Congress' findings deference in part because the institution 'is far better equipped than the judiciary to 'amass and evaluate the vast amounts of data' bearing upon' legislative questions,' id. at 195, and added that it 'owe[d] Congress' findings an additional measure of deference out of respect for its authority to exercise the legislative power.'. Id. at 196.

"(13) There exists substantial record evidence upon which Congress has reached its conclusion that a ban on partial-birth abortion is not required to contain a 'health' exception, because the facts indicate that a partial-birth abortion is never necessary to preserve the health of a woman, poses serious risks to a woman's health, and lies outside the standard of medical care. Congress was informed by extensive hearings held during the 104th, 105th, 107th, and 108th Congresses and passed a ban on partial-birth abortion in the 104th, 105th, and 106th Congresses. These findings reflect the very informed judgment of the Congress that a partial-birth abortion is never necessary to preserve the health of a woman, poses serious risks to a woman's health, and lies outside the standard of medical care, and should, therefore, be banned.

"(14) Pursuant to the testimony received during extensive legislative hearings during the 104th, 105th, 107th, and 108th Congresses, Congress finds and declares that:

"(A) Partial-birth abortion poses serious risks to the health of a woman undergoing the procedure. Those risks include, among other things: An increase in a woman's risk of suffering from cervical incompetence, a result of cervical dilation making it difficult or impossible for a woman to successfully carry a subsequent pregnancy to term; an increased risk of uterine rupture, abruption, amniotic fluid embolus, and trauma to the uterus as a result of converting the child to a footling breech position, a procedure which, according to a leading obstetrics textbook, 'there are very few, if any, indications for * * * other than for delivery of a second twin'; and a risk of lacerations and secondary hemorrhaging due to the doctor blindly forcing a sharp instrument into the base of the unborn child's skull while he or she is lodged in the birth canal, an act which could result in severe bleeding, brings with it the threat of shock, and could ultimately result in maternal death.

"(B) There is no credible medical evidence that partial-birth abortions are safe or are safer than other abortion procedures. No controlled studies of partial-birth abortions have been conducted nor have any comparative studies been conducted to demonstrate its safety and efficacy compared to other abortion methods. Furthermore, there have been no articles published in peer-reviewed journals that establish that partial-birth abortions are superior in any way to established abortion procedures. Indeed, unlike other more commonly used abortion procedures, there are currently no medical schools that provide instruction on abortions that include the instruction in partial-birth abortions in their curriculum.

"(C) A prominent medical association has concluded that partial-birth abortion is 'not an accepted medical practice', that it has 'never been subject to even a minimal amount of the normal medical practice development,' that 'the relative advantages and disadvantages of the procedure in specific circumstances remain unknown,' and that 'there is no consensus among obstetricians about its use'. The association has further noted that partial-birth abortion is broadly disfavored by both medical experts and the public, is 'ethically wrong,' and 'is never the only appropriate procedure'.

"(D) Neither the plaintiff in Stenberg v. Carhart, nor the experts who testified on his behalf, have identified a single circumstance during which a partial-birth abortion was necessary to preserve the health of a woman.

"(E) The physician credited with developing the partial-birth abortion procedure has testified that he has never encountered a situation where a partial-birth abortion was medically necessary to achieve the desired outcome and, thus, is never medically necessary to preserve the health of a woman.

"(F) A ban on the partial-birth abortion procedure will therefore advance the health interests of pregnant women seeking to terminate a pregnancy.

"(G) In light of this overwhelming evidence, Congress and the States have a compelling interest in prohibiting partial-birth abortions. In addition to promoting maternal health, such a prohibition will draw a bright line that clearly distinguishes abortion and infanticide, that preserves the integrity of the medical profession, and promotes respect for human life.

"(H) Based upon Roe v. Wade, 410 U.S. 113 (1973) and Planned Parenthood v. Casey, 505 U.S. 833 (1992), a governmental interest in protecting the life of a child during the delivery process arises by virtue of the fact that during a partial-birth abortion, labor is induced and the birth process has begun. This distinction was recognized in Roe when the Court noted, without comment, that the Texas parturition statute, which prohibited one from killing a child 'in a state of being born and before actual birth,' was not under attack. This interest becomes compelling as the child emerges from the maternal body. A child that is completely born is a full, legal person entitled to constitutional protections afforded a 'person' under the United States Constitution. Partial-birth abortions involve the killing of a child that is in the process, in fact mere inches away from, becoming a 'person'. Thus, the government has a heightened interest in protecting the life of the partially-born child.

"(I) This, too, has not gone unnoticed in the medical community, where a prominent medical association has recognized that partial-birth abortions are 'ethically different from other destructive abortion techniques because the fetus, normally twenty weeks or longer in gestation, is killed outside of the womb'. According to this medical association, the ' 'partial birth' gives the fetus an autonomy which separates it from the right of the woman to choose treatments for her own body'.

"(J) Partial-birth abortion also confuses the medical, legal, and ethical duties of physicians to preserve and promote life, as the physician acts directly against the physical life of a child, whom he or she had just delivered, all but the head, out of the womb, in order to end that life. Partial-birth abortion thus appropriates the terminology and techniques used by obstetricians in the delivery of living children—obstetricians who preserve and protect the life of the mother and the child—and instead uses those techniques to end the life of the partially-born child.

"(K) Thus, by aborting a child in the manner that purposefully seeks to kill the child after he or she has begun the process of birth, partial-birth abortion undermines the public's perception of the appropriate role of a physician during the delivery process, and perverts a process during which life is brought into the world, in order to destroy a partially-born child.

"(L) The gruesome and inhumane nature of the partial-birth abortion procedure and its disturbing similarity to the killing of a newborn infant promotes a complete disregard for infant human life that can only be countered by a prohibition of the procedure.

"(M) The vast majority of babies killed during partial-birth abortions are alive until the end of the procedure. It is a medical fact, however, that unborn infants at this stage can feel pain when subjected to painful stimuli and that their perception of this pain is even more intense than that of newborn infants and older children when subjected to the same stimuli. Thus, during a partial-birth abortion procedure, the child will fully experience the pain associated with piercing his or her skull and sucking out his or her brain.

"(N) Implicitly approving such a brutal and inhumane procedure by choosing not to prohibit it will further coarsen society to the humanity of not only newborns, but all vulnerable and innocent human life, making it increasingly difficult to protect such life. Thus, Congress has a compelling interest in acting—indeed it must act—to prohibit this inhumane procedure.

"(O) For these reasons, Congress finds that partial-birth abortion is never medically indicated to preserve the health of the mother; is in fact unrecognized as a valid abortion procedure by the mainstream medical community; poses additional health risks to the mother; blurs the line between abortion and infanticide in the killing of a partially-born child just inches from birth; and confuses the role of the physician in childbirth and should, therefore, be banned."

CHAPTER 75—PASSPORTS AND VISAS

§ 1541. Issuance without authority

Whoever, acting or claiming to act in any office or capacity under the United States, or a State, without lawful authority grants, issues, or verifies any passport or other instrument in the nature of a passport to or for any person whomsoever; or

Whoever, being a consular officer authorized to grant, issue, or verify passports, knowingly and willfully grants, issues, or verifies any such passport to or for any person not owing allegiance, to the United States, whether a citizen or not—

Shall be fined under this title, imprisoned not more than 25 years (if the offense was committed to facilitate an act of international terrorism (as defined in section 2331 of this title)), 20 years (if the offense was committed to facilitate a drug trafficking crime (as defined in section 929(a) of this title)), 10 years (in the case of the first or second such offense, if the offense was not committed to facilitate such an act of international terrorism or a drug trafficking crime), or 15 years (in the case of any other offense), or both.

For purposes of this section, the term "State" means a State of the United States, the District of Columbia, and any commonwealth, territory, or possession of the United States.

(June 25, 1948, c. 645, 62 Stat. 771; Sept. 13, 1994, Pub.L. 103–322, Title XIII, § 130009(a)(1), Title XXXIII, § 330016(1)(G), 108 Stat. 2030, 2147; Sept. 30, 1996, Pub.L. 104–208, Div. C, Title II, § 211(a)(2), 110 Stat. 3009–569; Oct. 11, 1996, Pub.L. 104–294, Title VI, § 607(n), 110 Stat. 3512; Nov. 2, 2002, Pub.L. 107–273, Div. B, Title IV, § 4002(a)(3), 116 Stat. 1806.)

HISTORICAL AND STATUTORY NOTES

Effective and Applicability Provisions

1996 Acts. Amendment by section 211(a)(2) of Pub.L. 104–208 applicable with respect to offenses occurring on or after Sept. 30, 1996, see section 211(c) of Pub.L. 104–208, set out as a note under section 1028 of this title.

Severability of Provisions

If any provision of Division C of Pub.L. 104–208 or the application of such provision to any person or circumstances is held to be unconstitutional, the remainder of Division C of Pub.L. 104–208 and the application of the provisions of Division C of Pub.L. 104–208 to any person or circumstance not to be affected thereby, see section 1(e) of Pub.L. 104–208, set out as a note under section 1101 of Title 8, Aliens and Nationality.

§ 1542. False statement in application and use of passport

Whoever willfully and knowingly makes any false statement in an application for passport with intent to induce or secure the issuance of a passport under the authority of the United States, either for his own use or the use of another, contrary to the laws regulating the issuance of passports or the rules prescribed pursuant to such laws; or

Whoever willfully and knowingly uses or attempts to use, or furnishes to another for use any passport the issue of which was secured in any way by reason of any false statement—

Shall be fined under this title, imprisoned not more than 25 years (if the offense was committed to facilitate an act of international terrorism (as defined in section 2331 of this title)), 20 years (if the offense was committed to facilitate a drug trafficking crime (as defined in section 929(a) of this title)), 10 years (in the case of the first or second such offense, if the offense was not committed to facilitate such an act of international terrorism or a drug trafficking crime), or 15 years (in the case of any other offense), or both.

(June 25, 1948, c. 645, 62 Stat. 771; Sept. 13, 1994, Pub.L. 103–322, Title XIII, § 130009(a)(2), Title XXXIII, § 330016(1)(I), 108 Stat. 2030, 2147; Sept. 30, 1996, Pub.L. 104–208, Div. C, Title II, § 211(a)(2), 110 Stat. 3009–569; Nov. 2, 2002, Pub.L. 107–273, Div. B, Title IV, § 4002(a)(3), 116 Stat. 1806.)

HISTORICAL AND STATUTORY NOTES

Effective and Applicability Provisions

1996 Acts. Amendment by section 211(a)(2) of Pub.L. 104–208 applicable with respect to offenses occurring on or after Sept. 30, 1996, see section 211(c) of Pub.L. 104–208, set out as a note under section 1028 of this title.

Severability of Provisions

If any provision of Division C of Pub.L. 104–208 or the application of such provision to any person or circumstances is held to be unconstitutional, the remainder of Division C of Pub.L. 104–208 and the application of the provisions of Division C of Pub.L. 104–208 to any person or circumstance not to be affected thereby, see section 1(e) of Pub.L. 104–208, set out as a note under section 1101 of Title 8, Aliens and Nationality.

§ 1543. Forgery or false use of passport

Whoever falsely makes, forges, counterfeits, mutilates, or alters any passport or instrument purporting to be a passport, with intent that the same may be used; or

Whoever willfully and knowingly uses, or attempts to use, or furnishes to another for use any such false, forged, counterfeited, mutilated, or altered passport or instrument purporting to be a passport, or any passport validly issued which has become void by the occurrence of any condition therein prescribed invalidating the same—

Shall be fined under this title, imprisoned not more than 25 years (if the offense was committed to facilitate an act of international terrorism (as defined in section 2331 of this title)), 20 years (if the offense was committed to facilitate a drug trafficking crime (as defined in section 929(a of this title)), 10 years (in the case of the first or second such offense, if the offense was not committed to facilitate such an act of international terrorism or a drug trafficking crime), or 15 years (in the case of any other offense), or both.
(June 25, 1948, c. 645, 62 Stat. 771; Sept. 13, 1994, Pub.L. 103–322, Title XIII, § 130009(a)(2), Title XXXIII, § 330016(1)(I), 108 Stat. 2030, 2147; Sept. 30, 1996, Pub.L. 104–208, Div. C, Title II, § 211(a)(2), 110 Stat. 3009–569; Nov. 2, 2002, Pub.L. 107–273, Div. B, Title IV, § 4002(a)(3), 116 Stat. 1806.)

HISTORICAL AND STATUTORY NOTES

Effective and Applicability Provisions

1996 Acts. Amendment by section 211(a)(2) of Pub.L. 104–208 applicable with respect to offenses occurring on or after Sept. 30, 1996, see section 211(c) of Pub.L. 104–208, set out as a note under section 1028 of this title.

Severability of Provisions

If any provision of Division C of Pub.L. 104–208 or the application of such provision to any person or circumstances is held to be unconstitutional, the remainder of Division C of Pub.L. 104–208 and the application of the provisions of Division C of Pub.L. 104–208 to any person or circumstance not to be affected thereby, see section 1(e) of Pub.L. 104–208, set out as a note under section 1101 of Title 8, Aliens and Nationality.

§ 1544. Misuse of passport

Whoever willfully and knowingly uses, or attempts to use, any passport issued or designed for the use of another; or

Whoever willfully and knowingly uses or attempts to use any passport in violation of the conditions or restrictions therein contained, or of the rules prescribed pursuant to the laws regulating the issuance of passports; or

Whoever willfully and knowingly furnishes, disposes of, or delivers a passport to any person, for use by another than the person for whose use it was originally issued and designed—

Shall be fined under this title, imprisoned not more than 25 years (if the offense was committed to facilitate an act of international terrorism (as defined in section 2331 of this title)), 20 years (if the offense was committed to facilitate a drug trafficking crime (as defined in section 929(a) of this title)), 10 years (in the case of the first or second such offense, if the offense was not committed to facilitate such an act of international terrorism or a drug trafficking crime), or 15 years (in the case of any other offense), or both.
(June 25, 1948, c. 645, 62 Stat. 771; Sept. 13, 1994, Pub.L. 103–322, Title XIII, § 130009(a)(2), Title XXXIII, § 330016(1)(I), 108 Stat. 2030, 2147; Sept. 30, 1996, Pub.L. 104–208, Div. C, Title II, § 211(a)(2), 110 Stat. 3009–569; Nov. 2, 2002, Pub.L. 107–273, Div. B, Title IV, § 4002(a)(3), 116 Stat. 1806.)

HISTORICAL AND STATUTORY NOTES

Effective and Applicability Provisions

1996 Acts. Amendment by section 211(a)(2) of Pub.L. 104–208 applicable with respect to offenses occurring on or after Sept. 30, 1996, see section 211(c) of Pub.L. 104–208, set out as a note under section 1028 of this title.

Severability of Provisions

If any provision of Division C of Pub.L. 104–208 or the application of such provision to any person or circumstances is held to be unconstitutional, the remainder of Division C of Pub.L. 104–208 and the application of the provisions of Division C of Pub.L. 104–208 to any person or circumstance not to be affected thereby, see section 1(e) of Pub.L. 104–208, set out as a note under section 1101 of Title 8, Aliens and Nationality.

§ 1545. Safe conduct violation

Whoever violates any safe conduct or passport duly obtained and issued under authority of the United States shall be fined under this title, imprisoned not more than 10 years, or both.
(June 25, 1948, c. 645, 62 Stat. 771; Sept. 13, 1994, Pub.L. 103–322, Title XIII, § 130009(a)(3), Title XXXIII, § 330016(1)(I), 108 Stat. 2030, 2147.)

§ 1546. Fraud and misuse of visas, permits, and other documents

(a) Whoever knowingly forges, counterfeits, alters, or falsely makes any immigrant or nonimmigrant visa, permit, border crossing card, alien registration receipt card, or other document prescribed by statute or regulation for entry into or as evidence of authorized stay or employment in the United States, or utters, uses, attempts to use, possesses, obtains, accepts, or receives any such visa, permit, border crossing card, alien registration receipt card, or other document prescribed by statute or regulation for entry into or as evidence of authorized stay or employment in the United States, knowing it to be forged, counterfeited, altered, or falsely made, or to have been procured by means of any false claim or statement, or to have been otherwise procured by fraud or unlawfully obtained; or

Whoever, except under direction of the Attorney General or the Commissioner of the Immigration and Naturalization Service, or other proper officer, knowingly possesses any blank permit, or engraves, sells, brings into the United States, or has in his control or possession any plate in the likeness of a plate designed for the printing of permits, or makes any print, photograph, or impression in the likeness of any immigrant or nonimmigrant visa, permit or other document required for entry into the United States, or has in his possession a distinctive paper which has been adopted by the Attorney General or the Commissioner of the Immigration and Naturalization Service for the printing of such visas, permits, or documents; or

Whoever, when applying for an immigrant or nonimmigrant visa, permit, or other document required for entry into the United States, or for admission to the United States personates another, or falsely appears in the name of a deceased individual, or evades or attempts to evade the immigration laws by appearing under an assumed or fictitious name without disclosing his true identity, or sells or otherwise disposes of, or offers to sell or otherwise dispose of, or utters, such visa, permit, or other document, to any person not authorized by law to receive such document; or

Whoever knowingly makes under oath, or as permitted under penalty of perjury under section 1746 of title 28, United States Code, knowingly subscribes as true, any false statement with respect to a material fact in any application, affidavit, or other document required by the immigration laws or regulations prescribed thereunder, or knowingly presents any such application, affidavit, or other document which contains any such false statement or which fails to contain any reasonable basis in law or fact—

Shall be fined under this title or imprisoned not more than 25 years (if the offense was committed to facilitate an act of international terrorism (as defined in section 2331 of this title)), 20 years (if the offense was committed to facilitate a drug trafficking crime (as defined in section 929(a) of this title)), 10 years (in the case of the first or second such offense, if the offense was not committed to facilitate such an act of international terrorism or a drug trafficking crime), or 15 years (in the case of any other offense), or both.

(b) Whoever uses—

(1) an identification document, knowing (or having reason to know) that the document was not issued lawfully for the use of the possessor,

(2) an identification document knowing (or having reason to know) that the document is false, or

(3) a false attestation,

for the purpose of satisfying a requirement of section 274A(b) of the Immigration and Nationality Act, shall be fined under this title, imprisoned not more than 5 years, or both.

(c) This section does not prohibit any lawfully authorized investigative, protective, or intelligence activity of a law enforcement agency of the United States, a State, or a subdivision of a State, or of an intelligence agency of the United States, or any activity authorized under title V of the Organized Crime Control Act of 1970 (18 U.S.C. note prec. 3481). For purposes of this section, the term "State" means a State of the United States, the District of Columbia, and any commonwealth, territory, or possession of the United States.

(June 25, 1948, c. 645, 62 Stat. 771; June 27, 1952, c. 477, Title IV, § 402(a), 66 Stat. 275; Oct. 18, 1976, Pub.L. 94–550, § 5, 90 Stat. 2535; Nov. 6, 1986, Pub.L. 99–603, Title I, § 103(a), 100 Stat. 3380; Oct. 24, 1988, Pub.L. 100–525, Title I, § 2(c), 102 Stat. 2610; Nov. 29, 1990, Pub.L. 101–647, Title XXXV, § 3550, 104 Stat. 4926; Sept. 13, 1994, Pub.L. 103–322, Title XIII, § 130009(a)(4), (5), Title XXXIII, § 330011(p), 108 Stat. 2030, 2145; Sept. 30, 1996, Pub.L. 104–208, Div. C, Title II, §§ 211(a)(2), 214, 110 Stat. 3009–569, 3009–572; Oct. 11, 1996, Pub.L. 104–294, Title VI, § 607(m), 110 Stat. 3512; Nov. 2, 2002, Pub.L. 107–273, Div. B, Title IV, § 4002(a)(3), 116 Stat. 1806.)

HISTORICAL AND STATUTORY NOTES

References in Text

The immigration laws, referred to in subsec. (a), are classified generally to chapter 12 (section 1101 et seq.) of Title 8, Aliens and Nationality. See also section 1101(a)(17) of Title 8.

Title V of the Organized Crime Control Act of 1970, referred to in subsec. (c), is Pub.L. 91–452, Title V, §§ 501 to 504, Oct. 15, 1970, 84 Stat. 933, which authorized the Attorney General to provide security and housing for Government witnesses and their families in proceedings against organized crime, and which was repealed by Pub.L. 98–473, Title II, c. XII, Part F, Subpart A, § 1209(b), Oct. 12, 1984, 98 Stat. 2163, effective Oct. 1, 1984. Prior to repeal Title V of the Organized Crime Control Act of 1970 was set out as a note preceding section 3481 of this title.

Effective and Applicability Provisions

1996 Acts. Amendment by section 211(a)(2) of Pub.L. 104–208 applicable with respect to offenses occurring on or after Sept. 30, 1996, see section 211(c) of Pub.L. 104–208, set out as a note under section 1028 of this title.

1994 Acts. Section 330011(p) of Pub.L. 103–322 provided in part that the amendment made by such section, amending directory language of section 3550 of Pub.L. 101–647 (which amended this section), was to take effect on the date section 3550 of Pub.L. 101–647 took effect; section 3550 of Pub.L. 101–647 took effect on the date of enactment of Pub.L. 101–647, which was approved Nov. 29, 1990.

Transfer of Functions

All functions vested by law in the Attorney General, the Department of Justice, or any other officer or any agency of that Department, with respect to the inspection at regular inspection locations at ports of entry of persons, and documents of persons, entering or leaving the United States, were to have been transferred to the Secretary of the Treasury by 1973 Reorg. Plan No. 2, § 2, eff. July 1, 1973, 38 F.R. 15932, 87 Stat. 1091, set out in Appendix 1 to Title 5, Government Organization and Employees. The transfer was negated by section 1(a)(1), (b) of Pub.L. 93–253, Mar. 16, 1974, 88 Stat. 50, which repealed section 2 of 1973 Reorg. Plan No. 2, eff. July 1, 1973.

Abolition of Immigration and Naturalization Service and Transfer of Functions

For abolition of Immigration and Naturalization Service, transfer of functions, and treatment of related references, see note set out under 8 U.S.C.A. § 1551.

Severability of Provisions

If any provision of Division C of Pub.L. 104–208 or the application of such provision to any person or circumstances is held to be unconstitutional, the remainder of Division C of Pub.L. 104–208 and the application of the provisions of Division C of Pub.L. 104–208 to any person or circumstance not to be affected thereby, see section 1(e) of Pub.L. 104–208, set out as a note under section 1101 of Title 8, Aliens and Nationality.

§ 1547. Alternative imprisonment maximum for certain offenses

Notwithstanding any other provision of this title, the maximum term of imprisonment that may be imposed for an offense under this chapter (other than an offense under section 1545)—

(1) if committed to facilitate a drug trafficking crime (as defined in 929(a)) is 15 years; and

(2) if committed to facilitate an act of international terrorism (as defined in section 2331) is 20 years.

(Added Pub.L. 103–322, Title XIII, § 130009(a)(6), Sept. 13, 1994, 108 Stat. 2030.)

CHAPTER 77—PEONAGE, SLAVERY, AND TRAFFICKING IN PERSONS

§ 1581. Peonage; obstructing enforcement

(a) Whoever holds or returns any person to a condition of peonage, or arrests any person with the intent of placing him in or returning him to a condition of peonage, shall be fined under this title or imprisoned not more than 20 years, or both. If death results from the violation of this section, or if the violation includes kidnapping or an attempt to kidnap, aggravated sexual abuse or the attempt to commit aggravated sexual abuse, or an attempt to kill, the defendant shall be fined under this title or imprisoned for any term of years or life, or both.

(b) Whoever obstructs, or attempts to obstruct, or in any way interferes with or prevents the enforcement of this section, shall be liable to the penalties prescribed in subsection (a).

(June 25, 1948, c. 645, 62 Stat. 772; Sept. 13, 1994, Pub.L. 103–322, Title XXXIII, § 330016(1)(K), 108 Stat. 2147; Sept. 30, 1996, Pub.L. 104–208, Div. C, Title II, § 218(a), 110 Stat. 3009–573; Oct. 28, 2000, Pub.L. 106–386, Div. A, § 112(a)(1), 114 Stat. 1486.)

HISTORICAL AND STATUTORY NOTES

Effective and Applicability Provisions

1996 Acts. Section 218(d) of Div. C of Pub.L. 104–208 provided that: "This section and the amendments made by this section [amending subsec. (a) of this section and sections 1583, 1584, and 1588 of this title and enacting a provision set out as a note under section 994 of Title 28, Judiciary and Judicial Procedure] shall apply with respect to offenses occurring on or after the date of the enactment of this Act [Sept. 30, 1996]."

Severability of Provisions

If any provision of Division C of Pub.L. 104–208 or the application of such provision to any person or circumstances is held to be unconstitutional, the remainder of Division C of Pub.L. 104–208 and the application of the provisions of Division C of Pub.L. 104–208 to any person or circumstance not to be affected thereby, see section 1(e) of Pub.L. 104–208, set out as a note under section 1101 of Title 8, Aliens and Nationality.

§ 1582. Vessels for slave trade

Whoever, whether as master, factor, or owner, builds, fits out, equips, loads, or otherwise prepares or sends away any vessel, in any port or place within the United States, or causes such vessel to sail from any such port or place, for the purpose of procuring any person from any foreign kingdom or country to be transported and held, sold, or otherwise disposed of as a slave, or held to service or labor, shall be fined under this title or imprisoned not more than seven years, or both.

(June 25, 1948, c. 645, 62 Stat. 772; Sept. 13, 1994, Pub.L. 103–322, Title XXXIII, § 330016(1)(K), 108 Stat. 2147.)

§ 1583. Enticement into slavery

Whoever kidnaps or carries away any other person, with the intent that such other person be sold into involuntary servitude, or held as a slave; or

Whoever entices, persuades, or induces any other person to go on board any vessel or to any other place with the intent that he may be made or held as a slave, or sent out of the country to be so made or held—

Shall be fined under this title or imprisoned not more than 20 years, or both.

If death results from the violation of this section, or if the violation includes kidnapping or an attempt to kidnap, aggravated sexual abuse or the attempt to commit aggravated sexual abuse, or an attempt to kill, the defendant shall be fined under this title or imprisoned for any term of years or life, or both.

(June 25, 1948, c. 645, 62 Stat. 772; Sept. 13, 1994, Pub.L. 103–322, Title XXXIII, § 330016(1)(K), 108 Stat. 2147; Sept. 30, 1996, Pub.L. 104–208, Div. C, Title II, § 218(a), 110 Stat. 3009–573; Oct. 28, 2000, Pub.L. 106–386, Div. A, § 112(a)(1), 114 Stat. 1486.)

HISTORICAL AND STATUTORY NOTES

Effective and Applicability Provisions

1996 Acts. Amendment by section 218(a) of Pub.L. 104–208 applicable with respect to offenses occurring on or after Sept. 30, 1996, see section 218(d) of Pub.L. 104–208, set out as a note under section 1581 of this title.

Severability of Provisions

If any provision of Division C of Pub.L. 104–208 or the application of such provision to any person or circumstances is held to be unconstitutional, the remainder of Division C of Pub.L. 104–208 and the application of the provisions of Division C of Pub.L. 104–208 to any person or circumstance not to be affected thereby, see section 1(e) of Pub.L. 104–208, set out as a note under section 1101 of Title 8, Aliens and Nationality.

§ 1584. Sale into involuntary servitude

Whoever knowingly and willfully holds to involuntary servitude or sells into any condition of involuntary servitude, any other person for any term, or brings within the United States any person so held, shall be fined under this title or imprisoned not more than 20 years, or both. If death results from the violation of this section, or if the violation includes kidnapping or an attempt to kidnap, aggravated sexual abuse or the attempt to commit aggravated sexual abuse, or an attempt to kill, the defendant shall be fined under this title or imprisoned for any term of years or life, or both.

(June 25, 1948, c. 645, 62 Stat. 773; Sept. 13, 1994, Pub.L. 103–322, Title XXXIII, § 330016(1)(K), 108 Stat. 2147; Sept. 30, 1996, Pub.L. 104–208, Div. C, Title II, § 218(a), 110 Stat. 3009–573; Oct. 28, 2000, Pub.L. 106–386, Div. A, § 112(a)(1), 114 Stat. 1486.)

HISTORICAL AND STATUTORY NOTES

Effective and Applicability Provisions

1996 Acts. Amendment by section 218(a) of Pub.L. 104–208 applicable with respect to offenses occurring on or after Sept. 30, 1996, see section 218(d) of Pub.L. 104–208, set out as a note under section 1581 of this title.

Severability of Provisions

If any provision of Division C of Pub.L. 104–208 or the application of such provision to any person or circumstances is held to be unconstitutional, the remainder of Division C of Pub.L. 104–208 and the application of the provisions of Division C of Pub.L. 104–208 to any person or circumstance not to be affected thereby, see section 1(e) of Pub.L. 104–208, set out as a note under section 1101 of Title 8, Aliens and Nationality.

§ 1585. Seizure, detention, transportation or sale of slaves

Whoever, being a citizen or resident of the United States and a member of the crew or ship's company of any foreign vessel engaged in the slave trade, or whoever, being of the crew or ship's company of any vessel owned in whole or in part, or navigated for, or in behalf of, any citizen of the United States, lands from such vessel, and on any foreign shore seizes any person with intent to make that person a slave, or decoys, or forcibly brings, carries, receives, confines, detains or transports any person as a slave on board such vessel, or, on board such vessel, offers or attempts to sell any such person as a slave, or on the high seas or anywhere on tide water, transfers or delivers to any other vessel any such person with intent to make such person a slave, or lands or delivers on shore from such vessel any person with intent to sell, or having previously sold, such person as a slave, shall be fined under this title or imprisoned not more than seven years, or both.

(June 25, 1948, c. 645, 62 Stat. 773; Sept. 13, 1994, Pub.L. 103–322, Title XXXIII, § 330016(1)(K), 108 Stat. 2147.)

§ 1586. Service on vessels in slave trade

Whoever, being a citizen or resident of the United States, voluntarily serves on board of any vessel employed or made use of in the transportation of slaves from any foreign country or place to another, shall be fined under this title or imprisoned not more than two years, or both.

(June 25, 1948, c. 645, 62 Stat. 773; Sept. 13, 1994, Pub.L. 103–322, Title XXXIII, § 330016(1)(I), 108 Stat. 2147.)

§ 1587. Possession of slaves aboard vessel

Whoever, being the captain, master, or commander of any vessel found in any river, port, bay, harbor, or on the high seas within the jurisdiction of the United States, or hovering off the coast thereof, and having on board any person for the purpose of selling such person as a slave, or with intent to land such person for such purpose, shall be fined under this title or imprisoned not more than four years, or both.

(June 25, 1948, c. 645, 62 Stat. 773; Sept. 13, 1994, Pub.L. 103–322, Title XXXIII, § 330016(1)(L), 108 Stat. 2147.)

§ 1588. Transportation of slaves from United States

Whoever, being the master or owner or person having charge of any vessel, receives on board any other person with the knowledge or intent that such person is to be carried from any place within the United States to any other place to be held or sold as a slave, or carries away from any place within the United States any such person with the intent that he may be so held or sold as a slave, shall be fined under this title or imprisoned not more than 10 years, or both.

(June 25, 1948, c. 645, 62 Stat. 773; Sept. 13, 1994, Pub.L. 103–322, Title XXXIII, § 330016(1)(K), 108 Stat. 2147; Sept. 30, 1996, Pub.L. 104–208, Div. C, Title II, § 218(a), 110 Stat. 3009–573.)

HISTORICAL AND STATUTORY NOTES

Effective and Applicability Provisions

1996 Acts. Amendment by section 218(a) of Pub.L. 104–208 applicable with respect to offenses occurring on or after Sept. 30, 1996, see section 218(d) of Pub.L. 104–208, set out as a note under section 1581 of this title.

Severability of Provisions

If any provision of Division C of Pub.L. 104–208 or the application of such provision to any person or circumstances is held to be unconstitutional, the remainder of Division C of Pub.L. 104–208 and the application of the provisions of Division C of Pub.L. 104–208 to any person or circumstance not to be affected thereby, see section 1(e) of Pub.L. 104–208, set out as a note under section 1101 of Title 8, Aliens and Nationality.

§ 1589. Forced labor

Whoever knowingly provides or obtains the labor or services of a person—

(1) by threats of serious harm to, or physical restraint against, that person or another person;

(2) by means of any scheme, plan, or pattern intended to cause the person to believe that, if the person did not perform such labor or services, that person or another person would suffer serious harm or physical restraint; or

(3) by means of the abuse or threatened abuse of law or the legal process,

shall be fined under this title or imprisoned not more than 20 years, or both. If death results from the violation of this section, or if the violation includes kidnapping or an attempt to kidnap, aggravated sexual abuse or the attempt to commit aggravated sexual abuse, or an attempt to kill, the defendant shall be fined under this title or imprisoned for any term of years or life, or both.

(Added Pub.L. 106–386, Div. A, § 112(a)(2), Oct. 28, 2000, 114 Stat. 1486.)

§ 1590. Trafficking with respect to peonage, slavery, involuntary servitude, or forced labor

Whoever knowingly recruits, harbors, transports, provides, or obtains by any means, any person for labor or services in violation of this chapter shall be fined under this title or imprisoned not more than 20 years, or both. If death results from the violation of this section, or if the violation includes kidnapping or an attempt to kidnap, aggravated sexual abuse, or the attempt to commit aggravated sexual abuse, or an attempt to kill, the defendant shall be fined under this title or imprisoned for any term of years or life, or both.

(Added Pub.L. 106–386, Div. A, § 112(a)(2), Oct. 28, 2000, 114 Stat. 1487.)

§ 1591. Sex trafficking of children or by force, fraud, or coercion

(a) Whoever knowingly—

(1) in or affecting interstate or foreign commerce, or within the special maritime and territorial jurisdiction of the United States, recruits, entices, harbors, transports, provides, or obtains by any means a person; or

(2) benefits, financially or by receiving anything of value, from participation in a venture which has engaged in an act described in violation of paragraph (1),

knowing that force, fraud, or coercion described in subsection (c)(2) will be used to cause the person to engage in a commercial sex act, or that the person has not attained the age of 18 years and will be caused to engage in a commercial sex act, shall be punished as provided in subsection (b).

(b) The punishment for an offense under subsection (a) is—

(1) if the offense was effected by force, fraud, or coercion or if the person recruited, enticed, harbored, transported, provided, or obtained had not attained the age of 14 years at the time of such offense, by a fine under this title and imprisonment for any term of years not less than 15 or for life; or

(2) if the offense was not so effected, and the person recruited, enticed, harbored, transported, provided, or obtained had attained the age of 14 years but had not attained the age of 18 years at the time of such offense, by a fine under this title and imprisonment for not less than 10 years or for life.

(c) In this section:

(1) The term "commercial sex act" means any sex act, on account of which anything of value is given to or received by any person.

(2) The term "coercion" means—

(A) threats of serious harm to or physical restraint against any person;

(B) any scheme, plan, or pattern intended to cause a person to believe that failure to perform an act would result in serious harm to or physical restraint against any person; or

(C) the abuse or threatened abuse of law or the legal process.

(3) The term "venture" means any group of two or more individuals associated in fact, whether or not a legal entity.

(Added Pub.L. 106–386, Div. A, § 112(a)(2), Oct. 28, 2000, 114 Stat. 1487, and amended Pub.L. 108–21, Title I, § 103(a)(3), Apr. 30, 2003, 117 Stat. 653; Pub.L. 108–193, § 5(a), Dec. 19, 2003, 117 Stat. 2879; Pub.L. 109–248, Title II, § 208, July 27, 2006, 120 Stat. 615.)

HISTORICAL AND STATUTORY NOTES

Codifications

Amendment by Pub.L. 109–248, Title II, § 208(2)(B), July 27, 2006, 120 Stat. 615, directing striking of ", or both" in subsec. (b)(2), was incapable of execution since ", or both" had already been stricken by prior amendment by Pub.L. 109–248, § 208(2)(A).

§ 1592. Unlawful conduct with respect to documents in furtherance of trafficking, peonage, slavery, involuntary servitude, or forced labor

(a) Whoever knowingly destroys, conceals, removes, confiscates, or possesses any actual or purported passport or other immigration document, or any other actual or purported government identification document, of another person—

(1) in the course of a violation of section 1581, 1583, 1584, 1589, 1590, 1591, or 1594(a);

(2) with intent to violate section 1581, 1583, 1584, 1589, 1590, or 1591; or

(3) to prevent or restrict or to attempt to prevent or restrict, without lawful authority, the person's liberty to move or travel, in order to maintain the labor or services of that person, when the person is or has been a victim of a severe form of trafficking in persons, as defined in section 103 of the Trafficking Victims Protection Act of 2000,

shall be fined under this title or imprisoned for not more than 5 years, or both.

(b) Subsection (a) does not apply to the conduct of a person who is or has been a victim of a severe form of trafficking in persons, as defined in section 103 of the Trafficking Victims Protection Act of 2000, if that conduct is caused by, or incident to, that trafficking.

(Added Pub.L. 106–386, Div. A, § 112(a)(2), Oct. 28, 2000, 114 Stat. 1488.)

HISTORICAL AND STATUTORY NOTES

References in Text

Section 103 of the Trafficking Victims Protection Act of 2000, referred to in text, means Pub.L. 106–386, Div. A, § 103, Oct. 28, 2000, 114 Stat. 1469, which enacted section 7102 of Title 22.

§ 1593. Mandatory restitution

(a) Notwithstanding section 3663 or 3663A, and in addition to any other civil or criminal penalties authorized by law, the court shall order restitution for any offense under this chapter.

(b)(1) The order of restitution under this section shall direct the defendant to pay the victim (through the appropriate court mechanism) the full amount of the victim's losses, as determined by the court under paragraph (3) of this subsection.

(2) An order of restitution under this section shall be issued and enforced in accordance with section 3664 in the same manner as an order under section 3663A.

(3) As used in this subsection, the term "full amount of the victim's losses" has the same meaning as provided in section 2259(b)(3) and shall in addition include the greater of the gross income or value to the defendant of the victim's services or labor or the value of the victim's labor as guaranteed under the minimum wage and overtime guarantees of the Fair Labor Standards Act (29 U.S.C. 201 et seq.).

(c) As used in this section, the term "victim" means the individual harmed as a result of a crime under this chapter, including, in the case of a victim who is under 18 years of age, incompetent, incapacitated, or deceased, the legal guardian of the victim or a representative of the victim's estate, or another family member, or any other person appointed as suitable by the court, but in no event shall the defendant be named such representative or guardian.

(Added Pub.L. 106–386, Div. A, § 112(a)(2), Oct. 28, 2000, 114 Stat. 1488.)

HISTORICAL AND STATUTORY NOTES

References in Text

The Fair Labor Standards Act, referred to in subsec. (a)(3), probably means the Fair Labor Standards Act of 1938, Act June 25, 1938, c. 676, 52 Stat. 1060, as amended, which is classified principally to chapter 8 (section 201 et seq.) of Title 29. See Tables for complete classification.

§ 1594. General provisions

(a) Whoever attempts to violate section 1581, 1583, 1584, 1589, 1590, or 1591 shall be punishable in the same manner as a completed violation of that section.

(b) The court, in imposing sentence on any person convicted of a violation of this chapter, shall order, in addition to any other sentence imposed and irrespective of any provision of State law, that such person shall forfeit to the United States—

(1) such person's interest in any property, real or personal, that was used or intended to be used to commit or to facilitate the commission of such violation; and

(2) any property, real or personal, constituting or derived from, any proceeds that such person obtained, directly or indirectly, as a result of such violation.

(c)(1) The following shall be subject to forfeiture to the United States and no property right shall exist in them:

(A) Any property, real or personal, used or intended to be used to commit or to facilitate the commission of any violation of this chapter.

(B) Any property, real or personal, which constitutes or is derived from proceeds traceable to any violation of this chapter.

(2) The provisions of chapter 46 of this title relating to civil forfeitures shall extend to any seizure or civil forfeiture under this subsection.

(d) Witness protection.—Any violation of this chapter shall be considered an organized criminal activity or other serious offense for the purposes of application of chapter 224 (relating to witness protection).

(Added Pub.L. 106–386, Div. A, § 112(a)(2), Oct. 28, 2000, 114 Stat. 1489.)

HISTORICAL AND STATUTORY NOTES

References in Text

Chapter 46 of this title, referred to in text, is classified to section 981 to 1000 of this title.

Chapter 224, referred to in text, probably means chapter 224 of this title, which is classified to sections 3521 to 3528 of this title.

§ 1595. Civil remedy

(a) An individual who is a victim of a violation of section 1589, 1590, or 1591 of this chapter may bring a civil action against the perpetrator in an appropriate district court of the United States and may recover damages and reasonable attorneys fees.

(b)(1) Any civil action filed under this section shall be stayed during the pendency of any criminal action arising out of the same occurrence in which the claimant is the victim.

(2) In this subsection, a "criminal action" includes investigation and prosecution and is pending until final adjudication in the trial court.

(Added Pub.L. 108–193, § 4(a)(4)(A), Dec. 19, 2003, 117 Stat. 2878.)

CHAPTER 79—PERJURY

§ 1621. Perjury generally

Whoever—

(1) having taken an oath before a competent tribunal, officer, or person, in any case in which a law of the United States authorizes an oath to be administered, that he will testify, declare, depose, or certify truly, or that any written testimony, declaration, deposition, or certificate by him subscribed, is true, willfully and contrary to such oath states or subscribes any material matter which he does not believe to be true; or

(2) in any declaration, certificate, verification, or statement under penalty of perjury as permitted under section 1746 of title 28, United States Code, willfully subscribes as true any material matter which he does not believe to be true;

is guilty of perjury and shall, except as otherwise expressly provided by law, be fined under this title or imprisoned not more than five years, or both. This section is applicable whether the statement or subscription is made within or without the United States.

(June 25, 1948, c. 645, 62 Stat. 773; Oct. 3, 1964, Pub.L. 88–619, § 1, 78 Stat. 995; Oct. 18, 1976, Pub.L. 94–550, § 2, 90 Stat. 2534; Sept. 13, 1994, Pub.L. 103–322, Title XXXIII, § 330016(1)(I), 108 Stat. 2147.)

§ 1622. Subornation of perjury

Whoever procures another to commit any perjury is guilty of subornation of perjury, and shall be fined under this title or imprisoned not more than five years, or both.

(June 25, 1948, c. 645, 62 Stat. 774; Sept. 13, 1994, Pub.L. 103–322, Title XXXIII, § 330016(1)(I), 108 Stat. 2147.)

§ 1623. False declarations before grand jury or court

(a) Whoever under oath (or in any declaration, certificate, verification, or statement under penalty of perjury as permitted under section 1746 of title 28, United States Code) in any proceeding before or ancillary to any court or grand jury of the United States knowingly makes any false material declaration or makes or uses any other information, including any book, paper, document, record, recording, or other material, knowing the same to contain any false material declaration, shall be fined under this title or imprisoned not more than five years, or both.

(b) This section is applicable whether the conduct occurred within or without the United States.

(c) An indictment or information for violation of this section alleging that, in any proceedings before or ancillary to any court or grand jury of the United States, the defendant under oath has knowingly made two or more declarations, which are inconsistent to the degree that one of them is necessarily false, need not specify which declaration is false if—

(1) each declaration was material to the point in question, and

(2) each declaration was made within the period of the statute of limitations for the offense charged under this section.

In any prosecution under this section, the falsity of a declaration set forth in the indictment or information shall be established sufficient for conviction by proof that the defendant while under oath made irreconcilably contradictory declarations material to the point in question in any proceeding before or ancillary to any court or grand jury. It shall be a defense to an indictment or information made pursuant to the first sentence of this subsection that the defendant at the time he made each declaration believed the declaration was true.

(d) Where, in the same continuous court or grand jury proceeding in which a declaration is made, the person making the declaration admits such declaration to be false, such admission shall bar prosecution under this section if, at the time the admission is made, the declaration has not substantially affected the proceeding, or it has not become manifest that such falsity has been or will be exposed.

(e) Proof beyond a reasonable doubt under this section is sufficient for conviction. It shall not be necessary that such proof be made by any particular number of witnesses or by documentary or other type of evidence.

(Added Pub.L. 91–452, Title IV, § 401(a), Oct. 15, 1970, 84 Stat. 932, and amended Pub.L. 94–550, § 6, Oct. 18, 1976, 90 Stat. 2535; Pub.L. 103–322, Title XXXIII, § 330016(1)(L), Sept. 13, 1994, 108 Stat. 2147.)

CHAPTER 81—PIRACY AND PRIVATEERING

§ 1651. Piracy under law of nations

Whoever, on the high seas, commits the crime of piracy as defined by the law of nations, and is afterwards brought into or found in the United States, shall be imprisoned for life.

(June 25, 1948, c. 645, 62 Stat. 774.)

§ 1652. Citizens as pirates

Whoever, being a citizen of the United States, commits any murder or robbery, or any act of hostility against the United States, or against any citizen thereof, on the high seas, under color of any commission from any foreign prince, or state, or on pretense of authority from any person, is a pirate, and shall be imprisoned for life.

(June 25, 1948, c. 645, 62 Stat. 774.)

§ 1653. Aliens as pirates

Whoever, being a citizen or subject of any foreign state, is found and taken on the sea making war upon the United States, or cruising against the vessels and property thereof, or of the citizens of the same, contrary to the provisions of any treaty existing between the United States and the state of which the offender is a citizen or subject, when by such treaty such acts are declared to be piracy, is a pirate, and shall be imprisoned for life.

(June 25, 1948, c. 645, 62 Stat. 774.)

§ 1654. Arming or serving on privateers

Whoever, being a citizen of the United States, without the limits thereof, fits out and arms, or attempts to fit out and arm or is concerned in furnishing, fitting out, or arming any private vessel of war or privateer, with intent that such vessel shall be employed to cruise or commit hostilities upon the citizens of the United States or their property; or

Whoever takes the command of or enters on board of any such vessel with such intent; or

Whoever purchases any interest in any such vessel with a view to share in the profits thereof—

Shall be fined under this title or imprisoned not more than ten years, or both.

(June 25, 1948, c. 645, 62 Stat. 774; Sept. 13, 1994, Pub.L. 103–322, Title XXXIII, § 330016(1)(L), 108 Stat. 2147.)

§ 1655. Assault on commander as piracy

Whoever, being a seaman, lays violent hands upon his commander, to hinder and prevent his fighting in defense of his vessel or the goods intrusted to him, is a pirate, and shall be imprisoned for life.

(June 25, 1948, c. 645, 62 Stat. 774.)

§ 1656. Conversion or surrender of vessel

Whoever, being a captain or other officer or mariner of a vessel upon the high seas or on any other waters within the admiralty and maritime jurisdiction of the United States, piratically or feloniously runs away with such vessel, or with any goods or merchandise thereof, to the value of $50 or over; or

Whoever yields up such vessel voluntarily to any pirate—

Shall be fined under this title or imprisoned not more than ten years, or both.

(June 25, 1948, c. 645, 62 Stat. 774; Sept. 13, 1994, Pub.L. 103–322, Title XXXIII, § 330016(1)(L), 108 Stat. 2147.)

§ 1657. Corruption of seamen and confederating with pirates

Whoever attempts to corrupt any commander, master, officer, or mariner to yield up or to run away with any vessel, or any goods, wares, or merchandise, or to turn pirate or to go over to or confederate with pirates, or in any wise to trade with any pirate, knowing him to be such; or

Whoever furnishes such pirate with any ammunition, stores, or provisions of any kind; or

Whoever fits out any vessel knowingly and, with a design to trade with, supply, or correspond with any pirate or robber upon the seas; or

Whoever consults, combines, confederates, or corresponds with any pirate or robber upon the seas, knowing him to be guilty of any piracy or robbery; or

Whoever, being a seaman, confines the master of any vessel—

Shall be fined under this title or imprisoned not more than three years, or both.

(June 25, 1948, c. 645, 62 Stat. 775; Sept. 13, 1994, Pub.L. 103–322, Title XXXIII, § 330016(1)(H), 108 Stat. 2147.)

HISTORICAL AND STATUTORY NOTES

Codifications

Pub.L. 101–647, Title XXV, § 2527(b), Nov. 29, 1990, 104 Stat. 4877, purported to amend this section by inserting "section 11, 12, or 13 of the Federal Deposit Insurance Act" after "consideration of any action brought under", which amendment could not be executed to the text of this section. Such amendment was probably intended to amend section 1657 of Title 28, Judiciary and Judicial Procedure.

§ 1658. Plunder of distressed vessel

(a) Whoever plunders, steals, or destroys any money, goods, merchandise, or other effects from or belonging to any vessel in distress, or wrecked, lost, stranded, or cast away, upon the sea, or upon any reef, shoal, bank, or rocks of the sea, or in any other place within the admiralty and maritime jurisdiction of the United States, shall be fined under this title or imprisoned not more than ten years, or both.

(b) Whoever willfully obstructs the escape of any person endeavoring to save his life from such vessel, or the wreck thereof; or

Whoever holds out or shows any false light, or extinguishes any true light, with intent to bring any vessel sailing upon the sea into danger or distress or shipwreck—

Shall be imprisoned not less than ten years and may be imprisoned for life.

(June 25, 1948, c. 645, 62 Stat. 775; Sept. 13, 1994, Pub.L. 103–322, Title XXXIII, § 330016(1)(K), 108 Stat. 2147.)

§ 1659. Attack to plunder vessel

Whoever, upon the high seas or other waters within the admiralty and maritime jurisdiction of the United States, by surprise or open force, maliciously attacks or sets upon any vessel belonging to another, with an intent unlawfully to plunder the same, or to despoil any owner thereof of any moneys, goods, or merchandise laden on board thereof, shall be fined under this title or imprisoned not more than ten years, or both.

(June 25, 1948, c. 645, 62 Stat. 775; Sept. 13, 1994, Pub.L. 103–322, Title XXXIII, § 330016(1)(K), 108 Stat. 2147.)

§ 1660. Receipt of pirate property

Whoever, without lawful authority, receives or takes into custody any vessel, goods, or other property, feloniously taken by any robber or pirate against the laws of the United States, knowing the same to have been feloniously taken, shall be imprisoned not more than ten years.

(June 25, 1948, c. 645, 62 Stat. 775.)

§ 1661. Robbery ashore

Whoever, being engaged in any piratical cruise or enterprise, or being of the crew of any piratical vessel, lands from such vessel and commits robbery on shore, is a pirate, and shall be imprisoned for life.

(June 25, 1948, c. 645, 62 Stat. 775.)

CHAPTER 83—POSTAL SERVICE

§ 1691. Laws governing postal savings

All the safeguards provided by law for the protection of public moneys, and all statutes relating to the embezzlement, conversion, improper handling, retention, use, or disposal of postal and money-order funds, false returns of postal and money-order business, forgery, counterfeiting, alteration, improper use or handling of postal and money-order blanks, forms, vouchers, accounts, and records, and the dies, plates, and engravings therefor, with the punishments provided for such offenses are extended and made applicable to postal savings depository business and funds and related matters.

(June 25, 1948, c. 645, 62 Stat. 776.)

§ 1692. Foreign mail as United States mail

Every foreign mail, while being transported across the territory of the United States under authority of law, is mail of the United States, and any depredation thereon, or offense in respect thereto, shall be punishable as though it were United States mail.

(June 25, 1948, c. 645, 62 Stat. 776.)

§ 1693. Carriage of mail generally

Whoever, being concerned in carrying the mail, collects, receives, or carries any letter or packet, contrary to law, shall be fined under this title or imprisoned not more than thirty days, or both.

(June 25, 1948, c. 645, 62 Stat. 776; Sept. 13, 1994, Pub.L. 103–322, Title XXXIII, § 330016(1)(A), 108 Stat. 2146.)

§ 1694. Carriage of matter out of mail over post routes

Whoever, having charge or control of any conveyance operating by land, air, or water, which regularly performs trips at stated periods on any post route, or from one place to another between which the mail is regularly carried, carries, otherwise than in the mail, any letters or packets, except such as relate to some part of the cargo of such conveyance, or to the current business of the carrier, or to some article carried at the same time by the same conveyance, shall, except as otherwise provided by law, be fined under this title.

(June 25, 1948, c. 645, 62 Stat. 776; Sept. 13, 1994, Pub.L. 103–322, Title XXXIII, § 330016(1)(A), 108 Stat. 2146.)

HISTORICAL AND STATUTORY NOTES

Study of Private Carriage of Mail; Reports to President and Congress

Congressional findings of need for study and reevaluation of restrictions on private carriage of letters and packets contained in this section and submission by United States Postal Service of reports to President and Congress for modernization of law, regulations, and administrative practices, see section 7 of Pub.L. 91–375, set out as a note under section 601 of Title 39, Postal Service.

§ 1695. Carriage of matter out of mail on vessels

Whoever carries any letter or packet on board any vessel which carries the mail, otherwise than in such mail, shall, except as otherwise provided by law, be fined under this title or imprisoned not more than thirty days, or both.

(June 25, 1948, c. 645, 62 Stat. 777; Sept. 13, 1994, Pub.L. 103–322, Title XXXIII, § 330016(1)(A), 108 Stat. 2146.)

HISTORICAL AND STATUTORY NOTES

Study of Private Carriage of Mail; Reports to President and Congress

Congressional findings of need for study and reevaluation of restrictions on private carriage of letters and packets contained in this section and submission by United States Postal Service of reports to President and Congress for modernization of law, regulations, and administrative practices, see section 7 of Pub.L. 91–375, set out as a note under section 601 of Title 39, Postal Service.

§ 1696. Private express for letters and packets

(a) Whoever establishes any private express for the conveyance of letters or packets, or in any manner causes or provides for the conveyance of the same by regular trips or at stated periods over any post route which is or may be established by law, or from any city, town, or place to any other city, town, or place, between which the mail is regularly carried, shall be fined not more than $500 or imprisoned not more than six months, or both.

This section shall not prohibit any person from receiving and delivering to the nearest post office, postal car, or other authorized depository for mail matter any mail matter properly stamped.

(b) Whoever transmits by private express or other unlawful means, or delivers to any agent thereof, or deposits at any appointed place, for the purpose of being so transmitted any letter or packet, shall be fined under this title.

(c) This chapter shall not prohibit the conveyance or transmission of letters or packets by private hands without compensation, or by special messenger employed for the particular occasion only. Whenever more than twenty-five such letters or packets are conveyed or transmitted by such special messenger, the requirements of section 601 of title 39, shall be observed as to each piece.

(June 25, 1948, c. 645, 62 Stat. 777; Aug. 12, 1970, Pub.L. 91–375, § 6(j)(14), 84 Stat. 778; Sept. 13, 1994, Pub.L. 103–322, Title XXXIII, § 330016(1)(A), 108 Stat. 2146.)

HISTORICAL AND STATUTORY NOTES

Study of Private Carriage of Mail; Reports to President and Congress

Congressional findings of need for study and reevaluation of restrictions on private carriage of letters and packets contained in this section and submission by United States Postal Service of reports to President and Congress for modernization of law, regulations, and administrative practices, see section 7 of Pub.L. 91–375, set out as a note under section 601 of Title 39, Postal Service.

§ 1697. Transportation of persons acting as private express

Whoever, having charge or control of any conveyance operating by land, air, or water, knowingly conveys or knowingly permits the conveyance of any person acting or employed as a private express for the conveyance of letters or packets, and actually in possession of the same for the purpose of conveying them contrary to law, shall be fined under this title.

(June 25, 1948, c. 645, 62 Stat. 777; Sept. 13, 1994, Pub.L. 103–322, Title XXXIII, § 330016(1)(C), 108 Stat. 2146.)

§ 1698. Prompt delivery of mail from vessel

Whoever, having charge or control of any vessel passing between ports or places in the United States, and arriving at any such port or place where there is a post office, fails to deliver to the postmaster or at the post office, within three hours after his arrival, if in the daytime, and if at night, within two hours after the next sunrise, all letters and packages brought by him or within his power or control and not relating to the cargo, addressed to or destined for such port or place, shall be fined under this title.

(June 25, 1948, c. 645, 62 Stat. 777; Sept. 13, 1994, Pub.L. 103–322, Title XXXIII, §§ 330004(10), 330016(1)(C), 108 Stat. 2141, 2146.)

§ 1699. Certification of delivery from vessel

No vessel arriving within a port or collection district of the United States shall be allowed to make entry or break bulk until all letters on board are delivered to the nearest post office, except where waybilled for discharge at other ports in the United States at which the vessel is scheduled to call and the Postal Service does not determine that unreasonable delay in the mails will occur, and the master or other person having charge or control thereof has signed and sworn to the following declaration before the collector or other proper customs officer:

I, A.B., master ______, of the ______, arriving from ______, and now lying in the port of ______, do solemnly swear (or affirm) that I have to the best of my knowledge and belief delivered to the post office at ______ every letter and every bag, packet, or parcel of letters on board the said vessel during her last voyage, or in my possession or under my power or control, except where waybilled for discharge at other ports in the United States at which the said vessel is scheduled to call and which the Postal Service has not determined will be unreasonably delayed by remaining on board the said vessel for delivery at such ports.

Whoever, being the master or other person having charge or control of such vessel, breaks bulk before he has arranged for such delivery or onward carriage, shall be fined under this title.

(June 25, 1948, c. 645, 62 Stat. 777; July 3, 1952, c. 553, 66 Stat. 325; Aug. 12, 1970, Pub.L. 91–375, § 6(j)(15), 84 Stat. 778; Sept. 13, 1994, Pub.L. 103–322, Title XXXIII, § 330016(1)(B), 108 Stat. 2146.)

HISTORICAL AND STATUTORY NOTES

Effective and Applicability Provisions

1970 Acts. Amendment by Pub.L. 91–375 effective within 1 year after Aug. 12, 1970, on date established therefor by the Board of Governors of the United States Postal Service and published by it in the Federal Register, see section 15(a) of Pub.L. 91–375, set out as an Effective Date note preceding section 101 of Title 39, Postal Service.

Transfer of Functions

All offices of collector of customs, comptroller of customs, surveyor of customs, and appraiser of merchandise in the Bureau of Customs of the Department of the Treasury to which appointments were required to be made by the President with the advice and consent of the Senate were ordered abolished, to be terminated not later than Dec. 31, 1966. All functions of the offices so eliminated were already vested in the Secretary of the Treasury.

§ 1700. Desertion of mails

Whoever, having taken charge of any mail, voluntarily quits or deserts the same before he has delivered it into the post office at the termination of the route, or to some known mail carrier, messenger, agent, or other employee in the Postal Service authorized to receive the same, shall be fined under this title or imprisoned not more than one year, or both.

(June 25, 1948, c. 645, 62 Stat. 778; Sept. 13, 1994, Pub.L. 103–322, Title XXXIII, § 330016(1)(G), 108 Stat. 2147.)

§ 1701. Obstruction of mails generally

Whoever knowingly and willfully obstructs or retards the passage of the mail, or any carrier or conveyance carrying the mail, shall be fined under this title or imprisoned not more than six months, or both.

(June 25, 1948, c. 645, 62 Stat. 778; Sept. 13, 1994, Pub.L. 103–322, Title XXXIII, § 330016(1)(B), 108 Stat. 2146.)

§ 1702. Obstruction of correspondence

Whoever takes any letter, postal card, or package out of any post office or any authorized depository for mail matter, or from any letter or mail carrier, or which has been in any post office or authorized depository, or in the custody of any letter or mail carrier, before it has been delivered to the person to whom it was directed, with design to obstruct the correspondence, or to pry into the business or secrets of another, or opens, secretes, embezzles, or destroys the same, shall be fined under this title or imprisoned not more than five years, or both.

(June 25, 1948, c. 645, 62 Stat. 778; Sept. 13, 1994, Pub.L. 103–322, Title XXXIII, § 330016(1)(I), 108 Stat. 2147.)

§ 1703. Delay or destruction of mail or newspapers

(a) Whoever, being a Postal Service officer or employee, unlawfully secretes, destroys, detains, delays, or opens any letter, postal card, package, bag, or mail entrusted to him or which shall come into his possession, and which was intended to be conveyed by mail, or carried or delivered by any carrier or other employee of the Postal Service, or forwarded through or delivered from any post office or station thereof established by authority of the Postmaster General or the Postal Service, shall be fined under this title or imprisoned not more than five years, or both.

(b) Whoever, being a Postal Service officer or employee, improperly detains, delays, or destroys any newspaper, or permits any other person to detain, delay, or destroy the same, or opens, or permits any other person to open, any mail or package of newspapers not directed to the office where he is employed; or

Whoever, without authority, opens, or destroys any mail or package of newspapers not directed to him, shall be fined under this title or imprisoned not more than one year, or both.

(June 25, 1948, c. 645, 62 Stat. 778; May 24, 1949, c. 139, § 37, 63 Stat. 95; Aug. 12, 1970, Pub.L. 91–375, § 6(j) (16), 84 Stat. 778; Sept. 13, 1994, Pub.L. 103–322, Title XXXIII, § 330016(1)(B), (G), 108 Stat. 2146, 2147.)

HISTORICAL AND STATUTORY NOTES

Effective and Applicability Provisions

1970 Acts. Amendment by Pub.L. 91–375 effective within 1 year after Aug. 12, 1970, on date established therefore by the Board of Governors of the United States Postal Service and published by it in the Federal Register, see section 15(a) of Pub.L. 91–375, set out as an Effective Date note preceding section 101 of Title 39, Postal Service.

§ 1704. Keys or locks stolen or reproduced

Whoever steals, purloins, embezzles, or obtains by false pretense any key suited to any lock adopted by the Post Office Department or the Postal Service and in use on any of the mails or bags thereof, or any key to any lock box, lock drawer, or other authorized receptacle for the deposit or delivery of mail matter; or

Whoever knowingly and unlawfully makes, forges, or counterfeits any such key, or possesses any such mail lock or key with the intent unlawfully or improperly to use, sell, or otherwise dispose of the same, or to cause the same to be unlawfully or improperly used, sold, or otherwise disposed of; or

Whoever, being engaged as a contractor or otherwise in the manufacture of any such mail lock or key, delivers any finished or unfinished lock or the interior part thereof, or key, used or designed for use by the department, to any person not duly authorized under the hand of the Postmaster General and the seal of the Post Office Department or the Postal Service, to receive the same, unless the person receiving it is the contractor for furnishing the same or engaged in the manufacture thereof in the manner authorized by the contract, or the agent of such manufacturer—

Shall be fined under this title or imprisoned not more than ten years, or both.

(June 25, 1948, c. 645, 62 Stat. 778; Aug. 12, 1970, Pub.L. 91–375, § 6(j) (17), 84 Stat. 778; Sept. 13, 1994, Pub.L. 103–322, Title XXXIII, § 330016(1)(G), 108 Stat. 2147.)

HISTORICAL AND STATUTORY NOTES

Effective and Applicability Provisions

1970 Acts. Amendment by Pub.L. 91–375 effective within 1 year after Aug. 12, 1970, on date established therefor by the Board of Governors of the United States Postal Service and published by it in the Federal Register, see section 15(a) of Pub.L. 91–375, set out as an Effective Date note preceding section 101 of Title 39, Postal Service.

§ 1705. Destruction of letter boxes or mail

Whoever willfully or maliciously injures, tears down or destroys any letter box or other receptacle intended or used for the receipt or delivery of mail on any mail route, or breaks open the same or willfully or maliciously injures, defaces or destroys any mail deposited therein, shall be fined under this title or imprisoned not more than three years, or both.

(June 25, 1948, c. 645, 62 Stat. 779; May 24, 1949, c. 139, § 38, 63 Stat. 95; Sept. 13, 1994, Pub.L. 103–322, Title XXXIII, § 330016(1)(H), 108 Stat. 2147; Nov. 2, 2002, Pub.L. 107–273, Div. B, Title III, § 3002(a)(2), 116 Stat. 1805.)

§ 1706. Injury to mail bags

Whoever tears, cuts, or otherwise injures any mail bag, pouch, or other thing used or designed for use in the conveyance of the mail, or draws or breaks any staple or loosens any part of any lock, chain, or strap attached thereto, with intent to rob or steal any such mail, or to render the same insecure, shall be fined under this title or imprisoned not more than three years, or both.

(June 25, 1948, c. 645, 62 Stat. 779; Sept. 13, 1994, Pub.L. 103–322, Title XXXIII, § 330016(1)(H), 108 Stat. 2147.)

§ 1707. Theft of property used by Postal Service

Whoever steals, purloins, or embezzles any property used by the Postal Service, or appropriates any such property to his own or any other than its proper use, or conveys away any such property to the hindrance or detriment of the public service, shall be fined under this title or imprisoned not more than three years, or both; but if the value of such property does not exceed $1,000, he shall be fined under this title or imprisoned not more than one year, or both.

(June 25, 1948, c. 645, 62 Stat. 779; Aug. 12, 1970, Pub.L. 91–375, § 6(j)(18), 84 Stat. 778; Sept. 13, 1994, Pub.L. 103–322, Title XXXIII, § 330016(1)(G), (H), 108 Stat. 2147; Oct. 11, 1996, Pub.L. 104–294, Title VI, § 606(a), 110 Stat. 3511.)

HISTORICAL AND STATUTORY NOTES

Effective and Applicability Provisions

1970 Acts. Amendment by Pub.L. 91–375 effective within 1 year after Aug. 12, 1970, on date established therefor by the Board of Governors of the United States Postal Service and published by it in the Federal Register, see section 15(a) of Pub.L. 91–375, set out as an Effective Date note preceding section 101 of Title 39, Postal Service.

§ 1708. Theft or receipt of stolen mail matter generally

Whoever steals, takes, or abstracts, or by fraud or deception obtains, or attempts so to obtain, from or out of any mail, post office, or station thereof, letter box, mail receptacle, or any mail route or other authorized depository for mail matter, or from a letter or mail carrier, any letter, postal card, package, bag, or mail, or abstracts or removes from any such letter, package, bag, or mail, any article or thing contained therein, or secretes, embezzles, or destroys any such letter, postal card, package, bag, or mail, or any article or thing contained therein; or

Whoever steals, takes, or abstracts, or by fraud or deception obtains any letter, postal card, package, bag, or mail, or any article or thing contained therein which has been left for collection upon or adjacent to a collection box or other authorized depository of mail matter; or

Whoever buys, receives, or conceals, or unlawfully has in his possession, any letter, postal card, package, bag, or mail, or any article or thing contained therein, which has been so stolen, taken, embezzled, or abstracted, as herein described, knowing the same to have been stolen, taken, embezzled, or abstracted—

Shall be fined under this title or imprisoned not more than five years, or both.

(June 25, 1948, c. 645, 62 Stat. 779; May 24, 1949, c. 139, § 39, 63 Stat. 95; July 1, 1952, c. 535, 66 Stat. 314; Sept. 13, 1994, Pub.L. 103–322, Title XXXIII, § 330016(1)(I), 108 Stat. 2147.)

§ 1709. Theft of mail matter by officer or employee

Whoever, being a Postal Service officer or employee, embezzles any letter, postal card, package, bag, or mail, or any article or thing contained therein entrusted to him or which comes into his possession intended to be conveyed by mail, or carried or delivered by any carrier, messenger, agent, or other person employed in any department of the Postal Service, or forwarded through or delivered from any post office or station thereof established by authority of the Postmaster

General or of the Postal Service; or steals, abstracts, or removes from any such letter, package, bag, or mail, any article or thing contained therein, shall be fined under this title or imprisoned not more than five years, or both.

(June 25, 1948, c. 645, 62 Stat. 780; Aug. 12, 1970, Pub.L. 91–375, § 6(j) (19) (A), 84 Stat. 778; Sept. 13, 1994, Pub.L. 103–322, Title XXXIII, § 330016(1)(I), 108 Stat. 2147.)

HISTORICAL AND STATUTORY NOTES

Effective and Applicability Provisions

1970 Acts. Amendment by Pub.L. 91–375 effective within 1 year after Aug. 12, 1970, on date established therefor by the Board of Governors of the United States Postal Service and published by it in the Federal Register, see section 15(a) of Pub.L. 91–375, set out as an Effective Date note preceding section 101 of Title 39, Postal Service.

§ 1710. Theft of newspapers

Whoever, being a Postal Service officer or employee, takes or steals any newspaper or package of newspapers from any post office or from any person having custody thereof, shall be fined under this title or imprisoned not more than one year, or both.

(June 25, 1948, c. 645, 62 Stat. 780; Aug. 12, 1970, Pub.L. 91–375, § 6(j) (20), 84 Stat. 778; Sept. 13, 1994, Pub.L. 103–322, Title XXXIII, § 330016(1)(B), 108 Stat. 2146.)

HISTORICAL AND STATUTORY NOTES

Effective and Applicability Provisions

1970 Acts. Amendment by Pub.L. 91–375 effective within 1 year after Aug. 12, 1970, on date established therefor by the Board of Governors of the United States Postal Service and published by it in the Federal Register, see section 15(a) of Pub.L. 91–375, set out as an Effective Date note preceding section 101 of Title 39, Postal Service.

§ 1711. Misappropriation of postal funds

Whoever, being a Postal Service officer or employee, loans, uses, pledges, hypothecates, or converts to his own use, or deposits in any bank, or exchanges for other funds or property, except as authorized by law, any money or property coming into his hands or under his control in any manner, in the execution or under color of his office, employment, or service, whether or not the same shall be the money or property of the United States; or fails or refuses to remit to or deposit in the Treasury of the United States or in a designated depository, or to account for or turn over to the proper officer or agent, any such money or property, when required to do so by law or the regulations of the Postal Service, or upon demand or order of the Postal Service, either directly or through a duly authorized officer or agent, is guilty of embezzlement; and every such person, as well as every other person advising or knowingly participating therein, shall be fined under this title or in a sum equal to the amount or value of the money or property embezzled, whichever is greater, or imprisoned not more than ten years, or both; but if the amount or value thereof does not exceed $1,000, he shall be fined under this title or imprisoned not more than one year, or both.

This section shall not prohibit any Postal Service officer or employee from depositing, under the direction of the Postal Service, in a national bank designated by the Secretary of the Treasury for that purpose, to his own credit as Postal Service officer or employee, any funds in his charge, nor prevent his negotiating drafts or other evidences of debt through such bank, or through United States disbursing officers, or otherwise, when instructed or required so to do by the Postal Service, for the purpose of remitting surplus funds from one post office to another.

(June 25, 1948, c. 645, 62 Stat. 780; Aug. 12, 1970, Pub.L. 91–375, § 6(j) (21), 84 Stat. 778; Sept. 13, 1994, Pub.L. 103–322, Title XXXIII, § 330016(1)(H), (2)(G), 108 Stat. 2147, 2148; Oct. 11, 1996, Pub.L. 104–294, Title VI, § 606(a), 110 Stat. 3511.)

HISTORICAL AND STATUTORY NOTES

Effective and Applicability Provisions

1970 Acts. Amendment by Pub.L. 91–375 effective within 1 year after Aug. 12, 1970, on date established therefor by the Board of Governors of the United States Postal Service and published by it in the Federal Register, see section 15(a) of Pub.L. 91–375, set out as an Effective Date note preceding section 101 of Title 39, Postal Service.

§ 1712. Falsification of postal returns to increase compensation

Whoever, being a Postal Service officer or employee, makes a false return, statement, or account to any officer of the United States, or makes a false entry in any record, book, or account, required by law or the rules or regulations of the Postal Service to be kept in respect of the business or operations of any post office or other branch of the Postal Service, for the purpose of fraudulently increasing his compensation or the compensation of the postmaster or any employee in a post office; or

Whoever, being a Postal Service officer or employee in any post office or station thereof, for the purpose of increasing the emoluments or compensation of his office, induces, or attempts to induce, any person to deposit mail matter in, or forward in any manner for mailing at, the office where such officer or employee is employed, knowing such matter to be properly mailable at another post office—

Shall be fined under this title or imprisoned not more than two years, or both.

(June 25, 1948, c. 645, 62 Stat. 780; Aug. 12, 1970, Pub.L. 91–375, § 6(j) (22), 84 Stat. 779; Sept. 13, 1994, Pub.L. 103–322, Title XXXIII, § 330016(1)(G), 108 Stat. 2147.)

HISTORICAL AND STATUTORY NOTES

Effective and Applicability Provisions

1970 Acts. Amendment by Pub.L. 91–375 effective within 1 year after Aug. 12, 1970, on date established therefor by the Board of Governors of the United States Postal Service and published by it in the Federal Register, see section 15(a) of Pub.L. 91–375, set out as an Effective Date note preceding section 101 of Title 39, Postal Service.

§ 1713. Issuance of money orders without payment

Whoever, being an officer or employee of the Postal Service, issues a money order without having previously received the money therefor, shall be fined under this title.

(June 25, 1948, c. 645, 62 Stat. 781; Aug. 12, 1970, Pub.L. 91–375, § 6(j)(23), 84 Stat. 779; Sept. 13, 1994, Pub.L. 103–322, Title XXXIII, § 330016(1)(G), 108 Stat. 2147.)

HISTORICAL AND STATUTORY NOTES

Effective and Applicability Provisions

1970 Acts. Amendment by Pub.L. 91–375 effective within 1 year after Aug. 12, 1970, on date established therefor by the Board of Governors of the United States Postal Service and published by it in the Federal Register, see section 15(a) of Pub.L. 91–375, set out as an Effective Date note preceding section 101 of Title 39, Postal Service.

[§ 1714. Repealed. Pub.L. 101–647, Title XII, § 1210(b), Nov. 29, 1990, 104 Stat. 4832]

HISTORICAL AND STATUTORY NOTES

Section, Act June 25, 1948, c. 645, 62 Stat. 781, prohibited information relating to foreign divorces from being conveyed through the mail, and set forth penalties for violations.

§ 1715. Firearms as nonmailable; regulations

Pistols, revolvers, and other firearms capable of being concealed on the person are nonmailable and shall not be deposited in or carried by the mails or delivered by any officer or employee of the Postal Service. Such articles may be conveyed in the mails, under such regulations as the Postal Service shall prescribe, for use in connection with their official duty, to officers of the Army, Navy, Air Force, Coast Guard, Marine Corps, or Organized Reserve Corps; to officers of the National Guard or Militia of a State, Territory, Commonwealth, Possession, or District; to officers of the United States or of a State, Territory, Commonwealth, Possession, or District whose official duty is to serve warrants of arrest or commitments; to employees of the Postal Service; to officers and employees of enforcement agencies of the United States; and to watchmen engaged in guarding the property of the United States, a State, Territory, Commonwealth, Possession, or District. Such articles also may be conveyed in the mails to manufacturers of firearms or bona fide dealers therein in customary trade shipments, including such articles for repairs or replacement of parts, from one to the other, under such regulations as the Postal Service shall prescribe.

Whoever knowingly deposits for mailing or delivery, or knowingly causes to be delivered by mail according to the direction thereon, or at any place to which it is directed to be delivered by the person to whom it is addressed, any pistol, revolver, or firearm declared nonmailable by this section, shall be fined under this title or imprisoned not more than two years, or both.

(June 25, 1948, c. 645, 62 Stat. 781; May 24, 1949, c. 139, § 40, 63 Stat. 95; Aug. 12, 1970, Pub.L. 91–375, § 6(j)(24), 84 Stat. 779; Sept. 13, 1994, Pub.L. 103–322, Title XXXIII, § 330016(1)(H), 108 Stat. 2147; Oct. 11, 1996, Pub.L. 104–294, Title VI, § 607(f), 110 Stat. 3511.)

HISTORICAL AND STATUTORY NOTES

Effective and Applicability Provisions

1970 Acts. Amendment by Pub.L. 91–375 effective within 1 year after Aug. 12, 1970, on date established therefor by the Board of Governors of the United States Postal Service and published by it in the Federal Register, see section 15(a) of Pub.L. 91–375, set out as an Effective Date note preceding section 101 of Title 39, Postal Service.

Modification of Other Laws

Section 104 of Pub.L. 90–618 provided that:

"Nothing in this title or the amendment made thereby [amending section 921 et seq. of this title] shall be construed as modifying or affecting any provision of—

"(a) the National Firearms Act (chapter 53 of the Internal Revenue Code of 1954) [section 5801 et seq. of Title 26];

"(b) section 414 of the Mutual Security Act of 1954 (22 U.S.C.1934) [section 1934 of Title 22], as amended, relating to munitions control; or

"(c) section 1715 of title 18, United States Code [this section], relating to nonmailable firearms."

Section 904 of Pub.L. 90–351 provided that:

"Nothing in this title or amendment made thereby [enacting section 921 et seq. of this title and provisions set out as notes under section 921 of this title] shall be construed as modifying or affecting any provision of—

"(a) the National Firearms Act (chapter 53 of the Internal Revenue Code of 1954); or

"(b) section 414 of the Mutual Security Act of 1954 (22 U.S.C.1934), as amended, relating to munitions control; or

"(c) section 1715 of title 18, United States Code [this section], relating to nonmailable firearms."

§ 1716. Injurious articles as nonmailable

(a) All kinds of poison, and all articles and compositions containing poison, and all poisonous animals, insects, reptiles, and all explosives, hazardous materials, inflammable materials, infernal machines, and mechanical, chemical, or other devices or compositions which may ignite or explode, and all disease germs or scabs, and all other natural or artificial articles, compositions, or material which may kill or injure another, or injure the mails or other property, whether or not sealed as first-class matter, are nonmailable matter and shall not be conveyed in the mails or delivered from any post office or station thereof, nor by any officer or employee of the Postal Service.

(b) The Postal Service may permit the transmission in the mails, under such rules and regulations as it shall prescribe as to preparation and packing, of any such articles which are not outwardly or of their own force dangerous or injurious to life, health, or property.

(c) The Postal Service is authorized and directed to permit the transmission in the mails, under regulations to be prescribed by it, of live scorpions which are to be used for purposes of medical research or for the manufacture of antivenom. Such regulations shall include such provisions with respect to the packaging of such live scorpions for transmission in the mails as the Postal Service deems necessary or desirable for the protection of Postal Service personnel and of the public generally and for ease of handling by such personnel and by any individual connected with such research or manufacture. Nothing contained in this paragraph shall be construed to authorize the transmission in the mails of live scorpions by means of aircraft engaged in the carriage of passengers for compensation or hire.

(d) The transmission in the mails of poisonous drugs and medicines may be limited by the Postal Service to shipments of such articles from the manufacturer thereof or dealer therein to licensed physicians, surgeons, dentists, pharmacists, druggists, cosmetologists, barbers, and veterinarians under such rules and regulations as it shall prescribe.

(e) The transmission in the mails of poisons for scientific use, and which are not outwardly dangerous or of their own force dangerous or injurious to life, health, or property, may be limited by the Postal Service to shipments of such articles between the manufacturers thereof, dealers therein, bona fide research or experimental scientific laboratories, and such other persons who are employees of the Federal, a State, or local government, whose official duties are comprised, in whole or in part, of the use of such poisons, and who are designated by the head of the agency in which they are employed to receive or send such articles, under such rules and regulations as the Postal Service shall prescribe.

(f) All spirituous, vinous, malted, fermented, or other intoxicating liquors of any kind are nonmailable and shall not be deposited in or carried through the mails.

(g) All knives having a blade which opens automatically (1) by hand pressure applied to a button or other device in the handle of the knife, or (2) by operation of inertia, gravity, or both, are nonmailable and shall not be deposited in or carried by the mails or delivered by any officer or employee of the Postal Service. Such knives may be conveyed in the mails, under such regulations as the Postal Service shall prescribe—

(1) to civilian or Armed Forces supply or procurement officers and employees of the Federal Government ordering, procuring, or purchasing such knives in connection with the activities of the Federal Government;

(2) to supply or procurement officers of the National Guard, the Air National Guard, or militia of a State ordering, procuring, or purchasing such knives in connection with the activities of such organizations;

(3) to supply or procurement officers or employees of any State, or any political subdivision of a State or Territory, ordering, procuring, or purchasing such knives in connection with the activities of such government; and

(4) to manufacturers of such knives or bona fide dealers therein in connection with any shipment made pursuant to an order from any person designated in paragraphs (1), (2), and (3).

The Postal Service may require, as a condition of conveying any such knife in the mails, that any person proposing to mail such knife explain in writing to the satisfaction of the Postal Service that the mailing of such knife will not be in violation of this section.

(h) Any advertising, promotional, or sales matter which solicits or induces the mailing of anything declared nonmailable by this section is likewise nonmailable unless such matter contains wrapping or packaging instructions which are in accord with regulations promulgated by the Postal Service.

(i)(1) Any ballistic knife shall be subject to the same restrictions and penalties provided under subsection (g) for knives described in the first sentence of that subsection.

(2) As used in this subsection, the term "ballistic knife" means a knife with a detachable blade that is propelled by a spring-operated mechanism.

(j)(1) Whoever knowingly deposits for mailing or delivery, or knowingly causes to be delivered by mail, according to the direction thereon, or at any place at which it is directed to be delivered by the person to whom it is addressed, anything declared nonmailable by this section, unless in accordance with the rules and regulations authorized to be prescribed by the Postal Service, shall be fined under this title or imprisoned not more than one year, or both.

(2) Whoever knowingly deposits for mailing or delivery, or knowingly causes to be delivered by mail, according to the direction thereon or at any place to which it is directed to be delivered by the person to whom it is addressed, anything declared nonmailable by this section, whether or not transmitted in accordance with the rules and regulations authorized to be prescribed by the Postal Service, with intent to kill or injure another, or injure the mails or other property, shall be fined under this title or imprisoned not more than twenty years, or both.

(3) Whoever is convicted of any crime prohibited by this section, which has resulted in the death of any person, shall be subject also to the death penalty or to imprisonment for life.

(k) For purposes of this section, the term "State" includes a State of the United States, the District of Columbia, and any commonwealth, territory, or possession of the United States.

(June 25, 1948, c. 645, 62 Stat. 781; May 8, 1952, c. 246, 66 Stat. 67; June 29, 1955, c. 224, 69 Stat. 191; Sept. 2, 1957, Pub.L. 85–268, 71 Stat. 594; Aug. 12, 1958, Pub.L. 85–623, § 5, 72 Stat. 562; Aug. 12, 1970, Pub.L. 91–375, § 6(j)(25), 84 Stat. 779; Dec. 15, 1971, Pub.L. 92–191, § 1, 85 Stat. 647; Oct. 27, 1986, Pub.L. 99–570, Title X, § 10003, 100 Stat. 3207–167; Sept. 13, 1994, Pub.L. 103–322, Title VI, § 60003(a)(7), Title XXXIII, § 330016(1)(H), 108 Stat. 1969, 2147; Oct. 11, 1996, Pub.L. 104–294, Title VI, § 607(g), 110 Stat. 3511; Nov. 2, 2002, Pub.L. 107–273, Div. B, Title IV, § 4002(b)(2), (6), 116 Stat. 1807; Dec. 20, 2006, Pub.L. 109–435, Title X, § 1008(d), 120 Stat. 3261.)

HISTORICAL AND STATUTORY NOTES

Effective and Applicability Provisions

2002 Acts. Amendment by section 4002(b)(2) of Pub.L. 107–273, as therein provided, effective Oct. 11, 1996, which is the date of enactment of Pub.L. 104–294, to which such amendment relates.

1986 Acts. Amendment by Pub.L. 99–570 effective 30 days after Oct. 27, 1986, see section 10004 of Pub.L. 99–570, set out as a note under section 1245 of Title 15, Commerce and Trade.

1971 Acts. Section 3 of Pub.L. 92–191 provided that: "The amendments made by this Act [adding subsec. (h) of this section and subsec. (g) of section 3001 of Title 39, Postal Service] shall become effective at the beginning of the third calendar month following the date of enactment of this Act [Dec. 15, 1971] or on the date section 3001 of title 39, United States Code [section 3001 of Title 39], becomes effective [July 1, 1971] pursuant to section 15(a) of Public Law 91–375 [set out as an Effective Date note preceding section 101 of Title 39], whichever is the later."

1970 Acts. Amendment by Pub.L. 91–375 effective within 1 year after Aug. 12, 1970, on date established therefor by the Board of Governors of the United States Postal Service and published by it in the Federal Register, see section 15(a) of Pub.L. 91–375, set out as an Effective Date note preceding section 101 of Title 39, Postal Service.

1958 Acts. Amendment by Pub.L. 85–623 effective on the sixtieth day after Aug. 12, 1958, see Effective Date note set out under section 1241 of Title 15, Commerce and Trade.

Hazardous Substances

Federal Hazardous Substances Act as not modifying this section, see Pub.L. 86–613, § 17, July 12, 1960, 74 Stat. 380, set out as a note under section 1261 of Title 15, Commerce and Trade.

§ 1716A. Nonmailable locksmithing devices and motor vehicle master keys

(a) Whoever knowingly deposits for mailing or delivery, or knowingly causes to be delivered by mail according to the direction thereon, or at any place to which it is directed to be delivered by the person to whom it is addressed, any matter declared to be nonmailable by section 3002 of title 39, shall be fined under this title or imprisoned not more than one year, or both.

(b) Whoever knowingly deposits for mailing or delivery, causes to be delivered by mail, or causes to be delivered by any interstate mailing or delivery other than by the United States Postal Service, any matter declared to be nonmailable by section 3002a of title 39, shall be fined under this title, imprisoned not more than one year, or both.

(Added Pub.L. 90–560, § 2(1), Oct. 12, 1968, 82 Stat. 997, and amended Pub.L. 91–375, § 6(j) (26), Aug. 12, 1970, 84 Stat. 780; Pub.L. 100–690, Title VII, § 7090(c), Nov. 18, 1988, 102 Stat. 4410; Pub.L. 101–647, Title XXXV, § 3551, Nov. 29, 1990, 104 Stat. 4926.)

HISTORICAL AND STATUTORY NOTES

Effective and Applicability Provisions

1970 Acts. Amendment by Pub.L. 91–375 effective within 1 year after Aug. 12, 1970, on date established therefor by the Board of Governors of the United States Postal Service and published by it in the Federal Register, see section 15(a) of Pub.L. 91–375, set out as an Effective Date note preceding section 101 of Title 39, Postal Service.

1968 Acts. Section 3 of Pub.L. 90–560 provided in part that this section is effective on the sixtieth day after Oct. 12, 1968.

§ 1716B. Nonmailable plants

Whoever knowingly deposits for mailing or delivery, or knowingly causes to be delivered by mail, according to the direction thereon, or at any place at which it is directed to be delivered by the person to whom it is addressed, anything declared nonmailable by section 3014(b) of title 39, unless in accordance with the rules and regulations prescribed by the Postal Service under section 3014(c) of such title, shall be fined under this title, or imprisoned not more than one year, or both.

(Added Pub.L. 100–574, § 1(b)(1), Oct. 31, 1988, 102 Stat. 2893.)

HISTORICAL AND STATUTORY NOTES

Effective and Applicability Provisions

1988 Acts. Section effective on the earlier of the 366th day after Oct. 31, 1988, or the first date as of which all required rules and regulations have been first published in the Federal Register, see section 4 of Pub.L. 100–574, set out as the note under section 3014 of Title 39, Postal Service.

§ 1716C. Forged agricultural certifications

Whoever forges or counterfeits any certification authorized under any rules or regulations prescribed under section 3014(c) of title 39 with intent to make it appear that such is a genuine certification, or makes or knowingly uses or sells, or possesses with intent to use or sell, any forged or counterfeited certification so authorized, or device for imprinting any such certification, shall be fined under this title, or imprisoned not more than one year, or both.

(Added Pub.L. 100–574, § 2(a), Oct. 31, 1988, 102 Stat. 2893.)

HISTORICAL AND STATUTORY NOTES

Effective and Applicability Provisions

1988 Acts. Section effective on the earlier of the 366th day after Oct. 31, 1988, or the first date as of which all required rules and regulations have been first published in the Federal Register, see section 4 of Pub.L. 100–574, set out as the note under section 3014 of Title 39, Postal Service.

§ 1716D. Nonmailable injurious animals, plant pests, plants, and illegally taken fish, wildlife, and plants

A person who knowingly deposits for mailing or delivery, or knowingly causes to be delivered by mail, according to the direction thereon, or at any place at which it is directed to be delivered by the person to whom it is addressed, anything that section 3015 of title 39 declares to be nonmailable matter shall be fined under this title, imprisoned not more than 1 year, or both.

(Added Pub.L. 103–322, Title XXXII, § 320108(b)(1), Sept. 13, 1994, 108 Stat. 2113.)

§ 1717. Letters and writings as nonmailable

(a) Every letter, writing, circular, postal card, picture, print, engraving, photograph, newspaper, pamphlet, book, or other publication, matter or thing, in violation of sections 499, 506, 793, 794, 915, 954, 956, 957, 960, 964, 1017, 1542, 1543, 1544 or 2388 of this title or which contains any matter advocating or urging treason, insurrection, or forcible resistance to any law of the United States is nonmailable and shall not be conveyed in the mails or delivered from any post office or by any letter carrier.

(b) Whoever uses or attempts to use the mails or Postal Service for the transmission of any matter declared by this section to be nonmailable, shall be fined under this title or imprisoned not more than ten years or both.

(June 25, 1948, c. 645, 62 Stat. 782; Sept. 2, 1960, Pub.L. 86–682, § 12(b), 74 Stat. 708; Aug. 12, 1970, Pub.L. 91–375, § 6(j) (27), 84 Stat. 780; Nov. 29, 1990, Pub.L. 101–647, Title XXXV, § 3552(a), 104 Stat. 4926; Sept. 13, 1994, Pub.L. 103–322, Title XXXIII, § 330016(1)(K), 108 Stat. 2147.)

HISTORICAL AND STATUTORY NOTES

Effective and Applicability Provisions

1970 Acts. Amended by Pub.L. 91–375 effective within 1 year after Aug. 12, 1970, on date established therefor by the Board of Governors of the United States Postal Service and published by it in the Federal Register, see section 15(a) of Pub.L. 91–375, set out as an Effective Date note preceding section 101 of Title 39, Postal Service.

[§ 1718. Repealed. Pub.L. 101–647, Title XII, § 1210(c), Nov. 29, 1990, 104 Stat. 4832]

HISTORICAL AND STATUTORY NOTES

Section, Act June 25, 1948, c. 645, 62 Stat. 782; Aug. 12, 1970, Pub.L. 91–375, § 6(j)(28), 84 Stat. 780, related to penalties for putting through the mail system envelopes or wrappers with libelous matters written on them.

§ 1719. Franking privilege

Whoever makes use of any official envelope, label, or indorsement authorized by law, to avoid the payment of postage or registry fee on his private letter, packet, package, or other matter in the mail, shall be fined under this title.

(June 25, 1948, c. 645, 62 Stat. 783; Sept. 13, 1994, Pub.L. 103–322, Title XXXIII, § 330016(1)(F), 108 Stat. 2147.)

§ 1720. Canceled stamps and envelopes

Whoever uses or attempts to use in payment of postage, any canceled postage stamp, whether the same has been used or not, or removes, attempts to remove, or assists in removing, the canceling or defacing marks from any postage stamp, or the superscription from any stamped envelope, or postal card, that has once been used in payment of postage, with the intent to use the same for a like purpose, or to sell or offer to sell the same, or knowingly possesses any such postage stamp, stamped envelope, or postal card, with intent to use the same or knowingly sells or offers to sell any such postage stamp, stamped envelope, or postal card, or uses or attempts to use the same in payment of postage; or

Whoever unlawfully and willfully removes from any mail matter any stamp attached thereto in payment of postage; or

Whoever knowingly uses in payment of postage, any postage stamp, postal card, or stamped envelope, issued in pursuance of law, which has already been used for a like purpose—

Shall be fined under this title or imprisoned not more than one year, or both; but if he is a person employed in the Postal Service, he shall be fined under this title or imprisoned not more than three years, or both.

(June 25, 1948, c. 645, 62 Stat. 783; Sept. 13, 1994, Pub.L. 103–322, Title XXXIII, § 330016(1)(G), 108 Stat. 2147.)

§ 1721. Sale or pledge of stamps

Whoever, being a Postal Service officer or employee, knowingly and willfully: uses or disposes of postage stamps, stamped envelopes, or postal cards entrusted to his care or custody in the payment of debts, or in the purchase of merchandise or other salable articles, or pledges or hypothecates the same or sells or disposes of them except for cash; or sells or disposes of postage stamps or postal cards for any larger or less sum than the values indicated on their faces; or sells or disposes of stamped envelopes for a larger or less sum than is charged therefor by the Postal Service for like quantities; or sells or disposes of postage stamps, stamped envelopes, or postal cards at any point or place outside of the delivery of the office where such officer or employee is employed; or for the purpose of increasing the emoluments, or compensation of any such officer or employee, inflates or induces the inflation of the receipts of any post office or any station or branch thereof; or sells or disposes of postage stamps, stamped envelopes, or postal cards, otherwise than as provided by law or the regulations of the Postal Service; shall be fined under this title or imprisoned not more than one year, or both.

(June 25, 1948, c. 645, 62 Stat. 783; Aug. 1, 1956, c. 818, 70 Stat. 784; Aug. 12, 1970, Pub.L. 91–375, § 6(j) (29), 84 Stat. 780; Sept. 13, 1994, Pub.L. 103–322, Title XXXIII, § 330016(1)(G), 108 Stat. 2147.)

HISTORICAL AND STATUTORY NOTES

Effective and Applicability Provisions

1970 Acts. Amendment by Pub.L. 91–375 effective within 1 year after Aug. 12, 1970, on date established therefor by the Board of Governors of the United States Postal Service and published by it in the Federal Register, see section 15(a) of Pub.L. 91–375, set out as an Effective Date note preceding section 101 of Title 39, Postal Service.

§ 1722. False evidence to secure second-class rate

Whoever knowingly submits to the Postal Service or to any officer or employee of the Postal Service, any false evidence relative to any publication for the purpose of securing the admission thereof at the second-class rate, for transportation in the mails, shall be fined under this title.

(June 25, 1948, c. 645, 62 Stat. 783; Aug. 12, 1970, Pub.L. 91–375, § 6(j) (30), 84 Stat. 780; Sept. 13, 1994, Pub.L. 103–322, Title XXXIII, § 330016(1)(G), 108 Stat. 2147.)

HISTORICAL AND STATUTORY NOTES

Effective and Applicability Provisions

1970 Acts. Amendment by Pub.L. 91–375 effective within 1 year after Aug. 12, 1970, on date established therefor by the Board of Governors of the United States Postal Service and published by it in the Federal Register, see section 15(a) of Pub.L. 91–375, set out as an Effective Date note preceding section 101 of Title 39, Postal Service.

§ 1723. Avoidance of postage by using lower class matter

Matter of the second, third, or fourth class containing any writing or printing in addition to the original matter, other than as authorized by law, shall not be admitted to the mails, nor delivered, except upon payment of postage for matter of the first class, deducting therefrom any amount which may have been prepaid by stamps affixed, unless by direction of a duly authorized officer of the Postal Service such postage shall be remitted.

Whoever knowingly conceals or incloses any matter of a higher class in that of a lower class, and deposits the same for conveyance by mail, at a less rate than would be charged for such higher class matter, shall be fined under this title.

(June 25, 1948, c. 645, 62 Stat. 784; Aug. 12, 1970, Pub.L. 91–375, § 6(j) (31), 84 Stat. 780; Sept. 13, 1994, Pub.L. 103–322, Title XXXIII, § 330016(1)(B), 108 Stat. 2146.)

HISTORICAL AND STATUTORY NOTES

Effective and Applicability Provisions

1970 Acts. Amendment by Pub.L. 91–375 effective within 1 year after Aug. 12, 1970, on date established therefor by the Board of Governors of the United States Postal Service and published by it in the Federal Register, see section 15(a) of Pub.L. 91–375, set out as an Effective Date note preceding section 101 of Title 39, Postal Service.

§ 1724. Postage on mail delivered by foreign vessels

Except as otherwise provided by treaty or convention the Postal Service may require the transportation by any steamship of mail between the United States and any foreign port at the compensation fixed under authority of law. Upon refusal by the master or the commander of such steamship or vessel to accept the mail, when tendered by the Postal Service or its representative, the collector or other officer of the port empowered to grant clearance, on notice of the refusal aforesaid, shall withhold clearance, until the collector or other officer of the port is informed by the Postal Service or its representative that the master or commander of the steamship or vessel has accepted the mail or that conveyance by his steamship or vessel is no longer required by the Postal Service.

(June 25, 1948, c. 645, 62 Stat. 784; Sept. 25, 1951, c. 413, § 1(4), 65 Stat. 336; Aug. 12, 1970, Pub.L. 91–375, § 6(j) (32), 84 Stat. 780.)

HISTORICAL AND STATUTORY NOTES

Effective and Applicability Provisions

1970 Acts. Amendment by Pub.L. 91–375 effective within 1 year after Aug. 12, 1970, on date established therefor by the Board of Governors of the United States Postal Service and published by it in the Federal Register, see section 15(a) of Pub.L. 91–375, set out as an Effective Date note preceding section 101 of Title 39, Postal Service.

§ 1725. Postage unpaid on deposited mail matter

Whoever knowingly and willfully deposits any mailable matter such as statements of accounts, circulars, sale bills, or other like matter, on which no postage has been paid, in any letter box established, approved, or accepted by the Postal Service for the receipt or delivery of mail matter on any mail route with intent to avoid payment of lawful postage thereon, shall for each such offense be fined under this title.

(June 25, 1948, c. 645, 62 Stat. 784; Aug. 12, 1970, Pub.L. 91–375, § 6(j) (33), 84 Stat. 780; Sept. 13, 1994, Pub.L. 103–322, Title XXXIII, § 330016(1)(F), 108 Stat. 2147.)

HISTORICAL AND STATUTORY NOTES

Effective and Applicability Provisions

1970 Acts. Amendment by Pub.L. 91–375 effective within 1 year after Aug. 12, 1970, on date established therefor by the Board of Governors of the United States Postal Service and published by it in the Federal Register, see section 15(a) of Pub.L. 91–375, set out as an Effective Date note preceding section 101 of Title 39, Postal Service.

§ 1726. Postage collected unlawfully

Whoever, being a postmaster or other person authorized to receive the postage of mail matter, fraudulently demands or receives any rate of postage or gratuity or reward other than is provided by law for the postage of such mail matter, shall be fined under this title or imprisoned not more than six months, or both.

(June 25, 1948, c. 645, 62 Stat. 784; Sept. 13, 1994, Pub.L. 103–322, Title XXXIII, § 330016(1)(B), 108 Stat. 2146.)

[§ 1727. Repealed. Pub.L. 90–384, § 1(a), July 5, 1968, 82 Stat. 292]

HISTORICAL AND STATUTORY NOTES

Section, Act June 25, 1948, c. 645, 62 Stat. 785, provided for a fine of not more than $50 for postage accounting violations.

Savings Provision

Section 2 of Pub.L. 90–384 provided that: "Nothing in this Act [repealing this section] shall be construed to affect in any way any prosecution for any offense occurring prior to the date of enactment of such Act [July 5, 1968]."

§ 1728. Weight of mail increased fraudulently

Whoever places any matter in the mails during the regular weighing period, for the purpose of increasing the weight of the mail, with intent to cause an increase in the compensation of the railroad mail carrier over whose route such mail may pass, shall be fined under this title or imprisoned not more than five years, or both.

(June 25, 1948, c. 645, 62 Stat. 785; Sept. 13, 1994, Pub.L. 103–322, Title XXXIII, § 330016(1)(N), 108 Stat. 2148.)

§ 1729. Post office conducted without authority

Whoever, without authority from the Postal Service, sets up or professes to keep any office or place of business bearing the sign, name, or title of post office, shall be fined under this title.

(June 25, 1948, c. 645, 62 Stat. 785; Aug. 12, 1970, Pub.L. 91–375, § 6(j) (34), 84 Stat. 780; Sept. 13, 1994, Pub.L. 103–322, Title XXXIII, § 330016(1)(G), 108 Stat. 2147.)

HISTORICAL AND STATUTORY NOTES

Effective and Applicability Provisions

1970 Acts. Amendment by Pub.L. 91–375 effective within 1 year after Aug. 12, 1970, on date established therefor by the Board of Governors of the United States Postal Service and published by it in the Federal Register, see section 15(a) of Pub.L. 91–375, set out as an Effective Date note preceding section 101 of Title 39, Postal Service.

§ 1730. Uniforms of carriers

Whoever, not being connected with the letter-carrier branch of the Postal Service, wears the uniform or badge which may be prescribed by the Postal Service to be worn by letter carriers, shall be fined under this title or imprisoned not more than six months, or both.

The provisions of the preceding paragraph shall not apply to an actor or actress in a theatrical, television, or motion-picture production who wears the uniform or badge of the letter-carrier branch of the Postal Service while portraying a member of that service.

(June 25, 1948, c. 645, 62 Stat. 785; July 21, 1968, Pub.L. 90–413, 82 Stat. 396; Aug. 12, 1970, Pub.L. 91–375, § 6(j) (35), 84 Stat. 780; Nov. 29, 1990, Pub.L. 101–647, Title XII, § 1210(a), 104 Stat. 4832; Sept. 13, 1994, Pub.L. 103–322, Title XXXIII, § 330016(1)(B), 108 Stat. 2146.)

HISTORICAL AND STATUTORY NOTES

Effective and Applicability Provisions

1970 Acts. Amendment by Pub.L. 91–375 effective within 1 year after Aug. 12, 1970, on date established therefor by the Board of Governors of the United States Postal Service and published by it in the Federal Register, see section 15(a) of Pub.L. 91–375, set out as an Effective Date note preceding section 101 of Title 39, Postal Service.

§ 1731. Vehicles falsely labeled as carriers

It shall be unlawful to paint, print, or in any manner to place upon or attach to any steamboat or other vessel, or any car, stagecoach, vehicle, or other conveyance, not actually used in carrying the mail, the words "United States Mail", or any words, letters, or characters of like import; or to give notice, by publishing in any newspaper or otherwise, that any steamboat or other vessel, or any car, stagecoach, vehicle, or other conveyance, is used in carrying the mail, when the same is not actually so used.

Whoever violates, and every owner, receiver, lessee, or managing operator who suffers, or permits the violation of, any provision of this section, shall be fined under this title or imprisoned not more than six months, or both.

(June 25, 1948, c. 645, 62 Stat. 785; Sept. 13, 1994, Pub.L. 103–322, Title XXXIII, § 330016(1)(G), 108 Stat. 2147.)

§ 1732. Approval of bond or sureties by postmaster

Whoever, being a postmaster, affixes his signature to the approval of any bond of a bidder, or to the certificate of sufficiency of sureties in any contract, before the said bond or contract is signed by the bidder or contractor and his sureties, or knowingly, or without the exercise of due diligence, approves any bond of a bidder with insufficient sureties, or knowingly makes any false or fraudulent certificate, shall be fined under this title or imprisoned not more than one year, or both; and shall be dismissed from office and disqualified from holding the office of postmaster.

(June 25, 1948, c. 645, 62 Stat. 785; Sept. 13, 1994, Pub.L. 103–322, Title XXXIII, § 330016(1)(K), 108 Stat. 2147.)

§ 1733. Mailing periodical publications without prepayment of postage

Whoever, except as permitted by law, knowingly mails any periodical publication without the prepayment of postage, or, being an officer or employee of the Postal Service, knowingly permits any periodical publication to be mailed without prepayment of postage, shall be fined under this title, or imprisoned not more than one year, or both.

(Added Pub.L. 86–682, § 7, Sept. 2, 1960, 74 Stat. 705, and amended Pub.L. 91–375, § 6(j) (36) (A), Aug. 12, 1970, 84 Stat. 780; Pub.L. 103–322, Title XXXIII, § 330016(1)(H), Sept. 13, 1994, 108 Stat. 2147.)

HISTORICAL AND STATUTORY NOTES

Effective and Applicability Provisions

1970 Acts. Amendment by Pub.L. 91–375 effective within 1 year after Aug. 12, 1970, on dates established therefor by the Board of Governors of the United States Postal Service and published by it in the Federal Register, see section 15(a) of Pub.L. 91–375, set out as an Effective Date note preceding section 101 of Title 39, Postal Service.

1960 Acts. Section 11 of Pub.L. 86–682 provided that this section shall be effective Sept. 1, 1960.

§ 1734. Editorials and other matter as "advertisements"

Whoever, being an editor or publisher, prints in a publication entered as second class mail, editorial or other reading matter for which he has been paid or promised a valuable consideration, without plainly marking the same "advertisement" shall be fined under this title.

(Added Pub.L. 86–682, § 7, Sept. 2, 1960, 74 Stat. 706, and amended Pub.L. 103–322, Title XXXIII, § 330016(1)(G), Sept. 13, 1994, 108 Stat. 2147.)

HISTORICAL AND STATUTORY NOTES

Effective and Applicability Provisions

1960 Acts. Section 11 of Pub.L. 86–682 provided that this section shall be effective Sept. 1, 1960.

§ 1735. Sexually oriented advertisements

(a) Whoever—

(1) willfully uses the mails for the mailing, carriage in the mails, or delivery of any sexually oriented advertisement in violation of section 3010 of title 39, or willfully violates any regulations of the Board of Governors issued under such section; or

(2) sells, leases, rents, lends, exchanges, or licenses the use of, or, except for the purpose expressly authorized by section 3010 of title 39, uses a mailing list maintained by the Board of Governors under such section;

shall be fined under this title or imprisoned not more than five years, or both, for the first offense, and shall be fined under this title or imprisoned not more than ten years, or both, for any second or subsequent offense.

(b) For the purposes of this section, the term "sexually oriented advertisement" shall have the same meaning as given it in section 3010(d) of title 39.

(Added Pub.L. 91–375, § 6(j)(37)(A), Aug. 12, 1970, 84 Stat. 781, and amended Pub.L. 103–322, Title XXXIII, § 330016(1)(K), (L), Sept. 13, 1994, 108 Stat. 2147.)

HISTORICAL AND STATUTORY NOTES

Effective and Applicability Provisions

1970 Acts. Section effective first day of sixth month which begins after Aug. 12, 1970, see section 15(b) of Pub.L. 91–375, set out as an Effective Date note preceding section 101 of Title 39, Postal Service.

§ 1736. Restrictive use of information

(a) No information or evidence obtained by reason of compliance by a natural person with any provision of section 3010 of title 39, or regulations issued thereunder, shall, except as provided in subsection (c) of this section, be used, directly or indirectly, as evidence against that person in a criminal proceeding.

(b) The fact of the performance of any act by an individual in compliance with any provision of section 3010 of title 39, or regulations issued thereunder, shall not be deemed the admission of any fact, or otherwise be used, directly or indirectly, as evidence against that person in a criminal proceeding, except as provided in subsection (c) of this section.

(c) Subsections (a) and (b) of this section shall not preclude the use of any such information or evidence in a prosecution or other action under any applicable provision of law with respect to the furnishing of false information.

(Added Pub.L. 91–375, § 6(j) (37) (A), Aug. 12, 1970, 84 Stat. 781.)

HISTORICAL AND STATUTORY NOTES

Effective and Applicability Provisions

1970 Acts. Section effective on first day of sixth month which begins after Aug. 12, 1970, see section 15(b) of Pub.L. 91–375, set out as an Effective Date note preceding section 101 of Title 39, Postal Service.

§ 1737. Manufacturer of sexually related mail matter

(a) Whoever shall print, reproduce, or manufacture any sexually related mail matter, intending or knowing that such matter will be deposited for mailing or delivery by mail in violation of section 3008 or 3010 of title 39, or in violation of any regulation of the Postal Service issued under such section, shall be fined under this title or imprisoned not more than five years, or both, for the first offense, and shall be fined under this title or imprisoned not more than ten years, or both, for any second or subsequent offense.

(b) As used in this section, the term "sexually related mail matter" means any matter which is within the scope of section 3008(a) or 3010(d) of title 39.

(Added Pub.L. 91–375, § 6(j)(37)(A), Aug. 12, 1970, 84 Stat. 781, and amended Pub.L. 103–322, Title XXXIII, § 330016(1)(K), (L), Sept. 13, 1994, 108 Stat. 2147.)

HISTORICAL AND STATUTORY NOTES

Effective and Applicability Provisions

1970 Acts. Section effective on first day of sixth month which begins after Aug. 12, 1970, see section 15(b) of Pub.L. 91–375, set out as an Effective Date note preceding section 101 of Title 39, Postal Service.

[§ 1738. Repealed. Pub.L. 106–578, § 4, Dec. 28, 2000, 114 Stat. 3076]

HISTORICAL AND STATUTORY NOTES

Section, Pub.L. 97–398, § 4(a), Dec. 31, 1982, 96 Stat. 2011, and amended Pub.L. 103–322, Title XXXIII, § 330016(1)(H), Sept. 13, 1994, 108 Stat. 2147, related to mailing private identification documents without a disclaimer.

Effective Date of Repeal

Amendment by Pub.L. 106–578, § 4, effective 90 days after December 28, 2000, see Pub.L. 106–578, § 5, set out as a note under section 1028 of this title.

CHAPTER 84—PRESIDENTIAL AND PRESIDENTIAL STAFF ASSASSINATION, KIDNAPPING AND ASSAULT

§ 1751. Presidential and Presidential staff assassination, kidnapping, and assault; penalties

(a) Whoever kills (1) any individual who is the President of the United States, the President-elect, the Vice President, or, if there is no Vice President, the officer next in the order of succession to the Office of the President of the United States, the Vice President-elect, or any person who is acting as President under the Constitution and laws of the United States, or (2) any person appointed under section 105(a)(2)(A) of title 3 employed in the Executive Office of the President or appointed under section 106(a)(1)(A) of title 3 employed in the Office of the Vice President, shall be punished as provided by sections 1111 and 1112 of this title.

(b) Whoever kidnaps any individual designated in subsection (a) of this section shall be punished (1) by imprisonment for any term of years or for life, or (2) by death or imprisonment for any term of years or for life, if death results to such individual.

(c) Whoever attempts to kill or kidnap any individual designated in subsection (a) of this section shall be punished by imprisonment for any term of years or for life.

(d) If two or more persons conspire to kill or kidnap any individual designated in subsection (a) of this section and one or more of such persons do any act to effect the object of the conspiracy, each shall be punished (1) by imprisonment for any term of years or for life, or (2) by death or imprisonment for any term of years or for life, if death results to such individual.

(e) Whoever assaults any person designated in subsection (a)(1) shall be fined under this title, or imprisoned not more than ten years, or both. Whoever assaults any person designated in subsection (a)(2) shall be fined under this title, or imprisoned not more than one year, or both; and if the assault involved the use of a dangerous weapon, or personal injury results, shall be fined under this title, or imprisoned not more than ten years, or both.

(f) The terms "President-elect" and "Vice-President-elect" as used in this section shall mean such persons as are the apparent successful candidates for the offices of President and Vice President, respectively, as ascertained from the results of the general elections held to determine the electors of President and Vice President in accordance with title 3, United States Code, sections 1 and 2.

(g) The Attorney General of the United States, in his discretion is authorized to pay an amount not to exceed $100,000 for information and services concerning a violation of subsection (a)(1). Any officer or employee of the United States or of any State or local government who furnishes information or renders service in the performance of his official duties shall not be eligible for payment under this subsection.

(h) If Federal investigative or prosecutive jurisdiction is asserted for a violation of this section, such assertion shall suspend the exercise of jurisdiction by a State or local authority, under any applicable State or local law, until Federal action is terminated.

(i) Violations of this section shall be investigated by the Federal Bureau of Investigation. Assistance may be requested from any Federal, State, or local agency, including the Army, Navy, and Air Force, any statute, rule, or regulation to the contrary notwithstanding.

(j) In a prosecution for an offense under this section the Government need not prove that the defendant knew that the victim of the offense was an official protected by this section.

(k) There is extraterritorial jurisdiction over the conduct prohibited by this section.

(Added Pub.L. 89–141, § 1, Aug. 28, 1965, 79 Stat. 580, and amended Pub.L. 97–285, §§ 3, 4(a), Oct. 6, 1982, 96 Stat. 1220; Pub.L. 103–322, Title XXXII, § 320101(e), Title XXXIII, §§ 330016(1)(K), (L), 330021(1), Sept. 13, 1994, 108 Stat. 2108, 2147, 2150; Pub.L. 104–294, Title VI, § 604(b)(12)(D), Oct. 11, 1996, 110 Stat. 3507.)

HISTORICAL AND STATUTORY NOTES

Effective and Applicability Provisions

1996 Acts. Amendment by section 604 of Pub.L. 104–294 effective Sept. 13, 1994, see section 604(d) of Pub.L. 104–294, set out as a note under section 13 of this title.

Repeals

Pub.L. 103–322, Title XXXII, § 320101(e)(1), (2), Sept. 13, 1994, 108 Stat. 2108, appearing in the credit of this section, was repealed by Pub.L. 104–294, Title VI, § 604(b)(12)(D), Oct. 11, 1996, 110 Stat. 3507.

§ 1752. Restricted building or grounds

(a) It shall be unlawful for any person or group of persons—

(1) willfully and knowingly to enter or remain in any posted, cordoned off, or otherwise restricted area of a building or grounds where the President or other person protected by the Secret Service is or will be temporarily visiting;

(2) willfully and knowingly to enter or remain in any posted, cordoned off, or otherwise restricted area of a building or grounds so restricted in conjunction with an event designated as a special event of national significance;

(3) willfully, knowingly, and with intent to impede or disrupt the orderly conduct of Government business or official functions, to engage in disorderly or disruptive conduct in, or within such proximity to, any building or grounds described in paragraph (1) or (2) when, or so that, such conduct, in fact, impedes or disrupts the orderly conduct of Government business or official functions;

(4) willfully and knowingly to obstruct or impede ingress or egress to or from any building, grounds, or area described in paragraph (1) or (2); or

(5) willfully and knowingly to engage in any act of physical violence against any person or property in any building, grounds, or area described in paragraph (1) or (2).

(b) Violation of this section, and attempts or conspiracies to commit such violations, shall be punishable by—

(1) a fine under this title or imprisonment for not more than 10 years, or both, if—

(A) the person, during and in relation to the offense, uses or carries a deadly or dangerous weapon or firearm; or

(B) the offense results in significant bodily injury as defined by section 2118(e)(3); and

(2) a fine under this title or imprisonment for not more than one year, or both, in any other case.

(c) Violation of this section, and attempts or conspiracies to commit such violations, shall be prosecuted by the United States attorney in the Federal district court having jurisdiction of the place where the offense occurred.

(d) None of the laws of the United States or of the several States and the District of Columbia shall be superseded by this section.

(e) As used in this section, the term "other person protected by the Secret Service" means any person whom the United States Secret Service is authorized to protect under section 3056 of this title when such person has not declined such protection.

[(f) Redesignated (e)]

(Added Pub.L. 91–644, Title V, § 18, Jan. 2, 1971, 84 Stat. 1891, and amended Pub.L. 97–308, § 1, Oct. 14, 1982, 96 Stat. 1451; Pub.L. 98–587, § 3(b), Oct. 30, 1984, 98 Stat. 3112; Pub.L. 103–322, Title XXXIII, § 330016(1)(G), Sept. 13, 1994, 108 Stat. 2147; Pub.L. 109–177, Title VI, § 602(a), (b)(1), Mar. 9, 2006, 120 Stat. 252.)

HISTORICAL AND STATUTORY NOTES

Transfer of Functions

For transfer of the functions, personnel, assets, and obligations of the United States Secret Service, including the functions of the Secretary of the Treasury relating thereto, to the Secretary of Homeland Security, and for treatment of related references, see 6 U.S.C.A. §§ 381, 551(d), 552(d), and 557, and the Department of Homeland Security Reorganization Plan of November 25, 2002, as modified, set out as a note under 6 U.S.C.A. § 542.

CHAPTER 85—PRISON-MADE GOODS

HISTORICAL AND STATUTORY NOTES

Savings Provisions of Pub.L. 98–473, Title II, c. II

See section 235 of Pub.L. 98–473, Title II, c. II, Oct. 12, 1984, 98 Stat. 2031, as amended, set out as a note under section 3551 of this title.

§ 1761. Transportation or importation

(a) Whoever knowingly transports in interstate commerce or from any foreign country into the United States any goods, wares, or merchandise manufactured, produced, or mined, wholly or in part by convicts or prisoners, except convicts or prisoners on parole, supervised release, or probation, or in any penal or reformatory institution, shall be fined under this title or imprisoned not more than two years, or both.

(b) This chapter shall not apply to agricultural commodities or parts for the repair of farm machinery, nor to commodities manufactured in a Federal, District of Columbia, or State institution for use by the Federal Government, or by the District of Columbia, or by any State or Political subdivision of a State or not-for-profit organizations.

(c) In addition to the exceptions set forth in subsection (b) of this section, this chapter shall not apply to goods, wares, or merchandise manufactured, produced, or mined by convicts or prisoners who—

(1) are participating in—one of not more than 50 non-Federal prison work pilot projects designated by the Director of the Bureau of Justice Assistance;

(2) have, in connection with such work, received wages at a rate which is not less than that paid for work of a similar nature in the locality in which the work was performed, except that such wages may be subject to deductions which shall not, in the aggregate, exceed 80 per centum of gross wages, and shall be limited as follows:

(A) taxes (Federal, State, local);

(B) reasonable charges for room and board, as determined by regulations issued by the chief State correctional officer, in the case of a State prisoner;

(C) allocations for support of family pursuant to State statute, court order, or agreement by the offender;

(D) contributions to any fund established by law to compensate the victims of crime of not more than 20 per centum but not less than 5 per centum of gross wages;

(3) have not solely by their status as offenders, been deprived of the right to participate in benefits made available by the Federal or State Government to other individuals on the basis of their employment, such as workmen's compensation. However, such convicts or prisoners shall not be qualified to receive any payments for unemployment compensation while incarcerated, notwithstanding any other provision of the law to the contrary; and

(4) have participated in such employment voluntarily and have agreed in advance to the specific deductions made from gross wages pursuant to this section, and all other financial arrangements as a result of participation in such employment.

(d) For the purposes of this section, the term "State" means a State of the United States and any commonwealth, territory, or possession of the United States.

(June 25, 1948, c. 645, 62 Stat. 785; June 19, 1968, Pub.L. 90–351, Title I, § 819(a), formerly § 827(a), as added Dec. 27, 1979, Pub.L. 96–157, § 2, 93 Stat. 1215, renumbered and amended Oct. 12, 1984, Pub.L. 98–473, Title II, §§ 223(c), 609B(f), 609K, 98 Stat. 2028, 2093, 2102; Apr. 2, 1987, Pub.L. 100–17, Title I, § 112(b)(3), 101 Stat. 149; Nov. 29, 1990, Pub.L. 101–647, Title XXIX, § 2906, 104 Stat. 647; Oct. 6, 1992, Pub.L. 102–393, Title V, § 535(a), 106 Stat. 1764; Sept. 13, 1994, Pub.L. 103–322, Title XXXIII, §§ 330010(11), 330016(1)(H), 108 Stat. 2144, 2147; Apr. 26, 1996, Pub.L. 104–134, Title I, § 101(b)[Title I, § 136], 110 Stat. 1321–93; renumbered Title I, Pub.L. 104–140, § 1(a), May 2, 1996, 110 Stat. 1327; Oct. 11, 1996, Pub.L. 104–294, Title VI, §§ 601(a)(7), 607(h), 110 Stat. 3498, 3512.)

HISTORICAL AND STATUTORY NOTES

Effective and Applicability Provisions

1984 Acts. Amendment by Pub.L. 98–473 effective on the first day of first calendar month beginning thirty six months after Oct. 12, 1984, applicable only to offenses committed after taking effect of sections 211 to 239 of Pub.L. 98–473, and except as otherwise provided for therein, see section 235 of Pub.L. 98–473, as amended, set out as a note under section 3551 of this title.

Reports by Secretary of Labor

Pub.L. 101–647, Title XXIX, § 2908, Nov. 29, 1990, 104 Stat. 4915, which required the Secretary of Labor to submit to Congress annual reports describing the extent and manner of compliance by State prison industry enhancement certification programs with the requirements set forth in 18

U.S.C. 1761(c), terminated, effective May 15, 2000, see Pub.L. 104–66, § 3003, as amended, set out as a note under 31 U.S.C.A. § 1113, and the 6th item on page 123 of House Document No. 103–7.

Exemptions to Federal Restrictions on Marketability of Prison Made Goods

Pub.L. 90–351, Title I, § 819(c), formerly § 827(c), as added Pub.L. 96–157, § 2, Dec. 27, 1979, 93 Stat. 1215; renumbered and amended Pub.L. 98–473, Title II, § 609B(f), (*o*), Oct. 12, 1984, 98 Stat. 2093, 2096, provided that:

"The provisions of section 1761 of title 18, United States Code, and of the first section of the Act of June 30, 1936 (49 Stat. 2036; 41 U.S.C. 35), commonly known as the Walsh–Healey Act, creating exemptions to Federal restrictions on marketability of prison made goods, as amended from time to time, shall not apply unless—

"(1) representatives of local union central bodies or similar labor union organizations have been consulted prior to the initiation of any project qualifying of any exemption created by this section; and

"(2) such paid inmate employment will not result in the displacement of employed workers, or be applied in skills, crafts, or trades in which there is a surplus of available gainful labor in the locality, or impair existing contracts for services."

§ 1762. Marking packages

(a) All packages containing any goods, wares, or merchandise manufactured, produced, or mined wholly or in part by convicts or prisoners, except convicts or prisoners on parole or probation, or in any penal or reformatory institution, when shipped or transported in interstate or foreign commerce shall be plainly and clearly marked, so that the name and address of the shipper, the name and address of the consignee, the nature of the contents, and the name and location of the penal or reformatory institution where produced wholly or in part may be readily ascertained on an inspection of the outside of such package.

(b) Whoever violates this section shall be fined under this title, and any goods, wares, or merchandise transported in violation of this section or section 1761 of this title shall be forfeited to the United States, and may be seized and condemned by like proceedings as those provided by law for the seizure and forfeiture of property imported into the United States contrary to law.

(June 25, 1948, c. 645, 62 Stat. 786; Oct. 6, 1992, Pub.L. 102–393, Title V, § 535(b), 106 Stat. 1764; Sept. 13, 1994, Pub.L. 103–322, Title XXXIII, § 330016(1)(H), 108 Stat. 2147; Oct. 11, 1996, Pub.L. 104–294, Title VI, § 601(a)(7), 110 Stat. 3498.)

CHAPTER 87—PRISONS

§ 1791. Providing or possessing contraband in prison

(a) Offense.—Whoever—

(1) in violation of a statute or a rule or order issued under a statute, provides to an inmate of a prison a prohibited object, or attempts to do so; or

(2) being an inmate of a prison, makes, possesses, or obtains, or attempts to make or obtain, a prohibited object;

shall be punished as provided in subsection (b) of this section.

(b) Punishment.—The punishment for an offense under this section is a fine under this title or—

(1) imprisonment for not more than 20 years, or both, if the object is specified in subsection (d)(1)(C) of this section;

(2) imprisonment for not more than 10 years, or both, if the object is specified in subsection (d)(1)(A) of this section;

(3) imprisonment for not more than 5 years, or both, if the object is specified in subsection (d)(1)(B) of this section;

(4) imprisonment for not more than one year, or both, if the object is specified in subsection (d)(1)(D) or (d)(1)(E) of this section; and

(5) imprisonment for not more than 6 months, or both, if the object is specified in subsection (d)(1)(F) of this section.

(c) Consecutive punishment required in certain cases.—Any punishment imposed under subsection (b) for a violation of this section involving a controlled substance shall be consecutive to any other sentence imposed by any court for an offense involving such a controlled substance. Any punishment imposed under subsection (b) for a violation of this section by an inmate of a prison shall be consecutive to the sentence being served by such inmate at the time the inmate commits such violation.

(d) Definitions.—As used in this section—

(1) the term "prohibited object" means—

(A) a firearm or destructive device or a controlled substance in schedule I or II, other than marijuana or a controlled substance referred to in subparagraph (C) of this subsection;

(B) marijuana or a controlled substance in schedule III, other than a controlled substance referred to in subparagraph (C) of this subsection, ammunition, a weapon (other than a firearm or destructive device), or an object that is designed or intended to be used as a weapon or to facilitate escape from a prison;

(C) a narcotic drug, methamphetamine, its salts, isomers, and salts of its isomers, lysergic acid diethylamide, or phencyclidine;

(D) a controlled substance (other than a controlled substance referred to in subparagraph (A), (B), or (C) of this subsection) or an alcoholic beverage;

(E) any United States or foreign currency; and

(F) any other object that threatens the order, discipline, or security of a prison, or the life, health, or safety of an individual;

(2) the terms "ammunition", "firearm", and "destructive device" have, respectively, the meanings given those terms in section 921 of this title;

(3) the terms "controlled substance" and "narcotic drug" have, respectively, the meanings given those terms in section 102 of the Controlled Substances Act (21 U.S.C. 802); and

(4) the term "prison" means a Federal correctional, detention, or penal facility or any prison, institution, or facility in which persons are held in custody by direction of or pursuant to a contract or agreement with the Attorney General.

(June 25, 1948, c. 645, 62 Stat. 786; Oct. 12, 1984, Pub.L. 98–473, Title II, § 1109(a), 98 Stat. 2147; Nov. 10, 1986, Pub.L. 99–646, § 52(a), 100 Stat. 3606; Nov. 18, 1988, Pub.L. 100–690, Title VI, § 6468(a), (b), 102 Stat. 4376; Sept. 13, 1994, Pub.L. 103–322, Title IX, § 90101, Title XXXIII, § 330003(a), 108 Stat. 1986, 2140; Oct. 11, 1996, Pub.L. 104–294, Title VI, § 601(m), 110 Stat. 3502; Jan. 5, 2006, Pub.L. 109–162, Title XI, § 1178, 119 Stat. 3126.)

HISTORICAL AND STATUTORY NOTES

References in Text

Section 102 of the Controlled Substances Act, referred to in subsec. (d)(3), is section 102 of Pub.L. 91–513, Title II, Oct. 27, 1970, 84 Stat. 1242, as amended, which is classified to section 802 of Title 21, Food and Drugs.

Effective and Applicability Provisions

1986 Acts. Section 52(b) of Pub.L. 99–646 provided that: "The amendment made by this section [amending this section] shall take effect 30 days after the date of the enactment of this Act [Nov. 10, 1986]."

§ 1792. Mutiny and riot prohibited

Whoever instigates, connives, willfully attempts to cause, assists, or conspires to cause any mutiny or riot, at any Federal penal, detention, or correctional facility, shall be imprisoned not more than ten years or fined under this title, or both.

(June 25, 1948, c. 645, 62 Stat. 786; Oct. 12, 1984, Pub.L. 98–473, Title II, § 1109(b), 98 Stat. 2148; Nov. 10, 1986, Pub.L. 99–646, § 53(a), 100 Stat. 3607; Sept. 13, 1994, Pub.L. 103–322, Title XXXIII, § 330016(1)(O), 108 Stat. 2148.)

HISTORICAL AND STATUTORY NOTES

Effective and Applicability Provisions

1986 Acts. Section 53(b) of Pub.L. 99–646, provided that: "The amendment made by this section [amending this section] shall take effect 30 days after the enactment of this Act [Nov. 10, 1986]."

§ 1793. Trespass on Bureau of Prisons reservations and land

Whoever, without lawful authority or permission, goes upon a reservation, land, or a facility of the Bureau of Prisons shall be fined under this title or imprisoned not more than six months, or both.

(Added Pub.L. 99–646, § 64(a), Nov. 10, 1986, 100 Stat. 3614, and amended Pub.L. 103–322, Title XXXIII, § 330016(1)(G), Sept. 13, 1994, 108 Stat. 2147.)

CHAPTER 88—PRIVACY

§ 1801. Video voyeurism

(a) Whoever, in the special maritime and territorial jurisdiction of the United States, has the intent to capture an image of a private area of an individual without their consent, and knowingly does so under circumstances in which the individual has a reasonable expectation of privacy, shall be fined under this title or imprisoned not more than one year, or both.

(b) In this section—

(1) the term "capture", with respect to an image, means to videotape, photograph, film, record by any means, or broadcast;

(2) the term "broadcast" means to electronically transmit a visual image with the intent that it be viewed by a person or persons;

(3) the term "a private area of the individual" means the naked or undergarment clad genitals, pubic area, buttocks, or female breast of that individual;

(4) the term "female breast" means any portion of the female breast below the top of the areola; and

(5) the term "under circumstances in which that individual has a reasonable expectation of privacy" means—

(A) circumstances in which a reasonable person would believe that he or she could disrobe in privacy, without being concerned that an image of a private area of the individual was being captured; or

(B) circumstances in which a reasonable person would believe that a private area of the individual would not be visible to the public, regardless of whether that person is in a public or private place .

(c) This section does not prohibit any lawful law enforcement, correctional, or intelligence activity.

(Added Pub.L. 108–495, § 2(a), Dec. 23, 2004, 118 Stat. 3999.)

HISTORICAL AND STATUTORY NOTES

Short Title

2004 Acts. Pub.L. 108–495, § 1, Dec. 23, 2004, 118 Stat. 3999, provided that: "This Act [enacting this chapter] may be cited as the 'Video Voyeurism Prevention Act of 2004'."

CHAPTER 89—PROFESSIONS AND OCCUPATIONS

§ 1821. Transportation of dentures

Whoever transports by mail or otherwise to or within the District of Columbia or any Possession of the United States or uses the mails or any instrumentality of interstate commerce for the purpose of sending or bringing into any State or Territory any set of artificial teeth or prosthetic dental appliance or other denture, constructed from any cast or impression made by any person other than, or without the authorization or prescription of, a person licensed to practice dentistry under the laws of the place into which such denture is sent or brought, where such laws prohibit;

(1) the taking of impressions or casts of the human mouth or teeth by a person not licensed under such laws to practice dentistry;

(2) the construction or supply of dentures by a person other than, or without the authorization or prescription of, a person licensed under such laws to practice dentistry; or

(3) the construction or supply of dentures from impressions or casts made by a person not licensed under such laws to practice dentistry—

Shall be fined under this title or imprisoned not more than one year, or both.

(June 25, 1948, c. 645, 62 Stat. 786; Oct. 11, 1996, Pub.L. 104–294, Title VI, § 601(a)(8), 110 Stat. 3498; Nov. 2, 2002, Pub.L. 107–273, Div. B, Title IV, § 4004(c), 116 Stat. 1812.)

HISTORICAL AND STATUTORY NOTES

References in Text

For definition of Canal Zone, referred to in text, see section 3602(b) of Title 22, Foreign Relations and Intercourse.

CHAPTER 90—PROTECTION OF TRADE SECRETS

§ 1831. Economic espionage

(a) In general.—Whoever, intending or knowing that the offense will benefit any foreign government, foreign instrumentality, or foreign agent, knowingly—

(1) steals, or without authorization appropriates, takes, carries away, or conceals, or by fraud, artifice, or deception obtains a trade secret;

(2) without authorization copies, duplicates, sketches, draws, photographs, downloads, uploads, alters, destroys, photocopies, replicates, transmits, delivers, sends, mails, communicates, or conveys a trade secret;

(3) receives, buys, or possesses a trade secret, knowing the same to have been stolen or appropriated, obtained, or converted without authorization;

(4) attempts to commit any offense described in any of paragraphs (1) through (3); or

(5) conspires with one or more other persons to commit any offense described in any of paragraphs (1) through (3), and one or more of such persons do any act to effect the object of the conspiracy,

shall, except as provided in subsection (b), be fined not more than $500,000 or imprisoned not more than 15 years, or both.

(b) Organizations.—Any organization that commits any offense described in subsection (a) shall be fined not more than $10,000,000.

(Added Pub.L. 104–294, Title I, § 101(a), Oct. 11, 1996, 110 Stat. 3488.)

§ 1832. Theft of trade secrets

(a) Whoever, with intent to convert a trade secret, that is related to or included in a product that is produced for or placed in interstate or foreign commerce, to the economic benefit of anyone other than the owner thereof, and intending or knowing that the offense will, injure any owner of that trade secret, knowingly—

(1) steals, or without authorization appropriates, takes, carries away, or conceals, or by fraud, artifice, or deception obtains such information;

(2) without authorization copies, duplicates, sketches, draws, photographs, downloads, uploads, alters, destroys, photocopies, replicates, transmits, delivers, sends, mails, communicates, or conveys such information;

(3) receives, buys, or possesses such information, knowing the same to have been stolen or appropriated, obtained, or converted without authorization;

(4) attempts to commit any offense described in paragraphs (1) through (3); or

(5) conspires with one or more other persons to commit any offense described in paragraphs (1) through (3), and one or more of such persons do any act to effect the object of the conspiracy,

shall, except as provided in subsection (b), be fined under this title or imprisoned not more than 10 years, or both.

(b) Any organization that commits any offense described in subsection (a) shall be fined not more than $5,000,000.

(Added Pub.L. 104–294, Title I, § 101(a), Oct. 11, 1996, 110 Stat. 3489.)

§ 1833. Exceptions to prohibitions

This chapter does not prohibit—

(1) any otherwise lawful activity conducted by a governmental entity of the United States, a State, or a political subdivision of a State; or

(2) the reporting of a suspected violation of law to any governmental entity of the United States, a State, or a political subdivision of a State, if such entity has lawful authority with respect to that violation.

(Added Pub.L. 104–294, Title I, § 101(a), Oct. 11, 1996, 110 Stat. 3489.)

§ 1834. Criminal forfeiture

(a) The court, in imposing sentence on a person for a violation of this chapter, shall order, in addition to any other sentence imposed, that the person forfeit to the United States—

(1) any property constituting, or derived from, any proceeds the person obtained, directly or indirectly, as the result of such violation; and

(2) any of the person's property used, or intended to be used, in any manner or part, to commit or facilitate the commission of such violation, if the court in its discretion so determines, taking into consideration the nature, scope, and proportionality of the use of the property in the offense.

(b) Property subject to forfeiture under this section, any seizure and disposition thereof, and any administrative or judicial proceeding in relation thereto, shall be governed by section 413 of the Comprehensive Drug Abuse Prevention and Control Act of 1970 (21 U.S.C. 853), except for subsections (d) and (j) of such section, which shall not apply to forfeitures under this section.

(Added Pub.L. 104–294, Title I, § 101(a), Oct. 11, 1996, 110 Stat. 3489.)

HISTORICAL AND STATUTORY NOTES

References in Text

Section 413 of the Comprehensive Drug Abuse Prevention and Control Act of 1970, referred to in subsec. (b), is section 413 of Pub.L. 91–513, as added and amended, which is classified to section 853 of Title 21, Food and Drugs.

§ 1835. Orders to preserve confidentiality

In any prosecution or other proceeding under this chapter, the court shall enter such orders and take such other action as may be necessary and appropriate to preserve the confidentiality of trade secrets, consistent with the requirements of the Federal Rules of Criminal and Civil Procedure, the Federal Rules of Evidence, and all other applicable laws. An interlocutory appeal by the United States shall lie from a decision or order of a district court authorizing or directing the disclosure of any trade secret.

(Added Pub.L. 104–294, Title I, § 101(a), Oct. 11, 1996, 110 Stat. 3490.)

§ 1836. Civil proceedings to enjoin violations

(a) The Attorney General may, in a civil action, obtain appropriate injunctive relief against any violation of this chapter.

(b) The district courts of the United States shall have exclusive original jurisdiction of civil actions under this section.

(Added Pub.L. 104–294, Title I, § 101(a), Oct. 11, 1996, 110 Stat. 3490, and amended Pub.L. 107–273, Title IV, § 4002(e)(9), Nov. 2, 2002, 116 Stat. 1810.)

§ 1837. Applicability to conduct outside the United States

This chapter also applies to conduct occurring outside the United States if—

(1) the offender is a natural person who is a citizen or permanent resident alien of the United States, or an organization organized under the laws of the United States or a State or political subdivision thereof; or

(2) an act in furtherance of the offense was committed in the United States.

(Added Pub.L. 104–294, Title I, § 101(a), Oct. 11, 1996, 110 Stat. 3490.)

§ 1838. Construction with other laws

This chapter shall not be construed to preempt or displace any other remedies, whether civil or criminal, provided by United States Federal, State, commonwealth, possession, or territory law for the misappropriation of a trade secret, or to affect the otherwise lawful disclosure of information by any Government employee under section 552 of title 5 (commonly known as the Freedom of Information Act).

(Added Pub.L. 104–294, Title I, § 101(a), Oct. 11, 1996, 110 Stat. 3490.)

§ 1839. Definitions

As used in this chapter—

(1) the term "foreign instrumentality" means any agency, bureau, ministry, component, institution, association, or any legal, commercial, or business organization, corporation, firm, or entity that is substantially owned, controlled, sponsored, commanded, managed, or dominated by a foreign government;

(2) the term "foreign agent" means any officer, employee, proxy, servant, delegate, or representative of a foreign government;

(3) the term "trade secret" means all forms and types of financial, business, scientific, technical, economic, or engineering information, including patterns, plans, compilations, program devices, formulas, designs, prototypes, methods, techniques, processes, procedures, programs, or codes, whether tangible or intangible, and whether or how stored, compiled, or memorialized physically, electronically, graphically, photographically, or in writing if—

(A) the owner thereof has taken reasonable measures to keep such information secret; and

(B) the information derives independent economic value, actual or potential, from not being generally known to, and not being readily ascertainable through proper means by, the public; and

(4) the term "owner", with respect to a trade secret, means the person or entity in whom or in which rightful legal or equitable title to, or license in, the trade secret is reposed.

(Added Pub.L. 104–294, Title I, § 101(a), Oct. 11, 1996, 110 Stat. 3490.)

CHAPTER 90A—PROTECTION OF UNBORN CHILDREN

§ 1841. Protection of unborn children

(a)(1) Whoever engages in conduct that violates any of the provisions of law listed in subsection (b) and thereby causes the death of, or bodily injury (as defined in section 1365) to, a child, who is in utero at the time the conduct takes place, is guilty of a separate offense under this section.

(2)(A) Except as otherwise provided in this paragraph, the punishment for that separate offense is the same as the punishment provided under Federal law for that conduct had that injury or death occurred to the unborn child's mother.

(B) An offense under this section does not require proof that—

(i) the person engaging in the conduct had knowledge or should have had knowledge that the victim of the underlying offense was pregnant; or

(ii) the defendant intended to cause the death of, or bodily injury to, the unborn child.

(C) If the person engaging in the conduct thereby intentionally kills or attempts to kill the unborn child, that person shall instead of being punished under subparagraph (A), be punished as provided under sections 1111, 1112, and 1113 of this title for intentionally killing or attempting to kill a human being.

(D) Notwithstanding any other provision of law, the death penalty shall not be imposed for an offense under this section.

(b) The provisions referred to in subsection (a) are the following:

(1) Sections 36, 37, 43, 111, 112, 113, 114, 115, 229, 242, 245, 247, 248, 351, 831, 844(d), (f), (h)(1), and (i), 924(j), 930, 1111, 1112, 1113, 1114, 1116, 1118, 1119, 1120, 1121, 1153(a), 1201(a), 1203, 1365(a), 1501, 1503, 1505, 1512, 1513, 1751, 1864, 1951, 1952 (a)(1)(B), (a) (2)(B), and (a)(3)(B), 1958, 1959, 1992, 2113, 2114, 2116, 2118, 2119, 2191, 2231, 2241(a), 2245, 2261, 2261A, 2280, 2281, 2332, 2332a, 2332b, 2340A, and 2441 of this title.

(2) Section 408(e) of the Controlled Substances Act of 1970 (21 U.S.C. 848(e)).

(3) Section 202 of the Atomic Energy Act of 1954 (42 U.S.C. 2283).

(c) Nothing in this section shall be construed to permit the prosecution—

(1) of any person for conduct relating to an abortion for which the consent of the pregnant woman, or a person authorized by law to act on her behalf,

has been obtained or for which such consent is implied by law;

(2) of any person for any medical treatment of the pregnant woman or her unborn child; or

(3) of any woman with respect to her unborn child.

(d) As used in this section, the term "unborn child" means a child in utero, and the term "child in utero" or "child, who is in utero" means a member of the species homo sapiens, at any stage of development, who is carried in the womb.

(Added Pub.L. 108–212, § 2(a), Apr. 1, 2004, 118 Stat. 568.)

HISTORICAL AND STATUTORY NOTES

References in Text

Section 202 of the Atomic Energy Act of 1954 (42 U.S.C. 2283), referred to in subsec. (b)(3), probably means section 235 of the Atomic Energy Act of 1954, Act Aug. 1, 1946, c. 724, Title I, as added by Pub.L. 96–295, Title II, § 202(a), June 30, 1980, 94 Stat. 786, which is classified to 42 U.S.C.A. § 2283. Section 202 of the Atomic Energy Act of 1954, which related to the authority of the Joint Committee on Atomic Energy, was classified to 42 U.S.C.A. § 2252 and was repealed by Act Aug. 1, 1946, c. 724, Title I, § 302(a), as added Act Aug. 30, 1954, c. 1073, § 1, as added Sept. 20, 1977, Pub.L. 95–110, § 1, 91 Stat. 884; renumbered Title I, Oct. 24, 1992, Pub.L. 102–486, Title IX, § 902(a)(8), 106 Stat. 2944.

Short Title

2004 Acts. Pub.L. 108–212, § 1, Apr. 1, 2004, 118 Stat. 568, provided that: "This Act [enacting this chapter and 10 U.S.C.A. § 919a] may be cited as the 'Unborn Victims of Violence Act of 2004' or 'Laci and Conner's Law'."

CHAPTER 91—PUBLIC LANDS

Sec.

§ 1851. Coal depredations

Whoever mines or removes coal of any character, whether anthracite, bituminous, or lignite, from beds or deposits in lands of, or reserved to the United States, with intent wrongfully to appropriate, sell, or dispose of the same, shall be fined under this title or imprisoned not more than one year, or both.

This section shall not interfere with any right or privilege conferred by existing laws of the United States.

(June 25, 1948, c. 645, 62 Stat. 787; Oct. 11, 1996, Pub.L. 104–294, Title VI, § 601(a)(8), 110 Stat. 3498.)

§ 1852. Timber removed or transported

Whoever cuts, or wantonly destroys any timber growing on the public lands of the United States; or

Whoever removes any timber from said public lands, with intent to export or to dispose of the same; or

Whoever, being the owner, master, pilot, operator, or consignee of any vessel, motor vehicle, or aircraft or the owner, director, or agent of any railroad, knowingly transports any timber so cut or removed from said lands, or lumber manufactured therefrom—

Shall be fined under this title or imprisoned not more than one year, or both.

This section shall not prevent any miner or agriculturist from clearing his land in the ordinary working of his mining claim, or in the preparation of his farm for tillage, or from taking the timber necessary to support his improvements, or the taking of timber for the use of the United States; nor shall it interfere with or take away any right or privilege under any existing law of the United States to cut or remove timber from any public lands.

(June 25, 1948, c. 645, 62 Stat. 787; Oct. 11, 1996, Pub.L. 104–294, Title VI, § 601(a)(8), 110 Stat. 3498.)

§ 1853. Trees cut or injured

Whoever unlawfully cuts, or wantonly injures or destroys any tree growing, standing, or being upon any land of the United States which, in pursuance of law, has been reserved or purchased by the United States for any public use, or upon any Indian reservation, or lands belonging to or occupied by any tribe of Indians under the authority of the United States, or any Indian allotment while the title to the same shall be held in trust by the Government, or while the same shall remain inalienable by the allottee without the consent of the United States, shall be fined under this title or imprisoned not more than one year, or both.

(June 25, 1948, c. 645, 62 Stat. 787; Oct. 11, 1996, Pub.L. 104–294, Title VI, § 601(a)(8), 110 Stat. 3498.)

§ 1854. Trees boxed for pitch or turpentine

Whoever cuts, chips, chops, or boxes any tree upon any lands belonging to the United States, or upon any lands covered by or embraced in any unperfected settlement, application, filing, entry, selection, or location, made under any law of the United States, for the purpose of obtaining from such tree any pitch, turpentine, or other substance; or

Whoever buys, trades for, or in any manner acquires any pitch, turpentine, or other substance, or any article or commodity made from any such pitch, turpentine, or other substance, with knowledge that the same has been so unlawfully obtained—

Shall be fined under this title or imprisoned not more than one year, or both.

(June 25, 1948, c. 645, 62 Stat. 788; Oct. 11, 1996, Pub.L. 104–294, Title VI, § 601(a)(8), 110 Stat. 3498.)

§ 1855. Timber set afire

Whoever, willfully and without authority, sets on fire any timber, underbrush, or grass or other inflammable material upon the public domain or upon any lands owned or leased by or under the partial, concurrent, or exclusive jurisdiction of the United States, or under contract for purchase or for the acquisition of which condemnation proceedings have been instituted, or upon any Indian reservation or lands belonging to or occupied by any tribe or group of Indians under authority of the United States, or upon any Indian allotment while the title to the same shall be held in trust by the Government, or while the same shall remain inalienable by the allottee without the consent of the United States, shall be fined under this title or imprisoned not more than five years, or both.

This section shall not apply in the case of a fire set by an allottee in the reasonable exercise of his proprietary rights in the allotment.

(June 25, 1948, c. 645, 62 Stat. 788; Nov. 18, 1988, Pub.L. 100–690, Title VI, § 6254(j), 102 Stat. 4368.)

§ 1856. Fires left unattended and unextinguished

Whoever, having kindled or caused to be kindled, a fire in or near any forest, timber, or other inflammable material upon any lands owned, controlled or leased by, or under the partial, concurrent, or exclusive jurisdiction of the United States, including lands under contract for purchase or for the acquisition of which condemnation proceedings have been instituted, and including any Indian reservation or lands belonging to or occupied by any tribe or group of Indians under the authority of the United States, or any Indian allotment while the title to the same is held in trust by the United States, or while the same shall remain inalienable by the allottee without the consent of the United States, leaves said fire without totally extinguishing the same, or permits or suffers said fire to burn or spread beyond his control, or leaves or suffers said fire to burn unattended, shall be fined under this title or imprisoned not more than six months, or both.

(June 25, 1948, c. 645, 62 Stat. 788; Sept. 13, 1994, Pub.L. 103–322, Title XXXIII, § 330016(1)(G), 108 Stat. 2147.)

§ 1857. Fences destroyed; livestock entering

Whoever knowingly and unlawfully breaks, opens, or destroys any gate, fence, hedge, or wall inclosing any lands of the United States reserved or purchased for any public use; or

Whoever drives any cattle, horses, hogs, or other livestock upon any such lands for the purposes of destroying the grass or trees on said lands, or where they may destroy the said grass or trees; or

Whoever knowingly permits his cattle, horses, hogs, or other livestock to enter through any such inclosure upon any such lands of the United States, where such cattle, horses, hogs, or other livestock may or can destroy the grass or trees or other property of the United States on the said lands—

Shall be fined under this title or imprisoned not more than one year, or both.

This section shall not apply to unreserved public lands.

(June 25, 1948, c. 645, 62 Stat. 788; Sept. 13, 1994, Pub.L. 103–322, Title XXXIII, § 330016(1)(G), 108 Stat. 2147.)

§ 1858. Survey marks destroyed or removed

Whoever willfully destroys, defaces, changes, or removes to another place any section corner, quarter-section corner, or meander post, on any Government line of survey, or willfully cuts down any witness tree or any tree blazed to mark the line of a Government survey, or willfully defaces, changes, or removes any monument or bench mark of any Government survey, shall be fined under this title or imprisoned not more than six months, or both.

(June 25, 1948, c. 645, 62 Stat. 789; Sept. 13, 1994, Pub.L. 103–322, Title XXXIII, § 330016(1)(E), 108 Stat. 2146.)

§ 1859. Surveys interrupted

Whoever, by threats or force, interrupts, hinders, or prevents the surveying of the public lands, or of any private land claim which has been or may be confirmed by the United States, by the persons authorized to survey the same in conformity with the instructions of the Director of the Bureau of Land Management, shall be fined under this title or imprisoned not more than three years, or both.

(June 25, 1948, c. 645, 62 Stat. 789; May 24, 1949, c. 139, § 42, 63 Stat. 95; Sept. 13, 1994, Pub.L. 103–322, Title XXXIII, § 330016(1)(J), 108 Stat. 2147.)

§ 1860. Bids at land sales

Whoever bargains, contracts, or agrees, or attempts to bargain, contract, or agree with another that such other shall not bid upon or purchase any parcel of lands of the United States offered at public sale; or

Whoever, by intimidation, combination, or unfair management, hinders, prevents, or attempts to hinder or prevent, any person from bidding upon or purchasing any tract of land so offered for sale—

Shall be fined not more than $1,000 or imprisoned not more than one year, or both.

(June 25, 1948, c. 645, 62 Stat. 789.)

§ 1861. Deception of prospective purchasers

Whoever, for a reward paid or promised to him in that behalf, undertakes to locate for an intending purchaser, settler, or entryman any public lands of the United States subject to disposition under the public-land laws, and who willfully and falsely represents to such intending purchaser, settler, or entryman that any tract of land shown to him is public land of the United States subject to sale, settlement, or entry, or that it is of a particular surveyed description, with intent to deceive the person to whom such representation is made, or who, in reckless disregard of the truth, falsely represents to any such person that any tract of land shown to him is public land of the United States subject to sale, settlement, or entry, or that it is of a particular surveyed description, thereby deceiving the person to whom such representation is made, shall be fined under this title or imprisoned not more than one year, or both.

(June 25, 1948, c. 645, 62 Stat. 789; Sept. 13, 1994, Pub.L. 103–322, Title XXXIII, § 330016(1)(F), 108 Stat. 2147.)

[§ 1862. Repealed. Pub.L. 95–200, § 3(c), Nov. 23, 1977, 91 Stat. 1428]

HISTORICAL AND STATUTORY NOTES

Section, Act June 25, 1948, c. 645, 62 Stat. 789, imposed a fine of not more than $500 or imprisonment of not more than six months as the penalty for knowingly trespassing upon the reserve known as the Bull Run National Forest in the Cascade Mountains. See note set out under section 482b of Title 16, Conservation, for the remainder of Pub.L. 95–200, including savings provisions therein, which in addition to repealing this section created the Bull Run Watershed Management Unit, Mount Hood National Forest.

§ 1863. Trespass on national forest lands

Whoever, without lawful authority or permission, goes upon any national-forest land while it is closed to the public pursuant to lawful regulation of the Secretary of Agriculture, shall be fined under this title or imprisoned not more than six months, or both.

(Added May 24, 1949, c. 139, § 43, 63 Stat. 95, and amended Sept. 13, 1994, Pub.L. 103–322, Title XXXIII, § 330016(1)(G), 108 Stat. 2147.)

§ 1864. Hazardous or injurious devices on Federal lands

(a) Whoever—

(1) with the intent to violate the Controlled Substances Act,

(2) with the intent to obstruct or harass the harvesting of timber, or

(3) with reckless disregard to the risk that another person will be placed in danger of death or bodily injury and under circumstances manifesting extreme indifference to such risk,

uses a hazardous or injurious device on Federal land, on an Indian reservation, or on an Indian allotment while the title to such allotment is held in trust by the United States or while such allotment remains inalienable by the allottee without the consent of the United States shall be punished under subsection (b).

(b) An individual who violates subsection (a) shall—

(1) if death of an individual results, be fined under this title or imprisoned for any term of years or for life, or both;

(2) if serious bodily injury to any individual results, be fined under this title or imprisoned for not more than 40 years, or both;

(3) if bodily injury to any individual results, be fined under this title or imprisoned for not more than 20 years, or both;

(4) if damage to the property of any individual results or if avoidance costs have been incurred exceeding $10,000, in the aggregate, be fined under this title or imprisoned for not more than 20 years, or both; and

(5) in any other case, be fined under this title or imprisoned for not more than one year.

(c) Any individual who is punished under subsection (b)(5) after one or more prior convictions under any such subsection shall be fined under this title or imprisoned for not more than 20 years, or both.

(d) As used in this section—

(1) the term "serious bodily injury" means bodily injury which involves—

(A) a substantial risk of death;

(B) extreme physical pain;

(C) protracted and obvious disfigurement; and

(D) protracted loss or impairment of the function of bodily member, organ, or mental faculty;

(2) the term "bodily injury" means—

(A) a cut, abrasion, bruise, burn, or disfigurement;

(B) physical pain;

(C) illness;

(D) impairment of the function of a bodily member, organ, or mental faculty; or

(E) any other injury to the body, no matter how temporary;

(3) the term "hazardous or injurious device" means a device, which when assembled or placed, is capable of causing bodily injury, or damage to property, by the action of any person making contact with such device subsequent to the assembly or placement. Such term includes guns attached to trip wires or other triggering mechanisms, ammunition attached to trip wires or other triggering mechanisms, or explosive devices attached to trip wires or other triggering mechanisms, sharpened stakes, lines or wires, lines or wires with hooks attached, nails placed so that the sharpened ends are positioned in an upright manner, or tree spiking devices including spikes, nails, or other objects hammered, driven, fastened, or otherwise placed into or on any timber, whether or not severed from the stump; and

(4) the term "avoidance costs" means costs incurred by any individual for the purpose of—

(A) detecting a hazardous or injurious device; or

(B) preventing death, serious bodily injury, bodily injury, or property damage likely to result from the use of a hazardous or injurious device in violation of subsection (a).

(e) Any person injured as the result of a violation of subsection (a) may commence a civil action on his own behalf against any person who is alleged to be in violation of subsection (a). The district courts shall have jurisdiction, without regard to the amount in controversy or the citizenship of the parties, in such civil actions. The court may award, in addition to monetary damages for any injury resulting from an alleged violation of subsection (a), costs of litigation, including reasonable attorney and expert witness fees, to any prevailing or substantially prevailing party, whenever the court determines such award is appropriate.

(Added Pub.L. 100–690, Title VI, § 6254(f), Nov. 18, 1988, 102 Stat. 4366, and amended Pub.L. 101–647, Title XXXV, § 3555, Nov. 29, 1990, 104 Stat. 4927; Pub.L. 103–322, Title XXXIII, § 330007, Sept. 13, 1994, 108 Stat. 2142; Pub.L. 104–134, Title I, § 101(c)[Title III, § 330], Apr. 26, 1996, 110 Stat. 1321–208; renumbered Title I, Pub.L. 104–140, § 1(a), May 2, 1996, 110 Stat. 1327.)

HISTORICAL AND STATUTORY NOTES

References in Text

The Controlled Substances Act, referred to in subsec. (a)(1), is Title II of Pub.L. 91–513, Oct. 27, 1970, 84 Stat. 1242, as amended, which is classified principally to subchapter I (section 801 et seq.) of chapter 13 of Title 21, Food and Drugs. For complete classification of this Act to the Code, see Short Title note set out under section 801 of Title 21 and Tables.

CHAPTER 93—PUBLIC OFFICERS AND EMPLOYEES

[1] So in original. Does not conform to section catchline.

§ 1901. Collecting or disbursing officer trading in public property

Whoever, being an officer of the United States concerned in the collection or the disbursement of the revenues thereof, carries on any trade or business in the funds or debts of the United States, or of any State, or in any public property of either, shall be fined under this title or imprisoned not more than one year, or both; and shall be removed from office, and be incapable of holding any office under the United States.

(June 25, 1948, c. 645, 62 Stat. 790; Sept. 13, 1994, Pub.L. 103–322, Title XXXIII, § 330016(1)(J), 108 Stat. 2147.)

§ 1902. Disclosure of crop information and speculation thereon

Whoever, being an officer, employee or person acting for or on behalf of the United States or any department or agency thereof, and having by virtue of his office, employment or position, become possessed of information which might influence or affect the market value of any product of the soil grown within the United States, which information is by law or by the rules of such department or agency required to be withheld from publication until a fixed time, willfully imparts, directly or indirectly, such information, or any part thereof, to any person not entitled under the law or the rules of the department or agency to receive the same; or, before such information is made public through regular official channels, directly or indirectly speculates in any such product by buying or selling the same in any quantity, shall be fined under this title or imprisoned not more than ten years, or both.

No person shall be deemed guilty of a violation of any such rules, unless prior to such alleged violation he shall have had actual knowledge thereof.

(June 25, 1948, c. 645, 62 Stat. 790; Sept. 13, 1994, Pub.L. 103–322, Title XXXIII, § 330016(1)(L), 108 Stat. 2147.)

§ 1903. Speculation in stocks or commodities affecting crop insurance

Whoever, while acting in any official capacity in the administration of any Act of Congress relating to crop insurance or to the Federal Crop Insurance Corporation speculates in any agricultural commodity or product thereof, to which such enactments apply, or in contracts relating thereto, or in the stock or membership interests of any association or corporation engaged in handling, processing, or disposing of any such commodity or product, shall be fined under this title or imprisoned not more than two years, or both.

(June 25, 1948, c. 645, 62 Stat. 790; Sept. 13, 1994, Pub.L. 103–322, Title XXXIII, § 330016(1)(L), 108 Stat. 2147.)

[§ 1904. Repealed. Pub.L. 103–322, Title XXXIII, § 330004(11), Sept. 13, 1994, 108 Stat. 2141]

HISTORICAL AND STATUTORY NOTES

Section, Acts June 25, 1948, c. 645, 62 Stat. 791; Sept. 13, 1994, Pub.L. 103–322, Title XXXIII, § 330016(1)(L), 108 Stat. 2147, related to disclosure of information or speculation in securities affecting Reconstruction Finance Corporation.

§ 1905. Disclosure of confidential information generally

Whoever, being an officer or employee of the United States or of any department or agency thereof, any person acting on behalf of the Office of Federal Housing Enterprise Oversight, or agent of the Department of Justice as defined in the Antitrust Civil Process Act (15 U.S.C. 1311–1314), or being an employee of a private sector organization who is or was assigned to an agency under chapter 37 of title 5, publishes, divulges, discloses, or makes known in any manner or to any extent not authorized by law any information coming to him in the course of his employment or official duties or by reason of any examination or investigation made by, or return, report or record made to or filed with, such department or agency or officer or employee thereof, which information concerns or relates to the trade secrets, processes, operations, style of work, or apparatus, or to the identity, confidential statistical data, amount or source of any income, profits, losses, or expenditures of any person, firm, partnership, corporation, or association; or permits any income return or copy thereof or any book containing any abstract or particulars thereof to be seen or examined by any person except as provided by law; shall be fined under this title, or imprisoned not more than one year, or both; and shall be removed from office or employment.

(June 25, 1948, c. 645, 62 Stat. 791; Sept. 12, 1980, Pub.L. 96–349, § 7(b), 94 Stat. 1158; Oct. 28, 1992, Pub.L. 102–550, Title XIII, § 1353, 106 Stat. 3970; Oct. 11, 1996, Pub.L. 104–294, Title VI, § 601(a)(8), 110 Stat. 3498; Dec. 17, 2002, Pub.L. 107–347, Title II, § 209(d)(2), 116 Stat. 2930.)

HISTORICAL AND STATUTORY NOTES

References in Text

The Antitrust Civil Process Act, referred to in text, is Pub.L. 87–664, Sept. 19, 1962, 76 Stat. 548, as amended, which is classified generally to chapter 34 (section 1311 et seq.) of Title 15, Commerce and Trade. For complete classification of this Act to the Code, see Short Title note set out under section 1311 of Title 15 and Tables volume.

Chapter 37 of title 5, referred to in text, is 5 U.S.C.A. § 3701 et seq.

Effective and Applicability Provisions

2002 Acts. Except as otherwise provided by section 402(a)(2) of Pub.L. 107–347, amendments made by Pub.L. 107–347, Titles I and II, §§ 101 to 216, effective 120 days after December 17, 2002, see section 402(a) of Pub.L. 107–347, set out as a note under 44 U.S.C.A. § 3601.

Short Title

1948 Acts. This section is popularly known as the Trade Secrets Act.

§ 1906. Disclosure of information from a bank examination report

Whoever, being an examiner, public or private, or a Government Accountability Office employee with access to bank examination report information under section 714 of title 31, discloses the names of borrowers or the collateral for loans of any member bank of the Federal Reserve System, any bank insured by the Federal Deposit Insurance Corporation, any branch or agency of a foreign bank (as such terms are defined in paragraphs (1) and (3) of section 1(b) of the International Banking Act of 1978), or any organization operating under section 25 or section 25(a) of the Federal Reserve Act, examined by him or subject to Government Accountability Office audit under section 714 of title 31 to other than the proper officers of such bank, branch, agency, or organization, without first having obtained the express permission in writing from the Comptroller of the Currency as to a national bank or a Federal branch or Federal agency (as such terms are defined in paragraphs (5) and (6) of section 1(b) of the International Banking Act of 1978), the Board of Governors of the Federal Reserve System as to a State member bank, an uninsured State branch or State agency (as such terms are defined in paragraphs (11) and (12) of section 1(b) of the International Banking Act of 1978), or an organization operating under section 25 or section 25(a) of the Federal Reserve Act, or the Federal Deposit Insurance Corporation as to any other insured bank, including any insured branch (as defined in section 3(s) of the Federal Deposit Insurance Act),, [1] or from the board of directors of such bank or organization, except when ordered to do so by a court of competent jurisdiction, or by direction of the Congress of the United States, or either House thereof, or any committee of Congress or either House duly authorized or as authorized by section 714 of title 31 shall be fined under this title or imprisoned not more than one year or both.

(June 25, 1948, c. 645, 62 Stat. 791; July 21, 1978, Pub.L. 95–320, § 3, 92 Stat. 393; Sept. 13, 1982, Pub.L. 97–258, § 3(e)(1), 96 Stat. 1064; Nov. 29, 1990, Pub.L. 101–647, Title XXV, § 2597(k), 104 Stat. 4911; Sept. 13, 1994, Pub.L. 103–322, Title XXXIII, § 330016(1)(K), 108 Stat. 2147; July 7, 2004, Pub.L. 108–271, § 8(b), 118 Stat. 814.)

[1] So in original.

HISTORICAL AND STATUTORY NOTES

References in Text

Section 1(b) of the International Banking Act of 1978, referred to in text, is classified to section 3101 of Title 12, Banks and Banking.

The Federal Reserve Act, referred to in text, is Act Dec. 23, 1913, c. 6, 38 Stat. 251, as amended, which is classified principally to chapter 3 of Title 12, 12 U.S.C.A. § 221 et seq. Section 25 of the Federal Reserve Act is classified to subchapter I of chapter 6 of Title 12, 12 U.S.C.A. § 601 et seq. Section 25(a) of the Federal Reserve Act, which is classified to subchapter II of chapter 6 of Title 12, 12 U.S.C.A. § 611 et seq., was renumbered section 25A by Pub.L. 102–242, Title I, § 142(e)(2), Dec. 10, 1991, 105 Stat. 2281. See Tables and 12 U.S.C.A. § 226 for complete classification.

Exception as to Transfer of Functions

Functions vested by any provision of law in the Comptroller of the Currency, referred to in this section, were not included in the transfer of functions of officers, agencies and employees of the Department of the Treasury to the Secretary of the Treasury, made by Reorg. Plan No. 26. of 1950, § 1, eff. July 31, 1950, 15 F.R. 4935, 64 Stat. 1280, set out in the Appendix to Title 5, Government Organization and Employees.

§ 1907. Disclosure of information by farm credit examiner

Whoever, being a farm credit examiner or any examiner, public or private, discloses the names of borrowers of any Federal land bank association or Federal land bank, or any organization examined by him under the provisions of law relating to Federal intermediate credit banks, to other than the proper officers of such institution or organization, without first having obtained express permission in writing from the Land Bank Commissioner or from the board of directors of such institution or organization, except when ordered to do so by a court of competent jurisdiction or by direction of the Congress of the United States or either House thereof, or any committee of Congress or either House duly authorized, shall be fined under this title or imprisoned not more than one year, or both; and shall be disqualified from holding office as a farm credit examiner.

(June 25, 1948, c. 645, 62 Stat. 791; Aug. 18, 1959, Pub.L. 86–168, Title I, § 104(h), 73 Stat. 387; Oct. 12, 1982, Pub.L. 97–297, § 4(c), 96 Stat. 1318; Sept. 13, 1994, Pub.L. 103–322, Title XXXIII, § 330016(1)(K), 108 Stat. 2147.)

HISTORICAL AND STATUTORY NOTES

Effective and Applicability Provisions

1959 Acts. Amendment by Pub.L. 86–168 effective Dec. 1, 1959, see section 104(k) of Pub.L. 86–168.

Abolishment of Office of Land Bank Commissioner

The office of Land Bank Commissioner was abolished by section 636f of Title 12, Banks and Banking.

[§ 1908. Repealed. Pub.L. 103–322, Title XXXIII, § 330004(11), Sept. 13, 1994, 108 Stat. 2141]

HISTORICAL AND STATUTORY NOTES

Section, Acts June 25, 1948, c. 645, 62 Stat. 792; Sept. 13, 1994, Pub.L. 103–322, Title XXXIII, § 330016(1)(K), 108 Stat. 2147, related to disclosure of information by National Agricultural Credit Corporation examiner.

§ 1909. Examiner performing other services

Whoever, being a national-bank examiner, Federal Deposit Insurance Corporation examiner, or farm credit examiner, performs any other service, for compensation, for any bank or banking or loan association, or for any officer, director, or employee thereof, or for any person connected therewith in any capacity, shall be fined under this title or imprisoned not more than one year, or both.

(June 25, 1948, c. 645, 62 Stat. 792; Sept. 13, 1994, Pub.L. 103–322, Title XXXIII, §§ 330004(12), 330016(1)(K), 108 Stat. 2142, 2147.)

§ 1910. Nepotism in appointment of receiver or trustee

Whoever, being a judge of any court of the United States, appoints as receiver, or trustee, any person related to such judge by consanguinity, or affinity, within the fourth degree—

Shall be fined under this title or imprisoned not more than five years, or both.

(June 25, 1948, c. 645, 62 Stat. 792; Sept. 13, 1994, Pub.L. 103–322, Title XXXIII, § 330016(1)(L), 108 Stat. 2147.)

§ 1911. Receiver mismanaging property

Whoever, being a receiver, trustee, or manager in possession of any property in any cause pending in any court of the United States, willfully fails to manage and operate such property according to the requirements of the valid laws of the State in which such property shall be situated, in the same manner that the owner or possessor thereof would be bound to do if in possession thereof, shall be fined under this title or imprisoned not more than one year, or both.

(June 25, 1948, c. 645, 62 Stat. 792; Sept. 13, 1994, Pub.L. 103–322, Title XXXIII, § 330016(1)(J), 108 Stat. 2147.)

§ 1912. Unauthorized fees for inspection of vessels

Whoever, being an officer, employee, or agent of the United States or any agency thereof, engaged in inspection of vessels, upon any pretense, receives any fee or reward for his services, except what is allowed to him by law, shall be fined under this title or imprisoned not more than six months, or both; and shall forfeit his office.

(June 25, 1948, c. 645, 62 Stat. 792; Sept. 13, 1994, Pub.L. 103–322, Title XXXIII, § 330016(1)(G), 108 Stat. 2147.)

§ 1913. Lobbying with appropriated moneys

No part of the money appropriated by any enactment of Congress shall, in the absence of express authorization by Congress, be used directly or indirectly to pay for any personal service, advertisement, telegram, telephone, letter, printed or written matter, or other device, intended or designed to influence in any manner a Member of Congress, a jurisdiction, or an official of any government, to favor, adopt, or oppose, by vote or otherwise, any legislation, law, ratification, policy or appropriation, whether before or after the introduction of any bill, measure, or resolution proposing such legislation, law, ratification, policy or appropriation; but this shall not prevent officers or employees of the United States or of its departments or agencies from communicating to any such Member or official, at his request, or to Congress or such official, through the proper official channels, requests for any legislation, law, ratification, policy or appropriations which they deem necessary for the efficient conduct of the public business, or from making any communication whose prohibition by this section might, in the opinion of the Attorney General, violate the Constitution or interfere with the conduct of foreign policy, counter-intelligence, intelligence, or national security activities. Violations of this section shall constitute violations of section 1352(a) of title 31.

(June 25, 1948, c. 645, 62 Stat. 792; Sept. 13, 1994, Pub.L. 103–322, Title XXXIII, § 330016(1)(G), 108 Stat. 2147; Nov. 2, 2002, Pub.L. 107–273, Div. A, Title II, § 205(b), 116 Stat. 1778.)

[§ 1914. Repealed. Pub.L. 87–849, § 2, Oct. 23, 1962, 76 Stat. 1126]

HISTORICAL AND STATUTORY NOTES

Section, Act June 25, 1948, c. 645, 62 Stat. 793, related to salary of government officials and employees payable only by United States, and is supplanted by section 209 of this title.

Effective Date of Repeal

Repeal of section effective 90 days after Oct. 23, 1962, see section 4 of Pub.L. 87–849, set out as an Effective Date note under section 201 of this title.

Exemptions

Exemptions from the provisions of this section heretofore created or authorized by statute which are in force on the effective date of the repeal of this section deemed to be exemptions from section 209 of this title except to the extent that they affect officers or employees of the executive branch of the United States Government, of any independent agency of the United States, or of the District of Columbia, as to whom they are no longer applicable, see section 2 of Pub.L. 87–849, set out as an Exemptions note under section 282 of this title.

§ 1915. Compromise of customs liabilities

Whoever, being an officer of the United States, without lawful authority compromises or abates or attempts to compromise or abate any claim of the United States arising under the customs laws for any fine, penalty or forfeiture, or in any manner relieves or attempts to relieve any person, vessel, vehicle, merchandise or baggage therefrom, shall be fined under this title or imprisoned not more than two years, or both.

(June 25, 1948, c. 645, 62 Stat. 793; Sept. 13, 1994, Pub.L. 103–322, Title XXXIII, § 330016(1)(K), 108 Stat. 2147.)

HISTORICAL AND STATUTORY NOTES

References in Text

The customs laws, referred to in text, are classified generally to Title 19, Customs Duties.

§ 1916. Unauthorized employment and disposition of lapsed appropriations

Whoever—

(1) violates the provision of section 3103 of title 5 that an individual may be employed in the civil service in an Executive department at the seat of

Government only for services actually rendered in connection with and for the purposes of the appropriation from which he is paid; or

(2) violates the provision of section 5501 of title 5 that money accruing from lapsed salaries or from unused appropriations for salaries shall be covered into the Treasury of the United States;

shall be fined under this title or imprisoned not more than one year, or both.

(Added Pub.L. 89–554, § 3(d), Sept. 6, 1966, 80 Stat. 608, and amended Pub.L. 104–294, Title VI, § 601(a)(8), Oct. 11, 1996, 110 Stat. 3498; Pub.L. 107–273, Div. B, Title III, § 3002(a)(3), Nov. 2, 2002, 116 Stat. 1805.)

§ 1917. Interference with civil service examinations

Whoever, being a member or employee of the United States Office of Personnel Management or an individual in the public service, willfully and corruptly—

(1) defeats, deceives, or obstructs an individual in respect of his right of examination according to the rules prescribed by the President under title 5 for the administration of the competitive service and the regulations prescribed by such Office under section 1302(a) of title 5;

(2) falsely marks, grades, estimates, or reports on the examination or proper standing of an individual examined;

(3) makes a false representation concerning the mark, grade, estimate, or report on the examination or proper standing of an individual examined, or concerning the individual examined; or

(4) furnishes to an individual any special or secret information for the purpose of improving or injuring the prospects or chances of an individual examined, or to be examined, being appointed, employed, or promoted;

shall, for each offense, be fined under this title not less than $100 or imprisoned not less than ten days nor more than one year, or both.

(Added Pub.L. 89–554, § 3(d), Sept. 6, 1966, 80 Stat. 609, and amended Sept. 13, 1994, Pub.L. 103–322, Title XXXIII, § 330010(2), 108 Stat. 2143; Oct. 11, 1996, Pub.L. 104–294, Title VI, § 601(a)(9), 110 Stat. 3498.)

HISTORICAL AND STATUTORY NOTES

Transfer of Functions

All functions vested by statute in the United States Civil Service Commission were transferred to the Director of the Office of Personnel Management (except as otherwise specified) by Reorg. Plan No. 2 of 1978, § 102, 43 F.R. 36037, 92 Stat. 3783, set out under section 1101 of Title 5, Government Organization and Employees, effective Jan. 1, 1979, as provided by section 1–102 of Ex. Ord. No. 12107, Dec. 28, 1978, 44 F.R. 1055, set out under section 1101 of Title 5.

§ 1918. Disloyalty and asserting the right to strike against the Government

Whoever violates the provision of section 7311 of title 5 that an individual may not accept or hold a position in the Government of the United States or the government of the District of Columbia if he—

(1) advocates the overthrow of our constitutional form of government;

(2) is a member of an organization that he knows advocates the overthrow of our constitutional form of government;

(3) participates in a strike, or asserts the right to strike, against the Government of the United States or the government of the District of Columbia; or

(4) is a member of an organization of employees of the Government of the United States or of individuals employed by the government of the District of Columbia that he knows asserts the right to strike against the Government of the United States or the government of the District of Columbia;

shall be fined under this title or imprisoned not more than one year and a day, or both.

(Added Pub.L. 89–554, § 3(d), Sept. 6, 1966, 80 Stat. 609, and amended Pub.L. 104–294, Title VI, § 601(a)(8), Oct. 11, 1996, 110 Stat. 3498.)

§ 1919. False statement to obtain unemployment compensation for Federal service

Whoever makes a false statement or representation of a material fact knowing it to be false, or knowingly fails to disclose a material fact, to obtain or increase for himself or for any other individual any payment authorized to be paid under chapter 85 of title 5 or under an agreement thereunder, shall be fined not more than $1,000 or imprisoned not more than one year, or both.

(Added Pub.L. 89–554, § 3(d), Sept. 6, 1966, 80 Stat. 609.)

§ 1920. False statement or fraud to obtain Federal employees' compensation

Whoever knowingly and willfully falsifies, conceals, or covers up a material fact, or makes a false, fictitious, or fraudulent statement or representation, or makes or uses a false statement or report knowing the same to contain any false, fictitious, or fraudulent statement or entry in connection with the application for or receipt of compensation or other benefit or payment under subchapter I or III of chapter 81 of title 5, shall be guilty of perjury, and on conviction thereof shall be punished by a fine under this title, or by imprisonment for not more than 5 years, or both; but if the amount of the benefits falsely obtained does not exceed $1,000, such person shall be punished by a fine under this title, or by imprisonment for not more than 1 year, or both.

(Added Pub.L. 89–554, § 3(d), Sept. 6, 1966, 80 Stat. 610, and amended Pub.L. 103–322, Title XXXIII, § 330016(1)(I), Sept. 13, 1994, 108 Stat. 2147; Pub.L. 103–333, Title I, § 101(b)(1), Sept. 30, 1994, 108 Stat. 2547; Pub.L. 104–294, Title VI, § 601(a)(10), Oct. 11, 1996, 110 Stat. 3498; Pub.L. 107–273, Div. B, Title IV, § 4002(f)(2), Nov. 2, 2002, 116 Stat. 1811.)

HISTORICAL AND STATUTORY NOTES

Effective and Applicability Provisions

1994 Acts. Amendment by section 101(b) of Pub.L. 103–333 effective Sept. 30, 1994, see section 101(c) of Pub.L. 103–333, set out as a note under section 8148 of Title 5, Government Organization and Employees.

§ 1921. Receiving Federal employees' compensation after marriage

Whoever, being entitled to compensation under sections 8107–8113 and 8133 of title 5 and whose compensation by the terms of those sections stops or is reduced on his marriage or on the marriage of his dependent, accepts after such marriage any compensation or payment to which he is not entitled shall be fined under this title or imprisoned not more than one year, or both.

(Added Pub.L. 89–554, § 3(d), Sept. 6, 1966, 80 Stat. 610, and amended Pub.L. 103–322, Title XXXIII, § 330016(1)(I), Sept. 13, 1994, 108 Stat. 2147.)

§ 1922. False or withheld report concerning Federal employees' compensation

Whoever, being an officer or employee of the United States charged with the responsibility for making the reports of the immediate superior specified by section 8120 of title 5, willfully fails, neglects, or refuses to make any of the reports, or knowingly files a false report, or induces, compels, or directs an injured employee to forego filing of any claim for compensation or other benefits provided under subchapter I of chapter 81 of title 5 or any extension or application thereof, or willfully retains any notice, report, claim, or paper which is required to be filed under that subchapter or any extension or application thereof, or regulations prescribed thereunder, shall be fined under this title or imprisoned not more than one year, or both.

(Added Pub.L. 89–554, § 3(d), Sept. 6, 1966, 80 Stat. 610, and amended Pub.L. 103–322, Title XXXIII, § 330016(1)(G), Sept. 13, 1994, 108 Stat. 2147.)

§ 1923. Fraudulent receipt of payments of missing persons

Whoever obtains or receives any money, check, or allotment under—

(1) subchapter VII of chapter 55 of title 5; or

(2) chapter 10 of title 37;

without being entitled thereto, with intent to defraud, shall be fined under this title or imprisoned not more than one year, or both.

(Added Pub.L. 89–554, § 3(d), Sept. 6, 1966, 80 Stat. 610, and amended Pub.L. 103–322, Title XXXIII § 330016(1)(I), Sept. 13, 1994, 108 Stat. 2147.)

§ 1924. Unauthorized removal and retention of classified documents or material

(a) Whoever, being an officer, employee, contractor, or consultant of the United States, and, by virtue of his office, employment, position, or contract, becomes possessed of documents or materials containing classified information of the United States, knowingly removes such documents or materials without authority and with the intent to retain such documents or materials at an unauthorized location shall be fined under this title or imprisoned for not more than one year, or both.

(b) For purposes of this section, the provision of documents and materials to the Congress shall not constitute an offense under subsection (a).

(c) In this section, the term "classified information of the United States" means information originated, owned, or possessed by the United States Government concerning the national defense or foreign relations of the United States that has been determined pursuant to law or Executive order to require protection against unauthorized disclosure in the interests of national security.

(Added Pub.L. 103–359, Title VIII, § 808(a), Oct. 14, 1994, 108 Stat. 3453, and amended Pub.L. 107–273, Div. B, Title IV, § 4002(d)(1)(C)(i), Nov. 2, 2002, 116 Stat. 1809.)

CHAPTER 95—RACKETEERING

4–Year Congressional Review; Expedited Consideration

Effective on and after the first day of fiscal year 2005, amendments by Title III (§§ 301 to 377) of Pub.L. 107–56 shall terminate if Congress enacts a joint resolution to that effect; such resolution shall be given expedited consideration, see Pub.L. 107–56 Title III, § 303, Oct. 26, 2001, 115 Stat. 298, set out as a note under 31 U.S.C.A. § 5311.

§ 1951. Interference with commerce by threats or violence

(a) Whoever in any way or degree obstructs, delays, or affects commerce or the movement of any article or commodity in commerce, by robbery or extortion or attempts or conspires so to do, or commits or threatens physical violence to any person or property in furtherance of a plan or purpose to do anything in violation of this section shall be fined under this title or imprisoned not more than twenty years, or both.

(b) As used in this section—

(1) The term "robbery" means the unlawful taking or obtaining of personal property from the person or in the presence of another, against his will, by means of actual or threatened force, or violence, or fear of injury, immediate or future, to his person or property, or property in his custody or possession, or the person or property of a relative or member of his family or of anyone in his company at the time of the taking or obtaining.

(2) The term "extortion" means the obtaining of property from another, with his consent, induced by wrongful use of actual or threatened force, violence, or fear, or under color of official right.

(3) The term "commerce" means commerce within the District of Columbia, or any Territory or Possession of the United States; all commerce between any point in a State, Territory, Possession, or the District of Columbia and any point outside thereof; all commerce between points within the same State through any place outside such State; and all other commerce over which the United States has jurisdiction.

(c) This section shall not be construed to repeal, modify or affect section 17 of Title 15, sections 52, 101–115, 151–166 of Title 29 or sections 151–188 of Title 45.

(June 25, 1948, c. 645, 62 Stat. 793; Sept. 13, 1994, Pub.L. 103–322, Title XXXIII, § 330016(1)(L), 108 Stat. 2147.)

HISTORICAL AND STATUTORY NOTES

References in Text

Sections 101 to 115 of Title 29, referred to in text of subsec. (c), is a reference to Act Mar. 23, 1932, c. 90, 47 Stat. 70, popularly known as the Norris-LaGuardia Act. For complete classification of this Act to the Code, see Short Title note set out under section 101 of Title 29, Labor, and Tables.

Section 11 of that act, formerly classified to section 111 of Title 29, was repealed and reenacted as section 3692 of this title by Act June 25, 1948, c. 645, § 21, 62 Stat. 862, eff. Sept. 1, 1948.

Section 12 of that act, formerly classified to section 112 of Title 29, was repealed by Act June 25, 1948, and is covered by rule 42(b), Federal Rules of Criminal Procedure, this title.

Section 164 of Title 45, included within the reference in subsec. (c) to sections 151 to 188 of Title 45, was repealed by Act Oct. 10, 1940, c. 851, § 4, 54 Stat. 1111. See section 5 of Title 41, Public Contracts.

Section 186 of Title 45, included within the reference in subsec. (c) to sections 151 to 188 of Title 45, was omitted from the Code.

Short Title

This section is commonly known as the "Hobbs Act."

§ 1952. Interstate and foreign travel or transportation in aid of racketeering enterprises

(a) Whoever travels in interstate or foreign commerce or uses the mail or any facility in interstate or foreign commerce, with intent to—

(1) distribute the proceeds of any unlawful activity; or

(2) commit any crime of violence to further any unlawful activity; or

(3) otherwise promote, manage, establish, carry on, or facilitate the promotion, management, establishment, or carrying on, of any unlawful activity,

and thereafter performs or attempts to perform—

(A) an act described in paragraph (1) or (3) shall be fined under this title, imprisoned not more than 5 years, or both; or

(B) an act described in paragraph (2) shall be fined under this title, imprisoned for not more than 20 years, or both, and if death results shall be imprisoned for any term of years or for life.

(b) As used in this section (i) "unlawful activity" means (1) any business enterprise involving gambling, liquor on which the Federal excise tax has not been paid, narcotics or controlled substances (as defined in section 102(6) of the Controlled Substances Act), or prostitution offenses in violation of the laws of the State in which they are committed or of the United States, (2) extortion, bribery, or arson in violation of the laws of the State in which committed or of the United States, or (3) any act which is indictable under subchapter II of chapter 53 of title 31, United States Code, or under section 1956 or 1957 of this title and (ii) the term "State" includes a State of the United States, the District of Columbia, and any commonwealth, territory, or possession of the United States.

(c) Investigations of violations under this section involving liquor shall be conducted under the supervision of the Attorney General.

(Added Pub.L. 87–228 § 1(a), Sept. 13, 1961, 75 Stat. 498, and amended Pub.L. 89–68, July 7, 1965, 79 Stat. 212; Pub.L. 91–513, Title II, § 701(i) (2), Oct. 27, 1970, 84 Stat. 1282; Pub.L. 99–570, Title XIII, § 1365(a), Oct. 27, 1986, 100 Stat. 3207–35; Pub.L. 101–647, Title XII, § 1205(i), Title XVI, § 1604, Nov. 29, 1990, 104 Stat. 4831, 4843; Pub.L. 103–322, Title XIV, § 140007(a), Title XXXIII, § 330016(1)(L), Sept. 13, 1994, 108 Stat. 2033, 2147; Pub.L. 107–296, Title XI, § 1112(h), Nov. 25, 2002, 116 Stat. 2277.)

HISTORICAL AND STATUTORY NOTES

References in Text

Section 102(6) of the Controlled Substances Act, referred to in subsec. (b) (1), is classified to section 802(6) of Title 21, Food and Drugs.

Effective and Applicability Provisions

2002 Acts. Amendment to this section by Pub.L. 107–296 effective 60 days after Nov. 25, 2002, see Pub.L. 107–296, § 4, set out as a note under 6 U.S.C.A. § 101.

1970 Acts. Amendment by Pub.L. 91–513 effective on the first day of the seventh calendar month that begins after Oct. 26, 1970, see section 704 of Pub.L. 91–513, set out as an Effective Date note under section 801 of Title 21, Food and Drugs.

Savings Provisions

Amendment of this section by Pub.L. 91–513 not to affect or abate any prosecutions for violation of law or any civil seizures or forfeitures and injunctive proceedings commenced prior to the effective date of such amendment, and all administrative proceedings pending before the former Bureau of Narcotics and Dangerous Drugs on Oct. 27, 1970, were to be continued and brought to final determination in accord with laws and regulations in effect prior to Oct. 27, 1970, see section 702 of Pub.L. 91–513, set out as a Savings Provision note under section 321 of Title 21, Food and Drugs.

Short Title

This section is commonly known as the "Travel Act."

[§ 1952A. Renumbered 1958]

[§ 1952B. Renumbered 1959]

§ 1953. Interstate transportation of wagering paraphernalia

(a) Whoever, except a common carrier in the usual course of its business, knowingly carries or sends in interstate or foreign commerce any record, paraphernalia, ticket, certificate, bills, slip, token, paper, writing, or other device used, or to be used, or adapted, devised, or designed for use in (a) bookmaking; or (b) wagering pools with respect to a sporting event; or (c) in a numbers, policy, bolita, or similar game shall be fined under this title or imprisoned for not more than five years or both.

(b) This section shall not apply to (1) parimutuel betting equipment, parimutuel tickets where legally acquired, or parimutuel materials used or designed for use at racetracks or other sporting events in connection with which betting is legal under applicable State law, or (2) the transportation of betting materials to be used in the placing of bets or wagers on a sporting event into a State in which such betting is legal under the statutes of that State, or (3) the carriage or transportation in interstate or foreign commerce of any newspaper or similar publication, or (4) equipment, tickets, or materials used or designed for use within a State in a lottery conducted by that State acting under authority of State law, or (5) the transportation in foreign commerce to a destination in a foreign country of equipment, tickets, or materials designed to be used within that foreign country in a lottery which is authorized by the laws of that foreign country.

(c) Nothing contained in this section shall create immunity from criminal prosecution under any laws of any State, Commonwealth of Puerto Rico, territory, possession, or the District of Columbia.

(d) For the purposes of this section (1) "State" means a State of the United States, the District of Columbia, the Commonwealth of Puerto Rico, or any territory or possession of the United States; and (2) "foreign country" means any empire, country, dominion, colony, or protectorate, or any subdivision thereof (other than the United States, its territories or possessions).

(e) For the purposes of this section "lottery" means the pooling of proceeds derived from the sale of tickets or chances and allotting those proceeds or parts thereof by chance to one or more chance takers or ticket purchasers. "Lottery" does not include the placing or accepting of bets or wagers on sporting events or contests.

(Added Pub.L. 87–218, § 1, Sept. 13, 1961, 75 Stat. 492, and amended Pub.L. 93–583, § 3, Jan. 2, 1975, 88 Stat. 1916; Pub.L. 96–90, § 2, Oct. 23, 1979, 93 Stat. 698; Pub.L. 103–322, Title XXXIII, § 330016(1)(L), Sept. 13, 1994, 108 Stat. 2147.)

§ 1954. Offer, acceptance, or solicitation to influence operations of employee benefit plan

Whoever being—

(1) an administrator, officer, trustee, custodian, counsel, agent, or employee of any employee welfare benefit plan or employee pension benefit plan; or

(2) an officer, counsel, agent, or employee of an employer or an employer any of whose employees are covered by such plan; or

(3) an officer, counsel, agent, or employee of an employee organization any of whose members are covered by such plan; or

(4) a person who, or an officer, counsel, agent, or employee of an organization which, provides benefit plan services to such plan

receives or agrees to receive or solicits any fee, kickback, commission, gift, loan, money, or thing of value because of or with intent to be influenced with respect to, any of the actions, decisions, or other duties relating to any question or matter concerning such plan or any person who directly or indirectly gives or offers, or promises to give or offer, any fee, kickback, commission, gift, loan, money, or thing of value prohibited by this section, shall be fined under this title or imprisoned not more than three years, or both: *Provided*, That this section shall not prohibit the payment to or acceptance by any person of bona fide salary, compensation, or other payments made for goods or facilities actually furnished or for services actually performed in the regular course of his duties as such person, administrator, officer, trustee, custodian, counsel, agent, or employee of such plan, employer, employee organization, or organization providing benefit plan services to such plan.

As used in this section, the term (a) "any employee welfare benefit plan" or "employee pension benefit plan" means any employee welfare benefit plan or employee pension benefit plan, respectively, subject to any provision of title I of the Employee Retirement Income Security Act of 1974, and (b) "employee organization" and "administrator" as defined respectively in sections 3(4) and (3)(16) of the Employee Retirement Income Security Act of 1974.

(Added Pub.L. 87–420, § 17(e), Mar. 20, 1962, 76 Stat. 42, and amended Pub.L. 91–452, Title II, § 225, Oct. 15, 1970, 84 Stat. 930; Pub.L. 93–406, Title I, § 111(a)(2)(C), Sept. 2, 1974, 88 Stat. 852; Pub.L. 103–322, Title XXXIII, § 330016(1)(L), Sept. 13, 1994, 108 Stat. 2147.)

HISTORICAL AND STATUTORY NOTES

References in Text

The Employee Retirement Income Security Act of 1974, referred to in text, is Pub.L. 93–406, Sept. 2, 1974, 88 Stat. 832, as amended. Title I of the Employee Retirement Income Security Act of 1974, referred to in text, is classified generally to subchapter I (section 1001 et seq.) of chapter 18 of Title 29, Labor. For complete classification of this Act to the Code, see Short Title note set out under section 1001 of Title 29 and Tables volume.

Section 3(4) of the Employee Retirement Income Security Act of 1974, referred to in text, is classified to section 1002(4) of Title 29.

Section (3)(16) of the Employee Retirement Income Security Act of 1974, referred to in text, probably means section 3(16) of the Employee Retirement Income Security Act of 1974, which is classified to section 1002(16) of Title 29.

Effective and Applicability Provisions

1974 Acts. Amendment by Pub.L. 93–406 effective Jan. 1, 1975, except as provided in section 1031(b)(2) of Title 29, Labor, see section 1031 of Title 29.

1970 Acts. Amendment by Pub.L. 91–452 effective the sixtieth day following Oct. 15, 1970, see section 260 of Pub.L. 91–452, set out as an Effective Date; Savings Provision note under section 6001 of this title.

1962 Acts. Section effective 90 days after Mar. 20, 1962, see section 19 of Pub.L. 87–420, set out as an Effective Date note under section 664 of this title.

Savings Provision

Amendment by Pub.L. 91–452 not to affect any immunity to which any individual is entitled under this section by reason of any testimony given before the sixtieth day following Oct. 15, 1970, see section 260 of Pub.L. 91–452, set out in part as an Effective Date; Savings Provision note section 6001 of this title.

§ 1955. Prohibition of illegal gambling businesses

(a) Whoever conducts, finances, manages, supervises, directs, or owns all or part of an illegal gambling business shall be fined under this title or imprisoned not more than five years, or both.

(b) As used in this section—

(1) "illegal gambling business" means a gambling business which—

(i) is a violation of the law of a State or political subdivision in which it is conducted;

(ii) involves five or more persons who conduct, finance, manage, supervise, direct, or own all or part of such business; and

(iii) has been or remains in substantially continuous operation for a period in excess of thirty days or has a gross revenue of $2,000 in any single day.

(2) "gambling" includes but is not limited to pool-selling, bookmaking, maintaining slot machines, roulette wheels or dice tables, and conducting lotteries, policy, bolita or numbers games, or selling chances therein.

(3) "State" means any State of the United States, the District of Columbia, the Commonwealth of Puerto Rico, and any territory or possession of the United States.

(c) If five or more persons conduct, finance, manage, supervise, direct, or own all or part of a gambling business and such business operates for two or more successive days, then, for the purpose of obtaining warrants for arrests, interceptions, and other searches and seizures, probable cause that the business receives gross revenue in excess of $2,000 in any single day shall be deemed to have been established.

(d) Any property, including money, used in violation of the provisions of this section may be seized and forfeited to the United States. All provisions of law relating to the seizures, summary, and judicial forfeiture procedures, and condemnation of vessels, vehicles, merchandise, and baggage for violation of the customs laws; the disposition of such vessels, vehicles, merchandise, and baggage or the proceeds from such sale; the remission or mitigation of such forfeitures; and the compromise of claims and the award of compensation to informers in respect of such forfeitures shall apply to seizures and forfeitures incurred or alleged to have been incurred under the provisions of this section, insofar as applicable and not inconsistent with such provisions. Such duties as are imposed upon the collector of customs or any other person in respect to the seizure and forfeiture of vessels, vehicles, merchandise, and baggage under the customs laws shall be performed with respect to seizures and forfeitures of property used or intended for use in violation of this section by such officers, agents, or other persons as may be designated for that purpose by the Attorney General.

(e) This section shall not apply to any bingo game, lottery, or similar game of chance conducted by an organization exempt from tax under paragraph (3) of subsection (c) of section 501 of the Internal Revenue Code of 1986, as amended, if no part of the gross receipts derived from such activity inures to the benefit of any private shareholder, member, or employee of such organization except as compensation for actual expenses incurred by him in the conduct of such activity.

(Added Pub.L. 91–452, Title VIII, § 803(a), Oct. 15, 1970, 84 Stat. 937, and amended Pub.L. 99–514, § 2, Oct. 22, 1986, 100 Stat. 2095; Pub.L. 103–322, Title XXXIII, § 330016(1)(N), Sept. 13, 1994, 108 Stat. 2148.)

HISTORICAL AND STATUTORY NOTES

References in Text

The customs laws, referred to in subsec. (d), are classified generally to Title 19, Customs Duties.

Paragraph (3) of subsection (c) of section 501 of the Internal Revenue Code of 1954, referred to in subsec. (e), is classified to section 501(c)(3) of Title 26, Internal Revenue Code of 1954.

Transfer of Functions

All offices of collector of customs, comptroller of customs, surveyor of customs, and appraiser of merchandise in the Bureau of Customs of the Department of the Treasury to which appointments were required to be made by the President with the advice and consent of the Senate were ordered abolished, with such offices to be terminated not later than Dec. 31, 1966, by Reorg. Plan No. 1 of 1965, eff. May 25, 1965, 30 F.R. 7035, 79 Stat. 1317, set out in the Appendix to Title 5, Government Organization and Employees. All functions of the offices eliminated were already vested in the Secretary of the Treasury by Reorg. Plan No. 26 of 1950, eff. July 31, 1950, 15 F.R. 4935, 64 Stat. 1280, set out in the Appendix to Title 5.

National Gambling Impact Study Commission

Pub.L. 104–169, Aug. 3, 1996, 110 Stat. 1482, as amended Pub.L. 105–30, § 1, July 25, 1997, 111 Stat. 248, provided that:

"Section 1. Short title.

"This Act [this note] may be cited as the 'National Gambling Impact Study Commission Act'.

"Sec. 2. Findings.

"The Congress finds that—

"(1) the most recent Federal study of gambling in the United States was completed in 1976;

"(2) legalization of gambling has increased substantially over the past 20 years, and State, local, and Native American tribal governments have established gambling as a source of jobs and additional revenue;

"(3) the growth of various forms of gambling, including electronic gambling and gambling over the Internet, could affect interstate and international matters under the jurisdiction of the Federal Government;

"(4) questions have been raised regarding the social and economic impacts of gambling, and Federal, State, local, and Native American tribal governments lack recent, comprehensive information regarding those impacts; and

"(5) a Federal commission should be established to conduct a comprehensive study of the social and economic impacts of gambling in the United States.

"Sec. 3. National Gambling Impact Study Commission.

"(a) Establishment of Commission.—There is established a commission to be known as the National Gambling Impact Study Commission (hereinafter referred to in this Act as 'the Commission'). The Commission shall—

"(1) be composed of 9 members appointed in accordance with subsection (b); and

"(2) conduct its business in accordance with the provisions of this Act.

"(b) Membership.—

"(1) In general.—The Commissioners shall be appointed for the life of the Commission as follows:

"(A) 3 shall be appointed by the President of the United States.

"(B) 3 shall be appointed by the Speaker of the House of Representatives.

"(C) 3 shall be appointed by the Majority Leader of the Senate.

"(2) Persons eligible.—The members of the Commission shall be individuals who have knowledge or expertise, whether by experience or training, in matters to be studied by the Commission under section 4. The members may be from the public or private sector, and may include Federal, State, local, or Native American tribal officers or employees, members of academia, non-profit organizations, or industry, or other interested individuals.

"(3) Consultation required.—The President, the Speaker of the House Representatives, and the Majority Leader of the Senate shall consult among themselves prior to the appointment of the members of the Commission in order to achieve, to the maximum extent possible, fair and equitable representation of various points of view with respect to the matters to be studied by the Commission under section 4.

"(4) Completion of appointments; vacancies.—The President, the Speaker of the House of Representatives, and the Majority Leader of the Senate shall conduct the consultation required under paragraph (3) and shall each make their respective appointments not later than 60 days after the date of enactment of this Act [Aug. 3, 1996]. Any vacancy that occurs during the life of the Commission shall not affect the powers of the Commission, and shall be filled in the same manner as the original appointment not later than 60 days after the vacancy occurs.

"(5) **Operation of the Commission.—**

"(A) **Chairmanship.**—The President, the Speaker of the House of Representatives, and the Majority Leader of the Senate shall jointly designate one member as the Chairman of the Commission. In the event of a disagreement among the appointing authorities, the Chairman shall be determined by a majority vote of the appointing authorities. The determination of which member shall be Chairman shall be made not later than 15 days after the appointment of the last member of the Commission, but in no case later than 75 days after the date of enactment of this Act [Aug. 3, 1996].

"(B) **Meetings.**—The Commission shall meet at the call of the Chairman. The initial meeting of the Commission shall be conducted not later than 30 days after the appointment of the last member of the Commission, or not later than 30 days after the date on which appropriated funds are available for the Commission, whichever is later.

"(C) **Quorum; voting; rules.**—A majority of the members of the Commission shall constitute a quorum to conduct business, but the Commission may establish a lesser quorum for conducting hearings scheduled by the Commission. Each member of the Commission shall have one vote, and the vote of each member shall be accorded the same weight. The Commission may establish by majority vote any other rules for the conduct of the Commission's business, if such rules are not inconsistent with this Act or other applicable law.

"**Sec. 4. Duties of the Commission.**

"(a) **Study.—**

"(1) **In general.**—It shall be the duty of the Commission to conduct a comprehensive legal and factual study of the social and economic impacts of gambling in the United States on—

"(A) Federal, State, local, and Native American tribal governments; and

"(B) communities and social institutions generally, including individuals, families, and businesses within such communities and institutions.

"(2) Matters to be studied.—The matters studied by the Commission under paragraph (1) shall at a minimum include—

"(A) a review of existing Federal, State, local, and Native American tribal government policies and practices with respect to the legalization or prohibition of gambling, including a review of the costs of such policies and practices;

"(B) an assessment of the relationship between gambling and levels of crime, and of existing enforcement and regulatory practices that are intended to address any such relationship;

"(C) an assessment of pathological or problem gambling, including its impact on individuals, families, businesses, social institutions, and the economy;

"(D) an assessment of the impacts of gambling on individuals, families, businesses, social institutions, and the economy generally, including the role of advertising in promoting gambling and the impact of gambling on depressed economic areas;

"(E) an assessment of the extent to which gambling provides revenues to State, local, and Native American tribal governments, and the extent to which possible alternative revenue sources may exist for such governments; and

"(F) an assessment of the interstate and international effects of gambling by electronic means, including the use of interactive technologies and the Internet.

"(b) **Report.**—No later than 2 years after the date on which the Commission first meets, the Commission shall submit to the President, the Congress, State Governors, and Native American tribal governments a comprehensive report of the Commission's findings and conclusions, together with any recommendations of the Commission. Such report shall include a summary of the reports submitted to the Commission by the Advisory Commission on Intergovernmental Relations and National Research Council under section 7, as well as a summary of any other material relied on by the Commission in the preparation of its report.

"**Sec. 5. Powers of the Commission.**

"(a) **Hearings.—**

"(1) **In general.**—The Commission may hold such hearings, sit and act at such times and places, administer such oaths, take such testimony, and receive such evidence as the Commission considers advisable to carry out its duties under section 4.

"(2) **Witness expenses.**—Witnesses requested to appear before the Commission shall be paid the same fees as are paid to witnesses under section 1821 of title 28, United States Code [28 U.S.C.A. § 1821]. The per diem and mileage allowances for witnesses shall be paid from funds appropriated to the Commission.

"(b) **Subpoenas.—**

"(1) **In general.**—If a person fails to supply information requested by the Commission, the Commission may by majority vote require by subpoena the production of any written or recorded information, document, report, answer, record, account, paper, computer file, or other data or documentary evidence necessary to carry out its duties under section 4. The Commission shall transmit to the Attorney General a confidential, written notice at least 10 days in advance of the issuance of any such subpoena. A subpoena under this paragraph may require the production of materials from any place within the United States.

"(2) **Interrogatories.**—The Commission may, with respect only to information necessary to understand any materials obtained through a subpoena under paragraph (1), issue a subpoena requiring the person producing such materials to answer, either through a sworn deposition or through written answers provided under oath (at the election of the person upon whom the subpoena is served), to interrogatories from the Commission regarding such information. A complete recording or transcription shall be made of any deposition made under this paragraph.

"(3) **Certification.**—Each person who submits materials or information to the Commission pursuant to a subpoena issued under paragraph (1) or (2) shall certify to the Commission the authenticity and completeness of all materials or information submitted. The provisions of section

1001 of title 18, United States Code [18 U.S.C.A. § 1001], shall apply to any false statements made with respect to the certification required under this paragraph.

"(4) Treatment of subpoenas.—Any subpoena issued by the Commission under paragraph (1) or (2) shall comply with the requirements for subpoenas issued by a United States district court under the Federal Rules of Civil Procedure.

"(5) Failure to obey a subpoena.—If a person refuses to obey a subpoena issued by the Commission under paragraph (1) or (2), the Commission may apply to a United States district court for an order requiring that person to comply with such subpoena. The application may be made within the judicial district in which that person is found, resides, or transacts business. Any failure to obey the order of the court may be punished by the court as civil contempt.

"(c) Information from Federal agencies.—The Commission may secure directly from any Federal department or agency such information as the Commission considers necessary to carry out its duties under section 4. Upon the request of the Commission, the head of such department or agency may furnish such information to the Commission.

"(d) Information to be kept confidential.—The Commission shall be considered an agency of the Federal Government for purposes of section 1905 of title 18, United States Code [18 U.S.C.A. § 1905], and any individual employed by an individual, entity, or organization under contract to the Commission under section 7 shall be considered an employee of the Commission for the purposes of section 1905 of title 18, United States Code [18 U.S.C.A. § 1905]. Information obtained by the Commission, other than information available to the public, shall not be disclosed to any person in any manner, except—

"(1) to Commission employees or employees of any individual, entity, or organization under contract to the Commission under section 7 for the purpose of receiving, reviewing, or processing such information;

"(2) upon court order; or

"(3) when publicly released by the Commission in an aggregate or summary form that does not directly or indirectly disclose—

"(A) the identity of any person or business entity; or

"(B) any information which could not be released under section 1905 of title 18, United States Code [18 U.S.C.A. § 1905].

"Sec. 6. Commission personnel matters.

"(a) Compensation of members.—Each member of the Commission who is not an officer or employee of the Federal Government, or whose compensation is not precluded by a State, local, or Native American tribal government position, shall be compensated at a rate equal to the daily equivalent of the annual rate of basic pay prescribed for Level IV of the Executive Schedule under section 5315 of title 5, United States Code [5 U.S.C.A. § 5315], for each day (including travel time) during which such member is engaged in the performance of the duties of the Commission. All members of the Commission who are officers or employees of the United States shall serve without compensation in addition to that received for their services as officers or employees of the United States.

"(b) Travel expenses.—The members of the Commission shall be allowed travel expenses, including per diem in lieu of subsistence, at rates authorized for employees of agencies under subchapter I of chapter 57 of title 5, United States Code [5 U.S.C.A. § 5701 et seq.], while away from their homes or regular places of business in the performance of service for the Commission.

"(c) Staff.—

"(1) In general.—The Chairman of the Commission may, without regard to the civil service laws and regulations, appoint and terminate an executive director and such other additional personnel as may be necessary to enable the Commission to perform its duties. The employment and termination of an executive director shall be subject to confirmation by a majority of the members of the Commission.

"(2) Compensation.—The executive director shall be compensated at a rate not to exceed the rate payable for Level V of the Executive Schedule under section 5316 of title 5, United States Code [5 U.S.C.A. § 5316]. The Chairman may fix the compensation of other personnel without regard to the provisions of chapter 51 and subchapter III of chapter 53 of title 5, United States Code [5 U.S.C.A. § 5101 et seq. and § 5331 et seq.], relating to classification of positions and General Schedule pay rates, except that the rate of pay for such personnel may not exceed the rate payable for Level V of the Executive Schedule under section 5316 of such title [5 U.S.C.A. § 5316 et seq.].

"(3) Detail of government employees.—Any Federal Government employee, with the approval of the head of the appropriate Federal agency, may be detailed to the Commission without reimbursement, and such detail shall be without interruption or loss of civil service status, benefits, or privilege.

"(d) Procurement of temporary and intermittent services.—The Chairman of the Commission may procure temporary and intermittent services under section 3109(b) of title 5, United States Code [5 U.S.C.A. § 3109(b)], at rates for individuals not to exceed the daily equivalent of the annual rate of basic pay prescribed for Level V of the Executive Schedule under section 5316 of such title [5 U.S.C.A. § 5316].

"(e) Applicability of Federal Tort Claims provisions.—For purposes of sections 1346(b) and 2401(b) and chapter 171 of title 28, United States Code, the Commission is a 'Federal agency' and each of the members and personnel of the Commission is an 'employee of the Government'.

"Sec. 7. Contracts for research.

"(a) Advisory Commission on Intergovernmental Relations.—

"(1) In general.—In carrying out its duties under section 4, the Commission shall contract with the Advisory Commission on Intergovernmental Relations for—

"(A) a thorough review and cataloging of all applicable Federal, State, local, and Native American tribal laws, regulations, and ordinances that pertain to gambling in the United States; and

"(B) assistance in conducting the studies required by the Commission under section 4(a), and in particular the review and assessments required in subparagraphs (A), (B), and (E) of paragraph (2) of such section.

"(2) **Report required.**—The contract entered into under paragraph (1) shall require that the Advisory Commission on Intergovernmental Relations submit a report to the Commission detailing the results of its efforts under the contract no later than 15 months after the date upon which the Commission first meets.

"(b) **National Research Council.**—

"(1) **In general.**—In carrying out its duties under section 4, the Commission shall contract with the National Research Council of the National Academy of Sciences for assistance in conducting the studies required by the Commission under section 4(a), and in particular the assessment required under subparagraph (C) of paragraph (2) of such section.

"(2) **Report required.**—The contract entered into under paragraph (1) shall require that the National Research Council submit a report to the Commission detailing the results of its efforts under the contract no later than 15 months after the date upon which the Commission first meets.

"(c) **Other organizations.**—Nothing in this section shall be construed to limit the ability of the Commission to enter into contracts with other entities or organizations for research necessary to carry out the Commission's duties under section 4.

"Sec. 8. Definitions.

"For the purposes of this Act:

"(1) **Gambling.**—The term 'gambling' means any legalized form of wagering or betting conducted in a casino, on a riverboat, on an Indian reservation, or at any other location under the jurisdiction of the United States. Such term includes any casino game, parimutuel betting, sports-related betting, lottery, pull-tab game, slot machine, any type of video gaming, computerized wagering or betting activities (including any such activity conducted over the Internet), and philanthropic or charitable gaming activities.

"(2) **Native American tribal government.**—The term 'Native American tribal government' means an Indian tribe, as defined under section 4(5) of the Indian Gaming Regulatory Act of 1988 (25 U.S.C. 2703(5)).

"(3) **State.**—The term 'State' means each of the several States of the United States, the District of Columbia, the Commonwealth of Puerto Rico, the Virgin Islands, Guam, American Samoa, and the Commonwealth of the Northern Mariana Islands.

"Sec. 9. Authorization of appropriations.

"(a) **In general.**—There are authorized to be appropriated to the Commission, the Advisory Commission on Intergovernmental Relations, and the National Academy of Sciences such sums as may be necessary to carry out the purposes of this Act. Any sums appropriated shall remain available, without fiscal year limitation, until expended.

"(b) **Limitation.**—No payment may be made under section 6 or 7 of this Act except to the extent provided for in advance in an appropriation Act.

"Sec. 10. Termination of the Commission.

"The Commission shall terminate 60 days after the Commission submits the report required under section 4(b)."

Applicability of Federal Tort Claims Provisions to National Gambling Impact Study Commission Act

Pub.L. 105–30, §§ 2, 3, July 25, 1997, 111 Stat. 248, provide that:

"Section 2. Construction.

"The amendment made by section 1 [which added subsec. (e) regarding applicability of Federal tort claims provisions to Sec. 6 of the National Gambling Impact Study Commission Act, set forth above as a note] shall not be construed to imply that any commission is not a 'Federal agency' or that any of the members or personnel of a commission is not an 'employee of the Government' for purposes of sections 1346(b) and 2401(b) and chapter 171 of title 28, United States Code.

"Sec. 3. Effective Date.

"The amendment made by section 1 shall be effective as of August 3, 1996."

Priority of State Laws

Enactment of this section as not indicating an intent on the part of the Congress to occupy the field in which this section operates to the exclusion of State or local law on the same subject matter, or to relieve any person of any obligation imposed by any State or local law, see section 811 of Pub.L. 91–452, set out as a Priority of State Laws note under section 1511 of this title.

Commission on the Review of the National Policy Toward Gambling

Sections 804 to 809 of Pub.L. 91–452 established the Commission on the Review of the National Policy Toward Gambling, provided for its membership and compensation of the members and the staff, empowered the Commission to subpoena witnesses and grant immunity, required the Commission to make a study of gambling in the United States and existing federal, state, and local policy and practices with respect to prohibition and taxation of gambling activities and to make a final report of its findings and recommendations to the President and to Congress within four years of its establishment, and provided for its termination sixty days after submission of the final report.

§ 1956. Laundering of monetary instruments

(a)(1) Whoever, knowing that the property involved in a financial transaction represents the proceeds of some form of unlawful activity, conducts or attempts to conduct such a financial transaction which in fact involves the proceeds of specified unlawful activity—

(A)(i) with the intent to promote the carrying on of specified unlawful activity; or

(ii) with intent to engage in conduct constituting a violation of section 7201 or 7206 of the Internal Revenue Code of 1986; or

(B) knowing that the transaction is designed in whole or in part—

(i) to conceal or disguise the nature, the location, the source, the ownership, or the control of the proceeds of specified unlawful activity; or

(ii) to avoid a transaction reporting requirement under State or Federal law, shall be sentenced to a fine of not more than $500,000 or twice the value of the property involved in the transaction, whichever is greater, or imprisonment for not more than twenty years, or both. For purposes of this paragraph, a financial transaction shall be considered to be one involving the proceeds of specified unlawful activity if it is part of a set of parallel or dependent transactions, any one of which involves the proceeds of specified unlawful activity, and all of which are part of a single plan or arrangement.

(2) Whoever transports, transmits, or transfers, or attempts to transport, transmit, or transfer a monetary instrument or funds from a place in the United States to or through a place outside the United States or to a place in the United States from or through a place outside the United States—

(A) with the intent to promote the carrying on of specified unlawful activity; or

(B) knowing that the monetary instrument or funds involved in the transportation, transmission, or transfer represent the proceeds of some form of unlawful activity and knowing that such transportation, transmission, or transfer is designed in whole or in part—

(i) to conceal or disguise the nature, the location, the source, the ownership, or the control of the proceeds of specified unlawful activity; or

(ii) to avoid a transaction reporting requirement under State or Federal law,

shall be sentenced to a fine of not more than $500,000 or twice the value of the monetary instrument or funds involved in the transportation, transmission, or transfer whichever is greater, or imprisonment for not more than twenty years, or both. For the purpose of the offense described in subparagraph (B), the defendant's knowledge may be established by proof that a law enforcement officer represented the matter specified in subparagraph (B) as true, and the defendant's subsequent statements or actions indicate that the defendant believed such representations to be true.

(3) Whoever, with the intent—

(A) to promote the carrying on of specified unlawful activity;

(B) to conceal or disguise the nature, location, source, ownership, or control of property believed to be the proceeds of specified unlawful activity; or

(C) to avoid a transaction reporting requirement under State or Federal law,

conducts or attempts to conduct a financial transaction involving property represented to be the proceeds of specified unlawful activity, or property used to conduct or facilitate specified unlawful activity, shall be fined under this title or imprisoned for not more than 20 years, or both. For purposes of this paragraph and paragraph (2), the term "represented" means any representation made by a law enforcement officer or by another person at the direction of, or with the approval of, a Federal official authorized to investigate or prosecute violations of this section.

(b) Penalties.—

(1) In general.—Whoever conducts or attempts to conduct a transaction described in subsection (a)(1) or (a)(3), or section 1957, or a transportation, transmission, or transfer described in subsection (a)(2), is liable to the United States for a civil penalty of not more than the greater of—

(A) the value of the property, funds, or monetary instruments involved in the transaction; or

(B) $10,000.

(2) Jurisdiction over foreign persons.—For purposes of adjudicating an action filed or enforcing a penalty ordered under this section, the district courts shall have jurisdiction over any foreign person, including any financial institution authorized under the laws of a foreign country, against whom the action is brought, if service of process upon the foreign person is made under the Federal Rules of Civil Procedure or the laws of the country in which the foreign person is found, and—

(A) the foreign person commits an offense under subsection (a) involving a financial transaction that occurs in whole or in part in the United States;

(B) the foreign person converts, to his or her own use, property in which the United States has an ownership interest by virtue of the entry of an order of forfeiture by a court of the United States; or

(C) the foreign person is a financial institution that maintains a bank account at a financial institution in the United States.

(3) Court authority over assets.—A court may issue a pretrial restraining order or take any other action necessary to ensure that any bank account or other property held by the defendant in the United States is available to satisfy a judgment under this section.

(4) Federal receiver.—

(A) In general.—A court may appoint a Federal Receiver, in accordance with subparagraph (B) of this paragraph, to collect, marshal, and take custody, control, and possession of all assets of the defendant, wherever located, to satisfy a civil judgment under this subsection, a forfeiture judgment under section 981 or 982, or a criminal sentence under section 1957 or subsection (a) of this section, including an order of restitution to any victim of a specified unlawful activity.

(B) Appointment and authority.—A Federal Receiver described in subparagraph (A)—

(i) may be appointed upon application of a Federal prosecutor or a Federal or State regulator, by the court having jurisdiction over the defendant in the case;

(ii) shall be an officer of the court, and the powers of the Federal Receiver shall include the powers set out in section 754 of title 28, United States Code; and

(iii) shall have standing equivalent to that of a Federal prosecutor for the purpose of submitting requests to obtain information regarding the assets of the defendant—

(I) from the Financial Crimes Enforcement Network of the Department of the Treasury; or

(II) from a foreign country pursuant to a mutual legal assistance treaty, multilateral agreement, or other arrangement for international law enforcement assistance, provided that such requests are in accordance with the policies and procedures of the Attorney General.

(c) As used in this section—

(1) the term "knowing that the property involved in a financial transaction represents the proceeds of some form of unlawful activity" means that the person knew the property involved in the transaction represented proceeds from some form, though not necessarily which form, of activity that constitutes a felony under State, Federal, or foreign law, regardless of whether or not such activity is specified in paragraph (7);

(2) the term "conducts" includes initiating, concluding, or participating in initiating, or concluding a transaction;

(3) the term "transaction" includes a purchase, sale, loan, pledge, gift, transfer, delivery, or other disposition, and with respect to a financial institution includes a deposit, withdrawal, transfer between accounts, exchange of currency, loan, extension of credit, purchase or sale of any stock, bond, certificate of deposit, or other monetary instrument, use of a safe deposit box, or any other payment, transfer, or delivery by, through, or to a financial institution, by whatever means effected;

(4) the term "financial transaction" means (A) a transaction which in any way or degree affects interstate or foreign commerce (i) involving the movement of funds by wire or other means or (ii) involving one or more monetary instruments, or (iii) involving the transfer of title to any real property, vehicle, vessel, or aircraft, or (B) a transaction involving the use of a financial institution which is engaged in, or the activities of which affect, interstate or foreign commerce in any way or degree;

(5) the term "monetary instruments" means (i) coin or currency of the United States or of any other country, travelers' checks, personal checks, bank checks, and money orders, or (ii) investment securities or negotiable instruments, in bearer form or otherwise in such form that title thereto passes upon delivery;

(6) the term "financial institution" includes—

(A) any financial institution, as defined in section 5312(a)(2) of title 31, United States Code, or the regulations promulgated thereunder; and

(B) any foreign bank, as defined in section 1 [1] of the International Banking Act of 1978 (12 U.S.C. 3101);

(7) the term "specified unlawful activity" means—

(A) any act or activity constituting an offense listed in section 1961(1) of this title except an act which is indictable under subchapter II of chapter 53 of title 31;

(B) with respect to a financial transaction occurring in whole or in part in the United States, an offense against a foreign nation involving—

(i) the manufacture, importation, sale, or distribution of a controlled substance (as such term is defined for the purposes of the Controlled Substances Act);

(ii) murder, kidnapping, robbery, extortion, destruction of property by means of explosive or fire, or a crime of violence (as defined in section 16);

(iii) fraud, or any scheme or attempt to defraud, by or against a foreign bank (as defined in paragraph 7 of section 1(b) of the International Banking Act of 1978)); [2]

(iv) bribery of a public official, or the misappropriation, theft, or embezzlement of public funds by or for the benefit of a public official;

(v) smuggling or export control violations involving—

(I) an item controlled on the United States Munitions List established under section 38 of the Arms Export Control Act (22 U.S.C. 2778); or

(II) an item controlled under regulations under the Export Administration Regulations (15 C.F.R. Parts 730–774);

(vi) an offense with respect to which the United States would be obligated by a multilateral treaty, either to extradite the alleged offender or to submit the case for prosecution, if the offender were found within the territory of the United States; or

(vii) trafficking in persons, selling or buying of children, sexual exploitation of children, or transporting, recruiting or harboring a person, including a child, for commercial sex acts;

(C) any act or acts constituting a continuing criminal enterprise, as that term is defined in section 408 of the Controlled Substances Act (21 U.S.C. 848);

(D) an offense under section 32 (relating to the destruction of aircraft), section 37 (relating to violence at international airports), section 115 (relating to influencing, impeding, or retaliating against a Federal official by threatening or injuring a family member), section 152 (relating to concealment of assets; false oaths and claims; bribery), section 175c (relating to the variola virus), section 215 (relating to commissions or gifts for procuring loans), section 351 (relating to congressional or Cabinet officer assassination), any of sections 500 through 503 (relating to certain counterfeiting offenses), section 513 (relating to securities of States and private entities), section 541 (relating to goods falsely classified), section 542 (relating to entry of goods by means of false statements), section 545 (relating to smuggling goods into the United States), section 549 (relating to removing goods from Customs custody), section 554 (relating to smuggling goods from the United States), section 641 (relating to public money, property, or records), section 656 (relating to theft, embezzlement, or misapplication by bank officer or employee), section 657 (relating to lending, credit, and insurance institutions), section 658 (relating to property mortgaged or pledged to farm credit agencies), section 666 (relating to theft or bribery concerning programs receiving Federal funds), section 793, 794, or 798 (relating to espionage), section 831 (relating to prohibited transactions involving nuclear materials), section 844(f) or (i) (relating to destruction by explosives or fire of Government property or property affecting interstate or foreign commerce), section 875 (relating to interstate communications), section 922(1) (relating to the unlawful importation of firearms), section 924(n) (relating to firearms trafficking), section 956 (relating to conspiracy to kill, kidnap, maim, or injure certain property in a foreign country), section 1005 (relating to fraudulent bank entries), 1006 [3] (relating to fraudulent Federal credit institution entries), 1007 [3] (relating to fraudulent Federal Deposit Insurance transactions), 1014 [3] (relating to fraudulent loan or credit applications), section 1030 (relating to computer fraud and abuse), 1032 [3] (relating to concealment of assets from conservator, receiver, or liquidating agent of financial institution), section 1111 (relating to murder), section 1114 (relating to murder of United States law enforcement officials), section 1116 (relating to murder of foreign officials, official guests, or internationally protected persons), section 1201 (relating to kidnaping), section 1203 (relating to hostage taking), section 1361 (relating to willful injury of Government property), section 1363 (relating to destruction of property within the special maritime and territorial jurisdiction), section 1708 (theft from the mail), section 1751 (relating to Presidential assassination), section 2113 or 2114 (relating to bank and postal robbery and theft), section 2280 (relating to violence against maritime navigation), section 2281 (relating to violence against maritime fixed platforms), section 2319 (relating to copyright infringement), section 2320 (relating to trafficking in counterfeit goods and services), section 2332 (relating to terrorist acts abroad against United States nationals), section 2332a (relating to use of weapons of mass destruction), section 2332b (relating to international terrorist acts transcending national boundaries), section 2332g (relating to missile systems designed to destroy aircraft), section 2332h (relating to radiological dispersal devices), section 2339A or 2339B (relating to providing material support to terrorists), section 2339C (relating to financing of terrorism), or section 2339D (relating to receiving military-type training from a foreign terrorist organization) of this title, section 46502 of title 49, United States Code, a felony violation of the Chemical Diversion and Trafficking Act of 1988 (relating to precursor and essential chemicals), section 590 of the Tariff Act of 1930 (19 U.S.C. 1590) (relating to aviation smuggling), section 422 of the Controlled Substances Act (relating to transportation of drug paraphernalia), section 38(c) (relating to criminal violations) of the Arms Export Control Act, section 11 (relating to violations) of the Export Administration Act of 1979, section 206 (relating to penalties) of the International Emergency Economic Powers Act, section 16 (relating to offenses and punishment) of the Trading with the Enemy Act, any felony violation of section 15 of the Food Stamp Act of 1977 [7 U.S.C.A. § 2024] (relating to food stamp fraud) involving a quantity of coupons having a value of not less than $5,000, any violation of section 543(a)(1) of the Housing Act of 1949 [42 U.S.C.A. § 1490s(a)(1)] (relating to equity skimming), any felony violation of the Foreign Agents Registration Act of 1938, any felony violation of the Foreign Corrupt Practices Act, or section 92 of the Atomic Energy Act of 1954 (42 U.S.C. 2122) (relating to prohibitions governing atomic weapons) [4]

ENVIRONMENTAL CRIMES

(E) a felony violation of the Federal Water Pollution Control Act (33 U.S.C. 1251 et seq.), the Ocean Dumping Act (33 U.S.C. 1401 et seq.), the

Act to Prevent Pollution from Ships (33 U.S.C. 1901 et seq.), the Safe Drinking Water Act (42 U.S.C. 300f et seq.), or the Resources Conservation and Recovery Act (42 U.S.C. 6901 et seq.); or

(F) any act or activity constituting an offense involving a Federal health care offense;

(8) the term "State" includes a State of the United States, the District of Columbia, and any commonwealth, territory, or possession of the United States.

(d) Nothing in this section shall supersede any provision of Federal, State, or other law imposing criminal penalties or affording civil remedies in addition to those provided for in this section.

(e) Violations of this section may be investigated by such components of the Department of Justice as the Attorney General may direct, and by such components of the Department of the Treasury as the Secretary of the Treasury may direct, as appropriate, and, with respect to offenses over which the Department of Homeland Security has jurisdiction, by such components of the Department of Homeland Security as the Secretary of Homeland Security may direct, and, with respect to offenses over which the United States Postal Service has jurisdiction, by the Postal Service. Such authority of the Secretary of the Treasury, the Secretary of Homeland Security, and the Postal Service shall be exercised in accordance with an agreement which shall be entered into by the Secretary of the Treasury, the Secretary of Homeland Security, the Postal Service, and the Attorney General. Violations of this section involving offenses described in paragraph (c)(7)(E) may be investigated by such components of the Department of Justice as the Attorney General may direct, and the National Enforcement Investigations Center of the Environmental Protection Agency.

(f) There is extraterritorial jurisdiction over the conduct prohibited by this section if—

(1) the conduct is by a United States citizen or, in the case of a non-United States citizen, the conduct occurs in part in the United States; and

(2) the transaction or series of related transactions involves funds or monetary instruments of a value exceeding $10,000.

(g) Notice of conviction of financial institutions.—If any financial institution or any officer, director, or employee of any financial institution has been found guilty of an offense under this section, section 1957 or 1960 of this title, or section 5322 or 5324 of title 31, the Attorney General shall provide written notice of such fact to the appropriate regulatory agency for the financial institution.

(h) Any person who conspires to commit any offense defined in this section or section 1957 shall be subject to the same penalties as those prescribed for the offense the commission of which was the object of the conspiracy.

(i) Venue.—**(1)** Except as provided in paragraph (2), a prosecution for an offense under this section or section 1957 may be brought in—

(A) any district in which the financial or monetary transaction is conducted; or

(B) any district where a prosecution for the underlying specified unlawful activity could be brought, if the defendant participated in the transfer of the proceeds of the specified unlawful activity from that district to the district where the financial or monetary transaction is conducted.

(2) A prosecution for an attempt or conspiracy offense under this section or section 1957 may be brought in the district where venue would lie for the completed offense under paragraph (1), or in any other district where an act in furtherance of the attempt or conspiracy took place.

(3) For purposes of this section, a transfer of funds from 1 place to another, by wire or any other means, shall constitute a single, continuing transaction. Any person who conducts (as that term is defined in subsection (c)(2)) any portion of the transaction may be charged in any district in which the transaction takes place.

(Added Pub.L. 99–570, Title XIII, § 1352(a), Oct. 27, 1986, 100 Stat. 3207–18, and amended Pub.L. 100–690, Title VI, §§ 6183, 6465, 6466, 6469(a)(1), 6471(a), (b), Title VII, § 7031, Nov. 18, 1988, 102 Stat. 4354, 4375, 4377, 4378, 4398; Pub.L. 101–647, Title I, §§ 105 to 108, Title XII, § 1205(j), Title XIV, §§ 1402, 1404, Title XXV, § 2506, Title XXXV, § 3557, Nov. 29, 1990, 104 Stat. 4791, 4792, 4831, 4835, 4862, 4927; Pub.L. 102–550, Title XV, §§ 1504(c), 1524, 1526(a), 1527(a), 1530, 1531, 1534, 1536, Oct. 28, 1992, 106 Stat. 4055, 4064 to 4067; Pub.L. 103–322, Title XXXII, § 320104(b), Title XXXIII, §§ 330008(2), 330011(*l*), 330012, 330019, 330021(1), Sept. 13, 1994, 108 Stat. 2111, 2142, 2145, 2146, 2149, 2150; Pub.L. 103–325, Title IV, §§ 411(c)(2)(E), 413(c)(1), (d), Sept. 23, 1994, 108 Stat. 2253, 2254, 2255; Pub.L. 104–132, Title VII, § 726, Apr. 24, 1996, 110 Stat. 1301; Pub.L. 104–191, Title II, § 246, Aug. 21, 1996, 110 Stat. 2018; Pub.L. 104–294, Title VI, §§ 601(f)(6), 604(b)(38), Oct. 11, 1996, 110 Stat. 3499, 3509; Pub.L. 106–569, Title VII, § 709(a), Dec. 27, 2000, 114 Stat. 3018; Pub.L. 107–56, Title III, §§ 315, 317, 318, 376, Title VIII, § 805(b), Title X, § 1004, Oct. 26, 2001, 115 Stat. 308, 310, 311, 342, 378, 392; Pub.L. 107–273, Div. B, Title IV, § 4002(a)(11), (b)(5), (c)(2), 4005(d)(1), (e), Nov. 2, 2002, 116 Stat. 1807, 1809, 1812, 1813; Pub.L. 108–458, Title VI, § 6909, Dec. 17, 2004, 118 Stat. 3774; Pub.L. 109–164, Title I, § 103(b), Jan. 10, 2006, 119 Stat. 3563; Pub.L. 109–177, Title III, § 311(c), Title IV, §§ 403(b), (c)(1), 405, 406(a)(2), 409, Mar. 9, 2006, 120 Stat. 242, 243, 244, 246.)

[1] So in original. Probably should read "section 1(b)".

[2] So in original. The second closing parenthesis probably should not appear.

3 So in original. Probably should be preceded by "section".

4 So in original. Probably should have a semicolon at the end.

HISTORICAL AND STATUTORY NOTES

References in Text

Section 7201 or 7206 of the Internal Revenue Code of 1986, referred to subsec. (a)(1)(A), is 26 U.S.C.A. § 7201 or 7206.

The Federal Rules of Civil Procedure, referred to in subsec. (b)(2), are set out in the Appendix to Title 28.

The International Banking Act of 1978, referred to in subsec. (c)(6)(B), (7)(B)(iii), is Pub.L. 95–369, Sept. 17, 1978, 92 Stat. 607, which enacted 42 U.S.C.A. §§ 347d, 611a, and 3101 to 3108, amended 12 U.S.C.A. §§ 72, 378, 614, 615, 618, 619, 1813, 1815, 1817, 1818, 1820, 1821, 1822, 1823, 1828, 1829b, 1831b, and 1841, and enacted provisions set out as notes under 12 U.S.C.A. §§ 36, 247, 601, 611a, and 3101. Section 1(b) of the Act is classified to 12 U.S.C.A. § 3101, and paragraph 7 of section 1(b) of the Act is classified to 12 U.S.C.A. § 3101(7). For complete classification, see Short Title note set out under 12 U.S.C.A. § 3101 and Tables.

The Controlled Substances Act, referred to in subsec. (c)(7)(B)(i), is Title II of Pub.L. 91–513, Oct. 27, 1970, 84 Stat. 1242, as amended, which is classified principally to subchapter I of chapter 13 of Title 21, 21 U.S.C.A. § 801. Section 422 of that Act, referred to in subsec. (c)(7)(D), is classified to 21 U.S.C.A. § 863. For complete classification, see Short Title note set out under 21 U.S.C.A. § 801 and Tables.

Section 38 of the Arms Export Control Act, referred to in subsec. (c)(7)(B)(v)(I), is Pub.L. 90–629, c. 3, § 38, as added Pub.L. 94–329, Title II, § 212(a)(1), June 30, 1976, 90 Stat. 744, as amended, which is classified to 22 U.S.C.A. § 2778.

The Chemical Diversion and Trafficking Act of 1988, referred to in subsec. (c)(7)(D), is Pub.L. 100–690, Title VI, §§ 6051 to 6061, Nov. 18, 1988, 102 Stat. 4312 to 4320. For complete classification, see Short Title note set out under 21 U.S.C.A. § 801 and Tables.

Section 11 of the Export Administration Act of 1979, referred to in subsec. (c)(7)(D), is classified to 50 App. U.S.C.A. § 2410.

Section 206 of the International Emergency Economic Powers Act, referred to in subsec. (c)(7)(D), is classified to 50 U.S.C.A. § 1705.

Section 16 of the Trading with the Enemy Act, referred to in subsec. (c)(7)(D), is classified to 50 App. U.S.C.A. § 16.

Section 15 of the Food Stamp Act of 1977, referred to in subsec. (c)(7)(D), is section 15 of Pub.L. 88–525, Aug. 31, 1964, 78 Stat. 705, as amended, which is classified to 7 U.S.C.A. § 2024.

The Housing Act of 1949, referred to in subsec. (c)(7)(D), is Act July 15, 1949, c. 338, 63 Stat. 413, as amended, which is classified principally to chapter 8A of Title 42 (42 U.S.C.A. § 1441 et seq.). For complete classification, see Short Title note set out under 42 U.S.C.A. § 1441 and Tables.

The Foreign Corrupt Practices Act, referred to in subsec. (c)(7)(D), probably means the Foreign Corrupt Practices Act of 1977, Pub.L. 95–213, Title I, Dec. 19, 1977, 91 Stat. 1494 to 1498, as amended, which enacted 15 U.S.C.A. §§ 78dd–1 and 78dd–2, and amended 15 U.S.C.A. §§ 78m and 78ff. For complete classification, see section 101 of Pub.L. 95–213, set out as a Short Title of 1977 Amendments note under 15 U.S.C.A. § 78a and Tables.

The Atomic Energy Act of 1954, referred to in subsec. (c)(7)(D), is Aug. 1, 1946, c. 724, 60 Stat. 755, as amended, which is classified principally to chapter 23 of Title 42, 42 U.S.C.A. § 2011 et seq. For complete classification, see short title note set out under 42 U.S.C.A. § 2011 and Tables.

The Foreign Agents Registration Act of 1938, referred to in subsec. (c)(7)(D), also known as the Propaganda Agency Act, is Act June 8, 1938, c. 327, 52 Stat. 631, as amended, which is classified generally to subchapter II of chapter 11 of Title 22, 22 U.S.C.A. § 611 et seq.

The Federal Water Pollution Control Act, referred to in subsec. (c)(7)(E), is Act June 30, 1948, c. 758, as amended generally by Pub.L. 92–500, § 2, Oct. 18, 1972, 86 Stat. 816, which is classified generally to chapter 26, 33 U.S.C.A. § 1251 et seq. For complete classification, see Short Title note set out under 33 U.S.C.A. § 1251 and Tables.

The Ocean Dumping Act, also known as the Marine Protection, Research and Sanctuaries Act of 1972, referred to in subsec. (c)(7)(E), is Pub.L. 92–532, Oct. 23, 1972, 86 Stat. 1052, as amended, which is classified principally to chapter 27, 33 U.S.C.A. § 1401 et seq. For complete classification, see Short Title note set out under 33 U.S.C.A. § 1401 and Tables.

The Act to Prevent Pollution from Ships, referred to in subsec. (c)(7)(E), is Pub.L. 96–478, Oct. 21, 1980, 94 Stat. 2297. For complete classification, see Short Title note under 33 U.S.C.A. § 1901 and Tables.

The Safe Drinking Water Act, referred to in subsec. (c)(7)(E), is Pub.L. 93–523, Dec. 16, 1974, 88 Stat. 1660, as amended, which is classified principally to subchapter XII of chapter 6A of Title 42, 42 U.S.C.A. § 300f. For complete classification, see Short Title note set out under 42 U.S.C.A. § 201 and Tables.

The Resource Conservation and Recovery Act of 1976, referred to in subsec. (c)(7)(E), is Pub.L. 94–580, Oct. 21, 1976, 90 Stat. 2796, as amended, which is classified generally to chapter 82 of Title 42, 42 U.S.C.A. § 6901 et seq. For complete classification, see Short Title note set out under 18 U.S.C.A. § 6901 and Tables.

Codifications

Amendment by Pub.L. 108–458, Title VI, § 6909(2), Dec. 17, 2004, 118 Stat. 3774, which directed insertion of text in subsec. (c)(7)(D) after "section 2332(b) (relating to international terrorist acts transcending national boundaries)," was executed by inserting text after "section 2332b (relating to international terrorist acts transcending national boundaries)," as the probable intent of Congress.

Amendment by Pub.L. 109–177, § 403(b), directing that subsec. (c)(7)(D) of this section be amended by striking "or any felony violation of the Foreign Corrupt Practices Act" and inserting "any felony violation of the Foreign Corrupt Practices Act", was not capable of execution due to prior amendment by Pub.L. 108–458, § 6909(3), which revised subsec. (c)(7)(D) and thus struck out "or" preceding "any felony violation of the Foreign Corrupt Practices Act". See 2004 Amendments notes under this section.

Effective and Applicability Provisions

2002 Acts. Amendment by section 4002(a)(11) of Pub.L. 107–273, as therein provided, effective Apr. 24, 1996, which is the date of enactment of Pub.L. 104–132, to which such amendment relates.

Amendment by section 4005(e) of Pub.L. 107–273, as therein provided, effective Oct. 26, 2001, which is the date of enactment of Pub.L. 107–56, to which such amendment relates.

1996 Acts. Amendment by section 604 of Pub.L. 104–294 effective Sept. 13, 1994, see section 604(d) of Pub.L. 104–294, set out as a note under section 13 of this title.

1994 Acts. Section 413(d) of Pub.L. 103–325 provided in part that the amendment made by such section, repealing section 3557(2)(E) of Pub.L. 101–647 (which amended this section), was to take effect on the date of enactment of section 3557(2)(E) of Pub.L. 101–647, which was approved Nov. 29, 1990.

Section 330011(*l*) of Pub.L. 103–322 provided in part that the amendment made by such section, repealing section 3557(2)(E) of Pub.L. 101–647 (which amended this section), was to take effect on the date of enactment of section 3557(2)(E) of Pub.L. 101–647, which was approved Nov. 29, 1990.

1992 Acts. Except as otherwise provided, amendment by Pub.L. 102–550 effective Oct. 28, 1992, see section 2 of Pub.L. 102–550, set out as a note under section 5301 of Title 42, The Public Health and Welfare.

Repeals

Section 805(b) of Pub.L. 107–56, cited in the credit of this section, was repealed by section 4005(e) of Pub.L. 107–273 effective Oct. 26, 2001.

Section 3557(2)(E) of Pub.L. 101–647, set out in the credit to this section, was repealed by section 330011(*l*) of Pub.L. 103–322 and also repealed by section 413(d) of Pub.L. 103–325.

Termination Date of 2001 Amendment

Effective on and after the first day of fiscal year 2005, amendments by Title III (§§ 301 to 377) of Pub.L. 107–56 shall terminate if Congress enacts a joint resolution to that effect; such resolution shall be given expedited consideration, see Pub.L. 107–56, Title III, § 303, Oct. 26, 2001, 115 Stat. 298, set out as a note under 31 U.S.C.A. § 5311.

§ 1957. Engaging in monetary transactions in property derived from specified unlawful activity

(a) Whoever, in any of the circumstances set forth in subsection (d), knowingly engages or attempts to engage in a monetary transaction in criminally derived property of a value greater than $10,000 and is derived from specified unlawful activity, shall be punished as provided in subsection (b).

(b)(1) Except as provided in paragraph (2), the punishment for an offense under this section is a fine under title 18, United States Code, or imprisonment for not more than ten years or both.

(2) The court may impose an alternate fine to that imposable under paragraph (1) of not more than twice the amount of the criminally derived property involved in the transaction.

(c) In a prosecution for an offense under this section, the Government is not required to prove the defendant knew that the offense from which the criminally derived property was derived was specified unlawful activity.

(d) The circumstances referred to in subsection (a) are—

(1) that the offense under this section takes place in the United States or in the special maritime and territorial jurisdiction of the United States; or

(2) that the offense under this section takes place outside the United States and such special jurisdiction, but the defendant is a United States person (as defined in section 3077 of this title, but excluding the class described in paragraph (2)(D) of such section).

(e) Violations of this section may be investigated by such components of the Department of Justice as the Attorney General may direct, and by such components of the Department of the Treasury as the Secretary of the Treasury may direct, as appropriate, and, with respect to offenses over which the Department of Homeland Security has jurisdiction, by such components of the Department of Homeland Security as the Secretary of Homeland Security may direct, and, with respect to offenses over which the United States Postal Service has jurisdiction, by the Postal Service. Such authority of the Secretary of the Treasury, the Secretary of Homeland Security, and the Postal Service shall be exercised in accordance with an agreement which shall be entered into by the Secretary of the Treasury, the Secretary of Homeland Security, the Postal Service, and the Attorney General.

(f) As used in this section—

(1) the term "monetary transaction" means the deposit, withdrawal, transfer, or exchange, in or affecting interstate or foreign commerce, of funds or a monetary instrument (as defined in section 1956(c)(5) of this title) by, through, or to a financial institution (as defined in section 1956 of this title), including any transaction that would be a financial transaction under section 1956(c)(4)(B) of this title, but such term does not include any transaction necessary to preserve a person's right to representation as guaranteed by the sixth amendment to the Constitution;

(2) the term "criminally derived property" means any property constituting, or derived from, proceeds obtained from a criminal offense; and

(3) the term "specified unlawful activity" has the meaning given that term in section 1956 of this title.

(Added Pub.L. 99–570, Title XIII, § 1352(a), Oct. 27, 1986, 100 Stat. 3207–21, and amended Pub.L. 100–690, Title VI, §§ 6182, 6184, 6469(a)(2), Nov. 18, 1988, 102 Stat. 4354, 4377; Pub.L. 102–550, Title XV, §§ 1526(b), 1527(b), Oct. 28, 1992, 106 Stat. 4065; Pub.L. 103–322, Title XXXIII, § 330020, Sept. 13, 1994, 108 Stat. 2149; Pub.L. 103–325, Title IV,

§ 413(c)(2), Sept. 23, 1994, 108 Stat. 2255; Pub.L. 109–177, Title IV, § 403(c)(2), Mar. 9, 2006, 120 Stat. 243.)

§ 1958. Use of interstate commerce facilities in the commission of murder-for-hire

(a) Whoever travels in or causes another (including the intended victim) to travel in interstate or foreign commerce, or uses or causes another (including the intended victim) to use the mail or any facility of interstate or foreign commerce, with intent that a murder be committed in violation of the laws of any State or the United States as consideration for the receipt of, or as consideration for a promise or agreement to pay, anything of pecuniary value, or who conspires to do so, shall be fined under this title or imprisoned for not more than ten years, or both; and if personal injury results, shall be fined under this title or imprisoned for not more than twenty years, or both; and if death results, shall be punished by death or life imprisonment, or shall be fined not more than $250,000, or both.

(b) As used in this section and section 1959—

(1) "anything of pecuniary value" means anything of value in the form of money, a negotiable instrument, a commercial interest, or anything else the primary significance of which is economic advantage;

(2) "facility of interstate or foreign commerce" includes means of transportation and communication; and

(3) "State" includes a State of the United States, the District of Columbia, and any commonwealth, territory, or possession of the United States.

(Added Pub.L. 98–473, Title II, § 1002(a), Oct. 12, 1984, 98 Stat. 2136, § 1952A; renumbered § 1958 and amended Pub.L. 100–690, Title VII, §§ 7053(a), 7058(b), Nov. 18, 1988, 102 Stat. 4402, 4403; Pub.L. 101–647, Title XII, § 1205(k), Title XXXV, § 3558, Nov. 29, 1990, 104 Stat. 4831, 4927; Pub.L. 103–322, Title VI, § 60003(a)(11), Title XIV, § 140007(b), Title XXXII, § 320105, Title XXXIII, § 330016(1)(L), (N), (Q), Sept. 13, 1994, 108 Stat. 1969, 2033, 2111; 2147, 2148; Pub.L. 104–294, Title VI, §§ 601(g)(3), 605(a), Oct. 11, 1996, 110 Stat. 3500, 3509; Pub.L. 108–458, Title VI, § 6704, Dec. 17, 2004, 118 Stat. 3766.)

HISTORICAL AND STATUTORY NOTES

Codifications

Amendment by section 7058(b) of Pub.L. 100–690 was executed to subsec. (a) as the probable intent of Congress despite lack of directory language that "section 1958 of title 18" be amended.

§ 1959. Violent crimes in aid of racketeering activity

(a) Whoever, as consideration for the receipt of, or as consideration for a promise or agreement to pay, anything of pecuniary value from an enterprise engaged in racketeering activity, or for the purpose of gaining entrance to or maintaining or increasing position in an enterprise engaged in racketeering activity, murders, kidnaps, maims, assaults with a dangerous weapon, commits assault resulting in serious bodily injury upon, or threatens to commit a crime of violence against any individual in violation of the laws of any State or the United States, or attempts or conspires so to do, shall be punished—

(1) for murder, by death or life imprisonment, or a fine under this title, or both; and for kidnapping, by imprisonment for any term of years or for life, or a fine under this title, or both;

(2) for maiming, by imprisonment for not more than thirty years or a fine under this title, or both;

(3) for assault with a dangerous weapon or assault resulting in serious bodily injury, by imprisonment for not more than twenty years or a fine under this title, or both;

(4) for threatening to commit a crime of violence, by imprisonment for not more than five years or a fine under this title, or both;

(5) for attempting or conspiring to commit murder or kidnapping, by imprisonment for not more than ten years or a fine under this title, or both; and

(6) for attempting or conspiring to commit a crime involving maiming, assault with a dangerous weapon, or assault resulting in serious bodily injury, by imprisonment for not more than three years or a fine of [1] under this title, or both.

(b) As used in this section—

(1) "racketeering activity" has the meaning set forth in section 1961 of this title; and

(2) "enterprise" includes any partnership, corporation, association, or other legal entity, and any union or group of individuals associated in fact although not a legal entity, which is engaged in, or the activities of which affect, interstate or foreign commerce.

(Added Pub.L. 98–473, Title II, § 1002(a), Oct. 12, 1984, 98 Stat. 2137, § 1952B; renumbered § 1959, Pub.L. 100–690, Title VII, § 7053(b), Nov. 18, 1988, 102 Stat. 4402, and amended Pub.L. 103–322, Title VI, § 60003(a)(12), Title XXXIII, §§ 330016(1)(J), (2)(C), 330021(1), Sept. 13, 1994, 108 Stat. 1969, 2147, 2148, 2150.)

[1] So in original. The word "of" probably should not appear.

§ 1960. Prohibition of unlicensed money transmitting businesses

(a) Whoever knowingly conducts, controls, manages, supervises, directs, or owns all or part of an unlicensed money transmitting business, shall be fined in accordance with this title or imprisoned not more than 5 years, or both.

(b) As used in this section—

(1) the term "unlicensed money transmitting business" means a money transmitting business which affects interstate or foreign commerce in any manner or degree and—

(A) is operated without an appropriate money transmitting license in a State where such operation is punishable as a misdemeanor or a felony under State law, whether or not the defendant knew that the operation was required to be licensed or that the operation was so punishable;

(B) fails to comply with the money transmitting business registration requirements under section 5330 of title 31, United States Code, or regulations prescribed under such section; or

(C) otherwise involves the transportation or transmission of funds that are known to the defendant to have been derived from a criminal offense or are intended to be used to be used[1] to promote or support unlawful activity;

(2) the term "money transmitting" includes transferring funds on behalf of the public by any and all means including but not limited to transfers within this country or to locations abroad by wire, check, draft, facsimile, or courier; and

(3) the term "State" means any State of the United States, the District of Columbia, the Northern Mariana Islands, and any commonwealth, territory, or possession of the United States.

(Added Pub.L. 102–550, Title XV, § 1512(a), Oct. 28, 1992, 106 Stat. 4057, and amended Pub.L. 103–325, Title IV, § 408(c), Sept. 23, 1994, 108 Stat. 2252; Pub.L. 107–56, Title III, § 373(a), Oct. 26, 2001, 115 Stat. 339; Pub.L. 109–162, Title XI, § 1171(a)(2), Jan. 5, 2006, 119 Stat. 3123.)

[1] So in original.

HISTORICAL AND STATUTORY NOTES

Termination Date of 2001 Amendment

Effective on and after the first day of fiscal year 2005, amendments by Title III (§§ 301 to 377) of Pub.L. 107–56 shall terminate if Congress enacts a joint resolution to that effect; such resolution shall be given expedited consideration, see Pub.L. 107–56, Title III, § 303, Oct. 26, 2001, 115 Stat. 298, set out as a note under 31 U.S.C.A. § 5311.

CHAPTER 96—RACKETEER INFLUENCED AND CORRUPT ORGANIZATIONS

Sec.

§ 1961. Definitions

As used in this chapter—

(1) "racketeering activity" means (A) any act or threat involving murder, kidnapping, gambling, arson, robbery, bribery, extortion, dealing in obscene matter, or dealing in a controlled substance or listed chemical (as defined in section 102 of the Controlled Substances Act), which is chargeable under State law and punishable by imprisonment for more than one year; (B) any act which is indictable under any of the following provisions of title 18, United States Code: Section 201 (relating to bribery), section 224 (relating to sports bribery), sections 471, 472, and 473 (relating to counterfeiting), section 659 (relating to theft from interstate shipment) if the act indictable under section 659 is felonious, section 664 (relating to embezzlement from pension and welfare funds), sections 891–894 (relating to extortionate credit transactions), section 1028 (relating to fraud and related activity in connection with identification documents), section 1029 (relating to fraud and related activity in connection with access devices), section 1084 (relating to the transmission of gambling information), section 1341 (relating to mail fraud), section 1343 (relating to wire fraud), section 1344 (relating to financial institution fraud), section 1425 (relating to the procurement of citizenship or nationalization unlawfully), section 1426 (relating to the reproduction of naturalization or citizenship papers), section 1427 (relating to the sale of naturalization or citizenship papers), sections 1461–1465 (relating to obscene matter), section 1503 (relating to obstruction of justice), section 1510 (relating to obstruction of criminal investigations), section 1511 (relating to the obstruction of State or local law enforcement), section 1512 (relating to tampering with a witness, victim, or an informant), section 1513 (relating to retaliating against a witness, victim, or an informant), section 1542 (relating to false statement in application and use of passport), section 1543 (relating to forgery or false use of passport), section 1544 (relating to misuse of passport), section 1546 (relating to fraud and misuse of visas, permits, and other documents), sections 1581–1592 (relating to peonage, slavery, and trafficking in persons).,[1] section 1951 (relating to interference with commerce, robbery, or extortion), section 1952 (relating to racketeering), section 1953 (relating to interstate transportation of wagering paraphernalia), section 1954 (relating to unlawful welfare fund payments), section 1955 (relating to the prohibition of illegal gambling businesses), section 1956 (relating to the laundering of monetary instruments), section 1957 (relating to engaging in monetary

transactions in property derived from specified unlawful activity), section 1958 (relating to use of interstate commerce facilities in the commission of murder-for-hire), section 1960 (relating to illegal money transmitters), sections 2251, 2251A, 2252, and 2260 (relating to sexual exploitation of children), sections 2312 and 2313 (relating to interstate transportation of stolen motor vehicles), sections 2314 and 2315 (relating to interstate transportation of stolen property), section 2318 (relating to trafficking in counterfeit labels for phonorecords, computer programs or computer program documentation or packaging and copies of motion pictures or other audiovisual works), section 2319 (relating to criminal infringement of a copyright), section 2319A (relating to unauthorized fixation of and trafficking in sound recordings and music videos of live musical performances), section 2320 (relating to trafficking in goods or services bearing counterfeit marks), section 2321 (relating to trafficking in certain motor vehicles or motor vehicle parts), sections 2341–2346 (relating to trafficking in contraband cigarettes), sections 2421–24 (relating to white slave traffic), sections 175–178 (relating to biological weapons), sections 229–229F (relating to chemical weapons), section 831 (relating to nuclear materials), (C) any act which is indictable under title 29, United States Code, section 186 (dealing with restrictions on payments and loans to labor organizations) or section 501(c) (relating to embezzlement from union funds), (D) any offense involving fraud connected with a case under title 11 (except a case under section 157 of this title), fraud in the sale of securities, or the felonious manufacture, importation, receiving, concealment, buying, selling, or otherwise dealing in a controlled substance or listed chemical (as defined in section 102 of the Controlled Substances Act), punishable under any law of the United States, (E) any act which is indictable under the Currency and Foreign Transactions Reporting Act, (F) any act which is indictable under the Immigration and Nationality Act, section 274 (relating to bringing in and harboring certain aliens), section 277 (relating to aiding or assisting certain aliens to enter the United States), or section 278 (relating to importation of alien for immoral purpose) if the act indictable under such section of such Act was committed for the purpose of financial gain, or (G) any act that is indictable under any provision listed in section 2332b(g)(5)(B);

(2) "State" means any State of the United States, the District of Columbia, the Commonwealth of Puerto Rico, any territory or possession of the United States, any political subdivision, or any department, agency, or instrumentality thereof;

(3) "person" includes any individual or entity capable of holding a legal or beneficial interest in property;

(4) "enterprise" includes any individual, partnership, corporation, association, or other legal entity, and any union or group of individuals associated in fact although not a legal entity;

(5) "pattern of racketeering activity" requires at least two acts of racketeering activity, one of which occurred after the effective date of this chapter and the last of which occurred within ten years (excluding any period of imprisonment) after the commission of a prior act of racketeering activity;

(6) "unlawful debt" means a debt (A) incurred or contracted in gambling activity which was in violation of the law of the United States, a State or political subdivision thereof, or which is unenforceable under State or Federal law in whole or in part as to principal or interest because of the laws relating to usury, and (B) which was incurred in connection with the business of gambling in violation of the law of the United States, a State or political subdivision thereof, or the business of lending money or a thing of value at a rate usurious under State or Federal law, where the usurious rate is at least twice the enforceable rate;

(7) "racketeering investigator" means any attorney or investigator so designated by the Attorney General and charged with the duty of enforcing or carrying into effect this chapter;

(8) "racketeering investigation" means any inquiry conducted by any racketeering investigator for the purpose of ascertaining whether any person has been involved in any violation of this chapter or of any final order, judgment, or decree of any court of the United States, duly entered in any case or proceeding arising under this chapter;

(9) "documentary material" includes any book, paper, document, record, recording, or other material; and

(10) "Attorney General" includes the Attorney General of the United States, the Deputy Attorney General of the United States, the Associate Attorney General of the United States, any Assistant Attorney General of the United States, or any employee of the Department of Justice or any employee of any department or agency of the United States so designated by the Attorney General to carry out the powers conferred on the Attorney General by this chapter. Any department or agency so designated may use in investigations authorized by this chapter either the investigative provisions of this chapter or the investigative power of such department or agency otherwise conferred by law.

(Added Pub.L. 91–452, Title IX, § 901(a), Oct. 15, 1970, 84 Stat. 941, and amended Pub.L. 95–575, § 3(c), Nov. 2, 1978, 92 Stat. 2465; Pub.L. 95–598, Title III, § 314(g), Nov. 6, 1978, 92 Stat. 2677; Pub.L. 98–473, Title II, §§ 901(g), 1020, Oct. 12, 1984, 98 Stat. 2136, 2143; Pub.L. 98–547, Title II, § 205, Oct. 25, 1984, 98 Stat. 2770; Pub.L. 99–570, Title XIII, § 1365(b), Oct. 27, 1986, 100 Stat. 3207–35; Pub.L. 99–646, § 50(a), Nov. 10, 1986, 100 Stat. 3605; Pub.L. 100–690, Title VII, §§ 7013, 7020(c), 7032, 7054, 7514, Nov. 18, 1988, 102 Stat. 4395, 4396, 4398, 4402, 4489; Pub.L. 101–73, Title IX, § 968, Aug. 9, 1989, 103 Stat. 506; Pub.L. 101–647, Title XXXV, § 3560, Nov. 29, 1990, 104 Stat. 4927; Pub.L. 103–322, Title IX, § 90104, Title XVI, § 160001(f), Title XXXIII, § 330021(1), Sept. 13, 1994, 108 Stat. 1987, 2037, 2150; Pub.L. 103–394, Title III, § 312(b), Oct. 22, 1994, 108 Stat. 4140; Pub.L. 104–132, Title IV, § 433, Apr. 24, 1996, 110 Stat. 1274; Pub.L. 104–153, § 3, July 2, 1996, 110 Stat. 1386; Pub.L. 104–208, Div. C, Title II, § 202, Sept. 30, 1996, 110 Stat. 3009–565; Pub.L. 104–294, Title VI, §§ 601(b)(3), (i)(3), 604(b)(6), Oct. 11, 1996, 110 Stat. 3499, 3501, 3506; Pub.L. 107–56, Title VIII, § 813, Oct. 26, 2001, 115 Stat. 382; Pub.L. 107–273, Div. B, Title IV, § 4005(f)(1), Nov. 2, 2002, 116 Stat. 1813; Pub.L. 108–193, § 5(b), Dec. 19, 2003, 117 Stat. 2879; Pub.L. 108–458, Title VI, § 6802(e), Dec. 17, 2004, 118 Stat. 3767; Pub.L. 109–164, Title I, § 103(c), Jan. 10, 2006, 119 Stat. 3563; Pub.L. 109–177, Title IV, § 403(a), Mar. 9, 2006, 120 Stat. 243.)

[1] So in original.

HISTORICAL AND STATUTORY NOTES

References in Text

Section 102 of the Controlled Substances Act, referred to in par. (1), is section 102 of Pub.L. 91–513, Title II, Oct. 27, 1970, 84 Stat. 1242, as amended, which is classified to section 802 of Title 21, Food and Drugs.

Sections 201, 224, 471, 472, 473, 659, 664, 891 to 894, 1028, 1029, 1084, 1341, 1343, 1344, 1461 to 1465, 1503, 1510, 1511, 1512, 1513, 1542, 1543, 1544, 1546, 1581 to 1591, 1951, 1952, 1953, 1954, 1955, 1956, 1957, 1958, 2251, 2252, 2312, 2313, 2314, 2315, 2321, 2341 to 2346, and 2421 to 2424 of title 18, United States Code, referred to in par. (1)(B), are sections 201, 224, 471, 472, 473, 659, 664, 891 to 894, 1028, 1029, 1084, 1341, 1343, 1344, 1461 to 1465, 1503, 1510, 1511, 1512, 1513, 1452, 1543, 1544, 1546, 1581 to 1591, 1951, 1952, 1953, 1954, 1955, 1956, 1957, 1958, 2251, 2252, 2312, 2313, 2314, 2315, 2321, 2341 to 2346, and 2421 to 2424 of this title, respectively.

The Currency and Foreign Transaction Reporting Act, as amended, referred to in par. (1)(E), was Pub.L. 91–508, Title II, Oct. 26, 1970, 84 Stat. 1118, which was classified generally to chapter 21 (section 1051 et seq.) of Title 31, Money and Finance prior to the revision of this title by Pub.L. 97–258, Sept. 12, 1982, 96 Stat. 995. For complete classification of this Act to the Code see section 5311 et seq. of revised Title 31 and Tables.

The Immigration and Nationality Act and such Act, referred to in par. (1)(F), is Act June 27, 1952, c. 477, 66 Stat. 163, as amended, which is classified principally to chapter 12 (section 1101 et seq.) of Title 8, Aliens and Nationality. Sections 274, 277 and 278 of such Act are classified to sections 1324, 1327 and 1328 of Title 8, respectively. For complete classification of this Act to the Code, see Tables.

The effective date of this chapter, referred to in par. (5), is Oct. 15, 1970.

Codifications

Section 5(b) of Pub.L. 108–193, which directed that paragraph (1)(A) of this section be amended by striking "sections 1581–1588 (relating to peonage and slavery)" and inserting "sections 1581–1591 (relating to peonage, slavery, and trafficking in persons)", was executed to paragraph (1)(B) of this section as the probable intent of Congress.

Effective and Applicability Provisions

2002 Acts. Amendment by section 4005(f)(1) of Pub.L. 107–273, as therein provided, effective Oct. 26, 2001, which is the date of enactment of Pub.L. 107–56, to which such amendment relates.

1996 Acts. Amendment by section 604 of Pub.L. 104–294 effective Sept. 13, 1994, see section 604(d) of Pub.L. 104–294, set out as a note under section 13 of this title.

1994 Acts. Amendment by Pub.L. 103–394 effective on Oct. 22, 1994, and not to apply with respect to cases commenced under Title 11 of the United States Code before Oct. 22, 1994, see section 702 of Pub.L. 103–394, set out as a note under section 101 of Title 11, Bankruptcy.

1978 Acts. Amendment by Pub.L. 95–598 effective Oct. 1, 1979, see section 402(a) of Pub.L. 95–598, set out as an Effective Date note preceding section 101 of Title 11, Bankruptcy.

Amendment by Pub.L. 95–575 effective Nov. 2, 1978, see section 4 of Pub.L. 95–575, set out as an Effective Date note under section 2341 of this title.

Severability of Provisions

If any provision of Division C of Pub.L. 104–208 or the application of such provision to any person or circumstances is held to be unconstitutional, the remainder of Division C of Pub.L. 104–208 and the application of the provisions of Division C of Pub.L. 104–208 to any person or circumstance not to be affected thereby, see section 1(e) of Pub.L. 104–208, set out as a note under section 1101 of Title 8, Aliens and Nationality.

Amendment by section 314 of Pub.L. 95–598 not to affect the application of chapter 9 [section 151 et seq.], chapter 96 [section 1961 et seq.], or section 2516, 3057, or 3284 of this title to any act of any person (1) committed before Oct. 1, 1979, or (2) committed after Oct. 1, 1979, in connection with a case commenced before such date, see section 403(d) of Pub.L. 95–598, set out preceding section 151 of this title.

If any provision of or amendment made by Pub.L. 103–394 or the application of such provision or amendment to any person or circumstance is held to be unconstitutional, the remaining provisions of and amendments made by Pub.L. 103–394 and the application of such provisions and amendments to any person or circumstance shall not be affected thereby, see section 701 of Pub.L. 103–394, set out as a note under section 101 of Title 11, Bankruptcy.

If any provision of Pub.L. 101–73 or the application thereof to any person or circumstance is held invalid, the remainder of Pub.L. 101–73 and the application of the provision to other persons not similarly situated or to other circumstances not to be affected thereby, see section 1221 of Pub.L. 101–73, set out as a note under section 1811 of Title 12, Banks and Banking.

Section 1301 of Pub.L. 91–452 provided that: "If the provisions of any part of this Act [see Short Title note set out above] or the application thereof to any person or circumstances be held invalid, the provisions of the other parts and their application to other persons or circumstances shall not be affected thereby."

Short Title

1984 Amendments. Pub.L. 98–473, Title II, § 301, Oct. 12, 1984, 98 Stat. 2040, provided that: "This title [probably means chapter III of title II of Pub.L. 98–473 which enacted sections 853, 854, and 970 of Title 21, Food and Drugs, and sections 1589, 1600, 1613a, and 1616 of Title 19, Customs Duties, amended section 1963 of this title and sections 1602, 1605, 1606, 1607, 1608, 1609, 1610, 1611, 1612, 1613, 1614, 1615, 1618, 1619, and 1644 of Title 19, sections 824, 848, and 881 of Title 21, and section 524 of Title 28, Judiciary and Judicial Procedure, and repealed section 7607 of Title 26, Internal Revenue Code] may be cited as the 'Comprehensive Forfeiture Act of 1984'."

1970 Acts. Section 1 of Pub.L. 91–452 provided in part that: "This Act [enacting sections 841 to 848, 1511, 1623, 1955, 1961 to 1968, 3331 to 3334, 3503, 3504, 3575 to 3578, and 6001 to 6005 of this title, and section 1826 of Title 28, Judiciary and Judicial Procedure, amending sections 835, 1073, 1505, 1954, 2424, 2516, 2517, 3148, 3486, and 3500 of this title, sections 15, 87f, 135c, 499m, and 2115 of Title 7, Agriculture, section 25 of Title 11, Bankruptcy, section 1820 of Title 12, Banks and Banking, sections 49, 77v, 78u, 79r, 80a–41, 80b–9, 155, 717m, 1271, and 1714 of Title 15, Commerce and Trade, section 825f of Title 16, Conservation, section 1333 of Title 19, Customs Duties, section 373 of Title 21, Food and Drugs, section 161 of Title 29, Labor, section 506 of Title 33, Navigation and Navigable Waters, sections 405 and 2201 of Title 42, The Public Health and Welfare, sections 157 and 362 of Title 45, Railroads, section 1124 of Title 46, Shipping, section 409 of Title 47, Telegraphs, Telephones, and Radio telegraphs, sections 9, 43, 46, 916, 1017, and 1484 of former Title 49, Transportation, section 792 of Title 50, War and National Defense, and sections 643a, 1152, 2026, and former section 2155 of Title 50, Appendix, repealing sections 837, 895, 1406, and 2514 of this title, sections 32 and 33 of Title 15; sections 4874 and 7493 of Title 26, Internal Revenue Code, section 827 of Title 46, sections 47 and 48 of former Title 49, and sections 121 to 144 of Title 50, enacting provisions set out as notes under this section and sections 841, 1511, 1955, preceding 3331, preceding 3481, 3504, and 6001 of this title, and repealing provisions set out as a note under section 2510 of this title] may be cited as the 'Organized Crime Control Act of 1970'."

This chapter is commonly known as the Racketeer Influenced and Corrupt Organizations Act or RICO.

President's Commission on Organized Crime; Taking of Testimony and Receipt of Evidence

Pub.L. 98–368, July 17, 1984, 98 Stat. 490, provided for the Commission established by Ex. Ord. No. 12435, formerly set out below, authority relating to taking of testimony, receipt of evidence, subpoena power, testimony of persons in custody, immunity, service of process, witness fees, access to other records and information, Federal protection for members and staff, closure of meetings, rules, and procedures, for the period of July 17, 1984, until the earlier of 2 years or the expiration of the Commission.

Congressional Statement of Findings and Purpose

Section 1 of Pub.L. 91–452 provided in part that: "The Congress finds that (1) organized crime in the United States is a highly sophisticated, diversified, and widespread activity that annually drains billions of dollars from America's economy by unlawful conduct and the illegal use of force, fraud, and corruption; (2) organized crime derives a major portion of its power through money obtained from such illegal endeavors as syndicated gambling, loan sharking, the theft and fencing of property, the importation and distribution of narcotics and other dangerous drugs, and other forms of social exploitation; (3) this money and power are increasingly used to infiltrate and corrupt legitimate business and labor unions and to subvert and corrupt our democratic processes; (4) organized crime activities in the United States weaken the stability of the Nation's economic system, harm innocent investors and competing organizations, interfere with free competition, seriously burden interstate and foreign commerce, threaten the domestic security, and undermine the general welfare of the Nation and its citizens; and (5) organized crime continues to grow because of defects in the evidence-gathering process of the law inhibiting the development of the legally admissible evidence necessary to bring criminal and other sanctions or remedies to bear the unlawful activities of those engaged in organized crime and because the sanctions and remedies available to the Government are unnecessarily limited in scope and impact.

"It is the purpose of this Act [see Short Title note above] to seek the eradication of organized crime in the United States by strengthening the legal tools in the evidence-gathering process, by establishing new penal prohibitions, and by providing enhanced sanctions and new remedies to deal with the unlawful activities of those engaged in organized crime."

Liberal Construction of Provisions; Supersedure of Federal or State Laws; Authority of Attorneys Representing United States

Section 904 of Pub.L. 91–452 provided that:

"**(a)** The provisions of this title [enacting this chapter and amending sections 1505, 2516, and 2517 of this title] shall be liberally construed to effectuate its remedial purposes.

"**(b)** Nothing in this title shall supersede any provision of Federal, State, or other law imposing criminal penalties or affording civil remedies in addition to those provided for in this title.

"**(c)** Nothing contained in this title shall impair the authority of any attorney representing the United States to—

"(1) lay before any grand jury impaneled by any district court of the United States any evidence concerning any alleged racketeering violation of law;

"(2) invoke the power of any such court to compel the production of any evidence before any such grand jury; or

"(3) institute any proceeding to enforce any order or process issued in execution of such power or to punish disobedience of any such order or process by any person."

EXECUTIVE ORDERS

EXECUTIVE ORDER NO. 12435

Ex. Ord. No. 12503, July 28, 1983, 48 F.R. 34723, as amended by Ex. Ord. No. 12507, March 22, 1985, 50 F.R. 11835, which related to the establishment, functions, administration and termination of the President's Commission on Organized Crime, was revoked by Ex. Ord. No. 12610, Sept. 30, 1987, 52 F.R. 36901.

§ 1962. Prohibited activities

(a) It shall be unlawful for any person who has received any income derived, directly or indirectly, from a pattern of racketeering activity or through collection of an unlawful debt in which such person has participated as a principal within the meaning of section 2, title 18, United States Code, to use or invest, directly or indirectly, any part of such income, or the proceeds of such income, in acquisition of any interest in, or the establishment or operation of, any enterprise which is engaged in, or the activities of which affect, interstate or foreign commerce. A purchase of securities on the open market for purposes of investment, and without the intention of controlling or participating in the control of the issuer, or of assisting another to do so, shall not be unlawful under this subsection if the securities of the issuer held by the purchaser, the members of his immediate family, and his or their accomplices in any pattern or racketeering activity or the collection of an unlawful debt after such purchase do not amount in the aggregate to one percent of the outstanding securities of any one class, and do not confer, either in law or in fact, the power to elect one or more directors of the issuer.

(b) It shall be unlawful for any person through a pattern of racketeering activity or through collection of an unlawful debt to acquire or maintain, directly or indirectly, any interest in or control of any enterprise which is engaged in, or the activities of which affect, interstate or foreign commerce.

(c) It shall be unlawful for any person employed by or associated with any enterprise engaged in, or the activities of which affect, interstate or foreign commerce, to conduct or participate, directly or indirectly, in the conduct of such enterprise's affairs through a pattern of racketeering activity or collection of unlawful debt.

(d) It shall be unlawful for any person to conspire to violate any of the provisions of subsection (a), (b), or (c) of this section.

(Added Pub.L. 91–452, Title IX, § 901(a), Oct. 15, 1970, 84 Stat. 942, and amended Pub.L. 100–690, Title VII, § 7033, Nov. 18, 1988, 102 Stat. 4398.)

§ 1963. Criminal penalties

(a) Whoever violates any provision of section 1962 of this chapter shall be fined under this title or imprisoned not more than 20 years (or for life if the violation is based on a racketeering activity for which the maximum penalty includes life imprisonment), or both, and shall forfeit to the United States, irrespective of any provision of State law—

(1) any interest the person has acquired or maintained in violation of section 1962;

(2) any—

(A) interest in;

(B) security of;

(C) claim against; or

(D) property or contractual right of any kind affording a source of influence over;

any enterprise which the person has established, operated, controlled, conducted, or participated in the conduct of, in violation of section 1962; and

(3) any property constituting, or derived from, any proceeds which the person obtained, directly or indirectly, from racketeering activity or unlawful debt collection in violation of section 1962.

The court, in imposing sentence on such person shall order, in addition to any other sentence imposed pursuant to this section, that the person forfeit to the United States all property described in this subsection. In lieu of a fine otherwise authorized by this section, a defendant who derives profits or other proceeds from an offense may be fined not more than twice the gross profits or other proceeds.

(b) Property subject to criminal forfeiture under this section includes—

(1) real property, including things growing on, affixed to, and found in land; and

(2) tangible and intangible personal property, including rights, privileges, interests, claims, and securities.

(c) All right, title, and interest in property described in subsection (a) vests in the United States upon the commission of the act giving rise to forfeiture under this section. Any such property that is subsequently transferred to a person other than the defendant may be the subject of a special verdict of forfeiture and thereafter shall be ordered forfeited to the United States, unless the transferee establishes in a hearing pursuant to subsection (*l*) that he is a bona fide purchaser for value of such property who at the time of purchase was reasonably without cause to believe that the property was subject to forfeiture under this section.

(d)(1) Upon application of the United States, the court may enter a restraining order or injunction, require the execution of a satisfactory performance bond, or take any other action to preserve the availability of property described in subsection (a) for forfeiture under this section—

(A) upon the filing of an indictment or information charging a violation of section 1962 of this chapter and alleging that the property with respect to which the order is sought would, in the event of conviction, be subject to forfeiture under this section; or

(B) prior to the filing of such an indictment or information, if, after notice to persons appearing to have an interest in the property and opportunity for a hearing, the court determines that—

(i) there is a substantial probability that the United States will prevail on the issue of forfeiture and that failure to enter the order will result in the property being destroyed, removed from the jurisdiction of the court, or otherwise made unavailable for forfeiture; and

(ii) the need to preserve the availability of the property through the entry of the requested order outweighs the hardship on any party against whom the order is to be entered:

Provided, however, That an order entered pursuant to subparagraph (B) shall be effective for not more than ninety days, unless extended by the court for good cause shown or unless an indictment or information described in subparagraph (A) has been filed.

(2) A temporary restraining order under this subsection may be entered upon application of the United States without notice or opportunity for a hearing when an information or indictment has not yet been filed with respect to the property, if the United States demonstrates that there is probable cause to believe that the property with respect to which the order is sought would, in the event of conviction, be subject to forfeiture under this section and that provision of notice will jeopardize the availability of the property for forfeiture. Such a temporary order shall expire not more than ten days after the date on which it is entered, unless extended for good cause shown or unless the party against whom it is entered consents to an extension for a longer period. A hearing requested concerning an order entered under this paragraph shall be held at the earliest possible time, and prior to the expiration of the temporary order.

(3) The court may receive and consider, at a hearing held pursuant to this subsection, evidence and information that would be inadmissible under the Federal Rules of Evidence.

(e) Upon conviction of a person under this section, the court shall enter a judgment of forfeiture of the property to the United States and shall also authorize the Attorney General to seize all property ordered forfeited upon such terms and conditions as the court shall deem proper. Following the entry of an order declaring the property forfeited, the court may, upon application of the United States, enter such appropriate restraining orders or injunctions, require the execution of satisfactory performance bonds, appoint receivers, conservators, appraisers, accountants, or trustees, or take any other action to protect the interest of the United States in the property ordered forfeited. Any income accruing to, or derived from, an enterprise or an interest in an enterprise which has been ordered forfeited under this section may be used to offset ordinary and necessary expenses to the enterprise which are required by law, or which are necessary to protect the interests of the United States or third parties.

(f) Following the seizure of property ordered forfeited under this section, the Attorney General shall direct the disposition of the property by sale or any other commercially feasible means, making due provision for the rights of any innocent persons. Any property right or interest not exercisable by, or transferable for value to, the United States shall expire and shall not revert to the defendant, nor shall the defendant or any person acting in concert with or on behalf of the defendant be eligible to purchase forfeited property at any sale held by the United States. Upon application of a person, other than the defendant or a person acting in concert with or on behalf of the defendant, the court may restrain or stay the sale or disposition of the property pending the conclusion of any appeal of the criminal case giving rise to the forfeiture, if the applicant demonstrates that proceeding with the sale or disposition of the property will result in irreparable injury, harm or loss to him. Notwithstanding 31 U.S.C. 3302(b), the proceeds of any sale or other disposition of property forfeited under this section and any moneys forfeited shall be used to pay all proper expenses for the forfeiture and the sale, including expenses of seizure, maintenance and custody of the property pending its disposition, advertising and court costs. The Attorney General shall deposit in the Treasury any amounts of such proceeds or moneys remaining after the payment of such expenses.

(g) With respect to property ordered forfeited under this section, the Attorney General is authorized to—

(1) grant petitions for mitigation or remission of forfeiture, restore forfeited property to victims of a violation of this chapter, or take any other action to protect the rights of innocent persons which is in the interest of justice and which is not inconsistent with the provisions of this chapter;

(2) compromise claims arising under this section;

(3) award compensation to persons providing information resulting in a forfeiture under this section;

(4) direct the disposition by the United States of all property ordered forfeited under this section by public sale or any other commercially feasible means, making due provision for the rights of innocent persons; and

(5) take appropriate measures necessary to safeguard and maintain property ordered forfeited under this section pending its disposition.

(h) The Attorney General may promulgate regulations with respect to—

(1) making reasonable efforts to provide notice to persons who may have an interest in property ordered forfeited under this section;

(2) granting petitions for remission or mitigation of forfeiture;

(3) the restitution of property to victims of an offense petitioning for remission or mitigation of forfeiture under this chapter;

(4) the disposition by the United States of forfeited property by public sale or other commercially feasible means;

(5) the maintenance and safekeeping of any property forfeited under this section pending its disposition; and

(6) the compromise of claims arising under this chapter.

Pending the promulgation of such regulations, all provisions of law relating to the disposition of property, or the proceeds from the sale thereof, or the remission or mitigation of forfeitures for violation of the customs laws, and the compromise of claims and the award of compensation to informers in respect of such forfeitures shall apply to forfeitures incurred, or alleged to have been incurred, under the provisions of this section, insofar as applicable and not inconsistent with the provisions hereof. Such duties as are imposed upon the Customs Service or any person with respect to the disposition of property under the customs law shall be performed under this chapter by the Attorney General.

(i) Except as provided in subsection (*l*), no party claiming an interest in property subject to forfeiture under this section may—

(1) intervene in a trial or appeal of a criminal case involving the forfeiture of such property under this section; or

(2) commence an action at law or equity against the United States concerning the validity of his alleged interest in the property subsequent to the filing of an indictment or information alleging that the property is subject to forfeiture under this section.

(j) The district courts of the United States shall have jurisdiction to enter orders as provided in this section without regard to the location of any property which may be subject to forfeiture under this section or which has been ordered forfeited under this section.

(k) In order to facilitate the identification or location of property declared forfeited and to facilitate the disposition of petitions for remission or mitigation of forfeiture, after the entry of an order declaring property forfeited to the United States the court may, upon application of the United States, order that the testimony of any witness relating to the property forfeited be taken by deposition and that any designated book, paper, document, record, recording, or other material not privileged be produced at the same time and place, in the same manner as provided for the taking of depositions under Rule 15 of the Federal Rules of Criminal Procedure.

(*l*)(1) Following the entry of an order of forfeiture under this section, the United States shall publish notice of the order and of its intent to dispose of the property in such manner as the Attorney General may direct. The Government may also, to the extent practicable, provide direct written notice to any person known to have alleged an interest in the property that is the subject of the order of forfeiture as a substitute for published notice as to those persons so notified.

(2) Any person, other than the defendant, asserting a legal interest in property which has been ordered forfeited to the United States pursuant to this section may, within thirty days of the final publication of notice or his receipt of notice under paragraph (1), whichever is earlier, petition the court for a hearing to adjudicate the validity of his alleged interest in the property. The hearing shall be held before the court alone, without a jury.

(3) The petition shall be signed by the petitioner under penalty of perjury and shall set forth the nature and extent of the petitioner's right, title, or interest in the property, the time and circumstances of the petitioner's acquisition of the right, title, or interest in the property, any additional facts supporting the petitioner's claim, and the relief sought.

(4) The hearing on the petition shall, to the extent practicable and consistent with the interests of justice, be held within thirty days of the filing of the petition. The court may consolidate the hearing on the petition with a hearing on any other petition filed by a person other than the defendant under this subsection.

(5) At the hearing, the petitioner may testify and present evidence and witnesses on his own behalf, and cross-examine witnesses who appear at the hearing. The United States may present evidence and witnesses in rebuttal and in defense of its claim to the property and cross-examine witnesses who appear at the hearing. In addition to testimony and evidence presented at the hearing, the court shall consider the relevant portions of the record of the criminal case which resulted in the order of forfeiture.

(6) If, after the hearing, the court determines that the petitioner has established by a preponderance of the evidence that—

(A) the petitioner has a legal right, title, or interest in the property, and such right, title, or interest renders the order of forfeiture invalid in whole or in part because the right, title, or interest was vested in the petitioner rather than the defendant or was superior to any right, title, or interest of the defendant at the time of the commission of the acts which gave rise to the forfeiture of the property under this section; or

(B) the petitioner is a bona fide purchaser for value of the right, title, or interest in the property and was at the time of purchase reasonably without cause to believe that the property was subject to forfeiture under this section;

the court shall amend the order of forfeiture in accordance with its determination.

(7) Following the court's disposition of all petitions filed under this subsection, or if no such petitions are filed following the expiration of the period provided in paragraph (2) for the filing of such petitions, the United States shall have clear title to property that is the subject of the order of forfeiture and may warrant good title to any subsequent purchaser or transferee.

(m) If any of the property described in subsection (a), as a result of any act or omission of the defendant—

(1) cannot be located upon the exercise of due diligence;

(2) has been transferred or sold to, or deposited with, a third party;

(3) has been placed beyond the jurisdiction of the court;

(4) has been substantially diminished in value; or

(5) has been commingled with other property which cannot be divided without difficulty;

the court shall order the forfeiture of any other property of the defendant up to the value of any property described in paragraphs (1) through (5).

(Added Pub.L. 91–452, Title IX, § 901(a), Oct. 15, 1970, 84 Stat. 943, and amended Pub.L. 98–473, Title II, §§ 302, 2301(a)–(c), Oct. 12, 1984, 98 Stat. 2040, 2192; Pub.L. 99–570, Title XI, § 1153(a), Oct. 27, 1986, 100 Stat. 3207–13; Pub.L. 99–646, § 23, Nov. 10, 1986, 100 Stat. 3597; Pub.L. 100–690, Title VII, §§ 7034, 7058(d), Nov. 18, 1988, 102 Stat. 4398, 4403; Pub.L. 101–647, Title XXXV, § 3561, Nov. 29, 1990, 104 Stat. 4927.)

HISTORICAL AND STATUTORY NOTES

Transfer of Functions

For transfer of the functions, personnel, assets, and liabilities of the United States Customs Service of the Department of the Treasury, including the functions of the Secretary of the Treasury relating thereto, to the Secretary of Homeland Security, and for treatment of related references, see 6 U.S.C.A. §§ 203(1), 551(d), 552(d) and 557, and the Department of Homeland Security Reorganization Plan of November 25, 2002, as modified, set out as a note under 6 U.S.C.A. § 542.

§ 1964. Civil remedies

(a) The district courts of the United States shall have jurisdiction to prevent and restrain violations of section 1962 of this chapter by issuing appropriate orders, including, but not limited to: ordering any person to divest himself of any interest, direct or indirect, in any enterprise; imposing reasonable restrictions on the future activities or investments of any person, including, but not limited to, prohibiting any person from engaging in the same type of endeavor as the enterprise engaged in, the activities of which affect interstate or foreign commerce; or ordering dissolution or reorganization of any enterprise, making due provision for the rights of innocent persons.

(b) The Attorney General may institute proceedings under this section. Pending final determination thereof, the court may at any time enter such restraining orders or prohibitions, or take such other actions, including the acceptance of satisfactory performance bonds, as it shall deem proper.

(c) Any person injured in his business or property by reason of a violation of section 1962 of this chapter may sue therefor in any appropriate United States district court and shall recover threefold the damages he sustains and the cost of the suit, including a reasonable attorney's fee, except that no person may rely upon any conduct that would have been actionable as fraud in the purchase or sale of securities to establish a violation of section 1962. The exception contained in the preceding sentence does not apply to an action against any person that is criminally convicted in connection with the fraud, in which case the statute of limitations shall start to run on the date on which the conviction becomes final.

(d) A final judgment or decree rendered in favor of the United States in any criminal proceeding brought by the United States under this chapter shall estop the defendant from denying the essential allegations of the criminal offense in any subsequent civil proceeding brought by the United States.

(Added Pub.L. 91–452, Title IX, § 901(a), Oct. 15, 1970, 84 Stat. 943, and amended Pub.L. 98–620, Title IV, § 402(24)(A), Nov. 8, 1984, 98 Stat. 3359; Pub.L. 104–67, Title I, § 107, Dec. 22, 1995, 109 Stat. 758.)

HISTORICAL AND STATUTORY NOTES

Effective and Applicability Provisions

1995 Acts. Amendment of this section by section 107 of Pub.L. 104–67 shall not affect or apply to any private action, arising under subchapter I (section 77a et seq.) of chapter 2A of Title 15, Commerce and Trade, or chapter 2B (section 78a et seq.) of Title 15, commenced before and pending on Dec. 22, 1995, see section 108 of Pub.L. 104–67, set out as a note under section 77*l* of Title 15.

1984 Acts. Amendment by Pub.L. 98–620 not to apply to cases pending on Nov. 8, 1984, see section 403 of Pub.L. 98–620, set out as a note under section 1657 of Title 28, Judiciary and Judicial Procedure.

Rule of Construction

Nothing in Pub.L. 104–67 or the amendment to this section by section 107 of Pub.L. 104–67 shall be deemed to create or ratify any implied private right of action, or to prevent the Commission, by rule or regulation, from restricting or otherwise regulating private actions under the Securities and Exchange Act of 1934, see section 203 of Pub.L. 104–67, set out as a note under section 78j–1 of this Title 15, Commerce and Trade.

§ 1965. Venue and process

(a) Any civil action or proceeding under this chapter against any person may be instituted in the district court of the United States for any district in which such person resides, is found, has an agent, or transacts his affairs.

(b) In any action under section 1964 of this chapter in any district court of the United States in which it is shown that the ends of justice require that other parties residing in any other district be brought before the court, the court may cause such parties to be summoned, and process for that purpose may be served in any judicial district of the United States by the marshal thereof.

(c) In any civil or criminal action or proceeding instituted by the United States under this chapter in the district court of the United States for any judicial district, subpenas issued by such court to compel the attendance of witnesses may be served in any other judicial district, except that in any civil action or proceeding no such subpena shall be issued for service upon any individual who resides in another district at a place more than one hundred miles from the place at which such court is held without approval given by a judge of such court upon a showing of good cause.

(d) All other process in any action or proceeding under this chapter may be served on any person in any judicial district in which such person resides, is found, has an agent, or transacts his affairs.

(Added Pub.L. 91–452, Title IX, § 901(a), Oct. 15, 1970, 84 Stat. 944.)

§ 1966. Expedition of actions

In any civil action instituted under this chapter by the United States in any district court of the United States, the Attorney General may file with the clerk of such court a certificate stating that in his opinion the case is of general public importance. A copy of that certificate shall be furnished immediately by such clerk to the chief judge or in his absence to the presiding district judge of the district in which such action is pending. Upon receipt of such copy, such judge shall designate immediately a judge of that district to hear and determine action.

(Added Pub.L. 91–452, Title IX, § 901(a), Oct. 15, 1970, 84 Stat. 944, and amended Pub.L. 98–620, Title IV, § 402(24)(B), Nov. 8, 1984, 98 Stat. 3359.)

HISTORICAL AND STATUTORY NOTES

Effective and Applicability Provisions

1984 Acts. Amendment by Pub.L. 98–620 not to apply to cases pending on Nov. 8, 1984, see section 403 of Pub.L. 98–620, set out as a note under section 1657 of Title 28, Judiciary and Judicial Procedure.

§ 1967. Evidence

In any proceeding ancillary to or in any civil action instituted by the United States under this chapter the proceedings may be open or closed to the public at the discretion of the court after consideration of the rights of affected persons.

(Added Pub.L. 91–452, Title IX, § 901(a), Oct. 15, 1970, 84 Stat. 944.)

§ 1968. Civil investigative demand

(a) Whenever the Attorney General has reason to believe that any person or enterprise may be in possession, custody, or control of any documentary materials relevant to a racketeering investigation, he may, prior to the institution of a civil or criminal proceeding thereon, issue in writing, and cause to be served upon such person, a civil investigative demand requiring such person to produce such material for examination.

(b) Each such demand shall—

(1) state the nature of the conduct constituting the alleged racketeering violation which is under investigation and the provision of law applicable thereto;

(2) describe the class or classes of documentary material produced thereunder with such definiteness and certainty as to permit such material to be fairly identified;

(3) state that the demand is returnable forthwith or prescribe a return date which will provide a reasonable period of time within which the material so demanded may be assembled and made available for inspection and copying or reproduction; and

(4) identify the custodian to whom such material shall be made available.

(c) No such demand shall—

(1) contain any requirement which would be held to be unreasonable if contained in a subpena duces tecum issued by a court of the United States in aid of a grand jury investigation of such alleged racketeering violation; or

(2) require the production of any documentary evidence which would be privileged from disclosure if demanded by a subpena duces tecum issued by a court of the United States in aid of a grand jury investigation of such alleged racketeering violation.

(d) Service of any such demand or any petition filed under this section may be made upon a person by—

(1) delivering a duly executed copy thereof to any partner, executive officer, managing agent, or general agent thereof, or to any agent thereof authorized by appointment or by law to receive service of process on behalf of such person, or upon any individual person;

(2) delivering a duly executed copy thereof to the principal office or place of business of the person to be served; or

(3) depositing such copy in the United States mail, by registered or certified mail duly addressed to such person at its principal office or place of business.

(e) A verified return by the individual serving any such demand or petition setting forth the manner of such service shall be prima facie proof of such service. In the case of service by registered or certified mail, such return shall be accompanied by the return post office receipt of delivery of such demand.

(f) (1) The Attorney General shall designate a racketeering investigator to serve as racketeer document custodian, and such additional racketeering investigators as he shall determine from time to time to be necessary to serve as deputies to such officer.

(2) Any person upon whom any demand issued under this section has been duly served shall make such material available for inspection and copying or reproduction to the custodian designated therein at the principal place of business of such person, or at such other place as such custodian and such person thereafter may agree and prescribe in writing or as the court may direct, pursuant to this section on the return date specified in such demand, or on such later date as such custodian may prescribe in writing. Such person may upon written agreement between such person and the custodian substitute for copies of all or any part of such material originals thereof.

(3) The custodian to whom any documentary material is so delivered shall take physical possession thereof, and shall be responsible for the use made thereof and for the return thereof pursuant to this chapter. The custodian may cause the preparation of such copies of such documentary material as may be required for official use under regulations which shall be promulgated by the Attorney General. While in the possession of the custodian, no material so produced shall be available for examination, without the consent of the person who produced such material, by any individual other than the Attorney General. Under such reasonable terms and conditions as the Attorney General shall prescribe, documentary material while in the possession of the custodian shall be available for examination by the person who produced such material or any duly authorized representatives of such person.

(4) Whenever any attorney has been designated to appear on behalf of the United States before any court or grand jury in any case or proceeding involving any alleged violation of this chapter, the custodian may deliver to such attorney such documentary material in the possession of the custodian as such attorney determines to be required for use in the presentation of such case or proceeding on behalf of the United States. Upon the conclusion of any such case or proceeding, such attorney shall return to the custodian any documentary material so withdrawn which has not passed into the control of such court or grand jury through the introduction thereof into the record of such case or proceeding.

(5) Upon the completion of—

(i) the racketeering investigation for which any documentary material was produced under this chapter, and

(ii) any case or proceeding arising from such investigation,

the custodian shall return to the person who produced such material all such material other than copies thereof made by the Attorney General pursuant to this subsection which has not passed into the control of any court or grand jury through the introduction thereof into the record of such case or proceeding.

(6) When any documentary material has been produced by any person under this section for use in any racketeering investigation, and no such case or proceeding arising therefrom has been instituted within a reasonable time after completion of the examination and analysis of all evidence assembled in the course of such investigation, such person shall be entitled, upon written demand made upon the Attorney General, to the return of all documentary material other than copies thereof made pursuant to this subsection so produced by such person.

(7) In the event of the death, disability, or separation from service of the custodian of any documentary material produced under any demand issued under this section or the official relief of such custodian from responsibility for the custody and control of such material, the Attorney General shall promptly—

(i) designate another racketeering investigator to serve as custodian thereof, and

(ii) transmit notice in writing to the person who produced such material as to the identity and address of the successor so designated.

Any successor so designated shall have with regard to such materials all duties and responsibilities imposed by this section upon his predecessor in office with regard thereto, except that he shall not be held responsible for any default or dereliction which occurred before his designation as custodian.

(g) Whenever any person fails to comply with any civil investigative demand duly served upon him under this section or whenever satisfactory copying or reproduction of any such material cannot be done and such person refuses to surrender such material, the Attorney General may file, in the district court of the United States for any judicial district in which such person resides, is found, or transacts business, and serve upon such person a petition for an order of such court for the enforcement of this section, except that if such person transacts business in more than one such district such petition shall be filed in the district in which such person maintains his principal place of business, or in such other district in which such person transacts business as may be agreed upon by the parties to such petition.

(h) Within twenty days after the service of any such demand upon any person, or at any time before the return date specified in the demand, whichever period is shorter, such person may file, in the district court of the United States for the judicial district within which such person resides, is found, or transacts business, and serve upon such custodian a petition for an order of such court modifying or setting aside such demand. The time allowed for compliance with the demand in whole or in part as deemed proper and ordered by the court shall not run during the pendency of such petition in the court. Such petition shall specify each ground upon which the petitioner relies in seeking such relief, and may be based upon any failure of such demand to comply with the provisions of this section or upon any constitutional or other legal right or privilege of such person.

(i) At any time during which any custodian is in custody or control of any documentary material delivered by any person in compliance with any such demand, such person may file, in the district court of the United States for the judicial district within which the office of such custodian is situated, and serve upon such custodian a petition for an order of such court requiring the performance by such custodian of any duty imposed upon him by this section.

(j) Whenever any petition is filed in any district court of the United States under this section, such court shall have jurisdiction to hear and determine the matter so presented, and to enter such order or orders as may be required to carry into effect the provisions of this section.

(Added Pub.L. 91–452, Title IX, § 901(a), Oct. 15, 1970, 84 Stat. 944.)

CHAPTER 97—RAILROAD CARRIERS AND MASS TRANSPORTATION SYSTEMS ON LAND, ON WATER, OR THROUGH THE AIR

§ 1991. Entering train to commit crime

Whoever, in any Territory or District, or within or upon any place within the exclusive jurisdiction of the United States, willfully and maliciously trespasses upon or enters upon any railroad train, railroad car, or railroad locomotive, with the intent to commit murder or robbery, shall be fined under this title or imprisoned not more than twenty years, or both.

Whoever, within such jurisdiction, willfully and maliciously trespasses upon or enters upon any railroad train, railroad car, or railroad locomotive, with intent to commit any unlawful violence upon or against any passenger on said train, or car, or upon or against any engineer, conductor, fireman, brakeman, or any officer or employee connected with said locomotive, train, or car, or upon or against any express messenger or mail agent on said train or in any car thereof, or to commit any crime or offense against any person or property thereon, shall be fined under this title or imprisoned not more than one year, or both.

Upon the trial of any person charged with any offense set forth in this section, it shall not be necessary to set forth or prove the particular person against whom it was intended to commit the offense, or that it was intended to commit such offense against any particular person.

(June 25, 1948, c. 645, 62 Stat. 794; Sept. 13, 1994, Pub.L. 103–322, Title XXXIII, § 330016(1)(K), 108 Stat. 2147; Oct. 11, 1996, Pub.L. 104–294, Title VI, § 601(a)(8), 110 Stat. 3498.)

§ 1992. Terrorist attacks and other violence against railroad carriers and against mass transportation systems on land, on water, or through the air

(a) General prohibitions.—Whoever, in a circumstance described in subsection (c), knowingly and without lawful authority or permission—

(1) wrecks, derails, sets fire to, or disables railroad on-track equipment or a mass transportation vehicle;

(2) places any biological agent or toxin, destructive substance, or destructive device in, upon, or near railroad on-track equipment or a mass transportation vehicle with intent to endanger the safety

of any person, or with a reckless disregard for the safety of human life;

(3) places or releases a hazardous material or a biological agent or toxin on or near any property described in subparagraph (A) or (B) of paragraph (4), with intent to endanger the safety of any person, or with reckless disregard for the safety of human life;

(4) sets fire to, undermines, makes unworkable, unusable, or hazardous to work on or use, or places any biological agent or toxin, destructive substance, or destructive device in, upon, or near any—

(A) tunnel, bridge, viaduct, trestle, track, electromagnetic guideway, signal, station, depot, warehouse, terminal, or any other way, structure, property, or appurtenance used in the operation of, or in support of the operation of, a railroad carrier, and with intent to, or knowing or having reason to know, such activity would likely, derail, disable, or wreck railroad on-track equipment; or

(B) garage, terminal, structure, track, electromagnetic guideway, supply, or facility used in the operation of, or in support of the operation of, a mass transportation vehicle, and with intent to, or knowing or having reason to know, such activity would likely, derail, disable, or wreck a mass transportation vehicle used, operated, or employed by a mass transportation provider;

(5) removes an appurtenance from, damages, or otherwise impairs the operation of a railroad signal system or mass transportation signal or dispatching system, including a train control system, centralized dispatching system, or highway-railroad grade crossing warning signal;

(6) with intent to endanger the safety of any person, or with a reckless disregard for the safety of human life, interferes with, disables, or incapacitates any dispatcher, driver, captain, locomotive engineer, railroad conductor, or other person while the person is employed in dispatching, operating, controlling, or maintaining railroad on-track equipment or a mass transportation vehicle;

(7) commits an act, including the use of a dangerous weapon, with the intent to cause death or serious bodily injury to any person who is on property described in subparagraph (A) or (B) of paragraph (4);

(8) surveils, photographs, videotapes, diagrams, or otherwise collects information with the intent to plan or assist in planning any of the acts described in paragraphs (1) through (6);

(9) conveys false information, knowing the information to be false, concerning an attempt or alleged attempt to engage in a violation of this subsection; or

(10) attempts, threatens, or conspires to engage in any violation of any of paragraphs (1) through (9),

shall be fined under this title or imprisoned not more than 20 years, or both, and if the offense results in the death of any person, shall be imprisoned for any term of years or for life, or subject to death, except in the case of a violation of paragraph (8), (9), or (10).

(b) Aggravated offense.—Whoever commits an offense under subsection (a) of this section in a circumstance in which—

(1) the railroad on-track equipment or mass transportation vehicle was carrying a passenger or employee at the time of the offense;

(2) the railroad on-track equipment or mass transportation vehicle was carrying high-level radioactive waste or spent nuclear fuel at the time of the offense; or

(3) the offense was committed with the intent to endanger the safety of any person, or with a reckless disregard for the safety of any person, and the railroad on-track equipment or mass transportation vehicle was carrying a hazardous material at the time of the offense that—

(A) was required to be placarded under subpart F of part 172 of title 49, Code of Federal Regulations; and

(B) is identified as class number 3, 4, 5, 6.1, or 8 and packing group I or packing group II, or class number 1, 2, or 7 under the hazardous materials table of section 172.101 of title 49, Code of Federal Regulations,

shall be fined under this title or imprisoned for any term of years or life, or both, and if the offense resulted in the death of any person, the person may be sentenced to death.

(c) Circumstances required for offense.—A circumstance referred to in subsection (a) is any of the following:

(1) Any of the conduct required for the offense is, or, in the case of an attempt, threat, or conspiracy to engage in conduct, the conduct required for the completed offense would be, engaged in, on, against, or affecting a mass transportation provider, or a railroad carrier engaged in interstate or foreign commerce.

(2) Any person travels or communicates across a State line in order to commit the offense, or transports materials across a State line in aid of the commission of the offense.

(d) Definitions.—In this section—

(1) the term "biological agent" has the meaning given to that term in section 178(1);

(2) the term "dangerous weapon" means a weapon, device, instrument, material, or substance, ani-

mate or inanimate, that is used for, or is readily capable of, causing death or serious bodily injury, including a pocket knife with a blade of less than 2 ½ inches in length and a box cutter;

(3) the term "destructive device" has the meaning given to that term in section 921(a)(4);

(4) the term "destructive substance" means an explosive substance, flammable material, infernal machine, or other chemical, mechanical, or radioactive device or material, or matter of a combustible, contaminative, corrosive, or explosive nature, except that the term "radioactive device" does not include any radioactive device or material used solely for medical, industrial, research, or other peaceful purposes;

(5) the term "hazardous material" has the meaning given to that term in chapter 51 of title 49;

(6) the term "high-level radioactive waste" has the meaning given to that term in section 2(12) of the Nuclear Waste Policy Act of 1982 (42 U.S.C. 10101(12));

(7) the term "mass transportation" has the meaning given to that term in section 5302(a)(7) of title 49, except that the term includes school bus, charter, and sightseeing transportation and passenger vessel as that term is defined in section 2101(22) of title 46, United States Code;

(8) the term "on-track equipment" means a carriage or other contrivance that runs on rails or electromagnetic guideways;

(9) the term "railroad on-track equipment" means a train, locomotive, tender, motor unit, freight or passenger car, or other on-track equipment used, operated, or employed by a railroad carrier;

(10) the term "railroad" has the meaning given to that term in chapter 201 of title 49;

(11) the term "railroad carrier" has the meaning given to that term in chapter 201 of title 49;

(12) the term "serious bodily injury" has the meaning given to that term in section 1365;

(13) the term "spent nuclear fuel" has the meaning given to that term in section 2(23) of the Nuclear Waste Policy Act of 1982 (42 U.S.C. 10101(23));

(14) the term "State" has the meaning given to that term in section 2266;

(15) the term "toxin" has the meaning given to that term in section 178(2); and

(16) the term "vehicle" means any carriage or other contrivance used, or capable of being used, as a means of transportation on land, on water, or through the air.

(Added Pub.L. 109–177, Title I, § 110(a), Mar. 9, 2006, 120 Stat. 208.)

HISTORICAL AND STATUTORY NOTES

References in Text

Chapter 51 of title 49, referred to in subsec. (c)(5), is Transportation of Hazardous Material, 49 U.S.C.A. § 5101 et seq.

Section 2 of the Nuclear Waste Policy Act of 1982, referred to in subsecs. (c)(6) and (d)(13), is Pub.L. 97–425, § 2, Jan. 7, 1983, 96 Stat. 2202, as amended, which is classified to 42 U.S.C.A. § 10101.

Chapter 201 of Title 49, referred to in subsec. (d)(10), (11), is 49 U.S.C.A. § 20101 et seq., relating to general railroad safety.

Prior Provisions

A prior section 1992, Act June 25, 1948, c. 645, 62 Stat. 794; Sept. 13, 1994, Pub.L. 103–322, Title VI, § 60003(a)(8), Title XXXIII, § 330016(1)(L), 108 Stat. 1969, 2147; Dec. 29, 1995, Pub.L. 104–88, Title IV, § 402(b), 109 Stat. 955; Oct. 26, 2001, Pub.L. 107–56, Title VIII, § 811(e), 115 Stat. 381; Nov. 2, 2002, Pub.L. 107–273, Div. B, Title IV, § 4002(a)(6), 116 Stat. 1807, relating to the offense of wrecking trains, was repealed by Pub.L. 109–177, Title I, § 110(a), Mar. 9, 2006, 120 Stat. 205.

[§ 1993. Repealed. Pub.L. 109–177, Title I, § 110(a), Mar. 9, 2006, 120 Stat. 205]

HISTORICAL AND STATUTORY NOTES

Section, added Pub.L. 107–56, Title VIII, § 801, Oct. 26, 2001, 115 Stat. 374, and amended Pub.L. 108–21, Title VI, § 609, Apr. 30, 2003, 117 Stat. 692; Pub.L. 109–59, Title III, § 3042(a), Aug. 10, 2005, 119 Stat. 1640, related to terrorist attacks and other acts of violence against public transportation systems. See, now, 18 U.S.C.A. § 1992.

[CHAPTER 99—Repealed]

[§ 2031. Repealed. Pub.L. 99–646, § 87(c)(1), Nov. 10, 1986, 100 Stat. 3623; Pub.L. 99–654, § 3(a)(1), Nov. 14, 1986, 100 Stat. 3663]

HISTORICAL AND STATUTORY NOTES

Section, Act June 25, 1948, c. 645, 62 Stat. 795, prescribed penalties for commission of rape within special maritime and territorial jurisdiction.

Effective Date of Repeal

Section repealed 30 days after Nov. 14, 1986, see section 4 of Pub.L. 99–654, set out as a note under section 2241 of this title.

Section repealed 30 days after Nov. 10, 1986, see section 87(e) of Pub.L. 99–646, set out as a note under section 2241 of this title.

[§ 2032. Repealed. Pub.L. 99–646, § 87(c)(1), Nov. 10, 1986, 100 Stat. 3623; Pub.L. 99–654, § 3(a)(1), Nov. 14, 1986, 100 Stat. 3663]

HISTORICAL AND STATUTORY NOTES

Section, Act June 25, 1948, c. 645, 62 Stat. 795, prescribed penalties for carnal knowledge of female under 16 within special maritime and territorial jurisdiction.

Effective Date of Repeal

Section repealed 30 days after Nov. 10, 1986, see section 87(e) of Pub.L. 99–646, set out as a note under section 2241 of this title.

CHAPTER 101—RECORDS AND REPORTS

Sec.

§ 2071. Concealment, removal, or mutilation generally

(a) Whoever willfully and unlawfully conceals, removes, mutilates, obliterates, or destroys, or attempts to do so, or, with intent to do so takes and carries away any record, proceeding, map, book, paper, document, or other thing, filed or deposited with any clerk or officer of any court of the United States, or in any public office, or with any judicial or public officer of the United States, shall be fined under this title or imprisoned not more than three years, or both.

(b) Whoever, having the custody of any such record, proceeding, map, book, document, paper, or other thing, willfully and unlawfully conceals, removes, mutilates, obliterates, falsifies, or destroys the same, shall be fined under this title or imprisoned not more than three years, or both; and shall forfeit his office and be disqualified from holding any office under the United States. As used in this subsection, the term "office" does not include the office held by any person as a retired officer of the Armed Forces of the United States.

(June 25, 1948, c. 645, 62 Stat. 795; Nov. 5, 1990, Pub.L. 101–510, Div. A, Title V, § 552(a), 104 Stat. 1566; Sept. 13, 1994, Pub.L. 103–322, Title XXXIII, § 330016(1)(I), 108 Stat. 2147.)

HISTORICAL AND STATUTORY NOTES

Effective and Applicability Provisions

1990 Acts. Section 552(b) of Pub.L. 101–510, provided that: "The amendment made by subsection (a) [amending this section] shall be effective as of January 1, 1989."

§ 2072. False crop reports

Whoever, being an officer or employee of the United States or any of its agencies, whose duties require the compilation or report of statistics or information relating to the products of the soil, knowingly compiles for issuance, or issues, any false statistics or information as a report of the United States or any of its agencies, shall be fined under this title or imprisoned not more than five years, or both.

(June 25, 1948, c. 645, 62 Stat. 795; Sept. 13, 1994, Pub.L. 103–322, Title XXXIII, § 330016(1)(K), 108 Stat. 2147.)

§ 2073. False entries and reports of moneys or securities

Whoever, being an officer, clerk, agent, or other employee of the United States or any of its agencies, charged with the duty of keeping accounts or records of any kind, with intent to deceive, mislead, injure, or defraud, makes in any such account or record any false or fictitious entry or record of any matter relating to or connected with his duties; or

Whoever, being an officer, clerk, agent, or other employee of the United States or any of its agencies, charged with the duty of receiving, holding, or paying over moneys or securities to, for, or on behalf of the United States, or of receiving or holding in trust for any person any moneys or securities, with like intent, makes a false report of such moneys or securities—

Shall be fined under this title or imprisoned not more than ten years, or both.

(June 25, 1948, c. 645, 62 Stat. 795; Sept. 13, 1994, Pub.L. 103–322, Title XXXIII, § 330016(1)(K), 108 Stat. 2147.)

§ 2074. False weather reports

Whoever knowingly issues or publishes any counterfeit weather forecast or warning of weather conditions falsely representing such forecast or warning to have been issued or published by the Weather Bureau, United States Signal Service, or other branch of the Government service, shall be fined under this title or imprisoned not more than ninety days, or both.

(June 25, 1948, c. 645, 62 Stat. 795; Sept. 13, 1994, Pub.L. 103–322, Title XXXIII, § 330016(1)(G), 108 Stat. 2147.)

HISTORICAL AND STATUTORY NOTES

References in Text

The United States Signal Service, referred to in text, is now the Signal Corps which is a branch of the Army, see section 3063 of Title 10, Armed Forces.

Transfer of Functions

The Weather Bureau of the Department of Commerce was consolidated with the Coast and Geodetic Survey to form a new agency in the Department of Commerce to be known as the Environmental Science Services Administration by Reorg. Plan No. 2 of 1965, eff. July 13, 1965, 30 F.R. 8819, 79 Stat. 1318, set out in the Appendix to Title 5, Government Organization and Employees. All functions of the Bureau were transferred to the Secretary of Commerce by the Plan.

The Environmental Science Services Administration was abolished by Reorg. Plan No. 4 of 1970, eff. Oct. 3, 1970, 35 F.R. 15627, 84 Stat. 2090, set out in the Appendix to Title 5, Government Organization and Employees, which created the National Oceanic and Atmospheric Administration in the Department of Commerce. By Department Organization Order 25–5A, republished 39 F.R. 27486, the Secretary of Commerce delegated to NOAA his functions relating to the Weather Bureau. By order of the Acting Associate Administrator of NOAA, the organization name of the Weather Bureau was changed to the National Weather Service. For further details, see the Codification note under section 311 of Title 15, Commerce and Trade.

§ 2075. Officer failing to make returns or reports

Every officer who neglects or refuses to make any return or report which he is required to make at stated times by any Act of Congress or regulation of the Department of the Treasury, other than his accounts, within the time prescribed by such Act or regulation, shall be fined under this title.

(June 25, 1948, c. 645, 62 Stat. 796; Nov. 2, 2002, Pub.L. 107–273, Div. B, Title IV, § 4002(d)(1)(C)(ii), 116 Stat. 1809.)

§ 2076. Clerk of United States District Court

Whoever, being a clerk of a district court of the United States, willfully refuses or neglects to make or forward any report, certificate, statement, or document as required by law, shall be fined under this title or imprisoned not more than one year, or both.

(June 25, 1948, c. 645, 62 Stat. 796; Oct. 11, 1996, Pub.L. 104–294, Title VI, § 601(a)(11), 110 Stat. 3498.)

CHAPTER 102—RIOTS

§ 2101. Riots

(a) Whoever travels in interstate or foreign commerce or uses any facility of interstate or foreign commerce, including, but not limited to, the mail, telegraph, telephone, radio, or television, with intent—

(1) to incite a riot; or

(2) to organize, promote, encourage, participate in, or carry on a riot; or

(3) to commit any act of violence in furtherance of a riot; or

(4) to aid or abet any person in inciting or participating in or carrying on a riot or committing any act of violence in furtherance of a riot;

and who either during the course of any such travel or use or thereafter performs or attempts to perform any other overt act for any purpose specified in subparagraph (A), (B), (C), or (D) of this paragraph [1]—

Shall be fined under this title, or imprisoned not more than five years, or both.

(b) In any prosecution under this section, proof that a defendant engaged or attempted to engage in one or more of the overt acts described in subparagraph (A), (B), (C), or (D) of paragraph (1) of subsection (a) [2] and (1) has traveled in interstate or foreign commerce, or (2) has use of or used any facility of interstate or foreign commerce, including but not limited to, mail, telegraph, telephone, radio, or television, to communicate with or broadcast to any person or group of persons prior to such overt acts, such travel or use shall be admissible proof to establish that such defendant traveled in or used such facility of interstate or foreign commerce.

(c) A judgment of conviction or acquittal on the merits under the laws of any State shall be a bar to any prosecution hereunder for the same act or acts.

(d) Whenever, in the opinion of the Attorney General or of the appropriate officer of the Department of Justice charged by law or under the instructions of the Attorney General with authority to act, any person shall have violated this chapter, the Department shall proceed as speedily as possible with a prosecution of such person hereunder and with any appeal which may lie from any decision adverse to the Government resulting from such prosecution.

(e) Nothing contained in this section shall be construed to make it unlawful for any person to travel in, or use any facility of, interstate or foreign commerce for the purpose of pursuing the legitimate objectives of organized labor, through orderly and lawful means.

(f) Nothing in this section shall be construed as indicating an intent on the part of Congress to prevent any State, any possession or Commonwealth of the United States, or the District of Columbia, from exercising jurisdiction over any offense over which it would have jurisdiction in the absence of this section; nor shall anything in this section be construed as depriving State and local law enforcement authorities of responsibility for prosecuting acts that may be violations of this section and that are violations of State and local law.

(Added Pub.L. 90–284, Title I, § 104(a), Apr. 11, 1968, 82 Stat. 75, and amended Pub.L. 99–386, Title I, § 106, Aug. 22, 1986, 100 Stat. 822; Pub.L. 103–322, Title XXXIII, § 330016(1)(L), Sept. 13, 1994, 108 Stat. 2147; Pub.L. 104–294, Title VI, § 601(f)(15), Oct. 11, 1996, 110 Stat. 3500.)

1 So in original. Probably should be "paragraph (1), (2), (3), or (4) of this subsection".

2 So in original. Probably should be "paragraph (1), (2), (3), or (4) of subsection (a)".

HISTORICAL AND STATUTORY NOTES

Savings Provisions of Pub.L. 98–473, Title II, c. II

See section 235 of Pub.L. 98–473, Title II, c. II, Oct. 12, 1984, 98 Stat. 2031, as amended, set out as a note under section 3551 of this title.

§ 2102. Definitions

(a) As used in this chapter, the term "riot" means a public disturbance involving (1) an act or acts of violence by one or more persons part of an assemblage of three or more persons, which act or acts shall constitute a clear and present danger of, or shall result in, damage or injury to the property of any other person or to the person of any other individual or (2) a threat or threats of the commission of an act or acts of violence by one or more persons part of an assemblage of three or more persons having, individually or collectively, the ability of immediate execution of such threat or threats, where the performance of the threatened act or acts of violence would constitute a clear and present danger of, or would result in, damage or injury to the property of any other person or to the person of any other individual.

(b) As used in this chapter, the term "to incite a riot", or "to organize, promote, encourage, participate in, or carry on a riot", includes, but is not limited to, urging or instigating other persons to riot, but shall not be deemed to mean the mere oral or written (1) advocacy of ideas or (2) expression of belief, not involving advocacy of any act or acts of violence or assertion of the rightness of, or the right to commit, any such act or acts.

(Added Pub.L. 90–284, Title I, § 104(a), Apr. 11, 1968, 82 Stat. 76.)

CHAPTER 103—ROBBERY AND BURGLARY

Sec.

§ 2111. Special maritime and territorial jurisdiction

Whoever, within the special maritime and territorial jurisdiction of the United States, by force and violence, or by intimidation, takes or attempts to take from the person or presence of another anything of value, shall be imprisoned not more than fifteen years.

(June 25, 1948, c. 645, 62 Stat. 796; Sept. 13, 1994, Pub.L. 103–322, Title XXXII, § 320903(a)(1), 108 Stat. 2124.)

HISTORICAL AND STATUTORY NOTES

§ 2112. Personal property of United States

Whoever robs or attempts to rob another of any kind or description of personal property belonging to the United States, shall be imprisoned not more than fifteen years.

(June 25, 1948, c. 645, 62 Stat. 796; Sept. 13, 1994, Pub.L. 103–322, Title XXXII, § 320903(a)(2), 108 Stat. 2124.)

§ 2113. Bank robbery and incidental crimes

(a) Whoever, by force and violence, or by intimidation, takes, or attempts to take, from the person or presence of another, or obtains or attempts to obtain by extortion any property or money or any other thing of value belonging to, or in the care, custody, control, management, or possession of, any bank, credit union, or any savings and loan association; or

Whoever enters or attempts to enter any bank, credit union, or any savings and loan association, or any building used in whole or in part as a bank, credit union, or as a savings and loan association, with intent to commit in such bank, credit union, or in such savings and loan association, or building, or part thereof, so used, any felony affecting such bank, credit union, or such savings and loan association and in violation of any statute of the United States, or any larceny—

Shall be fined under this title or imprisoned not more than twenty years, or both.

(b) Whoever takes and carries away, with intent to steal or purloin, any property or money or any other thing of value exceeding $1,000 belonging to, or in the care, custody, control, management, or possession of any bank, credit union, or any savings and loan association, shall be fined under this title or imprisoned not more than ten years, or both; or

Whoever takes and carries away, with intent to steal or purloin, any property or money or any other thing of value not exceeding $1,000 belonging to, or in the care, custody, control, management, or possession of any bank, credit union, or any savings and loan association, shall be fined under this title or imprisoned not more than one year, or both.

(c) Whoever receives, possesses, conceals, stores, barters, sells, or disposes of, any property or money or other thing of value which has been taken or stolen from a bank, credit union, or savings and loan association in violation of subsection (b), knowing the same to be property which has been stolen shall be subject to the punishment provided in subsection (b) for the taker.

(d) Whoever, in committing, or in attempting to commit, any offense defined in subsections (a) and (b) of this section, assaults any person, or puts in jeopardy the life of any person by the use of a dangerous weapon or device, shall be fined under this title or imprisoned not more than twenty-five years, or both.

(e) Whoever, in committing any offense defined in this section, or in avoiding or attempting to avoid apprehension for the commission of such offense, or in freeing himself or attempting to free himself from arrest or confinement for such offense, kills any person, or forces any person to accompany him without the consent of such person, shall be imprisoned not less than ten years, or if death results shall be punished by death or life imprisonment.

(f) As used in this section the term "bank" means any member bank of the Federal Reserve System, and any bank, banking association, trust company, savings bank, or other banking institution organized or operating under the laws of the United States, including a branch or agency of a foreign bank (as such terms are defined in paragraphs (1) and (3) of section 1(b) of the International Banking Act of 1978), and any institution the deposits of which are insured by the Federal Deposit Insurance Corporation.

(g) As used in this section the term "credit union" means any Federal credit union and any State-chartered credit union the accounts of which are insured by the National Credit Union Administration Board, and any "Federal Credit Union" as defined in section 2 of the Federal Credit Union Act. The term "State-chartered credit union" includes a credit union chartered under the laws of a State of the United States, the District of Columbia, or any commonwealth, territory, or possession of the United States.

(h) As used in this section, the term "savings and loan association" means—

(1) a Federal savings association or State savings association (as defined in section 3(b) of the Federal Deposit Insurance Act (12 U.S.C. 1813(b))) having accounts insured by the Federal Deposit Insurance Corporation; and

(2) a corporation described in section 3(b)(1)(C) of the Federal Deposit Insurance Act (12 U.S.C. 1813(b)(1)(C)) that is operating under the laws of the United States.

(June 25, 1948, c. 645, 62 Stat. 796; Aug. 3, 1950, c. 516, 64 Stat. 394; Apr. 8, 1952, c. 164, 66 Stat. 46; Sept. 22, 1959, Pub.L. 86–354, § 2, 73 Stat. 639; Oct. 19, 1970, Pub.L. 91–468, § 8, 84 Stat. 1017; Oct. 12, 1984, Pub. L. 98–473, Title II, § 1106, 98 Stat. 2145; Nov. 10, 1986, Pub.L. 99–646, § 68, 100 Stat. 3616; Aug. 9, 1989, Pub.L. 101–73, Title IX, §§ 962(a)(7), (d), 103 Stat. 502, 503; Pub.L. 101–647, Title XXV, § 2597(*l*), Nov. 29, 1990, 104 Stat. 4911; Sept. 13, 1994, Pub.L. 103–322, Title VI, § 60003(a)(9), Title XXXII, § 320608, Title XXXIII, § 330016(1)(K), (L), 108 Stat. 1969, 2120, 2147; Oct. 11, 1996, Pub.L. 104–294, Title VI, §§ 606(a), 607(d), 110 Stat. 3511; Nov. 2, 2002, Pub.L. 107–273, Div. B, Title IV, § 4002(d)(1)(C)(ii), 116 Stat. 1809.)

HISTORICAL AND STATUTORY NOTES

References in Text

Section 1(b) of the International Banking Act of 1978, referred to in subsec. (f), is classified to section 3101 of Title 12, Banks and Banking.

Section 2 of the Federal Credit Union Act, referred to in subsec. (g), is classified to section 1752 of Title 12.

Section 3(b) and 3(b)(1)(C) of the Federal Deposit Insurance Act, referred to in subsec. (h)(1) and (2), is section 1813(b) and (b)(1)(C) of Title 12, Banks and Banking.

2002 Acts. House Conference Report No. 107–685 and Statement by President, see 2002 U.S. Code Cong. and Adm. News, p. 1120.

Severability of Provisions

If any provision of Pub.L. 101–73 or the application thereof to any person or circumstance is held invalid, the remainder of Pub.L. 101–73 and the application of the provision to other persons not similarly situated or to other circumstances not to be affected thereby, see section 1221 of Pub.L. 101–73, set out as a note under section 1811 of Title 12, Banks and Banking.

§ 2114. Mail, money, or other property of United States

(a) Assault.—A person who assaults any person having lawful charge, control, or custody of any mail matter or of any money or other property of the United States, with intent to rob, steal, or purloin such mail matter, money, or other property of the United States, or robs or attempts to rob any such person of mail matter, or of any money, or other property of the United States, shall, for the first offense, be imprisoned not more than ten years; and if in effecting or attempting to effect such robbery he wounds the person having custody of such mail, money, or other property of the United States, or puts his life in jeopardy by the use of a dangerous weapon, or for a subsequent offense, shall be imprisoned not more than twenty-five years.

(b) Receipt, possession, concealment, or disposal of property.—A person who receives, possesses, conceals, or disposes of any money or other property that has been obtained in violation of this section, knowing the same to have been unlawfully obtained, shall be imprisoned not more than 10 years, fined under this title, or both.

(June 25, 1948, c. 645, 62 Stat. 797; Oct. 12, 1984, Pub.L. 98–473, Title II, § 223(d), 98 Stat. 2028; Nov. 29, 1990, Pub.L. 101–647, Title XXXV, § 3562, 104 Stat. 4927; Sept. 13, 1994, Pub.L. 103–322, Title XXXII, §§ 320602, 320903(a)(3), 108 Stat. 2115, 2124; Oct. 11, 1996, Pub.L. 104–294, Title VI, § 604(b)(17), 110 Stat. 3507.)

HISTORICAL AND STATUTORY NOTES

Effective and Applicability Provisions

1996 Acts. Amendment by section 604 of Pub.L. 104–294 effective Sept. 13, 1994, see section 604(d) of Pub.L. 104–294, set out as a note under section 13 of this title.

1984 Acts. Amendment by Pub.L. 98–473 effective on the first day of first calendar month beginning thirty six months after Oct. 12, 1984, applicable only to offenses committed after taking effect of sections 211 to 239 of Pub.L. 98–473, and except as otherwise provided for therein, see section 235 of Pub.L. 98–473, as amended, set out as a note under section 3551 of this title.

§ 2115. Post office

Whoever forcibly breaks into or attempts to break into any post office, or any building used in whole or in part as a post office, with intent to commit in such post office, or building or part thereof, so used, any larceny or other depredation, shall be fined under this title or imprisoned not more than five years, or both.

(June 25, 1948, c. 645, 62 Stat. 797; Oct. 11, 1996, Pub.L. 104–294, Title VI, § 601(a)(8), 110 Stat. 3498.)

§ 2116. Railway or steamboat post office

Whoever, by violence, enters a post-office car, or any part of any car, steamboat, or vessel, assigned to the use of the mail service, or willfully or maliciously assaults or interferes with any postal clerk in the discharge of his duties in connection with such car, steamboat, vessel, or apartment thereof, shall be fined under this title or imprisoned not more than three years, or both.

(June 25, 1948, c. 645, 62 Stat. 797; Oct. 11, 1996, Pub.L. 104–294, Title VI, § 601(a)(8), 110 Stat. 3498.)

§ 2117. Breaking or entering carrier facilities

Whoever breaks the seal or lock of any railroad car, vessel, aircraft, motortruck, wagon or other vehicle or of any pipeline system, containing interstate or foreign shipments of freight or express or other property, or enters any such vehicle or pipeline system with intent in either case to commit larceny therein, shall be fined under this title or imprisoned not more than ten years, or both.

A judgment of conviction or acquittal on the merits under the laws of any State shall be a bar to any prosecution under this section for the same act or acts. Nothing contained in this section shall be construed as indicating an intent on the part of Congress to occupy the field in which provisions of this section operate to the exclusion of State laws on the same subject matter, nor shall any provision of this section be construed as invalidating any provision of State law unless such provision is inconsistent with any of the purposes of this section or any provision thereof.

(June 25, 1948, c. 645, 62 Stat. 797; May 24, 1949, c. 139, § 44, 63 Stat. 96; Oct. 14, 1966, Pub.L. 89–654, § 2(a) to (c), 80 Stat. 904; Sept. 13, 1994, Pub.L. 103–322, Title XXXIII, § 330016(1)(K), 108 Stat. 2147.)

EXECUTIVE ORDERS

EXECUTIVE ORDER NO. 11836

Ex. Ord. No. 11836, Jan. 27, 1975, 40 F.R. 4255, relating to the Transportation Cargo Security Program, was revoked by Ex. Ord. No. 12553, Feb. 25, 1986, 51 F.R. 7237.

§ 2118. Robberies and burglaries involving controlled substances

(a) Whoever takes or attempts to take from the person or presence of another by force or violence or by intimidation any material or compound containing any quantity of a controlled substance belonging to or in the care, custody, control, or possession of a person registered with the Drug Enforcement Administration under section 302 of the Controlled Substances Act (21 U.S.C. 822) shall, except as provided in subsection (c), be fined under this title or imprisoned not more than twenty years, or both, if (1) the replacement cost of the material or compound to the registrant was not less than $500, (2) the person who engaged in such taking or attempted such taking traveled in interstate or foreign commerce or used any facility in interstate or foreign commerce to facilitate such taking or attempt, or (3) another person was killed or suffered significant bodily injury as a result of such taking or attempt.

(b) Whoever, without authority, enters or attempts to enter, or remains in, the business premises or property of a person registered with the Drug Enforcement Administration under section 302 of the Controlled Substances Act (21 U.S.C. 822) with the intent to steal any material or compound containing any quantity of a controlled substance shall, except as provided in subsection (c), be fined under this title or imprisoned not more than twenty years, or both, if (1) the replacement cost of the controlled substance to the registrant was not less than $500, (2) the person who engaged in such entry or attempted such entry or who remained in such premises or property traveled in interstate or foreign commerce or used any facility in interstate or foreign commerce to facilitate such entry or attempt or to facilitate remaining in such premises or property, or (3) another person was killed or suffered significant bodily injury as a result of such entry or attempt.

(c)(1) Whoever in committing any offense under subsection (a) or (b) assaults any person, or puts in jeopardy the life of any person, by the use of a dangerous weapon or device shall be fined under this title and imprisoned for not more than twenty-five years.

(2) Whoever in committing any offense under subsection (a) or (b) kills any person shall be fined under this title or imprisoned for any term of years or life, or both.

(d) If two or more persons conspire to violate subsection (a) or (b) of this section and one or more of such persons do any overt act to effect the object of the conspiracy, each shall be fined under this title or imprisoned not more than ten years or both.

(e) For purposes of this section—

(1) the term "controlled substance" has the meaning prescribed for that term by section 102 of the Controlled Substances Act;

(2) the term "business premises or property" includes conveyances and storage facilities; and

(3) the term "significant bodily injury" means bodily injury which involves a risk of death, significant physical pain, protracted and obvious disfigurement, or a protracted loss or impairment of the function of a bodily member, organ, or mental or sensory faculty.

(Added Pub.L. 98–305, § 2, May 31, 1984, 98 Stat. 221, and amended Pub.L. 103–322, Title XXXIII, §§ 330016(1)(O)-(Q), Sept. 13, 1994, 108 Stat. 2148.)

HISTORICAL AND STATUTORY NOTES

References in Text

Section 302 of the Controlled Substances Act, referred to in subsecs. (a) and (b), is classified to section 822 of Title 21, Food and Drugs.

Section 102 of the Controlled Substances Act, referred to in subsec. (e)(1), is classified to section 802 of Title 21, Food and Drugs.

Short Title

Section 1 of Pub.L. 98–305 provided: "That this Act [enacting this section and provisions set out as a note under section 522 of Title 28, Judiciary and Judicial Procedure] may be cited as the 'Controlled Substance Registrant Protection Act of 1984'."

Report to Congress

Attorney General, for first three years after May 31, 1984, to submit to Congress a report with respect to enforcement activities relating to offenses under this section, see section 4 of Pub.L. 98–305, set out as a note under section 522 of Title 28, Judiciary and Judicial Procedure.

§ 2119. Motor vehicles

Whoever, with the intent to cause death or serious bodily harm [1] takes a motor vehicle that has been transported, shipped, or received in interstate or foreign commerce from the person or presence of another by force and violence or by intimidation, or attempts to do so, shall—

(1) be fined under this title or imprisoned not more than 15 years, or both,

(2) if serious bodily injury (as defined in section 1365 of this title, including any conduct that, if the conduct occurred in the special maritime and territorial jurisdiction of the United States, would violate section 2241 or 2242 of this title) results, be fined under this title or imprisoned not more than 25 years, or both, and

(3) if death results, be fined under this title or imprisoned for any number of years up to life, or both, or sentenced to death.

(Added Pub.L. 102–519, Title I, § 101(a), Oct. 25, 1992, 106 Stat. 3384, and amended Pub.L. 103–322, Title VI, § 60003(a)(14), Sept. 13, 1994, 108 Stat. 1970; Pub.L. 104–217, § 2, Oct. 1, 1996, 110 Stat. 3020.)

[1] So in original. Probably should be followed by a comma.

HISTORICAL AND STATUTORY NOTES

Federal Cooperation to Prevent "Carjacking" and Motor Vehicle Theft

Section 101(b) of Pub.L. 102–519 provided that: "In view of the increase of motor vehicle theft with its growing threat to human life and to the economic well-being of the Nation, the Attorney General, acting through the Federal Bureau of Investigation and the United States Attorneys, is urged to work with State and local officials to investigate car thefts, including violations of section 2119 of title 18, United States Code [this section], for armed carjacking, and as appropriate and consistent with prosecutorial discretion, prosecute persons who allegedly violate such law and other relevant Federal statutes."

CHAPTER 105—SABOTAGE

[1] So in original. Does not conform to section catchline.

§ 2151. Definitions

As used in this chapter:

The words "war material" include arms, armament, ammunition, livestock, forage, forest products and standing timber, stores of clothing, air, water, food, foodstuffs, fuel, supplies, munitions, and all articles, parts or ingredients, intended for, adapted to, or suitable for the use of the United States or any associate nation, in connection with the conduct of war or defense activities.

The words "war premises" include all buildings, grounds, mines, or other places wherein such war material is being produced, manufactured, repaired, stored, mined, extracted, distributed, loaded, unloaded, or transported, together with all machinery and appliances therein contained; and all forts, arsenals, navy yards, camps, prisons, or other installations of the Armed Forces of the United States, or any associate nation.

The words "war utilities" include all railroads, railways, electric lines, roads of whatever description, any railroad or railway fixture, canal, lock, dam, wharf, pier, dock, bridge, building, structure, engine, machine, mechanical contrivance, car, vehicle, boat, aircraft, airfields, air lanes, and fixtures or appurtenances thereof, or any other means of transportation whatsoever, whereon or whereby such war material or any troops of the United States, or of any associate nation, are being or may be transported either within the limits of the United States or upon the high seas or elsewhere; and all air-conditioning systems, dams, reservoirs, aqueducts, water and gas mains and pipes, structures and buildings, whereby or in connection with which air, water or gas is being furnished, or may be furnished, to any war premises or to the Armed Forces of the United States, or any associate nation, and all electric light and power, steam or pneumatic power, telephone and telegraph plants, poles, wires, and fixtures, and wireless stations, and the buildings connected with the maintenance and operation thereof used to supply air, water, light, heat, power, or facilities of communication to any war premises or to the Armed Forces of the United States, or any associate nation.

The words "associate nation" mean any nation at war with any nation with which the United States is at war.

The words "national-defense material" include arms, armament, ammunition, livestock, forage, forest products and standing timber, stores of clothing, air, water, food, foodstuffs, fuel, supplies, munitions, and all other articles of whatever description and any part or ingredient thereof, intended for, adapted to, or suitable for the use of the United States in connection with the national defense or for use in or in connection with the producing, manufacturing, repairing, storing, mining, extracting, distributing, loading, unloading, or transporting of any of the materials or other articles hereinbefore mentioned or any part or ingredient thereof.

The words "national-defense premises" include all buildings, grounds, mines, or other places wherein such national-defense material is being produced, manufactured, repaired, stored, mined, extracted, distributed, loaded, unloaded, or transported, together with all machinery and appliances therein contained; and all forts, arsenals, navy yards, camps, prisons, or other installations of the Armed Forces of the United States.

The words "national-defense utilities" include all railroads, railways, electric lines, roads of whatever description, railroad or railway fixture, canal, lock, dam, wharf, pier, dock, bridge, building, structure, engine, machine, mechanical contrivance, car, vehicle, boat, aircraft, airfields, air lanes, and fixtures or appurtenances thereof, or any other means of transportation whatsoever, whereon or whereby such national-defense material, or any troops of the United States, are being or may be transported either within the limits of the United States or upon the high seas or elsewhere; and all air-conditioning systems, dams, reservoirs, aqueducts, water and gas mains and pipes, structures, and buildings, whereby or in connection with which air, water, or gas may be furnished to any national-defense premises or to the Armed Forces of the United States, and all electric light and power, steam or pneumatic power, telephone and telegraph plants, poles, wires, and fixtures and wireless stations, and the buildings connected with the maintenance and operation thereof used to supply air, water, light, heat, power, or facilities of communication to any national-defense premises or to the Armed Forces of the United States.

(June 25, 1948, c. 645, 62 Stat. 798; June 30, 1953, c. 175, § 2, 67 Stat. 133; Sept. 3, 1954, c. 1261, Title I, § 101, 68 Stat. 1216.)

HISTORICAL AND STATUTORY NOTES

Repeals

Section 7 of Act June 30, 1953, repealed Joint Res. July 3, 1952, c. 570, § 1(a)(29), 66 Stat. 333; Joint Res. Mar. 31, 1953, c. 13, § 1, 67 Stat. 18, formerly cited as credits to this section and also formerly set out as note under this section.

Short Title

1954 Acts. Section 1 of Act Sept. 3, 1954, provided that: "This Act [amending sections 794, 2151, and 2153 to 2156 of this title] may be cited as the 'Espionage and Sabotage Act of 1954'."

§ 2152. Fortifications, harbor defenses, or defensive sea areas

Whoever willfully trespasses upon, injures, or destroys any of the works or property or material of any submarine mine or torpedo or fortification or harbor-defense system owned or constructed or in process of construction by the United States; or

Whoever willfully interferes with the operation or use of any such submarine mine, torpedo, fortification, or harbor-defense system; or

Whoever knowingly, willfully, or wantonly violates any duly authorized and promulgated order or regulation of the President governing persons or vessels within the limits of defensive sea areas, which the President, for purposes of national defense, may from time to time establish by executive order—

Shall be fined under this title or imprisoned not more than five years, or both.

(June 25, 1948, c. 645, 62 Stat. 799; Sept. 13, 1994, Pub.L. 103–322, Title XXXIII, § 330016(1)(K), 108 Stat. 2147.)

EXECUTIVE ORDERS

EXECUTIVE ORDER NO. 10361

Ex. Ord. No. 10361, June 12, 1952, 17 F.R. 5357, formerly set out as a note under this section, which established the Whittier Defensive Sea Area, Alaska, was revoked by Ex. Ord. No. 11549, July 28, 1970, 35 F.R. 12191.

§ 2153. Destruction of war material, war premises, or war utilities

(a) Whoever, when the United States is at war, or in times of national emergency as declared by the President or by the Congress, with intent to injure, interfere with, or obstruct the United States or any associate nation in preparing for or carrying on the war or defense activities, or, with reason to believe that his act may injure, interfere with, or obstruct the United States or any associate nation in preparing for or carrying on the war or defense activities, willfully injures, destroys, contaminates or infects, or attempts to so injure, destroy, contaminate or infect any war material, war premises, or war utilities, shall be fined under this title or imprisoned not more than thirty years, or both.

(b) If two or more persons conspire to violate this section, and one or more of such persons do any act to effect the object of the conspiracy, each of the parties to such conspiracy shall be punished as provided in subsection (a) of this section.

(June 25, 1948, c. 645, 62 Stat. 799; June 30, 1953, c. 175, § 2, 67 Stat. 133; Sept. 3, 1954, c. 1261, Title I, § 102, 68 Stat. 1217; Sept. 13, 1994, Pub.L. 103–322, Title XXXIII, § 330016(1)(L), 108 Stat. 2147.)

HISTORICAL AND STATUTORY NOTES

Repeals

Section 7 of Act June 30, 1953, repealed Joint Res. July 3, 1952, c. 570, § 1(a)(29), 66 Stat. 333; Joint Res. Mar. 31, 1953, c. 13 § 1, 67 Stat. 18, formerly cited as credits to this section and also formerly set out as note under this section.

§ 2154. Production of defective war material, war premises, or war utilities

(a) Whoever, when the United States is at war, or in times of national emergency as declared by the President or by the Congress, with intent to injure, interfere with, or obstruct the United States or any associate nation in preparing for or carrying on the war or defense activities, or, with reason to believe that his act may injure, interfere with, or obstruct the United States or any associate nation in preparing for or carrying on the war or defense activities, willfully makes, constructs, or causes to be made or constructed in a defective manner, or attempts to make, construct, or cause to be made or constructed in a defective manner any war material, war premises or war utilities, or any tool, implement, machine, utensil, or receptacle used or employed in making, producing, manufacturing, or repairing any such war material, war premises or war utilities, shall be fined under this title or imprisoned not more than thirty years, or both.

(b) If two or more persons conspire to violate this section, and one or more of such persons do any act to effect the object of the conspiracy, each of the parties to such conspiracy shall be punished as provided in subsection (a) of this section.

(June 25, 1948, c. 645, 62 Stat. 799; June 30, 1953, c. 175, § 2, 67 Stat. 133; Sept. 3, 1954, c. 1261, Title I, § 103, 68 Stat. 1218; Sept. 13, 1994, Pub.L. 103–322, Title XXXIII, § 330016(1)(L), 108 Stat. 2147.)

HISTORICAL AND STATUTORY NOTES

Repeals

Section 7 of Act June 30, 1953, repealed Joint Res. July 3, 1952, c. 570, § 1(a)(29), 66 Stat. 333; Joint Res. Mar. 31, 1953, c. 13, § 1, 67 Stat. 18, formerly cited as credits to this section and also formerly set out as note under this section.

§ 2155. Destruction of national-defense materials, national-defense premises, or national-defense utilities

(a) Whoever, with intent to injure, interfere with, or obstruct the national defense of the United States, willfully injures, destroys, contaminates or infects, or attempts to so injure, destroy, contaminate or infect any national-defense material, national-defense premises, or national-defense utilities, shall be fined under this title or imprisoned not more than 20 years, or both, and, if death results to any person, shall be imprisoned for any term of years or for life.

(b) If two or more persons conspire to violate this section, and one or more of such persons do any act to effect the object of the conspiracy, each of the parties to such conspiracy shall be punished as provided in subsection (a) of this section.

(June 25, 1948, c. 645, 62 Stat. 799; Sept. 3, 1954, c. 1261, Title I, § 104, 68 Stat. 1218; Sept. 13, 1994, Pub.L. 103–322, Title XXXIII, § 330016(1)(L), 108 Stat. 2147; Oct. 11, 1996,

Pub.L. 104–294, Title VI, § 601(f)(12), 110 Stat. 3500; Oct. 26, 2001, Pub.L. 107–56, Title VIII, § 810(e), 115 Stat. 380.)

§ 2156. Production of defective national-defense material, national-defense premises, or national-defense utilities

(a) Whoever, with intent to injure, interfere with, or obstruct the national defense of the United States, willfully makes, constructs, or attempts to make or construct in a defective manner, any national-defense material, national-defense premises or national-defense utilities, or any tool, implement, machine, utensil, or receptacle used or employed in making, producing, manufacturing, or repairing any such national-defense material, national-defense premises or national-defense utilities, shall be fined under this title or imprisoned not more than ten years, or both.

(b) If two or more persons conspire to violate this section, and one or more of such persons do any act to effect the object of the conspiracy, each of the parties to such conspiracy shall be punished as provided in subsection (a) of this section.

(June 25, 1948, c. 645, 62 Stat. 800; Sept. 3, 1954, c. 1261, Title I, § 105, 68 Stat. 1218; Sept. 13, 1994, Pub.L. 103–322, Title XXXIII, § 330016(1)(L), 108 Stat. 2147; Oct. 11, 1996, Pub.L. 104–294, Title VI, § 601(f)(12), 110 Stat. 3500.)

[§ 2157. Repealed. Pub.L. 103–322, Title XXXIII, § 330004(13), Sept. 13, 1994, 108 Stat. 2142]

HISTORICAL AND STATUTORY NOTES

Section, Act June 30, 1953, c. 175, § 2, 67 Stat. 133, related to temporary extension of sections 2153 and 2154.

CHAPTER 107—SEAMEN AND STOWAWAYS

Sec.

§ 2191. Cruelty to seamen

Whoever, being the master or officer of a vessel of the United States, on the high seas, or on any other waters within the admiralty and maritime jurisdiction of the United States, flogs, beats, wounds, or without justifiable cause, imprisons any of the crew of such vessel, or withholds from them suitable food and nourishment, or inflicts upon them any corporal or other cruel and unusual punishment, shall be fined under this title or imprisoned not more than five years, or both.

(June 25, 1948, c. 645, 62 Stat. 800; Oct. 11, 1996, Pub.L. 104–294, Title VI, § 601(a)(8), 110 Stat. 3498.)

§ 2192. Incitation of seamen to revolt or mutiny

Whoever, being of the crew of a vessel of the United States, on the high seas, or on any other waters within the admiralty and maritime jurisdiction of the United States, endeavors to make a revolt or mutiny on board such vessel, or combines, conspires, or confederates with any other person on board to make such revolt or mutiny, or solicits, incites, or stirs up any other of the crew to disobey or resist the lawful orders of the master or other officer of such vessel, or to refuse or neglect his proper duty on board thereof, or to betray his proper trust, or assembles with others in a tumultuous and mutinous manner, or makes a riot on board thereof, or unlawfully confines the master or other commanding officer thereof, shall be fined under this title or imprisoned not more than five years, or both.

(June 25, 1948, c. 645, 62 Stat. 800; Oct. 11, 1996, Pub.L. 104–294, Title VI, § 601(a)(8), 110 Stat. 3498.)

§ 2193. Revolt or mutiny of seamen

Whoever, being of the crew of a vessel of the United States, on the high seas, or on any other waters within the admiralty and maritime jurisdiction of the United States, unlawfully and with force, or by fraud, or intimidation, usurps the command of such vessel from the master or other lawful officer in command thereof, or deprives him of authority and command on board, or resists or prevents him in the free and lawful exercise thereof, or transfers such authority and command to another not lawfully entitled thereto, is guilty of a revolt and mutiny, and shall be fined under this title or imprisoned not more than ten years, or both.

(June 25, 1948, c. 645, 62 Stat. 800; Sept. 13, 1994, Pub.L. 103–322, Title XXXIII, § 330016(1)(I), 108 Stat. 2147.)

§ 2194. Shanghaiing sailors

Whoever, with intent that any person shall perform service or labor of any kind on board of any vessel engaged in trade and commerce among the several States or with foreign nations, or on board of any vessel of the United States engaged in navigating the high seas or any navigable water of the United States, procures or induces, or attempts to procure or induce, another, by force or threats or by representations which he knows or believes to be untrue, or while the person so procured or induced is intoxicated or under the influence of any drug, to go on board of any such vessel, or to sign or in anywise enter into any agreement to go on board of any such vessel to perform service or labor thereon; or

Whoever knowingly detains on board of any such vessel any person so procured or induced to go on board, or to enter into any agreement to go on board, by any means herein defined—

Shall be fined under this title or imprisoned not more than one year, or both.

(June 25, 1948, c. 645, 62 Stat. 800; Oct. 11, 1996, Pub.L. 104–294, Title VI, § 601(a)(8), 110 Stat. 3498.)

§ 2195. Abandonment of sailors

Whoever, being master or commander of a vessel of the United States, while abroad, maliciously and without justifiable cause forces any officer or mariner of such vessel on shore, in order to leave him behind in any foreign port or place, or refuses to bring home again all such officers and mariners of such vessel whom he carried out with him, as are in a condition to return and willing to return, when he is ready to proceed on his homeward voyage, shall be fined under this title or imprisoned not more than six months, or both.

(June 25, 1948, c. 645, 62 Stat. 801; Sept. 13, 1994, Pub.L. 103–322, Title XXXIII, § 330016(1)(G), 108 Stat. 2147.)

§ 2196. Drunkenness or neglect of duty by seamen

Whoever, being a master, officer, radio operator, seaman, apprentice or other person employed on any merchant vessel, by willful breach of duty, or by reason of drunkenness, does any act tending to the immediate loss or destruction of, or serious damage to, such vessel, or tending immediately to endanger the life or limb of any person belonging to or on board of such vessel; or, by willful breach of duty or by neglect of duty or by reason of drunkenness, refuses or omits to do any lawful act proper and requisite to be done by him for preserving such vessel from immediate loss, destruction, or serious damage, or for preserving any person belonging to or on board of such ship from immediate danger to life or limb, shall be imprisoned not more than one year.

(June 25, 1948, c. 645, 62 Stat. 801.)

§ 2197. Misuse of Federal certificate, license or document

Whoever, not being lawfully entitled thereto, uses, exhibits, or attempts to use or exhibit, or, with intent unlawfully to use the same, receives or possesses any certificate, license, or document issued to vessels, or officers or seamen by any officer or employee of the United States authorized by law to issue the same; or

Whoever, without authority, alters or attempts to alter any such certificate, license, or document by addition, interpolation, deletion, or erasure; or

Whoever forges, counterfeits, or steals, or attempts to forge, counterfeit, or steal, any such certificate, license, or document; or unlawfully possesses or knowingly uses any such altered, changed, forged, counterfeit, or stolen certificate, license, or document; or

Whoever, without authority, prints or manufactures any blank form of such certificate, license, or document, or

Whoever possesses without lawful excuse, and with intent unlawfully to use the same, any blank form of such certificate, license, or document; or

Whoever, in any manner, transfers or negotiates such transfer of, any blank form of such certificate, license, or document, or any such altered, forged, counterfeit, or stolen certificate, license, or document, or any such certificate, license, or document to which the party transferring or receiving the same is not lawfully entitled—

Shall be fined under this title or imprisoned not more than five years, or both.

(June 25, 1948, c. 645, 62 Stat. 801; Sept. 13, 1994, Pub.L. 103–322, Title XXXIII, § 330016(1)(K), 108 Stat. 2147.)

[§ 2198. Repealed. Pub.L. 101–647, Title XII, 1207(b), Nov. 29, 1990, 104 Stat. 4832]

HISTORICAL AND STATUTORY NOTES

Section, June 25, 1948, c. 645, 62 Stat. 802, related to penalties for seducing a female passenger on an American vessel by employees of the vessel.

§ 2199. Stowaways on vessels or aircraft

Whoever, without the consent of the owner, charterer, master, or person in command of any vessel, or aircraft, with intent to obtain transportation, boards, enters or secretes himself aboard such vessel or aircraft and is thereon at the time of departure of said vessel or aircraft from a port, harbor, wharf, airport or other place within the jurisdiction of the United States; or

Whoever, with like intent, having boarded, entered or secreted himself aboard a vessel or aircraft at any place within or without the jurisdiction of the United States, remains aboard after the vessel or aircraft has left such place and is thereon at any place within the jurisdiction of the United States; or

Whoever, with intent to obtain a ride or transportation, boards or enters any aircraft owned or operated by the United States without the consent of the person in command or other duly authorized officer or agent—

(1) shall be fined under this title, imprisoned not more than 5 years, or both;

(2) if the person commits an act proscribed by this section, with the intent to commit serious bodily

injury, and serious bodily injury occurs (as defined under section 1365, including any conduct that, if the conduct occurred in the special maritime and territorial jurisdiction of the United States, would violate section 2241 or 2242) to any person other than a participant as a result of a violation of this section, shall be fined under this title or imprisoned not more than 20 years, or both; and

(3) if an individual commits an act proscribed by this section, with the intent to cause death, and if the death of any person other than a participant occurs as a result of a violation of this section, shall be fined under this title, imprisoned for any number of years or for life, or both.

The word "aircraft" as used in this section includes any contrivance for navigation or flight in the air.

(June 25, 1948, c. 645, 62 Stat. 802; Oct. 11, 1996, Pub.L. 104–294, Title VI, § 601(a)(8), 110 Stat. 3498; Mar. 9, 2006, Pub.L. 109–177, Title III, § 308, 120 Stat. 241.)

CHAPTER 109—SEARCHES AND SEIZURES

Sec.

§ 2231. Assault or resistance

(a) Whoever forcibly assaults, resists, opposes, prevents, impedes, intimidates, or interferes with any person authorized to serve or execute search warrants or to make searches and seizures while engaged in the performance of his duties with regard thereto or on account of the performance of such duties, shall be fined under this title or imprisoned not more than three years, or both; and—

(b) Whoever, in committing any act in violation of this section, uses any deadly or dangerous weapon, shall be fined under this title or imprisoned not more than ten years, or both.

(June 25, 1948, c. 645, 62 Stat. 802; Sept. 13, 1994, Pub.L. 103–322, Title XXXIII, § 330016(1)(K), (L), 108 Stat. 2147.)

§ 2232. Destruction or removal of property to prevent seizure

(a) Destruction or removal of property to prevent seizure.—Whoever, before, during, or after any search for or seizure of property by any person authorized to make such search or seizure, knowingly destroys, damages, wastes, disposes of, transfers, or otherwise takes any action, or knowingly attempts to destroy, damage, waste, dispose of, transfer, or otherwise take any action, for the purpose of preventing or impairing the Government's lawful authority to take such property into its custody or control or to continue holding such property under its lawful custody and control, shall be fined under this title or imprisoned not more than 5 years, or both.

(b) Impairment of in rem jurisdiction.—Whoever, knowing that property is subject to the in rem jurisdiction of a United States court for purposes of civil forfeiture under Federal law, knowingly and without authority from that court, destroys, damages, wastes, disposes of, transfers, or otherwise takes any action, or knowingly attempts to destroy, damage, waste, dispose of, transfer, or otherwise take any action, for the purpose of impairing or defeating the court's continuing in rem jurisdiction over the property, shall be fined under this title or imprisoned not more than 5 years, or both.

(c) Notice of search or execution of seizure warrant or warrant of arrest in rem.—Whoever, having knowledge that any person authorized to make searches and seizures, or to execute a seizure warrant or warrant of arrest in rem, in order to prevent the authorized seizing or securing of any person or property, gives notice or attempts to give notice in advance of the search, seizure, or execution of a seizure warrant or warrant of arrest in rem, to any person shall be fined under this title or imprisoned not more than 5 years, or both.

(d) Notice of certain electronic surveillance.—Whoever, having knowledge that a Federal investigative or law enforcement officer has been authorized or has applied for authorization under chapter 119 to intercept a wire, oral, or electronic communication, in order to obstruct, impede, or prevent such interception, gives notice or attempts to give notice of the possible interception to any person shall be fined under this title or imprisoned not more than five years, or both.

(e) Foreign intelligence surveillance.—Whoever, having knowledge that a Federal officer has been authorized or has applied for authorization to conduct electronic surveillance under the Foreign Intelligence Surveillance Act of 1978 (50 U.S.C. 1801, et seq.), in order to obstruct, impede, or prevent such activity, gives notice or attempts to give notice of the possible activity to any person shall be fined under this title or imprisoned not more than five years, or both.

(June 25, 1948, c. 645, 62 Stat. 802; Oct. 12, 1984, Pub.L. 98–473, Title II, § 1103, 98 Stat. 2143; Oct. 21, 1986, Pub.L. 99–508, Title I, § 109, 100 Stat. 1858; Nov. 10, 1986, Pub.L.

99–646, § 33, 100 Stat. 3598; Nov. 18, 1988, Pub.L. 100–690, Title VII, § 7066, 102 Stat. 4404; Sept. 13, 1994, Pub.L. 103–322, Title XXXIII, § 330016(1)(L), 108 Stat. 2147; Apr. 25, 2000, Pub.L. 106–185, § 12, 114 Stat. 218.)

HISTORICAL AND STATUTORY NOTES

References in Text

The Foreign Intelligence Surveillance Act of 1978, referred to in subsec. (e), is Pub.L. 95–511, Oct. 25, 1978, 92 Stat. 1783, as amended, which is classified generally to chapter 36 (section 1801 et seq.) of Title 50, War and National Defense. For complete classification of this Act to the Code, see Short Title note set out under section 1801 of Title 50 and Tables.

Effective and Applicability Provisions

2000 Acts. Amendments by Pub.L. 106–185, applicable to any forfeiture proceeding commenced on or after the date that is 120 days after April 25, 2000, see section 21 of Pub.L. 106–185, set out as a note under section 1324 of Title 8.

1986 Acts. Except as otherwise provided in section 111 of Pub.L. 99–508, amendment by Pub.L. 99–508 effective 90 days after Oct. 21, 1986, see section 111 of Pub.L. 99–508 set out as a note under section 2510 of this title.

§ 2233. Rescue of seized property

Whoever forcibly rescues, dispossesses, or attempts to rescue or dispossess any property, articles, or objects after the same shall have been taken, detained, or seized by any officer or other person under the authority of any revenue law of the United States, or by any person authorized to make searches and seizures, shall be fined under this title or imprisoned not more than two years, or both.

(June 25, 1948, c. 645, 62 Stat. 802; Sept. 13, 1994, Pub.L. 103–322, Title XXXIII, § 330016(1)(I), 108 Stat. 2147.)

§ 2234. Authority exceeded in executing warrant

Whoever, in executing a search warrant, willfully exceeds his authority or exercises it with unnecessary severity, shall be fined under this title or imprisoned not more than one year, or both.

(June 25, 1948, c. 645, 62 Stat. 803; Oct. 11, 1996, Pub.L. 104–294, Title VI, § 601(a)(8), 110 Stat. 3498; Nov. 2, 2002, Pub.L. 107–273, Div. B, Title III, § 3002(a)(3), 116 Stat. 1805.)

HISTORICAL AND STATUTORY NOTES

Canal Zone

Applicability of section to Canal Zone, see section 14 of this title.

§ 2235. Search warrant procured maliciously

Whoever maliciously and without probable cause procures a search warrant to be issued and executed, shall be fined under this title or imprisoned not more than one year, or both.

(June 25, 1948, c. 645, 62 Stat. 803; Oct. 11, 1996, Pub.L. 104–294, Title VI, § 601(a)(8), 110 Stat. 3498; Nov. 2, 2002, Pub.L. 107–273, Div. B, Title III, § 3002(a)(3), 116 Stat. 1805.)

§ 2236. Searches without warrant

Whoever, being an officer, agent, or employee of the United States or any department or agency thereof, engaged in the enforcement of any law of the United States, searches any private dwelling used and occupied as such dwelling without a warrant directing such search, or maliciously and without reasonable cause searches any other building or property without a search warrant, shall be fined under this title for a first offense; and, for a subsequent offense, shall be fined under this title or imprisoned not more than one year, or both.

This section shall not apply to any person—

(a) serving a warrant of arrest; or

(b) arresting or attempting to arrest a person committing or attempting to commit an offense in his presence, or who has committed or is suspected on reasonable grounds of having committed a felony; or

(c) making a search at the request or invitation or with the consent of the occupant of the premises.

(June 25, 1948, c. 645, 62 Stat. 803; Oct. 11, 1996, Pub.L. 104–294, Title VI, § 601(a)(8), 110 Stat. 3498; Nov. 2, 2002, Pub.L. 107–273, Div. B, Title IV, § 4002(d)(1)(C)(iii), 116 Stat. 1809.)

§ 2237. Criminal sanctions for failure to heave to, obstruction of boarding, or providing false information

(a)(1) It shall be unlawful for the master, operator, or person in charge of a vessel of the United States, or a vessel subject to the jurisdiction of the United States, to knowingly fail to obey an order by an authorized Federal law enforcement officer to heave to that vessel.

(2) It shall be unlawful for any person on board a vessel of the United States, or a vessel subject to the jurisdiction of the United States, to—

(A) forcibly resist, oppose, prevent, impede, intimidate, or interfere with a boarding or other law enforcement action authorized by any Federal law or to resist a lawful arrest; or

(B) provide materially false information to a Federal law enforcement officer during a boarding of a vessel regarding the vessel's destination, origin, ownership, registration, nationality, cargo, or crew.

(b) Any person who intentionally violates this section shall be fined under this title or imprisoned for not more than 5 years, or both.

(c) This section does not limit the authority of a customs officer under section 581 of the Tariff Act of 1930 (19 U.S.C. 1581), or any other provision of law enforced or administered by the Secretary of the Treasury or the Secretary of Homeland Security, or the authority of any Federal law enforcement officer under any law of the United States, to order a vessel to stop or heave to.

(d) A foreign nation may consent or waive objection to the enforcement of United States law by the United States under this section by radio, telephone, or similar oral or electronic means. Consent or waiver may be proven by certification of the Secretary of State or the designee of the Secretary of State.

(e) In this section—

(1) the term "Federal law enforcement officer" has the meaning given the term in section 115(c);

(2) the term "heave to" means to cause a vessel to slow, come to a stop, or adjust its course or speed to account for the weather conditions and sea state to facilitate a law enforcement boarding;

(3) the term "vessel subject to the jurisdiction of the United States" has the meaning given the term in section 2 of the Maritime Drug Law Enforcement Act (46 U.S.C. App. 1903); and

(4) the term "vessel of the United States" has the meaning given the term in section 2 of the Maritime Drug Law Enforcement Act (46 U.S.C. App. 1903).

(Added Pub.L. 109–177, Title III, § 303(a), Mar. 9, 2006, 120 Stat. 233.)

HISTORICAL AND STATUTORY NOTES

References in Text

Section 581 of the Tariff Act of 1930, referred to in subsec. (c), is Act June 17, 1930, c. 497, Title IV, § 581, 46 Stat. 747, as amended, which is classified to 19 U.S.C.A. § 1581.

Section 2 of the Maritime Drug Law Enforcement Act, referred to in subsec. (e)(3), (4), probably means section 3 of the Maritime Drug Law Enforcement Act, Pub.L. 96–350, § 3, Sept. 15, 1980, 94 Stat. 1160, as amended, which defines the terms "vessel subject to the jurisdiction of the United States" and "vessel of the United States" and is classified to 46 App. U.S.C.A. § 1903.

CHAPTER 109A—SEXUAL ABUSE

[1] So in original. Section heading amended without corresponding amendment of analysis.

§ 2241. Aggravated sexual abuse

(a) By force or threat.—Whoever, in the special maritime and territorial jurisdiction of the United States or in a Federal prison, or in any prison, institution, or facility in which persons are held in custody by direction of or pursuant to a contract or agreement with the Attorney General, knowingly causes another person to engage in a sexual act—

(1) by using force against that other person; or

(2) by threatening or placing that other person in fear that any person will be subjected to death, serious bodily injury, or kidnapping;

or attempts to do so, shall be fined under this title, imprisoned for any term of years or life, or both.

(b) By other means.—Whoever, in the special maritime and territorial jurisdiction of the United States or in a Federal prison, or in any prison, institution, or facility in which persons are held in custody by direction of or pursuant to a contract or agreement with the Attorney General, knowingly—

(1) renders another person unconscious and thereby engages in a sexual act with that other person; or

(2) administers to another person by force or threat of force, or without the knowledge or permission of that person, a drug, intoxicant, or other similar substance and thereby—

(A) substantially impairs the ability of that other person to appraise or control conduct; and

(B) engages in a sexual act with that other person;

or attempts to do so, shall be fined under this title, imprisoned for any term of years or life, or both.

(c) With children.—Whoever crosses a State line with intent to engage in a sexual act with a person who has not attained the age of 12 years, or in the special maritime and territorial jurisdiction of the United States or in a Federal prison, or in any prison, institution, or facility in which persons are held in custody by direction of or pursuant to a contract or agreement with the Attorney General, knowingly engages in a sexual act with another person who has not attained the age of 12 years, or knowingly engages in a sexual act under the circumstances described in subsections (a) and (b) with another person who has attained the age of 12 years but has not attained the age of 16 years (and is at least 4 years younger than the person so engaging), or attempts to do so, shall be fined under this title and imprisoned for not less than 30 years or for life. If the defendant has previously been convicted of another Federal offense under this subsection, or of a State offense that would have been an offense under either such provision had the offense occurred in a Federal prison, unless the death penalty is imposed, the defendant shall be sentenced to life in prison.

(d) State of mind proof requirement.—In a prosecution under subsection (c) of this section, the Government need not prove that the defendant knew that the other person engaging in the sexual act had not attained the age of 12 years.

(Added Pub.L. 99–646, § 87(b), Nov. 10, 1986, 100 Stat. 3620, and amended Pub.L. 103–322, Title XXXIII, § 330021(1), Sept. 13, 1994, 108 Stat. 2150; Pub.L. 104–208, Div. A, Title I, § 101(a) [Title I, § 121, subsection 7(b)], Sept. 30, 1996, 110 Stat. 3009–31; Pub.L. 105–314, Title III, § 301(a), Oct. 30, 1998, 112 Stat. 2978; Pub.L. 109–162, Title XI, § 1177(a)(1), (2), Jan. 5, 2006, 119 Stat. 3125; Pub.L. 109–248, Title II, §§ 206(a)(1), 207(2), July 27, 2006, 120 Stat. 613, 615.)

HISTORICAL AND STATUTORY NOTES

Codifications

Identical provision was enacted by Pub.L. 99–654, § 2, Nov. 14, 1986, 100 Stat. 3660.

Effective and Applicability Provisions

1986 Acts. Pub.L. 99–646, § 87(e), Nov. 10, 1986, provided that: "This section and the amendments made by this section [enacting this chapter; amending sections 113(a), (b), 1111(a), 1153, and 3185(12) of this title, sections 300w–3(a)(1)(G), 300w–4(c)(6), and 9511 of Title 42, The Public Health and Welfare, and section 1472(k)(1) of Title 49, Transportation]; and repealing chapter 99 (sections 2031 and 2032) of this title] shall take effect 30 days after the date of the enactment of this Act [Nov. 10, 1986]."

[Effective Date provision similar to Pub.L. 99–646, § 87(e), was enacted by Pub.L. 99–654, § 4, Nov. 14, 1986, 100 Stat. 3664.]

Short Title

1996 Amendments. Pub.L. 104–208, Div. A, Title I, § 101(a) [Title I, § 121, subsec. 7(a)], Sept. 30, 1996, 110 Stat. 3009–31, provided that: "This section [probably should be this subsection, which amended this section and section 2243 of this title] may be cited as the 'Amber Hagerman Child Protection Act of 1996'."

1986 Amendments. Pub.L. 99–646, § 87(a), Nov. 10, 1986, provided that: "This section [enacting this chapter; amending sections 113(a), (b), 1111(a), 1153, and 3185(12) of this title, sections 300w–3(a)(1)(G), 300w–4(c)(6), and 9511 of Title 42, The Public Health and Welfare, and section 1472(k)(1) of Title 49, Transportation; repealing chapter 99 (sections 2031 and 2032) of this title; and enacting note provision under this section] may be cited as the 'Sexual Abuse Act of 1986'."

[Short Title provision similar to Pub.L. 99–646, § 87(a), was enacted by Pub.L. 99–654, § 1, Nov. 14, 1986, 100 Stat. 3660.]

§ 2242. Sexual abuse

Whoever, in the special maritime and territorial jurisdiction of the United States or in a Federal prison, or in any prison, institution, or facility in which persons are held in custody by direction of or pursuant to a contract or agreement with the Attorney General, knowingly—

(1) causes another person to engage in a sexual act by threatening or placing that other person in fear (other than by threatening or placing that other person in fear that any person will be subjected to death, serious bodily injury, or kidnapping); or

(2) engages in a sexual act with another person if that other person is—

(A) incapable of appraising the nature of the conduct; or

(B) physically incapable of declining participation in, or communicating unwillingness to engage in, that sexual act;

or attempts to do so, shall be fined under this title and imprisoned for any term of years or for life.

(Added Pub.L. 99–646, § 87(b), Nov. 10, 1986, 100 Stat. 3621, and amended Pub.L. 103–322, Title XXXIII, § 330021(1), Sept. 13, 1994, 108 Stat. 2150; Pub.L. 109–162, Title XI, § 1177(a)(3), Jan. 5, 2006, 119 Stat. 3125; Pub.L. 109–248, Title II, §§ 205, 207(2), July 27, 2006, 120 Stat. 613, 615.)

HISTORICAL AND STATUTORY NOTES

Codifications

Identical provision was enacted by Pub.L. 99–654, § 2, Nov. 14, 1986, 100 Stat. 3661.

Effective and Applicability Provisions

1986 Acts. Section effective 30 days after Nov. 10, 1986, see section 87(e) of Pub.L. 99–646, set out as a note under section 2241 of this title.

§ 2243. Sexual abuse of a minor or ward

(a) Of a minor.—Whoever, in the special maritime and territorial jurisdiction of the United States or in a Federal prison, or in any prison, institution, or facility in which persons are held in custody by direction of or pursuant to a contract or agreement with the Attorney General, knowingly engages in a sexual act with another person who—

(1) has attained the age of 12 years but has not attained the age of 16 years; and

(2) is at least four years younger than the person so engaging;

or attempts to do so, shall be fined under this title, imprisoned not more than 15 years, or both.

(b) Of a ward.—Whoever, in the special maritime and territorial jurisdiction of the United States or in a Federal prison, or in any prison, institution, or facility in which persons are held in custody by direction of or pursuant to a contract or agreement with the Attorney General, knowingly engages in a sexual act with another person who is—

(1) in official detention; and

(2) under the custodial, supervisory, or disciplinary authority of the person so engaging;

or attempts to do so, shall be fined under this title, imprisoned not more than 15 years, or both.

(c) Defenses.—(1) In a prosecution under subsection (a) of this section, it is a defense, which the defendant must establish by a preponderance of the evidence, that the defendant reasonably believed that the other person had attained the age of 16 years.

(2) In a prosecution under this section, it is a defense, which the defendant must establish by a preponderance of the evidence, that the persons engaging in the sexual act were at that time married to each other.

(d) State of mind proof requirement.—In a prosecution under subsection (a) of this section, the Government need not prove that the defendant knew—

(1) the age of the other person engaging in the sexual act; or

(2) that the requisite age difference existed between the persons so engaging.

(Added Pub.L. 99–646, § 87(b), Nov. 10, 1986, 100 Stat. 3621, and amended Pub.L. 101–647, Title III, § 322, Nov. 29, 1990, 104 Stat. 4818; Pub.L. 104–208, Div. A, Title I, § 101(a) [Title I, § 121, subsection 7(c)], Sept. 30, 1996, 110 Stat. 3009–31; Pub.L. 105–314, Title III, § 301(b), Oct. 30, 1998, 112 Stat. 2978; Pub.L. 109–162, Title XI, § 1177(a)(4), (b)(1), Jan. 5, 2006, 119 Stat. 3125; Pub.L. 109–248, Title II, § 207, July 27, 2006, 120 Stat. 615.)

HISTORICAL AND STATUTORY NOTES

Codifications

Identical provision was enacted by Pub.L. 99–654, § 2, Nov. 14, 1986, 100 Stat. 3661.

Effective and Applicability Provisions

1986 Acts. Section effective 30 days after Nov. 10, 1986, see section 87(e) of Pub.L. 99–646, set out as a note under section 2241 of this title.

§ 2244. Abusive sexual contact

(a) Sexual conduct in circumstances where sexual acts are punished by this chapter.—Whoever, in the special maritime and territorial jurisdiction of the United States or in a Federal prison, or in any prison, institution, or facility in which persons are held in custody by direction of or pursuant to a contract or agreement with the Attorney General, knowingly engages in or causes sexual contact with or by another person, if so to do would violate—

(1) subsection (a) or (b) of section 2241 of this title had the sexual contact been a sexual act, shall be fined under this title, imprisoned not more than ten years, or both;

(2) section 2242 of this title had the sexual contact been a sexual act, shall be fined under this title, imprisoned not more than three years, or both;

(3) subsection (a) of section 2243 of this title had the sexual contact been a sexual act, shall be fined under this title, imprisoned not more than two years, or both;

(4) subsection (b) of section 2243 of this title had the sexual contact been a sexual act, shall be fined under this title, imprisoned not more than two years, or both; or

(5) subsection (c) of section 2241 of this title had the sexual contact been a sexual act, shall be fined under this title and imprisoned for any term of years or for life.

(b) In other circumstances.—Whoever, in the special maritime and territorial jurisdiction of the United States or in a Federal prison, or in any prison, institution, or facility in which persons are held in custody by direction of or pursuant to a contract or agreement with the Attorney General, knowingly engages in sexual contact with another person without that other person's permission shall be fined under this title, imprisoned not more than two years, or both.

(c) Offenses involving young children.—If the sexual contact that violates this section (other than subsection (a)(5)) is with an individual who has not attained the age of 12 years, the maximum term of imprisonment that may be imposed for the offense shall be twice that otherwise provided in this section.

(Added Pub.L. 99–646, § 87(b), Nov. 10, 1986, 100 Stat. 3622, and amended Pub.L. 100–690, Title VII, § 7058(a), Nov. 18, 1988, 102 Stat. 4403; Pub.L. 103–322, Title XXXIII, § 330016(1)(K), Sept. 13, 1994, 108 Stat. 2147; Pub.L. 105–314, Title III, § 302, Oct. 30, 1998., 112 Stat. 2979; Pub.L. 109–162, Title XI, § 1177(a)(5), (b)(2), Jan. 5, 2006, 119 Stat. 3125; Pub.L. 109–248, Title II, §§ 206(a)(2), 207(2), July 27, 2006, 120 Stat. 613, 615.)

HISTORICAL AND STATUTORY NOTES

Codifications

Identical provision was enacted by Pub.L. 99–654, § 2, Nov. 14, 1986, 100 Stat. 3661.

Effective and Applicability Provisions

1986 Acts. Section effective 30 days after Nov. 10, 1986, see section 87(e) of Pub.L. 99–646, set out as a note under section 2241 of this title.

§ 2245. Offenses resulting in death

(a) [1] **In general.**—A person who, in the course of an offense under this chapter, or section 1591, 2251, 2251A, 2260, 2421, 2422, 2423, or 2425, murders an individual, shall be punished by death or imprisoned for any term of years or for life.

(Added Pub.L. 103–322, Title VI, § 60010(a)(2), Sept. 13, 1994, 108 Stat. 1972, and amended Pub.L. 109–248, Title II, § 206(a)(3), July 27, 2006, 120 Stat. 613.)

[1] So in original. No subsec. (b) was enacted.

HISTORICAL AND STATUTORY NOTES

References in Text

This chapter, referred to in text, means chapter 109A of this title, Sexual abuse, 18 U.S.C.A. § 2241 et seq.

Prior Provisions

A prior section 2245 was renumbered section 2246 by Pub.L. 103–322, Title VI, § 60010(a)(1), Sept. 13, 1994, 108 Stat. 1972.

§ 2246. Definitions for chapter

As used in this chapter—

(1) the term "prison" means a correctional, detention, or penal facility;

(2) the term "sexual act" means—

(A) contact between the penis and the vulva or the penis and the anus, and for purposes of this subparagraph contact involving the penis occurs upon penetration, however, slight;

(B) contact between the mouth and the penis, the mouth and the vulva, or the mouth and the anus;

(C) the penetration, however slight, of the anal or genital opening of another by a hand or finger or by any object, with an intent to abuse, humiliate, harass, degrade, or arouse or gratify the sexual desire of any person; or

(D) the intentional touching, not through the clothing, of the genitalia of another person who has not attained the age of 16 years with an intent to abuse, humiliate, harass, degrade, or arouse or gratify the sexual desire of any person;

(3) the term "sexual contact" means the intentional touching, either directly or through the clothing, of the genitalia, anus, groin, breast, inner thigh, or buttocks of any person with an intent to abuse, humiliate, harass, degrade, or arouse or gratify the sexual desire of any person;

(4) the term "serious bodily injury" means bodily injury that involves a substantial risk of death, unconsciousness, extreme physical pain, protracted and obvious disfigurement, or protracted loss or impairment of the function of a bodily member, organ, or mental faculty;

(5) the term "official detention" means—

(A) detention by a Federal officer or employee, or under the direction of a Federal officer or employee, following arrest for an offense; following surrender in lieu of arrest for an offense; following a charge or conviction of an offense, or an allegation or finding of juvenile delinquency; following commitment as a material witness; following civil commitment in lieu of criminal proceedings or pending resumption of criminal proceedings that are being held in abeyance, or pending extradition, deportation, or exclusion; or

(B) custody by a Federal officer or employee, or under the direction of a Federal officer or employee, for purposes incident to any detention described in subparagraph (A) of this paragraph, including transportation, medical diagnosis or treatment, court appearance, work, and recreation;

but does not include supervision or other control (other than custody during specified hours or days) after release on bail, probation, or parole, or after release following a finding of juvenile delinquency; and

(6)the term "State" means a State of the United States, the District of Columbia, and any commonwealth, possession, or territory of the United States.

(Added Pub.L. 99–646, § 87(b), Nov. 10, 1986, 100 Stat. 3622, § 2245, renumbered § 2246 and amended Pub.L. 103–322, Title IV, § 40502, Title VI, § 60010(a)(1), Sept. 13, 1994, 108 Stat. 1945, 1972; Pub.L. 105–314, Title III, § 301(c), Oct. 30, 1998, 112 Stat. 2978.)

HISTORICAL AND STATUTORY NOTES

Codifications

Identical provision was enacted by Pub.L. 99–654, § 2, Nov. 14, 1986, 100 Stat. 3662.

Effective and Applicability Provisions

1986 Acts. Section effective 30 days after Nov. 10, 1986, see section 87(e) of Pub.L. 99–646, set out as a note under section 2241 of this title.

§ 2247. Repeat offenders

(a) Maximum Term of Imprisonment.—The maximum term of imprisonment for a violation of this chapter after a prior sex offense conviction shall be twice the term otherwise provided by this chapter, unless section 3559(e) applies.

(b) Prior Sex Offense Conviction Defined.—In this section, the term "prior sex offense conviction" has the meaning given that term in section 2426(b).

(Added Pub.L. 103–322, Title IV, § 40111(a), Sept. 13, 1994, 108 Stat. 1903, and amended Pub.L. 105–314, Title III, § 303, Oct. 30, 1998, 112 Stat. 2979; Pub.L. 108–21, Title I, § 106(b), Apr. 30, 2003, 117 Stat. 655.)

§ 2248. Mandatory restitution

(a) In general.—Notwithstanding section 3663 or 3663A, and in addition to any other civil or criminal penalty authorized by law, the court shall order restitution for any offense under this chapter.

(b) Scope and nature of order.—

(1) Directions.—The order of restitution under this section shall direct the defendant to pay to the victim (through the appropriate court mechanism) the full amount of the victim's losses as determined by the court pursuant to paragraph (2).

(2) Enforcement.—An order of restitution under this section shall be issued and enforced in accordance with section 3664 in the same manner as an order under section 3663A.

(3) Definition.—For purposes of this subsection, the term "full amount of the victim's losses" includes any costs incurred by the victim for—

(A) medical services relating to physical, psychiatric, or psychological care;

(B) physical and occupational therapy or rehabilitation;

(C) necessary transportation, temporary housing, and child care expenses;

(D) lost income;

(E) attorneys' fees, plus any costs incurred in obtaining a civil protection order; and

(F) any other losses suffered by the victim as a proximate result of the offense.

(4) Order mandatory.—(A) The issuance of a restitution order under this section is mandatory.

(B) A court may not decline to issue an order under this section because of—

(i) the economic circumstances of the defendant; or

(ii) the fact that a victim has, or is entitled to, receive compensation for his or her injuries from the proceeds of insurance or any other source.

(c) Definition.—For purposes of this section, the term "victim" means the individual harmed as a result of a commission of a crime under this chapter, including, in the case of a victim who is under 18 years of age, incompetent, incapacitated, or deceased, the legal guardian of the victim or representative of the victim's estate, another family member, or any other person appointed as suitable by the court, but in no event shall the defendant be named as such representative or guardian.

(Added Pub.L. 103–322, Title IV, § 40113(a)(1), Sept. 13, 1994, 108 Stat. 1904, and amended Pub.L. 104–132, Title II, § 205(b), Apr. 24, 1996, 110 Stat. 1231.)

HISTORICAL AND STATUTORY NOTES

Effective and Applicability Provisions

1996 Amendments. Section 211 of Pub.L. 104–132 provided that: "The amendments made by this subtitle [enacting sections 3613A and 3663A of this title, amending this section and sections 2259, 2264, 2327, 3013, 3556, 3563, 3572, 3611, 3612, 3613, 3614, 3663, and 3664 of this title and Rule 32 of the Federal Rules of Criminal Procedure, and enacting provisions set out as notes under this section, section 3551 of this title, and section 994 of Title 28, Judiciary and Judicial Procedure] shall, to the extent constitutionally permissible, be effective for sentencing proceedings in cases in which the defendant is convicted on or after the date of enactment of this Act [Apr. 24, 1996]."

CHAPTER 109B—SEX OFFENDER AND CRIMES AGAINST CHILDREN REGISTRY

§ 2250. Failure to register

(a) In general.—Whoever—

(1) is required to register under the Sex Offender Registration and Notification Act;

(2)(A) is a sex offender as defined for the purposes of the Sex Offender Registration and Notification Act by reason of a conviction under Federal law (including the Uniform Code of Military Justice), the law of the District of Columbia, Indian tribal law, or the law of any territory or possession of the United States; or

(B) travels in interstate or foreign commerce, or enters or leaves, or resides in, Indian country; and

(3) knowingly fails to register or update a registration as required by the Sex Offender Registration and Notification Act;

shall be fined under this title or imprisoned not more than 10 years, or both.

(b) Affirmative defense.—In a prosecution for a violation under subsection (a), it is an affirmative defense that—

(1) uncontrollable circumstances prevented the individual from complying;

(2) the individual did not contribute to the creation of such circumstances in reckless disregard of the requirement to comply; and

(3) the individual complied as soon as such circumstances ceased to exist.

(c) Crime of violence.—

(1) In general.—An individual described in subsection (a) who commits a crime of violence under Federal law (including the Uniform Code of Military Justice), the law of the District of Columbia, Indian tribal law, or the law of any territory or possession of the United States shall be imprisoned for not less than 5 years and not more than 30 years.

(2) Additional punishment.—The punishment provided in paragraph (1) shall be in addition and consecutive to the punishment provided for the violation described in subsection (a).

(Added Pub.L. 109–248, Title I, § 141(a)(1), July 27, 2006, 120 Stat. 602.)

HISTORICAL AND STATUTORY NOTES

References in Text

The Sex Offender Registration and Notification Act, referred to in subsec. (a)(1), (3), is Title I [§ 101 et seq.] of Pub.L. 109–248, July 27, 2006, 120 Stat. 590, which enacted subchapter I of Chapter 151 of Title 42, 42 U.S.C.A. § 16901 et seq.; for complete classification, see Short Title note set out under 42 U.S.C.A. § 16901 and Tables.

The Uniform Code of Military Justice, referred to in subsec. (c)(1), is classified to chapter 47 of Title 10, 10 U.S.C.A. § 801 et seq.

CHAPTER 110—SEXUAL EXPLOITATION AND OTHER ABUSE OF CHILDREN

Sec.

[1] So in original. Does not conform to section heading.

§ 2251. Sexual exploitation of children

(a) Any person who employs, uses, persuades, induces, entices, or coerces any minor to engage in, or who has a minor assist any other person to engage in, or who transports any minor in interstate or foreign commerce, or in any Territory or Possession of the United States, with the intent that such minor engage in, any sexually explicit conduct for the purpose of producing any visual depiction of such conduct, shall be punished as provided under subsection (e), if such person knows or has reason to know that such visual depiction will be transported in interstate or foreign commerce or mailed, if that visual depiction was produced using materials that have been mailed, shipped, or transported in interstate or foreign commerce by any means, including by computer, or if such visual depiction has actually been transported in interstate or foreign commerce or mailed.

(b) Any parent, legal guardian, or person having custody or control of a minor who knowingly permits such minor to engage in, or to assist any other person to engage in, sexually explicit conduct for the purpose of producing any visual depiction of such conduct shall be punished as provided under subsection (e) of this section, if such parent, legal guardian, or person knows or has reason to know that such visual depiction will be transported in interstate or foreign commerce or mailed, if that visual depiction was produced using materials that have been mailed, shipped, or transported in interstate or foreign commerce by any means, including by computer, or if such visual depiction has actually been transported in interstate or foreign commerce or mailed.

(c)(1) Any person who, in a circumstance described in paragraph (2), employs, uses, persuades, induces, entices, or coerces any minor to engage in, or who has a minor assist any other person to engage in, any sexually explicit conduct outside of the United States, its territories or possessions, for the purpose of producing any visual depiction of such conduct, shall be punished as provided under subsection (e).

(2) The circumstance referred to in paragraph (1) is that—

(A) the person intends such visual depiction to be transported to the United States, its territories or possessions, by any means, including by computer or mail; or

(B) the person transports such visual depiction to the United States, its territories or possessions, by any means, including by computer or mail.

(d)(1) Any person who, in a circumstance described in paragraph (2), knowingly makes, prints, or publishes, or causes to be made, printed, or published, any notice or advertisement seeking or offering—

(A) to receive, exchange, buy, produce, display, distribute, or reproduce, any visual depiction, if the production of such visual depiction involves the use of a minor engaging in sexually explicit conduct and such visual depiction is of such conduct; or

(B) participation in any act of sexually explicit conduct by or with any minor for the purpose of producing a visual depiction of such conduct:

shall be punished as provided under subsection (e).

(2) The circumstance referred to in paragraph (1) is that—

(A) such person knows or has reason to know that such notice or advertisement will be transported in interstate or foreign commerce by any means including by computer or mailed; or

(B) such notice or advertisement is transported in interstate or foreign commerce by any means including by computer or mailed.

(e) Any individual who violates, or attempts or conspires to violate, this section shall be fined under this title and imprisoned not less than 15 years nor more than 30 years, but if such person has one prior conviction under this chapter, section 1591, chapter 71, chapter 109A, or chapter 117, or under section 920 of title 10 (article 120 of the Uniform Code of Military Justice), or under the laws of any State relating to aggravated sexual abuse, sexual abuse, abusive sexual contact involving a minor or ward, or sex trafficking of children, or the production, possession, receipt, mailing, sale, distribution, shipment, or transportation of child pornography, such person shall be fined under this title and imprisoned for not less than 25 years nor more than 50 years, but if such person has 2 or more prior convictions under this chapter, chapter 71, chapter 109A, or chapter 117, or under section 920 of title 10 (article 120 of the Uniform Code of Military Justice), or under the laws of any State relating to the sexual exploitation of children, such person shall be fined under this title and imprisoned not less than 35 years nor more than life. Any organization that violates, or attempts or conspires to violate, this section shall be fined under this title. Whoever, in the course of an offense under this section, engages in conduct that results in the death of a person, shall be punished by death or imprisoned for not less than 30 years or for life.

(Added Pub.L. 95–225, § 2(a), Feb. 6, 1978, 92 Stat. 7, and amended Pub.L. 98–292, § 3, May 21, 1984, 98 Stat. 204; Pub.L. 99–500, Title I, § 101(b) [Title VII, § 704(a)], Oct. 18, 1986, 100 Stat. 1783–75; Pub.L. 99–591, Title I, § 101(b) [Title VII, § 704(a)] Oct. 30, 1986, 100 Stat. 3341–75; Pub.L. 99–628, §§ 2, 3, Nov. 7, 1986, 100 Stat. 3510; Pub.L. 100–690, Title VII, § 7511(a), Nov. 18, 1988, 102 Stat. 4485; Pub.L. 101–647, Title XXXV, § 3563, Nov. 29, 1990, 104 Stat. 4928; Pub.L. 103–322, Title VI, § 60011, Title XVI, § 160001(b)(2), (c), (e), Title XXXIII, § 330016(1)(S) to (U), Sept. 13, 1994, 108 Stat. 1973, 2037, 2148; Pub.L. 104–208, Div. A, Title I, § 101(a) [Title I, § 121, subsection 4], Sept. 30, 1996, 110 Stat. 3009–30; Pub.L. 105–314, Title II, § 201, Oct. 30, 1998, 112 Stat. 2977; Pub.L. 108–21, Title I, § 103(a)(1)(A), (b)(1)(A), Title V, §§ 506, 507, Apr. 30, 2003, 117 Stat. 652, 653, 683; Pub.L. 109–248, Title II, § 206(b)(1), July 27, 2006, 120 Stat. 614.)

HISTORICAL AND STATUTORY NOTES

References in Text

Chapter 71, referred to in subsec. (e), is 18 U.S.C.A. § 1460 et seq.

Chapter 109A, referred to in subsec. (e), is 18 U.S.C.A. § 2141 et seq.

Chapter 117, referred to in subsec. (e), is 18 U.S.C.A. § 2421 et seq.

Codifications

Pub.L. 99–591 is a corrected version of Pub.L. 99–500.

Amendment by section 3563 of Pub.L. 101–647 directed for the substitution of "in," for "in,,". Such substitution had already been editorially executed, therefore, no further change was required.

Short Title

2006 Amendments. Pub.L. 109–248, Title VII, § 707(a), July 27, 2006, 120 Stat. 650, provided that: "This section [amending 18 U.S.C.A. § 2255] may be cited as 'Masha's Law'."

1996 Amendments. Pub.L. 104–208, Div. A, Title I, § 101(a) [Title I, § 121], Sept. 30, 1996, 110 Stat. 3009–26, provided, in part, that: "This section [enacting section 2252a of this title, amending sections 2241, 2243, 2251, 2252, and 2256 of this title, and section 2000aa of Title 42, The Public Health and Welfare, and enacting provisions set out as notes under sections 2241 and 2251 of this title] may be cited as the 'Child Pornography Prevention Act of 1996'."

1990 Amendments. Pub.L. 101–647, Title III, § 301(a), Nov. 29, 1990, 104 Stat. 4816, provided that: "This title [amending sections 1460, 2243, 2252, and 2257 of this title and enacting provisions set out as notes under section 2257 of this title and section 994 of Title 28, Judiciary and Judicial Procedure] may be cited as the 'Child Protection Restoration and Penalties Enhancement Act of 1990'."

1988 Amendments. Section 7501 of Pub.L. 100–690 provided that: "This subtitle [subtitle N of Title VII, §§ 7501, 7511 to 7514, 7521 to 7526, of Pub.L. 100–690, enacting sections 1460, 1466, 1467, 1468, 1469, 2251A, and 2257 of this title, amending sections 1465, 1961, 2251, 2252, 2253, 2254, 2256, and 2516 of this title, section 1305 of Title 19, Customs Duties, and section 223 of Title 47, Telegraphs, Telephones, and Radiotelegraphs, and enacting a provision set out as a note under section 2257 of this title] may be cited as the 'Child Protection and Obscenity Enforcement Act of 1988'."

1986 Amendments. Section 1 of Pub.L. 99–628 provided that: "This Act [which enacted sections 2421 to 2423 of this title, amended chapter 117 heading and sections 2251, 2255, and 2424 of this title, and struck out former sections 2421 to 2423 of this title] may be cited as the 'Child Sexual Abuse and Pornography Act of 1986'."

Pub.L. 99–500, Title I, § 101(b) [Title VII, § 701], Oct. 18, 1986, 100 Stat. 1783–74; Pub.L. 99–591, Title I, § 101(b) [Title VII, § 701], Oct. 30, 1986, 100 Stat. 3341–74, provided that: "This Act [enacting section 2255, redesignating as section 2256 a prior section 2255, and amending sections 2251(c) and 2252(b) of this title and enacting note provisions under this section] may be cited as the 'Child Abuse Victims' Rights Act of 1986'."

1984 Amendments. Section 1 of Pub.L. 98–292 provided: "That this Act [enacting sections 2253 and 2254 of this title, amending this section and sections 2252, 2255, and 2516 of this title, and enacting provisions set out as notes under this section and section 522 of Title 28, Judiciary and Judicial Procedure] may be cited as the 'Child Protection Act of 1984'."

Section 1 of Pub.L. 95–225 provided: "That this Act [enacting this chapter and amending section 2423 of this title] may be cited as the 'Protection of Children Against Sexual Exploitation Act of 1977'."

Severability of Provisions

Pub.L. 104–208, Div. A, Title I, § 101(a) [Title I, § 121, subsec. 8], Sept. 30, 1996, 110 Stat. 3009–31, provided that: "If any provision of this Act [the Child Pornography Prevention Act of 1996, Pub.L. 104–208, Div. A, Title I, § 101(a) [Title I, § 121], Sept. 30, 1996, 110 Stat. 3009–26, for classification of which to the Code, see Short Title note set out under this section and Tables], including any provision or section of the definition of the term child pornography, an amendment made by this Act, or the application of such provision or amendment to any person or circumstance is held to be unconstitutional, the remainder of this Act, including any other provision or section of the definition of the term child pornography, the amendments made by this Act, and the application of such to any other person or circumstance shall not be affected thereby."

Section 4 of Pub.L. 95–225 provided that: "If any provision of this Act [see Short Title note set out above] or the application thereof to any person or circumstances is held invalid, the remainder of the Act and the application of this provision to other persons not similarly situated or to other circumstances shall not be affected thereby."

Child Pornography Prevention

Pub.L. 109–248, Title V, § 501, July 27, 2006, 120 Stat. 623, provided that:

"Congress makes the following findings:

"(1) The effect of the intrastate production, transportation, distribution, receipt, advertising, and possession of child pornography on the interstate market in child pornography:

"(A) The illegal production, transportation, distribution, receipt, advertising and possession of child pornography, as defined in section 2256(8) of title 18, United States Code, as well as the transfer of custody of children for the production of child pornography, is harmful to the physiological, emotional, and mental health of the children depicted in child pornography and has a substantial and detrimental effect on society as a whole.

"(B) A substantial interstate market in child pornography exists, including not only a multimillion dollar industry, but also a nationwide network of individuals openly advertising their desire to exploit children and to traffic in child pornography. Many of these individuals distribute child pornography with the expectation of receiving other child pornography in return.

"(C) The interstate market in child pornography is carried on to a substantial extent through the mails and other instrumentalities of interstate and foreign commerce, such as the Internet. The advent of the Internet has greatly increased the ease of transporting, distributing, receiving, and advertising child pornography in interstate commerce. The advent of digital cameras and digital video cameras, as well as videotape cameras, has greatly increased the ease of producing child pornography. The advent of inexpensive computer equipment with the capacity to store large numbers of digital images of child pornography has greatly increased the ease of possessing child pornography. Taken together, these technological advances have had the unfortunate result of greatly increasing the interstate market in child pornography.

"(D) Intrastate incidents of production, transportation, distribution, receipt, advertising, and possession of child pornography, as well as the transfer of custody of children for the production of child pornography, have a substantial and direct effect upon interstate commerce because:

"(i) Some persons engaged in the production, transportation, distribution, receipt, advertising, and possession of child pornography conduct such activities entirely within the boundaries of one state. These persons are unlikely to be content with the amount of child pornography they produce, transport, distribute, receive, advertise, or possess. These persons are therefore likely to enter the interstate market in child pornography in search of additional child pornography, thereby stimulating demand in the interstate market in child pornography.

"(ii) When the persons described in subparagraph (D)(i) enter the interstate market in search of additional child pornography, they are likely to distribute the child pornography they already produce, transport, distribute, receive, advertise, or possess to persons who will distribute additional child pornography to them, thereby stimulating supply in the interstate market in child pornography.

"(iii) Much of the child pornography that supplies the interstate market in child pornography is produced entirely within the boundaries of one state, is not traceable, and enters the interstate market surreptitiously. This child pornography supports demand in the interstate market in child pornography and is essential to its existence.

"(E) Prohibiting the intrastate production, transportation, distribution, receipt, advertising, and possession of child pornography, as well as the intrastate transfer of custody of children for the production of child pornography, will cause some persons engaged in such intrastate activities to cease all such activities, thereby reducing both supply and demand in the interstate market for child pornography.

"(F) Federal control of the intrastate incidents of the production, transportation, distribution, receipt, advertising, and possession of child pornography, as well as the intrastate transfer of children for the production of child pornography, is essential to the effective control of the interstate market in child pornography.

"(2) The importance of protecting children from repeat exploitation in child pornography:

"(A) The vast majority of child pornography prosecutions today involve images contained on computer hard drives, computer disks, and related media.

"(B) Child pornography is not entitled to protection under the First Amendment and thus may be prohibited.

"(C) The government has a compelling State interest in protecting children from those who sexually exploit them, and this interest extends to stamping out the vice of child pornography at all levels in the distribution chain.

"(D) Every instance of viewing images of child pornography represents a renewed violation of the privacy of the victims and a repetition of their abuse.

"(E) Child pornography constitutes prima facie contraband, and as such should not be distributed to, or copied by, child pornography defendants or their attorneys.

"(F) It is imperative to prohibit the reproduction of child pornography in criminal cases so as to avoid repeated violation and abuse of victims, so long as the government makes reasonable accommodations for the inspection, viewing, and examination of such material for the purposes of mounting a criminal defense."

Congressional Findings Relating to Obscenity and Child Pornography

Pub.L. 108–21, Title V, § 501, Apr. 30, 2003, 117 Stat. 676, provided that: "Congress finds the following:

"(1) Obscenity and child pornography are not entitled to protection under the First Amendment under Miller v. California, 413 U.S. 15 (1973) (obscenity), or New York v. Ferber, 458 U.S. 747 (1982) (child pornography) and thus may be prohibited.

"(2) The Government has a compelling state interest in protecting children from those who sexually exploit them, including both child molesters and child pornographers. 'The prevention of sexual exploitation and abuse of children constitutes a government objective of surpassing importance,' New York v. Ferber, 458 U.S. 747, 757 (1982), and this interest extends to stamping out the vice of child pornography at all levels in the distribution chain. Osborne v. Ohio, 495 U.S. 103, 110 (1990).

"(3) The Government thus has a compelling interest in ensuring that the criminal prohibitions against child pornography remain enforceable and effective. 'The most expeditious if not the only practical method of law enforcement may be to dry up the market for this material by imposing severe criminal penalties on persons selling, advertising, or otherwise promoting the product.' Ferber, 458 U.S. at 760.

"(4) In 1982, when the Supreme Court decided Ferber, the technology did not exist to:

"(A) computer generate depictions of children that are indistinguishable from depictions of real children;

"(B) use parts of images of real children to create a composite image that is unidentifiable as a particular child and in a way that prevents even an expert from concluding that parts of images of real children were used; or

"(C) disguise pictures of real children being abused by making the image look computer-generated.

"(5) Evidence submitted to the Congress, including from the National Center for Missing and Exploited Children, demonstrates that technology already exists to disguise depictions of real children to make them unidentifiable and to make depictions of real children appear computer-generated. The technology will soon exist, if it does not already, to computer generate realistic images of children.

"(6) The vast majority of child pornography prosecutions today involve images contained on computer hard drives, computer disks, and/or related media.

"(7) There is no substantial evidence that any of the child pornography images being trafficked today were made other than by the abuse of real children. Nevertheless, technological advances since Ferber have led many criminal defendants to suggest that the images of child pornography they possess are not those of real children, insisting that the government prove beyond a reasonable doubt that the images are not computer-generated. Such challenges increased significantly after the decision in Ashcroft v. Free Speech Coalition, 535 U.S. 234 (2002).

"(8) Child pornography circulating on the Internet has, by definition, been digitally uploaded or scanned into computers and has been transferred over the Internet, often in different file formats, from trafficker to trafficker. An image seized from a collector of child pornography is rarely a first-generation product, and the retransmission of images can alter the image so as to make it difficult for even an expert conclusively to opine that a particular image depicts a real child. If the original image has been scanned from a paper version into a digital format, this task can be even harder since proper forensic assessment may depend on the quality of the image scanned and the tools used to scan it.

"(9) The impact of the Free Speech Coalition decision on the Government's ability to prosecute child pornography offenders is already evident. The Ninth Circuit has seen a significant adverse effect on prosecutions since the 1999 Ninth Circuit Court of Appeals decision in Free Speech Coalition. After that decision, prosecutions generally have been brought in the Ninth Circuit only in the most clear-cut cases in which the government can specifically identify the child in the depiction or otherwise identify the origin of the image. This is a fraction of meritorious child pornography cases. The National Center for Missing and Exploited Children testified that, in light of the Supreme Court's affirmation of the Ninth Circuit decision, prosecutors in various parts of the country have expressed concern about the continued viability of previously indicted cases as well as declined potentially meritorious prosecutions.

"(10) Since the Supreme Court's decision in Free Speech Coalition, defendants in child pornography cases have almost universally raised the contention that the images in question could be virtual, thereby requiring the government, in nearly every child pornography prosecution, to find proof that the child is real. Some of these defense efforts have already been successful. In addition, the number of prosecutions being brought has been significantly and adversely affected as the resources required to be dedicated to each child pornography case now are significantly higher than ever before.

"(11) Leading experts agree that, to the extent that the technology exists to computer generate realistic images of child pornography, the cost in terms of time, money, and expertise is—and for the foreseeable future will remain—prohibitively expensive. As a result, for the foreseeable future, it will be more cost-effective to produce child pornography using real children. It will not, however, be difficult or expensive to use readily available technology to disguise those depictions of real children to make them unidentifiable or to make them appear computer-generated.

"(12) Child pornography results from the abuse of real children by sex offenders; the production of child pornography is a byproduct of, and not the primary reason for, the sexual abuse of children. There is no evidence that the future development of easy and inexpensive means of computer generating realistic images of children would stop or even reduce the sexual abuse of real children or the practice of visually recording that abuse.

"(13) In the absence of Congressional action, the difficulties in enforcing the child pornography laws will continue to grow increasingly worse. the mere prospect that the technology exists to create composite or computer-generated depictions that are indistinguishable from depictions of real children will allow defendants who possess images of real children to escape prosecution; for it threatens to create a reasonable doubt in every case of computer images even when a real child was abused. This threatens to render child pornography laws that protect real children unenforceable. Moreover, imposing an additional requirement that the Government prove beyond a reasonable doubt that the defendant knew that the image was in fact a real child—as some courts have done—threatens to result in the de facto legalization of the possession, receipt, and distribution of child pornography for all except the original producers of the material.

"(14) To avoid this grave threat to the Government's unquestioned compelling interest in effective enforcement of the child pornography laws that protect real children, a statute must be adopted that prohibits a narrowly-defined subcategory of images.

"(15) The Supreme Court's 1982 Ferber v. New York decision holding that child pornography was not protected drove child pornography off the shelves of adult bookstores. Congressional action is necessary now to ensure that open and notorious trafficking in such materials does not reappear, and even increase, on the Internet."

Congressional Findings

Pub.L. 104–208, Div. A, Title I, § 101(a) [Title I, § 121, subsec. 1], Sept. 30, 1996, 110 Stat. 3009–26, provided that: "Congress finds that—

"(1) the use of children in the production of sexually explicit material, including photographs, films, videos, computer images, and other visual depictions, is a form of sexual abuse which can result in physical or psychological harm, or both, to the children involved;

"(2) where children are used in its production, child pornography permanently records the victim's abuse, and its continued existence causes the child victims of sexual abuse continuing harm by haunting those children in future years;

"(3) child pornography is often used as part of a method of seducing other children into sexual activity; a child who is reluctant to engage in sexual activity with an adult, or to pose for sexually explicit photographs, can sometimes be convinced by viewing depictions of other children 'having fun' participating in such activity;

"(4) child pornography is often used by pedophiles and child sexual abusers to stimulate and whet their own sexual appetites, and as a model for sexual acting out with children; such use of child pornography can desensitize the viewer to the pathology of sexual abuse or exploitation of children, so that it can become acceptable to and even preferred by the viewer;

"(5) new photographic and computer imaging technologies make it possible to produce by electronic, mechanical, or other means, visual depictions of what appear to be children engaging in sexually explicit conduct that are virtually indistinguishable to the unsuspecting viewer from unretouched photographic images of actual children engaging in sexually explicit conduct;

"(6) computers and computer imaging technology can be used to—

"(A) alter sexually explicit photographs, films, and videos in such a way as to make it virtually impossible for unsuspecting viewers to identify individuals, or to determine if the offending material was produced using children;

"(B) produce visual depictions of child sexual activity designed to satisfy the preferences of individual child molesters, pedophiles, and pornography collectors; and

"(C) alter innocent pictures of children to create visual depictions of those children engaging in sexual conduct;

"(7) the creation or distribution of child pornography which includes an image of a recognizable minor invades the child's privacy and reputational interests, since images that are created showing a child's face or other identifiable feature on a body engaging in sexually explicit conduct can haunt the minor for years to come;

"(8) the effect of visual depictions of child sexual activity on a child molester or pedophile using that material to stimulate or whet his own sexual appetites, or on a child where the material is being used as a means of seducing or breaking down the child's inhibitions to sexual abuse or exploitation, is the same whether the child pornography consists of photographic depictions of actual children or visual depictions produced wholly or in part by electronic, mechanical, or other means, including by computer, which are virtually indistinguishable to the unsuspecting viewer from photographic images of actual children;

"(9) the danger to children who are seduced and molested with the aid of child sex pictures is just as great when the child pornographer or child molester uses visual depictions of child sexual activity produced wholly or in part by electronic, mechanical, or other means, including by computer, as when the material consists of unretouched photographic images of actual children engaging in sexually explicit conduct;

"(10)(A) the existence of and traffic in child pornographic images creates the potential for many types of harm in the community and presents a clear and present danger to all children; and

"(B) it inflames the desires of child molesters, pedophiles, and child pornographers who prey on children, thereby increasing the creation and distribution of child pornography and the sexual abuse and exploitation of actual children who are victimized as a result of the existence and use of these materials;

"(11)(A) the sexualization and eroticization of minors through any form of child pornographic images has a deleterious effect on all children by encouraging a societal perception of children as sexual objects and leading to further sexual abuse and exploitation of them; and

"(B) this sexualization of minors creates an unwholesome environment which affects the psychological, mental and emotional development of children and undermines the efforts of parents and families to encourage the sound mental, moral and emotional development of children;

"(12) prohibiting the possession and viewing of child pornography will encourage the possessors of such material to rid themselves of or destroy the material, thereby helping to protect the victims of child pornography and to eliminate the market for the sexual exploitative use of children; and

"(13) the elimination of child pornography and the protection of children from sexual exploitation provide a compelling governmental interest for prohibiting the production, distribution, possession, sale, or viewing of visual depictions of children engaging in sexually explicit conduct, including both photographic images of actual children engaging in such conduct and depictions produced by computer or other means which are virtually indistinguishable to the unsuspecting viewer from photographic images of actual children engaging in such conduct."

Pub.L. 99–500, Title I, § 101(b) [Title VII, § 702], Oct. 18, 1986, 100 Stat. 1783–74; Pub.L. 99–591, Title I, § 101(b) [Title VII, § 702], Oct. 30, 1986, 100 Stat. 3341–74, provided that:

"(1) child exploitation has become a multi-million dollar industry, infiltrated and operated by elements of organized crime, and by a nationwide network of individuals openly advertising their desire to exploit children;

"(2) Congress has recognized the physiological, psychological, and emotional harm caused by the production, distribution, and display of child pornography by strengthening laws prescribing such activity;

"(3) the Federal Government lacks sufficient enforcement tools to combat concerted efforts to exploit children prescribed by Federal law, and exploitation victims lack effective remedies under Federal law; and

"(4) current rules of evidence, criminal procedure, and civil procedure and other courtroom and investigative procedures inhibit the participation of child victims as witnesses and damage their credibility when they do testify, impairing the prosecution of child exploitation offenses."

Section 2 of Pub.L. 98–292 provided that: "The Congress finds that—

"(1) child pornography has developed into a highly organized, multi-million-dollar industry which operates on a nationwide scale;

"(2) thousands of children including large numbers of runaway and homeless youth are exploited in the production and distribution of pornographic materials; and

"(3) the use of children as subjects of pornographic materials is harmful to the physiological, emotional, and mental health of the individual child and to society."

Report to Congress by Attorney General

Pub.L. 99–500, Title I, § 101(b) [Title VII, § 705], Oct. 18, 1986, 100 Stat. 1783–75; Pub.L. 99–591, Title I, § 101(b) [Title VII, § 705], Oct. 30, 1986, 100 Stat. 3341–75, provided that:

"(a) Within one year after the date of enactment of this title, the Attorney General shall submit a report to Congress detailing possible changes in the Federal Rules of Evidence, the Federal Rules of Criminal Procedure, the Federal Rules of Civil Procedure, and other Federal courtroom, prosecutorial, and investigative procedures which would facilitate the participation of child witnesses in cases involving child abuse and sexual exploitation.

"(b) In preparing the report, the Attorney General shall consider, but not be limited to, such changes as—

"(1) use of closed-circuit cameras, two-way mirrors, and other out-of-court statements;

"(2) judicial discretion to circumscribe use of harassing, overly complex, and confusing questions against child witnesses;

"(3) use of videotape in investigations to reduce repetitions of interviews;

"(4) streamlining investigative procedures; and

"(5) improved training of prosecutorial and investigative staff in special problems of child witnesses, including handicapped children."

Annual Report to Congress

Attorney General to report annually to Congress on prosecutions, convictions, and forfeitures under this chapter, see section 9 of Pub.L. 98–292, set out as a note under section 522 of Title 28, Judiciary and Judicial Procedure.

§ 2251A. Selling or buying of children

(a) Any parent, legal guardian, or other person having custody or control of a minor who sells or otherwise transfers custody or control of such minor, or offers to sell or otherwise transfer custody of such minor either—

(1) with knowledge that, as a consequence of the sale or transfer, the minor will be portrayed in a visual depiction engaging in, or assisting another person to engage in, sexually explicit conduct; or

(2) with intent to promote either—

(A) the engaging in of sexually explicit conduct by such minor for the purpose of producing any visual depiction of such conduct; or

(B) the rendering of assistance by the minor to any other person to engage in sexually explicit conduct for the purpose of producing any visual depiction of such conduct;

shall be punished by imprisonment for not less than 30 years or for life and by a fine under this title, if any of the circumstances described in subsection (c) of this section exist.

(b) Whoever purchases or otherwise obtains custody or control of a minor, or offers to purchase or otherwise obtain custody or control of a minor either—

(1) with knowledge that, as a consequence of the purchase or obtaining of custody, the minor will be portrayed in a visual depiction engaging in, or assisting another person to engage in, sexually explicit conduct; or

(2) with intent to promote either—

(A) the engaging in of sexually explicit conduct by such minor for the purpose of producing any visual depiction of such conduct; or

(B) the rendering of assistance by the minor to any other person to engage in sexually explicit conduct for the purpose of producing any visual depiction of such conduct;

shall be punished by imprisonment for not less than 30 years or for life and by a fine under this title, if any of the circumstances described in subsection (c) of this section exist.

(c) The circumstances referred to in subsections (a) and (b) are that—

(1) in the course of the conduct described in such subsections the minor or the actor traveled in or was transported in interstate or foreign commerce;

(2) any offer described in such subsections was communicated or transported in interstate or foreign commerce by any means including by computer or mail; or

(3) the conduct described in such subsections took place in any territory or possession of the United States.

(Added Pub.L. 100–690, Title VII, § 7512(a), Nov. 18, 1988, 102 Stat. 4486, and amended Pub.L. 108–21, Title I, § 103(b)(1)(B), Apr. 30, 2003, 117 Stat. 653.)

§ 2252. Certain activities relating to material involving the sexual exploitation of minors

(a) Any person who—

(1) knowingly transports or ships in interstate or foreign commerce by any means including by computer or mails, any visual depiction, if—

(A) the producing of such visual depiction involves the use of a minor engaging in sexually explicit conduct; and

(B) such visual depiction is of such conduct;

(2) knowingly receives, or distributes, any visual depiction that has been mailed, or has been shipped or transported in interstate or foreign commerce, or which contains materials which have been mailed or so shipped or transported, by any means including by computer, or knowingly reproduces any visual depiction for distribution in interstate or foreign commerce or through the mails, if—

(A) the producing of such visual depiction involves the use of a minor engaging in sexually explicit conduct; and

(B) such visual depiction is of such conduct;

(3) either—

(A) in the special maritime and territorial jurisdiction of the United States, or on any land or building owned by, leased to, or otherwise used by or under the control of the Government of the United States, or in the Indian country as defined in section 1151 of this title, knowingly sells or possesses with intent to sell any visual depiction; or

(B) knowingly sells or possesses with intent to sell any visual depiction that has been mailed, or has been shipped or transported in interstate or foreign commerce, or which was produced using materials which have been mailed or so shipped or transported, by any means, including by computer, if—

(i) the producing of such visual depiction involves the use of a minor engaging in sexually explicit conduct; and

(ii) such visual depiction is of such conduct; or

(4) either—

(A) in the special maritime and territorial jurisdiction of the United States, or on any land or building owned by, leased to, or otherwise used by or under the control of the Government of the United States, or in the Indian country as defined in section 1151 of this title, knowingly possesses 1 or more books, magazines, periodicals, films, video tapes, or other matter which contain any visual depiction; or

(B) knowingly possesses 1 or more books, magazines, periodicals, films, video tapes, or other matter which contain any visual depiction that has been mailed, or has been shipped or transported in interstate or foreign commerce, or which was produced using materials which have been mailed or so shipped or transported, by any means including by computer, if—

(i) the producing of such visual depiction involves the use of a minor engaging in sexually explicit conduct; and

(ii) such visual depiction is of such conduct;

shall be punished as provided in subsection (b) of this section.

(b)(1) Whoever violates, or attempts or conspires to violate, paragraph (1), (2), or (3) of subsection (a) shall be fined under this title and imprisoned not less than 5 years and not more than 20 years, but if such person has a prior conviction under this chapter, section 1591, chapter 71, chapter 109A, chapter 117, or under section 920 of title 10 (article 120 of the Uniform Code of Military Justice), or under the laws of any State relating to aggravated sexual abuse, sexual abuse, or abusive sexual conduct involving a minor or ward, or the production, possession, receipt, mailing, sale, distribution, shipment, or transportation of child pornography, or sex trafficking of children, such person shall be fined under this title and imprisoned for not less than 15 years nor more than 40 years.

(2) Whoever violates, or attempts or conspires to violate, paragraph (4) of subsection (a) shall be fined under this title or imprisoned not more than 10 years, or both, but if such person has a prior conviction under this chapter, chapter 71, chapter 109A, or chapter 117, or under section 920 of Title 10 (article 120 of the Uniform Code of Military Justice), or under the laws of any State relating to aggravated sexual abuse, sexual abuse, or abusive sexual conduct involving a minor or ward, or the production, possession, receipt, mailing, sale, distribution, shipment, or transportation of child pornography, such person shall be fined under

this title and imprisoned for not less than 10 years nor more than 20 years.

(c) Affirmative defense.—It shall be an affirmative defense to a charge of violating paragraph (4) of subsection (a) that the defendant—

(1) possessed less than three matters containing any visual depiction proscribed by that paragraph; and

(2) promptly and in good faith, and without retaining or allowing any person, other than a law enforcement agency, to access any visual depiction or copy thereof—

(A) took reasonable steps to destroy each such visual depiction; or

(B) reported the matter to a law enforcement agency and afforded that agency access to each such visual depiction.

(Added Pub.L. 95–225, § 2(a), Feb. 6, 1978, 92 Stat. 7, and amended Pub.L. 98–292, § 4, May 21, 1984, 98 Stat. 204; Pub.L. 99–500, Title I, § 101(b) [Title VII, § 704(b)], Oct. 18, 1986, 100 Stat. 1783–75; Pub.L. 99–591, Title I, § 101(b) [Title VII, § 704(b)], Oct. 30, 1986, 100 Stat. 3341–75; Pub.L. 100–690, Title VII, § 7511(b), Nov. 18, 1988, 102 Stat. 4485; Pub.L. 101–647, Title III, § 323(a), (b), Nov. 29, 1990, 104 Stat. 4818, 4819; Pub.L. 103–322, Title XVI, § 160001(d), (e), Title XXXIII, § 330010(8), Sept. 13, 1994, 108 Stat. 2037, 2143; Pub.L. 104–208, Div. A, Title I, § 101(a) [Title I, § 121, subsection 5], Sept. 30, 1996, 110 Stat. 3009–30; Pub.L. 105–314, Title II, §§ 202(a), 203(a), Oct. 30, 1998., 112 Stat. 2977, 2978; Pub.L. 108–21, Title I, § 103(a)(1)(B), (C), (b)(1)(C), (D), Title V, § 507, Apr. 30, 2003, 117 Stat. 652, 653, 683; Pub.L. 109–248, Title II, § 206(b)(2), July 27, 2006, 120 Stat. 614.)

HISTORICAL AND STATUTORY NOTES

References in Text

Chapter 71, referred to in subsec. (b), is 18 U.S.C.A. § 1460 et seq.

Chapter 109A, referred to in subsec. (b), is 18 U.S.C.A. § 225 et seq.

Chapter 117, referred to in subsec. (b), is 18 U.S.C.A. § 2421 et seq.

Codifications

Pub.L. 99–591 is a corrected version of Pub.L. 99–500.

Confirmation of Intent of Congress in Enacting Sections 2252 and 2256

Section 160003 of Pub.L. 103–322 provided that:

"**(a) Declaration.**—The Congress declares that in enacting sections 2252 and 2256 of title 18, United States Code [this section and section 2256 of this title], it was and is the intent of Congress that—

"(1) the scope of 'exhibition of the genitals or pubic area' in section 2256(2)(E), in the definition of 'sexually explicit conduct', is not limited to nude exhibitions or exhibitions in which the outlines of those areas were discernible through clothing; and

"(2) the requirements in section 2252(a)(1)(A), (2)(A), (3)(B)(i), and (4)(B)(i) that the production of a visual depiction involve the use of a minor engaging in 'sexually explicit conduct' of the kind described in section 2256(2)(E) are satisfied if a person photographs a minor in such a way as to exhibit the child in a lascivious manner.

"**(b) Sense of the Congress.**—It is the sense of the Congress that in filing its brief in United States v. Knox, No. 92–1183, and thereby depriving the United States Supreme Court of the adverseness necessary for full and fair presentation of the issues arising in the case, the Department of Justice did not accurately reflect the intent of Congress in arguing that 'the videotapes in [the Knox case] constitute 'lascivious exhibition[s] of the genitals or pubic area' only if those body parts are visible in the tapes and the minors posed or acted lasciviously'."

§ 2252A. Certain activities relating to material constituting or containing child pornography

(a) Any person who—

(1) knowingly mails, or transports or ships in interstate or foreign commerce by any means, including by computer, any child pornography;

(2) knowingly receives or distributes—

(A) any child pornography that has been mailed, or shipped or transported in interstate or foreign commerce by any means, including by computer; or

(B) any material that contains child pornography that has been mailed, or shipped or transported in interstate or foreign commerce by any means, including by computer;

(3) knowingly—

(A) reproduces any child pornography for distribution through the mails, or in interstate or foreign commerce by any means, including by computer; or

(B) advertises, promotes, presents, distributes, or solicits through the mails, or in interstate or foreign commerce by any means, including by computer, any material or purported material in a manner that reflects the belief, or that is intended to cause another to believe, that the material or purported material is, or contains—

(i) an obscene visual depiction of a minor engaging in sexually explicit conduct; or

(ii) a visual depiction of an actual minor engaging in sexually explicit conduct;

(4) either—

(A) in the special maritime and territorial jurisdiction of the United States, or on any land or building owned by, leased to, or otherwise used by or under the control of the United States Government, or in the Indian country (as defined in section 1151), knowingly sells or possesses with the intent to sell any child pornography; or

(B) knowingly sells or possesses with the intent to sell any child pornography that has been mailed, or shipped or transported in interstate or foreign commerce by any means, including by computer, or that was produced using materials that have been mailed, or shipped or transported in interstate or foreign commerce by any means, including by computer;

(5) either—

(A) in the special maritime and territorial jurisdiction of the United States, or on any land or building owned by, leased to, or otherwise used by or under the control of the United States Government, or in the Indian country (as defined in section 1151), knowingly possesses any book, magazine, periodical, film, videotape, computer disk, or any other material that contains an image of child pornography; or

(B) knowingly possesses any book, magazine, periodical, film, videotape, computer disk, or any other material that contains an image of child pornography that has been mailed, or shipped or transported in interstate or foreign commerce by any means, including by computer, or that was produced using materials that have been mailed, or shipped or transported in interstate or foreign commerce by any means, including by computer; or

(6) knowingly distributes, offers, sends, or provides to a minor any visual depiction, including any photograph, film, video, picture, or computer generated image or picture, whether made or produced by electronic, mechanical, or other means, where such visual depiction is, or appears to be, of a minor engaging in sexually explicit conduct—

(A) that has been mailed, shipped, or transported in interstate or foreign commerce by any means, including by computer;

(B) that was produced using materials that have been mailed, shipped, or transported in interstate or foreign commerce by any means, including by computer; or

(C) which distribution, offer, sending, or provision is accomplished using the mails or by transmitting or causing to be transmitted any wire communication in interstate or foreign commerce, including by computer,

for purposes of inducing or persuading a minor to participate in any activity that is illegal.[1]

shall be punished as provided in subsection (b).

(b)(1) Whoever violates, or attempts or conspires to violate, paragraph (1), (2), (3), (4), or (6) of subsection (a) shall be fined under this title and imprisoned not less than 5 years and not more than 20 years, but, if such person has a prior conviction under this chapter, section 1591, chapter 71, chapter 109A, chapter 117, or under section 920 of title 10 (article 120 of the Uniform Code of Military Justice), or under the laws of any State relating to aggravated sexual abuse, sexual abuse, or abusive sexual conduct involving a minor or ward, or the production, possession, receipt, mailing, sale, distribution, shipment, or transportation of child pornography, or sex trafficking of children, such person shall be fined under this title and imprisoned for not less than 15 years nor more than 40 years.

(2) Whoever violates, or attempts or conspires to violate, subsection (a)(5) shall be fined under this title or imprisoned not more than 10 years, or both, but, if such person has a prior conviction under this chapter, chapter 71, chapter 109A, or chapter 117, or under section 920 of title 10 (article 120 of the Uniform Code of Military Justice), or under the laws of any State relating to aggravated sexual abuse, sexual abuse, or abusive sexual conduct involving a minor or ward, or the production, possession, receipt, mailing, sale, distribution, shipment, or transportation of child pornography, such person shall be fined under this title and imprisoned for not less than 10 years nor more than 20 years.

(c) It shall be an affirmative defense to a charge of violating paragraph (1), (2), (3)(A), (4), or (5) of subsection (a) that—

(1)(A) the alleged child pornography was produced using an actual person or persons engaging in sexually explicit conduct; and

(B) each such person was an adult at the time the material was produced; or

(2) the alleged child pornography was not produced using any actual minor or minors.

No affirmative defense under subsection (c)(2) shall be available in any prosecution that involves child pornography as described in section 2256(8)(C). A defendant may not assert an affirmative defense to a charge of violating paragraph (1), (2), (3)(A), (4), or (5) of subsection (a) unless, within the time provided for filing pretrial motions or at such time prior to trial as the judge may direct, but in no event later than 10 days before the commencement of the trial, the defendant provides the court and the United States with notice of the intent to assert such defense and the substance of any expert or other specialized testimony or evidence upon which the defendant intends to rely. If the defendant fails to comply with this subsection, the court shall, absent a finding of extraordinary circumstances that prevented timely compliance, prohibit the defendant from asserting such defense to a charge of violating paragraph (1), (2), (3)(A), (4), or (5) of subsection (a) or presenting any evidence for which the defendant has failed to provide proper and timely notice.

(d) Affirmative defense.—It shall be an affirmative defense to a charge of violating subsection (a)(5) that the defendant—

(1) possessed less than three images of child pornography; and

(2) promptly and in good faith, and without retaining or allowing any person, other than a law enforcement agency, to access any image or copy thereof—

(A) took reasonable steps to destroy each such image; or

(B) reported the matter to a law enforcement agency and afforded that agency access to each such image.

(e) Admissibility of evidence.—On motion of the government, in any prosecution under this chapter or section 1466A, except for good cause shown, the name, address, social security number, or other nonphysical identifying information, other than the age or approximate age, of any minor who is depicted in any child pornography shall not be admissible and may be redacted from any otherwise admissible evidence, and the jury shall be instructed, upon request of the United States, that it can draw no inference from the absence of such evidence in deciding whether the child pornography depicts an actual minor.

(f) Civil remedies.—

(1) In general.—Any person aggrieved by reason of the conduct prohibited under subsection (a) or (b) or section 1466A may commence a civil action for the relief set forth in paragraph (2).

(2) Relief.—In any action commenced in accordance with paragraph (1), the court may award appropriate relief, including—

(A) temporary, preliminary, or permanent injunctive relief;

(B) compensatory and punitive damages; and

(C) the costs of the civil action and reasonable fees for attorneys and expert witnesses.

(g) Child exploitation enterprises.—

(1) Whoever engages in a child exploitation enterprise shall be fined under this title and imprisoned for any term of years not less than 20 or for life.

(2) A person engages in a child exploitation enterprise for the purposes of this section if the person violates section 1591, section 1201 if the victim is a minor, or chapter 109A (involving a minor victim), 110 (except for sections 2257 and 2257A), or 117 (involving a minor victim), as a part of a series of felony violations constituting three or more separate incidents and involving more than one victim, and commits those offenses in concert with three or more other persons.

(Added Pub.L. 104–208, Div. A, Title I, § 101(a) [Title I, § 121, subsection 3(a)], Sept. 30, 1996, 110 Stat. 3009–28, and amended Pub.L. 105–314, Title II, §§ 202(b), 203(b), Oct. 30, 1998, 112 Stat. 2978; Pub.L. 107–273, Div. B, Title IV, § 4003(a)(5), Nov. 2, 2002, 116 Stat. 1811; Pub.L. 108–21, Title I, § 103(a)(1)(D), (E), (b)(1)(E), (F), Title V, §§ 502(d), 503, 505, 507, 510, Apr. 30, 2003, 117 Stat. 652, 653, 679, 680, 682 to 684; Pub.L. 109–248, Title II, § 206(b)(3), Title VII, § 701, July 27, 2006, 120 Stat. 614, 647.)

[1] So in original. The period probably should be a comma.

HISTORICAL AND STATUTORY NOTES

References in Text

Chapter 71, referred to in subsec. (b), is 18 U.S.C.A. § 1460 et seq.

Chapter 109A, referred to in subsec. (b), is 18 U.S.C.A. § 225 et seq.

Chapter 117, referred to in subsec. (b), is 18 U.S.C.A. § 2421 et seq.

§ 2252B. Misleading domain names on the Internet

(a) Whoever knowingly uses a misleading domain name on the Internet with the intent to deceive a person into viewing material constituting obscenity shall be fined under this title or imprisoned not more than 2 years, or both.

(b) Whoever knowingly uses a misleading domain name on the Internet with the intent to deceive a minor into viewing material that is harmful to minors on the Internet shall be fined under this title or imprisoned not more than 10 years, or both.

(c) For the purposes of this section, a domain name that includes a word or words to indicate the sexual content of the site, such as "sex" or "porn", is not misleading.

(d) For the purposes of this section, the term "material that is harmful to minors" means any communication, consisting of nudity, sex, or excretion, that, taken as a whole and with reference to its context—

(1) predominantly appeals to a prurient interest of minors;

(2) is patently offensive to prevailing standards in the adult community as a whole with respect to what is suitable material for minors; and

(3) lacks serious literary, artistic, political, or scientific value for minors.

(e) For the purposes of subsection (d), the term "sex" means acts of masturbation, sexual intercourse, or physcial[1] contact with a person's genitals, or the condition of human male or female genitals when in a state of sexual stimulation or arousal.

(Added Pub.L. 108–21, Title V, § 521(a), Apr. 30, 2003, Stat. 686, and amended Pub.L. 109–248, Title II, § 206(b)(4), July 27, 2006, 120 Stat. 614.)

[1] So in original. Probably should read "physical".

§ 2252C. Misleading words or digital images on the Internet

(a) In general.—Whoever knowingly embeds words or digital images into the source code of a website with the intent to deceive a person into viewing material constituting obscenity shall be fined under this title and imprisoned for not more than 10 years.

(b) Minors.—Whoever knowingly embeds words or digital images into the source code of a website with the intent to deceive a minor into viewing material harmful to minors on the Internet shall be fined under this title and imprisoned for not more than 20 years.

(c) Construction.—For the purposes of this section, a word or digital image that clearly indicates the sexual content of the site, such as "sex" or "porn", is not misleading.

(d) Definitions.—As used in this section—

(1) the terms "material that is harmful to minors" and "sex" have the meaning given such terms in section 2252B; and

(2) the term "source code" means the combination of text and other characters comprising the content, both viewable and nonviewable, of a web page, including any website publishing language, programming language, protocol or functional content, as well as any successor languages or protocols.

(Added Pub.L. 109–248, Title VII, § 703(a), July 27, 2006, 120 Stat. 648.)

§ 2253. Criminal forfeiture

(a) Property subject to criminal forfeiture.—A person who is convicted of an offense under this chapter involving a visual depiction described in section 2251, 2251A, 2252, 2252A, or 2260 of this chapter or who is convicted of an offense under section 2252B of this chapter,,[1] or who is convicted of an offense under chapter 109A, shall forfeit to the United States such person's interest in—

(1) any visual depiction described in section 2251, 2251A, or 2252[2] 2252A, 2252B, or 2260 of this chapter, or any book, magazine, periodical, film, videotape, or other matter which contains any such visual depiction, which was produced, transported, mailed, shipped or received in violation of this chapter;

(2) any property, real or personal, constituting or traceable to gross profits or other proceeds obtained from such offense; and

(3) any property, real or personal, used or intended to be used to commit or to promote the commission of such offense or any property traceable to such property.

(b) Section 413 of the Controlled Substances Act (21 U.S.C. 853) with the exception of subsections (a) and (d), applies to the criminal forfeiture of property pursuant to subsection (a).

[(c) to (*o*) Repealed. Pub.L. 109–248, Title V, § 505(c), July 27, 2006, 120 Stat. 630]

(Added Pub.L. 98–292, § 6, May 21, 1984, 98 Stat. 205, and amended Pub.L. 100–690, Title VII, § 7522(c), Nov. 18, 1988, 102 Stat. 4494; Pub.L. 101–647, Title XXXV, § 3564, Nov. 29, 1990, 104 Stat. 4928; Pub.L. 103–322, Title XXXIII, 330011(m)(1), Sept. 13, 1994, 108 Stat. 2145; Pub.L. 105–314, Title VI, § 602, Oct. 30, 1998, 112 Stat. 2982; Pub.L. 109–248, Title V, § 505(b), (c), July 27, 2006, 120 Stat. 630.)

[1] So in original. The first comma should probably follow "2260 of this chapter".

[2] So in original. A comma should probably follow "2252".

HISTORICAL AND STATUTORY NOTES

References in Text

Chapter 109A, referred to in subsec. (a), is chapter 109A of this title, Sexual Abuse, 18 U.S.C.A. § 2241 et seq.

Section 413 of the Controlled Substances Act, referred to in subsec. (b), is Pub.L. 91–513, Title II, § 413, as added Pub.L. 98–473, Title II, § 303, Oct. 12, 1984, 98 Stat. 2044, and amended, which is classified to 21 U.S.C.A. § 853.

Effective and Applicability Provisions

1994 Acts. Section 330011(m) of Pub.L. 103–322 provided in part that the amendment made by such section, amending sections 3564(1) and 3565(3)(A) of Pub.L. 101–647 (and thereby amending this section and section 2254 of this title), was to take effect on the date of enactment of Pub.L. 101–647, which was approved Nov. 29, 1990.

§ 2254. Civil forfeiture

Any property subject to forfeiture pursuant to section 2253 may be forfeited to the United States in a civil case in accordance with the procedures set forth in chapter 46.

(Added Pub.L. 98–292, § 6, May 21, 1984, 98 Stat. 205, and amended Pub.L. 99–500, Title I, § 101(m) [Title II, § 201(a), (c)], Oct. 18, 1986, 100 Stat. 1783–314, 1783–315; Pub.L. 99–591, Title I, § 101(m) [Title II, § 201(a), (c)], Oct. 30, 1986, 100 Stat. 3341–314, 3341–315; Pub.L. 100–690, Title VII, § 7522(c), Nov. 18, 1988, 102 Stat. 4498; Pub.L. 101–647, Title XX, § 2003, Title XXXV, § 3565, Nov. 29, 1990, 104 Stat. 4855, 4928; Pub.L. 103–322, Title XXXIII, § 330011(m)(2), Sept. 13, 1994, 108 Stat. 2145; Pub.L. 105–314, Title VI, § 603, Oct. 30, 1998, 112 Stat. 2982; Pub.L. 106–185, § 2(c)(4), Apr. 25, 2000, 114 Stat. 211; Pub.L. 107–273, Div. B, Title IV, § 4003(a)(6), Nov. 2, 2002, 116 Stat. 1811; Pub.L. 109–248, Title V, § 505(d), July 27, 2006, 120 Stat. 630.)

HISTORICAL AND STATUTORY NOTES

References in Text

Chapter 46, referred to in text, is chapter 46 of this title, Forfeiture, 18 U.S.C.A. § 981 et seq.

Effective and Applicability Provisions

2000 Acts. Amendments by Pub.L. 106–185, applicable to any forfeiture proceeding commenced on or after the date that is 120 days after April 25, 2000, see section 21 of Pub.L. 106–185, set out as a note under section 1324 of Title 8.

1994 Acts. Amendment by section 330011(m)(2) of Pub.L. 103–322 effective Nov. 29, 1990; see section 330011(m) of Pub.L. 103–322, set out as a note under section 2253 of this title.

§ 2255. Civil remedy for personal injuries

(a) In general.—Any person who, while a minor, was a victim of a violation of section 2241(c), 2242, 2243, 2251, 2251A, 2252, 2252A, 2260, 2421, 2422, or 2423 of this title and who suffers personal injury as a result of such violation, regardless of whether the injury occurred while such person was a minor, may sue in any appropriate United States District Court and shall recover the actual damages such person sustains and the cost of the suit, including a reasonable attorney's fee. Any person as described in the preceding sentence shall be deemed to have sustained damages of no less than $150,000 in value.

(b) Statute of limitations.—Any action commenced under this section shall be barred unless the complaint is filed within six years after the right of action first accrues or in the case of a person under a legal disability, not later than three years after the disability.

(Added Pub.L. 99–500, Title I, § 101(b) [Title VII, § 703(a)], Oct. 18, 1986, 100 Stat. 1783–75, and amended Pub.L. 99–591, Title I, § 101(b) [Title VII, § 703(a)], Oct. 30, 1986, 100 Stat. 3341–75; Pub.L. 105–314, Title VI, § 605, Oct. 30, 1998, 112 Stat. 2984; Pub.L. 109–248, Title VII, § 707(b), (c), July 27, 2006, 120 Stat. 650.)

HISTORICAL AND STATUTORY NOTES

Prior Provisions

Another section 2255 was renumbered section 2256 of this title.

§ 2256. Definitions for chapter

For the purposes of this chapter, the term—

(1) "minor" means any person under the age of eighteen years;

(2)(A) Except as provided in subparagraph (B), "sexually explicit conduct" means actual or simulated—

(i) sexual intercourse, including genital-genital, oral-genital, anal-genital, or oral-anal, whether between persons of the same or opposite sex;

(ii) bestiality;

(iii) masturbation;

(iv) sadistic or masochistic abuse; or

(v) lascivious exhibition of the genitals or pubic area of any person;

(B) For purposes of subsection 8(B)[1] of this section, "sexually explicit conduct" means—

(i) graphic sexual intercourse, including genital-genital, oral- genital, anal-genital, or oral-anal, whether between persons of the same or opposite sex, or lascivious simulated sexual intercourse where the genitals, breast, or pubic area of any person is exhibited;

(ii) graphic or lascivious simulated;

(I) bestiality;

(II) masturbation; or

(III) sadistic or masochistic abuse; or

(iii) graphic or simulated lascivious exhibition of the genitals or pubic area of any person;

(3) "producing" means producing, directing, manufacturing, issuing, publishing, or advertising;

(4) "organization" means a person other than an individual;

(5) "visual depiction" includes undeveloped film and videotape, and data stored on computer disk or by electronic means which is capable of conversion into a visual image;

(6) "computer" has the meaning given that term in section 1030 of this title;

(7) "custody or control" includes temporary supervision over or responsibility for a minor whether legally or illegally obtained;

(8) "child pornography" means any visual depiction, including any photograph, film, video, picture, or computer or computer-generated image or picture, whether made or produced by electronic, mechanical, or other means, of sexually explicit conduct, where—

(A) the production of such visual depiction involves the use of a minor engaging in sexually explicit conduct;

(B) such visual depiction is a digital image, computer image, or computer-generated image that is, or is indistinguishable from, that of a minor engaging in sexually explicit conduct; or

(C) such visual depiction has been created, adapted, or modified to appear that an identifiable minor is engaging in sexually explicit conduct.

[(D) Repealed. Pub.L. 108–21, Title V, § 502(a)(3), Apr. 30, 2003, 117 Stat. 678]

(9) "identifiable minor"—

(A) means a person—

(i)(I) who was a minor at the time the visual depiction was created, adapted, or modified; or

(II) whose image as a minor was used in creating, adapting, or modifying the visual depiction; and

(ii) who is recognizable as an actual person by the person's face, likeness, or other distinguishing characteristic, such as a unique birthmark or other recognizable feature; and

(B) shall not be construed to require proof of the actual identity of the identifiable minor.

(10) "graphic", when used with respect to a depiction of sexually explicit conduct, means that a viewer can observe any part of the genitals or pubic area of any depicted person or animal during any part of the time that the sexually explicit conduct is being depicted; and

(11) the term "indistinguishable" used with respect to a depiction, means virtually indistinguishable, in that the depiction is such that an ordinary person viewing the depiction would conclude that the depiction is of an actual minor engaged in sexually explicit conduct. This definition does not apply to depictions that are drawings, cartoons, sculptures, or paintings depicting minors or adults.

(Added Pub.L. 95–225, § 2(a), Feb. 6, 1978, 92 Stat. 8, § 2253; renumbered § 2255 and amended Pub.L. 98–292, §§ 5, May 21, 1984, 98 Stat. 205; renumbered § 2256, Pub.L. 99–500, Title I, § 101(b) [Title VII, § 703(a)], Oct. 18, 1986, 100 Stat. 1783–74; Pub.L. 99–591, Title I, § 101(b) [Title VII, § 703(a)], Oct. 30, 1986, 100 Stat. 3341–74, and amended Pub.L. 99–628, § 4, Nov. 7, 1986, 100 Stat. 3510; Pub.L. 100–690, Title VII, §§ 7511(c), 7512(b), Nov. 18, 1988, 102 Stat. 4485 to 4487; Pub.L. 104–208, Div. A, Title I, § 101(a) [Title I, § 121, subsection 2], Sept. 30, 1996, 110 Stat. 3009–27; Pub.L 108–21, Title V, § 502(a) to (c), Apr. 30, 2003, 117 Stat. 678, 679.)

1 So in original. Probably should be "(8)(B)".

HISTORICAL AND STATUTORY NOTES

Codifications

Amendment to this section by Pub.L. 99–628 has been executed to this section, as renumbered by Pub.L. 99–500, Title I, § 101(b) [Title VII, § 703(a)], Oct. 18, 1986, 100 Stat. 1783–74; Pub.L. 99–591, Title I, § 101(b) [Title VII, § 703(a)], Oct. 30, 1986, 100 Stat. 3341–74. Amendments were directed to be made to section 2255 of this title but were executed to this section as the probable intent of Congress.

§ 2257. Record keeping requirements

(a) Whoever produces any book, magazine, periodical, film, videotape, digital image, digitally- or computer-manipulated image of an actual human being, picture, or other matter which—

(1) contains one or more visual depictions made after November 1, 1990 of actual sexually explicit conduct; and

(2) is produced in whole or in part with materials which have been mailed or shipped in interstate or foreign commerce, or is shipped or transported or is intended for shipment or transportation in interstate or foreign commerce;

shall create and maintain individually identifiable records pertaining to every performer portrayed in such a visual depiction.

(b) Any person to whom subsection (a) applies shall, with respect to every performer portrayed in a visual depiction of actual sexually explicit conduct—

(1) ascertain, by examination of an identification document containing such information, the performer's name and date of birth, and require the performer to provide such other indicia of his or her identity as may be prescribed by regulations;

(2) ascertain any name, other than the performer's present and correct name, ever used by the performer including maiden name, alias, nickname, stage, or professional name; and

(3) record in the records required by subsection (a) the information required by paragraphs (1) and (2) of this subsection and such other identifying information as may be prescribed by regulation.

(c) Any person to whom subsection (a) applies shall maintain the records required by this section at his business premises, or at such other place as the Attorney General may by regulation prescribe and shall make such records available to the Attorney General for inspection at all reasonable times.

(d)(1) No information or evidence obtained from records required to be created or maintained by this section shall, except as provided in this section, directly or indirectly, be used as evidence against any person with respect to any violation of law.

(2) Paragraph (1) of this subsection shall not preclude the use of such information or evidence in a prosecution or other action for a violation of this chapter or chapter 71, or for a violation of any applicable provision of law with respect to the furnishing of false information.

(e)(1) Any person to whom subsection (a) applies shall cause to be affixed to every copy of any matter described in paragraph (1) of subsection (a) of this section, in such manner and in such form as the Attorney General shall by regulations prescribe, a statement describing where the records required by this section with respect to all performers depicted in that copy of the matter may be located. In this paragraph, the term "copy" includes every page of a website on which matter described in subsection (a) appears.

(2) If the person to whom subsection (a) of this section applies is an organization the statement required by this subsection shall include the name, title, and business address of the individual employed by such organization responsible for maintaining the records required by this section.

(f) It shall be unlawful—

(1) for any person to whom subsection (a) applies to fail to create or maintain the records as required by subsections (a) and (c) or by any regulation promulgated under this section;

(2) for any person to whom subsection (a) applies knowingly to make any false entry in or knowingly to fail to make an appropriate entry in, any record required by subsection (b) of this section or any regulation promulgated under this section;

(3) for any person to whom subsection (a) applies knowingly to fail to comply with the provisions of subsection (e) or any regulation promulgated pursuant to that subsection;

(4) for any person knowingly to sell or otherwise transfer, or offer for sale or transfer, any book, magazine, periodical, film, video, or other matter, produce in whole or in part with materials which have been mailed or shipped in interstate or foreign commerce or which is intended for shipment in interstate or foreign commerce, which—

(A) contains one or more visual depictions made after the effective date of this subsection of actual sexually explicit conduct; and

(B) is produced in whole or in part with materials which have been mailed or shipped in interstate or foreign commerce, or is shipped or transported or is intended for shipment or transportation in interstate or foreign commerce;

which does not have affixed thereto, in a manner prescribed as set forth in subsection (e)(1), a statement describing where the records required by this section may be located, but such person shall have no duty to determined the accuracy of the contents of the statement or the records required to be kept; and

(5) for any person to whom subsection (a) applies to refuse to permit the Attorney General or his or her designee to conduct an inspection under subsection (c).

(g) The Attorney General shall issue appropriate regulations to carry out this section.

(h) In this section—

(1) the term "actual sexually explicit conduct" means actual but not simulated conduct as defined in clauses (i) through (v) of section 2256(2)(A) of this title;

(2) the term "produces"—

(A) means—

(i) actually filming, videotaping, photographing, creating a picture, digital image, or digitally– or computer-manipulated image of an actual human being;

(ii) digitizing an image, of a visual depiction of sexually explicit conduct; or, assembling, manufacturing, publishing, duplicating, reproducing, or reissuing a book, magazine, periodical, film, videotape, digital image, or picture, or other matter intended for commercial distribution, that contains a visual depiction of sexually explicit conduct; or

(iii) inserting on a computer site or service a digital image of, or otherwise managing the sexually explicit content, of a computer site or service that contains a visual depiction of, sexually explicit conduct; and

(B) does not include activities that are limited to—

(i) photo or film processing, including digitization of previously existing visual depictions, as part of a commercial enterprise, with no other commercial interest in the sexually explicit material, printing, and video duplication;

(ii) distribution;

(iii) any activity, other than those activities identified in subparagraph (A), that does not involve the hiring, contracting for, managing, or otherwise arranging for the participation of the depicted performers;

(iv) the provision of a telecommunications service, or of an Internet access service or Internet information location tool (as those terms are defined in section 231 of the Communications Act of 1934 (47 U.S.C. 231)); or

(v) the transmission, storage, retrieval, hosting, formatting, or translation (or any combination thereof) of a communication, without selection or alteration of the content of the communication, except that deletion of a particular communication or material made by another person in a manner consistent with section 230(c) of the Communications Act of 1934 (47 U.S.C. 230(c)) shall not constitute such selection or alteration of the content of the communication; and

(3) the term "performer" includes any person portrayed in a visual depiction engaging in, or assisting another person to engage in, sexually explicit conduct.

(i) Whoever violates this section shall be imprisoned for not more than 5 years, and fined in accordance with the provisions of this title, or both. Whoever violates this section after having been convicted of a violation punishable under this section shall be imprisoned for any period of years not more than 10 years but not less than 2 years, and fined in accordance with the provisions of this title, or both.

(Added Pub.L. 100–690, Title VII, § 7513(a), Nov. 18, 1988, 102 Stat. 4487, and amended Pub.L. 101–647, Title III, §§ 301(b), 311, Nov. 29, 1990, 104 Stat. 4808; Pub.L. 103–322, Title XXXIII, § 330004(14), Sept. 13, 1994, 108 Stat. 2142; Pub.L. 108–21, Title V, § 511(a), Apr. 30, 2003, Stat. 684; Pub.L. 109–248, Title V, § 502(a), July 27, 2006, 120 Stat. 625.)

HISTORICAL AND STATUTORY NOTES

References in Text

Chapter 71, referred to in subsec. (d)(2), is 18 U.S.C.A. § 1460 et seq.

Section 231 of the Communications Act of 1934, referred to in subsec. (h)(2)(B)(iv), (v), is Act June 19, 1934, c. 652, Title II, § 231, as added Oct. 21, 1998, Pub.L. 105–277, Div. C, Title XIV, § 1403, 112 Stat. 2681-736, which is classified to 47 U.S.C.A. § 231.

Effective and Applicability Provisions

1990 Acts. Section 312 of Pub.L. 101–647 provided that: "Subsections (d), (f), (g), (h), and (i) of section 2257 of title 18, United States Code, as added by this title shall take effect 90 days after the date of the enactment of this Act [Nov. 29, 1990] except—

"(1) the Attorney General shall prepare the initial set of regulations required or authorized by subsections (d), (f), (g), (h), and (i) of section 2257 within 60 days of the date of the enactment of this Act; and

"(2) subsection (e) of section 2257 and of any regulation issued pursuant thereto shall take effect 90 days after the date of the enactment of this Act."

1988 Acts. Section 7513(c) of Pub.L. 100–690 provided that: "Section 2257 of title 18, United States Code, as added by this section [this section] shall take effect 180 days after the date of the enactment of this Act [Nov. 18, 1988] except—

"(1) the Attorney General shall prepare the initial set of regulations required or authorized by section 2257 [this section] within 90 days of the date of the enactment of this Act [Nov. 18, 1988]; and

"(2) subsection (e) of section 2257 of such title [subsec. (e) of this section] and of any regulation issued pursuant thereto shall take effect 270 days after the date of the enactment of this Act [Nov. 18, 1988]."

Construction

Pub.L. 109–248, Title V, § 502(b), July 27, 2006, 120 Stat. 626, provided that: "The provisions of section 2257 shall not apply to any depiction of actual sexually explicit conduct as described in clause (v) of section 2256(2)(A) of title 18, United States Code, produced in whole or in part, prior to the effective date of this section [Pub.L. 109–248, Title V, § 502, July 27, 2006, 120 Stat. 625, which amended this section and enacted provisions set out as this note] unless that depiction also includes actual sexually explicit conduct as described in clauses (i) through (iv) of section 2256(2)(A) of title 18, United States Code."

Report

Pub.L. 108–21, Title V, § 511(b), Apr. 30, 2003, 117 Stat. 685, provided that: "Not later than 1 year after enactment of this Act [1 year after Apr. 30, 2003], the Attorney General shall submit to Congress a report detailing the number of times since January 1993 that the Department of Justice has inspected the records of any producer of materials regulated pursuant to section 2257 of title 18, United States Code [this section], and section 75 of title 28 of the Code of Federal Regulations. The Attorney General shall indicate the number of violations prosecuted as a result of those inspections."

§ 2257A. Record keeping requirements for simulated sexual conduct

(a) Whoever produces any book, magazine, periodical, film, videotape, digital image, digitally- or computer-manipulated image of an actual human being, picture, or other matter that—

(1) contains 1 or more visual depictions of simulated sexually explicit conduct; and

(2) is produced in whole or in part with materials which have been mailed or shipped in interstate or foreign commerce, or is shipped or transported or is intended for shipment or transportation in interstate or foreign commerce;

shall create and maintain individually identifiable records pertaining to every performer portrayed in such a visual depiction.

(b) Any person to whom subsection (a) applies shall, with respect to every performer portrayed in a visual depiction of simulated sexually explicit conduct—

(1) ascertain, by examination of an identification document containing such information, the performer's name and date of birth, and require the performer to provide such other indicia of his or her identity as may be prescribed by regulations;

(2) ascertain any name, other than the performer's present and correct name, ever used by the performer including maiden name, alias, nickname, stage, or professional name; and

(3) record in the records required by subsection (a) the information required by paragraphs (1) and (2) and such other identifying information as may be prescribed by regulation.

(c) Any person to whom subsection (a) applies shall maintain the records required by this section at their business premises, or at such other place as the Attorney General may by regulation prescribe and shall make such records available to the Attorney General for inspection at all reasonable times.

(d)(1) No information or evidence obtained from records required to be created or maintained by this section shall, except as provided in this section, directly or indirectly, be used as evidence against any person with respect to any violation of law.

(2) Paragraph (1) shall not preclude the use of such information or evidence in a prosecution or other action for a violation of this chapter or chapter 71, or for a violation of any applicable provision of law with respect to the furnishing of false information.

(e)(1) Any person to whom subsection (a) applies shall cause to be affixed to every copy of any matter described in subsection (a)(1) in such manner and in such form as the Attorney General shall by regulations prescribe, a statement describing where the records required by this section with respect to all performers depicted in that copy of the matter may be located. In this paragraph, the term "copy" includes every page of a website on which matter described in subsection (a) appears.

(2) If the person to whom subsection (a) applies is an organization the statement required by this subsection shall include the name, title, and business address of the individual employed by such organization re-

sponsible for maintaining the records required by this section.

(f) It shall be unlawful—

(1) for any person to whom subsection (a) applies to fail to create or maintain the records as required by subsections (a) and (c) or by any regulation promulgated under this section;

(2) for any person to whom subsection (a) applies knowingly to make any false entry in or knowingly to fail to make an appropriate entry in, any record required by subsection (b) or any regulation promulgated under this section;

(3) for any person to whom subsection (a) applies knowingly to fail to comply with the provisions of subsection (e) or any regulation promulgated pursuant to that subsection; or

(4) for any person knowingly to sell or otherwise transfer, or offer for sale or transfer, any book, magazine, periodical, film, video, or other matter, produced in whole or in part with materials which have been mailed or shipped in interstate or foreign commerce or which is intended for shipment in interstate or foreign commerce, that—

(A) contains 1 or more visual depictions made after the date of enactment of this subsection of simulated sexually explicit conduct; and

(B) is produced in whole or in part with materials which have been mailed or shipped in interstate or foreign commerce, or is shipped or transported or is intended for shipment or transportation in interstate or foreign commerce;

which does not have affixed thereto, in a manner prescribed as set forth in subsection (e)(1), a statement describing where the records required by this section may be located, but such person shall have no duty to determine the accuracy of the contents of the statement or the records required to be kept.

(5) for any person to whom subsection (a) applies to refuse to permit the Attorney General or his or her designee to conduct an inspection under subsection (c).

(g) As used in this section, the terms "produces" and "performer" have the same meaning as in section 2257(h) of this title.

(h)(1) The provisions of this section and section 2257 shall not apply to matter, or any image therein, containing one or more visual depictions of simulated sexually explicit conduct, or actual sexually explicit conduct as described in clause (v) of section 2256(2)(A), if such matter—

(A)(i) is intended for commercial distribution;

(ii) is created as a part of a commercial enterprise by a person who certifies to the Attorney General that such person regularly and in the normal course of business collects and maintains individually identifiable information regarding all performers, including minor performers, employed by that person, pursuant to Federal and State tax, labor, and other laws, labor agreements, or otherwise pursuant to industry standards, where such information includes the name, address, and date of birth of the performer; and

(iii) is not produced, marketed or made available by the person described in clause (ii) to another in circumstances such than [1] an ordinary person would conclude that the matter contains a visual depiction that is child pornography as defined in section 2256(8); or

(B)(i) is subject to the authority and regulation of the Federal Communications Commission acting in its capacity to enforce section 1464 of this title, regarding the broadcast of obscene, indecent or profane programming; and

(ii) is created as a part of a commercial enterprise by a person who certifies to the Attorney General that such person regularly and in the normal course of business collects and maintains individually identifiable information regarding all performers, including minor performers, employed by that person, pursuant to Federal and State tax, labor, and other laws, labor agreements, or otherwise pursuant to industry standards, where such information includes the name, address, and date of birth of the performer.

(2) Nothing in subparagraphs (A) and (B) of paragraph (1) shall be construed to exempt any matter that contains any visual depiction that is child pornography, as defined in section 2256(8), or is actual sexually explicit conduct within the definitions in clauses (i) through (iv) of section 2256(2)(A).

(i)(1) Whoever violates this section shall be imprisoned for not more than 1 year, and fined in accordance with the provisions of this title, or both.

(2) Whoever violates this section in an effort to conceal a substantive offense involving the causing, transporting, permitting or offering or seeking by notice or advertisement, a minor to engage in sexually explicit conduct for the purpose of producing a visual depiction of such conduct in violation of this title, or to conceal a substantive offense that involved trafficking in material involving the sexual exploitation of a minor, including receiving, transporting, advertising, or possessing material involving the sexual exploitation of a minor with intent to traffic, in violation of this title, shall be imprisoned for not more than 5 years and fined in accordance with the provisions of this title, or both.

(3) Whoever violates paragraph (2) after having been previously convicted of a violation punishable under that paragraph shall be imprisoned for any period of years not more than 10 years but not less than 2 years, and fined in accordance with the provisions of this title, or both.

The provisions of this section shall not become effective until 90 days after the final regulations implementing this section are published in the Federal Register. The provisions of this section shall not apply to any matter, or image therein, produced, in whole or in part, prior to the effective date of this section.

(k)[2] On an annual basis, the Attorney General shall submit a report to Congress—

(1) concerning the enforcement of this section and section 2257 by the Department of Justice during the previous 12–month period; and

(2) including—

(A) the number of inspections undertaken pursuant to this section and section 2257;

(B) the number of open investigations pursuant to this section and section 2257;

(C) the number of cases in which a person has been charged with a violation of this section and section 2257; and

(D) for each case listed in response to subparagraph (C), the name of the lead defendant, the federal district in which the case was brought, the court tracking number, and a synopsis of the violation and its disposition, if any, including settlements, sentences, recoveries and penalties.

(Added Pub.L. 109–248, Title V, § 503(a), July 27, 2006, 120 Stat. 626.)

[1] So in original. Probably should read "that".

[2] So in original. No subsec. (j) enacted.

HISTORICAL AND STATUTORY NOTES

References in Text

Chapter 71, referred to in subsec. (d)(2), is chapter 71 of this title, Obscenity, 18 U.S.C.A. § 1460 et seq.

§ 2258. Failure to report child abuse

A person who, while engaged in a professional capacity or activity described in subsection (b) of section 226 of the Victims of Child Abuse Act of 1990 on Federal land or in a federally operated (or contracted) facility, learns of facts that give reason to suspect that a child has suffered an incident of child abuse, as defined in subsection (c) of that section, and fails to make a timely report as required by subsection (a) of that section, shall be fined under this title or imprisoned not more than 1 year or both.

(Added Pub.L. 101–647, Title II, § 226(g)(1), Nov. 29, 1990, 104 Stat. 4808, and amended Pub.L. 109–248, Title II, § 209, July 27, 2006, 120 Stat. 615.)

HISTORICAL AND STATUTORY NOTES

References in Text

Section 226 of the Victims of Child Abuse Act of 1990, referred to in text, is section 226 of Pub.L. 101–647, Nov. 29, 1990, 104 Stat. 4806, which is classified to section 13031 of Title 42, The Public Health and Welfare. For complete classification of this Act to the Code, see Short Title Note set out under section 1 of this title and Tables.

§ 2259. Mandatory restitution

(a) In general.—Notwithstanding section 3663 or 3663A, and in addition to any other civil or criminal penalty authorized by law, the court shall order restitution for any offense under this chapter.

(b) Scope and nature of order.—

(1) Directions.—The order of restitution under this section shall direct the defendant to pay the victim (through the appropriate court mechanism) the full amount of the victim's losses as determined by the court pursuant to paragraph (2).

(2) Enforcement.—An order of restitution under this section shall be issued and enforced in accordance with section 3664 in the same manner as an order under section 3663A.

(3) Definition.—For purposes of this subsection, the term "full amount of the victim's losses" includes any costs incurred by the victim for—

(A) medical services relating to physical, psychiatric, or psychological care;

(B) physical and occupational therapy or rehabilitation;

(C) necessary transportation, temporary housing, and child care expenses;

(D) lost income;

(E) attorneys' fees, as well as other costs incurred; and

(F) any other losses suffered by the victim as a proximate result of the offense.

(4) Order mandatory.—**(A)** The issuance of a restitution order under this section is mandatory.

(B) A court may not decline to issue an order under this section because of—

(i) the economic circumstances of the defendant; or

(ii) the fact that a victim has, or is entitled to, receive compensation for his or her injuries from the proceeds of insurance or any other source.

(c) Definition.—For purposes of this section, the term "victim" means the individual harmed as a result of a commission of a crime under this chapter, including, in the case of a victim who is under 18 years of age, incompetent, incapacitated, or deceased, the legal guardian of the victim or representative of the victim's estate, another family member, or any other person appointed as suitable by the court, but in no event shall the defendant be named as such representative or guardian.

(Added Pub.L. 103–322, Title IV, § 40113(b)(1), Sept. 13, 1994, 108 Stat. 1907, and amended Pub.L. 104–132, Title II, § 205(c), Apr. 24, 1996, 110 Stat. 1231.)

HISTORICAL AND STATUTORY NOTES

Effective and Applicability Provisions

1996 Acts. Amendment by Pub.L. 104–132 to be effective, to the extent constitutionally permissible, for sentencing proceedings in cases in which the defendant is convicted on or after Apr. 24, 1996, see section 211 of Pub.L. 104–132, set out as a note under section 2248 of this title.

§ 2260. Production of sexually explicit depictions of a minor for importation into the United States

(a) Use of minor.—A person who, outside the United States, employs, uses, persuades, induces, entices, or coerces any minor to engage in, or who has a minor assist any other person to engage in, or who transports any minor with the intent that the minor engage in any sexually explicit conduct for the purpose of producing any visual depiction of such conduct, intending that the visual depiction will be imported into the United States or into waters within 12 miles of the coast of the United States, shall be punished as provided in subsection (c).

(b) Use of visual depiction.—A person who, outside the United States, knowingly receives, transports, ships, distributes, sells, or possesses with intent to transport, ship, sell, or distribute any visual depiction of a minor engaging in sexually explicit conduct (if the production of the visual depiction involved the use of a minor engaging in sexually explicit conduct), intending that the visual depiction will be imported into the United States or into waters within a distance of 12 miles of the coast of the United States, shall be punished as provided in subsection (c).

(c) Penalties.—

(1) A person who violates subsection (a), or attempts or conspires to do so, shall be subject to the penalties provided in subsection (e) of section 2251 for a violation of that section, including the penalties provided for such a violation by a person with a prior conviction or convictions as described in that subsection.

(2) A person who violates subsection (b), or attempts or conspires to do so, shall be subject to the penalties provided in subsection (b)(1) of section 2252 for a violation of paragraph (1), (2), or (3) of subsection (a) of that section, including the penalties provided for such a violation by a person with a prior conviction or convictions as described in subsection (b)(1) of section 2252.

(Added Pub.L. 103–322, Title XVI, § 160001(a), Sept. 13, 1994, 108 Stat. 2036, § 2258, and renumbered § 2260, Pub.L. 104–294, Title VI, § 601(i)(1), Oct. 11, 1996, 110 Stat. 3501, and amended Pub.L. 109–248, Title II, § 206(b)(5), July 27, 2006, 120 Stat. 614.)

§ 2260A. Penalties for registered sex offenders

Whoever, being required by Federal or other law to register as a sex offender, commits a felony offense involving a minor under section 1201, 1466A, 1470, 1591, 2241, 2242, 2243, 2244, 2245, 2251, 2251A, 2260, 2421, 2422, 2423, or 2425, shall be sentenced to a term of imprisonment of 10 years in addition to the imprisonment imposed for the offense under that provision. The sentence imposed under this section shall be consecutive to any sentence imposed for the offense under that provision.

(Added Pub.L. 109–248, Title VII, § 702(a), July 27, 2006, 120 Stat. 648.)

CHAPTER 110A—DOMESTIC VIOLENCE AND STALKING

[1] So in original. Does not conform to section nameline.

[2] Editorially supplied. Section was enacted without corresponding amendment to analysis.

§ 2261. Interstate domestic violence

(a) Offenses.—

(1) Travel or conduct of offender.—A person who travels in interstate or foreign commerce or enters or leaves Indian country or within the special maritime and territorial jurisdiction of the United States with the intent to kill, injure, harass, or intimidate a spouse, intimate partner, or dating partner, and who, in the course of or as a result of such travel, commits or attempts to commit a crime of violence against that spouse or intimate partner, shall be punished as provided in subsection (b).

(2) Causing travel of victim.—A person who causes a spouse, intimate partner, or dating partner to travel in interstate or foreign commerce or to enter or leave Indian country by force, coercion, duress, or fraud, and who, in the course of, as a result of, or to facilitate such conduct or travel, commits or attempts to commit a crime of violence against that spouse or intimate partner, shall be punished as provided in subsection (b).

(b) Penalties.—A person who violates this section or section 2261A shall be fined under this title, imprisoned—

(1) for life or any term of years, if death of the victim results;

(2) for not more than 20 years if permanent disfigurement or life threatening bodily injury to the victim results;

(3) for not more than 10 years, if serious bodily injury to the victim results or if the offender uses a dangerous weapon during the offense;

(4) as provided for the applicable conduct under chapter 109A if the offense would constitute an offense under chapter 109A (without regard to whether the offense was committed in the special maritime and territorial jurisdiction of the United States or in a Federal prison); and

(5) for not more than 5 years, in any other case, or both fined and imprisoned.

(6) Whoever commits the crime of stalking in violation of a temporary or permanent civil or criminal injunction, restraining order, no-contact order, or other order described in section 2266 of title 18, United States Code, shall be punished by imprisonment for not less than 1 year.

(Added Pub.L. 103–322, Title IV, § 40221(a), Sept. 13, 1994, 108 Stat. 1926, and amended Pub.L. 104–201, Div. A, Title X, § 1069(b)(1), (2), Sept. 23, 1996, 110 Stat. 2656; Pub.L. 106–386, Div. B, Title I, § 1107(a), Oct. 28, 2000, 114 Stat. 1497; Pub.L. 109–162, Title I, §§ 114(b), 116(a), 117(a), Jan. 5, 2006, 119 Stat. 2988, 2989.)

§ 2261A. Stalking[1]

Whoever—

(1) travels in interstate or foreign commerce or within the special maritime and territorial jurisdiction of the United States, or enters or leaves Indian country, with the intent to kill, injure, harass, or place under surveillance with intent to kill, injure, harass, or intimidate another person, and in the course of, or as a result of, such travel places that person in reasonable fear of the death of, or serious bodily injury to, or causes substantial emotional distress to that person, a member of the immediate family (as defined in section 115) of that person, or the spouse or intimate partner of that person; or

(2) with the intent—

(A) to kill, injure, harass, or place under surveillance with intent to kill, injure, harass, or intimidate, or cause substantial emotional distress to a person in another State or tribal jurisdiction or within the special maritime and territorial jurisdiction of the United States; or

(B) to place a person in another State or tribal jurisdiction, or within the special maritime and territorial jurisdiction of the United States, in reasonable fear of the death of, or serious bodily injury to—

(i) that person;

(ii) a member of the immediate family (as defined in section 115 [2] of that person; or

(iii) a spouse or intimate partner of that person;

uses the mail, any interactive computer service, or any facility of interstate or foreign commerce to engage in a course of conduct that causes substantial emotional distress to that person or places that person in reasonable fear of the death of, or serious bodily injury to, any of the persons described in clauses (i) through (iii) of subparagraph (B);

shall be punished as provided in section 2261(b) of this title.

(Added Pub.L. 104–201, Div. A, Title X, § 1069(a), Sept. 23, 1996, 110 Stat. 2655, and amended Pub.L. 106–386, Div. B, Title I, § 1107(b)(1), Oct. 28, 2000, 114 Stat. 1498; Pub.L. 109–162, Title I, § 114(a), Jan. 5, 2006, 119 Stat. 2987.)

[1] Section was amended without corresponding amendment to analysis.

[2] So in original. Probably should be followed by ")".

HISTORICAL AND STATUTORY NOTES

Amendment of Federal Sentencing Guidelines Regarding Interstate Stalking

For provisions relating to amendment of the Guidelines regarding interstate stalking, see Pub.L.106–386, Div. B, Title I, § 1107(b)(2), Oct. 28, 2000, 114 Stat. 1498, set out as a note under 28 U.S.C.A. § 994.

§ 2262. Interstate violation of protection order

(a) Offenses.—

(1) Travel or conduct of offender.—A person who travels in interstate or foreign commerce, or enters or leaves Indian country or within the special maritime and territorial jurisdiction of the United States, with the intent to engage in conduct that violates the portion of a protection order that prohibits or provides protection against violence, threats, or harassment against, contact or communication with, or physical proximity to, another person, or that would violate such a portion of a protection order in the jurisdiction in which the order was issued, and subsequently engages in such conduct, shall be punished as provided in subsection (b).

(2) Causing travel of victim.—A person who causes another person to travel in interstate or foreign commerce or to enter or leave Indian country by force, coercion, duress, or fraud, and in the course of, as a result of, or to facilitate such conduct or travel engages in conduct that violates the portion of a protection order that prohibits or provides protection against violence, threats, or harassment against, contact or communication with, or physical proximity to, another person, or that would violate such a portion of a protection order in the jurisdiction in which the order was issued, shall be punished as provided in subsection (b).

(b) Penalties.—A person who violates this section shall be fined under this title, imprisoned—

(1) for life or any term of years, if death of the victim results;

(2) for not more than 20 years if permanent disfigurement or life threatening bodily injury to the victim results;

(3) for not more than 10 years, if serious bodily injury to the victim results or if the offender uses a dangerous weapon during the offense;

(4) as provided for the applicable conduct under chapter 109A if the offense would constitute an offense under chapter 109A (without regard to whether the offense was committed in the special maritime and territorial jurisdiction of the United States or in a Federal prison); and

(5) for not more than 5 years, in any other case, or both fined and imprisoned.

(Added Pub.L. 103–322, Title IV, § 40221(a), Sept. 13, 1994, 108 Stat. 1927, and amended Pub.L. 104–201, Div. A, Title X, § 1069(b)(2), Sept. 23, 1996, 110 Stat. 2656; Pub.L. 104–294, Title VI, § 605(d), Oct. 11, 1996, 110 Stat. 3509; Pub.L. 106–386, Div. B, Title I, § 1107(c), Oct. 28, 2000, 114 Stat. 1498; Pub.L. 109–162, Title I, § 117(b), Jan. 5, 2006, 119 Stat. 2989.)

§ 2263. Pretrial release of defendant

In any proceeding pursuant to section 3142 for the purpose of determining whether a defendant charged under this chapter shall be released pending trial, or for the purpose of determining conditions of such release, the alleged victim shall be given an opportunity to be heard regarding the danger posed by the defendant.

(Added Pub.L. 103–322, Title IV, § 40221(a), Sept. 13, 1994, 108 Stat. 1928.)

§ 2264. Restitution

(a) In general.—Notwithstanding section 3663 or 3663A, and in addition to any other civil or criminal penalty authorized by law, the court shall order restitution for any offense under this chapter.

(b) Scope and nature of order.—

(1) Directions.—The order of restitution under this section shall direct the defendant to pay the victim (through the appropriate court mechanism) the full amount of the victim's losses as determined by the court pursuant to paragraph (2).

(2) Enforcement.—An order of restitution under this section shall be issued and enforced in accordance with section 3664 in the same manner as an order under section 3663A.

(3) Definition.—For purposes of this subsection, the term "full amount of the victim's losses" includes any costs incurred by the victim for—

(A) medical services relating to physical, psychiatric, or psychological care;

(B) physical and occupational therapy or rehabilitation;

(C) necessary transportation, temporary housing, and child care expenses;

(D) lost income;

(E) attorneys' fees, plus any costs incurred in obtaining a civil protection order; and

(F) any other losses suffered by the victim as a proximate result of the offense.

(4) Order mandatory.—**(A)** The issuance of a restitution order under this section is mandatory.

(B) A court may not decline to issue an order under this section because of—

(i) the economic circumstances of the defendant; or

(ii) the fact that a victim has, or is entitled to, receive compensation for his or her injuries from the proceeds of insurance or any other source.

(c) Victim defined.—For purposes of this section, the term "victim" means the individual harmed as a result of a commission of a crime under this chapter, including, in the case of a victim who is under 18 years of age, incompetent, incapacitated, or deceased, the legal guardian of the victim or representative of the victim's estate, another family member, or any other person appointed as suitable by the court, but in no event shall the defendant be named as such representative or guardian.

(Added Pub.L. 103–322, Title IV, § 40221(a), Sept. 13, 1994, 108 Stat. 1928, and amended Pub.L. 104–132, Title II, § 205(d), Apr. 24, 1996, 110 Stat. 1231.)

HISTORICAL AND STATUTORY NOTES

Effective and Applicability Provisions

1996 Acts. Amendment by Pub.L. 104–132 to be effective, to the extent constitutionally permissible, for sentencing proceedings in cases in which the defendant is convicted on or after Apr. 24, 1996, see section 211 of Pub.L. 104–132, set out as a note under section 2248 of this title.

§ 2265. Full faith and credit given to protection orders

(a) Full faith and credit.—Any protection order issued that is consistent with subsection (b) of this section by the court of one State, Indian tribe, or territory (the issuing State, Indian tribe, or territory) shall be accorded full faith and credit by the court of another State, Indian tribe, or territory (the enforcing State, Indian tribe, or territory) and enforced by the court and law enforcement personnel of the other State, Indian tribal government or Territory as if it were the order of the enforcing State or tribe.

(b) Protection order.—A protection order issued by a State, tribal, or territorial court is consistent with this subsection if—

(1) such court has jurisdiction over the parties and matter under the law of such State, Indian tribe, or territory; and

(2) reasonable notice and opportunity to be heard is given to the person against whom the order is sought sufficient to protect that person's right to due process. In the case of ex parte orders, notice and opportunity to be heard must be provided within the time required by State, tribal, or territorial law, and in any event within a reasonable time after the order is issued, sufficient to protect the respondent's due process rights.

(c) Cross or counter petition.—A protection order issued by a State, tribal, or territorial court against one who has petitioned, filed a complaint, or otherwise filed a written pleading for protection against abuse by a spouse or intimate partner is not entitled to full faith and credit if—

(1) no cross or counter petition, complaint, or other written pleading was filed seeking such a protection order; or

(2) a cross or counter petition has been filed and the court did not make specific findings that each party was entitled to such an order.

(d) Notification and registration.—

(1) Notification.—A State, Indian tribe, or territory according full faith and credit to an order by a court of another State, Indian tribe, or territory shall not notify or require notification of the party against whom a protection order has been issued that the protection order has been registered or filed in that enforcing State, tribal, or territorial jurisdiction unless requested to do so by the party protected under such order.

(2) No prior registration or filing as prerequisite for enforcement.—Any protection order that is otherwise consistent with this section shall be accorded full faith and credit, notwithstanding failure to comply with any requirement that the order be registered or filed in the enforcing State, tribal, or territorial jurisdiction.

(3) Limits on Internet publication of registration information.—A State, Indian tribe, or territory shall not make available publicly on the Internet any information regarding the registration, filing of a petition for, or issuance of a protection order, restraining order or injunction, restraining order, or injunction[1] in either the issuing or enforcing State, tribal or territorial jurisdiction, if such publication would be likely to publicly reveal the identity or location of the party protected under such order. A State, Indian tribe, or territory may share court-generated and law enforcement-generated information contained in secure, governmental registries for protection order enforcement purposes.

(e) Tribal court jurisdiction.—For purposes of this section, a tribal court shall have full civil jurisdiction to enforce protection orders, including authority to enforce any orders through civil contempt proceedings, exclusion of violators from Indian lands, and other appropriate mechanisms, in matters arising within the authority of the tribe.

(Added Pub.L. 103–322, Title IV, § 40221(a), Sept. 13, 1994, 108 Stat. 1930, and amended Pub.L. 106–386, Div. B, Title I, § 1101(b)(4), Oct. 28, 2000, 114 Stat. 1493; Pub.L. 109–162, Title I, § 106(a) to (c), Jan. 5, 2006, 119 Stat. 2981, 2982; Pub.L. 109–271, § 2(n), Aug. 12, 2006, 120 Stat. 754.)

1 So in original.

§ 2265A. Repeat offenders[1]

(a) Maximum term of imprisonment.—The maximum term of imprisonment for a violation of this chapter after a prior domestic violence or stalking offense shall be twice the term otherwise provided under this chapter.

(b) Definition.—For purposes of this section—

(1) the term "prior domestic violence or stalking offense" means a conviction for an offense—

(A) under section 2261, 2261A, or 2262 of this chapter; or

(B) under State law for an offense consisting of conduct that would have been an offense under a section referred to in subparagraph (A) if the conduct had occurred within the special maritime and territorial jurisdiction of the United States, or in interstate or foreign commerce; and

(2) the term "State" means a State of the United States, the District of Columbia, or any commonwealth, territory, or possession of the United States.

(Added Pub.L. 109–162, Title I, § 115, Jan. 5, 2006, 119 Stat. 2988.)

1 Section was enacted without corresponding amendment to analysis.

§ 2266. Definitions

In this chapter:

(1) Bodily injury.—The term "bodily injury" means any act, except one done in self-defense, that results in physical injury or sexual abuse.

(2) Course of conduct.—The term "course of conduct" means a pattern of conduct composed of 2 or more acts, evidencing a continuity of purpose.

(3) Enter or leave Indian country.—The term "enter or leave Indian country" includes leaving the jurisdiction of 1 tribal government and entering the jurisdiction of another tribal government.

(4) Indian country.—The term "Indian country" has the meaning stated in section 1151 of this title.

(5) Protection order.—The term "protection order" includes—

(A) any injunction, restraining order, or any other order issued by a civil or criminal court for the purpose of preventing violent or threatening acts or harassment against, sexual violence, or contact or communication with or physical proximity to, another person, including any temporary or final order issued by a civil or criminal court whether obtained by filing an independent action or as a pendente lite order in another proceeding so long as any civil or criminal order was issued in response to a complaint, petition, or motion filed by or on behalf of a person seeking protection; and

(B) any support, child custody or visitation provisions, orders, remedies or relief issued as part of a protection order, restraining order, or injunction pursuant to State, tribal, territorial, or local law authorizing the issuance of protection orders, restraining orders, or injunctions for the protection of victims of domestic violence, sexual assault, dating violence, or stalking.

(6) Serious bodily injury.—The term "serious bodily injury" has the meaning stated in section 2119(2).

(7) Spouse or intimate partner.—The term "spouse or intimate partner" includes—

(A) for purposes of—

(i) sections other than 2261A—

(I) a spouse or former spouse of the abuser, a person who shares a child in common with the abuser, and a person who cohabits or has cohabited as a spouse with the abuser; or

(II) a person who is or has been in a social relationship of a romantic or intimate nature with the abuser, as determined by the length of the relationship, the type of relationship, and the frequency of interaction between the persons involved in the relationship; and

(ii) section 2261A—

(I) a spouse or former spouse of the target of the stalking, a person who shares a child in common with the target of the stalking, and a person who cohabits or has cohabited as a spouse with the target of the stalking; or

(II) a person who is or has been in a social relationship of a romantic or intimate nature with the target of the stalking, as determined by the length of the relationship, the type of the relationship, and the frequency of interaction between the persons involved in the relationship.

(B) any other person similarly situated to a spouse who is protected by the domestic or family violence laws of the State or tribal jurisdiction in which the injury occurred or where the victim resides.

(8) State.—The term "State" includes a State of the United States, the District of Columbia, and a commonwealth, territory, or possession of the United States.

(9) Travel in interstate or foreign commerce.—The term "travel in interstate or foreign commerce" does not include travel from 1 State to another by an individual who is a member of an Indian tribe and who remains at all times in the territory of the Indian tribe of which the individual is a member.

(10) Dating partner.—The term "dating partner"refers to a person who is or has been in a social relationship of a romantic or intimate nature with the abuser. The existence of such a relationship is based on a consideration of—

(A) the length of the relationship; and

(B) the type of relationship; and

(C) the frequency of interaction between the persons involved in the relationship.

(Added Pub.L. 103–322, Title IV, § 40221(a), Sept. 13, 1994, 108 Stat. 1931, and amended Pub.L. 106–386, Div. B, Title I, § 1107(d), Oct. 28, 2000, 114 Stat. 1499; Pub.L. 109–162, Title I, §§ 106(d), 116(b), Jan. 5, 2006, 119 Stat. 2982, 2988; Pub.L. 109–271, § 2(c), (i), Aug. 12, 2006, 120 Stat. 752.)

HISTORICAL AND STATUTORY NOTES

Codifications

Amendment by Pub.L. 109–162, Title I, § 106(d)(2), which directed in clauses (i) and (ii) of paragraph (7)(A) of this section to strike "2261A, a spouse or former spouse of the abuser, a person who shares a child in common with the abuser, and a person who cohabits or has cohabited as a spouse with the abuser" and insert specified language, was executed only to clause (ii) of paragraph (7)(A), since the quoted language specified to be deleted did not exist in clause (ii) of paragraph (7)(A).

CHAPTER 111—SHIPPING

[1] So in original. No section 2282 has been enacted.

[2] So in original. Does not conform to section catchline.

§ 2271. Conspiracy to destroy vessels

Whoever, on the high seas, or within the United States, willfully and corruptly conspires, combines, and confederates with any other person, such other person being either within or without the United States, to cast away or otherwise destroy any vessel, with intent to injure any person that may have underwritten or may thereafter underwrite any policy of insurance thereon or on goods on board thereof, or with intent to injure any person that has lent or advanced, or may lend or advance, any money on such vessel on bottomry or respondentia; or

Whoever, within the United States, builds, or fits out any vessel to be cast away or destroyed, with like intent—

Shall be fined under this title or imprisoned not more than ten years, or both.

(June 25, 1948, c. 645, 62 Stat. 803; Pub.L. 103–322, Title XXXIII, § 330016(1)(L), Sept. 13, 1994, 108 Stat. 2147.)

§ 2272. Destruction of vessel by owner

Whoever, upon the high seas or on any other waters within the admiralty and maritime jurisdiction of the United States, willfully and corruptly casts away or otherwise destroys any vessel of which he is owner, in whole or in part, with intent to injure any person that may underwrite any policy of insurance thereon, or any merchant that may have goods thereon, or any other owner of such vessel, shall be imprisoned for life or for any term of years.

(June 25, 1948, c. 645, 62 Stat. 803.)

§ 2273. Destruction of vessel by nonowner

Whoever, not being an owner, upon the high seas or on any other waters within the admiralty and maritime jurisdiction of the United States, willfully and corruptly casts away or otherwise destroys any vessel of the United States to which he belongs, or willfully attempts the destruction thereof, shall be imprisoned not more than ten years.

(June 25, 1948, c. 645, 62 Stat. 804.)

§ 2274. Destruction or misuse of vessel by person in charge

Whoever, being the owner, master or person in charge or command of any private vessel, foreign or domestic, or a member of the crew or other person, within the territorial waters of the United States, willfully causes or permits the destruction or injury of such vessel or knowingly permits said vessel to be used as a place of resort for any person conspiring with another or preparing to commit any offense against the United States, or any offense in violation of the treaties of the United States or of the obligations of the United States under the law of nations, or to defraud the United States; or knowingly permits such vessels to be used in violation of the rights and obligations of the United States under the law of nations, shall be fined under this title or imprisoned not more than ten years, or both.

In case such vessels are so used, with the knowledge of the owner or master or other person in charge or command thereof, the vessel, together with her tackle, apparel, furniture, and equipment, shall be subject to seizure and forfeiture to the United States in the same manner as merchandise is forfeited for violation of the customs revenue laws.

(June 25, 1948, c. 645, 62 Stat. 804; Pub.L. 103–322, Title XXXIII, § 330016(1)(L), Sept. 13, 1994, 108 Stat. 2147.)

HISTORICAL AND STATUTORY NOTES

References in Text

The customs revenue laws, referred to in text, are classified generally to Title 19, Customs Duties.

§ 2275. Firing or tampering with vessels

Whoever sets fire to any vessel of foreign registry, or any vessel of American registry entitled to engage in commerce with foreign nations, or to any vessel of the United States, or to the cargo of the same, or tampers with the motive power of instrumentalities of navigation of such vessel, or places bombs or explosives in or upon such vessel, or does any other act to or upon such vessel while within the jurisdiction of the United States, or, if such vessel is of American registry, while she is on the high sea, with intent to injure or endanger the safety of the vessel or of her cargo, or of persons on board, whether the injury or danger is so intended to take place within the jurisdiction of the United States, or after the vessel shall have departed therefrom and whoever attempts to do so shall be fined under this title or imprisoned not more than twenty years, or both.

(June 25, 1948, c. 645, 62 Stat. 804; Pub.L. 103–322, Title XXXIII, § 330016(1)(L), Sept. 13, 1994, 108 Stat. 2147.)

§ 2276. Breaking and entering vessel

Whoever, upon the high seas or on any other waters within the admiralty and maritime jurisdiction of the

United States, and out of the jurisdiction of any particular State, breaks or enters any vessel with intent to commit any felony, or maliciously cuts, spoils, or destroys any cordage, cable, buoys, buoy rope, head fast, or other fast, fixed to the anchor or moorings belonging to any vessel, shall be fined under this title or imprisoned not more than five years, or both.
(June 25, 1948, c. 645, 62 Stat. 804; Pub.L. 103–322, Title XXXIII, § 330016(1)(H), Sept. 13, 1994, 108 Stat. 2147.)

§ 2277. Explosives or dangerous weapons aboard vessels

(a) Whoever brings, carries, or possesses any dangerous weapon, instrument, or device, or any dynamite, nitroglycerin, or other explosive article or compound on board of any vessel documented under the laws of the United States, or any vessel purchased, requisitioned, chartered, or taken over by the United States pursuant to the provisions of Act June 6, 1941, ch. 174, 55 Stat. 242, as amended, without previously obtaining the permission of the owner or the master of such vessel; or

Whoever brings, carries, or possesses any such weapon or explosive on board of any vessel in the possession and under the control of the United States or which has been seized and forfeited by the United States or upon which a guard has been placed by the United States pursuant to the provisions of section 191 of Title 50, without previously obtaining the permission of the captain of the port in which such vessel is located, shall be fined under this title or imprisoned not more than one year, or both.

(b) This section shall not apply to the personnel of the Armed Forces of the United States or to officers or employees of the United States or of a State or of a political subdivision thereof, while acting in the performance of their duties, who are authorized by law or by rules or regulations to own or possess any such weapon or explosive.
(June 25, 1948, c. 645, 62 Stat. 804; Pub.L. 103–322, Title XXXIII, § 330016(1)(H), Sept. 13, 1994, 108 Stat. 2147; Oct. 6, 2006, Pub.L. 109–304, § 17(d)(6), 120 Stat. 1707.)

HISTORICAL AND STATUTORY NOTES

References in Text

Act June 6, 1941, c. 174, 55 Stat. 242, as amended, referred to in text of subsec. (a), expired July 1, 1953. For provisions covering the subject matter of that Act, see sections 196 to 198 of Title 50, War and National Defense.

§ 2278. Explosives on vessels carrying steerage passengers

Whoever, being the master of a steamship or other vessel referred to in section 151 of Title 46, except as otherwise expressly provided by law, takes, carries, or has on board of any such vessel any nitroglycerin, dynamite, or any other explosive article or compound, or any vitriol or like acids, or gunpowder, except for the ship's use, or any article or number of articles, whether as a cargo or ballast, which, by reason of the nature or quantity or mode of storage thereof, shall, either singly or collectively, be likely to endanger the health or lives of the passengers or the safety of the vessel, shall be fined under this title or imprisoned not more than one year, or both.
(June 25, 1948, c. 645, 62 Stat. 805; Pub.L. 103–322, Title XXXIII, § 330016(1)(H), Sept. 13, 1994, 108 Stat. 2147.)

HISTORICAL AND STATUTORY NOTES

References in Text

Section 151 of Title 46, referred to in text, was repealed by Pub.L. 98–89, § 4(b), Aug. 26, 1983, 97 Stat. 600.

§ 2279. Boarding vessels before arrival

Whoever, not being in the United States service, and not being duly authorized by law for the purpose, goes on board any vessel about to arrive at the place of her destination, before her actual arrival, and before she has been completely moored, shall be fined under this title or imprisoned not more than six months, or both.

The master of such vessel may take any such person into custody, and deliver him up forthwith to any law enforcement officer, to be by him taken before any committing magistrate, to be dealt with according to law.
(June 25, 1948, c. 645, 62 Stat. 805; Pub.L. 103–322, Title XXXIII, § 330016(1)(D), Sept. 13, 1994, 108 Stat. 2146.)

§ 2280. Violence against maritime navigation

(a) Offenses.—

(1) In general.—A person who unlawfully and intentionally—

(A) seizes or exercises control over a ship by force or threat thereof or any other form of intimidation;

(B) performs an act of violence against a person on board a ship if that act is likely to endanger the safe navigation of that ship;

(C) destroys a ship or causes damage to a ship or to its cargo which is likely to endanger the safe navigation of that ship;

(D) places or causes to be placed on a ship, by any means whatsoever, a device or substance which is likely to destroy that ship, or cause damage to that ship or its cargo which endangers or is likely to endanger the safe navigation of that ship;

(E) destroys or seriously damages maritime navigational facilities or seriously interferes with their operation, if such act is likely to endanger the safe navigation of a ship;

(F) communicates information, knowing the information to be false and under circumstances in which such information may reasonably be believed, thereby endangering the safe navigation of a ship;

(G) injures or kills any person in connection with the commission or the attempted commission of any of the offenses set forth in subparagraphs (A) through (F); or

(H) attempts or conspires to do any act prohibited under subparagraphs (A) through (G),

shall be fined under this title, imprisoned not more than 20 years, or both; and if the death of any person results from conduct prohibited by this paragraph, shall be punished by death or imprisoned for any term of years or for life.

(2) Threat to navigation.—A person who threatens to do any act prohibited under paragraph (1) (B), (C) or (E), with apparent determination and will to carry the threat into execution, if the threatened act is likely to endanger the safe navigation of the ship in question, shall be fined under this title, imprisoned not more than 5 years, or both.

(b) Jurisdiction.—There is jurisdiction over the activity prohibited in subsection (a)—

(1) in the case of a covered ship, if—

(A) such activity is committed—

(i) against or on board a ship flying the flag of the United States at the time the prohibited activity is committed;

(ii) in the United States; or

(iii) by a national of the United States or by a stateless person whose habitual residence is in the United States;

(B) during the commission of such activity, a national of the United States is seized, threatened, injured or killed; or

(C) the offender is later found in the United States after such activity is committed;

(2) in the case of a ship navigating or scheduled to navigate solely within the territorial sea or internal waters of a country other than the United States, if the offender is later found in the United States after such activity is committed; and

(3) in the case of any vessel, if such activity is committed in an attempt to compel the United States to do or abstain from doing any act.

(c) Bar to prosecution.—It is a bar to Federal prosecution under subsection (a) for conduct that occurred within the United States that the conduct involved was during or in relation to a labor dispute, and such conduct is prohibited as a felony under the law of the State in which it was committed. For purposes of this section, the term "labor dispute" has the meaning set forth in section 2(c) [1] of the Norris-LaGuardia Act, as amended (29 U.S.C. 113(c)).

(d) Delivery of suspected offender.—The master of a covered ship flying the flag of the United States who has reasonable grounds to believe that there is on board that ship any person who has committed an offense under Article 3 of the Convention for the Suppression of Unlawful Acts Against the Safety of Maritime Navigation may deliver such person to the authorities of a State Party to that Convention. Before delivering such person to the authorities of another country, the master shall notify in an appropriate manner the Attorney General of the United States of the alleged offense and await instructions from the Attorney General as to what action to take. When delivering the person to a country which is a State Party to the Convention, the master shall, whenever practicable, and if possible before entering the territorial sea of such country, notify the authorities of such country of the master's intention to deliver such person and the reasons therefor. If the master delivers such person, the master shall furnish to the authorities of such country the evidence in the master's possession that pertains to the alleged offense.

(e) Definitions.—In this section—

"covered ship" means a ship that is navigating or is scheduled to navigate into, through or from waters beyond the outer limit of the territorial sea of a single country or a lateral limit of that country's territorial sea with an adjacent country.

"national of the United States" has the meaning stated in section 101(a)(22) of the Immigration and Nationality Act (8 U.S.C. 1101(a)(22)).

"territorial sea of the United States" means all waters extending seaward to 12 nautical miles from the baselines of the United States determined in accordance with international law.

"ship" means a vessel of any type whatsoever not permanently attached to the sea-bed, including dynamically supported craft, submersibles or any other floating craft, but does not include a warship, a ship owned or operated by a government when being used as a naval auxiliary or for customs or police purposes, or a ship which has been withdrawn from navigation or laid up.

"United States", when used in a geographical sense, includes the Commonwealth of Puerto Rico, the Commonwealth of the Northern Mariana Islands and all territories and possessions of the United States.

(Added Pub.L. 103–322, Title VI, § 60019(a), Sept. 13, 1994, 108 Stat. 1975, and amended Pub.L. 104–132, Title VII, §§ 722, 723(a)(1), Apr. 24, 1996, 110 Stat. 1299, 1300.)

[1] So in original. Probably should be section "13(c)".

HISTORICAL AND STATUTORY NOTES

Effective and Applicability Provisions

1994 Acts. Section 60019(c) of Pub.L. 103–322 provided that: "This section and the amendments made by this section [enacting this section and section 2281 of this title] shall take effect on the later of—

"(1) the date of the enactment of this Act [Sept. 13, 1994]; or

"(2)(A) in the case of section 2280 of title 18, United States Code [this section]; the date the Convention for the Suppression of Unlawful Acts Against the Safety of Maritime Navigation has come into force and the United States has become a party to that Convention; and

"(B) in the case of section 2281 of title 18, United States Code [section 2281 of this title], the date the Protocol for the Suppression of Unlawful Acts Against the Safety of Fixed Platforms Located on the Continental Shelf has come into force and the United States has become a party to that Protocol."

[Convention and Protocol came into force Mar. 1, 1992, and entered into force with respect to the United States Mar. 6, 1995, Treaty Doc. 101-1.]

§ 2281. Violence against maritime fixed platforms

(a) Offenses.—

(1) In general.—A person who unlawfully and intentionally—

(A) seizes or exercises control over a fixed platform by force or threat thereof or any other form of intimidation;

(B) performs an act of violence against a person on board a fixed platform if that act is likely to endanger its safety;

(C) destroys a fixed platform or causes damage to it which is likely to endanger its safety;

(D) places or causes to be placed on a fixed platform, by any means whatsoever, a device or substance which is likely to destroy that fixed platform or likely to endanger its safety;

(E) injures or kills any person in connection with the commission or the attempted commission of any of the offenses set forth in subparagraphs (A) through (D); or

(F) attempts or conspires to do anything prohibited under subparagraphs (A) through (E),

shall be fined under this title, imprisoned not more than 20 years, or both; and if death results to any person from conduct prohibited by this paragraph, shall be punished by death or imprisoned for any term of years or for life.

(2) Threat to safety.—A person who threatens to do anything prohibited under paragraph (1) (B) or (C), with apparent determination and will to carry the threat into execution, if the threatened act is likely to endanger the safety of the fixed platform, shall be fined under this title, imprisoned not more than 5 years, or both.

(b) Jurisdiction.—There is jurisdiction over the activity prohibited in subsection (a) if—

(1) such activity is committed against or on board a fixed platform—

(A) that is located on the continental shelf of the United States;

(B) that is located on the continental shelf of another country, by a national of the United States or by a stateless person whose habitual residence is in the United States; or

(C) in an attempt to compel the United States to do or abstain from doing any act;

(2) during the commission of such activity against or on board a fixed platform located on a continental shelf, a national of the United States is seized, threatened, injured or killed; or

(3) such activity is committed against or on board a fixed platform located outside the United States and beyond the continental shelf of the United States and the offender is later found in the United States.

(c) Bar to prosecution.—It is a bar to Federal prosecution under subsection (a) for conduct that occurred within the United States that the conduct involved was during or in relation to a labor dispute, and such conduct is prohibited as a felony under the law of the State in which it was committed. For purposes of this section, the term "labor dispute" has the meaning set forth in section 2(c) [1] of the Norris-LaGuardia Act, as amended (29 U.S.C. 113(c)), and the term "State" includes a State of the United States, the District of Columbia, and any commonwealth, territory, or possession of the United States.

(d) Definitions.—In this section—

"continental shelf" means the sea-bed and subsoil of the submarine areas that extend beyond a country's territorial sea to the limits provided by customary international law as reflected in Article 76 of the 1982 Convention on the Law of the Sea.

"fixed platform" means an artificial island, installation or structure permanently attached to the seabed for the purpose of exploration or exploitation of resources or for other economic purposes.

"national of the United States" has the meaning stated in section 101(a)(22) of the Immigration and Nationality Act (8 U.S.C. 1101(a)(22)).

"territorial sea of the United States" means all waters extending seaward to 12 nautical miles from the baselines of the United States determined in accordance with international law.

"United States", when used in a geographical sense, includes the Commonwealth of Puerto Rico, the Commonwealth of the Northern Mariana Islands and all territories and possessions of the United States.

(Added Pub.L. 103-322, Title VI, § 60019(a), Sept. 13, 1994, 108 Stat. 1977, and amended Pub.L. 104-132, Title VII,

§ 723(a)(1), Apr. 24, 1996, 110 Stat. 1300; Pub.L. 104–294, Title VI, § 607(p), Oct. 11, 1996, 110 Stat. 3513.)

[1] So in original. Probably should be section 13(c).

HISTORICAL AND STATUTORY NOTES

Effective and Applicability Provisions

1994 Acts. Section to take effect on the later of Sept. 13, 1994 or the date the Protocol for the Suppression of Unlawful Acts Against the Safety of Fixed Platforms Located on the Continental Shelf has come into force and the United States has become a party to that Protocol, see section 60019(c)(1), (2)(B) of Pub.L. 103–322, set out as a note under section 2280 of this title.

§ 2282A. Devices or dangerous substances in waters of the United States likely to destroy or damage ships or to interfere with maritime commerce [1]

(a) A person who knowingly places, or causes to be placed, in navigable waters of the United States, by any means, a device or dangerous substance which is likely to destroy or cause damage to a vessel or its cargo, cause interference with the safe navigation of vessels, or interference with maritime commerce (such as by damaging or destroying marine terminals, facilities, or any other marine structure or entity used in maritime commerce) with the intent of causing such destruction or damage, interference with the safe navigation of vessels, or interference with maritime commerce shall be fined under this title or imprisoned for any term of years, or for life; or both.

(b) A person who causes the death of any person by engaging in conduct prohibited under subsection (a) may be punished by death.

(c) Nothing in this section shall be construed to apply to otherwise lawfully authorized and conducted activities of the United States Government.

(d) In this section:

(1) The term "dangerous substance" means any solid, liquid, or gaseous material that has the capacity to cause damage to a vessel or its cargo, or cause interference with the safe navigation of a vessel.

(2) The term "device" means any object that, because of its physical, mechanical, structural, or chemical properties, has the capacity to cause damage to a vessel or its cargo, or cause interference with the safe navigation of a vessel.

(Added Pub.L. 109–177, Title III, § 304(a)(1), Mar. 9, 2006, 120 Stat. 235.)

[1] So in original. No section 2282 of this title has been enacted.

§ 2282B. Violence against aids to maritime navigation

Whoever intentionally destroys, seriously damages, alters, moves, or tampers with any aid to maritime navigation maintained by the Saint Lawrence Seaway Development Corporation under the authority of section 4 of the Act of May 13, 1954 (33 U.S.C. 984), by the Coast Guard pursuant to section 81 of title 14, United States Code, or lawfully maintained under authority granted by the Coast Guard pursuant to section 83 of title 14, United States Code, if such act endangers or is likely to endanger the safe navigation of a ship, shall be fined under this title or imprisoned for not more than 20 years, or both.

(Added Pub.L. 109–177, Title III, § 304(b)(1), Mar. 9, 2006, 120 Stat. 235.)

HISTORICAL AND STATUTORY NOTES

References in Text

The Act of May 13, 1954, referred to in text, is Act May 13, 1954, c. 201, 68 Stat. 93, as amended, which is classified principally to chapter 19 of Title 33, 33 U.S.C.A. § 981 et seq. Section 4 of the Act is classified to 33 U.S.C.A. § 984.

§ 2283. Transportation of explosive, biological, chemical, or radioactive or nuclear materials

(a) In general.—Whoever knowingly transports aboard any vessel within the United States and on waters subject to the jurisdiction of the United States or any vessel outside the United States and on the high seas or having United States nationality an explosive or incendiary device, biological agent, chemical weapon, or radioactive or nuclear material, knowing that any such item is intended to be used to commit an offense listed under section 2332b(g)(5)(B), shall be fined under this title or imprisoned for any term of years or for life, or both.

(b) Causing death.—Any person who causes the death of a person by engaging in conduct prohibited by subsection (a) may be punished by death.

(c) Definitions.—In this section:

(1) Biological agent.—The term "biological agent" means any biological agent, toxin, or vector (as those terms are defined in section 178).

(2) By-product material.—The term "by-product material" has the meaning given that term in section 11(e) of the Atomic Energy Act of 1954 (42 U.S.C. 2014(e)).

(3) Chemical weapon.—The term "chemical weapon" has the meaning given that term in section 229F(1).

(4) Explosive or incendiary device.—The term "explosive or incendiary device" has the meaning given the term in section 232(5) and includes explosive materials, as that term is defined in section 841(c) and explosive as defined in section 844(j).

(5) Nuclear material.—The term "nuclear material" has the meaning given that term in section 831(f)(1).

(6) **Radioactive material.**—The term "radioactive material" means—

(A) source material and special nuclear material, but does not include natural or depleted uranium;

(B) nuclear by-product material;

(C) material made radioactive by bombardment in an accelerator; or

(D) all refined isotopes of radium.

(8) [1]**Source material.**—The term "source material" has the meaning given that term in section 11(z) of the Atomic Energy Act of 1954 (42 U.S.C. 2014(z)).

(9) **Special nuclear material.**—The term "special nuclear material" has the meaning given that term in section 11(aa) of the Atomic Energy Act of 1954 (42 U.S.C. 2014(aa)).

(Added Pub.L. 109–177, Title III, § 305(a), Mar. 9, 2006, 120 Stat. 236.)

1 So in original. No subsec. (7) was enacted.

HISTORICAL AND STATUTORY NOTES

References in Text

Section 11 of the Atomic Energy Act of 1954, referred to in subsec. (c)(2), (8), (9), is Act Aug. 1, 1946, c. 724, Title I, § 11, as added Aug. 30, 1954, c. 1073, § 1, 68 Stat. 922, as amended, which is classified to 42 U.S.C.A. § 2014.

§ 2284. Transportation of terrorists

(a) **In general.**—Whoever knowingly and intentionally transports any terrorist aboard any vessel within the United States and on waters subject to the jurisdiction of the United States or any vessel outside the United States and on the high seas or having United States nationality, knowing that the transported person is a terrorist, shall be fined under this title or imprisoned for any term of years or for life, or both.

(b) **Defined term.**—In this section, the term "terrorist" means any person who intends to commit, or is avoiding apprehension after having committed, an offense listed under section 2332b(g)(5)(B).

(Added Pub.L. 109–177, Title III, § 305(a), Mar. 9, 2006, 120 Stat. 237.)

HISTORICAL AND STATUTORY NOTES

References in Text

Section 101(a)(22) of the Immigration and Nationality Act, referred to in Subsec. (a)(2)(A), is Act June 27, 1952, c. 477, Title I, § 101(a)(22), 66 Stat. 167, as amended, which is classified to 8 U.S.C.A. § 1101(a)(22).

Section 2 of the Maritime Drug Law Enforcement Act, referred to in subsec. (a)(2)(C), probably means section 3 of the Maritime Drug Law Enforcement Act, Pub.L. 96–350, § 3, Sept. 15, 1980, 94 Stat. 1160, as amended, which defines the term "vessel of the United States" and is classified to 46 App. U.S.C.A. § 1903.

CHAPTER 111A—DESTRUCTION OF, OR INTERFERENCE WITH, VESSELS OR MARITIME FACILITIES

1 Editorially supplied. Section was enacted without corresponding amendment to section analysis.

§ 2290. Jurisdiction and scope

(a) **Jurisdiction.**—There is jurisdiction, including extraterritorial jurisdiction, over an offense under this chapter if the prohibited activity takes place—

(1) within the United States and within waters subject to the jurisdiction of the United States; or

(2) outside United States and—

(A) an offender or a victim is a national of the United States (as that term is defined under section 101(a)(22) of the Immigration and Nationality Act (8 U.S.C. 1101(a)(22));

(B) the activity involves a vessel in which a national of the United States was on board; or

(C) the activity involves a vessel of the United States (as that term is defined under section 2 of the Maritime Drug Law Enforcement Act (46 U.S.C. App. 1903).

(b) **Scope.**—Nothing in this chapter shall apply to otherwise lawful activities carried out by or at the direction of the United States Government.

(Added Pub.L. 109–177, Title III, § 306(a), Mar. 9, 2006, 120 Stat. 237.)

§ 2291. Destruction of vessel or maritime facility

(a) **Offense.**—Whoever knowingly—

(1) sets fire to, damages, destroys, disables, or wrecks any vessel;

(2) places or causes to be placed a destructive device, as defined in section 921(a)(4), destructive substance, as defined in section 31(a)(3), or an explosive, as defined in section 844(j) in, upon, or near, or otherwise makes or causes to be made unworkable or unusable or hazardous to work or use, any vessel, or any part or other materials used or intended to be used in connection with the operation of a vessel;

(3) sets fire to, damages, destroys, or disables or places a destructive device or substance in, upon, or near, any maritime facility, including any aid to

navigation, lock, canal, or vessel traffic service facility or equipment;

(4) interferes by force or violence with the operation of any maritime facility, including any aid to navigation, lock, canal, or vessel traffic service facility or equipment, if such action is likely to endanger the safety of any vessel in navigation;

(5) sets fire to, damages, destroys, or disables or places a destructive device or substance in, upon, or near, any appliance, structure, property, machine, or apparatus, or any facility or other material used, or intended to be used, in connection with the operation, maintenance, loading, unloading, or storage of any vessel or any passenger or cargo carried or intended to be carried on any vessel;

(6) performs an act of violence against or incapacitates any individual on any vessel, if such act of violence or incapacitation is likely to endanger the safety of the vessel or those on board;

(7) performs an act of violence against a person that causes or is likely to cause serious bodily injury, as defined in section 1365(h)(3), in, upon, or near, any appliance, structure, property, machine, or apparatus, or any facility or other material used, or intended to be used, in connection with the operation, maintenance, loading, unloading, or storage of any vessel or any passenger or cargo carried or intended to be carried on any vessel;

(8) communicates information, knowing the information to be false and under circumstances in which such information may reasonably be believed, thereby endangering the safety of any vessel in navigation; or

(9) attempts or conspires to do anything prohibited under paragraphs (1) through (8),

shall be fined under this title or imprisoned not more than 20 years, or both.

(b) Limitation.—Subsection (a) shall not apply to any person that is engaging in otherwise lawful activity, such as normal repair and salvage activities, and the transportation of hazardous materials regulated and allowed to be transported under chapter 51 of title 49.

(c) Penalty.—Whoever is fined or imprisoned under subsection (a) as a result of an act involving a vessel that, at the time of the violation, carried high-level radioactive waste (as that term is defined in section 2(12) of the Nuclear Waste Policy Act of 1982 (42 U.S.C. 10101(12)) or spent nuclear fuel (as that term is defined in section 2(23) of the Nuclear Waste Policy Act of 1982 (42 U.S.C. 10101(23)), shall be fined under this title, imprisoned for a term up to life, or both.

(d) Penalty when death results.—Whoever is convicted of any crime prohibited by subsection (a) and intended to cause death by the prohibited conduct, if the conduct resulted in the death of any person, shall be subject also to the death penalty or to a term of imprisonment for a period up to life.

(e) Threats.—Whoever knowingly and intentionally imparts or conveys any threat to do an act which would violate this chapter, with an apparent determination and will to carry the threat into execution, shall be fined under this title or imprisoned not more than 5 years, or both, and is liable for all costs incurred as a result of such threat.

(Added Pub.L. 109–177, Title III, § 306(a), Mar. 9, 2006, 120 Stat. 237.)

HISTORICAL AND STATUTORY NOTES

References in Text

Chapter 51 of title 49, referred to in subsec. (b), is Transportation of Hazardous Material, 49 U.S.C.A. § 5101 et seq.

Section 2 of the Nuclear Waste Policy Act of 1982, referred to in subsec. (c), is Pub.L. 97–425, § 2, Jan. 7, 1983, 96 Stat. 2202, as amended, which is classified to 42 U.S.C.A. § 10101.

§ 2292. Imparting or conveying false information

(a) In general.—Whoever imparts or conveys or causes to be imparted or conveyed false information, knowing the information to be false, concerning an attempt or alleged attempt being made or to be made, to do any act that would be a crime prohibited by this chapter or by chapter 111 of this title, shall be subject to a civil penalty of not more than $5,000, which shall be recoverable in a civil action brought in the name of the United States.

(b) Malicious conduct.—Whoever knowingly, intentionally, maliciously, or with reckless disregard for the safety of human life, imparts or conveys or causes to be imparted or conveyed false information, knowing the information to be false, concerning an attempt or alleged attempt to do any act which would be a crime prohibited by this chapter or by chapter 111 of this title, shall be fined under this title or imprisoned not more than 5 years.

(c) Jurisdiction.—

(1) **In general.**—Except as provided under paragraph (2), section 2290(a) shall not apply to any offense under this section.

(2) **Jurisdiction.**—Jurisdiction over an offense under this section shall be determined in accordance with the provisions applicable to the crime prohibited by this chapter, or by chapter 111 of this title, to which the imparted or conveyed false information relates, as applicable.

(Added Pub.L. 109–177, Title III, § 306(a), Mar. 9, 2006, 120 Stat. 239.)

HISTORICAL AND STATUTORY NOTES

References in Text

Chapter 111 of this title, referred to in text, is Shipping, 18 U.S.C.A. § 2271 et seq.

§ 2293. Bar to prosecution [1]

(a) In general.—It is a bar to prosecution under this chapter if—

(1) the conduct in question occurred within the United States in relation to a labor dispute, and such conduct is prohibited as a felony under the law of the State in which it was committed; or

(2) such conduct is prohibited as a misdemeanor, and not as a felony, under the law of the State in which it was committed.

(b) Definitions.—In this section:

(1) Labor dispute.—The term "labor dispute" has the same meaning given that term in section 13(c) of the Act to amend the Judicial Code and to define and limit the jurisdiction of courts sitting in equity, and for other purposes (29 U.S.C. 113(c), commonly known as the Norris–LaGuardia Act).

(2) State.—The term "State" means a State of the United States, the District of Columbia, and any commonwealth, territory, or possession of the United States.

(Added Pub.L. 109–177, Title III, § 306(a), Mar. 9, 2006, 120 Stat. 239.)

[1] Section was enacted without corresponding amendment to section analysis.

HISTORICAL AND STATUTORY NOTES

References in Text

Section 13(c) of the Act to amend the Judicial Code, referred to in subsec. (b)(1), is section 13(c) of the Act of March 23, 1932, commonly known as the Norris-LaGuardia Act, Act Mar. 23, 1932, c. 90, § 13, 47 Stat. 73, as amended, which is classified to 29 U.S.C.A. § 113(c).

CHAPTER 113—STOLEN PROPERTY

[1] So in original. Does not conform to section catchline.

§ 2311. Definitions

As used in this chapter:

"Aircraft" means any contrivance now known or hereafter invented, used, or designed for navigation of or for flight in the air;

"Cattle" means one or more bulls, steers, oxen, cows, heifers, or calves, or the carcass or carcasses thereof;

"Livestock" means any domestic animals raised for home use, consumption, or profit, such as horses, pigs, llamas, goats, fowl, sheep, buffalo, and cattle, or the carcasses thereof;

"Money" means the legal tender of the United States or of any foreign country, or any counterfeit thereof;

"Motor vehicle" includes an automobile, automobile truck, automobile wagon, motorcycle, or any other self-propelled vehicle designed for running on land but not on rails;

"Securities" includes any note, stock certificate, bond, debenture, check, draft, warrant, traveler's check, letter of credit, warehouse receipt, negotiable bill of lading, evidence of indebtedness, certificate of interest or participation in any profit-sharing agreement, collateral-trust certificate, preorganization certificate or subscription, transferable share, investment contract, voting-trust certificate; valid or blank motor vehicle title; certificate of interest in property, tangible or intangible; instrument or document or writing evidencing ownership of goods, wares, and merchandise, or transferring or assigning any right, title, or interest in or to goods, wares, and merchandise; or, in general, any instrument commonly known as a "security", or any certificate of interest or participation in, temporary or interim certificate for, receipt for, warrant, or right to subscribe to or purchase any of the foregoing, or any forged, counterfeited, or spurious representation of any of the foregoing;

"Tax stamp" includes any tax stamp, tax token, tax meter imprint, or any other form of evidence of an obligation running to a State, or evidence of the discharge thereof;

"Value" means the face, par, or market value, whichever is the greatest, and the aggregate value of all goods, wares, and merchandise, securities, and money referred to in a single indictment shall constitute the value thereof.

"Vessel" means any watercraft or other contrivance used or designed for transportation or navigation on, under, or immediately above, water.

(June 25, 1948, c. 645, 62 Stat. 805; Oct. 4, 1961, Pub.L. 87–371, 75 Stat. 802; Oct. 25, 1984, Pub.L. 98–547, Title II, § 202, 98 Stat. 2770; Sept. 13, 1994, Pub.L. 103–322, Title XXXII, § 320912, 108 Stat. 2128; Oct. 11, 1996, Pub.L. 104–294, Title VI, § 604(b)(20), 110 Stat. 3507; Nov. 2, 2002, Pub.L. 107–273, Div. B, Title IV, § 4002(b)(8), 116 Stat. 1808; Mar. 9, 2006, Pub.L. 109–177, Title III, § 307(b)(1), 120 Stat. 240.)

HISTORICAL AND STATUTORY NOTES

Effective and Applicability Provisions

1996 Acts. Amendment by section 604 of Pub.L. 104–294 effective Sept. 13, 1994, see section 604(d) of Pub.L. 104–294, set out as a note under section 13 of this title.

Short Title

2004 Acts. Pub.L. 108–482, Title I, § 101, Dec. 23, 2004, 118 Stat. 3912, provided that: "This title [amending 18 U.S.C.A. § 2318 and enacting provisions set out as a note under 18 U.S.C.A. § 2318] may be cited as the 'Anti-counterfeiting Amendments Act of 2004'."

1997 Amendments. Pub.L. 105–147, § 1, Dec. 16, 1997, 111 Stat. 2678, provided that: "This Act [amending sections 101, 506, and 507 of Title 17, sections 2319, 2319A, and 2320 of this title, and section 1498 of Title 28, and enacting provisions set out as a note under section 994 of Title 28] may be cited as the 'No Electronic Theft (NET) Act'."

1996 Amendments. Pub.L. 104–153, § 1, July 2, 1996, 110 Stat. 1386, provided that: "This Act [amending sections 1961, 2318, and 2320 of this title, sections 1116 and 1117 of Title 15, Commerce and Trade, section 603 of Title 17, Copyrights, sections 1431, 1484, and 1526 of Title 19, Customs Duties, and section 80302 of Title 49, Transportation, and enacting provisions set out as notes under this section and section 1431 of Title 19] may be cited as the 'Anticounterfeiting Consumer Protection Act of 1996'."

1992 Amendments. Pub.L. 102–519, § 1, Oct. 25, 1992, 106 Stat. 3384, provided that: "This Act [enacting sections 2026a to 2026c and 2041 to 2044 of this title, sections 2119 and 2322 of Title 18, Crimes and Criminal Procedure, sections 1646b and 1646c of Title 19, Customs Duties, sections 3750a to 3750d of Title 42, The Public Health and Welfare, amending sections 2021 to 2023, 2025, 2027 and 2034 of this title, sections 553, 981, 2312 and 2313 of Title 18, and enacting provisions set out as notes under sections 2026a and 2026b of this title, section 2119 of Title 18 and section 1646b of Title 19] may be cited as the 'Anti Car Theft Act of 1992'."

1984 Amendments. Section 1(a) of Pub.L. 98–547 provided that: "This Act [enacting sections 2021 to 2034 of this title, sections 511 to 513, 553, and 2320 [now 2321] of Title 18, Crimes and Criminal Procedure, and section 1627 of Title 19, Customs Duties, amending section 1901 of this title and sections 1961, 2311, and 2313 of Title 18, and enacting provisions set out as notes under sections 1901 and 2021 of this title] may be cited as the 'Motor Vehicle Theft Law Enforcement Act of 1984'."

Pub.L. 98–473, Title II, § 1501, Oct. 12, 1984, 98 Stat. 1501, provided that: "This chapter [enacting section 2320 of this title and amending sections 1116, 1117, and 1118 of Title 15, Commerce and Trade] may be cited as the 'Trademark Counterfeiting Act of 1984'."

1982 Amendments. Pub.L. 97–180, § 1, May 24, 1982, 96 Stat. 91, provided: "That this Act [enacting section 2319 of this title and amending section 2318 of this title and section 506 of Title 17, Copyrights] may be cited as the 'Piracy and Counterfeiting Amendments Act of 1982'."

Counterfeiting of Trademarked and Copyrighted Merchandise; Congressional Statement of Findings

Pub.L. 104–153, § 2, July 2, 1996, 110 Stat. 1386, provided that: "The counterfeiting of trademarked and copyrighted merchandise—

"(1) has been connected with organized crime;

"(2) deprives legitimate trademark and copyright owners of substantial revenues and consumer goodwill;

"(3) poses health and safety threats to United States consumers;

"(4) eliminates United States jobs; and

"(5) is a multibillion-dollar drain on the United States economy."

§ 2312. Transportation of stolen vehicles

Whoever transports in interstate or foreign commerce a motor vehicle, vessel, or aircraft, knowing the same to have been stolen, shall be fined under this title or imprisoned not more than 10 years, or both.

(June 25, 1948, c. 645, 62 Stat. 806; Oct. 25, 1992, Pub.L. 102–519, Title I, § 103, 106 Stat. 3385; Mar. 9, 2006, Pub.L. 109–177, Title III, § 307(b)(2)(A), 120 Stat. 240.)

§ 2313. Sale or receipt of stolen vehicles

(a) Whoever receives, possesses, conceals, stores, barters, sells, or disposes of any motor vehicle, vessel, or aircraft, which has crossed a State or United States boundary after being stolen, knowing the same to have been stolen, shall be fined under this title or imprisoned not more than 10 years, or both.

(b) For purposes of this section, the term "State" includes a State of the United States, the District of Columbia, and any commonwealth, territory, or possession of the United States.

(June 25, 1948, c. 645, 62 Stat. 806; Oct. 25, 1984, Pub.L. 98–547, Title II, § 203, 98 Stat. 2770; Nov. 29, 1990, Pub.L. 101–647, Title XII, § 1205(*l*)(1), (2), 104 Stat. 4831; Oct. 25,

1992, Pub.L. 102–519, Title I, § 103, 106 Stat. 3385; Mar. 9, 2006, Pub.L. 109–177, Title III, § 307(b)(2)(B), 120 Stat. 240.)

§ 2314. Transportation of stolen goods, securities, moneys, fraudulent State tax stamps, or articles used in counterfeiting

Whoever transports, transmits, or transfers in interstate or foreign commerce any goods, wares, merchandise, securities or money, of the value of $5,000 or more, knowing the same to have been stolen, converted or taken by fraud; or

Whoever, having devised or intending to devise any scheme or artifice to defraud, or for obtaining money or property by means of false or fraudulent pretenses, representations, or promises, transports or causes to be transported, or induces any person or persons to travel in, or to be transported in interstate or foreign commerce in the execution or concealment of a scheme or artifice to defraud that person or those persons of money or property having a value of $5,000 or more; or

Whoever, with unlawful or fraudulent intent, transports in interstate or foreign commerce any falsely made, forged, altered, or counterfeited securities or tax stamps, knowing the same to have been falsely made, forged, altered, or counterfeited; or

Whoever, with unlawful or fraudulent intent, transports in interstate or foreign commerce any traveler's check bearing a forged countersignature; or

Whoever, with unlawful or fraudulent intent, transports in interstate or foreign commerce, any tool, implement, or thing used or fitted to be used in falsely making, forging, altering, or counterfeiting any security or tax stamps, or any part thereof—

Shall be fined under this title or imprisoned not more than ten years, or both.

This section shall not apply to any falsely made, forged, altered, counterfeited or spurious representation of an obligation or other security of the United States, or of an obligation, bond, certificate, security, treasury note, bill, promise to pay or bank note issued by any foreign government. This section also shall not apply to any falsely made, forged, altered, counterfeited, or spurious representation of any bank note or bill issued by a bank or corporation of any foreign country which is intended by the laws or usage of such country to circulate as money.

(June 25, 1948, c. 645, 62 Stat. 806; May 24, 1949, c. 139, § 45, 63 Stat. 96; July 9, 1956, c. 519, 70 Stat. 507; Oct. 4, 1961, Pub.L. 87–371, § 2, 75 Stat. 802; Sept. 28, 1968, Pub.L. 90–535, 82 Stat. 885; Nov. 18, 1988, Pub.L. 100–690, Title VII, §§ 7057, 7080, 102 Stat. 4402, 4406; Nov. 29, 1990, Pub.L. 101–647, Title XII, § 1208, 104 Stat. 4832; Sept. 13, 1994, Pub.L. 103–322, Title XXXIII, § 330016(1)(K), (L), 108 Stat. 2147.)

§ 2315. Sale or receipt of stolen goods, securities, moneys, or fraudulent State tax stamps

Whoever receives, possesses, conceals, stores, barters, sells, or disposes of any goods, wares, or merchandise, securities, or money of the value of $5,000 or more, or pledges or accepts as security for a loan any goods, wares, or merchandise, or securities, of the value of $500 or more, which have crossed a State or United States boundary after being stolen, unlawfully converted, or taken, knowing the same to have been stolen, unlawfully converted, or taken; or

Whoever receives, possesses, conceals, stores, barters, sells, or disposes of any falsely made, forged, altered, or counterfeited securities or tax stamps, or pledges or accepts as security for a loan any falsely made, forged, altered, or counterfeited securities or tax stamps, moving as, or which are a part of, or which constitute interstate or foreign commerce, knowing the same to have been so falsely made, forged, altered, or counterfeited; or

Whoever receives in interstate or foreign commerce, or conceals, stores, barters, sells, or disposes of, any tool, implement, or thing used or intended to be used in falsely making, forging, altering, or counterfeiting any security or tax stamp, or any part thereof, moving as, or which is a part of, or which constitutes interstate or foreign commerce, knowing that the same is fitted to be used, or has been used, in falsely making, forging, altering, or counterfeiting any security or tax stamp, or any part thereof—

Shall be fined under this title or imprisoned not more than ten years, or both.

This section shall not apply to any falsely made, forged, altered, counterfeited, or spurious representation of an obligation or other security of the United States or of an obligation, bond, certificate, security, treasury note, bill, promise to pay, or bank note, issued by any foreign government. This section also shall not apply to any falsely made, forged, altered, counterfeited, or spurious representation of any bank note or bill issued by a bank or corporation of any foreign country which is intended by the laws or usage of such country to circulate as money.

For purposes of this section, the term "State" includes a State of the United States, the District of Columbia, and any commonwealth, territory, or possession of the United States.

(June 25, 1948, c. 645, 62 Stat. 806; Oct. 4, 1961, Pub.L. 87–371, § 3, 75 Stat. 802; Nov. 10, 1986, Pub.L. 99–646, § 76, 100 Stat. 3618; Nov. 18, 1988, Pub.L. 100–690, Title VII, §§ 7048, 7057(b), 102 Stat. 4401, 4402; Nov. 29, 1990, Pub.L. 101–647, Title XII, § 1205(m), 104 Stat. 4831; Sept. 13, 1994, Pub.L. 103–322, Title XXXIII, § 330016(1)(L), 108 Stat. 2147.)

§ 2316. Transportation of livestock

Whoever transports in interstate or foreign commerce any livestock, knowing the same to have been stolen, shall be fined under this title or imprisoned not more than five years, or both.

(June 25, 1948, c. 645, 62 Stat. 807; Oct. 12, 1984, Pub.L. 98–473, Title II, § 1113, 98 Stat. 2149; Sept. 13, 1994, Pub.L. 103–322, Title XXXIII, § 330016(1)(K), 108 Stat. 2147.)

§ 2317. Sale or receipt of livestock

Whoever receives, conceals, stores, barters, buys, sells, or disposes of any livestock, moving in or constituting a part of interstate or foreign commerce, knowing the same to have been stolen, shall be fined under this title or imprisoned not more than five years, or both.

(June 25, 1948, c. 645, 62 Stat. 807; Oct. 12, 1984, Pub.L. 98–473, Title II, § 1114, 98 Stat. 2149; Sept. 13, 1994, Pub.L. 103–322, Title XXXIII, § 330016(1)(K), 108 Stat. 2147.)

§ 2318. Trafficking in counterfeit labels, illicit labels, or counterfeit documentation or packaging

(a) Whoever, in any of the circumstances described in subsection (c), knowingly traffics in—

(1) a counterfeit label or illicit label affixed to, enclosing, or accompanying, or designed to be affixed to, enclose, or accompany—

(A) a phonorecord;

(B) a copy of a computer program;

(C) a copy of a motion picture or other audiovisual work;

(D) a copy of a literary work;

(E) a copy of a pictorial, graphic, or sculptural work;

(F) a work of visual art; or

(G) documentation or packaging; or

(2) counterfeit documentation or packaging,

shall be fined under this title or imprisoned for not more than 5 years, or both.

(b) As used in this section—

(1) the term "counterfeit label" means an identifying label or container that appears to be genuine, but is not;

(2) the term "traffic" has the same meaning as in section 2320(e) of this title;

(3) the terms "copy", "phonorecord", "motion picture", "computer program", and "audiovisual work", "literary work", "pictorial, graphic, or sculptural work", "sound recording", "work of visual art", and "copyright owner" have, respectively, the meanings given those terms in section 101 (relating to definitions) of title 17;

(4) the term "illicit label" means a genuine certificate, licensing document, registration card, or similar labeling component—

(A) that is used by the copyright owner to verify that a phonorecord, a copy of a computer program, a copy of a motion picture or other audiovisual work, a copy of a literary work, a copy of a pictorial, graphic, or sculptural work, a work of visual art, or documentation or packaging is not counterfeit or infringing of any copyright; and

(B) that is, without the authorization of the copyright owner—

(i) distributed or intended for distribution not in connection with the copy, phonorecord, or work of visual art to which such labeling component was intended to be affixed by the respective copyright owner; or

(ii) in connection with a genuine certificate or licensing document, knowingly falsified in order to designate a higher number of licensed users or copies than authorized by the copyright owner, unless that certificate or document is used by the copyright owner solely for the purpose of monitoring or tracking the copyright owner's distribution channel and not for the purpose of verifying that a copy or phonorecord is noninfringing;

(5) the term "documentation or packaging" means documentation or packaging, in physical form, for a phonorecord, copy of a computer program, copy of a motion picture or other audiovisual work, copy of a literary work, copy of a pictorial, graphic, or sculptural work, or work of visual art; and

(6) the term "counterfeit documentation or packaging" means documentation or packaging that appears to be genuine, but is not.

(c) The circumstances referred to in subsection (a) of this section are—

(1) the offense is committed within the special maritime and territorial jurisdiction of the United States; or within the special aircraft jurisdiction of the United States (as defined in section 46501 of title 49);

(2) the mail or a facility of interstate or foreign commerce is used or intended to be used in the commission of the offense;

(3) the counterfeit label or illicit label is affixed to, encloses, or accompanies, or is designed to be affixed to, enclose, or accompany—

(A) a phonorecord of a copyrighted sound recording or copyrighted musical work;

(B) a copy of a copyrighted computer program;

(C) a copy of a copyrighted motion picture or other audiovisual work;

(D) a copy of a literary work;

(E) a copy of a pictorial, graphic, or sculptural work;

(F) a work of visual art; or

(G) copyrighted documentation or packaging; or

(4) the counterfeited documentation or packaging is copyrighted.

(d) When any person is convicted of any violation of subsection (a), the court in its judgment of conviction shall in addition to the penalty therein prescribed, order the forfeiture and destruction or other disposition of all counterfeit labels or illicit labels and all articles to which counterfeit labels or illicit labels have been affixed or which were intended to have had such labels affixed, and of any equipment, device, or material used to manufacture, reproduce, or assemble the counterfeit labels or illicit labels.

(e) Except to the extent they are inconsistent with the provisions of this title, all provisions of section 509, title 17, United States Code, are applicable to violations of subsection (a).

(f) Civil remedies.—

(1) In general.—Any copyright owner who is injured, or is threatened with injury, by a violation of subsection (a) may bring a civil action in an appropriate United States district court.

(2) Discretion of court.—In any action brought under paragraph (1), the court—

(A) may grant 1 or more temporary or permanent injunctions on such terms as the court determines to be reasonable to prevent or restrain a violation of subsection (a);

(B) at any time while the action is pending, may order the impounding, on such terms as the court determines to be reasonable, of any article that is in the custody or control of the alleged violator and that the court has reasonable cause to believe was involved in a violation of subsection (a); and

(C) may award to the injured party—

(i) reasonable attorney fees and costs; and

(ii)(I) actual damages and any additional profits of the violator, as provided in paragraph (3); or

(II) statutory damages, as provided in paragraph (4).

(3) Actual damages and profits.—

(A) In general.—The injured party is entitled to recover—

(i) the actual damages suffered by the injured party as a result of a violation of subsection (a), as provided in subparagraph (B) of this paragraph; and

(ii) any profits of the violator that are attributable to a violation of subsection (a) and are not taken into account in computing the actual damages.

(B) Calculation of damages.—The court shall calculate actual damages by multiplying—

(i) the value of the phonorecords, copies, or works of visual art which are, or are intended to be, affixed with, enclosed in, or accompanied by any counterfeit labels, illicit labels, or counterfeit documentation or packaging, by

(ii) the number of phonorecords, copies, or works of visual art which are, or are intended to be, affixed with, enclosed in, or accompanied by any counterfeit labels, illicit labels, or counterfeit documentation or packaging.

(C) Definition.—For purposes of this paragraph, the "value" of a phonorecord, copy, or work of visual art is—

(i) in the case of a copyrighted sound recording or copyrighted musical work, the retail value of an authorized phonorecord of that sound recording or musical work;

(ii) in the case of a copyrighted computer program, the retail value of an authorized copy of that computer program;

(iii) in the case of a copyrighted motion picture or other audiovisual work, the retail value of an authorized copy of that motion picture or audiovisual work;

(iv) in the case of a copyrighted literary work, the retail value of an authorized copy of that literary work;

(v) in the case of a pictorial, graphic, or sculptural work, the retail value of an authorized copy of that work; and

(vi) in the case of a work of visual art, the retail value of that work.

(4) Statutory damages.—The injured party may elect, at any time before final judgment is rendered, to recover, instead of actual damages and profits, an award of statutory damages for each violation of subsection (a) in a sum of not less than $2,500 or more than $25,000, as the court considers appropriate.

(5) Subsequent violation.—The court may increase an award of damages under this subsection by 3 times the amount that would otherwise be awarded, as the court considers appropriate, if the court finds that a person has subsequently violated subsection (a) within 3 years after a final judgment was entered against that person for a violation of that subsection.

(6) Limitation on actions.—A civil action may not be commenced under section[1] unless it is commenced within 3 years after the date on which the claimant discovers the violation of subsection (a).

(Added Pub.L. 87–773, § 1, Oct. 9, 1962, 76 Stat. 775, and amended Pub.L. 93–573, Title I, § 103, Dec. 31, 1974, 88 Stat.

1873; Pub.L. 94–553, Title I, § 111, Oct. 19, 1976, 90 Stat. 2600; Pub.L. 97–180, § 2, May 24, 1982, 96 Stat. 91; Pub.L. 101–647, Title XXXV, § 3567, Nov. 29, 1990, 104 Stat. 4928; Pub.L. 103–272, § 5(e)(10), July 5, 1994, 108 Stat. 1374; Pub.L. 103–322, Title XXXIII, § 330016(1)(U), Sept. 13, 1994, 108 Stat. 2148; Pub.L. 104–153, § 4(a), (b)(1), July 2, 1996, 110 Stat. 1386, 1387; Pub.L. 108–482, Title I, § 102(a), (b), Dec. 23, 2004, 118 Stat. 3912, 3914; Pub.L. 109–181, § 2(c)(2), Mar. 16, 2006, 120 Stat. 288.)

[1] So in original. Probably should be "this subsection".

HISTORICAL AND STATUTORY NOTES

Effective and Applicability Provisions

1976 Acts. Amendment by Pub.L. 94–553 effective Jan. 1, 1978, see section 102 of Pub.L. 94–553, set out as a note preceding section 101 of Title 17, Copyrights.

Other Rights Not Affected

Pub.L. 108–482, Title I, § 103, Dec. 23, 2004, 118 Stat. 3915, provided that:

"(a) Chapters 5 and 12 of title 17; electronic transmissions.—The amendments made by this title [Anti-counterfeiting Amendments Act of 2004, Pub.L. 108–482, Title I, §§ 101 to 103, Dec. 23, 2004, 118 Stat. 3912, which amended this section]

"(1) shall not enlarge, diminish, or otherwise affect any liability or limitations on liability under sections 512, 1201 or 1202 of title 17, United States Code; and

"(2) Shall not be construed to apply—

"(A) in any case, to the electronic transmission of a genuine certificate, licensing document, registration card, similar labeling component, or documentation or packaging described in paragraph (4) or (5) of section 2318(b) of title 18, United States Code, as amended by this title; and

"(B) in the case of a civil action under section 2318(f) of title 18, United States Code, to the electronic transmission of a counterfeit label or counterfeit documentation or packaging defined in paragraph (1) or (6) of section 2318(b) of title 18, United States Code.

"(b) Fair use.—The amendments made by this title [Anti-counterfeiting Amendments Act of 2004, Pub.L. 108–482, Title I, §§ 101 to 103, Dec. 23, 2004, 118 Stat. 3912, which amended this section] shall not affect the fair use, under section 107 of title 17, United States Code, of a genuine certificate, licensing document, registration card, similar labeling component, or documentation or packaging described in paragraph (4) or (5) of section 2318(b) of title 18, United States Code [subsec. (b) of this section], as amended by this title."

§ 2319. Criminal infringement of a copyright

(a) Any person who violates section 506(a) (relating to criminal offenses) of title 17 shall be punished as provided in subsections (b), (c), and (d) and such penalties shall be in addition to any other provisions of title 17 or any other law.

(b) Any person who commits an offense under section 506(a)(1)(A) of title 17—

(1) shall be imprisoned not more than 5 years, or fined in the amount set forth in this title, or both, if the offense consists of the reproduction or distribution, including by electronic means, during any 180–day period, of at least 10 copies or phonorecords, of 1 or more copyrighted works, which have a total retail value of more than $2,500;

(2) shall be imprisoned not more than 10 years, or fined in the amount set forth in this title, or both, if the offense is a second or subsequent offense under paragraph (1); and

(3) shall be imprisoned not more than 1 year, or fined in the amount set forth in this title, or both, in any other case.

(c) Any person who commits an offense under section 506(a)(1)(B) of title 17—

(1) shall be imprisoned not more than 3 years, or fined in the amount set forth in this title, or both, if the offense consists of the reproduction or distribution of 10 or more copies or phonorecords of 1 or more copyrighted works, which have a total retail value of $2,500 or more;

(2) shall be imprisoned not more than 6 years, or fined in the amount set forth in this title, or both, if the offense is a second or subsequent offense under paragraph (1); and

(3) shall be imprisoned not more than 1 year, or fined in the amount set forth in this title, or both, if the offense consists of the reproduction or distribution of 1 or more copies or phonorecords of 1 or more copyrighted works, which have a total retail value of more than $1,000.

(d) Any person who commits an offense under section 506(a)(1)(C) of title 17—

(1) shall be imprisoned not more than 3 years, fined under this title, or both;

(2) shall be imprisoned not more than 5 years, fined under this title, or both, if the offense was committed for purposes of commercial advantage or private financial gain;

(3) shall be imprisoned not more than 6 years, fined under this title, or both, if the offense is a second or subsequent offense; and

(4) shall be imprisoned not more than 10 years, fined under this title, or both, if the offense is a second or subsequent offense under paragraph (2).

(e)(1) During preparation of the presentence report pursuant to Rule 32(c) of the Federal Rules of Criminal Procedure, victims of the offense shall be permitted to submit, and the probation officer shall receive, a victim impact statement that identifies the victim of the offense and the extent and scope of the injury and loss suffered by the victim, including the estimated economic impact of the offense on that victim.

(2) Persons permitted to submit victim impact statements shall include—

(A) producers and sellers of legitimate works affected by conduct involved in the offense;

(B) holders of intellectual property rights in such works; and

(C) the legal representatives of such producers, sellers, and holders.

(f) As used in this section—

(1) the terms "phonorecord" and "copies" have, respectively, the meanings set forth in section 101 (relating to definitions) of title 17;

(2) the terms "reproduction" and "distribution" refer to the exclusive rights of a copyright owner under clauses (1) and (3) respectively of section 106 (relating to exclusive rights in copyrighted works), as limited by sections 107 through 122, of title 17;

(3) the term "financial gain" has the meaning given the term in section 101 of title 17; and

(4) the term "work being prepared for commercial distribution" has the meaning given the term in section 506(a) of title 17.

(Added Pub.L. 97–180, § 3, May 24, 1982, 96 Stat. 92, and amended Pub.L. 102–561, Oct. 28, 1992, 106 Stat. 4233; Pub.L. 105–80, § 12(b)(2), Nov. 13, 1997, 111 Stat. 1536; Pub.L. 105–147, §§ 2(d), Dec. 16, 1997, 111 Stat. 2678; Pub.L. 107–273, Div. C, Title III, § 13211(a), Nov. 2, 2002, 116 Stat. 1910; Pub.L. 109–9, Title I, § 103(b), Apr. 27, 2005, 119 Stat. 220.)

HISTORICAL AND STATUTORY NOTES

Effective and Applicability Provisions

1997 Acts. Amendments by Pub.L. 105–80 effective Nov. 13, 1997, see section 13 of Pub.L. 105–80, set out as a note under section 119 of this title.

§ 2319A. Unauthorized fixation of and trafficking in sound recordings and music videos of live musical performances

(a) Offense.—Whoever, without the consent of the performer or performers involved, knowingly and for purposes of commercial advantage or private financial gain—

(1) fixes the sounds or sounds and images of a live musical performance in a copy or phonorecord, or reproduces copies or phonorecords of such a performance from an unauthorized fixation;

(2) transmits or otherwise communicates to the public the sounds or sounds and images of a live musical performance; or

(3) distributes or offers to distribute, sells or offers to sell, rents or offers to rent, or traffics in any copy or phonorecord fixed as described in paragraph (1), regardless of whether the fixations occurred in the United States;

shall be imprisoned for not more than 5 years or fined in the amount set forth in this title, or both, or if the offense is a second or subsequent offense, shall be imprisoned for not more than 10 years or fined in the amount set forth in this title, or both.

(b) Forfeiture and destruction.—When a person is convicted of a violation of subsection (a), the court shall order the forfeiture and destruction of any copies or phonorecords created in violation thereof, as well as any plates, molds, matrices, masters, tapes, and film negatives by means of which such copies or phonorecords may be made. The court may also, in its discretion, order the forfeiture and destruction of any other equipment by means of which such copies or phonorecords may be reproduced, taking into account the nature, scope, and proportionality of the use of the equipment in the offense.

(c) Seizure and forfeiture.—If copies or phonorecords of sounds or sounds and images of a live musical performance are fixed outside of the United States without the consent of the performer or performers involved, such copies or phonorecords are subject to seizure and forfeiture in the United States in the same manner as property imported in violation of the customs laws. The Secretary of the Treasury shall, not later than 60 days after the date of the enactment of the Uruguay Round Agreements Act, issue regulations to carry out this subsection, including regulations by which any performer may, upon payment of a specified fee, be entitled to notification by the United States Customs Service of the importation of copies or phonorecords that appear to consist of unauthorized fixations of the sounds or sounds and images of a live musical performance.

(d) Victim impact statement.—(1) During preparation of the presentence report pursuant to Rule 32(c) of the Federal Rules of Criminal Procedure, victims of the offense shall be permitted to submit, and the probation officer shall receive, a victim impact statement that identifies the victim of the offense and the extent and scope of the injury and loss suffered by the victim, including the estimated economic impact of the offense on that victim.

(2) Persons permitted to submit victim impact statements shall include—

(A) producers and sellers of legitimate works affected by conduct involved in the offense;

(B) holders of intellectual property rights in such works; and

(C) the legal representatives of such producers, sellers, and holders.

(e) Definitions.—As used in this section—

(1) the terms "copy", "fixed", "musical work", "phonorecord", "reproduce", "sound recordings",

and "transmit" mean those terms within the meaning of title 17; and

(2) the term "traffic" has the same meaning as in section 2320(e) of this title.

(f) Applicability.—This section shall apply to any Act or Acts that occur on or after the date of the enactment of the Uruguay Round Agreements Act.

(Added Pub.L. 103–465, Title V, § 513(a), Dec. 8, 1994, 108 Stat. 4974, and amended Pub.L. 105–147, § 2(e), Dec. 16, 1997, 111 Stat. 2679; Pub.L. 109–181, § 2(c)(1), Mar. 16, 2006, 120 Stat. 288.)

HISTORICAL AND STATUTORY NOTES

References in Text

The date of the enactment of the Uruguay Round Agreements Act, referred to in subsecs. (c) and (e), means the date of the enactment of Pub.L. 103–465, 108 Stat. 4809, which was approved Dec. 8, 1994.

Transfer of Functions

For transfer of the functions, personnel, assets, and liabilities of the United States Customs Service of the Department of the Treasury, including the functions of the Secretary of the Treasury relating thereto, to the Secretary of Homeland Security, and for treatment of related references, see 6 U.S.C.A. §§ 203(1), 551(d), 552(d) and 557, and the Department of Homeland Security Reorganization Plan of November 25, 2002, as modified, set out as a note under 6 U.S.C.A. § 542.

§ 2319B. Unauthorized recording of Motion pictures in a Motion picture exhibition facility

(a) Offense.—Any person who, without the authorization of the copyright owner, knowingly uses or attempts to use an audiovisual recording device to transmit or make a copy of a motion picture or other audiovisual work protected under title 17, or any part thereof, from a performance of such work in a motion picture exhibition facility, shall—

(1) be imprisoned for not more than 3 years, fined under this title, or both; or

(2) if the offense is a second or subsequent offense, be imprisoned for no more than 6 years, fined under this title, or both.

The possession by a person of an audiovisual recording device in a motion picture exhibition facility may be considered as evidence in any proceeding to determine whether that person committed an offense under this subsection, but shall not, by itself, be sufficient to support a conviction of that person for such offense.

(b) Forfeiture and destruction.—When a person is convicted of a violation of subsection (a), the court in its judgment of conviction shall, in addition to any penalty provided, order the forfeiture and destruction or other disposition of all unauthorized copies of motion pictures or other audiovisual works protected under title 17, or parts thereof, and any audiovisual recording devices or other equipment used in connection with the offense.

(c) Authorized activities.—This section does not prevent any lawfully authorized investigative, protective, or intelligence activity by an officer, agent, or employee of the United States, a State, or a political subdivision of a State, or by a person acting under a contract with the United States, a State, or a political subdivision of a State.

(d) Immunity for theaters.—With reasonable cause, the owner or lessee of a motion picture exhibition facility where a motion picture or other audiovisual work is being exhibited, the authorized agent or employee of such owner or lessee, the licensor of the motion picture or other audiovisual work being exhibited, or the agent or employee of such licensor—

(1) may detain, in a reasonable manner and for a reasonable time, any person suspected of a violation of this section with respect to that motion picture or audiovisual work for the purpose of questioning or summoning a law enforcement officer; and

(2) shall not be held liable in any civil or criminal action arising out of a detention under paragraph (1).

(e) Victim impact statement.—

(1) **In general.**—During the preparation of the presentence report under rule 32(c) of the Federal Rules of Criminal Procedure, victims of an offense under this section shall be permitted to submit to the probation officer a victim impact statement that identifies the victim of the offense and the extent and scope of the injury and loss suffered by the victim, including the estimated economic impact of the offense on that victim.

(2) **Contents.**—A victim impact statement submitted under this subsection shall include—

(A) producers and sellers of legitimate works affected by conduct involved in the offense;

(B) holders of intellectual property rights in the works described in subparagraph (A); and

(C) the legal representatives of such producers, sellers, and holders.

(f) State law not preempted.—Nothing in this section may be construed to annul or limit any rights or remedies under the laws of any State.

(g) Definitions.—In this section, the following definitions shall apply:

(1) **Title 17 definitions.**—The terms "audiovisual work", "copy", "copyright owner", "motion picture", "motion picture exhibition facility", and "transmit" have, respectively, the meanings given those terms in section 101 of title 17.

(2) **Audiovisual recording device.**—The term "audiovisual recording device" means a digital or

analog photographic or video camera, or any other technology or device capable of enabling the recording or transmission of a copyrighted motion picture or other audiovisual work, or any part thereof, regardless of whether audiovisual recording is the sole or primary purpose of the device.

(Added Pub.L. 109–9, Title I, § 102(a), Apr. 27, 2005, 119 Stat. 218.)

HISTORICAL AND STATUTORY NOTES

References in Text

Title 17, referred to in text, is 17 U.S.C.A. § 101 et seq.

§ 2320. Trafficking in counterfeit goods or services

(a) Whoever intentionally traffics or attempts to traffic in goods or services and knowingly uses a counterfeit mark on or in connection with such goods or services, or intentionally traffics or attempts to traffic in labels, patches, stickers, wrappers, badges, emblems, medallions, charms, boxes, containers, cans, cases, hangtags, documentation, or packaging of any type or nature, knowing that a counterfeit mark has been applied thereto, the use of which is likely to cause confusion, to cause mistake, or to deceive, shall, if an individual, be fined not more than $2,000,000 or imprisoned not more than 10 years, or both, and, if a person other than an individual, be fined not more than $5,000,000. In the case of an offense by a person under this section that occurs after that person is convicted of another offense under this section, the person convicted, if an individual, shall be fined not more than $5,000,000 or imprisoned not more than 20 years, or both, and if other than an individual, shall be fined not more than $15,000,000.

(b)(1) The following property shall be subject to forfeiture to the United States and no property right shall exist in such property:

(A) Any article bearing or consisting of a counterfeit mark used in committing a violation of subsection (a).

(B) Any property used, in any manner or part, to commit or to facilitate the commission of a violation of subsection (a).

(2) The provisions of chapter 46 of this title relating to civil forfeitures, including section 983 of this title, shall extend to any seizure or civil forfeiture under this section. At the conclusion of the forfeiture proceedings, the court, unless otherwise requested by an agency of the United States, shall order that any forfeited article bearing or consisting of a counterfeit mark be destroyed or otherwise disposed of according to law.

(3)(A) The court, in imposing sentence on a person convicted of an offense under this section, shall order, in addition to any other sentence imposed, that the person forfeit to the United States—

(i) any property constituting or derived from any proceeds the person obtained, directly or indirectly, as the result of the offense;

(ii) any of the person's property used, or intended to be used, in any manner or part, to commit, facilitate, aid, or abet the commission of the offense; and

(iii) any article that bears or consists of a counterfeit mark used in committing the offense.

(B) The forfeiture of property under subparagraph (A), including any seizure and disposition of the property and any related judicial or administrative proceeding, shall be governed by the procedures set forth in section 413 of the Comprehensive Drug Abuse Prevention and Control Act of 1970 (21 U.S.C. 853), other than subsection (d) of that section. Notwithstanding section 413(h) of that Act, at the conclusion of the forfeiture proceedings, the court shall order that any forfeited article or component of an article bearing or consisting of a counterfeit mark be destroyed.

(4) When a person is convicted of an offense under this section, the court, pursuant to sections 3556, 3663A, and 3664, shall order the person to pay restitution to the owner of the mark and any other victim of the offense as an offense against property referred to in section 3663A(c)(1)(A)(ii).

(5) The term "victim", as used in paragraph (4), has the meaning given that term in section 3663A(a)(2).

(c) All defenses, affirmative defenses, and limitations on remedies that would be applicable in an action under the Lanham Act shall be applicable in a prosecution under this section. In a prosecution under this section, the defendant shall have the burden of proof, by a preponderance of the evidence, of any such affirmative defense.

(d)(1) During preparation of the presentence report pursuant to Rule 32(c) of the Federal Rules of Criminal Procedure, victims of the offense shall be permitted to submit, and the probation officer shall receive, a victim impact statement that identifies the victim of the offense and the extent and scope of the injury and loss suffered by the victim, including the estimated economic impact of the offense on that victim.

(2) Persons permitted to submit victim impact statements shall include—

(A) producers and sellers of legitimate goods or services affected by conduct involved in the offense;

(B) holders of intellectual property rights in such goods or services; and

(C) the legal representatives of such producers, sellers, and holders.

(e) For the purposes of this section—

(1) the term "counterfeit mark" means—

(A) a spurious mark—

(i) that is used in connection with trafficking in any goods, services, labels, patches, stickers, wrappers, badges, emblems, medallions, charms, boxes, containers, cans, cases, hangtags, documentation, or packaging of any type or nature;

(ii) that is identical with, or substantially indistinguishable from, a mark registered on the principal register in the United States Patent and Trademark Office and in use, whether or not the defendant knew such mark was so registered;

(iii) that is applied to or used in connection with the goods or services for which the mark is registered with the United States Patent and Trademark Office, or is applied to or consists of a label, patch, sticker, wrapper, badge, emblem, medallion, charm, box, container, can, case, hangtag, documentation, or packaging of any type or nature that is designed, marketed, or otherwise intended to be used on or in connection with the goods or services for which the mark is registered in the United States Patent and Trademark Office; and

(iv) the use of which is likely to cause confusion, to cause mistake, or to deceive; or

(B) a spurious designation that is identical with, or substantially indistinguishable from, a designation as to which the remedies of the Lanham Act are made available by reason of section 220506 of title 36;

but such term does not include any mark or designation used in connection with goods or services, or a mark or designation applied to labels, patches, stickers, wrappers, badges, emblems, medallions, charms, boxes, containers, cans, cases, hangtags, documentation, or packaging of any type or nature used in connection with such goods or services, of which the manufacturer or producer was, at the time of the manufacture or production in question, authorized to use the mark or designation for the type of goods or services so manufactured or produced, by the holder of the right to use such mark or designation.

(2) the term "traffic" means to transport, transfer, or otherwise dispose of, to another, for purposes of commercial advantage or private financial gain, or to make, import, export, obtain control of, or possess, with intent to so transport, transfer, or otherwise dispose of;

(3) the term "financial gain" includes the receipt, or expected receipt, of anything of value; and

(4) the term "Lanham Act" means the Act entitled "An Act to provide for the registration and protection of trademarks used in commerce, to carry out the provisions of certain international conventions, and for other purposes", approved July 5, 1946 (15 U.S.C. 1051 et seq.).

(f) Nothing in this section shall entitle the United States to bring a criminal cause of action under this section for the repackaging of genuine goods or services not intended to deceive or confuse.

(g)(1) Beginning with the first year after the date of enactment of this subsection, the Attorney General shall include in the report of the Attorney General to Congress on the business of the Department of Justice prepared pursuant to section 522 of title 28, an accounting, on a district by district basis, of the following with respect to all actions taken by the Department of Justice that involve trafficking in counterfeit labels for phonorecords, copies of computer programs or computer program documentation or packaging, copies of motion pictures or other audiovisual works (as defined in section 2318 of this title), criminal infringement of copyrights (as defined in section 2319 of this title), unauthorized fixation of and trafficking in sound recordings and music videos of live musical performances (as defined in section 2319A of this title), or trafficking in goods or services bearing counterfeit marks (as defined in section 2320 of this title):

(A) The number of open investigations.

(B) The number of cases referred by the United States Customs Service.

(C) The number of cases referred by other agencies or sources.

(D) The number and outcome, including settlements, sentences, recoveries, and penalties, of all prosecutions brought under sections 2318, 2319, 2319A, and 2320 of this title.

(2)(A) The report under paragraph (1), with respect to criminal infringement of copyright, shall include the following:

(i) The number of infringement cases in these categories: audiovisual (videos and films); audio (sound recordings); literary works (books and musical compositions); computer programs; video games; and, others.

(ii) The number of online infringement cases.

(iii) The number and dollar amounts of fines assessed in specific categories of dollar amounts. These categories shall be: no fines ordered; fines under $500; fines from $500 to $1,000; fines from $1,000 to $5,000; fines from $5,000 to $10,000; and fines over $10,000.

(iv) The total amount of restitution ordered in all copyright infringement cases.

(B) In this paragraph, the term "online infringement cases" as used in paragraph (2) means those cases where the infringer—

(i) advertised or publicized the infringing work on the Internet; or

(ii) made the infringing work available on the Internet for download, reproduction, performance, or distribution by other persons.

(C) The information required under subparagraph (A) shall be submitted in the report required in fiscal year 2005 and thereafter.

(Added Pub.L. 98–473, Title II, § 1502(a), Oct. 12, 1984, 98 Stat. 2178, and amended Pub.L. 103–322, Title XXXII, § 320104(a), Title XXXIII, § 330016(1)(U), Sept. 13, 1994, 108 Stat. 2110, 2148; Pub.L. 104–153, § 5, July 2, 1996, 110 Stat. 1387; Pub.L. 105–147, § 2(f), Dec. 16, 1997, 111 Stat. 2679; Pub.L. 105–225, § 4(b), Aug. 12, 1998, 112 Stat. 1499; Pub.L. 105–354, § 2(c), Nov. 3, 1998, 112 Stat. 3244; Pub.L. 107–140, § 1, Feb. 8, 2002, 116 Stat. 12; Pub.L. 107–273, Div. A, Title II, § 205(e), Nov. 2, 2002, 116 Stat. 1778; Pub.L. 109–181, §§ 1(b), 2(b), Mar. 16, 2006, 120 Stat. 285, 288.)

HISTORICAL AND STATUTORY NOTES

References in Text

Chapter 46 of this title, referred to in subsec. (b)(2), is Forfeiture, 18 U.S.C.A. § 981 et seq.

Section 413 of the Comprehensive Drug Abuse Prevention and Control Act of 1970, referred to in subsec. (b)(3)(B), is Pub.L. 91–513, Title II, 413, as added Pub.L. 98–473, Title II, § 303, Oct. 12, 1984, 98 Stat. 2044, and amended Pub.L. 98–473, Title II, § 2301(d)–(f), Oct. 12, 1984, 98 Stat. 2192, 2193, which is classified to 21 U.S.C.A. § 853.

The Lanham Act, referred to in subsecs. (c), (d)(1)(B),(3), of this section, is Act July 5, 1946, c. 540, 60 Stat. 427, which is classified generally to chapter 22 (section 1051 et seq.) of Title 15, Commerce and Trade. For complete classification of this Act to the Code, see Short Title note set out under section 1051 of Title 15 and Tables.

Date of enactment of this subsection, referred to in subsec. (f)(1), is the date of enactment of Pub.L. 104–153, which was approved July 2, 1996.

Effective and Applicability Provisions

1998 Acts. Section 2(c) of Pub.L. 105–354 provided in part that amendments by that subsection were effective Aug. 12, 1998.

Transfer of Functions

For transfer of the functions, personnel, assets, and liabilities of the United States Customs Service of the Department of the Treasury, including the functions of the Secretary of the Treasury relating thereto, to the Secretary of Homeland Security, and for treatment of related references, see 6 U.S.C.A. §§ 203(1), 551(d), 552(d) and 557, and the Department of Homeland Security Reorganization Plan of November 25, 2002, as modified, set out as a note under 6 U.S.C.A. § 542.

Findings

Pub.L. 109–181, § 1(a)(2), Mar. 16, 2006, 120 Stat. 285, provided that:

"The Congress finds that—

"(A) the United States economy is losing millions of dollars in tax revenue and tens of thousands of jobs because of the manufacture, distribution, and sale of counterfeit goods;

"(B) the Bureau of Customs and Border Protection estimates that counterfeiting costs the United States $200 billion annually;

"(C) counterfeit automobile parts, including brake pads, cost the auto industry alone billions of dollars in lost sales each year;

"(D) counterfeit products have invaded numerous industries, including those producing auto parts, electrical appliances, medicines, tools, toys, office equipment, clothing, and many other products;

"(E) ties have been established between counterfeiting and terrorist organizations that use the sale of counterfeit goods to raise and launder money;

"(F) ongoing counterfeiting of manufactured goods poses a widespread threat to public health and safety; and

"(G) strong domestic criminal remedies against counterfeiting will permit the United States to seek stronger anti-counterfeiting provisions in bilateral and international agreements with trading partners."

§ 2321. Trafficking in certain motor vehicles or motor vehicle parts

(a) Whoever buys, receives, possesses, or obtains control of, with intent to sell or otherwise dispose of, a motor vehicle or motor vehicle part, knowing that an identification number for such motor vehicle or part has been removed, obliterated, tampered with, or altered, shall be fined under this title or imprisoned not more than ten years, or both.

(b) Subsection (a) does not apply if the removal, obliteration, tampering, or alteration—

(1) is caused by collision or fire; or

(2) is not a violation of section 511 of this title.

(c) As used in this section, the terms "identification number" and "motor vehicle" have the meaning given those terms in section 511 of this title.

(Added Pub.L. 98–547, Title II, § 204(a), Oct. 25, 1984, 98 Stat. 2770, and amended Pub.L. 99–646, § 42(a), Nov. 20, 1986, 100 Stat. 3601; Pub.L. 103–322, Title XXXIII, § 330016(1)(N), Sept. 13, 1994, 108 Stat. 2148.)

§ 2322. Chop shops

(a) In general.—

(1) Unlawful action.—Any person who knowingly owns, operates, maintains, or controls a chop shop or conducts operations in a chop shop shall be punished by a fine under this title or by imprisonment for not more than 15 years, or both. If a conviction of a person under this paragraph is for a violation committed after the first conviction of such person under this paragraph, the maximum punishment shall be doubled with respect to any fine and imprisonment.

(2) **Injunctions.**—The Attorney General shall, as appropriate, in the case of any person who violates paragraph (1), commence a civil action for permanent or temporary injunction to restrain such violation.

(b) **Definition.**—For purposes of this section, the term "chop shop" means any building, lot, facility, or other structure or premise where one or more persons engage in receiving, concealing, destroying, disassembling, dismantling, reassembling, or storing any passenger motor vehicle or passenger motor vehicle part which has been unlawfully obtained in order to alter, counterfeit, deface, destroy, disguise, falsify, forge, obliterate, or remove the identity, including the vehicle identification number or derivative thereof, of such vehicle or vehicle part and to distribute, sell, or dispose of such vehicle or vehicle part in interstate or foreign commerce.

(Added Pub.L. 102–519, Title I, § 105(a), Oct. 25, 1992, 106 Stat. 3385.)

CHAPTER 113A—TELEMARKETING FRAUD

§ 2325. Definition

In this chapter, "telemarketing"—

(1) means a plan, program, promotion, or campaign that is conducted to induce—

(A) purchases of goods or services;

(B) participation in a contest or sweepstakes; or,

(C) a charitable contribution, donation, or gift of money or any other thing of value,

by use of 1 or more interstate telephone calls initiated either by a person who is conducting the plan, program, promotion, or campaign or by a prospective purchaser or contest or sweepstakes participant or charitable contributor, or donor; but

(2) does not include the solicitation of sales through the mailing of a catalog that—

(A) contains a written description or illustration of the goods or services offered for sale;

(B) includes the business address of the seller;

(C) includes multiple pages of written material or illustration; and

(D) has been issued not less frequently than once a year,

if the person making the solicitation does not solicit customers by telephone but only receives calls initiated by customers in response to the catalog and during those calls takes orders without further solicitation.

(Added Pub.L. 103–322, Title XXV, § 250002(a)(2), Sept. 13, 1994, 108 Stat. 2082, and amended Pub.L. 107–56, Title X, § 1011(d), Oct. 26, 2001, 115 Stat. 396.)

HISTORICAL AND STATUTORY NOTES

Short Title

1994 Acts. Section 250001 of Pub.L. 103–322 provided that: "This Act [probably means this title, Title XXV of Pub.L. 103–322, which enacted this chapter, amended sections 1029, 1341, and 3059 of this title, and enacted provisions set out as notes under this section and section 994 of Title 28, Judiciary and Judicial Procedure] may be cited as the 'Senior Citizens Against Marketing Scams Act of 1994'."

Information Network

Section 250008 of Pub.L. 103–322, as amended Pub.L. 104–294, Title VI, § 604(b)(29), Oct. 11, 1996, 110 Stat. 3508, provided that:

"(a) **Hotline.**—The Attorney General shall, subject to the availability of appropriations, establish a national toll-free hotline for the purpose of—

"(1) providing general information on telemarketing fraud to interested persons; and

"(2) gathering information related to possible violations of provisions of law amended by this title [the Senior Citizens Against Marketing Scams Act of 1994, Title XXV of Pub.L. 103–322, see Short Title note set out under this section and Tables].

"(b) **Action on information gathered.**—The Attorney General shall work in cooperation with the Federal Trade Commission to ensure that information gathered through the hotline shall be acted on in an appropriate manner."

[Amendment by section 604 of Pub.L. 104–294 effective Sept. 13, 1994, see section 604(d) of Pub.L. 104–294, set out as a note under section 13 of this title.]

§ 2326. Enhanced penalties

A person who is convicted of an offense under section 1028, 1029, 1341, 1342, 1343, or 1344, or a conspiracy to commit such an offense, in connection with the conduct of telemarketing—

(1) shall be imprisoned for a term of up to 5 years in addition to any term of imprisonment imposed under any of those sections, respectively; and

(2) in the case of an offense under any of those sections that—

(A) victimized ten or more persons over the age of 55; or

(B) targeted persons over the age of 55,

shall be imprisoned for a term of up to 10 years in addition to any term of imprisonment imposed under any of those sections, respectively.

(Added Pub.L. 103–322, Title XXV, § 250002(a)(2), Sept. 13, 1994, 108 Stat. 2082; Pub.L. 105–184, §§ 3, 4, June 23, 1998, 112 Stat. 520.)

§ 2327. Mandatory restitution

(a) In general.—Notwithstanding section 3663 or 3663A, and in addition to any other civil or criminal penalty authorized by law, the court shall order restitution to all victims of any offense for which an enhanced penalty is provided under section 2326.

(b) Scope and nature of order.—

(1) Directions.—The order of restitution under this section shall direct the defendant to pay to the victim (through the appropriate court mechanism) the full amount of the victim's losses as determined by the court pursuant to paragraph (2).

(2) Enforcement.—An order of restitution under this section shall be issued and enforced in accordance with section 3664 in the same manner as an order under section 3663A.

(3) Definition.—For purposes of this subsection, the term "full amount of the victim's losses" means all losses suffered by the victim as a proximate result of the offense.

(4) Order mandatory.—**(A)** The issuance of a restitution order under this section is mandatory.

(B) A court may not decline to issue an order under this section because of—

(i) the economic circumstances of the defendant; or

(ii) the fact that a victim has, or is entitled to, receive compensation for his or her injuries from the proceeds of insurance or any other source.

(c) Victim defined.—In this section, the term "victim" has the meaning given that term in section 3663A(a)(2).

(Added Pub.L. 103–322, Title XXV, § 250002(a)(2), Sept. 13, 1994, 108 Stat. 2082, and amended Pub.L. 104–132, Title II, § 205(e), Apr. 24, 1996, 110 Stat. 1232; Pub.L. 104–294, Title VI, § 601(n), Oct. 11, 1996, 110 Stat. 3502; Pub.L. 105–184, § 5, June 23, 1998, 112 Stat. 520.)

HISTORICAL AND STATUTORY NOTES

Codifications

Section 601(n) of Pub.L. 104–294, which directed that subsec. (c) of this section be amended by substituting "designee" for "delegee", wherever appearing, was incapable of execution due to amendment by section 205(e)(3) and (4) of Pub.L. 104–132, which struck out former subsec. (c) and redesignated former subsec. (f) as (c), see 1996 Amendments notes set out under this section.

CHAPTER 113B—TERRORISM

[1] Editorially supplied. Section was enacted without corresponding amendment to analysis.

HISTORICAL AND STATUTORY NOTES

Codifications

Pub.L. 101–519, § 132, Nov. 5, 1990, 104 Stat. 2250, known as the "Antiterrorism Act of 1990", amended this chapter by adding sections 2331 and 2333 to 2338 and by amending former section 2331 and renumbering it as section 2332. Pub.L. 102–26, Title IV, § 402, Apr. 10, 1991, 105 Stat. 155, as amended Pub.L. 102–136, § 126, Oct. 25, 1991, 105 Stat. 643, repealed section 132 of Pub.L. 101–519, effective Nov. 5, 1990, and, also effective Nov. 5, 1990, amended this chapter to read as if section 132 of Pub.L. 101–519 had not been enacted.

§ 2331. Definitions

As used in this chapter—

(1) the term "international terrorism" means activities that—

(A) involve violent acts or acts dangerous to human life that are a violation of the criminal laws of the United States or of any State, or that would be a criminal violation if committed within the jurisdiction of the United States or of any State;

(B) appear to be intended—

(i) to intimidate or coerce a civilian population;

(ii) to influence the policy of a government by intimidation or coercion; or

(iii) to affect the conduct of a government by mass destruction, assassination, or kidnapping; and

(C) occur primarily outside the territorial jurisdiction of the United States, or transcend national boundaries in terms of the means by which they are accomplished, the persons they appear intended to intimidate or coerce, or the locale in which their perpetrators operate or seek asylum;

(2) the term "national of the United States" has the meaning given such term in section 101(a)(22) of the Immigration and Nationality Act;

(3) the term "person" means any individual or entity capable of holding a legal or beneficial interest in property;

(4) the term "act of war" means any act occurring in the course of—

(A) declared war;

(B) armed conflict, whether or not war has been declared, between two or more nations; or

(C) armed conflict between military forces of any origin; and

(5) the term "domestic terrorism" means activities that—

(A) involve acts dangerous to human life that are a violation of the criminal laws of the United States or of any State;

(B) appear to be intended—

(i) to intimidate or coerce a civilian population;

(ii) to influence the policy of a government by intimidation or coercion; or

(iii) to affect the conduct of a government by mass destruction, assassination, or kidnapping; and

(C) occur primarily within the territorial jurisdiction of the United States.

(Added Pub.L. 102–572, Title X, § 1003(a)(3), Oct. 29, 1992, 106 Stat. 4521, and amended Pub.L. 107–56, Title VIII, § 802(a), Oct. 26, 2001, 115 Stat. 376.)

HISTORICAL AND STATUTORY NOTES

References in Text

Section 101(a)(22) of the Immigration and Nationality Act, referred to in par. (2), is section 101(a)(22) of Act June 27, 1952, c. 477, Title I, 66 Stat. 166, as amended, which is classified to section 1101(a)(22) of Title 8, Aliens and Nationality.

Effective and Applicability Provisions

1992 Acts. Section 1003(c) of Pub.L. 102–572 provided that: "This section and the amendments made by this section [enacting this section and sections 2333 to 2338 of this title and amending section 2332 of this title] shall apply to any pending case or any cause of action arising on or after 4 years before the date of enactment of this Act [Oct. 29, 1992]."

Prior Provisions

A prior section 2331 was redesignated as 2332.

Another prior section 2331, added Pub.L. 101–519, § 132(b)(3), Nov. 5, 1990, 104 Stat. 2250, defining the terms used in this chapter as revised and expanded by the "Antiterrorism Act of 1990", was eliminated pursuant to Pub.L. 102–27, Title IV, § 402, Apr. 10, 1991, 105 Stat. 130, as amended Pub.L. 102–136, § 126, Oct. 25, 1991, 105 Stat. 643, which repealed section 132 of Pub.L. 101–519 and directed that, effective Nov. 5, 1990, chapter 113A of Title 18 (this chapter) read as if section 132 of Pub.L. 101–519 had not been enacted. Prior sections 2333 to 2338 were similarly eliminated pursuant to the repeal of section 132 of Pub.L. 101–519.

Short Title

2004 Amendments. Pub.L. 108–458, Title VI, § 6601, Dec. 17, 2004, 118 Stat. 3761, provided that: "This subtitle [Pub.L. 108–458, Title VI, Subtitle G, §§ 6601 to 6604, Dec. 17, 2004, 118 Stat. 3761, which enacted 18 U.S.C.A. § 2339D, amended 18 U.S.C.A. §§ 2332b and 2339A to 2339C, and enacted provisions set out as a note under 18 U.S.C.A. § 2332b] may be cited as the 'Material Support to Terrorism Prohibition Enhancement Act of 2004'."

2002 Amendments. Pub.L. 107–197, Title I, § 101, June 25, 2002, 116 Stat. 721, provided that: "This title [enacting 18 U.S.C.A. § 2332f and provisions set out as notes under that section] may be cited as the 'Terrorist Bombings Convention Implementation Act of 2002'."

Pub.L. 107–197, Title II, § 201, June 25, 2002, 116 Stat. 724, provided that: "This title [enacting 18 U.S.C.A. § 2339C and provisions set out as notes under that section] may be cited as the 'Suppression of the Financing of Terrorism Convention Implementation Act of 2002'."

§ 2332. Criminal penalties

(a) Homicide.—Whoever kills a national of the United States, while such national is outside the United States, shall—

(1) if the killing is murder (as defined in section 1111(a)), be fined under this title, punished by death or imprisonment for any term of years or for life, or both;

(2) if the killing is a voluntary manslaughter as defined in section 1112(a) of this title, be fined under this title or imprisoned not more than ten years, or both; and

(3) if the killing is an involuntary manslaughter as defined in section 1112(a) of this title, be fined under this title or imprisoned not more than three years, or both.

(b) Attempt or conspiracy with respect to homicide.—Whoever outside the United States attempts to kill, or engages in a conspiracy to kill, a national of the United States shall—

(1) in the case of an attempt to commit a killing that is a murder as defined in this chapter, be fined under this title or imprisoned not more than 20 years, or both; and

(2) in the case of a conspiracy by two or more persons to commit a killing that is a murder as defined in section 1111(a) of this title, if one or more of such persons do any overt act to effect the object of the conspiracy, be fined under this title or imprisoned for any term of years or for life, or both so fined and so imprisoned.

(c) Other conduct.—Whoever outside the United States engages in physical violence—

(1) with intent to cause serious bodily injury to a national of the United States; or

(2) with the result that serious bodily injury is caused to a national of the United States;

shall be fined under this title or imprisoned not more than ten years, or both.

(d) Limitation on prosecution.—No prosecution for any offense described in this section shall be undertaken by the United States except on written certification of the Attorney General or the highest ranking subordinate of the Attorney General with responsibility for criminal prosecutions that, in the judgment of the certifying official, such offense was intended to coerce, intimidate, or retaliate against a government or a civilian population.

(Added Pub.L. 99–399, Title XII, § 1202(a), Aug. 27, 1986, 100 Stat. 896, § 2331, and amended Pub.L. 102–572, Title X, § 1003(a)(1), Oct. 29, 1992, 106 Stat. 4521; renumbered § 2332 and amended Pub.L. 102–572, Title X, § 1003(a)(2), Oct. 29, 1992, 106 Stat. 4521; Pub.L. 103–322, Title VI, § 60022, Sept. 13, 1994, 108 Stat. 1980; Pub.L. 104–132, Title VII, § 705(a)(6), Apr. 24, 1996, 110 Stat. 1295.)

HISTORICAL AND STATUTORY NOTES

Effective and Applicability Provisions

1992 Acts. Amendment by Pub.L. 102–572 applicable to any pending case or any cause of action arising on or after 4 years before Oct. 29, 1992, see section 1003(c) of Pub.L. 102–572, set out as a note under section 2331 of this title.

Prior Provisions

Prior section 2332, which, prior to being renumbered by Pub.L. 101–519, § 132(b)(2), Nov. 5, 1990, 104 Stat. 2250, had been set out as § 2331, was returned to its § 2331 designation pursuant to the repeal of section 132 of Pub.L. 101–519.

Repeal of "Antiterrorism Act of 1990"

Section 402 of Pub.L. 102–27, as amended Pub.L. 102–136, § 126, Oct. 25, 1991, 105 Stat. 643, provided:

"(a)In Public Law 101–519, the Military Construction Appropriations Act, 1991, sections 131 [which enacted provisions set out as a note under section 1701 of Title 50, War and National Defense] and 132 [which enacted sections 1331 and 1333 to 1338 of this title, amended and renumbered as section 1332 former section 1331 of this title, and enacted provisions formerly set out under this section as notes authorizing the citation of section 132 of Pub.L. 101–519 as the 'Antiterrorism Act of 1990' and setting the effective date of the amendments made by that section as applying to pending cases and causes of action arising on or after 3 years before Nov. 5, 1990] are repealed effective November 5, 1990.

"(b)Effective November 5, 1990, chapter 113A of title 18, United States Code (this chapter) is amended to read as if section 132 of Public Law 101–519 had not been enacted."

§ 2332a. Use of weapons of mass destruction

(a) Offense against a national of the United States or within the United States.—A person who, without lawful authority, uses, threatens, or attempts or conspires to use, a weapon of mass destruction—

(1) against a national of the United States while such national is outside of the United States;

(2) against any person or property within the United States, and

(A) the mail or any facility of interstate or foreign commerce is used in furtherance of the offense;

(B) such property is used in interstate or foreign commerce or in an activity that affects interstate or foreign commerce;

(C) any perpetrator travels in or causes another to travel in interstate or foreign commerce in furtherance of the offense; or

(D) the offense, or the results of the offense, affect interstate or foreign commerce, or, in the case of a threat, attempt, or conspiracy, would have affected interstate or foreign commerce;

(3) against any property that is owned, leased or used by the United States or by any department or agency of the United States, whether the property is within or outside of the United States; or

(4) against any property within the United States that is owned, leased, or used by a foreign government,

shall be imprisoned for any term of years or for life, and if death results, shall be punished by death or imprisoned for any term of years or for life.

(b) Offense by national of the United States outside of the United States.—Any national of the United States who, without lawful authority, uses, or threatens, attempts, or conspires to use, a weapon of mass destruction outside of the United States shall be imprisoned for any term of years or for life, and if death results, shall be punished by death, or by imprisonment for any term of years or for life.

(c) Definitions.—For purposes of this section—

(1) the term "national of the United States" has the meaning given in section 101(a)(22) of the Immigration and Nationality Act (8 U.S.C. 1101(a)(22));

(2) the term "weapon of mass destruction" means—

(A) any destructive device as defined in section 921 of this title;

(B) any weapon that is designed or intended to cause death or serious bodily injury through the release, dissemination, or impact of toxic or poisonous chemicals, or their precursors;

(C) any weapon involving a biological agent, toxin, or vector (as those terms are defined in section 178 of this title); or

(D) any weapon that is designed to release radiation or radioactivity at a level dangerous to human life; and

(3) the term "property" includes all real and personal property.

(Added Pub.L. 103–322, Title VI, § 60023(a), Sept. 13, 1994, 108 Stat. 1980, and amended Pub.L. 104–132, Title V, § 511(c), Title VII, § 725, Apr. 24, 1996, 110 Stat. 1284, 1300; Pub.L. 104–294, Title VI, § 605(m), Oct. 11, 1996, 110 Stat. 3510; Pub.L. 105–277, Div. I, Title II, § 201(b)(1), Oct. 21, 1998, 112 Stat. 2681–871; Pub.L. 107–188, Title II, § 231(d), June 12, 2002, 116 Stat. 661; Pub.L. 108–458, Title VI, § 6802(a), (b), Dec. 17, 2004, 118 Stat. 3766, 3767.)

§ 2332b. Acts of terrorism transcending national boundaries

(a) Prohibited acts.—

(1) Offenses.—Whoever, involving conduct transcending national boundaries and in a circumstance described in subsection (b)—

(A) kills, kidnaps, maims, commits an assault resulting in serious bodily injury, or assaults with a dangerous weapon any person within the United States; or

(B) creates a substantial risk of serious bodily injury to any other person by destroying or damaging any structure, conveyance, or other real or personal property within the United States or by attempting or conspiring to destroy or damage any structure, conveyance, or other real or personal property within the United States;

in violation of the laws of any State, or the United States, shall be punished as prescribed in subsection (c).

(2) Treatment of threats, attempts and conspiracies.—Whoever threatens to commit an offense under paragraph (1), or attempts or conspires to do so, shall be punished under subsection (c).

(b) Jurisdictional bases.—

(1) Circumstances.—The circumstances referred to in subsection (a) are—

(A) the mail or any facility of interstate or foreign commerce is used in furtherance of the offense;

(B) the offense obstructs, delays, or affects interstate or foreign commerce, or would have so obstructed, delayed, or affected interstate or foreign commerce if the offense had been consummated;

(C) the victim, or intended victim, is the United States Government, a member of the uniformed services, or any official, officer, employee, or agent of the legislative, executive, or judicial branches, or of any department or agency, of the United States;

(D) the structure, conveyance, or other real or personal property is, in whole or in part, owned, possessed, or leased to the United States, or any department or agency of the United States;

(E) the offense is committed in the territorial sea (including the airspace above and the seabed and subsoil below, and artificial islands and fixed structures erected thereon) of the United States; or

(F) the offense is committed within the special maritime and territorial jurisdiction of the United States.

(2) Co-conspirators and accessories after the fact.—Jurisdiction shall exist over all principals and co-conspirators of an offense under this section, and accessories after the fact to any offense under this section, if at least one of the circumstances described in subparagraphs (A) through (F) of paragraph (1) is applicable to at least one offender.

(c) Penalties.—

(1) Penalties.—Whoever violates this section shall be punished—

(A) for a killing, or if death results to any person from any other conduct prohibited by this section, by death, or by imprisonment for any term of years or for life;

(B) for kidnapping, by imprisonment for any term of years or for life;

(C) for maiming, by imprisonment for not more than 35 years;

(D) for assault with a dangerous weapon or assault resulting in serious bodily injury, by imprisonment for not more than 30 years;

(E) for destroying or damaging any structure, conveyance, or other real or personal property, by imprisonment for not more than 25 years;

(F) for attempting or conspiring to commit an offense, for any term of years up to the maximum punishment that would have applied had the offense been completed; and

(G) for threatening to commit an offense under this section, by imprisonment for not more than 10 years.

(2) Consecutive sentence.—Notwithstanding any other provision of law, the court shall not place on probation any person convicted of a violation of this section; nor shall the term of imprisonment imposed under this section run concurrently with any other term of imprisonment.

(d) Proof requirements.—The following shall apply to prosecutions under this section:

(1) Knowledge.—The prosecution is not required to prove knowledge by any defendant of a jurisdictional base alleged in the indictment.

(2) State law.—In a prosecution under this section that is based upon the adoption of State law, only the elements of the offense under State law, and not any provisions pertaining to criminal procedure or evidence, are adopted.

(e) Extraterritorial jurisdiction.—There is extraterritorial Federal jurisdiction—

(1) over any offense under subsection (a), including any threat, attempt, or conspiracy to commit such offense; and

(2) over conduct which, under section 3, renders any person an accessory after the fact to an offense under subsection (a).

(f) Investigative authority.—In addition to any other investigative authority with respect to violations of this title, the Attorney General shall have primary investigative responsibility for all Federal crimes of terrorism, and any violation of section 351(e), 844(e), 844(f)(1), 956(b), 1361, 1366(b), 1366(c), 1751(e), 2152, or 2156 of this title, and the Secretary of the Treasury shall assist the Attorney General at the request of the Attorney General. Nothing in this section shall be construed to interfere with the authority of the United States Secret Service under section 3056.

(g) Definitions.—As used in this section—

(1) the term "conduct transcending national boundaries" means conduct occurring outside of the United States in addition to the conduct occurring in the United States;

(2) the term "facility of interstate or foreign commerce" has the meaning given that term in section 1958(b)(2);

(3) the term "serious bodily injury" has the meaning given that term in section 1365(g)(3);

(4) the term "territorial sea of the United States" means all waters extending seaward to 12 nautical miles from the baselines of the United States, determined in accordance with international law; and

(5) the term "Federal crime of terrorism" means an offense that—

(A) is calculated to influence or affect the conduct of government by intimidation or coercion, or to retaliate against government conduct; and

(B) is a violation of—

(i) section 32 (relating to destruction of aircraft or aircraft facilities), 37 (relating to violence at international airports), 81 (relating to arson within special maritime and territorial jurisdiction), 175 or 175b (relating to biological weapons), 175c (relating to variola virus), 229 (relating to chemical weapons), subsection (a), (b), (c), or (d) of section 351 (relating to congressional, cabinet, and Supreme Court assassination and kidnaping), 831 (relating to nuclear materials), 832 (relating to participation in nuclear and weapons of mass destruction threats to the United States) [1] 842(m) or (n) (relating to plastic explosives), 844(f)(2) or (3) (relating to arson and bombing of Government property risking or causing death), 844(i) (relating to arson and bombing of property used in interstate commerce), 930(c) (relating to killing or attempted killing during an attack on a Federal facility with a dangerous weapon), 956(a)(1) (relating to conspiracy to murder, kidnap, or maim persons abroad), 1030(a)(1) (relating to protection of computers), 1030(a)(5)(A)(i) resulting in damage as defined in 1030(a)(5)(B)(ii) through (v) (relating to protection of computers), 1114 (relating to killing or attempted killing of officers and employees of the United States), 1116 (relating to murder or manslaughter of foreign officials, official guests, or internationally protected persons), 1203 (relating to hostage taking), 1361 (relating to government property or contracts), 1362 (relating to destruction of communication lines, stations, or systems), 1363 (relating to injury to buildings or property within special maritime and territorial jurisdiction of the United States), 1366(a) (relating to destruction of an energy facility), 1751(a), (b), (c), or (d) (relating to Presidential and Presidential staff assassination and kidnaping), 1992 (relating to terrorist attacks and other acts of violence against railroad carriers and against mass transportation systems on land, on water, or through the air), 2155 (relating to destruction of national defense materials, premises, or utilities), 2156 (relating to national defense material, premises, or utilities), 2280 (relating to violence against maritime navigation), 2281 (relating to violence against maritime fixed platforms), 2332 (relating to certain homicides and other violence against United States nationals occurring outside of the United States), 2332a (relating to use of weapons of mass destruction), 2332b (relating to acts of terrorism transcending national boundaries), 2332f (relating to bombing of public places and facilities), 2332g (relating to missile systems designed to destroy aircraft), 2332h (relating to radiological dispersal devices), 2339 (relating to harboring terrorists), 2339A (relating to providing material support to terrorists), 2339B (relating to providing material support to terrorist organizations), 2339C (relating to financing of terrorism), 2339D (relating to military-type training from a foreign terrorist organization), or 2340A (relating to torture) of this title;

(ii) sections 92 (relating to prohibitions governing atomic weapons) or 236 (relating to sabotage of nuclear facilities or fuel) of the Atomic Energy Act of 1954 (42 U.S.C. 2122 or 2284);

(iii) section 46502 (relating to aircraft piracy), the second sentence of section 46504 (relating to assault on a flight crew with a dangerous weapon), section 46505(b)(3) or (c) (relating to explosive or incendiary devices, or endangerment of human life by means of weapons, on aircraft), section 46506 if homicide or attempted homicide is involved (relating to application of certain criminal laws to acts on aircraft), or section 60123(b) (relating to destruction of interstate gas or hazardous liquid pipeline facility) of title 49; or

(iv) section 1010A of the Controlled Substances Import and Export Act (relating to narco-terrorism).

(Added Pub.L. 104–132, Title VII, § 702(a), Apr. 24, 1996, 110 Stat. 1291, and amended Pub.L. 104–294, Title VI, § 601(s)(1), (3), Oct. 11, 1996, 110 Stat. 3502; Pub.L. 107–56, Title VIII, § 808, Oct. 26, 2001, 115 Stat. 378; Pub.L. 107–197, Title III, § 301(b), June 25, 2002, 116 Stat. 728; Pub.L. 108–458, Title VI, §§ 6603(a)(1), 6803(c)(3), 6908, Dec. 17, 2004, 118 Stat. 3762, 3769, 3774; Pub.L. 109–177, Title I, §§ 110(b)(3)(A), 112, Mar. 9, 2006, 120 Stat. 208, 209.)

[1] So in original. Probably should be followed by a comma.

Termination of Amendment

For termination of amendment by Pub.L. 108–458, § 6603(g), see Sunset Provisions note set out under this section.

HISTORICAL AND STATUTORY NOTES

References in Text

Section 1365(g)(3), referred to in subsec. (g)(3), was redesignated section 1365(h)(3) by Pub.L. 107–307, § 2(1), Dec. 2, 2002, 116 Stat. 2445.

Section 2332C of this title, referred to in subsec. (g)(5)(B)(i), was repealed by Pub.L. 105–277, Div. I, Title II, § 201(c)(1), Oct. 21, 1998, 112 Stat. 2681–871.

Section 236(a) of the Atomic Energy Act of 1954, referred to in subsec. (g)(5)(B)(ii), is Act, Aug. 1, 1946, c. 724, Title I, § 236(a), as added June 30, 1980, Pub.L. 96–295, Title II, § 204(a), 94 Stat. 787, as amended, which is classified to 42 U.S.C.A. § 2284(a).

Section 1010A of the Controlled Substances Import and Export Act, referred to in subsec. (g)(5)(B)(iv), is Pub.L. 91–513, Title III, § 1010A, as added by Pub.L. 109–177, Title I, § 122, Mar. 9, 2006, 120 Stat. 225, which is classified to 21 U.S.C.A. § 960a.

Sunset Provisions

Pub.L. 108–458, Title VI, § 6603(g), Dec. 17, 2004, 118 Stat. 3764, which provided that, except for offenses prohibited by Pub.L. 108–458, § 6603, which began or occurred before December 31, 2006, amendments made by Pub.L. 108–458, § 6603 to this section and 18 U.S.C.A. §§ 2339A and 2339B, shall cease to be effective on December 31, 2006, was repealed by Pub.L. 109–177, Title I, § 104, Mar. 9, 2006, 120 Stat. 195.

Transfer of Functions

For transfer of the functions, personnel, assets, and obligations of the United States Secret Service, including the functions of the Secretary of the Treasury relating thereto, to the Secretary of Homeland Security, and for treatment of related references, see 6 U.S.C.A. §§ 381, 551(d), 552(d) and 557, and the Department of Homeland Security Reorganization Plan of November 25, 2002, as modified, set out as a note under 6 U.S.C.A. § 542.

[§ 2332c. Repealed. Pub.L. 105–277, Div. I, Title II, § 201(c)(1), Oct. 21, 1998, 112 Stat. 2681–871]

HISTORICAL AND STATUTORY NOTES

Section, added Pub.L. 104–132, Title V, § 521(a), Apr. 24, 1996, 110 Stat. 1286, prohibited use of chemical weapons. See, now, chapter 11B of this title, 18 U.S.C.A. § 229 et seq.

§ 2332d. Financial transactions

(a) Offense.—Except as provided in regulations issued by the Secretary of the Treasury, in consultation with the Secretary of State, whoever, being a United States person, knowing or having reasonable cause to know that a country is designated under section 6(j) of the Export Administration Act of 1979 (50 U.S.C. App. 2405) as a country supporting international terrorism, engages in a financial transaction with the government of that country, shall be fined under this title, imprisoned for not more than 10 years, or both.

(b) Definitions.—As used in this section—

(1) the term "financial transaction" has the same meaning as in section 1956(c)(4); and

(2) the term "United States person" means any—

(A) United States citizen or national;

(B) permanent resident alien;

(C) juridical person organized under the laws of the United States; or

(D) any person in the United States.

(Added Pub.L. 104–132, Title III, § 321(a), Apr. 24, 1996, 110 Stat. 1254, and amended Pub.L. 107–273, Div. B, Title IV, § 4002(a)(5), Nov. 2, 2002, 116 Stat. 1806.)

HISTORICAL AND STATUTORY NOTES

References in Text

Section 6(j) of the Export Administration Act 1979, referred to in subsec. (a), is section 6(j) of Pub.L. 96–72, Sept. 29, 1979, 93 Stat. 513, as amended, which is classified to section 2405 of the Appendix to Title 50, War and National Defense.

Effective and Applicability Provisions

1996 Acts. Section 321(c) of Pub.L. 104–132 provided that: "The amendments made by this section [enacting this section] shall become effective 120 days after the date of enactment of this Act [Apr. 24, 1996]."

§ 2332e. Requests for military assistance to enforce prohibition in certain emergencies

The Attorney General may request the Secretary of Defense to provide assistance under section 382 of title 10 in support of Department of Justice activities relating to the enforcement of section 2332a of this title during an emergency situation involving a weapon of mass destruction. The authority to make such a request may be exercised by another official of the Department of Justice in accordance with section 382(f)(2) of title 10.

(Added Pub.L. 104–201, Div. A, Title XIV, § 1416(c)(2)(A), Sept. 23, 1996, 110 Stat. 2723, § 2332d; renumbered § 2332e, Pub.L. 104–294, Title VI, § 605(q), Oct. 11, 1996, 110 Stat. 3510, and amended Pub.L. 107–56, Title I, § 104, Oct. 26, 2001, 115 Stat. 277.)

§ 2332f. Bombings of places of public use, government facilities, public transportation systems and infrastructure facilities

(a) Offenses.—

(1) In general.—Whoever unlawfully delivers, places, discharges, or detonates an explosive or other lethal device in, into, or against a place of public use, a state or government facility, a public transportation system, or an infrastructure facility—

(A) with the intent to cause death or serious bodily injury, or

(B) with the intent to cause extensive destruction of such a place, facility, or system, where such destruction results in or is likely to result in major economic loss,

shall be punished as prescribed in subsection (c).

(2) Attempts and conspiracies.—Whoever attempts or conspires to commit an offense under paragraph (1) shall be punished as prescribed in subsection (c).

(b) Jurisdiction.—There is jurisdiction over the offenses in subsection (a) if—

(1) the offense takes place in the United States and—

(A) the offense is committed against another state or a government facility of such state, including its embassy or other diplomatic or consular premises of that state;

(B) the offense is committed in an attempt to compel another state or the United States to do or abstain from doing any act;

(C) at the time the offense is committed, it is committed—

(i) on board a vessel flying the flag of another state;

(ii) on board an aircraft which is registered under the laws of another state; or

(iii) on board an aircraft which is operated by the government of another state;

(D) a perpetrator is found outside the United States;

(E) a perpetrator is a national of another state or a stateless person; or

(F) a victim is a national of another state or a stateless person;

(2) the offense takes place outside the United States and—

(A) a perpetrator is a national of the United States or is a stateless person whose habitual residence is in the United States;

(B) a victim is a national of the United States;

(C) a perpetrator is found in the United States;

(D) the offense is committed in an attempt to compel the United States to do or abstain from doing any act;

(E) the offense is committed against a state or government facility of the United States, including an embassy or other diplomatic or consular premises of the United States;

(F) the offense is committed on board a vessel flying the flag of the United States or an aircraft which is registered under the laws of the United States at the time the offense is committed; or

(G) the offense is committed on board an aircraft which is operated by the United States.

(c) Penalties.—Whoever violates this section shall be punished as provided under section 2332a(a) of this title.

(d) Exemptions to jurisdiction.—This section does not apply to—

(1) the activities of armed forces during an armed conflict, as those terms are understood under the law of war, which are governed by that law,

(2) activities undertaken by military forces of a state in the exercise of their official duties; or

(3) offenses committed within the United States, where the alleged offender and the victims are United States citizens and the alleged offender is found in the United States, or where jurisdiction is predicated solely on the nationality of the victims or the alleged offender and the offense has no substantial effect on interstate or foreign commerce.

(e) Definitions.—As used in this section, the term—

(1) "serious bodily injury" has the meaning given that term in section 1365(g)(3) of this title;

(2) "national of the United States" has the meaning given that term in section 101(a)(22) of the Immigration and Nationality Act (8 U.S.C. 1101(a)(22));

(3) "state or government facility" includes any permanent or temporary facility or conveyance that is used or occupied by representatives of a state, members of Government, the legislature or the judiciary or by officials or employees of a state or any other public authority or entity or by employees or officials of an intergovernmental organization in connection with their official duties;

(4) "intergovernmental organization" includes international organization (as defined in section 1116(b)(5) of this title);

(5) "infrastructure facility" means any publicly or privately owned facility providing or distributing services for the benefit of the public, such as water, sewage, energy, fuel, or communications;

(6) "place of public use" means those parts of any building, land, street, waterway, or other location that are accessible or open to members of the public, whether continuously, periodically, or occasionally, and encompasses any commercial, business, cultural, historical, educational, religious, governmental, entertainment, recreational, or similar place that is so accessible or open to the public;

(7) "public transportation system" means all facilities, conveyances, and instrumentalities, whether publicly or privately owned, that are used in or for publicly available services for the transportation of persons or cargo;

(8) "explosive" has the meaning given in section 844(j) of this title insofar that it is designed, or has the capability, to cause death, serious bodily injury, or substantial material damage;

(9) "other lethal device" means any weapon or device that is designed or has the capability to cause death, serious bodily injury, or substantial damage to property through the release, dissemination, or impact of toxic chemicals, biological agents, or toxins (as those terms are defined in section 178 of this title) or radiation or radioactive material;

(10) "military forces of a state" means the armed forces of a state which are organized, trained, and equipped under its internal law for the primary purpose of national defense or security, and persons acting in support of those armed forces who are under their formal command, control, and responsibility;

(11) "armed conflict" does not include internal disturbances and tensions, such as riots, isolated and sporadic acts of violence, and other acts of a similar nature; and

(12) "state" has the same meaning as that term has under international law, and includes all political subdivisions thereof.

(Added Pub.L. 107–197, Title I, § 102(a), June 25, 2002, 116 Stat. 721.)

HISTORICAL AND STATUTORY NOTES

References in Text

Section 1365(g)(3), referred to in subsec. (e)(1), was redesignated section 1365(h)(3) by Pub.L. 107–307, § 2(1), Dec. 2, 2002, 116 Stat. 2445.

Section 101(a)(22) of the Immigration and Nationality Act, referred to in subsec. (e)(2), is Act June 27, 1952, c. 477, Title I, § 101(a)(22), 66 Stat. 169, as amended, which is classified to 8 U.S.C.A. § 1101(a)(22).

Effective and Applicability Provisions

2002 Acts. Pub.L. 107–197, Title I, § 103, June 25, 2002, 116 Stat. 724, provided that: "Section 102 [enacting this section and provisions set out as notes under this section] shall take effect on the date that the International Convention for the Suppression of Terrorist Bombings enters into force for the United States [July 26, 2002]."

Disclaimer

Pub.L. 107–197, Title I, § 102(c), June 25, 2002, 116 Stat. 724, provided that: "Nothing contained in this section is intended to affect the applicability of any other Federal or State law which might pertain to the underlying conduct."

§ 2332g. Missile systems designed to destroy aircraft

(a) Unlawful conduct.—

(1) In general.—Except as provided in paragraph (3), it shall be unlawful for any person to knowingly produce, construct, otherwise acquire, transfer directly or indirectly, receive, possess, import, export, or use, or possess and threaten to use—

(A) an explosive or incendiary rocket or missile that is guided by any system designed to enable the rocket or missile to—

(i) seek or proceed toward energy radiated or reflected from an aircraft or toward an image locating an aircraft; or

(ii) otherwise direct or guide the rocket or missile to an aircraft;

(B) any device designed or intended to launch or guide a rocket or missile described in subparagraph (A); or

(C) any part or combination of parts designed or redesigned for use in assembling or fabricating a rocket, missile, or device described in subparagraph (A) or (B).

(2) Nonweapon.—Paragraph (1)(A) does not apply to any device that is neither designed nor redesigned for use as a weapon.

(3) Excluded conduct.—This subsection does not apply with respect to—

(A) conduct by or under the authority of the United States or any department or agency thereof or of a State or any department or agency thereof; or

(B) conduct pursuant to the terms of a contract with the United States or any department or agency thereof or with a State or any department or agency thereof.

(b) Jurisdiction.—Conduct prohibited by subsection (a) is within the jurisdiction of the United States if—

(1) the offense occurs in or affects interstate or foreign commerce;

(2) the offense occurs outside of the United States and is committed by a national of the United States;

(3) the offense is committed against a national of the United States while the national is outside the United States;

(4) the offense is committed against any property that is owned, leased, or used by the United States or by any department or agency of the United States, whether the property is within or outside the United States; or

(5) an offender aids or abets any person over whom jurisdiction exists under this subsection in committing an offense under this section or conspires with any person over whom jurisdiction exists under this subsection to commit an offense under this section.

(c) Criminal penalties.—

(1) **In general.**—Any person who violates, or attempts or conspires to violate, subsection (a) shall be fined not more than $2,000,000 and shall be sentenced to a term of imprisonment not less than 25 years or to imprisonment for life.

(2) **Other circumstances.**—Any person who, in the course of a violation of subsection (a), uses, attempts or conspires to use, or possesses and threatens to use, any item or items described in subsection (a), shall be fined not more than $2,000,000 and imprisoned for not less than 30 years or imprisoned for life.

(3) **Special circumstances.**—If the death of another results from a person's violation of subsection (a), the person shall be fined not more than $2,000,000 and punished by imprisonment for life.

(d) Definition.—As used in this section, the term "aircraft" has the definition set forth in section 40102(a)(6) of title 49, United States Code.

(Added Pub.L. 108–458, Title VI, § 6903, Dec. 17, 2004, 118 Stat. 3770.)

§ 2332h. Radiological dispersal devices

(a) Unlawful conduct.—

(1) **In general.**—Except as provided in paragraph (2), it shall be unlawful for any person to knowingly produce, construct, otherwise acquire, transfer directly or indirectly, receive, possess, import, export, or use, or possess and threaten to use—

(A) any weapon that is designed or intended to release radiation or radioactivity at a level dangerous to human life; or

(B) any device or other object that is capable of and designed or intended to endanger human life through the release of radiation or radioactivity.

(2) **Exception.**—This subsection does not apply with respect to—

(A) conduct by or under the authority of the United States or any department or agency thereof; or

(B) conduct pursuant to the terms of a contract with the United States or any department or agency thereof.

(b) Jurisdiction.—Conduct prohibited by subsection (a) is within the jurisdiction of the United States if—

(1) the offense occurs in or affects interstate or foreign commerce;

(2) the offense occurs outside of the United States and is committed by a national of the United States;

(3) the offense is committed against a national of the United States while the national is outside the United States;

(4) the offense is committed against any property that is owned, leased, or used by the United States or by any department or agency of the United States, whether the property is within or outside the United States; or

(5) an offender aids or abets any person over whom jurisdiction exists under this subsection in committing an offense under this section or conspires with any person over whom jurisdiction exists under this subsection to commit an offense under this section.

(c) Criminal penalties.—

(1) **In general.**—Any person who violates, or attempts or conspires to violate, subsection (a) shall be fined not more than $2,000,000 and shall be sentenced to a term of imprisonment not less than 25 years or to imprisonment for life.

(2) **Other circumstances.**—Any person who, in the course of a violation of subsection (a), uses, attempts or conspires to use, or possesses and

threatens to use, any item or items described in subsection (a), shall be fined not more than $2,000,000 and imprisoned for not less than 30 years or imprisoned for life.

(3) Special circumstances.—If the death of another results from a person's violation of subsection (a), the person shall be fined not more than $2,000,000 and punished by imprisonment for life.

(Added Pub.L. 108–458, Title VI, § 6905, Dec. 17, 2004, 118 Stat. 3772.)

§ 2333. Civil remedies

(a) Action and jurisdiction.—Any national of the United States injured in his or her person, property, or business by reason of an act of international terrorism, or his or her estate, survivors, or heirs, may sue therefor in any appropriate district court of the United States and shall recover threefold the damages he or she sustains and the cost of the suit, including attorney's fees.

(b) Estoppel under United States law.—A final judgment or decree rendered in favor of the United States in any criminal proceeding under section 1116, 1201, 1203, or 2332 of this title or section 46314, 46502, 46505, or 46506 of title 49 shall estop the defendant from denying the essential allegations of the criminal offense in any subsequent civil proceeding under this section.

(c) Estoppel under foreign law.—A final judgment or decree rendered in favor of any foreign state in any criminal proceeding shall, to the extent that such judgment or decree may be accorded full faith and credit under the law of the United States, estop the defendant from denying the essential allegations of the criminal offense in any subsequent civil proceeding under this section.

(Added Pub.L. 102–572, Title X, § 1003(a)(4), Oct. 29, 1992, 106 Stat. 4522, and amended Pub.L. 103–429, § 2(1), Oct. 31, 1994, 108 Stat. 4377.)

HISTORICAL AND STATUTORY NOTES

Effective and Applicability Provisions

1992 Acts. Section applicable to any pending case or any cause of action arising on or after 4 years before Oct. 29, 1992, see section 1003(c) of Pub.L. 102–572, set out as a note under section 2331 of this title.

Prior Provisions

A prior section 2333, added Pub.L. 101–519, § 132(b)(4), Nov. 5, 1990, 104 Stat. 2251, which related to civil remedies, was eliminated pursuant to the repeal of section 132 of Pub.L. 101–519 by section 402 of Pub.L. 102–27, as amended.

§ 2334. Jurisdiction and venue

(a) General venue.—Any civil action under section 2333 of this title against any person may be instituted in the district court of the United States for any district where any plaintiff resides or where any defendant resides or is served, or has an agent. Process in such a civil action may be served in any district where the defendant resides, is found, or has an agent.

(b) Special maritime or territorial jurisdiction.—If the actions giving rise to the claim occurred within the special maritime and territorial jurisdiction of the United States, as defined in section 7 of this title, then any civil action under section 2333 of this title against any person may be instituted in the district court of the United States for any district in which any plaintiff resides or the defendant resides, is served, or has an agent.

(c) Service on witnesses.—A witness in a civil action brought under section 2333 of this title may be served in any other district where the defendant resides, is found, or has an agent.

(d) Convenience of the forum.—The district court shall not dismiss any action brought under section 2333 of this title on the grounds of the inconvenience or inappropriateness of the forum chosen, unless—

(1) the action may be maintained in a foreign court that has jurisdiction over the subject matter and over all the defendants;

(2) that foreign court is significantly more convenient and appropriate; and

(3) that foreign court offers a remedy which is substantially the same as the one available in the courts of the United States.

(Added Pub.L. 102–572, Title X, § 1003(a)(4), Oct. 29, 1992, 106 Stat. 4522.)

HISTORICAL AND STATUTORY NOTES

Effective and Applicability Provisions

1992 Acts. Section applicable to any pending case or any cause of action arising on or after 4 years before Oct. 29, 1992, see section 1003(c) of Pub.L. 102–572, set out as a note under section 2331 of this title.

Prior Provisions

A prior section 2334, added Pub.L. 101–519, § 132(b)(4), Nov. 5, 1990, 104 Stat. 2251, which related jurisdiction and venue, was eliminated pursuant to the repeal of section 132 of Pub.L. 101–519 by section 402 of Pub.L. 102–27, as amended.

§ 2335. Limitation of actions

(a) In general.—Subject to subsection (b), a suit for recovery of damages under section 2333 of this title shall not be maintained unless commenced within 4 years after the date the cause of action accrued.

(b) Calculation of period.—The time of the absence of the defendant from the United States or from any jurisdiction in which the same or a similar action arising from the same facts may be maintained by the plaintiff, or of any concealment of the defendant's whereabouts, shall not be included in the 4–year period set forth in subsection (a).

(Added Pub.L. 102–572, Title X, § 1003(a)(4), Oct. 29, 1992, 106 Stat. 4523.)

HISTORICAL AND STATUTORY NOTES

Effective and Applicability Provisions

1992 Acts. Section applicable to any pending case or cause of action arising on or after 4 years before Oct. 29, 1992, see section 1003(c) of Pub.L. 102–572, set out as a note under section 2331 of this title.

Prior Provisions

A prior section 2335, added Pub.L. 101–519, §132(b)(4), Nov. 5, 1990, 104 Stat. 2251, which related to limitation of actions, was eliminated pursuant to the repeal of section 132 of Pub.L. 102–519 by section 402 of Pub.L. 102–27, as amended.

§ 2336. Other limitations

(a) Acts of war.—No action shall be maintained under section 2333 of this title for injury or loss by reason of an act of war.

(b) Limitation on discovery.—If a party to an action under section 2333 seeks to discover the investigative files of the Department of Justice, the Assistant Attorney General, Deputy Attorney General, or Attorney General may object on the ground that compliance will interfere with a criminal investigation or prosecution of the incident, or a national security operation related to the incident, which is the subject of the civil litigation. The court shall evaluate any such objections in camera and shall stay the discovery if the court finds that granting the discovery request will substantially interfere with a criminal investigation or prosecution of the incident or a national security operation related to the incident. The court shall consider the likelihood of criminal prosecution by the Government and other factors it deems to be appropriate. A stay of discovery under this subsection shall constitute a bar to the granting of a motion to dismiss under rules 12(b)(6) and 56 of the Federal Rules of Civil Procedure. If the court grants a stay of discovery under this subsection, it may stay the action in the interests of justice.

(c) Stay of action for civil remedies.—(1) The Attorney General may intervene in any civil action brought under section 2333 for the purpose of seeking a stay of the civil action. A stay shall be granted if the court finds that the continuation of the civil action will substantially interfere with a criminal prosecution which involves the same subject matter and in which an indictment has been returned, or interfere with national security operations related to the terrorist incident that is the subject of the civil action. A stay may be granted for up to 6 months. The Attorney General may petition the court for an extension of the stay for additional 6–month periods until the criminal prosecution is completed or dismissed.

(2) In a proceeding under this subsection, the Attorney General may request that any order issued by the court for release to the parties and the public omit any reference to the basis on which the stay was sought.

(Added Pub.L. 102–572, Title X, § 1003(a)(4), Oct. 29, 1992, 106 Stat. 4523.)

HISTORICAL AND STATUTORY NOTES

References in Text

The Federal Rules of Civil Procedure, referred to in subsec. (b), are set out in Title 28, Judiciary and Judicial Procedure.

Effective and Applicability Provisions

1992 Acts. Section applicable to any pending case or cause of action arising on or after 4 years before Oct. 29, 1992, see section 1003(c) of Pub.L. 102–572, set out as a note under section 2331 of this title.

Prior Provisions

A prior section 2336, added Pub.L. 101–519, § 132(b)(4), Nov. 5, 1990, 104 Stat. 2252, which provided that no action be maintained under section 2333 for injury or loss by reason of an act of war, was eliminated pursuant to the repeal of section 132 of Pub.L. 101–519 by section 402 of Pub.L. 102–27, as amended.

§ 2337. Suits against Government officials

No action shall be maintained under section 2333 of this title against—

(1) the United States, an agency of the United States, or an officer or employee of the United States or any agency thereof acting within his or her official capacity or under color of legal authority; or

(2) a foreign state, an agency of a foreign state, or an officer or employee of a foreign state or an agency thereof acting within his or her official capacity or under color of legal authority.

(Added Pub.L. 102–572, Title X, § 1003(a)(4), Oct. 29, 1992, 106 Stat. 4523.)

HISTORICAL AND STATUTORY NOTES

Effective and Applicability Provisions

1992 Acts. Section applicable to any pending case or cause of action arising on or after 4 years before Oct. 29, 1992, see section 1003(c) of Pub.L. 102–572, set out as a note under section 2331 of this title.

Prior Provisions

A prior section 2337, added Pub.L. 101–519, § 132(b)(4), Nov. 5, 1990, 104 Stat. 2252, which related to suits against government officials, was eliminated pursuant to the repeal of section 132 of Pub.L. 101–519 by section 402 of Pub.L. 102–27, as amended.

§ 2338. Exclusive Federal jurisdiction

The district courts of the United States shall have exclusive jurisdiction over an action brought under this chapter.

(Added Pub.L. 102–572, Title X, § 1003(a)(4), Oct. 29, 1992, 106 Stat. 4524.)

HISTORICAL AND STATUTORY NOTES

Effective and Applicability Provisions

1992 Acts. Section applicable to any pending case or cause of action arising on or after 4 years before Oct. 29, 1992, see section 1003(c) of Pub.L. 102–572, set out as a note under section 2331 of this title.

Prior Provisions

A prior section 2338, added Pub.L. 101–519, § 132(b)(4), Nov. 5, 1990, 104 Stat. 2251, which related to exclusive Federal jurisdiction, was eliminated pursuant to repeal of section 132 of Pub.L. 101–519 by section 402 of Pub.L. 102–27, as amended.

§ 2339. Harboring or concealing terrorists

(a) Whoever harbors or conceals any person who he knows, or has reasonable grounds to believe, has committed, or is about to commit, an offense under section 32 (relating to destruction of aircraft or aircraft facilities), section 175 (relating to biological weapons), section 229 (relating to chemical weapons), section 831 (relating to nuclear materials), paragraph (2) or (3) of section 844(f) (relating to arson and bombing of government property risking or causing injury or death), section 1366(a) (relating to the destruction of an energy facility), section 2280 (relating to violence against maritime navigation), section 2332a (relating to weapons of mass destruction), or section 2332b (relating to acts of terrorism transcending national boundaries) of this title, section 236(a) (relating to sabotage of nuclear facilities or fuel) of the Atomic Energy Act of 1954 (42 U.S.C. 2284(a)), or section 46502 (relating to aircraft piracy) of title 49, shall be fined under this title or imprisoned not more than ten years, or both.

(b) A violation of this section may be prosecuted in any Federal judicial district in which the underlying offense was committed, or in any other Federal judicial district as provided by law.

(Added Pub.L. 107–56, Title VIII, § 803(a), Oct. 26, 2001, 115 Stat. 376, as amended Pub.L. 107–273, Div. B, Title IV, § 4005(d)(2), Nov. 2, 2002, 116 Stat. 1813.)

HISTORICAL AND STATUTORY NOTES

References in Text

Section 236(a) of the Atomic Energy Act of 1954, referred to in subsec. (a), is Act Aug. 1, 1946, c. 724, Title I, § 236(a), as added June 30, 1980, Pub.L. 96–295, Title II, § 204(a), 94 Stat. 787, as amended, which is classified to 42 U.S.C.A. § 2284(a).

Effective and Applicability Provisions

2002 Acts. Amendment by section 4005(d)(2) of Pub.L. 107–273, as therein provided, effective Oct. 26, 2001, which is the date of enactment of Pub.L. 107–56, to which such amendment relates.

§ 2339A. Providing material support to terrorists

(a) Offense.—Whoever provides material support or resources or conceals or disguises the nature, location, source, or ownership of material support or resources, knowing or intending that they are to be used in preparation for, or in carrying out, a violation of section 32, 37, 81, 175, 229, 351, 831, 842(m) or (n), 844(f) or (i), 930(c), 956, 1114, 1116, 1203, 1361, 1362, 1363, 1366, 1751, 1992, 2155, 2156, 2280, 2281, 2332, 2332a, 2332b, 2332f, or 2340A of this title, section 236 of the Atomic Energy Act of 1954 (42 U.S.C. 2284), section 46502 or 60123(b) of title 49, or any offense listed in section 2332b(g)(5)(B) (except for sections 2339A and 2339B) or in preparation for, or in carrying out, the concealment of an escape from the commission of any such violation, or attempts or conspires to do such an act, shall be fined under this title, imprisoned not more than 15 years, or both, and, if the death of any person results, shall be imprisoned for any term of years or for life. A violation of this section may be prosecuted in any Federal judicial district in which the underlying offense was committed, or in any other Federal judicial district as provided by law.

(b) Definitions.—As used in this section—

(1) the term "material support or resources" means any property, tangible or intangible, or service, including currency or monetary instruments or financial securities, financial services, lodging, training, expert advice or assistance, safehouses, false documentation or identification, communications equipment, facilities, weapons, lethal substances, explosives, personnel (1 or more individuals who may be or include oneself), and transportation, except medicine or religious materials;

(2) the term "training" means instruction or teaching designed to impart a specific skill, as opposed to general knowledge; and

(3) the term "expert advice or assistance" means advice or assistance derived from scientific, technical or other specialized knowledge.

(Added Pub.L. 103–322, Title XII, § 120005(a), Sept. 13, 1994, 108 Stat. 2022, and amended Pub.L. 104–132, Title III, § 323, Apr. 24, 1996, 110 Stat. 1255; Pub.L. 104–294, Title VI, §§ 601(b)(2), (s)(2), (3), 604(b)(5), Oct. 11, 1996, 110 Stat. 3498, 3502, 3506; Pub.L. 107–56, Title VIII, §§ 805(a), 810(c), 811(f), Oct. 26, 2001, 115 Stat. 377, 380, 381; Pub.L. 107–197, Title III, § 301(c), June 25, 2002, 116 Stat. 728; Pub.L. 107–273, Div. B, Title IV, § 4002(a)(7), (c)(1), (e)(11), Nov. 2, 2002, 116 Stat. 1807, 1808, 1811; Pub.L. 108–458, Title VI, § 6603(a)(2), (b), Dec. 17, 2004, 118 Stat. 3762; Pub.L. 109–177, Title I, § 110(b)(3)(B), Mar. 9, 2006, 120 Stat. 208.)

Termination of Amendment

For termination of amendment by Pub.L. 108–458, § 6603(g), see Sunset Provisions note set out under this section.

HISTORICAL AND STATUTORY NOTES

References in Text

Section 236(a) of the Atomic Energy Act of 1954, referred to in subsec. (a), is Act, Aug. 1, 1946, c. 724, Title I, § 236(a), as added June 30, 1980, Pub.L. 96–295, Title II, § 204(a), 94 Stat. 787, as amended, which is classified to 42 U.S.C.A. § 2284(a).

Codifications

Section 604(b)(5) of Pub.L. 104–294 amended directory language of section 120005(a) of Pub.L. 103–322, requiring no change in text.

Section 601(b)(2) of Pub.L. 104–294, which directed that subsec. (b) of this section be amended by substituting "2332", "2332a", "37", and "or an escape" for "2331", "2339", "36", and "of an escape", respectively, could not be executed to text as section had been completely revised by section 323 of Pub.L. 104–132. See 2002 and 1996 Amendments notes set out under this section.

Effective and Applicability Provisions

2002 Acts. Amendment by section 4002(c)(1) of Pub.L. 107–273, as therein provided, effective Oct. 11, 1996, which is the date of enactment of Pub.L. 104–294, to which such amendment relates.

1996 Acts. Amendment by section 604 of Pub.L. 104–294 effective Sept. 13, 1994, see section 604(d) of Pub.L. 104–294, set out as a note under section 13 of this title.

Sunset Provisions

Pub.L. 108–458, Title VI, § 6603(g), Dec. 17, 2004, 118 Stat. 3764, which provided that, except for offenses prohibited by Pub.L. 108–458, § 6603, which began or occurred before Dec. 31, 2006, amendments made by Pub.L. 108–458, § 6603, to this section and 18 U.S.C.A. §§ 2332b and 2339B, shall cease to be effective on Dec. 31, 2006, and was set out as a note under 18 U.S.C.A. § 2332b, was repealed by Pub.L. 109–177, Title I, § 104, Mar. 9, 2006, 120 Stat. 195.

Repeals

Section 601(b)(2) of Pub.L. 104–294, cited in the credit of this section, was repealed by section 4002(c)(1) of Pub.L. 107–273.

§ 2339B. Providing material support or resources to designated foreign terrorist organizations

(a) Prohibited activities.—

(1) Unlawful conduct.—Whoever knowingly provides material support or resources to a foreign terrorist organization, or attempts or conspires to do so, shall be fined under this title or imprisoned not more than 15 years, or both, and, if the death of any person results, shall be imprisoned for any term of years or for life. To violate this paragraph, a person must have knowledge that the organization is a designated terrorist organization (as defined in subsection (g)(6)), that the organization has engaged or engages in terrorist activity (as defined in section 212(a)(3)(B) of the Immigration and Nationality Act), or that the organization has engaged or engages in terrorism (as defined in section 140(d) (2) of the Foreign Relations Authorization Act, Fiscal Years 1988 and 1989).

(2) Financial institutions.—Except as authorized by the Secretary, any financial institution that becomes aware that it has possession of, or control over, any funds in which a foreign terrorist organization, or its agent, has an interest, shall—

(A) retain possession of, or maintain control over, such funds; and

(B) report to the Secretary the existence of such funds in accordance with regulations issued by the Secretary.

(b) Civil penalty.—Any financial institution that knowingly fails to comply with subsection (a)(2) shall be subject to a civil penalty in an amount that is the greater of—

(A) $50,000 per violation; or

(B) twice the amount of which the financial institution was required under subsection (a)(2) to retain possession or control.

(c) Injunction.—Whenever it appears to the Secretary or the Attorney General that any person is engaged in, or is about to engage in, any act that constitutes, or would constitute, a violation of this section, the Attorney General may initiate civil action in a district court of the United States to enjoin such violation.

(d) Extraterritorial jurisdiction.—

(1) In general.—There is jurisdiction over an offense under subsection (a) if—

(A) an offender is a national of the United States (as defined in section 101(a)(22) of the Immigration and Nationality Act (8 U.S.C. 1101(a)(22))) or an alien lawfully admitted for permanent residence in the United States (as defined in section 101(a)(20) of the Immigration and Nationality Act (8 U.S.C. 1101(a)(20)));

(B) an offender is a stateless person whose habitual residence is in the United States;

(C) after the conduct required for the offense occurs an offender is brought into or found in the United States, even if the conduct required for the offense occurs outside the United States;

(D) the offense occurs in whole or in part within the United States;

(E) the offense occurs in or affects interstate or foreign commerce; or

(F) an offender aids or abets any person over whom jurisdiction exists under this paragraph in committing an offense under subsection (a) or conspires with any person over whom jurisdiction exists under this paragraph to commit an offense under subsection (a).

(2) Extraterritorial jurisdiction.—There is extraterritorial Federal jurisdiction over an offense under this section.

(e) Investigations.—

(1) In general.—The Attorney General shall conduct any investigation of a possible violation of this section, or of any license, order, or regulation issued pursuant to this section.

(2) Coordination with the Department of the Treasury.—The Attorney General shall work in coordination with the Secretary in investigations relating to—

(A) the compliance or noncompliance by a financial institution with the requirements of subsection (a)(2); and

(B) civil penalty proceedings authorized under subsection (b).

(3) Referral.—Any evidence of a criminal violation of this section arising in the course of an investigation by the Secretary or any other Federal agency shall be referred immediately to the Attorney General for further investigation. The Attorney General shall timely notify the Secretary of any action taken on referrals from the Secretary, and may refer investigations to the Secretary for remedial licensing or civil penalty action.

(f) Classified information in civil proceedings brought by the United States.—

(1) Discovery of classified information by defendants.—

(A) Request by United States.—In any civil proceeding under this section, upon request made ex parte and in writing by the United States, a court, upon a sufficient showing, may authorize the United States to—

(i) redact specified items of classified information from documents to be introduced into evidence or made available to the defendant through discovery under the Federal Rules of Civil Procedure;

(ii) substitute a summary of the information for such classified documents; or

(iii) substitute a statement admitting relevant facts that the classified information would tend to prove.

(B) Order granting request.—If the court enters an order granting a request under this paragraph, the entire text of the documents to which the request relates shall be sealed and preserved in the records of the court to be made available to the appellate court in the event of an appeal.

(C) Denial of request.—If the court enters an order denying a request of the United States under this paragraph, the United States may take an immediate, interlocutory appeal in accordance with paragraph (5). For purposes of such an appeal, the entire text of the documents to which the request relates, together with any transcripts of arguments made ex parte to the court in connection therewith, shall be maintained under seal and delivered to the appellate court.

(2) Introduction of classified information; precautions by court.—

(A) Exhibits.—To prevent unnecessary or inadvertent disclosure of classified information in a civil proceeding brought by the United States under this section, the United States may petition the court ex parte to admit, in lieu of classified writings, recordings, or photographs, one or more of the following:

(i) Copies of items from which classified information has been redacted.

(ii) Stipulations admitting relevant facts that specific classified information would tend to prove.

(iii) A declassified summary of the specific classified information.

(B) Determination by court.—The court shall grant a request under this paragraph if the court finds that the redacted item, stipulation, or summary is sufficient to allow the defendant to prepare a defense.

(3) Taking of trial testimony.—

(A) Objection.—During the examination of a witness in any civil proceeding brought by the United States under this subsection, the United States may object to any question or line of inquiry that may require the witness to disclose classified information not previously found to be admissible.

(B) Action by court.—In determining whether a response is admissible, the court shall take precautions to guard against the compromise of any classified information, including—

(i) permitting the United States to provide the court, ex parte, with a proffer of the witness's response to the question or line of inquiry; and

(ii) requiring the defendant to provide the court with a proffer of the nature of the information that the defendant seeks to elicit.

(C) Obligation of defendant.—In any civil proceeding under this section, it shall be the defendant's obligation to establish the relevance and materiality of any classified information sought to be introduced.

(4) Appeal.—If the court enters an order denying a request of the United States under this subsection, the United States may take an immediate interlocutory appeal in accordance with paragraph (5).

(5) Interlocutory appeal.—

(A) Subject of appeal.—An interlocutory appeal by the United States shall lie to a court of appeals from a decision or order of a district court—

(i) authorizing the disclosure of classified information;

(ii) imposing sanctions for nondisclosure of classified information; or

(iii) refusing a protective order sought by the United States to prevent the disclosure of classified information.

(B) Expedited consideration.—

(i) In general.—An appeal taken pursuant to this paragraph, either before or during trial, shall be expedited by the court of appeals.

(ii) Appeals prior to trial.—If an appeal is of an order made prior to trial, an appeal shall be taken not later than 10 days after the decision or order appealed from, and the trial shall not commence until the appeal is resolved.

(iii) Appeals during trial.—If an appeal is taken during trial, the trial court shall adjourn the trial until the appeal is resolved, and the court of appeals—

(I) shall hear argument on such appeal not later than 4 days after the adjournment of the trial;

(II) may dispense with written briefs other than the supporting materials previously submitted to the trial court;

(III) shall render its decision not later than 4 days after argument on appeal; and

(IV) may dispense with the issuance of a written opinion in rendering its decision.

(C) Effect of ruling.—An interlocutory appeal and decision shall not affect the right of the defendant, in a subsequent appeal from a final judgment, to claim as error reversal by the trial court on remand of a ruling appealed from during trial.

(6) Construction.—Nothing in this subsection shall prevent the United States from seeking protective orders or asserting privileges ordinarily available to the United States to protect against the disclosure of classified information, including the invocation of the military and State secrets privilege.

(g) Definitions.—As used in this section—

(1) the term "classified information" has the meaning given that term in section 1(a) of the Classified Information Procedures Act (18 U.S.C. App.);

(2) the term "financial institution" has the same meaning as in section 5312(a)(2) of title 31, United States Code;

(3) the term "funds" includes coin or currency of the United States or any other country, traveler's checks, personal checks, bank checks, money orders, stocks, bonds, debentures, drafts, letters of credit, any other negotiable instrument, and any electronic representation of any of the foregoing;

(4) the term "material support or resources" has the same meaning given that term in section 2339A (including the definitions of "training" and "expert advice or assistance" in that section);

(5) the term "Secretary" means the Secretary of the Treasury; and

(6) the term "terrorist organization" means an organization designated as a terrorist organization under section 219 of the Immigration and Nationality Act.

(h) Provision of personnel.—No person may be prosecuted under this section in connection with the term "personnel" unless that person has knowingly provided, attempted to provide, or conspired to provide a foreign terrorist organization with 1 or more individuals (who may be or include himself) to work under that terrorist organization's direction or control or to organize, manage, supervise, or otherwise direct the operation of that organization. Individuals who act entirely independently of the foreign terrorist organization to advance its goals or objectives shall not be considered to be working under the foreign terrorist organization's direction and control.

(i) Rule of construction.—Nothing in this section shall be construed or applied so as to abridge the exercise of rights guaranteed under the First Amendment to the Constitution of the United States.

(j) Exception.—No person may be prosecuted under this section in connection with the term "personnel", "training", or "expert advice or assistance" if the provision of that material support or resources to a foreign terrorist organization was approved by the Secretary of State with the concurrence of the Attorney General. The Secretary of State may not approve the provision of any material support that may be used to carry out terrorist activity (as defined in section 212(a)(3)(B)(iii) of the Immigration and Nationality Act).

(Added Pub.L. 104–132, Title III, § 303(a), Apr. 24, 1996, 110 Stat. 1250, and amended Pub.L. 107–56, Title VIII, § 810(d), Oct. 26, 2001, 115 Stat. 380; Pub.L. 108–458, Title VI, § 6603(c) to (f), Dec. 17, 2004, 118 Stat. 3762, 3763.)

Termination of Amendment

For termination of amendment by Pub.L. 108–458, § 6603(g), see Sunset Provisions note set out under this section.

HISTORICAL AND STATUTORY NOTES

References in Text

Section 212(a)(3)(B) of the Immigration and Nationality Act, referred to in subsec. (a)(1), is Act June 27, 1952, c. 477, Title II, ch. 2, § 212(a)(3)(B), 66 Stat. 182, as amended, which is classified to 8 U.S.C.A. § 1182(a)(3)(B).

Section 140(d)(2) of the Foreign Relations Authorization Act, Fiscal Years 1988 and 1989, referred to in subsec. (a)(1), is Pub.L. 100–204, Title I, § 140, Dec. 22, 1987, 101 Stat. 1347, as amended, which is classified to 22 U.S.C.A. § 2656f(d)(2).

Section 101(a)(22) of the Immigration and Nationality Act, referred to in subsec. (d)(1)(A), is Act June 27, 1952, c. 477, Title I, § 101(a)(22), 66 Stat. 166, as amended, which is classified to 8 U.S.C.A. § 1101(a)(22).

Section 101(a)(20) of the Immigration and Nationality Act, referred to in subsec. (d)(1)(A), is Act June 27, 1952, c. 477, Title I, § 101(a)(20), 66 Stat. 166, as amended, which is classified to 8 U.S.C.A. § 1101(a)(20).

The Federal Rules of Civil Procedure, referred to in subsec. (f)(1)(A)(i), are set out in Title 28, Federal Rules of Civil Procedure.

Section 1(a) of the Classified Information Procedures Act, referred to in subsec. (g)(1), is section 1(a) of Pub.L. 95–456, Oct. 15, 1980, 94 Stat. 2025, as amended, which is classified to Appendix 3 to Title 18, Crimes and Criminal Procedure.

Section 219 of the Immigration and Nationality Act, referred to in subsec. (g)(6), is section 219 of Act June 27, 1952, c. 477, Title II, ch. 2, as added Apr. 24, 1996, Pub.L. 104–132, Title III, § 302(a), 110 Stat. 1248, as amended, which is classified to section 1189 of Title 8, Aliens and Nationality.

Section 212(a)(3)(B)(iii) of the Immigration and Nationality Act, referred to in subsec. (j), is Act June 27, 1952, c. 477, Title II, ch. 2, § 212(a)(3)(B)(iii), 66 Stat. 182, as amended, which is classified to 8 U.S.C.A. § 1182(a)(3)(B)(iii).

Sunset Provisions

Pub.L. 108–458, Title VI, § 6603(g), Dec. 17, 2004, 118 Stat. 3764, which provided that, except for offenses prohibited by Pub.L. 108–458, § 6603, which began or occurred before Dec. 31, 2006, amendments made by Pub.L. 108–458, § 6603, to this section and 18 U.S.C.A. §§ 2332b and 2339A, shall cease to be effective on Dec. 31, 2006, and was set out as a note under 18 U.S.C.A. § 2332b, was repealed by Pub.L. 109–177, Title I, § 104, Mar. 9, 2006, 120 Stat. 195.

International Terrorist Fundraising Prohibition; Findings and Purpose

Section 301 of Pub.L. 104–132 provided that:

"**(a) Findings.—The Congress finds that—**

"(1) international terrorism is a serious and deadly problem that threatens the vital interests of the United States;

"(2) the Constitution confers upon Congress the power to punish crimes against the law of nations and to carry out the treaty obligations of the United States, and therefore Congress may by law impose penalties relating to the provision of material support to foreign organizations engaged in terrorist activity;

"(3) the power of the United States over immigration and naturalization permits the exclusion from the United States of persons belonging to international terrorist organizations;

"(4) international terrorism affects the interstate and foreign commerce of the United States by harming international trade and market stability, and limiting international travel by United States citizens as well as foreign visitors to the United States;

"(5) international cooperation is required for an effective response to terrorism, as demonstrated by the numerous multilateral conventions in force providing universal prosecutive jurisdiction over persons involved in a variety of terrorist acts, including hostage taking, murder of an internationally protected person, and aircraft piracy and sabotage;

"(6) some foreign terrorist organizations, acting through affiliated groups or individuals, raise significant funds within the United States, or use the United States as a conduit for the receipt of funds raised in other nations; and

"(7) foreign organizations that engage in terrorist activity are so tainted by their criminal conduct that any contribution to such an organization facilitates that conduct.

"**(b) Purpose.**—The purpose of this subtitle [Subtitle A of Title III of Pub.L. 104–132, enacting this section and section 1189 of Title 8, Aliens and Nationality] is to provide the Federal Government the fullest possible basis, consistent with the Constitution, to prevent persons within the United States, or subject to the jurisdiction of the United States, from providing material support or resources to foreign organizations that engage in terrorist activities."

§ 2339C. Prohibitions against the financing of terrorism

(a) Offenses.—

(1) In general.—Whoever, in a circumstance described in subsection (b), by any means, directly or indirectly, unlawfully and willfully provides or collects funds with the intention that such funds be used, or with the knowledge that such funds are to be used, in full or in part, in order to carry out—

(A) an act which constitutes an offense within the scope of a treaty specified in subsection (e)(7), as implemented by the United States, or

(B) any other act intended to cause death or serious bodily injury to a civilian, or to any other person not taking an active part in the hostilities in a situation of armed conflict, when the purpose of such act, by its nature or context, is to intimidate a population, or to compel a government or an international organization to do or to abstain from doing any act,

shall be punished as prescribed in subsection (d)(1).

(2) Attempts and conspiracies.—Whoever attempts or conspires to commit an offense under paragraph (1) shall be punished as prescribed in subsection (d)(1).

(3) Relationship to predicate act.—For an act to constitute an offense set forth in this subsection, it shall not be necessary that the funds were actually used to carry out a predicate act.

(b) Jurisdiction.—There is jurisdiction over the offenses in subsection (a) in the following circumstances—

(1) the offense takes place in the United States and—

(A) a perpetrator was a national of another state or a stateless person;

(B) on board a vessel flying the flag of another state or an aircraft which is registered under the laws of another state at the time the offense is committed;

(C) on board an aircraft which is operated by the government of another state;

(D) a perpetrator is found outside the United States;

(E) was directed toward or resulted in the carrying out of a predicate act against—

(i) a national of another state; or

(ii) another state or a government facility of such state, including its embassy or other diplomatic or consular premises of that state;

(F) was directed toward or resulted in the carrying out of a predicate act committed in an attempt to compel another state or international organization to do or abstain from doing any act; or

(G) was directed toward or resulted in the carrying out of a predicate act—

(i) outside the United States; or

(ii) within the United States, and either the offense or the predicate act was conducted in, or the results thereof affected, interstate or foreign commerce;

(2) the offense takes place outside the United States and—

(A) a perpetrator is a national of the United States or is a stateless person whose habitual residence is in the United States;

(B) a perpetrator is found in the United States; or

(C) was directed toward or resulted in the carrying out of a predicate act against—

(i) any property that is owned, leased, or used by the United States or by any department or agency of the United States, including an embassy or other diplomatic or consular premises of the United States;

(ii) any person or property within the United States;

(iii) any national of the United States or the property of such national; or

(iv) any property of any legal entity organized under the laws of the United States, including any of its States, districts, commonwealths, territories, or possessions;

(3) the offense is committed on board a vessel flying the flag of the United States or an aircraft which is registered under the laws of the United States at the time the offense is committed;

(4) the offense is committed on board an aircraft which is operated by the United States; or

(5) the offense was directed toward or resulted in the carrying out of a predicate act committed in an attempt to compel the United States to do or abstain from doing any act.

(c) Concealment.—Whoever—

(1)(A) is in the United States; or

(B) is outside the United States and is a national of the United States or a legal entity organized under the laws of the United States (including any of its States, districts, commonwealths, territories, or possessions); and

(2) knowingly conceals or disguises the nature, location, source, ownership, or control of any material support or resources, or any funds or proceeds of such funds—

(A) knowing or intending that the support or resources are to be provided, or knowing that the support or resources were provided, in violation of section 2339B of this title; or

(B) knowing or intending that any such funds are to be provided or collected, or knowing that the funds were provided or collected, in violation of subsection (a),

shall be punished as prescribed in subsection (d)(2).

(d) Penalties.—

(1) Subsection (a)—Whoever violates subsection (a) shall be fined under this title, imprisoned for not more than 20 years, or both.

(2) Subsection (c)—Whoever violates subsection (c) shall be fined under this title, imprisoned for not more than 10 years, or both.

(e) Definitions.—In this section—

(1) the term "funds" means assets of every kind, whether tangible or intangible, movable or immovable, however acquired, and legal documents or instruments in any form, including electronic or digital, evidencing title to, or interest in, such assets, including coin, currency, bank credits, travelers checks, bank checks, money orders, shares, securities, bonds, drafts, and letters of credit;

(2) the term "government facility" means any permanent or temporary facility or conveyance that is used or occupied by representatives of a state, members of a government, the legislature, or the judiciary, or by officials or employees of a state or any other public authority or entity or by employees or officials of an intergovernmental organization in connection with their official duties;

(3) the term "proceeds" means any funds derived from or obtained, directly or indirectly, through the commission of an offense set forth in subsection (a);

(4) the term "provides" includes giving, donating, and transmitting;

(5) the term "collects" includes raising and receiving;

(6) the term "predicate act" means any act referred to in subparagraph (A) or (B) of subsection (a)(1);

(7) the term "treaty" means—

(A) the Convention for the Suppression of Unlawful Seizure of Aircraft, done at The Hague on December 16, 1970;

(B) the Convention for the Suppression of Unlawful Acts against the Safety of Civil Aviation, done at Montreal on September 23, 1971;

(C) the Convention on the Prevention and Punishment of Crimes against Internationally Protected Persons, including Diplomatic Agents, adopted by the General Assembly of the United Nations on December 14, 1973;

(D) the International Convention against the Taking of Hostages, adopted by the General Assembly of the United Nations on December 17, 1979;

(E) the Convention on the Physical Protection of Nuclear Material, adopted at Vienna on March 3, 1980;

(F) the Protocol for the Suppression of Unlawful Acts of Violence at Airports Serving International Civil Aviation, supplementary to the Convention for the Suppression of Unlawful Acts against the Safety of Civil Aviation, done at Montreal on February 24, 1988;

(G) the Convention for the Suppression of Unlawful Acts against the Safety of Maritime Navigation, done at Rome on March 10, 1988;

(H) the Protocol for the Suppression of Unlawful Acts against the Safety of Fixed Platforms located on the Continental Shelf, done at Rome on March 10, 1988; or

(I) the International Convention for the Suppression of Terrorist Bombings, adopted by the General Assembly of the United Nations on December 15, 1997;

(8) the term "intergovernmental organization" includes international organizations;

(9) the term "international organization" has the same meaning as in section 1116(b)(5) of this title;

(10) the term "armed conflict" does not include internal disturbances and tensions, such as riots, isolated and sporadic acts of violence, and other acts of a similar nature;

(11) the term "serious bodily injury" has the same meaning as in section 1365(g)(3) of this title;

(12) the term "national of the United States" has the meaning given that term in section 101(a)(22) of the Immigration and Nationality Act (8 U.S.C. 1101(a)(22));

(13) the term "material support or resources" has the same meaning given that term in section 2339B(g)(4) of this title; and

(14) the term "state" has the same meaning as that term has under international law, and includes all political subdivisions thereof.

(f) Civil penalty.—In addition to any other criminal, civil, or administrative liability or penalty, any legal entity located within the United States or organized under the laws of the United States, including any of the laws of its States, districts, commonwealths, territories, or possessions, shall be liable to the United States for the sum of at least $10,000, if a person responsible for the management or control of that legal entity has, in that capacity, committed an offense set forth in subsection (a).

(Added Pub.L. 107–197, Title II, § 202(a), June 25, 2002, 116 Stat. 724, and amended Pub.L. 107–273, Div. B, Title IV, § 4006, Nov. 2, 2002, 116 Stat. 1813; Pub.L. 108–458, Title VI, § 6604, Dec. 17, 2004, 118 Stat. 3764; Pub.L. 109–177, Title IV, § 408, Mar. 9, 2006, 120 Stat. 245.)

HISTORICAL AND STATUTORY NOTES

References in Text

Section 1365(g)(3), referred to in subsec. (e)(11), was redesignated section 1365(h)(3) by Pub.L. 107–307, §2(1), Dec. 2, 2002, 116 Stat. 2445.

Section 101(a)(22) of the Immigration and Nationality Act, referred to in subsec. (e)(12), is Act June 27, 1952, c. 477, Title I, § 101(a)(22), 66 Stat. 169, as amended, which is classified to 8 U.S.C.A. § 1101(a)(22).

Codifications

Amendment by Pub.L. 109–177, § 408, which directed that the directory language of Pub.L.108–458, § 6604, be amended by striking "Section 2339c(c)(2)" and inserting "Section 2339C(c)(2)"; and by striking "Section 2339c(e)" and inserting "Section 2339C(e)", effective on the date of enactment of that Act, required no change in text. See 2004 Amendments and Effective and Applicability Provisions notes under this section.

Effective and Applicability Provisions

2006 Acts. Pub.L. 109–177, Title IV, § 408, Mar. 9, 2006, 120 Stat. 245, provided in part that the directory language of section 6604 of the Intelligence Reform and Terrorism Prevention Act of 2004 [Pub.L.108–458, Title VI, § 6604, Dec. 17, 2004, 118 Stat. 3764, which amended this section] is amended "effective on the date of the enactment of that Act [Dec. 17, 2004]".

2002 Acts. Pub.L. 107–197, Title II, § 203, June 25, 2002, 116 Stat. 727, provided that: "Except for paragraphs (1)(D) and (2)(B) of section 2339C(b) of title 18, United States Code [subsecs. (b)(1)(D) and (b)(2)(B) of this section], which shall become effective on the date that the International Convention for the Suppression of the Financing of Terrorism enters into force for the United States [July 26, 2002], and for the provisions of section 2339C(e)(7)(I) of title 18, United States Code [subsec. (e)(7)(I) of this section], which shall become effective on the date that the International Convention for the Suppression of Terrorist Bombing enters into force for the United States [July 26, 2002], section 202 [enacting this section and provisions set out as notes under this section] shall take effect on the date of enactment of this Act [June 25, 2002]."

Disclaimer

Pub.L. 107–197, Title II, § 202(c), June 25, 2002, 116 Stat. 727, provided that: "Nothing contained in this section is intended to affect the scope or applicability of any other Federal or State law."

§ 2339D. Receiving military-type training from a foreign terrorist organization [1]

(a) Offense.—Whoever knowingly receives military-type training from or on behalf of any organization designated at the time of the training by the Secretary of State under section 219(a)(1) of the Immigration and Nationality Act as a foreign terrorist organization shall be fined under this title or imprisoned for ten years, or both. To violate this subsection, a person must have knowledge that the organization is a designated terrorist organization (as defined in subsection (c)(4)), that the organization has engaged or engages in terrorist activity (as defined in section 212 of the Immigration and Nationality Act), or that the organization has engaged or engages in terrorism (as defined in section 140(d)(2) of the Foreign Relations Authorization Act, Fiscal Years 1988 and 1989).

(b) Extraterritorial jurisdiction.—There is extraterritorial Federal jurisdiction over an offense under this section. There is jurisdiction over an offense under subsection (a) if—

(1) an offender is a national of the United States (as defined in 101(a)(22) [2] of the Immigration and Nationality Act) or an alien lawfully admitted for permanent residence in the United States (as defined in section 101(a)(20) of the Immigration and Nationality Act);

(2) an offender is a stateless person whose habitual residence is in the United States;

(3) after the conduct required for the offense occurs an offender is brought into or found in the United States, even if the conduct required for the offense occurs outside the United States;

(4) the offense occurs in whole or in part within the United States;

(5) the offense occurs in or affects interstate or foreign commerce; or

(6) an offender aids or abets any person over whom jurisdiction exists under this paragraph in committing an offense under subsection (a) or conspires with any person over whom jurisdiction exists under this paragraph to commit an offense under subsection (a).

(c) Definitions.—As used in this section—

(1) the term "military-type training" includes training in means or methods that can cause death or serious bodily injury, destroy or damage property, or disrupt services to critical infrastructure, or training on the use, storage, production, or assembly of any explosive, firearm or other weapon, including any weapon of mass destruction (as defined in section 2232a(c)(2)[3]);

(2) the term "serious bodily injury" has the meaning given that term in section 1365(h)(3);

(3) the term "critical infrastructure" means systems and assets vital to national defense, national security, economic security, public health or safety including both regional and national infrastructure. Critical infrastructure may be publicly or privately owned; examples of critical infrastructure include gas and oil production, storage, or delivery systems, water supply systems, telecommunications networks, electrical power generation or delivery systems, financing and banking systems, emergency services (including medical, police, fire, and rescue services), and transportation systems and services (including highways, mass transit, airlines, and airports); and

(4) the term "foreign terrorist organization" means an organization designated as a terrorist organization under section 219(a)(1) of the Immigration and Nationality Act.

(Added Pub.L. 108–458, Title VI, § 6602, Dec. 17, 2004, 118 Stat. 3761.)

[1] Section was enacted without corresponding amendment to analysis.

[2] So in original. Probably should be preceded by "section".

[3] So in original. Probably should be section "2332a(c)(2)".

HISTORICAL AND STATUTORY NOTES

References in Text

Section 219(a)(1) of the Immigration and Nationality Act, referred to in subsecs. (a) and (c)(4), is Act June 27, 1952, c. 477, Title II, ch. 2, § 219(a)(1), as added Apr. 24, 1996, Pub.L. 104–132, Title III, § 302(a), 110 Stat. 1248, as amended, which is classified to 8 U.S.C.A. § 1189(a)(1).

Section 212 of the Immigration and Nationality Act, referred to in subsec. (a), is Act June 27, 1952, c. 477, Title II, ch. 2, § 212, 66 Stat. 182, as amended, which is classified to 8 U.S.C.A. § 1182.

Section 140(d)(2) of the Foreign Relations Authorization Act, Fiscal Years 1988 and 1989, referred to in subsec. (a), is

Pub.L. 100–204, Title I, § 140(d)(2), Dec. 22, 1987, 101 Stat. 1347, as amended, which is classified to 22 U.S.C.A. § 2656f(d)(2).

101(a)(22) of the Immigration and Nationality Act, referred to in subsec. (b)(1), is Act June 27, 1952, c. 477, Title I, § 101(a)(22), 66 Stat. 166, as amended, which is classified to 8 U.S.C.A. § 1101(a)(22).

Section 101(a)(20) of the Immigration and Nationality Act, referred to in subsec. (b)(1), is Act June 27, 1952, c. 477, Title I, § 101(a)(20), 66 Stat. 166, as amended, which is classified to 8 U.S.C.A. § 1101(a)(20).

CHAPTER 113C—TORTURE

(Added Pub.L. 103–236, Title V, § 506(a), Apr. 30, 1994, 108 Stat. 463, and amended Pub.L. 103–415, § 1(k), Oct. 25, 1994, 108 Stat. 4301; Pub.L. 103–429, § 2(2), Oct. 31, 1994, 108 Stat. 4377; Pub.L. 108–375, Div. A, Title X, § 1089, Oct. 28, 2004, 118 Stat. 2067.)

HISTORICAL AND STATUTORY NOTES

Codifications

Pub.L. 104–294, Title VI, § 601(j)(1), Oct. 11, 1996, 110 Stat. 3501, which directed that chapter 113B, relating to torture, be redesignated chapter 113C, was incapable of execution due to prior identical amendment by section 303(c)(1) of Pub.L. 104–132.

Effective and Applicability Provisions

2002 Acts. Amendment by section 4002(c)(1) of Pub.L. 107–273, as therein provided, effective Oct. 11, 1996, which is the date of enactment of Pub.L. 104–294, to which such amendment relates.

HISTORICAL AND STATUTORY NOTES

Effective and Applicability Provisions

1994 Acts. Section 506(c) of Pub.L. 103–236 provided that: "The amendments made by this section [enacting this chapter] shall take effect on the later of—

"(1) the date of enactment of this Act [Apr. 30, 1994]; or

"(2) the date on which the United States has become a party to the Convention Against Torture and Other Cruel, Inhuman or Degrading Treatment or Punishment."

[Convention entered into force with respect to the United States Nov. 20, 1994, Treaty Doc. 100–20.]

§ 2340. Definitions

As used in this chapter—

(1) "torture" means an act committed by a person acting under the color of law specifically intended to inflict severe physical or mental pain or suffering (other than pain or suffering incidental to lawful sanctions) upon another person within his custody or physical control;

(2) "severe mental pain or suffering" means the prolonged mental harm caused by or resulting from—

(A) the intentional infliction or threatened infliction of severe physical pain or suffering;

(B) the administration or application, or threatened administration or application, of mind-altering substances or other procedures calculated to disrupt profoundly the senses or the personality;

(C) the threat of imminent death; or

(D) the threat that another person will imminently be subjected to death, severe physical pain or suffering, or the administration or application of mind-altering substances or other procedures calculated to disrupt profoundly the senses or personality; and

(3) "United States" means the several States of the United States, the District of Columbia, and the commonwealths, territories, and possessions of the United States.

§ 2340A. Torture

(a) Offense.—Whoever outside the United States commits or attempts to commit torture shall be fined under this title or imprisoned not more than 20 years, or both, and if death results to any person from conduct prohibited by this subsection, shall be punished by death or imprisoned for any term of years or for life.

(b) Jurisdiction.—There is jurisdiction over the activity prohibited in subsection (a) if—

(1) the alleged offender is a national of the United States; or

(2) the alleged offender is present in the United States, irrespective of the nationality of the victim or alleged offender.

(c) Conspiracy.—A person who conspires to commit an offense under this section shall be subject to the same penalties (other than the penalty of death) as the penalties prescribed for the offense, the commission of which was the object of the conspiracy.

(Added Pub.L. 103–236, Title V, § 506(a), Apr. 30, 1994, 108 Stat. 463, and amended Pub.L. 103–322, Title VI, § 60020, Sept. 13, 1994, 108 Stat. 1979; Pub.L. 107–56, Title VIII, § 811(g), Oct. 26, 2001, 115 Stat. 381.)

HISTORICAL AND STATUTORY NOTES

Effective and Applicability Provisions

1994 Acts. Section effective on the later of Apr. 30, 1994, or the date on which the United States has become a party to the Convention Against Torture and Other Cruel, Inhuman or Degrading Treatment or Punishment, see section 506(c) of Pub.L. 103–236, set out as a note under section 2340 of this title.

§ 2340B. Exclusive remedies

Nothing in this chapter shall be construed as precluding the application of State or local laws on the same subject, nor shall anything in this chapter be construed as creating any substantive or procedural right enforceable by law by any party in any civil proceeding.

(Added Pub.L. 103–236, Title V, § 506(a), Apr. 30, 1994, 108 Stat. 464.)

HISTORICAL AND STATUTORY NOTES

Effective and Applicability Provisions

1994 Acts. Section effective on the later of Apr. 30, 1994, or the date on which the United States has become a party to the Convention Against Torture and Other Cruel, Inhuman or Degrading Treatment or Punishment, see section 506(c) of Pub.L. 103–236, set out as a note under section 2340 of this title.

CHAPTER 114—TRAFFICKING IN CONTRABAND CIGARETTES AND SMOKELESS TOBACCO

Sec.

§ 2341. Definitions

As used in this chapter—

(1) the term "cigarette" means—

(A) any roll of tobacco wrapped in paper or in any substance not containing tobacco; and

(B) any roll of tobacco wrapped in any substance containing tobacco which, because of its appearance, the type of tobacco used in the filler, or its packaging and labeling, is likely to be offered to, or purchased by, consumers as a cigarette described in subparagraph (A);

(2) the term "contraband cigarettes" means a quantity in excess of 10,000 cigarettes, which bear no evidence of the payment of applicable State or local cigarette taxes in the State or locality where such cigarettes are found, if the State or local government requires a stamp, impression, or other indication to be placed on packages or other containers of cigarettes to evidence payment of cigarette taxes, and which are in the possession of any person other than—

(A) a person holding a permit issued pursuant to chapter 52 of the Internal Revenue Code of 1986 as a manufacturer of tobacco products or as an export warehouse proprietor, or a person operating a customs bonded warehouse pursuant to section 311 or 555 of the Tariff Act of 1930 (19 U.S.C. 1311 or 1555) or an agent of such person;

(B) a common or contract carrier transporting the cigarettes involved under a proper bill of lading or freight bill which states the quantity, source, and destination of such cigarettes;

(C) a person—

(i) who is licensed or otherwise authorized by the State where the cigarettes are found to account for and pay cigarette taxes imposed by such State; and

(ii) who has complied with the accounting and payment requirements relating to such license or authorization with respect to the cigarettes involved; or

(D) an officer, employee, or other agent of the United States or a State, or any department, agency, or instrumentality of the United States or a State (including any political subdivision of a State) having possession of such cigarettes in connection with the performance of official duties;

(3) the term "common or contract carrier" means a carrier holding a certificate of convenience and necessity, a permit for contract carrier by motor vehicle, or other valid operating authority under subtitle IV of title 49, or under equivalent operating authority from a regulatory agency of the United States or of any State;

(4) the term "State" means a State of the United States, the District of Columbia, the Commonwealth of Puerto Rico, or the Virgin Islands;

(5) the term "Attorney General" means the Attorney General of the United States;

(6) the term "smokeless tobacco" means any finely cut, ground, powdered, or leaf tobacco that is intended to be placed in the oral or nasal cavity or otherwise consumed without being combusted;

(7) the term "contraband smokeless tobacco" means a quantity in excess of 500 single-unit consumer-sized cans or packages of smokeless tobacco, or their equivalent, that are in the possession of any person other than—

(A) a person holding a permit issued pursuant to chapter 52 of the Internal Revenue Code of 1986 as manufacturer of tobacco products or as an export warehouse proprietor, a person operating a customs bonded warehouse pursuant to section 311 or 555 of the Tariff Act of 1930 (19 U.S.C. 1311, 1555), or an agent of such person;

(B) a common carrier transporting such smokeless tobacco under a proper bill of lading or freight bill which states the quantity, source, and designation of such smokeless tobacco;

(C) a person who—

(i) is licensed or otherwise authorized by the State where such smokeless tobacco is found to engage in the business of selling or distributing tobacco products; and

(ii) has complied with the accounting, tax, and payment requirements relating to such license or authorization with respect to such smokeless tobacco; or

(D) an officer, employee, or agent of the United States or a State, or any department, agency, or instrumentality of the United States or a State (including any political subdivision of a State), having possession of such smokeless tobacco in connection with the performance of official duties; [1]

(Added Pub.L. 95–575, § 1, Nov. 2, 1978, 92 Stat. 2463, and amended Pub.L. 97–449, § 5(c), Jan. 12, 1983, 96 Stat. 2442; Pub.L. 99–514, § 2, Oct. 22, 1986, 100 Stat. 2095; Pub.L. 107–296, Title XI, § 1112(i)(1), Nov. 25, 2002, 116 Stat. 2277; Pub.L. 109–177, Title I, § 121(a)(1), (b)(1), (6), Mar. 9, 2006, 120 Stat. 221, 222.)

1 So in original. The semicolon probably should be a period.

HISTORICAL AND STATUTORY NOTES

References in Text

Sections 311 and 555 of the Tariff Act of 1930, referred to in par. (2)(A), are classified to 19 U.S.C.A. §§ 1311 and 1555.

Chapter 52 of the Internal Revenue Code of 1986, referred to in pars. (2)(A) and (7)(A), is chapter 52 of Title 26, Tobacco Products and Cigarette Papers and Tubes, 26 U.S.C.A. § 5701 et seq.

Section 311 or 555 of the Tariff Act of 1930, referred to in par. (7)(A), is Act June 17, 1930, c. 497, Title III, § 311, or Title IV, § 555, 46 Stat. 743, which is classified to 19 U.S.C.A. § 1311 or 1555.

Codifications

Amendment by Pub.L. 109–177, § 121(b)(6), which directed that the matter preceding par. (2)(A) of this section be further amended by striking "State cigarette taxes in the State where such cigarettes are found, if the State" and inserting "State or local cigarette taxes in the State or locality where such cigarettes are found, if the State or local government", was executed by striking "State cigarette taxes in the State where such cigarettes are found, if such State" and inserting "State or local cigarette taxes in the State or locality where such cigarettes are found, if the State or local government", as the probable intent of Congress.

Amendment by Pub.L. 109–177, § 121(b)(1)(B), which directed that par. (5) of this section be amended "by striking the period at the end and inserting a semicolon", was executed by inserting a semicolon, as the probable intent of Congress.

Effective and Applicability Provisions

2002 Acts. Amendment by Pub.L. 107–296 effective 60 days after Nov. 25, 2002, see Pub.L. 107–296, § 4, set out as a note under 6 U.S.C.A. § 101.

1978 Acts. Section 4 of Pub.L. 95–575 provided that:

"**(a)** Except as provided in subsection (b), this Act [enacting this chapter, amending section 1961 of this title and sections 781 and 787 of Title 49, Transportation, and enacting provisions set out as a note under this section] shall take effect on the date of its enactment [Nov. 2, 1978].

"**(b)** Sections 2342(b) and 2343 of title 18, United States Code [section 2342(b) and 2343 of this title], as enacted by the first section of this Act, shall take effect on the first day of the first month beginning more than 120 days after the date of the enactment of this Act [Nov. 2, 1978]."

Authorization of Appropriations

Section 5 of Pub.L. 95–575 provided that: "There are hereby authorized to be appropriated such sums as may be necessary to carry out the provisions of chapter 114 of title 18, United States Code [this chapter], added by the first section of this Act."

§ 2342. Unlawful acts

(a) It shall be unlawful for any person knowingly to ship, transport, receive, possess, sell, distribute, or purchase contraband cigarettes or contraband smokeless tobacco.

(b) It shall be unlawful for any person knowingly to make any false statement or representation with respect to the information required by this chapter to be kept in the records of any person who ships, sells, or distributes any quantity of cigarettes in excess of 10,000 in a single transaction.

(Added Pub.L. 95–575, § 1, Nov. 2, 1978, 92 Stat. 2464, and amended Pub.L. 109–177, Title I, § 121(a)(2), (b)(2), Mar. 9, 2006, 120 Stat. 221, 222.)

HISTORICAL AND STATUTORY NOTES

Effective and Applicability Provisions

1978 Acts. Subsec. (a) of this section effective Nov. 2, 1978, and subsec. (b) of this section effective on the first day of the first month beginning more than 120 days after Nov. 2, 1978, see section 4 of Pub.L. 95–575, set out as a note under 18 U.S.C.A. § 2341.

§ 2343. Recordkeeping, reporting, and inspection

(a) Any person who ships, sells, or distributes any quantity of cigarettes in excess of 10,000, or any quantity of smokeless tobacco in excess of 500 single-unit consumer-sized cans or packages, in a single transaction shall maintain such information about the shipment, receipt, sale, and distribution of cigarettes as the Attorney General may prescribe by rule or regulation. The Attorney General may require such person to keep such information as the Attorney General considers appropriate for purposes of enforcement of this chapter, including—

(1) the name, address, destination (including street address), vehicle license number, driver's license number, signature of the person receiving such cigarettes, and the name of the purchaser;

(2) a declaration of the specific purpose of the receipt (personal use, resale, or delivery to another); and

(3) a declaration of the name and address of the recipient's principal in all cases when the recipient is acting as an agent.

Such information shall be contained on business records kept in the normal course of business.

(b) Any person, except for a tribal government, who engages in a delivery sale, and who ships, sells, or distributes any quantity in excess of 10,000 cigarettes, or any quantity in excess of 500 single-unit consumer-sized cans or packages of smokeless tobacco, or their equivalent, within a single month, shall submit to the Attorney General, pursuant to rules or regulations prescribed by the Attorney General, a report that sets forth the following:

(1) The person's beginning and ending inventory of cigarettes and cans or packages of smokeless tobacco (in total) for such month.

(2) The total quantity of cigarettes and cans or packages of smokeless tobacco that the person received within such month from each other person (itemized by name and address).

(3) The total quantity of cigarettes and cans or packages of smokeless tobacco that the person distributed within such month to each person (itemized by name and address) other than a retail purchaser.

(c) Upon the consent of any person who ships, sells, or distributes any quantity of cigarettes in excess of 10,000 in a single transaction, or pursuant to a duly issued search warrant, the Attorney General may enter the premises (including places of storage) of such person for the purpose of inspecting any records or information required to be maintained by such person under this chapter, and any cigarettes kept or stored by such person at such premises.

(d) Any report required to be submitted under this chapter to the Attorney General shall also be submitted to the Secretary of the Treasury and to the attorneys general and the tax administrators of the States from where the shipments, deliveries, or distributions both originated and concluded.

(e) In this section, the term "delivery sale" means any sale of cigarettes or smokeless tobacco in interstate commerce to a consumer if—

(1) the consumer submits the order for such sale by means of a telephone or other method of voice transmission, the mails, or the Internet or other online service, or by any other means where the consumer is not in the same physical location as the seller when the purchase or offer of sale is made; or

(2) the cigarettes or smokeless tobacco are delivered by use of the mails, common carrier, private delivery service, or any other means where the consumer is not in the same physical location as the seller when the consumer obtains physical possession of the cigarettes or smokeless tobacco.

(f) In this section, the term "interstate commerce" means commerce between a State and any place outside the State, or commerce between points in the same State but through any place outside the State.

(Added Pub.L. 95–575, § 1, Nov. 2, 1978, 92 Stat. 2464, and amended Pub.L. 107–296, Title XI, § 1112(i)(2), Nov. 25, 2002, 116 Stat. 2277; Pub.L. 109–177, Title I, § 121(a)(3), (b)(3), (c), (g)(1), Mar. 9, 2006, 120 Stat. 221, 222.)

HISTORICAL AND STATUTORY NOTES

Effective and Applicability Provisions

2002 Acts. Amendment to this section by Pub.L. 107–296 effective 60 days after Nov. 25, 2002, see Pub.L. 107–296, § 4, set out as a note under 6 U.S.C.A. § 101.

Section effective on the first day of the first month beginning more than 120 days after Nov. 2, 1978, see section 4 of Pub.L. 95–575, set out as a note under section 2341 of this title.

§ 2344. Penalties

(a) Whoever knowingly violates section 2342(a) of this title shall be fined under this title or imprisoned not more than five years, or both.

(b) Whoever knowingly violates any rule or regulation promulgated under section 2343(a) or 2346 of this title or violates section 2342(b) of this title shall be fined under this title or imprisoned not more than three years, or both.

(c) Any contraband cigarettes or contraband smokeless tobacco involved in any violation of the provisions of this chapter shall be subject to seizure and forfeiture, and all provisions of the Internal Revenue Code of 1986 relating to the seizure and forfeiture. The provisions of chapter 46 of title 18 relating to civil forfeitures shall extend to any seizure or civil forfeiture under this section. Any cigarettes or smokeless tobacco so seized and forfeited shall be either—

(1) destroyed and not resold; or

(2) used for undercover investigative operations for the detection and prosecution of crimes, and then destroyed and not resold.

(Added Pub.L. 95–575, § 1, Nov. 2, 1978, 92 Stat. 2464, and amended Pub.L. 99–514, § 2, Oct. 22, 1986, 100 Stat. 2095; Pub.L. 103–322, Title XXXIII, § 330016(1)(K), (S), Sept. 13, 1994, 108 Stat. 2147, 2148; Pub.L. 109–177, Title I, § 121(b)(4), (d), Mar. 9, 2006, 120 Stat. 222, 223.)

HISTORICAL AND STATUTORY NOTES

References in Text

The Internal Revenue Code of 1986, referred to in subsec. (c), is 26 U.S.C.A. § 1 et seq.

Chapter 46 of title 18, referred to in subsec. (c), is Forfeiture, 18 U.S.C.A. § 981 et seq.

Effective and Applicability Provisions

1978 Acts. Section effective Nov. 2, 1978, see section 4 of Pub.L. 95–575, set out as a note under section 2341 of this title.

§ 2345. Effect on State and local law

(a) Nothing in this chapter shall be construed to affect the concurrent jurisdiction of a State or local government to enact and enforce its own cigarette tax laws, to provide for the confiscation of cigarettes or smokeless tobacco and other property seized for violation of such laws, and to provide for penalties for the violation of such laws.

(b) Nothing in this chapter shall be construed to inhibit or otherwise affect any coordinated law enforcement effort by a number of State or local governments, through interstate compact or otherwise, to provide for the administration of State or local cigarette tax laws, to provide for the confiscation of cigarettes or smokeless tobacco and other property seized in violation of such laws, and to establish cooperative programs for the administration of such laws.

(Added Pub.L. 95–575, § 1, Nov. 2, 1978, 92 Stat. 2465, and amended Pub.L. 109–177, Title I, § 121(b)(5), (e), (g)(2), Mar. 9, 2006, 120 Stat. 222 to 224.)

HISTORICAL AND STATUTORY NOTES

Effective and Applicability Provisions

1978 Acts. Section effective Nov. 2, 1978, see section 4 of Pub.L. 95–575, set out as a note under section 2341 of this title.

§ 2346. Enforcement and regulations

(a) The Attorney General, subject to the provisions of section 2343(a) of this title, shall enforce the provisions of this chapter and may prescribe such rules and regulations as he deems reasonably necessary to carry out the provisions of this chapter.

(b)(1) A State, through its attorney general, a local government, through its chief law enforcement officer (or a designee thereof), or any person who holds a permit under chapter 52 of the Internal Revenue Code of 1986, may bring an action in the United States district courts to prevent and restrain violations of this chapter by any person (or by any person controlling such person), except that any person who holds a permit under chapter 52 of the Internal Revenue Code of 1986 may not bring such an action against a State or local government. No civil action may be commenced under this paragraph against an Indian tribe or an Indian in Indian country (as defined in section 1151).

(2) A State, through its attorney general, or a local government, through its chief law enforcement officer (or a designee thereof), may in a civil action under paragraph (1) also obtain any other appropriate relief for violations of this chapter from any person (or by any person controlling such person), including civil penalties, money damages, and injunctive or other equitable relief. Nothing in this chapter shall be deemed to abrogate or constitute a waiver of any sovereign immunity of a State or local government, or an Indian tribe against any unconsented lawsuit under this chapter, or otherwise to restrict, expand, or modify any sovereign immunity of a State or local government, or an Indian tribe.

(3) The remedies under paragraphs (1) and (2) are in addition to any other remedies under Federal, State, local, or other law.

(4) Nothing in this chapter shall be construed to expand, restrict, or otherwise modify any right of an authorized State official to proceed in State court, or take other enforcement actions, on the basis of an alleged violation of State or other law.

(5) Nothing in this chapter shall be construed to expand, restrict, or otherwise modify any right of an authorized local government official to proceed in State court, or take other enforcement actions, on the basis of an alleged violation of local or other law.

(Added Pub.L. 95–575, § 1, Nov. 2, 1978, 92 Stat. 2465, and amended Pub.L. 107–296, Title XI, § 1112(i)(2), Nov. 25, 2002, 116 Stat. 2277; Pub.L. 109–177, Title I, § 121(f), Mar. 9, 2006, 120 Stat. 223.)

HISTORICAL AND STATUTORY NOTES

References in Text

Chapter 52 of the Internal Revenue Code of 1986, referred to in subsec. (b)(1), is chapter 52 of Title 26, Tobacco Products and Cigarette Papers and Tubes, 26 U.S.C.A. § 5701 et seq.

Effective and Applicability Provisions

2002 Acts. Amendment to this section by Pub.L. 107–296 effective 60 days after Nov. 25, 2002, see Pub.L. 107–296, § 4, set out as a note under 6 U.S.C.A. § 101.

1978 Acts. Section effective Nov. 2, 1978, see section 4 of Pub.L. 95–575, set out as a note under section 2341 of this title.

CHAPTER 115—TREASON, SEDITION, AND SUBVERSIVE ACTIVITIES

§ 2381. Treason

Whoever, owing allegiance to the United States, levies war against them or adheres to their enemies, giving them aid and comfort within the United States or elsewhere, is guilty of treason and shall suffer death, or shall be imprisoned not less than five years and fined under this title but not less than $10,000; and shall be incapable of holding any office under the United States.

(June 25, 1948, c. 645, 62 Stat. 807; Sept. 13, 1994, Pub.L. 103–322, Title XXXIII, § 330016(2)(J), 108 Stat. 2148.)

HISTORICAL AND STATUTORY NOTES

Canal Zone

Applicability of section to Canal Zone, see § 14 of this title.

§ 2382. Misprision of treason

Whoever, owing allegiance to the United States and having knowledge of the commission of any treason against them, conceals and does not, as soon as may be, disclose and make known the same to the President or to some judge of the United States, or to the governor or to some judge or justice of a particular State, is guilty of misprision of treason and shall be fined under this title or imprisoned not more than seven years, or both.

(June 25, 1948, c. 645, 62 Stat. 807; Sept. 13, 1994, Pub.L. 103–322, Title XXXIII, § 330016(1)(H), 108 Stat. 2147.)

HISTORICAL AND STATUTORY NOTES

Canal Zone

Applicability of section to Canal Zone, see § 14 of this title.

§ 2383. Rebellion or insurrection

Whoever incites, sets on foot, assists, or engages in any rebellion or insurrection against the authority of the United States or the laws thereof, or gives aid or comfort thereto, shall be fined under this title or imprisoned not more than ten years, or both; and shall be incapable of holding any office under the United States.

(June 25, 1948, c. 645, 62 Stat. 808; Sept. 13, 1994, Pub.L. 103–322, Title XXXIII, § 330016(1)(L), 108 Stat. 2147.)

HISTORICAL AND STATUTORY NOTES

Canal Zone

Applicability of section to Canal Zone, see § 14 of this title.

§ 2384. Seditious conspiracy

If two or more persons in any State or Territory, or in any place subject to the jurisdiction of the United States, conspire to overthrow, put down, or to destroy by force the Government of the United States, or to levy war against them, or to oppose by force the authority thereof, or by force to prevent, hinder, or delay the execution of any law of the United States, or by force to seize, take, or possess any property of the United States contrary to the authority thereof, they shall each be fined under this title or imprisoned not more than twenty years, or both.

(June 25, 1948, c. 645, 62 Stat. 808; July 24, 1956, c. 678, § 1, 70 Stat. 623; Sept. 13, 1994, Pub.L. 103–322, Title XXXIII, § 330016(1)(N), 108 Stat. 2148.)

HISTORICAL AND STATUTORY NOTES

Effective and Applicability Provisions

1956 Acts. Section 3 of Act July 24, 1956 provided that the amendments to this section and § 2385 of this title by such Act July 24, 1956, shall be applicable only with respect to offenses committed on and after July 24, 1956.

Canal Zone

Applicability of section to Canal Zone see § 14 of this title.

§ 2385. Advocating overthrow of Government

Whoever knowingly or willfully advocates, abets, advises, or teaches the duty, necessity, desirability, or propriety of overthrowing or destroying the government of the United States or the government of any State, Territory, District or Possession thereof, or the government of any political subdivision therein, by force or violence, or by the assassination of any officer of any such government; or

Whoever, with intent to cause the overthrow or destruction of any such government, prints, publishes, edits, issues, circulates, sells, distributes, or publicly displays any written or printed matter advocating, advising, or teaching the duty, necessity, desirability, or propriety of overthrowing or destroying any government in the United States by force or violence, or attempts to do so; or

Whoever organizes or helps or attempts to organize any society, group, or assembly of persons who teach, advocate, or encourage the overthrow or destruction of any such government by force or violence; or becomes or is a member of, or affiliates with, any such society, group, or assembly of persons, knowing the purposes thereof—

Shall be fined under this title or imprisoned not more than twenty years, or both, and shall be ineligible for employment by the United States or any department or agency thereof, for the five years next following his conviction.

If two or more persons conspire to commit any offense named in this section, each shall be fined under this title or imprisoned not more than twenty years, or both, and shall be ineligible for employment by the United States or any department or agency thereof, for the five years next following his conviction.

As used in this section, the terms "organizes" and "organize", with respect to any society, group, or assembly of persons, include the recruiting of new members, the forming of new units, and the regrouping or expansion of existing clubs, classes, and other units of such society, group, or assembly of persons.

(June 25, 1948, c. 645, 62 Stat. 808; July 24, 1956, c. 678, § 2, 70 Stat. 623; June 19, 1962, Pub.L. 87–486, 76 Stat. 103; Sept. 13, 1994, Pub.L. 103–322, Title XXXIII, § 330016(1)(N), 108 Stat. 2148.)

HISTORICAL AND STATUTORY NOTES

Effective and Applicability Provisions

1956 Acts. Amendment of this section by Act July 24, 1956 as applicable only with respect to offenses committed on and after July 24, 1956, see note under § 2384 of this title.

Canal Zone

Applicability of section to Canal Zone, see § 14 of this title.

§ 2386. Registration of certain organizations

(A) For the purposes of this section:

"Attorney General" means the Attorney General of the United States;

"Organization" means any group, club, league, society, committee, association, political party, or combination of individuals, whether incorporated or otherwise, but such term shall not include any corporation, association, community chest, fund, or foundation, organized and operated exclusively for religious, charitable, scientific, literary, or educational purposes;

"Political activity" means any activity the purpose or aim of which, or one of the purposes or aims of which, is the control by force or overthrow of the Government of the United States or a political subdivision thereof, or any State or political subdivision thereof;

An organization is engaged in "civilian military activity" if:

(1) it gives instruction to, or prescribes instruction for, its members in the use of firearms or other weapons or any substitute therefor, or military or naval science; or

(2) it receives from any other organization or from any individual instruction in military or naval science; or

(3) it engages in any military or naval maneuvers or activities; or

(4) it engages, either with or without arms, in drills or parades of a military or naval character; or

(5) it engages in any other form of organized activity which in the opinion of the Attorney General constitutes preparation for military action;

An organization is "subject to foreign control" if:

(a) it solicits or accepts financial contributions, loans, or support of any kind, directly or indirectly, from, or is affiliated directly or indirectly with, a foreign government or a political subdivision thereof, or an agent, agency, or instrumentality of a foreign government or political subdivision thereof, or a political party in a foreign country, or an international political organization; or

(b) its policies, or any of them, are determined by or at the suggestion of, or in collaboration with, a foreign government or political subdivision thereof, or an agent, agency, or instrumentality of a foreign government or a political subdivision thereof, or a political party in a foreign country, or an international political organization.

(B)(1) The following organizations shall be required to register with the Attorney General:

Every organization subject to foreign control which engages in political activity;

Every organization which engages both in civilian military activity and in political activity;

Every organization subject to foreign control which engages in civilian military activity; and

Every organization, the purpose or aim of which, or one of the purposes or aims of which, is the establishment, control, conduct, seizure, or overthrow of a government or subdivision thereof by the use of force, violence, military measures, or threats of any one or more of the foregoing.

Every such organization shall register by filing with the Attorney General, on such forms and in such detail as the Attorney General may by rules and regulations prescribe, a registration statement containing the information and documents prescribed in subsection (B)(3) and shall within thirty days after the expiration of each period of six months succeeding the filing of such registration statement, file with the Attorney General, on such forms and in such detail as the Attorney General may by rules and regulations prescribe, a supplemental statement containing such information and documents as may be necessary to make the information and documents previously filed under this section accurate and current with respect to such preceding six months' period. Every statement required to be filed by this section shall be subscribed, under oath, by all of the officers of the organization.

(2) This section shall not require registration or the filing of any statement with the Attorney General by:

(a) The armed forces of the United States; or

(b) The organized militia or National Guard of any State, Territory, District, or possession of the United States; or

(c) Any law-enforcement agency of the United States or of any Territory, District or possession thereof, or of any State or political subdivision of a State, or of any agency or instrumentality of one or more States; or

(d) Any duly established diplomatic mission or consular office of a foreign government which is so recognized by the Department of State; or

(e) Any nationally recognized organization of persons who are veterans of the armed forces of the United States, or affiliates of such organizations.

(3) Every registration statement required to be filed by any organization shall contain the following information and documents:

(a) The name and post-office address of the organization in the United States, and the names and addresses of all branches, chapters, and affiliates of such organization;

(b) The name, address, and nationality of each officer, and of each person who performs the functions of an officer, of the organization, and of each branch, chapter, and affiliate of the organization;

(c) The qualifications for membership in the organization;

(d) The existing and proposed aims and purposes of the organization, and all the means by which these aims or purposes are being attained or are to be attained;

(e) The address or addresses of meeting places of the organization, and of each branch, chapter, or affiliate of the organization, and the times of meetings;

(f) The name and address of each person who has contributed any money, dues, property, or other thing of value to the organization or to any branch, chapter, or affiliate of the organization;

(g) A detailed statement of the assets of the organization, and of each branch, chapter, and affiliate of the organization, the manner in which such assets were acquired, and a detailed statement of the liabilities and income of the organization and of each branch, chapter, and affiliate of the organization;

(h) A detailed description of the activities of the organization, and of each chapter, branch, and affiliate of the organization;

(i) A description of the uniforms, badges, insignia, or other means of identification prescribed by the organization, and worn or carried by its officers or members, or any of such officers or members;

(j) A copy of each book, pamphlet, leaflet, or other publication or item of written, printed, or graphic matter issued or distributed directly or indirectly by the organization, or by any chapter, branch, or affiliate of the organization, or by any of the members of the organization under its authority or within its knowledge, together with the name of its author or authors and the name and address of the publisher;

(k) A description of all firearms or other weapons owned by the organization, or by any chapter, branch, or affiliate of the organization, identified by the manufacturer's number thereon;

(*l*) In case the organization is subject to foreign control, the manner in which it is so subject;

(m) A copy of the charter, articles of association, constitution, bylaws, rules, regulations, agreements, resolutions, and all other instruments relating to the organization, powers, and purposes of the organization and to the powers of the officers of the organization and of each chapter, branch, and affiliate of the organization; and

(n) Such other information and documents pertinent to the purposes of this section as the Attorney General may from time to time require.

All statements filed under this section shall be public records and open to public examination and inspection at all reasonable hours under such rules and regulations as the Attorney General may prescribe.

(C) The Attorney General is authorized at any time to make, amend, and rescind such rules and regulations as may be necessary to carry out this section, including rules and regulations governing the statements required to be filed.

(D) Whoever violates any of the provisions of this section shall be fined under this title or imprisoned not more than five years, or both.

Whoever in a statement filed pursuant to this section willfully makes any false statement or willfully omits to state any fact which is required to be stated, or which is necessary to make the statements made not misleading, shall be fined under this title or imprisoned not more than five years, or both.

(June 25, 1948, c. 645, 62 Stat. 808; Sept. 13, 1994, Pub.L. 103–322, Title XXXIII, § 330016(1)(I), (L), 108 Stat. 2147.)

Canal Zone

Applicability of section to Canal Zone, see § 14 of this title.

§ 2387. Activities affecting armed forces generally

(a) Whoever, with intent to interfere with, impair, or influence the loyalty, morale, or discipline of the military or naval forces of the United States:

(1) advises, counsels, urges, or in any manner causes or attempts to cause insubordination, disloyalty, mutiny, or refusal of duty by any member of the military or naval forces of the United States; or

(2) distributes or attempts to distribute any written or printed matter which advises, counsels, or urges insubordination, disloyalty, mutiny, or refusal of duty by any member of the military or naval forces of the United States—

Shall be fined under this title or imprisoned not more than ten years, or both, and shall be ineligible for employment by the United States or any department or agency thereof, for the five years next following his conviction.

(b) For the purposes of this section, the term "military or naval forces of the United States" includes the Army of the United States, the Navy, Air Force, Marine Corps, Coast Guard, Navy Reserve, Marine Corps Reserve, and Coast Guard Reserve of the United States; and, when any merchant vessel is commissioned in the Navy or is in the service of the Army or the Navy, includes the master, officers, and crew of such vessel.

(June 25, 1948, c. 645, 62 Stat. 811; May 24, 1949, c. 139, § 46, 63 Stat. 96; Sept. 13, 1994, Pub.L. 103–322, Title XXXIII, § 330016(1)(L), 108 Stat. 2147; Jan. 6, 2006, Pub.L. 109–163, Title V, § 515(f)(2), 119 Stat. 3236.)

HISTORICAL AND STATUTORY NOTES

Transfer of Functions

For transfer of authorities, functions, personnel, and assets of the Coast Guard, including the authorities and functions of the Secretary of Transportation relating thereto to the Department of Homeland Security, see 6 U.S.C.A. §§ 468(b), 551(d), 552(d) and 557, and the Department of Homeland Security Reorganization Plan of November 25, 2002, as modified, set out as a note under 6 U.S.C.A. § 542.

All functions of all officers of the Department of the Treasury, and all functions of all agencies and employees of such Department, were transferred, with certain exceptions, to the Secretary of the Treasury, with power vested in him to authorize their performance or the performance of any of his functions, by any of such officers, agencies, and employees, by 1950 Reorg. Plan No. 26, §§ 1, 2, eff. July 31, 1950, 15 F.R. 4935, 64 Stat. 1280, set out in the Appendix to Title 5, Government Organization and Employees. The Coast Guard, referred to in this section, is generally a service in the Transportation Department, but such Plan excepted, from the transfer, the functions of the Coast Guard, and of the Commandant thereof, when the Coast Guard is operating as a part of the Navy under §§ 1 and 3 of Title 14, Coast Guard.

§ 2388. Activities affecting armed forces during war

(a) Whoever, when the United States is at war, willfully makes or conveys false reports or false statements with intent to interfere with the operation or success of the military or naval forces of the United States or to promote the success of its enemies; or

Whoever, when the United States is at war, willfully causes or attempts to cause insubordination, disloyalty, mutiny, or refusal of duty, in the military or naval forces of the United States, or willfully obstructs the recruiting or enlistment service of the United States, to the injury of the service or the United States, or attempts to do so—

Shall be fined under this title or imprisoned not more than twenty years, or both.

(b) If two or more persons conspire to violate subsection (a) of this section and one or more such persons do any act to effect the object of the conspiracy, each of the parties to such conspiracy shall be punished as provided in said subsection (a).

(c) Whoever harbors or conceals any person who he knows, or has reasonable grounds to believe or suspect, has committed, or is about to commit, an offense under this section, shall be fined under this title or imprisoned not more than ten years, or both.

(d) This section shall apply within the admiralty and maritime jurisdiction of the United States, and on the high seas, as well as within the United States.

(June 25, 1948, c. 645, 62 Stat. 811; Sept. 13, 1994, Pub.L. 103–322, Title XXXIII, § 330016(1)(L), 108 Stat. 2147.)

HISTORICAL AND STATUTORY NOTES

Repeals

Section 7 of Act June 30, 1953, c. 175, 67 Stat. 133, repealed Joint Res. July 3, 1952, c. 570, § 1(a)(29), 66 Stat. 333; Joint Res. Mar. 31, 1953, c. 13, § 1, 67 Stat. 18, which had provided that this section should continue in force until six months after the termination of the national emergency proclaimed by 1950 Proc. No. 2914 which is set out as a note preceding § 1 of Appendix to Title 50, War and National Defense.

Section 6 of Joint Res. July 3, 1952, repealed Joint Res. Apr. 14, 1952, c. 204, 66 Stat. 54, as amended by Joint Res. May 28, 1952, c. 339, 66 Stat. 96. Intermediate extensions by Joint Res. June 14, 1952, c. 437, 66 Stat. 137, and Joint Res. June 30, 1952, ch. 526, 66 Stat. 296, which continued provisions until July 3, 1952, expired by their own terms.

Temporary Extension of Section

Temporary extension of section, see § 2391 of this title.

Canal Zone

Applicability of section to Canal Zone, see § 14 of this title.

§ 2389. Recruiting for service against United States

Whoever recruits soldiers or sailors within the United States, or in any place subject to the jurisdiction thereof, to engage in armed hostility against the same; or

Whoever opens within the United States, or in any place subject to the jurisdiction thereof, a recruiting station for the enlistment of such soldiers or sailors to serve in any manner in armed hostility against the United States—

Shall be fined under this title or imprisoned not more than five years, or both.

(June 25, 1948, c. 645, 62 Stat. 811; Sept. 13, 1994, Pub.L. 103–322, Title XXXIII, § 330016(1)(H), 108 Stat. 2147.)

HISTORICAL AND STATUTORY NOTES

Canal Zone

Applicability of section to Canal Zone, see § 14 of this title.

§ 2390. Enlistment to serve against United States

Whoever enlists or is engaged within the United States or in any place subject to the jurisdiction thereof, with intent to serve in armed hostility against the United States, shall be fined under this title or imprisoned not more than three years, or both.

(June 25, 1948, c. 645, 62 Stat. 812; Sept. 13, 1994, Pub.L. 103–322, Title XXXIII, § 330016(1)(B), 108 Stat. 2146.)

HISTORICAL AND STATUTORY NOTES

Canal Zone

Applicability of section to Canal Zone, see § 14 of this title.

[§ 2391. Repealed. Pub.L. 103–322, Title XXXIII, § 330004(13), Sept. 13, 1994, 108 Stat. 2142]

HISTORICAL AND STATUTORY NOTES

Section, Act June 30, 1953, c. 175, § 6, 67 Stat. 134, related to temporary extension of section 2388 of this title.

[§ 2401. Renumbered § 2441]

HISTORICAL AND STATUTORY NOTES

Codifications

Section 2401 was renumbered section 2441 of this title, by Pub.L. 104–294, § 605(p)(1), Oct. 11, 1996, 110 Stat. 3510.

CHAPTER 117—TRANSPORTATION FOR ILLEGAL SEXUAL ACTIVITY AND RELATED CRIMES

§ 2421. Transportation generally

Whoever knowingly transports any individual in interstate or foreign commerce, or in any Territory or Possession of the United States, with intent that such individual engage in prostitution, or in any sexual activity for which any person can be charged with a criminal offense, or attempts to do so, shall be fined under this title or imprisoned not more than 10 years, or both.

(June 25, 1948, c. 645, 62 Stat. 812; May 24, 1949, c. 139, § 47, 63 Stat. 96; Nov. 7, 1986, Pub.L. 99–628, § 5(b)(1), 100 Stat. 3511; Pub.L. 105–314, Title I, § 106, Oct. 30, 1998, 112 Stat. 2977.)

HISTORICAL AND STATUTORY NOTES

Canal Zone

Applicability of section to Canal Zone, see § 14 of this title.

§ 2422. Coercion and enticement

(a) Whoever knowingly persuades, induces, entices, or coerces any individual to travel in interstate or foreign commerce, or in any Territory or Possession of the United States, to engage in prostitution, or in any sexual activity for which any person can be charged with a criminal offense, or attempts to do so, shall be fined under this title or imprisoned not more than 20 years, or both.

(b) Whoever, using the mail or any facility or means of interstate or foreign commerce, or within the special maritime and territorial jurisdiction of the United States knowingly persuades, induces, entices, or coerces any individual who has not attained the age of 18 years, to engage in prostitution or any sexual activity for which any person can be charged with a criminal offense, or attempts to do so, shall be fined under this title and imprisoned not less than 10 years or for life.

(June 25, 1948, c. 645, 62 Stat. 812; Nov. 7, 1986, Pub.L. 99–628, § 5(b)(1), 100 Stat. 3511; Nov. 18, 1988, Pub.L. 100–690, Title VII, § 7070, 102 Stat. 4405; Feb. 8, 1996, Pub.L. 104–104, Title V, § 508, 110 Stat. 137; Oct. 30, 1998, Pub.L. 105–314, Title I, § 102, 112 Stat. 2975; Apr. 30, 2003, Pub.L. 108–21, Title I, § 103(a)(2)(A), (B), (b)(2)(A), 117 Stat. 652, 653; July 27, 2006, Pub.L. 109–248, Title II, § 203, 120 Stat. 613.)

HISTORICAL AND STATUTORY NOTES

Canal Zone

Applicability of section to Canal Zone, see § 14 of this title.

§ 2423. Transportation of minors

(a) Transportation with intent to engage in criminal sexual activity.—A person who knowingly transports an individual who has not attained the age of 18 years in interstate or foreign commerce, or in any commonwealth, territory or possession of the United States, with intent that the individual engage in prostitution, or in any sexual activity for which any person can be charged with a criminal offense, shall be fined under this title and imprisoned not less than 10 years or for life.

(b) Travel with intent to engage in illicit sexual conduct.—A person who travels in interstate commerce or travels into the United States, or a United States citizen or an alien admitted for permanent residence in the United States who travels in foreign commerce, for the purpose of engaging in any illicit sexual conduct with another person shall be fined under this title or imprisoned not more than 30 years, or both.

(c) Engaging in illicit sexual conduct in foreign places.—Any United States citizen or alien admitted for permanent residence who travels in foreign commerce, and engages in any illicit sexual conduct with another person shall be fined under this title or imprisoned not more than 30 years, or both.

(d) Ancillary offenses.—Whoever, for the purpose of commercial advantage or private financial gain, arranges, induces, procures, or facilitates the travel of a person knowing that such a person is traveling in interstate commerce or foreign commerce for the purpose of engaging in illicit sexual conduct shall be fined under this title, imprisoned not more than 30 years, or both.

(e) Attempt and conspiracy.—Whoever attempts or conspires to violate subsection (a), (b), (c), or (d) shall be punishable in the same manner as a completed violation of that subsection.

(f) Definition.—As used in this section, the term "illicit sexual conduct" means (1) a sexual act (as defined in section 2246) with a person under 18 years of age that would be in violation of chapter 109A if the sexual act occurred in the special maritime and territorial jurisdiction of the United States; or (2) any commercial sex act (as defined in section 1591) with a person under 18 years of age.

(g) Defense.—In a prosecution under this section based on illicit sexual conduct as defined in subsection (f)(2), it is a defense, which the defendant must establish by a preponderance of the evidence, that the defendant reasonably believed that the person with whom the defendant engaged in the commercial sex act had attained the age of 18 years.

(June 25, 1948, c. 645, 62 Stat. 812; Feb. 6, 1978, Pub.L. 95–225, § 3(a), 92 Stat. 8; Nov. 7, 1986, Pub.L. 99–628, § 5(b)(1), 100 Stat. 3511; Sept. 13, 1994, Pub.L. 103–322, Title XVI, § 160001(g), 108 Stat. 2037; Dec. 23, 1995, Pub.L. 104–71, § 5, 109 Stat. 774; Oct. 11, 1996, Pub.L. 104–294, Title VI, §§ 601(b)(4), 604(b)(33), 110 Stat. 3499, 3508; Oct. 30, 1998, Pub.L. 105–314, Title I, § 103, 112 Stat. 2976; Nov. 2, 2002, Pub.L. 107–273, Div. B, Title IV, § 4002(c)(1), 116 Stat. 1808; Apr. 30, 2003, Pub.L. 108–21, Title I, §§ 103(a)(2)(C), (b)(2)(B), 105, 117 Stat. 652, 653, 654; July 27, 2006, Pub.L. 109–248, Title II, § 204, 120 Stat. 613.)

HISTORICAL AND STATUTORY NOTES

References in Text

Chapter 109A, referred to in subsec. (f), is 18 U.S.C.A. § 2141 et seq.

Codifications

Section 601(b)(4) of Pub.L. 104–294, which directed that subsec. (b) of this section be amended by substituting "2246" for "2245", could not be executed to text due to a prior identical amendment by section 5 of Pub.L. 104–71. See also 2002, 1996, and 1995 Amendments notes set out under this section.

Effective and Applicability Provisions

2002 Acts. Amendment by section 4002(c)(1) of Pub.L. 107–273, as therein provided, effective Oct. 11, 1996, which is the date of enactment of Pub.L. 104–294, to which such amendment relates.

1996 Acts. Amendment by section 604 of Pub.L. 104–294 effective Sept. 13, 1994, see section 604(d) of Pub.L. 104–294, set out as a note under section 13 of this title.

Repeals

Section 601(b)(4) of Pub.L. 104–294, cited in the credit of this section, was repealed by section 4002(c)(1) of Pub.L. 107–273 effective Oct. 11, 1996.

Canal Zone

Applicability of section to Canal Zone, see § 14 of this title.

§ 2424. Filing factual statement about alien individual

(a) Whoever keeps, maintains, controls, supports, or harbors in any house or place for the purpose of prostitution, or for any other immoral purpose, any individual, knowing or in reckless disregard of the fact that the individual is an alien, shall file with the Commissioner of Immigration and Naturalization a statement in writing setting forth the name of such individual, the place at which that individual is kept, and all facts as to the date of that individual's entry into the United States, the port through which that individual entered, that individual's age, nationality, and parentage, and concerning that individual's procuration to come to this country within the knowledge of such person; and

Whoever fails within five business days after commencing to keep, maintain, control, support, or harbor in any house or place for the purpose of prostitution, or for any other immoral purpose, any alien individual to file such statement concerning such alien individual with the Commissioner of Immigration and Naturalization; or

Whoever knowingly and willfully states falsely or fails to disclose in such statement any fact within that person's knowledge or belief with reference to the age, nationality, or parentage of any such alien individual, or concerning that individual's procuration to come to this country—

Shall be fined under this title or imprisoned not more than 10 years, or both.

(b) In any prosecution brought under this section, if it appears that any such statement required is not on file in the office of the Commissioner of Immigration and Naturalization, the person whose duty it is to file such statement shall be presumed to have failed to file said statement, unless such person or persons shall prove otherwise. No person shall be excused from furnishing the statement, as required by this section, on the ground or for the reason that the statement so required by that person, or the information therein contained, might tend to criminate that person or subject that person to a penalty or forfeiture, but no information contained in the statement or any evidence which is directly or indirectly derived from such information may be used against any person making such statement in any criminal case, except a prosecution for perjury, giving a false statement or otherwise failing to comply with this section.

(June 25, 1948, c. 645, 62 Stat. 813; Oct. 15, 1970, Pub.L. 91–452, Title II, § 226, 84 Stat. 930; Nov. 7, 1986, Pub.L. 99–628, § 5(c), 100 Stat. 3511, 3512; Sept. 13, 1994, Pub.L. 103–322, Title XXXIII, § 330016(1)(I), 108 Stat. 2147; Sept. 30, 1996, Pub.L. 104–208, Div. C, Title III, § 325, 110 Stat. 3009–629.)

HISTORICAL AND STATUTORY NOTES

Effective and Applicability Provisions

1970 Acts. Amendment by Pub.L. 91–452 effective on the sixtieth day following the date of enactment of Pub.L. 91–452, which was approved Oct. 15, 1970, see section 260 of Pub.L. 91–452, set out as a note under section 6001 of this title.

Abolition of Immigration and Naturalization Service and Transfer of Functions

For abolition of Immigration and Naturalization Service, transfer of functions, and treatment of related references, see note set out under 8 U.S.C.A. § 1551.

Severability of Provisions

If any provision of Division C of Pub.L. 104–208 or the application of such provision to any person or circumstances is held to be unconstitutional, the remainder of Division C of Pub.L. 104–208 and the application of the provisions of Division C of Pub.L. 104–208 to any person or circumstance not to be affected thereby, see section 1(e) of Pub.L. 104–208, set out as a note under section 1101 of Title 8, Aliens and Nationality.

Amendment of this section by Pub.L. 91–452 not to affect any immunity to which any individual is entitled under this section by reason of any testimony given before the sixtieth day following Oct. 15, 1970, see section 260 of Pub.L. 91–452, set out as a note under section 6001 of this title.

Canal Zone

Applicability of section to Canal Zone, see § 14 of this title.

§ 2425. Use of interstate facilities to transmit information about a minor

Whoever, using the mail or any facility or means of interstate or foreign commerce, or within the special maritime and territorial jurisdiction of the United States, knowingly initiates the transmission of the name, address, telephone number, social security number, or electronic mail address of another individual, knowing that such other individual has not attained the age of 16 years, with the intent to entice, encourage, offer, or solicit any person to engage in any sexual activity for which any person can be charged with a criminal offense, or attempts to do so, shall be fined under this title, imprisoned not more than 5 years, or both.

(Added Pub.L. 105–314, Title I, § 101(a), Oct. 30, 1998., 112 Stat. 2975.)

§ 2426. Repeat offenders

(a) Maximum term of imprisonment.—The maximum term of imprisonment for a violation of this chapter after a prior sex offense conviction shall be twice the term of imprisonment otherwise provided by this chapter, unless section 3559(e) applies.

(b) Definitions.—In this section—

(1) the term "prior sex offense conviction" means a conviction for an offense—

(A) under this chapter, chapter 109A, or chapter 110; or

(B) under State law for an offense consisting of conduct that would have been an offense under a chapter referred to in paragraph (1) if the conduct had occurred within the special maritime and territorial jurisdiction of the United States; and

(2) the term "State" means a State of the United States, the District of Columbia, and any commonwealth, territory, or possession of the United States.

(Added Pub.L. 105–314, Title I, § 104(a), Oct. 30, 1998, 112 Stat. 2976, and amended Pub.L. 108–21, Title I, § 106(b), Apr. 30, 2003, 117 Stat. 655.)

HISTORICAL AND STATUTORY NOTES

References in Text

Chapter 109A, referred to in subsec. (b)(1)(A), is 18 U.S.C.A. § 2251 et seq.

Chapter 110, referred to in subsec. (b)(1)(A), is 18 U.S.C.A. § 2241 et seq.

§ 2427. Inclusion of offenses relating to child pornography in definition of sexual activity for which any person can be charged with a criminal offense

In this chapter, the term "sexual activity for which any person can be charged with a criminal offense" includes the production of child pornography, as defined in section 2256(8).

(Added Pub.L. 105–314, Title I, § 105(a), Oct. 30, 1998., 112 Stat. 2977.)

§ 2428. Forfeitures

(a) In general.—The court, in imposing sentence on any person convicted of a violation of this chapter, shall order, in addition to any other sentence imposed and irrespective of any provision of State law, that such person shall forfeit to the United States—

(1) such person's interest in any property, real or personal, that was used or intended to be used to commit or to facilitate the commission of such violation; and

(2) any property, real or personal, constituting or derived from any proceeds that such person obtained, directly or indirectly, as a result of such violation.

(b) Property subject to forfeiture.—

(1) In general.—The following shall be subject to forfeiture to the United States and no property right shall exist in them:

(A) Any property, real or personal, used or intended to be used to commit or to facilitate the commission of any violation of this chapter.

(B) Any property, real or personal, that constitutes or is derived from proceeds traceable to any violation of this chapter.

(2) Applicability of chapter 46.—The provisions of chapter 46 of this title relating to civil forfeitures shall apply to any seizure or civil forfeiture under this subsection.

(Added Pub.L. 109–164, Title I, § 103(d)(1), Jan. 10, 2006, 119 Stat. 3563.)

HISTORICAL AND STATUTORY NOTES

References in Text

Chapter 46 of this title, referred to in subsec. (b)(2), is Forfeiture, 18 U.S.C.A. § 981 et seq.

§§ 2429 to 2440. Reserved for future legislation

CHAPTER 118—WAR CRIMES

§ 2441. War crimes

(a) Offense.—Whoever, whether inside or outside the United States, commits a war crime, in any of the circumstances described in subsection (b), shall be fined under this title or imprisoned for life or any term of years, or both, and if death results to the victim, shall also be subject to the penalty of death.

(b) Circumstances.—The circumstances referred to in subsection (a) are that the person committing such war crime or the victim of such war crime is a member of the Armed Forces of the United States or a national of the United States (as defined in section 101 of the Immigration and Nationality Act).

(c) Definition.—As used in this section the term "war crime" means any conduct—

(1) defined as a grave breach in any of the international conventions signed at Geneva 12 August 1949, or any protocol to such convention to which the United States is a party;

(2) prohibited by Article 23, 25, 27, or 28 of the Annex to the Hague Convention IV, Respecting the Laws and Customs of War on Land, signed 18 October 1907;

(3) which constitutes a grave breach of common Article 3 (as defined in subsection (d)) when committed in the context of and in association with an armed conflict not of an international character; or

(4) of a person who, in relation to an armed conflict and contrary to the provisions of the Protocol on Prohibitions or Restrictions on the Use of Mines, Booby–Traps and Other Devices as amended at Geneva on 3 May 1996 (Protocol II as amended on 3 May 1996), when the United States is a party to such Protocol, willfully kills or causes serious injury to civilians.

(d) Common Article 3 violations.—

(1) Prohibited conduct.—In subsection (c)(3), the term "grave breach of common Article 3" means any conduct (such conduct constituting a grave breach of common Article 3 of the international conventions done at Geneva August 12, 1949), as follows:

(A) Torture.—The act of a person who commits, or conspires or attempts to commit, an act specifically intended to inflict severe physical or mental pain or suffering (other than pain or suffering incidental to lawful sanctions) upon another person within his custody or physical control for the purpose of obtaining information or a confession, punishment, intimidation, coercion, or any reason based on discrimination of any kind.

(B) Cruel or inhuman treatment.—The act of a person who commits, or conspires or attempts to commit, an act intended to inflict severe or serious physical or mental pain or suffering (other than pain or suffering incidental to lawful sanctions), including serious physical abuse, upon another within his custody or control.

(C) Performing biological experiments.—The act of a person who subjects, or conspires or attempts to subject, one or more persons within his custody or physical control to biological experiments without a legitimate medical or dental purpose and in so doing endangers the body or health of such person or persons.

(D) Murder.—The act of a person who intentionally kills, or conspires or attempts to kill, or kills whether intentionally or unintentionally in the course of committing any other offense under this subsection, one or more persons taking no active part in the hostilities, including those placed out of combat by sickness, wounds, detention, or any other cause.

(E) Mutilation or maiming.—The act of a person who intentionally injures, or conspires or attempts to injure, or injures whether intentionally or unintentionally in the course of committing any other offense under this subsection, one or more persons taking no active part in the hostilities, including those placed out of combat by sickness, wounds, detention, or any other cause, by disfiguring the person or persons by any mutilation thereof or by permanently disabling any member, limb, or organ of his body, without any legitimate medical or dental purpose.

(F) Intentionally causing serious bodily injury.—The act of a person who intentionally causes, or conspires or attempts to cause, serious bodily injury to one or more persons, including lawful combatants, in violation of the law of war.

(G) Rape.—The act of a person who forcibly or with coercion or threat of force wrongfully invades, or conspires or attempts to invade, the body of a person by penetrating, however slightly, the anal or genital opening of the victim with any part of the body of the accused, or with any foreign object.

(H) Sexual assault or abuse.—The act of a person who forcibly or with coercion or threat of force engages, or conspires or attempts to engage, in sexual contact with one or more persons, or causes, or conspires or attempts to cause, one or more persons to engage in sexual contact.

(I) Taking hostages.—The act of a person who, having knowingly seized or detained one or more persons, threatens to kill, injure, or continue to detain such person or persons with the intent of compelling any nation, person other than the hostage, or group of persons to act or refrain from acting as an explicit or implicit condition for the safety or release of such person or persons.

(2) Definitions.—In the case of an offense under subsection (a) by reason of subsection (c)(3)—

(A) the term "severe mental pain or suffering" shall be applied for purposes of paragraphs (1)(A) and (1)(B) in accordance with the meaning given that term in section 2340(2) of this title;

(B) the term "serious bodily injury" shall be applied for purposes of paragraph (1)(F) in accordance with the meaning given that term in section 113(b)(2) of this title;

(C) the term "sexual contact" shall be applied for purposes of paragraph (1)(G) in accordance with the meaning given that term in section 2246(3) of this title;

(D) the term "serious physical pain or suffering" shall be applied for purposes of paragraph (1)(B) as meaning bodily injury that involves—

(i) a substantial risk of death;

(ii) extreme physical pain;

(iii) a burn or physical disfigurement of a serious nature (other than cuts, abrasions, or bruises); or

(iv) significant loss or impairment of the function of a bodily member, organ, or mental faculty; and

(E) the term "serious mental pain or suffering" shall be applied for purposes of paragraph (1)(b) in accordance with the meaning given the term "severe mental pain or suffering" (as defined in section 2340(2) of this title), except that—

(i) the term "serious" shall replace the term "severe" where it appears; and

(ii) as to conduct occurring after the date of the enactment of the Military Commissions Act of 2006, the term "serious and non-transitory mental harm (which need not be prolonged)" shall replace the term "prolonged mental harm" where it appears.

(3) Inapplicability of certain provisions with respect to collateral damage or incident of lawful attack.—The intent specified for the conduct stated in subparagraphs (D), (E), and (F) or paragraph (1) precludes the applicability of those subparagraphs to an offense under subsection (a) by reasons of subsection (c)(3) with respect to—

(A) collateral damage; or

(B) death, damage, or injury incident to a lawful attack.

(4) Inapplicability of taking hostages to prisoner exchange.—Paragraph (1)(I) does not apply to an offense under subsection (a) by reason of subsection (c)(3) in the case of a prisoner exchange during wartime.

(5) Definition of grave breaches.—The definitions in this subsection are intended only to define the grave breaches of common Article 3 and not the full scope of United States obligations under that Article.

(Added Pub.L. 104–192, § 2(a), Aug. 21, 1996, 110 Stat. 2104, § 2401; renumbered § 2441, Pub.L. 104–294, § 605(p)(1), Oct. 11, 1996, 110 Stat. 3510, and amended Pub.L. 105–118, Title V, § 583, Nov. 26, 1997, 111 Stat. 2436; Pub.L. 107–273, Div. B, Title IV, § 4002(e)(7), Nov. 2, 2002, 116 Stat. 1810; Pub.L. 109–366, § 6(b)(1), Oct. 17, 2006, 120 Stat. 2633.)

HISTORICAL AND STATUTORY NOTES

References in Text

Section 101 of the Immigration and Nationality Act, referred to in subsec. (b), is section 101 of Act June 27, 1952, c. 477, Title I, 66 Stat. 166, which is classified to section 1101 of Title 8, Aliens and Nationality.

Common Article 3, referred to in subsec. (c)(3) and (d), probably means Common Article 3 of the Geneva Convention Relative to the Treatment of Prisoners of War, Aug. 12, 1949, 6 U.S.T. 3316, 75 U.N.T.S. 135; the text of Common Articles 3 of the Geneva Conventions is repeated in all four Geneva Conventions. See, generally, Geneva Convention for the Amelioration of the Condition of the Wounded and Sick in Armed Forces in the Field, Aug. 12, 1949, 6 U.S.T. 3114, 75 U.N.T.S. 31; Geneva Convention for the Amelioration of the Condition of Wounded, Sick and Shipwrecked Members of Armed Forces at Sea, Aug. 12, 1949, 6 U.S.T. 3217, 75 U.N.T.S. 85; Geneva Convention Relative to the Treatment of Prisoners of War, Aug. 12, 1949, 6 U.S.T. 3316, 75 U.N.T.S. 135; and, Geneva Convention Relative to the Protection of Civilian Persons in Time of War, Aug. 12, 1949, 6 U.S.T. 3516, 75 U.N.T.S. 287.

Codifications

Section 583 of Pub.L. 105–118, which directed that section 2401 of title 18 be amended, was executed to section 2441 of Title 18, despite parenthetical reference to "section 2401 of Title 18", as the probable intent of Congress. See also 2002 Amendments note under this section.

Effective and Applicability Provisions

2006 Acts. Pub.L. 109–366, § 6(b)(2), Oct. 17, 2006, 120 Stat. 2635, provided that: "The amendments made by this subsection [amending this section], except as specified in subsection (d)(2)(E) of section 2441 of title 18, United States Code [subsec. (d)(2)(E) of this section], shall take effect as of November 26, 1997, as if enacted immediately after the amendments made by section 583 of Public Law 105–118 (as amended by section 4002(e)(7) of Public Law 107–273) [Pub.L. 105–118, Title V, § 583, Nov. 26, 1997, 111 Stat. 2436, as amended by Pub.L. 107–273, Div. B, Title IV, § 4002(e)(7), Nov. 2, 2002, 116 Stat. 1810, which amended subsecs. (a) to (c) of this section]."

2002 Acts. Amendment by section 4002(e)(7) of Pub.L. 107–273, as therein provided, effective Nov. 26, 1997, which is the date of enactment of Pub.L. 105–118, to which such amendment relates.

Short Title

1996 Acts. Section 1 of Pub.L. 104–192 provided that: "This Act [enacting this section] may be cited as the 'War Crimes Act of 1996'."

Implementation of Treaty Obligations

Pub.L. 109–366, § 6(a), Oct. 17, 2006, 120 Stat. 2632, provided that:

"(1) In general.—The acts enumerated in subsection (d) of section 2441 of title 18, United States Code [subsec. (d) of this section], as added by subsection (b) of this section, and in subsection (c) of this section [enacting 42 U.S.C.A. § 2000dd–0], constitute violations of common Article 3 of the Geneva Conventions [the text of Common Articles 3 of the Geneva Conventions is repeated in all four Geneva Conventions, see, generally, Geneva Convention for the Amelioration of the Condition of the Wounded and Sick in Armed Forces in the Field, Aug. 12, 1949, 6 U.S.T. 3114, 75 U.N.T.S. 31; Geneva Convention for the Amelioration of the Condition of Wounded, Sick and Shipwrecked Members of Armed Forces at Sea, Aug. 12, 1949, 6 U.S.T. 3217, 75 U.N.T.S. 85; Geneva Convention Relative to the Treatment of Prisoners of War, Aug. 12, 1949, 6 U.S.T. 3316, 75 U.N.T.S. 135; and, Geneva Convention Relative to the Protection of Civilian Persons in Time of War, Aug. 12, 1949, 6 U.S.T. 3516, 75 U.N.T.S. 287] prohibited by United States law.

"(2) Prohibition on grave breaches.—The provisions of section 2441 of title 18, United States Code [this section], as amended by this section, fully satisfy the obligation under Article 129 of the Third Geneva Convention for the United States to provide effective penal sanctions for grave breaches which are encompassed in common Article 3 in the context of an armed conflict not of an international character. No foreign or international source of law shall supply a basis for a rule of decision in the courts of the United States in interpreting the prohibitions enumerated in subsection (d) of such section 2441 [subsec. (d) of this section].

"(3) Interpretation by the President.—

"(A) As provided by the Constitution and by this section [this note], the President has the authority for the United States to interpret the meaning and application of the Geneva Conventions and to promulgate higher standards and administrative regulations for violations of treaty obligations which are not grave breaches of the Geneva Conventions.

"(B) The President shall issue interpretations described by subparagraph (A) by Executive Order published in the Federal Register.

"(C) Any Executive Order published under this paragraph shall be authoritative (except as to grave breaches of common Article 3) as a matter of United States law, in the same manner as other administrative regulations.

"(D) Nothing in this section shall be construed to affect the constitutional functions and responsibilities of Congress and the judicial branch of the United States.

"(4) Definitions.—In this subsection:

"(A) Geneva Conventions.—The term 'Geneva Conventions' means—

"(i) the Convention for the Amelioration of the Condition of the Wounded and Sick in Armed Forces in the Field, done at Geneva August 12, 1949 (6 UST 3217);

"(ii) the Convention for the Amelioration of the Condition of the Wounded, Sick, and Shipwrecked Members of the Armed Forces at Sea, done at Geneva August 12, 1949 (6 UST 3217);

"(iii) the Convention Relative to the Treatment of Prisoners of War, done at Geneva August 12, 1949 (6 UST 3316); and

"(iv) the Convention Relative to the Protection of Civilian Persons in Time of War, done at Geneva August 12, 1949 (6 UST 3516).

"**(B) Third Geneva Convention.**—The term 'Third Geneva Convention' means the international convention referred to in subparagraph (A)(iii)."

CHAPTER 119—WIRE AND ELECTRONIC COMMUNICATIONS INTERCEPTION AND INTERCEPTION OF ORAL COMMUNICATIONS

§ 2510. Definitions

As used in this chapter—

(1) "wire communication" means any aural transfer made in whole or in part through the use of facilities for the transmission of communications by the aid of wire, cable, or other like connection between the point of origin and the point of reception (including the use of such connection in a switching station) furnished or operated by any person engaged in providing or operating such facilities for the transmission of interstate or foreign communications or communications affecting interstate or foreign commerce;

(2) "oral communication" means any oral communication uttered by a person exhibiting an expectation that such communication is not subject to interception under circumstances justifying such expectation, but such term does not include any electronic communication;

(3) "State" means any State of the United States, the District of Columbia, the Commonwealth of Puerto Rico, and any territory or possession of the United States;

(4) "intercept" means the aural or other acquisition of the contents of any wire, electronic, or oral communication through the use of any electronic, mechanical, or other device. [1]

(5) "electronic, mechanical, or other device" means any device or apparatus which can be used to intercept a wire, oral, or electronic communication other than—

(a) any telephone or telegraph instrument, equipment or facility, or any component thereof, (i) furnished to the subscriber or user by a provider of wire or electronic communication service in the ordinary course of its business and being used by the subscriber or user in the ordinary course of its business or furnished by such subscriber or user for connection to the facilities of such service and used in the ordinary course of its business; or (ii) being used by a provider of wire or electronic communication service in the ordinary course of its business, or by an investigative or law enforcement officer in the ordinary course of his duties;

(b) a hearing aid or similar device being used to correct subnormal hearing to not better than normal;

(6) "person" means any employee, or agent of the United States or any State or political subdivision thereof, and any individual, partnership, association, joint stock company, trust, or corporation;

(7) "Investigative or law enforcement officer" means any officer of the United States or of a State or political subdivision thereof, who is empowered by law to conduct investigations of or to make arrests for offenses enumerated in this chapter, and any attorney authorized by law to prosecute or participate in the prosecution of such offenses;

(8) "contents", when used with respect to any wire, oral, or electronic communication, includes any

information concerning the substance, purport, or meaning of that communication;

(9) "Judge of competent jurisdiction" means—

(a) a judge of a United States district court or a United States court of appeals; and

(b) a judge of any court of general criminal jurisdiction of a State who is authorized by a statute of that State to enter orders authorizing interceptions of wire, oral, or electronic communications;

(10) "communication common carrier" has the meaning given that term in section 3 of the Communications Act of 1934;

(11) "aggrieved person" means a person who was a party to any intercepted wire, oral, or electronic communication or a person against whom the interception was directed;

(12) "electronic communication" means any transfer of signs, signals, writing, images, sounds, data, or intelligence of any nature transmitted in whole or in part by a wire, radio, electromagnetic, photoelectronic or photooptical system that affects interstate or foreign commerce, but does not include—

(A) any wire or oral communication;

(B) any communication made through a tone-only paging device;

(C) any communication from a tracking device (as defined in section 3117 of this title); or

(D) electronic funds transfer information stored by a financial institution in a communications system used for the electronic storage and transfer of funds;

(13) "user" means any person or entity who—

(A) uses an electronic communication service; and

(B) is duly authorized by the provider of such service to engage in such use;

(14) "electronic communications system" means any wire, radio, electromagnetic, photooptical or photoelectronic facilities for the transmission of wire or electronic communications, and any computer facilities or related electronic equipment for the electronic storage of such communications;

(15) "electronic communication service" means any service which provides to users thereof the ability to send or receive wire or electronic communications;

(16) "readily accessible to the general public" means, with respect to a radio communication, that such communication is not—

(A) scrambled or encrypted;

(B) transmitted using modulation techniques whose essential parameters have been withheld from the public with the intention of preserving the privacy of such communication;

(C) carried on a subcarrier or other signal subsidiary to a radio transmission;

(D) transmitted over a communication system provided by a common carrier, unless the communication is a tone only paging system communication; or

(E) transmitted on frequencies allocated under part 25, subpart D, E, or F of part 74, or part 94 of the Rules of the Federal Communications Commission, unless, in the case of a communication transmitted on a frequency allocated under part 74 that is not exclusively allocated to broadcast auxiliary services, the communication is a two-way voice communication by radio;

(17) "electronic storage" means—

(A) any temporary, intermediate storage of a wire or electronic communication incidental to the electronic transmission thereof; and

(B) any storage of such communication by an electronic communication service for purposes of backup protection of such communication;

(18) "aural transfer" means a transfer containing the human voice at any point between and including the point of origin and the point of reception;

(19) "foreign intelligence information", for purposes of section 2517(6) of this title, means—

(A) information, whether or not concerning a United States person, that relates to the ability of the United States to protect against—

(i) actual or potential attack or other grave hostile acts of a foreign power or an agent of a foreign power;

(ii) sabotage or international terrorism by a foreign power or an agent of a foreign power; or

(iii) clandestine intelligence activities by an intelligence service or network of a foreign power or by an agent of a foreign power; or

(B) information, whether or not concerning a United States person, with respect to a foreign power or foreign territory that relates to—

(i) the national defense or the security of the United States; or

(ii) the conduct of the foreign affairs of the United States;

(20) "protected computer" has the meaning set forth in section 1030; and

(21) "computer trespasser"—

(A) means a person who accesses a protected computer without authorization and thus has no reasonable expectation of privacy in any communication transmitted to, through, or from the protected computer; and

(B) does not include a person known by the owner or operator of the protected computer to have an existing contractual relationship with the owner or operator of the protected computer for access to all or part of the protected computer.

(Added Pub.L. 90–351, Title III, § 802, June 19, 1968, 82 Stat. 212, and amended Pub.L. 99–508, Title I, § 101(a), (c)(1)(A), (4), Oct. 21, 1986, 100 Stat. 1848, 1851; Pub.L. 103–414, Title II, §§ 202(a), 203, Oct. 25, 1994, 108 Stat. 4290, 4291; Pub.L. 104–132, Title VII, § 731, Apr. 24, 1996, 110 Stat. 1303; Pub.L. 107–56, Title II, §§ 203(b)(2), 209(1), 217(1), Oct. 26, 2001, 115 Stat. 280, 283, 290; Pub.L. 107–108, Title III, § 314(b), Dec. 28, 2001, 115 Stat. 1402; Pub.L. 107–273, Div. B, Title IV, § 4002(e)(10), Nov. 2, 2002, 116 Stat. 1810.)

1 So in original. The period probably should be a semicolon.

HISTORICAL AND STATUTORY NOTES

References in Text

Section 3 of the Communications Act of 1934, referred to in par. (10), is Act June 19, 1934, c. 652, Title I, § 3, 48 Stat. 1065, as amended, which is classified to 47 U.S.C.A. § 153. The term "common carrier" is defined in par. (10) of such section 153.

Effective and Applicability Provisions

1986 Acts. Section 111 of Pub.L. 99–508 provided that:

"(a) In general.—Except as provided in subsection (b) or (c), this title and the amendments made by this title [enacting 18 U.S.C.A. §§ 2521 and 3117, amending this section and 18 U.S.C.A. §§ 2232, 2511 to 2513, 2516, 2517 to 2520, and enacting provisions set out as notes under this section] shall take effect 90 days after the date of the enactment of this Act [Oct. 21, 1986] and shall, in the case of conduct pursuant to a court order or extension, apply only with respect to court orders or extensions made after this title takes effect.

"(b) Special Rule for State Authorizations of Interceptions.—Any interception pursuant to section 2516(2) of title 18 of the United States Code which would be valid and lawful without regard to the amendments made by this title [enacting 18 U.S.C.A. §§ 2521 and 3117, amending this section and 18 U.S.C.A. §§ 2232, 2511 to 2513, 2516, 2517 to 2520, and enacting provisions set out as notes under this section] shall be valid and lawful notwithstanding such amendments if such interception occurs during the period beginning on the date such amendments take effect and ending on the earlier of—

"(1) the day before the date of the taking effect of State law conforming the applicable State statute with chapter 119 of title 18, United States Code, as so amended; or

"(2) the date two years after the date of the enactment of this Act [Oct. 21, 1986].

"(c) Effective Date for Certain Approvals by Justice Department Officials.—Section 104 of this Act [amending 18 U.S.C.A. § 2516(1)] shall take effect on the date of enactment of this Act [Oct. 21, 1986]."

Sunset Provisions

Pub.L. 107–56, Title II, § 224, Oct. 26, 2001, 115 Stat. 295, as amended Pub.L. 109–160, § 1, Dec. 30, 2005, 119 Stat. 2957; Pub.L. 109–170, § 1, Feb. 3, 3006, 120 Stat. 3, which provided that, except with respect to certain particular foreign intelligence investigations begun before Oct. 26, 2001, amendments made by Title II of Pub.L. 107–56 [enacting 18 U.S.C.A. § 2712, 22 U.S.C.A. § 7210, 50 U.S.C.A. §§ 403–5d, 1861 and 1862, amending this section and 18 U.S.C.A. §§ 2511, 2516, 2517, 2520, 2702, 2703, 2707, 2711, 3103a, 3121, 3123, 3124, and 3127, 22 U.S.C.A. §§ 7203 and 7205, 47 U.S.C.A. § 551, 50 U.S.C.A. §§ 1803 to 1805, 1823, 1824, 1842 and 1843, and Rules 6 and 41 of the Federal Rules of Criminal Procedure, repealing 50 U.S.C.A. §§ 1861 through 1863, and enacting provisions set out as notes under 18 U.S.C.A. §§ 2517 and 3124 and 28 U.S.C.A. § 532] (other than sections 203(a) [amending Rule 6 of the Federal Rules of Criminal Procedure], 203(c) [enacting provisions set out as a note under 18 U.S.C.A. § 2517], 205 [enacting provisions set out as a note under 28 U.S.C.A. § 532], 208 [amending 50 U.S.C.A. § 1803], 210 [amending 18 U.S.C.A. § 2703], 211 [amending 47 U.S.C.A. § 551], 213 [amending 18 U.S.C.A. § 3103a], 216 [amending 18 U.S.C.A. §§ 3121, 3123, 3124, and 3127], 219 [amending Rule 41 of the Federal Rules of Criminal Procedure], 221 [enacting 22 U.S.C.A. § 7210 and amending 22 U.S.C.A. §§ 7203 and 7205], and 222 [enacting provisions set out as a note under 18 U.S.C.A. § 3124], and the amendments made by those sections) shall cease to have effect on March 10, 2006, was repealed by Pub.L. 109–177, Title I, § 102(a), Mar. 9, 2006, 120 Stat. 194.

Repeals

Section 1212 of the Act of Oct. 15, 1970, Pub.L. 91–452, repealed section 804 of the Act of July 19, 1968, Pub.L. 90–351.

However, section 20 of the Act of Jan. 2, 1971, Pub.L. 91–644, repealed Section 1212 of Pub.L. 91–452 and contained certain amendments to section 804 of Pub.L. 90–351, which are set out above.

Short Title

1997 Amendments. Section 1 of Pub.L. 105–112, Nov. 21, 1997, 111 Stat. 2273, provided that: "This Act [amending section 2512 of this title] may be cited as the 'Law Enforcement Technology Advertisement Clarification Act of 1997'."

1986 Acts. Section 1 of Pub.L. 99–508 provided that: "This Act [enacting sections 1367, 2521, 2701 to 2710, 3117, and 3121 to 3126 of this title, amending this section and sections 2232, 2511 to 2513, and 2516 to 2520 of this title, and enacting provisions set out as notes under this section] may be cited as the 'Electronic Communications Privacy Act of 1986'."

Intelligence Activities

Section 107 of Pub.L. 99–508 provided that:

"(a) In general.—Nothing in this Act [Pub.L. 99–508, Oct. 21, 1986, 100 Stat. 1858] or the amendments made by this Act [for classification, see Short Title note set out above] constitutes authority for the conduct of any intelligence activity.

"(b) Certain Activities Under Procedures Approved by the Attorney General.—Nothing in chapter 119 or chapter 121 of title 18, United States Code, shall affect the conduct, by officers or employees of the United States Government in accordance with other applicable Federal law, under procedures approved by the Attorney General of activities intended to—

"(1) intercept encrypted or other official communications of United States executive branch entities or United

States Government contractors for communications security purposes;

"(2) intercept radio communications transmitted between or among foreign powers or agents of a foreign power as defined by the Foreign Intelligence Surveillance Act of 1978 [50 U.S.C.A. § 1801 et seq.]; or

"(3) access an electronic communication system used exclusively by a foreign power or agent of a foreign power as defined by the Foreign Intelligence Surveillance Act of 1978 [50 U.S.C.A. § 1801 et seq.]."

Congressional Findings

Section 801 of Pub.L. 90–351 provided that: "On the basis of its own investigations and of published studies, the Congress makes the following findings:

"**(a)** Wire communications are normally conducted through the use of facilities which form part of an interstate network. The same facilities are used for interstate and intrastate communications. There has been extensive wiretapping carried on without legal sanctions, and without the consent of any of the parties to the conversation. Electronic, mechanical, and other intercepting devices are being used to overhear oral conversations made in private, without the consent of any of the parties to such communications. The contents of these communications and evidence derived therefrom are being used by public and private parties as evidence in court and administrative proceedings and by persons whose activities affect interstate commerce. The possession, manufacture, distribution, advertising, and use of these devices are facilitated by interstate commerce.

"**(b)** In order to protect effectively the privacy of wire and oral communications, to protect the integrity of court and administrative proceedings, and to prevent the obstruction of interstate commerce, it is necessary for Congress to define on a uniform basis the circumstances and conditions under which the interception of wire and oral communications may be authorized, to prohibit any unauthorized interception of such communications, and the use of the contents thereof in evidence in courts and administrative proceedings.

"**(c)** Organized criminals make extensive use of wire and oral communications in their criminal activities. The interception of such communications to obtain evidence of the commission of crimes or to prevent their commission is an indispensable aid to law enforcement and the administration of justice.

"**(d)** To safeguard the privacy of innocent persons, the interception of wire or oral communications where none of the parties to the communication has consented to the interception should be allowed only when authorized by a court of competent jurisdiction and should remain under the control and supervision of the authorizing court. Interception of wire and oral communications should further be limited to certain major types of offenses and specific categories of crime with assurances that the interception is justified and that the information obtained thereby will not be misused."

National Commission for the Review of Federal and State Laws Relating to Wiretapping and Electronic Surveillance

Section 804 of Pub.L. 90–351, as amended Pub.L. 91–452, Title XII, § 1212, Oct. 15, 1970, 84 Stat. 961; Pub.L. 91–644, Title VI, § 20, Jan. 2, 1971, 84 Stat. 1892; Pub.L. 93–609, §§ 1–4, Jan. 2, 1975, 88 Stat. 1972, 1973; Pub.L. 94–176, Dec. 23, 1975, 89 Stat. 1031, established a National Commission for the Review of Federal and State Laws Relating to Wiretapping and Electronic Surveillance, provided for its membership, Chairman, powers and functions, compensation and allowances, required the Commission to study and review the operation of the provisions of this chapter to determine their effectiveness and to submit interim reports and a final report to the President and to the Congress of its findings and recommendations on or before Apr. 30, 1976, and also provided for its termination sixty days after submission of the final report.

§ 2511. Interception and disclosure of wire, oral, or electronic communications prohibited

(1) Except as otherwise specifically provided in this chapter any person who—

(a) intentionally intercepts, endeavors to intercept, or procures any other person to intercept or endeavor to intercept, any wire, oral, or electronic communication;

(b) intentionally uses, endeavors to use, or procures any other person to use or endeavor to use any electronic, mechanical, or other device to intercept any oral communication when—

(i) such device is affixed to, or otherwise transmits a signal through, a wire, cable, or other like connection used in wire communication; or

(ii) such device transmits communications by radio, or interferes with the transmission of such communication; or

(iii) such person knows, or has reason to know, that such device or any component thereof has been sent through the mail or transported in interstate or foreign commerce; or

(iv) such use or endeavor to use (A) takes place on the premises of any business or other commercial establishment the operations of which affect interstate or foreign commerce; or (B) obtains or is for the purpose of obtaining information relating to the operations of any business or other commercial establishment the operations of which affect interstate or foreign commerce; or

(v) such person acts in the District of Columbia, the Commonwealth of Puerto Rico, or any territory or possession of the United States;

(c) intentionally discloses, or endeavors to disclose, to any other person the contents of any wire, oral, or electronic communication, knowing or having reason to know that the information was obtained through the interception of a wire, oral, or electronic communication in violation of this subsection;

(d) intentionally uses, or endeavors to use, the contents of any wire, oral, or electronic communication, knowing or having reason to know that the information was obtained through the interception of a wire, oral, or electronic communication in violation of this subsection; or

(e) (i) intentionally discloses, or endeavors to disclose, to any other person the contents of any wire, oral, or electronic communication, intercepted by means authorized by sections 2511(2)(a)(ii), 2511(2)(b)–(c), 2511(2)(e), 2516, and 2518 of this chapter, (ii) knowing or having reason to know that the information was obtained through the interception of such a communication in connection with a criminal investigation, (iii) having obtained or received the information in connection with a criminal investigation, and (iv) with intent to improperly obstruct, impede, or interfere with a duly authorized criminal investigation,

shall be punished as provided in subsection (4) or shall be subject to suit as provided in subsection (5).

(2)(a)(i) It shall not be unlawful under this chapter for an operator of a switchboard, or an officer, employee, or agent of a provider of wire or electronic communication service, whose facilities are used in the transmission of a wire or electronic communication, to intercept, disclose, or use that communication in the normal course of his employment while engaged in any activity which is a necessary incident to the rendition of his service or to the protection of the rights or property of the provider of that service, except that a provider of wire communication service to the public shall not utilize service observing or random monitoring except for mechanical or service quality control checks.

(ii) Notwithstanding any other law, providers of wire or electronic communication service, their officers, employees, and agents, landlords, custodians, or other persons, are authorized to provide information, facilities, or technical assistance to persons authorized by law to intercept wire, oral, or electronic communications or to conduct electronic surveillance, as defined in section 101 of the Foreign Intelligence Surveillance Act of 1978, if such provider, its officers, employees, or agents, landlord, custodian, or other specified person, has been provided with—

(A) a court order directing such assistance signed by the authorizing judge, or

(B) a certification in writing by a person specified in section 2518(7) of this title or the Attorney General of the United States that no warrant or court order is required by law, that all statutory requirements have been met, and that the specified assistance is required,

setting forth the period of time during which the provision of the information, facilities, or technical assistance is authorized and specifying the information, facilities, or technical assistance required. No provider of wire or electronic communication service, officer, employee, or agent thereof, or landlord, custodian, or other specified person shall disclose the existence of any interception or surveillance or the device used to accomplish the interception or surveillance with respect to which the person has been furnished a court order or certification under this chapter, except as may otherwise be required by legal process and then only after prior notification to the Attorney General or to the principal prosecuting attorney of a State or any political subdivision of a State, as may be appropriate. Any such disclosure, shall render such person liable for the civil damages provided for in section 2520. No cause of action shall lie in any court against any provider of wire or electronic communication service, its officers, employees, or agents, landlord, custodian, or other specified person for providing information, facilities, or assistance in accordance with the terms of a court order, statutory authorization, or certification under this chapter.

(b) It shall not be unlawful under this chapter for an officer, employee, or agent of the Federal Communications Commission, in the normal course of his employment and in discharge of the monitoring responsibilities exercised by the Commission in the enforcement of chapter 5 of title 47 of the United States Code, to intercept a wire or electronic communication, or oral communication transmitted by radio, or to disclose or use the information thereby obtained.

(c) It shall not be unlawful under this chapter for a person acting under color of law to intercept a wire, oral, or electronic communication, where such person is a party to the communication or one of the parties to the communication has given prior consent to such interception.

(d) It shall not be unlawful under this chapter for a person not acting under color of law to intercept a wire, oral, or electronic communication where such person is a party to the communication or where one of the parties to the communication has given prior consent to such interception unless such communication is intercepted for the purpose of committing any criminal or tortious act in violation of the Constitution or laws of the United States or of any State.

(e) Notwithstanding any other provision of this title or section 705 or 706 of the Communications Act of 1934, it shall not be unlawful for an officer, employee, or agent of the United States in the normal course of his official duty to conduct electronic surveillance, as defined in section 101 of the Foreign Intelligence Surveillance Act of 1978, as authorized by that Act.

(f) Nothing contained in this chapter or chapter 121 or 206 of this title, or section 705 of the Communications Act of 1934, shall be deemed to affect the acquisition by the United States Government of foreign intelligence information from international or foreign communications, or foreign intelligence activities conducted in accordance with otherwise applicable

Federal law involving a foreign electronic communications system, utilizing a means other than electronic surveillance as defined in section 101 of the Foreign Intelligence Surveillance Act of 1978, and procedures in this chapter or chapter 121 and the Foreign Intelligence Surveillance Act of 1978 shall be the exclusive means by which electronic surveillance, as defined in section 101 of such Act, and the interception of domestic wire, oral, and electronic communications may be conducted.

(g) It shall not be unlawful under this chapter or chapter 121 of this title for any person—

(i) to intercept or access an electronic communication made through an electronic communication system that is configured so that such electronic communication is readily accessible to the general public;

(ii) to intercept any radio communication which is transmitted—

(I) by any station for the use of the general public, or that relates to ships, aircraft, vehicles, or persons in distress;

(II) by any governmental, law enforcement, civil defense, private land mobile, or public safety communications system, including police and fire, readily accessible to the general public;

(III) by a station operating on an authorized frequency within the bands allocated to the amateur, citizens band, or general mobile radio services; or

(IV) by any marine or aeronautical communications system;

(iii) to engage in any conduct which—

(I) is prohibited by section 633 of the Communications Act of 1934; or

(II) is excepted from the application of section 705(a) of the Communications Act of 1934 by section 705(b) of that Act;

(iv) to intercept any wire or electronic communication the transmission of which is causing harmful interference to any lawfully operating station or consumer electronic equipment, to the extent necessary to identify the source of such interference; or

(v) for other users of the same frequency to intercept any radio communication made through a system that utilizes frequencies monitored by individuals engaged in the provision or the use of such system, if such communication is not scrambled or encrypted.

(h) It shall not be unlawful under this chapter—

(i) to use a pen register or a trap and trace device (as those terms are defined for the purposes of chapter 206 (relating to pen registers and trap and trace devices) of this title); or

(ii) for a provider of electronic communication service to record the fact that a wire or electronic communication was initiated or completed in order to protect such provider, another provider furnishing service toward the completion of the wire or electronic communication, or a user of that service, from fraudulent, unlawful or abusive use of such service.

(i) It shall not be unlawful under this chapter for a person acting under color of law to intercept the wire or electronic communications of a computer trespasser transmitted to, through, or from the protected computer, if—

(I) the owner or operator of the protected computer authorizes the interception of the computer trespasser's communications on the protected computer;

(II) the person acting under color of law is lawfully engaged in an investigation;

(III) the person acting under color of law has reasonable grounds to believe that the contents of the computer trespasser's communications will be relevant to the investigation; and

(IV) such interception does not acquire communications other than those transmitted to or from the computer trespasser.

(3)(a) Except as provided in paragraph (b) of this subsection, a person or entity providing an electronic communication service to the public shall not intentionally divulge the contents of any communication (other than one to such person or entity, or an agent thereof) while in transmission on that service to any person or entity other than an addressee or intended recipient of such communication or an agent of such addressee or intended recipient.

(b) A person or entity providing electronic communication service to the public may divulge the contents of any such communication—

(i) as otherwise authorized in section 2511(2)(a) or 2517 of this title;

(ii) with the lawful consent of the originator or any addressee or intended recipient of such communication;

(iii) to a person employed or authorized, or whose facilities are used, to forward such communication to its destination; or

(iv) which were inadvertently obtained by the service provider and which appear to pertain to the commission of a crime, if such divulgence is made to a law enforcement agency.

(4)(a) Except as provided in paragraph (b) of this subsection or in subsection (5), whoever violates subsection (1) of this section shall be fined under this title or imprisoned not more than five years, or both.

(b) Conduct otherwise an offense under this subsection that consists of or relates to the interception of a satellite transmission that is not encrypted or scrambled and that is transmitted—

(i) to a broadcasting station for purposes of retransmission to the general public; or

(ii) as an audio subcarrier intended for redistribution to facilities open to the public, but not including data transmissions or telephone calls,

is not an offense under this subsection unless the conduct is for the purposes of direct or indirect commercial advantage or private financial gain.

[**(c)** Redesignated (b)]

(5)(a)(i) If the communication is—

(A) a private satellite video communication that is not scrambled or encrypted and the conduct in violation of this chapter is the private viewing of that communication and is not for a tortious or illegal purpose or for purposes of direct or indirect commercial advantage or private commercial gain; or

(B) a radio communication that is transmitted on frequencies allocated under subpart D of part 74 of the rules of the Federal Communications Commission that is not scrambled or encrypted and the conduct in violation of this chapter is not for a tortious or illegal purpose or for purposes of direct or indirect commercial advantage or private commercial gain,

then the person who engages in such conduct shall be subject to suit by the Federal Government in a court of competent jurisdiction.

(ii) In an action under this subsection—

(A) if the violation of this chapter is a first offense for the person under paragraph (a) of subsection (4) and such person has not been found liable in a civil action under section 2520 of this title, the Federal Government shall be entitled to appropriate injunctive relief; and

(B) if the violation of this chapter is a second or subsequent offense under paragraph (a) of subsection (4) or such person has been found liable in any prior civil action under section 2520, the person shall be subject to a mandatory $500 civil fine.

(b) The court may use any means within its authority to enforce an injunction issued under paragraph (ii)(A), and shall impose a civil fine of not less than $500 for each violation of such an injunction.

(Added Pub.L. 90–351, Title III, § 802, June 19, 1968, 82 Stat. 213, and amended Pub.L. 91–358, Title II, § 211(a), July 29, 1970, 84 Stat. 654; Pub.L. 95–511, Title II, § 201(a) to (c), Oct. 25, 1978, 92 Stat. 1796, 1797; Pub.L. 98–549, § 6(b)(2), Oct. 30, 1984, 98 Stat. 2804; Pub.L. 99–508, Title I, § 101(b), (c)(1), (5), (6), (d), (f), 102, Oct. 21, 1986, 100 Stat. 1849 to 1853; Pub.L. 103–322, Title XXXII, § 320901, Title XXXIII, § 330016(1)(G), Sept. 13, 1994, 108 Stat. 2123, 2147; Pub.L. 103–414, Title II, §§ 202(b), 204, 205, Oct. 25, 1994, 108 Stat. 4290, 4291; Pub.L. 104–294, Title VI, § 604(b)(42), Oct. 11, 1996, 110 Stat. 3509; Pub.L. 107–56, Title II, §§ 204, 217(2), Oct. 26, 2001, 115 Stat. 281, 291; Pub.L. 107–296, Title II, § 225(h)(2), (j)(1), Nov. 25, 2002, 116 Stat. 2158.)

HISTORICAL AND STATUTORY NOTES

References in Text

Chapter 5 of title 47 of the United States Code, referred to in par. (2)(b), is chapter 5 of Title 47, Telegraphs, Telephones, and Radiotelegraphs. Such chapter 5, set out as § 151 et seq. of Title 47, is the Communications Act of 1934.

Chapter 121 or 206 of this title, referred to in par. (2)(f), are 18 U.S.C.A. § 2701 et seq. or 3121 et seq.

Sections 705 and 706 of the Communications Act of 1934, referred to in par. (2)(e), (f), and (g), are classified to sections 605 and 606 of Title 47, Telegraphs, Telephones, and Radiotelegraphs, respectively.

The Foreign Intelligence Surveillance Act of 1978, referred to in pars. (2)(e) and (f), is Pub.L. 95–511, Oct. 25, 1978, 92 Stat. 1783, which is classified principally to chapter 36 (section 1801 et seq.) of Title 50, War and National Defense. Section 101 of the Foreign Intelligence Surveillance Act of 1978, referred to in pars. (2)(a)(ii), (e), and (f), is classified to section 1801 of Title 50. For complete classification of this Act to the Code, see Short Title note set out under section 1801 of Title 50 and Tables.

Section 633 of the Communications Act of 1934, referred to in par. (2)(g), is classified to section 553 of Title 47, Telegraphs, Telephones, and Radiotelegraphs.

Effective and Applicability Provisions

2002 Acts. Amendment to this section by Pub.L. 107–296 effective 60 days after Nov. 25, 2002, see Pub.L. 107–296, § 4, set out as a note under 6 U.S.C.A. § 101.

1996 Acts. Amendment by section 604 of Pub.L. 104–294 effective Sept. 13, 1994, see section 604(d) of Pub.L. 104–294, set out as a note under section 13 of this title.

1986 Acts. Except as otherwise provided in section 111 of Pub.L. 99–508, amendment by Pub.L. 99–508 effective 90 days after Oct. 21, 1986, see section 111 of Pub.L. 99–508 set out as a note under section 2510 of this title.

1984 Acts. Amendment by Pub.L. 98–549 to take effect 60 days after Oct. 30, 1984, except where otherwise expressly provided, see section 9(a) of Pub.L. 98–549, set out as a note under section 521 of Title 47, Telegraphs, Telephones and Radiotelegraphs.

1978 Acts. Amendment by Pub.L. 95–511 effective Oct. 25, 1978, except as specifically provided, see section 301 of Pub.L. 95–511, set out as an Effective Date note under section 1801 of Title 50, War and National Defense.

1970 Acts. Section 901(a) of Pub.L. 91–358 provided in part that the amendment of this section by Pub.L. 91–358 shall take effect on the first day of the seventh calendar month which begins after July 29, 1970.

Sunset Provisions

Provision that amendments by Pub.L. 107–56, Title II, Oct. 26, 2001, 115 Stat. 278, with certain exclusions, shall cease to have effect on March 10, 2006, except with respect to any particular foreign intelligence investigation that began before that date, or with respect to any particular offense or potential offense that began or occurred before that, such provisions to continue in effect, was repealed by Pub.L. 109–177, § 102(a), see Pub.L. 107–56, § 224, as amended, set out as a note under 18 U.S.C.A. § 2510.

§ 2512. Manufacture, distribution, possession, and advertising of wire, oral, or electronic communication intercepting devices prohibited

(1) Except as otherwise specifically provided in this chapter, any person who intentionally—

(a) sends through the mail, or sends or carries in interstate or foreign commerce, any electronic, mechanical, or other device, knowing or having reason to know that the design of such device renders it primarily useful for the purpose of the surreptitious interception of wire, oral, or electronic communications;

(b) manufactures, assembles, possesses, or sells any electronic, mechanical, or other device, knowing or having reason to know that the design of such device renders it primarily useful for the purpose of the surreptitious interception of wire, oral, or electronic communications, and that such device or any component thereof has been or will be sent through the mail or transported in interstate or foreign commerce; or

(c) places in any newspaper, magazine, handbill, or other publication or disseminates by electronic means any advertisement of—

(i) any electronic, mechanical, or other device knowing the content of the advertisement and knowing or having reason to know that the design of such device renders it primarily useful for the purpose of the surreptitious interception of wire, oral, or electronic communications; or

(ii) any other electronic, mechanical, or other device, where such advertisement promotes the use of such device for the purpose of the surreptitious interception of wire, oral, or electronic communications,

knowing the content of the advertisement and knowing or having reason to know that such advertisement will be sent through the mail or transported in interstate or foreign commerce,

shall be fined under this title or imprisoned not more than five years, or both.

(2) It shall not be unlawful under this section for—

(a) a provider of wire or electronic communication service or an officer, agent, or employee of, or a person under contract with, such a provider, in the normal course of the business of providing that wire or electronic communication service, or

(b) an officer, agent, or employee of, or a person under contract with, the United States, a State, or a political subdivision thereof, in the normal course of the activities of the United States, a State, or a political subdivision thereof,

to send through the mail, send or carry in interstate or foreign commerce, or manufacture, assemble, possess, or sell any electronic, mechanical, or other device knowing or having reason to know that the design of such device renders it primarily useful for the purpose of the surreptitious interception of wire, oral, or electronic communications.

(3) It shall not be unlawful under this section to advertise for sale a device described in subsection (1) of this section if the advertisement is mailed, sent, or carried in interstate or foreign commerce solely to a domestic provider of wire or electronic communication service or to an agency of the United States, a State, or a political subdivision thereof which is duly authorized to use such device.

(Added Pub.L. 90–351, Title III, § 802, June 19, 1968, 82 Stat. 214, and amended Pub.L. 99–508, Title I, § 101(c)(1)(A), (7), (f)(2), Oct. 21, 1986, 100 Stat. 1851, 1853; Pub.L. 103–322, Title XXXIII, §§ 330016(1)(L), 330022, Sept. 13, 1994, 108 Stat. 2147, 2150; Pub.L. 104–294, Title VI, § 604(b)(45), Oct. 11, 1996, 110 Stat. 3509; Pub.L. 105–112, § 2, Nov. 21, 1997, 111 Stat. 2273; Pub.L. 107–296, Title II, § 225(f), Nov. 25, 2002, 116 Stat. 2158.)

HISTORICAL AND STATUTORY NOTES

Effective and Applicability Provisions

2002 Acts. Amendment to this section by Pub.L. 107–296 effective 60 days after Nov. 25, 2002, see Pub.L. 107–296, § 4, set out as a note under 6 U.S.C.A. § 101.

1996 Acts. Amendment by section 604 of Pub.L. 104–294 effective Sept. 13, 1994, see section 604(d) of Pub.L. 104–294, set out as a note under section 13 of this title.

1986 Acts. Except as otherwise provided in section 111 of Pub.L. 99–508, amendment by Pub.L. 99–508 effective 90 days after Oct. 21, 1986, see section 111 of Pub.L. 99–508 set out as a note under section 2510 of this title.

Effect of Regulations Prohibiting Cellular Telecommunications Interception on Other Laws

For provision relating to the effect of regulations prohibiting manufacture of scanning receivers capable of receiving cellular telecommunications on other laws, see section 403(c) of Pub.L. 102–556, Oct. 28, 1992, 106 Stat. 4195, set out as a note under section 302a of Title 47, Telegraphs, Telephones, and Radiotelegraphs.

§ 2513. Confiscation of wire, oral, or electronic communication intercepting devices

Any electronic, mechanical, or other device used, sent, carried, manufactured, assembled, possessed, sold, or advertised in violation of section 2511 or section 2512 of this chapter may be seized and forfeited to the United States. All provisions of law relating to (1) the seizure, summary and judicial forfeiture, and condemnation of vessels, vehicles, merchandise, and baggage for violations of the customs laws contained in title 19 of the United States Code, (2) the disposition of such vessels, vehicles, merchandise, and baggage or the proceeds from the sale thereof, (3) the remission or mitigation of such forfeiture, (4) the compromise of claims, and (5) the award of compensation to informers in respect of such forfeitures, shall apply to seizures and forfeitures incurred, or alleged to have been incurred, under the provisions of this section, insofar as applicable and not inconsistent with the provisions of this section; except that such duties as are imposed upon the collector of customs or any other person with respect to the seizure and forfeiture of vessels, vehicles, merchandise, and baggage under the provisions of the customs laws contained in title 19 of the United States Code shall be performed with respect to seizure and forfeiture of electronic, mechanical, or other intercepting devices under this section by such officers, agents, or other persons as may be authorized or designated for that purpose by the Attorney General.

(Added Pub.L. 90–351, Title III, § 802, June 19, 1968, 82 Stat. 215, and amended Pub.L. 99–508, Title I, § 101(c)(1)(A), Oct. 21, 1986, 100 Stat. 1851.)

HISTORICAL AND STATUTORY NOTES

References in Text

Title 19 of the United States Code, referred to in text, is Title 19, Customs Duties.

Effective and Applicability Provisions

1986 Acts. Except as otherwise provided in section 111 of Pub.L. 99–508, amendment by Pub.L. 99–508 effective 90 days after Oct. 21, 1986, see section 111 of Pub.L. 99–508 set out as a note under section 2510 of this title.

[§ 2514. Repealed. Pub.L. 91–452, Title II, § 227(a), Oct. 15, 1970, 84 Stat. 930]

HISTORICAL AND STATUTORY NOTES

Section, Pub.L. 90–351, Title II, § 802, June 19, 1968, 82 Stat. 216, provided for immunity of witnesses giving testimony or producing evidence under compulsion in Federal grand jury or court proceedings. Subject matter is now covered in sections 6002 and 6003 of this title.

Effective Date of Repeal

Sections 227(a), 260 of Pub.L. 91–452 provided for repeal of this section effective four years following sixtieth day after date of enactment of Pub.L. 91–452, which was approved Oct. 15, 1970, such repeal not affecting any immunity to which any individual was entitled under this section by reason of any testimony or other information given before such date. See section 260 of Pub.L. 91–452, set out as a note under section 6001 of this title.

§ 2515. Prohibition of use as evidence of intercepted wire or oral communications

Whenever any wire or oral communication has been intercepted, no part of the contents of such communication and no evidence derived therefrom may be received in evidence in any trial, hearing, or other proceeding in or before any court, grand jury, department, officer, agency, regulatory body, legislative committee, or other authority of the United States, a State, or a political subdivision thereof if the disclosure of that information would be in violation of this chapter.

(Added Pub.L. 90–351, Title III, § 802, June 19, 1968, 82 Stat. 216.)

§ 2516. Authorization for interception of wire, oral, or electronic communications

(1) The Attorney General, Deputy Attorney General, Associate Attorney General [1], or any Assistant Attorney General, any acting Assistant Attorney General, or any Deputy Assistant Attorney General or acting Deputy Assistant Attorney General in the Criminal Division or National Security Division specially designated by the Attorney General, may authorize an application to a Federal judge of competent jurisdiction for, and such judge may grant in conformity with section 2518 of this chapter an order authorizing or approving the interception of wire or oral communications by the Federal Bureau of Investigation, or a Federal agency having responsibility for the investigation of the offense as to which the application is made, when such interception may provide or has provided evidence of—

(a) any offense punishable by death or by imprisonment for more than one year under sections 2122 and 2274 through 2277 of title 42 of the United States Code (relating to the enforcement of the Atomic Energy Act of 1954), section 2284 of title 42 of the United States Code (relating to sabotage of nuclear facilities or fuel), or under the following chapters of this title: chapter 10 (relating to biological weapons) [2] chapter 37 (relating to espionage), chapter 55 (relating to kidnapping), chapter 90 (relating to protection of trade secrets), chapter 105 (relating to sabotage), chapter 115 (relating to treason), chapter 102 (relating to riots), chapter 65 (relating to malicious mischief), chapter 111 (relating to destruction of vessels), or chapter 81 (relating to piracy);

(b) a violation of section 186 or section 501(c) of title 29, United States Code (dealing with restrictions on payments and loans to labor organizations), or any offense which involves murder, kidnapping, robbery, or extortion, and which is punishable under this title;

(c) any offense which is punishable under the following sections of this title: section 37 (relating to violence at international airports), section 43 (relating to animal enterprise terrorism), section 81 (arson within special maritime and territorial jurisdiction), section 201 (bribery of public officials and witnesses), section 215 (relating to bribery of bank officials), section 224 (bribery in sporting contests), subsection (d), (e), (f), (g), (h), or (i) of section 844 (unlawful use of explosives), section 1032 (relating to concealment of assets), section 1084 (transmission of wagering information), section 751 (relating to escape), section 832 (relating to nuclear and weapons of mass destruction threats), section 842 (relating to explosive materials), section 930 (relating to possession of weapons in Federal facilities), section 1014 (relating to loans and credit applications generally; renewals and discounts), section 1114 (relating to officers and employees of the United States), section 1116 (relating to protection of foreign officials), sections 1503, 1512, and 1513 (influencing or injuring an officer, juror, or witness generally), section 1510 (obstruction of criminal investigations), section 1511 (obstruction of State or local law enforcement), section 1591 (sex trafficking of children by force, fraud, or coercion), section 1751 (Presidential and Presidential staff assassination, kidnapping, and assault), section 1951 (interference with commerce by threats or violence), section 1952 (interstate and foreign travel or transportation in aid of racketeering enterprises), section 1958 (relating to use of interstate commerce facilities in the commission of murder for hire), section 1959 (relating to violent crimes in aid of racketeering activity), section 1954 (offer, acceptance, or solicitation to influence operations of employee benefit plan), section 1955 (prohibition of business enterprises of gambling), section 1956 (laundering of monetary instruments), section 1957 (relating to engaging in monetary transactions in property derived from specified unlawful activity), section 659 (theft from interstate shipment), section 664 (embezzlement from pension and welfare funds), section 1343 (fraud by wire, radio, or television), section 1344 (relating to bank fraud), section 1992 (relating to terrorist attacks against mass transportation), sections 2251 and 2252 (sexual exploitation of children), section 2251A (selling or buying of children), section 2252A (relating to material constituting or containing child pornography), section 1466A (relating to child obscenity), section 2260 (production of sexually explicit depictions of a minor for importation into the United States), sections 2421, 2422, 2423, and 2425 (relating to transportation for illegal sexual activity and related crimes), sections 2312, 2313, 2314, and 2315 (interstate transportation of stolen property), section 2321 (relating to trafficking in certain motor vehicles or motor vehicle parts), section 2340A (relating to torture), section 1203 (relating to hostage taking), section 1029 (relating to fraud and related activity in connection with access devices), section 3146 (relating to penalty for failure to appear), section 3521(b)(3) (relating to witness relocation and assistance), section 32 (relating to destruction of aircraft or aircraft facilities), section 38 (relating to aircraft parts fraud), section 1963 (violations with respect to racketeer influenced and corrupt organizations), section 115 (relating to threatening or retaliating against a Federal official), section 1341 (relating to mail fraud), a felony violation of section 1030 (relating to computer fraud and abuse), section 351 (violations with respect to congressional, Cabinet, or Supreme Court assassinations, kidnapping, and assault), section 831 (relating to prohibited transactions involving nuclear materials), section 33 (relating to destruction of motor vehicles or motor vehicle facilities), section 175 (relating to biological weapons), section 175c (relating to variola virus), section 956 (conspiracy to harm persons or property overseas), section [3] a felony violation of section 1028 (relating to production of false identification documentation), section 1425 (relating to the procurement of citizenship or nationalization unlawfully), section 1426 (relating to the reproduction of naturalization or citizenship papers), section 1427 (relating to the sale of naturalization or citizenship papers), section 1541 (relating to passport issuance without authority), section 1542 (relating to false statements in passport applications), section 1543 (relating to forgery or false use of passports), section 1544 (relating to misuse of passports), or section 1546 (relating to fraud and misuse of visas, permits, and other documents);

(d) any offense involving counterfeiting punishable under section 471, 472, or 473 of this title;

(e) any offense involving fraud connected with a case under title 11 or the manufacture, importation, receiving, concealment, buying, selling, or otherwise dealing in narcotic drugs, marihuana, or other dangerous drugs, punishable under any law of the United States;

(f) any offense including extortionate credit transactions under sections 892, 893, or 894 of this title;

(g) a violation of section 5322 of title 31, United States Code (dealing with the reporting of currency transactions), or section 5324 of title 31, United States Code (relating to structuring transactions to evade reporting requirement prohibited);

(h) any felony violation of sections 2511 and 2512 (relating to interception and disclosure of certain communications and to certain intercepting devices) of this title;

(i) any felony violation of chapter 71 (relating to obscenity) of this title;

(j) any violation of section 60123(b) (relating to destruction of a natural gas pipeline), section 46502 (relating to aircraft piracy), the second sentence of section 46504 (relating to assault on a flight crew with dangerous weapon), or section 46505(b)(3) or (c) (relating to explosive or incendiary devices, or endangerment of human life, by means of weapons on aircraft) of title 49;

(k) any criminal violation of section 2778 of title 22 (relating to the Arms Export Control Act);

(l) the location of any fugitive from justice from an offense described in this section;

(m) a violation of section 274, 277, or 278 of the Immigration and Nationality Act (8 U.S.C. 1324, 1327, or 1328) (relating to the smuggling of aliens);

(n) any felony violation of sections 922 and 924 of title 18, United States Code (relating to firearms);

(o) any violation of section 5861 of the Internal Revenue Code of 1986 (relating to firearms);

(p) a felony violation of section 1028 (relating to production of false identification documents), section 1542 (relating to false statements in passport applications), section 1546 (relating to fraud and misuse of visas, permits, and other documents, [4] section 1028A (relating to aggravated identity theft)) [5] of this title or a violation of section 274, 277, or 278 of the Immigration and Nationality Act (relating to the smuggling of aliens); or [6]

(q) any criminal violation of section 229 (relating to chemical weapons): or sections [7] 2332, 2332a, 2332b, 2332d, 2332f, 2332g, 2332h [8] 2339, 2339A, 2339B, 2339C, or 2339D of this title (relating to terrorism);

(r) any criminal violation of section 1 (relating to illegal restraints of trade or commerce), 2 (relating to illegal monopolizing of trade or commerce), or 3 (relating to illegal restraints of trade or commerce in territories or the District of Columbia) of the Sherman Act (15 U.S.C. 1, 2, 3); or

(s) any conspiracy to commit any offense described in any subparagraph of this paragraph.

(2) The principal prosecuting attorney of any State, or the principal prosecuting attorney of any political subdivision thereof, if such attorney is authorized by a statute of that State to make application to a State court judge of competent jurisdiction for an order authorizing or approving the interception of wire, oral, or electronic communications, may apply to such judge for, and such judge may grant in conformity with section 2518 of this chapter and with the applicable State statute an order authorizing, or approving the interception of wire, oral, or electronic communications by investigative or law enforcement officers having responsibility for the investigation of the offense as to which the application is made, when such interception may provide or has provided evidence of the commission of the offense of murder, kidnapping, gambling, robbery, bribery, extortion, or dealing in narcotic drugs, marihuana or other dangerous drugs, or other crime dangerous to life, limb, or property, and punishable by imprisonment for more than one year, designated in any applicable State statute authorizing such interception, or any conspiracy to commit any of the foregoing offenses.

(3) Any attorney for the Government (as such term is defined for the purposes of the Federal Rules of Criminal Procedure) may authorize an application to a Federal judge of competent jurisdiction for, and such judge may grant, in conformity with section 2518 of this title, an order authorizing or approving the interception of electronic communications by an investigative or law enforcement officer having responsibility for the investigation of the offense as to which the application is made, when such interception may provide or has provided evidence of any Federal felony.

(Added Pub.L. 90–351, Title III, § 802, June 19, 1968, 82 Stat. 216, and amended Pub.L. 91–452, Title VIII, § 810, Title IX, § 902(a), Title XI, § 1103, Oct. 15, 1970, 84 Stat. 940, 947, 959; Pub.L. 91–644, Title IV, § 16, Jan. 2, 1971, 84 Stat. 1891; Pub.L. 95–598, Title III, § 314(h), Nov. 6, 1978, 92 Stat. 2677; Pub.L. 97–285, §§ 2(e), 4(e), Oct. 6, 1982, 96 Stat. 1220, 1221; Pub.L. 98–292, § 8, May 21, 1984, 98 Stat. 206; Pub.L. 98–473, Title II, § 1203(c), Oct. 12, 1984, 98 Stat. 2152; Pub.L. 99–508, Title I, §§ 101(c)(1)(A), 104, 105, Oct. 21, 1986, 100 Stat. 1851, 1855; Pub.L. 99–570, Title I, § 1365(c), Oct. 27, 1986, 100 Stat. 3207–35; Pub.L. 100–690, Title VI, § 6461, Title VII, §§ 7036, 7053(d), 7525, Nov. 18, 1988, 102 Stat. 4374, 4399, 4402, 4502; Pub.L. 101–298, § 3(b), May 22, 1990, 104 Stat. 203; Pub.L. 101–647, Title XXV, § 2531, Title XXXV, § 3568, Nov. 29, 1990, 104 Stat. 4879, 4928; Pub.L. 103–272, § 5(e)(11), July 5, 1994, 108 Stat. 1374; Pub.L. 103–322, Title XXXIII, §§ 330011(c)(1), (q)(1), (r), 330021(1), Sept. 13, 1994, 108 Stat. 2144, 2145, 2150; Pub.L. 103–414, Title II, § 208, Oct. 25, 1994, 108 Stat. 4292; Pub.L. 103–429, § 7(a)(4)(A), Oct. 31, 1994, 108 Stat. 4389; Pub.L. 104–132, Title IV, § 434, Apr. 24, 1996, 110 Stat. 1274; Pub.L. 104–208, Div. C, Title II, § 201, Sept. 30, 1996, 110 Stat. 3009-564; Pub.L. 104–287, § 6(a)(2), Oct. 11, 1996, 110 Stat. 3398; Pub.L. 104–294, Title I, § 102, Title VI, § 601(d), Oct. 11, 1996, 110 Stat. 3491, 3499; Pub.L. 105–318, § 6(b), Oct. 30, 1998, 112 Stat. 3011; Pub.L. 106–181, Title V, § 506(c)(2)(B), Apr. 5, 2000, 114 Stat. 139; Pub.L. 107–56, Title II, §§ 201, 202, Oct. 26, 2001, 115 Stat. 278; Pub.L. 107–197, Title III, § 301(a), June 25, 2002, 116 Stat. 728; Pub.L. 107–273, Div. B, Title IV, §§ 4002(c)(1), 4005(a)(1), Nov. 2, 2002, 116 Stat. 1808, 1812; Pub.L. 108–21, Title II, § 201, Apr. 30, 2003, 117 Stat. 659; Pub.L. 108–458, Title VI, § 6907, Dec. 17, 2004, 118 Stat. 3774; Pub.L. 109–162, Title XI, § 1171(b), Jan. 5, 2006, 119 Stat. 3123; Pub.L. 109–177, Title I, §§ 110(b)(3)(C), 113, Title V, § 506(a)(6), Mar. 9, 2006, 120 Stat. 208, 209, 248.)

[1] See Codifications note set out under this section.

[2] So in original. A comma probably should appear.

[3] So in original. The word "section" probably should not appear.

[4] So in original. Probably should read "other documents),".

[5] So in original. The second closing parenthesis probably should not appear.

[6] So in original. The word "or" probably should not appear.

[7] So in original. Probably should be "weapons) or section".

[8] So in original. A comma probably should appear.

HISTORICAL AND STATUTORY NOTES

References in Text

The Atomic Energy Act of 1954, referred to in par. (1)(a), is classified generally to 42 U.S.C.A. § 2011 et seq.

Chapters 10, 37, 55, 90, 105, 115, 102, 65, 111, and 81, referred to in par. (1)(a), are 18 U.S.C.A. §§ 175 et seq., 791 et seq., 1201 et seq., 1831 et seq., 2151 et seq., 2381 et seq., 2101 et seq., 1361 et seq., 2271 et seq., and 1651 et seq., respectively.

The Arms Export Control Act, referred to in par. (1)(k), is Pub.L. 90–629, Oct. 22, 1968, 82 Stat. 1320, as amended, which is classified generally to chapter 39 of Title 22, Foreign Relations and Intercourse (22 U.S.C.A. § 2751 et seq.). For complete classification of this Act to the Code, see Short Title note set out under 22 U.S.C.A. § 2751 and Tables.

Sections 274, 277, and 278 of the Immigration and Nationality Act, referred to in par. (1)(m) and (p), are sections 274, 277, and 278 of Act June 27, 1952, c. 477, 66 Stat. 163, as amended, which are classified to 8 U.S.C.A. §§ 1324, 1327, and 1328.

Sections 1, 2, or 3 of the Sherman Act, referred to in par. (1)(r), are sections 1, 2, or 3, of Act July 2, 1890, c. 647, 26 Stat. 209, also known as the Sherman Anti-Trust Act, which are classified to 15 U.S.C.A. § 1, 2, or 3.

Codifications

Pub.L. 98–473, § 1203(c)(4), which directed the amendment of the first par. of par. (1) by inserting "Deputy Attorney General, Associate Attorney General," after "Attorney General." was executed by making the insertion after the first reference to "Attorney General," to reflect the probable intent of Congress.

Section 102 of Pub.L. 104–294, which directed that par. (1)(c) of this section be amended by inserting "chapter 90 (relating to protection of trade secrets)," following "chapter 37 (relating to espionage),", could not be executed to text, as par. (1)(c) does not contain phrase "chapter 37 (relating to espionage),".

Amendment to par. (1)(c) by section 1365(c) of Pub.L. 99–570 was executed by inserting "section 1956 (laundering of monetary instruments), section 1957 (relating to engaging in monetary transactions in property derived from specified unlawful activity)," after "section 1955 (prohibition of business enterprises of gambling)," as the probable intent of Congress.

Amendment by section 601(d)(1) of Pub.L. 104–294, which directed that "or" be struck out after the semicolon in par. (1)(*l*), could not be executed in view of prior identical amendment by section 201(2) of Pub.L. 104–208.

Amendment by section 601(d)(2) of Pub.L. 104–294, which directed that "or" be substituted for "and" following the semicolon in par. (1)(n), could not be executed as the word "and" does not appear at the end of par. (1)(n). See also 2002 Amendments notes set out under this section.

Effective and Applicability Provisions

2002 Acts. Amendment made by section 4002(c)(1) of Pub.L. 107–273, as therein provided, effective Oct. 11, 1996, which is the date of enactment of Pub.L. 104–294, to which such amendment relates.

2000 Acts. Amendment by Pub.L. 106–181 applicable only to fiscal years beginning after September 30, 1999, see section 3 of Pub.L. 106–181, set out as a note under section 106 of Title 49.

1996 Acts. Section 6(a) of Pub.L. 104–287 provided in part that amendment by such section 6(a), amending this section and section 6101 of Title 31, Money and Finance, was effective July 5, 1994.

1994 Acts. Section 7(a) of Pub.L. 103–429 provided in part that amendment of this section by section 7(a) of Pub.L. 103–429 is effective July 5, 1994.

Section 330011(c)(1) of Pub.L. 103–322 provided in part that the amendment made by such section, amending section 3(b) of Pub.L. 101–298, was to take effect on the date on which section 3(b) of Pub.L. 101–298 took effect [section 3(b) of Pub.L. 101–298 took effect on the date of enactment of Pub.L. 101–298, which was approved May 22, 1990].

Section 330011(q)(1) of Pub.L. 103–322 provided in part that the amendment made by such section, repealing section 3568 of Pub.L. 101–647, was to take effect on the date section 3568 of Pub.L. 101–647 took effect [section 3568 of Pub.L. 101–647 took effect on the date of enactment of Pub.L. 101–647, which was approved Nov. 29, 1990].

Section 330011(r) of Pub.L. 103–322 provided in part that the amendment made by such section, amending language of section 2531(3) of Pub.L. 101–647, was to take effect on the date section 2531(3) of Pub.L. 101–647 took effect [section 2531(3) of Pub.L. 101–647 took effect on the date of enactment of Pub.L. 101–647, which was approved Nov. 29, 1990].

1986 Acts. Except as otherwise provided in section 111 of Pub.L. 99–508, amendment by Pub.L. 99–508 effective 90 days after Oct. 21, 1986, see section 111 of Pub.L. 99–508 set out as a note under section 2510 of this title.

1978 Acts. Amendment by Pub.L. 95–598 effective Oct. 1, 1979, see section 402(a) of Pub.L. 95–598, set out as a note preceding section 101 of Title 11, Bankruptcy.

Sunset Provisions

Provision that amendments by Pub.L. 107–56, Title II, Oct. 26, 2001, 115 Stat. 278, with certain exclusions, shall cease to have effect on March 10, 2006, except with respect to any particular foreign intelligence investigation that began before that date, or with respect to any particular offense or potential offense that began or occurred before that, such provisions to continue in effect, was repealed by Pub.L. 109–177, § 102(a), see Pub.L. 107–56, § 224, as amended, set out as a note under 18 U.S.C.A. § 2510.

Repeals

Section 3568 of Pub.L. 101–647, which made an identical amendment to par. (1)(j) of this section as did section 2531(3) of Pub.L. 101–647, was repealed by section 330011(q)(1) of Pub.L. 103–322.

Paragraph (2) of section 601(d) of Pub.L. 104–294, cited in the credit of this section, was repealed by section 4002(c)(1) of Pub.L. 107–273, effective Oct. 11, 1996.

Severability of Provisions

If any provision of Division C of Pub.L. 104–208 or the application of such provision to any person or circumstances is held to be unconstitutional, the remainder of Division C of Pub.L. 104–208 and the application of the provisions of Division C of Pub.L. 104–208 to any person or circumstance not to be affected thereby, see section 1(e) of Pub.L. 104–208, set out as a note under section 1101 of Title 8, Aliens and Nationality.

Amendment by section 314 of Pub.L. 95–598 not to affect the application of this section to any act of any person (1) committed before Oct. 1, 1979, or (2) committed after Oct. 1, 1979, in connection with a case commenced before such date, see section 403(d) of Pub.L. 95–598, set out preceding section 101 of Title 11, Bankruptcy.

§ 2517. Authorization for disclosure and use of intercepted wire, oral, or electronic communications

(1) Any investigative or law enforcement officer who, by any means authorized by this chapter, has obtained knowledge of the contents of any wire, oral, or electronic communication, or evidence derived therefrom, may disclose such contents to another investigative or law enforcement officer to the extent that such disclosure is appropriate to the proper performance of the official duties of the officer making or receiving the disclosure.

(2) Any investigative or law enforcement officer who, by any means authorized by this chapter, has obtained knowledge of the contents of any wire, oral, or electronic communication or evidence derived therefrom may use such contents to the extent such use is appropriate to the proper performance of his official duties.

(3) Any person who has received, by any means authorized by this chapter, any information concerning a wire, oral, or electronic communication, or evidence derived therefrom intercepted in accordance with the provisions of this chapter may disclose the contents of that communication or such derivative evidence while giving testimony under oath or affirmation in any proceeding held under the authority of the United States or of any State or political subdivision thereof.

(4) No otherwise privileged wire, oral, or electronic communication intercepted in accordance with, or in violation of, the provisions of this chapter shall lose its privileged character.

(5) When an investigative or law enforcement officer, while engaged in intercepting wire, oral, or electronic communications in the manner authorized herein, intercepts wire, oral, or electronic communications relating to offenses other than those specified in the order of authorization or approval, the contents thereof, and evidence derived therefrom, may be disclosed or used as provided in subsections (1) and (2) of this section. Such contents and any evidence derived therefrom may be used under subsection (3) of this section when authorized or approved by a judge of competent jurisdiction where such judge finds on subsequent application that the contents were otherwise intercepted in accordance with the provisions of this chapter. Such application shall be made as soon as practicable.

(6) Any investigative or law enforcement officer, or attorney for the Government, who by any means authorized by this chapter, has obtained knowledge of the contents of any wire, oral, or electronic communication, or evidence derived therefrom, may disclose such contents to any other Federal law enforcement, intelligence, protective, immigration, national defense, or national security official to the extent that such contents include foreign intelligence or counterintelligence (as defined in section 3 of the National Security Act of 1947 (50 U.S.C. 401a)), or foreign intelligence information (as defined in subsection (19) of section 2510 of this title), to assist the official who is to receive that information in the performance of his official duties. Any Federal official who receives information pursuant to this provision may use that information only as necessary in the conduct of that person's official duties subject to any limitations on the unauthorized disclosure of such information.

(7) Any investigative or law enforcement officer, or other Federal official in carrying out official duties as such Federal official, who by any means authorized by this chapter, has obtained knowledge of the contents of any wire, oral, or electronic communication, or evidence derived therefrom, may disclose such contents or derivative evidence to a foreign investigative or law enforcement officer to the extent that such disclosure is appropriate to the proper performance of the official duties of the officer making or receiving the disclosure, and foreign investigative or law enforcement officers may use or disclose such contents or derivative evidence to the extent such use or disclosure is appropriate to the proper performance of their official duties.

(8) Any investigative or law enforcement officer, or other Federal official in carrying out official duties as such Federal official, who by any means authorized by this chapter, has obtained knowledge of the contents of any wire, oral, or electronic communication, or evidence derived therefrom, may disclose such contents or derivative evidence to any appropriate Federal, State, local, or foreign government official to the extent that such contents or derivative evidence reveals a threat of actual or potential attack or other grave hostile acts of a foreign power or an agent of a foreign power, domestic or international sabotage, domestic or international terrorism, or clandestine intelligence gathering activities by an intelligence service or network of a foreign power or by an agent of a foreign power, within the United States or elsewhere, for the purpose of preventing or responding to such a threat. Any official who receives information pursuant to this provision may use that information only as necessary in the conduct of that person's official duties subject to any limitations on the unauthorized disclo-

sure of such information, and any State, local, or foreign official who receives information pursuant to this provision may use that information only consistent with such guidelines as the Attorney General and Director of Central Intelligence shall jointly issue.

(Added Pub.L. 90–351, Title III, § 802, June 19, 1968, 82 Stat. 217, and amended Pub.L. 91–452, Title IX, § 902(b), Oct. 15, 1970, 84 Stat. 947; Pub.L. 99–508, Title I, § 101(c)(1)(A), Oct. 21, 1986, 100 Stat. 1851; Pub.L. 107–56, Title II, § 203(b)(1), Oct. 26, 2001, 115 Stat. 280; Pub.L. 107–296, Title VIII, § 896, Nov. 25, 2002, 116 Stat. 2257.)

HISTORICAL AND STATUTORY NOTES

References in Text

Section 3 of the National Security Act of 1947, referred to in par. (6), is Act July 26, 1947, c. 343, § 3, as added Oct. 24, 1992, Pub.L. 102–496, Title VII, § 702, 106 Stat. 3188, as amended, which is classified to 50 U.S.C.A. § 401a.

Effective and Applicability Provisions

2002 Acts. Amendment to this section by Pub.L. 107–296 effective 60 days after Nov. 25, 2002, see Pub.L. 107–296, § 4, set out as a note under 6 U.S.C.A. § 101.

1986 Acts. Except as otherwise provided in section 111 of Pub.L. 99–508, amendment by Pub.L. 99–508 effective 90 days after Oct. 21, 1986, see section 111 of Pub.L. 99–508 set out as a note under section 2510 of this title.

Sunset Provisions

Provision that amendments by Pub.L. 107–56, Title II, Oct. 26, 2001, 115 Stat. 278, with certain exclusions, shall cease to have effect on March 10, 2006, except with respect to any particular foreign intelligence investigation that began before that date, or with respect to any particular offense or potential offense that began or occurred before that, such provisions to continue in effect, was repealed by Pub.L. 109–177, § 102(a), see Pub.L. 107–56, § 224, as amended, set out as a note under 18 U.S.C.A. § 2510.

Change of Name

Reference to the Director of Central Intelligence or the Director of the Central Intelligence Agency in the Director's capacity as the head of the intelligence community deemed to be a reference to the Director of National Intelligence. Reference to the Director of Central Intelligence or the Director of the Central Intelligence Agency in the Director's capacity as the head of the Central Intelligence Agency deemed to be a reference to the Director of the Central Intelligence Agency. See Pub.L. 108–458, § 1081(a) and (b), set out as a note under 50 U.S.C.A. § 401.

Procedures

Pub.L. 107–56, Title II, § 203(c), Oct. 26, 2001, 115 Stat. 280, as amended Pub.L. 107–296, Title VIII, § 897(b), Nov. 25, 2002, 116 Stat. 2258; Pub.L. 108–458, Title VI, § 6501(b), Dec. 17, 2004, 118 Stat. 3760, provided that: "The Attorney General shall establish procedures for the disclosure of information pursuant to paragraphs (6) and (8) of section 2517 of title 18, United States Code, and Rule 6(e)(3)(D) of the Federal Rules of Criminal Procedure that identifies a United States person, as defined in section 101 of the Foreign Intelligence Surveillance Act of 1978 (50 U.S.C. 1801))."

[Amendment of this note by Pub.L. 107–296 effective 60 days after Nov. 25, 2002, see Pub.L. 107–296, § 4, set out as a note under 6 U.S.C.A. § 101.]

§ 2518. Procedure for interception of wire, oral, or electronic communications

(1) Each application for an order authorizing or approving the interception of a wire, oral, or electronic communication under this chapter shall be made in writing upon oath or affirmation to a judge of competent jurisdiction and shall state the applicant's authority to make such application. Each application shall include the following information:

(a) the identity of the investigative or law enforcement officer making the application, and the officer authorizing the application;

(b) a full and complete statement of the facts and circumstances relied upon by the applicant, to justify his belief that an order should be issued, including (i) details as to the particular offense that has been, is being, or is about to be committed, (ii) except as provided in subsection (11), a particular description of the nature and location of the facilities from which or the place where the communication is to be intercepted, (iii) a particular description of the type of communications sought to be intercepted, (iv) the identity of the person, if known, committing the offense and whose communications are to be intercepted;

(c) a full and complete statement as to whether or not other investigative procedures have been tried and failed or why they reasonably appear to be unlikely to succeed if tried or to be too dangerous;

(d) a statement of the period of time for which the interception is required to be maintained. If the nature of the investigation is such that the authorization for interception should not automatically terminate when the described type of communication has been first obtained, a particular description of facts establishing probable cause to believe that additional communications of the same type will occur thereafter;

(e) a full and complete statement of the facts concerning all previous applications known to the individual authorizing and making the application, made to any judge for authorization to intercept, or for approval of interceptions of, wire, oral, or electronic communications involving any of the same persons, facilities or places specified in the application, and the action taken by the judge on each such application; and

(f) where the application is for the extension of an order, a statement setting forth the results thus far obtained from the interception, or a reasonable explanation of the failure to obtain such results.

(2) The judge may require the applicant to furnish additional testimony or documentary evidence in support of the application.

(3) Upon such application the judge may enter an ex parte order, as requested or as modified, authorizing or approving interception of wire, oral, or electronic communications within the territorial jurisdiction of the court in which the judge is sitting (and outside that jurisdiction but within the United States in the case of a mobile interception device authorized by a Federal court within such jurisdiction), if the judge determines on the basis of the facts submitted by the applicant that—

(a) there is probable cause for belief that an individual is committing, has committed, or is about to commit a particular offense enumerated in section 2516 of this chapter;

(b) there is probable cause for belief that particular communications concerning that offense will be obtained through such interception;

(c) normal investigative procedures have been tried and have failed or reasonably appear to be unlikely to succeed if tried or to be too dangerous;

(d) except as provided in subsection (11), there is probable cause for belief that the facilities from which, or the place where, the wire, oral, or electronic communications are to be intercepted are being used, or are about to be used, in connection with the commission of such offense, or are leased to, listed in the name of, or commonly used by such person.

(4) Each order authorizing or approving the interception of any wire, oral, or electronic communication under this chapter shall specify—

(a) the identity of the person, if known, whose communications are to be intercepted;

(b) the nature and location of the communications facilities as to which, or the place where, authority to intercept is granted;

(c) a particular description of the type of communication sought to be intercepted, and a statement of the particular offense to which it relates;

(d) the identity of the agency authorized to intercept the communications, and of the person authorizing the application; and

(e) the period of time during which such interception is authorized, including a statement as to whether or not the interception shall automatically terminate when the described communication has been first obtained.

An order authorizing the interception of a wire, oral, or electronic communication under this chapter shall, upon request of the applicant, direct that a provider of wire or electronic communication service, landlord, custodian or other person shall furnish the applicant forthwith all information, facilities, and technical assistance necessary to accomplish the interception unobtrusively and with a minimum of interference with the services that such service provider, landlord, custodian, or person is according the person whose communications are to be intercepted. Any provider of wire or electronic communication service, landlord, custodian or other person furnishing such facilities or technical assistance shall be compensated therefor by the applicant for reasonable expenses incurred in providing such facilities or assistance. Pursuant to section 2522 of this chapter, an order may also be issued to enforce the assistance capability and capacity requirements under the Communications Assistance for Law Enforcement Act.

(5) No order entered under this section may authorize or approve the interception of any wire, oral, or electronic communication for any period longer than is necessary to achieve the objective of the authorization, nor in any event longer than thirty days. Such thirty-day period begins on the earlier of the day on which the investigative or law enforcement officer first begins to conduct an interception under the order or ten days after the order is entered. Extensions of an order may be granted, but only upon application for an extension made in accordance with subsection (1) of this section and the court making the findings required by subsection (3) of this section. The period of extension shall be no longer than the authorizing judge deems necessary to achieve the purposes for which it was granted and in no event for longer than thirty days. Every order and extension thereof shall contain a provision that the authorization to intercept shall be executed as soon as practicable, shall be conducted in such a way as to minimize the interception of communications not otherwise subject to interception under this chapter, and must terminate upon attainment of the authorized objective, or in any event in thirty days. In the event the intercepted communication is in a code or foreign language, and an expert in that foreign language or code is not reasonably available during the interception period, minimization may be accomplished as soon as practicable after such interception. An interception under this chapter may be conducted in whole or in part by Government personnel, or by an individual operating under a contract with the Government, acting under the supervision of an investigative or law enforcement officer authorized to conduct the interception.

(6) Whenever an order authorizing interception is entered pursuant to this chapter, the order may require reports to be made to the judge who issued the order showing what progress has been made toward achievement of the authorized objective and the need for continued interception. Such reports shall be made at such intervals as the judge may require.

(7) Notwithstanding any other provision of this chapter, any investigative or law enforcement officer, specially designated by the Attorney General, the Deputy Attorney General, the Associate Attorney General, or by the principal prosecuting attorney of any State or subdivision thereof acting pursuant to a statute of that State, who reasonably determines that—

(a) an emergency situation exists that involves—

(i) immediate danger of death or serious physical injury to any person,

(ii) conspiratorial activities threatening the national security interest, or

(iii) conspiratorial activities characteristic of organized crime,

that requires a wire, oral, or electronic communication to be intercepted before an order authorizing such interception can, with due diligence, be obtained, and

(b) there are grounds upon which an order could be entered under this chapter to authorize such interception,

may intercept such wire, oral, or electronic communication if an application for an order approving the interception is made in accordance with this section within forty-eight hours after the interception has occurred, or begins to occur. In the absence of an order, such interception shall immediately terminate when the communication sought is obtained or when the application for the order is denied, whichever is earlier. In the event such application for approval is denied, or in any other case where the interception is terminated without an order having been issued, the contents of any wire, oral, or electronic communication intercepted shall be treated as having been obtained in violation of this chapter, and an inventory shall be served as provided for in subsection (d) of this section on the person named in the application.

(8) (a) The contents of any wire, oral, or electronic communication intercepted by any means authorized by this chapter shall, if possible, be recorded on tape or wire or other comparable device. The recording of the contents of any wire, oral, or electronic communication under this subsection shall be done in such a way as will protect the recording from editing or other alterations. Immediately upon the expiration of the period of the order, or extensions thereof, such recordings shall be made available to the judge issuing such order and sealed under his directions. Custody of the recordings shall be wherever the judge orders. They shall not be destroyed except upon an order of the issuing or denying judge and in any event shall be kept for ten years. Duplicate recordings may be made for use or disclosure pursuant to the provisions of subsections (1) and (2) of section 2517 of this chapter for investigations. The presence of the seal provided for by this subsection, or a satisfactory explanation for the absence thereof, shall be a prerequisite for the use or disclosure of the contents of any wire, oral, or electronic communication or evidence derived therefrom under subsection (3) of section 2517.

(b) Applications made and orders granted under this chapter shall be sealed by the judge. Custody of the applications and orders shall be wherever the judge directs. Such applications and orders shall be disclosed only upon a showing of good cause before a judge of competent jurisdiction and shall not be destroyed except on order of the issuing or denying judge, and in any event shall be kept for ten years.

(c) Any violation of the provisions of this subsection may be punished as contempt of the issuing or denying judge.

(d) Within a reasonable time but not later than ninety days after the filing of an application for an order of approval under section 2518(7)(b) which is denied or the termination of the period of an order or extensions thereof, the issuing or denying judge shall cause to be served, on the persons named in the order or the application, and such other parties to intercepted communications as the judge may determine in his discretion that is in the interest of justice, an inventory which shall include notice of—

(1) the fact of the entry of the order or the application;

(2) the date of the entry and the period of authorized, approved or disapproved interception, or the denial of the application; and

(3) the fact that during the period wire, oral, or electronic communications were or were not intercepted.

The judge, upon the filing of a motion, may in his discretion make available to such person or his counsel for inspection such portions of the intercepted communications, applications and orders as the judge determines to be in the interest of justice. On an ex parte showing of good cause to a judge of competent jurisdiction the serving of the inventory required by this subsection may be postponed.

(9) The contents of any wire, oral, or electronic communication intercepted pursuant to this chapter or evidence derived therefrom shall not be received in evidence or otherwise disclosed in any trial, hearing, or other proceeding in a Federal or State court unless each party, not less than ten days before the trial, hearing, or proceeding, has been furnished with a copy of the court order, and accompanying application, under which the interception was authorized or approved. This ten-day period may be waived by the judge if he finds that it was not possible to furnish the party with the above information ten days before the trial, hearing, or proceeding and that the party will

not be prejudiced by the delay in receiving such information.

(10)(a) Any aggrieved person in any trial, hearing, or proceeding in or before any court, department, officer, agency, regulatory body, or other authority of the United States, a State, or a political subdivision thereof, may move to suppress the contents of any wire or oral communication intercepted pursuant to this chapter, or evidence derived therefrom, on the grounds that—

(i) the communication was unlawfully intercepted;

(ii) the order of authorization or approval under which it was intercepted is insufficient on its face; or

(iii) the interception was not made in conformity with the order of authorization or approval.

Such motion shall be made before the trial, hearing, or proceeding unless there was no opportunity to make such motion or the person was not aware of the grounds of the motion. If the motion is granted, the contents of the intercepted wire or oral communication, or evidence derived therefrom, shall be treated as having been obtained in violation of this chapter. The judge, upon the filing of such motion by the aggrieved person, may in his discretion make available to the aggrieved person or his counsel for inspection such portions of the intercepted communication or evidence derived therefrom as the judge determines to be in the interests of justice.

(b) In addition to any other right to appeal, the United States shall have the right to appeal from an order granting a motion to suppress made under paragraph (a) of this subsection, or the denial of an application for an order of approval, if the United States attorney shall certify to the judge or other official granting such motion or denying such application that the appeal is not taken for purposes of delay. Such appeal shall be taken within thirty days after the date the order was entered and shall be diligently prosecuted.

(c) The remedies and sanctions described in this chapter with respect to the interception of electronic communications are the only judicial remedies and sanctions for nonconstitutional violations of this chapter involving such communications.

(11) The requirements of subsections (1)(b)(ii) and (3)(d) of this section relating to the specification of the facilities from which, or the place where, the communication is to be intercepted do not apply if—

(a) in the case of an application with respect to the interception of an oral communication—

(i) the application is by a Federal investigative or law enforcement officer and is approved by the Attorney General, the Deputy Attorney General, the Associate Attorney General, an Assistant Attorney General, or an acting Assistant Attorney General;

(ii) the application contains a full and complete statement as to why such specification is not practical and identifies the person committing the offense and whose communications are to be intercepted; and

(iii) the judge finds that such specification is not practical; and

(b) in the case of an application with respect to a wire or electronic communication—

(i) the application is by a Federal investigative or law enforcement officer and is approved by the Attorney General, the Deputy Attorney General, the Associate Attorney General, an Assistant Attorney General, or an acting Assistant Attorney General;

(ii) the application identifies the person believed to be committing the offense and whose communications are to be intercepted and the applicant makes a showing that there is probable cause to believe that the person's actions could have the effect of thwarting interception from a specified facility;

(iii) the judge finds that such showing has been adequately made; and

(iv) the order authorizing or approving the interception is limited to interception only for such time as it is reasonable to presume that the person identified in the application is or was reasonably proximate to the instrument through which such communication will be or was transmitted.

(12) An interception of a communication under an order with respect to which the requirements of subsections (1)(b)(ii) and (3)(d) of this section do not apply by reason of subsection (11)(a) shall not begin until the place where the communication is to be intercepted is ascertained by the person implementing the interception order. A provider of wire or electronic communications service that has received an order as provided for in subsection (11)(b) may move the court to modify or quash the order on the ground that its assistance with respect to the interception cannot be performed in a timely or reasonable fashion. The court, upon notice to the government, shall decide such a motion expeditiously.

(Added Pub.L. 90–351, Title III, § 802, June 19, 1968, 82 Stat. 218, and amended Pub.L. 91–358, Title II, § 211(b), July 29, 1970, 84 Stat. 654; Pub.L. 95–511, Title II, § 201(d) to (g), Oct. 25, 1978, 92 Stat. 1797, 1798; Pub.L. 98–473, Title II, § 1203(a), (b), Oct. 12, 1984, 98 Stat. 2152; Pub.L. 99–508, Title I, §§ 101(c)(1)(A), (8), (e), 106(a) to (d)(3), Oct. 21, 1986, 100 Stat. 1851–1853, 1856, 1857; Pub.L. 103–414, Title II, § 201(b)(1), Oct. 25, 1994, 108 Stat. 4290; Pub.L. 105–272, Title VI, § 604, Oct. 20, 1998, 112 Stat. 2413.)

HISTORICAL AND STATUTORY NOTES

References in Text

The Communications Assistance for Law Enforcement Act, referred to in par. (4), is Pub.L. 103–414, Title I, Oct. 25, 1994, 108 Stat. 4279, which is classified generally to chapter 9 (section 1001 et seq.) of Title 47, Telegraphs, Telephones, and Radiotelegraphs. For complete classification of this Act to the Code, see Short Title note set out under section 1001 of Title 47 and Tables.

Effective and Applicability Provisions

1986 Acts. Except as otherwise provided in section 111 of Pub.L. 99–508, amendment by Pub.L. 99–508 effective 90 days after Oct. 21, 1986, see section 111 of Pub.L. 99–508 set out as a note under section 2510 of this title.

1978 Acts. Amendment by Pub.L. 95–511 effective Oct. 25, 1978, except as specifically provided, see section 301 of Pub.L. 95–511, set out as an Effective Date note under section 1801 of Title 50, War and National Defense.

1970 Acts. Section 901(a) of Pub.L. 91–358 provided in part that the amendment of this section by Pub.L. 91–358 shall take effect on the first day of the seventh calendar month which begins after July 29, 1970.

§ 2519. Reports concerning intercepted wire, oral, or electronic communications

(1) Within thirty days after the expiration of an order (or each extension thereof) entered under section 2518, or the denial of an order approving an interception, the issuing or denying judge shall report to the Administrative Office of the United States Courts—

(a) the fact that an order or extension was applied for;

(b) the kind of order or extension applied for (including whether or not the order was an order with respect to which the requirements of sections 2518(1)(b)(ii) and 2518(3)(d) of this title did not apply by reason of section 2518(11) of this title);

(c) the fact that the order or extension was granted as applied for, was modified, or was denied;

(d) the period of interceptions authorized by the order, and the number and duration of any extensions of the order;

(e) the offense specified in the order or application, or extension of an order;

(f) the identity of the applying investigative or law enforcement officer and agency making the application and the person authorizing the application; and

(g) the nature of the facilities from which or the place where communications were to be intercepted.

(2) In January of each year the Attorney General, an Assistant Attorney General specially designated by the Attorney General, or the principal prosecuting attorney of a State, or the principal prosecuting attorney for any political subdivision of a State, shall report to the Administrative Office of the United States Courts—

(a) the information required by paragraphs (a) through (g) of subsection (1) of this section with respect to each application for an order or extension made during the preceding calendar year;

(b) a general description of the interceptions made under such order or extension, including (i) the approximate nature and frequency of incriminating communications intercepted, (ii) the approximate nature and frequency of other communications intercepted, (iii) the approximate number of persons whose communications were intercepted, (iv) the number of orders in which encryption was encountered and whether such encryption prevented law enforcement from obtaining the plain text of communications intercepted pursuant to such order, and (v) the approximate nature, amount, and cost of the manpower and other resources used in the interceptions;

(c) the number of arrests resulting from interceptions made under such order or extension, and the offenses for which arrests were made;

(d) the number of trials resulting from such interceptions;

(e) the number of motions to suppress made with respect to such interceptions, and the number granted or denied;

(f) the number of convictions resulting from such interceptions and the offenses for which the convictions were obtained and a general assessment of the importance of the interceptions; and

(g) the information required by paragraphs (b) through (f) of this subsection with respect to orders or extensions obtained in a preceding calendar year.

(3) In April of each year the Director of the Administrative Office of the United States Courts shall transmit to the Congress a full and complete report concerning the number of applications for orders authorizing or approving the interception of wire, oral, or electronic communications pursuant to this chapter and the number of orders and extensions granted or denied pursuant to this chapter during the preceding calendar year. Such report shall include a summary and analysis of the data required to be filed with the Administrative Office by subsections (1) and (2) of this section. The Director of the Administrative Office of the United States Courts is authorized to issue binding regulations dealing with the content and form of the reports required to be filed by subsections (1) and (2) of this section.

(Added Pub.L. 90–351, Title III, § 802, June 19, 1968, 82 Stat. 222, and amended Pub.L. 95–511, Title II, § 201(h), Oct. 25, 1978, 92 Stat. 1798; Pub.L. 99–508, Title I, §§ 101(c)(1)(A), 106(d)(4), Oct. 21, 1986, 100 Stat. 1851, 1857; Pub.L. 106–197, § 2(a), May 2, 2000, 114 Stat. 247.)

HISTORICAL AND STATUTORY NOTES

Effective and Applicability Provisions

1986 Acts. Except as otherwise provided in section 111 of Pub.L. 99–508, amendment by Pub.L. 99–508 effective 90 days after Oct. 21, 1986, see section 111 of Pub.L. 99–508 set out as a note under section 2510 of this title.

1978 Acts. Amendment by Pub.L. 95–511 effective Oct. 25, 1978, except as specifically provided, see section 301 of Pub.L. 95–511, set out as an Effective Date note under section 1801 of Title 50, War and National Defense.

Termination of Reporting Requirements

Reporting requirement of par. (3) of this section excepted from termination under Pub.L. 104–66, § 3003(a)(1), as amended, set out in a note under 31 U.S.C.A. § 1113, see Pub.L. 106–197, § 1, set out as a note under 31 U.S.C.A. § 1113.

Report on Use of DCS 1000 (Carnivore) to Implement Orders Under 18 U.S.C. 2518

Pub.L. 107–273, Div. A, Title III, § 305(b), Nov. 2, 2002, 116 Stat. 1782, provided that: "At the same time that the Attorney General, or Assistant Attorney General specially designated by the Attorney General, submits to the Administrative Office of the United States Courts the annual report required by section 2519(2) of title 18, United States Code [18 U.S.C.A. § 2519(2)], that is respectively next due after the end of each of the fiscal years 2002 and 2003, the Attorney General shall also submit to the Chairmen and ranking minority members of the Committees on the Judiciary of the Senate and of the House of Representatives a report, covering the same respective time period, that contains the following information with respect to those orders described in that annual report that were applied for by law enforcement agencies of the Department of Justice and whose implementation involved the use of the DCS 1000 program (or any subsequent version of such program)—

"(1) the kind of order or extension applied for (including whether or not the order was an order with respect to which the requirements of sections 2518(1)(b)(ii) and 2518(3)(d) of title 18, United States Code, did not apply by reason of section 2518(11) of title 18 [18 U.S.C.A. § 2518]);

"(2) the period of interceptions authorized by the order, and the number and duration of any extensions of the order;

"(3) the offense specified in the order or application, or extension of an order;

"(4) the identity of the applying investigative or law enforcement officer and agency making the application and the person authorizing the application;

"(5) the nature of the facilities from which or place where communications were to be intercepted;

"(6) A general description of the interceptions made under such order or extension, including—

"(A) the approximate nature and frequency of incriminating communications intercepted;

"(B) the approximate nature and frequency of other communications intercepted;

"(C) the approximate number of persons whose communications were intercepted;

"(D) the number of orders in which encryption was encountered and whether such encryption prevented law enforcement from obtaining the plain text of communications intercepted pursuant to such order; and

"(E) the approximate nature, amount, and cost of the manpower and other resources used in the interceptions;

"(7) the number of arrests resulting from interceptions made under such order or extension, and the offenses for which arrests were made;

"(8) the number of trials resulting from such interceptions;

"(9) the number of motions to suppress made with respect to such interceptions, and the number granted or denied;

"(10) the number of convictions resulting from such interceptions and the offenses for which the convictions were obtained and a general assessment of the importance of the interceptions; and

"(11) the specific persons authorizing the use of the DCS 1000 program (or any subsequent version of such program) in the implementation of such order."

Encryption Reporting Requirements

Pub.L. 106–197, § 2(b), May 2, 2000, 114 Stat. 247, provided that: "The encryption reporting requirement in subsection (a) [amending par. (2)(b) of this section] shall be effective for the report transmitted by the Director of the Administrative Office of the Courts for calendar year 2000 and in subsequent reports."

§ 2520. Recovery of civil damages authorized

(a) In general.—Except as provided in section 2511(2)(a)(ii), any person whose wire, oral, or electronic communication is intercepted, disclosed, or intentionally used in violation of this chapter may in a civil action recover from the person or entity, other than the United States, which engaged in that violation such relief as may be appropriate.

(b) Relief.—In an action under this section, appropriate relief includes—

(1) such preliminary and other equitable or declaratory relief as may be appropriate;

(2) damages under subsection (c) and punitive damages in appropriate cases; and

(3) a reasonable attorney's fee and other litigation costs reasonably incurred.

(c) Computation of damages.—(1) In an action under this section, if the conduct in violation of this chapter is the private viewing of a private satellite video communication that is not scrambled or encrypted or if the communication is a radio communication that is transmitted on frequencies allocated under subpart D of part 74 of the rules of the Federal Communications Commission that is not scrambled or encrypted and the conduct is not for a tortious or illegal purpose or for purposes of direct or indirect commercial advantage or private commercial gain, then the court shall assess damages as follows:

(A) If the person who engaged in that conduct has not previously been enjoined under section

2511(5) and has not been found liable in a prior civil action under this section, the court shall assess the greater of the sum of actual damages suffered by the plaintiff, or statutory damages of not less than $50 and not more than $500.

(B) If, on one prior occasion, the person who engaged in that conduct has been enjoined under section 2511(5) or has been found liable in a civil action under this section, the court shall assess the greater of the sum of actual damages suffered by the plaintiff, or statutory damages of not less than $100 and not more than $1000.

(2) In any other action under this section, the court may assess as damages whichever is the greater of—

(A) the sum of the actual damages suffered by the plaintiff and any profits made by the violator as a result of the violation; or

(B) statutory damages of whichever is the greater of $100 a day for each day of violation or $10,000.

(d) Defense.—A good faith reliance on—

(1) a court warrant or order, a grand jury subpoena, a legislative authorization, or a statutory authorization;

(2) a request of an investigative or law enforcement officer under section 2518(7) of this title; or

(3) a good faith determination that section 2511(3) or 2511(2)(i) of this title permitted the conduct complained of;

is a complete defense against any civil or criminal action brought under this chapter or any other law.

(e) Limitation.—A civil action under this section may not be commenced later than two years after the date upon which the claimant first has a reasonable opportunity to discover the violation.

(f) Administrative discipline.—If a court or appropriate department or agency determines that the United States or any of its departments or agencies has violated any provision of this chapter, and the court or appropriate department or agency finds that the circumstances surrounding the violation raise serious questions about whether or not an officer or employee of the United States acted willfully or intentionally with respect to the violation, the department or agency shall, upon receipt of a true and correct copy of the decision and findings of the court or appropriate department or agency promptly initiate a proceeding to determine whether disciplinary action against the officer or employee is warranted. If the head of the department or agency involved determines that disciplinary action is not warranted, he or she shall notify the Inspector General with jurisdiction over the department or agency concerned and shall provide the Inspector General with the reasons for such determination.

(g) Improper disclosure is violation.—Any willful disclosure or use by an investigative or law enforcement officer or governmental entity of information beyond the extent permitted by section 2517 is a violation of this chapter for purposes of section 2520(a).

(Added Pub.L. 90–351, Title III, § 802, June 19, 1968, 82 Stat. 223, and amended Pub.L. 91–358, Title II, § 211(c), July 29, 1970, 84 Stat. 654; Pub.L. 99–508, Title I, § 103, Oct. 21, 1986, 100 Stat. 1853; Pub.L. 107–56, Title II, § 223(a), Oct. 26, 2001, 115 Stat. 293; Pub.L. 107–296, Title II, § 225(e), Nov. 25, 2002, 116 Stat. 2157.)

HISTORICAL AND STATUTORY NOTES

Effective and Applicability Provisions

2002 Acts. Amendment to this section by Pub.L. 107–296 effective 60 days after Nov. 25, 2002, see Pub.L. 107–296, § 4, set out as a note under 6 U.S.C.A. § 101.

1986 Acts. Except as otherwise provided in section 111 of pub.L. 99–508, amendment by Pub.L. 99–508 effective 90 days after Oct. 21, 1986, see section 111 of Pub.L. 99–508 set out as a note under section 2510 of this title.

1970 Acts. Section 901(a) of Pub.L. 91–358 provided in part that the amendment of this section by Pub.L. 91–358 shall take effect on the first day of the seventh calendar month which begins after July 29, 1970.

Sunset Provisions

Provision that amendments by Pub.L. 107–56, Title II, Oct. 26, 2001, 115 Stat. 278, with certain exclusions, shall cease to have effect on March 10, 2006, except with respect to any particular foreign intelligence investigation that began before that date, or with respect to any particular offense or potential offense that began or occurred before that, such provisions to continue in effect, was repealed by Pub.L. 109–177, § 102(a), see Pub.L. 107–56, § 224, as amended, set out as a note under 18 U.S.C.A. § 2510.

§ 2521. Injunction against illegal interception

Whenever it shall appear that any person is engaged or is about to engage in any act which constitutes or will constitute a felony violation of this chapter, the Attorney General may initiate a civil action in a district court of the United States to enjoin such violation. The court shall proceed as soon as practicable to the hearing and determination of such an action, and may, at any time before final determination, enter such a restraining order or prohibition, or take such other action, as is warranted to prevent a continuing and substantial injury to the United States or to any person or class of persons for whose protection the action is brought. A proceeding under this section is governed by the Federal Rules of Civil Procedure, except that, if an indictment has been returned against the respondent, discovery is governed by the Federal Rules of Criminal Procedure.

(Added Pub.L. 99–508, Title I, § 110(a), Oct. 21, 1986, 100 Stat. 1859.)

HISTORICAL AND STATUTORY NOTES

Effective and Applicability Provisions

1986 Acts. Section effective 90 days after Oct. 21, 1986 except as otherwise provided in section 111 of Pub.L. 99–508 with respect to conduct pursuant to court order or extension, see section 111 of Pub.L. 99–508, set out as a note under section 2510 of this title.

§ 2522. Enforcement of the Communications Assistance for Law Enforcement Act

(a) Enforcement by court issuing surveillance order.—If a court authorizing an interception under this chapter, a State statute, or the Foreign Intelligence Surveillance Act of 1978 (50 U.S.C. 1801 et seq.) or authorizing use of a pen register or a trap and trace device under chapter 206 or a State statute finds that a telecommunications carrier has failed to comply with the requirements of the Communications Assistance for Law Enforcement Act, the court may, in accordance with section 108 of such Act, direct that the carrier comply forthwith and may direct that a provider of support services to the carrier or the manufacturer of the carrier's transmission or switching equipment furnish forthwith modifications necessary for the carrier to comply.

(b) Enforcement upon application by Attorney General.—The Attorney General may, in a civil action in the appropriate United States district court, obtain an order, in accordance with section 108 of the Communications Assistance for Law Enforcement Act, directing that a telecommunications carrier, a manufacturer of telecommunications transmission or switching equipment, or a provider of telecommunications support services comply with such Act.

(c) Civil penalty.—

(1) In general.—A court issuing an order under this section against a telecommunications carrier, a manufacturer of telecommunications transmission or switching equipment, or a provider of telecommunications support services may impose a civil penalty of up to $10,000 per day for each day in violation after the issuance of the order or after such future date as the court may specify.

(2) Considerations.—In determining whether to impose a civil penalty and in determining its amount, the court shall take into account—

(A) the nature, circumstances, and extent of the violation;

(B) the violator's ability to pay, the violator's good faith efforts to comply in a timely manner, any effect on the violator's ability to continue to do business, the degree of culpability, and the length of any delay in undertaking efforts to comply; and

(C) such other matters as justice may require.

(d) Definitions.—As used in this section, the terms defined in section 102 of the Communications Assistance for Law Enforcement Act have the meanings provided, respectively, in such section.

(Added Pub.L. 103–414, Title II, § 201(a), Oct. 25, 1994, 108 Stat. 4289.)

HISTORICAL AND STATUTORY NOTES

References in Text

Communications Assistance for Law Enforcement Act and such Act, referred to in section heading and in subsecs. (a), (b), and (d), is Pub.L. 103–414, Title I, Oct. 25, 1994, 108 Stat. 4279, which is classified generally to chapter 9 (section 1001 et seq.) of Title 47, Telegraphs, Telephones, and Radiotelegraphs. Sections 102 and 108 of such Act are classified to sections 1001 and 1007 of Title 47, respectively. For complete classification of this Act to the Code, see Short Title note set out under section 1001 of Title 47 and Tables.

The Foreign Intelligence Surveillance Act of 1978, referred to in subsec. (a), is Pub.L. 95–511, Oct. 25, 1978, 92 Stat. 1783, as amended, which is classified principally to chapter 36 (section 1801 et seq.) of Title 50, War and National Defense. For complete classification of this Act to the Code, see Short Title note set out under section 1801 of Title 50 and Tables.

CHAPTER 121—STORED WIRE AND ELECTRONIC COMMUNICATIONS AND TRANSACTIONAL RECORDS ACCESS

Sec.

§ 2701. Unlawful access to stored communications

(a) Offense.—Except as provided in subsection (c) of this section whoever—

(1) intentionally accesses without authorization a facility through which an electronic communication service is provided; or

(2) intentionally exceeds an authorization to access that facility;

and thereby obtains, alters, or prevents authorized access to a wire or electronic communication while it is in electronic storage in such system shall be punished as provided in subsection (b) of this section.

(b) Punishment.—The punishment for an offense under subsection (a) of this section is—

(1) if the offense is committed for purposes of commercial advantage, malicious destruction or damage, or private commercial gain, or in furtherance of any criminal or tortious act in violation of the Constitution or laws of the United States or any State—

(A) a fine under this title or imprisonment for not more than 5 years, or both, in the case of a first offense under this subparagraph; and

(B) a fine under this title or imprisonment for not more than 10 years, or both, for any subsequent offense under this subparagraph; and

(2) in any other case—

(A) a fine under this title or imprisonment for not more than 1 year or both, in the case of a first offense under this paragraph; and

(B) a fine under this title or imprisonment for not more than 5 years, or both, in the case of an offense under this subparagraph that occurs after a conviction of another offense under this section.

(c) Exceptions.—Subsection (a) of this section does not apply with respect to conduct authorized—

(1) by the person or entity providing a wire or electronic communications service;

(2) by a user of that service with respect to a communication of or intended for that user; or

(3) in section 2703, 2704 or 2518 of this title.

(Added Pub.L. 99–508, Title II, § 201[a], Oct. 21, 1986, 100 Stat. 1860, and amended Pub.L. 103–322, Title XXXIII, §§ 330016(1)(K), (U), Sept. 13, 1994, 108 Stat. 2147, 2148; Pub.L. 104–294, Title VI, § 601(a)(3), Oct. 11, 1996, 110 Stat. 3498; Pub.L. 107–296, Title II, § 225(j)(2), Nov. 25, 2002, 116 Stat. 2158.)

HISTORICAL AND STATUTORY NOTES

Effective and Applicability Provisions

2002 Acts. Amendment to this section by Pub.L. 107–296 effective 60 days after Nov. 25, 2002, see Pub.L. 107–296, § 4, set out as a note under 6 U.S.C.A. § 101.

1986 Acts. Pub.L. 99–508, Title II, § 202, Oct. 21, 1986, 100 Stat. 1868, provided that: "This title and the amendments made by this title [enacting this chapter] shall take effect ninety days after the date of the enactment of this Act [Oct. 21, 1986] and shall, in the case of conduct pursuant to a court order or extension, apply only with respect to court orders or extensions made after this title takes effect.".

Short Title

1988 Acts. Pub.L. 100–618, § 1, Nov. 5, 1988, 102 Stat. 3195, provided that: "This Act [enacting section 2710 of this title and renumbering former section 2710 as 2711 of this title] may be cited as the 'Video Privacy Protection Act of 1988'."

§ 2702. Voluntary disclosure of customer communications or records

(a) Prohibitions.—Except as provided in subsection (b) or (c)—

(1) a person or entity providing an electronic communication service to the public shall not knowingly divulge to any person or entity the contents of a communication while in electronic storage by that service; and

(2) a person or entity providing remote computing service to the public shall not knowingly divulge to any person or entity the contents of any communication which is carried or maintained on that service—

(A) on behalf of, and received by means of electronic transmission from (or created by means of computer processing of communications received by means of electronic transmission from), a subscriber or customer of such service;

(B) solely for the purpose of providing storage or computer processing services to such subscriber or customer, if the provider is not authorized to access the contents of any such communications for purposes of providing any services other than storage or computer processing; and

(3) a provider of remote computing service or electronic communication service to the public shall not knowingly divulge a record or other information pertaining to a subscriber to or customer of such service (not including the contents of communications covered by paragraph (1) or (2)) to any governmental entity.

(b) Exceptions for disclosure of communications.— A provider described in subsection (a) may divulge the contents of a communication—

(1) to an addressee or intended recipient of such communication or an agent of such addressee or intended recipient;

(2) as otherwise authorized in section 2517, 2511(2)(a), or 2703 of this title;

(3) with the lawful consent of the originator or an addressee or intended recipient of such communication, or the subscriber in the case of remote computing service;

(4) to a person employed or authorized or whose facilities are used to forward such communication to its destination;

(5) as may be necessarily incident to the rendition of the service or to the protection of the rights or property of the provider of that service;

(6) to the National Center for Missing and Exploited Children, in connection with a report submitted thereto under section 227 of the Victims of Child Abuse Act of 1990 (42 U.S.C. 13032);

(7) to a law enforcement agency—

(A) if the contents—

(i) were inadvertently obtained by the service provider; and

(ii) appear to pertain to the commission of a crime; or

[**(B)** Repealed. Pub.L. 108–21, Title V, § 508(b)(1)(A), Apr. 30, 2003, 117 Stat. 684]

[**(C)** Repealed. Pub.L. 107–296, Title II, § 225(d)(1)(C), Nov. 25, 2002, 116 Stat. 2157]

(8) to a governmental entity, if the provider, in good faith, believes that an emergency involving danger of death or serious physical injury to any person requires disclosure without delay of communications relating to the emergency.

(c) Exceptions for disclosure of customer records.—A provider described in subsection (a) may divulge a record or other information pertaining to a subscriber to or customer of such service (not including the contents of communications covered by subsection (a)(1) or (a)(2))—

(1) as otherwise authorized in section 2703;

(2) with the lawful consent of the customer or subscriber;

(3) as may be necessarily incident to the rendition of the service or to the protection of the rights or property of the provider of that service;

(4) to a governmental entity, if the provider, in good faith, believes that an emergency involving danger of death or serious physical injury to any person requires disclosure without delay of information relating to the emergency;

(5) to the National Center for Missing and Exploited Children, in connection with a report submitted thereto under section 227 of the Victims of Child Abuse Act of 1990 (42 U.S.C. 13032); or

(6) to any person other than a governmental entity.

(d) Reporting of emergency disclosures.—On an annual basis, the Attorney General shall submit to the Committee on the Judiciary of the House of Representatives and the Committee on the Judiciary of the Senate a report containing—

(1) the number of accounts from which the Department of Justice has received voluntary disclosures under subsection (b)(8); and

(2) a summary of the basis for disclosure in those instances where—

(A) voluntary disclosures under subsection (b)(8) were made to the Department of Justice; and

(B) the investigation pertaining to those disclosures was closed without the filing of criminal charges.

(Added Pub.L. 99–508, Title II, § 201[a], Oct. 21, 1986, 100 Stat. 1860, and amended Pub.L. 100–690, Title VII, § 7037, Nov. 18, 1988, 102 Stat. 4399; Pub.L. 105–314, Title VI, § 604(b), Oct. 30, 1998, 112 Stat. 2984; Pub.L. 107–56, Title II, § 212(a)(1), Oct. 26, 2001, 115 Stat. 284; Pub.L. 107–296, Title II, § 225(d)(1), Nov. 25, 2002, 116 Stat. 2157; Pub.L. 108–21, Title V, § 508(b), Apr. 30, 2003, Stat. 684; Pub.L. 109–177, Title I, § 107(a), (b)(1), (c), Mar. 9, 2006, 120 Stat. 202, 203.)

HISTORICAL AND STATUTORY NOTES

References in Text

Section 227 of the Victims of Child Abuse Act of 1990, referred to in subsecs. (b)(6) and (c)(5), is Pub.L. 101–647, Title II, § 227, as added Pub.L. 105–314, Title VI, § 604(a), Oct. 30, 1998, 112 Stat. 2983, which is classified to 42 U.S.C.A. § 13032.

The Crime Control Act of 1990, referred to in subsec. (b)(6)(B) of the text, is Pub.L. 101–647, Nov. 29, 1990, 104 Stat. 4789, for complete classification of which, see Tables. Title II of that Act is entitled the Victims of Child Abuse Act of 1990. Thus, section 227 of the Crime Control Act of 1990, which enacted 42 U.S.C.A. § 13032, is also section 227 of the Victims of Child Abuse Act of 1990, Pub.L. 101–647, Title II, § 227, as added Pub.L. 105–314, Title VI, § 604(a), Oct. 30, 1998, 112 Stat. 2983.

Effective and Applicability Provisions

2002 Acts. Amendment to this section by Pub.L. 107–296 effective 60 days after Nov. 25, 2002, see Pub.L. 107–296, § 4, set out as a note under 6 U.S.C.A. § 101.

1986 Acts. Section effective 90 days after Oct. 21, 1986 except as otherwise provided in section 202 of Pub.L. 99–508 with respect to conduct pursuant to court order or extension, see section 202 of Pub.L. 99–508, set out as a note under 18 U.S.C.A. § 2701.

Sunset Provisions

Provision that amendments by Pub.L. 107–56, Title II, Oct. 26, 2001, 115 Stat. 278, with certain exclusions, shall cease to have effect on March 10, 2006, except with respect to any particular foreign intelligence investigation that began before that date, or with respect to any particular offense or potential offense that began or occurred before that, such provisions to continue in effect, was repealed by Pub.L. 109–177, § 102(a), see Pub.L. 107–56, § 224, as amended, set out as a note under 18 U.S.C.A. § 2510.

§ 2703. Required disclosure of customer communications or records

(a) Contents of wire or electronic communications in electronic storage.—A governmental entity may require the disclosure by a provider of electronic communication service of the contents of a wire or electronic communication, that is in electronic storage in an electronic communications system for one hundred and eighty days or less, only pursuant to a warrant issued using the procedures described in the Federal Rules of Criminal Procedure by a court with jurisdiction over the offense under investigation or equivalent State warrant. A governmental entity may require the disclosure by a provider of electronic communications services of the contents of a wire or electronic communication that has been in electronic storage in an electronic communications system for more than one hundred and eighty days by the means available under subsection (b) of this section.

(b) Contents of wire or electronic communications in a remote computing service.—(1) A governmental entity may require a provider of remote computing service to disclose the contents of any wire or electronic communication to which this paragraph is made applicable by paragraph (2) of this subsection—

(A) without required notice to the subscriber or customer, if the governmental entity obtains a warrant issued using the procedures described in the Federal Rules of Criminal Procedure by a court with jurisdiction over the offense under investigation or equivalent State warrant; or

(B) with prior notice from the governmental entity to the subscriber or customer if the governmental entity—

(i) uses an administrative subpoena authorized by a Federal or State statute or a Federal or State grand jury or trial subpoena; or

(ii) obtains a court order for such disclosure under subsection (d) of this section;

except that delayed notice may be given pursuant to section 2705 of this title.

(2) Paragraph (1) is applicable with respect to any wire or electronic communication that is held or maintained on that service—

(A) on behalf of, and received by means of electronic transmission from (or created by means of computer processing of communications received by means of electronic transmission from), a subscriber or customer of such remote computing service; and

(B) solely for the purpose of providing storage or computer processing services to such subscriber or customer, if the provider is not authorized to access the contents of any such communications for purposes of providing any services other than storage or computer processing.

(c) Records concerning electronic communication service or remote computing service.—(1) A governmental entity may require a provider of electronic communication service or remote computing service to disclose a record or other information pertaining to a subscriber to or customer of such service (not including the contents of communications) only when the governmental entity—

(A) obtains a warrant issued using the procedures described in the Federal Rules of Criminal Procedure by a court with jurisdiction over the offense under investigation or equivalent State warrant;

(B) obtains a court order for such disclosure under subsection (d) of this section;

(C) has the consent of the subscriber or customer to such disclosure;

(D) submits a formal written request relevant to a law enforcement investigation concerning telemarketing fraud for the name, address, and place of business of a subscriber or customer of such provider, which subscriber or customer is engaged in telemarketing (as such term is defined in section 2325 of this title); or

(E) seeks information under paragraph (2).

(2) A provider of electronic communication service or remote computing service shall disclose to a governmental entity the—

(A) name;

(B) address;

(C) local and long distance telephone connection records, or records of session times and durations;

(D) length of service (including start date) and types of service utilized;

(E) telephone or instrument number or other subscriber number or identity, including any temporarily assigned network address; and

(F) means and source of payment for such service (including any credit card or bank account number),

of a subscriber to or customer of such service when the governmental entity uses an administrative subpoena authorized by a Federal or State statute or a Federal or State grand jury or trial subpoena or any means available under paragraph (1).

(3) A governmental entity receiving records or information under this subsection is not required to provide notice to a subscriber or customer.

(d) Requirements for court order.—A court order for disclosure under subsection (b) or (c) may be issued by any court that is a court of competent jurisdiction and shall issue only if the governmental entity offers specific and articulable facts showing that there are reasonable grounds to believe that the contents of a wire or electronic communication, or the records or other information sought, are relevant and material to an ongoing criminal investigation. In the case of a State governmental authority, such a court order shall not issue if prohibited by the law of such State. A court issuing an order pursuant to this section, on a motion made promptly by the service provider, may quash or modify such order, if the information or records requested are unusually voluminous in nature or compliance with such order otherwise would cause an undue burden on such provider.

(e) No cause of action against a provider disclosing information under this chapter.—No cause of action shall lie in any court against any provider of wire or electronic communication service, its officers, employees, agents, or other specified persons for providing information, facilities, or assistance in accordance with the terms of a court order, warrant, subpoena, statutory authorization, or certification under this chapter.

(f) Requirement to preserve evidence.—

(1) In general.—A provider of wire or electronic communication services or a remote computing service, upon the request of a governmental entity, shall take all necessary steps to preserve records and other evidence in its possession pending the issuance of a court order or other process.

(2) Period of retention.—Records referred to in paragraph (1) shall be retained for a period of 90 days, which shall be extended for an additional 90-day period upon a renewed request by the governmental entity.

(g) Presence of officer not required.—Notwithstanding section 3105 of this title, the presence of an officer shall not be required for service or execution of a search warrant issued in accordance with this chapter requiring disclosure by a provider of electronic communications service or remote computing service of the contents of communications or records or other information pertaining to a subscriber to or customer of such service.

(Added Pub.L. 99–508, Title II, § 201[a], Oct. 21, 1986, 100 Stat. 1861, and amended Pub.L. 100–690, Title VII, §§ 7038, 7039, Nov. 18, 1988, 102 Stat. 4399; Pub.L. 103–322, Title XXXIII, § 330003(b), Sept. 13, 1994, 108 Stat. 2140; Pub.L. 103–414, Title II, § 207(a), Oct. 25, 1994, 108 Stat. 4292; Pub.L. 104–132, Title VIII, § 804, Apr. 24, 1996, 110 Stat. 1305; Pub.L. 104–293, Title VI, § 601(b), Oct. 11, 1996, 110 Stat. 3469; Pub.L. 104–294, Title VI, § 605(f), Oct. 11, 1996, 110 Stat. 3510; Pub.L. 105–184, § 8, June 23, 1998, 112 Stat. 522; Pub.L. 107–56, Title II, §§ 209(2), 210, 212(b)(1), 220(a)(1), (b), Oct. 26, 2001, 115 Stat. 283, 285, 291, 292; Pub.L. 107–273, Div. B, Title IV, § 4005(a)(2), Div. C, Title I, § 11010, Nov. 2, 2002, 116 Stat. 1812, 1822; Pub.L. 107–296, Title II, § 225(h)(1), Nov. 25, 2002, 116 Stat. 2158; Pub.L. 109–162, Title XI, § 1171(a)(1), Jan. 5, 2006, 119 Stat. 3123.)

HISTORICAL AND STATUTORY NOTES

Effective and Applicability Provisions

2002 Acts. Amendment to this section by Pub.L. 107–296 effective 60 days after Nov. 25, 2002, see Pub.L. 107–296, § 4, set out as a note under 6 U.S.C.A. § 101.

1986 Acts. Section effective 90 days after Oct. 21, 1986 except as otherwise provided in section 202 of Pub.L. 99–508 with respect to conduct pursuant to court order or extension, see section 202 of Pub.L. 99–508, set out as a note under section 2701 of this title.

Sunset Provisions

Provision that amendments by Pub.L. 107–56, Title II, Oct. 26, 2001, 115 Stat. 278, with certain exclusions, shall cease to have effect on March 10, 2006, except with respect to any particular foreign intelligence investigation that began before that date, or with respect to any particular offense or potential offense that began or occurred before that, such provisions to continue in effect, was repealed by Pub.L. 109–177, § 102(a), see Pub.L. 107–56, § 224, as amended, set out as a note under 18 U.S.C.A. § 2510.

§ 2704. Backup preservation

(a) Backup preservation.—(1) A governmental entity acting under section 2703(b)(2) may include in its subpoena or court order a requirement that the service provider to whom the request is directed create a backup copy of the contents of the electronic communications sought in order to preserve those communications. Without notifying the subscriber or customer of such subpoena or court order, such service provider shall create such backup copy as soon as practicable consistent with its regular business practices and shall confirm to the governmental entity that such backup copy has been made. Such backup copy shall be created within two business days after receipt by the service provider of the subpoena or court order.

(2) Notice to the subscriber or customer shall be made by the governmental entity within three days after receipt of such confirmation, unless such notice is delayed pursuant to section 2705(a).

(3) The service provider shall not destroy such backup copy until the later of—

(A) the delivery of the information; or

(B) the resolution of any proceedings (including appeals of any proceeding) concerning the government's subpoena or court order.

(4) The service provider shall release such backup copy to the requesting governmental entity no sooner than fourteen days after the governmental entity's notice to the subscriber or customer if such service provider—

(A) has not received notice from the subscriber or customer that the subscriber or customer has challenged the governmental entity's request; and

(B) has not initiated proceedings to challenge the request of the governmental entity.

(5) A governmental entity may seek to require the creation of a backup copy under subsection (a)(1) of this section if in its sole discretion such entity determines that there is reason to believe that notification under section 2703 of this title of the existence of the subpoena or court order may result in destruction of or tampering with evidence. This determination is not subject to challenge by the subscriber or customer or service provider.

(b) Customer challenges.—(1) Within fourteen days after notice by the governmental entity to the subscriber or customer under subsection (a)(2) of this section, such subscriber or customer may file a motion to quash such subpoena or vacate such court order, with copies served upon the governmental entity and with written notice of such challenge to the service provider. A motion to vacate a court order shall be filed in the court which issued such order. A motion to quash a subpoena shall be filed in the appropriate United States district court or State court. Such motion or application shall contain an affidavit or sworn statement—

(A) stating that the applicant is a customer or subscriber to the service from which the contents of electronic communications maintained for him have been sought; and

(B) stating the applicant's reasons for believing that the records sought are not relevant to a legitimate law enforcement inquiry or that there has not been substantial compliance with the provisions of this chapter in some other respect.

(2) Service shall be made under this section upon a governmental entity by delivering or mailing by registered or certified mail a copy of the papers to the person, office, or department specified in the notice which the customer has received pursuant to this chapter. For the purposes of this section, the term "delivery" has the meaning given that term in the Federal Rules of Civil Procedure.

(3) If the court finds that the customer has complied with paragraphs (1) and (2) of this subsection, the court shall order the governmental entity to file a sworn response, which may be filed in camera if the governmental entity includes in its response the reasons which make in camera review appropriate. If the court is unable to determine the motion or application on the basis of the parties' initial allegations and response, the court may conduct such additional proceedings as it deems appropriate. All such proceedings shall be completed and the motion or application decided as soon as practicable after the filing of the governmental entity's response.

(4) If the court finds that the applicant is not the subscriber or customer for whom the communications sought by the governmental entity are maintained, or that there is a reason to believe that the law enforcement inquiry is legitimate and that the communications sought are relevant to that inquiry, it shall deny the motion or application and order such process enforced. If the court finds that the applicant is the subscriber or customer for whom the communications sought by the governmental entity are maintained, and that there is not a reason to believe that the communications sought are relevant to a legitimate law enforcement inquiry, or that there has not been substantial compliance with the provisions of this chapter, it shall order the process quashed.

(5) A court order denying a motion or application under this section shall not be deemed a final order and no interlocutory appeal may be taken therefrom by the customer.

(Added Pub.L. 99–508, Title II, § 201[a], Oct. 21, 1986, 100 Stat. 1863.)

HISTORICAL AND STATUTORY NOTES

Effective and Applicability Provisions

1986 Acts. Section effective 90 days after Oct. 21, 1986 except as otherwise provided in section 202 of Pub.L. 99–508 with respect to conduct pursuant to court order or extension, see section 202 of Pub.L. 99–508, set out as a note under section 2701 of this title.

§ 2705. Delayed notice

(a) Delay of notification.—(1) A governmental entity acting under section 2703(b) of this title may—

(A) where a court order is sought, include in the application a request, which the court shall grant, for an order delaying the notification required under section 2703(b) of this title for a period not to exceed ninety days, if the court determines that there is reason to believe that notification of the existence of the court order may have an adverse result described in paragraph (2) of this subsection; or

(B) where an administrative subpoena authorized by a Federal or State statute or a Federal or State grand jury subpoena is obtained, delay the notification required under section 2703(b) of this title for a period not to exceed ninety days upon the execution of a written certification of a supervisory official that there is reason to believe that notification of the existence of the subpoena may have an adverse result described in paragraph (2) of this subsection.

(2) An adverse result for the purposes of paragraph (1) of this subsection is—

(A) endangering the life or physical safety of an individual;

(B) flight from prosecution;

(C) destruction of or tampering with evidence;

(D) intimidation of potential witnesses; or

(E) otherwise seriously jeopardizing an investigation or unduly delaying a trial.

(3) The governmental entity shall maintain a true copy of certification under paragraph (1)(B).

(4) Extensions of the delay of notification provided in section 2703 of up to ninety days each may be granted by the court upon application, or by certification by a governmental entity, but only in accordance with subsection (b) of this section.

(5) Upon expiration of the period of delay of notification under paragraph (1) or (4) of this subsection, the governmental entity shall serve upon, or deliver by registered or first-class mail to, the customer or subscriber a copy of the process or request together with notice that—

(A) states with reasonable specificity the nature of the law enforcement inquiry; and

(B) informs such customer or subscriber—

(i) that information maintained for such customer or subscriber by the service provider named in such process or request was supplied to or requested by that governmental authority and the date on which the supplying or request took place;

(ii) that notification of such customer or subscriber was delayed;

(iii) what governmental entity or court made the certification or determination pursuant to which that delay was made; and

(iv) which provision of this chapter allowed such delay.

(6) As used in this subsection, the term "supervisory official" means the investigative agent in charge or assistant investigative agent in charge or an equivalent of an investigating agency's headquarters or regional office, or the chief prosecuting attorney or the first assistant prosecuting attorney or an equivalent of a prosecuting attorney's headquarters or regional office.

(b) **Preclusion of notice to subject of governmental access.**—A governmental entity acting under section 2703, when it is not required to notify the subscriber or customer under section 2703(b)(1), or to the extent that it may delay such notice pursuant to subsection (a) of this section, may apply to a court for an order commanding a provider of electronic communications service or remote computing service to whom a warrant, subpoena, or court order is directed, for such period as the court deems appropriate, not to notify any other person of the existence of the warrant, subpoena, or court order. The court shall enter such an order if it determines that there is reason to believe that notification of the existence of the warrant, subpoena, or court order will result in—

(1) endangering the life or physical safety of an individual;

(2) flight from prosecution;

(3) destruction of or tampering with evidence;

(4) intimidation of potential witnesses; or

(5) otherwise seriously jeopardizing an investigation or unduly delaying a trial.

(Added Pub.L. 99–508, Title II, § 201[a], Oct. 21, 1986, 100 Stat. 1864.)

HISTORICAL AND STATUTORY NOTES

Effective and Applicability Provisions

1986 Acts. Section effective 90 days after Oct. 21, 1986 except as otherwise provided in section 202 of Pub.L. 99–508 with respect to conduct pursuant to court order or extension, see section 202 of Pub.L. 99–508, set out as a note under section 2701 of this title.

§ 2706. Cost reimbursement

(a) **Payment.**—Except as otherwise provided in subsection (c), a governmental entity obtaining the contents of communications, records, or other information under section 2702, 2703, or 2704 of this title shall pay to the person or entity assembling or providing such information a fee for reimbursement for such costs as are reasonably necessary and which have been directly incurred in searching for, assembling, reproducing, or otherwise providing such information. Such reimbursable costs shall include any costs due to necessary disruption of normal operations of any electronic communication service or remote computing service in which such information may be stored.

(b) **Amount.**—The amount of the fee provided by subsection (a) shall be as mutually agreed by the governmental entity and the person or entity providing the information, or, in the absence of agreement, shall be as determined by the court which issued the order for production of such information (or the court before which a criminal prosecution relating to such information would be brought, if no court order was issued for production of the information).

(c) **Exception.**— The requirement of subsection (a) of this section does not apply with respect to records or other information maintained by a communications common carrier that relate to telephone toll records and telephone listings obtained under section 2703 of this title. The court may, however, order a payment as described in subsection (a) if the court determines the information required is unusually voluminous in nature or otherwise caused an undue burden on the provider.

(Added Pub.L. 99–508, Title II, § 201[a], Oct. 21, 1986, 100 Stat. 1866, and amended Pub.L. 100–690, Title VII, § 7061, Nov. 18, 1988, 102 Stat. 4404.)

HISTORICAL AND STATUTORY NOTES

Effective and Applicability Provisions

1986 Acts. Section effective 90 days after Oct. 21, 1986 except as otherwise provided in section 202 of Pub.L. 99–508 with respect to conduct pursuant to court order or extension, see section 202 of Pub.L. 99–508, set out as a note under section 2701 of this title.

§ 2707. Civil action

(a) Cause of action.—Except as provided in section 2703(e), any provider of electronic communication service, subscriber, or other person aggrieved by any violation of this chapter in which the conduct constituting the violation is engaged in with a knowing or intentional state of mind may, in a civil action, recover from the person or entity, other than the United States, which engaged in that violation such relief as may be appropriate.

(b) Relief.—In a civil action under this section, appropriate relief includes—

(1) such preliminary and other equitable or declaratory relief as may be appropriate;

(2) damages under subsection (c); and

(3) a reasonable attorney's fee and other litigation costs reasonably incurred.

(c) Damages.—The court may assess as damages in a civil action under this section the sum of the actual damages suffered by the plaintiff and any profits made by the violator as a result of the violation, but in no case shall a person entitled to recover receive less than the sum of $1,000. If the violation is willful or intentional, the court may assess punitive damages. In the case of a successful action to enforce liability under this section, the court may assess the costs of the action, together with reasonable attorney fees determined by the court.

(d) Administrative discipline.—If a court or appropriate department or agency determines that the United States or any of its departments or agencies has violated any provision of this chapter, and the court or appropriate department or agency finds that the circumstances surrounding the violation raise serious questions about whether or not an officer or employee of the United States acted willfully or intentionally with respect to the violation, the department or agency shall, upon receipt of a true and correct copy of the decision and findings of the court or appropriate department or agency promptly initiate a proceeding to determine whether disciplinary action against the officer or employee is warranted. If the head of the department or agency involved determines that disciplinary action is not warranted, he or she shall notify the Inspector General with jurisdiction over the department or agency concerned and shall provide the Inspector General with the reasons for such determination.

(e) Defense.—A good faith reliance on—

(1) a court warrant or order, a grand jury subpoena, a legislative authorization, or a statutory authorization (including a request of a governmental entity under section 2703(f) of this title);

(2) a request of an investigative or law enforcement officer under section 2518(7) of this title; or

(3) a good faith determination that section 2511(3) of this title permitted the conduct complained of;

is a complete defense to any civil or criminal action brought under this chapter or any other law.

(f) Limitation.—A civil action under this section may not be commenced later than two years after the date upon which the claimant first discovered or had a reasonable opportunity to discover the violation.

(g) Improper disclosure.—Any willful disclosure of a 'record', as that term is defined in section 552a(a) of title 5, United States Code, obtained by an investigative or law enforcement officer, or a governmental entity, pursuant to section 2703 of this title, or from a device installed pursuant to section 3123 or 3125 of this title, that is not a disclosure made in the proper performance of the official functions of the officer or governmental entity making the disclosure, is a violation of this chapter. This provision shall not apply to information previously lawfully disclosed (prior to the commencement of any civil or administrative proceeding under this chapter) to the public by a Federal, State, or local governmental entity or by the plaintiff in a civil action under this chapter.

(Added Pub.L. 99–508, Title II, § 201[a], Oct. 21, 1986, 100 Stat. 1866, and amended Pub.L. 104–293, Title VI, § 601(c), Oct. 11, 1996, 110 Stat. 3469; Pub.L. 107–56, Title II, § 223(b), Title VIII, § 815, Oct. 26, 2001, 115 Stat. 293, 384; Pub.L. 107–273, Div. B, Title IV, § 4005(f)(2), Nov. 2, 2002, 116 Stat. 1813.)

HISTORICAL AND STATUTORY NOTES

Effective and Applicability Provisions

2002 Acts. Amendment by section 4005(f)(2) of Pub.L. 107–273, as therein provided, effective Oct. 26, 2001, which is the date of enactment of Pub.L. 107–56, to which such amendment relates.

1986 Acts. Section effective 90 days after Oct. 21, 1986 except as otherwise provided in section 202 of Pub.L. 99–508 with respect to conduct pursuant to court order or extension, see section 202 of Pub.L. 99–508, set out as a note under section 2701 of this title.

Sunset Provisions

Provision that amendments by Pub.L. 107–56, Title II, Oct. 26, 2001, 115 Stat. 278, with certain exclusions, shall cease to have effect on March 10, 2006, except with respect to any particular foreign intelligence investigation that began before that date, or with respect to any particular offense or potential offense that began or occurred before that, such provisions to continue in effect, was repealed by Pub.L. 109–177,

§ 102(a), see Pub.L. 107–56, § 224, as amended, set out as a note under 18 U.S.C.A. § 2510.

§ 2708. Exclusivity of remedies

The remedies and sanctions described in this chapter are the only judicial remedies and sanctions for nonconstitutional violations of this chapter.

(Added Pub.L. 99–508, Title II, § 201[a], Oct. 21, 1986, 100 Stat. 1867.)

HISTORICAL AND STATUTORY NOTES

Effective and Applicability Provisions

1986 Acts. Section effective 90 days after Oct. 21, 1986 except as otherwise provided in section 202 of Pub.L. 99–508 with respect to conduct pursuant to court order or extension, see section 202 of Pub.L. 99–508, set out as a note under section 2701 of this title.

§ 2709. Counterintelligence access to telephone toll and transactional records

(a) Duty to provide.—A wire or electronic communication service provider shall comply with a request for subscriber information and toll billing records information, or electronic communication transactional records in its custody or possession made by the Director of the Federal Bureau of Investigation under subsection (b) of this section.

(b) Required certification.—The Director of the Federal Bureau of Investigation, or his designee in a position not lower than Deputy Assistant Director at Bureau headquarters or a Special Agent in Charge in a Bureau field office designated by the Director, may—

(1) request the name, address, length of service, and local and long distance toll billing records of a person or entity if the Director (or his designee) certifies in writing to the wire or electronic communication service provider to which the request is made that the name, address, length of service, and toll billing records sought are relevant to an authorized investigation to protect against international terrorism or clandestine intelligence activities, provided that such an investigation of a United States person is not conducted solely on the basis of activities protected by the first amendment to the Constitution of the United States; and

(2) request the name, address, and length of service of a person or entity if the Director (or his designee) certifies in writing to the wire or electronic communication service provider to which the request is made that the information sought is relevant to an authorized investigation to protect against international terrorism or clandestine intelligence activities, provided that such an investigation of a United States person is not conducted solely upon the basis of activities protected by the first amendment to the Constitution of the United States.

(c) Prohibition of certain disclosure.—

(1) If the Director of the Federal Bureau of Investigation, or his designee in a position not lower than Deputy Assistant Director at Bureau headquarters or a Special Agent in Charge in a Bureau field office designated by the Director, certifies that otherwise there may result a danger to the national security of the United States, interference with a criminal, counterterrorism, or counterintelligence investigation, interference with diplomatic relations, or danger to the life or physical safety of any person, no wire or electronic communications service provider, or officer, employee, or agent thereof, shall disclose to any person (other than those to whom such disclosure is necessary to comply with the request or an attorney to obtain legal advice or legal assistance with respect to the request) that the Federal Bureau of Investigation has sought or obtained access to information or records under this section.

(2) The request shall notify the person or entity to whom the request is directed of the nondisclosure requirement under paragraph (1).

(3) Any recipient disclosing to those persons necessary to comply with the request or to an attorney to obtain legal advice or legal assistance with respect to the request shall inform such person of any applicable nondisclosure requirement. Any person who receives a disclosure under this subsection shall be subject to the same prohibitions on disclosure under paragraph (1).

(4) At the request of the Director of the Federal Bureau of Investigation or the designee of the Director, any person making or intending to make a disclosure under this section shall identify to the Director or such designee the person to whom such disclosure will be made or to whom such disclosure was made prior to the request, except that nothing in this section shall require a person to inform the Director or such designee of the identity of an attorney to whom disclosure was made or will be made to obtain legal advice or legal assistance with respect to the request under subsection (a).

(d) Dissemination by bureau.—The Federal Bureau of Investigation may disseminate information and records obtained under this section only as provided in guidelines approved by the Attorney General for foreign intelligence collection and foreign counterintelligence investigations conducted by the Federal Bureau of Investigation, and, with respect to dissemination to an agency of the United States, only if such information is clearly relevant to the authorized responsibilities of such agency.

(e) Requirement that certain congressional bodies be informed.—On a semiannual basis the Director of the Federal Bureau of Investigation shall fully inform the Permanent Select Committee on Intelligence of the House of Representatives and the Select Committee on Intelligence of the Senate, and the Committee on the Judiciary of the House of Representatives and the Committee on the Judiciary of the Senate, concerning all requests made under subsection (b) of this section.

(f) Libraries.—A library (as that term is defined in section 213(1) of the Library Services and Technology Act (20 U.S.C. 9122(1)), the services of which include access to the Internet, books, journals, magazines, newspapers, or other similar forms of communication in print or digitally by patrons for their use, review, examination, or circulation, is not a wire or electronic communication service provider for purposes of this section, unless the library is providing the services defined in section 2510(15) ("electronic communication service") of this title.

(Added Pub.L. 99–508, Title II, § 201[a], Oct. 21, 1986, 100 Stat. 1867, and amended Pub.L. 103–142, Nov. 17, 1993, 107 Stat. 1491; Pub.L. 104–293, Title VI, § 601(a), Oct. 11, 1996, 110 Stat. 3469; Pub.L. 107–56, Title V, § 505(a), Oct. 26, 2001, 115 Stat. 365; Pub.L. 109–177, Title I, § 116(a), Mar. 9, 2006, 120 Stat. 213; Pub.L. 109–178, §§ 4(b), 5, Mar. 9, 2006, 120 Stat. 280, 281.)

HISTORICAL AND STATUTORY NOTES

References in Text

Section 101 of the Foreign Intelligence Surveillance Act of 1978 (50 U.S.C. 1801), referred to in subsec. (b)(1)(B), (2)(B)(i), (ii), is classified to 50 U.S.C.A. § 1801.

Section 213(1) of the Library Services and Technology Act, referred to in subsec. (f), is section 213(1) of Pub.L. 104–208, which added section 213 to the Arts, Humanities, and Cultural Affairs Act of 1976, Pub.L. 94–462, Title II, § 213, as added Pub.L. 104–208, Div. A, Title I, § 101(e) [Title VII, § 702], Sept. 30, 1996, 110 Stat. 3009–296, which is classified to 20 U.S.C.A. § 9122(1).

2006 Acts. Amendments by Pub.L. 109–178 effective Mar. 9, 2006, see Pub.L. 109–178, 120 Stat. 282, set out as a note under 12 U.S.C.A. § 3414.

Termination of Reporting Requirements

Reporting requirement of subsec. (e) of this section excepted from termination under Pub.L. 104–66, § 3003(a)(1), as amended, set out in a note under 31 U.S.C.A. § 1113, see Pub.L. 106–197, § 1, set out as a note under 31 U.S.C.A. § 1113.

§ 2710. Wrongful disclosure of video tape rental or sale records

(a) Definitions.—For purposes of this section—

(1) the term "consumer" means any renter, purchaser, or subscriber of goods or services from a video tape service provider;

(2) the term "ordinary course of business" means only debt collection activities, order fulfillment, request processing, and the transfer of ownership;

(3) the term "personally identifiable information" includes information which identifies a person as having requested or obtained specific video materials or services from a video tape service provider; and

(4) the term "video tape service provider" means any person, engaged in the business, in or affecting interstate or foreign commerce, of rental, sale, or delivery of prerecorded video cassette tapes or similar audio visual materials, or any person or other entity to whom a disclosure is made under subparagraph (D) or (E) of subsection (b)(2), but only with respect to the information contained in the disclosure.

(b) Video tape rental and sale records.—(1) A video tape service provider who knowingly discloses, to any person, personally identifiable information concerning any consumer of such provider shall be liable to the aggrieved person for the relief provided in subsection (d).

(2) A video tape service provider may disclose personally identifiable information concerning any consumer—

(A) to the consumer;

(B) to any person with the informed, written consent of the consumer given at the time the disclosure is sought;

(C) to a law enforcement agency pursuant to a warrant issued under the Federal Rules of Criminal Procedure, an equivalent State warrant, a grand jury subpoena, or a court order;

(D) to any person if the disclosure is solely of the names and addresses of consumers and if—

(i) the video tape service provider has provided the consumer with the opportunity, in a clear and conspicuous manner, to prohibit such disclosure; and

(ii) the disclosure does not identify the title, description, or subject matter of any video tapes or other audio visual material; however, the subject matter of such materials may be disclosed if the disclosure is for the exclusive use of marketing goods and services directly to the consumer;

(E) to any person if the disclosure is incident to the ordinary course of business of the video tape service provider; or

(F) pursuant to a court order, in a civil proceeding upon a showing of compelling need for the information that cannot be accommodated by any other means, if—

(i) the consumer is given reasonable notice, by the person seeking the disclosure, of the court proceeding relevant to the issuance of the court order; and

(ii) the consumer is afforded the opportunity to appear and contest the claim of the person seeking the disclosure.

If an order is granted pursuant to subparagraph (C) or (F), the court shall impose appropriate safeguards against unauthorized disclosure.

(3) Court orders authorizing disclosure under subparagraph (C) shall issue only with prior notice to the consumer and only if the law enforcement agency shows that there is probable cause to believe that the records or other information sought are relevant to a legitimate law enforcement inquiry. In the case of a State government authority, such a court order shall not issue if prohibited by the law of such State. A court issuing an order pursuant to this section, on a motion made promptly by the video tape service provider, may quash or modify such order if the information or records requested are unreasonably voluminous in nature or if compliance with such order otherwise would cause an unreasonable burden on such provider.

(c) Civil action.—(1) Any person aggrieved by any act of a person in violation of this section may bring a civil action in a United States district court.

(2) The court may award—

(A) actual damages but not less than liquidated damages in an amount of $2,500;

(B) punitive damages;

(C) reasonable attorneys' fees and other litigation costs reasonably incurred; and

(D) such other preliminary and equitable relief as the court determines to be appropriate.

(3) No action may be brought under this subsection unless such action is begun within 2 years from the date of the act complained of or the date of discovery.

(4) No liability shall result from lawful disclosure permitted by this section.

(d) Personally identifiable information.—Personally identifiable information obtained in any manner other than as provided in this section shall not be received in evidence in any trial, hearing, arbitration, or other proceeding in or before any court, grand jury, department, officer, agency, regulatory body, legislative committee, or other authority of the United States, a State, or a political subdivision of a State.

(e) Destruction of old records.—A person subject to this section shall destroy personally identifiable information as soon as practicable, but no later than one year from the date the information is no longer necessary for the purpose for which it was collected and there are no pending requests or orders for access to such information under subsection (b)(2) or (c)(2) or pursuant to a court order.

(f) Preemption.—The provisions of this section preempt only the provisions of State or local law that require disclosure prohibited by this section.

(Added Pub.L. 100–618, § 2(a)(2), Nov. 5, 1988, 102 Stat. 3195.)

§ 2711. Definitions for chapter

As used in this chapter—

(1) the terms defined in section 2510 of this title have, respectively, the definitions given such terms in that section;

(2) the term "remote computing service" means the provision to the public of computer storage or processing services by means of an electronic communications system;

(3) the term "court of competent jurisdiction" has the meaning assigned by section 3127, and includes any Federal court within that definition, without geographic limitation; and

(4) the term "governmental entity" means a department or agency of the United States or any State or political subdivision thereof.

(Added Pub.L. 99–508, Title II, § 201[a], Oct. 21, 1986, 100 Stat. 1868, § 2710; renumbered § 2711, Pub.L. 100–618, § 2(a)(1), Nov. 5, 1988, 102 Stat. 3195, and amended Pub.L. 107–56, Title II, § 220(a)(2), Oct. 26, 2001, 115 Stat. 292; Pub.L. 109–177, Title I, § 107(b)(2), Mar. 9, 2006, 120 Stat. 202.)

HISTORICAL AND STATUTORY NOTES

Effective and Applicability Provisions

1986 Acts. Section effective 90 days after Oct. 21, 1986 except as otherwise provided in section 202 of Pub.L. 99–508 with respect to conduct pursuant to court order or extension, see section 202 of Pub.L. 99–508, set out as a note under section 2701 of this title.

Sunset Provisions

Provision that amendments by Pub.L. 107–56, Title II, Oct. 26, 2001, 115 Stat. 278, with certain exclusions, shall cease to have effect on March 10, 2006, except with respect to any particular foreign intelligence investigation that began before that date, or with respect to any particular offense or potential offense that began or occurred before that, such provisions to continue in effect, was repealed by Pub.L. 109–177, § 102(a), see Pub.L. 107–56, § 224, as amended, set out as a note under 18 U.S.C.A. § 2510.

§ 2712. Civil actions against the United States

(a) In general.—Any person who is aggrieved by any willful violation of this chapter or of chapter 119 of this title or of sections 106(a), 305(a), or 405(a) of the Foreign Intelligence Surveillance Act of 1978 (50 U. S.C. 1801 et seq.) may commence an action in United States District Court against the United States to recover money damages. In any such action, if a person who is aggrieved successfully establishes such a violation of this chapter or of chapter 119 of this title or of the above specific provisions of title 50, the Court may assess as damages—

(1) actual damages, but not less than $10,000, whichever amount is greater; and

(2) litigation costs, reasonably incurred.

(b) Procedures.—(1) Any action against the United States under this section may be commenced only after a claim is presented to the appropriate department or agency under the procedures of the Federal Tort Claims Act, as set forth in title 28, United States Code.

(2) Any action against the United States under this section shall be forever barred unless it is presented in writing to the appropriate Federal agency within 2 years after such claim accrues or unless action is begun within 6 months after the date of mailing, by certified or registered mail, of notice of final denial of the claim by the agency to which it was presented. The claim shall accrue on the date upon which the claimant first has a reasonable opportunity to discover the violation.

(3) Any action under this section shall be tried to the court without a jury.

(4) Notwithstanding any other provision of law, the procedures set forth in section 106(f), 305(g), or 405(f) of the Foreign Intelligence Surveillance Act of 1978 (50 U.S.C. 1801 et seq.) shall be the exclusive means by which materials governed by those sections may be reviewed.

(5) An amount equal to any award against the United States under this section shall be reimbursed by the department or agency concerned to the fund described in section 1304 of title 31, United States Code, out of any appropriation, fund, or other account (excluding any part of such appropriation, fund, or account that is available for the enforcement of any Federal law) that is available for the operating expenses of the department or agency concerned.

(c) Administrative discipline.—If a court or appropriate department or agency determines that the United States or any of its departments or agencies has violated any provision of this chapter, and the court or appropriate department or agency finds that the circumstances surrounding the violation raise serious questions about whether or not an officer or employee of the United States acted willfully or intentionally with respect to the violation, the department or agency shall, upon receipt of a true and correct copy of the decision and findings of the court or appropriate department or agency promptly initiate a proceeding to determine whether disciplinary action against the officer or employee is warranted. If the head of the department or agency involved determines that disciplinary action is not warranted, he or she shall notify the Inspector General with jurisdiction over the department or agency concerned and shall provide the Inspector General with the reasons for such determination.

(d) Exclusive remedy.—Any action against the United States under this subsection shall be the exclusive remedy against the United States for any claims within the purview of this section.

(e) Stay of proceedings.—(1) Upon the motion of the United States, the court shall stay any action commenced under this section if the court determines that civil discovery will adversely affect the ability of the Government to conduct a related investigation or the prosecution of a related criminal case. Such a stay shall toll the limitations periods of paragraph (2) of subsection (b).

(2) In this subsection, the terms "related criminal case" and "related investigation" mean an actual prosecution or investigation in progress at the time at which the request for the stay or any subsequent motion to lift the stay is made. In determining whether an investigation or a criminal case is related to an action commenced under this section, the court shall consider the degree of similarity between the parties, witnesses, facts, and circumstances involved in the 2 proceedings, without requiring that any one or more factors be identical.

(3) In requesting a stay under paragraph (1), the Government may, in appropriate cases, submit evidence ex parte in order to avoid disclosing any matter that may adversely affect a related investigation or a related criminal case. If the Government makes such an ex parte submission, the plaintiff shall be given an opportunity to make a submission to the court, not ex parte, and the court may, in its discretion, request further information from either party.

(Added Pub.L. 107–56, Title II, § 223(c)(1), Oct. 26, 2001, 115 Stat. 294.)

HISTORICAL AND STATUTORY NOTES

References in Text

Chapter 119 of this title, referred to in subsec. (a), is 18 U.S.C.A. § 2510 et seq.

The Foreign Intelligence Surveillance Act of 1978, referred to in subsecs. (a) and (b)(4), is Pub.L. 95–511, Oct. 25, 1978, 92 Stat. 1793, as amended, which is principally classified to 50 U.S.C.A. § 1801 et seq. Section 106(a) of the Act is Pub.L. 95–511, Title I, § 106(a), Oct. 25, 1978, 92 Stat. 1793, which is classified to 50 U.S.C.A. § 1806(a). Section 305(a) of the Act is Pub.L. 95–511, Title III, § 305, as added Pub.L. 103–359, Title VIII, § 807(a)(3), Oct. 14, 1994, 108 Stat. 3449, which is classified to 50 U.S.C.A. § 1825(a). Section 405(a) of the Act is Pub.L. 95–511, Title IV, § 405, as added Pub.L. 105–272, Title VI, § 601(2), Oct. 20, 1998, 112 Stat. 2408, which is classified to 50 U.S.C.A. § 1845(a). See Tables for complete classification.

The Federal Torts Claims Act, referred to in subsec. (b)(1), is classified generally to 28 U.S.C.A. § 1346(b) and chapter 171 of Title 28 [28 U.S.C.A. § 2671 et seq.].

Sunset Provisions

Provision that amendments by Pub.L. 107–56, Title II, Oct. 26, 2001, 115 Stat. 278, with certain exclusions, shall cease to have effect on March 10, 2006, except with respect to any particular foreign intelligence investigation that began before that date, or with respect to any particular offense or potential offense that began or occurred before that, such provisions to continue in effect, was repealed by Pub.L. 109–177, § 102(a), see Pub.L. 107–56, § 224, as amended, set out as a note under 18 U.S.C.A. § 2510.

CHAPTER 123—PROHIBITION ON RELEASE AND USE OF CERTAIN PERSONAL INFORMATION FROM STATE MOTOR VEHICLE RECORDS

Sec.

§ 2721. Prohibition on release and use of certain personal information from State motor vehicle records

(a) In general.—A State department of motor vehicles, and any officer, employee, or contractor thereof, shall not knowingly disclose or otherwise make available to any person or entity:

(1) personal information, as defined in 18 U.S.C. 2725(3), about any individual obtained by the department in connection with a motor vehicle record, except as provided in subsection (b) of this section; or

(2) highly restricted personal information, as defined in 18 U.S.C. 2725(4), about any individual obtained by the department in connection with a motor vehicle record, without the express consent of the person to whom such information applies, except uses permitted in subsections (b)(1), (b)(4), (b)(6), and (b)(9): *Provided,* That subsection (a)(2) shall not in any way affect the use of organ donation information on an individual's driver's license or affect the administration of organ donation initiatives in the States.

(b) Permissible uses.—Personal information referred to in subsection (a) shall be disclosed for use in connection with matters of motor vehicle or driver safety and theft, motor vehicle emissions, motor vehicle product alterations, recalls, or advisories, performance monitoring of motor vehicles and dealers by motor vehicle manufacturers, and removal of non-owner records from the original owner records of motor vehicle manufacturers to carry out the purposes of titles I and IV of the Anti Car Theft Act of 1992, the Automobile Information Disclosure Act (15 U.S.C. 1231 et seq.), the Clean Air Act (42 U.S.C. 7401 et seq.), and chapters 301, 305, and 321–331 of title 49, and, subject to subsection (a)(2), may be disclosed as follows:

(1) For use by any government agency, including any court or law enforcement agency, in carrying out its functions, or any private person or entity acting on behalf of a Federal, State, or local agency in carrying out its functions.

(2) For use in connection with matters of motor vehicle or driver safety and theft; motor vehicle emissions; motor vehicle product alterations, recalls, or advisories; performance monitoring of motor vehicles, motor vehicle parts and dealers; motor vehicle market research activities, including survey research; and removal of non-owner records from the original owner records of motor vehicle manufacturers.

(3) For use in the normal course of business by a legitimate business or its agents, employees, or contractors, but only—

(A) to verify the accuracy of personal information submitted by the individual to the business or its agents, employees, or contractors; and

(B) if such information as so submitted is not correct or is no longer correct, to obtain the correct information, but only for the purposes of preventing fraud by, pursuing legal remedies against, or recovering on a debt or security interest against, the individual.

(4) For use in connection with any civil, criminal, administrative, or arbitral proceeding in any Federal, State, or local court or agency or before any self-regulatory body, including the service of process, investigation in anticipation of litigation, and the execution or enforcement of judgments and orders, or pursuant to an order of a Federal, State, or local court.

(5) For use in research activities, and for use in producing statistical reports, so long as the personal information is not published, redisclosed, or used to contact individuals.

(6) For use by any insurer or insurance support organization, or by a self-insured entity, or its agents, employees, or contractors, in connection with claims investigation activities, antifraud activities, rating or underwriting.

(7) For use in providing notice to the owners of towed or impounded vehicles.

(8) For use by any licensed private investigative agency or licensed security service for any purpose permitted under this subsection.

(9) For use by an employer or its agent or insurer to obtain or verify information relating to a holder of a commercial driver's license that is required under chapter 313 of title 49.

(10) For use in connection with the operation of private toll transportation facilities.

(11) For any other use in response to requests for individual motor vehicle records if the State has obtained the express consent of the person to whom such personal information pertains.

(12) For bulk distribution for surveys, marketing or solicitations if the State has obtained the express consent of the person to whom such personal information pertains.

(13) For use by any requester, if the requester demonstrates it has obtained the written consent of the individual to whom the information pertains.

(14) For any other use specifically authorized under the law of the State that holds the record, if such use is related to the operation of a motor vehicle or public safety.

(c) Resale or redisclosure.—An authorized recipient of personal information (except a recipient under subsection (b)(11) or (12)) may resell or redisclose the information only for a use permitted under subsection (b) (but not for uses under subsection (b) (11) or (12)). An authorized recipient under subsection (b)(11) may resell or redisclose personal information for any purpose. An authorized recipient under subsection (b)(12) may resell or redisclose personal information pursuant to subsection (b)(12). Any authorized recipient (except a recipient under subsection (b) (11)) that resells or rediscloses personal information covered by this chapter must keep for a period of 5 years records identifying each person or entity that receives information and the permitted purpose for which the information will be used and must make such records available to the motor vehicle department upon request.

(d) Waiver procedures.—A State motor vehicle department may establish and carry out procedures under which the department or its agents, upon receiving a request for personal information that does not fall within one of the exceptions in subsection (b), may mail a copy of the request to the individual about whom the information was requested, informing such individual of the request, together with a statement to the effect that the information will not be released unless the individual waives such individual's right to privacy under this section.

(e) Prohibition on conditions.—No State may condition or burden in any way the issuance of an individual's motor vehicle record as defined in 18 U.S.C. 2725(1) to obtain express consent. Nothing in this paragraph shall be construed to prohibit a State from charging an administrative fee for issuance of a motor vehicle record.

(Added Pub.L. 103–322, Title XXX, § 300002(a), Sept. 13, 1994, 108 Stat. 2099, and amended Pub.L. 104–287, § 1, Oct. 11, 1996, 110 Stat. 3388; Pub.L. 104–294, Title VI, § 604(b)(46), Oct. 11, 1996, 110 Stat. 3509; Pub.L. 106–69, Title III, § 350(c), (d), Oct. 9, 1999, 113 Stat. 1025; Pub.L. 106–346, § 101(a) [Title III, § 309(c) to (e)], Oct. 23, 2000, 114 Stat. 1356, 1356A–24.)

HISTORICAL AND STATUTORY NOTES

References in Text

Titles I and IV of the Anti Car Theft Act of 1992, referred to in subsec. (b), are Titles I and IV of Pub.L. 102–519, Oct. 25, 1992, 106 Stat. 3384. For complete classification of this Act to the Code, see Short Title note set out under section 1901 of Title 15, Commerce and Trade, and Tables.

The Automobile Information Disclosure Act, referred to in subsec. (b), is Pub.L. 85–506, July 7, 1958, 72 Stat. 325, as amended, which is classified generally to chapter 28 (section 1231 et seq.) of Title 15, Commerce and Trade. For complete classification of this Act to the Code, see Short Title note set out under section 1231 of Title 15 and Tables.

The Clean Air Act, referred to in subsec. (b), is Act July 14, 1955, c. 360, as amended generally by Pub.L. 88–206, Dec. 17, 1963, 77 Stat. 392, and later by Pub.L. 95–95, Aug. 7, 1977, 91 Stat. 685. The Clean Air Act was originally classified to chapter 15B (section 1857 et seq.) of Title 42, The Public Health and Welfare. On enactment of Pub.L. 95–95, the Act was reclassified to chapter 85 (section 7401 et seq.) of Title 42. For complete classification of this Act to the Code, see Short Title note set out under section 7401 of Title 42 and Tables.

Effective and Applicability Provisions

1999 Acts. Section 350(g)(2) of Pub.L. 106–69 provided that: "Subsections (b) [not classified to the Code], (c) [amending subsec. (b)(11) of this section], and (d) [amending subsec. (b)(12) of this section] shall be effective on June 1, 2000, excluding the States of Arkansas, Montana, Nevada, North Dakota, Oregon, and Texas that shall be in compliance with subsections (b), (c), and (d) within 90 days of the next convening of the State legislature and excluding the States of Wisconsin, South Carolina, and Oklahoma that shall be in compliance within 90 days following the day of issuance of a final decision on Reno vs. Condon [120 S.Ct. 666, 145 L.Ed. 2d 587, decided Jan. 12, 2000] by the United States Supreme Court if the State legislature is in session, or within 90 days of the next convening of the State legislature following the issuance of such final decision if the State legislature is not in session."

1996 Acts. Amendment by section 604 of Pub.L. 104–294 effective Sept. 13, 1994, see section 604(d) of Pub.L. 104–294, set out as a note under section 13 of this title.

1994 Acts. Section 300003 of Pub.L. 103–322 provided that: "The amendments made by section 300002 [enacting this chapter] shall become effective on the date that is 3 years after the date of enactment of this Act [Sept. 13, 1994]. After the effective date, if a State has implemented a procedure under section 2721(b) (11) and (12) of title 18, United States Code, as added by section 2902 [subsec. (b)(11) and (12) of this section as added by section 300002(a) of Pub.L. 103–322], for prohibiting disclosures or uses of personal information, and the procedure otherwise meets the requirements of subsection (b)(11) and (12), the State shall be in compliance with subsection (b)(11) and (12) even if the procedure is not available to individuals until they renew their license, title, registration or identification card, so long as the State provides some other procedure for individuals to contact the State on their own initiative to prohibit such uses or disclosures. Prior to the effective date, personal information covered by the amendment made by section 300002 may be released consistent with State law or practice."

Short Title

1994 Acts. Section 300001 of Pub.L. 103–322 provided that: "This title [enacting this chapter and provisions set out as notes under this section] may be cited as the 'Driver's Privacy Protection Act of 1994'."

§ 2722. Additional unlawful acts

(a) Procurement for unlawful purpose.—It shall be unlawful for any person knowingly to obtain or disclose personal information, from a motor vehicle record, for any use not permitted under section 2721(b) of this title.

(b) False representation.—It shall be unlawful for any person to make false representation to obtain any personal information from an individual's motor vehicle record.

(Added Pub.L. 103–322, Title XXX, § 300002(a), Sept. 13, 1994, 108 Stat. 2101.)

HISTORICAL AND STATUTORY NOTES

Effective and Applicability Provisions

1994 Acts. Section effective on the date which is 3 years after Sept. 13, 1994, provided that, after such effective date, if a State has implemented a procedure under section 2721(b)(11) and (12) of this title for prohibiting disclosures or uses of personal information, and the procedure otherwise meets the requirements of such subsection (b)(11) and (12), the State shall be in compliance with such subsection even if the procedure is not available to individuals until they renew their license, title, registration or identification card, so long as the State provides some other procedure for individuals to contact the State on their own initiative to prohibit such uses or disclosures and provided further, that prior to such effective date, personal information covered by this chapter may be released consistent with State law or practice, see section 300003 of Pub.L. 103–322, set out as a note under section 2721 of this title.

§ 2723. Penalties

(a) Criminal fine.—A person who knowingly violates this chapter shall be fined under this title.

(b) Violations by State department of motor vehicles.—Any State department of motor vehicles that has a policy or practice of substantial noncompliance with this chapter shall be subject to a civil penalty imposed by the Attorney General of not more than $5,000 a day for each day of substantial noncompliance.

(Added Pub.L. 103–322, Title XXX, § 300002(a), Sept. 13, 1994, 108 Stat. 2101.)

HISTORICAL AND STATUTORY NOTES

Effective and Applicability Provisions

1994 Acts. Section effective on the date which is 3 years after Sept. 13, 1994, provided that, after such effective date, if a State has implemented a procedure under section 2721(b)(11) and (12) of this title for prohibiting disclosures or uses of personal information, and the procedure otherwise meets the requirements of such subsection (b)(11) and (12), the State shall be in compliance with such subsection even if the procedure is not available to individuals until they renew their license, title, registration or identification card, so long as the State provides some other procedure for individuals to contact the State on their own initiative to prohibit such uses or disclosures and provided further, that prior to such effective date, personal information covered by this chapter may be released consistent with State law or practice, see section 300003 of Pub.L. 103–322, set out as a note under section 2721 of this title.

§ 2724. Civil action

(a) Cause of action.—A person who knowingly obtains, discloses or uses personal information, from a motor vehicle record, for a purpose not permitted under this chapter shall be liable to the individual to whom the information pertains, who may bring a civil action in a United States district court.

(b) Remedies.—The court may award—

(1) actual damages, but not less than liquidated damages in the amount of $2,500;

(2) punitive damages upon proof of willful or reckless disregard of the law;

(3) reasonable attorneys' fees and other litigation costs reasonably incurred; and

(4) such other preliminary and equitable relief as the court determines to be appropriate.

(Added Pub.L. 103–322, Title XXX, § 300002(a), Sept. 13, 1994, 108 Stat. 2101.)

HISTORICAL AND STATUTORY NOTES

Effective and Applicability Provisions

1994 Acts. Section effective on the date which is 3 years after Sept. 13, 1994, provided that, after such effective date, if a State has implemented a procedure under section 2721(b)(11) and (12) of this title for prohibiting disclosures or uses of personal information, and the procedure otherwise meets the requirements of such subsection (b)(11) and (12), the State shall be in compliance with such subsection even if the procedure is not available to individuals until they renew their license, title, registration or identification card, so long as the State provides some other procedure for individuals to contact the State on their own initiative to prohibit such uses or disclosures and provided further, that prior to such effective date, personal information covered by this chapter may be released consistent with State law or practice, see section 300003 of Pub.L. 103–322, set out as a note under section 2721 of this title.

§ 2725. Definitions

In this chapter—

(1) "motor vehicle record" means any record that pertains to a motor vehicle operator's permit, motor vehicle title, motor vehicle registration, or identification card issued by a department of motor vehicles;

(2) "person" means an individual, organization or entity, but does not include a State or agency thereof;

(3) "personal information" means information that identifies an individual, including an individual's photograph, social security number, driver identification number, name, address (but not the 5-digit zip code), telephone number, and medical or disability information, but does not include information on vehicular accidents, driving violations, and driver's status.[1]

(4) "highly restricted personal information" means an individual's photograph or image, social security number, medical or disability information; and

(5) "express consent" means consent in writing, including consent conveyed electronically that bears an electronic signature as defined in section 106(5) of Public Law 106–229.

(Added Pub.L. 103–322, Title XXX, § 300002(a), Sept. 13, 1994, 108 Stat. 2102, and amended Pub.L. 106–346, § 101(a) [Title III, § 309(b)], Oct. 23, 2000, 114 Stat. 1356, 1356A–24.)

[1] So in original. The period probably should be replaced with a semicolon.

HISTORICAL AND STATUTORY NOTES

References in Text

Section 106(5) of Public Law 106–229, referred to in text, is section 106(5) of Pub.L. 106–229, June 30, 2000, 114 Stat. 472, classified to section 7006(5) of Title 15.

Effective and Applicability Provisions

1994 Acts. Section effective on the date which is 3 years after Sept. 13, 1994, provided that, after such effective date, if a State has implemented a procedure under section 2721(b)(11) and (12) of this title for prohibiting disclosures or uses of personal information, and the procedure otherwise meets the requirements of such subsection (b)(11) and (12), the State shall be in compliance with such subsection even if the procedure is not available to individuals until they renew their license, title, registration or identification card, so long as the State provides some other procedure for individuals to contact the State on their own initiative to prohibit such uses or disclosures and provided further, that prior to such effective date, personal information covered by this chapter may be released consistent with State law or practice, see section 300003 of Pub.L. 103–322, set out as a note under section 2721 of this title.

PART II—CRIMINAL PROCEDURE

[1] So in original. Only the first word of item should be capitalized.

[2] So in original. Does not conform to section catchline, and only the first word of item should be capitalized.

HISTORICAL AND STATUTORY NOTES

Effective and Applicability Provisions

1984 Acts. Addition of item for chapter 232 effective 30 days after Oct. 12, 1984, pursuant to section 1409(a) of Pub.L. 98–473, set out as a note under section 10601 of Title 42, The Public Health and Welfare.

For applicability of sentencing provisions to offenses, see Effective Date and Savings Provisions, etc., note, section 235 of Pub.L. 98–473, as amended, set out under section 3551 of this title.

CHAPTER 201—GENERAL PROVISIONS

HISTORICAL AND STATUTORY NOTES

Effective and Applicability Provisions

1984 Acts. Addition of item 3013 effective 30 days after Oct. 12, 1984, pursuant to section 1409(a) of Pub.L. 98–473, set out as a note under section 10601 of Title 42, The Public Health and Welfare.

Savings Provisions of Pub.L. 98–473, Title II, c. II

See section 235 of Pub.L. 98–473, Title II, c. II, Oct. 12, 1984, 98 Stat. 2031, as amended, set out as a note under section 3551 of this title.

Law Enforcement Assistance Act of 1965

Pub.L. 89–197, §§ 1 to 11, Sept. 22, 1965, 79 Stat. 828, as amended by Pub.L. 89–798, Nov. 8, 1966, 80 Stat. 1506, was repealed by Pub.L. 90–351, Title I, § 405, June 19, 1968, 82 Stat. 204, subject to the provisions of section 3745 of Title 42, and is now covered by section 3701 et seq. (chapter 46) of Title 42, The Public Health and Welfare. Such Act had provided for grants and contracts for improvement of quality of state and local personnel through professional training; grants and contracts to improve state and local law enforcement techniques; delegation and redelegation of powers; contributions to program by recipients, rules and regulations, necessary stipends, and allowances; studies by Attorney General and technical assistance to states; prohibition against control over local agencies; advisory committees, compensation, and expenses; term of program; appropriations; and reports to President and Congress.

Coordination of Federal Law Enforcement and Crime Prevention Programs

Designation of Attorney General to coordinate Federal law enforcement and crime prevention program, see Ex. Ord. No. 11396, Feb. 7, 1968, 33 F.R. 2689, set out as a note preceding section 1 of this title.

§ 3001. Procedure governed by rules; scope, purpose and effect; definition of terms; local rules; forms—(Rule)

SEE FEDERAL RULES OF CRIMINAL PROCEDURE

Scope, Rule 1.

Purpose and construction, Rule 2.

Proceedings to which rules apply, Rules 54 and 59.

Definitions, Rule 54(c).

Rules of District Courts and Circuit Courts of Appeal, Rule 57.

Forms, Rule 58.

Effective date, Rule 59.

Citation of rule, Rule 60.

(June 25, 1948, c. 645, 62 Stat. 814.)

§ 3002. Courts always open—(Rule)

SEE FEDERAL RULES OF CRIMINAL PROCEDURE

Business hours, Rule 56.

(June 25, 1948, c. 645, 62 Stat. 814.)

§ 3003. Calendars—(Rule)

SEE FEDERAL RULES OF CRIMINAL PROCEDURE

Preference to criminal cases, Rule 50.

(June 25, 1948, c. 645, 62 Stat. 814.)

§ 3004. Decorum in court room—(Rule)

SEE FEDERAL RULES OF CRIMINAL PROCEDURE

Photographing or radio broadcasting prohibited, Rule 53.

(June 25, 1948, c. 645, 62 Stat. 814.)

§ 3005. Counsel and witnesses in capital cases

Whoever is indicted for treason or other capital crime shall be allowed to make his full defense by counsel; and the court before which the defendant is to be tried, or a judge thereof, shall promptly, upon the defendant's request, assign 2 such counsel, of whom at least 1 shall be learned in the law applicable to capital cases, and who shall have free access to the accused at all reasonable hours. In assigning counsel under this section, the court shall consider the recommendation of the Federal Public Defender organization, or, if no such organization exists in the district, of the Administrative Office of the United States Courts. The defendant shall be allowed, in his defense to make any proof that he can produce by lawful witnesses, and shall have the like process of the court to compel his witnesses to appear at his trial, as is usually granted to compel witnesses to appear on behalf of the prosecution.

(June 25, 1948, c. 645, 62 Stat. 814; Sept. 13, 1994, Pub.L. 103–322, Title VI, § 60026, 108 Stat. 1982.)

§ 3006. Assignment of counsel—(Rule)

SEE FEDERAL RULES OF CRIMINAL PROCEDURE

Appointment by court, Rule 44.

Accused to be informed of right to counsel, Rules 5 and 44.

(June 25, 1948, c. 645, 62 Stat. 814.)

§ 3006A. Adequate representation of defendants

(a) Choice of plan.—Each United States district court, with the approval of the judicial council of the circuit, shall place in operation throughout the district a plan for furnishing representation for any person financially unable to obtain adequate representation in accordance with this section. Representation under each plan shall include counsel and investigative, expert, and other services necessary for adequate representation. Each plan shall provide the following:

(1) Representation shall be provided for any financially eligible person who—

(A) is charged with a felony or a Class A misdemeanor;

(B) is a juvenile alleged to have committed an act of juvenile delinquency as defined in section 5031 of this title;

(C) is charged with a violation of probation;

(D) is under arrest, when such representation is required by law;

(E) is charged with a violation of supervised release or faces modification, reduction, or enlargement of a condition, or extension or revocation of a term of supervised release;

(F) is subject to a mental condition hearing under chapter 313 of this title;

(G) is in custody as a material witness;

(H) is entitled to appointment of counsel under the sixth amendment to the Constitution;

(I) faces loss of liberty in a case, and Federal law requires the appointment of counsel; or

(J) is entitled to the appointment of counsel under section 4109 of this title.

(2) Whenever the United States magistrate judge or the court determines that the interests of justice so require, representation may be provided for any financially eligible person who—

(A) is charged with a Class B or C misdemeanor, or an infraction for which a sentence to confinement is authorized; or

(B) is seeking relief under section 2241, 2254, or 2255 of title 28.

(3) Private attorneys shall be appointed in a substantial proportion of the cases. Each plan may include, in addition to the provisions for private attorneys, either of the following or both:

(A) Attorneys furnished by a bar association or a legal aid agency,

(B) Attorneys furnished by a defender organization established in accordance with the provisions of subsection (g).

Prior to approving the plan for a district, the judicial council of the circuit shall supplement the plan with provisions for representation on appeal. The district court may modify the plan at any time with the approval of the judicial council of the circuit. It shall modify the plan when directed by the judicial council of the circuit. The district court shall notify the Administrative Office of the United States Courts of any modification of its plan.

(b) Appointment of counsel.—Counsel furnishing representation under the plan shall be selected from a panel of attorneys designated or approved by the court, or from a bar association, legal aid agency, or defender organization furnishing representation pursuant to the plan. In every case in which a person entitled to representation under a plan approved under subsection (a) appears without counsel, the United States magistrate judge or the court shall advise the person that he has the right to be represented by counsel and that counsel will be appointed to represent him if he is financially unable to obtain counsel. Unless the person waives representation by counsel, the United States magistrate judge or the court, if satisfied after appropriate inquiry that the person is financially unable to obtain counsel, shall appoint counsel to represent him. Such appointment may be made retroactive to include any representation furnished pursuant to the plan prior to appointment. The United States magistrate judge or the court shall appoint separate counsel for persons having interests that cannot properly be represented by the same counsel, or when other good cause is shown.

(c) Duration and substitution of appointments.—A person for whom counsel is appointed shall be represented at every stage of the proceedings from his initial appearance before the United States magistrate judge or the court through appeal, including ancillary matters appropriate to the proceedings. If at any time after the appointment of counsel the United States magistrate judge or the court finds that the person is financially able to obtain counsel or to make partial payment for the representation, it may terminate the appointment of counsel or authorize payment as provided in subsection (f), as the interests of justice may dictate. If at any stage of the proceedings, including an appeal, the United States magistrate judge or the court finds that the person is financially unable to pay counsel whom he had retained, it may appoint counsel as provided in subsection (b) and authorize payment as provided in subsection (d), as the interests of justice may dictate. The United States magistrate judge or the court may, in the interests of justice, substitute one appointed counsel for another at any stage of the proceedings.

(d) Payment for representation.—

(1) Hourly rate.—Any attorney appointed pursuant to this section or a bar association or legal aid agency or community defender organization which has provided the appointed attorney shall, at the conclusion of the representation or any segment thereof, be compensated at a rate not exceeding $60 per hour for time expended in court or before a United States magistrate judge and $40 per hour for time reasonably expended out of court, unless the Judicial Conference determines that a higher rate of not in excess of $75 per hour is justified for a circuit or for particular districts within a circuit, for time expended in court or before a United States magistrate judge and for time expended out of court. The Judicial Conference shall develop guidelines for determining the maximum hourly rates for each circuit in accordance with the preceding sentence, with variations by district, where appropriate, taking into account such factors as the minimum range of the prevailing hourly rates for qualified attorneys in the district in which the representation is provided and the recommendations of the judicial councils of the circuits. Not less than 3 years after the effective date of the Criminal Justice Act Revision of 1986, the Judicial Conference is authorized to raise the maximum hourly rates specified in this paragraph up to the aggregate of the overall average percentages of the adjustments in the rates of pay under the General Schedule made pursuant to section 5305 of title 5 on or after such effective date. After the rates are raised under the preceding sentence, such maximum hourly rates may be raised at intervals of not less than 1 year each, up to the aggregate of the overall average percentages of such adjustments made since the last raise was made under this paragraph. Attorneys may be reimbursed for expenses reasonably incurred, including the costs of transcripts authorized by the United States magistrate [1] or the court, and the costs of defending actions alleging malpractice of counsel in furnishing representational services under this section. No reimbursement for expenses in defending against malpractice claims shall be made if a judgment of malpractice is rendered against the counsel furnishing representational services under this section. The United States magistrate [1] or the court shall make determinations relating to reimbursement of expenses under this paragraph.

(2) Maximum amounts.—For representation of a defendant before the United States magistrate judge or the district court, or both, the compensation to be paid to an attorney or to a bar association or legal aid agency or community defender organization shall not exceed $7,000 for each attorney in a case in which one or more felonies are charged, and $2,000 for each attorney in a case in which only misdemeanors are charged. For representation of a defendant in an appellate court, the compensation to be paid to an attorney or to a bar association or legal aid agency or community defender organization shall not exceed $5,000 for each attorney in each court. For representation of a petitioner in a non-capital habeas corpus proceeding, the compensation for each attorney shall not exceed the amount applicable to a felony in this paragraph for representation of a defendant before a judicial officer of the district court. For representation of such petitioner in an appellate court, the compensation for each attorney shall not exceed the amount applicable for representation of a defendant in an appellate court. For representation of an offender before the United States Parole Commission in a proceeding under section 4106A of this title, the compensation shall not exceed $1,500 for each attorney in each proceeding; for representation of an offender in an appeal from a determination of such Commission under such section, the compensation shall not exceed $5,000 for each attorney in each court. For any other representation required or authorized by this section, the compensation shall not exceed $1,500 for each attorney in each proceeding.

(3) Waiving maximum amounts.—Payment in excess of any maximum amount provided in paragraph (2) of this subsection may be made for extended or complex representation whenever the court in which the representation was rendered, or the United States magistrate judge if the representation was furnished exclusively before him, certifies that the amount of the excess payment is necessary to provide fair compensation and the payment is approved by the chief judge of the circuit. The chief judge of the circuit may delegate such approval authority to an active circuit judge.

(4) Disclosure of fees.—

(A) In general.—Subject to subparagraphs (B) through (E), the amounts paid under this subsection for services in any case shall be made available to the public by the court upon the court's approval of the payment.

(B) Pre–trial or trial in progress.—If a trial is in pre-trial status or still in progress and after considering the defendant's interests as set forth in subparagraph (D), the court shall—

(i) redact any detailed information on the payment voucher provided by defense counsel to justify the expenses to the court; and

(ii) make public only the amounts approved for payment to defense counsel by dividing those amounts into the following categories:

(I) Arraignment and or plea.

(II) Bail and detention hearings.

(III) Motions.

(IV) Hearings.

(V) Interviews and conferences.

(VI) Obtaining and reviewing records.

(VII) Legal research and brief writing.

(VIII) Travel time.

(IX) Investigative work.

(X) Experts.

(XI) Trial and appeals.

(XII) Other.

(C) Trial completed.—

(i) In general.—If a request for payment is not submitted until after the completion of the trial and subject to consideration of the defendant's interests as set forth in subparagraph (D), the court shall make available to the public an unredacted copy of the expense voucher.

(ii) Protection of the rights of the defendant.—If the court determines that defendant's interests as set forth in subparagraph (D) require a limited disclosure, the court shall disclose amounts as provided in subparagraph (B).

(D) Considerations.—The interests referred to in subparagraphs (B) and (C) are—

(i) to protect any person's 5th amendment right against self-incrimination;

(ii) to protect the defendant's 6th amendment rights to effective assistance of counsel;

(iii) the defendant's attorney-client privilege;

(iv) the work product privilege of the defendant's counsel;

(v) the safety of any person; and

(vi) any other interest that justice may require, except that the amount of the fees shall not be considered a reason justifying any limited disclosure under section 3006A(d)(4) of title 18, United States Code.

(E) Notice.—The court shall provide reasonable notice of disclosure to the counsel of the defendant prior to the approval of the payments in order to allow the counsel to request redaction based on the considerations set forth in subparagraph (D). Upon completion of the trial, the court shall release unredacted copies of the vouchers provided by defense counsel to justify the expenses to the court. If there is an appeal, the court shall not release unredacted copies of the vouchers provided by defense counsel to justify the expenses to the court until such time as the appeals process is completed, unless the court determines that none of the defendant's interests set forth in subparagraph (D) will be compromised.

(F) Effective date.—The amendment made by paragraph (4) shall become effective 60 days after enactment of this Act, will apply only to cases filed on or after the effective date, and shall be in effect for no longer than 24 months after the effective date.

(5) Filing claims.—A separate claim for compensation and reimbursement shall be made to the district court for representation before the United States magistrate judge and the court, and to each appellate court before which the attorney provided representation to the person involved. Each claim shall be supported by a sworn written statement specifying the time expended, services rendered, and expenses incurred while the case was pending before the United States magistrate judge and the court, and the compensation and reimbursement applied for or received in the same case from any other source. The court shall fix the compensation and reimbursement to be paid to the attorney or to the bar association or legal aid agency or community defender organization which provided the appointed attorney. In cases where representation is furnished exclusively before a United States magistrate judge, the claim shall be submitted to him and he shall fix the compensation and reimbursement to be paid. In cases where representation is furnished other than before the United States magistrate judge, the district court, or an appellate court, claims shall be submitted to the district court which shall fix the compensation and reimbursement to be paid.

(6) New trials.—For purposes of compensation and other payments authorized by this section, an order by a court granting a new trial shall be deemed to initiate a new case.

(7) Proceedings before appellate courts.—If a person for whom counsel is appointed under this section appeals to an appellate court or petitions for a writ of certiorari, he may do so without prepayment of fees and costs or security therefor and without filing the affidavit required by section 1915(a) of title 28.

(e) Services other than counsel.—

(1) Upon request.—Counsel for a person who is financially unable to obtain investigative, expert, or other services necessary for adequate representation may request them in an ex parte application. Upon finding, after appropriate inquiry in an ex parte proceeding, that the services are necessary and that the person is financially unable to obtain them, the court, or the United States magistrate judge if the services are required in connection with a matter over which he has jurisdiction, shall authorize counsel to obtain the services.

(2) Without prior request.—**(A)** Counsel appointed under this section may obtain, subject to later review, investigative, expert, and other services without prior authorization if necessary for adequate representation. Except as provided in subparagraph (B) of this paragraph, the total cost of services obtained without prior authorization may not exceed $500 and expenses reasonably incurred.

(B) The court, or the United States magistrate judge (if the services were rendered in a case disposed of entirely before the United States magistrate judge), may, in the interest of justice, and upon the finding that timely procurement of necessary services could not await prior authorization, approve payment for such services after they have been obtained, even if the cost of such services exceeds $500.

(3) Maximum amounts.—Compensation to be paid to a person for services rendered by him to a person under this subsection, or to be paid to an organization for services rendered by an employee thereof, shall not exceed $1,600, exclusive of reimbursement for expenses reasonably incurred, unless payment in excess of that limit is certified by the court, or by the United States magistrate judge if the services were rendered in connection with a case disposed of entirely before him, as necessary to provide fair compensation for services of an unusual character or duration, and the amount of the excess payment is approved by the chief judge of the circuit. The chief judge of the circuit may delegate such approval authority to an active circuit judge.

(4) Disclosure of fees.—The amounts paid under this subsection for services in any case shall be made available to the public.

(f) Receipt of other payments.—Whenever the United States magistrate judge or the court finds that funds are available for payment from or on behalf of a person furnished representation, it may authorize or direct that such funds be paid to the appointed attorney, to the bar association or legal aid agency or community defender organization which provided the appointed attorney, to any person or organization authorized pursuant to subsection (e) to render investigative, expert, or other services, or to the court for deposit in the Treasury as a reimbursement to the appropriation, current at the time of payment, to carry out the provisions of this section. Except as so authorized or directed, no such person or organization may request or accept any payment or promise of payment for representing a defendant.

(g) Defender organization.—

(1) Qualifications.—A district or a part of a district in which at least two hundred persons annually require the appointment of counsel may establish a defender organization as provided for either under subparagraphs (A) or (B) of paragraph (2) of this subsection or both. Two adjacent districts or parts of districts may aggregate the number of persons required to be represented to establish eligibility for a defender organization to serve both areas. In the event that adjacent districts or parts of districts are located in different circuits, the plan for furnishing representation shall be approved by the judicial council of each circuit.

(2) Types of defender organizations.—

(A) Federal Public Defender Organization.—A Federal Public Defender Organization shall consist of one or more full-time salaried attorneys. An organization for a district or part of a district or two adjacent districts or parts of districts shall be supervised by a Federal Public Defender appointed by the court of appeals of the circuit, without regard to the provisions of title 5 governing appointments in the competitive service, after considering recommendations from the district court or courts to be served. Nothing contained herein shall be deemed to authorize more than one Federal Public Defender within a single judicial district. The Federal Public Defender shall be appointed for a term of four years, unless sooner removed by the court of appeals of the circuit for incompetency, misconduct in office, or neglect of duty. Upon the expiration of his term, a Federal Public Defender may, by a majority vote of the judges of the court of appeals, continue to perform the duties of his office until his successor is appointed, or until one year after the expiration of such Defender's term, whichever is earlier. The compensation of the Federal Public Defender shall be fixed by the court of appeals of the circuit at a rate not to exceed the compensation received by the United States attorney for the district where representation is furnished or, if two districts or parts of districts are involved, the compensation of the higher paid United States attorney of the districts. The Federal Public Defender may appoint, without regard to the provisions of title 5 governing appointments in the competitive service, full-time attorneys in such number as may be approved by the court of appeals of the circuit and other personnel in such number as may be approved by the Director of the Administrative Office of the United States Courts. Compensation paid to such attorneys and other personnel of the organization shall be fixed by the Federal Public Defender at a rate not to exceed that paid to attorneys and other personnel of similar qualifications and experience in the Office of the United States attorney in the district where representation is furnished or, if two districts or parts of districts are involved, the higher compensation paid to persons of similar qualifications and experience in the districts. Neither the Federal Public Defender nor any attorney so appointed by him may engage in the private practice of law. Each organization shall submit to the Director of the Administrative Office of the United States Courts, at the time and in the form prescribed by him, reports of its activities and financial position and its proposed budget. The Director of the Administrative Office shall submit, in accordance with section 605 of title 28, a budget for each organization for each fiscal year and shall out of the appropriations therefor make payments to and on behalf of each organization. Payments under this subparagraph to an organization shall be in lieu of payments under subsection (d) or (e).

(B) Community Defender Organization.—A Community Defender Organization shall be a nonprofit defense counsel service established and administered by any group authorized by the plan to provide representation. The organization shall be eligible to furnish attorneys and receive payments under this section if its bylaws are set forth in the plan of the district or districts in which it will serve. Each organization shall submit to the Judicial Conference of the United States an annual report setting forth its activities and financial position and the anticipated caseload and expenses for the next fiscal year. Upon application an organization may, to the extent approved by the Judicial Conference of the United States:

(i) receive an initial grant for expenses necessary to establish the organization; and

(ii) in lieu of payments under subsection (d) or (e), receive periodic sustaining grants to provide representation and other expenses pursuant to this section.

(3) Malpractice and negligence suits.—The Director of the Administrative Office of the United States Courts shall, to the extent the Director considers appropriate, provide representation for and hold harmless, or provide liability insurance for, any person who is an officer or employee of a Federal Public Defender Organization established under this subsection, or a Community Defender Organization established under this subsection which is receiving periodic sustaining grants, for money damages for injury, loss of liberty, loss of property, or personal injury or death arising from malpractice or negligence of any such officer or employee in furnishing representational services under this section while acting within the scope of that person's office or employment.

(h) Rules and reports.—Each district court and court of appeals of a circuit shall submit a report on the appointment of counsel within its jurisdiction to the Administrative Office of the United States Courts in such form and at such times as the Judicial Conference of the United States may specify. The Judicial Conference of the United States may, from time to time, issue rules and regulations governing the operation of plans formulated under this section.

(i) Appropriations.—There are authorized to be appropriated to the United States courts, out of any money in the Treasury not otherwise appropriated, sums necessary to carry out the provisions of this section, including funds for the continuing education and training of persons providing representational services under this section. When so specified in appropriation acts, such appropriations shall remain available until expended. Payments from such appropriations shall be made under the supervision of the Director of the Administrative Office of the United States Courts.

(j) Districts included.—As used in this section, the term "district court" means each district court of the United States created by chapter 5 of title 28, the District Court of the Virgin Islands, the District Court for the Northern Mariana Islands, and the District Court of Guam.

(k) Applicability in the District of Columbia.—The provisions of this section shall apply in the United States District Court for the District of Columbia and the United States Court of Appeals for the District of Columbia Circuit. The provisions of this section shall not apply to the Superior Court of the District of Columbia and the District of Columbia Court of Appeals.

(Added Pub.L. 88–455, § 2, Aug. 20, 1964, 78 Stat. 552, and amended Pub.L. 90–578, Title III, § 301(a)(1), Oct. 17, 1968, 82 Stat. 1115; Pub.L. 91–447, § 1, Oct. 14, 1970, 84 Stat. 916; Pub.L. 93–412, § 3, Sept. 3, 1974, 88 Stat. 1093; Pub.L. 97–164, Title II, § 206(a), (b), Apr. 2, 1982, 96 Stat. 53; Pub.L. 98–473, Title II, §§ 223(e), 405, 1901, Oct. 12, 1984, 98 Stat. 2028, 2067, 2185; Pub.L. 99–651, Title I, §§ 102, 103, Nov. 14, 1986, 100 Stat. 3642, 3645; Pub.L. 100–182, § 19, Dec. 7, 1987, 101 Stat. 1270; Pub.L. 100–690, Title VII, § 7101(f), Nov. 18, 1988, 102 Stat. 4416; Pub.L. 101–650, Title III, § 321, Dec. 1, 1990, 104 Stat. 5117; Pub.L. 104–132, Title IX, § 903(a), Apr. 24, 1996, 110 Stat. 1318; Pub.L. 105–119, Title III, § 308(a), Nov. 26, 1997, 111 Stat. 2493, 2494; Pub.L. 106–113, § 1000(a)(1) [Title III, § 308(a)], Nov. 29. 1999, 113 Stat. 1535, 1501A–37; Pub.L. 106–518, Title II, §§ 210, 211, Nov. 13, 2000, 114 Stat. 2415; Pub.L. 108–447, Div. B, Title III, § 304, Dec. 8, 2004, 118 Stat. 2894.)

[1] So in original. Probably should be "United States magistrate judge".

HISTORICAL AND STATUTORY NOTES

References in Text

The General Schedule, referred to in subsec. (d)(1), is set out under 5 U.S.C.A. § 5332.

The effective date of the Criminal Justice Act Revision of 1986, referred to in subsec. (d)(1), is, with qualifications, 120 days after the date of enactment of Pub.L. 99–651, which was approved Nov. 14, 1986. See section 105 of Pub.L. 99–651, set out as a note under this section.

Section 5305 of Title 5, referred to in subsec. (d)(1), was amended generally by Pub.L. 101–509, Title V, § 529 [Title I, § 101(a)(1)], Nov. 5, 1990, 104 Stat. 1427, 1436, and, as so amended, does not relate to adjustments in the rate of pay under the General Schedule. See 5 U.S.C.A. § 5303.

The enactment of this Act, referred to in subsec. (d)(4)(F), means the enactment of Pub.L.105–119, which was approved Nov. 26, 1997.

The provisions of title 5 governing appointments in the competitive service, referred to in subsec. (g)(2)(A), are classified to section 3301 et seq. of Title 5, Government Organization and Employees.

Title 28, United States Code, section 605, referred to in subsec. (g) (2) (A), is section 605 of Title 28, Judiciary and Judicial Procedure.

Chapter 5 of title 28, United States Code, referred to in subsec. (j), is chapter 5 of Title 28, Judiciary and Judicial Procedure.

Codifications

Subsection (d)(4)(F) refers to "The amendment made by paragraph (4)". Section 308 of Pub.L. 105–119 struck out former paragraph (4) of subsection (d) and inserted the new paragraph (4), of which subpar. (F) is part. Section 308 of Pub.L. 105–119 contained no other paragraph designated as paragraph (4).

Effective and Applicability Provisions

1999 Acts. Pub.L. 106–113, § 1000(a)(1) [Title III, § 308(b)], Nov. 29, 1999, 113 Stat. 1535, 1501A–37 provided that: "This section [amending subsec. (d)(4)(D) of this section] shall apply to all disclosures made under section 3006A(d) of title 18, United States Code, related to any criminal trial or appeal involving a sentence of death where the underlying alleged criminal conduct took place on or after April 19, 1995."

1996 Acts. Section 903(c) of Pub.L. 104–132 provided that: "The amendments made by this section [amending this section and section 848 of Title 21, Food and Drugs] apply to—

"(1) cases commenced on or after the date of the enactment of this Act [Apr. 24, 1996]; and

"(2) appellate proceedings, in which an appeal is perfected, on or after the date of the enactment of this Act [Apr. 24, 1996]."

1987 Acts. Section 26 of Pub.L. 100–182 provided that: "The amendments made by this Act [amending this section and sections 3551 note, 3553, 3561, 3563, 3564, 3583, 3663, 3672, 3742, and 4106 of this title, section 994 of Title 28, Judiciary and Judicial Procedure, and sections 504 and 1111 of Title 29, Labor, and enacting provisions set out as notes under sections 3551 and 3553 of this title, section 994 of Title 28, and rule 35, Federal Rules of Criminal Procedure] shall apply with respect to offenses committed after enactment of this Act [Dec. 7, 1987]."

1986 Acts. Section 105 of Pub.L. 99–651 provided that: "This title and the amendments made by this title [amending this section and section 1825 of Title 28, Judiciary and

Judicial Procedure and enacting provisions set out as a note under this section] shall take effect one hundred and twenty days after the date of enactment of this Act. [Nov. 14, 1986]. The maximum hourly rates provided in section 3006A(d)(1) of title 18, United States Code, as amended by section 102(a)(3)(A) of this Act [subsec. (d)(1) of this section] shall apply only to services performed on or after the effective date of this title. The maximum allowed for compensation for a case, as provided in section 3006A(d)(2) of title 18, United States Code, as amended by section 102(a)(3)(B) of this Act [subsec. (d)(2) of this section], shall apply only to compensation claims in which some portion of the claim is for services performed on or after the effective date of this title. The maximum compensation allowed pursuant to section 3006A(e) of title 18, United States Code [subsec. (e) of this section], as amended by subparagraphs (B) and (C) of section 102(a)(4) of this Act [subsec. (e)(2), (3) of this section], shall apply only to services obtained on or after the effective date of this title."

1984 Acts. Amendment by Pub.L. 98–473 effective on the first day of first calendar month beginning thirty-six months after Oct. 12, 1984, applicable only to offenses committed after taking effect of sections 211 to 239 of Pub.L. 98–473, and except as otherwise provided for therein, see section 235 of Pub.L. 98–473, as amended, set out as a note under section 3551 of this title.

1982 Acts. Amendment by Pub.L. 97–164 effective Oct. 1, 1982, see section 402 of Pub.L. 97–164, set out as an Effective Date of 1982 Amendment note under section 171 of Title 28, Judiciary and Judicial Procedure.

1974 Acts. Section 4 of Pub.L. 93–412 provided in part that the amendment of subsec. (*l*) by Pub.L. 93–412 shall take effect on Sept. 3, 1974.

1970 Acts. Section 3 of Pub.L. 91–447 provided that: "The amendments made by section 1 of this Act [amending this section] shall become effective one hundred and twenty days after the date of enactment [Oct. 14, 1970]."

1968 Acts. Amendment by Pub.L. 90–578 effective Oct. 17, 1968, except when a later effective date is applicable, which is the earlier of date when implementation of amendment by appointment of magistrates and assumption of office takes place or third anniversary of enactment of Pub.L. 90–578 on Oct. 17, 1968, see section 403 of Pub.L. 90–578, set out as an Effective Date of 1968 Amendment note under section 631 of Title 28, Judiciary and Judicial Procedure.

Change of Name

"United States magistrate judge" substituted for "United States magistrate" in text pursuant to section 321 of Pub.L. 101–650, set out as a note under 28 U.S.C.A. § 631.

Savings Provisions

Section 206(c) of Pub.L. 97–164 provided that: "The amendments made by subsection (a) of this section [amending subsec. (h)(2)(A) of this section] shall not affect the term of existing appointments."

Short Title

1986 Amendments. Section 101 of Pub.L. 99–651 provided that: "This title [amending this section and section 1825 of Title 28, Judiciary and Judicial Procedure and enacting provisions set out as a note under this section] may be referred to as the 'Criminal Justice Act Revision of 1986'."

1984 Amendments. Section 1901 of Pub.L. 98–473 provided that: "This chapter [amending this section] may be cited as the 'Criminal Justice Act Revision of 1984'."

1964 Acts. Section 1 of Pub.L. 88–455 provided: "That this Act [enacting this section and provisions set out as a note under this section] may be cited as the 'Criminal Justice Act of 1964.' "

Attorney Fees and Litigation Expenses to Defense

Pub.L. 105–119, Title VI, § 617, Nov. 26, 1997, 111 Stat. 2519, provided that: "During fiscal year 1998 and in any fiscal year thereafter, the court, in any criminal case (other than a case in which the defendant is represented by assigned counsel paid for by the public) pending on or after the date of the enactment of this Act [Nov. 26, 1997], may award to a prevailing party, other than the United States, a reasonable attorney's fee and other litigation expenses, where the court finds that the position of the United States was vexatious, frivolous, or in bad faith, unless the court finds that special circumstances make such an award unjust. Such awards shall be granted pursuant to the procedures and limitations (but not the burden of proof) provided for an award under section 2412 of title 28, United States Code. To determine whether or not to award fees and costs under this section, the court, for good cause shown, may receive evidence ex parte and in camera (which shall include the submission of classified evidence or evidence that reveals or might reveal the identity of an informant or undercover agent or matters occurring before a grand jury) and evidence or testimony so received shall be kept under seal. Fees and other expenses awarded under this provision to a party shall be paid by the agency over which the party prevails from any funds made available to the agency by appropriation. No new appropriations shall be made as a result of this provision."

Government Rates of Travel for Criminal Justice Act Attorneys and Experts

Pub.L. 102–572, Title VII, § 702, Oct. 29, 1992, 106 Stat. 4515, provided that: "The Administrator of General Services, in entering into contracts providing for special rates to be charged by Federal Government sources of supply, including common carriers and hotels (or other commercial providers of lodging) for official travel and accommodation of Federal Government employees, shall provide for charging the same rates for attorneys, experts, and other persons traveling primarily in connection with carrying out responsibilities under section 3006A of title 18, United States Code [this section], including community defender organizations established under subsection (g) of that section [subsec. (g) of this section]."

Study of Federal Defender Program; Report to Congress

Pub.L. 101–650, Title III, § 318, Dec. 1, 1990, 104 Stat. 5116, as amended Pub.L. 102–198, § 9, Dec. 9, 1991, 105 Stat. 1626, directed the Judicial Conference of the United States to conduct a study of the effectiveness of the Federal defender program and to transmit a report on the results of the study to the Committees on the Judiciary of the Senate and the House of Representatives no later than March 31, 1993, with the report to include recommendations for legislation, a proposed formula for compensation of Federal defender program counsel, and suggestions for procedural and operational changes by the courts.

Certification by Attorney General to Administrative Office of United States Courts of Payment of Obligated Expenses

Pub.L. 95–144, § 5(c), Oct. 28, 1977, 91 Stat. 1222, provided that: "The Attorney General shall certify to the Administrative Office of the United States Courts those expenses which it is obligated to pay on behalf of an indigent offender under section 3006A of title 18, United States Code [this section], and similar statutes."

Funds For Payment of Compensation and Reimbursement

Pub.L. 101–45, Title II, § 102, June 30, 1989, 103 Stat. 122, provided: "That compensation and reimbursement of attorneys and others as authorized under section 3006A of title 18, United States Code [this section], and section 1875(d) of title 28, United States Code [section 1875(d) of Title 28, Judiciary and Judicial Procedure], may hereinafter be paid from funds appropriated for "Defender Services" in the year in which payment is required."

Power and Function of a United States Commissioner

Section 2 of Pub.L. 91–447 provided that: "A United States commissioner [now magistrate] for a district may exercise any power, function, or duty authorized to be performed by a United States magistrate under the amendments made by section 1 of this Act [amending this section] if such commissioner had authority to perform such power, function, or duty prior to the enactment of such amendments."

Submission of Plans

Section 3 of Pub.L. 88–455 directed each district court to submit a plan in accord with section 3006A of this title and the rules of the Judicial Conference of the United States to the judicial council of the circuit within 6 months from Aug. 20, 1964, further directed each judicial council to approve and send to the Administrative Office of the United States courts a plan for each district in its circuit within 9 months from Aug. 20, 1964, and also directed each district court and court of appeals to place its approved plan in operation within 1 year from Aug. 20, 1964.

§ 3007. Motions—(Rule)

SEE FEDERAL RULES OF CRIMINAL PROCEDURE

Motions substituted for pleas in abatement and special pleas in bar, Rule 12.

Form and contents, Rule 47.

(June 25, 1948, c. 645, 62 Stat. 814.)

§ 3008. Service and filing of papers—(Rule)

SEE FEDERAL RULES OF CRIMINAL PROCEDURE

Requirement and manner of service; notice of orders; filing papers, Rule 49.

(June 25, 1948, c. 645, 62 Stat. 815.)

§ 3009. Records—(Rule)

SEE FEDERAL RULES OF CRIMINAL PROCEDURE

Keeping of records by district court clerks and magistrate judges, Rule 55.

(June 25, 1948, c. 645, 62 Stat. 815; Oct. 17, 1968, Pub.L. 90–578, Title III, § 301(a)(4), 82 Stat. 1115; Amended Dec. 1, 1990, Pub.L. 101–650, Title III, § 321, 104 Stat. 5117.)

HISTORICAL AND STATUTORY NOTES

Change of Name

Words "magistrate judge" substituted for "magistrate" in text pursuant to section 321 of Pub.L. 101–650, set out as a note under 28 U.S.C.A. § 631.

§ 3010. Exceptions unnecessary—(Rule)

SEE FEDERAL RULES OF CRIMINAL PROCEDURE

Objections substituted for exceptions, Rule 51.

(June 25, 1948, c. 645, 62 Stat. 815.)

§ 3011. Computation of time—(Rule)

SEE FEDERAL RULES OF CRIMINAL PROCEDURE

Computation: enlargement; expiration of term; motions and affidavits; service by mail, Rule 45.

(June 25, 1948, c. 645, 62 Stat. 815.)

[§ 3012. Repealed. Pub.L. 98–473, Title II, § 218(a)(2), Oct. 12, 1984, 98 Stat. 2027]

HISTORICAL AND STATUTORY NOTES

Prior to repeal this section read as follows:

"Orders respecting persons in custody

"Prisoners or persons in custody shall be brought into court or returned on order of the Court or of the United States Attorney, for which no fee shall be charged and no writ required."

Effective Date of Repeal

Repeal by Pub.L. 98–473 effective on the first day of first calendar month beginning thirty-six months after Oct. 12, 1984, applicable only to offenses committed after taking effect of sections 211 to 239 of Pub.L. 98–473, and except as otherwise provided for therein, see section 235 of Pub.L. 98–473, as amended, set out as a note under section 3551 of this title.

§ 3013. Special assessment on convicted persons

(a) The court shall assess on any person convicted of an offense against the United States—

(1) in the case of an infraction or a misdemeanor—

(A) if the defendant is an individual—

(i) the amount of $5 in the case of an infraction or a class C misdemeanor;

(ii) the amount of $10 in the case of a class B misdemeanor; and

(iii) the amount of $25 in the case of a class A misdemeanor; and

(B) if the defendant is a person other than an individual—

(i) the amount of $25 in the case of an infraction or a class C misdemeanor;

(ii) the amount of $50 in the case of a class B misdemeanor; and

(iii) the amount of $125 in the case of a class A misdemeanor;

(2) in the case of a felony—

(A) the amount of $100 if the defendant is an individual; and

(B) the amount of $400 if the defendant is a person other than an individual.

(b) Such amount so assessed shall be collected in the manner that fines are collected in criminal cases.

(c) The obligation to pay an assessment ceases five years after the date of the judgment. This subsection shall apply to all assessments irrespective of the date of imposition.

(d) For the purposes of this section, an offense under section 13 of this title is an offense against the United States.

(Added Pub.L. 98–473, Title II, § 1405(a), Oct. 12, 1984, 98 Stat. 2174, and amended Pub.L. 100–185, § 3, Dec. 11, 1987, 101 Stat. 1279; Pub.L. 100–690, Title VII, §§ 7082(b), 7085, Nov. 18, 1988, 102 Stat. 4407, 4408; Pub.L. 101–647, Title XXXV, § 3569, Nov. 29, 1990, 104 Stat. 4928; Pub.L. 104–132, Title II, § 210, Apr. 24, 1996, 110 Stat. 1240; Pub.L. 104–294, Title VI, § 601(r)(4), Oct. 11, 1996, 110 Stat. 3502.)

HISTORICAL AND STATUTORY NOTES

Effective and Applicability Provisions

1996 Acts. Amendment by Pub.L. 104–132 to be effective, to the extent constitutionally permissible, for sentencing proceedings in cases in which the defendant is convicted on or after Apr. 24, 1996, see section 211 of Pub.L. 104–132, set out as a note under section 2248 of this title.

1984 Acts. Section effective 30 days after Oct. 12, 1984, see section 1409(a) of Pub.L. 98–473, set out as a note under section 10601 of Title 42, Public Health and Welfare.

CHAPTER 203—ARREST AND COMMITMENT

Sec.

Sec.

[1] So in original. Does not conform to section catchline.

[2] So in original. The words "Special Agents" probably should not be capitalized.

[3] So in original. Section was repealed without a corresponding change in the table of sections under this chapter.

§ 3041. Power of courts and magistrates

For any offense against the United States, the offender may, by any justice or judge of the United States, or by any United States magistrate judge, or by any chancellor, judge of a supreme or superior court, chief or first judge of the common pleas, mayor of a city, justice of the peace, or other magistrate, of any state where the offender may be found, and at the expense of the United States, be arrested and imprisoned or released as provided in chapter 207 of this title, as the case may be, for trial before such court of the United States as by law has cognizance of the offense. Copies of the process shall be returned as speedily as may be into the office of the clerk of such court, together with the recognizances of the witnesses for their appearances to testify in the case.

A United States judge or magistrate judge shall proceed under this section according to rules promulgated by the Supreme Court of the United States. Any state judge or magistrate acting hereunder may proceed according to the usual mode of procedure of his state but his acts and orders shall have no effect beyond determining, pursuant to the provisions of section 3142 of this title, whether to detain or conditionally release the prisoner prior to trial or to discharge him from arrest.

(June 25, 1948, c. 645, 62 Stat. 815; June 22, 1966, Pub.L. 89–465, § 5(a), 80 Stat. 217; Oct. 17, 1968, Pub.L. 90–578, Title III, § 301(a)(1), (3), 82 Stat. 1115; Oct. 12, 1984, Pub.L. 98–473, Title II, § 204(a), 98 Stat. 1985; Dec. 1, 1990, Pub.L. 101–650, Title III, § 321, 104 Stat. 5117.)

HISTORICAL AND STATUTORY NOTES

Change of Name

United States magistrate appointed under section 631 of Title 28, Judiciary and Judicial Procedure, to be known as United States magistrate judge after Dec. 1, 1990, with any reference to United States magistrate or magistrate in Title 28, in any other Federal statute, etc., deemed a reference to United States magistrate judge appointed under section 631 of Title 28, see section 321 of Pub.L. 101–650, set out as a note under section 631 of Title 28.

Effective and Applicability Provisions

1968 Acts. Amendment by Pub.L. 90–578 effective Oct. 17, 1968, except when a later effective date is applicable, which is the earlier of date when implementation of amendment by appointment of magistrates and assumption of office takes place or third anniversary of enactment of Pub.L. 90–578 on Oct. 17, 1968, see section 403 of Pub.L. 90–578, set out as an Effective Date of 1968 Amendment note under section 631 of Title 28, Judiciary and Judicial Procedure.

1966 Acts. Amendment by Pub.L. 89–465 effective 90 days after June 22, 1966, see section 6 of Pub.L. 89–465, set out as an Effective Date note under section 3146 of this title.

Change of Name

"United States magistrate judge" substituted for "United States magistrate" in text pursuant to section 321 of Pub.L. 101–650, set out as a note under 28 U.S.C.A. § 631.

Savings Provisions of Pub.L. 98–473, Title II, c. II

See section 235 of Pub.L. 98–473, Title II, c. II, Oct. 12, 1984, 98 Stat. 2031, set out as a note under section 3551 of this title.

§ 3042. Extraterritorial jurisdiction

Section 3041 of this title shall apply in any country where the United States exercises extraterritorial jurisdiction for the arrest and removal therefrom to the United States of any citizen or national of the United States who is a fugitive from justice charged with or convicted of the commission of any offense against the United States, and shall also apply throughout the United States for the arrest and removal therefrom to the jurisdiction of any officer or representative of the United States vested with judicial authority in any country in which the United States exercises extraterritorial jurisdiction, of any citizen or national of the United States who is a fugitive from justice charged with or convicted of the commission of any offense against the United States in any country where it exercises extraterritorial jurisdiction.

Such fugitive first mentioned may, by any officer or representative of the United States vested with judicial authority in any country in which the United States exercises extraterritorial jurisdiction and agreeably to the usual mode of process against offenders subject to such jurisdiction, be arrested and detained or conditionally released pursuant to section 3142 of this title, as the case may be, pending the issuance of a warrant for his removal, which warrant the principal officer or representative of the United States vested with judicial authority in the country where the fugitive shall be found shall seasonably issue, and the United States marshal or corresponding officer shall execute.

Such marshal or other officer, or the deputies of such marshal or officer, when engaged in executing such warrant without the jurisdiction of the court to which they are attached, shall have all the powers of a marshal of the United States so far as such powers are requisite for the prisoner's safekeeping and the execution of the warrant.

(June 25, 1948, c. 645, 62 Stat. 815; Oct. 12, 1984, Pub.L. 98–473, Title II, § 204(b), 98 Stat. 1985.)

[§ 3043. Repealed. Pub.L. 98–473, Title II, § 204(c), Oct. 12, 1984, 98 Stat. 1986]

HISTORICAL AND STATUTORY NOTES

Section, Act June 25, 1948, c. 645, § 1, 62 Stat. 816; Oct. 17, 1968, Pub.L. 90–578, Title III, § 301(a)(2), 82 Stat. 1115, related to authority of federal and State judges and magistrates [now magistrate judges] to hold to security of the peace and for good behavior. See section 3142 of this title.

§ 3044. Complaint—(Rule)

SEE FEDERAL RULES OF CRIMINAL PROCEDURE

Contents of complaint; oath, Rule 3.

(June 25, 1948, c. 645, 62 Stat. 816.)

§ 3045. Internal revenue violations

Warrants of arrest for violations of internal revenue laws may be issued by United States magistrate judges upon the complaint of a United States attorney, assistant United States attorney, collector, or deputy collector of internal revenue or revenue agent, or private citizen; but no such warrant of arrest shall be issued upon the complaint of a private citizen unless first approved in writing by a United States attorney.

(June 25, 1948, c. 645, 62 Stat. 816; Oct. 17, 1968, Pub.L. 90–578, Title III, § 301(a)(2), 82 Stat. 1115; Dec. 1, 1990, Pub.L. 101–650, Title III, § 321, 104 Stat. 5117.)

HISTORICAL AND STATUTORY NOTES

References in Text

The internal revenue laws, referred to in text, are classified generally to Title 26, Internal Revenue Code.

Change of Name

United States magistrate appointed under section 631 of Title 28, Judiciary and Judicial Procedure, to be known as United States magistrate judge after Dec. 1, 1990, with any reference to United States magistrate or magistrate in Title 28, in any other Federal statute, etc., deemed a reference to United States magistrate judge appointed under section 631 of Title 28, see section 321 of Pub.L. 101–650, set out as a note under section 631 of Title 28.

Effective and Applicability Provisions

1968 Amendments. Amendment by Pub.L. 90–578 effective Oct. 17, 1968, except when a later effective date is applicable, which is the earlier of date when implementation of amendment by appointment of magistrates and assumption of office takes place or third anniversary of enactment of Pub.L. 90–578 on Oct. 17, 1968, see section 403 of Pub.L. 90–578, set out as an Effective Date of 1968 Amendment note under section 631 of Title 28, Judiciary and Judicial Procedure.

Change of Name

"United States magistrate judges" substituted for "United States magistrates" in text pursuant to section 321 of Pub.L. 101–650, set out as a note under 28 U.S.C.A. § 631.

Abolition of Offices of Collector and Deputy Collector of Internal Revenue

The offices of Collector and Deputy Collector of Internal Revenue were abolished by Reorg. Plan No. 1 of 1952, § 1, eff. Mar. 14, 1952, 17 F.R. 2243, 66 Stat. 823, set out in Appendix 1 to Title 5, Government Organization and Employees, and the offices of "district commissioner of internal revenue", and so many other offices, with titles to be determined by the Secretary of the Treasury, were established by section 2(a) of the Plan.

§ 3046. Warrant or summons—(Rule)

SEE FEDERAL RULES OF CRIMINAL PROCEDURE

Issuance upon complaint, Rule 4.

Issuance upon indictment, Rule 9.

Summons on request of government; form; contents; service; return, Rules 4, 9.

(June 25, 1948, c. 645, 62 Stat. 816.)

§ 3047. Multiple warrants unnecessary

When two or more charges are made, or two or more indictments are found against any person, only one writ or warrant shall be necessary to commit him for trial. It shall be sufficient to state in the writ the name or general character of the offenses, or to refer to them only in general terms.

(June 25, 1948, c. 645, 62 Stat. 816.)

§ 3048. Commitment to another district; removal—(Rule)

SEE FEDERAL RULES OF CRIMINAL PROCEDURE

Arrest in nearby or distant districts; informative statement by judge or magistrate judge; hearing and removal; warrant; Rule 40.

(June 25, 1948, c. 645, 62 Stat. 817; Oct. 17, 1968, Pub.L. 90–578, Title III, § 301(a)(3), 82 Stat. 1115; Dec. 1, 1990, Pub.L. 101–650, Title III, § 321, 104 Stat. 5117.)

HISTORICAL AND STATUTORY NOTES

Change of Name

"Magistrate judge" substituted for "magistrate" in text pursuant to section 321 of Pub.L. 101–650, set out as a note under 28 U.S.C.A. § 631.

§ 3049. Warrant for removal

Only one writ or warrant is necessary to remove a prisoner from one district to another. One copy thereof may be delivered to the sheriff or jailer from whose custody the prisoner is taken, and another to the sheriff or jailer to whose custody he is committed, and the original writ, with the marshal's return thereon, shall be returned to the clerk of the district to which he is removed.

(June 25, 1948, c. 645, 62 Stat. 817.)

§ 3050. Bureau of Prisons employees' powers

An officer or employee of the Bureau of Prisons may—

(1) make arrests on or off of Bureau of Prisons property without warrant for violations of the following provisions regardless of where the violation may occur: sections 111 (assaulting officers), 751 (escape), and 752 (assisting escape) of title 18, United States Code, and section 1826(c) (escape) of title 28, United States Code;

(2) make arrests on Bureau of Prisons premises or reservation land of a penal, detention, or correctional facility without warrant for violations occurring thereon of the following provisions: sections 661 (theft), 1361 (depredation of property), 1363 (destruction of property), 1791 (contraband), 1792 (mutiny and riot), and 1793 (trespass) of title 18, United States Code; and

(3) arrest without warrant for any other offense described in title 18 or 21 of the United States Code, if committed on the premises or reservation of a penal or correctional facility of the Bureau of Prisons if necessary to safeguard security, good order, or government property;

if such officer or employee has reasonable grounds to believe that the arrested person is guilty of such offense, and if there is likelihood of such person's escaping before an arrest warrant can be obtained. If the arrested person is a fugitive from custody, such prisoner shall be returned to custody. Officers and employees of the said Bureau of Prisons may carry firearms under such rules and regulations as the Attorney General may prescribe.

(June 25, 1948, c. 645, 62 Stat. 817; Nov. 10, 1986, Pub.L. 99–646, § 65, 100 Stat. 3615.)

HISTORICAL AND STATUTORY NOTES

Transfer of Functions

All functions of all other officers of the Department of Justice and all functions of all agencies and employees of such Department were, with a few exceptions, transferred to the Attorney General, with power vested in him to authorize their performance or the performance of any of his functions by any of such officers, agencies, and employees, by Reorg. Plan No. 2 of 1950, §§ 1, 2, eff. May 24, 1950, 15 F.R. 3173, 64 Stat. 1261, set out in Appendix 1 to Title 5, Government Organization and Employees.

§ 3051. Powers of Special Agents[1] of Bureau of Alcohol, Tobacco, Firearms, and Explosives

(a) Special agents of the Bureau of Alcohol, Tobacco, Firearms, and Explosives, as well as any other investigator or officer charged by the Attorney General with the duty of enforcing any of the criminal, seizure, or forfeiture provisions of the laws of the United States, may carry firearms, serve warrants and subpoenas issued under the authority of the United States and make arrests without warrant for any offense against the United States committed in their presence, or for any felony cognizable under the laws of the United States if they have reasonable grounds to believe that the person to be arrested has committed or is committing such felony.

(b) Any special agent of the Bureau of Alcohol, Tobacco, Firearms, and Explosives may, in respect to the performance of his or her duties, make seizures of property subject to forfeiture to the United States.

(c)(1) Except as provided in paragraphs (2) and (3), and except to the extent that such provisions conflict with the provisions of section 983 of title 18, United States Code, insofar as section 983 applies, the provisions of the Customs laws relating to—

(A) the seizure, summary and judicial forfeiture, and condemnation of property;

(B) the disposition of such property;

(C) the remission or mitigation of such forfeiture; and

(D) the compromise of claims,

shall apply to seizures and forfeitures incurred, or alleged to have been incurred, under any applicable provision of law enforced or administered by the Bureau of Alcohol, Tobacco, Firearms, and Explosives.

(2) For purposes of paragraph (1), duties that are imposed upon a customs officer or any other person with respect to the seizure and forfeiture of property under the customs laws of the United States shall be performed with respect to seizures and forfeitures of property under this section by such officers, agents, or any other person as may be authorized or designated for that purpose by the Attorney General.

(3) Notwithstanding any other provision of law, the disposition of firearms forfeited by reason of a violation of any law of the United States shall be governed by the provisions of section 5872(b) of the Internal Revenue Code of 1986.

(Added Pub.L. 107–296, Title XI, § 1113, Nov. 25, 2002, 116 Stat. 2279.)

[1] So in original. The words "Special Agents" probably should not be capitalized.

HISTORICAL AND STATUTORY NOTES

References in Text

The customs laws, referred to in subsec. (c)(1), (2), are classified generally to Title 19.

Section 5872(b) of the Internal Revenue Code of 1986, referred to in subsec. (c)(3), is 26 U.S.C.A. § 5872(b).

Effective and Applicability Provisions

2002 Acts. This section effective 60 days after Nov. 25, 2002, see Pub.L. 107–296, § 4, set out as a note under 6 U.S.C.A. § 101.

Prior Provisions

Prior section 3051, Act June 25, 1948, c. 645, § 1, 62 Stat. 817, repealed Oct. 31, 1951, c. 655, § 56(f), 65 Stat. 729, related to powers of extradition agents. Substantially identical provisions are contained in section 3193 of this title.

Subsec. (*l*) of section 56 of Act Oct. 31, 1951, c. 655, 65 Stat. 730, provided that the repeal of the prior section 3051 should not affect any rights or liabilities existing hereunder on the effective date of the repeal (Oct. 31 1951).

§ 3052. Powers of Federal Bureau of Investigation

The Director, Associate Director, Assistant to the Director, Assistant Directors, inspectors, and agents of the Federal Bureau of Investigation of the Department of Justice may carry firearms, serve warrants and subpoenas issued under the authority of the United States and make arrests without warrant for any offense against the United States committed in their presence, or for any felony cognizable under the laws of the United States if they have reasonable grounds to believe that the person to be arrested has committed or is committing such felony.

(June 25, 1948, c. 645, 62 Stat. 817; Jan. 10, 1951, c. 1221, § 1, 64 Stat. 1239.)

HISTORICAL AND STATUTORY NOTES

Transfer of Functions

All functions of all other officers of the Department of Justice and all functions of all agencies and employees of such Department were, with a few exceptions, transferred to the Attorney General, with power vested in him to authorize their performance or the performance of any of his functions by any of such officers, agencies, and employees, by Reorg. Plan No. 2 of 1950, §§ 1, 2, eff. May 24, 1950, 15 F.R. 3173, 64 Stat. 1261, set out in Appendix 1 to Title 5, Government Organization and Employees.

§ 3053. Powers of marshals and deputies

United States marshals and their deputies may carry firearms and may make arrests without warrant for any offense against the United States committed in their presence, or for any felony cognizable under the laws of the United States if they have reasonable grounds to believe that the person to be arrested has committed or is committing such felony.

(June 25, 1948, c. 645, 62 Stat. 817.)

HISTORICAL AND STATUTORY NOTES

Transfer of Functions

All functions of all other officers of the Department of Justice and all functions of all agencies and employees of such Department were, with a few exceptions, transferred to the Attorney General, with power vested in him to authorize their performance or the performance of any of his functions by any of such officers, agencies, and employees, by Reorg. Plan No. 2 of 1950, §§ 1, 2, eff. May 24, 1950, 15 F.R. 3173, 64 Stat. 1261, set out in Appendix 1 to Title 5, Government Organization and Employees.

[§ 3054. Repealed. Pub.L. 97–79, § 9(b)(3), Nov. 16, 1981, 95 Stat. 1079]

HISTORICAL AND STATUTORY NOTES

Section, Acts June 25, 1948, c. 645, 62 Stat. 817; Dec. 5, 1969, Pub.L. 91–135, § 7(b), 83 Stat. 281, provided for an officer's power to act in enforcing sections 42, 43, and 44 of this title relating to animals and birds. See section 3375 of Title 16, Conservation.

§ 3055. Officers' powers to suppress Indian liquor traffic

The chief special officer for the suppression of the liquor traffic among Indians and duly authorized officers working under his supervision whose appointments are made or affirmed by the Commissioner of Indian Affairs or the Secretary of the Interior may execute all warrants of arrest and other lawful precepts issued under the authority of the United States and in the execution of his duty he may command all necessary assistance.

(June 25, 1948, c. 645, 62 Stat. 817.)

§ 3056. Powers, authorities, and duties of United States Secret Service

(a) Under the direction of the Secretary of Homeland Security, the United States Secret Service is authorized to protect the following persons:

(1) The President, the Vice President (or other officer next in the order of succession to the Office of President), the President-elect, and the Vice President-elect.

(2) The immediate families of those individuals listed in paragraph (1).

(3) Former Presidents and their spouses for their lifetimes, except that protection of a spouse shall terminate in the event of remarriage unless the former President did not serve as President prior to January 1, 1997, in which case, former Presidents and their spouses for a period of not more than ten years from the date a former President leaves office, except that—

(A) protection of a spouse shall terminate in the event of remarriage or the divorce from, or death of a former President; and

(B) should the death of a President occur while in office or within one year after leaving office, the spouse shall receive protection for one year from the time of such death:

Provided, That the Secretary of Homeland Security shall have the authority to direct the Secret Service to provide temporary protection for any of these individuals at any time if the Secretary of Homeland Security or designee determines that information or conditions warrant such protection.

(4) Children of a former President who are under 16 years of age for a period not to exceed ten years or upon the child becoming 16 years of age, whichever comes first.

(5) Visiting heads of foreign states or foreign governments.

(6) Other distinguished foreign visitors to the United States and official representatives of the United States performing special missions abroad when the President directs that such protection be provided.

(7) Major Presidential and Vice Presidential candidates and, within 120 days of the general Presidential election, the spouses of such candidates. As used in this paragraph, the term "major Presidential and Vice Presidential candidates" means those individuals identified as such by the Secretary of Homeland Security after consultation with an advisory committee consisting of the Speaker of the House of Representatives, the minority leader of the House of Representatives, the majority and minority leaders of the Senate, and one additional member selected by the other members of the

committee. The Committee shall not be subject to the Federal Advisory Committee Act (5 U.S.C. App. 2).

The protection authorized in paragraphs (2) through (7) may be declined.

(b) Under the direction of the Secretary of Homeland Security, the Secret Service is authorized to detect and arrest any person who violates—

(1) section 508, 509, 510, 871, or 879 of this title or, with respect to the Federal Deposit Insurance Corporation, Federal land banks, and Federal land bank associations, section 213, 216, 433, 493, 657, 709, 1006, 1007, 1011, 1013, 1014, 1907, or 1909 of this title;

(2) any of the laws of the United States relating to coins, obligations, and securities of the United States and of foreign governments; or

(3) any of the laws of the United States relating to electronic fund transfer frauds, access device frauds, false identification documents or devices, and any fraud or other criminal or unlawful activity in or against any federally insured financial institution; except that the authority conferred by this paragraph shall be exercised subject to the agreement of the Attorney General and the Secretary of Homeland Security and shall not affect the authority of any other Federal law enforcement agency with respect to those laws.

(c)(1) Under the direction of the Secretary of Homeland Security, officers and agents of the Secret Service are authorized to—

(A) execute warrants issued under the laws of the United States;

(B) carry firearms;

(C) make arrests without warrant for any offense against the United States committed in their presence, or for any felony cognizable under the laws of the United States if they have reasonable grounds to believe that the person to be arrested has committed or is committing such felony;

(D) offer and pay rewards for services and information leading to the apprehension of persons involved in the violation or potential violation of those provisions of law which the Secret Service is authorized to enforce;

(E) pay expenses for unforeseen emergencies of a confidential nature under the direction of the Secretary of Homeland Security and accounted for solely on the Secretary's certificate; and

(F) perform such other functions and duties as are authorized by law.

(2) Funds expended from appropriations available to the Secret Service for the purchase of counterfeits and subsequently recovered shall be reimbursed to the appropriations available to the Secret Service at the time of the reimbursement.

(d) Whoever knowingly and willfully obstructs, resists, or interferes with a Federal law enforcement agent engaged in the performance of the protective functions authorized by this section or by section 1752 of this title shall be fined not more than $1,000 or imprisoned not more than one year, or both.

(e)(1) When directed by the President, the United States Secret Service is authorized to participate, under the direction of the Secretary of Homeland Security, in the planning, coordination, and implementation of security operations at special events of national significance, as determined by the President.

(2) At the end of each fiscal year, the President through such agency or office as the President may designate, shall report to the Congress—

(A) what events, if any, were designated special events of national significance for security purposes under paragraph (1); and

(B) the criteria and information used in making each designation.

(f) Under the direction of the Secretary of Homeland Security, the Secret Service is authorized, at the request of any State or local law enforcement agency, or at the request of the National Center for Missing and Exploited Children, to provide forensic and investigative assistance in support of any investigation involving missing or exploited children.

(g) The United States Secret Service shall be maintained as a distinct entity within the Department of Homeland Security and shall not be merged with any other Department function. No personnel and operational elements of the United States Secret Service shall report to an individual other than the Director of the United States Secret Service, who shall report directly to the Secretary of Homeland Security without being required to report through any other official of the Department.

(June 25, 1948, c. 645, 62 Stat. 818; July 16, 1951, c. 226, § 4, 65 Stat. 122; Aug. 31, 1954, c. 1143, § 2, 68 Stat. 999; Aug. 18, 1959, Pub.L. 86–168, Title I, § 104(h), 73 Stat. 387; Oct. 10, 1962, Pub.L. 87–791, 76 Stat. 809; Oct. 15, 1962, Pub.L. 87–829, § 3, 76 Stat. 956; Sept. 15, 1965, Pub.L. 89–186, 79 Stat. 791; Sept. 29, 1965, Pub.L. 89–218, 79 Stat. 890; Oct. 21, 1968, Pub.L. 90–608, c. XI, § 1101, 82 Stat. 1198; Jan. 2, 1971, Pub.L. 91–644, Title V, § 19, 84 Stat. 1892; Jan. 5, 1971, Pub.L. 91–651, § 4, 84 Stat. 1941; July 12, 1974, Pub.L. 93–346, § 8, as added Dec. 27, 1974, Pub.L. 93–552, Title VI, § 609(a), 88 Stat. 1765; Sept. 11, 1976, Pub.L. 94–408, § 2, 90 Stat. 1239; Oct. 12, 1982, Pub.L. 97–297, § 3, 96 Stat. 1318; Oct. 14, 1982, Pub.L. 97–308, § 2, 96 Stat. 1452; Nov. 14, 1983, Pub.L. 98–151, § 115(b), 97 Stat. 977; Oct. 30, 1984, Pub.L. 98–587, § 1(a), 98 Stat. 3110; Sept. 30, 1994, Pub.L. 103–329, Title V, § 530, 108 Stat. 2412; Oct. 11, 1996, Pub.L. 104–294, Title VI, § 605(i), 110 Stat. 3510; Dec. 19, 2000, Pub.L. 106–544, § 3, 114 Stat. 2716; Oct. 26, 2001, Pub.L.

107–56, Title V, § 506(b), 115 Stat. 367; Nov. 25, 2002, Pub.L. 107–296, Title XVII, § 1703(a)(1), 116 Stat. 2313; Apr. 30, 2003, Pub.L. 108–21, Title III, § 322, 117 Stat. 665; Mar. 9, 2006, Pub.L. 109–177, Title VI, §§ 604, 607, 608(a), 120 Stat. 253, 256.)

HISTORICAL AND STATUTORY NOTES

References in Text

The Federal Advisory Committee Act, referred to in subsec. (a)(7), is Pub.L. 92–463, Oct. 6, 1972, 86 Stat. 770, as amended, also known as "FACA", which is classified principally to 5 U.S.C.A. App. 2. See Tables for complete classification.

Section 216 of this title, referred to in subsec. (b)(1), was repealed by Pub.L. 98–473, Title II, § 1107(b), Oct. 12, 1984, 98 Stat. 2146.

Effective and Applicability Provisions

2002 Acts. Amendment by section 1703(a) of Pub.L. 107–296 effective on the date of transfer of the United States Secret Service to the Department of Homeland Security, see section 1703(b) of Pub.L. 107–296, set out as a note under 3 U.S.C.A. § 202.

1974 Acts. Amendment by Pub.L. 93–552 effective July 12, 1974, see section 609(b) of Pub.L. 93–552, set out as an Effective Date of 1974 Amendment note under section 202 of Title 3, The President.

1959 Acts. Amendment by Pub.L. 86–168 effective Dec. 31, 1959, see section 104(k) of Pub.L. 86–168.

Transfer of Functions

For transfer of the functions, personnel, assets, and obligations of the United States Secret Service, including the functions of the Secretary of the Treasury relating thereto, to the Secretary of Homeland Security, and for treatment of related references, see 6 U.S.C.A. §§ 381, 551(d), 552(d) and 557, and the Department of Homeland Security Reorganization Plan of November 25, 2002, as modified, set out as a note under 6 U.S.C.A. § 542.

Funds for Protection; Reimbursement for Protection of Undesignated Persons

Pub.L. 109–295, Title V, § 517(b), Oct. 4, 2006, 120 Stat. 1380, provided that: "Beginning in fiscal year 2008, none of the funds appropriated by this or any other Act to the United States Secret Service shall be made available for the protection of a person, other than persons granted protection under section 3056(a) of title 18, United States Code [subsec. (a) of this section], and the Secretary of Homeland Security: *Provided*, That the Director of the United States Secret Service may enter into an agreement to perform such protection on a fully reimbursable basis for protectees not designated under section 3056(a) of title 18, United States Code."

Secret Service Training

Pub.L. 108–90, Title II, Oct. 1, 2003, 117 Stat. 1145, provided in part: "That in fiscal year 2004 and thereafter, subject to the reimbursement of actual costs to this account, funds appropriated in this account [United States Secret Service; Salaries and Expenses] shall be available, at the discretion of the Director, for the following: training United States Postal Service law enforcement personnel and Postal police officers, training Federal law enforcement officers, training State and local government law enforcement officers on a space-available basis, and training private sector security officials on a space-available basis".

Expansion of National Electronic Crime Task Force Initiative

Pub.L. 107–56, Title I, § 105, Oct. 26, 2001, 115 Stat. 277, as amended Pub.L. 109–177, Title VI, § 608(b), Mar. 9, 2006, 120 Stat. 256, provided that: "The Director of the United States Secret Service shall take appropriate actions to develop a national network of electronic crime task forces, based on the New York Electronic Crimes Task Force model, throughout the United States, for the purpose of preventing, detecting, and investigating various forms of electronic crimes, including potential terrorist attacks against critical infrastructure and financial payment systems. The electronic crimes task forces shall not be subject to the Federal Advisory Committee Act (5 U.S.C. App. 2) [Pub.L. 92–463, Oct. 6, 1972, 86 Stat. 770, as amended, also known as "FACA", which is classified principally to 5 U.S.C.A. App. 2; see Tables for complete classification]."

National Threat Assessment Center.

Pub.L. 106–544, § 4, Dec. 19, 2000, 114 Stat. 2716, provided that:

"**(a) Establishment.**—The United States Secret Service (hereafter in this section referred to as the 'Service'), at the direction of the Secretary of the Treasury, may establish the National Threat Assessment Center (hereafter in this section referred to as the 'Center') as a unit within the Service.

"**(b) Functions.**—The Service may provide the following to Federal, State, and local law enforcement agencies through the Center:

"(1) Training in the area of threat assessment.

"(2) Consultation on complex threat assessment cases or plans.

"(3) Research on threat assessment and the prevention of targeted violence.

"(4) Facilitation of information sharing among all such agencies with protective or public safety responsibilities.

"(5) Programs to promote the standardization of Federal, State, and local threat assessments and investigations involving threats.

"(6) Any other activities the Secretary determines are necessary to implement a comprehensive threat assessment capability.

"**(c) Report.**—Not later than 1 year after the date of the enactment of this Act [Dec. 19, 2000], the Service shall submit a report to the Committees on the Judiciary of the Senate and the House of Representatives detailing the manner in which the Center will operate."

Telecommunications Support to United States Secret Service by White House Communications Agency

Pub.L. 104–208, Div. A, Title I, § 101(b) [Title VIII, § 8100], Sept. 30, 1996, 110 Stat. 3009–108, provided that: "Beginning in fiscal year 1997 and thereafter, and notwithstanding any other provision of law, fixed and mobile telecommunications support shall be provided by the White House Communications Agency (WHCA) to the United States Secret Service (USSS), without reimbursement, in connection with the Secret Service's duties directly related to the protection of the President or the Vice President or other officer immediately next in order of succession to the office of the President at the White House Security Complex in the Washington, D.C. Metropolitan Area and Camp David, Maryland. For these purposes, the White House Security Complex includes the White House, the White House grounds, the Old Executive Office Building, the New Executive Office Building, the Blair House, the Treasury Building, and the Vice President's Residence at the Naval Observatory."

[Any reference in a law, map, regulation, document, paper, or other record of the United States to the building referred to as the Old Executive Office Building shall be deemed to be a reference to the Dwight D. Eisenhower Executive Office Building, see section 2 of Pub.L. 106–92, set out as a note under section 101 of Title 3.]

Off-Set of Costs of Protecting Former Presidents and Spouses

Pub.L. 104–208, Div. A, Title I, § 101(f) [Title V, § 509], Sept. 30, 1996, 110 Stat. 3009–345, provided that: "The United States Secret Service may, during the fiscal year ending September 30, 1997, and hereafter, accept donations of money to off-set costs incurred while protecting former Presidents and spouses of former Presidents when the former President or spouse travels for the purpose of making an appearance or speech for a payment of money or any thing of value."

Similar provisions were contained in the following prior appropriations Acts:

Pub.L. 104–52, Title V, § 509, Nov. 19, 1995, 109 Stat. 492.

Pub.L. 103–329, Title V, § 514, Sept. 30, 1994, 108 Stat. 2410.

Pub.L. 103–123, Title V, § 515, Oct. 28, 1993, 107 Stat. 1253.

Former Vice President or Spouse; Protection

Pub.L. 103–1, Jan. 15, 1993, 107 Stat. 3, provided: "That—

"(1) the United States Secret Service, in addition to other duties now provided by law, is authorized to furnish protection to—

"(A) the person occupying the Office of Vice President of the United States immediately preceding January 20, 1993, or

"(B) his spouse,

if the President determines that such person may thereafter be in significant danger; and

"(2) protection of any such person, pursuant to the authority provided in paragraph (1), shall continue only for such period as the President determines, except that such protection shall not continue beyond July 20, 1993, unless otherwise permitted by law."

Pub.L. 96–503, Dec. 5, 1980, 94 Stat. 2740, provided: "That the United States Secret Service, in addition to other duties now provided by law, is authorized to furnish protection to (a) the person occupying the Office of Vice President of the United States immediately preceding January 20, 1981, or (b) his spouse, if the President determines that such person may thereafter be in significant danger: *Provided, however,* That protection of any such person shall continue only for such period as the President determines and shall not continue beyond July 20, 1981, unless otherwise permitted by law."

Personal Protection of Major Presidential or Vice-Presidential Candidates and Spouses

Pub.L. 90–331, June 6, 1968, 82 Stat. 170, as amended Pub.L. 94–408, § 1, Sept. 11, 1976, 90 Stat. 1239; Pub.L. 94–524, § 11, Oct. 17, 1976, 90 Stat. 2477; Pub.L. 96–329, Aug. 11, 1980, 94 Stat. 1029, which authorized the Secret Service to protect major presidential or vice-presidential candidates and their spouses, was repealed by Pub.L. 98–587, § 2, Oct. 30, 1984, 98 Stat. 3111.

Presidential Protection Assistance Act of 1976

Pub.L. 94–524, Oct. 17, 1976, 90 Stat. 2475, as amended Pub.L. 99–190, § 143, Dec. 19, 1985, 99 Stat. 1324; Pub.L. 101–136, Title V, § 527, Nov. 3, 1989, 103 Stat. 815; Pub.L. 101–509, Title V, § 531(a), Nov. 5, 1990, 104 Stat. 1469; Pub.L. 102–141, Title V, § 533, Oct. 28, 1991, 105 Stat. 867; Pub.L. 104–52, Title V, § 529, Nov. 19, 1995, 109 Stat. 496; Pub.L. 104–316, Title I, § 109(a), Oct. 19, 1996, 110 Stat. 3832, provided: "That this Act may be cited as the 'Presidential Protection Assistance Act of 1976'."

"**Sec. 2.** As used in this Act the term—

"(1) 'Secret Service' means the United States Secret Service, the Department of the Treasury;

"(2) 'Director' means the Director of the Secret Service;

"(3) 'protectee' means any person eligible to receive the protection authorized by section 3056 of title 18, United States Code [this section], or Public Law 90–331 (82 Stat. 170) [set out as a note under this section];

"(4) 'Executive departments' has the same meaning as provided in section 101 of title 5, United States Code;

"(5) 'Executive agencies' has the same meaning as provided in section 105 of title 5, United States Code;

"(6) 'Coast Guard' means the United States Coast Guard, Department of Transportation or such other Executive department or Executive agency to which the United States Coast Guard may subsequently be transferred;

"(7) 'duties' means all responsibilities of an Executive department or Executive agency relating to the protection of any protectee; and

"(8) 'non–Governmental property' means any property owned, leased, occupied, or otherwise utilized by a protectee which is not owned or controlled by the Government of the United States of America.

"**Sec. 3.** (a) Each protectee may designate one non-governmental property to be fully secured by the Secret Service on a permanent basis.

"(b) A protectee may thereafter designate a different non–Governmental property in lieu of the non–Governmental property previously designated under subsection (a) (hereinafter in this Act referred to as the 'previously designated property') as the one non–Governmental property to be fully secured by the Secret Service on a permanent basis under subsection (a). Thereafter, any expenditures by the Secret Service to maintain a permanent guard detail or for permanent facilities, equipment, and services to secure the non–Governmental property previously designated under subsection (a) shall be subject to the limitations imposed under section 4.

"(c) For the purposes of this section, where two or more protectees share the same domicile, such protectees shall be deemed a single protectee.

"Sec. 4. Expenditures by the Secret Service for maintaining a permanent guard detail and for permanent facilities, equipment, and services to secure any non–Governmental property in addition to the one non–Governmental property designated by each protectee under subsection 3(a) or 3(b) may not exceed a cumulative total of $200,000 at each such additional non–Governmental property, unless expenditures in excess of that amount are specifically approved by resolutions adopted by the Committees on Appropriations of the House and Senate, respectively.

"Sec. 5. (a) All improvements and other items acquired by the Federal Government and used for the purpose of securing any non–Governmental property in the performance of the duties of the Secret Service shall be the property of the United States.

"(b) Upon termination of Secret Service protection at any non-Governmental property all such improvements and other items shall be removed from the non-Governmental property unless the Director determines that it would not be economically feasible to do so; except that such improvements and other items shall be removed and the non-Governmental property shall be restored to its original state if the owner of such property at the time of termination requests the removal of such improvements or other items. If any such improvements or other items are not removed, the owner of the non-Governmental property at the time of termination shall compensate the United States for the original cost of such improvements or other items or for the amount by which they have increased the fair market value of the property, as determined by the Director, as of the date of termination, whichever is less.

"(c) In the event that any non–Governmental property becomes a previously designated property and Secret Service protection at that property has not been terminated, all such improvements and other items which the Director determines are not necessary to secure the previously designated property within the limitations imposed under section 4 shall be removed or compensated for in accordance with the procedures set forth under Subsection (b) of this section.

"Sec. 6. Executive departments and Executive agencies shall assist the Secret Service in the performance of its duties by providing services, equipment, and facilities on a temporary and reimbursable basis when requested by the Director and on a permanent and reimbursable basis upon advance written request of the Director; except that the Department of Defense and the Coast Guard shall provide such assistance on a temporary basis without reimbursement when assisting the Secret Service in its duties directly related to the protection of the President or the Vice President or other officer immediately next in order of succession to the office of the President.

"Sec. 7. No services, equipment, or facilities may be ordered, purchased, leased, or otherwise procured for the purposes of carrying out the duties of the Secret Service by persons other than officers or employees of the Federal Government duly authorized by the Director to make such orders, purchases, leases, or procurements.

"Sec. 8. No funds may be expended or obligated for the purpose of carrying out the purposes of section 3056 of title 18, United States Code, and section 1 of Public Law 90–331 [set out as a note under this section] other than funds specifically appropriated to the Secret Service for those purposes with the exception of—

"(1) expenditures made by the Department of Defense or the Coast Guard from funds appropriated to the Department of Defense or the Coast Guard in providing assistance on a temporary basis to the Secret Service in the performance of its duties directly related to the protection of the President or the Vice President or other officer next in order of succession to the office of the President; and

"(2) expenditures made by Executive departments and agencies, in providing assistance at the request of the Secret Service in the performance of its duties, and which will be reimbursed by the Secret Service under section 6 of this Act.

"Sec. 9. The Director, the Secretary of Defense, and the Commandant of the Coast Guard shall each transmit a detailed semi-annual report of expenditures made pursuant to this Act during the six-month period immediately preceding such report by the Secret Service, the Department of Defense, and the Coast Guard, respectively, to the Committees on Appropriations, Committees on the Judiciary, and Committees on Government Operations of the House of Representatives and the Senate, respectively, on March 31 and September 30, of each year.

"Sec. 10. Expenditures made pursuant to this Act shall be subject to audit by the Comptroller General and his authorized representatives, who shall have access to all records relating to such expenditures. The Comptroller General shall transmit a report of the results of any such audit to the Committees on Appropriations, Committees on the Judiciary, and Committees on Government Operations of the House of Representatives and the Senate, respectively." [Senate Committee redesignated Senate Committee on Governmental Affairs, eff. Feb. 11, 1977]

"Sec. 11. Section 2 of Public Law 90–331 (82 Stat. 170) [formerly set out as a note under this section] is repealed.

"Sec. 12. In carrying out the protection of the President of the United States, pursuant to section 3056(a) of title 18 [subsec. (a) of this section], at the one non-governmental property designated by the President of the United States to be fully secured by the United States Secret Service on a permanent basis, as provided in section 3(a) of Public Law 94–524 [section 3(a) of this note], or at an airport facility used for travel en route to or from such property the Secretary of the Treasury may utilize, with their consent, the law enforcement services, personnel, equipment, and facilities of the affected State and local governments. Further, the Secretary of the Treasury is authorized to reimburse such State and local governments for the utilization of such services, personnel, equipment, and facilities. All claims for such reimbursement by the affected governments will be submitted to the Secretary of the Treasury on a quarterly basis. Expenditures for this reimbursement are authorized not to exceed $300,000 at the one nongovernmental property, and $70,000 at the airport facility, in any one fiscal year: *Provided*, That the designated site is located in a municipality or political subdivision of any State where the permanent resident population is 7,000 or less and where the absence of such Federal assistance would place an undue economic burden on the affected State and local governments: *Provided further*, That the airport facility is wholly or partially located in a municipality or political subdivision of any State where the permanent resident population is 7,000 or less, the airport is located within 25 nautical miles of the designated nongovernmental property, and where the absence of such Federal assistance would place an undue economic burden on the affected State and local governments."

[For transfer of the functions, personnel, assets, and obligations of the United States Secret Service, including the functions of the Secretary of the Treasury relating thereto, to the Secretary of Homeland Security, and for treatment of related references, see 6 U.S.C.A. §§ 381, 551(d), 552(d) and 557, and the Department of Homeland Security Reorganization Plan of November 25, 2002, as modified, set out as a note under 6 U.S.C.A. § 542.]

[Amendment of section 5(b) of Pub.L. 94–524 by Pub.L. 104–316 effective Oct. 19, 1996, see section 101(e) of Pub.L. 104–316, set out as a note under section 130c of Title 2, The Congress.]

[Any reference in any provision of law enacted before Jan. 4, 1995, to the Committee on Government Operations of the House of Representatives treated as referring to the Committee on Government Reform and Oversight of the House of Representatives, except that any reference in any provision of law enacted before Jan. 4, 1995, to the Committee on Government Operations of the House of Representatives treated as referring to the Committee on the Budget of the House of Representatives in the case of a provision of law relating to the establishment, extension, and enforcement of special controls over the Federal budget, see section 1(a)(6) and (c)(2) of Pub.L. 104–14, set out as a note preceding section 21 of Title 2, The Congress.]

Secret Service Protection of Former Federal Officials

Pub.L. 95–1, Jan. 19, 1977, 91 Stat. 3, provided: "That the United States Secret Service, in addition to other duties now provided by law, is authorized to furnish protection to a person who (a) as a Federal Government official has been receiving protection by the United States Secret Service for a period immediately preceding January 20, 1977, or (b) as a member of such official's immediate family has been receiving protection by either the United States Secret Service or other security personnel of the official's department immediately preceding January 20, 1977, if the President determines that such person may thereafter be in significant danger: *Provided, however,* That protection of any such person shall continue only for such period as the President determines and shall not continue beyond July 20, 1977, unless otherwise permitted by law."

Extension of Protection of President's Widow and Children

Pub.L. 90–145, Nov. 17, 1967, 81 Stat. 466, extended until Mar. 1, 1969, the authority vested in the United States Secret Service by section 3056 of this title, as it existed prior to the amendment in 1968 by Pub.L. 90–608, to protect the widow and minor children of a former President who were receiving such protection on Nov. 17, 1967.

Applicability of Reorg. Plan No. 26 of 1950

Section 5 of Pub.L. 91–651 provided that: "Section 3056 of title 18, United States Code, as amended by section 4 of this Act, shall be subject to Reorganization Plan Numbered 26 of 1950 (64 Stat. 1280) [set out in Appendix 1 to Title 5, Government Organization and Employees]."

§ 3056A. Powers, authorities, and duties of United States Secret Service Uniformed Division

(a) There is hereby created and established a permanent police force, to be known as the "United States Secret Service Uniformed Division". Subject to the supervision of the Secretary of Homeland Security, the United States Secret Service Uniformed Division shall perform such duties as the Director, United States Secret Service, may prescribe in connection with the protection of the following:

(1) The White House in the District of Columbia.

(2) Any building in which Presidential offices are located.

(3) The Treasury Building and grounds.

(4) The President, the Vice President (or other officer next in the order of succession to the Office of President), the President-elect, the Vice President-elect, and their immediate families.

(5) Foreign diplomatic missions located in the metropolitan area of the District of Columbia.

(6) The temporary official residence of the Vice President and grounds in the District of Columbia.

(7) Foreign diplomatic missions located in metropolitan areas (other than the District of Columbia) in the United States where there are located twenty or more such missions headed by full-time officers, except that such protection shall be provided only—

(A) on the basis of extraordinary protective need;

(B) upon request of an affected metropolitan area; and

(C) when the extraordinary protective need arises at or in association with a visit to—

(i) a permanent mission to, or an observer mission invited to participate in the work of, an international organization of which the United States is a member; or

(ii) an international organization of which the United States is a member;

except that such protection may also be provided for motorcades and at other places associated with any such visit and may be extended at places of temporary domicile in connection with any such visit.

(8) Foreign consular and diplomatic missions located in such areas in the United States, its territories and possessions, as the President, on a case-by-case basis, may direct.

(9) Visits of foreign government officials to metropolitan areas (other than the District of Columbia) where there are located twenty or more consular or diplomatic missions staffed by accredited personnel, including protection for motorcades and at other places associated with such visits when such officials are in the United States to conduct official business with the United States Government.

(10) Former Presidents and their spouses, as provided in section 3056(a)(3) of title 18.

(11) An event designated under section 3056(e) of title 18 as a special event of national significance.

(12) Major Presidential and Vice Presidential candidates and, within 120 days of the general Presidential election, the spouses of such candidates, as provided in section 3056(a)(7) of title 18.

(13) Visiting heads of foreign states or foreign governments.

(b)(1) Under the direction of the Director of the Secret Service, members of the United States Secret Service Uniformed Division are authorized to—

(A) carry firearms;

(B) make arrests without warrant for any offense against the United States committed in their presence, or for any felony cognizable under the laws of the United States if they have reasonable grounds to believe that the person to be arrested has committed or is committing such felony; and

(C) perform such other functions and duties as are authorized by law.

(2) Members of the United States Secret Service Uniformed Division shall possess privileges and powers similar to those of the members of the Metropolitan Police of the District of Columbia.

(c) Members of the United States Secret Service Uniformed Division shall be furnished with uniforms and other necessary equipment.

(d) In carrying out the functions pursuant to paragraphs (7) and (9) of subsection (a), the Secretary of Homeland Security may utilize, with their consent, on a reimbursable basis, the services, personnel, equipment, and facilities of State and local governments, and is authorized to reimburse such State and local governments for the utilization of such services, personnel, equipment, and facilities. The Secretary of Homeland Security may carry out the functions pursuant to paragraphs (7) and (9) of subsection (a) by contract. The authority of this subsection may be transferred by the President to the Secretary of State. In carrying out any duty under paragraphs (7) and (9) of subsection (a), the Secretary of State is authorized to utilize any authority available to the Secretary under title II of the State Department Basic Authorities Act of 1956.

(Added Pub.L. 109–177, Title VI, § 605(a), Mar. 9, 2006, 120 Stat. 253.)

HISTORICAL AND STATUTORY NOTES

References in Text

Title II of the State Department Basic Authorities Act of 1956, referred to in subsec. (d), is Act Aug. 1, 1956, c. 841, Title II, as added Aug. 24, 1982, Pub.L. 97–241, title II, § 202(b), 96 Stat. 283, known as the Foreign Missions Act, which is classified principally to chapter 53 of Title 22, Foreign Relations and Intercourse, 22 U.S.C.A. § 4301 et seq. For complete classification of this Act to the Code, see Short Title of 1982 Acts note set out under 22 U.S.C.A. § 4301 and Tables

Savings Provisions

Pub.L. 109–177, Title VI, § 606, Mar. 9, 2006, 120 Stat. 256, provided that:

"(a) This title [Pub.L. 109–177, Title VI [§§ 601 to 608], Mar. 9, 2006, 120 Stat. 251, enacting 18 U.S.C.A. § 3056A, amending 5 U.S.C.A. App. 3 §§ 8D and 8I, 12 U.S.C.A. § 3414, 18 U.S.C.A. §§ 1028, 1752, and 3056, 22 U.S.C.A. §§ 2709, 4304, and 4314, and 31 U.S.C.A. § 1537, repealing Chapter 3 of Title 3 (3 U.S.C.A. § 201 et seq.), and amending provisions set out as a note under 18 U.S.C.A. § 3056] does not affect the retirement benefits of current employees or annuitants that existed on the day before the effective date of this Act [Mar. 9, 2006].

"(b) This title [Pub.L. 109–177, Title VI [§§ 601 to 608], Mar. 9, 2006, 120 Stat. 251, enacting 18 U.S.C.A. § 3056A, amending 5 U.S.C.A. App. 3 §§ 8D and 8I, 12 U.S.C.A. § 3414, 18 U.S.C.A. §§ 1028, 1752, and 3056, 22 U.S.C.A. §§ 2709, 4304, and 4314, and 31 U.S.C.A. § 1537, repealing Chapter 3 of Title 3 (3 U.S.C.A. § 201 et seq.), and amending provisions set out as a note under 18 U.S.C.A. § 3056] does not affect any Executive order transferring to the Secretary of State the authority of section 208 of title 3 (now section 3056A(d) of title 18) in effect on the day before the effective date of this Act [Mar. 9, 2006]."

§ 3057. Bankruptcy investigations

(a) Any judge, receiver, or trustee having reasonable grounds for believing that any violation under chapter 9 of this title or other laws of the United States relating to insolvent debtors, receiverships or reorganization plans has been committed, or that an investigation should be had in connection therewith, shall report to the appropriate United States attorney all the facts and circumstances of the case, the names of the witnesses and the offense or offenses believed to have been committed. Where one of such officers has made such report, the others need not do so.

(b) The United States attorney thereupon shall inquire into the facts and report thereon to the judge, and if it appears probable that any such offense has been committed, shall without delay, present the matter to the grand jury, unless upon inquiry and examination he decides that the ends of public justice do not require investigation or prosecution, in which case he shall report the facts to the Attorney General for his direction.

(June 25, 1948, c. 645, 62 Stat. 818; May 24, 1949, c. 139, § 48, 63 Stat. 96; Nov. 6, 1978, Pub.L. 95–598, Title III, § 314(i), 92 Stat. 2677.)

HISTORICAL AND STATUTORY NOTES

Effective and Applicability Provisions

1978 Acts. Amendment by Pub.L. 95–598 effective Oct. 1, 1979, see section 402(a) of Pub.L. 95–598, set out as an Effective Dates note preceding section 101 of Title 11, Bankruptcy.

Savings Provisions of Pub.L. 95–598

Amendment by section 314 of Pub.L. 95–598 not to affect the application of chapter 9 [§ 151 et seq.], chapter 96 [§ 1961 et seq.], or section 2516, 3057, or 3284 of this title to any act of any person (1) committed before Oct. 1, 1979, or (2) committed after Oct. 1, 1979, in connection with a case commenced before such date, see section 403(d) of Pub.L. 95–598, set out preceding section 151 of this title.

Transfer of Functions

All functions of all other officers of the Department of Justice and all functions of all agencies and employees of such Department were, with a few exceptions, transferred to the Attorney General, with power vested in him to authorize their performance or the performance of any of his functions by any of such officers, agencies, and employees, by Reorg. Plan No. 2, of 1950, §§ 1, 2, eff. May 24, 1950, 15 F.R. 3173, 64 Stat. 1261, set out in Appendix 1 to Title 5, Government Organization and Employees.

§ 3058. Interned belligerent nationals

Whoever, belonging to the armed land or naval forces of a belligerent nation or belligerent faction and being interned in the United States, in accordance with the law of nations, leaves or attempts to leave said jurisdiction, or leaves or attempts to leave the limits of internment without permission from the proper official of the United States in charge, or willfully overstays a leave of absence granted by such official, shall be subject to arrest by any marshal or deputy marshal of the United States, or by the military or naval authorities thereof, and shall be returned to the place of internment and there confined and safely kept for such period of time as the official of the United States in charge shall direct.

(June 25, 1948, c. 645, 62 Stat. 818; Nov. 29, 1990, Pub.L. 101–647, Title XXXV, § 3571, 104 Stat. 4928.)

[§ 3059. Repealed. Pub.L. 107–273, Div. A, Title III, § 301(c)(2), Nov. 2, 2002, 116 Stat. 1781]

HISTORICAL AND STATUTORY NOTES

Section, Act June 25, 1948, c. 645, 62 Stat. 818; Sept. 13, 1982, Pub.L. 97–258, § 2(d)(2), 96 Stat. 1058; Sept. 13, 1994, Pub.L. 103–322, Title XXV, § 250004, 108 Stat. 2086, related to rewards for the capture of anyone who is charged with violation of criminal laws of the United States or any State or of the District of Columbia and authorization of appropriations therefor.

Spending Limitations Lifted

Pub.L. 107–77, Title I, § 106, Nov. 28, 2001, 115 Stat. 765, provided that: "Notwithstanding any other provision of law, not to exceed $10,000,000 of the funds made available in this Act [the Departments of Commerce, Justice, and State, the Judiciary, and Related Agencies Appropriations Act, 2002, Pub.L. 107–77, Nov. 28, 2001, 115 Stat. 748; see Tables for complete classification] may be used to establish and publicize a program under which publicly advertised, extraordinary rewards may be paid, which shall not be subject to spending limitations contained in sections 3059 and 3072 of title 18, United States Code: *Provided,* That any reward of $100,000 or more, up to a maximum of $2,000,000, may not be made without the personal approval of the President or the Attorney General and such approval may not be delegated: *Provided further,* That rewards made pursuant to section 501 of Public Law 107–56 [18 U.S.C.A. § 3071 note] shall not be subject to this section."

Similar provisions were contained in the following prior Appropriations Acts:

Pub.L. 106–553, § 1(a)(2) [Title I, § 106], Dec. 21, 2000, 114 Stat. 2762, 2762A–67.

Pub.L. 106–113, Div. B, § 1000(a)(1) [Title I, § 106], Nov. 29, 1999, 113 Stat. 1535, 1501A–19.

Pub.L. 105–277, Div. A, § 101(b) [Title I, § 106], Oct. 21, 1998, 112 Stat.2681–66.

Pub.L. 105–119, Title I, § 106, Nov. 26, 1997, 111 Stat. 2457.

Pub.L. 104–208, Div. A, Title I, § 101(a) [Title I, § 106], Sept. 30, 1996, 110 Stat. 3009–17.

Pub.L. 104–19, Title III, § 3001, July 27, 1995, 109 Stat. 250.

[§ 3059A. Repealed. Pub.L. 107–273, Div. A, Title III, § 301(c)(2), Nov. 2, 2002, 116 Stat. 1781]

HISTORICAL AND STATUTORY NOTES

Section, added Pub.L. 101–647, Title XXV, § 2587(a), Nov. 29, 1990, 104 Stat. 4904, and amended Pub.L. 103–322, Title XXXII, § 320607, Title XXXIII, § 330010(10), (17), Sept. 13, 1994, 108 Stat. 2120, 2143, 2144; Pub.L. 104–294, Title VI, §§ 601(f)(4), 604(b)(24), Oct. 11, 1996, 110 Stat. 3499, 3508, provided for special rewards for information relating to certain financial institution offenses.

[§ 3059B. Repealed. Pub.L. 107–273, Div. A, Title III, § 301(c)(2), Nov. 2, 2002, 116 Stat. 1781]

HISTORICAL AND STATUTORY NOTES

Section, added Pub.L. 104–132, Title VIII, § 815(e)(1), Apr. 24, 1996, 110 Stat. 1315, related to general reward authority.

§ 3060. Preliminary examination

(a) Except as otherwise provided by this section, a preliminary examination shall be held within the time set by the judge or magistrate judge pursuant to subsection (b) of this section, to determine whether there is probable cause to believe that an offense has been committed and that the arrested person has committed it.

(b) The date for the preliminary examination shall be fixed by the judge or magistrate judge at the initial appearance of the arrested person. Except as provided by subsection (c) of this section, or unless the arrested person waives the preliminary examination, such examination shall be held within a reasonable time following initial appearance, but in any event not later than—

(1) the tenth day following the date of the initial appearance of the arrested person before such officer if the arrested person is held in custody without any provision for release, or is held in custody for failure to meet the conditions of release imposed, or is released from custody only during specified hours of the day; or

(2) the twentieth day following the date of the initial appearance if the arrested person is released from custody under any condition other than a condition described in paragraph (1) of this subsection.

(c) With the consent of the arrested person, the date fixed by the judge or magistrate judge for the preliminary examination may be a date later than that prescribed by subsection (b), or may be continued one or more times to a date subsequent to the date initially fixed therefor. In the absence of such consent of the accused, the judge or magistrate judge may extend the time limits only on a showing that extraordinary circumstances exist and justice requires the delay.

(d) Except as provided by subsection (e) of this section, an arrested person who has not been accorded the preliminary examination required by subsection (a) within the period of time fixed by the judge or magistrate judge in compliance with subsections (b) and (c), shall be discharged from custody or from the requirement of bail or any other condition of release, without prejudice, however, to the institution of further criminal proceedings against him upon the charge upon which he was arrested.

(e) No preliminary examination in compliance with subsection (a) of this section shall be required to be accorded an arrested person, nor shall such arrested person be discharged from custody or from the requirement of bail or any other condition of release pursuant to subsection (d), if at any time subsequent to the initial appearance of such person before a judge or magistrate judge and prior to the date fixed for the preliminary examination pursuant to subsections (b) and (c) an indictment is returned or, in appropriate cases, an information is filed against such person in a court of the United States.

(f) Proceedings before United States magistrate judges under this section shall be taken down by a court reporter or recorded by suitable sound recording equipment. A copy of the record of such proceeding shall be made available at the expense of the United States to a person who makes affidavit that he is unable to pay or give security therefor, and the expense of such copy shall be paid by the Director of the Administrative Office of the United States Courts.

(June 25, 1948, c. 645, 62 Stat. 819; Oct. 17, 1968, Pub.L. 90–578, Title III, § 303(a), 82 Stat. 1117; Dec. 1, 1990, Pub.L. 101–650, Title III, § 321, 104 Stat. 5117; Jan. 5, 2006, Pub.L. 109–162, Title XI, § 1179, 119 Stat. 3126.)

HISTORICAL AND STATUTORY NOTES

Change of Name

Words "magistrate judge" and "United States magistrate judges" substituted for "magistrate" and "United States magistrates" in text pursuant to section 321 of Pub.L. 101–650, set out as a note under 28 U.S.C.A. § 631.

Effective and Applicability Provisions

1968 Acts. Amendment by Pub.L. 90–578 effective Oct. 17, 1968, except when a later effective date is applicable, which is the earlier of date when implementation of amendment by appointment of magistrates and assumption of office takes place or third anniversary of enactment of Pub.L. 90–578 on Oct. 17, 1968, see section 403 of Pub.L. 90–578, set out as an Effective Date of 1968 Amendment note under section 631 of Title 28, Judiciary and Judicial Procedure.

§ 3061. Investigative powers of Postal Service personnel

(a) Subject to subsection (b) of this section, Postal Inspectors and other agents of the United States Postal Service designated by the Board of Governors to investigate criminal matters related to the Postal Service and the mails may—

(1) serve warrants and subpoenas issued under the authority of the United States;

(2) make arrests without warrant for offenses against the United States committed in their presence;

(3) make arrests without warrant for felonies cognizable under the laws of the United States if they have reasonable grounds to believe that the person to be arrested has committed or is committing such a felony;

(4) carry firearms; and

(5) make seizures of property as provided by law.

(b) The powers granted by subsection (a) of this section shall be exercised only—

(1) in the enforcement of laws regarding property in the custody of the Postal Service, property of the Postal Service, the use of the mails, and other postal offenses; and

(2) to the extent authorized by the Attorney General pursuant to agreement between the Attorney General and the Postal Service, in the enforcement of other laws of the United States, if the Attorney General determines that violations of such laws have a detrimental effect upon the operations of the Postal Service.

(c)(1) The Postal Service may employ police officers for duty in connection with the protection of property owned or occupied by the Postal Service or under the charge and control of the Postal Service, and persons on that property, including duty in areas outside the property to the extent necessary to protect the property and persons on the property.

(2) With respect to such property, such officers shall have the power to—

(A) enforce Federal laws and regulations for the protection of persons and property;

(B) carry firearms; and

(C) make arrests without a warrant for any offense against the Unites States committed in the presence of the officer or for any felony cognizable under the laws of the United States if the officer has reasonable grounds to believe that the person to be arrested has committed or is committing a felony.

(3) With respect to such property, such officers may have, to such extent as the Postal Service may by regulations prescribe, the power to—

(A) serve warrants and subpoenas issued under the authority of the United States; and

(B) conduct investigations, on and off the property in question, of offenses that may have been committed against property owned or occupied by the Postal Service or persons on the property.

(4)(A) As to such property, the Postmaster General may prescribe regulations necessary for the protection and administration of property owned or occupied by the Postal Service and persons on the property. The regulations may include reasonable penalties, within the limits prescribed in subparagraph (B), for violations of the regulations. The regulations shall be posted and remain posted in a conspicuous place on the property.

(B) A person violating a regulation prescribed under this subsection shall be fined under this title, imprisoned for not more than 30 days, or both.

(Added Pub.L. 90–560, § 5(a), Oct. 12, 1968, 82 Stat. 998, and amended Pub.L. 91–375, § 6(j)(38)(A), Aug. 12, 1970, 84 Stat. 781; Pub.L. 100–690, Title VI, § 6251(a), Nov. 18, 1988, 102 Stat. 4362; Pub.L. 109–435, Title X, § 1001, Dec. 20, 2006, 120 Stat. 3254.)

HISTORICAL AND STATUTORY NOTES

Effective and Applicability Provisions

1970 Acts. Amendment by Pub.L. 91–375 effective within 1 year after Aug. 12, 1970, on date established therefor by the Board of Governors of the United States Postal Service and published by it in the Federal Register, see section 15(a) of Pub.L. 91–375, set out as an Effective Date note preceding section 101 of Title 39, Postal Service.

§ 3062. General arrest authority for violation of release conditions

A law enforcement officer, who is authorized to arrest for an offense committed in his presence, may arrest a person who is released pursuant to chapter 207 if the officer has reasonable grounds to believe that the person is violating, in his presence, a condition imposed on the person pursuant to section 3142(c)(1)(B)(iv), (v), (viii), (ix), or (xiii), or, if the violation involves a failure to remain in a specified institution as required, a condition imposed pursuant to section 3142(c)(1)(B)(x).

(Added Pub.L. 98–473, Title II, § 204(d), Oct. 12, 1984, 98 Stat. 1986, and amended Pub.L. 100–690, Title VII, § 7052, Nov. 18, 1988, 102 Stat. 4401.)

§ 3063. Powers of Environmental Protection Agency

(a) Upon designation by the Administrator of the Environmental Protection Agency, any law enforcement officer of the Environmental Protection Agency with responsibility for the investigation of criminal violations of a law administered by the Environmental Protection Agency, may—

(1) carry firearms;

(2) execute and serve any warrant or other processes issued under the authority of the United States; and

(3) make arrests without warrant for—

(A) any offense against the United States committed in such officer's presence; or

(B) any felony offense against the United States if such officer has probable cause to believe that the person to be arrested has committed or is committing that felony offense.

(b) The powers granted under subsection (a) of this section shall be exercised in accordance with guidelines approved by the Attorney General.

(Added Pub.L. 100–582, § 4(a), Nov. 1, 1988, 102 Stat. 2958.)

§ 3064. Powers of Federal Motor Carrier Safety Administration

Authorized employees of the Federal Motor Carrier Safety Administration may direct a driver of a commercial motor vehicle (as defined in section 31132 of title 49) to stop for inspection of the vehicle, driver, cargo, and required records at or in the vicinity of an inspection site.

(Added Pub.L. 109–59, Title IV, § 4143(b), Aug. 10, 2005, 119 Stat. 1748.)

CHAPTER 204—REWARDS FOR INFORMATION CONCERNING TERRORIST ACTS AND ESPIONAGE

[1] So in original. Section was amended without a corresponding change in the table of sections under this chapter.

[2] So in original. Section was repealed without a corresponding change in the table of sections under this chapter.

§ 3071. Information for which rewards authorized

(a) With respect to acts of terrorism primarily within the territorial jurisdiction of the United States, the Attorney General may reward any individual who furnishes information—

(1) leading to the arrest or conviction, in any country, of any individual or individuals for the commission of an act of terrorism against a United States person or United States property; or

(2) leading to the arrest or conviction, in any country, of any individual or individuals for conspiring or attempting to commit an act of terrorism against a United States person or property; or

(3) leading to the prevention, frustration, or favorable resolution of an act of terrorism against a United States person or property.

(b) With respect to acts of espionage involving or directed at the United States, the Attorney General may reward any individual who furnishes information—

(1) leading to the arrest or conviction, in any country, of any individual or individuals for commission of an act of espionage against the United States;

(2) leading to the arrest or conviction, in any country, of any individual or individuals for conspiring or attempting to commit an act of espionage against the United States; or

(3) leading to the prevention or frustration of an act of espionage against the United States.

(Added Pub.L. 98–533, Title I, § 101(a), Oct. 19, 1984, 98 Stat. 2706, and amended Pub.L. 103–359, Title VIII, § 803(a), Oct. 14, 1994, 108 Stat. 3438.)

HISTORICAL AND STATUTORY NOTES

Short Title

1984 Acts. Section 1 of Pub.L. 98–533 provided that: "This Act [enacting this chapter and section 2708 of Title 22, Foreign Relations and Intercourse, amending sections 2669, 2678 and 2704 of Title 22, Foreign Relations and Intercourse, enacting provisions set out as a note under section 5928 of Title 5, Government Organizations and Employees and amending provisions set out as a note preceding section 2651 of Title 22, Foreign Relations and Intercourse] may be cited as the '1984 Act to Combat International Terrorism'."

Attorney General's Authority to Pay Rewards to Combat Terrorism

Pub.L. 107–56, Title V, § 501, Oct. 26, 2001, 115 Stat. 363, which authorized the Attorney General to use available funds for payment of rewards to combat terrorism, was repealed by Pub.L. 107–273, Div. A, Title III, § 301(c)(1), Nov. 2, 2002, 116 Stat. 1781.

§ 3072. Determination of entitlement; maximum amount; Presidential approval; conclusiveness [1]

The Attorney General shall determine whether an individual furnishing information described in section 3071 is entitled to a reward and the amount to be paid.

(Added Pub.L. 98–533, Title I, § 101(a), Oct. 19, 1984, 98 Stat. 2707, and amended Pub.L. 107–273, Div. A, Title III, § 301(c)(2), Nov. 2, 2002, 116 Stat. 1781.)

[1] So in original. Text of section was amended without corresponding change in the section heading.

HISTORICAL AND STATUTORY NOTES

Spending Limitations Lifted

Any funds made available to the Attorney General before or after July 27, 1995, as not subject to the spending limitations contained in this section and section 3059 of this title, but with a proviso that any reward of $100,000 or more, up to a maximum of $2,000,000, not to be made without the personal approval of the President or the Attorney General, with such approval not to be delegated, see section 106 of Pub.L. 107–77, set out as a note under section 3059 of this title.

§ 3073. Protection of identity

Any reward granted under this chapter shall be certified for payment by the Attorney General. If it is determined that the identity of the recipient of a reward or of the members of the recipient's immediate family must be protected, the Attorney General may take such measures in connection with the payment of the reward as deemed necessary to effect such protection.

(Added Pub.L. 98–533, Title I, § 101(a), Oct. 19, 1984, 98 Stat. 2707.)

§ 3074. Exception of governmental officials

No officer or employee of any governmental entity who, while in the performance of his or her official duties, furnishes the information described in section 3071 shall be eligible for any monetary reward under this chapter.

(Added Pub.L. 98–533, Title I, § 101(a), Oct. 19, 1984, 98 Stat. 2707.)

[§ 3075. Repealed. Pub.L. 107–273, Div. A, Title III, § 301(c)(2), Nov. 2, 2002, 116 Stat. 1781]

HISTORICAL AND STATUTORY NOTES

Section, added Pub.L. 98–533, Title I, § 101(a), Oct. 19, 1984, 98 Stat. 2707, authorized appropriations of $5,000,000, without fiscal year limitation, for the purpose of implementing this chapter.

Pub.L. 107–273, § 301(c)(2), which directed the repeal of section 3075 of chapter 203, was executed to this section which is in chapter 204.

§ 3076. Eligibility for witness security program

Any individual (and the immediate family of such individual) who furnishes information which would justify a reward by the Attorney General under this chapter or by the Secretary of State under section 36 of the State Department Basic Authorities Act of 1956 may, in the discretion of the Attorney General, participate in the Attorney General's witness security program authorized under chapter 224 of this title.

(Added Pub.L. 98–533, Title I, § 101(a), Oct. 19, 1984, 98 Stat. 2707, and amended Pub.L. 99–646, § 45, Nov. 10, 1986, 100 Stat. 3601.)

HISTORICAL AND STATUTORY NOTES

References in Text

Section 36 of the State Department Basic Authorities Act of 1956, referred to in text, is classified to section 2708 of Title 22, Foreign Relations and Intercourse.

§ 3077. Definitions

As used in this chapter, the term—

(1) "act of terrorism" means an act of domestic or international terrorism as defined in section 2331;

(2) "United States person" means—

(A) a national of the United States as defined in section 101(a)(22) of the Immigration and Nationality Act (8 U.S.C. 1101(a)(22));

(B) an alien lawfully admitted for permanent residence in the United States as defined in section 101(a)(20) of the Immigration and Nationality Act (8 U.S.C. 1101(a)(20));

(C) any person within the United States;

(D) any employee or contractor of the United States Government, regardless of nationality, who is the victim or intended victim of an act of terrorism by virtue of that employment;

(E) a sole proprietorship, partnership, company, or association composed principally of nationals or permanent resident aliens of the United States; and

(F) a corporation organized under the laws of the United States, any State, the District of Columbia, or any territory or possession of the United States, and a foreign subsidiary of such corporation;

(3) "United States property" means any real or personal property which is within the United States or, if outside the United States, the actual or beneficial ownership of which rests in a United States person or any Federal or State governmental entity of the United States;

(4) "United States", when used in a geographical sense, includes Puerto Rico and all territories and possessions of the United States;

(5) "State" includes any State of the United States, the District of Columbia, the Commonwealth of Puerto Rico, and any other possession or territory of the United States;

(6) "government entity" includes the Government of the United States, any State or political subdivision thereof, any foreign country, and any state, provincial, municipal, or other political subdivision of a foreign country;

(7) "Attorney General" means the Attorney General of the United States or that official designated by the Attorney General to perform the Attorney General's responsibilities under this chapter; and

(8) "act of espionage" means an activity that is a violation of—

(A) section 793, 794, or 798 of this title; or

(B) section 4 of the Subversive Activities Control Act of 1950.

(Added Pub.L. 98–533, Title I, § 101(a), Oct. 19, 1984, 98 Stat. 2707, and amended Pub.L. 100–690, Title VII, § 7051, Nov. 18, 1988, 102 Stat. 4401; Pub.L. 101–647, Title XXXV, § 3572, Nov. 29, 1990, 104 Stat. 4929; Pub.L. 103–322, Title XXXIII, § 330021(1), Sept. 13, 1994, 108 Stat. 2150; Pub.L. 103–359, Title VIII, § 803(b), Oct. 14, 1994, 108 Stat. 3439; Pub.L. 104–294, Title VI, § 605(g), Oct. 11, 1996, 110 Stat. 3510; Pub.L. 107–56, Title VIII, § 802(b), Oct. 26, 2001, 115 Stat. 376.)

HISTORICAL AND STATUTORY NOTES

References in Text

The Immigration and Nationality Act, referred to in pars. (2)(A) and (B) is Act June 27, 1952, c. 477, 66 Stat. 163, as amended, which is classified principally to chapter 12 (section 1101 et seq.) of Title 8, Aliens and Nationality. Section 101(a)(20) and (22) of the Immigration and Nationality Act is classified to section 1101(a)(20) and (22), respectively of Title 8. For complete classification of this Act to the Code, see Short Title note set out under section 1101 of Title 8 and Tables.

The Subversive Activities Control Act of 1950, referred to in par. (8)(B), is Act Sept. 23, 1950, c. 1024, Title I, 64 Stat. 987, as amended, which is classified principally to subchapter I (section 781 et seq.) of chapter 23 of Title 50, War and National Defense. Section 4 of such Act is classified to section 783 of Title 50. For complete classification of this Act to the Code, see Short Title note set out under section 781 of Title 50 and Tables.

CHAPTER 205—SEARCHES AND SEIZURES

§ 3101. Effect of rules of court—(Rule)

SEE FEDERAL RULES OF CRIMINAL PROCEDURE

Rules generally applicable throughout United States, Rule 54.

Acts of Congress superseded, Rule 41(g).

(June 25, 1948, c. 645, 62 Stat. 819.)

HISTORICAL AND STATUTORY NOTES

References in Text

Rule 41(g), referred to in text, was relettered 41(h).

§ 3102. Authority to issue search warrant—(Rule)

SEE FEDERAL RULES OF CRIMINAL PROCEDURE

Federal, State or Territorial Judges, or U.S. magistrate judges authorized to issue search warrants, Rule 41(a).

(June 25, 1948, c. 645, 62 Stat. 819; Oct. 17, 1968, Pub.L. 90–578, Title III, § 301(a)(4), 82 Stat. 1115; Dec. 1, 1990, Pub.L. 101–650, Title III, § 321, 104 Stat. 5117.)

HISTORICAL AND STATUTORY NOTES

Effective and Applicability Provisions

1968 Acts. Amendment by Pub.L. 90–578 effective Oct. 17, 1968, except when a later effective date is applicable, which is the earlier of date when implementation of amendment by appointment of magistrates and assumption of office takes place or third anniversary of enactment of Pub.L. 90–578 on Oct. 17, 1968, see section 403 of Pub.L. 90–578, set out as a note under section 631 of Title 28, Judiciary and Judicial Procedure.

Change of Name

"U.S. magistrate judges" substituted for "U.S. magistrates" in text pursuant to section 321 of Pub.L. 101–650, set out as a note under 28 U.S.C.A. § 631.

§ 3103. Grounds for issuing search warrant—(Rule)

SEE FEDERAL RULES OF CRIMINAL PROCEDURE

Grounds prescribed for issuance of search warrant, Rule 41(b).

(June 25, 1948, c. 645, 62 Stat. 819.)

§ 3103a. Additional grounds for issuing warrant

(a) In general.—In addition to the grounds for issuing a warrant in section 3103 of this title, a warrant may be issued to search for and seize any property that constitutes evidence of a criminal offense in violation of the laws of the United States.

(b) Delay.—With respect to the issuance of any warrant or court order under this section, or any other rule of law, to search for and seize any property or material that constitutes evidence of a criminal offense in violation of the laws of the United States, any notice required, or that may be required, to be given may be delayed if—

(1) the court finds reasonable cause to believe that providing immediate notification of the execution of the warrant may have an adverse result (as defined in section 2705, except if the adverse results consist only of unduly delaying a trial);

(2) the warrant prohibits the seizure of any tangible property, any wire or electronic communication (as defined in section 2510), or, except as expressly provided in chapter 121, any stored wire or electronic information, except where the court finds reasonable necessity for the seizure; and

(3) the warrant provides for the giving of such notice within a reasonable period not to exceed 30 days after the date of its execution, or on a later date certain if the facts of the case justify a longer period of delay.

(c) Extensions of delay.—Any period of delay authorized by this section may be extended by the court for good cause shown, subject to the condition that extensions should only be granted upon an updated showing of the need for further delay and that each additional delay should be limited to periods of 90 days or less, unless the facts of the case justify a longer period of delay.

(d) Reports.—

(1) Report by judge.—Not later than 30 days after the expiration of a warrant authorizing delayed notice (including any extension thereof) entered under this section, or the denial of such warrant (or request for extension), the issuing or denying judge shall report to the Administrative Office of the United States Courts—

(A) the fact that a warrant was applied for;

(B) the fact that the warrant or any extension thereof was granted as applied for, was modified, or was denied;

(C) the period of delay in the giving of notice authorized by the warrant, and the number and duration of any extensions; and

(D) the offense specified in the warrant or application.

(2) Report by Administrative Office of the United States Courts.—Beginning with the fiscal year ending September 30, 2007, the Director of the Administrative Office of the United States Courts shall transmit to Congress annually a full and complete report summarizing the data required to be filed with the Administrative Office by paragraph (1), including the number of applications for warrants and extensions of warrants authorizing delayed notice, and the number of such warrants and extensions granted or denied during the preceding fiscal year.

(3) Regulations.—The Director of the Administrative Office of the United States Courts, in consultation with the Attorney General, is authorized to issue binding regulations dealing with the content and form of the reports required to be filed under paragraph (1).

(Added Pub.L. 90–351, Title IX, § 1401(a), June 19, 1968, 82 Stat. 238, and amended Pub.L. 107–56, Title II, § 213, Oct. 26, 2001, 115 Stat. 285; Pub.L. 109–177, Title I, § 114, Mar. 9, 2006, 120 Stat. 210.)

HISTORICAL AND STATUTORY NOTES

Codifications

Pub.L. 90–351 enacted section 3103a of this title as part of chapter 204, and Pub.L. 90–462, § 3, Aug. 8, 1968, 82 Stat. 638, corrected the chapter designation from 204 to 205.

References in Text

Chapter 121, referred to in subsec. (b), is 18 U.S.C.A. § 2701 et seq.

§ 3104. Issuance of search warrant; contents—(Rule)

SEE FEDERAL RULES OF CRIMINAL PROCEDURE

Issuance of search warrant on affidavit; contents to identify persons or place; command to search forthwith, Rule 41(c).

(June 25, 1948, c. 645, 62 Stat. 819.)

§ 3105. Persons authorized to serve search warrant

A search warrant may in all cases be served by any of the officers mentioned in its direction or by an officer authorized by law to serve such warrant, but by no other person, except in aid of the officer on his requiring it, he being present and acting in its execution.

(June 25, 1948, c. 645, 62 Stat. 819.)

§ 3106. Officer authorized to serve search warrant—(Rule)

SEE FEDERAL RULES OF CRIMINAL PROCEDURE

Officer to whom search warrant shall be directed, Rule 41(c).

(June 25, 1948, c. 645, 62 Stat. 819.)

§ 3107. Service of warrants and seizures by Federal Bureau of Investigation

The Director, Associate Director, Assistant to the Director, Assistant Directors, agents, and inspectors of the Federal Bureau of Investigation of the Department of Justice are empowered to make seizures under warrant for violation of the laws of the United States.

(June 25, 1948, c. 645, 62 Stat. 819; Jan. 10, 1951, c. 1221, § 2, 64 Stat. 1239.)

HISTORICAL AND STATUTORY NOTES

Transfer of Functions

All functions of all other officers of the Department of Justice and all functions of all agencies and employees of such Department were, with a few exceptions, transferred to the Attorney General, with power vested in him to authorize their performance or the performance of any of his functions by any of such officers, agencies, and employees, by 1950 Reorg. Plan No. 2, §§ 1, 2, eff. May 24, 1950, 15 F.R. 3173, 64 Stat. 1261, set out in Appendix 1 to Title 5, Government Organization and Employees.

§ 3108. Execution, service, and return—(Rule)

SEE FEDERAL RULES OF CRIMINAL PROCEDURE

Method and time for execution, service and return of search warrant, Rule 41(c), (d).

(June 25, 1948, c. 645, 62 Stat. 819.)

§ 3109. Breaking doors or windows for entry or exit

The officer may break open any outer or inner door or window of a house, or any part of a house, or anything therein, to execute a search warrant, if, after notice of his authority and purpose, he is refused admittance or when necessary to liberate himself or a person aiding him in the execution of the warrant.
(June 25, 1948, c. 645, 62 Stat. 820.)

§ 3110. Property defined—(Rule)

SEE FEDERAL RULES OF CRIMINAL PROCEDURE

Term "property" as used in Rule 41 includes documents, books, papers and any other tangible objects, Rule 41(g).
(June 25, 1948, c. 645, 62 Stat. 820).

HISTORICAL AND STATUTORY NOTES

References in Text

Rule 41(g), referred to in text, was relettered 41(h).

§ 3111. Property seizable on search warrant—(Rule)

SEE FEDERAL RULES OF CRIMINAL PROCEDURE

Specified property seizable on search warrant, Rule 41(b).
(June 25, 1948, c. 645, 62 Stat. 820.)

[§ 3112. Repealed. Pub.L. 97–79, § 9(b)(3), Nov. 16, 1981, 95 Stat. 1079.]

HISTORICAL AND STATUTORY NOTES

Section, Acts June 25, 1948, p. 645, 62 Stat. 820; Dec. 5, 1969, Pub.L. 91–135, § 7(c), 83 Stat. 281; Nov. 8, 1978, Pub.L. 95–616, § 3(j) (1), 92 Stat. 3112, provided for the issuance of search warrants for seizure of animals, birds, and eggs. See section 3375 of Title 16, Conservation.

§ 3113. Liquor violations in Indian country

If any superintendent of Indian affairs, or commanding officer of a military post, or special agent of the Office of Indian Affairs for the suppression of liquor traffic among Indians and in the Indian country and any authorized deputies under his supervision has probable cause to believe that any person is about to introduce or has introduced any spirituous liquor, beer, wine or other intoxicating liquors named in sections 1154 and 1156 of this title into the Indian country in violation of law, he may cause the places, conveyances, and packages of such person to be searched. If any such intoxicating liquor is found therein, the same, together with such conveyances and packages of such person, shall be seized and delivered to the proper officer, and shall be proceeded against by libel in the proper court, and forfeited, one-half to the informer and one-half to the use of the United States. If such person be a trader, his license shall be revoked and his bond put in suit.

Any person in the service of the United States authorized by this section to make searches and seizures, or any Indian may take and destroy any ardent spirits or wine found in the Indian country, except such as are kept or used for scientific, sacramental, medicinal, or mechanical purposes or such as may be introduced therein by the Department of the Army.
(June 25, 1948, c. 645, 62 Stat. 820; Oct. 31, 1951, c. 655, § 30, 65 Stat. 721; Sept. 13, 1994, Pub.L. 103–322, Title XXXIII, § 330004(15), 108 Stat. 2142.)

§ 3114. Return of seized property and suppression of evidence; motion—(Rule)

SEE FEDERAL RULES OF CRIMINAL PROCEDURE

Return of property and suppression of evidence upon motion, Rule 41(e).
(June 25, 1948, c. 645, 62 Stat. 820.)

§ 3115. Inventory upon execution and return of search warrant—(Rule)

SEE FEDERAL RULES OF CRIMINAL PROCEDURE

Inventory of property seized under search warrant, and copies to persons affected, Rule 41(d).
(June 25, 1948, c. 645, 62 Stat. 820.)

§ 3116. Records of examining magistrate judge; return to clerk of court—(Rule)

SEE FEDERAL RULES OF CRIMINAL PROCEDURE

Magistrate judges and clerks of court to keep records as prescribed by Director of the Administrative Office of the United States Courts, Rule 55.

Return or filing of records with clerk, Rule 41(f).
(June 25, 1948, c. 645, 62 Stat. 821; Oct. 17, 1968, Pub.L. 90–578, Title III, § 301(a)(4), 82 Stat. 1115; Dec. 1, 1990, Pub.L. 101–650, Title III, § 321, 104 Stat. 5117.)

HISTORICAL AND STATUTORY NOTES

References in Text

Rule 41(f), referred to in text, was relettered 41(g).

Effective and Applicability Provisions

1968 Amendments. Amendment by Pub.L. 90–578 effective Oct. 17, 1968, except when a later effective date is applicable, which is the earlier of date when implementation of amendment by appointment of magistrates and assumption of office takes place or third anniversary of enactment of Pub.L. 90–578 on Oct. 17, 1968, see section 403 of Pub.L.

90–578, set out as a note under section 631 of Title 28, Judiciary and Judicial Procedure.

Change of Name

Words "magistrate judge" substituted for "magistrate" in section catchline and "Magistrate judges" substituted for "Magistrates" in text pursuant to section 321 of Pub.L. 101–650, set out as a note under 28 U.S.C.A. § 631.

§ 3117. Mobile tracking devices

(a) In general.—If a court is empowered to issue a warrant or other order for the installation of a mobile tracking device, such order may authorize the use of that device within the jurisdiction of the court, and outside that jurisdiction if the device is installed in that jurisdiction.

(b) Definition.—As used in this section, the term "tracking device" means an electronic or mechanical device which permits the tracking of the movement of a person or object.

(Added Pub.L. 99–508, Title I, § 108(a), Oct. 21, 1986, 100 Stat. 1858.)

HISTORICAL AND STATUTORY NOTES

Effective and Applicability Provisions

1986 Acts. Section effective 90 days after Oct. 21, 1986 except as otherwise provided in section 111 of Pub.L. 99–508 with respect to conduct pursuant to court order or extension, see section 111 of Pub.L. 99–508, set out as a note under section 2510 of this title.

Prior Provisions

Another section 3117 of this title, as added Pub.L. 100–690, § 6477(b)(1), was renumbered section 3118 of this title.

§ 3118. Implied consent for certain tests

(a) Consent.—Whoever operates a motor vehicle in the special maritime and territorial jurisdiction of the United States consents thereby to a chemical test or tests of such person's blood, breath, or urine, if arrested for any offense arising from such person's driving while under the influence of a drug or alcohol in such jurisdiction. The test or tests shall be administered upon the request of a police officer having reasonable grounds to believe the person arrested to have been driving a motor vehicle upon the special maritime and territorial jurisdiction of the United States while under the influence of drugs or alcohol in violation of the laws of a State, territory, possession, or district.

(b) Effect of Refusal.—Whoever, having consented to a test or tests by reason of subsection (a), refuses to submit to such a test or tests, after having first been advised of the consequences of such a refusal, shall be denied the privilege of operating a motor vehicle upon the special maritime and territorial jurisdiction of the United States during the period of a year commencing on the date of arrest upon which such test or tests was refused, and such refusal may be admitted into evidence in any case arising from such person's driving while under the influence of a drug or alcohol in such jurisdiction. Any person who operates a motor vehicle in the special maritime and territorial jurisdiction of the United States after having been denied such privilege under this subsection shall be treated for the purposes of any civil or criminal proceedings arising out of such operation as operating such vehicle without a license to do so.

(Added Pub.L. 100–690, Title VI, § 6477(b)(1), Nov. 18, 1988, 102 Stat. 4381, § 3117, renumbered § 3118, Pub.L. 101–647, Title XXXV, § 3574, Nov. 29, 1990, 104 Stat. 4929.)

CHAPTER 206—PEN REGISTERS AND TRAP AND TRACE DEVICES

Sec.

§ 3121. General prohibition on pen register and trap and trace device use; exception

(a) In general.—Except as provided in this section, no person may install or use a pen register or a trap and trace device without first obtaining a court order under section 3123 of this title or under the Foreign Intelligence Surveillance Act of 1978 (50 U.S.C. 1801 et seq.).

(b) Exception.—The prohibition of subsection (a) does not apply with respect to the use of a pen register or a trap and trace device by a provider of electronic or wire communication service—

(1) relating to the operation, maintenance, and testing of a wire or electronic communication service or to the protection of the rights or property of such provider, or to the protection of users of that service from abuse of service or unlawful use of service; or

(2) to record the fact that a wire or electronic communication was initiated or completed in order to protect such provider, another provider furnishing service toward the completion of the wire com-

munication, or a user of that service, from fraudulent, unlawful or abusive use of service; or (3) where the consent of the user of that service has been obtained.

(c) Limitation.—A government agency authorized to install and use a pen register or trap and trace device under this chapter or under State law shall use technology reasonably available to it that restricts the recording or decoding of electronic or other impulses to the dialing, routing, addressing, and signaling information utilized in the processing and transmitting of wire or electronic communications so as not to include the contents of any wire or electronic communications.

(d) Penalty.—Whoever knowingly violates subsection (a) shall be fined under this title or imprisoned not more than one year, or both.

(Added Pub.L. 99–508, Title III, § 301(a), Oct. 21, 1986, 100 Stat. 1868, and amended Pub.L. 103–414, Title II, § 207(b), Oct. 25, 1994, 108 Stat. 4292; Pub.L. 107–56, Title II, § 216(a), Oct. 26, 2001, 115 Stat. 288.)

HISTORICAL AND STATUTORY NOTES

References in Text

The Foreign Intelligence Surveillance Act (50 U.S.C. 1801 et seq.), referred to in subsec. (a), is Pub.L. 95–511, Oct. 25, 1978, 92 Stat. 1783, as amended, which is classified generally to chapter 36 (section 1801 et seq.) of Title 50, War and National Defense.

Effective and Applicability Provisions

1986 Acts. Pub.L. 99–508, Title III, § 302, Oct. 21, 1986, 100 Stat. 1872, provided that:

"**(a) In general.**—Except as provided in subsection (b), this title and the amendments made by this title [enacting this chapter and section 1367 of this title] shall take effect ninety days after the date of the enactment of this Act [Oct. 21, 1986] and shall, in the case of conduct pursuant to a court order or extension, apply only with respect to court orders or extensions made after this title takes effect.

"**(b) Special rule for state authorizations of interceptions.**—Any pen register or trap and trace device order or installation which would be valid and lawful without regard to the amendments made by this title [enacting this chapter and section 1367 of this title] shall be valid and lawful notwithstanding such amendments if such order or installation occurs during the period beginning on the date such amendments take effect and ending on the earlier of—

"(1) the day before the date of the taking effect of changes in State law required in order to make orders or installations under Federal law as amended by this title; or

"(2) the date two years after the date of the enactment of this Act [Oct. 21, 1986]."

§ 3122. Application for an order for a pen register or a trap and trace device

(a) Application.—(1) An attorney for the Government may make application for an order or an extension of an order under section 3123 of this title authorizing or approving the installation and use of a pen register or a trap and trace device under this chapter, in writing under oath or equivalent affirmation, to a court of competent jurisdiction.

(2) Unless prohibited by State law, a State investigative or law enforcement officer may make application for an order or an extension of an order under section 3123 of this title authorizing or approving the installation and use of a pen register or a trap and trace device under this chapter, in writing under oath or equivalent affirmation, to a court of competent jurisdiction of such State.

(b) Contents of application.—An application under subsection (a) of this section shall include—

(1) the identity of the attorney for the Government or the State law enforcement or investigative officer making the application and the identity of the law enforcement agency conducting the investigation; and

(2) a certification by the applicant that the information likely to be obtained is relevant to an ongoing criminal investigation being conducted by that agency.

(Added Pub.L. 99–508, Title III, § 301(a), Oct. 21, 1986, 100 Stat. 1869.)

HISTORICAL AND STATUTORY NOTES

Effective and Applicability Provisions

1986 Acts. Section effective 90 days after Oct. 21, 1986 except as otherwise provided in section 302 of Pub.L. 99–508 with respect to conduct pursuant to court order or extension, see section 302 of Pub.L. 99–508, set out as a note under section 3121 of this title.

§ 3123. Issuance of an order for a pen register or a trap and trace device

(a) In general.—

(1) Attorney for the Government.—Upon an application made under section 3122(a)(1), the court shall enter an ex parte order authorizing the installation and use of a pen register or trap and trace device anywhere within the United States, if the court finds that the attorney for the Government has certified to the court that the information likely to be obtained by such installation and use is relevant to an ongoing criminal investigation. The order, upon service of that order, shall apply to any person or entity providing wire or electronic communication service in the United States whose assistance may facilitate the execution of the order. Whenever such an order is served on any person or entity not specifically named in the order, upon request of such person or entity, the attorney for the Government or law enforcement or investigative officer that is serving the order shall provide written or electronic certification that the order applies to the person or entity being served.

(2) State investigative or law enforcement officer.—Upon an application made under section 3122(a)(2), the court shall enter an ex parte order authorizing the installation and use of a pen register or trap and trace device within the jurisdiction of the court, if the court finds that the State law enforcement or investigative officer has certified to the court that the information likely to be obtained by such installation and use is relevant to an ongoing criminal investigation.

(3)(A) Where the law enforcement agency implementing an ex parte order under this subsection seeks to do so by installing and using its own pen register or trap and trace device on a packet-switched data network of a provider of electronic communication service to the public, the agency shall ensure that a record will be maintained which will identify—

(i) any officer or officers who installed the device and any officer or officers who accessed the device to obtain information from the network;

(ii) the date and time the device was installed, the date and time the device was uninstalled, and the date, time, and duration of each time the device is accessed to obtain information;

(iii) the configuration of the device at the time of its installation and any subsequent modification thereof; and

(iv) any information which has been collected by the device.

To the extent that the pen register or trap and trace device can be set automatically to record this information electronically, the record shall be maintained electronically throughout the installation and use of such device.

(B) The record maintained under subparagraph (A) shall be provided ex parte and under seal to the court which entered the ex parte order authorizing the installation and use of the device within 30 days after termination of the order (including any extensions thereof).

(b) Contents of order.—An order issued under this section—

(1) shall specify—

(A) the identity, if known, of the person to whom is leased or in whose name is listed the telephone line or other facility to which the pen register or trap and trace device is to be attached or applied;

(B) the identity, if known, of the person who is the subject of the criminal investigation;

(C) the attributes of the communications to which the order applies, including the number or other identifier and, if known, the location of the telephone line or other facility to which the pen register or trap and trace device is to be attached or applied, and, in the case of an order authorizing installation and use of a trap and trace device under subsection (a)(2), the geographic limits of the order; and".

(D) a statement of the offense to which the information likely to be obtained by the pen register or trap and trace device relates; and

(2) shall direct, upon the request of the applicant, the furnishing of information, facilities, and technical assistance necessary to accomplish the installation of the pen register or trap and trace device under section 3124 of this title.

(c) Time period and extensions.—(1) An order issued under this section shall authorize the installation and use of a pen register or a trap and trace device for a period not to exceed sixty days.

(2) Extensions of such an order may be granted, but only upon an application for an order under section 3122 of this title and upon the judicial finding required by subsection (a) of this section. The period of extension shall be for a period not to exceed sixty days.

(d) Nondisclosure of existence of pen register or a trap and trace device.—An order authorizing or approving the installation and use of a pen register or a trap and trace device shall direct that—

(1) the order be sealed until otherwise ordered by the court; and

(2) the person owning or leasing the line or other facility to which the pen register or a trap and trace device is attached, or applied, or who is obligated by the order to provide assistance to the applicant, not disclose the existence of the pen register or trap and trace device or the existence of the investigation to the listed subscriber, or to any other person, unless or until otherwise ordered by the court.

(Added Pub.L. 99–508, Title III, § 301(a), Oct. 21, 1986, 100 Stat. 1869, and amended Pub.L. 107–56, Title II, § 216(b), Oct. 26, 2001, 115 Stat. 288.)

HISTORICAL AND STATUTORY NOTES

Effective and Applicability Provisions

1986 Acts. Section effective 90 days after Oct. 21, 1986 except as otherwise provided in section 302 of Pub.L. 99–508 with respect to conduct pursuant to court order or extension, see section 302 of Pub.L. 99–508, set out as a note under section 3121 of this title.

§ 3124. Assistance in installation and use of a pen register or a trap and trace device

(a) Pen registers.—Upon the request of an attorney for the Government or an officer of a law enforcement agency authorized to install and use a pen register under this chapter, a provider of wire or electronic communication service, landlord, custodian, or other person shall furnish such investigative or law enforcement officer forthwith all information, facilities, and technical assistance necessary to accomplish the installation of the pen register unobtrusively and with a minimum of interference with the services that the person so ordered by the court accords the party with respect to whom the installation and use is to take place, if such assistance is directed by a court order as provided in section 3123(b)(2) of this title.

(b) Trap and trace device.—Upon the request of an attorney for the Government or an officer of a law enforcement agency authorized to receive the results of a trap and trace device under this chapter, a provider of a wire or electronic communication service, landlord, custodian, or other person shall install such device forthwith on the appropriate line or other facility and shall furnish such investigative or law enforcement officer all additional information, facilities and technical assistance including installation and operation of the device unobtrusively and with a minimum of interference with the services that the person so ordered by the court accords the party with respect to whom the installation and use is to take place, if such installation and assistance is directed by a court order as provided in section 3123(b)(2) of this title. Unless otherwise ordered by the court, the results of the trap and trace device shall be furnished, pursuant to section 3123(b) or section 3125 of this title, to the officer of a law enforcement agency, designated in the court order, at reasonable intervals during regular business hours for the duration of the order.

(c) Compensation.—A provider of a wire or electronic communication service, landlord, custodian, or other person who furnishes facilities or technical assistance pursuant to this section shall be reasonably compensated for such reasonable expenses incurred in providing such facilities and assistance.

(d) No cause of action against a provider disclosing information under this chapter.—No cause of action shall lie in any court against any provider of a wire or electronic communication service, its officers, employees, agents, or other specified persons for providing information, facilities, or assistance in accordance with a court order under this chapter or request pursuant to section 3125 of this title.

(e) Defense.—A good faith reliance on a court order under this chapter, a request pursuant to section 3125 of this title, a legislative authorization, or a statutory authorization is a complete defense against any civil or criminal action brought under this chapter or any other law.

(f) Communications assistance enforcement orders.—Pursuant to section 2522, an order may be issued to enforce the assistance capability and capacity requirements under the Communications Assistance for Law Enforcement Act.

(Added Pub.L. 99–508, Title III, § 301(a), Oct. 21, 1986, 100 Stat. 1870, and amended Pub.L. 100–690, Title VII, §§ 7040, 7092(b), (d), Nov. 18, 1988, 102 Stat. 4399, 4411; Pub.L. 101–647, Title XXXV, § 3575, Nov. 29, 1990, 104 Stat. 4929; Pub.L. 103–414, Title II, § 201(b)(2), Oct. 25, 1994, 108 Stat. 4290; Pub.L. 107–56, Title II, § 216(c)(5), (6), Oct. 26, 2001, 115 Stat. 290.)

HISTORICAL AND STATUTORY NOTES

References in Text

The Communications Assistance for Law Enforcement Act, referred to in subsec. (f), is Pub.L. 103–414, Title I, Oct. 25, 1994, 108 Stat. 4279, which is classified generally to chapter 9 (section 1001 et seq.) of Title 47, Telegraphs, Telephones, and Radiotelegraphs. For complete classification of this Act to the Code, see Short Title note set out under section 1001 of Title 47 and Tables.

Effective and Applicability Provisions

1986 Acts. Section effective 90 days after Oct. 21, 1986 except as otherwise provided in section 302 of Pub.L. 99–508 with respect to conduct pursuant to court order or extension, see section 302 of Pub.L. 99–508, set out as a note under section 3121 of this title.

Assistance to Law Enforcement Agencies

Pub.L. 107–56, Title II, § 222, Oct. 26, 2001, 115 Stat. 292, provided that: "Nothing in this Act [the Uniting and Strengthening America by Providing Appropriate Tools Required to Intercept and Obstruct Terrorism (USA PATRIOT ACT) Act of 2001, Pub.L. 107–56, Oct. 26, 2001, 115 Stat. 272; see Tables for complete classification] shall impose any additional technical obligation or requirement on a provider of a wire or electronic communication service or other person to furnish facilities or technical assistance. A provider of a wire or electronic communication service, landlord, custodian, or other person who furnishes facilities or technical assistance pursuant to section 216 shall be reasonably compensated for such reasonable expenditures incurred in providing such facilities or assistance."

§ 3125. Emergency pen register and trap and trace device installation

(a) Notwithstanding any other provision of this chapter, any investigative or law enforcement officer, specially designated by the Attorney General, the Deputy Attorney General, the Associate Attorney General, any Assistant Attorney General, any acting Assistant Attorney General, or any Deputy Assistant Attorney General, or by the principal prosecuting attorney of any State or subdivision thereof acting pursuant to a statute of that State, who reasonably determines that—

(1) an emergency situation exists that involves—

(A) immediate danger of death or serious bodily injury to any person;

(B) conspiratorial activities characteristic of organized crime;

(C) an immediate threat to a national security interest; or

(D) an ongoing attack on a protected computer (as defined in section 1030) that constitutes a crime punishable by a term of imprisonment greater than one year;

that requires the installation and use of a pen register or a trap and trace device before an order authorizing such installation and use can, with due diligence, be obtained, and

(2) there are grounds upon which an order could be entered under this chapter to authorize such installation and use;

may have installed and use a pen register or trap and trace device if, within forty-eight hours after the installation has occurred, or begins to occur, an order approving the installation or use is issued in accordance with section 3123 of this title.

(b) In the absence of an authorizing order, such use shall immediately terminate when the information sought is obtained, when the application for the order is denied or when forty-eight hours have lapsed since the installation of the pen register or trap and trace device, whichever is earlier.

(c) The knowing installation or use by any investigative or law enforcement officer of a pen register or trap and trace device pursuant to subsection (a) without application for the authorizing order within forty-eight hours of the installation shall constitute a violation of this chapter.

(d) A provider of a wire or electronic service, landlord, custodian, or other person who furnished facilities or technical assistance pursuant to this section shall be reasonably compensated for such reasonable expenses incurred in providing such facilities and assistance.

(Added Pub.L. 100–690, Title VII, § 7092(a)(2), Nov. 18, 1988, 102 Stat. 4410, and amended Pub.L. 103–322, Title XXXIII, § 330008(3), Sept. 13, 1994, 108 Stat. 2142; Pub.L. 104–294, Title VI, § 601(f)(5), Oct. 11, 1996, 110 Stat. 3499; Pub.L. 107–296, Title II, § 225(i), Nov. 25, 2002, 116 Stat. 2158.)

HISTORICAL AND STATUTORY NOTES

Effective and Applicability Provisions

2002 Acts. Amendment to this section by Pub.L. 107–296 effective 60 days after Nov. 25, 2002, see Pub.L. 107–296, § 4, set out as a note under 6 U.S.C.A. § 101.

Prior Provisions

A prior section 3125 was renumbered section 3126 by Pub.L. 100–690, Title VII, § 7029(a)(1), Nov. 18, 1988, 102 Stat. 4410.

§ 3126. Reports concerning pen registers and trap and trace devices

The Attorney General shall annually report to Congress on the number of pen register orders and orders for trap and trace devices applied for by law enforcement agencies of the Department of Justice, which report shall include information concerning—

(1) the period of interceptions authorized by the order, and the number and duration of any extensions of the order;

(2) the offense specified in the order or application, or extension of an order;

(3) the number of investigations involved;

(4) the number and nature of the facilities affected; and

(5) the identity, including district, of the applying investigative or law enforcement agency making the application and the person authorizing the order.

(Added Pub.L. 99–508, Title III, § 301(a), Oct. 21, 1986, 100 Stat. 1871, § 3125, renumbered § 3126, Pub.L. 100–690, Title VII, § 7092(a)(1), Nov. 18, 1988, 102 Stat. 4410, and amended Pub.L. 106–197, § 3, May 2, 2000, 114 Stat. 247.)

HISTORICAL AND STATUTORY NOTES

Effective and Applicability Provisions

1986 Acts. Section effective 90 days after Oct. 21, 1986 except as otherwise provided in section 302 of Pub.L. 99–508 with respect to conduct pursuant to court order or extension, see section 302 of Pub.L. 99–508 set out as a note under section 3121 of this title.

Termination of Reporting Requirements

Reporting requirement of this section excepted from termination under Pub.L. 104–66, § 3003(a)(1), as amended, set out in a note under 31 U.S.C.A. § 1113, see Pub.L. 106–197, § 1, set out as a note under 31 U.S.C.A. § 1113.

Prior Provisions

A prior section 3126 was renumbered section 3127 by Pub.L. 100–690, Title VII, § 7092(a)(1), Nov. 18, 1988, 102 Stat. 4410.

Report on Use of DCS 1000 (Carnivore) to Implement Orders Under 18 U.S.C. 3123

Pub.L. 107–273, Div. A, Title III, § 305(a), Nov. 2, 2002, 116 Stat. 1782, provided that: "At the same time that the Attorney General submits to Congress the annual reports required by section 3126 of title 18, United States Code [18 U.S.C.A. § 3126], that are respectively next due after the end of each of the fiscal years 2002 and 2003, the Attorney General shall also submit to the Chairmen and ranking minority members of the Committees on the Judiciary of the Senate and of the House of Representatives a report, covering the same respective time period, on the number of orders under section 3123 [18 U.S.C.A. § 3123] applied for by law enforcement agencies of the Department of Justice whose implementation involved the use of the DCS 1000 program (or any subsequent version of such program), which report shall include information concerning—

"(1) the period of interceptions authorized by the order, and the number and duration of any extensions of the order;

"(2) the offense specified in the order or application, or extension of an order;

"(3) the number of investigations involved;

"(4) the number and nature of the facilities affected;

"(5) the identity of the applying investigative or law enforcement agency making the application for an order; and

"(6) the specific persons authorizing the use of the DCS 1000 program (or any subsequent version of such program) in the implementation of such order."

§ 3127. Definitions for chapter

As used in this chapter—

(1) the terms "wire communication", "electronic communication", "electronic communication service", and "contents" have the meanings set forth for such terms in section 2510 of this title;

(2) the term "court of competent jurisdiction" means—

(A) any district court of the United States (including a magistrate judge of such a court) or any United States court of appeals having jurisdiction over the offense being investigated; or

(B) a court of general criminal jurisdiction of a State authorized by the law of that State to enter orders authorizing the use of a pen register or a trap and trace device;

(3) the term "pen register" means a device or process which records or decodes dialing, routing, addressing, or signaling information transmitted by an instrument or facility from which a wire or electronic communication is transmitted, provided, however, that such information shall not include the contents of any communication, but such term does not include any device or process used by a provider or customer of a wire or electronic communication service for billing, or recording as an incident to billing, for communications services provided by such provider or any device or process used by a provider or customer of a wire communication service for cost accounting or other like purposes in the ordinary course of its business;

(4) the term "trap and trace device" means a device or process which captures the incoming electronic or other impulses which identify the originating number or other dialing, routing, addressing, and signaling information reasonably likely to identify the source of a wire or electronic communication, provided, however, that such information shall not include the contents of any communication;

(5) the term "attorney for the Government" has the meaning given such term for the purposes of the Federal Rules of Criminal Procedure; and

(6) the term "State" means a State, the District of Columbia, Puerto Rico, and any other possession or territory of the United States.

(Added Pub.L. 99–508, Title III, § 301(a), Oct. 21, 1986, 100 Stat. 1871, § 3126, and renumbered § 3127, Pub.L. 100–690, Title VII, § 7092(a)(1), Nov. 18, 1988, 102 Stat. 4410, and amended Pub.L. 101–650, Title III, § 321, Dec. 1, 1990, 104 Stat. 5117; Pub.L. 107–56, Title II, § 216(c)(1) to (4), Oct. 26, 2001, 115 Stat. 290.)

HISTORICAL AND STATUTORY NOTES

Effective and Applicability Provisions

1986 Acts. Section effective 90 days after Oct. 21, 1986 except as otherwise provided in section 302 of Pub.L. 99–508 with respect to conduct pursuant to court order or extension, see section 302 of Pub.L. 99–508, set out as a note under section 3121 of this title.

Change of Name

Words "magistrate judge" substituted for "magistrate" in par. (2)(A) pursuant to section 321 of Pub.L. 101–650, set out as a note under 28 U.S.C.A. § 631.

CHAPTER 207—RELEASE AND DETENTION PENDING JUDICIAL PROCEEDINGS

HISTORICAL AND STATUTORY NOTES

Savings Provisions of Pub.L. 98–473, Title II, c. II

See section 235 of Pub.L. 98–473, Title II, c. II, Oct. 12, 1984, 98 Stat. 2031, set out as a note under section 3551 of this title.

§ 3141. Release and detention authority generally

(a) Pending trial.—A judicial officer authorized to order the arrest of a person under section 3041 of this title before whom an arrested person is brought shall order that such person be released or detained, pending judicial proceedings, under this chapter.

(b) Pending sentence or appeal.—A judicial officer of a court of original jurisdiction over an offense, or a judicial officer of a Federal appellate court, shall order that, pending imposition or execution of sen-

tence, or pending appeal of conviction or sentence, a person be released or detained under this chapter.
(Added Pub.L. 98–473, Title II, § 203(a), Oct. 12, 1984, 98 Stat. 1976, and amended Pub.L. 99–646, § 55(a), (b), Nov. 10, 1986, 100 Stat. 3607.)

HISTORICAL AND STATUTORY NOTES

Effective and Applicability Provisions

1986 Acts. Section 55(j) of Pub.L. 99–646 provided that: "The amendments made by this section [amending sections 3141 to 3144, 3146 to 3148, and 3156 of this title] shall take effect 30 days after the date of enactment of this Act [Nov. 10, 1986]."

Prior Provisions

A prior section, 3141, Act June 25, 1948, c. 645, 62 Stat. 821; June 22, 1966, Pub.L. 89–465, § 5(b), 80 Stat. 217, which related to bail power of courts and magistrates, was repealed by Pub.L. 98–473, Title II, c. 1, § 203(a), Oct. 12, 1984, 98 Stat. 1976.

Short Title

2004 Amendments. Pub.L. 108–458, Title VI, § 6951, Dec. 17, 2004, 118 Stat. 3775, provided that: "This subtitle [Pub.L. 108–458, Title VI, Subtitle K, §§ 6951, 6952, Dec. 17, 2004, 118 Stat. 3775, amending 18 U.S.C.A. § 3142] may be cited as the 'Pretrial Detention of Terrorists Act of 2004'."

1990 Amendments. Pub.L. 101–647, Title IX, § 901, Nov. 29, 1990, 104 Stat. 4826, provided that: "This title [amending 18 U.S.C.A. §§ 3143 and 3145] may be cited as the 'Mandatory Detention for Offenders Convicted of Serious Crimes Act'."

1984 Amendments. Section 202 of Pub.L. 98–473 provided that: "This chapter [enacting sections 3062 and 3141 to 3150 of this title, amending sections 3041, 3042, 3154, 3156, 3731, 3772, and 4282 of this title, rules 5, 15, 40, 46 and 54 of the Federal Rules of Criminal Procedure, this title, section 636 of Title 28, Judiciary and Judicial Procedure, rule 9 of the Federal Rules of Appellate Procedure, and repealing section 3043 of this title and former sections 3141 to 3151 of this title] may be cited as the 'Bail Reform Act of 1984'."

1982 Amendments. Pub.L. 97–267, § 1, Sept. 27, 1982, 96 Stat. 1136, provided: "That this Act [amending sections 3152 to 3155 of this title and section 604 of Title 28, Judiciary and Judicial Procedure, and enacting provisions set out as notes under sections 3141 and 3152 of this title] may be cited as the 'Pretrial Services Act of 1982'."

1966 Amendments. Section 1 of Pub.L. 89–465 provided: "That this Act [enacting sections 3146 to 3152 of this title, amending sections 3041, 3141 to 3143, and 3568 of this title, and enacting provisions set out as a note below] may be cited as the 'Bail Reform Act of 1966'."

Purpose of Bail Reform Act of 1966

Section 2 of Pub.L. 89–465 provided that: "The purpose of this Act [enacting sections 3146 to 3152 of this title, amending sections 3041, 3141 to 3143, and 3568 of this title and enacting provisions set out as a note above] is to revise the practices relating to bail to assure that all persons, regardless of their financial status, shall not needlessly be detained pending their appearance to answer charges, to testify, or pending appeal, when detention serves neither the ends of justice nor the public interest."

§ 3142. Release or detention of a defendant pending trial

(a) In general.—Upon the appearance before a judicial officer of a person charged with an offense, the judicial officer shall issue an order that, pending trial, the person be—

(1) released on personal recognizance or upon execution of an unsecured appearance bond, under subsection (b) of this section;

(2) released on a condition or combination of conditions under subsection (c) of this section;

(3) temporarily detained to permit revocation of conditional release, deportation, or exclusion under subsection (d) of this section; or

(4) detained under subsection (e) of this section.

(b) Release on personal recognizance or unsecured appearance bond.—The judicial officer shall order the pretrial release of the person on personal recognizance, or upon execution of an unsecured appearance bond in an amount specified by the court, subject to the condition that the person not commit a Federal, State, or local crime during the period of release and subject to the condition that the person cooperate in the collection of a DNA sample from the person if the collection of such a sample is authorized pursuant to section 3 of the DNA Analysis Backlog Elimination Act of 2000 (42 U.S.C. 14135a), unless the judicial officer determines that such release will not reasonably assure the appearance of the person as required or will endanger the safety of any other person or the community.

(c) Release on conditions.—(1) If the judicial officer determines that the release described in subsection (b) of this section will not reasonably assure the appearance of the person as required or will endanger the safety of any other person or the community, such judicial officer shall order the pretrial release of the person—

(A) subject to the condition that the person not commit a Federal, State, or local crime during the period of release and subject to the condition that the person cooperate in the collection of a DNA sample from the person if the collection of such a sample is authorized pursuant to section 3 of the DNA Analysis Backlog Elimination Act of 2000 (42 U.S.C. 14135a); and

(B) subject to the least restrictive further condition, or combination of conditions, that such judicial officer determines will reasonably assure the appearance of the person as required and the safety of any other person and the community, which may include the condition that the person—

(i) remain in the custody of a designated person, who agrees to assume supervision and to report any violation of a release condition to the court, if the designated person is able reasonably to assure the judicial officer that the person will appear as required and will not pose a danger to the safety of any other person or the community;

(ii) maintain employment, or, if unemployed, actively seek employment;

(iii) maintain or commence an educational program;

(iv) abide by specified restrictions on personal associations, place of abode, or travel;

(v) avoid all contact with an alleged victim of the crime and with a potential witness who may testify concerning the offense;

(vi) report on a regular basis to a designated law enforcement agency, pretrial services agency, or other agency;

(vii) comply with a specified curfew;

(viii) refrain from possessing a firearm, destructive device, or other dangerous weapon;

(ix) refrain from excessive use of alcohol, or any use of a narcotic drug or other controlled substance, as defined in section 102 of the Controlled Substances Act (21 U.S.C. 802), without a prescription by a licensed medical practitioner;

(x) undergo available medical, psychological, or psychiatric treatment, including treatment for drug or alcohol dependency, and remain in a specified institution if required for that purpose;

(xi) execute an agreement to forfeit upon failing to appear as required, property of a sufficient unencumbered value, including money, as is reasonably necessary to assure the appearance of the person as required, and shall provide the court with proof of ownership and the value of the property along with information regarding existing encumbrances as the judicial office may require;

(xii) execute a bail bond with solvent sureties; who will execute an agreement to forfeit in such amount as is reasonably necessary to assure appearance of the person as required and shall provide the court with information regarding the value of the assets and liabilities of the surety if other than an approved surety and the nature and extent of encumbrances against the surety's property; such surety shall have a net worth which shall have sufficient unencumbered value to pay the amount of the bail bond;

(xiii) return to custody for specified hours following release for employment, schooling, or other limited purposes; and

(xiv) satisfy any other condition that is reasonably necessary to assure the appearance of the person as required and to assure the safety of any other person and the community.

In any case that involves a minor victim under section 1201, 1591, 2241, 2242, 2244(a)(1), 2245, 2251, 2251A, 2252(a)(1), 2252(a)(2), 2252(a)(3), 2252A(a)(1), 2252A(a)(2), 2252A(a)(3), 2252A(a)(4), 2260, 2421, 2422, 2423, or 2425 of this title, or a failure to register offense under section 2250 of this title, any release order shall contain, at a minimum, a condition of electronic monitoring and each of the conditions specified at subparagraphs (iv), (v), (vi), (vii), and (viii).

(2) The judicial officer may not impose a financial condition that results in the pretrial detention of the person.

(3) The judicial officer may at any time amend the order to impose additional or different conditions of release.

(d) Temporary detention to permit revocation of conditional release, deportation, or exclusion.—If the judicial officer determines that—

(1) such person—

(A) is, and was at the time the offense was committed, on—

(i) release pending trial for a felony under Federal, State, or local law;

(ii) release pending imposition or execution of sentence, appeal of sentence or conviction, or completion of sentence, for any offense under Federal, State, or local law; or

(iii) probation or parole for any offense under Federal, State, or local law; or

(B) is not a citizen of the United States or lawfully admitted for permanent residence, as defined in section 101(a)(20) of the Immigration and Nationality Act (8 U.S.C. 1101(a)(20)); and

(2) such person may flee or pose a danger to any other person or the community;

such judicial officer shall order the detention of such person, for a period of not more than ten days, excluding Saturdays, Sundays, and holidays, and direct the attorney for the Government to notify the appropriate court, probation or parole official, or State or local law enforcement official, or the appropriate official of the Immigration and Naturalization Service. If the official fails or declines to take such person into custody during that period, such person shall be treated in accordance with the other provisions of this section, notwithstanding the applicability of other provisions of law governing release pending trial or deportation or exclusion proceedings. If temporary detention is sought under paragraph (1)(B) of this subsection, such person has the burden of proving to the court such person's United States citizenship or lawful admission for permanent residence.

(e) Detention.—If, after a hearing pursuant to the provisions of subsection (f) of this section, the judicial officer finds that no condition or combination of conditions will reasonably assure the appearance of the person as required and the safety of any other person and the community, such judicial officer shall order the detention of the person before trial. In a case described in subsection (f)(1) of this section, a rebuttable presumption arises that no condition or combination of conditions will reasonably assure the safety of any other person and the community if such judicial officer finds that—

(1) the person has been convicted of a Federal offense that is described in subsection (f)(1) of this section, or of a State or local offense that would have been an offense described in subsection (f)(1) of this section if a circumstance giving rise to Federal jurisdiction had existed;

(2) the offense described in paragraph (1) of this subsection was committed while the person was on release pending trial for a Federal, State, or local offense; and

(3) a period of not more than five years has elapsed since the date of conviction, or the release of the person from imprisonment, for the offense described in paragraph (1) of this subsection, whichever is later.

Subject to rebuttal by the person, it shall be presumed that no condition or combination of conditions will reasonably assure the appearance of the person as required and the safety of the community if the judicial officer finds that there is probable cause to believe that the person committed an offense for which a maximum term of imprisonment of ten years or more is prescribed in the Controlled Substances Act (21 U.S.C. 801 et seq.), the Controlled Substances Import and Export Act (21 U.S.C. 951 et seq.), or chapter 705 of title 46, an offense under section 924(c), 956(a), or 2332b of this title, or an offense listed in section 2332b(g)(5)(B) of title 18, United States Code, for which a maximum term of imprisonment of 10 years or more is prescribed or an offense involving a minor victim under section 1201, 1591, 2241, 2242, 2244(a)(1), 2245, 2251, 2251A, 2252(a)(1), 2252(a)(2), 2252(a)(3), 2252A(a)(1), 2252A(a)(2), 2252A(a)(3), 2252A(a)(4), 2260, 2421, 2422, 2423, or 2425 of this title.

(f) Detention hearing.—The judicial officer shall hold a hearing to determine whether any condition or combination of conditions set forth in subsection (c) of this section will reasonably assure the appearance of such person as required and the safety of any other person and the community—

(1) upon motion of the attorney for the Government, in a case that involves—

(A) a crime of violence, or an offense listed in section 2332b(g)(5)(B) for which a maximum term of imprisonment of 10 years or more is prescribed;

(B) an offense for which the maximum sentence is life imprisonment or death;

(C) an offense for which a maximum term of imprisonment of ten years or more is prescribed in the Controlled Substances Act (21 U.S.C. 801 et seq.), the Controlled Substances Import and Export Act (21 U.S.C. 951 et seq.), or chapter 705 of title 46;

(D) any felony if such person has been convicted of two or more offenses described in subparagraphs (A) through (C) of this paragraph, or two or more State or local offenses that would have been offenses described in subparagraphs (A) through (C) of this paragraph if a circumstance giving rise to Federal jurisdiction had existed, or a combination of such offenses; or

(E) any felony that is not otherwise a crime of violence that involves a minor victim or that involves the possession or use of a firearm or destructive device (as those terms are defined in section 921), or any other dangerous weapon, or involves a failure to register under section 2250 of title 18, United States Code; or

(2) Upon motion of the attorney for the Government or upon the judicial officer's own motion, in a case that involves—

(A) a serious risk that such person will flee; or

(B) a serious risk that such person will obstruct or attempt to obstruct justice, or threaten, injure, or intimidate, or attempt to threaten, injure, or intimidate, a prospective witness or juror.

The hearing shall be held immediately upon the person's first appearance before the judicial officer unless that person, or the attorney for the Government, seeks a continuance. Except for good cause, a continuance on motion of such person may not exceed five days (not including any intermediate Saturday, Sunday, or legal holiday), and a continuance on motion of the attorney for the Government may not exceed three days (not including any intermediate Saturday, Sunday, or legal holiday). During a continuance, such person shall be detained, and the judicial officer, on motion of the attorney for the Government or sua sponte, may order that, while in custody, a person who appears to be a narcotics addict receive a medical examination to determine whether such person is an addict. At the hearing, such person has the right to be represented by counsel, and, if financially unable to obtain adequate representation, to have counsel appointed. The person shall be afforded an opportunity to testify, to present witnesses, to cross-examine witnesses who appear at the hearing, and to present information by proffer or otherwise. The rules concerning admissibility of evidence in criminal trials do not apply to the presentation and consideration of information at the hearing. The facts the judicial officer uses to support a finding pursuant to subsection (e) that no condition or combination of conditions will reasonably assure the safety of any other person and the community shall be supported by clear and convincing evidence. The person may be detained pending completion of the hearing. The hearing may be reopened, before or after a determination by the judicial officer, at any time before trial if the judicial officer finds that information exists that was not known to the movant at the time of the hearing and that has a material bearing on the issue whether there are conditions of release that will reasonably assure the appearance of such person as required and the safety of any other person and the community.

(g) Factors to be considered.—The judicial officer shall, in determining whether there are conditions of release that will reasonably assure the appearance of the person as required and the safety of any other person and the community, take into account the available information concerning—

(1) the nature and circumstances of the offense charged, including whether the offense is a crime of violence, a Federal crime of terrorism, or involves a minor victim or a controlled substance, firearm, explosive, or destructive device;

(2) the weight of the evidence against the person;

(3) the history and characteristics of the person, including—

(A) the person's character, physical and mental condition, family ties, employment, financial resources, length of residence in the community, community ties, past conduct, history relating to drug or alcohol abuse, criminal history, and record concerning appearance at court proceedings; and

(B) whether, at the time of the current offense or arrest, the person was on probation, on parole, or on other release pending trial, sentencing, appeal, or completion of sentence for an offense under Federal, State, or local law; and

(4) the nature and seriousness of the danger to any person or the community that would be posed by the person's release. In considering the conditions of release described in subsection (c)(1)(B)(xi) or (c)(1)(B)(xii) of this section, the judicial officer may upon his own motion, or shall upon the motion of the Government, conduct an inquiry into the source of the property to be designated for potential forfeiture or offered as collateral to secure a bond, and shall decline to accept the designation, or the use as collateral, of property that, because of its source, will not reasonably assure the appearance of the person as required.

(h) Contents of release order.—In a release order issued under subsection (b) or (c) of this section, the judicial officer shall—

(1) include a written statement that sets forth all the conditions to which the release is subject, in a manner sufficiently clear and specific to serve as a guide for the person's conduct; and

(2) advise the person of—

(A) the penalties for violating a condition of release, including the penalties for committing an offense while on pretrial release;

(B) the consequences of violating a condition of release, including the immediate issuance of a warrant for the person's arrest; and

(C) sections 1503 of this title (relating to intimidation of witnesses, jurors, and officers of the court), 1510 (relating to obstruction of criminal investigations), 1512 (tampering with a witness, victim, or an informant), and 1513 (retaliating against a witness, victim, or an informant).

(i) Contents of detention order.—In a detention order issued under subsection (e) of this section, the judicial officer shall—

(1) include written findings of fact and a written statement of the reasons for the detention;

(2) direct that the person be committed to the custody of the Attorney General for confinement in a corrections facility separate, to the extent practicable, from persons awaiting or serving sentences or being held in custody pending appeal;

(3) direct that the person be afforded reasonable opportunity for private consultation with counsel; and

(4) direct that, on order of a court of the United States or on request of an attorney for the Government, the person in charge of the corrections facility in which the person is confined deliver the person to a United States marshal for the purpose of an appearance in connection with a court proceeding.

The judicial officer may, by subsequent order, permit the temporary release of the person, in the custody of a United States marshal or another appropriate person, to the extent that the judicial officer determines such release to be necessary for preparation of the person's defense or for another compelling reason.

(j) Presumption of innocence.—Nothing in this section shall be construed as modifying or limiting the presumption of innocence.

(Added Pub.L. 98–473, Title II, § 203(a), Oct. 12, 1984, 98 Stat. 1976, and amended Pub.L. 99–646, §§ 55(a), (c), 72, Nov. 10, 1986, 100 Stat. 3607, 3617; Pub.L. 100–690, Title VII, § 7073, Nov. 18, 1988, 102 Stat. 4405; Pub.L. 101–647, Title X, § 1001(b), Title XXXVI, §§ 3622–3624, Nov. 29, 1990, 104 Stat. 4827, 4965; Pub.L. 104–132, Title VII, §§ 702(d), 729, Apr. 24, 1996, 110 Stat. 1294, 1302; Pub.L. 108–21, Title II, § 203, Apr. 30, 2003, 117 Stat. 660; Pub.L. 108–458, Title VI, § 6952, Dec. 17, 2004, 118 Stat. 3775; Pub.L. 109–162, Title X, § 1004(b), Jan. 5, 2006, 119 Stat.

3085; Pub.L. 109–248, Title II, § 216, July 27, 2006, 120 Stat. 617; Pub.L. 109–304, § 17(d)(7), Oct. 6, 2006, 120 Stat. 1707.)

HISTORICAL AND STATUTORY NOTES

References in Text

Section 102 of the Controlled Substances Act, referred to in subsec. (c)(1)(B)(ix), is classified to section 802 of Title 21, Food and Drugs.

Section 101(a)(20) of the Immigration and Nationality Act, referred to in subsec. (d)(1)(B), is classified to section 1101(a)(20) of Title 8, Aliens and Nationality.

The Controlled Substances Act, referred to in subsecs. (e) and (f)(1)(C), is Title II of Pub.L. 91–513, Oct. 27, 1970, 84 Stat. 1242, which is classified principally to subchapter I (section 801 et seq.) of chapter 13 of Title 21, Food and Drugs. For complete classification of this Act to the Code, see Short Title note set out under section 801 of Title 21 and Tables volume.

The Controlled Substances Import and Export Act, referred to in subsecs. (e) and (f)(1)(C), is Title III of Pub.L. 91–513, Oct. 27, 1970, 84 Stat. 1285, which is classified principally to subchapter II (section 951 et seq.) of chapter 13 of Title 21. For complete classification of this Act to the Code, see Short Title note set out under section 951 of Title 21 and Tables volume.

Chapter 705 of title 46, referred to in subsecs. (e) and (f)(1)(C), is Maritime Drug Law Enforcement, 46 U.S.C.A. § 70501 et seq.

Effective and Applicability Provisions

1990 Acts. Amendment by sections 3622, 3623 and 3624 of Pub.L. 101–647 effective 180 days after Nov. 29, 1990, see section 3631 of Pub.L. 101–647, set out as a note under section 3001 of Title 28, Judiciary and Judicial Procedure.

1986 Acts. Amendment by section 55 of Pub.L. 99–646 effective 30 days after Nov. 10, 1986, see section 55(j) of Pub.L. 99–646, set out as a note under section 3141 of this title.

Abolition of Immigration and Naturalization Service and Transfer of Functions

For abolition of Immigration and Naturalization Service, transfer of functions, and treatment of related references, see note set out under 8 U.S.C.A. § 1551.

Prior Provisions

A prior section 3142, Act June 25, 1948, c. 645, 62 Stat. 821; June 22, 1966, Pub.L. 89–465, § 5(c), 80 Stat. 217, relating to surrender by bail, was repealed by Pub.L. 98–473, Title II, c. 1, § 203(a), Oct. 12, 1984, 98 Stat. 1976. See section 3149 of this title.

§ 3143. Release or detention of a defendant pending sentence or appeal

(a) Release or detention pending sentence.—(1) Except as provided in paragraph (2), the judicial officer shall order that a person who has been found guilty of an offense and who is awaiting imposition or execution of sentence, other than a person for whom the applicable guideline promulgated pursuant to 28 U.S.C. 994 does not recommend a term of imprisonment, be detained, unless the judicial officer finds by clear and convincing evidence that the person is not likely to flee or pose a danger to the safety of any other person or the community if released under section 3142(b) or (c). If the judicial officer makes such a finding, such judicial officer shall order the release of the person in accordance with section 3142(b) or (c).

(2) The judicial officer shall order that a person who has been found guilty of an offense in a case described in subparagraph (A), (B), or (C) of subsection (f)(1) of section 3142 and is awaiting imposition or execution of sentence be detained unless—

(A)(i) the judicial officer finds there is a substantial likelihood that a motion for acquittal or new trial will be granted; or

(ii) an attorney for the Government has recommended that no sentence of imprisonment be imposed on the person; and

(B) the judicial officer finds by clear and convincing evidence that the person is not likely to flee or pose a danger to any other person or the community.

(b) Release or detention pending appeal by the defendant.—(1) Except as provided in paragraph (2), the judicial officer shall order that a person who has been found guilty of an offense and sentenced to a term of imprisonment, and who has filed an appeal or a petition for a writ of certiorari, be detained, unless the judicial officer finds—

(A) by clear and convincing evidence that the person is not likely to flee or pose a danger to the safety of any other person or the community if released under section 3142(b) or (c) of this title; and

(B) that the appeal is not for the purpose of delay and raises a substantial question of law or fact likely to result in—

(i) reversal,

(ii) an order for a new trial,

(iii) a sentence that does not include a term of imprisonment, or

(iv) a reduced sentence to a term of imprisonment less than the total of the time already served plus the expected duration of the appeal process.

If the judicial officer makes such findings, such judicial officer shall order the release of the person in accordance with section 3142(b) or (c) of this title, except that in the circumstance described in subparagraph (B)(iv) of this paragraph, the judicial officer shall order the detention terminated at the expiration of the likely reduced sentence.

(2) The judicial officer shall order that a person who has been found guilty of an offense in a case described in subparagraph (A), (B), or (C) of subsection (f)(1) of section 3142 and sentenced to a term of imprisonment, and who has filed an appeal or a petition for a writ of certiorari, be detained.

(c) Release or detention pending appeal by the government.—The judicial officer shall treat a defendant in a case in which an appeal has been taken by the United States under section 3731 of this title, in accordance with section 3142 of this title, unless the defendant is otherwise subject to a release or detention order.

Except as provided in subsection (b) of this section, the judicial officer, in a case in which an appeal has been taken by the United States under section 3742, shall—

(1) if the person has been sentenced to a term of imprisonment, order that person detained; and

(2) in any other circumstance, release or detain the person under section 3142.

(Added Pub.L. 98–473, Title II, § 203(a), Oct. 12, 1984, 98 Stat. 1981, and amended Pub.L. 98–473, Title II, § 223(f), Oct. 12, 1986, 98 Stat. 2028; Pub.L. 99–646, §§ 51(a), 55(a), (d), Nov. 10, 1986, 100 Stat. 3605, 3607, 3609; Pub.L. 100–690, Title VII, § 7091, Nov. 18, 1988, 102 Stat. 4410; Pub.L. 101–647, Title IX, § 902(a), (b), Title X, § 1001(a), Nov. 29, 1990, 104 Stat. 4826, 4827; Pub.L. 102–572, Title VII, § 703, Oct. 29, 1992, 106 Stat. 4515.)

HISTORICAL AND STATUTORY NOTES

Effective and Applicability Provisions

1992 Acts. Amendment by Pub.L. 102–572 effective Jan. 1, 1993, see section 1101 of Pub.L. 102–572, set out as a note under section 905 of Title 2, The Congress.

1986 Acts. Amendment by section 55 of Pub.L. 99–646 effective 30 days after Nov. 10, 1986, see section 55(j) of Pub.L. 99–646, set out as a note under section 3141 of this title.

1984 Amendments. Amendment by Pub.L. 98–473 effective on the first day of first calendar month beginning thirty-six months after Oct. 12, 1984, applicable only to offenses committed after taking effect of sections 211 to 239 of Pub.L. 98–473, and except as otherwise provided for therein, see section 235 of Pub.L. 98–473, as amended, set out as a note under section 3551 of this title.

Repeals

Section 51(b) of Pub.L. 99–646 provided that amendment by section 223(f)(2) of Pub.L. 98–473 shall not take effect, such amendment having added a concluding sentence to subsec. (c), eff. Nov. 1, 1987 pursuant to section 235(a)(1) of Pub.L. 98–473, which read: "The judge shall treat a defendant in a case in which an appeal has been taken by the United States pursuant to the provisions of section 3742 in accordance with the provisions of—

"(1) subsection (a) if the person has been sentenced to a term of imprisonment; or

"(2) section 3142 if the person has not been sentenced to a term of imprisonment."

Prior Provisions

A prior section 3143, Act June 25, 1948, c. 645, 62 Stat. 821; June 22, 1966, Pub.L. 89–465, § 5(d), 80 Stat. 217, providing for additional bail in cases where it appeared that a person was about to abscond and that the person's bail was insufficient, was repealed by Pub.L. 98–473, Title II, c. 1, § 203(a), Oct. 12, 1984, 98 Stat. 1976.

§ 3144. Release or detention of a material witness

If it appears from an affidavit filed by a party that the testimony of a person is material in a criminal proceeding, and if it is shown that it may become impracticable to secure the presence of the person by subpoena, a judicial officer may order the arrest of the person and treat the person in accordance with the provisions of section 3142 of this title. No material witness may be detained because of inability to comply with any condition of release if the testimony of such witness can adequately be secured by deposition, and if further detention is not necessary to prevent a failure of justice. Release of a material witness may be delayed for a reasonable period of time until the deposition of the witness can be taken pursuant to the Federal Rules of Criminal Procedure.

(Added Pub.L. 98–473, Title II, § 203(a), Oct. 12, 1984, 98 Stat. 1982, and amended Pub.L. 99–646, § 55(e), Nov. 10, 1986, 100 Stat. 3609.)

HISTORICAL AND STATUTORY NOTES

Effective and Applicability Provisions

1986 Acts. Amendment by section 55 of Pub.L. 99–646 effective 30 days after Nov. 10, 1986, see section 55(j) of Pub.L. 99–646, set out as a note under section 3141 of this title.

Prior Provisions

A prior section 3144, Act June 25, 1948, c. 645, 62 Stat. 821, providing for bail in cases removed from State courts and brought to the Supreme Court of the United States, was repealed by Pub.L. 98–473, Title II, c. 1, § 203(a), Oct. 12, 1984, 98 Stat. 1976. See section 3150 of this title.

§ 3145. Review and appeal of a release or detention order

(a) Review of a release order.—If a person is ordered released by a magistrate judge, or by a person other than a judge of a court having original jurisdiction over the offense and other than a Federal appellate court—

(1) the attorney for the Government may file, with the court having original jurisdiction over the offense, a motion for revocation of the order or amendment of the conditions of release; and

(2) the person may file, with the court having original jurisdiction over the offense, a motion for amendment of the conditions of release.

The motion shall be determined promptly.

(b) Review of a detention order.—If a person is ordered detained by a magistrate judge, or by a person other than a judge of a court having original jurisdiction over the offense and other than a Federal appellate court, the person may file, with the court having original jurisdiction over the offense, a motion for revocation or amendment of the order. The motion shall be determined promptly.

(c) Appeal from a release or detention order.—An appeal from a release or detention order, or from a decision denying revocation or amendment of such an order, is governed by the provisions of section 1291 of title 28 and section 3731 of this title. The appeal shall be determined promptly. A person subject to detention pursuant to section 3143(a)(2) or (b)(2), and who meets the conditions of release set forth in section 3143(a)(1) or (b)(1), may be ordered released, under appropriate conditions, by the judicial officer, if it is clearly shown that there are exceptional reasons why such person's detention would not be appropriate.

(Added Pub.L. 98–473, Title II, § 203(a), Oct. 12, 1984, 98 Stat. 1982, and amended Pub.L. 101–647, Title IX, § 902(c), Nov. 29, 1990, 104 Stat. 4827; Pub.L. 101–650, Title III, § 321, Dec. 1, 1990, 104 Stat. 5117.)

HISTORICAL AND STATUTORY NOTES

Change of Name

Words "magistrate judge" substituted for "magistrate" in subsecs. (a) and (b) pursuant to section 321 of Pub.L. 101–650, set out as a note under 28 U.S.C.A. § 631.

Prior Provisions

A prior section 3145, Act June 25, 1948, c. 645, 62 Stat. 821, carrying the section heading "Parties and witnesses" and referring the user to the Federal Rules of Criminal Procedure, was repealed by Pub.L. 98–473, Title II, c. 1, § 203(a), Oct. 12, 1984, 98 Stat. 1976.

§ 3146. Penalty for failure to appear

(a) Offense.—Whoever, having been released under this chapter knowingly—

(1) fails to appear before a court as required by the conditions of release; or

(2) fails to surrender for service of sentence pursuant to a court order;

shall be punished as provided in subsection (b) of this section.

(b) Punishment.—**(1)** The punishment for an offense under this section is—

(A) if the person was released in connection with a charge of, or while awaiting sentence, surrender for service of sentence, or appeal or certiorari after conviction for—

(i) an offense punishable by death, life imprisonment, or imprisonment for a term of 15 years or more, a fine under this title or imprisonment for not more than ten years, or both;

(ii) an offense punishable by imprisonment for a term of five years or more, a fine under this title or imprisonment for not more than five years, or both;

(iii) any other felony, a fine under this title or imprisonment for not more than two years, or both; or

(iv) a misdemeanor, a fine under this title or imprisonment for not more than one year, or both; and

(B) if the person was released for appearance as a material witness, a fine under this chapter or imprisonment for not more than one year, or both.

(2) A term of imprisonment imposed under this section shall be consecutive to the sentence of imprisonment for any other offense.

(c) Affirmative defense.—It is an affirmative defense to a prosecution under this section that uncontrollable circumstances prevented the person from appearing or surrendering, and that the person did not contribute to the creation of such circumstances in reckless disregard of the requirement to appear or surrender, and that the person appeared or surrendered as soon as such circumstances ceased to exist.

(d) Declaration of forfeiture.—If a person fails to appear before a court as required, and the person executed an appearance bond pursuant to section 3142(b) of this title or is subject to the release condition set forth in clause (xi) or (xii) of section 3142(c)(1)(B) of this title, the judicial officer may, regardless of whether the person has been charged with an offense under this section, declare any property designated pursuant to that section to be forfeited to the United States.

(Added Pub.L. 98–473, Title II, § 203(a), Oct. 12, 1984, 98 Stat. 1982, and amended Pub.L. 99–646, § 55(f), Nov. 10, 1986, 100 Stat. 3609; Pub.L. 103–322, Title XXXIII, § 330016(2)(K), Sept. 13, 1994, 108 Stat. 2148; Pub.L. 104–294, Title VI, § 601(a)(4), Oct. 11, 1996, 110 Stat. 3498.)

HISTORICAL AND STATUTORY NOTES

Effective and Applicability Provisions

1986 Acts. Amendment by section 55 of Pub.L. 99–646 effective 30 days after Nov. 10, 1986, see section 55(j) of Pub.L. 99–646, set out as a note under section 3141 of this title.

Prior Provisions

A prior section 3146, added Pub.L. 89–465, § 3(a), June 22, 1966, 80 Stat. 214, and amended Pub.L. 97–291, § 8, Oct. 12, 1982, 96 Stat. 1257, relating to release in noncapital cases prior to trial, was repealed by Pub.L. 98–473, Title II, c. 1, § 203(a), Oct. 12, 1984, 98 Stat. 1976. See section 3142 of this title.

Another prior section 3146, Act Aug. 20, 1954, c. 772, § 1, 68 Stat. 747, which prescribed penalties for jumping bail, was repealed by Pub.L. 89–465, § 3(a), June 22, 1966, 80 Stat. 214. See section 3148 of this title.

§ 3147. Penalty for an offense committed while on release

A person convicted of an offense committed while released under this chapter shall be sentenced, in addition to the sentence prescribed for the offense to—

(1) a term of imprisonment of not more than ten years if the offense is a felony; or

(2) a term of imprisonment of not more than one year if the offense is a misdemeanor.

A term of imprisonment imposed under this section shall be consecutive to any other sentence of imprisonment.

(Added Pub.L. 98–473, Title II, § 203(a), Oct. 12, 1984, 98 Stat. 1983, and amended Pub.L. 98–473, Title II, § 223(g), Oct. 12, 1984, 98 Stat. 2028; Pub.L. 99–646, § 55(g), Nov. 10, 1986, 100 Stat. 3610.)

HISTORICAL AND STATUTORY NOTES

Effective and Applicability Provisions

1986 Acts. Amendment by section 55 of Pub.L. 99–646 effective 30 days after Nov. 10, 1986, see section 55(j) of Pub.L. 99–646, set out as a note under section 3141 of this title.

1984 Acts. Amendment by Pub.L. 98–473 effective Nov. 1, 1987, and applicable only to offenses committed after the taking effect of such amendment, see section 235(a)(1) of Pub.L. 98–473, set out as a note under section 3551 of this title.

Savings Provisions

Amendment by Pub.L. 98–473 effective on the first day of first calendar month beginning thirty-six months after Oct. 12, 1984, applicable only to offenses committed after taking effect of sections 211 to 239 of Pub.L. 98–473, and except as otherwise provided for therein, see section 235 of Pub.L. 98–473, as amended, set out as a note under section 3551 of this title.

Prior Provisions

A prior section 3147, added Pub.L. 89–465, § 3(a), June 22, 1966, 80 Stat. 215, providing for an appeal from the conditions of release was repealed by Pub.L. 98–473, Title II, c. 1, § 203(a), Oct. 12, 1984, 98 Stat. 1976. See section 3145 of this title.

§ 3148. Sanctions for violation of a release condition

(a) Available sanctions.—A person who has been released under section 3142 of this title, and who has violated a condition of his release, is subject to a revocation of release, an order of detention, and a prosecution for contempt of court.

(b) Revocation of release.—The attorney for the Government may initiate a proceeding for revocation of an order of release by filing a motion with the district court. A judicial officer may issue a warrant for the arrest of a person charged with violating a condition of release, and the person shall be brought before a judicial officer in the district in which such person's arrest was ordered for a proceeding in accordance with this section. To the extent practicable, a person charged with violating the condition of release that such person not commit a Federal, State, or local crime during the period of release, shall be brought before the judicial officer who ordered the release and whose order is alleged to have been violated. The judicial officer shall enter an order of revocation and detention if, after a hearing, the judicial officer—

(1) finds that there is—

(A) probable cause to believe that the person has committed a Federal, State, or local crime while on release; or

(B) clear and convincing evidence that the person has violated any other condition of release; and

(2) finds that—

(A) based on the factors set forth in section 3142(g) of this title, there is no condition or combination of conditions of release that will assure that the person will not flee or pose a danger to the safety of any other person or the community; or

(B) the person is unlikely to abide by any condition or combination of conditions of release.

If there is probable cause to believe that, while on release, the person committed a Federal, State, or local felony, a rebuttable presumption arises that no condition or combination of conditions will assure that the person will not pose a danger to the safety of any other person or the community. If the judicial officer finds that there are conditions of release that will assure that the person will not flee or pose a danger to the safety of any other person or the community, and that the person will abide by such conditions, the judicial officer shall treat the person in accordance with the provisions of section 3142 of this title and may amend the conditions of release accordingly.

(c) Prosecution for contempt.—The judicial officer may commence a prosecution for contempt, under section 401 of this title, if the person has violated a condition of release.

(Added Pub.L. 98–473, Title II, § 203(a), Oct. 12, 1984, 98 Stat. 1983, and amended Pub.L. 99–646, § 55(a), (h), Nov. 10, 1986, 100 Stat. 3607, 3610.)

HISTORICAL AND STATUTORY NOTES

Effective and Applicability Provisions

1986 Acts. Amendment by section 55 of Pub.L. 99–646 effective 30 days after Nov. 10, 1986, see section 55(j) of Pub.L. 99–646, set out as a note under section 3141 of this title.

Prior Provisions

A prior section 3148, added Pub.L. 89–465, § 3(a), June 22, 1966, 80 Stat. 215, and amended Pub.L. 91–452, Title X, § 1002, Oct. 15, 1970, 84 Stat. 952, relating to release in capital cases and after conviction, was repealed by Pub.L. 98–473, Title II, c. 1, § 203(a), Oct. 12, 1984, 98 Stat. 1976. See section 3143 of this title.

§ 3149. Surrender of an offender by a surety

A person charged with an offense, who is released upon the execution of an appearance bond with a surety, may be arrested by the surety, and if so arrested, shall be delivered promptly to a United States marshal and brought before a judicial officer. The judicial officer shall determine in accordance with the provisions of section 3148(b) whether to revoke the release of the person, and may absolve the surety of responsibility to pay all or part of the bond in accordance with the provisions of Rule 46 of the Federal Rules of Criminal Procedure. The person so committed shall be held in official detention until released pursuant to this chapter or another provision of law.

(Added Pub.L. 98–473, Title II, § 203(a), Oct. 12, 1984, 98 Stat. 1984.)

HISTORICAL AND STATUTORY NOTES

Prior Provisions

A prior section 3149, added Pub.L. 89–465, § 3(a), June 22, 1966, 80 Stat. 216, providing for the release of material witnesses, was repealed by Pub.L. 98–473, Title II, c. 1, § 203(a), Oct. 12, 1984, 98 Stat. 1976. See section 3144 of this title.

§ 3150. Applicability to a case removed from a State court

The provisions of this chapter apply to a criminal case removed to a Federal court from a State court.

(Added Pub.L. 98–473, Title II, § 203(a), Oct. 12, 1984, 98 Stat. 1984.)

HISTORICAL AND STATUTORY NOTES

Codifications

Section 1410 of Pub.L. 98–433, Title II, ch. XIV, Oct. 12, 1984, 98 Stat. 2178, purported to delete "the general fund of" in subsec. (a) but was incapable of execution.

Prior Provisions

A prior section 3150, added Pub.L. 89–465, § 3(a), June 22, 1966, 80 Stat. 216, providing for penalties for failure to appear, was repealed by Pub.L. 98–473, Title II, c. 1, § 203(a), Oct. 12, 1984, 98 Stat. 1976. See section 3146 of this title.

[§ 3150a. Repealed. Pub.L. 98–473, Title II, § 203(a), Oct. 12, 1984, 98 Stat. 1976]

HISTORICAL AND STATUTORY NOTES

Section, added Pub.L. 97–258, § 2(d)(3)(B), Sept. 13, 1982, 96 Stat. 1058, related to refund of forfeited bail.

Section 49 of Pub.L. 99–646, § 49, Nov. 10, 1986, 100 Stat. 3605 struck out section 1410 of Pub.L. 98–473, amending former section 3150a of this title.

§ 3151. Refund of forfeited bail

Appropriations available to refund money erroneously received and deposited in the Treasury are available to refund any part of forfeited bail deposited into the Treasury and ordered remitted under the Federal Rules of Criminal Procedure.

(Added Pub.L. 100–690, Title VII, § 7084(a), Nov. 18, 1988, 102 Stat. 4408.)

HISTORICAL AND STATUTORY NOTES

References in Text

The Federal Rules of Criminal Procedure, referred to in text, are set out in this title.

Prior Provisions

A prior section 3151, added Pub.L. 89–465, § 3(a), June 22, 1966, 80 Stat. 216, which provided that nothing in this chapter should interfere with or prevent the exercise by any court of the United States of its power to punish for contempt, was repealed by Pub.L. 98–473, Title II, § 203(a), Oct. 12, 1984, 98 Stat. 1976.

§ 3152. Establishment of pretrial services

(a) On and after the date of the enactment of the Pretrial Services Act of 1982, the Director of the Administrative Office of the United States Courts (hereinafter in this chapter referred to as the "Director") shall, under the supervision and direction of the Judicial Conference of the United States, provide directly, or by contract or otherwise (to such extent and in such amounts as are provided in appropriation Acts), for the establishment of pretrial services in each judicial district (other than the District of Columbia). Pretrial services established under this section shall be supervised by a chief probation officer appointed under section 3654 of this title or by a chief pretrial services officer selected under subsection (c) of this section.

(b) Beginning eighteen months after the date of the enactment of the Pretrial Services Act of 1982, if an appropriate United States district court and the circuit judicial council jointly recommend the establishment under this subsection of pretrial services in a particular district, pretrial services shall be established under the general authority of the Administrative Office of the United States Courts.

(c) The pretrial services established under subsection (b) of this section shall be supervised by a chief pretrial services officer selected by a panel consisting of the chief judge of the circuit, the chief judge of the district, and a magistrate judge of the district or their designees. The chief pretrial services officer appointed under this subsection shall be an individual other than one serving under authority of section 3654 of this title.

(Added Pub.L. 93–619, Title II, § 201, Jan. 3, 1975, 88 Stat. 2086, and amended Pub.L. 97–267, § 2, Sept. 27, 1982, 96

Stat. 1136; Pub.L. 101–650, Title III, § 321, Dec. 1, 1990, 104 Stat. 5117.)

HISTORICAL AND STATUTORY NOTES

References in Text

The date of enactment of the Pretrial Services Act of 1982, referred to in subsecs. (a) and (b), is the date of enactment of Pub.L. 97–267, which was approved on Sept. 27, 1982.

Change of Name

Words "magistrate judge" substituted for "magistrate" in subsec. (c) pursuant to section 321 of Pub.L. 101–650, set out as a note under 28 U.S.C.A. § 631.

Prior Provisions

A prior section 3152, as added by Pub.L. 89–465, § 3(a), June 22, 1966, 80 Stat. 216, defined the terms "judicial officer" and "offense", and was repealed by Pub.L. 93–619, Title II, § 201, Jan. 3, 1975, 88 Stat. 2086. See section 3156 of this title.

Status of Pretrial Services Agencies in Effect Prior to September 27, 1982

Section 8 of Pub.L. 97–267 provided that: "During the period beginning on the date of enactment of this Act [Sept. 27, 1982] and ending eighteen months after the date of the enactment of this Act, the pretrial services agencies established under section 3152 of title 18 of the United States Code [this section] in effect before the date of enactment of this Act [Sept. 27, 1982] may continue to operate, employ staff, provide pretrial services, and perform such functions and powers as are authorized under chapter 207 of title 18 of the United States Code [this chapter]."

Authorization of Appropriations

Section 9 of Pub.L. 97–267 provided that:

"(a) There are authorized to be appropriated, for the fiscal year ending September 30, 1984, and each succeeding fiscal year thereafter, such sums as may be necessary to carry out the functions and powers of pretrial services established under section 3152(b) of title 18, United States Code [subsec. (b) of this section].

"(b) There are authorized to be appropriated for the fiscal year ending September 30, 1983, and the fiscal year ending September 30, 1984, such sums as may be necessary to carry out the functions and powers of the pretrial services agencies established under section 3152 of title 18 of the United States Code [this section] in effect before the date of enactment of this Act [Sept. 27, 1982]."

§ 3153. Organization and administration of pretrial services

(a)(1) With the approval of the district court, the chief pretrial services officer in districts in which pretrial services are established under section 3152(b) of this title shall appoint such other personnel as may be required. The position requirements and rate of compensation of the chief pretrial services officer and such other personnel shall be established by the Director with the approval of the Judicial Conference of the United States, except that no such rate of compensation shall exceed the rate of basic pay in effect and then payable for grade GS–16 of the General Schedule under section 5332 of title 5, United States Code.

(2) The chief pretrial services officer in districts in which pretrial services are established under section 3152(b) of this title is authorized, subject to the general policy established by the Director and the approval of the district court, to procure temporary and intermittent services to the extent authorized by section 3109 of title 5, United States Code. The staff, other than clerical staff, may be drawn from law school students, graduate students, or such other available personnel.

(b) The chief probation officer in all districts in which pretrial services are established under section 3152(a) of this title shall designate personnel appointed under chapter 231 of this title to perform pretrial services under this chapter.

(c)(1) Except as provided in paragraph (2) of this subsection, information obtained in the course of performing pretrial services functions in relation to a particular accused shall be used only for the purposes of a bail determination and shall otherwise be confidential. Each pretrial services report shall be made available to the attorney for the accused and the attorney for the Government.

(2) The Director shall issue regulations establishing the policy for release of information made confidential by paragraph (1) of this subsection. Such regulations shall provide exceptions to the confidentiality requirements under paragraph (1) of this subsection to allow access to such information—

(A) by qualified persons for purposes of research related to the administration of criminal justice;

(B) by persons under contract under section 3154(4) of this title;

(C) by probation officers for the purpose of compiling presentence reports;

(D) insofar as such information is a pretrial diversion report, to the attorney for the accused and the attorney for the Government; and

(E) in certain limited cases, to law enforcement agencies for law enforcement purposes.

(3) Information made confidential under paragraph (1) of this subsection is not admissible on the issue of guilt in a criminal judicial proceeding unless such proceeding is a prosecution for a crime committed in the course of obtaining pretrial release or a prosecution for failure to appear for the criminal judicial proceeding with respect to which pretrial services were provided.

(Added Pub.L. 93–619, Title II, § 201, Jan. 3, 1975, 88 Stat. 2086, and amended Pub.L. 97–267, § 3, Sept. 27, 1982, 96 Stat. 1136.)

§ 3154. Functions and powers relating to pretrial services

Pretrial services functions shall include the following:

(1) Collect, verify, and report to the judicial officer, prior to the pretrial release hearing, information pertaining to the pretrial release of each individual charged with an offense, including information relating to any danger that the release of such person may pose to any other person or the community, and, where appropriate, include a recommendation as to whether such individual should be released or detained and, if release is recommended, recommend appropriate conditions of release; except that a district court may direct that information not be collected, verified, or reported under this paragraph on individuals charged with Class A misdemeanors as defined in section 3559(a)(6) of this title.

(2) Review and modify the reports and recommendations specified in paragraph (1) of this section for persons seeking release pursuant to section 3145 of this chapter.

(3) Supervise persons released into its custody under this chapter.

(4) Operate or contract for the operation of appropriate facilities for the custody or care of persons released under this chapter including residential halfway houses, addict and alcoholic treatment centers, and counseling services.

(5) Inform the court and the United States attorney of all apparent violations of pretrial release conditions, arrests of persons released to the custody of providers of pretrial services or under the supervision of providers of pretrial services, and any danger that any such person may come to pose to any other person or the community, and recommend appropriate modifications of release conditions.

(6) Serve as coordinator for other local agencies which serve or are eligible to serve as custodians under this chapter and advise the court as to the eligibility, availability, and capacity of such agencies.

(7) Assist persons released under this chapter in securing any necessary employment, medical, legal, or social services.

(8) Prepare, in cooperation with the United States marshal and the United States attorney such pretrial detention reports as are required by the provisions of the Federal Rules of Criminal Procedure relating to the supervision of detention pending trial.

(9) Develop and implement a system to monitor and evaluate bail activities, provide information to judicial officers on the results of bail decisions, and prepare periodic reports to assist in the improvement of the bail process.

(10) To the extent provided for in an agreement between a chief pretrial services officer in districts in which pretrial services are established under section 3152(b) of this title, or the chief probation officer in all other districts, and the United States attorney, collect, verify, and prepare reports for the United States attorney's office of information pertaining to the pretrial diversion of any individual who is or may be charged with an offense, and perform such other duties as may be required under any such agreement.

(11) Make contracts, to such extent and in such amounts as are provided in appropriation Acts, for the carrying out of any pretrial services functions.

(12)(A) As directed by the court and to the degree required by the regimen of care or treatment ordered by the court as a condition of release, keep informed as to the conduct and provide supervision of a person conditionally released under the provisions of section 4243 or 4246 of this title, and report such person's conduct and condition to the court ordering release and the Attorney General or his designee.

(B) Any violation of the conditions of release shall immediately be reported to the court and the Attorney General or his designee.

(13) If approved by the district court, be authorized to carry firearms under such rules and regulations as the Director of the Administrative Office of the United States Courts may prescribe.

(14) Perform such other functions as specified under this chapter.

(Added Pub.L. 93–619, Title II, § 201, Jan. 3, 1975, 88 Stat. 2087, and amended Pub.L. 97–267, § 4, Sept. 27, 1982, 96 Stat. 1137; Pub.L. 98–437, Title II, § 203(b), Oct. 12, 1984, 98 Stat. 1984; Pub.L. 101–647, Title XXXV, § 3576, Nov. 29, 1990, 104 Stat. 4929; Pub.L. 102–572, Title VII, § 701(b), Title X, § 1002, Oct. 29, 1992, 106 Stat. 4515, 4521; Pub.L. 104–317, Title I, § 101(b), Oct. 19, 1996, 110 Stat. 3848.)

HISTORICAL AND STATUTORY NOTES

Codifications

Section 203(b)(1) of Pub.L. 98–473, Title II, c. 1, Oct. 12, 1984, 98 Stat.1984, which directed the substitution in par. (1) of "and, where appropriate, include a recommendation as to whether such individual should be released or detained and, if release is recommended, recommend appropriate conditions of release" for "and recommend appropriate release conditions for each such person" was executed by inserting the substituted phrase for "and recommend appropriate release conditions for such individual" as the probable intent of Congress.

Effective and Applicability Provisions

1992 Acts. Amendment by Pub.L. 102–572 effective Jan. 1, 1993, see section 1101 of Pub.L. 102–572, set out as a note under section 905 of Title 2, The Congress.

Demonstration Program For Drug Testing of Arrested Persons and Defendants on Probation or Supervised Release

Pub.L. 100–690, Title VII, § 7304, Nov. 18, 1988, 102 Stat. 4464, provided that:

"**(a) Establishment.**—The Director of the Administrative Office of the United States Courts shall establish a demonstration program of mandatory testing of criminal defendants.

"**(b) Length of Program.**—The demonstration program shall begin not later than January 1, 1989, and shall last two years.

"**(c) Selection of Districts.**—The Judicial Conference of the United States shall select 8 Federal judicial districts in which to carry out the demonstration program, so that the group selected represents a mix of districts on the basis of criminal caseload and the types of cases in that caseload.

"**(d) Inclusion in Pretrial Services.**—In each of the districts in which the demonstration program takes place, pretrial services under chapter 207 of title 18, United States Code [this chapter], shall arrange for the drug testing of defendants in criminal cases. To the extent feasible, such testing shall be completed before the defendant makes the defendant's initial appearance in the case before a judicial officer. The results of such testing shall be included in the report to the judicial officer under section 3154 of title 18, United States Code [this section].

"**(e) Mandatory Condition of Probation and Supervised Release.**—In each of the judicial districts in which the demonstration program is in effect, it shall be an additional, mandatory condition of probation, and an additional mandatory condition of supervised release for offenses occurring or completed on or after January 1, 1989, for any defendant convicted of a felony, that such defendant refrain from any illegal use of any controlled substance (as defined in section 102 of the Controlled Substances Act [section 802 of Title 21, Food and Drugs]) and submit to periodic drug tests for use of controlled substances at least once every 60 days. The requirement that drug tests be administered at least once every 60 days may be suspended upon motion of the Director of the Administrative Office, or the Director's designee, if, after at least one year of probation or supervised release, the defendant has passed all drug tests administered pursuant to this section. No action may be taken against a defendant pursuant to a drug test administered in accordance with this subsection unless the drug test confirmation is a urine drug test confirmed using gas chromatography techniques or such test as the Secretary of Health and Human Services may determine to be of equivalent accuracy.

"**(f) Report to Congress.**—Not later than 90 days after the first year of the demonstration program and not later than 90 days after the end of the demonstration program, the Director of the Administrative Office of the United States Courts shall report to Congress on the effectiveness of the demonstration program and include in such report recommendations as to whether mandatory drug testing of defendants should be made more general and permanent."

§ 3155. Annual reports

Each chief pretrial services officer in districts in which pretrial services are established under section 3152(b) of this title, and each chief probation officer in all other districts, shall prepare an annual report to the chief judge of the district court and the Director concerning the administration and operation of pretrial services. The Director shall be required to include in the Director's annual report to the Judicial Conference under section 604 of title 28 a report on the administration and operation of the pretrial services for the previous year.

(Added Pub.L. 93–619, Title II, § 201, Jan. 3, 1975, 88 Stat. 2088, and amended Pub.L. 97–267, § 5, Sept. 27, 1982, 96 Stat. 1138.)

§ 3156. Definitions

(a) As used in sections 3141–3150 of this chapter—

(1) the term "judicial officer" means, unless otherwise indicated, any person or court authorized pursuant to section 3041 of this title, or the Federal Rules of Criminal Procedure, to detain or release a person before trial or sentencing or pending appeal in a court of the United States, and any judge of the Superior Court of the District of Columbia;

(2) the term "offense" means any criminal offense, other than an offense triable by court-martial, military commission, provost court, or other military tribunal, which is in violation of an Act of Congress and is triable in any court established by Act of Congress;

(3) the term "felony" means an offense punishable by a maximum term of imprisonment of more than one year;

(4) the term "crime of violence" means—

(A) an offense that has an element of the offense the use, attempted use, or threatened use of physical force against the person or property of another;

(B) any other offense that is a felony and that, by its nature, involves a substantial risk that physical force against the person or property of another may be used in the course of committing the offense; or

(C) any felony under chapter 109A, 110, or 117; and

(5) the term "State" includes a State of the United States, the District of Columbia, and any commonwealth, territory, or possession of the United States.

(b) As used in sections 3152–3155 of this chapter—

(1) the term "judicial officer" means, unless otherwise indicated, any person or court authorized pursuant to section 3041 of this title, or the Federal Rules of Criminal Procedure, to detain or release a person before trial or sentencing or pending appeal in a court of the United States, and

(2) the term "offense" means any Federal criminal offense which is in violation of any Act of Congress and is triable by any court established by Act of Congress (other than a Class B or C misdemeanor or an infraction, or an offense triable by court-martial, military commission, provost court, or other military tribunal).

(Added Pub.L. 93–619, Title II, § 201, Jan. 3, 1975, 88 Stat. 2088, and amended Pub.L. 98–473, Title II, § 203(c), 223(h), Oct. 12, 1984, 98 Stat. 1985, 2029; Pub.L. 99–646, § 55(i), Nov. 10, 1986, 100 Stat. 3611; Pub.L. 103–322, Title IV, § 40501, Sept. 13, 1994, 108 Stat. 1945; Pub.L. 104–294, Title VI, § 607(i), Oct. 11, 1996, 110 Stat. 3512; Pub.L. 105–314, Title VI, § 601, Oct. 30, 1998, 112 Stat. 2982.)

HISTORICAL AND STATUTORY NOTES

References in Text

Chapter 109A, referred to in subsec. (a)(4)(C), is 18 U.S.C.A. § 2241 et seq.

Chapter 110, referred to in subsec. (a)(4)(C), is 18 U.S.C.A. § 2251 et seq.

Chapter 117, referred to in subsec. (a)(4)(C), is 18 U.S.C.A. § 2421 et seq.

Effective and Applicability Provisions

1986 Acts. Amendment by section 55 of Pub.L. 99–646 effective 30 days after Nov. 10, 1986, see section 55(j) of Pub.L. 99–646, set out as a note under section 3141 of this title.

1984 Acts. Amendment by section 223(h) of Pub.L. 98–473 effective Nov. 1, 1987, and applicable only to offenses committed after the taking effect of such amendment, see section 235(a)(1) of Pub.L. 98–473, set out as a note under section 3551 of this title.

Savings Provisions

Amendment by Pub.L. 98–473 effective on the first day of first calendar month beginning thirty-six months after Oct. 12, 1984, applicable only to offenses committed after taking effect of sections 211 to 239 of Pub.L. 98–473, and except as otherwise provided for therein, see section 235 of Pub.L. 98–473, as amended, set out as a note under section 3551 of this title.

CHAPTER 208—SPEEDY TRIAL

Sec.

§ 3161. Time limits and exclusions

(a) In any case involving a defendant charged with an offense, the appropriate judicial officer, at the earliest practicable time, shall, after consultation with the counsel for the defendant and the attorney for the Government, set the case for trial on a day certain, or list it for trial on a weekly or other short-term trial calendar at a place within the judicial district, so as to assure a speedy trial.

(b) Any information or indictment charging an individual with the commission of an offense shall be filed within thirty days from the date on which such individual was arrested or served with a summons in connection with such charges. If an individual has been charged with a felony in a district in which no grand jury has been in session during such thirty-day period, the period of time for filing of the indictment shall be extended an additional thirty days.

(c)(1) In any case in which a plea of not guilty is entered, the trial of a defendant charged in an information or indictment with the commission of an offense shall commence within seventy days from the filing date (and making public) of the information or indictment, or from the date the defendant has appeared before a judicial officer of the court in which such charge is pending, whichever date last occurs. If a defendant consents in writing to be tried before a magistrate judge on a complaint, the trial shall commence within seventy days from the date of such consent.

(2) Unless the defendant consents in writing to the contrary, the trial shall not commence less than thirty days from the date on which the defendant first appears through counsel or expressly waives counsel and elects to proceed pro se.

(d)(1) If any indictment or information is dismissed upon motion of the defendant, or any charge contained in a complaint filed against an individual is dismissed or otherwise dropped, and thereafter a complaint is filed against such defendant or individual charging him with the same offense or an offense based on the same conduct or arising from the same criminal episode, or an information or indictment is filed charging such defendant with the same offense or an offense based on the same conduct or arising from the same criminal episode, the provisions of subsections (b) and (c) of this section shall be applicable with respect to such subsequent complaint, indictment, or information, as the case may be.

(2) If the defendant is to be tried upon an indictment or information dismissed by a trial court and reinstated following an appeal, the trial shall commence within seventy days from the date the action occasioning the trial becomes final, except that the court retrying the case may extend the period for trial not to exceed one hundred and eighty days from the date the action occasioning the trial becomes final if the unavailability of witnesses or other factors resulting from the passage of time shall make trial within seventy days impractical. The periods of delay enumerated in section 3161(h) are excluded in computing the time limitations specified in this section. The sanctions of section 3162 apply to this subsection.

(e) If the defendant is to be tried again following a declaration by the trial judge of a mistrial or following an order of such judge for a new trial, the trial shall commence within seventy days from the date the action occasioning the retrial becomes final. If the defendant is to be tried again following an appeal or a collateral attack, the trial shall commence within seventy days from the date the action occasioning the retrial becomes final, except that the court retrying the case may extend the period for retrial not to exceed one hundred and eighty days from the date the action occasioning the retrial becomes final if unavailability of witnesses or other factors resulting from passage of time shall make trial within seventy days impractical. The periods of delay enumerated in section 3161(h) are excluded in computing the time limitations specified in this section. The sanctions of section 3162 apply to this subsection.

(f) Notwithstanding the provisions of subsection (b) of this section, for the first twelve-calendar-month period following the effective date of this section as set forth in section 3163(a) of this chapter the time limit imposed with respect to the period between arrest and indictment by subsection (b) of this section shall be sixty days, for the second such twelve-month period such time limit shall be forty-five days and for the third such period such time limit shall be thirty-five days.

(g) Notwithstanding the provisions of subsection (c) of this section, for the first twelve-calendar-month period following the effective date of this section as set forth in section 3163(b) of this chapter, the time limit with respect to the period between arraignment and trial imposed by subsection (c) of this section shall be one hundred and eighty days, for the second such twelve-month period such time limit shall be one hundred and twenty days, and for the third such period such time limit with respect to the period between arraignment and trial shall be eighty days.

(h) The following periods of delay shall be excluded in computing the time within which an information or an indictment must be filed, or in computing the time within which the trial of any such offense must commence:

(1) Any period of delay resulting from other proceedings concerning the defendant, including but not limited to—

(A) delay resulting from any proceeding, including any examinations, to determine the mental competency or physical capacity of the defendant;

(B) delay resulting from any proceeding, including any examination of the defendant, pursuant to section 2902 of title 28, United States Code;

(C) delay resulting from deferral of prosecution pursuant to section 2902 of title 28, United States Code;

(D) delay resulting from trial with respect to other charges against the defendant;

(E) delay resulting from any interlocutory appeal;

(F) delay resulting from any pretrial motion, from the filing of the motion through the conclusion of the hearing on, or other prompt disposition of, such motion;

(G) delay resulting from any proceeding relating to the transfer of a case or the removal of any defendant from another district under the Federal Rules of Criminal Procedure;

(H) delay resulting from transportation of any defendant from another district, or to and from places of examination or hospitalization, except that any time consumed in excess of ten days from the date an order of removal or an order directing such transportation, and the defendant's arrival at the destination shall be presumed to be unreasonable;

(I) delay resulting from consideration by the court of a proposed plea agreement to be entered into by the defendant and the attorney for the Government; and

(J) delay reasonably attributable to any period, not to exceed thirty days, during which any proceeding concerning the defendant is actually under advisement by the court.

(2) Any period of delay during which prosecution is deferred by the attorney for the Government pursuant to written agreement with the defendant, with the approval of the court, for the purpose of allowing the defendant to demonstrate his good conduct.

(3)(A) Any period of delay resulting from the absence or unavailability of the defendant or an essential witness.

(B) For purposes of subparagraph (A) of this paragraph, a defendant or an essential witness shall be considered absent when his whereabouts are unknown and, in addition, he is attempting to avoid apprehension or prosecution or his whereabouts cannot be determined by due diligence. For purposes of such subparagraph, a defendant or an essential witness shall be considered unavailable whenever his whereabouts are known but his presence for trial cannot be obtained by due diligence or he resists appearing at or being returned for trial.

(4) Any period of delay resulting from the fact that the defendant is mentally incompetent or physically unable to stand trial.

(5) Any period of delay resulting from the treatment of the defendant pursuant to section 2902 of title 28, United States Code.

(6) If the information or indictment is dismissed upon motion of the attorney for the Government and thereafter a charge is filed against the defendant for the same offense, or any offense required to be joined with that offense, any period of delay from the date the charge was dismissed to the date the time limitation would commence to run as to the subsequent charge had there been no previous charge.

(7) A reasonable period of delay when the defendant is joined for trial with a codefendant as to whom the time for trial has not run and no motion for severance has been granted.

(8)(A) Any period of delay resulting from a continuance granted by any judge on his own motion or at the request of the defendant or his counsel or at the request of the attorney for the Government, if the judge granted such continuance on the basis of his findings that the ends of justice served by taking such action outweigh the best interest of the public and the defendant in a speedy trial. No such period of delay resulting from a continuance granted by the court in accordance with this paragraph shall be excludable under this subsection unless the court sets forth, in the record of the case, either orally or in writing, its reasons for finding that the ends of justice served by the granting of such continuance outweigh the best interests of the public and the defendant in a speedy trial.

(B) The factors, among others, which a judge shall consider in determining whether to grant a continuance under subparagraph (A) of this paragraph in any case are as follows:

(i) Whether the failure to grant such a continuance in the proceeding would be likely to make a continuation of such proceeding impossible, or result in a miscarriage of justice.

(ii) Whether the case is so unusual or so complex, due to the number of defendants, the nature of the prosecution, or the existence of novel questions of fact or law, that it is unreasonable to expect adequate preparation for pretrial proceedings or for the trial itself within the time limits established by this section.

(iii) Whether, in a case in which arrest precedes indictment, delay in the filing of the indictment is caused because the arrest occurs at a time such that it is unreasonable to expect return and filing of the indictment within the period specified in section 3161(b), or because the facts upon which the grand jury must base its determination are unusual or complex.

(iv) Whether the failure to grant such a continuance in a case which, taken as a whole, is not so unusual or so complex as to fall within clause (ii), would deny the defendant reasonable time to obtain counsel, would unreasonably deny the defendant or the Government continuity of counsel, or would deny counsel for the defendant or the attorney for the Government the reasonable time necessary for effective preparation, taking into account the exercise of due diligence.

(C) No continuance under subparagraph (A) of this paragraph shall be granted because of general congestion of the court's calendar, or lack of diligent preparation or failure to obtain available witnesses on the part of the attorney for the Government.

(9) Any period of delay, not to exceed one year, ordered by a district court upon an application of a party and a finding by a preponderance of the evidence that an official request, as defined in section 3292 of this title, has been made for evidence of any such offense and that it reasonably appears, or reasonably appeared at the time the request was made, that such evidence is, or was, in such foreign country.

(i) If trial did not commence within the time limitation specified in section 3161 because the defendant had entered a plea of guilty or nolo contendere subsequently withdrawn to any or all charges in an indictment or information, the defendant shall be deemed indicted with respect to all charges therein contained within the meaning of section 3161, on the day the order permitting withdrawal of the plea becomes final.

(j)(1) If the attorney for the Government knows that a person charged with an offense is serving a term of imprisonment in any penal institution, he shall promptly—

(A) undertake to obtain the presence of the prisoner for trial; or

(B) cause a detainer to be filed with the person having custody of the prisoner and request him to so advise the prisoner and to advise the prisoner of his right to demand trial.

(2) If the person having custody of such prisoner receives a detainer, he shall promptly advise the prisoner of the charge and of the prisoner's right to demand trial. If at any time thereafter the prisoner informs the person having custody that he does demand trial, such person shall cause notice to that effect to be sent promptly to the attorney for the Government who caused the detainer to be filed.

(3) Upon receipt of such notice, the attorney for the Government shall promptly seek to obtain the presence of the prisoner for trial.

(4) When the person having custody of the prisoner receives from the attorney for the Government a properly supported request for temporary custody of such prisoner for trial, the prisoner shall be made available to that attorney for the Government (subject, in cases of interjurisdictional transfer, to any right of the prisoner to contest the legality of his delivery).

(k)(1) If the defendant is absent (as defined by subsection (h)(3)) on the day set for trial, and the defendant's subsequent appearance before the court on a bench warrant or other process or surrender to the court occurs more than 21 days after the day set for trial, the defendant shall be deemed to have first appeared before a judicial officer of the court in which the information or indictment is pending within the meaning of subsection (c) on the date of the defendant's subsequent appearance before the court.

(2) If the defendant is absent (as defined by subsection (h)(3)) on the day set for trial, and the defendant's subsequent appearance before the court on a bench warrant or other process or surrender to the court occurs not more than 21 days after the day set for trial, the time limit required by subsection (c), as extended by subsection (h), shall be further extended by 21 days.

(Added Pub.L. 93–619, Title I, § 101, Jan. 3, 1975, 88 Stat. 2076, and amended Pub.L. 96–43, §§ 2–5, Aug. 2, 1979, 93 Stat. 327, 328; Pub.L. 98–473, Title II, § 1219, Oct. 12, 1984, 98 Stat. 2167; Pub.L. 100–690, Title VI, § 6476, Nov. 18, 1988, 102 Stat. 4380; Pub.L. 101–650, Title III, § 321, Dec. 1, 1990, 104 Stat. 5117.)

HISTORICAL AND STATUTORY NOTES

References in Text

Section 2902 of Title 28, referred to in subsec. (h)(1)(B), (C), (5), was repealed by Pub.L. 106–310, Div. B, Title XXIV, § 3405(c)(1), Oct. 17, 2000, 114 Stat. 1221.

Change of Name

Words "magistrate judge" substituted for "magistrate" in subsec. (c)(1) pursuant to section 321 of Pub.L. 101–650, set out as a note under 28 U.S.C.A. § 631.

Short Title

1979 Amendments. Section 1 of Pub.L. 96–43 provided: "That this Act [amending this section and sections 3163 to 3168, 3170 and 3174 of this title] may be cited as the 'Speedy Trial Act Amendments Act of 1979'."

1974 Acts. Section 1 of Pub.L. 93–619 provided: "That this Act [enacting this chapter and sections 3153 to 3156 of this title, and amending section 3152 of this title, and section 604 of Title 28, Judiciary and Judicial Procedure] may be cited as the 'Speedy Trial Act of 1974'."

§ 3162. Sanctions

(a)(1) If, in the case of any individual against whom a complaint is filed charging such individual with an offense, no indictment or information is filed within the time limit required by section 3161(b) as extended by section 3161(h) of this chapter, such charge against that individual contained in such complaint shall be dismissed or otherwise dropped. In determining whether to dismiss the case with or without prejudice, the court shall consider, among others, each of the following factors: the seriousness of the offense; the facts and circumstances of the case which led to the dismissal; and the impact of a reprosecution on the administration of this chapter and on the administration of justice.

(2) If a defendant is not brought to trial within the time limit required by section 3161(c) as extended by section 3161(h), the information or indictment shall be dismissed on motion of the defendant. The defendant shall have the burden of proof of supporting such motion but the Government shall have the burden of going forward with the evidence in connection with any exclusion of time under subparagraph 3161(h) (3). In determining whether to dismiss the case with or without prejudice, the court shall consider, among others, each of the following factors: the seriousness of the offense; the facts and circumstances of the case which led to the dismissal; and the impact of a reprosecution on the administration of this chapter and on the administration of justice. Failure of the defendant to move for dismissal prior to trial or entry of a plea of guilty or nolo contendere shall constitute a waiver of the right to dismissal under this section.

(b) In any case in which counsel for the defendant or the attorney for the Government (1) knowingly allows the case to be set for trial without disclosing the fact that a necessary witness would be unavailable for trial; (2) files a motion solely for the purpose of delay which he knows is totally frivolous and without merit; (3) makes a statement for the purpose of obtaining a continuance which he knows to be false and which is material to the granting of a continuance; or (4) otherwise willfully fails to proceed to trial without justification consistent with section 3161 of this chapter, the court may punish any such counsel or attorney, as follows:

(A) in the case of an appointed defense counsel, by reducing the amount of compensation that otherwise would have been paid to such counsel pursuant to section 3006A of this title in an amount not to exceed 25 per centum thereof;

(B) in the case of a counsel retained in connection with the defense of a defendant, by imposing on such counsel a fine of not to exceed 25 per centum of the compensation to which he is entitled in connection with his defense of such defendant;

(C) by imposing on any attorney for the Government a fine of not to exceed $250;

(D) by denying any such counsel or attorney for the Government the right to practice before the court considering such case for a period of not to exceed ninety days; or

(E) by filing a report with an appropriate disciplinary committee.

The authority to punish provided for by this subsection shall be in addition to any other authority or power available to such court.

(c) The court shall follow procedures established in the Federal Rules of Criminal Procedure in punishing any counsel or attorney for the Government pursuant to this section.

(Added Pub.L. 93–619, Title I, § 101, Jan. 3, 1975, 88 Stat. 2079.)

§ 3163. Effective dates

(a) The time limitation in section 3161(b) of this chapter—

(1) shall apply to all individuals who are arrested or served with a summons on or after the date of expiration of the twelve-calendar-month period following July 1, 1975; and

(2) shall commence to run on such date of expiration to all individuals who are arrested or served with a summons prior to the date of expiration of such twelve-calendar-month period, in connection with the commission of an offense, and with respect to which offense no information or indictment has been filed prior to such date of expiration.

(b) The time limitation in section 3161(c) of this chapter—

(1) shall apply to all offenses charged in informations or indictments filed on or after the date of expiration of the twelve-calendar-month period following July 1, 1975; and

(2) shall commence to run on such date of expiration as to all offenses charged in informations or indictments filed prior to that date.

(c) Subject to the provisions of section 3174(c), section 3162 of this chapter shall become effective and apply to all cases commenced by arrest or summons, and all informations or indictments filed, on or after July 1, 1980.

(Added Pub.L. 93–619, Title I, § 101, Jan. 3, 1975, 88 Stat. 2080, and amended Pub.L. 96–43, § 6, Aug. 2, 1979, 93 Stat. 328.)

§ 3164. Persons detained or designated as being of high risk

(a) The trial or other disposition of cases involving—

(1) a detained person who is being held in detention solely because he is awaiting trial, and

(2) a released person who is awaiting trial and has been designated by the attorney for the Government as being of high risk,

shall be accorded priority.

(b) The trial of any person described in subsection (a)(1) or (a)(2) of this section shall commence not later than ninety days following the beginning of such continuous detention or designation of high risk by the attorney for the Government. The periods of delay enumerated in section 3161(h) are excluded in computing the time limitation specified in this section.

(c) Failure to commence trial of a detainee as specified in subsection (b), through no fault of the accused or his counsel, or failure to commence trial of a designated releasee as specified in subsection (b), through no fault of the attorney for the Government, shall result in the automatic review by the court of the conditions of release. No detainee, as defined in subsection (a), shall be held in custody pending trial after the expiration of such ninety-day period required for the commencement of his trial. A designated releasee, as defined in subsection (a), who is found by the court to have intentionally delayed the trial of his case shall be subject to an order of the court modifying his nonfinancial conditions of release under this title to insure that he shall appear at trial as required.

(Added Pub.L. 93–619, Title I, § 101, Jan. 3, 1975, 88 Stat. 2081, and amended Pub.L. 96–43, § 7, Aug. 2, 1979, 93 Stat. 329.)

§ 3165. District plans—generally

(a) Each district court shall conduct a continuing study of the administration of criminal justice in the district court and before United States magistrate judges of the district and shall prepare plans for the disposition of criminal cases in accordance with this chapter. Each such plan shall be formulated after consultation with, and after considering the recommendations of, the Federal Judicial Center and the planning group established for that district pursuant to section 3168. The plans shall be prepared in accordance with the schedule set forth in subsection (e) of this section.

(b) The planning and implementation process shall seek to accelerate the disposition of criminal cases in the district consistent with the time standards of this chapter and the objectives of effective law enforcement, fairness to accused persons, efficient judicial administration, and increased knowledge concerning the proper functioning of the criminal law. The process shall seek to avoid underenforcement, overenforcement and discriminatory enforcement of the law, prejudice to the prompt disposition of civil litigation, and undue pressure as well as undue delay in the trial of criminal cases.

(c) The plans prepared by each district court shall be submitted for approval to a reviewing panel consisting of the members of the judicial council of the circuit and either the chief judge of the district court whose plan is being reviewed or such other active judge of that court as the chief judge of that district court may designate. If approved by the reviewing panel, the plan shall be forwarded to the Administrative Office of the United States Courts, which office shall report annually on the operation of such plans to the Judicial Conference of the United States.

(d) The district court may modify the plan at any time with the approval of the reviewing panel. It shall modify the plan when directed to do so by the reviewing panel or the Judicial Conference of the United States. Modifications shall be reported to the Administrative Office of the United States Courts.

(e)(1) Prior to the expiration of the twelve-calendar-month period following July 1, 1975, each United States district court shall prepare and submit a plan in accordance with subsections (a) through (d) above to govern the trial or other disposition of offenses within the jurisdiction of such court during the second and third twelve-calendar-month periods following the effective date of subsection 3161(b) and subsection 3161(c).

(2) Prior to the expiration of the thirty-six calendar month period following July 1, 1975, each United States district court shall prepare and submit a plan in accordance with subsections (a) through (d) above to govern the trial or other disposition of offenses within the jurisdiction of such court during the fourth and fifth twelve-calendar-month periods following the effective date of subsection 3161(b) and subsection 3161(c).

(3) Not later than June 30, 1980, each United States district court with respect to which implementation has not been ordered under section 3174(c) shall prepare and submit a plan in accordance with subsections (a) through (d) to govern the trial or other disposition of offenses within the jurisdiction of such court during the sixth and subsequent twelve-calendar-month periods following the effective date of subsection 3161(b) and subsection 3161(c) in effect prior to the date of enactment of this paragraph.

(f) Plans adopted pursuant to this section shall, upon adoption, and recommendations of the district planning group shall, upon completion, become public documents.

(Added Pub.L. 93–619, Title I, § 101, Jan. 3, 1975, 88 Stat. 2081, and amended Pub.L. 96–43, § 8, Aug. 2, 1979, 93 Stat. 329; Pub.L. 101–647, Title XXXV, § 3577, Nov. 29, 1990, 104 Stat. 4929; Pub.L. 101–650, Title III, § 321, Dec. 1, 1990, 104 Stat. 5117.)

HISTORICAL AND STATUTORY NOTES

References in Text

For the effective date of subsection 3161(b) and subsection 3161(c) referred to in subsec. (e)(3), see section 3163(a) and (b) of this title. The date of enactment of par. (3) of subsec. (e) of this section is the date of enactment of Pub.L. 96-43, which was approved Aug. 2, 1979. Subsecs. (a) and (b) of section 3163 of this title were not amended by Pub.L. 96–43.

Change of Name

"United States magistrate judges" substituted for "United States magistrates" in subsec. (a) pursuant to section 321 of Pub.L. 101–650, set out as a note under 28 U.S.C.A. § 631.

§ 3166. District plans—contents

(a) Each plan shall include a description of the time limits, procedural techniques, innovations, systems and other methods, including the development of reliable methods for gathering and monitoring information and statistics, by which the district court, the United States attorney, the Federal public defender, if any, and private attorneys experienced in the defense of criminal cases, have expedited or intend to expedite the trial or other disposition of criminal cases, consistent with the time limits and other objectives of this chapter.

(b) Each plan shall include information concerning the implementation of the time limits and other objectives of this chapter, including:

(1) the incidence of and reasons for, requests or allowances of extensions of time beyond statutory or district standards;

(2) the incidence of, and reasons for, periods of delay under section 3161(h) of this title;

(3) the incidence of, and reasons for, the invocation of sanctions for noncompliance with time standards, or the failure to invoke such sanctions, and the nature of the sanction, if any invoked for noncompliance;

(4) the new timetable set, or requested to be set, for an extension;

(5) the effect on criminal justice administration of the prevailing time limits and sanctions, including the effects on the prosecution, the defense, the courts, the correctional process, costs, transfers and appeals;

(6) the incidence and length of, reasons for, and remedies for detention prior to trial, and information required by the provisions of the Federal Rules of Criminal Procedure relating to the supervision of detention pending trial;

(7) the identity of cases which, because of their special characteristics, deserve separate or different time limits as a matter of statutory classifications;

(8) the incidence of, and reasons for each thirty-day extension under section 3161(b) with respect to an indictment in that district; and

(9) the impact of compliance with the time limits of subsections (b) and (c) of section 3161 upon the civil case calendar in the district.

(c) Each district plan required by section 3165 shall include information and statistics concerning the administration of criminal justice within the district, including, but not limited to:

(1) the time span between arrest and indictment, indictment and trial, and conviction and sentencing;

(2) the number of matters presented to the United States Attorney for prosecution, and the numbers of such matters prosecuted and not prosecuted;

(3) the number of matters transferred to other districts or to States for prosecution;

(4) the number of cases disposed of by trial and by plea;

(5) the rates of nolle prosequi, dismissal, acquittal, conviction, diversion, or other disposition;

(6) the extent of preadjudication detention and release, by numbers of defendants and days in custody or at liberty prior to disposition; and

(7)(A) the number of new civil cases filed in the twelve-calendar-month period preceding the submission of the plan;

(B) the number of civil cases pending at the close of such period; and

(C) the increase or decrease in the number of civil cases pending at the close of such period, compared to the number pending at the close of the previous twelve-calendar-month period, and the length of time each such case has been pending.

(d) Each plan shall further specify the rule changes, statutory amendments, and appropriations needed to effectuate further improvements in the administration of justice in the district which cannot be accomplished without such amendments or funds.

(e) Each plan shall include recommendations to the Administrative Office of the United States Courts for reporting forms, procedures, and time requirements. The Director of the Administrative Office of the United States Courts, with the approval of the Judicial Conference of the United States, shall prescribe such forms and procedures and time requirements consistent with section 3170 after consideration of the recommendations contained in the district plan and the need to reflect both unique local conditions and uniform national reporting standards.

(f) Each plan may be accompanied by guidelines promulgated by the judicial council of the circuit for use by all district courts within that circuit to implement and secure compliance with this chapter.

(Added Pub.L. 93–619, Title I, § 101, Jan. 3, 1975, 88 Stat. 2082, and amended Pub.L. 96–43, § 9(a)–(c), Aug. 2, 1979, 93 Stat. 329; Pub.L. 101–647, Title XXXV, § 3578, Nov. 29, 1990, 104 Stat. 4929.)

§ 3167. Reports to Congress

(a) The Administrative Office of the United States Courts, with the approval of the Judicial Conference, shall submit periodic reports to Congress detailing the plans submitted pursuant to section 3165. The reports shall be submitted within three months following the final dates for the submission of plans under section 3165(e) of this title.

(b) Such reports shall include recommendations for legislative changes or additional appropriations to achieve the time limits and objectives of this chapter. The report shall also contain pertinent information such as the state of the criminal docket at the time of the adoption of the plan; the extent of pretrial detention and release; and a description of the time limits, procedural techniques, innovations, systems, and other methods by which the trial or other disposition of criminal cases have been expedited or may be expedited in the districts. Such reports shall also include the following:

(1) The reasons why, in those cases not in compliance with the time limits of subsections (b) and (c) of section 3161, the provisions of section 3161(h) have not been adequate to accommodate reasonable periods of delay.

(2) The category of offenses, the number of defendants, and the number of counts involved in those cases which are not meeting the time limits specified in subsections (b) and (c) of section 3161.

(3) The additional judicial resources which would be necessary in order to achieve compliance with the time limits specified in subsections (b) and (c) of section 3161.

(4) The nature of the remedial measures which have been employed to improve conditions and practices in those districts with low compliance experience under this chapter or to promote the adoption of practices and procedures which have been successful in those districts with high compliance experience under this chapter.

(5) If a district has experienced difficulty in complying with this chapter, but an application for relief under section 3174 has not been made, the reason why such application has not been made.

(6) The impact of compliance with the time limits of subsections (b) and (c) of section 3161 upon the civil case calendar in each district as demonstrated

by the information assembled and statistics compiled and submitted under sections 3166 and 3170.

(c) Not later than December 31, 1979, the Department of Justice shall prepare and submit to the Congress a report which sets forth the impact of the implementation of this chapter upon the office of the United States Attorney in each district and which shall also include—

(1) the reasons why, in those cases not in compliance, the provisions of section 3161(h) have not been adequate to accommodate reasonable periods of delay;

(2) the nature of the remedial measures which have been employed to improve conditions and practices in the offices of the United States Attorneys in those districts with low compliance experience under this chapter or to promote the adoption of practices and procedures which have been successful in those districts with high compliance experience under this chapter;

(3) the additional resources for the offices of the United States Attorneys which would be necessary to achieve compliance with the time limits of subsections (b) and (c) of section 3161;

(4) suggested changes in the guidelines or other rules implementing this chapter or statutory amendments which the Department of Justice deems necessary to further improve the administration of justice and meet the objectives of this chapter; and

(5) the impact of compliance with the time limits of subsections (b) and (c) of section 3161 upon the litigation of civil cases by the offices of the United States Attorneys and the rule changes, statutory amendments, and resources necessary to assure that such litigation is not prejudiced by full compliance with this chapter.

(Added Pub.L. 93–619, Title I, § 101, Jan. 3, 1975, 88 Stat. 2083, and amended Pub.L. 96–43, § 9(e), Aug. 2, 1979, 93 Stat. 330.)

§ 3168. Planning process

(a) Within sixty days after July 1, 1975, each United States district court shall convene a planning group consisting at minimum of the Chief Judge, a United States magistrate judge, if any designated by the Chief Judge, the United States Attorney, the Clerk of the district court, the Federal Public Defender, if any, two private attorneys, one with substantial experience in the defense of criminal cases in the district and one with substantial experience in civil litigation in the district, the Chief United States Probation Officer for the district, and a person skilled in criminal justice research who shall act as reporter for the group. The group shall advise the district court with respect to the formulation of all district plans and shall submit its recommendations to the district court for each of the district plans required by section 3165. The group shall be responsible for the initial formulation of all district plans and of the reports required by this chapter and in aid thereof, it shall be entitled to the planning funds specified in section 3171.

(b) The planning group shall address itself to the need for reforms in the criminal justice system, including but not limited to changes in the grand jury system, the finality of criminal judgments, habeas corpus and collateral attacks, pretrial diversion, pretrial detention, excessive reach of Federal criminal law, simplification and improvement of pretrial and sentencing procedures, and appellate delay.

(c) Members of the planning group with the exception of the reporter shall receive no additional compensation for their services, but shall be reimbursed for travel, subsistence and other necessary expenses incurred by them in carrying out the duties of the advisory group in accordance with the provisions of title 5, United States Code, chapter 57. The reporter shall be compensated in accordance with section 3109 of title 5, United States Code, and notwithstanding other provisions of law he may be employed for any period of time during which his services are needed.

(Added Pub.L. 93–619, Title I, § 101, Jan. 3, 1975, 88 Stat. 2083, and amended Pub.L. 96–43, § 9(d), Aug. 2, 1979, 93 Stat. 330; Pub.L. 101–650, Title III, § 321, Dec. 1, 1990, 104 Stat. 5117.)

HISTORICAL AND STATUTORY NOTES

Change of Name

"United States magistrate judge" substituted for "United States magistrate" in subsec. (a) pursuant to section 321 of Pub.L. 101–650, set out as a note under 28 U.S.C.A. § 631.

§ 3169. Federal Judicial Center

The Federal Judicial Center shall advise and consult with the planning groups and the district courts in connection with their duties under this chapter.

(Added Pub.L. 93–619, Title I, § 101, Jan. 3, 1975, 88 Stat. 2084.)

§ 3170. Speedy trial data

(a) To facilitate the planning process, the implementation of the time limits, and continuous and permanent compliance with the objectives of this chapter, the clerk of each district court shall assemble the information and compile the statistics described in sections 3166(b) and 3166(c) of this title. The clerk of each district court shall assemble such information and compile such statistics on such forms and under such regulations as the Administrative Office of the United States Courts shall prescribe with the approval of the Judicial Conference and after consultation with the Attorney General.

(b) The clerk of each district court is authorized to obtain the information required by sections 3166(b) and 3166(c) from all relevant sources including the United States Attorney, Federal Public Defender, private defense counsel appearing in criminal cases in the district, United States district court judges, and the chief Federal Probation Officer for the district. This subsection shall not be construed to require the release of any confidential or privileged information.

(c) The information and statistics compiled by the clerk pursuant to this section shall be made available to the district court, the planning group, the circuit council, and the Administrative Office of the United States Courts.

(Added Pub.L. 93–619, Title I, § 101, Jan. 3, 1975, 88 Stat. 2084, and amended Pub.L. 96–43, § 9(f), Aug. 2, 1979, 93 Stat. 331; Pub.L. 101–647, Title XXXV, § 3579, Nov. 29, 1990, 104 Stat. 4929.)

§ 3171. Planning appropriations

(a) There is authorized to be appropriated for the fiscal year ending June 30, 1975, to the Federal judiciary the sum of $2,500,000 to be allocated by the Administrative Office of the United States Courts to Federal judicial districts to carry out the initial phases of planning and implementation of speedy trial plans under this chapter. The funds so appropriated shall remain available until expended.

(b) No funds appropriated under this section may be expended in any district except by two-thirds vote of the planning group. Funds to the extent available may be expended for personnel, facilities, and any other purpose permitted by law.

(Added Pub.L. 93–619, Title I, § 101, Jan. 3, 1975, 88 Stat. 2084.)

§ 3172. Definitions

As used in this chapter—

(1) the terms "judge" or "judicial officer" mean, unless otherwise indicated, any United States magistrate judge, Federal district judge, and

(2) the term "offense" means any Federal criminal offense which is in violation of any Act of Congress and is triable by any court established by Act of Congress (other than a Class B or C misdemeanor or an infraction, or an offense triable by court-martial, military commission, provost court, or other military tribunal).

(Added Pub.L. 93–619, Title I, § 101, Jan. 3, 1975, 88 Stat. 2085, and amended Pub.L. 98–473, Title II, § 223(i), Oct. 12, 1984, 98 Stat. 2029; Pub.L. 101–650, Title III, § 321, Dec. 1, 1990, 104 Stat. 5117.)

HISTORICAL AND STATUTORY NOTES

Effective and Applicability Provisions

1984 Acts. Amendment by Pub.L. 98–473 effective Nov. 1, 1987, and applicable only to offenses committed after the taking effect of such amendment, see section 235(a)(1) of Pub.L. 98–473, set out as a note under section 3551 of this title.

Change of Name

"United States magistrate judge" substituted for "United States magistrate" in par. (1) pursuant to section 321 of Pub.L. 101–650, set out as a note under 28 U.S.C.A. § 631.

Savings Provisions

1984 Amendments. Amendment by Pub.L. 98–473 effective on the first day of first calendar month beginning thirty-six months after Oct. 12, 1984, applicable only to offenses committed after taking effect of sections 211 to 239 of Pub.L. 98–473, and except as otherwise provided for therein, see section 235 of Pub.L. 98–473, as amended, set out as a note under section 3551 of this title.

§ 3173. Sixth amendment rights

No provision of this chapter shall be interpreted as a bar to any claim of denial of speedy trial as required by amendment VI of the Constitution.

(Added by Pub.L. 93–619, Title I, § 101, Jan. 3, 1975, 88 Stat. 2085.)

§ 3174. Judicial emergency and implementation

(a) In the event that any district court is unable to comply with the time limits set forth in section 3161(c) due to the status of its court calendars, the chief judge, where the existing resources are being efficiently utilized, may, after seeking the recommendations of the planning group, apply to the judicial council of the circuit for a suspension of such time limits as provided in subsection (b). The judicial council of the circuit shall evaluate the capabilities of the district, the availability of visiting judges from within and without the circuit, and make any recommendations it deems appropriate to alleviate calendar congestion resulting from the lack of resources.

(b) If the judicial council of the circuit finds that no remedy for such congestion is reasonably available, such council may, upon application by the chief judge of a district, grant a suspension of the time limits in section 3161(c) in such district for a period of time not to exceed one year for the trial of cases for which indictments or informations are filed during such one-year period. During such period of suspension, the time limits from arrest to indictment, set forth in section 3161(b), shall not be reduced, nor shall the sanctions set forth in section 3162 be suspended; but such time limits from indictment to trial shall not be increased to exceed one hundred and eighty days. The time limits for the trial of cases of detained persons who are being detained solely because they are awaiting trial shall not be affected by the provisions of this section.

(c)(1) If, prior to July 1, 1980, the chief judge of any district concludes, with the concurrence of the planning group convened in the district, that the district is prepared to implement the provisions of section 3162 in their entirety, he may apply to the judicial council of the circuit in which the district is located to implement such provisions. Such application shall show the degree of compliance in the district with the time limits set forth in subsections (b) and (c) of section 3161 during the twelve-calendar-month period preceding the date of such application and shall contain a proposed order and schedule for such implementation, which includes the date on which the provisions of section 3162 are to become effective in the district, the effect such implementation will have upon such district's practices and procedures, and provision for adequate notice to all interested parties.

(2) After review of any such application, the judicial council of the circuit shall enter an order implementing the provisions of section 3162 in their entirety in the district making application, or shall return such application to the chief judge of such district, together with an explanation setting forth such council's reasons for refusing to enter such order.

(d)(1) The approval of any application made pursuant to subsection (a) or (c) by a judicial council of a circuit shall be reported within ten days to the Director of the Administrative Office of the United States Courts, together with a copy of the application, a written report setting forth in sufficient detail the reasons for granting such application, and, in the case of an application made pursuant to subsection (a), a proposal for alleviating congestion in the district.

(2) The Director of the Administrative Office of the United States Courts shall not later than ten days after receipt transmit such report to the Congress and to the Judicial Conference of the United States. The judicial council of the circuit shall not grant a suspension to any district within six months following the expiration of a prior suspension without the consent of the Congress by Act of Congress. The limitation on granting a suspension made by this paragraph shall not apply with respect to any judicial district in which the prior suspension is in effect on the date of the enactment of the Speedy Trial Act Amendments Act of 1979.

(e) If the chief judge of the district court concludes that the need for suspension of time limits in such district under this section is of great urgency, he may order the limits suspended for a period not to exceed thirty days. Within ten days of entry of such order, the chief judge shall apply to the judicial council of the circuit for a suspension pursuant to subsection (a).

(Added Pub.L. 93–619, Title I, § 101, Jan. 3, 1975, 88 Stat. 2085, and amended Pub.L. 96–43, § 10, Aug. 2, 1979, 93 Stat. 331.)

HISTORICAL AND STATUTORY NOTES

References in Text

The date of enactment of the Speedy Trial Act Amendments Act of 1979, referred to in subsec. (d) (2), means the date of enactment of Pub.L. 96–43, which was approved Aug. 2, 1979.

Termination of Reporting Requirements

For termination, effective May 15, 2000, of reporting provisions in subsec. (d)(2) of this section pertaining to suspension of time limits provided through the Speedy Trial Act, see Pub.L. 104–66, § 3003, as amended, set out as a note under 31 U.S.C.A. § 1113, and the 5th item on page 12 of House Document No. 103–7.

CHAPTER 209—EXTRADITION

Sec.

§ 3181. Scope and limitation of chapter

(a) The provisions of this chapter relating to the surrender of persons who have committed crimes in foreign countries shall continue in force only during the existence of any treaty of extradition with such foreign government.

(b) The provisions of this chapter shall be construed to permit, in the exercise of comity, the surrender of persons, other than citizens, nationals, or permanent residents of the United States, who have committed crimes of violence against nationals of the United States in foreign countries without regard to the existence of any treaty of extradition with such foreign government if the Attorney General certifies, in writing, that—

(1) evidence has been presented by the foreign government that indicates that had the offenses been committed in the United States, they would

constitute crimes of violence as defined under section 16 of this title; and

(2) the offenses charged are not of a political nature.

(c) As used in this section, the term "national of the United States" has the meaning given such term in section 101(a)(22) of the Immigration and Nationality Act (8 U.S.C. 1101(a)(22)).

(June 25, 1948, c. 645, 62 Stat. 822; Apr. 24, 1996, Pub.L. 104–132, Title IV, § 443(a), 110 Stat. 1280.)

HISTORICAL AND STATUTORY NOTES

References in Text

Section 101(a)(22) of the Immigration and Nationality Act, referred to in subsec. (c), is section 101(a)(22) of Act June 27, 1952, c. 477, 66 Stat. 166, which is classified to section 1101(a)(22) of Title 8, Aliens and Nationality.

Extradition Treaties Interpretation Act of 1998

Pub.L. 105–323, Title II, §§ 201 to 203, Oct. 30, 1998, 112 Stat. 3033, provided that:

"Sec. 201. Short title

"This title [Title II of Pub.L. 105–323, which enacted this note] may be cited as the 'Extradition Treaties Interpretation Act of 1998'.

"Sec. 202. Findings

"Congress finds that—

"(1) each year, several hundred children are kidnapped by a parent in violation of law, court order, or legally binding agreement and brought to, or taken from, the United States;

"(2) until the mid–1970's, parental abduction generally was not considered a criminal offense in the United States;

"(3) since the mid–1970's, United States criminal law has evolved such that parental abduction is now a criminal offense in each of the 50 States and the District of Columbia;

"(4) in enacting the International Parental Kidnapping Crime Act of 1993 (Public Law 103–173; 107 Stat. 1998; 18 U.S.C. 1204), Congress recognized the need to combat parental abduction by making the act of international parental kidnapping a Federal criminal offense;

"(5) many of the extradition treaties to which the United States is a party specifically list the offenses that are extraditable and use the word 'kidnapping', but it has been the practice of the United States not to consider the term to include parental abduction because these treaties were negotiated by the United States prior to the development in United States criminal law described in paragraphs (3) and (4);

"(6) the more modern extradition treaties to which the United States is a party contain dual criminality provisions, which provide for extradition where both parties make the offense a felony, and therefore it is the practice of the United States to consider such treaties to include parental abduction if the other foreign state party also considers the act of parental abduction to be a criminal offense; and

"(7) this circumstance has resulted in a disparity in United States extradition law which should be rectified to better protect the interests of children and their parents.

"Sec. 203. Interpretation of extradition treaties

"For purposes of any extradition treaty to which the United States is a party, Congress authorizes the interpretation of the terms 'kidnaping' and 'kidnapping' to include parental kidnapping."

Judicial Assistance to the International Tribunal for Yugoslavia and to the International Tribunal for Rwanda

Pub.L. 104–106, Div. A, Title XIII, § 1342, Feb. 10, 1996, 110 Stat. 486, provided that:

"(a) Surrender of persons.—

"(1) Application of United States extradition laws.— Except as provided in paragraphs (2) and (3), the provisions of chapter 209 of title 18, United States Code [18 U.S.C.A. § 3181 et seq.], relating to the extradition of persons to a foreign country pursuant to a treaty or convention for extradition between the United States and a foreign government, shall apply in the same manner and extent to the surrender of persons, including United States citizens, to—

"(A) the International Tribunal for Yugoslavia, pursuant to the Agreement Between the United States and the International Tribunal for Yugoslavia; and

"(B) the International Tribunal for Rwanda, pursuant to the Agreement Between the United States and the International Tribunal for Rwanda.

"(2) Evidence on hearings.—For purposes of applying section 3190 of title 18, United States Code [18 U.S.C.A. § 3190], in accordance with paragraph (1), the certification referred to in that section may be made by the principal diplomatic or consular officer of the United States resident in such foreign countries where the International Tribunal for Yugoslavia or the International Tribunal for Rwanda may be permanently or temporarily situated.

"(3) Payment of fees and costs.—(A) The provisions of the Agreement Between the United States and the International Tribunal for Yugoslavia and of the Agreement Between the United States and the International Tribunal for Rwanda shall apply in lieu of the provisions of section 3195 of title 18, United States Code [18 U.S.C.A. § 3195], with respect to the payment of expenses arising from the surrender by the United States of a person to the International Tribunal for Yugoslavia or the International Tribunal for Rwanda, respectively, or from any proceedings in the United States relating to such surrender.

"(B) The authority of subparagraph (A) may be exercised only to the extent and in the amounts provided in advance in appropriations Acts.

"(4) Nonapplicability of the Federal Rules.—The Federal Rules of Evidence and the Federal Rules of Criminal Procedure do not apply to proceedings for the surrender of persons to the International Tribunal for Yugoslavia or the International Tribunal for Rwanda.

"(b) Assistance to foreign and international tribunals and to litigants before such tribunals.—[Amends section 1782 of Title 28, Judiciary and Judicial Procedure.].

"(c) Definitions.—For purposes of this section:

"(1) International Tribunal for Yugoslavia.—The term 'International Tribunal for Yugoslavia' means the International Tribunal for the Prosecution of Persons Responsible for Serious Violations of International Humanitarian Law in the Territory of the Former Yugoslavia, as established by United Nations Security Council Resolution 827 of May 25, 1993.

"(2) **International Tribunal for Rwanda.**—The term 'International Tribunal for Rwanda' means the International Tribunal for the Prosecution of Persons Responsible for Genocide and Other Serious Violations of International Humanitarian Law Committed in the Territory of Rwanda and Rwandan Citizens Responsible for Genocide and Other Such Violations Committed in the Territory of Neighboring States, as established by United Nations Security Council Resolution 955 of November 8, 1994.

"(3) **Agreement Between the United States and the International Tribunal for Yugoslavia.**—The term 'Agreement Between the United States and the International Tribunal for Yugoslavia' means the Agreement on Surrender of Persons Between the Government of the United States and the International Tribunal for the Prosecution of Persons Responsible for Serious Violations of International Law in the Territory of the Former Yugoslavia, signed at The Hague, October 5, 1994.

"(4) **Agreement Between the United States and the International Tribunal for Rwanda.**—The term 'Agreement between [sic] the United States and the International Tribunal for Rwanda' means the Agreement on Surrender of Persons Between the Government of the United States and the International Tribunal for the Prosecution of Persons Responsible for Genocide and Other Serious Violations of International Humanitarian Law Committed in the Territory of Rwanda and Rwandan Citizens Responsible for Genocide and Other Such Violations Committed in the Territory of Neighboring States, signed at The Hague, January 24, 1995."

Extradition and Mutual Legal Assistance Treaties and Model Comprehensive Antidrug Laws

Pub.L. 100–690, Title IV, § 4605, Nov. 18, 1988, 102 Stat. 4290, which directed greater emphasis on updating of extradition treaties and on negotiating mutual legal assistance treaties with major drug producing and drug-transit countries, and called for development of model treaties and antinarcotics legislation, was repealed by Pub.L. 102–583, § 6(e)(1), Nov. 2, 1992, 106 Stat. 4933.

Requirement That Extradition of Drug Traffickers Be A Priority Issue of United States Missions in Major Illicit Drug Producing or Transit Countries

Pub.L. 100–204, Title VIII, § 803, Dec. 22, 1987, 101 Stat. 1397, provided that:

"The Secretary of State shall ensure that the Country Plan for the United States diplomatic mission in each major illicit drug producing country and in each major drug-transit country (as those terms are defined in section 481(i) of the Foreign Assistance Act of 1961) includes, as an objective to be pursued by the mission—

"(1) negotiating an updated extradition treaty which ensures that drug traffickers can be extradited to the United States, or

"(2) if an existing treaty provides for such extradition, taking such steps as may be necessary to ensure that the treaty is effectively implemented."

Updated Extradition Treaties With Major Drug-Producing Countries

Pub.L. 99–93, Title I, § 133, Aug. 16, 1985, 99 Stat. 420, provided that: "The Secretary of State, with the assistance of the National Drug Enforcement Policy Board, shall increase United States efforts to negotiate updated extradition treaties relating to narcotics offenses with each major drug-producing country, particularly those in Latin America."

Treaties of Extradition

The United States has entered into the following bilateral treaties of extradition with the following countries:

Country	Date signed	Entered into force	Citation
Albania	Mar. 1, 1933	Nov. 14, 1935	49 Stat. 3313.
Antigua and Barbuda	June 3, 1996	July 1, 1999	
Argentina	June 10, 1997	June 15, 2000	
Australia	May 14, 1974	May 8, 1976	27 UST 957.
	Sept. 4, 1990	Dec. 21, 1992	—
Austria	Jan. 8, 1998	Jan. 1, 2000	
	May 19, 1934	Sept. 5, 1934	49 Stat. 2710.
Bahamas	Dec. 22, 1931	June 24, 1935	47 Stat. 2122.
		Aug. 17, 1978	30 UST 187.
	Mar. 9, 1990	Sept. 22, 1994	TIAS
Barbados	Feb. 28, 1996	Mar. 3, 2000	Senate Treaty Doc. 104–7, 104th Cong., 1st Sess.
Belgium	Apr. 27, 1987	Sept. 1, 1997	(1995).
Belize	Mar. 30, 2000	Mar. 27, 2001	Senate Treaty Doc. 104–22, 104th Cong., 2nd Sess.
Bolivia	June 27, 1995	Nov. 21, 1996	(1995).
Brazil	Jan. 13, 1961	Dec. 17, 1964	15 UST 2093.
	June 18, 1962	Dec. 17, 1964	15 UST 2112.
Bulgaria	Mar. 19, 1924	June 24, 1924	43 Stat. 1886.
	June 8, 1934	Aug. 15, 1935	49 Stat. 3250.
Burma	Dec. 22, 1931	Nov. 1, 1941	47 Stat. 2122.
Canada	Dec. 3, 1971	Mar. 22, 1976	27 UST 983.
	June 28, July 9, 1974	Mar. 22, 1976	27 UST 1017.
	Jan. 11, 1988	Nov. 26, 1991	TIAS.
	Jan. 12, 2001	Apr. 30, 2003	
Chile	Apr. 17, 1900	June 26, 1902	32 Stat. 1850.
Colombia	Sept. 14, 1979	Mar. 4, 1982	TIAS.
Congo	Jan. 6, 1909	July 27, 1911	37 Stat. 1526.
	Jan. 15, 1929	May 19, 1929	46 Stat. 2276.
	Apr. 23, 1936	Sept. 24, 1936	50 Stat. 1117.
		Aug. 5, 1961	13 UST 2065.
Costa Rica	Dec. 4, 1982	Oct. 11, 1991	TIAS.
Cuba	Apr. 6, 1904	Mar. 2, 1905	33 Stat. 2265.
	Dec. 6, 1904	Mar. 2, 1905	33 Stat. 2273.
	Jan. 14, 1926	June 18, 1926	44 Stat. 2392.
Cyprus	June 17, 1996	Sept. 14, 1999	
Czechoslovakia	July 2, 1925	Mar. 29, 1926	44 Stat. 2367.
	Apr. 29, 1935	Aug. 28, 1935	49 Stat. 3253.
Denmark	June 22, 1972	July 31, 1974	25 UST 1293.
Dominica	Oct. 10, 1996	May 25, 2000	
Dominican Republic	June 19, 1909	Aug. 2, 1910	36 Stat. 2468.
Ecuador	June 28, 1872	Nov. 12, 1873	18 Stat. 199.
	Sept. 22, 1939	May 29, 1941	55 Stat. 1196.
Egypt	Aug. 11, 1874	Apr. 22, 1875	19 Stat. 572.
El Salvador	Apr. 18, 1911	July 10, 1911	37 Stat. 1516.
Estonia	Nov. 8, 1923	Nov. 15, 1924	43 Stat. 1849.

Country	Date signed	Entered into force	Citation
	Oct. 10, 1934	May 7, 1935	49 Stat. 3190.
Fiji	Dec. 22, 1931	June 24, 1935	47 Stat. 2122.
		Aug. 17, 1973	24 UST 1965.
Finland	June 11, 1976	May 11, 1980	31 UST 944.
France	Apr. 23, 1996	Feb. 1, 2002	
	Feb. 12, 1970	Apr. 3, 1971	22 UST 407.
Gambia	Dec. 22, 1931	June 24, 1935	47 Stat. 2122.
Germany	June 20, 1978	Aug. 29, 1980	32 UST 1485.
	Oct. 21, 1986	Mar. 11, 1993	—.
Ghana	Dec. 22, 1931	June 24, 1935	47 Stat. 2122.
Greece	May 6, 1931	Nov. 1, 1932	47 Stat. 2185.
	Sept. 2, 1937	Sept. 2, 1937	51 Stat. 357.
Grenada	May 30, 1996	Sept. 14, 1999	
Guatemala	Feb. 27, 1903	Aug. 15, 1903	33 Stat. 2147.
	Feb. 20, 1940	Mar. 13, 1941	55 Stat. 1097.
Guyana	Dec. 22, 1931	June 24, 1935	47 Stat. 2122.
Haiti	Aug. 9, 1904	June 28, 1905	34 Stat. 2858.
Honduras	Jan. 15, 1909	July 10, 1912	37 Stat. 1616.
	Feb. 21, 1927	June 5, 1928	45 Stat. 2489.
Hong Kong	Dec. 20, 1996	Jan. 21, 1998	
Hungary	Dec. 1, 1994	Mar. 18, 1997	Senate Treaty Doc. 104–5, 104th Cong., 1st Sess. (1995).
Iceland	Jan. 6, 1902		32 Stat. 1096.
	Nov. 6, 1905	Feb. 19, 1906	34 Stat. 2887.
India	June 25, 1997	July 21, 1999	
Iraq	June 7, 1934	Apr. 23, 1936	49 Stat. 3380.
Ireland	July 13, 1983	Dec. 15, 1984	TIAS 10813.
Israel	Dec. 10, 1962	Dec. 5, 1963	14 UST 1707.
		Apr. 11, 1967	18 UST 382.
Italy	Oct. 13, 1983	Sept. 24, 1984	TIAS 10837.
Jamaica	June 14, 1983	July 7, 1991	Senate Treaty Doc. 98–18, 98th Cong., 2nd Sess. (1984).
Japan	Mar. 3, 1978	Mar. 26, 1980	31 UST 892.
Jordan	Mar. 28, 1995	July 29, 1995	Senate Treaty Doc. 104–3, 104th Cong., 2nd Sess. (1995).
Kenya	Dec. 22, 1931	June 24, 1935	47 Stat. 2122.
		Aug. 19, 1965	16 UST 1866.
Kiribati	June 8, 1972	Jan. 21, 1977	28 UST 227.
Korea	June 9, 1998	Dec. 20, 1999	
Latvia	Oct. 16, 1923	Mar. 1, 1924	43 Stat. 1738.
	Oct. 10, 1934	Mar. 29, 1935	49 Stat. 3131.
Lesotho	Dec. 22, 1931	June 24, 1935	47 Stat. 2122.
Liberia	Nov. 1, 1937	Nov. 21, 1939	54 Stat. 1733.
Liechtenstein	May 20, 1936	June 28, 1937	50 Stat. 1337.
Lithuania	Apr. 9, 1924	Aug. 23, 1924	43 Stat. 1835.
	May 17, 1934	Jan. 8, 1935	49 Stat. 3077.
	Oct. 23, 2001	Mar. 31, 2003	
Luxembourg	Oct. 1, 1996	Feb. 1, 2002	
	Apr. 24, 1935	Mar. 3, 1936	49 Stat. 3355.
Lithuania	Oct. 23, 2001	Mar. 31, 2003	
Malawi	Dec. 22, 1931	June 24, 1935	47 Stat. 2122.
		Apr. 4, 1967	18 UST 1822.
Malaysia	Aug. 3, 1995	June 2, 1997	Senate Treaty Doc. 104–26, 104th Cong., 2nd Sess. (1996).
Malta	Dec. 22, 1931	June 24, 1935	47 Stat. 2122.
Mauritius	Dec. 22, 1931	June 24, 1935	47 Stat. 2122.
Mexico	May 4, 1978	Jan. 25, 1980	31 UST 5059.
	Nov. 13, 1997	May. 21, 2001.	
Monaco	Feb. 15, 1939	Mar. 28, 1940	54 Stat. 1780.
Nauru	Dec. 22, 1931	Aug. 30, 1935	47 Stat. 2122.
Netherlands	June 24, 1980	Sept. 15, 1983	TIAS 10733.
New Zealand	Jan. 12, 1970	Dec. 8, 1970	22 UST 1.
Nicaragua	Mar. 1, 1905	July 14, 1907	35 Stat. 1869.
Nigeria	Dec. 22, 1931	June 24, 1935	47 Stat. 2122.
Norway	June 9, 1977	Mar. 7, 1980	31 UST 5619.
Pakistan	Dec. 22, 1931	Mar. 9, 1942	47 Stat. 2122.
Panama	May 25, 1904	May 8, 1905	34 Stat. 2851.
Papua New Guinea	Dec. 22, 1931	Aug. 30, 1935	47 Stat. 2122.
	Feb. 2, 23, 1988	Feb. 23, 1988	TIAS.
Paraguay	Nov. 9, 1998	Mar. 9, 2001	
Peru	July 26, 2001	Aug. 25, 2003	
Philippines	Nov. 13, 1994	Nov. 22, 1996	Senate Treaty Doc. 104–16, 104th Cong., 1st Sess. (1995).
Poland	July 10, 1996	Sept. 17, 1999	
	Apr. 5, 1935	June 5, 1936	49 Stat. 3394.
Portugal	May 7, 1908	Nov. 14, 1908	35 Stat. 2071.
Romania	July 23, 1924	Apr. 7, 1925	44 Stat. 2020.
	Nov. 10, 1936	July 27, 1937	50 Stat. 1349.
Saint Christopher and Nevis	Sept. 18, 1996	Feb. 23, 2000	
Saint Lucia	Apr. 18, 1996	Feb. 2, 2000	
Saint Vincent and the Grenadines	Aug. 15, 1996	Sept. 8, 1999	
San Marino	Jan. 10, 1906	July 8, 1908	35 Stat. 1971.
	Oct. 10, 1934	June 28, 1935	49 Stat. 3198.
Seychelles	Dec. 22, 1931	June 24, 1935	47 Stat. 2122.
Sierra Leone	Dec. 22, 1931	June 24, 1935	47 Stat. 2122.
Singapore	Dec. 22, 1931	June 24, 1935	47 Stat. 2122.
		June 10, 1969	20 UST 2764.
Slovac Republic	July 2, 1925	Mar. 29, 1926	44 Stat. 2367.
	Apr. 29, 1935	Aug. 28, 1935	49 Stat. 3253.
Solomon Islands	June 8, 1972	Jan. 21, 1977	28 UST 277.
South Africa	Sept. 16, 1999	June 25, 2001	
Spain	May 29, 1970	June 16, 1971	22 UST 737.
	Jan. 25, 1975	June 2, 1978	29 UST 2283.
	Feb. 9, 1988	July 2, 1993	—
	March 12, 1996	July 25, 1999	—
Sri Lanka	Sept. 30, 1999	Jan. 12, 2001	
Suriname	June 2, 1887	July 11, 1889	26 Stat. 1481.
	Jan. 18, 1904	Aug. 28, 1904	33 Stat. 2257.
Swaziland	Dec. 22, 1931	June 24, 1935	47 Stat. 2122.
		July 28, 1970	21 UST 1930.
Sweden	Oct. 24, 1961	Dec. 3, 1963	14 UST 1845.
	Mar. 14, 1983	Sept. 24, 1984	TIAS 10812.
Switzerland	Nov. 14, 1990	Sept. 10, 1997	Senate Treaty Doc. 104–9, 104th Cong., 1st Sess. (1995).
Tanzania	Dec. 22, 1931	June 24, 1935	47 Stat. 2122.
		Dec. 6, 1965	16 UST 2066.
Thailand	Dec. 30, 1922	Mar. 24, 1924	43 Stat. 1749.
Tonga	Dec. 22, 1931	Aug. 1, 1966	47 Stat. 2122.
		Apr. 13, 1977	28 UST 5290.
Trinidad and Tobago	Mar. 4, 1996	Nov. 29, 1999	
Turkey	June 7, 1979	Jan. 1, 1981	32 UST 3111.
Tuvalu	June 8, 1972	Jan. 21, 1977	28 UST 227.
		Apr. 25, 1980	32 UST 1310.
United Kingdom	June 8, 1972	Jan. 21, 1977	28 UST 227.

Country	Date signed	Entered into force	Citation
	June 25, 1985	Dec. 23, 1986	TIAS.
Uruguay	Apr. 6, 1973	Apr. 11, 1984	TIAS 10850.
Venezuela	Jan. 19, 21, 1922.	Apr. 14, 1923	43 Stat. 1698.
Yugoslavia [1]	Oct. 25, 1901	June 12, 1902	32 Stat. 1890.
Zambia	Dec. 22, 1931	June 24, 1935	47 Stat. 2122.
Zimbabwe	July 25, 1997	Apr. 26, 2000	

[1] For the successor States of Yugoslavia, inquire of the Treaty Office of the United States Department of State.

Convention on Extradition

The United States is a party to the Multilateral Convention on Extradition [1] signed at Montevideo on Dec. 26, 1933, entered into force for the United States on Jan. 25, 1935. 49 Stat. 3111.

Other states which have become parties: Argentina, Chile,[2] Colombia, Dominican Republic, Ecuador,[2] El Salvador,[2] Guatemala, Honduras,[2] Mexico,[2] Nicaragua, Panama.

[1] Article 21 provides that the convention "does not abrogate or modify the bilateral or collective treaties, which at the present date are in force between the signatory States. Nevertheless, if any of said treaties lapse, the present Convention will take effect and become applicable immediately among the respective States . . .." Since the United States has bilateral extradition treaties with each of the other parties which antedate the convention, except for those with Argentina, Colombia, and Mexico, the multilateral convention is presently inoperative for the United States.

[2] With reservation.

Extradition of United States Citizens. See section 3196 of Title 18, Crimes and Criminal Procedure, for authority of Secretary of State to order extradition of U.S. citizens where applicable treaty or convention does not obligate U.S. to extradite.

§ 3182. Fugitives from State or Territory to State, District, or Territory

Whenever the executive authority of any State or Territory demands any person as a fugitive from justice, of the executive authority of any State, District, or Territory to which such person has fled, and produces a copy of an indictment found or an affidavit made before a magistrate of any State or Territory, charging the person demanded with having committed treason, felony, or other crime, certified as authentic by the governor or chief magistrate of the State or Territory from whence the person so charged has fled, the executive authority of the State, District, or Territory to which such person has fled shall cause him to be arrested and secured, and notify the executive authority making such demand, or the agent of such authority appointed to receive the fugitive, and shall cause the fugitive to be delivered to such agent when he shall appear. If no such agent appears within thirty days from the time of the arrest, the prisoner may be discharged.

(June 25, 1948, c. 645, 62 Stat. 822; Oct. 11, 1996, Pub.L. 104–294, Title VI, § 601(f)(9), 110 Stat. 3500.)

§ 3183. Fugitives from State, Territory, or Possession into extraterritorial jurisdiction of United States

Whenever the executive authority of any State, Territory, District, or possession of the United States demands any American citizen or national as a fugitive from justice who has fled to a country in which the United States exercises extraterritorial jurisdiction, and produces a copy of an indictment found or an affidavit made before a magistrate of the demanding jurisdiction, charging the fugitive so demanded with having committed treason, felony, or other offense, certified as authentic by the Governor or chief magistrate of such demanding jurisdiction, or other person authorized to act, the officer or representative of the United States vested with judicial authority to whom the demand has been made shall cause such fugitive to be arrested and secured, and notify the executive authorities making such demand, or the agent of such authority appointed to receive the fugitive, and shall cause the fugitive to be delivered to such agent when he shall appear.

If no such agent shall appear within three months from the time of the arrest, the prisoner may be discharged.

The agent who receives the fugitive into his custody shall be empowered to transport him to the jurisdiction from which he has fled.

(June 25, 1948, c. 645, 62 Stat. 822; Nov. 2, 2002, Pub.L. 107–273, Div. B, Title IV, § 4004(d), 116 Stat. 1812.)

§ 3184. Fugitives from foreign country to United States

Whenever there is a treaty or convention for extradition between the United States and any foreign government, or in cases arising under section 3181(b), any justice or judge of the United States, or any magistrate judge authorized so to do by a court of the United States, or any judge of a court of record of general jurisdiction of any State, may, upon complaint made under oath, charging any person found within his jurisdiction, with having committed within the jurisdiction of any such foreign government any of the crimes provided for by such treaty or convention, or provided for under section 3181(b), issue his warrant for the apprehension of the person so charged, that he may be brought before such justice, judge, or magistrate judge, to the end that the evidence of criminality may be heard and considered. Such complaint may be filed before and such warrant may be issued by a judge or magistrate judge of the United States District Court for the District of Columbia if the whereabouts within the United States of the person charged are not known or, if there is reason to believe the person will shortly enter the United States. If, on such hearing, he deems the evidence sufficient to sustain the charge under the provisions of the proper treaty or convention, or under section 3181(b), he shall certify the same, together with a copy of all the testimony taken before him, to the Secretary of State, that a warrant may issue upon the requisition of the proper authorities of such foreign government, for the surrender of such person, according to the stipulations of the treaty or convention; and he shall issue his warrant for the commitment of the person so charged to the proper jail, there to remain until such surrender shall be made.

(June 25, 1948, c. 645, 62 Stat. 822; Oct. 17, 1968, Pub.L. 90–578, Title III, § 301(a)(3), 82 Stat. 1115; Nov. 18, 1988, Pub.L. 100–690, Title VII, § 7087, 102 Stat. 4409; Nov. 29, 1990, Pub.L. 101–647, Title XVI, § 1605, 104 Stat. 4843; Dec. 1, 1990, Pub.L. 101–650, Title III, § 321, 104 Stat. 5117; Apr. 24, 1996, Pub.L. 104–132, Title IV, § 443(b), 110 Stat. 1281.)

HISTORICAL AND STATUTORY NOTES

Effective and Applicability Provisions

1968 Acts. Amendment by Pub.L. 90–578 effective Oct. 17, 1968, except when a later effective date is applicable, which is the earlier of date when implementation of amendment by appointment of magistrates and assumption of office takes place or third anniversary of enactment of Pub.L. 90–578 on Oct. 17, 1968, see section 403 of Pub.L. 90–578, set out as a note under section 631 of Title 28, Judiciary and Judicial Procedure.

Change of Name

Words "magistrate judge" substituted for "magistrate" in text pursuant to section 321 of Pub.L. 101–650, set out as a note under 28 U.S.C.A. § 631.

§ 3185. Fugitives from country under control of United States into the United States

Whenever any foreign country or territory, or any part thereof, is occupied by or under the control of the United States, any person who, having violated the criminal laws in force therein by the commission of any of the offenses enumerated below, departs or flees from justice therein to the United States, shall, when found therein, be liable to arrest and detention by the authorities of the United States, and on the written request or requisition of the military governor or other chief executive officer in control of such foreign country or territory shall be returned and surrendered as hereinafter provided to such authorities for trial under the laws in force in the place where such offense was committed.

(1) Murder and assault with intent to commit murder;

(2) Counterfeiting or altering money, or uttering or bringing into circulation counterfeit or altered money;

(3) Counterfeiting certificates or coupons of public indebtedness, bank notes, or other instruments of public credit, and the utterance or circulation of the same;

(4) Forgery or altering and uttering what is forged or altered;

(5) Embezzlement or criminal malversation of the public funds, committed by public officers, employees, or depositaries;

(6) Larceny or embezzlement of an amount not less than $100 in value;

(7) Robbery;

(8) Burglary, defined to be the breaking and entering by nighttime into the house of another person with intent to commit a felony therein;

(9) Breaking and entering the house or building of another, whether in the day or nighttime, with the intent to commit a felony therein;

(10) Entering, or breaking and entering the offices of the Government and public authorities, or the offices of banks, banking houses, savings banks, trust companies, insurance or other companies, with the intent to commit a felony therein;

(11) Perjury or the subornation of perjury;

(12) A felony under chapter 109A of this title;

(13) Arson;

(14) Piracy by the law of nations;

(15) Murder, assault with intent to kill, and manslaughter, committed on the high seas, on board a ship owned by or in control of citizens or residents of such foreign country or territory and not under the flag of the United States, or of some other government;

(16) Malicious destruction of or attempt to destroy railways, trams, vessels, bridges, dwellings, public edifices, or other buildings, when the act endangers human life.

This chapter, so far as applicable, shall govern proceedings authorized by this section. Such proceedings shall be had before a judge of the courts of the United States only, who shall hold such person on evidence establishing probable cause that he is guilty of the offense charged.

No return or surrender shall be made of any person charged with the commission of any offense of a political nature.

If so held, such person shall be returned and surrendered to the authorities in control of such foreign country or territory on the order of the Secretary of State of the United States, and such authorities shall secure to such a person a fair and impartial trial.

(June 25, 1948, c. 645, 62 Stat. 823; May 24, 1949, c. 139, § 49, 63 Stat. 96; Nov. 10, 1986, Pub.L. 99–646, § 87(c)(6), 100 Stat. 3623; Nov. 14, 1986, Pub.L. 99–654, § 3(a)(6), 100 Stat. 3663.)

HISTORICAL AND STATUTORY NOTES

Effective and Applicability Provisions

1986 Acts. Amendment by Pub.L. 99–654, effective 30 days after Nov. 14, 1986, see section 4 of Pub.L. 99–654, set out as a note under section 2241 of this title.

Amendment by section 87 of Pub.L. 99–646 effective 30 days after Nov. 10, 1986, see section 87(e) of Pub.L. 99–646, set out as a note under section 2241 of this title.

§ 3186. Secretary of State to surrender fugitive

The Secretary of State may order the person committed under sections 3184 or 3185 of this title to be delivered to any authorized agent of such foreign government, to be tried for the offense of which charged.

Such agent may hold such person in custody, and take him to the territory of such foreign government, pursuant to such treaty.

A person so accused who escapes may be retaken in the same manner as any person accused of any offense.

(June 25, 1948, c. 645, 62 Stat. 824.)

§ 3187. Provisional arrest and detention within extraterritorial jurisdiction

The provisional arrest and detention of a fugitive, under sections 3042 and 3183 of this title, in advance of the presentation of formal proofs, may be obtained by telegraph upon the request of the authority competent to request the surrender of such fugitive addressed to the authority competent to grant such surrender. Such request shall be accompanied by an express statement that a warrant for the fugitive's arrest has been issued within the jurisdiction of the authority making such request charging the fugitive with the commission of the crime for which his extradition is sought to be obtained.

No person shall be held in custody under telegraphic request by virtue of this section for more than ninety days.

(June 25, 1948, c. 645, 62 Stat. 824.)

§ 3188. Time of commitment pending extradition

Whenever any person who is committed for rendition to a foreign government to remain until delivered up in pursuance of a requisition, is not so delivered up and conveyed out of the United States within two calendar months after such commitment, over and above the time actually required to convey the prisoner from the jail to which he was committed, by the readiest way, out of the United States, any judge of the United States, or of any State, upon application made to him by or on behalf of the person so committed, and upon proof made to him that reasonable notice of the intention to make such application has been given to the Secretary of State, may order the person so committed to be discharged out of custody, unless sufficient cause is shown to such judge why such discharge ought not to be ordered.

(June 25, 1948, c. 645, 62 Stat. 824.)

§ 3189. Place and character of hearing

Hearings in cases of extradition under treaty stipulation or convention shall be held on land, publicly, and in a room or office easily accessible to the public.

(June 25, 1948, c. 645, 62 Stat. 824.)

§ 3190. Evidence on hearing

Depositions, warrants, or other papers or copies thereof offered in evidence upon the hearing of any extradition case shall be received and admitted as evidence on such hearing for all the purposes of such hearing if they shall be properly and legally authenticated so as to entitle them to be received for similar purposes by the tribunals of the foreign country from which the accused party shall have escaped, and the certificate of the principal diplomatic or consular officer of the United States resident in such foreign country shall be proof that the same, so offered, are authenticated in the manner required.

(June 25, 1948, c. 645, 62 Stat. 824.)

§ 3191. Witnesses for indigent fugitives

On the hearing of any case under a claim of extradition by a foreign government, upon affidavit being filed by the person charged setting forth that there are witnesses whose evidence is material to his defense, that he cannot safely go to trial without them, what he expects to prove by each of them, and that he is not possessed of sufficient means, and is actually unable to pay the fees of such witnesses, the judge or magistrate judge hearing the matter may order that such witnesses be subpenaed; and the costs incurred by the process, and the fees of witnesses, shall be paid in the same manner as in the case of witnesses subpenaed in behalf of the United States.

(June 25, 1948, c. 645, 62 Stat. 825; Oct. 17, 1968, Pub.L. 90–578, Title III, § 301(a)(3), 82 Stat. 1115; Dec. 1, 1990, Pub.L. 101–650, Title III, § 321, 104 Stat. 5117.)

HISTORICAL AND STATUTORY NOTES

Effective and Applicability Provisions

1968 Acts. Amendment by Pub.L. 90–578 effective Oct. 17, 1968, except when a later effective date is applicable, which is the earlier of date when implementation of amendment by appointment of magistrates and assumption of office takes place or third anniversary of enactment of Pub.L. 90–578 on Oct. 17, 1968, see section 403 of Pub.L. 90–578, set out as a note under section 631 of Title 28, Judiciary and Judicial Procedure.

Change of Name

Words "magistrate judge" substituted for "magistrate" in text pursuant to section 321 of Pub.L. 101–650, set out as a note under 28 U.S.C.A. § 631.

§ 3192. Protection of accused

Whenever any person is delivered by any foreign government to an agent of the United States, for the purpose of being brought within the United States and tried for any offense of which he is duly accused, the President shall have power to take all necessary measures for the transportation and safekeeping of such accused person, and for his security against lawless violence, until the final conclusion of his trial for the offenses specified in the warrant of extradition, and until his final discharge from custody or imprisonment for or on account of such offenses, and for a reasonable time thereafter, and may employ such portion of the land or naval forces of the United States, or of the militia thereof, as may be necessary for the safekeeping and protection of the accused.

(June 25, 1948, c. 645, 62 Stat. 825.)

§ 3193. Receiving agent's authority over offenders

A duly appointed agent to receive, in behalf of the United States, the delivery, by a foreign government, of any person accused of crime committed within the United States, and to convey him to the place of his trial, shall have all the powers of a marshal of the United States, in the several districts through which it may be necessary for him to pass with such prisoner, so far as such power is requisite for the prisoner's safe-keeping.

(June 25, 1948, c. 645, 62 Stat. 825.)

EXECUTIVE ORDERS

EXECUTIVE ORDER NO. 11517

Mar. 19, 1970, 35 F.R. 4937

ISSUANCE AND SIGNATURE BY SECRETARY OF STATE OF WARRANTS APPOINTING AGENTS TO RETURN FUGITIVES FROM JUSTICE EXTRADITED TO UNITED STATES

WHEREAS the President of the United States, under section 3192 of Title 18, United States Code [section 3192 of this title], has been granted the power to take all necessary measures for the transportation, safekeeping and security against lawless violence of any person delivered by any foreign government to an agent of the United States for return to the United States for trial for any offense of which he is duly accused; and

WHEREAS fugitives from justice in the United States whose extradition from abroad has been requested by the Government of the United States and granted by a foreign government are to be returned in the custody of duly appointed agents in accordance with the provisions of section 3193 of Title 18, United States Code [this section]; and

WHEREAS such duly appointed agents under the provisions of the law mentioned above, being authorized to receive delivery of the fugitive in behalf of the United States and to convey him to the place of his trial, are given the powers of a marshal of the United States in the several districts of the United States through which it may be necessary for them to pass with such prisoner, so far as such power is requisite for the prisoner's safekeeping; and

WHEREAS such warrants serve as a certification to the foreign government delivering the fugitives to any other foreign country through which such agents may pass, and to authorities in the United States of the powers therein conferred upon the agents; and

WHEREAS it is desirable by delegation of functions heretofore performed by the President to simplify and thereby expedite the issuance of such warrants to agents in the interests of the prompt return of fugitives to the United States:

NOW, THEREFORE, by virtue of the authority vested in me by section 301 of Title 3 of the United States Code [section 301 of Title 3, The President], and as President of the United States, it is ordered as follows:

Section 1. The Secretary of State is hereby designated and empowered to issue and sign all warrants appointing agents to receive, in behalf of the United States, the delivery in extradition by a foreign government of any person accused of a crime committed within the United States, and to convey such person to the place of his trial.

Sec. 2. Agents appointed in accordance with section 1 of this order shall have all the powers conferred in respect of such agents by applicable treaties of the United States and by section 3193 of Title 18, United States Code [this section], or by any other provisions of United States law.

Sec. 3. Executive Order No. 10347. April 18, 1952, as amended by Executive Order No. 11354, May 23, 1967, [set out as a note under section 42 of Title 4, Flag and Seal, Seat of Government, and the States], is further amended by deleting numbered paragraph 4 and renumbering paragraphs 5 and 6 as paragraphs 4 and 5, respectively.

RICHARD NIXON

§ 3194. Transportation of fugitive by receiving agent

Any agent appointed as provided in section 3182 of this title who receives the fugitive into his custody is empowered to transport him to the State or Territory from which he has fled.

(June 25, 1948, c. 645, 62 Stat. 825.)

§ 3195. Payment of fees and costs

All costs or expenses incurred in any extradition proceeding in apprehending, securing, and transmitting a fugitive shall be paid by the demanding authority.

All witness fees and costs of every nature in cases of international extradition, including the fees of the magistrate judge, shall be certified by the judge or magistrate judge before whom the hearing shall take place to the Secretary of State of the United States, and the same shall be paid out of appropriations to defray the expenses of the judiciary or the Department of Justice as the case may be.

The Attorney General shall certify to the Secretary of State the amounts to be paid to the United States on account of said fees and costs in extradition cases by the foreign government requesting the extradition, and the Secretary of State shall cause said amounts to be collected and transmitted to the Attorney General for deposit in the Treasury of the United States.

(June 25, 1948, c. 645, 62 Stat. 825; Oct. 17, 1968, Pub.L. 90–578, Title III, § 301(a)(3), 82 Stat. 1115; Dec. 1, 1990, Pub.L. 101–650, Title III, § 321, 104 Stat. 5117.)

HISTORICAL AND STATUTORY NOTES

Effective and Applicability Provisions

1968 Acts. Amendment by Pub.L. 90–578 effective Oct. 17, 1968, except when a later effective date is applicable, which is the earlier of date when implementation of amendment by appointment of magistrates and assumption of office takes place or third anniversary of enactment of Pub.L. 90–578 on Oct. 17, 1968, see section 403 of Pub.L. 90–578, set out as a note under section 631 of Title 28, Judiciary and Judicial Procedure.

Change of Name

Words "magistrate judge" substituted for "magistrate" in text pursuant to section 321 of Pub.L. 101–650, set out as a note under 28 U.S.C.A. § 631.

§ 3196. Extradition of United States citizens

If the applicable treaty or convention does not obligate the United States to extradite its citizens to a foreign country, the Secretary of State may, nevertheless, order the surrender to that country of a United States citizen whose extradition has been requested by that country if the other requirements of that treaty or convention are met.

(Added Pub.L. 101–623, § 11(a), Nov. 21, 1990, 104 Stat. 3356.)

CHAPTER 211—JURISDICTION AND VENUE

§ 3231. District courts

The district courts of the United States shall have original jurisdiction, exclusive of the courts of the States, of all offenses against the laws of the United States.

Nothing in this title shall be held to take away or impair the jurisdiction of the courts of the several States under the laws thereof.

(June 25, 1948, c. 645, 62 Stat. 826.)

§ 3232. District of offense—(Rule)

SEE FEDERAL RULES OF CRIMINAL PROCEDURE

Proceedings to be in district and division in which offense committed, Rule 18.

(June 25, 1948, c. 645, 62 Stat. 826.)

§ 3233. Transfer within district—(Rule)

SEE FEDERAL RULES OF CRIMINAL PROCEDURE

Arraignment, plea, trial, sentence in district of more than one division, Rule 19.

(June 25, 1948, c. 645, 62 Stat. 826.)

HISTORICAL AND STATUTORY NOTES

References in Text

Rule 19 of the Federal Rules of Criminal Procedure, referred to in text, was rescinded Feb. 28, 1966, eff. July 1, 1966.

§ 3234. Change of venue to another district—(Rule)

SEE FEDERAL RULES OF CRIMINAL PROCEDURE

Plea or disposal of case in district other than that in which defendant was arrested, Rule 20.

(June 25, 1948, c. 645, 62 Stat. 826.)

§ 3235. Venue in capital cases

The trial of offenses punishable with death shall be had in the county where the offense was committed, where that can be done without great inconvenience.

(June 25, 1948, c. 645, 62 Stat. 826.)

§ 3236. Murder or manslaughter

In all cases of murder or manslaughter, the offense shall be deemed to have been committed at the place where the injury was inflicted, or the poison administered or other means employed which caused the death, without regard to the place where the death occurs.

(June 25, 1948, c. 645, 62 Stat. 826.)

§ 3237. Offenses begun in one district and completed in another

(a) Except as otherwise expressly provided by enactment of Congress, any offense against the United States begun in one district and completed in another, or committed in more than one district, may be inquired of and prosecuted in any district in which such offense was begun, continued, or completed.

Any offense involving the use of the mails, transportation in interstate or foreign commerce, or the importation of an object or person into the United States is a continuing offense and, except as otherwise expressly provided by enactment of Congress, may be inquired of and prosecuted in any district from, through, or into which such commerce, mail matter, or imported object or person moves.

(b) Notwithstanding subsection (a), where an offense is described in section 7203 of the Internal Revenue Code of 1986, or where venue for prosecution of an offense described in section 7201 or 7206(1), (2), or (5) of such Code (whether or not the offense is also described in another provision of law) is based solely on a mailing to the Internal Revenue Service, and prosecution is begun in a judicial district other than the judicial district in which the defendant resides, he may upon motion filed in the district in which the prosecution is begun, elect to be tried in the district in which he was residing at the time the alleged offense was committed: *Provided,* That the motion is filed within twenty days after arraignment of the defendant upon indictment or information.

(June 25, 1948, c. 645, 62 Stat. 826; Aug. 6, 1958, Pub.L. 85–595, 72 Stat. 512; Nov. 2, 1966, Pub.L. 89–713, § 2, 80 Stat. 1108; July 18, 1984, Pub.L. 98–369, Title I, § 162, 98 Stat. 697; Oct. 12, 1984, Pub.L. 98–473, Title II, § 1204(a), 98 Stat. 2152.)

HISTORICAL AND STATUTORY NOTES

References in Text

Section 7203 of the Internal Revenue Code of 1954, referred to in subsec. (b), is classified to section 7203 of Title 26, Internal Revenue Code.

Section 7201 or 7206(1), (2) or (5) of such Code, referred to in subsec. (b), are classified respectively to sections 7201 and 7206(1), (2), (5) of Title 26, Internal Revenue Code.

Effective and Applicability Provisions

1966 Acts. Amendment by Pub.L. 89–713 effective Nov. 2, 1966, see section 6 of Pub.L. 89–713, set out as an Effective Date of 1966 Amendment note under section 6091 of Title 26, Internal Revenue Code.

§ 3238. Offenses not committed in any district

The trial of all offenses begun or committed upon the high seas, or elsewhere out of the jurisdiction of any particular State or district, shall be in the district in which the offender, or any one of two or more joint offenders, is arrested or is first brought; but if such offender or offenders are not so arrested or brought into any district, an indictment or information may be filed in the district of the last known residence of the offender or of any one of two or more joint offenders, or if no such residence is known the indictment or information may be filed in the District of Columbia.

(June 25, 1948, c. 645, 62 Stat. 826; May 23, 1963, Pub.L. 88–27, 77 Stat. 48.)

§ 3239. Optional venue for espionage and related offenses

The trial for any offense involving a violation, begun or committed upon the high seas or elsewhere out of the jurisdiction of any particular State or district, of—

(1) section 793, 794, 798, or section 1030(a)(1) of this title;

(2) section 601 of the National Security Act of 1947 (50 U.S.C. 421); or

(3) section 4(b) or 4(c) of the Subversive Activities Control Act of 1950 (50 U.S.C. 783(b) or (c));

may be in the District of Columbia or in any other district authorized by law.

(Added Pub.L. 103–322, Title XXXII, § 320909(a), Sept. 13, 1994, 108 Stat. 2127.)

HISTORICAL AND STATUTORY NOTES

References in Text

Section 601 of the National Security Act of 1947 (50 U.S.C. 421), referred to in par. (2), is section 601 of Act July 26, 1947, c. 343, as added, which is classified to section 421 of Title 50, War and National Defense.

Section 4(b) or (c) of the Subversive Activities Control Act of 1950 (50 U.S.C. 783(b) or (c)), referred to in par. (3), is section 4(b) or (c) of Act Sept. 23, 1950, c. 1024, as amended, which is classified to section 783(b) or (c) of Title 50, War and National Defense.

Prior Provisions

A prior section 3239, Act June 25, 1948, c. 645, 62 Stat. 827, which related to threatening communications, was repealed by Pub.L. 98–473, Title II, § 1204(b), Oct. 12, 1984, 98 Stat. 2152.

§ 3240. Creation of new district or division

Whenever any new district or division is established, or any county or territory is transferred from one district or division to another district or division, prosecutions for offenses committed within such district, division, county, or territory prior to such transfer, shall be commenced and proceeded with the same as if such new district or division had not been created, or such county or territory had not been transferred, unless the court, upon the application of the defendant, shall order the case to be removed to the new district or division for trial.

(June 25, 1948, c. 645, 62 Stat. 827; May 24, 1949, c. 139, § 50, 63 Stat. 96.)

§ 3241. Jurisdiction of offenses under certain sections

The District Court of the Virgin Islands shall have jurisdiction of offenses under the laws of the United States, not locally inapplicable, committed within the territorial jurisdiction of such courts, and jurisdiction, concurrently with the district courts of the United States, of offenses against the laws of the United States committed upon the high seas.

(June 25, 1948, c. 645, 62 Stat. 827; July 7, 1958, Pub.L. 85–508, § 12(i), 72 Stat. 348; Nov. 2, 2002, Pub.L. 107–273, Div. B, Title IV, § 4004(e), 116 Stat. 1812.)

HISTORICAL AND STATUTORY NOTES

Effective and Applicability Provisions

1958 Acts. Amendment by Pub.L. 85–508 effective Jan. 3, 1959 upon admission of Alaska into the Union pursuant to Proc. No. 3269, Jan. 5, 1959, 24 F.R. 81, 73 Stat. c16, as required by sections 1 and 8(c) of Pub.L. 85–508, see notes set out under section 81A of Title 28, Judiciary and Judicial Procedure and preceding section 21 of Title 48, Territories and Insular Possessions.

§ 3242. Indians committing certain offenses; acts on reservations

All Indians committing any offense listed in the first paragraph of and punishable under section 1153 (relating to offenses committed within Indian country) of this title shall be tried in the same courts and in the same manner as are all other persons committing such offense within the exclusive jurisdiction of the United States.

(June 25, 1948, c. 645, 62 Stat. 827; May 24, 1949, c. 139, § 51, 63 Stat. 96; Nov. 2, 1966, Pub.L. 89–707, § 2, 80 Stat. 1101; May 29, 1976, Pub.L. 94–297, § 4, 90 Stat. 586.)

§ 3243. Jurisdiction of State of Kansas over offenses committed by or against Indians on Indian reservations

Jurisdiction is conferred on the State of Kansas over offenses committed by or against Indians on Indian reservations, including trust or restricted allotments, within the State of Kansas, to the same extent as its courts have jurisdiction over offenses committed elsewhere within the State in accordance with the laws of the State.

This section shall not deprive the courts of the United States of jurisdiction over offenses defined by the laws of the United States committed by or against Indians on Indian reservations.

(June 25, 1948, c. 645, 62 Stat. 827.)

§ 3244. Jurisdiction of proceedings relating to transferred offenders

When a treaty is in effect between the United States and a foreign country providing for the transfer of convicted offenders—

(1) the country in which the offender was convicted shall have exclusive jurisdiction and competence over proceedings seeking to challenge, modify, or set aside convictions or sentences handed down by a court of such country;

(2) all proceedings instituted by or on behalf of an offender transferred from the United States to a foreign country seeking to challenge, modify, or set aside the conviction or sentence upon which the transfer was based shall be brought in the court which would have jurisdiction and competence if the offender had not been transferred;

(3) all proceedings instituted by or on behalf of an offender transferred to the United States pertaining to the manner of execution in the United States of the sentence imposed by a foreign court shall be brought in the United States district court for the district in which the offender is confined or in which supervision is exercised and shall name the Attorney General and the official having immediate custody or exercising immediate supervision of the offender as respondents. The Attorney General shall defend against such proceedings;

(4) all proceedings instituted by or on behalf of an offender seeking to challenge the validity or legality of the offender's transfer from the United States shall be brought in the United States district court of the district in which the proceedings to determine the validity of the offender's consent were held and shall name the Attorney General as respondent; and

(5) all proceedings instituted by or on behalf of an offender seeking to challenge the validity or legality of the offender's transfer to the United States shall be brought in the United States district court of the district in which the offender is confined or of the district in which supervision is exercised and shall name the Attorney General and the official having immediate custody or exercising immediate supervision of the offender as respondents. The Attorney General shall defend against such proceedings.

(Added Pub.L. 95–144, § 3, Oct. 28, 1977, 91 Stat. 1220, Title 28, § 2256; renumbered Pub.L. 95–598, Title III, § 314(j)(1), Nov. 6, 1978, 92 Stat. 2677.)

HISTORICAL AND STATUTORY NOTES

Codifications

Section was formerly classified to section 2256 of Title 28, Judiciary and Judicial Procedure.

Savings Provisions

Amendment by section 314 of Pub.L. 95–598 not to affect the application of chapter 9 [§ 151 et seq.], chapter 96 [§ 1961 et seq.], or section 2516, 3057, or 3284 of this title to any act of any person (1) committed before Oct. 1, 1979, or (2) committed after Oct. 1, 1979, in connection with a case commenced before such date, see section 403(d) of Pub.L. 95–598, set out preceding section 101 of Title 11, Bankruptcy.

CHAPTER 212—MILITARY EXTRATERRITORIAL JURISDICTION

§ 3261. Criminal offenses committed by certain members of the Armed Forces and by persons employed by or accompanying the Armed Forces outside the United States

(a) Whoever engages in conduct outside the United States that would constitute an offense punishable by imprisonment for more than 1 year if the conduct had been engaged in within the special maritime and territorial jurisdiction of the United States—

(1) while employed by or accompanying the Armed Forces outside the United States; or

(2) while a member of the Armed Forces subject to chapter 47 of title 10 (the Uniform Code of Military Justice),

shall be punished as provided for that offense.

(b) No prosecution may be commenced against a person under this section if a foreign government, in accordance with jurisdiction recognized by the United States, has prosecuted or is prosecuting such person for the conduct constituting such offense, except upon the approval of the Attorney General or the Deputy Attorney General (or a person acting in either such capacity), which function of approval may not be delegated.

(c) Nothing in this chapter may be construed to deprive a court-martial, military commission, provost court, or other military tribunal of concurrent jurisdiction with respect to offenders or offenses that by statute or by the law of war may be tried by a court-martial, military commission, provost court, or other military tribunal.

(d) No prosecution may be commenced against a member of the Armed Forces subject to chapter 47 of title 10 (the Uniform Code of Military Justice) under this section unless—

(1) such member ceases to be subject to such chapter; or

(2) an indictment or information charges that the member committed the offense with one or more other defendants, at least one of whom is not subject to such chapter.

(Added Pub.L. 106–523, § 2(a), Nov. 22, 2000, 114 Stat. 2488.)

HISTORICAL AND STATUTORY NOTES

References in Text

Chapter 47 of title 10, referred to in subsec. (a)(2) and (d), is 10 U.S.C.A. § 801 et seq.

Short Title

2000 Acts. Pub.L. 106–523, § 1, Nov. 22, 2000, 114 Stat. 2488, provided that: "This Act [enacting chapter 212 of this title] may be cited as the 'Military Extraterritorial Jurisdiction Act of 2000'."

§ 3262. Arrest and commitment

(a) The Secretary of Defense may designate and authorize any person serving in a law enforcement position in the Department of Defense to arrest, in accordance with applicable international agreements, outside the United States any person described in section 3261(a) if there is probable cause to believe that such person violated section 3261(a).

(b) Except as provided in sections 3263 and 3264, a person arrested under subsection (a) shall be delivered as soon as practicable to the custody of civilian law enforcement authorities of the United States for removal to the United States for judicial proceedings in relation to conduct referred to in such subsection unless such person has had charges brought against him or her under chapter 47 of title 10 for such conduct.

(Added Pub.L. 106–523, § 2(a), Nov. 22, 2000, 114 Stat. 2489.)

HISTORICAL AND STATUTORY NOTES

References in Text

Chapter 47 of title 10, referred to in subsec. (b), is 10 U.S.C.A. § 801 et seq.

§ 3263. Delivery to authorities of foreign countries

(a) Any person designated and authorized under section 3262(a) may deliver a person described in section 3261(a) to the appropriate authorities of a foreign country in which such person is alleged to have violated section 3261(a) if—

(1) appropriate authorities of that country request the delivery of the person to such country for trial for such conduct as an offense under the laws of that country; and

(2) the delivery of such person to that country is authorized by a treaty or other international agreement to which the United States is a party.

(b) The Secretary of Defense, in consultation with the Secretary of State, shall determine which officials of a foreign country constitute appropriate authorities for purposes of this section.

(Added Pub.L. 106–523, § 2(a), Nov. 22, 2000, 114 Stat. 2489.)

§ 3264. Limitation on removal

(a) Except as provided in subsection (b), and except for a person delivered to authorities of a foreign country under section 3263, a person arrested for or charged with a violation of section 3261(a) shall not be removed—

(1) to the United States; or

(2) to any foreign country other than a country in which such person is believed to have violated section 3261(a).

(b) The limitation in subsection (a) does not apply if—

(1) a Federal magistrate judge orders the person to be removed to the United States to be present at a detention hearing held pursuant to section 3142(f);

(2) a Federal magistrate judge orders the detention of the person before trial pursuant to section 3142(e), in which case the person shall be promptly removed to the United States for purposes of such detention;

(3) the person is entitled to, and does not waive, a preliminary examination under the Federal Rules of Criminal Procedure, in which case the person shall be removed to the United States in time for such examination;

(4) a Federal magistrate judge otherwise orders the person to be removed to the United States; or

(5) the Secretary of Defense determines that military necessity requires that the limitations in subsection (a) be waived, in which case the person shall be removed to the nearest United States military installation outside the United States adequate to detain the person and to facilitate the initial appearance described in section 3265(a).

(Added Pub.L. 106–523, § 2(a), Nov. 22, 2000, 114 Stat. 2489.)

HISTORICAL AND STATUTORY NOTES

References in Text

The Federal Rules of Criminal Procedure, referred to in subsec. (b)(3), are set out following this title.

§ 3265. Initial proceedings

(a)(1) In the case of any person arrested for or charged with a violation of section 3261(a) who is not delivered to authorities of a foreign country under section 3263, the initial appearance of that person under the Federal Rules of Criminal Procedure—

(A) shall be conducted by a Federal magistrate judge; and

(B) may be carried out by telephony or such other means that enables voice communication among the participants, including any counsel representing the person.

(2) In conducting the initial appearance, the Federal magistrate judge shall also determine whether there is probable cause to believe that an offense under section 3261(a) was committed and that the person committed it.

(3) If the Federal magistrate judge determines that probable cause exists that the person committed an offense under section 3261(a), and if no motion is made seeking the person's detention before trial, the Federal magistrate judge shall also determine at the initial appearance the conditions of the person's release before trial under chapter 207 of this title.

(b) In the case of any person described in subsection (a), any detention hearing of that person under section 3142(f)—

(1) shall be conducted by a Federal magistrate judge; and

(2) at the request of the person, may be carried out by telephony or such other means that enables voice communication among the participants, including any counsel representing the person.

(c)(1) If any initial proceeding under this section with respect to any such person is conducted while the person is outside the United States, and the person is entitled to have counsel appointed for purposes of such proceeding, the Federal magistrate judge may appoint as such counsel for purposes of such hearing a qualified military counsel.

(2) For purposes of this subsection, the term "qualified military counsel" means a judge advocate made available by the Secretary of Defense for purposes of such proceedings, who—

(A) is a graduate of an accredited law school or is a member of the bar of a Federal court or of the highest court of a State; and

(B) is certified as competent to perform such duties by the Judge Advocate General of the armed force of which he is a member.

(Added Pub.L. 106–523, § 2(a), Nov. 22, 2000, 114 Stat. 2490.)

HISTORICAL AND STATUTORY NOTES

References in Text

The Federal Rules of Criminal Procedure, referred to in subsec. (a)(1), are set out following this title.

Chapter 207 of this title, referred to in subsec. (a)(3), is 18 U.S.C.A. § 3141 et seq.

§ 3266. Regulations

(a) The Secretary of Defense, after consultation with the Secretary of State and the Attorney General, shall prescribe regulations governing the apprehension, detention, delivery, and removal of persons under this chapter and the facilitation of proceedings under section 3265. Such regulations shall be uniform throughout the Department of Defense.

(b)(1) The Secretary of Defense, after consultation with the Secretary of State and the Attorney General, shall prescribe regulations requiring that, to the maximum extent practicable, notice shall be provided to any person employed by or accompanying the Armed Forces outside the United States who is not a national of the United States that such person is potentially subject to the criminal jurisdiction of the United States under this chapter.

(2) A failure to provide notice in accordance with the regulations prescribed under paragraph (1) shall not defeat the jurisdiction of a court of the United States or provide a defense in any judicial proceeding arising under this chapter.

(c) The regulations prescribed under this section, and any amendments to those regulations, shall not take effect before the date that is 90 days after the date on which the Secretary of Defense submits a report containing those regulations or amendments (as the case may be) to the Committee on the Judiciary of the House of Representatives and the Committee on the Judiciary of the Senate.

(Added Pub.L. 106–523, § 2(a), Nov. 22, 2000, 114 Stat. 2491.)

§ 3267. Definitions

As used in this chapter:

(1) The term "employed by the Armed Forces outside the United States" means—

(A) employed as—

(i) a civilian employee of—

(I) the Department of Defense (including a nonappropriated fund instrumentality of the Department); or

(II) any other Federal agency, or any provisional authority, to the extent such employment relates to supporting the mission of the Department of Defense overseas;

(ii) a contractor (including a subcontractor at any tier) of—

(I) the Department of Defense (including a nonappropriated fund instrumentality of the Department); or

(II) any other Federal agency, or any provisional authority, to the extent such employment relates to supporting the mission of the Department of Defense overseas; or

(iii) an employee of a contractor (or subcontractor at any tier) of—

(I) the Department of Defense (including a nonappropriated fund instrumentality of the Department); or

(II) any other Federal agency, or any provisional authority, to the extent such employment relates to supporting the mission of the Department of Defense overseas;

(B) present or residing outside the United States in connection with such employment; and

(C) not a national of or ordinarily resident in the host nation.

(2) The term "accompanying the Armed Forces outside the United States" means—

(A) A dependent of—

(i) a member of the Armed Forces;

(ii) a civilian employee of the Department of Defense (including a nonappropriated fund instrumentality of the Department); or

(iii) a Department of Defense contractor (including a subcontractor at any tier) or an employee of a Department of Defense contractor (including a subcontractor at any tier);

(B) residing with such member, civilian employee, contractor, or contractor employee outside the United States; and

(C) not a national of or ordinarily resident in the host nation.

(3) The term "Armed Forces" has the meaning given the term "armed forces" in section 101(a)(4) of title 10.

(4) The terms "Judge Advocate General" and "judge advocate" have the meanings given such terms in section 801 of title 10.

(Added Pub.L. 106–523, § 2(a), Nov. 22, 2000, 114 Stat. 2491; Pub.L. 108–375, Div. A, Title X, § 1088, Oct. 28, 2004, 118 Stat. 2066.)

CHAPTER 212A—EXTRATERRITORIAL JURISDICTION OVER CERTAIN TRAFFICKING IN PERSONS OFFENSES

§ 3271. Trafficking in persons offenses committed by persons employed by or accompanying the Federal Government outside the United States

(a) Whoever, while employed by or accompanying the Federal Government outside the United States, engages in conduct outside the United States that would constitute an offense under chapter 77 or 117 of this title if the conduct had been engaged in within the United States or within the special maritime and territorial jurisdiction of the United States shall be punished as provided for that offense.

(b) No prosecution may be commenced against a person under this section if a foreign government, in accordance with jurisdiction recognized by the United States, has prosecuted or is prosecuting such person for the conduct constituting such offense, except upon the approval of the Attorney General or the Deputy Attorney General (or a person acting in either such capacity), which function of approval may not be delegated.

(Added Pub.L. 109–164, Title I, § 103(a)(1), Jan. 10, 2006, 119 Stat. 3562.)

HISTORICAL AND STATUTORY NOTES

References in Text

Chapter 77 of this title, referred to in subsec. (a), is Peonage, Slavery, and Trafficking in Persons, 18 U.S.C.A. § 1581 et seq.

Chapter 117 of this title, referred to in subsec. (a), is Transportation for Illegal Sexual Activity and Related Crimes, 18 U.S.C.A. § 2421 et seq.

§ 3272. Definitions

As used in this chapter:

(1) The term "employed by the Federal Government outside the United States" means—

(A) employed as a civilian employee of the Federal Government, as a Federal contractor (including a subcontractor at any tier), or as an employee of a Federal contractor (including a subcontractor at any tier);

(B) present or residing outside the United States in connection with such employment; and

(C) not a national of or ordinarily resident in the host nation.

(2) The term "accompanying the Federal Government outside the United States" means—

(A) a dependant of—

(i) a civilian employee of the Federal Government; or

(ii) a Federal contractor (including a subcontractor at any tier) or an employee of a Federal contractor (including a subcontractor at any tier);

(B) residing with such civilian employee, contractor, or contractor employee outside the United States; and

(C) not a national of or ordinarily resident in the host nation.

(Added Pub.L. 109–164, Title I, § 103(a)(1), Jan. 10, 2006, 119 Stat. 3562.)

CHAPTER 213—LIMITATIONS

[1] Section catchline amended by Pub.L. 108–21 without corresponding amendment of chapter analysis.

HISTORICAL AND STATUTORY NOTES

Effective and Applicability Provisions

1984 Acts. Addition of item 3292 effective 30 days after Oct. 12, 1984, see section 1220 of Pub.L. 98–473, Title II, Oct. 12, 1984, 98 Stat. 2167, set out as a note under section 3505 of this title.

§ 3281. Capital offenses

An indictment for any offense punishable by death may be found at any time without limitation.

(June 25, 1948, c. 645, 62 Stat. 827; Sept. 13, 1994, Pub.L. 103–322, Title XXXIII, § 330004(16), 108 Stat. 2142.)

§ 3282. Offenses not capital

(a) In general.—Except as otherwise expressly provided by law, no person shall be prosecuted, tried, or punished for any offense, not capital, unless the indictment is found or the information is instituted within five years next after such offense shall have been committed.

(b) DNA profile indictment.—

(1) In general.—In any indictment for an offense under chapter 109A for which the identity of the accused is unknown, it shall be sufficient to describe the accused as an individual whose name is unknown, but who has a particular DNA profile.

(2) Exception.—Any indictment described under paragraph (1), which is found not later than 5 years after the offense under chapter 109A is committed, shall not be subject to—

(A) the limitations period described under subsection (a); and

(B) the provisions of chapter 208 until the individual is arrested or served with a summons in connection with the charges contained in the indictment.

(3) Defined term.—For purposes of this subsection, the term "DNA profile" means a set of DNA identification characteristics.

(June 25, 1948, c. 645, 62 Stat. 828; Sept. 1, 1954, c. 1214, § 12(a), formerly § 10(a), 68 Stat. 1145, renumbered Sept. 26, 1961, Pub.L. 87–299, § 1, 75 Stat. 648; Apr. 30, 2003, Pub.L. 108–21, Title VI, § 610(a), 117 Stat. 692.)

HISTORICAL AND STATUTORY NOTES

References in Text

Chapter 109A, referred to in subsec. (b)(1), (2), is 18 U.S.C.A. § 2241 et seq.

Chapter 208, referred to in subsec. (b)(2)(B), is 18 U.S.C.A. § 3161 et seq.

Effective and Applicability Provisions

1954 Acts. Section 12(b) of Act Sept. 1, 1954, formerly section 10(b), as renumbered by Pub.L. 87–299, § 1, provided that: "The amendment made by subsection (a) [amending this section] shall be effective with respect to offenses (1) committed on or after September 1, 1954, or (2) committed prior to such date, if on such date prosecution therefor is not barred by provisions of law in effect prior to such date."

§ 3283. Offenses against children

No statute of limitations that would otherwise preclude prosecution for an offense involving the sexual or physical abuse, or kidnaping, of a child under the age of 18 years shall preclude such prosecution during the life of the child, or for ten years after the offense, whichever is longer.

(June 25, 1948, c. 645, 62 Stat. 828; Sept. 13, 1994, Pub.L. 103–322, Title XXXIII, § 330018(a), 108 Stat. 2149; Apr. 30, 2003, Pub.L. 108–21, Title II, § 202, 117 Stat. 660; Jan. 5, 2006, Pub.L. 109–162, Title XI, § 1182(c), 119 Stat. 3126.)

§ 3284. Concealment of bankrupt's assets

The concealment of assets of a debtor in a case under title 11 shall be deemed to be a continuing offense until the debtor shall have been finally discharged or a discharge denied, and the period of limitations shall not begin to run until such final discharge or denial of discharge.

(June 25, 1948, c. 645, 62 Stat. 828; Nov. 6, 1978, Pub.L. 95–598, Title III, § 314(k), 92 Stat. 2678.)

HISTORICAL AND STATUTORY NOTES

Effective and Applicability Provisions

1978 Acts. Amendment by Pub.L. 95–598 effective Oct. 1, 1979, see section 402(a) of Pub.L. 95–598, set out as an Effective Date note preceding section 101 of Title 11, Bankruptcy.

Savings Provisions

Amendment by section 314 of Pub.L. 95–598 not to affect the application of this section to any act of any person (1) committed before Oct. 1, 1979, or (2) committed after Oct. 1, 1979, in connection with a case commenced before such date, see section 403(d) of Pub.L. 95–598, set out preceding section 101 of Title 11, Bankruptcy.

§ 3285. Criminal contempt

No proceeding for criminal contempt within section 402 of this title shall be instituted against any person, corporation or association unless begun within one year from the date of the act complained of; nor shall any such proceeding be a bar to any criminal prosecution for the same act.

(June 25, 1948, c. 645, 62 Stat. 828.)

§ 3286. Extension of statute of limitation for certain terrorism offenses

(a) Eight-year limitation.—Notwithstanding section 3282, no person shall be prosecuted, tried, or punished for any noncapital offense involving a violation of any provision listed in section 2332b(g)(5)(B), or a violation of section 112, 351(e), 1361, or 1751(e) of this title, or section 46504, 46505, or 46506 of title 49, unless the indictment is found or the information is instituted within 8 years after the offense was committed. Notwithstanding the preceding sentence, offenses listed in section 3295 are subject to the statute of limitations set forth in that section.

(b) No limitation.—Notwithstanding any other law, an indictment may be found or an information instituted at any time without limitation for any offense listed in section 2332b(g)(5)(B), if the commission of such offense resulted in, or created a forseeable risk of, death or serious bodily injury to another person.

(Added Pub.L. 103–322, Title XII, § 120001(a), Sept. 13, 1994, 108 Stat. 2021, and amended Pub.L. 104–132, Title VII, § 702(c), Apr. 24, 1996, 110 Stat. 1294; Pub.L. 104–294, Title VI, § 601(b)(1), Oct. 11, 1996, 110 Stat. 3498; Pub.L. 107–56, Title VIII, § 809(a), Oct. 26, 2001, 115 Stat. 379; Pub.L.

107–273, Div. B, Title IV, § 4002(c)(1), Nov. 2, 2002, 116 Stat. 1808.)

HISTORICAL AND STATUTORY NOTES

Codifications

Section 601(b)(1) of Pub.L. 104–294, which directed that this section be amended by substituting "2332", "2332a", and "37" for "2331", "2339", and "36", respectively, could not be executed to text due to a prior identical amendment by section 702(c)(2) through (4) of Pub.L. 104–132. See 1996 Amendments note set out under this section.

Effective and Applicability Provisions

2002 Acts. Amendment by section 4002(c)(1) of Pub.L. 107–273, as therein provided, effective Oct. 11, 1996, which is the date of enactment of Pub.L. 104–294, to which such amendment relates.

2001 Acts. Pub.L. 107–56, Title VIII, § 809(b), Oct. 26, 2001, 115 Stat. 380, provided that: "The amendments made by this section [amending this section] shall apply to the prosecution of any offense committed before, on, or after the date of the enactment of this section [Oct. 26, 2001].

1994 Acts. Section 120001(b) of Pub.L. 103–322 provided that: "The amendment made by subsection (a) [enacting this section] shall not apply to any offense committed more than 5 years prior to the date of enactment of this Act [Sept. 13, 1994]."

Repeals

Section 601(b)(1) of Pub.L. 104–294, cited in the credit of this section, was repealed by section 4002(c)(1) of Pub.L. 107–273, effective Oct. 11, 1996.

Prior Provisions

A prior section 3286, Act June 25, 1948, c. 645, 62 Stat. 828, relating to seduction on vessel of United States, was repealed by Pub.L. 101–647, Title XII, § 1207(b), Nov. 29, 1990, 104 Stat. 4832.

§ 3287. Wartime suspension of limitations

When the United States is at war the running of any statute of limitations applicable to any offense (1) involving fraud or attempted fraud against the United States or any agency thereof in any manner, whether by conspiracy or not, or (2) committed in connection with the acquisition, care, handling, custody, control or disposition of any real or personal property of the United States, or (3) committed in connection with the negotiation, procurement, award, performance, payment for, interim financing, cancelation, or other termination or settlement, of any contract, subcontract, or purchase order which is connected with or related to the prosecution of the war, or with any disposition of termination inventory by any war contractor or Government agency, shall be suspended until three years after the termination of hostilities as proclaimed by the President or by a concurrent resolution of Congress.

Definitions of terms in section 103 of title 41 shall apply to similar terms used in this section.

(June 25, 1948, c. 645, 62 Stat. 828.)

§ 3288. Indictments and information dismissed after period of limitations

Whenever an indictment or information charging a felony is dismissed for any reason after the period prescribed by the applicable statute of limitations has expired, a new indictment may be returned in the appropriate jurisdiction within six calendar months of the date of the dismissal of the indictment or information, or, in the event of an appeal, within 60 days of the date the dismissal of the indictment or information becomes final, or, if no regular grand jury is in session in the appropriate jurisdiction when the indictment or information is dismissed, within six calendar months of the date when the next regular grand jury is convened, which new indictment shall not be barred by any statute of limitations. This section does not permit the filing of a new indictment or information where the reason for the dismissal was the failure to file the indictment or information within the period prescribed by the applicable statute of limitations, or some other reason that would bar a new prosecution.

(June 25, 1948, c. 645, 62 Stat. 828; Oct. 16, 1963, Pub.L. 88–139, § 2, 77 Stat. 248; Aug. 30, 1964, Pub.L. 88–520, § 1, 78 Stat. 699; Nov. 18, 1988, Pub.L. 100–690, Title VII, § 7081(a), 102 Stat. 4407.)

§ 3289. Indictments and information dismissed before period of limitations

Whenever an indictment or information charging a felony is dismissed for any reason before the period prescribed by the applicable statute of limitations has expired, and such period will expire within six calendar months of the date of the dismissal of the indictment or information, a new indictment may be returned in the appropriate jurisdiction within six calendar months of the expiration of the applicable statute of limitations, or, in the event of an appeal, within 60 days of the date the dismissal of the indictment or information becomes final, or, if no regular grand jury is in session in the appropriate jurisdiction at the expiration of the applicable statute of limitations, within six calendar months of the date when the next regular grand jury is convened, which new indictment shall not be barred by any statute of limitations. This section does not permit the filing of a new indictment or information where the reason for the dismissal was the failure to file the indictment or information within the period prescribed by the applicable statute of limitations, or some other reason that would bar a new prosecution.

(June 25, 1948, c. 645, 62 Stat. 829; Oct. 16, 1963, Pub.L. 88–139, § 2, 77 Stat. 248; Aug. 30, 1964, Pub.L. 88–520, § 2, 78 Stat. 699; Nov. 18, 1988, Pub.L. 100–690, Title VII, § 7081(b), 102 Stat. 4407; Nov. 29, 1990, Pub.L. 101–647, Title XII, § 1213, Title XXV, § 2595(b), Title XXXV, § 3580, 104 Stat. 4833, 4907, 4929; Sept. 13, 1994, Pub.L. 103–322, Title XXXIII, § 330011(q)(2), 108 Stat. 2145.)

HISTORICAL AND STATUTORY NOTES

Effective and Applicability Provisions

1994 Acts. Section 330011(q)(2) of Pub.L. 103–322 provided in part that the amendment made by such section, repealing section 1213 of Pub.L. 101–647 (which amended this section), was to take effect on the date section 1213 of Pub.L. 101–647 took effect; section 1213 of Pub.L. 101–647 took effect on the date of enactment of Pub.L. 101–647, which was approved Nov. 29, 1990.

Repeals

Section 1213 of Pub.L. 101–647, amending this section, was repealed by section 330011(q)(2) of Pub.L. 103–322.

§ 3290. Fugitives from justice

No statute of limitations shall extend to any person fleeing from justice.

(June 25, 1948, c. 645, 62 Stat. 829.)

§ 3291. Nationality, citizenship and passports

No person shall be prosecuted, tried, or punished for violation of any provision of sections 1423 to 1428, inclusive, of chapter 69 and sections 1541 to 1544, inclusive, of chapter 75 of title 18 of the United States Code, or for conspiracy to violate any of such sections, unless the indictment is found or the information is instituted within ten years after the commission of the offense.

(Added June 30, 1951, c. 194, § 1, 65 Stat. 107, and amended Sept. 13, 1994, Pub.L. 103–322, Title XXXIII, § 330008(9), 108 Stat. 2143.)

§ 3292. Suspension of limitations to permit United States to obtain foreign evidence

(a)(1) Upon application of the United States, filed before return of an indictment, indicating that evidence of an offense is in a foreign country, the district court before which a grand jury is impaneled to investigate the offense shall suspend the running of the statute of limitations for the offense if the court finds by a preponderance of the evidence that an official request has been made for such evidence and that it reasonably appears, or reasonably appeared at the time the request was made, that such evidence is, or was, in such foreign country.

(2) The court shall rule upon such application not later than thirty days after the filing of the application.

(b) Except as provided in subsection (c) of this section, a period of suspension under this section shall begin on the date on which the official request is made and end on the date on which the foreign court or authority takes final action on the request.

(c) The total of all periods of suspension under this section with respect to an offense—

(1) shall not exceed three years; and

(2) shall not extend a period within which a criminal case must be initiated for more than six months if all foreign authorities take final action before such period would expire without regard to this section.

(d) As used in this section, the term "official request" means a letter rogatory, a request under a treaty or convention, or any other request for evidence made by a court of the United States or an authority of the United States having criminal law enforcement responsibility, to a court or other authority of a foreign country.

(Added Pub.L. 98–473, Title II, § 1218(a), Oct. 12, 1984, 98 Stat. 2167.)

HISTORICAL AND STATUTORY NOTES

Effective and Applicability Provisions

1984 Acts. Section effective 30 days after Oct. 12, 1984, see section 1220 of Pub.L. 98–473 set out as a note under section 3505 of this title.

§ 3293. Financial institution offenses

No person shall be prosecuted, tried, or punished for a violation of, or a conspiracy to violate—

(1) section 215, 656, 657, 1005, 1006, 1007, 1014, 1033, or 1344;

(2) section 1341 or 1343, if the offense affects a financial institution; or

(3) section 1963, to the extent that the racketeering activity involves a violation of section 1344;

unless the indictment is returned or the information is filed within 10 years after the commission of the offense.

(Added Pub.L. 101–73, Title IX, § 961(*l*)(1), Aug. 9, 1989, 103 Stat. 501, and amended Pub.L. 101–647, Title XXV, § 2505(a), Nov. 29, 1990, 104 Stat. 4862; Pub.L. 103–322, Title XXXII, § 320604(b), Title XXXIII, § 330002(e), Sept. 13, 1994, 108 Stat. 2119, 2140.)

HISTORICAL AND STATUTORY NOTES

Effective and Applicability Provisions

1990 Acts. Section 2505(b) of Pub.L. 101–647 provided that: "The amendments made by subsection (a) [amending this section] shall apply to any offense committed before the date of the enactment of this section [Nov. 29, 1990], if the statute of limitations applicable to that offense had not run as of such date."

Separability of Provisions

If any provision of Pub.L. 101–73 or the application thereof to any person or circumstance is held invalid, the remainder of Pub.L. 101–73 and the application of the provision to other persons not similarly situated or to other circumstances not to be affected thereby, see section 1221 of Pub.L. 101–73, set out as a note under section 1811 of Title 12, Banks and Banking.

Effect of This Section on Offenses for Which Period of Limitations Had Not Run

Section 961(*l*)(3) of Pub.L. 101–73 provided that: "The amendments made by this subsection [enacting this section] shall apply to an offense committed before the effective date of this section [Aug. 9, 1989], if the statute of limitations applicable to that offense under this chapter had not run as of such date."

§ 3294. Theft of major artwork

No person shall be prosecuted, tried, or punished for a violation of or conspiracy to violate section 668 unless the indictment is returned or the information is filed within 20 years after the commission of the offense.

(Added Pub.L. 103–322, Title XXXII, § 320902(b), Sept. 13, 1994, 108 Stat. 2124.)

§ 3295. Arson offenses

No person shall be prosecuted, tried, or punished for any non-capital offense under section 81 or subsection (f), (h), or (i) of section 844 unless the indictment is found or the information is instituted not later than 10 years after the date on which the offense was committed.

(Added Pub.L. 104–132, Title VII, § 708(c)(1), Apr. 24, 1996, 110 Stat. 1297.)

§ 3296. Counts dismissed pursuant to a plea agreement

(a) In general.—Notwithstanding any other provision of this chapter, any counts of an indictment or information that are dismissed pursuant to a plea agreement shall be reinstated by the District Court if—

(1) the counts sought to be reinstated were originally filed within the applicable limitations period;

(2) the counts were dismissed pursuant to a plea agreement approved by the District Court under which the defendant pled guilty to other charges;

(3) the guilty plea was subsequently vacated on the motion of the defendant; and

(4) the United States moves to reinstate the dismissed counts within 60 days of the date on which the order vacating the plea becomes final.

(b) Defenses; objections.—Nothing in this section shall preclude the District Court from considering any defense or objection, other than statute of limitations, to the prosecution of the counts reinstated under subsection (a).

(Added Pub.L. 107–273, Div. B, Title III, § 3003(a), Nov. 2, 2002, 116 Stat. 1805.)

§ 3297. Cases involving DNA evidence

In a case in which DNA testing implicates an identified person in the commission of a felony, no statute of limitations that would otherwise preclude prosecution of the offense shall preclude such prosecution until a period of time following the implication of the person by DNA testing has elapsed that is equal to the otherwise applicable limitation period.

(Added Pub.L. 108–405, Title II, § 204(a), Oct. 30, 2004, 118 Stat. 2271, and amended Pub.L. 109–162, Title X, § 1005, Jan. 5, 2006, 119 Stat. 3086.)

HISTORICAL AND STATUTORY NOTES

Effective and Applicability Provisions

2004 Acts. Pub.L. 108–405, Title II, § 204(c), Oct. 30, 2004, 118 Stat. 2271, provided that: "The amendments made by this section [enacting this section] shall apply to the prosecution of any offense committed before, on, or after the date of the enactment of this section [Oct. 30, 2004] if the applicable limitation period has not yet expired."

§ 3298. Trafficking-related offenses

No person shall be prosecuted, tried, or punished for any non-capital offense or conspiracy to commit a non-capital offense under section 1581 (Peonage; Obstructing Enforcement), 1583 (Enticement into Slavery), 1584 (Sale into Involuntary Servitude), 1589 (Forced Labor), 1590 (Trafficking with Respect to Peonage, Slavery, Involuntary Servitude, or Forced Labor), or 1592 (Unlawful Conduct with Respect to Documents in furtherance of Trafficking, Peonage, Slavery, Involuntary Servitude, or Forced Labor) of this title or under section 274(a) of the Immigration and Nationality Act unless the indictment is found or the information is instituted not later than 10 years after the commission of the offense.

(Added Pub.L. 109–162, Title XI, § 1182(a), Jan. 5, 2006, 119 Stat. 3126.)

HISTORICAL AND STATUTORY NOTES

References in Text

Section 274(a) of the Immigration and Nationality Act, referred to in text, is June 27, 1952, c. 477, Title II, ch. 8, § 274, 66 Stat. 228, as amended, which is classified to 8 U.S.C.A. § 1324(c).

§ 3299. Child abduction and sex offenses

Notwithstanding any other law, an indictment may be found or an information instituted at any time without limitation for any offense under section 1201 involving a minor victim, and for any felony under chapter 109A, 110 (except for section 2257 and 2257A), or 117, or section 1591.

(Added Pub.L. 109–248, Title II, § 211(1), July 27, 2006, 120 Stat. 616.)

HISTORICAL AND STATUTORY NOTES

References in Text

Chapters 109A, 110, or 117, referred to in text, are chapters 109A, Sexual Abuse, 110, Sexual exploitation and other abuse of children, and 117, Transportation for illegal sexual activity and related crimes, of this title, 18 U.S.C.A. § 2241 et seq., § 2251 et seq., and § 2421 et seq., respectively.

CHAPTER 215—GRAND JURY

§ 3321. Number of grand jurors; summoning additional jurors

Every grand jury impaneled before any district court shall consist of not less than sixteen nor more than twenty-three persons. If less than sixteen of the persons summoned attend, they shall be placed on the grand jury, and the court shall order the marshal to summon, either immediately or for a day fixed, from the body of the district, and not from the bystanders, a sufficient number of persons to complete the grand jury. Whenever a challenge to a grand juror is allowed, and there are not in attendance other jurors sufficient to complete the grand jury, the court shall make a like order to the marshal to summon a sufficient number of persons for that purpose.

(June 25, 1948, c. 645, 62 Stat. 829.)

§ 3322. Disclosure of certain matters occurring before grand jury

(a) A person who is privy to grand jury information—

(1) received in the course of duty as an attorney for the government; or

(2) disclosed under rule 6(e)(3)(A)(ii) of the Federal Rules of Criminal Procedure;

may disclose that information to an attorney for the government for use in enforcing section 951 of the Financial Institutions Reform, Recovery and Enforcement Act of 1989 or for use in connection with any civil forfeiture provision of Federal law.

(b)(1) Upon motion of an attorney for the government, a court may direct disclosure of matters occurring before a grand jury during an investigation of a banking law violation to identified personnel of a Federal or State financial institution regulatory agency—

(A) for use in relation to any matter within the jurisdiction of such regulatory agency; or

(B) to assist an attorney for the government to whom matters have been disclosed under subsection (a).

(2) A court may issue an order under paragraph (1) at any time during or after the completion of the investigation of the grand jury, upon a finding of a substantial need.

(c) A person to whom matter has been disclosed under this section shall not use such matter other than for the purpose for which such disclosure was authorized.

(d) As used in this section—

(1) the term "banking law violation" means a violation of, or a conspiracy to violate—

(A) section 215, 656, 657, 1005, 1006, 1007, 1014, 1344, 1956, or 1957;

(B) section 1341 or 1343 affecting a financial institution; or

(C) any provision of subchapter II of chapter 53 of title 31, United States Code;

(2) the term "attorney for the government" has the meaning given such term in the Federal Rules of Criminal Procedure; and

(3) the term "grand jury information" means matters occurring before a grand jury other than the deliberations of the grand jury or the vote of any grand juror.

(Added Pub.L. 101–73, Title IX, § 964(a), Aug. 9, 1989, 103 Stat. 505, and amended Pub.L. 106–102, Title VII, § 740, Nov. 12, 1999, 113 Stat. 1480; Pub.L. 106–185, § 10, Apr. 25, 2000, 114 Stat. 217; Pub.L. 107–273, Div. C, Title I, § 11002, Nov. 2, 2002, 116 Stat. 1816.)

HISTORICAL AND STATUTORY NOTES

References in Text

Section 951 of the Financial Institutions Reform, Recovery and Enforcement Act of 1989, referred to in subsec. (a), is section 951 of Pub.L. 101–73, Title IX, Aug. 9, 1989, 103 Stat. 498, which is classified to section 1833a of Title 12, Banks and Banking.

Subchapter II of chapter 53 of Title 31, referred to in text, is 31 U.S.C.A. § 5311 et seq.

The Federal Rules of Criminal Procedure, referred to in subsec. (d)(2), are set out in this title.

Effective and Applicability Provisions

2000 Acts. Amendments by Pub.L. 106–185 applicable to any forfeiture proceeding commenced on or after the date that is 120 days after April 25, 2000, see section 21 of Pub.L. 106–185, set out as a note under section 1324 of Title 8.

Severability of Provisions

If any provision of Pub.L. 101–73 or the application thereof to any person or circumstance is held invalid, the remainder of Pub.L. 101–73 and the application of the provision to other persons not similarly situated or to other circumstances not to be affected thereby, see section 1221 of Pub.L. 101–73, set out as a note under section 1811 of Title 12, Banks and Banking.

Prior Provisions

A prior section 3322, Act June 25, 1948, c. 645, 62 Stat. 829, which related to the summoning of and number of grand jurors, was repealed by Pub.L. 101–73, Title IX, § 964(a),

Aug. 9, 1989, 103 Stat. 505. See Rule 6(a), Federal Rules of Criminal Procedure, this title.

[§§ 3323 to 3328. Repealed. Pub.L. 101–73, Title IX, § 964(a), Aug. 9, 1989, 103 Stat. 505]

HISTORICAL AND STATUTORY NOTES

Section 3323, Act June 25, 1948, c. 645, 62 Stat. 829, related to challenging the array of grand jurors or individual grand jurors and motions to dismiss. See Rule 6(b), Federal Rules of Criminal Procedure, this title.

Section 3324, Act June 25, 1948, c. 645, 62 Stat. 829, related to the appointment of the grand jury foreman and deputy foreman, oaths, affirmations and indictments, and records of jurors concurring. See Rule 6(c), Federal Rules of Criminal Procedure, this title.

Section 3325, Act June 25, 1948, c. 645, 62 Stat. 829, related to persons who may be present while the grand jury is in session, and exclusion while the jury is deliberating or voting. See Rule 6(d), Federal Rules of Criminal Procedure, this title.

Section 3326, Act June 25, 1948, c. 645, 62 Stat. 829, related to disclosure of proceedings to government attorneys, disclosure by direction of the court or permission of the defendant, and secrecy of the indictment. See Rule 6(e), Federal Rules of Criminal Procedure, this title.

Section 3327, Act June 25, 1948, c. 645, 62 Stat. 830, related to concurrence of 12 or more jurors in the indictment, and return of the indictment to the judge in open court. See Rule 6(f), Federal Rules of Criminal Procedure, this title.

Section 3328, Act June 25, 1948, c. 645, 62 Stat. 830, related to discharge of the grand jury by the court, limitation of service, and excusing jurors for cause. See Rule 6(g), Federal Rules of Criminal Procedure, this title.

CHAPTER 216—SPECIAL GRAND JURY

HISTORICAL AND STATUTORY NOTES

National Commission on Individual Rights

Pub.L. 91–452, Title XII, §§ 1201 to 1211, Oct. 15, 1970, 84 Stat. 960, provided for the establishment, membership, functions, etc., of the National Commission on Individual Rights, which terminated sixty days after submission of its final report six years following Jan. 1, 1972.

§ 3331. Summoning and term

(a) In addition to such other grand juries as shall be called from time to time, each district court which is located in a judicial district containing more than four million inhabitants or in which the Attorney General, the Deputy Attorney General, the Associate Attorney General or any designated Assistant Attorney General, certifies in writing to the chief judge of the district that in his judgment a special grand jury is necessary because of criminal activity in the district shall order a special grand jury to be summoned at least once in each period of eighteen months unless another special grand jury is then serving. The grand jury shall serve for a term of eighteen months unless an order for its discharge is entered earlier by the court upon a determination of the grand jury by majority vote that its business has been completed. If, at the end of such term or any extension thereof, the district court determines the business of the grand jury has not been completed, the court may enter an order extending such term for an additional period of six months. No special grand jury term so extended shall exceed thirty-six months, except as provided in subsection (e) of section 3333 of this chapter.

(b) If a district court within any judicial circuit fails to extend the term of a special grand jury or enters an order for the discharge of such grand jury before such grand jury determines that it has completed its business, the grand jury, upon the affirmative vote of a majority of its members, may apply to the chief judge of the circuit for an order for the continuance of the term of the grand jury. Upon the making of such an application by the grand jury, the term thereof shall continue until the entry upon such application by the chief judge of the circuit of an appropriate order. No special grand jury term so extended shall exceed thirty-six months, except as provided in subsection (e) of section 3333 of this chapter.

(Added Pub.L. 91–452, Title I, § 101(a), Oct. 15, 1970, 84 Stat. 923, and amended Pub.L. 100–690, Title VII, § 7020(d), Nov. 18, 1988, 102 Stat. 4396.)

§ 3332. Powers and duties

(a) It shall be the duty of each such grand jury impaneled within any judicial district to inquire into offenses against the criminal laws of the United States alleged to have been committed within that district. Such alleged offenses may be brought to the attention of the grand jury by the court or by any attorney appearing on behalf of the United States for the presentation of evidence. Any such attorney receiving information concerning such an alleged offense from any other person shall, if requested by such other person, inform the grand jury of such alleged offense, the identity of such other person, and such attorney's action or recommendation.

(b) Whenever the district court determines that the volume of business of the special grand jury exceeds the capacity of the grand jury to discharge its obligations, the district court may order an additional special grand jury for that district to be impaneled.

(Added Pub.L. 91–452, Title I, § 101(a), Oct. 15, 1970, 84 Stat. 924.)

HISTORICAL AND STATUTORY NOTES

References in Text

The criminal laws of the United States, referred to in subsec. (a), are classified generally to this title.

§ 3333. Reports

(a) A special grand jury impaneled by any district court, with the concurrence of a majority of its members, may, upon completion of its original term, or each extension thereof, submit to the court a report—

(1) concerning noncriminal misconduct, malfeasance, or misfeasance in office involving organized criminal activity by an appointed public officer or employee as the basis for a recommendation of removal or disciplinary action; or

(2) regarding organized crime conditions in the district.

(b) The court to which such report is submitted shall examine it and the minutes of the special grand jury and, except as otherwise provided in subsections (c) and (d) of this section, shall make an order accepting and filing such report as a public record only if the court is satisfied that it complies with the provisions of subsection (a) of this section and that—

(1) the report is based upon facts revealed in the course of an investigation authorized by subsection (a) of section 3332 and is supported by the preponderance of the evidence; and

(2) when the report is submitted pursuant to paragraph (1) of subsection (a) of this section, each person named therein and any reasonable number of witnesses in his behalf as designated by him to the foreman of the grand jury were afforded an opportunity to testify before the grand jury prior to the filing of such report, and when the report is submitted pursuant to paragraph (2) of subsection (a) of this section, it is not critical of an identified person.

(c)(1) An order accepting a report pursuant to paragraph (1) of subsection (a) of this section and the report shall be sealed by the court and shall not be filed as a public record or be subject to subpena or otherwise made public (i) until at least thirty-one days after a copy of the order and report are served upon each public officer or employee named therein and an answer has been filed or the time for filing an answer has expired, or (ii) if an appeal is taken, until all rights of review of the public officer or employee named therein have expired or terminated in an order accepting the report. No order accepting a report pursuant to paragraph (1) of subsection (a) of this section shall be entered until thirty days after the delivery of such report to the public officer or body pursuant to paragraph (3) of subsection (c) of this section. The court may issue such orders as it shall deem appropriate to prevent unauthorized publication of a report. Unauthorized publication may be punished as contempt of the court.

(2) Such public officer or employee may file with the clerk a verified answer to such a report not later than twenty days after service of the order and report upon him. Upon a showing of good cause, the court may grant such public officer or employee an extension of time within which to file such answer and may authorize such limited publication of the report as may be necessary to prepare such answer. Such an answer shall plainly and concisely state the facts and law constituting the defense of the public officer or employee to the charges in said report, and, except for those parts thereof which the court determines to have been inserted scandalously, prejudiciously, or unnecessarily, such answer shall become an appendix to the report.

(3) Upon the expiration of the time set forth in paragraph (1) of subsection (c) of this section, the United States attorney shall deliver a true copy of such report, and the appendix, if any, for appropriate action to each public officer or body having jurisdiction, responsibility, or authority over each public officer or employee named in the report.

(d) Upon the submission of a report pursuant to subsection (a) of this section, if the court finds that the filing of such report as a public record may prejudice fair consideration of a pending criminal matter, it shall order such report sealed and such report shall not be subject to subpena or public inspection during the pendency of such criminal matter, except upon order of the court.

(e) Whenever the court to which a report is submitted pursuant to paragraph (1) of subsection (a) of this section is not satisfied that the report complies with the provisions of subsection (b) of this section, it may direct that additional testimony be taken before the same grand jury, or it shall make an order sealing such report, and it shall not be filed as a public record or be subject to subpena or otherwise made public until the provisions of subsection (b) of this section are met. A special grand jury term may be extended by the district court beyond thirty-six months in order that such additional testimony may be taken or the provisions of subsection (b) of this section may be met.

(f) As used in this section, "public officer or employee" means any officer or employee of the United States, any State, the District of Columbia, the Commonwealth of Puerto Rico, any territory or possession of the United States, or any political subdivision, or any department, agency, or instrumentality thereof.

(Added Pub.L. 91–452, Title I, § 101(a), Oct. 15, 1970, 84 Stat. 924.)

§ 3334. General provisions

The provisions of chapter 215, title 18, United States Code, and the Federal Rules of Criminal Procedure applicable to regular grand juries shall apply to special grand juries to the extent not inconsistent with sections 3331, 3332, or 3333 of this chapter.

(Added Pub.L. 91–452, Title I, § 101(a), Oct. 15, 1970, 84 Stat. 926.)

CHAPTER 217—INDICTMENT AND INFORMATION

Sec.

§ 3361. Form and contents—(Rule)

SEE FEDERAL RULES OF CRIMINAL PROCEDURE

Contents and form; striking surplusage, Rule 7(a), (c), (d).

(June 25, 1948, c. 645, 62 Stat. 830.)

§ 3362. Waiver of indictment and prosecution on information—(Rule)

SEE FEDERAL RULES OF CRIMINAL PROCEDURE

Waiver of indictment for offenses not punishable by death, Rule 7(b).

(June 25, 1948, c. 645, 62 Stat. 830.)

§ 3363. Joinder of offenses—(Rule)

SEE FEDERAL RULES OF CRIMINAL PROCEDURE

Joinder of two or more offenses in same indictment, Rule 8(a).

Trial together of indictments or informations, Rule 13.

(June 25, 1948, c. 645, 62 Stat. 830.)

§ 3364. Joinder of defendants—(Rule)

SEE FEDERAL RULES OF CRIMINAL PROCEDURE

Joinder of two or more defendants charged in same indictment, Rule 8(b).

Relief from prejudicial joinder, Rule 14.

(June 25, 1948, c. 645, 62 Stat. 830.)

§ 3365. Amendment of information—(Rule)

SEE FEDERAL RULES OF CRIMINAL PROCEDURE

Amendment of information, time and conditions, Rule 7(e).

(June 25, 1948, c. 645, 62 Stat. 830.)

§ 3366. Bill of particulars—(Rule)

SEE FEDERAL RULES OF CRIMINAL PROCEDURE

Bill of particulars for cause; motion after arraignment; time; amendment, Rule 7(f).

(June 25, 1948, c. 645, 62 Stat. 830.)

§ 3367. Dismissal—(Rule)

SEE FEDERAL RULES OF CRIMINAL PROCEDURE

Dismissal filed by Attorney General or United States Attorney, Rule 48.

Dismissal on objection to array of grand jury or lack of legal qualification of individual grand juror, Rule 6(b)(2).

(June 25, 1948, c. 645, 62 Stat. 830.)

CHAPTER 219—TRIAL BY UNITED STATES MAGISTRATES

Sec.

HISTORICAL AND STATUTORY NOTES

Savings Provisions

See section 235 of Pub.L. 98–473, Title II, c. II, Oct. 12, 1984, 98 Stat. 2031, as amended, set out as a note under section 3551 of this title.

§ 3401. Misdemeanors; application of probation laws

(a) When specially designated to exercise such jurisdiction by the district court or courts he serves, any United States magistrate judge shall have jurisdiction to try persons accused of, and sentence persons convicted of, misdemeanors committed within that judicial district.

(b) Any person charged with a misdemeanor, other than a petty offense may elect, however, to be tried before a district judge for the district in which the offense was committed. The magistrate judge shall carefully explain to the defendant that he has a right to trial, judgment, and sentencing by a district judge and that he may have a right to trial by jury before a district judge or magistrate judge. The magistrate judge may not proceed to try the case unless the defendant, after such explanation, expressly consents to be tried before the magistrate judge and expressly and specifically waives trial, judgment, and sentencing by a district judge. Any such consent and waiver shall be made in writing or orally on the record.

(c) A magistrate judge who exercises trial jurisdiction under this section, and before whom a person is convicted or pleads either guilty or nolo contendere, may, with the approval of a judge of the district court, direct the probation service of the court to conduct a presentence investigation on that person and render a report to the magistrate judge prior to the imposition of sentence.

(d) The probation laws shall be applicable to persons tried by a magistrate judge under this section, and such officer shall have power to grant probation and to revoke, modify, or reinstate the probation of any person granted probation by a magistrate judge.

(e) Proceedings before United States magistrate judges under this section shall be taken down by a court reporter or recorded by suitable sound recording equipment. For purposes of appeal a copy of the record of such proceedings shall be made available at the expense of the United States to a person who makes affidavit that he is unable to pay or give security therefor, and the expense of such copy shall be paid by the Director of the Administrative Office of the United States Courts.

(f) The district court may order that proceedings in any misdemeanor case be conducted before a district judge rather than a United States magistrate judge upon the court's own motion or, for good cause shown, upon petition by the attorney for the Government. Such petition should note the novelty, importance, or complexity of the case, or other pertinent factors, and be filed in accordance with regulations promulgated by the Attorney General.

(g) The magistrate judge may, in a petty offense case involving a juvenile, exercise all powers granted to the district court under chapter 403 of this title. The magistrate judge may, in the case of any misdemeanor, other than a petty offense, involving a juvenile in which consent to trial before a magistrate judge has been filed under subsection (b), exercise all powers granted to the district court under chapter 403 of this title. For purposes of this subsection, proceedings under chapter 403 of this title may be instituted against a juvenile by a violation notice or complaint, except that no such case may proceed unless the certification referred to in section 5032 of this title has been filed in open court at the arraignment.

(h) The magistrate judge shall have power to modify, revoke, or terminate supervised release of any person sentenced to a term of supervised release by a magistrate judge.

(i) A district judge may designate a magistrate judge to conduct hearings to modify, revoke, or terminate supervised release, including evidentiary hearings, and to submit to the judge proposed findings of fact and recommendations for such modification, revocation, or termination by the judge, including, in the case of revocation, a recommended disposition under section 3583(e) of this title. The magistrate judge shall file his or her proposed findings and recommendations.

(June 25, 1948, c. 645, 62 Stat. 830; July 7, 1958, Pub.L. 85–508, § 12(j), 72 Stat. 348; Oct. 17, 1968, Pub.L. 90–578, Title III, § 302(a), 82 Stat. 1115; Oct. 10, 1979, Pub.L. 96–82, § 7(a), (b), 93 Stat. 645, 646; Oct. 12, 1984, Pub.L. 98–473, Title II, § 223(j), 98 Stat. 2029; Nov. 18, 1988, Pub.L. 100–690, Title VII, § 7072(a), 102 Stat. 4405; Dec. 1, 1990, Pub.L. 101–650, Title III, § 321, 104 Stat. 5117; Oct. 29, 1992, Pub.L. 102–572, Title I, § 103, 106 Stat. 4507; Oct. 19, 1996, Pub.L. 104–317, Title II, § 202(a), 110 Stat. 3848, 3849; Nov. 13, 2000, Pub.L. 106–518, Title II, § 203(a), 114 Stat. 2414.)

HISTORICAL AND STATUTORY NOTES

References in Text

Chapter 403 of this title, referred to in subsec. (g), is 18 U.S.C.A. § 5031 et seq.

Codifications

Amendment of subsec. (g) by Pub.L. 100–690, Title VII, § 7072(a), Nov. 18, 1988, 102 Stat. 4405, directing "and section 4216" be struck out, was executed to subsec. (g) applicable to offenses committed prior to Nov. 1, 1987, as the probable intent of Congress, in view of the amendment by section 223(j) of Pub.L. 98–473.

Amendment by section 223(j)(2) of Pub.L. 98–473 has been executed to subsec. (g) as the probable intent of Congress in view of redesignation of subsec. (h) as (g) by section 223(j)(1) and notwithstanding directory language of section 223(j)(2) calling for amendment of subsec. (h).

Effective and Applicability Provisions

1992 Acts. Amendment by Pub.L. 102–572 effective Jan. 1, 1993, see section 1101 of Pub.L. 102–572, set out as a note under section 905 of Title 2, The Congress.

1984 Acts. Amendment by Pub.L. 98–473 effective Nov. 1, 1987, and applicable only to offenses committed after the taking effect of such amendment, see section 235(a)(1) of Pub.L. 98–473, set out as a note under section 3551 of this title.

1968 Acts. Amendment by Pub.L. 90–578 effective Oct. 17, 1968, except when a later effective date is applicable, which is the earlier of date when implementation of amendment by appointment of magistrates and assumption of office takes place or third anniversary of enactment of Pub.L. 90–578 on Oct. 17, 1968, see section 403 of Pub.L. 90–578, set out as an Effective Date of 1968 Amendment note under section 631 of Title 28, Judiciary and Judicial Procedure.

1958 Acts. Amendment by Pub.L. 85–508 effective Jan. 3, 1959 upon admission of Alaska into the Union pursuant to Proc.No. 3269, Jan. 5, 1959, 24 F.R. 81, 73 Stat. c16, as required by sections 1 and 8(c) of Pub.L. 85–508, see notes set out under section 81A of Title 28, Judiciary and Judicial Procedure and preceding former section 21 of Title 48, Territories and Insular Possessions.

Change of Name

"United States magistrate judge", "magistrate judge", and "magistrate judges" substituted for "United States magistrate", "magistrate", and "magistrates" in subsecs. (a), (c), (e), and (f), and "magistrate judge under" substituted for "magistrate under" in subsec. (d) pursuant to section 321 of Pub.L. 101–650, set out as a note under 28 U.S.C.A. § 631.

Savings Provisions

Amendment by Pub.L. 98–473 effective on the first day of first calendar month beginning thirty-six months after October 12, 1984, applicable only to offenses committed after taking effect of sections 211 to 239 of Pub.L. 98–473, and except as otherwise provided for therein, see section 235 of Pub.L. 98–473, as amended, set out as a note under section 3551 of this title.

§ 3402. Rules of procedure, practice and appeal [1]

In all cases of conviction by a United States magistrate judge an appeal of right shall lie from the judgment of the magistrate judge to a judge of the district court of the district in which the offense was committed.

(June 25, 1948, c. 645, 62 Stat. 831; Oct. 17, 1968, Pub.L. 90–578, Title III, § 302(b), 82 Stat. 1116; Nov. 19, 1988, Pub.L. 100–702, Title IV, § 404(b)(2), 102 Stat. 4651; Dec. 1, 1990, Pub.L. 101–650, Title III, § 321, 104 Stat. 5117.)

[1] Section catchline was not amended to conform to change in text made by Pub.L. 100–702.

HISTORICAL AND STATUTORY NOTES

Effective and Applicability Provisions

1988 Amendments. Amendment by Pub.L. 100–702 effective Dec. 1, 1988, see section 407 of Pub.L. 100–702, set out as a note under section 2071 of Title 28, Judiciary and Judicial Procedure.

1968 Amendments. Amendment by Pub.L. 90–578 effective Oct. 17, 1968, except when a later effective date is applicable, which is the earlier of date when implementation of amendment by appointment of magistrates and assumption of office takes place or third anniversary of enactment of Pub.L. 90–578 on Oct. 17, 1968, see section 403 of Pub.L. 90–578, set out as an Effective Date of 1968 Amendment note under section 631 of Title 28, Judiciary and Judicial Procedure.

Change of Name

"United States magistrate judge" and "magistrate judge" substituted for "United States magistrate" and "magistrate" in text pursuant to section 321 of Pub.L. 101–650, set out as a note under 28 U.S.C.A. § 631.

CHAPTER 221—ARRAIGNMENT, PLEAS AND TRIAL

§ 3431. Term of court; power of court unaffected by expiration—(Rule)

SEE FEDERAL RULES OF CRIMINAL PROCEDURE

Expiration of term without significance in criminal cases, Rule 45(c).

(June 25, 1948, c. 645, 62 Stat. 831.)

HISTORICAL AND STATUTORY NOTES

References in Text

Rule 45(c) of the Federal Rules of Criminal Procedure, referred to in text, was rescinded, Feb. 28, 1966, eff. July 1, 1966.

§ 3432. Indictment and list of jurors and witnesses for prisoner in capital cases

A person charged with treason or other capital offense shall at least three entire days before commencement of trial be furnished with a copy of the indictment and a list of the veniremen, and of the witnesses to be produced on the trial for proving the indictment, stating the place of abode of each venireman and witness, except that such list of the veniremen and witnesses need not be furnished if the court finds by a preponderance of the evidence that providing the list may jeopardize the life or safety of any person.

(June 25, 1948, c. 645, 62 Stat. 831; Sept. 13, 1994, Pub.L. 103–322, Title VI, § 60025, 108 Stat. 1982.)

§ 3433. Arraignment—(Rule)

SEE FEDERAL RULES OF CRIMINAL PROCEDURE

Reading and furnishing copy of indictment to accused, Rule 10.

(June 25, 1948, c. 645, 62 Stat. 831.)

§ 3434. Presence of defendant—(Rule)

SEE FEDERAL RULES OF CRIMINAL PROCEDURE

Right of defendant to be present generally; corporation; waiver, Rule 43.

(June 25, 1948, c. 645, 62 Stat. 831.)

§ 3435. Receiver of stolen property triable before or after principal

A person charged with receiving or concealing stolen property may be tried either before or after the trial of the principal offender.

(June 25, 1948, c. 645, 62 Stat. 831.)

§ 3436. Consolidation of indictments or informations—(Rule)

SEE FEDERAL RULES OF CRIMINAL PROCEDURE

Two or more indictments or informations triable together, Rule 13.

(June 25, 1948, c. 645, 62 Stat. 832.)

§ 3437. Severance—(Rule)

SEE FEDERAL RULES OF CRIMINAL PROCEDURE

Relief from prejudicial joinder of defendants or offenses, Rule 14.

(June 25, 1948, c. 645, 62 Stat. 832.)

§ 3438. Pleas—(Rule)

SEE FEDERAL RULES OF CRIMINAL PROCEDURE

Plea of guilty, not guilty, or nolo contendere; acceptance by court; refusal to plead; corporation failing to appear, Rule 11.

Withdrawal of plea of guilty, Rule 32.

(June 25, 1948, c. 645, 62 Stat. 832.)

§ 3439. Demurrers and special pleas in bar or abatement abolished; relief on motion—(Rule)

SEE FEDERAL RULES OF CRIMINAL PROCEDURE

Motion to dismiss or for appropriate relief substituted for demurrer or dilatory plea or motion to quash, Rule 12.

(June 25, 1948, c. 645, 62 Stat. 832.)

§ 3440. Defenses and objections determined on motion—(Rule)

SEE FEDERAL RULES OF CRIMINAL PROCEDURE

Defenses or objections which may or must be raised before trial; time; hearing; effect of determination; limitations by law unaffected, Rule 12(b).

(June 25, 1948, c. 645, 62 Stat. 832.)

§ 3441. Jury; number of jurors; waiver—(Rule)

SEE FEDERAL RULES OF CRIMINAL PROCEDURE

Jury trial, waiver, twelve jurors or less by written stipulation, trial by court on general or special findings, Rule 23.

(June 25, 1948, c. 645, 62 Stat. 832.)

§ 3442. Jurors, examination, peremptory challenges; alternates—(Rule)

SEE FEDERAL RULES OF CRIMINAL PROCEDURE

Examination and peremptory challenges of trial jurors; alternate jurors, Rule 24.

(June 25, 1948, c. 645, 62 Stat. 832.)

§ 3443. Instructions to jury—(Rule)

SEE FEDERAL RULES OF CRIMINAL PROCEDURE

Court's instructions to jury, written requests and copies, objections, Rule 30.

(June 25, 1948, c. 645, 62 Stat. 832.)

§ 3444. Disability of judge—(Rule)

SEE FEDERAL RULES OF CRIMINAL PROCEDURE

Disability of judge after verdict or finding of guilt, Rule 25.

(June 25, 1948, c. 645, 62 Stat. 832.)

§ 3445. Motion for judgment of acquittal—(Rule)

SEE FEDERAL RULES OF CRIMINAL PROCEDURE

Motions for directed verdict abolished.

Motions for judgment of acquittal adopted; court may reserve decision; renewal, Rule 29.

(June 25, 1948, c. 645, 62 Stat. 832.)

§ 3446. New trial—(Rule)

SEE FEDERAL RULES OF CRIMINAL PROCEDURE

Granting of new trial, grounds, and motion, Rule 33.

(June 25, 1948, c. 645, 62 Stat. 832.)

§§ 3447 to 3480. Reserved for future legislation

CHAPTER 223—WITNESSES AND EVIDENCE

HISTORICAL AND STATUTORY NOTES

Effective and Applicability Provisions

1984 Amendments. Addition of items 3505 to 3507 effective 30 days after Oct. 12, 1984, see section 1220 of Pub.L. 98–473, Title II, Oct. 12, 1984, 98 Stat. 2167, set out as a note under section 3505 of this title.

Protected Facilities for Housing Government Witnesses

Pub.L. 91–452, Title V, §§ 501–504, Oct. 15, 1970, 84 Stat. 933, which authorized the Attorney General to provide security and housing for Government witnesses, potential Government witnesses, and their families in proceedings against organized crime, was repealed by Pub.L. 98–473, Title II, c. XII, Part F, Subpart A, § 1209(b), Oct. 12, 1984, 98 Stat. 2163, effective Oct. 1, 1984, pursuant to section 1210 of Pub.L. 98–473.

§ 3481. Competency of accused

In trial of all persons charged with the commission of offenses against the United States and in all proceedings in courts martial and courts of inquiry in any State, District, Possession or Territory, the person charged shall, at his own request, be a competent witness. His failure to make such request shall not create any presumption against him.

(June 25, 1948, c. 645, 62 Stat. 833.)

HISTORICAL AND STATUTORY NOTES

Short Title

1997 Amendments. Pub.L. 105–6, § 1, Mar. 19, 1997, 111 Stat. 12, provided that: "This Act [enacting section 3510 of this title, amending section 3593(c) of this title, and enacting provisions set out as a note under section 3510 of this title] may be cited as the 'Victim Rights Clarification Act of 1997'."

§ 3482. Evidence and witnesses—(Rule)

SEE FEDERAL RULES OF CRIMINAL PROCEDURE

Competency and privileges of witnesses and admissibility of evidence governed by principles of common law, Rule 26.

(June 25, 1948, c. 645, 62 Stat. 833.)

HISTORICAL AND STATUTORY NOTES

References in Text

Rule 26 of the Federal Rules of Criminal Procedure, referred to in text, was amended in 1972. The subject matter is covered by the Federal Rules of Evidence, Title 28, Judiciary and Judicial Procedure.

§ 3483. Indigent defendants, process to produce evidence—(Rule)

SEE FEDERAL RULES OF CRIMINAL PROCEDURE

Subpoena for indigent defendants, motion, affidavit, costs, Rule 17(b).

(June 25, 1948, c. 645, 62 Stat. 833.)

§ 3484. Subpoenas—(Rule)

SEE FEDERAL RULES OF CRIMINAL PROCEDURE

Form, contents and issuance of subpoena, Rule 17(a).

Service in United States, Rule 17(d), (e,1)[1].

Service in foreign country, Rule 17(d), (e,2)[1].

Indigent defendants, Rule 17(b).

On taking depositions, Rule 17(f).

Papers and documents, Rule 17(c).

Disobedience of subpoena as contempt of court, Rule 17(g).

(June 25, 1948, c. 645, 62 Stat. 833.)

[1] So in original.

§ 3485. Expert witnesses—(Rule)

SEE FEDERAL RULES OF CRIMINAL PROCEDURE

Selection and appointment of expert witnesses by court or parties; compensation, Rule 28.

(June 25, 1948, c. 645, 62 Stat. 833.)

HISTORICAL AND STATUTORY NOTES

References in Text

Rule 28 of the Federal Rules of Criminal Procedure, referred to in text, was amended in 1972. The subject matter of this reference is covered by Federal Rules of Evidence, Title 28, Judiciary and Judicial Procedure.

§ 3486. Administrative subpoenas

(a) Authorization.—(1)(A) In any investigation relating of—

(i)(I) a Federal health care offense; or (II) a Federal offense involving the sexual exploitation or abuse of children, the Attorney General; or

(ii) an offense under section 871 or 879, or a threat against a person protected by the United States Secret Service under paragraph (5) or (6) of section 3056,[1] if the Director of the Secret Service determines that the threat constituting the offense or the threat against the person protected is imminent, the Secretary of the Treasury,

may issue in writing and cause to be served a subpoena requiring the production and testimony described in subparagraph (B).

(B) Except as provided in subparagraph (C), a subpoena issued under subparagraph (A) may require—

(i) the production of any records or other things relevant to the investigation; and

(ii) testimony by the custodian of the things required to be produced concerning the production and authenticity of those things.

(C) A subpoena issued under subparagraph (A) with respect to a provider of electronic communication service or remote computing service, in an investigation of a Federal offense involving the sexual exploitation or abuse of children shall not extend beyond—

(i) requiring that provider to disclose the information specified in section 2703(c)(2), which may be relevant to an authorized law enforcement inquiry; or

(ii) requiring a custodian of the records of that provider to give testimony concerning the production and authentication of such records or information.

(D) As used in this paragraph, the term "Federal offense involving the sexual exploitation or abuse of children" means an offense under section 1201, 2241(c), 2242, 2243, 2251, 2251A, 2252, 2252A, 2260, 2421, 2422, or 2423, in which the victim is an individual who has not attained the age of 18 years.

(2) A subpoena under this subsection shall describe the objects required to be produced and prescribe a return date within a reasonable period of time within which the objects can be assembled and made available.

(3) The production of records relating to a Federal health care offense shall not be required under this section at any place more than 500 miles distant from the place where the subpoena for the production of such records is served. The production of things in any other case may be required from any place within the United States or subject to the laws or jurisdiction of the United States.

(4) Witnesses subpoenaed under this section shall be paid the same fees and mileage that are paid witnesses in the courts of the United States.

(5) At any time before the return date specified in the summons, the person or entity summoned may, in the United States district court for the district in which that person or entity does business or resides, petition for an order modifying or setting aside the summons, or a prohibition of disclosure ordered by a court under paragraph (6).

(6)(A) A United State[2] district court for the district in which the summons is or will be served, upon application of the United States, may issue an ex parte order that no person or entity disclose to any other person or entity (other than to an attorney in order to obtain legal advice) the existence of such summons for a period of up to 90 days.

(B) Such order may be issued on a showing that the things being sought may be relevant to the investigation and there is reason to believe that such disclosure may result in—

(i) endangerment to the life or physical safety of any person;

(ii) flight to avoid prosecution;

(iii) destruction of or tampering with evidence; or

(iv) intimidation of potential witnesses.

(C) An order under this paragraph may be renewed for additional periods of up to 90 days upon a showing that the circumstances described in subparagraph (B) continue to exist.

(7) A summons issued under this section shall not require the production of anything that would be protected from production under the standards applicable to a subpoena duces tecum issued by a court of the United States.

(8) If no case or proceeding arises from the production of records or other things pursuant to this section within a reasonable time after those records or things are produced, the agency to which those records or things were delivered shall, upon written demand made by the person producing those records or things, return them to that person, except where the production required was only of copies rather than originals.

(9) A subpoena issued under paragraph (1)(A)(i)(II) or (1)(A)(ii) may require production as soon as possible, but in no event less than 24 hours after service of the subpoena.

(10) As soon as practicable following the issuance of a subpoena under paragraph (1)(A)(ii), the Secretary of the Treasury shall notify the Attorney General of its issuance.

(b) Service.—A subpoena issued under this section may be served by any person who is at least 18 years of age and is designated in the subpoena to serve it. Service upon a natural person may be made by personal delivery of the subpoena to him. Service may be made upon a domestic or foreign corporation or upon a partnership or other unincorporated association which is subject to suit under a common name, by delivering the subpoena to an officer, to a managing or general agent, or to any other agent authorized by appointment or by law to receive service of process. The affidavit of the person serving the subpoena entered on a true copy thereof by the person serving it shall be proof of service.

(c) Enforcement.—In the case of contumacy by or refusal to obey a subpoena issued to any person, the Attorney General may invoke the aid of any court of the United States within the jurisdiction of which the investigation is carried on or of which the subpoenaed person is an inhabitant, or in which he carries on business or may be found, to compel compliance with the subpoena. The court may issue an order requiring the subpoenaed person to appear before the Attorney General to produce records, if so ordered, or to give testimony concerning the production and authentication of such records. Any failure to obey the order of the court may be punished by the court as a contempt thereof. All process in any such case may be served in any judicial district in which such person may be found.

(d) Immunity from civil liability.—Notwithstanding any Federal, State, or local law, any person, including officers, agents, and employees, receiving a subpoena under this section, who complies in good faith with the subpoena and thus produces the materials sought, shall not be liable in any court of any State or the United States to any customer or other person for such production or for nondisclosure of that production to the customer.

(e) Limitation on use.—**(1)** Health information about an individual that is disclosed under this section may not be used in, or disclosed to any person for use in, any administrative, civil, or criminal action or investigation directed against the individual who is the subject of the information unless the action or investigation arises out of and is directly related to receipt of health care or payment for health care or action involving a fraudulent claim related to health; or if authorized by an appropriate order of a court of competent jurisdiction, granted after application showing good cause therefor.

(2) In assessing good cause, the court shall weigh the public interest and the need for disclosure against the injury to the patient, to the physician-patient relationship, and to the treatment services.

(3) Upon the granting of such order, the court, in determining the extent to which any disclosure of all or any part of any record is necessary, shall impose appropriate safeguards against unauthorized disclosure.

(Added Pub.L. 104–191, Title II, § 248(a), Aug. 21, 1996, 110 Stat. 2018, and amended Pub.L. 105–277, Div. A, § 101(b) [Title I, § 122], Oct. 21, 1998, 112 Stat. 2681–72; Pub.L. 105–314, Title VI, § 606(a)(1), Oct. 30, 1998, 112 Stat. 2984; Pub.L. 106–544, § 5(a), (b)(1), (c), Dec. 19, 2000, 114 Stat. 2717, 2718; Pub.L. 108–21, Title V, § 509, Apr. 30, 2003, 117 Stat. 684.)

1 So in original. Probably should be "section 3056(a),".

2 So in original. Probably should be "States".

HISTORICAL AND STATUTORY NOTES

Transfer of Functions

For transfer of the functions, personnel, assets, and obligations of the United States Secret Service, including the functions of the Secretary of the Treasury relating thereto, to the Secretary of Homeland Security, and for treatment of related references, see 6 U.S.C.A. §§ 381, 551(d), 552(d) and 557, and the Department of Homeland Security Reorganization Plan of November 25, 2002, as modified, set out as a note under 6 U.S.C.A. § 542.

Prior Provisions

A prior section 3486, Acts June 25, 1948, ch. 645, 62 Stat. 833; Aug. 20, 1954, ch. 769, § 1, 68 Stat. 745; Aug. 28, 1965, Pub.L. 89–141, § 2, 79 Stat. 581, related to procedures for granting immunity to witnesses compelled to testify or produce evidence in any Congressional investigation, or case or proceeding before any grand jury or court of the United States, involving interference with or endangering of national security or defense of the United States, prior to repeal by Pub.L. 91–452, Title II, § 228(a), Oct. 15, 1970, 84 Stat. 930, effective on the sixtieth day following Oct. 15, 1970. See section 6001 et seq. of this title.

[§ 3486A. Repealed. Pub.L. 106–544, § 5(b)(3), Dec. 19, 2000, 114 Stat. 2718]

HISTORICAL AND STATUTORY NOTES

Section, Pub.L. 105–314, Title VI, § 606(a)(2), Oct. 30, 1998, 112 Stat. 2984, related to administrative subpoenas in cases involving child abuse and child sexual exploitation.

§ 3487. Refusal to pay as evidence of embezzlement

The refusal of any person, whether in or out of office, charged with the safe-keeping, transfer, or disbursement of the public money to pay any draft, order, or warrant, drawn upon him by the Government Accountability Office, for any public money in his hands belonging to the United States, no matter in what capacity the same may have been received, or may be held, or to transfer or disburse any such money, promptly, upon the legal requirement of any authorized officer, shall be deemed, upon the trial of any indictment against such person for embezzlement, prima facie evidence of such embezzlement.

(June 25, 1948, c. 645, 62 Stat. 833; July 7, 2004, Pub.L. 108–271, § 8(b), 118 Stat. 814.)

§ 3488. Intoxicating liquor in Indian country as evidence of unlawful introduction

The possession by a person of intoxicating liquors in Indian country where the introduction is prohibited by treaty or Federal statute shall be prima facie evidence of unlawful introduction.

(June 25, 1948, c. 645, 62 Stat. 834.)

§ 3489. Discovery and inspection—(Rule)

SEE FEDERAL RULES OF CRIMINAL PROCEDURE

Inspection of documents and papers taken from defendant, Rule 16.

(June 25, 1948, c. 645, 62 Stat. 834.)

§ 3490. Official record or entry—(Rule)

SEE FEDERAL RULES OF CRIMINAL PROCEDURE

Proof of official record or entry as in civil actions, Rule 27.

(June 25, 1948, c. 645, 62 Stat. 834.)

§ 3491. Foreign documents

Any book, paper, statement, record, account, writing, or other document, or any portion thereof, of whatever character and in whatever form, as well as any copy thereof equally with the original, which is not in the United States shall, when duly certified as provided in section 3494 of this title, be admissible in evidence in any criminal action or proceeding in any court of the United States if the court shall find, from all the testimony taken with respect to such foreign document pursuant to a commission executed under section 3492 of this title, that such document (or the original thereof in case such document is a copy) satisfies the authentication requirements of the Federal Rules of Evidence, unless in the event that the genuineness of such document is denied, any party to such criminal action or proceeding making such denial shall establish to the satisfaction of the court that such document is not genuine. Nothing contained herein shall be deemed to require authentication under the provisions of section 3494 of this title of any such foreign documents which may otherwise be properly authenticated by law.

(June 25, 1948, c. 645, 62 Stat. 834; May 24, 1949, c. 139, § 52, 63 Stat. 96; Oct. 3, 1964, Pub.L. 88–619, § 2, 78 Stat. 995; Dec. 12, 1975, Pub.L. 94–149, § 3, 89 Stat. 806.)

HISTORICAL AND STATUTORY NOTES

References in Text

The Federal Rules of Evidence, referred to in text, are classified to Title 28, Judiciary and Judicial Procedure.

§ 3492. Commission to consular officers to authenticate foreign documents

(a) The testimony of any witness in a foreign country may be taken either on oral or written interrogatories, or on interrogatories partly oral and partly written, pursuant to a commission issued, as hereinafter provided, for the purpose of determining whether any foreign documents sought to be used in any criminal action or proceeding in any court of the United States are genuine, and whether the authentication requirements of the Federal Rules of Evidence are satisfied with respect to any such document (or the original thereof in case such document is a copy). Application for the issuance of a commission for such purpose may be made to the court in which such action or proceeding is pending by the United States or any other party thereto, after five days' notice in writing by the applicant party, or his attorney, to the opposite party, or his attorney of record, which notice shall state the names and addresses of witnesses whose testimony is to be taken and the time when it is desired to take such testimony. In granting such application the court shall issue a commission for the purpose of taking the testimony sought by the applicant addressed to any consular officer of the United States conveniently located for the purpose. In cases of testimony taken on oral or partly oral interrogatories, the court shall make provisions in the commission for the selection as hereinafter provided of foreign counsel to represent each party (except the United States) to the criminal action or proceeding in which the foreign documents in question are to be used, unless such party has, prior to the issuance of the commission, notified the court that he does not desire the selection of foreign counsel to represent him at the time of taking of such testimony. In cases of testimony taken on written interrogatories, such provision shall be made only upon the request of any such party prior to the issuance of such commission. Selection of foreign counsel shall be made by the party whom such foreign counsel is to represent within ten days prior to the taking of testimony or by the court from which the commission issued, upon the request of such party made within such time.

(b) Any consular officer to whom a commission is addressed to take testimony, who is interested in the outcome of the criminal action or proceeding in which the foreign documents in question are to be used or has participated in the prosecution of such action or proceeding, whether by investigations, preparation of evidence, or otherwise, may be disqualified on his own motion or on that of the United States or any other party to such criminal action or proceeding made to the court from which the commission issued at any time prior to the execution thereof. If after notice and hearing, the court grants the motion, it shall instruct the consular officer thus disqualified to send the commission to any other consular officer of the United States named by the court, and such other officer shall execute the commission according to its terms and shall for all purposes be deemed the officer to whom the commission is addressed.

(c) The provisions of this section and sections 3493–3496 of this title applicable to consular officers shall be applicable to diplomatic officers pursuant to such regulations as may be prescribed by the President. For purposes of this section and sections 3493 through 3496 of this title, the term "consular officers" includes any United States citizen who is designated to perform notarial functions pursuant to section 1750 of the Revised Statutes, as amended (22 U.S.C. 4221).

(June 25, 1948, c. 645, 62 Stat. 834; May 24, 1949, c. 139, § 53, 63 Stat. 96; Dec. 12, 1975, Pub.L. 94–149, § 4, 89 Stat. 806; Oct. 21, 1998, Pub.L. 105–277, Div. G, Title XXII, § 2222(c)(2), 112 Stat. 2681–818.)

HISTORICAL AND STATUTORY NOTES

References in Text

The Federal Rules of Evidence, referred to in subsec. (a), are classified to Title 28, Judiciary and Judicial Procedure.

§ 3493. Deposition to authenticate foreign documents

The consular officer to whom any commission authorized under section 3492 of this title is addressed shall take testimony in accordance with its terms. Every person whose testimony is taken shall be cautioned and sworn to testify the whole truth and carefully examined. His testimony shall be reduced to writing or typewriting by the consular officer taking the testimony, or by some person under his personal supervision, or by the witness himself, in the presence of the consular officer and by no other person, and shall, after it has been reduced to writing or typewriting, be subscribed by the witness. Every foreign document, with respect to which testimony is taken, shall be annexed to such testimony and subscribed by each witness who appears for the purpose of establishing the genuineness of such document. When counsel for all the parties attend the examination of any witness whose testimony is to be taken on written interrogatories, they may consent that oral interrogatories in addition to those accompanying the commission may be put to the witness. The consular officer taking any testimony shall require an interpreter to be present when his services are needed or are requested by any party or his attorney.

(June 25, 1948, c. 645, 62 Stat. 835.)

§ 3494. Certification of genuineness of foreign document

If the consular officer executing any commission authorized under section 3492 of this title shall be satisfied, upon all the testimony taken, that a foreign document is genuine, he shall certify such document to be genuine under the seal of his office. Such certification shall include a statement that he is not subject to disqualification under the provisions of section 3492 of this title. He shall thereupon transmit, by mail, such foreign documents, together with the record of all testimony taken and the commission which has been executed, to the clerk of the court from which such commission issued, in the manner in which his official dispatches are transmitted to the Government. The clerk receiving any executed commission shall open it and shall make any foreign documents and record of testimony, transmitted with such commission, available for inspection by the parties to the criminal action or proceeding in which such documents are to be used, and said parties shall be furnished copies of such documents free of charge.

(June 25, 1948, c. 645, 62 Stat. 835.)

§ 3495. Fees and expenses of consuls, counsel, interpreters and witnesses

(a) The consular fees prescribed under section 1201 of Title 22, for official services in connection with the taking of testimony under sections 3492–3494 of this title, and the fees of any witness whose testimony is taken shall be paid by the party who applied for the commission pursuant to which such testimony was taken. Every witness under section 3493 of this title shall be entitled to receive, for each day's attendance, fees prescribed under section 3496 of this title. Every foreign counsel selected pursuant to a commission issued on application of the United States, and every interpreter whose services are required by a consular officer under section 3493 of this title, shall be paid by the United States, such compensation, together with such personal and incidental expense upon verified statements filed with the consular officer, as he may allow. Compensation and expenses of foreign counsel selected pursuant to a commission issued on application of any party other than the United States shall be paid by the party whom such counsel represents and shall be allowed in the same manner.

(b) Whenever any party makes affidavit, prior to the issuance of a commission for the purpose of taking testimony, that he is not possessed of sufficient means and is actually unable to pay any fees and costs incurred under this section, such fees and costs shall, upon order of the court, be paid in the same manner as fees and costs are paid which are chargeable to the United States.

(c) Any appropriation available for the payment of fees and costs in the case of witnesses subpenaed in behalf of the United States in criminal cases shall be available for any fees or costs which the United States is required to pay under this section.

(June 25, 1948, c. 645, 62 Stat. 836; May 24, 1949, c. 139, § 54, 63 Stat. 96.)

HISTORICAL AND STATUTORY NOTES

References in Text

Section 1201 of Title 22, referred to in subsec. (a), was transferred to section 4219 of Title 22, Foreign Relations and Intercourse.

§ 3496. Regulations by President as to commissions, fees of witnesses, counsel and interpreters

The President is authorized to prescribe regulations governing the manner of executing and returning commissions by consular officers under the provisions of sections 3492–3494 of this title and schedules of fees allowable to witnesses, foreign counsel, and interpreters under section 3495 of this title.

(June 25, 1948, c. 645, 62 Stat. 836.)

EXECUTIVE ORDERS

EXECUTIVE ORDER NO. 10307

Nov. 23, 1951, 16 F.R. 11907

DELEGATION OF AUTHORITY

By virtue of the authority vested in me by the act of August 8, 1950, 64 Stat. 419 (3 U.S.C.Supp. 301–303), I hereby delegate to the Secretary of State (1) the authority vested in the President by section 3496 of title 18 of the United States Code (62 Stat. 836) to prescribe regulations governing the manner of executing and returning commissions by consular officers under the provisions of sections 3492–3494 of the said title, and schedules of fees allowable to witnesses, foreign counsel, and interpreters under section 3495 of the said title, and (2) the authority vested in the President by section 3492(c) of title 18 of the United States Code (62 Stat. 835) to prescribe regulations making the provisions of sections 3492–3496 of the said title applicable to diplomatic officers.

Executive Order No. 8298 of December 4, 1939, entitled "Regulations Governing the Manner of Executing and Returning Commissions by Officers of the Foreign Service in Criminal Cases, and Schedule of Fees and Compensation in Such Cases", is hereby revoked.

§ 3497. Account as evidence of embezzlement

Upon the trial of any indictment against any person for embezzling public money it shall be sufficient evidence, prima facie, for the purpose of showing a balance against such person, to produce a transcript from the books and proceedings of the Government Accountability Office.

(June 25, 1948, c. 645, 62 Stat. 836; July 7, 2004, Pub.L. 108–271, § 8(b), 118 Stat. 814.)

§ 3498. Depositions—(Rule)

SEE FEDERAL RULES OF CRIMINAL PROCEDURE

Time, manner and conditions of taking depositions; costs; notice; use; objections; written interrogatories, Rule 15.

Subpoenas on taking depositions, Rule 17(f).

(June 25, 1948, c. 645, 62 Stat. 836.)

§ 3499. Contempt of court by witness—(Rule)

SEE FEDERAL RULES OF CRIMINAL PROCEDURE

Disobedience of subpoena without excuse as contempt, Rule 17(g).

(June 25, 1948, c. 645, 62 Stat. 836.)

§ 3500. Demands for production of statements and reports of witnesses

(a) In any criminal prosecution brought by the United States, no statement or report in the possession of the United States which was made by a Government witness or prospective Government witness (other than the defendant) shall be the subject of subpena, discovery, or inspection until said witness has testified on direct examination in the trial of the case.

(b) After a witness called by the United States has testified on direct examination, the court shall, on motion of the defendant, order the United States to produce any statement (as hereinafter defined) of the witness in the possession of the United States which relates to the subject matter as to which the witness has testified. If the entire contents of any such statement relate to the subject matter of the testimony of the witness, the court shall order it to be delivered directly to the defendant for his examination and use.

(c) If the United States claims that any statement ordered to be produced under this section contains matter which does not relate to the subject matter of the testimony of the witness, the court shall order the United States to deliver such statement for the inspection of the court in camera. Upon such delivery the court shall excise the portions of such statement which do not relate to the subject matter of the testimony of the witness. With such material excised, the court shall then direct delivery of such statement to the defendant for his use. If, pursuant to such procedure, any portion of such statement is withheld from the defendant and the defendant objects to such withholding, and the trial is continued to an adjudication of the guilt of the defendant, the entire text of such statement shall be preserved by the United States and, in the event the defendant appeals, shall be made available to the appellate court for the purpose of determining the correctness of the ruling of the trial judge. Whenever any statement is delivered to a defendant pursuant to this section, the court in its discretion, upon application of said defendant, may recess proceedings in the trial for such time as it may determine to be reasonably required for the examination of such statement by said defendant and his preparation for its use in the trial.

(d) If the United States elects not to comply with an order of the court under subsection (b) or (c) hereof to deliver to the defendant any such statement, or such portion thereof as the court may direct, the court shall strike from the record the testimony of the witness, and the trial shall proceed unless the court in its discretion shall determine that the interests of justice require that a mistrial be declared.

(e) The term "statement", as used in subsections (b), (c), and (d) of this section in relation to any witness called by the United States, means—

(1) a written statement made by said witness and signed or otherwise adopted or approved by him;

(2) a stenographic, mechanical, electrical, or other recording, or a transcription thereof, which is a substantially verbatim recital of an oral statement made by said witness and recorded contemporaneously with the making of such oral statement; or

(3) a statement, however taken or recorded, or a transcription thereof, if any, made by said witness to a grand jury.

(Added Pub.L. 85–269, Sept. 2, 1957, 71 Stat. 595, and amended Pub.L. 91–452, Title I, § 102, Oct. 15, 1970, 84 Stat. 926.)

HISTORICAL AND STATUTORY NOTES

Canal Zone

Applicability of section to Canal Zone, see section 14 of this title.

§ 3501. Admissibility of confessions

(a) In any criminal prosecution brought by the United States or by the District of Columbia, a confession, as defined in subsection (e) hereof, shall be admissible in evidence if it is voluntarily given. Before such confession is received in evidence, the trial judge shall, out of the presence of the jury, determine any issue as to voluntariness. If the trial judge determines that the confession was voluntarily made it shall be admitted in evidence and the trial judge shall permit the jury to hear relevant evidence on the issue of voluntariness and shall instruct the jury to give such weight to the confession as the jury feels it deserves under all the circumstances.

(b) The trial judge in determining the issue of voluntariness shall take into consideration all the circumstances surrounding the giving of the confession, including (1) the time elapsing between arrest and arraignment of the defendant making the confession, if it was made after arrest and before arraignment, (2) whether such defendant knew the nature of the offense with which he was charged or of which he was suspected at the time of making the confession, (3) whether or not such defendant was advised or knew that he was not required to make any statement and that any such statement could be used against him, (4) whether or not such defendant had been advised prior to questioning of his right to the assistance of counsel; and (5) whether or not such defendant was without the assistance of counsel when questioned and when giving such confession.

The presence or absence of any of the above-mentioned factors to be taken into consideration by the judge need not be conclusive on the issue of voluntariness of the confession.

(c) In any criminal prosecution by the United States or by the District of Columbia, a confession made or given by a person who is a defendant therein, while such person was under arrest or other detention in the custody of any law-enforcement officer or law-enforcement agency, shall not be inadmissible solely because of delay in bringing such person before a magistrate judge or other officer empowered to commit persons charged with offenses against the laws of the United States or of the District of Columbia if such confession is found by the trial judge to have been made voluntarily and if the weight to be given the confession is left to the jury and if such confession was made or given by such person within six hours immediately following his arrest or other detention: *Provided,* That the time limitation contained in this subsection shall not apply in any case in which the delay in bringing such person before such magistrate judge or other officer beyond such six-hour period is found by the trial judge to be reasonable considering the means of transportation and the distance to be traveled to the nearest available such magistrate judge or other officer.

(d) Nothing contained in this section shall bar the admission in evidence of any confession made or given voluntarily by any person to any other person without interrogation by anyone, or at any time at which the person who made or gave such confession was not under arrest or other detention.

(e) As used in this section, the term "confession" means any confession of guilt of any criminal offense or any self-incriminating statement made or given orally or in writing.

(Added Pub.L. 90–351, Title II, § 701(a), June 19, 1968, 82 Stat. 210, and amended Pub.L. 90–578, Title III, § 301(a)(3), Oct. 17, 1968, 82 Stat. 1115; Pub.L. 101–650, Title III, § 321, Dec. 1, 1990, 104 Stat. 5117.)

Unconstitutionality of Section

The United States Supreme Court, in Dickerson v. United States, 120 S.Ct. 2326, 530 U.S. 428, 147 L.Ed. 2d 405 (2000), held that Miranda announced a constitutional rule that Congress could not supersede legislatively by enacting this section.

HISTORICAL AND STATUTORY NOTES

Change of Name

Words "magistrate judge" substituted for "magistrate" in subsec. (c) pursuant to section 321 of Pub.L. 101–650, set out as a note under 28 U.S.C.A. § 631.

§ 3502. Admissibility in evidence of eye witness testimony

The testimony of a witness that he saw the accused commit or participate in the commission of the crime for which the accused is being tried shall be admissible in evidence in a criminal prosecution in any trial court ordained and established under article III of the Constitution of the United States.

(Added Pub.L. 90–351, Title II, § 701(a), June 19, 1968, 82 Stat. 211.)

[§ 3503. Repealed. Pub.L. 107–273, Div. B, Title IV, § 4002(c)(3)(A), Nov. 2, 2002, 116 Stat. 1809]

HISTORICAL AND STATUTORY NOTES

Section, added Pub.L. 91–452, Title VI, § 601(a), Oct. 15, 1970, 84 Stat. 934, related to depositions to preserve testimony.

§ 3504. Litigation concerning sources of evidence

(a) In any trial, hearing, or other proceeding in or before any court, grand jury, department, officer, agency, regulatory body, or other authority of the United States—

(1) upon a claim by a party aggrieved that evidence is inadmissible because it is the primary product of an unlawful act or because it was obtained by the exploitation of an unlawful act, the opponent of the claim shall affirm or deny the occurrence of the alleged unlawful act;

(2) disclosure of information for a determination if evidence is inadmissible because it is the primary product of an unlawful act occurring prior to June 19, 1968, or because it was obtained by the exploitation of an unlawful act occurring prior to June 19, 1968, shall not be required unless such information may be relevant to a pending claim of such inadmissibility; and

(3) no claim shall be considered that evidence of an event is inadmissible on the ground that such evidence was obtained by the exploitation of an unlawful act occurring prior to June 19, 1968, if such event occurred more than five years after such allegedly unlawful act.

(b) As used in this section "unlawful act" means any act the use of any electronic, mechanical, or other device (as defined in section 2510(5) of this title) in violation of the Constitution or laws of the United States or any regulation or standard promulgated pursuant thereto.

(Added Pub.L. 91–452, Title VII, § 702(a), Oct. 15, 1970, 84 Stat. 935.)

HISTORICAL AND STATUTORY NOTES

Congressional Statement of Findings

Section 701 of Pub.L. 91–452 provided that: "The Congress finds that claims that evidence offered in proceedings was obtained by the exploitation of unlawful acts, and is therefore inadmissible in evidence, (1) often cannot reliably be determined when such claims concern evidence of events occurring years after the allegedly unlawful act, and (2) when the allegedly unlawful act has occurred more than five years prior to the event in question, there is virtually no likelihood that the evidence offered to prove the event has been obtained by the exploitation of that allegedly unlawful act."

Applicability to Proceedings

Section 703 of Pub.L. 91–452 provided that: "This title [enacting this section and provisions set as notes under this section] shall apply to all proceedings, regardless of when commenced, occurring after the date of its enactment [Oct. 15, 1970]. Paragraph (3) of subsection (a) of section 3504, chapter 223, title 18, United States Code, shall not apply to any proceeding in which all information to be relied upon to establish inadmissibility was possessed by the party making such claim and adduced in such proceeding prior to such enactment."

§ 3505. Foreign records of regularly conducted activity

(a)(1) In a criminal proceeding in a court of the United States, a foreign record of regularly conducted activity, or a copy of such record, shall not be excluded as evidence by the hearsay rule if a foreign certification attests that—

(A) such record was made, at or near the time of the occurrence of the matters set forth, by (or from information transmitted by) a person with knowledge of those matters;

(B) such record was kept in the course of a regularly conducted business activity;

(C) the business activity made such a record as a regular practice; and

(D) if such record is not the original, such record is a duplicate of the original;

unless the source of information or the method or circumstances of preparation indicate lack of trustworthiness.

(2) A foreign certification under this section shall authenticate such record or duplicate.

(b) At the arraignment or as soon after the arraignment as practicable, a party intending to offer in evidence under this section a foreign record of regularly conducted activity shall provide written notice of that intention to each other party. A motion opposing admission in evidence of such record shall be made by the opposing party and determined by the court before trial. Failure by a party to file such motion before trial shall constitute a waiver of objection to such record or duplicate, but the court for cause shown may grant relief from the waiver.

(c) As used in this section, the term—

(1) "foreign record of regularly conducted activity" means a memorandum, report, record, or data compilation, in any form, of acts, events, conditions, opinions, or diagnoses, maintained in a foreign country;

(2) "foreign certification" means a written declaration made and signed in a foreign country by the custodian of a foreign record of regularly conducted activity or another qualified person that, if falsely made, would subject the maker to criminal penalty under the laws of that country; and

(3) "business" includes business, institution, association, profession, occupation, and calling of every kind, whether or not conducted for profit.

(Added Pub.L. 98–473, Title II, § 1217(a), Oct. 12, 1984, 98 Stat. 2165.)

HISTORICAL AND STATUTORY NOTES

Effective and Applicability Provisions

1984 Acts. Section 1220 of Pub.L. 98–473 provided that: "This part and the amendments made by this part [part K of chapter XII of Title II of Pub.L. 98–473, enacting this section and sections 3506, 3507, and 3292 of this title and amending section 3161 of this title] shall take effect thirty days after the date of the enactment of this Act [Oct. 12, 1984]."

§ 3506. Service of papers filed in opposition to official request by United States to foreign government for criminal evidence

(a) Except as provided in subsection (b) of this section, any national or resident of the United States who submits, or causes to be submitted, a pleading or other document to a court or other authority in a foreign country in opposition to an official request for evidence of an offense shall serve such pleading or other document on the Attorney General at the time such pleading or other document is submitted.

(b) Any person who is a party to a criminal proceeding in a court of the United States who submits, or causes to be submitted, a pleading or other document to a court or other authority in a foreign country in opposition to an official request for evidence of an offense that is a subject of such proceeding shall serve such pleading or other document on the appropriate attorney for the Government, pursuant to the Federal Rules of Criminal Procedure, at the time such pleading or other document is submitted.

(c) As used in this section, the term "official request" means a letter rogatory, a request under a treaty or convention, or any other request for evidence made by a court of the United States or an authority of the United States having criminal law enforcement responsibility, to a court or other authority of a foreign country.

(Added Pub.L. 98–473, Title II, § 1217(a), Oct. 12, 1984, 98 Stat. 2166.)

HISTORICAL AND STATUTORY NOTES

References in Text

The Federal Rules of Criminal Procedure, referred to in subsec. (b), are set out in this title.

Effective and Applicability Provisions

1984 Acts. Section effective 30 days after Oct. 12, 1984, see section 1220 of Pub.L. 98–473 set out as a note under section 3505 of this title.

§ 3507. Special master at foreign deposition

Upon application of a party to a criminal case, a United States district court before which the case is pending may, to the extent permitted by a foreign country, appoint a special master to carry out at a deposition taken in that country such duties as the court may direct, including presiding at the deposition or serving as an advisor on questions of United States law. Notwithstanding any other provision of law, a special master appointed under this section shall not decide questions of privilege under foreign law. The refusal of a court to appoint a special master under this section, or of the foreign country to permit a special master appointed under this section to carry out a duty at a deposition in that country, shall not affect the admissibility in evidence of a deposition taken under the provisions of the Federal Rules of Criminal Procedure.

(Added Pub.L. 98–473, Title II, § 1217(a), Oct. 12, 1984, 98 Stat. 2166.)

HISTORICAL AND STATUTORY NOTES

References in Text

The Federal Rules of Criminal Procedure, referred to in text, are set out in this title.

Effective and Applicability Provisions

1984 Acts. Section effective 30 days after Oct. 12, 1984, see section 1220 of Pub.L. 98–473 set out as a note under section 3505 of this title.

§ 3508. Custody and return of foreign witnesses

(a) When the testimony of a person who is serving a sentence, is in pretrial detention, or is otherwise being held in custody, in a foreign country, is needed in a State or Federal criminal proceeding, the Attorney General shall, when he deems it appropriate in the exercise of his discretion, have the authority to request the temporary transfer of that person to the United States for the purposes of giving such testimony, to transport such person to the United States in custody, to maintain the custody of such person while he is in the United States, and to return such person to the foreign country.

(b) Where the transfer to the United States of a person in custody for the purposes of giving testimony is provided for by treaty or convention, by this section, or both, that person shall be returned to the foreign country from which he is transferred. In no event shall the return of such person require any request for extradition or extradition proceedings, or proceedings under the immigration laws.

(c) Where there is a treaty or convention between the United States and the foreign country in which the witness is being held in custody which provides for the transfer, custody and return of such witnesses, the terms and conditions of that treaty shall apply. Where there is no such treaty or convention, the Attorney General may exercise the authority described in paragraph (a) if both the foreign country and the witness give their consent.

(Added Pub.L. 100–690, Title VI, § 6484(a), Nov. 18, 1988, 102 Stat. 4384.)

HISTORICAL AND STATUTORY NOTES

References in Text

The immigration laws, referred to in subsec. (b), are classified generally to Title 8, Aliens and Nationality.

§ 3509. Child victims' and child witnesses' rights

(a) Definitions.—For purposes of this section—

(1) the term "adult attendant" means an adult described in subsection (i) who accompanies a child throughout the judicial process for the purpose of providing emotional support;

(2) the term "child" means a person who is under the age of 18, who is or is alleged to be—

(A) a victim of a crime of physical abuse, sexual abuse, or exploitation; or

(B) a witness to a crime committed against another person;

(3) the term "child abuse" means the physical or mental injury, sexual abuse or exploitation, or negligent treatment of a child;

(4) the term "physical injury" includes lacerations, fractured bones, burns, internal injuries, severe bruising or serious bodily harm;

(5) the term "mental injury" means harm to a child's psychological or intellectual functioning which may be exhibited by severe anxiety, depression, withdrawal or outward aggressive behavior, or a combination of those behaviors, which may be demonstrated by a change in behavior, emotional response, or cognition;

(6) the term "exploitation" means child pornography or child prostitution;

(7) the term "multidisciplinary child abuse team" means a professional unit composed of representatives from health, social service, law enforcement, and legal service agencies to coordinate the assistance needed to handle cases of child abuse;

(8) the term "sexual abuse" includes the employment, use, persuasion, inducement, enticement, or coercion of a child to engage in, or assist another person to engage in, sexually explicit conduct or the rape, molestation, prostitution, or other form of sexual exploitation of children, or incest with children;

(9) the term "sexually explicit conduct" means actual or simulated—

(A) sexual intercourse, including sexual contact in the manner of genital-genital, oral-genital, anal-genital, or oral-anal contact, whether between persons of the same or of opposite sex; sexual contact means the intentional touching, either directly or through clothing, of the genitalia, anus, groin, breast, inner thigh, or buttocks of any person with an intent to abuse, humiliate, harass, degrade, or arouse or gratify sexual desire of any person;

(B) bestiality;

(C) masturbation;

(D) lascivious exhibition of the genitals or pubic area of a person or animal; or

(E) sadistic or masochistic abuse;

(10) the term "sex crime" means an act of sexual abuse that is a criminal act;

(11) the term "negligent treatment" means the failure to provide, for reasons other than poverty, adequate food, clothing, shelter, or medical care so as to seriously endanger the physical health of the child; and

(12) the term "child abuse" does not include discipline administered by a parent or legal guardian to his or her child provided it is reasonable in manner and moderate in degree and otherwise does not constitute cruelty.

(b) Alternatives to live in-court testimony.—

(1) Child's live testimony by 2–way closed circuit television.—

(A) In a proceeding involving an alleged offense against a child, the attorney for the Government, the child's attorney, or a guardian ad litem appointed under subsection (h) may apply for an order that the child's testimony be taken in a room outside the courtroom and be televised by 2–way closed circuit television. The person seeking such an order shall apply for such an order at least 5 days before the trial date, unless the court finds on the record that the need for such an order was not reasonably foreseeable.

(B) The court may order that the testimony of the child be taken by closed-circuit television as provided in subparagraph (A) if the court finds that the child is unable to testify in open court in the presence of the defendant, for any of the following reasons:

(i) The child is unable to testify because of fear.

(ii) There is a substantial likelihood, established by expert testimony, that the child would suffer emotional trauma from testifying.

(iii) The child suffers a mental or other infirmity.

(iv) Conduct by defendant or defense counsel causes the child to be unable to continue testifying.

(C) The court shall support a ruling on the child's inability to testify with findings on the record. In determining whether the impact on an individual child of one or more of the factors described in subparagraph (B) is so substantial as to justify an order under subparagraph (A), the court may question the minor in chambers, or at some other comfortable place other than the courtroom, on the record for a reasonable period of time with the child attendant, the prosecutor, the child's attorney, the guardian ad litem, and the defense counsel present.

(D) If the court orders the taking of testimony by television, the attorney for the Government and the attorney for the defendant not including an attorney pro se for a party shall be present in a room outside the courtroom with the child and the child shall be subjected to direct and cross-examination. The only other persons who may be permitted in the room with the child during the child's testimony are—

(i) the child's attorney or guardian ad litem appointed under subsection (h);

(ii) Persons necessary to operate the closed-circuit television equipment;

(iii) A judicial officer, appointed by the court; and

(iv) Other persons whose presence is determined by the court to be necessary to the welfare and well-being of the child, including an adult attendant.

The child's testimony shall be transmitted by closed circuit television into the courtroom for viewing and hearing by the defendant, jury, judge, and public. The defendant shall be provided with the means of private, contemporaneous communication with the defendant's attorney during the testimony. The closed circuit television transmission shall relay into the room in which the child is testifying the defendant's image, and the voice of the judge.

(2) Videotaped deposition of child.—(A) In a proceeding involving an alleged offense against a child, the attorney for the Government, the child's attorney, the child's parent or legal guardian, or the guardian ad litem appointed under subsection (h) may apply for an order that a deposition be taken of the child's testimony and that the deposition be recorded and preserved on videotape.

(B)(i) Upon timely receipt of an application described in subparagraph (A), the court shall make a preliminary finding regarding whether at the time of trial the child is likely to be unable to testify in open court in the physical presence of the defendant, jury, judge, and public for any of the following reasons:

(I) The child will be unable to testify because of fear.

(II) There is a substantial likelihood, established by expert testimony, that the child would suffer emotional trauma from testifying in open court.

(III) The child suffers a mental or other infirmity.

(IV) Conduct by defendant or defense counsel causes the child to be unable to continue testifying.

(ii) If the court finds that the child is likely to be unable to testify in open court for any of the reasons stated in clause (i), the court shall order that the child's deposition be taken and preserved by videotape.

(iii) The trial judge shall preside at the videotape deposition of a child and shall rule on all questions as if at trial. The only other persons who may be permitted to be present at the proceeding are—

(I) the attorney for the Government;

(II) the attorney for the defendant;

(III) the child's attorney or guardian ad litem appointed under subsection (h);

(IV) persons necessary to operate the videotape equipment;

(V) subject to clause (iv), the defendant; and

(VI) other persons whose presence is determined by the court to be necessary to the welfare and well-being of the child.

The defendant shall be afforded the rights applicable to defendants during trial, including the right to an attorney, the right to be confronted with the witness against the defendant, and the right to cross-examine the child.

(iv) If the preliminary finding of inability under clause (i) is based on evidence that the child is unable to testify in the physical presence of the defendant, the court may order that the defendant, including a defendant represented pro se, be excluded from the room in which the deposition is conducted. If the court orders that the defendant be excluded from the deposition room, the court shall order that 2–way closed circuit television equipment relay the defendant's image into the room in which the child is testifying, and the child's testimony into the room in which the defendant is viewing the proceeding, and that the defendant be provided with a means of private, contemporaneous communication with the defendant's attorney during the deposition.

(v) Handling of videotape.—The complete record of the examination of the child, including the image and voices of all persons who in any way participate in the examination, shall be made and preserved on video tape in addition to being stenographically recorded. The videotape shall be transmitted to the clerk of the court in which the action is pending and shall be made available for viewing to the prosecuting attorney, the defendant, and the defendant's attorney during ordinary business hours.

(C) If at the time of trial the court finds that the child is unable to testify as for a reason described in subparagraph (B)(i), the court may admit into evidence the child's videotaped deposition in lieu of the child's testifying at the trial. The court shall support a ruling under this subparagraph with findings on the record.

(D) Upon timely receipt of notice that new evidence has been discovered after the original videotaping and before or during trial, the court, for good cause shown, may order an additional videotaped deposition. The testimony of the child shall be restricted to the matters specified by the court as the basis for granting the order.

(E) In connection with the taking of a videotaped deposition under this paragraph, the court may enter a protective order for the purpose of protecting the privacy of the child.

(F) The videotape of a deposition taken under this paragraph shall be destroyed 5 years after the date on which the trial court entered its judgment, but not before a final judgment is entered on appeal including Supreme Court review. The videotape shall become part of the court record and be kept by the court until it is destroyed.

(c) Competency examinations.—

(1) Effect on Federal Rules of Evidence.—Nothing in this subsection shall be construed to abrogate rule 601 of the Federal Rules of Evidence.

(2) Presumption.—A child is presumed to be competent.

(3) Requirement of written motion.—A competency examination regarding a child witness may be conducted by the court only upon written motion and offer of proof of incompetency by a party.

(4) Requirement of compelling reasons.—A competency examination regarding a child may be conducted only if the court determines, on the record, that compelling reasons exist. A child's age alone is not a compelling reason.

(5) Persons permitted to be present.—The only persons who may be permitted to be present at a competency examination are—

(A) the judge;

(B) the attorney for the Government;

(C) the attorney for the defendant;

(D) a court reporter; and

(E) persons whose presence, in the opinion of the court, is necessary to the welfare and well-being of the child, including the child's attorney, guardian ad litem, or adult attendant.

(6) Not before jury.—A competency examination regarding a child witness shall be conducted out of the sight and hearing of a jury.

(7) Direct examination of child.—Examination of a child related to competency shall normally be conducted by the court on the basis of questions submitted by the attorney for the Government and the attorney for the defendant including a party acting as an attorney pro se. The court may permit an attorney but not a party acting as an attorney pro se to examine a child directly on competency if the court is satisfied that the child will not suffer emotional trauma as a result of the examination.

(8) Appropriate questions.—The questions asked at the competency examination of a child shall be appropriate to the age and developmental level of the child, shall not be related to the issues at trial, and shall focus on determining the child's ability to understand and answer simple questions.

(9) Psychological and psychiatric examinations.—Psychological and psychiatric examinations to assess the competency of a child witness shall not be ordered without a showing of compelling need.

(d) Privacy protection.—

(1) Confidentiality of information.—(A) A person acting in a capacity described in subparagraph (B) in connection with a criminal proceeding shall—

(i) keep all documents that disclose the name or any other information concerning a child in a secure place to which no person who does not have reason to know their contents has access; and

(ii) disclose documents described in clause (i) or the information in them that concerns a child only to persons who, by reason of their participation in the proceeding, have reason to know such information.

(B) Subparagraph (A) applies to—

(i) all employees of the Government connected with the case, including employees of the Department of Justice, any law enforcement agency involved in the case, and any person hired by the Government to provide assistance in the proceeding;

(ii) employees of the court;

(iii) the defendant and employees of the defendant, including the attorney for the defendant and persons hired by the defendant or the attorney for the defendant to provide assistance in the proceeding; and

(iv) members of the jury.

(2) Filing under seal.—All papers to be filed in court that disclose the name of or any other information concerning a child shall be filed under seal without necessity of obtaining a court order. The person who makes the filing shall submit to the clerk of the court—

(A) the complete paper to be kept under seal; and

(B) the paper with the portions of it that disclose the name of or other information concerning a child redacted, to be placed in the public record.

(3) Protective orders.—(A) On motion by any person the court may issue an order protecting a child from public disclosure of the name of or any other information concerning the child in the course of the proceedings, if the court determines that there is a significant possibility that such disclosure would be detrimental to the child.

(B) A protective order issued under subparagraph (A) may—

(i) provide that the testimony of a child witness, and the testimony of any other witness, when the attorney who calls the witness has reason to anticipate that the name of or any other information concerning a child may be divulged in the testimony, be taken in a closed courtroom; and

(ii) provide for any other measures that may be necessary to protect the privacy of the child.

(4) Disclosure of information.—This subsection does not prohibit disclosure of the name of or other information concerning a child to the defendant, the attorney for the defendant, a multidisciplinary child abuse team, a guardian ad litem, or an adult attendant, or to anyone to whom, in the opinion of the court, disclosure is necessary to the welfare and well-being of the child.

(e) Closing the courtroom.—When a child testifies the court may order the exclusion from the courtroom of all persons, including members of the press, who do not have a direct interest in the case. Such an order may be made if the court determines on the record that requiring the child to testify in open court would cause substantial psychological harm to the child or would result in the child's inability to effectively communicate. Such an order shall be narrowly tailored to serve the Government's specific compelling interest.

(f) Victim impact statement.—In preparing the presentence report pursuant to rule 32(c) of the Federal Rules of Criminal Procedure, the probation officer shall request information from the multidisciplinary child abuse team and other appropriate sources to determine the impact of the offense on the child victim and any other children who may have been affected. A guardian ad litem appointed under subsection (h) shall make every effort to obtain and report information that accurately expresses the child's and the family's views concerning the child's victimization. A guardian ad litem shall use forms that permit the child to express the child's views concerning the personal consequences of the child's victimization, at a level and in a form of communication commensurate with the child's age and ability.

(g) Use of multidisciplinary child abuse teams.—

(1) In general.—A multidisciplinary child abuse team shall be used when it is feasible to do so. The court shall work with State and local governments that have established multidisciplinary child abuse teams designed to assist child victims and child witnesses, and the court and the attorney for the Government shall consult with the multidisciplinary child abuse team as appropriate.

(2) Role of multidisciplinary child abuse teams.—The role of the multidisciplinary child abuse team shall be to provide for a child services that the members of the team in their professional roles are capable of providing, including—

(A) medical diagnoses and evaluation services, including provision or interpretation of x-rays, laboratory tests, and related services, as needed, and documentation of findings;

(B) telephone consultation services in emergencies and in other situations;

(C) medical evaluations related to abuse or neglect;

(D) psychological and psychiatric diagnoses and evaluation services for the child, parent or parents, guardian or guardians, or other caregivers, or any other individual involved in a child victim or child witness case;

(E) expert medical, psychological, and related professional testimony;

(F) case service coordination and assistance, including the location of services available from public and private agencies in the community; and

(G) training services for judges, litigators, court officers and others that are involved in child victim and child witness cases, in handling child victims and child witnesses.

(h) Guardian ad litem.—

(1) In general.—The court may appoint, and provide reasonable compensation and payment of expenses for, a guardian ad litem for a child who was a victim of, or a witness to, a crime involving abuse or exploitation to protect the best interests of the child. In making the appointment, the court shall consider a prospective guardian's background in, and familiarity with, the judicial process, social service programs, and child abuse issues. The guardian ad litem shall not be a person who is or may be a witness in a proceeding involving the child for whom the guardian is appointed.

(2) Duties of guardian ad litem.—A guardian ad litem may attend all the depositions, hearings, and trial proceedings in which a child participates, and make recommendations to the court concerning the welfare of the child. The guardian ad litem may have access to all reports, evaluations and records, except attorney's work product, necessary to effectively advocate for the child. (The extent of access to grand jury materials is limited to the access routinely provided to victims and their representatives.) A guardian ad litem shall marshal and coordinate the delivery of resources and special services to the child. A guardian ad litem shall not be compelled to testify in any court action or proceeding concerning any information or opinion received from the child in the course of serving as a guardian ad litem.

(3) Immunities.—A guardian ad litem shall be presumed to be acting in good faith and shall be immune from civil and criminal liability for complying with the guardian's lawful duties described in paragraph (2).

(i) Adult attendant.—A child testifying at or attending a judicial proceeding shall have the right to be accompanied by an adult attendant to provide emotional support to the child. The court, at its discretion, may allow the adult attendant to remain in close physical proximity to or in contact with the child while the child testifies. The court may allow the adult attendant to hold the child's hand or allow the child to sit on the adult attendant's lap throughout the course of the proceeding. An adult attendant shall not provide the child with an answer to any question directed to the child during the course of the child's testimony or otherwise prompt the child. The image of the child attendant, for the time the child is testifying or being deposed, shall be recorded on videotape.

(j) Speedy trial.—In a proceeding in which a child is called to give testimony, on motion by the attorney for the Government or a guardian ad litem, or on its own motion, the court may designate the case as being of special public importance. In cases so designated, the court shall, consistent with these rules, expedite the proceeding and ensure that it takes precedence over any other. The court shall ensure a speedy trial in order to minimize the length of time the child must endure the stress of involvement with the criminal process. When deciding whether to grant a continuance, the court shall take into consideration the age of

Complete Annotation Materials, see Title 18 U.S.C.A.

the child and the potential adverse impact the delay may have on the child's well-being. The court shall make written findings of fact and conclusions of law when granting a continuance in cases involving a child.

(k) Stay of civil action.—If, at any time that a cause of action for recovery of compensation for damage or injury to the person of a child exists, a criminal action is pending which arises out of the same occurrence and in which the child is the victim, the civil action shall be stayed until the end of all phases of the criminal action and any mention of the civil action during the criminal proceeding is prohibited. As used in this subsection, a criminal action is pending until its final adjudication in the trial court.

(*l*) Testimonial aids.—The court may permit a child to use anatomical dolls, puppets, drawings, mannequins, or any other demonstrative device the court deems appropriate for the purpose of assisting a child in testifying.

(m) Prohibition on reproduction of child pornography.—

(1) In any criminal proceeding, any property or material that constitutes child pornography (as defined by section 2256 of this title) shall remain in the care, custody, and control of either the Government or the court.

(2)(A) Notwithstanding Rule 16 of the Federal Rules of Criminal Procedure, a court shall deny, in any criminal proceeding, any request by the defendant to copy, photograph, duplicate, or otherwise reproduce any property or material that constitutes child pornography (as defined by section 2256 of this title), so long as the Government makes the property or material reasonably available to the defendant.

(B) For the purposes of subparagraph (A), property or material shall be deemed to be reasonably available to the defendant if the Government provides ample opportunity for inspection, viewing, and examination at a Government facility of the property or material by the defendant, his or her attorney, and any individual the defendant may seek to qualify to furnish expert testimony at trial.

(Added Pub.L. 101–647, Title II, § 225(a), Nov. 29, 1990, 104 Stat. 4798, and amended Pub.L. 103–322, Title XXXIII, §§ 330010(6), (7), 330011(e), 330018(b), Sept. 13, 1994, 108 Stat. 2143, 2145, 2149; Pub.L. 104–294, Title VI, § 605(h), Oct. 11, 1996, 110 Stat. 3510; Pub.L. 109–248, Title V, §§ 504, 507, July 27, 2006, 120 Stat. 629, 631.)

HISTORICAL AND STATUTORY NOTES

References in Text

The Federal Rules of Evidence, referred to in subsec. (c)(1), are set out in Title 28.

The Federal Rules of Criminal Procedure, referred to in subsec. (f), are set out in Title 18.

§ 3510. Rights of victims to attend and observe trial

(a) Non-capital cases.—Notwithstanding any statute, rule, or other provision of law, a United States district court shall not order any victim of an offense excluded from the trial of a defendant accused of that offense because such victim may, during the sentencing hearing, make a statement or present any information in relation to the sentence.

(b) Capital cases.—Notwithstanding any statute, rule, or other provision of law, a United States district court shall not order any victim of an offense excluded from the trial of a defendant accused of that offense because such victim may, during the sentencing hearing, testify as to the effect of the offense on the victim and the victim's family or as to any other factor for which notice is required under section 3593(a).

(c) Definition.—As used in this section, the term "victim" includes all persons defined as victims in section 503(e)(2) of the Victims' Rights and Restitution Act of 1990.

(Added Pub.L. 105–6, § 2(a), Mar. 19, 1997, 111 Stat. 12.)

HISTORICAL AND STATUTORY NOTES

References in Text

Section 503(e)(2) of the Victims' Rights and Restitution Act of 1990, referred to in subsec. (c), is classified to section 10607(e)(2) of Title 42, The Public Health and Welfare.

Effective and Applicability Provisions

1997 Acts. Section 3510(d) of Pub.L. 105–6 provided that: "The amendments made by this section [enacting this section, amending section 3593(c) of this title, and enacting provisions set out as a note under section 3481 of this title] shall apply in cases pending on the date of the enactment of this Act [Mar. 19, 1997]."

§ 3511. Judicial review of requests for information

(a) The recipient of a request for records, a report, or other information under section 2709(b) of this title, section 626(a) or (b) or 627(a) of the Fair Credit Reporting Act, section 1114(a)(5)(A) of the Right to Financial Privacy Act, or section 802(a) of the National Security Act of 1947 may, in the United States district court for the district in which that person or entity does business or resides, petition for an order modifying or setting aside the request. The court may modify or set aside the request if compliance would be unreasonable, oppressive, or otherwise unlawful.

(b)(1) The recipient of a request for records, a report, or other information under section 2709(b) of this title, section 626(a) or (b) or 627(a) of the Fair Credit Reporting Act, section 1114(a)(5)(A) of the Right to Financial Privacy Act, or section 802(a) of the National Security Act of 1947, may petition any court described in subsection (a) for an order modifying or setting aside a nondisclosure requirement imposed in connection with such a request.

(2) If the petition is filed within one year of the request for records, a report, or other information under section 2709(b) of this title, section 626(a) or (b) or 627(a) of the Fair Credit Reporting Act, section 1114(a)(5)(A) of the Right to Financial Privacy Act, or section 802(a) of the National Security Act of 1947, the court may modify or set aside such a nondisclosure requirement if it finds that there is no reason to believe that disclosure may endanger the national security of the United States, interfere with a criminal, counterterrorism, or counterintelligence investigation, interfere with diplomatic relations, or endanger the life or physical safety of any person. If, at the time of the petition, the Attorney General, Deputy Attorney General, an Assistant Attorney General, or the Director of the Federal Bureau of Investigation, or in the case of a request by a department, agency, or instrumentality of the Federal Government other than the Department of Justice, the head or deputy head of such department, agency, or instrumentality, certifies that disclosure may endanger the national security of the United States or interfere with diplomatic relations, such certification shall be treated as conclusive unless the court finds that the certification was made in bad faith.

(3) If the petition is filed one year or more after the request for records, a report, or other information under section 2709(b) of this title, section 626(a) or (b) or 627(a) of the Fair Credit Reporting Act, section 1114(a)(5)(A) of the Right to Financial Privacy Act, or section 802(a) of the National Security Act of 1947, the Attorney General, Deputy Attorney General, an Assistant Attorney General, or the Director of the Federal Bureau of Investigation, or his designee in a position not lower than Deputy Assistant Director at Bureau headquarters or a Special Agent in Charge in a Bureau field office designated by the Director, or in the case of a request by a department, agency, or instrumentality of the Federal Government other than the Federal Bureau of Investigation, the head or deputy head of such department, agency, or instrumentality, within ninety days of the filing of the petition, shall either terminate the nondisclosure requirement or re-certify that disclosure may result in a danger to the national security of the United States, interference with a criminal, counterterrorism, or counterintelligence investigation, interference with diplomatic relations, or danger to the life or physical safety of any person. In the event of re-certification, the court may modify or set aside such a nondisclosure requirement if it finds that there is no reason to believe that disclosure may endanger the national security of the United States, interfere with a criminal, counterterrorism, or counterintelligence investigation, interfere with diplomatic relations, or endanger the life or physical safety of any person. If the recertification that disclosure may endanger the national security of the United States or interfere with diplomatic relations is made by the Attorney General, Deputy Attorney General, an Assistant Attorney General, or the Director of the Federal Bureau of Investigation, such certification shall be treated as conclusive unless the court finds that the recertification was made in bad faith. If the court denies a petition for an order modifying or setting aside a nondisclosure requirement under this paragraph, the recipient shall be precluded for a period of one year from filing another petition to modify or set aside such nondisclosure requirement.

(c) In the case of a failure to comply with a request for records, a report, or other information made to any person or entity under section 2709(b) of this title, section 626(a) or (b) or 627(a) of the Fair Credit Reporting Act, section 1114(a)(5)(A) of the Right to Financial Privacy Act, or section 802(a) of the National Security Act of 1947, the Attorney General may invoke the aid of any district court of the United States within the jurisdiction in which the investigation is carried on or the person or entity resides, carries on business, or may be found, to compel compliance with the request. The court may issue an order requiring the person or entity to comply with the request. Any failure to obey the order of the court may be punished by the court as contempt thereof. Any process under this section may be served in any judicial district in which the person or entity may be found.

(d) In all proceedings under this section, subject to any right to an open hearing in a contempt proceeding, the court must close any hearing to the extent necessary to prevent an unauthorized disclosure of a request for records, a report, or other information made to any person or entity under section 2709(b) of this title, section 626(a) or (b) or 627(a) of the Fair Credit Reporting Act, section 1114(a)(5)(A) of the Right to Financial Privacy Act, or section 802(a) of the National Security Act of 1947. Petitions, filings, records, orders, and subpoenas must also be kept under seal to the extent and as long as necessary to prevent the unauthorized disclosure of a request for records, a report, or other information made to any person or entity under section 2709(b) of this title, section 626(a) or (b) or 627(a) of the Fair Credit Reporting Act, section 1114(a)(5)(A) of the Right to Financial Privacy Act, or section 802(a) of the National Security Act of 1947.

(e) In all proceedings under this section, the court shall, upon request of the government, review ex parte and in camera any government submission or portions thereof, which may include classified information.

(Added Pub.L. 109–177, Title I, § 115(2), Mar. 9, 2006, 120 Stat. 211.)

HISTORICAL AND STATUTORY NOTES

References in Text

The Fair Credit Reporting Act, referred to in text, is Pub.L. 90–321, Title VI, as added by Pub.L. 91–508, Title VI, § 601, Oct. 26, 1970, 84 Stat. 1127, as amended, which is classified principally to subchapter III of chapter 41 of Title 15, 15 U.S.C.A. § 1681 et seq. Sections 626 and 627 of the Fair Credit Reporting Act are classified to 15 U.S.C.A. §§ 1681u and 1681v, respectively. For complete classification, see Short Title note set out under 15 U.S.C.A. § 1601 and Tables.

Section 1114 of the Right to Financial Privacy Act, referred to in text, is Pub.L. 95–630, Title XI, § 1114, Nov. 10, 1978, 92 Stat. 3707, which is classified to 12 U.S.C.A. § 3414.

Section 802 of the National Security Act of 1947, referred to in text, is July 26, 1947, c. 343, Title VIII, § 802, as added Oct. 14, 1994, Pub.L. 103–359, Title VIII, § 802(a), 108 Stat. 3436, which is classified to 50 U.S.C.A. § 436.

Reports on National Security Letters

Pub.L. 109–177, Title I, § 118, Mar. 9, 2006, 120 Stat. 217, provided that:

"(a) **Existing reports.**—Any report made to a committee of Congress regarding national security letters under section 2709(c)(1) of title 18, United States Code, section 626(d) or 627(c) of the Fair Credit Reporting Act (15 U.S.C. 1681u(d) or 1681v(c)), section 1114(a)(3) or 1114(a)(5)(D) of the Right to Financial Privacy Act (12 U.S.C. 3414(a)(3) or 3414(a)(5)(D)), or section 802(b) of the National Security Act of 1947 (50 U.S.C. 436(b)) shall also be made to the Committees on the Judiciary of the House of Representatives and the Senate.

"(b) **[Omitted; amended 15 § 1681v]**

"(c) **Report on requests for national security letters.**—

"(1) **In general.**—In April of each year, the Attorney General shall submit to Congress an aggregate report setting forth with respect to the preceding year the total number of requests made by the Department of Justice for information concerning different United States persons under—

"(A) section 2709 of title 18, United States Code (to access certain communication service provider records), excluding the number of requests for subscriber information;

"(B) section 1114 of the Right to Financial Privacy Act (12 U.S.C. 3414) (to obtain financial institution customer records);

"(C) section 802 of the National Security Act of 1947 (50 U.S.C. 436) (to obtain financial information, records, and consumer reports);

"(D) section 626 of the Fair Credit Reporting Act (15 U.S.C. 1681u) (to obtain certain financial information and consumer reports); and

"(E) section 627 of the Fair Credit Reporting Act (15 U.S.C. 1681v) (to obtain credit agency consumer records for counterterrorism investigations).

"(2) **Unclassified form.**—The report under this section [this note] shall be submitted in unclassified form.

"(d) **National security letter defined.**—In this section [this note], the term 'national security letter' means a request for information under one of the following provisions of law:

"(1) Section 2709(a) of title 18, United States Code (to access certain communication service provider records).

"(2) Section 1114(a)(5)(A) of the Right to Financial Privacy Act (12 U.S.C. 3414(a)(5)(A)) (to obtain financial institution customer records).

"(3) Section 802 of the National Security Act of 1947 (50 U.S.C. 436) (to obtain financial information, records, and consumer reports).

"(4) Section 626 of the Fair Credit Reporting Act (15 U.S.C. 1681u) (to obtain certain financial information and consumer reports).

"(5) Section 627 of the Fair Credit Reporting Act (15 U.S.C. 1681v) (to obtain credit agency consumer records for counterterrorism investigations)."

CHAPTER 224—PROTECTION OF WITNESSES

§ 3521. Witness relocation and protection

(a)(1) The Attorney General may provide for the relocation and other protection of a witness or a potential witness for the Federal Government or for a State government in an official proceeding concerning an organized criminal activity or other serious offense, if the Attorney General determines that an offense involving a crime of violence directed at the witness with respect to that proceeding, an offense set forth in chapter 73 of this title directed at the witness, or a State offense that is similar in nature to either such offense, is likely to be committed. The Attorney General may also provide for the relocation and other protection of the immediate family of, or a person otherwise closely associated with, such witness or potential witness if the family or person may also be endangered on account of the participation of the witness in the judicial proceeding.

(2) The Attorney General shall issue guidelines defining the types of cases for which the exercise of the authority of the Attorney General contained in paragraph (1) would be appropriate.

(3) The United States and its officers and employees shall not be subject to any civil liability on account

of any decision to provide or not to provide protection under this chapter.

(b)(1) In connection with the protection under this chapter of a witness, a potential witness, or an immediate family member or close associate of a witness or potential witness, the Attorney General shall take such action as the Attorney General determines to be necessary to protect the person involved from bodily injury and otherwise to assure the health, safety, and welfare of that person, including the psychological well-being and social adjustment of that person, for as long as, in the judgment of the Attorney General, the danger to that person exists. The Attorney General may, by regulation—

(A) provide suitable documents to enable the person to establish a new identity or otherwise protect the person;

(B) provide housing for the person;

(C) provide for the transportation of household furniture and other personal property to a new residence of the person;

(D) provide to the person a payment to meet basic living expenses, in a sum established in accordance with regulations issued by the Attorney General, for such times as the Attorney General determines to be warranted;

(E) assist the person in obtaining employment;

(F) provide other services necessary to assist the person in becoming self-sustaining;

(G) disclose or refuse to disclose the identity or location of the person relocated or protected, or any other matter concerning the person or the program after weighing the danger such a disclosure would pose to the person, the detriment it would cause to the general effectiveness of the program, and the benefit it would afford to the public or to the person seeking the disclosure, except that the Attorney General shall, upon the request of State or local law enforcement officials or pursuant to a court order, without undue delay, disclose to such officials the identity, location, criminal records, and fingerprints relating to the person relocated or protected when the Attorney General knows or the request indicates that the person is under investigation for or has been arrested for or charged with an offense that is punishable by more than one year in prison or that is a crime of violence;

(H) protect the confidentiality of the identity and location of persons subject to registration requirements as convicted offenders under Federal or State law, including prescribing alternative procedures to those otherwise provided by Federal or State law for registration and tracking of such persons; and

(I) exempt procurement for services, materials, and supplies, and the renovation and construction of safe sites within existing buildings from other provisions of law as may be required to maintain the security of protective witnesses and the integrity of the Witness Security Program.

The Attorney General shall establish an accurate, efficient, and effective system of records concerning the criminal history of persons provided protection under this chapter in order to provide the information described in subparagraph (G).

(2) Deductions shall be made from any payment made to a person pursuant to paragraph (1)(D) to satisfy obligations of that person for family support payments pursuant to a State court order.

(3) Any person who, without the authorization of the Attorney General, knowingly discloses any information received from the Attorney General under paragraph (1)(G) shall be fined $5,000 or imprisoned five years, or both.

(c) Before providing protection to any person under this chapter, the Attorney General shall, to the extent practicable, obtain information relating to the suitability of the person for inclusion in the program, including the criminal history, if any, and a psychological evaluation of, the person. The Attorney General shall also make a written assessment in each case of the seriousness of the investigation or case in which the person's information or testimony has been or will be provided and the possible risk of danger to other persons and property in the community where the person is to be relocated and shall determine whether the need for that person's testimony outweighs the risk of danger to the public. In assessing whether a person should be provided protection under this chapter, the Attorney General shall consider the person's criminal record, alternatives to providing protection under this chapter, the possibility of securing similar testimony from other sources, the need for protecting the person, the relative importance of the person's testimony, results of psychological examinations, whether providing such protection will substantially infringe upon the relationship between a child who would be relocated in connection with such protection and that child's parent who would not be so relocated, and such other factors as the Attorney General considers appropriate. The Attorney General shall not provide protection to any person under this chapter if the risk of danger to the public, including the potential harm to innocent victims, outweighs the need for that person's testimony. This subsection shall not be construed to authorize the disclosure of the written assessment made pursuant to this subsection.

(d)(1) Before providing protection to any person under this chapter, the Attorney General shall enter into a memorandum of understanding with that person. Each such memorandum of understanding shall set forth the responsibilities of that person, including—

(A) the agreement of the person, if a witness or potential witness, to testify in and provide information to all appropriate law enforcement officials concerning all appropriate proceedings;

(B) the agreement of the person not to commit any crime;

(C) the agreement of the person to take all necessary steps to avoid detection by others of the facts concerning the protection provided to that person under this chapter;

(D) the agreement of the person to comply with legal obligations and civil judgments against that person;

(E) the agreement of the person to cooperate with all reasonable requests of officers and employees of the Government who are providing protection under this chapter;

(F) the agreement of the person to designate another person to act as agent for the service of process;

(G) the agreement of the person to make a sworn statement of all outstanding legal obligations, including obligations concerning child custody and visitation;

(H) the agreement of the person to disclose any probation or parole responsibilities, and if the person is on probation or parole under State law, to consent to Federal supervision in accordance with section 3522 of this title; and

(I) the agreement of the person to regularly inform the appropriate program official of the activities and current address of such person.

Each such memorandum of understanding shall also set forth the protection which the Attorney General has determined will be provided to the person under this chapter, and the procedures to be followed in the case of a breach of the memorandum of understanding, as such procedures are established by the Attorney General. Such procedures shall include a procedure for filing and resolution of grievances of persons provided protection under this chapter regarding the administration of the program. This procedure shall include the opportunity for resolution of a grievance by a person who was not involved in the case.

(2) The Attorney General shall enter into a separate memorandum of understanding pursuant to this subsection with each person protected under this chapter who is eighteen years of age or older. The memorandum of understanding shall be signed by the Attorney General and the person protected.

(3) The Attorney General may delegate the responsibility initially to authorize protection under this chapter only to the Deputy Attorney General, to the Associate Attorney General, to any Assistant Attorney General in charge of the Criminal Division or National Security Division of the Department of Justice, to the Assistant Attorney General in charge of the Civil Rights Division of the Department of Justice (insofar as the delegation relates to a criminal civil rights case), and to one other officer or employee of the Department of Justice.

(e) If the Attorney General determines that harm to a person for whom protection may be provided under section 3521 of this title is imminent or that failure to provide immediate protection would otherwise seriously jeopardize an ongoing investigation, the Attorney General may provide temporary protection to such person under this chapter before making the written assessment and determination required by subsection (c) of this section or entering into the memorandum of understanding required by subsection (d) of this section. In such a case the Attorney General shall make such assessment and determination and enter into such memorandum of understanding without undue delay after the protection is initiated.

(f) The Attorney General may terminate the protection provided under this chapter to any person who substantially breaches the memorandum of understanding entered into between the Attorney General and that person pursuant to subsection (d), or who provides false information concerning the memorandum of understanding or the circumstances pursuant to which the person was provided protection under this chapter, including information with respect to the nature and circumstances concerning child custody and visitation. Before terminating such protection, the Attorney General shall send notice to the person involved of the termination of the protection provided under this chapter and the reasons for the termination. The decision of the Attorney General to terminate such protection shall not be subject to judicial review.

(Added Pub.L. 98–473, Title II, § 1208, Oct. 12, 1984, 98 Stat. 2153, and amended Pub.L. 101–647, Title XXXV, § 3582, Nov. 29, 1990, 104 Stat. 4929; Pub.L. 105–119, Title I, § 115(a)(9), Nov. 26, 1997, 111 Stat. 2467; Pub.L. 109–177, Title V, § 506(a)(7), Mar. 9, 2006, 120 Stat. 248.)

HISTORICAL AND STATUTORY NOTES

Effective and Applicability Provisions

1997 Amendments. Amendment by section 115 of Pub.L. 105–119 to take effect on Nov. 26, 1997, except that States shall have 3 years from Nov. 26, 1997, to implement amendments made by Pub.L. 104–119 which impose new requirements under subchapter VI (section 14071 et seq.) of chapter 136 of Title 42, The Public Health and Welfare, and the Attorney General may grant an additional 2 years to a State that is making good faith efforts to implement these amendments, see section 115(c) of Pub.L. 105–119, set out as a note under section 14071 of Title 42.

1984 Amendments. Section 1210 of Pub.L. 98–473 provided that: "This subpart [subpart A of part F of chapter XII of Title II of Pub.L. 98–473, enacting this chapter] and the amendments made by this subpart [repealing provisions formerly set out as a note preceding section 3481 of this title] shall take effect on October 1, 1984."

Short Title

1984 Acts. Section 1207 of Pub.L. 98–473 provided that: "This subpart [subpart A of part F of chapter XII of Title II of Pub.L. 98–473, enacting this chapter, repealing provisions formerly set out as a note preceding section 3481 of this title, and enacting provisions set out as a note under section] may be cited as the 'Witness Security Reform Act of 1984'."

§ 3522. Probationers and parolees

(a) A probation officer may, upon the request of the Attorney General, supervise any person provided protection under this chapter who is on probation or parole under State law, if the State involved consents to such supervision. Any person so supervised shall be under Federal jurisdiction during the period of supervision and shall, during that period be subject to all laws of the United States which pertain to probationers or parolees, as the case may be.

(b) The failure by any person provided protection under this chapter who is supervised under subsection (a) to comply with the memorandum of understanding entered into by that person pursuant to section 3521(d) of this title shall be grounds for the revocation of probation or parole, as the case may be.

(c) The United States Parole Commission and the Chairman of the Commission shall have the same powers and duties with respect to a probationer or parolee transferred from State supervision pursuant to this section as they have with respect to an offender convicted in a court of the United States and paroled under chapter 311 of this title. The provisions of sections 4201 through 4204, 4205(a), (e), and (h), 4206 through 4215, and 4218 of this title shall apply following a revocation of probation or parole under this section.

(d) If a person provided protection under this chapter who is on probation or parole and is supervised under subsection (a) of this section has been ordered by the State court which imposed sentence on the person to pay a sum of money to the victim of the offense involved for damage caused by the offense, that penalty or award of damages may be enforced as though it were a civil judgment rendered by a United States district court. Proceedings to collect the moneys ordered to be paid may be instituted by the Attorney General in any United States district court. Moneys recovered pursuant to such proceedings shall be distributed to the victim.

(Added Pub.L. 98–473, Title II, § 1208, Oct. 12, 1984, 98 Stat. 2157, and amended Pub.L. 99–646, § 75, Nov. 10, 1986, 100 Stat. 3618; Pub.L. 100–690, Title VII, § 7072(b), Nov. 18, 1988, 102 Stat. 4405.)

HISTORICAL AND STATUTORY NOTES

References in Text

Chapter 311 of this title, referred to in subsec. (c), which consisted of 18 U.S.C.A. §§ 4201 to 4218, was repealed effective Nov. 1, 1987, by Pub.L. 98–473, Title II, §§ 218(a)(5), 235(a)(1), (b)(1), Oct. 12, 1984, 98 Stat. 2027, 2031, 2032, subject to remaining effective for five years after Nov. 1, 1987, in certain circumstances.

Effective and Applicability Provisions

1984 Acts. Section effective on Oct. 1, 1984, see section 1210 of Pub.L. 98–473 set out as a note under section 3521 of this title.

§ 3523. Civil judgments

(a) If a person provided protection under this chapter is named as a defendant in a civil cause of action arising prior to or during the period in which the protection is provided, process in the civil proceeding may be served upon that person or an agent designated by that person for that purpose. The Attorney General shall make reasonable efforts to serve a copy of the process upon the person protected at the person's last known address. The Attorney General shall notify the plaintiff in the action whether such process has been served. If a judgment in such action is entered against that person the Attorney General shall determine whether the person has made reasonable efforts to comply with the judgment. The Attorney General shall take appropriate steps to urge the person to comply with the judgment. If the Attorney General determines that the person has not made reasonable efforts to comply with the judgment, the Attorney General may, after considering the danger to the person and upon the request of the person holding the judgment disclose the identity and location of the person to the plaintiff entitled to recovery pursuant to the judgment. Any such disclosure of the identity and location of the person shall be made upon the express condition that further disclosure by the plaintiff of such identity or location may be made only if essential to the plaintiff's efforts to recover under the judgment, and only to such additional persons as is necessary to effect the recovery. Any such disclosure or nondisclosure by the Attorney General shall not subject the United States and its officers or employees to any civil liability.

(b)(1) Any person who holds a judgment entered by a Federal or State court in his or her favor against a person provided protection under this chapter may, upon a decision by the Attorney General to deny disclosure of the current identity and location of such protected person, bring an action against the protected person in the United States district court in the district where the person holding the judgment (hereinafter in this subsection referred to as the "petitioner") resides. Such action shall be brought within one hundred and twenty days after the petitioner requested the Attorney General to disclose the identity and location of the protected person. The complaint in such action shall contain statements that the petitioner holds a valid judgment of a Federal or State court against a person provided protection under this chapter and that the petitioner sought to enforce the judgment by requesting the Attorney General to disclose the identity and location of the protected person.

(2) The petitioner in an action described in paragraph (1) shall notify the Attorney General of the action at the same time the action is brought. The Attorney General shall appear in the action and shall affirm or deny the statements in the complaint that the person against whom the judgment is allegedly held is provided protection under this chapter and that the petitioner requested the Attorney General to disclose the identity and location of the protected person for the purpose of enforcing the judgment.

(3) Upon a determination (A) that the petitioner holds a judgment entered by a Federal or State court and (B) that the Attorney General has declined to disclose to the petitioner the current identity and location of the protected person against whom the judgment was entered, the court shall appoint a guardian to act on behalf of the petitioner to enforce the judgment. The clerk of the court shall forthwith furnish the guardian with a copy of the order of appointment. The Attorney General shall disclose to the guardian the current identity and location of the protected person and any other information necessary to enable the guardian to carry out his or her duties under this subsection.

(4) It is the duty of the guardian to proceed with all reasonable diligence and dispatch to enforce the rights of the petitioner under the judgment. The guardian shall, however, endeavor to carry out such enforcement duties in a manner that maximizes, to the extent practicable, the safety and security of the protected person. In no event shall the guardian disclose the new identity or location of the protected person without the permission of the Attorney General, except that such disclosure may be made to a Federal or State court in order to enforce the judgment. Any good faith disclosure made by the guardian in the performance of his or her duties under this subsection shall not create any civil liability against the United States or any of its officers or employees.

(5) Upon appointment, the guardian shall have the power to perform any act with respect to the judgment which the petitioner could perform, including the initiation of judicial enforcement actions in any Federal or State court or the assignment of such enforcement actions to a third party under applicable Federal or State law. The Federal Rules of Civil Procedure shall apply in any action brought under this subsection to enforce a Federal or State court judgment.

(6) The costs of any action brought under this subsection with respect to a judgment, including any enforcement action described in paragraph (5), and the compensation to be allowed to a guardian appointed in any such action shall be fixed by the court and shall be apportioned among the parties as follows: the petitioner shall be assessed in the amount the petitioner would have paid to collect on the judgment in an action not arising under the provisions of this subsection; the protected person shall be assessed the costs which are normally charged to debtors in similar actions and any other costs which are incurred as a result of an action brought under this subsection. In the event that the costs and compensation to the guardian are not met by the petitioner or by the protected person, the court may, in its discretion, enter judgment against the United States for costs and fees reasonably incurred as a result of the action brought under this subsection.

(7) No officer or employee of the Department of Justice shall in any way impede the efforts of a guardian appointed under this subsection to enforce the judgment with respect to which the guardian was appointed.

(c) The provisions of this section shall not apply to a court order to which section 3524 of this title applies.

(Added Pub.L. 98–473, Title II, § 1208, Oct. 12, 1984, 98 Stat. 2157.)

HISTORICAL AND STATUTORY NOTES

References in Text

The Federal Rules of Civil Procedure, referred to in subsec. (b)(5), are set out in Title 28, Judiciary and Judicial Procedure.

Effective and Applicability Provisions

1984 Acts. Section effective on Oct. 1, 1984, see section 1210 of Pub.L. 98–473 set out as a note under section 3521 of this title.

§ 3524. Child custody arrangements

(a) The Attorney General may not relocate any child in connection with protection provided to a person under this chapter if it appears that a person other than that protected person has legal custody of that child.

(b) Before protection is provided under this chapter to any person (1) who is a parent of a child of whom that person has custody, and (2) who has obligations to another parent of that child with respect to custody or visitation of that child under a court order, the

Attorney General shall obtain and examine a copy of such order for the purpose of assuring that compliance with the order can be achieved. If compliance with a visitation order cannot be achieved, the Attorney General may provide protection under this chapter to the person only if the parent being relocated initiates legal action to modify the existing court order under subsection (e)(1) of this section. The parent being relocated must agree in writing before being provided protection to abide by any ensuing court orders issued as a result of an action to modify.

(c) With respect to any person provided protection under this chapter (1) who is the parent of a child who is relocated in connection with such protection and (2) who has obligations to another parent of that child with respect to custody or visitation of that child under a State court order, the Attorney General shall, as soon as practicable after the person and child are so relocated, notify in writing the child's parent who is not so relocated that the child has been provided protection under this chapter. The notification shall also include statements that the rights of the parent not so relocated to visitation or custody, or both, under the court order shall not be infringed by the relocation of the child and the Department of Justice responsibility with respect thereto. The Department of Justice will pay all reasonable costs of transportation and security incurred in insuring that visitation can occur at a secure location as designated by the United States Marshals Service, but in no event shall it be obligated to pay such costs for visitation in excess of thirty days a year, or twelve in number a year. Additional visitation may be paid for, in the discretion of the Attorney General, by the Department of Justice in extraordinary circumstances. In the event that the unrelocated parent pays visitation costs, the Department of Justice may, in the discretion of the Attorney General, extend security arrangements associated with such visitation.

(d)(1) With respect to any person provided protection under this chapter (A) who is the parent of a child who is relocated in connection with such protection and (B) who has obligations to another parent of that child with respect to custody or visitation of that child under a court order, an action to modify that court order may be brought by any party to the court order in the District Court for the District of Columbia or in the district court for the district in which the child's parent resides who has not been relocated in connection with such protection.

(2) With respect to actions brought under paragraph (1), the district courts shall establish a procedure to provide a reasonable opportunity for the parties to the court order to mediate their dispute with respect to the order. The court shall provide a mediator for this purpose. If the dispute is mediated, the court shall issue an order in accordance with the resolution of the dispute.

(3) If, within sixty days after an action is brought under paragraph (1) to modify a court order, the dispute has not been mediated, any party to the court order may request arbitration of the dispute. In the case of such a request, the court shall appoint a master to act as arbitrator, who shall be experienced in domestic relations matters. Rule 53 of the Federal Rules of Civil Procedure shall apply to masters appointed under this paragraph. The court and the master shall, in determining the dispute, give substantial deference to the need for maintaining parent-child relationships, and any order issued by the court shall be in the best interests of the child. In actions to modify a court order brought under this subsection, the court and the master shall apply the law of the State in which the court order was issued or, in the case of the modification of a court order issued by a district court under this section, the law of the State in which the parent resides who was not relocated in connection with the protection provided under this chapter. The costs to the Government of carrying out a court order may be considered in an action brought under this subsection to modify that court order but shall not outweigh the relative interests of the parties themselves and the child.

(4) Until a court order is modified under this subsection, all parties to that court order shall comply with their obligations under that court order subject to the limitations set forth in subsection (c) of this section.

(5) With respect to any person provided protection under this chapter who is the parent of a child who is relocated in connection with such protection, the parent not relocated in connection with such protection may bring an action, in the District Court for the District of Columbia or in the district court for the district in which that parent resides, for violation by that protected person of a court order with respect to custody or visitation of that child. If the court finds that such a violation has occurred, the court may hold in contempt the protected person. Once held in contempt, the protected person shall have a maximum of sixty days, in the discretion of the Attorney General, to comply with the court order. If the protected person fails to comply with the order within the time specified by the Attorney General, the Attorney General shall disclose the new identity and address of the protected person to the other parent and terminate any financial assistance to the protected person unless otherwise directed by the court.

(6) The United States shall be required by the court to pay litigation costs, including reasonable attorneys' fees, incurred by a parent who prevails in enforcing a custody or visitation order; but shall retain the right to recover such costs from the protected person.

(e)(1) In any case in which the Attorney General determines that, as a result of the relocation of a person and a child of whom that person is a parent in connection with protection provided under this chapter, the implementation of a court order with respect to custody or visitation of that child would be substantially impossible, the Attorney General may bring, on behalf of the person provided protection under this chapter, an action to modify the court order. Such action may be brought in the district court for the district in which the parent resides who would not be or was not relocated in connection with the protection provided under this chapter. In an action brought under this paragraph, if the Attorney General establishes, by clear and convincing evidence, that implementation of the court order involved would be substantially impossible, the court may modify the court order but shall, subject to appropriate security considerations, provide an alternative as substantially equivalent to the original rights of the nonrelocating parent as feasible under the circumstances.

(2) With respect to any State court order in effect to which this section applies, and with respect to any district court order in effect which is issued under this section, if the parent who is not relocated in connection with protection provided under this chapter intentionally violates a reasonable security requirement imposed by the Attorney General with respect to the implementation of that court order, the Attorney General may bring an action in the district court for the district in which that parent resides to modify the court order. The court may modify the court order if the court finds such an intentional violation.

(3) The procedures for mediation and arbitration provided under subsection (d) of this section shall not apply to actions for modification brought under this subsection.

(f) In any case in which a person provided protection under this chapter is the parent of a child of whom that person has custody and has obligations to another parent of that child concerning custody and visitation of that child which are not imposed by court order, that person, or the parent not relocated in connection with such protection, may bring an action in the district court of the district in which that parent not relocated resides to obtain an order providing for custody or visitation, or both, of that child. In any such action, all the provisions of subsection (d) of this section shall apply.

(g) In any case in which an action under this section involves court orders from different States with respect to custody or visitation of the same child, the court shall resolve any conflicts by applying the rules of conflict of laws of the State in which the court is sitting.

(h)(1) Subject to paragraph (2), the costs of any action described in subsection (d), (e), or (f) of this section shall be paid by the United States.

(2) The Attorney General shall insure that any State court order in effect to which this section applies and any district court order in effect which is issued under this section are carried out. The Department of Justice shall pay all costs and fees described in subsections (c) and (d) of this section.

(i) As used in this section, the term "parent" includes any person who stands in the place of a parent by law.

(Added Pub.L. 98–473, Title II, § 1208, Oct. 12, 1984, 98 Stat. 2159.)

HISTORICAL AND STATUTORY NOTES

References in Text

Rule 53 of the Federal Rules of Civil Procedure, referred to in subsec. (d)(3), is set out in Title 28, Judiciary and Judicial Procedure.

Effective and Applicability Provisions

1984 Acts. Section effective on Oct. 1, 1984, see section 1210 of Pub.L. 98–473 set out as a note under section 3521 of this title.

§ 3525. Victims Compensation Fund

(a) The Attorney General may pay restitution to, or in the case of death, compensation for the death of any victim of a crime that causes or threatens death or serious bodily injury and that is committed by any person during a period in which that person is provided protection under this chapter.

(b) Not later than four months after the end of each fiscal year, the Attorney General shall transmit to the Congress a detailed report on payments made under this section for such year.

(c) There are authorized to be appropriated for the fiscal year 1985 and for each fiscal year thereafter, $1,000,000 for payments under this section.

(d) The Attorney General shall establish guidelines and procedures for making payments under this section. The payments to victims under this section shall be made for the types of expenses provided for in section 3579(b) of this title, except that in the case of the death of the victim, an amount not to exceed

$50,000 may be paid to the victim's estate. No payment may be made under this section to a victim unless the victim has sought restitution and compensation provided under Federal or State law or by civil action. Such payments may be made only to the extent the victim, or the victim's estate, has not otherwise received restitution and compensation, including insurance payments, for the crime involved. Payments may be made under this section to victims of crimes occurring on or after the date of the enactment of this chapter. In the case of a crime occurring before the date of the enactment of this chapter, a payment may be made under this section only in the case of the death of the victim, and then only in an amount not exceeding $25,000, and such a payment may be made notwithstanding the requirements of the third sentence of this subsection.

(e) Nothing in this section shall be construed to create a cause of action against the United States.

(Added Pub.L. 98–473, Title II, § 1208, Oct. 12, 1984, 98 Stat. 2162.)

HISTORICAL AND STATUTORY NOTES

Effective and Applicability Provisions

1984 Acts. Section effective on Oct. 1, 1984, see section 1210 of Pub.L. 98–473 set out as a note under section 3521 of this title.

Termination of Reporting Requirements

Reporting requirement of subsec. (b) of this section excepted from termination under Pub.L. 104–66, § 3003(a)(1), as amended, set out in a note under 31 U.S.C.A. § 1113, see Pub.L. 106–197, § 1, set out as a note under 31 U.S.C.A. § 1113.

Restitution to Estate of Victims Killed Before October 12, 1984; Limitation

Pub.L. 99–180, Title II, § 200, Dec. 13, 1985, 99 Stat. 1142, provided: "That restitution of not to exceed $25,000 shall be paid to the estate of victims killed before October 12, 1984 as a result of crimes committed by persons who have been enrolled in the Federal witness protection program, if such crimes were committed within two years after protection was terminated, notwithstanding any limitations contained in part (a) of section 3525 of title 18 of the United States Code [subsec. (a) of this section]."

Similar provisions were contained in the following prior appropriation Act:

Pub.L. 99–88, Title I, § 100, Aug. 15, 1985, 99 Stat. 303.

§ 3526. Cooperation of other Federal agencies and State governments; reimbursement of expenses

(a) Each Federal agency shall cooperate with the Attorney General in carrying out the provisions of this chapter and may provide, on a reimbursable basis, such personnel and services as the Attorney General may request in carrying out those provisions.

(b) In any case in which a State government requests the Attorney General to provide protection to any person under this chapter—

(1) the Attorney General may enter into an agreement with that State government in which that government agrees to reimburse the United States for expenses incurred in providing protection to that person under this chapter; and

(2) the Attorney General shall enter into an agreement with that State government in which that government agrees to cooperate with the Attorney General in carrying out the provisions of this chapter with respect to all persons.

(Added Pub.L. 98–473, Title II, § 1208, Oct. 12, 1984, 98 Stat. 2162.)

HISTORICAL AND STATUTORY NOTES

Effective and Applicability Provisions

1984 Acts. Section effective on Oct. 1, 1984, see section 1210 of Pub.L. 98–473 set out as a note under section 3521 of this title.

§ 3527. Additional authority of Attorney General

The Attorney General may enter into such contracts or other agreements as may be necessary to carry out this chapter. Any such contract or agreement which would result in the United States being obligated to make outlays may be entered into only to the extent and in such amount as may be provided in advance in an appropriation Act.

(Added Pub.L. 98–473, Title II, § 1208, Oct. 12, 1984, 98 Stat. 2163.)

HISTORICAL AND STATUTORY NOTES

Effective and Applicability Provisions

1984 Acts. Section effective on Oct. 1, 1984, see section 1210 of Pub.L. 98–473 set out as a note under section 3521 of this title.

§ 3528. Definition

For purposes of this chapter, the term "State" means each of the several States, the District of Columbia, the Commonwealth of Puerto Rico, and any territory or possession of the United States.

(Added Pub.L. 98–473, Title II, § 1208, Oct. 12, 1984, 98 Stat. 2163.)

HISTORICAL AND STATUTORY NOTES

Effective and Applicability Provisions

1984 Acts. Section effective on Oct. 1, 1984, see section 1210 of Pub.L. 98–473 set out as a note under section 3521 of this title.

CHAPTER 225—VERDICT

§ 3531. Return; several defendants; conviction of less offense; poll of jury—(Rule)

SEE FEDERAL RULES OF CRIMINAL PROCEDURE

Verdict to be unanimous; return; several defendants; disagreement; conviction of less offense; poll of jury, Rule 31.

(June 25, 1948, c. 645, 62 Stat. 837.)

§ 3532. Setting aside verdict of guilty; judgment notwithstanding verdict—(Rule)

SEE FEDERAL RULES OF CRIMINAL PROCEDURE

Setting aside verdict of guilty on motion for judgment of acquittal, entering of such judgment, or ordering new trial; absence of verdict, Rule 29(b).

(June 25, 1948, c. 645, 62 Stat. 837.)

CHAPTER 227—SENTENCES

[1] Editorially supplied.

HISTORICAL AND STATUTORY NOTES

Prior Provisions

A prior chapter 227 (§ 3561 et seq.) was repealed by Pub.L. 98–473, Title II, §§ 212(a)(1), (2), 235(a)(1), Oct. 12, 1984, 98 Stat. 1987, 2031, as amended, (except sections 3577 to 3580 which were renumbered sections 3661 to 3664, respectively), effective Nov. 1, 1987, and applicable only to offenses committed after the taking effect of such repeal. Section 235 of Pub.L. 98–473, as amended, relating to effective dates, is set out as a note under section 3551 of this title. Prior to repeal, the provisions of this chapter read as follows:

§ 3561. Judgment form and entry—(Rule)

SEE FEDERAL RULES OF CRIMINAL PROCEDURE

Judgment to be signed by judge and entered by clerk, Rule 32(b).

(June 25, 1948, c. 645, 62 Stat. 837.)

§ 3562. Sentence—(Rule)

SEE FEDERAL RULES OF CRIMINAL PROCEDURE

Imposition of sentence; commitment; bail; presentence investigation and report, Rule 32(a, c).

(June 25, 1948, c. 645, 62 Stat. 837.)

§ 3563. Corruption of blood or forfeiture of estate

No conviction or judgment shall work corruption of blood or any forfeiture of estate.

(June 25, 1948, c. 645, 62 Stat. 837.)

§ 3564. Pillory and whipping

The punishment of whipping and of standing in the pillory shall not be inflicted.

(June 25, 1948, c. 645, 62 Stat. 837.)

§ 3565. Collection and payment of fines and penalties

(a)(1) Except as provided in paragraph (2) of this subsection, in all criminal cases in which judgment or sentence is rendered, imposing the payment of a fine or penalty, whether alone or with any other kind of punishment, such judgment, so far as the fine or penalty is concerned, may be enforced by execution against the property of the defendant in like manner as judgments in civil cases. If the court finds by a preponderance of the information relied upon in imposing sentence that the defendant has the present ability to pay a fine or penalty, the judgment may direct imprisonment until the fine or penalty is paid, and the issue of execution on the judgment shall not discharge the defendant from imprisonment until the amount of the judgment is paid.

(2) A judgment imposing the payment of a fine or penalty shall, upon the filing of notice of lien in the manner in which a notice of tax lien would be filed under section 6323(f) of the Internal Revenue Code of 1986, be a lien in favor of the United States upon all property and rights of property belonging to the defendant, except with respect to properties or transactions specified in subsections (b), (c) or (d) of section 6323 of the Internal Revenue Code of 1986 for which a notice of tax lien properly filed on the same date would not be valid and except with respect to property that would be exempt from levy for taxes under section 6334(a) of the Code. Such lien shall be valid against any subsequent purchaser, holder of a security interest, mechanic's lienor or judgment creditor. A writ of execution may be issued with respect to any property or rights to property subject to such lien.

(3) Such lien is valid against property referred to in paragraph (2) of this subsection if, but for such paragraph, applicable law would permit enforcement of the lien.

(4) The effect of any execution, whether by attachment, garnishment, levy or other means, on salary, wages or other income payable to or receivable by a defendant shall be continuous from the date such execution is first made until the liability for the fine or penalty to which the execution relates is satisfied, the liability ceases to exist or becomes unenforceable, or the execution is released. Salaries, wages and other income shall be exempt from execution only to the extent of the exemptions from levy for taxes provided in section 6334(d) of the Internal Revenue Code of 1986.

(5) For the purposes of any State or local law providing for the filing of a notice of a tax lien, a notice of lien for a judgment imposing the payment of a fine or penalty shall be

considered a notice of lien for taxes payable to the United States. If such notice is not accepted for filing, the registration, recording, docketing, or indexing, of the judgment imposing payment of a fine or penalty in accordance with section 1962 of title 28, United States Code shall be considered for all purposes as the filing prescribed by this subsection.

(b)(1) A judgment imposing the payment of a fine or penalty shall—

(A) provide for immediate payment unless, in the interest of justice, the court specifies payment on a date certain or in installments;

(B) include the name and address of the defendant, the docket number of the case, the amount of the fine, and the schedule of payments (if other than immediate payment is specified); and

(C) if other than immediate payment is specified, require the defendant to notify the appropriate United States Attorney of any change in the name or address of the defendant.

(2) If the judgment specifies other than immediate payment of a fine or penalty, the period provided for payment shall not exceed five years, excluding any period served by the defendant as imprisonment for the offense. The defendant shall pay interest on any amount payment of which is deferred under this paragraph. The interest shall be computed on the unpaid balance at the rate of 1.5 percent per month for each full calendar month for which such amount is unpaid.

(3) If the judgment specifies other than immediate payment of a fine or penalty, and the defendant does not pay an amount due, at the discretion of the Attorney General, the entire unpaid balance shall be payable immediately.

(c)(1) The defendant shall pay interest on any amount of a fine or penalty (other than a penalty under paragraph (2) of this subsection) that is past due. The interest shall be computed on the unpaid balance at the rate of 1.5 percent per month.

(2) If an amount owed by a defendant as a fine or penalty is past due for more than 90 days, the defendant shall pay, in addition to any amount otherwise payable, a penalty equal to 25 percent of the amount past due.

(d)(1) Except as provided in paragraph (2) of this subsection, the defendant shall pay to the Attorney General any amount due as a fine or penalty.

(2) The Attorney General and the Director of the Administrative Office of the United States Courts may jointly provide by regulation that fines and penalties for specified categories of offenses shall be paid to the clerk of the court.

(e) If a fine or penalty exceeds $500, the clerk of the court shall furnish to the Attorney General a certified copy of the judgment.

(f) If a fine or penalty is imposed on an organization, it is the duty of each individual authorized to make disbursements for the organization to make payment from assets of the organization. If a fine or penalty is imposed on a director, officer, employee, or agent of an organization, payment shall not be made, directly or indirectly, from assets of the organization, unless the court finds that such payment is expressly permissible under applicable State law.

(g) When a fine or penalty is satisfied as provided by law, the Attorney General shall file with the court a notice of satisfaction of judgment if the defendant makes a written request to the Attorney General for such filing, or if the amount of the fine or penalty exceeds $500. Upon request of the defendant, the clerk shall furnish to the defendant a certified copy of the notice.

(h) The obligation to pay a fine or penalty ceases upon the death of the defendant or the expiration of twenty years after the date of the entry of the judgment, whichever occurs earlier. The defendant and the Attorney General may agree in writing to extend such twenty-year period.

(June 25, 1948, c. 645, 62 Stat. 837; Oct. 12, 1984, Pub.L. 98–473, Title II, §§ 235(a)(1), 238(g)(1), (i), 98 Stat. 2031, 2039; Oct. 30, 1984, Pub.L. 98–596, §§ 2, 12(a)(7)(A), (9), (b), 98 Stat. 3134, 3139, 3140; Oct. 22, 1986, Pub.L. 99–514, § 2, 100 Stat. 2095.)

§ 3566. Execution of death sentence

The manner of inflicting the punishment of death shall be that prescribed by the laws of the place within which the sentence is imposed. The United States marshal charged with the execution of the sentence may use available local facilities and the services of an appropriate local official or employ some other person for such purpose, and pay the costs thereof in an amount approved by the Attorney General. If the laws of the place within which sentence is imposed make no provision for the infliction of the penalty of death, then the court shall designate some other place in which such sentence shall be executed in the manner prescribed by the laws thereof.

(June 25, 1948, c. 645, 62 Stat. 837.)

§ 3567. Death sentence may prescribe dissection

The court before which any person is convicted of murder in the first degree, or rape, may, in its discretion, add to the judgment of death, that the body of the offender be delivered to a surgeon for dissection; and the marshal who executes such judgment shall deliver the body, after execution, to such surgeon as the court may direct; and such surgeon, or some person appointed by him, shall receive and take away the body at the time of execution.

(June 25, 1948, c. 645, 62 Stat. 838.)

§ 3568. Effective date of sentence; credit for time in custody prior to the imposition of sentence

The sentence of imprisonment of any person convicted of an offense shall commence to run from the date on which such person is received at the penitentiary, reformatory, or jail for service of such sentence. The Attorney General shall give any such person credit toward service of his sentence for any days spent in custody in connection with the offense or acts for which sentence was imposed. As used in this section, the term "offense" means any criminal offense, other than an offense triable by court-martial, military commission, provost court, or other military tribunal, which is in violation of an Act of Congress and is triable in any court established by Act of Congress.

If any such person shall be committed to a jail or other place of detention to await transportation to the place at which his sentence is to be served, his sentence shall commence to run from the date on which he is received at such jail or other place of detention.

No sentence shall prescribe any other method of computing the term.

(June 25, 1948, c. 645, 62 Stat. 838; Sept. 2, 1960, Pub.L. 86–691, § 1(a), 74 Stat. 738; June 22, 1966, Pub.L. 89–465, § 4, 80 Stat. 217.)

§ 3569. Discharge of indigent prisoner

When a poor convict, sentenced for violation of any law of the United States by any court established by enactment of Congress, to be imprisoned and pay a fine, or fine and costs, or to pay a fine, or fine and costs, has been confined in prison, solely for the nonpayment of such fine, or fine and costs, such convict may make application in writing to the nearest United States magistrate in the district where he is imprisoned setting forth his inability to pay such fine, or fine and costs, and after notice to the district attorney of the United States, who may appear, offer evidence, and be heard, the magistrate shall proceed to hear and determine the matter.

If on examination it shall appear to him that such convict is unable to pay such fine, or fine and costs, and that he has not any property exceeding $20 in value, except such as is by law exempt from being taken on execution for debt, the magistrate shall administer to him the following oath: "I do solemnly swear that I have not any property, real or personal, exceeding $20, except such as is by law exempt from being taken on civil process for debt; and that I have no property in any way conveyed or concealed, or in any way disposed of, for my future use or benefit. So help me God." Upon taking such oath such convict shall be discharged; and the magistrate shall file with the institution in which the convict is confined, a certificate setting forth the facts. In case the convict is found by the magistrate to possess property valued at an amount in excess of said exemption, nevertheless, if the Attorney General finds that the retention by such convict of all such property is reasonably necessary for his support or that of his family, such convict shall be released without further imprisonment solely for the nonpayment of such fine, or fine and costs; or if he finds that the retention by such convict of any part of such property is reasonably necessary for his support or that of his family, such convict shall be released without further imprisonment solely for nonpayment of such fine or fine and costs upon payment on account of his fine and costs, of that portion of his property in excess of the amount found to be reasonably necessary for his support or that of his family.

(June 25, 1948, c. 645, 62 Stat. 838; Oct. 17, 1968, Pub.L. 90–578, Title III, § 301(a)(1), (3), 82 Stat. 1115; Oct. 12, 1984, Pub.L. 98–473, Title II, §§ 235(a)(1), 238(h), (i), 98 Stat. 2031, 2039; Oct. 30, 1984, Pub.L. 98–596, §§ 3, 12(a)(8), (9), (b), 98 Stat. 3136, 3139, 3140.)

§ 3570. Presidential remission as affecting unremitted part

Whenever, by the judgment of any court or judicial officer of the United States, in any criminal proceeding, any person is sentenced to two kinds of punishment, the one pecuniary and the other corporal, the President's remission in whole or in part of either kind shall not impair the legal validity of the other kind, or of any portion of either kind, not remitted.

(June 25, 1948, c. 645, 62 Stat. 839.)

§ 3571. Clerical mistakes—(Rule)

SEE FEDERAL RULES OF CRIMINAL PROCEDURE

Court empowered to correct clerical mistakes in judgments, orders, or record, Rule 36.

(June 25, 1948, c. 645, 62 Stat. 839.)

§ 3572. Correction or reduction of sentence—(Rule)

SEE FEDERAL RULES OF CRIMINAL PROCEDURE

Court empowered to correct or reduce sentence; time; Rule 35.

(June 25, 1948, c. 645, 62 Stat. 839.)

§ 3573. Arrest or setting aside of judgment—(Rule)

SEE FEDERAL RULES OF CRIMINAL PROCEDURE

Arrest of judgment, grounds and motion, time, Rule 34.

Setting aside judgment and permitting withdrawal of plea of guilty, Rule 32(d).

(June 25, 1948, c. 645, 62 Stat. 839.)

§ 3574. Stay of execution; supersedeas—(Rule)

SEE FEDERAL RULES OF CRIMINAL PROCEDURE

Death or imprisonment sentence, fines stayed on appeal; conditions and power of court, Rule 38(a).

(June 25, 1948, c. 645, 62 Stat. 839.)

§ 3575. Increased sentence for dangerous special offenders

(a) Whenever an attorney charged with the prosecution of a defendant in a court of the United States for an alleged felony committed when the defendant was over the age of twenty-one years has reason to believe that the defendant is a dangerous special offender such attorney, a reasonable time before trial or acceptance by the court of a plea of guilty or nolo contendere, may sign and file with the court, and may amend, a notice (1) specifying that the defendant is a dangerous special offender who upon conviction for such felony is subject to the imposition of a sentence under subsection (b) of this section, and (2) setting out with particularity the reasons why such attorney believes the defendant to be a dangerous special offender. In no case shall the fact that the defendant is alleged to be a dangerous special offender be an issue upon the trial of such felony, be disclosed to the jury, or be disclosed before any plea of guilty or nolo contendere or verdict or finding of guilty to the presiding judge without the consent of the parties. If the court finds that the filing of the notice as a public record may prejudice fair consideration of a pending criminal matter, it may order the notice sealed and the notice shall not be subject to subpena or public inspection during the pendency of such criminal matter, except on order of the court, but shall be subject to inspection by the defendant alleged to be a dangerous special offender and his counsel.

(b) Upon any plea of guilty or nolo contendere or verdict or finding of guilty of the defendant of such felony, a hearing shall be held, before sentence is imposed, by the court sitting without a jury. The court shall fix a time for the hearing, and notice thereof shall be given to the defendant and the United States at least ten days prior thereto. The court shall permit the United States and counsel for the defendant, or the defendant if he is not represented by counsel, to inspect the presentence report sufficiently prior to the hearing as to afford a reasonable opportunity for verification. In extraordinary cases, the court may withhold material not relevant to a proper sentence, diagnostic opinion which might seriously disrupt a program of rehabilitation, any source of information obtained on a promise of confidentiality, and material previously disclosed in open court. A court withholding all or part of a presentence report shall inform the parties of its action and place in the record the reasons therefor. The court may require parties inspecting all or part of a presentence report to give notice of any part thereof intended to be controverted. In connection with the hearing, the defendant and the United States shall be entitled to assistance of counsel, compulsory process, and cross-examination of such witnesses as appear at the hearing. A duly authenticated copy of a former judgment or commitment shall be prima facie evidence of such former judgment or commitment. If it appears by a preponderance of the information, including information submitted during the trial of such felony and the sentencing hearing and so much of the presentence report as the court relies upon, that the defendant is a dangerous special offender, the court shall sentence the defendant to imprisonment for an appropriate term not to exceed twenty-five years and not disproportionate in severity to the maximum term otherwise authorized by law for such felony. Otherwise it shall sentence the defendant in accordance with the law prescribing penalties for such felony. The court shall place in the record its findings, including an identification of the information relied upon in making such findings, and its reasons for the sentence imposed.

(c) This section shall not prevent the imposition and execution of a sentence of death or of imprisonment for life or for a term exceeding twenty-five years upon any person convicted of an offense so punishable.

(d) Notwithstanding any other provision of this section, the court shall not sentence a dangerous special offender to less than any mandatory minimum penalty prescribed by law for such felony. This section shall not be construed as creating any mandatory minimum penalty.

(e) A defendant is a special offender for purposes of this section if—

(1) the defendant has previously been convicted in courts of the United States, a State, the District of Columbia, the Commonwealth of Puerto Rico, a territory or possession of the United States, any political subdivision, or any department, agency, or instrumentality thereof for two or more offenses committed on occasions different from one another and from such felony and punishable in such courts by death or imprisonment in excess of one year, for one or more of such convictions the defendant has been imprisoned prior to the commission of such felony, and less than five years have elapsed between the commission of such felony and either the defendant's release, on parole or otherwise, from imprisonment for one such conviction or his commission of the last such previous offense or another offense punishable by death or imprisonment in excess of one year under applicable laws of the United States, a State, the District of Columbia, the Commonwealth of Puerto Rico, a territory or possession of the United States, any political subdivision, or any department, agency or instrumentality thereof; or

(2) the defendant committed such felony as part of a pattern of conduct which was criminal under applicable laws of any jurisdiction, which constituted a substantial source of his income, and in which he manifested special skill or expertise; or

(3) such felony was, or the defendant committed such felony in furtherance of, a conspiracy with three or more other persons to engage in a pattern of conduct criminal under applicable laws of any jurisdiction, and the defendant did, or agreed that he would, initiate, organize, plan, finance, direct, manage, or supervise all or part of such conspiracy or conduct, or give or receive a bribe or use force as all or part of such conduct.

A conviction shown on direct or collateral review or at the hearing to be invalid or for which the defendant has been pardoned on the ground of innocence shall be disregarded for purposes of paragraph (1) of this subsection. In support of findings under paragraph (2) of this subsection, it may be shown that the defendant has had in his own name or under his control income or property not explained as derived from a source other than such conduct. For purposes of paragraph (2) of this subsection, a substantial source of income means a source of income which for any period of one year or more exceeds the minimum wage, determined on the basis of a forty-hour week and a fifty-week year, without reference to exceptions, under section 6(a)(1) of the Fair Labor Standards Act of 1938 (52 Stat. 1602, as amended 80 Stat. 838), and as hereafter amended, for an employee engaged in commerce or in the production of goods for commerce, and which for the same period exceeds fifty percent of the defendant's declared adjusted gross income under section 62 of the Internal Revenue Act of 1954 (68A Stat. 17, as amended 83 Stat. 655), and as hereafter amended. For purposes of paragraph (2) of this subsection, special skill or expertise in criminal conduct includes unusual knowledge, judgment or ability, including manual dexterity, facilitating the initiation, organizing, planning, financing, direction, management, supervision, execution or concealment of criminal conduct, the enlistment of accomplices in such conduct, the escape from detection or apprehension for such conduct, or the disposition of the fruits or proceeds of such conduct. For purposes of paragraphs (2) and (3) of this subsection, criminal conduct forms a pattern if it embraces criminal acts that have the same or similar purposes, results, participants, victims, or methods of commission, or otherwise are interrelated by distinguishing characteristics and are not isolated events.

(f) A defendant is dangerous for purposes of this section if a period of confinement longer than that provided for such felony is required for the protection of the public from further criminal conduct by the defendant.

(g) The time for taking an appeal from a conviction for which sentence is imposed after proceedings under this section shall be measured from imposition of the original sentence.

(Added Pub.L. 91–452, Title X, § 1001(a), Oct. 15, 1970, 84 Stat. 948.)

§ 3576. Review of sentence

With respect to the imposition, correction, or reduction of a sentence after proceedings under section 3575 of this chapter, a review of the sentence on the record of the sentencing court may be taken by the defendant or the United States to a court of appeals. Any review of the sentence taken by the United States shall be taken at least five days before expiration of the time for taking a review of the sentence or appeal of the conviction by the defendant and shall be diligently prosecuted. The sentencing court may, with or without motion and notice, extend the time for taking a review of the sentence for a period not to exceed thirty days from the expiration of the time otherwise prescribed by law. The court shall not extend the time for taking a review of the sentence by the United States after the time has expired. A court extending the time for taking a review of the sentence by the United States shall extend the time for taking a review of the sentence or appeal of the conviction by the defendant for the same period. The taking of a review of the sentence by the United States shall be deemed the taking of a review of the sentence and an appeal of the conviction by the defendant. Review of the sentence shall include review of whether the procedure employed was lawful, the findings made were clearly erroneous, or the sentencing court's discretion was abused. The court of appeals on review of the sentence may, after considering the record, including the entire presentence report, information submitted during the trial of such felony and the sentencing hearing, and the findings and reasons of the sentencing court, affirm the sentence, impose or direct the imposition of any sentence which the sentencing court could originally have imposed, or remand for further sentencing proceedings and imposition of sentence, except that a sentence may be made more severe only on review of the sentence taken by the United States and after hearing. Failure of the United States to take a review of the imposition of the sentence shall, upon review taken by the United States of the correction or reduction of the sentence, foreclose imposition of a sentence more severe than that previously imposed. Any withdrawal or dismissal of review of the sentence taken by the United States shall foreclose imposition of a sentence more severe than that reviewed but shall not otherwise foreclose the review of the sentence or the appeal of the conviction. The court of appeals shall state in writing the reasons for its disposition of the review of the sentence. Any review of the sentence taken by the United States may be dismissed on a showing of abuse of the right of the United States to take such review.

(Added Pub.L. 91–452, Title X, § 1001(a), Oct. 15, 1970, 84 Stat. 950.)

§ 3577. Use of information for sentencing

No limitation shall be placed on the information concerning the background, character, and conduct of a person convicted of an offense which a court of the United States may receive and consider for the purpose of imposing an appropriate sentence.

(Added Pub.L. 91–452, Title X, § 1001(a), Oct. 15, 1970, 84 Stat. 951.)

§ 3578. Conviction records

(a) The Attorney General of the United States is authorized to establish in the Department of Justice a repository for records of convictions and determinations of the validity of such convictions.

(b) Upon the conviction thereafter of a defendant in a court of the United States, the District of Columbia, the Commonwealth of Puerto Rico, a territory or possession of the United States, any political subdivision, or any department, agency, or instrumentality thereof for an offense punishable in such court by death or imprisonment in excess of one year, or a judicial determination of the validity of such conviction on collateral review, the court shall cause a certified record of the conviction or determination to be made to the repository in such form and containing such information as the Attorney General of the United States shall by regulation prescribe.

(c) Records maintained in the repository shall not be public records. Certified copies thereof—

(1) may be furnished for law enforcement purposes on request of a court or law enforcement or corrections officer of the United States, the District of Columbia, the Commonwealth of Puerto Rico, a territory or possession of the United States, any political subdivision, or any department, agency, or instrumentality thereof;

(2) may be furnished for law enforcement purposes on request of a court or law enforcement or corrections officer of a State, any political subdivision, or any department, agency, or instrumentality thereof, if a statute of such State requires that, upon the conviction of a defendant in a court of the State or any political subdivision thereof for an offense punishable in such court by death or imprisonment in excess of one year, or a judicial determination of the validity of such conviction on collateral review, the court cause a certified record of the conviction or determination to be made to the repository in such form and containing such information as the Attorney General of the United States shall by regulation prescribe; and

(3) shall be prima facie evidence in any court of the United States, the District of Columbia, the Commonwealth of Puerto Rico, a territory or possession of the United States, any political subdivision, or any department, agency, or instrumentality thereof, that the convictions occurred and whether they have been judicially determined to be invalid on collateral review.

(d) The Attorney General of the United States shall give reasonable public notice, and afford to interested parties opportunity for hearing, prior to prescribing regulations under this section.

(Added Pub.L. 91–452, Title X, § 1001(a), Oct. 15, 1970, 84 Stat. 951.)

§ 3579. Order of restitution

(a)(1) The court, when sentencing a defendant convicted of an offense under this title or under subsection (h), (i), (j), or (n) of section 902, of the Federal Aviation Act of 1958 (49 U.S.C. 1472), may order, in addition to or in lieu of any other penalty authorized by law, that the defendant make restitution to any victim of such offense.

(2) If the court does not order restitution, or orders only partial restitution, under this section, the court shall state on the record the reasons therefor.

(b) The order may require that such defendant—

(1) in the case of an offense resulting in damage to or loss or destruction of property of a victim of the offense—

(A) return the property to the owner of the property or someone designated by the owner, or

(B) if return of the property under subparagraph (A) is impossible, impractical, or inadequate, pay an amount equal to the greater of—

(i) the value of the property on the date of the damage, loss, or destruction, or

(ii) the value of the property on the date of sentencing,

less the value (as of the date the property is returned) of any part of the property that is returned;

(2) in the case of an offense resulting in bodily injury to a victim—

(A) pay an amount equal to the cost of necessary medical and related professional services and devices relating to physical, psychiatric, and psychological care, including nonmedical care and treatment rendered in accordance with a method of healing recognized by the law of the place of treatment;

(B) pay an amount equal to the cost of necessary physical and occupational therapy and rehabilitation; and

(C) reimburse the victim for income lost by such victim as a result of such offense;

(3) in the case of an offense resulting in bodily injury also results in the death of a victim, pay an amount equal to the cost of necessary funeral and related services; and

(4) in any case, if the victim (or if the victim is deceased, the victim's estate) consents, make restitution in services in lieu of money, or make restitution to a person or organization designated by the victim or the estate.

(c) If the court decides to order restitution under this section, the court shall, if the victim is deceased, order that the restitution be made to the victim's estate.

(d) To the extent that the court determines that the complication and prolongation of the sentencing process resulting from the fashioning of an order of restitution under this section outweighs the need to provide restitution to any victims, the court may decline to make such an order.

(e)(1) The court shall not impose restitution with respect to a loss for which the victim has received or is to receive compensation, except that the court may, in the interest of justice, order restitution to any person who has compensated the victim for such loss to the extent that such person paid the compensation. An order of restitution shall require that all restitution to victims under such order be made before any restitution to any other person under such order is made.

(2) Any amount paid to a victim under an order of restitution shall be set off against any amount later recovered as compensatory damages by such victim in—

(A) any Federal civil proceeding; and

(B) any State civil proceeding, to the extent provided by the law of that State.

(f)(1) The court may require that such defendant make restitution under this section within a specified period or in specified installments.

(2) The end of such period or the last such installment shall not be later than—

(A) the end of the period of probation, if probation is ordered;

(B) five years after the end of the term of imprisonment imposed, if the court does not order probation; and

(C) five years after the date of sentencing in any other case.

(3) If not otherwise provided by the court under this subsection, restitution shall be made immediately.

(4) The order of restitution shall require the defendant to make restitution directly to the victim or other person eligible under this section, or to deliver the amount or property due as restitution to the Attorney General for transfer to such victim or person.

(g) If such defendant is placed on probation or paroled under this title, any restitution ordered under this section shall be a condition of such probation or parole. The court may revoke probation and the Parole Commission may revoke parole if the defendant fails to comply with such order. In determining whether to revoke probation or parole, the court or Parole Commission shall consider the defendant's employment status, earning ability, financial resources, the willfulness of the defendant's failure to pay, and any other special circumstances that may have a bearing on the defendant's ability to pay.

(h) An order of restitution may be enforced by the United States in the manner provided for the collection of fines and penalties by section 3565 or by a victim named in the order to receive the restitution in the same manner as a judgment in a civil action.

(Added Pub.L. 97–291, § 5(a), Oct. 12, 1982, 96 Stat. 1253, and amended Pub.L. 98–596, § 9, Oct. 30, 1984, 98 Stat. 3138; Pub.L. 99–646, §§ 77(a), 78(a), 79(a), Nov. 10, 1986, 100 Stat. 3618, 3619.)

§ 3580. Procedure for issuing order of restitution

(a) The court, in determining whether to order restitution under section 3579 of this title and the amount of such restitution, shall consider the amount of the loss sustained by any victim as a result of the offense, the financial resources of the defendant, the financial needs and earning ability of the defendant and the defendant's dependents, and such other factors as the court deems appropriate.

(b) The court may order the probation service of the court to obtain information pertaining to the factors set forth in subsection (a) of this section. The probation service of the court shall include the information collected in the report of presentence investigation or in a separate report, as the court directs.

(c) The court shall disclose to both the defendant and the attorney for the Government all portions of the presentence or other report pertaining to the matters described in subsection (a) of this section.

(d) Any dispute as the the proper amount or type of restitution shall be resolved by the court by the preponderance of the evidence. The burden of demonstrating the amount of the loss sustained by a victim as a result of the offense shall be on the attorney for the Government. The burden of demonstrating the financial resources of the defendant and the financial needs of the defendant and such defendant's dependents shall be on the defendant. The burden of demonstrating such other matters as the court deems appropriate shall be upon the party designated by the court as justice requires.

(e) A conviction of a defendant for an offense involving the act giving rise to restitution under this section shall estop the defendant from denying the essential allegations of that offense in any subsequent Federal civil proceeding or State civil proceeding, to the extent consistent with State law, brought by the victim.

(Added Pub.L. 97–291, § 5(a), Oct. 12, 1982, 96 Stat. 1255.)

SUBCHAPTER A—GENERAL PROVISIONS

SUBCHAPTER A—GENERAL PROVISIONS [1]

[1] So in original. Subchapter analysis probably should appear at the chapter head.

§ 3551. Authorized sentences

(a) In general.—Except as otherwise specifically provided, a defendant who has been found guilty of an offense described in any Federal statute, including sections 13 and 1153 of this title, other than an Act of Congress applicable exclusively in the District of Columbia or the Uniform Code of Military Justice, shall be sentenced in accordance with the provisions of this chapter so as to achieve the purposes set forth in subparagraphs (A) through (D) of section 3553(a)(2) to the extent that they are applicable in light of all the circumstances of the case.

(b) Individuals.—An individual found guilty of an offense shall be sentenced, in accordance with the provisions of section 3553, to—

(1) a term of probation as authorized by subchapter B;

(2) a fine as authorized by subchapter C; or

(3) a term of imprisonment as authorized by subchapter D.

A sentence to pay a fine may be imposed in addition to any other sentence. A sanction authorized by section 3554, 3555, or 3556 may be imposed in addition to the sentence required by this subsection.

(c) Organizations.—An organization found guilty of an offense shall be sentenced, in accordance with the provisions of section 3553, to—

(1) a term of probation as authorized by subchapter B; or

(2) a fine as authorized by subchapter C.

A sentence to pay a fine may be imposed in addition to a sentence to probation. A sanction authorized by section 3554, 3555, or 3556 may be imposed in addition to the sentence required by this subsection.

(Added Pub.L. 98–473, Title II, § 212(a)(2), Oct. 12, 1984, 98 Stat. 1988, and amended Pub.L. 101–647, Title XVI, § 1602, Nov. 29, 1990, 104 Stat. 4843.)

HISTORICAL AND STATUTORY NOTES

Effective and Applicability Provisions

1998 Acts. Pub.L. 98–473, Title II, § 235, Oct. 12, 1984, 98 Stat. 2032, as amended Pub.L. 99–217, §§ 2, 4, Dec. 26, 1985, 99 Stat. 1728; Pub.L. 99–646, § 35, Nov. 10, 1986, 100 Stat. 3599; Pub.L. 100–182, § 2, Dec. 7, 1987, 101 Stat. 1266; Pub.L. 104–232, § 4, Oct. 2, 1996, 110 Stat. 3056, provided that:

"**(a)(1)** This chapter [see Short Title note under this section] shall take effect on the first day of the first calendar month beginning 36 months after the date of enactment [Oct. 12, 1984] and shall apply only to offenses committed after the taking effect of this chapter, except that—

"**(A)** the repeal of chapter 402 of title 18, United States Code [section 5005 et seq. of this title], shall take effect on the date of enactment;

"**(B)(i)** chapter 58 of title 28, United States Code [section 991 et seq. of Title 28, Judiciary and Judicial Procedure], shall take effect on the date of enactment of this Act [Oct. 12, 1984] or October 1, 1983, whichever occurs later, and the United States Sentencing Commission shall submit the initial sentencing guidelines promulgated under section 994(a)(1) of title 28 to the Congress within 30 months of the effective date of such chapter 58; and

"**(ii)** the sentencing guidelines promulgated pursuant to section 994(a)(1) shall not go into effect until—

"**(I)** the United States Sentencing Commission has submitted the initial set of sentencing guidelines to the Congress pursuant to subparagraph (B)(i), along with a report stating the reasons for the Commission's recommendations;

"**(II)** the General Accounting Office [now Government Accountability Office] has undertaken a study of the guidelines, and their potential impact in comparison with the operation of the existing sentencing and parole release system, and has, within one hundred and fifty days of submission of the guidelines, reported to the Congress the results of its study; and

"**(III)** the day after the Congress has had six months after the date described in subclause (I) in which to examine the guidelines and consider the reports; and

"**(IV)** section 212(a)(2) [enacting chapter 227, sentences, comprised of sections 3551 to 3559, 3561 to 3566, 3571 to 3574, and 3581 to 3586; and chapter 229, post-sentence administration, comprised of sections 3601 to 3607, 3611 to 3615, and 3621 to 3625 of this title; and repealing former chapter 227, sentence, judgment, and execution, comprised of sections 3561 to 3580; former chapter 229, fines, penalties, and forfeitures, comprised of sections 3611 to 3620; and former chapter 231, probation, comprised of sections 3651 to 3656 of this title] takes effect, in the case of the initial sentencing guidelines so promulgated.

"**(2)** For the purposes of section 992(a) of title 28, the terms of the first members of the United States Sentencing Commission shall not begin to run until the sentencing guidelines go into effect pursuant to paragraph (1)(B)(ii).

"**(b)(1)** The following provisions of law in effect on the day before the effective date of this Act shall remain in effect for five years after the effective date as to an individual who committed an offense or an act of juvenile delinquency before the effective date and as to a term of imprisonment during the period described in subsection (a)(1)(B):

"**(A)** Chapter 311 of title 18, United States Code.

"**(B)** Chapter 309 of title 18, United States Code.

"**(C)** Sections 4251 through 4255 of title 18, United States Code.

"**(D)** Sections 5041 and 5042 of title 18, United States Code.

"**(E)** Sections 5017 through 5020 of title 18, United States Code, as to a sentence imposed before the date of enactment [Oct. 12, 1984].

"**(F)** The maximum term of imprisonment in effect on the effective date for an offense committed before the effective date.

"**(G)** Any other law relating to a violation of a condition of release or to arrest authority with regard to a person who violates a condition of release.

["(2) Repealed. Pub.L. 104–232, § 4, Oct. 2, 1996, 110 Stat. 3056]

"(3) The United States Parole Commission shall set a release date, for an individual who will be in its jurisdiction the day before the expiration of five years after the effective date of this Act, pursuant to section 4206 of title 18, United States Code. A release date set pursuant to this paragraph shall be set early enough to permit consideration of an appeal of the release date, in accordance with Parole Commission procedures, before the expiration of five years following the effective date of this Act.

"(4) Notwithstanding the other provisions of this subsection, all laws in effect on the day before the effective date of this Act pertaining to an individual who is—

"(A) released pursuant to a provision listed in paragraph (1); and

"(B)(i) subject to supervision on the day before the expiration of the five-year period following the effective date of this Act; or

"(ii) released on a date set pursuant to paragraph (3);

"including laws pertaining to terms and conditions of release, revocation of release, provision of counsel, and payment of transportation costs, shall remain in effect as to the individual until the expiration of his sentence, except that the district court shall determine, in accord with the Federal Rules of Criminal Procedure, whether release should be revoked or the conditions of release amended for violation of a condition of release.

"(5) Notwithstanding the provisions of section 991 of title 28, United States Code, and sections 4351 and 5002 of title 18, United States Code, the Chairman of the United States Parole Commission or his designee shall be a member of the National Institute of Corrections, and the Chairman of the United States Parole Commission shall be a member of the Advisory Corrections Council and a nonvoting member of the United States Sentencing Commission, ex officio, until the expiration of the five-year period following the effective date of this Act. Notwithstanding the provisions of section 4351 of title 18, during the five-year period the National Institute of Corrections shall have seventeen members, including seven ex officio members. Notwithstanding the provisions of section 991 of title 28, during the five-year period the United States Sentencing Commission shall consist of nine members, including two ex officio, nonvoting members."

[Pub.L. 107–273, Div. C, Title I, § 11017(a), Nov. 2, 2002, 116 Stat. 1824, provided that: "For purposes of section 235(b) of the Sentencing Reform Act of 1984 (98 Stat. 2032) [section 235(b) of Pub.L. 98–473, set out as a note under this section], as such section relates to chapter 311 of title 18, United States Code [18 U.S.C.A. § 4201 et seq. (repealed)], and the Parole Commission, each reference in such section to 'fifteen years' or 'fifteen-year period' shall be deemed to be a reference to 'eighteen years' or 'eighteen-year period', respectively." See also section 11017(b) and (c) of Pub.L. 107–273, set out as a note under 18 U.S.C.A. § 4202]

[Pub.L. 104–232, § 3(b)(2), Oct. 2, 1996, 110 Stat. 3056, provided that: "Effective on the date such plan [an alternative plan by the Attorney General for the transfer of the United States Parole Commission's functions to another entity within the Department of Justice pursuant to section 3 of Pub.L. 104–232, set out as a note under section 4201 of this title] takes effect, paragraphs (3) and (4) of section 235 (b) of the Sentencing Reform Act of 1984 (98 Stat. 2032) [section 235(b)(3) and (4) of Pub.L. 98–473, set out above] are repealed."]

[Pub.L. 104–232, § 2(a), Oct. 2, 1996, 110 Stat. 3055, provided that: "For purposes of section 235(b) of the Sentencing Reform Act of 1984 (98 Stat. 2032) [section 235(b) of Pub.L. 98–473, set out as a note under this section], as it related to chapter 311 of title 18, United States Code [18 U.S.C.A. § 4201 et seq. (repealed)], and the Parole Commission, each reference in such section to 'ten years' or 'ten-year period' shall be deemed to be a reference to 'fifteen years' or 'fifteen-year period', respectively."]

[Pub.L. 101–650, Title III, § 316, Dec. 1, 1990, 104 Stat. 5115, provided that: "For the purposes of section 235(b) of Public Law 98–473 [set out as a note under this section] as it relates to chapter 311 of title 18, United States Code [18 U.S.C.A. § 4201 et seq. (repealed)], and the United States Parole Commission, each reference in such section to 'five years' or a 'five-year period', shall be deemed a reference to 'ten years' or a 'ten-year period', respectively."]

[For termination, effective May 15, 2000, of reporting provisions of Pub.L. 98–473, § 235(a)(1)(B)(ii)(II), relating to U.S. Sentencing Commission guidelines study, set out above, see Pub.L. 104–66, § 3003, as amended, set out as a note under 31 U.S.C.A. § 1113, and the 8th item on page 5 of House Document No. 103–7.]

Short Title

2005 Amendments. Pub.L. 109–76, § 1, Sept. 29, 2005, 119 Stat. 2035, provided that: "This Act [enacting provisions set out as notes under this section and 28 U.S.C.A. § 994] may be cited as the 'United States Parole Commission Extension and Sentencing Commission Authority Act of 2005'."

1998 Amendments. Section 211 of Pub.L. 98–473 provided that: "This chapter [enacting this chapter, chapters 229 and 232 and section 3742 of this title, sections 991 to 998 of Title 28, Judiciary and Judicial Procedure, and rule 9 of the Rules of Procedure for the Trial of Misdemeanors Before United States Magistrates, amending sections 924, 1161, 1761, 2114, 3006A, 3143, 3147, 3156, 3172, 3401, 3670, 4004, 4082, 4101, 4105, 4106, 4108, 4321, 4351, 5002, 5037, and 5042 of this title, rules 6, 32, 35, 38, 40, and 54 of the Federal Rules of Criminal Procedure, sections 1182 and 1252 of Title 8, Aliens and Nationality, sections 460k–3 and 460n–8 of Title 16, Conservation, sections 841, 844, 845, 848, 960, and 962 of Title 21, Food and Drugs, section 114 of Title 23, Highways, section 5871 of Title 26, Internal Revenue Code, sections 509, 591, and 2901 of Title 28, Judiciary and Judicial Procedure, sections 504, 1111, and 1695 of Title 29, Labor, sections 257 and 259 of Title 42, The Public Health and Welfare, sections 1472 and 11507 of Title 49, Transportation, and section 460 of the Appendix to Title 50, War and National Defense, redesignating sections 3577–3580, 3611, 3612, 3615, 3617–3620, and 3656 of this title, repealing sections 1, 3012, 3561–3576, 3613, 3614, 3651–3655, 4084, 4085, 4161–4166, 4201–4218, 4251–4255, 4281, 4283, 4284, 5005, 5006, 5010–5026, and 5041 of this title and section 849 of Title 21, and enacting provisions set out as notes under this section and sections 3612 of this title and 994 of title 28] may be cited as the 'Sentencing Reform Act of 1984'."

1996 Amendments. Pub.L. 104–132, Title II, § 201, Apr. 24, 1996, 110 Stat. 1227, provided that: "This subtitle [enacting sections 3613A and 3663A of this title, amending sections 2248, 2259, 2264, 2327, 3013, 3556, 3563, 3572, 3611, 3612, 3613, 3614, 3663, and 3664 of this title and Rule 32 of the Federal Rules of Criminal Procedure, and enacting provisions set out as notes under this section, section 2248 of this title and section 994 of Title 28, Judiciary and Judicial Procedure] may be cited as the 'Mandatory Victims Restitution Act of 1996'."

1987 Amendments. Pub.L. 100–182, § 1, Dec. 7, 1987, 101 Stat. 1266, provided that: "This Act [amending sections 3006A, 3551 note, 3553, 3561, 3563, 3564, 3583, 3663, 3672, 3742, and 4106 of this title, section 994 of Title 28, Judiciary and Judicial Procedure, and sections 504 and 1111 of Title 29, Labor, and enacting provisions set out as notes under this section and section 3553 of this title, section 994 of Title 28, and rule 35, Federal Rules of Criminal Procedure] may be cited as the 'Sentencing Act of 1987'."

1985 Amendments. Pub.L. 99–217, § 1, Dec. 26, 1985, 99 Stat. 1728, provided that: "This Act [amending section 994 of Title 28, Judiciary and Judicial Procedure, and a provision set out as a note under this section] may be cited as the 'Sentencing Reform Amendments Act of 1985'."

Extension of Existence of the Parole Commission

Pub.L. 109–76, § 2, Sept. 29, 2005, 119 Stat. 2035, provided that: "For purposes of section 235(b) of the Sentencing Reform Act of 1984 (98 Stat. 2032) [Pub.L. 98–473, Title II, § 235, Oct. 12, 1984, 98 Stat. 2032, as amended, set out as a note under this section] as such section relates to chapter 311 of title 18, United States Code, [18 U.S.C.A. § 4201 et seq.] and the United States Parole Commission, each reference in such section to 'eighteen years' or 'eighteen-year period' shall be deemed a reference to '21 years' or '21-year period', respectively."

Mandatory Victim Restitution; Promulgation of Regulations by Attorney General

Pub.L. 104–132, Title II, § 209, Apr. 24, 1996, 110 Stat. 1240, provided that: "Not later than 90 days after the date of enactment of this subtitle [Apr. 24, 1996], the Attorney General shall promulgate guidelines, or amend existing guidelines, to carry out this subtitle and the amendments made by this subtitle [see Short Title of 1996 Amendments note set out under this section] and to ensure that—

"(1) in all plea agreements negotiated by the United States, consideration is given to requesting that the defendant provide full restitution to all victims of all charges contained in the indictment or information, without regard to the counts to which the defendant actually pleaded; and

"(2) orders of restitution made pursuant to the amendments made by this subtitle are enforced to the fullest extent of the law."

[Provisions of section 209 of Pub.L. 104–132 to be effective, to the extent constitutionally permissible, for sentencing proceedings in cases in which the defendant is convicted on or after Apr. 24, 1996, see section 211 of Pub.L. 104–132, set out as a note under section 2248 of this title.]

Sentencing of Nonviolent and Nonserious Offenders; Sense of Congress

Section 239 of Pub.L. 98–473 provided that:

"Since, due to an impending crisis in prison overcrowding, available Federal prison space must be treated as a scarce resource in the sentencing of criminal defendants;

"Since, sentencing decisions should be designed to ensure that prison resources are, first and foremost, reserved for those violent and serious criminal offenders who pose the most dangerous threat to society;

"Since, in cases of nonviolent and nonserious offenders, the interests of society as a whole as well as individual victims of crime can continue to be served through the imposition of alternative sentences, such as restitution and community service;

"Since, in the two years preceding the enactment of sentencing guidelines, Federal sentencing practice should ensure that scarce prison resources are available to house violent and serious criminal offenders by the increased use of restitution, community service, and other alternative sentences in cases of nonviolent and nonserious offenders: Now, therefore, be it

"Declared, That it is the sense of the Senate that in the two years preceding the enactment of the sentencing guidelines, Federal judges, in determining the particular sentence to be imposed, consider—

"(1) the nature and circumstances of the offense and the history and characteristics of the defendant;

"(2) the general appropriateness of imposing a sentence other than imprisonment in cases in which the defendant has not been convicted of a crime of violence or otherwise serious offense; and

"(3) the general appropriateness of imposing a sentence of imprisonment in cases in which the defendant has been convicted of a crime of violence or otherwise serious offense."

§ 3552. Presentence reports

(a) Presentence investigation and report by probation officer.—A United States probation officer shall make a presentence investigation of a defendant that is required pursuant to the provisions of Rule 32(c) of the Federal Rules of Criminal Procedure, and shall, before the imposition of sentence, report the results of the investigation to the court.

(b) Presentence study and report by bureau of prisons.—If the court, before or after its receipt of a report specified in subsection (a) or (c), desires more information than is otherwise available to it as a basis for determining the sentence to be imposed on a defendant found guilty of a misdemeanor or felony, it may order a study of the defendant. The study shall be conducted in the local community by qualified consultants unless the sentencing judge finds that there is a compelling reason for the study to be done by the Bureau of Prisons or there are no adequate professional resources available in the local community to perform the study. The period of the study shall be no more than sixty days. The order shall specify the additional information that the court needs before determining the sentence to be imposed. Such an order shall be treated for administrative purposes as a provisional sentence of imprisonment for the maximum term authorized by section 3581(b) for the offense committed. The study shall inquire into such matters as are specified by the court and any other matters that the Bureau of Prisons or the professional consultants believe are pertinent to the factors set forth in section 3553(a). The period of the study may, in the discretion of the court, be extended for an additional period of not more than sixty days. By the expiration of the period of the study, or by the expiration of any extension granted by the court, the United States marshal shall, if the defendant is in custody, return the defendant to the court for final sentencing. The Bureau of Prisons or the professional consultants shall provide the court with a written report of the pertinent results of the study and make to the court whatever recommendations the Bureau or the consultants believe will be helpful to a proper resolution of the case. The report shall include recommendations of the Bureau or the consultants concerning the guidelines and policy statements, promulgated by the Sentencing Commission pursuant to 28 U.S.C. 994(a), that they believe are applicable to the defendant's case. After receiving the report and the recommendations, the court shall proceed finally to sentence the defendant in accordance with the sentencing alternatives and procedures available under this chapter.

(c) Presentence examination and report by psychiatric or psychological examiners.—If the court, before or after its receipt of a report specified in subsection (a) or (b) desires more information than is otherwise available to it as a basis for determining the mental condition of the defendant, the court may order the same psychiatric or psychological examination and report thereon as may be ordered under section 4244(b) of this title.

(d) Disclosure of presentence reports.—The court shall assure that a report filed pursuant to this section is disclosed to the defendant, the counsel for the defendant, and the attorney for the Government at least ten days prior to the date set for sentencing, unless this minimum period is waived by the defendant. The court shall provide a copy of the presentence report to the attorney for the Government to use in collecting an assessment, criminal fine, forfeiture or restitution imposed.

(Added Pub.L. 98–473, Title II, § 212(a)(2), Oct. 12, 1984, 98 Stat. 1988, and amended Pub.L. 99–646, § 7(a), Nov. 10, 1986, 100 Stat. 3593; Pub.L. 101–647, Title XXXVI, § 3625, Nov. 29, 1990, 104 Stat. 4965.)

HISTORICAL AND STATUTORY NOTES

Effective and Applicability Provisions

1998 Acts. Section effective on the first day of first calendar month beginning thirty-six months after October 12, 1984, applicable only to offenses committed after taking effect of sections 211 to 239 of Pub.L. 98–473, and except as otherwise provided for therein, see section 235 of Pub.L. 98–473, as amended, set out as a note under section 3551 of this title.

1990 Acts. Amendment by section 3625 of Pub.L. 101–647 effective 180 days after Nov. 29, 1990, see section 3631 of Pub.L. 101–647, set out as a note under section 3001 of Title 28, Judiciary and Judicial Procedure.

1986 Acts. Section 7(b) of Pub.L. 99–646 provided that: "The amendments made by this section [amending this section] shall take effect on the date of the taking effect of section 3552 of title 18, United States Code [this section]."

Use of Certain Technology to Facilitate Criminal Conduct

Pub.L. 104–294, Title V, § 501, Oct. 11, 1996, 110 Stat. 3497, provided that:

"(a) **Information.**—The Administrative Office of the United States courts shall establish policies and procedures for the inclusion in all presentence reports of information that specifically identifies and describes any use of encryption or scrambling technology that would be relevant to an enhancement under section 3C1.1 (dealing with Obstructing or Impeding the Administration of Justice) of the Sentencing Guidelines [set out in this title] or to offense conduct under the Sentencing Guidelines.

"(b) **Compiling and report.**—The United States Sentencing Commission shall—

"(1) compile and analyze any information contained in documentation described in subsection (a) relating to the use of encryption or scrambling technology to facilitate or conceal criminal conduct; and

"(2) based on the information compiled and analyzed under paragraph (1), annually report to the Congress on the nature and extent of the use of encryption or scrambling technology to facilitate or conceal criminal conduct."

§ 3553. Imposition of a sentence

(a) Factors to be considered in imposing a sentence.—The court shall impose a sentence sufficient, but not greater than necessary, to comply with the purposes set forth in paragraph (2) of this subsection. The court, in determining the particular sentence to be imposed, shall consider—

(1) the nature and circumstances of the offense and the history and characteristics of the defendant;

(2) the need for the sentence imposed—

(A) to reflect the seriousness of the offense, to promote respect for the law, and to provide just punishment for the offense;

(B) to afford adequate deterrence to criminal conduct;

(C) to protect the public from further crimes of the defendant; and

(D) to provide the defendant with needed educational or vocational training, medical care, or other correctional treatment in the most effective manner;

(3) the kinds of sentences available;

(4) the kinds of sentence and the sentencing range established for—

(A) the applicable category of offense committed by the applicable category of defendant as set forth in the guidelines—

(i) issued by the Sentencing Commission pursuant to section 994(a)(1) of title 28, United States Code, subject to any amendments made to such guidelines by act of Congress (regardless of whether such amendments have yet to be incorporated by the Sentencing Commission into amendments issued under section 994(p) of title 28); and

(ii) that, except as provided in section 3742(g), are in effect on the date the defendant is sentenced; or

(B) in the case of a violation of probation or supervised release, the applicable guidelines or policy statements issued by the Sentencing Commission pursuant to section 994(a)(3) of title 28, United States Code, taking into account any amendments made to such guidelines or policy statements by act of Congress (regardless of whether such amendments have yet to be incorporated by the Sentencing Commission into amendments issued under section 994(p) of title 28);

(5) any pertinent policy statement—

(A) issued by the Sentencing Commission pursuant to section 994(a)(2) of title 28, United States Code, subject to any amendments made to such policy statement by act of Congress (regardless of whether such amendments have yet to be incorporated by the Sentencing Commission into amendments issued under section 994(p) of title 28); and

(B) that, except as provided in section 3742(g), is in effect on the date the defendant is sentenced.[1]

(6) the need to avoid unwarranted sentence disparities among defendants with similar records who have been found guilty of similar conduct; and

(7) the need to provide restitution to any victims of the offense.

(b) Application of guidelines in imposing a sentence.—

(1) In general.—Except as provided in paragraph (2), the court shall impose a sentence of the kind, and within the range, referred to in subsection (a)(4) unless the court finds that there exists an aggravating or mitigating circumstance of a kind, or to a degree, not adequately taken into consideration by the Sentencing Commission in formulating the guidelines that should result in a sentence different from that described. In determining whether a circumstance was adequately taken into consideration, the court shall consider only the sentencing guidelines, policy statements, and official commentary of the Sentencing Commission. In the absence of an applicable sentencing guideline, the court shall impose an appropriate sentence, having due regard for the purposes set forth in subsection (a)(2). In the absence of an applicable sentencing guideline in the case of an offense other than a petty offense, the court shall also have due regard for the relationship of the sentence imposed to sentences prescribed by guidelines applicable to similar offenses and offenders, and to the applicable policy statements of the Sentencing Commission.

(2) Child crimes and sexual offenses.—

(A)[2] **Sentencing.**—In sentencing a defendant convicted of an offense under section 1201 involving a minor victim, an offense under section 1591, or an offense under chapter 71, 109A, 110, or 117, the court shall impose a sentence of the kind, and within the range, referred to in subsection (a)(4) unless—

(i) the court finds that there exists an aggravating circumstance of a kind, or to a degree, not adequately taken into consideration by the Sentencing Commission in formulating the guidelines that should result in a sentence greater than that described;

(ii) the court finds that there exists a mitigating circumstance of a kind or to a degree, that—

(I) has been affirmatively and specifically identified as a permissible ground of downward departure in the sentencing guidelines or policy statements issued under section 994(a) of title 28, taking account of any amendments to such sentencing guidelines or policy statements by Congress;

(II) has not been taken into consideration by the Sentencing Commission in formulating the guidelines; and

(III) should result in a sentence different from that described; or

(iii) the court finds, on motion of the Government, that the defendant has provided substantial assistance in the investigation or prosecution of another person who has committed an offense and that this assistance established a mitigating circumstance of a kind, or to a degree, not adequately taken into consideration by the Sentencing Commission in formulating the guidelines that should result in a sentence lower than that described.

In determining whether a circumstance was adequately taken into consideration, the court shall consider only the sentencing guidelines, policy statements, and official commentary of the Sentencing Commission, together with any amendments thereto by act of Congress. In the absence of an applicable sentencing guideline, the court shall impose an appropriate sentence, having due regard for the purposes set forth in subsection (a)(2). In the absence of an applicable sentencing guideline in the case of an offense other than a petty offense, the court shall also have due regard for the relationship of the sentence imposed to sentences prescribed by guidelines applicable to similar offenses and offenders, and to the applicable policy statements of the Sentencing Commission, together with any amendments to such guidelines or policy statements by act of Congress.

(c) Statement of reasons for imposing a sentence.—The court, at the time of sentencing, shall state in open court the reasons for its imposition of the particular sentence, and, if the sentence—

(1) is of the kind, and within the range, described in subsection (a)(4) and that range exceeds 24 months, the reason for imposing a sentence at a particular point within the range; or

(2) is not of the kind, or is outside the range, described in subsection (a)(4), the specific reason for the imposition of a sentence different from that described, which reasons must also be stated with specificity in the written order of judgment and commitment, except to the extent that the court relies upon statements received in camera in accordance with Federal Rule of Criminal Procedure 32. In the event that the court relies upon statements received in camera in accordance with Federal Rule of Criminal Procedure 32 the court shall state that such statements were so received and that it relied upon the content of such statements.

If the court does not order restitution, or orders only partial restitution, the court shall include in the statement the reason therefor. The court shall provide a transcription or other appropriate public record of the court's statement of reasons, together with the order of judgment and commitment, to the Probation System and to the Sentencing Commission,,[3] and, if the sentence includes a term of imprisonment, to the Bureau of Prisons.

(d) Presentence procedure for an order of notice.—Prior to imposing an order of notice pursuant to section 3555, the court shall give notice to the defendant and the Government that it is considering imposing such an order. Upon motion of the defendant or the Government, or on its own motion, the court shall—

(1) permit the defendant and the Government to submit affidavits and written memoranda addressing matters relevant to the imposition of such an order;

(2) afford counsel an opportunity in open court to address orally the appropriateness of the imposition of such an order; and

(3) include in its statement of reasons pursuant to subsection (c) specific reasons underlying its determinations regarding the nature of such an order.

Upon motion of the defendant or the Government, or on its own motion, the court may in its discretion employ any additional procedures that it concludes will not unduly complicate or prolong the sentencing process.

(e) Limited authority to impose a sentence below a statutory minimum.—Upon motion of the Government, the court shall have the authority to impose a sentence below a level established by statute as a minimum sentence so as to reflect a defendant's substantial assistance in the investigation or prosecution of another person who has committed an offense. Such sentence shall be imposed in accordance with the guidelines and policy statements issued by the Sentencing Commission pursuant to section 994 of title 28, United States Code.

(f) Limitation on applicability of statutory minimums in certain cases.—Notwithstanding any other provision of law, in the case of an offense under section 401, 404, or 406 of the Controlled Substances Act (21 U.S.C. 841, 844, 846) or section 1010 or 1013 of the Controlled Substances Import and Export Act (21 U.S.C. 960, 963), the court shall impose a sentence pursuant to guidelines promulgated by the United States Sentencing Commission under section 994 of title 28 without regard to any statutory minimum sentence, if the court finds at sentencing, after the Government has been afforded the opportunity to make a recommendation, that—

(1) the defendant does not have more than 1 criminal history point, as determined under the sentencing guidelines;

(2) the defendant did not use violence or credible threats of violence or possess a firearm or other dangerous weapon (or induce another participant to do so) in connection with the offense;

(3) the offense did not result in death or serious bodily injury to any person;

(4) the defendant was not an organizer, leader, manager, or supervisor of others in the offense, as determined under the sentencing guidelines and was not engaged in a continuing criminal enterprise, as defined in section 408 of the Controlled Substances Act; and

(5) not later than the time of the sentencing hearing, the defendant has truthfully provided to the Government all information and evidence the defendant has concerning the offense or offenses that were part of the same course of conduct or of a common scheme or plan, but the fact that the defendant has no relevant or useful other information to provide or that the Government is already aware of the information shall not preclude a deter-

mination by the court that the defendant has complied with this requirement.

(Added Pub.L. 98–473, Title II, § 212(a)(2), Oct. 12, 1984, 98 Stat. 1989, and amended Pub.L. 99–570, Title I, § 1007(a), Oct. 27, 1986, 100 Stat. 3207–7; Pub.L. 99–646, §§ 8(a), 9(a), 80(a), 81(a), Nov. 10, 1986, 100 Stat. 3593, 3619; Pub.L. 100–182, §§ 3, 16(a), 17, Dec. 7, 1987, 101 Stat. 1266, 1269, 1270; Pub.L. 100–690, Title VII, § 7102, Nov. 18, 1988, 102 Stat. 4416; Pub.L. 103–322, Title VIII, § 80001(a), Title XXVIII, § 280001, Sept. 13, 1994, 108 Stat. 1985, 2095; Pub.L. 104–294, Title VI, § 601(b)(5), (6), (h), Oct. 11, 1996, 110 Stat. 3499, 3500; Pub.L. 107–273, Div. B, Title IV, § 4002(a)(8), Nov. 2, 2002, 116 Stat. 1807; Pub.L. 108–21, Title IV, § 401(a), (c), (j)(5), Apr. 30, 2003, 117 Stat. 667, 669, 673.)

[1] So in original. The period probably should be a semicolon.

[2] So in original. No subpar. (B) has been enacted.

[3] So in original. The second comma probably should not appear.

Unconstitutionality of Subsec. (b)(1)

Mandatory aspect of subsec. (b)(1) of this section held unconstitutional by United States v. Booker, 543 U.S. 220, 125 S.Ct. 738, 160 L.Ed.2d 621 (2005).

HISTORICAL AND STATUTORY NOTES

References in Text

Chapters 71, 109A, 110, and 117, referred to in subsec. (b)(2), are 18 U.S.C.A. § 1460 et seq., 18 U.S.C.A. § 2241 et seq., 18 U.S.C.A. § 2251 et seq., and 18 U.S.C.A. § 2421 et seq., respectively.

Federal Rule of Criminal Procedure 32, referred to in subsec. (c)(2), is set out in the Appendix to this title.

The Controlled Substances Act, referred to in subsec. (f), is Pub.L. 91–513, Title II, Oct. 27, 1970, 84 Stat. 1242, as amended, which is classified principally to subchapter I (section 801 et seq.) of chapter 13 of Title 21, Food and Drugs. Sections 401, 404, 406, and 408 of such Act are classified to sections 841, 844, 846, and 848, respectively, of Title 21. For complete classification of this Act to the Code, see Short Title note set out under section 801 of Title 21 and Tables.

The Controlled Substances Import and Export Act, referred to in subsec. (f), is Pub.L. 91–513, Title III, Oct. 27, 1970, 84 Stat. 1285, as amended, which is classified principally to subchapter II (section 951 et seq.) of chapter 13 of Title 21, Food and Drugs. Sections 1010 and 1013 of such Act are classified to sections 960 and 963, respectively, of Title 21. For complete classification of this Act to the Code, see Short Title note set out under section 951 of Title 21 and Tables.

Effective and Applicability Provisions

1994 Acts. Section 80001(c) of Pub.L. 103–322 provided that: "The amendment made by subsection (a) [enacting subsec. (f) of this section] shall apply to all sentences imposed on or after the 10th day beginning after the date of enactment of this Act [Sept. 13, 1994]."

1987 Acts. Amendment by Pub.L. 100–182 applicable with respect to offenses committed after enactment of Pub.L. 100–182, which was approved Dec. 7, 1987, see section 26 of Pub.L. 100–182, set out as a note under section 3006A of this title.

1986 Acts. Section 8(c) of Pub.L. 99–646 provided that: "The amendments made by this section [amending subsec. (a) of this section and section 3663 of this title] shall take effect on the date of the taking effect of section 3553 of title 18, United States Code [this section]."

Section 9(b) of Pub.L. 99–646 provided that: "The amendments made by this section [amending subsec. (b) of this section] shall take effect on the date of the taking effect of section 3553 of title 18, United States Code [this section]."

Section 80(b) of Pub.L. 99–646 provided that: "The amendments made by this section [amending subsec. (d) of this section] shall take effect on the date of the taking effect of section 212(a)(2) of the Sentencing Reform Act of 1984 [set out as a note under this section]".

Section 81(b) of Pub.L. 99–646 provided that: "The amendments made by this section [amending subsec. (a) of this section] shall take effect on the date of the taking effect of section 212(a)(2) of the Sentencing Reform Act of 1984 [set out as a note under this section]".

Section 1007(b) of Pub.L. 99–570 provided that: "The amendment made by this section [enacting subsec. (e) of this section] shall take effect on the date of the taking effect of section 3553 of title 18, United States Code [this section]."

1984 Acts. Section effective on the first day of first calendar month beginning thirty-six months after Oct. 12, 1984, applicable only to offenses committed after taking effect of sections 211 to 239 of Pub.L. 98–473, and except as otherwise provided for therein, see section 235 of Pub.L. 98–473, as amended, set out as a note under section 3551 of this title.

Report by Attorney General

Pub.L. 108–21, Title IV, § 401(*l*), Apr. 30, 2003, 117 Stat. 674, provided that:

"(1) **Defined term.**—For purposes of this section [section 401 of Pub.L. 108–21, amending this section, 18 U.S.C.A. § 3742, and 28 U.S.C.A. §§ 991 and 994, and enacting provisions set out as notes under this section and 28 U.S.C.A. §§ 991 and 994], the term 'report described in paragraph (3)' means a report, submitted by the Attorney General, which states in detail the policies and procedures that the Department of Justice has adopted subsequent to the enactment of this Act [Apr. 30, 2003]—

"(A) to ensure that Department of Justice attorneys oppose sentencing adjustments, including downward departures, that are not supported by the facts and the law;

"(B) to ensure that Department of Justice attorneys in such cases make a sufficient record so as to permit the possibility of an appeal;

"(C) to delineate objective criteria, specified by the Attorney General, as to which such cases may warrant consideration of an appeal, either because of the nature or magnitude of the sentencing error, its prevalence in the district, or its prevalence with respect to a particular judge;

"(D) to ensure that Department of Justice attorneys promptly notify the designated Department of Justice component in Washington concerning such adverse sentencing decisions; and

"(E) to ensure the vigorous pursuit of appropriate and meritorious appeals of such adverse decisions.

"(2) **Report required.**—

"(A) **In general.**—Not later than 15 days after a district court's grant of a downward departure in any case, other than a case involving a downward departure for substantial assistance to authorities pursuant to section 5K1.1 of the United States Sentencing Guidelines [set out in this title], the Attorney General shall submit a report to the Committees on the Judiciary of the House of Representatives and the Senate containing the information described under subparagraph (B).

"(B) **Contents.**—The report submitted pursuant to subparagraph (A) shall set forth—

"(i) the case;

"(ii) the facts involved;

"(iii) the identity of the district court judge;

"(iv) the district court's stated reasons, whether or not the court provided the United States with advance notice of its intention to depart; and

"(v) the position of the parties with respect to the downward departure, whether or not the United States has filed, or intends to file, a motion for reconsideration.

"(C) **Appeal of the departure.**—Not later than 5 days after a decision by the Solicitor General regarding the authorization of an appeal of the departure, the Attorney General shall submit a report to the Committees on the Judiciary of the House of Representatives and the Senate that describes the decision of the Solicitor General and the basis for such decision.

"(3) **Effective date.**—Paragraph (2) shall take effect on the day that is 91 days after the date of enactment of this Act [Apr. 30, 2003], except that such paragraph shall not take effect if not more than 90 days after the date of enactment of this Act [Apr. 30, 2003] the Attorney General has submitted to the Judiciary Committees of the House of Representatives and the Senate the report described in paragraph (3)."

Authority to Lower Sentences Below Statutory Minimum for Old Offenses

Section 24 of Pub.L. 100–182 provided that: "Notwithstanding section 235 of the Comprehensive Crime Control Act of 1984 [section 235 of Pub.L. 98–473, set out as a note under section 3551 of this title]—

"(1) section 3553(e) of title 18, United States Code [subsec. (e) of this section];

"(2) rule 35(b) of the Federal Rules of Criminal Procedure as amended by section 215(b) of such Act; and

"(3) rule 35(b) as in effect before the taking effect of the initial set of guidelines promulgated by the United States Sentencing Commission pursuant to chapter 58 of title 28, United States Code [sections 991 et seq. of Title 28, Judiciary and Judicial Procedure],

shall apply in the case of an offense committed before the taking effect of such guidelines."

§ 3554. Order of criminal forfeiture

The court, in imposing a sentence on a defendant who has been found guilty of an offense described in section 1962 of this title or in title II or III of the Comprehensive Drug Abuse Prevention and Control Act of 1970 shall order, in addition to the sentence that is imposed pursuant to the provisions of section 3551, that the defendant forfeit property to the United States in accordance with the provisions of section 1963 of this title or section 413 of the Comprehensive Drug Abuse and Control Act of 1970.

(Added Pub.L. 98–473, Title II, § 212(a)(2), Oct. 12, 1984, 98 Stat. 1990.)

HISTORICAL AND STATUTORY NOTES

References in Text

The Comprehensive Drug Abuse Protection and Control Act of 1970, referred to in text, is Pub.L. 91–513, Oct. 27, 1970, 84 Stat. 1236, as amended. Titles II and III of such Act are classified principally to subchapters I (section 801 et seq.) and II (section 951 et seq.), respectively, of chapter 13 of Title 21, Food and Drugs. Section 413 of such Act is classified to section 853 of Title 21. For complete classification of this Act to the Code, see Short Title note set out under section 801 of Title 21 and Tables volume.

Effective and Applicability Provisions

1984 Acts. Section effective on the first day of first calendar month beginning thirty-six months after October 12, 1984, applicable only to offenses committed after taking effect of sections 211 to 239 of Pub.L. 98–473, and except as otherwise provided for therein, see section 235 of Pub.L. 98–473, as amended, set out as a note under section 3551 of this title.

§ 3555. Order of notice to victims

The court, in imposing a sentence on a defendant who has been found guilty of an offense involving fraud or other intentionally deceptive practices, may order, in addition to the sentence that is imposed pursuant to the provisions of section 3551, that the defendant give reasonable notice and explanation of the conviction, in such form as the court may approve, to the victims of the offense. The notice may be ordered to be given by mail, by advertising in designated areas or through designated media, or by other appropriate means. In determining whether to require the defendant to give such notice, the court shall consider the factors set forth in section 3553(a) to the extent that they are applicable and shall consider the cost involved in giving the notice as it relates to the loss caused by the offense, and shall not require the defendant to bear the costs of notice in excess of $20,000.

(Added Pub.L. 98–473, Title II, § 212(a)(2), Oct. 12, 1984, 98 Stat. 1991.)

§ 3556. Order of restitution

The court, in imposing a sentence on a defendant who has been found guilty of an offense shall order restitution in accordance with section 3663A, and may order restitution in accordance with section 3663. The procedures under section 3664 shall apply to all orders of restitution under this section.

(Added Pub.L. 98–473, Title II, § 212(a)(2), Oct. 12, 1984, 98 Stat. 1991, and amended Pub.L. 99–646, § 20(b), Nov. 10, 1986, 100 Stat. 3596; Pub.L. 104–132, Title II, § 202, Apr. 24, 1996, 110 Stat. 1227.)

HISTORICAL AND STATUTORY NOTES

Effective and Applicability Provisions

1996 Acts. Amendment by Pub.L. 104–132 to be effective, to the extent constitutionally permissible, for sentencing proceedings in cases in which the defendant is convicted on or after Apr. 24, 1996, see section 211 of Pub.L. 104–132, set out as a note under section 2248 of this title.

1986 Acts. Section 20(c) of Pub.L. 99–646 provided that: "The amendments made by this section [amending this section and section 3663 of this title] shall take effect on the date of the taking effect of section 212(a)(2) of the Sentencing Reform Act of 1984 [see Effective Date note below]."

1984 Acts. Section effective on the first day of first calendar month beginning thirty-six months after Oct. 12, 1984, applicable only to offenses committed after taking effect of sections 211 to 239 of Pub.L. 98–473, and except as otherwise provided for therein, see section 235 of Pub.L. 98–473 as amended, set out as a note under section 3551 of this title.

§ 3557. Review of a sentence

The review of a sentence imposed pursuant to section 3551 is governed by the provisions of section 3742.

(Added Pub.L. 98–473, Title II, § 212(a)(2), Oct. 12, 1984, 98 Stat. 1991.)

HISTORICAL AND STATUTORY NOTES

Effective and Applicability Provisions

1984 Acts. Section effective on the first day of first calendar month beginning thirty-six months after Oct. 12, 1984, applicable only to offenses committed after taking effect of sections 211 to 239 of Pub.L. 98–473, and except as otherwise provided for therein, see section 235 of Pub.L. 98–473, as amended, set out as a note under section 3551 of this title.

§ 3558. Implementation of a sentence

The implementation of a sentence imposed pursuant to section 3551 is governed by the provisions of chapter 229.

(Added Pub.L. 98–473, Title II, § 212(a)(2), Oct. 12, 1984, 98 Stat. 1991.)

HISTORICAL AND STATUTORY NOTES

Effective and Applicability Provisions

1984 Acts. Section effective on the first day of first calendar month beginning thirty-six months after Oct. 12, 1984, applicable only to offenses committed after taking effect of sections 211 to 239 of Pub.L. 98–473, and except as otherwise provided for therein, see section 235 of Pub.L. 98–473, as amended, set out as a note under section 3551 of this title.

§ 3559. Sentencing classification of offenses

(a) Classification.—An offense that is not specifically classified by a letter grade in the section defining it, is classified if the maximum term of imprisonment authorized is—

(1) life imprisonment, or if the maximum penalty is death, as a Class A felony;

(2) twenty-five years or more, as a Class B felony;

(3) less than twenty-five years but ten or more years, as a Class C felony;

(4) less than ten years but five or more years, as a Class D felony;

(5) less than five years but more than one year, as a Class E felony;

(6) one year or less but more than six months, as a Class A misdemeanor;

(7) six months or less but more than thirty days, as a Class B misdemeanor;

(8) thirty days or less but more than five days, as a Class C misdemeanor; or

(9) five days or less, or if no imprisonment is authorized, as an infraction.

(b) Effect of classification.—Except as provided in subsection (c), an offense classified under subsection (a) carries all the incidents assigned to the applicable letter designation, except that the maximum term of imprisonment is the term authorized by the law describing the offense.

(c) Imprisonment of certain violent felons.—

(1) Mandatory life imprisonment.—Notwithstanding any other provision of law, a person who is convicted in a court of the United States of a serious violent felony shall be sentenced to life imprisonment if—

(A) the person has been convicted (and those convictions have become final) on separate prior occasions in a court of the United States or of a State of—

(i) 2 or more serious violent felonies; or

(ii) one or more serious violent felonies and one or more serious drug offenses; and

(B) each serious violent felony or serious drug offense used as a basis for sentencing under this subsection, other than the first, was committed after the defendant's conviction of the preceding serious violent felony or serious drug offense.

(2) Definitions.—For purposes of this subsection—

(A) the term "assault with intent to commit rape" means an offense that has as its elements engaging in physical contact with another person or using or brandishing a weapon against another person with intent to commit aggravated sexual abuse or sexual abuse (as described in sections 2241 and 2242);

(B) the term "arson" means an offense that has as its elements maliciously damaging or destroying any building, inhabited structure, vehicle, vessel, or real property by means of fire or an explosive;

(C) the term "extortion" means an offense that has as its elements the extraction of anything of value from another person by threatening or placing that person in fear of injury to any person or kidnapping of any person;

(D) the term "firearms use" means an offense that has as its elements those described in section 924(c) or 929(a), if the firearm was brandished, discharged, or otherwise used as a weapon and the crime of violence or drug trafficking crime during and relation to which the firearm was used was subject to prosecution in a court of the United States or a court of a State, or both;

(E) the term "kidnapping" means an offense that has as its elements the abduction, restraining, confining, or carrying away of another person by force or threat of force;

(F) the term "serious violent felony" means—

(i) a Federal or State offense, by whatever designation and wherever committed, consisting of murder (as described in section 1111); manslaughter other than involuntary manslaughter (as described in section 1112); assault with intent to commit murder (as described in section 113(a)); assault with intent to commit rape; aggravated sexual abuse and sexual abuse (as described in sections 2241 and 2242); abusive sexual contact (as described in sections 2244 (a)(1) and (a)(2)); kidnapping; aircraft piracy (as described in section 46502 of Title 49); robbery (as described in section 2111, 2113, or 2118); carjacking (as described in section 2119); extortion; arson; firearms use; firearms possession (as described in section 924(c)); or attempt, conspiracy, or solicitation to commit any of the above offenses; and

(ii) any other offense punishable by a maximum term of imprisonment of 10 years or more that has as an element the use, attempted use, or threatened use of physical force against the person of another or that, by its nature, involves a substantial risk that physical force against the person of another may be used in the course of committing the offense;

(G) the term "State" means a State of the United States, the District of Columbia, and a commonwealth, territory, or possession of the United States; and

(H) the term "serious drug offense" means—

(i) an offense that is punishable under section 401(b)(1)(A) or 408 of the Controlled Substances Act (21 U.S.C. 841(b)(1)(A), 848) or section 1010(b)(1)(A) of the Controlled Substances Import and Export Act (21 U.S.C. 960(b)(1)(A)); or

(ii) an offense under State law that, had the offense been prosecuted in a court of the United States, would have been punishable under section 401(b)(1)(A) or 408 of the Controlled Substances Act (21 U.S.C. 841(b)(1)(A), 848) or section 1010(b)(1)(A) of the Controlled Substances Import and Export Act (21 U.S.C. 960(b)(1)(A)).

(3) Nonqualifying felonies.—

(A) Robbery in certain cases.—Robbery, an attempt, conspiracy, or solicitation to commit robbery; or an offense described in paragraph (2)(F)(ii) shall not serve as a basis for sentencing under this subsection if the defendant establishes by clear and convincing evidence that—

(i) no firearm or other dangerous weapon was used in the offense and no threat of use of a firearm or other dangerous weapon was involved in the offense; and

(ii) the offense did not result in death or serious bodily injury (as defined in section 1365) to any person.

(B) Arson in certain cases.—Arson shall not serve as a basis for sentencing under this subsection if the defendant establishes by clear and convincing evidence that—

(i) the offense posed no threat to human life; and

(ii) the defendant reasonably believed the offense posed no threat to human life.

(4) Information filed by United States Attorney.—The provisions of section 411(a) of the Controlled Substances Act (21 U.S.C. 851(a)) shall apply to the imposition of sentence under this subsection.

(5) Rule of construction.—This subsection shall not be construed to preclude imposition of the death penalty.

(6) Special provision for Indian country.—No person subject to the criminal jurisdiction of an Indian tribal government shall be subject to this subsection for any offense for which Federal jurisdiction is solely predicated on Indian country (as defined in section 1151) and which occurs within the boundaries of such Indian country unless the governing body of the tribe has elected that this subsection have effect over land and persons subject to the criminal jurisdiction of the tribe.

(7) Resentencing upon overturning of prior conviction.—If the conviction for a serious violent felony or serious drug offense that was a basis for sentencing under this subsection is found, pursuant to any appropriate State or Federal procedure, to be unconstitutional or is vitiated on the explicit basis of innocence, or if the convicted person is pardoned on the explicit basis of innocence, the person serving a sentence imposed under this subsection shall be resentenced to any sentence that was available at the time of the original sentencing.

(d) Death or imprisonment for crimes against children.—

(1) In general.—Subject to paragraph (2) and notwithstanding any other provision of law, a person who is convicted of a Federal offense that is a serious violent felony (as defined in subsection (c)) or a violation of section 2422, 2423, or 2251 shall, unless the sentence of death is imposed, be sentenced to imprisonment for life, if—

(A) the victim of the offense has not attained the age of 14 years;

(B) the victim dies as a result of the offense; and

(C) the defendant, in the course of the offense, engages in conduct described in section 3591(a)(2).

(2) Exception.—With respect to a person convicted of a Federal offense described in paragraph (1), the court may impose any lesser sentence that is authorized by law to take into account any substantial assistance provided by the defendant in the investigation or prosecution of another person who has committed an offense, in accordance with the Federal Sentencing Guidelines and the policy statements of the Federal Sentencing Commission pursuant to section 994(p) of title 28, or for other good cause.

(e) Mandatory life imprisonment for repeated sex offenses against children.—

(1) In general.—A person who is convicted of a Federal sex offense in which a minor is the victim shall be sentenced to life imprisonment if the person has a prior sex conviction in which a minor was the victim, unless the sentence of death is imposed.

(2) Definitions.—For the purposes of this subsection—

(A) the term "Federal sex offense" means an offense under section 1591 (relating to sex trafficking of children), 2241 (relating to aggravated sexual abuse), 2242 (relating to sexual abuse), 2244(a)(1) (relating to abusive sexual contact), 2245 (relating to sexual abuse resulting in death), 2251 (relating to sexual exploitation of children), 2251A (relating to selling or buying of children), 2422(b) (relating to coercion and enticement of a minor into prostitution), or 2423(a) (relating to transportation of minors);

(B) the term "State sex offense" means an offense under State law that is punishable by more than one year in prison and consists of conduct that would be a Federal sex offense if, to the extent or in the manner specified in the applicable provision of this title—

(i) the offense involved interstate or foreign commerce, or the use of the mails; or

(ii) the conduct occurred in any commonwealth, territory, or possession of the United States, within the special maritime and territorial jurisdiction of the United States, in a Federal prison, on any land or building owned by, leased to, or otherwise used by or under the control of the Government of the United States, or in the Indian country (as defined in section 1151);

(C) the term "prior sex conviction" means a conviction for which the sentence was imposed before the conduct occurred constituting the subsequent Federal sex offense, and which was for a Federal sex offense or a State sex offense;

(D) the term "minor" means an individual who has not attained the age of 17 years; and

(E) the term "state" has the meaning given that term in subsection (c)(2).

(3) Nonqualifying felonies.—An offense described in section 2422(b) or 2423(a) shall not serve as a basis for sentencing under this subsection if the defendant establishes by clear and convincing evidence that—

(A) the sexual act or activity was consensual and not for the purpose of commercial or pecuniary gain;

(B) the sexual act or activity would not be punishable by more than one year in prison under the law of the State in which it occurred; or

(C) no sexual act or activity occurred.

(f) Mandatory minimum terms of imprisonment for violent crimes against children.—A person who is convicted of a Federal offense that is a crime of violence against the person of an individual who has not attained the age of 18 years shall, unless a greater mandatory minimum sentence of imprisonment is otherwise provided by law and regardless of any maximum term of imprisonment otherwise provided for the offense—

(1) if the crime of violence is murder, be imprisoned for life or for any term of years not less than 30, except that such person shall be punished by death or life imprisonment if the circumstances satisfy any of subparagraphs (A) through (D) of section 3591(a)(2) of this title;

(2) if the crime of violence is kidnapping (as defined in section 1201) or maiming (as defined in section 114), be imprisoned for life or any term of years not less than 25; and

(3) if the crime of violence results in serious bodily injury (as defined in section 1365), or if a dangerous weapon was used during and in relation to the crime of violence, be imprisoned for life or for any term of years not less than 10.

(g)(1) If a defendant who is convicted of a felony offense (other than offense of which an element is the false registration of a domain name) knowingly falsely registered a domain name and knowingly used that domain name in the course of that offense, the maximum imprisonment otherwise provided by law for that offense shall be doubled or increased by 7 years, whichever is less.

(2) As used in this section—

(A) the term "falsely registers" means registers in a manner that prevents the effective identification of or contact with the person who registers; and

(B) the term "domain name" has the meaning given that term is [1] section 45 of the Act entitled "An Act to provide for the registration and protection of trademarks used in commerce, to carry out the provisions of certain international conventions, and for other purposes" approved July 5, 1946 (commonly referred to as the "Trademark Act of 1946") (15 U.S.C. 1127).

(Added Pub.L. 98–473, Title II, § 212(a)(2), Oct. 12, 1984, 98 Stat. 1991, and amended Pub.L. 100–185, § 5, Dec. 11, 1987, 101 Stat. 1279; Pub.L. 100–690, Title VII, § 7041, Nov. 18, 1988, 102 Stat. 4399; Pub.L. 103–322, Title VII, § 70001, Sept. 13, 1994, 108 Stat. 1982; Pub.L. 105–314, Title V, § 501, Oct. 30, 1998, 112 Stat. 2980; Pub.L. 105–386, § 1(b), Nov. 13, 1998, 112 Stat. 3470; Pub.L. 108–21, Title I, § 106(a), Apr. 30, 2003, 117 Stat. 654; Pub.L. 108–482, Title II, § 204(a), Dec. 23, 2004, 118 Stat. 3917; Pub.L. 109–248, Title II, §§ 202, 206(c), July 27, 2006, 120 Stat. 612, 614.)

[1] So in original. Probably should be the word "in".

HISTORICAL AND STATUTORY NOTES

References in Text

Section 45 of the Act entitled "An Act to provide for he registration and protection of trademarks used in commerce, to carry out the provisions of certain international conventions, and for other purposes" approved July 5, 1946 (commonly referred to as the "Trademark Act of 1946"; 15 U.S.C.A. § 1127) referred to in subsec. (g)(2)(B), is Act July 5, 1946, c. 540, Title X, § 45, 60 Stat. 443, as amended, which is classified to 15 U.S.C.A. § 1127.

Effective and Applicability Provisions

1984 Acts. Section effective on the first day of first calendar month beginning thirty-six months after Oct. 12, 1984, applicable only to offenses committed after taking effect of sections 211 to 239 of Pub.L. 98–473, and except as otherwise provided for therein, see section 235 of Pub.L. 98–473, as amended, set out as a note under section 3551 of this title.

Short Title

2003 Amendments. Subsec. (e), as enacted by Pub.L. 108–21, Title I, § 106(a), Apr. 30, 2003, 117 Stat. 654, is known as the Two Strikes You're Out Act.

SUBCHAPTER B—PROBATION

SUBCHAPTER B—PROBATION [1]

[1] So in original. Subchapter analysis probably should appear at the chapter head.

HISTORICAL AND STATUTORY NOTES

1994 Amendments

Pub.L. 103–322, Title XXXIII, § 330010(3), Sept. 13, 1994, 108 Stat. 2143, directed that the analysis of sections be moved to a position below the subchapter heading. The amendment served to correct a technical error in Pub.L. 98–473 which, in enacting this subchapter, had placed the analysis above the subchapter heading.

§ 3561. Sentence of probation

(a) In general.—A defendant who has been found guilty of an offense may be sentenced to a term of probation unless—

(1) the offense is a Class A or Class B felony and the defendant is an individual;

(2) the offense is an offense for which probation has been expressly precluded; or

(3) the defendant is sentenced at the same time to a term of imprisonment for the same or a different offense that is not a petty offense.

(b) Domestic violence offenders.—A defendant who has been convicted for the first time of a domestic violence crime shall be sentenced to a term of probation if not sentenced to a term of imprisonment. The term "domestic violence crime" means a crime of violence for which the defendant may be prosecuted in a court of the United States in which the victim or intended victim is the spouse, former spouse, intimate partner, former intimate partner, child, or former child of the defendant, or any other relative of the defendant.

(c) Authorized terms.—The authorized terms of probation are—

(1) for a felony, not less than one nor more than five years;

(2) for a misdemeanor, not more than five years; and

(3) for an infraction, not more than one year.

(Added Pub.L. 98–473, Title II, § 212(a)(2), Oct. 12, 1984, 98 Stat. 1992, and amended Pub.L. 99–646, § 10(a), Nov. 10, 1986, 100 Stat. 3593; Pub.L. 100–182, § 7, Dec. 7, 1987, 101 Stat. 1267; Pub.L. 103–322, Title XXVIII, § 280004, Title XXXII, § 320921(a), Sept. 13, 1994, 108 Stat. 2096, 2130; Pub.L. 104–294, Title VI, § 604(c)(1), Oct. 11, 1996, 110 Stat. 3509.)

HISTORICAL AND STATUTORY NOTES

Effective and Applicability Provisions

1996 Acts. Amendment by section 604 of Pub.L. 104–294 effective Sept. 13, 1994, see section 604(d) of Pub.L. 104–294, set out as a note under section 13 of this title.

1987 Acts. Amendment by Pub.L. 100–182 applicable with respect to offenses committed after enactment of Pub.L. 100–182, which was approved Dec. 7, 1987, see section 26 of Pub.L. 100–182, set out as a note under section 3006A of this title.

1986 Acts. Section 10(b) of Pub.L. 99–646 provided that: "The amendment made by this section [amending subsec. (a) of this section] shall take effect on the date of the taking effect of such section 3561(a) [subsec. (a) of this section]."

1984 Acts. Section effective on the first day of first calendar month beginning thirty-six months after Oct. 12, 1984,. applicable only to offenses committed after taking effect of sections 211 to 239 of Pub.L. 98–473, and except as otherwise provided for therein, see section 235 of Pub.L. 98–473, as amended, set out as a note under section 3551 of this title.

Prior Provisions

For a prior section 3561, applicable to offenses committed prior to Nov. 1, 1987, see note set out preceding section 3551 of this title.

§ 3562. Imposition of a sentence of probation

(a) Factors to be considered in imposing a term of probation.—The court, in determining whether to impose a term of probation, and, if a term of probation is to be imposed, in determining the length of the term and the conditions of probation, shall consider the factors set forth in section 3553(a) to the extent that they are applicable.

(b) Effect of finality of judgment.—Notwithstanding the fact that a sentence of probation can subsequently be—

(1) modified or revoked pursuant to the provisions of section 3564 or 3565;

(2) corrected pursuant to the provisions of rule 35 of the Federal Rules of Criminal Procedure and section 3742; or

(3) appealed and modified, if outside the guideline range, pursuant to the provisions of section 3742;

a judgment of conviction that includes such a sentence constitutes a final judgment for all other purposes.

(Added Pub.L. 98–473, Title II, § 212(a)(2), Oct. 12, 1984, 98 Stat. 1992, and amended Pub.L. 101–647, Title XXXV, § 3583, Nov. 29, 1990, 104 Stat. 4930.)

HISTORICAL AND STATUTORY NOTES

References in Text

The Federal Rules of Criminal Procedure, referred to in text, are set out in Title 18.

Effective and Applicability Provisions

1984 Acts. Section effective on the first day of first calendar month beginning thirty-six months after Oct. 12, 1984, applicable only to offenses committed after taking effect of sections 211 to 239 of Pub.L. 98–473, and except as otherwise provided for therein, see section 235 of Pub.L. 98–473, as amended, set out as a note under section 3551 of this title.

Prior Provisions

For a prior section 3562, applicable to offenses committed prior to Nov. 1, 1987, see note set out preceding section 3551 of this title.

§ 3563. Conditions of probation

(a) Mandatory conditions.—The court shall provide, as an explicit condition of a sentence of probation—

(1) for a felony, a misdemeanor, or an infraction, that the defendant not commit another Federal, State, or local crime during the term of probation;

(2) for a felony, that the defendant also abide by at least one condition set forth in subsection (b)(2), (b)(3), or (b)(13), unless the court finds on the record that extraordinary circumstances exist that would make such a condition plainly unreasonable, in which event the court shall impose one or more of the other conditions set forth under subsection (b);

(3) for a felony, a misdemeanor, or an infraction, that the defendant not unlawfully possess a controlled substance;

(4) for a domestic violence crime as defined in section 3561(b) by a defendant convicted of such an offense for the first time that the defendant attend a public, private, or private nonprofit offender rehabilitation program that has been approved by the court, in consultation with a State Coalition Against Domestic Violence or other appropriate experts, if an approved program is readily available within a 50-mile radius of the legal residence of the defendant; and

(5) for a felony, a misdemeanor, or an infraction, that the defendant refrain from any unlawful use of a controlled substance and submit to one drug test within 15 days of release on probation and at least 2 periodic drug tests thereafter (as determined by the court) for use of a controlled substance, but the condition stated in this paragraph may be ameliorated or suspended by the court for any individual defendant if the defendant's presentence report or other reliable sentencing information indicates a low risk of future substance abuse by the defendant;

(6) that the defendant—

(A) make restitution in accordance with sections 2248, 2259, 2264, 2327, 3663, 3663A, and 3664; and

(B) pay the assessment imposed in accordance with section 3013;

(7) that the defendant will notify the court of any material change in the defendant's economic circumstances that might affect the defendant's ability to pay restitution, fines, or special assessments;

(8) for a person required to register under the Sex Offender Registration and Notification Act, that the person comply with the requirements of that Act; and

(9) that the defendant cooperate in the collection of a DNA sample from the defendant if the collection of such a sample is authorized pursuant to section 3 of the DNA Analysis Backlog Elimination Act of 2000.

If the court has imposed and ordered execution of a fine and placed the defendant on probation, payment of the fine or adherence to the court-established installment schedule shall be a condition of the probation.

(b) Discretionary conditions.—The court may provide, as further conditions of a sentence of probation, to the extent that such conditions are reasonably related to the factors set forth in section 3553(a)(1) and (a)(2) and to the extent that such conditions involve only such deprivations of liberty or property as are reasonably necessary for the purposes indicated in section 3553(a)(2), that the defendant—

(1) support his dependents and meet other family responsibilities;

(2) make restitution to a victim of the offense under section 3556 (but not subject to the limitation of section 3663(a) or 3663A(c)(1)(A));

(3) give to the victims of the offense the notice ordered pursuant to the provisions of section 3555;

(4) work conscientiously at suitable employment or pursue conscientiously a course of study or vocational training that will equip him for suitable employment;

(5) refrain, in the case of an individual, from engaging in a specified occupation, business, or profession bearing a reasonably direct relationship to the conduct constituting the offense, or engage in such a specified occupation, business, or profession only to a stated degree or under stated circumstances;

(6) refrain from frequenting specified kinds of places or from associating unnecessarily with specified persons;

(7) refrain from excessive use of alcohol, or any use of a narcotic drug or other controlled substance, as defined in section 102 of the Controlled Substances Act (21 U.S.C. 802), without a prescription by a licensed medical practitioner;

(8) refrain from possessing a firearm, destructive device, or other dangerous weapon;

(9) undergo available medical, psychiatric, or psychological treatment, including treatment for drug or alcohol dependency, as specified by the court, and remain in a specified institution if required for that purpose;

(10) remain in the custody of the Bureau of Prisons during nights, weekends, or other intervals of time, totaling no more than the lesser of one year or the term of imprisonment authorized for the offense, during the first year of the term of probation;

(11) reside at, or participate in the program of, a community corrections facility (including a facility maintained or under contract to the Bureau of Prisons) for all or part of the term of probation;

(12) work in community service as directed by the court;

(13) reside in a specified place or area, or refrain from residing in a specified place or area;

(14) remain within the jurisdiction of the court, unless granted permission to leave by the court or a probation officer;

(15) report to a probation officer as directed by the court or the probation officer;

(16) permit a probation officer to visit him at his home or elsewhere as specified by the court;

(17) answer inquiries by a probation officer and notify the probation officer promptly of any change in address or employment;

(18) notify the probation officer promptly if arrested or questioned by a law enforcement officer;

(19) remain at his place of residence during nonworking hours and, if the court finds it appropriate, that compliance with this condition be monitored by telephonic or electronic signaling devices, except that a condition under this paragraph may be imposed only as an alternative to incarceration;

(20) comply with the terms of any court order or order of an administrative process pursuant to the law of a State, the District of Columbia, or any other possession or territory of the United States, requiring payments by the defendant for the support and maintenance of a child or of a child and the parent with whom the child is living;

(21) be ordered deported by a United States district court, or United States magistrate judge, pursuant to a stipulation entered into by the defendant and the United States under section 238(d)(5) of the Immigration and Nationality Act, except that, in the absence of a stipulation, the United States district court or a United States magistrate judge, may order deportation as a condition of probation, if, after notice and hearing pursuant to such section,

the Attorney General demonstrates by clear and convincing evidence that the alien is deportable;

(22) satisfy such other conditions as the court may impose or;

(23) if required to register under the Sex Offender Registration and Notification Act, submit his person, and any property, house, residence, vehicle, papers, computer, other electronic communication or data storage devices or media, and effects to search at any time, with or without a warrant, by any law enforcement or probation officer with reasonable suspicion concerning a violation of a condition of probation or unlawful conduct by the person, and by any probation officer in the lawful discharge of the officer's supervision functions.

(c) Modifications of conditions.—The court may modify, reduce, or enlarge the conditions of a sentence of probation at any time prior to the expiration or termination of the term of probation, pursuant to the provisions of the Federal Rules of Criminal Procedure relating to the modification of probation and the provisions applicable to the initial setting of the conditions of probation.

(d) Written statement of conditions.—The court shall direct that the probation officer provide the defendant with a written statement that sets forth all the conditions to which the sentence is subject, and that is sufficiently clear and specific to serve as a guide for the defendant's conduct and for such supervision as is required.

(e) Results of drug testing.—The results of a drug test administered in accordance with subsection (a)(5) shall be subject to confirmation only if the results are positive, the defendant is subject to possible imprisonment for such failure, and either the defendant denies the accuracy of such test or there is some other reason to question the results of the test. A defendant who tests positive may be detained pending verification of a positive drug test result. A drug test confirmation shall be a urine drug test confirmed using gas chromatography/mass spectrometry techniques or such test as the Director of the Administrative Office of the United States Courts after consultation with the Secretary of Health and Human Services may determine to be of equivalent accuracy. The court shall consider whether the availability of appropriate substance abuse treatment programs, or an individual's current or past participation in such programs, warrants an exception in accordance with United States Sentencing Commission guidelines from the rule of section 3565(b), when considering any action against a defendant who fails a drug test administered in accordance with subsection (a)(5).

(Added Pub.L. 98–473, Title II, § 212(a)(2), Oct. 12, 1984, 98 Stat. 1993, and amended Pub.L. 99–646, §§ 11(a), 12(a), Nov. 10, 1986, 100 Stat. 3594; Pub.L. 100–182, §§ 10, 18, Dec. 7, 1987, 101 Stat. 1267, 1270; Pub.L. 100–690, Title VII, §§ 7086, 7110, 7303(a)(1), 7305(a), Nov. 18, 1988, 102 Stat. 4408, 4419, 4464, 4465; Pub.L. 101–647, Title XXXV, § 3584, Nov. 29, 1990, 104 Stat. 4930; Pub.L. 102–521, § 3, Oct. 25, 1992, 106 Stat. 3404; Pub.L. 103–322, Title II, § 20414(b), Title XXVIII, § 280002, Title XXXII, § 320921(b), Sept. 13, 1994, 108 Stat. 1830, 2096, 2130; Pub.L. 104–132, Title II, § 203, Apr. 24, 1996, 110 Stat. 1227; Pub.L. 104–208, Div. C, Title III, §§ 308(g)(10)(E), 374(b), Sept. 30, 1996, 110 Stat. 3009–625, 3009–647; Pub.L. 104–294, Title VI, § 601(k), Oct. 11, 1996, 110 Stat. 3501; Pub.L. 105–119, Title I, § 115(a)(8)(B)(i) to (iii), Nov. 26, 1997, 111 Stat. 2465; Pub.L. 106–546, § 7(a), Dec. 19, 2000, 114 Stat. 2734; Pub.L. 107–273, Div. B, Title IV, § 4002(c)(1), (e)(12), Nov. 2, 2002, 116 Stat. 1808, 1811; Pub.L. 109–248, Title I, § 141(d), Title II, § 210(a), July 27, 2006, 120 Stat. 603, 615.)

HISTORICAL AND STATUTORY NOTES

References in Text

The Sex Offender Registration and Notification Act, referred to in subsec. (a)(8), is Title I [§ 101 et seq.] of Pub.L. 109–248, July 27, 2006, 120 Stat. 590, which enacted subchapter I of Chapter 151 of Title 42, 42 U.S.C.A. § 16901 et seq.; for complete classification, see Short Title note set out under 42 U.S.C.A. § 16901 and Tables.

Section 3 of the DNA Analysis Backlog Elimination Act of 2000, referred to in subsec. (a)(9), is Pub.L. 106–546, § 3, Dec. 19, 2000, 114 Stat. 2728, which is classified to section 14135a of Title 42.

Section 238(d)(5) of the Immigration and Nationality Act, referred to in subsec. (b)(21), is section 238(d)(5) of Act June 27, 1952, as added, amended, and redesignated, which is classified to section 1228(c)(5) of Title 8, Aliens and Nationality.

The Sex Offender Registration and Notification Act, referred to in subsec. (b)(23), is Pub.L. 109–248, Title I [§ 101 et seq.], July 27, 2006, 120 Stat. 590, which is classified principally to chapter 151 of Title 42, 42 U.S.C.A. § 16901 et seq. For complete classification, see Short Title note set out under 42 U.S.C.A. § 16901 and Tables.

The Federal Rules of Criminal Procedure, referred to in subsec. (c), are set out in this title.

The United States Sentencing Commission guidelines, referred to in subsec. (e), are the Federal Sentencing Guidelines, set out in this title.

Codifications

Amendment by section 3584(1) of Pub.L. 101–647 directed the substitution of "defendant" for "defendent" in subsec. (a)(3). Such substitution had already been editorially executed, therefore, no further change was required.

Section 601(k) of Pub.L. 104–294, which directed that subsec. (a) of be amended by striking "and" at the end of par. (3); by striking the period at the end of first par. (4) and inserting "; and"; by redesignating the second par. (4) as (5); and by placing pars. (4) and (5), as so amended and redesignated, in numerical order, was incapable of execution except for insertion of "; and" due to prior amendment by section 203(1)(A) to (C) of Pub.L. 104–132. See also 2002 and 1996 Amendments notes set out under this section.

Amendment by section 115(a)(8)(B)(i) of Pub.L. 105–119 was executed to the matter following subsec. (a)(7), as the probable intent of Congress, despite directory language purporting to require the execution of such amendment "at the end" of par. (7).

Amendment by section 115(a)(8)(B)(ii) of Pub.L. 105–119, which directed that "The matter inserted by subparagraph (A)" at the end of this section be amended, was executed to "the matter inserted by subparagraph (B)(i)" at the end of this section, as the probable intent of Congress.

Amendment by section 115(a)(8)(B)(iii)(IV) of Pub.L. 105–119, enacting subsec. (a)(8), was executed by inserting par. (8) immediately following par. (7), as the probable intent of Congress, despite directory language purporting to amend by making such insertion following par. (7) "as moved by clause (i) [section 115(a)(8)(B)(i) of Pub.L. 105–119]" which would, if followed literally, result in insertion of par. (8) following subsec. (e) of this section. See 1997 Amendments notes for subsecs. (a) and (e) of this section.

Effective and Applicability Provisions

2002 Acts. Amendment by section 4002(c)(1) of Pub.L. 107–273, as therein provided, effective Oct. 11, 1996, which is the date of enactment of Pub.L. 104–294, to which such amendment relates.

Amendment by section 4002(e)(12) of Pub.L. 107–273, as therein provided, effective Nov. 26, 1997, which is the date of enactment of Pub.L. 105–119, to which such amendment relates.

1997 Acts. Amendment by section 115 of Pub.L. 105–119 to take effect 1 year after Nov. 26, 1997, except that States shall have 3 years from Nov. 26, 1997, to implement amendments made by Pub.L. 104–119 which impose new requirements under subchapter VI (section 14071 et seq.) of chapter 136 of Title 42, The Public Health and Welfare, and the Attorney General may grant an additional 2 years to a State that is making good faith efforts to implement these amendments, see section 115(c) of Pub.L. 105–119, set out as a note under section 14071 of Title 42.

1996 Acts. Amendment by section 308(g)(10)(E) of Div. C of Pub.L. 104–208 effective, with certain exceptions and subject to certain transitional rules, on the first day of the first month beginning more than 180 days after Sept. 30, 1996, see section 309 of Div. C of Pub.L. 104–208, set out as a note under section 1101 of Title 8, Aliens and Nationality.

Amendment by Pub.L. 104–132 to be effective, to the extent constitutionally permissible, for sentencing proceedings in cases in which the defendant is convicted on or after Apr. 24, 1996, see section 211 of Pub.L. 104–132, set out as a note under section 2248 of this title.

1988 Acts. Section 7303(d) of Pub.L. 100–690 provided that: "The amendments made by this section [amending this section and sections 3565, 3583, 4209, and 4214 of this title] shall apply with respect to persons whose probation, supervised release, or parole begins after December 31, 1988."

1987 Acts. Amendment by Pub.L. 100–182 applicable with respect to offenses committed after enactment of Pub.L. 100–182, which was approved Dec. 7, 1987, see section 26 of Pub.L. 100–182, set out as a note under section 3006A of this title.

1986 Acts. Section 11(b) of Pub.L. 99–646 provided that: "The amendment made by this section [amending subsec. (b)(11) of this section] shall take effect on the date of the taking effect of such section 3563(b)(11) [subsec. (b)(11) of this section]."

Section 12(c)(1) of Pub.L. 99–646 provided that: "The amendments made by subsection (a) [amending subsec. (c) of this section] shall take effect on the date of the taking effect of such section 3563(c) [subsec. (c) of this section]."

1984 Acts. Section effective on the first day of first calendar month beginning thirty-six months after Oct. 12, 1984, applicable only to offenses committed after taking effect of sections 211 to 239 of Pub.L. 98–473, and except as otherwise provided for therein, see section 235 of Pub.L. 98–473, as amended, set out as a note under section 3551 of this title.

Repeals

Section 601(k) of Pub.L. 104–294, cited in the credit of this section, was repealed by section 4002(c)(1) of Pub.L. 107–273, effective Oct. 11, 1996.

Severability of Provisions

If any provision of Division C of Pub.L. 104–208 or the application of such provision to any person or circumstances is held to be unconstitutional, the remainder of Division C of Pub.L. 104–208 and the application of the provisions of Division C of Pub.L. 104–208 to any person or circumstance not to be affected thereby, see section 1(e) of Pub.L. 104–208, set out as a note under section 1101 of Title 8, Aliens and Nationality.

Prior Provisions

For a prior section 3563, applicable to offenses committed prior to Nov. 1, 1987, see note set out preceding section 3551 of this title.

§ 3564. Running of a term of probation

(a) Commencement.—A term of probation commences on the day that the sentence of probation is imposed, unless otherwise ordered by the court.

(b) Concurrence with other sentences.—Multiple terms of probation, whether imposed at the same time or at different times, run concurrently with each other. A term of probation runs concurrently with any Federal, State, or local term of probation, supervised release, or parole for another offense to which the defendant is subject or becomes subject during the term of probation. A term of probation does not run while the defendant is imprisoned in connection with a conviction for a Federal, State, or local crime unless the imprisonment is for a period of less than thirty consecutive days.

(c) Early termination.—The court, after considering the factors set forth in section 3553(a) to the extent that they are applicable, may, pursuant to the provisions of the Federal Rules of Criminal Procedure relating to the modification of probation, terminate a term of probation previously ordered and discharge the defendant at any time in the case of a misdemeanor or an infraction or at any time after the expiration of one year of probation in the case of a felony, if it is satisfied that such action is warranted by the conduct of the defendant and the interest of justice.

(d) Extension.—The court may, after a hearing, extend a term of probation, if less than the maximum authorized term was previously imposed, at any time prior to the expiration or termination of the term of probation, pursuant to the provisions applicable to the initial setting of the term of probation.

(e) Subject to revocation.—A sentence of probation remains conditional and subject to revocation until its expiration or termination.

(Added Pub.L. 98–473, Title II, § 212(a)(2), Oct. 12, 1984, 98 Stat. 1994, and amended Pub.L. 99–646, § 13(a), Nov. 10, 1986, 100 Stat. 3594; Pub.L. 100–182, § 11, Dec. 7, 1987, 101 Stat. 1268.)

HISTORICAL AND STATUTORY NOTES

Effective and Applicability Provisions

1987 Acts. Amendment by Pub.L. 100–182 applicable with respect to offenses committed after enactment of Pub.L. 100–182, which was approved Dec. 7, 1987, see section 26 of Pub.L. 100–182, set out as a note under section 3006A of this title.

1986 Acts. Section 13(b) of Pub.L. 99–646 provided that: "The amendments made by this section [amending subsec. (b) of this section] shall take effect on the date of the taking effect of such section 3564 [this section]."

1984 Acts. Section effective on the first day of first calendar month beginning thirty-six months after Oct. 12, 1984, applicable only to offenses committed after taking effect of sections 211 to 239 of Pub.L. 98–473, and except as otherwise provided for therein, see section 235 of Pub.L. 98–473, as amended, set out as a note under section 3551 of this title.

Prior Provisions

For a prior section 3564, applicable to offenses committed prior to Nov. 1, 1987, see note set out preceding section 3551 of this title.

§ 3565. Revocation of probation

(a) Continuation or revocation.—If the defendant violates a condition of probation at any time prior to the expiration or termination of the term of probation, the court may, after a hearing pursuant to Rule 32.1 of the Federal Rules of Criminal Procedure, and after considering the factors set forth in section 3553(a) to the extent that they are applicable—

(1) continue him on probation, with or without extending the term or modifying or enlarging the conditions; or

(2) revoke the sentence of probation and resentence the defendant under subchapter A.

(b) Mandatory revocation for possession of controlled substance or firearm or refusal to comply with drug testing.—If the defendant—

(1) possesses a controlled substance in violation of the condition set forth in section 3563(a)(3);

(2) possesses a firearm, as such term is defined in section 921 of this title, in violation of Federal law, or otherwise violates a condition of probation prohibiting the defendant from possessing a firearm;

(3) refuses to comply with drug testing, thereby violating the condition imposed by section 3563(a)(4); or

(4) as a part of drug testing, tests positive for illegal controlled substances more than 3 times over the course of 1 year;

the court shall revoke the sentence of probation and resentence the defendant under subchapter A to a sentence that includes a term of imprisonment.

(c) Delayed revocation.—The power of the court to revoke a sentence of probation for violation of a condition of probation, and to impose another sentence, extends beyond the expiration of the term of probation for any period reasonably necessary for the adjudication of matters arising before its expiration if, prior to its expiration, a warrant or summons has been issued on the basis of an allegation of such a violation.

(Added Pub.L. 98–473, Title II, § 212(a)(2), Oct. 12, 1984, 98 Stat. 1995, and amended Pub.L. 100–690, Title VI, § 6214, Title VII, § 7303(a)(2), Nov. 18, 1988, 102 Stat. 4361, 4464; Pub.L. 101–647, Title XXXV, § 3585, Nov. 29, 1990, 104 Stat. 4930; Pub.L. 103–322, Title XI, § 110506, Sept. 13, 1994, 108 Stat. 2017; Pub.L. 107–273, Div. B, Title II, § 2103(a), Nov. 2, 2002, 116 Stat. 1793.)

HISTORICAL AND STATUTORY NOTES

References in Text

The Federal Rules of Criminal Procedure, referred to in subsec. (a), are set out in this title.

Section 3563(a)(4), referred to in subsec. (b)(3), probably means par. (4) of section 3563(a) added by Pub.L. 103–322, § 20414(b)(3), which was renumbered par. (5) by Pub.L. 104–132, Title II, § 203(1)(C), Apr. 24, 1996, 110 Stat. 1227.

Effective and Applicability Provisions

1988 Acts. Amendment by section 7303(a)(2) of Pub.L. 100–690 applicable with respect to persons whose probation, supervised release, or parole begins after Dec. 31, 1988, see section 7303(d) of Pub.L. 100–690, set out as a note under section 3563 of this title.

1984 Acts. Section effective on the first day of first calendar month beginning thirty-six months after Oct. 12, 1984, applicable only to offenses committed after taking effect of sections 211 to 239 of Pub.L. 98–473, and except as otherwise provided for therein, see section 235 of Pub.L. 98–473, as amended, set out as a note under section 3551 of this title.

Prior Provisions

For a prior section 3565, applicable to offenses committed prior to Nov. 1, 1987, see note set out preceding section 3551 of this title.

§ 3566. Implementation of a sentence of probation

The implementation of a sentence of probation is governed by the provisions of subchapter A of chapter 229.

(Added Pub.L. 98–473, Title II, § 212(a)(2), Oct. 12, 1984, 98 Stat. 1995.)

HISTORICAL AND STATUTORY NOTES

Effective and Applicability Provisions

1984 Acts. Section effective on the first day of first calendar month beginning thirty-six months after Oct. 12, 1984, applicable only to offenses committed after taking effect of sections 211 to 239 of Pub.L. 98–473, and except as otherwise provided for therein, see section 235 of Pub.L. 98–473, as amended, set out as a note under section 3551 of this title.

Prior Provisions

For a prior section 3566, applicable to offenses committed prior to Nov. 1, 1987, see note set out preceding section 3551 of this title.

SUBCHAPTER C—FINES

SUBCHAPTER C—FINES[1]

[1] So in original. Subchapter analysis probably should appear at the chapter head.

§ 3571. Sentence of fine

(a) In general.—A defendant who has been found guilty of an offense may be sentenced to pay a fine.

(b) Fines for individuals.—Except as provided in subsection (e) of this section, an individual who has been found guilty of an offense may be fined not more than the greatest of—

(1) the amount specified in the law setting forth the offense;

(2) the applicable amount under subsection (d) of this section;

(3) for a felony, not more than $250,000;

(4) for a misdemeanor resulting in death, not more than $250,000;

(5) for a Class A misdemeanor that does not result in death, not more than $100,000;

(6) for a Class B or C misdemeanor that does not result in death, not more than $5,000; or

(7) for an infraction, not more than $5,000.

(c) Fines for organizations.—Except as provided in subsection (e) of this section, an organization that has been found guilty of an offense may be fined not more than the greatest of—

(1) the amount specified in the law setting forth the offense;

(2) the applicable amount under subsection (d) of this section;

(3) for a felony, not more than $500,000;

(4) for a misdemeanor resulting in death, not more than $500,000;

(5) for a Class A misdemeanor that does not result in death, not more than $200,000;

(6) for a Class B or C misdemeanor that does not result in death, not more than $10,000; and

(7) for an infraction, not more than $10,000.

(d) Alternative fine based on gain or loss.—If any person derives pecuniary gain from the offense, or if the offense results in pecuniary loss to a person other than the defendant, the defendant may be fined not more than the greater of twice the gross gain or twice the gross loss, unless imposition of a fine under this subsection would unduly complicate or prolong the sentencing process.

(e) Special rule for lower fine specified in substantive provision.—If a law setting forth an offense specifies no fine or a fine that is lower than the fine otherwise applicable under this section and such law, by specific reference, exempts the offense from the applicability of the fine otherwise applicable under this section, the defendant may not be fined more than the amount specified in the law setting forth the offense.

(Added Pub.L. 98–473, Title II, § 212(a)(2), Oct. 12, 1984, 98 Stat. 1995, and amended Pub.L. 100–185, § 6, Dec. 11, 1987, 101 Stat. 1280.)

HISTORICAL AND STATUTORY NOTES

Effective and Applicability Provisions

1984 Acts. Section effective on the first day of first calendar month beginning thirty-six months after Oct. 12, 1984, applicable only to offenses committed after taking effect of sections 211 to 239 of Pub.L. 98–473, and except as otherwise provided for therein, see section 235 of Pub.L. 98–473, as amended, set out as a note under section 3551 of this title.

Prior Provisions

For a prior section 3571, applicable to offenses committed prior to Nov. 1, 1987, see note set out preceding section 3551 of this title.

§ 3572. Imposition of a sentence of fine and related matters

(a) Factors to be considered.—In determining whether to impose a fine, and the amount, time for payment, and method of payment of a fine, the court shall consider, in addition to the factors set forth in section 3553(a)—

(1) the defendant's income, earning capacity, and financial resources;

(2) the burden that the fine will impose upon the defendant, any person who is financially dependent on the defendant, or any other person (including a government) that would be responsible for the welfare of any person financially dependent on the

defendant, relative to the burden that alternative punishments would impose;

(3) any pecuniary loss inflicted upon others as a result of the offense;

(4) whether restitution is ordered or made and the amount of such restitution;

(5) the need to deprive the defendant of illegally obtained gains from the offense;

(6) the expected costs to the government of any imprisonment, supervised release, or probation component of the sentence;

(7) whether the defendant can pass on to consumers or other persons the expense of the fine; and

(8) if the defendant is an organization, the size of the organization and any measure taken by the organization to discipline any officer, director, employee, or agent of the organization responsible for the offense and to prevent a recurrence of such an offense.

(b) Fine not to impair ability to make restitution.—If, as a result of a conviction, the defendant has the obligation to make restitution to a victim of the offense, other than the United States, the court shall impose a fine or other monetary penalty only to the extent that such fine or penalty will not impair the ability of the defendant to make restitution.

(c) Effect of finality of judgment.—Notwithstanding the fact that a sentence to pay a fine can subsequently be—

(1) modified or remitted under section 3573;

(2) corrected under rule 35 of the Federal Rules of Criminal Procedure and section 3742; or

(3) appealed and modified under section 3742;

a judgment that includes such a sentence is a final judgment for all other purposes.

(d) Time, method of payment, and related items.—(1) A person sentenced to pay a fine or other monetary penalty, including restitution, shall make such payment immediately, unless, in the interest of justice, the court provides for payment on a date certain or in installments. If the court provides for payment in installments, the installments shall be in equal monthly payments over the period provided by the court, unless the court establishes another schedule.

(2) If the judgment, or, in the case of a restitution order, the order, permits other than immediate payment, the length of time over which scheduled payments will be made shall be set by the court, but shall be the shortest time in which full payment can reasonably be made.

(3) A judgment for a fine which permits payments in installments shall include a requirement that the defendant will notify the court of any material change in the defendant's economic circumstances that might affect the defendant's ability to pay the fine. Upon receipt of such notice the court may, on its own motion or the motion of any party, adjust the payment schedule, or require immediate payment in full, as the interests of justice require.

(e) Alternative sentence precluded.—At the time a defendant is sentenced to pay a fine, the court may not impose an alternative sentence to be carried out if the fine is not paid.

(f) Responsibility for payment of monetary obligation relating to organization.—If a sentence includes a fine, special assessment, restitution, or other monetary obligation (including interest) with respect to an organization, each individual authorized to make disbursements for the organization has a duty to pay the obligation from assets of the organization. If such an obligation is imposed on a director, officer, shareholder, employee, or agent of an organization, payments may not be made, directly or indirectly, from assets of the organization, unless the court finds that such payment is expressly permissible under applicable State law.

(g) Security for stayed fine.—If a sentence imposing a fine is stayed, the court shall, absent exceptional circumstances (as determined by the court)—

(1) require the defendant to deposit, in the registry of the district court, any amount of the fine that is due;

(2) require the defendant to provide a bond or other security to ensure payment of the fine; or

(3) restrain the defendant from transferring or dissipating assets.

(h) Delinquency.—A fine or payment of restitution is delinquent if a payment is more than 30 days late.

(i) Default.—A fine or payment of restitution is in default if a payment is delinquent for more than 90 days. Notwithstanding any installment schedule, when a fine or payment of restitution is in default, the entire amount of the fine or restitution is due within 30 days after notification of the default, subject to the provisions of section 3613A.

(Added Pub.L. 98–473, Title II, § 212(a)(2), Oct. 12, 1984, 98 Stat. 1995, and amended Pub.L. 100–185, § 7, Dec. 11, 1987, 101 Stat. 1280; Pub.L. 101–647, Title XXXV, § 3587, Nov. 29, 1990, 104 Stat. 4930; Pub.L. 103–322, Title II, § 20403(a), Sept. 13, 1994, 108 Stat. 1825; Pub.L. 104–132, Title II, § 207(b), Apr. 24, 1996, 110 Stat. 1236.)

HISTORICAL AND STATUTORY NOTES

References in Text

The Federal Rules of Criminal Procedure, referred to in subsec. (c), are set out in Title 18.

Effective and Applicability Provisions

1996 Acts. Amendment by Pub.L. 104–132 to be effective, to the extent constitutionally permissible, for sentencing proceedings in cases in which the defendant is convicted on or after Apr. 24, 1996, see section 211 of Pub.L. 104–132, set out as a note under section 2248 of this title.

1984 Acts. Section effective on the first day of first calendar month beginning thirty six months after Oct. 12, 1984, applicable only to offenses committed after taking effect of sections 211 to 239 of Pub.L. 98–473, and except as otherwise provided for therein, see section 235 of Pub.L. 98–473, as amended, set out as a note under section 3551 of this title.

Prior Provisions

For a prior section 3572, applicable to offenses committed prior to Nov. 1, 1987, see note set out preceding section 3551 of this title.

§ 3573. Petition of the Government for modification or remission

Upon petition of the Government showing that reasonable efforts to collect a fine or assessment are not likely to be effective, the court may, in the interest of justice—

(1) remit all or part of the unpaid portion of the fine or special assessment, including interest and penalties;

(2) defer payment of the fine or special assessment to a date certain or pursuant to an installment schedule; or

(3) extend a date certain or an installment schedule previously ordered.

A petition under this subsection shall be filed in the court in which sentence was originally imposed, unless the court transfers jurisdiction to another court. This section shall apply to all fines and assessments irrespective of the date of imposition.

(Added Pub.L. 98–473, Title II, § 212(a)(2), Oct. 12, 1984, 98 Stat. 1997, and amended Pub.L. 100–185, § 8(a), Dec. 11, 1987, 101 Stat. 1282; Pub.L. 100–690, Title VII, § 7082(a), Nov. 18, 1988, 102 Stat. 4407.)

HISTORICAL AND STATUTORY NOTES

Effective and Applicability Provisions

1984 Acts. Section effective on the first day of first calendar month beginning thirty-six months after Oct. 12, 1984, applicable only to offenses committed after taking effect of sections 211 to 239 of Pub.L. 98–473, and except as otherwise provided for therein, see section 235 of Pub.L. 98–473, as amended, set out as a note under section 3551 of this title.

Prior Provisions

For a prior section 3573, applicable to offenses committed prior to Nov. 1, 1987, see note set out preceding section 3551 of this title.

§ 3574. Implementation of a sentence of fine

The implementation of a sentence to pay a fine is governed by the provisions of subchapter B of chapter 229.

(Added Pub.L. 98–473, Title II, § 212(a)(2), Oct. 12, 1984, 98 Stat. 1997.)

HISTORICAL AND STATUTORY NOTES

Effective and Applicability Provisions

1984 Acts. Section effective on the first day of first calendar month beginning thirty-six months after Oct. 12, 1984, applicable only to offenses committed after taking effect of sections 211 to 239 of Pub.L. 98–473, and except as otherwise provided for therein, see section 235 of Pub.L. 98–473, as amended, set out as a note under section 3551 of this title.

Prior Provisions

For a prior section 3574, applicable to offenses committed prior to Nov. 1, 1987, see note set out preceding section 3551 of this title.

SUBCHAPTER D—IMPRISONMENT

SUBCHAPTER D—IMPRISONMENT[1]

[1] So in original. Subchapter analysis probably should appear at the chapter head.

§ 3581. Sentence of imprisonment

(a) In general.—A defendant who has been found guilty of an offense may be sentenced to a term of imprisonment.

(b) Authorized terms.—The authorized terms of imprisonment are—

(1) for a Class A felony, the duration of the defendant's life or any period of time;

(2) for a Class B felony, not more than twenty-five years;

(3) for a Class C felony, not more than twelve years;

(4) for a Class D felony, not more than six years;

(5) for a Class E felony, not more than three years;

(6) for a Class A misdemeanor, not more than one year;

(7) for a Class B misdemeanor, not more than six months;

(8) for a Class C misdemeanor, not more than thirty days; and

(9) for an infraction, not more than five days.

(Added Pub.L. 98–473, Title II, § 212(a)(2), Oct. 12, 1984, 98 Stat. 1998.)

HISTORICAL AND STATUTORY NOTES

Effective and Applicability Provisions

1984 Acts. Section effective on the first day of first calendar month beginning thirty-six months after Oct. 12, 1984, applicable only to offenses committed after taking effect of sections 211 to 239 of Pub.L. 98–473, and except as otherwise provided for therein, see section 235 of Pub.L. 98–473, as amended, set out as a note under section 3551 of this title.

§ 3582. Imposition of a sentence of imprisonment

(a) Factors to be considered in imposing a term of imprisonment.—The court, in determining whether to impose a term of imprisonment, and, if a term of imprisonment is to be imposed, in determining the length of the term, shall consider the factors set forth in section 3553(a) to the extent that they are applicable, recognizing that imprisonment is not an appropriate means of promoting correction and rehabilitation. In determining whether to make a recommendation concerning the type of prison facility appropriate for the defendant, the court shall consider any pertinent policy statements issued by the Sentencing Commission pursuant to 28 U.S.C. 994(a)(2).

(b) Effect of finality of judgment.—Notwithstanding the fact that a sentence to imprisonment can subsequently be—

(1) modified pursuant to the provisions of subsection (c);

(2) corrected pursuant to the provisions of rule 35 of the Federal Rules of Criminal Procedure and section 3742; or

(3) appealed and modified, if outside the guideline range, pursuant to the provisions of section 3742;

a judgment of conviction that includes such a sentence constitutes a final judgment for all other purposes.

(c) Modification of an imposed term of imprisonment.—The court may not modify a term of imprisonment once it has been imposed except that—

(1) in any case—

(A) the court, upon motion of the Director of the Bureau of Prisons, may reduce the term of imprisonment (and may impose a term of probation or supervised release with or without conditions that does not exceed the unserved portion of the original term of imprisonment), after considering the factors set forth in section 3553(a) to the extent that they are applicable, if it finds that—

(i) extraordinary and compelling reasons warrant such a reduction; or

(ii) the defendant is at least 70 years of age, has served at least 30 years in prison, pursuant to a sentence imposed under section 3559(c), for the offense or offenses for which the defendant is currently imprisoned, and a determination has been made by the Director of the Bureau of Prisons that the defendant is not a danger to the safety of any other person or the community, as provided under section 3142(g);

and that such a reduction is consistent with applicable policy statements issued by the Sentencing Commission; and

(B) the court may modify an imposed term of imprisonment to the extent otherwise expressly permitted by statute or by Rule 35 of the Federal Rules of Criminal Procedure; and

(2) in the case of a defendant who has been sentenced to a term of imprisonment based on a sentencing range that has subsequently been lowered by the Sentencing Commission pursuant to 28 U.S.C. 994(*o*), upon motion of the defendant or the Director of the Bureau of Prisons, or on its own motion, the court may reduce the term of imprisonment, after considering the factors set forth in section 3553(a) to the extent that they are applicable, if such a reduction is consistent with applicable policy statements issued by the Sentencing Commission.

(d) Inclusion of an order to limit criminal association of organized crime and drug offenders.—The court, in imposing a sentence to a term of imprisonment upon a defendant convicted of a felony set forth in chapter 95 (racketeering) or 96 (racketeer influenced and corrupt organizations) of this title or in the Comprehensive Drug Abuse Prevention and Control Act of 1970 (21 U.S.C. 801 et seq.), or at any time thereafter upon motion by the Director of the Bureau of Prisons or a United States attorney, may include as a part of the sentence an order that requires that the defendant not associate or communicate with a specified person, other than his attorney, upon a showing of probable cause to believe that association or communication with such person is for the purpose of enabling the defendant to control, manage, direct, finance, or otherwise participate in an illegal enterprise.

(Added Pub.L. 98–473, Title II, § 212(a)(2), Oct. 12, 1984, 98 Stat. 1998, and amended Pub.L. 100–690, Title VII, § 7107, Nov. 18, 1988, 102 Stat. 4418; Pub.L. 101–647, Title XXXV, § 3588, Nov. 29, 1990, 104 Stat. 4930; Pub.L. 103–322, Title VII, § 70002, Sept. 13, 1994, 108 Stat. 1984; Pub.L. 104–294, Title VI, § 604(b)(3), Oct. 11, 1996, 110 Stat. 3506; Pub.L. 107–273, Div. B, Title III, § 3006, Nov. 2, 2002, 116 Stat. 1806.)

HISTORICAL AND STATUTORY NOTES

References in Text

The Federal Rules of Criminal Procedure, referred to in text, are set out in Title 18.

The Comprehensive Drug Abuse Prevention and Control Act of 1970, referred to in subsec. (d), is Pub.L. 91–513, Oct. 27, 1970, 84 Stat. 1236, as amended, which is classified principally to chapter 13 of Title 21, Food and Drugs [21 U.S.C.A. § 801 et seq.]. For complete classification of this Act to the Code, see Short Title note set out under section 801 of Title 21 and Tables.

Effective and Applicability Provisions

1996 Acts. Amendment by section 604 of Pub.L. 104–294 effective Sept. 13, 1994, see section 604(d) of Pub.L. 104–294, set out as a note under section 13 of this title.

1984 Acts. Section effective on the first day of first calendar month beginning thirty-six months after Oct. 12, 1984, applicable only to offenses committed after taking effect of sections 211 to 239 of Pub.L. 98–473, and except as otherwise provided for therein, see section 235 of Pub.L. 98–473, as amended, set out as a note under section 3551 of this title.

§ 3583. Inclusion of a term of supervised release after imprisonment

(a) In general.—The court, in imposing a sentence to a term of imprisonment for a felony or a misdemeanor, may include as a part of the sentence a requirement that the defendant be placed on a term of supervised release after imprisonment, except that the court shall include as a part of the sentence a requirement that the defendant be placed on a term of supervised release if such a term is required by statute or if the defendant has been convicted for the first time of a domestic violence crime as defined in section 3561(b).

(b) Authorized terms of supervised release.—Except as otherwise provided, the authorized terms of supervised release are—

(1) for a Class A or Class B felony, not more than five years;

(2) for a Class C or Class D felony, not more than three years; and

(3) for a Class E felony, or for a misdemeanor (other than a petty offense), not more than one year.

(c) Factors to be considered in including a term of supervised release.—The court, in determining whether to include a term of supervised release, and, if a term of supervised release is to be included, in determining the length of the term and the conditions of supervised release, shall consider the factors set forth in section 3553(a)(1), (a)(2)(B), (a)(2)(C), (a)(2)(D), (a)(4), (a)(5), (a)(6), and (a)(7).

(d) Conditions of supervised release.—The court shall order, as an explicit condition of supervised release, that the defendant not commit another Federal, State, or local crime during the term of supervision and that the defendant not unlawfully possess a controlled substance. The court shall order as an explicit condition of supervised release for a defendant convicted for the first time of a domestic violence crime as defined in section 3561(b) that the defendant attend a public, private, or private nonprofit offender rehabilitation program that has been approved by the court, in consultation with a State Coalition Against Domestic Violence or other appropriate experts, if an approved program is readily available within a 50-mile radius of the legal residence of the defendant. The court shall order, as an explicit condition of supervised release for a person required to register under the Sex Offender Registration and Notification Act, that the person comply with the requirements of that Act. The court shall order, as an explicit condition of supervised release, that the defendant cooperate in the collection of a DNA sample from the defendant, if the collection of such a sample is authorized pursuant to section 3 of the DNA Analysis Backlog Elimination Act of 2000. The court shall also order, as an explicit condition of supervised release, that the defendant refrain from any unlawful use of a controlled substance and submit to a drug test within 15 days of release on supervised release and at least 2 periodic drug tests thereafter (as determined by the court) for use of a controlled substance. The condition stated in the preceding sentence may be ameliorated or suspended by the court as provided in section 3563(a)(4). The results of a drug test administered in accordance with the preceding subsection shall be subject to confirmation only if the results are positive, the defendant is subject to possible imprisonment for such failure, and either the defendant denies the accuracy of such test or there is some other reason to question the results of the test. A drug test confirmation shall be a urine drug test confirmed using gas chromatography/mass spectrometry techniques or such test as the Director of the Administrative Office of the United States Courts after consultation with the Secretary of Health and Human Services may determine to be of equivalent accuracy. The court shall consider whether the availability of appropriate substance abuse treatment programs, or an individual's current or past participation in such programs, warrants an exception in accordance with United States Sentencing Commission guidelines from the rule of section 3583(g) when considering any action against a defendant who fails a drug test. The court may order, as a further condition of supervised release, to the extent that such condition—

(1) is reasonably related to the factors set forth in section 3553(a)(1), (a)(2)(B), (a)(2)(C), and (a)(2)(D);

(2) involves no greater deprivation of liberty than is reasonably necessary for the purposes set forth in section 3553(a)(2)(B), (a)(2)(C), and (a)(2)(D); and

(3) is consistent with any pertinent policy statements issued by the Sentencing Commission pursuant to 28 U.S.C. 994(a);

any condition set forth as a discretionary condition of probation in section 3563(b)(1) through (b)(10) and (b)(12) through (b)(20), and any other condition it considers to be appropriate. If an alien defendant is subject to deportation, the court may provide, as a condition of supervised release, that he be deported and remain outside the United States, and may order that he be delivered to a duly authorized immigration official for such deportation. The court may order, as an explicit condition of supervised release for a person who is a felon and required to register under the Sex Offender Registration and Notification Act, that the person submit his person, and any property, house, residence, vehicle, papers, computer, other electronic communications or data storage devices or media, and effects to search at any time, with or without a warrant, by any law enforcement or probation officer with reasonable suspicion concerning a violation of a condition of supervised release or unlawful conduct by the person, and by any probation officer in the lawful discharge of the officer's supervision functions.

(e) Modification of conditions or revocation.—The court may, after considering the factors set forth in section 3553(a)(1), (a)(2)(B), (a)(2)(C), (a)(2)(D), (a)(4), (a)(5), (a)(6), and (a)(7)—

(1) terminate a term of supervised release and discharge the defendant released at any time after the expiration of one year of supervised release, pursuant to the provisions of the Federal Rules of Criminal Procedure relating to the modification of probation, if it is satisfied that such action is warranted by the conduct of the defendant released and the interest of justice;

(2) extend a term of supervised release if less than the maximum authorized term was previously imposed, and may modify, reduce, or enlarge the conditions of supervised release, at any time prior to the expiration or termination of the term of supervised release, pursuant to the provisions of the Federal Rules of Criminal Procedure relating to the modification of probation and the provisions applicable to the initial setting of the terms and conditions of post-release supervision;

(3) revoke a term of supervised release, and require the defendant to serve in prison all or part of the term of supervised release authorized by statute for the offense that resulted in such term of supervised release without credit for time previously served on postrelease supervision, if the court, pursuant to the Federal Rules of Criminal Procedure applicable to revocation of probation or supervised release, finds by a preponderance of the evidence that the defendant violated a condition of supervised release, except that a defendant whose term is revoked under this paragraph may not be required to serve on any such revocation more than 5 years in prison if the offense that resulted in the term of supervised release is a class A felony, more than 3 years in prison if such offense is a class B felony, more than 2 years in prison if such offense is a class C or D felony, or more than one year in any other case; or

(4) order the defendant to remain at his place of residence during nonworking hours and, if the court so directs, to have compliance monitored by telephone or electronic signaling devices, except that an order under this paragraph may be imposed only as an alternative to incarceration.

(f) Written statement of conditions.—The court shall direct that the probation officer provide the defendant with a written statement that sets forth all the conditions to which the term of supervised release is subject, and that is sufficiently clear and specific to serve as a guide for the defendant's conduct and for such supervision as is required.

(g) Mandatory revocation for possession of controlled substance or firearm or for refusal to comply with drug testing.—If the defendant—

(1) possesses a controlled substance in violation of the condition set forth in subsection (d);

(2) possesses a firearm, as such term is defined in section 921 of this title, in violation of Federal law, or otherwise violates a condition of supervised release prohibiting the defendant from possessing a firearm;

(3) refuses to comply with drug testing imposed as a condition of supervised release; or

(4) as a part of drug testing, tests positive for illegal controlled substances more than 3 times over the course of 1 year;

the court shall revoke the term of supervised release and require the defendant to serve a term of imprisonment not to exceed the maximum term of imprisonment authorized under subsection (e)(3).

(h) Supervised release following revocation.—When a term of supervised release is revoked and the defendant is required to serve a term of imprisonment, the court may include a requirement that the defendant be placed on a term of supervised release after imprisonment. The length of such a term of supervised release shall not exceed the term of supervised release authorized by statute for the offense that resulted in the original term of supervised release, less any term of imprisonment that was imposed upon revocation of supervised release.

(i) Delayed revocation.—The power of the court to revoke a term of supervised release for violation of a condition of supervised release, and to order the defendant to serve a term of imprisonment and, subject to the limitations in subsection (h), a further term of supervised release, extends beyond the expiration of the term of supervised release for any period reasonably necessary for the adjudication of matters arising before its expiration if, before its expiration, a warrant or summons has been issued on the basis of an allegation of such a violation.

(j) Supervised release terms for terrorism predicates.—Notwithstanding subsection (b), the authorized term of supervised release for any offense listed in section 2332b(g)(5)(B) is any term of years or life.

(k) Notwithstanding subsection (b), the authorized term of supervised release for any offense under section 1201 involving a minor victim, and for any offense under section 1591, 2241, 2242, 2243, 2244, 2245, 2250, 2251, 2251A, 2252, 2252A, 2260, 2421, 2422, 2423, or 2425, is any term of years not less than 5, or life. If a defendant required to register under the Sex Offender Registration and Notification Act commits any criminal offense under chapter 109A, 110, or 117, or section 1201 or 1591, for which imprisonment for a term longer than 1 year can be imposed, the court shall revoke the term of supervised release and require the defendant to serve a term of imprisonment under subsection (e)(3) without regard to the exception contained therein. Such term shall be not less than 5 years.

(Added Pub.L. 98–473, Title II, § 212(a)(2), Oct. 12, 1984, 98 Stat. 1999, and amended Pub.L. 99–570, Title I, § 1006(a)(1) to (3), Oct. 27, 1986, 100 Stat. 3207–6, 3207–7; Pub.L. 99–646, § 14(a), Nov. 10, 1986, 100 Stat. 3594; Pub.L. 100–182, §§ 8, 9, 12, 25, Dec. 7, 1987, 101 Stat. 1267, 1268, 1272; Pub.L. 100–690, Title VII, §§ 7108, 7303(b), 7305(b), Nov. 18, 1988, 102 Stat. 4418, 4419, 4464 to 4466; Pub.L. 101–647, Title XXXV, § 3589, Nov. 29, 1990, 104 Stat. 4930; Pub.L. 103–322, Title II, § 20414(c), Title XI, § 110505, Title XXXII, § 320921(c), Sept. 13, 1994, 108 Stat. 1831, 2016, 2130; Pub.L. 105–119, Title I, § 115(a)(8)(B)(iv), Nov. 26, 1997, 111 Stat. 2465; Pub.L. 106–546, § 7(b), Dec. 19, 2000, 114 Stat. 2734; Pub.L. 107–56, Title VIII, § 812, Oct. 26, 2001, 115 Stat. 382; Pub.L. 107–273, Div. B, Title II, § 2103(b), Title III, § 3007, Nov. 2, 2002, 116 Stat. 1793, 1806; Pub.L. 108–21, Title I, § 101, Apr. 30, 2003, 117 Stat. 651; Pub.L. 109–177, Title II, § 212, Mar. 9, 2006, 120 Stat. 230; Pub.L. 109–248, Title I, § 141(e), Title II, § 210(b), July 27, 2006, 120 Stat. 603, 615.)

HISTORICAL AND STATUTORY NOTES

References in Text

The Sex Offender Registration and Notification Act, referred to in subsecs. (d), (k), is Title I [§ 101 et seq.] of Pub.L. 109–248, July 27, 2006, 120 Stat. 590, which enacted subchapter I of Chapter 151 of Title 42, 42 U.S.C.A. § 16901 et seq.; for complete classification, see Short Title note set out under 42 U.S.C.A. § 16901 and Tables.

Section 3 of the DNA Analysis Backlog Elimination Act of 2000, referred to in subsec. (d), is Pub.L. 106–546, § 3, Dec. 19, 2000, 114 Stat. 2728, which is classified to section 42 U.S.C.A. § 14135a.

Section 3563(a)(4), referred to in subsec. (d), probably means par. (4) of section 3563(a) added by Pub.L. 103–322, § 20414(b)(3), which was renumbered par. (5) by Pub.L. 104–132, Title II, § 203(1)(C), Apr. 24, 1996, 110 Stat. 1227.

Section 3563(b), referred to in subsec. (d), was amended by Pub.L. 105–132, Title II, § 203(2)(A), (B), Apr. 24, 1996, 110 Stat. 1227, which struck out par. (2) and redesignated former pars. (3) to (20) as (2) to (19), respectively.

The United States Sentencing Commission guidelines, referred to in subsec. (d), are the Federal Sentencing Guidelines, which are set out in this title.

The Federal Rules of Criminal Procedure, referred to in subsec. (e), are set out under this title.

Chapter 109A, referred to in subsec. (k), is chapter 109A of this title, entitled Sexual Abuse, 18 U.S.C.A. § 2241 et seq.

Chapter 110, referred to in subsec. (k), is chapter 110 of this title, entitled Sexual Exploitation and Other Abuse of Children, 18 U.S.C.A. § 2251 et seq.

Chapter 117, referred to in subsec. (k), is chapter 117 of this title, entitled Transportation for Illegal Sexual Activity and Related Crimes, 18 U.S.C.A. § 2421 et seq.

Codifications

Amendment by section 14(a)(1) of Pub.L. 99–646 to subsec. (e) catchline duplicates amendment to such subsection catchline by Pub.L. 99–570, § 1006(a)(3)(A).

Effective and Applicability Provisions

1997 Acts. Amendment by section 115 of Pub.L. 105–119 to take effect 1 year after Nov. 26, 1997, except that States shall have 3 years from Nov. 26, 1997, to implement amendments made by Pub.L. 104–119 which impose new requirements under subchapter VI (section 14071 et seq.) of chapter 136 of Title 42, The Public Health and Welfare, and the Attorney General may grant an additional 2 years to a State that is making good faith efforts to implement these amendments, see section 115(c) of Pub.L. 105–119, set out as a note under section 14071 of Title 42.

1988 Acts. Amendment by section 7303(b) of Pub.L. 100–690 applicable with respect to persons whose probation, supervised release, or parole begins after Dec. 31, 1988, see section 7303(d) of Pub.L. 100–690, set out as a note under section 3563 of this title.

1987 Acts. Amendment by Pub.L. 100–182 applicable with respect to offenses committed after enactment of Pub.L. 100–182, which was approved Dec. 7, 1987, see section 26 of Pub.L. 100–182, set out as a note under section 3006A of this title.

1986 Acts. Section 14(b) of Pub.L. 99–646 provided that: "The amendments made by this section [amending subsec. (e) of this section] shall take effect on the date of the taking effect of section 3583 of title 18, United States Code [this section]."

Section 1006(a)(4) of Pub.L. 99–570 provided that: "The amendments made by this subsection [amending subsecs. (a), (b) and (e) of this section] shall take effect on the date of the taking effect of section 3583 of title 18, United States Code [this section]."

1984 Acts. Section effective on the first day of first calendar month beginning thirty-six months after Oct. 12, 1984, applicable only to offenses committed after taking effect of sections 211 to 239 of Pub.L. 98–473, and except as otherwise provided for therein, see section 235 of Pub.L. 98–473, as amended, set out as a note under section 3551 of this title.

§ 3584. Multiple sentences of imprisonment

(a) Imposition of concurrent or consecutive terms.—If multiple terms of imprisonment are imposed on a defendant at the same time, or if a term of imprisonment is imposed on a defendant who is already subject to an undischarged term of imprisonment, the terms may run concurrently or consecutively, except that the terms may not run consecutively for an attempt and for another offense that was the sole objective of the attempt. Multiple terms of imprisonment imposed at the same time run concurrently unless the court orders or the statute mandates that the terms are to run consecutively. Multiple terms of imprisonment imposed at different times run consecutively unless the court orders that the terms are to run concurrently.

(b) Factors to be considered in imposing concurrent or consecutive terms.—The court, in determining whether the terms imposed are to be ordered to run concurrently or consecutively, shall consider, as to each offense for which a term of imprisonment is being imposed, the factors set forth in section 3553(a).

(c) Treatment of multiple sentence as an aggregate.—Multiple terms of imprisonment ordered to run consecutively or concurrently shall be treated for administrative purposes as a single, aggregate term of imprisonment.

(Added Pub.L. 98–473, Title II, § 212(a)(2), Oct. 12, 1984, 98 Stat. 2000.)

HISTORICAL AND STATUTORY NOTES

Effective and Applicability Provisions

1984 Acts. Section effective on the first day of first calendar month beginning thirty-six months after Oct. 12, 1984, applicable only to offenses committed after taking effect of sections 211 to 239 of Pub.L. 98–473, and except as otherwise provided for therein, see section 235 of Pub.L. 98–473, as amended, set out as a note under section 3551 of this title.

§ 3585. Calculation of a term of imprisonment

(a) Commencement of sentence.—A sentence to a term of imprisonment commences on the date the defendant is received in custody awaiting transportation to, or arrives voluntarily to commence service of sentence at, the official detention facility at which the sentence is to be served.

(b) Credit for prior custody.—A defendant shall be given credit toward the service of a term of imprisonment for any time he has spent in official detention prior to the date the sentence commences—

(1) as a result of the offense for which the sentence was imposed; or

(2) as a result of any other charge for which the defendant was arrested after the commission of the offense for which the sentence was imposed;

that has not been credited against another sentence.

(Added Pub.L. 98–473, Title II, § 212(a)(2), Oct. 12, 1984, 98 Stat. 2001.)

HISTORICAL AND STATUTORY NOTES

Effective and Applicability Provisions

1984 Acts. Section effective on the first day of first calendar month beginning thirty-six months after Oct. 12, 1984, applicable only to offenses committed after taking effect of sections 211 to 239 of Pub.L. 98–473, and except as otherwise provided for therein, see section 235 of Pub.L. 98–473, as amended, set out as a note under section 3551 of this title.

§ 3586. Implementation of a sentence of imprisonment

The implementation of a sentence of imprisonment is governed by the provisions of subchapter C of chapter 229 and, if the sentence includes a term of supervised release, by the provisions of subchapter A of chapter 229.

(Added Pub.L. 98–473, Title II, § 212(a)(2), Oct. 12, 1984, 98 Stat. 2001.)

HISTORICAL AND STATUTORY NOTES

Effective and Applicability Provisions

1984 Acts. Section effective on the first day of first calendar month beginning thirty-six months after Oct. 12, 1984, applicable only to offenses committed after taking effect of sections 211 to 239 of Pub.L. 98–473, and except as otherwise provided for therein, see section 235 of Pub.L. 98–473, as amended, set out as a note under section 3551 of this title.

CHAPTER 228—DEATH SENTENCE

Sec.

HISTORICAL AND STATUTORY NOTES

Codifications

A prior chapter 228 entitled "IMPOSITION, PAYMENT, AND COLLECTION OF FINES", consisting of sections 3591 to 3599, was enacted by Pub.L. 98–473, Title II, § 238(a), Oct. 12, 1984, 98 Stat. 2034, to be effective, pursuant to section 235 of Pub.L. 98–473 (set out as a note under section 3551 of this title), on Nov. 1, 1986 (effective date extended by Pub.L. 99–217, § 4, Dec. 26, 1985, 99 Stat. 1728, to Nov. 1, 1987). However, that chapter was repealed by Pub.L. 98–596, § 12(a)(1), Oct. 30, 1984, 98 Stat. 3139, which repeal, pursuant to section 12(b) of Pub.L. 98–596, was effective on Oct. 12, 1984. See Prior Provisions note under sections 3591 to 3598 for subject matter of prior sections 3591 to 3599. The chapter 228, which was to have gone into effect on Nov. 1, 1986 (extended to Nov. 1, 1987), but for the repeal by section 12(a)(1) of Pub.L. 98–596.

§ 3591. Sentence of death

(a) A defendant who has been found guilty of—

(1) an offense described in section 794 or section 2381; or

(2) any other offense for which a sentence of death is provided, if the defendant, as determined beyond a reasonable doubt at the hearing under section 3593—

(A) intentionally killed the victim;

(B) intentionally inflicted serious bodily injury that resulted in the death of the victim;

(C) intentionally participated in an act, contemplating that the life of a person would be taken or intending that lethal force would be used in connection with a person, other than one of the participants in the offense, and the victim died as a direct result of the act; or

(D) intentionally and specifically engaged in an act of violence, knowing that the act created a grave risk of death to a person, other than one of the participants in the offense, such that participation in the act constituted a reckless disregard for human life and the victim died as a direct result of the act,

shall be sentenced to death if, after consideration of the factors set forth in section 3592 in the course of a hearing held pursuant to section 3593, it is determined that imposition of a sentence of death is justified, except that no person may be sentenced to death who was less than 18 years of age at the time of the offense.

(b) A defendant who has been found guilty of—

(1) an offense referred to in section 408(c)(1) of the Controlled Substances Act (21 U.S.C. 848(c)(1)), committed as part of a continuing criminal enterprise offense under the conditions described in subsection (b) of that section which involved not less than twice the quantity of controlled substance described in subsection (b)(2)(A) or twice the gross receipts described in subsection (b)(2)(B); or

(2) an offense referred to in section 408(c)(1) of the Controlled Substances Act (21 U.S.C. 848(c)(1)), committed as part of a continuing criminal enterprise offense under that section, where the defendant is a principal administrator, organizer, or leader of such an enterprise, and the defendant, in order to obstruct the investigation or prosecution of the enterprise or an offense involved in the enterprise, attempts to kill or knowingly directs, advises, authorizes, or assists another to attempt to kill any public officer, juror, witness, or members of the family or household of such a person,

shall be sentenced to death if, after consideration of the factors set forth in section 3592 in the course of a hearing held pursuant to section 3593, it is determined that imposition of a sentence of death is justified, except that no person may be sentenced to death who was less than 18 years of age at the time of the offense.

(Added Pub.L. 103–322, Title VI, § 60002(a), Sept. 13, 1994, 108 Stat. 1959.)

HISTORICAL AND STATUTORY NOTES

Prior Provisions

A prior section 3591 provided for imposition of fines. See Codification note preceding this section.

Short Title

1994 Acts. Section 60001 of Pub.L. 103–322 provided that: "This title [enacting this chapter (section 3591 et seq.) and sections 36, 37, 1118, 1119, 1120, 1121, 2245, 2280, 2281, and 2332a of this title, amending sections 34, 241, 242, 245, 247, 794, 844, 924, 930, 1091, 1111, 1114, 1116, 1117, 1201, 1203, 1503, 1512, 1513, 1716, 1958, 1959, 1992, 2113, 2119, 2251, 2332, 2340A, 3005, and 3432 of this title, and section 1324 of Title 8, Aliens and Nationality, redesignating former section 2245 of this title as 2246, repealing section 46503 of Title 49, Transportation, and enacting provisions set out as notes under this section and sections 36, 37, and 2280 of this title] may be cited as the 'Federal Death Penalty Act of 1994'."

Applicability to Uniform Code of Military Justice

Section 60004 of Pub.L. 103–322 provided that: "Chapter 228 of title 18, United States Code, as added by this title [this chapter], shall not apply to prosecutions under the Uniform Code of Military Justice (10 U.S.C. 801) [section 801 et seq. of Title 10, Armed Forces]."

§ 3592. Mitigating and aggravating factors to be considered in determining whether a sentence of death is justified

(a) **Mitigating factors.**—In determining whether a sentence of death is to be imposed on a defendant, the finder of fact shall consider any mitigating factor, including the following:

(1) **Impaired capacity.**—The defendant's capacity to appreciate the wrongfulness of the defendant's conduct or to conform conduct to the requirements of law was significantly impaired, regardless of whether the capacity was so impaired as to constitute a defense to the charge.

(2) **Duress.**—The defendant was under unusual and substantial duress, regardless of whether the

duress was of such a degree as to constitute a defense to the charge.

(3) Minor participation.—The defendant is punishable as a principal in the offense, which was committed by another, but the defendant's participation was relatively minor, regardless of whether the participation was so minor as to constitute a defense to the charge.

(4) Equally culpable defendants.—Another defendant or defendants, equally culpable in the crime, will not be punished by death.

(5) No prior criminal record.—The defendant did not have a significant prior history of other criminal conduct.

(6) Disturbance.—The defendant committed the offense under severe mental or emotional disturbance.

(7) Victim's consent.—The victim consented to the criminal conduct that resulted in the victim's death.

(8) Other factors.—Other factors in the defendant's background, record, or character or any other circumstance of the offense that mitigate against imposition of the death sentence.

(b) Aggravating factors for espionage and treason.—In determining whether a sentence of death is justified for an offense described in section 3591(a)(1), the jury, or if there is no jury, the court, shall consider each of the following aggravating factors for which notice has been given and determine which, if any, exist:

(1) Prior espionage or treason offense.—The defendant has previously been convicted of another offense involving espionage or treason for which a sentence of either life imprisonment or death was authorized by law.

(2) Grave risk to national security.—In the commission of the offense the defendant knowingly created a grave risk of substantial danger to the national security.

(3) Grave risk of death.—In the commission of the offense the defendant knowingly created a grave risk of death to another person.

The jury, or if there is no jury, the court, may consider whether any other aggravating factor for which notice has been given exists.

(c) Aggravating factors for homicide.—In determining whether a sentence of death is justified for an offense described in section 3591(a)(2), the jury, or if there is no jury, the court, shall consider each of the following aggravating factors for which notice has been given and determine which, if any, exist:

(1) Death during commission of another crime.—The death, or injury resulting in death, occurred during the commission or attempted commission of, or during the immediate flight from the commission of, an offense under section 32 (destruction of aircraft or aircraft facilities), section 33 (destruction of motor vehicles or motor vehicle facilities), section 37 (violence at international airports), section 351 (violence against Members of Congress, Cabinet officers, or Supreme Court Justices), an offense under section 751 (prisoners in custody of institution or officer), section 794 (gathering or delivering defense information to aid foreign government), section 844(d) (transportation of explosives in interstate commerce for certain purposes), section 844(f) (destruction of Government property by explosives), section 1118 (prisoners serving life term), section 1201 (kidnapping), section 844(i) (destruction of property affecting interstate commerce by explosives), section 1116 (killing or attempted killing of diplomats), section 1203 (hostage taking), section 1992 (wrecking trains), section 2245 (offenses resulting in death), section 2280 (maritime violence), section 2281 (maritime platform violence), section 2332 (terrorist acts abroad against United States nationals), section 2332a (use of weapons of mass destruction), or section 2381 (treason) of this title, or section 46502 of title 49, United States Code (aircraft piracy).

(2) Previous conviction of violent felony involving firearm.—For any offense, other than an offense for which a sentence of death is sought on the basis of section 924(c), the defendant has previously been convicted of a Federal or State offense punishable by a term of imprisonment of more than 1 year, involving the use or attempted or threatened use of a firearm (as defined in section 921) against another person.

(3) Previous conviction of offense for which a sentence of death or life imprisonment was authorized.—The defendant has previously been convicted of another Federal or State offense resulting in the death of a person, for which a sentence of life imprisonment or a sentence of death was authorized by statute.

(4) Previous conviction of other serious offenses.—The defendant has previously been convicted of 2 or more Federal or State offenses, punishable by a term of imprisonment of more than 1 year, committed on different occasions, involving the infliction of, or attempted infliction of, serious bodily injury or death upon another person.

(5) Grave risk of death to additional persons.—The defendant, in the commission of the offense, or in escaping apprehension for the violation of the offense, knowingly created a grave risk of death to 1 or more persons in addition to the victim of the offense.

(6) Heinous, cruel, or depraved manner of committing offense.—The defendant committed the offense in an especially heinous, cruel, or depraved manner in that it involved torture or serious physical abuse to the victim.

(7) Procurement of offense by payment.—The defendant procured the commission of the offense by payment, or promise of payment, of anything of pecuniary value.

(8) Pecuniary gain.—The defendant committed the offense as consideration for the receipt, or in the expectation of the receipt, of anything of pecuniary value.

(9) Substantial planning and premeditation.—The defendant committed the offense after substantial planning and premeditation to cause the death of a person or commit an act of terrorism.

(10) Conviction for two felony drug offenses.—The defendant has previously been convicted of 2 or more State or Federal offenses punishable by a term of imprisonment of more than one year, committed on different occasions, involving the distribution of a controlled substance.

(11) Vulnerability of victim.—The victim was particularly vulnerable due to old age, youth, or infirmity.

(12) Conviction for serious Federal drug offenses.—The defendant had previously been convicted of violating title II or III of the Comprehensive Drug Abuse Prevention and Control Act of 1970 for which a sentence of 5 or more years may be imposed or had previously been convicted of engaging in a continuing criminal enterprise.

(13) Continuing criminal enterprise involving drug sales to minors.—The defendant committed the offense in the course of engaging in a continuing criminal enterprise in violation of section 408(c) of the Controlled Substances Act (21 U.S.C. 848(c)), and that violation involved the distribution of drugs to persons under the age of 21 in violation of section 418 of that Act (21 U.S.C. 859).

(14) High public officials.—The defendant committed the offense against—

(A) the President of the United States, the President-elect, the Vice President, the Vice President-elect, the Vice President-designate, or, if there is no Vice President, the officer next in order of succession to the office of the President of the United States, or any person who is acting as President under the Constitution and laws of the United States;

(B) a chief of state, head of government, or the political equivalent, of a foreign nation;

(C) a foreign official listed in section 1116(b)(3)(A), if the official is in the United States on official business; or

(D) a Federal public servant who is a judge, a law enforcement officer, or an employee of a United States penal or correctional institution—

(i) while he or she is engaged in the performance of his or her official duties;

(ii) because of the performance of his or her official duties; or

(iii) because of his or her status as a public servant.

For purposes of this subparagraph, a "law enforcement officer" is a public servant authorized by law or by a Government agency or Congress to conduct or engage in the prevention, investigation, or prosecution or adjudication of an offense, and includes those engaged in corrections, parole, or probation functions.

(15) Prior conviction of sexual assault or child molestation.—In the case of an offense under chapter 109A (sexual abuse) or chapter 110 (sexual abuse of children), the defendant has previously been convicted of a crime of sexual assault or crime of child molestation.

(16) Multiple killings or attempted killings.—The defendant intentionally killed or attempted to kill more than one person in a single criminal episode.

The jury, or if there is no jury, the court, may consider whether any other aggravating factor for which notice has been given exists.

(d) Aggravating factors for drug offense death penalty.—In determining whether a sentence of death is justified for an offense described in section 3591(b), the jury, or if there is no jury, the court, shall consider each of the following aggravating factors for which notice has been given and determine which, if any, exist:

(1) Previous conviction of offense for which a sentence of death or life imprisonment was authorized.—The defendant has previously been convicted of another Federal or State offense resulting in the death of a person, for which a sentence of life imprisonment or death was authorized by statute.

(2) Previous conviction of other serious offenses.—The defendant has previously been convicted of two or more Federal or State offenses, each punishable by a term of imprisonment of more than one year, committed on different occasions, involving the importation, manufacture, or distribution of a controlled substance (as defined in section 102 of the Controlled Substances Act (21 U.S.C. 802)) or the infliction of, or attempted infliction of, serious bodily injury or death upon another person.

(3) **Previous serious drug felony conviction.**—The defendant has previously been convicted of another Federal or State offense involving the manufacture, distribution, importation, or possession of a controlled substance (as defined in section 102 of the Controlled Substances Act (21 U.S.C. 802)) for which a sentence of five or more years of imprisonment was authorized by statute.

(4) **Use of firearm.**—In committing the offense, or in furtherance of a continuing criminal enterprise of which the offense was a part, the defendant used a firearm or knowingly directed, advised, authorized, or assisted another to use a firearm to threaten, intimidate, assault, or injure a person.

(5) **Distribution to persons under 21.**—The offense, or a continuing criminal enterprise of which the offense was a part, involved conduct proscribed by section 418 of the Controlled Substances Act (21 U.S.C. 859) which was committed directly by the defendant.

(6) **Distribution near schools.**—The offense, or a continuing criminal enterprise of which the offense was a part, involved conduct proscribed by section 419 of the Controlled Substances Act (21 U.S.C. 860) which was committed directly by the defendant.

(7) **Using minors in trafficking.**—The offense, or a continuing criminal enterprise of which the offense was a part, involved conduct proscribed by section 420 of the Controlled Substances Act (21 U.S.C. 861) which was committed directly by the defendant.

(8) **Lethal adulterant.**—The offense involved the importation, manufacture, or distribution of a controlled substance (as defined in section 102 of the Controlled Substances Act (21 U.S.C. 802)), mixed with a potentially lethal adulterant, and the defendant was aware of the presence of the adulterant.

The jury, or if there is no jury, the court, may consider whether any other aggravating factor for which notice has been given exists.

(Added Pub.L. 103–322, Title VI, § 60002(a), Sept. 13, 1994, 108 Stat. 1960, and amended Pub.L. 103–322, Title XXXIII, § 330021(1), Sept. 13, 1994, 108 Stat. 1960, 2150; Pub.L. 104–132, Title VII, § 728, Apr. 24, 1996, 110 Stat. 1302; Pub.L. 104–294, Title VI, §§ 601(b)(7), 604(b)(35), Oct. 11, 1996, 110 Stat. 3499, 3508; Pub.L. 107–273, Div. B, Title IV, § 4002(e)(2), Nov. 2, 2002, 116 Stat. 1810; Pub.L. 109–248, Title II, § 206(a)(4), July 27, 2006, 120 Stat. 614.)

HISTORICAL AND STATUTORY NOTES

References in Text

Title II or III of the Comprehensive Drug Abuse Prevention and Control Act of 1970, referred to in subsec. (c)(12), means Title II or III of Pub.L. 91–513, Oct. 27, 1970, 84 Stat. 1236, as amended, Title II of which is classified principally to subchapter I (section 801 et seq.) of chapter 13 of Title 21, Food and Drugs, and is popularly known as the Controlled Substances Act, and Title III of which is classified principally to subchapter II (section 951 et seq.) of chapter 13 of Title 21 and is popularly known as the Controlled Substances Import and Export Act. For complete classification of these Acts to the Code, see Short Title notes set out under sections 801 and 951 of Title 21, Food and Drugs, and Tables.

Effective and Applicability Provisions

1996 Acts. Amendment by section 604 of Pub.L. 104–294 effective Sept. 13, 1994, see section 604(d) of Pub.L. 104–294, set out as a note under section 13 of this title.

Prior Provisions

A prior section 3592 provided for payment, delinquency, and default of fines. See Codification note preceding section 3591.

Applicability to Uniform Code of Military Justice

Section not to apply to prosecutions under the Uniform Code of Military Justice (chapter 47 [section 801 et seq.] of Title 10, Armed Forces), see section 60004 of Pub.L. 103–322, set out as a note under section 3591 of this title.

§ 3593. Special hearing to determine whether a sentence of death is justified

(a) **Notice by the government.**—If, in a case involving an offense described in section 3591, the attorney for the government believes that the circumstances of the offense are such that a sentence of death is justified under this chapter, the attorney shall, a reasonable time before the trial or before acceptance by the court of a plea of guilty, sign and file with the court, and serve on the defendant, a notice—

(1) stating that the government believes that the circumstances of the offense are such that, if the defendant is convicted, a sentence of death is justified under this chapter and that the government will seek the sentence of death; and

(2) setting forth the aggravating factor or factors that the government, if the defendant is convicted, proposes to prove as justifying a sentence of death.

The factors for which notice is provided under this subsection may include factors concerning the effect of the offense on the victim and the victim's family, and may include oral testimony, a victim impact statement that identifies the victim of the offense and the extent and scope of the injury and loss suffered by the victim and the victim's family, and any other relevant information. The court may permit the attorney for the government to amend the notice upon a showing of good cause.

(b) **Hearing before a court or jury.**—If the attorney for the government has filed a notice as required under subsection (a) and the defendant is found guilty of or pleads guilty to an offense described in section 3591, the judge who presided at the trial or before whom the guilty plea was entered, or another judge if that judge is unavailable, shall conduct a separate sentencing hearing to determine the punishment to be imposed. The hearing shall be conducted—

(1) before the jury that determined the defendant's guilt;

(2) before a jury impaneled for the purpose of the hearing if—

(A) the defendant was convicted upon a plea of guilty;

(B) the defendant was convicted after a trial before the court sitting without a jury;

(C) the jury that determined the defendant's guilt was discharged for good cause; or

(D) after initial imposition of a sentence under this section, reconsideration of the sentence under this section is necessary; or

(3) before the court alone, upon the motion of the defendant and with the approval of the attorney for the government.

A jury impaneled pursuant to paragraph (2) shall consist of 12 members, unless, at any time before the conclusion of the hearing, the parties stipulate, with the approval of the court, that it shall consist of a lesser number.

(c) Proof of mitigating and aggravating factors.—Notwithstanding rule 32 of the Federal Rules of Criminal Procedure, when a defendant is found guilty or pleads guilty to an offense under section 3591, no presentence report shall be prepared. At the sentencing hearing, information may be presented as to any matter relevant to the sentence, including any mitigating or aggravating factor permitted or required to be considered under section 3592. Information presented may include the trial transcript and exhibits if the hearing is held before a jury or judge not present during the trial, or at the trial judge's discretion. The defendant may present any information relevant to a mitigating factor. The government may present any information relevant to an aggravating factor for which notice has been provided under subsection (a). Information is admissible regardless of its admissibility under the rules governing admission of evidence at criminal trials except that information may be excluded if its probative value is outweighed by the danger of creating unfair prejudice, confusing the issues, or misleading the jury. For the purposes of the preceding sentence, the fact that a victim, as defined in section 3510, attended or observed the trial shall not be construed to pose a danger of creating unfair prejudice, confusing the issues, or misleading the jury. The government and the defendant shall be permitted to rebut any information received at the hearing, and shall be given fair opportunity to present argument as to the adequacy of the information to establish the existence of any aggravating or mitigating factor, and as to the appropriateness in the case of imposing a sentence of death. The government shall open the argument. The defendant shall be permitted to reply. The government shall then be permitted to reply in rebuttal. The burden of establishing the existence of any aggravating factor is on the government, and is not satisfied unless the existence of such a factor is established beyond a reasonable doubt. The burden of establishing the existence of any mitigating factor is on the defendant, and is not satisfied unless the existence of such a factor is established by a preponderance of the information.

(d) Return of special findings.—The jury, or if there is no jury, the court, shall consider all the information received during the hearing. It shall return special findings identifying any aggravating factor or factors set forth in section 3592 found to exist and any other aggravating factor for which notice has been provided under subsection (a) found to exist. A finding with respect to a mitigating factor may be made by 1 or more members of the jury, and any member of the jury who finds the existence of a mitigating factor may consider such factor established for purposes of this section regardless of the number of jurors who concur that the factor has been established. A finding with respect to any aggravating factor must be unanimous. If no aggravating factor set forth in section 3592 is found to exist, the court shall impose a sentence other than death authorized by law.

(e) Return of a finding concerning a sentence of death.—If, in the case of—

(1) an offense described in section 3591(a)(1), an aggravating factor required to be considered under section 3592(b) is found to exist;

(2) an offense described in section 3591(a)(2), an aggravating factor required to be considered under section 3592(c) is found to exist; or

(3) an offense described in section 3591(b), an aggravating factor required to be considered under section 3592(d) is found to exist,

the jury, or if there is no jury, the court, shall consider whether all the aggravating factor or factors found to exist sufficiently outweigh all the mitigating factor or factors found to exist to justify a sentence of death, or, in the absence of a mitigating factor, whether the aggravating factor or factors alone are sufficient to justify a sentence of death. Based upon this consideration, the jury by unanimous vote, or if there is no jury, the court, shall recommend whether the defendant should be sentenced to death, to life imprisonment without possibility of release or some other lesser sentence.

(f) Special precaution to ensure against discrimination.—In a hearing held before a jury, the court, prior to the return of a finding under subsection (e), shall instruct the jury that, in considering whether a sentence of death is justified, it shall not consider the race, color, religious beliefs, national origin, or sex of the defendant or of any victim and that the jury is not to recommend a sentence of death unless it has concluded that it would recommend a sentence of death for the crime in question no matter what the race, color, religious beliefs, national origin, or sex of the defendant or of any victim may be. The jury, upon return of a finding under subsection (e), shall also return to the court a certificate, signed by each juror, that consideration of the race, color, religious beliefs, national origin, or sex of the defendant or any victim was not involved in reaching his or her individual decision and that the individual juror would have made the same recommendation regarding a sentence for the crime in question no matter what the race, color, religious beliefs, national origin, or sex of the defendant or any victim may be.

(Added Pub.L. 103–322, Title VI, § 60002(a), Sept. 13, 1994, 108 Stat. 1964, and amended Pub.L. 105–6, § 2(c), Mar. 19, 1997, 111 Stat. 12; Pub.L. 107–273, Div. B, Title IV, § 4002(e)(8), Nov. 2, 2002, 116 Stat. 1810.)

HISTORICAL AND STATUTORY NOTES

References in Text

Rule 32 of the Federal Rules of Criminal Procedure, referred to in subsec. (c), is set out in the Federal Rules of Criminal Procedure, this title.

Effective and Applicability Provisions

1997 Acts. Amendment by Pub.L. 105–6 applicable to cases pending on Mar. 19, 1997, see section 2(d) of Pub.L. 105–6, set out as a note under section 3510 of this title.

Prior Provisions

A prior section 3593 provided for modification or remission of fines. See Codification note preceding section 3591.

Applicability to Uniform Code of Military Justice

Section not to apply to prosecutions under the Uniform Code of Military Justice (chapter 47 [section 801 et seq.] of Title 10, Armed Forces), see section 60004 of Pub.L. 103–322, set out as a note under section 3591 of this title.

§ 3594. Imposition of a sentence of death

Upon a recommendation under section 3593(e) that the defendant should be sentenced to death or life imprisonment without possibility of release, the court shall sentence the defendant accordingly. Otherwise, the court shall impose any lesser sentence that is authorized by law. Notwithstanding any other law, if the maximum term of imprisonment for the offense is life imprisonment, the court may impose a sentence of life imprisonment without possibility of release.

(Added Pub.L. 103–322, Title VI, § 60002(a), Sept. 13, 1994, 108 Stat. 1966.)

HISTORICAL AND STATUTORY NOTES

Prior Provisions

A prior section 3594 required clerks to forward fine payments to the United States Treasury and to notify the Attorney General of receipt and sentencing courts to certify to the Attorney General the imposition of and changes in fines. See Codification note preceding section 3591.

Applicability to Uniform Code of Military Justice

Section not to apply to prosecutions under the Uniform Code of Military Justice (chapter 47 [section 801 et seq.] of Title 10, Armed Forces), see section 60004 of Pub.L. 103–322, set out as a note under section 3591 of this title.

§ 3595. Review of a sentence of death

(a) Appeal.—In a case in which a sentence of death is imposed, the sentence shall be subject to review by the court of appeals upon appeal by the defendant. Notice of appeal must be filed within the time specified for the filing of a notice of appeal. An appeal under this section may be consolidated with an appeal of the judgment of conviction and shall have priority over all other cases.

(b) Review.—The court of appeals shall review the entire record in the case, including—

(1) the evidence submitted during the trial;

(2) the information submitted during the sentencing hearing;

(3) the procedures employed in the sentencing hearing; and

(4) the special findings returned under section 3593(d).

(c) Decision and disposition.—

(1) The court of appeals shall address all substantive and procedural issues raised on the appeal of a sentence of death, and shall consider whether the sentence of death was imposed under the influence of passion, prejudice, or any other arbitrary factor and whether the evidence supports the special finding of the existence of an aggravating factor required to be considered under section 3592.

(2) Whenever the court of appeals finds that—

(A) the sentence of death was imposed under the influence of passion, prejudice, or any other arbitrary factor;

(B) the admissible evidence and information adduced does not support the special finding of the existence of the required aggravating factor; or

(C) the proceedings involved any other legal error requiring reversal of the sentence that was properly preserved for appeal under the rules of criminal procedure,

the court shall remand the case for reconsideration under section 3593 or imposition of a sentence other than death. The court of appeals shall not reverse or vacate a sentence of death on account of any error which can be harmless, including any erroneous special finding of an aggravating factor, where the Government establishes beyond a reasonable doubt that the error was harmless.

(3) The court of appeals shall state in writing the reasons for its disposition of an appeal of a sentence of death under this section.

(Added Pub.L. 103–322, Title VI, § 60002(a), Sept. 13, 1994, 108 Stat. 1967.)

HISTORICAL AND STATUTORY NOTES

Prior Provisions

A prior section 3595 provided for interest and monetary penalties for delinquency and default of fines. See Codification note preceding section 3591.

Applicability to Uniform Code of Military Justice

Section not to apply to prosecutions under the Uniform Code of Military Justice (chapter 47 [section 801 et seq.] of Title 10, Armed Forces), see section 60004 of Pub.L. 103–322, set out as a note under section 3591 of this title.

§ 3596. Implementation of a sentence of death

(a) In general.—A person who has been sentenced to death pursuant to this chapter shall be committed to the custody of the Attorney General until exhaustion of the procedures for appeal of the judgment of conviction and for review of the sentence. When the sentence is to be implemented, the Attorney General shall release the person sentenced to death to the custody of a United States marshal, who shall supervise implementation of the sentence in the manner prescribed by the law of the State in which the sentence is imposed. If the law of the State does not provide for implementation of a sentence of death, the court shall designate another State, the law of which does provide for the implementation of a sentence of death, and the sentence shall be implemented in the latter State in the manner prescribed by such law.

(b) Pregnant woman.—A sentence of death shall not be carried out upon a woman while she is pregnant.

(c) Mental capacity.—A sentence of death shall not be carried out upon a person who is mentally retarded. A sentence of death shall not be carried out upon a person who, as a result of mental disability, lacks the mental capacity to understand the death penalty and why it was imposed on that person.

(Added Pub.L. 103–322, Title VI, § 60002(a), Sept. 13, 1994, 108 Stat. 1967.)

HISTORICAL AND STATUTORY NOTES

Prior Provisions

A prior section 3596 provided civil remedies for satisfaction of unpaid fines. See Codification note preceding section 3591.

Applicability to Uniform Code of Military Justice

Section not to apply to prosecutions under the Uniform Code of Military Justice (chapter 47 [section 801 et seq.] of Title 10, Armed Forces), see section 60004 of Pub.L. 103–322, set out as a note under section 3591 of this title.

§ 3597. Use of State facilities

(a) In general.—A United States marshal charged with supervising the implementation of a sentence of death may use appropriate State or local facilities for the purpose, may use the services of an appropriate State or local official or of a person such an official employs for the purpose, and shall pay the costs thereof in an amount approved by the Attorney General.

(b) Excuse of an employee on moral or religious grounds.—No employee of any State department of corrections, the United States Department of Justice, the Federal Bureau of Prisons, or the United States Marshals Service, and no employee providing services to that department, bureau, or service under contract shall be required, as a condition of that employment or contractual obligation, to be in attendance at or to participate in any prosecution or execution under this section if such participation is contrary to the moral or religious convictions of the employee. In this subsection, "participation in executions" includes personal preparation of the condemned individual and the apparatus used for execution and supervision of the activities of other personnel in carrying out such activities.

(Added Pub.L. 103–322, Title VI, § 60002(a), Sept. 13, 1994, 108 Stat. 1968.)

HISTORICAL AND STATUTORY NOTES

Prior Provisions

A prior section 3597 authorized resentencing a person upon the failure to pay a fine. See Codification note preceding section 3591.

Applicability to Uniform Code of Military Justice

Section not to apply to prosecutions under the Uniform Code of Military Justice (chapter 47 [section 801 et seq.] of Title 10, Armed Forces), see section 60004 of Pub.L. 103–322, set out as a note under section 3591 of this title.

§ 3598. Special provisions for Indian country

Notwithstanding sections 1152 and 1153, no person subject to the criminal jurisdiction of an Indian tribal government shall be subject to a capital sentence under this chapter for any offense the Federal jurisdiction for which is predicated solely on Indian country (as defined in section 1151 of this title) and which has occurred within the boundaries of Indian country, unless the governing body of the tribe has elected that this chapter have effect over land and persons subject to its criminal jurisdiction.

(Added Pub.L. 103–322, Title VI, § 60002(a), Sept. 13, 1994, 108 Stat. 1968.)

HISTORICAL AND STATUTORY NOTES

Prior Provisions

A prior section 3598 established a statute of limitations on the liability to pay fines.

A prior section 3599 established penalties for the willful failure to pay fines.

See Codification note preceding section 3591.

Applicability to Uniform Code of Military Justice

Section not to apply to prosecutions under the Uniform Code of Military Justice (chapter 47 [section 801 et seq.] of Title 10, Armed Forces), see section 60004 of Pub.L. 103–322, set out as a note under section 3591 of this title.

§ 3599. Counsel for financially unable defendants

(a)(1) Notwithstanding any other provision of law to the contrary, in every criminal action in which a defendant is charged with a crime which may be punishable by death, a defendant who is or becomes financially unable to obtain adequate representation or investigative, expert, or other reasonably necessary services at any time either—

(A) before judgment; or

(B) after the entry of a judgment imposing a sentence of death but before the execution of that judgment;

shall be entitled to the appointment of one or more attorneys and the furnishing of such other services in accordance with subsections (b) through (f).

(2) In any post conviction proceeding under section 2254 or 2255 of title 28, United States Code, seeking to vacate or set aside a death sentence, any defendant who is or becomes financially unable to obtain adequate representation or investigative, expert, or other reasonably necessary services shall be entitled to the appointment of one or more attorneys and the furnishing of such other services in accordance with subsections (b) through (f).

(b) If the appointment is made before judgment, at least one attorney so appointed must have been admitted to practice in the court in which the prosecution is to be tried for not less than five years, and must have had not less than three years experience in the actual trial of felony prosecutions in that court.

(c) If the appointment is made after judgment, at least one attorney so appointed must have been admitted to practice in the court of appeals for not less than five years, and must have had not less than three years experience in the handling of appeals in that court in felony cases.

(d) With respect to subsections (b) and (c), the court, for good cause, may appoint another attorney whose background, knowledge, or experience would otherwise enable him or her to properly represent the defendant, with due consideration to the seriousness of the possible penalty and to the unique and complex nature of the litigation.

(e) Unless replaced by similarly qualified counsel upon the attorney's own motion or upon motion of the defendant, each attorney so appointed shall represent the defendant throughout every subsequent stage of available judicial proceedings, including pretrial proceedings, trial, sentencing, motions for new trial, appeals, applications for writ of certiorari to the Supreme Court of the United States, and all available post-conviction process, together with applications for stays of execution and other appropriate motions and procedures, and shall also represent the defendant in such competency proceedings and proceedings for executive or other clemency as may be available to the defendant.

(f) Upon a finding that investigative, expert, or other services are reasonably necessary for the representation of the defendant, whether in connection with issues relating to guilt or the sentence, the court may authorize the defendant's attorneys to obtain such services on behalf of the defendant and, if so authorized, shall order the payment of fees and expenses therefor under subsection (g). No ex parte proceeding, communication, or request may be considered pursuant to this section unless a proper showing is made concerning the need for confidentiality. Any such proceeding, communication, or request shall be transcribed and made a part of the record available for appellate review.

(g)(1) Compensation shall be paid to attorneys appointed under this subsection at a rate of not more than $125 per hour for in-court and out-of-court time. The Judicial Conference is authorized to raise the maximum for hourly payment specified in the paragraph up to the aggregate of the overall average percentages of the adjustments in the rates of pay for the General Schedule made pursuant to section 5305 of title 5 on or after such date. After the rates are raised under the preceding sentence, such hourly range may be raised at intervals of not less than one year, up to the aggregate of the overall average percentages of such adjustments made since the last raise under this paragraph.

(2) Fees and expenses paid for investigative, expert, and other reasonably necessary services authorized under subsection (f) shall not exceed $7,500 in any case, unless payment in excess of that limit is certified by the court, or by the United States magistrate judge, if the services were rendered in connection with the case disposed of entirely before such magistrate judge, as necessary to provide fair compensation for services of an unusual character or duration, and the amount of the excess payment is approved by the chief judge of the circuit. The chief judge of the circuit may delegate such approval authority to an active circuit judge.

(3) The amounts paid under this paragraph for services in any case shall be disclosed to the public, after the disposition of the petition.

(Added Pub.L. 109–177, Title II, § 222(a), Mar. 9, 2006, 120 Stat. 231.)

HISTORICAL AND STATUTORY NOTES

References in Text

The General Schedule, referred to in subsec. (g)(1), is set out under 5 U.S.C.A. § 5332.

CHAPTER 228A—POST-CONVICTION DNA TESTING

§ 3600. DNA testing

(a) In general.—Upon a written motion by an individual under a sentence of imprisonment or death pursuant to a conviction for a Federal offense (referred to in this section as the "applicant"), the court that entered the judgment of conviction shall order DNA testing of specific evidence if the court finds that all of the following apply:

(1) The applicant asserts, under penalty of perjury, that the applicant is actually innocent of—

(A) the Federal offense for which the applicant is under a sentence of imprisonment or death; or

(B) another Federal or State offense, if—

(i) evidence of such offense was admitted during a Federal death sentencing hearing and exoneration of such offense would entitle the applicant to a reduced sentence or new sentencing hearing; and

(ii) in the case of a State offense—

(I) the applicant demonstrates that there is no adequate remedy under State law to permit DNA testing of the specified evidence relating to the State offense; and

(II) to the extent available, the applicant has exhausted all remedies available under State law for requesting DNA testing of specified evidence relating to the State offense.

(2) The specific evidence to be tested was secured in relation to the investigation or prosecution of the Federal or State offense referenced in the applicant's assertion under paragraph (1).

(3) The specific evidence to be tested—

(A) was not previously subjected to DNA testing and the applicant did not—

(i) knowingly and voluntarily waive the right to request DNA testing of that evidence in a court proceeding after the date of enactment of the Innocence Protection Act of 2004; or

(ii) knowingly fail to request DNA testing of that evidence in a prior motion for postconviction DNA testing; or

(B) was previously subjected to DNA testing and the applicant is requesting DNA testing using a new method or technology that is substantially more probative than the prior DNA testing.

(4) The specific evidence to be tested is in the possession of the Government and has been subject to a chain of custody and retained under conditions sufficient to ensure that such evidence has not been substituted, contaminated, tampered with, replaced, or altered in any respect material to the proposed DNA testing.

(5) The proposed DNA testing is reasonable in scope, uses scientifically sound methods, and is consistent with accepted forensic practices.

(6) The applicant identifies a theory of defense that—

(A) is not inconsistent with an affirmative defense presented at trial; and

(B) would establish the actual innocence of the applicant of the Federal or State offense referenced in the applicant's assertion under paragraph (1).

(7) If the applicant was convicted following a trial, the identity of the perpetrator was at issue in the trial.

(8) The proposed DNA testing of the specific evidence may produce new material evidence that would—

(A) support the theory of defense referenced in paragraph (6); and

(B) raise a reasonable probability that the applicant did not commit the offense.

(9) The applicant certifies that the applicant will provide a DNA sample for purposes of comparison.

(10) The motion is made in a timely fashion, subject to the following conditions:

(A) There shall be a rebuttable presumption of timeliness if the motion is made within 60 months of enactment of the Justice For All Act of 2004 or within 36 months of conviction, whichever comes later. Such presumption may be rebutted upon a showing—

(i) that the applicant's motion for a DNA test is based solely upon information used in a previously denied motion; or

(ii) of clear and convincing evidence that the applicant's filing is done solely to cause delay or harass.

(B) There shall be a rebuttable presumption against timeliness for any motion not satisfying subparagraph (A) above. Such presumption may be rebutted upon the court's finding—

(i) that the applicant was or is incompetent and such incompetence substantially contributed to the delay in the applicant's motion for a DNA test;

(ii) the evidence to be tested is newly discovered DNA evidence;

(iii) that the applicant's motion is not based solely upon the applicant's own assertion of innocence and, after considering all relevant facts and circumstances surrounding the motion, a denial would result in a manifest injustice; or

(iv) upon good cause shown.

(C) For purposes of this paragraph—

(i) the term "incompetence" has the meaning as defined in section 4241 of title 18, United States Code;

(ii) the term "manifest" means that which is unmistakable, clear, plain, or indisputable and requires that the opposite conclusion be clearly evident.

(b) Notice to the Government; preservation order; appointment of counsel.—

(1) Notice.—Upon the receipt of a motion filed under subsection (a), the court shall—

(A) notify the Government; and

(B) allow the Government a reasonable time period to respond to the motion.

(2) Preservation order.—To the extent necessary to carry out proceedings under this section, the court shall direct the Government to preserve the specific evidence relating to a motion under subsection (a).

(3) Appointment of counsel.—The court may appoint counsel for an indigent applicant under this section in the same manner as in a proceeding under section 3006A(a)(2)(B).

(c) Testing procedures.—

(1) In general.—The court shall direct that any DNA testing ordered under this section be carried out by the Federal Bureau of Investigation.

(2) Exception.—Notwithstanding paragraph (1), the court may order DNA testing by another qualified laboratory if the court makes all necessary orders to ensure the integrity of the specific evidence and the reliability of the testing process and test results.

(3) Costs.—The costs of any DNA testing ordered under this section shall be paid—

(A) by the applicant; or

(B) in the case of an applicant who is indigent, by the Government.

(d) Time limitation in capital cases.—In any case in which the applicant is sentenced to death—

(1) any DNA testing ordered under this section shall be completed not later than 60 days after the date on which the Government responds to the motion filed under subsection (a); and

(2) not later than 120 days after the date on which the DNA testing ordered under this section is completed, the court shall order any post-testing procedures under subsection (f) or (g), as appropriate.

(e) Reporting of test results.—

(1) In general.—The results of any DNA testing ordered under this section shall be simultaneously disclosed to the court, the applicant, and the Government.

(2) NDIS.—The Government shall submit any test results relating to the DNA of the applicant to the National DNA Index System (referred to in this subsection as "NDIS").

(3) Retention of DNA sample.—

(A) Entry into NDIS.—If the DNA test results obtained under this section are inconclusive or show that the applicant was the source of the DNA evidence, the DNA sample of the applicant may be retained in NDIS.

(B) Match with other offense.—If the DNA test results obtained under this section exclude the applicant as the source of the DNA evidence, and a comparison of the DNA sample of the applicant results in a match between the DNA sample of the applicant and another offense, the Attorney General shall notify the appropriate agency and preserve the DNA sample of the applicant.

(C) No match.—If the DNA test results obtained under this section exclude the applicant as the source of the DNA evidence, and a comparison of the DNA sample of the applicant does not result in a match between the DNA sample of the applicant and another offense, the Attorney General shall destroy the DNA sample of the applicant and ensure that such information is not retained in NDIS if there is no other legal authority to retain the DNA sample of the applicant in NDIS.

(f) Post-testing procedures; inconclusive and inculpatory results.—

(1) Inconclusive results.—If DNA test results obtained under this section are inconclusive, the court may order further testing, if appropriate, or may deny the applicant relief.

(2) Inculpatory results.—If DNA test results obtained under this section show that the applicant was the source of the DNA evidence, the court shall—

(A) deny the applicant relief; and

(B) on motion of the Government—

(i) make a determination whether the applicant's assertion of actual innocence was false, and, if the court makes such a finding, the court may hold the applicant in contempt;

(ii) assess against the applicant the cost of any DNA testing carried out under this section;

(iii) forward the finding to the Director of the Bureau of Prisons, who, upon receipt of such a finding, may deny, wholly or in part, the good conduct credit authorized under section 3632 on the basis of that finding;

(iv) if the applicant is subject to the jurisdiction of the United States Parole Commission, forward the finding to the Commission so that the Commission may deny parole on the basis of that finding; and

(v) if the DNA test results relate to a State offense, forward the finding to any appropriate State official.

(3) Sentence.—In any prosecution of an applicant under chapter 79 for false assertions or other conduct in proceedings under this section, the court, upon conviction of the applicant, shall sentence the applicant to a term of imprisonment of not less than 3 years, which shall run consecutively to any other term of imprisonment the applicant is serving.

(g) Post-testing procedures; motion for new trial or resentencing.—

(1) In general.—Notwithstanding any law that would bar a motion under this paragraph as untimely, if DNA test results obtained under this section exclude the applicant as the source of the DNA evidence, the applicant may file a motion for a new trial or resentencing, as appropriate. The court shall establish a reasonable schedule for the applicant to file such a motion and for the Government to respond to the motion.

(2) Standard for granting motion for new trial or resentencing.—The court shall grant the motion of the applicant for a new trial or resentencing, as appropriate, if the DNA test results, when considered with all other evidence in the case (regardless of whether such evidence was introduced at trial), establish by compelling evidence that a new trial would result in an acquittal of—

(A) in the case of a motion for a new trial, the Federal offense for which the applicant is under a sentence of imprisonment or death; and

(B) in the case of a motion for resentencing, another Federal or State offense, if evidence of such offense was admitted during a Federal death sentencing hearing and exoneration of such offense would entitle the applicant to a reduced sentence or a new sentencing proceeding.

(h) Other laws unaffected.—

(1) Post-conviction relief.—Nothing in this section shall affect the circumstances under which a person may obtain DNA testing or post-conviction relief under any other law.

(2) Habeas corpus.—Nothing in this section shall provide a basis for relief in any Federal habeas corpus proceeding.

(3) Not a motion under section 2255.—A motion under this section shall not be considered to be a motion under section 2255 for purposes of determining whether the motion or any other motion is a second or successive motion under section 2255.

(Added Pub.L. 108–405, Title IV, § 411(a)(1), Oct. 30, 2004, 118 Stat. 2279.)

HISTORICAL AND STATUTORY NOTES

References in Text

The date of enactment of the Innocence Protection Act of 2004, referred to in subsec. (a)(3)(A)(i), is Oct. 30, 2004, the approval date of Pub.L. 108–405, Title IV, §§ 401 to 432, 118 Stat. 2278, known as the Innocence Protection Act of 2004, which enacted this section.

Enactment of the Justice For All Act of 2004, referred to in subsec. (a)(10)(A), is the enactment of Pub.L. 108–405, which was approved Oct. 30, 2004.

Effective and Applicability Provisions

2004 Acts. Pub.L. 108–405, Title IV, § 411(c), Oct. 30, 2004, 118 Stat. 2284, provided that: "This section and the amendments made by this section [enacting this chapter and provisions set out as a note under this section] shall take effect on the date of enactment of this Act [Oct. 30, 2004] and shall apply with respect to any offense committed, and to any judgment of conviction entered, before, on, or after that date of enactment."

Short Title

2004 Acts. Pub.L. 108–405, Title IV, § 401, Oct. 30, 2004, 118 Stat. 2278, provided that: "This title [enacting this section, 18 U.S.C.A. § 3600A, and 42 U.S.C.A. §§ 14136e, 14163, and 14163a to 14163e, amending 28 U.S.C.A. § 2513, and enacting provisions set out as notes under this section and 42 U.S.C.A. § 14136] may be cited as the 'Innocence Protection Act of 2004'."

System For Reporting Motions

Pub.L. 108–405, Title IV, § 411(b), Oct. 30, 2004, 118 Stat. 2284, provided that:

"(1) Establishment.—The Attorney General shall establish a system for reporting and tracking motions filed in accordance with section 3600 of title 18, United States Code [this section].

"(2) **Operation.**—In operating the system established under paragraph (1), the Federal courts shall provide to the Attorney General any requested assistance in operating such a system and in ensuring the accuracy and completeness of information included in that system.

"(3) **Report.**—Not later than 2 years after the date of enactment of this Act [Oct. 30, 2004], the Attorney General shall submit a report to Congress that contains—

"(A) a list of motions filed under section 3600 of title 18, United States Code, as added by this title [the Innocence Protection Act of 2004, Pub.L. 108–405, Title IV, §§ 401 to 432, Oct. 30, 2004, 118 Stat. 2278, enacting this section, 42 U.S.C.A. § 3600A, 42 U.S.C.A. §§ 14136e, 14163, and 14163a to 14163e, amending 28 U.S.C.A. § 2513, and enacting provisions set out as notes under this section and 42 U.S.C.A. § 14136];

"(B) whether DNA testing was ordered pursuant to such a motion;

"(C) whether the applicant obtained relief on the basis of DNA test results; and

"(D) whether further proceedings occurred following a granting of relief and the outcome of such proceedings.

"(4) **Additional information.**—The report required to be submitted under paragraph (3) may include any other information the Attorney General determines to be relevant in assessing the operation, utility, or costs of section 3600 of title 18, United States Code, as added by this title, and any recommendations the Attorney General may have relating to future legislative action concerning that section."

§ 3600A. Preservation of biological evidence

(a) In general.—Notwithstanding any other provision of law, the Government shall preserve biological evidence that was secured in the investigation or prosecution of a Federal offense, if a defendant is under a sentence of imprisonment for such offense.

(b) Defined term.—For purposes of this section, the term "biological evidence" means—

(1) a sexual assault forensic examination kit; or

(2) semen, blood, saliva, hair, skin tissue, or other identified biological material.

(c) Applicability.—Subsection (a) shall not apply if—

(1) a court has denied a request or motion for DNA testing of the biological evidence by the defendant under section 3600, and no appeal is pending;

(2) the defendant knowingly and voluntarily waived the right to request DNA testing of the biological evidence in a court proceeding conducted after the date of enactment of the Innocence Protection Act of 2004;

(3) after a conviction becomes final and the defendant has exhausted all opportunities for direct review of the conviction, the defendant is notified that the biological evidence may be destroyed and the defendant does not file a motion under section 3600 within 180 days of receipt of the notice;

(4)(A) the evidence must be returned to its rightful owner, or is of such a size, bulk, or physical character as to render retention impracticable; and

(B) the Government takes reasonable measures to remove and preserve portions of the material evidence sufficient to permit future DNA testing; or

(5) the biological evidence has already been subjected to DNA testing under section 3600 and the results included the defendant as the source of such evidence.

(d) Other preservation requirement.—Nothing in this section shall preempt or supersede any statute, regulation, court order, or other provision of law that may require evidence, including biological evidence, to be preserved.

(e) Regulations.—Not later than 180 days after the date of enactment of the Innocence Protection Act of 2004, the Attorney General shall promulgate regulations to implement and enforce this section, including appropriate disciplinary sanctions to ensure that employees comply with such regulations.

(f) Criminal penalty.—Whoever knowingly and intentionally destroys, alters, or tampers with biological evidence that is required to be preserved under this section with the intent to prevent that evidence from being subjected to DNA testing or prevent the production or use of that evidence in an official proceeding, shall be fined under this title, imprisoned for not more than 5 years, or both.

(g) Habeas corpus.—Nothing in this section shall provide a basis for relief in any Federal habeas corpus proceeding.

(Added Pub.L. 108–405, Title IV, § 411(a)(1), Oct. 30, 2004, 118 Stat. 2283.)

HISTORICAL AND STATUTORY NOTES

References in Text

The date of enactment of the Innocence Protection Act of 2004, referred to in subsecs. (c)(2) and (e), is Oct. 30, 2004, the approval date of Pub.L. 108–405, Title IV, §§ 401 to 432, 118 Stat. 2278, known as the Innocence Protection Act of 2004, which enacted this section.

Effective and Applicability Provisions

2004 Acts. This section effective Oct. 30, 2004, and applicable to any offense committed, and any judgment of conviction entered, before, on, or after Oct. 30, 2004, see Pub.L. 108–405, § 411(c), set out as a note under 18 U.S.C.A. § 3600.

CHAPTER 229—POSTSENTENCE ADMINISTRATION

[1] Editorially supplied.

HISTORICAL AND STATUTORY NOTES

Prior Provisions

A prior chapter 229 (§ 3611 et seq.) was repealed by Pub.L. 98–473, Title II, c. II, § 212(a)(1), (2), 235(a)(1), Oct. 12, 1984, 98 Stat. 1987, (except sections 3611, 3612, 3615, and 3617 to 3620, which were renumbered as sections 3665 to 3671, respectively) effective Nov. 1, 1987, and applicable only to offenses committed after the taking effect of such repeal. Section 235 of Pub.L. 98–473, as amended, relating to effective dates, is set out as a note under section 3551 of this title. Prior to repeal, the provisions of such chapter 229, "Fines, Penalties, and Forfeitures", read as follows:

§ 3611. Firearms possessed by convicted felons

A judgment of conviction for transporting a stolen motor vehicle in interstate or foreign commerce or for committing or attempting to commit a felony in violation of any law of the United States involving the use of threats, force, or violence or perpetrated in whole or in part by the use of firearms, may, in addition to the penalty provided by law for such offense, order the confiscation and disposal of firearms and ammunition found in the possession or under the immediate control of the defendant at the time of his arrest.

The court may direct the delivery of such firearms or ammunition to the law-enforcement agency which apprehended such person, for its use or for any other disposition in its discretion.

(June 25, 1948, c. 645, 62 Stat. 839.)

§ 3612. Bribe moneys

Moneys received or tendered in evidence in any United States Court, or before any officer thereof, which have been paid to or received by any official as a bribe, shall, after the final disposition of the case, proceeding or investigation, be deposited in the registry of the court to be disposed of in accordance with the order of the court, to be subject, however, to the provisions of section 2042 of Title 28.

(June 25, 1948, c. 645, 62 Stat. 840; May 24, 1949, c. 139, § 55, 63 Stat. 96.)

§ 3613. Fines for setting grass and timber fires

In all cases arising under sections 1855 and 1856 of this title the fines collected shall be paid into the public-school fund of the county in which the lands where the offense was committed are situated.

(June 25, 1948, c. 645, 62 Stat. 840.)

§ 3614. Fine for seduction

When a person is convicted of a violation of section 2198 of this title and fined, the court may direct that the amount of the fine, when paid, be paid for the use of the female seduced, or her child, if she have any.

(June 25, 1948, c. 645, 62 Stat. 840.)

§ 3615. Liquors and related property; definitions

All liquor involved in any violation of sections 1261–1265 of this title, the containers of such liquor, and every vehicle or vessel used in the transportation thereof, shall be seized and forfeited and such property or its proceeds disposed of in accordance with the laws relating to seizures, forfeitures, and dispositions of property or proceeds, for violation of the internal-revenue laws.

As used in this section, "vessel" includes every description of watercraft used, or capable of being used, as a means of transportation in water or in water and air; "vehicle" includes animals and every description of carriage or other contrivance used, or capable of being used, as a means of transportation on land or through the air.

(June 25, 1948, c. 645, 62 Stat. 840.)

[§ 3616. Repealed. Pub.L. 91–513, Title III, § 1101(b)(2)(A), Oct. 27, 1970, 84 Stat. 1292]

§ 3617. Remission or mitigation of forfeitures under liquor laws; possession pending trial

(a) Jurisdiction of court

Whenever, in any proceeding in court for the forfeiture, under the internal-revenue laws, of any vehicle or aircraft seized for a violation of the internal-revenue laws relating to liquors, such forfeiture is decreed, the court shall have exclusive jurisdiction to remit or mitigate the forfeiture.

(b) Conditions precedent to remission or mitigation

In any such proceeding the court shall not allow the claim of any claimant for remission or mitigation unless and until he proves (1) that he has an interest in such vehicle or aircraft, as owner or otherwise, which he acquired in good faith, (2) that he had at no time any knowledge or reason to believe that it was being or would be used in the violation of laws of the United States or of any State relating to liquor, and (3) if it appears that the interest asserted by the claimant arises out of or is in any way subject to any contract or agreement under which any person having a record or reputation for violating laws of the United States or of any State relating to liquor has a right with respect to such vehicle or aircraft, that, before such claimant acquired his interest, or such other person acquired his right under such contract or agreement, whichever occurred later, the claimant, his officer or agent, was informed in answer to his inquiry, at the headquarters of the sheriff, chief of police, principal Federal internal-revenue officer engaged in the enforcement of the liquor laws, or other principal local or Federal law-enforcement officer of the locality in which such other person acquired his right under such contract or agreement, of the locality in which such other person then resided, and of each locality in which the claimant has made any other inquiry as to the character or financial standing of such other person, that such other person had no such record or reputation.

(c) Claimants first entitled to delivery

Upon the request of any claimant whose claim for remission or mitigation is allowed and whose interest is first in the order of priority among such claims allowed in such proceeding and is of an amount in excess of, or equal to, the appraised value of such vehicle or aircraft, the court shall order its return to him; and, upon the joint request of any two or more claimants whose claims are allowed and whose interests are not subject to any prior or intervening interests claimed and allowed in such proceedings, and are of a total amount in excess of, or equal to, the appraised value of such vehicle or aircraft, the court shall order its return to such of the joint requesting claimants as is designated in such request. Such return shall be made only upon payment of all expenses incident to the seizure and forfeiture incurred by the United States. In all other cases the court shall order disposition of such vehicle or aircraft as provided in sections 304f–304m of Title 40 [see now 40 U.S.C.A. § 1306], and if such disposition be by public sale, payment from the proceeds thereof, after satisfaction of all such expenses, of any such claim in its order of priority among the claims allowed in such proceedings.

(d) Delivery on bond pending trial

In any proceeding in court for the forfeiture under the internal-revenue laws of any vehicle or aircraft seized for a violation of the internal-revenue laws relating to liquor, the court shall order delivery thereof to any claimant who shall establish his right to the immediate possession thereof, and shall execute, with one or more sureties approved by the court, and deliver to the court, a bond to the United States for the payment of a sum equal to the appraised value of such vehicle or aircraft. Such bond shall be conditioned to return such vehicle or aircraft at the time of the trial and to pay the difference between the appraised value of such vehicle or aircraft as of the time it shall have been so released on bond and the appraised value thereof as of the time of trial; and conditioned further that, if the vehicle or aircraft be not returned at the time of trial, the bond shall stand in lieu of, and be forfeited in the same manner as, such vehicle or aircraft. Notwithstanding this subsection or any other provisions of law relating to the delivery of possession on bond of vehicles or aircraft sought to be forfeited under the internal-revenue laws, the court may, in its discretion and upon good cause shown by the United States, refuse to order such delivery of possession.

(June 25, 1948, c. 645, 62 Stat. 840.)

§ 3618. Conveyances carrying liquor

Any conveyance, whether used by the owner or another in introducing or attempting to introduce intoxicants into the Indian country, or into other places where the introduction is prohibited by treaty or enactment of Congress, shall be subject to seizure, libel, and forfeiture.

(June 25, 1948, c. 645, 62 Stat. 841.)

§ 3619. Disposition of conveyances seized for violation of the Indian liquor laws

The provisions of section 3617 of this title shall apply to any conveyances seized, proceeded against by libel, or forfeited under the provisions of section 3113 or 3618 of this title for having been used in introducing or attempting to introduce intoxicants into the Indian country or into other places where such introduction is prohibited by treaty or enactment of Congress.

(Added Oct. 24, 1951, c. 546, § 2, 65 Stat. 609.)

§ 3620. Vessels carrying explosives and steerage passengers

The amount of any fine imposed upon the master of a steamship or other vessel under the provisions of section 2278 of this title shall be a lien upon such vessel, and such vessel may be libeled therefor in the district court of the United States for any district in which such vessel shall arrive or from which it shall depart.

(Added Sept. 3, 1954, c. 1263, § 36, 68 Stat. 1239.)

§ 3621. Criminal default on fine

(a) Whoever, having been sentenced to pay a fine or penalty, willfully does not pay an amount due—

(1) in the case of an individual, shall be fined not more than the greater of $100,000 or twice the unpaid balance of the fine or penalty, or imprisoned not more than one year, or both; and

(2) in the case of a person other than an individual, shall be fined not more than the greater of $250,000 or twice the unpaid balance of the fine or penalty.

(b) It is a defense to a prosecution under subsection (a)(1) of this section that the individual was unable to make the payment because of such individual's responsibility to provide necessities for such individual or other individuals financially dependent upon such individual. The defendant has the burden of establishing the defense under this subsection by a preponderance of the evidence.

(Added Pub.L. 98–596, § 6(a), Oct. 30, 1984, 98 Stat. 3136.)

§ 3622. Factors relating to imposition of fines

(a) In determining whether to impose a fine and the amount of a fine, the court shall consider, in addition to other relevant factors—

(1) the nature and circumstances of the offense;

(2) the history and characteristics of the defendant;

(3) the defendant's income, earning capacity, and financial resources;

(4) the burden that the fine will impose upon the defendant, any person who is financially dependent on the defendant, or any other person (including a government) that would be responsible for the welfare of any person financially dependent on the defendant, relative to the burden that alternative punishments would impose;

(5) any pecuniary loss inflicted upon others as a result of the offense;

(6) whether restitution is ordered and the amount of such restitution;

(7) the need to deprive the defendant of illegally obtained gains from the offense;

(8) whether the defendant can pass on to consumers or other persons the expense of the fine; and

(9) if the defendant is an organization, the size of the organization and any measure taken by the organization to discipline any officer, director, employee, or agent of the organization responsible for the offense and to prevent a recurrence of such an offense.

(b) If, as a result of a conviction, the defendant has the obligation to make restitution to a victim of the offense, the court shall impose a fine or penalty only to the extent that such fine or penalty will not impair the ability of the defendant to make restitution.

(Added Pub.L. 98–596, § 6(a), Oct. 30, 1984, 98 Stat. 3136.)

§ 3623. Alternative fines

(a) An individual convicted of an offense may be fined not more than the greatest of—

(1) the amount specified in the law setting forth the offense;

(2) the applicable amount under subsection (c) of this section;

(3) in the case of a felony, $250,000;

(4) in the case of a misdemeanor resulting in death, $250,000; or

(5) in the case of a misdemeanor punishable by imprisonment for more than six months, $100,000.

(b) A person (other than an individual) convicted of an offense may be fined not more than the greatest of—

(1) the amount specified in the law setting forth the offense;

(2) the applicable amount under subsection (c) of this section;

(3) in the case of a felony, $500,000;

(4) in the case of a misdemeanor resulting in death, $500,000; or

(5) in the case of a misdemeanor punishable by imprisonment for more than six months, $100,000.

(c)(1) If the defendant derives pecuniary gain from the offense, or if the offense results in pecuniary loss to another person, the defendant may be fined not more than the greater of twice the gross gain or twice the gross loss, unless imposition of a fine under this subsection would unduly complicate or prolong the sentencing process.

(2) Except as otherwise expressly provided, the aggregate of fines that a court may impose on a defendant at the same time for different offenses that arise from a common scheme or plan, and that do not cause separable or distinguishable kinds of harm or damage, is twice the amount imposable for the most serious offense.

(Added Pub.L. 98–596, § 6(a), Oct. 30, 1984, 98 Stat. 3137.)

§ 3624. Security for stayed fine

If a sentence imposing a fine is stayed, the court shall, absent exceptional circumstances (as determined by the court)—

(1) require the defendant to deposit, in the registry of the district court, any amount of the fine that is due;

(2) require the defendant to provide a bond or other security to ensure payment of the fine; or

(3) restrain the defendant from transferring or dissipating assets.

(Added Pub.L. 98–596, § 6(a), Oct. 30, 1984, 98 Stat. 3138.)

SUBCHAPTER A—PROBATION

SUBCHAPTER A—PROBATION [1]

[1] So in original. Subchapter analysis probably should appear at the chapter head.

§ 3601. Supervision of probation

A person who has been sentenced to probation pursuant to the provisions of subchapter B of chapter 227, or placed on probation pursuant to the provisions of chapter 403, or placed on supervised release pursuant to the provisions of section 3583, shall, during the term imposed, be supervised by a probation officer to the degree warranted by the conditions specified by the sentencing court.

(Added Pub.L. 98–473, Title II, § 212(a)(2), Oct. 12, 1984, 98 Stat. 2001.)

HISTORICAL AND STATUTORY NOTES

Effective and Applicability Provisions

1984 Acts. Section effective on the first day of first calendar month beginning thirty six months after Oct. 12, 1984, applicable only to offenses committed after taking effect of sections 211 to 239 of Pub.L. 98–473, and except as otherwise provided for therein, see section 235 of Pub.L. 98–473, as amended, set out as a note under section 3551 of this title.

Short Title

1996 Amendments. Pub.L. 104–134, Title I, § 101[(a)][Title VIII, § 801], Apr. 26, 1996, 110 Stat. 1321–66; renumbered Title I Pub.L. 104–140, § 1(a), May 2, 1996, 110 Stat. 1327, provided that: "This title [enacting sections 1915A and 1932 of Title 28, Judiciary and Judicial Procedure, amending sections 3624 and 3636 of this title, section 523 of Title 11, Bankruptcy, sections 1346 and 1915 of Title 28, and sections 1997a, 1997b, 1997c, 1997e, 1997f, and 1997h of Title 42, The Public Health and Welfare, enacting notes under section 3626 of this title, and repealing notes under section 3626 of this title] may be cited as the 'Prison Litigation Reform Act of 1995'."

Post Incarceration Vocational and Remedial Educational Opportunities for Inmates

Pub.L. 107–273, Div. B, Title II, § 2411, Nov. 2, 2002, 116 Stat. 1799, provided that:

"(a) **Federal Reentry Center Demonstration.**—

"(1) **Authority and establishment of Demonstration Project.**—The Attorney General, in consultation with the Director of the Administrative Office of the United States Courts, shall establish the Federal Reentry Center Demonstration project. The project shall involve appropriate prisoners from the Federal prison population and shall utilize community corrections facilities, home confinement, and a coordinated response by Federal agencies to assist participating prisoners in preparing for and adjusting to reentry into the community.

"(2) **Project elements.**—The project authorized by paragraph (1) shall include the following core elements:

"(A) A Reentry Review Team for each prisoner, consisting of a representative from the Bureau of Prisons, the United States Probation System, the United States Parole Commission, and the relevant community corrections facility, who shall initially meet with the prisoner to develop a reentry plan tailored to the needs of the prisoner.

"(B) A system of graduated levels of supervision with the community corrections facility to promote community safety, provide incentives for prisoners to complete the reentry plan, including victim restitution, and provide a reasonable method for imposing sanctions for a prisoner's violation of the conditions of participation in the project.

"(C) Substance abuse treatment and aftercare, mental and medical health treatment and aftercare, vocational and educational training, life skills instruction, conflict resolution skills training, batterer intervention programs, assistance obtaining suitable affordable housing, and other programming to promote effective reintegration into the community as needed.

"(3) **Probation officers.**—From funds made available to carry out this section [this note], the Director of the Administrative Office of the United States Courts shall assign 1 or more probation officers from each participating judicial district to the Reentry Demonstration project. Such officers shall be assigned to and stationed at the community corrections facility and shall serve on the Reentry Review Teams.

"(4) **Project duration.**—The Reentry Center Demonstration project shall begin not later than 6 months following the availability of funds to carry out this subsection, and shall last 3 years.

"(b) **Definitions.**—In this section [this note], the term 'appropriate prisoner' shall mean a person who is considered by prison authorities—

"(1) to pose a medium to high risk of committing a criminal act upon reentering the community; and

"(2) to lack the skills and family support network that facilitate successful reintegration into the community.

"(c) **Authorization of appropriations.**—To carry out this section [this note], there are authorized to be appropriated, to remain available until expended—

"(1) to the Federal Bureau of Prisons—

"(A) $1,375,000 for fiscal year 2003;

"(B) $1,110,000 for fiscal year 2004;

"(C) $1,130,000 for fiscal year 2005;

"(D) $1,155,000 for fiscal year 2006; and

"(E) $1,230,000 for fiscal year 2007; and

"(2) to the Federal Judiciary—

"(A) $3,380,000 for fiscal year 2003;

"(B) $3,540,000 for fiscal year 2004;

"(C) $3,720,000 for fiscal year 2005;

"(D) $3,910,000 for fiscal year 2006; and

"(E) $4,100,000 for fiscal year 2007."

§ 3602. Appointment of probation officers

(a) Appointment.—A district court of the United States shall appoint qualified persons to serve, with or without compensation, as probation officers within the jurisdiction and under the direction of the court making the appointment. The court may, for cause, remove a probation officer appointed to serve with compensation, and may, in its discretion, remove a probation officer appointed to serve without compensation.

(b) Record of appointment.—The order of appointment shall be entered on the records of the court, a copy of the order shall be delivered to the officer appointed, and a copy shall be sent to the Director of the Administrative Office of the United States Courts.

(c) Chief probation officer.—If the court appoints more than one probation officer, one may be designated by the court as chief probation officer and shall direct the work of all probation officers serving in the judicial district.

(Added Pub.L. 98–473, Title II, § 212(a)(2), Oct. 12, 1984, 98 Stat. 2001.)

HISTORICAL AND STATUTORY NOTES

Effective and Applicability Provisions

1984 Acts. Section effective on the first day of first calendar month beginning thirty-six months after Oct. 12, 1984, applicable only to offenses committed after taking effect of sections 211 to 239 of Pub.L. 98–473, and except as otherwise provided for therein, see section 235 of Pub.L. 98–473, as amended, set out as a note under section 3551 of this title.

§ 3603. Duties of probation officers

A probation officer shall—

(1) instruct a probationer or a person on supervised release, who is under his supervision, as to the conditions specified by the sentencing court, and provide him with a written statement clearly setting forth all such conditions;

(2) keep informed, to the degree required by the conditions specified by the sentencing court, as to the conduct and condition of a probationer or a person on supervised release, who is under his supervision, and report his conduct and condition to the sentencing court;

(3) use all suitable methods, not inconsistent with the conditions specified by the court, to aid a probationer or a person on supervised release who is under his supervision, and to bring about improvements in his conduct and condition;

(4) be responsible for the supervision of any probationer or a person on supervised release who is known to be within the judicial district;

(5) keep a record of his work, and make such reports to the Director of the Administrative Office of the United States Courts as the Director may require;

(6) upon request of the Attorney General or his designee, assist in the supervision of and furnish information about, a person within the custody of the Attorney General while on work release, furlough, or other authorized release from his regular place of confinement, or while in prerelease custody pursuant to the provisions of section 3624(c);

(7) keep informed concerning the conduct, condition, and compliance with any condition of probation, including the payment of a fine or restitution of each probationer under his supervision and report thereon to the court placing such person on probation and report to the court any failure of a probationer under his supervision to pay a fine in default within thirty days after notification that it is in default so that the court may determine whether probation should be revoked;

(8)(A) when directed by the court, and to the degree required by the regimen of care or treatment ordered by the court as a condition of release, keep informed as to the conduct and provide supervision of a person conditionally released under the provisions of section 4243 or 4246 of this title, and report such person's conduct and condition to the court ordering release and to the Attorney General or his designee; and

(B) immediately report any violation of the conditions of release to the court and the Attorney General or his designee;

(9) if approved by the district court, be authorized to carry firearms under such rules and regulations as the Director of the Administrative Office of the United States Courts may prescribe; and

(10) perform any other duty that the court may designate.

(Added Pub.L. 98–473, Title II, § 212(a)(2), Oct. 12, 1984, 98 Stat. 2002, and amended Pub.L. 99–646, § 15(a), Nov. 10, 1986, 100 Stat. 3595; Pub.L. 102–572, Title VII, § 701(a), Oct. 29, 1992, 106 Stat. 4514; Pub.L. 104–317, Title I, § 101(a), Oct. 19, 1996, 110 Stat. 3848.)

HISTORICAL AND STATUTORY NOTES

Effective and Applicability Provisions

1992 Acts. Amendment by Pub.L. 102–572 effective Jan. 1, 1993, see section 1101 of Pub.L. 102–572, set out as a note under section 905 of Title 2, The Congress.

1986 Acts. Section 15(b) of Pub.L. 99–646 provided that: "The amendments made by this section [amending this section] shall take effect on the date of the taking effect of section 3603 of title 18, United States Code [this section]."

1984 Acts. Section effective on the first day of first calendar month beginning thirty six months after Oct. 12, 1984, applicable only to offenses committed after taking effect of sections 211 to 239 of Pub.L. 98–473, and except as otherwise provided for therein, see section 235 of Pub.L. 98–473, as amended, set out as a note under section 3551 of this title.

§ 3604. Transportation of a probationer

A court, after imposing a sentence of probation, may direct a United States marshal to furnish the probationer with—

(a) transportation to the place to which he is required to proceed as a condition of his probation; and

(b) money, not to exceed such amount as the Attorney General may prescribe, for subsistence expenses while traveling to his destination.

(Added Pub.L. 98–473, Title II, § 212(a)(2), Oct. 12, 1984, 98 Stat. 2002.)

HISTORICAL AND STATUTORY NOTES

Effective and Applicability Provisions

1984 Acts. Section effective on the first day of first calendar month beginning thirty six months after Oct. 12, 1984, applicable only to offenses committed after taking effect of sections 211 to 239 of Pub.L. 98–473, and except as otherwise provided for therein, see section 235 of Pub.L. 98–473, as amended, set out as a note under section 3551 of this title.

§ 3605. Transfer of jurisdiction over a probationer

A court, after imposing a sentence, may transfer jurisdiction over a probationer or person on supervised release to the district court for any other district to which the person is required to proceed as a condition of his probation or release, or is permitted to proceed, with the concurrence of such court. A later transfer of jurisdiction may be made in the same manner. A court to which jurisdiction is transferred under this section is authorized to exercise all powers over the probationer or releasee that are permitted by this subchapter or subchapter B or D of chapter 227.

(Added Pub.L. 98–473, Title II, § 212(a)(2), Oct. 12, 1984, 98 Stat. 2003.)

HISTORICAL AND STATUTORY NOTES

Effective and Applicability Provisions

1984 Acts. Section effective on the first day of first calendar month beginning thirty six months after Oct. 12, 1984, applicable only to offenses committed after taking effect of sections 211 to 239 of Pub.L. 98–473, and except as otherwise provided for therein, see section 235 of Pub.L. 98–473, as amended, set out as a note under section 3551 of this title.

§ 3606. Arrest and return of a probationer

If there is probable cause to believe that a probationer or a person on supervised release has violated a condition of his probation or release, he may be arrested, and, upon arrest, shall be taken without unnecessary delay before the court having jurisdiction over him. A probation officer may make such an arrest wherever the probationer or releasee is found, and may make the arrest without a warrant. The court having supervision of the probationer or releasee, or, if there is no such court, the court last having supervision of the probationer or releasee, may issue a warrant for the arrest of a probationer or releasee for violation of a condition of release, and a probation officer or United States marshal may execute the warrant in the district in which the warrant was issued or in any district in which the probationer or releasee is found.

(Added Pub.L. 98–473, Title II, § 212(a)(2), Oct. 12, 1984, 98 Stat. 2003.)

HISTORICAL AND STATUTORY NOTES

Effective and Applicability Provisions

1984 Acts. Section effective on the first day of first calendar month beginning thirty six months after Oct. 12, 1984, applicable only to offenses committed after taking effect of sections 211 to 239 of Pub.L. 98–473, and except as otherwise provided for therein, see section 235 of Pub.L. 98–473, as amended, set out as a note under section 3551 of this title.

§ 3607. Special probation and expungement procedures for drug possessors

(a) Pre-judgment probation.—If a person found guilty of an offense described in section 404 of the Controlled Substances Act (21 U.S.C. 844)—

(1) has not, prior to the commission of such offense, been convicted of violating a Federal or State law relating to controlled substances; and

(2) has not previously been the subject of a disposition under this subsection;

the court may, with the consent of such person, place him on probation for a term of not more than one year without entering a judgment of conviction. At any time before the expiration of the term of probation, if the person has not violated a condition of his probation, the court may, without entering a judgment of conviction, dismiss the proceedings against the person and discharge him from probation. At the expiration of the term of probation, if the person has not violated a condition of his probation, the court shall, without entering a judgment of conviction, dismiss the proceedings against the person and discharge him from probation. If the person violates a condition of his probation, the court shall proceed in accordance with the provisions of section 3565.

(b) Record of disposition.—A nonpublic record of a disposition under subsection (a), or a conviction that is the subject of an expungement order under subsection (c), shall be retained by the Department of Justice solely for the purpose of use by the courts in determining in any subsequent proceeding whether a person qualifies for the disposition provided in subsection (a) or the expungement provided in subsection (c). A disposition under subsection (a), or a conviction that is the subject of an expungement order under subsection (c), shall not be considered a conviction for the purpose of a disqualification or a disability imposed by law upon conviction of a crime, or for any other purpose.

(c) Expungement of record of disposition.—If the case against a person found guilty of an offense under section 404 of the Controlled Substances Act (21 U.S.C. 844) is the subject of a disposition under subsection (a), and the person was less than twenty-one years old at the time of the offense, the court shall enter an expungement order upon the application of such person. The expungement order shall direct that there be expunged from all official records, except the nonpublic records referred to in subsection (b), all references to his arrest for the offense, the institution of criminal proceedings against him, and the results thereof. The effect of the order shall be to restore such person, in the contemplation of the law, to the status he occupied before such arrest or institution of criminal proceedings. A person concerning whom such an order has been entered shall not be held thereafter under any provision of law to be guilty of perjury, false swearing, or making a false statement by reason of his failure to recite or acknowledge such arrests or institution of criminal proceedings, or the results thereof, in response to an inquiry made of him for any purpose.

(Added Pub.L. 98–473, Title II, § 212(a)(2), Oct. 12, 1984, 98 Stat. 2003.)

HISTORICAL AND STATUTORY NOTES

Effective and Applicability Provisions

1984 Acts. Section effective on the first day of first calendar month beginning thirty six months after Oct. 12, 1984, applicable only to offenses committed after taking effect of sections 211 to 239 of Pub.L. 98–473, and except as otherwise provided for therein, see section 235 of Pub.L. 98–473, as amended, set out as a note under section 3551 of this title.

Short Title

1984 Acts. This section is popularly known as the Federal First Offender Act or FFOA.

§ 3608. Drug testing of Federal offenders on post-conviction release

The Director of the Administrative Office of the United States Courts, in consultation with the Attorney General and the Secretary of Health and Human Services, shall, subject to the availability of appropriations, establish a program of drug testing of Federal offenders on post-conviction release. The program shall include such standards and guidelines as the Director may determine necessary to ensure the reliability and accuracy of the drug testing programs. In each judicial district the chief probation officer shall arrange for the drug testing of defendants on post-conviction release pursuant to a conviction for a felony or other offense described in section 3563(a)(4).

(Added Pub.L. 103–322, Title II, § 20414(a)(1), Sept. 13, 1994, 108 Stat. 1830.)

HISTORICAL AND STATUTORY NOTES

References in Text

Section 3563(a)(4), referred to in text, probably means par. (4) of section 3563(a) added by section 20414(b)(3) of Pub.L. 103–322, which was renumbered par. (5) by Pub.L. 104–132, Title II, § 203(1)(C), Apr. 24, 1996, 110 Stat. 1227.

SUBCHAPTER B—FINES

SUBCHAPTER B—FINES [1]

[1] So in original. Subchapter analysis probably should appear at the chapter head.

[2] So in original. Does not conform to section catchline.

§ 3611. Payment of a fine or restitution

A person who is sentenced to pay a fine, assessment, or restitution, shall pay the fine, assessment, or restitution (including any interest or penalty), as specified by the Director of the Administrative Office of the United States Courts. Such Director may specify that such payment be made to the clerk of the court or in the manner provided for under section 604(a)(18) of title 28, United States Code.

(Added Pub.L. 98–473, Title II, § 212(a)(2), Oct. 12, 1984, 98 Stat. 2004, and amended Pub.L. 100–185, § 10(a), Dec. 11, 1987, 101 Stat. 1283; Pub.L. 101–647, Title XXXV, § 3591, Nov. 29, 1990, 104 Stat. 4931; Pub.L. 104–132, Title II, § 207(c)(1), Apr. 24, 1996, 110 Stat. 1237.)

HISTORICAL AND STATUTORY NOTES

Effective and Applicability Provisions

1996 Acts. Amendment by Pub.L. 104–132 to be effective, to the extent constitutionally permissible, for sentencing proceedings in cases in which the defendant is convicted on or after Apr. 24, 1996, see section 211 of Pub.L. 104–132, set out as a note under section 2248 of this title.

1987 Acts. Section 10(b) of Pub.L. 100–185 provided that: "The amendment made by this section [amending this section] shall apply with respect to any fine imposed after October 31, 1988. Such amendment shall also apply with respect to any fine imposed on or before October 31, 1988, if the fine remains uncollected as of February 1, 1989, unless the Director of the Administrative Office of the United States Courts determines further delay is necessary. If the Director so determines, the amendment made by this section shall apply with respect to any such fine imposed on or before October 31, 1988, if the fine remains uncollected as of May 1, 1989."

1984 Acts. Section effective on the first day of first calendar month beginning thirty six months after Oct. 12, 1984, applicable only to offenses committed after taking effect of sections 211 to 239 of Pub.L. 98–473, and except as otherwise provided for therein, see section 235 of Pub.L. 98–473, as amended, set out as a note under section 3551 of this title.

Prior Provisions

For a prior section 3611, applicable to offenses committed prior to Nov. 1, 1987, see note set out preceding section 3601 of this title.

Receipt of Fines; Interim Provisions

Section 9 of Pub.L. 100–185 provided that:

"**(a) November 1, 1987, to April 30, 1988.**—Notwithstanding section 3611 of title 18, United States Code [this section], a person who, during the period beginning on November 1, 1987, and ending on April 30, 1988, is sentenced to pay a fine or assessment shall pay the fine or assessment (including any interest or penalty) to the clerk of the court, with respect to an offense committed on or before December 31, 1984, and to the Attorney General, with respect to an offense committed after December 31, 1984.

"**(b) May 1, 1988, to October 31, 1988.**—(1) Notwithstanding section 3611 of title 18, United States Code [this section], a person who during the period beginning on May 1, 1988, and ending on October 31, 1988, is sentenced to pay a fine or assessment shall pay the fine or assessment in accordance with this subsection.

"(2) In a case initiated by citation or violation notice, such person shall pay the fine or assessment (including any interest or penalty), as specified by the Director of the Administrative Office of the United States Courts. Such Director may specify that such payment be made to the clerk of the court or in the manner provided for under section 604(a)(17) of title 28, United States Code [section 604(a)(17) of Title 28, Judiciary and Judicial Procedure].

"(3) In any other case, such person shall pay the fine or assessment (including any interest or penalty) to the clerk of the court, with respect to an offense committed on or before December 31, 1984, and to the Attorney General, with respect to an offense committed after December 31, 1984."

§ 3612. Collection of unpaid fine or restitution

(a) Notification of receipt and related matters.—The clerk or the person designated under section 604(a)(18) of title 28 shall notify the Attorney General of each receipt of a payment with respect to which a certification is made under subsection (b), together with other appropriate information relating to such payment. The notification shall be provided—

(1) in such manner as may be agreed upon by the Attorney General and the Director of the Administrative Office of the United States Courts; and

(2) within 15 days after the receipt or at such other time as may be determined jointly by the Attorney General and the Director of the Administrative Office of the United States Courts.

If the fifteenth day under paragraph (2) is a Saturday, Sunday, or legal public holiday, the clerk, or the person designated under section 604(a)(18) of title 28, shall provide notification not later than the next day that is not a Saturday, Sunday, or legal public holiday.

(b) Information to be included in judgment; judgment to be transmitted to Attorney General.—**(1)** A judgment or order imposing, modifying, or remitting a fine or restitution order of more than $100 shall include—

(A) the name, social security account number, mailing address, and residence address of the defendant;

(B) the docket number of the case;

(C) the original amount of the fine or restitution order and the amount that is due and unpaid;

(D) the schedule of payments (if other than immediate payment is permitted under section 3572(d));

(E) a description of any modification or remission;

(F) if other than immediate payment is permitted, a requirement that, until the fine or restitution order is paid in full, the defendant notify the Attorney General of any change in the mailing address or residence address of the defendant not later than thirty days after the change occurs; and

(G) in the case of a restitution order, information sufficient to identify each victim to whom restitution is owed. It shall be the responsibility of each victim to notify the Attorney General, or the appropriate entity of the court, by means of a form to be provided by the Attorney General or the court, of any change in the victim's mailing address while restitution is still owed the victim. The confidentiality of any information relating to a victim shall be maintained.

(2) Not later than ten days after entry of the judgment or order, the court shall transmit a certified copy of the judgment or order to the Attorney General.

(c) Responsibility for collection.—The Attorney General shall be responsible for collection of an unpaid fine or restitution concerning which a certification has been issued as provided in subsection (b). An order of restitution, pursuant to section 3556, does not create any right of action against the United States by the person to whom restitution is ordered to be paid. Any money received from a defendant shall be disbursed so that each of the following obligations is paid in full in the following sequence:

(1) A penalty assessment under section 3013 of title 18, United States Code.

(2) Restitution of all victims.

(3) All other fines, penalties, costs, and other payments required under the sentence.

(d) Notification of delinquency.—Within ten working days after a fine or restitution is determined to be delinquent as provided in section 3572(h), the Attorney General shall notify the person whose fine or restitution is delinquent, to inform the person of the delinquency.

(e) Notification of default.—Within ten working days after a fine or restitution is determined to be in default as provided in section 3572(i), the Attorney General shall notify the person defaulting to inform the person that the fine or restitution is in default and the entire unpaid balance, including interest and penalties, is due within thirty days.

(f) Interest on fines and restitution.—

(1) In general.—The defendant shall pay interest on any fine or restitution of more than $2,500, unless the fine is paid in full before the fifteenth day after the date of the judgment. If that day is a Saturday, Sunday, or legal public holiday, the defendant shall be liable for interest beginning with the next day that is not a Saturday, Sunday, or legal public holiday.

(2) Computation.—Interest on a fine shall be computed—

(A) daily (from the first day on which the defendant is liable for interest under paragraph (1)); and

(B) at a rate equal to the weekly average 1-year constant maturity Treasury yield, as published by the Board of Governors of the Federal Reserve System, for the calendar week preceding the first day on which the defendant is liable for interest under paragraph (1).

(3) Modification of interest by court.—If the court determines that the defendant does not have the ability to pay interest under this subsection, the court may—

(A) waive the requirement for interest;

(B) limit the total of interest payable to a specific dollar amount; or

(C) limit the length of the period during which interest accrues.

(g) Penalty for delinquent fine.—If a fine or restitution becomes delinquent, the defendant shall pay, as a penalty, an amount equal to 10 percent of the principal amount that is delinquent. If a fine or restitution becomes in default, the defendant shall pay, as a penalty, an additional amount equal to 15 percent of the principal amount that is in default.

(h) Waiver of interest or penalty by Attorney General.—The Attorney General may waive all or part of any interest or penalty under this section or any interest or penalty relating to a fine imposed under any prior law if, as determined by the Attorney General, reasonable efforts to collect the interest or penalty are not likely to be effective.

(i) Application of payments.—Payments relating to fines and restitution shall be applied in the following order: (1) to principal; (2) to costs; (3) to interest; and (4) to penalties.

(Added Pub.L. 98–473, Title II, § 212(a)(2), Oct. 12, 1984, 98 Stat. 2004, and amended Pub.L. 100–185, § 11, Dec. 11, 1987, 101 Stat. 1283, 1284; Pub.L. 100–690, Title VII, § 7082(c), (d), Nov. 18, 1988, 102 Stat. 4408; Pub.L. 101–647, Title XXXV, § 3592, Nov. 29, 1990, 104 Stat. 4931; Pub.L. 104–132, Title II, § 207(c)(2), Apr. 24, 1996, 110 Stat. 1237; Pub.L. 106–554, § 1(a)(7) [Title III, § 307(b)], Dec. 21, 2000, 114 Stat. 2763, 2763A–635; Pub.L. 107–273, Div. B, Title IV, § 4002(b)(15), Nov. 2, 2002, 116 Stat. 1808.)

HISTORICAL AND STATUTORY NOTES

Effective and Applicability Provisions

1996 Acts. Amendment by Pub.L. 104–132 to be effective, to the extent constitutionally permissible, for sentencing proceedings in cases in which the defendant is convicted on or after Apr. 24, 1996, see section 211 of Pub.L. 104–132, set out as a note under section 2248 of this title.

1984 Acts. Section effective on the first day of first calendar month beginning thirty six months after Oct. 12, 1984, applicable only to offenses committed after taking effect of sections 211 to 239 of Pub.L. 98–473, and except as otherwise provided for therein, see section 235 of Pub.L. 98–473, as amended, set out as a note under section 3551 of this title.

Prior Provisions

For a prior section 3612, applicable to offenses committed prior to Nov. 1, 1987, see note set out preceding section 3601 of this title.

Notice to Pay Fine in Full or by Installment

Section 237 of Pub.L. 98–473 provided:

"(a)(1) Except as provided in paragraph (2), for each criminal fine for which the unpaid balance exceeds $100 as of the effective date of this Act [see section 235 of Pub.L. 98–473 set out as a note under section 3551 of this title], the Attorney General shall, within one hundred and twenty days, notify the person by certified mail of his obligation, within thirty days after notification, to—

"(A) pay the fine in full;

"(B) specify, and demonstrate compliance with, an installment schedule established by a court before enactment of the amendments made by this Act [the Sentencing Reform Act of 1984 (Pub.L. 98–473, Title II, c. II)], specifying the dates on which designated partial payments will be made; or

"(C) establish with the concurrence of the Attorney General, a new installment schedule of a duration not exceeding two years, except in special circumstances, and specifying the dates on which designated partial payments will be made.

"(2) This subsection shall not apply in cases in which—

"(A) the Attorney General believes the likelihood of collection is remote; or

"(B) criminal fines have been stayed pending appeal.

"(b) The Attorney General shall, within one hundred and eighty days after the effective date of this Act, declare all fines for which this obligation is unfulfilled to be in criminal default, subject to the civil and criminal remedies established by amendments made by this Act. No interest or monetary penalties shall be charged on any fines subject to this section.

"(c) Not later than one year following the effective date of this Act, the Attorney General shall include in the annual crime report steps taken to implement this Act and the progress achieved in criminal fine collection, including collection data for each judicial district."

§ 3613. Civil remedies for satisfaction of an unpaid fine

(a) Enforcement.—The United States may enforce a judgment imposing a fine in accordance with the practices and procedures for the enforcement of a civil judgment under Federal law or State law. Notwithstanding any other Federal law (including section 207 of the Social Security Act), a judgment imposing a fine may be enforced against all property or rights to property of the person fined, except that—

(1) property exempt from levy for taxes pursuant to section 6334(a)(1), (2), (3), (4), (5), (6), (7), (8), (10), and (12) of the Internal Revenue Code of 1986 shall be exempt from enforcement of the judgment under Federal law;

(2) section 3014 of chapter 176 of title 28 shall not apply to enforcement under Federal law; and

(3) the provisions of section 303 of the Consumer Credit Protection Act (15 U.S.C. 1673) shall apply to enforcement of the judgment under Federal law or State law.

(b) Termination of liability.—The liability to pay a fine shall terminate the later of 20 years from the entry of judgment or 20 years after the release from imprisonment of the person fined, or upon the death of the individual fined.

(c) Lien.—A fine imposed pursuant to the provisions of subchapter C of chapter 227 of this title, or an order of restitution made pursuant to sections[1] 2248, 2259, 2264, 2327, 3663, 3663A, or 3664 of this title, is a lien in favor of the United States on all property and rights to property of the person fined as if the liability of the person fined were a liability for a tax assessed under the Internal Revenue Code of 1986. The lien arises on the entry of judgment and continues for 20 years or until the liability is satisfied, remitted, set aside, or is terminated under subsection (b).

(d) Effect of filing notice of lien.—Upon filing of a notice of lien in the manner in which a notice of tax lien would be filed under section 6323(f)(1) and (2) of the Internal Revenue Code of 1986, the lien shall be valid against any purchaser, holder of a security interest, mechanic's lienor or judgment lien creditor, except with respect to properties or transactions specified in subsection (b), (c), or (d) of section 6323 of the Internal Revenue Code of 1986 for which a notice of tax lien properly filed on the same date would not be valid. The notice of lien shall be considered a notice of lien for taxes payable to the United States for the purpose of any State or local law providing for the filing of a notice of a tax lien. A notice of lien that is registered, recorded, docketed, or indexed in accordance with the rules and requirements relating to judgments of the courts of the State where the notice of lien is registered, recorded, docketed, or indexed shall be considered for all purposes as the filing prescribed by this section. The provisions of section 3201(e) of chapter 176 of title 28 shall apply to liens filed as prescribed by this section.

(e) Discharge of debt inapplicable.—No discharge of debts in a proceeding pursuant to any chapter of title 11, United States Code, shall discharge liability to pay a fine pursuant to this section, and a lien filed as prescribed by this section shall not be voided in a bankruptcy proceeding.

(f) Applicability to order of restitution.—In accordance with section 3664(m)(1)(A) of this title, all provisions of this section are available to the United States for the enforcement of an order of restitution.

(Added Pub.L. 98–473, Title II, § 212(a)(2), Oct. 12, 1984, 98 Stat. 2005, and amended Pub.L. 101–647, Title XXXV, § 3593, Nov. 29, 1990, 104 Stat. 4931; Pub.L. 104–132, Title II, § 207(c)(3), Apr. 24, 1996, 110 Stat. 1238.)

[1] So in original. Probably should be "section".

HISTORICAL AND STATUTORY NOTES

References in Text

Section 207 of the Social Security Act, referred to in subsec. (a), is classified to section 407 of Title 42, The Public Health and Welfare.

The Internal Revenue Code of 1986, referred to in subsecs. (a), (c) and (d), is classified generally to Title 26, Internal Revenue Code.

Effective and Applicability Provisions

1996 Acts. Amendment by Pub.L. 104–132 to be effective, to the extent constitutionally permissible, for sentencing proceedings in cases in which the defendant is convicted on or after Apr. 24, 1996, see section 211 of Pub.L. 104–132, set out as a note under section 2248 of this title.

1984 Acts. Section effective on the first day of first calendar month beginning thirty six months after Oct. 12, 1984, applicable only to offenses committed after taking effect of sections 211 to 239 of Pub.L. 98–473, and except as otherwise provided for therein, see section 235 of Pub.L. 98–473, as amended, set out as a note under section 3551 of this title.

Prior Provisions

For a prior section 3613, applicable to offenses committed prior to Nov. 1, 1987, see note set out preceding section 3601 of this title.

§ 3613A. Effect of default

(a)(1) Upon a finding that the defendant is in default on a payment of a fine or restitution, the court may, pursuant to section 3565, revoke probation or a term of supervised release, modify the terms or conditions of probation or a term of supervised release, resentence a defendant pursuant to section 3614, hold the defendant in contempt of court, enter a restraining order or injunction, order the sale of property of the defendant, accept a performance bond, enter or adjust a payment schedule, or take any other action necessary to obtain compliance with the order of a fine or restitution.

(2) In determining what action to take, the court shall consider the defendant's employment status, earning ability, financial resources, the willfulness in failing to comply with the fine or restitution order, and any other circumstances that may have a bearing on the defendant's ability or failure to comply with the order of a fine or restitution.

(b)(1) Any hearing held pursuant to this section may be conducted by a magistrate judge, subject to de novo review by the court.

(2) To the extent practicable, in a hearing held pursuant to this section involving a defendant who is confined in any jail, prison, or other correctional facility, proceedings in which the prisoner's participation is required or permitted shall be conducted by telephone, video conference, or other communications technology without removing the prisoner from the facility in which the prisoner is confined.

(Added Pub.L. 104–132, Title II, § 207(c)(4), Apr. 24, 1996, 110 Stat. 1239.)

HISTORICAL AND STATUTORY NOTES

Effective and Applicability Provisions

1996 Acts. Section to be effective, to the extent constitutionally permissible, for sentencing proceedings in cases in which the defendant is convicted on or after Apr. 24, 1996, see section 211 of Pub.L. 104–132, set out as a note under section 2248 of this title.

§ 3614. Resentencing upon failure to pay a fine or restitution

(a) Resentencing.—Subject to the provisions of subsection (b), if a defendant knowingly fails to pay a delinquent fine or restitution the court may resentence the defendant to any sentence which might originally have been imposed.

(b) Imprisonment.—The defendant may be sentenced to a term of imprisonment under subsection (a) only if the court determines that—

(1) the defendant willfully refused to pay the delinquent fine or had failed to make sufficient bona fide efforts to pay the fine; or

(2) in light of the nature of the offense and the characteristics of the person, alternatives to imprisonment are not adequate to serve the purposes of punishment and deterrence.

(c) Effect of indigency.—In no event shall a defendant be incarcerated under this section solely on the basis of inability to make payments because the defendant is indigent.

(Added Pub.L. 98–473, Title II, § 212(a)(2), Oct. 12, 1984, 98 Stat. 2006, and amended Pub.L. 104–132, Title II, § 207(c)(5), Apr. 24, 1996, 110 Stat. 1240.)

HISTORICAL AND STATUTORY NOTES

Effective and Applicability Provisions

1996 Acts. Amendment by Pub.L. 104–132 to be effective, to the extent constitutionally permissible, for sentencing proceedings in cases in which the defendant is convicted on or after Apr. 24, 1996, see section 211 of Pub.L. 104–132, set out as a note under section 2248 of this title.

1984 Acts. Section effective on the first day of first calendar month beginning thirty six months after Oct. 12, 1984, applicable only to offenses committed after taking effect of sections 211 to 239 of Pub.L. 98–473, and except as otherwise provided for therein, see section 235 of Pub.L. 98–473, as amended, set out as a note under section 3551 of this title.

Prior Provisions

For a prior section 3614, applicable to offenses committed prior to Nov. 1, 1987, see note set out preceding section 3601 of this title.

§ 3615. Criminal default

Whoever, having been sentenced to pay a fine, willfully fails to pay the fine, shall be fined not more than twice the amount of the unpaid balance of the fine or $10,000, whichever is greater, imprisoned not more than one year, or both.

(Added Pub.L. 98–473, Title II, § 212(a)(2), Oct. 12, 1984, 98 Stat. 2006.)

HISTORICAL AND STATUTORY NOTES

Effective and Applicability Provisions

1984 Acts. Section effective on the first day of first calendar month beginning thirty six months after Oct. 12, 1984, applicable only to offenses committed after taking effect of sections 211 to 239 of Pub.L. 98–473, and except as otherwise provided for therein, see section 235 of Pub.L. 98–473, as amended, set out as a note under section 3551 of this title.

Prior Provisions

For a prior section 3615, applicable to offenses committed prior to Nov. 1, 1987, see note set out preceding section 3601 of this title.

SUBCHAPTER C—IMPRISONMENT

SUBCHAPTER C—IMPRISONMENT [1]

Sec.

[1] So in original. Subchapter analysis probably should appear at the chapter head.

HISTORICAL AND STATUTORY NOTES

Codifications

Amendment by Pub.L. 104–134, Title I, § 101[(a)][Title VIII, § 802(c)], Apr. 26, 1996, 110 Stat. 1321–70; renumbered Title I Pub.L. 104–140, § 1(a), May 2, 1996, 110 Stat. 1327, which directed that subchapter C analysis be amended, was executed by making amendment to item 3626 as the probable intent of Congress.

§ 3621. Imprisonment of a convicted person

(a) Commitment to custody of Bureau of Prisons.—A person who has been sentenced to a term of imprisonment pursuant to the provisions of subchapter D of chapter 227 shall be committed to the custody of the Bureau of Prisons until the expiration of the term imposed, or until earlier released for satisfactory behavior pursuant to the provisions of section 3624.

(b) Place of imprisonment.—The Bureau of Prisons shall designate the place of the prisoner's imprisonment. The Bureau may designate any available penal or correctional facility that meets minimum standards of health and habitability established by the Bureau, whether maintained by the Federal Government or otherwise and whether within or without the judicial district in which the person was convicted, that the Bureau determines to be appropriate and suitable, considering—

(1) the resources of the facility contemplated;

(2) the nature and circumstances of the offense;

(3) the history and characteristics of the prisoner;

(4) any statement by the court that imposed the sentence—

(A) concerning the purposes for which the sentence to imprisonment was determined to be warranted; or

(B) recommending a type of penal or correctional facility as appropriate; and

(5) any pertinent policy statement issued by the Sentencing Commission pursuant to section 994(a)(2) of title 28.

In designating the place of imprisonment or making transfers under this subsection, there shall be no favoritism given to prisoners of high social or economic status. The Bureau may at any time, having regard for the same matters, direct the transfer of a prisoner from one penal or correctional facility to another. The Bureau shall make available appropriate substance abuse treatment for each prisoner the Bureau determines has a treatable condition of substance addiction or abuse.

(c) Delivery of order of commitment.—When a prisoner, pursuant to a court order, is placed in the custody of a person in charge of a penal or correctional facility, a copy of the order shall be delivered to such person as evidence of this authority to hold the prisoner, and the original order, with the return endorsed thereon, shall be returned to the court that issued it.

(d) Delivery of prisoner for court appearances.—The United States marshal shall, without charge, bring a prisoner into court or return him to a prison facility on order of a court of the United States or on written request of an attorney for the Government.

(e) Substance abuse treatment.—

(1) Phase-in.—In order to carry out the requirement of the last sentence of subsection (b) of this section, that every prisoner with a substance abuse problem have the opportunity to participate in appropriate substance abuse treatment, the Bureau of Prisons shall, subject to the availability of appropriations, provide residential substance abuse treatment (and make arrangements for appropriate aftercare)—

(A) for not less than 50 percent of eligible prisoners by the end of fiscal year 1995, with priority for such treatment accorded based on an eligible prisoner's proximity to release date;

(B) for not less than 75 percent of eligible prisoners by the end of fiscal year 1996, with priority for such treatment accorded based on an eligible prisoner's proximity to release date; and

(C) for all eligible prisoners by the end of fiscal year 1997 and thereafter, with priority for such treatment accorded based on an eligible prisoner's proximity to release date.

(2) Incentive for prisoners' successful completion of treatment program.—

(A) Generally.—Any prisoner who, in the judgment of the Director of the Bureau of Prisons, has successfully completed a program of residential substance abuse treatment provided under paragraph (1) of this subsection, shall remain in the custody of the Bureau under such conditions as the Bureau deems appropriate. If the conditions of confinement are different from those the prisoner would have experienced absent the successful completion of the treatment, the Bureau shall periodically test the prisoner for substance abuse and discontinue such conditions on determining that substance abuse has recurred.

(B) Period of custody.—The period a prisoner convicted of a nonviolent offense remains in custody after successfully completing a treatment program may be reduced by the Bureau of Prisons, but such reduction may not be more than one year from the term the prisoner must otherwise serve.

(3) Report.—The Bureau of Prisons shall transmit to the Committees on the Judiciary of the Senate and the House of Representatives on January 1, 1995, and on January 1 of each year thereafter, a report. Such report shall contain—

(A) a detailed quantitative and qualitative description of each substance abuse treatment program, residential or not, operated by the Bureau;

(B) a full explanation of how eligibility for such programs is determined, with complete information on what proportion of prisoners with substance abuse problems are eligible; and

(C) a complete statement of to what extent the Bureau has achieved compliance with the requirements of this title.

(4) Authorization of appropriations.—There are authorized to carry out this subsection such sums as may be necessary for each of fiscal years 2007 through 2011.

(5) Definitions.—As used in this subsection—

(A) the term "residential substance abuse treatment" means a course of individual and group activities, lasting between 6 and 12 months, in residential treatment facilities set apart from the general prison population—

(i) directed at the substance abuse problems of the prisoner;

(ii) intended to develop the prisoner's cognitive, behavioral, social, vocational, and other skills so as to solve the prisoner's substance abuse and related problems; and

(iii) which may include the use of pharmacotherapies [1], if appropriate, that may extend beyond the treatment period;

(B) the term "eligible prisoner" means a prisoner who is—

(i) determined by the Bureau of Prisons to have a substance abuse problem; and

(ii) willing to participate in a residential substance abuse treatment program; and

(C) the term "aftercare" means placement, case management and monitoring of the participant in a community-based substance abuse treatment program when the participant leaves the custody of the Bureau of Prisons.

(6) Coordination of Federal assistance.—The Bureau of Prisons shall consult with the Department of Health and Human Services concerning substance abuse treatment and related services and the incorporation of applicable components of existing comprehensive approaches including relapse prevention and aftercare services.

(f) Sex offender management.—

(1) In general.—The Bureau of Prisons shall make available appropriate treatment to sex offenders who are in need of and suitable for treatment, as follows:

(A) Sex offender management programs.—The Bureau of Prisons shall establish non-residential sex offender management programs to provide appropriate treatment, monitoring, and supervision of sex offenders and to provide aftercare during pre-release custody.

(B) Residential sex offender treatment programs.—The Bureau of Prisons shall establish residential sex offender treatment programs to provide treatment to sex offenders who volunteer for such programs and are deemed by the Bureau of Prisons to be in need of and suitable for residential treatment.

(2) Regions.—At least 1 sex offender management program under paragraph (1)(A), and at least one residential sex offender treatment program under paragraph (1)(B), shall be established in each region within the Bureau of Prisons.

(3) Authorization of appropriations.—There are authorized to be appropriated to the Bureau of Prisons for each fiscal year such sums as may be necessary to carry out this subsection.

(Added Pub.L. 98–473, Title II, § 212(a)(2), Oct. 12, 1984, 98 Stat. 2007, and amended Pub.L. 101–647, Title XXIX, § 2903, Nov. 29, 1990, 104 Stat. 4913; Pub.L. 103–322, Title II, § 20401, Title III, § 32001, Sept. 13, 1994, 108 Stat. 1824, 1896; Pub.L. 109–162, Title XI, § 1146, Jan. 5, 2006, 119 Stat. 3112; Pub.L. 109–248, Title VI, § 622, July 27, 2006, 120 Stat. 634.)

1 So in enrolled.

HISTORICAL AND STATUTORY NOTES

Effective and Applicability Provisions

1984 Acts. Section effective on the first day of first calendar month beginning thirty six months after Oct. 12, 1984, applicable only to offenses committed after taking effect of sections 211 to 239 of Pub.L. 98–473, and except as otherwise provided for therein, see section 235 of Pub.L. 98–473, as amended, set out as a note under section 3551 of this title.

Prior Provisions

For a prior section 3621, applicable to offenses committed prior to Nov. 1, 1987, see note set out preceding section 3601 of this title.

§ 3622. Temporary release of a prisoner

The Bureau of Prisons may release a prisoner from the place of his imprisonment for a limited period if such release appears to be consistent with the purpose for which the sentence was imposed and any pertinent policy statement issued by the Sentencing Commission pursuant to 28 U.S.C. 994(a)(2), if such release otherwise appears to be consistent with the public interest and if there is reasonable cause to believe that a prisoner will honor the trust to be imposed in him, by authorizing him, under prescribed conditions, to—

(a) visit a designated place for a period not to exceed thirty days, and then return to the same or another facility, for the purpose of—

(1) visiting a relative who is dying;

(2) attending a funeral of a relative;

(3) obtaining medical treatment not otherwise available;

(4) contacting a prospective employer;

(5) establishing or reestablishing family or community ties; or

(6) engaging in any other significant activity consistent with the public interest;

(b) participate in a training or educational program in the community while continuing in official detention at the prison facility; or

(c) work at paid employment in the community while continuing in official detention at the penal or correctional facility if—

(1) the rates of pay and other conditions of employment will not be less than those paid or provided for work of a similar nature in the community; and

(2) the prisoner agrees to pay to the Bureau such costs incident to official detention as the Bureau finds appropriate and reasonable under all the circumstances, such costs to be collected by the Bureau and deposited in the Treasury to the credit of the appropriation available for such costs at the time such collections are made.

(Added Pub.L. 98–473, Title II, § 212(a)(2), Oct. 12, 1984, 98 Stat. 2007.)

HISTORICAL AND STATUTORY NOTES

Effective and Applicability Provisions

1984 Acts. Section effective on the first day of first calendar month beginning thirty six months after Oct. 12, 1984, applicable only to offenses committed after taking effect of sections 211 to 239 of Pub.L. 98–473, and except as otherwise provided for therein, see section 235 of Pub.L. 98–473, as amended, set out as a note under section 3551 of this title.

Prior Provisions

For a prior section 3622, applicable to offenses committed prior to Nov. 1, 1987, see note set out preceding section 3601 of this title.

EXECUTIVE ORDERS

EXECUTIVE ORDER NO. 11755

Dec. 29, 1973, 39 F.R. 779, as amended by Ex.Ord.No. 12608, Sept. 9, 1987, 52 F.R. 34617; Ex. Ord. No. 12943, Dec. 13, 1994, 59 F.R. 64553

PRISON LABOR

The development of the occupational and educational skills of prison inmates is essential to their rehabilitation and to their ability to make an effective return to free society. Meaningful employment serves to develop those skills. It is also true, however, that care must be exercised to avoid either the exploitation of convict labor or any unfair competition between convict labor and free labor in the production of goods and services.

Under sections 3621 and 3622 of title 18, United States Code, the Bureau of Prisons is empowered to authorize Federal prisoners to work at paid employment in the community during their terms of imprisonment under conditions that protect against both the exploitation of convict labor and unfair competition with free labor.

Several states and other jurisdictions have similar laws or regulations under which individuals confined for violations of the laws of those places may be authorized to work at paid employment in the community.

Executive Order No. 325A, which was originally issued by President Theodore Roosevelt in 1905, prohibits the employment, in the performance of Federal contracts, of any person who is serving a sentence of imprisonment at hard labor imposed by a court of a State, territory, or municipality.

I have now determined that Executive Order No. 325A should be replaced with a new Executive order which would permit the employment of non-Federal prison inmates in the performance of Federal contracts under terms and conditions that are comparable to those now applicable to inmates of Federal prisons.

Now, THEREFORE, pursuant to the authority vested in me as President of the United States, it is hereby ordered as follows:

Section 1. (a) All contracts involving the use of appropriated funds which shall hereafter be entered into by any department or agency of the executive branch for performance in any State, the District of Columbia, the Commonwealth of Puerto Rico, the Virgin Islands, Guam, American Samoa, the Commonwealth of the Northern Mariana Islands, or the Trust Territory of the Pacific Islands shall, unless otherwise provided by law, contain a stipulation forbidding in the performance of such contracts, the employment of persons undergoing sentences of imprisonment which have been imposed by any court of a State, the District of Columbia, the Commonwealth of Puerto Rico, the Virgin Islands, Guam, American Samoa, the Commonwealth of the Northern Mariana Islands, or the Trust Territory of the Pacific Islands. This limitation, however, shall not prohibit the employment by a contractor in the performance of such contracts of persons on parole or probation to work at paid employment during the term of their sentence or persons who have been pardoned or who have served their terms. Nor shall it prohibit the employment by a contractor in the performance of such contracts of persons confined for violation of the laws of any of the States, the District of Columbia, the Commonwealth of Puerto Rico, the Virgin Islands, Guam, American Samoa, the Commonwealth of the Northern Mariana Islands, or the Trust Territory of the Pacific Islands who are authorized to work at paid employment in the community under the laws of such jurisdiction, if

(1)(A) The worker is paid or is in an approved work training program on a voluntary basis;

(B) Representatives of local union central bodies or similar labor union organizations have been consulted;

(C) Such paid employment will not result in the displacement of employed workers, or be applied in skills, crafts, or trades in which there is a surplus of available gainful labor in the locality, or impair existing contracts for services; and

(D) The rates of pay and other conditions of employment will not be less than those paid or provided for work of a similar nature in the locality in which the work is being performed; and

(2) The Attorney General has certified that the work-release laws or regulations of the jurisdiction involved are in conformity with the requirements of this order.

(b) After notice and opportunity for hearing, the Attorney General shall revoke any such certification under section 1(a)(2) if he finds that the work-release program of the jurisdiction involved is not being conducted in conformity with the requirements of this order or with its intent or purposes.

(c) The provisions of this order do not apply to purchases made under the micropurchase authority contained in section 32 of the Office of Federal Procurement Policy Act, as amended [section 428 of Title 41, Public Contracts].

Sec. 2. The Federal Procurement Regulations, the Armed Services Procurement Regulations, and to the extent necessary, any supplemental or comparable regulations issued by any agency of the executive branch shall be revised to reflect the policy prescribed by this order.

Sec. 3. Executive Order No. 325A is hereby superseded.

Sec. 4. This order shall be effective as of January 1, 1974.

RICHARD NIXON

§ 3623. Transfer of a prisoner to State authority

The Director of the Bureau of Prisons shall order that a prisoner who has been charged in an indictment or information with, or convicted of, a State felony, be transferred to an official detention facility within such State prior to his release from a Federal prison facility if—

(1) the transfer has been requested by the Governor or other executive authority of the State;

(2) the State has presented to the Director a certified copy of the indictment, information, or judgment of conviction; and

(3) the Director finds that the transfer would be in the public interest.

If more than one request is presented with respect to a prisoner, the Director shall determine which request should receive preference. The expenses of such transfer shall be borne by the State requesting the transfer.

(Added Pub.L. 98–473, Title II, § 212(a)(2), Oct. 12, 1984, 98 Stat. 2008.)

HISTORICAL AND STATUTORY NOTES

Effective and Applicability Provisions

1984 Acts. Section effective on the first day of first calendar month beginning thirty six months after Oct. 12, 1984, applicable only to offenses committed after taking effect of sections 211 to 239 of Pub.L. 98–473, and except as otherwise provided for therein, see section 235 of Pub.L. 98–473, as amended, set out as a note under section 3551 of this title.

Prior Provisions

For a prior section 3623, applicable to offenses committed prior to Nov. 1, 1987, see note set out preceding section 3601 of this title.

§ 3624. Release of a prisoner

(a) Date of release.—A prisoner shall be released by the Bureau of Prisons on the date of the expiration of the prisoner's term of imprisonment, less any time credited toward the service of the prisoner's sentence as provided in subsection (b). If the date for a prisoner's release falls on a Saturday, a Sunday, or a legal holiday at the place of confinement, the prisoner may be released by the Bureau on the last preceding weekday.

(b) Credit toward service of sentence for satisfactory behavior.—

(1) Subject to paragraph (2), a prisoner who is serving a term of imprisonment of more than 1 year [1] other than a term of imprisonment for the duration of the prisoner's life, may receive credit toward the service of the prisoner's sentence, beyond the time served, of up to 54 days at the end of each year of the prisoner's term of imprisonment, beginning at the end of the first year of the term, subject to determination by the Bureau of Prisons that, during that year, the prisoner has displayed exemplary compliance with institutional disciplinary regulations. Subject to paragraph (2), if the Bureau determines that, during that year, the prisoner has not satisfactorily complied with such institutional regulations, the prisoner shall receive no such credit toward service of the prisoner's sentence or shall receive such lesser credit as the Bureau determines to be appropriate. In awarding credit under this section, the Bureau shall consider whether the prisoner, during the relevant period, has earned, or is making satisfactory progress toward earning, a high school diploma or an equivalent degree. Credit that has not been earned may not later be granted. Subject to paragraph (2), credit for the last year or portion of a year of the term of imprisonment shall be prorated and credited within the last six weeks of the sentence.

(2) Notwithstanding any other law, credit awarded under this subsection after the date of enactment of the Prison Litigation Reform Act shall vest on the date the prisoner is released from custody.

(3) The Attorney General shall ensure that the Bureau of Prisons has in effect an optional General Educational Development program for inmates who have not earned a high school diploma or its equivalent.

(4) Exemptions to the General Educational Development requirement may be made as deemed appropriate by the Director of the Federal Bureau of Prisons.

(c) Pre-release custody.—The Bureau of Prisons shall, to the extent practicable, assure that a prisoner serving a term of imprisonment spends a reasonable part, not to exceed six months, of the last 10 per centum of the term to be served under conditions that will afford the prisoner a reasonable opportunity to adjust to and prepare for the prisoner's re-entry into the community. The authority provided by this subsection may be used to place a prisoner in home confinement. The United States Probation System shall, to the extent practicable, offer assistance to a prisoner during such pre-release custody.

(d) Allotment of clothing, funds, and transportation.—Upon the release of a prisoner on the expiration of the prisoner's term of imprisonment, the Bureau of Prisons shall furnish the prisoner with—

(1) suitable clothing;

(2) an amount of money, not more than $500, determined by the Director to be consistent with the needs of the offender and the public interest, unless the Director determines that the financial position of the offender is such that no sum should be furnished; and

(3) transportation to the place of the prisoner's conviction, to the prisoner's bona fide residence within the United States, or to such other place within the United States as may be authorized by the Director.

(e) Supervision after release.—A prisoner whose sentence includes a term of supervised release after imprisonment shall be released by the Bureau of Prisons to the supervision of a probation officer who shall, during the term imposed, supervise the person released to the degree warranted by the conditions specified by the sentencing court. The term of supervised release commences on the day the person is released from imprisonment and runs concurrently with any Federal, State, or local term of probation or supervised release or parole for another offense to which the person is subject or becomes subject during the term of supervised release. A term of supervised release does not run during any period in which the person is imprisoned in connection with a conviction for a Federal, State, or local crime unless the imprisonment is for a period of less than 30 consecutive days. No prisoner shall be released on supervision unless such prisoner agrees to adhere to an installment schedule, not to exceed two years except in special circumstances, to pay for any fine imposed for the offense committed by such prisoner.

(f) Mandatory functional literacy requirement.—

(1) The Attorney General shall direct the Bureau of Prisons to have in effect a mandatory functional literacy program for all mentally capable inmates who are not functionally literate in each Federal correctional institution within 6 months from the date of the enactment of this Act.

(2) Each mandatory functional literacy program shall include a requirement that each inmate participate in such program for a mandatory period sufficient to provide the inmate with an adequate opportunity to achieve functional literacy, and appropriate incentives which lead to successful completion of such programs shall be developed and implemented.

(3) As used in this section, the term "functional literacy" means—

(A) an eighth grade equivalence in reading and mathematics on a nationally recognized standardized test;

(B) functional competency or literacy on a nationally recognized criterion-referenced test; or

(C) a combination of subparagraphs (A) and (B).

(4) Non-English speaking inmates shall be required to participate in an English-As-A-Second-Language program until they function at the equivalence of the eighth grade on a nationally recognized educational achievement test.

(5) The Chief Executive Officer of each institution shall have authority to grant waivers for good cause as determined and documented on an individual basis.

(Added Pub.L. 98–473, Title II, § 212(a)(2), Oct. 12, 1984, 98 Stat. 2008, and amended Pub.L. 99–646, §§ 16(a), 17(a), Nov. 10, 1986, 100 Stat. 3595; Pub.L. 101–647, Title XXIX, §§ 2902(a), 2904, Nov. 29, 1990, 104 Stat. 4913; Pub.L. 103–322, Title II, §§ 20405, 20412, Sept. 13, 1994, 108 Stat. 1825, 1828; Pub.L. 104–66, Title I, § 1091(c), Dec. 21, 1995, 109 Stat. 722; Pub.L. 104–134, Title I, § 101[(a)][Title VIII, § 809(c)], Apr. 26, 1996, 110 Stat.1321–76; renumbered Title I Pub.L. 104–140, § 1(a), May 2, 1996, 110 Stat. 1327.)

[1] So in original. Probably should be followed by a comma.

HISTORICAL AND STATUTORY NOTES

References in Text

The date of enactment of the Prison Litigation Reform Act, referred to in subsec. (b)(2), is the date of enactment of Title VIII of Pub.L. 104–134, which was approved Apr. 26, 1996.

The date of enactment of this Act, referred to in subsec. (f)(1), probably means the date of enactment of Pub.L. 101–647, Nov. 29, 1990, 104 Stat. 4789, which was approved Nov. 29, 1990.

Effective and Applicability Provisions

1990 Acts. Section 2902(b) of Pub.L. 101–647 provided that: "Section 3624(c) of title 18, United States Code, as amended by this section [subsec. (c) of this section] shall apply with respect to all inmates, regardless of the date of their offense."

1986 Acts. Section 16(b) of Pub.L. 99–646 provided that: "The amendment made by this section [amending subsec. (b) of this section] shall take effect on the date of the taking effect of such section 3624 [this section]."

Section 17(a) of Pub.L. 99–646 provided that: "The amendment made by this section [amending subsec. (e) of this section] shall take effect on the date of the taking effect of such section 3624 [this section]."

1984 Acts. Section effective on the first day of first calendar month beginning thirty-six months after Oct. 12, 1984, applicable only to offenses committed after taking effect of sections 211 to 239 of Pub.L. 98–473, and except as otherwise provided for therein, see section 235 of Pub.L. 98–473, as amended, set out as a note under section 3551 of this title.

Severability of Provisions

If any provision of section 101[a] [Title VIII] of Pub.L. 104–134, an amendment made by such Title, or the application of such provision or amendment to any person or circumstance is held to be unconstitutional, the remainder of such Title, the amendments made by such Title, and the application of the provisions of such Title to any person or circumstance not affected thereby, see section 101[a] [Title VIII, § 810] of Pub.L. 104–134, set out as a note under section 3626 of this title.

Prior Provisions

For a prior section 3624, applicable to offenses committed prior to Nov. 1, 1987, see note set out preceding section 3601 of this title.

§ 3625. Inapplicability of the Administrative Procedure Act

The provisions of sections 554 and 555 and 701 through 706 of title 5, United States Code, do not apply to the making of any determination, decision, or order under this subchapter.

(Added Pub.L. 98–473, Title II, § 212(a)(2), Oct. 12, 1984, 98 Stat. 2010.)

HISTORICAL AND STATUTORY NOTES

Effective and Applicability Provisions

1984 Acts. Section effective on the first day of first calendar month beginning thirty-six months after Oct. 12, 1984, applicable only to offenses committed after taking effect of sections 211 to 239 of Pub.L. 98–473, and except as otherwise provided for therein, see section 235 of Pub.L. 98–473, as amended, set out as a note under section 3551 of this title.

§ 3626. Appropriate remedies with respect to prison conditions

(a) Requirements for relief.—

(1) Prospective relief.—(A) Prospective relief in any civil action with respect to prison conditions shall extend no further than necessary to correct the violation of the Federal right of a particular plaintiff or plaintiffs. The court shall not grant or approve any prospective relief unless the court finds that such relief is narrowly drawn, extends no further than necessary to correct the violation of the Federal right, and is the least intrusive means necessary to correct the violation of the Federal right. The court shall give substantial weight to any adverse impact on public safety or the operation of a criminal justice system caused by the relief.

(B) The court shall not order any prospective relief that requires or permits a government official to exceed his or her authority under State or local law or otherwise violates State or local law, unless—

(i) Federal law requires such relief to be ordered in violation of State or local law;

(ii) the relief is necessary to correct the violation of a Federal right; and

(iii) no other relief will correct the violation of the Federal right.

(C) Nothing in this section shall be construed to authorize the courts, in exercising their remedial powers, to order the construction of prisons or the raising of taxes, or to repeal or detract from otherwise applicable limitations on the remedial powers of the courts.

(2) Preliminary injunctive relief.—In any civil action with respect to prison conditions, to the extent otherwise authorized by law, the court may enter a temporary restraining order or an order for preliminary injunctive relief. Preliminary injunctive relief must be narrowly drawn, extend no further than necessary to correct the harm the court finds requires preliminary relief, and be the least intrusive means necessary to correct that harm. The court shall give substantial weight to any adverse impact on public safety or the operation of a criminal justice system caused by the preliminary relief and shall respect the principles of comity set out in paragraph (1)(B) in tailoring any preliminary relief. Preliminary injunctive relief shall automatically expire on the date that is 90 days after its entry, unless the court makes the findings required under subsection (a)(1) for the entry of prospective relief and makes the order final before the expiration of the 90-day period.

(3) Prisoner release order.—**(A)** In any civil action with respect to prison conditions, no court shall enter a prisoner release order unless—

(i) a court has previously entered an order for less intrusive relief that has failed to remedy the deprivation of the Federal right sought to be remedied through the prisoner release order; and

(ii) the defendant has had a reasonable amount of time to comply with the previous court orders.

(B) In any civil action in Federal court with respect to prison conditions, a prisoner release order shall be entered only by a three-judge court in accordance with section 2284 of title 28, if the requirements of subparagraph (E) have been met.

(C) A party seeking a prisoner release order in Federal court shall file with any request for such relief, a request for a three-judge court and materials sufficient to demonstrate that the requirements of subparagraph (A) have been met.

(D) If the requirements under subparagraph (A) have been met, a Federal judge before whom a civil action with respect to prison conditions is pending who believes that a prison release order should be considered may sua sponte request the convening of a three-judge court to determine whether a prisoner release order should be entered.

(E) The three-judge court shall enter a prisoner release order only if the court finds by clear and convincing evidence that—

(i) crowding is the primary cause of the violation of a Federal right; and

(ii) no other relief will remedy the violation of the Federal right.

(F) Any State or local official including a legislator or unit of government whose jurisdiction or function includes the appropriation of funds for the construction, operation, or maintenance of prison facilities, or the prosecution or custody of persons who may be released from, or not admitted to, a prison as a result of a prisoner release order shall have standing to oppose the imposition or continuation in effect of such relief and to seek termination of such relief, and shall have the right to intervene in any proceeding relating to such relief.

(b) Termination of relief.—

(1) Termination of prospective relief.—**(A)** In any civil action with respect to prison conditions in which prospective relief is ordered, such relief shall be terminable upon the motion of any party or intervener—

(i) 2 years after the date the court granted or approved the prospective relief;

(ii) 1 year after the date the court has entered an order denying termination of prospective relief under this paragraph; or

(iii) in the case of an order issued on or before the date of enactment of the Prison Litigation Reform Act, 2 years after such date of enactment.

(B) Nothing in this section shall prevent the parties from agreeing to terminate or modify relief before the relief is terminated under subparagraph (A).

(2) Immediate termination of prospective relief.—In any civil action with respect to prison conditions, a defendant or intervener shall be entitled to the immediate termination of any prospective relief if the relief was approved or granted in the absence of a finding by the court that the relief is narrowly drawn, extends no further than necessary to correct the violation of the Federal right, and is the least intrusive means necessary to correct the violation of the Federal right.

(3) Limitation.—Prospective relief shall not terminate if the court makes written findings based on the record that prospective relief remains necessary to correct a current and ongoing violation of the Federal right, extends no further than necessary to correct the violation of the Federal right, and that the prospective relief is narrowly drawn and the least intrusive means to correct the violation.

(4) Termination or modification of relief.—Nothing in this section shall prevent any party or intervener from seeking modification or termination before the relief is terminable under paragraph (1) or (2), to the extent that modification or termination would otherwise be legally permissible.

(c) Settlements.—

(1) Consent decrees.—In any civil action with respect to prison conditions, the court shall not enter or approve a consent decree unless it complies with the limitations on relief set forth in subsection (a).

(2) Private settlement agreements.—(A) Nothing in this section shall preclude parties from entering into a private settlement agreement that does not comply with the limitations on relief set forth in subsection (a), if the terms of that agreement are not subject to court enforcement other than the reinstatement of the civil proceeding that the agreement settled.

(B) Nothing in this section shall preclude any party claiming that a private settlement agreement has been breached from seeking in State court any remedy available under State law.

(d) State law remedies.—The limitations on remedies in this section shall not apply to relief entered by a State court based solely upon claims arising under State law.

(e) Procedure for motions affecting prospective relief.—

(1) Generally.—The court shall promptly rule on any motion to modify or terminate prospective relief in a civil action with respect to prison conditions. Mandamus shall lie to remedy any failure to issue a prompt ruling on such a motion.

(2) Automatic stay.—Any motion to modify or terminate prospective relief made under subsection (b) shall operate as a stay during the period—

(A)(i) beginning on the 30th day after such motion is filed, in the case of a motion made under paragraph (1) or (2) of subsection (b); or

(ii) beginning on the 180th day after such motion is filed, in the case of a motion made under any other law; and

(B) ending on the date the court enters a final order ruling on the motion.

(3) Postponement of automatic stay.—The court may postpone the effective date of an automatic stay specified in subsection (e)(2)(A) for not more than 60 days for good cause. No postponement shall be permissible because of general congestion of the court's calendar.

(4) Order blocking the automatic stay.—Any order staying, suspending, delaying, or barring the operation of the automatic stay described in paragraph (2) (other than an order to postpone the effective date of the automatic stay under paragraph (3)) shall be treated as an order refusing to dissolve or modify an injunction and shall be appealable pursuant to section 1292(a)(1) of title 28, United States Code, regardless of how the order is styled or whether the order is termed a preliminary or a final ruling.

(f) Special masters.—

(1) In general.—(A) In any civil action in a Federal court with respect to prison conditions, the court may appoint a special master who shall be disinterested and objective and who will give due regard to the public safety, to conduct hearings on the record and prepare proposed findings of fact.

(B) The court shall appoint a special master under this subsection during the remedial phase of the action only upon a finding that the remedial phase will be sufficiently complex to warrant the appointment.

(2) Appointment.—(A) If the court determines that the appointment of a special master is necessary, the court shall request that the defendant institution and the plaintiff each submit a list of not more than 5 persons to serve as a special master.

(B) Each party shall have the opportunity to remove up to 3 persons from the opposing party's list.

(C) The court shall select the master from the persons remaining on the list after the operation of subparagraph (B).

(3) Interlocutory appeal.—Any party shall have the right to an interlocutory appeal of the judge's selection of the special master under this subsection, on the ground of partiality.

(4) Compensation.—The compensation to be allowed to a special master under this section shall be based on an hourly rate not greater than the hourly rate established under section 3006A for payment of court-appointed counsel, plus costs reasonably incurred by the special master. Such compensation and costs shall be paid with funds appropriated to the Judiciary.

(5) Regular review of appointment.—In any civil action with respect to prison conditions in which a special master is appointed under this subsection, the court shall review the appointment of the special master every 6 months to determine whether the services of the special master continue to be required under paragraph (1). In no event shall the appointment of a special master extend beyond the termination of the relief.

(6) Limitations on powers and duties.—A special master appointed under this subsection—

(A) may be authorized by a court to conduct hearings and prepare proposed findings of fact, which shall be made on the record;

(B) shall not make any findings or communications ex parte;

(C) may be authorized by a court to assist in the development of remedial plans; and

(D) may be removed at any time, but shall be relieved of the appointment upon the termination of relief.

(g) Definitions.—As used in this section—

(1) the term "consent decree" means any relief entered by the court that is based in whole or in part upon the consent or acquiescence of the parties but does not include private settlements;

(2) the term "civil action with respect to prison conditions" means any civil proceeding arising under Federal law with respect to the conditions of confinement or the effects of actions by government officials on the lives of persons confined in prison, but does not include habeas corpus proceedings challenging the fact or duration of confinement in prison;

(3) the term "prisoner" means any person subject to incarceration, detention, or admission to any facility who is accused of, convicted of, sentenced for, or adjudicated delinquent for, violations of criminal law or the terms and conditions of parole, probation, pretrial release, or diversionary program;

(4) the term "prisoner release order" includes any order, including a temporary restraining order or preliminary injunctive relief, that has the purpose or effect of reducing or limiting the prison population, or that directs the release from or nonadmission of prisoners to a prison;

(5) the term "prison" means any Federal, State, or local facility that incarcerates or detains juveniles or adults accused of, convicted of, sentenced for, or adjudicated delinquent for, violations of criminal law;

(6) the term "private settlement agreement" means an agreement entered into among the parties that is not subject to judicial enforcement other than the reinstatement of the civil proceeding that the agreement settled;

(7) the term "prospective relief" means all relief other than compensatory monetary damages;

(8) the term "special master" means any person appointed by a Federal court pursuant to Rule 53 of the Federal Rules of Civil Procedure or pursuant to any inherent power of the court to exercise the powers of a master, regardless of the title or description given by the court; and

(9) the term "relief" means all relief in any form that may be granted or approved by the court, and includes consent decrees but does not include private settlement agreements.

(Added Pub.L. 103–322, Title II, § 20409(a), Sept. 13, 1994, 108 Stat. 1827, and amended Pub.L. 104–134, Title I, § 101[(a)][Title VIII, § 802(a)], Apr. 26, 1996, 110 Stat. 1321–66; renumbered Title I Pub.L. 104–140, May 2, 1996, 110 Stat. 1327, and amended Pub.L. 105–119, Title I, § 123(a), Nov. 26, 1997, 111 Stat. 2470.)

HISTORICAL AND STATUTORY NOTES

References in Text

The date of enactment of the Prison Litigation Reform Act, referred to in subsec. (b)(1)(A)(iii), is the date of enactment of Pub.L. 104–134, which was approved April 26, 1996.

The Federal Rules of Civil Procedure, referred to in subsec. (g)(8), are set out in the Appendix to Title 28.

Effective and Applicability Provisions

1997 Acts. Section 123(b) of Pub.L. 105–119 provided that: "The amendments made by this Act [sic][probably means section 123 of Pub.L. 105–119, which amended subsecs. (a), (b), and (e) of this section] shall take effect upon the date of the enactment of this Act [Nov. 26, 1997] and shall apply to pending cases."

1996 Acts. Pub.L. 104–134, Title I, § 101[(a)][Title VIII, § 802(b)(1)], Apr. 26, 1996, 110 Stat. 1321–70; renumbered Title I Pub.L. 104–140, § 1(a), May 2, 1996, 110 Stat. 1327, provided that: "Section 3626 of title 18, United States Code [this section], as amended by this section, shall apply with respect to all prospective relief whether such relief was originally granted or approved before, on, or after the date of the enactment of this title [Apr. 26, 1996]."

1994 Acts. Section 20409(b) of Pub.L. 103–322, which provided that this section applied to all court orders outstanding on Sept. 13, 1994, was repealed by Pub.L. 104–134, Title I, § 101[(a)][Title VIII, § 802(b)(2)], Apr. 26, 1996, 110 Stat. 1321–70; renumbered Pub.L. 104–140, § 1(a), May 2, 1996, 110 Stat. 1327.

Section 20409(d) of Pub.L. 103–322, which provided for the repeal of this section 5 years after Sept. 13, 1994, was repealed by Pub.L. 104–134, Title I, § 101[(a)][Title VIII, § 802(b)(2)], Apr. 26, 1996, 110 Stat. 1321–70; renumbered Title I Pub.L. 104–140, § 1(a), May 2, 1996, 110 Stat. 1327.

Severability of Provisions

Pub.L. 104–134, Title I, § 101[(a)][Title VIII, § 810], Apr. 26, 1996, 110 Stat. 1321–77; renumbered Title I Pub.L. 104–140, § 1(a), May 2, 1996, 110 Stat. 1327, provided that: "If any provision of this title [for distribution of which to the Code, see Short Title of 1996 Amendments note set out under section 3601 of this title and Tables], an amendment made by this title, or the application of such provision or amendment to any person or circumstance is held to be unconstitutional, the remainder of this title, the amendments made by this title, and the application of the provisions of such [sic] to any person or circumstance shall not be affected thereby."

Notice to Crime Victims of Pending Damage Award

Pub.L. 104–134, Title I, § 101[(a)][Title VIII, § 808], Apr. 26, 1996, 110 Stat. 1321–76; renumbered Title I Pub.L. 104–140, § 1(a), May 2, 1996, 110 Stat. 1327, provided that: "Prior to payment of any compensatory damages awarded to a prisoner in connection with a civil action brought against any Federal, State, or local jail, prison, or correctional facility or against any official or agent of such jail, prison, or correctional facility, reasonable efforts shall be made to notify the victims of the crime for which the prisoner was convicted and incarcerated concerning the pending amount of any such compensatory damages."

Payment of Damage Award in Satisfaction of Pending Restitution Orders

Pub.L. 104–134, § 101[(a)][Title VIII, § 807], Apr. 26, 1996, 110 Stat. 1321–75; renumbered Title I Pub.L. 104–140, § 1(a), May 2, 1996, 110 Stat. 1327, provided that: "Any compensatory damages awarded to a prisoner in connection with a civil action brought against any Federal, State, or local jail, prison, or correctional facility or against any official or agent of such jail, prison, or correctional facility, shall be paid directly to satisfy any outstanding restitution orders pending against the prisoner. The remainder of any such award after full payment of all pending restitution orders shall be forwarded to the prisoner."

Special Masters Appointed Prior to Apr. 26, 1996; Prohibition on Use of Funds

Pub.L. 104–208, Div. A, Title I, § 101(a) [Title III, § 306], Sept. 30, 1996, 110 Stat. 3009–45, provided that: "None of the funds available to the Judiciary in fiscal years 1996 and 1997 and hereafter shall be available for expenses authorized pursuant to section 802(a) of title VIII of section 101(a) of title I of the Omnibus Consolidated Rescissions and Appropriations Act of 1996, Public Law 104–134 [enacting this section], for costs related to the appointment of Special Masters prior to April 26, 1996."

[CHAPTER 231—REPEALED]

[§§ 3651 to 3656. Repealed or Renumbered. Pub.L. 98–473, Title II, § 212(a)(1), (2), Oct. 12, 1984, 98 Stat. 1987]

HISTORICAL AND STATUTORY NOTES

Effective Date of Repeal

Pub.L. 98–473, Title II, §§ 212(a)(1), (2), 235(a)(1), Oct. 12, 1984, 98 Stat. 1987, 2031, as amended, repealed this chapter (except section 3656 which was renumbered section 3672), effective Nov. 1, 1987, and applicable only to offenses committed after the taking effect of such repeal. Section 235 of Pub.L. 98–473, as amended, relating to effective dates, is set out as an Effective Date note under section 3551 of this title. Prior to repeal, the provisions of this chapter read as follows:

§ 3651. Suspension of sentence and probation

Upon entering a judgment of conviction of any offense not punishable by death or life imprisonment, any court having jurisdiction to try offenses against the United States when satisfied that the ends of justice and the best interest of the public as well as the defendant will be served thereby, may suspend the imposition or execution of sentence and place the defendant on probation for such period and upon such terms and conditions as the court deems best.

Upon entering a judgment of conviction of any offense not punishable by death or life imprisonment, if the maximum punishment provided for such offense is more than six months, any court having jurisdiction to try offenses against the United States, when satisfied that the ends of justice and the best interest of the public as well as the defendant will be served thereby, may impose a sentence in excess of six months and provide that the defendant be confined in a jail-type institution or a treatment institution for a period not exceeding six months and that the execution of the remainder of the sentence be suspended and the defendant placed on probation for such period and upon such terms and conditions as the court deems best.

Probation may be granted whether the offense is punishable by fine or imprisonment or both. If an offense is punishable by both fine and imprisonment, the court may impose a fine and place the defendant on probation as to imprisonment. Probation may be limited to one or more counts or indictments, but, in the absence of express limitation, shall extend to the entire sentence and judgment.

The court may revoke or modify any condition of probation, or may change the period of probation.

The period of probation, together with any extension thereof, shall not exceed five years.

While on probation and among the conditions thereof, the defendant—

May be required to pay a fine in one or several sums; and

May be required to make restitution or reparation to aggrieved parties for actual damages or loss caused by the offense for which conviction was had; and

May be required to provide for the support of any persons, for whose support he is legally responsible.

The court may require a person as conditions of probation to reside in or participate in the program of a residential community treatment center, or both, for all or part of the period of probation: *Provided*, That the Attorney General certifies that adequate treatment facilities, personnel, and programs are available. If the Attorney General determines that the person's residence in the center or participation in its program, or both, should be terminated, because the person can derive no further significant benefits from such residence or participation, or both, or because his such residence or participation adversely affects the rehabilitation of other residents or participants, he shall so notify the court, which shall thereupon, by order, make such other provision with respect to the person on probation as it deems appropriate.

A person residing in a residential community treatment center may be required to pay such costs incident to residence as the Attorney General deems appropriate.

The court may require a person who is an addict within the meaning of section 4251(a) of this title, or a drug dependent person within the meaning of section 2(q) of the Public Health Service Act, as amended (42 U.S.C. 201), as a condition of probation, to participate in the community supervision programs authorized by section 4255 of this title for all or part of the period of probation.

The defendant's liability for any punishment (other than a fine) imposed as to which probation is granted, shall be fully discharged by the fulfillment of the terms and conditions of probation. If at the end of the period of probation, the defendant has not complied with a condition of probation, the court may nevertheless terminate proceedings against the defendant, but no such termination shall affect the defendant's obligation to pay a fine imposed or made a condition of probation, and such fine shall be collected in the manner provided in section 3565 of this title.

(June 25, 1948, c. 645, 62 Stat. 842; June 20, 1958, Pub.L. 85–463, § 1, 72 Stat. 216; Aug. 23, 1958, Pub.L. 85–741, 72 Stat. 834; Oct. 22, 1970, Pub.L. 91–492, § 1, 84 Stat. 1090; May 11, 1972, Pub.L. 92–293, § 1, 86 Stat. 136; Oct. 27, 1978, Pub.L. 95–537, § 2, 92 Stat. 2038; Oct. 12, 1984, Pub.L. 98–473, Title II, §§ 235(a)(1), 238(b), (c), (i), 98 Stat. 2031, 2038, 2039; Oct. 30, 1984, Pub.L. 98–596, §§ 4, 12(a)(2), (3), (9), (b), 98 Stat. 3136, 3139, 3140.)

§ 3652. Probation—(Rule)

SEE FEDERAL RULES OF CRIMINAL PROCEDURE

Probation as provided by law, Rule 32(e).

Presentence investigation, Rule 32(c).

(June 25, 1948, c. 645, 62 Stat. 842.)

§ 3653. Report of probation officer and arrest of probationer

When directed by the court, the probation officer shall report to the court, with a statement of the conduct of the probationer while on probation. The court may thereupon discharge the probationer from further supervision and may terminate the proceedings against him, or may extend the probation, as shall seem advisable.

Whenever during the period of his probation, a probationer heretofore or hereafter placed on probation, goes from the district in which he is being supervised to another district, jurisdiction over him may be transferred, in the discretion of the court, from the court for the district from which he goes to the court for the other district, with the concurrence of the latter court. Thereupon the court for the district to which jurisdiction is transferred shall have all power with respect to the probationer that was previously possessed by the court for the district from which the transfer is made, except that the period of probation shall not be changed without the consent of the sentencing court. This process under the same conditions may be repeated whenever during the period of his probation the probationer goes from the district in which he is being supervised to another district.

At any time within the probation period, the probation officer may for cause arrest the probationer wherever found, without a warrant. At any time within the probation period, or within the maximum probation period permitted by section 3651 of this title, the court for the district in which the probationer is being supervised or if he is no longer under supervision, the court for the district in which he was last under supervision, may issue a warrant for his arrest for violation of probation occurring during the probation period. Such warrant may be executed in any district by the probation officer or the United States marshal of the district in which the warrant was issued or of any district in which the probationer is found. If the probationer shall be arrested in any district other than that in which he was last supervised, he shall be returned to the district in which the warrant was issued, unless jurisdiction over him is transferred as above provided to the district in which he is found, and in that case he shall be detained pending further proceedings in such district.

As speedily as possible after arrest the probationer shall be taken before the court for the district having jurisdiction over him. Thereupon the court may revoke the probation and require him to serve the sentence imposed, or any lesser sentence, and, if imposition of sentence was suspended, may impose any sentence which might originally have been imposed.

(June 25, 1948, c. 645, 62 Stat. 842; May 24, 1949, c. 139, § 56, 63 Stat. 96.)

§ 3654. Appointment and removal of probation officers

Any court having original jurisdiction to try offenses against the United States may appoint one or more suitable persons to serve as probation officers within the jurisdiction and under the direction of the court making such appointment.

All such probation officers shall serve without compensation except that in case it shall appear to the court that the needs of the service require that there should be salaried probation officers, such court may appoint such officers.

Such court may in its discretion remove a probation officer serving in such court.

The appointment of a probation officer shall be in writing and shall be entered on the records of the court, and a copy of the order of appointment shall be delivered to the officer so appointed and a copy sent to the Director of the Administrative Office of the United States Courts.

Whenever such court shall have appointed more than one probation officer, one may be designated chief probation officer and shall direct the work of all probation officers serving in such court.

(June 25, 1948, c. 645, 62 Stat. 843; Aug. 2, 1949, c. 383, § 2, 63 Stat. 491.)

§ 3655. Duties of probation officers

The probation officer shall furnish to each probationer under his supervision a written statement of the conditions of probation and shall instruct him regarding the same.

He shall keep informed concerning the conduct and condition of each probationer under his supervision and shall report thereon to the court placing such person on probation.

He shall use all suitable methods, not inconsistent with the conditions imposed by the court, to aid probationers and to bring about improvements in their conduct and condition.

He shall keep records of his work; shall keep accurate and complete accounts of all moneys collected from persons under his supervision; shall give receipts therefor, and shall make at least monthly returns thereof; shall make such reports to the Director of the Administrative Office of the United States Courts as he may at any time require; and shall perform such other duties as the court may direct.

He shall report to the court any failure of a probationer under his supervision to pay an amount due as a fine or as restitution.

Each probation officer shall perform such duties with respect to persons on parole as the United States Parole Commission shall request.

(June 25, 1948, c. 645, 62 Stat. 843; March 15, 1976, Pub.L. 94–233, § 14, 90 Stat. 233; Oct. 12, 1984, Pub.L. 98–473, Title II, §§ 235(a)(1), 238(d), (i), 98 Stat. 2031, 2038, 2039; Oct. 30, 1984, Pub.L. 98–596, §§ 5, 12(a)(4), (9), (b), 98 Stat. 3136, 3139, 3140.)

§ 3656. Duties of Director of Administrative Office of the United States Courts

The Director of the Administrative Office of the United States Courts, or his authorized agent, shall investigate the work of the probation officers and make recommendations concerning the same to the respective judges and shall have access to the records of all probation officers.

He shall collect for publication statistical and other information concerning the work of the probation officers.

He shall prescribe record forms and statistics to be kept by the probation officers and shall formulate general rules for the proper conduct of the probation work.

He shall endeavor by all suitable means to promote the efficient administration of the probation system and the enforcement of the probation laws in all United States courts.

He shall, under the supervision and direction of the Judicial Conference of the United States, fix the salaries of probation officers and shall provide for their necessary expenses including clerical service and travel expenses.

He shall incorporate in his annual report a statement concerning the operation of the probation system in such courts.

(June 25, 1948, c. 645, 62 Stat. 843; May 24, 1949, c. 139, § 57, 63 Stat. 97.)

CHAPTER 232—MISCELLANEOUS SENTENCING PROVISIONS

§ 3661. Use of information for sentencing

No limitation shall be placed on the information concerning the background, character, and conduct of a person convicted of an offense which a court of the United States may receive and consider for the purpose of imposing an appropriate sentence.

(June 25, 1948, c. 645, § 1, 62 Stat. 683, § 3577 as added Pub.L. 91–452, Title X, § 1001(a), Oct. 15, 1970, 84 Stat. 951, § 3577, and renumbered Pub.L. 98–473, Title II, § 212(a)(1), Oct. 12, 1984, 98 Stat. 1987.)

HISTORICAL AND STATUTORY NOTES

Effective and Applicability Provisions

1984 Acts. Amendment by Pub.L. 98–473 effective on the first day of first calendar month beginning thirty six months after Oct. 12, 1984, applicable only to offenses committed after taking effect of sections 211 to 239 of Pub.L. 98–473, and except as otherwise provided for therein, see section 235 of Pub.L. 98–473, as amended, set out as a note under section 3551 of this title.

Short Title

1990 Amendments. Pub.L. 101–421, § 1, Oct. 12, 1990, 104 Stat. 909, provided that: "This Act [amending provisions set out as a note under section 3672 of this title] may be cited as the 'Drug and Alcohol Dependent Offenders Treatment Act of 1989'."

1986 Amendments. Pub.L. 99–570, Title I, § 1861(a), Oct. 27, 1986, 100 Stat. 3207–53, provided that: "This section [amending sections 3672 and 4255 of this title, enacting provisions set out as a note under section 3672 of this title, and amending provisions set out as a note under section 3672 of this title] may be cited as the 'Drug and Alcohol Dependent Offenders Treatment Act of 1986'."

§ 3662. Conviction records

(a) The Attorney General of the United States is authorized to establish in the Department of Justice a repository for records of convictions and determinations of the validity of such convictions.

(b) Upon the conviction thereafter of a defendant in a court of the United States, the District of Columbia, the Commonwealth of Puerto Rico, a territory or possession of the United States, any political subdivision, or any department, agency, or instrumentality thereof for an offense punishable in such court by death or imprisonment in excess of one year, or a judicial determination of the validity of such conviction on collateral review, the court shall cause a certified record of the conviction or determination to be made to the repository in such form and containing such information as the Attorney General of the United States shall by regulation prescribe.

(c) Records maintained in the repository shall not be public records. Certified copies thereof—

(1) may be furnished for law enforcement purposes on request of a court or law enforcement or corrections officer of the United States, the District of Columbia, the Commonwealth of Puerto Rico, a territory or possession of the United States, any political subdivision, or any department, agency, or instrumentality thereof;

(2) may be furnished for law enforcement purposes on request of a court or law enforcement or corrections officer of a State, any political subdivision, or any department, agency, or instrumentality thereof, if a statute of such State requires that, upon the conviction of a defendant in a court of the State or any political subdivision thereof for an offense punishable in such court by death or imprisonment in excess of one year, or a judicial determination of the validity of such conviction on collateral review, the court cause a certified record of the conviction or determination to be made to the repository in such form and containing such information as the Attorney General of the United States shall by regulation prescribe; and

(3) shall be prima facie evidence in any court of the United States, the District of Columbia, the Commonwealth of Puerto Rico, a territory or possession of the United States, any political subdivision, or any department, agency, or instrumentality thereof, that the convictions occurred and whether they have been judicially determined to be invalid on collateral review.

(d) The Attorney General of the United States shall give reasonable public notice, and afford to interested parties opportunity for hearing, prior to prescribing regulations under this section.

(June 25, 1948, c. 645, § 1, 62 Stat. 683, § 3578 as added Pub.L. 91–452, Title X, § 1001(a), Oct. 15, 1970, 84 Stat. 951, § 3578, and renumbered Pub.L. 98–473, Title II, § 212(a)(1), Oct. 12, 1984, 98 Stat. 1987.)

HISTORICAL AND STATUTORY NOTES

Effective and Applicability Provisions

1984 Acts. Amendment by Pub.L. 98–473 effective on the first day of first calendar month beginning thirty six months after Oct. 12, 1984, applicable only to offenses committed after taking effect of sections 211 to 239 of Pub.L. 98–473, and except as otherwise provided for therein, see section 235 of Pub.L. 98–473, as amended, set out as a note under section 3551 of this title.

§ 3663. Order of restitution

(a)(1)(A) The court, when sentencing a defendant convicted of an offense under this title, section 401, 408(a), 409, 416, 420, or 422(a) of the Controlled Substances Act (21 U.S.C. 841, 848(a), 849, 856, 861, 863) (but in no case shall a participant in an offense under such sections be considered a victim of such offense under this section), or section 5124, 46312, 46502, or 46504 of title 49, other than an offense described in section 3663A(c), may order, in addition to or, in the case of a misdemeanor, in lieu of any other penalty authorized by law, that the defendant make restitution to any victim of such offense, or if the victim is deceased, to the victim's estate. The court may also order, if agreed to by the parties in a plea agreement, restitution to persons other than the victim of the offense.

(B)(i) The court, in determining whether to order restitution under this section, shall consider—

(I) the amount of the loss sustained by each victim as a result of the offense; and

(II) the financial resources of the defendant, the financial needs and earning ability of the defendant and the defendant's dependents, and such other factors as the court deems appropriate.

(ii) To the extent that the court determines that the complication and prolongation of the sentencing process resulting from the fashioning of an order of restitution under this section outweighs the need to provide restitution to any victims, the court may decline to make such an order.

(2) For the purposes of this section, the term "victim" means a person directly and proximately harmed as a result of the commission of an offense for which restitution may be ordered including, in the case of an offense that involves as an element a scheme, conspiracy, or pattern of criminal activity, any person directly harmed by the defendant's criminal conduct in the course of the scheme, conspiracy, or pattern. In the case of a victim who is under 18 years of age, incompetent, incapacitated, or deceased, the legal guardian of the victim or representative of the victim's estate, another family member, or any other person appointed as suitable by the court, may assume the victim's rights under this section, but in no event shall the defendant be named as such representative or guardian.

(3) The court may also order restitution in any criminal case to the extent agreed to by the parties in a plea agreement.

(b) The order may require that such defendant—

(1) in the case of an offense resulting in damage to or loss or destruction of property of a victim of the offense—

(A) return the property to the owner of the property or someone designated by the owner; or

(B) if return of the property under subparagraph (A) is impossible, impractical, or inadequate, pay an amount equal to the greater of—

(i) the value of the property on the date of the damage, loss, or destruction, or

(ii) the value of the property on the date of sentencing,

less the value (as of the date the property is returned) of any part of the property that is returned;

(2) in the case of an offense resulting in bodily injury to a victim including an offense under chapter 109A or chapter 110—

(A) pay an amount equal to the cost of necessary medical and related professional services and devices relating to physical, psychiatric, and psychological care, including nonmedical care and treatment rendered in accordance with a method of healing recognized by the law of the place of treatment;

(B) pay an amount equal to the cost of necessary physical and occupational therapy and rehabilitation; and

(C) reimburse the victim for income lost by such victim as a result of such offense;

(3) in the case of an offense resulting in bodily injury also results in the death of a victim, pay an amount equal to the cost of necessary funeral and related services;

(4) in any case, reimburse the victim for lost income and necessary child care, transportation, and other expenses related to participation in the investigation or prosecution of the offense or attendance at proceedings related to the offense; and

(5) in any case, if the victim (or if the victim is deceased, the victim's estate) consents, make restitution in services in lieu of money, or make restitution to a person or organization designated by the victim or the estate.

(c)(1) Notwithstanding any other provision of law (but subject to the provisions of subsections (a)(1)(B)(i)(II) and (ii), [1] when sentencing a defendant convicted of an offense described in section 401, 408(a), 409, 416, 420, or 422(a) of the Controlled Substances Act (21 U.S.C. 841, 848(a), 849, 856, 861, 863), in which there is no identifiable victim, the court may order that the defendant make restitution in accordance with this subsection.

(2)(A) An order of restitution under this subsection shall be based on the amount of public harm caused by the offense, as determined by the court in accordance with guidelines promulgated by the United States Sentencing Commission.

(B) In no case shall the amount of restitution ordered under this subsection exceed the amount of the fine which may be ordered for the offense charged in the case.

(3) Restitution under this subsection shall be distributed as follows:

(A) 65 percent of the total amount of restitution shall be paid to the State entity designated to administer crime victim assistance in the State in which the crime occurred.

(B) 35 percent of the total amount of restitution shall be paid to the State entity designated to receive Federal substance abuse block grant funds.

(4) The court shall not make an award under this subsection if it appears likely that such award would interfere with a forfeiture under chapter 46 or chapter 96 of this title or under the Controlled Substances Act (21 U.S.C. 801 et seq.).

(5) Notwithstanding section 3612(c) or any other provision of law, a penalty assessment under section 3013 or a fine under subchapter C of chapter 227 shall take precedence over an order of restitution under this subsection.

(6) Requests for community restitution under this subsection may be considered in all plea agreements negotiated by the United States.

(7)(A) The United States Sentencing Commission shall promulgate guidelines to assist courts in determining the amount of restitution that may be ordered under this subsection.

(B) No restitution shall be ordered under this subsection until such time as the Sentencing Commission promulgates guidelines pursuant to this paragraph.

(d) An order of restitution made pursuant to this section shall be issued and enforced in accordance with section 3664.

(June 25, 1948, c. 645, § 1, 62 Stat. 683, § 3579 as added Pub.L. 97–291, § 5(a), Oct. 12, 1982, 96 Stat. 1253; renumbered and amended Pub.L. 98–473, Title II, § 212(a)(1), (3), Oct. 12, 1984, 98 Stat. 1987, 2010; Pub.L. 98–596, § 9, Oct. 30, 1984, 98 Stat. 3138; Nov. 10, 1986, Pub.L. 99–646, §§ 8(b), 20(a), 77(a), 78(a), 79(a), 100 Stat. 3593, 3596, 3618, 3619; Dec. 7, 1987, Pub.L. 100–182, § 13, 101 Stat. 1268; Dec. 11, 1987, Pub.L. 100–185, § 12, 101 Stat. 1285; Nov. 18, 1988, Pub.L. 100–690, Title VII, § 7042, 102 Stat. 4399; Nov. 29, 1990, Pub.L. 101–647, Title XXV, § 2509, Title XXXV, § 3595, 104 Stat. 4863, 4931; July 5, 1994, Pub.L. 103–272, § 5(e)(12), 108 Stat. 1374; Sept. 13, 1994, Pub.L. 103–322, Title IV, §§ 40504, 40505, 108 Stat. 1947; Apr. 24, 1996, Pub.L. 104–132, Title II, § 205(a), 110 Stat. 1229; Oct. 11, 1996, Pub.L. 104–294, Title VI, §§ 601(r)(1),(2), 605(*l*), 110 Stat. 3502, 3510; Oct. 17, 2000, Pub.L. 106–310, Div. B, Title XXXVI, § 3613(c), 114 Stat. 1230; Aug. 10, 2005, Pub.L. 109–59, Title VII, § 7128(b), 119 Stat. 1910.)

[1] So in original. Probably should be "(ii))".

HISTORICAL AND STATUTORY NOTES

References in Text

The Controlled Substances Act, referred to in subsec. (c)(1), (4), is Title II of Pub.L. 91–513, Oct. 27, 1970, 84 Stat. 1242, as amended, which is classified principally to subchapter I (section 801 et seq.) of chapter 13 of Title 21, Food and Drugs. For complete classification of this Act to the Code, see Short Title note set out under section 801 of Title 21 and Tables.

Effective and Applicability Provisions

1996 Acts. Amendment by Pub.L. 104–132 to be effective, to the extent constitutionally permissible, for sentencing proceedings in cases in which the defendant is convicted on or after Apr. 24, 1996, see section 211 of Pub.L. 104–132, set out as a note under section 2248 of this title.

1987 Acts. Amendment by Pub.L. 100–182 applicable with respect to offenses committed after enactment of Pub.L. 100–182, which was approved Dec. 7, 1987, see section 26 of Pub.L. 100–182, set out as a note under section 3006A of this title.

1986 Acts. Amendment of subsec. (a) by section 8(b) of Pub.L. 99–646, effective on the day section 3553 takes effect, Nov. 1, 1987, see section 8(c) of Pub.L. 99–646, set out as a note under section 3553 of this title.

Amendment of subsec. (a)(1) by section 20(a) of Pub.L. 99–646, effective on the date of taking effect of section

212(a)(2) of Pub.L. 98–473, Nov. 1, 1987, see section 20(c) of Pub.L. 99–646, set out as a note under section 3556 of this title.

Section 77(b) of Pub.L. 99–646 provided: "The amendment made by this section [amending this section] shall take effect on the 30th day after the date of the enactment of this Act [Nov. 10, 1986]."

Section 78(b) of Pub.L. 99–646 provided that: "The amendment made by this section [amending this section] shall take effect on the 30th day after the date of the enactment of this Act [Nov. 10, 1986]."

Section 79(b) of Pub.L. 99–646 provided that: "The amendment made by this section [amending this section] shall take effect on the date of the enactment of this Act [Nov. 10, 1986]."

1984 Acts. Amendment by section 9 of Pub.L. 98–596 applicable with respect to offenses committed after Dec. 31, 1984, see section 10 of Pub.L. 98–596, set out as a note under section 1 of this title.

1984 Acts. Amendment by Pub.L. 98–473 effective on the first day of first calendar month beginning thirty six months after Oct. 12, 1984, applicable only to offenses committed after taking effect of sections 211 to 239 of Pub.L. 98–473, and except as otherwise provided for therein, see section 235 of Pub.L. 98–473, as amended, set out as a note under section 3551 of this title.

Offenses After January 1, 1983

Section effective with respect to offenses occurring after Jan. 1, 1983, pursuant to section 9(b)(2) of Pub.L. 97–291.

Profit by a Criminal from Sale of His Story

Section 7 of Pub.L. 97–291 provided that: "Within one year after the date of enactment of this Act [Oct. 12, 1982], the Attorney General shall report to Congress regarding any laws that are necessary to ensure that no Federal felon derives any profit from the sale of the recollections, thoughts, and feelings of such felon with regards to the offense committed by the felon until any victim of the offense receives restitution."

§ 3663A. Mandatory restitution to victims of certain crimes

(a)(1) Notwithstanding any other provision of law, when sentencing a defendant convicted of an offense described in subsection (c), the court shall order, in addition to, or in the case of a misdemeanor, in addition to or in lieu of, any other penalty authorized by law, that the defendant make restitution to the victim of the offense or, if the victim is deceased, to the victim's estate.

(2) For the purposes of this section, the term "victim" means a person directly and proximately harmed as a result of the commission of an offense for which restitution may be ordered including, in the case of an offense that involves as an element a scheme, conspiracy, or pattern of criminal activity, any person directly harmed by the defendant's criminal conduct in the course of the scheme, conspiracy, or pattern. In the case of a victim who is under 18 years of age, incompetent, incapacitated, or deceased, the legal guardian of the victim or representative of the victim's estate, another family member, or any other person appointed as suitable by the court, may assume the victim's rights under this section, but in no event shall the defendant be named as such representative or guardian.

(3) The court shall also order, if agreed to by the parties in a plea agreement, restitution to persons other than the victim of the offense.

(b) The order of restitution shall require that such defendant—

(1) in the case of an offense resulting in damage to or loss or destruction of property of a victim of the offense—

(A) return the property to the owner of the property or someone designated by the owner; or

(B) if return of the property under subparagraph (A) is impossible, impracticable, or inadequate, pay an amount equal to—

(i) the greater of—

(I) the value of the property on the date of the damage, loss, or destruction; or

(II) the value of the property on the date of sentencing, less

(ii) the value (as of the date the property is returned) of any part of the property that is returned;

(2) in the case of an offense resulting in bodily injury to a victim—

(A) pay an amount equal to the cost of necessary medical and related professional services and devices relating to physical, psychiatric, and psychological care, including nonmedical care and treatment rendered in accordance with a method of healing recognized by the law of the place of treatment;

(B) pay an amount equal to the cost of necessary physical and occupational therapy and rehabilitation; and

(C) reimburse the victim for income lost by such victim as a result of such offense;

(3) in the case of an offense resulting in bodily injury that results in the death of the victim, pay an amount equal to the cost of necessary funeral and related services; and

(4) in any case, reimburse the victim for lost income and necessary child care, transportation, and other expenses incurred during participation in the investigation or prosecution of the offense or attendance at proceedings related to the offense.

(c)(1) This section shall apply in all sentencing proceedings for convictions of, or plea agreements relating to charges for, any offense—

(A) that is—

(i) a crime of violence, as defined in section 16;

(ii) an offense against property under this title, or under section 416(a) of the Controlled Substances Act (21 U.S.C. 856(a)), including any offense committed by fraud or deceit; or

(iii) an offense described in section 1365 (relating to tampering with consumer products); and

(B) in which an identifiable victim or victims has suffered a physical injury or pecuniary loss.

(2) In the case of a plea agreement that does not result in a conviction for an offense described in paragraph (1), this section shall apply only if the plea specifically states that an offense listed under such paragraph gave rise to the plea agreement.

(3) This section shall not apply in the case of an offense described in paragraph (1)(A)(ii) if the court finds, from facts on the record, that—

(A) the number of identifiable victims is so large as to make restitution impracticable; or

(B) determining complex issues of fact related to the cause or amount of the victim's losses would complicate or prolong the sentencing process to a degree that the need to provide restitution to any victim is outweighed by the burden on the sentencing process.

(d) An order of restitution under this section shall be issued and enforced in accordance with section 3664.

(Added Pub.L. 104–132, Title II, § 204(a), Apr. 24, 1996, 110 Stat. 1227, and amended Pub.L. 106–310, Div. B, Title XXXVI, § 3613(d), Oct. 17, 2000, 114 Stat. 1230.)

HISTORICAL AND STATUTORY NOTES

Effective and Applicability Provisions

1996 Acts. Section to be effective, to the extent constitutionally permissible, for sentencing proceedings in cases in which the defendant is convicted on or after Apr. 24, 1996, see section 211 of Pub.L. 104–132, set out as a note under section 2248 of this title.

§ 3664. Procedure for issuance and enforcement of order of restitution

(a) For orders of restitution under this title, the court shall order the probation officer to obtain and include in its presentence report, or in a separate report, as the court may direct, information sufficient for the court to exercise its discretion in fashioning a restitution order. The report shall include, to the extent practicable, a complete accounting of the losses to each victim, any restitution owed pursuant to a plea agreement, and information relating to the economic circumstances of each defendant. If the number or identity of victims cannot be reasonably ascertained, or other circumstances exist that make this requirement clearly impracticable, the probation officer shall so inform the court.

(b) The court shall disclose to both the defendant and the attorney for the Government all portions of the presentence or other report pertaining to the matters described in subsection (a) of this section.

(c) The provisions of this chapter, chapter 227, and Rule 32(c) of the Federal Rules of Criminal Procedure shall be the only rules applicable to proceedings under this section.

(d)(1) Upon the request of the probation officer, but not later than 60 days prior to the date initially set for sentencing, the attorney for the Government, after consulting, to the extent practicable, with all identified victims, shall promptly provide the probation officer with a listing of the amounts subject to restitution.

(2) The probation officer shall, prior to submitting the presentence report under subsection (a), to the extent practicable—

(A) provide notice to all identified victims of—

(i) the offense or offenses of which the defendant was convicted;

(ii) the amounts subject to restitution submitted to the probation officer;

(iii) the opportunity of the victim to submit information to the probation officer concerning the amount of the victim's losses;

(iv) the scheduled date, time, and place of the sentencing hearing;

(v) the availability of a lien in favor of the victim pursuant to subsection (m)(1)(B); and

(vi) the opportunity of the victim to file with the probation officer a separate affidavit relating to the amount of the victim's losses subject to restitution; and

(B) provide the victim with an affidavit form to submit pursuant to subparagraph (A)(vi).

(3) Each defendant shall prepare and file with the probation officer an affidavit fully describing the financial resources of the defendant, including a complete listing of all assets owned or controlled by the defendant as of the date on which the defendant was arrested, the financial needs and earning ability of the defendant and the defendant's dependents, and such other information that the court requires relating to such other factors as the court deems appropriate.

(4) After reviewing the report of the probation officer, the court may require additional documentation or hear testimony. The privacy of any records filed, or testimony heard, pursuant to this section shall be maintained to the greatest extent possible, and such records may be filed or testimony heard in camera.

(5) If the victim's losses are not ascertainable by the date that is 10 days prior to sentencing, the attorney for the Government or the probation officer

shall so inform the court, and the court shall set a date for the final determination of the victim's losses, not to exceed 90 days after sentencing. If the victim subsequently discovers further losses, the victim shall have 60 days after discovery of those losses in which to petition the court for an amended restitution order. Such order may be granted only upon a showing of good cause for the failure to include such losses in the initial claim for restitutionary relief.

(6) The court may refer any issue arising in connection with a proposed order of restitution to a magistrate judge or special master for proposed findings of fact and recommendations as to disposition, subject to a de novo determination of the issue by the court.

(e) Any dispute as to the proper amount or type of restitution shall be resolved by the court by the preponderance of the evidence. The burden of demonstrating the amount of the loss sustained by a victim as a result of the offense shall be on the attorney for the Government. The burden of demonstrating the financial resources of the defendant and the financial needs of the defendant's dependents, shall be on the defendant. The burden of demonstrating such other matters as the court deems appropriate shall be upon the party designated by the court as justice requires.

(f)(1)(A) In each order of restitution, the court shall order restitution to each victim in the full amount of each victim's losses as determined by the court and without consideration of the economic circumstances of the defendant.

(B) In no case shall the fact that a victim has received or is entitled to receive compensation with respect to a loss from insurance or any other source be considered in determining the amount of restitution.

(2) Upon determination of the amount of restitution owed to each victim, the court shall, pursuant to section 3572, specify in the restitution order the manner in which, and the schedule according to which, the restitution is to be paid, in consideration of—

(A) the financial resources and other assets of the defendant, including whether any of these assets are jointly controlled;

(B) projected earnings and other income of the defendant; and

(C) any financial obligations of the defendant; including obligations to dependents.

(3)(A) A restitution order may direct the defendant to make a single, lump-sum payment, partial payments at specified intervals, in-kind payments, or a combination of payments at specified intervals and in-kind payments.

(B) A restitution order may direct the defendant to make nominal periodic payments if the court finds from facts on the record that the economic circumstances of the defendant do not allow the payment of any amount of a restitution order, and do not allow for the payment of the full amount of a restitution order in the foreseeable future under any reasonable schedule of payments.

(4) An in-kind payment described in paragraph (3) may be in the form of—

(A) return of property;

(B) replacement of property; or

(C) if the victim agrees, services rendered to the victim or a person or organization other than the victim.

(g)(1) No victim shall be required to participate in any phase of a restitution order.

(2) A victim may at any time assign the victim's interest in restitution payments to the Crime Victims Fund in the Treasury without in any way impairing the obligation of the defendant to make such payments.

(h) If the court finds that more than 1 defendant has contributed to the loss of a victim, the court may make each defendant liable for payment of the full amount of restitution or may apportion liability among the defendants to reflect the level of contribution to the victim's loss and economic circumstances of each defendant.

(i) If the court finds that more than 1 victim has sustained a loss requiring restitution by a defendant, the court may provide for a different payment schedule for each victim based on the type and amount of each victim's loss and accounting for the economic circumstances of each victim. In any case in which the United States is a victim, the court shall ensure that all other victims receive full restitution before the United States receives any restitution.

(j)(1) If a victim has received compensation from insurance or any other source with respect to a loss, the court shall order that restitution be paid to the person who provided or is obligated to provide the compensation, but the restitution order shall provide that all restitution of victims required by the order be paid to the victims before any restitution is paid to such a provider of compensation.

(2) Any amount paid to a victim under an order of restitution shall be reduced by any amount later recovered as compensatory damages for the same loss by the victim in—

(A) any Federal civil proceeding; and

(B) any State civil proceeding, to the extent provided by the law of the State.

(k) A restitution order shall provide that the defendant shall notify the court and the Attorney General of any material change in the defendant's economic circumstances that might affect the defendant's ability to pay restitution. The court may also accept notification of a material change in the defendant's economic circumstances from the United States or from the victim. The Attorney General shall certify to the court that the victim or victims owed restitution by the defendant have been notified of the change in circumstances. Upon receipt of the notification, the court may, on its own motion, or the motion of any party, including the victim, adjust the payment schedule, or require immediate payment in full, as the interests of justice require.

(*l*) A conviction of a defendant for an offense involving the act giving rise to an order of restitution shall estop the defendant from denying the essential allegations of that offense in any subsequent Federal civil proceeding or State civil proceeding, to the extent consistent with State law, brought by the victim.

(m)(1)(A)(i) An order of restitution may be enforced by the United States in the manner provided for in subchapter C of chapter 227 and subchapter B of chapter 229 of this title; or

(ii) by all other available and reasonable means.

(B) At the request of a victim named in a restitution order, the clerk of the court shall issue an abstract of judgment certifying that a judgment has been entered in favor of such victim in the amount specified in the restitution order. Upon registering, recording, docketing, or indexing such abstract in accordance with the rules and requirements relating to judgments of the court of the State where the district court is located, the abstract of judgment shall be a lien on the property of the defendant located in such State in the same manner and to the same extent and under the same conditions as a judgment of a court of general jurisdiction in that State.

(2) An order of in-kind restitution in the form of services shall be enforced by the probation officer.

(n) If a person obligated to provide restitution, or pay a fine, receives substantial resources from any source, including inheritance, settlement, or other judgment, during a period of incarceration, such person shall be required to apply the value of such resources to any restitution or fine still owed.

(*o*) A sentence that imposes an order of restitution is a final judgment notwithstanding the fact that—

(1) such a sentence can subsequently be—

(A) corrected under Rule 35 of the Federal Rules of Criminal Procedure and section 3742 of chapter 235 of this title;

(B) appealed and modified under section 3742;

(C) amended under subsection (d)(5); or

(D) adjusted under section 3664(k), 3572, or 3613A; or

(2) the defendant may be resentenced under section 3565 or 3614.

(p) Nothing in this section or sections 2248, 2259, 2264, 2327, 3663, and 3663A and arising out of the application of such sections, shall be construed to create a cause of action not otherwise authorized in favor of any person against the United States or any officer or employee of the United States.

(Added Pub.L. 97–291, § 5(a), Oct. 12, 1982, 96 Stat. 1255, § 3580, renumbered § 3664, Pub.L. 98–473, Title II, § 212(a)(1), Oct. 12, 1984, 98 Stat. 1987, and amended Pub.L. 101–647, Title XXXV, § 3596, Nov. 29, 1990, 104 Stat. 4931; Pub.L. 104–132, Title II, § 206(a), Apr. 24, 1996, 110 Stat. 1232; Pub.L. 107–273, Div. B, Title IV, § 4002(e)(1), Nov. 2, 2002, 116 Stat. 1810.)

HISTORICAL AND STATUTORY NOTES

References in Text

The Federal Rules of Criminal Procedure, referred to in subsecs. (c) and (*o*)(1)(A), are set out in this title.

Effective and Applicability Provisions

1996 Acts. Amendment by Pub.L. 104–132 to be effective, to the extent constitutionally permissible, for sentencing proceedings in cases in which the defendant is convicted on or after Apr. 24, 1996, see section 211 of Pub.L. 104–132, set out as a note under 18 U.S.C.A. § 2248.

1984 Acts. Amendment by Pub.L. 98–473, except as otherwise provided, effective on the first day of first calendar month beginning thirty six months after Oct. 12, 1984, and applicable only to offenses committed after taking effect of sections 211 to 239 of Pub.L. 98–473, see section 235 of Pub.L. 98–473, as amended, set out as a note under 18 U.S.C.A. § 3551.

1982 Acts. Section effective with respect to offenses occurring after Jan. 1, 1983, see section 9(b)(2) of Pub.L. 97–291, set out as an Effective and Applicability note under 18 U.S.C.A. § 1512.

§ 3665. Firearms possessed by convicted felons

A judgment of conviction for transporting a stolen motor vehicle in interstate or foreign commerce or for committing or attempting to commit a felony in violation of any law of the United States involving the use of threats, force, or violence or perpetrated in whole or in part by the use of firearms, may, in addition to the penalty provided by law for such offense, order the confiscation and disposal of firearms and ammunition found in the possession or under the immediate control of the defendant at the time of his arrest.

The court may direct the delivery of such firearms or ammunition to the law-enforcement agency which apprehended such person, for its use or for any other disposition in its discretion.

(June 25, 1948, c. 645, § 1, 62 Stat. 839, § 3611; renumbered § 3665, Oct. 12, 1984, Pub.L. 98–473, Title II, § 212(a)(1), 98 Stat. 1987.)

HISTORICAL AND STATUTORY NOTES

Effective and Applicability Provisions

1984 Acts. Amendment by Pub.L. 98–473 effective on the first day of first calendar month beginning thirty-six months after Oct. 12, 1984, applicable only to offenses committed after taking effect of sections 211 to 239 of Pub.L. 98–473, and except as otherwise provided for therein, see section 235 of Pub.L. 98–473, as amended, set out as a note under section 3551 of this title.

§ 3666. Bribe moneys

Moneys received or tendered in evidence in any United States Court, or before any officer thereof, which have been paid to or received by any official as a bribe, shall, after the final disposition of the case, proceeding or investigation, be deposited in the registry of the court to be disposed of in accordance with the order of the court, to be subject, however, to the provisions of section 2042 of Title 28.

(June 25, 1948, c. 645, 62 Stat. 840, § 3612; May 24, 1949, c. 139, § 55, 63 Stat. 96; renumbered § 3666, Oct. 12, 1984, Pub.L. 98–473, Title II, § 212(a)(1), 98 Stat. 1987.)

HISTORICAL AND STATUTORY NOTES

Effective and Applicability Provisions

1984 Acts. Amendment by Pub.L. 98–473 effective on the first day of first calendar month beginning thirty-six months after Oct. 12, 1984, applicable only to offenses committed after taking effect of sections 211 to 239 of Pub.L. 98–473, and except as otherwise provided for therein, see section 235 of Pub.L. 98–473, as amended, set out as a note under section 3551 of this title.

§ 3667. Liquors and related property; definitions

All liquor involved in any violation of sections 1261–1265 of this title, the containers of such liquor, and every vehicle or vessel used in the transportation thereof, shall be seized and forfeited and such property or its proceeds disposed of in accordance with the laws relating to seizures, forfeitures, and dispositions of property or proceeds, for violation of the internal-revenue laws.

As used in this section, "vessel" includes every description of watercraft used, or capable of being used, as a means of transportation in water or in water and air; "vehicle" includes animals and every description of carriage or other contrivance used, or capable of being used, as a means of transportation on land or through the air.

(June 25, 1948, c. 645, 62 Stat. 840, § 3615; renumbered § 3667, Oct. 12, 1984, Pub.L. 98–473, Title II, § 212(a)(1), 98 Stat. 1987.)

HISTORICAL AND STATUTORY NOTES

Effective and Applicability Provisions

1984 Acts. Amendment by Pub.L. 98–473 effective on the first day of first calendar month beginning thirty six months after Oct. 12, 1984, applicable only to offenses committed after taking effect of sections 211 to 239 of Pub.L. 98–473, and except as otherwise provided for therein, see section 235 of Pub.L. 98–473, as amended, set out as a note under section 3551 of this title.

§ 3668. Remission or mitigation of forfeitures under liquor laws; possession pending trial

(a) Jurisdiction of court

Whenever, in any proceeding in court for the forfeiture, under the internal-revenue laws, of any vehicle or aircraft seized for a violation of the internal-revenue laws relating to liquors, such forfeiture is decreed, the court shall have exclusive jurisdiction to remit or mitigate the forfeiture.

(b) Conditions precedent to remission or mitigation

In any such proceeding the court shall not allow the claim of any claimant for remission or mitigation unless and until he proves (1) that he has an interest in such vehicle or aircraft, as owner or otherwise, which he acquired in good faith, (2) that he had at no time any knowledge or reason to believe that it was being or would be used in the violation of laws of the United States or of any State relating to liquor, and (3) if it appears that the interest asserted by the claimant arises out of or is in any way subject to any contract or agreement under which any person having a record or reputation for violating laws of the United States or of any State relating to liquor has a right with respect to such vehicle or aircraft, that, before such claimant acquired his interest, or such other person acquired his right under such contract or agreement, whichever occurred later, the claimant, his officer or agent, was informed in answer to his inquiry, at the headquarters of the sheriff, chief of police, principal Federal internal-revenue officer engaged in the enforcement of the liquor laws, or other principal local or Federal law-enforcement officer of the locality in which such other person acquired his right under such contract or agreement, of the locality in which such other person then resided, and of each locality in which the claimant has made any other inquiry as to the character or financial standing of such other person, that such other person had no such record or reputation.

(c) Claimants first entitled to delivery

Upon the request of any claimant whose claim for remission or mitigation is allowed and whose interest is first in the order of priority among such claims allowed in such proceeding and is of an amount in excess of, or equal to, the appraised value of such vehicle or aircraft, the court shall order its return to him; and, upon the joint request of any two or more claimants whose claims are allowed and whose interests are not subject to any prior or intervening interests claimed and allowed in such proceedings, and are of a total amount in excess of, or equal to, the appraised value of such vehicle or aircraft, the court shall order its return to such of the joint requesting claimants as is designated in such request. Such return shall be made only upon payment of all expenses incident to the seizure and forfeiture incurred by the United States. In all other cases the court shall order disposition of such vehicle or aircraft as provided in section 1306 of title 40, and if such disposition be by public sale, payment from the proceeds thereof, after satisfaction of all such expenses, of any such claim in its order of priority among the claims allowed in such proceedings.

(d) Delivery on bond pending trial

In any proceeding in court for the forfeiture under the internal-revenue laws of any vehicle or aircraft seized for a violation of the internal-revenue laws relating to liquor, the court shall order delivery thereof to any claimant who shall establish his right to the immediate possession thereof, and shall execute, with one or more sureties approved by the court, and deliver to the court, a bond to the United States for the payment of a sum equal to the appraised value of such vehicle or aircraft. Such bond shall be conditioned to return such vehicle or aircraft at the time of the trial and to pay the difference between the appraised value of such vehicle or aircraft as of the time it shall have been so released on bond and the appraised value thereof as of the time of trial; and conditioned further that, if the vehicle or aircraft be not returned at the time of trial, the bond shall stand in lieu of, and be forfeited in the same manner as, such vehicle or aircraft. Notwithstanding this subsection or any other provisions of law relating to the delivery of possession on bond of vehicles or aircraft sought to be forfeited under the internal-revenue laws, the court may, in its discretion and upon good cause shown by the United States, refuse to order such delivery of possession.

(June 25, 1948, c. 645, 62 Stat. 840, § 3617; renumbered § 3668, Oct. 12, 1984, Pub.L. 98–473, Title II, § 212(a)(1), 98 Stat. 1987; Aug. 21, 2002, Pub.L. 107–217, § 3(d), 116 Stat. 1299.)

HISTORICAL AND STATUTORY NOTES

Effective and Applicability Provisions

1984 Acts. Amendment by Pub.L. 98–473 effective on the first day of first calendar month beginning thirty six months after Oct. 12, 1984, applicable only to offenses committed after taking effect of sections 211 to 239 of Pub.L. 98–473, and except as otherwise provided for therein, see section 235 of Pub.L. 98–473, as amended, set out as a note under section 3551 of this title.

§ 3669. Conveyances carrying liquor

Any conveyance, whether used by the owner or another in introducing or attempting to introduce intoxicants into the Indian country, or into other places where the introduction is prohibited by treaty or enactment of Congress, shall be subject to seizure, libel, and forfeiture.

(June 25, 1948, c. 645, 62 Stat. 841, § 3618; renumbered § 3669, Oct. 12, 1984, Pub.L. 98–473, Title II, § 212(a)(1), 98 Stat. 1989.)

HISTORICAL AND STATUTORY NOTES

Effective and Applicability Provisions

1984 Acts. Amendment by Pub.L. 98–473 effective on the first day of first calendar month beginning thirty six months after Oct. 12, 1984, applicable only to offenses committed after taking effect of sections 211 to 239 of Pub.L. 98–473, and except as otherwise provided for therein, see section 235 of Pub.L. 98–473, as amended, set out as a note under section 3551 of this title.

§ 3670. Disposition of conveyances seized for violation of the Indian liquor laws

The provisions of section 3668 of this title shall apply to any conveyances seized, proceeded against by libel, or forfeited under the provisions of section 3113 or 3669 of this title for having been used in introducing or attempting to introduce intoxicants into the Indian country or into other places where such introduction is prohibited by treaty or enactment of Congress.

(Added Oct. 24, 1951, c. 546, § 2, 65 Stat. 609, § 3619, renumbered § 3670 and amended Oct. 12, 1984, Pub.L. 98–473, Title II, §§ 212(a)(1), 223(k), 98 Stat. 1987, 2029.)

HISTORICAL AND STATUTORY NOTES

Effective and Applicability Provisions

1984 Acts. Amendment by Pub.L. 98–473 effective on the first day of first calendar month beginning thirty six months after Oct. 12, 1984, applicable only to offenses committed after taking effect of sections 211 to 239 of Pub.L. 98–473, and except as otherwise provided for therein, see section 235 of Pub.L. 98–473, as amended, set out as a note under section 3551 of this title.

§ 3671. Vessels carrying explosives and steerage passengers

The amount of any fine imposed upon the master of a steamship or other vessel under the provisions of section 2278 of this title shall be a lien upon such vessel, and such vessel may be libeled therefor in the district court of the United States for any district in which such vessel shall arrive or from which it shall depart.

(Added Sept. 3, 1954, c. 1263, § 36, 68 Stat. 1239, § 3620, renumbered § 3671, Oct. 12, 1984, Pub.L. 98–473, Title II, § 212(a)(1), 98 Stat. 1989.)

HISTORICAL AND STATUTORY NOTES

Effective and Applicability Provisions

1984 Acts. Amendment by Pub.L. 98–473 effective on the first day of first calendar month beginning thirty six months after Oct. 12, 1984, applicable only to offenses committed after taking effect of sections 211 to 239 of Pub.L. 98–473, and except as otherwise provided for therein, see section 235 of Pub.L. 98–473, as amended, set out as a note under section 3551 of this title.

§ 3672. Duties of Director of Administrative Office of the United States Courts

The Director of the Administrative Office of the United States Courts, or his authorized agent, shall investigate the work of the probation officers and make recommendations concerning the same to the respective judges and shall have access to the records of all probation officers.

He shall collect for publication statistical and other information concerning the work of the probation officers.

He shall prescribe record forms and statistics to be kept by the probation officers and shall formulate general rules for the proper conduct of the probation work.

He shall endeavor by all suitable means to promote the efficient administration of the probation system and the enforcement of the probation laws in all United States courts.

He shall, under the supervision and direction of the Judicial Conference of the United States, fix the salaries of probation officers and shall provide for their necessary expenses including clerical service and travel expenses.

He shall incorporate in his annual report a statement concerning the operation of the probation system in such courts.

He shall have the authority to contract with any appropriate public or private agency or person for the detection of and care in the community of an offender who is an alcohol-dependent person, an addict or a drug-dependent person, or a person suffering from a psychiatric disorder within the meaning of section 2 of the Public Health Service Act. This authority shall include the authority to provide equipment and supplies; testing; medical, educational, social, psychological and vocational services; corrective and preventative guidance and training; and other rehabilitative services designed to protect the public and benefit the alcohol-dependent person, addict or drug-dependent person, or a person suffering from a psychiatric disorder by eliminating his dependence on alcohol or addicting drugs, by controlling his dependence and his susceptibility to addiction, or by treating his psychiatric disorder. He may negotiate and award such contracts without regard to section 3709 of the Revised Statutes of the United States.

He shall pay for presentence studies and reports by qualified consultants and presentence examinations and reports by psychiatric or psychological examiners ordered by the court under subsection (b) or (c) of section 3552, except for studies conducted by the Bureau of Prisons.

Whenever the court finds that funds are available for payment by or on behalf of a person furnished such services, training, or guidance, the court may direct that such funds be paid to the Director. Any moneys collected under this paragraph shall be used to reimburse the appropriations obligated and disbursed in payment for such services, training, or guidance.

(June 25, 1948, c. 645, 62 Stat. 843, § 3656; May 24, 1949, c. 139, § 57, 63 Stat. 97; renumbered § 3672, Oct. 12, 1984, Pub.L. 98–473, Title II, § 212(a)(1), 98 Stat. 1987, and amended Oct. 27, 1986, Pub.L. 99–570, Title I, § 1861(b)(1), 100 Stat. 3207–53; Nov. 10, 1986, Pub.L. 99–646, § 18(a), 100 Stat. 3595; Dec. 7, 1987, Pub.L. 100–182, § 20, 101 Stat. 1270.)

HISTORICAL AND STATUTORY NOTES

References in Text

Section 2 of the Public Health Service Act, referred to in text, is section 2 of Act July 1, 1944, c. 373, Title I, 58 Stat. 682, as amended, which is classified to section 201 of Title 42, The Public Health and Welfare.

Section 3709 of the Revised Statutes, referred to in the seventh undesignated par., is classified to section 5 of Title 41, Public Contracts.

Codifications

Pub.L. 99–570 and Pub.L. 99–646 made identical amendments to text by addition of final two unnumbered paragraphs.

Effective and Applicability Provisions

1987 Acts. Amendment by Pub.L. 100–182 applicable with respect to offenses committed after enactment of Pub.L. 100–182, which was approved Dec. 7, 1987, see section 26 of Pub.L. 100–182, set out as a note under section 3006A of this title.

1986 Acts. Section 18(b) of Pub.L. 99–646 provided that: "The amendment made by this section [amending this section] shall take effect on the date of the taking effect of such redesignation [Nov. 1, 1987]."

Section 1861(b)(2) of Pub.L. 99–570 provided that: "The amendment made by this section [amending this section] shall take effect on the date of the taking effect of such redesignation [Nov. 1, 1987]."

1984 Acts. Amendment by Pub.L. 98–473 effective on the first day of first calendar month beginning thirty six months after Oct. 12, 1984, applicable only to offenses committed after taking effect of sections 211 to 239 of Pub.L. 98–473, and except as otherwise provided for therein, see section 235 of Pub.L. 98–473, as amended, set out as a note under section 3551 of this title.

Authorization of Appropriations

Section 4(a) of Pub.L. 95–537, as amended by Pub.L. 98–236, § 2, Mar. 20, 1984, 98 Stat. 66; Pub.L. 99–570, § 1861(d), Oct. 27, 1986, 100 Stat. 3207–54; Pub.L. 100–690, Title VI, § 6291, Nov. 18, 1988, 102 Stat. 4369; Pub.L. 101–421, § 2, Oct. 12, 1990, 104 Stat. 909, provided that: "To carry out the purposes of this Act [amending former sections 3651 and 4255 of this title] and the 7th paragraph of section 3672 of title 18, United States Code [this section], there are authorized to be appropriated sums not to exceed $3,500,000 for the fiscal year ending September 30, 1980; $3,645,000 for the fiscal year ending September 30, 1981; $3,750,000 for the fiscal year ending September 30, 1982; $5,000,000 for the fiscal year ending September 30, 1984; $5,500,000 for the fiscal year ending September 30, 1985; $6,500,000 for the fiscal year ending September 30, 1986; $12,000,000 for the fiscal year ending September 30, 1987; $24,000,000 for the fiscal year ending September 30, 1988; $26,000,000 for the fiscal year ending September 30, 1989; $30,000,000 for the fiscal year ending September 30, 1990; $40,000,000 for the fiscal year ending September 30, 1991; and $45,000,000 for the fiscal year ending September 30, 1992."

Increase in Compensation Rates

Increase in compensation rates fixed under this section, see notes set out under section 603 of Title 28, Judiciary and Judicial Procedure.

§ 3673. Definitions for sentencing provisions

As used in chapters 227 and 229—

(1) the term "found guilty" includes acceptance by a court of a plea of guilty or nolo contendere;

(2) the term "commission of an offense" includes the attempted commission of an offense, the consummation of an offense, and any immediate flight after the commission of an offense; and

(3) the term "law enforcement officer" means a public servant authorized by law or by a government agency to engage in or supervise the prevention, detection, investigation, or prosecution of an offense.

(Added Pub.L. 98–473, Title II, § 212(a)(4), Oct. 12, 1984, 98 Stat. 2010, and amended Pub.L. 99–646, § 2(a), Nov. 10, 1986, 100 Stat. 3592.)

HISTORICAL AND STATUTORY NOTES

Effective and Applicability Provisions

1986 Acts. Section 2(b) of Pub.L. 99–646 provided that: "The amendments made by this section [amending this section] shall take effect on the date of the taking effect of section 3673 of title 18, United States Code [this section]."

1984 Acts. Section effective on the first day of first calendar month beginning thirty-six months after Oct. 12, 1984, applicable only to offenses committed after taking effect of sections 211 to 239 of Pub.L. 98–473, and except as otherwise provided for therein, see section 235 of Pub.L. 98–473, as amended, set as a note under section 3551 of this title.

CHAPTER 232A—SPECIAL FORFEITURE OF COLLATERAL PROFITS OF CRIME

§ 3681. Order of special forfeiture

(a) Upon the motion of the United States attorney made at any time after conviction of a defendant for an offense under section 794 of this title or for an offense against the United States resulting in physical harm to an individual, and after notice to any interested party, the court shall, if the court determines that the interest of justice or an order of restitution under this title so requires, order such defendant to forfeit all or any part of proceeds received or to be received by that defendant, or a transferee of that defendant, from a contract relating to a depiction of such crime in a movie, book, newspaper, magazine, radio or television production, or live entertainment of any kind, or an expression of that defendant's thoughts, opinions, or emotions regarding such crime.

(b) An order issued under subsection (a) of this section shall require that the person with whom the defendant contracts pay to the Attorney General any proceeds due the defendant under such contract.

(c)(1) Proceeds paid to the Attorney General under this section shall be retained in escrow in the Crime Victims Fund in the Treasury by the Attorney General for five years after the date of an order under this section, but during that five year period may—

(A) be levied upon to satisfy—

(i) a money judgment rendered by a United States district court in favor of a victim of an offense for which such defendant has been convicted, or a legal representative of such victim; and

(ii) a fine imposed by a court of the United States; and

(B) if ordered by the court in the interest of justice, be used to—

(i) satisfy a money judgment rendered in any court in favor of a victim of any offense for which such defendant has been convicted, or a legal representative of such victim; and

(ii) pay for legal representation of the defendant in matters arising from the offense for which such defendant has been convicted, but no more than 20 percent of the total proceeds may be so used.

(2) The court shall direct the disposition of all such proceeds in the possession of the Attorney General at the end of such five years and may require that all or any part of such proceeds be released from escrow and paid into the Crime Victims Fund in the Treasury.

(d) As used in this section, the term "interested party" includes the defendant and any transferee of proceeds due the defendant under the contract, the person with whom the defendant has contracted, and any person physically harmed as a result of the offense for which the defendant has been convicted.

(Added Pub.L. 98–473, Title II, § 1406(a), Oct. 12, 1984, 98 Stat. 2175, § 3671, and amended Pub.L. 99–399, Title XIII, § 1306(c), Aug. 27, 1986, 100 Stat. 899; renumbered and amended Pub.L. 99–646, §§ 40, 41(a), Nov. 10, 1986, 100 Stat. 3600.)

HISTORICAL AND STATUTORY NOTES

Effective and Applicability Provisions

1984 Acts. Section effective 30 days after Oct. 12, 1984, pursuant to section 1409(a) of Pub.L. 98–473.

§ 3682. Notice to victims of order of special forfeiture

The United States attorney shall, within thirty days after the imposition of an order under this chapter and at such other times as the Attorney General may require, publish in a newspaper of general circulation in the district in which the offense for which a defendant was convicted occurred, a notice that states—

(1) the name of, and other identifying information about, the defendant;

(2) the offense for which the defendant was convicted; and

(3) that the court has ordered a special forfeiture of certain proceeds that may be used to satisfy a judgment obtained against the defendant by a victim of an offense for which the defendant has been convicted.

(Added Pub.L. 98–473, Title II, § 1406(a), Oct. 12, 1984, 98 Stat. 2176, § 3672, and renumbered Pub.L. 99–646, § 41(a), Nov. 10, 1986, 100 Stat. 3600.)

HISTORICAL AND STATUTORY NOTES

Effective and Applicability Provisions

1984 Acts. Section effective 30 days after Oct. 12, 1984, pursuant to section 1409(a) of Pub.L. 98–473.

CHAPTER 233—CONTEMPTS

Sec.

§ 3691. Jury trial of criminal contempts

Whenever a contempt charged shall consist in willful disobedience of any lawful writ, process, order, rule, decree, or command of any district court of the United States by doing or omitting any act or thing in violation thereof, and the act or thing done or omitted also constitutes a criminal offense under any Act of Congress, or under the laws of any state in which it was done or omitted, the accused, upon demand therefor, shall be entitled to trial by a jury, which shall conform as near as may be to the practice in other criminal cases.

This section shall not apply to contempts committed in the presence of the court, or so near thereto as to obstruct the administration of justice, nor to contempts committed in disobedience of any lawful writ, process, order, rule, decree, or command entered in any suit or action brought or prosecuted in the name of, or on behalf of, the United States.

(June 25, 1948, c. 645, 62 Stat. 844.)

HISTORICAL AND STATUTORY NOTES

Savings Provisions

See section 235 of Pub.L. 98–473, Title II, c. II, Oct. 12, 1984, 98 Stat. 2031, as amended, set out as a note under section 3551 of this title.

§ 3692. Jury trial for contempt in labor dispute cases

In all cases of contempt arising under the laws of the United States governing the issuance of injunctions or restraining orders in any case involving or growing out of a labor dispute, the accused shall enjoy the right to a speedy and public trial by an impartial jury of the State and district wherein the contempt shall have been committed.

This section shall not apply to contempts committed in the presence of the court or so near thereto as to interfere directly with the administration of justice nor to the misbehavior, misconduct, or disobedience of any officer of the court in respect to the writs, orders or process of the court.

(June 25, 1948, c. 645, 62 Stat. 844.)

HISTORICAL AND STATUTORY NOTES

Taft-Hartley Injunctions

Former section 111 of Title 29, Labor, upon which this section is based, as inapplicable to injunctions issued under the Taft-Hartley Act, see section 178 of Title 29.

§ 3693. Summary disposition or jury trial; notice—(Rule)

SEE FEDERAL RULES OF CRIMINAL PROCEDURE

Summary punishment; certificate of judge; order; notice; jury trial; bail; disqualification of judge, Rule 42.

(June 25, 1948, c. 645, 62 Stat. 844.)

CHAPTER 235—APPEAL

HISTORICAL AND STATUTORY NOTES

Savings Provisions

See section 235 of Pub.L. 98–473, Title II, c. II, Oct. 12, 1984, 98 Stat. 2031, as amended, set out as a note under section 3551 of this title.

§ 3731. Appeal by United States

In a criminal case an appeal by the United States shall lie to a court of appeals from a decision, judgment, or order of a district court dismissing an indictment or information or granting a new trial after verdict or judgment, as to any one or more counts, or any part thereof, except that no appeal shall lie where the double jeopardy clause of the United States Constitution prohibits further prosecution.

An appeal by the United States shall lie to a court of appeals from a decision or order of a district court suppressing or excluding evidence or requiring the return of seized property in a criminal proceeding, not made after the defendant has been put in jeopardy and before the verdict or finding on an indictment or information, if the United States attorney certifies to the district court that the appeal is not taken for purpose of delay and that the evidence is a substantial proof of a fact material in the proceeding.

An appeal by the United States shall lie to a court of appeals from a decision or order, entered by a district court of the United States, granting the release of a person charged with or convicted of an offense, or denying a motion for revocation of, or modification of the conditions of, a decision or order granting release.

The appeal in all such cases shall be taken within thirty days after the decision, judgment or order has been rendered and shall be diligently prosecuted.

The provisions of this section shall be liberally construed to effectuate its purposes.

(June 25, 1948, c. 645, 62 Stat. 844; May 24, 1949, c. 139, § 58, 63 Stat. 97; June 19, 1968, Pub.L. 90–351, Title VIII, § 1301, 82 Stat. 237; Jan. 2, 1971, Pub.L. 91–644, Title III, § 14(a), 84 Stat. 1890; Oct. 12, 1984, Pub.L. 98–473, Title II, §§ 205, 1206, 98 Stat. 1986, 2153; Nov. 10, 1986, Pub.L. 99–646, § 32, 100 Stat. 3598; Sept. 13, 1994, Pub.L. 103–322, Title XXXIII, § 330008(4), 108 Stat. 2142; Nov. 2, 2002, Pub.L. 107–273, Div. B, Title III, § 3004, 116 Stat. 1805.)

HISTORICAL AND STATUTORY NOTES

Savings Provision

Section 14(b) of Pub.L. 91–644 provided that: "The amendments made by this section [to this section] shall not apply with respect to any criminal case begun in any district court before the effective date of this section [Jan. 2, 1971]."

§ 3732. Taking of appeal; notice; time—(Rule)

SEE FEDERAL RULES OF CRIMINAL PROCEDURE

Taking appeal; notice, contents, signing; time, Rule 37(a).

(June 25, 1948, c. 645, 62 Stat. 845.)

HISTORICAL AND STATUTORY NOTES

References in Text

Rule 37 of the Federal Rules of Criminal Procedure was abrogated Dec. 4, 1967, eff. July 1, 1968, and is covered by rules 3, 4, Federal Rules of Appellate Procedure, Title 28, Judiciary and Judicial Procedure.

§ 3733. Assignment of errors—(Rule)

SEE FEDERAL RULES OF CRIMINAL PROCEDURE

Assignments of error on appeal abolished, Rule 37(a)(1).

Necessity of specific objection in order to assign error in instructions, Rule 30.

(June 25, 1948, c. 645, 62 Stat. 845.)

HISTORICAL AND STATUTORY NOTES

References in Text

Rule 37 of the Federal Rules of Criminal Procedure was abrogated Dec. 4, 1967, eff. July 1, 1968, and is covered by rule 3, Federal Rules of Appellate Procedure, Title 28, Judiciary and Judicial Procedure

§ 3734. Bill of exceptions abolished—(Rule)

SEE FEDERAL RULES OF CRIMINAL PROCEDURE

Exceptions abolished, Rule 51.

Bill of exceptions not required, Rule 37(a)(1).

(June 25, 1948, c. 645, 62 Stat. 845.)

HISTORICAL AND STATUTORY NOTES

References in Text

Rule 37 of the Federal Rules of Criminal Procedure was abrogated Dec. 4, 1967, eff. July 1, 1968, and is covered by rule 3, Federal Rules of Appellate Procedure, Title 28, Judiciary and Judicial Procedure.

§ 3735. Bail on appeal or certiorari—(Rule)

SEE FEDERAL RULES OF CRIMINAL PROCEDURE

Bail on appeal or certiorari; application, Rules 38(c) and 46(a)(2).

(June 25, 1948, c. 645, 62 Stat. 845.)

HISTORICAL AND STATUTORY NOTES

References in Text

Rule 38(c) of the Federal Rules of Criminal Procedure was abrogated Dec. 4, 1967, eff. July 1, 1968, and is covered by rule 9, Federal Rules of Appellate Procedure, Title 28, Judiciary and Judicial Procedure.

Rule 46 was amended as part of the Bail Reform Act in 1966 and in 1972, and some provisions originally contained in Rule 46 are covered by this chapter, see Notes of Advisory Committee on Rules and Amendment notes under Rule 46, this title.

§ 3736. Certiorari—(Rule)

SEE FEDERAL RULES OF CRIMINAL PROCEDURE

Petition to Supreme Court, time, Rule 37(b).

(June 25, 1948, c. 645, 62 Stat. 845.)

HISTORICAL AND STATUTORY NOTES

References in Text

Rule 37 of the Federal Rules of Criminal Procedure was abrogated Dec. 4, 1967, eff. July 1, 1968. Provisions of such former rule for certiorari are covered by rule 19 et seq., of the Rules of the United States Supreme Court, Title 28, Judiciary and Judicial Procedure.

§ 3737. Record—(Rule)

SEE FEDERAL RULES OF CRIMINAL PROCEDURE

Preparation, form; typewritten record, Rule 39(b).

Exceptions abolished, Rule 51.

Bill of exceptions unnecessary, Rule 37(a)(1).

(June 25, 1948, c. 645, 62 Stat. 846.)

HISTORICAL AND STATUTORY NOTES

References in Text

Rule 37 and 39 of the Federal Rules of Criminal Procedure was abrogated Dec. 4, 1967, eff. July 1, 1968, and are covered by rules 10, Federal Rules of Appellate Procedure, Title 28, Judiciary and Judicial Procedure.

§ 3738. Docketing appeal and record—(Rule)

SEE FEDERAL RULES OF CRIMINAL PROCEDURE

Filing record on appeal and docketing proceeding; time, Rule 39(c).

(June 25, 1948, c. 645, 62 Stat. 846.)

HISTORICAL AND STATUTORY NOTES

References in Text

Rule 39 of the Federal Rules of Criminal Procedure was abrogated Dec. 4, 1967, eff. July 1, 1968, and is covered by rules 10 to 12, Federal Rules of Appellate Procedure, Title 28, Judiciary and Judicial Procedure.

§ 3739. Supervision—(Rule)

SEE FEDERAL RULES OF CRIMINAL PROCEDURE

Control and supervision in appellate court, Rule 39(a).

(June 25, 1948, c. 645, 62 Stat. 846.)

HISTORICAL AND STATUTORY NOTES

References in Text

Rule 39 of the Federal Rules of Criminal Procedure was abrogated Dec. 4, 1967, eff. July 1, 1968, and is covered by rule 27, Federal Rules of Appellate Procedure, Title 28, Judiciary and Judicial Procedure.

§ 3740. Argument—(Rule)

SEE FEDERAL RULES OF CRIMINAL PROCEDURE

Setting appeal for argument; preference to criminal appeals, Rule 39(d).

(June 25, 1948, c. 645, 62 Stat. 846.)

HISTORICAL AND STATUTORY NOTES

References in Text

Rule 39 of the Federal Rules of Criminal Procedure was abrogated Dec. 4, 1967, eff. July 1, 1968, and is covered by rule 34, Federal Rules of Appellate Procedure, Title 28, Judiciary and Judicial Procedure.

§ 3741. Harmless error and plain error—(Rule)

SEE FEDERAL RULES OF CRIMINAL PROCEDURE

Error or defect as affecting substantial rights, Rule 52.

Defects in indictment, Rule 7.

Waiver of error, Rules 12(b)(2) and 30.

(June 25, 1948, c. 645, 62 Stat. 846.)

§ 3742. Review of a sentence

(a) Appeal by a defendant.—A defendant may file a notice of appeal in the district court for review of an otherwise final sentence if the sentence—

(1) was imposed in violation of law;

(2) was imposed as a result of an incorrect application of the sentencing guidelines; or

(3) is greater than the sentence specified in the applicable guideline range to the extent that the

sentence includes a greater fine or term of imprisonment, probation, or supervised release than the maximum established in the guideline range, or includes a more limiting condition of probation or supervised release under section 3563(b)(6) or (b)(11) than the maximum established in the guideline range; or

(4) was imposed for an offense for which there is no sentencing guideline and is plainly unreasonable.

(b) Appeal by the Government.—The Government may file a notice of appeal in the district court for review of an otherwise final sentence if the sentence—

(1) was imposed in violation of law;

(2) was imposed as a result of an incorrect application of the sentencing guidelines;

(3) is less than the sentence specified in the applicable guideline range to the extent that the sentence includes a lesser fine or term of imprisonment, probation, or supervised release than the minimum established in the guideline range, or includes a less limiting condition of probation or supervised release under section 3563(b)(6) or (b)(11) than the minimum established in the guideline range; or

(4) was imposed for an offense for which there is no sentencing guideline and is plainly unreasonable.

The Government may not further prosecute such appeal without the personal approval of the Attorney General, the Solicitor General, or a deputy solicitor general designated by the Solicitor General.

(c) Plea agreements.—In the case of a plea agreement that includes a specific sentence under rule 11(e)(1)(C) of the Federal Rules of Criminal Procedure—

(1) a defendant may not file a notice of appeal under paragraph (3) or (4) of subsection (a) unless the sentence imposed is greater than the sentence set forth in such agreement; and

(2) the Government may not file a notice of appeal under paragraph (3) or (4) of subsection (b) unless the sentence imposed is less than the sentence set forth in such agreement.

(d) Record on review.—If a notice of appeal is filed in the district court pursuant to subsection (a) or (b), the clerk shall certify to the court of appeals—

(1) that portion of the record in the case that is designated as pertinent by either of the parties;

(2) the presentence report; and

(3) the information submitted during the sentencing proceeding.

(e) Consideration.—Upon review of the record, the court of appeals shall determine whether the sentence—

(1) was imposed in violation of law;

(2) was imposed as a result of an incorrect application of the sentencing guidelines;

(3) is outside the applicable guideline range, and

(A) the district court failed to provide the written statement of reasons required by section 3553(c);

(B) the sentence departs from the applicable guideline range based on a factor that—

(i) does not advance the objectives set forth in section 3553(a)(2); or

(ii) is not authorized under section 3553(b); or

(iii) is not justified by the facts of the case; or

(C) the sentence departs to an unreasonable degree from the applicable guidelines range, having regard for the factors to be considered in imposing a sentence, as set forth in section 3553(a) of this title and the reasons for the imposition of the particular sentence, as stated by the district court pursuant to the provisions of section 3553(c); or

(4) was imposed for an offense for which there is no applicable sentencing guideline and is plainly unreasonable.

The court of appeals shall give due regard to the opportunity of the district court to judge the credibility of the witnesses, and shall accept the findings of fact of the district court unless they are clearly erroneous and, except with respect to determinations under subsection (3)(A) or (3)(B), shall give due deference to the district court's application of the guidelines to the facts. With respect to determinations under subsection (3)(A) or (3)(B), the court of appeals shall review de novo the district court's application of the guidelines to the facts.

(f) Decision and disposition.—If the court of appeals determines that—

(1) the sentence was imposed in violation of law or imposed as a result of an incorrect application of the sentencing guidelines, the court shall remand the case for further sentencing proceedings with such instructions as the court considers appropriate;

(2) the sentence is outside the applicable guideline range and the district court failed to provide the required statement of reasons in the order of judgment and commitment, or the departure is based on an impermissible factor, or is to an unreasonable degree, or the sentence was imposed for an offense for which there is no applicable sentencing guideline and is plainly unreasonable, it shall state specific reasons for its conclusions and—

(A) if it determines that the sentence is too high and the appeal has been filed under subsection (a), it shall set aside the sentence and remand the case for further sentencing proceedings with such instructions as the court considers appropriate, subject to subsection (g);

(B) if it determines that the sentence is too low and the appeal has been filed under subsection (b), it shall set aside the sentence and remand the case for further sentencing proceedings with such instructions as the court considers appropriate, subject to subsection (g);

(3) the sentence is not described in paragraph (1) or (2), it shall affirm the sentence.

(g) Sentencing upon remand.—A district court to which a case is remanded pursuant to subsection (f)(1) or (f)(2) shall resentence a defendant in accordance with section 3553 and with such instructions as may have been given by the court of appeals, except that—

(1) In determining the range referred to in subsection 3553(a)(4), the court shall apply the guidelines issued by the Sentencing Commission pursuant to section 994(a)(1) of title 28, United States Code, and that were in effect on the date of the previous sentencing of the defendant prior to the appeal, together with any amendments thereto by any act of Congress that was in effect on such date; and

(2) The court shall not impose a sentence outside the applicable guidelines range except upon a ground that—

(A) was specifically and affirmatively included in the written statement of reasons required by section 3553(c) in connection with the previous sentencing of the defendant prior to the appeal; and

(B) was held by the court of appeals, in remanding the case, to be a permissible ground of departure.

(h) Application to a sentence by a magistrate judge.—An appeal of an otherwise final sentence imposed by a United States magistrate judge may be taken to a judge of the district court, and this section shall apply (except for the requirement of approval by the Attorney General or the Solicitor General in the case of a Government appeal) as though the appeal were to a court of appeals from a sentence imposed by a district court.

(i) Guideline not expressed as a range.—For the purpose of this section, the term "guideline range" includes a guideline range having the same upper and lower limits.

(j) Definitions.—For purposes of this section—

(1) a factor is a "permissible" ground of departure if it—

(A) advances the objectives set forth in section 3553(a)(2); and

(B) is authorized under section 3553(b); and

(C) is justified by the facts of the case; and

(2) a factor is an "impermissible" ground of departure if it is not a permissible factor within the meaning of subsection (j)(1).

(Added Pub.L. 98–473, Title II, § 213(a), Oct. 12, 1984, 98 Stat. 2011, and amended Pub.L. 99–646, § 73(a), Nov. 10, 1986, 100 Stat. 3617; Pub.L. 100–182, §§ 4 to 6, Dec. 7, 1987, 101 Stat. 1266, 1267; Pub.L. 100–690, Title VII, § 7103(a), Nov. 18, 1988, 102 Stat. 4416, 4417; Pub.L. 101–647, Title XXXV, §§ 3501, 3503, Nov. 29, 1990, 104 Stat. 4921; Pub.L. 101–650, Title III, § 321, Dec. 1, 1990, 104 Stat. 5117; Pub.L. 103–322, Title XXXIII, § 330002(k), Sept. 13, 1994, 108 Stat. 2140; Pub.L. 108–21, Title IV, § 401(d) to (f), Apr. 30, 2003, 117 Stat. 670, 671.)

Unconstitutionality of Subsec. (e)

Mandatory aspect of subsec. (e) of this section held unconstitutional by United States v. Booker, 543 U.S. 220, 125 S.Ct. 738, 160 L.Ed.2d 621 (2005).

HISTORICAL AND STATUTORY NOTES

References in Text

Section 3563(b)(6) and (b)(11), referred to in subsecs. (a)(3) and (b)(3), were renumbered section 3563(b)(5) and (b)(10) by Pub.L. 104–132, Title II, § 203(2)(B), April 24, 1996, 110 Stat. 1227.

The Federal Rules of Criminal Procedure, referred to in subsec. (c), are set out in this title.

Effective and Applicability Provisions

1987 Acts. Amendment by Pub.L. 100–182 applicable with respect to offenses committed after enactment of Pub.L. 100–182, which was approved Dec. 7, 1987, see section 26 of Pub.L. 100–182, set out as a note under section 3006A of this title.

1984 Acts. Section effective on the first day of first calendar month beginning thirty six months after Oct. 12, 1984, applicable only to offenses committed after taking effect of sections 211 to 239 of Pub.L. 98–473, and except as otherwise provided for therein, see section 235 of Pub.L. 98–473, as amended, set out as a note under section 3551 of this title.

Change of Name

Words "magistrate judge" and "United States magistrate judge" substituted for "magistrate" and "United States magistrate" in subsec. (g) pursuant to section 321 of Pub.L. 101–650, set out as a note under 28 U.S.C.A. § 631.

Change of Name

United States magistrate appointed under section 631 of Title 28, Judiciary and Judicial Procedure, to be known as United States magistrate judge after Dec. 1, 1990, with any reference to United States magistrate or magistrate in Title 28, in any other Federal statute, etc., deemed a reference to United States magistrate judge appointed under section 631 of Title 28, see section 321 of Pub.L. 101–650, set out as a note under section 631 of Title 28.

CHAPTER 237—CRIME VICTIMS' RIGHTS

Sec.

HISTORICAL AND STATUTORY NOTES

This chapter, enacted by Pub.L. 108–405, Title I, § 102(a), Oct. 30, 2004, 118 Stat. 2261, was previously repealed. See Prior Provisions note set out under this chapter.

Prior Provisions

Prior chapter 237, 18 U.S.C.A. §§ 3771 and 3772, was repealed by Pub.L. 100–702, Title IV, § 404(a)(1), Nov. 19, 1988, 102 Stat. 4651, effective Dec. 1, 1988. See 28 U.S.C.A. §§ 2071 to 2074

Prior section 3771, Acts June 25, 1948, c. 645, 62 Stat. 846; May 24, 1949, c. 139, § 59, 63 Stat. 98; May 10, 1950, c. 174, § 1, 64 Stat. 158; July 7, 1958, Pub.L. 85–508, § 12(k), 72 Stat. 348; Mar. 18, 1959, Pub.L. 86–3, § 14(g), 73 Stat. 11; Oct. 17, 1968, Pub.L. 90–578, Title III, § 301(a)(2), 82 Stat. 1115, which related to procedure up to and including verdict, was repealed by Pub.L. 100–702, Title IV, § 404(a)(1), Nov. 19, 1988, 102 Stat. 4651, effective Dec. 1, 1988, see Pub.L. 100–702, § 407, set out as a note under 28 U.S.C.A. § 2071.

Prior section 3772, Acts June 25, 1948, c. 645, 62 Stat. 846; May 24, 1949, c. 139, § 60, 63 Stat. 98; July 7, 1958, Pub.L. 85–508, § 12(*l*), 72 Stat. 348; Mar. 18, 1959, Pub.L. 86–3, § 14(h), 73 Stat. 11; Oct. 12, 1984, Pub.L. 98–473, Title II, § 206, 98 Stat. 1986, which related to procedure after verdict, was repealed by Pub.L. 100–702, Title IV, § 404(a)(1), Nov. 19, 1988, 102 Stat. 4651, effective Dec. 1, 1988, see Pub.L. 100–702, § 407, set out as a note under 28 U.S.C.A. § 2071.

§ 3771. Crime victims' rights

(a) Rights of crime victims.—A crime victim has the following rights:

(1) The right to be reasonably protected from the accused.

(2) The right to reasonable, accurate, and timely notice of any public court proceeding, or any parole proceeding, involving the crime or of any release or escape of the accused.

(3) The right not to be excluded from any such public court proceeding, unless the court, after receiving clear and convincing evidence, determines that testimony by the victim would be materially altered if the victim heard other testimony at that proceeding.

(4) The right to be reasonably heard at any public proceeding in the district court involving release, plea, sentencing, or any parole proceeding.

(5) The reasonable right to confer with the attorney for the Government in the case.

(6) The right to full and timely restitution as provided in law.

(7) The right to proceedings free from unreasonable delay.

(8) The right to be treated with fairness and with respect for the victim's dignity and privacy.

(b) Rights afforded.—

(1) In general.—In any court proceeding involving an offense against a crime victim, the court shall ensure that the crime victim is afforded the rights described in subsection (a). Before making a determination described in subsection (a)(3), the court shall make every effort to permit the fullest attendance possible by the victim and shall consider reasonable alternatives to the exclusion of the victim from the criminal proceeding. The reasons for any decision denying relief under this chapter shall be clearly stated on the record.

(2) Habeas corpus proceedings.—

(A) In general.—In a Federal habeas corpus proceeding arising out of a State conviction, the court shall ensure that a crime victim is afforded the rights described in paragraphs (3), (4), (7), and (8) of subsection (a).

(B) Enforcement.—

(i) In general.—These rights may be enforced by the crime victim or the crime victim's lawful representative in the manner described in paragraphs (1) and (3) of subsection (d).

(ii) Multiple victims.—In a case involving multiple victims, subsection (d)(2) shall also apply.

(C) Limitation.—This paragraph relates to the duties of a court in relation to the rights of a crime victim in Federal habeas corpus proceedings arising out of a State conviction, and does not give rise to any obligation or requirement applicable to personnel of any agency of the Executive Branch of the Federal Government.

(D) Definition.—For purposes of this paragraph, the term "crime victim" means the person against whom the State offense is committed or, if that person is killed or incapacitated, that person's family member or other lawful representative.

(c) Best efforts to accord rights.—

(1) Government.—Officers and employees of the Department of Justice and other departments and agencies of the United States engaged in the detection, investigation, or prosecution of crime shall make their best efforts to see that crime victims are notified of, and accorded, the rights described in subsection (a).

(2) Advice of attorney.—The prosecutor shall advise the crime victim that the crime victim can seek the advice of an attorney with respect to the rights described in subsection (a).

(3) **Notice.**—Notice of release otherwise required pursuant to this chapter shall not be given if such notice may endanger the safety of any person.

(d) **Enforcement and limitations.**—

(1) **Rights.**—The crime victim or the crime victim's lawful representative, and the attorney for the Government may assert the rights described in subsection (a). A person accused of the crime may not obtain any form of relief under this chapter.

(2) **Multiple crime victims.**—In a case where the court finds that the number of crime victims makes it impracticable to accord all of the crime victims the rights described in subsection (a), the court shall fashion a reasonable procedure to give effect to this chapter that does not unduly complicate or prolong the proceedings.

(3) **Motion for relief and writ of mandamus.**—The rights described in subsection (a) shall be asserted in the district court in which a defendant is being prosecuted for the crime or, if no prosecution is underway, in the district court in the district in which the crime occurred. The district court shall take up and decide any motion asserting a victim's right forthwith. If the district court denies the relief sought, the movant may petition the court of appeals for a writ of mandamus. The court of appeals may issue the writ on the order of a single judge pursuant to circuit rule or the Federal Rules of Appellate Procedure. The court of appeals shall take up and decide such application forthwith within 72 hours after the petition has been filed. In no event shall proceedings be stayed or subject to a continuance of more than five days for purposes of enforcing this chapter. If the court of appeals denies the relief sought, the reasons for the denial shall be clearly stated on the record in a written opinion.

(4) **Error.**—In any appeal in a criminal case, the Government may assert as error the district court's denial of any crime victim's right in the proceeding to which the appeal relates.

(5) **Limitation on relief.**—In no case shall a failure to afford a right under this chapter provide grounds for a new trial. A victim may make a motion to re-open a plea or sentence only if—

(A) the victim has asserted the right to be heard before or during the proceeding at issue and such right was denied;

(B) the victim petitions the court of appeals for a writ of mandamus within 10 days; and

(C) in the case of a plea, the accused has not pled to the highest offense charged.

This paragraph does not affect the victim's right to restitution as provided in title 18, United States Code.

(6) **No cause of action.**—Nothing in this chapter shall be construed to authorize a cause of action for damages or to create, to enlarge, or to imply any duty or obligation to any victim or other person for the breach of which the United States or any of its officers or employees could be held liable in damages. Nothing in this chapter shall be construed to impair the prosecutorial discretion of the Attorney General or any officer under his direction.

(e) **Definitions.**—For the purposes of this chapter, the term "crime victim" means a person directly and proximately harmed as a result of the commission of a Federal offense or an offense in the District of Columbia. In the case of a crime victim who is under 18 years of age, incompetent, incapacitated, or deceased, the legal guardians of the crime victim or the representatives of the crime victim's estate, family members, or any other persons appointed as suitable by the court, may assume the crime victim's rights under this chapter, but in no event shall the defendant be named as such guardian or representative.

(f) **Procedures to promote compliance.**—

(1) **Regulations.**—Not later than 1 year after the date of enactment of this chapter, the Attorney General of the United States shall promulgate regulations to enforce the rights of crime victims and to ensure compliance by responsible officials with the obligations described in law respecting crime victims.

(2) **Contents.**—The regulations promulgated under paragraph (1) shall—

(A) designate an administrative authority within the Department of Justice to receive and investigate complaints relating to the provision or violation of the rights of a crime victim;

(B) require a course of training for employees and offices of the Department of Justice that fail to comply with provisions of Federal law pertaining to the treatment of crime victims, and otherwise assist such employees and offices in responding more effectively to the needs of crime victims;

(C) contain disciplinary sanctions, including suspension or termination from employment, for employees of the Department of Justice who willfully or wantonly fail to comply with provisions of Federal law pertaining to the treatment of crime victims; and

(D) provide that the Attorney General, or the designee of the Attorney General, shall be the final arbiter of the complaint, and that there shall be no judicial review of the final decision of the Attorney General by a complainant.

(Added Pub.L. 108–405, Title I, § 102(a), Oct. 30, 2004, 118 Stat. 2261, and amended Pub.L. 109–248, Title II, § 212, July 27, 2006, 120 Stat. 616.)

HISTORICAL AND STATUTORY NOTES

References in Text

The Federal Rules of Appellate Procedure, referred to in subsec. (d)(3), are set out in the Appendix to Title 28.

The date of enactment of this chapter, referred to in subsec. (f)(1), is the date of enactment of Pub.L. 108–405, which was approved Oct. 30, 2004.

Prior Provisions

Section, Acts June 25, 1948, c. 645, 62 Stat. 846; May 24, 1949, c. 139, § 59, 63 Stat. 98; May 10, 1950, c. 174, § 1, 64 Stat. 158; July 7, 1958, Pub.L. 85–508, § 12(k), 72 Stat. 348; Mar. 18, 1959, Pub.L. 86–3, § 14(g), 73 Stat. 11; Oct. 17, 1968, Pub.L. 90–578, Title III, § 301(a)(2), 82 Stat. 1115, relating to criminal procedure, including verdicts, was repealed by Pub.L. 100–702, Title IV, § 404(a)(1), Nov. 19, 1988, 102 Stat. 4651 eff. Dec. 1, 1988, see Pub.L. 100–702, § 407, set out as a note under 28 U.S.C.A. § 2071.

Short Title

2004 Acts. Pub.L. 108–405, Title I, § 101, Oct. 30, 2004, 118 Stat. 2261, provided that: "This title [enacting this section and 42 U.S.C.A. §§ 10603d and 10603e, repealing 42 U.S.C.A. § 10606, and enacting provisions set out as a note under this section] may be cited as the 'Scott Campbell, Stephanie Roper, Wendy Preston, Louarna Gillis, and Nila Lynn Crime Victims' Rights Act'."

Reports to Congress

Pub.L. 108–405, Title I, § 104(a), Oct. 30, 2004, 118 Stat. 2265, provided that: "Not later than 1 year after the date of enactment of this Act [Oct. 30, 2004] and annually thereafter, the Administrative Office of the United States Courts, for each Federal court, shall report to Congress the number of times that a right established in chapter 237 of title 18, United States Code [18 U.S.C.A. § 3771 et seq.], is asserted in a criminal case and the relief requested is denied and, with respect to each such denial, the reason for such denial, as well as the number of times a mandamus action is brought pursuant to chapter 237 of title 18, and the result reached."

[§ 3772. Repealed. Pub.L. 100–702, Title IV, § 404(a)(1), Nov. 19, 1988, 102 Stat. 4651]

HISTORICAL AND STATUTORY NOTES

Section, Acts June 25, 1948, c. 645, 62 Stat. 846; May 24, 1949, c. 139, § 60, 63 Stat. 98; July 7, 1958, Pub.L. 85–508, § 12(*l*), 72 Stat. 348; Mar. 18, 1959, Pub.L. 86–3, § 14(h), 73 Stat. 11; Oct. 12, 1984, Pub.L. 98–473, Title II, § 206, 98 Stat. 1986, related to procedure after verdict. See Sections 2071 to 2074 of Title 28, Judiciary and Judicial Procedure.

Effective Date of Repeal

Sections repealed effective Dec. 1, 1988, see section 407 of Pub.L. 100–702, set out as a note under section 2071 of Title 28, Judiciary and Judicial Procedure.

PART III—PRISONS AND PRISONERS

1 Chapter heading added without corresponding amendment of part analysis.

HISTORICAL AND STATUTORY NOTES

Effective and Applicability Provisions

For applicability of sentencing provisions to offenses, see Effective Date and Savings Provisions, etc., note, section 235 of Pub.L. 98–473, as amended, set out under section 3551 of this title.

Savings Provisions

See section 235 of Pub.L. 98–473, Title II, c. II, Oct. 12, 1984, 98 Stat. 2031, as amended, set out as a note under section 3551 of this title.

CHAPTER 301—GENERAL PROVISIONS

§ 4001. Limitation on detention; control of prisons

(a) No citizen shall be imprisoned or otherwise detained by the United States except pursuant to an Act of Congress.

(b)(1) The control and management of Federal penal and correctional institutions, except military or naval institutions, shall be vested in the Attorney General, who shall promulgate rules for the government thereof, and appoint all necessary officers and employees in accordance with the civil-service laws, the Classification Act, as amended and the applicable regulations.

(2) The Attorney General may establish and conduct industries, farms, and other activities and classify the inmates; and provide for their proper government, discipline, treatment, care, rehabilitation, and reformation.

(June 25, 1948, c. 645, 62 Stat. 847; Sept. 25, 1971, Pub.L. 92–128, § 1(a), (b), 85 Stat. 347.)

HISTORICAL AND STATUTORY NOTES

References in Text

The civil-service laws, referred to in subsec. (b)(1), are set forth in Title 5, Government Organization and Employees. See, particularly, section 3301 et seq. of that Title.

The Classification Act, as amended, referred to in subsec. (b)(1), originally was the Classification Act of 1923, Mar. 4, 1923, c. 265, 42 Stat. 1488, as amended, which was repealed by section 1202 of the Classification Act of 1949, Oct. 28, 1949, c. 782, 63 Stat. 972. Section 1106(a) of the 1949 Act provided that references in other laws to the Classification Act of 1923 shall be held and considered to mean the Classification Act of 1949. The Classification Act of 1949 was in turn repealed by Pub.L. 89–554, § 8(a), Sept. 6, 1966, 80 Stat. 632, and reenacted by the first section thereof as chapter 51 and subchapter III of chapter 53 of Title 5, Government Organization and Employees.

Short Title

2000 Amendments. Pub.L. 106–294, § 1, Oct. 12, 2000, 114 Stat. 1038, provided that: "This Act [enacting section 4048 of this title and amending section 4013 of this title] may be cited as the 'Federal Prisoner Health Care Copayment Act of 2000'."

1998 Acts. Pub.L. 105–370, § 1, Nov. 12, 1998, 112 Stat. 3374, provided that: "This Act [enacting section 4014 of this title and provisions set out as a note under section 4042 of this title] may be cited as the 'Correction Officers Health and Safety Act of 1998'."

Placement of Prisoners in Privately Operated Prisons

Pub.L. 106–553, § 1(a)(2) [Title I, § 114, formerly § 115], Dec. 21, 2000, 114 Stat. 2762, 2762A–68; renumbered § 114, Pub.L. 106–554, § 1(a)(4) [Div. A, § 213(a)(2)], Dec. 21, 2000, 114 Stat. 2763, 2763A–179, provided that: "Beginning in fiscal year 2001 and thereafter, funds appropriated to the Federal Prison System may be used to place in privately operated prisons only such persons sentenced to incarceration under the District of Columbia Code as the Director, Bureau of Prisons, may determine to be appropriate for such placement consistent with Federal classification standards, after consideration of all relevant factors, including the threat of danger to public safety."

Fee to Recover the Cost of Incarceration

Pub.L. 102–395, Title I, § 111(a), Oct. 6, 1992, 106 Stat. 1842, provided that:

"(1) For fiscal year 1993 and thereafter the Attorney General shall establish and collect a fee to cover the costs of confinement from any person convicted in a United States District Court and committed to the Attorney General's custody.

"(2) Such fee shall be equivalent to the average cost of one year of incarceration, and the Attorney General shall credit or rebate a prorated portion of the fee with respect to any such person incarcerated for 334 days or fewer in a given fiscal year.

"(3) The calculation of the number of days of incarceration in a given fiscal year for the purpose of such fee shall include time served prior to conviction.

"(4) The Attorney General shall not collect such fee from any person with respect to whom a fine was imposed or waived by a judge of a United States District Court pursuant to section 5E1.2(f) and (i) of the United States Sentencing Guidelines [section 5E1.2(f) and (i) of the Federal Sentencing Guidelines set out as part of Title 18], or any successor provisions.

"(5) In cases in which the Attorney General has authority to collect the fee, the Attorney General shall have discretion to waive the fee or impose a lesser fee if the person under confinement establishes that (1) he or she is not able and, even with the use of a reasonable installment schedule, is not likely to become able to pay all or part of the fee, or (2) imposition of a fine would unduly burden the defendant's dependents.

"(6) For fiscal year 1993 only, fees collected in accordance with this section shall be deposited as offsetting receipts to the Treasury.

"(7) For fiscal year 1994 and thereafter, fees collected in accordance with this section shall be deposited as offsetting collections to the appropriation Federal Prison System, 'Salaries and expenses', and shall be available, inter alia, to enhance alcohol and drug abuse prevention programs."

Use of Inactive Department of Defense Facilities as Prisons

Pub.L. 95–624, § 9, Nov. 9, 1978, 92 Stat. 3463, provided that: "The Attorney General shall consult with the Secretary of Defense in order to develop a plan to assure that such suitable facilities as the Department of Defense operates which are not in active use shall be made available for operation by the Department of Justice for the confinement of United States prisoners. Such plan shall provide for the return to the management of the Department of Defense of any such facility upon a finding by the Secretary of Defense that such return is necessary to the operation of the Department."

§ 4002. Federal prisoners in State institutions; employment

For the purpose of providing suitable quarters for the safekeeping, care, and subsistence of all persons held under authority of any enactment of Congress, the Attorney General may contract, for a period not exceeding three years, with the proper authorities of any State, Territory, or political subdivision thereof, for the imprisonment, subsistence, care, and proper employment of such persons.

Such Federal prisoners shall be employed only in the manufacture of articles for, the production of supplies for, the construction of public works for, and the maintenance and care of the institutions of, the State or political subdivision in which they are imprisoned.

The rates to be paid for the care and custody of said persons shall take into consideration the character of the quarters furnished, sanitary conditions, and quality of subsistence and may be such as will permit and encourage the proper authorities to provide reasonably decent, sanitary, and healthful quarters and subsistence for such persons.

(June 25, 1948, c. 645, 62 Stat. 847; Nov. 9, 1978, Pub.L. 95–624, § 8, 92 Stat. 3463.)

§ 4003. Federal institutions in States without appropriate facilities

If by reason of the refusal or inability of the authorities having control of any jail, workhouse, penal, correctional, or other suitable institution of any State or Territory, or political subdivision thereof, to enter into a contract for the imprisonment, subsistence, care, or proper employment of United States prisoners, or if there are no suitable or sufficient facilities available at reasonable cost, the Attorney General may select a site either within or convenient to the State, Territory, or judicial district concerned and cause to be erected thereon a house of detention, workhouse, jail, prison-industries project, or camp, or other place of confinement, which shall be used for the detention of persons held under authority of any Act of Congress, and of such other persons as in the opinion of the Attorney General are proper subjects for confinement in such institutions.

(June 25, 1948, c. 645, 62 Stat. 848.)

§ 4004. Oaths and acknowledgments

The wardens and superintendents, associate wardens and superintendents, chief clerks, and record clerks, of Federal penal or correctional institutions, may administer oaths to and take acknowledgments of officers, employees, and inmates of such institutions, but shall not demand or accept any fee or compensation therefor.

(June 25, 1948, c. 645, 62 Stat. 848; July 7, 1955, c. 282, 69 Stat. 282; Oct. 12, 1984, Pub.L. 98–473, Title II, § 223(*l*), 98 Stat. 2029.)

HISTORICAL AND STATUTORY NOTES

Effective and Applicability Provisions

1984 Acts. Amendment by Pub.L. 98–473 effective on the first day of first calendar month beginning thirty six months after Oct. 12, 1984, applicable only to offenses committed after taking effect of sections 211 to 239 of Pub.L. 98–473, and except as otherwise provided for therein, see section 235 of Pub.L. 98–473, as amended, set out as a note under section 3551 of this title.

§ 4005. Medical relief; expenses

(a) Upon request of the Attorney General and to the extent consistent with the Assisted Suicide Funding Restriction Act of 1997, the Federal Security Administrator shall detail regular and reserve commissioned officers of the Public Health Service, pharmacists, acting assistant surgeons, and other employees of the Public Health Service to the Department of Justice for the purpose of supervising and furnishing medical, psychiatric, and other technical and scientific services to the Federal penal and correctional institutions.

(b) The compensation, allowances, and expenses of the personnel detailed under this section may be paid from applicable appropriations of the Public Health Service in accordance with the law and regulations governing the personnel of the Public Health Service, such appropriations to be reimbursed from applicable appropriations of the Department of Justice; or the Attorney General may make allotments of funds and transfer of credit to the Public Health Service in such amounts as are available and necessary, for payment of compensation, allowances, and expenses of personnel so detailed, in accordance with the law and regulations governing the personnel of the Public Health Service.

(June 25, 1948, c. 645, 62 Stat. 848; Apr. 30, 1997, Pub.L. 105–12, § 9(k), 111 Stat. 28.)

HISTORICAL AND STATUTORY NOTES

References in Text

The Assisted Suicide Funding Restriction Act of 1997, referred to in subsec. (a), is Pub.L. 105–12, Apr. 30, 1997, 111 Stat. 23, which is classified principally to chapter 138 (section 14401 et seq.) of Title 42, The Public Health and Welfare. For complete classification of this Act to the Code, see Short Title note set out under section 14401 of Title 42 and Tables.

Effective and Applicability Provisions

1997 Acts. Amendment by Pub.L. 105–12 effective Apr. 30, 1997, to apply to Federal payments made pursuant to obligations incurred after Apr. 30, 1997, for items and services provided on or after such date, and also to apply with respect to contracts entered into, renewed, or extended after Apr. 30, 1997, as well as contracts entered into before Apr. 30, 1997, to the extent permitted by such contracts, see section 11 of Pub.L. 105–12, set out as a note under section 14401 of Title 42, The Public Health and Welfare.

Transfer of Functions

All functions of the Federal Security Administrator were transferred to the Secretary of Health, Education, and Welfare, and the office of Federal Security Administrator was abolished by sections 5 and 8 of Reorg. Plan No. 1 of 1953, as amended, eff. Apr. 11, 1953, 18 F.R. 2053, 67 Stat. 631, set out in the Appendix to Title 5, Government Organization and Employees.

All functions of the Public Health Service, of the Surgeon General of the Public Health Service, and of all other officers and employees of the Public Health Service, and all functions of all agencies of or in the Public Health Service transferred to Secretary of Health, Education, and Welfare by 1966 Reorg. Plan No. 3, 31 F.R. 8855, 80 Stat. 1610, effective June 25, 1966, set out in the Appendix to Title 5.

The Secretary of Health, Education, and Welfare was redesignated the Secretary of Health and Human Services by Pub.L. 96–88, Title V, § 509(b), Oct. 17, 1979, 93 Stat. 695, which is classified to section 3508(b) of Title 20, Education.

§ 4006. Subsistence for prisoners

(a) In general.—The Attorney General or the Secretary of Homeland Security, as applicable, shall allow and pay only the reasonable and actual cost of the subsistence of prisoners in the custody of any marshal of the United States, and shall prescribe such regulations for the government of the marshals as will enable him to determine the actual and reasonable expenses incurred.

(b) Health care items and services.—

(1) In general.—Payment for costs incurred for the provision of health care items and services for individuals in the custody of the United States Marshals Service, the Federal Bureau of Investigation and the Department of Homeland Security shall be the amount billed, not to exceed the amount that would be paid for the provision of similar health care items and services under the Medicare program under title XVIII of the Social Security Act.

(2) Full and final payment.—Any payment for a health care item or service made pursuant to this subsection, shall be deemed to be full and final payment.

(June 25, 1948, c. 645, 62 Stat. 848; Nov. 29, 1999, Pub.L. 106–113, Div. B, § 1000(a)(1) [Title I, § 114], 113 Stat. 1535, 1501A–20; Dec. 21, 2000, Pub.L. 106–553, § 1(a)(2) [Title VI, § 626], 114 Stat. 2762, 2762A–108; Jan. 5, 2006, Pub.L. 109–162, Title XI, § 1157, 119 Stat. 3114.)

HISTORICAL AND STATUTORY NOTES

References in Text

The Medicare program under title XVIII of the Social Security Act, referred to in subsec. (b)(1), is 42 U.S.C.A. § 1395 et seq.

Abolition of Immigration and Naturalization Service and Transfer of Functions

For abolition of Immigration and Naturalization Service, transfer of functions, and treatment of related references, see note set out under 8 U.S.C.A. § 1551.

§ 4007. Expenses of prisoners

The expenses attendant upon the confinement of persons arrested or committed under the laws of the United States, as well as upon the execution of any sentence of a court thereof respecting them, shall be paid out of the Treasury of the United States in the manner provided by law.

(June 25, 1948, c. 645, 62 Stat. 848.)

HISTORICAL AND STATUTORY NOTES

Payment of Costs of Incarceration by Federal Prisoners

Pub.L. 100–690, Title VII, § 7301, Nov. 18, 1988, 102 Stat. 4463, provided that: "Not later than 1 year after the date of enactment of this section, the United States Sentencing Commission shall study the feasibility of requiring prisoners incarcerated in Federal correctional institutions to pay some or all of the costs incident to the prisoner's confinement, including, but not limited to, the costs of food, housing, and shelter. The study shall review measures which would allow prisoners unable to pay such costs to work at paid employment within the community, during incarceration or after release, in order to pay the costs incident to the prisoner's confinement."

§ 4008. Transportation expenses

Prisoners shall be transported by agents designated by the Attorney General or his authorized representative.

The reasonable expense of transportation, necessary subsistence, and hire and transportation of guards and agents shall be paid by the Attorney General from such appropriation for the Department of Justice as he shall direct.

Upon conviction by a consular court or court martial the prisoner shall be transported from the court to the place of confinement by agents of the Department of State, the Army, Navy, or Air Force, as the case may be, the expense to be paid out of the Treasury of the United States in the manner provided by law.

(June 25, 1948, c. 645, 62 Stat. 849; May 24, 1949, c. 139, § 61, 63 Stat. 98.)

§ 4009. Appropriations for sites and buildings

The Attorney General may authorize the use of a sum not to exceed $100,000 in each instance, payable from any unexpended balance of the appropriation "Support of United States prisoners" for the purpose of leasing or acquiring a site, preparation of plans, and erection of necessary buildings under section 4003 of this title.

If in any instance it shall be impossible or impracticable to secure a proper site and erect the necessary buildings within the above limitation the Attorney General may authorize the use of a sum not to exceed $10,000 in each instance, payable from any unexpended balance of the appropriation "Support of United States prisoners" for the purpose of securing options and making preliminary surveys or sketches.

Upon selection of an appropriate site the Attorney General shall submit to Congress an estimate of the cost of purchasing same and of remodeling, constructing, and equipping the necessary buildings thereon.

(June 25, 1948, c. 645, 62 Stat. 849.)

§ 4010. Acquisition of additional land

The Attorney General may, when authorized by law, acquire land adjacent to or in the vicinity of a Federal penal or correctional institution if he considers the additional land essential to the protection of the health or safety of the inmates of the institution.

(Added Pub.L. 89–554, § 3(f), Sept. 6, 1966, 80 Stat. 610.)

§ 4011. Disposition of cash collections for meals, laundry, etc.

Collections in cash for meals, laundry, barber service, uniform equipment, and other items for which payment is made originally from appropriations for the maintenance and operation of Federal penal and correctional institutions, may be deposited in the Treasury to the credit of the appropriation currently available for those items when the collection is made.

(Added Pub.L. 89–554, § 3(f), Sept. 6, 1966, 80 Stat. 610.)

§ 4012. Summary seizure and forfeiture of prison contraband

An officer or employee of the Bureau of Prisons may, pursuant to rules and regulations of the Director of the Bureau of Prisons, summarily seize any object introduced into a Federal penal or correctional facility or possessed by an inmate of such a facility in violation of a rule, regulation or order promulgated by the Director, and such object shall be forfeited to the United States.

(Added Pub.L. 98–473, Title II, § 1109(d), Oct. 12, 1984, 98 Stat. 2148.)

§ 4013. Support of United States prisoners in non–Federal institutions

(a) The Attorney General, in support of United States prisoners in non-Federal institutions, is authorized to make payments from funds appropriated for Federal prisoner detention for—

(1) necessary clothing;

(2) medical care and necessary guard hire; and

(3) the housing, care, and security of persons held in custody of a United States marshal pursuant to Federal law under agreements with State or local units of government or contracts with private entities.

[(4) Redesignated (b)]

(b) The Attorney General, in support of Federal prisoner detainees in non-Federal institutions, is authorized to make payments, from funds appropriated for State and local law enforcement assistance, for entering into contracts or cooperative agreements with any State, territory, or political subdivision thereof, for the necessary construction, physical renovation, acquisition of equipment, supplies, or materials required to establish acceptable conditions of confinement and detention services in any State or local jurisdiction which agrees to provide guaranteed bed space for Federal detainees within that correctional system, in accordance with regulations which are issued by the Attorney General and are comparable to the regulations issued under section 4006 of this title, except that—

(1) amounts made available for purposes of this paragraph shall not exceed the average per-inmate cost of constructing similar confinement facilities for the Federal prison population,

(2) the availability of such federally assisted facility shall be assured for housing Federal prisoners, and

(3) the per diem rate charged for housing such Federal prisoners shall not exceed allowable costs or other conditions specified in the contract or cooperative agreement.

(c)(1) The United States Marshals Service may designate districts that need additional support from private detention entities under subsection (a)(3) based on—

(A) the number of Federal detainees in the district; and

(B) the availability of appropriate Federal, State, and local government detention facilities.

(2) In order to be eligible for a contract for the housing, care, and security of persons held in custody of the United States Marshals pursuant to Federal law and funding under subsection (a)(3), a private entity shall—

(A) be located in a district that has been designated as needing additional Federal detention facilities pursuant to paragraph (1);

(B) meet the standards of the American Correctional Association;

(C) comply with all applicable State and local laws and regulations;

(D) have approved fire, security, escape, and riot plans; and

(E) comply with any other regulations that the Marshals Service deems appropriate.

(3) The United States Marshals Service shall provide an opportunity for public comment on a contract under subsection (a)(3).

(d) Health care fees for Federal prisoners in non-Federal institutions.—

(1) In general.—Notwithstanding amounts paid under subsection (a)(3), a State or local government may assess and collect a reasonable fee from the trust fund account (or institutional equivalent) of a Federal prisoner for health care services, if—

(A) the prisoner is confined in a non-Federal institution pursuant to an agreement between the Federal Government and the State or local government;

(B) the fee—

(i) is authorized under State law; and

(ii) does not exceed the amount collected from State or local prisoners for the same services; and

(C) the services—

(i) are provided within or outside of the institution by a person who is licensed or certified under State law to provide health care services and who is operating within the scope of such license;

(ii) constitute a health care visit within the meaning of section 4048(a)(4) of this title; and

(iii) are not preventative health care services, emergency services, prenatal care, diagnosis or treatment of chronic infectious diseases, mental health care, or substance abuse treatment.

(2) No refusal of treatment for financial reasons.—Nothing in this subsection may be construed to permit any refusal of treatment to a prisoner on the basis that—

(A) the account of the prisoner is insolvent; or

(B) the prisoner is otherwise unable to pay a fee assessed under this subsection.

(3) Notice to prisoners of law.—Each person who is or becomes a prisoner shall be provided with written and oral notices of the provisions of this subsection and the applicability of this subsection to the prisoner. Notwithstanding any other provision of this subsection, a fee under this section may not be assessed against, or collected from, such person—

(A) until the expiration of the 30–day period beginning on the date on which each prisoner in the prison system is provided with such notices; and

(B) for services provided before the expiration of such period.

(4) Notice to prisoners of State or local implementation.—The implementation of this subsection by the State or local government, and any amendment to that implementation, shall not take effect until the expiration of the 30–day period beginning on the date on which each prisoner in the prison system is provided with written and oral notices of the provisions of that implementation (or amendment, as the case may be). A fee under this subsection may not be assessed against, or collected from, a prisoner pursuant to such implementation (or amendments, as the case may be) for services provided before the expiration of such period.

(5) Notice before public comment period.—Before the beginning of any period a proposed implementation under this subsection is open to public comment, written and oral notice of the provisions of that proposed implementation shall be provided to groups that advocate on behalf of Federal prisoners and to each prisoner subject to such proposed implementation.

(6) Comprehensive HIV/AIDS services required.—Any State or local government assessing or collecting a fee under this subsection shall provide comprehensive coverage for services relating to human immunodeficiency virus (HIV) and acquired immune deficiency syndrome (AIDS) to each Federal prisoner in the custody of such State or local government when medically appropriate. The State or local government may not assess or collect a fee under this subsection for providing such coverage.

(Added Pub.L. 100–690, Title VII, § 7608(d)(1), Nov. 18, 1988, 102 Stat. 4516, and amended Pub.L. 101–647, Title XVII, § 1701, Title XXXV, § 3599, Nov. 29, 1990, 104 Stat. 4843, 4931; Pub.L. 103–322, Title XXXIII, § 330011(*o*), Sept. 13, 1994, 108 Stat. 2145; Pub.L. 106–294, § 3, Oct. 12, 2000, 114 Stat. 1040; Pub.L. 107–273, Div. A, Title III, § 302(2), Nov. 2, 2002, 116 Stat. 1781.)

HISTORICAL AND STATUTORY NOTES

Effective and Applicability Provisions

1994 Acts. Section 330011(*o*) of Pub.L. 103–322 provided in part that the amendment made by such section, repealing section 3599 of Pub.L. 101–647 (which amended this section), was to take effect on the date of enactment of section 3599 of Pub.L. 101–647, which was approved Nov. 29, 1990.

Repeals

Section 3599 of Pub.L. 101–647, which amended this section, was repealed by section 330011(*o*) of Pub.L. 103–322.

Justice Prisoner and Alien Transportation System Fund, United States Marshals Service

Pub.L. 106–553, § 1(a)(2) [Title I], Dec. 21, 2000, 114 Stat. 2762, 2762A–55, provided in part that: "Beginning in fiscal year 2000 and thereafter, payment shall be made from the Justice Prisoner and Alien Transportation System Fund for necessary expenses related to the scheduling and transportation of United States prisoners and illegal and criminal aliens in the custody of the United States Marshals Service, as authorized in 18 U.S.C. 4013 [this section], including, without limitation, salaries and expenses, operations, and the acquisition, lease, and maintenance of aircraft and support facilities: *Provided,* That the Fund shall be reimbursed or credited with advance payments from amounts available to the Department of Justice, other Federal agencies, and other sources at rates that will recover the expenses of Fund operations, including, without limitation, accrual of annual leave and depreciation of plant and equipment of the Fund: *Provided further,* That proceeds from the disposal of Fund aircraft shall be credited to the Fund: *Provided further,* That amounts in the Fund shall be available without fiscal year limitation, and may be used for operating equipment lease agreements that do not exceed 10 years."

Pub.L. 106–113, Div. B, § 1000(a)(1) [Title I], Nov. 29, 1999, 113 Stat. 1535, 1501A–7, provided in part that: "Beginning in fiscal year 2000 and thereafter, payment shall be made from the Justice Prisoner and Alien Transportation System Fund for necessary expenses related to the scheduling and transportation of United States prisoners and illegal and criminal aliens in the custody of the United States Marshals Service, as authorized in 18 U.S.C. 4013, including, without limitation, salaries and expenses, operations, and the acquisition, lease, and maintenance of aircraft and support facilities: *Provided,* That the Fund shall be reimbursed or credited with advance payments from amounts available to the Department of Justice, other Federal agencies, and other sources at rates that will recover the expenses of Fund operations, including, without limitation, accrual of annual leave and depreciation of plant and equipment of the Fund: *Provided further,* That proceeds from the disposal of Fund aircraft shall be credited to the Fund: *Provided further,* That amounts in the Fund shall be available without fiscal year limitation, and may be used for operating equipment lease agreements that do not exceed 5 years."

Pub.L. 105–277, Div. A, § 101(b) [Title I], Oct. 21, 1998, 112 Stat. 2681–54, provided in part that: "There is hereby established a Justice Prisoner and Alien Transportation System Fund for the payment of necessary expenses related to the scheduling and transportation of United States prisoners and illegal and criminal aliens in the custody of the United States Marshals Service, as authorized in 18 U.S.C. 4013, including, without limitation, salaries and expenses, operations, and the acquisition, lease, and maintenance of aircraft and support facilities: *Provided,* That the Fund shall be reimbursed or credited with advance payments from amounts available to the Department of Justice, other Federal agencies, and other sources at rates that will recover the expenses of Fund operations, including, without limitation, accrual of annual leave and depreciation of plant and equipment of the Fund: *Provided further,* That proceeds from the disposal of Fund aircraft shall be credited to the Fund: *Provided further,* That amounts in the Fund shall be available without fiscal year limitation, and may be used for operating equipment lease agreements that do not exceed 5 years."

Contracts and Agreements for Detention and Incarceration Space or Facilities

Pub.L. 106–553, § 1(a)(2) [Title I, § 118, formerly § 119], Dec. 21, 2000, 114 Stat. 2762, 2762A–69; renumbered § 118, Pub.L. 106–554, § 1(a)(4) [Div. A, § 213(a)(2)], Dec. 21, 2000, 114 Stat. 2763, 2763A–179, provided that: "Notwithstanding any other provision of law, including section 4(d) of the Service Contract Act of 1965 (41 U.S.C. 353(d)), the Attorney General hereafter may enter into contracts and other agreements, of any reasonable duration, for detention or incarceration space or facilities, including related services, on any reasonable basis."

§ 4014. Testing for human immunodeficiency virus

(a) The Attorney General shall cause each individual convicted of a Federal offense who is sentenced to incarceration for a period of 6 months or more to be tested for the presence of the human immunodeficiency virus, as appropriate, after the commencement of that incarceration, if such individual is determined to be at risk for infection with such virus in accordance with the guidelines issued by the Bureau of Prisons relating to infectious disease management.

(b) If the Attorney General has a well-founded reason to believe that a person sentenced to a term of imprisonment for a Federal offense, or ordered detained before trial under section 3142(e), may have intentionally or unintentionally transmitted the human immunodeficiency virus to any officer or employee of the United States, or to any person lawfully present in a correctional facility who is not incarcerated there, the Attorney General shall—

(1) cause the person who may have transmitted the virus to be tested promptly for the presence of such virus and communicate the test results to the person tested; and

(2) consistent with the guidelines issued by the Bureau of Prisons relating to infectious disease management, inform any person (in, as appropriate, confidential consultation with the person's physician) who may have been exposed to such virus, of the potential risk involved and, if warranted by the circumstances, that prophylactic or other treatment should be considered.

(c) If the results of a test under subsection (a) or (b) indicate the presence of the human immunodeficiency virus, the Attorney General shall provide appropriate access for counselling, health care, and support services to the affected officer, employee, or other person, and to the person tested.

(d) The results of a test under this section are inadmissible against the person tested in any Federal or State civil or criminal case or proceeding.

(e) Not later than 1 year after the date of the enactment of this section, the Attorney General shall issue rules to implement this section. Such rules shall require that the results of any test are communicated only to the person tested, and, if the results of the test indicate the presence of the virus, to correctional facility personnel consistent with guidelines issued by the Bureau of Prisons. Such rules shall also provide for procedures designed to protect the privacy of a person requesting that the test be performed and the privacy of the person tested.

(Added Pub.L. 105–370, § 2(a), Nov. 12, 1998, 112 Stat. 3374.)

HISTORICAL AND STATUTORY NOTES

References in Text

The date of the enactment of this section, referred to in subsec. (e), is the date of enactment of the Correction Officers Health and Safety Act of 1998, Pub.L. 105–370, Nov. 12, 1998, 112 Stat. 3374, which was approved November 12, 1998.

CHAPTER 303—BUREAU OF PRISONS

§ 4041. Bureau of Prisons; director and employees

The Bureau of Prisons shall be in charge of a director appointed by and serving directly under the Attorney General. The Attorney General may appoint such additional officers and employees as he deems necessary.

(June 25, 1948, c. 645, 62 Stat. 849; Nov. 2, 2002, Pub.L. 107–273, Div. A, Title III, § 302(1), 116 Stat. 1781.)

HISTORICAL AND STATUTORY NOTES

Compensation of Director

Annual rate of basic pay of Director, see section 5315 of Title 5, Government Organization and Employees.

§ 4042. Duties of Bureau of Prisons

(a) In general.—The Bureau of Prisons, under the direction of the Attorney General, shall—

(1) have charge of the management and regulation of all Federal penal and correctional institutions;

(2) provide suitable quarters and provide for the safekeeping, care, and subsistence of all persons charged with or convicted of offenses against the United States, or held as witnesses or otherwise;

(3) provide for the protection, instruction, and discipline of all persons charged with or convicted of offenses against the United States;

(4) provide technical assistance to State and local governments in the improvement of their correctional systems; and

(5) provide notice of release of prisoners in accordance with subsections (b) and (c).

(b) Notice of release of prisoners.—(1) At least 5 days prior to the date on which a prisoner described in paragraph (3) is to be released on supervised release, or, in the case of a prisoner on supervised release, at least 5 days prior to the date on which the prisoner changes residence to a new jurisdiction, written notice of the release or change of residence shall be provided to the chief law enforcement officer of the State and of the local jurisdiction in which the prisoner will reside. Notice prior to release shall be provided by the Director of the Bureau of Prisons. Notice concerning a change of residence following release shall be provided by the probation officer responsible for the supervision of the released prisoner, or in a manner specified by the Director of the Administrative Office of the United States Courts. The notice requirements under this subsection do not apply in relation to a prisoner being protected under chapter 224.

(2) A notice under paragraph (1) shall disclose—

(A) the prisoner's name;

(B) the prisoner's criminal history, including a description of the offense of which the prisoner was convicted; and

(C) any restrictions on conduct or other conditions to the release of the prisoner that are imposed by law, the sentencing court, or the Bureau of Prisons or any other Federal agency.

(3) A prisoner is described in this paragraph if the prisoner was convicted of—

(A) a drug trafficking crime, as that term is defined in section 924(c)(2); or

(B) a crime of violence (as defined in section 924(c)(3)).

(c) Notice of sex offender release.—(1) In the case of a person described in paragraph (3), or any other person in a category specified by the Attorney General, who is released from prison or sentenced to probation, notice shall be provided to—

(A) the chief law enforcement officer of the State and of the local jurisdiction in which the person will reside; and

(B) a State or local agency responsible for the receipt or maintenance of sex offender registration information in the State or local jurisdiction in which the person will reside.

The notice requirements under this subsection do not apply in relation to a person being protected under chapter 224.

(2) Notice provided under paragraph (1) shall include the information described in subsection (b)(2), the place where the person will reside, and the information that the person shall register as required by the Sex Offender Registration and Notification Act. For a person who is released from the custody of the Bureau of Prisons whose expected place of residence following release is known to the Bureau of Prisons, notice shall be provided at least 5 days prior to release by the Director of the Bureau of Prisons. For a person who is sentenced to probation, notice shall be provided promptly by the probation officer responsible for the supervision of the person, or in a manner specified by the Director of the Administrative Office of the United States Courts. Notice concerning a subsequent change of residence by a person described in paragraph (3) during any period of probation, supervised release, or parole shall also be provided to the agencies and officers specified in paragraph (1) by the probation officer responsible for the supervision of the person, or in a manner specified by the Director of the Administrative Office of the United States Courts.

(3) The Director of the Bureau of Prisons shall inform a person who is released from prison and required to register under the Sex Offender Registration and Notification Act of the requirements of that Act as they apply to that person and the same information shall be provided to a person sentenced to probation by the probation officer responsible for supervision of that person.

[(4) Repealed. Pub.L. 109–248, Title I, § 141(h), July 27, 2006, 120 Stat. 604]

(5) The United States and its agencies, officers, and employees shall be immune from liability based on good faith conduct in carrying out this subsection and subsection (b).

(d) Application of section.—This section shall not apply to military or naval penal or correctional institutions or the persons confined therein.

(June 25, 1948, c. 645, 62 Stat. 849; July 1, 1968, Pub.L. 90–371, 82 Stat. 280; Sept. 13, 1994, Pub.L. 103–322, Title II, § 20417, 108 Stat. 1834; Nov. 26, 1997, Pub.L. 105–119, Title I, § 115(a)(8)(A), 111 Stat. 2464; July 27, 2006, Pub.L. 109–248, Title I, § 141(f) to (h), 120 Stat. 603.)

HISTORICAL AND STATUTORY NOTES

References In Text

The Sex Offender Registration and Notification Act, referred to in subsec. (c)(2), (3), is Title I [§ 101 et seq.] of Pub.L. 109–248, July 27, 2006, 120 Stat. 590, which enacted subchapter I of Chapter 151 of Title 42, 42 U.S.C.A. § 16901 et seq.; for complete classification, see Short Title note set out under 42 U.S.C.A. § 16901 and Tables.

Effective and Applicability Provisions

1997 Acts. Amendment by section 115 of Pub.L. 105–119 to take effect 1 year after Nov. 26, 1997, except that States shall have 3 years from Nov. 26, 1997, to implement amendments made by Pub.L. 104–119 which impose new requirements under subchapter VI (section 14071 et seq.) of chapter 136 of Title 42, The Public Health and Welfare, and the Attorney General may grant an additional 2 years to a State that is making good faith efforts to implement these amendments, see section 115(c) of Pub.L. 105–119, set out as a note under section 14071 of Title 42.

Restrictions on Spending for Amenities or Personal Comforts in Federal Prison System

Pub.L. 107–77, Title VI, § 611, Nov. 28, 2001, 115 Stat. 800, provided that: "Hereafter, none of the funds appropriated or otherwise made available to the Bureau of Prisons shall be used to provide the following amenities or personal comforts in the Federal prison system—

"(1) in-cell television viewing except for prisoners who are segregated from the general prison population for their own safety;

"(2) the viewing of R, X, and NC–17 rated movies, through whatever medium presented;

"(3) any instruction (live or through broadcasts) or training equipment for boxing, wrestling, judo, karate, or other martial art, or any bodybuilding or weightlifting equipment of any sort;

"(4) possession of in-cell coffee pots, hot plates or heating elements; or

"(5) the use or possession of any electric or electronic musical instrument."

Similar provisions were contained in the following prior Appropriations Acts:

Pub.L. 106–553, § 1(a)(2) [§ 611], Dec. 21, 2000, 114 Stat. 2762A–105.

Pub.L. 106–113, Div. B, § 1000(a)(1) [Title VI, § 612], Nov. 29, 1999, 113 Stat. 1501A–54.

Pub.L. 105–277, Div. A, § 101(b) [Title VI, § 611], Oct. 21, 1998, 112 Stat. 2681–113.

Pub.L. 105–119, Title VI, § 611, Nov. 26, 1997, 111 Stat. 2517.

Pub.L. 104–208, Div. A, § 101(a) [Title VI, § 611], Sept. 30, 1996, 110 Stat. 3009–66.

Pub.L. 104–134, Title I, § 101(a) [Title VI, § 611], April 26, 1996, 110 Stat. 1321–64.

Proscriptions on Distribution of Sexually Explicit Materials

Pub.L. 107–77, Title VI, § 614, Nov. 28, 2001, 115 Stat. 801, provided that: "Hereafter, none of the funds appropriated or otherwise made available to the Federal Bureau of Prisons may be used to distribute or make available any commercially published information or material to a prisoner when it is made known to the Federal official having authority to obligate or expend such funds that such information or material is sexually explicit or features nudity."

Similar provisions were contained in the following prior Appropriations Acts:

Pub.L. 106–553, § 1(a)(2) [§ 614], Dec. 21, 2000, 114 Stat. 2762A–106.

Pub.L. 106–113, Div. B, § 1000(a)(1) [Title VI, § 615], Nov. 29, 1999, 113 Stat. 1501A–54.

Pub.L. 105–277, Div. A, § 101(b) [Title VI, § 614], Oct. 21, 1998, 112 Stat. 2681–113.

Pub.L. 105–119, Title VI, § 614, Nov. 26, 1997, 111 Stat. 2518.

Pub.L. 104–208, Div. A, § 101(a) [Title VI, § 614], Sept. 30, 1996, 110 Stat. 3009–66.

Federal Prisoner Detention Appropriations Availability Regarding Prisoners Awaiting Trial or Sentencing

Pub.L. 106–553, § 1(a)(2) [Title I], Dec. 21, 2000, 114 Stat. 2762, 2762A–55, provided in part that: "That hereafter amounts appropriated for Federal Prisoner Detention shall be available to reimburse the Federal Bureau of Prisons for salaries and expenses of transporting, guarding and providing medical care outside of Federal penal and correctional institutions to prisoners awaiting trial or sentencing."

Guidelines for States Regarding Infectious Diseases in Correctional institutions

Pub.L. 105–370, § 2(c), Nov. 12, 1998, 112 Stat. 3375, provided that: "Not later than 1 year after the date of enactment of this Act [the Correction Officers Health and Safety Act of 1998, Pub.L. 105–370, Nov. 12, 1998, 112 Stat. 3374, which enacted section 4014 of this title and this note, and which was approved Nov. 12, 1998] the Attorney General, in consultation with the Secretary of Health and Human Services, shall provide to the several States proposed guidelines for the prevention, detection, and treatment of incarcerated persons and correctional employees who have, or may be exposed to, infectious diseases in correctional institutions."

Prisoner Access

Pub.L. 105–314, Title VIII, § 801, Oct. 30, 1998, 112 Stat. 2990, provided that: "Notwithstanding any other provision of law, no agency, officer, or employee of the United States shall implement, or provide any financial assistance to, any Federal program or Federal activity in which a Federal prisoner is allowed access to any electronic communication service or remote computing service without the supervision of an official of the Federal Government."

Application of Subsec. (b) to Prisoners to Whom Prior Law Applies

Section 20404 of Pub.L. 103–322 provided that: "In the case of a prisoner convicted of an offense committed prior to November 1, 1987, the reference to supervised release in section 4042(b) of title 18, United States Code [subsec. (b) of this section], shall be deemed to be a reference to probation or parole."

Cost Savings Measures

Pub.L. 101–647, Title XXIX, § 2907, Nov. 29, 1990, 104 Stat. 4915, provided that: "The Director of the Federal Bureau of Prisons (referred to as the 'Director') shall, to the extent practicable, take such measures as are appropriate to cut costs of construction. Such measures may include reducing expenditures for amenities including, for example, color television or pool tables."

Administration of Confinement Facilities Located on Military Installations by Bureau of Prisons

Pub.L. 100–690, Title VII, § 7302, Nov. 18, 1988, 102 Stat. 4463, provided that: "In conjunction with the Department of Defense and the Commission on Alternative Utilization of Military Facilities as established in the National Defense Authorization Act of Fiscal Year 1989 [Pub.L. 100–456, Sept.

29, 1988, 102 Stat. 1918], the Bureau of Prisons shall be responsible for—

"(1) administering Bureau of Prisons confinement facilities for civilian nonviolent prisoners located on military installations in cooperation with the Secretary of Defense, with an emphasis on placing women inmates in such facilities, or in similar minimum security confinement facilities not located on military installations, so that the percentage of eligible women equals the percentage of eligible men housed in such or similar minimum security confinement facilities (i.e., prison camps);

"(2) establishing and regulating drug treatment programs for inmates held in such facilities in coordination and cooperation with the National Institute on Drug Abuse; and

"(3) establishing and managing work programs in accordance with guidelines under the Bureau of Prisons for persons held in such facilities and in cooperation with the installation commander."

§ 4043. Acceptance of gifts and bequests to the Commissary Funds, Federal Prisons

The Attorney General may accept gifts or bequests of money for credit to the "Commissary Funds, Federal Prisons". A gift or bequest under this section is a gift or bequest to or for the use of the United States under the Internal Revenue Code of 1986 (26 U.S.C. 1 et seq.).

(Added Pub.L. 97–258, § 2(d)(4)(B), Sept. 13, 1982, 96 Stat. 1059, and amended Pub.L. 99–514, § 2, Oct. 22, 1986, 100 Stat. 2095.)

HISTORICAL AND STATUTORY NOTES

References in Text

The Internal Revenue Code of 1954 [now Internal Revenue Code of 1986], referred to in text, is classified generally to Title 26, U.S.C.A. Internal Revenue Code.

Deposit or Investment of Excess Amounts in Federal Prison Commissary Fund

Pub.L. 105–277, Div. A, § 101(b) [Title I, § 108], Oct. 21, 1998, 112 Stat. 2681–67, provided that: "For fiscal year 1999 and thereafter, the Director of the Bureau of Prisons may make expenditures out of the Commissary Fund of the Federal Prison System, regardless of whether any such expenditure is security-related, for programs, goods, and services for the benefit of inmates (to the extent the provision of those programs, goods, or services to inmates is not otherwise prohibited by law), including—

"(1) the installation, operation, and maintenance of the Inmate Telephone System;

"(2) the payment of all the equipment purchased or leased in connection with the Inmate Telephone System; and

"(3) the salaries, benefits, and other expenses of personnel who install, operate, and maintain the Inmate Telephone System."

Similar provisions were contained in the following prior appropriation Acts:

Pub.L. 104–91, Title I, § 101(a), Jan. 6, 1996, 110 Stat. 11; Pub.L. 104–99, Title II, § 211, Jan. 26, 1996, 110.

Pub.L. 103–317, Title I, § 107, Aug. 26, 1994, 108 Stat. 1735.

§ 4044. Donations on behalf of the Bureau of Prisons

The Attorney General may, in accordance with rules prescribed by the Attorney General, accept in the name of the Department of Justice any form of devise, bequest, gift or donation of money or property for use by the Bureau of Prisons or Federal Prison Industries. The Attorney General may take all appropriate steps to secure possession of such property and may sell, assign, transfer, or convey such property other than money.

(Added Pub.L. 99–646, § 67(a), Nov. 10, 1986, 100 Stat. 3616.)

§ 4045. Authority to conduct autopsies

A chief executive officer of a Federal penal or correctional facility may, pursuant to rules prescribed by the Director, order an autopsy and related scientific or medical tests to be performed on the body of a deceased inmate of the facility in the event of homicide, suicide, fatal illness or accident, or unexplained death, when it is determined that such autopsy or test is necessary to detect a crime, maintain discipline, protect the health or safety of other inmates, remedy official misconduct, or defend the United States or its employees from civil liability arising from the administration of the facility. To the extent consistent with the needs of the autopsy or of specific scientific or medical tests, provisions of State and local law protecting religious beliefs with respect to such autopsies shall be observed. Such officer may also order an autopsy or post-mortem operation, including removal of tissue for transplanting, to be performed on the body of a deceased inmate of the facility, with the written consent of a person authorized to permit such an autopsy or post-mortem operation under the law of the State in which the facility is located.

(Added Pub.L. 99–646, § 67(a), Nov. 10, 1986, 100 Stat. 3616.)

§ 4046. Shock incarceration program

(a) The Bureau of Prisons may place in a shock incarceration program any person who is sentenced to a term of imprisonment of more than 12, but not more than 30, months, if such person consents to that placement.

(b) For such initial portion of the term of imprisonment as the Bureau of Prisons may determine, not to exceed 6 months, an inmate in the shock incarceration program shall be required to—

(1) adhere to a highly regimented schedule that provides the strict discipline, physical training, hard labor, drill, and ceremony characteristic of military basic training; and

(2) participate in appropriate job training and educational programs (including literacy programs) and drug, alcohol, and other counseling programs.

(c) An inmate who in the judgment of the Director of the Bureau of Prisons has successfully completed the required period of shock incarceration shall remain in the custody of the Bureau for such period (not to exceed the remainder of the prison term otherwise required by law to be served by that inmate), and under such conditions, as the Bureau deems appropriate.

(Added Pub.L. 101–647, Title XXX, § 3001(a), Nov. 29, 1990, 104 Stat. 4915.)

HISTORICAL AND STATUTORY NOTES

Authorization of Appropriations

Section 3002 of Pub.L. 101–647 provided that: "There are authorized to be appropriated for fiscal year 1990 and each fiscal year thereafter such sums as may be necessary to carry out the shock incarceration program established under the amendments made by this Act [enacting this section]."

§ 4047. Prison impact assessments

(a) Any submission of legislation by the Judicial or Executive branch which could increase or decrease the number of persons incarcerated in Federal penal institutions shall be accompanied by a prison impact statement (as defined in subsection (b)).

(b) The Attorney General shall, in consultation with the Sentencing Commission and the Administrative Office of the United States Courts, prepare and furnish prison impact assessments under subsection (c) of this section, and in response to requests from Congress for information relating to a pending measure or matter that might affect the number of defendants processed through the Federal criminal justice system. A prison impact assessment on pending legislation must be supplied within 21 days of any request. A prison impact assessment shall include—

(1) projections of the impact on prison, probation, and post prison supervision populations;

(2) an estimate of the fiscal impact of such population changes on Federal expenditures, including those for construction and operation of correctional facilities for the current fiscal year and 5 succeeding fiscal years;

(3) an analysis of any other significant factor affecting the cost of the measure and its impact on the operations of components of the criminal justice system; and

(4) a statement of the methodologies and assumptions utilized in preparing the assessment.

(c) The Attorney General shall prepare and transmit to the Congress, by March 1 of each year, a prison impact assessment reflecting the cumulative effect of all relevant changes in the law taking effect during the preceding calendar year.

(Added Pub.L. 103–322, Title II, § 20402(a), Sept. 13, 1994, 108 Stat. 1824.)

§ 4048. Fees for health care services for prisoners

(a) Definitions.—In this section—

(1) the term "account" means the trust fund account (or institutional equivalent) of a prisoner;

(2) the term "Director" means the Director of the Bureau of Prisons;

(3) the term "health care provider" means any person who is—

(A) authorized by the Director to provide health care services; and

(B) operating within the scope of such authorization;

(4) the term "health care visit"—

(A) means a visit, as determined by the Director, by a prisoner to an institutional or noninstitutional health care provider; and

(B) does not include a visit initiated by a prisoner—

(i) pursuant to a staff referral; or

(ii) to obtain staff-approved follow-up treatment for a chronic condition; and

(5) the term "prisoner" means—

(A) any individual who is incarcerated in an institution under the jurisdiction of the Bureau of Prisons; or

(B) any other individual, as designated by the Director, who has been charged with or convicted of an offense against the United States.

(b) Fees for health care services.—

(1) **In general.**—The Director, in accordance with this section and with such regulations as the Director shall promulgate to carry out this section, may assess and collect a fee for health care services provided in connection with each health care visit requested by a prisoner.

(2) **Exclusion.**—The Director may not assess or collect a fee under this section for preventative health care services, emergency services, prenatal care, diagnosis or treatment of chronic infectious diseases, mental health care, or substance abuse treatment, as determined by the Director.

(c) Persons subject to fee.—Each fee assessed under this section shall be collected by the Director from the account of—

(1) the prisoner receiving health care services in connection with a health care visit described in subsection (b)(1); or

(2) in the case of health care services provided in connection with a health care visit described in subsection (b)(1) that results from an injury inflicted on a prisoner by another prisoner, the prisoner who inflicted the injury, as determined by the Director.

(d) Amount of fee.—Any fee assessed and collected under this section shall be in an amount of not less than $1.

(e) No consent required.—Notwithstanding any other provision of law, the consent of a prisoner shall not be required for the collection of a fee from the account of the prisoner under this section. However, each such prisoner shall be given a reasonable opportunity to dispute the amount of the fee or whether the prisoner qualifies under an exclusion under this section.

(f) No refusal of treatment for financial reasons.—Nothing in this section may be construed to permit any refusal of treatment to a prisoner on the basis that—

(1) the account of the prisoner is insolvent; or

(2) the prisoner is otherwise unable to pay a fee assessed under this section.

(g) Use of amounts.—

(1) **Restitution of specific victims.**—Amounts collected by the Director under this section from a prisoner subject to an order of restitution issued pursuant to section 3663 or 3663A shall be paid to victims in accordance with the order of restitution.

(2) **Allocation of other amounts.**—Of amounts collected by the Director under this section from prisoners not subject to an order of restitution issued pursuant to section 3663 or 3663A—

(A) 75 percent shall be deposited in the Crime Victims Fund established under section 1402 of the Victims of Crime Act of 1984 (42 U.S.C. 10601); and

(B) 25 percent shall be available to the Attorney General for administrative expenses incurred in carrying out this section.

(h) Notice to prisoners of law.—Each person who is or becomes a prisoner shall be provided with written and oral notices of the provisions of this section and the applicability of this section to the prisoner. Notwithstanding any other provision of this section, a fee under this section may not be assessed against, or collected from, such person—

(1) until the expiration of the 30–day period beginning on the date on which each prisoner in the prison system is provided with such notices; and

(2) for services provided before the expiration of such period.

(i) Notice to prisoners of regulations.—The regulations promulgated by the Director under subsection (b)(1), and any amendments to those regulations, shall not take effect until the expiration of the 30–day period beginning on the date on which each prisoner in the prison system is provided with written and oral notices of the provisions of those regulations (or amendments, as the case may be). A fee under this section may not be assessed against, or collected from, a prisoner pursuant to such regulations (or amendments, as the case may be) for services provided before the expiration of such period.

(j) Notice before public comment period.—Before the beginning of any period a proposed regulation under this section is open to public comment, the Director shall provide written and oral notice of the provisions of that proposed regulation to groups that advocate on behalf of Federal prisoners and to each prisoner subject to such proposed regulation.

(k) Reports to Congress.—Not later than 1 year after the date of the enactment of the Federal Prisoner Health Care Copayment Act of 2000, and annually thereafter, the Director shall transmit to Congress a report, which shall include—

(1) a description of the amounts collected under this section during the preceding 12–month period;

(2) an analysis of the effects of the implementation of this section, if any, on the nature and extent of health care visits by prisoners;

(3) an itemization of the cost of implementing and administering the program;

(4) a description of current inmate health status indicators as compared to the year prior to enactment; and

(5) a description of the quality of health care services provided to inmates during the preceding 12–month period, as compared with the quality of those services provided during the 12–month period ending on the date of the enactment of such Act.

(*l*) Comprehensive HIV/AIDS services required.—The Bureau of Prisons shall provide comprehensive coverage for services relating to human immunodeficiency virus (HIV) and acquired immune deficiency syndrome (AIDS) to each Federal prisoner in the custody of the Bureau of Prisons when medically appropriate. The Bureau of Prisons may not assess or collect a fee under this section for providing such coverage.

(Added Pub.L. 106–294, § 2(a), Oct. 12, 2000, 114 Stat. 1038.)

HISTORICAL AND STATUTORY NOTES

References in Text

The date of the enactment of the Federal Prisoner Health Care Copayment Act of 2000, referred to in subsec. (k), is the date of enactment of Pub.L. 106–294, which was approved Oct. 12, 2000. For complete classification of this Act to the Code, see Short Title note set out under section 4001 of this title and Tables.

CHAPTER 305—COMMITMENT AND TRANSFER

HISTORICAL AND STATUTORY NOTES

Effective and Applicability Provisions

For applicability of sentencing provisions to offenses, see Effective Date and Savings Provisions, etc., note, section 235 of Pub.L. 98–473, as amended, set out under section 3551 of this title.

Savings Provisions

See section 235 of Pub.L. 98–473, Title II, c. II, Oct. 12, 1984, 98 Stat. 2031, as amended, set out as a note under section 3551 of this title.

§ 4081. Classification and treatment of prisoners

The Federal penal and correctional institutions shall be so planned and limited in size as to facilitate the development of an integrated system which will assure the proper classification and segregation of Federal prisoners according to the nature of the offenses committed, the character and mental condition of the prisoners, and such other factors as should be considered in providing an individualized system of discipline, care, and treatment of the persons committed to such institutions.

(June 25, 1948, c. 645, 62 Stat. 850.)

§ 4082. Commitment to Attorney General; residential treatment centers; extension of limits of confinement; work furlough

(a) The willful failure of a prisoner to remain within the extended limits of his confinement, or to return within the time prescribed to an institution or facility designated by the Attorney General, shall be deemed an escape from the custody of the Attorney General punishable as provided in chapter 35 of this title.

(b)(1) The Attorney General shall, upon the request of the head of any law enforcement agency of a State or of a unit of local government in a State, make available as expeditiously as possible to such agency, with respect to prisoners who have been convicted of felony offenses against the United States and who are confined at a facility which is a residential community treatment center located in the geographical area in which such agency has jurisdiction, the following information maintained by the Bureau of Prisons (to the extent that the Bureau of Prisons maintains such information)—

(A) the names of such prisoners;

(B) the community treatment center addresses of such prisoners;

(C) the dates of birth of such prisoners;

(D) the Federal Bureau of Investigation numbers assigned to such prisoners;

(E) photographs and fingerprints of such prisoners; and

(F) the nature of the offenses against the United States of which each such prisoner has been convicted and the factual circumstances relating to such offenses.

(2) Any law enforcement agency which receives information under this subsection shall not disseminate such information outside of such agency.

(c) As used in this section—

the term "facility" shall include a residential community treatment center; and

the term "relative" shall mean a spouse, child (including stepchild, adopted child or child as to whom the prisoner, though not a natural parent, has acted in the place of a parent), parent (including a person who, though not a natural parent, has acted in the place of a parent), brother, or sister.

(June 25, 1948, c. 645, 62 Stat. 850; Sept. 10, 1965, Pub.L. 89–176, § 1, 79 Stat. 674; Dec. 28, 1973, Pub.L. 93–209, 87 Stat. 907; Oct. 12, 1984, Pub.L. 98–473, Title II, § 218(a)(3), 98 Stat. 2027; Nov. 10, 1986, Pub.L. 99–646, § 57(a), 100 Stat. 3611.)

HISTORICAL AND STATUTORY NOTES

Effective and Applicability Provisions

1984 Acts. Amendment by Pub.L. 98–473 effective on the first day of first calendar month beginning thirty-six months after Oct. 12, 1984, applicable only to offenses committed after taking effect of sections 211 to 239 of Pub.L. 98–473, and except as otherwise provided for therein, see section 235 of Pub.L. 98–473, as amended, set out as a note under section 3551 of this title.

National Training School for Boys

The National Training School for Boys was governed and managed by a Board of Trustees until July 1, 1939, at which time 1939 Reorg.Plan No. 2 (4 F.R. 2731, 53 Stat. 1431) abolished the Board of Trustees and transferred the School and its functions (including the functions of the Board of Trustees) to the Department of Justice, to be administered by the Director of the Bureau of Prisons, under the direction and supervision of the Attorney General. The School was so operated until May 15, 1968, when it was closed pursuant to order of the Attorney General.

EXECUTIVE ORDERS

EXECUTIVE ORDER NO. 11755

Dec. 29, 1973, 39 F.R. 779, as amended by Ex.Ord.No. 12608, Sept. 9, 1987, 52 F.R. 34617; Ex. Ord. No. 12943, Dec. 13, 1994, 59 F.R. 64553

PRISON LABOR

[Executive Order No. 11755, as amended, has been moved and is set out under section 3622 of this title.]

§ 4083. Penitentiary imprisonment; consent

Persons convicted of offenses against the United States or by courts-martial punishable by imprisonment for more than one year may be confined in any United States penitentiary.

A sentence for an offense punishable by imprisonment for one year or less shall not be served in a penitentiary without the consent of the defendant.

(June 25, 1948, c. 645, 62 Stat. 850; Sept. 14, 1959, Pub.L. 86–256, 73 Stat. 518.)

[§§ 4084, 4085. Repealed. Pub.L. 98–473, Title II, § 218(a)(3), Oct. 12, 1984, 98 Stat. 2027]

HISTORICAL AND STATUTORY NOTES

Prior to repeal, these sections, June 25, 1948, c. 645, 62 Stat. 850, read:

"§ 4084. Copy of commitment delivered with prisoner

"Whenever a prisoner is committed to a warden, sheriff or jailer by virtue of a writ, or warrant, a copy thereof shall be delivered to such officer as his authority to hold the prisoner, and the original shall be returned to the proper court or officer, with the officer's return endorsed thereon."

"§ 4085. Transfer for state offense; expense

"**(a)** Whenever any federal prisoner has been indicted, informed against, or convicted of a felony in a court of record of any State or the District of Columbia, the Attorney General shall, if he finds it in the public interest to do so, upon the request of the Governor or the executive authority thereof, and upon the presentation of a certified copy of such indictment, information or judgment of conviction, cause such person, prior to his release, to be transferred to a penal or correctional institution within such State or District.

"If more than one such request is presented in respect to any prisoner, the Attorney General shall determine which request should receive preference.

"The expense of personnel and transportation incurred shall be chargeable to the appropriation for the "Support of United States prisoners."

"**(b)** This section shall not limit the authority of the Attorney General to transfer prisoners pursuant to other provisions of law."

Effective Date of Repeal; Savings Provisions

Repeal by Pub.L. 98–473 effective on the first day of first calendar month beginning thirty six months after Oct. 12, 1984, applicable only to offenses committed after taking effect of sections 211 to 239 of Pub.L. 98–473, and except as otherwise provided for therein, see section 235 of Pub.L. 98–473, as amended, set out as a note under section 3551 of this title.

§ 4086. Temporary safe-keeping of federal offenders by marshals

United States marshals shall provide for the safekeeping of any person arrested, or held under authority of any enactment of Congress pending commitment to an institution.

(June 25, 1948, c. 645, 62 Stat. 851.)

CHAPTER 306—TRANSFER TO OR FROM FOREIGN COUNTRIES

HISTORICAL AND STATUTORY NOTES

Savings Provisions

See section 235 of Pub.L. 98–473, Title II, c. II, Oct. 12, 1984, 98 Stat. 2031, as amended, set out as a note under section 3551 of this title.

§ 4100. Scope and limitation of chapter

(a) The provisions of this chapter relating to the transfer of offenders shall be applicable only when a treaty providing for such a transfer is in force, and shall only be applicable to transfers of offenders to and from a foreign country pursuant to such a treaty. A sentence imposed by a foreign country upon an offender who is subsequently transferred to the United States pursuant to a treaty shall be subject to being fully executed in the United States even though the treaty under which the offender was transferred is no longer in force.

(b) An offender may be transferred from the United States pursuant to this chapter only to a country of which the offender is a citizen or national. Only an offender who is a citizen or national of the United States may be transferred to the United States. An offender may be transferred to or from the United States only with the offender's consent, and only if the offense for which the offender was sentenced satisfies the requirement of double criminality as defined in this chapter. Once an offender's consent to transfer has been verified by a verifying officer, that consent shall be irrevocable. If at the time of transfer the offender is under eighteen years of age, or is deemed by the verifying officer to be mentally incompetent or otherwise incapable of knowingly and voluntarily consenting to the transfer, the transfer shall not be accomplished unless consent to the transfer be given by a parent or guardian, guardian ad litem, or by an appropriate court of the sentencing country. The appointment of a guardian ad litem shall be independent of the appointment of counsel under section 4109 of this title.

(c) An offender shall not be transferred to or from the United States if a proceeding by way of appeal or of collateral attack upon the conviction or sentence be pending.

(d) The United States upon receiving notice from the country which imposed the sentence that the offender has been granted a pardon, commutation, or amnesty, or that there has been an ameliorating modification or a revocation of the sentence shall give the offender the benefit of the action taken by the sentencing country.

(Added Pub.L. 95–144, § 1, Oct. 28, 1977, 91 Stat. 1212, and amended Pub.L. 100–690, Title VII, § 7101(e), Nov. 18, 1988, 102 Stat. 4416.)

HISTORICAL AND STATUTORY NOTES

Prisoner Transfer Treaties

Pub.L. 104–208, Div. C, Title III, § 330, Sept. 30, 1996, 110 Stat. 3009–631, provided that:

"(a) Negotiations with other countries.—(1) Congress advises the President to begin to negotiate and renegotiate, not later than 90 days after the date of enactment of this Act [Sept. 30, 1996], bilateral prisoner transfer treaties, providing for the incarceration, in the country of the alien's nationality, of any alien who—

"(A) is a national of a country that is party to such a treaty; and

"(B) has been convicted of a criminal offense under Federal or State law and who—

"(i) is not in lawful immigration status in the United States, or

"(ii) on the basis of conviction for a criminal offense under Federal or State law, or on any other basis, is subject to deportation or removal under the Immigration and Nationality Act [8 U.S.C.A. § 1101 et seq.],

for the duration of the prison term to which the alien was sentenced for the offense referred to in subparagraph (B). Any such agreement may provide for the release of such alien pursuant to parole procedures of that country.

"(2) In entering into negotiations under paragraph (1), the President may consider providing for appropriate compensation, subject to the availability of appropriations, in cases where the United States is able to independently verify the adequacy of the sites where aliens will be imprisoned and the length of time the alien is actually incarcerated in the foreign country under such a treaty.

"(b) Sense of Congress.—It is the sense of the Congress that—

"(1) the focus of negotiations for such agreements should be—

"(A) to expedite the transfer of aliens unlawfully in the United States who are (or are about to be) incarcerated in United States prisons,

"(B) to ensure that a transferred prisoner serves the balance of the sentence imposed by the United States courts,

"(C) to eliminate any requirement of prisoner consent to such a transfer, and

"(D) to allow the Federal Government or the States to keep their original prison sentences in force so that transferred prisoners who return to the United States prior to the completion of their original United States sentences can be returned to custody for the balance of their prison sentences;

"(2) the Secretary of State should give priority to concluding an agreement with any country for which the President determines that the number of aliens described in subsection (a) who are nationals of that country in the United States represents a significant percentage of all such aliens in the United States; and

"(3) no new treaty providing for the transfer of aliens from Federal, State, or local incarceration facilities to a foreign incarceration facility should permit the alien to refuse the transfer.

"(c) Prisoner consent.—Notwithstanding any other provision of law, except as required by treaty, the transfer of an alien from a Federal, State, or local incarceration facility under an agreement of the type referred to in subsection (a) shall not require consent of the alien.

"(d) Annual report.—Not later than 90 days after the date of the enactment of this Act [Sept. 30, 1996], and annually thereafter, the Attorney General shall submit a report to the Committees on the Judiciary of the House of Representatives and of the Senate stating whether each prisoner transfer treaty to which the United States is a party has been effective in the preceding 12 months in bringing about the return of deportable incarcerated aliens to the country of which they are nationals and in ensuring that they serve the balance of their sentences.

"(e) Training foreign law enforcement personnel.—(1) Subject to paragraph (2), the President shall direct the Border Patrol Academy and the Customs Service Academy to enroll for training an appropriate number of foreign law enforcement personnel, and shall make appointments of foreign law enforcement personnel to such academies, as necessary to further the following United States law enforcement goals:

"**(A)** Preventing of drug smuggling and other cross-border criminal activity.

"**(B)** Preventing illegal immigration.

"**(C)** Preventing the illegal entry of goods into the United States (including goods the sale of which is illegal in the United States, the entry of which would cause a quota to be exceeded, or the appropriate duty or tariff for which has not been paid).

"**(2)** The appointments described in paragraph (1) shall be made only to the extent there is capacity in such academies beyond what is required to train United States citizens needed in the Border Patrol and Customs Service, and only of personnel from a country with which the prisoner transfer treaty has been stated to be effective in the most recent report referred to in subsection (d).

"**(f) Authorization of appropriations.**—There are authorized to be appropriated such sums as may be necessary to carry out this section."

[For transfer of the functions, personnel, assets, and liabilities of the United States Customs Service of the Department of the Treasury, including the functions of the Secretary of the Treasury relating thereto, to the Secretary of Homeland Security, and for treatment of related references, see 6 U.S.C.A. §§ 203(1), 551(d), 552(d) and 557, and the Department of Homeland Security Reorganization Plan of November 25, 2002, as modified, set out as a note under 6 U.S.C.A. § 542.]

Authorization of Appropriations

Section 5(a) of Pub.L. 95–144 provided that: "There is authorized to be appropriated such funds as may be required to carry out the purposes of this Act [which enacted this chapter, section 955 of Title 10, Armed Forces, and section 2256 of Title 28, Judiciary and Judicial Procedure, amended section 636 of Title 28, and enacted provisions set out as notes under sections 3006A, 4100, and 4102 of this title]".

§ 4101. Definitions

As used in this chapter the term—

(a) "double criminality" means that at the time of transfer of an offender the offense for which he has been sentenced is still an offense in the transferring country and is also an offense in the receiving country. With regard to a country which has a federal form of government, an act shall be deemed to be an offense in that country if it is an offense under the federal laws or the laws of any state or province thereof;

(b) "imprisonment" means a penalty imposed by a court under which the individual is confined to an institution;

(c) "juvenile" means—

(1) a person who is under eighteen years of age; or

(2) for the purpose of proceedings and disposition under chapter 403 of this title because of an act of juvenile delinquency, a person who is under twenty-one years of age;

(d) "juvenile delinquency" means—

(1) a violation of the laws of the United States or a State thereof or of a foreign country committed by a juvenile which would have been a crime if committed by an adult; or

(2) noncriminal acts committed by a juvenile for which supervision or treatment by juvenile authorities of the United States, a State thereof, or of the foreign country concerned is authorized;

(e) "offender" means a person who has been convicted of an offense or who has been adjudged to have committed an act of juvenile delinquency;

(f) "parole" means any form of release of an offender from imprisonment to the community by a releasing authority prior to the expiration of his sentence, subject to conditions imposed by the releasing authority and to its supervision, including a term of supervised release pursuant to section 3583;

(g) "probation" means any form of a sentence under which the offender is permitted to remain at liberty under supervision and subject to conditions for the breach of which a penalty of imprisonment may be ordered executed;

(h) "sentence" means not only the penalty imposed but also the judgment of conviction in a criminal case or a judgment of acquittal in the same proceeding, or the adjudication of delinquency in a juvenile delinquency proceeding or dismissal of allegations of delinquency in the same proceedings;

(i) "State" means any State of the United States, the District of Columbia, the Commonwealth of Puerto Rico, and any territory or possession of the United States;

(j) "transfer" means a transfer of an individual for the purpose of the execution in one country of a sentence imposed by the courts of another country; and

(k) "treaty" means a treaty under which an offender sentenced in the courts of one country may be transferred to the country of which he is a citizen or national for the purpose of serving the sentence.

(Added Pub.L. 95–144, § 1, Oct. 28, 1977, 91 Stat. 1213, and amended Pub.L. 98–473, Title II, § 223(m)(1), Oct. 12, 1984, 98 Stat. 2029.)

HISTORICAL AND STATUTORY NOTES

Effective and Applicability Provisions

1984 Acts. Amendment by Pub.L. 98–473 effective on the first day of first calendar month beginning thirty six months after Oct. 12, 1984, applicable only to offenses committed after taking effect of sections 211 to 239 of Pub.L. 98–473, and except as otherwise provided for therein, see section 235 of Pub.L. 98–473, as amended, set out as a note under section 3551 of this title.

§ 4102. Authority of the Attorney General

The Attorney General is authorized—

(1) to act on behalf of the United States as the authority referred to in a treaty;

(2) to receive custody of offenders under a sentence of imprisonment, on parole, or on probation who are citizens or nationals of the United States transferred from foreign countries and as appropriate confine them in penal or correctional institutions, or assign them to the parole or probation authorities for supervision;

(3) to transfer offenders under a sentence of imprisonment, on parole, or on probation to the foreign countries of which they are citizens or nationals;

(4) to make regulations for the proper implementation of such treaties in accordance with this chapter and to make regulations to implement this chapter;

(5) to render to foreign countries and to receive from them the certifications and reports required to be made under such treaties;

(6) to make arrangements by agreement with the States for the transfer of offenders in their custody who are citizens or nationals of foreign countries to the foreign countries of which they are citizens or nationals and for the confinement, where appropriate, in State institutions of offenders transferred to the United States;

(7) to make agreements and establish regulations for the transportation through the territory of the United States of offenders convicted in a foreign country who are being transported to a third country for the execution of their sentences, the expenses of which shall be paid by the country requesting the transportation;

(8) to make agreements with the appropriate authorities of a foreign country and to issue regulations for the transfer and treatment of juveniles who are transferred pursuant to treaty, the expenses of which shall be paid by the country of which the juvenile is a citizen or national;

(9) in concert with the Secretary of Health, Education, and Welfare, to make arrangements with the appropriate authorities of a foreign country and to issue regulations for the transfer and treatment of individuals who are accused of an offense but who have been determined to be mentally ill; the expenses of which shall be paid by the country of which such person is a citizen or national;

(10) to designate agents to receive, on behalf of the United States, the delivery by a foreign government of any citizen or national of the United States being transferred to the United States for the purpose of serving a sentence imposed by the courts of the foreign country, and to convey him to the place designated by the Attorney General. Such agent shall have all the powers of a marshal of the United States in the several districts through which it may be necessary for him to pass with the offender, so far as such power is requisite for the offender's transfer and safekeeping; within the territory of a foreign country such agent shall have such powers as the authorities of the foreign country may accord him;

(11) to delegate the authority conferred by this chapter to officers of the Department of Justice.

(Added Pub.L. 95–144, § 1, Oct. 28, 1977, 91 Stat. 1214.)

HISTORICAL AND STATUTORY NOTES

Change of Name

The Secretary and Department of Health, Education, and Welfare was redesignated the Secretary and Department of Health and Human Services by Pub.L. 96–88, Title V, § 509(b), Oct. 17, 1979, 93 Stat. 695, which is classified to section 3508(b) of Title 20, Education.

Certification by Attorney General to Secretary of State for Reimbursement of Expenses Incurred Under Transfer Treaty

Section 5(b) of Pub.L. 95–144 provided that: "The Attorney General shall certify to the Secretary of State the expenses of the United States related to the return of an offender to the foreign country of which the offender is a citizen or national for which the United States is entitled to seek reimbursement from that country under a treaty providing for transfer and reimbursement."

§ 4103. Applicability of United States laws

All laws of the United States, as appropriate, pertaining to prisoners, probationers, parolees, and juvenile offenders shall be applicable to offenders transferred to the United States, unless a treaty or this chapter provides otherwise.

(Added Pub.L. 95–144, § 1, Oct. 28, 1977, 91 Stat. 1215.)

§ 4104. Transfer of offenders on probation

(a) Prior to consenting to the transfer to the United States of an offender who is on probation, the Attorney General shall determine that the appropriate United States district court is willing to undertake the supervision of the offender.

(b) Upon the receipt of an offender on probation from the authorities of a foreign country, the Attorney General shall cause the offender to be brought before the United States district court which is to exercise supervision over the offender.

(c) The court shall place the offender under supervision of the probation officer of the court. The offender shall be supervised by a probation officer, under such conditions as are deemed appropriate by the court as though probation had been imposed by the United States district court.

(d) The probation may be revoked in accordance with section 3565 of this title and the applicable provisions of the Federal Rules of Criminal Procedure. A violation of the conditions of probation shall constitute grounds for revocation. If probation is revoked the suspended sentence imposed by the sentencing court shall be executed.

(e) The provisions of sections 4105 and 4106 of this title shall be applicable following a revocation of probation.

(f) Prior to consenting to the transfer from the United States of an offender who is on probation, the Attorney General shall obtain the assent of the court exercising jurisdiction over the probationer.

(Added Pub.L. 95–144, § 1, Oct. 28, 1977, 91 Stat. 1215, and amended Pub.L. 107–273, Div. C, Title IV, § 4002(e)(6), Nov. 2, 2002, 116 Stat. 1810.)

§ 4105. Transfer of offenders serving sentence of imprisonment

(a) Except as provided elsewhere in this section, an offender serving a sentence of imprisonment in a foreign country transferred to the custody of the Attorney General shall remain in the custody of the Attorney General under the same conditions and for the same period of time as an offender who had been committed to the custody of the Attorney General by a court of the United States for the period of time imposed by the sentencing court.

(b) The transferred offender shall be given credit toward service of the sentence for any days, prior to the date of commencement of the sentence, spent in custody in connection with the offense or acts for which the sentence was imposed.

(c)(1) The transferred offender shall be entitled to all credits for good time, for labor, or any other credit toward the service of the sentence which had been given by the transferring country for time served as of the time of the transfer. Subsequent to the transfer, the offender shall in addition be entitled to credits toward service of sentence for satisfactory behavior, computed on the basis of the time remaining to be served at the time of the transfer and at the rate provided in section 3624(b) of this title for a sentence of the length of the total sentence imposed and certified by the foreign authorities. These credits shall be combined to provide a release date for the offender pursuant to section 3624(a) of this title.

(2) If the country from which the offender is transferred does not give credit for good time, the basis of computing the deduction from the sentence shall be the sentence imposed by the sentencing court and certified to be served upon transfer, at the rate provided in section 3624(b) of this title.

(3) Credit toward service of sentence may be withheld as provided in section 3624(b) of this title.

(4) Any sentence for an offense against the United States, imposed while the transferred offender is serving the sentence of imprisonment imposed in a foreign country, shall be aggregated with the foreign sentence, in the same manner as if the foreign sentence was one imposed by a United States district court for an offense against the United States.

(Added Pub.L. 95–144, § 1, Oct. 28, 1977, 91 Stat. 1215, and amended Pub.L. 98–473, Title II, § 223(m)(2), Oct. 12, 1984, 98 Stat. 2029.)

HISTORICAL AND STATUTORY NOTES

Effective and Applicability Provisions

1984 Acts. Amendment by Pub.L. 98–473 effective on the first day of first calendar month beginning thirty six months after Oct. 12, 1984, applicable only to offenses committed after taking effect of sections 211 to 239 of Pub.L. 98–473, and except as otherwise provided for therein, see section 235 of Pub.L. 98–473, as amended, set out as a note under section 3551 of this title.

§ 4106. Transfer of offenders on parole; parole of offenders transferred

(a) Upon the receipt of an offender who is on parole from the authorities of a foreign country, the Attorney General shall assign the offender to the United States Parole Commission for supervision.

(b) The United States Parole Commission and the Chairman of the Commission shall have the same powers and duties with reference to an offender transferred to the United States to serve a sentence of imprisonment or who at the time of transfer is on parole as they have with reference to an offender convicted in a court of the United States except as otherwise provided in this chapter or in the pertinent treaty. Sections 4201 through 4204; 4205(d), (e), and (h); 4206 through 4215; and 4218 of this title shall be applicable.

(c) An offender transferred to the United States to serve a sentence of imprisonment may be released on parole at such time as the Parole Commission may determine.

(d) This section shall apply only to offenses committed before November 1, 1987, and the Parole Commission's performance of its responsibilities under this section shall be subject to section 235 of the Comprehensive Crime Control Act of 1984.

(Added Pub.L. 95–144, § 1, Oct. 28, 1977, 91 Stat. 1216, and amended Pub.L. 98–473, Title II, § 223(m)(3), Oct. 12, 1984, 98 Stat. 2029; Pub.L. 100–182, § 14, Dec. 7, 1987, 101 Stat. 1268; Pub.L. 100–690, Title VII, § 7072(c), Nov. 18, 1988, 102 Stat. 4405.)

HISTORICAL AND STATUTORY NOTES

References in Text

Sections 4201 through 4204; 4205(d), (e), and (h); 4206 through 4215; and 4218 of this title, referred to in subsec. (b), were repealed effective Nov. 1, 1987, by Pub.L. 98–473, Title II, §§ 218(a)(5), 235(a)(1), (b)(1), Oct. 12, 1984, 98 Stat. 2027, 2031, 2032, subject to remaining effective for five years after Nov. 1, 1987, in certain circumstances.

Section 235 of the Comprehensive Crime Control Act of 1984, referred to in subsec. (d), is set out as an Effective and Applicability Provisions note under 18 U.S.C.A. § 3551.

Effective and Applicability Provisions

1984 Acts. Amendment by Pub.L. 98–473 effective on the first day of first calendar month beginning thirty six months after Oct. 12, 1984, applicable only to offenses committed after taking effect of sections 211 to 239 of Pub.L. 98–473, and except as otherwise provided for therein, see section 235 of Pub.L. 98–473, as amended, set out as a note under section 3551 of this title.

§ 4106A. Transfer of offenders on parole; parole of offenders transferred

(a) Upon the receipt of an offender who is on parole from the authorities of a foreign country, the Attorney General shall assign the offender to the United States Parole Commission for supervision.

(b)(1)(A) The United States Parole Commission shall, without unnecessary delay, determine a release date and a period and conditions of supervised release for an offender transferred to the United States to serve a sentence of imprisonment, as though the offender were convicted in a United States district court of a similar offense.

(B) In making such determination, the United States Parole Commission shall consider—

(i) any recommendation of the United States Probation Service, including any recommendation as to the applicable guideline range; and

(ii) any documents provided by the transferring country; relating to that offender.

(C) The combined periods of imprisonment and supervised release that result from such determination shall not exceed the term of imprisonment imposed by the foreign court on that offender.

(D) The duties conferred on a United states probation officer with respect to a defendant by section 3552 of this title shall, with respect to an offender so transferred, be carried out by the United States Probation Service.

(2)(A) A determination by the United States Parole Commission under this subsection may be appealed to the United States court of appeals for the circuit in which the offender is imprisoned at the time of the determination of such Commission. Notice of appeal must be filed not later than 45 days after receipt of notice of such determination.

(B) The court of appeals shall decide and dispose of the appeal in accordance with section 3742 of this title as though the determination appealed had been a sentence imposed by a United States district court.

(3) During the supervised release of an offender under this subsection, the United States district court for the district in which the offender resides shall supervise the offender.

(c) This section shall apply only to offenses committed on or after November 1, 1987.

(Added Pub.L. 100–690, Title VII, § 7101(a), Nov. 18, 1988, 102 Stat. 4415, and amended Pub.L. 101–647, Title XXXV, §§ 3599B, 3599C, Nov. 29, 1990, 104 Stat. 4931, 4932.)

HISTORICAL AND STATUTORY NOTES

Codification

Amendment by section 3599C of Pub.L. 101–647 directed the insertion of a period at the end of subsec. (b)(1)(C). Such period had already been editorially supplied, therefore, no further change was required.

§ 4107. Verification of consent of offender to transfer from the United States

(a) Prior to the transfer of an offender from the United States, the fact that the offender consents to such transfer and that such consent is voluntary and with full knowledge of the consequences thereof shall be verified by a United States magistrate judge or a judge as defined in section 451 of title 28, United States Code.

(b) The verifying officer shall inquire of the offender whether he understands and agrees that the transfer will be subject to the following conditions:

(1) only the appropriate courts in the United States may modify or set aside the conviction or sentence, and any proceedings seeking such action may only be brought in such courts;

(2) the sentence shall be carried out according to the laws of the country to which he is to be transferred and that those laws are subject to change;

(3) if a court in the country to which he is transferred should determine upon a proceeding initiated by him or on his behalf that his transfer was not accomplished in accordance with the treaty or laws of that country, he may be returned to the United States for the purpose of completing the sentence if the United States requests his return; and

(4) his consent to transfer, once verified by the verifying officer, is irrevocable.

(c) The verifying officer, before determining that an offender's consent is voluntary and given with full knowledge of the consequences, shall advise the offender of his right to consult with counsel as provided by this chapter. If the offender wishes to consult with counsel before giving his consent, he shall be advised that the proceedings will be continued until he has had an opportunity to consult with counsel.

(d) The verifying officer shall make the necessary inquiries to determine that the offender's consent is voluntary and not the result of any promises, threats, or other improper inducements, and that the offender accepts the transfer subject to the conditions set forth in subsection (b). The consent and acceptance shall be on an appropriate form prescribed by the Attorney General.

(e) The proceedings shall be taken down by a reporter or recorded by suitable sound recording equipment. The Attorney General shall maintain custody of the records.

(Added Pub.L. 95–144, § 1, Oct. 28, 1977, 91 Stat. 1216, and amended Pub.L. 101–650, Title III, § 321, Dec. 1, 1990, 104 Stat. 5117.)

HISTORICAL AND STATUTORY NOTES

Change of Name

"United States magistrate judge" substituted for "United States magistrate" in subsec. (a) pursuant to section 321 of Pub.L. 101–650, set out as a note under 28 U.S.C.A. § 631.

§ 4108. Verification of consent of offender to transfer to the United States

(a) Prior to the transfer of an offender to the United States, the fact that the offender consents to such transfer and that such consent is voluntary and with full knowledge of the consequences thereof, shall be verified in the country in which the sentence was imposed by a United States magistrate judge, or by a citizen specifically designated by a judge of the United States as defined in section 451 of title 28, United States Code. The designation of a citizen who is an employee or officer of a department or agency of the United States shall be with the approval of the head of that department or agency.

(b) The verifying officer shall inquire of the offender whether he understands and agrees that the transfer will be subject to the following conditions:

(1) only the country in which he was convicted and sentenced can modify or set aside the conviction or sentence, and any proceedings seeking such action may only be brought in that country;

(2) the sentence shall be carried out according to the laws of the United States and that those laws are subject to change;

(3) if a United States court should determine upon a proceeding initiated by him or on his behalf that his transfer was not accomplished in accordance with the treaty or laws of the United States, he may be returned to the country which imposed the sentence for the purpose of completing the sentence if that country requests his return; and

(4) his consent to transfer, once verified by the verifying officer, is irrevocable.

(c) The verifying officer, before determining that an offender's consent is voluntary and given with full knowledge of the consequences, shall advise the offender of his right to consult with counsel as provided by this chapter. If the offender wishes to consult with counsel before giving his consent, he shall be advised that the proceedings will be continued until he has had an opportunity to consult with counsel.

(d) The verifying officer shall make the necessary inquiries to determine that the offender's consent is voluntary and not the result of any promises, threats, or other improper inducements, and that the offender accepts the transfer subject to the conditions set forth in subsection (b). The consent and acceptance shall be on an appropriate form prescribed by the Attorney General.

(e) The proceedings shall be taken down by a reporter or recorded by suitable sound recording equipment. The Attorney General shall maintain custody of the records.

(Added Pub.L. 95–144, § 1, Oct. 28, 1977, 91 Stat. 1217, and amended Pub.L. 98–473, Title II, § 223(m)(4), Oct. 12, 1984, 98 Stat. 2030; Pub.L. 100–690, Title VII, § 7101(b), Nov. 18, 1988, 102 Stat. 4415; Pub.L. 101–650, Title III, § 321, Dec. 1, 1990, 104 Stat. 5117.)

HISTORICAL AND STATUTORY NOTES

Effective and Applicability Provisions

1984 Acts. Amendment by Pub.L. 98–473 effective on the first day of first calendar month beginning thirty six months after Oct. 12, 1984, applicable only to offenses committed after taking effect of sections 211 to 239 of Pub.L. 98–473, and except as otherwise provided for therein, see section 235 of Pub.L. 98–473, as amended, set out as a note under section 3551 of this title.

Change of Name

"United States magistrate judge" substituted for "United States magistrate" in subsec. (a) pursuant to section 321 of Pub.L. 101–650, set out as a note under 28 U.S.C.A. § 631.

§ 4109. Right to counsel, appointment of counsel

(a) In proceedings to verify consent of an offender for transfer, the offender shall have the right to advice of counsel. If the offender is financially unable to obtain counsel—

(1) counsel for proceedings conducted under section 4107 shall be appointed in accordance with section 3006A of this title. Such appointment shall be considered an appointment in a misdemeanor case for purposes of compensation under the Act; [1]

(2) counsel for proceedings conducted under section 4108 shall be appointed by the verifying officer pursuant to such regulations as may be prescribed by the Director of the Administrative Office of the

United States Courts. The Secretary of State shall make payments of fees and expenses of the appointed counsel, in amounts approved by the verifying officer, which shall not exceed the amounts authorized under section 3006A of this title for representation in a misdemeanor case. Payment in excess of the maximum amount authorized may be made for extended or complex representation whenever the verifying officer certifies that the amount of the excess payment is necessary to provide fair compensation, and the payment is approved by the chief judge of the United States court of appeals for the appropriate circuit. Counsel from other agencies in any branch of the Government may be appointed: *Provided,* That in such cases the Secretary of State shall pay counsel directly, or reimburse the employing agency for travel and transportation expenses. Notwithstanding section 3324(a) and (b) of title 31, the Secretary may make advance payments of travel and transportation expenses to counsel appointed under this subsection.

(b) Guardians ad litem appointed by the verifying officer under section 4100 of this title to represent offenders who are financially unable to provide for compensation and travel expenses of the guardian ad litem shall be compensated and reimbursed under subsection (a)(1) of this section.

(c) The offender shall have the right to advice of counsel in proceedings before the United States Parole Commission under section 4106A of this title and in an appeal from a determination of such Commission under such section. If the offender is financially unable to obtain counsel, counsel for such proceedings and appeal shall be appointed under section 3006A of this title.

(Added Pub.L. 95–144, § 1, Oct. 28, 1977, 91 Stat. 1218, and amended Pub.L. 97–258, § 3(e) (2), Sept. 13, 1982, 96 Stat. 1064; Pub.L. 100–690, Title VII, § 7101(d), Nov. 18, 1988, 102 Stat. 4416; Pub.L. 101–647, Title XXXV, § 3598, Nov. 29, 1990, 104 Stat. 4931.)

[1] So in original. Probably should be "section 3006A of this title;".

§ 4110. Transfer of juveniles

An offender transferred to the United States because of an act which would have been an act of juvenile delinquency had it been committed in the United States or any State thereof shall be subject to the provisions of chapter 403 of this title except as otherwise provided in the relevant treaty or in an agreement pursuant to such treaty between the Attorney General and the authority of the foreign country.

(Added Pub.L. 95–144, § 1, Oct. 28, 1977, 91 Stat. 1218.)

§ 4111. Prosecution barred by foreign conviction

An offender transferred to the United States shall not be detained, prosecuted, tried, or sentenced by the United States, or any State thereof for any offense the prosecution of which would have been barred if the sentence upon which the transfer was based had been by a court of the jurisdiction seeking to prosecute the transferred offender, or if prosecution would have been barred by the laws of the jurisdiction seeking to prosecute the transferred offender if the sentence on which the transfer was based had been issued by a court of the United States or by a court of another State.

(Added Pub.L. 95–144, § 1, Oct. 28, 1977, 91 Stat. 1218.)

§ 4112. Loss of rights, disqualification

An offender transferred to the United States to serve a sentence imposed by a foreign court shall not incur any loss of civil, political, or civic rights nor incur any disqualification other than those which under the laws of the United States or of the State in which the issue arises would result from the fact of the conviction in the foreign country.

(Added Pub.L. 95–144, § 1, Oct. 28, 1977, 91 Stat. 1218.)

§ 4113. Status of alien offender transferred to a foreign country

(a) An alien who is deportable from the United States but who has been granted voluntary departure pursuant to section 240B of the Immigration and Nationality Act and who is transferred to a foreign country pursuant to this chapter shall be deemed for all purposes to have voluntarily departed from this country.

(b) An alien who is the subject of an order of removal from the United States pursuant to section 240 of the Immigration and Nationality Act who is transferred to a foreign country pursuant to this chapter shall be deemed for all purposes to have been removed from this country.

(c) An alien who is the subject of an order of removal from the United States pursuant to section 240 of the Immigration and Nationality Act, who is transferred to a foreign country pursuant to this chapter shall be deemed for all purposes to have been excluded from admission and removed from the United States.

(Added Pub.L. 95–144, § 1, Oct. 28, 1977, 91 Stat. 1219, and amended Pub.L. 104–208, Div. C, Title III, § 308(d)(4)(U), (e)(1)(Q), (2)(I), (g)(3)(B), (5)(A)(iv), Sept. 30, 1996, 110 Stat. 3009–619, 3009–620, 3009–622, 3009–623.)

HISTORICAL AND STATUTORY NOTES

References in Text

The Immigration and Nationality Act, referred to in text, is Act June 27, 1952, c. 477, 66 Stat. 163, as amended, which is classified principally to chapter 12 (section 1101 et seq.) of Title 8, Aliens and Nationality. Sections 240 and 240B of such Act are classified to sections 1229a and 1229c, respectively, of Title 8. For complete classification of this Act to the Code, see Short Title note set out under section 1101 of Title 8 and Tables.

Effective and Applicability Provisions

1996 Acts. Amendment by section 308(d)(4)(U), (e)(1)(Q), (2)(I), and (g)(5)(iv) of Div. C. of Pub.L. 104–208, effective, with certain exceptions and subject to certain transitional rules, on the first day of the first month beginning more than 180 days after Sept. 30, 1996, see section 309 of Pub.L. 104–208, set out as a note under section 1101 of Title, Aliens and Nationality.

Severability of Provisions

If any provision of Division C of Pub.L. 104–208 or the application of such provision to any person or circumstances is held to be unconstitutional, the remainder of Division C of Pub.L. 104–208 and the application of the provisions of Division C of Pub.L. 104–208 to any person or circumstance not to be affected thereby, see section 1(e) of Pub.L. 104–208, set out as a note under section 1101 of Title 8, Aliens and Nationality.

§ 4114. Return of transferred offenders

(a) Upon a final decision by the courts of the United States that the transfer of the offender to the United States was not in accordance with the treaty or the laws of the United States and ordering the offender released from serving the sentence in the United States the offender may be returned to the country from which he was transferred to complete the sentence if the country in which the sentence was imposed requests his return. The Attorney General shall notify the appropriate authority of the country which imposed the sentence, within ten days, of a final decision of a court of the United States ordering the offender released. The notification shall specify the time within which the sentencing country must request the return of the offender which shall be no longer than thirty days.

(b) Upon receiving a request from the sentencing country that the offender ordered released be returned for the completion of his sentence, the Attorney General may file a complaint for the return of the offender with any justice or judge of the United States or any authorized magistrate judge within whose jurisdiction the offender is found. The complaint shall be upon oath and supported by affidavits establishing that the offender was convicted and sentenced by the courts of the country to which his return is requested; the offender was transferred to the United States for the execution of his sentence; the offender was ordered released by a court of the United States before he had completed his sentence because the transfer of the offender was not in accordance with the treaty or the laws of the United States; and that the sentencing country has requested that he be returned for the completion of the sentence. There shall be attached to the complaint a copy of the sentence of the sentencing court and of the decision of the court which ordered the offender released.

A summons or a warrant shall be issued by the justice, judge or magistrate judge ordering the offender to appear or to be brought before the issuing authority. If the justice, judge, or magistrate judge finds that the person before him is the offender described in the complaint and that the facts alleged in the complaint are true, he shall issue a warrant for commitment of the offender to the custody of the Attorney General until surrender shall be made. The findings and a copy of all the testimony taken before him and of all documents introduced before him shall be transmitted to the Secretary of State, that a Return Warrant may issue upon the requisition of the proper authorities of the sentencing country, for the surrender of offender.

(c) A complaint referred to in subsection (b) must be filed within sixty days from the date on which the decision ordering the release of the offender becomes final.

(d) An offender returned under this section shall be subject to the jurisdiction of the country to which he is returned for all purposes.

(e) The return of an offender shall be conditioned upon the offender being given credit toward service of the sentence for the time spent in the custody of or under the supervision of the United States.

(f) Sections 3186, 3188 through 3191, and 3195 of this title shall be applicable to the return of an offender under this section. However, an offender returned under this section shall not be deemed to have been extradited for any purpose.

(g) An offender whose return is sought pursuant to this section may be admitted to bail or be released on his own recognizance at any stage of the proceedings.

(Added Pub.L. 95–144, § 1, Oct. 28, 1977, 91 Stat. 1219, and amended Pub.L. 101–650, Title III, § 321, Dec. 1, 1990, 104 Stat. 5117.)

HISTORICAL AND STATUTORY NOTES

Change of Name

Words "magistrate judge" substituted for "magistrate" in subsec. (b) pursuant to section 321 of Pub.L. 101–650, set out as a note under 28 U.S.C.A. § 631.

§ 4115. Execution of sentences imposing an obligation to make restitution or reparations

If in a sentence issued in a penal proceeding of a transferring country an offender transferred to the United States has been ordered to pay a sum of money to the victim of the offense for damage caused by the offense, that penalty or award of damages may be enforced as though it were a civil judgment rendered by a United States district court. Proceedings to collect the moneys ordered to be paid may be instituted by the Attorney General in any United States district court. Moneys recovered pursuant to such proceedings shall be transmitted through diplomatic channels to the treaty authority of the transferring country for distribution to the victim.

(Added Pub.L. 95–144, § 1, Oct. 28, 1977, 91 Stat. 1220.)

CHAPTER 307—EMPLOYMENT

1990 Amendment

Pub.L. 101–647, Title XXXV, § 3599A, Nov. 29, 1990, 104 Stat. 4931, substituted in item 4126A "Fund" for "fund".

1988 Amendment

Pub.L. 100–690, Title VII, § 7093(b), Nov. 18, 1988, 102 Stat. 4412, added item 4129.

§ 4121. Federal Prison Industries; board of directors

"Federal Prison Industries", a government corporation of the District of Columbia, shall be administered by a board of six directors, appointed by the President to serve at the will of the President without compensation.

The directors shall be representatives of (1) industry, (2) labor, (3) agriculture, (4) retailers and consumers, (5) the Secretary of Defense, and (6) the Attorney General, respectively.

(June 25, 1948, c. 645, 62 Stat. 851; May 24, 1949, c. 139, § 62, 63 Stat. 98.)

HISTORICAL AND STATUTORY NOTES

Transfer of Functions

The Federal Prison Industries, Inc. (together with its Board of Directors), and its functions were transferred to the Department of Justice to be administered under the general direction and supervision of the Attorney General, by Reorg. Plan No. II of 1939, § 3(a), eff. July 1, 1939, 4 F.R. 2731, 53 Stat. 1431, set out in the Appendix to Title 5, Government Organization and Employees. See, also, Reorg. Plan No. 2 of 1950, § 1, eff. May 24, 1950, 15 F.R. 3173, 64 Stat. 1261, and section 509 of Title 28, Judiciary and Judicial Procedure.

Mandatory Work Requirement for All Prisoners

Pub.L. 101–647, Title XXIX, § 2905, Nov. 29, 1990, 104 Stat. 4914, provided that:

"**(a) In general.—(1)** It is the policy of the Federal Government that convicted inmates confined in Federal prisons, jails, and other detention facilities shall work. The type of work in which they will be involved shall be dictated by appropriate security considerations and by the health of the prisoner involved.

"**(2)** A Federal prisoner may be excused from the requirement to work only as necessitated by—

"**(A)** security considerations;

"**(B)** disciplinary action;

"**(C)** medical certification of disability such as would make it impracticable for prison officials to arrange useful work for the prisoner to perform; or

"**(D)** a need for the prisoner to work less than a full work schedule in order to participate in literacy training, drug rehabilitation, or similar programs in addition to the work program."

Closure of McNeil Island Penitentiary; Report on Status of Federal Prison Industries

Pub.L. 95–624, § 10, Nov. 9, 1978, 92 Stat. 3463, provided that:

"**(a)** On or before September 1, 1979, the Attorney General shall submit to the Congress—

"**(1)** a plan to assure the closure of the United States Penitentiary on McNeil Island, Steilacoom, Washington, on or before January 1, 1982; and

"**(2)** a report on the status of the Federal Prison Industries.

"**(b)** The report made under this section shall include a long-range plan for the improvement of meaningful employment training, and the methods which could be undertaken to employ a greater number of United States prisoners in the program. Such report may include recommendations for legislation."

§ 4122. Administration of Federal Prison Industries

(a) Federal Prison Industries shall determine in what manner and to what extent industrial operations shall be carried on in Federal penal and correctional institutions for the production of commodities for consumption in such institutions or for sale to the departments or agencies of the United States, but not for sale to the public in competition with private enterprise.

(b)(1) Its board of directors shall provide employment for the greatest number of those inmates in the United States penal and correctional institutions who are eligible to work as is reasonably possible, diversify, so far as practicable, prison industrial operations and so operate the prison shops that no single private industry shall be forced to bear an undue burden of competition from the products of the prison workshops, and to reduce to a minimum competition with private industry or free labor.

(2) Federal Prison Industries shall conduct its operations so as to produce products on an economic basis, but shall avoid capturing more than a reasonable share of the market among Federal departments, agencies, and institutions for any specific product. Federal Prison Industries shall concentrate on providing to the Federal Government only those products which permit employment of the greatest number of those inmates who are eligible to work as is reasonably possible.

(3) Federal Prison Industries shall diversify its products so that its sales are distributed among its industries as broadly as possible.

(4) Any decision by Federal Prison Industries to produce a new product or to significantly expand the production of an existing product shall be made by the board of directors of the corporation.

Before the board of directors makes a final decision, the corporation shall do the following:

(A) The corporation shall prepare a detailed written analysis of the probable impact on industry and free labor of the plans for new production or expanded production. In such written analysis the corporation shall, at a minimum, identify and consider—

(i) the number of vendors currently meeting the requirements of the Federal Government for the product;

(ii) the proportion of the Federal Government market for the product currently served by small businesses, small disadvantaged businesses, or businesses operating in labor surplus areas;

(iii) the size of the Federal Government and non-Federal Government markets for the product;

(iv) the projected growth in the Federal Government demand for the product; and

(v) the projected ability of the Federal Government market to sustain both Federal Prison Industries and private vendors.

(B) The corporation shall announce in a publication designed to most effectively provide notice to potentially affected private vendors the plans to produce any new product or to significantly expand production of an existing product. The announcement shall also indicate that the analysis prepared under subparagraph (A) is available through the corporation and shall invite comments from private industry regarding the new production or expanded production.

(C) The corporation shall directly advise those affected trade associations that the corporation can reasonably identify the plans for new production or expanded production, and the corporation shall invite such trade associations to submit comments on those plans.

(D) The corporation shall provide to the board of directors—

(i) the analysis prepared under subparagraph (A) on the proposal to produce a new product or to significantly expand the production of an existing product,

(ii) comments submitted to the corporation on the proposal, and

(iii) the corporation's recommendations for action on the proposal in light of such comments.

In addition, the board of directors, before making a final decision under this paragraph on a proposal, shall, upon the request of an established trade association or other interested representatives of private industry, provide a reasonable opportunity to such trade association or other representatives to present comments directly to the board of directors on the proposal.

(5) Federal Prison Industries shall publish in the manner specified in paragraph (4)(B) the final decision of the board with respect to the production of a new product or the significant expansion of the production of an existing product.

(6) Federal Prison Industries shall publish, after the end of each 6-month period, a list of sales by the corporation for that 6-month period. Such list shall be made available to all interested parties.

(c) Its board of directors may provide for the vocational training of qualified inmates without regard to their industrial or other assignments.

(d)(1) The provisions of this chapter shall apply to the industrial employment and training of prisoners convicted by general courts-martial and confined in any institution under the jurisdiction of any department or agency comprising the Department of Defense, to the extent and under terms and conditions agreed upon by the Secretary of Defense, the Attorney General and the Board of Directors of Federal Prison Industries.

(2) Any department or agency of the Department of Defense may, without exchange of funds, transfer to Federal Prison Industries any property or equipment suitable for use in performing the functions and duties covered by agreement entered into under paragraph (1) of this subsection.

(e)(1) The provisions of this chapter shall apply to the industrial employment and training of prisoners confined in any penal or correctional institution under the direction of the Commissioner of the District of Columbia to the extent and under terms and conditions agreed upon by the Commissioner, the Attorney General, and the Board of Directors of Federal Prison Industries.

(2) The Commissioner of the District of Columbia may, without exchange of funds, transfer to the Fed-

eral Prison Industries any property or equipment suitable for use in performing the functions and duties covered by an agreement entered into under subsection (e)(1) of this section.

(3) Nothing in this chapter shall be construed to affect the provisions of the Act approved October 3, 1964 (D.C.Code, sections 24–451 et seq.), entitled "An Act to establish in the Treasury a correctional industries fund for the government of the District of Columbia, and for other purposes."

(June 25, 1948, c. 645, 62 Stat. 851; May 24, 1949, c. 139, § 63, 63 Stat. 98; Oct. 31, 1951, c. 655, § 31, 65 Stat. 722; Dec. 27, 1967, Pub.L. 90–226, Title VIII, § 802, 81 Stat. 741; Nov. 18, 1988, Pub.L. 100–690, Title VII, § 7096, 102 Stat. 4413.)

HISTORICAL AND STATUTORY NOTES

References in Text

The Act approved October 3, 1964 (D.C.Code, sections 24–451 et seq.), entitled "An Act to establish in the Treasury a correctional institution industries fund for the government of the District of Columbia, and for other purposes", referred to in subsec. (e)(3), is Pub.L. 88–622, Oct. 3, 1964, 78 Stat. 1000, which is not classified to this Code.

Transfer of Functions

The Office of Commissioner of the District of Columbia, as established by Reorg. Plan No. 3 of 1967, was abolished as of noon Jan. 2, 1975, by Pub.L. 93–198, Title VII, § 711, Dec. 24, 1973, 87 Stat. 818, and replaced by the Office of Mayor of the District of Columbia by section 421 of Pub.L. 93–198, classified to section 1–241 of the District of Columbia Code.

Utilization of Surplus Property

Act June 29, 1948, c. 719, § 4, 62 Stat. 1100, provided that: "For its own use in the industrial employment and training of prisoners and not for transfer or disposition, transfers of surplus property under the Surplus Property Act of 1944 [former sections 1611 to 1646 of Appendix to Title 50, War and National Defense] may be made to Federal Prison Industries, Incorporated, without reimbursement or transfer of funds."

§ 4123. New industries

Any industry established under this chapter shall be so operated as not to curtail the production of any existing arsenal, navy yard, or other Government workshop.

Such forms of employment shall be provided as will give the inmates of all Federal penal and correctional institutions a maximum opportunity to acquire a knowledge and skill in trades and occupations which will provide them with a means of earning a livelihood upon release.

The industries may be either within the precincts of any penal or correctional institution or in any convenient locality where an existing property may be obtained by lease, purchase, or otherwise.

(June 25, 1948, c. 645, 62 Stat. 851.)

§ 4124. Purchase of prison-made products by Federal departments

(a) The several Federal departments and agencies and all other Government institutions of the United States shall purchase at not to exceed current market prices, such products of the industries authorized by this chapter as meet their requirements and may be available.

(b) Disputes as to the price, quality, character, or suitability of such products shall be arbitrated by a board consisting of the Attorney General, the Administrator of General Services, and the President, or their representatives. Their decision shall be final and binding upon all parties.

(c) Each Federal department, agency, and institution subject to the requirements of subsection (a) shall separately report acquisitions of products and services from Federal Prison Industries to the Federal Procurement Data System (as referred to in section 6(d)(4) of the Office of Federal Procurement Policy Act) in the same manner as it reports other acquisitions. Each report published by the Federal Procurement Data System that contains the information collected by the System shall include a statement to accompany the information reported by the department, agency, or institution under the preceding sentence as follows: "Under current law, sales by Federal Prison Industries are considered intragovernmental transfers. The purpose of reporting sales by Federal Prison Industries is to provide a complete overview of acquisitions by the Federal Government during the reporting period.".

(d) Within 90 days after the date of the enactment of this subsection, Federal Prison Industries shall publish a catalog of all products and services which it offers for sale. This catalog shall be updated periodically to the extent necessary to ensure that the information in the catalog is complete and accurate.

(June 25, 1948, c. 645, 62 Stat. 851; Oct. 31, 1951, c. 655, § 32, 65 Stat. 723; Feb. 14, 1984, Pub.L. 98–216, § 3(b)(2), 98 Stat. 6; Nov. 29, 1990, Pub.L. 101–647, Title XXIX, § 2901, 104 Stat. 4912; Oct. 28, 1992, Pub.L. 102–564, Title III, § 303(b), 106 Stat. 4262; Oct. 19, 1996, Pub.L. 104–316, Title I, § 109(b), 110 Stat. 3832.)

HISTORICAL AND STATUTORY NOTES

References in Text

Section 6(d)(4) of the Office of Federal Procurement Policy Act, referred to in subsec. (c), is classified to section 405(d)(4) of Title 41, Public Contracts.

The date of enactment of this subsection, referred to in subsec. (d), probably means the date of enactment of Pub.L. 101–647, Nov. 29, 1990, 104 Stat. 4789, which was approved Nov. 29, 1990.

Effective and Applicability Provisions

1996 Acts. Amendment by Pub.L. 104–316 effective Oct. 19, 1996, see section 101(e) of Pub.L. 104–316, set out as a note under section 130c of Title 2, The Congress.

Savings Provisions

For savings provisions relating to amendment by Pub.L. 98–216, see section 4(d) of Pub.L. 98–216, set out as a note preceding section 101 of Title 31, Money and Finance.

Funding for Purchases

Pub.L. 108–447, Div. H, Title VI, § 637, 118 Stat. 3281, provided that: "None of the funds made available under this or any other Act for fiscal year 2005 and each fiscal year thereafter shall be expended for the purchase of a product or service offered by Federal Prison Industries, Inc., unless the agency making such purchase determines that such offered product or service provides the best value to the buying agency pursuant to governmentwide procurement regulations, issued pursuant to section 25(c)(1) of the Office of Federal Procurement Act [Office of Federal Procurement Policy Act, Pub.L. 93–400, § 25, as added Pub.L. 100–679, § 4, Nov. 17, 1988, 102 Stat. 4056, and amended] (41 U.S.C. 421(c)(1)) that impose procedures, standards, and limitations of section 2410n of title 10, United States Code."

Similar provisions were contained in the following prior appropriations Acts:

Pub.L. 108–199, Div. F, Title VI, § 637, 118 Stat. 358.

Purchases by the Central Intelligence Agency of Products of Federal Prison Industries

Pub.L. 108–177, Title IV, § 404, Dec. 13, 2003, 117 Stat. 2632, as amended Pub.L. 108–458, Title I, § 1071(g)(3)(C), Dec. 17, 2004, 118 Stat. 3692, provided that: "Notwithstanding section 4124 of title 18, United States Code [this section], purchases by the Central Intelligence Agency from Federal Prison Industries shall be made only if the Director of the Central Intelligence Agency determines that the product or service to be purchased from Federal Prison Industries best meets the needs of the Agency."

[Except as otherwise expressly provided, amendments by Pub.L. 108–458, Title I, to take effect not later than six months after Dec. 17, 2004, see Pub.L. 108–458, Title I, § 1097(a), set out in the Transfer, Termination, Implementation, Transition, and Effective Dates of the National Security Intelligence Reform Act of 2004 note under 50 U.S.C.A. § 401.]

§ 4125. Public works; prison camps

(a) The Attorney General may make available to the heads of the several departments the services of United States prisoners under terms, conditions, and rates mutually agreed upon, for constructing or repairing roads, clearing, maintaining and reforesting public lands, building levees, and constructing or repairing any other public ways or works financed wholly or in major part by funds appropriated by Congress.

(b) The Attorney General may establish, equip, and maintain camps upon sites selected by him elsewhere than upon Indian reservations, and designate such camps as places for confinement of persons convicted of an offense against the laws of the United States.

(c) The expenses of transferring and maintaining prisoners at such camps and of operating such camps shall be paid from the appropriation "Support of United States prisoners", which may, in the discretion of the Attorney General, be reimbursed for such expenses.

(d) As part of the expense of operating such camps the Attorney General is authorized to provide for the payment to the inmates or their dependents such pecuniary earnings as he may deem proper, under such rules and regulations as he may prescribe.

(e) All other laws of the United States relating to the imprisonment, transfer, control, discipline, escape, release of, or in any way affecting prisoners, shall apply to prisoners transferred to such camps.

(June 25, 1948, c. 645, 62 Stat. 852.)

§ 4126. Prison Industries Fund; use and settlement of accounts

(a) All moneys under the control of Federal Prison Industries, or received from the sale of the products or by-products of such Industries, or for the services of federal prisoners, shall be deposited or covered into the Treasury of the United States to the credit of the Prison Industries Fund and withdrawn therefrom only pursuant to accountable warrants or certificates of settlement issued by the Government Accountability Office.

(b) All valid claims and obligations payable out of said fund shall be assumed by the corporation.

(c) The corporation, in accordance with the laws generally applicable to the expenditures of the several departments, agencies, and establishments of the Government, is authorized to employ the fund, and any earnings that may accrue to the corporation—

(1) as operating capital in performing the duties imposed by this chapter;

(2) in the lease, purchase, other acquisition, repair, alteration, erection, and maintenance of industrial buildings and equipment;

(3) in the vocational training of inmates without regard to their industrial or other assignments;

(4) in paying, under rules and regulations promulgated by the Attorney General, compensation to inmates employed in any industry, or performing outstanding services in institutional operations, and compensation to inmates or their dependents for injuries suffered in any industry or in any work activity in connection with the maintenance or operation of the institution in which the inmates are confined.

In no event may compensation for such injuries be paid in an amount greater than that provided in chapter 81 of title 5.

(d) Accounts of all receipts and disbursements of the corporation shall be rendered to the Government Accountability Office for settlement and adjustment, as required by the Comptroller General.

(e) Such accounting shall include all fiscal transactions of the corporation, whether involving appropriated moneys, capital, or receipts from other sources.

(f) Funds available to the corporation may be used for the lease, purchase, other acquisition, repair, alteration, erection, or maintenance of facilities only to the extent such facilities are necessary for the industrial operations of the corporation under this chapter. Such funds may not be used for the construction or acquisition of penal or correctional institutions, including camps described in section 4125.

(June 25, 1948, c. 645, 62 Stat. 852; May 24, 1949, c. 139, § 64, 63 Stat. 99; Sept. 26, 1961, Pub.L. 87–317, 75 Stat. 681; Nov. 18, 1988, Pub.L. 100–690, Title VII, § 7094, 102 Stat. 4412; July 7, 2004, Pub.L. 108–271, § 8(b), 118 Stat. 814.)

§ 4127. Prison Industries report to Congress

The board of directors of Federal Prison Industries shall submit an annual report to the Congress on the conduct of the business of the corporation during each fiscal year, and on the condition of its funds during such fiscal year. Such report shall include a statement of the amount of obligations issued under section 4129(a)(1) during such fiscal year, and an estimate of the amount of obligations that will be so issued in the following fiscal year.

(June 25, 1948, c. 645, 62 Stat. 852; Nov. 18, 1988, Pub.L. 100–690, Title VII, § 7095, 102 Stat. 4413.)

HISTORICAL AND STATUTORY NOTES

Termination of Reporting Requirements

For termination of reporting provisions of this section, effective May 15, 2000, see Pub.L. 104–66, § 3003, as amended, set out as a note under 31 U.S.C.A. § 1113, and page 117 of House Document No. 103–7.

For termination, effective May 15, 2000, of reporting provisions in this section, see Pub.L. 104–66, § 3003, as amended, set out as a note under 31 U.S.C.A. § 1113 and page 117 of House Document No. 103–7.

§ 4128. Enforcement by Attorney General

In the event of any failure of Federal Prison Industries to act, the Attorney General shall not be limited in carrying out the duties conferred upon him by law.

(June 25, 1948, c. 645, 62 Stat. 853.)

§ 4129. Authority to borrow and invest

(a)(1) As approved by the board of directors, Federal Prison Industries, to such extent and in such amounts as are provided in appropriations Acts, is authorized to issue its obligations to the Secretary of the Treasury, and the Secretary of the Treasury, in the Secretary's discretion, may purchase or agree to purchase any such obligations, except that the aggregate amount of obligations issued by Federal Prison Industries under this paragraph that are outstanding at any time may not exceed 25 percent of the net worth of the corporation. For purchases of such obligations by the Secretary of the Treasury, the Secretary is authorized to use as a public debt transaction the proceeds of the sale of any securities issued under chapter 31 of title 31 after the date of the enactment of this section, and the purposes for which securities may be issued under that chapter are extended to include such purchases. Each purchase of obligations by the Secretary of the Treasury under this subsection shall be upon such terms and conditions as to yield a return at a rate not less than a rate determined by the Secretary of the Treasury, taking into consideration the current average yield on outstanding marketable obligations of the United States of comparable maturity. For purposes of the first sentence of this paragraph, the net worth of Federal Prison Industries is the amount by which its assets (including capital) exceed its liabilities.

(2) The Secretary of the Treasury may sell, upon such terms and conditions and at such price or prices as the Secretary shall determine, any of the obligations acquired by the Secretary under this subsection. All purchases and sales by the Secretary of the Treasury of such obligations under this subsection shall be treated as public debt transactions of the United States.

(b) Federal Prison Industries may request the Secretary of the Treasury to invest excess moneys from the Prison Industries Fund. Such investments shall be in public debt securities with maturities suitable to the needs of the corporation as determined by the board of directors, and bearing interest at rates determined by the Secretary of the Treasury, taking into consideration current market yields on outstanding marketable obligations of the United States of comparable maturities.

(Added Pub.L. 100–690, Title VII, § 7093(a), Nov. 18, 1988, 102 Stat. 4411.)

HISTORICAL AND STATUTORY NOTES

References in Text

The date of enactment of this section, referred to in subsec. (a), is the date of enactment of section 7093(a) of Pub.L. 100–690, which enacted this section, and which was approved Nov. 18, 1988.

[CHAPTER 309—REPEALED]

[§ 4161 to 4166. Repealed. Pub.L. 98–473, Title II, § 218(a)(4), Oct. 12, 1984, 98 Stat. 2027]

HISTORICAL AND STATUTORY NOTES

Section 235(a)(1) of Pub.L. 98–473, set out as a note under section 3551 of this title, provided that the repeal of this chapter is effective Nov. 1, 1987, and applicable only to offenses committed after the taking effect of such repeal. Section 235(b)(1)(B) of Pub.L. 98–473 provided that the provisions of this chapter in effect before Nov. 1, 1987, shall remain in effect for five years after Nov. 1, 1987, as to an individual who committed an offense or an act of juvenile delinquency before Nov. 1, 1987, and as to a term of imprisonment during the period described in section 235(a)(1)(B) of Pub.L. 98–473. Prior to repeal, the provisions of this chapter, June 25, 1948, c. 645, 62 Stat. 853; June 29, 1951, c. 176, 65 Stat. 98; Pub.L. 86–259, Sept. 14, 1959, 73 Stat. 546; – Pub.L. 87–665, Sept. 19, 1962, 76 Stat. 552, read as follows:

§ 4161. Computation generally

Each prisoner convicted of an offense against the United States and confined in a penal or correctional institution for a definite term other than for life, whose record of conduct shows that he has faithfully observed all the rules and has not been subjected to punishment, shall be entitled to a deduction from the term of his sentence beginning with the day on which the sentence commences to run, as follows:

Five days for each month, if the sentence is not less than six months and not more than one year.

Six days for each month, if the sentence is more than one year and less than three years.

Seven days for each month, if the sentence is not less than three years and less than five years.

Eight days for each month, if the sentence is not less than five years and less than ten years.

Ten days for each month, if the sentence is ten years or more.

When two or more consecutive sentences are to be served, the aggregate of the several sentences shall be the basis upon which the deduction shall be computed.

§ 4162. Industrial good time

A prisoner may, in the discretion of the Attorney General, be allowed a deduction from his sentence of not to exceed three days for each month of actual employment in an industry or camp for the first year or any part thereof, and not to exceed five days for each month of any succeeding year or part thereof.

In the discretion of the Attorney General such allowance may also be made to a prisoner performing exceptionally meritorious service or performing duties of outstanding importance in connection with institutional operations.

Such allowance shall be in addition to commutation of time for good conduct, and under the same terms and conditions and without regard to length of sentence.

§ 4163. Discharge

Except as hereinafter provided a prisoner shall be released at the expiration of his term of sentence less the time deducted for good conduct. A certificate of such deduction shall be entered on the commitment by the warden or keeper. If such release date falls upon a Saturday, a Sunday, or on a Monday which is a legal holiday at the place of confinement, the prisoner may be released at the discretion of the warden or keeper on the preceding Friday. If such release date falls on a holiday which falls other than on a Saturday, Sunday, or Monday, the prisoner may be released at the discretion of the warden or keeper on the day preceding the holiday.

§ 4164. Released prisoner as parolee

A prisoner having served his term or terms less good–time deductions shall, upon release, be deemed as if released on parole until the expiration of the maximum term or terms for which he was sentenced less one hundred and eighty days.

This section shall not prevent delivery of a prisoner to the authorities of any State otherwise entitled to his custody.

§ 4165. Forfeiture for offense

If during the term of imprisonment a prisoner commits any offense or violates the rules of the institution, all or any part of his earned good time may be forfeited.

§ 4166. Restoration of forfeited commutation

The Attorney General may restore any forfeited or lost good time or such portion thereof as he deems proper upon recommendation of the Director of the Bureau of Prisons.

[CHAPTER 311—REPEALED]

HISTORICAL AND STATUTORY NOTES

Prior Provisions

A prior chapter 311, consisting of sections 4201–4210, act June 25, 1948, ch. 645, 62 Stat. 854, 855, as amended, was repealed by section 2 of Pub. L. 94–233 as part of the general revision of this chapter by Pub. L. 94–233.

[§§ 4201 to 4218. Repealed. Pub.L. 98–473, Title II, § 218(a)(5), Oct. 12, 1984, 98 Stat. 2027]

EFFECTIVE DATE OF REPEAL; CHAPTER TO REMAIN IN EFFECT FOR EIGHTEEN YEARS AFTER NOV. 1, 1987

Section 235(a)(1) of Pub.L. 98–473, set out as a note under section 3551 of this title, provided that the repeal of this chapter is effective Nov. 1, 1987, and applicable only to offenses committed after the taking effect of such repeal. Section 235(b)(1)(A) of Pub.L. 98–473 provided that the provisions of this chapter in effect before Nov. 1, 1987, shall remain in effect for five years after Nov. 1, 1987, as to an individual who committed an offense or an act of juvenile delinquency before Nov. 1, 1987, and as to a term of imprisonment during the period described in section 235(a)(1)(B) of Pub.L. 98–473. Pub.L. 101–650, Title III, § 316, Dec. 1, 1990, 104 Stat. 5115, extended the period that this chapter remains in effect after Nov. 1, 1987, from five years to ten years. Pub.L. 104–232, section 2(a), Oct. 2, 1996, 110 Stat. 3055, extended the period that this chapter remains in effect after November 1, 1987, from ten years to fifteen years. Pub.L. 107–273, § 11017, set out as a note under 18 U.S.C.A. § 4202, deemed references to "fifteen" to be "eighteen" in Pub.L. 98–473, § 235(b), as it relates to 18 U.S.C.A. § 4201 et seq. The provisions of this chapter as in effect prior to repeal, and as amended subsequent to repeal, read as follows:

§ 4201. Definitions

As used in this chapter—

(1) "Commission" means the United States Parole Commission;

(2) "Commissioner" means any member of the United States Parole Commission;

(3) "Director" means the Director of the Bureau of Prisons;

(4) "Eligible prisoner" means any Federal prisoner who is eligible for parole pursuant to this title or any other law including any Federal prisoner whose parole has been revoked and who is not otherwise ineligible for parole;

(5) "Parolee" means any eligible prisoner who has been released on parole or deemed as if released on parole under section 4164 or section 4205(f); and

(6) "Rules and regulations" means rules and regulations promulgated by the Commission pursuant to section 4203 and section 553 of title 5, United States Code.

(Added Pub.L. 94–233, § 2, Mar. 15, 1976, 90 Stat. 219.)

Parole Commission Phaseout

Pub.L. 104–232, §§ 1 to 3, Oct. 2, 1996, 110 Stat. 3055, as amended Pub.L. 105–33, Title XI, § 11231(d), Aug. 5, 1997, 111 Stat. 745, provided that:

"Section 1. Short title.

"This Act [enacting this note and a provision set out as a note under section 3551 of this title and amending a provision set out as a note under section 3551 of this title] may be cited as the 'Parole Commission Phaseout Act of 1996'.

"Sec. 2. Extension of Parole Commission.

"(a) In general.—For purposes of section 235(b) of the Sentencing Reform Act of 1984 (98 Stat. 2032) [section 235(b) of Pub.L. 98–473, set out as a note under section 3551 of this title] as it related to chapter 311 of title 18, United States Code [this chapter], and the Parole Commission, each reference in such section to 'ten years' or 'ten-year period' shall be deemed to be a reference to 'fifteen years' or 'fifteen-year period', respectively.

"(b) Powers and duties of Parole Commission.—Notwithstanding section 4203 of title 18, United States Code [section 4203 of this title], the United States Parole Commission may perform its functions with any quorum of Commissioners, or Commissioner, as the Commission may prescribe by regulation.

(c) The United States Parole Commission shall have no more than five members.

"Sec. 3. Reports by the Attorney General.

"(a) In general.—Beginning in the year 1998, the Attorney General shall report to the Congress not later than May 1 of each year through the year 2002 on the status of the United States Parole Commission. Unless the Attorney General, in such report, certifies that the continuation of the Commission is the most effective and cost-efficient manner for carrying out the Commission's functions, the Attorney General shall include in such report an alternative plan for a transfer of the Commission's functions to another entity.

"(b) Transfer within the Department of Justice.—

"(1) Effect of plan.—If the Attorney General includes such a plan in the report, and that plan provides for the transfer of the Commission's functions and powers to another entity within the Department of Justice, such plan shall take effect according to its terms on November 1 of that year in which the report is made, unless Congress by law provides otherwise. In the event such plan takes effect, all laws pertaining to the authority and jurisdiction of the Commission with respect to individual offenders shall remain in effect notwithstanding the expiration of the period specified in section 2 of this Act.

"(2) Conditional repeal.—Effective on the date such plan takes effect, paragraphs (3) and (4) of section 235(b) of the Sentencing Reform Act of 1984 (98 Stat. 2032) [section 235 (b)(3) and (4) of Pub.L. 98–473, set out as a note under section 3551 of this title] are repealed."

[Pub.L. 105–33, Title XI, §§ 11231(d), 11721, Aug. 5, 1997, 111 Stat. 745, 786, amended Sec. 2(c) of the above note, effective on the later of Oct. 1, 1997 or the day the District of Columbia Financial Responsibility and Management Assistance Authority certifies that the financial plan and budget for the District government for fiscal year 1998 meet certain requirements. For effective date information regarding this amendment, see section 11721 of Pub.L. 105–33, set out as a note under 18 U.S.C.A. § 4246.]

§ 4202. Parole Commission created

There is hereby established, as an independent agency in the Department of Justice, a United States Parole Commission which shall be comprised of nine members appointed by the President, by and with the advice and consent of the Senate. The President shall designate from among the Commissioners one to serve as Chairman. The term of office of a Commissioner shall be six years, except that the term of a person appointed as a Commissioner to fill a vacancy shall expire six years from the date upon which such person was appointed and qualified. Upon the expiration of a term of office of a Commissioner, the Commissioner shall continue to act until a successor has been appointed and qualified, except that no Commissioner may serve in excess of twelve years. Commissioners shall be compensated at the highest rate now or hereafter prescribed for grade 18 of the General Schedule pay rates (5 U.S.C. 5332).

(Added Pub.L. 94–233, § 2, Mar. 15, 1976, 90 Stat. 219.)

Extension of Term of Commissioner

Section 235(b)(2) of Pub. L. 98–473, which provided that notwithstanding the provisions of section 4202 of this title as in effect on the day before Nov. 1, 1987 [set out above], the term of office of a Commissioner who is in office on Nov. 1, 1987, is extended to the end of the fifteen-year period after Nov. 1, 1987, and which pursuant to Pub.L. 101–650, Title III, § 316, Dec. 1, 1990, 104 Stat. 5115, further extended the term of office of a Commissioner to a ten–year period after

Nov. 1, 1987, was repealed by Pub.L. 104–232, § 4, Oct. 2, 1996, 110 Stat. 3056.

United States Parole Commission Extension

Pub.L. 107–273, Div. C, Title I, § 11017, Nov. 2, 2002, 116 Stat. 1824, provided that:

"(a) **Extension of the Parole Commission.**—For purposes of section 235(b) of the Sentencing Reform Act of 1984 (98 Stat. 2032) [section 235(b) of Pub.L. 98–473, set out as a note under 18 U.S.C.A. § 3551] as such section relates to chapter 311 of title 18, United States Code [18 U.S.C.A. § 4201 et seq. (repealed)], and the Parole Commission, each reference in such section to 'fifteen years' or 'fifteen-year period' shall be deemed to be a reference to 'eighteen years' or 'eighteen-year period', respectively.

"(b) **Study by Attorney General.**—The Attorney General, not later than 60 days after the enactment of this Act [Nov. 2, 2002], should establish a committee within the Department of Justice to evaluate the merits and feasibility of transferring the United States Parole Commission's functions regarding the supervised release of District of Columbia offenders to another entity or entities outside the Department of Justice. This committee should consult with the District of Columbia Superior Court and the District of Columbia Court Services and Offender Supervision Agency, and should report its findings and recommendations to the Attorney General. The Attorney General, in turn, should submit to Congress, not later than 18 months after the enactment of this Act [Nov. 2, 2002], a long-term plan for the most effective and cost-efficient assignment of responsibilities relating to the supervised release of District of Columbia offenders.

"(c) **Service as Commissioner.**—Notwithstanding subsection (a) [of this note], the final clause of the fourth sentence of section 4202 of title 18, United States Code [this section], which begins 'except that', shall not apply to a person serving as a Commissioner of the United States Parole Commission when this Act [Pub.L. 107–273, Nov. 2, 2002, 116 Stat. 1758; see Tables for complete classification] takes effect."

§ 4203. Powers and duties of the Commission

(a) The Commission shall meet at lease quarterly, and by majority vote shall—

(1) promulgate rules and regulations establishing guidelines for the powers enumerated in subsection (b) of this section and such other rules and regulations as are necessary to carry out a national parole policy and the purposes of this chapter;

(2) create such regions as are necessary to carry out the provisions of this chapter; and

(3) ratify, revise, or deny any request for regular, supplemental, or deficiency appropriations, prior to the submission of the requests to the Office of Management and Budget by the Chairman, which requests shall be separate from those of any other agency of the Department of Justice.

(b) The Commission, by majority vote, and pursuant to the procedures set out in this chapter, shall have the power to—

(1) grant or deny an application or recommendation to parole any eligible prisoner;

(2) impose reasonable conditions on an order granting parole;

(3) modify or revoke an order paroling any eligible prisoner; and

(4) request probation officers and other individuals, organizations, and public or private agencies to perform such duties with respect to any parolee as the Commission deems necessary for maintaining proper supervision of and assistance to such parolees; and so as to assure that no probation officers, individuals, organizations, or agencies shall bear excessive caseloads.

(c) The Commission, by majority vote, and pursuant to rules and regulations—

(1) may delegate to any Commissioner or commissioners powers enumerated in subsection (b) of this section;

(2) may delegate to hearing examiners any powers necessary to conduct hearings and proceedings, take sworn testimony, obtain and make a record of pertinent information, make findings of probable cause and issue subpenas for witnesses or evidence in parole revocation proceedings, and recommend disposition of any matters enumerated in subsection (b) of this section, except that any such findings or recommendations shall be based upon the concurrence of not less than two hearing examiners;

(3) may delegate authority to conduct hearings held pursuant to section 4214 to any officer or employee of the executive or judicial branch of Federal or State government; and

(4) may review, or may delegate to the National Appeals Board the power to review, any decision made pursuant to subparagraph (1) of this subsection except that any such decision so reviewed must be reaffirmed, modified or reversed within thirty days of the date the decision is rendered, and, in case of such review, the individual to whom the decision applies shall be informed in writing of the Commission's actions with respect thereto and the reasons for such actions.

(d) Except as otherwise provided by law, any action taken by the Commission pursuant to subsection (a) of this section shall be taken by a majority vote of all individuals currently holding office as members of the Commission which shall maintain and make available for public inspection a record of the final vote of each member on statements of policy and interpretations adopted by it. In so acting, each Commissioner shall have equal responsibility and authority, shall have full access to all information relating to the performance of such duties and responsibilities, and shall have one vote.

(e)(1) The Commission shall, upon the request of the head of any law enforcement agency of a State or of a unit of local government in a State, make available as expeditiously as possible to such agency, with respect to individuals who are under the jurisdiction of the Commission, who have been convicted of felony offenses against the United States, and who reside, are employed, or are supervised in the geographical area in which such agency has jurisdiction, the following information maintained by the Commission (to the extent that the Commission maintains such information)—

(A) the names of such individuals;

(B) the addresses of such individuals;

(C) the dates of birth of such individuals;

(D) the Federal Bureau of Investigation numbers assigned to such individuals;

(E) photographs and fingerprints of such individuals; and

(F) the nature of the offenses against the United States of which each such individual has been convicted and the factual circumstances relating to such offense.

(2) Any law enforcement agency which receives information under this subsection shall not disseminate such information outside of such agency.

(Added Pub.L. 94–233, § 2, Mar. 15, 1976, 90 Stat. 220, and amended Pub.L. 99–646, § 57(b), (c), Nov. 10, 1986, 100 Stat. 3611, 3612.)

§ 4204. Powers and duties of the Chairman

(a) The Chairman shall—

(1) convene and preside at meetings of the Commission pursuant to section 4203 and such additional meetings of the Commission as the Chairman may call or as may be requested in writing by at least three Commissioners;

(2) appoint, fix the compensation of, assign, and supervise all personnel employed by the Commission except that—

(A) the appointment of any hearing examiner shall be subject to approval of the Commission within the first year of such hearing examiner's employment; and

(B) regional Commissioners shall appoint and supervise such personnel employed regularly and full time in their respective regions as are compensated at a rate up to and including grade 9 of the General Schedule pay rates (5 U.S.C. 5332);

(3) assign duties among officers and employees of the Commission, including Commissioners, so as to balance the workload and provide for orderly administration;

(4) direct the preparation of requests for appropriations for the Commission, and the use of funds made available to the Commission;

(5) designate not fewer than three Commissioners to serve on the National Appeals Board of whom one shall be so designated to serve as vice chairman of the Commission (who shall act as Chairman of the Commission in the absence or disability of the Chairman or in the event of the vacancy of the Chairmanship), and designate, for each such region established pursuant to section 4203, one Commissioner to serve as regional Commissioner in each such region; except that in each such designation the Chairman shall consider years of service, personal preference and fitness, and no such designation shall take effect unless concurred in by the President, or his designee;

(6) serve as spokesman for the Commission and report annually to each House of Congress on the activities of the Commission; and

(7) exercise such other powers and duties and perform such other functions as may be necessary to carry out the purposes of this chapter or as may be provided under any other provision of law.

(b) The Chairman shall have the power to—

(1) without regard to section 3324(a) and (b) of title 31, enter into and perform such contracts, leases, cooperative agreements, and other transactions as may be necessary in the conduct of the functions of the Commission, with any public agency, or with any person, firm, association, corporation, educational institution, or nonprofit organization;

(2) accept voluntary and uncompensated services, notwithstanding the provisions of section 1342 of title 31;

(3) procure for the Commission temporary and intermittent services to the same extent as is authorized by section 3109(b) of title 5, United States Code;

(4) collect systematically the data obtained from studies, research, and the empirical experience of public and private agencies concerning the parole process;

(5) carry out programs of research concerning the parole process to develop classification systems which describe types of offenders, and to develop theories and practices which can be applied to the different types of offenders;

(6) publish data concerning the parole process;

(7) devise and conduct, in various geographical locations, seminars, workshops and training programs providing continuing studies and instruction for personnel of Federal, State and local agencies and private and public organizations working with parolees and connected with the parole process; and

(8) utilize the services, equipment, personnel, information, facilities, and instrumentalities with or without reimbursement therefor of other Federal, State, local, and private agencies with their consent.

(c) In carrying out his functions under this section, the Chairman shall be governed by the national parole policies promulgated by the Commission.

(Added Pub.L. 94–233, § 2, Mar. 15, 1976, 90 Stat. 221, and amended Pub.L. 97–258, § 3(e)(3), (4), Sept. 13, 1982, 96 Stat. 1064; Pub.L. 99–646, § 58(a), Nov. 10, 1986, 100 Stat. 3612.)

Delegation of Presidential Authority To Concur in Designations of Commissioners

Ex. Ord. No. 11919, June 9, 1976, 41 F.R. 23663, provided:

By virtue of the authority vested in me by section 301 of title 3, United States Code, and section 4204(a)(5) of title 18, United States Code, as enacted by the Parole Commission and Reorganization Act(Public Law 94–233), and as President of the United States of America, it is hereby ordered that the Attorney General shall serve as the President's designee for purposes of concurring in designations of Commissioners of the United States Parole Commission to serve on the National Appeals Board, as vice chairman of the Commission, and as regional Commissioner.

GERALD R. FORD

§ 4205. Time of eligibility for release on parole

(a) Whenever confined and serving a definite term or terms of more than one year, a prisoner shall be eligible for release on parole after serving one-third of such term or terms or after serving ten years of a life sentence or of a sentence of over thirty years, except to the extent otherwise provided by law.

(b) Upon entering a judgment of conviction, the court having jurisdiction to impose sentence, when in its opinion the ends of justice and best interest of the public require that the defendant be sentenced to imprisonment for a term exceeding one year, may (1) designate in the sentence of imprisonment imposed a minimum term at the expiration of which the prisoner shall become eligible for parole, which term may be less than but shall not be more than one-third of the maximum sentence imposed by the court, or (2) the court may fix the maximum sentence of imprisonment to be served in which event the court may specify that the prisoner may be released on parole at such time as the Commission may determine.

(c) If the court desires more detailed information as a basis for determining the sentence to be imposed, the court may commit the defendant to the custody of the Attorney General, which commitment shall be deemed to be for the maximum sentence of imprisonment prescribed by law, for a study as described in subsection (d) of this section. The results of such study, together with any recommendations which the Director of the Bureau of Prisons believes would be helpful in determining the disposition of the case, shall be furnished to the court within three months unless the court grants time, not to exceed an additional three months, for further study. After receiving such reports and recommendations, the court may in its discretion: (1) place the offender on probation as authorized by section 3651; or (2) affirm the sentence of imprisonment originally imposed, or reduce the sentence of imprisonment, and commit the offender under any applicable provision of law. The term of the sentence shall run from the date of original commitment under this section.

(d) Upon commitment of a prisoner sentenced to imprisonment under the provisions of subsection (a) or (b) of this section, the Director, under such regulations as the Attorney General may prescribe, shall cause a complete study to be made of the prisoner and shall furnish to the Commission a summary report together with any recommendations which in his opinion would be helpful in determining the suitability of the prisoner for parole. This report may include but shall not be limited to data regarding the prisoner's previous delinquency or criminal experience, pertinent circumstances of his social background, his capabilities, his mental and physical health, and such other factors as may be considered pertinent. The Commission may make such other investigation as it may deem necessary.

(e) Upon request of the Commission, it shall be the duty of the various probation officers and government bureaus and agencies to furnish the Commission information available to such officer, bureau, or agency, concerning any eligible prisoner or parolee and whenever not incompatible with the public interest, their views and recommendation with respect to any matter within the jurisdiction of the Commission.

(f) Any prisoner sentenced to imprisonment for a term or terms of not less than six months but not more than one year shall be released at the expiration of such sentence less good time deductions provided by law, unless the court which imposed sentence, shall, at the time of sentencing provide for the prisoner's release as if on parole after service of one-third of such term or terms notwithstanding the provisions of section 4164. This subsection shall not prevent delivery of any person released on parole to the authorities of any State otherwise entitled to his custody.

(g) At any time upon motion of the Bureau of Prisons, the court may reduce any minimum term to the time the defendant has served. The court shall have jurisdiction to act upon the application at any time and no hearing shall be required.

(h) Nothing in this chapter shall be construed to provide that any prisoner shall be eligible for release on parole if such prisoner is ineligible for such release under any other provision of law.

(Added Pub.L. 94–233, § 2, Mar. 15, 1976, 90 Stat. 222.)

§ 4206. Parole determination criteria

(a) If an eligible prisoner has substantially observed the rules of the institution or institutions to which he has been confined, and if the Commission, upon consideration of the nature and circumstances of the offense and the history and characteristics of the prisoner, determines:

(1) that release would not depreciate the seriousness of his offense or promote disrespect for the law; and

(2) that release would not jeopardize the public welfare; subject to the provisions of subsections (b) and (c) of this section, and pursuant to guidelines promulgated by the Commission pursuant to section 4203(a)(1), such prisoner shall be released.

(b) The Commission shall furnish the eligible prisoner with a written notice of its determination not later than twenty-one days, excluding holidays, after the date of the parole determination proceeding. If parole is denied such notice shall state with particularity the reasons for such denial.

(c) The Commission may grant or deny release on parole notwithstanding the guidelines referred to in subsection (a) of this section if it determines there is good cause for so doing: *Provided*, That the prisoner is furnished written notice stating with particularity the reasons for its determination, including a summary of the information relied upon.

(d) Any prisoner, serving a sentence of five years or longer, who is not earlier released under this section or any other applicable provision of law, shall be released on parole after having served two-thirds of each consecutive term or terms, or after serving thirty years of each consecutive term or terms of more than forty-five years including any life term, whichever is earlier: *Provided, however*, That the Commission shall not release such prisoner if it determines that he has seriously or frequently violated institution rules and regulations or that there is a reasonable probability that he will commit any Federal, State, or local crime.

(Added Pub.L. 94–233, § 2, Mar. 15, 1976, 90 Stat. 223.)

§ 4207. Information considered

In making a determination under this chapter (relating to release on parole) the Commission shall consider, if available and relevant:

(1) reports and recommendations which the staff of the facility in which such prisoner is confined may make;

(2) official reports of the prisoner's prior criminal record, including a report or record of earlier probation and parole experiences;

(3) presentence investigation reports;

(4) recommendations regarding the prisoner's parole made at the time of sentencing by the sentencing judge;

(5) [1] a statement, which may be presented orally or otherwise, by any victim of the offense for which the prisoner is imprisoned about the financial, social, psychological, and emotional harm done to, or loss suffered by such victim; and

(5) [1] reports of physical, mental, or psychiatric examination of the offender.

There shall also be taken into consideration such additional relevant information concerning the prisoner (including information submitted by the prisoner) as may be reasonably available.

(Added Pub.L. 94–233, § 2, Mar. 15, 1976, 90 Stat. 224, and amended Pub.L. 98–473, Title II, § 1408(a), Oct. 12, 1984, 98 Stat. 2177.)

[1] So in original. Two paragraphs (5) were enacted.

§ 4208. Parole determination proceeding; time

(a) In making a determination under this chapter (relating to parole) the Commission shall conduct a parole determination proceeding unless it determines on the basis of the prisoner's record that the prisoner will be released on parole. Whenever feasible, the initial parole determination proceeding for a prisoner eligible for parole pursuant to subsections (a) and (b)(1) of section 4205 shall be held not later than thirty days before the date of such eligibility for parole. Whenever feasible, the initial parole determination proceeding for a prisoner eligible for parole pursuant to subsection (b)(2) of section 4205 or released on parole and whose parole has been revoked shall be held not later than one hundred and twenty days following such prisoner's imprisonment or reimprisonment in a Federal institution, as the case may be. An eligible prisoner may knowingly and intelligently waive any proceeding.

(b) At least thirty days prior to any parole determination proceeding, the prisoner shall be provided with (1) written notice of the time and place of the proceeding, and (2) reasonable access to a report or other document to be used by the Commission in making its determination. A prisoner may waive such notice, except that if notice is not waived the proceeding shall be held during the next regularly scheduled proceedings by the Commission at the institution in which the prisoner is confined.

(c) Subparagraph (2) of subsection (b) shall not apply to—

(1) diagnostic opinions which, if made known to the eligible prisoner, could lead to a serious disruption of his institutional program;

(2) any document which reveals sources of information obtained upon a promise of confidentiality; or

(3) any other information which, if disclosed, might result in harm, physical or otherwise, to any person.

If any document is deemed by either the Commission, the Bureau of Prisons, or any other agency to fall within the exclusionary provisions of subparagraphs (1), (2), or (3) of this subsection, then it shall become the duty of the Commission, the Bureau, or such other agency, as the case may be, to summarize the basic contents of the material withheld, bearing in mind the need for confidentiality or the impact on the inmate, or both, and furnish such summary to the inmate.

(d)(1) During the period prior to the parole determination proceeding as provided in subsection (b) of this section, a prisoner may consult, as provided by the director, with a representative as referred to in subparagraph (2) of this subsection, and by mail or otherwise with any person concerning such proceeding.

(2) The prisoner shall, if he chooses, be represented at the parole determination proceeding by a representative who qualifies under rules and regulations promulgated by the Commission. Such rules shall not exclude attorneys as a class.

(e) The prisoner shall be allowed to appear and testify on his own behalf at the parole determination proceeding.

(f) A full and complete record of every proceeding shall be retained by the Commission. Upon request, the Commission shall make available to any eligible prisoner such record as the Commission may retain of the proceeding.

(g) If parole is denied, a personal conference to explain the reasons for such denial shall be held, if feasible, between the prisoner and a representative of the Commission at the conclusion of the proceeding. When feasible, the conference shall include advice to the prisoner as to what steps may be taken to enhance his chance of being released at a subsequent proceeding.

(h) In any case in which release on parole is not granted, subsequent parole determination proceedings shall be held not less frequently than:

(1) eighteen months in the case of a prisoner with a term or terms of more than one year but less than seven years; and

(2) twenty-four months in the case of a prisoner with a term or terms of seven years or longer.

(Added Pub.L. 94–233, § 2, Mar. 15, 1976, 90 Stat. 224, and amended Pub.L. 99–646, § 581(b), Nov. 10, 1986, 100 Stat. 3612.)

§ 4209. Conditions of parole

(a) In every case, the Commission shall impose as conditions of parole that the parolee not commit another Federal, State, or local crime, that the parolee not possess illegal controlled substances, and, if a fine was imposed, that the parolee make a diligent effort to pay the fine in accordance with the judgment. In every case, the Commission shall impose as a condition of parole for a person required to register under the Sex Offender Registration and Notification Act that the person comply with the requirements of that Act. In every case, the Commission shall impose as a condition of parole that the parolee cooperate in the collection of a DNA sample from the parolee, if the collection of such a sample is authorized pursuant to section 3 or section 4 of the DNA Analysis Backlog Elimination Act of 2000 or section 1565 of title 10. In every case, the Commission shall also impose as a condition of parole that the parolee pass a drug test prior to release and refrain from any unlawful use of a controlled substance and submit to at least 2 periodic drug tests (as determined by the Commission) for use of a controlled substance. The condition stated in the preceding sentence may be ameliorated or suspended by the Commission for any individual parolee if it determines that there is good cause for doing so. The results of a drug test administered in accordance with the provisions of the preceding sentence shall be subject to confirmation only if the results are positive, the defendant is subject to possible imprisonment for such failure, and either the defendant denies the accuracy of such test or there is some other reason to question the results of the test. A drug test confirmation shall be a urine drug test confirmed using gas chromatography/mass spectrometry techniques or such test as the Director of the Administrative Office of the United States Courts after consultation with the Secretary of Health and Human Services may determine to be of equivalent accuracy. The Commission shall consider whether the availability of appropriate substance abuse treatment programs, or an individual's current or past participation in such programs, warrants an exception in accordance with United States Sentencing Commission guidelines from the rule of section 4214(f) when considering any action against a defendant who fails a drug test. The Commission may impose or modify other conditions of parole to the extent that such conditions are reasonably related to—

(1) the nature and circumstances of the offense; and

(2) the history and characteristics of the parolee;

and may provide for such supervision and other limitations as are reasonable to protect the public welfare.

(b) The conditions of parole should be sufficiently specific to serve as a guide to supervision and conduct, and upon release on parole the parolee shall be given a certificate setting forth the conditions of his parole. An effort shall be made to make certain that the parolee understands the conditions of his parole.

(c) Release on parole or release as if on parole (or probation, or supervised release where applicable) may as a condition of such release require—

(1) a parolee to reside in or participate in the program of a residential community treatment center, or both, for all or part of the period of such parole; or

(2) a parolee to remain at his place of residence during nonworking hours and, if the Commission so directs, to have compliance with this condition monitored by telephone or electronic signaling devices, except that a condition under this paragraph may be imposed only as an alternative to incarceration.

A parolee residing in a residential community treatment center pursuant to paragraph (1) of this subsection may be required to pay such costs incident to such residence as the Commission deems appropriate.

(d)(1) The Commission may modify conditions of parole pursuant to this section on its own motion, or on the motion of a United States probation officer supervising a parolee: Provided, That the parolee receives notice of such action and has ten days after receipt of such notice to express his views on the proposed modification. Following such ten-day period, the Commission shall have twenty-one days, exclusive of holidays, to act upon such motion or application. Notwithstanding any other provision of this paragraph, the Commission may modify conditions of parole, without regard to such ten-day period, on any such motion if the Commission determines that the immediate modification of conditions of parole is required to prevent harm to the parolee or to the public.

(2) A parolee may petition the Commission on his own behalf for a modification of conditions pursuant to this section.

(3) The provisions of this subsection shall not apply to modifications of parole conditions pursuant to a revocation proceeding under section 4214.

(Added Pub.L. 94–233, § 2, Mar. 15, 1976, 90 Stat. 225, and amended Pub.L. 98–473, Title II, §§ 235(a)(1), 238(e), (i), Oct. 12, 1984, 98 Stat. 2031, 2039; Pub.L. 98–596, §§ 7, 12(a)(5), (9), (b), Oct. 30, 1984, 98 Stat. 3138, 3139, 3140; Pub.L. 99–646, § 58(c), Nov. 10, 1986, 100 Stat. 3612; Pub.L. 100–690, Title VII, §§ 7303(c)(1), (2), 7305(c), Nov. 18, 1988, 102 Stat. 4464, 4466; Pub.L. 103–322, Title II, § 20414(d), Sept. 13, 1994, 108 Stat. 1832; Pub.L. 105–119, Title I, § 115(a)(8)(B)(v), Nov. 26, 1997, 111 Stat. 2466; Pub.L. 106–546, § 7(c), Dec. 19, 2000, 114 Stat. 2734; Pub.L. 109–248, Title I, § 141(j), July 27, 2006, 120 Stat. 604.)

References in Text

Section 3 or section 4 of the DNA Analysis Backlog Elimination Act of 2000, referred to in text, is Pub.L. 106–546, §§ 3, 4, Dec. 19, 2000, 114 Stat. 2728, 2730, which are classified to section 14135a or section 14132b of Title 42.

The Sex Offender Registration and Notification Act, referred to in subsec. (a), is Title I [§ 101 et seq.] of Pub.L. 109–248, July 27, 2006, 120 Stat. 590, which enacted subchapter I of Chapter 151 of Title 42, 42 U.S.C.A. § 16901 et seq.; for complete classification, see Short Title note set out under 42 U.S.C.A. § 16901 and Tables.

Codifications

Pub.L. 98–473, §§ 235(a)(1), 238(e), (i), and Pub.L. 98–596, § 12(a)(5), (9), (b), amended section as follows: Section 238(e) of Pub.L. 98–473 amended provisions of subsec. (a) preceding par. (1) effective, pursuant to section 235(a)(1) of Pub.L. 98–473, the first day of the first calendar month beginning twenty-four months after Oct. 12, 1984. Section 12(a)(5) of Pub.L. 98–596 amended provisions of subsec. (a) preceding par. (1) to read as they had before amendment by Pub. L.98–473, applicable pursuant to section 12(b) of Pub.L. 98–596 on and after the date of enactment of Pub.L. 98–473 [Oct. 12, 1984]. Section 238(i) of Pub.L. 98–473, which repealed section 238 of Pub.L. 98–473 on the same date established by section 235(a)(1) of Pub.L. 98–473, was repealed by section 12(a)(9) of Pub.L. 98–596. The cumulative effect of the amendments resulted in no change in the text of this section.

Effective and Applicability Provisions

1997 Acts. Amendment by section 115(a)(8)(B)(v) of Pub.L. 105–119, which amended subsec. (a) of section 4209 of this title insofar as such section remains in effect with respect to certain individuals by inserting after the first sentence, which at the time of amendment ended with the phrase "that the parolee make a diligent effort to pay the fine in accordance with the judgment.", provision reading "In every case, the Commission shall impose as a condition of parole for a person described in section 4042(c)(4), that the parolee report the address where the parolee will reside and any subsequent change of residence to the probation officer responsible for supervision, and that the parolee register in any State where the parolee resides, is employed, carries on a vocation, or is a student (as such terms are defined under section 170101(a)(3) of the Violent Crime Control and Law Enforcement Act of 1994).", to take effect 1 year after Nov. 26, 1997, except that States shall have 3 years from Nov. 26, 1997 to implement amendments made by Pub.L. 104–119 which impose new requirements under subchapter VI (section 14071 et seq.) of chapter 136 of Title 42, The Public Health and Welfare, and the Attorney General may grant an additional 2 years to a State that is making good faith efforts to implement these amendments, see section 115(c) of Pub.L. 105–119, set out as a note under section 14071 of Title 42.

1988 Acts. Amendment by section 7303(c)(1), (2) of Pub.L. 100–690 applicable with respect to persons whose probation, supervised release, or parole begins after Dec. 31, 1988, see section 7303(d) of Pub.L. 100–690, set out as a note under section 3563 of this title.

§ 4210. Jurisdiction of Commission

(a) A parolee shall remain in the legal custody and under the control of the Attorney General, until the expiration of the maximum term or terms for which such parolee was sentenced.

(b) Except as otherwise provided in this section, the jurisdiction of the Commission over the parolee shall terminate no later than the date of the expiration of the maximum term or terms for which he was sentenced, except that—

(1) such jurisdiction shall terminate at an earlier date to the extent provided under section 4164 (relating to mandatory release) or section 4211 (relating to early termination of parole supervision), and

(2) in the case of a parolee who has been convicted of any criminal offense committed subsequent to his release on parole, and such offense is punishable by a term of imprisonment, detention or incarceration in any penal facility, the Commission shall determine, in accordance with the provisions of section 4214(b) or (c), whether all or any part of the unexpired term being served at the time of parole shall run concurrently or consecutively with the sentence imposed for the new offense, but in no case shall such service together with such time as the parolee has previously served in connection with the offense for which he was paroled, be longer than the maximum term for which he was sentenced in connection with such offense.

(c) In the case of any parolee found to have intentionally refused or failed to respond to any reasonable request, order, summons, or warrant of the Commission or any member or agent thereof, the jurisdiction of the Commission may be extended for the period during which the parolee so refused or failed to respond.

(d) The parole of any parolee shall run concurrently with the period of parole or probation under any other Federal, State, or local sentence.

(e) Upon the termination of the jurisdiction of the Commission over any parolee, the Commission shall issue a certificate of discharge to such parolee and to such other agencies as it may determine.

(Added Pub.L. 94–233, § 2, Mar. 15, 1976, 90 Stat. 226, and amended Pub.L. 99–646, § 58(d)(e), Nov. 10, 1986, 100 Stat. 3612).

§ 4211. Early termination of parole

(a) Upon its own motion or upon request of the parolee, the Commission may terminate supervision over a parolee prior to the termination of jurisdiction under section 4210.

(b) Two years after each parolee's release on parole, and at least annually thereafter, the Commission shall review the status of the parolee to determine the need for continued supervision. In calculating such two-year period there shall not be included any period of release on parole prior to the most recent such release, nor any period served in confinement on any other sentence.

(c)(1) Five years after each parolee's release on parole, the Commission shall terminate supervision over such parolee unless it is determined, after a hearing conducted in accordance with the procedures prescribed in section 4214(a)(2), that such supervision should not be terminated because there is a likelihood that the parolee will engage in conduct violating any criminal law.

(2) If supervision is not terminated under subparagraph (1) of this subsection the parolee may request a hearing annually thereafter, and a hearing, with procedures as provided in subparagraph (1) of this subsection shall be conducted with respect to such termination of supervision not less frequently than biennially.

(3) In calculating the five-year period referred to in subparagraph (1), there shall not be included any period of release on parole prior to the most recent such release, nor any period served in confinement on any other sentence.

(Added Pub.L. 94–233, § 2, Mar. 15, 1976, 90 Stat. 227.)

§ 4212. Aliens

When an alien prisoner subject to deportation becomes eligible for parole, the Commission may authorize the release of such prisoner on condition that such person be deported and remain outside the United States.

Such prisoner when his parole becomes effective, shall be delivered to the duly authorized immigration official for deportation.

(Added Pub.L. 94–233, § 2, Mar. 15, 1976, 90 Stat. 227.)

§ 4213. Summons to appear or warrant for retaking of parolee

(a) If any parolee is alleged to have violated his parole, the Commission may—

(1) summon such parolee to appear at a hearing conducted pursuant to section 4214; or

(2) issue a warrant and retake the parolee as provided in this section.

(b) Any summons or warrant issued under this section shall be issued by the Commission as soon as practicable after discovery of the alleged violation, except when delay is deemed necessary. Imprisonment in an institution shall not be deemed grounds for delay of such issuance, except that, in the case of any parolee charged with a criminal offense, issuance of a summons or warrant may be suspended pending disposition of the charge.

(c) Any summons or warrant issued pursuant to this section shall provide the parolee with written notice of—

(1) the conditions of parole he is alleged to have violated as provided under section 4209;

(2) his rights under this chapter; and

(3) the possible action which may be taken by the Commission.

(d) Any officer of any Federal penal or correctional institution, or any Federal officer authorized to serve criminal process within the United States, to whom a warrant issued under this section is delivered, shall execute such warrant by taking such parolee and returning him to the custody of the regional commissioner, or to the custody of the Attorney General, if the Commission shall so direct.

(Added Pub.L. 94–233, § 2, Mar. 15, 1976, 90 Stat. 227.)

§ 4214. Revocation of parole

(a)(1) Except as provided in subsections (b) and (c), any alleged parole violator summoned or retaken under section 4213 shall be accorded the opportunity to have—

(A) a preliminary hearing at or reasonably near the place of the alleged parole violation or arrest, without unnecessary delay, to determine if there is probable cause to believe that he has violated a condition of his parole; and upon a finding of probable cause a digest shall be prepared by the Commission setting forth in writing the factors considered and the reasons for the decision, a copy of which shall be given to the parolee within a reasonable period of time; except that after a finding of probable cause the Commission may restore any parolee to parole supervision if:

(i) continuation of revocation proceedings is not warranted; or

(ii) incarceration of the parolee pending further revocation proceedings is not warranted by the alleged frequency or seriousness of such violation or violations;

(iii) the parolee is not likely to fail to appear for further proceedings; and

(iv) the parolee does not constitute a danger to himself or others.

(B) upon a finding of probable cause under subparagraph (1)(A), a revocation hearing at or reasonably near the place of the alleged parole violation or arrest within sixty days of such determination of probable cause except that a revocation hearing may be held at the same time and place set for the preliminary hearing.

(2) Hearings held pursuant to subparagraph (1) of this subsection shall be conducted by the Commission in accordance with the following procedures:

(A) notice to the parolee of the conditions of parole alleged to have been violated, and the time, place, and purposes of the scheduled hearing;

(B) opportunity for the parolee to be represented by an attorney (retained by the parolee, or if he is financially unable to retain counsel, counsel shall be provided pursuant to section 3006A) or, if he so chooses, a representative as provided by rules and regulations, unless the parolee knowingly and intelligently waives such representation.

(C) opportunity for the parolee to appear and testify, and present witnesses and relevant evidence on his own behalf; and

(D) opportunity for the parolee to be apprised of the evidence against him and, if he so requests, to confront and cross-examine adverse witnesses, unless the Commission specifically finds substantial reason for not so allowing.

For the purposes of subparagraph (1) of this subsection, the Commission may subpena witnesses and evidence, and pay witness fees as established for the courts of the United States. If a person refuses to obey such a subpena, the Commission may petition a court of the United States for the judicial district in which such parole proceeding is being conducted, or in which such person may be found, to request such person to attend, testify, and produce evidence. The court may issue an order requiring such person to appear before the Commission, when the court finds such information, thing, or testimony directly related to a matter with respect to which the Commission is empowered to make a determination under this section. Failure to obey such an order is punishable by such court as a contempt. All process in such a case may be served in the judicial district in which such a parole proceeding is being conducted, or in which such person may be found.

(b)(1) Conviction for any criminal offense committed subsequent to release on parole shall constitute probable cause for purposes of subsection (a) of this section. In cases in which a parolee has been convicted of such an offense and is serving a new sentence in an institution, a parole revocation warrant or summons issued pursuant to section 4213 may be placed against him as a detainer. Such detainer shall be reviewed by the Commission within one hundred and eighty days of notification to the Commission of placement. The parolee shall receive notice of the pending review, have an opportunity to submit a written application containing information relative to the disposition of the detainer, and, unless waived, shall have counsel as provided in subsection (a)(2)(B) of this section to assist him in the preparation of such application.

(2) If the Commission determines that additional information is needed to review a detainer, a dispositional hearing may be held at the institution where the parolee is confined. The parolee shall have notice of such hearing, be allowed to appear and testify on his own behalf, and, unless waived, shall have counsel as provided in subsection (a)(2)(B) of this section.

(3) Following the disposition review, the Commission may:

(A) let the detainer stand; or

(B) withdraw the detainer.

(c) Any alleged parole violator who is summoned or retaken by warrant under section 4213 who knowingly and intelligently waives his right to a hearing under subsection (a) of this section, or who knowingly and intelligently admits violation at a preliminary hearing held pursuant to subsection (a)(1)(A) of this section, or who is retaken pursuant to subsection (b) of this section, shall receive a revocation hearing within ninety days of the date of retaking. The Commission may conduct such hearing at the institution to which he has been returned, and the alleged parole violator shall have notice of such hearing, be allowed to appear and testify on his own behalf, and, unless waived, shall have counsel or another representative as provided in subsection (a)(2)(B) of this section.

(d) Whenever a parolee is summoned or retaken pursuant to section 4213, and the Commission finds pursuant to the procedures of this section and by a preponderance of the evidence that the parolee has violated a condition of his parole the Commission may take any of the following actions:

(1) restore the parolee to supervision;

(2) reprimand the parolee;

(3) modify the parolee's conditions of the parole;

(4) refer the parolee to a residential community treatment center for all or part of the remainder of his original sentence; or

(5) formally revoke parole or release as if on parole pursuant to this title.

The Commission may take any such action provided it has taken into consideration whether or not the parolee has been convicted of any Federal, State, or local crime subsequent to his release on parole, and the seriousness thereof, or whether such action is warranted by the frequency or seriousness of the parolee's violation of any other condition or conditions of his parole.

(e) The Commission shall furnish the parolee with a written notice of its determination not later than twenty-one days, excluding holidays, after the date of the revocation hearing. If parole is revoked, a digest shall be prepared by the Commission setting forth in writing the factors considered and reasons for such action, a copy of which shall be given to the parolee.

(f) Notwithstanding any other provision of this section, a parolee who is found by the Commission to be in possession of a controlled substance shall have his parole revoked. (Added Pub.L. 94–233, § 2, Mar. 15, 1976, 90 Stat. 228, and amended Pub.L. 98–473, Title II, §§ 235(a)(1), 238(f), (i), Oct. 12, 1984, 98 Stat. 2031, 2039; Pub.L. 98–596, § 12(a)(6), (9), (b), Oct. 30, 1984, 98 Stat. 3139, 3140; Pub.L. 99–646, § 58(f), Nov. 10, 1986, 100 Stat. 3612; Pub.L. 100–690, Title VII, § 7303(c)(3), Nov. 18, 1988, 102 Stat. 4464.)

Codifications

Pub.L. 98–473, §§ 235(a)(1), 238(f), (i), and Pub.L. 98–596, § 12(a)(6), (9), (b), amended section as follows: Section 238(f) of Pub.L. 98–473 amended par. (1) effective pursuant to section 235(a)(1) of Pub.L. 98–473 the first day of the first calendar month beginning twenty-four months after Oct. 12, 1984. Section 12(a)(6) of Pub. L. 98–596 amended par. (1) to read as it had before amendment by Pub.L. 98–473, applicable pursuant to section 12(b) of Pub.L. 98–596 on and after the date of enactment of Pub.L. 98–473 [Oct. 12, 1984]. Section 238(i) of Pub.L. 98–473, which repealed section 238 of Pub.L. 98–473 on the same date established by section 235(a)(1) of Pub.L. 98–473, was repealed by section 12(a)(9) of Pub.L. 98–596. The cumulative effect of the amendments resulted in no change in the text of this section.

Effective and Applicability Provisions

1988 Acts. Amendment by section 7303(c)(3) of Pub.L. 100–690 applicable with respect to persons whose probation, supervised release, or parole begins after Dec. 31, 1988, see section 7303(d) of Pub.L. 100–690, set out as a note under section 3563 of this title.

§ 4215. Appeal

(a) Whenever parole release is denied under section 4206, parole conditions are imposed or modified under section 4209, parole discharge is denied under section 4211(c), or parole is modified or revoked under section 4214, the individual to whom any such decision applies may appeal such decision by submitting a written application to the National Appeal [Appeals] Board not later than thirty days following the date on which the decision is rendered.

(b) The National Appeals Board, upon receipt of the appellant's papers, must act pursuant to rules and regulations within sixty days to reaffirm, modify, or reverse the decision and shall inform the appellant in writing of the decision and the reasons therefor.

(c) The National Appeals Board may review any decision of a regional commissioner upon the written request of the Attorney General filed not later than thirty days following the decision and, by majority vote, shall reaffirm, modify, or reverse the decision within sixty days of the receipt of the Attorney General's request. The Board shall inform the Attorney General and the individual to whom the decision applies in writing of its decision and the reasons therefor.

(Added Pub.L. 94–233, § 2, Mar. 15, 1976, 90 Stat. 230, and amended Pub.L. 98–473, Title II, § 1408(c), Oct. 12, 1984, 98 Stat. 2178.)

[§ 4216. Repealed. Pub.L. 99–646, § 3(a), Nov. 10, 1986, 100 Stat. 3592]

Section, Pub.L. 94–233, § 2, Mar. 15, 1976, 90 Stat. 239, authorized imposition of sentence on young adult offenders pursuant to the Federal Youth Corrections Act.

[§ 4217. Repealed. Pub.L. 99–646, § 58(g)(1), Nov. 10, 1986, 100 Stat. 3612, as amended Pub.L. 100–690, Title VII, § 7014, Nov. 18, 1988, 102 Stat. 4935]

Section, added Pub.L. 94–233, § 2, Mar. 15, 1976, 90 Stat. 231, authorized execution of warrants to retake Canal Zone parole violators.

§ 4218. Applicability of Administrative Procedure Act

(a) For purposes of the provisions of chapter 5 of title 5, United States Code, other than sections 554, 555, 556, and 557, the Commission is an "agency" as defined in such chapter.

(b) For purposes of subsection (a) of this section, section 553(b)(3)(A) of title 5, United States Code, relating to rulemaking, shall be deemed not to include the phrase "general statements of policy".

(c) To the extent that actions of the Commission pursuant to section 4203(a)(1) are not in accord with the provisions of section 553 of title 5, United States Code, they shall be reviewable in accordance with the provisions of sections 701 through 706 of title 5, United States Code.

(d) Actions of the Commission pursuant to paragraphs (1), (2), and (3) of section 4203(b) shall be considered actions committed to agency discretion for purposes of section 701(a)(2) of title 5, United States Code.

(Added Pub.L. 94–233, § 2, Mar. 15, 1976, 90 Stat. 231.)

CHAPTER 313—OFFENDERS WITH MENTAL DISEASE OR DEFECT

§ 4241. Determination of mental competency to stand trial to undergo postrelease proceedings

(a) Motion to determine competency of defendant.—At any time after the commencement of a prosecution for an offense and prior to the sentencing of the defendant, or at any time after the commencement of probation or supervised release and prior to the completion of the sentence, the defendant or the attorney for the Government may file a motion for a hearing to determine the mental competency of the defendant. The court shall grant the motion, or shall order such a hearing on its own motion, if there is reasonable cause to believe that the defendant may presently be suffering from a mental disease or defect rendering him mentally incompetent to the extent that he is unable to understand the nature and consequences of the proceedings against him or to assist properly in his defense.

(b) Psychiatric or psychological examination and report.—Prior to the date of the hearing, the court may order that a psychiatric or psychological examination of the defendant be conducted, and that a psychiatric or psychological report be filed with the court, pursuant to the provisions of section 4247 (b) and (c).

(c) Hearing.—The hearing shall be conducted pursuant to the provisions of section 4247(d).

(d) Determination and disposition.—If, after the hearing, the court finds by a preponderance of the evidence that the defendant is presently suffering from a mental disease or defect rendering him mentally incompetent to the extent that he is unable to understand the nature and consequences of the proceedings against him or to assist properly in his defense, the court shall commit the defendant to the custody of the Attorney General. The Attorney General shall hospitalize the defendant for treatment in a suitable facility—

(1) for such a reasonable period of time, not to exceed four months, as is necessary to determine whether there is a substantial probability that in the foreseeable future he will attain the capacity to permit the proceedings to go forward; and

(2) for an additional reasonable period of time until—

(A) his mental condition is so improved that trial may proceed, if the court finds that there is a substantial probability that within such additional period of time he will attain the capacity to permit the proceedings to go forward; or

(B) the pending charges against him are disposed of according to law;

whichever is earlier.

If, at the end of the time period specified, it is determined that the defendant's mental condition has not so improved as to permit proceedings to go forward, the defendant is subject to the provisions of sections 4246 and 4248.

(e) Discharge.—When the director of the facility in which a defendant is hospitalized pursuant to subsection (d) determines that the defendant has recovered to such an extent that he is able to understand the nature and consequences of the proceedings against him and to assist properly in his defense, he shall promptly file a certificate to that effect with the clerk of the court that ordered the commitment. The clerk shall send a copy of the certificate to the defendant's counsel and to the attorney for the Government. The court shall hold a hearing, conducted pursuant to the provisions of section 4247(d), to determine the competency of the defendant. If, after the hearing, the court finds by a preponderance of the evidence that the defendant has recovered to such an extent that he is able to understand the nature and consequences of the proceedings against him and to assist properly in his defense, the court shall order his immediate discharge from the facility in which he is hospitalized and shall set the date for trial or other proceedings. Upon discharge, the defendant is subject to the provisions of chapters 207 and 227.

(f) Admissibility of finding of competency.—A finding by the court that the defendant is mentally competent to stand trial shall not prejudice the defendant in raising the issue of his insanity as a defense to the offense charged, and shall not be admissible as evidence in a trial for the offense charged.

(June 25, 1948, c. 645, 62 Stat. 855; Oct. 12, 1984, Pub.L. 98–473, Title II, § 403(a), 98 Stat. 2057; July 27, 2006, Pub.L. 109–248, Title III, § 302(2), 120 Stat. 619.)

HISTORICAL AND STATUTORY NOTES

References in Text

Chapters 207 and 227, referred to in subsec. (e), are chapters 207, Release and detention pending judicial proceedings, and 227, Sentences, of this title, 18 U.S.C.A. § 3141 et seq. and § 3551 et seq., respectively.

Short Title

1984 Acts. Section 401 of Pub.L. 98–473 provided that: "This chapter [amending this chapter, section 3006A of this title, rule 12.2 of the Federal Rules of Criminal Procedure and rule 704 of the Federal Rules of Evidence] may be sited [sic] as the 'Insanity Defense Reform Act of 1984'."

§ 4242. Determination of the existence of insanity at the time of the offense

(a) Motion for pretrial psychiatric or psychological examination.—Upon the filing of a notice, as provided in Rule 12.2 of the Federal Rules of Criminal Procedure, that the defendant intends to rely on the defense of insanity, the court, upon motion of the attorney for the Government, shall order that a psychiatric or psychological examination of the defendant be conducted, and that a psychiatric or psychological report be filed with the court, pursuant to the provisions of section 4247(b) and (c).

(b) Special verdict.—If the issue of insanity is raised by notice as provided in Rule 12.2 of the Federal Rules of Criminal Procedure on motion of the defendant or of the attorney for the Government, or on the court's own motion, the jury shall be instructed to find, or, in the event of a nonjury trial, the court shall find the defendant—

(1) guilty;

(2) not guilty; or

(3) not guilty only by reason of insanity.

(June 25, 1948, c. 645, 62 Stat. 855; Oct. 12, 1984, Pub.L. 98–473, Title II, § 403(a), 98 Stat. 2059.)

§ 4243. Hospitalization of a person found not guilty only by reason of insanity

(a) Determination of present mental condition of acquitted person.—If a person is found not guilty only by reason of insanity at the time of the offense charged, he shall be committed to a suitable facility until such time as he is eligible for release pursuant to subsection (e).

(b) Psychiatric or psychological examination and report.—Prior to the date of the hearing, pursuant to subsection (c), the court shall order that a psychiatric or psychological examination of the defendant be conducted, and that a psychiatric or psychological report be filed with the court, pursuant to the provisions of section 4247(b) and (c).

(c) Hearing.—A hearing shall be conducted pursuant to the provisions of section 4247(d) and shall take place not later than forty days following the special verdict.

(d) Burden of proof.—In a hearing pursuant to subsection (c) of this section, a person found not guilty only by reason of insanity of an offense involving bodily injury to, or serious damage to the property of, another person, or involving a substantial risk of such injury or damage, has the burden of proving by clear and convincing evidence that his release would not create a substantial risk of bodily injury to another person or serious damage of property of another due to a present mental disease or defect. With respect to any other offense, the person has the burden of such proof by a preponderance of the evidence.

(e) Determination and disposition.—If, after the hearing, the court fails to find by the standard specified in subsection (d) of this section that the person's release would not create a substantial risk of bodily injury to another person or serious damage of property of another due to a present mental disease or defect, the court shall commit the person to the custody of the Attorney General. The Attorney General shall release the person to the appropriate official of the State in which the person is domiciled or was tried if such State will assume responsibility for his custody, care, and treatment. The Attorney General shall make all reasonable efforts to cause such a State to assume such responsibility. If, notwithstanding such efforts, neither such State will assume such responsibility, the Attorney General shall hospitalize the person for treatment in a suitable facility until—

(1) such a State will assume such responsibility; or

(2) the person's mental condition is such that his release, or his conditional release under a prescribed regimen of medical, psychiatric, or psychological care or treatment, would not create a substantial risk of bodily injury to another person or serious damage to property of another;

whichever is earlier. The Attorney General shall continue periodically to exert all reasonable efforts to cause such a State to assume such responsibility for the person's custody, care, and treatment.

(f) Discharge.—When the director of the facility in which an acquitted person is hospitalized pursuant to subsection (e) determines that the person has recovered from his mental disease or defect to such an extent that his release, or his conditional release under a prescribed regimen of medical, psychiatric, or psychological care or treatment, would no longer create a substantial risk of bodily injury to another person or serious damage to property of another, he shall promptly file a certificate to that effect with the clerk of the court that ordered the commitment. The clerk shall send a copy of the certificate to the person's counsel and to the attorney for the Government. The court shall order the discharge of the acquitted person or, on the motion of the attorney for the Government or on its own motion, shall hold a hearing, conducted pursuant to the provisions of section 4247(d), to determine whether he should be released. If, after the hearing, the court finds by the standard specified in subsection (d) that the person has recovered from his mental disease or defect to such an extent that—

(1) his release would no longer create a substantial risk of bodily injury to another person or serious damage to property of another, the court shall order that he be immediately discharged; or

(2) his conditional release under a prescribed regimen of medical, psychiatric, or psychological care or treatment would no longer create a substantial risk of bodily injury to another person or serious damage to property of another, the court shall—

(A) order that he be conditionally discharged under a prescribed regimen of medical, psychiatric, or psychological care or treatment that has been prepared for him, that has been certified to the court as appropriate by the director of the facility in which he is committed, and that has been found by the court to be appropriate; and

(B) order, as an explicit condition of release, that he comply with the prescribed regimen of medical, psychiatric, or psychological care or treatment.

The court at any time may, after a hearing employing the same criteria, modify or eliminate the regimen of medical, psychiatric, or psychological care or treatment.

(g) Revocation of conditional discharge.—The director of a medical facility responsible for administering a regimen imposed on an acquitted person conditionally discharged under subsection (f) shall notify the Attorney General and the court having jurisdiction over the person of any failure of the person to comply with the regimen. Upon such notice, or upon other probable cause to believe that the person has failed to comply with the prescribed regimen of medical, psychiatric, or psychological care or treatment, the person may be arrested, and, upon arrest, shall be taken without unnecessary delay before the court having jurisdiction over him. The court shall, after a hearing, determine whether the person should be remanded to a suitable facility on the ground that, in light of his failure to comply with the prescribed regimen of medical, psychiatric, or psychological care or treatment, his continued release would create a substantial risk of bodily injury to another person or serious damage to property of another.

(h) Limitations on furloughs.—An individual who is hospitalized under subsection (e) of this section after being found not guilty only by reason of insanity of an offense for which subsection (d) of this section creates a burden of proof of clear and convincing evidence, may leave temporarily the premises of the facility in which that individual is hospitalized only—

(1) with the approval of the committing court, upon notice to the attorney for the Government and such individual, and after opportunity for a hearing;

(2) in an emergency; or

(3) when accompanied by a Federal law enforcement officer (as defined in section 115 of this title).

(i) Certain persons found not guilty by reason of insanity in the District of Columbia.—

(1) Transfer to custody of the Attorney General.—Notwithstanding section 301(h) of title 24 of the District of Columbia Code, and notwithstanding subsection 4247(j) of this title, all persons who have been committed to a hospital for the mentally ill pursuant to section 301(d)(1) of title 24 of the District of Columbia Code, and for whom the United States has continuing financial responsibility, may be transferred to the custody of the Attorney General, who shall hospitalize the person for treatment in a suitable facility.

(2) Application.—

(A) In general.—The Attorney General may establish custody over such persons by filing an application in the United States District Court for the District of Columbia, demonstrating that the person to be transferred is a person described in this subsection.

(B) Notice.—The Attorney General shall, by any means reasonably designed to do so, provide written notice of the proposed transfer of custody to such person or such person's guardian, legal representative, or other lawful agent. The person to be transferred shall be afforded an opportunity, not to exceed 15 days, to respond to the proposed transfer of custody, and may, at the court's discretion, be afforded a hearing on the proposed transfer of custody. Such hearing, if granted, shall be limited to a determination of whether the constitutional rights of such person would be violated by the proposed transfer of custody.

(C) Order.—Upon application of the Attorney General, the court shall order the person transferred to the custody of the Attorney General, unless, pursuant to a hearing under this paragraph, the court finds that the proposed transfer would violate a right of such person under the United States Constitution.

(D) Effect.—Nothing in this paragraph shall be construed to—

(i) create in any person a liberty interest in being granted a hearing or notice on any matter;

(ii) create in favor of any person a cause of action against the United States or any officer or employee of the United States; or

(iii) limit in any manner or degree the ability of the Attorney General to move, transfer, or otherwise manage any person committed to the custody of the Attorney General.

(3) Construction with other sections.—Subsections (f) and (g) and section 4247 shall apply to any person transferred to the custody of the Attorney General pursuant to this subsection.

(June 25, 1948, c. 645, 62 Stat. 855; Pub.L. 98–473, Title II, § 403(a), Oct. 12, 1984, 98 Stat. 2059; Nov. 18, 1988, Pub.L. 100–690, Title VII, § 7043, 102 Stat. 4400; Oct. 11, 1996, Pub.L. 104–294, Title III, § 301(a), 110 Stat. 3494.)

HISTORICAL AND STATUTORY NOTES

Severability of Provisions

Section 301(d) of Pub.L. 104–294 provided that: "If any provision of this section [section 301 of Pub.L. 104–294, which amended this section and enacted provisions set out as notes under this section], an amendment made by this section, or the application of such provision or amendment to any person or circumstance is held to be unconstitutional, the remainder of this section and the amendments made by this section shall not be affected thereby."

Transfer of Records

Section 301(b) of Pub.L. 104–294 provided that: "Notwithstanding any provision of the District of Columbia Code or any other provision of law, the District of Columbia and St. Elizabeth's Hospital—

"(1) not later than 30 days after the date of enactment of this Act [Oct. 11, 1996], shall provide to the Attorney General copies of all records in the custody or control of the District or the Hospital on such date of enactment pertaining to persons described in section 4243(i) of title 18, United States Code (as added by subsection (a)) [subsec. (i) of this section];

"(2) not later than 30 days after the creation of any records by employees, agents, or contractors of the District of Columbia or of St. Elizabeth's Hospital pertaining to persons described in section 4243(i) of title 18, United States Code [subsec. (i) of this section], provide to the Attorney General copies of all such records created after the date of enactment of this Act [Oct. 11, 1996];

"(3) shall not prevent or impede any employee, agent, or contractor of the District of Columbia or of St. Elizabeth's Hospital who has obtained knowledge of the persons described in section 4243(i) of title 18, United States Code [subsec. (i) of this section], in the employee's professional capacity from providing that knowledge to the Attorney General, nor shall civil or criminal liability attach to such employees, agents, or contractors who provide such knowledge; and

"(4) shall not prevent or impede interviews of persons described in section 4243(i) of title 18, United States Code [subsec. (i) of this section], by representatives of the Attorney General, if such persons voluntarily consent to such interviews."

Clarification of Effect on Certain Testimonial Privileges

Section 301(c) of Pub.L. 104–294 provided that: "The amendments made by this section [amending this section] shall not be construed to affect in any manner any doctor-patient or psychotherapist-patient testimonial privilege that may be otherwise applicable to persons found not guilty by reason of insanity and affected by this section [section 301 of Pub.L. 104–294, which amended this section and enacted provisions set out as notes under this section]."

§ 4244. Hospitalization of a convicted person suffering from mental disease or defect

(a) Motion to determine present mental condition of convicted defendant.—A defendant found guilty of an offense, or the attorney for the Government, may, within ten days after the defendant is found guilty, and prior to the time the defendant is sentenced, file a motion for a hearing on the present mental condition of the defendant if the motion is supported by substantial information indicating that the defendant may presently be suffering from a mental disease or defect for the treatment of which he is in need of custody for care or treatment in a suitable facility. The court shall grant the motion, or at any time prior to the sentencing of the defendant shall order such a hearing on its own motion, if it is of the opinion that there is reasonable cause to believe that the defendant may presently be suffering from a mental disease or defect for the treatment of which he is in need of custody for care or treatment in a suitable facility.

(b) Psychiatric or psychological examination and report.—Prior to the date of the hearing, the court may order that a psychiatric or psychological examination of the defendant be conducted, and that a psychiatric or psychological report be filed with the court, pursuant to the provisions of section 4247(b) and (c). In addition to the information required to be included in the psychiatric or psychological report pursuant to the provisions of section 4247(c), if the report includes an opinion by the examiners that the defendant is presently suffering from a mental disease or defect but that it is not such as to require his custody for care or treatment in a suitable facility, the report shall also include an opinion by the examiner concerning the sentencing alternatives that could best accord the defendant the kind of treatment he does need.

(c) Hearing.—The hearing shall be conducted pursuant to the provisions of section 4247(d).

(d) Determination and disposition.—If, after the hearing, the court finds by a preponderance of the evidence that the defendant is presently suffering from a mental disease or defect and that he should, in lieu of being sentenced to imprisonment, be committed to a suitable facility for care or treatment, the court shall commit the defendant to the custody of the Attorney General. The Attorney General shall hospitalize the defendant for care or treatment in a suitable facility. Such a commitment constitutes a provisional sentence of imprisonment to the maximum term authorized by law for the offense for which the defendant was found guilty.

(e) Discharge.—When the director of the facility in which the defendant is hospitalized pursuant to subsection (d) determines that the defendant has recovered from his mental disease or defect to such an extent that he is no longer in need of custody for care or treatment in such a facility, he shall promptly file a certificate to that effect with the clerk of the court that ordered the commitment. The clerk shall send a copy of the certificate to the defendant's counsel and to the attorney for the Government. If, at the time of the filing of the certificate, the provisional sentence imposed pursuant to subsection (d) has not expired, the court shall proceed finally to sentencing and may modify the provisional sentence.

(Added Sept. 7, 1949, c. 535, § 1, 63 Stat. 686, and amended Oct. 12, 1984, Pub.L. 98–473, Title II, § 403(a), 98 Stat. 2061.)

HISTORICAL AND STATUTORY NOTES

Severability of Provisions

Section 4 of Act Sept. 7, 1949, provided that: "If any provision of title 18, United States Code, sections 4244 to 4248, inclusive, or the application thereof to any person or circumstance shall be held invalid, the remainder of the said sections and the application of such provision to persons or circumstances other than those as to which it is held invalid shall not be affected thereby."

Use of Appropriations

Section 3 of Act Sept. 7, 1949, provided that: "The Attorney General may authorize the use of any unexpended balance of the appropriation for 'Support of United States prisoners' for carrying out the purposes of title 18, United States Code, sections 4244 to 4248, inclusive, or in payment of any expenses incidental thereto and not provided for by other specific appropriations."

§ 4245. Hospitalization of an imprisoned person suffering from mental disease or defect

(a) Motion to determine present mental condition of imprisoned person.—If a person serving a sentence of imprisonment objects either in writing or through his attorney to being transferred to a suitable facility for care or treatment, an attorney for the Government, at the request of the director of the facility in which the person is imprisoned, may file a motion with the court for the district in which the facility is located for a hearing on the present mental condition of the person. The court shall grant the motion if there is reasonable cause to believe that the person may presently be suffering from a mental disease or defect for the treatment of which he is in need of custody for care or treatment in a suitable facility. A motion filed under this subsection shall stay the transfer of the person pending completion of procedures contained in this section.

(b) Psychiatric or psychological examination and report.—Prior to the date of the hearing, the court may order that a psychiatric or psychological examination of the person may be conducted, and that a psychiatric or psychological report be filed with the court, pursuant to the provisions of section 4247(b) and (c).

(c) Hearing.—The hearing shall be conducted pursuant to the provisions of section 4247(d).

(d) Determination and disposition.—If, after the hearing, the court finds by a preponderance of the evidence that the person is presently suffering from a mental disease or defect for the treatment of which he is in need of custody for care or treatment in a suitable facility, the court shall commit the person to the custody of the Attorney General. The Attorney General shall hospitalize the person for treatment in a suitable facility until he is no longer in need of such custody for care or treatment or until the expiration of the sentence of imprisonment, whichever occurs earlier.

(e) Discharge.—When the director of the facility in which the person is hospitalized pursuant to subsection (d) determines that the person has recovered from his mental disease or defect to such an extent that he is no longer in need of custody for care or treatment in such a facility, he shall promptly file a certificate to that effect with the clerk of the court that ordered the commitment. The clerk shall send a copy of the certificate to the person's counsel and to the attorney for the Government. If, at the time of the filing of the certificate, the term of imprisonment imposed upon the person has not expired, the court shall order that the person be reimprisoned until the expiration of his sentence of imprisonment.

(Added Sept. 7, 1949, c. 535, § 1, 63 Stat. 687, and amended Oct. 12, 1984, Pub.L. 98–473, Title II, § 403(a), 98 Stat. 2062.)

§ 4246. Hospitalization of a person due for release but suffering from mental disease or defect

(a) Institution of proceeding.—If the director of a facility in which a person is hospitalized certifies that a person in the custody of the Bureau of Prisons whose sentence is about to expire, or who has been committed to the custody of the Attorney General pursuant to section 4241(d), or against whom all criminal charges have been dismissed solely for reasons related to the mental condition of the person, is presently suffering from a mental disease or defect as a result of which his release would create a substantial risk of bodily injury to another person or serious damage to property of another, and that suitable arrangements for State custody and care of the person are not available, he shall transmit the certificate to the clerk of the court for the district in which the person is confined. The clerk shall send a copy of the certificate to the person, and to the attorney for the Government, and, if the person was committed pursuant to section 4241(d), to the clerk of the court that ordered the commitment. The court shall order a hearing to determine whether the person is presently suffering from a mental disease or defect as a result of which his release would create a substantial risk of bodily injury to another person or serious damage to property of another. A certificate filed under this subsection shall stay the release of the person pending completion of procedures contained in this section.

(b) Psychiatric or psychological examination and report.—Prior to the date of the hearing, the court may order that a psychiatric or psychological examination of the defendant be conducted, and that a psychiatric or psychological report be filed with the court, pursuant to the provisions of section 4247(b) and (c).

(c) Hearing.—The hearing shall be conducted pursuant to the provisions of section 4247(d).

(d) Determination and disposition.—If, after the hearing, the court finds by clear and convincing evidence that the person is presently suffering from a mental disease or defect as a result of which his release would create a substantial risk of bodily injury to another person or serious damage to property of another, the court shall commit the person to the custody of the Attorney General. The Attorney General shall release the person to the appropriate official of the State in which the person is domiciled or was tried if such State will assume responsibility for his custody, care, and treatment. The Attorney General shall make all reasonable efforts to cause such a State to assume such responsibility. If, notwithstanding such efforts, neither such State will assume such responsibility, the Attorney General shall hospitalize the person for treatment in a suitable facility, until—

(1) such a State will assume such responsibility; or

(2) the person's mental condition is such that his release, or his conditional release under a prescribed regimen of medical, psychiatric, or psycho-

logical care or treatment would not create a substantial risk of bodily injury to another person or serious damage to property of another;

whichever is earlier. The Attorney General shall continue periodically to exert all reasonable efforts to cause such a State to assume such responsibility for the person's custody, care, and treatment.

(e) Discharge.—When the director of the facility in which a person is hospitalized pursuant to subsection (d) determines that the person has recovered from his mental disease or defect to such an extent that his release would no longer create a substantial risk of bodily injury to another person or serious damage to property of another, he shall promptly file a certificate to that effect with the clerk of the court that ordered the commitment. The clerk shall send a copy of the certificate to the person's counsel and to the attorney for the Government. The court shall order the discharge of the person or, on the motion of the attorney for the Government or on its own motion, shall hold a hearing, conducted pursuant to the provisions of section 4247(d), to determine whether he should be released. If, after the hearing, the court finds by a preponderance of the evidence that the person has recovered from his mental disease or defect to such an extent that—

(1) his release would no longer create a substantial risk of bodily injury to another person or serious damage to property of another, the court shall order that he be immediately discharged; or

(2) his conditional release under a prescribed regimen of medical, psychiatric, or psychological care or treatment would no longer create a substantial risk of bodily injury to another person or serious damage to property of another, the court shall—

(A) order that he be conditionally discharged under a prescribed regimen of medical, psychiatric, or psychological care or treatment that has been prepared for him, that has been certified to the court as appropriate by the director of the facility in which he is committed, and that has been found by the court to be appropriate; and

(B) order, as an explicit condition of release, that he comply with the prescribed regimen of medical, psychiatric, or psychological care or treatment.

The court at any time may, after a hearing employing the same criteria, modify or eliminate the regimen of medical, psychiatric, or psychological care or treatment.

(f) Revocation of conditional discharge.—The director of a medical facility responsible for administering a regimen imposed on a person conditionally discharged under subsection (e) shall notify the Attorney General and the court having jurisdiction over the person of any failure of the person to comply with the regimen. Upon such notice, or upon other probable cause to believe that the person has failed to comply with the prescribed regimen of medical, psychiatric, or psychological care or treatment, the person may be arrested, and, upon arrest, shall be taken without unnecessary delay before the court having jurisdiction over him. The court shall, after a hearing, determine whether the person should be remanded to a suitable facility on the ground that, in light of his failure to comply with the prescribed regimen of medical, psychiatric, or psychological care or treatment, his continued release would create a substantial risk of bodily injury to another person or serious damage to property of another.

(g) Release to state of certain other persons.—If the director of a facility in which a person is hospitalized pursuant to this chapter certifies to the Attorney General that a person, against whom all charges have been dismissed for reasons not related to the mental condition of the person, is presently suffering from a mental disease or defect as a result of which his release would create a substantial risk of bodily injury to another person or serious damage to property of another, the Attorney General shall release the person to the appropriate official of the State in which the person is domiciled or was tried for the purpose of institution of State proceedings for civil commitment. If neither such State will assume such responsibility, the Attorney General shall release the person upon receipt of notice from the State that it will not assume such responsibility, but not later than ten days after certification by the director of the facility.

(h) Definition.—As used in this chapter the term "State" includes the District of Columbia.

(Added Sept. 7, 1949, c. 535, § 1, 63 Stat. 687, and amended Oct. 12, 1984, Pub.L. 98–473, Title II, § 403(a), 98 Stat. 2062; Nov. 29, 1990, Pub.L. 101–647, Title XXXV, § 3599D, 104 Stat. 4932; Aug. 5, 1997, Pub.L. 105–33, Title XI, § 11204(1), 111 Stat. 739.)

HISTORICAL AND STATUTORY NOTES

Effective and Applicability Provisions

1997 Acts. Section 11721 of Title XI of Pub.L. 105–33 provided that: "Except as otherwise provided in this title, the provisions of this title [amending this section and section 4247 of this title, sections 6103 and 7213 of Title 26 and section 715 of Title 31, enacting section 138 of Title 40, amending provision set out as a note under section 4201 of Title 18, and enacting provisions set out as notes under section 4201 of this title and section 6103 of Title 26] shall take effect on the later of October 1, 1997, or the day the District of Columbia Financial Responsibility and Management Assistance Authority certifies that the financial plan and budget for the District government for fiscal year 1998 meet the requirements of section 201(c)(1) of the District of Columbia Financial Responsibility and Management Assistance Act of 1995 [not classified to the Code], as amended by this title."

§ 4247. General provisions for chapter

(a) Definitions.—As used in this chapter—

(1) "rehabilitation program" includes—

(A) basic educational training that will assist the individual in understanding the society to which he will return and that will assist him in understanding the magnitude of his offense and its impact on society;

(B) vocational training that will assist the individual in contributing to, and in participating in, the society to which he will return;

(C) drug, alcohol, and sex offender treatment programs, and other treatment programs that will assist the individual in overcoming a psychological or physical dependence or any condition that makes the individual dangerous to others; and

(D) organized physical sports and recreation programs;

(2) "suitable facility" means a facility that is suitable to provide care or treatment given the nature of the offense and the characteristics of the defendant;

(3) "State" includes the District of Columbia;

(4) "bodily injury" includes sexual abuse;

(5) "sexually dangerous person" means a person who has engaged or attempted to engage in sexually violent conduct or child molestation and who is sexually dangerous to others; and

(6) "sexually dangerous to others" with respect a person, means that the person suffers from a serious mental illness, abnormality, or disorder as a result of which he would have serious difficulty in refraining from sexually violent conduct or child molestation if released.

(b) Psychiatric or psychological examination.—A psychiatric or psychological examination ordered pursuant to this chapter shall be conducted by a licensed or certified psychiatrist or psychologist, or, if the court finds it appropriate, by more than one such examiner. Each examiner shall be designated by the court, except that if the examination is ordered under section 4245, 4246, or 4248, upon the request of the defendant an additional examiner may be selected by the defendant. For the purposes of an examination pursuant to an order under section 4241, 4244, or 4245, the court may commit the person to be examined for a reasonable period, but not to exceed thirty days, and under section 4242, 4243, 4246, or 4248 for a reasonable period, but not to exceed forty-five days, to the custody of the Attorney General for placement in a suitable facility. Unless impracticable, the psychiatric or psychological examination shall be conducted in the suitable facility closest to the court. The director of the facility may apply for a reasonable extension, but not to exceed fifteen days under section 4241, 4244, or 4245, and not to exceed thirty days under section 4242, 4243, 4246, or 4248 upon a showing of good cause that the additional time is necessary to observe and evaluate the defendant.

(c) Psychiatric or psychological reports.—A psychiatric or psychological report ordered pursuant to this chapter shall be prepared by the examiner designated to conduct the psychiatric or psychological examination, shall be filed with the court with copies provided to the counsel for the person examined and to the attorney for the Government, and shall include—

(1) the person's history and present symptoms;

(2) a description of the psychiatric, psychological, and medical tests that were employed and their results;

(3) the examiner's findings; and

(4) the examiner's opinions as to diagnosis, prognosis, and—

(A) if the examination is ordered under section 4241, whether the person is suffering from a mental disease or defect rendering him mentally incompetent to the extent that he is unable to understand the nature and consequences of the proceedings against him or to assist properly in his defense;

(B) if the examination is ordered under section 4242, whether the person was insane at the time of the offense charged;

(C) if the examination is ordered under section 4243 or 4246, whether the person is suffering from a mental disease or defect as a result of which his release would create a substantial risk of bodily injury to another person or serious damage to property of another;

(D) if the examination is ordered under section 4248, whether the person is a sexually dangerous person;

(E) if the examination is ordered under section 4244 or 4245, whether the person is suffering from a mental disease or defect as a result of which he is in need of custody for care or treatment in a suitable facility; or

(F) if the examination is ordered as a part of a presentence investigation, any recommendation the examiner may have as to how the mental condition of the defendant should affect the sentence.

(d) Hearing.—At a hearing ordered pursuant to this chapter the person whose mental condition is the subject of the hearing shall be represented by counsel and, if he is financially unable to obtain adequate representation, counsel shall be appointed for him pursuant to section 3006A. The person shall be afforded an opportunity to testify, to present evidence, to subpoena witnesses on his behalf, and to confront and cross-examine witnesses who appear at the hearing.

(e) Periodic report and information requirements.—(1) The director of the facility in which a person is committed pursuant to—

(A) section 4241 shall prepare semiannual reports; or

(B) section 4243, 4244, 4245, 4246, or 4248 shall prepare annual reports concerning the mental condition of the person and containing recommendations concerning the need for his continued commitment. The reports shall be submitted to the court that ordered the person's commitment to the facility and copies of the reports shall be submitted to such other persons as the court may direct. A copy of each such report concerning a person committed after the beginning of a prosecution of that person for violation of section 871, 879, or 1751 of this title shall be submitted to the Director of the United States Secret Service. Except with the prior approval of the court, the Secret Service shall not use or disclose the information in these copies for any purpose other than carrying out protective duties under section 3056(a) of this title.

(2) The director of the facility in which a person is committed pursuant to section 4241, 4243, 4244, 4245, 4246, or 4248 shall inform such person of any rehabilitation programs that are available for persons committed in that facility.

(f) Videotape record.—Upon written request of defense counsel, the court may order a videotape record made of the defendant's testimony or interview upon which the periodic report is based pursuant to subsection (e). Such videotape record shall be submitted to the court along with the periodic report.

(g) Habeas corpus unimpaired.—Nothing contained in section 4243, 4246, or 4248 precludes a person who is committed under either of such sections from establishing by writ of habeas corpus the illegality of his detention.

(h) Discharge.—Regardless of whether the director of the facility in which a person is committed has filed a certificate pursuant to the provisions of subsection (e) of section 4241, 4244, 4245, 4246, or 4248 or subsection (f) of section 4243, counsel for the person or his legal guardian may, at any time during such person's commitment, file with the court that ordered the commitment a motion for a hearing to determine whether the person should be discharged from such facility, but no such motion may be filed within one hundred and eighty days of a court determination that the person should continue to be committed. A copy of the motion shall be sent to the director of the facility in which the person is committed and to the attorney for the Government.

(i) Authority and responsibility of the Attorney General.—The Attorney General—

(A) may contract with a State, a political subdivision, a locality, or a private agency for the confinement, hospitalization, care, or treatment of, or the provision of services to, a person committed to his custody pursuant to this chapter;

(B) may apply for the civil commitment, pursuant to State law, of a person committed to his custody pursuant to section 4243, 4246, or 4248;

(C) shall, before placing a person in a facility pursuant to the provisions of section 4241, 4243, 4244, 4245, 4246, or 4248 consider the suitability of the facility's rehabilitation programs in meeting the needs of the person; and

(D) shall consult with the Secretary of the Department of Health and Human Services in the general implementation of the provisions of this chapter and in the establishment of standards for facilities used in the implementation of this chapter.

(j) Sections 4241, 4242, 4243, and 4244 do not apply to a prosecution under an Act of Congress applicable exclusively to the District of Columbia or the Uniform Code of Military Justice.

(Added Sept. 7, 1949, c. 535, § 1, 63 Stat. 687, and amended Oct. 12, 1984, Pub.L. 98–473, Title II, § 403(a), 98 Stat. 2065; Nov. 18, 1988, Pub.L. 100–690, Title VII, §§ 7044, 7047(a), 102 Stat. 4400, 4401; Sept. 13, 1994, Pub.L. 103–322, Title XXXIII, § 330003(d), 108 Stat. 2141; Aug. 5, 1997, Pub.L. 105–33, Title XI, § 11204(2), (3), 111 Stat. 739; July 27, 2006, Pub.L. 109–248, Title III, § 302(3), 120 Stat. 619.)

HISTORICAL AND STATUTORY NOTES

Effective and Applicability Provisions

1997 Acts. Amendment of subsecs. (a) and (j) by Pub.L. 105–33 effective on the later of October 1, 1997, or the day the District of Columbia Financial Responsibility and Management Assistance Authority certifies that the financial plan and budget for the District government for fiscal year 1998 meet certain requirements, see section 11721 of Pub.L. 105–33, set out as a note under § 4246 of this title.

Transfer of Functions

For transfer of the functions, personnel, assets, and obligations of the United States Secret Service, including the functions of the Secretary of the Treasury relating thereto, to the Secretary of Homeland Security, and for treatment of related references, see 6 U.S.C.A. §§ 381, 551(d), 552(d) and 557, and the Department of Homeland Security Reorganization Plan of November 25, 2002, as modified, set out as a note under 6 U.S.C.A. § 542.

§ 4248. Civil commitment of a sexually dangerous person

(a) Institution of proceedings.—In relation to a person who is in the custody of the Bureau of Prisons, or who has been committed to the custody of the Attorney General pursuant to section 4241(d), or against whom all criminal charges have been dismissed solely for reasons relating to the mental condition of the person, the Attorney General or any individual authorized by the Attorney General or the Director of the Bureau of Prisons may certify that the person is a sexually dangerous person, and transmit the certificate to the clerk of the court for the district in which the person is confined. The clerk shall send a copy of the certificate to the person, and to the attorney for the Government, and, if the person was committed pursuant to section 4241(d), to the clerk of the court that ordered the commitment. The court shall order a hearing to determine whether the person is a sexually dangerous person. A certificate filed under this subsection shall stay the release of the person pending completion of procedures contained in this section.

(b) Psychiatric or psychological examination and report.—Prior to the date of the hearing, the court may order that a psychiatric or psychological examination of the defendant be conducted, and that a psychiatric or psychological report be filed with the court, pursuant to the provisions of section 4247(b) and (c).

(c) Hearing.—The hearing shall be conducted pursuant to the provisions of section 4247(d).

(d) Determination and disposition.—If, after the hearing, the court finds by clear and convincing evidence that the person is a sexually dangerous person, the court shall commit the person to the custody of the Attorney General. The Attorney General shall release the person to the appropriate official of the State in which the person is domiciled or was tried if such State will assume responsibility for his custody, care, and treatment. The Attorney General shall make all reasonable efforts to cause such a State to assume such responsibility. If, notwithstanding such efforts, neither such State will assume such responsibility, the Attorney General shall place the person for treatment in a suitable facility, until—

(1) such a State will assume such responsibility; or

(2) the person's condition is such that he is no longer sexually dangerous to others, or will not be sexually dangerous to others if released under a prescribed regimen of medical, psychiatric, or psychological care or treatment;

whichever is earlier.

(e) Discharge.—When the Director of the facility in which a person is placed pursuant to subsection (d) determines that the person's condition is such that he is no longer sexually dangerous to others, or will not be sexually dangerous to others if released under a prescribed regimen of medical, psychiatric, or psychological care or treatment, he shall promptly file a certificate to that effect with the clerk of the court that ordered the commitment. The clerk shall send a copy of the certificate to the person's counsel and to the attorney for the Government. The court shall order the discharge of the person or, on motion of the attorney for the Government or on its own motion, shall hold a hearing, conducted pursuant to the provisions of section 4247(d), to determine whether he should be released. If, after the hearing, the court finds by a preponderance of the evidence that the person's condition is such that—

(1) he will not be sexually dangerous to others if released unconditionally, the court shall order that he be immediately discharged; or

(2) he will not be sexually dangerous to others if released under a prescribed regimen of medical, psychiatric, or psychological care or treatment, the court shall—

(A) order that he be conditionally discharged under a prescribed regimen of medical, psychiatric, or psychological care or treatment that has been prepared for him, that has been certified to the court as appropriate by the Director of the facility in which he is committed, and that has been found by the court to be appropriate; and

(B) order, as an explicit condition of release, that he comply with the prescribed regimen of medical, psychiatric, or psychological care or treatment.

The court at any time may, after a hearing employing the same criteria, modify or eliminate the regimen of medical, psychiatric, or psychological care or treatment.

(f) Revocation of conditional discharge.—The director of a facility responsible for administering a regimen imposed on a person conditionally discharged under subsection (e) shall notify the Attorney General and the court having jurisdiction over the person of any failure of the person to comply with the regimen. Upon such notice, or upon other probable cause to believe that the person has failed to comply with the prescribed regimen of medical, psychiatric, or psychological care or treatment, the person may be arrested, and, upon arrest, shall be taken without unnecessary delay before the court having jurisdiction over him. The court shall, after a hearing, determine whether the person should be remanded to a suitable facility on the ground that he is sexually dangerous to others in light of his failure to comply with the prescribed regimen of medical, psychiatric, or psychological care or treatment.

(g) Release to State of certain other persons.—If the director of the facility in which a person is hospitalized or placed pursuant to this chapter certifies to the Attorney General that a person, against whom all charges have been dismissed for reasons not related to the mental condition of the person, is a sexually dangerous person, the Attorney General shall release the person to the appropriate official of the State in which the person is domiciled or was tried for the purpose of institution of State proceedings for civil commitment. If neither such State will assume such responsibility, the Attorney General shall release the person upon receipt of notice from the State that it will not assume such responsibility, but not later than 10 days after certification by the director of the facility.

(Added Pub.L. 109–248, Title III, § 302(4), July 27, 2006, 120 Stat. 620.)

HISTORICAL AND STATUTORY NOTES

Prior Provisions

A prior section 4248, Sept. 7, 1949, c. 535, § 1, 63 Stat. 686, which related to the termination of custody by release or transfer, was omitted in the general amendment of this chapter by Pub.L. 98–473, Title II, c. IV, § 403(a), Oct. 12, 1984, 98 Stat. 2057.

[CHAPTER 314—REPEALED]

[§§ 4251 to 4255. Repealed. Pub.L. 98–473, Title II, § 218(a)(6), Oct. 12, 1984, 98 Stat. 2027]

HISTORICAL AND STATUTORY NOTES

Pub.L. 98–473, Title II, § 218(a)(6), Oct. 12, 1984, 98 Stat. 2027, repealed this chapter, effective Nov. 1, 1987. This chapter, which remains applicable for five years to individual who committed offense or act of juvenile delinquency prior to Nov. 1, 1987, and as to term of imprisonment under section 235(a)(1)(B) of Pub.L. 98–473, read as follows prior to repeal by Pub.L. 98–473:

§ 4251. Definitions

As used in this chapter—

(a) "Addict" means any individual who habitually uses any narcotic drug as defined in section 102(16) of the Controlled Substances Act so as to endanger the public morals, health, safety, or welfare, or who is or has been so far addicted to the use of such narcotic drugs as to have lost the power of self-control with reference to his addiction.

(b) "Crime of violence" includes voluntary manslaughter, murder, rape, mayhem, kidnapping, robbery, burglary or housebreaking in the nighttime, extortion accompanied by threats of violence, assault with a dangerous weapon or assault with intent to commit any offense punishable by imprisonment for more than one year, arson punishable as a felony, or an attempt or conspiracy to commit any of the foregoing offenses.

(c) "Treatment" includes confinement and treatment in an institution and under supervised aftercare in the community and includes, but is not limited to, medical, educational, social, psychological, and vocational services, corrective and preventive guidance and training, and other rehabilitative services designed to protect the public and benefit the addict by eliminating his dependence on addicting drugs, or by controlling his dependence, and his susceptibility to addiction.

(d) "Felony" includes any offense in violation of a law of the United States classified as a felony under section 1 of title 18 of the United States Code, and further includes any offense in violation of a law of any State, any possession or territory of the United States, the District of Columbia, the Canal Zone, or the Commonwealth of Puerto Rico, which at the time of the offense was classified as a felony by the law of the place where that offense was committed.

(e) "Conviction" and "convicted" mean the final judgment on a verdict or finding of guilty, a plea of guilty, or a plea of nolo contendere, and do not include a final judgment which has been expunged by pardon, reversed, set aside, or otherwise rendered nugatory.

(f) "Eligible offender" means any individual who is convicted of an offense against the United States, but does not include—

(1) an offender who is convicted of a crime of violence.

(2) an offender who is convicted of unlawfully importing or selling or conspiring to import or sell a narcotic drug, unless the court determines that such sale was for the primary purpose of enabling the offender to obtain a narcotic drug which he requires for his personal use because of his addiction to such drug.

(3) an offender against whom there is pending a prior charge of a felony which has not been finally determined or who is on probation or whose sentence following conviction on such a charge, including any time on parole or mandatory release, has not been fully served: *Provided,* That an offender on probation, parole, or mandatory release shall be included if the authority authorized to require his return to custody consents to his commitment.

(4) an offender who has been convicted of a felony on two or more prior occasions.

(5) an offender who has been committed under Title I of the Narcotic Addict Rehabilitation Act of 1966, under this chapter, under the District of Columbia Code, or under any State proceeding because of narcotic addiction on three or more occasions.

(Added Pub.L. 89–793, Title II, § 201, Nov. 8, 1966, 80 Stat. 1442, and amended Pub.L. 91–513, Title III, § 1102(s), Oct. 27, 1970, 84 Stat. 1294; Pub.L. 92–420, § 3, Sept. 16, 1972, 86 Stat. 677; Pub.L. 103–322, Title XXXIII, § 330021(1), Sept. 13, 1994, 108 Stat. 2150.)

§ 4252. Examination

If the court believes that an eligible offender is an addict, it may place him in the custody of the Attorney General for an examination to determine whether he is an addict and is likely to be rehabilitated through treatment. The Attorney General shall report to the court within thirty days; or any additional period granted by the court, the results of such examination and make any recommendations he deems desirable. An offender shall receive full credit toward the service of his sentence for any time spent in custody for an examination.

(Added Pub.L. 89–793, Title II, § 201, Nov. 8, 1966, 80 Stat. 1443.)

§ 4253. Commitment

(a) Following the examination provided for in section 4252, if the court determines that an eligible offender is an addict and is likely to be rehabilitated through treatment, it shall commit him to the custody of the Attorney General for treatment under this chapter, except that no offender shall be committed under this chapter if the Attorney General certifies that adequate facilities or personnel for treatment are unavailable. Such commitment shall be for an indeterminate period of time not to exceed ten years, but in no event shall it exceed the maximum sentence that could otherwise have been imposed.

(b) If, following the examination provided for in section 4252, the court determines that an eligible offender is not an addict, or is an addict not likely to be rehabilitated through treatment, it shall impose such other sentence as may be authorized or required by law.

(Added Pub.L. 89–793, Title II, § 201, Nov. 8, 1966, 80 Stat. 1443.)

§ 4254. Conditional release

An offender committed under section 4253(a) may not be conditionally released until he has been treated for six months following such commitment in an institution maintained or approved by the Attorney General for treatment. The Attorney General may then or at any time thereafter report to the Board of Parole whether the offender should be conditionally released under supervision. After receipt of the Attorney General's report, and certification from the Surgeon General of the Public Health Service that the offender has made sufficient progress to warrant his conditional release under supervision, the Board may in its discretion order such a release. In determining suitability for release, the Board may make any investigation it deems necessary. If the Board does not conditionally release the offender, or if a conditional release is revoked, the Board may thereafter grant a release on receipt of a further report from the Attorney General.

(Added Pub.L. 89–793, Title II, § 201, Nov. 8, 1966, 80 Stat. 1443.)

§ 4255. Supervision in the community

An offender who has been conditionally released shall be under the jurisdiction of the United States Parole Commission as if on parole, pursuant to chapter 311 of this title.

The Director of the Administrative Office of the United States Courts shall have the authority to contract with any appropriate public or private agency or person for the detection of and care in the community of an offender who is an alcohol-dependent person, or an addict or a drug-dependent person within the meaning of section 2 of the Public Health Service Act (42 U.S.C. 201). Such authority includes the authority to provide equipment and supplies; testing; medical, educational, social, psychological, and vocational services; corrective and preventive guidance and training; and other rehabilitative services designed to protect the public and benefit the alcohol-dependent person, addict, or drug-dependent person by eliminating that person's or addict's dependence on alcohol or addicting drugs, or by controlling that person's or addict's dependence and susceptibility to addiction. Such Director may negotiate and award such contracts without regard to section 3709 of the Revised Statutes (41 U.S.C. 5).

(Added Pub.L. 89–793, Title II, § 201, Nov. 8, 1966, 80 Stat. 1443, and amended Pub.L. 95–537, § 3, Oct. 27, 1978, 92 Stat. 2038; Pub.L. 99–570, Title I, § 1861(c), Oct. 27, 1986, 100 Stat. 3207–53; Pub.L. 99–646, § 19, Nov. 10, 1986, 100 Stat. 3596.)

Effective Date of Repeal; Savings Provisions

Repeal by Pub.L. 98–473 effective on the first day of first calendar month beginning thirty six months after Oct. 12, 1984, applicable only to offenses committed after taking effect of sections 211 to 239 of Pub.L. 98–473, applicable for five years after repeal pursuant to the provisions of section 235(b)(1) of Pub.L. 98–473, and except as otherwise provided for therein, see section 235 of Pub.L. 98–473, as amended, set out as a note under section 3551 of this title.

CHAPTER 315—DISCHARGE AND RELEASE PAYMENTS

[§ 4281. Repealed. Pub.L. 98–473, Title II, § 218(a)(7), Oct. 12, 1984, 98 Stat. 2027]

HISTORICAL AND STATUTORY NOTES

This section as in effect prior to repeal by Pub.L. 98–473 read as follows:

§ 4281. Discharge from prison

A person convicted under the laws of the United States shall, upon discharge from imprisonment, or release on parole, be furnished with transportation to the place of conviction or bona fide residence within the United States at the time of his commitment or to such place within the United states as may be authorized by the Attorney General.

He shall also be furnished with such suitable clothing as may be authorized by the Attorney General, and, in the discretion of the Attorney General, an amount of money not to exceed $100.

(June 25, 1948, c. 645, 62 Stat. 856; Sept. 19, 1962, Pub.L. 87–672, 76 Stat. 557.)

Effective Date of Repeal; Savings Provisions

Repeal by Pub.L. 98–473 effective on the first day of first calendar month beginning thirty six months after Oct. 12, 1984, applicable only to offenses committed after taking effect of sections 211 to 239 of Pub.L. 98–473, and except as otherwise provided for therein, see section 235 of Pub.L. 98–473, as amended, set out as a note under section 3551 of this title.

§ 4282. Arrested but unconvicted persons

On the release from custody of a person arrested on a charge of violating any law of the United States or of the Territory of Alaska, but not indicted nor informed against, or indicted or informed against but not convicted, and detained pursuant to chapter 207, or a person held as a material witness, the court in its discretion may direct the United States marshal for the district wherein he is released, pursuant to regulations promulgated by the Attorney General, to furnish the person so released with transportation and subsistence to the place of his arrest, or, at his election, to the place of his bona fide residence if such cost is not greater than to the place of arrest.

(June 25, 1948, c. 645, 62 Stat. 856; Oct. 12, 1984, Pub.L. 98–473, Title II, § 207, 98 Stat. 1986.)

HISTORICAL AND STATUTORY NOTES

Admission of Alaska as State

Admission of Alaska into the Union was accomplished Jan. 3, 1959, upon issuance of Proc.No. 3269, Jan. 3, 1959, 24 F.R. 81, 73 Stat. c16, as required by sections 1 and 8(c) of Pub.L. 85–508, July 7, 1958, 72 Stat. 339, set out as notes preceding section 21 of Title 48, Territories and Insular Possessions.

[§§ 4283, 4284. Repealed. Pub.L. 98–473, Title II, § 218(a)(7), Oct. 12, 1984, 98 Stat. 2027]

HISTORICAL AND STATUTORY NOTES

These sections as in effect prior to repeal by Pub.L. 98–473 read as follows:

§ 4283. Probation

A court of the United States when placing a defendant on probation, may direct the United States marshal to furnish the defendant with transportation to the place to which the defendant is required to proceed under the terms of his probation and, in addition, may also direct the marshal to furnish the defendant with an amount of money, not to exceed $30, for subsistence expense to his destination. In such event, such expenses shall be paid by the marshal.

(June 25, 1948, c. 645, 62 Stat. 856.)

§ 4284. Advances for rehabilitation

(a) The Attorney General, under such regulations as he prescribes, acting for himself or through such officers and employees as he designates, may use so much of the trust funds designated as "Commissary Funds, Federal Prisons" in section 1321(a)(22) of title 31, as may be surplus to other needs of the trust, to provide advances to prisoners at the time of their release, as an aid to their rehabilitation.

(b) An advance made hereunder shall in no instance exceed $150 except with the specific approval of the Attorney General, and shall in every case be secured by the personal note of the prisoner conditioned to make repayment monthly when employed, or otherwise possessed of funds, with interest at a rate not to exceed 6 per centum per annum and subject to an agreement on the part of the prisoner that the funds so advanced shall be expended only for the purposes designated in the loan agreement. Repayments of principal and interest shall be credited to the trust fund from which the advance was made. Any unpaid principal or interest on said note shall be considered as a debt due the United States.

(Added May 15, 1952, c. 289, § 1, 66 Stat. 72, and amended Sept. 13, 1982, Pub.L. 97–258, § 3(e)(5), 96 Stat. 1064.)

For applicability of sentencing provisions to offenses, see Effective Date and Savings Provisions, etc., note, section 235 of Pub.L. 98–473, as amended, set out under section 3551 of this title.

Effective Date of Repeal

Repeal by Pub.L. 98–473 effective on the first day of first calendar month beginning thirty six months after Oct. 12, 1984, applicable only to offenses committed after taking effect of sections 211 to 239 of Pub.L. 98–473, and except as otherwise provided for therein, see section 235 of Pub.L. 98–473, as amended, set out as a note under section 3551 of this title.

§ 4285. Persons released pending further judicial proceedings

Any judge or magistrate judge of the United States, when ordering a person released under chapter 207 on a condition of his subsequent appearance before that court, any division of that court, or any court of the United States in another judicial district in which criminal proceedings are pending, may, when the interests of justice would be served thereby and the United States judge or magistrate judge is satisfied, after appropriate inquiry, that the defendant is financially unable to provide the necessary transportation to appear before the required court on his own, direct the United States marshal to arrange for that person's means of noncustodial transportation or furnish the fare for such transportation to the place where his appearance is required, and in addition may direct the United States marshal to furnish that person with an amount of money for subsistence expenses to his destination, not to exceed the amount authorized as a per diem allowance for travel under section 5702(a) of title 5, United States Code. When so ordered, such expenses shall be paid by the marshal out of funds authorized by the Attorney General for such expenses.

(Added Pub.L. 95–503, § 1, Oct. 24, 1978, 92 Stat. 1704, and amended Pub.L. 101–647, Title XXXV, § 3599E, Nov. 29, 1990, 104 Stat. 4932; Pub.L. 101–650, Title III, § 321, Dec. 1, 1990, 104 Stat. 5117.)

HISTORICAL AND STATUTORY NOTES

Effective and Applicability Provisions

1978 Acts. Section 3 of Pub.L. 95–503 provided that: "The amendments made by this Act [enacting this section] shall take effect on October 1, 1978."

Change of Name

Words "magistrate judge" substituted for "magistrate" in text pursuant to section 321 of Pub.L. 101–650, set out as a note under 28 U.S.C.A. § 631.

CHAPTER 317—INSTITUTIONS FOR WOMEN

HISTORICAL AND STATUTORY NOTES

Savings Provisions of Pub.L. 98–473, Title II, c. II

See section 235 of Pub.L. 98–473, Title II, c. II, Oct. 12, 1984, 98 Stat. 2031, as amended, set out as a note under section 3551 of this title.

§ 4321. Board of Advisers

Four citizens of the United States of prominence and distinction, appointed by the President to serve without compensation, for terms of four years, together with the Attorney General of the United States, the Director of the Bureau of Prisons and the warden of the Federal Reformatory for Women, shall constitute a Board of Advisers of said Federal Reformatory for Women, which shall recommend ways and means for the discipline and training of the inmates, to fit them for suitable employment upon their discharge.

Any person chosen to fill a vacancy shall be appointed only for the unexpired term of the citizen whom he shall succeed.

(June 25, 1948, c. 645, 62 Stat. 856; Oct. 12, 1984, Pub.L. 98–473, Title II, § 223(n), 98 Stat. 2030.)

HISTORICAL AND STATUTORY NOTES

Effective and Applicability Provisions

1984 Acts. Amendment by Pub.L. 98–473 effective on the first day of first calendar month beginning thirty six months after Oct. 12, 1984, applicable only to offenses committed after taking effect of sections 211 to 239 of Pub.L. 98–473, and except as otherwise provided for therein, see section 235 of Pub.L. 98–473, as amended, set out as a note under section 3551 of this title.

CHAPTER 319—NATIONAL INSTITUTE OF CORRECTIONS

[1] Editorially supplied. Sections 4351 to 4353 added by Pub.L. 93–415 without corresponding enactment of chapter analysis.

HISTORICAL AND STATUTORY NOTES

Savings Provisions of Pub.L. 98–473, Title II, c. II

See section 235 of Pub.L. 98–473, Title II, c. II, Oct. 12, 1984, 98 Stat. 2031, as amended, set out as a note under section 3551 of this title.

§ 4351. Establishment; Advisory Board; appointment of members; compensation; officers; committees; delegation of powers; Director, appointment and powers [1]

(a) There is hereby established within the Bureau of Prisons a National Institute of Corrections.

(b) The overall policy and operations of the National Institute of Corrections shall be under the supervision of an Advisory Board. The Board shall consist of sixteen members. The following six individuals shall serve as members of the Commission ex officio: the Director of the Federal Bureau of Prisons or his designee, the Director of the Bureau of Justice Assistance or his designee, Chairman of the United States Sentencing Commission or his designee, the Director of the Federal Judicial Center or his designee, the Associate Administrator for the Office of Juvenile Justice and Delinquency Prevention or his designee, and the Assistant Secretary for Human Development of the Department of Health, Education, and Welfare or his designee.

(c) The remaining ten members of the Board shall be selected as follows:

(1) Five shall be appointed initially by the Attorney General of the United States for staggered terms; one member shall serve for one year, one member for two years, and three members for three years. Upon the expiration of each member's term, the Attorney General shall appoint successors who will each serve for a term of three years. Each member selected shall be qualified as a practitioner (Federal, State, or local) in the field of corrections, probation, or parole.

(2) Five shall be appointed initially by the Attorney General of the United States for staggered terms, one member shall serve for one year, three members for two years, and one member for three years. Upon the expiration of each member's term the Attorney General shall appoint successors who will each serve for a term of three years. Each member selected shall be from the private sector, such as business, labor, and education, having demonstrated an active interest in corrections, probation, or parole.

(d) The members of the Board shall not, by reason of such membership, be deemed officers or employees of the United States. Members of the Commission who are full-time officers or employees of the United States shall serve without additional compensation, but shall be reimbursed for travel, subsistence, and other necessary expenses incurred in the performance of the duties vested in the Board. Other members of the Board shall, while attending meetings of the Board or while engaged in duties related to such meetings or in other activities of the Commission pursuant to this title, be entitled to receive compensation at the rate not to exceed the daily equivalent of the rate authorized for GS–18 by section 5332 of title 5, United States Code, including traveltime, and while away from their homes or regular places of business may be allowed travel expenses, including per diem in lieu of subsistence equal to that authorized by section 5703 of title 5, United States Code, for persons in the Government service employed intermittently.

(e) The Board shall elect a chairman from among its members who shall serve for a term of one year. The members of the Board shall also elect one or more members as a vice-chairman.

(f) The Board is authorized to appoint, without regard to the civil service laws, technical, or other advisory committees to advise the Institute with respect to the administration of this title as it deems appropriate. Members of these committees not otherwise employed by the United States, while engaged in advising the Institute or attending meetings of the committees, shall be entitled to receive compensation at the rate fixed by the Board but not to exceed the daily equivalent of the rate authorized for GS–18 by section 5332 of title 5, United States Code, and while away from their homes or regular places of business may be allowed travel expenses, including per diem in lieu of subsistence equal to that authorized by section 5703 of title 5, United States Code, for persons in the Government service employed intermittently.

(g) The Board is authorized to delegate its powers under this title to such persons as it deems appropriate.

(h) The Institute shall be under the supervision of an officer to be known as the Director, who shall be appointed by the Attorney General after consultation with the Board. The Director shall have authority to supervise the organization, employees, enrollees, financial affairs, and all other operations of the Institute and may employ such staff, faculty, and administrative personnel, subject to the civil service and classification laws, as are necessary to the functioning of the Institute. The Director shall have the power to acquire and hold real and personal property for the Institute and may receive gifts, donations, and trusts on behalf of the Institute. The Director shall also have the power to appoint such technical or other advisory councils comprised of consultants to guide and advise the Board. The Director is authorized to delegate his powers under this title to such persons as he deems appropriate.

(Added Pub.L. 93–415, Title V, § 521, Sept. 7, 1974, 88 Stat. 1139, and amended Pub.L. 95–115, § 8(a), Oct. 3, 1977, 91 Stat. 1060; Pub.L. 98–473, Title II, § 223(*o*), Oct. 12, 1984, 98 Stat. 2030; Pub.L. 103–322, Title XXXIII, § 330001(i), Sept. 13, 1994, 108 Stat. 2140.)

1 Section catchline editorially supplied.

HISTORICAL AND STATUTORY NOTES

References in Text

The Office of Juvenile Justice and Delinquency Prevention, referred to in subsec. (b), as created by 42 U.S.C.A. § 5611, was formerly headed by an Associate Administrator. Pub.L. 98–473 amended 42 U.S.C.A. § 5611 to establish the Office of Juvenile Justice and Delinquency Prevention as headed by an Administrator.

The civil service laws, referred to in subsecs. (f) and (h), are set forth in Title 5, Government Organization and Employees. See, particularly, section 3301 et seq. of that Title.

The classification laws, referred to in subsec. (h), are classified generally to chapter 51 and subchapter III of chapter 53 of Title 5.

Change of Name

The Department of Health, Education, and Welfare was redesignated the Department of Health and Human Services by Pub.L. 96–88, Title V, § 509(b), Oct. 17, 1979, 93 Stat. 695, which is classified to section 3508(b) of Title 20, Education.

Effective and Applicability Provisions

1984 Acts. Amendment by Pub.L. 98–473 effective on the first day of first calendar month beginning thirty six months after Oct. 12, 1984, applicable only to offenses committed after taking effect of sections 211 to 239 of Pub.L. 98–473, and except as otherwise provided for therein, see section 235 of Pub.L. 98–473, as amended, set out as a note under section 3551 of this title.

1977 Acts. Amendment by Pub.L. 95–115 effective on Oct. 1, 1977, see section 263(c) of Pub.L. 93–415, as added by Pub.L. 95–115, set out as an Effective Date of 1977 Amendment note under section 5601 of Title 42, The Public Health and Welfare.

Termination of Advisory Boards

Advisory Boards established after Jan. 5, 1973, to terminate not later than the expiration of the two-year period beginning on the date of their establishment, unless, in the case of a board established by the President or an officer of the Federal Government, such board is renewed by appropriate action prior to the expiration of such two-year period, or in the case of a board established by the Congress, its duration is otherwise provided for by law, see sections 3(2) and 14 of Pub.L. 92–463, Oct. 6, 1972, 86 Stat. 770, 776, set out in the Appendix to Title 5, Government Organization and Employees.

Membership of National Institute of Corrections

See section 235(b)(5) of Pub.L. 98–473, Title II, c. II, Oct. 12, 1984, 98 Stat. 2033, set out as a note under section 3551 of this title.

§ 4352. Authority of Institute; time; records of recipients; access; scope of section[1]

(a) In addition to the other powers, express and implied, the National Institute of Corrections shall have authority—

(1) to receive from or make grants to and enter into contracts with Federal, State, and general units of local government, public and private agencies, educational institutions, organizations, and individuals to carry out the purposes of this chapter;

(2) to serve as a clearinghouse and information center for the collection, preparation, and dissemination of information on corrections, including, but not limited to, programs for prevention of crime and recidivism, training of corrections personnel, and rehabilitation and treatment of criminal and juvenile offenders;

(3) to assist and serve in a consulting capacity to Federal, State, and local courts, departments, and agencies in the development, maintenance, and coordination of programs, facilities, and services, training, treatment, and rehabilitation with respect to criminal and juvenile offenders;

(4) to encourage and assist Federal, State, and local government programs and services, and programs and services of other public and private agencies, institutions, and organizations in their efforts to develop and implement improved corrections programs;

(5) to devise and conduct, in various geographical locations, seminars, workshops, and training programs for law enforcement officers, judges, and judicial personnel, probation and parole personnel, correctional personnel, welfare workers, and other persons, including lay ex-offenders, and paraprofessional personnel, connected with the treatment and rehabilitation of criminal and juvenile offenders;

(6) to develop technical training teams to aid in the development of seminars, workshops, and training programs within the several States and with the State and local agencies which work with prisoners, parolees, probationers, and other offenders;

(7) to conduct, encourage, and coordinate research relating to corrections, including the causes, prevention, diagnosis, and treatment of criminal offenders;

(8) to formulate and disseminate correctional policy, goals, standards, and recommendations for Federal, State, and local correctional agencies, organizations, institutions, and personnel;

(9) to conduct evaluation programs which study the effectiveness of new approaches, techniques, systems, programs, and devices employed to improve the corrections system;

(10) to receive from any Federal department or agency such statistics, data, program reports, and other material as the Institute deems necessary to carry out its functions. Each such department or agency is authorized to cooperate with the Institute and shall, to the maximum extent practicable, consult with and furnish information to the Institute;

(11) to arrange with and reimburse the heads of Federal departments and agencies for the use of personnel, facilities, or equipment of such departments and agencies;

(12) to confer with and avail itself of the assistance, services, records, and facilities of State and local governments or other public or private agencies, organizations, or individuals;

(13) to enter into contracts with public or private agencies, organizations, or individuals, for the performance of any of the functions of the Institute; and

(14) to procure the services of experts and consultants in accordance with section 3109 of title 5 of the United States Code, at rates of compensation not to exceed the daily equivalent of the rate authorized for GS–18 by section 5332 of title 5 of the United States Code.

[(b) Repealed. Pub.L. 97–375, Title I, § 109(a), Dec. 21, 1982, 96 Stat. 1820]

(c) Each recipient of assistance under this chapter shall keep such records as the Institute shall prescribe, including records which fully disclose the amount and disposition by such recipient of the proceeds of such assistance, the total cost of the project or undertaking in connection with which such assistance is given or used, and the amount of that portion of the cost of the project or undertaking supplied by other sources, and such other records as will facilitate an effective audit.

(d) The Institute, and the Comptroller General of the United States, or any of their duly authorized representatives, shall have access for purposes of audit and examinations to any books, documents, papers, and records of the recipients that are pertinent to the grants received under this chapter.

(e) The provision of this section shall apply to all recipients of assistance under this title, whether by direct grant or contract from the Institute or by subgrant or subcontract from primary grantees or contractors of the Institute.

(Added Pub.L. 93–415, Title V, § 521, Sept. 7, 1974, 88 Stat. 1140, and amended Pub.L. 97–375, Title I, § 109(a), Dec. 21, 1982, 96 Stat. 1820; Pub.L. 101–647, Title XXXV, § 3599F, Nov. 29, 1990, 104 Stat. 4932.)

[1] Section catchline editorially supplied.

HISTORICAL AND STATUTORY NOTES

Inclusion of National Institute of Corrections in Federal Prison System Salaries and Expenses Budget

Pub.L. 104–208, Div. A, Title I, § 101(a) [Title I], Sept. 30, 1996, 110 Stat. 3009–11, provided in part: "That the National Institute of Corrections hereafter shall be included in the FPS Salaries and Expenses budget, in the Contract Confinement program and shall continue to perform its current functions under 18 U.S.C. 4351, et seq. [section 4351 et seq. of this title], with the exception of its grant program and shall collect reimbursement for services whenever possible."

National Training Center For Prison Drug Rehabilitation Program Personnel

Pub.L. 100–690, Title VI, § 6292, Nov. 18, 1988, 102 Stat. 4369, provided that:

"**(a) In general.**—The Director of the National Institute of Corrections, in consultation with persons with expertise in the field of community-based drug rehabilitation, shall establish and operate, at any suitable location, a national training center (hereinafter in this section referred to as the "center") for training Federal, State, and local prison or jail officials to conduct drug rehabilitation programs for criminals convicted of drug-related crimes and for drug-dependent criminals. Programs conducted at the center shall include training for correctional officers, administrative staff, and correctional mental health professionals (including subcontracting agency personnel).

"**(b) Design and construction of facilities.**—The Director of the National Institute of Corrections shall design and construct facilities for the center.

"**(c) Authorization of appropriations.**—In addition to amounts otherwise authorized to be appropriated with respect to the National Institute of Corrections, there are authorized to be appropriated to the Director of the National Institute of Corrections—

"(1) for establishment and operation of the center, for curriculum development for the center, and for salaries and expenses of personnel at the center, not more than $4,000,000 for each of fiscal years 1989, 1990, and 1991; and

"(2) for design and construction of facilities for the center, not more than $10,000,000 for fiscal years 1989, 1990, and 1991."

[§ 4353. Pub.L. 107–273, Div. A, Title III, § 301(a), Nov. 2, 2002, 116 Stat. 1780]

HISTORICAL AND STATUTORY NOTES

Section, added Pub.L. 93–415, Title V, § 521, Sept. 7, 1974, 88 Stat. 1141, related to authorization of appropriations required to carry out the purposes of this chapter.

PART IV—CORRECTION OF YOUTHFUL OFFENDERS

HISTORICAL AND STATUTORY NOTES

1984 Amendment

Pub.L. 98–473, Title II, § 218(g), substituted "Repealed" for "Federal Youth Corrections Act" in item for chapter 402.

1950 Amendment

Act Sept. 30, 1950, c. 1115, § 5(a), 64 Stat. 1090, added item for chapter 402.

CHAPTER 401—GENERAL PROVISIONS

1996 Amendments

Pub.L. 104–134, Title I, § 101[a][Title VI, § 614(a)(2)], Apr. 26, 1996, 110 Stat. 1321–65; renumbered Title I Pub.L. 104–140, § 1(a), May 2, 1996, 110 Stat. 1327, struck out item 5002, which established an Advisory Corrections Council.

1952 Amendment

Act May 9, 1952, c. 253, § 2, 66 Stat. 68, added item "5003".

1950 Amendment

Act Sept. 30, 1950, c. 1115, § 5(b), 64 Stat. 1090, added item "5002".

Savings Provisions of Pub.L. 98–473, Title II, c. II

See section 235 of Pub.L. 98–473, Title II, c. II, Oct. 12, 1984, 98 Stat. 2031, as amended, set out as a note under section 3551 of this title.

§ 5001. Surrender to State authorities; expenses

Whenever any person under twenty-one years of age has been arrested, charged with the commission of an offense punishable in any court of the United States or of the District of Columbia, and, after investigation by the Department of Justice, it appears that such person has committed an offense or is a delinquent under the laws of any State or of the District of Columbia which can and will assume jurisdiction over such juvenile and will take him into custody and deal with him according to the laws of such State or of the District of Columbia, and that it will be to the best interest of the United States and of the juvenile offender, the United States attorney of the district in which such person has been arrested may forego his prosecution and surrender him as herein provided, unless such surrender is precluded under section 5032 of this title.

The United States marshal of such district upon written order of the United States attorney shall convey such person to such State or the District of Columbia, or, if already therein, to any other part thereof and deliver him into the custody of the proper authority thereof.

Before any person is conveyed from one State to another or from or to the District of Columbia under this section, he shall signify his willingness to be so returned, or there shall be presented to the United States attorney a demand from the executive authority of such State or the District of Columbia, to which the prisoner is to be returned, supported by indictment or affidavit as prescribed by section 3182 of this title.

The expense incident to the transportation of any such person, as herein authorized, shall be paid from the appropriation "Salaries, Fees, and Expenses, United States Marshals."

(June 25, 1948, c. 645, 62 Stat. 857; Nov. 18, 1988, Pub.L. 100–690, Title VI, § 6467(b), 102 Stat. 4376.)

[§ 5002. Repealed. Pub.L. 104–134, Title I, § 101[(a)][Title VI, § 614(a)(1)], Apr. 26, 1996, 110 Stat. 1321–65; renumbered Title I Pub.L. 104–140, § 1(a), May 2, 1996, 110 Stat. 1327]

HISTORICAL AND STATUTORY NOTES

Section, added Sept. 30, 1950, c.1115, § 4, 64 Stat. 1090, and amended Oct. 12, 1984, Pub.L. 98–473, Title II, § 223(p), 98 Stat. 2030, provided for the creation of an Advisory Corrections Council.

Effective Date of Repeal

Pub.L. 104–134, Title I, § 101[(a)][Title VI, § 614(b)], Apr. 26, 1996, 110 Stat. 1321–65; renumbered Title I Pub.L. 104–140, § 1(a), May 2, 1996, 110 Stat. 1327, provided that: "This section [repealing this section] shall take effect 30 days after the date of the enactment of this Act [Apr. 26, 1996]."

§ 5003. Custody of State offenders

(a)(1) The Director of the Bureau of Prisons when proper and adequate facilities and personnel are available may contract with proper officials of a State or territory, for the custody, care, subsistence, education, treatment, and training of persons convicted of criminal offenses in the courts of such State or territory.

(2) Any such contract shall provide—

(A) for reimbursing the United States in full for all costs or expenses involved;

(B) for receiving in exchange persons convicted of criminal offenses in the courts of the United States, to serve their sentence in appropriate institutions or facilities of the State or territory by designation as provided in section 4082(b) of this title, this exchange to be made according to formulas or conditions which may be negotiated in the contract; or

(C) for compensating the United States by means of a combination of monetary payment and of receipt of persons convicted of criminal offenses in the courts of the United States, according to formulas or conditions which may be negotiated in the contract.

(3) No such contract shall provide for the receipt of more State or territory prisoners by the United States than are transferred to that State or territory by such contract.

(b) Funds received under such contract may be deposited in the Treasury to the credit of the appropriation or appropriations from which the payments for such service were originally made.

(c) Unless otherwise specifically provided in the contract, a person committed to the Attorney General hereunder shall be subject to all the provisions of law and regulations applicable to persons committed for violations of laws of the United States not inconsistent with the sentence imposed.

(d) The term "State" as used in this section includes any State, territory, or possession of the United States, and the Canal Zone.

(Added May 9, 1952, c. 253, § 1, 66 Stat. 68, and amended Oct. 19, 1965, Pub.L. 89–267, § 1, 79 Stat. 990; Nov. 10, 1986, Pub.L. 99–646, § 66, 100 Stat. 3615.)

HISTORICAL AND STATUTORY NOTES

References in Text

Section 4082(b) of this title, referred to in subsec. (a)(2)(B), was repealed, and subsec. (f) was redesignated 18 U.S.C.A. § 4082(b), by Pub.L. 98–473, Title II, § 218(a), Oct. 12, 1984, 98 Stat. 2027.

For definition of Canal Zone, referred to in subsec. (d), see section 3602(b) of Title 22, Foreign Relations and Intercourse.

[CHAPTER 402—REPEALED]

HISTORICAL AND STATUTORY NOTES

Codification

This chapter was repealed by Pub.L. 98–473, Title II, § 218(a)(8), Oct. 12, 1984, 98 Stat. 2027, effective Oct. 12, 1984, pursuant to section 235(a)(1)(A) of Pub.L. 98–473, set out as an Effective Date note under section 3551 of this title, with sections 5017 to 5020 subject to remain in effect as provided in section 235(b) of Pub.L. 98–473, set out as a Savings Provision of Pub.L. 98–473 note under section 3551 of this title. For sentencing guidelines required to take age into consideration as a factor, see section 994(d) of Title 28, Judiciary and Judicial Procedure.

[§§ 5005, 5006. Repealed. Pub.L. 98–473, Title II, § 218(a)(8), Oct. 12, 1984, 98 Stat. 2027]

HISTORICAL AND STATUTORY NOTES

Section 5005, added Sept. 30, 1950, c. 1115, § 2, 64 Stat. 1086, and amended Mar. 15, 1976, Pub.L. 94–233, § 3, 90 Stat. 231, related to the making of youth correction decisions by the United States Parole Commission.

Section 5006, added Sept. 30, 1950, c. 1115, § 2, 64 Stat. 1086, and amended May 15, 1976, Pub.L. 94–233, § 4, 90 Stat. 231, defined the terms used in this chapter.

Effective Date of Repeal

Sections repealed effective on Oct. 12, 1984, pursuant to section 235(a)(1)(A) of Pub.L. 98–473, set out as a note under section 3551 of this title.

[§§ 5007 to 5009. Repealed. Pub.L. 94–233, § 5, Mar. 15, 1976, 90 Stat. 231]

HISTORICAL AND STATUTORY NOTES

Section 5007, added Act Sept. 30, 1950, c. 1115, § 2, 64 Stat. 1086, provided for meetings and duties of members of the Youth Correction Division.

Section 5008, added Act Sept. 30, 1950, c. 1115, § 2, 64 Stat. 1086, provided for the appointment of officers and employees by the Attorney General.

Section 5009, added Act Sept. 30, 1950, c. 1115, § 2, 64 Stat. 1086, provided for the adoption and promulgation of rules governing procedure by the Youth Correction Division.

Effective Date of Repeal

Repeal of sections effective on the 60th day following Mar. 15, 1976, see section 16(b) of Pub.L. 94–233, set out as a note under section 4201 of this title.

[§§ 5010 to 5016. Repealed. Pub.L. 98–473, Title II, § 218(a)(8), Oct. 12, 1984, 98 Stat. 2027]

HISTORICAL AND STATUTORY NOTES

Section 5010, added Sept. 30, 1950, c. 1115, § 2, 64 Stat. 1087, and amended Mar. 15, 1976, Pub.L. 94–233, § 9, 90

Stat. 232, provided for the imposition of a suspended sentence or sentence to the custody of the Attorney General in the case of youthful offenders.

Section 5011, added Sept. 30, 1950, c. 1115, § 2, 64 Stat. 1087, provided for the treatment of youthful offenders.

Section 5012, added Sept. 30, 1950, c. 1115, § 2, 64 Stat. 1087, provided for the Director's certification of the availability of proper and adequate treatment facilities for youthful offenders.

Section 5013, added Sept. 30, 1950, c. 1115, § 2, 64 Stat. 1087, authorized the Director of the Bureau of Prisons to contract for the maintenance of youthful offenders.

Section 5014, added Sept. 30, 1950, c. 1115, § 2, 64 Stat. 1087, and amended July 17, 1970, Pub.L. 91–339, § 1, 84 Stat. 437; Mar. 15, 1976, Pub.L. 94–233, § 6, 90 Stat. 231, related to classification studies and reports.

Section 5015, added Sept. 30, 1950, c. 1115, § 2, 64 Stat. 1088, and amended Mar. 15, 1976, Pub.L. 94–233, § 9, 90 Stat. 232, related to the power of the Director as to placement of youthful offenders.

Section 5016, added Sept. 30, 1950, c. 1115, § 2, 64 Stat. 1088, and amended Mar. 15, 1976, Pub.L. 94–233, § 9, 90 Stat. 232, related to the periodic reports which the Director was required to make on all committed youthful offenders.

Effective Date of Repeal

Sections repealed effective Oct. 12, 1984, pursuant to section 235(a)(1)(A) of Pub.L. 98–473, set out as a note under section 3551 of this title.

[§ 5017. Repealed. Pub.L. 98–473, Title II, § 218(a)(8), Oct. 12, 1984, 98 Stat. 2027]

HISTORICAL AND STATUTORY NOTES

Section 5017 was repealed, effective Oct. 12, 1984, pursuant to section 235(a)(1)(A) of Pub.L. 98–473, set out as an Effective Date note under section 3551 of this title, subject to remain in effect as provided in section 235(b) of Pub.L. 98–473, set out as a Savings Provision of Pub.L. 98–473 note under section 3551 of this title. Section 5017 read as follows:

§ 5017. Release of youth offenders

(a) The Commission may at any time after reasonable notice to the Director release conditionally under supervision a committed youth offender in accordance with the provisions of section 4206 of this title. When, in the judgment of the Director, a committed youth offender should be released conditionally under supervision he shall so report and recommend to the Commission.

(b) The Commission may discharge a committed youth offender unconditionally at the expiration of one year from the date of conditional release.

(c) A youth offender committed under section 5010(b) of this chapter shall be released conditionally under supervision on or before the expiration of four years from the date of his conviction and shall be discharged unconditionally on or before six years from the date of his conviction.

(d) A youth offender committed under section 5010(c) of this chapter shall be released conditionally under supervision not later than two years before the expiration of the term imposed by the court. He may be discharged unconditionally at the expiration of not less than one year from the date of his conditional release. He shall be discharged unconditionally on or before the expiration of the maximum sentence imposed, computed uninterruptedly from the date of conviction.

(e) Commutation of sentence authorized by any Act of Congress shall not be granted as a matter of right to committed youth offenders but only in accordance with rules prescribed by the Director with the approval of the Commission.

(Added Sept. 30, 1950, c. 1115, § 2, 64 Stat. 1088, and amended Mar. 15, 1976, Pub.L. 94–233, §§ 7, 9, 90 Stat. 232.)

[§ 5018. Repealed. Pub.L. 98–473, Title II, § 218(a)(8), Oct. 12, 1984, 98 Stat. 2027]

HISTORICAL AND STATUTORY NOTES

Section 5018 was repealed, effective Oct. 12, 1984, pursuant to section 235(a)(1)(A) of Pub.L. 98–473, set out as an Effective Date note under section 3551 of this title, subject to remain in effect as provided in section 235(b) of Pub.L. 98–473, set out as a Savings Provision of Pub.L. 98–473 note under section 3551 of this title. Section 5018 read as follows:

§ 5018. Revocation of Commission orders

The Commission may revoke or modify any of its previous orders respecting a committed youth offender except an order of unconditional discharge.

(Added Sept. 30, 1950, c. 1115, § 2, 64 Stat. 1089, and amended Mar. 15, 1976, Pub.L. 94–233, § 9, 90 Stat. 232.)

[§ 5019. Repealed. Pub.L. 98–473, Title II, § 218(a)(8), Oct. 12, 1984, 98 Stat. 2027]

HISTORICAL AND STATUTORY NOTES

Section 5019 was repealed, effective Oct. 12, 1984, pursuant to section 235(a)(1)(A) of Pub.L. 98–473, set out as an Effective Date note under section 3551 of this title, subject to remain in effect as provided in section 235(b) of Pub.L. 98–473, set out as a Savings Provision note under section 3551 of this title. Section 5019 read as follows:

§ 5019. Supervision of released youth offenders

Committed youth offenders permitted to remain at liberty under supervision or conditionally released shall be under the supervision of United States probation officers, supervisory agents appointed by the Attorney General, and voluntary supervisory agents approved by the Commission. The Commission is authorized to encourage the formation of voluntary organizations composed of members who will serve without compensation as voluntary supervisory agents and sponsors. The powers and duties of voluntary supervisory agents and sponsors shall be limited and defined by regulations adopted by the Commission.

(Added Sept. 30, 1950, c. 1115, § 2, 64 Stat. 1089, and amended Mar. 15, 1976, Pub.L. 94–233, § 9, 90 Stat. 232.)

[§ 5020. Repealed. Pub.L. 98–473, Title II, § 218(a)(8), Oct. 12, 1984, 98 Stat. 2027]

HISTORICAL AND STATUTORY NOTES

Section 5020 was repealed, effective Oct. 12, 1984, pursuant to section 235(a)(1)(A) of Pub.L. 98–473, set out as an Effective Date note under section 3551 of this title, subject to remain in effect as provided in section 235(b) of Pub.L. 98–473, set out as a Savings Provision of Pub.L. 98–473 note under section 3551 of this title. Section 5020 read as follows:

§ 5020. Apprehension of released offenders

If, at any time before the unconditional discharge of a committed youth offender, the Commission is of the opinion that such youth offender will be benefited by further treatment in an institution or other facility the Commission may direct his return to custody or if necessary may issue a warrant for the apprehension and return to custody of such youthful offender and cause such warrant to be executed by a United States probation officer, an appointed supervisory agent, a United States marshal, or any officer of a Federal penal or correctional institution. Upon return to custody, such youth offender shall be given a revocation hearing by the Commission.

(Added Sept. 30, 1950, c. 1115, § 2, 64 Stat. 1089, and amended July 17, 1970, Pub.L. 91–339, § 2, 84 Stat. 437; Mar. 15, 1976, Pub.L. 94–233, § 8, 90 Stat. 232.)

[§§ 5021 to 5026. Repealed. Pub.L. 98–473, Title II, § 218(a)(8), Oct. 12, 1984, 98 Stat. 2027]

HISTORICAL AND STATUTORY NOTES

Section 5021, added Sept. 30, 1950, c. 1115, § 2, 64 Stat. 1089, and amended Oct. 3, 1961, Pub.L. 87–336, 75 Stat. 750; Mar. 15, 1976, Pub.L. 94–233, § 9, 90 Stat. 232, related to the issuance of certificates setting aside the convictions of youthful offenders.

Section 5022, added Sept. 30, 1950, c. 1115, § 2, 64 Stat. 1089, provided that this chapter would not apply to offenses committed before its enactment.

Section 5023, added Sept. 30, 1950, c. 1115, § 2, 64 Stat. 1089, and amended Apr. 8, 1952, c. 163, § 1, 66 Stat. 45, related to the relationship between this chapter and the Probation and Juvenile Delinquency Acts.

Section 5024, added Sept. 30, 1950, c. 1115, § 2, 64 Stat. 1089, and amended Apr. 8, 1952, c. 163, § 2, 66 Stat. 45; June 25, 1959, Pub.L. 86–70, § 17(a), 73 Stat. 144; July 12, 1960, Pub.L. 86–624, § 13(b), 74 Stat. 413; Dec. 27, 1967, Pub.L. 90–226, Title VIII, § 801(a), 81 Stat. 741, provided that this chapter was applicable to the States of the United States and to the District of Columbia.

Section 5025, added Apr. 8, 1952, c. 163, § 3(a), 66 Stat. 46, and amended Dec. 27, 1967, Pub.L. 90–226, Title VIII, § 801(b), 81 Stat. 741, related to the applicability of this chapter to the District of Columbia.

Section 5026, added Apr. 8, 1952, c. 163, § 3(a), 66 Stat. 46, provided that this chapter did not affect the parole of other offenders.

Effective Date of Repeal

Sections repealed effective Oct. 12, 1984, pursuant to section 235(a)(1)(A) of Pub.L. 98–473, set out as a note under section 3551 of this title.

CHAPTER 403—JUVENILE DELINQUENCY

Sec.

HISTORICAL AND STATUTORY NOTES

Codification

Amendment by section 3599H of Pub.L. 101–647 directed the substitution of "probation" for "Probation" in item 5042. Prior amendment by Pub.L. 98–473 directed the substitution of "5042. Revocation of Probation." for "5042. Revocation of probation.", however, such amendment was not executed to item 5042, and further change is not required.

1990 Amendment

Pub.L. 101–647, Title XXXV, § 3599H, Nov. 29, 1990, 104 Stat. 4932, substituted in item 5042 "probation" for "Probation".

1984 Amendment

Pub.L. 98–473, Title II, § 214(d), Oct. 12, 1984, 98 Stat. 2013, struck out item 5041 "Parole" and in item 5042 struck out "parole or" following "of".

1974 Amendment

Pub.L. 93–415, Title V, § 513, Sept. 7, 1974, 88 Stat. 1138, substituted "Delinquency proceedings in district courts; transfer for criminal prosecution." for "Proceeding against juvenile delinquent." in item 5032; "Custody prior to appearance before magistrate." for "Jurisdiction; written consent; jury trial precluded." in item 5033; "Duties of magistrate." for "Probation; commitment to custody of Attorney General; support." in item 5034; "Detention prior to disposition." for "Arrest, detention and bail." in item 5035; "Speedy trial." for "Contracts for support; payment." in item 5036; "Dispositional hearing." for "Parole." in item 5037; and added items 5038 to 5042.

§ 5031. Definitions

For the purposes of this chapter, a "juvenile" is a person who has not attained his eighteenth birthday, or for the purpose of proceedings and disposition under this chapter for an alleged act of juvenile delinquency, a person who has not attained his twenty-first birthday, and "juvenile delinquency" is the violation of a law of the United States committed by a person prior to his eighteenth birthday which would have been a crime if committed by an adult or a violation by such a person of section 922(x).

(June 25, 1948, c. 645, 62 Stat. 857; Sept. 7, 1974, Pub.L. 93–415, Title V, § 501, 88 Stat. 1133; Sept. 13, 1994, Pub.L. 103–322, Title XI, § 110201(c)(1), 108 Stat. 2012.)

HISTORICAL AND STATUTORY NOTES

Codifications

Another section 501 of Title V of Pub.L. 93–415, as added by Pub.L. 107–273, Div. C, Title II, § 12222(a), Nov. 2, 2002, 116 Stat. 1894, is set out as a note under 42 U.S.C.A. § 5601.

Another section 501 of Title V of Pub.L. 93–415, as added by Pub.L. 102–586, § 5(a), Nov. 4, 1992, 106 Stat. 5027, was set out as a note under 42 U.S.C.A. § 5601, prior to the general amendment of that Title V by Pub.L. 107–273.

§ 5032. Delinquency proceedings in district courts; transfer for criminal prosecution

A juvenile alleged to have committed an act of juvenile delinquency, other than a violation of law committed within the special maritime and territorial jurisdiction of the United States for which the maximum authorized term of imprisonment does not exceed six months, shall not be proceeded against in any court of the United States unless the Attorney General, after investigation, certifies to the appropriate district court of the United States that (1) the juvenile court or other appropriate court of a State does not have jurisdiction or refuses to assume jurisdiction over said juvenile with respect to such alleged act of juvenile delinquency, (2) the State does not have available programs and services adequate for the needs of juveniles, or (3) the offense charged is a crime of violence that is a felony or an offense described in section 401 of the Controlled Substances Act (21 U.S.C. 841), or section 1002(a), 1003, 1005, 1009, or 1010(b)(1), (2), or (3) of the Controlled Substances Import and Export Act (21 U.S.C. 952(a), 953, 955, 959, 960(b)(1), (2), (3)), section 922(x) or section 924(b), (g), or (h) of this title, and that there is a substantial Federal interest in the case or the offense to warrant the exercise of Federal jurisdiction.

If the Attorney General does not so certify, such juvenile shall be surrendered to the appropriate legal authorities of such State. For purposes of this section, the term "State" includes a State of the United States, the District of Columbia, and any commonwealth, territory, or possession of the United States.

If an alleged juvenile delinquent is not surrendered to the authorities of a State pursuant to this section, any proceedings against him shall be in an appropriate district court of the United States. For such purposes, the court may be convened at any time and place within the district, in chambers or otherwise. The Attorney General shall proceed by information or as authorized under section 3401(g) of this title, and no criminal prosecution shall be instituted for the alleged act of juvenile delinquency except as provided below.

A juvenile who is alleged to have committed an act of juvenile delinquency and who is not surrendered to State authorities shall be proceeded against under this chapter unless he has requested in writing upon advice of counsel to be proceeded against as an adult, except that, with respect to a juvenile fifteen years and older alleged to have committed an act after his fifteenth birthday which if committed by an adult would be a felony that is a crime of violence or an offense described in section 401 of the Controlled Substances Act (21 U.S.C. 841), or section 1002(a), 1005, or 1009 of the Controlled Substances Import and Export Act (21 U.S.C. 952(a), 955, 959), or section 922(x) of this title, or in section 924(b), (g), or (h) of this title, criminal prosecution on the basis of the alleged act may be begun by motion to transfer of the Attorney General in the appropriate district court of the United States, if such court finds, after hearing, such transfer would be in the interest of justice. In the application of the preceding sentence, if the crime of violence is an offense under section 113(a), 113(b), 113(c), 1111, 1113, or, if the juvenile possessed a firearm during the offense, section 2111, 2113, 2241(a), or 2241(c), "thirteen" shall be substituted for "fifteen" and "thirteenth" shall be substituted for "fifteenth". Notwithstanding sections 1152 and 1153, no person subject to the criminal jurisdiction of an Indian tribal government shall be subject to the preceding sentence for any offense the Federal jurisdiction for which is predicated solely on Indian country (as defined in section 1151), and which has occurred within the boundaries of such Indian country, unless the governing body of the tribe has elected that the preceding sentence have effect over land and persons subject to its criminal jurisdiction. However, a juvenile who is alleged to have committed an act after his sixteenth birthday which if committed by an adult would be a felony offense that has as an element thereof the use, attempted use, or threatened use of physical force against the person of another, or that, by its very nature, involves a substantial risk that physical force against the person of another may be used in committing the offense, or would be an offense described in section 32, 81, 844(d), (e), (f), (h), (i) or 2275 of this title, subsection (b)(1) (A), (B), or (C), (d), or (e) of section 401 of the Controlled Substances Act, or section 1002(a), 1003, 1009, or 1010(b) (1), (2), or (3) of the Controlled Substances Import and Export Act (21 U.S.C. 952(a), 953, 959, 960(b) (1), (2), (3)), and who has previously been found guilty of an act which if committed by an adult would have been one of the offenses set forth in this paragraph or an offense in violation of a State felony statute that would have been such an offense if a circumstance giving rise to Federal jurisdiction had existed, shall be transferred to the appropriate district court of the United States for criminal prosecution.

Evidence of the following factors shall be considered, and findings with regard to each factor shall be made in the record, in assessing whether a transfer would be in the interest of justice: the age and social background of the juvenile; the nature of the alleged offense; the extent and nature of the juvenile's prior delinquency record; the juvenile's present intellectual development and psychological maturity; the nature of past treatment efforts and the juvenile's response to such efforts; the availability of programs designed to treat the juvenile's behavioral problems. In considering the nature of the offense, as required by this paragraph, the court shall consider the extent to which the juvenile played a leadership role in an organization, or otherwise influenced other persons to take part in criminal activities, involving the use or distribution of controlled substances or firearms. Such a factor, if found to exist, shall weigh in favor of a transfer to adult status, but the absence of this factor shall not preclude such a transfer.

Reasonable notice of the transfer hearing shall be given to the juvenile, his parents, guardian, or custodian and to his counsel. The juvenile shall be assisted by counsel during the transfer hearing, and at every other critical stage of the proceedings.

Once a juvenile has entered a plea of guilty or the proceeding has reached the stage that evidence has begun to be taken with respect to a crime or an alleged act of juvenile delinquency subsequent criminal prosecution or juvenile proceedings based upon such alleged act of delinquency shall be barred.

Statements made by a juvenile prior to or during a transfer hearing under this section shall not be admissible at subsequent criminal prosecutions.

Whenever a juvenile transferred to district court under this section is not convicted of the crime upon which the transfer was based or another crime which would have warranted transfer had the juvenile been initially charged with that crime, further proceedings concerning the juvenile shall be conducted pursuant to the provisions of this chapter.

A juvenile shall not be transferred to adult prosecution nor shall a hearing be held under section 5037 (disposition after a finding of juvenile delinquency) until any prior juvenile court records of such juvenile have been received by the court, or the clerk of the juvenile court has certified in writing that the juvenile has no prior record, or that the juvenile's record is unavailable and why it is unavailable.

Whenever a juvenile is adjudged delinquent pursuant to the provisions of this chapter, the specific acts which the juvenile has been found to have committed shall be described as part of the official record of the proceedings and part of the juvenile's official record.

(June 25, 1948, c. 645, 62 Stat. 857; Sept. 7, 1974, Pub.L. 93–415, Title V, § 502, 88 Stat. 1134; Oct. 12, 1984, Pub.L. 98–473, Title II, § 1201, 98 Stat. 2149; Nov. 18, 1988, Pub.L. 100–690, Title VI, § 6467(a), 102 Stat. 4375; Nov. 29, 1990, Pub.L. 101–647, Title XII, § 1205(n), Title XXXV, § 3599G, 104 Stat. 4831, 4932; Sept. 13, 1994, Pub.L. 103–322, Title XI, § 110201(c)(2), Title XIV, §§ 140001, 140002, Title XV, § 150002, 108 Stat. 2012, 2031, 2035; Oct. 11, 1996, Pub.L. 104–294, Title VI, § 601(c)(1), (g)(1), 110 Stat. 3499, 3500.)

HISTORICAL AND STATUTORY NOTES

References in Text

Section 401 of the Controlled Substances Act, referred to in text, is section 401 of Pub.L. 91–513, Title II, Oct. 27, 1970, 84 Stat. 1260, which is classified to section 841 of Title 21, Food and Drugs.

Sections 1002, 1003, 1005, 1009, and 1010 of the Controlled Substances Import and Export Act, referred to in text, are sections 1002, 1003, 1005, 1009, and 1010 of Pub. L. 91–513, Title III, Oct. 27, 1970, 84 Stat. 1285, 1286, 1287, 1289, 1290, respectively, which are classified to sections 952, 953, 955, 959, and 960 of Title 21, respectively.

Codifications

Another section 502 of Title V of Pub.L. 93–415, as added by Pub.L. 107–273, Div. C, Title II, § 12222(a), Nov. 2, 2002, 116 Stat. 1894, is classified to 42 U.S.C.A. § 5781.

Another section 502 of Title V of Pub.L. 93–415, as added by Pub.L. 102–586, § 5(a), Nov. 4, 1992, 106 Stat. 5027, was classified to 42 U.S.C.A. § 5781, prior to the general amendment of that Title V by Pub.L. 107–273.

In the fourth paragraph, "that is a crime of violence or an offense described in section 841, 952(a), 955, or 959 of title 21," was substituted for "punishable by a maximum penalty of ten years imprisonment or more, life imprisonment, or death," instead of for "punishable by a maximum term of ten years imprisonment or more, life imprisonment or death," as directed by Pub.L. 98–473, Title II, § 1201(b)(1), Oct. 12, 1984, 98 Stat. 2150, as the probable intent of Congress.

§ 5033. Custody prior to appearance before magistrate judge

Whenever a juvenile is taken into custody for an alleged act of juvenile delinquency, the arresting officer shall immediately advise such juvenile of his legal rights, in language comprehensive to a juvenile, and shall immediately notify the Attorney General and the juvenile's parents, guardian, or custodian of such custody. The arresting officer shall also notify the parents, guardian, or custodian of the rights of the juvenile and of the nature of the alleged offense.

The juvenile shall be taken before a magistrate judge forthwith. In no event shall the juvenile be detained for longer than a reasonable period of time before being brought before a magistrate judge.

(June 25, 1948, c. 645, 62 Stat. 857; Sept. 7, 1974, Pub.L. 93–415, Title V, § 503, 88 Stat. 1135; Dec. 1, 1990, Pub.L. 101–650, Title III, § 321, 104 Stat. 5117.)

HISTORICAL AND STATUTORY NOTES

Codifications

Another section 503 of Title V of Pub.L. 93–415, as added by Pub.L. 107–273, Div. C, Title II, § 12222(a), Nov. 2, 2002, 116 Stat. 1894, is classified to 42 U.S.C.A. § 5782.

Another section 503 of Title V of Pub.L. 93–415, as added by Pub.L. 102–586, § 5(a), Nov. 4, 1992, 106 Stat. 5027, was classified to 42 U.S.C.A. § 5782, prior to the general amendment of that Title V by Pub.L. 107–273.

Change of Name

Words "magistrate judge" substituted for "magistrate" in section catchline and text pursuant to section 321 of Pub.L. 101–650, set out as a note under 28 U.S.C.A. § 631.

§ 5034. Duties of magistrate judge

The magistrate judge shall insure that the juvenile is represented by counsel before proceeding with critical stages of the proceedings. Counsel shall be assigned to represent a juvenile when the juvenile and his parents, guardian, or custodian are financially unable to obtain adequate representation. In cases where the juvenile and his parents, guardian, or custodian are financially able to obtain adequate representation but have not retained counsel, the magistrate judge may assign counsel and order the payment of reasonable attorney's fees or may direct the juvenile, his parents, guardian, or custodian to retain private counsel within a specified period of time.

The magistrate judge may appoint a guardian ad litem if a parent or guardian of the juvenile is not present, or if the magistrate judge has reason to believe that the parents or guardian will not cooperate with the juvenile in preparing for trial, or that the interests of the parents or guardian and those of the juvenile are adverse.

If the juvenile has not been discharged before his initial appearance before the magistrate judge, the magistrate judge shall release the juvenile to his parents, guardian, custodian, or other responsible party (including, but not limited to, the director of a shelter-care facility) upon their promise to bring such juvenile before the appropriate court when requested by such court unless the magistrate judge determines, after hearing, at which the juvenile is represented by counsel, that the detention of such juvenile is required to secure his timely appearance before the appropriate court or to insure his safety or that of others.

(June 25, 1948, c. 645, 62 Stat. 858; Mar. 31, 1962, Pub.L. 87–428, 76 Stat. 52; Sept. 7, 1974, Pub.L. 93–415, Title V, § 504, 88 Stat. 1135; Nov. 18, 1988, Pub. L. 100–690, Title VII, § 7045, 102 Stat. 4400; Dec. 1, 1990, Pub.L. 101–650, Title III, § 321, 104 Stat. 5117.)

HISTORICAL AND STATUTORY NOTES

Codifications

Another section 504 of Title V of Pub.L. 93–415, as added by Pub.L. 107–273, Div. C, Title II, § 12222(a), Nov. 2, 2002, 116 Stat. 1895, is classified to 42 U.S.C.A. § 5783.

Another section 504 of Title V of Pub.L. 93–415, as added by Pub.L. 102–586, § 5(a), Nov. 4, 1992, 106 Stat. 5027, was classified to 42 U.S.C.A. § 5783, prior to the general amendment of that Title V by Pub.L. 107–273.

Change of Name

Words "magistrate judge" substituted for "magistrate" in section catchline and text pursuant to section 321 of Pub.L. 101–650, set out as a note under 28 U.S.C.A. § 631.

§ 5035. Detention prior to disposition

A juvenile alleged to be delinquent may be detained only in a juvenile facility or such other suitable place as the Attorney General may designate. Whenever possible, detention shall be in a foster home or community based facility located in or near his home community. The Attorney General shall not cause any juvenile alleged to be delinquent to be detained or confined in any institution in which the juvenile has regular contact with adult persons convicted of a crime or awaiting trial on criminal charges. Insofar as possible, alleged delinquents shall be kept separate from adjudicated delinquents. Every juvenile in custody shall be provided with adequate food, heat, light, sanitary facilities, bedding, clothing, recreation, education, and medical care, including necessary psychiatric, psychological, or other care and treatment.

(June 25, 1948, c. 645, 62 Stat. 858; Sept. 7, 1974, Pub.L. 93–415, Title V, § 505, 88 Stat. 1135.)

HISTORICAL AND STATUTORY NOTES

Codifications

Another section 505 of Title V of Pub.L. 93–415, as added by Pub.L. 107–273, Div. C, Title II, § 12222(a), Nov. 2, 2002, 116 Stat. 1896, is classified to 42 U.S.C.A. § 5784.

Another section 505 of Title V of Pub.L. 93–415, as added by Pub.L. 102–586, § 5(a), Nov. 4, 1992, 106 Stat. 5028, was classified to 42 U.S.C.A. § 5784, prior to the general amendment of that Title V by Pub.L. 107–273.

§ 5036. Speedy trial

If an alleged delinquent who is in detention pending trial is not brought to trial within thirty days from the date upon which such detention was begun, the information shall be dismissed on motion of the alleged delinquent or at the direction of the court, unless the Attorney General shows that additional delay was caused by the juvenile or his counsel, or consented to by the juvenile and his counsel, or would be in the interest of justice in the particular case. Delays attributable solely to court calendar congestion may not be considered in the interest of justice. Except in extraordinary circumstances, an information dismissed under this section may not be reinstituted.

(June 25, 1948, c. 645, 62 Stat. 858; Sept. 7, 1974, Pub.L. 93–415, Title V, § 506, 88 Stat. 1136.)

HISTORICAL AND STATUTORY NOTES

Codifications

Another section 506 of Title V of Pub.L. 93–415, as added by Pub.L. 102–586, § 5(a), Nov. 4, 1992, 106 Stat. 5029, was classified to 42 U.S.C.A. § 5785, prior to the general amendment of that Title V by Pub.L. 107–273.

§ 5037. Dispositional hearing

(a) If the court finds a juvenile to be a juvenile delinquent, the court shall hold a disposition hearing concerning the appropriate disposition no later than twenty court days after the juvenile delinquency hearing unless the court has ordered further study pursuant to subsection (d). After the disposition hearing, and after considering any pertinent policy statements promulgated by the Sentencing Commission pursuant to 28 U.S.C. 994, the court may suspend the findings of juvenile delinquency, place him on probation, or commit him to official detention which may include a term of juvenile delinquent supervision to follow detention. In addition, the court may enter an order of restitution pursuant to section 3556. With respect to release or detention pending an appeal or a petition for a writ of certiorari after disposition, the court shall proceed pursuant to the provisions of chapter 207.

(b) The term for which probation may be ordered for a juvenile found to be a juvenile delinquent may not extend—

(1) in the case of a juvenile who is less than eighteen years old, beyond the lesser of—

(A) the date when the juvenile becomes twenty-one years old; or

(B) the maximum term that would be authorized by section 3561(c) if the juvenile had been tried and convicted as an adult; or

(2) in the case of a juvenile who is between eighteen and twenty-one years old, beyond the lesser of—

(A) three years; or

(B) the maximum term that would be authorized by section 3561(c) if the juvenile had been tried and convicted as an adult.

The provisions dealing with probation set forth in sections 3563 and 3564 are applicable to an order placing a juvenile on probation. If the juvenile violates a condition of probation at any time prior to the expiration or termination of the term of probation, the court may, after a dispositional hearing and after considering any pertinent policy statements promulgated by the Sentencing Commission pursuant to section 994 of title 28, revoke the term of probation and order a term of official detention. The term of official detention authorized upon revocation of probation shall not exceed the terms authorized in section 5037(c)(2) (A) and (B). The application of sections 5037(c)(2) (A) and (B) shall be determined based upon the age of the juvenile at the time of the disposition of the revocation proceeding. If a juvenile is over the age of 21 years old at the time of the revocation proceeding, the mandatory revocation provisions of section 3565(b) are applicable. A disposition of a juvenile who is over the age of 21 years shall be in accordance with the provisions of section 5037(c)(2), except that in the case of a juvenile who if convicted as an adult would be convicted of a Class A, B, or C felony, no term of official detention may continue beyond the juvenile's 26th birthday, and in any other case, no term of official detention may continue beyond the juvenile's 24th birthday. A term of official detention may include a term of juvenile delinquent supervision.

(c) The term for which official detention may be ordered for a juvenile found to be a juvenile delinquent may not extend—

(1) in the case of a juvenile who is less than eighteen years old, beyond the lesser of—

(A) the date when the juvenile becomes twenty-one years old;

(B) the maximum of the guideline range, pursuant to section 994 of title 28, applicable to an otherwise similarly situated adult defendant unless the court finds an aggravating factor to warrant an upward departure from the otherwise applicable guideline range; or

(C) the maximum term of imprisonment that would be authorized if the juvenile had been tried and convicted as an adult; or

(2) in the case of a juvenile who is between eighteen and twenty-one years old—

(A) who if convicted as an adult would be convicted of a Class A, B, or C felony, beyond the lesser of—

(i) five years; or

(ii) the maximum of the guideline range, pursuant to section 994 of title 28, applicable to an otherwise similarly situated adult defendant unless the court finds an aggravating factor to warrant an upward departure from the otherwise applicable guideline range; or

(B) in any other case beyond the lesser of—

(i) three years;

(ii) the maximum of the guideline range, pursuant to section 994 of title 28, applicable to an otherwise similarly situated adult defendant unless the court finds an aggravating factor to warrant an upward departure from the otherwise applicable guideline range; or

(iii) the maximum term of imprisonment that would be authorized if the juvenile had been tried and convicted as an adult.

Section 3624 is applicable to an order placing a juvenile under detention.

(d)(1) The court, in ordering a term of official detention, may include the requirement that the juvenile be placed on a term of juvenile delinquent supervision after official detention.

(2) The term of juvenile delinquent supervision that may be ordered for a juvenile found to be a juvenile delinquent may not extend—

(A) in the case of a juvenile who is less than 18 years old, a term that extends beyond the date when the juvenile becomes 21 years old; or

(B) in the case of a juvenile who is between 18 and 21 years old, a term that extends beyond the maximum term of official detention set forth in section 5037(c)(2) (A) and (B), less the term of official detention ordered.

(3) The provisions dealing with probation set forth in sections 3563 and 3564 are applicable to an order placing a juvenile on juvenile delinquent supervision.

(4) The court may modify, reduce, or enlarge the conditions of juvenile delinquent supervision at any time prior to the expiration or termination of the term of supervision after a dispositional hearing and after consideration of the provisions of section 3563 regarding the initial setting of the conditions of probation.

(5) If the juvenile violates a condition of juvenile delinquent supervision at any time prior to the expiration or termination of the term of supervision, the court may, after a dispositional hearing and after considering any pertinent policy statements promulgated by the Sentencing Commission pursuant to section 994 of title 18,[1] revoke the term of supervision and order a term of official detention. The term of official detention which is authorized upon revocation of juvenile delinquent supervision shall not exceed the term authorized in section 5037(c)(2)(A) and (B), less any term of official detention previously ordered. The application of sections 5037(c)(2) (A) and (B) shall be determined based upon the age of the juvenile at the time of the disposition of the revocation proceeding. If a juvenile is over the age of 21 years old at the time of the revocation proceeding, the mandatory revocation provisions of section 3565(b) are applicable. A disposition of a juvenile who is over the age of 21 years old shall be in accordance with the provisions of section 5037(c)(2), except that in the case of a juvenile who if convicted as an adult would be convicted of a Class A, B, or C felony, no term of official detention may continue beyond the juvenile's 26th birthday, and in any other case, no term of official detention may continue beyond the juvenile's 24th birthday.

(6) When a term of juvenile delinquent supervision is revoked and the juvenile is committed to official detention, the court may include a requirement that the juvenile be placed on a term of juvenile delinquent supervision. Any term of juvenile delinquent supervision ordered following revocation for a juvenile who is over the age of 21 years old at the time of the revocation proceeding shall be in accordance with the provisions of section 5037(d)(1), except that in the case of a juvenile who if convicted as an adult would be convicted of a Class A, B, or C felony, no term of juvenile delinquent supervision may continue beyond the juvenile's 26th birthday, and in any other case, no term of juvenile delinquent supervision may continue beyond the juvenile's 24th birthday.

(e) If the court desires more detailed information concerning an alleged or adjudicated delinquent, it may commit him, after notice and hearing at which the juvenile is represented by counsel, to the custody of the Attorney General for observation and study by an appropriate agency. Such observation and study shall be conducted on an outpatient basis, unless the court determines that inpatient observation and study are necessary to obtain the desired information. In the case of an alleged juvenile delinquent, inpatient study may be ordered only with the consent of the juvenile and his attorney. The agency shall make a complete study of the alleged or adjudicated delinquent to ascertain his personal traits, his capabilities, his background, any previous delinquency or criminal experience, any mental or physical defect, and any other relevant factors. The Attorney General shall submit to the court and the attorneys for the juvenile and the Government the results of the study within thirty days after the commitment of the juvenile, unless the court grants additional time.

(June 25, 1948, c. 645, 62 Stat. 858; Sept. 7, 1974, Pub.L. 93–415, Title V, § 507, 88 Stat. 1136; Oct. 12, 1984, Pub.L. 98–473, Title II, § 214(a), 98 Stat. 2013; Nov. 10, 1986, Pub.L. 99–646, § 21(a), 100 Stat. 3596; Oct. 11, 1996, Pub.L. 104–294, Title VI, § 604(b)(40), 110 Stat. 3509; Nov. 2, 2002, Pub.L. 107–273, Div. C, Title II, § 12301, 116 Stat. 1896.)

[1] So in original. Probably should be "title 28".

HISTORICAL AND STATUTORY NOTES

Effective and Applicability Provisions

1996 Acts. Amendment by section 604 of Pub.L. 104–294 effective Sept. 13, 1994, see section 604(d) of Pub.L. 104–294, set out as a note under section 13 of this title.

1986 Acts. Section 21(b) of Pub.L. 99–646 provided that: "The amendments made by this section [amending this section] shall take effect on the date of the amendments made by such section 214 [of Pub.L. 98–473] take effect [Nov. 1, 1987]."

1984 Acts. Amendment by Pub.L. 98–473 effective on the first day of first calendar month beginning thirty six months after Oct. 12, 1984, applicable only to offenses committed after taking effect of sections 211 to 239 of Pub.L. 98–473, and except as otherwise provided for therein, see section 235 of Pub.L. 98–473, as amended, set out as a note under section 3551 of this title.

§ 5038. Use of juvenile records

(a) Throughout and upon the completion of the juvenile delinquency proceeding, the records shall be safeguarded from disclosure to unauthorized persons. The records shall be released to the extent necessary to meet the following circumstances:

(1) inquiries received from another court of law;

(2) inquiries from an agency preparing a presentence report for another court;

(3) inquiries from law enforcement agencies where the request for information is related to the investigation of a crime or a position within that agency;

(4) inquiries, in writing, from the director of a treatment agency or the director of a facility to which the juvenile has been committed by the court;

(5) inquiries from an agency considering the person for a position immediately and directly affecting the national security; and

(6) inquiries from any victim of such juvenile delinquency, or if the victim is deceased from the immediate family of such victim, related to the final disposition of such juvenile by the court in accordance with section 5037.

Unless otherwise authorized by this section, information about the juvenile record may not be released when the request for information is related to an application for employment, license, bonding, or any civil right or privilege. Responses to such inquiries shall not be different from responses made about persons who have never been involved in a delinquency proceeding.

(b) District courts exercising jurisdiction over any juvenile shall inform the juvenile, and his parent or guardian, in writing in clear and nontechnical language, of rights relating to his juvenile record.

(c) During the course of any juvenile delinquency proceeding, all information and records relating to the proceeding, which are obtained or prepared in the discharge of an official duty by an employee of the court or an employee of any other governmental agency, shall not be disclosed directly or indirectly to anyone other than the judge, counsel for the juvenile and the Government, or others entitled under this section to receive juvenile records.

(d) Whenever a juvenile is found guilty of committing an act which if committed by an adult would be a felony that is a crime of violence or an offense described in section 401 of the Controlled Substances Act or section 1001(a), 1005, or 1009 of the Controlled Substances Import and Export Act, such juvenile shall be fingerprinted and photographed. Except a juvenile described in subsection (f), fingerprints and photographs of a juvenile who is not prosecuted as an adult shall be made available only in accordance with the provisions of subsection (a) of this section. Fingerprints and photographs of a juvenile who is prosecuted as an adult shall be made available in the manner applicable to adult defendants.

(e) Unless a juvenile who is taken into custody is prosecuted as an adult neither the name nor picture of any juvenile shall be made public in connection with a juvenile delinquency proceeding.

(f) Whenever a juvenile has on two separate occasions been found guilty of committing an act which if committed by an adult would be a felony crime of violence or an offense described in section 401 of the Controlled Substances Act or section 1001(a), 1005, or 1009 of the Controlled Substances Import and Export Act, or whenever a juvenile has been found guilty of committing an act after his 13th birthday which if committed by an adult would be an offense described in the second sentence of the fourth paragraph of section 5032 of this title, the court shall transmit to the Federal Bureau of Investigation the information concerning the adjudications, including name, date of adjudication, court, offenses, and sentence, along with the notation that the matters were juvenile adjudications.

(Added Pub.L. 93–415, Title V, § 508, Sept. 7, 1974, 88 Stat. 1137, and amended Pub.L. 95–115, § 8(b), Oct. 3, 1977, 91 Stat. 1060; Pub.L. 98–473, Title II, § 1202, Oct. 12, 1984, 98 Stat. 2150; Pub.L. 103–322, Title XIV, § 140005, Sept. 13, 1994, 108 Stat. 2032; Pub.L. 104–294, Title VI, § 601(f)(16), (*o*), Oct. 11, 1996, 110 Stat. 3500, 3502.)

HISTORICAL AND STATUTORY NOTES

References in Text

The Controlled Substances Act, referred to in subsecs. (d) and (f), is Pub.L. 91–513, Title II, Oct. 27, 1970, 84 Stat. 1242, as amended, which is classified principally to subchapter I (section 801 et seq.) of chapter 13 of Title 21, Food and Drugs. Section 401 of such Act is classified to section 841 of Title 21. For complete classification of this Act to the Code, see Short Title note set out under section 801 of Title 21 and Tables.

The Controlled Substances Import and Export Act, referred to in subsecs. (d) and (f), is Pub.L. 91–513, Title III, Oct. 27, 1970, 84 Stat. 1285, as amended, which is classified principally to subchapter II (section 951 et seq.) of chapter 13 of Title 21, Food and Drugs. Sections 1001(a), 1005, and 1009 of such Act are classified to sections 951(a), 955, and 959, respectively, of Title 21. For complete classification of this Act to the Code, see Short Title note set out under section 951 of Title 21 and Tables.

Effective and Applicability Provisions

1977 Acts. Amendment by Pub.L. 95–115 to take effect on Oct. 1, 1977, see section 263(c) of Pub.L. 93–415, as added by Pub.L. 95–115, set out as a note under section 5601 of Title 42, The Public Health and Welfare.

§ 5039. Commitment

No juvenile committed, whether pursuant to an adjudication of delinquency or conviction for an offense, to the custody of the Attorney General may be placed or retained in an adult jail or correctional institution in which he has regular contact with adults incarcerated because they have been convicted of a crime or are awaiting trial on criminal charges.

Every juvenile who has been committed shall be provided with adequate food, heat, light, sanitary facilities, bedding, clothing, recreation, counseling, education, training, and medical care including necessary psychiatric, psychological, or other care and treatment.

Whenever possible, the Attorney General shall commit a juvenile to a foster home or community-based facility located in or near his home community.

(Added Pub.L. 93–415, Title V, § 509, Sept. 7, 1974, 88 Stat. 1138, and amended Pub.L. 103–322, Title XIV, § 140003, Sept. 13, 1994, 108 Stat. 2032.)

§ 5040. Support

The Attorney General may contract with any public or private agency or individual and such community-based facilities as halfway houses and foster homes for the observation and study and the custody and care of juveniles in his custody. For these purposes, the Attorney General may promulgate such regulations as are necessary and may use the appropriation for "support of United States prisoners" or such other appropriations as he may designate.

(Added Pub.L. 93–415, Title V, § 510, Sept. 7, 1974, 88 Stat. 1138.)

[§ 5041. Repealed. Pub.L. 98–473, Title II, § 214(b), Oct. 12, 1984, 98 Stat. 2014]

HISTORICAL AND STATUTORY NOTES

Prior to repeal this section read:

§ 5041. Parole

A juvenile delinquent who has been committed may be released on parole at any time under such conditions and regulations as the United States Parole Commission deems proper in accordance with the provisions in section 4206 of this title.

(Added Pub.L. 93–415, Title V, § 511, Sept. 7, 1974, 88 Stat. 1138, and amended Pub.L. 94–233, § 11, Mar. 15, 1976, 90 Stat. 233.)

Effective Date of Repeal

Repeal by Pub.L. 98–473 effective on the first day of first calendar month beginning thirty six months after Oct. 12, 1984, applicable only to offenses committed after taking effect of sections 211 to 239 of Pub.L. 98–473, applicable for five years after repeal pursuant to the provisions of section 235(b)(1) of Pub.L. 98–473, and except as otherwise provided for therein, see section 235 of Pub.L. 98–473, as amended, set out as a note under section 3551 of this title.

§ 5042. Revocation of probation

Any juvenile probationer shall be accorded notice and a hearing with counsel before his probation can be revoked.

(Added Pub.L. 93–415, Title V, § 512, Sept. 7, 1974, 88 Stat. 1138, and amended Pub.L. 98–473, Title II, § 214(c), Oct. 12, 1984, 98 Stat. 2014.)

HISTORICAL AND STATUTORY NOTES

Effective and Applicability Provisions

1984 Acts. Amendment by Pub.L. 98–473 effective on the first day of first calendar month beginning thirty six months after Oct. 12, 1984, applicable only to offenses committed after taking effect of sections 211 to 239 of Pub.L. 98–473, applicable for five years after amendment pursuant to the provisions of section 235(b)(1) of Pub.L. 98–473, and except as otherwise provided for therein, see section 235 of Pub.L. 98–473, as amended, set out as a note under section 3551 of this title.

PART V—IMMUNITY OF WITNESSES

HISTORICAL AND STATUTORY NOTES

1970 Amendment

Pub.L. 91–452, Title II, § 201(a), Oct. 15, 1970, 84 Stat. 926, added Part V and items 6001 to 6005.

CHAPTER 601—IMMUNITY OF WITNESSES

HISTORICAL AND STATUTORY NOTES

1994 Amendments

Pub.L. 103–322, Title XXXIII, § 330013(1), Sept. 13, 1994, 108 Stat. 2146, added chapter heading.

§ 6001. Definitions

As used in this chapter—

(1) "agency of the United States" means any executive department as defined in section 101 of title 5, United States Code, a military department as defined in section 102 of title 5, United States Code, the Nuclear Regulatory Commission, the Board of Governors of the Federal Reserve System, the China Trade Act registrar appointed under 53 Stat. 1432 (15 U.S.C. sec. 143), the Commodity Futures Trading Commission, the Federal Communications Commission, the Federal Deposit Insurance Corporation, the Federal Maritime Commission, the Federal Power Commission, the Federal Trade Commission, the Surface Transportation Board, the National Labor Relations Board, the National Transportation Safety Board, the Railroad Retirement Board, an arbitration board established under 48 Stat. 1193 (45 U.S.C. sec. 157), the Securities and Exchange Commission, or a board established under 49 Stat. 31 (15 U.S.C. sec. 715d);

(2) "other information" includes any book, paper, document, record, recording, or other material;

(3) "proceeding before an agency of the United States" means any proceeding before such an agency with respect to which it is authorized to issue subpenas and to take testimony or receive other information from witnesses under oath; and

(4) "court of the United States" means any of the following courts: the Supreme Court of the United States, a United States court of appeals, a United States district court established under chapter 5, title 28, United States Code, a United States bankruptcy court established under chapter 6, title 28, United States Code, the District of Columbia Court of Appeals, the Superior Court of the District of Columbia, the District Court of Guam, the District Court of the Virgin Islands, the United States Court of Federal Claims, the Tax Court of the United States, the Court of International Trade, and the Court of Appeals for the Armed Forces.

(Added Pub.L. 91–452, Title II, § 201(a), Oct. 15, 1970, 84 Stat. 926, and amended Pub.L. 95–405, § 25, Sept. 30, 1978, 92 Stat. 877; Pub.L. 95–598, Title III, § 314(*l*), Nov. 6, 1978, 92 Stat. 2678; Pub.L. 96–417, Title VI, § 601(1), Oct. 10, 1980, 94 Stat. 1744; Pub.L. 97–164, Title I, § 164(1), Apr. 2, 1982, 96 Stat. 50; Pub.L. 102–550, Title XV, § 1543, Oct. 28, 1992, 106 Stat. 4069; Pub.L. 102–572, Title IX, § 902(b)(1), Oct. 29, 1992, 106 Stat. 4519; Pub.L. 103–272, § 4(d), July 5, 1994, 108 Stat. 1361; Pub.L. 103–322, Title XXXIII, § 330013(2), (3), Sept. 13, 1994, 108 Stat. 2146; Pub.L. 103–337, Div. A, Title IX, § 924(d)(1)(B), Oct. 5, 1994, 108 Stat. 2832; Pub.L. 104–88, Title III, § 303(2), Dec. 29, 1995, 109 Stat. 943.)

HISTORICAL AND STATUTORY NOTES

Effective and Applicability Provisions

1995 Acts. Amendment by Pub.L. 104–88 effective Jan. 1, 1996, see section 2 of Pub.L. 104–88, set out as a note under section 701 of Title 49, Transportation.

1992 Acts. Except as otherwise provided, amendment by Pub.L. 102–550 effective Oct. 28, 1992, see section 2 of Pub.L. 102–550, set out as a note under section 5301 of Title 42, The Public Health and Welfare.

1982 Acts. Amendment by Pub.L. 97–164 effective Oct. 1, 1982, see section 402 of Pub.L. 97–164, set out as an Effective Date of 1982 Amendment note under section 171 of Title 28, Judiciary and Judicial Procedure.

1980 Acts. Amendment by Pub.L. 96–417 effective Nov. 1, 1980, and applicable with respect to civil actions pending on or commenced on or after such date, see section 701(a) of Pub.L. 96–417, set out as an Effective Date of 1980 Amendment note under section 251 of Title 28, Judiciary and Judicial Procedure.

1978 Acts. Amendment by Pub.L. 95–598 effective Oct. 1, 1979, see section 402(a) of Pub.L. 95–598, set out as an Effective Dates note preceding section 101 of Title 11, Bankruptcy.

Amendment by Pub.L. 95–405 effective Oct. 1, 1978, see section 28 of Pub.L. 95–405, set out as an Effective Date of 1978 Amendment note under section 2 of Title 7, Agriculture.

1970 Acts. Section 260 of Pub.L. 91–452 provided that: "The provisions of part V of title 18, United States Code, added by title II of this Act [this part], and the amendments and repeals made by title II of this Act [sections 835, 895, 1406, 1954, 2424, 2514 and 3486 of this title, sections 15, 87(f), 135c, 499m(f), and 2115 of Title 7, Agriculture, section 25 of former Title 11, Bankruptcy, section 1820 of Title 12, Banks and Banking, sections 32, 33, 49, 77v, 78u(d), 79r(e), 80a–41, 80b–9, 155, 717m, 1271, and 1714 of Title 15, Commerce and Trade, section 825f of Title 16, Conservation, section 1333 of Title 19, Customs Duties, section 373 of Title 21, Food and Drugs, sections 4874 and 7493 of Title 26, Internal Revenue Code, section 161(3) of Title 29, Labor, section 506 of Title 33, Navigation and Navigable Waters, sections 405(f) and 2201 of Title 42, The Public Health and Welfare, sections 157 and 362 of Title 45, Railroads, sections 827 and 1124 of Title 46, Shipping, section 409(*l*) of Title 47, Telegraphs, Telephones, and Radiotelegraphs, sections 9, 43, 46, 47, 48, 916, and 1017 of former Title 49, Transportation, and section 1484 of Title 49, Appendix, section 792 of Title 50, War and National Defense, and sections 643a, 1152, 2026, and 2155(b) of Title 50, Appendix], shall take effect on the sixtieth day following the date of the enactment of this Act [Oct. 15, 1970]. No amendment to or repeal of any provision of law under title II of this Act shall affect any immunity to which any individual is entitled under such provision by reason of any testimony or other information given before such day."

Change of Name

References to United States Claims Court deemed to refer to United States Court of Federal Claims and references to Claims Court deemed to refer to Court of Federal Claims, see section 902(b) of Pub.L. 102–572, set out as a note under section 171 of Title 28, Judiciary and Judicial Procedure.

Savings Provisions

Amendment by section 314 of Pub.L. 95–598 not to affect the application of chapter 9 [§ 151 et seq.], chapter 96 [§ 1961 et seq.], or section 2516, 3057, or 3284 of this title to any act of any person (1) committed before Oct. 1, 1979, or (2) committed after Oct. 1, 1979, in connection with a case commenced before such date, see section 403(d) of Pub.L. 95–598, set out preceding section 101 of Title 11, Bankruptcy.

Amendment or Repeal of Inconsistent Provisions

Section 259 of Pub.L. 91–452 provided that: "In addition to the provisions of law specifically amended or specifically repealed by this title [see Effective Date note set out under this section], any other provision of law inconsistent with the provisions of part V of title 18, United States Code (added by title II of this Act) [this part], is to that extent amended or repealed."

Abolition of the Atomic Energy Commission

The Atomic Energy Commission was abolished and all functions were transferred to the Administrator of the Energy Research and Development Administration (unless otherwise specifically provided) by section 5814 of Title 42, The Public Health and Welfare. The Energy Research and Development Administration was terminated and functions vested by law in the Administrator thereof were transferred to the Secretary of Energy (unless otherwise specifically provided) by sections 7151(a) and 7293 of Title 42.

Termination of Civil Aeronautics Board and Transfer of Certain Functions

All functions, powers, and duties of the Civil Aeronautics Board were terminated or transferred by former section 1551 of Title 49, Transportation, effective in part on Dec. 31, 1981, in part on Jan. 1, 1983, and in part on Jan. 1, 1985.

Termination of Federal Power Commission

The Federal Power Commission, referred to in par. (1) was terminated and the functions, personnel, property, funds, etc., thereof were transferred to the Secretary of Energy (except for certain functions which were transferred to the Federal Energy Regulatory Commission) by sections 7151(b), 7171(a), 7172(a), 7291, and 7293 of Title 42, The Public Health and Welfare.

Subversive Activities Control Board

The Subversive Activities Control Board was established by Act Sept. 23, 1950, c. 1024, § 12, 64 Stat. 997, and ceased to operate June 30, 1973.

§ 6002. Immunity generally

Whenever a witness refuses, on the basis of his privilege against self-incrimination, to testify or provide other information in a proceeding before or ancillary to—

(1) a court or grand jury of the United States,

(2) an agency of the United States, or

(3) either House of Congress, a joint committee of the two Houses, or a committee or a subcommittee of either House,

and the person presiding over the proceeding communicates to the witness an order issued under this title, the witness may not refuse to comply with the order on the basis of his privilege against self-incrimination; but no testimony or other information compelled under the order (or any information directly or indirectly derived from such testimony or other information) may be used against the witness in any criminal case, except a prosecution for perjury, giving a false statement, or otherwise failing to comply with the order.

(Added Pub.L. 91–452, Title II, § 201(a), Oct. 15, 1970, 84 Stat. 927, and amended Pub.L. 103–322, Title XXXIII, § 330013(4), Sept. 13, 1994, 108 Stat. 2146.)

§ 6003. Court and grand jury proceedings

(a) In the case of any individual who has been or may be called to testify or provide other information at any proceeding before or ancillary to a court of the United States or a grand jury of the United States, the United States district court for the judicial district in which the proceeding is or may be held shall issue, in accordance with subsection (b) of this section, upon the request of the United States attorney for such district, an order requiring such individual to give testimony or provide other information which he refuses to give or provide on the basis of his privilege against self-incrimination, such order to become effective as provided in section 6002 of this title.

(b) A United States attorney may, with the approval of the Attorney General, the Deputy Attorney General, the Associate Attorney General, or any designated Assistant Attorney General or Deputy Assistant Attorney General, request an order under subsection (a) of this section when in his judgment—

(1) the testimony or other information from such individual may be necessary to the public interest; and

(2) such individual has refused or is likely to refuse to testify or provide other information on the basis of his privilege against self-incrimination.

(Added Pub.L. 91–452, Title II, § 201(a), Oct. 15, 1970, 84 Stat. 927, and amended Pub.L. 100–690, Title VII, § 7020(e), Nov. 18, 1988, 102 Stat. 4396; Pub.L. 103–322, Title XXXIII, § 330013(4), Sept. 13, 1994, 108 Stat. 2146.)

§ 6004. Certain administrative proceedings

(a) In the case of any individual who has been or who may be called to testify or provide other information at any proceeding before an agency of the United States, the agency may, with the approval of the Attorney General, issue, in accordance with subsection (b) of this section, an order requiring the individual to give testimony or provide other information which he refuses to give or provide on the basis of his privilege against self-incrimination, such order to become effective as provided in section 6002 of this title.

(b) An agency of the United States may issue an order under subsection (a) of this section only if in its judgment—

(1) the testimony or other information from such individual may be necessary to the public interest; and

(2) such individual has refused or is likely to refuse to testify or provide other information on the basis of his privilege against self-incrimination.

(Added Pub.L. 91–452, Title II, § 201(a), Oct. 15, 1970, 84 Stat. 927, and amended Pub.L. 103–322, Title XXXIII, § 330013(4), Sept. 13, 1994, 108 Stat. 2146.)

§ 6005. Congressional proceedings

(a) In the case of any individual who has been or may be called to testify or provide other information at any proceeding before or ancillary to either House of Congress, or any committee, or any subcommittee of either House, or any joint committee of the two Houses, a United States district court shall issue, in accordance with subsection (b) of this section, upon the request of a duly authorized representative of the House of Congress or the committee concerned, an order requiring such individual to give testimony or provide other information which he refuses to give or provide on the basis of his privilege against self-incrimination, such order to become effective as provided in section 6002 of this title.

(b) Before issuing an order under subsection (a) of this section, a United States district court shall find that—

(1) in the case of a proceeding before or ancillary to either House of Congress, the request for such an order has been approved by an affirmative vote of a majority of the Members present of that House;

(2) in the case of a proceeding before or ancillary to a committee or a subcommittee of either House of Congress or a joint committee of both Houses, the request for such an order has been approved by an affirmative vote of two-thirds of the members of the full committee; and

(3) ten days or more prior to the day on which the request for such an order was made, the Attorney General was served with notice of an intention to request the order.

(c) Upon application of the Attorney General, the United States district court shall defer the issuance of any order under subsection (a) of this section for such period, not longer than twenty days from the date of the request for such order, as the Attorney General may specify.

(Added Pub.L. 91–452, Title II, § 201(a), Oct. 15, 1970, 84 Stat. 928, and amended Pub.L. 103–322, Title XXXIII, § 330013(4), Sept. 13, 1994, 108 Stat. 2146; Pub.L. 104–292, § 5, Oct. 11, 1996, 110 Stat. 3460; Pub.L. 104–294, Title VI, § 605(*o*), Oct. 11, 1996, 110 Stat. 3510.)

APPENDIX 1
UNLAWFUL POSSESSION OR RECEIPT OF FIREARMS

Pub.L. 91–538, §§ 1–9, Dec. 9, 1970, 84 Stat. 1397–1403

[§ 1201. Repealed. Pub.L. 99–308, § 104(b), May 19, 1986, 100 Stat. 459.]

HISTORICAL AND STATUTORY NOTES

Section, Pub.L. 90–351, Title VII, § 1201, June 19, 1968, 82 Stat. 236; Pub.L. 90–618, Title III, § 301(a)(1), Oct. 22, 1968, 82 Stat. 1236, related to Congressional findings and statement of policy with respect to receipt, possession, or transportation of a firearm by felons, veterans who are discharged under dishonorable conditions, mental incompetents, aliens who are illegally in this country, and former citizens who have renounces their citizenship.

Effective Date of Repeal

Section repealed effective 180 days after May 19, 1986, see section 110(a) of Pub.L. 99–308, set out as a note under section 921 of this title.

[§ 1202. Repealed. Pub.L. 99–308, § 104(b), May 19, 1986, 100 Stat. 459.]

HISTORICAL AND STATUTORY NOTES

Section, Pub.L. 90–351, Title VII, § 1202, June 19, 1968, 82 Stat. 236; Pub.L. 90–618, Title III, § 301(a)(2), (b), Oct. 22, 1968, 82 Stat. 1236; Pub.L. 98–373, Title II, §§ 1802, 1803, Oct. 12, 1984, 98 Stat. 2185, provided penalties for receipt, possession, or transportation of firearms in commerce or affecting commerce by a convicted felon, dishonorably discharged veteran, mental incompetent, former citizen, illegal alien, or any individual employed by such a person and defined terms as used in Title VII of Pub.L. 90–351.

Effective Date of Repeal

Section repealed effective 180 days after May 19, 1986, see section 110(a) of Pub.L. 99–308, set out as a note under section 921 of this title.

[§ 1203. Repealed. Pub.L. 99–308, § 104(b), May 19, 1986, 100 Stat. 459.]

HISTORICAL AND STATUTORY NOTES

Section, Pub.L. 90–351, Title VII, § 1203, June 19, 1968, 82 Stat. 236, related to person exempt from the provisions of Title VII of Pub.L. 90–351.

Effective Date of Repeal

Section repealed effective 180 days after May 19, 1986, see section 110(a) of Pub.L. 99–308, set out as a note under section 921 of this title.

APPENDIX 2

INTERSTATE AGREEMENT ON DETAINERS

Pub.L. 91–538, §§ 1–9, Dec. 9, 1970, 84 Stat. 1397–1403

§ 1. Short title

This Act may be cited as the "Interstate Agreement on Detainers Act".

(Pub.L. 91–538, § 1, Dec. 9, 1970, 84 Stat. 1397.)

HISTORICAL AND STATUTORY NOTES

Complementary Laws:

Ala.—Code 1975, § 15–9–81.
Alaska—AS 33.35.010 to 33.35.040.
Ariz.—A.R.S. §§ 31–481, 31–482.
Ark.—A.C.A. §§ 16–95–101 to 16–95–107.
Cal.—West's Ann.Cal.Penal Code, §§ 1389 to 1389.8.
Colo.—West's C.R.S.A. §§ 24–60–501 to 24–60–507.
Conn.—C.G.S.A. §§ 54–186 to 54–192.
Del.—11 Del.C. §§ 2540 to 2550.
D.C.—D.C. Official Code, 2001 Ed. §§ 24–801 to 24–805.
Fla.—West's F.S.A. §§ 941.45 to 941.50.
Ga.—O.C.G.A. §§ 42–6–20 to 42–6–25.
Hawaii—H R S §§ 834–1 to 834–6.
Idaho—I.C. §§ 19–5001 to 19–5008.
Ill.—S.H.A. 730 ILCS 5/3–8–9.
Ind.—West's A.I.C. 35–33–10–4.
Iowa—I.C.A. §§ 821.1 to 821.8.
Kan.—K.S.A. 22–4401 to 22–4408.
Ky.—KRS 440.450 to 440.510.
Maine—34–A M.R.S.A. §§ 9601 to 9609.
Md.—Code, Correctional Services, §§ 8–401 to 8–417.
Mass.—M.G.L.A. c. 276 App., §§ 1–1 to 1–8.
Mich.—M.C.L.A. §§ 780.601 to 780.608.
Minn.—M.S.A. § 629.294.
Mo.—V.A.M.S. §§ 217.490.
Mt.—M.C.A. 46–31–101 to 46–31–204.
Neb.—R.R.S. 1943, §§ 29–759 to 29–765.
Nev.—N.R.S. 178.620 to 178.640.
N.H.—RSA 606–A:1 to 606–A:6.
N.J.—N.J.S.A. 2A:159A–1 to 2A:159A–15.
N.M.—NMSA 1978, § 31–5–12 to 31–5–16.
N.Y.—McKinney's CPL § 580.20.
N.C.—G.S. §§ 15A–761 to 15A–767.
N.D.—NDCC 29–34–01 to 29–34–08.
Ohio—R.C. §§ 2963.30 to 2963.35.
Okl.—22 Okl.St.Ann. §§ 1345 to 1349.
Ore.—ORS 135.775 to 135.793.
Pa.—42 Pa.C.S.A. §§ 9101 to 9108.
R.I.—Gen.Laws 1956, §§ 13–13–1 to 13–13–8.
S.C.—Code 1976, §§ 17–11–10 to 17–11–80.
S.D.—SDCL 23–24A–1 to 23–24A–34.
Tenn.—T.C.A. §§ 40–31–101 to 40–31–108.
Tex.—Vernon's Ann.C.C.P. art. 51.14.
U.S.—18 U.S.C.A. App.
Utah—U.C.A. 1953, 77–29–5 to 77–29–11.
Vt.—28 V.S.A. §§ 1501 to 1509, 1531 to 1537.
Va.—Code 1950, §§ 53.1–210 to 53.1–215.
Wash.—West's RCWA 9.100.010 to 9.100.080.
W.Va.—Code, 62–14–1 to 62–14–7.
Wis.—W.S.A. 976.05, 976.06.
Wyo.—Wyo.Stat.Ann. §§ 7–15–101 to 7–15–105.

§ 2. Enactment into law of Interstate Agreement on Detainers

The Interstate Agreement on Detainers is hereby enacted into law and entered into by the United States on its own behalf and on behalf of the District of Columbia with all jurisdictions legally joining in substantially the following form:

"The contracting States solemnly agree that:

"Article I

"The party States find that charges outstanding against a prisoner, detainers based on untried indictments, informations, or complaints and difficulties in securing speedy trial of persons already incarcerated in other jurisdictions, produce uncertainties which obstruct programs of prisoner treatment and rehabilitation. Accordingly, it is the policy of the party States and the purpose of this agreement to encourage the expeditious and orderly disposition of such charges and determination of the proper status of any and all detainers based on untried indictments, informations, or complaints. The party States also find that proceedings with reference to such charges and detainers, when emanating from another jurisdiction, cannot properly be had in the absence of cooperative procedures. It is the further purpose of this agreement to provide such cooperative procedures.

"Article II

"As used in this agreement:

"(a) 'State' shall mean a State of the United States; the United States of America; a territory or possession of the United States; the District of Columbia; the Commonwealth of Puerto Rico.

"(b) 'Sending State' shall mean a State in which a prisoner is incarcerated at the time that he initiates a request for final disposition pursuant to article III hereof or at the time that a request for custody or availability is initiated pursuant to article IV hereof.

"(c) 'Receiving State' shall mean the State in which trial is to be had on an indictment, information, or complaint pursuant to article III or article IV hereof.

"Article III

"(a) Whenever a person has entered upon a term of imprisonment in a penal or correctional institution of a party State, and whenever during the continuance of the term of imprisonment there is pending in any other party State any untried indictment, information, or complaint on the basis of which a detainer has been lodged against the prisoner, he shall be brought to trial within one hundred and eighty days after he shall have caused to be delivered to the prosecuting officer and the appropriate court of the prosecuting officer's jurisdiction written notice of the place of his imprisonment and his request for a final disposition to be made of the indictment, information, or complaint: *Provided*, That, for good cause shown in open court, the prisoner or his counsel being present, the court having jurisdiction of the matter may grant any necessary or reasonable continuance. The request of the prisoner shall be accompanied by a certificate of the appropriate official having custody of the prisoner, stating the term of commitment under which the prisoner is being held, the time already served, the time remaining to be served on the sentence, the amount of good time earned, the time of parole eligibility of the prisoner, and any decision of the State parole agency relating to the prisoner.

"(b) The written notice and request for final disposition referred to in paragraph (a) hereof shall be given or sent by the prisoner to the warden, commissioner of corrections, or other official having custody of him, who shall promptly forward it together with the certificate to the appropriate prosecuting official and court by registered or certified mail, return receipt requested.

"(c) The warden, commissioner of corrections, or other official having custody of the prisoner shall promptly inform him of the source and contents of any detainer lodged against him and shall also inform him of his right to make a request for final disposition of the indictment, information, or complaint on which the detainer is based.

"(d) Any request for final disposition made by a prisoner pursuant to paragraph (a) hereof shall operate as a request for final disposition of all untried indictments, informations, or complaints on the basis of which detainers have been lodged against the prisoner from the State to whose prosecuting official the request for final disposition is specifically directed. The warden, commissioner of corrections, or other official having custody of the prisoner shall forthwith notify all appropriate prosecuting officers and courts in the several jurisdictions within the State to which the prisoner's request for final disposition is being sent of the proceeding being initiated by the prisoner. Any notification sent pursuant to this paragraph shall be accompanied by copies of the prisoner's written notice, request, and the certificate. If trial is not had on any indictment, information, or complaint contemplated hereby prior to the return of the prisoner to the original place of imprisonment, such indictment, information, or complaint shall not be of any further force or effect, and the court shall enter an order dismissing the same with prejudice.

"(e) Any request for final disposition made by a prisoner pursuant to paragraph (a) hereof shall also be deemed to be a waiver of extradition with respect to any charge or proceeding contemplated thereby or included therein by reason of paragraph (d) hereof, and a waiver of extradition to the receiving State to serve any sentence there imposed upon him, after completion of his term of imprisonment in the sending State. The request for final disposition shall also constitute a consent by the prisoner to the production of his body in any court where his presence may be required in order to effectuate the purposes of this agreement and a further consent voluntarily to be returned to the original place of imprisonment in accordance with the provisions of this agreement. Nothing in this paragraph shall prevent the imposition of a concurrent sentence if otherwise permitted by law.

"(f) Escape from custody by the prisoner subsequent to his execution of the request for final disposition referred to in paragraph (a) hereof shall void the request.

"Article IV

"(a) The appropriate officer of the jurisdiction in which an untried indictment, information, or complaint is pending shall be entitled to have a prisoner against whom he has lodged a detainer and who is serving a term of imprisonment in any party State made available in accordance with article V(a) hereof upon presentation of a written request for temporary custody or availability to the appropriate authorities of the State in which the prisoner is incarcerated: *Provided*, That the court having jurisdiction of such indictment, information, or complaint shall have duly approved, recorded, and transmitted the request: *And provided further*, That there shall be a period of thirty days after receipt by the appropriate authorities before the request be honored, within which period the Governor of the sending State may disapprove the request for temporary custody or availability, either upon his own motion or upon motion of the prisoner.

"**(b)** Upon request of the officer's written request as provided in paragraph (a) hereof, the appropriate authorities having the prisoner in custody shall furnish the officer with a certificate stating the term of commitment under which the prisoner is being held, the time already served, the time remaining to be served on the sentence, the amount of good time earned, the time of parole eligibility of the prisoner, and any decisions of the State parole agency relating to the prisoner. Said authorities simultaneously shall furnish all other officers and appropriate courts in the receiving State who has lodged detainers against the prisoner with similar certificates and with notices informing them of the request for custody or availability and of the reasons therefor.

"**(c)** In respect of any proceeding made possible by this article, trial shall be commenced within one hundred and twenty days of the arrival of the prisoner in the receiving State, but for good cause shown in open court, the prisoner or his counsel being present, the court having jurisdiction of the matter may grant any necessary or reasonable continuance.

"**(d)** Nothing contained in this article shall be construed to deprive any prisoner of any right which he may have to contest the legality of his delivery as provided in paragraph (a) hereof, but such delivery may not be opposed or denied on the ground that the executive authority of the sending State has not affirmatively consented to or ordered such delivery.

"**(e)** If trial is not had on any indictment, information, or complaint contemplated hereby prior to the prisoner's being returned to the original place of imprisonment pursuant to article V(e) hereof, such indictment, information, or complaint shall not be of any further force or effect, and the court shall enter an order dismissing the same with prejudice.

"Article V

"**(a)** In response to a request made under article III or article IV hereof, the appropriate authority in a sending State shall offer to deliver temporary custody of such prisoner to the appropriate authority in the State where such indictment, information, or complaint is pending against such person in order that speedy and efficient prosecution may be had. If the request for final disposition is made by the prisoner, the offer of temporary custody shall accompany the written notice provided for in article III of this agreement. In the case of a Federal prisoner, the appropriate authority in the receiving State shall be entitled to temporary custody as provided by this agreement or to the prisoner's presence in Federal custody at the place of trial, whichever custodial arrangement may be approved by the custodian.

"**(b)** The officer or other representative of a State accepting an offer of temporary custody shall present the following upon demand:

"**(1)** Proper identification and evidence of his authority to act for the State into whose temporary custody this prisoner is to be given.

"**(2)** A duly certified copy of the indictment, information, or complaint on the basis of which the detainer has been lodged and on the basis of which the request for temporary custody of the prisoner has been made.

"**(c)** If the appropriate authority shall refuse or fail to accept temporary custody of said person, or in the event that an action on the indictment, information, or complaint on the basis of which the detainer has been lodged is not brought to trial within the period provided in article III or article IV hereof, the appropriate court of the jurisdiction where the indictment, information, or complaint has been pending shall enter an order dismissing the same with prejudice, and any detainer based thereon shall cease to be of any force or effect.

"**(d)** The temporary custody referred to in this agreement shall be only for the purpose of permitting prosecution on the charge or charges contained in one or more untried indictments, informations, or complaints which form the basis of the detainer or detainers or for prosecution on any other charge or charges arising out of the same transaction. Except for his attendance at court and while being transported to or from any place at which his presence may be required, the prisoner shall be held in a suitable jail or other facility regularly used for persons awaiting prosecution.

"**(e)** At the earliest practicable time consonant with the purposes of this agreement, the prisoner shall be returned to the sending State.

"**(f)** During the continuance of temporary custody or while the prisoner is otherwise being made available for trial as required by this agreement, time being served on the sentence shall continue to run but good time shall be earned by the prisoner only if, and to the extent that, the law and practice of the jurisdiction which imposed the sentence may allow.

"**(g)** For all purposes other than that for which temporary custody as provided in this agreement is exercised, the prisoner shall be deemed to remain in the custody of and subject to the jurisdiction of the sending State and any escape from temporary custody may be dealt with in the same manner as an escape from the original place of imprisonment or in any other manner permitted by law.

"**(h)** From the time that a party State receives custody of a prisoner pursuant to this agreement until such prisoner is returned to the territory and custody of the sending State, the State in which the one or more untried indictments, informations, or complaints are pending or in which trial is being had shall be responsible for the prisoner and shall also pay all costs of transporting, caring for, keeping, and returning the prisoner. The provisions of this paragraph shall govern unless the States concerned shall have entered into a supplementary agreement providing for a different allocation of costs and responsibilities as between or among themselves. Nothing herein contained shall be construed to alter or affect any internal relationship among the departments, agencies, and officers of and in the government of a party State, or between a party State and its subdivisions, as to the payment of costs, or responsibilities therefor.

"Article VI

"**(a)** In determining the duration and expiration dates of the time periods provided in articles III and IV of this agreement, the running of said time periods shall be tolled whenever and for as long as the prisoner is unable to stand trial, as determined by the court having jurisdiction of the matter.

"**(b)** No provision of this agreement, and no remedy made available by this agreement shall apply to any person who is adjudged to be mentally ill.

"Article VII

"Each State party to this agreement shall designate an officer who, acting jointly with like officers of other party States, shall promulgate rules and regulations to carry out more effectively the terms and provisions of this agreement, and who shall provide, within and without the State, information necessary to the effective operation of this agreement.

"Article VIII

"This agreement shall enter into full force and effect as to a party State when such State has enacted the same into law. A State party to this agreement may withdraw herefrom by enacting a statute repealing the same. However, the withdrawal of any State shall not affect the status of any proceedings already initiated by inmates or by State officers at the time such withdrawal takes effect, nor shall it affect their rights in respect thereof.

"Article IX

"This agreement shall be liberally construed so as to effectuate its purposes. The provisions of this agreement shall be severable and if any phrase, clause, sentence, or provision of this agreement is declared to be contrary to the constitution of any party State or of the United States or the applicability thereof to any government, agency, person, or circumstance is held invalid, the validity of the remainder of this agreement and the applicability thereof to any government, agency, person, or circumstance shall not be affected thereby. If this agreement shall be held contrary to the constitution of any State party hereto, the agreement shall remain in full force and effect as to the remaining States and in full force and effect as to the State affected as to all severable matters."

(Pub.L. 91–538, § 2, Dec. 9, 1970, 84 Stat. 1397.)

§ 3. Definition of term "Governor" for purposes of United States and District of Columbia

The term "Governor" as used in the agreement on detainers shall mean with respect to the United States, the Attorney General, and with respect to the District of Columbia, the Mayor of the District of Columbia.

(Pub.L. 91–538, § 3, Dec. 9, 1970, 84 Stat. 1402.)

HISTORICAL AND STATUTORY NOTES

Transfer of Functions

"Mayor of the District of Columbia" was substituted for "Commissioner of the District of Columbia" pursuant to section 421 of Pub.L. 93–198. The Office of Commissioner of the District of Columbia, as established by Reorg. Plan No. 3 of 1967, was abolished as of noon Jan. 2, 1975, by Pub.L. 93–198, Title VII, § 711, Dec. 24, 1973, 87 Stat. 818, and replaced by the Office of Mayor of the District of Columbia by section 421 of Pub.L. 93–198, classified to section 1–241 of the District of Columbia Code.

§ 4. Definition of term "appropriate court"

The term "appropriate court" as used in the agreement on detainers shall mean with respect to the United States, the courts of the United States, and with respect to the District of Columbia, the courts of the District of Columbia, in which indictments, informations, or complaints, for which disposition is sought, are pending.

(Pub.L. 91–538, § 4, Dec. 9, 1970, 84 Stat. 1402.)

§ 5. Enforcement and cooperation by courts, departments, agencies, officers, and employees of United States and District of Columbia

All courts, departments, agencies, officers, and employees of the United States and of the District of Columbia are hereby directed to enforce the agreement on detainers and to cooperate with one another and with all party States in enforcing the agreement and effectuating its purpose.

(Pub.L. 91–538, § 5, Dec. 9, 1970, 84 Stat. 1402.)

§ 6. Regulations, forms, and instructions

For the United States, the Attorney General, and for the District of Columbia, the Mayor of the District of Columbia, shall establish such regulations, prescribe such forms, issue such instructions, and perform such other acts as he deems necessary for carrying out the provisions of this Act.

(Pub.L. 91–538, § 6, Dec. 9, 1970, 84 Stat. 1403.)

HISTORICAL AND STATUTORY NOTES

References in Text

This Act, referred to in text, is Pub.L. 91–538, Dec. 9, 1970, 84 Stat. 1397, known as the "Interstate Agreement on Detainers Act".

Transfer of Functions

"Mayor of the District of Columbia" was substituted for "Commissioner of the District of Columbia" pursuant to section 421 of Pub.L. 93–198. The Office of Commissioner of the District of Columbia, as established by Reorg. Plan No. 3 of 1967, was abolished as of noon Jan. 2, 1975, by Pub.L. 93–198, Title VII, § 711, Dec. 24, 1973, 87 Stat. 818, and replaced by the Office of Mayor of the District of Columbia by section 421 of Pub.L. 93–198, classified to section 1–241 of the District of Columbia Code.

§ 7. Reservation of right to alter, amend, or repeal

The right to alter, amend, or repeal this Act is expressly reserved.

(Pub.L. 91–538, § 7, Dec. 9, 1970, 84 Stat. 1403.)

HISTORICAL AND STATUTORY NOTES

References in Text

This Act, referred to in text, is Pub.L. 91–538, Dec. 9, 1970, 84 Stat. 1397, known as the "Interstate Agreement on Detainers Act".

§ 8. Effective date

This Act shall take effect on the ninetieth day after the date of its enactment.

(Pub.L. 91–538, § 8, Dec. 9, 1970, 84 Stat. 1403.)

HISTORICAL AND STATUTORY NOTES

References in Text

This Act, referred to in text, is Pub.L. 91–538, Dec. 9, 1970, 84 Stat. 1397, known as the "Interstate Agreement on Detainers Act".

The date of its enactment, referred to in text, means Dec. 9, 1970.

§ 9. Special provisions when United States is a receiving State

Notwithstanding any provision of the agreement on detainers to the contrary, in a case in which the United States is a receiving State—

(1) any order of a court dismissing any indictment, information, or complaint may be with or without prejudice. In determining whether to dismiss the case with or without prejudice, the court shall consider, among others, each of the following factors: The seriousness of the offense; the facts and circumstances of the case which led to the dismissal; and the impact of a reprosecution on the administration of the agreement on detainers and on the administration of justice; and

(2) it shall not be a violation of the agreement on detainers if prior to trial the prisoner is returned to the custody of the sending State pursuant to an order of the appropriate court issued after reasonable notice to the prisoner and the United States and an opportunity for a hearing.

(Pub.L. 91–538, § 9, as added Pub.L. 100–690, Title VII, § 7059, Nov. 18, 1988, 102 Stat. 4403.)

APPENDIX 3
CLASSIFIED INFORMATION PROCEDURES ACT

Pub.L. 96–456, Oct. 15, 1980, 94 Stat. 2025

§ 1. Definitions

(a) "Classified information", as used in this Act, means any information or material that has been determined by the United States Government pursuant to an Executive order, statute, or regulation, to require protection against unauthorized disclosure for reasons of national security and any restricted data, as defined in paragraph r. of section 11 of the Atomic Energy Act of 1954 (42 U.S.C. 2014(y)).

(b) "National security", as used in this Act, means the national defense and foreign relations of the United States.

(Pub.L. 96–456, § 1, Oct. 15, 1980, 94 Stat. 2025.)

HISTORICAL AND STATUTORY NOTES

References in Text

This Act, referred to in text, is Pub.L. 96–456, Oct. 15, 1980, 94 Stat. 2025, known as the "Classified Information Procedures Act".

§ 2. Pretrial conference

At any time after the filing of the indictment or information, any party may move for a pretrial conference to consider matters relating to classified information that may arise in connection with the prosecution. Following such motion, or on its own motion, the court shall promptly hold a pretrial conference to establish the timing of requests for discovery, the provision of notice required by section 5 of this Act, and the initiation of the procedure established by section 6 of this Act. In addition, at the pretrial conference the court may consider any matters which relate to classified information or which may promote a fair and expeditious trial. No admission made by the defendant or by any attorney for the defendant at such a conference may be used against the defendant unless the admission is in writing and is signed by the defendant and by the attorney for the defendant.

(Pub.L. 96–456, § 2, Oct. 15, 1980, 94 Stat. 2025.)

§ 3. Protective orders

Upon motion of the United States, the court shall issue an order to protect against the disclosure of any classified information disclosed by the United States to any defendant in any criminal case in a district court of the United States.

(Pub.L. 96–456, § 3, Oct. 15, 1980, 94 Stat. 2025.)

§ 4. Discovery of classified information by defendants

The court, upon a sufficient showing, may authorize the United States to delete specified items of classified information from documents to be made available to the defendant through discovery under the Federal Rules of Criminal Procedure, to substitute a summary of the information for such classified documents, or to substitute a statement admitting relevant facts that the classified information would tend to prove. The court may permit the United States to make a request for such authorization in the form of a written statement to be inspected by the court alone. If the court enters an order granting relief following such an ex parte showing, the entire text of the statement of the United States shall be sealed and preserved in the records of the court to be made available to the appellate court in the event of an appeal.

§ 5. Notice of defendant's intention to disclose classified information

(a) Notice by defendant

If a defendant reasonably expects to disclose or to cause the disclosure of classified information in any manner in connection with any trial or pretrial proceeding involving the criminal prosecution of such defendant, the defendant shall, within the time specified by the court or, where no time is specified, within thirty days prior to trial, notify the attorney for the United States and the court in writing. Such notice shall include a brief description of the classified information. Whenever a defendant learns of additional classified information he reasonably expects to disclose at any such proceeding, he shall notify the attorney for the United States and the court in writing as soon as possible thereafter and shall include a brief description of the classified information. No defendant shall disclose any information known or believed to be classified in connection with a trial or pretrial proceeding until notice has been given under this subsection and until the United States has been afforded a reasonable opportunity to seek a determination pursuant to the procedure set forth in section 6 of this Act, and until the time for the United States to appeal such determination under section 7 has expired or any appeal under section 7 by the United States is decided.

(b) Failure to comply

If the defendant fails to comply with the requirements of subsection (a) the court may preclude disclosure of any classified information not made the subject of notification and may prohibit the examination by the defendant of any witness with respect to any such information.

(Pub.L. 96–456, § 5, Oct. 15, 1980, 94 Stat. 2026.)

§ 6. Procedure for cases involving classified information

(a) Motion for hearing

Within the time specified by the court for the filing of a motion under this section, the United States may request the court to conduct a hearing to make all determinations concerning the use, relevance, or admissibility of classified information that would otherwise be made during the trial or pretrial proceeding. Upon such a request, the court shall conduct such a hearing. Any hearing held pursuant to this subsection (or any portion of such hearing specified in the request of the Attorney General) shall be held in camera if the Attorney General certifies to the court in such petition that a public proceeding may result in the disclosure of classified information. As to each item of classified information, the court shall set forth in writing the basis for its determination. Where the United States' motion under this subsection is filed prior to the trial or pretrial proceeding, the court shall rule prior to the commencement of the relevant proceeding.

(b) Notice

(1) Before any hearing is conducted pursuant to a request by the United States under subsection (a), the United States shall provide the defendant with notice of the classified information that is at issue. Such notice shall identify the specific classified information at issue whenever that information previously has been made available to the defendant by the United States. When the United States has not previously made the information available to the defendant in connection with the case, the information may be described by generic category, in such form as the court may approve, rather than by identification of the specific information of concern to the United States.

(2) Whenever the United States requests a hearing under subsection (a), the court, upon request of the defendant, may order the United States to provide the defendant, prior to trial, such details as to the portion of the indictment or information at issue in the hearing as are needed to give the defendant fair notice to prepare for the hearing.

(c) Alternative procedure for disclosure of classified information

(1) Upon any determination by the court authorizing the disclosure of specific classified information under the procedures established by this section, the United States may move that, in lieu of the disclosure of such specific classified information, the court order—

(A) the substitution for such classified information of a statement admitting relevant facts that the specific classified information would tend to prove; or

(B) the substitution for such classified information of a summary of the specific classified information.

The court shall grant such a motion of the United States if it finds that the statement or summary will provide the defendant with substantially the same ability to make his defense as would disclosure of the specific classified information. The court shall hold a hearing on any motion under this section. Any such hearing shall be held in camera at the request of the Attorney General.

(2) The United States may, in connection with a motion under paragraph (1), submit to the court an affidavit of the Attorney General certifying that disclosure of classified information would cause identifiable damage to the national security of the United States and explaining the basis for the classification of such information. If so requested by the United States, the court shall examine such affidavit in camera and ex parte.

(d) Sealing of records of in camera hearings

If at the close of an in camera hearing under this Act (or any portion of a hearing under this Act that is held in camera) the court determines that the classified information at issue may not be disclosed or elicited at the trial or pretrial proceeding, the record of such in camera hearing shall be sealed and preserved by the court for use in the event of an appeal. The defendant may seek reconsideration of the court's determination prior to or during trial.

(e) Prohibition on disclosure of classified information by defendant, relief for defendant when United States opposes disclosure

(1) Whenever the court denies a motion by the United States that it issue an order under subsection (c) and the United States files with the court an affidavit of the Attorney General objecting to disclosure of the classified information at issue, the court shall order that the defendant not disclose or cause the disclosure of such information.

(2) Whenever a defendant is prevented by an order under paragraph (1) from disclosing or causing the disclosure of classified information, the court shall dismiss the indictment or information; except that, when the court determines that the interests of justice would not be served by dismissal of the indictment or information, the court shall order such other action, in lieu of dismissing the indictment or information, as the court determines is appropriate. Such action may include, but need not be limited to—

(A) dismissing specified counts of the indictment or information;

(B) finding against the United States on any issue as to which the excluded classified information relates; or

(C) striking or precluding all or part of the testimony of a witness.

An order under this paragraph shall not take effect until the court has afforded the United States an opportunity to appeal such order under section 7, and thereafter to withdraw its objection to the disclosure of the classified information at issue.

(f) Reciprocity

Whenever the court determines pursuant to subsection (a) that classified information may be disclosed in connection with a trial or pretrial proceeding, the court shall, unless the interests of fairness do not so require, order the United States to provide the defendant with the information it expects to use to rebut the classified information. The court may place the United States under a continuing duty to disclose such rebuttal information. If the United States fails to comply with its obligation under this subsection, the court may exclude any evidence not made the subject of a required disclosure and may prohibit the examination by the United States of any witness with respect to such information.

(Pub.L. 96–456, § 6, Oct. 15, 1980, 94 Stat. 2026.)

HISTORICAL AND STATUTORY NOTES

References in Text

This Act, referred to in subsec. (d), is Pub.L. 96–456, Oct. 15, 1980, 94 Stat. 2025, known as the "Classified Information Procedures Act".

§ 7. Interlocutory appeal

(a) An interlocutory appeal by the United States taken before or after the defendant has been placed in jeopardy shall lie to a court of appeals from a decision or order of a district court in a criminal case authorizing the disclosure of classified information, imposing sanctions for nondisclosure of classified information, or refusing a protective order sought by the United States to prevent the disclosure of classified information.

(b) An appeal taken pursuant to this section either before or during trial shall be expedited by the court of appeals. Prior to trial, an appeal shall be taken within ten days after the decision or order appealed from and the trial shall not commence until the appeal is resolved. If an appeal is taken during trial, the trial court shall adjourn the trial until the appeal is resolved and the court of appeals (1) shall hear argument on such appeal within four days of the adjournment of the trial, (2) may dispense with written briefs other than the supporting materials previously submitted to the trial court, (3) shall render its decision within four days of argument on appeal, and (4) may dispense with the issuance of a written opinion in rendering its decision. Such appeal and decision shall not affect the right of the defendant, in a subsequent appeal from a judgment of conviction, to claim as error reversal by the trial court on remand of a ruling appealed from during trial.

(Pub.L. 96–456, § 7, Oct. 15, 1980, 94 Stat. 2028.)

§ 8. Introduction of classified information

(a) Classification status

Writings, recordings, and photographs containing classified information may be admitted into evidence without change in their classification status.

(b) Precautions by court

The court, in order to prevent unnecessary disclosure of classified information involved in any criminal proceeding, may order admission into evidence of only part of a writing, recording, or photograph, or may order admission into evidence of the whole writing, recording, or photograph with excision of some or all of the classified information contained therein, unless the whole ought in fairness be considered.

(c) Taking of testimony

During the examination of a witness in any criminal proceeding, the United States may object to any question or line of inquiry that may require the witness to disclose classified information not previously found to be admissible. Following such an objection, the court shall take such suitable action to determine whether the response is admissible as will safeguard against the compromise of any classified information. Such action may include requiring the United States to provide the court with a proffer of the witness' response to the question or line of inquiry and requiring the defendant to provide the court with a proffer of the nature of the information he seeks to elicit.

(Pub.L. 96–456, § 8, Oct. 15, 1980, 94 Stat. 2028.)

§ 9. Security procedures

(a) Within one hundred and twenty days of the date of the enactment of this Act, the Chief Justice of the United States, in consultation with the Attorney General, the Director of National Intelligence, and the Secretary of Defense, shall prescribe rules establishing procedures for the protection against unauthorized disclosure of any classified information in the custody of the United States district courts, courts of appeal, or Supreme Court. Such rules, and any changes in such rules, shall be submitted to the appropriate committees of Congress and shall become effective forty-five days after such submission.

(b) Until such time as rules under subsection (a) first become effective, the Federal courts shall in each case involving classified information adopt procedures to protect against the unauthorized disclosure of such information.

(Pub.L. 96–456, § 9, Oct. 15, 1980, 94 Stat. 2029; Pub.L. 108–458, Title I, § 1071(f), Dec. 17, 2004, 118 Stat. 3691.)

HISTORICAL AND STATUTORY NOTES

References in Text

The date of the enactment of this Act, referred to in subsec. (a), means Oct. 15, 1980.

Effective and Applicability Provisions

2004 Acts. Except as otherwise expressly provided, amendments by Pub.L. 108–458, Title I, to take effect not later than six months after Dec. 17, 2004, see Pub.L. 108–458, Title I, § 1097(a), set out in the Transfer, Termination, Implementation, Transition, and Effective Dates of the National Security Intelligence Reform Act of 2004 note under 50 U.S.C.A. § 401.

SECURITY PROCEDURES ESTABLISHED PURSUANT TO PUB.L. 96–456, 94 STAT. 2025, BY THE CHIEF JUSTICE OF THE UNITED STATES FOR THE PROTECTION OF CLASSIFIED INFORMATION

1. Purpose. The purpose of these procedures is to meet the requirements of Section 9(a) of the Classified Information Procedures Act of 1980, Pub.L. 96–456, 94 Stat. 2025, which in pertinent part provides that:

> ". . . [T]he Chief Justice of the United States, in consultation with the Attorney General, the Director of Central Intelligence, and the Secretary of Defense, shall prescribe rules establishing procedures for the protection against unauthorized disclosure of any classified information in the custody of the United States district courts, courts of appeal, or Supreme Court. . . ."

These procedures apply in all proceedings in criminal cases involving classified information, and appeals therefrom, before the United States district courts, the courts of appeal and the Supreme Court.

2. Court Security Officer. In any proceeding in a criminal case or appeal therefrom in which classified information is within, or reasonably expected to be within, the custody of the court, the court shall designate a court security officer. The Attorney General or the Department of Justice Security Officer, with the concurrence of the head of the agency or agencies from which the classified information originates, or their representatives, shall recommend to the court persons qualified to serve as court security officer. The court security officer shall be selected from among those persons so recommended.

The court security officer shall be an individual with demonstrated competence in security matters, and shall, prior to designation, have been certified to the court in writing by the Department of Justice Security Officer as cleared for the level and category of classified information that will be involved. The court security officer may be an employee of the Executive Branch of the Government detailed to the court for this purpose. One or more alternate court security officers, who have been recommended and cleared in the manner specified above, may be designated by the court as required.

The court security officer shall be responsible to the court for document, physical, personnel and communications security, and shall take measures reasonably necessary to fulfill these responsibilities. The court security officer shall notify the court and the Department of Justice Security Officer of any actual, attempted, or potential violation of security procedures.

3. Secure Quarters. Any *in camera* proceeding—including a pretrial conference, motion hearing, or appellate hearing—concerning the use, relevance, or admissibility of classified information, shall be held in secure quarters recommended by the court security officer and approved by the court.

The secure quarters shall be located within the Federal courthouse, unless it is determined that none of the quarters available in the courthouse meets, or can reasonably be made equivalent to, security requirements of the Executive Branch applicable to the level and category of classified information involved. In that event, the court shall designate the facilities of another United States Government agency, recommended by the court security officer, which is located within the vicinity of the courthouse, as the site of the proceedings.

The court security officer shall make necessary arrangements to ensure that the applicable Executive Branch standards are met and shall conduct or arrange for such inspection of the quarters as may be necessary. The court security officer shall, in consultation with the United States Marshal, arrange for the installation of security devices and take such other measures as may be necessary to protect against any unauthorized access to classified information. All of the aforementioned activity shall be conducted in a manner which does not interfere with the orderly proceedings of the court. Prior to any hearing or other proceeding, the court security officer shall certify in writing to the court that the quarters are secure.

4. Personnel Security—Court Personnel. No person appointed by the court or designated for service therein shall be given access to any classified information in the custody of the court, unless such person has received a security clearance as provided herein and unless access to such information is necessary for the performance of an official function. A security clearance for justices and judges is not required, but such clearance shall be provided upon the request of any judicial officer who desires to be cleared.

The court shall inform the court security officer or the attorney for the government of the names of court personnel who may require access to classified information. That person shall then notify the Department of Justice Security Officer, who shall promptly make arrangements to obtain any necessary security clearances and shall approve such clearances under standards of the Executive Branch applicable to the level and category of classified information involved. The Department of Justice Security Officer shall advise the court in writing when the necessary security clearances have been obtained.

If security clearances cannot be obtained promptly, personnel in the Executive Branch having the necessary clearances may be temporarily assigned to assist the court. If a proceeding is required to be recorded and an official court reporter having the necessary security clearance is unavailable, the court may request the court security officer or the attorney for the government to have a cleared reporter from the Executive Branch designated to act as reporter in the proceedings. The reporter so designated shall take the oath of office as prescribed by 28 U.S.C. § 753(a).

Justices, judges and cleared court personnel shall not disclose classified information to anyone who does not have a security clearance and who does not require the information in the discharge of an official function. However, nothing contained in these procedures shall preclude a judge from discharging his official duties, including giving appropriate instructions to the jury.

Any problem of security involving court personnel or persons acting for the court shall be referred to the court for appropriate action.

5. Persons Acting for the Defendant. The government may obtain information by any lawful means concerning the trustworthiness of persons associated with the defense and may bring such information to the attention of the court for the court's consideration in framing an appropriate protective order pursuant to Section 3 of the Act.

6. Jury. Nothing contained in these procedures shall be construed to require an investigation or security clearance of the members of the jury or interfere with the functions of a jury, including access to classified information introduced as evidence in the trial of a case.

After a verdict has been rendered by a jury, the trial judge should consider a government request for a cautionary instruction to jurors regarding the release or disclosure of classified information contained in documents they have reviewed during the trial.

7. Custody and Storage of Classified Materials.

a. Materials Covered. These security procedures apply to all papers, documents, motions, pleadings, briefs, notes, records of statements involving classified information, notes relating to classified information taken during *in camera* proceedings, orders, affidavits, transcripts, untranscribed notes of a court reporter, magnetic recordings, or any other submissions or records which contain classified information as the term is defined in Section 1(a) of the Act, and which are in the custody of the court. This includes, but is not limited to (1) any motion made in connection with a pretrial conference held pursuant to Section 2 of the Act, (2) written statements submitted by the United States pursuant to Section 4 of the Act, (3) any written statement or written notice submitted to the court by the defendant pursuant to Section 5(a) of the Act, (4) any petition or written motion made pursuant to Section 6 of the Act, (5) any description of, or reference to, classified information contained in papers filed in an appeal, pursuant to Section 7 of the Act and (6) any written statement provided by the United States or by the defendant pursuant to Section 8(c) of the Act.

b. Safekeeping. Classified information submitted to the court shall be placed in the custody of the court security officer who shall be responsible for its safekeeping. When not in use, the court security officer shall store all classified materials in a safe or safe-type steel file container with built-in, dial-type, three position, changeable combinations which conform to the General Services Administration standards for security containers. Classified information shall be segregated from other information unrelated to the case at hand by securing it in a separate security container. If the court does not possess a storage container which meets the required standards, the necessary storage container or containers are to be supplied to the court on a temporary basis by the appropriate Executive Branch agency as determined by the Department of Justice Security Officer. Only the court security officer and alternate court security officer(s) shall have access to the combination and the contents of the container unless the court, after consultation with the security officer, determines that a cleared person other than the court security officer may also have access.

For other than temporary storage (*e.g.*, brief court recess), the court security officer shall insure that the storage area in which these containers shall be located meets Executive Branch standards applicable to the level and category of classified information involved. The secure storage area may be located within either the Federal courthouse or the facilities of another United States Government agency.

c. Transmittal of Classified Information. During the pendency of a trial or appeal, classified materials stored in the facilities of another United States Government agency shall be transmitted in the manner prescribed by the Executive Branch security regulations applicable to the level and category of classified information involved. A trust receipt shall accompany all classified materials transmitted and shall be signed by the recipient and returned to the court security officer.

8. Operating Routine.

a. Access to Court Records. Court personnel shall have access to court records only as authorized. Access to classified information by court personnel shall be limited to the minimum number of cleared persons necessary for operating purposes. Access includes presence at an *in camera* hearing or any other proceeding during which classified information may be disclosed. Arrangements for access to classified information in the custody of the court by court personnel and persons acting for the defense shall be approved in advance by the court, which may issue a protective order concerning such access.

Except as otherwise authorized by a protective order, persons acting for the defendant will not be given custody of classified information provided by the government. They may, at the discretion of the court, be afforded access to classified information provided by the government in secure quarters which have been approved in accordance with § 3 of these procedures, but such classified information shall remain in the control of the court security officer.

b. Telephone Security. Classified information shall not be discussed over standard commercial telephone instruments or office intercommunication systems.

c. Disposal of Classified Material. The court security officer shall be responsible for the secure disposal of all classified materials which are not otherwise required to be retained.

9. Records Security.

a. Classification Markings. The court security officer, after consultation with the attorney for the government, shall be responsible for the marking of all court documents containing classified information with the appropriate level of classification and for indicating thereon any special access controls that also appear on the face of the document from which the classified information was obtained or that are otherwise applicable.

Every document filed by the defendant in the case shall be filed under seal and promptly turned over to the court security officer. The court security officer shall promptly examine the document and, in consultation with the attorney for the government or representative of the appropriate agency, determine whether it contains classified information. If it is determined that the document does contain classified information, the court security officer shall ensure that it is marked with the appropriate classification marking. If it is determined that the document does not contain classified information, it shall be unsealed and placed in the public record. Upon the request of the government, the court may direct that any document containing classified information shall thereafter be protected in accordance with § 7 of these procedures.

b. Accountability System. The court security officer shall be responsible for the establishment and maintenance of a control and accountability system for all classified information received by or transmitted from the court.

10. Transmittal of the Record on Appeal. The record on appeal, or any portion thereof, which contains classified information shall be transmitted to the court of appeals or to the Supreme Court in the manner specified in § 7(c) of these procedures.

11. Final Disposition. Within a reasonable time after all proceedings in the case have been concluded, including appeals, the court shall release to the court security officer all materials containing classified information. The court security officer shall then transmit them to the Department of Justice Security Officer who shall consult with the originating agency to determine the appropriate disposition of such materials. Upon the motion of the government, the court may order the return of the classified documents and materials to the department or agency which originated them. The materials shall be transmitted in the manner specified in § 7(c) of these procedures and shall be accompanied by the appropriate accountability records required by § 9(b) of these procedures.

12. Expenses. Expenses of the United States Government which arise in connection with the implementation of these procedures shall be borne by the Department of Justice or other appropriate Executive Branch agency.

13. Interpretation. Any question concerning the interpretation of any security requirement contained in these procedures shall be resolved by the court in consultation with the Department of Justice Security Officer and the appropriate Executive Branch agency security officer.

14. Term. These procedures shall remain in effect until modified in writing by The Chief Justice after consultation with the Attorney General of the United States, the Director of Central Intelligence, and the Secretary of Defense.

15. Effective Date. These procedures shall become effective forty-five days after the date of submission to the appropriate Congressional Committees, as required by the Act.

Issued this 12th day of February, 1981, after taking into account the views of the Attorney General of the United States, the Director of Central Intelligence, and the Secretary of Defense, as required by law.

/s/WARREN E. BURGER
Chief Justice of the United States

§ 9A. Coordination requirements relating to the prosecution of cases involving classified information

(a) Briefings required.—The Assistant Attorney General for the Criminal Division or the Assistant Attorney General for National Security, as appropriate, and the appropriate United States attorney, or the designees of such officials, shall provide briefings to the senior agency official, or the designee of such official, with respect to any case involving classified information that originated in the agency of such senior agency official.

(b) Timing of briefings.—Briefings under subsection (a) with respect to a case shall occur—

(1) as soon as practicable after the Department of Justice and the United States attorney concerned determine that a prosecution or potential prosecution could result; and

(2) at such other times thereafter as are necessary to keep the senior agency official concerned fully and currently informed of the status of the prosecution.

(c) Senior agency official defined.—In this section, the term "senior agency official" has the meaning given that term in section 1.1 of Executive Order No. 12958.

(Pub.L. 96–456, § 9A, as added Pub.L. 106–567, Title VI, § 607, Dec. 27, 2000, 114 Stat. 2855, and amended Pub.L. 109–177, Title V, § 506(a)(8), Mar. 9, 2006, 120 Stat. 248.)

§ 10. Identification of information related to national defense

In any prosecution in which the United States must establish that material relates to the national defense or constitutes classified information, the United States shall notify the defendant, within the time before trial specified by the court, of the portions of the material that it reasonably expects to rely upon to establish the national defense or classified information element of the offense.

(Pub.L. 96–456, § 10, Oct. 15, 1980, 94 Stat. 2029.)

§ 11. Amendments to Act

Sections 1 through 10 of this Act may be amended as provided in section 2076, Title 28, United States Code.

(Pub.L. 96–456, § 11, Oct. 15, 1980, 94 Stat. 2029.)

HISTORICAL AND STATUTORY NOTES

References in Text

This Act, referred to in catchline, is Pub.L. 96–456, Oct. 15, 1980, 94 Stat. 2025, known as the "Classified Information Procedures Act".

§ 12. Attorney General guidelines

(a) Within one hundred and eighty days of enactment of this Act, the Attorney General shall issue guidelines specifying the factors to be used by the Department of Justice in rendering a decision whether to prosecute a violation of Federal law in which, in the judgment of the Attorney General, there is a possibility that classified information will be revealed. Such guidelines shall be transmitted to the appropriate committees of Congress.

(b) When the Department of Justice decides not to prosecute a violation of Federal law pursuant to subsection (a), an appropriate official of the Department of Justice shall prepare written findings detailing the reasons for the decision not to prosecute. The findings shall include—

(1) the intelligence information which the Department of Justice officials believe might be disclosed,

(2) the purpose for which the information might be disclosed,

(3) the probability that the information would be disclosed, and

(4) the possible consequences such disclosure would have on the national security.

(Pub.L. 96–456, § 12, Oct. 15, 1980, 94 Stat. 2029.)

HISTORICAL AND STATUTORY NOTES

References in Text

The enactment of this Act, referred to in subsec. (a), means Oct. 15, 1980.

§ 13. Reports to Congress

(a) Consistent with applicable authorities and duties, including those conferred by the Constitution upon the executive and legislative branches, the Attorney General shall report orally or in writing semiannually to the Permanent Select Committee on Intelligence of the United States House of Representatives, the Select Committee on Intelligence of the United States Senate, and the chairmen and ranking minority members of the Committees on the Judiciary of the Senate and House of Representatives on all cases where a decision not to prosecute a violation of Federal law pursuant to section 12(a) has been made.

(b) In the case of the semiannual reports (whether oral or written) required to be submitted under subsection (a) to the Permanent Select Committee on Intelligence of the House of Representatives and the Select Committee on Intelligence of the Senate, the submittal dates for such reports shall be as provided in section 507 of the National Security Act of 1947.

(c) The Attorney General shall deliver to the appropriate committees of Congress a report concerning the operation and effectiveness of this Act and including suggested amendments to this Act. For the first three years this Act is in effect, there shall be a report each year. After three years, such reports shall be delivered as necessary.

(Pub.L. 96–456, § 13, Oct. 15, 1980, 94 Stat. 2030, and amended Pub.L. 107–306, Title VIII, § 811(b)(3), Nov. 27, 2002, 116 Stat. 2423.)

HISTORICAL AND STATUTORY NOTES

References in Text

Section 507 of the National Security Act of 1947, referred to in subsec. (b), is Act July 26, 1947, c. 343, Title V, § 507, as added Nov. 27, 2002, Pub.L. 107–306, Title VIII, § 811(a)(1), 116 Stat. 2418, which is classified to 50 U.S.C.A. § 415b.

This Act, referred to in subsec. (c), is Pub.L. 96–456, Oct. 15, 1980, 94 Stat. 2025, known as the "Classified Information Procedures Act".

Termination of Reporting Requirements

Reporting requirement of subsec. (a) of this section excepted from termination under Pub.L. 104–66, § 3003(a)(1), as amended, set out in a note under 31 U.S.C.A. § 1113, see Pub.L. 106–197, § 1, set out as a note under 31 U.S.C.A. § 1113.

§ 14. Functions of Attorney General exercised by Deputy Attorney General, the Associate Attorney General, or designated Assistant Attorney General

The functions and duties of the Attorney General under this Act may be exercised by the Deputy Attorney General, the Associate Attorney General, or by an Assistant Attorney General designated by the Attorney General for such purpose and may not be delegated to any other official.

(Pub.L. 96–456, § 14, Oct. 15, 1980, 94 Stat. 2030; Pub.L. 100–690, Title VII, § 7020(g), Nov. 18, 1988, 102 Stat. 4396.)

HISTORICAL AND STATUTORY NOTES

References in Text

This Act, referred to in text, is known as the "Classified Information Procedures Act" and is classified as this appendix to Title 18.

§ 15. Effective date

The provisions of this Act shall become effective upon the date of the enactment of this Act, but shall not apply to any prosecution in which an indictment or information was filed before such date.

(Pub.L. 96–456, § 15, Oct. 15, 1980, 94 Stat. 2030.)

HISTORICAL AND STATUTORY NOTES

References in Text

This Act, referred to in text, is Pub.L. 96–456, Oct. 15, 1980, 94 Stat. 2025, known as the "Classified Information Procedures Act".

The date of the enactment of this Act, referred to in text, means Oct. 15, 1980.

§ 16. Short title

That this Act may be cited as the "Classified Information Procedures Act".

(Pub.L. 96–456, § 16, Oct. 15, 1980, 94 Stat. 2031.)

CONSTITUTION OF THE UNITED STATES

PREAMBLE

WE THE PEOPLE of the United States, in Order to form a more perfect Union, establish Justice, insure domestic Tranquility, provide for the common defence, promote the general Welfare, and secure the Blessings of Liberty to ourselves and our Posterity, do ordain and establish this CONSTITUTION for the United States of America.

ARTICLE I

Section. 1. All legislative Powers herein granted shall be vested in a Congress of the United States, which shall consist of a Senate and House of Representatives.

Section. 2. The House of Representatives shall be composed of Members chosen every second Year by the People of the several States, and the Electors in each State shall have the Qualifications requisite for Electors of the most numerous Branch of the State Legislature.

No Person shall be a Representative who shall not have attained to the Age of twenty five Years, and been seven Years a Citizen of the United States, and who shall not, when elected, be an Inhabitant of that State in which he shall be chosen.

[Representatives and direct Taxes shall be apportioned among the several States which may be included within this Union, according to their respective Numbers, which shall be determined by adding to the whole Number of free Persons, including those bound to Service for a Term of Years, and excluding Indians not taxed, three fifths of all other Persons.] [1] The actual Enumeration shall be made within three Years after the first Meeting of the Congress of the United States, and within every subsequent Term of ten Years, in such Manner as they shall by Law direct. The Number of Representatives shall not exceed one for every thirty Thousand, but each State shall have at Least one Representative; and until such enumeration shall be made, the State of New Hampshire shall be entitled to chuse three, Massachusetts eight, Rhode-Island and Providence Plantations one, Connecticut five, New-York six, New Jersey four, Pennsylvania eight, Delaware one, Maryland six, Virginia ten, North Carolina five, South Carolina five, and Georgia three.

When vacancies happen in the Representation from any State, the Executive Authority thereof shall issue Writs of Election to fill such Vacancies.

The House of Representatives shall chuse their Speaker and other Officers; and shall have the sole Power of Impeachment.

[1] The clause of this paragraph inclosed in brackets was amended, as to the mode of apportionment of representatives among the several states, by the Fourteenth Amendment, § 2, and as to taxes on incomes without apportionment, by the Sixteenth Amendment.

Section. 3. [The Senate of the United States shall be composed of two Senators from each State, chosen by the Legislature thereof, for six Years; and each Senator shall have one Vote.] [1]

Immediately after they shall be assembled in Consequence of the first Election, they shall be divided as equally as may be into three Classes. The Seats of the Senators of the first Class shall be vacated at the Expiration of the second Year, of the second Class at the Expiration of the fourth Year, and of the third Class at the Expiration of the sixth Year, so that one third may be chosen every second Year; [and if Vacancies happen by Resignation, or otherwise, during the Recess of the Legislature of any State, the Executive thereof may make temporary Appointments until the next Meeting of the Legislature, which shall then fill such Vacancies.] [2]

No Person shall be a Senator who shall not have attained to the Age of thirty Years, and been nine Years a Citizen of the United States, and who shall not, when elected, be an Inhabitant of that State for which he shall be chosen.

The Vice President of the United States shall be President of the Senate, but shall have no Vote, unless they be equally divided.

The Senate shall chuse their other Officers, and also a President pro tempore, in the Absence of the Vice

President, or when he shall exercise the Office of President of the United States.

The Senate shall have the sole Power to try all Impeachments. When sitting for that Purpose, they shall be on Oath or Affirmation. When the President of the United States is tried, the Chief Justice shall preside: And no Person shall be convicted without the Concurrence of two thirds of the Members present.

Judgment in Cases of Impeachment shall not extend further than to removal from Office, and disqualification to hold and enjoy any Office of honor, Trust or Profit under the United States: but the Party convicted shall nevertheless be liable and subject to Indictment, Trial, Judgment and Punishment, according to Law.

1 This paragraph, inclosed in brackets, was superseded by the Seventeenth Amendment.

2 The clause of this paragraph inclosed in brackets was superseded by the Seventeenth Amendment.

Section. 4. The Times, Places and Manner of holding Elections for Senators and Representatives, shall be prescribed in each State by the Legislature thereof; but the Congress may at any time by Law make or alter such Regulations, except as to the Places of chusing Senators.

The Congress shall assemble at least once in every Year, and such Meeting shall be on the [first Monday in December],[1] unless they shall by Law appoint a different Day.

1 The clause of this paragraph inclosed in brackets was superseded by the Twentieth Amendment.

Section. 5. Each House shall be the Judge of the Elections, Returns and Qualifications of its own Members, and a Majority of each shall constitute a Quorum to do Business; but a smaller Number may adjourn from day to day, and may be authorized to compel the Attendance of absent Members, in such Manner, and under such Penalties as each House may provide.

Each House may determine the Rules of its Proceedings, punish its Members for disorderly Behaviour, and, with the Concurrence of two thirds, expel a Member.

Each House shall keep a Journal of its Proceedings, and from time to time publish the same, excepting such Parts as may in their Judgment require Secrecy; and the Yeas and Nays of the Members of either House on any question shall, at the Desire of one fifth of those Present, be entered on the Journal.

Neither House, during the Session of Congress, shall, without the Consent of the other, adjourn for more than three days, nor to any other Place than that in which the two Houses shall be sitting.

Section. 6. The Senators and Representatives shall receive a Compensation for their Services, to be ascertained by Law, and paid out of the Treasury of the United States. They shall in all Cases, except Treason, Felony and Breach of the Peace, be privileged from Arrest during their Attendance at the Session of their respective Houses, and in going to and returning from the same; and for any Speech or Debate in either House, they shall not be questioned in any other Place.

No Senator or Representative shall, during the Time for which he was elected, be appointed to any civil Office under the Authority of the United States, which shall have been created, or the Emoluments whereof shall have been encreased during such time; and no Person holding any Office under the United States, shall be a Member of either House during his Continuance in Office.

Section. 7. All Bills for raising Revenue shall originate in the House of Representatives; but the Senate may propose or concur with Amendments as on other Bills.

Every Bill which shall have passed the House of Representatives and the Senate, shall, before it becomes a Law, be presented to the President of the United States; If he approve he shall sign it, but if not he shall return it, with his Objections to that House in which it shall have originated, who shall enter the Objections at large on their Journal, and proceed to reconsider it. If after such Reconsideration two thirds of that House shall agree to pass the Bill, it shall be sent, together with the Objections, to the other House, by which it shall likewise be reconsidered, and if approved by two thirds of that House, it shall become a Law. But in all such Cases the Votes of both Houses shall be determined by Yeas and Nays, and the Names of the Persons voting for and against the Bill shall be entered on the Journal of each House respectively. If any Bill shall not be returned by the President within ten Days (Sundays excepted) after it shall have been presented to him, the Same shall be a Law, in like Manner as if he had signed it, unless the Congress by their Adjournment prevent its Return, in which Case it shall not be a Law.

Every Order, Resolution, or Vote to which the Concurrence of the Senate and House of Representatives may be necessary (except on a question of Adjournment) shall be presented to the President of the United States; and before the Same shall take Effect, shall be approved by him, or being disapproved by him, shall be repassed by two thirds of the Senate and House of Representatives, according to the Rules and Limitations prescribed in the Case of a Bill.

Section. 8. The Congress shall have Power To lay and collect Taxes, Duties, Imposts and Excises, to pay the Debts and provide for the common Defence and general Welfare of the United States; but all Duties, Imposts and Excises shall be uniform throughout the United States;

To borrow Money on the credit of the United States;

To regulate Commerce with foreign Nations, and among the several States, and with the Indian Tribes;

To establish an uniform Rule of Naturalization, and uniform Laws on the subject of Bankruptcies throughout the United States;

To coin Money, regulate the Value thereof, and of foreign Coin, and fix the Standard of Weights and Measures;

To provide for the Punishment of counterfeiting the Securities and current Coin of the United States;

To establish Post Offices and post Roads;

To promote the Progress of Science and useful Arts, by securing for limited Times to Authors and Inventors the exclusive Right to their respective Writings and Discoveries;

To constitute Tribunals inferior to the supreme Court;

To define and punish Piracies and Felonies committed on the high Seas, and Offences against the Law of Nations;

To declare War, grant Letters of Marque and Reprisal, and make Rules concerning Captures on Land and Water;

To raise and support Armies, but no Appropriation of Money to that Use shall be for a longer Term than two Years;

To provide and maintain a Navy;

To make Rules for the Government and Regulation of the land and naval Forces;

To provide for calling forth the Militia to execute the Laws of the Union, suppress Insurrections and repel Invasions;

To provide for organizing, arming, and disciplining, the Militia, and for governing such Part of them as may be employed in the Service of the United States, reserving to the States respectively, the Appointment of the Officers, and the Authority of training the Militia according to the discipline prescribed by Congress;

To exercise exclusive Legislation in all Cases whatsoever, over such District (not exceeding ten Miles square) as may, by Cession of particular States, and the Acceptance of Congress, become the Seat of the Government of the United States, and to exercise like Authority over all Places purchased by the Consent of the Legislature of the State in which the Same shall be, for the Erection of Forts, Magazines, Arsenals, dock-Yards, and other needful Buildings;—And

To make all Laws which shall be necessary and proper for carrying into Execution the foregoing Powers, and all other Powers vested by this Constitution in the Government of the United States, or in any Department or Officer thereof.

Section. 9. The Migration or Importation of such Persons as any of the States now existing shall think proper to admit, shall not be prohibited by the Congress prior to the Year one thousand eight hundred and eight, but a Tax or duty may be imposed on such Importation, not exceeding ten dollars for each Person.

The Privilege of the Writ of Habeas Corpus shall not be suspended, unless when in Cases of Rebellion or Invasion the public Safety may require it.

No Bill of Attainder or ex post facto Law shall be passed.

No Capitation, or other direct, Tax shall be laid, unless in Proportion to the Census or Enumeration herein before directed to be taken.[1]

No Tax or Duty shall be laid on Articles exported from any State.

No Preference shall be given by any Regulation of Commerce or Revenue to the Ports of one State over those of another; nor shall Vessels bound to, or from, one State, be obliged to enter, clear, or pay Duties in another.

No Money shall be drawn from the Treasury, but in Consequence of Appropriations made by Law; and a regular Statement and Account of the Receipts and Expenditures of all public Money shall be published from time to time.

No Title of Nobility shall be granted by the United States: And no Person holding any Office of Profit or Trust under them, shall, without the Consent of the Congress, accept of any present, Emolument, Office, or Title, of any kind whatever, from any King, Prince, or foreign State.

[1] This paragraph has been affected by the Sixteenth Amendment.

Section. 10. No State shall enter into any Treaty, Alliance, or Confederation; grant Letters of Marque and Reprisal; coin Money; emit Bills of Credit; make any Thing but gold and silver Coin a Tender in Payment of Debts; pass any Bill of Attainder, ex post facto Law, or Law impairing the Obligation of Contracts, or grant any Title of Nobility.

No State shall, without the Consent of the Congress, lay any Imposts or Duties on Imports or Exports, except what may be absolutely necessary for executing it's inspection Laws: and the net Produce of all Duties and Imposts, laid by any State on Imports or Exports, shall be for the Use of the Treasury of the United States; and all such Laws shall be subject to the Revision and Controul of the Congress.

No State shall, without the Consent of Congress, lay any Duty of Tonnage, keep Troops, or Ships of War in time of Peace, enter into any Agreement or Compact with another State, or with a foreign Power, or engage in War, unless actually invaded, or in such imminent Danger as will not admit of delay.

ARTICLE II

Section. 1. The executive Power shall be vested in a President of the United States of America. He shall hold his Office during the Term of four Years, and, together with the Vice President, chosen for the same Term, be elected, as follows:

Each State shall appoint, in such Manner as the Legislature thereof may direct, a Number of Electors, equal to the whole Number of Senators and Representatives to which the State may be entitled in the Congress: but no Senator or Representative, or Person holding an Office of Trust or Profit under the United States, shall be appointed an Elector.

[The Electors shall meet in their respective States, and vote by Ballot for two Persons, of whom one at least shall not be an Inhabitant of the same State with themselves. And they shall make a List of all the Persons voted for, and of the Number of Votes for each; which List they shall sign and certify, and transmit sealed to the Seat of the Government of the United States, directed to the President of the Senate. The President of the Senate shall, in the Presence of the Senate and House of Representatives, open all the Certificates, and the Votes shall then be counted. The Person having the greatest Number of Votes shall be the President, if such Number be a Majority of the whole Number of Electors appointed; and if there be more than one who have such Majority, and have an equal Number of Votes, then the House of Representatives shall immediately chuse by Ballot one of them for President; and if no Person have a Majority, then from the five highest on the List the said House shall in like Manner chuse the President. But in chusing the President, the Votes shall be taken by States, the Representation from each State having one Vote; A quorum for this Purpose shall consist of a Member or Members from two thirds of the States, and a Majority of all the States shall be necessary to a Choice. In every Case, after the Choice of the President, the Person having the greatest Number of Votes of the Electors shall be the Vice President. But if there should remain two or more who have equal Votes, the Senate shall chuse from them by Ballot the Vice President.] [1]

The Congress may determine the Time of chusing the Electors, and the Day on which they shall give their Votes; which Day shall be the same throughout the United States.

No Person except a natural born Citizen, or a Citizen of the United States, at the time of the Adoption of this Constitution, shall be eligible to the Office of President; neither shall any Person be eligible to that Office who shall not have attained to the Age of thirty five Years, and been fourteen Years a Resident within the United States.

In Case of the Removal of the President from Office, or of his Death, Resignation, or Inability to discharge the Powers and Duties of the said Office, the Same shall devolve on the Vice President, and the Congress may by Law provide for the Case of Removal, Death, Resignation or Inability, both of the President and Vice President, declaring what Officer shall then act as President, and such Officer shall act accordingly, until the Disability be removed, or a President shall be elected.

The President shall, at stated Times, receive for his Services, a Compensation, which shall neither be encreased nor diminished during the Period for which he shall have been elected, and he shall not receive within that Period any other Emolument from the United States, or any of them.

Before he enter on the Execution of his Office, he shall take the following Oath or Affirmation:—"I do solemnly swear (or affirm) that I will faithfully execute the Office of President of the United States, and will to the best of my Ability, preserve, protect and defend the Constitution of the United States."

[1] This paragraph, inclosed in brackets, was superseded by the Twelfth Amendment, post.

Section. 2. The President shall be Commander in Chief of the Army and Navy of the United States, and of the Militia of the several States, when called into the actual Service of the United States; he may require the Opinion, in writing, of the principal Officer in each of the executive Departments, upon any Subject relating to the Duties of their respective Offices, and he shall have Power to grant Reprieves and Pardons for Offences against the United States, except in Cases of Impeachment.

He shall have Power, by and with the Advice and Consent of the Senate, to make Treaties, provided two thirds of the Senators present concur; and he shall nominate, and by and with the Advice and Consent of the Senate, shall appoint Ambassadors, other public Ministers and Consuls, Judges of the supreme Court, and all other Officers of the United States, whose Appointments are not herein otherwise provided for, and which shall be established by Law: but the Congress may by Law vest the Appointment of such inferior Officers, as they think proper, in the President alone, in the Courts of Law, or in the Heads of Departments.

The President shall have Power to fill up all Vacancies that may happen during the Recess of the Senate, by granting Commissions which shall expire at the End of their next Session.

Section. 3. He shall from time to time give to the Congress Information of the State of the Union, and recommend to their Consideration such Measures as he shall judge necessary and expedient; he may, on extraordinary Occasions, convene both Houses, or either of them, and in Case of Disagreement between them, with Respect to the Time of Adjournment, he may adjourn them to such Time as he shall think proper; he shall receive Ambassadors and other public Ministers; he shall take Care that the Laws be faithfully executed, and shall Commission all the Officers of the United States.

Section. 4. The President, Vice President and all civil Officers of the United States, shall be removed from Office on Impeachment for, and Conviction of, Treason, Bribery, or other high Crimes and Misdemeanors.

ARTICLE III

Section. 1. The judicial Power of the United States, shall be vested in one supreme Court, and in such inferior Courts as the Congress may from time to time ordain and establish. The Judges, both of the supreme and inferior Courts, shall hold their Offices during good Behaviour, and shall, at stated Times, receive for their Services, a Compensation, which shall not be diminished during their Continuance in Office.

Section. 2. The judicial Power shall extend to all Cases, in Law and Equity, arising under this Constitution, the Laws of the United States, and Treaties made, or which shall be made, under their Authority;—to all Cases affecting Ambassadors, other public Ministers and Consuls;—to all Cases of admiralty and maritime Jurisdiction;—to Controversies to which the United States shall be a Party;—to Controversies between two or more States;—between a State and Citizens of another State;—between citizens of different States;—between Citizens of the same State claiming Lands under Grants of different States, and between a State, or the Citizens thereof, and foreign States, Citizens or Subjects.[1]

In all Cases affecting Ambassadors, other public Ministers and Consuls, and those in which a State shall be Party, the supreme Court shall have original Jurisdiction. In all the other Cases before mentioned, the supreme Court shall have appellate Jurisdiction, both as to Law and Fact, with such Exceptions, and under such Regulations as the Congress shall make.

The Trial of all Crimes, except in Cases of Impeachment, shall be by Jury; and such Trial shall be held in the State where the said Crimes shall have been committed; but when not committed within any State, the Trial shall be at such Place or Places as the Congress may by Law have directed.

1 This section has been affected by the Eleventh Amendment.

Section. 3. Treason against the United States, shall consist only in levying War against them, or in adhering to their Enemies, giving them Aid and Comfort. No Person shall be convicted of Treason unless on the Testimony of two Witnesses to the same overt Act, or on Confession in open Court.

The Congress shall have Power to declare the Punishment of Treason, but no Attainder of Treason shall work Corruption of Blood, or Forfeiture except during the Life of the Person attainted.

ARTICLE IV

Section. 1. Full Faith and Credit shall be given in each State to the public Acts, Records, and judicial Proceedings of every other State. And the Congress may by general Laws prescribe the Manner in which such Acts, Records and Proceedings shall be proved, and the Effect thereof.

Section. 2. The Citizens of each State shall be entitled to all Privileges and Immunities of Citizens in the several States.

A Person charged in any State with Treason, Felony, or other Crime, who shall flee from Justice, and be found in another State, shall on Demand of the executive Authority of the State from which he fled, be delivered up, to be removed to the State having Jurisdiction of the Crime.

No Person held to Service or Labour in one State, under the Laws thereof, escaping into another, shall, in Consequence of any Law or Regulation therein, be discharged from such Service or Labour, but shall be delivered up on Claim of the Party to whom such Service or Labour may be due.[1]

1 This clause was affected by the Thirteenth Amendment.

Section. 3. New States may be admitted by the Congress into this Union; but no new State shall be formed or erected within the Jurisdiction of any other State; nor any State be formed by the Junction of two or more States, or Parts of States, without the Consent of the Legislatures of the States concerned as well as of the Congress.

The Congress shall have Power to dispose of and make all needful Rules and Regulations respecting the Territory or other Property belonging to the United States; and nothing in this Constitution shall be so construed as to Prejudice any Claims of the United States, or of any particular State.

Section. 4. The United States shall guarantee to every State in this Union a Republican Form of Government, and shall protect each of them against Invasion; and on Application of the Legislature, or of the Executive (when the Legislature cannot be convened) against domestic Violence.

ARTICLE V

The Congress, whenever two thirds of both Houses shall deem it necessary, shall propose Amendments to this Constitution, or, on the Application of the Legislatures of two thirds of the several States, shall call a Convention for proposing Amendments, which, in either Case, shall be valid to all Intents and Purposes, as Part of this Constitution, when ratified by the Legislatures of three fourths of the several States, or by Conventions in three fourths thereof, as the one or the other Mode of Ratification may be proposed by the Congress; Provided that no Amendment which may be made prior to the Year One thousand eight hundred and eight shall in any Manner affect the first and fourth Clauses in the Ninth Section of the first Article; and that no State, without its Consent, shall be deprived of its equal Suffrage in the Senate.

ARTICLE VI

All Debts contracted and Engagements entered into, before the Adoption of this Constitution, shall be as valid against the United States under this Constitution, as under the Confederation.

This Constitution, and the Laws of the United States which shall be made in Pursuance thereof; and all Treaties made, or which shall be made, under the Authority of the United States, shall be the supreme Law of the Land; and the Judges in every State shall be bound thereby, any Thing in the Constitution or Laws of any State to the Contrary notwithstanding.

The Senators and Representatives before mentioned, and the Members of the several State Legislatures, and all executive and judicial Officers, both of the United States and of the several States, shall be bound by Oath or Affirmation, to support this Constitution; but no religious Test shall ever be required as a Qualification to any Office or public Trust under the United States.

ARTICLE VII

The Ratification of the Conventions of nine States, shall be sufficient for the Establishment of this Constitution between the States so ratifying the Same.

DONE in Convention by the Unanimous Consent of the States present the Seventeenth Day of September in the Year of Our Lord one thousand seven hundred and Eighty seven and of the Independence of the United States of America the Twelfth. IN WITNESS whereof We have hereunto subscribed our Names.

GO. WASHINGTON—*Presidt. and deputy from Virginia*

Attest WILLIAM JACKSON *Secretary*

New Hampshire

JOHN LANGDON NICHOLAS GILMAN

Massachusetts

NATHANIEL GORHAM RUFUS KING

Connecticut

WM. SAML. JOHNSON ROGER SHERMAN

New York

ALEXANDER HAMILTON

New Jersey

WIL: LIVINGSTON WM. PATERSON.
DAVID BREARLEY. JONA: DAYTON

Pennsylvania

B FRANKLIN THOS. FITZSIMONS
THOMAS MIFFLIN JARED INGERSOLL
ROBT MORRIS JAMES WILSON
GEO. CLYMER GOUV MORRIS

Delaware

GEO: READ RICHARD BASSETT
GUNNING BEDFORD jun JACO: BROOM
JOHN DICKINSON

Maryland

JAMES MCHENRY DANL CARROLL
DAN OF ST THOS. JENIFER

Virginia

JOHN BLAIR— JAMES MADISON JR.

North Carolina

WM. BLOUNT HU WILLIAMSON
RICHD. DOBBS SPAIGHT

South Carolina

J. RUTLEDGE CHARLES PINCKNEY
CHARLES COTESWORTH PINCKNEY PIERCE BUTLER

Georgia

WILLIAM FEW ABR BALDWIN

Articles in Addition to, and Amendment of, the Constitution of the United States of America, Proposed by Congress, and Ratified by the Legislatures of the Several States Pursuant to the Fifth Article of the Original Constitution

ARTICLE [I]

Congress shall make no law respecting an establishment of religion, or prohibiting the free exercise thereof; or abridging the freedom of speech, or of the press; or the right of the people peaceably to assemble, and to petition the Government for a redress of grievances.

ARTICLE [II]

A well regulated Militia, being necessary to the security of a free State, the right of the people to keep and bear Arms, shall not be infringed.

ARTICLE [III]

No Soldier shall, in time of peace be quartered in any house, without the consent of the Owner, nor in time of war, but in a manner to be prescribed by law.

ARTICLE [IV]

The right of the people to be secure in their persons, houses, papers, and effects, against unreasonable searches and seizures, shall not be violated, and no Warrants shall issue, but upon probable cause, supported by Oath or affirmation, and particularly describing the place to be searched, and the persons or things to be seized.

ARTICLE [V]

No person shall be held to answer for a capital, or otherwise infamous crime, unless on a presentment or indictment of a Grand Jury, except in cases arising in the land or naval forces, or in the Militia, when in actual service in time of War or public danger; nor shall any person be subject for the same offence to be twice put in jeopardy of life or limb; nor shall be compelled in any criminal case to be a witness against himself, nor be deprived of life, liberty, or property, without due process of law; nor shall private property be taken for public use, without just compensation.

ARTICLE [VI]

In all criminal prosecutions, the accused shall enjoy the right to a speedy and public trial, by an impartial jury of the State and district wherein the crime shall have been committed, which district shall have been previously ascertained by law, and to be informed of the nature and cause of the accusation; to be confronted with the witnesses against him; to have compulsory process for obtaining witnesses in his favor, and to have the Assistance of Counsel for his defence.

ARTICLE [VII]

In Suits at common law, where the value in controversy shall exceed twenty dollars, the right of trial by jury shall be preserved, and no fact tried by a jury, shall be otherwise reexamined in any Court of the United States, than according to the rules of the common law.

ARTICLE [VIII]

Excessive bail shall not be required, nor excessive fines imposed, nor cruel and unusual punishments inflicted.

ARTICLE [IX]

The enumeration in the Constitution, of certain rights, shall not be construed to deny or disparage others retained by the people.

ARTICLE [X]

The powers not delegated to the United States by the Constitution, nor prohibited by it to the States, are reserved to the States respectively, or to the people.

ARTICLE [XI]

The Judicial power of the United States shall not be construed to extend to any suit in law or equity, commenced or prosecuted against one of the United States by Citizens of another State, or by Citizens or Subjects of any Foreign State.

ARTICLE [XII]

The Electors shall meet in their respective states, and vote by ballot for President and Vice-President, one of whom, at least, shall not be an inhabitant of the same state with themselves; they shall name in their ballots the person voted for as President, and in distinct ballots the person voted for as Vice-President, and they shall make distinct lists of all persons voted for as President, and of all persons voted for as Vice-President, and of the number of votes for each, which lists they shall sign and certify, and transmit sealed to the seat of the government of the United States, directed to the President of the Senate;—The President of the Senate shall, in the presence of the Senate and House of Representatives, open all the certificates and the votes shall then be counted;—The person having the greatest number of votes for President, shall be the President, if such number be a majority of the whole number of Electors appointed; and if no person have such majority, then from the persons having the highest numbers not exceeding three on the list of those voted for as President, the House of Representatives shall choose immediately, by ballot, the President. But in choosing the President, the votes shall be taken by states, the representation from each state having one vote; a quorum for this purpose shall consist of a member or members from two-thirds of the states, and a majority of all the states shall be necessary to a choice. And if the House of Representatives shall not choose a President whenever the right of choice shall devolve upon them, before the fourth day of March next following, then the Vice-President shall act as President, as in the case of the death or other constitutional disability of the President.—The person having the greatest number of votes as Vice-President, shall be the Vice-President, if such number be a majority of the whole number of Electors appointed, and if no person have a majority, then from the two highest numbers on the list, the Senate shall choose the Vice-President; a quorum for the purpose shall consist of two-thirds of the whole number of Senators, and a majority of the whole number shall be necessary to a choice. But no person constitutionally ineligible to the office of President shall be eligible to that of Vice-President of the United States.[1]

[1] This Amendment was affected by the Twentieth Amendment.

ARTICLE XIII

Section 1. Neither slavery nor involuntary servitude, except as a punishment for crime whereof the party shall have been duly convicted, shall exist within the United States, or any place subject to their jurisdiction.

Section 2. Congress shall have power to enforce this article by appropriate legislation.

ARTICLE XIV

Section 1. All persons born or naturalized in the United States, and subject to the jurisdiction thereof, are citizens of the United States and of the State wherein they reside. No State shall make or enforce any law which shall abridge the privileges or immunities of citizens of the United States; nor shall any State deprive any person of life, liberty, or property, without due process of law; nor deny to any person within its jurisdiction the equal protection of the laws.

Section 2. Representatives shall be apportioned among the several States according to their respective numbers, counting the whole number of persons in each State, excluding Indians not taxed. But when the right to vote at any election for the choice of electors for President and Vice President of the United States, Representatives in Congress, the Executive and Judicial officers of a State, or the members of the Legislature thereof, is denied to any of the male inhabitants of such State, being twenty-one years of age, and citizens of the United States, or in any way abridged, except for participation in rebellion, or other crime, the basis of representation therein shall be reduced in the proportion which the number of such male citizens shall bear to the whole number of male citizens twenty-one years of age in such State.

Section 3. No person shall be a Senator or Representative in Congress, or elector of President and Vice President, or hold any office, civil or military, under the United States, or under any State, who, having previously taken an oath, as a member of Congress, or as an officer of the United States, or as a member of any State legislature, or as an executive or judicial officer of any State, to support the Constitution of the United States, shall have engaged in insurrection or rebellion against the same, or given aid or comfort to the enemies thereof. But Congress may by a vote of two-thirds of each House, remove such disability.

Section 4. The validity of the public debt of the United States, authorized by law, including debts incurred for payment of pensions and bounties for services in suppressing insurrection or rebellion, shall not be questioned. But neither the United States nor any State shall assume or pay any debt or obligation incurred in aid of insurrection or rebellion against the United States, or any claim for the loss or emancipation of any slave; but all such debts, obligations and claims shall be held illegal and void.

Section 5. The Congress shall have power to enforce, by appropriate legislation, the provisions of this article.

ARTICLE XV

Section 1. The right of citizens of the United States to vote shall not be denied or abridged by the United States or by any State on account of race, color, or previous condition of servitude.

Section 2. The Congress shall have power to enforce this article by appropriate legislation.

ARTICLE XVI

The Congress shall have power to lay and collect taxes on incomes, from whatever source derived, without apportionment among the several States, and without regard to any census or enumeration.

ARTICLE [XVII]

The Senate of the United States shall be composed of two Senators from each state, elected by the people thereof, for six years; and each Senator shall have one vote. The electors in each State shall have the qualifications requisite for electors of the most numerous branch of the State legislatures.

When vacancies happen in the representation of any State in the Senate, the executive authority of such State shall issue writs of election to fill such vacancies: *Provided,* That the legislature of any State may empower the executive thereof to make temporary appointments until the people fill the vacancies by election as the legislature may direct.

This amendment shall not be so construed as to affect the election or term of any Senator chosen before it becomes valid as part of the Constitution.

ARTICLE [XVIII] [Repealed. See Article XXI]

Section 1. After one year from the ratification of this article the manufacture, sale, or transportation of intoxicating liquors within, the importation thereof into, or the exportation thereof from the United States and all territory subject to the jurisdiction thereof for beverage purposes is hereby prohibited.

Section 2. The Congress and the several States shall have concurrent power to enforce this article by appropriate legislation.

Section 3. This article shall be inoperative unless it shall have been ratified as an amendment to the Constitution by the legislatures of the several States, as provided in the Constitution, within seven years from the date of the submission hereof to the States by the Congress.

ARTICLE [XIX]

The right of citizens of the United States to vote shall not be denied or abridged by the United States or by any State on account of sex.

Congress shall have power to enforce this article by appropriate legislation.

ARTICLE [XX]

Section 1. The terms of the President and Vice President shall end at noon on the 20th day of January, and the terms of Senators and Representatives at noon on the 3d day of January, of the years in which such terms would have ended if this article had not been ratified; and the terms of their successors shall then begin.

Sec. 2. The Congress shall assemble at least once in every year, and such meeting shall begin at noon on the 3d day of January, unless they shall by law appoint a different day.

Sec. 3. If, at the time fixed for the beginning of the term of the President, the President elect shall have died, the Vice President elect shall become President. If a President shall not have been chosen before the time fixed for the beginning of his term, or if the President elect shall have failed to qualify, then the Vice President elect shall act as President until a President shall have qualified; and the Congress may by law provide for the case wherein neither a President elect nor a Vice President elect shall have qualified, declaring who shall then act as President, or the manner in which one who is to act shall be selected, and such person shall act accordingly until a President or Vice President shall have qualified.

Sec. 4. The Congress may by law provide for the case of the death of any of the persons from whom the House of Representatives may choose a President whenever the right of choice shall have devolved upon them, and for the case of the death of any of the persons from whom the Senate may choose a Vice President whenever the right of choice shall have devolved upon them.

Sec. 5. Sections 1 and 2 shall take effect on the 15th day of October following the ratification of this article.

Sec. 6. This article shall be inoperative unless it shall have been ratified as an amendment to the Constitution by the legislatures of three-fourths of the several States within seven years from the date of its submission.

ARTICLE [XXI]

Section 1. The eighteenth article of amendment to the Constitution of the United States is hereby repealed.

Sec. 2. The transportation or importation into any State, Territory, or possession of the United States for delivery or use therein of intoxicating liquors, in violation of the laws thereof, is hereby prohibited.

Sec. 3. This article shall be inoperative unless it shall have been ratified as an amendment to the Constitution by conventions in the several States, as provided in the Constitution, within seven years from the date of the submission hereof to the States by the Congress.

ARTICLE [XXII]

Section 1. No person shall be elected to the office of the President more than twice, and no person who has held the office of President, or acted as President, for more than two years of a term to which some other person was elected President shall be elected to the office of the President more than once. But this Article shall not apply to any person holding the office of President when this Article was proposed by the Congress, and shall not prevent any person who may be holding the office of President, or acting as President, during the term within which this Article becomes operative from holding the office of President or acting as President during the remainder of such term.

Sec. 2. This Article shall be inoperative unless it shall have been ratified as an amendment to the Constitution by the legislatures of three-fourths of the several States within seven years from the date of its submission to the States by the Congress.

ARTICLE [XXIII]

Section 1. The District constituting the seat of Government of the United States shall appoint in such manner as the Congress may direct:

A number of electors of President and Vice President equal to the whole number of Senators and Representatives in Congress to which the District would be entitled if it were a State, but in no event more than the least populous State; they shall be in addition to those appointed by the States, but they shall be considered, for the purposes of the election of President and Vice President, to be electors appointed by a State; and they shall meet in the District and perform such duties as provided by the twelfth article of amendment.

Sec. 2. The Congress shall have power to enforce this article by appropriate legislation.

ARTICLE [XXIV]

Section 1. The right of citizens of the United States to vote in any primary or other election for President or Vice President, for electors for President or Vice President, or for Senator or Representative in Congress, shall not be denied or abridged by the United States or any State by reason of failure to pay any poll tax or other tax.

Sec. 2. The Congress shall have power to enforce this article by appropriate legislation.

ARTICLE [XXV]

Section 1. In case of the removal of the President from office or of his death or resignation, the Vice President shall become President.

Sec. 2. Whenever there is a vacancy in the office of the Vice President, the President shall nominate a Vice President who shall take office upon confirmation by a majority vote of both Houses of Congress.

Sec. 3. Whenever the President transmits to the President pro tempore of the Senate and the Speaker of the House of Representatives his written declaration that he is unable to discharge the powers and duties of his office, and until he transmits to them a written declaration to the contrary, such powers and duties shall be discharged by the Vice President as Acting President.

Sec. 4. Whenever the Vice President and a majority of either the principal officers of the executive departments or of such other body as Congress may by law provide, transmit to the President pro tempore of the Senate and the Speaker of the House of Representatives their written declaration that the President is unable to discharge the powers and duties of his office, the Vice President shall immediately assume the powers and duties of the office as Acting President.

Thereafter, when the President transmits to the President pro tempore of the Senate and the Speaker of the House of Representatives his written declaration that no inability exists, he shall resume the powers and duties of his office unless the Vice President and a majority of either the principal officers of the executive department or of such other body as Congress may by law provide, transmit within four days to the President pro tempore of the Senate and the Speaker of the House of Representatives their written declaration that the President is unable to discharge the powers and duties of his office. Thereupon Congress shall decide the issue, assembling within forty-eight hours for that purpose if not in session. If the Congress, within twenty-one days after receipt of the latter written declaration, or, if Congress is not in session, within twenty-one days after Congress is required to assemble, determines by two-thirds vote of both Houses that the President is unable to discharge the powers and duties of his office, the Vice President shall continue to discharge the same as Acting President; otherwise, the President shall resume the powers and duties of his office.

ARTICLE [XXVI]

Section 1. The right of citizens of the United States, who are eighteen years of age or older, to vote shall not be denied or abridged by the United States or by any State on account of age.

Sec. 2. The Congress shall have power to enforce this article by appropriate legislation.

ARTICLE [XXVII][1]

No law, varying the compensation for the services of the Senators and Representatives, shall take effect, until an election of Representatives shall have intervened.

1 "Article [XXVII]" editorially added. Originally read "Article the second".

TITLE 8
ALIENS AND NATIONALITY

CHAPTER 12—IMMIGRATION AND NATIONALITY

SUBCHAPTER II—IMMIGRATION

PART VIII—GENERAL PENALTY PROVISIONS

SUBCHAPTER II—IMMIGRATION

PART VIII—GENERAL PENALTY PROVISIONS

§ 1321. Prevention of unauthorized landing of aliens

(a) Failure to report; penalties

It shall be the duty of every person, including the owners, masters, officers, and agents of vessels, aircraft, transportation lines, or international bridges or toll roads, other than transportation lines which may enter into a contract as provided in section 1223 of this title, bringing an alien to, or providing a means for an alien to come to, the United States (including an alien crewman whose case is not covered by section 1284(a) of this title) to prevent the landing of such alien in the United States at a port of entry other than as designated by the Attorney General or at any time or place other than as designated by the immigration officers. Any such person, owner, master, officer, or agent who fails to comply with the foregoing requirements shall be liable to a penalty to be imposed by the Attorney General of $3,000 for each such violation, which may, in the discretion of the Attorney General, be remitted or mitigated by him in accordance with such proceedings as he shall by regulation prescribe. Such penalty shall be a lien upon the vessel or aircraft whose owner, master, officer, or agent violates the provisions of this section, and such vessel or aircraft may be libeled therefor in the appropriate United States court.

(b) Prima facie evidence

Proof that the alien failed to present himself at the time and place designated by the immigration officers shall be prima facie evidence that such alien has landed in the United States at a time or place other than as designated by the immigration officers.

(c) Liability of owners and operators of international bridges and toll roads

(1) Any owner or operator of a railroad line, international bridge, or toll road who establishes to the satisfaction of the Attorney General that the person has acted diligently and reasonably to fulfill the duty imposed by subsection (a) of this section shall not be liable for the penalty described in such subsection, notwithstanding the failure of the person to prevent the unauthorized landing of any alien.

(2)(A) At the request of any person described in paragraph (1), the Attorney General shall inspect any facility established, or any method utilized, at a point of entry into the United States by such person for the purpose of complying with subsection (a) of this section. The Attorney General shall approve any such facility or method (for such period of time as the Attorney General may prescribe) which the Attorney General determines is satisfactory for such purpose.

(B) Proof that any person described in paragraph (1) has diligently maintained any facility, or utilized any method, which has been approved by the Attorney General under subparagraph (A) (within the period for which the approval is effective) shall be prima facie evidence that such person acted diligently and reasonably to fulfill the duty imposed by subsection (a) of this section (within the meaning of paragraph (1) of this subsection).

(June 27, 1952, c. 477, Title II, ch. 8, § 271, 66 Stat. 226; Nov. 6, 1986, Pub.L. 99–603, Title I, § 114, 100 Stat. 3383; Nov. 29, 1990, Pub.L. 101–649, Title V, § 543(a)(8), 104 Stat. 5058; Sept. 30, 1996, Pub.L. 104–208, Div. C, Title III, § 308(g)(1), 110 Stat. 3009–622.)

HISTORICAL AND STATUTORY NOTES

Effective and Applicability Provisions

1996 Acts. Amendment by section 308 of Div. C of Pub.L. 104–208 effective, with certain exceptions and subject to certain transitional rules, on the first day of the first month beginning more than 180 days after Sept. 30, 1996, see section 309 of Div. C of Pub.L. 104–208, set out as a note under section 1101 of this title.

1990 Acts. Amendment by section 543(a)(8) of Pub.L. 101–649 applicable to actions taken after Nov. 29, 1990, see section 543(c) of Pub.L. 101–649, set out as a note under section 1221 of this title.

Abolition of Immigration and Naturalization Service and Transfer of Functions

For abolition of Immigration and Naturalization Service, transfer of functions, and treatment of related references, see note set out under 8 U.S.C.A. § 1551.

Severability of Provisions

If any provision of Division C of Pub.L. 104–208 or the application of such provision to any person or circumstances is held to be unconstitutional, the remainder of Division C of Pub.L. 104–208 and the application of the provisions of Division C of Pub.L. 104–208 to any person or circumstance not to be affected thereby, see section 1(e) of Pub.L. 104–208, set out as a note under section 1101 of this title.

§ 1322. Bringing in aliens subject to denial of admission on a health-related ground; persons liable; clearance papers; exceptions; "person" defined

(a) Any person who shall bring to the United States an alien (other than an alien crewman) who is inadmissible under section 1182(a)(1) of this title shall pay to the Commissioner for each and every alien so afflicted the sum of $3,000 unless (1) the alien was in possession of a valid, unexpired immigrant visa, or (2) the alien was allowed to land in the United States, or (3) the alien was in possession of a valid unexpired nonimmigrant visa or other document authorizing such alien to apply for temporary admission to the United States or an unexpired reentry permit issued to him, and (A) such application was made within one hundred and twenty days of the date of issuance of the visa or other document, or in the case of an alien in possession of a reentry permit, within one hundred and twenty days of the date on which the alien was last examined and admitted by the Service, or (B) in the event the application was made later than one hundred and twenty days of the date of issuance of the visa or other document or such examination and admission, if such person establishes to the satisfaction of the Attorney General that the existence of the condition causing inadmissibility could not have been detected by the exercise of due diligence prior to the alien's embarkation.

(b) No vessel or aircraft shall be granted clearance papers pending determination of the question of liability to the payment of any fine under this section, or while the fines remain unpaid, nor shall such fines be remitted or refunded; but clearance may be granted prior to the determination of such question upon the deposit of a sum sufficient to cover such fines or of a bond with sufficient surety to secure the payment thereof, approved by the Commissioner.

(c) Nothing contained in this section shall be construed to subject transportation companies to a fine for bringing to ports of entry in the United States aliens who are entitled by law to exemption from the provisions of section 1182(a) of this title.

(d) As used in this section, the term "person" means the owner, master, agent, commanding officer, charterer, or consignee of any vessel or aircraft.

(June 27, 1952, c. 477, Title II, ch. 8, § 272, 66 Stat. 226; Oct. 3, 1965, Pub.L. 89–236, § 18, 79 Stat. 920; Nov. 29, 1990, Pub.L. 101–649, Title V, § 543(a)(9), Title VI, § 603(a)(15), 104 Stat. 5058, 5083; Dec. 12, 1991, Pub.L. 102–232, Title III, § 307(*l*)(7), 105 Stat. 1757; Oct. 25, 1994, Pub.L. 103–416, Title II, § 219(*o*), 108 Stat. 4317; Sept. 30, 1996, Pub.L. 104–208, Div. C, Title III, § 308(d)(3)(A), (4)(I)(i), 110 Stat. 3009–617, 3009–618.)

HISTORICAL AND STATUTORY NOTES

Effective and Applicability Provisions

1996 Acts. Amendment by section 308 of Div. C of Pub.L. 104–208 effective, with certain exceptions and subject to certain transitional rules, on the first day of the first month beginning more than 180 days after Sept. 30, 1996, see section 309 of Div. C of Pub.L. 104–208, set out as a note under section 1101 of this title.

1994 Acts. Amendment by section 219 of Pub.L. 103–416 effective as if included in the enactment of the Immigration Act of 1990, Pub.L. 101–649, 104 Stat. 4978, which was approved Nov. 29, 1990, except as otherwise specifically provided, see section 219(dd) of Pub.L. 103–416, set out as a note under section 1101 of this title.

1991 Acts. Amendments by sections 302 through 308 of Pub.L. 102–232, except as otherwise specifically provided, effective as if included in the enactment of Pub.L. 101–649, see section 310(1) of Pub.L. 102–232, set out as a note under section 1101 of this title.

Amendment by section 307(*l*)(7) of Pub.L. 102–232 effective as if included in section 603(a) of Pub.L. 101–649, see section 307(*l*) of Pub.L. 102–232, set out as a note under section 1157 of this title.

1990 Acts. Amendment by section 543(a)(9) of Pub.L. 101–649 applicable to actions taken after Nov. 29, 1990, see section 543(c) of Pub.L. 101–649, set out as a note under section 1221 of this title.

Amendment by section 603(a)(15) of Pub.L. 101–649 applicable to individuals entering the United States on or after June 1, 1991, see section 601(e)(1) of Pub.L. 101–649, set out as a note under section 1101 of this title.

1965 Acts. Amendment of section by Pub.L. 89–236 effective, except as otherwise provided, on the first day of the first month after the expiration of thirty days following the date of enactment of Pub.L. 89–236, which was approved on Oct. 3, 1965, see § 20 of Pub.L. 89–236, set out as a note under § 1151 of this title.

Abolition of Immigration and Naturalization Service and Transfer of Functions

For abolition of Immigration and Naturalization Service, transfer of functions, and treatment of related references, see note set out under 8 U.S.C.A. § 1551.

Severability of Provisions

If any provision of Division C of Pub.L. 104–208 or the application of such provision to any person or circumstances is held to be unconstitutional, the remainder of Division C of Pub.L. 104–208 and the application of the provisions of Division C of Pub.L. 104–208 to any person or circumstance not to be affected thereby, see section 1(e) of Pub.L. 104–208, set out as a note under section 1101 of this title.

§ 1323. Unlawful bringing of aliens into United States

(a) Persons liable

(1) It shall be unlawful for any person, including any transportation company, or the owner, master, commanding officer, agent, charterer, or consignee of any vessel or aircraft, to bring to the United States from any place outside thereof (other than from foreign contiguous territory) any alien who does not have a valid passport and an unexpired visa, if a visa was required under this chapter or regulations issued thereunder.

(2) It is unlawful for an owner, agent, master, commanding officer, person in charge, purser, or consignee of a vessel or aircraft who is bringing an alien (except an alien crewmember) to the United States to take any consideration to be kept or returned contingent on whether an alien is admitted to, or ordered removed from, the United States.

(b) Evidence

If it appears to the satisfaction of the Attorney General that any alien has been so brought, such person, or transportation company, or the master, commanding officer, agent, owner, charterer, or consignee of any such vessel or aircraft, shall pay to the Commissioner a fine of $3,000 for each alien so brought and, except in the case of any such alien who is admitted, or permitted to land temporarily, in addition, an amount equal to that paid by such alien for his transportation from the initial point of departure, indicated in his ticket, to the port of arrival, such latter fine to be delivered by the Commissioner to the alien on whose account the assessment is made. No vessel or aircraft shall be granted clearance pending the determination of the liability to the payment of such fine or while such fine remains unpaid, except that clearance may be granted prior to the determination of such question upon the deposit of an amount sufficient to cover such fine, or of a bond with sufficient surety to secure the payment thereof approved by the Commissioner.

(c) Remission or refund

Except as provided in subsection (e) of this section, such fine shall not be remitted or refunded, unless it appears to the satisfaction of the Attorney General that such person, and the owner, master, commanding officer, agent, charterer, and consignee of the vessel or aircraft, prior to the departure of the vessel or aircraft from the last port outside the United States, did not know, and could not have ascertained by the exercise of reasonable diligence, that the individual transported was an alien and that a valid passport or visa was required.

(d) Repealed. Pub.L. 104–208, Div. C, Title III, § 308(e)(13), Sept. 30, 1996, 110 Stat. 3009–620

(e) Reduction, refund, or waiver

A fine under this section may be reduced, refunded, or waived under such regulations as the Attorney General shall prescribe in cases in which—

(1) the carrier demonstrates that it had screened all passengers on the vessel or aircraft in accordance with procedures prescribed by the Attorney General, or

(2) circumstances exist that the Attorney General determines would justify such reduction, refund, or waiver.

(June 27, 1952, c. 477, Title II, ch. 8, § 273, 66 Stat. 227; Nov. 29, 1990, Pub.L. 101–649, Title II, § 201(b), Title V, § 543(a)(10), 104 Stat. 5014, 5058; Dec. 12, 1991, Pub.L. 102–232, Title III, § 306(c)(4)(D), 105 Stat. 1752; Oct. 25, 1994, Pub.L. 103–416, Title II, §§ 209(a), 216, 219(p), 108 Stat. 4312, 4315, 4317; Sept. 30, 1996, Pub.L. 104–208, Div. C, Title III, §§ 308(c)(3), (e)(13), 371(b)(8), Title VI, § 671(b)(6), (7), 110 Stat. 3009–616, 3009–620, 3009–645, 3009–722.)

HISTORICAL AND STATUTORY NOTES

Effective and Applicability Provisions

1996 Acts. Amendment by section 308 of Div. C of Pub.L. 104–208 effective, with certain exceptions and subject to certain transitional rules, on the first day of the first month beginning more than 180 days after Sept. 30, 1996, see section 309 of Div. C of Pub.L. 104–208, set out as a note under section 1101 of this title.

Amendment by section 371(b)(8) of Div. C of Pub.L. 104–208 effective Sept. 30, 1996, see section 371(d)(1) of Div. C of Pub.L. 104–208, set out as a note under section 1101 of this title.

Amendment by section 671(b)(6), (7) of Div. C of Pub.L. 104–208 effective as if included in the enactment of Pub.L. 103–416, which was approved Oct. 25, 1994, see section 671(b)(14) of Div. C of Pub.L. 104–208, set out as a note under section 1101 of this title.

1994 Acts. Section 209(b) of Pub.L. 103–416, as amended Pub.L. 104–208, Div. C, Title VI, § 671(b)(8), Sept. 30, 1996, 110 Stat. 3009–722, provided that: "The amendments made by this section [amending this section] shall apply with respect to aliens brought to the United States more than 60 days after the date of enactment of this Act [Oct. 25, 1994]."

[Amendment by section 671(b)(8) of Div. C of Pub.L. 104–208 effective as if included in the enactment of Pub.L. 103–416, which was approved Oct. 25, 1994, see section 671(b)(14) of Div. C of Pub.L. 104–208, set out as a note under section 1101 of this title.]

Amendment by section 219 of Pub.L. 103–416 effective as if included in the enactment of the Immigration Act of 1990, Pub.L. 101–649, 104 Stat. 4978, which was approved Nov. 29, 1990, except as otherwise specifically provided, see section 219(dd) of Pub.L. 103–416, set out as a note under section 1101 of this title.

1991 Acts. Amendments by sections 302 through 308 of Pub.L. 102–232, except as otherwise specifically provided, effective as if included in the enactment of Pub.L. 101–649, see section 310(1) of Pub.L. 102–232, set out as a note under section 1101 of this title.

1990 Acts. Amendment by Pub.L. 101–649 effective as of Nov. 29, 1990, see section 201(d) of Pub.L. 101–649, set out as a note under section 1187 of this title.

Amendment by section 543(a)(10) of Pub.L. 101–649 applicable to actions taken after Nov. 29, 1990, see section 543(c) of Pub.L. 101–649, set out as a note under section 1221 of this title.

Abolition of Immigration and Naturalization Service and Transfer of Functions

For abolition of Immigration and Naturalization Service, transfer of functions, and treatment of related references, see note set out under 8 U.S.C.A. § 1551.

Severability of Provisions

If any provision of Division C of Pub.L. 104–208 or the application of such provision to any person or circumstances is held to be unconstitutional, the remainder of Division C of Pub.L. 104–208 and the application of the provisions of Division C of Pub.L. 104–208 to any person or circumstance not to be affected thereby, see section 1(e) of Pub.L. 104–208, set out as a note under section 1101 of this title.

§ 1324. Bringing in and harboring certain aliens

(a) Criminal penalties

(1)(A) Any person who—

(i) knowing that a person is an alien, brings to or attempts to bring to the United States in any manner whatsoever such person at a place other than a designated port of entry or place other than as designated by the Commissioner, regardless of whether such alien has received prior official authorization to come to, enter, or reside in the United States and regardless of any future official action which may be taken with respect to such alien;

(ii) knowing or in reckless disregard of the fact that an alien has come to, entered, or remains in the United States in violation of law, transports, or moves or attempts to transport or move such alien within the United States by means of transportation or otherwise, in furtherance of such violation of law;

(iii) knowing or in reckless disregard of the fact that an alien has come to, entered, or remains in the United States in violation of law, conceals, harbors, or shields from detection, or attempts to conceal, harbor, or shield from detection, such alien in any place, including any building or any means of transportation;

(iv) encourages or induces an alien to come to, enter, or reside in the United States, knowing or in reckless disregard of the fact that such coming to, entry, or residence is or will be in violation of law; or

(v)(I) engages in any conspiracy to commit any of the preceding acts, or

(II) aids or abets the commission of any of the preceding acts,

shall be punished as provided in subparagraph (B).

(B) A person who violates subparagraph (A) shall, for each alien in respect to whom such a violation occurs—

(i) in the case of a violation of subparagraph (A)(i) or (v)(I) or in the case of a violation of subparagraph (A)(ii), (iii), or (iv) in which the offense was done for the purpose of commercial advantage or private financial gain, be fined under Title 18, imprisoned not more than 10 years, or both;

(ii) in the case of a violation of subparagraph (A)(ii), (iii), (iv), or (v)(II), be fined under Title 18, imprisoned not more than 5 years, or both;

(iii) in the case of a violation of subparagraph (A)(i), (ii), (iii), (iv), or (v) during and in relation to which the person causes serious bodily injury (as defined in section 1365 of Title 18) to, or places in jeopardy the life of, any person, be fined under Title 18, imprisoned not more than 20 years, or both; and

(iv) in the case of a violation of subparagraph (A)(i), (ii), (iii), (iv), or (v) resulting in the death of any person, be punished by death or imprisoned for any term of years or for life, fined under Title 18, or both.

(C) It is not a violation of clauses (ii) or (iii) of subparagraph (A), or of clause (iv) of subparagraph (A) except where a person encourages or induces an alien to come to or enter the United States, for a religious denomination having a bona fide nonprofit, religious organization in the United States, or the agents or officers of such denomination or organization, to encourage, invite, call, allow, or enable an alien who is present in the United States to perform the vocation of a minister or missionary for the denomination or organization in the United States as a volunteer who is not compensated as an employee, notwithstanding the provision of room, board, travel, medical assistance, and other basic living expenses, provided the minister or missionary has been a member of the denomination for at least one year.

(2) Any person who, knowing or in reckless disregard of the fact that an alien has not received prior official authorization to come to, enter, or reside in the United States, brings to or attempts to bring to the United States in any manner whatsoever, such alien, regardless of any official action which may later be taken with respect to such alien shall, for each alien in respect to whom a violation of this paragraph occurs—

(A) be fined in accordance with Title 18 or imprisoned not more than one year, or both; or

(B) in the case of—

(i) an offense committed with the intent or with reason to believe that the alien unlawfully brought into the United States will commit an offense against the United States or any State punishable by imprisonment for more than 1 year,

(ii) an offense done for the purpose of commercial advantage or private financial gain, or

(iii) an offense in which the alien is not upon arrival immediately brought and presented to an appropriate immigration officer at a designated port of entry,

be fined under Title 18 and shall be imprisoned, in the case of a first or second violation of subparagraph (B)(iii), not more than 10 years, in the case of a first or second violation of subparagraph (B)(i) or (B)(ii), not less than 3 nor more than 10 years, and for any other violation, not less than 5 nor more than 15 years.

(3)(A) Any person who, during any 12-month period, knowingly hires for employment at least 10 individuals with actual knowledge that the individuals are aliens described in subparagraph (B) shall be fined under Title 18 or imprisoned for not more than 5 years, or both.

(B) An alien described in this subparagraph is an alien who—

(i) is an unauthorized alien (as defined in section 1324a(h)(3) of this title), and

(ii) has been brought into the United States in violation of this subsection.

(4) In the case of a person who has brought aliens into the United States in violation of this subsection, the sentence otherwise provided for may be increased by up to 10 years if—

(A) the offense was part of an ongoing commercial organization or enterprise;

(B) aliens were transported in groups of 10 or more; and

(C)(i) aliens were transported in a manner that endangered their lives; or

(ii) the aliens presented a life-threatening health risk to people in the United States.

(b) Seizure and forfeiture

(1) In general

Any conveyance, including any vessel, vehicle, or aircraft, that has been or is being used in the commission of a violation of subsection (a) of this section, the gross proceeds of such violation, and any property traceable to such conveyance or proceeds, shall be seized and subject to forfeiture.

(2) Applicable procedures

Seizures and forfeitures under this subsection shall be governed by the provisions of chapter 46 of Title 18, relating to civil forfeitures, including section 981(d) of such title, except that such duties as are imposed upon the Secretary of the Treasury under the customs laws described in that section shall be performed by such officers, agents, and other persons as may be designated for that purpose by the Attorney General.

(3) Prima facie evidence in determinations of violations

In determining whether a violation of subsection (a) of this section has occurred, any of the following shall be prima facie evidence that an alien involved in the alleged violation had not received prior official authorization to come to, enter, or reside in the United States or that such alien had come to, entered, or remained in the United States in violation of law:

(A) Records of any judicial or administrative proceeding in which that alien's status was an issue and in which it was determined that the alien had not received prior official authorization to come to, enter, or reside in the United States or that such alien had come to, entered, or remained in the United States in violation of law.

(B) Official records of the Service or of the Department of State showing that the alien had not received prior official authorization to come to, enter, or reside in the United States or that such alien had come to, entered, or remained in the United States in violation of law.

(C) Testimony, by an immigration officer having personal knowledge of the facts concerning that alien's status, that the alien had not received prior official authorization to come to, enter, or reside in the United States or that such alien had come to, entered, or remained in the United States in violation of law.

(c) Authority to arrest

No officer or person shall have authority to make any arrests for a violation of any provision of this section except officers and employees of the Service designated by the Attorney General, either individually or as a member of a class, and all other officers whose duty it is to enforce criminal laws.

(d) Admissibility of videotaped witness testimony

Notwithstanding any provision of the Federal Rules of Evidence, the videotaped (or otherwise audiovisually preserved) deposition of a witness to a violation of subsection (a) of this section who has been deported or otherwise expelled from the United States, or is otherwise unable to testify, may be admitted into evidence in an action brought for that violation if the witness was available for cross examination and the deposition otherwise complies with the Federal Rules of Evidence.

(e) Outreach program

The Secretary of Homeland Security, in consultation with the Attorney General and the Secretary of State, as appropriate, shall develop and implement an outreach program to educate the public in the United States and abroad about the penalties for bringing in and harboring aliens in violation of this section.

(June 27, 1952, c. 477, Title II, ch. 8, § 274, 66 Stat. 228; Nov. 2, 1978, Pub.L. 95–582, § 2, 92 Stat. 2479; Dec. 29, 1981, Pub.L. 97–116, § 12, 95 Stat. 1617; Nov. 6, 1986, Pub.L. 99–603, Title I, Part B, § 112, 100 Stat. 3381; Oct. 24, 1988, Pub.L. 100–525, § 2(d), 102 Stat. 2610; Sept. 13, 1994, Pub.L. 103–322, Title VI, § 60024, 108 Stat. 1981; Sept. 30, 1996, Pub.L. 104–208, Div. C, Title II, §§ 203(a) to (d), 219, Title VI, § 671(a)(1), 110 Stat. 3009–565, 3009–566, 3009–574, 3009–721; Apr. 25, 2000, Pub.L. 106–185, § 18(a), 114 Stat. 222; Dec. 17, 2004, Pub.L. 108–458, Title V, § 5401, 118 Stat. 3737; Nov. 10, 2005, Pub.L. 109–97, Title VII, § 796, 119 Stat. 2165.)

HISTORICAL AND STATUTORY NOTES

References in Text

Chapter 46, of Title 18, referred to in subsec. (b), is classified to 18 U.S.C.A. § 981 et seq.

The Federal rules of Evidence, referred to in subsec. (d) are set out in Title 28, Judiciary and Judicial Procedure.

Effective and Applicability Provisions

2000 Acts. Pub.L. 106–185, § 21, Apr. 25, 2000, 114 Stat. 225, provided that: "Except as provided in section 14(c) [enacting a note provision under section 2466 of Title 28 relating to the enactment of 28 U.S.C.A. § 2466 applicable to cases pending on or after Apr. 25, 2000], this Act and the amendments made by this Act [Civil Asset Forfeiture Reform Act of 2000, Pub.L. 106–185, Apr. 25, 2000, 114 Stat. 202, enacting sections 983 and 985 of Title 18, section 2467 of Title 28, amending this section, and sections 981, 982, 984, 986, 2232, 2254, and 3322 of this title, section 1621 of Title 19, section 881 of Title 21, sections 524, 2461, 2465, and 2680 of Title 28, and section 2996f of Title 42, repealing section 888 of Title 21, and enacting provisions set out as notes under section 3724 of Title 31] shall apply to any forfeiture proceeding commenced on or after the date that is 120 days after the date of the enactment of this Act [Apr. 25, 2000]."

1996 Acts. Section 203(f) of Div. C of Pub.L. 104–208 provided that: "This section and the amendments made by this section [amending this section and enacting a provision set out as a note under section 994 of Title 28, Judiciary and Judicial Procedure] shall apply with respect to offenses occurring on or after the date of the enactment of this Act [Sept. 30, 1996]."

Amendment by section 671(a)(1) of Div. C of Pub.L. 104–208 effective as if included in the enactment of Pub.L. 103–322, which was approved Sept. 13, 1994, see section 671(a)(7) of Div. C of Pub.L. 104–208, set out as a note under section 1101 of this title.

1988 Acts. Amendments by section 2(d) of Pub.L. 100–525 effective as if included in the enactment of Pub.L. 99–603, pursuant to section 2(s) of Pub.L. 100–525, set out as a note under section 1101 of this title.

1981 Acts. Amendment by Pub.L. 97–116 effective on Dec. 29, 1981, see section 21(a) of Pub.L. 97–116, set out as a note under section 1101 of this title.

Abolition of Immigration and Naturalization Service and Transfer of Functions

For abolition of Immigration and Naturalization Service, transfer of functions, and treatment of related references, see note set out under 8 U.S.C.A. § 1551.

Severability of Provisions

If any provision of Division C of Pub.L. 104–208 or the application of such provision to any person or circumstances is held to be unconstitutional, the remainder of Division C of Pub.L. 104–208 and the application of the provisions of Division C of Pub.L. 104–208 to any person or circumstance not to be affected thereby, see section 1(e) of Pub.L. 104–208, set out as a note under section 1101 of this title.

§ 1324a. Unlawful employment of aliens

(a) Making employment of unauthorized aliens unlawful

(1) In general

It is unlawful for a person or other entity—

(A) to hire, or to recruit or refer for a fee, for employment in the United States an alien knowing the alien is an unauthorized alien (as defined in subsection (h)(3) of this section) with respect to such employment, or

(B) (i) to hire for employment in the United States an individual without complying with the requirements of subsection (b) of this section or (ii) if the person or entity is an agricultural association, agricultural employer, or farm labor contractor (as defined in section 1802 of Title 29), to hire, or to recruit or refer for a fee, for employment in the United States an individual without complying with the requirements of subsection (b) of this section.

(2) Continuing employment

It is unlawful for a person or other entity, after hiring an alien for employment in accordance with paragraph (1), to continue to employ the alien in the United States knowing the alien is (or has become)

an unauthorized alien with respect to such employment.

(3) Defense

A person or entity that establishes that it has complied in good faith with the requirements of subsection (b) of this section with respect to the hiring, recruiting, or referral for employment of an alien in the United States has established an affirmative defense that the person or entity has not violated paragraph (1)(A) with respect to such hiring, recruiting, or referral.

(4) Use of labor through contract

For purposes of this section, a person or other entity who uses a contract, subcontract, or exchange, entered into, renegotiated, or extended after November 6, 1986, to obtain the labor of an alien in the United States knowing that the alien is an unauthorized alien (as defined in subsection (h)(3) of this section) with respect to performing such labor, shall be considered to have hired the alien for employment in the United States in violation of paragraph (1)(A).

(5) Use of State employment agency documentation

For purposes of paragraphs (1)(B) and (3), a person or entity shall be deemed to have complied with the requirements of subsection (b) of this section with respect to the hiring of an individual who was referred for such employment by a State employment agency (as defined by the Attorney General), if the person or entity has and retains (for the period and in the manner described in subsection (b)(3) of this section) appropriate documentation of such referral by that agency, which documentation certifies that the agency has complied with the procedures specified in subsection (b) of this section with respect to the individual's referral.

(6) Treatment of documentation for certain employees

(A) In general

For purposes of this section, if—

(i) an individual is a member of a collective-bargaining unit and is employed, under a collective bargaining agreement entered into between one or more employee organizations and an association of two or more employers, by an employer that is a member of such association, and

(ii) within the period specified in subparagraph (B), another employer that is a member of the association (or an agent of such association on behalf of the employer) has complied with the requirements of subsection (b) of this section with respect to the employment of the individual,

the subsequent employer shall be deemed to have complied with the requirements of subsection (b) of this section with respect to the hiring of the employee and shall not be liable for civil penalties described in subsection (e)(5) of this section.

(B) Period

The period described in this subparagraph is 3 years, or, if less, the period of time that the individual is authorized to be employed in the United States.

(C) Liability

(i) In general

If any employer that is a member of an association hires for employment in the United States an individual and relies upon the provisions of subparagraph (A) to comply with the requirements of subsection (b) of this section and the individual is an alien not authorized to work in the United States, then for the purposes of paragraph (1)(A), subject to clause (ii), the employer shall be presumed to have known at the time of hiring or afterward that the individual was an alien not authorized to work in the United States.

(ii) Rebuttal of presumption

The presumption established by clause (i) may be rebutted by the employer only through the presentation of clear and convincing evidence that the employer did not know (and could not reasonably have known) that the individual at the time of hiring or afterward was an alien not authorized to work in the United States.

(iii) Exception

Clause (i) shall not apply in any prosecution under subsection (f)(1) of this section.

(7) Application to Federal Government

For purposes of this section, the term "entity" includes an entity in any branch of the Federal Government.

(b) Employment verification system

The requirements referred to in paragraphs (1)(B) and (3) of subsection (a) of this section are, in the case of a person or other entity hiring, recruiting, or referring an individual for employment in the United States, the requirements specified in the following three paragraphs:

(1) Attestation after examination of documentation

(A) In general

The person or entity must attest, under penalty of perjury and on a form designated or established by the Attorney General by regulation, that it has verified that the individual is not an unauthorized alien by examining—

(i) a document described in subparagraph (B), or

(ii) a document described in subparagraph (C) and a document described in subparagraph (D).

Such attestation may be manifested by either a hand-written or an electronic signature. A person or entity has complied with the requirement of this paragraph with respect to examination of a document if the document reasonably appears on its face to be genuine. If an individual provides a document or combination of documents that reasonably appears on its face to be genuine and that is sufficient to meet the requirements of the first sentence of this paragraph, nothing in this paragraph shall be construed as requiring the person or entity to solicit the production of any other document or as requiring the individual to produce such another document.

(B) Documents establishing both employment authorization and identity

A document described in this subparagraph is an individual's—

(i) United States passport;[1]

(ii) resident alien card, alien registration card, or other document designated by the Attorney General, if the document—

(I) contains a photograph of the individual and such other personal identifying information relating to the individual as the Attorney General finds, by regulation, sufficient for purposes of this subsection,

(II) is evidence of authorization of employment in the United States, and

(III) contains security features to make it resistant to tampering, counterfeiting, and fraudulent use.

(C) Documents evidencing employment authorization

A document described in this subparagraph is an individual's—

(i) social security account number card (other than such a card which specifies on the face that the issuance of the card does not authorize employment in the United States); or

(ii) other documentation evidencing authorization of employment in the United States which the Attorney General finds, by regulation, to be acceptable for purposes of this section.

(D) Documents establishing identity of individual

A document described in this subparagraph is an individual's—

(i) driver's license or similar document issued for the purpose of identification by a State, if it contains a photograph of the individual or such other personal identifying information relating to the individual as the Attorney General finds, by regulation, sufficient for purposes of this section; or

(ii) in the case of individuals under 16 years of age or in a State which does not provide for issuance of an identification document (other than a driver's license) referred to in clause (i), documentation of personal identity of such other type as the Attorney General finds, by regulation, provides a reliable means of identification.

(E) Authority to prohibit use of certain documents

If the Attorney General finds, by regulation, that any document described in subparagraph (B), (C), or (D) as establishing employment authorization or identity does not reliably establish such authorization or identity or is being used fraudulently to an unacceptable degree, the Attorney General may prohibit or place conditions on its use for purposes of this subsection.

(2) Individual attestation of employment authorization

The individual must attest, under penalty of perjury on the form designated or established for purposes of paragraph (1), that the individual is a citizen or national of the United States, an alien lawfully admitted for permanent residence, or an alien who is authorized under this chapter or by the Attorney General to be hired, recruited, or referred for such employment. Such attestation may be manifested by either a hand-written or an electronic signature.

(3) Retention of verification form

After completion of such form in accordance with paragraphs (1) and (2), the person or entity must retain a paper, microfiche, microfilm, or electronic version of the form and make it available for inspection by officers of the Service, the Special Counsel for Immigration-Related Unfair Employment Practices, or the Department of Labor during a period beginning on the date of the hiring, recruiting, or referral of the individual and ending—

(A) in the case of the recruiting or referral for a fee (without hiring) of an individual, three years after the date of the recruiting or referral, and

(B) in the case of the hiring of an individual—

(i) three years after the date of such hiring, or

(ii) one year after the date the individual's employment is terminated,

whichever is later.

(4) Copying of documentation permitted

Notwithstanding any other provision of law, the person or entity may copy a document presented by an individual pursuant to this subsection and may retain the copy, but only (except as otherwise permitted under law) for the purpose of complying with the requirements of this subsection.

(5) Limitation on use of attestation form

A form designated or established by the Attorney General under this subsection and any information contained in or appended to such form, may not be used for purposes other than for enforcement of this chapter and sections 1001, 1028, 1546, and 1621 of Title 18.

(6) Good faith compliance

(A) In general

Except as provided in subparagraphs (B) and (C), a person or entity is considered to have complied with a requirement of this subsection notwithstanding a technical or procedural failure to meet such requirement if there was a good faith attempt to comply with the requirement.

(B) Exception if failure to correct after notice

Subparagraph (A) shall not apply if—

(i) the Service (or another enforcement agency) has explained to the person or entity the basis for the failure,

(ii) the person or entity has been provided a period of not less than 10 business days (beginning after the date of the explanation) within which to correct the failure, and

(iii) the person or entity has not corrected the failure voluntarily within such period.

(C) Exception for pattern or practice violators

Subparagraph (A) shall not apply to a person or entity that has or is engaging in a pattern or practice of violations of subsection (a)(1)(A) or (a)(2) of this section.

(c) No authorization of national identification cards

Nothing in this section shall be construed to authorize, directly or indirectly, the issuance or use of national identification cards or the establishment of a national identification card.

(d) Evaluation and changes in employment verification system

(1) Presidential monitoring and improvements in system

(A) Monitoring

The President shall provide for the monitoring and evaluation of the degree to which the employment verification system established under subsection (b) of this section provides a secure system to determine employment eligibility in the United States and shall examine the suitability of existing Federal and State identification systems for use for this purpose.

(B) Improvements to establish secure system

To the extent that the system established under subsection (b) of this section is found not to be a secure system to determine employment eligibility in the United States, the President shall, subject to paragraph (3) and taking into account the results of any demonstration projects conducted under paragraph (4), implement such changes in (including additions to) the requirements of subsection (b) of this section as may be necessary to establish a secure system to determine employment eligibility in the United States. Such changes in the system may be implemented only if the changes conform to the requirements of paragraph (2).

(2) Restrictions on changes in system

Any change the President proposes to implement under paragraph (1) in the verification system must be designed in a manner so the verification system, as so changed, meets the following requirements:

(A) Reliable determination of identity

The system must be capable of reliably determining whether—

(i) a person with the identity claimed by an employee or prospective employee is eligible to work, and

(ii) the employee or prospective employee is claiming the identity of another individual.

(B) Using of counterfeit-resistant documents

If the system requires that a document be presented to or examined by an employer, the document must be in a form which is resistant to counterfeiting and tampering.

(C) **Limited use of system**

Any personal information utilized by the system may not be made available to Government agencies, employers, and other persons except to the extent necessary to verify that an individual is not an unauthorized alien.

(D) **Privacy of information**

The system must protect the privacy and security of personal information and identifiers utilized in the system.

(E) **Limited denial of verification**

A verification that an employee or prospective employee is eligible to be employed in the United States may not be withheld or revoked under the system for any reason other than that the employee or prospective employee is an unauthorized alien.

(F) **Limited use for law enforcement purposes**

The system may not be used for law enforcement purposes, other than for enforcement of this chapter or sections 1001, 1028, 1546, and 1621 of Title 18.

(G) **Restriction on use of new documents**

If the system requires individuals to present a new card or other document (designed specifically for use for this purpose) at the time of hiring, recruitment, or referral, then such document may not be required to be presented for any purpose other than under this chapter (or enforcement of sections 1001, 1028, 1546, and 1621 of Title 18) nor to be carried on one's person.

(3) **Notice to Congress before implementing changes**

(A) **In general**

The President may not implement any change under paragraph (1) unless at least—

(i) 60 days,

(ii) one year, in the case of a major change described in subparagraph (D)(iii), or

(iii) two years, in the case of a major change described in clause (i) or (ii) of subparagraph (D),

before the date of implementation of the change, the President has prepared and transmitted to the Committee on the Judiciary of the House of Representatives and to the Committee on the Judiciary of the Senate a written report setting forth the proposed change. If the President proposes to make any change regarding social security account number cards, the President shall transmit to the Committee on Ways and Means of the House of Representatives and to the Committee on Finance of the Senate a written report setting forth the proposed change. The President promptly shall cause to have printed in the Federal Register the substance of any major change (described in subparagraph (D)) proposed and reported to Congress.

(B) **Contents of report**

In any report under subparagraph (A) the President shall include recommendations for the establishment of civil and criminal sanctions for unauthorized use or disclosure of the information or identifiers contained in such system.

(C) **Congressional review of major changes**

(i) **Hearings and review**

The Committees on the Judiciary of the House of Representatives and of the Senate shall cause to have printed in the Congressional Record the substance of any major change described in subparagraph (D), shall hold hearings respecting the feasibility and desirability of implementing such a change, and, within the two year period before implementation, shall report to their respective Houses findings on whether or not such a change should be implemented.

(ii) **Congressional action**

No major change may be implemented unless the Congress specifically provides, in an appropriations or other Act, for funds for implementation of the change.

(D) **Major changes defined**

As used in this paragraph, the term "major change" means a change which would—

(i) require an individual to present a new card or other document (designed specifically for use for this purpose) at the time of hiring, recruitment, or referral,

(ii) provide for a telephone verification system under which an employer, recruiter, or referrer must transmit to a Federal official information concerning the immigration status of prospective employees and the official transmits to the person, and the person must record, a verification code, or

(iii) require any change in any card used for accounting purposes under the Social Security Act [42 U.S.C.A. § 301 et seq.]; including any change requiring that the only social security account number cards which may be presented in order to comply with subsection (b)(1)(C)(i) of this section are such cards as are in a counterfeit-resistant form consistent with the second sentence of section 205(c)(2)(D) of the Social Security Act [42 U.S.C.A. § 405(c)(2)(D)].

(E) General revenue funding of social security card changes

Any costs incurred in developing and implementing any change described in subparagraph (D)(iii) for purposes of this subsection shall not be paid for out of any trust fund established under the Social Security Act [42 U.S.C.A. § 301 et seq.].

(4) Demonstration projects

(A) Authority

The President may undertake demonstration projects (consistent with paragraph (2)) of different changes in the requirements of subsection (b) of this section. No such project may extend over a period of longer than five years.

(B) Reports on projects

The President shall report to the Congress on the results of demonstration projects conducted under this paragraph.

(e) Compliance

(1) Complaints and investigations

The Attorney General shall establish procedures—

(A) for individuals and entities to file written, signed complaints respecting potential violations of subsection (a) or (g)(1) of this section,

(B) for the investigation of those complaints which, on their face, have a substantial probability of validity,

(C) for the investigation of such other violations of subsection (a) or (g)(1) of this section as the Attorney General determines to be appropriate, and

(D) for the designation in the Service of a unit which has, as its primary duty, the prosecution of cases of violations of subsection (a) or (g)(1) of this section under this subsection.

(2) Authority in investigations

In conducting investigations and hearings under this subsection—

(A) immigration officers and administrative law judges shall have reasonable access to examine evidence of any person or entity being investigated,

(B) administrative law judges, may, if necessary, compel by subpoena the attendance of witnesses and the production of evidence at any designated place or hearing, and

(C) immigration officers designated by the Commissioner may compel by subpoena the attendance of witnesses and the production of evidence at any designated place prior to the filing of a complaint in a case under paragraph (2).

In case of contumacy or refusal to obey a subpoena lawfully issued under this paragraph and upon application of the Attorney General, an appropriate district court of the United States may issue an order requiring compliance with such subpoena and any failure to obey such order may be punished by such court as a contempt thereof.

(3) Hearing

(A) In general

Before imposing an order described in paragraph (4), (5), or (6) against a person or entity under this subsection for a violation of subsection (a) or (g)(1) of this section, the Attorney General shall provide the person or entity with notice and, upon request made within a reasonable time (of not less than 30 days, as established by the Attorney General) of the date of the notice, a hearing respecting the violation.

(B) Conduct of hearing

Any hearing so requested shall be conducted before an administrative law judge. The hearing shall be conducted in accordance with the requirements of section 554 of Title 5. The hearing shall be held at the nearest practicable place to the place where the person or entity resides or of the place where the alleged violation occurred. If no hearing is so requested, the Attorney General's imposition of the order shall constitute a final and unappealable order.

(C) Issuance of orders

If the administrative law judge determines, upon the preponderance of the evidence received, that a person or entity named in the complaint has violated subsection (a) or (g)(1) of this section, the administrative law judge shall state his findings of fact and issue and cause to be served on such person or entity an order described in paragraph (4), (5), or (6).

(4) Cease and desist order with civil money penalty for hiring, recruiting, and referral violations

With respect to a violation of subsection (a)(1)(A) or (a)(2) of this section, the order under this subsection—

(A) shall require the person or entity to cease and desist from such violations and to pay a civil penalty in an amount of—

(i) not less than $250 and not more than $2,000 for each unauthorized alien with respect to whom a violation of either such subsection occurred.

(ii) not less than $2,000 and not more than $5,000 for each such alien in the case of a person or entity previously subject to one order under this paragraph, or

(iii) not less than $3,000 and not more than $10,000 for each such alien in the case of a person or entity previously subject to more than one order under this paragraph; and

(B) may require the person or entity—

(i) to comply with the requirements of subsection (b) of this section (or subsection (d) of this section if applicable) with respect to individuals hired (or recruited or referred for employment for a fee) during a period of up to three years, and

(ii) to take such other remedial action as is appropriate.

In applying this subsection in the case of a person or entity composed of distinct, physically separate subdivisions each of which provides separately for the hiring, recruiting, or referring for employment, without reference to the practices of, and not under the control of or common control with, another subdivision, each such subdivision shall be considered a separate person or entity.

(5) Order for civil money penalty for paperwork violations

With respect to a violation of subsection (a)(1)(B) of this section, the order under this subsection shall require the person or entity to pay a civil penalty in an amount of not less than $100 and not more than $1,000 for each individual with respect to whom such violation occurred. In determining the amount of the penalty, due consideration shall be given to the size of the business of the employer being charged, the good faith of the employer, the seriousness of the violation, whether or not the individual was an unauthorized alien, and the history of previous violations.

(6) Order for prohibited indemnity bonds

With respect to a violation of subsection (g)(1) of this section, the order under this subsection may provide for the remedy described in subsection (g)(2) of this section.

(7) Administrative appellate review

The decision and order of an administrative law judge shall become the final agency decision and order of the Attorney General unless either (A) within 30 days, an official delegated by regulation to exercise review authority over the decision and order modifies or vacates the decision and order, or (B) within 30 days of the date of such a modification or vacation (or within 60 days of the date of decision and order of an administrative law judge if not so modified or vacated) the decision and order is referred to the Attorney General pursuant to regulations, in which case the decision and order of the Attorney General shall become the final agency decision and order under this subsection. The Attorney General may not delegate the Attorney General's authority under this paragraph to any entity which has review authority over immigration-related matters.

(8) Judicial review

A person or entity adversely affected by a final order respecting an assessment may, within 45 days after the date the final order is issued, file a petition in the Court of Appeals for the appropriate circuit for review of the order.

(9) Enforcement of orders

If a person or entity fails to comply with a final order issued under this subsection against the person or entity, the Attorney General shall file a suit to seek compliance with the order in any appropriate district court of the United States. In any such suit, the validity and appropriateness of the final order shall not be subject to review.

(f) Criminal penalties and injunctions for pattern or practice violations

(1) Criminal penalty

Any person or entity which engages in a pattern or practice of violations of subsection (a)(1)(A) or (a)(2) of this section shall be fined not more than $3,000 for each unauthorized alien with respect to whom such a violation occurs, imprisoned for not more than six months for the entire pattern or practice, or both, notwithstanding the provisions of any other Federal law relating to fine levels.

(2) Enjoining of pattern or practice violations

Whenever the Attorney General has reasonable cause to believe that a person or entity is engaged in a pattern or practice of employment, recruitment, or referral in violation of paragraph (1)(A) or (2) of subsection (a) of this section, the Attorney General may bring a civil action in the appropriate district court of the United States requesting such relief, including a permanent or temporary injunction, restraining order, or other order against the person or entity, as the Attorney General deems necessary.

(g) Prohibition of indemnity bonds

(1) Prohibition

It is unlawful for a person or other entity, in the hiring, recruiting, or referring for employment of any individual, to require the individual to post a bond or security, to pay or agree to pay an amount, or otherwise to provide a financial guarantee or indemnity, against any potential liability arising under this section relating to such hiring, recruiting, or referring of the individual.

(2) Civil penalty

Any person or entity which is determined, after notice and opportunity for an administrative hearing under subsection (e) of this section, to have violated paragraph (1) shall be subject to a civil penalty of $1,000 for each violation and to an administrative order requiring the return of any amounts received in violation of such paragraph to the employee or, if the employee cannot be located, to the general fund of the Treasury.

(h) Miscellaneous provisions

(1) Documentation

In providing documentation or endorsement of authorization of aliens (other than aliens lawfully admitted for permanent residence) authorized to be employed in the United States, the Attorney General shall provide that any limitations with respect to the period or type of employment or employer shall be conspicuously stated on the documentation or endorsement.

(2) Preemption

The provisions of this section preempt any State or local law imposing civil or criminal[1] sanctions (other than through licensing and similar laws) upon those who employ, or recruit or refer for a fee for employment, unauthorized aliens.

(3) Definition of unauthorized alien

As used in this section, the term "unauthorized alien" means, with respect to the employment of an alien at a particular time, that the alien is not at that time either (A) an alien lawfully admitted for permanent residence, or (B) authorized to be so employed by this chapter or by the Attorney General.

(June 27, 1952, c. 477, Title II, ch. 8, § 274A, as added Nov. 6, 1986, Pub.L. 99–603, Title I, § 101(a)(1), 100 Stat. 3360, and amended Oct. 24, 1988, Pub.L. 100–525, § 2(a)(1), 102 Stat. 2609; Nov. 29, 1990, Pub.L. 101–649, Title V, §§ 521(a), 538(a), 104 Stat. 5053, 5056; Dec. 12, 1991, Pub.L. 102–232, Title III, §§ 306(b)(2), 309(b)(11), 105 Stat. 1752, 1759; Oct. 25, 1994, Pub.L. 103–416, Title II, §§ 213, 219(z)(4), 108 Stat. 4314, 4318; Sept. 30, 1996, Pub.L. 104–208, Div. C, Title III, § 379(a), Title IV, §§ 411(a), 412(a) to (d), 416, 110 Stat. 3009–649, 3009–666 to 3009–668, 3009–669; Pub.L. 108–390, § 1(a), Oct. 30, 2004, 118 Stat. 2242.)

[1] So in original. Probably should be followed by "or".

HISTORICAL AND STATUTORY NOTES

References in Text

The Social Security Act, referred to in subsec. (d)(3)(E), is Act Aug. 14, 1935, c. 531, 49 Stat. 620, as amended, which is classified generally to chapter 7 (§ 301 et seq.) of Title 42, The Public Health and Welfare. For complete classification of this Act to the Code, see section 1305 of Title 42 and Tables.

Effective and Applicability Provisions

2004 Acts. Pub.L. 108–390, § 1(b), Oct. 30, 2004, 118 Stat. 2242, provided that:

"The amendments made by subsection (a) [amending subsec. (b)(1) to (3) of this section] shall take effect on the earlier of—

"(1) the date on which final regulations implementing such amendments take effect; or

"(2) 180 days after the date of the enactment of this Act [Oct. 30, 2004]."

1996 Acts. Section 379(b) of Div. C of Pub.L. 104–208 provided that: "The amendments made by subsection (a) [amending this section and section 1324c of this title] shall apply to orders issued on or after the date of the enactment of this Act [Sept. 30, 1996]."

Section 411(b) of Div. C of Pub.L. 104–208 provided that: "The amendment made by subsection (a) [amending this section] shall apply to failures occurring on or after the date of the enactment of this Act [Sept. 30, 1996]."

Section 412(e) of Div. C of Pub.L. 104–208, as amended Pub.L. 105–54, § 3(a), Oct. 6, 1997, 111 Stat. 1175; Pub.L. 108–156, § 3(d), Dec. 3, 2003, 117 Stat. 1945, provided that:

"(1) The amendments made by subsection (a) [amending this section] shall apply with respect to hiring (or recruitment or referral) occurring on or after such date (not later than 18 months after the date of the enactment of this Act [Sept. 30, 1996]) as the Secretary of Homeland Security shall designate.

"(2) The amendment made by subsection (b) [amending this section] shall apply to individuals hired on or after 60 days after the date of the enactment of this Act [Sept. 30, 1996].

"(3) The amendment made by subsection (c) [amending this section] shall take effect on the date of the enactment of this Act [Sept. 30, 1996].

"(4) The amendment made by subsection (d) [amending this section] applies to hiring occurring before, on, or after the date of the enactment of this Act [Sept. 30, 1996], but no penalty shall be imposed under subsection (e) or (f) of section 274A of the Immigration and Nationality Act [subsec. (e) or (f) of this section] for such hiring occurring before such date [Sept. 30, 1996]."

[Section 3(b) of Pub.L. 105–54 provided that: "The amendment made by subsection (a) [amending section 412(e)(1) of Pub.L. 104–208, set out as a note under this section] shall take effect as if included in the enactment of the Illegal Immigration Reform and Immigrant Responsibility Act of 1996 [Pub.L. 104–208, Div. C, Sept. 30, 1996, 110 Stat. 3009–546. For complete classification of this Act to the Code, see Short Title note set out under section 1101 of this title and Tables.]."]

1994 Acts. Section 219(z) of Pub.L. 103–416 provided in part that the amendment by section 219(z)(4) of Pub.L. 103–416 is effective as if included in the amendment by section 306(b)(2) of Pub.L. 102–232, see section 310 of Pub.L. 102–232, set out as a note under section 1101 of this title.

1991 Acts. Amendments by sections 302 through 308 of Pub.L. 102–232, except as otherwise specifically provided, effective as if included in the enactment of Pub.L. 101–649, see section 310(1) of Pub.L. 102–232, set out as a note under section 1101 of this title.

Amendment by section 309(b) of Pub.L. 102–232 to take effect Dec. 12, 1991, see section 310(2) of Pub.L. 103–232, as amended, set out as a note under section 1101 of this title.

1990 Acts. Section 521(b) of Pub.L. 101–649 provided that: "The amendments made by subsection (a) [amending this section] shall apply to recruiting and referring occurring on or after the date of the enactment of this Act [Nov. 29, 1990]."

Section 538(b) of Pub.L. 101–649 provided that: "The amendment made by subsection (a) [amending this section] shall take effect on the date of the enactment of this Act [Nov. 29, 1990]."

1988 Acts. Amendments by section 2(a)(1) of Pub.L. 100–525 effective as if included in the enactment of Pub.L. 99–603, pursuant to section 2(s) of Pub.L. 100–525, set out as a note under section 1101 of this title.

Abolition of Immigration and Naturalization Service and Transfer of Functions

For abolition of Immigration and Naturalization Service, transfer of functions, and treatment of related references, see note set out under 8 U.S.C.A. § 1551.

Severability of Provisions

If any provision of Division C of Pub.L. 104–208 or the application of such provision to any person or circumstances is held to be unconstitutional, the remainder of Division C of Pub.L. 104–208 and the application of the provisions of Division C of Pub.L. 104–208 to any person or circumstance not to be affected thereby, see section 1(e) of Pub.L. 104–208, set out as a note under section 1101 of this title.

Delegation of Functions

The authority conferred upon the President by subsec.(d)(4) of this section, to undertake demonstration projects of different changes in the requirements of the employment verification system, is delegated to the Attorney General, with demonstration projects to be conducted consistent with the restrictions in subsec. (d)(2) of this section, and not to extend for a period longer than 3 years, with the Attorney General authorized to redelegate such authority, see Ex. Ord. No. 12781, Nov. 20, 1991, 56 F.R. 59203, set out as a note under section 301 of Title 3, The President.

The Attorney General shall perform the functions vested in the President by section 402 of Pub.L. 99–603 [set out as a note under this section], except for those vested in the President by par. (3)(A) thereof, which functions shall be performed by the Secretary of Labor, see Ex. Ord. No. 12789, Feb. 10, 1992, 57 F.R. 5225, set out as a note under section 1364 of this title.

Pilot Programs for Employment Eligibility Confirmation

Pub.L. 104–208, Div. C, Title IV, Subtitle A, §§ 401 to 405, Sept. 30, 1996, 110 Stat. 3009–655 to 3009–665, as amended Pub.L. 107–128, § 2, Jan. 16, 2002, 115 Stat. 2407; Pub.L. 108–156, §§ 2, 3, Dec. 3, 2003, 117 Stat. 1944, provided that:

"Sec. 401. Establishment of programs.

"(a) In general.—The Secretary of Homeland Security shall conduct 3 pilot programs of employment eligibility confirmation under this subtitle [this note].

"(b) Implementation deadline; termination.—The Secretary of Homeland Security shall implement the pilot programs in a manner that permits persons and other entities to have elections under section 402 of this division made and in effect no later than 1 year after the date of the enactment of this Act [Sept. 30, 1996]. Unless the Congress otherwise provides, the Secretary of Homeland Security shall terminate a pilot program at the end of the 11–year period beginning on the first day the pilot program is in effect.

"(c) Scope of operation of pilot programs.—The Secretary of Homeland Security shall provide for the operation—

"(1) of the basic pilot program (described in section 403(a) of this division) in, at a minimum, 5 of the 7 States with the highest estimated population of aliens who are not lawfully present in the United States, and the Secretary of Homeland Security shall expand the operation of the program to all 50 States not later than December 1, 2004;

"(2) of the citizen attestation pilot program (described in section 403(b) of this division) in at least 5 States (or, if fewer, all of the States) that meet the condition described in section 403(b)(2)(A) of this division; and

"(3) of the machine-readable-document pilot program (described in section 403(c) of this division) in at least 5 States (or, if fewer, all of the States) that meet the condition described in section 403(c)(2) of this division.

"(d) References in subtitle.—In this subtitle [this note]—

"(1) Pilot program references.—The terms 'program' or 'pilot program' refer to any of the 3 pilot programs provided for under this subtitle [this note].

"(2) Confirmation system.—The term 'confirmation system' means the confirmation system established under section 404 of this division.

"(3) References to section 274A.—Any reference in this subtitle [this note] to section 274A (or a subdivision of such section) is deemed a reference to such section (or subdivision thereof) of the Immigration and Nationality Act [this section].

"(4) I–9 or similar form.—The term 'I–9 or similar form' means the form used for purposes of section 274A(b)(1)(A) [subsec. (b)(1)(A) of this section] or such other form as the Secretary of Homeland Security determines to be appropriate.

"(5) Limited application to recruiters and referrers.—Any reference to recruitment or referral (or a recruiter or referrer) in relation to employment is deemed a reference only to such recruitment or referral (or recruiter or referrer) that is subject to section 274A(a)(1)(B)(ii) [subsec. (a)(1)(B)(ii) of this section].

"(6) United States citizenship.—The term 'United States citizenship' includes United States nationality.

"(7) State.—The term 'State' has the meaning given such term in section 101(a)(36) of the Immigration and Nationality Act [section 110(a)(36) of this title].

"Sec. 402. Voluntary election to participate in a pilot program.

"(a) Voluntary election.—Subject to subsection (c)(3)(B), any person or other entity that conducts any hiring (or recruitment or referral) in a State in which a pilot program is operating may elect to participate in that pilot program. Except as specifically provided in subsection (e), the Secretary of Homeland Security may not require any person or other entity to participate in a pilot program.

"(b) Benefit of rebuttable presumption.—

"(1) In general.—If a person or other entity is participating in a pilot program and obtains confirmation of identity and employment eligibility in compliance with the terms and conditions of the program with respect to the hiring (or recruitment or referral) of an individual for employment in the United States, the person or entity has established a rebuttable presumption that the person or entity has not violated section 274A(a)(1)(A) [subsec. (a)(1)(A) of this section] with respect to such hiring (or such recruitment or referral).

"(2) Construction.—Paragraph (1) shall not be construed as preventing a person or other entity that has an election in effect under subsection (a) from establishing an affirmative defense under section 274A(a)(3) [subsec. (a)(3) of this section] if the person or entity complies with the requirements of section 274A(a)(1)(B) [subsec. (a)(1)(B) of this section] but fails to obtain confirmation under paragraph (1).

"(c) General terms of elections.—

"(1) In general.—An election under subsection (a) shall be in such form and manner, under such terms and conditions, and shall take effect, as the Secretary of Homeland Security shall specify. The Secretary of Homeland Security may not impose any fee as a condition of making an election or participating in a pilot program.

"(2) Scope of election.—

"(A) In general.—Subject to paragraph (3), any electing person or other entity may provide that the election under subsection (a) shall apply (during the period in which the election is in effect)—

"(i) to all its hiring (and all recruitment or referral) in the State (or States) in which the pilot program is operating, or

"(ii) to its hiring (or recruitment or referral) in one or more pilot program States or one or more places of hiring (or recruitment or referral, as the case may be) in the pilot program States.

"(B) Application of programs in non-pilot program States.—In addition, the Secretary of Homeland Security may permit a person or entity electing the citizen attestation pilot program (described in 403(b) of this division) or the machine-readable-document pilot program (described in section 403(c) of this division) to provide that the election applies to its hiring (or recruitment or referral) in one or more States or places of hiring (or recruitment or referral) in which the pilot program is not otherwise operating but only if such States meet the requirements of 403(b)(2)(A) and 403(c)(2) of this division, respectively.

"(3) Termination of elections.—The Secretary of Homeland Security may terminate an election by a person or other entity under this section because the person or entity has substantially failed to comply with its obligations under the pilot program. A person or other entity may terminate an election in such form and manner as the Secretary of Homeland Security shall specify.

"(d) Consultation, education, and publicity.—

"(1) Consultation.—The Secretary of Homeland Security shall closely consult with representatives of employers (and recruiters and referrers) in the development and implementation of the pilot programs, including the education of employers (and recruiters and referrers) about such programs.

"(2) Publicity.—The Secretary of Homeland Security shall widely publicize the election process and pilot programs, including the voluntary nature of the pilot programs and the advantages to employers (and recruiters and referrers) of making an election under this section.

"(3) Assistance through District offices.—The Secretary of Homeland Security shall designate one or more individuals in each District office of the Immigration and Naturalization Service for a Service District in which a pilot program is being implemented—

"(A) to inform persons and other entities that seek information about pilot programs of the voluntary nature of such programs, and

"(B) to assist persons and other entities in electing and participating in any pilot programs in effect in the District, in complying with the requirements of section 274A [this section], and in facilitating confirmation of the identity and employment eligibility of individuals consistent with such section.

"(e) Select entities required to participate in a pilot program.—

"(1) Federal Government.—

"(A) Executive Departments.—

"(i) In general.—Each Department of the Federal Government shall elect to participate in a pilot program and shall comply with the terms and conditions of such an election.

"(ii) Election.—Subject to clause (iii), the Secretary of each such Department—

"(I) shall elect the pilot program (or programs) in which the Department shall participate, and

"(II) may limit the election to hiring occurring in certain States (or geographic areas) covered by the program (or programs) and in specified divisions within the Department, so long as all hiring by such divisions and in such locations is covered.

"(iii) Role of Secretary of Homeland Security.—The Secretary of Homeland Security shall assist and coordinate elections under this subparagraph in such manner as assures that—

"(I) a significant portion of the total hiring within each Department within States covered by a pilot program is covered under such a program, and

"(II) there is significant participation by the Federal Executive branch in each of the pilot programs.

"(B) Legislative branch.—Each Member of Congress, each officer of Congress, and the head of each agency of the legislative branch, that conducts hiring in a State in which a pilot program is operating shall elect to participate in a pilot program, may specify which pilot program or programs (if there is more than one) in which the Member, officer, or agency will participate, and shall comply with the terms and conditions of such an election.

"(2) Application to certain violators.—An order under section 274A(e)(4) [subsec. (e)(4) of this section] or section 274B(g) of the Immigration and Nationality Act [section 1324b(g) of this title] may require the subject of the order to participate in, and comply with the terms of, a pilot program with respect to the subject's hiring (or recruitment or referral) of individuals in a State covered by such a program.

"(3) Consequence of failure to participate.—If a person or other entity is required under this subsection to participate in a pilot program and fails to comply with the requirements of such program with respect to an individual—

"(A) such failure shall be treated as a violation of section 274A(a)(1)(B) [subsec. (a)(1)(B) of this section] with respect to that individual, and

"(B) a rebuttable presumption is created that the person or entity has violated section 274A(a)(1)(A) [subsec. (a)(1)(A) of this section].

Subparagraph (B) shall not apply in any prosecution under section 274A(f)(1) [subsec. (f)(1) of this section].

"(f) Construction.—This subtitle [this note] shall not affect the authority of the Secretary of Homeland Security under any other law (including section 274A(d)(4) [subsec. (d)(4) of this section) to conduct demonstration projects in relation to section 274A [this section].

"Sec. 403. Procedures for participants in pilot programs.

"(a) Basic pilot program.—A person or other entity that elects to participate in the basic pilot program described in this subsection agrees to conform to the following procedures in the case of the hiring (or recruitment or referral) for employment in the United States of each individual covered by the election:

"(1) Provision of additional information.—The person or entity shall obtain from the individual (and the individual shall provide) and shall record on the I–9 or similar form—

"(A) the individual's social security account number, if the individual has been issued such a number, and

"(B) if the individual does not attest to United States citizenship under section 274A(b)(2) [subsec. (b)(2) of this section], such identification or authorization number established by the Immigration and Naturalization Service for the alien as the Secretary of Homeland Security shall specify,

and shall retain the original form and make it available for inspection for the period and in the manner required of I–9 forms under section 274A(b)(3) [subsec. (b)(3) of this section].

"(2) Presentation of documentation.—

"(A) In general.—The person or other entity, and the individual whose identity and employment eligibility are being confirmed, shall, subject to subparagraph (B), fulfill the requirements of section 274A(b) [subsec. (b) of this section] with the following modifications:

"(i) A document referred to in section 274A(b)(1)(B)(ii) (as redesignated by section 412(a) of this division) [subsec. (b)(1)(B)(ii) of this section, as redesignated by section 412(a) of Div. C of Pub.L. 104–208] must be designated by the Secretary of Homeland Security as suitable for the purpose of identification in a pilot program.

"(ii) A document referred to in section 274A(b)(1)(D) [subsec. (b)(1)(D) of this section] must contain a photograph of the individual.

"(iii) The person or other entity has complied with the requirements of section 274A(b)(1) [subsec. (b)(1) of this section] with respect to examination of a document if the document reasonably appears on its face to be genuine and it reasonably appears to pertain to the individual whose identity and work eligibility is being confirmed.

"(B) Limitation of requirement to examine documentation.—If the Secretary of Homeland Security finds that a pilot program would reliably determine with respect to an individual whether—

"(i) the person with the identity claimed by the individual is authorized to work in the United States, and

"(ii) the individual is claiming the identity of another person,

if a person or entity could fulfill the requirement to examine documentation contained in subparagraph (A) of section 274A(b)(1) [subsec. (b)(1)(A) of this section] by examining a document specified in either subparagraph (B) or (D) of such section [subsec. (b)(1)(B) or (D) of this section], the Secretary of Homeland Security may provide that, for purposes of such requirement, only such a document need be examined. In such case, any reference in section 274A(b)(1)(A) [subsec. (b)(1)(A) of this section] to a verification that an individual is not an unauthorized alien shall be deemed to be a verification of the individual's identity.

"(3) Seeking confirmation.—

"(A) In general.—The person or other entity shall make an inquiry, as provided in section 404(a)(1) of this division, using the confirmation system to seek confirmation of the identity and employment eligibility of an individual, by not later than the end of 3 working days (as specified by the Secretary of Homeland Security) after the date of the hiring (or recruitment or referral, as the case may be).

"(B) Extension of time period.—If the person or other entity in good faith attempts to make an inquiry during such 3 working days and the confirmation system has registered that not all inquiries were received during such time, the person or entity can make an inquiry in the first subsequent working day in which the confirmation system registers that it has received all inquiries. If the confirmation system cannot receive inquiries at all times during a day, the person or entity merely has to assert that the entity attempted to make the inquiry on that day for the previous sentence to apply to such an inquiry, and does not have to provide any additional proof concerning such inquiry.

"(4) Confirmation or nonconfirmation.—

"(A) Confirmation upon initial inquiry.—If the person or other entity receives an appropriate confirmation of an individual's identity and work eligibility under the confirmation system within the time period specified under section 404(b) of this division, the person or entity shall record on the I–9 or similar form an appropriate code that is provided under the system and that indicates a final confirmation of such identity and work eligibility of the individual.

"(B) Nonconfirmation upon initial inquiry and secondary verification.—

"(i) Nonconfirmation.—If the person or other entity receives a tentative nonconfirmation of an individual's identity or work eligibility under the confirmation system within the time period specified under 404(b) of this division, the person or entity shall so inform the individual for whom the confirmation is sought.

"(ii) No contest.—If the individual does not contest the nonconfirmation within the time period specified in section 404(c) of this division, the nonconfirmation shall be considered final. The person or entity shall then record on the I–9 or similar form an appropriate code which has been provided under the system to indicate a tentative nonconfirmation.

"(iii) Contest.—If the individual does contest the nonconfirmation, the individual shall utilize the process for secondary verification provided under section 404(c) of this division. The nonconfirmation will remain tentative until a final confirmation or nonconfirmation is provided by the confirmation system within the time period specified in such section. In no case shall an employer terminate employment of an individual because of a failure of the individual to have identity and work eligibility confirmed under this section until a nonconfirmation becomes final. Nothing in this clause shall apply to a termination of employment for any reason other than because of such a failure.

"(iv) Recording of conclusion on form.—If a final confirmation or nonconfirmation is provided by the confirmation system under section 404(c) of this division regarding an individual, the person or entity shall record on the I–9 or similar form an appropriate code that is provided under the system and that indicates a confirmation or nonconfirmation of identity and work eligibility of the individual.

"(C) Consequences of nonconfirmation.—

"(i) Termination or notification of continued employment.—If the person or other entity has received a final nonconfirmation regarding an individual under subparagraph (B), the person or entity may terminate employment (or recruitment or referral) of the individual. If the person or entity does not terminate employment (or recruitment or referral) of the individual, the person or entity shall notify the Secretary of Homeland Security of such fact through the confirmation system or in such other manner as the Attorney General may specify.

"(ii) Failure to notify.—If the person or entity fails to provide notice with respect to an individual as required under clause (i), the failure is deemed to constitute a violation of section 274A(a)(1)(B) [subsec. (a)(1)(B) of this section] with respect to that individual and the applicable civil monetary penalty under section 274A(e)(5) [subsec. (e)(5) of this section] shall be (notwithstanding the amounts specified in such section) no less than $500 and no more than $1,000 for each individual with respect to whom such violation occurred.

"(iii) Continued employment after final nonconfirmation.—If the person or other entity continues to employ (or to recruit or refer) an individual after receiving final nonconfirmation, a rebuttable presumption is created that the person or entity has violated section 274A(a)(1)(A) [subsec. (a)(1)(A) of this section]. The previous sentence shall not apply in any prosecution under section 274A(f)(1) [subsec. (f)(1) of this section].

"(b) Citizen attestation pilot program.—

"(1) In general.—Except as provided in paragraphs (3) through (5), the procedures applicable under the citizen attestation pilot program under this subsection shall be the same procedures as those under the basic pilot program under subsection (a).

"(2) Restrictions.—

"(A) State document requirement to participate in pilot program.—The Secretary of Homeland Security may not provide for the operation of the citizen attestation pilot program in a State unless each driver's license or similar identification document described in section 274A(b)(1)(D)(i) [subsec. (b)(1)(D)(i) of this section] issued by the State—

"(i) contains a photograph of the individual involved, and

"(ii) has been determined by the Secretary of Homeland Security to have security features, and to have been issued through application and issuance procedures, which make such document sufficiently resistant to counterfeiting, tampering, and fraudulent use that it is a reliable means of identification for purposes of this section.

"(B) Authorization to limit employer participation.—The Attorney General may restrict the number of persons or other entities that may elect to participate in the citizen attestation pilot program under this subsection as the Secretary of Homeland Security determines to be necessary to produce a representative sample of employers and to reduce the potential impact of fraud.

"(3) No confirmation required for certain individuals attesting to U.S. citizenship.—In the case of a person or other entity hiring (or recruiting or referring) an individual under the citizen attestation pilot program, if the individual attests to United States citizenship (under penalty of perjury on an I–9 or similar form which form states on its face the criminal and other penalties provided under law for a false representation of United States citizenship)—

"(A) the person or entity may fulfill the requirement to examine documentation contained in subparagraph (A) of section 274A(b)(1) [subsec. (b)(1)(A) of this section] by examining a document specified in either subparagraph (B)(i) or (D) of such section [subsec. (b)(1)(B)(i) or (D) of this section]; and

"(B) the person or other entity is not required to comply with respect to such individual with the procedures described in paragraphs (3) and (4) of subsection (a), but only if the person or entity retains the form and makes it available for inspection in the same manner as in the case of an I–9 form under section 274A(b)(3) [subsec. (b)(3) of this section].

"(4) Waiver of document presentation requirement in certain cases.—

"(A) In general.—In the case of a person or entity that elects, in a manner specified by the Secretary of Homeland Security consistent with subparagraph (B), to participate in the pilot program under this paragraph, if an individual being hired (or recruited or referred) attests (in the manner described in paragraph (3)) to United States citizenship and the person or entity retains the form on which the attestation is made and makes it available for inspection in the same manner as in the case of an I–9 form under section 274A(b)(3) [subsec. (b)(3) of this section], the person or entity is not required to comply with the procedures described in section 274A(b) [subsec. (b) of this section].

"(B) Restriction.—The Secretary of Homeland Security shall restrict the election under this paragraph to no more than 1,000 employers and, to the extent practicable, shall select among employers seeking to make such election in a manner that provides for such an election by a representative sample of employers.

"(5) Nonreviewable determinations.—The determinations of the Secretary of Homeland Security under paragraphs (2) and (4) are within the discretion of the Secretary of Homeland Security and are not subject to judicial or administrative review.

"(c) Machine-readable-document pilot program.—

"(1) In general.—Except as provided in paragraph (3), the procedures applicable under the machine-readable-document pilot program under this subsection shall be the same procedures as those under the basic pilot program under subsection (a).

"(2) State document requirement to participate in pilot program.—The Secretary of Homeland Security may not provide for the operation of the machine-readable-document pilot program in a State unless driver's licenses and similar identification documents described in section 274A(b)(1)(D)(i) [subsec. (b)(1)(D)(i) of this section] issued by the State include a machine-readable social security account number.

"(3) Use of machine-readable documents.—If the individual whose identity and employment eligibility must be confirmed presents to the person or entity hiring (or recruiting or referring) the individual a license or other document described in paragraph (2) that includes a machine-readable social security account number, the person or entity must make an inquiry through the confirmation system by using a machine-readable feature of such document. If the individual does not attest to United States citizenship under section 274A(b)(2) [subsec. (b)(2) of this section], the individual's identification or authorization number described in subsection (a)(1)(B) shall be provided as part of the inquiry.

"(d) Protection from liability for actions taken on the basis of information provided by the confirmation system.—No person or entity participating in a pilot program shall be civilly or criminally liable under any law for any action taken in good faith reliance on information provided through the confirmation system.

"Sec. 404. Employment eligibility confirmation system.

"(a) In general.—The Secretary of Homeland Security shall establish a pilot program confirmation system through which the Attorney General (or a designee of the Secretary of Homeland Security, which may be a nongovernmental entity)—

"(1) responds to inquiries made by electing persons and other entities (including those made by the transmittal of data from machine-readable documents under the machine-readable pilot program) at any time through a toll-free telephone line or other toll-free electronic media concerning an individual's identity and whether the individual is authorized to be employed, and

"(2) maintains records of the inquiries that were made, of confirmations provided (or not provided), and of the codes provided to inquirers as evidence of their compliance with their obligations under the pilot programs.

To the extent practicable, the Secretary of Homeland Security shall seek to establish such a system using one or more nongovernmental entities.

"(b) Initial response.—The confirmation system shall provide confirmation or a tentative nonconfirmation of an individual's identity and employment eligibility within 3 working days of the initial inquiry. If providing confirmation or tentative nonconfirmation, the confirmation system shall provide an appropriate code indicating such confirmation or such nonconfirmation.

"(c) Secondary verification process in case of tentative nonconfirmation.—In cases of tentative nonconfirmation, the Attorney General shall specify, in consultation with the Commissioner of Social Security and the Commissioner of the Immigration and Naturalization Service, an available secondary verification process to confirm the validity of information provided and to provide a final confirmation or nonconfirmation within 10 working days after the date of the tentative nonconfirmation. When final confirmation or nonconfirmation is provided, the confirmation system shall provide an appropriate code indicating such confirmation or nonconfirmation.

"(d) Design and operation of system.—The confirmation system shall be designed and operated—

"(1) to maximize its reliability and ease of use by persons and other entities making elections under section 402(a) of this division consistent with insulating and protecting the privacy and security of the underlying information;

"(2) to respond to all inquiries made by such persons and entities on whether individuals are authorized to be employed and to register all times when such inquiries are not received;

"(3) with appropriate administrative, technical, and physical safeguards to prevent unauthorized disclosure of personal information; and

"(4) to have reasonable safeguards against the system's resulting in unlawful discriminatory practices based on national origin or citizenship status, including—

"(A) the selective or unauthorized use of the system to verify eligibility;

"(B) the use of the system prior to an offer of employment; or

"(C) the exclusion of certain individuals from consideration for employment as a result of a perceived likelihood that additional verification will be required, beyond what is required for most job applicants.

"(e) Responsibilities of the Commissioner of Social Security.—As part of the confirmation system, the Commissioner of Social Security, in consultation with the entity responsible for administration of the system, shall establish a reliable, secure method, which, within the time periods specified under subsections (b) and (c), compares the name and social security account number provided in an inquiry against such information maintained by the Commissioner in order to confirm (or not confirm) the validity of the information provided regarding an individual whose identity and employment eligibility must be confirmed, the correspondence of the name and number, and whether the individual has presented a social security account number that is not valid for employment. The Commissioner shall not disclose or release social security information (other than such confirmation or nonconfirmation).

"(f) Responsibilities of the Commissioner of the Immigration and Naturalization Service.—As part of the confirmation system, the Commissioner of the Immigration and Naturalization Service, in consultation with the entity responsible for administration of the system, shall establish a reliable, secure method, which, within the time periods specified under subsections (b) and (c), compares the name and alien identification or authorization number described in section 403(a)(1)(B) of this division which are provided in an inquiry against such information maintained by the Commissioner in order to confirm (or not confirm) the validity of the information provided, the correspondence of the name and number, and whether the alien is authorized to be employed in the United States.

"(g) Updating information.—The Commissioners of Social Security and the Immigration and Naturalization Service shall update their information in a manner that promotes the maximum accuracy and shall provide a process for the prompt correction of erroneous information, including instances in which it is brought to their attention in the secondary verification process described in subsection (c).

"(h) Limitation on use of the confirmation system and any related systems.—

"(1) In general.—Notwithstanding any other provision of law, nothing in this subtitle [this note] shall be construed to permit or allow any department, bureau, or other agency of the United States Government to utilize any information, data base, or other records assembled under this subtitle [this note] for any other purpose other than as provided for under a pilot program.

"(2) No national identification card.—Nothing in this subtitle [this note] shall be construed to authorize, directly or indirectly, the issuance or use of national identification cards or the establishment of a national identification card.

"Sec. 405. Reports.

"(a) In general.—The Secretary of Homeland Security shall submit to the Committees on the Judiciary of the House of Representatives and of the Senate reports on the pilot programs within 3 months after the end of the third and fourth years in which the programs are in effect. Such reports shall—

"(1) assess the degree of fraudulent attesting of United States citizenship,

"(2) include recommendations on whether or not the pilot programs should be continued or modified, and

"(3) assess the benefits of the pilot programs to employers and the degree to which they assist in the enforcement of section 274A [this section]."

"(b) Report on expansion.—Not later than June 1, 2004, the Secretary of Homeland Security shall submit to the Committees on the Judiciary of the House of Representatives and the Senate a report—

"(1) evaluating whether the problems identified by the report submitted under subsection (a) have been substantially resolved; and

"(2) describing what actions the Secretary of Homeland Security shall take before undertaking the expansion of the basic pilot program to all 50 States in accordance with section 401(c)(1) [of this note], in order to resolve any outstanding problems raised in the report filed under subsection (a)."

[Pub.L. 107–128, § 3, Jan. 16, 2002, 115 Stat. 2407, provided that: "The amendment made by this Act [amending provisions set out as a note under this section and enacting provisions set out as a note under section 1101 of this title] shall take effect on the date of the enactment of this Act [Jan. 16, 2002]."]

Report on Additional Authority or Resources Needed for Enforcement of Employer Sanctions Provisions

Section 413(a) of Div. C of Pub.L. 104–208, as amended Pub.L. 108–156, § 3(d), Dec. 3, 2003, 117 Stat. 1945, provided that: "Not later than 1 year after the date of the enactment of this Act [Sept. 30, 1996], the Secretary of Homeland Security shall submit to the Committees on the Judiciary of the House of Representatives and of the Senate a report on any additional authority or resources needed—

"(1) by the Immigration and Naturalization Service in order to enforce section 274A of the Immigration and Nationality Act [this section], or

"(2) by Federal agencies in order to carry out the Executive Order of February 13, 1996 (entitled 'Economy and Efficiency in Government Procurement Through Compliance with Certain Immigration and Naturalization Act Provisions') [Ex. Ord. No. 12989, set out under this section] and to expand the restrictions in such order to cover agricultural subsidies, grants, job training programs, and other Federally subsidized assistance programs."

Pilot Projects for Secure Documents

Pub.L. 101–238, § 5, Dec. 18, 1989, 103 Stat. 2104, provided that:

"(a) Consultation.—Before June 1, 1991, the Attorney General shall consult with State governments on any proper State initiative to improve the security of State or local documents which would satisfy the requirements of section 274A(b)(1) of the Immigration and Nationality Act (8 U.S.C. 1324a) [subsec. (b)(1) of this section]. The result of such consultations shall be reported, before September 1, 1991, to the Committees on the Judiciary of the Senate and House of Representatives of the United States.

"(b) Assistance for State Initiatives.—After such consultation described in subsection (a), the Attorney General shall make grants to, and enter into contracts with (to such extent or in such amounts as are provided in an appropriation Act), the State of California and at least 2 other States with large immigrant populations to promote any State initiatives to improve the security of State or local documents which would satisfy the requirements of section 274A(b)(1) of the Immigration and Nationality Act [subsec. (b)(1) of this section].

"(c) Authorization of Appropriations.—There are authorized to be appropriated to the Attorney General $10,000,000 for fiscal year 1992 to carry out subsection (b).

"(d) Report Required.—The Attorney General shall report to the Committees on the Judiciary of the Senate and House of Representatives not later than August 1, 1993, on the security of State or local documents which would satisfy the requirements of section 274A(b)(1) of the Immigration and Nationality Act (8 U.S.C. 1324a) [subsec. (b)(1) of this section], and any improvements in such documents that have occurred as a result of this section."

Date of Enactment of This Section For Aliens Employed Under Section 8704 of Title 46, Shipping

Date of enactment of this section with respect to aliens deemed employed under section 8704 of Title 46, Shipping, as the date 180 days after Jan. 11, 1988, see section 5(f)(3) of Pub.L. 100–239, set out as a note under section 8704 of Title 46.

Promulgation of Regulations

Section 101(a)(2) of Pub.L. 99–603 provided that: "The Attorney General shall, not later than the first day of the seventh month beginning after the date of the enactment of this Act [Nov. 6, 1986], first issue, on an interim or other basis, such regulations as may be necessary in order to implement this section [enacting this section, amending sections 1802, 1813 and 1851 of Title 29, Labor, repealing section 1816 of Title 29 and enacting provisions set out as notes under this section and section 1802 of Title 29 and section 405 of Title 42, The Public Health and Welfare]."

Persons Hired, Recruited or Referred Before Nov. 6, 1986

Section 101(a)(3)(A) of Pub.L. 99–603 provided that: "Section 274A(a)(1) of the Immigration and Nationality Act [subsec. (a)(1) of this section] shall not apply to the hiring, or recruiting or referring of an individual for employment which has occurred before the date of the enactment of this Act [Nov. 6, 1986]."

Continuing Employment of Persons Hired Before Nov. 6, 1986

Section 101(a)(3)(B) of Pub.L. 99–603 provided that: "Section 274A(a)(2) of the Immigration and Nationality Act [subsec. (a)(2) of this section] shall not apply to continuing employment of an alien who was hired before the date of the enactment of this Act [Nov. 6, 1986]."

Study on Use of Telephone Verification System for Determining Employment Eligibility of Aliens

Section 101(d) of Pub.L. 99–603 provided that:

"(1) The Attorney General, in consultation with the Secretary of Labor and the Secretary of Health and Human Services, shall conduct a study for use by the Department of Justice in determining employment eligibility of aliens in the United States. Such study shall concentrate on those data bases that are currently available to the Federal Government which through the use of a telephone and computation capability could be used to verify instantly the employment eligibility status of job applicants who are aliens.

"(2) Such study shall be conducted in conjunction with any existing Federal program which is designed for the purpose of providing information on the resident or employment status of aliens for employers. The study shall include an analysis of costs and benefits which shows the differences in costs and efficiency of having the Federal Government or a contractor perform this service. Such comparisons should include reference to such technical capabilities as processing techniques and time, verification techniques and time, backup safeguards, and audit trail performance.

"(3) Such study shall also concentrate on methods of phone verification which demonstrate the best safety and service standards, the least burden for the employer, the best capability for effective enforcement, and procedures which are within the boundaries of the Privacy Act of 1974 [5 U.S.C.A. § 552a].

"(4) Such study shall be conducted within twelve months of the date of enactment of this Act [Nov. 6, 1986].

"(5) The Attorney General shall prepare and transmit to the Congress a report—

"(A) not later than six months after the date of enactment of this Act [Nov. 6, 1986], describing the status of such study; and

"(B) not later than twelve months after such date, setting forth the findings of such study."

Feasibility Study of Social Security Number Validation System

Section 101(e) of Pub.L. 99–603 provided that: "The Secretary of Health and Human Services, acting through the Social Security Administration and in cooperation with the Attorney General and the Secretary of Labor, shall conduct a study of the feasibility and costs of establishing a social security number validation system to assist in carrying out the purposes of section 274A of the Immigration and Nationality Act [this section], and of the privacy concerns that would be raised by the establishment of such a system. The Secretary shall submit to the Committees on Ways and Means and Judiciary of the House of Representatives and to the Committees on Finance and Judiciary of the Senate, within 2 years after the date of the enactment of this Act [Nov. 6, 1986], a full and complete report on the results of the study together with such recommendations as may be appropriate."

Reports on Unauthorized Alien Employment

Section 402 of Pub.L. 99–603 provided that: "The President shall transmit to Congress annual reports on the implementation of section 274A of the Immigration and Nationality Act [this section] (relating to unlawful employment of aliens) during the first three years after its implementation. Each report shall include—

"(1) an analysis of the adequacy of the employment verification system provided under subsection (b) of that section;

"(2) a description of the status of the development and implementation of changes in that system under subsection (d) of that section, including the results of any demonstration projects conducted under paragraph (4) of such subsection; and

"(3) an analysis of the impact of the enforcement of that section on—

"(A) the employment, wages, and working conditions of United States workers and on the economy of the United States,

"(B) the number of aliens entering the United States illegally or who fail to maintain legal status after entry, and

"(C) the violation of terms and conditions of nonimmigrant visas by foreign visitors."

[Functions of President under section 402 of Pub.L. 99–603 delegated to Secretary of Homeland Security, except functions in section 402(3)(A) which were delegated to Secretary of Labor, by sections 1(b) and 2(a) of Ex. Ord. No. 12789, Feb. 10, 1992, 57 F.R. 5225, set out as a note under 8 U.S.C.A. § 1364.]

EXECUTIVE ORDERS

EXECUTIVE ORDER NO. 12989

Feb. 13, 1996, 61 F.R. 6091, as amended Ex. Ord. No. 13286, Sec. 19, Feb. 28, 2003, 68 F.R. 10623

ECONOMY AND EFFICIENCY IN GOVERNMENT PROCUREMENT THROUGH COMPLIANCE WITH CERTAIN IMMIGRATION AND NATIONALITY ACT PROVISIONS

This order is designed to promote economy and efficiency in Government procurement. Stability and dependability are important elements of economy and efficiency. A contractor whose work force is less stable will be less likely to produce goods and services economically and efficiently than a contractor whose work force is more stable. It remains the policy of this Administration to enforce the immigration laws to the fullest extent, including the detection and deportation of illegal aliens. In these circumstances, contractors cannot rely on the continuing availability and service of illegal aliens, and contractors that choose to employ unauthorized aliens inevitably will have a less stable and less dependable work force than contractors that do not employ such persons. Because of this Administration's vigorous enforcement policy, contractors that employ unauthorized alien workers are necessarily less stable and dependable procurement sources than contractors that do not hire such persons. I find, therefore, that adherence to the general policy of not contracting with providers that knowingly employ unauthorized alien workers will promote economy and efficiency in Federal procurement.

NOW, THEREFORE, to ensure the economical and efficient administration and completion of Federal Government contracts, and by the authority vested in me as President by the Constitution and the laws of the United States of America, including 40 U.S.C. 486(a) [see now 40 U.S.C.A. § 121(a)] and 3 U.S.C. 301 [section 301 of Title 3, The President], it is hereby ordered as follows:

Section 1. **(a)** It is the policy of the executive branch in procuring goods and services that, to ensure the economical and efficient administration and completion of Federal Government contracts, contracting agencies should not contract with employers that have not complied with section 274A(a)(1)(A) and 274A(a)(2) of the Immigration and Nationality Act (8 U.S.C. 1324a(a)(1)(A), 1324a(a)(2)) [subsec. (a)(1), (2) of this section] (the "INA employment provisions") prohibiting the unlawful employment of aliens. All discretion under this Executive order shall be exercised consistent with this policy.

(b) It remains the policy of this Administration to fully and aggressively enforce the antidiscrimination provisions of the Immigration and Nationality Act to the fullest extent. Nothing in this order relieves employers from their obligation to avoid unfair immigration-related employment practices as required by the antidiscrimination provisions of section 1324(b) of the INA (8 U.S.C. 1324b) [probably means section 274B of the INA, which is section 1324b of this title] and all other antidiscrimination requirements of applicable law, including the requirements of 8 U.S.C. 1324b(a)(6) [section 1324b(a)(6) of this title] concerning the treatment of certain documentary practices as unfair immigration-related employment practices.

Sec. 2. Contractor, as used in this Executive order, shall have the same meaning as defined in subpart 9.4 of the Federal Acquisition Regulation.

Sec. 3. Using the procedures established pursuant to 8 U.S.C. 1324a(e) [subsec. (e) of this section]: (a) the Secretary of Homeland Security may investigate to determine whether a contractor or an organizational unit thereof is not in compliance with the INA employment provisions;

(b) the Secretary of Homeland Security shall receive and may investigate complaints by employees of any entity covered under section 3(a) of this order where such complaints allege noncompliance with the INA employment provisions; and

(c) the Attorney General shall hold such hearings as are required under 8 U.S.C. 1324a(e) [subsec. (e) of this section] to determine whether an entity covered under section 3(a) is not in compliance with the INA employment provisions.

Sec. 4. **(a)** Whenever the Secretary of Homeland Security or the Attorney General determines that a contractor or an organizational unit thereof is not in compliance with the INA employment provisions, the Secretary of Homeland Security or the Attorney General shall transmit that determination to the appropriate contracting agency and such other Federal agencies as the Secretary of Homeland Security or the Attorney General may determine. Upon receipt of such determination from the Secretary of Homeland Security or the Attorney General, the head of the appropriate contracting agency shall consider the contractor or an organizational unit thereof for debarment as well as for such other action as may be appropriate in accordance with the procedures and standards prescribed by the Federal Acquisition Regulation.

(b) The head of the contracting agency may debar the contractor or an organizational unit thereof based on the determination of the Secretary of Homeland Security or the Attorney General that it is not in compliance with the INA employment provisions. Such determination shall not be reviewable in the debarment proceedings.

(c) The scope of the debarment generally should be limited to those organizational units of a Federal contractor that the Secretary of Homeland Security or the Attorney General finds are not in compliance with the INA employment provisions.

(d) The period of the debarment shall be for 1 year and may be extended for additional periods of 1 year if, using the procedures established pursuant to 8 U.S.C. 1324a(e) [subsec. (e) of this section], the Secretary of Homeland Security or the Attorney General determines that the organizational unit of the Federal contractor continues to be in violation of the INA employment provisions.

(e) The Administrator of General Services shall list a debarred contractor or an organizational unit thereof on the List of Parties Excluded from Federal Procurement and Nonprocurement Programs and the contractor or an organizational unit thereof shall be ineligible to participate in any procurement or nonprocurement activities.

Sec. 5. (a) The Secretary of Homeland Security and Attorney General shall be responsible for the administration and enforcement of this order, except for the debarment procedures. The Secretary of Homeland Security and Attorney General may adopt such additional rules and regulations and issue such orders as may be deemed necessary and appropriate to carry out their respective responsibilities under this order. If the Secretary of Homeland Security or the Attorney General proposes to issue rules, regulations, or orders that affect the contracting departments and agencies, the Secretary of Homeland Security or the Attorney General shall consult with the Secretary of Defense, the Secretary of Labor, the Administrator of General Services, the Administrator of the National Aeronautics and Space Administration, the Administrator for Federal Procurement Policy, and such other agencies as may be appropriate.

(b) The Secretary of Defense, the Administrator of General Services, and the Administrator of the National Aeronautics and Space Administration shall amend the Federal Acquisition Regulation to the extent necessary and appropriate to implement the debarment responsibility and other related responsibilities assigned to heads of contracting departments and agencies under this order.

Sec. 6. Each contracting department and agency shall cooperate with and provide such information and assistance to the Secretary of Homeland Security and the Attorney General as may be required in the performance of their respective functions under this order.

Sec. 7. The Secretary of Homeland Security, the Attorney General, the Secretary of Defense, the Administrator of General Services, the Administrator of the National Aeronautics and Space Administration, and the heads of contracting departments and agencies may delegate any of their functions or duties under this order to any officer or employee of their respective agencies.

Sec. 8. This order shall be implemented in a manner intended to least burden the procurement process. This order neither authorizes nor requires any additional certification provision, clause, or requirement to be included in any contract or contract solicitation.

Sec. 9. This order is not intended, and should not be construed, to create any right or benefit, substantive or procedural, enforceable at law by a party against the United States, its agencies, its officers, or its employees. This order is not intended, however, to preclude judicial review of final agency decisions in accordance with the Administrative Procedure Act, 5 U.S.C. 701 *et seq.* [section 701 et seq. of Title 5, Government Organization and Employees].

William J. Clinton

§ 1324b. Unfair immigration-related employment practices

(a) Prohibition of discrimination based on national origin or citizenship status

(1) General rule

It is an unfair immigration-related employment practice for a person or other entity to discriminate against any individual (other than an unauthorized alien, as defined in section 1324a(h)(3) of this title) with respect to the hiring, or recruitment or referral for a fee, of the individual for employment or the discharging of the individual from employment—

(A) because of such individual's national origin, or

(B) in the case of a protected individual (as defined in paragraph (3)), because of such individual's citizenship status.

(2) Exceptions

Paragraph (1) shall not apply to—

(A) a person or other entity that employs three or fewer employees,

(B) a person's or entity's discrimination because of an individual's national origin if the discrimination with respect to that person or entity and that individual is covered under section 703 of the Civil Rights Act of 1964 [42 U.S.C.A. § 2000e–2], or

(C) discrimination because of citizenship status which is otherwise required in order to comply with law, regulation, or executive order, or required by Federal, State, or local government contract, or which the Attorney General determines to be essential for an employer to do business with an agency or department of the Federal, State, or local government.

(3) "Protected individual" defined

As used in paragraph (1), the term "protected individual" means an individual who—

(A) is a citizen or national of the United States, or

(B) is an alien who is lawfully admitted for permanent residence, is granted the status of an alien lawfully admitted for temporary residence under section 1160(a) or 1255a(a)(1) of this title, is admitted as a refugee under section 1157 of this title, or is granted asylum under section 1158 of this title; but does not include (i) an alien who fails to apply for naturalization within six months of the date the alien first becomes eligible (by virtue of period of lawful permanent residence) to apply for naturalization or, if later, within six months after November 6, 1986, and (ii) an alien who has applied on a timely basis, but has not been naturalized as a citizen within 2 years after the date of the application, unless the alien can establish that the alien is actively pursuing naturalization, except that time consumed in the Service's processing the application shall not be counted toward the 2–year period.

(4) Additional exception providing right to prefer equally qualified citizens

Notwithstanding any other provision of this section, it is not an unfair immigration-related employment practice for a person or other entity to prefer to hire, recruit, or refer an individual who is a citizen or national of the United States over another individual who is an alien if the two individuals are equally qualified.

(5) Prohibition of intimidation or retaliation

It is also an unfair immigration-related employment practice for a person or other entity to intimidate, threaten, coerce, or retaliate against any individual for the purpose of interfering with any right or privilege secured under this section or because the individual intends to file or has filed a charge or a complaint, testified, assisted, or participated in any manner in an investigation, proceeding, or hearing under this section. An individual so intimidated, threatened, coerced, or retaliated against shall be considered, for purposes of subsections (d) and (g) of this section, to have been discriminated against.

(6) Treatment of certain documentary practices as employment practices

A person's or other entity's request, for purposes of satisfying the requirements of section 1324a(b) of this title, for more or different documents than are required under such section or refusing to honor documents tendered that on their face reasonably appear to be genuine shall be treated as an unfair immigration-related employment practice if made for the purpose or with the intent of discriminating against an individual in violation of paragraph (1).

(b) Charges of violations

(1) In general

Except as provided in paragraph (2), any person alleging that the person is adversely affected directly by an unfair immigration-related employment practice (or a person on that person's behalf) or an officer of the Service alleging that an unfair immigration-related employment practice has occurred or is occurring may file a charge respecting such practice or violation with the Special Counsel (appointed under subsection (c) of this section). Charges shall be in writing under oath or affirmation and shall contain such information as the Attorney General requires. The Special Counsel by certified mail shall serve a notice of the charge (including the date, place, and circumstances of the alleged unfair immigration-related employment practice) on the person or entity involved within 10 days.

(2) No overlap with EEOC complaints

No charge may be filed respecting an unfair immigration-related employment practice described in subsection (a)(1)(A) of this section if a charge with respect to that practice based on the same set of facts has been filed with the Equal Employment Opportunity Commission under title VII of the Civil Rights Act of 1964 [42 U.S.C.A. § 2000e et seq.], unless the charge is dismissed as being outside the scope of such title. No charge respecting an employment practice may be filed with the Equal Employment Opportunity Commission under such title if a charge with respect to such practice based on the same set of facts has been filed under this subsection, unless the charge is dismissed under this section as being outside the scope of this section.

(c) Special Counsel

(1) Appointment

The President shall appoint, by and with the advice and consent of the Senate, a Special Counsel for Immigration-Related Unfair Employment Practices (hereinafter in this section referred to as the "Special Counsel") within the Department of Justice to serve for a term of four years. In the case of a vacancy in the office of the Special Counsel the President may designate the officer or employee who shall act as Special Counsel during such vacancy.

(2) Duties

The Special Counsel shall be responsible for investigation of charges and issuance of complaints under this section and in respect of the prosecution of all such complaints before administrative law judges and the exercise of certain functions under subsection (j)(1) of this section.

(3) Compensation

The Special Counsel is entitled to receive compensation at a rate not to exceed the rate now or hereafter provided for grade GS–17 of the General Schedule, under section 5332 of Title 5.

(4) Regional offices

The Special Counsel, in accordance with regulations of the Attorney General, shall establish such regional offices as may be necessary to carry out his duties.

(d) Investigation of charges

(1) By Special Counsel

The Special Counsel shall investigate each charge received and, within 120 days of the date of the receipt of the charge, determine whether or not there is reasonable cause to believe that the charge is true and whether or not to bring a complaint with respect to the charge before an administrative law judge. The Special Counsel may, on his own initiative, conduct investigations respecting unfair immigration-related employment practices and, based on such an investigation and subject to paragraph (3), file a complaint before such a judge.

(2) Private actions

If the Special Counsel, after receiving such a charge respecting an unfair immigration-related employment practice which alleges knowing and intentional discriminatory activity or a pattern or practice of discriminatory activity, has not filed a complaint before an administrative law judge with respect to such charge within such 120-day period, the Special Counsel shall notify the person making the charge of the determination not to file such a complaint during such period and the person making the charge may (subject to paragraph (3)) file a complaint directly before such a judge within 90 days after the date of receipt of the notice. The Special Counsel's failure to file such a complaint within such 120–day period shall not affect the right of the Special Counsel to investigate the charge or to bring a complaint before an administrative law judge during such 90–day period.

(3) Time limitations on complaints

No complaint may be filed respecting any unfair immigration-related employment practice occurring more than 180 days prior to the date of the filing of the charge with the Special Counsel. This subparagraph shall not prevent the subsequent amending of a charge or complaint under subsection (e)(1) of this section.

(e) Hearings

(1) Notice

Whenever a complaint is made that a person or entity has engaged in or is engaging in any such unfair immigration-related employment practice, an administrative law judge shall have power to issue and cause to be served upon such person or entity a copy of the complaint and a notice of hearing before the judge at a place therein fixed, not less than five days after the serving of the complaint. Any such complaint may be amended by the judge conducting the hearing, upon the motion of the party filing the complaint, in the judge's discretion at any time prior to the issuance of an order based thereon. The person or entity so complained of shall have the right to file an answer to the original or amended complaint and to appear in person or otherwise and give testimony at the place and time fixed in the complaint.

(2) Judges hearing cases

Hearings on complaints under this subsection shall be considered before administrative law judges who are specially designated by the Attorney General as having special training respecting employment discrimination and, to the extent practicable, before such judges who only consider cases under this section.

(3) Complainant as party

Any person filing a charge with the Special Counsel respecting an unfair immigration-related employment practice shall be considered a party to any complaint before an administrative law judge respecting such practice and any subsequent appeal respecting that complaint. In the discretion of the judge conducting the hearing, any other person may be allowed to intervene in the proceeding and to present testimony.

(f) Testimony and authority of hearing officers

(1) Testimony

The testimony taken by the administrative law judge shall be reduced to writing. Thereafter, the judge, in his discretion, upon notice may provide for the taking of further testimony or hear argument.

(2) Authority of administrative law judges

In conducting investigations and hearings under this subsection [1] and in accordance with regulations of the Attorney General, the Special Counsel and administrative law judges shall have reasonable access to examine evidence of any person or entity being investigated. The administrative law judges by subpoena may compel the attendance of witnesses and the production of evidence at any designated place or hearing. In case of contumacy or refusal to obey a subpoena lawfully issued under this paragraph and upon application of the administrative law judge, an appropriate district court of the United States may issue an order requiring compliance with such subpoena and any failure to obey such order may be punished by such court as a contempt thereof.

(g) Determinations

(1) Order

The administrative law judge shall issue and cause to be served on the parties to the proceeding an order, which shall be final unless appealed as provided under subsection (i) of this section.

(2) Orders finding violations

(A) In general

If, upon the preponderance of the evidence, an administrative law judge determines that any person or entity named in the complaint has engaged in or is engaging in any such unfair immigration-related employment practice, then the judge shall state his findings of fact and shall issue and cause to be served on such person or entity an order which requires such person or entity to cease and desist from such unfair immigration-related employment practice.

(B) Contents of order

Such an order also may require the person or entity—

(i) to comply with the requirements of section 1324a(b) of this title with respect to individuals hired (or recruited or referred for employment for a fee) during a period of up to three years;

(ii) to retain for the period referred to in clause (i) and only for purposes consistent with section 1324a(b)(5) of this title, the name and address of each individual who applies, in person or in writing, for hiring for an existing position, or for recruiting or referring for a fee, for employment in the United States;

(iii) to hire individuals directly and adversely affected, with or without back pay;

(iv)(I) except as provided in subclauses (II) through (IV), to pay a civil penalty of not less than $250 and not more than $2,000 for each individual discriminated against,

(II) except as provided in subclauses (III) and (IV), in the case of a person or entity previously subject to a single order under this paragraph, to pay a civil penalty of not less than $2,000 and not more than $5,000 for each individual discriminated against,

(III) except as provided in subclause (IV), in the case of a person or entity previously subject to more than one order under this paragraph, to pay a civil penalty of not less than $3,000 and not more than $10,000 for each individual discriminated against, and

(IV) in the case of an unfair immigration-related employment practice described in subsection (a)(6) of this section, to pay a civil penalty of not less than $100 and not more than $1,000 for each individual discriminated against;

(v) to post notices to employees about their rights under this section and employers' obligations under section 1324a of this title;

(vi) to educate all personnel involved in hiring and complying with this section or section 1324a of this title about the requirements of this section or such section;

(vii) to remove (in an appropriate case) a false performance review or false warning from an employee's personnel file; and

(viii) to lift (in an appropriate case) any restrictions on an employee's assignments, work shifts, or movements.

(C) Limitation on back pay remedy

In providing a remedy under subparagraph (B)(iii), back pay liability shall not accrue from a date more than two years prior to the date of the filing of a charge with the Special Counsel. Interim earnings or amounts earnable with reasonable diligence by the individual or individuals discriminated against shall operate to reduce the back pay otherwise allowable under such paragraph. No order shall require the hiring of an individual as an employee or the payment to an individual of any back pay, if the individual was refused employment for any reason other than discrimination on account of national origin or citizenship status.

(D) Treatment of distinct entities

In applying this subsection in the case of a person or entity composed of distinct, physically separate subdivisions each of which provides separately for the hiring, recruiting, or referring for employment, without reference to the practices of, and not under the control of or common control with, another subdivision, each such subdivision shall be considered a separate person or entity.

(3) Orders not finding violations

If upon the preponderance of the evidence an administrative law judge determines that the person or entity named in the complaint has not engaged and is not engaging in any such unfair immigration-related employment practice, then the judge shall state his findings of fact and shall issue an order dismissing the complaint.

(h) Awarding of attorneys' fees

In any complaint respecting an unfair immigration-related employment practice, an administrative law judge, in the judge's discretion, may allow a prevailing party, other than the United States, a reasonable attorney's fee, if the losing party's argument is without reasonable foundation in law and fact.

(i) Review of final orders

(1) In general

Not later than 60 days after the entry of such final order, any person aggrieved by such final order may seek a review of such order in the United States court of appeals for the circuit in which the violation is alleged to have occurred or in which the employer resides or transacts business.

(2) Further review

Upon the filing of the record with the court, the jurisdiction of the court shall be exclusive and its judgment shall be final, except that the same shall be subject to review by the Supreme Court of the United States upon writ of certiorari or certification as provided in section 1254 of Title 28.

(j) Court enforcement of administrative orders

(1) In general

If an order of the agency is not appealed under subsection (i)(1) of this section, the Special Counsel (or, if the Special Counsel fails to act, the person filing the charge) may petition the United States district court for the district in which a violation of the order is alleged to have occurred, or in which the respondent resides or transacts business, for the enforcement of the order of the administrative law judge, by filing in such court a written petition praying that such order be enforced.

(2) Court enforcement order

Upon the filing of such petition, the court shall have jurisdiction to make and enter a decree enforcing the order of the administrative law judge. In such a proceeding, the order of the administrative law judge shall not be subject to review.

(3) Enforcement decree in original review

If, upon appeal of an order under subsection (i)(1) of this section, the United States court of appeals does not reverse such order, such court shall have the jurisdiction to make and enter a decree enforcing the order of the administrative law judge.

(4) Awarding of attorney's fees

In any judicial proceeding under subsection (i) of this section or this subsection, the court, in its discretion, may allow a prevailing party, other than the United States, a reasonable attorney's fee as part of costs but only if the losing party's argument is without reasonable foundation in law and fact.

(k) Termination dates

(1) This section shall not apply to discrimination in hiring, recruiting, or referring, or discharging of individuals occurring after the date of any termination of the provisions of section 1324a of this title, under subsection (*l*) of that section.

(2) The provisions of this section shall terminate 30 calendar days after receipt of the last report required to be transmitted under section 1324a(j) of this title if—

(A) the Comptroller General determines, and so reports in such report that—

(i) no significant discrimination has resulted, against citizens or nationals of the United States or against any eligible workers seeking employment, from the implementation of section 1324a of this title, or

(ii) such section has created an unreasonable burden on employers hiring such workers; and

(B) there has been enacted, within such period of 30 calendar days, a joint resolution stating in substance that the Congress approves the findings of the Comptroller General contained in such report. The provisions of subsections (m) and (n) of section 1324a of this title shall apply to any joint resolution under subparagraph (B) in the same manner as they apply to a joint resolution under subsection (*l*) of such section.

(*l*) Dissemination of information concerning anti-discrimination provisions

(1) Not later than 3 months after November 29, 1990, the Special Counsel, in cooperation with the chairman of the Equal Employment Opportunity Commission, the Secretary of Labor, and the Administrator of the Small Business Administration, shall conduct a campaign to disseminate information respecting the rights and remedies prescribed under this section and under title VII of the Civil Rights Act of 1964 [42 U.S.C.A. § 2000e et seq.] in connection with unfair immigration-related employment practices. Such campaign shall be aimed at increasing the knowledge of employers, employees, and the general public concerning employer and employee rights, responsibilities, and remedies under this section and such title.

(2) In order to carry out the campaign under this subsection, the Special Counsel—

(A) may, to the extent deemed appropriate and subject to the availability of appropriations, contract with public and private organizations for outreach activities under the campaign, and

(B) shall consult with the Secretary of Labor, the chairman of the Equal Employment Opportunity Commission, and the heads of such other agencies as may be appropriate.

(3) There are authorized to be appropriated to carry out this subsection $10,000,000 for each fiscal year (beginning with fiscal year 1991).

(June 27, 1952, c. 477, Title II, ch. 8, § 274B, as added Nov. 6, 1986, Pub.L. 99–603, Title I, 102(a), 100 Stat. 3374, and amended Oct. 24, 1988, Pub.L. 100–525, § 2(b), 102 Stat. 2610; Nov. 29, 1990, Pub.L. 101–649, Title V, §§ 531, 532(a), 533(a), 534(a), 535(a), 536(a), 537(a), 539(a), 104 Stat. 5054, 5055, 5056; Dec. 12, 1991, Pub.L. 102–232, Title III, § 306(b)(1),(3),(c)(1), 105 Stat. 1752; Oct. 25, 1994, Pub.L. 103–416, Title II, § 219(q), 108 Stat. 4317; Sept. 30, 1996, Pub.L. 104–208, Div. C, Title IV, § 421(a), Title VI, § 671(d)(1)(B), 110 Stat. 3009–670, 3009–723.)

[1] So in original. Probably should be "section".

HISTORICAL AND STATUTORY NOTES

References in Text

The Civil Rights Act of 1964, referred to in subsecs. (b)(2) and (*l*)(1), is Pub.L. 88–352, July 2, 1964, 78 Stat. 241, as amended, which is classified principally to subchapters II to IX (section 2000a et seq.) of chapter 21 of Title 42, The Public Health and Welfare. Title VII of that Act is classified to subchapter VI (section 2000e et seq.) of chapter 21 of Title 42.

Subsections (j), (*l*), (m), and (n) of section 1324a of this title, referred to in subsec. (k), were repealed by Pub.L.

104–208, Div. C, Title IV, § 412(c), Sept. 30, 1996, 110 Stat. 3009–668.

Effective and Applicability Provisions

1996 Acts. Section 421(b) of Div. C of Pub.L. 104–208 provided that: "The amendments made by subsection (a) [amending this section] shall apply to requests made on or after the date of the enactment of this Act [Sept. 30, 1996]."

1994 Acts. Amendment by section 219 of Pub.L. 103–416 effective as if included in the enactment of the Immigration Act of 1990, Pub.L. 101–649, 104 Stat. 4978, which was approved Nov. 29, 1990, except as otherwise specifically provided, see section 219(dd) of Pub.L. 103–416, set out as a note under section 1101 of this title.

1991 Acts. Amendments by sections 302 through 308 of Pub.L. 102–232, except as otherwise specifically provided, effective as if included in the enactment of Pub.L. 101–649, see section 310(1) of Pub.L. 102–232, set out as a note under section 1101 of this title.

1990 Acts. Section 532(b) of Pub.L. 101–649 provided that: "The amendment made by subsection (a) [amending subsec. (a)(3)(B)(i) of this section] shall apply to actions occurring on or after the date of the enactment of this Act [Nov. 29, 1990]."

Section 533(b) of Pub.L. 101–649 provided that: "The amendments made by subsection (a) [amending subsec. (a)(1) and (3) of this section] shall apply to unfair immigration-related employment practices occurring before, on, or after the date of the enactment of this Act [Nov. 29, 1990]."

Section 534(b) of Pub.L. 101–649 provided that: "The amendment made by subsection (a) [enacting subsec. (a)(5) of this section] shall apply to actions occurring on or after the date of the enactment of this Act [Nov. 29, 1990]."

Section 535(b) of Pub.L. 101–649 provided that: "The amendment made by subsection (a) [enacting subsec. (a)(6) of this section] shall take effect on the date of the enactment of this Act, but shall apply to actions occurring on or after such date [Nov. 29, 1990]."

Section 536(b) of Pub.L. 101–649 provided that: "The amendments made by this section [amending subsec. (g)(2)(B)(iv) of this section] shall apply to unfair immigration-related employment practices occurring after the date of the enactment of this Act [Nov. 29, 1990]."

Section 537(b) of Pub.L. 101–649 provided that: "The amendments made by subsection (a) [amending subsec. (d)(2) of this section] shall apply to charges received on or after the date of the enactment of this Act [Nov. 29, 1990]."

Section 539(b) of Pub.L. 101–649 provided that: "The amendments made by subsection (a) [enacting subsec. (g)(2)(B)(v) to (viii) of this section] shall apply to orders with respect to unfair immigration-related employment practices occurring on or after the date of the enactment of this Act [Nov. 29, 1990]."

Abolition of Immigration and Naturalization Service and Transfer of Functions

For abolition of Immigration and Naturalization Service, transfer of functions, and treatment of related references, see note set out under 8 U.S.C.A. § 1551.

Severability of Provisions

If any provision of Division C of Pub.L. 104–208 or the application of such provision to any person or circumstances is held to be unconstitutional, the remainder of Division C of Pub.L. 104–208 and the application of the provisions of Division C of Pub.L. 104–208 to any person or circumstance not to be affected thereby, see section 1(e) of Pub.L. 104–208, set out as a note under section 1101 of this title.

Unlicensed Individuals Employed on Fishing, Fish Processing, or Fish Tender Vessels

Aliens deemed to be employed in the United States for purposes of this section if they are unlicensed individuals employed on fishing, fish processing, or fish tender vessels, with the term "November 6, 1986" in subsec. (i) of this section to mean, with respect to such aliens, "the date 180 days after January 11, 1986", see section 8704 of Title 46, Shipping.

Authority of Equal Employment Opportunity Commission Unaffected

Section 102(b) of Pub.L. 99–603 provided that: Except as may be specifically provided in this section [enacting this section], nothing in this section shall be construed to restrict the authority of the Equal Employment Opportunity Commission to investigate allegations, in writing and under oath or affirmation, of unlawful employment practices, as provided in section 706 of the Civil Rights Act of 1964 (42 U.S.C. 2000e–5) [42 U.S.C.A. § 2000e–5], or any other authority provided therein."

§ 1324c. Penalties for document fraud

(a) Activities prohibited

It is unlawful for any person or entity knowingly—

(1) to forge, counterfeit, alter, or falsely make any document for the purpose of satisfying a requirement of this chapter or to obtain a benefit under this chapter,

(2) to use, attempt to use, possess, obtain, accept, or receive or to provide any forged, counterfeit, altered, or falsely made document in order to satisfy any requirement of this chapter or to obtain a benefit under this chapter,

(3) to use or attempt to use or to provide or attempt to provide any document lawfully issued to or with respect to a person other than the possessor (including a deceased individual) for the purpose of satisfying a requirement of this chapter or obtaining a benefit under this chapter,

(4) to accept or receive or to provide any document lawfully issued to or with respect to a person other than the possessor (including a deceased individual) for the purpose of complying with section 1324a(b) of this title or obtaining a benefit under this chapter, or

(5) to prepare, file, or assist another in preparing or filing, any application for benefits under this chapter, or any document required under this chapter, or any document submitted in connection with

such application or document, with knowledge or in reckless disregard of the fact that such application or document was falsely made or, in whole or in part, does not relate to the person on whose behalf it was or is being submitted, or

(6) (A) to present before boarding a common carrier for the purpose of coming to the United States a document which relates to the alien's eligibility to enter the United States, and (B) to fail to present such document to an immigration officer upon arrival at a United States port of entry.

(b) Exception

This section does not prohibit any lawfully authorized investigative, protective, or intelligence activity of a law enforcement agency of the United States, a State, or a subdivision of a State, or of an intelligence agency of the United States, or any activity authorized under chapter 224 of Title 18.

(c) Construction

Nothing in this section shall be construed to diminish or qualify any of the penalties available for activities prohibited by this section but proscribed as well in Title 18.

(d) Enforcement

(1) Authority in investigations

In conducting investigations and hearings under this subsection—

(A) immigration officers and administrative law judges shall have reasonable access to examine evidence of any person or entity being investigated,

(B) administrative law judges, may, if necessary, compel by subpoena the attendance of witnesses and the production of evidence at any designated place or hearing, and

(C) immigration officers designated by the Commissioner may compel by subpoena the attendance of witnesses and the production of evidence at any designated place prior to the filing of a complaint in a case under paragraph (2).

In case of contumacy or refusal to obey a subpoena lawfully issued under this paragraph and upon application of the Attorney General, an appropriate district court of the United States may issue an order requiring compliance with such subpoena and any failure to obey such order may be punished by such court as a contempt thereof.

(2) Hearing

(A) In general

Before imposing an order described in paragraph (3) against a person or entity under this subsection for a violation of subsection (a) of this section, the Attorney General shall provide the person or entity with notice and, upon request made within a reasonable time (of not less than 30 days, as established by the Attorney General) of the date of the notice, a hearing respecting the violation.

(B) Conduct of hearing

Any hearing so requested shall be conducted before an administrative law judge. The hearing shall be conducted in accordance with the requirements of section 554 of Title 5. The hearing shall be held at the nearest practicable place to the place where the person or entity resides or of the place where the alleged violation occurred. If no hearing is so requested, the Attorney General's imposition of the order shall constitute a final and unappealable order.

(C) Issuance of orders

If the administrative law judge determines, upon the preponderance of the evidence received, that a person or entity has violated subsection (a) of this section, the administrative law judge shall state his findings of fact and issue and cause to be served on such person or entity an order described in paragraph (3).

(3) Cease and desist order with civil money penalty

With respect to a violation of subsection (a) of this section, the order under this subsection shall require the person or entity to cease and desist from such violations and to pay a civil penalty in an amount of—

(A) not less than $250 and not more than $2,000 for each document that is the subject of a violation under subsection (a) of this section, or

(B) in the case of a person or entity previously subject to an order under this paragraph, not less than $2,000 and not more than $5,000 for each document that is the subject of a violation under subsection (a) of this section.

In applying this subsection in the case of a person or entity composed of distinct, physically separate subdivisions each of which provides separately for the hiring, recruiting, or referring for employment, without reference to the practices of, and not under the control of or common control with, another subdivision, each such subdivision shall be considered a separate person or entity.

(4) Administrative appellate review

The decision and order of an administrative law judge shall become the final agency decision and order of the Attorney General unless either (A) within 30 days, an official delegated by regulation to exercise review authority over the decision and order modifies or vacates the decision and order, or (B) within 30 days of the date of such a modification or vacation (or within 60 days of the date of decision and order of an administrative law judge if not so modified or vacated) the decision and order is referred to the Attorney General pursuant to regulations, in which case the decision and order of the Attorney General shall become the final agency decision and order under this subsection.

(5) Judicial review

A person or entity adversely affected by a final order under this section may, within 45 days after the date the final order is issued, file a petition in the Court of Appeals for the appropriate circuit for review of the order.

(6) Enforcement of orders

If a person or entity fails to comply with a final order issued under this section against the person or entity, the Attorney General shall file a suit to seek compliance with the order in any appropriate district court of the United States. In any such suit, the validity and appropriateness of the final order shall not be subject to review.

(7) Waiver by Attorney General

The Attorney General may waive the penalties imposed by this section with respect to an alien who knowingly violates subsection (a)(6) of this section if the alien is granted asylum under section 1158 of this title or withholding of removal under section 1231(b)(3) of this title.

(e) Criminal penalties for failure to disclose role as document preparer

(1) Whoever, in any matter within the jurisdiction of the Service, knowingly and willfully fails to disclose, conceals, or covers up the fact that they have, on behalf of any person and for a fee or other remuneration, prepared or assisted in preparing an application which was falsely made (as defined in subsection (f) of this section) for immigration benefits, shall be fined in accordance with Title 18, imprisoned for not more than 5 years, or both, and prohibited from preparing or assisting in preparing, whether or not for a fee or other remuneration, any other such application.

(2) Whoever, having been convicted of a violation of paragraph (1), knowingly and willfully prepares or assists in preparing an application for immigration benefits pursuant to this chapter, or the regulations promulgated thereunder, whether or not for a fee or other remuneration and regardless of whether in any matter within the jurisdiction of the Service, shall be fined in accordance with Title 18, imprisoned for not more than 15 years, or both, and prohibited from preparing or assisting in preparing any other such application.

(f) Falsely make

For purposes of this section, the term "falsely make" means to prepare or provide an application or document, with knowledge or in reckless disregard of the fact that the application or document contains a false, fictitious, or fraudulent statement or material representation, or has no basis in law or fact, or otherwise fails to state a fact which is material to the purpose for which it was submitted.

(June 27, 1952, c. 477, Title II, ch. 8, § 274C, as added Nov. 29, 1990, Pub.L. 101–649, Title V, § 544(a), 104 Stat. 5059, and amended Dec. 12, 1991, Pub.L. 102–232, Title III, § 306(c)(5)(A), 105 Stat. 1752; Oct. 25, 1994, Pub.L. 103–416, Title II, § 219(r), 108 Stat. 4317; Sept. 30, 1996, Pub.L. 104–208, Div. C, Title II, §§ 212(a) to (d), 213, 220, Title III, §§ 308(g)(10)(D), 379(a), 110 Stat. 3009–570, 3009–571, 3009–575, 3009–625, 3009–649.)

HISTORICAL AND STATUTORY NOTES

References in Text

This chapter, referred to in subsecs. (a)(1) to (5) and (e), was in the original, "this Act", meaning act June 27, 1952, c. 477, 66 Stat. 163, as amended, known as the Immigration and Nationality Act, which is classified principally to this chapter. For complete classification of this Act to the Code, see Tables.

Effective and Applicability Provisions

1996 Acts. Section 212(e) of Div. C of Pub.L. 104–208 provided that: "Section 274C(f) of the Immigration and Nationality Act, as added by subsection (b) [subsec. (f) of this section], applies to the preparation of applications before, on, or after the date of the enactment of this Act [Sept. 30, 1996]."

Amendment by section 308 of Div. C of Pub.L. 104–208 effective, with certain exceptions and subject to certain transitional rules, on the first day of the first month beginning more than 180 days after Sept. 30, 1996, see section 309 of Div. C of Pub.L. 104–208, set out as a note under section 1101 of this title.

Amendment by section 379(a) of Div. C of Pub.L. 104–208 applicable to orders issued on or after Sept. 30, 1996, see section 379(b) of Div. C of Pub.L. 104–208, set out as a note under section 1324a of this title.

1994 Acts. Amendment by section 219 of Pub.L. 103–416 effective as if included in the enactment of the Immigration Act of 1990, Pub.L. 101–649, 104 Stat. 4978, which was approved Nov. 29, 1990, except as otherwise specifically provided, see section 219(dd) of Pub.L. 103–416, set out as a note under section 1101 of this title.

1991 Acts. Amendments by sections 302 through 308 of Pub.L. 102–232, except as otherwise specifically provided, effective as if included in the enactment of Pub.L. 101–649, see section 310(1) of Pub.L. 102–232, set out as a note under section 1101 of this title.

1990 Acts. Section applicable to persons or entities that have committed violations on or after Nov. 29, 1990, see section 544(c) of Pub.L. 101–649, set out as a note under section 1251 of this title.

Abolition of Immigration and Naturalization Service and Transfer of Functions

For abolition of Immigration and Naturalization Service, transfer of functions, and treatment of related references, see note set out under 8 U.S.C.A. § 1551.

Severability of Provisions

If any provision of Division C of Pub.L. 104–208 or the application of such provision to any person or circumstances is held to be unconstitutional, the remainder of Division C of Pub.L. 104–208 and the application of the provisions of Division C of Pub.L. 104–208 to any person or circumstance not to be affected thereby, see section 1(e) of Pub.L. 104–208, set out as a note under section 1101 of this title.

§ 1324d. Civil penalties for failure to depart

(a) In general

Any alien subject to a final order of removal who—

(1) willfully fails or refuses to—

(A) depart from the United States pursuant to the order,

(B) make timely application in good faith for travel or other documents necessary for departure, or

(C) present for removal at the time and place required by the Attorney General; or

(2) conspires to or takes any action designed to prevent or hamper the alien's departure pursuant to the order,

shall pay a civil penalty of not more than $500 to the Commissioner for each day the alien is in violation of this section.

(b) Construction

Nothing in this section shall be construed to diminish or qualify any penalties to which an alien may be subject for activities proscribed by section 1253(a) of this title or any other section of this chapter.

(June 27, 1952, c. 477, Title II, ch. 8, § 274D, as added Sept. 30, 1996, Pub.L. 104–208, Div. C, Title III, § 380(a), 110 Stat. 3009–650.)

HISTORICAL AND STATUTORY NOTES

Effective and Applicability Provisions

1996 Acts. Section 380(c) of Div. C of Pub.L. 104–208 provided that: "The amendment made by subsection (a) [enacting this section] shall apply to actions occurring on or after the title III–A effective date (as defined in section 309(a) of this division) [the effective date of Title III–A of Div. C of Pub.L. 104–208, as defined in section 309(a) of Div. C of Pub.L. 104–208 [which is set out as a note under section 1101 of this title] as the first day of the first month beginning more than 180 days after Sept. 30, 1996]."

Abolition of Immigration and Naturalization Service and Transfer of Functions

For abolition of Immigration and Naturalization Service, transfer of functions, and treatment of related references, see note set out under 8 U.S.C.A. § 1551.

Severability of Provisions

If any provision of Division C of Pub.L. 104–208 or the application of such provision to any person or circumstances is held to be unconstitutional, the remainder of Division C of Pub.L. 104–208 and the application of the provisions of Division C of Pub.L. 104–208 to any person or circumstance not to be affected thereby, see section 1(e) of Pub.L. 104–208, set out as a note under section 1101 of this title.

References to Order of Removal Deemed to Include Order of Exclusion and Deportation

For purposes of this chapter, any reference in law to an order of removal is deemed to include a reference to an order of exclusion and deportation or an order of deportation, see section 309(d)(2) of Pub.L. 104–208, set out in an Effective Date of 1996 Amendments note under section 1101 of this title.

§ 1325. Improper entry by alien

(a) Improper time or place; avoidance of examination or inspection; misrepresentation and concealment of facts

Any alien who (1) enters or attempts to enter the United States at any time or place other than as designated by immigration officers, or (2) eludes examination or inspection by immigration officers, or (3) attempts to enter or obtains entry to the United States by a willfully false or misleading representation or the willful concealment of a material fact, shall, for the first commission of any such offense, be fined under Title 18 or imprisoned not more than 6 months, or both, and, for a subsequent commission of any such offense, be fined under Title 18, or imprisoned not more than 2 years, or both.

(b) Improper time or place; civil penalties

Any alien who is apprehended while entering (or attempting to enter) the United States at a time or place other than as designated by immigration officers shall be subject to a civil penalty of—

(1) at least $50 and not more than $250 for each such entry (or attempted entry); or

(2) twice the amount specified in paragraph (1) in the case of an alien who has been previously subject to a civil penalty under this subsection.

Civil penalties under this subsection are in addition to, and not in lieu of, any criminal or other civil penalties that may be imposed.

(c) Marriage fraud

Any individual who knowingly enters into a marriage for the purpose of evading any provision of the immigration laws shall be imprisoned for not more than 5 years, or fined not more than $250,000, or both.

(d) Immigration-related entrepreneurship fraud

Any individual who knowingly establishes a commercial enterprise for the purpose of evading any provision of the immigration laws shall be imprisoned for not more than 5 years, fined in accordance with Title 18, or both.

(June 27, 1952, c. 477, Title II, ch. 8, § 275, 66 Stat. 229; Nov. 10, 1986, Pub.L. 99–639, § 2(d), 100 Stat. 3542; Nov. 29, 1990, Pub.L. 101–649, Title I, § 121(b)(3), Title V, § 543(b)(2), 104 Stat. 4994, 5059; Dec. 12, 1991, Pub.L. 102–232, Title III, § 306(c)(3), 105 Stat. 1752; Sept. 30, 1996, Pub.L. 104–208, Div. C, Title I, § 105(a), 110 Stat. 3009–556.)

HISTORICAL AND STATUTORY NOTES

Effective and Applicability Provisions

1996 Acts. Section 105(b) of Pub.L. 104–208 provided that: "The amendments made by subsection (a) [enacting subsec. (b) of this section and redesignating subsecs. (b) and (c) as (c) and (d) of this section] shall apply to illegal entries or attempts to enter occurring on or after the first day of the sixth month beginning after the date of the enactment of this Act [Sept. 30, 1996]."

1991 Acts. Amendments by sections 302 through 308 of Pub.L. 102–232, except as otherwise specifically provided, effective as if included in the enactment of Pub.L. 101–649, see section 310(1) of Pub.L. 102–232, set out as a note under section 1101 of this title.

1990 Acts. Amendment by section 121(b)(3) of Pub.L. 101–649 effective Oct. 1, 1991, and applicable beginning with fiscal year 1992, with general transition provisions, admissibility standards, and construction provisions, see section 161 of Pub.L. 101–649, set out as a note under section 1101 of this title.

Amendment by section 543(b)(2) of Pub.L. 101–649 applicable to actions taken after Nov. 29, 1990, see section 543(c) of Pub.L. 101–649, set out as a note under section 1221 of this title.

Abolition of Immigration and Naturalization Service and Transfer of Functions

For abolition of Immigration and Naturalization Service, transfer of functions, and treatment of related references, see note set out under 8 U.S.C.A. § 1551.

Severability of Provisions

If any provision of Division C of Pub.L. 104–208 or the application of such provision to any person or circumstances is held to be unconstitutional, the remainder of Division C of Pub.L. 104–208 and the application of the provisions of Division C of Pub.L. 104–208 to any person or circumstance not to be affected thereby, see section 1(e) of Pub.L. 104–208, set out as a note under section 1101 of this title.

§ 1326. Reentry of removed aliens

(a) In general

Subject to subsection (b) of this section, any alien who—

(1) has been denied admission, excluded, deported, or removed or has departed the United States while an order of exclusion, deportation, or removal is outstanding, and thereafter

(2) enters, attempts to enter, or is at any time found in, the United States, unless (A) prior to his reembarkation at a place outside the United States or his application for admission from foreign contiguous territory, the Attorney General has expressly consented to such alien's reapplying for admission; or (B) with respect to an alien previously denied admission and removed, unless such alien shall establish that he was not required to obtain such advance consent under this chapter or any prior Act,

shall be fined under Title 18, or imprisoned not more than 2 years, or both.

(b) Criminal penalties for reentry of certain removed aliens

Notwithstanding subsection (a) of this section, in the case of any alien described in such subsection—

(1) whose removal was subsequent to a conviction for commission of three or more misdemeanors involving drugs, crimes against the person, or both, or a felony (other than an aggravated felony), such alien shall be fined under Title 18, imprisoned not more than 10 years, or both;

(2) whose removal was subsequent to a conviction for commission of an aggravated felony, such alien shall be fined under such Title, imprisoned not more than 20 years, or both;

(3) who has been excluded from the United States pursuant to section 1225(c) of this title because the alien was excludable under section 1182(a)(3)(B) of this title or who has been removed from the United States pursuant to the provisions of subchapter V of this chapter, and who thereafter, without the permission of the Attorney General, enters the United States, or attempts to do so, shall be fined under Title 18 and imprisoned for a period of 10 years, which sentence shall not run concurrently with any other sentence.[1] or

(4) who was removed from the United States pursuant to section 1231(a)(4)(B) of this title who thereafter, without the permission of the Attorney General, enters, attempts to enter, or is at any time found in, the United States (unless the Attorney General has expressly consented to such alien's reentry) shall be fined under Title 18, imprisoned for not more than 10 years, or both.

For the purposes of this subsection, the term "removal" includes any agreement in which an alien stipulates to removal during (or not during) a criminal trial under either Federal or State law.

(c) Reentry of alien deported prior to completion of term of imprisonment

Any alien deported pursuant to section 1252(h)(2)[2] of this title who enters, attempts to enter, or is at any time found in, the United States (unless the Attorney General has expressly consented to such alien's reentry) shall be incarcerated for the remainder of the sentence of imprisonment which was pending at the time of deportation without any reduction for parole or supervised release. Such alien shall be subject to such other penalties relating to the reentry of deported aliens as may be available under this section or any other provision of law.

(d) Limitation on collateral attack on underlying deportation order

In a criminal proceeding under this section, an alien may not challenge the validity of the deportation order described in subsection (a)(1) of this section or subsection (b) of this section unless the alien demonstrates that—

(1) the alien exhausted any administrative remedies that may have been available to seek relief against the order;

(2) the deportation proceedings at which the order was issued improperly deprived the alien of the opportunity for judicial review; and

(3) the entry of the order was fundamentally unfair.

(June 27, 1952, c. 477, Title II, ch. 8, § 276, 66 Stat. 229; Nov. 18, 1988, Pub.L. 100–690, Title VII, § 7345(a), 102 Stat. 4471; Nov. 29, 1990, Pub.L. 101–649, Title V, § 543(b)(3), 104 Stat. 5059; Sept. 13, 1994, Pub.L. 103–322, Title XIII, § 130001(b), 108 Stat. 2023; Apr. 24, 1996, Pub.L. 104–132, Title IV, §§ 401(c), 438(b), 441(a), 110 Stat. 1267, 1276, 1279; Sept. 30, 1996, Pub.L. 104–208, Div. C, Title III, §§ 305(b), 308(d)(4)(J), (e)(1)(K), (14)(A), 324(a), (b), 110 Stat. 3009–606, 3009–618, 3009–619, 3009–620, 3009–629.)

1 So in original. The period probably should be a semicolon.

2 See References in Text note below.

HISTORICAL AND STATUTORY NOTES

References in Text

Section 1252 of this title, referred to in subsec. (c), was amended by Pub.L. 104–208, div. C, title III, § 306(a)(2), Sept. 30, 1996, 110 Stat. 3009–607, and as so amended, does not contain a subsec. (h). For provisions similar to those formerly contained in section 1252(h)(2)of this title, see section 1231(a)(4) of this title.

Codifications

Amendment by section 543(b)(3) of Pub.L. 101–649, directing that "section 276(8 U.S.C. 1326)" be amended, without specifying any subsection designation, has been executed to subsec. (a) of this section as the probable intent of Congress.

Effective and Applicability Provisions

1996 Acts. Amendment by sections 305 and 308 of Div. C of Pub.L. 104–208 effective, with certain exceptions and subject to certain transitional rules, on the first day of the first month beginning more than 180 days after Sept. 30, 1996, see section 309 of Div. C of Pub.L. 104–208, set out as a note under section 1101 of this title.

Section 324(c) of Div. C of Pub.L. 104–208 provided that: "The amendment made by subsection (a) [amending this section] shall apply to departures that occurred before, on, or after the date of the enactment of this Act [Sept. 30, 1996], but only with respect to entries (and attempted entries) occurring on or after such date."

Amendment by section 401(c) of Pub.L. 104–132 effective Apr. 24, 1996 and applicable to all aliens without regard to date of entry or attempted entry into United States, see section 401(f) of Pub.L. 104–132, set out as a note under section 1105a of this title.

Section 441(b) of Pub.L. 104–132 provided that: "The amendment made by subsection (a) [enacting subsec. (d) of this section] shall apply to criminal proceedings initiated after the date of enactment of this Act [Apr. 24, 1996]."

1990 Acts. Amendment by section 543(b)(3) of Pub.L. 101–649 applicable to actions taken after Nov. 29, 1990, see section 543(c) of Pub.L. 101–649, set out as a note under section 1221 of this title.

1988 Acts. Section 7345(b) of Pub.L. 100–690 provided that: "The amendments made by subsection (a) [amending this section] shall apply to any alien who enters, attempts to enter, or is found in, the United States on or after the date of the enactment of this Act [Nov. 18, 1988]."

Abolition of Immigration and Naturalization Service and Transfer of Functions

For abolition of Immigration and Naturalization Service, transfer of functions, and treatment of related references, see note set out under 8 U.S.C.A. § 1551.

Severability of Provisions

If any provision of Division C of Pub.L. 104–208 or the application of such provision to any person or circumstances is held to be unconstitutional, the remainder of Division C of Pub.L. 104–208 and the application of the provisions of Division C of Pub.L. 104–208 to any person or circumstance not to be affected thereby, see section 1(e) of Pub.L. 104–208, set out as a note under section 1101 of this title.

References to Order of Removal Deemed to Include Order of Exclusion and Deportation

For purposes of this chapter, any reference in law to an order of removal is deemed to include a reference to an order of exclusion and deportation or an order of deportation, see section 309(d)(2) of Pub.L. 104–208, set out in an Effective Date of 1996 Amendments note under section 1101 of this title.

§ 1327. Aiding or assisting certain aliens to enter

Any person who knowingly aids or assists any alien inadmissible under section 1182(a)(2) (insofar as an alien inadmissible under such section has been convicted of an aggravated felony) or 1182(a)(3) (other than subparagraph (E) thereof) of this title to enter the United States, or who connives or conspires with any person or persons to allow, procure, or permit any such alien to enter the United States, shall be fined under Title 18, or imprisoned not more than 10 years, or both.

(June 27, 1952, c. 477, Title II, ch. 8, § 277, 66 Stat. 229; Nov. 18, 1988, Pub.L. 100–690, Title VII, § 7346(a), (c)(1), 102 Stat. 4471; Nov. 29, 1990, Pub.L. 101–649, Title V, § 543(b)(4), Title VI, § 603(a)(16), 104 Stat. 5059, 5084; Sept.

30, 1996, Pub.L. 104–208, Div. C, Title III, § 308(d)(3)(A), 110 Stat. 3009–617.)

HISTORICAL AND STATUTORY NOTES

Effective and Applicability Provisions

1996 Acts. Amendment by section 308 of Div. C of Pub.L. 104–208 effective, with certain exceptions and subject to certain transitional rules, on the first day of the first month beginning more than 180 days after Sept. 30, 1996, see section 309 of Div. C of Pub.L. 104–208, set out as a note under section 1101 of this title.

1990 Acts. Amendment by section 543(b)(4) of Pub.L. 101–649 applicable to actions taken after Nov. 29, 1990, see section 543(c) of Pub.L. 101–649, set out as a note under section 1221 of this title.

Amendment by section 603(a)(16) of Pub.L. 101–649 applicable to individuals entering the United States on or after June 1, 1991, see section 601(e)(1) of Pub.L. 101–649, set out as a note under section 1101 of this title.

1988 Acts. Section 7346(b) of Pub.L. 100–690 provided that: "The amendment made by subsection (a) [amending this section] shall apply to any aid or assistance which occurs on or after the date of the enactment of this Act [Nov. 18, 1988]."

Severability of Provisions

If any provision of Division C of Pub.L. 104–208 or the application of such provision to any person or circumstances is held to be unconstitutional, the remainder of Division C of Pub.L. 104–208 and the application of the provisions of Division C of Pub.L. 104–208 to any person or circumstance not to be affected thereby, see section 1(e) of Pub.L. 104–208, set out as a note under section 1101 of this title.

§ 1328. Importation of alien for immoral purpose

The importation into the United States of any alien for the purpose of prostitution, or for any other immoral purpose, is forbidden. Whoever shall, directly or indirectly, import, or attempt to import into the United States any alien for the purpose of prostitution or for any other immoral purpose, or shall hold or attempt to hold any alien for any such purpose in pursuance of such illegal importation, or shall keep, maintain, control, support, employ, or harbor in any house or other place, for the purpose of prostitution or for any other immoral purpose, any alien, in pursuance of such illegal importation, shall be fined under Title 18, or imprisoned not more than 10 years, or both. The trial and punishment of offenses under this section may be in any district to or into which such alien is brought in pursuance of importation by the person or persons accused, or in any district in which a violation of any of the provisions of this section occurs. In all prosecutions under this section, the testimony of a husband or wife shall be admissible and competent evidence against each other.

(June 27, 1952, c. 477, Title II, ch. 8, § 278, 66 Stat. 230; Nov. 29, 1990, Pub.L. 101–649, Title V, § 543(b)(5), 104 Stat. 5059.)

HISTORICAL AND STATUTORY NOTES

Effective and Applicability Provisions

1990 Acts. Amendment by section 543(b)(5) of Pub.L. 101–649 applicable to actions taken after Nov. 29, 1990, see section 543(c) of Pub.L. 101–649, set out as a note under section 1221 of this title.

§ 1329. Jurisdiction of district courts

The district courts of the United States shall have jurisdiction of all causes, civil and criminal, brought by the United States that arise under the provisions of this subchapter. It shall be the duty of the United States attorney of the proper district to prosecute every such suit when brought by the United States. Notwithstanding any other law, such prosecutions or suits may be instituted at any place in the United States at which the violation may occur or at which the person charged with a violation under section 1325 or 1326 of this title may be apprehended. No suit or proceeding for a violation of any of the provisions of this subchapter shall be settled, compromised, or discontinued without the consent of the court in which it is pending and any such settlement, compromise, or discontinuance shall be entered of record with the reasons therefor. Nothing in this section shall be construed as providing jurisdiction for suits against the United States or its agencies or officers.

(June 27, 1952, c. 477, Title II, ch. 8, § 279, 66 Stat. 230; Sept. 30, 1996, Pub.L. 104–208, Div. C, Title III, § 381(a), 110 Stat. 3009–650.)

HISTORICAL AND STATUTORY NOTES

Effective and Applicability Provisions

1996 Acts. Section 381(b) of Div. C of Pub.L. 104–208 provided that: "The amendments made by subsection (a) [amending this section] shall apply to actions filed after the date of the enactment of this Act [Sept. 30, 1996]."

Severability of Provisions

If any provision of Division C of Pub.L. 104–208 or the application of such provision to any person or circumstances is held to be unconstitutional, the remainder of Division C of Pub.L. 104–208 and the application of the provisions of Division C of Pub.L. 104–208 to any person or circumstance not to be affected thereby, see section 1(e) of Pub.L. 104–208, set out as a note under section 1101 of this title.

§ 1330. Collection of penalties and expenses

(a) Notwithstanding any other provisions of this subchapter, the withholding or denial of clearance of or a lien upon any vessel or aircraft provided for in section 1221, 1224, 1253(c)(2), 1281, 1283, 1284, 1285, 1286, 1321, 1322, or 1323 of this title shall not be regarded as the sole and exclusive means or remedy for the enforcement of payments of any fine, penalty or expenses imposed or incurred under such sections, but, in the discretion of the Attorney General, the amount thereof may be recovered by civil suit, in the name of the United States, from any person made liable under any of such sections.

(b)(1) There is established in the general fund of the Treasury a separate account which shall be known as the "Immigration Enforcement Account". Notwithstanding any other section of this subchapter, there shall be deposited as offsetting receipts into the Immigration Enforcement Account amounts described in paragraph (2) to remain available until expended.

(2) The amounts described in this paragraph are the following:

(A) The increase in penalties collected resulting from the amendments made by sections 203(b) and 543(a) of the Immigration Act of 1990.

(B) Civil penalties collected under sections 1229c(d), 1324c, 1324d, and 1325(b) of this title.

(3)(A) The Secretary of the Treasury shall refund out of the Immigration Enforcement Account to any appropriation the amount paid out of such appropriation for expenses incurred by the Attorney General for activities that enhance enforcement of provisions of this subchapter. Such activities include—

(i) the identification, investigation, apprehension, detention, and removal of criminal aliens;

(ii) the maintenance and updating of a system to identify and track criminal aliens, deportable aliens, inadmissible aliens, and aliens illegally entering the United States; and

(iii) for the repair, maintenance, or construction on the United States border, in areas experiencing high levels of apprehensions of illegal aliens, of structures to deter illegal entry into the United States.

(B) The amounts which are required to be refunded under subparagraph (A) shall be refunded at least quarterly on the basis of estimates made by the Attorney General of the expenses referred to in subparagraph (A). Proper adjustments shall be made in the amounts subsequently refunded under subparagraph (A) to the extent prior estimates were in excess of, or less than, the amount required to be refunded under subparagraph (A).

(C) The amounts required to be refunded from the Immigration Enforcement Account for fiscal year 1996 and thereafter shall be refunded in accordance with estimates made in the budget request of the Attorney General for those fiscal years. Any proposed changes in the amounts designated in such budget requests shall only be made after notification to the Committees on Appropriations of the House of Representatives and the Senate in accordance with section 605 of Public Law 104–134.

(D) The Attorney General shall prepare and submit annually to the Congress statements of financial condition of the Immigration Enforcement Account, including beginning account balance, revenues, withdrawals, and ending account balance and projection for the ensuing fiscal year.

(June 27, 1952, c. 477, Title II, ch. 8, § 280, 66 Stat. 230; Nov. 29, 1990, Pub.L. 101–649, Title V, § 542(a), 104 Stat. 5057; Oct. 25, 1994, Pub.L. 103–416, Title II, § 219(s), 108 Stat. 4317; Sept. 30, 1996, Pub.L. 104–208, Div. C, Title III, §§ 308(g)(4)(C), 382(a), 110 Stat. 3009–623, 3009–651.)

HISTORICAL AND STATUTORY NOTES

References in Text

Section 203(b) of the Immigration Act of 1990, referred to in subsec. (b)(2)(A), is section 203(b) of Pub.L. 101–649, which amended section 1281(d) of this title.

Section 543(a) of the Immigration Act of 1990, referred to in subsec. (b)(2)(A), is section 543(a) of Pub.L. 101–649, which amended sections 1221, 1227, 1229, 1284, 1285, 1286, 1287, 1321, 1322, and 1323 of this title.

Section 605 of Public Law 104–134, referred to in subsec. (b)(3)(C), is Pub.L.104–134, Title I, § 101[a] [Title VI, § 605], Apr. 26, 1996, 110 Stat. 1321–63, as amended Pub.L. 104–140, § 1(a), May 2, 1996, 110 Stat. 1327, which was not classified to the Code.

Effective and Applicability Provisions

1996 Acts. Amendment by section 308 of Div. C of Pub.L. 104–208 effective, with certain exceptions and subject to certain transitional rules, on the first day of the first month beginning more than 180 days after Sept. 30, 1996, see section 309 of Div. C of Pub.L. 104–208, set out as a note under section 1101 of this title.

Section 382(c) of Div. C of Pub.L. 104–208 provided that: "The amendments made by this section [amending this section and section 1356 of this title] shall apply to fines and penalties collected on or after the date of the enactment of this Act [Sept. 30, 1996]."

1994 Acts. Amendment by section 219 of Pub.L. 103–416 effective as if included in the enactment of the Immigration Act of 1990, Pub.L. 101–649, 104 Stat. 4978, which was approved Nov. 29, 1990, except as otherwise specifically provided, see section 219(dd) of Pub.L. 103–416, set out as a note under section 1101 of this title.

1990 Acts. Section 542(b) of Pub.L. 101–649 provided that: "The amendment made by subsection (a) [designating existing provision as subsec. (a) and adding subsec. (b)] shall apply to fines and penalties collected on or after January 1, 1991."

Abolition of Immigration and Naturalization Service and Transfer of Functions

For abolition of Immigration and Naturalization Service, transfer of functions, and treatment of related references, see note set out under 8 U.S.C.A. § 1551.

Severability of Provisions

If any provision of Division C of Pub.L. 104–208 or the application of such provision to any person or circumstances is held to be unconstitutional, the remainder of Division C of

Pub.L. 104–208 and the application of the provisions of Division C of Pub.L. 104–208 to any person or circumstance not to be affected thereby, see section 1(e) of Pub.L. 104–208, set out as a note under section 1101 of this title.

TITLE 15
COMMERCE AND TRADE

CHAPTER 41—CONSUMER CREDIT PROTECTION

§ 1644. Fraudulent use of credit cards; penalties

(a) Use, attempt or conspiracy to use card in transaction affecting interstate or foreign commerce

Whoever knowingly in a transaction affecting interstate or foreign commerce, uses or attempts or conspires to use any counterfeit, fictitious, altered, forged, lost, stolen, or fraudulently obtained credit card to obtain money, goods, services, or anything else of value which within any one-year period has a value aggregating $1,000 or more; or

(b) Transporting, attempting or conspiring to transport card in interstate commerce

Whoever, with unlawful or fraudulent intent, transports or attempts or conspires to transport in interstate or foreign commerce a counterfeit, fictitious, altered, forged, lost, stolen, or fraudulently obtained credit card knowing the same to be counterfeit, fictitious, altered, forged, lost, stolen, or fraudulently obtained; or

(c) Use of interstate commerce to sell or transport card

Whoever, with unlawful or fraudulent intent, uses any instrumentality of interstate or foreign commerce to sell or transport a counterfeit, fictitious, altered, forged, lost, stolen, or fraudulently obtained credit card knowing the same to be counterfeit, fictitious, altered, forged, lost, stolen, or fraudulently obtained; or

(d) Receipt, concealment, etc., of goods obtained by use of card

Whoever knowingly receives, conceals, uses, or transports money, goods, services, or anything else of value (except tickets for interstate or foreign transportation) which (1) within any one-year period has a value aggregating $1,000 or more, (2) has moved in or is part of, or which constitutes interstate or foreign commerce, and (3) has been obtained with a counterfeit, fictitious, altered, forged, lost, stolen, or fraudulently obtained credit card; or

(e) Receipt, concealment, etc., of tickets for interstate or foreign transportation obtained by use of card

Whoever knowingly receives, conceals, uses, sells, or transports in interstate or foreign commerce one or more tickets for interstate or foreign transportation, which (1) within any one-year period have a value aggregating $500 or more, and (2) have been purchased or obtained with one or more counterfeit, fictitious, altered, forged, lost, stolen, or fraudulently obtained credit cards; or

(f) Furnishing of money, etc., through use of card

Whoever in a transaction affecting interstate or foreign commerce furnishes money, property, services, or anything else of value, which within any one-year period has a value aggregating $1,000 or more, through the use of any counterfeit, fictitious, altered, forged, lost, stolen, or fraudulently obtained credit card knowing the same to be counterfeit, fictitious, altered, forged, lost, stolen, or fraudulently obtained—

shall be fined not more than $10,000 or imprisoned not more than ten years, or both.

(Pub.L. 90–321, Title I, § 134, as added Pub.L. 91–508, Title V, § 502(a), Oct. 26, 1970, 84 Stat. 1127, and amended Pub.L. 93–495, Title IV, § 414, Oct. 28, 1974, 88 Stat. 1520.)

HISTORICAL AND STATUTORY NOTES

Effective and Applicability Provisions

1974 Acts. Amendment by Pub.L. 93–495 effective Oct. 28, 1974, see § 416 of Pub.L. 93–495, set out as an Effective Date note under § 1665a of this title.

1970 Acts. Section 503(3) of Pub.L. 91–508 provided that: "Section 134 of such Act [this section] applies to offenses committed on or after such date of enactment [Oct. 26, 1970]."

TITLE 21

FOOD AND DRUGS

CHAPTER 13—DRUG ABUSE PREVENTION AND CONTROL

SUBCHAPTER I—CONTROL AND ENFORCEMENT

PART A—INTRODUCTORY PROVISIONS

PART B—AUTHORITY TO CONTROL; STANDARDS AND SCHEDULES

PART C—REGISTRATION OF MANUFACTURERS, DISTRIBUTORS, AND DISPENSERS OF CONTROLLED SUBSTANCES

PART D—OFFENSES AND PENALTIES

PART E—ADMINISTRATIVE AND ENFORCEMENT PROVISIONS

UNIFORM CONTROLLED SUBSTANCES ACT

Table of Jurisdictions Wherein the 1970, 1990, or 1994 Versions of the Uniform Controlled Substances Act or a Combination Thereof have been Adopted [1]

For text of the 1970, 1990, and 1994 versions of the Uniform Controlled Substances Act, and annotation materials for adopting jurisdictions, see Uniform Laws Annotated, Master Edition, Volume 9, Parts II, III, and IV.

Jurisdiction	Statutory Citation
Alabama	Code 1975, §§ 20–2–1 to 20–2–190.
Alaska	AS 11.71.010 to 11.71.900, 17.30.010 to 17.30.900.
Arizona	A.R.S. §§ 36–2501 to 36–2553.
Arkansas [2]	A.C.A. §§ 5–64–101 to 5–64–608.
California	West's Ann.Cal. Health & Safety Code, §§ 11000 to 11657.
Colorado	West's C.R.S.A. §§ 18–18–101 to 18–18–605.
Connecticut	C.G.S.A. §§ 21a–240 to 21a–283.
Delaware	16 Del.C. §§ 4701 to 4796.
District of Columbia	D.C. Official Code, 2001 Ed. §§ 48–901.01 to 48–931.02.
Florida	West's F.S.A. §§ 893.01 to 893.165.
Georgia	O.C.G.A. §§ 16–13–20 to 16–13–56.
Hawaii	HRS §§ 329–1 to 329–128.
Idaho	I.C. §§ 37–2701 to 37–2751.
Illinois	S.H.A. 720 ILCS 570/100 to 570/603.
Indiana	West's A.I.C. 35–48–1–1 to 35–48–7–15.
Iowa	I.C.A. §§ 124.101 to 124.602.
Kansas	K.S.A. 65–4101 to 65–4166.
Kentucky	KRS 218A.010 to 218A.993.
Louisiana	LSA–R.S. 40:961 to 40:995.
Maine	17–A M.R.S.A. §§ 1101 to 1118; 22 M.R.S.A. §§ 2383, 2383–A, 2383–B.
Maryland	Criminal Law, §§ 5–101 to 5–1101.
Massachusetts	M.G.L.A. c. 94C, §§ 1 to 48.
Michigan	M.C.L.A. §§ 333.7101 to 333.7545.
Minnesota	M.S.A. §§ 152.01 to 152.20.
Mississippi	Code 1972, §§ 41–29–101 to 41–29–185.
Missouri	V.A.M.S. §§ 195.010 to 195.320.
Montana	MCA 50–32–101 to 50–32–405.
Nebraska	R.R.S.1943, §§ 28–401 to 28–457.
Nevada	N.R.S. 453.011 et seq.
New Jersey	N.J.S.A. 2C:35–1 to 2C:35–24, 2C:36–1 to 2C:36–10, 24:21–1 to 24:21–53.
New Mexico	NMSA 1978, §§ 30–31–1 to 30–31–41.
New York	McKinney's Public Health Law §§ 3300 to 3396.
North Carolina	G.S. §§ 90–86 to 90–113.8.
North Dakota	NDCC 19–03.1–01 to 19–03.1–46.
Ohio	R.C. §§ 3719.01 to 3719.99.
Oklahoma	63 Okl.St.Ann. §§ 2–101 to 2–610.
Oregon	ORS 475.005 to 475.285, 475.295, 475.940 to 475.999.
Pennsylvania	35 P.S. §§ 780–101 to 780–144.
Puerto Rico	24 L.P.R.A. §§ 2101 to 2607.
Rhode Island	Gen.Laws 1956, §§ 21–28–1.01 to 21–28–6.02.
South Carolina	Code 1976, §§ 44–53–110 to 44–53–590.
South Dakota	SDCL 34–20B–1 to 34–20B–114.
Tennessee	T.C.A. §§ 39–17–401 to 39–17–434, 53–11–301 to 53–11–452.
Texas	V.T.C.A. Health and Safety Code, §§ 481.001 to 482.005.
Utah	U.C.A.1953, 58–37–1 to 58–37–21.
Virgin Islands	19 V.I.C. §§ 591 to 631.
Virginia	Code 1950, § 54.1–3400 to 54.1–3472.
Washington	West's RCWA §§ 69.50.101 to 69.50.609.
West Virginia	Code, 60A–1–101 to 60A–6–605.
Wisconsin	W.S.A. 961.001 to 961.62.
Wyoming	Wyo.Stat.Ann. §§ 35–7–1001 to 35–7–1060.

[1] The 1970, 1990, and 1994 versions of the Uniform Controlled Substances Act, while different, are similar in many of their provisions. The acts of the adopting jurisdictions will, therefore, generally contain many provisions common to all to those versions. Thus, it is often difficult to say with certitude that a jurisdiction has adopted one version of the act rather than another.

[2] Arkansas has adopted and retains the major provisions of both the Uniform Narcotic Drug Act and the Uniform Controlled Substances Act.

SUBCHAPTER I—CONTROL AND ENFORCEMENT

PART A—INTRODUCTORY PROVISIONS

§ 801. Congressional findings and declarations: controlled substances

The Congress makes the following findings and declarations:

(1) Many of the drugs included within this subchapter have a useful and legitimate medical purpose and are necessary to maintain the health and general welfare of the American people.

(2) The illegal importation, manufacture, distribution, and possession and improper use of controlled substances have a substantial and detrimental effect on the health and general welfare of the American people.

(3) A major portion of the traffic in controlled substances flows through interstate and foreign commerce. Incidents of the traffic which are not an integral part of the interstate or foreign flow, such as manufacture, local distribution, and possession, nonetheless have a substantial and direct effect upon interstate commerce because—

(A) after manufacture, many controlled substances are transported in interstate commerce,

(B) controlled substances distributed locally usually have been transported in interstate commerce immediately before their distribution, and

(C) controlled substances possessed commonly flow through interstate commerce immediately prior to such possession.

(4) Local distribution and possession of controlled substances contribute to swelling the interstate traffic in such substances.

(5) Controlled substances manufactured and distributed intrastate cannot be differentiated from controlled substances manufactured and distributed interstate. Thus, it is not feasible to distinguish, in terms of controls, between controlled substances manufactured and distributed interstate and controlled substances manufactured and distributed intrastate.

(6) Federal control of the intrastate incidents of the traffic in controlled substances is essential to the effective control of the interstate incidents of such traffic.

(7) The United States is a party to the Single Convention on Narcotic Drugs, 1961, and other international conventions designed to establish effective control over international and domestic traffic in controlled substances.

(Pub.L. 91–513, Title II, § 101, Oct. 27, 1970, 84 Stat. 1242.)

HISTORICAL AND STATUTORY NOTES

References in Text

"This subchapter", referred to in text, was in the original "this title" which is Title II of Pub.L. 91–513, Oct. 27, 1970, 84 Stat. 1242, and is popularly known as the "Controlled Substances Act". For complete classification of Title II to the Code, see Short Title note below and Tables.

Effective and Applicability Provisions

1970 Acts. Section 704 of Pub.L. 91–513 provided that:

"**(a)** Except as otherwise provided in this section, this title [see Short Title note below] shall become effective on the first day of the seventh calendar month that begins after the day immediately preceding the date of enactment [Oct. 27, 1970].

"**(b)** Parts A, B, E, and F of this title [Parts A, B, E, and F of this subchapter], section 702 [set out as a note under section 321 of this title], this section, and sections 705 through 709 [set out as sections 901 to 904 of this title and as a note under this section] shall become effective upon enactment [Oct. 27, 1970].

"**(c)** Sections 305 (relating to labels and labeling) [section 825 of this title], and 306 (relating to manufacturing quotas) [section 826 of this title] shall become effective on the date specified in subsection (a) of this section, except that the Attorney General may by order published in the Federal Register postpone the effective date of either or both of these sections for such period as he may determine to be necessary for the efficient administration of this title [this subchapter]."

Severability

Pub.L. 106–310, Div. B, Title XXXVI, § 3673, Oct. 17, 2000, 114 Stat. 1246, provided that: "Any provision of this title [Title XXXVI (§§ 3601 to 3673) of Pub.L. 106–310; see Tables for complete classification] held to be invalid or unenforceable by its terms, or as applied to any person or circumstance, shall be construed as to give the maximum effect permitted by law, unless such provision is held to be utterly invalid or unenforceable, in which event such provision shall be severed from this title and shall not affect the applicability of the remainder of this title, or of such provision, to other persons not similarly situated or to other, dissimilar circumstances."

Short Title

2006 Amendments. Pub.L. 109–177, Title VII, § 701, Mar. 9, 2006, 120 Stat. 256, provided that: "This title [enacting 21 U.S.C.A. §§ 860a, 865, and 871a, and 42 U.S.C.A. §§ 3797cc, 3797cc–1, 3797cc–2, and 3797cc–3; amending 21 U.S.C.A. §§ 802, 814, 823, 826, 830, 841, 842, 844, 848, 853, 952, 960, and 971, 22 U.S.C.A. §§ 2291h, 2291j, and 2291j–1, 28 U.S.C.A. § 994, 42 U.S.C.A. §§ 3793, 3797u, and 6921, and 49 U.S.C.A. § 5103; enacting provisions set out as notes under 21 U.S.C.A. §§ 802, 826, 830, 844 and 853, and 22 U.S.C.A. §§ 2291 and 2291h; and repealing a provision set out as a note under 21 U.S.C.A. § 802] may be cited as the 'Combat Methamphetamine Epidemic Act of 2005'."

2005 Amendments. Pub.L. 109–57, § 1(a), Aug. 2, 2005, 119 Stat. 592, provided that: "This Act [amending 21 U.S.C.A. § 953] may be cited as the 'Controlled Substances Export Reform Act of 2005'."

2004 Amendments. Pub.L. 108–358, § 1, Oct. 22, 2004, 118 Stat. 1661, provided that: "This Act [enacting 42 U.S.C.A. § 290bb–25f, amending 21 U.S.C.A. §§ 802 and 811, enacting provisions set out as notes under 21 U.S.C.A. § 802 and 42 U.S.C.A. § 290aa–4, and amending provisions set out as a note under 21 U.S.C.A. § 802 and listed in a table relating to sentencing guidelines set out as a note under 28 U.S.C.A. § 994] may be cited as the 'Anabolic Steroid Control Act of 2004'."

2003 Amendments. Pub.L. 108–21, Title VI, § 608(a), Apr. 30, 2003, 117 Stat. 691, provided that: "This section [amending 21 U.S.C.A. §§ 843 and 856, and amending provisions set out as a note under 28 U.S.C.A. § 994] may be cited as the 'Illicit Drug Anti-Proliferation Act of 2003'."

2000 Amendments. Pub.L. 106–310, Div. B, Title XXXV, § 3501, Oct. 17, 2000, 114 Stat. 1222, provided that: "This title [amending sections 823 and 824 of this title] may be cited as the 'Drug Addiction Treatment Act of 2000'."

Pub.L. 106–310, Div. B, Title XXXVI, § 3601, Oct. 17, 2000, 114 Stat. 1227, provided that: "This title [Title XXXVI (§§ 3601 to 3673) of Pub.L. 106–310; see Tables for complete classification] may be cited as the 'Methamphetamine Anti-Proliferation Act of 2000'."

Pub.L. 106–172, § 1, Feb. 18, 2000, 114 Stat. 7, provided that: "This Act [amending sections 802, 827, 841, and 960 of this title, and enacting provisions set out as notes under this section and section 812 of this title] may be cited as the 'Hillory J. Farias and Samantha Reid Date-Rape Drug Prohibition Act of 2000'."

1998 Amendments. Pub.L. 105–357, § 1, Nov. 10, 1998, 112 Stat. 3271, provided that: "This Act [amending section 956 of this title and enacting provisions set out as notes under section 956 of this title] may be cited as the 'Controlled Substances Trafficking Prohibition Act'."

Pub.L. 105–277, Div. C, Title VIII, § 801(a), Oct. 21, 1998, 112 Stat. 2681–693, provided that: "This title [enacting section 1713 of this title and section 2291–5 of Title 22, amending section 956 of this title, and enacting provisions set out as notes under sections 801 and 956 of this title and section 2291 of Title 22] may be cited as the 'Western Hemisphere Drug Elimination Act'."

Pub.L. 105–277, Div. C, Title VIII, § 871, Oct. 21, 1998, 112 Stat. 2681–707, provided that: "This subtitle [amending section 956 of this title and enacting provisions set out as notes under section 956 of this title] may be cited as the 'Controlled Substances Trafficking Prohibition Act'."

Pub.L. 105–277, Div. E, § 1, Oct. 21, 1998, 112 Stat. 2681–759, provided that: "This division [Division E (§§ 1 to 3) of Pub.L. 105–277, Oct. 21, 1998, 112 Stat. 2681–759, amending sections 841 and 960 of this title and section 13705 of Title 42] may be cited as the 'Methamphetamine Trafficking Penalty Enhancement Act of 1998'."

1996 Amendments. Pub.L. 104–305, § 1, Oct. 13, 1996, 110 Stat. 3807, provided that: "This Act [amending sections 841, 844, 959, and 960 of this title and enacting provisions set out as notes under section 872 of this Title and 994 of Title 28, Judiciary and Judicial Procedure] may be cited as the 'Drug-Induced Rape Prevention and Punishment Act of 1996'."

Pub.L. 104–237, § 1(a), Oct. 3, 1996, 110 Stat. 3099, provided that: "This Act [enacting section 872a of this title, amending sections 802, 814, 830, 841, 842, 843, 844, 853, 881, 959, and 960 of this title and section 1607 of Title 19, Customs Duties, and enacting provisions set out as notes under this section and sections 872, and 971 of this title, section 994 of Title 28, Judiciary and Judicial Procedure, and section 290aa–4 of Title 42, The Public Health and Welfare] may be cited as the 'Comprehensive Methamphetamine Control Act of 1996'."

1994 Amendments. Pub.L. 103–322, Title XVIII, § 180201(a), Sept. 13, 1994, 108 Stat. 2046, provided that: "This section [enacting section 849 of this title, amending section 841 of this title, and enacting provisions set out as a note under section 994 of this title] may be cited as the 'Drug Free Truck Stop Act'."

1993 Amendments. Pub.L. 103–200, § 1, Dec. 17, 1993, 107 Stat. 2333, provided that: "This Act [enacting section 814 of this title, amending sections 802, 821, 822, 823, 824, 830, 843, 880, 957, 958, 960, and 971 of this title and enacting provisions set out as a note under section 802 of this title] may be cited as the 'Domestic Chemical Diversion Control Act of 1993'."

1990 Amendments. Pub.L. 101–647, Title XIX, § 1901, Nov. 29, 1990, 104 Stat. 4851, provided that: "This Act [enacting sections 802(41), 812(c), Schedule III (e), and 333(e) of this title and section 290aa–6(b)(12) of Title 42, The Public Health and Welfare, amending section 844 of this title, repealing section 333a of this title and enacting provisions set out as notes under sections 802 and 829 of this title] may be cited as the 'Anabolic Steroids Control Act of 1990'."

1988 Amendments. Pub.L. 100–690, Title VI, § 6001, Nov. 18, 1988, 102 Stat. 4312, provided that: "This title [enacting sections 844a, 858, 881–1, 887, 972, and 1509 of this title, section 559g of Title 16, Conservation, sections 930, 1864, 3117, and 3508 of Title 18, Crimes and Criminal Procedure, section 530A of Title 28, Judiciary and Judicial Procedure, sections 5325 and 5326 of Title 31, Money and Finance, and sections 3741, 3742, 3750 to 3658, 3760 to 3764, 3766 to 3766b, 3796h, and 3796a–1 of Title 42, The Public Health and Welfare, amending sections 802, 813, 830, 841, 842, 843, 844, 845, 845a, 845b, 846, 848, 857, 872, 876, 881, 886, 960, 961, and 963 of this title, sections 1730d, 1829b, 1953, 1955, 3403, 3412, 3413, 3417, and 3420 of Title 12, Banks and Banking, section 1245 of Title 15, Commerce and Trade, sections 1 note, 559, and 559e of Title 16, sections 13, 111, 112, 115, 341, 342, 343, 842, 844, 924, 981, 1791, 1855, 1956, 1957, 2516, 3061, 3161, 3565, 3672 note, 5001, and 5032 of Title 18, section 1594 of Title 19, Customs Duties, section 524 of Title 28, sections 5312, 5318, and 5321 of Title 31, section 2003 of Title 39, Postal Service, sections 1396c, 3732, 3791, 3793, 3796, and 3796b of Title 42, The Public Health and Welfare, and section 782 of the Appendix to Title 49, Transportation, and enacting provisions set out as notes under this section and sections 802, 881, and 972 of this title, sections 5315 and 5541 of Title 5, Government Organization and Employees, sections 1 and 559b of Title 16, sections 981, 982, and 4352 of Title 18, section 994 of Title 28, section 3796 of Title 42, and section 2 of Title 43, Public Lands] may be cited as the 'Anti-Drug Abuse Amendments Act of 1988'."

Pub.L. 100–690, Title VI, § 6071, Nov. 18, 1988, 102 Stat. 4320, provided that: "This subtitle [enacting sections 887 and 1509 of this title, amending section 881 of this title, section 1594 of Title 19, Customs Duties, section 524 of Title 28, Judiciary and Judicial Procedure, and section 782 of the Appendix to Title 49, Transportation, and enacting provisions set out as a note under section 881 of this title] may be cited as the 'Asset Forfeiture Amendments Act of 1988'."

Pub.L. 100–690, Title VI, § 6051, Nov. 18, 1988, 102 Stat. 4312, provided that: "This subtitle [enacting section 972 of this title, amending sections 802, 830, 841, 842, 843, 872, 876, 881, 960, and 961 of this title, and enacting provisions set out as notes under sections 802 and 972 of this title] may be cited as the 'Chemical Diversion and Trafficking Act of 1988'."

1986 Amendments. Pub.L. 99–570, § 1, Oct. 27, 1986, 100 Stat. 3207, provided that: "This Act [see Tables for classification] may be cited as the 'Anti-Drug Abuse Act of 1986'."

Pub.L. 99–570, Title I, Subtitle A, § 1001, Oct. 27, 1986, 100 Stat. 3207–2, provided that: "This subtitle [amending sections 802, 841, 845, 848, 881 and 960 of this title, sections 3553 and 3583 of Title 18, Crimes and Criminal Procedure, and rule 35 of Title 18, Federal Rules of Criminal Procedure, and section 994 of Title 28, Judiciary and Judicial Procedure, and enacting provisions set out as notes under section 841 of this title and sections 3553 and 3583 of Title 18, and rule 35 of Title 18, Federal Rules of Criminal Procedure] may be cited as the 'Narcotics Penalties and Enforcement Act of 1986'."

Pub.L. 99–570, Title I, Subtitle B, § 1051, Oct. 27, 1986, 100 Stat. 3207–8, provided that: "This subtitle [amending section 844 of this title] may be cited as the 'Drug Possession Penalty Act of 1986'."

Pub.L. 99–570, Title I, Subtitle C, § 1101, Oct. 27, 1986, 100 Stat. 3207–10, provided that: "This subtitle [enacting section 845b of this title and amending sections 841, 845 and 845a of this title] may be cited as the 'Juvenile Drug Trafficking Act of 1986'."

Pub.L. 99–570, Title I, Subtitle E, § 1201, Oct. 27, 1986, 100 Stat. 3207–13, provided that: "This subtitle [enacting section 813 of this title, and amending section 802 of this title] may be cited as the 'Controlled Substance Analogue Enforcement Act of 1986'."

Pub.L. 99–570, Title I, Subtitle F, § 1251, Oct. 27, 1986, 100 Stat. 3207–14, provided that: "This subtitle [amending section 848 of this title] may be cited as the 'Continuing Drug Enterprises Act of 1986'."

Pub.L. 99–570, Title I, Subtitle G, § 1301, Oct. 27, 1986, 100 Stat. 3207–15, provided that: "This subtitle [amending section 960 of this title] may be cited as the 'Controlled Substances Import and Export Penalties Enhancement Act of 1986'."

Pub.L. 99–570, Title I, Subtitle O, § 1821, Oct. 27, 1986, 100 Stat. 3207–51, which had provided that: "This subtitle [enacting section 857 of this title and note thereunder] may be cited as the 'Mail Order Drug Paraphernalia Control Act'.", was repealed by Pub.L. 101–647, Title XXIV, § 2401(d), Nov. 29, 1990, 104 Stat. 4859.

Pub.L. 99–570, Title I, § 1991, Oct. 27, 1986, 100 Stat. 3207–59, provided that: "This subtitle [amending section 881 of this title] may be cited as the 'Federal Drug Law Enforcement Agent Protection Act of 1986'."

1984 Amendments. Pub.L. 98–473, Title II, § 501, Oct. 12, 1984, 98 Stat. 2068, provided that: "This chapter [chapter V, §§ 501 to 525 of Pub.L. 98–473, enacting section 845a of this title, amending sections 802, 811, 812, 822, 823, 824, 827, 841, 843, 845, 873, 881, 952, 953, 957, 958, 960, and 962 of this title, and enacting provisions set out as a note under this section] may be cited as the 'Controlled Substances Penalties Amendments Act of 1984'."

Pub.L. 98–473, Title II, § 506(a), Oct. 12, 1984, 98 Stat. 2070, provided that: "This part [Part B of Chapter V, §§ 506 to 525, amending sections 802, 811, 812, 822, 823, 824, 827, 843, 873, 881, 952, 953, 957, and 958 of this title] may be cited as the 'Dangerous Drug Diversion Control Act of 1984'."

1978 Amendments. Pub.L. 95–633, § 1, Nov. 11, 1978, 92 Stat. 3768 provided: "That this Act [enacting sections 801a, 830 and 852 of this title, amending sections 352, 802, 811, 812, 823, 827, 841 to 843, 872, 881, 952, 953 and 965 of this title and section 242a of Title 42, The Public Health and Welfare, repealing former section 830 of this title, and enacting provisions set out as notes under sections 801a, 812 and 830 of this title] may be cited as the 'Psychotropic Substances Act of 1978'."

1974 Amendments. Pub.L. 93–281, § 1, May 14, 1974, 88 Stat. 124 provided: "That this Act [amending sections 802, 823, 824, and 827 of this title] may be cited as the 'Narcotic Addict Treatment Act of 1974'."

1970 Acts. Pub.L. 91–513, in the provisions preceding § 1 immediately following the enacting clause, provided: "That this Act [enacting this chapter and sections 257a, 2688*l*–1, 2688n–1 and 3509 of Title 42, The Public Health and Welfare, amending sections 162, 198a, 321, 331, 333, 334, 360, 372, and 381 of this title, sections 1114, 1952, and 4251 of Title 18, Crimes and Criminal Procedure, section 1581 of Title 19, Customs Duties, sections 4901, 4905, 6808, 7012, 7103, 7326, 7607, 7609, 7641, 7651, and 7655 of Title 26, Internal Revenue Code, section 2901 of Title 28, Judiciary and Judicial Procedure, sections 529d, 529e, and 529f of Title 31, Money and Finance, section 304m of Title 40, Public Buildings, Property, and Works, sections 201, 225a, 242, 242a, 246, 257, 258, 259, 260, 261, 261a, 2688k, 2688*l*, 2688m, 2688n, 2688*o*, 2688r, and 3411 of Title 42, The Public Health and Welfare, section 239a of Title 46, Shipping, and section 787 of Title 49, Transportation, repealing sections 171, 172, 173, 173a, 174, 176, 176a, 176b, 177 to 184, 184a, 185, 188 to 188n, 191, 192, 193, 197, 198, 199, 360a, and 501 to 517 of this title, sections 1401 to 1407, and 3616 of Title 18, Crimes and Criminal Procedure, sections 4701 to 4707, 4711 to 4716, 4721 to 4726, 4731 to 4736, 4741 to 4746, 4751 to 4757, 4761, 4762, 4771 to 4776, 7237, 7238, and 7491 of Title 26, Internal Revenue Code, sections 529a and 529g of Title 31, Money and Finance, and section 1421m of Title 48, Territories and Insular Possessions, and enacting provisions set out as notes under this section and sections 171, 321, 822, 951, and 957 of this title] may be cited as the 'Comprehensive Drug Abuse Prevention and Control Act of 1970'."

Section 100 of Pub.L. 91–513 provided that: "This title [enacting this subchapter, amending sections 321, 331, 333, 334, 360, 372, and 381 of this title, sections 1114 and 1952 of Title 18, Crimes and Criminal Procedure, and section 242a of Title 42, The Public Health and Welfare, repealing section 360a of this title, and enacting provisions set out as notes under this section and sections 321 and 822 of this title] may be cited as the 'Controlled Substances Act'."

Anti-drug Message on Internet Sites

Pub.L. 106–391, Title III, § 320, Oct. 30, 2000, 114 Stat. 1597, provided that: "Not later than 90 days after the date of the enactment of this Act [Oct. 30, 2000], the Administrator, in consultation with the Director of the Office of National

Drug Control Policy, shall place anti-drug messages on Internet sites controlled by the National Aeronautics and Space Administration."

Antidrug Messages on Federal Government Internet Websites

Pub.L. 106–310, Div. B, Title XXXVI, § 3671, Oct. 17, 2000, 114 Stat. 1245, provided that: "Not later than 90 days after the date of the enactment of this Act [Oct. 17, 2000], the head of each department, agency, and establishment of the Federal Government shall, in consultation with the Director of the Office of National Drug Control Policy, place antidrug messages on appropriate Internet websites controlled by such department, agency, or establishment which messages shall, where appropriate, contain an electronic hyperlink to the Internet website, if any, of the Office."

Annual Report Regarding Date-Rape Drugs; National Awareness Campaign

Pub.L. 106–172, § 7, Feb. 18, 2000, 114 Stat. 11, provided that:

"**(a) Annual report.**—The Secretary of Health and Human Services (in this section referred to as the 'Secretary') shall periodically submit to Congress reports each of which provides an estimate of the number of incidents of the abuse of date-rape drugs (as defined in subsection (c)) that occurred during the most recent 1-year period for which data are available. The first such report shall be submitted not later than January 15, 2000, and subsequent reports shall be submitted annually thereafter.

"**(b) National awareness campaign.**—

"**(1) Development of plan; recommendations of advisory committee.**—

"**(A) In general.**—The Secretary, in consultation with the Attorney General, shall develop a plan for carrying out a national campaign to educate individuals described in subparagraph (B) on the following:

"(i) The dangers of date-rape drugs.

"(ii) The applicability of the Controlled Substances Act [this subchapter] to such drugs, including penalties under such Act.

"(iii) Recognizing the symptoms that indicate an individual may be a victim of such drugs, including symptoms with respect to sexual assault.

"(iv) Appropriately responding when an individual has such symptoms.

"**(B) Intended population.**—The individuals referred to in subparagraph (A) are young adults, youths, law enforcement personnel, educators, school nurses, counselors of rape victims, and emergency room personnel in hospitals.

"**(C) Advisory committee.**—Not later than 180 days after the date of the enactment of this Act [Feb. 18, 2000], the Secretary shall establish an advisory committee to make recommendations to the Secretary regarding the plan under subparagraph (A). The committee shall be composed of individuals who collectively possess expertise on the effects of date-rape drugs and on detecting and controlling the drugs.

"**(2) Implementation of plan.**—Not later than 180 days after the date on which the advisory committee under paragraph (1) is established, the Secretary, in consultation with the Attorney General, shall commence carrying out the national campaign under such paragraph in accordance with the plan developed under such paragraph. The campaign may be carried out directly by the Secretary and through grants and contracts.

"**(3) Evaluation by General Accounting Office [now Government Accountability Office].**—Not later than 2 years after the date on which the national campaign under paragraph (1) is commenced, the Comptroller General of the United States shall submit to Congress an evaluation of the effects with respect to date-rape drugs of the national campaign.

"**(c) Definition.**—For purposes of this section, the term 'date-rape drugs' means gamma hydroxybutyric acid and its salts, isomers, and salts of isomers and such other drugs or substances as the Secretary, after consultation with the Attorney General, determines to be appropriate."

Development of Model Protocols, Training Materials, Forensic Field Tests, and Coordination Mechanism for Investigations and Prosecutions Relating to Gamma Hydroxybutyric Acid, Other Controlled Substances, and Designer Drugs

Pub.L. 106–172, § 6, Feb. 18, 2000, 114 Stat. 11, provided that:

"**(a) In general.**—The Attorney General, in consultation with the Administrator of the Drug Enforcement Administration and the Director of the Federal Bureau of Investigation, shall—

"(1) Develop—

"(A) model protocols for the collection of toxicology specimens and the taking of victim statements in connection with investigations into and prosecutions related to possible violations of the Controlled Substances Act [this subchapter] or other Federal or State laws that result in or contribute to rape, other crimes of violence, or other crimes involving abuse of gamma hydroxybutyric acid, other controlled substances, or so-called 'designer drugs'; and

"(B) model training materials for law enforcement personnel involved in such investigations; and

"(2) make such protocols and training materials available to Federal, State, and local personnel responsible for such investigations.

"**(b) Grant.**—

"**(1) In general.**—The Attorney General shall make a grant, in such amount and to such public or private person or entity as the Attorney General considers appropriate, for the development of forensic field tests to assist law enforcement officials in detecting the presence of gamma hydroxybutyric acid and related substances.

"**(2) Authorization of appropriations.**—There are authorized to be appropriated such sums as may be necessary to carry out this subsection.

"**(c) Report.**—Not later than 180 days after the date of the enactment of this Act [Feb. 18, 2000], the Attorney General shall submit to the Committees on the Judiciary of the Senate and House of Representatives a report on current mechanisms for coordinating Federal, State, and local investigations into and prosecutions related to possible violations of the Controlled Substances Act [this subchapter] or other Federal or State laws that result in or contribute to rape, other crimes of violence, or other crimes involving the abuse of gamma hydroxybutyric acid, other controlled substances, or so-called 'designer drugs'. The report shall also include recommendations for the improvement of such mechanisms."

Congressional Findings Regarding Methamphetamine Manufacture and Abuse

Pub.L. 104–237, § 2, Oct. 3, 1996, 110 Stat. 3100, provided that: "The Congress finds the following:

"(1) Methamphetamine is a very dangerous and harmful drug. It is highly addictive and is associated with permanent brain damage in long-term users.

"(2) The abuse of methamphetamine has increased dramatically since 1990. This increased use has led to devastating effects on individuals and the community, including—

"(A) a dramatic increase in deaths associated with methamphetamine ingestion;

"(B) an increase in the number of violent crimes associated with methamphetamine ingestion; and

"(C) an increase in criminal activity associated with the illegal importation of methamphetamine and precursor compounds to support the growing appetite for this drug in the United States.

"(3) Illegal methamphetamine manufacture and abuse presents an imminent public health threat that warrants aggressive law enforcement action, increased research on methamphetamine and other substance abuse, increased coordinated efforts to prevent methamphetamine abuse, and increased monitoring of the public health threat methamphetamine presents to the communities of the United States."

Support for International Efforts to Control Methamphetamine and Precursor Chemicals

Pub.L. 104–237, Title I, § 101, Oct. 3, 1996, 110 Stat. 3100, provided that: "The Attorney General, in consultation with the Secretary of State, shall coordinate international drug enforcement efforts to decrease the movement of methamphetamine and methamphetamine precursors into the United States."

Interagency Methamphetamine Task Force

Pub.L. 104–237, Title V, § 501, Oct. 3, 1996, 110 Stat. 3111, provided that:

"(a) **Establishment.**—There is established a 'Methamphetamine Interagency Task Force' (referred to as the 'interagency task force') which shall consist of the following members:

"(1) The Attorney General, or a designee, who shall serve as chair.

"(2) 2 representatives selected by the Attorney General.

"(3) The Secretary of Education or a designee.

"(4) The Secretary of Health and Human Services or a designee.

"(5) 2 representatives of State and local law enforcement and regulatory agencies, to be selected by the Attorney General.

"(6) 2 representatives selected by the Secretary of Health and Human Services.

"(7) 5 nongovernmental experts in drug abuse prevention and treatment to be selected by the Attorney General.

"(b) **Responsibilities.**—The interagency task force shall be responsible for designing, implementing, and evaluating the education and prevention and treatment practices and strategies of the Federal Government with respect to methamphetamine and other synthetic stimulants.

"(c) **Meetings.**—The interagency task force shall meet at least once every 6 months.

"(d) **Funding.**—The administrative expenses of the interagency task force shall be paid out of existing Department of Justice appropriations.

"(e) **FACA.**—The Federal Advisory Committee Act (5 U.S.C. App. 2) shall apply to the interagency task force.

"(f) **Termination.**—The interagency task force shall terminate 4 years after the date of enactment of this Act [Oct. 3, 1996]."

Suspicious Orders Task Force

Pub.L. 104–237, Title V, § 504, Oct. 3, 1996, 110 Stat. 3112, provided that:

"(a) **In general.**—The Attorney General shall establish a 'Suspicious Orders Task Force' (the 'Task Force') which shall consist of—

"(1) appropriate personnel from the Drug Enforcement Administration (the 'DEA') and other Federal, State, and local law enforcement and regulatory agencies with the experience in investigating and prosecuting illegal transactions of listed chemicals and supplies; and

"(2) representatives from the chemical and pharmaceutical industry.

"(b) **Responsibilities.**—The Task Force shall be responsible for developing proposals to define suspicious orders of listed chemicals, and particularly to develop quantifiable parameters which can be used by registrants in determining if an order is a suspicious order which must be reported to DEA. The quantifiable parameters to be addressed will include frequency of orders, deviations from prior orders, and size of orders. The Task Force shall also recommend provisions as to what types of payment practices or unusual business practices shall constitute prima facie suspicious orders. In evaluating the proposals, the Task Force shall consider effectiveness, cost and feasibility for industry and government, and other relevant factors.

"(c) **Meetings.**—The Task Force shall meet at least two times per year and at such other times as may be determined necessary by the Task Force.

"(d) **Report.**—The Task Force shall present a report to the Attorney General on its proposals with regard to suspicious orders and the electronic reporting of suspicious orders within one year of the date of enactment of this Act [Oct. 3, 1996]. Copies of the report shall be forwarded to the Committees of the Senate and House of Representatives having jurisdiction over the regulation of listed chemical and controlled substances.

"(e) **Funding.**—The administrative expenses of the Task Force shall be paid out of existing Department of Justice funds or appropriations.

"(f) **FACA.**—The Federal Advisory Committee Act (5 U.S.C.App. 2) shall apply to the Task Force.

"(g) **Termination.**—The Task Force shall terminate upon presentation of its report to the Attorney General, or two years after the date of enactment of this Act [Oct. 3, 1996], whichever is sooner."

Joint Federal Task Force on Illegal Drug Laboratories

Pub.L. 100–690, Title II, § 2405, Nov. 18, 1988, 102 Stat. 4231, provided that:

"**(a) Establishment of Task Force.**—There is established the Joint Federal Task Force on Illegal Drug Laboratories (hereafter in this section referred to as the 'Task Force').

"**(b) Appointment and membership of Task Force.**—The members of the Task Force shall be appointed by the Administrators of the Environmental Protection Agency and the Drug Enforcement Administration (hereafter in this section referred to as the 'Administrators'). The Task Force shall consist of at least 6 and not more than 20 members. Each Administrator shall appoint one-half of the members as follows: (1) the Administrator of the Environmental Protection Agency shall appoint members from among Emergency Response Technicians and other appropriate employees of the Agency; and (2) the Administrator of the Drug Enforcement Administration [sic] shall appoint members from among Special Agents assigned to field divisions and other appropriate employees of the Administration.

"**(c) Duties of Task Force.**—The Task Force shall formulate, establish, and implement a program for the cleanup and disposal of hazardous waste produced by illegal drug laboratories. In formulating such program, the Task Force shall consider the following factors:

"(1) The volume of hazardous waste produced by illegal drug laboratories.

"(2) The cost of cleaning up and disposing of hazardous waste produced by illegal drug laboratories.

"(3) The effectiveness of the various methods of cleaning up and disposing of hazardous waste produced by illegal drug laboratories.

"(4) The coordination of the efforts of the Environmental Protection Agency and the Drug Enforcement Administration in cleaning up and disposing of hazardous waste produced by illegal drug laboratories.

"(5) The dissemination of information to law enforcement agencies that have responsibility for enforcement of drug laws.

"**(d) Guidelines.**—The Task Force shall recommend to the Administrators guidelines for cleanup of illegal drug laboratories to protect the public health and environment. Not later than 180 days after the date of the enactment of this subtitle [Nov. 18, 1988], the Administrators shall formulate and publish such guidelines.

"**(e) Demonstration projects.**—

"(1) The Attorney General shall make grants to, and enter into contracts with, State and local governments for demonstration projects to clean up and safely dispose of substances associated with illegal drug laboratories which may present a danger to public health or the environment.

"(2) The Attorney General may not under this subsection make a grant or enter into a contract unless the applicant for such assistance agrees to comply with the guidelines issued pursuant to subsection (d).

"(3) The Attorney General shall, through grant or contract, provide for independent evaluations of the activities carried out pursuant to this subsection and shall recommend appropriate legislation to the Congress.

"**(f) Funding.**—Of the amounts made available to carry out the Controlled Substances Act [21 U.S.C.A. § 801 et seq.] for fiscal year 1989, not less than $5,000,000 shall be made available to carry out subsections (d) and (e).

"**(g) Reports.**—After consultation with the Task Force, the Administrators shall—

"(1) transmit to the President and to each House of Congress not later the 270 days after the date of the enactment of this subtitle [Nov. 18, 1988] a report describing the program established by the Task Force under subsection (c) (including an analysis of the factors specified in paragraphs (1) through (5) of that subsection);.

"(2) periodically transmit to the President and to each House of Congress reports describing the implementation of the program established by the Task Force under subsection (c) (including an analysis of the factors specified in paragraphs (1) through (5) of that subsection) and the progress made in the cleanup and disposal of hazardous waste produced by illegal drug laboratories; and

"(3) transmit to each House of Congress a report describing the findings made as a result of the evaluations referred to in subsection (e)(3)."

[For termination, effective May 15, 2000, of reporting provisions of Pub.L. 100–690, Title II, § 2405, set out above, see Pub.L. 104–66, § 3003, as amended, set out as a note under 31 U.S.C.A. § 1113, and the 10th item on page 147 of House Document No. 103–7.]

Great Lakes Drug Interdiction

Pub. L. 100–690, Title VII, § 7404, Nov. 18, 1988, 102 Stat. 4484, provided that:

"**(a) Interagency agreement.**—The Secretary of Transportation and the Secretary of the Treasury shall enter into an agreement for the purpose of increasing the effectiveness of maritime drug interdiction activities of the Coast Guard and the Customs Service in the Great Lakes area.

"**(b) Negotiations with Canada on drug enforcement cooperation.**—The Secretary of State is encouraged to enter into negotiations with appropriate officials of the Government of Canada for the purpose of establishing an agreement between the United States and Canada which provides for increased cooperation and sharing of information between United States and Canadian law enforcement officials with respect to law enforcement efforts conducted on the Great Lakes between the United States and Canada."

[For transfer of authorities, functions, personnel, and assets of the Coast Guard, including the authorities and functions of the Secretary of Transportation relating thereto, to the Department of Homeland Security, and for treatment of related references, see 6 U.S.C.A. §§ 468(b), 551(d), 552(d) and 557, and the Department of Homeland Security Reorganization Plan of November 25, 2002, as modified, set out as a note under 6 U.S.C.A. § 542.]

[For transfer of functions, personnel, assets, and liabilities of the United States Customs Service of the Department of the Treasury, including functions of the Secretary of the Treasury relating thereto, to the Secretary of Homeland Security, and for treatment of related references, see 6 U.S.C.A. §§ 203(1), 551(d), 552(d) and 557, and the Department of Homeland Security Reorganization Plan of November 25, 2002, as modified, set out as a note under 6 U.S.C.A. § 542.]

GAO Study of Capabilities of United States to Control Drug Smuggling into United States

Pub.L. 100–180, Div. A, Title XII, § 1241, Dec. 4, 1987, 101 Stat. 1162, provided that:

"**(a) Study requirement.**—The Comptroller General of the United States shall conduct a comprehensive study regarding smuggling of illegal drugs into the United States and the current capabilities of the United States to deter such smuggling. In carrying out such study, the Comptroller General shall—

"(1) assess the national security implications of the smuggling of illegal drugs into the United States;

"(2) assess the magnitude, nature, and operational impact that current resource limitations have on the drug smuggling interdiction efforts of Federal law enforcement agencies and the capability of the Department of Defense to respond to requests for assistance from those law enforcement agencies;

"(3) assess the effect on military readiness, the costs that would be incurred, the operational effects on military and civilian agencies, the potential for improving drug interdiction operations, and the methods for implementing increased drug law enforcement assistance by the Department of Defense under section 825 of H.R. 1748 as passed the House of Representatives on May 20, 1987, as if such section were enacted into law and were to become effective on January 1, 1988;

"(4) assess results of a cooperative drug enforcement operation between the United States Customs Service and National Guard units from the States of Arizona, Utah, Missouri, and Wisconsin conducted along the United States-Mexico border beginning on August 29, 1987, and include in the assessment information relating to the cost of conducting the operation, the personnel and equipment used in such operation, the command and control relationships in such operation, and the legal issues involved in such operation;

"(5) determine whether giving the Armed Forces a more direct, active role in drug interdiction activities would enhance the morale and readiness of the Armed Forces;

"(6) determine what assets are currently available to and under consideration for the Department of Defense, the Department of Transportation, the Department of Justice, and the Department of the Treasury for the detection of airborne drug smugglers;

"(7) assess the current plan of the Customs Service for the coordinated use of such assets;

"(8) determine the cost effectiveness and the capability of the Customs Service to use effectively the information generated by the systems employed by or planned for the Department of Defense, the Coast Guard, and the Customs Service, respectively, to detect airborne drug smugglers;

"(9) determine the availability of current and anticipated tracking, pursuit, and apprehension resources to use the capabilities of such systems; and

"(10) at a minimum, assess the detection capabilities of the Over-the-Horizon Backscatter radar (OTH–B), ROTHR, aerostats, airships, and the E–3A, E–2C, P–3, and P–3 Airborne Early Warning aircraft (including any variant of the P–3 Airborne Early Warning aircraft).

"**(b) Reports.**—(1) Not later than April 30, 1988, the Comptroller General shall, as provided in paragraph (3), submit a report on the results of the study required by subsection (a) with respect to the elements of the study specified in paragraphs (1) through (5) of that subsection.

"(2) As soon as practicable after the report under paragraph (1) is submitted, and not later than March 31, 1989, the Comptroller General shall, as provided in paragraph (3), submit a report on the results of the study required by subsection (a) with respect to the elements of the study specified in paragraphs (6) through (10) of that subsection.

"(3) The reports under paragraphs (1) and (2) shall be submitted to—

"(A) the Committees on Armed Services, the Judiciary, Foreign Relations, and Appropriations of the Senate;

"(B) the Committees on Armed Services, the Judiciary, Foreign Affairs, and Appropriations of the House of Representatives;

"(C) the members of the Senate Caucus on International Narcotics Control; and

"(D) the Select Committee on Narcotics Abuse and Control of the House of Representatives.

"(4) The reports under this subsection shall be submitted in both classified and unclassified forms and shall include such comments and recommendations as the Comptroller General considers appropriate."

[Any reference in any provision of law enacted before Jan. 4, 1995, to the Committee on Armed Services of the House of Representatives treated as referring to the Committee on National Security of the House of Representatives, see section 1(a)(1) of Pub.L. 104–14, set out as a note preceding section 21 of Title 2, The Congress.]

Compliance With Budget Act

Pub.L. 99–570, § 3, Oct. 27, 1986, 100 Stat. 3207–1, provided that: "Notwithstanding any other provision of this Act [see Tables for classification], any spending authority and any credit authority provided under this Act shall be effective for any fiscal year only to such extent or in such amounts as are provided in appropriation Acts. For purposes of this Act, the term 'spending authority' has the meaning provided in section 401(c)(2) of the Congressional Budget Act of 1974 [2 U.S.C.A. § 651(c)(2)] and the term 'credit authority' has the meaning provided in section 3(10) of the Congresional [sic] Budget Act of 1974 [2 U.S.C.A. § 622(10)]."

Drug Interdiction

Pub.L. 99–570, Title III, §§ 3001 to 3003, 3301, Oct. 27, 1986, 100 Stat. 3207–73, 3207–74, 3207–98, as amended Pub.L. 104–66, Title I, § 1091(a), Dec. 21, 1995, 109 Stat. 722, provided that:

"Sec. 3001. Short title

"This title [enacting section 379 of Title 10, Armed Forces, sections 1590, 1628, 1629, and 2081 of Title 19, Customs Duties, and section 312a of Title 47, Telegraphs, Telephones, and Radiotelegraphs, amending section 959 of this title, sections 374 and 911 of Title 10, sections 507, 1401, 1433, 1436, 1454, 1459, 1497, 1509, 1584, 1585, 1586, 1594, 1595, 1595a, 1613, 1613b, 1619, and 1622 of Title 19, section 5316 of Title 31, Money and Finance, sections 1901, 1902, 1903, 1904, and 12109 of Title 46, Shipping, and sections 1401, 1472, 1474, and 1509 of Title 49, Transportation, repealing section 1460 of Title 19, enacting provisions set out as notes under this section, sections 371, 374, 525, and 9441 of Title 10, sections

1613b and 1654 of Title 19, section 403 of Title 23, Highways, section 1901 of Title 46, and sections 1509 and 11344 of Title 49, and repealing a provision set out as a note under section 89 of Title 14, Coast Guard] may be cited as the 'National Drug Interdiction Improvement Act of 1986'.

"Sec. 3002. Findings

"The Congress hereby finds that—

"(1) a balanced, coordinated, multifaceted strategy for combating the growing drug abuse and drug trafficking problem in the United States is essential in order to stop the flow and abuse of drugs within our borders;

"(2) a balanced, coordinated, multifaceted strategy for combating the narcotics drug abuse and trafficking in the United States should include—

"(A) increased investigations of large networks of drug smuggler organizations;

"(B) source country drug eradication;

"(C) increased emphasis on stopping narcotics traffickers in countries through which drugs are transshipped;

"(D) increased emphasis on drug education programs in the schools and workplace;

"(E) increased Federal Government assistance to State and local agencies, civic groups, school systems, and officials in their efforts to combat the drug abuse and trafficking problem at the local level; and

"(F) increased emphasis on the interdiction of drugs and drug smugglers at the borders of the United States, in the air, at sea, and on the land;

"(3) funds to support the interdiction of narcotics smugglers who threaten the transport of drugs through the air, on the sea, and across the land borders of the United States should be emphasized in the Federal Government budget process to the same extent as the other elements of a comprehensive antidrug effort are emphasized;

"(4) the Department of Defense and the use of its resources should be an integral part of a comprehensive, natonal [sic] drug interdiction program;

"(5) the Federal Government civilian agencies engaged in drug interdiction, particularly the United States Customs Service and the Coast Guard, currently lack the aircraft, ships, radar, command, control, communications, and intelligence (C3I) system, and manpower resources necessary to mount a comprehensive attack on the narcotics traffickers who threaten the United States;

"(6) the civilian drug interdiction agencies of the United States are currently interdicting only a small percentage of the illegal, drug smuggler penetrations in the United States every year;

"(7) the budgets for our civilian drug interdiction agencies, primarily the United States Customs Service and the Coast Guard, have not kept pace with those of the traditional investigative law enforcement agencies of the Department of Justice; and

"(8) since the amendment of the Posse Comitatus Act (18 U.S.C. 1385) in 1981, the Department of Defense has assisted in the effort to interdict drugs, but they can do more.

"Sec. 3003. Purposes

"It is the purpose of this title—

"(1) to increase the level of funding and resources available to civilian drug interdiction agencies of the Federal Government;

"(2) to increase the level of support from the Department of Defense as consistent with the Posse Comitatus Act [section 1385 of Title 18, Crimes and Criminal Procedure], for interdiction of the narcotics traffickers before such traffickers penetrate the borders of the United States; and

"(3) to improve other drug interdiction programs of the Federal Government.

"Sec. 3301. Establishment of United States–Bahamas Drug Interdiction Task Force

"(a) Authorization of appropriations.—

"(1) Establishment of United States–Bahamas Drug Interdiction Task Force.—(A) There is authorized to be established a United States–Bahamas Drug Interdiction Task Force to be operated jointly by the United States Government and the government of the Bahamas.

"(B) The Secretary of State, the Commandant of the Coast Guard, the Commissioner of Customs, the Attorney General, and the head of the National Narcotics Border Interdiction System (NNBIS), shall upon enactment of this Act [Oct. 27, 1986], immediately commence negotiations with the Government of the Bahamas to enter into a detailed agreement for the establishment and operation of a new drug interdiction task force, including plans for (i) the joint operation and maintenance of any drug interdiction assets authorized for the task force in this section and section 3141 [not classified to the Code], and (ii) any training and personnel enhancements authorized in this section and section 3141 [not classified to the Code].

"(C) [Repealed. Pub.L. 104–66, Title I, § 1091(a), Dec. 21, 1995, 109 Stat. 722]

"(2) Amounts authorized.—There are authorized to be appropriated, in addition to any other amounts authorized to be appropriated in this title, $10,000,000 for the following:

"(A) $9,000,000 for 3 drug interdiction pursuit helicopters for use primarily for operations of the United States–Bahamas Drug Interdiction Task Force established under this section; and

"(B) $1,000,000 to enhance communications capabilities for the operation of a United States–Bahamas Drug Interdiction Task Force established under this section.

"(3) Coast Guard–Bahamas drug interdiction docking facility.—(A) There is authorized to be appropriated for acquisition, construction, and improvements for the Coast Guard for fiscal year 1987, $5,000,000, to be used for initial design engineering, and other activities for construction of a drug interdiction docking facility in the Bahamas to facilitate Coast Guard and Bahamian drug interdiction operations in and through the Bahama Islands. Of the amounts authorized to be appropriated in this subsection, such sums as may be necessary shall be available for necessary communication and air support.

"(B) The Commandant of the Coast Guard shall use such amounts appropriated pursuant to the authorization in this paragraph as may be necessary to establish a repair, maintenance, and boat lift facility to provide repair and maintenance services for both Coast Guard and Bahamian marine drug interdiction equipment, vessels, and related assets.

"(b) **Concurrence by Secretary of State.**—Programs authorized by this section may be carried out only with the concurrence of the Secretary of State."

[For termination of reporting provisions pertaining to the progress of the United States–Bahamas Interdiction Task Force, effective May 15, 2000, see Pub.L. 104–66, § 3003, as amended, set out as a note under 31 U.S.C.A. § 1113, and the 9th item on page 118 of House Document No. 103–7.]

Information on Drug Abuse at the Workplace

Pub.L. 99–570, Title IV, § 4303, Oct. 27, 1986, 100 Stat. 3207–154, provided that:

"(a) The Secretary of Labor shall collect such information as is available on the incidence of drug abuse in the workplace and efforts to assist workers, including counseling, rehabilitation and employee assistance programs. The Secretary shall conduct such additional research as is necessary to assess the impact and extent of drug abuse and remediation efforts. The Secretary shall submit the findings of such collection and research to the House Committee on Education and Labor and the Senate Committee on Labor and Human Services no later that two years from the date of enactment of this Act [Oct. 27, 1986].

"(b) There is authorized to be appropriated the aggregate sum of $3,000,000 for fiscal years 1987 and 1988, to remain available until expended, to enable the Secretary of Labor to carry out the purposes of this section."

[Any reference in any provision of law enacted before Jan. 4, 1995, to the Committee on Education and Labor of the House of Representatives treated as referring to the Committee on Economic and Educational Opportunities of the House of Representatives, see section 1(a)(3) of Pub.L. 104–14, set out as a note preceding section 21 of Title 2, The Congress.]

Coordination of Interagency Drug Abuse Prevention Activities

Pub.L. 99–570, Title IV, § 4304, Oct. 27, 1986, 100 Stat. 3207–154, provided that:

"(a) The Secretary of Education, the Secretary of Health and Human Services, and the Secretary of Labor shall each designate an officer or employee of the Departments of Education, Health and Human Services, and Labor, respectively, to coordinate interagency drug abuse prevention activities to prevent duplication of effort.

"(b) Within one year after enactment of this Act [Oct. 27, 1986], a report shall be jointly submitted to the Congress by such Secretaries concerning the extent to which States and localities have been able to implement non-duplicative drug abuse prevention activities."

Substance Abuse Insurance Coverage Study

Pub.L. 99–570, Title VI, § 6005, Oct. 27, 1986, 100 Stat. 3207–160, as amended Pub. L. 100–690, Title II, § 2058(c), Nov.18, 1988, 102 Stat. 4213, provided:

"(a) **Study.**—The Secretary of Health and Human Services shall contract with the Institute of Medicine of the National Academy of Sciences to conduct a study of (1) the extent to which the cost of drug abuse treatment is covered by private insurance, public programs, and other sources of payment, and (2) the adequacy of such coverage for the rehabilitation of drug abusers.

"(b) **Report.**—Not later than 18 months after the execution of the contract referred to in subsec. (a), the Secretary of Health and Human Services shall transmit to the Congress a report of the results of the study conducted under subsection (a). The report shall include recommendations of means to meet the needs identified in such study."

Health Insurance Coverage for Drug and Alcohol Treatment

Pub.L. 99–570, Title VI, § 6006, Oct. 27, 1986, 100 Stat. 3207–160, provided:

"(a) **Findings.**—The Congress finds that—

"(1) drug and alcohol abuse are problems of grave concern and consequence in American society;

"(2) over 500,000 individuals are known heroin addicts; 5 million individuals use cocaine, and at least 7 million individuals regularly use prescription drugs, mostly addictive ones, without medical supervision;

"(3) 10 million adults and 3 million children and adolescents abuse alcohol, and an additional 30 to 40 million people are adversely affected because of close family ties to alcoholics;

"(4) the total cost of drug abuse to the Nation in 1983 was over $60,000,000,000; and

"(5) the vast majority of health benefits plans provide only limited coverage for treatment of drug and alcohol addiction, which is a fact that can discourage the abuser from seeking treatment or, if the abuser does seek treatment, can cause the abuser to face significant out of pocket expenses for the treatment.

"(b) **Sense of Congress.**—It is the sense of Congress that—

"(1) all employers providing health insurance policies should ensure that the policies provide adequate coverage for treatment of drug and alcohol addiction in recognition that the health consequences and costs for individuals and society can be as formidable as those resulting from other diseases and illnesses for which insurance coverage is much more adequate; and

"(2) State insurance commissioners should encourage employers providing health benefits plans to ensure that the policies provide more adequate coverage for treatment of drug and alcohol addiction."

Continuation of Orders, Rules, and Regulations

Section 705 of Pub.L. 91–513 provided that: "Any orders, rules, and regulations which have been promulgated under any law affected by this title [this subchapter] and which are in effect on the day preceding enactment of this title [Oct. 27, 1970] shall continue in effect until modified, superseded, or repealed."

Commission on Marihuana and Drug Abuse

Section 601 of Pub.L. 91–513, as amended Pub.L. 92–13, May 14, 1971, 85 Stat. 37, provided that:

"(a) **[Establishment; composition]** There is established a commission to be known as the Commission on Marihuana and Drug Abuse (hereafter in this section referred to as the 'Commission'). The Commission shall be composed of—

"(1) two Members of the Senate appointed by the President of the Senate;

"(2) two Members of the House of Representatives appointed by the Speaker of the House of Representatives; and

"(3) nine members appointed by the President of the United States.

At no time shall more than one of the members appointed under paragraph (1), or more than one of the members appointed under paragraph (2), or more than five of the members appointed under paragraph (3) be members of the same political party.

"(b) [Chairman; Vice Chairman; compensation of members; meetings] (1) The President shall designate one of the members of the Commission as Chairman, and one as VICE CHAIRMAN. Seven members of the Commission shall constitute a quorum, but a lesser number may conduct hearings.

"(2) Members of the Commission who are Members of Congress or full-time officers or employees of the United States shall serve without additional compensation but shall be reimbursed for travel, subsistence, and other necessary expenses incurred in the performance of the duties vested in the Commission. Members of the Commission from private life shall receive $100 per diem while engaged in the actual performance of the duties vested in the Commission, plus reimbursement for travel, subsistence, and other necessary expenses incurred in the performance of such duties.

"(3) The Commission shall meet at the call of the Chairman or at the call of a majority of the members thereof.

"(c) [Personnel; experts; information from departments and agencies] (1) The Commission shall have the power to appoint and fix the compensation of such personnel as it deems advisable, without regard to the provisions of title 5, United States Code, governing appointments in the competitive service, and the provisions of chapter 51 and subchapter III of chapter 53 of such title, relating to classification and General Schedule pay rates.

"(2) The Commission may procure, in accordance with the provisions of section 3109 of title 5, United States Code,the temporary or intermittent services of experts or consultants. Persons so employed shall receive compensation at a rate to be fixed by the Commission, but not in excess of $75 per diem, including traveltime. While away from his home or regular place of business in the performance of services for the Commission, any such person may be allowed travel expenses, including per diem in lieu of subsistence, as authorized by section 5703(b) of title 5, United States Code, for persons in the Government service employed intermittently.

"(3) The Commission may secure directly from any department or agency of the United States information necessary to enable it to carry out its duties under this section. Upon request of the Chairman of the Commission, such department or agency shall furnish such information to the Commission.

"(d) [Marihuana study; report to the President and the Congress] (1) The Commission shall conduct a study of marihuana including, but not limited to, the following areas:

"(A) the extent of use of marihuana in the United States to include its various sources, the number of users, number of arrests, number of convictions, amount of marihuana seized, type of user, nature of use;

"(B) an evaluation of the efficacy of existing marihuana laws;

"(C) a study of the pharmacology of marihuana and its immediate and long-term effects, both physiological and psychological;

"(D) the relationship of marihuana use to aggressive behavior and crime;

"(E) the relationship between marihuana and the use of other drugs; and

"(F) the international control of marihuana.

"(2) Within one year after the date on which funds first become available to carry out this section, the Commission shall submit to the President and the Congress a comprehensive report on its study and investigation under this subsection which shall include its recommendations and such proposals for legislation and administrative action as may be necessary to carry out its recommendations.

"(e) [Study and investigation of causes of drug abuse; report to the President and the Congress; termination of Commission] The Commission shall conduct a comprehensive study and investigation of the causes of drug abuse and their relative significance. The Commission shall submit to the President and the Congress such interim reports as it deems advisable and shall within two years after the date on which funds first become available to carry out this section submit to the President and the Congress a final report which shall contain a detailed statement of its findings and conclusions and also such recommendations for legislation and administrative actions as it deems appropriate. The Commission shall cease to exist sixty days after the final report is submitted under this subsection.

"(f) [Limitation on expenditures] Total expenditures of the Commission shall not exceed $4,000,000."

EXECUTIVE ORDERS

EXECUTIVE ORDER NO. 11599

Ex. Ord. No. 11599, June 17, 1971, 36 F.R. 11793, formerly set out as a note under this section, which established the Special Action Office for Drug Abuse Prevention, was superseded by former section 1111 et seq. of this title and is now covered by section 1111 et seq. of this title, which established the Office of Drug Abuse Policy.

EXECUTIVE ORDER NO. 11641

Ex. Ord. No. 11641, Jan. 28, 1972, 37 F.R. 2421, formerly set out as a note under this section, which established the Office for Drug Abuse Law Enforcement, was revoked by Ex. Ord. No. 11727, July 6, 1973, 38 F.R. 18357, set out below.

EXECUTIVE ORDER NO. 11676

Ex. Ord. No. 11676, July 27, 1972, 37 F.R. 15125, formerly set out as a note under this section, which established the Office of National Narcotics Intelligence, was revoked by Ex. Ord. No. 11727, July 6, 1973, 38 F.R. 18357 set out below.

EXECUTIVE ORDER NO. 11727
July 6, 1973, 38 F.R. 18357

DRUG LAW ENFORCEMENT

Reorganization Plan No. 2 of 1973 [set out in the Appendix to Title 5, Government Organization and Employees], which becomes effective on July 1, 1973, among other things establishes a Drug Enforcement Administration in the Department of Justice. In my message to the Congress transmitting that plan, I stated that all functions of the Office for Drug Abuse Law Enforcement (established pursuant to Executive Order No. 11641 of January 28, 1972) and the Office of National Narcotics Intelligence (established pursuant to Executive Order No. 11676 of July 27, 1972) would, together with other related functions, be merged in the new Drug Enforcement Administration.

NOW, THEREFORE, by virtue of the authority vested in me by the Constitution and laws of the United States, including section 5317 of title 5 of the United States Code, as amended [section 5317 of Title 5, Government Organization and Employees], it is hereby ordered as follows:

Section 1. The Attorney General, to the extent permitted by law, is authorized to coordinate all activities of executive branch departments and agencies which are directly related to the enforcement of laws respecting narcotics and dangerous drugs. Each department and agency of the Federal Government shall, upon request and to the extent permitted by law, assist the Attorney General in the performance of functions assigned to him pursuant to this order, and the Attorney General may, in carrying out those functions, utilize the services of any other agencies, Federal and State, as may be available and appropriate.

Sec. 2. Executive Order No. 11641 of January 28, 1972, is revoked and the Attorney General shall provide for the reassignment of the functions of the Office for Drug Abuse Law Enforcement and for the abolishment of that Office.

Sec. 3. Executive Order No. 11676 of July 27, 1972, is hereby revoked and the Attorney General shall provide for the reassignment of the functions of the Office of National Narcotics Intelligence and for the abolishment of that Office.

Sec. 4. Section 1 of Executive Order No. 11708 of March 23, 1973, as amended [set out as a note under section 5317 of Title 5, Government Organization and Employees], placing certain positions in level IV of the Executive Schedule is hereby further amended by deleting—

(1) "(6) Director, Office for Drug Abuse Law Enforcement, Department of Justice."; and

(2) "(7) Director, Office of National Narcotics Intelligence, Department of Justice."

Sec. 5. The Attorney General shall provide for the winding up of the affairs of the two offices and for the reassignment of their functions.

Sec. 6. This order shall be effective as of July 1, 1973.

RICHARD NIXON

§ 801a. Congressional findings and declarations: psychotropic substances

The Congress makes the following findings and declarations:

(1) The Congress has long recognized the danger involved in the manufacture, distribution, and use of certain psychotropic substances for nonscientific and nonmedical purposes, and has provided strong and effective legislation to control illicit trafficking and to regulate legitimate uses of psychotropic substances in this country. Abuse of psychotropic substances has become a phenomenon common to many countries, however, and is not confined to national borders. It is, therefore, essential that the United States cooperate with other nations in establishing effective controls over international traffic in such substances.

(2) The United States has joined with other countries in executing an international treaty, entitled the Convention on Psychotropic Substances and signed at Vienna, Austria, on February 21, 1971, which is designed to establish suitable controls over the manufacture, distribution, transfer, and use of certain psychotropic substances. The Convention is not self-executing, and the obligations of the United States thereunder may only be performed pursuant to appropriate legislation. It is the intent of the Congress that the amendments made by this Act, together with existing law, will enable the United States to meet all of its obligations under the Convention and that no further legislation will be necessary for that purpose.

(3) In implementing the Convention on Psychotropic Substances, the Congress intends that, consistent with the obligations of the United States under the Convention, control of psychotropic substances in the United States should be accomplished within the framework of the procedures and criteria for classification of substances provided in the Comprehensive Drug Abuse Prevention and Control Act of 1970 [21 U.S.C.A. § 801 et seq.]. This will insure that (A) the availability of psychotropic substances to manufacturers, distributors, dispensers, and researchers for useful and legitimate medical and scientific purposes will not be unduly restricted; (B) nothing in the Convention will interfere with bona fide research activities; and (C) nothing in the Convention will interfere with ethical medical practice in this country as determined by the Secretary of Health and Human Services on the basis of a consensus of the views of the American medical and scientific community.

(Pub.L. 95–633, Title I, § 101, Nov. 10, 1978, 92 Stat. 3768; Pub.L. 96–88, Title V, § 509(b), Oct. 17, 1979, 93 Stat. 695.)

HISTORICAL AND STATUTORY NOTES

References in Text

This Act, referred to in par. (2), is Pub.L. 95–633, Nov. 10, 1978, 92 Stat. 2768, known as the Psychotropic Substances Act of 1978, which enacted this section and §§ 830, and 852 of this title, amended §§ 352, 802, 811, 812, 823, 827, 841 to 843, 872, 881, 952, 953, and 965 of this title and § 242 of Title 42, The Public Health and Welfare, and enacted provisions set out as notes under this section and §§ 801, 812, and 830 of this title. For complete classification of this Act to the Code, see Short Title of 1978 Amendment note set out under § 801 of this title and Tables.

The Comprehensive Drug Abuse Prevention and Control Act of 1970, referred to in par. (3), is Pub.L. 91–513, Oct. 27, 1970, 84 Stat. 1236, as amended, which is classified principally to this chapter [§ 801 et seq. of this title]. For complete classification of this Act to the Code, see Short Title note set out under § 801 of this title and Tables.

Codifications

Section was enacted as part of the Psychotropic Substances Act of 1978 and not as part of the Controlled Substances Act, which comprises this subchapter.

Effective and Applicability Provisions

Section 112 of Pub.L. 95–633 provided that: "This title [which enacted this section and section 852 of this title, amended sections 352, 802, 811, 812, 823, 827, 872, 952 and 953 of this title and section 242a of Title 42, The Public Health and Welfare, and enacted provisions set out as notes under sections 801 and 812 of this title] and the amendments made by this title shall take effect on the date the Convention on Psychotropic Substances, signed at Vienna, Austria on February 21, 1971, enters into force in respect to the United States." [The Convention entered into force in respect to the United States on July 15, 1980.]

Change of Name

"Secretary of Health and Human Services" was substituted for "Secretary of Health, Education, and Welfare" on authority of Pub.L. 96–88, Title V, § 509, Oct. 17, 1979, 93 Stat. 695, which is classified to § 3508 of Title 20, Education.

§ 802. Definitions

As used in this subchapter:

(1) The term "addict" means any individual who habitually uses any narcotic drug so as to endanger the public morals, health, safety, or welfare, or who is so far addicted to the use of narcotic drugs as to have lost the power of self-control with reference to his addiction.

(2) The term "administer" refers to the direct application of a controlled substance to the body of a patient or research subject by—

(A) a practitioner (or, in his presence, by his authorized agent), or

(B) the patient or research subject at the direction and in the presence of the practitioner,

whether such application be by injection, inhalation, ingestion, or any other means.

(3) The term "agent" means an authorized person who acts on behalf of or at the direction of a manufacturer, distributor, or dispenser; except that such term does not include a common or contract carrier, public warehouseman, or employee of the carrier or warehouseman, when acting in the usual and lawful course of the carrier's or warehouseman's business.

(4) The term "Drug Enforcement Administration" means the Drug Enforcement Administration in the Department of Justice.

(5) The term "control" means to add a drug or other substance, or immediate precursor, to a schedule under part B of this subchapter, whether by transfer from another schedule or otherwise.

(6) The term "controlled substance" means a drug or other substance, or immediate precursor, included in schedule I, II, III, IV, or V of part B of this subchapter. The term does not include distilled spirits, wine, malt beverages, or tobacco, as those terms are defined or used in subtitle E of the Internal Revenue Code of 1986.

(7) The term "counterfeit substance" means a controlled substance which, or the container or labeling of which, without authorization, bears the trademark, trade name, or other identifying mark, imprint, number, or device, or any likeness thereof, of a manufacturer, distributor, or dispenser other than the person or persons who in fact manufactured, distributed, or dispensed such substance and which thereby falsely purports or is represented to be the product of, or to have been distributed by, such other manufacturer, distributor, or dispenser.

(8) The terms "deliver" or "delivery" mean the actual, constructive, or attempted transfer of a controlled substance or a listed chemical, whether or not there exists an agency relationship.

(9) The term "depressant or stimulant substance" means—

(A) a drug which contains any quantity of barbituric acid or any of the salts of barbituric acid; or

(B) a drug which contains any quantity of (i) amphetamine or any of its optical isomers; (ii) any salt of amphetamine or any salt of an optical isomer of amphetamine; or (iii) any substance which the Attorney General, after investigation, has found to be, and by regulation designated as, habit forming because of its stimulant effect on the central nervous system; or

(C) lysergic acid diethylamide; or

(D) any drug which contains any quantity of a substance which the Attorney General, after investigation, has found to have, and by regulation designated as having, a potential for abuse because of its depressant or stimulant effect on the central nervous system or its hallucinogenic effect.

(10) The term "dispense" means to deliver a controlled substance to an ultimate user or research subject by, or pursuant to the lawful order of, a practitioner, including the prescribing and administering of a controlled substance and the packaging, labeling or compounding necessary to prepare the substance for such delivery. The term "dispenser" means a practitioner who so delivers a controlled substance to an ultimate user or research subject.

(11) The term "distribute" means to deliver (other than by administering or dispensing) a controlled substance or a listed chemical. The term "distribu-

tor" means a person who so delivers a controlled substance or a listed chemical.

(12) The term "drug" has the meaning given that term by section 321(g)(1) of this title.

(13) The term "felony" means any Federal or State offense classified by applicable Federal or State law as a felony.

(14) The term "isomer" means the optical isomer, except as used in schedule I(c) and schedule II(a)(4). As used in schedule I(c), the term "isomer" means any optical, positional, or geometric isomer. As used in schedule II(a)(4), the term "isomer" means any optical or geometric isomer.

(15) The term "manufacture" means the production, preparation, propagation, compounding, or processing of a drug or other substance, either directly or indirectly or by extraction from substances of natural origin, or independently by means of chemical synthesis or by a combination of extraction and chemical synthesis, and includes any packaging or repackaging of such substance or labeling or relabeling of its container; except that such term does not include the preparation, compounding, packaging, or labeling of a drug or other substance in conformity with applicable State or local law by a practitioner as an incident to his administration or dispensing of such drug or substance in the course of his professional practice. The term "manufacturer" means a person who manufactures a drug or other substance.

(16) The term "marihuana" means all parts of the plant Cannabis sativa L., whether growing or not; the seeds thereof; the resin extracted from any part of such plant; and every compound, manufacture, salt, derivative, mixture, or preparation of such plant, its seeds or resin. Such term does not include the mature stalks of such plant, fiber produced from such stalks, oil or cake made from the seeds of such plant, any other compound, manufacture, salt, derivative, mixture, or preparation of such mature stalks (except the resin extracted therefrom), fiber, oil, or cake, or the sterilized seed of such plant which is incapable of germination.

(17) The term "narcotic drug" means any of the following whether produced directly or indirectly by extraction from substances of vegetable origin, or independently by means of chemical synthesis, or by a combination of extraction and chemical synthesis:

(A) Opium, opiates, derivatives of opium and opiates, including their isomers, esters, ethers, salts, and salts of isomers, esters, and ethers, whenever the existence of such isomers, esters, ethers, and salts is possible within the specific chemical designation. Such term does not include the isoquinoline alkaloids of opium.

(B) Poppy straw and concentrate of poppy straw.

(C) Coca leaves, except coca leaves and extracts of coca leaves from which cocaine, ecgonine, and derivatives of ecgonine or their salts have been removed.

(D) Cocaine, its salts, optical and geometric isomers, and salts of isomers.

(E) Ecgonine, its derivatives, their salts, isomers, and salts of isomers.

(F) Any compound, mixture, or preparation which contains any quantity of any of the substances referred to in subparagraphs (A) through (E).

(18) The term "opiate" means any drug or other substance having an addiction-forming or addiction-sustaining liability similar to morphine or being capable of conversion into a drug having such addiction-forming or addiction-sustaining liability.

(19) The term "opium poppy" means the plant of the species Papaver somniferum L., except the seed thereof.

(20) The term "poppy straw" means all parts, except the seeds, of the opium poppy, after mowing.

(21) The term "practitioner" means a physician, dentist, veterinarian, scientific investigator, pharmacy, hospital, or other person licensed, registered, or otherwise permitted, by the United States or the jurisdiction in which he practices or does research, to distribute, dispense, conduct research with respect to, administer, or use in teaching or chemical analysis, a controlled substance in the course of professional practice or research.

(22) The term "production" includes the manufacture, planting, cultivation, growing, or harvesting of a controlled substance.

(23) The term "immediate precursor" means a substance—

(A) which the Attorney General has found to be and by regulation designated as being the principal compound used, or produced primarily for use, in the manufacture of a controlled substance;

(B) which is an immediate chemical intermediary used or likely to be used in the manufacture of such controlled substance; and

(C) the control of which is necessary to prevent, curtail, or limit the manufacture of such controlled substance.

(24) The term "Secretary", unless the context otherwise indicates, means the Secretary of Health and Human Services.

(25) The term "serious bodily injury" means bodily injury which involves—

(A) a substantial risk of death;

(B) protracted and obvious disfigurement; or

(C) protracted loss or impairment of the function of a bodily member, organ, or mental faculty.

(26) The term "State" means a State of the United States, the District of Columbia, and any commonwealth, territory, or possession of the United States.

(27) The term "ultimate user" means a person who has lawfully obtained, and who possesses, a controlled substance for his own use or for the use of a member of his household or for an animal owned by him or by a member of his household.

(28) The term "United States", when used in a geographic sense, means all places and waters, continental or insular, subject to the jurisdiction of the United States.

(29) The term "maintenance treatment" means the dispensing, for a period in excess of twenty-one days, of a narcotic drug in the treatment of an individual for dependence upon heroin or other morphine-like drugs.

(30) The term "detoxification treatment" means the dispensing, for a period not in excess of one hundred and eighty days, of a narcotic drug in decreasing doses to an individual in order to alleviate adverse physiological or psychological effects incident to withdrawal from the continuous or sustained use of a narcotic drug and as a method of bringing the individual to a narcotic drug-free state within such period.

(31) The term "Convention on Psychotropic Substances" means the Convention on Psychotropic Substances signed at Vienna, Austria, on February 21, 1971; and the term "Single Convention on Narcotic Drugs" means the Single Convention on Narcotic Drugs signed at New York, New York, on March 30, 1961.

(32)(A) Except as provided in subparagraph (C), the term "controlled substance analogue" means a substance—

(i) the chemical structure of which is substantially similar to the chemical structure of a controlled substance in schedule I or II;

(ii) which has a stimulant, depressant, or hallucinogenic effect on the central nervous system that is substantially similar to or greater than the stimulant, depressant, or hallucinogenic effect on the central nervous system of a controlled substance in schedule I or II; or

(iii) with respect to a particular person, which such person represents or intends to have a stimulant, depressant, or hallucinogenic effect on the central nervous system that is substantially similar to or greater than the stimulant, depressant, or hallucinogenic effect on the central nervous system of a controlled substance in schedule I or II.

(B) The designation of gamma butyrolactone or any other chemical as a listed chemical pursuant to paragraph (34) or (35) does not preclude a finding pursuant to subparagraph (A) of this paragraph that the chemical is a controlled substance analogue.

(C) Such term does not include—

(i) a controlled substance;

(ii) any substance for which there is an approved new drug application;

(iii) with respect to a particular person any substance, if an exemption is in effect for investigational use, for that person, under section 355 of this title to the extent conduct with respect to such substance is pursuant to such exemption; or

(iv) any substance to the extent not intended for human consumption before such an exemption takes effect with respect to that substance.

(33) The term "listed chemical" means any list I chemical or any list II chemical.

(34) The term "list I chemical" means a chemical specified by regulation of the Attorney General as a chemical that is used in manufacturing a controlled substance in violation of this subchapter and is important to the manufacture of the controlled substances, and such term includes (until otherwise specified by regulation of the Attorney General, as considered appropriate by the Attorney General or upon petition to the Attorney General by any person) the following:

(A) Anthranilic acid, its esters, and its salts.

(B) Benzyl cyanide.

(C) Ephedrine, its salts, optical isomers, and salts of optical isomers.

(D) Ergonovine and its salts.

(E) Ergotamine and its salts.

(F) N-Acetylanthranilic acid, its esters, and its salts.

(G) Norpseudoephedrine, its salts, optical isomers, and salts of optical isomers.

(H) Phenylacetic acid, its esters, and its salts.

(I) Phenylpropanolamine, its salts, optical isomers, and salts of optical isomers.

(J) Piperidine and its salts.

(K) Pseudoephedrine, its salts, optical isomers, and salts of optical isomers.

(L) 3,4–Methylenedioxyphenyl–2–propanone.

(M) Methylamine.

(N) Ethylamine.

(O) Propionic anhydride.

(P) Isosafrole.

(Q) Safrole.

(R) Piperonal.

(S) N-Methylephedrine.

(T) N-methylpseudoephedrine.

(U) Hydriodic acid.

(V) Benzaldehyde.

(W) Nitroethane.

(X) Gamma butyrolactone.

(Y) Any salt, optical isomer, or salt of an optical isomer of the chemicals listed in subparagraphs (M) through (U) of this paragraph.

(35) The term "list II chemical" means a chemical (other than a list I chemical) specified by regulation of the Attorney General as a chemical that is used in manufacturing a controlled substance in violation of this subchapter, and such term includes (until otherwise specified by regulation of the Attorney General, as considered appropriate by the Attorney General or upon petition to the Attorney General by any person) the following chemicals:

(A) Acetic anhydride.

(B) Acetone.

(C) Benzyl chloride.

(D) Ethyl ether.

(E) Repealed. Pub.L. 101–647, Title XXIII, § 2301(b), Nov. 29, 1990, 104 Stat. 4858

(F) Potassium permanganate.

(G) 2–Butanone (or Methyl Ethyl Ketone).

(H) Toluene.

(I) Iodine.

(J) Hydrochloric gas.

(36) The term "regular customer" means, with respect to a regulated person, a customer with whom the regulated person has an established business relationship that is reported to the Attorney General.

(37) The term "regular importer" means, with respect to a listed chemical, a person that has an established record as an importer of that listed chemical that is reported to the Attorney General.

(38) The term "regulated person" means a person who manufactures, distributes, imports, or exports a listed chemical, a tableting machine, or an encapsulating machine or who acts as a broker or trader for an international transaction involving a listed chemical, a tableting machine, or an encapsulating machine.

(39) The term "regulated transaction" means—

(A) a distribution, receipt, sale, importation, or exportation of, or an international transaction involving shipment of, a listed chemical, or if the Attorney General establishes a threshold amount for a specific listed chemical, a threshold amount, including a cumulative threshold amount for multiple transactions (as determined by the Attorney General, in consultation with the chemical industry and taking into consideration the quantities normally used for lawful purposes), of a listed chemical, except that such term does not include—

(i) a domestic lawful distribution in the usual course of business between agents or employees of a single regulated person;

(ii) a delivery of a listed chemical to or by a common or contract carrier for carriage in the lawful and usual course of the business of the common or contract carrier, or to or by a warehouseman for storage in the lawful and usual course of the business of the warehouseman, except that if the carriage or storage is in connection with the distribution, importation, or exportation of a listed chemical to a third person, this clause does not relieve a distributor, importer, or exporter from compliance with section 830 of this title;

(iii) any category of transaction or any category of transaction for a specific listed chemical or chemicals specified by regulation of the Attorney General as excluded from this definition as unnecessary for enforcement of this subchapter or subchapter II of this chapter;

(iv) any transaction in a listed chemical that is contained in a drug that may be marketed or distributed lawfully in the United States under the Federal Food, Drug, and Cosmetic Act, subject to clause (v), unless—

(I) the Attorney General has determined under section 814 of this title that the drug or group of drugs is being diverted to obtain the listed chemical for use in the illicit production of a controlled substance; and

(II) the quantity of the listed chemical contained in the drug included in the transaction or multiple transactions equals or exceeds the threshold established for that chemical by the Attorney General;

(v) any transaction in a scheduled listed chemical product that is a sale at retail by a regulated seller or a distributor required to submit reports under section 830(b)(3) of this title; or

(vi) any transaction in a chemical mixture which the Attorney General has by regulation designated as exempt from the application of this subchapter and subchapter II of this chapter based on a finding that the mixture is formulated in such a way that it cannot be easily used in the illicit production of a controlled substance and that the listed chemical or chemicals contained in the mixture cannot be readily recovered; and

(B) a distribution, importation, or exportation of a tableting machine or encapsulating machine.

(40) The term "chemical mixture" means a combination of two or more chemical substances, at least one of which is not a list I chemical or a list II chemical, except that such term does not include any combination of a list I chemical or a list II chemical with another chemical that is present solely as an impurity.

(41)(A) The term "anabolic steroid" means any drug or hormonal substance, chemically and pharmacologically related to testosterone (other than estrogens, progestins, corticosteroids, and dehydroepiandrosterone), and includes

(i) androstanediol—

(I) 3B,17B–dihydroxy–5α– androstane; and

(II) 3α,17B–dihydroxy–5α– androstane;

(ii) androstanedione (5α–androstan–3,17–dione);

(iii) androstenediol—

(I) 1–androstenediol (3B,17B–dihydroxy–5α–androst–1–ene);

(II) 1–androstenediol (3α,17B–dihydroxy–5α–androst–1–ene);

(III) 4–androstenediol (3B,17B–dihydroxy–androst–4–ene); and

(IV) 5–androstenediol (3B,17B–dihydroxy–androst–5–ene);

(iv) androstenedione—

(I) 1–androstenedione ([5α]–androst–1–en–3,17–dione);

(II) 4–androstenedione (androst–4–en–3,17–dione); and

(III) 5–androstenedione (androst–5–en–3,17–dione);

(v) bolasterone (7α,17α– dimethyl–17B–hydroxyandrost–4–en–3–one);

(vi) boldenone (17B–hydroxyandrost–1,4,–diene–3–one);

(vii) calusterone (7B, 17α–dimethyl–17B–hydroxyandrost–4–en–3–one);

(viii) clostebol (4–chloro–17B–hydroxyandrost–4–en–3–one);

(ix) dehydrochloromethyltestosterone (4–chloro–17B–hydroxy–17α–methyl–androst–1, 4–dien–3–one);

(x) Δ 1–dihydrotestosterone (a.k.a. "1–testosterone") (17B–hydroxy–5α–androst–1–en–3–one);

(xi) 4–dihydrotestosterone (17B–hydroxy–androstan–3–one);

(xii) drostanolone (17B–hydroxy–2α– methyl–5α–androstan–3–one);

(xiii) ethylestrenol (17α–ethyl–17B–hydroxyestr–4–ene);

(xiv) fluoxymesterone (9–fluoro–17α–methyl–11B, 17B–dihydroxyandrost–4–en–3–one);

(xv) formebolone (2–formyl–17α–methyl–11α, 17B–dihydroxyandrost–1,4–dien–3–one);

(xvi) furazabol (17α–methyl–17B–hydroxyandrostano[2,3–c]–furazan);

(xvii) 13β–ethyl–17β–hydroxygon–4–en–3–one;

(xviii) 4–hydroxytestosterone (4,17B–dihydroxy–androst–4–en–3–one);

(xix) 4–hydroxy–19–nortestosterone (4,17B–dihydroxy–estr–4–en–3–one);

(xx) mestanolone (17α–methyl– 17B–hydroxy–5α–androstan–3–one);

(xxi) mesterolone (1α–methyl–17B–hydroxy–[5α] –androstan–3–one);

(xxii) methandienone (17α–methyl–17B–hydroxyandrost–1,4–dien–3–one);

(xxiii) methandriol (17α–methyl– 3B,17B–dihydroxyandrost–5–ene);

(xxiv) methenolone (1–methyl–17B–hydroxy–5α–androst–1–en–3–one);

(xxv) 17α–methyl–3B, 17B–dihydroxy–5α–androstane;

(xxvi) 17α–methyl–3α, 17B–dihydroxy–5α–androstane;

(xxvii) 17α–methyl–3B, 17B–dihydroxyandrost–4–ene.

(xxviii) 17α–methyl–4–hydroxynandrolone (17α–methyl–4–hydroxy–17B–hydroxyestr–4–en–3–one);

(xxix) methyldienolone (17α–methyl–17B–hydroxyestra–4,9(10)–dien–3–one);

(xxx) methyltrienolone (17α–methyl–17B–hydroxyestra–4,9–11–trien–3–one);

(xxxi) methyltestosterone (17α–methyl–17B–hydroxyandrost–4–en–3–one);

(xxxii) mibolerone (7α, 17α–dimethyl–17B–hydroxyestr–4–en–3–one);

(xxxiii) 17α–methyl–Δ 1–dihydrotestosterone (17B–hydroxy–17α–methyl–5α– androst–1–en–3–one) (a.k.a. "17–α–methyl–1–testosterone");

(xxxiv) nandrolone (17B–hydroxyestr–4–en–3–one);

(xxxv) norandrostenediol—

(I) 19–nor–4–androstenediol (3B, 17B–dihydroxyestr–4–ene);

(II) 19–nor–4–androstenediol (3α, 17B–dihydroxyestr–4–ene);

(III) 19–nor–5–androstenediol (3B, 17B–dihydroxyestr–5–ene); and

(IV) 19–nor–5–androstenediol (3α, 17B–dihydroxyestr–5–ene);

(xxxvi) norandrostenedione—

(I) 19–nor–4–androstenedione (estr–4–en–3,17–dione); and

(II) 19–nor–5–androstenedione (estr–5–en–3,17–dione;

(xxxvii) norbolethone (13B, 17α–diethyl–17B–hydroxygon–4–en–3–one);

(xxxviii) norclostebol (4–chloro–17B–hydroxyestr–4–en–3–one);

(xxxix) norethandrolone (17α–ethyl–17B–hydroxyestr–4–en–3–one);

(xl) normethandrolone (17α–methyl–17B–hydroxyestr–4–en–3–one);

(xli) oxandrolone (17α–methyl–17B–hydroxy–2–oxa–[5α]– androstan–3–one);

(xlii) oxymesterone (17α–methyl–4,17B–dihydroxyandrost–4–en–3–one);

(xliii) oxymetholone (17α–methyl–2–hydroxymethylene–17B–hydroxy– [5α]–androstan–3–one);

(xliv) stanozolol (17α–methyl– 17β–hydroxy–[5α]–androst–2–eno[3,2–c]–pyrazole);

(xlv) stenbolone (17B–hydroxy–2–methyl–[5α] –androst–1–en–3–one);

(xlvi) testolactone (13–hydroxy–3–oxo–13,17–secoandrosta–1,4–dien–17–oic acid lactone);

(xlvii) testosterone (17B–hydroxyandrost–4–en–3–one);

(xlviii) tetrahydrogestrinone (13B,17α–diethyl–17B–hydroxygon–4,9, 11–trien–3–one);

(xlix) trenbolone (17B–hydroxyestr–4,9,11–trien–3–one); and

(xlx)[1] any salt, ester, or ether of a drug or substance described in this paragraph.

The substances excluded under this subparagraph may at any time be scheduled by the Attorney General in accordance with the authority and requirements of subsections (a) through (c) of section 811 of this title.

(B)(i) Except as provided in clause (ii), such term does not include an anabolic steroid which is expressly intended for administration through implants to cattle or other nonhuman species and which has been approved by the Secretary of Health and Human Services for such administration.

(ii) If any person prescribes, dispenses, or distributes such steroid for human use, such person shall be considered to have prescribed, dispensed, or distributed an anabolic steroid within the meaning of subparagraph (A).

(42) The term "international transaction" means a transaction involving the shipment of a listed chemical across an international border (other than a United States border) in which a broker or trader located in the United States participates.

(43) The terms "broker" and "trader" mean a person that assists in arranging an international transaction in a listed chemical by—

(A) negotiating contracts;

(B) serving as an agent or intermediary; or

(C) bringing together a buyer and seller, a buyer and transporter, or a seller and transporter.

(44) The term "felony drug offense" means an offense that is punishable by imprisonment for more than one year under any law of the United States or of a State or foreign country that prohibits or restricts conduct relating to narcotic drugs, marihuana, anabolic steroids, or depressant or stimulant substances.

(45)(A) The term "scheduled listed chemical product" means, subject to subparagraph (b), a product that—

(i) contains ephedrine, pseudoephedrine, or phenylpropanolamine; and

(ii) may be marketed or distributed lawfully in the United States under the Federal, Food, Drug, and Cosmetic Act as a nonprescription drug.

Each reference in clause (i) to ephedrine, pseudoephedrine, or phenylpropanolamine includes each of the salts, optical isomers, and salts of optical isomers of such chemical.

(B) Such term does not include a product described in subparagraph (A) if the product contains a chemical specified in such subparagraph that the Attorney General has under section 811(a) of this title added to any of the schedules under section 812(c) of this title. In the absence of such scheduling by the Attorney General, a chemical specified in such subparagraph may not be considered to be a controlled substance.

(46) The term "regulated seller" means a retail distributor (including a pharmacy or a mobile retail vendor), except that such term does not include an employee or agent of such distributor.

(47) The term "mobile retail vendor" means a person or entity that makes sales at retail from a stand that is intended to be temporary, or is capable of being moved from one location to another, whether the stand is located within or on the premises of a fixed facility (such as a kiosk at a shopping center or an airport) or whether the stand is located on unimproved real estate (such as a lot or field leased for retail purposes).

(48) The term "at retail", with respect to the sale or purchase of a scheduled listed chemical product, means a sale or purchase for personal use, respectively.

(49)(A) The term "retail distributor" means a grocery store, general merchandise store, drug store, or other entity or person whose activities as a distributor relating to ephedrine, pseudoephedrine, or phenylpropanolamine products are limited almost exclusively to sales for personal use, both in number of sales and volume of sales, either directly to walk-in customers or in face-to-face transactions by direct sales.

(B) For purposes of this paragraph, entities are defined by reference to the Standard Industrial Classification (SIC) code, as follows:

(i) A grocery store is an entity within SIC code 5411.

(ii) A general merchandise store is an entity within SIC codes 5300 through 5399 and 5499.

(iii) A drug store is an entity within SIC code 5912.

(C) Redesignated (B)

(Pub.L. 91–513, Title II, § 102, Oct. 27, 1970, 84 Stat. 1242; Pub.L. 93–281, § 2, May 14, 1974, 88 Stat. 124; Pub.L. 95–633, Title I, § 102(b), Nov. 10, 1978, 92 Stat. 3772; Pub.L. 96–88, Title V, § 509(b), Oct. 17, 1979, 93 Stat. 695; Pub.L. 96–132, § 16(a), Nov. 30, 1979, 93 Stat. 1049; Pub.L. 98–473, Title II, § 507(a), (b), Oct. 12, 1984, 98 Stat. 2071; Pub.L. 98–509, Title III, § 301(a), Oct. 19, 1984, 98 Stat. 2364; Pub.L. 99–570, Title I, §§ 1003(b), 1203, 1870, Oct. 27, 1986, 100 Stat. 3207–6, 3207–13, 3207–56; Pub.L. 99–646, § 83, Nov. 10, 1986, 100 Stat. 3619; Pub.L. 100–690, Title VI, § 6054, Nov. 18, 1988, 102 Stat. 4316; Pub.L. 101–647, Title XIX, § 1902(b), Title XXIII, § 2301, Title XXXV, § 3599I, Nov. 29, 1990, 104 Stat. 4852, 4858, 4932; Pub.L. 103–200, §§ 2(a), 7 to 9(a), Dec. 17, 1993, 107 Stat. 2333, 2340; Pub.L. 103–322, Title IX, § 90105(d), Title XXXIII, § 330024(a), (b), (d)(1), Sept. 13, 1994, 108 Stat. 1988, 2150; Pub.L. 104–237, Title II, §§ 204(a), 209, Title IV, § 401(a), (b), Oct. 3, 1996, 110 Stat. 3102, 3104, 3106, 3107; Pub.L. 104–294, Title VI, §§ 604(b)(4), 607(j), Oct. 11, 1996, 110 Stat. 3506, 3512; Pub.L. 105–115, Title I, § 126(c)(3), Nov. 21, 1997, 111 Stat. 2328; Pub.L. 106–172, §§ 3(c), 5(a), Feb. 18, 2000, 114 Stat. 9, 10; Pub.L. 106–310, Div. B, Title XXXVI, § 3622(a), Oct. 17, 2000, 114 Stat. 1231; Pub.L. 107–273, Div. B, Title IV, § 4002(c)(1), Nov. 2, 2002, 116 Stat. 1808; Pub.L. 108–358, § 2(a), Oct. 22, 2004, 118 Stat. 1661; Pub.L. 109–162, Title XI, § 1180, Jan. 5, 2006, 119 Stat. 3126; Pub.L. 109–177, Title VII, §§ 711(a)(1), (2)(A), 712(a)(1), Mar. 9, 2006, 120 Stat. 256, 263.)

[1] So in original. Probably should be "(*l*)".

HISTORICAL AND STATUTORY NOTES

References in Text

"This subchapter", referred to in text, was in the original "this title" which is Title II of Pub.L. 91–513, Oct. 27, 1970, 84 Stat. 1242, and is popularly known as the "Controlled Substances Act". For complete classification of Title II to the Code, see Short Title note set out under section 801 of this title and Tables.

"Subchapter II of this chapter", referred to in text, was in the original "title III", meaning Title III of Pub.L. 91–513, Oct. 27, 1970, 84 Stat. 1285. Part A of Title III comprises subchapter II of this chapter. For classification of Part B, consisting of sections 1101 to 1105 of Title III, see Tables.

Subtitle E of the Internal Revenue Code of 1986, referred to in par. (6), is classified to § 5001 et seq. of Title 26, Internal Revenue Code.

Schedule I or II, referred to in par. (32)(A), are set out in section 812(c) of this title.

Section 401(d) of the Comprehensive Methamphetamine Control Act of 1996, referred to in par. (39)(A)(iv), is section 401(d) of Pub.L. 104–237, Title IV, Oct. 3, 1996, 110 Stat. 3108, which is set out as a note under this section.

The Federal Food, Drug, and Cosmetic Act, referred to in pars. (39)(A)(iv) and (45)(A)(ii), also known as the Federal Food, Drug, and Cosmetic Act, FFDCA, the Copeland Pure Food and Drugs Act, the Food, Drug, and Cosmetic Act, FDCA, and the Humphrey-Durham Act, is Act June 25, 1938, c. 675, 52 Stat. 1040, as amended, which is classified principally to chapter 9 of this title, 21 U.S.C.A. § 301 et seq. For complete classification, see 21 U.S.C.A. § 301 and Tables.

Codifications

Amendment by section 83 of Pub.L. 99–646 to par. (14) was not capable of execution in view of prior identical amendment by Pub.L. 99–570.

Amendment by Pub.L. 98–509 was executed to par. (29) of this section notwithstanding directory language of Pub.L. 98–509 that the amendment be executed to "section 102(28) of the Controlled Substances Act", since par. (28) was redesignated (29) by Pub.L. 98–473.

Sections 604(b)(4) and 607(j)(2) of Pub.L. 104–294, both of which directed that this section be amended by redesignating the second par. (43) as par. (44), could not be executed to text because of prior identical amendment by section 401(b)(3) of Pub.L. 104–237. See also 2002 Amendments note set out under this section.

Effective and Applicability Provisions

2004 Acts. Pub.L. 108–358, § 2(d), Oct. 22, 2004, 118 Stat. 1664, provided that: "The amendments made by this section [amending pars. (41) and (44) of this section, 21 U.S.C.A. § 811, and provisions set out as a note under this section] shall take effect 90 days after the date of enactment of this Act [Oct. 22, 2004]."

2002 Acts. Amendment by section 4002(c)(1) of Pub.L. 107–273, as therein provided, effective Oct. 11, 1996, which is the date of enactment of Pub.L. 104–294, to which such amendment relates.

2000 Acts. Pub.L. 106–310, Div. B, Title XXXVI, § 3622(b), Oct. 17, 2000, 114 Stat. 1231, provided that: "The amendments made by subsection (a) [amending par. (39)(A)(iv)(II) of this section] shall take effect 1 year after the date of the enactment of this Act [Oct. 17, 2000]."

1997 Acts. Amendments by Pub.L. 105–115, the Food and Drug Administration Modernization Act of 1997, effective 90 days after November 21, 1997, except as otherwise provided, see section 501 of Pub.L. 105–115, set out as a note under section 321 of this title.

1996 Acts. Amendment by section 604 of Pub.L. 104–294 effective Sept. 13, 1994, see section 604(d) of Pub.L. 104–294, set out as a note under 18 U.S.C.A. § 13.

Section 401(g) of Pub.L. 104–237 provided that: "Notwithstanding any other provision of this Act [enacting section 872a of this title, amending this section and sections 814, 830, 841, 842, 843, 844, 853, 881, 959, and 960 of this title and section 1607 of Title 19, Customs Duties, and enacting provisions set out as notes under this section and sections 801, 872 and 971 of this title, section 994 of Title 28, Judiciary and Judicial Procedure, and section 290aa–4 of Title 42, The Public Health and Welfare], this section shall not apply to the sale of any pseudoephedrine or phenylpropanolamine product prior to 12 months after the date of enactment of this Act [Oct. 3, 1996], except that, on application of a manufacturer of a particular pseudoephedrine or phenylpropanolamine drug product, the Attorney General may, in her sole discretion, extend such effective date up to an additional six months. Notwithstanding any other provision of law, the decision of the Attorney General on such an application shall not be subject to judicial review."

1994 Acts. Section 330024(f) of Pub.L. 103–322 provided that: "The amendments made by this section [amending this section and sections 824, 960, and 971 of this title] shall take effect as of the date that is 120 days after the date of enactment of the Domestic Chemical Diversion Control Act of 1993 [Dec. 17, 1993]."

1993 Acts. Section 11 of Pub.L. 103–200 provided that: "This Act and the amendments made by this Act [enacting section 814 of this title, amending this section and sections 821, 822, 823, 824, 830, 843, 880, 957, 958, 960, and 971 of this title and enacting provisions set out as notes under this section and section 801 of this title] shall take effect on the date that is 120 days after the date of enactment of this Act [Dec. 17, 1993]."

1990 Acts. Section 1902(d) of Pub.L. 101–647 provided that: "This section and the amendment made by this section [enacting par. (41) of this section and section 812(c) Schedule III(e) and note provision set out under section 829 of this title] shall take effect 90 days after the date of enactment of this Act [Nov. 29, 1990']."

1988 Acts. Section 6061 of Pub.L. 100–690 provided that: "Except as otherwise provided in this subtitle, this subtitle [enacting section 972 of this title, amending sections 802, 830, 841, 842, 843, 872, 876, 881, 960, and 961 of this title] shall take effect 120 days after the enactment of this Act [Nov. 18, 1988]."

1978 Acts. Amendment by Pub.L. 95–633 effective on the date the Convention on Psychotropic Substances enters into force in the United States [July 15, 1980], see § 112 of Pub.L. 95–633, set out as a note under § 801a of this title.

1970 Acts. Section effective Oct. 27, 1970, see § 704(b) of Pub.L. 91–513, set out as a note under § 801 of this title.

Change of Name

"Secretary of Health and Human Services" was substituted for "Secretary of Health, Education, and Welfare" on authority of Pub.L. 96–88, Title V, § 509, Oct. 17, 1979, 93 Stat. 695, which is classified to 20 U.S.C.A. § 3508.

Repeals

Sections 604(b)(4) and 607(j)(2) of Pub.L. 104–294, cited in the credit of this section, were repealed by section 4002(c)(1) of Pub.L. 107–273, effective Oct. 11, 1996.

Preservation of State Authority to Regulate Scheduled Listed Chemicals

Pub.L. 109–177, Title VII, § 711(g), Mar. 9, 2006, 120 Stat. 263, provided that: "This section and the amendments made by this section [Pub.L. 109–177, Title VII, § 711, Mar. 9, 2006, 120 Stat. 256, amending this section and 21 U.S.C.A. §§ 830, 841, 842, 844 and enacting provisions set out as notes under 21 U.S.C.A. §§ 830 and 844] may not be construed as having any legal effect on section 708 of the Controlled Substances Act [Pub.L. 91–513, Title II, § 708, Oct. 27, 1970, 84 Stat. 1284, which is classified to 21 U.S.C.A. § 903] as applied to the regulation of scheduled listed chemicals (as defined in section 102(45) of such Act [Pub.L. 91–513, Title II, § 102(45), Oct. 27, 1970, 84 Stat. 1242, which is classified to par. (45) of this section."

Report on Diversion of Ordinary, Over-the-counter Pseudoephedrine and Phenylpropanolamine Products

Pub.L. 106–310, Div. B, Title XXXVI, § 3642, Oct. 17, 2000, 114 Stat. 1237, provided that:

"**(a) Study.**—The Attorney General shall conduct a study of the use of ordinary, over-the-counter pseudoephedrine and phenylpropanolamine products in the clandestine production of illicit drugs. Sources of data for the study shall include the following:

"(1) Information from Federal, State, and local clandestine laboratory seizures and related investigations identifying the source, type, or brand of drug products being utilized and how they were obtained for the illicit production of methamphetamine and amphetamine.

"(2) Information submitted voluntarily from the pharmaceutical and retail industries involved in the manufacture, distribution, and sale of drug products containing ephedrine, pseudoephedrine, and phenylpropanolamine, including information on changes in the pattern, volume, or both, of sales of ordinary, over-the-counter pseudoephedrine and phenylpropanolamine products.

"**(b) Report.**—

"**(1) Requirement.**—Not later than 1 year after the date of the enactment of this Act [Oct. 17, 2000], the Attorney General shall submit to Congress a report on the study conducted under subsection (a).

"**(2) Elements.**—The report shall include—

"(A) the findings of the Attorney General as a result of the study; and

"(B) such recommendations on the need to establish additional measures to prevent diversion of ordinary, over-the-counter pseudoephedrine and phenylpropanolamine (such as a threshold on ordinary, over-the-counter pseudoephedrine and phenylpropanolamine products) as the Attorney General considers appropriate.

"**(3) Matters considered.**—In preparing the report, the Attorney General shall consider the comments and recommendations including the comments on the Attorney General's proposed findings and recommendations, of State and local law enforcement and regulatory officials and of representatives of the industry described in subsection (a)(2).

"**(c) Regulation of retail sales.**—

"**(1) In general.**—Notwithstanding section 401(d) of the Comprehensive Methamphetamine Control Act of 1996 (21 U.S.C. 802 note) and subject to paragraph (2), the Attorney General shall establish by regulation a single-transaction limit of not less than 24 grams of ordinary, over-the-counter pseudoephedrine or phenylpropanolamine (as the case may be) for retail distributors, if the Attorney General finds, in the report under subsection (b), that—

"(A) there is a significant number of instances (as set forth in paragraph (3)(A) of such section 401(d) [set out as a note under this section] for purposes of such section) where ordinary, over-the-counter pseudoephedrine products, phenylpropanolamine products, or both such products that were purchased from retail distributors were widely used in the clandestine production of illicit drugs; and

"(B) the best practical method of preventing such use is the establishment of single-transaction limits for retail distributors of either or both of such products.

"(2) Due process.—The Attorney General shall establish the single-transaction limit under paragraph (1) only after notice, comment, and an informal hearing."

Regulation of Retail Sales of Certain Precursor Chemicals; Effect on Thresholds; Combination Ephedrine Products

Section 401(d) to (f) of Pub.L. 104–237, which related to regulation of retail sales of certain precursor chemicals, was repealed by Pub.L. 109–177, Title VII, § 712(b), Mar. 9, 2006, 120 Stat. 264.

Exemption for Substances in Paragraph 41

Pub.L. 101–647, Title XIX, § 1903, Nov. 29, 1990, 104 Stat. 4853, as amended Pub.L. 108–358, § 2(c), Oct. 22, 2004, 118 Stat. 1663, provided that:

"(a) Drugs for treatment of rare diseases.—If the Attorney General finds that a drug listed in paragraph (41) of section 102 of the Controlled Substances Act (as added by section 2 of this Act [sic]) is—

"(1) approved by the Food and Drug Administration as an accepted treatment for a rare disease or condition, as defined in section 526 of the Federal Food, Drug, and Cosmetic Act (21 U.S.C. 360bb) [21 U.S.C.A. § 360bb]; and

"(2) does not have a significant potential for abuse, the Attorney General may exempt such drug from any production regulations otherwise issued under the Controlled Substances Act [21 U.S.C.A. § 801 et seq.] as may be necessary to ensure adequate supplies of such drug for medical purposes.

"(b) Date of issuance of regulations.—The Attorney General shall issue regulations implementing this section not later than 45 days after the date of enactment of this Act [Nov. 29, 1990], except that the regulations required under section 3(a) [sic] shall be issued not later than 180 days after the date of enactment of this Act [Nov. 29, 1990]."

[Amendments made by Pub.L. 108–358, § 2(c), amending this note, to take effect 90 days after Oct. 22, 2003, see Pub.L. 108–356, § 2(d), set out as an 2004 Effective and Applicability Provisions note under this section.]

Promulgation of Regulations for Administration of Amendment by Alcohol Abuse, Drug Abuse, and Mental Health Amendments of 1984; Inclusion of Findings in Report

Section 301(b) of Pub.L. 98–509 provided that: "The Secretary of Health and Human Services shall, within ninety days of the date of the enactment of this Act [Oct. 19, 1984], promulgate regulations for the administration of section 102(28) of the Controlled Substances Act [par. (29) of this section] as amended by subsection (a) and shall include in the first report submitted under section 505(b) of the Public Health Service Act [section 290aa–4 of Title 42] after the expiration of such ninety days the findings of the Secretary with respect to the effect of the amendment made by subsection (a) [amending par. (29) of this section]."

§ 803. Repealed. Pub.L. 95–137, § 1(b), Oct. 18, 1977, 91 Stat. 1169

HISTORICAL AND STATUTORY NOTES

Section, Pub.L. 95–513, Title II, § 103, Oct. 27, 1970, 84 Stat. 1245, authorized the Bureau of Narcotics and Dangerous Drugs to add, during the fiscal year 1971, 300 agents, together with necessary supporting personnel, and provided for appropriations of $6,000,000 to carry out such addition.

PART B—AUTHORITY TO CONTROL; STANDARDS AND SCHEDULES

§ 811. Authority and criteria for classification of substances

(a) Rules and regulations of Attorney General; hearing

The Attorney General shall apply the provisions of this subchapter to the controlled substances listed in the schedules established by section 812 of this title and to any other drug or other substance added to such schedules under this subchapter. Except as provided in subsections (d) and (e) of this section, the Attorney General may by rule—

(1) add to such a schedule or transfer between such schedules any drug or other substance if he—

(A) finds that such drug or other substance has a potential for abuse, and

(B) makes with respect to such drug or other substance the findings prescribed by subsection (b) of section 812 of this title for the schedule in which such drug is to be placed; or

(2) remove any drug or other substance from the schedules if he finds that the drug or other substance does not meet the requirements for inclusion in any schedule.

Rules of the Attorney General under this subsection shall be made on the record after opportunity for a hearing pursuant to the rulemaking procedures prescribed by subchapter II of chapter 5 of Title 5. Proceedings for the issuance, amendment, or repeal of such rules may be initiated by the Attorney General (1) on his own motion, (2) at the request of the Secretary, or (3) on the petition of any interested party.

(b) Evaluation of drugs and other substances

The Attorney General shall, before initiating proceedings under subsection (a) of this section to control a drug or other substance or to remove a drug or other substance entirely from the schedules, and after gathering the necessary data, request from the Secretary a scientific and medical evaluation, and his recommendations, as to whether such drug or other substance should be so controlled or removed as a controlled substance. In making such evaluation and recommendations, the Secretary shall consider the factors listed in paragraphs (2), (3), (6), (7), and (8) of subsection (c) of this section and any scientific or medical considerations involved in paragraphs (1), (4), and (5) of such subsection. The recommendations of the Secretary shall include recommendations with respect to the appropriate schedule, if any, under which such drug or other substance should be listed. The evaluation and the recommendations of the Secretary shall be made in writing and submitted to the Attorney General within a reasonable time. The recommendations of the Secretary to the Attorney General shall be binding on the Attorney General as to such scientific and medical matters, and if the Secretary recommends that a drug or other substance not be controlled, the Attorney General shall not control the drug or other substance. If the Attorney General determines that these facts and all other relevant data constitute substantial evidence of potential for abuse such as to warrant control or substantial evidence that the drug or other substance should be removed entirely from the schedules, he shall initiate proceedings for control or removal, as the case may be, under subsection (a) of this section.

(c) Factors determinative of control or removal from schedules

In making any finding under subsection (a) of this section or under subsection (b) of section 812 of this title, the Attorney General shall consider the following factors with respect to each drug or other substance proposed to be controlled or removed from the schedules:

(1) Its actual or relative potential for abuse.

(2) Scientific evidence of its pharmacological effect, if known.

(3) The state of current scientific knowledge regarding the drug or other substance.

(4) Its history and current pattern of abuse.

(5) The scope, duration, and significance of abuse.

(6) What, if any, risk there is to the public health.

(7) Its psychic or physiological dependence liability.

(8) Whether the substance is an immediate precursor of a substance already controlled under this subchapter.

(d) International treaties, conventions, and protocols requiring control; procedures respecting changes in drug schedules of Convention on Psychotropic Substances

(1) If control is required by United States obligations under international treaties, conventions, or protocols in effect on October 27, 1970, the Attorney General shall issue an order controlling such drug under the schedule he deems most appropriate to carry out such obligations, without regard to the findings required by subsection (a) of this section or section 812(b) of this title and without regard to the procedures prescribed by subsections (a) and (b) of this section.

(2)(A) Whenever the Secretary of State receives notification from the Secretary-General of the United Nations that information has been transmitted by or to the World Health Organization, pursuant to article 2 of the Convention on Psychotropic Substances, which may justify adding a drug or other substance to one of the schedules of the Convention, transferring a drug or substance from one schedule to another, or deleting it from the schedules, the Secretary of State shall immediately transmit the notice to the Secretary of Health and Human Services who shall publish it in the Federal Register and provide opportunity to interested persons to submit to him comments respecting the scientific and medical evaluations which he is to prepare respecting such drug or substance. The Secretary of Health and Human Services shall prepare for transmission through the Secretary of State to the World Health Organization such medical and scientific evaluations as may be appropriate regarding the possible action that could be proposed by the World Health Organization respecting the drug or substance with respect to which a notice was transmitted under this subparagraph.

(B) Whenever the Secretary of State receives information that the Commission on Narcotic Drugs of the United Nations proposes to decide whether to add a drug or other substance to one of the schedules of the Convention, transfer a drug or substance from one schedule to another, or delete it from the schedules, the Secretary of State shall transmit timely notice to the Secretary of Health and Human Services of such information who shall publish a summary of such information in the Federal Register and provide opportunity to interested persons to submit to him comments respecting the recommendation which he is to furnish, pursuant to this subparagraph, respecting such proposal. The Secretary of Health and Human Services shall evaluate the proposal and furnish a recommendation to the Secretary of State which shall be binding on the representative of the United States in discussions and negotiations relating to the proposal.

(3) When the United States receives notification of a scheduling decision pursuant to article 2 of the Convention on Psychotropic Substances that a drug or other substance has been added or transferred to a schedule specified in the notification or receives notification (referred to in this subsection as a "schedule notice") that existing legal controls applicable under this subchapter to a drug or substance and the controls required by the Federal Food, Drug, and Cosmetic Act [21 U.S.C.A. § 301 et seq.] do not meet the requirements of the schedule of the Convention in which such drug or substance has been placed, the Secretary of Health and Human Services after consultation with the Attorney General, shall first determine whether existing legal controls under this subchapter applicable to the drug or substance and the controls required by the Federal Food, Drug, and Cosmetic Act, meet the requirements of the schedule specified in the notification or schedule notice and shall take the following action:

(A) If such requirements are met by such existing controls but the Secretary of Health and Human Services nonetheless believes that more stringent controls should be applied to the drug or substance, the Secretary shall recommend to the Attorney General that he initiate proceedings for scheduling the drug or substance, pursuant to subsections (a) and (b) of this section, to apply to such controls.

(B) If such requirements are not met by such existing controls and the Secretary of Health and Human Services concurs in the scheduling decision or schedule notice transmitted by the notification, the Secretary shall recommend to the Attorney General that he initiate proceedings for scheduling the drug or substance under the appropriate schedule pursuant to subsections (a) and (b) of this section.

(C) If such requirements are not met by such existing controls and the Secretary of Health and Human Services does not concur in the scheduling decision or schedule notice transmitted by the notification, the Secretary shall—

(i) if he deems that additional controls are necessary to protect the public health and safety, recommend to the Attorney General that he initiate proceedings for scheduling the drug or substance pursuant to subsections (a) and (b) of this section, to apply such additional controls;

(ii) request the Secretary of State to transmit a notice of qualified acceptance, within the period specified in the Convention, pursuant to paragraph 7 of article 2 of the Convention, to the Secretary-General of the United Nations;

(iii) request the Secretary of State to transmit a notice of qualified acceptance as prescribed in clause (ii) and request the Secretary of State to ask for a review by the Economic and Social Council of the United Nations, in accordance with paragraph 8 of article 2 of the Convention, of the scheduling decision; or

(iv) in the case of a schedule notice, request the Secretary of State to take appropriate action under the Convention to initiate proceedings to remove the drug or substance from the schedules under the Convention or to transfer the drug or substance to a schedule under the Convention different from the one specified in the schedule notice.

(4)(A) If the Attorney General determines, after consultation with the Secretary of Health and Human Services, that proceedings initiated under recommendations made under paragraph [1] (B) or (C)(i) of paragraph (3) will not be completed within the time period required by paragraph 7 of article 2 of the Convention, the Attorney General, after consultation with the Secretary and after providing interested persons opportunity to submit comments respecting the requirements of the temporary order to be issued under this sentence, shall issue a temporary order controlling the drug or substance under schedule IV or V, whichever is most appropriate to carry out the minimum United States obligations under paragraph 7 of article 2 of the Convention. As a part of such order, the Attorney General shall, after consultation with the Secretary, except such drug or substance from the application of any provision of part C of this subchapter which he finds is not required to carry out the United States obligations under paragraph 7 of article 2 of the Convention. In the case of proceedings initiated under subparagraph (B) of paragraph (3), the Attorney General, concurrently with the issuance of such order, shall request the Secretary of State to transmit a notice of qualified acceptance to the Secretary-General of the United Nations pursuant to paragraph 7 of article 2 of the Convention. A temporary order issued under this subparagraph controlling a drug or other substance subject to proceedings initiated under subsections (a) and (b) of this section shall expire upon the effective date of the application to the drug or substance of the controls resulting from such proceedings.

(B) After a notice of qualified acceptance of a scheduling decision with respect to a drug or other substance is transmitted to the Secretary-General of the United Nations in accordance with clause (ii) or (iii) of paragraph (3)(C) or after a request has been made under clause (iv) of such paragraph with respect to a drug or substance described in a schedule notice, the Attorney General, after consultation with the Secretary of Health and Human Services and after providing interested persons opportunity to submit comments respecting the requirements of the order to be issued under this sentence, shall issue an order controlling the drug or substance under schedule IV or V, whichever is most appropriate to carry out the minimum United States obligations under paragraph 7 of article 2 of the Convention in the case of a drug or substance for which a notice of qualified acceptance was transmitted or whichever the Attorney General determines is appropriate in the case of a drug or substance described in a schedule notice. As a part of such order, the Attorney General shall, after consultation with the Secretary, except such drug or substance from the application of any provision of part C of this subchapter which he finds is not required to carry out the United States obligations under paragraph 7 of article 2 of the Convention. If, as a result of a review under paragraph 8 of article 2 of the Convention of the scheduling decision with respect to which a notice of qualified acceptance was transmitted in accordance with clause (ii) or (iii) of paragraph (3)(C)—

(i) the decision is reversed, and

(ii) the drug or substance subject to such decision is not required to be controlled under schedule IV or V to carry out the minimum United States obligations under paragraph 7 of article 2 of the Convention,

the order issued under this subparagraph with respect to such drug or substance shall expire upon receipt by the United States of the review decision. If, as a result of action taken pursuant to action initiated under a request transmitted under clause (iv) of paragraph (3)(C), the drug or substance with respect to which such action was taken is not required to be controlled under schedule IV or V, the order issued under this paragraph with respect to such drug or substance shall expire upon receipt by the United States of a notice of the action taken with respect to such drug or substance under the Convention.

(C) An order issued under subparagraph (A) or (B) may be issued without regard to the findings required by subsection (a) of this section or by section 812(b) of this title and without regard to the procedures prescribed by subsection (a) or (b) of this section.

(5) Nothing in the amendments made by the Psychotropic Substances Act of 1978 or the regulations or orders promulgated thereunder shall be construed to preclude requests by the Secretary of Health and Human Services or the Attorney General through the Secretary of State, pursuant to article 2 or other applicable provisions of the Convention, for review of scheduling decisions under such Convention, based on new or additional information.

(e) Immediate precursors

The Attorney General may, without regard to the findings required by subsection (a) of this section or section 812(b) of this title and without regard to the procedures prescribed by subsections (a) and (b) of this section, place an immediate precursor in the same schedule in which the controlled substance of which it is an immediate precursor is placed or in any other schedule with a higher numerical designation. If the Attorney General designates a substance as an immediate precursor and places it in a schedule, other substances shall not be placed in a schedule solely because they are its precursors.

(f) Abuse potential

If, at the time a new-drug application is submitted to the Secretary for any drug having a stimulant, depressant, or hallucinogenic effect on the central nervous system, it appears that such drug has an abuse potential, such information shall be forwarded by the Secretary to the Attorney General.

(g) Exclusion of non-narcotic substances sold over the counter without a prescription; dextromethorphan; exemption of substances lacking abuse potential

(1) The Attorney General shall by regulation exclude any non-narcotic drug which contains a controlled substance from the application of this subchapter and subchapter II of this chapter if such drug may, under the Federal Food, Drug, and Cosmetic Act [21 U.S.C.A. § 301 et seq.], be lawfully sold over the counter without a prescription.

(2) Dextromethorphan shall not be deemed to be included in any schedule by reason of enactment of this subchapter unless controlled after October 27, 1970 pursuant to the foregoing provisions of this section.

(3) The Attorney General may, by regulation, exempt any compound, mixture, or preparation containing a controlled substance from the application of all or any part of this subchapter if he finds such compound, mixture, or preparation meets the requirements of one of the following categories:

(A) A mixture, or preparation containing a nonnarcotic controlled substance, which mixture or preparation is approved for prescription use, and which contains one or more other active ingredients which are not listed in any schedule and which are included therein in such combinations, quantity, proportion, or concentration as to vitiate the potential for abuse.

(B) A compound, mixture, or preparation which contains any controlled substance, which is not for administration to a human being or animal, and which is packaged in such form or concentration, or with adulterants or denaturants, so that as packaged it does not present any significant potential for abuse.

(C) Upon the recommendation of the Secretary of Health and Human Services, a compound, mixture, or preparation which contains any anabolic steroid, which is intended for administration to a human being or an animal, and which, because of its concentration, preparation, formulation or delivery system, does not present any significant potential for abuse.

(h) Temporary scheduling to avoid imminent hazards to public safety

(1) If the Attorney General finds that the scheduling of a substance in schedule I on a temporary basis is necessary to avoid an imminent hazard to the public safety, he may, by order and without regard to the requirements of subsection (b) of this section relating to the Secretary of Health and Human Services, schedule such substance in schedule I if the substance is not listed in any other schedule in section 812 of this title or if no exemption or approval is in effect for the substance under section 505 of the Federal Food, Drug, and Cosmetic Act [21 U.S.C.A. § 355]. Such an order may not be issued before the expiration of thirty days from—

(A) the date of the publication by the Attorney General of a notice in the Federal Register of the intention to issue such order and the grounds upon which such order is to be issued, and

(B) the date the Attorney General has transmitted the notice required by paragraph (4).

(2) The scheduling of a substance under this subsection shall expire at the end of one year from the date of the issuance of the order scheduling such substance, except that the Attorney General may, during the pendency of proceedings under subsection (a)(1) of this section with respect to the substance, extend the temporary scheduling for up to six months.

(3) When issuing an order under paragraph (1), the Attorney General shall be required to consider, with respect to the finding of an imminent hazard to the public safety, only those factors set forth in paragraphs (4), (5), and (6) of subsection (c) of this section, including actual abuse, diversion from legitimate channels, and clandestine importation, manufacture, or distribution.

(4) The Attorney General shall transmit notice of an order proposed to be issued under paragraph (1) to the Secretary of Health and Human Services. In issuing an order under paragraph (1), the Attorney General shall take into consideration any comments submitted by the Secretary in response to a notice transmitted pursuant to this paragraph.

(5) An order issued under paragraph (1) with respect to a substance shall be vacated upon the conclusion of a subsequent rulemaking proceeding initiated under subsection (a) of this section with respect to such substance.

(6) An order issued under paragraph (1) is not subject to judicial review.

(Pub.L. 91–513, Title II, § 201, Oct. 27, 1970, 84 Stat. 1245; Pub.L. 95–633, Title I, § 102(a), Nov. 10, 1978, 92 Stat. 3769; Pub.L. 96–88, Title V, § 509(b), Oct. 17, 1979, 93 Stat. 695; Pub.L. 98–473, Title II, §§ 508, 509(a), Oct. 12, 1984, 98 Stat. 2071, 2072; Pub.L. 108–358, § 2(b), Oct. 22, 2004, 118 Stat. 1663.)

1 So in original. Probably should be "subparagraph".

HISTORICAL AND STATUTORY NOTES

References in Text

"This subchapter", referred to in subsecs. (a), (c)(8), (d)(3), (4)(A), (B), and (g)(2), was in the original "this title" which is Title II of Pub.L. 91–513, Oct. 27, 1970, 84 Stat. 1242, and is popularly known as the "Controlled Substances Act". For complete classification of Title II to the Code, see Short Title note set out under § 801 of this title and Tables.

The Federal Food, Drug, and Cosmetic Act, referred to in subsecs. (d)(3) and (g)(1), is Act June 25, 1938, c. 675, 52 Stat. 1040, as amended, which is classified generally to chapter 9 (§ 301 et seq.) of this title. For complete classification of this Act to the Code, see § 301 of this title and Tables.

Schedules IV and V, referred to in subsec. (d)(4)(A), (B), are set out in § 812(c) of this title.

The Psychotropic Substances Act of 1978, referred to in subsec. (d)(5), is Pub.L. 95–633, Nov. 11, 1978, 92 Stat. 3768, which enacted §§ 801a, 830, and 852 of this title, amended this section and §§ 352, 802, 812, 823, 827, 841 to 843, 872, 881, 952, 953, and 965 of this title and § 242a of Title 42, The Public Health and Welfare, and enacted provisions set out as notes under §§ 801, 801a, 812, and 830 of this title. For complete classification of the Act to the Code, see Short Title of 1978 Amendment note set out under § 801 of this title and Tables volume.

This subchapter and subchapter II of this chapter, referred to in subsec. (g)(1), was in the original "Titles II and III of the Comprehensive Drug Abuse Prevention and Control Act", meaning Comprehensive Drug Abuse Prevention and Control Act of 1970, Pub.L. 91–513, Title II, § 101 et seq., Title III, § 1001 et seq., Oct. 27, 1970, 84 Stat. 1242, 1285. Title II of the Act, which is popularly known as the Controlled Substances Act, is classified principally to this subchapter, 21 U.S.C.A. § 801 et seq. Title III of the Act, which is popularly known as the Controlled Substances Import and Export Act, is classified principally to subchapter II of chapter 13 of this title, 21 U.S.C.A. § 951 et seq. For complete classification, see Short Title notes set out under 21 U.S.C.A. §§ 801 and 951 and Tables.

Effective and Applicability Provisions

2004 Acts. Amendments made by Pub.L. 108–358, § 2(b), amending subsec. (g)(1), (3)(C) of this section, to take effect 90 days after Oct. 22, 2004, see Pub.L. 108–358, § 2(d), set out as a note under 21 U.S.C.A. § 802.

1978 Acts. Amendment by Pub.L. 95–633 effective on the date the Convention on Psychotropic Substances enters into force in the United States [July 15, 1980], see § 112 of Pub.L. 95–633, set out as a note under § 801a of this title.

Section effective Oct. 27, 1970, see § 704(b) of Pub.L. 91–513, set out as a note under § 801 of this title.

Change of Name

"Secretary of Health and Human Services" was substituted for "Secretary of Health, Education, and Welfare" on authority of Pub.L. 96–88, Title V, § 509, Oct. 17, 1979, 93 Stat. 695, which is classified to § 3508 of Title 20, Education.

§ 812. Schedules of controlled substances

(a) Establishment

There are established five schedules of controlled substances, to be known as schedules I, II, III, IV, and V. Such schedules shall initially consist of the substances listed in this section. The schedules established by this section shall be updated and republished on a semiannual basis during the two-year period beginning one year after October 27, 1970, and shall be updated and republished on an annual basis thereafter.

(b) Placement on schedules; findings required

Except where control is required by United States obligations under an international treaty, convention, or protocol, in effect on October 27, 1970, and except in the case of an immediate precursor, a drug or other substance may not be placed in any schedule unless the findings required for such schedule are made with respect to such drug or other substance. The findings required for each of the schedules are as follows:

(1) Schedule I.—

(A) The drug or other substance has a high potential for abuse.

(B) The drug or other substance has no currently accepted medical use in treatment in the United States.

(C) There is a lack of accepted safety for use of the drug or other substance under medical supervision.

(2) Schedule II.—

(A) The drug or other substance has a high potential for abuse.

(B) The drug or other substance has a currently accepted medical use in treatment in the United States or a currently accepted medical use with severe restrictions.

(C) Abuse of the drug or other substances may lead to severe psychological or physical dependence.

(3) Schedule III.—

(A) The drug or other substance has a potential for abuse less than the drugs or other substances in schedules I and II.

(B) The drug or other substance has a currently accepted medical use in treatment in the United States.

(C) Abuse of the drug or other substance may lead to moderate or low physical dependence or high psychological dependence.

(4) Schedule IV.—

(A) The drug or other substance has a low potential for abuse relative to the drugs or other substances in schedule III.

(B) The drug or other substance has a currently accepted medical use in treatment in the United States.

(C) Abuse of the drug or other substance may lead to limited physical dependence or psychological dependence relative to the drugs or other substances in schedule III.

(5) Schedule V.—

(A) The drug or other substance has a low potential for abuse relative to the drugs or other substances in schedule IV.

(B) The drug or other substance has a currently accepted medical use in treatment in the United States.

(C) Abuse of the drug or other substance may lead to limited physical dependence or psychological dependence relative to the drugs or other substances in schedule IV.

(c) Initial schedules of controlled substances

Schedules I, II, III, IV, and V shall, unless and until amended [1] pursuant to section 811 of this title, consist of the following drugs or other substances, by whatever official name, common or usual name, chemical name, or brand name designated:

Schedule I

(a) Unless specifically excepted or unless listed in another schedule, any of the following opiates, including their isomers, esters, ethers, salts, and salts of isomers, esters, and ethers, whenever the existence of such isomers, esters, ethers, and salts is possible within the specific chemical designation:

(1) Acetylmethadol.

(2) Allylprodine.

(3) Alphacetylmathadol.[2]

(4) Alphameprodine.

(5) Alphamethadol.

(6) Benzethidine.

(7) Betacetylmethadol.

(8) Betameprodine.

(9) Betamethadol.

(10) Betaprodine.

(11) Clonitazene.

(12) Dextromoramide.

(13) Dextrorphan.

(14) Diampromide.

(15) Diethylthiambutene.

(16) Dimenoxadol.

(17) Dimepheptanol.

(18) Dimethylthiambutene.

(19) Dioxaphetyl butyrate.

(20) Dipipanone.

(21) Ethylmethylthiambutene.

(22) Etonitazene.

(23) Etoxeridine.

(24) Furethidine.

(25) Hydroxypethidine.

(26) Ketobemidone.

(27) Levomoramide.

(28) Levophenacylmorphan.

(29) Morpheridine.

(30) Noracymethadol.

(31) Norlevorphanol.

(32) Normethadone.

(33) Norpipanone.

(34) Phenadoxone.

(35) Phenampromide.

(36) Phenomorphan.

(37) Phenoperidine.

(38) Piritramide.

(39) Proheptazine.

(40) Properidine.

(41) Racemoramide.

(42) Trimeperidine.

(b) Unless specifically excepted or unless listed in another schedule, any of the following opium derivatives, their salts, isomers, and salts of isomers whenever the existence of such salts, isomers, and salts of isomers is possible within the specific chemical designation:

(1) Acetorphine.

(2) Acetyldihydrocodeine.

(3) Benzylmorphine.

(4) Codeine methylbromide.

(5) Codeine-N-Oxide.

(6) Cyprenorphine.

(7) Desomorphine.

(8) Dihydromorphine.

(9) Etorphine.

(10) Heroin.

(11) Hydromorphinol.

(12) Methyldesorphine.

(13) Methylhydromorphine.

(14) Morphine methylbromide.

(15) Morphine methylsulfonate.

(16) Morphine-N-Oxide.

(17) Myrophine.

(18) Nicocodeine.

(19) Nicomorphine.

(20) Normorphine.

(21) Pholcodine.

(22) Thebacon.

(c) Unless specifically excepted or unless listed in another schedule, any material, compound, mixture, or preparation, which contains any quantity of the following hallucinogenic substances, or which contains any of their salts, isomers, and salts of isomers whenever the existence of such salts, isomers, and salts of isomers is possible within the specific chemical designation:

(1) 3,4-methylenedioxy amphetamine.

(2) 5-methoxy-3,4-methylenedioxy amphetamine.

(3) 3,4,5-trimethoxy amphetamine.

(4) Bufotenine.

(5) Diethyltryptamine.

(6) Dimethyltryptamine.

(7) 4-methyl-2,5-dimethoxyamphetamine.

(8) Ibogaine.

(9) Lysergic acid diethylamide.

(10) Marihuana.

(11) Mescaline.

(12) Peyote.

(13) N-ethyl-3-piperidyl benzilate.

(14) N-methyl-3-piperidyl benzilate.

(15) Psilocybin.

(16) Psilocyn.

(17) Tetrahydrocannabinols.

Schedule II

(a) Unless specifically excepted or unless listed in another schedule, any of the following substances whether produced directly or indirectly by extraction from substances of vegetable origin, or independently by means of chemical synthesis, or by a combination of extraction and chemical synthesis:

(1) Opium and opiate, and any salt, compound, derivative, or preparation of opium or opiate.

(2) Any salt, compound, derivative, or preparation thereof which is chemically equivalent or identical with any of the substances referred to in clause (1), except that these substances shall not include the isoquinoline alkaloids of opium.

(3) Opium poppy and poppy straw.

(4) coca [3] leaves, except coca leaves and extracts of coca leaves from which cocaine, ecgonine, and derivatives of ecgonine or their salts have been removed; cocaine, its salts, optical and geometric isomers, and salts of isomers; ecgonine, its derivatives, their salts, isomers, and salts of isomers; or any compound, mixture, or preparation which contains any quantity of any of the substances referred to in this paragraph.

(b) Unless specifically excepted or unless listed in another schedule, any of the following opiates, including their isomers, esters, ethers, salts, and salts of isomers, esters and ethers, whenever the existence of such isomers, esters, ethers, and salts is possible within the specific chemical designation:

(1) Alphaprodine.

(2) Anileridine.

(3) Bezitramide.

(4) Dihydrocodeine.

(5) Diphenoxylate.

(6) Fentanyl.

(7) Isomethadone.

(8) Levomethorphan.

(9) Levorphanol.

(10) Metazocine.

(11) Methadone.

(12) Methadone-Intermediate, 4-cyano-2-dimethylamino-4, 4-diphenyl butane.

(13) Moramide-Intermediate, 2-methyl-3-morpholino-1, 1-diphenylpropane-carboxylic acid.

(14) Pethidine.

(15) Pethidine-Intermediate-A, 4-cyano-1-methyl-4-phenylpiperidine.

(16) Pethidine-Intermediate-B, ethyl-4-phenylpiperidine-4-carboxylate.

(17) Pethidine-Intermediate-C, 1-methyl-4-phenylpiperidine-4-carboxylic acid.

(18) Phenazocine.

(19) Piminodine.

(20) Racemethorphan.

(21) Racemorphan.

(c) Unless specifically excepted or unless listed in another schedule, any injectable liquid which contains any quantity of methamphetamine, including its salts, isomers, and salts of isomers.

Schedule III

(a) Unless specifically excepted or unless listed in another schedule, any material, compound, mixture, or preparation which contains any quantity of the following substances having a stimulant effect on the central nervous system:

(1) Amphetamine, its salts, optical isomers, and salts of its optical isomers.

(2) Phenmetrazine and its salts.

(3) Any substance (except an injectable liquid) which contains any quantity of methamphetamine, including its salts, isomers, and salts of isomers.

(4) Methylphenidate.

(b) Unless specifically excepted or unless listed in another schedule, any material, compound, mixture, or preparation which contains any quantity of the following substances having a depressant effect on the central nervous system:

(1) Any substance which contains any quantity of a derivative of barbituric acid, or any salt of a derivative of barbituric acid.

(2) Chorhexadol.

(3) Glutethimide.

(4) Lysergic acid.

(5) Lysergic acid amide.

(6) Methyprylon.

(7) Phencyclidine.

(8) Sulfondiethylmethane.

(9) Sulfonethylmethane.

(10) Sulfonmethane.

(c) Nalorphine.

(d) Unless specifically excepted or unless listed in another schedule, any material, compound, mixture, or preparation containing limited quantities of any of the following narcotic drugs, or any salts thereof:

(1) Not more than 1.8 grams of codeine per 100 milliliters or not more than 90 milligrams per dosage unit, with an equal or greater quantity of an isoquinoline alkaloid of opium.

(2) Not more than 1.8 grams of codeine per 100 milliliters or not more than 90 milligrams per dosage unit, with one or more active, non-narcotic ingredients in recognized therapeutic amounts.

(3) Not more than 300 milligrams of dihydrocodeinone per 100 milliliters or not more than 15 milligrams per dosage unit, with a fourfold or greater quantity of an isoquinoline alkaloid of opium.

(4) Not more than 300 milligrams of dihydrocodeinone per 100 milliliters or not more than 15 milligrams per dosage unit, with one or more active, nonnarcotic ingredients in recognized therapeutic amounts.

(5) Not more than 1.8 grams of dihydrocodeine per 100 milliliters or not more than 90 milligrams per dosage unit, with one or more active, nonnarcotic ingredients in recognized therapeutic amounts.

(6) Not more than 300 milligrams of ethylmorphine per 100 milliliters or not more than 15 milligrams per dosage unit, with one or more active, nonnarcotic ingredients in recognized therapeutic amounts.

(7) Not more than 500 milligrams of opium per 100 milliliters or per 100 grams, or not more than 25 milligrams per dosage unit, with one or more active,

nonnarcotic ingredients in recognized therapeutic amounts.

(8) Not more than 50 milligrams of morphine per 100 milliliters or per 100 grams with one or more active, nonnarcotic ingredients in recognized therapeutic amounts.

(e) Anabolic steroids.

Schedule IV

(1) Barbital.

(2) Chloral betaine.

(3) Chloral hydrate.

(4) Ethchlorvynol.

(5) Ethinamate.

(6) Methohexital.

(7) Meprobamate.

(8) Methylphenobarbital.

(9) Paraldehyde.

(10) Petrichloral.

(11) Phenobarbital.

Schedule V

Any compound, mixture, or preparation containing any of the following limited quantities of narcotic drugs, which shall include one or more nonnarcotic active medicinal ingredients in sufficient proportion to confer upon the compound, mixture, or preparation valuable medicinal qualities other than those possessed by the narcotic drug alone:

(1) Not more than 200 milligrams of codeine per 100 milliliters or per 100 grams.

(2) Not more than 100 milligrams of dihydrocodeine per 100 milliliters or per 100 grams.

(3) Not more than 100 milligrams of ethylmorphine per 100 milliliters or per 100 grams.

(4) Not more than 2.5 milligrams of diphenoxylate and not less than 25 micrograms of atropine sulfate per dosage unit.

(5) Not more than 100 milligrams of opium per 100 milliliters or per 100 grams.

(Pub.L. 91–513, Title II, § 202, Oct. 27, 1970, 84 Stat. 1247; Pub.L. 95–633, Title I, § 103, Nov. 10, 1978, 92 Stat. 3772; Pub.L. 98–473, Title II, §§ 507(c), 509(b), Oct. 12, 1984, 98 Stat. 2071, 2072; Pub.L. 99–570, Title I, § 1867, Oct. 27, 1986, 100 Stat. 3207–55; Pub.L. 99–646, § 84, Nov. 10, 1986, 100 Stat. 3619; Pub.L. 101–647, Title XIX, § 1902(a), Nov. 29, 1990, 104 Stat. 4851.)

1 Revised schedules are published in the Code of Federal Regulations, Part 1308 of Title 21, Food and Drugs.

2 So in original. Probably should be "Alphacetylmethadol".

3 So in original. Probably should be capitalized.

HISTORICAL AND STATUTORY NOTES

Effective and Applicability Provisions

1990 Acts. Amendment by Pub.L. 101–647 effective 90 days after Nov. 29, 1990, see section 1902 of Pub.L. 101–647, set out as a note under section 802 of this title.

1978 Acts. Amendment by Pub.L. 95–633 effective on the date the Convention on Psychotropic Substances enters into force in the United States [July 15, 1980], see § 112 of Pub.L. 95–633, set out as a note under § 801a of this title.

1970 Acts. Section effective Oct. 27, 1970, see § 704(b) of Pub.L. 91–513, set out as a note under § 801 of this title.

Emergency Scheduling of Gamma Hydroxybutyric Acid and Listing of Gamma Butyrolactone as List I Chemical

Pub.L. 106–172, § 3(a), Feb. 18, 2000, 114 Stat. 8, provided that:

"(a) Emergency scheduling of GHB.—

"(1) In general.—The Congress finds that the abuse of illicit gamma hydroxybutyric acid is an imminent hazard to the public safety. Accordingly, the Attorney General, notwithstanding sections 201(a), 201(b), 201(c), and 202 of the Controlled Substances Act [21 U.S.C.A. §§ 811(a), 811(b), 811(c), and this section], shall issue, not later than 60 days after the date of the enactment of this Act [Feb. 18, 2000], a final order that schedules such drug (together with its salts, isomers, and salts of isomers) in the same schedule under section 202(c) of the Controlled Substances Act [subsec. (c) of this section] as would apply to a scheduling of a substance by the Attorney General under section 201(h)(1) of such Act [21 U.S.C.A. § 811(h)(1)] (relating to imminent hazards to the public safety), except as follows:

"(A) For purposes of any requirements that relate to the physical security of registered manufacturers and registered distributors, the final order shall treat such drug, when the drug is manufactured, distributed, or possessed in accordance with an exemption under section 505(i) of the Federal Food, Drug, and Cosmetic Act [21 U.S.C.A. § 355(i)] (whether the exemption involved is authorized before, on, or after the date of the enactment of this Act [Feb. 18, 2000]), as being in the same schedule as that recommended by the Secretary of Health and Human Services for the drug when the drug is the subject of an authorized investigational new drug application (relating to such section 505(i) [21 U.S.C.A. § 355(i)]). The recommendation referred to in the preceding sentence is contained in the first paragraph of the letter transmitted on May 19, 1999, by such Secretary (acting through the Assistant Secretary for Health) to the Attorney General (acting through the Deputy Administrator of the Drug Enforcement Administration), which letter was in response to the letter transmitted by the Attorney General (acting through such Deputy Administrator) on September 16, 1997. In publishing the final order in the Federal Register, the Attorney General shall publish a copy of the letter that was transmitted by the Secretary of Health and Human Services.

"(B) In the case of gamma hydroxybutyric acid that is contained in a drug product for which an application is approved under section 505 of the Federal Food, Drug, and Cosmetic Act [21 U.S.C.A. § 355] (whether the application involved is approved before, on, or after the date of the enactment of this Act [Feb. 18, 2000]), the final order shall schedule such drug in the same schedule as that recommended by the Secretary of Health and Human Services for authorized formulations of the drug. The recommendation referred to in the preceding sentence is contained in the last sentence of the fourth paragraph of the letter referred to in subparagraph (A) with respect to May 19, 1999.

"(2) **Failure to issue order.**—If the final order is not issued within the period specified in paragraph (1), gamma hydroxybutyric acid (together with its salts, isomers, and salts of isomers) is deemed to be scheduled under section 202(c) of the Controlled Substances Act [subsec. (c) of this section] in accordance with the policies described in paragraph (1), as if the Attorney General had issued a final order in accordance with such paragraph."

Congressional Findings Regarding Gamma Hydroxybutyric Acid

Pub.L. 106–172, § 2, Feb. 18, 2000, 114 Stat. 7, provided that:

"Congress finds as follows:

"(1) Gamma hydroxybutyric acid (also called G, Liquid X, Liquid Ecstasy, Grievous Bodily Harm, Georgia Home Boy, Scoop) has become a significant and growing problem in law enforcement. At least 20 States have scheduled such drug in their drug laws and law enforcement officials have been experiencing an increased presence of the drug in driving under the influence, sexual assault, and overdose cases especially at night clubs and parties.

"(2) A behavioral depressant and a hypnotic, gamma hydroxybutyric acid ('GHB') is being used in conjunction with alcohol and other drugs with detrimental effects in an increasing number of cases. It is difficult to isolate the impact of such drug's ingestion since it is so typically taken with an ever-changing array of other drugs and especially alcohol which potentiates its impact.

"(3) GHB takes the same path as alcohol, processes via alcohol dehydrogenase, and its symptoms at high levels of intake and as impact builds are comparable to alcohol ingestion/intoxication. Thus, aggression and violence can be expected in some individuals who use such drug.

"(4) If taken for human consumption, common industrial chemicals such as gamma butyrolactone and 1.4–butanediol are swiftly converted by the body into GHB. Illicit use of these and other GHB analogues and precursor chemicals is a significant and growing law enforcement problem.

"(5) A human pharmaceutical formulation of gamma hydroxybutyric acid is being developed as a treatment for cataplexy, a serious and debilitating disease. Cataplexy, which causes sudden and total loss of muscle control, affects about 65 percent of the estimated 180,000 Americans with narcolepsy, a sleep disorder. People with cataplexy often are unable to work, drive a car, hold their children or live a normal life.

"(6) Abuse of illicit GHB is an imminent hazard to public safety that requires immediate regulatory action under the Controlled Substances Act (21 U.S.C. 801 et seq.)."

Placement of Pipradrol and SPA in Schedule IV to Carry Out Obligation Under Convention on Psychotropic Substances

Section 102(c) of Pub.L. 95–633 provided that: "For the purpose of carrying out the minimum United States obligations under paragraph 7 of article 2 of the Convention on Psychotropic Substances, signed at Vienna, Austria, on February 21, 1971, with respect to pipradrol and SPA (also known as (-)-1-dimethylamino-1,2-diphenylethane), the Attorney General shall by order, made without regard to sections 201 and 202 of the Controlled Substances Act [this section and section 811 of this title], place such drugs in schedule IV of such Act [see subsec. (c) of this section]."

Provision of § 102(c) of Pub.L. 95–633, set out above, effective on the date the Convention on Psychotrophic Substances enters into force in the United States [July 15, 1980], see § 112 of Pub.L. 95–633, set out as an Effective Date note under § 801a of this title.

§ 813. Treatment of controlled substance analogues

A controlled substance analogue shall, to the extent intended for human consumption, be treated, for the purposes of any Federal law as a controlled substance in schedule I.

(Pub.L. 91–513, Title II, § 203, as added Pub.L. 99–570, Title I, § 1202, Oct. 27, 1986, 100 Stat. 3207–13, and amended Pub.L. 100–690, Title VI, § 6470(c), Nov. 18, 1988, 102 Stat. 4378.)

HISTORICAL AND STATUTORY NOTES

References in Text

Schedule I, referred to in text, is set out in section 812(c) of this title.

§ 814. Removal of exemption of certain drugs

(a) Removal of exemption

The Attorney General shall by regulation remove from exemption under section 802(39)(A)(iv) of this title a drug or group of drugs that the Attorney General finds is being diverted to obtain a listed chemical for use in the illicit production of a controlled substance.

(b) Factors to be considered

In removing a drug or group of drugs from exemption under subsection (a) of this section, the Attorney General shall consider, with respect to a drug or group of drugs that is proposed to be removed from exemption—

(1) the scope, duration, and significance of the diversion;

(2) whether the drug or group of drugs is formulated in such a way that it cannot be easily used in the illicit production of a controlled substance; and

(3) whether the listed chemical can be readily recovered from the drug or group of drugs.

(c) Specificity of designation

The Attorney General shall limit the designation of a drug or a group of drugs removed from exemption under subsection (a) of this section to the most particularly identifiable type of drug or group of drugs for which evidence of diversion exists unless there is evidence, based on the pattern of diversion and other relevant factors, that the diversion will not be limited to that particular drug or group of drugs.

(d) Reinstatement of exemption with respect to particular drug products

(1) Reinstatement

On application by a manufacturer of a particular drug product that has been removed from exemption under subsection (a) of this section, the Attorney General shall by regulation reinstate the exemption with respect to that particular drug product if the Attorney General determines that the particular drug product is manufactured and distributed in a manner that prevents diversion.

(2) Factors to be considered

In deciding whether to reinstate the exemption with respect to a particular drug product under paragraph (1), the Attorney General shall consider—

(A) the package sizes and manner of packaging of the drug product;

(B) the manner of distribution and advertising of the drug product;

(C) evidence of diversion of the drug product;

(D) any actions taken by the manufacturer to prevent diversion of the drug product; and

(E) such other factors as are relevant to and consistent with the public health and safety, including the factors described in subsection (b) of this section as applied to the drug product.

(3) Status pending application for reinstatement

A transaction involving a particular drug product that is the subject of a bona fide pending application for reinstatement of exemption filed with the Attorney General not later than 60 days after a regulation removing the exemption is issued pursuant to subsection (a) of this section shall not be considered to be a regulated transaction if the transaction occurs during the pendency of the application and, if the Attorney General denies the application, during the period of 60 days following the date on which the Attorney General denies the application, unless—

(A) the Attorney General has evidence that, applying the factors described in subsection (b) of this section to the drug product, the drug product is being diverted; and

(B) the Attorney General so notifies the applicant.

(4) Amendment and modification

A regulation reinstating an exemption under paragraph (1) may be modified or revoked with respect to a particular drug product upon a finding that—

(A) applying the factors described in subsection (b) of this section to the drug product, the drug product is being diverted; or

(B) there is a significant change in the data that led to the issuance of the regulation.

(e) Repealed. Pub.L. 109–177, Title VII, § 712(a)(2), Mar. 9, 2006, 120 Stat. 263

(Pub.L. 91–513, Title II, § 204, as added Pub.L. 103–200, § 2(b)(1), Dec. 17, 1993, 107 Stat. 2334, and amended Pub.L. 104–237, Title IV, § 401(c), Oct. 3, 1996, 110 Stat. 3108; Pub.L. 109–177, Title VII, § 712(a)(2), Mar. 9, 2006, 120 Stat. 263.)

HISTORICAL AND STATUTORY NOTES

Effective and Applicability Provisions

1996 Acts. Amendment by section 401(c) of Pub.L. 104–237 not to apply, notwithstanding any other provision of Pub.L. 104–237, to the sale of any pseudoephedrine or phenylpropanolamine product prior to 12 months after Oct. 3, 1996, except that, on application of a manufacturer of a particular drug product, the Attorney General may exercise exclusive, and judicially unreviewable, discretion to extend such effective date up to an additional 6 months, see section 401(g) of Pub.L. 104–237, set out as a note under 21 U.S.C.A. § 802.

1993 Acts. Section effective on the day that is 120 days after Dec. 17, 1993, see section 11 of Pub.L. 103–200, set out as a note under section 802 of this title.

PART C—REGISTRATION OF MANUFACTURERS, DISTRIBUTORS, AND DISPENSERS OF CONTROLLED SUBSTANCES

§ 821. Rules and regulations

The Attorney General is authorized to promulgate rules and regulations and to charge reasonable fees relating to the registration and control of the manufacture, distribution, and dispensing of controlled substances and to listed chemicals.

(Pub.L. 91–513, Title II, § 301, Oct. 27, 1970, 84 Stat. 1253; Pub.L. 103–200, § 3(a), Dec. 17, 1993, 107 Stat. 2336; Pub.L. 108–447, Div. B, Title VI, § 633(b), Dec. 8, 2004, 118 Stat. 2922.)

HISTORICAL AND STATUTORY NOTES

Effective and Applicability Provisions

1993 Acts. Amendment to this section by Pub.L. 103–200 to take effect on the date that is 120 days after the date of enactment of Pub.L. 103–200, which was approved Dec. 17, 1993, see section 11 of Pub.L. 103–200, set out as a note under section 802 of this title.

1970 Acts. Section effective the first day of the seventh calendar month that begins after the day immediately preceding Oct. 27, 1970, see § 704(a) of Pub.L. 91–513, set out as a note under § 801 of this title.

§ 822. Persons required to register

(a) Period of registration

(1) Every person who manufactures or distributes any controlled substance or list I chemical, or who proposes to engage in the manufacture or distribution of any controlled substance or list I chemical, shall obtain annually a registration issued by the Attorney General in accordance with the rules and regulations promulgated by him.

(2) Every person who dispenses, or who proposes to dispense, any controlled substance, shall obtain from the Attorney General a registration issued in accordance with the rules and regulations promulgated by him. The Attorney General shall, by regulation, determine the period of such registrations. In no event, however, shall such registrations be issued for less than one year nor for more than three years.

(b) Authorized activities

Persons registered by the Attorney General under this subchapter to manufacture, distribute, or dispense controlled substances or list I chemicals are authorized to possess, manufacture, distribute, or dispense such substances or chemicals (including any such activity in the conduct of research) to the extent authorized by their registration and in conformity with the other provisions of this subchapter.

(c) Exceptions

The following persons shall not be required to register and may lawfully possess any controlled substance or list I chemical under this subchapter:

(1) An agent or employee of any registered manufacturer, distributor, or dispenser of any controlled substance or list I chemical if such agent or employee is acting in the usual course of his business or employment.

(2) A common or contract carrier or warehouseman, or an employee thereof, whose possession of the controlled substance or list I chemical is in the usual course of his business or employment.

(3) An ultimate user who possesses such substance for a purpose specified in section 802(25) of this title.

(d) Waiver

The Attorney General may, by regulation, waive the requirement for registration of certain manufacturers, distributors, or dispensers if he finds it consistent with the public health and safety.

(e) Separate registration

A separate registration shall be required at each principal place of business or professional practice where the applicant manufactures, distributes, or dispenses controlled substances or list I chemicals.

(f) Inspection

The Attorney General is authorized to inspect the establishment of a registrant or applicant for registration in accordance with the rules and regulations promulgated by him.

(Pub.L. 91–513, Title II, § 302, Oct. 27, 1970, 84 Stat. 1253; Pub.L. 98–473, Title II, § 510, Oct. 12, 1984, 98 Stat. 2072; Pub.L. 103–200, § 3(b), Dec. 17, 1993, 107 Stat. 2336.)

HISTORICAL AND STATUTORY NOTES

References in Text

"This subchapter", referred to in subsecs. (b) and (c), was in the original "this title" which is Title II of Pub.L. 91–513, Oct. 27, 1970, 84 Stat. 1242, and is popularly known as the "Controlled Substances Act". For complete classification of Title II to the Code, see Short Title note set out under § 801 of this title and Tables.

Section 802(25) of this title, referred to in subsec. (c)(3) of this section, was redesignated 802(26) by Pub.L. 98–473, § 507(a), Oct. 12, 1984, 98 Stat. 2071, and was further redesignated 802(27) by Pub.L. 99–570, Title I, § 1003(b)(2), Oct. 27, 1986, 100 Stat. 3207–6, without amending this section to conform to the redesignations.

Effective and Applicability Provisions

1993 Acts. Amendment to this section by Pub.L. 103–200, to take effect on the date that is 120 days after the date of enactment of Pub.L. 103–200, which was approved Dec. 17, 1993, see section 11 of Pub.L. 103–200, set out as a note under section 802 of this title.

1970 Acts. Section effective the first day of the seventh calendar month that begins after the day immediately preceding Oct. 27, 1970, see § 704(a) of Pub.L. 91–513, set out as a note under § 801 of this title.

Provisional Registration

Section 703 of Pub.L. 91–513 provided that:

"(a)(1) Any person who—

"(A) is engaged in manufacturing, distributing, or dispensing any controlled substance on the day before the effective date of section 302 [this section], and

"(B) is registered on such day under section 510 of the Federal Food, Drug, and Cosmetic Act [section 360 of this title] or under section 4722 of the Internal Revenue Code of 1954 [former section 4722 of Title 261],

shall, with respect to each establishment for which such registration is in effect under any such section, be deemed to have a provisional registration under section 303 [section 823 of this title] for the manufacture, distribution, or dispensing (as the case may be) of controlled substances.

"(2) During the period his provisional registration is in effect under this section, the registration number assigned such person under such section 510 [section 360 of this title] or under such section 4722 [former section 4722 of Title 26] (as the case may be) shall be his registration number for purposes of section 303 of this title [section 823 of this title].

"(b) The provisions of section 304 [section 824 of this title], relating to suspension and revocation of registration, shall apply to a provisional registration under this section.

"(c) Unless sooner suspended or revoked under subsection (b), a provisional registration of a person under subsection (a)(1) of this section shall be in effect until—

"(1) the date on which such person has registered with the Attorney General under section 303 [section 823 of this title] or has had his registration denied under such section, or

"(2) such date as may be prescribed by the Attorney General for registration of manufacturers, distributors, or dispensers, as the case may be,

whichever occurs first."

§ 823. Registration requirements

(a) Manufacturers of controlled substances in schedule I or II

The Attorney General shall register an applicant to manufacture controlled substances in schedule I or II if he determines that such registration is consistent with the public interest and with United States obligations under international treaties, conventions, or protocols in effect on May 1, 1971. In determining the public interest, the following factors shall be considered:

(1) maintenance of effective controls against diversion of particular controlled substances and any controlled substance in schedule I or II compounded therefrom into other than legitimate medical, scientific, research, or industrial channels, by limiting the importation and bulk manufacture of such controlled substances to a number of establishments which can produce an adequate and uninterrupted supply of these substances under adequately competitive conditions for legitimate medical, scientific, research, and industrial purposes;

(2) compliance with applicable State and local law;

(3) promotion of technical advances in the art of manufacturing these substances and the development of new substances;

(4) prior conviction record of applicant under Federal and State laws relating to the manufacture, distribution, or dispensing of such substances;

(5) past experience in the manufacture of controlled substances, and the existence in the establishment of effective control against diversion; and

(6) such other factors as may be relevant to and consistent with the public health and safety.

(b) Distributors of controlled substances in schedule I or II

The Attorney General shall register an applicant to distribute a controlled substance in schedule I or II unless he determines that the issuance of such registration is inconsistent with the public interest. In determining the public interest, the following factors shall be considered:

(1) maintenance of effective control against diversion of particular controlled substances into other than legitimate medical, scientific, and industrial channels;

(2) compliance with applicable State and local law;

(3) prior conviction record of applicant under Federal or State laws relating to the manufacture, distribution, or dispensing of such substances;

(4) past experience in the distribution of controlled substances; and

(5) such other factors as may be relevant to and consistent with the public health and safety.

(c) Limits of authorized activities

Registration granted under subsections (a) and (b) of this section shall not entitle a registrant to (1) manufacture or distribute controlled substances in schedule I or II other than those specified in the registration, or (2) manufacture any quantity of those controlled substances in excess of the quota assigned pursuant to section 826 of this title.

(d) Manufacturers of controlled substances in schedule III, IV, or V

The Attorney General shall register an applicant to manufacture controlled substances in schedule III, IV, or V, unless he determines that the issuance of such registration is inconsistent with the public interest. In determining the public interest, the following factors shall be considered:

(1) maintenance of effective controls against diversion of particular controlled substances and any controlled substance in schedule III, IV, or V compounded therefrom into other than legitimate medical, scientific, or industrial channels;

(2) compliance with applicable State and local law;

(3) promotion of technical advances in the art of manufacturing these substances and the development of new substances;

(4) prior conviction record of applicant under Federal or State laws relating to the manufacture, distribution, or dispensing of such substances;

(5) past experience in the manufacture, distribution, and dispensing of controlled substances, and the existence in the establishment of effective controls against diversion; and

(6) such other factors as may be relevant to and consistent with the public health and safety.

(e) Distributors of controlled substances in schedule III, IV, or V

The Attorney General shall register an applicant to distribute controlled substances in schedule III, IV, or V, unless he determines that the issuance of such registration is inconsistent with the public interest. In determining the public interest, the following factors shall be considered:

(1) maintenance of effective controls against diversion of particular controlled substances into other than legitimate medical, scientific, and industrial channels;

(2) compliance with applicable State and local law;

(3) prior conviction record of applicant under Federal or State laws relating to the manufacture, distribution, or dispensing of such substances;

(4) past experience in the distribution of controlled substances; and

(5) such other factors as may be relevant to and consistent with the public health and safety.

(f) Research by practitioners; pharmacies; research applications; construction of Article 7 of the Convention on Psychotropic Substances

The Attorney General shall register practitioners (including pharmacies, as distinguished from pharmacists) to dispense, or conduct research with, controlled substances in schedule II, III, IV, or V, if the applicant is authorized to dispense, or conduct research with respect to, controlled substances under the laws of the State in which he practices. The Attorney General may deny an application for such registration if he determines that the issuance of such registration would be inconsistent with the public interest. In determining the public interest, the following factors shall be considered:

(1) The recommendation of the appropriate State licensing board or professional disciplinary authority.

(2) The applicant's experience in dispensing, or conducting research with respect to controlled substances.

(3) The applicant's conviction record under Federal or State laws relating to the manufacture, distribution, or dispensing of controlled substances.

(4) Compliance with applicable State, Federal, or local laws relating to controlled substances.

(5) Such other conduct which may threaten the public health and safety.

Separate registration under this part for practitioners engaging in research with controlled substances in schedule II, III, IV, or V, who are already registered under this part in another capacity, shall not be required. Registration applications by practitioners wishing to conduct research with controlled substances in schedule I shall be referred to the Secretary, who shall determine the qualifications and competency of each practitioner requesting registration, as well as the merits of the research protocol. The Secretary, in determining the merits of each research protocol, shall consult with the Attorney General as to effective procedures to adequately safeguard against diversion of such controlled substances from legitimate medical or scientific use. Registration for the purpose of bona fide research with controlled substances in schedule I by a practitioner deemed qualified by the Secretary may be denied by the Attorney General only on a ground specified in section 824(a) of this title. Article 7 of the Convention on Psychotropic Substances shall not be construed to prohibit, or impose additional restrictions upon, research involving drugs or other substances scheduled under the convention which is conducted in conformity with this subsection and other applicable provisions of this subchapter.

(g) Practitioners dispensing narcotic drugs for narcotic treatment; annual registration; separate registration; qualifications; waiver

(1) Except as provided in paragraph (2), practitioners who dispense narcotic drugs to individuals for maintenance treatment or detoxification treatment shall obtain annually a separate registration for that purpose. The Attorney General shall register an applicant to dispense narcotic drugs to individuals for maintenance treatment or detoxification treatment (or both)

(A) if the applicant is a practitioner who is determined by the Secretary to be qualified (under standards established by the Secretary) to engage in the treatment with respect to which registration is sought;

(B) if the Attorney General determines that the applicant will comply with standards established by the Attorney General respecting (i) security of stocks of narcotic drugs for such treatment, and (ii) the maintenance of records (in accordance with section 827 of this title) on such drugs; and

(C) if the Secretary determines that the applicant will comply with standards established by the Secretary (after consultation with the Attorney General) respecting the quantities of narcotic drugs which may be provided for unsupervised use by individuals in such treatment.

(2)(A) Subject to subparagraphs (D) and (J), the requirements of paragraph (1) are waived in the case of the dispensing (including the prescribing), by a practitioner, of narcotic drugs in schedule III, IV, or V or combinations of such drugs if the practitioner meets the conditions specified in subparagraph (B) and the narcotic drugs or combinations of such drugs meet the conditions specified in subparagraph (C).

(B) For purposes of subparagraph (A), the conditions specified in this subparagraph with respect to a practitioner are that, before the initial dispensing of narcotic drugs in schedule III, IV, or V or combinations of such drugs to patients for maintenance or detoxification treatment, the practitioner submit to the Secretary a notification of the intent of the practitioner to begin dispensing the drugs or combinations for such purpose, and that the notification contain the following certifications by the practitioner:

(i) The practitioner is a qualifying physician (as defined in subparagraph (G)).

(ii) With respect to patients to whom the practitioner will provide such drugs or combinations of drugs, the practitioner has the capacity to refer the patients for appropriate counseling and other appropriate ancillary services.

(iii) The total number of such patients of the practitioner at any one time will not exceed the applicable number. For purposes of this clause, the applicable number is 30, unless, not sooner than 1 year after the date on which the practitioner submitted the initial notification, the practitioner submits a second notification to the Secretary of the need and intent of the practitioner to treat up to 100 patients. A second notification under this clause shall contain the certifications required by clauses (i) and (ii) of this subparagraph. The Secretary may by regulation change such total number.

(iv) Repealed. Pub.L. 109–56, § 1(a), Aug. 2, 2005, 119 Stat. 591

(C) For purposes of subparagraph (A), the conditions specified in this subparagraph with respect to narcotic drugs in schedule III, IV, or V or combinations of such drugs are as follows:

(i) The drugs or combinations of drugs have, under the Federal Food, Drug, and Cosmetic Act [21 U.S.C.A. § 301 et seq.] or section 262 of Title 42, been approved for use in maintenance or detoxification treatment.

(ii) The drugs or combinations of drugs have not been the subject of an adverse determination. For purposes of this clause, an adverse determination is a determination published in the Federal Register and made by the Secretary, after consultation with the Attorney General, that the use of the drugs or combinations of drugs for maintenance or detoxification treatment requires additional standards respecting the qualifications of practitioners to provide such treatment, or requires standards respecting the quantities of the drugs that may be provided for unsupervised use.

(D)(i) A waiver under subparagraph (A) with respect to a practitioner is not in effect unless (in addition to conditions under subparagraphs (B) and (C)) the following conditions are met:

(I) The notification under subparagraph (B) is in writing and states the name of the practitioner.

(II) The notification identifies the registration issued for the practitioner pursuant to subsection (f) of this section.

(III) If the practitioner is a member of a group practice, the notification states the names of the other practitioners in the practice and identifies the registrations issued for the other practitioners pursuant to subsection (f) of this section.

(ii) Upon receiving a notification under subparagraph (B), the Attorney General shall assign the practitioner involved an identification number under this paragraph for inclusion with the registration issued for the practitioner pursuant to subsection (f) of this section. The identification number so assigned shall be appropriate to preserve the confidentiality of patients for whom the practitioner has dispensed narcotic drugs under a waiver under subparagraph (A).

(iii) Not later than 45 days after the date on which the Secretary receives a notification under subparagraph (B), the Secretary shall make a determination of whether the practitioner involved meets all requirements for a waiver under subparagraph (B). If the Secretary fails to make such determination by the end of the such 45–day period, the Attorney General shall assign the physician an identification number described in clause (ii) at the end of such period.

(E)(i) If a practitioner is not registered under paragraph (1) and, in violation of the conditions specified in subparagraphs (B) through (D), dispenses narcotic drugs in schedule III, IV, or V or combinations of such drugs for maintenance treatment or detoxification treatment, the Attorney General may, for purposes of section 824(a)(4) of this title, consider the practitioner to have committed an act that renders the registration of the practitioner pursuant to subsection (f) of this section to be inconsistent with the public interest.

(ii)(I) Upon the expiration of 45 days from the date on which the Secretary receives a notification under subparagraph (B), a practitioner who in good faith submits a notification under subparagraph (B) and reasonably believes that the conditions specified in subparagraphs (B) through (D) have been met shall, in dispensing narcotic drugs in schedule III, IV, or V or combinations of such drugs for maintenance treatment or detoxification treatment, be considered to have a waiver under subparagraph (A) until notified otherwise by the Secretary, except that such a practitioner may commence to prescribe or dispense such narcotic drugs for such purposes prior to the expiration of such 45–day period if it facilitates the treatment of an individual patient and both the Secretary and the Attorney General are notified by the practitioner of the intent to commence prescribing or dispensing such narcotic drugs.

(II) For purposes of subclause (I), the publication in the Federal Register of an adverse determination by the Secretary pursuant to subparagraph (C)(ii) shall (with respect to the narcotic drug or combination involved) be considered to be a notification provided by the Secretary to practitioners, effective upon the expiration of the 30–day period beginning on the date on which the adverse determination is so published.

(F)(i) With respect to the dispensing of narcotic drugs in schedule III, IV, or V or combinations of such drugs to patients for maintenance or detoxification treatment, a practitioner may, in his or her discretion, dispense such drugs or combinations for such treatment under a registration under paragraph (1) or a waiver under subparagraph (A) (subject to meeting the applicable conditions).

(ii) This paragraph may not be construed as having any legal effect on the conditions for obtaining a registration under paragraph (1), including with respect to the number of patients who may be served under such a registration.

(G) For purposes of this paragraph:

(i) The term "group practice" has the meaning given such term in section 1395nn(h)(4) of Title 42.

(ii) The term "qualifying physician" means a physician who is licensed under State law and who meets one or more of the following conditions:

(I) The physician holds a subspecialty board certification in addiction psychiatry from the American Board of Medical Specialties.

(II) The physician holds an addiction certification from the American Society of Addiction Medicine.

(III) The physician holds a subspecialty board certification in addiction medicine from the American Osteopathic Association.

(IV) The physician has, with respect to the treatment and management of opiate-dependent patients, completed not less than eight hours of training (through classroom situations, seminars at professional society meetings, electronic communications, or otherwise) that is provided by the American Society of Addiction Medicine, the American Academy of Addiction Psychiatry, the American Medical Association, the American Osteopathic Association, the American Psychiatric Association, or any other organization that the Secretary determines is appropriate for purposes of this subclause.

(V) The physician has participated as an investigator in one or more clinical trials leading to the approval of a narcotic drug in schedule III, IV, or V for maintenance or detoxification treatment, as demonstrated by a statement submitted to the Secretary by the sponsor of such approved drug.

(VI) The physician has such other training or experience as the State medical licensing board (of the State in which the physician will provide maintenance or detoxification treatment) considers to demonstrate the ability of the physician to treat and manage opiate-dependent patients.

(VII) The physician has such other training or experience as the Secretary considers to demonstrate the ability of the physician to treat and manage opiate-dependent patients. Any criteria of the Secretary under this subclause shall be established by regulation. Any such criteria are effective only for 3 years after the date on which the criteria are promulgated, but may be extended for such additional discrete 3–year periods as the Secretary considers appropriate for purposes of this subclause. Such an extension of criteria may only be effectuated through a statement published in the Federal Register by the Secretary during the 30–day period preceding the end of the 3–year period involved.

(H)(i) In consultation with the Administrator of the Drug Enforcement Administration, the Administrator of the Substance Abuse and Mental Health Services Administration, the Director of the National Institute on Drug Abuse, and the Commissioner of Food and Drugs, the Secretary shall issue regulations (through notice and comment rulemaking) or issue practice guidelines to address the following:

(I) Approval of additional credentialing bodies and the responsibilities of additional credentialing bodies.

(II) Additional exemptions from the requirements of this paragraph and any regulations under this paragraph.

Nothing in such regulations or practice guidelines may authorize any Federal official or employee to exercise supervision or control over the practice of medicine or the manner in which medical services are provided.

(ii) Not later than 120 days after October 17, 2000, the Secretary shall issue a treatment improvement protocol containing best practice guidelines for the treatment and maintenance of opiate-dependent patients. The Secretary shall develop the protocol in consultation with the Director of the National Institute on Drug Abuse, the Administrator of the Drug Enforcement Administration, the Commissioner of Food and Drugs, the Administrator of the Substance Abuse and Mental Health Services Administration and other substance abuse disorder professionals. The protocol shall be guided by science.

(I) During the 3–year period beginning on the date of approval by the Food and Drug Administration of a drug in schedule III, IV, or V, a State may not preclude a practitioner from dispensing or prescribing such drug, or combination of such drugs, to patients for maintenance or detoxification treatment in accordance with this paragraph unless, before the expiration of that 3–year period, the State enacts a law prohibiting a practitioner from dispensing such drugs or combinations of drug.[1]

(J)(i) This paragraph takes effect on the date referred to in subparagraph (I), and remains in effect thereafter.

(ii) For purposes relating to clause (iii), the Secretary and the Attorney General may, during the 3–year period beginning on December 29, 2006, make determinations in accordance with the following:

(I) The Secretary may make a determination of whether treatments provided under waivers under subparagraph (A) have been effective forms of maintenance treatment and detoxification treatment in clinical settings; may make a determination of whether such waivers have significantly increased (relative to the beginning of such period) the availability of maintenance treatment and detoxification treatment; and may make a determination of whether such waivers have adverse consequences for the public health.

(II) The Attorney General may make a determination of the extent to which there have been violations of the numerical limitations established under subparagraph (B) for the number of individuals to whom a practitioner may provide treatment; may make a determination of whether waivers under subparagraph (A) have increased (relative to the beginning of such period) the extent to which narcotic drugs in schedule III, IV, or V or combinations of such drugs are being dispensed or possessed in violation of this chapter; and may make a determination of whether such waivers have adverse consequences for the public health.

(iii) If, before the expiration of the period specified in clause (ii), the Secretary or the Attorney General publishes in the Federal Register a decision, made on the basis of determinations under such clause, that subparagraph (B)(iii) should be applied by limiting the total number of patients a practitioner may treat to 30, then the provisions in such subparagraph (B)(iii) permitting more than 30 patients shall not apply, effective 60 days after the date on which the decision is so published. The Secretary shall in making any such decision consult with the Attorney General, and shall in publishing the decision in the Federal Register include any comments received from the Attorney General for inclusion in the publication. The Attorney General shall in making any such decision consult with the Secretary, and shall in publishing the decision in the Federal Register include any comments received from the Secretary for inclusion in the publication.

(h) Applicants for distribution of list I chemicals

The Attorney General shall register an applicant to distribute a list I chemical unless the Attorney General determines that registration of the applicant is inconsistent with the public interest. Registration under this subsection shall not be required for the distribution of a drug product that is exempted under clause (iv) or (v) of section 802(39)(A) of this title. In determining the public interest for the purposes of this subsection, the Attorney General shall consider—

(1) maintenance by the applicant of effective controls against diversion of listed chemicals into other than legitimate channels;

(2) compliance by the applicant with applicable Federal, State, and local law;

(3) any prior conviction record of the applicant under Federal or State laws relating to controlled substances or to chemicals controlled under Federal or State law;

(4) any past experience of the applicant in the manufacture and distribution of chemicals; and

(5) such other factors as are relevant to and consistent with the public health and safety.

(Pub.L. 91–513, Title II, § 303, Oct. 27, 1970, 84 Stat. 1253; Pub.L. 93–281, § 3, May 14, 1974, 88 Stat. 124; Pub.L. 95–633, Title I, § 109, Nov. 10, 1978, 92 Stat. 3773; Pub.L. 98–473, Title II, § 511, Oct. 12, 1984, 98 Stat. 2073; Pub.L. 103–200, § 3(c), Dec. 17, 1993, 107 Stat. 2336; Pub.L. 106–310, Div. B, Title XXXV, § 3502(a), Oct. 17, 2000, 114 Stat. 1222; Pub.L. 107–273, Div. B, Title II, § 2501, Nov. 2, 2002, 116 Stat. 1803; Pub.L. 109–56, § 1(a), (b), Aug. 2, 2005, 119 Stat. 591; Pub.L. 109–177, Title VII, § 712(a)(3), Mar. 9, 2006, 120 Stat. 263; Pub.L. 109–469, Title XI, § 1102, Dec. 29, 2006, 120 Stat. 3540.)

[1] So in original. Probably should be "drugs".

HISTORICAL AND STATUTORY NOTES

References in Text

Schedules I, II, III, IV, and V, referred to in text, are set out in § 812(c) of this title.

The Federal Food, Drug, and Cosmetic Act, referred to subsec. (g)(2)(C)(i), is Act June 25, 1938, c. 675, 52 Stat. 1040, as amended, which is classified principally to chapter 9 of this title (21 U.S.C.A. § 301 et seq.).

This chapter, referred to subsec. (g)(2)(J)(2)(ii)(II), was in the original "this Act", meaning the Controlled Substances Act, Title II of Pub.L. 91–513, Oct. 27, 1970, 84 Stat. 1242, as amended, which enacted this chapter. For complete classification of this Act to the Code, see Short Title note set out under section 801 of this title and Tables.

Effective and Applicability Provisions

2005 Acts. Pub.L 109–56, § 1(c), Aug. 2, 2005, 119 Stat. 591, provided that: "This section [amending this section]

shall take effect on the date of enactment of this Act [Aug. 2, 2005]."

1993 Acts. Amendment to this section by Pub.L. 103–200, to take effect on the date that is 120 days after the date of enactment of Pub.L. 103–200, which was approved Dec. 17, 1993, see section 11 of Pub.L. 103–200, set out as a note under section 802 of this title.

1978 Acts. Amendment by Pub.L. 95–633 effective on the date the Convention on Psychotropic Substances enters into force in the United States [July 15, 1980], see § 112 of Pub.L. 95–633, set out as a note under § 801a of this title.

Section effective the first day of the seventh calendar month that begins after the day immediately preceding Oct. 27, 1970, see § 704(a) of Pub.L. 91–513, set out as a note under § 801 of this title.

Provisional Registration

For provisional registration of persons engaged in manufacturing, distributing, or dispensing of controlled substances on the day before the effective date of § 822 of this title who are registered on such date under § 360 of this title or former § 4722 of Title 26, see § 703 of Pub.L. 91–513, set out as a note under § 822 of this title.

§ 824. Denial, revocation, or suspension of registration

(a) Grounds

A registration pursuant to section 823 of this title to manufacture, distribute, or dispense a controlled substance or a list I chemical may be suspended or revoked by the Attorney General upon a finding that the registrant—

(1) has materially falsified any application filed pursuant to or required by this subchapter or subchapter II of this chapter;

(2) has been convicted of a felony under this subchapter or subchapter II of this chapter or any other law of the United States, or of any State, relating to any substance defined in this subchapter as a controlled substance or a list I chemical;

(3) has had his State license or registration suspended, revoked, or denied by competent State authority and is no longer authorized by State law to engage in the manufacturing, distribution, or dispensing of controlled substances or list I chemicals or has had the suspension, revocation, or denial of his registration recommended by competent State authority;

(4) has committed such acts as would render his registration under section 823 of this title inconsistent with the public interest as determined under such section; or

(5) has been excluded (or directed to be excluded) from participation in a program pursuant to section 1320a–7(a) of Title 42.

A registration pursuant to section 823(g)(1) of this title to dispense a narcotic drug for maintenance treatment or detoxification treatment may be suspended or revoked by the Attorney General upon a finding that the registrant has failed to comply with any standard referred to in section 823(g)(1) of this title.

(b) Limits of revocation or suspension

The Attorney General may limit revocation or suspension of a registration to the particular controlled substance or list I chemical with respect to which grounds for revocation or suspension exist.

(c) Service of show cause order; proceedings

Before taking action pursuant to this section, or pursuant to a denial of registration under section 823 of this title, the Attorney General shall serve upon the applicant or registrant an order to show cause why registration should not be denied, revoked, or suspended. The order to show cause shall contain a statement of the basis thereof and shall call upon the applicant or registrant to appear before the Attorney General at a time and place stated in the order, but in no event less than thirty days after the date of receipt of the order. Proceedings to deny, revoke, or suspend shall be conducted pursuant to this section in accordance with subchapter II of chapter 5 of Title 5. Such proceedings shall be independent of, and not in lieu of, criminal prosecutions or other proceedings under this subchapter or any other law of the United States.

(d) Suspension of registration in cases of imminent danger

The Attorney General may, in his discretion, suspend any registration simultaneously with the institution of proceedings under this section, in cases where he finds that there is an imminent danger to the public health or safety. A failure to comply with a standard referred to in section 823(g)(1) of this title may be treated under this subsection as grounds for immediate suspension of a registration granted under such section. A suspension under this subsection shall continue in effect until the conclusion of such proceedings, including judicial review thereof, unless sooner withdrawn by the Attorney General or dissolved by a court of competent jurisdiction.

(e) Suspension and revocation of quotas

The suspension or revocation of a registration under this section shall operate to suspend or revoke any quota applicable under section 826 of this title.

(f) Disposition of controlled substances or list I chemicals

In the event the Attorney General suspends or revokes a registration granted under section 823 of this title, all controlled substances or list I chemicals owned or possessed by the registrant pursuant to such registration at the time of suspension or the effective date of the revocation order, as the case may be, may, in the discretion of the Attorney General, be placed under seal. No disposition may be made of any controlled substances or list I chemicals under seal until the time for taking an appeal has elapsed or until all appeals have been concluded except that a court, upon application therefor, may at any time order the sale of perishable controlled substances or list I chemicals. Any such order shall require the deposit of the proceeds of the sale with the court. Upon a revocation order becoming final, all such controlled substances or list I chemicals (or proceeds of sale deposited in court) shall be forfeited to the United States; and the Attorney General shall dispose of such controlled substances or list I chemicals in accordance with section 881(e) of this title. All right, title, and interest in such controlled substances or list I chemicals shall vest in the United States upon a revocation order becoming final.

(g) Seizure or placement under seal of controlled substances or list I chemicals

The Attorney General may, in his discretion, seize or place under seal any controlled substances or list I chemicals owned or possessed by a registrant whose registration has expired or who has ceased to practice or do business in the manner contemplated by his registration. Such controlled substances or list I chemicals shall be held for the benefit of the registrant, or his successor in interest. The Attorney General shall notify a registrant, or his successor in interest, who has any controlled substance or list I chemical seized or placed under seal of the procedures to be followed to secure the return of the controlled substance or list I chemical and the conditions under which it will be returned. The Attorney General may not dispose of any controlled substance or list I chemical seized or placed under seal under this subsection until the expiration of one hundred and eighty days from the date such substance or chemical was seized or placed under seal.

(Pub.L. 91–513, Title II, § 304, Oct. 27, 1970, 84 Stat. 1255; Pub.L. 93–281, § 4, May 14, 1974, 88 Stat. 125; Pub.L. 98–473, Title II, §§ 304, 512, 513, Oct. 12, 1984, 98 Stat. 2050, 2073; Pub.L. 100–93, § 8(j), Aug. 18, 1987, 101 Stat. 695; Pub.L. 103–200, § 3(d), Dec. 17, 1993, 107 Stat. 2337; Pub.L. 103–322, Title XXXIII, § 330024(e), Sept. 13, 1994, 108 Stat. 2151; Pub.L. 106–310, Div. B, Title XXXV, § 3502(b), Oct. 17, 2000, 114 Stat. 1227.)

HISTORICAL AND STATUTORY NOTES

References in Text

"This subchapter", referred to in subsecs. (a)(1), (2), and (c), was in the original "this title" which is Title II of Pub.L. 91–513, Oct. 27, 1970, 84 Stat. 1242, and is popularly known as the "Controlled Substances Act". For complete classification of Title II to the Code, see Short Title note set out under § 801 of this title and Tables.

"Subchapter II of this chapter", referred to in subsec. (a)(1), (2), was in the original "title III", meaning Title III of Pub.L. 91–513, Oct. 27, 1970, 84 Stat. 1285. Part A of Title III comprises subchapter II of this chapter. For classification of Part B, consisting of §§ 1101 to 1105 of Title III, see Tables.

Effective and Applicability Provisions

1994 Acts. Amendment by Pub.L. 103–322 effective 120 days after Dec. 17, 1993, see section 330024(f) of Pub.L. 103–322, set out as a note under section 802 of this title.

1993 Acts. Amendment to this section by Pub.L. 103–200, to take effect on the date that is 120 days after the date of enactment of Pub.L. 103–200, which was approved Dec. 17, 1993, see section 11 of Pub.L. 103–200, set out as a note under section 802 of this title.

1987 Acts. Amendment by Pub.L. 100–93 effective at the end of the fourteen-day period beginning on Aug. 18, 1987, and inapplicable to administrative proceedings commenced before the end of such period, see section 15(a) of Pub.L. 100–93, set out as a note under section 1320a–7 of Title 42, the Public Health and Welfare.

1970 Acts. Section effective the first day of the seventh calendar month that begins after the day immediately preceding Oct. 27, 1970, see § 704(a) of Pub.L. 91–513, set out as a note under § 801 of this title.

Provisional Registration

Applicability of this section to provisional registrations, see § 703 of Pub.L. 91–513, set out as a note under § 822 of this title.

§ 825. Labeling and packaging

(a) Symbol

It shall be unlawful to distribute a controlled substance in a commercial container unless such container, when and as required by regulations of the Attorney General, bears a label (as defined in section 321(k) of this title) containing an identifying symbol for such substance in accordance with such regulations. A different symbol shall be required for each schedule of controlled substances.

(b) Unlawful distribution without identifying symbol

It shall be unlawful for the manufacturer of any controlled substance to distribute such substance unless the labeling (as defined in section 321(m) of this title) of such substance contains, when and as required by regulations of the Attorney General, the identifying symbol required under subsection (a) of this section.

(c) Warning on label

The Secretary shall prescribe regulations under section 353(b) of this title which shall provide that the label of a drug listed in schedule II, III, or IV shall, when dispensed to or for a patient, contain a clear, concise warning that it is a crime to transfer the drug to any person other than the patient.

(d) Containers to be securely sealed

It shall be unlawful to distribute controlled substances in schedule I or II, and narcotic drugs in schedule III or IV, unless the bottle or other container, stopper, covering, or wrapper thereof is securely sealed as required by regulations of the Attorney General.

(Pub.L. 91–513, Title II, § 305, Oct. 27, 1970, 84 Stat. 1256.)

HISTORICAL AND STATUTORY NOTES

References in Text

Schedules I, II, III, and IV, referred to in subsecs. (c) and (d), are set out in § 812(c) of this title.

Effective and Applicability Provisions

1970 Acts. Section effective the first day of the seventh calendar month that begins after the day immediately preceding Oct. 27, 1970, but with the Attorney General authorized to postpone such effective date for such period as he might determine to be necessary for the efficient administration of this subchapter, see § 704(c) of Pub.L. 91–513, set out as a note under § 801 of this title.

§ 826. Production quotas for controlled substances

(a) Establishment of total annual needs

The Attorney General shall determine the total quantity and establish production quotas for each basic class of controlled substance in schedules I and II and for ephedrine, pseudoephedrine, and phenylpropanolamine to be manufactured each calendar year to provide for the estimated medical, scientific, research, and industrial needs of the United States, for lawful export requirements, and for the establishment and maintenance of reserve stocks. Production quotas shall be established in terms of quantities of each basic class of controlled substance and not in terms of individual pharmaceutical dosage forms prepared from or containing such a controlled substance.

(b) Individual production quotas; revised quotas

The Attorney General shall limit or reduce individual production quotas to the extent necessary to prevent the aggregate of individual quotas from exceeding the amount determined necessary each year by the Attorney General under subsection (a) of this section. The quota of each registered manufacturer for each basic class of controlled substance in schedule I or II or for ephedrine, pseudoephedrine, or phenylpropanolamine shall be revised in the same proportion as the limitation or reduction of the aggregate of the quotas. However, if any registrant, before the issuance of a limitation or reduction in quota, has manufactured in excess of his revised quota, the amount of the excess shall be subtracted from his quota for the following year.

(c) Manufacturing quotas for registered manufacturers

On or before October 1 of each year, upon application therefor by a registered manufacturer, the Attorney General shall fix a manufacturing quota for the basic classes of controlled substances in schedules I and II and for ephedrine, pseudoephedrine, and phenylpropanolamine that the manufacturer seeks to produce. The quota shall be subject to the provisions of subsections (a) and (b) of this section. In fixing such quotas, the Attorney General shall determine the manufacturer's estimated disposal, inventory, and other requirements for the calendar year; and, in making his determination, the Attorney General shall consider the manufacturer's current rate of disposal, the trend of the national disposal rate during the preceding calendar year, the manufacturer's production cycle and inventory position, the economic availability of raw materials, yield and stability problems, emergencies such as strikes and fires, and other factors.

(d) Quotas for registrants who have not manufactured controlled substance during one or more preceding years

The Attorney General shall, upon application and subject to the provisions of subsections (a) and (b) of this section, fix a quota for a basic class of controlled substance in schedule I or II for any registrant who has not manufactured that basic class of controlled substance or ephedrine, pseudoephedrine, or phenylpropanolamine during one or more preceding calendar years. In fixing such quota, the Attorney General shall take into account the registrant's reasonably anticipated requirements for the current year; and, in making his determination of such requirements, he shall consider such factors specified in subsection (c) of this section as may be relevant.

(e) Quota increases

At any time during the year any registrant who has applied for or received a manufacturing quota for a basic class of controlled substance in schedule I or II or for ephedrine, pseudoephedrine, or phenylpropanolamine may apply for an increase in that quota to meet his estimated disposal, inventory, and other requirements during the remainder of that year. In passing upon the application the Attorney General shall take into consideration any occurrences since the filing of the registrant's initial quota application that may require an increased manufacturing rate by the registrant during the balance of the year. In passing upon the application the Attorney General may also take into account the amount, if any, by which the determination of the Attorney General under subsection (a) of this section exceeds the aggregate of the quotas of all registrants under this section.

(f) Incidental production exception

Notwithstanding any other provisions of this subchapter, no registration or quota may be required for the manufacture of such quantities of controlled substances in schedules I and II or ephedrine, pseudoephedrine, or phenylpropanolamine as incidentally and necessarily result from the manufacturing process used for the manufacture of a controlled substance or of ephedrine, pseudoephedrine, or phenylpropanolamine with respect to which its manufacturer is duly registered under this subchapter. The Attorney General may, by regulation, prescribe restrictions on the retention and disposal of such incidentally produced substances or chemicals.

(g) Each reference in this section to ephedrine, pseudoephedrine, or phenylpropanolamine includes each of the salts, optical isomers, and salts of optical isomers of such chemical.

(Pub.L. 91–513, Title II, § 306, Oct. 27, 1970, 84 Stat. 1257; Pub.L. 94–273, § 3(16), Apr. 21, 1976, 90 Stat. 377; Pub.L. 109–177, Title VII, § 713, Mar. 9, 2006, 120 Stat. 264.)

HISTORICAL AND STATUTORY NOTES

References in Text

Schedules I and II, referred to in text, are set out in § 812(c) of this title.

"This subchapter", referred to in subsec. (f), was in the original "this title" which is Title II of Pub.L. 91–513, Oct. 27, 1970, 84 Stat. 1242, and is popularly known as the "Controlled Substances Act". For complete classification of Title II to the Code, see Short Title note set out under § 801 of this title and Tables volume.

Effective and Applicability Provisions

1970 Acts. Section effective the first day of the seventh calendar month that begins after the day immediately preceding Oct. 27, 1970, but with the Attorney General authorized to postpone such effective date for such period as he might determine to be necessary for the efficient administration of this subchapter, see § 704(c) of Pub.L. 91–513, set out as a note under § 801 of this title.

Coordination with United States Trade Representative

Pub.L. 109–177, Title VII, § 718, Mar. 9, 2006, 120 Stat. 267, provided that: "In implementing sections 713 through 717 and section 721 of this title [Title VII of Pub.L. 109–177, Title VII [§§ 701 to 756], Mar. 9, 2006, 120 Stat. 256, the Combat Methamphetamine Epidemic Act of 2005, sections 713 through 717 and section 721 of which amended this section and 21 U.S.C.A. §§ 830, 842, 952, 960, and 971], the Attorney General shall consult with the United States Trade Representative to ensure implementation complies with all applicable international treaties and obligations of the United States."

§ 827. Records and reports of registrants

(a) Inventory

Except as provided in subsection (c) of this section—

(1) every registrant under this subchapter shall, on May 1, 1971, or as soon thereafter as such registrant first engages in the manufacture, distribution, or dispensing of controlled substances, and every second year thereafter, make a complete and accurate record of all stocks thereof on hand, except that the regulations prescribed under this section shall permit each such biennial inventory (following the initial inventory required by this paragraph) to be prepared on such registrant's regular general physical inventory date (if any) which is nearest to and does not vary by more than six months from the biennial date that would otherwise apply;

(2) on the effective date of each regulation of the Attorney General controlling a substance that immediately prior to such date was not a controlled substance, each registrant under this subchapter manufacturing, distributing, or dispensing such substance shall make a complete and accurate record of all stocks thereof on hand; and

(3) on and after May 1, 1971, every registrant under this subchapter manufacturing, distributing, or dispensing a controlled substance or substances shall maintain, on a current basis, a complete and accurate record of each such substance manufactured, received, sold, delivered, or otherwise disposed of by him, except that this paragraph shall not require the maintenance of a perpetual inventory.

(b) Availability of records

Every inventory or other record required under this section (1) shall be in accordance with, and contain such relevant information as may be required by, regulations of the Attorney General, (2) shall (A) be maintained separately from all other records of the registrant, or (B) alternatively, in the case of nonnarcotic controlled substances, be in such form that information required by the Attorney General is readily retrievable from the ordinary business records of the registrant, and (3) shall be kept and be available, for at least two years, for inspection and copying by officers or employees of the United States authorized by the Attorney General.

(c) Nonapplicability

The foregoing provisions of this section shall not apply—

(1)(A) to the prescribing of controlled substances in schedule II, III, IV, or V by practitioners acting in the lawful course of their professional practice unless such substance is prescribed in the course of maintenance or detoxification treatment of an individual; or

(B) to the administering of a controlled substance in schedule II, III, IV, or V unless the practitioner regularly engages in the dispensing or administering of controlled substances and charges his patients, either separately or together with charges for other professional services, for substances so dispensed or administered or unless such substance is administered in the course of maintenance treatment or detoxification treatment of an individual;

(2)(A) to the use of controlled substances, at establishments registered under this subchapter which keep records with respect to such substances, in research conducted in conformity with an exemption granted under section 355(i) or 360b(j) of this title;

(B) to the use of controlled substances, at establishments registered under this subchapter which keep records with respect to such substances, in preclinical research or in teaching; or

(3) to the extent of any exemption granted to any person, with respect to all or part of such provisions, by the Attorney General by or pursuant to regulation on the basis of a finding that the application of such provisions (or part thereof) to such person is not necessary for carrying out the purposes of this subchapter.

Nothing in the Convention on Psychotropic Substances shall be construed as superseding or otherwise affecting the provisions of paragraph (1)(B), (2), or (3) of this subsection.

(d) Periodic reports to Attorney General

Every manufacturer registered under section 823 of this title shall, at such time or times and in such form as the Attorney General may require, make periodic reports to the Attorney General of every sale, delivery or other disposal by him of any controlled substance, and each distributor shall make such reports with respect to narcotic controlled substances, identifying by the registration number assigned under this subchapter the person or establishment (unless exempt from registration under section 822(d) of this title) to whom such sale, delivery, or other disposal was made.

(e) Reporting and recordkeeping requirements of drug conventions

In addition to the reporting and recordkeeping requirements under any other provision of this subchapter, each manufacturer registered under section 823 of this title shall, with respect to narcotic and nonnarcotic controlled substances manufactured by it, make such reports to the Attorney General, and maintain such records, as the Attorney General may require to enable the United States to meet its obligations under articles 19 and 20 of the Single Convention on Narcotic Drugs and article 16 of the Convention on Psychotropic Substances. The Attorney General shall administer the requirements of this subsection in such a manner as to avoid the unnecessary imposition of duplicative requirements under this subchapter on manufacturers subject to the requirements of this subsection.

(f) Investigational uses of drugs; procedures

Regulations under sections 355(i) and 360(j) of this title, relating to investigational use of drugs, shall include such procedures as the Secretary, after consultation with the Attorney General, determines are necessary to insure the security and accountability of controlled substances used in research to which such regulations apply.

(g) Change of address

Every registrant under this subchapter shall be required to report any change of professional or business address in such manner as the Attorney General shall by regulation require.

(h) Reporting requirements for GHB

In the case of a drug product containing gamma hydroxybutyric acid for which an application has been approved under section 355 of this title, the Attorney General may, in addition to any other requirements that apply under this section with respect to such a drug product, establish any of the following as reporting requirements:

(1) That every person who is registered as a manufacturer of bulk or dosage form, as a packager, repackager, labeler, relabeler, or distributor shall report acquisition and distribution transactions quarterly, not later than the 15th day of the month succeeding the quarter for which the report is submitted, and annually report end-of-year inventories.

(2) That all annual inventory reports shall be filed no later than January 15 of the year following that for which the report is submitted and include data on the stocks of the drug product, drug substance, bulk drug, and dosage forms on hand as of the close of business December 31, indicating whether materials reported are in storage or in process of manufacturing.

(3) That every person who is registered as a manufacturer of bulk or dosage form shall report all manufacturing transactions both inventory increases, including purchases, transfers, and returns, and reductions from inventory, including sales, transfers, theft, destruction, and seizure, and shall provide data on material manufactured, manufactured from other material, use in manufacturing other material, and use in manufacturing dosage forms.

(4) That all reports under this section must include the registered person's registration number as well as the registration numbers, names, and other identifying information of vendors, suppliers, and customers, sufficient to allow the Attorney General to track the receipt and distribution of the drug.

(5) That each dispensing practitioner shall maintain for each prescription the name of the prescribing practitioner, the prescribing practitioner's Federal and State registration numbers, with the expiration dates of these registrations, verification that the prescribing practitioner possesses the appropriate registration to prescribe this controlled substance, the patient's name and address, the name of the patient's insurance provider and documentation by a medical practitioner licensed and registered to prescribe the drug of the patient's medical need for the drug. Such information shall be available for inspection and copying by the Attorney General.

(6) That section 830(b)(3) of this title (relating to mail order reporting) applies with respect to gamma hydroxybutyric acid to the same extent and in the same manner as such section applies with respect to the chemicals and drug products specified in subparagraph (A)(i) of such section.

(Pub.L. 91–513, Title II, § 307, Oct. 27, 1970, 84 Stat. 1258; Pub.L. 93–281, § 5, May 14, 1974, 88 Stat. 125; Pub.L. 95–633, Title I, §§ 104, 110, Nov. 10, 1978, 92 Stat. 3772, 3773; Pub.L. 98–473, Title II, §§ 514, 515, Oct. 12, 1984, 98 Stat. 2074; Pub.L. 106–172, § 4, Feb. 18, 2000, 114 Stat. 9.)

HISTORICAL AND STATUTORY NOTES

References in Text

"This subchapter", referred to in subsecs. (a), (c)(2), (3), (d) and (e), was in the original "this title" which is Title II of Pub.L. 91–513, Oct. 27, 1970, 84 Stat. 1242, and is popularly known as the "Controlled Substances Act". For complete classification of Title II to the Code, see Short Title note set out under § 801 of this title and Tables volume.

Schedules II, III, IV, and V, referred to in subsec. (c)(1), are set out in § 812(c) of this title.

Effective and Applicability Provisions

1978 Acts. Amendment by Pub.L. 95–633 effective on the date the Convention on Psychotropic Substances enters into force in the United States [July 15, 1980], see § 112 of Pub.L. 95–633, set out as a note under § 801a of this title.

1970 Acts. Section effective the first day of the seventh calendar month that begins after the day immediately preceding Oct. 27, 1970, see § 704(a) of Pub.L. 91–513, set out as a note under § 801 of this title.

§ 828. Order forms

(a) Unlawful distribution of controlled substances

It shall be unlawful for any person to distribute a controlled substance in schedule I or II to another except in pursuance of a written order of the person to whom such substance is distributed, made on a form to be issued by the Attorney General in blank in accordance with subsection (d) of this section and regulations prescribed by him pursuant to this section.

(b) Nonapplicability of provisions

Nothing in subsection (a) of this section shall apply to—

(1) the exportation of such substances from the United States in conformity with subchapter II of this chapter;

(2) the delivery of such a substance to or by a common or contract carrier for carriage in the lawful and usual course of its business, or to or by a warehouseman for storage in the lawful and usual course of its business; but where such carriage or storage is in connection with the distribution by the owner of the substance to a third person, this paragraph shall not relieve the distributor from compliance with subsection (a) of this section.

(c) Preservation and availability

(1) Every person who in pursuance of an order required under subsection (a) of this section distributes a controlled substance shall preserve such order for a period of two years, and shall make such order available for inspection and copying by officers and employees of the United States duly authorized for that purpose by the Attorney General, and by officers or employees of States or their political subdivisions who are charged with the enforcement of State or local laws regulating the production, or regulating the distribution or dispensing, of controlled substances and who are authorized under such laws to inspect such orders.

(2) Every person who gives an order required under subsection (a) of this section shall, at or before the time of giving such order, make or cause to be made a duplicate thereof on a form to be issued by the Attorney General in blank in accordance with subsection (d) of this section and regulations prescribed by him pursuant to this section, and shall, if such order is accepted, preserve such duplicate for a period of two years and make it available for inspection and copying by the officers and employees mentioned in paragraph (1) of this subsection.

(d) Issuance

(1) The Attorney General shall issue forms pursuant to subsections (a) and (c)(2) of this section only to persons validly registered under section 823 of this title (or exempted from registration under section 822(d) of this title). Whenever any such form is issued to a person, the Attorney General shall, before delivery thereof, insert therein the name of such person, and it shall be unlawful for any other person (A) to use such form for the purpose of obtaining controlled substances or (B) to furnish such form to any person with intent thereby to procure the distribution of such substances.

(2) The Attorney General may charge reasonable fees for the issuance of such forms in such amounts as

he may prescribe for the purpose of covering the cost to the United States of issuing such forms, and other necessary activities in connection therewith.

(e) Unlawful acts

It shall be unlawful for any person to obtain by means of order forms issued under this section controlled substances for any purpose other than their use, distribution, dispensing, or administration in the conduct of a lawful business in such substances or in the course of his professional practice or research.
(Pub.L. 91–513, Title II, § 308, Oct. 27, 1970, 84 Stat. 1259.)

HISTORICAL AND STATUTORY NOTES

References in Text

Schedules I and II, referred to in subsec. (a), are set out in § 812(c) of this title.

"Subchapter II of this chapter", referred to in subsec. (b)(1), was in the original "title III", meaning Title III of Pub.L. 91–513, Oct. 27, 1970, 84 Stat. 1285. Part A of Title III comprises subchapter II of this chapter. For classification of Part B, consisting of §§ 1101 to 1105 of Title III, see Tables.

Effective and Applicability Provisions

Section effective the first day of the seventh calendar month that begins after the day immediately preceding Oct. 27, 1970, see § 704(a) of Pub.L. 91–513, set out as a note under § 801 of this title.

§ 829. Prescriptions

(a) Schedule II substances

Except when dispensed directly by a practitioner, other than a pharmacist, to an ultimate user, no controlled substance in schedule II, which is a prescription drug as determined under the Federal Food, Drug, and Cosmetic Act [21 U.S.C.A. § 301 et seq.], may be dispensed without the written prescription of a practitioner, except that in emergency situations, as prescribed by the Secretary by regulation after consultation with the Attorney General, such drug may be dispensed upon oral prescription in accordance with section 503(b) of that Act [21 U.S.C.A. § 353(b)]. Prescriptions shall be retained in conformity with the requirements of section 827 of this title. No prescription for a controlled substance in schedule II may be refilled.

(b) Schedule III and IV substances

Except when dispensed directly by a practitioner, other than a pharmacist, to an ultimate user, no controlled substance in schedule III or IV, which is a prescription drug as determined under the Federal Food, Drug, and Cosmetic Act [21 U.S.C.A. § 301 et seq.], may be dispensed without a written or oral prescription in conformity with section 503(b) of that Act [21 U.S.C.A. § 353(b)]. Such prescriptions may not be filled or refilled more than six months after the date thereof or be refilled more than five times after the date of the prescription unless renewed by the practitioner.

(c) Schedule V substances

No controlled substance in schedule V which is a drug may be distributed or dispensed other than for a medical purpose.

(d) Non-prescription drugs with abuse potential

Whenever it appears to the Attorney General that a drug not considered to be a prescription drug under the Federal Food, Drug, and Cosmetic Act [21 U.S.C.A. § 301 et seq.] should be so considered because of its abuse potential, he shall so advise the Secretary and furnish to him all available data relevant thereto.
(Pub.L. 91–513, Title II, § 309, Oct. 27, 1970, 84 Stat. 1260.)

HISTORICAL AND STATUTORY NOTES

References in Text

Schedules II, III, IV, and V, referred to in text, are set out in § 812(c) of this title.

The Federal Food, Drug, and Cosmetic Act, referred to in subsecs. (a), (b), and (d), is Act June 25, 1938, c. 675, 52 Stat. 1040, as amended, which is classified generally to chapter 9 (§ 301 et seq.) of this title. Section 503(b) of that Act is classified to § 353(b) of this title. For complete classification of this Act to the Code, see § 301 of this title and Tables volume.

Effective and Applicability Provisions

1970 Acts. Section effective the first day of the seventh calendar month that begins after the day immediately preceding Oct. 27, 1970, see § 704(a) of Pub.L. 91–513, set out as a note under § 801 of this title.

Effect of Scheduling on Prescriptions

Pub.L. 101–647, Title XIX, § 1902(c), Nov. 29, 1990, 104 Stat. 4852, provided that: "Any prescription for anabolic steroids subject to refill on or after the date of enactment of the amendments made by this section [Nov. 29, 1990] may be refilled without restriction under section 309(a) of the Controlled Substances Act 921 U.S.C. 829(a) [subsec. (a) of this section]."

§ 830. Regulation of listed chemicals and certain machines

(a) Record of regulated transactions

(1) Each regulated person who engages in a regulated transaction involving a listed chemical, a tableting machine, or an encapsulating machine shall keep a record of the transaction for two years after the date of the transaction.

(2) A record under this subsection shall be retrievable and shall include the date of the regulated transaction, the identity of each party to the regulated transaction, a statement of the quantity and form of the listed chemical, a description of the tableting machine or encapsulating machine, and a description of the

method of transfer. Such record shall be available for inspection and copying by the Attorney General.

(3) It is the duty of each regulated person who engages in a regulated transaction to identify each other party to the transaction. It is the duty of such other party to present proof of identity to the regulated person. The Attorney General shall specify by regulation the types of documents and other evidence that constitute proof of identity for purposes of this paragraph.

(b) Reports to Attorney General

(1) Each regulated person shall report to the Attorney General, in such form and manner as the Attorney General shall prescribe by regulation—

(A) any regulated transaction involving an extraordinary quantity of a listed chemical, an uncommon method of payment or delivery, or any other circumstance that the regulated person believes may indicate that the listed chemical will be used in violation of this subchapter;

(B) any proposed regulated transaction with a person whose description or other identifying characteristic the Attorney General furnishes in advance to the regulated person;

(C) any unusual or excessive loss or disappearance of a listed chemical under the control of the regulated person; and

(D) any regulated transaction in a tableting machine or an encapsulating machine.

Each report under subparagraph (A) shall be made at the earliest practicable opportunity after the regulated person becomes aware of the circumstance involved. A regulated person may not complete a transaction with a person whose description or identifying characteristic is furnished to the regulated person under subparagraph (B) unless the transaction is approved by the Attorney General. The Attorney General shall make available to regulated persons guidance documents describing transactions and circumstances for which reports are required under subparagraph (A) and subparagraph (C).

(2) A regulated person that manufactures a listed chemical shall report annually to the Attorney General, in such form and manner and containing such specific data as the Attorney General shall prescribe by regulation, information concerning listed chemicals manufactured by the person. The requirement of the preceding sentence shall not apply to the manufacture of a drug product that is exempted under section 802(39)(A)(iv) of this title.

(3) Mail order reporting

(A) As used in this paragraph:

(i) The term "drug product" means an active ingredient in dosage form that has been approved or otherwise may be lawfully marketed under the Food, Drug, and Cosmetic Act [21 U.S.C.A. § 301 et seq.] for distribution in the United States.

(ii) The term "valid prescription" means a prescription which is issued for a legitimate medical purpose by an individual practitioner licensed by law to administer and prescribe the drugs concerned and acting in the usual course of the practitioner's professional practice.

(B) Each regulated person who engages in a transaction with a nonregulated person or who engages in an export transaction which—

(i) involves ephedrine, pseudoephedrine, or phenylpropanolamine (including drug products containing these chemicals); and

(ii) uses or attempts to use the Postal Service or any private or commercial carrier;

shall, on a monthly basis, submit a report of each such transaction conducted during the previous month to the Attorney General in such form, containing such data, and at such times as the Attorney General shall establish by regulation.

(C) The data required for such reports shall include—

(i) the name of the purchaser;

(ii) the quantity and form of the ephedrine, pseudoephedrine, or phenylpropanolamine purchased; and

(iii) the address to which such ephedrine, pseudoephedrine, or phenylpropanolamine was sent.

(D) Except as provided in subparagraph (E), the following distributions to a nonregulated person, and the following export transactions, shall not be subject to the reporting requirement in subparagraph (B):

(i) Distributions of sample packages of drug products when such packages contain not more than two solid dosage units or the equivalent of two dosage units in liquid form, not to exceed 10 milliliters of liquid per package, and not more than one package is distributed to an individual or residential address in any 30–day period.

(ii) Distributions of drug products by retail distributors that may not include face-to-face transactions to the extent that such distributions are consistent with the activities authorized for a retail distributor as specified in section 802(49) of this title, except that this clause does not apply to sales of scheduled listed chemical products at retail.

(iii) Distributions of drug products to a resident of a long term care facility (as that term is defined in regulations prescribed by the Attorney General) or distributions of drug products to a long term care facility for dispensing to or for use by a resident of that facility.

(iv) Distributions of drug products pursuant to a valid prescription.

(v) Exports which have been reported to the Attorney General pursuant to section 954 or 971 of this title or which are subject to a waiver granted under section 971(f)(2) of this title.

(vi) Any quantity, method, or type of distribution or any quantity, method, or type of distribution of a specific listed chemical (including specific formulations or drug products) or of a group of listed chemicals (including specific formulations or drug products) which the Attorney General has excluded by regulation from such reporting requirement on the basis that such reporting is not necessary for the enforcement of this subchapter or subchapter II of this chapter.

(E) The Attorney General may revoke any or all of the exemptions listed in subparagraph (D) for an individual regulated person if he finds that drug products distributed by the regulated person are being used in violation of this subchapter or subchapter II of this chapter. The regulated person shall be notified of the revocation, which will be effective upon receipt by the person of such notice, as provided in section 971(c)(1) of this title, and shall have the right to an expedited hearing as provided in section 971(c)(2) of this title.

(c) Confidentiality of information obtained by Attorney General; non-disclosure; exceptions

(1) Except as provided in paragraph (2), any information obtained by the Attorney General under this section which is exempt from disclosure under section 552(a) of Title 5, by reason of section 552(b)(4) of such title, is confidential and may not be disclosed to any person.

(2) Information referred to in paragraph (1) may be disclosed only—

(A) to an officer or employee of the United States engaged in carrying out this subchapter, subchapter II of this chapter, or the customs laws;

(B) when relevant in any investigation or proceeding for the enforcement of this subchapter, subchapter II of this chapter, or the customs laws;

(C) when necessary to comply with an obligation of the United States under a treaty or other international agreement; or

(D) to a State or local official or employee in conjunction with the enforcement of controlled substances laws or chemical control laws.

(3) The Attorney General shall—

(A) take such action as may be necessary to prevent unauthorized disclosure of information by any person to whom such information is disclosed under paragraph (2); and

(B) issue guidelines that limit, to the maximum extent feasible, the disclosure of proprietary business information, including the names or identities of United States exporters of listed chemicals, to any person to whom such information is disclosed under paragraph (2).

(4) Any person who is aggrieved by a disclosure of information in violation of this section may bring a civil action against the violator for appropriate relief.

(5) Notwithstanding paragraph (4), a civil action may not be brought under such paragraph against investigative or law enforcement personnel of the Drug Enforcement Administration.

(d) Scheduled listed chemicals; restrictions on sales quantity; requirements regarding nonliquid forms

With respect to ephedrine base, pseudoephedrine base, or phenylpropanolamine base in a scheduled listed chemical product—

(1) the quantity of such base sold at retail in such a product by a regulated seller, or a distributor required to submit reports by subsection (b)(3) of this section may not, for any purchaser, exceed a daily amount of 3.6 grams, without regard to the number of transactions; and

(2) such a seller or distributor may not sell such a product in nonliquid form (including gel caps) at retail unless the product is packaged in blister packs, each blister containing not more than 2 dosage units, or where the use of blister packs is technically infeasible, the product is packaged in unit dose packets or pouches.

(e) Scheduled listed chemicals; behind-the-counter access; logbook requirement; training of sales personnel; privacy protections

(1) Requirements regarding retail transactions

(A) In general

Each regulated seller shall ensure that, subject to subparagraph (F), sales by such seller of a scheduled listed chemical product at retail are made in accordance with the following:

(i) In offering the product for sale, the seller places the product such that customers do not have direct access to the product before the sale is made (in this paragraph referred to as "behind-the-counter" placement). For purposes of this paragraph, a behind-the-counter placement of a product includes circumstances in which the product is stored in a locked cabinet that is located in an area of the facility involved to which customers do have direct access.

(ii) The seller delivers the product directly into the custody of the purchaser.

(iii) The seller maintains, in accordance with criteria issued by the Attorney General, a written or electronic list of such sales that identifies the products by name, the quantity sold, the names and addresses of purchasers, and the dates and times of the sales (which list is referred to in this subsection as the 'logbook'), except that such requirement does not apply to any purchase by an individual of a single sales package if that package contains not more than 60 milligrams of pseudoephedrine.

(iv) In the case of a sale to which the requirement of clause (iii) applies, the seller does not sell such a product unless—

(I) the prospective purchaser—

(aa) presents an identification card that provides a photograph and is issued by a State or the Federal Government, or a document that, with respect to identification, is considered acceptable for purposes of sections 274a.2(b)(1)(v)(A) and 274a.2(b)(1)(v)(B) of title 8, Code of Federal Regulations (as in effect on or after March 9, 2006; and

(bb) signs the logbook and enters in the logbook his or her name, address, and the date and time of the sale; and

(II) the seller—

(aa) determines that the name entered in the logbook corresponds to the name provided on such identification and that the date and time entered are correct; and

(bb) enters in the logbook the name of the product and the quantity sold.

(v) The logbook includes, in accordance with criteria of the Attorney General, a notice to purchasers that entering false statements or misrepresentations in the logbook may subject the purchasers to criminal penalties under section 1001 of Title 18, which notice specifies the maximum fine and term of imprisonment under such section.

(vi) The seller maintains each entry in the logbook for not fewer than two years after the date on which the entry is made.

(vii) In the case of individuals who are responsible for delivering such products into the custody of purchasers or who deal directly with purchasers by obtaining payments for the products, the seller has submitted to the Attorney General a self-certification that all such individuals have, in accordance with criteria under subparagraph (B)(ii), undergone training provided by the seller to ensure that the individuals understand the requirements that apply under this subsection and subsection (d) of this section.

(viii) The seller maintains a copy of such certification and records demonstrating that individuals referred to in clause (vii) have undergone the training.

(ix) If the seller is a mobile retail vendor:

(I) The seller complies with clause (i) by placing the product in a locked cabinet.

(II) The seller does not sell more than 7.5 grams of ephedrine base, pseudoephedrine base, or phenylpropanolamine base in such products per customer during a 30-day period.

(B) Additional provisions regarding certifications and training

(i) In general

A regulated seller may not sell any scheduled listed chemical product at retail unless the seller has submitted to the Attorney General the self-certification referred to in subparagraph (A)(vii). The certification is not effective for purposes of the preceding sentence unless, in addition to provisions regarding the training of individuals referred to in such subparagraph, the certification includes a statement that the seller understands each of the requirements that apply under this paragraph and under subsection (d) of this section and agrees to comply with the requirements.

(ii) Issuance of criteria; self-certification

The Attorney General shall by regulation establish criteria for certifications under this paragraph. The criteria shall—

(I) provide that the certifications are self-certifications provided through the program under clause (iii);

(II) provide that a separate certification is required for each place of business at which a regulated seller sells scheduled listed chemical products at retail; and

(III) include criteria for training under subparagraph (A)(vii).

(iii) Program for regulated sellers

The Attorney General shall establish a program regarding such certifications and training in accordance with the following:

(I) The program shall be carried out through an Internet site of the Department of Justice and such other means as the Attorney General determines to be appropriate.

(II) The program shall inform regulated sellers that section 1001 of Title 18 applies to such certifications.

(III) The program shall make available to such sellers an explanation of the criteria under clause (ii).

(IV) The program shall be designed to permit the submission of the certifications through such Internet site.

(V) The program shall be designed to automatically provide the explanation referred to in subclause (III), and an acknowledgement that the Department has received a certification, without requiring direct interactions of regulated sellers with staff of the Department (other than the provision of technical assistance, as appropriate).

(iv) Availability of certification to State and local officials

Promptly after receiving a certification under subparagraph (A)(vii), the Attorney General shall make available a copy of the certification to the appropriate State and local officials.

(C) Privacy protections

In order to protect the privacy of individuals who purchase scheduled listed chemical products, the Attorney General shall by regulation establish restrictions on disclosure of information in logbooks under subparagraph (A)(iii). Such regulations shall—

(i) provide for the disclosure of the information as appropriate to the Attorney General and to State and local law enforcement agencies; and

(ii) prohibit accessing, using, or sharing information in the logbooks for any purpose other than to ensure compliance with this subchapter or to facilitate a product recall to protect public health and safety.

(D) False statements or misrepresentations by purchasers

For purposes of section 1001 of Title 18 entering information in the logbook under subparagraph (A)(iii) shall be considered a matter within the jurisdiction of the executive, legislative, or judicial branch of the Government of the United States.

(E) Good faith protection

A regulated seller who in good faith releases information in a logbook under subparagraph (A)(iii) to Federal, State, or local law enforcement authorities is immune from civil liability for such release unless the release constitutes gross negligence or intentional, wanton, or willful misconduct.

(F) Inapplicability of requirements to certain sales

Subparagraph (A) does not apply to the sale at retail of a scheduled listed chemical product if a report on the sales transaction is required to be submitted to the Attorney General under subsection (b)(3) of this section.

(G) Certain measures regarding theft and diversion

A regulated seller may take reasonable measures to guard against employing individuals who may present a risk with respect to the theft and diversion of scheduled listed chemical products, which may include, notwithstanding State law, asking applicants for employment whether they have been convicted of any crime involving or related to such products or controlled substances.

(2) Mail-order reporting; verification of identity of purchaser; 30-day restriction on quantities for individual purchasers

Each regulated person who makes a sale at retail of a scheduled listed chemical product and is required under subsection (b)(3) of this section to submit a report of the sales transaction to the Attorney General is subject to the following:

(A) The person shall, prior to shipping the product, confirm the identity of the purchaser in accordance with procedures established by the Attorney General. The Attorney General shall by regulation establish such procedures.

(B) The person may not sell more than 7.5 grams of ephedrine base, pseudoephedrine base, or phenylpropanolamine base in such products per customer during a 30-day period.

(3) Exemptions for certain products

Upon the application of a manufacturer of a scheduled listed chemical product, the Attorney General may by regulation provide that the product is exempt from the provisions of subsection (d) of this section and paragraphs (1) and (2) of this subsection if the Attorney General determines that the product cannot be used in the illicit manufacture of methamphetamine.

(Pub.L. 91–513, Title II, § 310, as added Pub.L. 95–633, Title II, § 202(a), Nov. 10, 1978, 92 Stat. 3774, and amended Pub.L. 100–690, Title VI, § 6052(a), Nov. 18, 1988, 102 Stat. 4312; Pub.L. 103–200, §§ 2(c), 10, Dec. 17, 1993, 107 Stat. 2336, 2341; Pub.L. 104–237, Title II, § 208, Title IV, § 402, Oct. 3, 1996, 110 Stat. 3104, 3111; Pub.L. 106–310, Div. B, Title XXXVI, § 3652, Oct. 17, 2000, 114 Stat. 1239; Pub.L.

109–177, Title VII, §§ 711(a)(2)(B), (b)(1), (c)(1), (2), (d), 716(b)(2), Mar. 9, 2006, 120 Stat. 257, 261, 267.)

HISTORICAL AND STATUTORY NOTES

References in Text

The Food, Drug, and Cosmetic Act, referred to in subsec. (b)(3)(A)(i), is Act June 25, 1938, c. 675, 52 Stat. 1040, as amended, which is classified principally to chapter 9 of this title (21 U.S.C.A. § 301 et seq.). For complete classification of this Act to the Code, see Tables.

"This subchapter", referred to in subsecs. (b)(3)(D)(vi) and (E) and (e)(1)(C)(ii), was in the original "this title" which is Title II of Pub.L. 91–513, Oct. 27, 1970, 84 Stat. 1242, as amended, known as the "Controlled Substances Act". For complete classification, see Short Title note set out under 21 U.S.C.A. § 801 and Tables.

Subchapter II of this chapter, referred to in subsec. (b)(3)(D)(vi) and (E), was in the original "title III", meaning Title III of Pub.L. 91–513, Oct. 27, 1970, 84 Stat. 1285. Part A of Title III comprises subchapter II of this chapter. For classification of Part B, consisting of sections 1101 to 1105 of Title III, see Tables.

Effective and Applicability Provisions

2006 Acts. Pub.L. 109–177, Title VII, § 711(b)(2), Mar. 9, 2006, 120 Stat. 261, provided that:

"With respect to subsections (d) and (e)(1) of section 310 of the Controlled Substances Act, as added by paragraph (1) of this subsection [Pub.L. 109–177, Title VII, § 711(b)(1), Mar. 9, 2006, 120 Stat. 257, amending Pub.L. 91–513, Title II, § 310, as added by Pub.L. 95–633, Title II, § 202(a), Nov. 10, 1978, 92 Stat. 3774, which is classified to this section, by adding subsections (d) and (e)(1)]:

"(A) Such subsection (d) applies on and after the expiration of the 30–day period beginning on the date of the enactment of this Act [March 9, 2006].

"(B) Such subsection (e)(1) applies on and after September 30, 2006."

Pub.L. 109–177, Title VII, § 711(c)(3), Mar. 9, 2006, 120 Stat. 261, provided that: "The amendments made by paragraphs (1) and (2) [Pub.L. 109–177, Title VII, § 711(c)(1) and (2), Mar. 9, 2006, 120 Stat. 261, amending subsections (b)(3)(D)(ii) and (e)(2) of this section]apply on and after the expiration of the 30–day period beginning on the date of the enactment of this Act [March 9, 2006]."

1993 Acts. Amendment to this section by Pub.L. 103–200, to take effect on the date that is 120 days after the date of enactment of Pub.L. 103–200, which was approved Dec. 17, 1993, see section 11 of Pub.L. 103–200, set out as a note under section 802 of this title.

1988 Acts. Amendment by section 6052 of Pub.L. 100–690 effective 120 days after Nov. 18, 1988, see section 6061 of Pub.L. 100–690, set out as a note under section 802 of this title.

Effective Date; Time to Submit Piperidine Report; Required Information

Section 203(a) of Pub.L. 95–633 provided that:

"(1) Except as provided under paragraph (2), the amendments made by this title [enacting this section and amending sections 841 to 843 of this title] shall take effect on the date of the enactment of this Act [Nov. 10, 1978].

"(2) Any person required to submit a report under section 310(a)(1) of the Controlled Substances Act [subsec. (a)(1) of this section] respecting a distribution, sale, or importation of piperidine during the 90 days after the date of the enactment of this Act [Nov. 10, 1978] may submit such report any time up to 97 days after such date of enactment.

"(3) Until otherwise provided by the Attorney General by regulation, the information required to be reported by a person under section 310(a)(1) of the Controlled Substances Act [subsec. (a)(1) of this section] (as added by section 202(a)(2) of this title) with respect to the person's distribution, sale, or importation of piperidine shall—

"(A) be the information described in subparagraphs (A) and (B) of such section, and

"(B) except as provided in paragraph (2) of this subsection, be reported not later than seven days after the date of such distribution, sale, or importation."

Effective Date of Repeal

Pub.L. 96–359, § 8(b), Sept. 26, 1980, 94 Stat. 1194, repealed § 203(d) of Pub.L. 95–633, formerly set out under this section, which had provided for the repeal of this section effective Jan. 1, 1981.

Combat Methamphetamine Epidemic Act of 2005—Coordination with United States Trade Representative

Pub.L. 109–177, Title VII, § 718, Mar. 9, 2006, 120 Stat. 267, provided that in implementing sections 713 though 717 and section 721 of the Combat Methamphetamine Epidemic Act of 2005, the Attorney General shall consult with the United States Trade Representative to insure compliance with all applicable international treaties and obligations of the United States, see Pub.L. 109–177, § 718, set out as a note under 21 U.S.C.A. § 826.

Regulations for Piperidine Reporting

Section 203(b) of Pub.L. 95–633 provided that: "The Attorney General shall—

"(1) first publish proposed interim regulations to carry out the requirements of section 310(a) of the Controlled Substances Act [subsec. (a) of this section] (as added by section 202(a)(2) of this title) not later than 30 days after the date of the enactment of this Act [Nov. 10, 1978], and

"(2) first promulgate final interim regulations to carry out such requirements not later than 75 days after the date of the enactment of this Act [Nov. 10, 1978], such final interim regulations to be effective with respect to distributions, sales, and importations of piperidine on and after the ninety-first day after the date of the enactment of this Act [Nov. 10, 1978]."

Report to President and Congress on Effectiveness of Title II of Pub.L. 95–633

Section 203(c) of Pub.L. 95–633 required the Attorney General, after consultation with the Secretary of Health, Education, and Welfare [now Secretary of Health and Human Services], to analyze and evaluate the impact and effectiveness of the amendments made by Title II of Pub.L. 95–633 [enacting this section and amending sections 841 to 843 of this title], including the impact on the illicit manufacture and use of phencyclidine and the impact of the requirements imposed by such amendments on legitimate distributions and uses of piperidine, and, not later than Mar. 1, 1980, to report to the President and the Congress on such analysis and evaluation and to include in such report such recommendations as he deemed appropriate.

PART D—OFFENSES AND PENALTIES

§ 841. Prohibited acts A

(a) Unlawful acts

Except as authorized by this subchapter, it shall be unlawful for any person knowingly or intentionally—

(1) to manufacture, distribute, or dispense, or possess with intent to manufacture, distribute, or dispense, a controlled substance; or

(2) to create, distribute, or dispense, or possess with intent to distribute or dispense, a counterfeit substance.

(b) Penalties

Except as otherwise provided in section 859, 860, or 861 of this title, any person who violates subsection (a) of this section shall be sentenced as follows:

(1)(A) In the case of a violation of subsection (a) of this section involving—

(i) 1 kilogram or more of a mixture or substance containing a detectable amount of heroin;

(ii) 5 kilograms or more of a mixture or substance containing a detectable amount of—

(I) coca leaves, except coca leaves and extracts of coca leaves from which cocaine, ecgonine, and derivatives of ecgonine or their salts have been removed;

(II) cocaine, its salts, optical and geometric isomers, and salts of isomers;

(III) ecgonine, its derivatives, their salts, isomers, and salts of isomers; or

(IV) any compound, mixture, or preparation which contains any quantity of any of the substances referred to in subclauses (I) through (III);

(iii) 50 grams or more of a mixture or substance described in clause (ii) which contains cocaine base;

(iv) 100 grams or more of phencyclidine (PCP) or 1 kilogram or more of a mixture or substance containing a detectable amount of phencyclidine (PCP);

(v) 10 grams or more of a mixture or substance containing a detectable amount of lysergic acid diethylamide (LSD);

(vi) 400 grams or more of a mixture or substance containing a detectable amount of N-phenyl-N-[1-(2-phenylethyl)-4-piperidinyl] propanamide or 100 grams or more of a mixture or substance containing a detectable amount of any analogue of N-phenyl-N-[1-(2-phenylethyl)-4-piperidinyl] propanamide;

(vii) 1000 kilograms or more of a mixture or substance containing a detectable amount of marijuana, or 1,000 or more marijuana plants regardless of weight; or

(viii) 50 grams or more of methamphetamine, its salts, isomers, and salts of its isomers or 500 grams or more of a mixture or substance containing a detectable amount of methamphetamine, its salts, isomers, or salts of its isomers;

such person shall be sentenced to a term of imprisonment which may not be less than 10 years or more than life and if death or serious bodily injury results from the use of such substance shall be not less than 20 years or more than life, a fine not to exceed the greater of that authorized in accordance with the provisions of Title 18, or $4,000,000 if the defendant is an individual or $10,000,000 if the defendant is other than an individual, or both. If any person commits such a violation after a prior conviction for a felony drug offense has become final, such person shall be sentenced to a term of imprisonment which may not be less than 20 years and not more than life imprisonment and if death or serious bodily injury results from the use of such substance shall be sentenced to life imprisonment, a fine not to exceed the greater of twice that authorized in accordance with the provisions of Title 18, or $8,000,000 if the defendant is an individual or $20,000,000 if the defendant is other than an individual, or both. If any person commits a violation of this subparagraph or of section 849, 859, 860, or 861 of this title after two or more prior convictions for a felony drug offense have become final, such person shall be sentenced to a mandatory term of life imprisonment without release and fined in accordance with the preceding sentence. Notwithstanding section 3583 of Title 18, any sentence under this subparagraph shall, in the absence of such a prior conviction, impose a term of supervised release of at least 5 years in addition to such term of imprisonment and shall, if there was such a prior conviction, impose a term of supervised release of at least 10 years in addition to such term of imprisonment. Notwithstanding any other provision of law, the court shall not place on probation or suspend the sentence of any person sentenced under this subparagraph. No person sentenced under this subparagraph shall be eligible for parole during the term of imprisonment imposed therein.

(B) In the case of a violation of subsection (a) of this section involving—

(i) 100 grams or more of a mixture or substance containing a detectable amount of heroin;

(ii) 500 grams or more of a mixture or substance containing a detectable amount of—

(I) coca leaves, except coca leaves and extracts of coca leaves from which cocaine, ecgonine, and derivatives of ecgonine or their salts have been removed;

(II) cocaine, its salts, optical and geometric isomers, and salts of isomers;

(III) ecgonine, its derivatives, their salts, isomers, and salts of isomers; or

(IV) any compound, mixture, or preparation which contains any quantity of any of the substances referred to in subclauses (I) through (III);

(iii) 5 grams or more of a mixture or substance described in clause (ii) which contains cocaine base;

(iv) 10 grams or more of phencyclidine (PCP) or 100 grams or more of a mixture or substance containing a detectable amount of phencyclidine (PCP);

(v) 1 gram or more of a mixture or substance containing a detectable amount of lysergic acid diethylamide (LSD);

(vi) 40 grams or more of a mixture or substance containing a detectable amount of N–phenyl–N–[1–(2–phenylethyl)–4–piperidinyl] propanamide or 10 grams or more of a mixture or substance containing a detectable amount of any analogue of N–phenyl–N–[1–(2–phenylethyl)–4–piperidinyl] propanamide;

(vii) 100 kilograms or more of a mixture or substance containing a detectable amount of marijuana, or 100 or more marijuana plants regardless of weight; or

(viii) 5 grams or more of methamphetamine, its salts, isomers, and salts of its isomers or 50 grams or more of a mixture or substance containing a detectable amount of methamphetamine, its salts, isomers, or salts of its isomers;

such person shall be sentenced to a term of imprisonment which may not be less than 5 years and not more than 40 years and if death or serious bodily injury results from the use of such substance shall be not less than 20 years or more than life, a fine not to exceed the greater of that authorized in accordance with the provisions of Title 18, or $2,000,000 if the defendant is an individual or $5,000,000 if the defendant is other than an individual, or both. If any person commits such a violation after a prior conviction for a felony drug offense has become final, such person shall be sentenced to a term of imprisonment which may not be less than 10 years and not more than life imprisonment and if death or serious bodily injury results from the use of such substance shall be sentenced to life imprisonment, a fine not to exceed the greater of twice that authorized in accordance with the provisions of Title 18, or $4,000,000 if the defendant is an individual or $10,000,000 if the defendant is other than an individual, or both. Notwithstanding section 3583 of Title 18, any sentence imposed under this subparagraph shall, in the absence of such a prior conviction, include a term of supervised release of at least 4 years in addition to such term of imprisonment and shall, if there was such a prior conviction, include a term of supervised release of at least 8 years in addition to such term of imprisonment. Notwithstanding any other provision of law, the court shall not place on probation or suspend the sentence of any person sentenced under this subparagraph. No person sentenced under this subparagraph shall be eligible for parole during the term of imprisonment imposed therein.

(C) In the case of a controlled substance in schedule I or II, gamma hydroxybutyric acid (including when scheduled as an approved drug product for purposes of section 3(a)(1)(B) of the Hillory J. Farias and Samantha Reid Date–Rape Drug Prohibition Act of 2000), or 1 gram of flunitrazepam, except as provided in subparagraphs (A), (B), and (D), such person shall be sentenced to a term of imprisonment of not more than 20 years and if death or serious bodily injury results from the use of such substance shall be sentenced to a term of imprisonment of not less than twenty years or more than life, a fine not to exceed the greater of that authorized in accordance with the provisions of Title 18, or $1,000,000 if the defendant is an individual or $5,000,000 if the defendant is other than an individual, or both. If any person commits such a violation after a prior conviction for a felony drug offense has become final, such person shall be sentenced to a term of imprisonment of not more than 30 years and if death or serious bodily injury results from the use of such substance shall be sentenced to life imprisonment, a fine not to exceed the greater of twice that authorized in accordance with the provisions of Title 18, or $2,000,000 if the defendant is an individual or $10,000,000 if the defendant is other than an individual, or both. Notwithstanding section 3583 of Title 18, any sentence imposing a term of imprisonment under this paragraph shall, in the absence of such a prior conviction, impose a term of supervised release of at least 3 years in addition to such term of imprisonment and shall, if there was such a prior conviction, impose a term of supervised release of at least 6 years in addition to such term of imprisonment. Notwithstanding any other provision of law, the court shall not place on probation or suspend the sentence of any person sentenced under the provisions of this subparagraph which provide for a mandatory term of imprisonment if death or serious bodily injury results, nor shall a person so sentenced be eligible for parole during the term of such a sentence.

(D) In the case of less than 50 kilograms of marihuana, except in the case of 50 or more marihuana plants regardless of weight, 10 kilograms of hashish, or one kilogram of hashish oil or in the case of any controlled substance in schedule III (other than gamma hydroxybutyric acid), or 30 milligrams of flunitrazepam, such person shall, except as provided in paragraphs (4) and (5) of this subsection, be sentenced to a term of imprisonment of not more than 5 years, a fine not to exceed the greater of that authorized in accordance with the provisions of Title 18, or $250,000 if the defendant is an individual or $1,000,000 if the defendant is other than an individual, or both. If any person commits such a violation after a prior conviction for a felony drug offense has become final, such person shall be sentenced to a term of imprisonment of not more than 10 years, a fine not to exceed the greater of twice that authorized in accordance with the provisions of Title 18, or $500,000 if the defendant is an individual or $2,000,000 if the defendant is other than an individual, or both. Notwithstanding section 3583 of Title 18, any sentence imposing a term of imprisonment under this paragraph shall, in the absence of such a prior conviction, impose a term of supervised release of at least 2 years in addition to such term of imprisonment and shall, if there was such a prior conviction, impose a term of supervised release of at least 4 years in addition to such term of imprisonment.

(2) In the case of a controlled substance in schedule IV, such person shall be sentenced to a term of imprisonment of not more than 3 years, a fine not to exceed the greater of that authorized in accordance with the provisions of Title 18, or $250,000 if the defendant is an individual or $1,000,000 if the defendant is other than an individual, or both. If any person commits such a violation after one or more prior convictions of him for an offense punishable under this paragraph, or for a felony under any other provision of this subchapter or subchapter II of this chapter or other law of a State, the United States, or a foreign country relating to narcotic drugs, marihuana, or depressant or stimulant substances, have become final, such person shall be sentenced to a term of imprisonment of not more than 6 years, a fine not to exceed the greater of twice that authorized in accordance with the provisions of Title 18, or $500,000 if the defendant is an individual or $2,000,000 if the defendant is other than an individual, or both. Any sentence imposing a term of imprisonment under this paragraph shall, in the absence of such a prior conviction, impose a term of supervised release of at least one year in addition to such term of imprisonment and shall, if there was such a prior conviction, impose a term of supervised release of at least 2 years in addition to such term of imprisonment.

(3) In the case of a controlled substance in schedule V, such person shall be sentenced to a term of imprisonment of not more than one year, a fine not to exceed the greater of that authorized in accordance with the provisions of Title 18, or $100,000 if the defendant is an individual or $250,000 if the defendant is other than an individual, or both. If any person commits such a violation after one or more convictions of him for an offense punishable under this paragraph, or for a crime under any other provision of this subchapter or subchapter II of this chapter or other law of a State, the United States, or a foreign country relating to narcotic drugs, marihuana, or depressant or stimulant substances, have become final, such persons shall be sentenced to a term of imprisonment of not more than 2 years, a fine not to exceed the greater of twice that authorized in accordance with the provisions of Title 18, or $200,000 if the defendant is an individual or $500,000 if the defendant is other than an individual, or both.

(4) Notwithstanding paragraph (1)(D) of this subsection, any person who violates subsection (a) of this section by distributing a small amount of marihuana for no remuneration shall be treated as provided in section 844 of this title and section 3607 of Title 18.

(5) Any person who violates subsection (a) of this section by cultivating or manufacturing a controlled substance on Federal property shall be imprisoned as provided in this subsection and shall be fined any amount not to exceed—

(A) the amount authorized in accordance with this section;

(B) the amount authorized in accordance with the provisions of Title 18;

(C) $500,000 if the defendant is an individual; or

(D) $1,000,000 if the defendant is other than an individual;

or both.

(6) Any person who violates subsection (a), or attempts to do so, and knowingly or intentionally uses a poison, chemical, or other hazardous substance on Federal land, and, by such use—

(A) creates a serious hazard to humans, wildlife, or domestic animals,

(B) degrades or harms the environment or natural resources, or

(C) pollutes an aquifer, spring, stream, river, or body of water,

shall be fined in accordance with title 18, United States Code, or imprisoned not more than five years, or both.

(7) Penalties for distribution. (A) In general. Whoever, with intent to commit a crime of violence, as defined in section 16 of Title 18 (including rape), against an individual, violates subsection (a) of this section by distributing a controlled substance or controlled substance analogue to that individual without that individual's knowledge, shall be imprisoned not more than 20 years and fined in accordance with Title 18.

(B) Definitions. For purposes of this paragraph, the term "without that individual's knowledge" means that the individual is unaware that a substance with the ability to alter that individual's ability to appraise conduct or to decline participation in or communicate unwillingness to participate in conduct is administered to the individual.

(c) Offenses involving listed chemicals

Any person who knowingly or intentionally—

(1) possesses a listed chemical with intent to manufacture a controlled substance except as authorized by this subchapter;

(2) possesses or distributes a listed chemical knowing, or having reasonable cause to believe, that the listed chemical will be used to manufacture a controlled substance except as authorized by this subchapter; or

(3) with the intent of causing the evasion of the recordkeeping or reporting requirements of section 830 of this title, or the regulations issued under that section, receives or distributes a reportable amount of any listed chemical in units small enough so that the making of records or filing of reports under that section is not required;

shall be fined in accordance with Title 18 or imprisoned not more than 20 years in the case of a violation of paragraph (1) or (2) involving a list I chemical or not more than 10 years in the case of a violation of this subsection other than a violation of paragraph (1) or (2) involving a list I chemical, or both.

(d) Boobytraps on Federal property; penalties; "boobytrap" defined

(1) Any person who assembles, maintains, places, or causes to be placed a boobytrap on Federal property where a controlled substance is being manufactured, distributed, or dispensed shall be sentenced to a term of imprisonment for not more than 10 years or fined under Title 18, or both.

(2) If any person commits such a violation after 1 or more prior convictions for an offense punishable under this subsection, such person shall be sentenced to a term of imprisonment of not more than 20 years or fined under Title 18, or both.

(3) For the purposes of this subsection, the term "boobytrap" means any concealed or camouflaged device designed to cause bodily injury when triggered by any action of any unsuspecting person making contact with the device. Such term includes guns, ammunition, or explosive devices attached to trip wires or other triggering mechanisms, sharpened stakes, and lines or wires with hooks attached.

(e) Ten-year injunction as additional penalty

In addition to any other applicable penalty, any person convicted of a felony violation of this section relating to the receipt, distribution, manufacture, exportation, or importation of a listed chemical may be enjoined from engaging in any transaction involving a listed chemical for not more than ten years.

(f) Wrongful distribution or possession of listed chemicals

(1) Whoever knowingly distributes a listed chemical in violation of this subchapter (other than in violation of a recordkeeping or reporting requirement of section 830 of this title) shall, except to the extent that paragraph (12), (13), or (14) of section 842(a) of this title applies, be fined under Title 18 or imprisoned not more than 5 years, or both.

(2) Whoever possesses any listed chemical, with knowledge that the recordkeeping or reporting requirements of section 830 of this title have not been adhered to, if, after such knowledge is acquired, such person does not take immediate steps to remedy the violation shall be fined under Title 18 or imprisoned not more than one year, or both.

(g) Internet sales of date rape drugs

(1) Whoever knowingly uses the Internet to distribute a date rape drug to any person, knowing or with reasonable cause to believe that—

(A) the drug would be used in the commission of criminal sexual conduct; or

(B) the person is not an authorized purchaser;

shall be fined under this subchapter or imprisoned not more than 20 years, or both.

(2) As used in this subsection:

(A) The term "date rape drug" means—

(i) gamma hydroxybutyric acid (GHB) or any controlled substance analogue of GHB, including gamma butyrolactone (GBL) or 1,4-butanediol;

(ii) ketamine;

(iii) flunitrazepam; or

(iv) any substance which the Attorney General designates, pursuant to the rulemaking procedures prescribed by section 553 of Title 5, to be used in committing rape or sexual assault.

The Attorney General is authorized to remove any substance from the list of date rape drugs pursuant to the same rulemaking authority.

(B) The term "authorized purchaser" means any of the following persons, provided such person has acquired the controlled substance in accordance with this chapter:

(i) A person with a valid prescription that is issued for a legitimate medical purpose in the usual course of professional practice that is based upon a qualifying medical relationship by a practitioner registered by the Attorney General. A "qualifying medical relationship" means a medical relationship that exists when the practitioner has conducted at least 1 medical evaluation with the authorized purchaser in the physical presence of the practitioner, without regard to whether portions of the evaluation are conducted by other heath professionals. The preceding sentence shall not be construed to imply that 1 medical evaluation demonstrates that a prescription has been issued for a legitimate medical purpose within the usual course of professional practice.

(ii) Any practitioner or other registrant who is otherwise authorized by their registration to dispense, procure, purchase, manufacture, transfer, distribute, import, or export the substance under this chapter.

(iii) A person or entity providing documentation that establishes the name, address, and business of the person or entity and which provides a legitimate purpose for using any "date rape drug" for which a prescription is not required.

(3) The Attorney General is authorized to promulgate regulations for record-keeping and reporting by persons handling 1,4–butanediol in order to implement and enforce the provisions of this section. Any record or report required by such regulations shall be considered a record or report required under this chapter.

(Pub.L. 91–513, Title II, § 401, Oct. 27, 1970, 84 Stat. 1260; Pub.L. 95–633, Title II, § 201, Nov. 10, 1978, 92 Stat. 3774; Pub.L. 96–359, § 8(c), Sept. 26, 1980, 94 Stat. 1194; Pub.L. 98–473, Title II, §§ 224(a), 502, 503(b)(1), (2), Oct. 12, 1984, 98 Stat. 2030, 2068, 2070; Pub.L. 99–570, Title I, §§ 1002, 1003(a), 1004(a), 1005(a), 1103, Title XV, § 15005, Oct. 27, 1986, 100 Stat. 3207–2, 3207–5, 3207–6, 3207–11, 3207–192; Pub.L. 100–690, Title VI, §§ 6055, 6254(h), 6452(a), 6470(g), (h), 6479, Nov. 18, 1988, 102 Stat. 4318, 4367, 4371, 4378, 4381; Pub.L. 101–647, Title X, § 1002(e), Title XII, § 1202, Title XXXV, § 3599K, Nov. 29, 1990, 104 Stat. 4828, 4830, 4932; Pub.L. 103–322, Title IX, § 90105(a), (c), Title XVIII, § 180201(b)(2)(A), Sept. 13, 1994, 108 Stat. 1987, 1988, 2047; Pub.L. 104–237, Title II, § 206(a), Title III, § 302(a), Oct. 3, 1996, 110 Stat. 3103, 3105; Pub.L. 104–305, § 2(a), (b)(1), Oct. 13, 1996, 110 Stat. 3807; Pub.L. 105–277, Div. E, § 2(a), Oct. 21, 1998, 112 Stat. 2681–759; Pub.L. 106–172, §§ 3(b)(1), 5(b), 9, Feb. 18, 2000, 114 Stat. 9, 10, 13; Pub.L. 107–273, Div. B, Title III, § 3005(a), Title IV, § 4002(d)(2)(A), Nov. 2, 2002, 116 Stat. 1805, 1809; Pub.L. 109–177, Title VII, §§ 711(f)(1)(B), 732, Mar. 9, 2006, 120 Stat. 262, 270; Pub.L. 109–248, Title II, § 201, July 27, 2006, 120 Stat. 611.)

HISTORICAL AND STATUTORY NOTES

References in Text

Subchapter II of this chapter, referred to in text, was in the original "title III", meaning of Title III of Pub.L. 91–513, Oct. 27, 1970, 84 Stat. 1285. Part A of Title III comprises subchapter II of this chapter. For classification of Part B, consisting of sections 1101 to 1105 of Title III, see U.S.C.A. Tables.

This subchapter, referred to in subsecs. (a), (b) (1) to (3), (c), (f), and (g)(1)(B), originally read "this title", meaning Pub.L. 91–513, Title II, Oct. 27, 1970, 84 Stat. 1242, as amended, popularly known as the "Controlled Substances Act", which is principally classified to this subchapter. For complete classification of Title II, see Short Title note set out under 21 U.S.C.A. § 801 and Tables.

Schedules I, II, III, IV, and V, referred to in subsec. (b)(1), (2), and (3), are set out in section 812(c) of this title.

"Section 3(a)(1)(B) of the Hillory J. Farias and Samantha Reid Date–Rape Drug Prohibition Act of 2000", referred to in subsec. (b)(1)(C), is classified as a note under section 812 of this title.

This chapter, referred to in subsec. (g), originally read "this Act", meaning the Controlled Substances Act, Pub.L. 91–513, Title II, Oct. 27, 1970, 84 Stat. 1242, as amended, which is classified principally to subchapter I of chapter 13 of this title, 21 U.S.C.A. § 801 et seq. For complete classification, see Short Title note set out under 21 U.S.C.A. § 801 and Tables.

Codifications

Amendment by section 224(a)(5) of Pub.L. 98–473 deleting the last sentence of subsec. (b)(5), which read "Any sentence imposing a term of imprisonment under this paragraph shall, in the absence of such a prior conviction, impose a special parole term of at least 2 years in addition to such term of imprisonment and shall, if there was such a prior conviction, impose a special parole term of at least 4 years in addition to such term of imprisonment", did not take into account repeal of such subsec. (b)(5) by section 502(5) of Pub.L. 98–473 and addition of a new subsec. (b)(5) by section 502(6) of Pub.L. 98–473, thereby resulting in the deletion of a provision of subsec. (b)(5) which had been previously repealed. Section 224(a)(5) of Pub.L. 98–473 was repealed by section 1005(a)(2) of Pub.L. 99–570.

The amendment to former subsec. (c) by Pub.L. 99–570, § 1004(a), directing the substitution of "term of supervised release" for "special parole term" wherever appearing has not been executed to such subsec. (c) in view of repeal by Pub.L. 98–473, § 224(a)(2), eff. Nov. 1, 1987.

The amendment to former subsec. (c) by Pub.L. 101–647, § 1002(e)(2), directing the substitution of "418, 419, or 420" for "405, 405A, or 405B", which for purposes of codification were translated as "859, 860, or 861" and "845, 845a, or 845b", respectively has not been executed to such subsec. in view of repeal by Pub.L. 98–473. See text set out as note above.

Effective and Applicability Provisions

1988 Acts. Amendment by section 6055 of Pub.L. 100–690 effective 120 days after Nov. 18, 1988, see section 6061 of Pub.L. 100–690, set out as a note under section 802 of this title.

1986 Acts. Section 1004(b) of Pub.L. 99–570 provided that: "The amendments made by this section [amending this section and sections 845, 845a, 960 and 962 of this title] shall take effect on the date of the taking effect of section 3583 of title 18, United States Code [Nov. 1, 1987]."

1978 Acts. Amendment by Pub.L. 95–633 effective Nov. 10, 1978, see § 203(a) of Pub.L. 95–633 set out as a note under § 830 of this title.

1970 Acts. Section effective the first day of the seventh calendar month that begins after the day immediately preceding Oct. 27, 1970, see § 704(a) of Pub.L. 91–513, set out as a note under § 801 of this title.

Effective Date and Savings Provisions of 1984 Amendments. Amendment by Pub.L. 98–473, § 224(a), effective on the first day of first calendar month beginning thirty-six months after Oct. 12, 1984, applicable only to offenses committed after taking effect of sections 211 to 239 of Pub.L. 98–473, and except as otherwise provided for therein, see section 235 of Pub.L. 98–473, as amended, set out as a note under section 3551 of Title 18, Crimes and Criminal Procedure.

Effective and Applicability Provisions of Repeal

Section 224(a)(1), (2), (3), and (5) of Pub.L. 98–473, cited to credit, was repealed by section 1005(a)(2) of Pub.L. 99–570. Such provisions of section 224(a) of Pub.L. 98–473, which were to take effect Nov. 1, 1987, as a result of repeal were never executed to text of section.

Pub.L. 96–359, § 8(b), Sept. 26, 1980, 94 Stat. 1194, repealed § 203(d) of Pub.L. 95–633, formerly set out under this section, which had provided for the repeal of subsec. (d) of this section effective Jan. 1, 1981.

§ 842. Prohibited acts B

(a) Unlawful acts

It shall be unlawful for any person—

(1) who is subject to the requirements of part C to distribute or dispense a controlled substance in violation of section 829 of this title;

(2) who is a registrant to distribute or dispense a controlled substance not authorized by his registration to another registrant or other authorized person or to manufacture a controlled substance not authorized by his registration;

(3) who is a registrant to distribute a controlled substance in violation of section 825 of this title;

(4) to remove, alter, or obliterate a symbol or label required by section 825 of this title;

(5) to refuse or negligently fail to make, keep, or furnish any record, report, notification, declaration, order or order form, statement, invoice, or information required under this subchapter or subchapter II of this chapter;

(6) to refuse any entry into any premises or inspection authorized by this subchapter or subchapter II of this chapter;

(7) to remove, break, injure, or deface a seal placed upon controlled substances pursuant to section 824(f) or 881 of this title or to remove or dispose of substances so placed under seal;

(8) to use, to his own advantage, or to reveal, other than to duly authorized officers or employees of the United States, or to the courts when relevant in any judicial proceeding under this subchapter or subchapter II of this chapter, any information acquired in the course of an inspection authorized by this subchapter concerning any method or process which as a trade secret is entitled to protection, or to use to his own advantage or reveal (other than as authorized by section 830 of this title) any information that is confidential under such section;

(9) who is a regulated person to engage in a regulated transaction without obtaining the identification required by [1] 830(a)(3) of this title;

(10) negligently to fail to keep a record or make a report under section 830 of this title;

(11) to distribute a laboratory supply to a person who uses, or attempts to use, that laboratory supply to manufacture a controlled substance or a listed chemical, in violation of this subchapter or subchapter II of this chapter, with reckless disregard for the illegal uses to which such a laboratory supply will be put;

(12) who is a regulated seller, or a distributor required to submit reports under subsection (b)(3) of section 830 of this title—

(A) to sell at retail a scheduled listed chemical product in violation of paragraph (1) of subsection (d) of such section, knowing at the time of the transaction involved (independent of consulting the logbook under subsection (e)(1)(A)(iii) of such section) that the transaction is a violation; or

(B) to knowingly or recklessly sell at retail such a product in violation of paragraph (2) of such subsection (d);

(13) who is a regulated seller to knowingly or recklessly sell at retail a scheduled listed chemical product in violation of subsection (e) of such section; or

(14) who is a regulated seller or an employee or agent of such seller to disclose, in violation of regulations under subparagraph (C) of section 830(e)(1) of this title, information in logbooks under subparagraph (A)(iii) of such section, or to refuse to provide such a logbook to Federal, State, or local law enforcement authorities.

As used in paragraph (11), the term "laboratory supply" means a listed chemical or any chemical, substance, or item on a special surveillance list published by the Attorney General, which contains chemicals, products, materials, or equipment used in the manufacture of controlled substances and listed chemicals. For purposes of paragraph (11), there is a rebuttable presumption of reckless disregard at trial if the Attorney General notifies a firm in writing that a laboratory supply sold by the firm, or any other person or firm, has been used by a customer of the notified firm, or distributed further by that customer, for the unlawful production of controlled substances or listed chemicals a firm distributes and 2 weeks or more after the notification the notified firm distributes a laboratory supply to the customer.

(b) Manufacture

It shall be unlawful for any person who is a registrant to manufacture a controlled substance in schedule I or II, or ephedrine, pseudoephedrine, or phenylpropanolamine or any of the salts, optical isomers, or salts of optical isomers of such chemical, which is—

(1) not expressly authorized by his registration and by a quota assigned to him pursuant to section 826 of this title; or

(2) in excess of a quota assigned to him pursuant to section 826 of this title.

(c) Penalties

(1)(A) Except as provided in subparagraph (B) of this paragraph and paragraph (2), any person who violates this section shall, with respect to any such violation, be subject to a civil penalty of not more than $25,000. The district courts of the United States (or, where there is no such court in the case of any territory or possession of the United States, then the court in such territory or possession having the jurisdiction of a district court of the United States in cases arising under the Constitution and laws of the United States) shall have jurisdiction in accordance with section 1355 of Title 28 to enforce this paragraph.

(B) In the case of a violation of paragraph (5) or (10) of subsection (a) of this section, the civil penalty shall not exceed $10,000.

(2)(A) If a violation of this section is prosecuted by an information or indictment which alleges that the violation was committed knowingly and the trier of fact specifically finds that the violation was so committed, such person shall, except as otherwise provided in subparagraph (B) of this paragraph, be sentenced to imprisonment of not more than one year or a fine under Title 18, or both.

(B) If a violation referred to in subparagraph (A) was committed after one or more prior convictions of the offender for an offense punishable under this paragraph (2), or for a crime under any other provision of this subchapter or subchapter II of this chapter or other law of the United States relating to narcotic drugs, marihuana, or depressant or stimulant substances, have become final, such person shall be sentenced to a term of imprisonment of not more than 2 years, a fine under Title 18, or both.

(C) In addition to the penalties set forth elsewhere in this subchapter or subchapter II of this chapter, any business that violates paragraph (11) of subsection (a) of this section shall, with respect to the first such violation, be subject to a civil penalty of not more than $250,000, but shall not be subject to criminal penalties under this section, and shall, for any succeeding violation, be subject to a civil fine of not more than $250,000 or double the last previously imposed penalty, whichever is greater.

(3) Except under the conditions specified in paragraph (2) of this subsection, a violation of this section does not constitute a crime, and a judgment for the United States and imposition of a civil penalty pursuant to paragraph (1) shall not give rise to any disability or legal disadvantage based on conviction for a criminal offense.

(4)(A) If a regulated seller, or a distributor required to submit reports under section 830(b)(3) of this title, violates paragraph (12) of subsection (a) of this section, or if a regulated seller violates paragraph (13) of such subsection, the Attorney General may by order prohibit such seller or distributor (as the case may be) from selling any scheduled listed chemical product. Any sale of such a product in violation of such an order is subject to the same penalties as apply under paragraph (2).

(B) An order under subparagraph (A) may be imposed only through the same procedures as apply under section 824(c) of this title for an order to show cause.

(Pub.L. 91–513, Title II, § 402, Oct. 27, 1970, 84 Stat. 1262; Pub.L. 95–633, Title II, § 202(b)(1), (2), Nov. 10, 1978, 92 Stat. 3776; Pub.L. 100–690, Title VI, § 6056, Nov. 18, 1988, 102 Stat. 4318; Pub.L. 104–237, Title II, § 205, Oct. 3, 1996, 110 Stat. 3103; Pub.L. 105–277, Div. A, § 101(b) [Title I, § 117], Oct. 21, 1998, 112 Stat. 2681–68; Pub.L. 107–273, Div. B, Title IV, § 4002(b)(16), (d)(2)(B), Nov. 2, 2002, 116 Stat. 1808, 1809; Pub.L. 109–177, Title VII, §§ 711(f)(1)(A), (2), 714, Mar. 9, 2006, 120 Stat. 262, 263, 264.)

[1] So in original. The word "section" probably should follow.

HISTORICAL AND STATUTORY NOTES

References in Text

"This subchapter", referred to in subsecs. (a)(5), (6), (8), (11), and (c)(2)(B), (C), was in the original "this title" which is Title II of Pub.L. 91–513, Oct. 27, 1970, 84 Stat. 1242, and is popularly known as the "Controlled Substances Act". For complete classification of Title II to the Code, see Short Title note set out under section 801 of this title and Tables.

Subchapter II of this chapter, referred to in subsecs. (a)(5), (6), (8), (11), and (c)(2)(B), (C), was in the original "title III", meaning Title III of Pub.L. 91–513, Oct. 27, 1970, 84 Stat. 1285. Part A of Title III comprises subchapter II of this chapter. For classification of Part B, consisting of sections 1101 to 1105 of Title III, see Tables.

Schedules I and II, referred to in subsec. (b), are set out in § 812(c) of this title.

Effective and Applicability Provisions

1988 Acts. Amendment by section 6056 of Pub.L. 100–690, effective 120 days after Nov. 18, 1988, see section 6061 of Pub.L. 100–690, set out as a note under section 802 of this title.

1978 Acts. Amendment by Pub.L. 95–633 effective Nov. 10, 1978, see § 203(a) of Pub.L. 95–633, set out as a note under § 830 of this title.

1970 Acts. Section effective the first day of the seventh calendar month that begins after the day immediately preceding Oct. 27, 1970, see § 704(a) of Pub.L. 91–513, set out as a note under § 801 of this title.

Effective Date of Repeal

Pub.L. 96–359, § 8(b), Sept. 26, 1980, 94 Stat. 1194, repealed § 203(d) of Pub.L. 95–633, formerly set out under this section, which had provided for the repeal of subsecs. (a)(9) and (c)(2)(C) of this section effective Jan. 1, 1981.

Combat Methamphetamine Epidemic Act of 2005—Coordination with United States Trade Representative

Pub.L. 109–177, Title VII, § 718, Mar. 9, 2006, 120 Stat. 267, provided that in implementing sections 713 though 717 and section 721 of the Combat Methamphetamine Epidemic Act of 2005, the Attorney General shall consult with the United States Trade Representative to insure compliance with all applicable international treaties and obligations of the United States, see Pub.L. 109–177, § 718, set out as a note under 21 U.S.C.A. § 826.

§ 843. Prohibited acts C

(a) Unlawful acts

It shall be unlawful for any person knowingly or intentionally—

(1) who is a registrant to distribute a controlled substance classified in schedule I or II, in the course of his legitimate business, except pursuant to an order or an order form as required by section 828 of this title;

(2) to use in the course of the manufacture, distribution, or dispensing of a controlled substance, or to use for the purpose of acquiring or obtaining a controlled substance, a registration number which is fictitious, revoked, suspended, expired, or issued to another person;

(3) to acquire or obtain possession of a controlled substance by misrepresentation, fraud, forgery, deception, or subterfuge;

(4) (A) to furnish false or fraudulent material information in, or omit any material information from, any application, report, record, or other document required to be made, kept, or filed under this subchapter or subchapter II of this chapter, or (B) to present false or fraudulent identification where the person is receiving or purchasing a listed chemical and the person is required to present identification under section 830(a) of this title;

(5) to make, distribute, or possess any punch, die, plate, stone, or other thing designed to print, imprint, or reproduce the trademark, trade name, or other identifying mark, imprint, or device of another or any likeness of any of the foregoing upon any drug or container or labeling thereof so as to render such drug a counterfeit substance;

(6) to possess any three-neck round-bottom flask, tableting machine, encapsulating machine, or gelatin capsule, or any equipment, chemical, product, or material which may be used to manufacture a controlled substance or listed chemical, knowing, intending, or having reasonable cause to believe, that it will be used to manufacture a controlled substance or listed chemical in violation of this subchapter or subchapter II of this chapter;

(7) to manufacture, distribute, export, or import any three-neck round-bottom flask, tableting machine, encapsulating machine, or gelatin capsule, or any equipment, chemical, product, or material which may be used to manufacture a controlled substance or listed chemical, knowing, intending, or having reasonable cause to believe, that it will be used to manufacture a controlled substance or listed chemical in violation of this subchapter or subchapter II of this chapter or, in the case of an exportation, in violation of this subchapter or subchapter II of this chapter or of the laws of the country to which it is exported;

(8) to create a chemical mixture for the purpose of evading a requirement of section 830 of this title or to receive a chemical mixture created for that purpose; or

(9) to distribute, import, or export a list I chemical without the registration required by this subchapter or subchapter II of this chapter.

(b) Communication facility

It shall be unlawful for any person knowingly or intentionally to use any communication facility in committing or in causing or facilitating the commission of any act or acts constituting a felony under any provision of this subchapter or subchapter II of this chapter. Each separate use of a communication facility shall be a separate offense under this subsection. For purposes of this subsection, the term "communication facility" means any and all public and private instrumentalities used or useful in the transmission of writing, signs, signals, pictures, or sounds of all kinds and includes mail, telephone, wire, radio, and all other means of communication.

(c) Advertisement

It shall be unlawful for any person to place in any newspaper, magazine, handbill, or other publications, any written advertisement knowing that it has the purpose of seeking or offering illegally to receive, buy, or distribute a Schedule [1] I controlled substance. As used in this section the term "advertisement" includes, in addition to its ordinary meaning, such advertisements as those for a catalog of Schedule [1] I controlled substances and any similar written advertisement that has the purpose of seeking or offering illegally to receive, buy, or distribute a Schedule [1] I controlled substance. The term "advertisement" does not include material which merely advocates the use of a similar material, which advocates a position or practice, and does not attempt to propose or facilitate an actual transaction in a Schedule [1] I controlled substance.

(d) Penalties

(1) Except as provided in paragraph (2), any person who violates this section shall be sentenced to a term of imprisonment of not more than 4 years, a fine under Title 18, or both; except that if any person commits such a violation after one or more prior convictions of him for violation of this section, or for a felony under any other provision of this subchapter or subchapter II of this chapter or other law of the United States relating to narcotic drugs, marihuana, or depressant or stimulant substances, have become final, such person shall be sentenced to a term of imprisonment of not more than 8 years, a fine under Title 18, or both.

(2) Any person who, with the intent to manufacture or to facilitate the manufacture of methamphetamine, violates paragraph (6) or (7) of subsection (a) of this section, shall be sentenced to a term of imprisonment of not more than 10 years, a fine under Title 18, or both; except that if any person commits such a violation after one or more prior convictions of that person—

(A) for a violation of paragraph (6) or (7) of subsection (a) of this section;

(B) for a felony under any other provision of this subchapter or subchapter II of this chapter; or

(C) under any other law of the United States or any State relating to controlled substances or listed chemicals,

has become final, such person shall be sentenced to a term of imprisonment of not more than 20 years, a fine under Title 18, or both.

(e) Additional penalties

In addition to any other applicable penalty, any person convicted of a felony violation of this section relating to the receipt, distribution, manufacture, exportation, or importation of a listed chemical may be enjoined from engaging in any transaction involving a listed chemical for not more than ten years.

(f) Injunctions

(1) In addition to any penalty provided in this section, the Attorney General is authorized to commence a civil action for appropriate declaratory or injunctive relief relating to violations of this section, section 842, or 856 [2] of this title.

(2) Any action under this subsection may be brought in the district court of the United States for the district in which the defendant is located or resides or is doing business.

(3) Any order or judgment issued by the court pursuant to this subsection shall be tailored to restrain violations of this section or section 842 of this title.

(4) The court shall proceed as soon as practicable to the hearing and determination of such an action. An action under this subsection is governed by the Federal Rules of Civil Procedure except that, if an indictment has been returned against the respondent, discovery is governed by the Federal Rules of Criminal Procedure.

(Pub.L. 91–513, Title II, § 403, Oct. 27, 1970, 84 Stat. 1263; Pub.L. 95–633, Title II, § 202(b)(3), Nov. 10, 1978, 92 Stat. 3776; Pub.L. 98–473, Title II, § 516, Oct. 12, 1984, 98 Stat. 2074; Pub. L. 99–570, Title I, § 1866(a), Oct. 27, 1986, 100 Stat. 3207–54; Pub.L. 100–690, Title VI, § 6057, Nov. 18, 1988, 102 Stat. 4319; Pub.L. 103–200, § 3(g), Dec. 17, 1993, 107 Stat. 2337; Pub.L. 103–322, Title IX, § 90106, Sept. 13, 1994, 108 Stat. 1988; Pub.L. 104–237, Title II, §§ 203(a), 206(b), Oct. 3, 1996, 110 Stat. 3102, 3103; Pub.L. 107–273, Div. B, Title IV, § 4002(d)(2)(C), Nov. 2, 2002, 116 Stat. 1810; Pub.L. 108–21, Title VI, § 608(d), Apr. 30, 2003, 117 Stat. 691.)

[1] So in original. Probably should not be capitalized.

[2] So in original. Probably should be preceded by "section".

HISTORICAL AND STATUTORY NOTES

References in Text

Schedules I and II, referred to in subsec. (a)(1), are set out in § 812(c) of this title.

"This subchapter", referred to in subsecs. (a)(4)(A), (6), (7), (9), (b), and (c), was in the original "this title" which is Title II of Pub.L. 91–513, Oct. 27, 1970, 84 Stat. 1242, and is popularly known as the "Controlled Substances Act". For complete classification of Title II to the Code, see Short Title note set out under section 801 of this title and Tables.

"Subchapter II of this chapter", referred to in subsecs. (a)(4)(A), (6), (7), (9), (b), and (c), was in the original "title III", meaning Title III of Pub.L. 91–513, Oct. 27, 1970, 84 Stat. 1285. Part A of Title III comprises subchapter II of this chapter. For classification of Part B, consisting of sections 1101 to 1105 of Title III, see Tables volume.

The Federal Rules of Civil Procedure, referred to in subsec. (f)(4), are set out in Title 28, Judiciary and Judicial Procedure.

The Federal Rules of Criminal Procedure, referred to in subsec. (f)(4), are set out in Title 18, Crimes and Criminal Procedure.

Effective and Applicability Provisions

1993 Acts. Amendment to this section by Pub.L. 103–200, to take effect on the date that is 120 days after the date of enactment of Pub.L. 103–200, which was approved Dec. 17, 1993, see section 11 of Pub.L. 103–200, set out as a note under section 802 of this title.

1988 Acts. Amendment by section 6057 of Pub.L. 100–690 effective 120 days after Nov. 18, 1988, see section 6061 of Pub.L. 100–690, set out as a note under section 802 of this title.

1978 Acts. Amendment by Pub.L. 95–633 effective Nov. 10, 1978, except as otherwise provided, see § 203(a) of Pub.L. 95–633, set out as a note under § 830 of this title.

1970 Acts. Section effective the first day of the seventh calendar month that begins after the day immediately preceding Oct. 27, 1970, see § 704(a) of Pub.L. 91–513, set out as a note under § 801 of this title.

Effective Date of Repeal

Pub.L. 96–359, § 8(b), Sept. 26, 1980, 94 Stat. 1194, repealed § 203(d) of Pub.L. 95–633, formerly set out as a note under this section, which had provided for the repeal of subsec. (a)(4)(B) of this section effective Jan. 1, 1981.

§ 844. Penalties for simple possession

(a) Unlawful acts; penalties

It shall be unlawful for any person knowingly or intentionally to possess a controlled substance unless such substance was obtained directly, or pursuant to a valid prescription or order, from a practitioner, while acting in the course of his professional practice, or except as otherwise authorized by this subchapter or subchapter II of this chapter. It shall be unlawful for any person knowingly or intentionally to possess any list I chemical obtained pursuant to or under authority of a registration issued to that person under section 823 of this title or section 958 of this title if that registration has been revoked or suspended, if that registration has expired, or if the registrant has ceased to do business in the manner contemplated by his registration. It shall be unlawful for any person to knowingly or intentionally purchase at retail during a 30 day period more than 9 grams of ephedrine base, pseudoephedrine base, or phenylpropanolamine base in a scheduled listed chemical product, except that, of such 9 grams, not more than 7.5 grams may be imported by means of shipping through any private or commercial carrier or the Postal Service. Any person who violates this subsection may be sentenced to a term of imprisonment of not more than 1 year, and shall be fined a minimum of $1,000, or both, except that if he commits such offense after a prior conviction under this subchapter or subchapter II of this chapter, or a prior conviction for any drug, narcotic, or chemical offense chargeable under the law of any State, has become final, he shall be sentenced to a term of imprisonment for not less than 15 days but not more than 2 years, and shall be fined a minimum of $2,500, except, further, that if he commits such offense after two or more prior convictions under this subchapter or subchapter II of this chapter, or two or more prior convictions for any drug, narcotic, or chemical offense chargeable under the law of any State, or a combination of two or more such offenses have become final, he shall be sentenced to a term of imprisonment for not less than 90 days but not more than 3 years, and shall be fined a minimum of $5,000. Notwithstanding the preceding sentence, a person convicted under this subsection for the possession of a mixture or substance which contains cocaine base shall be imprisoned not less than 5 years and not more than 20 years, and fined a minimum of $1,000, if the conviction is a first conviction under this subsection and the amount of the mixture or substance exceeds 5 grams, if the conviction is after a prior conviction for the possession of such a mixture or substance under this subsection becomes final and the amount of the mixture or substance exceeds 3 grams, or if the conviction is after 2 or more prior convictions for the possession of such a mixture or substance under this subsection become final and the amount of the mixture or substance exceeds 1 gram. Notwithstanding any penalty provided in this subsection, any person convicted under this subsection for the possession of flunitrazepam shall be imprisoned for not more than 3 years, shall be fined as otherwise provided in this section, or both. The imposition or execution of a minimum sentence required to be imposed under this subsection shall not be suspended or deferred. Further, upon conviction, a person who violates this subsection shall be fined the reasonable costs of the investigation and prosecution of the offense, including the costs of prosecution of an offense as defined in sections 1918 and 1920 of Title 28, except that this sentence shall not apply and a fine under this section need not be imposed if the court determines under the provision of Title 18 that the defendant lacks the ability to pay.

(b) Repealed. Pub.L. 98–473, Title II, § 219(a), Oct. 12, 1984, 98 Stat. 2027

(c) "Drug, narcotic, or chemical offense" defined

As used in this section, the term "drug, narcotic, or chemical offense" means any offense which proscribes the possession, distribution, manufacture, cultivation, sale, transfer, or the attempt or conspiracy to possess, distribute, manufacture, cultivate, sell or transfer any substance the possession of which is prohibited under this subchapter.

(Pub.L. 91–513, Title II, § 404, Oct. 27, 1970, 84 Stat. 1264; Pub.L. 98–473, Title II, § 219, Oct. 12, 1984, 98 Stat. 2027; Pub.L. 99–570, Title I, § 1052, Oct. 27, 1986, 100 Stat. 3207–8; Pub.L. 100–690, Title VI, §§ 6371, 6480, Nov. 18, 1988, 102 Stat. 4370, 4382; Pub.L. 101–647, Title XII, § 1201, Title XIX, § 1907, Nov. 29, 1990, 104 Stat. 4829, 4854; Pub.L. 104–237, Title II, § 201(a), Oct. 3, 1996, 110 Stat. 3101; Pub.L. 104–305, § 2(c), Oct. 13, 1996, 110 Stat. 3808; Pub.L. 109–177, Title VII, § 711(e)(1), Mar. 9, 2006, 120 Stat. 262.)

HISTORICAL AND STATUTORY NOTES

References in Text

"This subchapter", referred to in subsec. (a), was in the original "this title" which is Title II of Pub.L. 91–513, Oct. 27,

1970, 84 Stat. 1242, and is popularly known as the "Controlled Substances Act". For complete classification of Title II to the Code, see Short Title note set out under section 801 of this title and Tables.

"Subchapter II of this chapter", referred to in subsec. (a), was in the original "title III", meaning Title III of Pub.L. 91–513, Oct. 27, 1970, 84 Stat. 1285. Part A of Title III comprises subchapter II of this chapter. For classification of Part B, consisting of sections 1101 to 1105 of Title III, see Tables.

Effective and Applicability Provisions

2006 Acts. Pub.L. 109–177, Title VII, § 711(e)(2), Mar. 9, 2006, 120 Stat. 262, provided that: "The amendment made by paragraph (1) [Pub.L. 109–177, Title VII, § 711(e)(1), Mar. 9, 2006, 120 Stat. 262, amending subsection (a) of this section] applies on and after the expiration of the 30–day period beginning on the date of the enactment of this Act [March 9, 2006]."

1970 Acts. Section effective the first day of the seventh calendar month that begins after the day immediately preceding Oct. 27, 1970, see § 704(a) of Pub.L. 91–513, set out as a note under § 801 of this title.

§ 844a. Civil penalty for possession of small amounts of certain controlled substances

(a) In general

Any individual who knowingly possesses a controlled substance that is listed in section 841(b)(1)(A) of this title in violation of section 844 of this title in an amount that, as specified by regulation of the Attorney General, is a personal use amount shall be liable to the United States for a civil penalty in an amount not to exceed $10,000 for each such violation.

(b) Income and net assets

The income and net assets of an individual shall not be relevant to the determination whether to assess a civil penalty under this section or to prosecute the individual criminally. However, in determining the amount of a penalty under this section, the income and net assets of an individual shall be considered.

(c) Prior conviction

A civil penalty may not be assessed under this section if the individual previously was convicted of a Federal or State offense relating to a controlled substance.

(d) Limitation on number of assessments

A civil penalty may not be assessed on an individual under this section on more than two separate occasions.

(e) Assessment

A civil penalty under this section may be assessed by the Attorney General only by an order made on the record after opportunity for a hearing in accordance with section 554 of Title 5. The Attorney General shall provide written notice to the individual who is the subject of the proposed order informing the individual of the opportunity to receive such a hearing with respect to the proposed order. The hearing may be held only if the individual makes a request for the hearing before the expiration of the 30–day period beginning on the date such notice is issued.

(f) Compromise

The Attorney General may compromise, modify, or remit, with or without conditions, any civil penalty imposed under this section.

(g) Judicial review

If the Attorney General issues an order pursuant to subsection (e) of this section after a hearing described in such subsection, the individual who is the subject of the order may, before the expiration of the 30–day period beginning on the date the order is issued, bring a civil action in the appropriate district court of the United States. In such action, the law and the facts of the violation and the assessment of the civil penalty shall be determined de novo, and shall include the right of a trial by jury, the right to counsel, and the right to confront witnesses. The facts of the violation shall be proved beyond a reasonable doubt.

(h) Civil action

If an individual does not request a hearing pursuant to subsection (e) of this section and the Attorney General issues an order pursuant to such subsection, or if an individual does not under subsection (g) of this section seek judicial review of such an order, the Attorney General may commence a civil action in any appropriate district court of the United States for the purpose of recovering the amount assessed and an amount representing interest at a rate computed in accordance with section 1961 of Title 28. Such interest shall accrue from the expiration of the 30–day period described in subsection (g) of this section. In such an action, the decision of the Attorney General to issue the order, and the amount of the penalty assessed by the Attorney General, shall not be subject to review.

(i) Limitation

The Attorney General may not under this subsection[1] commence proceeding against an individual after the expiration of the 5–year period beginning on the date on which the individual allegedly violated subsection (a) of this section.

(j) Expungement procedures

The Attorney General shall dismiss the proceedings under this section against an individual upon application of such individual at any time after the expiration of 3 years if—

(1) the individual has not previously been assessed a civil penalty under this section;

(2) the individual has paid the assessment;

(3) the individual has complied with any conditions imposed by the Attorney General;

(4) the individual has not been convicted of a Federal or State offense relating to a controlled substance; and

(5) the individual agrees to submit to a drug test, and such test shows the individual to be drug free.

A nonpublic record of a disposition under this subsection shall be retained by the Department of Justice solely for the purpose of determining in any subsequent proceeding whether the person qualified for a civil penalty or expungement under this section. If a record is expunged under this subsection, an individual concerning whom such an expungement has been made shall not be held thereafter under any provision of law to be guilty of perjury, false swearing, or making a false statement by reason of his failure to recite or acknowledge a proceeding under this section or the results thereof in response to an inquiry made of him for any purpose.

(Pub.L. 91–513, Title II, § 405, formerly Pub.L. 100–690, Title VI, § 6486, Nov. 18, 1988, 102 Stat. 4384, renumbered § 405 and amended Pub.L. 101–647, Title X, § 1002(g)(1), (2), Nov. 29, 1990, 104 Stat. 4828.)

[1]So in original. Probably should be "section".

HISTORICAL AND STATUTORY NOTES

Prior Provisions

A prior section 405 of Pub.L. 91–513, Title II, Oct. 27, 1970, 84 Stat. 1265, was redesignated section 418 by Pub.L. 101–647, § 1002(a)(1).

§ 845. Transferred to § 859

§ 845a. Transferred to § 860

§ 845b. Transferred to § 861

§ 846. Attempt and conspiracy

Any person who attempts or conspires to commit any offense defined in this subchapter shall be subject to the same penalties as those prescribed for the offense, the commission of which was the object of the attempt or conspiracy.

(Pub.L. 91–513, Title II, § 406, Oct. 27, 1970, 84 Stat. 1265; Pub.L. 100–690, Title VI, § 6470(a), Nov. 18, 1988, 102 Stat. 4377.)

HISTORICAL AND STATUTORY NOTES

References in Text

"This subchapter", referred to in text, was in the original "this title", which is Title II of Pub.L. 91–513, Oct. 27, 1970, 84 Stat. 1242, and is popularly known as the "Controlled Substances Act". For complete classification of Title II to the Code, see Short Title note set out under § 801 of This title and Tables.

Effective and Applicability Provisions

1970 Acts. Section effective the first day of the seventh calendar month that begins after the day immediately preceding Oct. 27, 1970, see § 704(a) of Pub.L. 95–513, set out as a note under § 801 of this title.

§ 847. Additional penalties

Any penalty imposed for violation of this subchapter shall be in addition to, and not in lieu of, any civil or administrative penalty or sanction authorized by law.

(Pub.L. 91–513, Title II, § 407, Oct. 27, 1970, 84 Stat. 1265.)

HISTORICAL AND STATUTORY NOTES

References in Text

"This subchapter", referred to in text, was in the original "this title" which is Title II of Pub.L. 91–513, Oct. 27, 1970, 84 Stat. 1242, and is popularly known as the "Controlled Substances Act". For complete classification of Title II to the Code, see Short Title note set out under § 801 of this title and Tables.

Effective and Applicability Provisions

1970 Acts. Section effective the first day of the seventh calendar month that begins after the day immediately preceding Oct. 27, 1970, see § 704(a) of Pub.L. 91–513, set out as a note under § 801 of this title.

§ 848. Continuing criminal enterprise

(a) Penalties; forfeitures

Any person who engages in a continuing criminal enterprise shall be sentenced to a term of imprisonment which may not be less than 20 years and which may be up to life imprisonment, to a fine not to exceed the greater of that authorized in accordance with the provisions of Title 18, or $2,000,000 if the defendant is an individual or $5,000,000 if the defendant is other than an individual, and to the forfeiture prescribed in section 853 of this title; except that if any person engages in such activity after one or more prior convictions of him under this section have become final, he shall be sentenced to a term of imprisonment which may not be less than 30 years and which may be up to life imprisonment, to a fine not to exceed the greater of twice the amount authorized in accordance with the provisions of Title 18, or $4,000,000 if the defendant is an individual or $10,000,000 if the defendant is other than an individual, and to the forfeiture prescribed in section 853 of this title.

(b) Life imprisonment for engaging in continuing criminal enterprise

Any person who engages in a continuing criminal enterprise shall be imprisoned for life and fined in accordance with subsection (a) of this section, if—

(1) such person is the principal administrator, organizer, or leader of the enterprise or is one of

several such principal administrators, organizers, or leaders; and

(2)(A) the violation referred to in subsection (c)(1) of this section involved at least 300 times the quantity of a substance described in subsection 841(b)(1)(B) of this title, or

(B) the enterprise, or any other enterprise in which the defendant was the principal or one of several principal administrators, organizers, or leaders, received $10 million dollars in gross receipts during any twelve-month period of its existence for the manufacture, importation, or distribution of a substance described in section 841(b)(1)(B) of this title.

(c) "Continuing criminal enterprise" defined

For purposes of subsection (a) of this section, a person is engaged in a continuing criminal enterprise if—

(1) he violates any provision of this subchapter or subchapter II of this chapter the punishment for which is a felony, and

(2) such violation is a part of a continuing series of violations of this subchapter or subchapter II of this chapter—

(A) which are undertaken by such person in concert with five or more other persons with respect to whom such person occupies a position of organizer, a supervisory position, or any other position of management, and

(B) from which such person obtains substantial income or resources.

(d) Suspension of sentence and probation prohibited

In the case of any sentence imposed under this section, imposition or execution of such sentence shall not be suspended, probation shall not be granted, and the Act of July 15, 1932 (D.C.Code, secs. 24–203 to 24–207), shall not apply.

(e) Death penalty

(1) In addition to the other penalties set forth in this section—

(A) any person engaging in or working in furtherance of a continuing criminal enterprise, or any person engaging in an offense punishable under section 841(b)(1)(A) of this title or section 960(b)(1) of this title who intentionally kills or counsels, commands, induces, procures, or causes the intentional killing of an individual and such killing results, shall be sentenced to any term of imprisonment, which shall not be less than 20 years, and which may be up to life imprisonment, or may be sentenced to death; and

(B) any person, during the commission of, in furtherance of, or while attempting to avoid apprehension, prosecution or service of a prison sentence for, a felony violation of this subchapter or subchapter II of this chapter who intentionally kills or counsels, commands, induces, procures, or causes the intentional killing of any Federal, State, or local law enforcement officer engaged in, or on account of, the performance of such officer's official duties and such killing results, shall be sentenced to any term of imprisonment, which shall not be less than 20 years, and which may be up to life imprisonment, or may be sentenced to death.

(2) As used in paragraph (1)(B), the term "law enforcement officer" means a public servant authorized by law or by a Government agency or Congress to conduct or engage in the prevention, investigation, prosecution or adjudication of an offense, and includes those engaged in corrections, probation, or parole functions.

(g)[1] to (p) Repealed. Pub.L. 109–177, Title II, § 221(2), Mar. 9, 2006, 120 Stat. 231

(q) Repealed. Pub.L. 109–177, Title II, §§ 221(4), 222(c), Mar. 9, 2006, 120 Stat. 231, 232

(r) Repealed. Pub.L. 109–177, Title II, § 221(3), Mar. 9, 2006, 120 Stat. 231

(s) Special provision for methamphetamine

For the purposes of subsection (b) of this section, in the case of continuing criminal enterprise involving methamphetamine or its salts, isomers, or salts of isomers, paragraph (2)(A) shall be applied by substituting "200" for "300", and paragraph (2)(B) shall be applied by substituting "$5,000,000" for "$10 million dollars".

(Pub.L. 91–513, Title II, § 408, Oct. 27, 1970, 84 Stat. 1265; Pub.L. 98–473, Title II, §§ 224(b), 305, Oct. 12, 1984, 98 Stat. 2030, 2050; Pub.L. 98–473, § 224(b), formerly § 224(c), as amended Pub.L. 99–570, Title I, § 1005(b)(2), Oct. 27, 1987, 100 Stat. 3207–6; Pub.L. 99–570, Title I, §§ 1252, 1253, Oct. 27, 1986, 100 Stat. 3207–14, 3207–15; Pub.L. 100–690, Titles VI, VII, §§ 6481, 7001, Nov. 18, 1988, 102 Stat. 4382, 4387; Pub.L. 103–322, Title XXXIII, §§ 330003(e), 330009(d), 330014, Sept. 13, 1994, 108 Stat. 2141, 2143, 2146; Pub.L. 104–132, Title I, § 108, Title IX, § 903(b), Apr. 24, 1996, 110 Stat. 1226, 1318; Pub.L. 109–177, Title II, §§ 221, 222(c), Title VII, § 733, Mar. 9, 2006, 120 Stat. 231, 232, 270.)

[1] So in original. Section does not contain a subsec. (f).

HISTORICAL AND STATUTORY NOTES

References in Text

"This subchapter", referred to in subsecs. (c) and (e)(1)(B), was in the original "this title", which is Title II of Pub.L. 91–513, Oct. 27, 1970, 84 Stat. 1242, as amended, popularly known as the "Controlled Substances Act". For complete classification of such Title II to the Code, see Short Title note set out under 21 U.S.C.A. § 801 and Tables.

"Subchapter II of this chapter", referred to in subsecs. (c) and (e)(1)(B), was in the original "title III", meaning Title III of Pub.L. 91–513, Oct. 27, 1970, 84 Stat. 1285. Part A of Title III comprises subchapter II of this chapter. For classification of Part B, consisting of sections 1101 to 1105 of Title III, see Tables.

Act of July 15, 1932 (D.C. Code, secs. 24–203—24–207), referred to in subsec. (d), is act July 15, 1932, ch. 492, 47 Stat. 696, as amended, which appears in sections 24–203 to 24–209 of Title 24, Prisoners and Their Treatment, and section 22–2601 of Title 22, Criminal Offenses, of the District of Columbia Code.

Codifications

Directory language of section 7001(a)(1) of Pub.L. 100–690, calling for the redesignation of subsec. (e) of this section as (f), was incapable of execution since, after the earlier redesignation of subsec. (e) as (d) by section 6481(b) of Pub.L. 100–690, no subsection (e) remained to be redesignated.

Effective and Applicability Provisions

1996 Acts. Amendment by section 903(b) of Pub.L. 104–132 effective as to cases commenced or appeals perfected on or after Apr. 24, 1996, see section 903(c) of Pub.L. 104–132, set out as a note under section 3006A of Title 18, Crimes and Criminal Procedure.

Effective Date and Savings Provisions of 1984 Amendments. Amendment by Pub.L. 98–473, § 224(b), effective on the first day of first calendar month beginning thirty-six months after Oct. 12, 1984, applicable only to offenses committed after taking effect of sections 211 to 239 of Pub.L. 98–473, and except as otherwise provided for therein, see section 235 of Pub.L. 98–473, as amended, set out as a note under section 3551 of Title 18, Crimes and Criminal Procedure.

1970 Acts. Section effective the first day of the seventh calendar month that begins after the day immediately preceding Oct. 27, 1970, see § 704(a) of Pub.L. 91–513, set out as a note under § 801 of this title.

Change of Name

"General Accounting Office" was changed to "Government Accountability Office" by Pub.L. 108–271, § 8(b), set out as a note under 31 U.S.C.A. § 702, which provided that any reference to the General Accounting Office in any law, rule, regulation, certificate, directive, instruction, or other official paper in force on July 17, 2004, was considered to refer and apply to the Government Accountability Office.

GAO Study of the Cost of Executions

Section 7002 of Pub.L. 100–690, which related to the study by the Comptroller General of the cost of executions, was repealed by Pub.L. 104–66, Title I, § 1091(d), Dec. 21, 1995, 109 Stat. 722.

§ 849. Transportation safety offenses

(a) Definitions

In this section—

"safety rest area" means a roadside facility with parking facilities for the rest or other needs of motorists.

"truck stop" means a facility (including any parking lot appurtenant thereto) that—

(A) has the capacity to provide fuel or service, or both, to any commercial motor vehicle (as defined in section 31301 of Title 49), operating in commerce (as defined in that section); and

(B) is located within 2,500 feet of the National System of Interstate and Defense Highways or the Federal-Aid Primary System.

(b) First offense

A person who violates section 841(a)(1) of this title or section 856 of this title by distributing or possessing with intent to distribute a controlled substance in or on, or within 1,000 feet of, a truck stop or safety rest area is (except as provided in subsection (b) of this section)[1] subject to—

(1) twice the maximum punishment authorized by section 841(b) of this title; and

(2) twice any term of supervised release authorized by section 841(b) of this title for a first offense.

(c) Subsequent offense

A person who violates section 841(a)(1) of this title or section 856 of this title by distributing or possessing with intent to distribute a controlled substance in or on, or within 1,000 feet of, a truck stop or a safety rest area after a prior conviction or convictions under subsection (a)[2] of this section have become final is subject to—

(1) 3 times the maximum punishment authorized by section 841(b) of this title; and

(2) 3 times any term of supervised release authorized by section 841(b) of this title for a first offense.

(Pub.L. 91–513, Title II, § 409, as added Pub.L. 103–322, Title XVIII, § 180201(b)(1), Sept. 13, 1994, 108 Stat. 2046.)

[1] So in original. Probably should be subsection "(c)".

[2] So in original. Probably should be subsection "(b)".

HISTORICAL AND STATUTORY NOTES

Prior Provisions

A prior section 849, Pub.L. 91–513, Title II, § 409, Oct. 27, 1970, 84 Stat. 1266, relating to the sentencing of dangerous special drug offenders, was repealed by Pub.L. 98–473, Title II, § 219(a), Oct. 12, 1984, 98 Stat. 2027.

For applicability of sentencing provisions of former section 849 to offenses, see Effective Date and Savings Provisions, etc., note, section 235 of Pub.L. 98–473, as amended, set out under section 3551 of Title 18, Crimes and Criminal Procedure.

Repeal of former section 849 by Pub.L. 98–473, Title II, § 219(a), Oct. 12, 1984, 98 Stat. 2027, to be effective on the first day of first calendar month beginning thirty six months after Oct. 12, 1984, and to apply only to offenses committed after taking effect of sections 211 to 239 of Pub.L. 98–473, except as otherwise provided for therein, see section 235 of Pub.L. 98–473, as amended, set out as a note under section 3551 of Title 18, Crimes and Criminal Procedure.

§ 850. Information for sentencing

Except as otherwise provided in this subchapter or section 242a(a) of Title 42, no limitation shall be placed on the information concerning the background, character, and conduct of a person convicted of an offense which a court of the United States may receive and consider for the purpose of imposing an appropriate sentence under this subchapter or subchapter II of this chapter.

(Pub.L. 91–513, Title II, § 410, Oct. 27, 1970, 84 Stat. 1269.)

HISTORICAL AND STATUTORY NOTES

References in Text

"This subchapter", referred to in text, was in the original "this title" which is Title II of Pub.L. 91–513, Oct. 27, 1970, 84 Stat. 1242, and is popularly known as the "Controlled Substances Act". For complete classification of Title II to the Code, see Short Title note set out under § 801 of this title and Tables.

Section 242a of this title, referred to in text, was repealed by Pub.L. 106–310, Div. B, Title XXXII, § 3201(b)(1), Oct. 17, 2000, 114 Stat. 1190.

"Subchapter II of this chapter", referred to in text, was in the original "title III", meaning Title III of Pub.L. 91–513, Oct. 27, 1970, 84 Stat. 1285. Part A of Title III comprises subchapter II of this chapter. For classification of Part B, consisting of §§ 1101 to 1105 of Title III, see Tables.

Effective and Applicability Provisions

1970 Acts. Section effective the first day of the seventh calendar month that begins after the day immediately preceding Oct. 27, 1970, see § 704(a) of Pub.L. 91–513, set out as a note under § 801 of this title.

§ 851. Proceedings to establish prior convictions

(a) Information filed by United States Attorney

(1) No person who stands convicted of an offense under this part shall be sentenced to increased punishment by reason of one or more prior convictions, unless before trial, or before entry of a plea of guilty, the United States attorney files an information with the court (and serves a copy of such information on the person or counsel for the person) stating in writing the previous convictions to be relied upon. Upon a showing by the United States attorney that facts regarding prior convictions could not with due diligence be obtained prior to trial or before entry of a plea of guilty, the court may postpone the trial or the taking of the plea of guilty for a reasonable period for the purpose of obtaining such facts. Clerical mistakes in the information may be amended at any time prior to the pronouncement of sentence.

(2) An information may not be filed under this section if the increased punishment which may be imposed is imprisonment for a term in excess of three years unless the person either waived or was afforded prosecution by indictment for the offense for which such increased punishment may be imposed.

(b) Affirmation or denial of previous conviction

If the United States attorney files an information under this section, the court shall after conviction but before pronouncement of sentence inquire of the person with respect to whom the information was filed whether he affirms or denies that he has been previously convicted as alleged in the information, and shall inform him that any challenge to a prior conviction which is not made before sentence is imposed may not thereafter be raised to attack the sentence.

(c) Denial; written response; hearing

(1) If the person denies any allegation of the information of prior conviction, or claims that any conviction alleged is invalid, he shall file a written response to the information. A copy of the response shall be served upon the United States attorney. The court shall hold a hearing to determine any issues raised by the response which would except the person from increased punishment. The failure of the United States attorney to include in the information the complete criminal record of the person or any facts in addition to the convictions to be relied upon shall not constitute grounds for invalidating the notice given in the information required by subsection (a)(1) of this section. The hearing shall be before the court without a jury and either party may introduce evidence. Except as otherwise provided in paragraph (2) of this subsection, the United States attorney shall have the burden of proof beyond a reasonable doubt on any issue of fact. At the request of either party, the court shall enter findings of fact and conclusions of law.

(2) A person claiming that a conviction alleged in the information was obtained in violation of the Constitution of the United States shall set forth his claim, and the factual basis therefor, with particularity in his response to the information. The person shall have the burden of proof by a preponderance of the evidence on any issue of fact raised by the response. Any challenge to a prior conviction, not raised by response to the information before an increased sentence is imposed in reliance thereon, shall be waived unless good cause be shown for failure to make a timely challenge.

(d) Imposition of sentence

(1) If the person files no response to the information, or if the court determines, after hearing, that the person is subject to increased punishment by reason of prior convictions, the court shall proceed to impose sentence upon him as provided by this part.

(2) If the court determines that the person has not been convicted as alleged in the information, that a conviction alleged in the information is invalid, or that the person is otherwise not subject to an increased sentence as a matter of law, the court shall, at the request of the United States attorney, postpone sentence to allow an appeal from that determination. If no such request is made, the court shall impose sentence as provided by this part. The person may appeal from an order postponing sentence as if sentence had been pronounced and a final judgment of conviction entered.

(e) Statute of limitations

No person who stands convicted of an offense under this part may challenge the validity of any prior conviction alleged under this section which occurred more than five years before the date of the information alleging such prior conviction.

(Pub.L. 91–513, Title II, § 411, Oct. 27, 1970, 84 Stat. 1269.)

HISTORICAL AND STATUTORY NOTES

Effective and Applicability Provisions

1970 Acts. Section effective the first day of the seventh calendar month that begins after the day immediately preceding Oct. 27, 1970, see § 704(a) of Pub.L. 91–513, set out as a note under § 801 of this title.

§ 852. Application of treaties and other international agreements

Nothing in the Single Convention on Narcotic Drugs, the Convention on Psychotropic Substances, or other treaties or international agreements shall be construed to limit the provision of treatment, education, or rehabilitation as alternatives to conviction or criminal penalty for offenses involving any drug or other substance subject to control under any such treaty or agreement.

(Pub.L. 91–513, Title II, § 412, as added Pub.L. 95–633, Title I, § 107(a), Nov. 10, 1978, 92 Stat. 3773.)

HISTORICAL AND STATUTORY NOTES

Effective and Applicability Provisions

1980 Acts. Section effective on the date the Convention on Psychotropic Substances enters into force in the United States [July 15, 1980], see § 112 of Pub.L. 95–633, set out as a note under § 801a of this title.

§ 853. Criminal forfeitures

(a) Property subject to criminal forfeiture

Any person convicted of a violation of this subchapter or subchapter II of this chapter punishable by imprisonment for more than one year shall forfeit to the United States, irrespective of any provision of State law—

(1) any property constituting, or derived from, any proceeds the person obtained, directly or indirectly, as the result of such violation;

(2) any of the person's property used, or intended to be used, in any manner or part, to commit, or to facilitate the commission of, such violation; and

(3) in the case of a person convicted of engaging in a continuing criminal enterprise in violation of section 848 of this title, the person shall forfeit, in addition to any property described in paragraph (1) or (2), any of his interest in, claims against, and property or contractual rights affording a source of control over, the continuing criminal enterprise.

The court, in imposing sentence on such person, shall order, in addition to any other sentence imposed pursuant to this subchapter or subchapter II of this chapter, that the person forfeit to the United States all property described in this subsection. In lieu of a fine otherwise authorized by this part, a defendant who derives profits or other proceeds from an offense may be fined not more than twice the gross profits or other proceeds.

(b) Meaning of term "property"

Property subject to criminal forfeiture under this section includes—

(1) real property, including things growing on, affixed to, and found in land; and

(2) tangible and intangible personal property, including rights, privileges, interests, claims, and securities.

(c) Third party transfers

All right, title, and interest in property described in subsection (a) of this section vests in the United States upon the commission of the act giving rise to forfeiture under this section. Any such property that is subsequently transferred to a person other than the defendant may be the subject of a special verdict of forfeiture and thereafter shall be ordered forfeited to the United States, unless the transferee establishes in a hearing pursuant to subsection (n) of this section that he is a bona fide purchaser for value of such property who at the time of purchase was reasonably without cause to believe that the property was subject to forfeiture under this section.

(d) Rebuttable presumption

There is a rebuttable presumption at trial that any property of a person convicted of a felony under this subchapter or subchapter II of this chapter is subject to forfeiture under this section if the United States establishes by a preponderance of the evidence that—

(1) such property was acquired by such person during the period of the violation of this subchapter or subchapter II of this chapter or within a reasonable time after such period; and

(2) there was no likely source for such property other than the violation of this subchapter or subchapter II of this chapter.

(e) Protective orders

(1) Upon application of the United States, the court may enter a restraining order or injunction, require the execution of a satisfactory performance bond, or take any other action to preserve the availability of property described in subsection (a) of this section for forfeiture under this section—

(A) upon the filing of an indictment or information charging a violation of this subchapter or subchapter II of this chapter for which criminal forfeiture may be ordered under this section and alleging that the property with respect to which the order is sought would, in the event of conviction, be subject to forfeiture under this section; or

(B) prior to the filing of such an indictment or information, if, after notice to persons appearing to have an interest in the property and opportunity for a hearing, the court determines that—

(i) there is a substantial probability that the United States will prevail on the issue of forfeiture and that failure to enter the order will result in the property being destroyed, removed from the jurisdiction of the court, or otherwise made unavailable for forfeiture; and

(ii) the need to preserve the availability of the property through the entry of the requested order outweighs the hardship on any party against whom the order is to be entered:

Provided, however, That an order entered pursuant to subparagraph (B) shall be effective for not more than ninety days, unless extended by the court for good cause shown or unless an indictment or information described in subparagraph (A) has been filed.

(2) A temporary restraining order under this subsection may be entered upon application of the United States without notice or opportunity for a hearing when an information or indictment has not yet been filed with respect to the property, if the United States demonstrates that there is probable cause to believe that the property with respect to which the order is sought would, in the event of conviction, be subject to forfeiture under this section and that provision of notice will jeopardize the availability of the property for forfeiture. Such a temporary order shall expire not more than ten days after the date on which it is entered, unless extended for good cause shown or unless the party against whom it is entered consents to an extension for a longer period. A hearing requested concerning an order entered under this paragraph shall be held at the earliest possible time and prior to the expiration of the temporary order.

(3) The court may receive and consider, at a hearing held pursuant to this subsection, evidence and information that would be inadmissible under the Federal Rules of Evidence.

(4) Order to repatriate and deposit

(A) In general

Pursuant to its authority to enter a pretrial restraining order under this section, the court may order a defendant to repatriate any property that may be seized and forfeited, and to deposit that property pending trial in the registry of the court, or with the United States Marshals Service or the Secretary of the Treasury, in an interest-bearing account, if appropriate.

(B) Failure to comply

Failure to comply with an order under this subsection, or an order to repatriate property under subsection (p) of this section, shall be punishable as a civil or criminal contempt of court, and may also result in an enhancement of the sentence of the defendant under the obstruction of justice provision of the Federal Sentencing Guidelines.

(f) Warrant of seizure

The Government may request the issuance of a warrant authorizing the seizure of property subject to forfeiture under this section in the same manner as provided for a search warrant. If the court determines that there is probable cause to believe that the property to be seized would, in the event of conviction, be subject to forfeiture and that an order under subsection (e) of this section may not be sufficient to assure the availability of the property for forfeiture, the court shall issue a warrant authorizing the seizure of such property.

(g) Execution

Upon entry of an order of forfeiture under this section, the court shall authorize the Attorney General to seize all property ordered forfeited upon such terms and conditions as the court shall deem proper. Following entry of an order declaring the property forfeited, the court may, upon application of the United States, enter such appropriate restraining orders or injunctions, require the execution of satisfactory performance bonds, appoint receivers, conservators, appraisers, accountants, or trustees, or take any other action to protect the interest of the United States in the property ordered forfeited. Any income accruing to or derived from property ordered forfeited under this section may be used to offset ordinary and necessary expenses to the property which are required by law, or which are necessary to protect the interests of the United States or third parties.

(h) Disposition of property

Following the seizure of property ordered forfeited under this section, the Attorney General shall direct the disposition of the property by sale or any other commercially feasible means, making due provision for the rights of any innocent persons. Any property right or interest not exercisable by, or transferable for value to, the United States shall expire and shall not revert to the defendant, nor shall the defendant or any person acting in concert with him or on his behalf be eligible to purchase forfeited property at any sale held by the United States. Upon application of a person, other than the defendant or a person acting in concert with him or on his behalf, the court may restrain or stay the sale or disposition of the property pending the conclusion of any appeal of the criminal case giving rise to the forfeiture, if the applicant demonstrates that proceeding with the sale or disposition of the property will result in irreparable injury, harm, or loss to him.

(i) Authority of the Attorney General

With respect to property ordered forfeited under this section, the Attorney General is authorized to—

(1) grant petitions for mitigation or remission of forfeiture, restore forfeited property to victims of a violation of this subchapter, or take any other action to protect the rights of innocent persons which is in the interest of justice and which is not inconsistent with the provisions of this section;

(2) compromise claims arising under this section;

(3) award compensation to persons providing information resulting in a forfeiture under this section;

(4) direct the disposition by the United States, in accordance with the provisions of section 881(e) of this title, of all property ordered forfeited under this section by public sale or any other commercially feasible means, making due provision for the rights of innocent persons; and

(5) take appropriate measures necessary to safeguard and maintain property ordered forfeited under this section pending its disposition.

(j) Applicability of civil forfeiture provisions

Except to the extent that they are inconsistent with the provisions of this section, the provisions of section 881(d) of this title shall apply to a criminal forfeiture under this section.

(k) Bar on intervention

Except as provided in subsection (n) of this section, no party claiming an interest in property subject to forfeiture under this section may—

(1) intervene in a trial or appeal of a criminal case involving the forfeiture of such property under this section; or

(2) commence an action at law or equity against the United States concerning the validity of his alleged interest in the property subsequent to the filing of an indictment or information alleging that the property is subject to forfeiture under this section.

(*l*) Jurisdiction to enter orders

The district courts of the United States shall have jurisdiction to enter orders as provided in this section without regard to the location of any property which may be subject to forfeiture under this section or which has been ordered forfeited under this section.

(m) Depositions

In order to facilitate the identification and location of property declared forfeited and to facilitate the disposition of petitions for remission or mitigation of forfeiture, after the entry of an order declaring property forfeited to the United States, the court may, upon application of the United States, order that the testimony of any witness relating to the property forfeited be taken by deposition and that any designated book, paper, document, record, recording, or other material not privileged be produced at the same time and place, in the same manner as provided for the taking of depositions under Rule 15 of the Federal Rules of Criminal Procedure.

(n) Third party interests

(1) Following the entry of an order of forfeiture under this section, the United States shall publish notice of the order and of its intent to dispose of the property in such manner as the Attorney General may direct. The Government may also, to the extent practicable, provide direct written notice to any person known to have alleged an interest in the property that is the subject of the order of forfeiture as a substitute for published notice as to those persons so notified.

(2) Any person, other than the defendant, asserting a legal interest in property which has been ordered forfeited to the United States pursuant to this section may, within thirty days of the final publication of notice or his receipt of notice under paragraph (1), whichever is earlier, petition the court for a hearing to adjudicate the validity of his alleged interest in the property. The hearing shall be held before the court alone, without a jury.

(3) The petition shall be signed by the petitioner under penalty of perjury and shall set forth the nature and extent of the petitioner's right, title, or interest in the property, the time and circumstances of the petitioner's acquisition of the right, title, or interest in the property, any additional facts supporting the petitioner's claim, and the relief sought.

(4) The hearing on the petition shall, to the extent practicable and consistent with the interests of justice, be held within thirty days of the filing of the petition. The court may consolidate the hearing on the petition with a hearing on any other petition filed by a person other than the defendant under this subsection.

(5) At the hearing, the petitioner may testify and present evidence and witnesses on his own behalf, and cross-examine witnesses who appear at the hearing. The United States may present evidence and witnesses in rebuttal and in defense of its claim to the property and cross-examine witnesses who appear at the hearing. In addition to testimony and evidence presented at the hearing, the court shall consider the relevant portions of the record of the criminal case which resulted in the order of forfeiture.

(6) If, after the hearing, the court determines that the petitioner has established by a preponderance of the evidence that—

(A) the petitioner has a legal right, title, or interest in the property, and such right, title, or interest renders the order of forfeiture invalid in whole or in part because the right, title, or interest was vested in the petitioner rather than the defendant or was superior to any right, title, or interest of the defendant at the time of the commission of the acts which gave rise to the forfeiture of the property under this section; or

(B) the petitioner is a bona fide purchaser for value of the right, title, or interest in the property and was at the time of purchase reasonably without cause to believe that the property was subject to forfeiture under this section;

the court shall amend the order of forfeiture in accordance with its determination.

(7) Following the court's disposition of all petitions filed under this subsection, or if no such petitions are filed following the expiration of the period provided in paragraph (2) for the filing of such petitions, the United States shall have clear title to property that is the subject of the order of forfeiture and may warrant good title to any subsequent purchaser or transferee.

(*o*) Construction

The provisions of this section shall be liberally construed to effectuate its remedial purposes.

(p) Forfeiture of substitute property

(1) In general

Paragraph (2) of this subsection shall apply, if any property described in subsection (a), as a result of any act or omission of the defendant—

(A) cannot be located upon the exercise of due diligence;

(B) has been transferred or sold to, or deposited with, a third party;

(C) has been placed beyond the jurisdiction of the court;

(D) has been substantially diminished in value; or

(E) has been commingled with other property which cannot be divided without difficulty.

(2) Substitute property

In any case described in any of subparagraphs (A) through (E) of paragraph (1), the court shall order the forfeiture of any other property of the defendant, up to the value of any property described in subparagraphs (A) through (E) of paragraph (1), as applicable.

(3) Return of property to jurisdiction

In the case of property described in paragraph (1)(C), the court may, in addition to any other action authorized by this subsection, order the defendant to return the property to the jurisdiction of the court so that the property may be seized and forfeited.

(q) Restitution for cleanup of clandestine laboratory sites

The court, when sentencing a defendant convicted of an offense under this subchapter or subchapter II of this chapter involving the manufacture, the possession, or the possession with intent to distribute, of amphetamine or methamphetamine, shall—

(1) order restitution as provided in sections 3612 and 3664 of Title 18;

(2) order the defendant to reimburse the United States, the State or local government concerned, or both the United States and the State or local government concerned for the costs incurred by the United States or the State or local government concerned, as the case may be, for the cleanup associated with the manufacture of amphetamine or methamphetamine by the defendant, or on premises or in property that the defendant owns, resides, or does business in; and

(3) order restitution to any person injured as a result of the offense as provided in section 3663A of Title 18.

(Pub.L. 91–513, Title II, § 413, as added Pub.L. 98–473, Title II, § 303, Oct. 12, 1984, 98 Stat. 2044, and amended Pub.L. 98–473, Title II, § 2301(d)–(f), Oct. 12, 1984, 98 Stat. 2192, 2193; Pub.L. 99–570, Title I, §§ 1153(b), 1864, Oct. 27, 1986, 100 Stat. 3207–13, 3207–54; Pub.L. 104–237, Title II, § 207, Oct. 3, 1996, 110 Stat. 3104; Pub.L. 106–310, Div. B, Title XXXVI, § 3613(a), Oct. 17, 2000, 114 Stat. 1229; Pub.L. 107–56, Title III, § 319(d), Oct. 26, 2001, 115 Stat. 314; Pub.L. 109–177, Title VII, § 743(a), Mar. 9, 2006, 120 Stat. 272.)

Termination Date of 2001 Amendment

Amendments by Title III of Pub.L. 107–56 to terminate effective on and after the first day of fiscal year 2005 if Congress enacts a joint resolution that such amendments no longer have the force of law, see Pub.L. 107–56, § 303, set out as a Four-Year Congressional Review; Expedited Consideration note under 31 U.S.C.A. § 5311.

HISTORICAL AND STATUTORY NOTES

References in Text

This subchapter, referred to in text, was in the original "this title", meaning is Title II of Pub.L. 91–513, Oct. 27, 1970, 84 Stat. 1242, as amended, known as the Controlled Substances Act. For complete classification of Title II to the Code, see Short Title note set out under section 801 of this title and Tables.

Subchapter II of this chapter, referred to in subsecs. (a), (d), (e)(1)(A), and (q), was in the original "title III", meaning Title III of Pub.L. 91–513, Oct. 27, 1970, 84 Stat. 1285, as amended. Part A of such Title III is classified to subchapter II of this chapter. For classification of Part B (§§ 1101 to 1105) of Title III of Pub.L. 91–513, see Tables.

Codifications

Amendment by section 1153(b) of Pub.L. 99–570 was executed to section 413 of the Comprehensive Drug Abuse Prevention and Control Act of 1970 (this section) as the probable intent of Congress, despite directory language purporting to require the amendment of section 413 of title II of the "Comprehensive Drug Abuse Prevention and Control Act of 1975".

The language of section 1153(b) of Pub.L. 99–570, amending this section by redesignating former subsec. (p) as (q) and inserting a new subsec. (p) was executed by only inserting a new subsec. (p) since prior subsec. (p) had already been redesignated subsec. (*o*) by Pub.L. 98–473, Title II, § 2301(e)(2), Oct. 12, 1984, 98 Stat. 2193.

Amendment by section 1864(1) of Pub.L. 99–570, directing the substitution of "subsection (n)" for "subsection (*o*)" in the second subsection (h) [originally enacted as subsec. (n) and redesignated subsec. (h) by section 2301(e)(2) of Pub.L. 98–473] was incapable of execution. Such subsec. (h) was subsequently redesignated subsec. (k) by section 1864(4) of Pub.L. 99–570.

Amendment by section 1864(3) of Pub.L. 99–570, directing the substitution of "this subchapter" for "this chapter" in subsec. (i)(1), was executed by substituting "this subchapter" for "this section", as the probable intent of Congress.

Savings Provisions

Pub.L. 109–177, Title VII, § 743(b), Mar. 9, 2006, 120 Stat. 273, provided that: "Nothing in this section [Pub.L. 109–177, Title VII, § 743, Mar. 9, 2006, 120 Stat. 273, which amended this section and enacted this note] shall be interpreted or construed to amend, alter, or otherwise affect the obligations, liabilities and other responsibilities of any person under any Federal or State environmental laws."

Severability of Provisions

For severability of provisions of Title XXXVI (§§ 3601 to 3673) of Pub.L. 106–310, see section 3673 of Pub.L. 106–310, set out as a note under section 801 of this title.

4–Year Congressional Review; Expedited Consideration

Effective on and after the first day of fiscal year 2005, amendments by Title III (§§ 301 to 377) of Pub.L. 107–56 shall terminate if Congress enacts a joint resolution to that effect; such resolution shall be given expedited consideration, see Pub.L. 107–56, Title III, § 303, Oct. 26, 2001, 115 Stat. 298, set out as a note under 31 U.S.C.A. § 5311.

§ 853a. Transferred to § 862

§ 854. Investment of illicit drug profits

(a) Prohibition

It shall be unlawful for any person who has received any income derived, directly or indirectly, from a violation of this subchapter or subchapter II of this chapter punishable by imprisonment for more than one year in which such person has participated as a principal within the meaning of section 2 of Title 18 to use or invest, directly or indirectly, any part of such income, or the proceeds of such income, in acquisition of any interest in, or the establishment or operation of, any enterprise which is engaged in, or the activities of which affect interstate or foreign commerce. A purchase of securities on the open market for purposes of investment, and without the intention of controlling or participating in the control of the issuer, or of assisting another to do so, shall not be unlawful under this section if the securities of the issuer held by the purchaser, the members of his immediate family, and his or their accomplices in any violation of this subchapter or subchapter II of this chapter after such purchase do not amount in the aggregate to 1 per centum of the outstanding securities of any one class, and do not confer, either in law or in fact, the power to elect one or more directors of the issuer.

(b) Penalty

Whoever violates this section shall be fined not more than $50,000 or imprisoned not more than ten years, or both.

(c) "Enterprise" defined

As used in this section, the term "enterprise" includes any individual, partnership, corporation, association, or other legal entity, and any union or group of individuals associated in fact although not a legal entity.

(d) Construction

The provisions of this section shall be liberally construed to effectuate its remedial purposes.

(Pub.L. 91–513, Title II, § 414, as added Pub.L. 98–473, Title II, § 303, Oct. 12, 1984, 98 Stat. 2049.)

§ 855. Alternative fine

In lieu of a fine otherwise authorized by this part, a defendant who derives profits or other proceeds from an offense may be fined not more than twice the gross profits or other proceeds.

(Pub.L. 91–513, Title II, § 415, as added Pub.L. 98–473, Title II, § 2302, Oct. 12, 1984, 98 Stat. 2193.)

§ 856. Maintaining drug-involved premises

(a) Unlawful acts

Except as authorized by this subchapter, it shall be unlawful to—

(1) knowingly open, lease, rent, use, or maintain any place, whether permanently or temporarily, for the purpose of manufacturing, distributing, or using any controlled substance;

(2) manage or control any place, whether permanently or temporarily, either as an owner, lessee, agent, employee, occupant, or mortgagee, and knowingly and intentionally rent, lease, profit from, or make available for use, with or without compensation, the place for the purpose of unlawfully manufacturing, storing, distributing, or using a controlled substance.

(b) Penalties

Any person who violates subsection (a) of this section shall be sentenced to a term of imprisonment of not more than 20 years or a fine of not more than $500,000, or both, or a fine of $2,000,000 for a person other than an individual.

(c) Violation as offense against property

A violation of subsection (a) of this section shall be considered an offense against property for purposes of section 3663A(c)(1)(A)(ii) of Title 18.

(d)(1) Any person who violates subsection (a) of this section shall be subject to a civil penalty of not more than the greater of

(A) $250,000; or

(B) 2 times the gross receipts, either known or estimated, that were derived from each violation that is attributable to the person.

(2) If a civil penalty is calculated under paragraph (1)(B), and there is more than 1 defendant, the court may apportion the penalty between multiple violators, but each violator shall be jointly and severally liable for the civil penalty under this subsection.

(e) Any person who violates subsection (a) of this section shall be subject to declaratory and injunctive remedies as set forth in section 843(f) of this title.

(Pub.L. 91–513, Title II, § 416, as added Pub.L. 99–570, Title I, § 1841(a), Oct. 27, 1986, 100 Stat. 3207–52, and amended Pub.L. 106–310, Div. B, Title XXXVI, § 3613(e), Oct. 17, 2000, 114 Stat. 1230; Pub.L. 108–21, Title VI, § 608(b)(1), (2), (c), Apr. 30, 2003, 117 Stat. 691.)

HISTORICAL AND STATUTORY NOTES

Short Title

1986 Amendments. This section is commonly known as the Crack House Statute.

§ 857. Repealed. Pub.L. 101–647, Title XXIV, § 2401(d), Nov. 29, 1990, 104 Stat. 4859

HISTORICAL AND STATUTORY NOTES

Section (i.e. subsec. (a)), Pub.L. 99–570, Title I, § 1822(a), Oct. 27, 1986, 100 Stat. 3207–51, made unlawful sale of drug paraphernalia in interstate and foreign commerce, through use of the Postal Service or other interstate conveyance or in importation or exportation of drug paraphernalia. See section 863 of this title.

Section (i.e. subsecs. (b)–(f)), Pub.L. 99–570, Title I, § 1822(b)–(f), Oct. 27, 1986, 100 Stat. 3207–51; Pub.L. 100–690, Title VI, § 6485, Nov. 18, 1988, 102 Stat. 4384, were transferred by Pub.L. 101–647, § 2401(b), and appear as subsecs. (b)–(f) of section 863 of this title.

Effective and Applicability Provisions

1986 Acts. Section 1823 of Pub.L. 99–570, which had provided that: "This subtitle [enacting this section] shall become effective 90 days after the date of enactment of this Act [Oct. 27, 1986]", was repealed by Pub.L. 101–647, Title XXIV, § 2401(d), Nov. 29, 1990, 104 Stat. 4859.

§ 858. Endangering human life while illegally manufacturing controlled substance

Whoever, while manufacturing a controlled substance in violation of this subchapter, or attempting to do so, or transporting or causing to be transported materials, including chemicals, to do so, creates a substantial risk of harm to human life shall be fined in accordance with Title 18, or imprisoned not more than 10 years, or both.

(Pub.L. 91–513, Title II, § 417, as added Pub.L. 100–690, Title VI, § 6301(a), Nov. 18, 1988, 102 Stat. 4370.)

HISTORICAL AND STATUTORY NOTES

References in Text

This subchapter, referred to in text, was in the original "this title" which is Title II of Pub.L. 91–513, Oct. 27, 1970, 84 Stat. 1242, and is popularly known as the "Controlled Substances Act". For complete classification of Title II to the Code, see Short Title note set out under section 801 of this title and Tables.

§ 859. Distribution to persons under age twenty-one

(a) First offense

Except as provided in section 860 of this title, any person at least eighteen years of age who violates section 841(a)(1) of this title by distributing a controlled substance to a person under twenty-one years of age is (except as provided in subsection (b) of this section) subject to (1) twice the maximum punishment authorized by section 841(b) of this title, and (2) at least twice any term of supervised release authorized by section 841(b) of this title, for a first offense involving the same controlled substance and schedule. Except to the extent a greater minimum sentence is otherwise provided by section 841(b) of this title, a term of imprisonment under this subsection shall be not less than one year. The mandatory minimum sentencing provisions of this subsection shall not apply to offenses involving 5 grams or less of marihuana.

(b) Second offense

Except as provided in section 860 of this title, any person at least eighteen years of age who violates section 841(a)(1) of this title by distributing a controlled substance to a person under twenty-one years of age after a prior conviction under subsection (a) of this section (or under section 333(b) of this title as in effect prior to May 1, 1971) has become final, is subject to (1) three times the maximum punishment authorized by section 841(b) of this title, and (2) at least three times any term of supervised release authorized by section 841(b) of this title, for a second or subsequent offense involving the same controlled substance and schedule. Except to the extent a greater minimum sentence is otherwise provided by section 841(b) of this title, a term of imprisonment under this subsection shall be not less than one year. Penalties for third and subsequent convictions shall be governed by section 841(b)(1)(A) of this title.

(Pub.L. 91–513, Title II, § 418, formerly § 405, Oct. 27, 1970, 84 Stat. 1265; Pub.L. 98–473, Title II, §§ 224(b), 503(b)(3), Oct. 12, 1984, 98 Stat. 2030, 2070; Pub.L. 98–473, § 224(b), as amended Pub.L. 99–570, Title I, § 1005(b)(1), Oct. 27, 1986, 100 Stat. 3207–6; Pub.L. 99–570, Title I, §§ 1004(a), 1105(a), (b), Oct. 27, 1986, 100 Stat. 3207–6, 3207–11; Pub.L. 100–690, Title VI, §§ 6452(b), 6455, 6456, Nov. 18, 1988, 102 Stat. 4371, 4372; renumbered § 418 and amended by Pub.L. 101–647, Title X, §§ 1002(a), 1003(a), Title XXXV, § 3599L, Nov. 29, 1990, 104 Stat. 4827, 4828, 4932.)

HISTORICAL AND STATUTORY NOTES

Codifications

Section was formerly classified to section 845 of this title.

Effective and Applicability Provisions

1986 Acts. Amendment by section 1004(a) of Pub.L. 99–570 to take effect on the date of the taking of effect of section 3583 of Title 18, Crimes and Criminal Procedure, Nov. 1, 1987, see section 1004(b) of Pub.L. 99–570, set out as a note under section 841 of this title.

Effective Date and Savings Provisions of 1984 Amendments. Amendment by Pub.L. 98–473, § 224(b), effective on the first day of first calendar month beginning thirty-six months after Oct. 12, 1984, applicable only to offenses committed after taking effect of sections 211 to 239 of Pub.L. 98–473, and except as otherwise provided for therein, see section 235 of Pub.L. 98–473, as amended, set out as a note under section 3551 of Title 18, Crimes and Criminal Procedure.

Repeals

Section 224(b) of Pub.L. 98–473, cited to credit, was repealed by section 1005(b)(1) of Pub.L. 99–570. Such provisions of section 224(b) of Pub.L. 98–473, which were to take effect Nov. 1, 1987, as a result of repeal were never executed to text of section.

§ 860. Distribution or manufacturing in or near schools and colleges

(a) Penalty

Any person who violates section 841(a)(1) of this title or section 856 of this title by distributing, possessing with intent to distribute, or manufacturing a controlled substance in or on, or within one thousand feet of, the real property comprising a public or private elementary, vocational, or secondary school or a public or private college, junior college, or university, or a playground, or housing facility owned by a public housing authority, or within 100 feet of a public or private youth center, public swimming pool, or video arcade facility, is (except as provided in subsection (b) of this section) subject to (1) twice the maximum punishment authorized by section 841(b) of this title; and (2) at least twice any term of supervised release authorized by section 841(b) of this title for a first offense. A fine up to twice that authorized by section 841(b) of this title may be imposed in addition to any term of imprisonment authorized by this subsection. Except to the extent a greater minimum sentence is otherwise provided by section 841(b) of this title, a person shall be sentenced under this subsection to a term of imprisonment of not less than one year. The mandatory minimum sentencing provisions of this paragraph shall not apply to offenses involving 5 grams or less of marihuana.

(b) Second offenders

Any person who violates section 841(a)(1) of this title or section 856 of this title by distributing, possessing with intent to distribute, or manufacturing a controlled substance in or on, or within one thousand feet of, the real property comprising a public or private elementary, vocational, or secondary school or a public or private college, junior college, or university, or a playground, or housing facility owned by a public housing authority, or within 100 feet of a public or private youth center, public swimming pool, or video arcade facility, after a prior conviction under subsection (a) of this section has become final is punishable (1) by the greater of (A) a term of imprisonment of not less than three years and not more than life imprisonment or (B) three times the maximum punishment authorized by section 841(b) of this title for a first offense, and (2) at least three times any term of supervised release authorized by section

841(b) of this title for a first offense. A fine up to three times that authorized by section 841(b) of this title may be imposed in addition to any term of imprisonment authorized by this subsection. Except to the extent a greater minimum sentence is otherwise provided by section 841(b) of this title, a person shall be sentenced under this subsection to a term of imprisonment of not less than three years. Penalties for third and subsequent convictions shall be governed by section 841(b)(1)(A) of this title.

(c) Employing children to distribute drugs near schools or playgrounds

Notwithstanding any other law, any person at least 21 years of age who knowingly and intentionally—

(1) employs, hires, uses, persuades, induces, entices, or coerces a person under 18 years of age to violate this section; or

(2) employs, hires, uses, persuades, induces, entices, or coerces a person under 18 years of age to assist in avoiding detection or apprehension for any offense under this section by any Federal, State, or local law enforcement official,

is punishable by a term of imprisonment, a fine, or both, up to triple those authorized by section 841 of this title.

(d) Suspension of sentence; probation; parole

In the case of any mandatory minimum sentence imposed under this section, imposition or execution of such sentence shall not be suspended and probation shall not be granted. An individual convicted under this section shall not be eligible for parole until the individual has served the mandatory minimum term of imprisonment as provided by this section.

(e) Definitions

For the purposes of this section—

(1) The term "playground" means any outdoor facility (including any parking lot appurtenant thereto) intended for recreation, open to the public, and with any portion thereof containing three or more separate apparatus intended for the recreation of children including, but not limited to, sliding boards, swingsets, and teeterboards.

(2) The term "youth center" means any recreational facility and/or gymnasium (including any parking lot appurtenant thereto), intended primarily for use by persons under 18 years of age, which regularly provides athletic, civic, or cultural activities.

(3) The term "video arcade facility" means any facility, legally accessible to persons under 18 years of age, intended primarily for the use of pinball and video machines for amusement containing a minimum of ten pinball and/or video machines.

(4) The term "swimming pool" includes any parking lot appurtenant thereto.

(Pub.L. 91–513, Title II, § 419, formerly § 405A, as added Pub.L. 98–473, Title II, § 503(a), Oct. 12, 1984, 98 Stat. 2069, and amended Pub.L. 99–570, Title I, §§ 1004(a), 1104, 1105(c), 1841(b), 1866(b), (c), Oct. 27, 1986, 100 Stat. 3207–6, 3207–11, 3207–52, 3207–55; Pub.L. 99–646, § 28, Nov. 10, 1986, 100 Stat. 3598; Pub.L. 100–690, Title VI, §§ 6452(b)(1), 6457, 6458, Nov. 18, 1988, 102 Stat. 4371, 4373; renumbered § 419 and amended Pub.L. 101–647, Title X, §§ 1002(b), 1003(b), Title XII, § 1214, Title XV, § 1502, Title XXXV, § 3599L, Nov. 29, 1990, 104 Stat. 4827, 4829, 4833, 4932; Pub.L. 103–322, Title XIV, § 140006, Title XXXII, § 320107, Title XXXIII, § 330009(a), Sept. 13, 1994, 108 Stat. 2032, 2111, 2143.)

HISTORICAL AND STATUTORY NOTES

Codifications

Section was formerly classified to section 845a of this title.

Section 1003(b)(1) of Pub.L. 101–647 in amending subsec. (a) struck out "or a fine" as part of such amendment. Subsec. (a) contained "or fine" which language was struck out as the probable intent of Congress.

Pub.L. 101–647, § 1214(1), directed that section 405A(a) of the Controlled Substances Act (21 U.S.C. 845a(a)) as redesignated by this Act, be amended. Section 405A was redesignated section 419 and classified to this section for codification purposes. The amendment was executed to this section as the probable intent of Congress.

Amendment by Pub.L. 101–647, § 1214(1)(A), to subsec. (a)(1), directed that ", or a fine, or both," be struck out. The amendment executed as part of amendment by section 1003(b)(1) of Pub.L. 101–647, was executed as striking out ", or fine, or both" as the probable intent of Congress. See note above.

Pub.L. 101–647, § 1214(2), directed that section 405A(b) of the Controlled Substances Act (21 U.S.C. 845a(b)), as redesignated by this Act, be amended. Section 405A was redesignated section 419 and classified to this section for codification purposes. The amendment was executed to this section as the probable intent of Congress.

Section 1214(2)(A) of Pub.L. 101–647, which struck out "or a fine up to three times that authorized by section 841(b) of this title for a first offense, or both" was incapable of execution in view of prior amendment to subsec. (b)(1)(B) by section 1003(b)(2) of Pub.L. 101–647 which totally amended subsec. (b)(1)(B) of this section.

Amendments to subsec. (b) of this section by Pub.L. 99–570, § 1866(b), which struck out "special term" and inserted in lieu thereof "term of supervised release", and by Pub.L. 99–646, § 28, which inserted "parole" after "(2) at least three times any special" were incapable of execution to the text. Amendment by Pub.L. 99–570, § 1004, is also incapable of execution to the text.

Effective and Applicability Provisions

1986 Acts. Amendment by section 1004(a) of Pub.L. 99–570 to take effect on the date of the taking of effect of section 3583 of Title 18, Crimes and Criminal Procedure, Nov. 1, 1987, see section 1004(b) of Pub.L. 99–570, set out as a note under section 841 of this title.

§ 860a. Consecutive sentence for manufacturing or distributing, or possessing with intent to manufacture or distribute, methamphetamine on premises where children are present or reside

Whoever violates section 841(a)(1) of this title by manufacturing or distributing, or possessing with intent to manufacture or distribute, methamphetamine or its salts, isomers or salts of isomers on premises in which an individual who is under the age of 18 years is present or resides, shall, in addition to any other sentence imposed, be imprisoned for a period of any term of years but not more than 20 years, subject to a fine, or both.

(Pub.L. 109–177, Title VII, § 734(a), Mar. 9, 2006, 120 Stat. 270.)

§ 861. Employment or use of persons under 18 years of age in drug operations

(a) Unlawful acts

It shall be unlawful for any person at least eighteen years of age to knowingly and intentionally—

(1) employ, hire, use, persuade, induce, entice, or coerce, a person under eighteen years of age to violate any provision of this subchapter or subchapter II of this chapter;

(2) employ, hire, use, persuade, induce, entice, or coerce, a person under eighteen years of age to assist in avoiding detection or apprehension for any offense of this subchapter or subchapter II of this chapter by any Federal, State, or local law enforcement official; or

(3) receive a controlled substance from a person under 18 years of age, other than an immediate family member, in violation of this subchapter or subchapter II of this chapter.

(b) Penalty for first offense

Any person who violates subsection (a) of this section is subject to twice the maximum punishment otherwise authorized and at least twice any term of supervised release otherwise authorized for a first offense. Except to the extent a greater minimum sentence is otherwise provided, a term of imprisonment under this subsection shall not be less than one year.

(c) Penalty for subsequent offenses

Any person who violates subsection (a) of this section after a prior conviction under subsection (a) of this section has become final, is subject to three times the maximum punishment otherwise authorized and at least three times any term of supervised release otherwise authorized for a first offense. Except to the extent a greater minimum sentence is otherwise provided, a term of imprisonment under this subsection shall not be less than one year. Penalties for third and subsequent convictions shall be governed by section 841(b)(1)(A) of this title.

(d) Penalty for providing or distributing controlled substance to underage person

Any person who violates subsection (a)(1) or (2) of this section [1]

(1) by knowingly providing or distributing a controlled substance or a controlled substance analogue to any person under eighteen years of age; or

(2) if the person employed, hired, or used is fourteen years of age or younger,

shall be subject to a term of imprisonment for not more than five years or a fine of not more than $50,000, or both, in addition to any other punishment authorized by this section.

(e) Suspension of sentence; probation; parole

In any case of any sentence imposed under this section, imposition or execution of such sentence shall not be suspended and probation shall not be granted. An individual convicted under this section of an offense for which a mandatory minimum term of imprisonment is applicable shall not be eligible for parole under section 4202 of Title 18 until the individual has served the mandatory term of imprisonment as enhanced by this section.

(f) Distribution of controlled substance to pregnant individual

Except as authorized by this subchapter, it shall be unlawful for any person to knowingly or intentionally provide or distribute any controlled substance to a pregnant individual in violation of any provision of this subchapter. Any person who violates this subsection shall be subject to the provisions of subsections (b), (c), and (e) of this section.

(Pub.L. 91–513, Title II, § 420, formerly § 405B, as added Pub.L. 99–570, Title I, § 1102, Oct. 27, 1986, 100 Stat. 3207–10, and amended Pub.L. 100–690, Title VI, §§ 6452(b)(1), 6459, 6470(d), Nov. 18, 1988, 102 Stat. 4371, 4373, 4378; renumbered § 420 and amended Pub.L. 101–647, Title X, §§ 1002(c), 1003(c), Title XXXV, § 3599L, Nov. 29, 1990, 104 Stat. 4827, 4829, 4932.)

[1] So in original. Probably should be followed by a dash.

HISTORICAL AND STATUTORY NOTES

References in Text

"This subchapter", referred to in subsecs. (a) and (f), was in the original "this title" which is Title II of Pub.L. 91–513, Oct. 27, 1970, 84 Stat. 1242, and is popularly known as the "Controlled Substances Act". For complete classification of Title II to the Code, see Short Title note set out under section 801 of this title and Tables.

"Subchapter II of this chapter", referred to in subsec. (a), was in the original "title III", meaning Title III of Pub.L. 91–513, Oct. 27, 1970, 84 Stat. 1285. Part A of Title III comprises subchapter II of this chapter. For classification of Part B, consisting of sections 1101 to 1105 of Title III, see Tables.

Section 4202 of title 18, referred to in subsec. (e), which, as originally enacted in Title 18, Crimes and Criminal Procedure, related to eligibility of prisoners for parole, was repealed and a new section 4202 enacted as part of the repeal and enactment of a new chapter 311 (§ 4201 et seq.) of Title 18, by Pub.L. 94–233, § 2, Mar. 15, 1976, 90 Stat. 219. For provisions relating to the eligibility of prisoners for parole, see §§ 218(a)(5), 235(a)(1), (b)(1), Oct. 12, 1984, 98 Stat. 2027, 2031, 2032, as amended, provided that, effective on the first day of the first calendar month beginning 36 months after Oct. 12, 1984 (Nov. 1, 1987), chapter 311 of Title 18 is repealed, subject to remaining effective for five years after Nov. 1, 1987, in certain circumstances. See Effective Date note set out under section 3551 of Title 18.

Codifications

Section was formerly classified to section 845b of this title.

§ 862. Denial of Federal benefits to drug traffickers and possessors

(a) Drug traffickers

(1) Any individual who is convicted of any Federal or State offense consisting of the distribution of controlled substances shall—

(A) at the discretion of the court, upon the first conviction for such an offense be ineligible for any or all Federal benefits for up to 5 years after such conviction;

(B) at the discretion of the court, upon a second conviction for such an offense be ineligible for any or all Federal benefits for up to 10 years after such conviction; and

(C) upon a third or subsequent conviction for such an offense be permanently ineligible for all Federal benefits.

(2) The benefits which are denied under this subsection shall not include benefits relating to long-term drug treatment programs for addiction for any person who, if there is a reasonable body of evidence to substantiate such declaration, declares himself to be an addict and submits himself to a long-term treatment program for addiction, or is deemed to be rehabilitated pursuant to rules established by the Secretary of Health and Human Services.

(b) Drug possessors

(1) Any individual who is convicted of any Federal or State offense involving the possession of a controlled substance (as such term is defined for purposes of this subchapter) shall—

(A) upon the first conviction for such an offense and at the discretion of the court—

(i) be ineligible for any or all Federal benefits for up to one year;

(ii) be required to successfully complete an approved drug treatment program which includes periodic testing to insure that the individual remains drug free;

(iii) be required to perform appropriate community service; or

(iv) any combination of clause (i), (ii), or (iii); and

(B) upon a second or subsequent conviction for such an offense be ineligible for all Federal benefits for up to 5 years after such conviction as determined by the court. The court shall continue to have the discretion in subparagraph (A) above. In imposing penalties and conditions under subparagraph (A), the court may require that the completion of the conditions imposed by clause (ii) or (iii) be a requirement for the reinstatement of benefits under clause (i).

(2) The penalties and conditions which may be imposed under this subsection shall be waived in the case of a person who, if there is a reasonable body of evidence to substantiate such declaration, declares himself to be an addict and submits himself to a long-term treatment program for addiction, or is deemed to be rehabilitated pursuant to rules established by the Secretary of Health and Human Services.

(c) Suspension of period of ineligibility

The period of ineligibility referred to in subsections (a) and (b) of this section shall be suspended if the individual—

(A) completes a supervised drug rehabilitation program after becoming ineligible under this section;

(B) has otherwise been rehabilitated; or

(C) has made a good faith effort to gain admission to a supervised drug rehabilitation program, but is unable to do so because of inaccessibility or unavailability of such a program, or the inability of the individual to pay for such a program.

(d) Definitions

As used in this section—

(1) the term "Federal benefit"—

(A) means the issuance of any grant, contract, loan, professional license, or commercial license provided by an agency of the United States or by appropriated funds of the United States; and

(B) does not include any retirement, welfare, Social Security, health, disability, veterans benefit, public housing, or other similar benefit, or any other benefit for which payments or services are required for eligibility; and

(2) the term "veterans benefit" means all benefits provided to veterans, their families, or survivors by virtue of the service of a veteran in the Armed Forces of the United States.

(e) **Inapplicability of this section to Government witnesses**

The penalties provided by this section shall not apply to any individual who cooperates or testifies with the Government in the prosecution of a Federal or State offense or who is in a Government witness protection program.

(f) **Indian provision**

Nothing in this section shall be construed to affect the obligation of the United States to any Indian or Indian tribe arising out of any treaty, statute, Executive order, or the trust responsibility of the United States owing to such Indian or Indian tribe. Nothing in this subsection shall exempt any individual Indian from the sanctions provided for in this section, provided that no individual Indian shall be denied any benefit under Federal Indian programs comparable to those described in subsection (d)(1)(B) or (d)(2) of this section.

(g) **Presidential report**

(1) On or before May 1, 1989, the President shall transmit to the Congress a report—

(A) delineating the role of State courts in implementing this section;

(B) describing the manner in which Federal agencies will implement and enforce the requirements of this section;

(C) detailing the means by which Federal and State agencies, courts, and law enforcement agencies will exchange and share the data and information necessary to implement and enforce the withholding of Federal benefits; and

(D) recommending any modifications to improve the administration of this section or otherwise achieve the goal of discouraging the trafficking and possession of controlled substances.

(2) No later than September 1, 1989, the Congress shall consider the report of the President and enact such changes as it deems appropriate to further the goals of this section.

(h) **Effective date**

The denial of Federal benefits set forth in this section shall take effect for convictions occurring after September 1, 1989.

(Pub.L. 91–513, Title II, § 421, formerly Pub.L. 100–690, Title V, § 5301, Nov. 18, 1988, 102 Stat. 4310, renumbered § 421 and amended Pub.L. 101–647, Title X, § 1002(d), Nov. 29, 1990, 104 Stat. 4827.)

HISTORICAL AND STATUTORY NOTES

References in Text

This subchapter, referred to in subsec. (b)(1), was in the original "this title", which is Title II of Pub.L. 91–513, Oct. 27, 1970, 84 Stat. 1242, and is popularly known as the "Controlled Substances Act". For complete classification of Title II to the Code, see Short Title note set out under section 801 of this title and Tables.

Codifications

Section was enacted as part of the Anti-Drug Abuse Act of 1988 and not as part of the Comprehensive Drug Abuse Prevention and Control Act of 1970, which enacted this chapter, or the Controlled Substances Act, which comprises this subchapter.

Section was formerly classified to section 853a of this title.

§ 862a. Denial of assistance and benefits for certain drug-related convictions

(a) **In general**

An individual convicted (under Federal or State law) of any offense which is classified as a felony by the law of the jurisdiction involved and which has as an element the possession, use, or distribution of a controlled substance (as defined in section 802(6) of this title) shall not be eligible for—

(1) assistance under any State program funded under part A of title IV of the Social Security Act [42 U.S.C.A. § 601 et seq.], or

(2) benefits under the food stamp program (as defined in section 3(h) of the Food Stamp Act of 1977 [7 U.S.C.A. § 2012(h)]) or any State program carried out under the Food Stamp Act of 1977 [7 U.S.C.A. § 2011 et seq.].

(b) **Effects on assistance and benefits for others**

(1) **Program of temporary assistance for needy families**

The amount of assistance otherwise required to be provided under a State program funded under part A of title IV of the Social Security Act [42 U.S.C.A. § 601 et seq.] to the family members of an individual to whom subsection (a) of this section applies shall be reduced by the amount which would have otherwise been made available to the individual under such part.

(2) **Benefits under the Food Stamp Act of 1977**

The amount of benefits otherwise required to be provided to a household under the food stamp program (as defined in section 3(h) of the Food Stamp Act of 1977 [7 U.S.C.A. § 2012(h)]), or any State program carried out under the Food Stamp Act of 1977 [7 U.S.C.A. § 2011 et seq.], shall be determined by considering the individual to whom subsection (a) of this section applies not to be a member of such household, except that the income and resources of the individual shall be considered to be income and resources of the household.

(c) Enforcement

A State that has not exercised its authority under subsection (d)(1)(A) of this section shall require each individual applying for assistance or benefits referred to in subsection (a) of this section, during the application process, to state, in writing, whether the individual, or any member of the household of the individual, has been convicted of a crime described in subsection (a) of this section.

(d) Limitations

(1) State elections

(A) Opt out

A State may, by specific reference in a law enacted after August 22, 1996, exempt any or all individuals domiciled in the State from the application of subsection (a) of this section.

(B) Limit period of prohibition

A State may, by law enacted after August 22, 1996, limit the period for which subsection (a) of this section shall apply to any or all individuals domiciled in the State.

(2) Inapplicability to a conviction if the conviction is for conduct occurring on or before August 22, 1996

Subsection (a) of this section shall not apply to a conviction if the conviction is for conduct occurring on or before August 22, 1996.

(e) "State" defined

For purposes of this section, the term "State" has the meaning given it—

(1) in section 419(5) of the Social Security Act [42 U.S.C.A. § 619(5)], when referring to assistance provided under a State program funded under part A of title IV of the Social Security Act [42 U.S.C.A. § 601 et seq.], and

(2) in section 3(m) of the Food Stamp Act of 1977 [7 U.S.C.A. § 2012(m)], when referring to the food stamp program (as defined in section 3(h) of the Food Stamp Act of 1977 [7 U.S.C.A. § 2012(h)]) or any State program carried out under the Food Stamp Act of 1977 [7 U.S.C.A. § 2011 et seq.].

(f) Rule of interpretation

Nothing in this section shall be construed to deny the following Federal benefits:

(1) Emergency medical services under title XIX of the Social Security Act [42 U.S.C.A. § 1396 et seq.].

(2) Short-term, noncash, in-kind emergency disaster relief.

(3)(A) Public health assistance for immunizations.

(B) Public health assistance for testing and treatment of communicable diseases if the Secretary of Health and Human Services determines that it is necessary to prevent the spread of such disease.

(4) Prenatal care.

(5) Job training programs.

(6) Drug treatment programs.

(Pub.L. 104–193, Title I, § 115, Aug. 22, 1996, 110 Stat. 2180; Pub.L. 105–33, Title V, § 5516(a), Aug. 5, 1997, 111 Stat 620.)

HISTORICAL AND STATUTORY NOTES

References in Text

The Food Stamp Act of 1977, referred to in subsecs. (a)(2), (b)(2), and (e)(2), is Pub.L. 88–525, Aug. 31, 1964, 78 Stat. 703, as amended, which is classified generally to chapter 51 (section 2011 et seq.) of Title 7, Agriculture. Section 3(h) and (m) of such Act is classified to section 2012(h) and (m), respectively, of Title 7. For complete classification of this Act to the Code, see Short Title note set out under section 2011 of Title 7 and Tables.

The Social Security Act, referred to in subsecs. (a)(1), (b)(1), (e)(1), and (f)(1), is Act Aug. 14, 1935, c. 531, 49 Stat. 620, as amended, which is classified generally to chapter 7 (section 301 et seq.) of Title 42, The Public Health and Welfare. Part A of Title IV of such Act is classified to part A (section 601 et seq.) of subchapter IV of chapter 7 of Title 42; section 419(5) of such Act is classified to section 619(5) of Title 42; Title XIX of such Act is classified to subchapter XIX (section 1396 et seq.) of chapter 7 of Title 42. For complete classification of this Act to the Code, see section 1305 of Title 42 and Tables.

Codifications

Section was enacted as part of the Personal Responsibility and Work Opportunity Reconciliation Act of 1996 and not as part of the Comprehensive Drug Abuse Prevention and Control Act of 1970, which enacted this chapter, or the Controlled Substances Act, which comprises this subchapter.

Effective and Applicability Provisions

1997 Acts. Section 5518(d) of Pub.L. 105–33 provided: "The amendments made by this chapter to a provision of the Personal Responsibility and Work Opportunity Reconciliation Act of 1996 [Pub.L. 104–193, Aug. 22, 1996, 110 Stat. 2105] that have not become part of another statute [amending section 9910d of Title 42, Public Health and Welfare, and provisions set out as notes under sections 601 and 613 of Title 42 and section 612c of Title 7, Agriculture] shall take effect as if the amendments had been included in the provision at the time the provision became law."

1996 Acts. Section effective July 1, 1997, except as otherwise provided, see section 116 of Pub.L. 104–193, set out as note under section 601 of Title 42, The Public Health and Welfare.

§ 862b. Sanctioning for testing positive for controlled substances

Notwithstanding any other provision of law, States shall not be prohibited by the Federal Government from testing welfare recipients for use of controlled substances nor from sanctioning welfare recipients who test positive for use of controlled substances.

(Pub.L. 104–193, Title IX, § 902, Aug. 22, 1996, 110 Stat. 2347.)

HISTORICAL AND STATUTORY NOTES

Codifications

Section was enacted as part of the Personal Responsibility and Work Opportunity Reconciliation Act of 1996 and not as part of the Comprehensive Drug Abuse Prevention and Control Act of 1970, which enacted this chapter, or the Controlled Substances Act, which comprises this subchapter.

§ 863. Drug paraphernalia

(a) In general

It is unlawful for any person—

(1) to sell or offer for sale drug paraphernalia;

(2) to use the mails or any other facility of interstate commerce to transport drug paraphernalia; or

(3) to import or export drug paraphernalia.

(b) Penalties

Anyone convicted of an offense under subsection (a) of this section shall be imprisoned for not more than three years and fined under Title 18.

(c) Seizure and forfeiture

Any drug paraphernalia involved in any violation of subsection (a) of this section shall be subject to seizure and forfeiture upon the conviction of a person for such violation. Any such paraphernalia shall be delivered to the Administrator of General Services, General Services Administration, who may order such paraphernalia destroyed or may authorize its use for law enforcement or educational purposes by Federal, State, or local authorities.

(d) "Drug paraphernalia" defined

The term "drug paraphernalia" means any equipment, product, or material of any kind which is primarily intended or designed for use in manufacturing, compounding, converting, concealing, producing, processing, preparing, injecting, ingesting, inhaling, or otherwise introducing into the human body a controlled substance, possession of which is unlawful under this subchapter. It includes items primarily intended or designed for use in ingesting, inhaling, or otherwise introducing marijuana,[1] cocaine, hashish, hashish oil, PCP, methamphetamine, or amphetamines into the human body, such as—

(1) metal, wooden, acrylic, glass, stone, plastic, or ceramic pipes with or without screens, permanent screens, hashish heads, or punctured metal bowls;

(2) water pipes;

(3) carburetion tubes and devices;

(4) smoking and carburetion masks;

(5) roach clips: meaning objects used to hold burning material, such as a marihuana cigarette, that has become too small or too short to be held in the hand;

(6) miniature spoons with level capacities of one-tenth cubic centimeter or less;

(7) chamber pipes;

(8) carburetor pipes;

(9) electric pipes;

(10) air-driven pipes;

(11) chillums;

(12) bongs;

(13) ice pipes or chillers;

(14) wired cigarette papers; or

(15) cocaine freebase kits.

(e) Matters considered in determination of what constitutes drug paraphernalia

In determining whether an item constitutes drug paraphernalia, in addition to all other logically relevant factors, the following may be considered:

(1) instructions, oral or written, provided with the item concerning its use;

(2) descriptive materials accompanying the item which explain or depict its use;

(3) national and local advertising concerning its use;

(4) the manner in which the item is displayed for sale;

(5) whether the owner, or anyone in control of the item, is a legitimate supplier of like or related items to the community, such as a licensed distributor or dealer of tobacco products;

(6) direct or circumstantial evidence of the ratio of sales of the item(s) to the total sales of the business enterprise;

(7) the existence and scope of legitimate uses of the item in the community; and

(8) expert testimony concerning its use.

(f) Exemptions

This section shall not apply to—

(1) any person authorized by local, State, or Federal law to manufacture, possess, or distribute such items; or

(2) any item that, in the normal lawful course of business, is imported, exported, transported, or sold through the mail or by any other means, and traditionally intended for use with tobacco products, including any pipe, paper, or accessory.

(Pub.L. 91–513, Title II, § 422(a), as added Pub.L. 101–647, Title XXIV, § 2401(a), Nov. 29, 1990, 104 Stat. 4858, renumbered Title II, § 422(b) to (f), formerly Title I, § 1822(b) to (f), Pub.L. 99–570, Oct. 27, 1986, 100 Stat. 3207–51, and amended Pub.L. 100–690, Title VI, § 6485, Nov. 18, 1988, 102 Stat. 4384; renumbered Title II, § 422(b) to (f), and amended Pub.L. 101–647, Title XXIV, § 2401(b), (c), Nov. 29, 1990, 104 Stat. 4859; Pub.L. 106–310, Div. B, Title XXXVI, § 3614, Oct. 17, 2000, 114 Stat. 1230.)

[1] So in original. Probably should be "marihuana". Compare 21 U.S.C.A. § 802(16).

HISTORICAL AND STATUTORY NOTES

References in Text

This subchapter, referred to in subsec. (d), was in the original "this title", which is Title II of Pub.L. 91–513, Oct. 27, 1970, 84 Stat. 1242, popularly known as the "Controlled Substances Act". For complete classification of this Act to the Code, see Short Title note set out under section 801 of this title and Tables.

Codifications

Subsecs. (b) to (f) of this section were formerly classified to section 857(b) to (f) of this title.

Subsec. (f) introductory text, which read in the original "This subtitle" and had been codified to read "This section" was also amended by Pub.L. 101–647, § 2401(c)(2), to read "This section".

Prior Provisions

Provisions similar to those comprising subsec. (a) of this section were contained in section 1822(a) of Pub.L. 99–570, Title I, Oct. 27, 1986, 100 Stat. 3207–51 (formerly classified to section 857(a) of this title) prior to repeal of the provision by Pub.L. 101–647, Title XXIV, § 2401(d), Nov. 29, 1990, 104 Stat. 1859.

§ 864. Anhydrous ammonia

(a) It is unlawful for any person—

(1) to steal anhydrous ammonia, or

(2) to transport stolen anhydrous ammonia across State lines,

knowing, intending, or having reasonable cause to believe that such anhydrous ammonia will be used to manufacture a controlled substance in violation of this part.

(b) Any person who violates subsection (a) of this section shall be imprisoned or fined, or both, in accordance with section 843(d) of this title as if such violation were a violation of a provision of section 843 of this title.

(Pub.L. 91–513, Title II, § 423, as added Pub.L. 106–310, Div. B, Title XXXVI, § 3653(a), Oct. 17, 2000, 114 Stat. 1240.)

§ 865. Smuggling methamphetamine or methamphetamine precursor chemicals into the United States while using facilitated entry programs

(a) Enhanced prison sentence

The sentence of imprisonment imposed on a person convicted of an offense under the Controlled Substances Act (21 U.S.C. 801 et seq.) or the Controlled Substances Import and Export Act (21 U.S.C. 951 et seq.), involving methamphetamine or any listed chemical that is defined in section 102(33) of the Controlled Substances Act (21 U.S.C. 802(33) , shall, if the offense is committed under the circumstance described in subsection (b) of this section, be increased by a consecutive term of imprisonment of not more than 15 years.

(b) Circumstances

For purposes of subsection (a) of this section, the circumstance described in this subsection is that the offense described in subsection (a) of this section was committed by a person who—

(1) was enrolled in, or who was acting on behalf of any person or entity enrolled in, any dedicated commuter lane, alternative or accelerated inspection system, or other facilitated entry program administered or approved by the Federal Government for use in entering the United States; and

(2) committed the offense while entering the United States, using such lane, system, or program.

(c) Permanent ineligibility

Any person whose term of imprisonment is increased under subsection (a) of this section shall be permanently and irrevocably barred from being eligible for or using any lane, system, or program described in subsection (b)(1) of this section.

(Pub.L. 109–177, Title VII, § 731, Mar. 9, 2006, 120 Stat. 270.)

HISTORICAL AND STATUTORY NOTES

References in Text

The Controlled Substances Act, referred to in subsec. (a), is Title II of Pub.L. 91–513, Oct. 27, 1970, 84 Stat. 1242, as amended, which is classified principally to this subchapter, 21 U.S.C.A. § 801 et seq.; section 102(33) of the Controlled Substances Act is classified to 21 U.S.C.A. § 802(33). For complete classification, see Short Title note set out under 21 U.S.C.A. § 801 and Tables.

The Controlled Substances Import and Export Act, referred to in subsec. (a), is Title III of Pub.L. 91–513, Oct. 27, 1970, 84 Stat. 1285, as amended, which is classified principally to subchapter II of chapter 13 of this title, 21 U.S.C.A. § 951 et seq. For complete classification, see Short Title note under 21 U.S.C.A. § 951 and Tables.

Codifications

Section was enacted as part of the Combat Methamphetamine Epidemic Act of 2005 and not as part of the Controlled Substances Act, which comprises this subchapter.

PART E—ADMINISTRATIVE AND ENFORCEMENT PROVISIONS

§ 871. Attorney General

(a) Delegation of functions

The Attorney General may delegate any of his functions under this subchapter to any officer or employee of the Department of Justice.

(b) Rules and regulations

The Attorney General may promulgate and enforce any rules, regulations, and procedures which he may deem necessary and appropriate for the efficient execution of his functions under this subchapter.

(c) Acceptance of devises, bequests, gifts, and donations

The Attorney General may accept in the name of the Department of Justice any form of devise, bequest, gift, or donation where the donor intends to donate property for the purpose of preventing or controlling the abuse of controlled substances. He may take all appropriate steps to secure possession of such property and may sell, assign, transfer, or convey any such property other than moneys.

(Pub.L. 91–513, Title II, § 501, Oct. 27, 1970, 84 Stat. 1270.)

HISTORICAL AND STATUTORY NOTES

References in Text

"This subchapter", referred to in subsecs. (a) and (b), was in the original "this title" which is Title II of Pub.L. 91–513, Oct. 27, 1970, 84 Stat. 1242, and is popularly known as the "Controlled Substances Act". For complete classification of Title II to the Code, see Short Title note set out under § 801 of this title and Tables.

Effective and Applicability Provisions

1970 Acts. Section effective Oct. 27, 1970, see § 704(b) of Pub.L. 91–513, set out as a note under § 801 of this title.

§ 871a. Semiannual reports to Congress

(a) In general

The Attorney General shall, on a semiannual basis, submit to the congressional committees and organizations specified in subsection (b) of this section reports that—

(1) describe the allocation of the resources of the Drug Enforcement Administration and the Federal Bureau of Investigation for the investigation and prosecution of alleged violations of the Controlled Substances Act involving methamphetamine; and

(2) the measures being taken to give priority in the allocation of such resources to such violations involving—

(A) persons alleged to have imported into the United States substantial quantities of methamphetamine or scheduled listed chemicals (as defined pursuant to the amendment made by section 711(a)(1));

(B) persons alleged to have manufactured methamphetamine; and

(C) circumstances in which the violations have endangered children.

(b) Congressional committees

The congressional committees and organizations referred to in subsection (a) of this section are—

(1) in the House of Representatives, the Committee on the Judiciary, the Committee on Energy and Commerce, and the Committee on Government Reform; and

(2) in the Senate, the Committee on the Judiciary, the Committee on Commerce, Science, and Transportation, and the Caucus on International Narcotics Control.

(Pub.L. 109–177, Title VII, § 736, Mar. 9, 2006, 120 Stat. 271.)

HISTORICAL AND STATUTORY NOTES

References in Text

The Controlled Substances Act, referred to in subsec. (a)(1), is Title II of Pub.L. 91–513, Oct. 27, 1970, 84 Stat. 1242, as amended, which is classified principally to this subchapter, 21 U.S.C.A. § 801 et seq. For complete classification, see Short Title note set out under 21 U.S.C.A. § 801 and Tables.

The amendment made by section 711(a)(1), referred to in subsec. (a)(2)(A), probably means Pub.L. 109–177, Title VII, § 711(a)(1), Mar. 9, 2006, 120 Stat. 256, which amended section 102(45), to (49) of the Controlled Substances Act, Pub.L. 91–513, Title II, § 102, Oct. 27, 1970, 84 Stat. 1242, as amended, which is classified to 21 U.S.C.A. § 802(45) to (49).

Codifications

Section was enacted as part of the Combat Methamphetamine Epidemic Act of 2005 and not as part of the Controlled Substances Act, which comprises this subchapter.

§ 872. Education and research programs of Attorney General

(a) Authorization

The Attorney General is authorized to carry out educational and research programs directly related to enforcement of the laws under his jurisdiction concerning drugs or other substances which are or may be subject to control under this subchapter. Such programs may include—

(1) educational and training programs on drug abuse and controlled substances law enforcement for local, State, and Federal personnel;

(2) studies or special projects designed to compare the deterrent effects of various enforcement strategies on drug use and abuse;

(3) studies or special projects designed to assess and detect accurately the presence in the human body of drugs or other substances which are or may be subject to control under this subchapter, including the development of rapid field identification methods which would enable agents to detect microquantities of such drugs or other substances;

(4) studies or special projects designed to evaluate the nature and sources of the supply of illegal drugs throughout the country;

(5) studies or special projects to develop more effective methods to prevent diversion of controlled substances into illegal channels; and

(6) studies or special projects to develop information necessary to carry out his functions under section 811 of this title.

(b) Contracts

The Attorney General may enter into contracts for such educational and research activities without performance bonds and without regard to section 5 of Title 41.

(c) Identification of research populations; authorization to withhold

The Attorney General may authorize persons engaged in research to withhold the names and other identifying characteristics of persons who are the subjects of such research. Persons who obtain this authorization may not be compelled in any Federal, State, or local civil, criminal, administrative, legislative, or other proceeding to identify the subjects of research for which such authorization was obtained.

(d) Affect of treaties and other international agreements on confidentiality

Nothing in the Single Convention on Narcotic Drugs, the Convention on Psychotropic Substances, or other treaties or international agreements shall be construed to limit, modify, or prevent the protection of the confidentiality of patient records or of the names and other identifying characteristics of research subjects as provided by any Federal, State, or local law or regulation.

(e) Use of controlled substances in research

The Attorney General, on his own motion or at the request of the Secretary, may authorize the possession, distribution, and dispensing of controlled substances by persons engaged in research. Persons who obtain this authorization shall be exempt from State or Federal prosecution for possession, distribution, and dispensing of controlled substances to the extent authorized by the Attorney General.

(f) Program to curtail diversion of precursor and essential chemicals

The Attorney General shall maintain an active program, both domestic and international, to curtail the diversion of precursor chemicals and essential chemicals used in the illicit manufacture of controlled substances.

(Pub.L. 91–513, Title II, § 502, Oct. 27, 1970, 84 Stat. 1271; Pub.L. 95–633, Title I, § 108(a), Nov. 10, 1978, 92 Stat. 3773; Pub.L. 100–690, Title VI, § 6060, Nov. 18, 1988, 102 Stat. 4320.)

HISTORICAL AND STATUTORY NOTES

References in Text

"This subchapter", referred to in subsec. (a), was in the original "this title" which is Title II of Pub.L. 91–513, Oct. 27, 1970, 84 Stat. 1242, and is popularly known as the "Controlled Substances Act". For complete classification of Title II to the Code, see Short Title note set out under § 801 of this title and Tables.

Effective and Applicability Provisions

1988 Acts. Amendment by section 6060 of Pub.L. 100–690 effective 120 days after Nov. 18, 1988, see section 6061 of Pub.L. 100–690, set out as a note under section 802 of this title.

1978 Acts. Amendment by Pub.L. 95–633 effective on the date the Convention on Psychotropic Substances enters into force in the United States [July 15, 1980], see § 112 of Pub.L. 95–633, set out as an Effective Date note under § 801a of this title.

1970 Acts. Section effective Oct. 27, 1970, see § 704(b) of Pub.L. 91–513, set out as a note under § 801 of this title.

Training for Drug Enforcement Administration and State and Local Law Enforcement Personnel Relating to Clandestine Laboratories

Pub.L. 106–310, Div. B, Title XXXVI, § 3623, Oct. 17, 2000, 114 Stat. 1231, provided that:

"**(a) In general.**—

"**(1) Requirement.**—The Administrator of the Drug Enforcement Administration shall carry out the programs described in subsection (b) with respect to the law enforcement personnel of States and localities determined by the Administrator to have significant levels of methamphetamine-related or amphetamine-related crime or projected by the Administrator to have the potential for such levels of crime in the future.

"**(2) Duration.**—The duration of any program under that subsection may not exceed 3 years.

"**(b) Covered programs.**—The programs described in this subsection are as follows:

"**(1) Advanced mobile clandestine laboratory training teams.**—A program of advanced mobile clandestine laboratory training teams, which shall provide information and training to State and local law enforcement personnel in techniques utilized in conducting undercover investigations and conspiracy cases, and other information designed to assist in the investigation of the illegal manufacturing and trafficking of amphetamine and methamphetamine.

"(2) Basic clandestine laboratory certification training.—A program of basic clandestine laboratory certification training, which shall provide information and training—

"(A) to Drug Enforcement Administration personnel and State and local law enforcement personnel for purposes of enabling such personnel to meet any certification requirements under law with respect to the handling of wastes created by illegal amphetamine and methamphetamine laboratories; and

"(B) to State and local law enforcement personnel for purposes of enabling such personnel to provide the information and training covered by subparagraph (A) to other State and local law enforcement personnel.

"(3) Clandestine laboratory recertification and awareness training.—A program of clandestine laboratory recertification and awareness training, which shall provide information and training to State and local law enforcement personnel for purposes of enabling such personnel to provide recertification and awareness training relating to clandestine laboratories to additional State and local law enforcement personnel.

"(c) Authorization of appropriations.—There are authorized to be appropriated for each of fiscal years 2000, 2001, and 2002 amounts as follows:

"(1) $1,500,000 to carry out the program described in subsection (b)(1).

"(2) $3,000,000 to carry out the program described in subsection (b)(2).

"(3) $1,000,000 to carry out the program described in subsection (b)(3)."

Educational Program for Police Departments

Pub.L. 104–305, § 4, Oct. 13, 1996, 110 Stat. 3809, provided that: "The Attorney General may—

"(1) create educational materials regarding the use of controlled substances (as that term is defined in section 102 of the Controlled Substances Act) [section 802 of this title] in the furtherance of rapes and sexual assaults; and

"(2) disseminate those materials to police departments throughout the United States."

Study and Report on Measures to Prevent Sales of Agents Used in Methamphetamine Production

Pub.L. 104–237, Title II, § 202, Oct. 3, 1996, 110 Stat. 3101, provided that:

"(a) Study.—The Attorney General of the United States shall conduct a study on possible measures to effectively prevent the diversion of red phosphorous, iodine, hydrochloric gas, and other agents for use in the production of methamphetamine. Nothing in this section shall preclude the Attorney General from taking any action the Attorney General already is authorized to take with regard to the regulation of listed chemicals under current law.

"(b) Report.—Not later than January 1, 1998, the Attorney General shall submit a report to the Congress of its findings pursuant to the study conducted under subsection (a) on the need for and advisability of preventive measures.

"(c) Considerations.—In developing recommendations under subsection (b), the Attorney General shall consider—

"(1) the use of red phosphorous, iodine, hydrochloric gas, and other agents in the illegal manufacture of methamphetamine;

"(2) the use of red phosphorous, iodine, hydrochloric gas, and other agents for legitimate, legal purposes, and the impact any regulations may have on these legitimate purposes; and

"(3) comments and recommendations from law enforcement, manufacturers of such chemicals, and the consumers of such chemicals for legitimate, legal purposes."

§ 872a. Public-private education program

(a) Advisory panel

The Attorney General shall establish an advisory panel consisting of an appropriate number of representatives from Federal, State, and local law enforcement and regulatory agencies with experience in investigating and prosecuting illegal transactions of precursor chemicals. The Attorney General shall convene the panel as often as necessary to develop and coordinate educational programs for wholesale and retail distributors of precursor chemicals and supplies.

(b) Continuation of current efforts

The Attorney General shall continue to—

(1) maintain an active program of seminars and training to educate wholesale and retail distributors of precursor chemicals and supplies regarding the identification of suspicious transactions and their responsibility to report such transactions; and

(2) provide assistance to State and local law enforcement and regulatory agencies to facilitate the establishment and maintenance of educational programs for distributors of precursor chemicals and supplies.

(Pub.L. 104–237, Title V, § 503, Oct. 3, 1996, 110 Stat. 3112.)

HISTORICAL AND STATUTORY NOTES

Codifications

Section was enacted as part of the Comprehensive Methamphetamine Control Act of 1996, Pub.L. 104–237, and not as part of the Controlled Substances Act, Pub.L. 91–513, which comprises this subchapter.

§ 873. Cooperative arrangements

(a) Cooperation of Attorney General with local, State, and Federal agencies

The Attorney General shall cooperate with local, State, and Federal agencies concerning traffic in controlled substances and in suppressing the abuse of controlled substances. To this end, he is authorized to—

(1) arrange for the exchange of information between governmental officials concerning the use and abuse of controlled substances;

(2) cooperate in the institution and prosecution of cases in the courts of the United States and before the licensing boards and courts of the several States;

(3) conduct training programs on controlled substance law enforcement for local, State, and Federal personnel;

(4) maintain in the Department of Justice a unit which will accept, catalog, file, and otherwise utilize all information and statistics, including records of controlled substance abusers and other controlled substance law offenders, which may be received from Federal, State, and local agencies, and make such information available for Federal, State, and local law enforcement purposes;

(5) conduct programs of eradication aimed at destroying wild or illicit growth of plant species from which controlled substances may be extracted;

(6) assist State and local governments in suppressing the diversion of controlled substances from legitimate medical, scientific, and commercial channels by—

(A) making periodic assessments of the capabilities of State and local governments to adequately control the diversion of controlled substances;

(B) providing advice and counsel to State and local governments on the methods by which such governments may strengthen their controls against diversion; and

(C) establishing cooperative investigative efforts to control diversion; and

(7) notwithstanding any other provision of law, enter into contractual agreements with State and local law enforcement agencies to provide for cooperative enforcement and regulatory activities under this chapter.

(b) Requests by Attorney General for assistance from Federal agencies or instrumentalities

When requested by the Attorney General, it shall be the duty of any agency or instrumentality of the Federal Government to furnish assistance, including technical advice, to him for carrying out his functions under this subchapter; except that no such agency or instrumentality shall be required to furnish the name of, or other identifying information about, a patient or research subject whose identity it has undertaken to keep confidential.

(c) Descriptive and analytic reports by Attorney General to State agencies of distribution patterns of schedule II substances having highest rates of abuse

The Attorney General shall annually (1) select the controlled substance (or controlled substances) contained in schedule II which, in the Attorney General's discretion, is determined to have the highest rate of abuse, and (2) prepare and make available to regulatory, licensing, and law enforcement agencies of States descriptive and analytic reports on the actual distribution patterns in such States of each such controlled substance.

(d) Grants by Attorney General

(1) The Attorney General may make grants, in accordance with paragraph (2), to State and local governments to assist in meeting the costs of—

(A) collecting and analyzing data on the diversion of controlled substances,

(B) conducting investigations and prosecutions of such diversions,

(C) improving regulatory controls and other authorities to control such diversions,

(D) programs to prevent such diversions,

(E) preventing and detecting forged prescriptions, and

(F) training law enforcement and regulatory personnel to improve the control of such diversions.

(2) No grant may be made under paragraph (1) unless an application therefor is submitted to the Attorney General in such form and manner as the Attorney General may prescribe. No grant may exceed 80 per centum of the costs for which the grant is made, and no grant may be made unless the recipient of the grant provides assurances satisfactory to the Attorney General that it will obligate funds to meet the remaining 20 per centum of such costs. The Attorney General shall review the activities carried out with grants under paragraph (1) and shall report annually to Congress on such activities.

(3) To carry out this subsection there is authorized to be appropriated $6,000,000 for fiscal year 1985 and $6,000,000 for fiscal year 1986.

(Pub.L. 91–513, Title II, § 503, Oct. 27, 1970, 84 Stat. 1271; Pub.L. 96–359, § 8(a), Sept. 26, 1980, 94 Stat. 1194; Pub.L. 98–473, Title II, § 517, Oct. 12, 1984, 98 Stat. 2074; Pub.L. 99–570, Title I, § 1868, Oct. 27, 1986, 100 Stat. 3207–55; Pub.L. 99–646, § 85, Nov. 10, 1986, 100 Stat. 3620.)

HISTORICAL AND STATUTORY NOTES

References in Text

This chapter, referred to in subsec. (a)(7), was in the original as added by Pub.L. 99–646 "this act", meaning Pub.L. 91–513, Oct. 27, 1970, 84 Stat. 1236, as amended. In the subsec. (a)(7) added by Pub.L. 99–570, the reference was "this title", meaning title II of Pub.L. 91–513 which is popularly known as the "Controlled Substances Act" and is classified principally to this subchapter. For complete classification of this Act and title II to the Code, see Short Title note set out under section 801 of this title and Tables.

Schedule II, referred to in subsec. (c), is set out in section 812(c) of this title.

Codifications

Pub.L. 99–570 and Pub.L. 99–646 made similar amendments by adding a new par. (7) to subsec. (a). As originally enacted, Pub.L. 99–646 referred to "this Act" and Pub.L. 99–570 referred to "this title" and both have been editorially translated as "this Subchapter" in view of prior editorial treatment of references to the Controlled Substances Act.

Effective and Applicability Provisions

1970 Acts. Section effective Oct. 27, 1970, see § 704(b) of Pub.L. 91–513, set out as a note under § 801 of this title.

Annual Report on Counterdrug Intelligence Matters

Pub.L. 107–306, Title VIII, § 826, Nov. 27, 2002, 116 Stat. 2429, provided that:

"**(a) Annual report.**—The Counterdrug Intelligence Coordinating Group shall submit to the appropriate committees of Congress each year a report on current counterdrug intelligence matters. The report shall include the recommendations of the Counterdrug Intelligence Coordinating Group on the appropriate number of permanent staff, and of detailed personnel, for the staff of the Counterdrug Intelligence Executive Secretariat.

"**(b) Submittal date.**—The date of the submittal each year of the report required by subsection (a) shall be the date provided in section 507 of the National Security Act of 1947 [50 U.S.C.A. § 415b], as added by section 811 of this Act.

"**(c) Appropriate committees of Congress defined.**—In this section [this note], the term 'appropriate committees of Congress' means—

"(1) the Committees on Appropriations of the Senate and House of Representatives; and

"(2) the congressional intelligence committees (as defined in section 3 of the National Security Act of 1947 (50 U.S.C. § 401a))."

National Drug Intelligence Center

Pub.L. 108–487, Title I, § 104(e), Dec. 23, 2004, 118 Stat. 3942, provided that:

"**(1) In general.**—Of the amount authorized to be appropriated in subsection (a) [Pub.L. 108–487, Title I, § 104(a), Dec. 23, 2004, 118 Stat. 3941, which is not classified to the Code], $42,322,000 shall be available for the National Drug Intelligence Center. Within such amount, funds provided for research, development, testing, and evaluation purposes shall remain available until September 30, 2006, and funds provided for procurement purposes shall remain available until September 30, 2007.

"**(2) Transfer of funds.**—The Director of National Intelligence shall transfer to the Attorney General funds available for the National Drug Intelligence Center under paragraph (1). The Attorney General shall utilize funds so transferred for the activities of the National Drug Intelligence Center.

"**(3) Limitation.**—Amounts available for the National Drug Intelligence Center may not be used in contravention of the provisions of section 103(d)(1) of the National Security Act of 1947 (50 U.S.C. 403–3(d)(1)).

"**(4) Authority.**—Notwithstanding any other provision of law, the Attorney General shall retain full authority over the operations of the National Drug Intelligence Center."

[Except as otherwise expressly provided, amendments made by Pub.L. 108–487 to this note to take effect on Dec. 23, 2004, see Pub.L. 108–487, § 801, set out as a note under 22 U.S.C.A. § 2656f.]

[Except as otherwise provided, any reference in the Intelligence Authorization Act for Fiscal Year 2005, Pub.L. 108–487, Dec. 23, 2004, 118 Stat. 3939, to Director of Central Intelligence deemed to be a reference to Director of Central Intelligence as head of the intelligence community, see Pub.L. 108–487, § 802, set out as a note under 50 U.S.C.A. § 401.]

Similar provisions were contained in the following prior appropriations Acts:

Pub.L. 108–177, Title I, § 104(e), Dec. 13, 2003, 117 Stat. 2602.

Pub.L. 107–306, Title I, § 104(e), Nov. 27, 2002, 116 Stat. 2387.

Pub.L. 107–108, Title I, § 104(e), Dec. 28, 2001, 115 Stat. 1396.

Pub.L. 106–567, Title I, § 104(e), Dec. 27, 2000, 114 Stat. 2834.

Pub.L. 106–120, Title I, § 104(e), Dec. 3, 1999, 113 Stat. 1609.

Pub.L. 105–272, Title I, § 104(e), Oct. 20, 1998, 112 Stat. 2398.

Pub.L. 105–107, Title I, § 104(e), Nov. 20, 1997, 111 Stat. 2250

Pub.L. 104–293, Title I, § 104(d), Oct. 11, 1996, 110 Stat. 3464

Pub.L. 103–139, Title VIII, § 8056, Nov. 11, 1993, 107 Stat. 1452, provided that: "During the current fiscal year and thereafter, there is established, under the direction and control of the Attorney General, the National Drug Intelligence Center, whose mission it shall be to coordinate and consolidate drug intelligence from all national security and law enforcement agencies, and produce information regarding the structure, membership, finances, communications, and activities of drug trafficking organizations: *Provided*, That funding for the operation of the National Drug Intelligence Center, including personnel costs associated therewith, shall be provided from the funds appropriated to the Department of Defense."

Similar provisions were contained in the following prior appropriations Act:

Pub.L. 102–396, Title IX, § 9078, Oct. 6, 1992, 106 Stat. 1919.

Combating Amphetamine and Methamphetamine Manufacturing and Trafficking

Pub.L. 106–310, Div. B, Title XXXVI, § 3625, Oct. 17, 2000, 114 Stat. 1233, provided that:

"**(a) Activities.**—In order to combat the illegal manufacturing and trafficking in amphetamine and methamphetamine, the Administrator of the Drug Enforcement Administration may—

"(1) assist State and local law enforcement in small and mid- sized communities in all phases of investigations related to such manufacturing and trafficking, including assistance with foreign-language interpretation;

"(2) staff additional regional enforcement and mobile enforcement teams related to such manufacturing and trafficking;

"(3) establish additional resident offices and posts of duty to assist State and local law enforcement in rural areas in combating such manufacturing and trafficking;

"(4) provide the Special Operations Division of the Administration with additional agents and staff to collect, evaluate, interpret, and disseminate critical intelligence targeting the command and control operations of major amphetamine and methamphetamine manufacturing and trafficking organizations;

"(5) enhance the investigative and related functions of the Chemical Control Program of the Administration to implement more fully the provisions of the Comprehensive Methamphetamine Control Act of 1996 (Public Law 104–237);

"(6) design an effective means of requiring an accurate accounting of the import and export of list I chemicals, and coordinate investigations relating to the diversion of such chemicals;

"(7) develop a computer infrastructure sufficient to receive, process, analyze, and redistribute time-sensitive enforcement information from suspicious order reporting to field offices of the Administration and other law enforcement and regulatory agencies, including the continuing development of the Suspicious Order Reporting and Tracking System (SORTS) and the Chemical Transaction Database (CTRANS) of the Administration;

"(8) establish an education, training, and communication process in order to alert the industry to current trends and emerging patterns in the illegal manufacturing of amphetamine and methamphetamine; and

"(9) carry out such other activities as the Administrator considers appropriate.

"(b) Additional positions and personnel.—

"(1) In general.—In carrying out activities under subsection (a), the Administrator may establish in the Administration not more than 50 full-time positions, including not more than 31 special-agent positions, and may appoint personnel to such positions.

"(2) Particular positions.—In carrying out activities under paragraphs (5) through (8) of subsection (a), the Administrator may establish in the Administration not more than 15 full-time positions, including not more than 10 diversion investigator positions, and may appoint personnel to such positions. Any positions established under this paragraph are in addition to any positions established under paragraph (1).

"(c) Authorization of appropriations.—There are authorized to be appropriated for the Drug Enforcement Administration for each fiscal year after fiscal year 1999, $9,500,000 for purposes of carrying out the activities authorized by subsection (a) and employing personnel in positions established under subsection (b), of which $3,000,000 shall be available for activities under paragraphs (5) through (8) of subsection (a) and for employing personnel in positions established under subsection (b)(2)."

§ 874. Advisory committees

The Attorney General may from time to time appoint committees to advise him with respect to preventing and controlling the abuse of controlled substances. Members of the committees may be entitled to receive compensation at the rate of $100 for each day (including traveltime) during which they are engaged in the actual performance of duties. While traveling on official business in the performance of duties for the committees, members of the committees shall be allowed expenses of travel, including per diem instead of subsistence, in accordance with subchapter I of chapter 57 of Title 5.

(Pub.L. 91–513, Title II, § 504, Oct. 27, 1970, 84 Stat. 1272.)

HISTORICAL AND STATUTORY NOTES

Effective and Applicability Provisions

1970 Acts. Section effective Oct. 27, 1970, see § 704(b) of Pub.L. 91–513, set out as a note under § 801 of this title.

Termination of Advisory Committees

Advisory committees in existence on Jan. 5, 1973, to terminate not later than the expiration of two year period following Jan. 5, 1973, and advisory committees established after Jan. 5, 1973, to terminate not later than the expiration of two year period beginning on the date of their establishment, unless in the case of a committee established by the President or an officer of the Federal Government, such committee is renewed by appropriate action prior to the expiration of such two year period, or in the case of a committee established by Congress, its duration is otherwise provided by law, see § 14 of Pub.L. 92–463, Oct. 6, 1972, 86 Stat. 776, set out in the Appendix to Title 5, Government Organization and Employees.

§ 875. Administrative hearings

(a) Power of Attorney General

In carrying out his functions under this subchapter, the Attorney General may hold hearings, sign and issue subpenas, administer oaths, examine witnesses, and receive evidence at any place in the United States.

(b) Procedures applicable

Except as otherwise provided in this subchapter, notice shall be given and hearings shall be conducted under appropriate procedures of subchapter II of chapter 5 of Title 5.

(Pub.L. 91–513, Title II, § 505, Oct. 27, 1970, 84 Stat. 1272.)

HISTORICAL AND STATUTORY NOTES

References in Text

"This subchapter", referred to in text, was in the original "this title" which is Title II of Pub.L. 91–513, Oct. 27, 1970, 84 Stat. 1242, and is popularly known as the "Controlled Substances Act". For complete classification of Title II to the Code, see Short Title note set out under § 801 of this title and Tables.

Effective and Applicability Provisions

1970 Acts. Section effective Oct. 27, 1970, see § 704(b) of Pub.L. 91–513, set out as a note under § 801 of this title.

§ 876. Subpenas

(a) Authorization of use by Attorney General

In any investigation relating to his functions under this subchapter with respect to controlled substances, listed chemicals, tableting machines, or encapsulating machines, the Attorney General may subpena witnesses, compel the attendance and testimony of witnesses, and require the production of any records (including books, papers, documents, and other tangible things which constitute or contain evidence) which the Attorney General finds relevant or material to the investigation. The attendance of witnesses and the production of records may be required from any place in any State or in any territory or other place subject to the jurisdiction of the United States at any designated place of hearing; except that a witness shall not be required to appear at any hearing more than 500 miles distant from the place where he was served with a subpena. Witnesses summoned under this section shall be paid the same fees and mileage that are paid witnesses in the courts of the United States.

(b) Service

A subpena issued under this section may be served by any person designated in the subpena to serve it. Service upon a natural person may be made by personal delivery of the subpena to him. Service may be made upon a domestic or foreign corporation or upon a partnership or other unincorporated association which is subject to suit under a common name, by delivering the subpena to an officer, to a managing or general agent, or to any other agent authorized by appointment or by law to receive service of process. The affidavit of the person serving the subpena entered on a true copy thereof by the person serving it shall be proof of service.

(c) Enforcement

In the case of contumacy by or refusal to obey a subpena issued to any person, the Attorney General may invoke the aid of any court of the United States within the jurisdiction of which the investigation is carried on or of which the subpenaed person is an inhabitant, or in which he carries on business or may be found, to compel compliance with the subpena. The court may issue an order requiring the subpenaed person to appear before the Attorney General to produce records, if so ordered, or to give testimony touching the matter under investigation. Any failure to obey the order of the court may be punished by the court as a contempt thereof. All process in any such case may be served in any judicial district in which such person may be found.

(Pub.L. 91–513, Title II, § 506, Oct. 27, 1970, 84 Stat. 1272; Pub.L. 100–690, Title VI, § 6058, Nov. 18, 1988, 102 Stat. 4319.)

HISTORICAL AND STATUTORY NOTES

References in Text

"This subchapter", referred to in subsec. (a), was in the original "this title" which is Title II of Pub.L. 91–513, Oct. 27, 1970, 84 Stat. 1242, and is popularly known as the "Controlled Substances Act". For complete classification of Title II to the Code, see Short Title note set out under § 801 of this title and Tables.

Effective and Applicability Provisions

1988 Acts. Amendment by section 6058 of Pub.L. 100–690 effective 120 days after Nov. 18, 1988, see section 6061 of Pub.L. 100–690, set out as a note under section 802 of this title.

1970 Acts. Section effective Oct. 27, 1970, see § 704(b) of Pub.L. 91–513, set out as a note under § 801 of this title.

§ 877. Judicial review

All final determinations, findings, and conclusions of the Attorney General under this subchapter shall be final and conclusive decisions of the matters involved, except that any person aggrieved by a final decision of the Attorney General may obtain review of the decision in the United States Court of Appeals for the District of Columbia or for the circuit in which his principal place of business is located upon petition filed with the court and delivered to the Attorney General within thirty days after notice of the decision. Findings of fact by the Attorney General, if supported by substantial evidence, shall be conclusive.

(Pub.L. 91–513, Title II, § 507, Oct. 27, 1970, 84 Stat. 1273.)

HISTORICAL AND STATUTORY NOTES

References in Text

"This subchapter", referred to in text, was in the original "this title" which is Title II of Pub.L. 91–513, Oct. 27, 1970, 84 Stat. 1242, and is popularly known as the "Controlled Substances Act". For complete classification of Title II to the Code, see Short Title note set out under § 801 of this title and Tables.

Effective Date

1970 Acts. Section effective Oct. 27, 1970, see § 704(b) of Pub.L. 91–513, set out as a note under § 801 of this title.

§ 878. Powers of enforcement personnel

(a) Any officer or employee of the Drug Enforcement Administration or any State or local law enforcement officer designated by the Attorney General may—

(1) carry firearms;

(2) execute and serve search warrants, arrest warrants, administrative inspection warrants, subpenas, and summonses issued under the authority of the United States;

(3) make arrests without warrant (A) for any offense against the United States committed in his presence, or (B) for any felony, cognizable under the laws of the United States, if he has probable cause to believe that the person to be arrested has committed or is committing a felony;

(4) make seizures of property pursuant to the provisions of this subchapter; and

(5) perform such other law enforcement duties as the Attorney General may designate.

(b) State and local law enforcement officers performing functions under this section shall not be deemed Federal employees and shall not be subject to provisions of law relating to Federal employees, except that such officers shall be subject to section 3374(c) of Title 5.

(Pub.L. 91–513, Title II, § 508, Oct. 27, 1970, 84 Stat. 1273; Pub.L. 96–132, § 16(b), Nov. 30, 1979, 93 Stat. 1049; Pub.L. 99–570, Title I, § 1869, Oct. 27, 1986, 100 Stat. 3207–55; Pub.L. 99–646, § 86, Nov. 10, 1986, 100 Stat. 3620.)

HISTORICAL AND STATUTORY NOTES

References in Text

"This subchapter", referred to in subsec. (a)(4), was in the original "this title" which is Title II of Pub.L. 91–513, Oct. 27, 1970, 84 Stat. 1242, and is popularly known as the "Controlled Substances Act". For complete classification of Title II to the Code, see Short Title note set out under section 801 of this title and Tables.

Codifications

Amendment by section 1869(2) of Pub.L. 99–570, which directed that in subsec. (a) "or (with respect to offenses under this subchapter or subchapter II of this chapter) and State or local law enforcement officer" be inserted after "Drug Enforcement Administration" was not executed as the probable intent of Congress, in view of the subsequent amendment to subsec. (a) by section 86(2) of Pub.L. 99–646, which directed that "or any State or local law enforcement officer" be inserted after "Drug Enforcement Administration".

Effective and Applicability Provisions

1970 Acts. Section effective Oct. 27, 1970, see § 704(b) of Pub.L. 91–513, set out as an note under 801 of this title.

§ 879. Search warrants

A search warrant relating to offenses involving controlled substances may be served at any time of the day or night if the judge or United States magistrate judge issuing the warrant is satisfied that there is probable cause to believe that grounds exist for the warrant and for its service at such time.

(Pub.L. 91–513, Title II, § 509, Oct. 27, 1970, 84 Stat. 1274; Pub.L. 93–481, § 3, Oct. 26, 1974, 88 Stat. 1455; Pub.L. 101–650, Title III, § 321, Dec. 1, 1990, 104 Stat. 5117.)

HISTORICAL AND STATUTORY NOTES

Effective and Applicability Provisions

1970 Acts. Section effective Oct. 27, 1970, see § 704(b) of Pub.L. 91–513, set out as a note under § 801 of this title.

Change of Name

United States magistrate appointed under section 631 of Title 28, Judiciary and Judicial Procedure, to be known as United States magistrate judge after Dec. 1, 1990, with any reference to United States magistrate or magistrate in Title 28, in any other Federal statute, etc., deemed a reference to United States magistrate judge appointed under section 631 of Title 28, see section 321 of Pub.L. 101–650, set out as a note under section 631 of Title 28.

§ 880. Administrative inspections and warrants

(a) "Controlled premises" defined

As used in this section, the term "controlled premises" means—

(1) places where original or other records or documents required under this subchapter are kept or required to be kept, and

(2) places, including factories, warehouses, and other establishments, and conveyances, where persons registered under section 823 of this title (or exempt from registration under section 822(d) of this title or by regulation of the Attorney General) or regulated persons may lawfully hold, manufacture, distribute, dispense, administer, or otherwise dispose of controlled substances or listed chemicals or where records relating to those activities are maintained.

(b) Grant of authority; scope of inspections

(1) For the purpose of inspecting, copying, and verifying the correctness of records, reports, or other documents required to be kept or made under this subchapter and otherwise facilitating the carrying out of his functions under this subchapter, the Attorney General is authorized, in accordance with this section, to enter controlled premises and to conduct administrative inspections thereof, and of the things specified in this section, relevant to those functions.

(2) Such entries and inspections shall be carried out through officers or employees (hereinafter referred to as "inspectors") designated by the Attorney General. Any such inspector, upon stating his purpose and presenting to the owner, operator, or agent in charge of such premises (A) appropriate credentials and (B) a written notice of his inspection authority (which notice in the case of an inspection requiring, or in fact supported by, an administrative inspection warrant shall consist of such warrant), shall have the right to enter such premises and conduct such inspection at reasonable times.

(3) Except as may otherwise be indicated in an applicable inspection warrant, the inspector shall have the right—

(A) to inspect and copy records, reports, and other documents required to be kept or made under this subchapter;

(B) to inspect, within reasonable limits and in a reasonable manner, controlled premises and all pertinent equipment, finished and unfinished drugs, listed chemicals, and other substances or materials, containers, and labeling found therein, and, except as provided in paragraph (4) of this subsection, all other things therein (including records, files, papers, processes, controls, and facilities) appropriate for verification of the records, reports, and documents referred to in clause (A) or otherwise bearing on the provisions of this subchapter; and

(C) to inventory any stock of any controlled substance or listed chemical therein and obtain samples of any such substance or chemical.

(4) Except when the owner, operator, or agent in charge of the controlled premises so consents in writing, no inspection authorized by this section shall extend to—

(A) financial data;

(B) sales data other than shipment data; or

(C) pricing data.

(c) Situations not requiring warrants

A warrant under this section shall not be required for the inspection of books and records pursuant to an administrative subpena issued in accordance with section 876 of this title, nor for entries and administrative inspections (including seizures of property)—

(1) with the consent of the owner, operator, or agent in charge of the controlled premises;

(2) in situations presenting imminent danger to health or safety;

(3) in situations involving inspection of conveyances where there is reasonable cause to believe that the mobility of the conveyance makes it impracticable to obtain a warrant;

(4) in any other exceptional or emergency circumstance where time or opportunity to apply for a warrant is lacking; or

(5) in any other situations where a warrant is not constitutionally required.

(d) Administrative inspection warrants; issuance; execution; probable cause

Issuance and execution of administrative inspection warrants shall be as follows:

(1) Any judge of the United States or of a State court of record, or any United States magistrate judge, may, within his territorial jurisdiction, and upon proper oath or affirmation showing probable cause, issue warrants for the purpose of conducting administrative inspections authorized by this subchapter or regulations thereunder, and seizures of property appropriate to such inspections. For the purposes of this section, the term "probable cause" means a valid public interest in the effective enforcement of this subchapter or regulations thereunder sufficient to justify administrative inspections of the area, premises, building, or conveyance, or contents thereof, in the circumstances specified in the application for the warrant.

(2) A warrant shall issue only upon an affidavit of an officer or employee having knowledge of the facts alleged, sworn to before the judge or magistrate judge and establishing the grounds for issuing the warrant. If the judge or magistrate judge is satisfied that grounds for the application exist or that there is probable cause to believe they exist, he shall issue a warrant identifying the area, premises, building, or conveyance to be inspected, the purpose of such inspection, and, where appropriate, the type of property to be inspected, if any. The warrant shall identify the items or types of property to be seized, if any. The warrant shall be directed to a person authorized under subsection (b)(2) of this section to execute it. The warrant shall state the grounds for its issuance and the name of the person or persons whose affidavit has been taken in support thereof. It shall command the person to whom it is directed to inspect the area, premises, building, or conveyance identified for the purpose specified, and, where appropriate, shall direct the seizure of the property specified. The warrant shall direct that it be served during normal business hours. It shall designate the judge or magistrate judge to whom it shall be returned.

(3) A warrant issued pursuant to this section must be executed and returned within ten days of its date unless, upon a showing by the United States of a need therefor, the judge or magistrate judge allows additional time in the warrant. If property is seized pursuant to a warrant, the person executing the warrant shall give to the person from whom or from whose premises the property was taken a copy of the warrant and a receipt for the property taken or shall leave the copy and receipt at the place from which the property was taken. The return of the warrant shall be made promptly and shall be accompanied by a written inventory of any property taken. The inventory shall be made in the presence of the person executing the warrant and of the person from whose possession or premises the property was taken, if they are present, or in the presence of at least one credible person other than the person making such inventory, and shall be verified by the person executing the warrant. The judge or magistrate judge, upon request, shall deliver a copy of the inventory to the person from whom

or from whose premises the property was taken and to the applicant for the warrant.

(4) The judge or magistrate judge who has issued a warrant under this section shall attach to the warrant a copy of the return and all papers filed in connection therewith and shall file them with the clerk of the district court of the United States for the judicial district in which the inspection was made.

(Pub.L. 91–513, Title II, § 510, Oct. 27, 1970, 84 Stat. 1274; Pub.L. 101–647, Title XXXV, § 3599M, Nov. 29, 1990, 104 Stat. 4932; Pub.L. 101–650, Title III, § 321, Dec. 1, 1990, 104 Stat. 5117; Pub.L. 103–200, § 6, Dec. 17, 1993, 107 Stat. 2339.)

HISTORICAL AND STATUTORY NOTES

References in Text

"This subchapter", referred to in subsecs. (a)(1), (b)(1), (3)(A), (B), and (d)(1), was in the original "this title" which is Title II of Pub.L. 91–513, Oct. 27, 1970, 84 Stat. 1242, and is popularly known as the "Controlled Substances Act". For complete classification of Title II to the Code, see Short Title note set out under § 801 of this title and Tables.

Effective and Applicability Provisions

1993 Acts. Amendment to this section by Pub.L. 103–200, to take effect on the date that is 120 days after the date of enactment of Pub.L. 103–200, which was approved Dec. 17, 1993, see section 11 of Pub.L. 103–200, set out as a note under section 802 of this title.

1970 Acts. Section effective Oct. 27, 1970, see § 704(b) of Pub.L. 91–513, set out as a note under § 801 of this title.

Change of Name

United States magistrate appointed under section 631 of Title 28, Judiciary and Judicial Procedure, to be known as United States magistrate judge after Dec. 1, 1990, with any reference to United States magistrate or magistrate in Title 28, in any other Federal statute, etc., deemed a reference to United States magistrate judge appointed under section 631 of Title 28, see section 321 of Pub.L. 101–650, set out as a note under section 631 of Title 28.

§ 881. Forfeitures

(a) Subject property

The following shall be subject to forfeiture to the United States and no property right shall exist in them:

(1) All controlled substances which have been manufactured, distributed, dispensed, or acquired in violation of this subchapter.

(2) All raw materials, products, and equipment of any kind which are used, or intended for use, in manufacturing, compounding, processing, delivering, importing, or exporting any controlled substance or listed chemical in violation of this subchapter.

(3) All property which is used, or intended for use, as a container for property described in paragraph (1), (2), or (9).

(4) All conveyances, including aircraft, vehicles, or vessels, which are used, or are intended for use, to transport, or in any manner to facilitate the transportation, sale, receipt, possession, or concealment of property described in paragraph (1), (2), or (9).

(5) All books, records, and research, including formulas, microfilm, tapes, and data which are used, or intended for use, in violation of this subchapter.

(6) All moneys, negotiable instruments, securities, or other things of value furnished or intended to be furnished by any person in exchange for a controlled substance or listed chemical in violation of this subchapter, all proceeds traceable to such an exchange, and all moneys, negotiable instruments, and securities used or intended to be used to facilitate any violation of this subchapter.

(7) All real property, including any right, title, and interest (including any leasehold interest) in the whole of any lot or tract of land and any appurtenances or improvements, which is used, or intended to be used, in any manner or part, to commit, or to facilitate the commission of, a violation of this subchapter punishable by more than one year's imprisonment.

(8) All controlled substances which have been possessed in violation of this subchapter.

(9) All listed chemicals, all drug manufacturing equipment, all tableting machines, all encapsulating machines, and all gelatin capsules, which have been imported, exported, manufactured, possessed, distributed, dispensed, acquired, or intended to be distributed, dispensed, acquired, imported, or exported, in violation of this subchapter or subchapter II of this chapter.

(10) Any drug paraphernalia (as defined in section 863 of this title).

(11) Any firearm (as defined in section 921 of Title 18) used or intended to be used to facilitate the transportation, sale, receipt, possession, or concealment of property described in paragraph (1) or (2) and any proceeds traceable to such property.

(b) Seizure procedures

Any property subject to forfeiture to the United States under this section may be seized by the Attorney General in the manner set forth in section 981(b) of Title 18.

(c) Custody of Attorney General

Property taken or detained under this section shall not be repleviable, but shall be deemed to be in the custody of the Attorney General, subject only to the orders and decrees of the court or the official having jurisdiction thereof. Whenever property is seized under any of the provisions of this subchapter, the Attorney General may—

(1) place the property under seal;

(2) remove the property to a place designated by him; or

(3) require that the General Services Administration take custody of the property and remove it, if practicable, to an appropriate location for disposition in accordance with law.

(d) Other laws and proceedings applicable

The provisions of law relating to the seizure, summary and judicial forfeiture, and condemnation of property for violation of the customs laws; the disposition of such property or the proceeds from the sale thereof; the remission or mitigation of such forfeitures; and the compromise of claims shall apply to seizures and forfeitures incurred, or alleged to have been incurred, under any of the provisions of this subchapter, insofar as applicable and not inconsistent with the provisions hereof; except that such duties as are imposed upon the customs officer or any other person with respect to the seizure and forfeiture of property under the customs laws shall be performed with respect to seizures and forfeitures of property under this subchapter by such officers, agents, or other persons as may be authorized or designated for that purpose by the Attorney General, except to the extent that such duties arise from seizures and forfeitures effected by any customs officer.

(e) Disposition of forfeited property

(1) Whenever property is civilly or criminally forfeited under this subchapter the Attorney General may—

(A) retain the property for official use or, in the manner provided with respect to transfers under section 1616a of Title 19, transfer the property to any Federal agency or to any State or local law enforcement agency which participated directly in the seizure or forfeiture of the property;

(B) except as provided in paragraph (4), sell, by public sale or any other commercially feasible means, any forfeited property which is not required to be destroyed by law and which is not harmful to the public;

(C) require that the General Services Administration take custody of the property and dispose of it in accordance with law;

(D) forward it to the Bureau of Narcotics and Dangerous Drugs for disposition (including delivery for medical or scientific use to any Federal or State agency under regulations of the Attorney General); or

(E) transfer the forfeited personal property or the proceeds of the sale of any forfeited personal or real property to any foreign country which participated directly or indirectly in the seizure or forfeiture of the property, if such a transfer—

(i) has been agreed to by the Secretary of State;

(ii) is authorized in an international agreement between the United States and the foreign country; and

(iii) is made to a country which, if applicable, has been certified under section 2291j(b) of Title 22.

(2)(A) The proceeds from any sale under subparagraph (B) of paragraph (1) and any moneys forfeited under this title shall be used to pay—

(i) all property expenses of the proceedings for forfeiture and sale including expenses of seizure, maintenance of custody, advertising, and court costs; and

(ii) awards of up to $100,000 to any individual who provides original information which leads to the arrest and conviction of a person who kills or kidnaps a Federal drug law enforcement agent.

Any award paid for information concerning the killing or kidnapping of a Federal drug law enforcement agent, as provided in clause (ii), shall be paid at the discretion of the Attorney General.

(B) The Attorney General shall forward to the Treasurer of the United States for deposit in accordance with section 524(c) of Title 28, any amounts of such moneys and proceeds remaining after payment of the expenses provided in subparagraph (A), except that, with respect to forfeitures conducted by the Postal Service, the Postal Service shall deposit in the Postal Service Fund, under section 2003(b)(7) of Title 39, such moneys and proceeds.

(3) The Attorney General shall assure that any property transferred to a State or local law enforcement agency under paragraph (1)(A)—

(A) has a value that bears a reasonable relationship to the degree of direct participation of the State or local agency in the law enforcement effort resulting in the forfeiture, taking into account the total value of all property forfeited and the total law enforcement effort with respect to the violation of law on which the forfeiture is based; and

(B) will serve to encourage further cooperation between the recipient State or local agency and Federal law enforcement agencies.

(4)(A) With respect to real property described in subparagraph (B), if the chief executive officer of the State involved submits to the Attorney General a request for purposes of such subparagraph, the authority established in such subparagraph is in lieu of the authority established in paragraph (1)(B).

(B) In the case of property described in paragraph (1)(B) that is civilly or criminally forfeited under this subchapter, if the property is real property that is appropriate for use as a public area reserved for recreational or historic purposes or for the preservation of natural conditions, the Attorney General, upon the request of the chief executive officer of the State in which the property is located, may transfer title to the property to the State, either without charge or for a nominal charge, through a legal instrument providing that—

(i) such use will be the principal use of the property; and

(ii) title to the property reverts to the United States in the event that the property is used otherwise.

(f) Forfeiture and destruction of schedule I and II substances

(1) All controlled substances in schedule I or II that are possessed, transferred, sold, or offered for sale in violation of the provisions of this subchapter; all dangerous, toxic, or hazardous raw materials or products subject to forfeiture under subsection (a)(2) of this section; and any equipment or container subject to forfeiture under subsection (a)(2) or (3) of this section which cannot be separated safely from such raw materials or products shall be deemed contraband and seized and summarily forfeited to the United States. Similarly, all substances in schedule I or II, which are seized or come into the possession of the United States, the owners of which are unknown, shall be deemed contraband and summarily forfeited to the United States.

(2) The Attorney General may direct the destruction of all controlled substances in schedule I or II seized for violation of this subchapter; all dangerous, toxic, or hazardous raw materials or products subject to forfeiture under subsection (a)(2) of this section; and any equipment or container subject to forfeiture under subsection (a)(2) or (3) of this section which cannot be separated safely from such raw materials or products under such circumstances as the Attorney General may deem necessary.

(g) Plants

(1) All species of plants from which controlled substances in schedules I and II may be derived which have been planted or cultivated in violation of this subchapter, or of which the owners or cultivators are unknown, or which are wild growths, may be seized and summarily forfeited to the United States.

(2) The failure, upon demand by the Attorney General or his duly authorized agent, of the person in occupancy or in control of land or premises upon which such species of plants are growing or being stored, to produce an appropriate registration, or proof that he is the holder thereof, shall constitute authority for the seizure and forfeiture.

(3) The Attorney General, or his duly authorized agent, shall have authority to enter upon any lands, or into any dwelling pursuant to a search warrant, to cut, harvest, carry off, or destroy such plants.

(h) Vesting of title in United States

All right, title, and interest in property described in subsection (a) of this section shall vest in the United States upon commission of the act giving rise to forfeiture under this section.

(i) Stay of civil forfeiture proceedings

The provisions of section 981(g) of Title 18 regarding the stay of a civil forfeiture proceeding shall apply to forfeitures under this section.

(j) Venue

In addition to the venue provided for in section 1395 of Title 28 or any other provision of law, in the case of property of a defendant charged with a violation that is the basis for forfeiture of the property under this section, a proceeding for forfeiture under this section may be brought in the judicial district in which the defendant owning such property is found or in the judicial district in which the criminal prosecution is brought.

(*l*)[1] Agreement between Attorney General and Postal Service for performance of functions

The functions of the Attorney General under this section shall be carried out by the Postal Service pursuant to such agreement as may be entered into between the Attorney General and the Postal Service.

(Pub.L. 91–513, Title II, § 511, Oct. 27, 1970, 84 Stat. 1276; Pub.L. 95–633, Title III, § 301(a), Nov. 10, 1978, 92 Stat. 3777; Pub.L. 96–132, § 14, Nov. 30, 1979, 93 Stat. 1048; Pub.L. 98–473, Title II, §§ 306, 309, 518, Oct. 12, 1984, 98 Stat. 2050, 2051, 2075; Pub.L. 99–570, Title I, §§ 1006(c), 1865, 1992, Oct. 27, 1986, 100 Stat. 3207–7, 3207–54, 3207–60; Pub.L. 99–646, § 74, Nov. 10, 1986, 100 Stat. 3618; Pub.L. 100–690, Titles V, VI, §§ 5105, 6059, 6074, 6075, 6077(a), (b), 6253, Nov. 18, 1988, 102 Stat. 4301, 4319, 4323–4325, 4363; Pub.L. 101–189, Div. A, Title XII, § 1215(a), Nov. 29, 1989, 103 Stat. 1569; Pub.L. 101–647, Title XX, §§ 2003, 2004, 2007, 2008, Nov. 29, 1990, 104 Stat. 4855, 4856; Pub.L. 102–239, § 2, Dec. 17, 1991, 105 Stat. 1912; Pub.L. 102–583, § 6(a), Nov. 2, 1992, 106 Stat. 4932; Pub.L. 103–447, Title I, §§ 102(d), 103(a), Nov. 2, 1994, 108 Stat. 4693; Pub.L. 104–237, Title II, § 201(b), Oct. 3, 1996, 110 Stat. 3101; Pub.L. 106–185, §§ 2(c)(2), 5(b), 8(b), Apr. 25, 2000, 114 Stat. 210, 214, 216; Pub.L. 107–273, Div. B, Title IV, § 4002(e)(3), Nov. 2, 2002, 116 Stat. 1810.)

[1] So in original. No subsec. (k) has been enacted.

HISTORICAL AND STATUTORY NOTES

References in Text

"This subchapter", referred to in text, was in the original "this title" which is Title II of Pub.L. 91–513, Oct. 27, 1970, 84 Stat. 1242, and is popularly known as the "Controlled Substances Act". For complete classification of Title II to the Code, see Short Title note set out under § 801 of this title and Tables.

The customs laws, referred to in subsec. (d), are classified generally to Title 19, Customs Duties.

Schedules I and II, referred to in subsecs. (f) and (g)(1), are set out in section 812(c) of this title.

Transfer of Functions

Bureau of Narcotics and Dangerous Drugs, including office of Director thereof, in Department of Justice abolished by Reorg. Plan No. 2 of 1973, eff. July 1, 1973, 38 F.R. 15932, 87 Stat. 1091, set out in the Appendix to Title 5, Government Organization and Employees. Reorg. Plan No. 2 of 1973 also created in Department of Justice a single, comprehensive agency for enforcement of drug laws to be known as Drug Enforcement Administration, empowered Attorney General to authorize performance by officers, employees, and agencies of Department of functions transferred to him, and directed Attorney General to coordinate all drug law enforcement functions to assure maximum cooperation between Drug Enforcement Administration, Federal Bureau of Investigation, and other units of Department of Justice involved in drug law enforcement.

Effective and Applicability Provisions

2000 Acts. Amendments by Pub.L. 106–185, applicable to any forfeiture proceeding commenced on or after the date that is 120 days after April 25, 2000, see section 21 of Pub.L. 106–185, set out as a note under section 1324 of Title 8.

1992 Acts. Substitution in subsec. (e)(1)(iii) of "section 2291j of Title 22" for "section 2291(h) of Title 22" by Pub.L. 102–583 effective Oct. 1, 1992, see section 6(a) of Pub.L. 102–583, set out as a note under section 2291h of Title 22, Foreign Relations and Intercourse.

1989 Acts. Section 1215(b) of Pub.L. 101–189 provided that: "The amendment made by subsection (a) [amending subsec. (e)(3)(B) of this section] shall take effect as of October 1, 1989."

1988 Acts. Section 6077(c) of Pub.L. 100–690, as amended Pub.L. 101–162, Title II, § 208, Nov. 21, 1989, 103 Stat. 1005, provided that: "Section 551(e)(3)(B) [probably means 511(e)(3)(B)] of the Controlled Substances Act, as enacted by subsection (a) [subsec. (e)(3)(B) of this section], shall apply with respect to fiscal years beginning after September 30, 1991."

Amendment by section 6059 of Pub.L. 100–690 effective 120 days after Nov. 18, 1988, see section 6061 of Pub.L. 100–690, set out as a note under section 802 of this title.

1970 Acts. Section effective Oct. 27, 1970, see § 704(b) of Pub.L. 91–513, set out as a note under § 801 of this title.

Constructive Seizure Procedures

Pub.L. 101–225, Title II, § 210, Dec. 12, 1989, 103 Stat. 1913, provided that: "Not later than 6 months after the date of enactment of this Act [Dec. 12, 1989], the Secretary of Transportation and the Secretary of the Treasury, in order to avoid the devastating economic effects on innocent owners of seizures of their vessels, shall develop a procedure for constructive seizure of vessels of the United States engaged in commercial service as defined in section 2101 of title 46, United States Code [46 U.S.C.A. § 2101], that are suspected of being used for committing violations of law involving personal use quantities of controlled substances."

Regulations for Expedited Administrative Forfeiture Procedures

Section 6079 of Pub.L. 100–690 provided that:

"**(a) In general.**—Not later than 90 days after the date of enactment of this Act [Nov. 18, 1988], the Attorney General and the Secretary of the Treasury shall consult, and after providing a 30–day public comment period, shall prescribe regulations for expedited administrative procedures for seizures under section 511(a)(4), (6), and (7) of the Controlled Substances Act (21 U.S.C. 881(a)(4), (6), and (7)); section 596 of the Tariff Act of 1930 (19 U.S.C. 1595a(a)); and section 2 of the Act of August 9, 1939 (53 Stat. 1291; 49 U.S.C. App. 782) for violations involving the possession of personal use quantities of a controlled substance.

"**(b) Specifications.**—The regulations prescribed pursuant to subsection (a) shall—

"(1) minimize the adverse impact caused by prolonged detention, and

"(2) provide for a final administrative determination of the case within 21 days of seizure, or provide a procedure by which the defendant can obtain release of the property pending a final determination of the case. Such regulations shall provide that the appropriate agency official rendering a final determination shall immediately return the property if the following conditions are established:

"(A) the owner or interested party did not know of or consent to the violation;

"(B) the owner establishes a valid, good faith interest in the seized property as owner or otherwise; and

"(C)(1) the owner establishes that the owner at no time had any knowledge or reason to believe that the property in which the owner claims an interest was being or would be used in a violation of the law; and

"(2) if the owner at any time had, or should have had, knowledge or reason to believe that the property in which the owner claims an interest was being or would be used in a violation of the law, that the owner did what reasonably could be expected to prevent the violation.

An owner shall not have the seized property returned under this subsection if the owner had not acted in a normal and customary manner to ascertain how the property would be used.

"**(c) Notice.**—At the time of seizure or upon issuance of a summons to appear under subsection (d), the officer making the seizure shall furnish to any person in possession of the conveyance a written notice specifying the procedures under this section. At the earliest practicable opportunity after determining ownership of the seized conveyance, the head of the department or agency that seizes the conveyance shall furnish a written notice to the legal and factual basis of the seizure.

"**(d) Summons in lieu of seizure of commercial fishing industry vessels.**—Not later than 90 days after the enactment of this Act [Nov. 18, 1988], the Attorney General, the

Secretary of the Treasury, and the Secretary of Transportation shall prescribe joint regulations, after a public comment period of at least 30 days, providing for issuance of a summons to appear in lieu of seizure of a commercial fishing industry vessel as defined in section 2101 (11a), (11b), and (11c) of title 46, United States Code [46 U.S.C.A. § 2101 (11a), (11b), (11c)], for violations involving the possession of personal use quantities of a controlled substance. These regulations shall apply when the violation is committed on a commercial fishing industry vessel that is proceeding to or from a fishing area or intermediate port of call, or is actively engaged in fishing operations. The authority provided under this section shall not affect existing authority to arrest an individual for drug-related offenses or to release that individual into the custody of the vessel's master. Upon answering a summons to appear, the procedures set forth in subsections (a), (b), and (c) of this section shall apply. The jurisdiction of the district court for any forfeiture incurred shall not be affected by the use of a summons under this section.

"**(e) Personal use quantities of a controlled substance.**—For the purposes of this section, personal use quantities of a controlled substance shall not include sweepings or other evidence of nonpersonal use amounts."

§ 881–1. Transferred § 888

HISTORICAL AND STATUTORY NOTES

Codifications

Section, Pub.L. 91–513, Title II, 518, formerly 511A, as added Pub.L. 100–690, Title VI, § 6080(a), Nov. 18, 1988, 102 Stat. 4326; renumbered 518, Pub.L. 101–647, Title X, § 1002(h)(1), Nov. 29, 1990, 104 Stat. 4828, relating to expedited procedures for seized conveyances, was transferred to 21 U.S.C.A. § 888 prior to repeal by Pub.L. 106–185, applicable to any forfeiture proceeding commenced on or after the date that is 120 days after April 25, 2000, see section 21 of Pub.L. 106–185, set out as a note under 8 U.S.C.A. § 1324.

§ 881a. Transferred to § 889

§ 882. Injunctions

(a) Jurisdiction

The district courts of the United States and all courts exercising general jurisdiction in the territories and possessions of the United States shall have jurisdiction in proceedings in accordance with the Federal Rules of Civil Procedure to enjoin violations of this subchapter.

(b) Jury trial

In case of an alleged violation of an injunction or restraining order issued under this section, trial shall, upon demand of the accused, be by a jury in accordance with the Federal Rules of Civil Procedure.

(Pub.L. 91–513, Title II, § 512, Oct. 27, 1970, 84 Stat. 1278.)

HISTORICAL AND STATUTORY NOTES

References in Text

The Federal Rules of Civil Procedure, referred to in text, are set out in Title 28, Judiciary and Judicial Procedure.

"This subchapter", referred to in subsec. (a), was in the original "this title" which is Title II of Pub.L. 91–513, Oct. 27, 1970, 84 Stat. 1242, and is popularly known as the "Controlled Substances Act". For complete classification of Title II to the Code, see Short Title note set out under § 801 of this title and Tables.

Effective and Applicability Provisions

1970 Acts. Section effective Oct. 27, 1970, see § 704(b) of Pub.L. 91–513, set out as a note under § 801 of this title.

§ 883. Enforcement proceedings

Before any violation of this subchapter is reported by the Administrator of the Drug Enforcement Administration to any United States attorney for institution of a criminal proceeding, the Administrator may require that the person against whom such proceeding is contemplated is given appropriate notice and an opportunity to present his views, either orally or in writing, with regard to such contemplated proceeding.

(Pub.L. 91–513, Title II, § 513, Oct. 27, 1970, 84 Stat. 1278; Pub.L. 96–132, § 16(c), Nov. 30, 1979, 93 Stat. 1049.)

HISTORICAL AND STATUTORY NOTES

References in Text

"This subchapter", referred to in text, was in the original "this title" which is Title II of Pub.L. 91–513, Oct. 27, 1970, 84 Stat. 1242, and is popularly known as the "Controlled Substances Act". For complete classification of Title II to the Code, see Short Title note set out under § 801 of this title and Tables.

Effective and Applicability Provisions

1970 Acts. Section effective Oct. 27, 1970, see § 704(b) of Pub.L. 91–513, set out as a note under § 801 of this title.

§ 884. Immunity and privilege

(a) Refusal to testify

Whenever a witness refuses, on the basis of his privilege against self-incrimination, to testify or provide other information in a proceeding before a court or grand jury of the United States, involving a violation of this subchapter, and the person presiding over the proceeding communicates to the witness an order issued under this section, the witness may not refuse to comply with the order on the basis of his privilege against self-incrimination. But no testimony or other information compelled under the order issued under subsection (b) of this section or any information obtained by the exploitation of such testimony or other information, may be used against the witness in any criminal case, including any criminal case brought in a court of a State, except a prosecution for perjury, giving a false statement, or otherwise failing to comply with the order.

(b) Order of United States district court

In the case of any individual who has been or may be called to testify or provide other information at any proceeding before a court or grand jury of the United

States, the United States district court for the judicial district in which the proceeding is or may be held shall issue, upon the request of the United States attorney for such district, an order requiring such individual to give any testimony or provide any other information which he refuses to give or provide on the basis of his privilege against self-incrimination.

(c) Request by United States attorney

A United States attorney may, with the approval of the Attorney General or the Deputy Attorney General, the Associate Attorney General, or any Assistant Attorney General designated by the Attorney General, request an order under subsection (b) of this section when in his judgment—

(1) the testimony or other information from such individual may be necessary to the public interest; and

(2) such individual has refused or is likely to refuse to testify or provide other information on the basis of his privilege against self-incrimination.

(Pub.L. 91–513, Title II, § 514, Oct. 27, 1970, 84 Stat. 1278; Pub.L. 100–690, Title VII, § 7020(f), Nov. 18, 1988, 102 Stat. 4396.)

HISTORICAL AND STATUTORY NOTES

References in Text

"This subchapter", referred to in subsec. (a), was in the original "this title" which is Title II of Pub.L. 91–513, Oct. 27, 1970, 84 Stat. 1242, and is popularly known as the "Controlled Substances Act". For complete classification of Title II to the Code, see Short Title note set out under § 801 of this title and Tables.

Effective and Applicability Provisions

1970 Acts. Section effective Oct. 27, 1970, see § 704(b) of Pub.L. 91–513, set out as a note under § 801 of this title.

§ 885. Burden of proof; liabilities

(a) Exemptions and exceptions; presumption in simple possession offenses

(1) It shall not be necessary for the United States to negative any exemption or exception set forth in this subchapter in any complaint, information, indictment, or other pleading or in any trial, hearing, or other proceeding under this subchapter, and the burden of going forward with the evidence with respect to any such exemption or exception shall be upon the person claiming its benefit.

(2) In the case of a person charged under section 844(a) of this title with the possession of a controlled substance, any label identifying such substance for purposes of section 353(b)(2) of this title shall be admissible in evidence and shall be prima facie evidence that such substance was obtained pursuant to a valid prescription from a practitioner while acting in the course of his professional practice.

(b) Registration and order forms

In the absence of proof that a person is the duly authorized holder of an appropriate registration or order form issued under this subchapter, he shall be presumed not to be the holder of such registration or form, and the burden of going forward with the evidence with respect to such registration or form shall be upon him.

(c) Use of vehicles, vessels, and aircraft

The burden of going forward with the evidence to establish that a vehicle, vessel, or aircraft used in connection with controlled substances in schedule I was used in accordance with the provisions of this subchapter shall be on the persons engaged in such use.

(d) Immunity of Federal, State, local and other officials

Except as provided in sections 2234 and 2235 of Title 18, no civil or criminal liability shall be imposed by virtue of this subchapter upon any duly authorized Federal officer lawfully engaged in the enforcement of this subchapter, or upon any duly authorized officer of any State, territory, political subdivision thereof, the District of Columbia, or any possession of the United States, who shall be lawfully engaged in the enforcement of any law or municipal ordinance relating to controlled substances.

(Pub.L. 91–513, Title II, § 515, Oct. 27, 1970, 84 Stat. 1279.)

HISTORICAL AND STATUTORY NOTES

References in Text

"This subchapter", referred to in subsecs. (a)(1), (b), (c), and (d), was in the original "this title" which is Title II of Pub.L. 91–513, Oct. 27, 1970, 84 Stat. 1242, and is popularly known as the "Controlled Substances Act". For complete classification of Title II to the Code, see Short Title note set out under § 801 of this title and Tables.

Schedule I, referred to in subsec. (c), is set out in § 812(c) of this title.

Effective and Applicability Provisions

1970 Acts. Section effective Oct. 27, 1970, see § 704(b) of Pub.L. 91–513, set out as a note under § 801 of this title.

§ 886. Payments and advances

(a) Payment to informers

The Attorney General is authorized to pay any person, from funds appropriated for the Drug Enforcement Administration, for information concerning a violation of this subchapter, such sum or sums of money as he may deem appropriate, without reference to any moieties or rewards to which such person may otherwise be entitled by law.

(b) Reimbursement for purchase of controlled substances

Moneys expended from appropriations of the Drug Enforcement Administration for purchase of controlled substances and subsequently recovered shall be reimbursed to the current appropriation for the Administration.

(c) Advance of funds for enforcement purposes

The Attorney General is authorized to direct the advance of funds by the Treasury Department in connection with the enforcement of this subchapter.

(d) Drug Pollution Fund

(1) There is established in the Treasury a trust fund to be known as the "Drug Pollution Fund" (hereinafter referred to in this subsection as the "Fund"), consisting of amounts appropriated or credited to such Fund under section 841(b)(6) of this title.

(2) There are hereby appropriated to the Fund amounts equivalent to the fines imposed under section 841(b)(6) of this title.

(3) Amounts in the Fund shall be available, as provided in appropriations Acts, for the purpose of making payments in accordance with paragraph (4) for the clean up of certain pollution resulting from the actions referred to in section 841(b)(6) of this title.

(4)(A) The Secretary of the Treasury, after consultation with the Attorney General, shall make payments under paragraph (3), in such amounts as the Secretary determines appropriate, to the heads of executive agencies or departments that meet the requirements of subparagraph (B).

(B) In order to receive a payment under paragraph (3), the head of an executive agency or department shall submit an application in such form and containing such information as the Secretary of the Treasury shall by regulation require. Such application shall contain a description of the fine imposed under section 841(b)(6) of this title, the circumstances surrounding the imposition of such fine, and the type and severity of pollution that resulted from the actions to which such fine applies.

(5) For purposes of subchapter B of chapter 98 of Title 26, the Fund established under this paragraph shall be treated in the same manner as a trust fund established under subchapter A of such chapter.

(Pub.L. 91–513, Title II, § 516, Oct. 27, 1970, 84 Stat. 1279; Pub.L. 96–132, § 16(b), Nov. 30, 1979, 93 Stat. 1049; Pub.L. 100–690, Title VI, § 6254(i), Nov. 18, 1988, 102 Stat. 4367.)

HISTORICAL AND STATUTORY NOTES

References in Text

"This subchapter", referred to in subsecs. (a) and (c), was in the original "this title" which is Title II of Pub.L. 91–513, Oct. 27, 1970, 84 Stat. 1242, and is popularly known as the "Controlled Substances Act". For complete classification of Title II to the Code, see Short Title note set out under § 801 of this title and Tables.

Codifications

"Administration" was substituted for "Bureau" in subsec. (b) as the probable intent of Congress in view of amendment by Pub.L. 96–132, which substituted "Drug Enforcement Administration" for "Bureau of Narcotics and Dangerous Drugs" in subsecs. (a) and (b).

Effective and Applicability Provisions

1970 Acts. Section effective Oct. 27, 1970, see section 704(b) of Pub.L. 91–513, set out as a note under section 801 of this title.

Reimbursement by Drug Enforcement Administration of Expenses Incurred to Remediate Methamphetamine Laboratories

Pub.L. 106–310, Div. B, Title XXXVI, § 3672, Oct. 17, 2000, 114 Stat. 1246, provided that:

"**(a) Reimbursement authorized.**—The Attorney General, acting through the Administrator of the Drug Enforcement Administration, may reimburse States, units of local government, Indian tribal governments, other public entities, and multi-jurisdictional or regional consortia thereof for expenses incurred to clean up and safely dispose of substances associated with clandestine methamphetamine laboratories which may present a danger to public health or the environment.

"**(b) Additional DEA personnel.**—From amounts appropriated or otherwise made available to carry out this section, the Attorney General may hire not more than five additional Drug Enforcement Administration personnel to administer this section.

"**(c) Authorization of appropriations.**—There is authorized to be appropriated to the Attorney General to carry out this section $20,000,000 for fiscal year 2001."

§ 886a. Diversion Control Fee Account

(1) In general

There is established in the general fund of the Treasury a separate account which shall be known as the Diversion Control Fee Account. For fiscal year 1993 and thereafter:

(A) There shall be deposited as offsetting receipts into that account all fees collected by the Drug Enforcement Administration, in excess of $15,000,000, for the operation of its diversion control program.

(B) Such amounts as are deposited into the Diversion Control Fee Account shall remain available until expended and shall be refunded out of that account by the Secretary of the Treasury, at least on a quarterly basis, to reimburse the Drug Enforcement Administration for expenses incurred in the operation of the diversion control program. Such reimbursements shall be made without distinguishing between expenses related to controlled substance activities and expenses related to chemical activities.

(C) Fees charged by the Drug Enforcement Administration under its diversion control program shall be set at a level that ensures the recovery of the full costs of operating the various aspects of that program.

(D) The amount required to be refunded from the Diversion Control Fee Account for fiscal year 1994 and thereafter shall be refunded in accordance with estimates made in the budget request of the Attorney General for those fiscal years. Any proposed changes in the amounts designated in said budget requests shall only be made after notification to the Committees on Appropriations of the House of Representatives and the Senate fifteen days in advance.

(2) Definitions

In this section:

(A) Diversion control program

The term "diversion control program" means the controlled substance and chemical diversion control activities of the Drug Enforcement Administration.

(B) Controlled substance and chemical diversion control activities

The term "controlled substance and chemical diversion control activities" means those activities related to the registration and control of the manufacture, distribution, dispensing, importation, and exportation of controlled substances and listed chemicals.

(Pub.L. 102–395, Title I, § 111(b), Oct. 6, 1992, 106 Stat. 1843; Pub.L. 105–362, Title X, § 1001(b), Nov. 10, 1998, 112 Stat. 3291; Pub.L. 108–447, Div. B, Title VI, § 633(a), Dec. 8, 2004, 118 Stat. 2921.)

HISTORICAL AND STATUTORY NOTES

Codifications

Section was enacted as part of the Departments of Commerce, Justice, and State, the Judiciary, and Related Agencies Appropriations Act, 1993, and not as part of the Controlled Substances Act, which enacted this subchapter.

Pub.L. 108–447, Div. B, Title VI, § 633(a)(1), which directed redesignation of pars. (1) to (5) as subpars. (A) to (E) of par. (1), was executed by redesignating pars. (1) to (4) as subpars. (A) to (D) of par. (1), as the probable intent of Congress, since no par. (5) existed. See 2004 Amendments notes set out under this section.

§ 887. Coordination and consolidation of post-seizure administration

The Attorney General and the Secretary of the Treasury shall take such action as may be necessary to develop and maintain a joint plan to coordinate and consolidate post-seizure administration of property seized under this subchapter, subchapter II of this chapter, or provisions of the customs laws relating to controlled substances.

(Pub.L. 91–513, Title II, § 517, as added Pub.L. 100–690, Title VI, § 6078(a), Nov. 18, 1988, 102 Stat. 4325.)

HISTORICAL AND STATUTORY NOTES

References in Text

"This subchapter", referred to in text, was in the original "this title" which is Title II of Pub.L. 91–513, Oct. 27, 1970, 84 Stat. 1242, and is popularly known as the "Controlled Substances Act". For complete classification of Title II to the Code, see Short Title note set out under section 801 of this title and Tables.

"Subchapter II of this chapter", referred to in text, was in the original "title III", meaning Title III of Pub.L. 91–513, Oct. 27, 1970, 84 Stat. 1285. Part A of Title III comprises subchapter II of this chapter. For classification of Part B, consisting of sections 1101 to 1105 of Title III, see Tables.

§ 888. Repealed. Pub.L. 106–185, § 2(c)(3), Apr. 25, 2000, 114 Stat. 210

HISTORICAL AND STATUTORY NOTES

Section, Pub.L. 91–513, Title II, § 518, formerly § 511A, as added Pub.L. 100–690, Title VI, § 6080(a), Nov. 18, 1988, 102 Stat. 4326; renumbered § 518, Pub.L. 101–647, Title X, § 1002(h)(1), Nov. 29, 1990, 104 Stat. 4828, related to expedited procedures for seized conveyances.

Effective Date of Repeal

Repeal by Pub.L. 106–185, applicable to any forfeiture proceeding commenced on or after the date that is 120 days after April 25, 2000, see section 21 of Pub.L. 106–185, set out as a note under 8 U.S.C.A. § 1324.

§ 889. Production control of controlled substances

(a) Definitions

As used in this section:

(1) The term "controlled substance" has the same meaning given such term in section 802(6) of this title.

(2) The term "Secretary" means the Secretary of Agriculture.

(3) The term "State" means each of the fifty States, the District of Columbia, the Commonwealth of Puerto Rico, Guam, the Virgin Islands of the United States, American Samoa, the Commonwealth of the Northern Mariana Islands, or the Trust Territory of the Pacific Islands.

(b) Persons ineligible for Federal agricultural program benefits

Notwithstanding any other provision of law, following December 23, 1985, any person who is convicted under Federal or State law of planting, cultivation, growing, producing, harvesting, or storing a controlled substance in any crop year shall be ineligible for—

(1) as to any commodity produced during that crop year, and the four succeeding crop years, by such person—

(A) any price support or payment made available under the Agricultural Act of 1949 (7 U.S.C. 1421 et seq.), the Commodity Credit Corporation

Charter Act (15 U.S.C. 714 et seq.), or any other Act;

(B) a farm storage facility loan made under section 4(h) of the Commodity Credit Corporation Charter Act (15 U.S.C. 714b(h));

(C) crop insurance under the Federal Crop Insurance Act (7 U.S.C. 1501 et seq.);

(D) a disaster payment made under the Agricultural Act of 1949 (7 U.S.C. 1421 et seq.); or

(E) a loan made, insured or guaranteed under the Consolidated Farm and Rural Development Act (7 U.S.C. 1921 et seq.) or any other provision of law administered by the Farmers Home Administration; or

(2) a payment made under section 4 or 5 of the Commodity Credit Corporation Charter Act (15 U.S.C. 714b or 714c) for the storage of an agricultural commodity that is—

(A) produced during that crop year, or any of the four succeeding crop years, by such person; and

(B) acquired by the Commodity Credit Corporation.

(c) Regulations

Not later than 180 days after December 23, 1985, the Secretary shall issue such regulations as the Secretary determines are necessary to carry out this section, including regulations that—

(1) define the term "person";

(2) govern the determination of persons who shall be ineligible for program benefits under this section; and

(3) protect the interests of tenants and sharecroppers.

(Pub.L. 91–513, Title II, § 519, formerly Pub.L. 99–198, Title XVII, § 1764, Dec. 23, 1985, 99 Stat. 1652; renumbered § 519, Pub.L. 101–647, Title X, § 1002(h)(2), Nov. 29, 1990, 104 Stat. 4828.)

HISTORICAL AND STATUTORY NOTES

Codifications

Section was formerly classified to section 881a of this title.

§ 890. Review of Federal sales of chemicals usable to manufacture controlled substances

A Federal department or agency may not sell from the stocks of the department or agency any chemical which, as determined by the Administrator of the Drug Enforcement Administration, could be used in the manufacture of a controlled substance unless the Administrator certifies in writing to the head of the department or agency that there is no reasonable cause to believe that the sale of the chemical would result in the illegal manufacture of a controlled substance.

(Pub.L. 91–513, Title II, § 520, as added Pub.L. 104–201, Div. A, Title X, § 1034(a), Sept. 23, 1996, 110 Stat. 2640.)

PART F—GENERAL PROVISIONS

HISTORICAL AND STATUTORY NOTES

Codifications

The letter designation for this Part F was, in the original, Part G. The original Part F of Title II of Pub.L. 91–513, consisting of § 601 thereof, is set out as a note under § 801 of this title. The original Part G of Title II of Pub.L. 91–513 consisted of §§ 701 to 709. Sections 701 to 705 amended and repealed sections in this title and in Title 18, Crimes and Criminal Procedure, and Title 42, The Public Health and Welfare, and enacted provisions set out as notes under §§ 321, 801, and 822 of this title. See Tables volume for classifications of said §§ 701 to 705. Sections 706 to 709 of Pub.L. 91–513 are set out as §§ 901 to 904 of this title and, for purposes of codification, comprise this Part F.

§ 901. Severability

If a provision of this chapter is held invalid, all valid provisions that are severable shall remain in effect. If a provision of this chapter is held invalid in one or more of its applications, the provision shall remain in effect in all its valid applications that are severable.

(Pub.L. 91–513, Title II, § 706, Oct. 27, 1970, 84 Stat. 1284.)

HISTORICAL AND STATUTORY NOTES

References in Text

This chapter, referred to in text, was, in the original, this Act, meaning Pub.L. 91–513, Oct. 27, 1970, 84 Stat. 1236. For complete classification of this Act to the Code, see Short Title note set out under § 801 of this title and Tables.

Effective Date

Section effective Oct. 27, 1970, see § 704(b) of Pub.L. 91–513, set out as a note under § 801 of this title.

§ 902. Savings provisions

Nothing in this chapter, except this part and, to the extent of any inconsistency, sections 827(e) and 829 of this title, shall be construed as in any way affecting, modifying, repealing, or superseding the provisions of the Federal Food, Drug, and Cosmetic Act [21 U.S.C.A. § 301 et seq.].

(Pub.L. 91–513, Title II, § 707, Oct. 27, 1970, 84 Stat. 1284.)

HISTORICAL AND STATUTORY NOTES

References in Text

This chapter, referred to in text, was, in the original, this Act, meaning Pub.L. 91–513, Oct. 27, 1970, 84 Stat. 1236. For complete classification of this Act to the Code, see Short Title not set out under § 801 of this title and Tables.

The Federal Food, Drug, and Cosmetic Act, referred to in text, is Act June 25, 1938, c. 675, 52 Stat. 1040, which is classified generally to chapter 9 (§ 301 et seq.) of this title. For complete classification of this Act to the Code, see § 301 of this title and Tables volume.

Effective Date

1970 Acts. Section effective Oct. 27, 1970, see § 704(b) of Pub.L. 91–513, set out as a note under § 801 of this title.

§ 903. Application of State law

No provision of this subchapter shall be construed as indicating an intent on the part of the Congress to occupy the field in which that provision operates, including criminal penalties, to the exclusion of any State law on the same subject matter which would otherwise be within the authority of the State, unless there is a positive conflict between that provision of this subchapter and that State law so that the two cannot consistently stand together.

(Pub.L. 91–513, Title II, § 708, Oct. 27, 1970, 84 Stat. 1284.)

HISTORICAL AND STATUTORY NOTES

References in Text

"This subchapter", referred to in text, was in the original "this title" which is Title II of Pub.L. 91–513, Oct. 27, 1970, 84 Stat. 1242, and is popularly known as the "Controlled Substances Act". For complete classification of Title II to the Code, see Short Title note set out under § 801 of this title and Tables.

Effective Date

1970 Acts. Section effective Oct. 27, 1970, see § 704(b) of Pub.L. 91–513, set out as a note under § 801 of this title.

§ 904. Payment of tort claims

Notwithstanding section 2680(k) of Title 28, the Attorney General, in carrying out the functions of the Department of Justice under this subchapter, is authorized to pay tort claims in the manner authorized by section 2672 of Title 28, when such claims arise in a foreign country in connection with the operations of the Drug Enforcement Administration abroad.

(Pub.L. 91–513, Title II, § 709, Oct. 27, 1970, 84 Stat. 1284; Pub.L. 93–481, § 1, Oct. 26, 1974, 88 Stat. 1455; Pub.L. 95–137, § 1(a), Oct. 18, 1977, 91 Stat. 1169; Pub.L. 96–132, §§ 13, 15, Nov. 30, 1979, 93 Stat. 1048; Pub.L. 97–414, § 9(g)(1), Jan. 4, 1983, 96 Stat. 2064.)

HISTORICAL AND STATUTORY NOTES

References in Text

"This subchapter", referred to in text, was in the original "this title" which, is Title II of Pub.L. 91–513, Oct. 27, 1970, 84 Stat. 1242, and is popularly known as the "Controlled Substances Act". For complete classification of Title II to the Code, see Short Title note set out under § 801 of this title and Tables.

Effective and Applicability Provisions

1970 Acts. Section effective Oct. 27, 1970, see § 704(b) of Pub.L. 91–513, set out as a note under § 801 of this title.

SUBCHAPTER II—IMPORT AND EXPORT

HISTORICAL AND STATUTORY NOTES

Codifications

This subchapter is comprised of Part A of Title III of Pub.L. 91–513, Oct. 27, 1970, 84 Stat. 1285. Part B of Title III contains amendatory, repealing, and transitional provisions generally classified elsewhere.

§ 951. Definitions

(a) For purposes of this subchapter—

(1) The term "import" means, with respect to any article, any bringing in or introduction of such article into any area (whether or not such bringing in or introduction constitutes an importation within the meaning of the tariff laws of the United States).

(2) The term "customs territory of the United States" has the meaning assigned to such term by general note 2 of the Harmonized Tariff Schedule of the United States.

(b) Each term defined in section 802 of this title shall have the same meaning for purposes of this subchapter as such term has for purposes of subchapter I of this chapter.

(Pub.L. 91–513, Title III, § 1001, Oct. 27, 1970, 84 Stat. 1285; Pub.L. 100–418, Title I, § 1214(m), Aug. 23, 1988, 102 Stat. 1158.)

HISTORICAL AND STATUTORY NOTES

References in Text

The Tariff Schedules of the United States, referred to in subsec. (a)(2), are no longer set out in the Code. See Notice set out under section 1202 of Title 19.

"This subchapter" referred to in subsec. (b), was in the original "this title" meaning Title III of Pub.L. 91–513, Oct. 27, 1970, 84 Stat. 1285. Part A of Title III comprises this subchapter. For classification of Part B (sections 1101 to 1105) of Title III of Pub.L. 91–513, see Tables.

Effective and Applicability Provisions

1988 Acts. Amendment by Pub.L. 100–418 effective Jan. 1, 1989, and applicable with respect to articles entered on or after such date, see section 1217(b)(1) of Pub.L. 100–418, set out as a note under section 3001 of Title 19, Customs Duties.

1970 Acts. Section 1105(a) to (c) of Pub.L. 91–513 provided that:

"(a) Except as otherwise provided in this section, this title [see Short Title Note under this section] shall become effective on the first day of the seventh calendar month that begins after the day immediately preceding the date of enactment [Oct. 27, 1970].

"(b) Sections 1000, 1001, 1006, 1015, 1016, 1103, 1104 [this section and Short Title Note under this section and sections 171 note, 956, 957 note, 965, and 966 of this title], and this section shall become effective upon enactment [Oct. 27, 1970].

"(c)(1) If the Attorney General, pursuant to the authority of section 704(c) of title II [set out as a note under section 801 of this title], postpones the effective date of section 306 (relating to manufacturing quotas) [section 826 of this title] for any period beyond the date specified in section 704(a) [set out as a note under section 801 of this title], and such postponement applies to narcotic drugs, the repeal of the Narcotics Manufacturing Act of 1960 [sections 501 to 517 of this title] by paragraph (10) of section 1101(a) of this title is hereby postponed for the same period, except that the postponement made by this paragraph shall not apply to the repeal of sections 4, 5, 13, 15, and 16 of that Act [which were classified to sections 182, 503, 511, and 513 of this title and sections 4702, 4731, and 4731 note of Title 26, Internal Revenue Code].

"(2) Effective for any period of postponement, by paragraph (1) of this subsection, of the repeal of provisions of the Narcotics Manufacturing Act of 1960 [sections 501 to 517 of this title], that Act shall be applied subject to the following modifications:

"(A) The term 'narcotic drug' shall mean a narcotic drug as defined in section 102(16) of title II [section 802(16) of this title], and all references, in the Narcotics Manufacturing Act of 1960 [sections 501 to 517 of this title], to a narcotic drug as defined by section 4731 of the Internal Revenue Code of 1954 [section 4731 of Title 26] are amended to refer to a narcotic drug as defined by such section 102(16) [section 802(16) of this title].

"(B) On and after the date prescribed by the Attorney General pursuant to clause (2) of section 703(c) of title II [set out as a note under section 822 of this title], the requirements of a manufacturer's license with respect to a basic class of narcotic drug under the Narcotics Manufacturing Act of 1960 [sections 501 to 517 of this title], and of a registration under section 4722 of the Internal Revenue Code of 1954 [section 4722 of Title 26] as a prerequisite to issuance of such a license, shall be superseded by a requirement of actual registration (as distinguished from provisional registration) as a manufacturer of that class of drug under section 303(a) of title II [section 823(a) of this title].

"(C) On and after the effective date of the repeal of such section 4722 [section 4722 of Title 26] by section 1101(b)(3) of this title, but prior to the date specified in subparagraph (B) of this paragraph, the requirement of registration under such section 4722 as a prerequisite of a manufacturer's license under the Narcotics Manufacturing Act of 1960 [sections 501 to 517 of this title] shall be superseded by a requirement of either (i) actual registration as a manufacturer under section 303 of title II [section 823 of this title] or (ii) provisional registration (by virtue of a preexisting registration under such section 4722) under section 703 of title II [set out as a note under section 822 of this title]."

Short Title

1970 Acts. Section 1000 of Pub.L. 91–513 provided that: "This title [enacting this subchapter, amending section 198a and 162 of this title, section 4251 of Title 18, section 1584 of Title 19, sections 4901, 4905, 6808, 7012, 7103, 7326, 7607, 7609, 7641, 7651, and 7655 of Title 26, section 2901 of Title 28, sections 529d, 529e, and 529f of Title 31, section 304m of Title 40, section 3411 of Title 42, section 239a of Title 46, and section 787 of Title 49, repealing sections 171 to 174, 176 to 185, 188 to 188n, 191 to 193, 197, 198, 199, and 501 to 517 of this title, sections 1401 to 1407, and 3616 of Title 18, sections 4701 to 4707, 4711 to 4716, 4721 to 4726, 4731 to 4736, 4741 to 4746, 4751 to 4757, 4761, 4762, 4771 to 4776, 7237, 7238, and 7491 of Title 26, sections 529a and 529g of Title 31, section 1421m of Title 48, and enacting provisions set out as notes under this section and sections 171 and 957 of this title] may be cited as the 'Controlled Substances Import and Export Act'."

Rules and Regulations

Section 1105(d) of Pub.L. 91–513 provided that: "Any orders, rules, and regulations which have been promulgated under any law affected by this title [see Short Title note above] and which are in effect on the day preceding enactment of this title [Oct. 27, 1970] shall continue in effect until modified, superseded, or repealed."

§ 952. Importation of controlled substances

(a) Controlled substances in schedule I or II and narcotic drugs in schedule III, IV, or V; exceptions

It shall be unlawful to import into the customs territory of the United States from any place outside thereof (but within the United States), or to import into the United States from any place outside thereof, any controlled substance in schedule I or II of subchapter I of this chapter, or ephedrine, pseudoephedrine, or phenylpropanolamine, or any narcotic drug in schedule III, IV, or V of subchapter I of this chapter, except that—

(1) such amounts of crude opium, poppy straw, concentrate of poppy straw, and coca leaves, and of ephedrine, pseudoephedrine, and phenylpropanolamine, as the Attorney General finds to be necessary to provide for medical, scientific, or other legitimate purposes, and

(2) such amounts of any controlled substance in schedule I or II or any narcotic drug in schedule III, IV, or V that the Attorney General finds to be necessary to provide for the medical, scientific, or other legitimate needs of the United States—

(A) during an emergency in which domestic supplies of such substance or drug are found by the Attorney General to be inadequate,

(B) In any case in which the Attorney General finds that competition among domestic manufacturers of the controlled substance is inadequate and will not be rendered adequate by the registration of additional manufacturers under section 823 of this title, or

(C) in any case in which the Attorney General finds that such controlled substance is in limited quantities exclusively for scientific, analytical, or research uses,

may be so imported under such regulations as the Attorney General shall prescribe. No crude opium may be so imported for the purpose of manufacturing heroin or smoking opium.

(b) Nonnarcotic controlled substances in schedule III, IV, or V

It shall be unlawful to import into the customs territory of the United States from any place outside thereof (but within the United States), or to import into the United States from any place outside thereof, any nonnarcotic controlled substance in schedule III,

IV, or V, unless such nonnarcotic controlled substance—

(1) is imported for medical, scientific, or other legitimate uses, and

(2) is imported pursuant to such notification, or declaration, or in the case of any nonnarcotic controlled substance in schedule III, such import permit, notification, or declaration, as the Attorney General may by regulation prescribe, except that if a nonnarcotic controlled substance in schedule IV or V is also listed in schedule I or II of the Convention on Psychotropic Substances it shall be imported pursuant to such import permit requirements, prescribed by regulation of the Attorney General, as are required by the Convention.

(c) Coca leaves

In addition to the amount of coca leaves authorized to be imported into the United States under subsection (a) of this section, the Attorney General may permit the importation of additional amounts of coca leaves. All cocaine and ecgonine (and all salts, derivatives, and preparations from which cocaine or ecgonine may be synthesized or made) contained in such additional amounts of coca leaves imported under this subsection shall be destroyed under the supervision of an authorized representative of the Attorney General.

(d)(1) With respect to a registrant under section 958 of this title who is authorized under subsection (a)(1) to import ephedrine, pseudoephedrine, or phenylpropanolamine, at any time during the year the registrant may apply for an increase in the amount of such chemical that the registrant is authorized to import, and the Attorney General may approve the application if the Attorney General determines that the approval is necessary to provide for medical, scientific, or other legitimate purposes regarding the chemical.

(2) With respect to the application under paragraph (1):

(A) Not later than 60 days after receiving the application, the Attorney General shall approve or deny the application.

(B) In approving the application, the Attorney General shall specify the period of time for which the approval is in effect, or shall provide that the approval is effective until the registrant involved is notified in writing by the Attorney General that the approval is terminated.

(C) If the Attorney General does not approve or deny the application before the expiration of the 60-day period under subparagraph (A), the application is deemed to be approved, and such approval remains in effect until the Attorney General notifies the registrant in writing that the approval is terminated.

(e) Each reference in this section to ephedrine, pseudoephedrine, or phenylpropanolamine includes each of the salts, optical isomers, and salts of optical isomers of such chemical.

(Pub.L. 91–513, Title III, § 1002, Oct. 27, 1970, 84 Stat. 1285; Pub.L. 95–633, Title I, § 105, Nov. 10, 1978, 92 Stat. 3772; Pub.L. 98–473, Title II, §§ 519 to 521, Oct. 12, 1984, 98 Stat. 2075; Pub.L. 109–177, Title VII, § 715, Mar. 9, 2006, 120 Stat. 264.)

HISTORICAL AND STATUTORY NOTES

References in Text

"Subchapter I of this chapter", referred to in subsec. (a), was in the original "Title II" which is Title II of Pub.L. 91–513, Oct. 27, 1970, 84 Stat. 1242, as amended, known as the "Controlled Substances Act". For complete classification, see Short Title note set out under 21 U.S.C.A. § 801 and Tables.

Effective and Applicability Provisions

1978 Acts. Amendment by Pub.L. 95–633 effective on the date the Convention on Psychotropic Substances enters into force in the United States [July 15, 1980], see section 112 of Pub.L. 95–633, set out a note under section 801a of this title.

1970 Acts. Section effective the first day of the seventh calendar month that begins after the day immediately preceding Oct. 27, 1970, see section 1105(a) of Pub.L. 91–513, set out as a note under section 951 of this title.

Combat Methamphetamine Epidemic Act of 2005—Coordination with United States Trade Representative

Pub.L. 109–177, Title VII, § 718, Mar. 9, 2006, 120 Stat. 267, provided that in implementing sections 713 though 717 and section 721 of the Combat Methamphetamine Epidemic Act of 2005, the Attorney General shall consult with the United States Trade Representative to insure compliance with all applicable international treaties and obligations of the United States, see Pub.L. 109–177, § 718, set out as a note under 21 U.S.C.A. § 826.

§ 953. Exportation of controlled substances

(a) Narcotic drugs in schedule I, II, III, or IV

It shall be unlawful to export from the United States any narcotic drug in schedule I, II, III, or IV unless—

(1) it is exported to a country which is a party to—

(A) the International Opium Convention of 1912 for the Suppression of the Abuses of Opium, Morphine, Cocaine, and Derivative Drugs, or to the International Opium Convention signed at Geneva on February 19, 1925; or

(B) the Convention for Limiting the Manufacture and Regulating the Distribution of Narcotic Drugs concluded at Geneva, July 13, 1931, as amended by the protocol signed at Lake Success on December 11, 1946, and the protocol bringing under international control drugs outside the scope of the convention of July 13, 1931, for limiting the manufacture and regulating the distribution of narcotic drugs (as amended by the protocol signed at Lake Success on December 11, 1946), signed at Paris, November 19, 1948; or

(C) the Single Convention on Narcotic Drugs, 1961, signed at New York, March 30, 1961;

(2) such country has instituted and maintains, in conformity with the conventions to which it is a party, a system for the control of imports of narcotic drugs which the Attorney General deems adequate;

(3) the narcotic drug is consigned to a holder of such permits or licenses as may be required under the laws of the country of import, and a permit or license to import such drug has been issued by the country of import;

(4) substantial evidence is furnished to the Attorney General by the exporter that (A) the narcotic drug is to be applied exclusively to medical or scientific uses within the country of import, and (B) there is an actual need for the narcotic drug for medical or scientific uses within such country; and

(5) a permit to export the narcotic drug in each instance has been issued by the Attorney General.

(b) Exception for exportation for special scientific purposes

Notwithstanding subsection (a) of this section, the Attorney General may authorize any narcotic drug (including crude opium and coca leaves) in schedule I, II, III, or IV to be exported from the United States to a country which is a party to any of the international instruments mentioned in subsection (a) of this section if the particular drug is to be applied to a special scientific purpose in the country of destination and the authorities of such country will permit the importation of the particular drug for such purpose.

(c) Nonnarcotic controlled substances in schedule I or II

It shall be unlawful to export from the United States any nonnarcotic controlled substance in schedule I or II unless—

(1) it is exported to a country which has instituted and maintains a system which the Attorney General deems adequate for the control of imports of such substances;

(2) the controlled substance is consigned to a holder of such permits or licenses as may be required under the laws of the country of import;

(3) substantial evidence is furnished to the Attorney General that (A) the controlled substance is to be applied exclusively to medical, scientific, or other legitimate uses within the country to which exported, (B) it will not be exported from such country, and (C) there is an actual need for the controlled substance for medical, scientific, or other legitimate uses within the country; and

(4) a permit to export the controlled substance in each instance has been issued by the Attorney General.

(d) Exception for exportation for special scientific purposes

Notwithstanding subsection (c) of this section, the Attorney General may authorize any nonnarcotic controlled substance in schedule I or II to be exported from the United States if the particular substance is to be applied to a special scientific purpose in the country of destination and the authorities of such country will permit the importation of the particular drug for such purpose.

(e) Nonnarcotic controlled substances in schedule III or IV; controlled substances in schedule V

It shall be unlawful to export from the United States to any other country any nonnarcotic controlled substance in schedule III or IV or any controlled substances in schedule V unless—

(1) there is furnished (before export) to the Attorney General documentary proof that importation is not contrary to the laws or regulations of the country of destination for consumption for medical, scientific, or other legitimate purposes;

(2) it is exported pursuant to such notification or declaration, or in the case of any nonnarcotic controlled substance in schedule III, such export permit, notification, or declaration as the Attorney General may by regulation prescribe; and

(3) in the case of a nonnarcotic controlled substance in schedule IV or V which is also listed in schedule I or II of the Convention on Psychotropic Substances, it is exported pursuant to such export permit requirements, prescribed by regulation of the Attorney General, as are required by the Convention.

(f) Notwithstanding subsections (a)(4) and (c)(3), the Attorney General may authorize any controlled substance that is in schedule I or II, or is a narcotic drug in schedule III or IV, to be exported from the United States to a country for subsequent export from that country to another country, if each of the following conditions is met:

(1) Both the country to which the controlled substance is exported from the United States (referred to in this subsection as the "first country") and the country to which the controlled substance is exported from the first country (referred to in this subsection as the "second country") are parties to the Single Convention on Narcotic Drugs, 1961, and the Convention on Psychotropic Substances, 1971.

(2) The first country and the second country have each instituted and maintain, in conformity with such Conventions, a system of controls of imports of controlled substances which the Attorney General deems adequate.

(3) With respect to the first country, the controlled substance is consigned to a holder of such permits or licenses as may be required under the laws of such country, and a permit or license to import the controlled substance has been issued by the country.

(4) With respect to the second country, substantial evidence is furnished to the Attorney General by the person who will export the controlled substance from the United States that—

(A) the controlled substance is to be consigned to a holder of such permits or licenses as may be required under the laws of such country, and a permit or license to import the controlled substance is to be issued by the country; and

(B) the controlled substance is to be applied exclusively to medical, scientific, or other legitimate uses within the country.

(5) The controlled substance will not be exported from the second country.

(6) Within 30 days after the controlled substance is exported from the first country to the second country, the person who exported the controlled substance from the United States delivers to the Attorney General documentation certifying that such export from the first country has occurred.

(7) A permit to export the controlled substance from the United States has been issued by the Attorney General.

(Pub.L. 91–513, Title III, § 1003, Oct. 27, 1970, 84 Stat. 1286; Pub.L. 95–633, Title I, § 106, Nov. 10, 1978, 92 Stat. 3772; Pub.L. 98–473, Title II, § 522, Oct. 12, 1984, 98 Stat. 2076; Pub.L. 109–57, § 1(b), Aug. 2, 2005, 119 Stat. 592.)

HISTORICAL AND STATUTORY NOTES

References in Text

Schedules I, II, III, IV, and V, referred to in text, are set out in section 812(c) of this title.

Effective and Applicability Provisions

1978 Acts. Amendment by Pub.L. 95–633 effective on the date the Convention on Psychotropic Substances enters into force in the United States [July 15, 1980], see section 112 of Pub.L. 95–633, set out as a note under section 801a of this title.

1970 Acts. Section effective the first day of the seventh calendar month that begins after the day immediately preceding Oct. 27, 1970, see section 1105(a) of Pub.L. 91–513, set out as a note under section 951 of this title.

§ 954. Transshipment and in-transit shipment of controlled substances

Notwithstanding sections 952, 953, and 957 of this title—

(1) A controlled substance in schedule I may—

(A) be imported into the United States for transshipment to another country, or

(B) be transferred or transshipped from one vessel, vehicle, or aircraft to another vessel, vehicle, or aircraft within the United States for immediate exportation,

if and only if it is so imported, transferred, or transshipped (i) for scientific, medical, or other legitimate purposes in the country of destination, and (ii) with the prior written approval of the Attorney General (which shall be granted or denied within 21 days of the request).

(2) A controlled substance in schedule II, III, or IV may be so imported, transferred, or transshipped if and only if advance notice is given to the Attorney General in accordance with regulations of the Attorney General.

(Pub.L. 91–513, Title III, § 1004, Oct. 27, 1970, 84 Stat. 1287.)

HISTORICAL AND STATUTORY NOTES

References in Text

Schedules I, II, III, and IV, referred to in text, are set out in section 812(c) of this title.

Effective and Applicability Provisions

1970 Acts. Section effective the first day of the seventh calendar month that begins after the day immediately preceding Oct. 27, 1970, see section 1105(a) of Pub.L. 91–513, set out as a note under section 951 of this title.

§ 955. Possession on board vessels, etc., arriving in or departing from United States

It shall be unlawful for any person to bring or possess on board any vessel or aircraft, or on board any vehicle of a carrier, arriving in or departing from the United States or the customs territory of the United States, a controlled substance in schedule I or II or a narcotic drug in schedule III or IV, unless such substance or drug is a part of the cargo entered in the manifest or part of the official supplies of the vessel, aircraft, or vehicle.

(Pub.L. 91–513, Title III, § 1005, Oct. 27, 1970, 84 Stat. 1287.)

HISTORICAL AND STATUTORY NOTES

References in Text

Schedules I, II, III, and IV, referred to in text, are set out in section 812(c) of this title.

Effective and Applicability Provisions

1970 Acts. Section effective the first day of the seventh calendar month that begins after the day immediately preceding Oct. 27, 1970, see section 1105(a) of Pub.L. 91–513, set out as a note under section 951 of this title.

§§ 955a to 955d. Transferred

HISTORICAL AND STATUTORY NOTES

Codifications

Sections, Pub.L. 96–350, §§ 1-4, Sept. 15, 1980, 94 Stat. 1159, 1160, relating to maritime drug law enforcement, were transferred to 46 U.S.C.A. §§ 1901 to 1904.

§ 956. Exemption authority

(a) Individual possessing controlled substance

(1) Subject to paragraph (2), the Attorney General may by regulation exempt from sections 952(a) and (b), 953, 954, and 955 of this title any individual who has a controlled substance (except a substance in schedule I) in his possession for his personal medical use, or for administration to an animal accompanying him, if he lawfully obtained such substance and he makes such declaration (or gives such other notification) as the Attorney General may by regulation require.

(2) Notwithstanding any exemption under paragraph (1), a United States resident who enters the United States through an international land border with a controlled substance (except a substance in schedule I) for which the individual does not possess a valid prescription issued by a practitioner (as defined in section 802 of this title) in accordance with applicable Federal and State law (or documentation that verifies the issuance of such a prescription to that individual) may not import the controlled substance into the United States in an amount that exceeds 50 dosage units of the controlled substance.

(b) Compound, mixture, or preparation

The Attorney General may by regulation except any compound, mixture, or preparation containing any depressant or stimulant substance listed in paragraph (a) or (b) of schedule III or in schedule IV or V from the application of all or any part of this subchapter if (1) the compound, mixture, or preparation contains one or more active medicinal ingredients not having a depressant or stimulant effect on the central nervous system, and (2) such ingredients are included therein in such combinations, quantity, proportion, or concentration as to vitiate the potential for abuse of the substances which do have a depressant or stimulant effect on the central nervous system.

(Pub.L. 91–513, Title III, § 1006, Oct. 27, 1970, 84 Stat. 1288; Pub.L. 105–277, Div. C, Title VIII, § 872, Oct. 21, 1998, 112 Stat. 2681–707; Pub.L. 105–357, § 2(a), Nov. 10, 1998, 112 Stat. 3271.)

HISTORICAL AND STATUTORY NOTES

References in Text

Schedules I, III, IV, and V, referred to in text, are set out in § 812(c) of this title.

Codifications

Amendment by section 2(a) of Pub.L. 105–357 directed the substitution of "(1) Subject to paragraph (2), the Attorney General" for "The Attorney General" in subsec. (a)(1), and the addition of par. (2) to subsec. (a). Prior amendment by Pub.L. 105–277 resulted in the substitution of "(1) Subject to paragraph (2), the Attorney General" for "The Attorney General" in subsec. (a)(1), and the addition of par. (2) to subsec. (a), thus requiring no further change in text.

Effective and Applicability Provisions

1970 Acts. Section effective Oct. 27, 1970, see section 1105(b) of Pub.L. 91–513, set out as a note under section 951 of this title.

Construction of Section as Amended by Pub.L. 105–277

Pub.L. 105–277, Div. C, Title VIII, § 872(b), (c), Oct. 21, 1998, 112 Stat. 2681–707, provided that:

"(b) Federal minimum requirement.—Section 1006(a)(2) of the Controlled Substances Import and Export Act [subsec. (a)(2) of this section], as added by subsection (a) [Pub.L. 105–277, Div. C, Title VIII, § 872(a), Oct. 21, 1998, 112 Stat. 2681–707, which amended this section], is a minimum Federal requirement and shall not be construed to limit a State from imposing any additional requirement.

"(c) Extent.—The amendment made by subsection (a) [amending this section] shall not be construed to affect the jurisdiction of the Secretary of Health and Human Services under the Federal Food, Drug and Cosmetic Act (21 U.S.C. 301 et seq.)".

Construction of Section as Amended by Pub.L. 105–357

Pub.L. 105–357, § 2(b), (c), Nov. 10, 1998, 112 Stat. 3271, provided that:

"(b) Federal minimum requirement.—Section 1006(a)(2) of the Controlled Substances Import and Export Act, as added by this section [subsec. (a)(2) of this section], is a minimum Federal requirement and shall not be construed to limit a State from imposing any additional requirement.

"(c) Extent.—The amendment made by subsection (a) [amending this section] shall not be construed to affect the jurisdiction of the Secretary of Health and Human Services under the Federal Food, Drug and Cosmetic Act (21 U.S.C. 301 et seq.)."

§ 957. Persons required to register

(a) Coverage

No person may—

(1) import into the customs territory of the United States from any place outside thereof (but within the United States), or import into the United States from any place outside thereof, any controlled substance or list I chemical, or

(2) export from the United States any controlled substance or list I chemical,

unless there is in effect with respect to such person a registration issued by the Attorney General under section 958 of this title, or unless such person is exempt from registration under subsection (b) of this section.

(b) Exemptions

(1) The following persons shall not be required to register under the provisions of this section and may lawfully possess a controlled substance or list I chemical:

(A) An agent or an employee of any importer or exporter registered under section 958 of this title if such agent or employee is acting in the usual course of his business or employment.

(B) A common or contract carrier or warehouseman, or an employee thereof, whose possession of any controlled substance or list I chemical is in the usual course of his business or employment.

(C) An ultimate user who possesses such substance for a purpose specified in section 802(25) of this title and in conformity with an exemption granted under section 956(a) of this title.

(2) The Attorney General may, by regulation, waive the requirement for registration of certain importers and exporters if he finds it consistent with the public health and safety; and may authorize any such importer or exporter to possess controlled substances or list I chemicals for purposes of importation and exportation.

(Pub.L. 91–513, Title III, § 1007, Oct. 27, 1970, 84 Stat. 1288; Pub.L. 98–473, Title II, § 523, Oct. 12, 1984, 98 Stat. 2076; Pub.L. 103–200, § 3(e), Dec. 17, 1993, 107 Stat. 2337.)

HISTORICAL AND STATUTORY NOTES

References in Text

Section 802(25) of this title, referred to in subsec. (b)(1)(C), was redesignated section 802(26) of this title by Pub.L. 98–473, title II, § 507(a), Oct. 12, 1984, 98 Stat. 2071, and was further redesignated section 802(27) of this title by Pub.L. 99–570, title I, § 1003(b)(2), Oct. 27, 1986, 100 Stat. 3207-6.

Effective and Applicability Provisions

Amendment to this section by Pub.L. 103–200 to take effect on the date that is 120 days after the date of enactment of Pub.L. 103–200, which was approved Dec. 17, 1993, see section 11 of Pub.L. 103–200, set out as a note under section 802 of this title.

1970 Acts. Section effective the first day of the seventh calendar month that begins after the day immediately preceding Oct. 27, 1970, see section 1105(a) of Pub.L. 91–513, set out as a note under section 951 of this title.

Provisional Registration

Section 1104 of Pub.L. 91–513 provided that:

"(a)(1) Any person—

"(A) who is engaged in importing or exporting any controlled substance on the day before the effective date of section 1007 [May 1, 1971],

"(B) who notifies the Attorney General that he is so engaged, and

"(C) who is registered on such day under section 510 of the Federal Food, Drug, and Cosmetic Act [section 360 of this title] or under section 4722 of the Internal Revenue Code of 1954 [former section 4722 of Title 26],

shall, with respect to each establishment for which such registration is in effect under any such section, be deemed to have a provisional registration under section 1008 [section 958 of this title] for the import or export (as the case may be) of controlled substances.

"(2) During the period his provisional registration is in effect under this section, the registration number assigned such person under such section 510 or under such section 4722 (as the case may be) shall be his registration number for purposes of part A of this title [this subchapter].

"(b) The provisions of section 304 [section 824 of this title], relating to suspension and revocation of registration, shall apply to a provisional registration under this section.

"(c) Unless sooner suspended or revoked under subsection (b), a provisional registration of a person under subsection (a)(1) of this section shall be in effect until—

"(1) the date on which such person has registered with the Attorney General under section 1008 [section 958 of this title] or has had his registration denied under such section, or

"(2) such date as may be prescribed by the Attorney General for registration of importers or exporters, as the case may be,

whichever occurs first."

§ 958. Registration requirements

(a) Applicants to import or export controlled substances in schedule I or II

The Attorney General shall register an applicant to import or export a controlled substance in schedule I or II if he determines that such registration is consistent with the public interest and with United States obligations under international treaties, conventions, or protocols in effect on May 1, 1971. In determining the public interest, the factors enumerated in paragraph (1) through (6) of section 823(a) of this title shall be considered.

(b) Activity limited to specified substances

Registration granted under this section shall not entitle a registrant to import or export controlled substances other than specified in the registration.

(c) Applicants to import controlled substances in schedule III, IV, or V or to export controlled substances in schedule III or IV; applicants to import or export list I chemicals

(1) The Attorney General shall register an applicant to import a controlled substance in schedule III, IV, or V or to export a controlled substance in schedule III or IV, unless he determines that the issuance

of such registration is inconsistent with the public interest. In determining the public interest, the factors enumerated in paragraphs (1) through (6) of section 823(d) of this title shall be considered.

(2)(A) The Attorney General shall register an applicant to import or export a list I chemical unless the Attorney General determines that registration of the applicant is inconsistent with the public interest. Registration under this subsection shall not be required for the import or export of a drug product that is exempted under section 802(39)(A)(iv) of this title.

(B) In determining the public interest for the purposes of subparagraph (A), the Attorney General shall consider the factors specified in section 823(h) of this title.

(d) Denial of application

(1) The Attorney General may deny an application for registration under subsection (a) of this section if he is unable to determine that such registration is consistent with the public interest (as defined in subsection (a) of this section) and with the United States obligations under international treaties, conventions, or protocols in effect on May 1, 1971.

(2) The Attorney General may deny an application for registration under subsection (c) of this section, or revoke or suspend a registration under subsection (a) or (c) of this section, if he determines that such registration is inconsistent with the public interest (as defined in subsection (a) or (c) of this section) or with the United States obligations under international treaties, conventions, or protocols in effect on May 1, 1971.

(3) The Attorney General may limit the revocation or suspension of a registration to the particular controlled substance, or substances, or list I chemical or chemicals, with respect to which grounds for revocation or suspension exist.

(4) Before taking action pursuant to this subsection, the Attorney General shall serve upon the applicant or registrant an order to show cause as to why the registration should not be denied, revoked, or suspended. The order to show cause shall contain a statement of the basis thereof and shall call upon the applicant or registrant to appear before the Attorney General, or his designee, at a time and place stated in the order, but in no event less than thirty days after the date of receipt of the order. Proceedings to deny, revoke, or suspend shall be conducted pursuant to this subsection in accordance with subchapter II of chapter 5 of Title 5. Such proceedings shall be independent of, and not in lieu of, criminal prosecutions or other proceedings under this subchapter or any other law of the United States.

(5) The Attorney General may, in his discretion, suspend any registration simultaneously with the institution of proceedings under this subsection, in cases where he finds that there is an imminent danger to the public health and safety. Such suspension shall continue in effect until the conclusion of such proceedings, including judicial review thereof, unless sooner withdrawn by the Attorney General or dissolved by a court of competent jurisdiction.

(6) In the event that the Attorney General suspends or revokes a registration granted under this section, all controlled substances or list I chemicals owned or possessed by the registrant pursuant to such registration at the time of suspension or the effective date of the revocation order, as the case may be, may, in the discretion of the Attorney General, be seized or placed under seal. No disposition may be made of any controlled substances or list I chemicals under seal until the time for taking an appeal has elapsed or until all appeals have been concluded, except that a court, upon application therefor, may at any time order the sale of perishable controlled substances or list I chemicals. Any such order shall require the deposit of the proceeds of the sale with the court. Upon a revocation order becoming final, all such controlled substances or list I chemicals (or proceeds of the sale thereof which have been deposited with the court) shall be forfeited to the United States; and the Attorney General shall dispose of such controlled substances or list I chemicals in accordance with section 881(e) of this title.

(e) Registration period

No registration shall be issued under this subchapter for a period in excess of one year. Unless the regulations of the Attorney General otherwise provide, sections 822(f), 825, 827, and 830 of this title shall apply to persons registered under this section to the same extent such sections apply to persons registered under section 823 of this title.

(f) Rules and regulations

The Attorney General is authorized to promulgate rules and regulations and to charge reasonable fees relating to the registration and control of importers and exporters of controlled substances or listed chemicals.

(g) Scope of authorized activity

Persons registered by the Attorney General under this section to import or export controlled substances or list I chemicals may import or export (and for the purpose of so importing or exporting, may possess) such substances to the extent authorized by their registration and in conformity with the other provisions of this subchapter and subchapter I of this chapter.

(h) Separate registrations for each principal place of business

A separate registration shall be required at each principal place of business where the applicant imports or exports controlled substances or list I chemicals.

(i) Emergency situations

Except in emergency situations as described in section 952(a)(2)(A) of this title, prior to issuing a registration under this section to a bulk manufacturer of a controlled substance in schedule I or II, and prior to issuing a regulation under section 952(a) of this title authorizing the importation of such a substance, the Attorney General shall give manufacturers holding registrations for the bulk manufacture of the substance an opportunity for a hearing.

(Pub.L. 91–513, Title III, § 1008, Oct. 27, 1970, 84 Stat. 1289; Pub.L. 98–473, Title II, §§ 524, 525, Oct. 12, 1984, 98 Stat. 2076; Pub.L. 99–570, Title I, § 1866(d), Oct. 27, 1986, 100 Stat. 3207–55; Pub.L. 103–200, § 3(f), Dec. 17, 1993, 107 Stat. 2337; Pub.L. 108–447, Div. B, Title VI, § 633(c), Dec. 8, 2004, 118 Stat. 2922.)

HISTORICAL AND STATUTORY NOTES

References in Text

Schedules I, II, III, IV, and V, referred to in subsecs. (a), (c), and (i) are set out in section 812(c) of this title.

This subchapter, referred to in subsecs. (d)(4) and (g), was in the original "this title" meaning Title III of Pub.L. 91–513, Oct. 27, 1970, 84 Stat. 1285. Part A of Title III comprises this subchapter. For classification of Part B, consisting of sections 1101 to 1105 of Title III of Pub.L. 91–513, see Tables.

Codifications

In subsec. (a) "May 1, 1971" was substituted for "effective date of this section" and in subsec. (d)(1) and (2) "May 1, 1971" was substituted for "effective date of this part".

Amendment by section 663(c) of Pub.L. 108–447, Div. B, Title VI, was executed to subsec. (f) of this section, which is section 1008(f) of the Controlled Substances Import and Export Act, as the probable intent of Congress despite directory language purporting to amend "Section 1088(f) of the Controlled Substances Import and Export Act".

Effective and Applicability Provisions

1993 Acts. Amendment to this section by Pub.L. 103–200 to take effect on the date that is 120 days after the date of enactment of Pub.L. 103–200, which was approved Dec. 17, 1993, see section 11 of Pub.L. 103–200, set out as a note under section 802 of this title.

1970 Acts. Section effective the first day of the seventh calendar month that begins after the day immediately preceding Oct. 27, 1970, see section 1105(a) of Pub.L. 91–513, set out as a note under section 951 of this title.

§ 959. Possession, manufacture, or distribution of controlled substance

(a) Manufacture or distribution for purpose of unlawful importation

It shall be unlawful for any person to manufacture or distribute a controlled substance in schedule I or II or flunitrazepam or listed chemical—

(1) intending that such substance or chemical will be unlawfully imported into the United States or into waters within a distance of 12 miles of the coast of the United States; or

(2) knowing that such substance or chemical will be unlawfully imported into the United States or into waters within a distance of 12 miles of the coast of the United States.

(b) Possession, manufacture, or distribution by person on board aircraft

It shall be unlawful for any United States citizen on board any aircraft, or any person on board an aircraft owned by a United States citizen or registered in the United States, to—

(1) manufacture or distribute a controlled substance or listed chemical; or

(2) possess a controlled substance or listed chemical with intent to distribute.

(c) Acts committed outside territorial jurisdiction of United States; venue

This section is intended to reach acts of manufacture or distribution committed outside the territorial jurisdiction of the United States. Any person who violates this section shall be tried in the United States district court at the point of entry where such person enters the United States, or in the United States District Court for the District of Columbia.

(Pub.L. 91–513, Title III, § 1009, Oct. 27, 1970, 84 Stat. 1289; Pub.L. 99–570, Title III, § 3161(a), Oct. 27, 1986, 100 Stat. 3207–94; Pub.L. 104–237, Title I, § 102(a), (b), Oct. 3, 1996, 110 Stat. 3100; Pub.L. 104–305, § 2(b)(2)(A), Oct. 13, 1996, 110 Stat. 3807.)

HISTORICAL AND STATUTORY NOTES

References in Text

Schedules I and II, referred to in text, are set out in section 812(c) of this title.

Effective and Applicability Provisions

1970 Acts. Section effective the first day of the seventh calendar month that begins after the day immediately preceding Oct. 27, 1970, see section 1105(a) of Pub.L. 91–513, set out as a note under section 951 of this title.

§ 960. Prohibited acts A

(a) Unlawful acts

Any person who—

(1) contrary to section 952, 953, or 957 of this title, knowingly or intentionally imports or exports a controlled substance,

(2) contrary to section 955 of this title, knowingly or intentionally brings or possesses on board a vessel, aircraft, or vehicle a controlled substance, or

(3) contrary to section 959 of this title, manufactures, possesses with intent to distribute, or distributes a controlled substance,

shall be punished as provided in subsection (b) of this section.

(b) Penalties

(1) In the case of a violation of subsection (a) of this section involving—

(A) 1 kilogram or more of a mixture or substance containing a detectable amount of heroin;

(B) 5 kilograms or more of a mixture or substance containing a detectable amount of—

(i) coca leaves, except coca leaves and extracts of coca leaves from which cocaine, ecgonine, and derivatives of ecgonine or their salts have been removed;

(ii) cocaine, its salts, optical and geometric isomers, and salts or isomers;

(iii) ecgonine, its derivatives, their salts, isomers, and salts of isomers; or

(iv) any compound, mixture, or preparation which contains any quantity of any of the substances referred to in clauses (i) through (iii);

(C) 50 grams or more of a mixture or substance described in subparagraph (B) which contains cocaine base;

(D) 100 grams or more of phencyclidine (PCP) or 1 kilogram or more of a mixture or substance containing a detectable amount of phencyclidine (PCP);

(E) 10 grams or more of a mixture or substance containing a detectable amount of lysergic acid diethylamide (LSD);

(F) 400 grams or more of a mixture or substance containing a detectable amount of N-phenyl-N-[1-(2-phenylethyl)-4-piperidinyl] propanamide or 100 grams or more of a mixture or substance containing a detectable amount of any analogue of N-phenyl-N-[1-(2-phenylethyl)-4-piperidinyl] propanamide;

(G) 1000 kilograms or more of a mixture or substance containing a detectable amount of marihuana; or

(H) 50 grams or more of methamphetamine, its salts, isomers, and salts of its isomers or 500 grams or more of a mixture or substance containing a detectable amount of methamphetamine, its salts, isomers, or salts of its isomers.

the person committing such violation shall be sentenced to a term of imprisonment of not less than 10 years and not more than life and if death or serious bodily injury results from the use of such substance shall be sentenced to a term of imprisonment of not less than 20 years and not more than life, a fine not to exceed the greater of that authorized in accordance with the provisions of Title 18, or $4,000,000 if the defendant is an individual or $10,000,000 if the defendant is other than an individual, or both. If any person commits such a violation after a prior conviction for a felony drug offense has become final, such person shall be sentenced to a term of imprisonment of not less than 20 years and not more than life imprisonment and if death or serious bodily injury results from the use of such substance shall be sentenced to life imprisonment, a fine not to exceed the greater of twice that authorized in accordance with the provisions of Title 18, or $8,000,000 if the defendant is an individual or $20,000,000 if the defendant is other than an individual, or both. Notwithstanding section 3583 of Title 18, any sentence under this paragraph shall, in the absence of such a prior conviction, impose a term of supervised release of at least 5 years in addition to such term of imprisonment and shall, if there was such a prior conviction, impose a term of supervised release of at least 10 years in addition to such term of imprisonment. Notwithstanding any other provision of law, the court shall not place on probation or suspend the sentence of any person sentenced under this paragraph. No person sentenced under this paragraph shall be eligible for parole during the term of imprisonment imposed therein.

(2) In the case of a violation of subsection (a) of this section involving—

(A) 100 grams or more of a mixture or substance containing a detectable amount of heroin;

(B) 500 grams or more of a mixture or substance containing a detectable amount of—

(i) coca leaves, except coca leaves and extracts of coca leaves from which cocaine, ecgonine, and derivatives of ecgonine or their salts have been removed;

(ii) cocaine, its salts, optical and geometric isomers, and salts or isomers;

(iii) ecgonine, its derivatives, their salts, isomers, and salts of isomers; or

(iv) any compound, mixture, or preparation which contains any quantity of any of the substances referred to in clauses (i) through (iii);

(C) 5 grams or more of a mixture or substance described in subparagraph (B) which contains cocaine base;

(D) 10 grams or more of phencyclidine (PCP) or 100 grams or more of a mixture or substance containing a detectable amount of phencyclidine (PCP);

(E) 1 gram or more of a mixture or substance containing a detectable amount of lysergic acid diethylamide (LSD);

(F) 40 grams or more of a mixture or substance containing a detectable amount of N-phenyl-

N-[1-(2-phenylethyl)-4-piperidinyl] propanamide or 10 grams or more of a mixture or substance containing a detectable amount of any analogue of N-phenyl-N-[1-(2-phenylethyl)-4-piperidinyl] propanamide;

(G) 100 kilograms or more of a mixture or substance containing a detectable amount of marihuana; or

(H) 5 grams or more of methamphetamine, its salts, isomers, and salts of its isomers or 50 grams or more of a mixture or substance containing a detectable amount of methamphetamine, its salts, isomers, or salts of its isomers.

the person committing such violation shall be sentenced to a term of imprisonment of not less than 5 years and not more than 40 years and if death or serious bodily injury results from the use of such substance shall be sentenced to a term of imprisonment of not less than twenty years and not more than life, a fine not to exceed the greater of that authorized in accordance with the provisions of Title 18 or $2,000,000 if the defendant is an individual or $5,000,000 if the defendant is other than an individual, or both. If any person commits such a violation after a prior conviction for a felony drug offense has become final, such person shall be sentenced to a term of imprisonment of not less than 10 years and not more than life imprisonment and if death or serious bodily injury results from the use of such substance shall be sentenced to life imprisonment, a fine not to exceed the greater of twice that authorized in accordance with the provisions of Title 18 or $4,000,000 if the defendant is an individual or $10,000,000 if the defendant is other than an individual, or both. Notwithstanding section 3583 of Title 18, any sentence imposed under this paragraph shall, in the absence of such a prior conviction, include a term of supervised release of at least 4 years in addition to such term of imprisonment and shall, if there was such a prior conviction, include a term of supervised release of at least 8 years in addition to such term of imprisonment. Notwithstanding any other provision of law, the court shall not place on probation or suspend the sentence of any person sentenced under this paragraph. No person sentenced under this paragraph shall be eligible for parole during the term of imprisonment imposed therein.

(3) In the case of a violation under subsection (a) of this section involving a controlled substance in schedule I or II, gamma hydroxybutyric acid (including when scheduled as an approved drug product for purposes of section 3(a)(1)(B) of the Hillory J. Farias and Samantha Reid Date-Rape Drug Prohibition Act of 2000), or flunitrazepam, the person committing such violation shall, except as provided in paragraphs (1), (2), and (4), be sentenced to a term of imprisonment of not more than 20 years and if death or serious bodily injury results from the use of such substance shall be sentenced to a term of imprisonment of not less than twenty years and not more than life, a fine not to exceed the greater of that authorized in accordance with the provisions of Title 18 or $1,000,000 if the defendant is an individual or $5,000,000 if the defendant is other than an individual, or both. If any person commits such a violation after a prior conviction for a felony drug offense has become final, such person shall be sentenced to a term of imprisonment of not more than 30 years and if death or serious bodily injury results from the use of such substance shall be sentenced to life imprisonment, a fine not to exceed the greater of twice that authorized in accordance with the provisions of Title 18 or $2,000,000 if the defendant is an individual or $10,000,000 if the defendant is other than an individual, or both. Notwithstanding section 3583 of Title 18, any sentence imposing a term of imprisonment under this paragraph shall, in the absence of such a prior conviction, impose a term of supervised release of at least 3 years in addition to such term of imprisonment and shall, if there was such a prior conviction, impose a term of supervised release of at least 6 years in addition to such term of imprisonment. Notwithstanding the prior sentence, and notwithstanding any other provision of law, the court shall not place on probation or suspend the sentence of any person sentenced under the provisions of this paragraph which provide for a mandatory term of imprisonment if death or serious bodily injury results, nor shall a person so sentenced be eligible for parole during the term of such a sentence.

(4) In the case of a violation under subsection (a) of this section with respect to less than 50 kilograms of marihuana, except in the case of 100 or more marihuana plants regardless of weight, less than 10 kilograms of hashish, less than one kilogram of hashish oil, or any quantity of a controlled substance in schedule III, IV, or V,[1] (except a violation involving flunitrazepam and except a violation involving gamma hydroxybutyric acid) the person committing such violation shall be imprisoned not more than five years, or be fined not to exceed the greater of that authorized in accordance with the provisions of Title 18 or $250,000 if the defendant is an individual or $1,000,000 if the defendant is other than an individual, or both. If a sentence under this paragraph provides for imprisonment, the sentence shall, notwithstanding section 3583 of Title 18, in addition to such term of imprisonment, include (A) a term of supervised release of not less than two years if such controlled substance is in schedule I, II, III, or (B) a term of supervised release of not less than one year if such controlled substance is in schedule IV.

(c) Repealed. Pub.L. 98–473, Title II, § 225, formerly § 225(a), Oct. 12, 1984, 98 Stat. 2030, as amended by Pub.L. 99–570, Title I, § 1005(c), Oct. 27, 1986, 100 Stat. 3201–6.

(d) Penalty for importation or exportation

A person who knowingly or intentionally—

(1) imports or exports a listed chemical with intent to manufacture a controlled substance in violation of this subchapter or subchapter I of this chapter;

(2) exports a listed chemical in violation of the laws of the country to which the chemical is exported or serves as a broker or trader for an international transaction involving a listed chemical, if the transaction is in violation of the laws of the country to which the chemical is exported;

(3) imports or exports a listed chemical knowing, or having reasonable cause to believe, that the chemical will be used to manufacture a controlled substance in violation of this subchapter or subchapter I of this chapter;

(4) exports a listed chemical, or serves as a broker or trader for an international transaction involving a listed chemical, knowing, or having reasonable cause to believe, that the chemical will be used to manufacture a controlled substance in violation of the laws of the country to which the chemical is exported;

(5) imports or exports a listed chemical, with the intent to evade the reporting or recordkeeping requirements of section 971 of this title applicable to such importation or exportation by falsely representing to the Attorney General that the importation or exportation qualifies for a waiver of the 15–day notification requirement granted pursuant to paragraph (2) or (3) of section 971(f) of this title by misrepresenting the actual country of final destination of the listed chemical or the actual listed chemical being imported or exported;

(6) imports a listed chemical in violation of section 952 of this title, imports or exports such a chemical in violation of section 957 or 971 of this title, or transfers such a chemical in violation of section 971(d) of this title; or

(7) manufactures, possesses with intent to distribute, or distributes a listed chemical in violation of section 959 of this title.[2]

shall be fined in accordance with Title 18, imprisoned not more than 20 years in the case of a violation of paragraph (1) or (3) involving a list I chemical or not more than 10 years in the case of a violation of this subsection other than a violation of paragraph (1) or (3) involving a list I chemical, or both.

(Pub.L. 91–513, Title III, § 1010, Oct. 27, 1970, 84 Stat. 1290; Pub.L. 98–473, Title II, § 225 (formerly § 225(a)), Title V, § 504, Oct. 12, 1984, 98 Stat. 2030, 2070; renumbered § 225 and amended Pub.L. 99–570, Title I, §§ 1004(a), 1005(c), 1302, 1866(e), Oct. 27, 1986, 100 Stat. 3207–6, 3207–15, 3207–55; Pub.L. 100–690, Title VI, §§ 6053(c), 6475, Nov. 18, 1988, 102 Stat. 4315, 4380; Pub.L. 101–647, Title XII, § 1204, Title XXXV, § 3599J, Nov. 29, 1990, 104 Stat. 4830, 4932; Pub.L. 103–200, §§ 4(b), 5(b), Dec. 17, 1993, 107 Stat. 2338, 2339; Pub.L. 103–322, Title IX, § 90105(a), Title XXXIII, § 330024(d)(2), Sept. 13, 1994, 108 Stat. 1987, 2151; Pub.L. 104–237, Title I, § 102(c), Title III, § 302(b), Oct. 3, 1996, 110 Stat. 3100, 3105; Pub.L. 104–305, § 2(b)(2)(B), (C), Oct. 13, 1996, 110 Stat. 3807; Pub.L. 105–277, Div. E, § 2(b), Oct. 21, 1998, 112 Stat. 2681–759; Pub.L. 106–172, § 3(b)(2), Feb. 18, 2000, 114 Stat. 9; Pub.L. 107–273, Div. B, Title III, § 3005(b), Nov. 2, 2002, 116 Stat. 1806; Pub.L. 109–177, Title VII, §§ 716(b)(1)(A), 717, Mar. 9, 2006, 120 Stat. 267.)

1 So in original.

2 So in original. The period probably should be a comma.

HISTORICAL AND STATUTORY NOTES

References in Text

Schedules I, II, III and IV, referred to in subsec. (b), are set out in section 812(c) of this title.

"Section 3(a)(1)(B) of the Hillory J. Farias and Samantha Reid Date–Rape Drug Prohibition Act of 2000", referred to in subsec. (b)(3), is classified as a note under section 812 of this title.

"This subchapter", referred to in subsec. (d)(1), (3), was in the original "this title", which is Title III of Pub.L. 91–513, Oct. 27, 1970, 84 Stat. 1285, popularly known as the "Controlled Substances Import and Export Act". Part A of Title III comprises this subchapter. Sections 1101 to 1105 of Title III comprises Part B. For complete classification of Title III of Pub.L. 91–513 to the Code, see Short Title note set out under 951 of this title and Tables.

"Subchapter I of this chapter", referred to in subsec. (d)(1), (3), was in the original "title II", meaning Title II of Pub.L. 91–513, Oct. 27, 1970, 84 Stat. 1242, popularly known as the "Controlled Substances Act". For complete classification of Title II of Pub.L. 91–513 to the Code, see Short Title note set out under 801 of this title and Tables.

Codifications

Amendment by section 1005(c) of Pub.L. 99–570, directing that section "1515 of the Controlled Substances Import and Export Act (21 U.S.C. 960)" be amended, was executed to section 1010 of such Act (21 U.S.C.A. § 960), as the probable intent of Congress.

Amendment of subsec. (b)(3) [now (b)(4)] by section 1866(e) of Pub.L. 99–570, directing the striking of "except as provided in paragraph (4)" was previously effected by section 1302(a), (b)(1) of Pub.L. 99–570, which also redesignated subsec. (b)(3) as (b)(4).

The amendment by section 1004(a) of Pub.L. 99–570, which directed the substitution of "term of supervised release" for "special parole term" wherever appearing in subsec. (c), was not executed due to repeal by Pub.L. 98–473, § 225, eff. Nov. 1, 1987.

Effective and Applicability Provisions

1994 Acts. Amendment by Pub.L. 103–322 effective 120 days after Dec. 17, 1993, see section 330024(f) of Pub.L. 103–322, set out as a note under section 802 of this title.

1993 Acts. Amendment to this section by Pub.L. 103–200 to take effect on the date that is 120 days after the date of enactment of Pub.L. 103–200, which was approved Dec. 17, 1993, see section 11 of Pub.L. 103–200, set out as a note under section 802 of this title.

1988 Acts. Amendment of section by section 6053(c) of Pub.L. 100–690 effective 120 days after Nov. 18, 1988, see section 6061 of Pub.L. 100–690, set out as a note under section 802 of this title.

1986 Acts. Amendment by section 1004(a) of Pub.L. 99–570 to take effect on the date section 3583 of Title 18 becomes effective (Nov. 1, 1987), see section 1004(b) of Pub.L. 99–570, set out as a note under section 841 of this title.

1984 Acts. Amendment by Pub.L. 98–473, § 225, effective on the first day of first calendar month beginning thirty six months after Oct. 12, 1984 [Nov. 1, 1987], applicable only to offenses committed after taking effect of sections 211 to 239 of Pub.L. 98–473, and except as otherwise provided for therein, see section 235 of Pub.L. 98–473, as amended, set out as a note under section 3551 of Title 18.

1970 Acts. Section effective the first day of the seventh calendar month that begins after the day immediately preceding Oct. 27, 1970, see section 1105(a) of Pub.L. 91–513, set out as a note under section 951 of this title.

Repeals

Section 225(a)(1) to (3) of Pub.L. 98–473, cited to credit, was amended by section 1005(c) of Pub.L. 99–570 to repeal pars. (1) and (2) and renumber par. (3) as section 225(a) of Pub.L. 98–473. Such provisions of section 225(a) of Pub.L. 98–473, which were to take effect Nov. 1, 1987, as a result of repeal were never executed to text of section. See 1984 Amendment notes above.

Combat Methamphetamine Epidemic Act of 2005—Coordination with United States Trade Representative

Pub.L. 109–177, Title VII, § 718, Mar. 9, 2006, 120 Stat. 267, provided that in implementing sections 713 though 717 and section 721 of the Combat Methamphetamine Epidemic Act of 2005, the Attorney General shall consult with the United States Trade Representative to insure compliance with all applicable international treaties and obligations of the United States, see Pub.L. 109–177, § 718, set out as a note under 21 U.S.C.A. § 826.

§ 960a. Foreign terrorist organizations, terrorist persons and groups

(a) Prohibited acts

Whoever engages in conduct that would be punishable under section 841(a) of this title if committed within the jurisdiction of the United States, or attempts or conspires to do so, knowing or intending to provide, directly or indirectly, anything of pecuniary value to any person or organization that has engaged or engages in terrorist activity (as defined in section 1182(a)(3)(B) of Title 8) or terrorism (as defined in section 2656f(d)(2) of Title 22), shall be sentenced to a term of imprisonment of not less than twice the minimum punishment under section 841(b)(1) of this title, and not more than life, a fine in accordance with the provisions of Title 18, or both. Notwithstanding section 3583 of Title 18, any sentence imposed under this subsection shall include a term of supervised release of at least 5 years in addition to such term of imprisonment.

(b) Jurisdiction

There is jurisdiction over an offense under this section if—

(1) the prohibited drug activity or the terrorist offense is in violation of the criminal laws of the United States;

(2) the offense, the prohibited drug activity, or the terrorist offense occurs in or affects interstate or foreign commerce;

(3) an offender provides anything of pecuniary value for a terrorist offense that causes or is designed to cause death or serious bodily injury to a national of the United States while that national is outside the United States, or substantial damage to the property of a legal entity organized under the laws of the United States (including any of its States, districts, commonwealths, territories, or possessions) while that property is outside of the United States;

(4) the offense or the prohibited drug activity occurs in whole or in part outside of the United States (including on the high seas), and a perpetrator of the offense or the prohibited drug activity is a national of the United States or a legal entity organized under the laws of the United States (including any of its States, districts, commonwealths, territories, or possessions); or

(5) after the conduct required for the offense occurs an offender is brought into or found in the United States, even if the conduct required for the offense occurs outside the United States.

(c) Proof requirements

To violate subsection (a) of this section, a person must have knowledge that the person or organization has engaged or engages in terrorist activity (as defined in section 1182(a)(3)(B) of Title 8) or terrorism (as defined in section 2656f(d)(2) of Title 22).

(d) Definitions

As used in this section, the term "anything of pecuniary value" has the meaning given the term in section 1958(b)(1) of Title 18.

(Pub.L. 91–513, Title III, § 1010A, as added Pub.L. 109–177, Title I, § 122, Mar. 9, 2006, 120 Stat. 225.)

§ 961. Prohibited acts B

Any person who violates section 954 of this title or fails to notify the Attorney General of an importation or exportation under section 971 of this title shall be subject to the following penalties:

(1) Except as provided in paragraph (2), any such person shall, with respect to any such violation, be subject to a civil penalty of not more than $25,000. Sections 842(c)(1) and (c)(3) of this title shall apply to any civil penalty assessed under this paragraph.

(2) If such a violation is prosecuted by an information or indictment which alleges that the violation was committed knowingly or intentionally and the trier of fact specifically finds that the violation was so committed, such person shall be sentenced to imprisonment for not more than one year or a fine of not more than $25,000 or both.

(Pub.L. 91–513, Title III, § 1011, Oct. 27, 1970, 84 Stat. 1290; Pub.L. 100–690, Title VI, § 6053(d), Nov. 18, 1988, 102 Stat. 4316.)

HISTORICAL AND STATUTORY NOTES

Effective and Applicability Provisions

1988 Acts. Amendment by section 6053(d) of Pub.L. 100–690 effective 120 days after Nov. 18, 1988, see section 6061 of Pub.L. 100–690, set out as a note under section 802 of this title.

1970 Acts. Section effective the first day of the seventh calendar month that begins after the day immediately preceding Oct. 27, 1970, see § 1105(a) of Pub.L. 91–513, set out as a note under section 951 of this title.

§ 962. Second or subsequent offenses

(a) Term of imprisonment and fine

Any person convicted of any offense under this subchapter is, if the offense is a second or subsequent offense, punishable by a term of imprisonment twice that otherwise authorized, by twice the fine otherwise authorized, or by both. If the conviction is for an offense punishable under section 960(b) of this title, and if it is the offender's second or subsequent offense, the court shall impose, in addition to any term of imprisonment and fine, twice the term of supervised release otherwise authorized.

(b) Determination of status

For purposes of this section, a person shall be considered convicted of a second or subsequent offense if, prior to the commission of such offense, one or more prior convictions of such person for a felony drug offense have become final.

(c) Procedures applicable

Section 851 of this title shall apply with respect to any proceeding to sentence a person under this section.

(Pub.L. 91–513, Title III, § 1012, Oct. 27, 1970, 84 Stat. 1290; Pub.L. 98–473, Title II, §§ 225(b), 505, Oct. 12, 1984, 98 Stat. 2030, 2070; Pub.L 99–570, Title I, §§ 1004(a), 1005(c), Oct. 27, 1986, 100 Stat. 3207–6; Pub.L. 103–322, Title IX, § 90105(b), Sept. 13, 1994, 108 Stat. 1988.)

HISTORICAL AND STATUTORY NOTES

References in Text

"This subchapter" referred to in subsec. (b), was in the original "this title" meaning Title III of Pub.L. 91–513, Oct. 27, 1970, 84 Stat. 1285. Part A of Title III comprises this subchapter. For classification of Part B (sections 1101 to 1105) of Title III of Pub.L. 91–513, see Tables.

Effective and Applicability Provisions

1986 Acts. Amendment by section 1004(a) of Pub.L. 99–570 shall take effect on the effective date of section 3583 of Title 18 (Nov. 1, 1987), see section 1004(b) of Pub.L. 99–570, set out as a note under section 841 of this title.

1984 Acts. Amendment by Pub.L. 98–473, § 225(b), effective on the first day of first calendar month beginning thirty six months after Oct. 12, 1984 [Nov. 1, 1987], applicable only to offenses committed after taking effect of sections 211 to 239 of Pub.L. 98–473, and except as otherwise provided for therein, see section 235 of Pub.L. 98–473, as amended, set out as a note under section 3551 of Title 18.

1970 Acts. Section effective the first day of the seventh calendar month that beings after the day immediately preceding Oct. 27, 1970, see section 1105(a) of Pub.L. 91–513, set out as a note under section 951 of this title.

Repeals

Section 225(b) of Pub.L. 98–473, cited to credit, was repealed by section 1005(c) of Pub.L. 99–570. Such provisions of section 225(b) of Pub.L. 98–473, which were to take effect Nov. 1, 1987, as a result of repeal were never executed to text of section. See 1984 Amendments note under this section.

§ 963. Attempt and conspiracy

Any person who attempts or conspires to commit any offense defined in this subchapter shall be subject to the same penalties as those prescribed for the offense, the commission of which was the object of the attempt or conspiracy.

(Pub.L. 91–513, Title III, § 1013, Oct. 27, 1970, 84 Stat. 1291; Pub.L. 100–690, Title VI, § 6470(a), Nov. 18, 1988, 102 Stat. 4377.)

HISTORICAL AND STATUTORY NOTES

References in Text

"This subchapter" referred to in text, was in the original "this title" meaning Title III of Pub.L. 91–513, Oct. 27, 1970, 84 Stat. 1285. Part A of Title III comprises this subchapter. For classification of Part B (sections 1101 to 1105) of Title III of Pub.L. 91–513, see Tables.

Effective and Applicability Provisions

1970 Acts. Section effective the first day of the seventh calendar month that begins after the day immediately preceding Oct. 27, 1970, see section 1105(a) of Pub.L. 91–513, set out as a note under section 951 of this title.

§ 964. Additional penalties

Any penalty imposed for violation of this subchapter shall be in addition to, and not in lieu of, any civil or administrative penalty or sanction authorized by law.

(Pub.L. 91–513, Title III, § 1014, Oct. 27, 1970, 84 Stat. 1291.)

HISTORICAL AND STATUTORY NOTES

References in Text

"This subchapter" referred to in text, was in the original "this title" meaning Title III of Pub.L. 91–513, Oct. 27, 1970, 84 Stat. 1285. Part A of Title III comprises this subchapter. For classification of Part B (sections 1101 to 1105) of Title III of Pub.L. 91–513, see Tables.

Effective and Applicability Provisions

1970 Acts. Section effective the first day of the seventh calendar month that begins after the day immediately preceding Oct. 27, 1970, see section 1105(a) of Pub.L. 91–513, set out as a note under section 951 of this title.

§ 965. Applicability of Part E of subchapter I

Part E of subchapter I of this chapter shall apply with respect to functions of the Attorney General (and of officers and employees of the Bureau of Narcotics and Dangerous Drugs) under this subchapter, to administrative and judicial proceedings under this subchapter, and to violations of this subchapter, to the same extent that such part applies to functions of the Attorney General (and such officers and employees) under subchapter I of this chapter, to such proceedings under subchapter I of this chapter, and to violations of subchapter I of this chapter. For purposes of the application of this section to section 880 or 881 of this title, any reference in such section 880 or 881 of this title to "this subchapter" shall be deemed to be a reference to this subchapter, any reference to section 823 of this title shall be deemed to be a reference to section 958 of this title, and any reference to section 822(d) of this title shall be deemed to be a reference to section 957(b)(2) of this title.

(Pub.L. 91–513, Title III, § 1015, Oct. 27, 1970, 84 Stat. 1291; Pub.L. 95–633, Title III, § 301(b), Nov. 10, 1978, 92 Stat. 3778.)

HISTORICAL AND STATUTORY NOTES

Reference in Text

"This subchapter" referred to in text, was in the original "this title", meaning Title III of Pub.L. 91–513, Oct. 27, 1970, 84 Stat. 1285. Part A of Title III comprises this subchapter. For classification of Part B (sections 1101 to 1105) of Title III of Pub.L. 91–513, see Tables.

Effective and Applicability Provisions

Section effective Oct. 27, 1970, see section 1105(b) of Pub.L. 91–513, set out as a note under section 951 of this title.

Transfer of Functions

The Bureau of Narcotics and Dangerous Drugs, including the office of Director thereof, in the Department of Justice was abolished by Reorg. Plan No. 2 of 1973, eff. July 1, 1973, 38 F.R. 15932, 87 Stat. 1091, set out in the Appendix to Title 5. Reorg. Plan No. 2 of 1973 also created in the Department of Justice a single, comprehensive agency for the enforcement of drug laws to be known as the Drug Enforcement Administration, empowered the Attorney General to authorize the performance by officers, employees, and agencies of the Department of functions transferred to him, and directed the Attorney General to coordinate all drug law enforcement functions to assure maximum cooperation between the Drug Enforcement Administration, the Federal Bureau of Investigation, and the other units of the Department of Justice involved in drug law enforcement.

§ 966. Authority of Secretary of the Treasury

Nothing in this chapter shall derogate from the authority of the Secretary of the Treasury under the customs and related laws.

(Pub.L. 91–513, Title III, § 1016, Oct. 27, 1970, 84 Stat. 1291.)

HISTORICAL AND STATUTORY NOTES

References in Text

This chapter, referred to in text, was, in the original "this Act", meaning Pub.L. 91–513, Oct. 27, 1970, 84 Stat. 1236. For complete classification of this Act to the Code, see Short Title note set out under section 801 of this title and Tables.

The customs laws, referred to in text, are classified generally to Title 19.

Effective and Applicability Provisions

1970 Acts. Section effective Oct. 27, 1970, see section 1105(b) of Pub.L. 91–513, set out as a note under section 951 of this title.

§ 967. Smuggling of controlled substances; investigations; oaths; subpenas; witnesses; evidence; production of records; territorial limits; fees and mileage of witnesses

For the purpose of any investigation which, in the opinion of the Secretary of the Treasury, is necessary and proper to the enforcement of section 545 of Title 18 (relating to smuggling goods into the United States) with respect to any controlled substance (as defined in section 802 of this title), the Secretary of the Treasury may administer oaths and affirmations, subpena witnesses, compel their attendance, take evidence, and require the production of records (including books, papers, documents and tangible things which constitute or contain evidence) relevant or material to the investigation. The attendance of witnesses and the production of records may be required from any place within the customs territory of the United States, except that a witness shall not be required to appear at any hearing distant more than 100 miles from the place where he was served with subpena. Witnesses summoned by the Secretary shall be paid the same fees and mileage that are paid witnesses in the courts of the United States. Oaths and affirmations may be made at any place subject to the jurisdiction of the United States.

(Aug. 11, 1955, c. 800, § 1, 69 Stat. 684; Oct. 27, 1970, Pub.L. 91–513, Title III, § 1102(t), 84 Stat. 1294.)

HISTORICAL AND STATUTORY NOTES

Codifications

This section was formerly classified to section 1034 of Title 31 prior to the general revision and enactment of Title 31 by Pub.L. 97–258, § 1, Sept. 13, 1982, 96 Stat. 877.

Section was also formerly classified to section 198a of this title.

Section was not enacted as part of the Comprehensive Drug Abuse Prevention and Control Act of 1970 (Pub.L. 91–513, Oct. 27, 1970, 84 Stat. 1236) which comprises this chapter.

Effective and Applicability Provisions

1970 Acts. Amendment by Pub.L. 91–513 effective the first day of the seventh calendar month that begins after Oct. 26, 1970, see section 1105(a) of Pub.L. 91–513, set out as a note under section 951 of this title.

Savings Provisions

Prosecutions for any violation of law occurring, and civil seizures or forfeitures and injunctive proceedings commenced, prior to the effective date of amendment of this section by section 1102 of Pub.L. 91–513, not to be affected or abated by reason thereof, see section 1103 of Pub.L. 91–513, set out as a Savings Provisions note under sections 171 to 174 to this title.

§ 968. Service of subpena; proof of service

A subpena of the Secretary of the Treasury may be served by any person designated in the subpena to serve it. Service upon a natural person may be made by personal delivery of the subpena to him. Service may be made upon a domestic or foreign corporation or upon a partnership or other unincorporated association which is subject to suit under a common name, by delivering the subpena to an officer, a managing or general agent, or to any other agent authorized by appointment or by law to receive service of process. The affidavit of the person serving the subpena entered on a true copy thereof by the person serving it shall be proof of service.

(Aug. 11, 1955, c. 800, § 2, 69 Stat. 685.)

HISTORICAL AND STATUTORY NOTES

Codifications

This section was formerly classified to section 1035 of Title 31 prior to the general revision and enactment of Title 31 by Pub.L. 97–258, § 1, Sept. 13, 1982, 96 Stat. 877.

Section was also formerly classified to section 198b of this title.

Section was not enacted as part of the Comprehensive Drug Abuse Prevention and Control Act of 1970 (Pub.L. 91–513, Oct. 27, 1970, 84 Stat. 1236) which comprises this chapter.

§ 969. Contempt proceedings

In case of contumacy by, or refusal to obey a subpena issued to, any person, the Secretary of the Treasury may invoke the aid of any court of the United States within the jurisdiction of which the investigation is carried on or of which the subpenaed person is an inhabitant, carries on business or may be found, to compel compliance with the subpena of the Secretary of the Treasury. The court may issue an order requiring the subpenaed person to appear before the Secretary of the Treasury there to produce records, if so ordered, or to give testimony touching the matter under investigation. Any failure to obey the order of the court may be punished by the court as a contempt thereof. All process in any such case may be served in the judicial district whereof the subpenaed person is an inhabitant or wherever he may be found.

(Aug. 11, 1955, c. 800, § 3, 69 Stat. 685.)

HISTORICAL AND STATUTORY NOTES

Codifications

This section was formerly classified to section 1036 of Title 31 prior to the general revision and enactment of Title 31 by Pub.L. 97–258, § 1, Sept. 13, 1982, 96 Stat. 877.

Section was also formerly classified to section 198c of this title.

Section was not enacted as part of the Comprehensive Drug Abuse Prevention and Control Act of 1970 (Pub.L. 91–513, Oct. 27, 1970, 84 Stat. 1236) which comprises this chapter.

§ 970. Criminal forfeitures

Section 853 of this title, relating to criminal forfeitures, shall apply in every respect to a violation of this subchapter punishable by imprisonment for more than one year.

(Pub.L. 91–513, Title III, § 1017, as added Pub.L. 98–473, Title II, § 307, Oct. 12, 1984, 98 Stat. 2051.)

HISTORICAL AND STATUTORY NOTES

References in Text

This subchapter, referred to in text, was in the original "this title" meaning Title III of Pub.L. 91–513, Oct. 27, 1970, 84 Stat. 1285. Part A of Title III comprises this subchapter. For classification of Part B (sections 1101 to 1105) of Title III of Pub.L. 91–513, see Tables.

§ 971. Notification, suspension of shipment, and penalties with respect to importation and exportation of listed chemicals

(a) Notification prior to transaction

Each regulated person who imports or exports a listed chemical shall notify the Attorney General of the importation or exportation not later than 15 days before the transaction is to take place.

(b) Regular customers or importers

(1) The Attorney General shall provide by regulation for circumstances in which the requirement of subsection (a) of this section does not apply to a transaction between a regulated person and a regular

customer or to a transaction that is an importation by a regular importer. At the time of any importation or exportation constituting a transaction referred to in the preceding sentence, the regulated person shall notify the Attorney General of the transaction.

(2) The regulations under this subsection shall provide that the initial notification under subsection (a) of this section with respect to a customer of a regulated person or to an importer shall, upon the expiration of the 15–day period, qualify the customer as a regular customer or the importer as a regular importer, unless the Attorney General otherwise notifies the regulated person in writing.

(c) Suspension of importation or exportation; disqualification of regular customers or importers; hearing

(1) The Attorney General may order the suspension of any importation or exportation of a listed chemical (other than a regulated transaction to which the requirement of subsection (a) of this section does not apply by reason of subsection (b) of this section) or may disqualify any regular customer or regular importer on the ground that the chemical may be diverted to the clandestine manufacture of a controlled substance (without regard to the form of the chemical that may be diverted, including the diversion of a finished drug product to be manufactured from bulk chemicals to be transferred). From and after the time when the Attorney General provides written notice of the order (including a statement of the legal and factual basis for the order) to the regulated person, the regulated person may not carry out the transaction.

(2) Upon written request to the Attorney General, a regulated person to whom an order applies under paragraph (1) is entitled to an agency hearing on the record in accordance with subchapter II of chapter 5 of Title 5. The hearing shall be held on an expedited basis and not later than 45 days after the request is made, except that the hearing may be held at a later time, if so requested by the regulated person.

(d)(1)(A) Information provided in a notice under subsection (a) or (b) of this section shall include the name of the person to whom the importer or exporter involved intends to transfer the listed chemical involved, and the quantity of such chemical to be transferred.

(B) In the case of a notice under subsection (b) of this section submitted by a regular importer, if the transferee identified in the notice is not a regular customer, such importer may not transfer the listed chemical until after the expiration of the 15–day period beginning on the date on which the notice is submitted to the Attorney General.

(C) After a notice under subsection (a) or (b) of this section is submitted to the Attorney General, if circumstances change and the importer or exporter will not be transferring the listed chemical to the transferee identified in the notice, or will be transferring a greater quantity of the chemical than specified in the notice, the importer or exporter shall update the notice to identify the most recent prospective transferee or the most recent quantity or both (as the case may be) and may not transfer the listed chemical until after the expiration of the 15–day period beginning on the date on which the update is submitted to the Attorney General, except that such 15–day restriction does not apply if the prospective transferee identified in the update is a regular customer. The preceding sentence applies with respect to changing circumstances regarding a transferee or quantity identified in an update to the same extent and in the same manner as such sentence applies with respect to changing circumstances regarding a transferee or quantity identified in the original notice under subsection (a) or (b) of this section.

(D) In the case of a transfer of a listed chemical that is subject to a 15–day restriction under subparagraph (B) or (C), the transferee involved shall, upon the expiration of the 15–day period, be considered to qualify as a regular customer, unless the Attorney General otherwise notifies the importer or exporter involved in writing.

(2) With respect to a transfer of a listed chemical with which a notice or update referred to in paragraph (1) is concerned:

(A) The Attorney General, in accordance with the same procedures as apply under subsection (c)(2) of this section—

(i) may order the suspension of the transfer of the listed chemical by the importer or exporter involved, except for a transfer to a regular customer, on the ground that the chemical may be diverted to the clandestine manufacture of a controlled substance (without regard to the form of the chemical that may be diverted, including the diversion of a finished drug product to be manufactured from bulk chemicals to be transferred), subject to the Attorney General ordering such suspension before the expiration of the 15–day period referred to in paragraph (1) with respect to the importation or exportation (in any case in which such a period applies); and

(ii) may, for purposes of clause (i) and paragraph (1), disqualify a regular customer on such ground.

(B) From and after the time when the Attorney General provides written notice of the order under subparagraph (A) (including a statement of the legal and factual basis for the order) to the importer or exporter, the importer or exporter may not carry out the transfer.

(3) For purposes of this subsection:

(A) The terms "importer" and "exporter" mean a regulated person who imports or exports a listed chemical, respectively.

(B) The term "transfer", with respect to a listed chemical, includes the sale of the chemical.

(C) The term "transferee" means a person to whom an importer or exporter transfers a listed chemical.

(e) Broker or trader for international transaction in listed chemical

A person located in the United States who is a broker or trader for an international transaction in a listed chemical that is a regulated transaction solely because of that person's involvement as a broker or trader shall, with respect to that transaction, be subject to all of the notification, reporting, recordkeeping, and other requirements placed upon exporters of listed chemicals by this subchapter and subchapter I of this chapter.

(f) Application of notification requirement to exports of listed chemical; waiver

(1) The Attorney General may by regulation require that the 15-day notification requirement of subsection (a) of this section apply to all exports of a listed chemical to a specified country, regardless of the status of certain customers in such country as regular customers, if the Attorney General finds that such notification is necessary to support effective chemical diversion control programs or is required by treaty or other international agreement to which the United States is a party.

(2) The Attorney General may by regulation waive the 15-day notification requirement for exports of a listed chemical to a specified country if the Attorney General determines that such notification is not required for effective chemical diversion control. If the notification requirement is waived, exporters of the listed chemical shall be required to submit to the Attorney General reports of individual exportations or periodic reports of such exportation of the listed chemical, at such time or times and containing such information as the Attorney General shall establish by regulation.

(3) The Attorney General may by regulation waive the 15-day notification requirement for the importation of a listed chemical if the Attorney General determines that such notification is not necessary for effective chemical diversion control. If the notification requirement is waived, importers of the listed chemical shall be required to submit to the Attorney General reports of individual importations or periodic reports of the importation of the listed chemical, at such time or times and containing such information as the Attorney General shall establish by regulation.

(g) Within 30 days after a transaction covered by this section is completed, the importer or exporter shall send the Attorney General a return declaration containing particulars of the transaction, including the date, quantity, chemical, container, name of transferees, and such other information as the Attorney General may specify in regulations. For importers, a single return declaration may include the particulars of both the importation and distribution. If the importer has not distributed all chemicals imported by the end of the initial 30-day period, the importer shall file supplemental return declarations no later than 30 days from the date of any further distribution, until the distribution or other disposition of all chemicals imported pursuant to the import notification or any update are accounted for.

(h)(1) With respect to a regulated person importing ephedrine, pseudoephedrine, or phenylpropanolamine (referred to in this section as an "importer"), a notice of importation under subsection (a) or (b) of this section shall include all information known to the importer on the chain of distribution of such chemical from the manufacturer to the importer.

(2) For the purpose of preventing or responding to the diversion of ephedrine, pseudoephedrine, or phenylpropanolamine for use in the illicit production of methamphetamine, the Attorney General may, in the case of any person who is a manufacturer or distributor of such chemical in the chain of distribution referred to in paragraph (1) (which person is referred to in this subsection as a "foreign-chain distributor"), request that such distributor provide to the Attorney General information known to the distributor on the distribution of the chemical, including sales.

(3) If the Attorney General determines that a foreign-chain distributor is refusing to cooperate with the Attorney General in obtaining the information referred to in paragraph (2), the Attorney General may, in accordance with procedures that apply under subsection (c) of this section, issue an order prohibiting the importation of ephedrine, pseudoephedrine, or phenylpropanolamine in any case in which such distributor is part of the chain of distribution for such chemical. Not later than 60 days prior to issuing the order, the Attorney General shall publish in the Federal Register a notice of intent to issue the order. During such 60-day period, imports of the chemical with respect to such distributor may not be restricted under this paragraph.

(Pub.L. 91–513, Title III, § 1018, as added Pub.L. 100–690, Title VI, § 6053(a), Nov. 18, 1988, 102 Stat. 4314, and amended Pub.L. 103–200, §§ 4(a), 5(a), 9(b), Dec. 17, 1993, 107 Stat. 2338 to 2340; Pub.L. 103–322, Title XXXIII, § 330024(c),

Sept. 13, 1994, 108 Stat. 2150; Pub.L. 109–177, Title VII, §§ 716(a), (b)(1)(B), 721, Mar. 9, 2006, 120 Stat. 265, 267.)

HISTORICAL AND STATUTORY NOTES

References in Text

"This subchapter", referred to in subsec. (d), was in the original "this title" which is Title III of Pub.L. 91–513, Oct. 27, 1970, 84 Stat. 1285, known as the "Controlled Substances Import and Export Act". Part A of such Title III comprises this subchapter. For complete classification of Title III of Pub.L. 91–513 to the Code, see Short Title note set out under section 951 of this title and Tables.

"Subchapter I of this chapter", referred to in subsec. (d), was in the original "title II", meaning Title II of Pub.L. 91–513, Oct. 27, 1970, 84 Stat. 1242, known as the "Controlled Substances Act". For complete classification of Title II of Pub.L. 91–513 to the Code, see Short Title note set out under section 801 of this title and Tables.

Effective and Applicability Provisions

Amendment by Pub.L. 103–322 effective 120 days after Dec. 17, 1993, see section 330024(f) of Pub.L. 103–322, set out as a note under section 802 of this title.

1993 Acts. Amendment to this section by Pub.L. 103–200 to take effect on the date that is 120 days after the date of enactment of Pub.L. 103–200, which was approved Dec. 17, 1993, see section 11 of Pub.L. 103–200, set out as a note under section 802 of this title.

1988 Acts. Section 6053(b) of Pub.L. 100–690 provided that:

"(1) Not later than 45 days after the date of the enactment of this Act [Nov. 18, 1988], the Attorney General shall forward to the Director of the Office of Management and Budget proposed regulations required by the amendment made by subsection (a) [which enacted this section].

"(2) Not later than 55 days after the date of the enactment of this Act [Nov. 18, 1988], the Director of the Office of Management and Budget shall—

"(A) review such proposed regulations of the Attorney General; and

"(B) forward any comments and recommendations for modifications to the Attorney General.

"(3) Not later than 60 days after the date of the enactment of this Act [Nov. 18, 1988], the Attorney General shall publish the proposed final regulations required by the amendment made by subsection (a) [which enacted this section].

"(4) Not later than 120 days after the date of the enactment of this Act [Nov. 18, 1988], the Attorney General shall promulgate final regulations required by the amendment made by subsection (a) [which enacted this section].

"(5) Subsection (a) of section 1018 of the Controlled Substances Import and Export Act, as added by subsection (a) of this section, shall take effect 90 days after the promulgation of the final regulations under paragraph (4).

"(6) Each regulated person shall provide to the Attorney General the identity of any regular customer or regular supplier of the regulated person not later than 30 days after the promulgation of the final regulations under paragraph (4). Not later than 60 days after the end of such 30–day period, each regular customer and regular supplier so identified shall be a regular customer or regular supplier for purposes of any applicable exception from the requirement of subsection (a) of such section 1018 [subsec. (a) of this section], unless the the [sic] Attorney General otherwise notifies the regulated person in writing."

Section effective 120 days after Nov. 18, 1988, see section 6061 of Pub.L. 100–690, set out as a note under section 802 of this title.

Combat Methamphetamine Epidemic Act of 2005—Coordination with United States Trade Representative

Pub.L. 109–177, Title VII, § 718, Mar. 9, 2006, 120 Stat. 267, provided that in implementing sections 713 though 717 and section 721 of the Combat Methamphetamine Epidemic Act of 2005, the Attorney General shall consult with the United States Trade Representative to insure compliance with all applicable international treaties and obligations of the United States, see Pub.L. 109–177, § 718, set out as a note under 21 U.S.C.A. § 826.

Exception for Iodine to Importation and Exportation Requirements for Listed Chemicals

Pub.L. 104–237, Title II, § 204(b), Oct. 3, 1996, 110 Stat. 3102, provided that:

"(1) Iodine shall not be subject to the requirements for listed chemicals provided in section 1018 of the Controlled Substances Import and Export Act (21 U.S.C. 971) [this section].

"(2) **Effect of exception.**—The exception made by paragraph (1) shall not limit the authority of the Attorney General to impose the requirements for listed chemicals provided in section 1018 of the Controlled Substances Import and Export Act (21 U.S.C. 971) [this section]."

TITLE 26

INTERNAL REVENUE CODE

CHAPTER 53—MACHINE GUNS, DESTRUCTIVE DEVICES, AND CERTAIN OTHER FIREARMS

HISTORICAL AND STATUTORY NOTES

Prior Provisions

A prior chapter 53, Act Aug. 16, 1954, c. 736, 68A Stat. 721, was generally revised by Pub.L. 90–618, Title II, § 201, Oct. 22, 1968, 82 Stat. 1227. The analysis reflects the following changes by way of substitution:

"Machine Guns, Destructive Devices, and Certain Other Firearms" for "Machine Guns and Certain Other Firearms" in the chapter heading;

"General provisions and exemptions" for "General provisions" in subch. B;

"Prohibited acts" for "Unlawful acts" in subch. C.

SUBCHAPTER A—TAXES

HISTORICAL AND STATUTORY NOTES

Prior Provisions

A prior subchapter A, consisting of parts I to IV, was omitted from the Code upon the general revision of this chapter by Pub.L. 90–618, Title II, § 201, Oct. 22, 1968, 82 Stat. 1227.

PART I—SPECIAL (OCCUPATIONAL) TAXES

HISTORICAL AND STATUTORY NOTES

Prior Provisions

A prior part I, Act Aug. 16, 1964, c. 736, 68A Stat. 721, and amended thereafter, consisted of §§ 5801 to 5803, prior to the general revision of this chapter by Pub.L. 90–618, Title II, § 201, Oct. 22, 1968, 82 Stat. 1228.

§ 5801. Imposition of tax

(a) General rule.—On 1st engaging in business and thereafter on or before July 1 of each year, every importer, manufacturer, and dealer in firearms shall pay a special (occupational) tax for each place of business at the following rates:

(1) Importers and manufacturers: $1,000 a year or fraction thereof.

(2) Dealers: $500 a year or fraction thereof.

(b) Reduced rates of tax for small importers and manufacturers.—

(1) In general.—Paragraph (1) of subsection (a) shall be applied by substituting "$500" for "$1,000" with respect to any taxpayer the gross receipts of which (for the most recent taxable year ending before the 1st day of the taxable period to which the tax imposed by subsection (a) relates) are less than $500,000.

(2) Controlled group rules.—All persons treated as 1 taxpayer under section 5061(e)(3) shall be treated as 1 taxpayer for purposes of paragraph (1).

(3) Certain rules to apply.—For purposes of paragraph (1), rules similar to the rules of subparagraphs (B) and (C) of section 448(c)(3) shall apply.

(Added Pub.L. 90–618, Title II, § 201, Oct. 22, 1968, 82 Stat. 1227, and amended Pub.L. 100–203, Title X, § 10512(g)(1), Dec. 22, 1987, 101 Stat. 1330–449.)

HISTORICAL AND STATUTORY NOTES

Effective and Applicability Provisions

1987 Acts. Amendment by Pub.L. 100–203 effective Jan. 1, 1988, see section 10512(h) of Pub.L. 100–203, set out as a note under 26 U.S.C.A. § 5081.

1968 Acts. Section 207 of Pub.L. 90–618 provided that:

"**(a)** Section 201 of this title [enacting this chapter] shall take effect on the first day of the first month following the month in which it is enacted [October, 1968].

"**(b)** Notwithstanding the provisions of subsection (a) or any other provision of law, any person possessing a firearm as defined in section 5845(a) of the Internal Revenue Code of 1954 [26 U.S.C.A. § 5845(a)] (as amended by this title) which is not registered to him in the National Firearms Registration and Transfer Record shall register each firearm so possessed with the Secretary of the Treasury or his delegate in such form and manner as the Secretary or his delegate may require within the thirty days immediately following the effective date of section 201 of this Act [see subsec. (a) of this section]. Such registrations shall become a part of the National Firearms Registration and Transfer Record required to be maintained by section 5841 of the Internal Revenue Code of 1954 [26 U.S.C.A. § 5841] (as amended by this title). No information or evidence required to be submitted or retained by a natural person to register a firearm under this section shall be used, directly or indirectly, as evidence against such person in any criminal proceeding with respect to a prior or concurrent violation of law.

"**(c)** The amendments made by sections 202 through 206 of this title [amending 26 U.S.C.A. §§ 6806 and 7273, repealing 26 U.S.C.A. §§ 5692 and 6107, and enacting provisions set out as a note under this section] shall take effect on the date of enactment [Oct. 22, 1968].

"**(d)** The Secretary of the Treasury, after publication in the Federal Register of his intention to do so, is authorized to establish such periods of amnesty, not to exceed ninety days in the case of any single period, and immunity from liability during any such period, as the Secretary determines will contribute to the purposes of this title [enacting this chapter, amending 26 U.S.C.A. §§ 6806 and 7273, repealing 26 U.S.C.A. §§ 5692 and 6107, and enacting provisions set out as notes under this section]."

Prior Provisions

A prior section 5801, Act Aug. 16, 1954, c. 736, 68A Stat. 721, as amended Sept. 2, 1958, Pub.L. 85–859, Title II, § 203(a), 72 Stat. 1427; June 1, 1960, Pub.L. 86–478, § 1, 74 Stat. 149, consisted of provisions similar to those comprising this section, before the general revision of this chapter by Pub.L. 90–618.

§ 5802. Registration of importers, manufacturers, and dealers

On first engaging in business and thereafter on or before the first day of July of each year, each importer, manufacturer, and dealer in firearms shall register with the Secretary in each internal revenue district in which such business is to be carried on, his name, including any trade name, and the address of each location in the district where he will conduct such business. An individual required to register under this section shall include a photograph and fingerprints of the individual with the initial application. Where there is a change during the taxable year in the location of, or the trade name used in, such business, the importer, manufacturer, or dealer shall file an application with the Secretary to amend his registration. Firearms operations of an importer, manufacturer, or dealer may not be commenced at the new location or under a new trade name prior to approval by the Secretary of the application.

(Added Pub.L. 90–618, Title II, § 201, Oct. 22, 1968, 82 Stat. 1227, and amended Pub.L. 94–455, Title XIX, § 1906(b)(13)(A), Oct. 4, 1976, 90 Stat. 1834; Pub.L. 103–322, Title XI, § 110301(b), Sept. 13, 1994, 108 Stat. 2012.)

HISTORICAL AND STATUTORY NOTES

Effective and Applicability Provisions

1968 Acts. Section effective the first day of the first month following October, 1968, see section 207 of Pub.L. 90–618, set out as a note under 26 U.S.C.A. § 5801.

Prior Provisions

A prior section 5802, Act Aug. 16, 1954, c. 736, 68A Stat. 721, consisted of provisions similar to those comprising this section, before the general revision of this chapter by Pub.L. 90–618.

A prior section 5803, Act Aug. 16, 1954, c. 736, 68A Stat. 722, setting forth a cross reference to § 5812 exempting certain transfers, before the general revision of this chapter by Pub.L. 90–618.

PART II—TAX ON TRANSFERRING FIREARMS

HISTORICAL AND STATUTORY NOTES

Prior Provisions

A prior part II, consisted of §§ 5811 to 5814, prior to the general revision of this chapter by Pub.L. 90–618, Title II, § 201, Oct. 22, 1968, 82 Stat. 1227.

§ 5811. Transfer tax

(a) Rate.—There shall be levied, collected, and paid on firearms transferred a tax at the rate of $200 for each firearm transferred, except, the transfer tax on any firearm classified as any other weapon under section 5845(e) shall be at the rate of $5 for each such firearm transferred.

(b) By whom paid.—The tax imposed by subsection (a) of this section shall be paid by the transferor.

(c) Payment.—The tax imposed by subsection (a) of this section shall be payable by the appropriate stamps prescribed for payment by the Secretary.

(Added Pub.L. 90–618, Title II, § 201, Oct. 22, 1968, 82 Stat. 1228, and amended Pub.L. 94–455, Title XIX, § 1906(b)(13)(A), Oct. 4, 1976, 90 Stat. 1834.)

HISTORICAL AND STATUTORY NOTES

Effective and Applicability Provisions

1968 Acts. Section effective the first day of the first month following October, 1968, see section 207 of Pub.L. 90–618, set out as a note under 26 U.S.C.A. § 5801.

Prior Provisions

A prior section 5811, Act Aug. 16, 1954, c. 736, 68A Stat. 722, as amended Sept. 2, 1958, Pub.L. 85–859, Title II, § 203(b), 72 Stat. 1427; June 1, 1960, Pub.L. 86–478, § 2, 74 Stat. 149, consisted of provisions similar to those comprising this section, before the general revision of this chapter by Pub.L. 90–618.

§ 5812. Transfers

(a) Application.—A firearm shall not be transferred unless (1) the transferor of the firearm has filed with the Secretary a written application, in duplicate, for the transfer and registration of the firearm to the transferee on the application form prescribed by the Secretary; (2) any tax payable on the transfer is paid as evidenced by the proper stamp affixed to the original application form; (3) the transferee is identified in the application form in such manner as the Secretary may by regulations prescribe, except that, if such person is an individual, the identification must include his fingerprints and his photograph; (4) the transferor of the firearm is identified in the application form in such manner as the Secretary may by regulations prescribe; (5) the firearm is identified in the application form in such manner as the Secretary may by regulations prescribe; and (6) the application form shows that the Secretary has approved the transfer and the registration of the firearm to the transferee. Applications shall be denied if the transfer, receipt, or possession of the firearm would place the transferee in violation of law.

(b) Transfer of possession.—The transferee of a firearm shall not take possession of the firearm unless the Secretary has approved the transfer and registration of the firearm to the transferee as required by subsection (a) of this section.

(Added Pub.L. 90–618, Title II, § 201, Oct. 22, 1968, 82 Stat. 1228, and amended Pub.L. 94–455, Title XIX, § 1906(b)(13)(A), Oct. 4, 1976, 90 Stat. 1834.)

HISTORICAL AND STATUTORY NOTES

Effective and Applicability Provisions

1968 Acts. Section effective the first day of the first month following October, 1968, see section 207 of Pub.L. 90–618, set out as a note under 26 U.S.C.A. § 5801.

Prior Provisions

A prior section 5812, Act Aug. 16, 1954, c. 736, 68A Stat. 722, consisted of provisions similar to those comprising this section, before the general revision of this chapter by Pub.L. 90–618.

A prior section 5813, Act Aug. 16, 1954, c. 736, 68A Stat. 723, related to the affixing of the required stamps to the order form for the firearm, before the general revision of this chapter by Pub.L. 90–618.

A prior section 5814, Act Aug. 16, 1954, c. 736, 68A Stat. 723, as amended Sept. 2, 1958, Pub.L. 85–859, Title II, § 203(c), 72 Stat. 1427, related to the order forms required for the transfer of a firearm, before the general revision of this chapter by Pub.L. 90–618.

PART III—TAX ON MAKING FIREARMS

HISTORICAL AND STATUTORY NOTES

Prior Provisions

A prior part III, consisted of a prior § 5821, prior to the general revision of this chapter by Pub.L. 90–618, Title II, § 201, Oct. 22, 1968, 82 Stat. 1227.

A prior part IV, consisted of a prior § 5831, prior to the general revision of this chapter by Pub.L. 90–618, Title II, § 201, Oct. 22, 1968, 82 Stat. 1227.

§ 5821. Making tax

(a) Rate.—There shall be levied, collected, and paid upon the making of a firearm a tax at the rate of $200 for each firearm made.

(b) By whom paid.—The tax imposed by subsection (a) of this section shall be paid by the person making the firearm.

(c) Payment.—The tax imposed by subsection (a) of this section shall be payable by the stamp prescribed for payment by the Secretary.

(Added Pub.L. 90–618, Title II, § 201, Oct. 22, 1968, 82 Stat. 1228, and amended Pub.L. 94–455, Title XIX, § 1906(b)(13)(A), Oct. 4, 1976, 90 Stat. 1834.)

HISTORICAL AND STATUTORY NOTES

Effective and Applicability Provisions

1968 Acts. Section effective the first day of the first month following October, 1968, see section 207 of Pub.L. 90–618, set out as a note under 26 U.S.C.A. § 5801.

Prior Provisions

A prior section 5821, Act Aug. 16, 1954, c. 736, 68A Stat. 724, as amended Sept. 2, 1958, Pub.L. 85–859, Title II, § 203(d), 72 Stat. 1427, consisted of provisions similar to those comprising this section, before the general revision of this chapter by Pub.L. 90–618.

§ 5822. Making

No person shall make a firearm unless he has (a) filed with the Secretary a written application, in duplicate, to make and register the firearm on the form prescribed by the Secretary; (b) paid any tax payable on the making and such payment is evidenced by the proper stamp affixed to the original application form; (c) identified the firearm to be made in the application form in such manner as the Secretary may by regulations prescribe; (d) identified himself in the application form in such manner as the Secretary may by regulations prescribe, except that, if such person is an individual, the identification must include his fingerprints and his photograph; and (e) obtained the approval of the Secretary to make and register the firearm and the application form shows such approval. Applications shall be denied if the making or possession of the firearm would place the person making the firearm in violation of law.

(Added Pub.L. 90–618, Title II, § 201, Oct. 22, 1968, 82 Stat. 1228, and amended Pub.L. 94–455, Title XIX, § 1906(b)(13)(A), Oct. 4, 1976, 90 Stat. 1834.)

HISTORICAL AND STATUTORY NOTES

Effective and Applicability Provisions

1968 Acts. Section effective the first day of the first month following October, 1968, see section 207(a) of Pub.L. 90–618, set out as a note under 26 U.S.C.A. § 5801.

Prior Provisions

A prior section 5831, Act Aug. 16, 1954, c. 736, 68A Stat. 724, set forth a cross reference to 26 U.S.C.A. § 4181, relating to an excise tax on pistols, revolvers, and firearms, before the general revision of this chapter by Pub.L. 90–618, Title II, § 201, Oct. 22, 1968, 82 Stat. 1227.

SUBCHAPTER B—GENERAL PROVISIONS AND EXEMPTIONS

HISTORICAL AND STATUTORY NOTES

Prior Provisions

A prior subchapter B, consisted of §§ 5841 to 5848, prior to the general revision of this chapter by Pub.L. 90–618, Title II, § 201, Oct. 22, 1968, 82 Stat. 1227.

PART I—GENERAL PROVISIONS

[1] So in original. Does not conform to section catchline.

§ 5841. Registration of firearms

(a) Central registry.—The Secretary shall maintain a central registry of all firearms in the United States which are not in the possession or under the control of the United States. This registry shall be known as the National Firearms Registration and Transfer Record. The registry shall include—

(1) identification of the firearm;

(2) date of registration; and

(3) identification and address of person entitled to possession of the firearm.

(b) By whom registered.—Each manufacturer, importer, and maker shall register each firearm he manufactures, imports, or makes. Each firearm transferred shall be registered to the transferee by the transferor.

(c) How registered.—Each manufacturer shall notify the Secretary of the manufacture of a firearm in such manner as may by regulations be prescribed and such notification shall effect the registration of the firearm required by this section. Each importer, maker, and transferor of a firearm shall, prior to importing, making, or transferring a firearm, obtain authorization in such manner as required by this chapter or regulations issued thereunder to import, make, or transfer the firearm, and such authorization shall effect the registration of the firearm required by this section.

(d) Firearms registered on effective date of this Act.—A person shown as possessing a firearm by the records maintained by the Secretary pursuant to the National Firearms Act in force on the day immediately prior to the effective date of the National Firearms Act of 1968 shall be considered to have registered under this section the firearms in his possession which are disclosed by that record as being in his possession.

(e) Proof of registration.—A person possessing a firearm registered as required by this section shall retain proof of registration which shall be made available to the Secretary upon request.

(Added Pub.L. 90–618, Title II, § 201, Oct. 22, 1968, 82 Stat. 1229, and amended Pub.L. 94–455, Title XIX, § 1906(b)(13)(A), Oct. 4, 1976, 90 Stat. 1834.)

HISTORICAL AND STATUTORY NOTES

References in Text

The National Firearms Act in force prior to the effective date of the National Firearms Act of 1968, referred to in subsec. (d), is Act Aug. 16, 1954, c. 736, 68A Stat. 721, which was classified generally to prior chapter 53 (prior § 5801 et seq.) of this title. For complete classification of this Act to the Code, see Tables.

The National Firearms Act of 1968, referred to in subsec. (d), is Pub.L. 90–618, Title II, Oct. 22, 1968, 82 Stat. 1227, which is classified generally to chapter 53 of this title (26 U.S.C.A. § 5801 et seq.). For complete classification of this Act to the Code, see Short Title note set out under 26 U.S.C.A. § 5849 and Tables.

The effective date of this Act and the effective date of the National Firearms Act of 1968, referred to in subsec. (d) heading and text, means the effective date of the National Firearms Act of 1968, which is Nov. 1, 1968. See section 207(a) of Pub.L. 90–618, set out as a note under 26 U.S.C.A. § 5801.

Effective and Applicability Provisions

1968 Acts. Section effective the first day of the first month following October, 1968, see section 207 of Pub.L. 90–618, set out as a note under 26 U.S.C.A. § 5801.

Prior Provisions

A prior section 5841, Act Aug. 16, 1954, c. 736, 68A Stat. 725, consisted of provisions similar to those comprising this section, before the general revision of this chapter by Pub.L. 90–618.

§ 5842. Identification of firearms

(a) Identification of firearms other than destructive devices.—Each manufacturer and importer and anyone making a firearm shall identify each firearm, other than a destructive device, manufactured, imported, or made by a serial number which may not be readily removed, obliterated, or altered, the name of the manufacturer, importer, or maker, and such other identification as the Secretary may by regulations prescribe.

(b) Firearms without serial number.—Any person who possesses a firearm, other than a destructive device, which does not bear the serial number and other information required by subsection (a) of this section shall identify the firearm with a serial number assigned by the Secretary and any other information the Secretary may by regulations prescribe.

(c) Identification of destructive device.—Any firearm classified as a destructive device shall be identified in such manner as the Secretary may by regulations prescribe.

(Added Pub.L. 90–618, Title II, § 201, Oct. 22, 1968, 82 Stat. 1230, and amended Pub.L. 94–455, Title XIX, § 1906(b)(13)(A), Oct. 4, 1976, 90 Stat. 1834.)

HISTORICAL AND STATUTORY NOTES

Effective and Applicability Provisions

1968 Acts. Section effective the first day of the first month following October, 1968, see section 207 of Pub.L. 90–618, set out as a note under 26 U.S.C.A. § 5801.

Similar Provisions

Provisions similar to those comprising this section were contained in a prior section 5843, Act Aug. 16, 1954, c. 736, 68A Stat. 725, as amended Sept. 2, 1958, Pub.L. 85–859, Title II, § 203(e), 72 Stat. 1427, before the general revision of this chapter by Pub.L. 90–618.

Prior Provisions

A prior section 5842, Act Aug. 16, 1954, c. 736, 68A Stat. 725, related to books, records, and returns, before the general revision of this chapter by Pub.L. 90–618.

§ 5843. Records and returns

Importers, manufacturers, and dealers shall keep such records of, and render such returns in relation to, the importation, manufacture, making, receipt, and sale, or other disposition, of firearms as the Secretary may by regulations prescribe.

(Added Pub.L. 90–618, Title II, § 201, Oct. 22, 1968, 82 Stat. 1230, and amended Pub.L. 94–455, Title XIX, § 1906(b)(13)(A), Oct. 4, 1976, 90 Stat. 1834.)

HISTORICAL AND STATUTORY NOTES

Effective and Applicability Provisions

1968 Acts. Section effective the first day of the first month following October, 1968, see section 207 of Pub.L. 90–618, set out as a note under 26 U.S.C.A. § 5801.

Similar Provisions

Provisions similar to those comprising this section were contained in prior section 5842, Act Aug. 16, 1954, 68A Stat. 725, before the general revision of this chapter by Pub.L. 90–618.

Prior Provisions

A prior section 5843, Act Aug. 16, 1954, c. 736, 68A Stat. 725, as amended Sept. 2, 1958, Pub.L. 85–859, Title II, § 203(e), 72 Stat. 1427, related to identification of firearms, before the general revision of this chapter by Pub.L. 90–618. See, now, 26 U.S.C.A. § 5842.

§ 5844. Importation

No firearm shall be imported or brought into the United States or any territory under its control or jurisdiction unless the importer establishes, under regulations as may be prescribed by the Secretary, that the firearm to be imported or brought in is—

(1) being imported or brought in for the use of the United States or any department, independent establishment, or agency thereof or any State or possession or any political subdivision thereof; or

(2) being imported or brought in for scientific or research purposes; or

(3) being imported or brought in solely for testing or use as a model by a registered manufacturer or solely for use as a sample by a registered importer or registered dealer;

except that, the Secretary may permit the conditional importation or bringing in of a firearm for examination and testing in connection with classifying the firearm.

(Added Pub.L. 90–618, Title II, § 201, Oct. 22, 1968, 82 Stat. 1230, and amended Pub.L. 94–455, Title XIX, § 1906(b)(13)(A), Oct. 4, 1976, 90 Stat. 1834.)

HISTORICAL AND STATUTORY NOTES

Effective and Applicability Provisions

1968 Acts. Section effective the first day of the first month following October, 1968, see section 207 of Pub.L. 90–618, set out as a note under 26 U.S.C.A. § 5801.

Similar Provisions

Provisions similar to those comprising this section were contained in a prior section 5845, Act Aug. 16, 1954, c. 736, 68A Stat. 725, before the general revision of this chapter by Pub.L. 90–618.

Prior Provisions

A prior section 5844, Act Aug. 16, 1954, c. 736, 68A Stat. 725, related to exportation, before the general revision of this chapter by Pub.L. 90–618.

§ 5845. Definitions

For the purpose of this chapter—

(a) Firearm.—The term "firearm" means (1) a shotgun having a barrel or barrels of less than 18 inches in length; (2) a weapon made from a shotgun if such weapon as modified has an overall length of less than 26 inches or a barrel or barrels of less than 18 inches in length; (3) a rifle having a barrel or barrels of less than 16 inches in length; (4) a weapon made from a rifle if such weapon as modified has an overall length of less than 26 inches or a barrel or barrels of less than 16 inches in length; (5) any other weapon, as defined in subsection (e); (6) a machinegun; (7) any silencer (as defined in section 921 of title 18, United States Code); and (8) a destructive device. The term "firearm" shall not include an antique firearm or any device (other than a machinegun or destructive device) which, although designed as a weapon, the Secretary finds by reason of the date of its manufacture, value, design, and other characteristics is primarily a collector's item and is not likely to be used as a weapon.

(b) Machinegun.—The term "machinegun" means any weapon which shoots, is designed to shoot, or can be readily restored to shoot, automatically more than one shot, without manual reloading, by a single function of the trigger. The term shall also include the frame or receiver of any such weapon, any part designed and intended solely and exclusively, or combination of parts designed and intended, for use in converting a weapon into a machinegun, and any combination of parts from which a machinegun can be assembled if such parts are in the possession or under the control of a person.

(c) Rifle.—The term "rifle" means a weapon designed or redesigned, made or remade, and intended to be fired from the shoulder and designed or redesigned and made or remade to use the energy of the explosive in a fixed cartridge to fire only a single projectile through a rifled bore for each single pull of the trigger, and shall include any such weapon which may be readily restored to fire a fixed cartridge.

(d) Shotgun.—The term "shotgun" means a weapon designed or redesigned, made or remade, and intended to be fired from the shoulder and designed or redesigned and made or remade to use the energy of the explosive in a fixed shotgun shell to fire through a smooth bore either a number of projectiles (ball shot) or a single projectile for each pull of the trigger, and shall include any such weapon which may be readily restored to fire a fixed shotgun shell.

(e) Any other weapon.—The term "any other weapon" means any weapon or device capable of being concealed on the person from which a shot can be discharged through the energy of an explosive, a pistol or revolver having a barrel with a smooth bore designed or redesigned to fire a fixed shotgun shell, weapons with combination shotgun and rifle barrels 12 inches or more, less than 18 inches in length, from which only a single discharge can be made from either barrel without manual reloading, and shall include any such weapon which may be readily restored to fire. Such term shall not include a pistol or a revolver having a rifled bore, or rifled bores, or weapons designed, made, or intended to be fired from the shoulder and not capable of firing fixed ammunition.

(f) Destructive device.—The term "destructive device" means (1) any explosive, incendiary, or poison gas (A) bomb, (B) grenade, (C) rocket having a propellent charge of more than four ounces, (D) missile having an explosive or incendiary charge of more than one-quarter ounce, (E) mine, or (F) similar device; (2) any type of weapon by whatever name known which will, or which may be readily converted to, expel a projectile by the action of an explosive or other propellant, the barrel or barrels of which have a bore of more than one-half inch in diameter, except a shotgun or shotgun shell which the Secretary finds is generally recognized as particularly suitable for sporting purposes; and (3) any combination of parts either designed or intended for use in converting any device into a destructive device as defined in subparagraphs (1) and (2) and from which a destructive device may be readily assembled. The term "destructive device" shall not include any device which is neither designed nor redesigned for use as a weapon; any device, although originally designed for use as a weapon, which is redesigned for use as a signaling, pyrotechnic, line throwing, safety, or similar device; surplus ordnance sold, loaned, or given by the Secretary of the Army pursuant to the provisions of section 4684(2), 4685, or 4686 of title 10 of the United States Code; or any other device which the Secretary finds is not likely to be used as a weapon, or is an antique or is a rifle which the owner intends to use solely for sporting purposes.

(g) Antique firearm.—The term "antique firearm" means any firearm not designed or redesigned for using rim fire or conventional center fire ignition with fixed ammunition and manufactured in or before 1898 (including any matchlock, flintlock, percussion cap, or similar type of ignition system or replica thereof, whether actually manufactured before or after the year 1898) and also any firearm using fixed ammunition manufactured in or before 1898, for which ammunition is no longer manufactured in the United States and is not readily available in the ordinary channels of commercial trade.

(h) Unserviceable firearm.—The term "unserviceable firearm" means a firearm which is incapable of discharging a shot by means of an explosive and incapable of being readily restored to a firing condition.

(i) Make.—The term "make", and the various derivatives of such word, shall include manufacturing (other than by one qualified to engage in such business under this chapter), putting together, altering, any combination of these, or otherwise producing a firearm.

(j) Transfer.—The term "transfer" and the various derivatives of such word, shall include selling, assigning, pledging, leasing, loaning, giving away, or otherwise disposing of.

(k) Dealer.—The term "dealer" means any person, not a manufacturer or importer, engaged in the business of selling, renting, leasing, or loaning firearms and shall include pawnbrokers who accept firearms as collateral for loans.

(*l*) Importer.—The term "importer" means any person who is engaged in the business of importing or bringing firearms into the United States.

(m) Manufacturer.—The term "manufacturer" means any person who is engaged in the business of manufacturing firearms.

(Added Pub.L. 90–618, Title II, § 201, Oct. 22, 1968, 82 Stat. 1230, and amended Pub.L. 94–455, Title XIX, § 1906(b)(13)(A), (J), Oct. 4, 1976, 90 Stat. 1834, 1835; Pub.L. 99–308, § 109, May 19, 1986, 100 Stat. 460.)

HISTORICAL AND STATUTORY NOTES

References in Text

Section 4684(2), 4685, or 4686 of title 10 of the United States Code, referred to in subsec. (f), are 10 U.S.C.A. §§ 4684(2), 4685, and 4686.

Effective and Applicability Provisions

1986 Acts. Amendment by Pub.L. 99–308 effective 180 days after May 19, 1986, see section 110(a) of Pub.L. 99–308, set out as a note under 18 U.S.C.A. § 921.

1968 Acts. Section effective the first day of the first month following October, 1968, except as to persons possessing firearms as defined in subsec. (a) which are not registered to such persons in the National Firearms Registration and Transfer Record, see section 207 of Pub.L. 90–618, set out as a note 26 U.S.C.A. § 5801.

Similar Provisions

Provisions similar to those comprising this section were contained in prior section 5848, Act Aug. 16, 1954, c. 736, 68A Stat. 727, as amended Sept. 2, 1958, Pub.L. 85–859, Title II, § 203(f), 72 Stat. 1427; June 1, 1960, Pub.L. 86–478, § 3, 74 Stat. 149, before the general revision of this chapter by Pub.L. 90-618.

Prior Provisions

A prior section 5845, Act Aug. 16, 1954, c. 736, 68A Stat. 725, related to the importation of firearms into the United States or its territory, before the general revision of this chapter by Pub.L. 90–618.

§ 5846. Other laws applicable

All provisions of law relating to special taxes imposed by chapter 51 and to engraving, issuance, sale, accountability, cancellation, and distribution of stamps for tax payment shall, insofar as not inconsistent with the provisions of this chapter, be applicable with respect to the taxes imposed by sections 5801, 5811, and 5821.

(Added Pub.L. 90–618, Title II, § 201, Oct. 22, 1968, 82 Stat. 1232.)

HISTORICAL AND STATUTORY NOTES

Effective and Applicability Provisions

1986 Acts. Section effective the first day of the first month following October, 1968, see section 207 of Pub.L. 90–618, set out as a note under 26 U.S.C.A. § 5801.

Prior Provisions

A prior section 5846, Act Aug. 16, 1954, c. 736, 68A Stat. 726, consisted of provisions similar to those comprising this section, before the general revision of this chapter by Pub.L. 90–618.

Modification of Other Laws

Firearms provisions of 10 U.S.C.A. § 921 et seq., as not modifying or affecting this chapter, see section 104 of Pub.L. 90–618, set out as a note under 10 U.S.C.A. § 921.

§ 5847. Effect on other laws

Nothing in this chapter shall be construed as modifying or affecting the requirements of section 414 of the Mutual Security Act of 1954, as amended, with respect to the manufacture, exportation, and importation of arms, ammunition, and implements of war.

(Added Pub.L. 90–618, Title II, § 201, Oct. 22, 1968, 82 Stat. 1232.)

HISTORICAL AND STATUTORY NOTES

References in Text

Section 414 of the Mutual Security Act of 1954, as amended, referred to in text, was classified to 22 U.S.C.A. § 1934, and was repealed by section 212(b)(1) of Pub.L. 94–329, Title II, 90 Stat. 745. Section 212(b)(1) of Pub.L. 94–329 also provided that any reference to section 414 of the Mutual Security Act of 1954 shall be deemed a reference to section 38 of the Arms Export Control Act. Section 38 of the Arms Export Control Act is classified to 22 U.S.C.A. § 2778.

Effective and Applicability Provisions

1968 Acts. Section effective the first day of the first month following October, 1968, see section 207 of Pub.L. 90–618, set out as a note under 26 U.S.C.A. § 5801.

Prior Provisions

A prior section 5847, Act Aug. 16, 1954, c. 736, 68A Stat. 726, related to regulations which the Secretary or his delegate may prescribe, before the general revision of this chapter by Pub.L. 90–618.

§ 5848. Restrictive use of information

(a) General rule.—No information or evidence obtained from an application, registration, or records required to be submitted or retained by a natural person in order to comply with any provision of this chapter or regulations issued thereunder, shall, except as provided in subsection (b) of this section, be used, directly or indirectly, as evidence against that person in a criminal proceeding with respect to a violation of law occurring prior to or concurrently with the filing of the application or registration, or the compiling of the records containing the information or evidence.

(b) Furnishing false information.—Subsection (a) of this section shall not preclude the use of any such information or evidence in a prosecution or other action under any applicable provision of law with respect to the furnishing of false information.

(Added Pub.L. 90–618, Title II, § 201, Oct. 22, 1968, 82 Stat. 1232.)

HISTORICAL AND STATUTORY NOTES

Effective and Applicability Provisions

1968 Acts. Section effective the first day of the first month following October, 1968, see section 207 of Pub.L. 90–618, set out as a note under 26 U.S.C.A. § 5801.

Prior Provisions

A prior section 5848, Act Aug. 16, 1954, c. 736, 68A Stat. 727, as amended Sept. 2, 1958, Pub.L. 85–859, Title II, § 203(f), 72 Stat. 1427; June 1, 1960, Pub.L. 86–478, § 3, 74 Stat. 149, related to definition of a firearm, machine gun, rifle, shotgun, other weapon, importer, manufacturer, dealer, interstate commerce, transfer and person, before the general revisions of this chapter by Pub.L. 90–618. See 26 U.S.C.A. § 5845.

§ 5849. Citation of chapter

This chapter may be cited as the "National Firearms Act" and any reference in any other provision of law to the "National Firearms Act" shall be held to refer to the provisions of this chapter.

(Added Pub.L. 90–618, Title II, § 201, Oct. 22, 1968, 82 Stat. 1232.)

HISTORICAL AND STATUTORY NOTES

Effective and Applicability Provisions

1968 Acts. Section effective the first day of the first month following October, 1968, see section 207 of Pub.L. 90–618, set out as a note under 26 U.S.C.A. § 5801.

Prior Provisions

A prior section 5849, Pub.L. 85–859, Title II, § 203(g)(1), Sept. 2, 1958, 72 Stat. 1427, consisted of provisions similar to those comprising this section, before the general revision of this chapter by Pub.L. 90–618.

Short Title

Section 202 of Pub.L. 90–618 provided that: "The amendments made by section 201 of this title [enacting this chapter] shall be cited as the 'National Firearms Act Amendments of 1968'."

PART II—EXEMPTIONS

[1] So in original. Does not conform to section catchline.

§ 5851. Special (occupational) tax exemption

(a) Business with United States.—Any person required to pay special (occupational) tax under section 5801 shall be relieved from payment of that tax if he establishes to the satisfaction of the Secretary that his business is conducted exclusively with, or on behalf of, the United States or any department, independent establishment, or agency thereof. The Secretary may relieve any person manufacturing firearms for, or on behalf of, the United States from compliance with any provision of this chapter in the conduct of such business.

(b) Application.—The exemption provided for in subsection (a) of this section may be obtained by filing with the Secretary an application on such form and containing such information as may by regulations be prescribed. The exemptions must thereafter be renewed on or before July 1 of each year. Approval of the application by the Secretary shall entitle the applicant to the exemptions stated on the approved application.

(Added Pub.L. 90–618, Title II, § 201, Oct. 22, 1968, 82 Stat. 1233, and amended Pub.L. 94–455, Title XIX, § 1906(b)(13)(A), Oct. 4, 1976, 90 Stat. 1834.)

HISTORICAL AND STATUTORY NOTES

Effective and Applicability Provisions

1968 Acts. Section effective the first day of the first month following October, 1968, see section 207 of Pub.L. 90–618, set out as a note under 26 U.S.C.A. § 5801.

Prior Provisions

A prior section 5851, Act Aug. 16, 1954, c. 736, 68A Stat. 728, as amended Sept. 2, 1958, Pub.L. 85–859, Title II, § 203(h)(1), (2), 72 Stat. 1428, related to possessing firearms illegally, before the general revision of this chapter by Pub.L. 90–618. See 26 U.S.C.A. § 5861(b), (c).

Similar Provisions

Provisions similar to those comprising this section were contained in a prior section 5812, Act Aug. 16, 1954, c. 736, 68A Stat. 722, before the general revision of this chapter by Pub.L. 90–618.

§ 5852. General transfer and making tax exemption

(a) Transfer.—Any firearm may be transferred to the United States or any department, independent establishment, or agency thereof, without payment of the transfer tax imposed by section 5811.

(b) Making by a person other than a qualified manufacturer.—Any firearm may be made by, or on behalf of, the United States, or any department, independent establishment, or agency thereof, without payment of the making tax imposed by section 5821.

(c) Making by a qualified manufacturer.—A manufacturer qualified under this chapter to engage in such business may make the type of firearm which he is qualified to manufacture without payment of the making tax imposed by section 5821.

(d) Transfers between special (occupational) taxpayers.—A firearm registered to a person qualified under this chapter to engage in business as an importer, manufacturer, or dealer may be transferred by that person without payment of the transfer tax imposed by section 5811 to any other person qualified under this chapter to manufacture, import, or deal in that type of firearm.

(e) Unserviceable firearm.—An unserviceable firearm may be transferred as a curio or ornament without payment of the transfer tax imposed by section 5811, under such requirements as the Secretary may by regulations prescribe.

(f) Right to exemption.—No firearm may be transferred or made exempt from tax under the provisions of this section unless the transfer or making is performed pursuant to an application in such form and manner as the Secretary may by regulations prescribe.

(Added Pub.L. 90–618, Title II, § 201, Oct. 22, 1968, 82 Stat. 1233, and amended Pub.L. 94–455, Title XIX, § 1906(b)(13)(A), Oct. 4, 1976, 90 Stat. 1834.)

HISTORICAL AND STATUTORY NOTES

Effective and Applicability Provisions

1968 Acts. Section effective the first day of the first month following October, 1968, see section 207 of Pub.L. 90–618, set out as a note under 26 U.S.C.A. § 5801.

Similar Provisions

Provisions similar to those comprising this section were contained in a prior section 5814, Act Aug. 16, 1954, c. 736, 68A Stat. 723, as amended Sept. 2, 1958, Pub.L. 85–859, Title II, § 203(c), 72 Stat. 1427, before the general revision of this chapter by Pub.L. 90–618.

Prior Provisions

A prior section 5852, Act Aug. 16, 1954, c. 736, 68A Stat. 728, related to removing or changing identification marks, before the general revision of this chapter by Pub.L. 90–618. See 26 U.S.C.A. § 5861(g) and 18 U.S.C.A. § 922(k).

§ 5853. Transfer and making tax exemption available to certain governmental entities

(a) Transfer.—A firearm may be transferred without the payment of the transfer tax imposed by section 5811 to any State, possession of the United States, any political subdivision thereof, or any official police organization of such a government entity engaged in criminal investigations.

(b) Making.—A firearm may be made without payment of the making tax imposed by section 5821 by, or on behalf of, any State, or possession of the United States, any political subdivision thereof, or any official police organization of such a government entity engaged in criminal investigations.

(c) Right to exemption.—No firearm may be transferred or made exempt from tax under this section unless the transfer or making is performed pursuant to an application in such form and manner as the Secretary may by regulations prescribe.

(Added Pub.L. 90–618, Title II, § 201, Oct. 22, 1968, 82 Stat. 1233, and amended Pub.L. 94–455, Title XIX, § 1906(b)(13)(A), Oct. 4, 1976, 90 Stat. 1834.)

HISTORICAL AND STATUTORY NOTES

Effective and Applicability Provisions

1968 Acts. Section effective the first day of the first month following October, 1968, see section 207 of Pub.L. 90–618, set out as a note under 26 U.S.C.A. § 5801.

Similar Provisions

Provisions similar to those comprising this section were contained in a prior section 5821, Act Aug. 16, 1954, c. 736, 68A Stat. 724, as amended Sept. 2, 1958, Pub.L. 85–859, Title II, § 203(d), 72 Stat. 1427, before the general revision of this chapter by Pub.L. 90–618.

Prior Provisions

A prior section 5853, Act Aug. 16, 1954, c. 736, 68A Stat. 728, related to importing firearms illegally, before the general revision of this chapter by Pub.L. 90–618. See 26 U.S.C.A. § 5861(k) and 18 U.S.C.A. § 922(a).

§ 5854. Exportation of firearms exempt from transfer tax

A firearm may be exported without payment of the transfer tax imposed under section 5811 provided that proof of the exportation is furnished in such form and manner as the Secretary may by regulations prescribe.

(Added Pub.L. 90–618, Title II, § 201, Oct. 22, 1968, 82 Stat. 1234, and amended Pub.L. 94–455, Title XIX, § 1906(b)(13)(A), Oct. 4, 1976, 90 Stat. 1834.)

HISTORICAL AND STATUTORY NOTES

Effective and Applicability Provisions

1968 Acts. Section effective the first day of the first month following October, 1968, see section 207 of Pub.L. 90–618, set out as a note under 26 U.S.C.A. § 5801.

Similar Provisions

Provisions similar to those comprising this section were contained in a prior section 5844, Act Aug. 16, 1954, c. 736, 68A Stat. 725, before the general revision of this chapter by Pub.L. 90–618.

Prior Provisions

A prior section 5854, Pub.L. 85–859, Title II, § 203(i)(1), Sept. 2, 1958, 72 Stat. 1428, related to failure to register and pay special tax, before the general revision of this chapter by Pub.L. 90–618. See 26 U.S.C.A. § 5861(a), (d) and 18 U.S.C.A. § 923.

A prior section 5855, Pub.L. 85–859, Title II, § 203(i)(1), Sept. 2, 1958, 72 Stat. 1428, made it unlawful for any person required to comply with the provisions of 26 U.S.C.A. §§ 5814, 5821, and 5841, to ship, carry or deliver any firearm in interstate commerce if such sections have not been complied with, before the general revision of this chapter by Pub.L. 90–618. See 26 U.S.C.A. § 5861(j) and 18 U.S.C.A. § 922(e), (f), (i) and (j).

SUBCHAPTER C—PROHIBITED ACTS

1 Editorially supplied. Subchapter added by Pub.L. 90–618 without a subchapter analysis.

HISTORICAL AND STATUTORY NOTES

Prior Provisions

A prior subchapter C consisted of sections 5851 to 5854, prior to the general revision of this chapter by Pub.L. 90–618, Title II, § 201, Oct. 22, 1968, 82 Stat. 1227.

§ 5861. Prohibited acts

It shall be unlawful for any person—

(a) to engage in business as a manufacturer or importer of, or dealer in, firearms without having paid the special (occupational) tax required by section 5801 for his business or having registered as required by section 5802; or

(b) to receive or possess a firearm transferred to him in violation of the provisions of this chapter; or

(c) to receive or possess a firearm made in violation of the provisions of this chapter; or

(d) to receive or possess a firearm which is not registered to him in the National Firearms Registration and Transfer Record; or

(e) to transfer a firearm in violation of the provisions of this chapter; or

(f) to make a firearm in violation of the provisions of this chapter; or

(g) to obliterate, remove, change, or alter the serial number or other identification of a firearm required by this chapter; or

(h) to receive or possess a firearm having the serial number or other identification required by this chapter obliterated, removed, changed, or altered; or

(i) to receive or possess a firearm which is not identified by a serial number as required by this chapter; or

(j) to transport, deliver, or receive any firearm in interstate commerce which has not been registered as required by this chapter; or

(k) to receive or possess a firearm which has been imported or brought into the United States in violation of section 5844; or

(*l*) to make, or cause the making of, a false entry on any application, return, or record required by this chapter, knowing such entry to be false.

(Added Pub.L. 90–618, Title II, § 201, Oct. 22, 1968, 82 Stat. 1234.)

HISTORICAL AND STATUTORY NOTES

Effective and Applicability Provisions

1968 Acts. Section effective the first day of the first month following October, 1968, see section 207 of Pub.L. 90–618, set out as a note under 26 U.S.C.A. § 5801.

Similar Provisions

Provisions similar to those comprising subsecs. (a), (b), (d), (g), (k), and (j) of this section were contained in prior sections of I.R.C.1954, before the general revision of this chapter by Pub.L. 90–618, as follows:

Present subsecs.:	Prior sections:
(a)	5854.
(b)	5851.
(d)	5854.
(g)	5852.
(k)	5853.
(j)	5855.

Prior sections 5851 to 5853, Act Aug. 16, 1954, c. 736, are set out in 68A Stat. 728.

Prior sections 5854 and 5855, Pub.L. 85–859, Title II, § 203(i)(1), Sept. 2, 1958, are set out in 72 Stat. 1428.

Prior Provisions

A prior section 5861, Act Aug. 16, 1954, c. 736, 68A Stat. 729, related to penalties, before the general revision of this chapter by Pub.L. 90–618. See 26 U.S.C.A. § 5871.

A prior section 5862, Act Aug. 16, 1954, c. 736, 68A Stat. 729, related to the forfeiture and disposal of any firearm involved in any violation of the provisions of this chapter or any regulation promulgated thereunder, before the general revision of this chapter by Pub.L. 90–618. See 26 U.S.C.A. § 5872.

SUBCHAPTER D—PENALTIES AND FORFEITURES

HISTORICAL AND STATUTORY NOTES

Prior Provisions

A prior subchapter D, consisted of sections 5861 and 5862, prior to the general revision of this chapter by Pub.L. 90–618, Title II, § 201, Oct. 22, 1968, 82 Stat. 1227.

§ 5871. Penalties

Any person who violates or fails to comply with any provision of this chapter shall, upon conviction, be fined not more than $10,000, or be imprisoned not more than ten years, or both.

(Added Pub.L. 90–618, Title II, § 201, Oct. 22, 1968, 82 Stat. 1234, and amended Pub.L. 98–473, Title II, § 227, Oct. 12, 1984, 98 Stat. 2030.)

HISTORICAL AND STATUTORY NOTES

Effective and Applicability Provisions

1984 Acts. Section 235(a)(1)(B)(ii)(IV) of Pub.L. 98–473 had provided that the amendment made by section 227 of Pub.L. 98–473 was to be effective Oct. 12, 1984. Pub.L. 99–646, § 35(2)(D), Nov. 10, 1986, 100 Stat. 3599, amended section 235(a)(1)(B)(ii)(IV) of Pub.L. 98–473, making it inapplicable to section 227. Amendment by Pub.L. 98–473 effective the first day of the first calendar month beginning 36 months after Oct. 12, 1984, see section 235(a)(1) of Pub.L. 98–473, as amended, set out as a note under 18 U.S.C.A. § 3551.

1968 Acts. Section effective the first day of the first month following October, 1968, see section 207(a) of Pub.L. 90–618, set out as a note under 26 U.S.C.A. § 5801.

Similar Provisions

Provisions similar to those comprising this section were contained in prior section 5861, Act Aug. 16, 1954, c. 736, 68A Stat. 729, before the general revision of this chapter by Pub.L. 90–618.

Prior Provisions

A prior section 5871, Act Aug. 16, 1954, c. 736, 68A Stat. 729, consisted of provisions similar to those comprising this section, before the general revision of this chapter by Pub.L. 90–618.

§ 5872. Forfeitures

(a) Laws applicable.—Any firearm involved in any violation of the provisions of this chapter shall be subject to seizure and forfeiture, and (except as provided in subsection (b)) all the provisions of internal revenue laws relating to searches, seizures, and forfeitures of unstamped articles are extended to and made to apply to the articles taxed under this chapter, and the persons to whom this chapter applies.

(b) Disposal.—In the case of the forfeiture of any firearm by reason of a violation of this chapter, no notice of public sale shall be required; no such firearm shall be sold at public sale; if such firearm is forfeited for a violation of this chapter and there is no remission or mitigation of forfeiture thereof, it shall be delivered by the Secretary to the Administrator of General Services, General Services Administration, who may order such firearm destroyed or may sell it to any State, or possession, or political subdivision thereof, or at the request of the Secretary, may authorize its retention for official use of the Treasury Department, or may transfer it without charge to any executive department or independent establishment of the Government for use by it.

(Added Pub.L. 90–618, Title II, § 201, Oct. 22, 1968, 82 Stat. 1235, and amended Pub.L. 94–455, Title XIX, § 1906(b)(13)(A), Oct. 4, 1976, 90 Stat. 1834.)

HISTORICAL AND STATUTORY NOTES

Effective and Applicability Provisions

1968 Acts. Section effective the first day of the first month following October, 1968, see section 207(a) of Pub.L. 90–618, set out as a note under 26 U.S.C.A. § 5801.

Similar Provisions

Provisions similar to those comprising this section were contained in prior section 5862, Act Aug. 16, 1954, c. 736, 68A Stat. 729, before the general revision of this chapter by Pub.L. 90–618.

CHAPTER 75—CRIMES, OTHER OFFENSES, AND FORFEITURES

SUBCHAPTER A—CRIMES

PART I—GENERAL PROVISIONS

Sec.

§ 7201. Attempt to evade or defeat tax

Any person who willfully attempts in any manner to evade or defeat any tax imposed by this title or the payment thereof shall, in addition to other penalties provided by law, be guilty of a felony and, upon conviction thereof, shall be fined not more than $100,000 ($500,000 in the case of a corporation), or imprisoned not more than 5 years, or both, together with the costs of prosecution.

(Aug. 16, 1954, c. 736, 68A Stat. 851; Sept. 3, 1982, Pub.L. 97–248, Title III, § 329(a), 96 Stat. 618.)

HISTORICAL AND STATUTORY NOTES

Effective and Applicability Provisions

1982 Acts. Section 329(e) of Pub.L. 97–248 provided that: "The amendments made by this section [amending this section and sections 7203, 7206, and 7207 of this title] shall apply to offenses committed after the date of the enactment of this Act [Sept. 3, 1982]."

§ 7202. Willful failure to collect or pay over tax

Any person required under this title to collect, account for, and pay over any tax imposed by this title who willfully fails to collect or truthfully account for and pay over such tax shall, in addition to other penalties provided by law, be guilty of a felony and, upon conviction thereof, shall be fined not more than $10,000, or imprisoned not more than 5 years, or both, together with the costs of prosecution.

(Aug. 16, 1954, c. 736, 68A Stat. 851.)

§ 7203. Willful failure to file return, supply information, or pay tax

Any person required under this title to pay any estimated tax or tax, or required by this title or by regulations made under authority thereof to make a return, keep any records, or supply any information, who willfully fails to pay such estimated tax or tax, make such return, keep such records, or supply such information, at the time or times required by law or regulations, shall, in addition to other penalties provided by law, be guilty of a misdemeanor and, upon conviction thereof, shall be fined not more than $25,000 ($100,000 in the case of a corporation), or imprisoned not more than 1 year, or both, together with the costs of prosecution. In the case of any person with respect to whom there is a failure to pay any estimated tax, this section shall not apply to such person with respect to such failure if there is no addition to tax under section 6654 or 6655 with respect to such failure. In the case of a willful violation of any provision of section 6050I, the first sentence of this section shall be applied by substituting "felony" for "misdemeanor" and "5 years" for "1 year".

(Aug. 16, 1954, c. 736, 68A Stat. 851; June 28, 1968, Pub.L. 90–364, Title I, § 103(e)(5), 82 Stat. 264; Sept. 3, 1982, Pub.L. 97–248, Title III, §§ 327, 329(b), 96 Stat. 617, 618; July 18, 1984, Pub.L. 98–369, Div. A, Title IV, § 412(b)(9), 98 Stat. 792; Nov. 18, 1988, Pub.L. 100–690, Title VII, § 7601(a)(2)(B), 102 Stat. 4504; Nov. 29, 1990, Pub.L. 101–647, Title XXXIII, § 3303(a), 104 Stat. 4918.)

HISTORICAL AND STATUTORY NOTES

Effective and Applicability Provisions

1990 Acts. Section 3303(c) of Pub.L. 101–647 provided that: "The amendment made by subsection (a) [amending this section] shall apply to actions, and failures to act, occurring after the date of the enactment of this Act [Nov. 29, 1990]."

1988 Acts. Amendment by Pub.L. 100–690 applicable to actions after Nov. 18, 1988, see section 7601(a)(3) of Pub.L. 100–690, set out as a note under section 6050I of this title.

1984 Acts. Amendment by Pub.L. 98–369 applicable with respect to taxable years beginning after Dec. 31, 1984, see section 414(a) of Pub.L. 98–369, set out as a note under section 6654 of this title.

1982 Acts. Amendment by Pub.L. 97–248 applicable to offenses committed after Sept. 3, 1982, see section 329(e) of Pub.L. 97–248 set out as a note under section 7201 of this title.

1968 Acts. Amendment by Pub.L. 90–364, applicable with respect to taxable years beginning after Dec. 31, 1967, except as provided by section 104 of Pub.L. 90–364, set out as notes under sections 51 and 6154 of this title, see section 103(f) of Pub.L. 90–364.

§ 7204. Fraudulent statement or failure to make statement to employees

In lieu of any other penalty provided by law (except the penalty provided by section 6674) any person required under the provisions of section 6051 to furnish a statement who willfully furnishes a false or fraudulent statement or who willfully fails to furnish a statement in the manner, at the time, and showing the information required under section 6051, or regulations prescribed thereunder, shall, for each such offense, upon conviction thereof, be fined not more than $1,000, or imprisoned not more than 1 year, or both.

(Aug. 16, 1954, c. 736, 68A Stat. 852.)

§ 7205. Fraudulent withholding exemption certificate or failure to supply information

(a) Withholding on wages.—Any individual required to supply information to his employer under section 3402 who willfully supplies false or fraudulent information, or who willfully fails to supply information thereunder which would require an increase in the tax to be withheld under section 3402, shall, in addition to any other penalty provided by law, upon conviction thereof, be fined not more than $1,000, or imprisoned not more than 1 year, or both.

(b) Backup withholding on interest and dividends.—If any individual willfully makes a false certification under paragraph (1) or (2)(C) of section 3406(d), then such individual shall, in addition to any other penalty provided by law, upon conviction thereof, be fined not more than $1,000, or imprisoned not more than 1 year, or both.

(Aug. 16, 1954, c. 736, 68A Stat. 852; Mar. 15, 1966, Pub.L. 89–368, Title I, § 101(e)(5), 80 Stat. 62; Aug. 13, 1981, Pub.L. 97–34, Title VII, § 721(b), 95 Stat. 341; Sept. 3, 1982, Pub.L. 97–248, Title III, §§ 306(b), 308(a), 96 Stat. 589, 591; Aug. 5, 1983, Pub.L. 98–67, Title I, §§ 102(a), 107(b), 97 Stat. 369, 382; July 18, 1984, Pub.L. 98–369, Div. A, Title I, § 159(a), 98 Stat. 696; Dec. 19, 1989, Pub.L. 101–239, Title VII, § 7711(b)(2), 103 Stat. 2393.)

HISTORICAL AND STATUTORY NOTES

Effective and Applicability Provisions

1989 Acts. Amendment to subsec. (b) of this section by section 7711(b)(2) of Pub.L. 101–239 to apply to returns and statements the due date for which (determined without regard to extensions) is after December 31, 1989, see section 7711(c) of Pub.L. 101–239, set out as a note under section 6721 of this title.

1984 Acts. Section 159(b) of Pub.L. 98–369 provided that: "The amendments made by this section [amending this section] shall apply to actions and failures to act occurring after the date of the enactment of this Act [July 18, 1984]."

1983 Acts. Amendment by Pub. L. 98–67 effective Aug. 5, 1983, see section 110(c) of Pub. L. 98–67, set out as a note under section 31 of this title.

1982 Acts. Section 308 of Pub. L. 97–248, formerly set out as a note under section 3451 of this title, had provided, prior to its repeal, that the amendment of this section by Pub. L. 97–248 would apply to interest, dividends, and patronage dividends paid or credited after June 30, 1983.

1981 Acts. Amendment by Pub.L. 97–34 applicable to acts and failures to act after Dec. 31, 1981, see section 721(d) of Pub.L. 97–34, set out as a note under section 6682 of this title.

Repeals

Pub. L. 97–248, Title III, § 306(b), Sept. 3, 1982, 96 Stat. 589, set out in the credit of this section, was repealed by Pub. L. 98–67, Title I, § 102(a), Aug. 5, 1983, 97 Stat. 369. That repeal served to cancel out a 1982 amendment which was to have been applicable to payments of interest, dividends, and patronage dividends paid or credited after June 30, 1983.

§ 7206. Fraud and false statements

Any person who—

(1) Declaration under penalties of perjury.—Willfully makes and subscribes any return, statement, or other document, which contains or is verified by a written declaration that it is made under the penalties of perjury, and which he does not believe to be true and correct as to every material matter; or

(2) Aid or assistance.—Willfully aids or assists in, or procures, counsels, or advises the preparation or presentation under, or in connection with any matter arising under, the internal revenue laws, of a return, affidavit, claim, or other document, which is fraudulent or is false as to any material matter, whether or not such falsity or fraud is with the knowledge or consent of the person authorized or required to present such return, affidavit, claim, or document; or

(3) Fraudulent bonds, permits, and entries.—Simulates or falsely or fraudulently executes or signs any bond, permit, entry, or other document required by the provisions of the internal revenue laws, or by any regulation made in pursuance thereof, or procures the same to be falsely or fraudulently executed, or advises, aids in, or connives at such execution thereof; or

(4) Removal or concealment with intent to defraud.—Removes, deposits, or conceals, or is concerned in removing, depositing, or concealing, any goods or commodities for or in respect whereof any tax is or shall be imposed, or any property upon which levy is authorized by section 6331, with intent to evade or defeat the assessment or collection of any tax imposed by this title; or

(5) Compromises and closing agreements.—In connection with any compromise under section 7122, or offer of such compromise, or in connection with any closing agreement under section 7121, or offer to enter into any such agreement, willfully—

(A) Concealment of property.—Conceals from any officer or employee of the United States any property belonging to the estate of a taxpayer or other person liable in respect of the tax, or

(B) Withholding, falsifying, and destroying records.—Receives, withholds, destroys, mutilates, or falsifies any book, document, or record, or makes any false statement, relating to the estate or financial condition of the taxpayer or other person liable in respect of the tax;

shall be guilty of a felony and, upon conviction thereof, shall be fined not more than $100,000 ($500,000 in the case of a corporation), or imprisoned not more than 3 years, or both, together with the costs of prosecution.

(Aug. 16, 1954, c. 736, 68A Stat. 852; Sept. 3, 1982, Pub.L. 97–248, Title III, § 329(c), 96 Stat. 618.)

HISTORICAL AND STATUTORY NOTES

Effective and Applicability Provisions

1982 Acts. Amendment by Pub.L. 97–248 applicable to offenses committed after Sept. 3, 1982, see section 329(e) of Pub.L. 97–248 set out as a note under section 7201 of this title.

§ 7207. Fraudulent returns, statements, or other documents

Any person who willfully delivers or discloses to the Secretary any list, return, account, statement, or other document, known by him to be fraudulent or to be false as to any material matter, shall be fined not more than $10,000 ($50,000 in the case of a corporation), or imprisoned not more than 1 year, or both. Any person required pursuant to section 6047(b), section 6104(d), or subsection (i) or (j) of section 527 to furnish any information to the Secretary or any other person who willfully furnishes to the Secretary or such other person any information known by him to be fraudulent or to be false as to any material matter shall be fined not more than $10,000 ($50,000 in the case of a corporation), or imprisoned not more than 1 year, or both.

(Aug. 16, 1954, c. 736, 68A Stat. 853; Oct. 10, 1962, Pub.L. 87–792, § 7(m)(3), 76 Stat. 831; Dec. 30, 1969, Pub.L. 91–172, Title I, § 101(e)(5), 83 Stat. 524; Oct. 4, 1976, Pub.L. 94–455, Title XIX, § 1906(b)(13)(A), 90 Stat. 1834; Dec. 28, 1980, Pub.L. 96–603, § 1(d)(5), 94 Stat. 3505; Sept. 3, 1982, Pub.L. 97–248, Title III, § 329(d), 96 Stat. 619; July 18, 1984, Pub.L. 98–369, Div. A, Title IV, § 491(d)(51), 98 Stat. 852; Dec. 22, 1987, Pub.L. 100–203, Title X, § 10704(c), 101 Stat. 1330–463; Oct. 21, 1998, Pub.L. 105–277, Div. J, Title I, § 1004(b)(2)(E), 112 Stat. 2681–890; Nov. 2, 2002, Pub.L. 107–276, § 6(d), 116 Stat. 1933.)

HISTORICAL AND STATUTORY NOTES

Effective and Applicability Provisions

2002 Acts. Pub.L. 107–276, § 6(h)(3), Nov. 2, 2002, 116 Stat. 1934, provided that: "The amendment made by subsection (d) [amending this section] shall apply to reports and notices required to be filed on or after the date of the enactment of this Act [Nov. 2, 2002]."

1998 Acts. Amendment by section 1004(b) of Pub.L. 105–277 applicable to requests made after the later of December 31, 1998, or the 60th day after the Secretary of the Treasury first issues the regulations referred to in section 6104(d)(4) of this title, except section 6104(d) of this title, as in effect before the amendments made by section 1004(b) of Pub.L. 105–277, shall not apply to any return the due date for which is after the date such amendments take effect, see section 1004(b)(3) of Pub.L. 105–277, set out as a note under section 6104 of this title.

1987 Acts. Amendment by Pub.L. 100–203 applicable to returns for years beginning after Dec. 31, 1986, and on and after Dec. 22, 1987 in case of applications submitted after July 15, 1987 or on or before July 15, 1987 if the organization has a copy of the application on July 15, 1987, see section 10704(d) of Pub.L. 100–203, set out as a note under section 6652 of this title.

1984 Acts. Amendment by Pub.L. 98–369 applicable to obligations issued after Dec. 31, 1983, see section 491(f)(1) of Pub.L. 98–369, set out as a note under section 62 of this title.

1982 Acts. Amendment by Pub.L. 97–248 applicable to offenses committed after Sept. 3, 1982, see section 329(e) of Pub.L. 97–248 set out as a note under section 7201 of this title.

1980 Acts. Amendment by Pub.L. 96–603 applicable to taxable years beginning after Dec. 31, 1980, see section 1(f) of Pub.L. 96–603, set out as a note under section 6033 of this title.

1976 Acts. Amendment by Pub.L. 94–455 effective the first day of the first month which begins more than 90 days after Oct. 4, 1976, see section 1906(d) of Pub.L. 94–455, set out as a note under section 6013 of this title.

1969 Acts. Amendment by Pub.L. 91–172 effective on Jan. 1, 1970, see section 101(h)(1) of Pub.L. 91–172, set out as a note under section 4940 of this title.

1962 Acts. Amendment of section by Pub.L. 87–792 applicable to taxable years beginning after Dec. 31, 1962, see section 8 of Pub.L. 87–792, set out as a note under section 22 of this title.

Effect of Amendments on Existing Disclosures

Notices, reports, or returns that were required to be filed with the Secretary of the Treasury before the date of the enactment of the amendments made by Pub.L. 107–276 (November 2, 2002) and that were disclosed by the Secretary of the Treasury consistent with the law in effect at the time of disclosure shall remain subject on and after such date to the disclosure provisions of 26 U.S.C.A. § 6104, see Pub.L. 107–276, § 7, Nov. 2, 2002, 116 Stat. 1935, set out as a note under 26 U.S.C.A. § 6104.

§ 7208. Offenses relating to stamps

Any person who—

(1) Counterfeiting.—With intent to defraud, alters, forges, makes, or counterfeits any stamp, coupon, ticket, book, or other device prescribed under authority of this title for the collection or payment of any tax imposed by this title, or sells, lends, or has in his possession any such altered, forged, or counterfeited stamp, coupon, ticket, book, or other device, or makes, uses, sells, or has in his possession any material in imitation of the material used in the manufacture of such stamp, coupon, ticket, book, or other device; or

(2) Mutilation or removal.—Fraudulently cuts, tears, or removes from any vellum, parchment, paper, instrument, writing, package, or article, upon which any tax is imposed by this title, any adhesive stamp or the impression of any stamp, die, plate, or other article provided, made, or used in pursuance of this title; or

(3) Use of mutilated, insufficient, or counterfeited stamps.—Fraudulently uses, joins, fixes, or places to, with, or upon any vellum, parchment, paper, instrument, writing, package, or article, upon which any tax is imposed by this title,

(A) any adhesive stamp, or the impression of any stamp, die, plate, or other article, which has been cut, torn, or removed from any other vellum, parchment, paper, instrument, writing, package, or article, upon which any tax is imposed by this title; or

(B) any adhesive stamp or the impression of any stamp, die, plate, or other article of insufficient value; or

(C) any forged or counterfeited stamp, or the impression of any forged or counterfeited stamp, die, plate, or other article; or

(4) Reuse of stamps.—

(A) Preparation for reuse.—Willfully removes, or alters the cancellation or defacing marks of, or otherwise prepares, any adhesive stamp, with intent to use, or cause the same to be used, after it has already been used; or

(B) Trafficking.—Knowingly or willfully buys, sells, offers for sale, or gives away, any such washed or restored stamp to any person for use, or knowingly uses the same; or

(C) Possession.—Knowingly and without lawful excuse (the burden of proof of such excuse being on the accused) has in possession any washed, restored, or altered stamp, which has been removed from any vellum, parchment, paper, instrument, writing, package, or article; or

(5) Emptied stamped packages.—Commits the offense described in section 7271 (relating to disposal and receipt of stamped packages) with intent to defraud the revenue, or to defraud any person;

shall be guilty of a felony and, upon conviction thereof, shall be fined not more than $10,000, or imprisoned not more than 5 years, or both.

(Aug. 16, 1954, c. 736, 68A Stat. 853.)

§ 7209. Unauthorized use or sale of stamps

Any person who buys, sells, offers for sale, uses, transfers, takes or gives in exchange, or pledges or gives in pledge, except as authorized in this title or in regulations made pursuant thereto, any stamp, coupon, ticket, book, or other device prescribed by the Secretary under this title for the collection or payment of any tax imposed by this title, shall, upon conviction thereof, be fined not more than $1,000, or imprisoned not more than 6 months, or both.

(Aug. 16, 1954, c. 736, 68A Stat. 854; Oct. 4, 1976, Pub.L. 94–455, Title XIX, § 1906(b) (13) (A), 90 Stat. 1834.)

HISTORICAL AND STATUTORY NOTES

Effective and Applicability Provisions

1976 Acts. Amendment by Pub.L. 94–455 effective the first day of the first month which begins more than 90 days after Oct. 4, 1976, see section 1906(d) of Pub.L. 94–455, set out as a note under section 6013 of this title.

§ 7210. Failure to obey summons

Any person who, being duly summoned to appear to testify, or to appear and produce books, accounts, records, memoranda, or other papers, as required under sections 6420(e)(2), 6421(g)(2), 6427(j)(2), 7602, 7603, and 7604(b), neglects to appear or to produce such books, accounts, records, memoranda, or other papers, shall, upon conviction thereof, be fined not more than $1,000, or imprisoned not more than 1 year, or both, together with costs of prosecution.

(Aug. 16, 1954, c. 736, 68A Stat. 854; Apr. 2, 1956, c. 160, § 4(h), 70 Stat. 91; June 29, 1956, c. 462, Title II, § 208(d)(3), 70 Stat. 396; June 21, 1965, Pub.L. 89–44, Title II, § 202(c)(4), 79 Stat. 139; May 21, 1970, Pub.L. 91–258, Title II, § 207(d)(9), 84 Stat. 249; Oct. 17, 1976, Pub.L. 94–530, § 1(c)(6), 90 Stat. 2488; Nov. 6, 1978, Pub.L. 95–599, Title V, § 505(c)(5), 92 Stat. 2760; Apr. 2, 1980, Pub.L. 96–223, Title II, § 232(d)(4)(E), 94 Stat. 278; Jan. 6, 1983, Pub.L. 97–424, Title V, § 515(b)(12), 96 Stat. 2182; July 18, 1984, Pub.L. 98–369, Div. A, Title IX, § 911(d)(2)(G), 98 Stat. 1007; Oct. 22, 1986, Pub.L. 99–514, Title XVII, § 1703(e)(2)(G), 100 Stat. 2778, as amended Nov. 10, 1988, Pub.L. 100–647, Title I, § 1017(c)(12), 102 Stat. 3577; Nov. 10, 1988, Pub.L. 100–647, Title I, § 1017(c)(9), 102 Stat. 3576.)

HISTORICAL AND STATUTORY NOTES

Effective and Applicability Provisions

1988 Acts. Amendment by section 1017(c)(9), (12) of Pub.L. 100–647 effective as if included in the provisions of Pub.L. 99–514 to which such amendment relates, except that no addition to tax shall be made under section 6654 or 6655 of this title for any period before Apr. 16, 1989 (Mar. 16, 1989 in the case of a taxpayer subject to section 6655 of this title) with respect to any underpayment to the extent such underpayment was created or increased by any provision of Titles I or II of Pub.L. 100–647, see section 1019 of Pub.L. 100–647, set out as a note under section 1 of this title.

1986 Acts. Amendment by Pub.L. 99–514 applicable to gasoline removed, as defined in section 4082 of this title, after Dec. 31, 1987, see section 1703(h) of Pub.L. 99–514, set out as a note under section 4081 of this title.

1984 Acts. Amendment by section 911(d)(2)(G) of Pub.L. 98–369 effective Aug. 1, 1984, see section 911(e) of Pub.L. 98–369, set out as a note under section 6427 of this title.

1983 Acts. Amendment by section 515 of Pub.L. 97–424 applicable to articles sold after Jan. 6, 1983, see section 515(c) of Pub.L. 97–424 set out as a note under section 34 of this title.

1980 Acts. Amendment by Pub.L. 96–223 effective Jan. 1, 1979, see section 232(h) (2) of Pub.L. 96–223, set out as a note under section 6427 of this title.

1978 Acts. Amendment by Pub.L. 95–599 effective Jan. 1, 1979, see section 505(d) of Pub.L. 95–599, set out as a note under section 6427 of this title.

1976 Acts. Amendment by Pub.L. 94–530 effective Oct. 1, 1976, see section 1(d) of Pub.L. 94–530, set out as a note under section 4041 of this title.

1970 Acts. Amendment by Pub.L. 91–258 effective July 1, 1970, see section 211(a) of Pub.L. 91–258, set out as a note under section 4041 of this title.

1965 Acts. Amendment of section by Pub.L. 89–44 effective Jan. 1, 1966, see § 701(a)(1), (2), of Pub.L. 89–44, set out as a note under § 4161 of this title.

1956 Acts. Amendment of section by Act June 29, 1956 effective June 29, 1956, see § 211 of Act June 29, 1956, set out as a note under § 4041 of this title.

§ 7211. False statements to purchasers or lessees relating to tax

Whoever in connection with the sale or lease, or offer for sale or lease, of any article, or for the purpose of making such sale or lease, makes any statement, written or oral—

(1) intended or calculated to lead any person to believe that any part of the price at which such article is sold or leased, or offered for sale or lease,

consists of a tax imposed under the authority of the United States, or

(2) ascribing a particular part of such price to a tax imposed under the authority of the United States,

knowing that such statement is false or that the tax is not so great as the portion of such price ascribed to such tax, shall be guilty of a misdemeanor and, upon conviction thereof, shall be punished by a fine of not more than $1,000, or by imprisonment for not more than 1 year, or both.

(Aug. 16, 1954, c. 736, 68A Stat. 854.)

§ 7212. Attempts to interfere with administration of internal revenue laws

(a) Corrupt or forcible interference.—Whoever corruptly or by force or threats of force (including any threatening letter or communication) endeavors to intimidate or impede any officer or employee of the United States acting in an official capacity under this title, or in any other way corruptly or by force or threats of force (including any threatening letter or communication) obstructs or impedes, or endeavors to obstruct or impede, the due administration of this title, shall, upon conviction thereof, be fined not more than $5,000, or imprisoned not more than 3 years, or both, except that if the offense is committed only by threats of force, the person convicted thereof shall be fined not more than $3,000, or imprisoned not more than 1 year, or both. The term "threats of force", as used in this subsection, means threats of bodily harm to the officer or employee of the United States or to a member of his family.

(b) Forcible rescue of seized property.—Any person who forcibly rescues or causes to be rescued any property after it shall have been seized under this title, or shall attempt or endeavor so to do, shall, excepting in cases otherwise provided for, for every such offense, be fined not more than $500, or not more than double the value of the property so rescued, whichever is the greater, or be imprisoned not more than 2 years.

(Aug. 16, 1954, c. 736, 68A Stat. 855.)

§ 7213. Unauthorized disclosure of information

(a) Returns and return information.—

(1) Federal employees and other persons.—It shall be unlawful for any officer or employee of the United States or any person described in section 6103(n) (or an officer or employee of any such person), or any former officer or employee, willfully to disclose to any person, except as authorized in this title, any return or return information (as defined in section 6103(b)). Any violation of this paragraph shall be a felony punishable upon conviction by a fine in any amount not exceeding $5,000, or imprisonment of not more than 5 years, or both, together with the costs of prosecution, and if such offense is committed by any officer or employee of the United States, he shall, in addition to any other punishment, be dismissed from office or discharged from employment upon conviction for such offense.

(2) State and other employees.—It shall be unlawful for any person (not described in paragraph (1)) willfully to disclose to any person, except as authorized in this title, any return or return information (as defined in section 6103(b)) acquired by him or another person under subsection (d), (i)(3)(B)(i) or (7)(A)(ii), (*l*)(6), (7), (8), (9), (10), (12), (15), (16), (19), or (20) or (m)(2), (4), (5), (6), or (7) of section 6103 or under section 6104(c). Any violation of this paragraph shall be a felony punishable by a fine in any amount not exceeding $5,000, or imprisonment of not more than 5 years, or both, together with the costs of prosecution.

(3) Other persons.—It shall be unlawful for any person to whom any return or return information (as defined in section 6103(b)) is disclosed in a manner unauthorized by this title thereafter willfully to print or publish in any manner not provided by law any such return or return information. Any violation of this paragraph shall be a felony punishable by a fine in any amount not exceeding $5,000, or imprisonment of not more than 5 years, or both, together with the costs of prosecution.

(4) Solicitation.—It shall be unlawful for any person willfully to offer any item of material value in exchange for any return or return information (as defined in section 6103(b)) and to receive as a result of such solicitation any such return or return information. Any violation of this paragraph shall be a felony punishable by a fine in any amount not exceeding $5,000, or imprisonment of not more than 5 years, or both, together with the costs of prosecution.

(5) Shareholders.—It shall be unlawful for any person to whom a return or return information (as defined in section 6103(b)) is disclosed pursuant to the provisions of section 6103(e)(1)(D)(iii) willfully to disclose such return or return information in any manner not provided by law. Any violation of this paragraph shall be a felony punishable by a fine in any amount not to exceed $5,000, or imprisonment of not more than 5 years, or both, together with the costs of prosecution.

(b) Disclosure of operations of manufacturer or producer.—Any officer or employee of the United States who divulges or makes known in any manner whatever not provided by law to any person the operations, style of work, or apparatus of any manufacturer or producer visited by him in the discharge of his official duties shall be guilty of a misdemeanor and, upon conviction thereof, shall be fined not more than $1,000, or imprisoned not more than 1 year, or both, together with the costs of prosecution; and the offender shall be dismissed from office or discharged from employment.

(c) Disclosures by certain delegates of Secretary.—All provisions of law relating to the disclosure of information, and all provisions of law relating to penalties for unauthorized disclosure of information, which are applicable in respect of any function under this title when performed by an officer or employee of the Treasury Department are likewise applicable in respect of such function when performed by any person who is a "delegate" within the meaning of section 7701(a)(12)(B).

(d) Disclosure of software.—Any person who willfully divulges or makes known software (as defined in section 7612(d)(1)) to any person in violation of section 7612 shall be guilty of a felony and, upon conviction thereof, shall be fined not more than $5,000, or imprisoned not more than 5 years, or both, together with the costs of prosecution.

(e) Cross references.—

(1) Penalties for disclosure of information by preparers of returns.—

For penalty for disclosure or use of information by preparers of returns, see section 7216.

(2) Penalties for disclosure of confidential information.—

For penalties for disclosure of confidential information by any officer or employee of the United States or any department or agency thereof, see 18 U.S.C. 1905.

(Aug. 16, 1954, c. 736, 68A Stat. 855; Sept. 2, 1958, Pub.L. 85–866, Title I, § 90(c), 72 Stat. 1666; Sept. 13, 1960, Pub.L. 86–778, Title I, § 103(s), 74 Stat. 940; Oct. 4, 1976, Pub.L. 94–455, Title XII, § 1202(d), (h)(3), 90 Stat. 1686, 1688; Nov. 6, 1978, Pub.L. 95–600, Title VII, § 701(bb)(1)(C), (6), 92 Stat. 2922, 2923; May 26, 1980, Pub.L. 96–249, Title I, § 127(a)(2)(D), 94 Stat. 366; June 9, 1980, Pub.L. 96–265, Title IV, § 408(a)(2)(D), 94 Stat. 468; Dec. 5, 1980, Pub.L. 96–499, Title III, § 302(b), 94 Stat. 2604; Dec. 28, 1980, Pub.L. 96–611, § 11(a)(2)(B)(iv), (4)(A), 94 Stat. 3574; Sept. 3, 1982, Pub.L. 97–248, Title III, § 356(b)(2), 96 Stat. 645; Oct. 25, 1982, Pub.L. 97–365, § 8(c)(2), 96 Stat. 1754; July 18, 1984, Pub.L. 98–369, Div. A, Title IV, § 453(b)(4), Div. B, Title VI, § 2653(b)(4), 98 Stat. 820, 1156; Aug. 16, 1984, Pub.L. 98–378, § 21(f)(5), 98 Stat. 1326; Oct. 13, 1988, Pub.L. 100–485, Title VII, § 701(b)(2)(C), 102 Stat. 2426; Nov. 10, 1988, Pub.L. 100–647, Title VIII, § 8008(c)(2)(B), 102 Stat. 3787; Dec. 19, 1989, Pub.L. 101–239, Title VI, § 6202(a)(1)(C), 103 Stat. 2228; Nov. 5, 1990, Pub.L. 101–508, Title V, § 5111(b)(3), 104 Stat. 1388–273; July 30, 1996, Pub.L. 104–168, Title XII, § 1206(b)(5), 110 Stat. 1473; Aug. 5, 1997, Pub.L. 105–33, Title XI, § 11024(b)(8), 111 Stat. 722; Aug. 5, 1997, Pub.L. 105–35, § 2(b)(1), 111 Stat. 1105; July 22, 1998, Pub.L. 105–206, Title III, § 3413(b), 112 Stat. 754; Jan. 23, 2002, Pub.L. 107–134, Title II, § 201(c)(10), 115 Stat. 2444; Dec. 8, 2003, Pub.L. 108–173, Title I, § 105(e)(4), Title VIII, § 811(c)(2)(C), 117 Stat. 2167, 2369; Aug. 17, 2006, Pub.L. 109–280, Title XII, § 1224(b)(5), 120 Stat. 1093.)

HISTORICAL AND STATUTORY NOTES

Codifications

Pub.L. 109–280, Title XII, § 1224(b)(5), Aug. 17, 2006, 120 Stat. 1093, which directed amendment of paragraph (2) of section 7213(a), was executed by amending paragraph (2) of subsec. (a) of this section, which is paragraph (2) of section 7213(a) of the Internal Revenue Code of 1986, as the probable intent of Congress.

The addition of the reference in subsec. (a)(2) of this section to subsection (*l*)(8) of section 6103 was achieved by Pub.L. 96–611 in two ways: first, under section 11(a)(2)(B)(iv) of Pub.L. 96–611, by amending the directory language of section 408(a)(2)(D) of Pub.L. 96–265 which had previously amended subsec. (a)(2) of this section and, second, under section 11(a)(4)(A) of Pub.L. 96–611, by a direct amendment of subsec. (a)(2) of this section. Both amendments served to achieve an identical change in the text of subsec. (a)(2) of this section. See Effective Date of 1980 Amendments note set out under this section for the different effective dates of these two approaches to the same amendment.

Effective and Applicability Provisions

2006 Acts. Amendments by Pub.L. 109–280, § 1224, effective Aug. 17, 2006, but not applicable to requests made before Aug. 17, 2006, see Pub.L. 109–280, § 1224(c), set out as a note under 26 U.S.C.A. § 6103.

2002 Acts. Amendments by section 201 of Pub.L. 107–134, applicable to disclosures made on or after Jan. 23, 2002, see section 201(d) of Pub.L. 107–134, set out as a note under 26 U.S.C.A. § 6103.

1998 Acts. Amendments by section 3413 of Pub.L. 105–206 to apply to summonses issued, and software acquired, after July 22, 1998, with separate requirements for software acquired on or before such date, see section 3413(e) of Pub.L. 105–206, set out as a note under section 7612 of this title.

1997 Acts. Amendment of subsec. (a)(2) by Pub.L. 105–33 effective on the later of October 1, 1997, or the day the District of Columbia Financial Responsibility and Management Assistance Authority certifies that the financial plan and budget for the District government for fiscal year 1998 meet certain requirements, see section 11721 of Pub.L. 105–33, set out as a note under § 4246 of this title.

Section 2(c) of Pub.L. 105–35 provided that: "The amendments made by this section [amending this section and enacting section 7213A of this title] shall apply to violations occurring on and after the date of the enactment of this Act [Aug. 5, 1997]."

1996 Acts. Amendment by section 1206(b)(5) of Pub.L. 104–168 effective July 30, 1996, see section 1206(c) of Pub.L. 104–168, set out as a note under section 6103 of this title.

1989 Acts. Amendment to subsec. (a)(2) of this section by section 6202(a)(1)(C) of Pub.L. 101–239 to take effect on Dec.

19, 1989, see section 6202(a)(1)(D) of Pub.L. 101–239, set out as a note under section 6103 of this title.

1988 Acts. Amendments by Pub.L. 100–647 effective as if included in the provisions of Pub.L. 99–514 to which such amendments relate, except that no addition to tax shall be made under section 6654 or 6655 of this title for any period before Apr. 16, 1989 (Mar. 16, 1989 in the case of a taxpayer subject to section 6655 of this title) with respect to any underpayment to the extent such underpayment was created or increased by any provision of Titles I or II of Pub.L. 100–647, see section 1019 of Pub.L. 100–647, set out as a note under section 1 of this title.

Amendment by Pub.L. 100–485 effective Oct. 13, 1988, see section 701(b)(3) of Pub.L. 100–485, set out as a note under section 6103 of this title.

1984 Acts. Amendment by Pub.L. 98–378 applicable to refunds payable under section 6402 of this title after Dec. 31, 1985, see section 21(g) of Pub.L. 98–378, set out as a note under section 6103 of this title.

Amendment by section 2653 of Pub.L. 98–369 applicable to refunds payable under section 6402 of this title after Dec. 31, 1985, see section 2653(c) of Pub.L. 98–369, as amended, set out as a note under section 6402 of this title.

Amendment by Section 453(b)(4) of Pub.L. 98–369 effective the first day of the first calendar month which begins more than 90 days after July 18, 1984, see section 456(a) of Pub.L. 98–369, set out as a note under section 5101 of this title.

1982 Acts. Amendment by Pub.L. 97–365 effective Oct. 25, 1982, see section 8(d) of Pub.L. 97–365, set out as a note under section 6103 of this title.

Amendment by Pub.L. 97–248 effective the day after Sept. 3, 1982, see section 356(c) of Pub.L. 97–248, set out as a note under section 6103 of this title.

1980 Acts. Section 11(a)(4)(B) of Pub.L. 96–611 provided that: "The amendment made by subparagraph (A) [amending this section] shall take effect on December 5, 1980."

Amendment by Pub.L. 96–499 effective Dec. 5, 1980, see section 302(c) of Pub.L. 96–499, set out as a note under section 6103 of this title.

Amendment by Pub.L. 96–265, as amended by section 11(a)(2)(B)(iv) of Pub.L. 96–611 effective June 9, 1980, the date of enactment of Pub.L. 96–265, see section 11(a)(3) of Pub.L. 96–611, set out as a note under section 6103 of this title.

Amendment by Pub.L. 96–249 effective May 26, 1980, see section 127(a)(3) of Pub.L. 96–249, set out as a note under section 6103 of this title.

1978 Acts. Amendment by Pub.L. 95–600 effective Jan. 1, 1977, see section 701(bb)(8) of Pub.L. 95–600, set out as a note under section 6103 of this title.

1976 Acts. Amendment by Pub.L. 94–455 effective Jan. 1, 1977, see section 1202(i) of Pub.L. 94–455, set out as a note under section 6103 of this title.

1960 Acts. Subsec. (d) of this section effective Sept. 13, 1960, see section 103(v)(1) of Pub.L. 86–778, set out as a note under section 402 of Title 42, The Public Health and Welfare.

1958 Acts. Subsec. (c) of this section effective Aug. 17, 1954, see section 1(c) of Pub.L. 85–866, set out as a note under section 165 of this title.

Confidentiality of Information

The Secretary may issue regulations governing the confidentiality of information obtained pursuant to the provisions of subsec. (a)(2) of this section, as amended by section 11024(b)(8) of Pub.L. 105–33, see section 11024(c) of Pub.L. 105–33, set out as a note under section 6103 of this title.

Clarification of Congressional Intent as to Scope of Amendment by Section 2653 of Pub.L. 98–369

For provisions that nothing in the amendment to this section by section 2653 of Pub.L. 98–369 shall be construed as exempting debts of corporations or any other category of persons from the application of such amendments, or other amendments by section 2653 of Pub.L. 98–369, with such amendments to extend to all Federal agencies as defined by section 2653 of Pub.L. 98–369, see section 9402(b) of Pub.L. 100–203, set out as a note under section 6402 of this title.

§ 7213A. Unauthorized inspection of returns or return information

(a) Prohibitions.—

(1) Federal employees and other persons.—It shall be unlawful for—

(A) any officer or employee of the United States, or

(B) any person described in subsection (*l*)(18) or (n) of section 6103 or an officer or employee of any such person,

willfully to inspect, except as authorized in this title, any return or return information.

(2) State and other employees.—It shall be unlawful for any person (not described in paragraph (1)) willfully to inspect, except as authorized in this title, any return or return information acquired by such person or another person under a provision of section 6103 referred to in section 7213(a)(2) or under section 6104(c).

(b) Penalty.—

(1) In general.—Any violation of subsection (a) shall be punishable upon conviction by a fine in any amount not exceeding $1,000, or imprisonment of not more than 1 year, or both, together with the costs of prosecution.

(2) Federal officers or employees.—An officer or employee of the United States who is convicted of any violation of subsection (a) shall, in addition to any other punishment, be dismissed from office or discharged from employment.

(c) Definitions.—For purposes of this section, the terms "inspect", "return", and "return information" have the respective meanings given such terms by section 6103(b).

(Added Pub.L. 105–35, § 2(a), Aug. 5, 1997, 111 Stat. 1104, and amended Pub.L. 107–210, Div. A, Title II, § 202(b)(3), Aug. 6, 2002, 116 Stat. 961; Pub.L. 109–280, Title XII, § 1224(b)(6), Aug. 17, 2006, 120 Stat. 1093.)

HISTORICAL AND STATUTORY NOTES

Codifications

Pub.L. 109–280, Title XII, § 1224(b)(6), Aug. 17, 2006, 120 Stat. 1093, which directed amendment of paragraph (2) of section 7213A(a), was executed by amending paragraph (2) of subsec. (a) of this section, which is paragraph (2) of section 7213A(a) of the Internal Revenue Code of 1986, as the probable intent of Congress.

Effective and Applicability Provisions

2006 Acts. Amendments by Pub.L. 109–280, § 1224, effective Aug. 17, 2006, but not applicable to requests made before Aug. 17, 2006, see Pub.L. 109–280, § 1224(c), set out as a note under 26 U.S.C.A. § 6103.

2002 Acts. Amendments made by Pub.L. 107–210, § 202, effective Aug. 6, 2002, see section 202(e) of Pub.L. 107–210, set out as a note under 26 U.S.C.A. § 6050T.

Except as otherwise provided by sections 123(c), 141(b), and 151(b) to (d) of Pub.L. 107–210, amendments made by Division A of Pub.L. 107–210, Titles I to III, §§ 101 to 383, shall apply to petitions for certification filed under parts 2 or 3 of subchapter II of chapter 12 of Title 19 [19 U.S.C.A. § 2271 et seq. or § 2341 et seq.] on or after 90 days after August 6, 2002, see section 151 of Pub.L. 107–210, set out as a note preceding 19 U.S.C.A. § 2271.

1997 Acts. Enactment of this section by section (2)(a) of Pub.L. 105–35 to apply to violations occurring on and after August 5, 1997, see section 2(c) of Pub.L. 105–35 set out as a note under section 7213 of this title.

Rule of Construction for Title II of Pub.L. 107–210

Nothing in Pub.L. 107–210, Div. A, Title II, § 201 et seq., Aug. 6, 2002, 116 Stat. 954, other than provisions relating to COBRA continuation coverage and reporting requirements, shall be construed as creating any new mandate on any party regarding health insurance coverage, see section 203(f) of Pub.L. 107–210, set out as a note under 29 U.S.C.A. § 2918.

§ 7214. Offenses by officers and employees of the United States

(a) Unlawful acts of revenue officers or agents.—Any officer or employee of the United States acting in connection with any revenue law of the United States—

(1) who is guilty of any extortion or willful oppression under color of law; or

(2) who knowingly demands other or greater sums than are authorized by law, or receives any fee, compensation, or reward, except as by law prescribed, for the performance of any duty; or

(3) who with intent to defeat the application of any provision of this title fails to perform any of the duties of his office or employment; or

(4) who conspires or colludes with any other person to defraud the United States; or

(5) who knowingly makes opportunity for any person to defraud the United States; or

(6) who does or omits to do any act with intent to enable any other person to defraud the United States; or

(7) who makes or signs any fraudulent entry in any book, or makes or signs any fraudulent certificate, return, or statement; or

(8) who, having knowledge or information of the violation of any revenue law by any person, or of fraud committed by any person against the United States under any revenue law, fails to report, in writing, such knowledge or information to the Secretary; or

(9) who demands, or accepts, or attempts to collect, directly or indirectly as payment or gift, or otherwise, any sum of money or other thing of value for the compromise, adjustment, or settlement of any charge or complaint for any violation or alleged violation of law, except as expressly authorized by law so to do;

shall be dismissed from office or discharged from employment and, upon conviction thereof, shall be fined not more than $10,000, or imprisoned not more than 5 years, or both. The court may in its discretion award out of the fine so imposed an amount, not in excess of one-half thereof, for the use of the informer, if any, who shall be ascertained by the judgment of the court. The court also shall render judgment against the said officer or employee for the amount of damages sustained in favor of the party injured, to be collected by execution.

(b) Interest of internal revenue officer or employee in tobacco or liquor production.—Any internal revenue officer or employee interested, directly or indirectly, in the manufacture of tobacco, snuff, or cigarettes, or in the production, rectification, or redistillation of distilled spirits, shall be dismissed from office; and each such officer or employee so interested in any such manufacture or production, rectification, or redistillation or production of fermented liquors shall be fined not more than $5,000.

(c) Cross reference.—

For penalty on collecting or disbursing officers trading in public funds or debts or property, see 18 U.S.C. 1901.

(Aug. 16, 1954, c. 736, 68A Stat. 856; Sept. 2, 1958, Pub.L. 85–859, Title II, § 204(5), 72 Stat. 1429; Oct. 4, 1976, Pub.L. 94–455, Title XIX, § 1906(b) (13) (A), 90 Stat. 1834.)

HISTORICAL AND STATUTORY NOTES

Effective and Applicability Provisions

1976 Acts. Amendment by Pub.L. 94–455 effective the first day of the first month which begins more than 90 days after Oct. 4, 1976, see section 1906(d) of Pub.L. 94–455, set out as a note under section 6013 of this title.

1958 Acts. Amendment by Pub.L. 85–859 effective Sept. 3, 1958, see § 210(a)(1) of Pub.L. 85–859, set out as a note under § 5001 of this title.

§ 7215. Offenses with respect to collected taxes

(a) Penalty.—Any person who fails to comply with any provision of section 7512(b) shall, in addition to any other penalties provided by law, be guilty of a misdemeanor, and, upon conviction thereof, shall be fined not more than $5,000, or imprisoned not more than one year, or both, together with the costs of prosecution.

(b) Exceptions.—This section shall not apply—

(1) to any person, if such person shows that there was reasonable doubt as to (A) whether the law required collection of tax, or (B) who was required by law to collect tax, and

(2) to any person, if such person shows that the failure to comply with the provisions of section 7512(b) was due to circumstances beyond his control.

For purposes of paragraph (2), a lack of funds existing immediately after the payment of wages (whether or not created by the payment of such wages) shall not be considered to be circumstances beyond the control of a person.

(Added Pub.L. 85–321, § 2, Feb. 11, 1958, 72 Stat. 6, and amended Pub.L. 97–248, Title III, §§ 307(a)(15), 308(a), Sept. 3, 1982, 96 Stat. 590, 591; Pub.L. 98–67, Title I, § 102(a), Aug. 5, 1983, 97 Stat. 369.)

HISTORICAL AND STATUTORY NOTES

Effective and Applicability Provisions

1982 Acts. Section 308 of Pub. L. 97–248, formerly set out as a note under section 3451 of this title, had provided, prior to its repeal, that the amendment of this section by Pub. L. 97–248 would apply to interest, dividends, and patronage dividends paid or credited after June 30, 1983.

Repeals

Pub. L. 97–248, Title III, § 307(a)(15), Sept. 3, 1982, 96 Stat. 590, set out in the credit of this section, was repealed by Pub. L. 98–67, Title I, § 102(a), Aug. 5, 1983, 97 Stat. 369. That repeal served to cancel out a 1982 amendment which was to have been applicable to payments of interest, dividends, and patronage dividends paid or credited after June 30, 1983.

§ 7216. Disclosure or use of information by preparers of returns

(a) General rule.—Any person who is engaged in the business of preparing, or providing services in connection with the preparation of, returns of the tax imposed by chapter 1, or any person who for compensation prepares any such return for any other person, and who knowingly or recklessly—

(1) discloses any information furnished to him for, or in connection with, the preparation of any such return, or

(2) uses any such information for any purpose other than to prepare, or assist in preparing, any such return,

shall be guilty of a misdemeanor, and, upon conviction thereof, shall be fined not more than $1,000, or imprisoned not more than 1 year, or both, together with the costs of prosecution.

(b) Exceptions.—

(1) Disclosure.—Subsection (a) shall not apply to a disclosure of information if such disclosure is made—

(A) pursuant to any other provision of this title, or

(B) pursuant to an order of a court.

(2) Use.—Subsection (a) shall not apply to the use of information in the preparation of, or in connection with the preparation of, State and local tax returns and declarations of estimated tax of the person to whom the information relates.

(3) Regulations.—Subsection (a) shall not apply to a disclosure or use of information which is permitted by regulations prescribed by the Secretary under this section. Such regulations shall permit (subject to such conditions as such regulations shall provide) the disclosure or use of information for quality or peer reviews.

(Added Pub.L. 92–178, Title III, § 316(a), Dec. 10, 1971, 85 Stat. 529, and amended Pub.L. 94–455, Title XIX, § 1906(b)(13)(A), Oct. 4, 1976, 90 Stat. 1834; Pub.L. 98–369, Div. A, Title IV, § 412(b)(10), July 18, 1984, 98 Stat. 792; Pub.L. 100–647, Title VI, § 6242(b), Nov. 10, 1988, 102 Stat. 3749; Pub.L. 101–239, Title VII, § 7739(a), Dec. 19, 1989, 103 Stat. 2404.)

HISTORICAL AND STATUTORY NOTES

Effective and Applicability Provisions

1989 Acts. Section 7739(b) of Pub.L. 101–239 provided that: "The amendment made by subsection (a) [amending subsec. (b)(3) of this section] shall take effect on the date of the enactment of this Act [Dec. 19, 1989]."

1988 Acts. Amendment by Pub.L. 100–647 applicable to disclosures or uses after Dec. 31, 1988, see section 6242(d) of Pub.L. 100–647, set out as a note under section 6712 of this title.

1984 Acts. Amendment by Pub.L. 98–369 applicable with respect to taxable years beginning after Dec. 31, 1984, see section 414(a) of Pub.L. 98–369, set out as a note under section 6654 of this title.

1976 Acts. Amendment by Pub.L. 94–455 effective the first day of the first month which begins more than 90 days after Oct. 4, 1976, see section 1900(d) of Pub.L. 94–455, set out as a note under section 6013 of this title.

1971 Acts. Section 316(c) of Pub.L. 92–178 provided that: "The amendments made by this section [enacting this section] shall take effect on the first day of the first month which begins after the date of the enactment of this Act [Dec. 10, 1971.]"

§ 7217. Prohibition on executive branch influence over taxpayer audits and other investigations

(a) Prohibition.—It shall be unlawful for any applicable person to request, directly or indirectly, any officer or employee of the Internal Revenue Service to conduct or terminate an audit or other investigation of any particular taxpayer with respect to the tax liability of such taxpayer.

(b) Reporting requirement.—Any officer or employee of the Internal Revenue Service receiving any request prohibited by subsection (a) shall report the receipt of such request to the Treasury Inspector General for Tax Administration.

(c) Exceptions.—Subsection (a) shall not apply to any written request made—

(1) to an applicable person by or on behalf of the taxpayer and forwarded by such applicable person to the Internal Revenue Service;

(2) by an applicable person for disclosure of return or return information under section 6103 if such request is made in accordance with the requirements of such section; or

(3) by the Secretary of the Treasury as a consequence of the implementation of a change in tax policy.

(d) Penalty.—Any person who willfully violates subsection (a) or fails to report under subsection (b) shall be punished upon conviction by a fine in any amount not exceeding $5,000, or imprisonment of not more than 5 years, or both, together with the costs of prosecution.

(e) Applicable person.—For purposes of this section, the term "applicable person" means—

(1) the President, the Vice President, any employee of the executive office of the President, and any employee of the executive office of the Vice President; and

(2) any individual (other than the Attorney General of the United States) serving in a position specified in section 5312 of title 5, United States Code.

(Added July 22, 1998, Pub.L. 105–206, Title I, § 1105(a), 112 Stat. 711.)

HISTORICAL AND STATUTORY NOTES

Effective Dates

1998 Acts. Section 1105(c) of Pub.L. 105–206 provided that: "The amendments made by this section [adding this section] shall apply to requests made after the date of the enactment of this Act [July 22, 1998]."

Prior Provisions

Another section 7217, added Pub.L. 94–455, Title XII, § 1202(e) (1), Oct. 4, 1976, 90 Stat. 1687, and amended Pub.L. 95–600, Title VII, § 701(bb)(7), Nov. 6, 1978, 92 Stat. 2923, related to civil damages for unauthorized disclosure of returns and return information, was repealed by Pub.L. 97–248, Title III, § 357(b) (1), Sept. 3, 1982, 96 Stat. 646, applicable with respect to disclosures made after Sept. 3, 1982, see section 357(c) of Pub.L. 97–248, set out as a note under section 7431 of this title.

TITLE 28

JUDICIARY AND JUDICIAL PROCEDURE

Act June 25, 1948, c. 646, § 1, 62 Stat. 869

CHAPTER 58—UNITED STATES SENTENCING COMMISSION

Sec.

§ 991. United States Sentencing Commission; establishment and purposes

(a) There is established as an independent commission in the judicial branch of the United States a United States Sentencing Commission which shall consist of seven voting members and one nonvoting member. The President, after consultation with representatives of judges, prosecuting attorneys, defense attorneys, law enforcement officials, senior citizens, victims of crime, and others interested in the criminal justice process, shall appoint the voting members of the Commission, by and with the advice and consent of the Senate, one of whom shall be appointed, by and with the advice and consent of the Senate, as the Chair and three of whom shall be designated by the President as Vice Chairs. Not more than 3 of the members shall be Federal judges selected after considering a list of six judges recommended to the President by the Judicial Conference of the United States. Not more than four of the members of the Commission shall be members of the same political party, and of the three Vice Chairs, no more than two shall be members of the same political party. The Attorney General, or the Attorney General's designee, shall be an ex officio, nonvoting member of the Commission. The Chair, Vice Chairs, and members of the Commission shall be subject to removal from the Commission by the President only for neglect of duty or malfeasance in office or for other good cause shown.

(b) The purposes of the United States Sentencing Commission are to—

(1) establish sentencing policies and practices for the Federal criminal justice system that—

(A) assure the meeting of the purposes of sentencing as set forth in section 3553(a)(2) of title 18, United States Code;

(B) provide certainty and fairness in meeting the purposes of sentencing, avoiding unwarranted sentencing disparities among defendants with similar records who have been found guilty of similar criminal conduct while maintaining sufficient flexibility to permit individualized sentences when warranted by mitigating or aggravating factors not taken into account in the establishment of general sentencing practices; and

(C) reflect, to the extent practicable, advancement in knowledge of human behavior as it relates to the criminal justice process; and

(2) develop means of measuring the degree to which the sentencing, penal, and correctional practices are effective in meeting the purposes of sentencing as set forth in section 3553(a)(2) of title 18, United States Code.

(Added Pub.L. 98–473, Title II, § 217(a), Oct. 12, 1984, 98 Stat. 2017, and amended Pub.L. 99–22, § 1(1), Apr. 15, 1985, 99 Stat. 46; Pub.L. 103–322, Title XXVIII, § 280005(a), (c)(1), (2), Sept. 13, 1994, 108 Stat. 2096, 2097; Pub.L. 104–294, Title VI, § 604(b)(11), Oct. 11, 1996, 110 Stat. 3507; Pub.L. 108–21, Title IV, § 401(n)(1), Apr. 30, 2003, 117 Stat. 676.)

HISTORICAL AND STATUTORY NOTES

Effective and Applicability Provisions

2003 Acts. Pub.L. 108–21, Title IV, § 401(n)(2), Apr. 30, 2003, 117 Stat. 676, provided that: "The amendment made under paragraph (1) [amending subsec. (a) of this section] shall not apply to any person who is serving, or who has been nominated to serve, as a member of the Sentencing Commission on the date of enactment of this Act [Apr. 30, 2003]."

1996 Acts. Amendment by section 604 of Pub.L. 104–294 effective Sept. 13, 1994, see section 604(d) of Pub.L. 104–294, set out as a note under section 13 of Title 18, Crimes and Criminal Procedure.

1984 Acts. Section effective Oct. 12, 1984, see section 235(a)(1)(B)(i) of Pub.L. 98–473, as amended, set out as a note under section 3551 of Title 18, Crimes and Criminal Procedure.

Composition of Members of Commission During First Five-Year Period

For provisions directing that, notwithstanding the provisions of this section, during the five-year period following Oct. 12, 1984, the United States Sentencing Commission shall consist of nine members, including two ex officio, nonvoting members, see section 235(b)(5) of Pub.L. 98–473, set out as an Effective Date note under section 3551 of Title 18, Crimes and Criminal Procedure.

§ 992. Terms of office; compensation

(a) The voting members of the United States Sentencing Commission shall be appointed for six-year terms, except that the initial terms of the first members of the Commission shall be staggered so that—

(1) two members, including the Chair, serve terms of six years;

(2) three members serve terms of four years; and

(3) two members serve terms of two years.

(b)(1) Subject to paragraph (2)—

(A) no voting member of the Commission may serve more than two full terms; and

(B) a voting member appointed to fill a vacancy that occurs before the expiration of the term for which a predecessor was appointed shall be appointed only for the remainder of such term.

(2) A voting member of the Commission whose term has expired may continue to serve until the earlier of—

(A) the date on which a successor has taken office; or

(B) the date on which the Congress adjourns sine die to end the session of Congress that commences after the date on which the member's term expired.

(c) The Chair and Vice Chairs of the Commission shall hold full-time positions and shall be compensated during their terms of office at the annual rate at which judges of the United States courts of appeals are compensated. The voting members of the Commission, other than the Chair and Vice Chairs, shall hold full-time positions until the end of the first six years after the sentencing guidelines go into effect pursuant to section 235(a)(1)(B)(ii) of the Sentencing Reform Act of 1984, and shall be compensated at the annual rate at which judges of the United States courts of appeals are compensated. Thereafter, the voting members of the Commission, other than the Chair and Vice Chairs,,[1] shall hold part-time positions and shall be paid at the daily rate at which judges of the United States courts of appeals are compensated. A Federal judge may serve as a member of the Commission without resigning the judge's appointment as a Federal judge.

(d) Sections 44(c) and 134(b) of this title (relating to the residence of judges) do not apply to any judge holding a full-time position on the Commission under subsection (c) of this section.

(Added Pub.L. 98–473, Title II, § 217(a), Oct. 12, 1984, 98 Stat. 2018, and amended Pub.L. 99–646, §§ 4, 6(a), Nov. 10, 1986, 100 Stat. 3592; Pub.L. 102–349, § 1, Aug. 26, 1992, 106 Stat. 933; Pub.L. 103–322, Title XXVIII, § 280005(b), (c)(1), (3), Sept. 13, 1994, 108 Stat. 2096, 2097.)

[1] So in original.

HISTORICAL AND STATUTORY NOTES

References in Text

Section 235(a)(1)(B)(ii) of the Sentencing Reform Act of 1984, referred to in subsec. (c), is section 235(a)(1)(B)(ii) of Pub.L. 98–473, which is set out as a note under section 3551 of Title 18, Crimes and Criminal Procedure.

Effective and Applicability Provisions

1984 Acts. Section effective Oct. 12, 1984, see section 235(a)(1)(B)(i) of Pub.L. 98–473, as amended, set out as a note under section 3551 of Title 18, Crimes and Criminal Procedure.

Commencement of Terms of First Members of Commission

For provisions directing that, for purposes of subsec. (a) of this section, the terms of the first members of the United States Sentencing Commission shall not begin to run until the sentencing guidelines go into effect pursuant to section 235(a)(1)(B)(ii) of Pub.L. 98–473, set out as an Effective Date note under section 3551 of Title 18, Crimes and Criminal Procedure, see section 235(a)(2) of Pub.L. 98–473, as amended, set out as an Effective Date note under section 3551 of Title 18.

§ 993. Powers and duties of Chair

The Chair shall—

(a) call and preside at meetings of the Commission, which shall be held for at least two weeks in each quarter after the members of the Commission hold part-time positions; and

(b) direct—

(1) the preparation of requests for appropriations for the Commission; and

(2) the use of funds made available to the Commission.

(Added Pub.L. 98–473, Title II, § 217(a), Oct. 12, 1984, 98 Stat. 2019, and amended Pub.L. 99–22, § 1(2), Apr. 15, 1985, 99 Stat. 46; Pub.L. 99–646, § 5, Nov. 10, 1986, 100 Stat. 3592; Pub.L. 103–322, Title XXVIII, § 280005(c)(1), Sept. 13, 1994, 108 Stat. 2097.)

HISTORICAL AND STATUTORY NOTES

Effective and Applicability Provisions

1984 Acts. Section effective Oct. 12, 1984, see section 235(a)(1)(B)(i) of Pub.L. 98–473, as amended, set out as a note under section 3551 of Title 18, Crimes and Criminal Procedure.

§ 994. Duties of the Commission

(a) The Commission, by affirmative vote of at least four members of the Commission, and pursuant to its rules and regulations and consistent with all pertinent provisions of any Federal statute shall promulgate and distribute to all courts of the United States and to the United States Probation System—

(1) guidelines, as described in this section, for use of a sentencing court in determining the sentence to be imposed in a criminal case, including—

(A) a determination whether to impose a sentence to probation, a fine, or a term of imprisonment;

(B) a determination as to the appropriate amount of a fine or the appropriate length of a term of probation or a term of imprisonment;

(C) a determination whether a sentence to a term of imprisonment should include a requirement that the defendant be placed on a term of supervised release after imprisonment, and, if so, the appropriate length of such a term;

(D) a determination whether multiple sentences to terms of imprisonment should be ordered to run concurrently or consecutively; and

(E) a determination under paragraphs (6) and (11) of section 3563(b) of title 18;

(2) general policy statements regarding application of the guidelines or any other aspect of sentencing or sentence implementation that in the view of the Commission would further the purposes set forth in section 3553(a)(2) of title 18, United States Code, including the appropriate use of—

(A) the sanctions set forth in sections 3554, 3555, and 3556 of title 18;

(B) the conditions of probation and supervised release set forth in sections 3563(b) and 3583(d) of title 18;

(C) the sentence modification provisions set forth in sections 3563(c), 3564, 3573, and 3582(c) of title 18;

(D) the fine imposition provisions set forth in section 3572 of title 18;

(E) the authority granted under rule 11(e)(2) of the Federal Rules of Criminal Procedure to accept or reject a plea agreement entered into pursuant to rule 11(e)(1); and

(F) the temporary release provisions set forth in section 3622 of title 18, and the prerelease custody provisions set forth in section 3624(c) of title 18; and

(3) guidelines or general policy statements regarding the appropriate use of the provisions for revocation of probation set forth in section 3565 of title 18, and the provisions for modification of the term or conditions of supervised release and revocation of supervised release set forth in section 3583(e) of title 18.

(b)(1) The Commission, in the guidelines promulgated pursuant to subsection (a)(1), shall, for each category of offense involving each category of defendant, establish a sentencing range that is consistent with all pertinent provisions of title 18, United States Code.

(2) If a sentence specified by the guidelines includes a term of imprisonment, the maximum of the range established for such a term shall not exceed the minimum of that range by more than the greater of 25 percent or 6 months, except that, if the minimum term of the range is 30 years or more, the maximum may be life imprisonment.

(c) The Commission, in establishing categories of offenses for use in the guidelines and policy statements governing the imposition of sentences of probation, a fine, or imprisonment, governing the imposition of other authorized sanctions, governing the size of a fine or the length of a term of probation, imprisonment, or supervised release, and governing the conditions of probation, supervised release, or imprisonment, shall consider whether the following matters, among others, have any relevance to the nature, extent, place of service, or other incidents [1] of an appropriate sentence, and shall take them into account only to the extent that they do have relevance—

(1) the grade of the offense;

(2) the circumstances under which the offense was committed which mitigate or aggravate the seriousness of the offense;

(3) the nature and degree of the harm caused by the offense, including whether it involved property, irreplaceable property, a person, a number of persons, or a breach of public trust;

(4) the community view of the gravity of the offense;

(5) the public concern generated by the offense;

(6) the deterrent effect a particular sentence may have on the commission of the offense by others; and

(7) the current incidence of the offense in the community and in the Nation as a whole.

(d) The Commission in establishing categories of defendants for use in the guidelines and policy statements governing the imposition of sentences of probation, a fine, or imprisonment, governing the imposition of other authorized sanctions, governing the size of a fine or the length of a term of probation, imprisonment, or supervised release, and governing the conditions of probation, supervised release, or imprisonment, shall consider whether the following matters, among others, with respect to a defendant, have any relevance to the nature, extent, place of service, or other incidents [1] of an appropriate sentence, and shall take them into account only to the extent that they do have relevance—

(1) age;

(2) education;

(3) vocational skills;

(4) mental and emotional condition to the extent that such condition mitigates the defendant's culpability or to the extent that such condition is otherwise plainly relevant;

(5) physical condition, including drug dependence;

(6) previous employment record;

(7) family ties and responsibilities;

(8) community ties;

(9) role in the offense;

(10) criminal history; and

(11) degree of dependence upon criminal activity for a livelihood.

The Commission shall assure that the guidelines and policy statements are entirely neutral as to the race, sex, national origin, creed, and socioeconomic status of offenders.

(e) The Commission shall assure that the guidelines and policy statements, in recommending a term of imprisonment or length of a term of imprisonment, reflect the general inappropriateness of considering the education, vocational skills, employment record, family ties and responsibilities, and community ties of the defendant.

(f) The Commission, in promulgating guidelines pursuant to subsection (a)(1), shall promote the purposes set forth in section 991(b)(1), with particular attention to the requirements of subsection 991(b)(1)(B) for providing certainty and fairness in sentencing and reducing unwarranted sentence disparities.

(g) The Commission, in promulgating guidelines pursuant to subsection (a)(1) to meet the purposes of sentencing as set forth in section 3553(a)(2) of title 18, United States Code, shall take into account the nature and capacity of the penal, correctional, and other facilities and services available, and shall make recommendations concerning any change or expansion in the nature or capacity of such facilities and services that might become necessary as a result of the guidelines promulgated pursuant to the provisions of this chapter. The sentencing guidelines prescribed under this chapter shall be formulated to minimize the likelihood that the Federal prison population will exceed the capacity of the Federal prisons, as determined by the Commission.

(h) The Commission shall assure that the guidelines specify a sentence to a term of imprisonment at or near the maximum term authorized for categories of defendants in which the defendant is eighteen years old or older and—

(1) has been convicted of a felony that is—

(A) a crime of violence; or

(B) an offense described in section 401 of the Controlled Substances Act (21 U.S.C. 841), sections 1002(a), 1005, and 1009 of the Controlled Substances Import and Export Act (21 U.S.C. 952(a), 955, and 959), and chapter 705 of title 46; and

(2) has previously been convicted of two or more prior felonies, each of which is—

(A) a crime of violence; or

(B) an offense described in section 401 of the Controlled Substances Act (21 U.S.C. 841), sections 1002(a), 1005, and 1009 of the Controlled Substances Import and Export Act (21 U.S.C. 952(a), 955, and 959), and chapter 705 of title 46.

(i) The Commission shall assure that the guidelines specify a sentence to a substantial term of imprisonment for categories of defendants in which the defendant—

(1) has a history of two or more prior Federal, State, or local felony convictions for offenses committed on different occasions;

(2) committed the offense as part of a pattern of criminal conduct from which the defendant derived a substantial portion of the defendant's income;

(3) committed the offense in furtherance of a conspiracy with three or more persons engaging in a pattern of racketeering activity in which the defendant participated in a managerial or supervisory capacity;

(4) committed a crime of violence that constitutes a felony while on release pending trial, sentence, or appeal from a Federal, State, or local felony for which he was ultimately convicted; or

(5) committed a felony that is set forth in section 401 or 1010 of the Comprehensive Drug Abuse Prevention and Control Act of 1970 (21 U.S.C. 841 and 960), and that involved trafficking in a substantial quantity of a controlled substance.

(j) The Commission shall insure that the guidelines reflect the general appropriateness of imposing a sentence other than imprisonment in cases in which the defendant is a first offender who has not been convicted of a crime of violence or an otherwise serious offense, and the general appropriateness of imposing a term of imprisonment on a person convicted of a crime of violence that results in serious bodily injury.

(k) The Commission shall insure that the guidelines reflect the inappropriateness of imposing a sentence to a term of imprisonment for the purpose of rehabilitating the defendant or providing the defendant with needed educational or vocational training, medical care, or other correctional treatment.

(*l*) The Commission shall insure that the guidelines promulgated pursuant to subsection (a)(1) reflect—

(1) the appropriateness of imposing an incremental penalty for each offense in a case in which a defendant is convicted of—

(A) multiple offenses committed in the same course of conduct that result in the exercise of ancillary jurisdiction over one or more of the offenses; and

(B) multiple offenses committed at different times, including those cases in which the subsequent offense is a violation of section 3146 (penalty for failure to appear) or is committed while the person is released pursuant to the provisions of section 3147 (penalty for an offense committed while on release) of title 18; and

(2) the general inappropriateness of imposing consecutive terms of imprisonment for an offense of conspiring to commit an offense or soliciting commission of an offense and for an offense that was the sole object of the conspiracy or solicitation.

(m) The Commission shall insure that the guidelines reflect the fact that, in many cases, current sentences do not accurately reflect the seriousness of the offense. This will require that, as a starting point in its development of the initial sets of guidelines for particular categories of cases, the Commission ascertain the average sentences imposed in such categories of cases prior to the creation of the Commission, and in cases involving sentences to terms of imprisonment, the length of such terms actually served. The Commission shall not be bound by such average sentences, and shall independently develop a sentencing range that is consistent with the purposes of sentencing described in section 3553(a)(2) of title 18, United States Code.

(n) The Commission shall assure that the guidelines reflect the general appropriateness of imposing a lower sentence than would otherwise be imposed, including a sentence that is lower than that established by statute as a minimum sentence, to take into account a defendant's substantial assistance in the investigation or prosecution of another person who has committed an offense.

(*o*) The Commission periodically shall review and revise, in consideration of comments and data coming to its attention, the guidelines promulgated pursuant to the provisions of this section. In fulfilling its duties and in exercising its powers, the Commission shall consult with authorities on, and individual and institutional representatives of, various aspects of the Federal criminal justice system. The United States Probation System, the Bureau of Prisons, the Judicial Conference of the United States, the Criminal Division of the United States Department of Justice, and a representative of the Federal Public Defenders shall submit to the Commission any observations, comments, or questions pertinent to the work of the Commission whenever they believe such communication would be useful, and shall, at least annually, submit to the Commission a written report commenting on the operation of the Commission's guidelines, suggesting changes in the guidelines that appear to be warranted, and otherwise assessing the Commission's work.

(p) The Commission, at or after the beginning of a regular session of Congress, but not later than the first day of May, may promulgate under subsection (a) of this section and submit to Congress amendments to the guidelines and modifications to previously submitted amendments that have not taken effect, including modifications to the effective dates of such amendments. Such an amendment or modification shall be accompanied by a statement of the reasons therefor and shall take effect on a date specified by the Commission, which shall be no earlier than 180 days after being so submitted and no later than the first day of November of the calendar year in which the amendment or modification is submitted, except to the extent that the effective date is revised or the amendment is otherwise modified or disapproved by Act of Congress.

(q) The Commission and the Bureau of Prisons shall submit to Congress an analysis and recommendations concerning maximum utilization of resources to deal effectively with the Federal prison population. Such report shall be based upon consideration of a variety of alternatives, including—

(1) modernization of existing facilities;

(2) inmate classification and periodic review of such classification for use in placing inmates in the least restrictive facility necessary to ensure adequate security; and

(3) use of existing Federal facilities, such as those currently within military jurisdiction.

(r) The Commission, not later than two years after the initial set of sentencing guidelines promulgated under subsection (a) goes into effect, and thereafter whenever it finds it advisable, shall recommend to the Congress that it raise or lower the grades, or otherwise modify the maximum penalties, of those offenses for which such an adjustment appears appropriate.

(s) The Commission shall give due consideration to any petition filed by a defendant requesting modification of the guidelines utilized in the sentencing of such defendant, on the basis of changed circumstances unrelated to the defendant, including changes in—

(1) the community view of the gravity of the offense;

(2) the public concern generated by the offense; and

(3) the deterrent effect particular sentences may have on the commission of the offense by others.

(t) The Commission, in promulgating general policy statements regarding the sentencing modification provisions in section 3582(c)(1)(A) of title 18, shall describe what should be considered extraordinary and compelling reasons for sentence reduction, including the criteria to be applied and a list of specific examples. Rehabilitation of the defendant alone shall not be considered an extraordinary and compelling reason.

(u) If the Commission reduces the term of imprisonment recommended in the guidelines applicable to a particular offense or category of offenses, it shall specify in what circumstances and by what amount the sentences of prisoners serving terms of imprisonment for the offense may be reduced.

(v) The Commission shall ensure that the general policy statements promulgated pursuant to subsection (a)(2) include a policy limiting consecutive terms of imprisonment for an offense involving a violation of a general prohibition and for an offense involving a violation of a specific prohibition encompassed within the general prohibition.

(w)(1) The Chief Judge of each district court shall ensure that, within 30 days following entry of judgment in every criminal case, the sentencing court submits to the Commission, in a format approved and required by the Commission, a written report of the sentence, the offense for which it is imposed, the age, race, sex of the offender, and information regarding factors made relevant by the guidelines. The report shall also include—

(A) the judgment and commitment order;

(B) the written statement of reasons for the sentence imposed (which shall include the reason for any departure from the otherwise applicable guideline range and which shall be stated on the written statement of reasons form issued by the Judicial Conference and approved by the United States Sentencing Commission);

(C) any plea agreement;

(D) the indictment or other charging document;

(E) the presentence report; and

(F) any other information as the Commission finds appropriate.

The information referred to in subparagraphs (A) through (F) shall be submitted by the sentencing court in a format approved and required by the Commission.

(2) The Commission shall, upon request, make available to the House and Senate Committees on the Judiciary, the written reports and all underlying records accompanying those reports described in this section, as well as other records received from courts.

(3) The Commission shall submit to Congress at least annually an analysis of these documents, any recommendations for legislation that the Commission concludes is warranted by that analysis, and an accounting of those districts that the Commission believes have not submitted the appropriate information and documents required by this section.

(4) The Commission shall make available to the Attorney General, upon request, such data files as the Commission itself may assemble or maintain in electronic form as a result of the information submitted under paragraph (1). Such data files shall be made available in electronic form and shall include all data fields requested, including the identity of the sentencing judge.

(x) The provisions of section 553 of title 5, relating to publication in the Federal Register and public hearing procedure, shall apply to the promulgation of guidelines pursuant to this section.

(y) The Commission, in promulgating guidelines pursuant to subsection (a)(1), may include, as a component of a fine, the expected costs to the Government of any imprisonment, supervised release, or probation sentence that is ordered.

(Added Pub.L. 98–473, Title II, § 217(a), Oct. 12, 1984, 98 Stat. 2019, and amended Pub.L. 99–217, § 3, Dec. 26, 1985, 99 Stat. 1728; Pub.L. 99–363, § 2, July 11, 1986, 100 Stat. 770; Pub.L. 99–570, Title I, §§ 1006(b), 1008, Oct. 27, 1986, 100 Stat. 3207–7; Pub.L. 99–646, §§ 6(b), 56, Nov. 10, 1986, 100 Stat. 3592, 3611; Pub.L. 100–182, §§ 16(b), 23, Dec. 7, 1987, 101 Stat. 1269, 1271; Pub.L. 100–690, Title VII, §§ 7083, 7103(b), 7109, Nov. 18, 1988, 102 Stat. 4408, 4417, 4419; Pub.L. 103–322, Title II, § 20403(b), Title XXVIII, § 280005(c)(4), Title XXXIII, § 330003(f)(1), Sept. 13, 1994, 108 Stat. 1825, 2097, 2141; Pub.L. 108–21, Title IV, § 401(h), (k), Apr. 30, 2003, 117 Stat. 672, 674; Pub.L. 109–177, Title VII, § 735, Mar. 9, 2006, 120 Stat. 271; Pub.L. 109–304, § 17(f)(1), Oct. 6, 2006, 120 Stat. 1708.)

[1] So in original. Probably should be "incidence".

Application of Sentencing Guidelines

See Blakely v. Washington, 124 S.Ct. 2531 (2004); U.S. v. Booker, U.S. v. Fanfan, 125 S.Ct. 738 (2005).

HISTORICAL AND STATUTORY NOTES

References in Text

Paragraphs (6) and (11) of section 3563(b) of Title 18, referred to in subsec. (a)(1)(E), were renumbered paragraphs (5) and (10), respectively, of section 3563(b) by Pub.L. 104–132, Title II, § 203(2)(B), Apr. 24, 1996, 110 Stat. 1227.

The Federal Rules of Criminal Procedure, referred to in subsec. (a)(2)(E), are set out in Title 18, Crimes and Criminal Procedure.

Chapter 705 of Title 46, referred to in subsecs. (h)(1)(B), (2)(B), is Maritime Drug Law Enforcement, 46 U.S.C.A. § 70501 et seq.

Codifications

Amendment by Pub.L. 99–646 to subsec. (t) of this section has been executed to subsec. (u) as the probable intent of Congress in view of prior redesignation of subsec. (t) as (u) by Pub.L. 99–570.

Effective and Applicability Provisions

1987 Acts. Amendment by Pub.L. 100–182 applicable with respect to offenses committed after Dec. 7, 1987, see section 26 of Pub.L. 100–182, set out as a note under section 3006A of Title 18, Crimes and Criminal Procedure.

1984 Acts. Section effective Oct. 12, 1984, see section 235(a)(1)(B)(i) of Pub.L. 98–473, as amended, set out as a note under section 3551 of Title 18, Crimes and Criminal Procedure.

Termination of Reporting Requirements

For termination of reporting provisions of subsec. (p) of this section, relating to amendments to guidelines in determining the sentence to be imposed in a criminal case, effective May 15, 2000, see Pub.L. 104–66, § 3003, as amended, set out as a note under 31 U.S.C.A. § 1113, and the 13th item on page 13 of House Document No. 103–7, which references subsec. (*o*) of this section, which was subsequently renumbered subsec. (p) of this section.

For termination, effective May 15, 2000, of reporting provisions of this section, pertaining to the U.S. Sentencing Commission, Bureau of Prisons, analysis and recommendations concerning maximum utilization of resources to deal with Federal prison population, see Pub.L. 104–66, § 3003, as amended, set out as a note under 31 U.S.C.A. § 1113, and the 9th item on page 147 of House Document No. 103–7, which references subsec. (p) of this section, which was subsequently renumbered as subsec. (q).

For termination, effective May 15, 2000, of provisions in subsec. (w) of this section relating to requirement that the Commission submit to Congress at least annually an analysis of reports and recommendations for legislation that the Commission concludes is warranted by that analysis, see Pub.L. 104–66, § 3003, as amended, set out as a note under 31 U.S.C.A. § 1113 and House Document No. 103–7, page 13.

Short Title

1997 Amendments. Pub.L. 105–101, § 1, Nov. 19, 1997, 111 Stat. 2202, provided that: "This Act [enacting a provision set out as a note under this section] may be cited as the 'Veterans' Cemetery Protection Act of 1997'."

1995 Acts. Pub.L. 104–71, § 1, Dec. 23, 1995, 109 Stat. 774, provided that: "This Act [amending section 2423 of Title 18, Crimes and Criminal Procedure, and enacting provisions set out as a note under this section] may be cited as the 'Sex Crimes Against Children Prevention Act of 1995'."

Provisions for Review, Promulgation, or Amendment of Federal Sentencing Guidelines

Pub.L. 109–476, § 4, Jan. 12, 2007, 120 Stat. 3571.—Offenses involving obtaining confidential phone records information by fraud or related activity.

Pub.L. 109–295, Title V, § 551(d), Oct. 4, 2006, 120 Stat. 1390.—Offenses involving border tunnels and passages under 18 U.S.C.A. § 554 (set out second).

Pub.L. 109–248, Title I, § 141(b), July 27, 2006, 120 Stat. 602.—Offenses involving failure to register as a sex offender.

Pub.L. 109–181, § 1(c), Mar. 16, 2006, 120 Stat. 287.—Offenses involving trafficking in counterfeit labels, illicit labels, counterfeit documentation or packaging, or counterfeit goods or services.

Pub.L. 109–177, Title III, § 307(c), Mar. 9, 2006, 120 Stat. 240.—Goods or chattel within interstate or foreign shipment or commerce (any offense under 18 U.S.C.A. § 659 or 2311).

Pub.L. 109–162, Title XI, § 1191(c), Jan. 5, 2006, 119 Stat. 3129.—Federal offense while wearing or displaying insignia and uniform received in violation of 18 U.S.C.A. § 716.

Pub.L. 109–9, Title I, § 105, Apr. 27, 2005, 119 Stat. 222.—Intellectual property rights crimes, including any offense under 17 U.S.C.A. §§ 506, 1201, or 1202, or 18 U.S.C.A. §§ 2318, 2319, 2319A, 2319B, or 2320.

Pub.L. 108–482, Title II, § 204(b), Dec. 23, 2004, 118 Stat. 3917.—Felony offense carried out online that may be facilitated through use of a domain name registered with materially false contact information.

Pub.L. 108–458, Title VI, § 6703(b), Dec. 17, 2004, 118 Stat. 3766.—Offenses involving international or domestic terrorism.

Pub.L. 108–358, § 3, Oct. 22, 2004, 118 Stat. 1664.—Offenses involving anabolic steroids.

Pub.L. 108–275, § 5, July 15, 2004, 118 Stat. 833.—Identity theft offenses involving an abuse of position.

Pub.L. 108–187, § 4(b), Dec. 16, 2003, 117 Stat. 2705.—Electronic mail fraud.

Pub.L. 108–21, Title I, § 104(a), Apr. 30, 2003, 117 Stat. 653.—Kidnapping.

Pub.L. 108–21, Title IV, § 401(b), (g), (i), (j)(1) to (4), and (m), Apr. 30, 2003, 117 Stat. 668 to 675.—Child crimes and sexual offenses, child pornography, downward departures, and acceptance of responsibility.

Pub.L. 108–21, Title V, § 504(c)(2), Apr. 30, 2003, 117 Stat. 682.—Offenses involving obscene visual representations of sexual abuse of children.

Pub.L. 108–21, Title V, § 512, Apr. 30, 2003, 117 Stat. 685.—Offenses involving interstate travel to engage in sexual act with a juvenile.

Pub.L. 108–21, Title V, § 513(c), Apr. 30, 2003, 117 Stat. 685.—Offenses involving distribution of images, whether real or computer generated, that contain, or appear to contain, obscene visual depictions of a minor engaging in sexually explicit conduct.

Pub.L. 108–21, Title VI, § 608(e), Apr. 30, 2003, 117 Stat. 691.—Offenses involving gamma hydroxybutyric acid (GHB).

Pub.L. 107–296, Title II, § 225(b), Nov. 25, 2002, 116 Stat. 2156.—Computer fraud and abuse.

Pub.L. 107–273, Div. C, Title I, § 11008(e), Nov. 2, 2002, 116 Stat. 1819.—Threats.

Pub.L. 107–204, Title VIII, § 805, July 30, 2002, 116 Stat. 802.—Destruction, alteration, or falsification of records.

Pub.L. 107–204, Title IX, § 905, July 30, 2002, 116 Stat. 805.—White-collar crimes.

Pub.L. 107–204, Title XI, § 1104, July 30, 2002, 116 Stat. 808.—Securities and accounting fraud and related offenses.

Pub.L. 107–155, § 314, Mar. 27, 2002, 116 Stat. 107.—Violations of Federal Election Campaign Act of 1971 and related election laws.

Pub.L. 107–56, Title VIII, § 814(f), Oct. 26, 2001, 115 Stat. 384.—Computer fraud and abuse.

Pub.L. 106–420, § 3, Nov. 1, 2000, 114 Stat. 1868.—Higher education financial assistance fraud.

Pub.L. 106–386, Div. B, Title I, § 1107(b)(2), Oct. 28, 2000, 114 Stat. 1498.—Interstate stalking.

Pub.L. 106–310, Div. B, Title XXXVI, § 3611, Oct. 17, 2000, 114 Stat. 1228.—Manufacture of and trafficking in amphetamine.

Pub.L. 106–310, Div. B, Title XXXVI, § 3612, Oct. 17, 2000, 114 Stat. 1228.—Manufacture of amphetamine or methamphetamine.

Pub.L. 106–310, Div. B, Title XXXVI, § 3651, Oct. 17, 2000, 114 Stat. 1238.—Trafficking in list I chemicals.

Pub.L. 106–310, Div. B, Title XXXVI, §§ 3663, 3664, Oct. 17, 2000, 114 Stat. 1242, 1244.—Manufacture of or trafficking in Ecstasy.

Pub.L. 106–160, § 3, Dec. 9, 1999, 113 Stat. 1774.—Electronic theft offenses.

Pub.L. 105–318, § 4, Oct. 30, 1998, 112 Stat. 3009.—Crimes against intellectual property.

Pub.L. 105–314, Title V, Oct. 30, 1998, 112 Stat. 2980.—Sexual abuse, transportation for illegal sexual activity, and distribution of pornography.

Pub.L. 105–184, § 6, June 23, 1998, 112 Stat. 521.—Telemarketing fraud.

Pub.L. 105–172, § 2(e), Apr. 24, 1998, 112 Stat. 55.—Wireless telephone cloning.

Pub.L. 105–147, § 2(g), Dec. 16, 1997, 111 Stat. 2680.—Crimes against intellectual property.

Pub.L. 105–101, Nov. 19, 1997, 111 Stat. 2202; Pub. L. 105–368, Title IV, § 403(d)(1), Nov. 11, 1998, 112 Stat. 3339.—Offenses against property at national cemeteries.

Pub.L. 104–305, § 2(b)(3), Oct. 13, 1996, 110 Stat. 3808.—Offenses involving flunitrazepam.

Pub.L. 104–237, Title II, § 203(b), Oct. 3, 1996, 110 Stat. 3102.—Manufacture of methamphetamine.

Pub.L. 104–237, Title III, § 301, Oct. 3, 1996, 110 Stat. 3105.—Manufacture of and trafficking in methamphetamine.

Pub.L. 104–237, Title III, § 302(c), Oct. 3, 1996, 110 Stat. 3105.—Offenses involving list I chemicals.

Pub.L. 104–237, Title III, § 303, Oct. 3, 1996, 110 Stat. 3106.—Dangerous handling of controlled substances.

Pub.L. 104–208, Div. C, Title II, § 203(e), Sept. 30, 1996, 110 Stat. 3009–566.—Smuggling, transporting, harboring, and inducing aliens.

Pub.L. 104–208, Div. C, Title II, § 211(b), Sept. 30, 1996, 110 Stat. 3009–569.—Fraudulent acquisition and use of government-issued documents.

Pub.L. 104–208, Div. C, Title II, § 218(b), (c), Sept. 30, 1996, 110 Stat. 3009–573, 3009–574.—Involuntary servitude.

Pub.L. 104–208, Div. C, Title III, § 333, Sept. 30, 1996, 110 Stat. 3009–634.—Conspiring with or assisting an alien to import, export, possess, manufacture, or distribute a controlled substance.

Pub.L. 104–208, Div. C, Title III, § 334, Sept. 30, 1996, 110 Stat. 3009–635.—Failure to depart, illegal reentry, and passport and visa fraud.

Pub.L. 104–201, Div. A, Title XIV, § 1423, Sept. 23, 1996, 110 Stat. 2725; Pub. L. 105–261, Div. A, Title X, § 1069(c)(1), Oct. 17, 1998, 112 Stat. 2136.—Offenses relating to importation and exportation of nuclear, biological, or chemical weapons or technologies.

Pub.L. 104–132, Title II, § 208, Apr. 24, 1996, 110 Stat. 1240.—Mandatory victim restitution.

Pub.L. 104–132, Title VII, § 730, Apr. 24, 1996, 110 Stat. 1303.—International terrorism.

Pub.L. 104–132, Title VIII, § 805, Apr. 24, 1996, 110 Stat. 1305.—Terrorist activity damaging Federal interest computer.

Pub.L. 104–132, Title VIII, § 807(h), Apr. 24, 1996, 110 Stat. 1308.—International counterfeiting of United States currency; codified at 18 U.S.C.A. § 470 note.

Pub.L. 104–71, §§ 1–4, Dec. 23, 1995, 109 Stat. 774.—Sex crimes against children.

Pub.L. 103–322, Title IV, § 40111(b), Sept. 13, 1994, 108 Stat. 1903.—Sexual abuse by repeat sex offender.

Pub.L. 103–322, Title IV, § 40112, Sept. 13, 1994, 108 Stat. 1903.—Aggravated sexual abuse or sexual abuse.

Pub.L. 103–322, Title IV, § 40503(c), Sept. 13, 1994, 108 Stat. 1947.—Intentional transmission of HIV; codified at 42 U.S.C.A. § 10607(c).

Pub.L. 103–322, Title VIII, § 80001(b), Sept. 13, 1994, 108 Stat. 1986.—Importing, exporting, possessing, manufacturing, and distributing a controlled substance.

Pub.L. 103–322, Title IX, § 90102, Sept. 13, 1994, 108 Stat. 1987.—Drug-dealing in "drug-free" zones; codified at 42 U.S.C.A. § 14051.

Pub.L. 103–322, Title IX, § 90103(b), Sept. 13, 1994, 108 Stat. 1987.—Use or distribution of illegal drugs in the Federal prisons; codified at 42 U.S.C.A. § 14052(b).

Pub.L. 103–322, Title XI, § 110501, Sept. 13, 1994, 108 Stat. 2015.—Use of semiautomatic firearm during crime of violence or drug trafficking.

Pub.L. 103–322, Title XI, § 110502, Sept. 13, 1994, 108 Stat. 2015.—Second offense of using explosive to commit felony.

Pub.L. 103–322, Title XI, § 110512, Sept. 13, 1994, 108 Stat. 2019.—Using firearm in commission of counterfeiting or forgery.

Pub.L. 103–322, Title XI, § 110513, Sept. 13, 1994, 108 Stat. 2019.—Firearms possession by violent felons and serious drug offenders.

Pub.L. 103–322, Title XII, § 120004, Sept. 13, 1994, 108 Stat. 2022.—Felonies promoting international terrorism.

Pub.L. 103–322, Title XIV, § 140008, Sept. 13, 1994, 108 Stat. 2033.—Solicitation of minor to commit crime.

Pub.L. 103–322, Title XVIII, § 180201(c), Sept. 13, 1994, 108 Stat. 2047.—Possession or distribution of drugs at truck stops or safety rest areas.

Pub.L. 103–322, Title XXIV, § 240002, Sept. 13, 1994, 108 Stat. 2081, as amended Pub.L. 104–294, Title VI,

§ 604(b)(10), Oct. 11, 1996, 110 Stat. 3507.—Crimes against elderly victims.

Pub.L. 103–322, Title XXV, § 250003, Sept. 13, 1994, 108 Stat. 2085.—Fraud against older victims.

Pub.L. 103–322, Title XXVIII, § 280003, Sept. 13, 1994, 108 Stat. 2096.—Hate crimes.

Pub.L. 102–141, Title VI, § 632, Oct. 28, 1991, 105 Stat. 876.—Sexual abuse or exploitation of minors.

Pub.L. 101–647, Title III, § 321, Nov. 29, 1990, 104 Stat. 4817.—Sexual crimes against children.

Pub.L. 101–647, Title XXV, § 2507, Nov. 29, 1990, 104 Stat. 4862.—Major bank crimes.

Pub.L. 101–647, Title XXVII, § 2701, Nov. 29, 1990, 104 Stat. 4912.—Methamphetamine offenses.

Pub.L. 101–73, Title IX, § 961(m), Aug. 9, 1989, 103 Stat. 501.—Offenses substantially jeopardizing safety and soundness of federally insured financial institutions.

Pub.L. 100–700, § 2(b), Nov. 19, 1988, 102 Stat. 4631.—Major fraud against the United States.

Pub.L. 100–690, Title VI, § 6453, Nov. 18, 1988, 102 Stat. 4371.—Importation of controlled substances by aircraft and other vessels.

Pub.L. 100–690, Title VI, § 6454, Nov. 18, 1988, 102 Stat. 4372.—Drug offenses involving children.

Pub.L. 100–690, Title VI, § 6468(c), (d), Nov. 18, 1988, 102 Stat. 4376.—Drug offenses within Federal prisons.

Pub.L. 100–690, Title VI, § 6482(c), Nov. 18, 1988, 102 Stat. 4382.—Common carrier operation under influence of alcohol or drugs.

[Except as otherwise provided, amendments by Pub.L. 107–155 generally effective Nov. 6, 2002, see Pub.L. 107–155, § 402, set out as a note under 2 U.S.C.A. § 431, for effective date provisions, modification of contribution limits applicability to run off elections, applicability and transitional rules for spending of soft money of national political parties and promulgation of regulation provisions.]

[Amendments by Pub.L. 108–187 effective Jan. 1, 2004, see section 16 of Pub.L. 108–187, set out as a note under 15 U.S.C.A. § 7701.]

Provision of Emergency Amendment Authority for Sentencing Commission

Pub.L. 109–76, § 3, Sept. 29, 2005, 119 Stat. 2035, provided that:

"In accordance with the procedure set forth in section 21(a) of the Sentencing Act of 1987 (Public Law 100–182) [Pub.L. 100–182, § 21(a), Dec. 7, 1987, 101 Stat. 1271, set out as a note under this section], as though the authority under that Act had not expired, the United States Sentencing Commission shall—

"**(1)** not later than 60 days after the date of the enactment of this Act [Sept. 29, 2005], amend the Federal sentencing guidelines, commentary, and policy statements to implement section 6703 of the Intelligence Reform and Terrorism Prevention Act of 2004 (Public Law 108–458) [Pub.L. 108–458, Title VI, § 6703, Dec. 17, 2004, 118 Stat. 3766, amending 18 U.S.C.A. §§ 1001 and 1505 and enacting a provision referenced in a table under this section]; and

"**(2)** not later than 180 days after the date of the enactment of this Act [Sept. 29, 2005], amend the Federal sentencing guidelines, commentary, and policy statements to implement section 3 of the Anabolic Steroid Control Act of 2004 (Public Law 108–358) [Pub.L. 108–358, § 3, Oct. 22, 2004, 118 Stat. 1664, enacting a provision referenced in a table under this section]."

Cocaine and Crack Sentences and Sentences for Money Laundering and Other Unlawful Activity; Reduction of Sentencing Disparities

Pub.L. 104–38, Oct. 30, 1995, 109 Stat. 334, provided that:

"**Section 1. Disapproval of Amendments Relating to Lowering of Crack Sentences and Sentences for Money Laundering and Transactions in Property Derived From Unlawful Activity.**

"In accordance with section 994(p) of title 28, United States Code [subsec. (p) of this section], amendments numbered 5 and 18 of the 'Amendments to the Sentencing Guidelines, Policy Statements, and Official Commentary', submitted by the United States Sentencing Commission to Congress on May 1, 1995, are hereby disapproved and shall not take effect.

"**Sec. 2. Reduction of Sentencing Disparity.**

"**(a) Recommendations.**—

"**(1) In general.**—The United States Sentencing Commission shall submit to Congress recommendations (and an explanation therefor), regarding changes to the statutes and sentencing guidelines governing sentences for unlawful manufacturing, importing, exporting, and trafficking of cocaine, and like offenses, including unlawful possession, possession with intent to commit any of the forgoing offenses, and attempt and conspiracy to commit any of the forgoing offenses. The recommendations shall reflect the following considerations—

"**(A)** the sentence imposed for trafficking in a quantity of crack cocaine should generally exceed the sentence imposed for trafficking in a like quantity of powder cocaine;

"**(B)** high-level wholesale cocaine traffickers, organizers, and leaders, of criminal activities should generally receive longer sentences than low-level retail cocaine traffickers and those who played a minor or minimal role in such criminal activity;

"**(C)** if the Government establishes that a defendant who traffics in powder cocaine has knowledge that such cocaine will be converted into crack cocaine prior to its distribution to individual users, the defendant should be treated at sentencing as though the defendant had trafficked in crack cocaine; and

"**(D)** an enhanced sentence should generally be imposed on a defendant who, in the course of an offense described in this subsection—

"**(i)** murders or causes serious bodily injury to an individual;

"**(ii)** uses a dangerous weapon;

"**(iii)** uses or possesses a firearm;

"**(iv)** involves a juvenile or a woman who the defendant knows or should know to be pregnant;

"**(v)** engages in a continuing criminal enterprise or commits other criminal offenses in order to facilitate his drug trafficking activities;

"**(vi)** knows, or should know, that he is involving an unusually vulnerable person;

"(vii) restrains a victim;

"(viii) traffics in cocaine within 500 feet of a school;

"(ix) obstructs justice;

"(x) has a significant prior criminal record; or

"(xi) is an organizer or leader of drug trafficking activities involving five or more persons.

"(2) Ratio.—The recommendations described in the preceding subsection shall propose revision of the drug quantity ratio of crack cocaine to powder cocaine under the relevant statutes and guidelines in a manner consistent with the ratios set for other drugs and consistent with the objectives set forth in section 3553(a) of title 28 United States Code [reference to section 3553(a) of Title 18, Crimes and Criminal Procedure, was probably intended].

"(b) Study.—No later than May 1, 1996, the Department of Justice shall submit to the Judiciary Committees of the Senate and House of Representatives a report on the charging and plea practices of Federal prosecutors with respect to the offense of money laundering. Such study shall include an account of the steps taken or to be taken by the Justice Department to ensure consistency and appropriateness in the use of the money laundering statute. The Sentencing Commission shall submit to the Judiciary Committees comments on the study prepared by the Department of Justice."

Emergency Guidelines Promulgation Authority

Pub.L. 100–182, § 21, Dec. 7, 1987, 101 Stat. 1271, provided that:

"(a) In general.—In the case of—

"(1) an invalidated sentencing guideline;

"(2) the creation of a new offense or amendment of an existing offense; or

"(3) any other reason relating to the application of a previously established sentencing guideline, and determined by the United States Sentencing Commission to be urgent and compelling;

the Commission, by affirmative vote of at least four members of the Commission, and pursuant to its rules and regulations and consistent with all pertinent provisions of title 28 and title 18, United States Code, shall promulgate and distribute to all courts of the United States and to the United States Probation System a temporary guideline or amendment to an existing guideline, to remain in effect until and during the pendency of the next report to Congress under section 994(p) of title 28, United States Code [subsec. (p) of this section].

"(b) Expiration of authority.—The authority of the Commission under paragraphs (1) and (2) of subsection (a) shall expire on November 1, 1989. The authority of the Commission to promulgate and distribute guidelines under paragraph (3) of subsection (a) shall expire on May 1, 1988."

Submission to Congress of Initial Sentencing Guidelines

Provisions directing that the United States Sentencing Commission submit to Congress within 30 months of Oct. 12, 1984, the initial sentencing guidelines promulgated pursuant to subsec. (a)(1) of this section, see section 235(a)(1)(B)(i) of Pub.L. 98–473, as amended, set out as an Effective Date note under 18 U.S.C.A. § 3551.

Effective Date of Sentencing Guidelines

Sentencing guidelines promulgated pursuant to this section effective when U.S. Sentencing Commission has submitted the initial set of sentencing guidelines to Congress, the General Accounting Office has studied and reported to Congress on the guidelines, Congress has examined the guidelines, and section 212(a)(2) of Pub.L. 98–473 takes effect [Nov. 1, 1987], see section 235(a)(1)(B)(ii) of Pub.L. 98–473, as amended, set out as an Effective and Applicability Provisions note under 18 U.S.C.A. § 3551.

Studies of Impact and Operation of Sentencing Guideline System; Reporting Requirements

Pub.L. 98–473, Title II, § 236, Oct. 11, 1984, 98 Stat. 2033, provided that:

"(a)(1) Four years after the sentencing guidelines promulgated pursuant to section 994(a)(1) [subsec. (a)(1) of this section], and the provisions of sections 3581, 3583, and 3624 of title 18, United States Code, go into effect, the General Accounting Office [now Government Accountability Office] shall undertake a study of the guidelines in order to determine their impact and compare the guidelines system with the operation of the previous sentencing and parole release system, and, within six months of the undertaking of such study, report to the Congress the results of its study.

"(2) Within one month of the start of the study required under subsection (a), the United States Sentencing Commission shall submit a report to the General Accounting Office [now Government Accountability Office], all appropriate courts, the Department of Justice, and the Congress detailing the operation of the sentencing guideline system and discussing any problems with the system or reforms needed. The report shall include an evaluation of the impact of the sentencing guidelines on prosecutorial discretion, plea bargaining, disparities in sentencing, and the use of incarceration, and shall be issued by affirmative vote of a majority of the voting members of the Commission.

"(b) The Congress shall review the study submitted pursuant to subsection (a) in order to determine—

"(1) whether the sentencing guideline system has been effective;

"(2) whether any changes should be made in the sentencing guideline system; and

"(3) whether the parole system should be reinstated in some form and the life of the Parole Commission extended."

[For termination, effective May 15, 2000, of reporting provisions of above note, see Pub.L. 104–66, § 3003, as amended, set out as a note under 31 U.S.C.A. § 1113, and the 12th item on page 13 of House Document No. 103–7.]

§ 995. Powers of the Commission

(a) The Commission, by vote of a majority of the members present and voting, shall have the power to—

(1) establish general policies and promulgate such rules and regulations for the Commission as are necessary to carry out the purposes of this chapter;

(2) appoint and fix the salary and duties of the Staff Director of the Sentencing Commission, who shall serve at the discretion of the Commission and who shall be compensated at a rate not to exceed the highest rate now or hereafter prescribed for

Level 6 of the Senior Executive Service Schedule (5 U.S.C. 5382);

(3) deny, revise, or ratify any request for regular, supplemental, or deficiency appropriations prior to any submission of such request to the Office of Management and Budget by the Chair;

(4) procure for the Commission temporary and intermittent services to the same extent as is authorized by section 3109(b) of title 5, United States Code;

(5) utilize, with their consent, the services, equipment, personnel, information, and facilities of other Federal, State, local, and private agencies and instrumentalities with or without reimbursement therefor;

(6) without regard to 31 U.S.C. 3324, enter into and perform such contracts, leases, cooperative agreements, and other transactions as may be necessary in the conduct of the functions of the Commission, with any public agency, or with any person, firm, association, corporation, educational institution, or non-profit organization;

(7) accept and employ, in carrying out the provisions of this title, voluntary and uncompensated services, notwithstanding the provisions of 31 U.S.C. 1342, however, individuals providing such services shall not be considered Federal employees except for purposes of chapter 81 of title 5, United States Code, with respect to job-incurred disability and title 28, United States Code, with respect to tort claims;

(8) request such information, data, and reports from any Federal agency or judicial officer as the Commission may from time to time require and as may be produced consistent with other law;

(9) monitor the performance of probation officers with regard to sentencing recommendations, including application of the Sentencing Commission guidelines and policy statements;

(10) issue instructions to probation officers concerning the application of Commission guidelines and policy statements;

(11) arrange with the head of any other Federal agency for the performance by such agency of any function of the Commission, with or without reimbursement;

(12) establish a research and development program within the Commission for the purpose of—

(A) serving as a clearinghouse and information center for the collection, preparation, and dissemination of information on Federal sentencing practices; and

(B) assisting and serving in a consulting capacity to Federal courts, departments, and agencies in the development, maintenance, and coordination of sound sentencing practices;

(13) collect systematically the data obtained from studies, research, and the empirical experience of public and private agencies concerning the sentencing process;

(14) publish data concerning the sentencing process;

(15) collect systematically and disseminate information concerning sentences actually imposed, and the relationship of such sentences to the factors set forth in section 3553(a) of title 18, United States Code;

(16) collect systematically and disseminate information regarding effectiveness of sentences imposed;

(17) devise and conduct, in various geographical locations, seminars and workshops providing continuing studies for persons engaged in the sentencing field;

(18) devise and conduct periodic training programs of instruction in sentencing techniques for judicial and probation personnel and other persons connected with the sentencing process;

(19) study the feasibility of developing guidelines for the disposition of juvenile delinquents;

(20) make recommendations to Congress concerning modification or enactment of statutes relating to sentencing, penal, and correctional matters that the Commission finds to be necessary and advisable to carry out an effective, humane and rational sentencing policy;

(21) hold hearings and call witnesses that might assist the Commission in the exercise of its powers or duties;

(22) perform such other functions as are required to permit Federal courts to meet their responsibilities under section 3553(a) of title 18, United States Code, and to permit others involved in the Federal criminal justice system to meet their related responsibilities;

(23) retain private attorneys to provide legal advice to the Commission in the conduct of its work, or to appear for or represent the Commission in any case in which the Commission is authorized by law to represent itself, or in which the Commission is representing itself with the consent of the Department of Justice; and the Commission may in its discretion pay reasonable attorney's fees to private attorneys employed by it out of its appropriated funds. When serving as officers or employees of the United States, such private attorneys shall be considered special government employees as defined in section 202(a) of title 18; and

(24) grant incentive awards to its employees pursuant to chapter 45 of title 5, United States Code.

(b) The Commission shall have such other powers and duties and shall perform such other functions as may be necessary to carry out the purposes of this chapter, and may delegate to any member or designated person such powers as may be appropriate other than the power to establish general policy statements and guidelines pursuant to section 994(a)(1) and (2), the issuance of general policies and promulgation of rules and regulations pursuant to subsection (a)(1) of this section, and the decisions as to the factors to be considered in establishment of categories of offenses and offenders pursuant to section 994(b). The Commission shall, with respect to its activities under subsections (a)(9), (a)(10), (a)(11), (a)(12), (a)(13), (a)(14), (a)(15), (a)(16), (a)(17), and (a)(18), to the extent practicable, utilize existing resources of the Administrative Office of the United States Courts and the Federal Judicial Center for the purpose of avoiding unnecessary duplication.

(c) Upon the request of the Commission, each Federal agency is authorized and directed to make its services, equipment, personnel, facilities, and information available to the greatest practicable extent to the Commission in the execution of its functions.

(d) A simple majority of the membership then serving shall constitute a quorum for the conduct of business. Other than for the promulgation of guidelines and policy statements pursuant to section 994, the Commission may exercise its powers and fulfill its duties by the vote of a simple majority of the members present.

(e) Except as otherwise provided by law, the Commission shall maintain and make available for public inspection a record of the final vote of each member on any action taken by it.

(Added Pub.L. 98–473, Title II, § 217(a), Oct. 12, 1984, 98 Stat. 2024, and amended Pub.L. 100–690, Title VII, §§ 7104, 7105, 7106(b), Nov. 18, 1988, 102 Stat. 4418; Pub.L. 101–650, Title III, § 325(b)(5), Dec. 1, 1990, 104 Stat. 5121; Pub.L. 103–322, Title XXVIII, § 280005(c)(1), Sept. 13, 1994, 108 Stat. 2097.)

HISTORICAL AND STATUTORY NOTES

References in Text

The provisions of title 28, United States Code, with respect to tort claims, referred to in subsec. (a)(7), are classified generally to section 1346(b) and chapter 171 (section 2671 et seq.) of this title.

Effective and Applicability Provisions

1984 Acts. Section effective Oct. 12, 1984, see section 235(a)(1)(B)(i) of Pub.L. 98–473, as amended, set out as a note under section 3551 of Title 18, Crimes and Criminal Procedure.

§ 996. Director and staff

(a) The Staff Director shall supervise the activities of persons employed by the Commission and perform other duties assigned to the Staff Director by the Commission.

(b) The Staff Director shall, subject to the approval of the Commission, appoint such officers and employees as are necessary in the execution of the functions of the Commission. The officers and employees of the Commission shall be exempt from the provisions of part III of title 5, except the following: chapters 45 (Incentive Awards), 63 (Leave), 81 (Compensation for Work Injuries), 83 (Retirement), 85 (Unemployment Compensation), 87 (Life Insurance), and 89 (Health Insurance), and subchapter VI of chapter 55 (Payment for accumulated and accrued leave).

(Added Pub.L. 98–473, Title II, § 217(a), Oct. 12, 1984, 98 Stat. 2026, and amended Pub.L. 100–690, Title VII, § 7106(c), Nov. 18, 1988, 102 Stat. 4418; Pub.L. 101–650, Title III, § 325(b)(6), Dec. 1, 1990, 104 Stat. 5121; Pub.L. 103–322, Title XXVIII, § 280005(c)(5), Sept. 13, 1994, 108 Stat. 2097; Pub.L. 106–518, Title III, § 302(a), Nov. 13, 2000, 114 Stat. 2416.)

HISTORICAL AND STATUTORY NOTES

References in Text

Part III of title 5, referred to in subsec. (b), is 5 U.S.C.A. § 2101 et seq.

Chapter 45 of title 5, referred to in subsec. (b), is 5 U.S.C.A. § 4501 et seq.

Chapter 63 of title 5, referred to in subsec. (b), is 5 U.S.C.A. § 6301 et seq.

Chapter 81 of title 5, referred to in subsec. (b), is 5 U.S.C.A. § 8101 et seq.

Chapter 83 of title 5, referred to in subsec. (b), is 5 U.S.C.A. § 8301 et seq.

Chapter 85 of title 5, referred to in subsec. (b), is 5 U.S.C.A. § 8501 et seq.

Chapter 87 of title 5, referred to in subsec. (b), is 5 U.S.C.A. § 8701 et seq.

Chapter 89 of title 5, referred to in subsec. (b), is 5 U.S.C.A. § 8901 et seq.

Subchapter VI of chapter 55, referred to in subsec. (b), is 5 U.S.C.A. § 5551 et seq.

Effective and Applicability Provisions

1984 Acts. Section effective Oct. 12, 1984, see section 235(a)(1)(B)(i) of Pub.L. 98–473, as amended, set out as a note under section 3551 of Title 18, Crimes and Criminal Procedure.

Accrued or Accumulated Leave

Pub.L. 106–518, § 302(b), Nov. 13, 2000, 114 Stat. 2417, provided that: "Any leave that an individual accrued or accumulated (or that otherwise became available to such individual) under the leave system of the United States Sentencing Commission and that remains unused as of the date of the enactment of this Act shall, on and after such date, be treated as leave accrued or accumulated (or that otherwise became available to such individual) under chapter 63 of title 5, United States Code [5 U.S.C.A. § 6301 et seq.]."

§ 997. Annual report

The Commission shall report annually to the Judicial Conference of the United States, the Congress, and the President of the United States on the activities of the Commission.

(Added Pub.L. 98–473, Title II, § 217(a), Oct. 12, 1984, 98 Stat. 2026.)

HISTORICAL AND STATUTORY NOTES

Effective and Applicability Provisions

1984 Acts. Section effective Oct. 12, 1984, see section 235(a)(1)(B)(i) of Pub.L. 98–473, as amended, set out as a note under section 3551 of Title 18, Crimes and Criminal Procedure.

Termination of Reporting Requirements

For termination, effective May 15, 2000, of provisions of this section relating to requirement to report annually to Congress, see Pub.L. 104–66, § 3003, as amended, set out as a note under 31 U.S.C.A. § 1113, and page 13 of House Document No. 103–7.

§ 998. Definitions

As used in this chapter—

(a) "Commission" means the United States Sentencing Commission;

(b) "Commissioner" means a member of the United States Sentencing Commission;

(c) "guidelines" means the guidelines promulgated by the Commission pursuant to section 994(a) of this title; and

(d) "rules and regulations" means rules and regulations promulgated by the Commission pursuant to section 995 of this title.

(Added Pub.L. 98–473, Title II, § 217(a), Oct. 12, 1984, 98 Stat. 2026.)

HISTORICAL AND STATUTORY NOTES

Effective and Applicability Provisions

1984 Acts. Section effective Oct. 12, 1984, see section 235(a)(1)(B)(i) of Pub.L. 98–473, as amended, set out as a note under section 3551 of Title 18, Crimes and Criminal Procedure.

CHAPTER 83—COURTS OF APPEALS

HISTORICAL AND STATUTORY NOTES

§ 1291. Final decisions of district courts

The courts of appeals (other than the United States Court of Appeals for the Federal Circuit) shall have jurisdiction of appeals from all final decisions of the district courts of the United States, the United States District Court for the District of the Canal Zone, the District Court of Guam, and the District Court of the Virgin Islands, except where a direct review may be had in the Supreme Court. The jurisdiction of the United States Court of Appeals for the Federal Circuit shall be limited to the jurisdiction described in sections 1292(c) and (d) and 1295 of this title.

(June 25, 1948, c. 646, 62 Stat. 929; Oct. 31, 1951, c. 655, § 48, 65 Stat. 726; July 7, 1958, Pub.L. 85–508, § 12(e), 72 Stat. 348; Apr. 2, 1982, Pub.L. 97–164, Title I, § 124, 96 Stat. 36.)

HISTORICAL AND STATUTORY NOTES

Effective and Applicability Provisions

1982 Acts. Amendment by Pub.L. 97–164 effective Oct. 1, 1982, see section 402 of Pub.L. 97–164, set out as a note under section 171 of this title.

1958 Acts. Amendment of section by Pub.L. 85–508 effective Jan. 3, 1959, upon admission of Alaska into the Union pursuant to Proc. No. 3269, Jan. 3, 1959, 24 F.R. 81, 73 Stat. c16, as required by sections 1 and 8(c) of Pub.L. 85–508, see notes set out under section 81A of this title and preceding section 21 of Title 48, Territories and Insular Possessions.

Termination of United States District Court for the District of the Canal Zone

For termination of the United States District Court for the District of the Canal Zone at end of the "transition period", being the 30-month period beginning Oct. 1, 1979, and ending midnight Mar. 31, 1982, see Paragraph 5 of Article XI of the Panama Canal Treaty of 1977 and sections 3831 and 3841 to 3843 of Title 22, Foreign Relations and Intercourse.

CHAPTER 153—HABEAS CORPUS

HISTORICAL AND STATUTORY NOTES

Codifications

The table of sections for chapter 153 was amended by Pub.L. 95–598, Title II, § 250(b), Nov. 6, 1978, 92 Stat. 2672, effective June 28, 1984, pursuant to Pub.L. 95–598, Title IV, § 402(b), Nov. 6, 1978, 92 Stat. 2682, as amended by Pub.L. 98–249, § 1(a), Mar. 31, 1984, 98 Stat. 116; Pub.L. 98–271, § 1(a), Apr. 30, 1984, 98 Stat. 163; Pub.L. 98–299, § 1(a), May 25, 1984, 98 Stat. 214; Pub.L. 98–325, § 1(a), June 20, 1984, 98 Stat. 268, set out as an Effective and Applicability Provisions note preceding section 101 of Title 11, Bankruptcy, by adding:

"2256. Habeas corpus from bankruptcy courts.".

Section 402(b) of Pub.L. 95–598 was amended by section 113 of Pub.L. 98–353, Title I, July 10, 1984, 98 Stat. 343, by substituting "shall not be effective" for "shall take effect on June 28, 1984", thereby eliminating the amendment by section 250(b) of Pub.L. 95–598, effective June 27, 1984, pursuant to section 122(c) of Pub.L. 98–353, set out as an Effective and Applicability Provisions note under section 151 of this title.

Section 121(a) of Pub.L. 98–353 directed that section 402(b) of Pub.L. 95–598 be amended by substituting "the date of enactment of the Bankruptcy Amendments and Federal Judgeship Act of 1984 [i.e. July 10, 1984]" for "June 28, 1984". This amendment was not executed in view of the prior amendment to section 402(b) of Pub.L. 95–598 by section 113 of Pub.L. 98–353.

Rules Governing Section 2254 Cases in the United States District Courts and Rules Governing Proceedings in the United States District Courts under Section 2255 of Title 28, United States Code, are set out in this pamphlet, ante.

§ 2241. Power to grant writ

(a) Writs of habeas corpus may be granted by the Supreme Court, any justice thereof, the district courts and any circuit judge within their respective jurisdictions. The order of a circuit judge shall be entered in the records of the district court of the district wherein the restraint complained of is had.

(b) The Supreme Court, any justice thereof, and any circuit judge may decline to entertain an application for a writ of habeas corpus and may transfer the application for hearing and determination to the district court having jurisdiction to entertain it.

(c) The writ of habeas corpus shall not extend to a prisoner unless—

(1) He is in custody under or by color of the authority of the United States or is committed for trial before some court thereof; or

(2) He is in custody for an act done or omitted in pursuance of an Act of Congress, or an order, process, judgment or decree of a court or judge of the United States; or

(3) He is in custody in violation of the Constitution or laws or treaties of the United States; or

(4) He, being a citizen of a foreign state and domiciled therein is in custody for an act done or omitted under any alleged right, title, authority, privilege, protection, or exemption claimed under the commission, order or sanction of any foreign state, or under color thereof, the validity and effect of which depend upon the law of nations; or

(5) It is necessary to bring him into court to testify or for trial.

(d) Where an application for a writ of habeas corpus is made by a person in custody under the judgment and sentence of a State court of a State which contains two or more Federal judicial districts, the application may be filed in the district court for the district wherein such person is in custody or in the district court for the district within which the State court was held which convicted and sentenced him and each of such district courts shall have concurrent jurisdiction to entertain the application. The district court for the district wherein such an application is filed in the exercise of its discretion and in furtherance of justice may transfer the application to the other district court for hearing and determination.

(e)(1) No court, justice, or judge shall have jurisdiction to hear or consider an application for a writ of habeas corpus filed by or on behalf of an alien detained by the United States who has been determined by the United States to have been properly detained as an enemy combatant or is awaiting such determination.

(2) Except as provided in paragraphs (2) and (3) of section 1005(e) of the Detainee Treatment Act of 2005 (10 U.S.C. 801 note), no court, justice, or judge shall have jurisdiction to hear or consider any other action against the United States or its agents relating to any aspect of the detention, transfer, treatment, trial, or conditions of confinement of an alien who is or was detained by the United States and has been determined by the United States to have been properly detained as an enemy combatant or is awaiting such determination.

(June 25, 1948, c. 646, 62 Stat. 964; May 24, 1949, c. 139, § 112, 63 Stat. 105; Sept. 19, 1966, Pub.L. 89–590, 80 Stat. 811; Dec. 30, 2005, Pub.L. 109–148, Div. A, Title X, § 1005(e)(1), 119 Stat. 2742; Jan. 6, 2006, Pub.L. 109–163, Title XIV, § 1405(e)(1), 119 Stat. 3477; Oct. 17, 2006, Pub.L. 109–366, § 7(a), 120 Stat. 2635.)

HISTORICAL AND STATUTORY NOTES

References in Text

Section 1005(e) of the Detainee Treatment Act of 2005, referred to in subsec. (e)(2), probably means Pub.L. 109–148,

Div. A, Title X, § 1005, Dec. 30, 2005, 119 Stat. 2740, which is set out in a note under 10 U.S.C.A. § 801 note. Pub.L. 109–163, Div. A, Title XIV, Jan. 6, 2006, 119 Stat. 3474, also enacted a "Detainee Treatment Act of 2005", see Short Title note under 42 U.S.C.A. § 2000dd and Tables, but that Act contains no section 1005(e).

Effective and Applicability Provisions

2006 Acts. Pub.L. 109–366, § 7(b), Oct. 17, 2006, 120 Stat. 2635, provided that: "The amendment made by subsection (a) [amending this section] shall take effect on the date of the enactment of this Act [Oct. 17, 2006], and shall apply to all cases, without exception, pending on or after the date of the enactment of this Act which relate to any aspect of the detention, transfer, treatment, trial, or conditions of detention of an alien detained by the United States since September 11, 2001."

Treaty Obligations not Establishing Grounds for Certain Claims

Pub.L. 109–366, § 5, Oct. 17, 2006, 120 Stat. 2631, provided that:

"**(a) In general.**—No person may invoke the Geneva Conventions or any protocols thereto in any habeas corpus or other civil action or proceeding to which the United States, or a current or former officer, employee, member of the Armed Forces, or other agent of the United States is a party as a source of rights in any court of the United States or its States or territories.

"**(b) Geneva conventions defined.**—In this section, the term 'Geneva Conventions' means—

"(1) the Convention for the Amelioration of the Condition of the Wounded and Sick in Armed Forces in the Field, done at Geneva August 12, 1949 (6 UST 3114);

"(2) the Convention for the Amelioration of the Condition of the Wounded, Sick, and Shipwrecked Members of the Armed Forces at Sea, done at Geneva August 12, 1949 (6 UST 3217);

"(3) the Convention Relative to the Treatment of Prisoners of War, done at Geneva August 12, 1949 (6 UST 3316); and

"(4) the Convention Relative to the Protection of Civilian Persons in Time of War, done at Geneva August 12, 1949 (6 UST 3516)."

§ 2242. Application

Application for a writ of habeas corpus shall be in writing signed and verified by the person for whose relief it is intended or by someone acting in his behalf.

It shall allege the facts concerning the applicant's commitment or detention, the name of the person who has custody over him and by virtue of what claim or authority, if known.

It may be amended or supplemented as provided in the rules of procedure applicable to civil actions.

If addressed to the Supreme Court, a justice thereof or a circuit judge it shall state the reasons for not making application to the district court of the district in which the applicant is held.

(June 25, 1948, c. 646, 62 Stat. 965.)

§ 2243. Issuance of writ; return; hearing; decision

A court, justice or judge entertaining an application for a writ of habeas corpus shall forthwith award the writ or issue an order directing the respondent to show cause why the writ should not be granted, unless it appears from the application that the applicant or person detained is not entitled thereto.

The writ, or order to show cause shall be directed to the person having custody of the person detained. It shall be returned within three days unless for good cause additional time, not exceeding twenty days, is allowed.

The person to whom the writ or order is directed shall make a return certifying the true cause of the detention.

When the writ or order is returned a day shall be set for hearing, not more than five days after the return unless for good cause additional time is allowed.

Unless the application for the writ and the return present only issues of law the person to whom the writ is directed shall be required to produce at the hearing the body of the person detained.

The applicant or the person detained may, under oath, deny any of the facts set forth in the return or allege any other material facts.

The return and all suggestions made against it may be amended, by leave of court, before or after being filed.

The court shall summarily hear and determine the facts, and dispose of the matter as law and justice require.

(June 25, 1948, c. 646, 62 Stat. 965.)

§ 2244. Finality of determination

(a) No circuit or district judge shall be required to entertain an application for a writ of habeas corpus to inquire into the detention of a person pursuant to a judgment of a court of the United States if it appears that the legality of such detention has been determined by a judge or court of the United States on a prior application for a writ of habeas corpus, except as provided in section 2255.

(b)(1) A claim presented in a second or successive habeas corpus application under section 2254 that was presented in a prior application shall be dismissed.

(2) A claim presented in a second or successive habeas corpus application under section 2254 that was not presented in a prior application shall be dismissed unless—

(A) the applicant shows that the claim relies on a new rule of constitutional law, made retroactive to cases on collateral review by the Supreme Court, that was previously unavailable; or

(B)(i) the factual predicate for the claim could not have been discovered previously through the exercise of due diligence; and

(ii) the facts underlying the claim, if proven and viewed in light of the evidence as a whole, would be sufficient to establish by clear and convincing evidence that, but for constitutional error, no reasonable factfinder would have found the applicant guilty of the underlying offense.

(3)(A) Before a second or successive application permitted by this section is filed in the district court, the applicant shall move in the appropriate court of appeals for an order authorizing the district court to consider the application.

(B) A motion in the court of appeals for an order authorizing the district court to consider a second or successive application shall be determined by a three-judge panel of the court of appeals.

(C) The court of appeals may authorize the filing of a second or successive application only if it determines that the application makes a prima facie showing that the application satisfies the requirements of this subsection.

(D) The court of appeals shall grant or deny the authorization to file a second or successive application not later than 30 days after the filing of the motion.

(E) The grant or denial of an authorization by a court of appeals to file a second or successive application shall not be appealable and shall not be the subject of a petition for rehearing or for a writ of certiorari.

(4) A district court shall dismiss any claim presented in a second or successive application that the court of appeals has authorized to be filed unless the applicant shows that the claim satisfies the requirements of this section.

(c) In a habeas corpus proceeding brought in behalf of a person in custody pursuant to the judgment of a State court, a prior judgment of the Supreme Court of the United States on an appeal or review by a writ of certiorari at the instance of the prisoner of the decision of such State court, shall be conclusive as to all issues of fact or law with respect to an asserted denial of a Federal right which constitutes ground for discharge in a habeas corpus proceeding, actually adjudicated by the Supreme Court therein, unless the applicant for the writ of habeas corpus shall plead and the court shall find the existence of a material and controlling fact which did not appear in the record of the proceeding in the Supreme Court and the court shall further find that the applicant for the writ of habeas corpus could not have caused such fact to appear in such record by the exercise of reasonable diligence.

(d)(1) A 1-year period of limitation shall apply to an application for a writ of habeas corpus by a person in custody pursuant to the judgment of a State court. The limitation period shall run from the latest of—

(A) the date on which the judgment became final by the conclusion of direct review or the expiration of the time for seeking such review;

(B) the date on which the impediment to filing an application created by State action in violation of the Constitution or laws of the United States is removed, if the applicant was prevented from filing by such State action;

(C) the date on which the constitutional right asserted was initially recognized by the Supreme Court, if the right has been newly recognized by the Supreme Court and made retroactively applicable to cases on collateral review; or

(D) the date on which the factual predicate of the claim or claims presented could have been discovered through the exercise of due diligence.

(2) The time during which a properly filed application for State post-conviction or other collateral review with respect to the pertinent judgment or claim is pending shall not be counted toward any period of limitation under this subsection.

(June 25, 1948, c. 646, 62 Stat. 965; Nov. 2, 1966, Pub.L. 89–711, § 1, 80 Stat. 1104; Apr. 24, 1996, Pub.L. 104–132, Title I, §§ 101, 106, 110 Stat. 1217, 1220.)

§ 2245. Certificate of trial judge admissible in evidence

On the hearing of an application for a writ of habeas corpus to inquire into the legality of the detention of a person pursuant to a judgment the certificate of the judge who presided at the trial resulting in the judgment, setting forth the facts occurring at the trial, shall be admissible in evidence. Copies of the certificate shall be filed with the court in which the application is pending and in the court in which the trial took place.

(June 25, 1948, c. 646, 62 Stat. 966.)

§ 2246. Evidence; depositions; affidavits

On application for a writ of habeas corpus, evidence may be taken orally or by deposition, or, in the discretion of the judge, by affidavit. If affidavits are admitted any party shall have the right to propound written interrogatories to the affiants, or to file answering affidavits.

(June 25, 1948, c. 646, 62 Stat. 966.)

§ 2247. Documentary evidence

On application for a writ of habeas corpus documentary evidence, transcripts of proceedings upon arraignment, plea and sentence and a transcript of the oral testimony introduced on any previous similar application by or in behalf of the same petitioner, shall be admissible in evidence.

(June 25, 1948, c. 646, 62 Stat. 966.)

§ 2248. Return or answer; conclusiveness

The allegations of a return to the writ of habeas corpus or of an answer to an order to show cause in a habeas corpus proceeding, if not traversed, shall be accepted as true except to the extent that the judge finds from the evidence that they are not true.

(June 25, 1948, c. 646, 62 Stat. 966.)

§ 2249. Certified copies of indictment, plea and judgment; duty of respondent

On application for a writ of habeas corpus to inquire into the detention of any person pursuant to a judgment of a court of the United States, the respondent shall promptly file with the court certified copies of the indictment, plea of petitioner and the judgment, or such of them as may be material to the questions raised, if the petitioner fails to attach them to his petition, and same shall be attached to the return to the writ, or to the answer to the order to show cause.

(June 25, 1948, c. 646, 62 Stat. 966.)

§ 2250. Indigent petitioner entitled to documents without cost

If on any application for a writ of habeas corpus an order has been made permitting the petitioner to prosecute the application in forma pauperis, the clerk of any court of the United States shall furnish to the petitioner without cost certified copies of such documents or parts of the record on file in his office as may be required by order of the judge before whom the application is pending.

(June 25, 1948, c. 646, 62 Stat. 966.)

§ 2251. Stay of State court proceedings

(a) In general.—

(1) Pending matters.—A justice or judge of the United States before whom a habeas corpus proceeding is pending, may, before final judgment or after final judgment of discharge, or pending appeal, stay any proceeding against the person detained in any State court or by or under the authority of any State for any matter involved in the habeas corpus proceeding.

(2) Matter not pending.—For purposes of this section, a habeas corpus proceeding is not pending until the application is filed.

(3) Application for appointment of counsel.—If a State prisoner sentenced to death applies for appointment of counsel pursuant to section 3599(a)(2) of title 18 in a court that would have jurisdiction to entertain a habeas corpus application regarding that sentence, that court may stay execution of the sentence of death, but such stay shall terminate not later than 90 days after counsel is appointed or the application for appointment of counsel is withdrawn or denied.

(b) No further proceedings.—After the granting of such a stay, any such proceeding in any State court or by or under the authority of any State shall be void. If no stay is granted, any such proceeding shall be as valid as if no habeas corpus proceedings or appeal were pending.

(June 25, 1948, c. 646, 62 Stat. 966; Mar. 9, 2006, Pub.L. 109–177, Title V, § 507(f), 120 Stat. 251.)

HISTORICAL AND STATUTORY NOTES

Application to Pending Cases

Pub.L. 109–177, Title V, § 507(d), Mar. 9, 2006, 120 Stat. 251, provided that:

"(1) **In general.**—This section and the amendments made by this section [enacting 28 U.S.C.A. § 2265, amending 28 U.S.C.A. §§ 2251, 2261, and 2266, and repealing 28 U.S.C.A. § 2265] shall apply to cases pending on or after the date of enactment of this Act [Mar. 9, 2006].

"(2) **Time limits.**—In a case pending on the date of enactment of this Act [Mar. 9, 2006], if the amendments made by this section [enacting 28 U.S.C.A. § 2265, amending 28 U.S.C.A. §§ 2251, 2261, and 2266, and repealing 28 U.S.C.A. § 2265] establish a time limit for taking certain action, the period of which began on the date of an event that occurred prior to the date of enactment of this Act [Mar. 9, 2006], the period of such time limit shall instead begin on the date of enactment of this Act [Mar. 9, 2006]."

§ 2252. Notice

Prior to the hearing of a habeas corpus proceeding in behalf of a person in custody of State officers or by virtue of State laws notice shall be served on the attorney general or other appropriate officer of such State as the justice or judge at the time of issuing the writ shall direct.

(June 25, 1948, c. 646, 62 Stat. 967.)

§ 2253. Appeal

(a) In a habeas corpus proceeding or a proceeding under section 2255 before a district judge, the final order shall be subject to review, on appeal, by the court of appeals for the circuit in which the proceeding is held.

(b) There shall be no right of appeal from a final order in a proceeding to test the validity of a warrant to remove to another district or place for commitment or trial a person charged with a criminal offense against the United States, or to test the validity of such person's detention pending removal proceedings.

(c)(1) Unless a circuit justice or judge issues a certificate of appealability, an appeal may not be taken to the court of appeals from—

(A) the final order in a habeas corpus proceeding in which the detention complained of arises out of process issued by a State court; or

(B) the final order in a proceeding under section 2255.

(2) A certificate of appealability may issue under paragraph (1) only if the applicant has made a substantial showing of the denial of a constitutional right.

(3) The certificate of appealability under paragraph (1) shall indicate which specific issue or issues satisfy the showing required by paragraph (2).

(June 25, 1948, c. 646, 62 Stat. 967; May 24, 1949, c. 139, § 113, 63 Stat. 105; Oct. 31, 1951, c. 655, § 52, 65 Stat. 727; Apr. 24, 1996, Pub.L. 104–132, Title I, § 102, 110 Stat. 1217.)

§ 2254. State custody; remedies in Federal courts

(a) The Supreme Court, a Justice thereof, a circuit judge, or a district court shall entertain an application for a writ of habeas corpus in behalf of a person in custody pursuant to the judgment of a State court only on the ground that he is in custody in violation of the Constitution or laws or treaties of the United States.

(b)(1) An application for a writ of habeas corpus on behalf of a person in custody pursuant to the judgment of a State court shall not be granted unless it appears that—

(A) the applicant has exhausted the remedies available in the courts of the State; or

(B)(i) there is an absence of available State corrective process; or

(ii) circumstances exist that render such process ineffective to protect the rights of the applicant.

(2) An application for a writ of habeas corpus may be denied on the merits, notwithstanding the failure of the applicant to exhaust the remedies available in the courts of the State.

(3) A State shall not be deemed to have waived the exhaustion requirement or be estopped from reliance upon the requirement unless the State, through counsel, expressly waives the requirement.

(c) An applicant shall not be deemed to have exhausted the remedies available in the courts of the State, within the meaning of this section, if he has the right under the law of the State to raise, by any available procedure, the question presented.

(d) An application for a writ of habeas corpus on behalf of a person in custody pursuant to the judgment of a State court shall not be granted with respect to any claim that was adjudicated on the merits in State court proceedings unless the adjudication of the claim—

(1) resulted in a decision that was contrary to, or involved an unreasonable application of, clearly established Federal law, as determined by the Supreme Court of the United States; or

(2) resulted in a decision that was based on an unreasonable determination of the facts in light of the evidence presented in the State court proceeding.

(e)(1) In a proceeding instituted by an application for a writ of habeas corpus by a person in custody pursuant to the judgment of a State court, a determination of a factual issue made by a State court shall be presumed to be correct. The applicant shall have the burden of rebutting the presumption of correctness by clear and convincing evidence.

(2) If the applicant has failed to develop the factual basis of a claim in State court proceedings, the court shall not hold an evidentiary hearing on the claim unless the applicant shows that—

(A) the claim relies on—

(i) a new rule of constitutional law, made retroactive to cases on collateral review by the Supreme Court, that was previously unavailable; or

(ii) a factual predicate that could not have been previously discovered through the exercise of due diligence; and

(B) the facts underlying the claim would be sufficient to establish by clear and convincing evidence that but for constitutional error, no reasonable factfinder would have found the applicant guilty of the underlying offense.

(f) If the applicant challenges the sufficiency of the evidence adduced in such State court proceeding to support the State court's determination of a factual issue made therein, the applicant, if able, shall produce that part of the record pertinent to a determination of the sufficiency of the evidence to support such determination. If the applicant, because of indigency or other reason is unable to produce such part of the record, then the State shall produce such part of the record and the Federal court shall direct the State to do so by order directed to an appropriate State official. If the State cannot provide such pertinent part of the record, then the court shall determine under the existing facts and circumstances what weight shall be given to the State court's factual determination.

(g) A copy of the official records of the State court, duly certified by the clerk of such court to be a true and correct copy of a finding, judicial opinion, or other reliable written indicia showing such a factual determination by the State court shall be admissible in the Federal court proceeding.

(h) Except as provided in section 408 of the Controlled Substances Act, in all proceedings brought under this section, and any subsequent proceedings on review, the court may appoint counsel for an applicant who is or becomes financially unable to afford counsel, except as provided by a rule promulgated by the Supreme Court pursuant to statutory authority. Appointment of counsel under this section shall be governed by section 3006A of title 18.

(i) The ineffectiveness or incompetence of counsel during Federal or State collateral post-conviction proceedings shall not be a ground for relief in a proceeding arising under section 2254.

(June 25, 1948, c. 646, 62 Stat. 967; Nov. 2, 1966, Pub.L. 89–711, § 2, 80 Stat. 1105; Apr. 24, 1996, Pub.L. 104–132, Title I, § 104, 110 Stat. 1218.)

HISTORICAL AND STATUTORY NOTES

Senate Revision Amendments

Senate amendment to this section, Senate Report No. 1559, amendment No. 47, has three declared purposes, set forth as follows:

"The first is to eliminate from the prohibition of the section applications in behalf of prisoners in custody under authority of a State officer but whose custody has not been directed by the judgment of a State court. If the section were applied to applications by persons detained solely under authority of a State officer it would unduly hamper Federal courts in the protection of Federal officers prosecuted for acts committed in the course of official duty.

"The second purpose is to eliminate, as a ground of Federal jurisdiction to review by habeas corpus judgments of State courts, the proposition that the State court has denied a prisoner a 'fair adjudication of the legality of his detention under the Constitution and laws of the United States.' The Judicial Conference believes that this would be an undesirable ground for Federal jurisdiction in addition to exhaustion of State remedies or lack of adequate remedy in the State courts because it would permit proceedings in the Federal court on this ground before the petitioner had exhausted his State remedies. This ground would, of course, always be open to a petitioner to assert in the Federal court after he had exhausted his State remedies or if he had no adequate State remedy.

"The third purpose is to substitute detailed and specific language for the phrase 'no adequate remedy available.' That phrase is not sufficiently specific and precise, and its meaning should, therefore, be spelled out in more detail in the section as is done by the amendment."

1966 Acts. Senate Report No. 1797, see 1966 U.S. Code Cong. and Adm. News, p. 3663.

References in Text

Section 408 of the Controlled Substances Act, referred to in subsec. (h), is classified to section 848 of Title 21, Food and Drugs.

§ 2255. Federal custody; remedies on motion attacking sentence

A prisoner in custody under sentence of a court established by Act of Congress claiming the right to be released upon the ground that the sentence was imposed in violation of the Constitution or laws of the United States, or that the court was without jurisdiction to impose such sentence, or that the sentence was in excess of the maximum authorized by law, or is otherwise subject to collateral attack, may move the court which imposed the sentence to vacate, set aside or correct the sentence.

Unless the motion and the files and records of the case conclusively show that the prisoner is entitled to no relief, the court shall cause notice thereof to be served upon the United States attorney, grant a prompt hearing thereon, determine the issues and make findings of fact and conclusions of law with respect thereto. If the court finds that the judgment was rendered without jurisdiction, or that the sentence imposed was not authorized by law or otherwise open to collateral attack, or that there has been such a denial or infringement of the constitutional rights of the prisoner as to render the judgment vulnerable to collateral attack, the court shall vacate and set the judgment aside and shall discharge the prisoner or resentence him or grant a new trial or correct the sentence as may appear appropriate.

A court may entertain and determine such motion without requiring the production of the prisoner at the hearing.

An appeal may be taken to the court of appeals from the order entered on the motion as from a final judgment on application for a writ of habeas corpus.

An application for a writ of habeas corpus in behalf of a prisoner who is authorized to apply for relief by motion pursuant to this section, shall not be entertained if it appears that the applicant has failed to apply for relief, by motion, to the court which sentenced him, or that such court has denied him relief, unless it also appears that the remedy by motion is inadequate or ineffective to test the legality of his detention.

A 1-year period of limitation shall apply to a motion under this section. The limitation period shall run from the latest of—

(1) the date on which the judgment of conviction becomes final;

(2) the date on which the impediment to making a motion created by governmental action in violation of the Constitution or laws of the United States is removed, if the movant was prevented from making a motion by such governmental action;

(3) the date on which the right asserted was initially recognized by the Supreme Court, if that right has been newly recognized by the Supreme Court and made retroactively applicable to cases on collateral review; or

(4) the date on which the facts supporting the claim or claims presented could have been discovered through the exercise of due diligence.

Except as provided in section 408 of the Controlled Substances Act, in all proceedings brought under this section, and any subsequent proceedings on review, the court may appoint counsel, except as provided by a rule promulgated by the Supreme Court pursuant to statutory authority. Appointment of counsel under this section shall be governed by section 3006A of title 18.

A second or successive motion must be certified as provided in section 2244 by a panel of the appropriate court of appeals to contain—

(1) newly discovered evidence that, if proven and viewed in light of the evidence as a whole, would be sufficient to establish by clear and convincing evidence that no reasonable factfinder would have found the movant guilty of the offense; or

(2) a new rule of constitutional law, made retroactive to cases on collateral review by the Supreme Court, that was previously unavailable.

(June 25, 1948, c. 646, 62 Stat. 967; May 24, 1949, c. 139, § 114, 63 Stat. 105; Apr. 24, 1996, Pub.L. 104–132, Title I, § 105, 110 Stat. 1220.)

HISTORICAL AND STATUTORY NOTES

References in Text

Section 408 of the Controlled Substances Act, referred to in text, is classified to section 848 of Title 21, Food and Drugs.

[§ 2256. Omitted]

HISTORICAL AND STATUTORY NOTES

Codifications

This section as added by Pub. L. 95–598, Title II, § 250(a), Nov. 6, 1978, 92 Stat. 2672, effective June 28, 1984, pursuant to Pub. L. 95–598, Title IV, § 402(b), Nov. 6, 1978, 92 Stat. 2682, as amended by Pub. L. 98–249, § 1(a), Mar. 31, 1984, 98 Stat. 116; Pub. L. 98–271, § 1(a), Apr. 30, 1984, 98 Stat. 163; Pub. L. 98–299, § 1(a), May 25, 1984, 98 Stat. 214; Pub. L. 98–325, § 1(a), June 20, 1984, 98 Stat. 268 [set out as an Effective and Applicability Provisions note preceding section 101 of Title 11, Bankruptcy], read as follows:

§ 2256. Habeas corpus from bankruptcy courts

A bankruptcy court may issue a writ of habeas corpus—

(1) when appropriate to bring a person before the court—

(A) for examination;

(B) to testify; or

(C) to perform a duty imposed on such person under this title; or

(2) ordering the release of a debtor in a case under title 11 in custody under the judgment of a Federal or State court if—

(A) such debtor was arrested or imprisoned on process in any civil action;

(B) such process was issued for the collection of a debt—

(i) dischargeable under title 11; or

(ii) that is or will be provided for in a plan under chapter 11 or 13 of title 11; and

(C) before the issuance of such writ, notice and a hearing have been afforded the adverse party of such debtor in custody to contest the issuance of such writ.

Prior Provisions

A prior section 2256, added Pub. L. 95–144, § 3, Oct. 28, 1977, 91 Stat. 1220, which related to jurisdiction of proceedings relating to transferred offenders, was transferred to section 3244 of Title 18, Crimes and Criminal Procedure, by Pub. L. 95–598, Title III, § 314(j), Nov. 6, 1978, 92 Stat. 2677.

CHAPTER 154—SPECIAL HABEAS CORPUS PROCEDURES IN CAPITAL CASES

Sec.

§ 2261. Prisoners in State custody subject to capital sentence; appointment of counsel; requirement of rule of court or statute; procedures for appointment

(a) This chapter shall apply to cases arising under section 2254 brought by prisoners in State custody who are subject to a capital sentence. It shall apply only if the provisions of subsections (b) and (c) are satisfied.

(b) **Counsel.**—This chapter is applicable if—

(1) the Attorney General of the United States certifies that a State has established a mechanism for providing counsel in postconviction proceedings as provided in section 2265; and

(2) counsel was appointed pursuant to that mechanism, petitioner validly waived counsel, petitioner retained counsel, or petitioner was found not to be indigent.

(c) Any mechanism for the appointment, compensation, and reimbursement of counsel as provided in subsection (b) must offer counsel to all State prisoners under capital sentence and must provide for the entry of an order by a court of record—

(1) appointing one or more counsels to represent the prisoner upon a finding that the prisoner is indigent and accepted the offer or is unable compe-

tently to decide whether to accept or reject the offer;

(2) finding, after a hearing if necessary, that the prisoner rejected the offer of counsel and made the decision with an understanding of its legal consequences; or

(3) denying the appointment of counsel upon a finding that the prisoner is not indigent.

(d) No counsel appointed pursuant to subsections (b) and (c) to represent a State prisoner under capital sentence shall have previously represented the prisoner at trial in the case for which the appointment is made unless the prisoner and counsel expressly request continued representation.

(e) The ineffectiveness or incompetence of counsel during State or Federal post-conviction proceedings in a capital case shall not be a ground for relief in a proceeding arising under section 2254. This limitation shall not preclude the appointment of different counsel, on the court's own motion or at the request of the prisoner, at any phase of State or Federal post-conviction proceedings on the basis of the ineffectiveness or incompetence of counsel in such proceedings.

(Added Pub.L. 104–132, Title I, § 107(a), Apr. 24, 1996, 110 Stat. 1221, and amended Pub.L. 109–177, Title V, § 507(a), (b), Mar. 9, 2006, 120 Stat. 250.)

HISTORICAL AND STATUTORY NOTES

Effective and Applicability Provisions

1996 Acts. Section 107(c) of Pub.L. 104–132 provided that: "Chapter 154 of title 28, United States Code (as added by subsection (a)) [this chapter] shall apply to cases pending on or after the date of enactment of this Act [Apr. 24, 1996]."

§ 2262. Mandatory stay of execution; duration; limits on stays of execution; successive petitions

(a) Upon the entry in the appropriate State court of record of an order under section 2261(c), a warrant or order setting an execution date for a State prisoner shall be stayed upon application to any court that would have jurisdiction over any proceedings filed under section 2254. The application shall recite that the State has invoked the post-conviction review procedures of this chapter and that the scheduled execution is subject to stay.

(b) A stay of execution granted pursuant to subsection (a) shall expire if—

(1) a State prisoner fails to file a habeas corpus application under section 2254 within the time required in section 2263;

(2) before a court of competent jurisdiction, in the presence of counsel, unless the prisoner has competently and knowingly waived such counsel, and after having been advised of the consequences, a State prisoner under capital sentence waives the right to pursue habeas corpus review under section 2254; or

(3) a State prisoner files a habeas corpus petition under section 2254 within the time required by section 2263 and fails to make a substantial showing of the denial of a Federal right or is denied relief in the district court or at any subsequent stage of review.

(c) If one of the conditions in subsection (b) has occurred, no Federal court thereafter shall have the authority to enter a stay of execution in the case, unless the court of appeals approves the filing of a second or successive application under section 2244(b).

(Added Pub.L. 104–132, Title I, § 107(a), Apr. 24, 1996, 110 Stat. 1222.)

HISTORICAL AND STATUTORY NOTES

Effective and Applicability Provisions

1996 Acts. Section applicable to cases pending on or after Apr. 24, 1996, see section 107(c) of Pub.L. 104–132, set out as a note under section 2261 of this title.

§ 2263. Filing of habeas corpus application; time requirements; tolling rules

(a) Any application under this chapter for habeas corpus relief under section 2254 must be filed in the appropriate district court not later than 180 days after final State court affirmance of the conviction and sentence on direct review or the expiration of the time for seeking such review.

(b) The time requirements established by subsection (a) shall be tolled—

(1) from the date that a petition for certiorari is filed in the Supreme Court until the date of final disposition of the petition if a State prisoner files the petition to secure review by the Supreme Court of the affirmance of a capital sentence on direct review by the court of last resort of the State or other final State court decision on direct review;

(2) from the date on which the first petition for post-conviction review or other collateral relief is filed until the final State court disposition of such petition; and

(3) during an additional period not to exceed 30 days, if—

(A) a motion for an extension of time is filed in the Federal district court that would have jurisdiction over the case upon the filing of a habeas corpus application under section 2254; and

(B) a showing of good cause is made for the failure to file the habeas corpus application within the time period established by this section.

(Added Pub.L. 104–132, Title I, § 107(a), Apr. 24, 1996, 110 Stat. 1223.)

HISTORICAL AND STATUTORY NOTES

Effective and Applicability Provisions

1996 Acts. Section applicable to cases pending on or after Apr. 24, 1996, see section 107(c) of Pub.L. 104–132, set out as a note under section 2261 of this title.

§ 2264. Scope of Federal review; district court adjudications

(a) Whenever a State prisoner under capital sentence files a petition for habeas corpus relief to which this chapter applies, the district court shall only consider a claim or claims that have been raised and decided on the merits in the State courts, unless the failure to raise the claim properly is—

(1) the result of State action in violation of the Constitution or laws of the United States;

(2) the result of the Supreme Court's recognition of a new Federal right that is made retroactively applicable; or

(3) based on a factual predicate that could not have been discovered through the exercise of due diligence in time to present the claim for State or Federal post-conviction review.

(b) Following review subject to subsections (a), (d), and (e) of section 2254, the court shall rule on the claims properly before it.

(Added Pub.L. 104–132, Title I, § 107(a), Apr. 24, 1996, 110 Stat. 1223.)

HISTORICAL AND STATUTORY NOTES

Effective and Applicability Provisions

1996 Acts. Section applicable to cases pending on or after Apr. 24, 1996, see section 107(c) of Pub.L. 104–132, set out as a note under section 2261 of this title.

§ 2265. Certification and judicial review

(a) Certification.—

(1) In general.—If requested by an appropriate State official, the Attorney General of the United States shall determine—

(A) whether the State has established a mechanism for the appointment, compensation, and payment of reasonable litigation expenses of competent counsel in State postconviction proceedings brought by indigent prisoners who have been sentenced to death;

(B) the date on which the mechanism described in subparagraph (A) was established; and

(C) whether the State provides standards of competency for the appointment of counsel in proceedings described in subparagraph (A).

(2) Effective date.—The date the mechanism described in paragraph (1)(A) was established shall be the effective date of the certification under this subsection.

(3) Only express requirements.—There are no requirements for certification or for application of this chapter other than those expressly stated in this chapter.

(b) Regulations.—The Attorney General shall promulgate regulations to implement the certification procedure under subsection (a).

(c) Review of certification.—

(1) In general.—The determination by the Attorney General regarding whether to certify a State under this section is subject to review exclusively as provided under chapter 158 of this title.

(2) Venue.—The Court of Appeals for the District of Columbia Circuit shall have exclusive jurisdiction over matters under paragraph (1), subject to review by the Supreme Court under section 2350 of this title.

(3) Standard of review.—The determination by the Attorney General regarding whether to certify a State under this section shall be subject to de novo review.

(Added Pub.L. 109–177, Title V, § 507(c)(1), Mar. 9, 2006, 120 Stat. 250.)

HISTORICAL AND STATUTORY NOTES

References in Text

Chapter 158 of this title, referred to in subsec. (c)(1), is Orders of Federal Agencies; Review, 28 U.S.C.A. § 2341 et seq.

Prior Provisions

A prior section 2265, added Pub.L. 104–132, Title I, § 107(a), Apr. 24, 1996, 110 Stat. 1223, relating to application to State unitary review procedure, was repealed by Pub.L. 109–177, Title V, § 507(c)(1), Mar. 9, 2006, 120 Stat. 250.

§ 2266. Limitation periods for determining applications and motions

(a) The adjudication of any application under section 2254 that is subject to this chapter, and the adjudication of any motion under section 2255 by a person under sentence of death, shall be given priority by the district court and by the court of appeals over all noncapital matters.

(b)(1)(A) A district court shall render a final determination and enter a final judgment on any application for a writ of habeas corpus brought under this chapter in a capital case not later than 450 days after the date on which the application is filed, or 60 days after the date on which the case is submitted for decision, whichever is earlier.

(B) A district court shall afford the parties at least 120 days in which to complete all actions, including the preparation of all pleadings and briefs, and if necessary, a hearing, prior to the submission of the case for decision.

(C)(i) A district court may delay for not more than one additional 30–day period beyond the period specified in subparagraph (A), the rendering of a determination of an application for a writ of habeas corpus if the court issues a written order making a finding, and stating the reasons for the finding, that the ends of justice that would be served by allowing the delay outweigh the best interests of the public and the applicant in a speedy disposition of the application.

(ii) The factors, among others, that a court shall consider in determining whether a delay in the disposition of an application is warranted are as follows:

(I) Whether the failure to allow the delay would be likely to result in a miscarriage of justice.

(II) Whether the case is so unusual or so complex, due to the number of defendants, the nature of the prosecution, or the existence of novel questions of fact or law, that it is unreasonable to expect adequate briefing within the time limitations established by subparagraph (A).

(III) Whether the failure to allow a delay in a case that, taken as a whole, is not so unusual or so complex as described in subclause (II), but would otherwise deny the applicant reasonable time to obtain counsel, would unreasonably deny the applicant or the government continuity of counsel, or would deny counsel for the applicant or the government the reasonable time necessary for effective preparation, taking into account the exercise of due diligence.

(iii) No delay in disposition shall be permissible because of general congestion of the court's calendar.

(iv) The court shall transmit a copy of any order issued under clause (i) to the Director of the Administrative Office of the United States Courts for inclusion in the report under paragraph (5).

(2) The time limitations under paragraph (1) shall apply to—

(A) an initial application for a writ of habeas corpus;

(B) any second or successive application for a writ of habeas corpus; and

(C) any redetermination of an application for a writ of habeas corpus following a remand by the court of appeals or the Supreme Court for further proceedings, in which case the limitation period shall run from the date the remand is ordered.

(3)(A) The time limitations under this section shall not be construed to entitle an applicant to a stay of execution, to which the applicant would otherwise not be entitled, for the purpose of litigating any application or appeal.

(B) No amendment to an application for a writ of habeas corpus under this chapter shall be permitted after the filing of the answer to the application, except on the grounds specified in section 2244(b).

(4)(A) The failure of a court to meet or comply with a time limitation under this section shall not be a ground for granting relief from a judgment of conviction or sentence.

(B) The State may enforce a time limitation under this section by petitioning for a writ of mandamus to the court of appeals. The court of appeals shall act on the petition for a writ of mandamus not later than 30 days after the filing of the petition.

(5)(A) The Administrative Office of the United States Courts shall submit to Congress an annual report on the compliance by the district courts with the time limitations under this section.

(B) The report described in subparagraph (A) shall include copies of the orders submitted by the district courts under paragraph (1)(B)(iv).

(c)(1)(A) A court of appeals shall hear and render a final determination of any appeal of an order granting or denying, in whole or in part, an application brought under this chapter in a capital case not later than 120 days after the date on which the reply brief is filed, or if no reply brief is filed, not later than 120 days after the date on which the answering brief is filed.

(B)(i) A court of appeals shall decide whether to grant a petition for rehearing or other request for rehearing en banc not later than 30 days after the date on which the petition for rehearing is filed unless a responsive pleading is required, in which case the court shall decide whether to grant the petition not later than 30 days after the date on which the responsive pleading is filed.

(ii) If a petition for rehearing or rehearing en banc is granted, the court of appeals shall hear and render a final determination of the appeal not later than 120 days after the date on which the order granting rehearing or rehearing en banc is entered.

(2) The time limitations under paragraph (1) shall apply to—

(A) an initial application for a writ of habeas corpus;

(B) any second or successive application for a writ of habeas corpus; and

(C) any redetermination of an application for a writ of habeas corpus or related appeal following a remand by the court of appeals en banc or the Supreme Court for further proceedings, in which case the limitation period shall run from the date the remand is ordered.

(3) The time limitations under this section shall not be construed to entitle an applicant to a stay of execution, to which the applicant would otherwise not be entitled, for the purpose of litigating any application or appeal.

(4)(A) The failure of a court to meet or comply with a time limitation under this section shall not be a ground for granting relief from a judgment of conviction or sentence.

(B) The State may enforce a time limitation under this section by applying for a writ of mandamus to the Supreme Court.

(5) The Administrative Office of the United States Courts shall submit to Congress an annual report on the compliance by the courts of appeals with the time limitations under this section.

(Added Pub.L. 104–132, Title I, § 107(a), Apr. 24, 1996, 110 Stat. 1224, and amended Pub.L. 109–177, Title V, § 507(e), Mar. 9, 2006, 120 Stat. 251.)

HISTORICAL AND STATUTORY NOTES

Effective and Applicability Provisions

1996 Acts. Section applicable to cases pending on or after Apr. 24, 1996, see section 107(c) of Pub.L. 104–132, set out as a note under section 2261 of this title.

CHAPTER 175—CIVIL COMMITMENT AND REHABILITATION OF NARCOTIC ADDICTS [REPEALED]

[§§ 2901 to 2906. Repealed. Pub.L. 106–310, Div. B, Title XXXIV, § 3405(c)(1), Oct. 17, 2000, 114 Stat. 1221]

HISTORICAL AND STATUTORY NOTES

Section 2901, added Pub.L. 89–793, Title I, § 101, Nov. 8, 1966, 80 Stat. 1438, and amended Pub.L. 91–513, Title III, § 1102(*l*), Oct. 27, 1970, 84 Stat. 1293; Pub.L. 92–420, § 2, Sept. 16, 1972, 86 Stat. 677; Pub.L. 98–473, Title II, § 228(c), Oct. 12, 1984, 98 Stat. 2030, related to definitions under this chapter.

Section 2902, added Pub.L. 89–793, Title I, § 101, Nov. 8, 1966, 80 Stat. 1439, related to discretionary authority of court; examination, report, and determination by court; termination of civil commitment.

Section 2903, added Pub.L. 89–793, Title I, § 101, Nov. 8, 1966, 80 Stat. 1440, related to authority and responsibilities of the Surgeon General; institutional custody; aftercare; maximum period of civil commitment; credit toward sentence.

Section 2904, added Pub.L. 89–793, Title I, § 101, Nov. 8, 1966, 80 Stat. 1441, related to civil commitment not a conviction; use of test results.

Section 2905, added Pub.L. 89–793, Title I, § 101, Nov. 8, 1966, 80 Stat. 1441, related to delegation of functions by Surgeon General; use of Federal, State, and private facilities.

Section 2906, added Pub.L. 89–793, Title I, § 101, Nov. 8, 1966, 80 Stat. 1441, provided that absence of offer by the court to a defendant of an election under section 2902(a) or any determination as to civil commitment, not reviewable on appeal or otherwise.

Effective and Applicability Provisions

1972 Acts. Section 5 of Pub.L. 92–420 provided that: "This Act [amending section 2901(d) of this title, section 4251(c) of Title 18, and section 3411(b) of Title 42] shall take effect immediately upon enactment [Sept. 16, 1972]. Sections 2 and 3 [amending section 4251(c) of Title 18 and section 3411(b) of Title 42, respectively] shall apply to any case pending in a district court of the United States in which an appearance has not been made prior to the effective date [Sept. 16, 1972]."

TITLE 31
MONEY AND FINANCE

CHAPTER 53—MONETARY TRANSACTIONS

Pub.L. 108–458, Title VI, § 6203(i), Dec. 17, 2004, 118 Stat. 3747, rewrote item 5318A, which formerly read: "Special measures for jurisdictions, financial institutions, or international transactions of primary money laundering concern.".

SUBCHAPTER II—RECORDS AND REPORTS ON MONETARY INSTRUMENTS TRANSACTIONS

§ 5311. Declaration of purpose

It is the purpose of this subchapter (except section 5315) to require certain reports or records where they have a high degree of usefulness in criminal, tax, or regulatory investigations or proceedings, or in the conduct of intelligence or counterintelligence activities, including analysis, to protect against international terrorism.

(Pub.L. 97–258, Sept. 13, 1982, 96 Stat. 995; Pub.L. 107–56, Title III, § 358(a), Oct. 26, 2001, 115 Stat. 326.)

HISTORICAL AND STATUTORY NOTES

Effective and Applicability Provisions

2001 Acts. Amendments by section 358 of Pub.L. 107–56 applicable with respect to reports filed or records maintained on, before, or after Oct. 26, 2001, see section 358(h) of Pub.L. 107–56, set out as a note under 12 U.S.C.A. § 1829b.

Short Title

1970 Acts. This subchapter and chapter 21 of Title 12, 12 U.S.C.A. § 1951 et seq., are each popularly known as the Bank Secrecy Act. See Short Title note set out under 12 U.S.C.A. § 1951.

Improving International Standards and Cooperation to Fight Terrorist Financing; Definitions; Coordination of United States Government Efforts

Pub.L. 108–458, Title VII, §§ 7701, 7702, 7704, Dec. 17, 2004, 118 Stat. 3858 to 3860, provided that:

"Sec. 7701. Improving International Standards and Cooperation to Fight Terrorist Financing.

"(a) Findings.—Congress makes the following findings:

"(1) The global war on terrorism and cutting off terrorist financing is a policy priority for the United States and its partners, working bilaterally and multilaterally through the United Nations, the United Nations Security Council and its committees, such as the 1267 and 1373 Committees, the Financial Action Task Force (FATF), and various international financial institutions, including the International Monetary Fund (IMF), the International Bank for Reconstruction and Development (IBRD), and the regional multilateral development banks, and other multilateral fora.

"(2) The international financial community has become engaged in the global fight against terrorist financing. The Financial Action Task Force has focused on the new threat posed by terrorist financing to the international financial system, resulting in the establishment of the FATF's Eight Special Recommendations on Terrorist Financing as the international standard on combating terrorist financing. The Group of Seven and the Group of Twenty Finance Ministers are developing action plans to curb the financing of terror. In addition, other economic and regional fora, such as the Asia-Pacific Economic Cooperation (APEC) Forum, and the Western Hemisphere Financial Ministers, have been used to marshal political will and actions in support of combating the financing of terrorism (CFT) standards.

"(3) FATF's Forty Recommendations on Money Laundering and the Eight Special Recommendations on Terrorist Financing are the recognized global standards for fighting money laundering and terrorist financing. The FATF has engaged in an assessment process for jurisdictions based on their compliance with these standards.

"(4) In March 2004, the IMF and IBRD Boards agreed to make permanent a pilot program of collaboration with the FATF to assess global compliance with the FATF Forty Recommendations on Money Laundering and the Eight Special Recommendations on Terrorist Financing. As a result, anti-money laundering (AML) and combating the financing of terrorism (CFT) assessments are now a regular part of their Financial Sector Assessment Program (FSAP) and Offshore Financial Center assessments, which provide for a comprehensive analysis of the strength of a jurisdiction's financial system. These reviews assess potential systemic vulnerabilities, consider sectoral development needs and priorities, and review the state of implementation of and compliance with key financial codes and regulatory standards, among them the AML and CFT standards.

"(5) To date, 70 FSAPs have been conducted, with over 24 of those incorporating AML and CFT assessments. The international financial institutions (IFIs), the FATF, and the FATF-style regional bodies together are expected to assess AML and CFT regimes in up to 40 countries or jurisdictions per year. This will help countries and jurisdictions identify deficiencies in their AML and CFT regimes and help focus technical assistance efforts.

"(6) Technical assistance programs from the United States and other nations, coordinated with the Department of State and other departments and agencies, are playing an important role in helping countries and jurisdictions address shortcomings in their AML and CFT regimes and bringing their regimes into conformity with international standards. Training is coordinated within the United States Government, which leverages multilateral organizations and bodies and international financial institutions to internationalize the conveyance of technical assistance.

"(7) In fulfilling its duties in advancing incorporation of AML and CFT standards into the IFIs as part of the IFIs' work on protecting the integrity of the international monetary system, the Department of the Treasury, under the guidance of the Secretary of the Treasury, has effectively brought together all of the key United States Government agencies. In particular, United States Government agencies continue to work together to foster broad support for this important undertaking in various multilateral fora, and United States Government agencies recognize the need for close coordination and communication within our own Government.

"**(b) Sense of Congress regarding success in multilateral organizations.**—It is the sense of Congress that the Secretary of the Treasury should continue to promote the dissemination of international AML and CFT standards, and to press for full implementation of the FATF 40 + 8 Recommendations by all countries in order to curb financial risks and hinder terrorist financing around the globe. The efforts of the Secretary in this regard should include, where necessary or appropriate, multilateral action against countries whose counter-money laundering regimes and efforts against the financing of terrorism fall below recognized international standards.

"Sec. 7702. Definitions.

"In this subtitle [Pub.L. 108–458, Title VII, Subtitle G (§§ 7701 to 7704), Dec. 17, 2004, 118 Stat. 3858; enacting this note and amending 22 U.S.C.A. §§ 262*o*–2 and 262r–4]—

"(1) the term 'international financial institutions' has the same meaning as in section 1701(c)(2) of the International Financial Institutions Act [22 U.S.C.A. § 262r(c)(2)];

"(2) the term 'Financial Action Task Force' means the international policy-making and standard-setting body dedicated to combating money laundering and terrorist financing that was created by the Group of Seven in 1989; and

"(3) the terms 'Interagency Paper on Sound Practices to Strengthen the Resilience of the U.S. Financial System' and 'Interagency Paper' mean the interagency paper prepared by the Board of Governors of the Federal Reserve System, the Comptroller of the Currency, and the Securities and Exchange Commission that was announced in the Federal Register on April 8, 2003."

"Sec. 7704. Coordination of United States Government Efforts.

"The Secretary of the Treasury, or the designee of the Secretary, as the lead United States Government official to the Financial Action Task Force (FATF), shall continue to convene the interagency United States Government FATF working group. This group, which includes representatives from all relevant Federal agencies, shall meet at least once a year to advise the Secretary on policies to be pursued by the United States regarding the development of common international AML and CFT standards, to assess the adequacy and implementation of such standards, and to recommend to the Secretary improved or new standards, as necessary."

Findings and Purposes

Pub.L. 107–56, Title III, § 302, Oct. 26, 2001, 115 Stat. 296, as amended Pub.L. 108–458, Title VI, § 6202(c), Dec. 17, 2004, 118 Stat. 3745, provided that:

"(a) **Findings.**—The Congress finds that—

"(1) money laundering, estimated by the International Monetary Fund to amount to between 2 and 5 percent of global gross domestic product, which is at least $600,000,000,000 annually, provides the financial fuel that permits transnational criminal enterprises to conduct and expand their operations to the detriment of the safety and security of American citizens;

"(2) money laundering, and the defects in financial transparency on which money launderers rely, are critical to the financing of global terrorism and the provision of funds for terrorist attacks;

"(3) money launderers subvert legitimate financial mechanisms and banking relationships by using them as protective covering for the movement of criminal proceeds and the financing of crime and terrorism, and, by so doing, can threaten the safety of United States citizens and undermine the integrity of United States financial institutions and of the global financial and trading systems upon which prosperity and growth depend;

"(4) certain jurisdictions outside of the United States that offer 'offshore' banking and related facilities designed to provide anonymity, coupled with weak financial supervisory and enforcement regimes, provide essential tools to disguise ownership and movement of criminal funds derived from, or used to commit, offenses ranging from narcotics trafficking, terrorism, arms smuggling, and trafficking in human beings, to financial frauds that prey on law-abiding citizens;

"(5) transactions involving such offshore jurisdictions make it difficult for law enforcement officials and regulators to follow the trail of money earned by criminals, organized international criminal enterprises, and global terrorist organizations;

"(6) correspondent banking facilities are one of the banking mechanisms susceptible in some circumstances to manipulation by foreign banks to permit the laundering of funds by hiding the identity of real parties in interest to financial transactions;

"(7) private banking services can be susceptible to manipulation by money launderers, for example corrupt foreign government officials, particularly if those services include the creation of offshore accounts and facilities for large personal funds transfers to channel funds into accounts around the globe;

"(8) United States anti-money laundering efforts are impeded by outmoded and inadequate statutory provisions that make investigations, prosecutions, and forfeitures more difficult, particularly in cases in which money laundering involves foreign persons, foreign banks, or foreign countries;

"(9) the ability to mount effective counter-measures to international money launderers requires national, as well as bilateral and multilateral action, using tools specially designed for that effort; and

"(10) the Basle Committee on Banking Regulation and Supervisory Practices and the Financial Action Task Force on Money Laundering, of both of which the United States is a member, have each adopted international anti-money laundering principles and recommendations.

"(b) **Purposes.**—The purposes of this title [the International Money Laundering Abatement and Financial Anti-Terrorism Act of 2001, Pub.L. 107–56, Title III, §§ 301 to 377; see Tables for classification] are—

"(1) to increase the strength of United States measures to prevent, detect, and prosecute international money laundering and the financing of terrorism;

"(2) To ensure that—

"(A) banking transactions and financial relationships and the conduct of such transactions and relationships, do not contravene the purposes of subchapter II of chapter 53 of title 31, United States Code [this subchapter], section 21 of the Federal Deposit Insurance Act [12 U.S.C.A. § 1829b], or chapter 2 of title I of Public Law 91–508 (84 Stat. 1116) [12 U.S.C.A. § 1951 et seq.], or facilitate the evasion of any such provision; and

"(B) the purposes of such provisions of law continue to be fulfilled, and such provisions of law are effectively and efficiently administered;

"(3) to strengthen the provisions put into place by the Money Laundering Control Act of 1986 (18 U.S.C. 981 note) [Pub.L. 99–570, Title I, Subtitle H, Oct. 27, 1986, 100 Stat. 3207–18, which enacted sections 981, 982, 1956 and 1957 of this title, section 5324 of Title 31, amended sections 1952, 1961 and 2516 of this title, sections 1464, 1730, 1786, 1817, 1818, 3403 and 3413 of Title 12, sections 5312, 5316, 5317, 5318, 5321 and 5322 of Title 31, and enacted provisions set out as notes under section 981 of this title, sections 1464 and 1730 of Title 12, sections 5315, 5316, 5317, 5321 and 5324 of Title 31], especially with respect to crimes by non-United States nationals and foreign financial institutions;

"(4) to provide a clear national mandate for subjecting to special scrutiny those foreign jurisdictions, financial institutions operating outside of the United States, and classes of international transactions or types of accounts that pose particular, identifiable opportunities for criminal abuse;

"(5) to provide the Secretary of the Treasury (in this title referred to as the 'Secretary') with broad discretion, subject to the safeguards provided by the Administrative Procedure Act under title 5, United States Code [5 U.S.C.A. §§ 551 et seq., 701 et seq.], to take measures tailored to the particular money laundering problems presented by specific foreign jurisdictions, financial institutions operating outside of the United States, and classes of international transactions or types of accounts;

"(6) to ensure that the employment of such measures by the Secretary permits appropriate opportunity for comment by affected financial institutions;

"(7) to provide guidance to domestic financial institutions on particular foreign jurisdictions, financial institutions operating outside of the United States, and classes of international transactions or types of accounts that are of primary money laundering concern to the United States Government;

"(8) to ensure that the forfeiture of any assets in connection with the anti-terrorist efforts of the United States permits for adequate challenge consistent with providing due process rights;

"(9) to clarify the terms of the safe harbor from civil liability for filing suspicious activity reports;

"(10) to strengthen the authority of the Secretary to issue and administer geographic targeting orders, and to clarify that violations of such orders or any other requirement imposed under the authority contained in chapter 2 of title I of Public Law 91–508 [12 U.S.C.A. § 1951 et seq.] and subchapter II chapter 53 of title 31, United States Code [this subchapter], may result in criminal and civil penalties;

"(11) to ensure that all appropriate elements of the financial services industry are subject to appropriate requirements to report potential money laundering transactions to proper authorities, and that jurisdictional disputes do not hinder examination of compliance by financial institutions with relevant reporting requirements;

"(12) to strengthen the ability of financial institutions to maintain the integrity of their employee population; and

"(13) to strengthen measures to prevent the use of the United States financial system for personal gain by corrupt foreign officials and to facilitate the repatriation of any stolen assets to the citizens of countries to whom such assets belong."

[Amendments by Pub.L. 108–458, Title VI, Subtitle C, to Public Law 107–56, the United States Code, the Federal Deposit Insurance Act, and any other provision of law to take effect as if such amendments had been included in Public Law 107–56, as of Oct. 26, 2001, and no amendment made by such Public Law that is inconsistent with an amendment made by this subtitle to be deemed to have taken effect, see Pub.L. 108–458, § 6205, set out as a note under 12 U.S.C.A. § 1828.]

4–Year Congressional Review; Expedited Consideration

Pub.L. 107–56, Title III, § 303, Oct. 26, 2001, 115 Stat. 298, as amended Pub.L. 108–458, Title VI, § 6202(d), Dec. 17, 2004, 118 Stat. 3745, which related to 4–Year Congressional review; expedited consideration, was repealed by Pub.L. 108–458, Title VI, § 6204, Dec. 17, 2004, 118 Stat. 3747. Prior to repeal, the note read:

"**(a) In general.**—Effective on and after the first day of fiscal year 2005, the provisions of this title and the amendments made by this title [the International Money Laundering Abatement and Financial Anti-Terrorism Act of 2001, enacting 15 U.S.C.A. § 1681v, 22 U.S.C.A. § 262p–4r, and 31 U.S.C.A. §§ 310, 5318A, 5319, 5331, and 5332, amending 12 U.S.C.A. §§ 248, 1828, 1829b, 1842, 1953, 3412, 3414, and 3420, 15 U.S.C.A. § 1681u, 18 U.S.C.A. §§ 470 to 474, 476 to 484, 493, 981, 982, 1029, 1956, 1960, and 2466, 21 U.S.C.A. § 853, 28 U.S.C.A. § 2467, and 31 U.S.C.A. §§ 5312, 5317, 5318, 5321, 5322, 5324, 5326, 5328, 5330, and 5341, redesignating former 31 U.S.C.A. § 310 as § 311, enacting provisions set out as notes under 12 U.S.C.A. §§ 1828, 1829b, and 1842, 18 U.S.C.A. § 983, and 31 U.S.C.A. §§ 310, 5311, 5313, 5314, 5318, 5331, and 5332] shall terminate if the Congress enacts a joint resolution, the text after the resolving clause of which is as follows: 'That provisions of the International Money Laundering Abatement and Financial Antiterrorism [sic; probably should be 'Anti-Terrorism'] Act of 2001 [this title; see classifications above], and the amendments made thereby, shall no longer have the force of law.'.

"**(b) Expedited consideration.**—Any joint resolution submitted pursuant to this section should be considered by the Congress expeditiously. In particular, it shall be considered in the Senate in accordance with the provisions of section 601(b) of the International Security Assistance and Arms Control Act of 1976 [Pub.L. 94–329, Title IV, § 601(b), June 30, 1976, 90 Stat. 765, which is not classified to the Code]."

[Amendments by Pub.L. 108–458, Title VI, Subtitle C, to Public Law 107–56, the United States Code, the Federal Deposit Insurance Act, and any other provision of law to take effect as if such amendments had been included in Public Law 107–56, as of Oct. 26, 2001, and no amendment made by such Public Law that is inconsistent with an amendment made by this subtitle to be deemed to have taken effect, see Pub.L. 108–458, § 6205, set out as a note under 12 U.S.C.A. § 1828.]

Cooperative Efforts to Deter Money Laundering

Pub.L. 107–56, Title III, § 314, Oct. 26, 2001, 115 Stat. 307, as amended Pub.L. 108–458, Title VI, § 6202(f), Dec. 17, 2004, 118 Stat. 3745, provided that:

"**(a) Cooperation among financial institutions, regulatory authorities, and law enforcement authorities.**—

"**(1) Regulations.**—The Secretary shall, within 120 days after the date of enactment of this Act [Oct. 26, 2001], adopt regulations to encourage further cooperation among financial institutions, their regulatory authorities, and law enforcement authorities, with the specific purpose of encouraging regulatory authorities and law enforcement authorities to share with financial institutions information regarding individuals, entities, and organizations engaged in, or reasonably suspected based on credible evidence of engaging in, terrorist acts or money laundering activities.

"**(2) Cooperation and information sharing procedures.**—The regulations adopted under paragraph (1) may include or create procedures for cooperation and information sharing focusing on—

"**(A)** matters specifically related to the finances of terrorist groups, the means by which terrorist groups transfer funds around the world and within the United States, including through the use of charitable organizations, nonprofit organizations, and nongovernmental organizations, the extent to which financial institutions in the United States are unwittingly involved in such finances, and the extent to which such institutions are at risk as a result;

"**(B)** the relationship, particularly the financial relationship, between international narcotics traffickers and foreign terrorist organizations, the extent to which their memberships overlap and engage in joint activities, and the extent to which they cooperate with each other in raising and transferring funds for their respective purposes; and

"**(C)** means of facilitating the identification of accounts and transactions involving terrorist groups and facilitating the exchange of information concerning such accounts and transactions between financial institutions and law enforcement organizations.

"**(3) Contents.**—The regulations adopted pursuant to paragraph (1) may—

"**(A)** require that each financial institution designate 1 or more persons to receive information concerning, and monitor accounts of individuals, entities, and organizations identified pursuant to paragraph (1); and

"**(B)** further establish procedures for the protection of the shared information, consistent with the capacity, size, and nature of the financial institution to which the particular procedures apply.

"(4) **Rule of construction.**—The receipt of information by a financial institution pursuant to this section shall not relieve or otherwise modify the obligations of the financial institution with respect to any other person or account.

"(5) **Use of information.**—Information received by a financial institution pursuant to this section shall not be used for any purpose other than identifying and reporting on activities that may involve terrorist acts or money laundering activities.

"(b) **Cooperation among financial institutions.**—Upon notice provided to the Secretary, 2 or more financial institutions and any association of financial institutions may share information with one another regarding individuals, entities, organizations, and countries suspected of possible terrorist or money laundering activities. A financial institution or association that transmits, receives, or shares such information for the purposes of identifying and reporting activities that may involve terrorist acts or money laundering activities shall not be liable to any person under any law or regulation of the United States, any constitution, law, or regulation of any State or political subdivision thereof, or under any contract or other legally enforceable agreement (including any arbitration agreement), for such disclosure or for any failure to provide notice of such disclosure to the person who is the subject of such disclosure, or any other person identified in the disclosure, except where such transmission, receipt, or sharing violates this section or regulations promulgated pursuant to this section.

"(c) **Rule of construction.**—Compliance with the provisions of this title [Pub.L. 107–56, Title III, §§ 301 to 377; see Tables for classification] requiring or allowing financial institutions and any association of financial institutions to disclose or share information regarding individuals, entities, and organizations engaged in or suspected of engaging in terrorist acts or money laundering activities shall not constitute a violation of the provisions of title V of the Gramm–Leach–Bliley Act (Public Law 106–102) [Pub.L. 106–102, Title V, Nov. 12, 1999, 113 Stat. 1436, which is classified to 15 U.S.C.A. § 6801 et seq.].

"(d) **Reports to the financial services industry on suspicious financial activities.**—At least semiannually, the Secretary shall—

"(1) publish a report containing a detailed analysis identifying patterns of suspicious activity and other investigative insights derived from suspicious activity reports and investigations conducted by Federal, State, and local law enforcement agencies to the extent appropriate; and

"(2) distribute such report to financial institutions (as defined in section 5312 of title 31, United States Code [31 U.S.C.A. § 5312])."

[Amendments by Pub.L. 108–458, Title VI, Subtitle C, to Public Law 107–56, the United States Code, the Federal Deposit Insurance Act, and any other provision of law to take effect as if such amendments had been included in Public Law 107–56, as of Oct. 26, 2001, and no amendment made by such Public Law that is inconsistent with an amendment made by this subtitle to be deemed to have taken effect, see Pub.L. 108–458, § 6205, set out as a note under 12 U.S.C.A. § 1828.]

Report and Recommendation

Pub.L. 107–56, Title III, § 324, Oct. 26, 2001, 115 Stat. 316, provided that: "Not later than 30 months after the date of enactment of this Act [Oct. 26, 2001], the Secretary, in consultation with the Attorney General, the Federal banking agencies (as defined at section 3 of the Federal Deposit Insurance Act [Act Sept. 21, 1950, c. 967, § 2[3], 64 Stat. 873, which is classified to 12 U.S.C.A. § 1813]), the National Credit Union Administration Board, the Securities and Exchange Commission, and such other agencies as the Secretary may determine, at the discretion of the Secretary, shall evaluate the operations of the provisions of this subtitle [Pub.L. 107–56, Title III, Subtitle A, §§ 311 to 330; see Tables for classification] and make recommendations to Congress as to any legislative action with respect to this subtitle as the Secretary may determine to be necessary or advisable."

International Cooperation on Identification of Originators of Wire Transfers

Pub.L. 107–56, Title III, § 328, Oct. 26, 2001, 115 Stat. 319, provided that:

"The Secretary shall—

"(1) in consultation with the Attorney General and the Secretary of State, take all reasonable steps to encourage foreign governments to require the inclusion of the name of the originator in wire transfer instructions sent to the United States and other countries, with the information to remain with the transfer from its origination until the point of disbursement; and

"(2) Report annually to the committee on financial services of the House of Representatives and the committee on banking, housing, and urban affairs of the Senate on—

"(A) progress toward the goal enumerated in paragraph (1), as well as impediments to implementation and an estimated compliance rate; and

"(B) impediments to instituting a regime in which all appropriate identification, as defined by the Secretary, about wire transfer recipients shall be included with wire transfers from their point of origination until disbursement."

Criminal Penalties

Pub.L. 107–56, Title III, § 329, Oct. 26, 2001, 115 Stat. 319, provided that: "Any person who is an official or employee of any department, agency, bureau, office, commission, or other entity of the Federal Government, and any other person who is acting for or on behalf of any such entity, who, directly or indirectly, in connection with the administration of this title [the International Money Laundering Abatement and Financial Anti-Terrorism Act of 2001, Pub.L. 107–56, Title III, §§ 301 to 377, Oct. 26, 2001, 115 Stat. 296; for complete classification, see Short Title note set out under 31 U.S.C.A. § 5301 and Tables], corruptly demands, seeks, receives, accepts, or agrees to receive or accept anything of value personally or for any other person or entity in return for—

"(1) being influenced in the performance of any official act;

"(2) being influenced to commit or aid in the committing, or to collude in, or allow, any fraud, or make opportunity for the commission of any fraud, on the United States; or

"(3) being induced to do or omit to do any act in violation of the official duty of such official or person, shall be fined in an amount not more than 3 times the monetary equivalent of the thing of value, or imprisoned for not more than 15 years, or both. A violation of this section shall be subject to chapter 227 of title 18, United States Code [18 U.S.C.A. § 3551 et seq.], and the provisions of the United States Sentencing Guidelines."

Report on Investment Companies

Pub.L. 107–56, Title III, § 356(c), Oct. 26, 2001, 115 Stat. 324, as amended Pub.L. 108–458, Title VI, § 6202(j), Dec. 17, 2004, 118 Stat. 3746, provided that:

"(1) **In general.**—Not later than 1 year after the date of enactment of this Act [Oct. 26, 2001], the Secretary, the Board of Governors of the Federal Reserve System, and the Securities and Exchange Commission shall jointly submit a report to the Congress on recommendations for effective regulations to apply the requirements of subchapter II of chapter 53 of title 31, United States Code [this subchapter], to investment companies pursuant to section 5312(a)(2)(I) of title 31, United States Code.

"(2) **Definition.**—For purposes of this subsection, the term 'investment company'—

"(A) has the same meaning as in section 3 of the Investment Company Act of 1940 (15 U.S.C. 80a–3); and

"(B) includes any person that, but for the exceptions provided for in paragraph (1) or (7) of section 3(c) of the Investment Company Act of 1940 (15 U.S.C. 80a–3(c)), would be an investment company.

"(3) **Additional recommendations.**—The report required by paragraph (1) may make different recommendations for different types of entities covered by this subsection.

"(4) **Beneficial ownership of personal holding companies.**—The report described in paragraph (1) shall also include recommendations as to whether the Secretary should promulgate regulations to treat any corporation, business trust, or other grantor trust whose assets are predominantly securities, bank certificates of deposit, or other securities or investment instruments (other than such as relate to operating subsidiaries of such corporation or trust) and that has 5 or fewer common shareholders or holders of beneficial or other equity interest, as a financial institution within the meaning of that phrase in section 5312(a)(2)(I) and whether to require such corporations or trusts to disclose their beneficial owners when opening accounts or initiating funds transfers at any domestic financial institution."

Report on Need for Additional Legislation Relating to Informal Money Transfer Systems

Pub.L. 107–56, Title III, § 359(d), Oct. 26, 2001, 115 Stat. 329, provided that: ""(d) **Report.**—Not later than 1 year after the date of enactment of this Act [Oct. 26, 2001], the Secretary of the Treasury shall report to Congress on the need for any additional legislation relating to persons who engage as a business in an informal money transfer system or any network of people who engage as a business in facilitating the transfer of money domestically or internationally outside of the conventional financial institutions system, counter money laundering and regulatory controls relating to underground money movement and banking systems, including whether the threshold for the filing of suspicious activity reports under section 5318(g) of title 31, United States Code should be lowered in the case of such systems."

Uniform State Licensing and Regulation of Check Cashing, Currency Exchange, and Money Transmitting Businesses

Pub.L. 103–325, Title IV, § 407, Sept. 23, 1994, 108 Stat. 2247, provided that:

"(a) **Uniform laws and enforcement.**—For purposes of preventing money laundering and protecting the payment system from fraud and abuse, it is the sense of the Congress that the several States should—

"(1) establish uniform laws for licensing and regulating businesses which—

"(A) provide check cashing, currency exchange, or money transmitting or remittance services, or issue or redeem money orders, travelers' checks, and other similar instruments; and

"(B) are not depository institutions (as defined in section 5313(g) of title 31, United States Code) [section 5313(g) of this title]; and

"(2) provide sufficient resources to the appropriate State agency to enforce such laws and regulations prescribed pursuant to such laws.

"(b) **Model statute.**—It is the sense of the Congress that the several States should develop, through the auspices of the National Conference of Commissioners on Uniform State Laws, the American Law Institute, or such other forum as the States may determine to be appropriate, a model statute to carry out the goals described in subsection (a) which would include the following:

"(1) **Licensing requirements.**—A requirement that any business described in subsection (a)(1) be licensed and regulated by an appropriate State agency in order to engage in any such activity within the State.

"(2) **Licensing standards.**—A requirement that—

"(A) in order for any business described in subsection (a)(1) to be licensed in the State, the appropriate State agency shall review and approve—

"(i) the business record and the capital adequacy of the business seeking the license; and

"(ii) the competence, experience, integrity, and financial ability of any individual who—

"(I) is a director, officer, or supervisory employee of such business; or

"(II) owns or controls such business; and

"(B) any record, on the part of any business seeking the license or any person referred to in subparagraph (A)(ii), of—

"(i) any criminal activity;

"(ii) any fraud or other act of personal dishonesty;

"(iii) any act, omission, or practice which constitutes a breach of a fiduciary duty; or

"(iv) any suspension or removal, by any agency or department of the United States or any State, from participation in the conduct of any federally or State licensed or regulated business,

may be grounds for the denial of any such license by the appropriate State agency.

"(3) **Reporting requirements.**—A requirement that any business described in subsection (a)(1)—

"(A) disclose to the appropriate State agency the fees charged to consumers for services described in subsection (a)(1)(A); and

"(B) conspicuously disclose to the public, at each location of such business, the fees charged to consumers for such services.

"(4) **Procedures to ensure compliance with Federal cash transaction reporting requirements.**—A civil or criminal penalty for operating any business referred to in paragraph (1) without establishing and complying with appropriate procedures to ensure compliance with subchapter II of chapter 53 of title 31, United States Code (relating to records and reports on monetary instruments transactions) [this subchapter].

"(5) **Criminal penalties for operation of business without a license.**—A criminal penalty for operating any business referred to in paragraph (1) without a license within the State after the end of an appropriate transition period beginning on the date of enactment of such model statute by the State.

"(c) **Study required.**—The Secretary of the Treasury shall conduct a study of—

"(1) the progress made by the several States in developing an enacting a model statute which—

"(A) meets the requirements of subsection (b); and

"(B) furthers the goals of—

"(i) preventing money laundering by businesses which are required to be licensed under any such statute; and

"(ii) protecting the payment system, including the receipt, payment, collection, and clearing of checks, from fraud and abuse by such businesses; and

"(2) the adequacy of—

"(A) the activity of the several States in enforcing the requirements of such statute; and

"(B) the resources made available to the appropriate State agencies for such enforcement activity.

"(d) **Report required.**—Not later than the end of the 3-year period beginning on the date of enactment of this Act [Sept. 23, 1994] and not later than the end of each of the first two 1-year periods beginning after the end of such 3-year period, the Secretary of the Treasury shall submit a report to the Congress containing the findings and recommendations of the Secretary in connection with the study under subsection (c), together with such recommendations for legislative and administrative action as the Secretary may determine to be appropriate.

"(e) **Recommendations in cases of inadequate regulation and enforcement by States.**—If the Secretary of the Treasury determines that any State has been unable to—

"(1) enact a statute which meets the requirements described in subsection (b);

"(2) undertake adequate activity to enforce such statute; or

"(3) make adequate resources available to the appropriate State agency for such enforcement activity,

the report submitted pursuant to subsection (d) shall contain recommendations of the Secretary which are designed to facilitate the enactment and enforcement by the State of such a statute.

"(f) **Federal funding study.**—

"(1) **Study required.**—The Secretary of the Treasury shall conduct a study to identify possible available sources of Federal funding to cover costs which will be incurred by the States in carrying out the purposes of this section.

"(2) **Report.**—The Secretary of the Treasury shall submit a report to the Congress on the study conducted pursuant to paragraph (1) not later than the end of the 18-month period beginning on the date of enactment of this Act [Sept. 23, 1994]."

Anti-Money Laundering Training Team

Pub.L. 102-550, Title XV, § 1518, Oct. 28, 1992, 106 Stat. 4060, provided that: "The Secretary of the Treasury and the Attorney General shall jointly establish a team of experts to assist and provide training to foreign governments and agencies thereof in developing and expanding their capabilities for investigating and prosecuting violations of money laundering and related laws."

Advisory Group on Reporting Requirements

Pub.L. 102-550, Title XV, § 1564, Oct. 28, 1992, 106 Stat. 4073, provided that:

"(a) **Establishment.**—Not later than 90 days after the date of the enactment of this Act [Oct. 28, 1992], the Secretary of the Treasury shall establish a Bank Secrecy Act Advisory Group consisting of representatives of the Department of the Treasury, the Department of Justice, and the Office of National Drug Control Policy and of other interested persons and financial institutions subject to the reporting requirements of subchapter II of chapter 53 of title 31, United States Code [this subchapter], or section 6050I of the Internal Revenue Code of 1986 [section 6050I of Title 26, Internal Revenue Code].

"(b) **Purposes.**—The Advisory Group shall provide a means by which the Secretary—

"(1) informs private sector representatives, on a regular basis, of the ways in which the reports submitted pursuant to the requirements referred to in subsection (a) have been used;

"(2) informs private sector representatives, on a regular basis, of how information regarding suspicious financial transactions provided voluntarily by financial institutions has been used; and

"(3) receives advice on the manner in which the reporting requirements referred to in subsection (a) should be modified to enhance the ability of law enforcement agencies to use the information provided for law enforcement purposes.

"(c) **Inapplicability of Federal Advisory Committee Act.**—The Federal Advisory Committee Act [Appendix 2 to Title 5, Government Organization and Employees] shall not apply to the Bank Secrecy Act Advisory Group established pursuant to subsection (a)."

GAO Feasibility Study of the Financial Crimes Enforcement Network

Pub.L. 102-550, Title XV, § 1565, Oct. 28, 1992, 106 Stat. 4074, provided that:

"(a) **Study required.**—The Comptroller General of the United States shall conduct a feasibility study of the Financial Crimes Enforcement Network (popularly referred to as 'Fincen') established by the Secretary of the Treasury in cooperation with other agencies and departments of the United States and appropriate Federal banking agencies.

"(b) **Specific requirements.**—In conducting the study required under subsection (a), the Comptroller General shall examine and evaluate—

"(1) the extent to which Federal, State, and local governmental and nongovernmental organizations are voluntarily providing information which is necessary for the system to be useful for law enforcement purposes;

"(2) the extent to which the operational guidelines established for the system provide for the coordinated and efficient entry of information into, and withdrawal of information from, the system;

"(3) the extent to which the operating procedures established for the system provide appropriate standards or guidelines for determining—

"(A) who is to be given access to the information in the system;

"(B) what limits are to be imposed on the use of such information; and

"(C) how information about activities or relationships which involve or are closely associated with the exercise of constitutional rights is to be screened out of the system; and

"(4) the extent to which the operating procedures established for the system provide for the prompt verification of the accuracy and completeness of information entered into the system and the prompt deletion or correction of inaccurate or incomplete information.

"(c) **Report to Congress.**—Before the end of the 1-year period, beginning on the date of the enactment of this Act [Oct. 28, 1992], the Comptroller General of the United States shall submit a report to the Congress containing the findings and conclusions of the Comptroller General in connection with the study conducted pursuant to subsection (a), together with such recommendations for legislative or administrative action as the Comptroller General may determine to be appropriate."

[For termination, effective May 15, 2000, of reporting provisions of Pub.L. 102–550, § 1565(c), set out above, see Pub.L. 104–66, § 3003, as amended, set out as a note under 31 U.S.C.A. § 1113, and the 10th item on page 5 of House Document No. 103–7.]

Reports on Uses Made of Currency Transaction Reports

Pub.L.101–647, Title I, § 101, Nov. 29, 1990, 104 Stat. 4789, which provided for a biennial report to Congress, through 1995, relating to uses made of currency transaction reports, terminated, effective May 15, 2000, pursuant to Pub.L. 104–66, § 3003, as amended, set out as a note under 31 U.S.C.A. § 1113, and the 15th item on page 141 of House Document No. 103–7.

International Currency Transaction Reporting

Pub.L. 100–690, Title IV, § 4701, Nov. 18, 1988, 102 Stat. 4290, which related to Congressional findings concerning success of cash transaction and money laundering control statutes in the United States and desirability of the United States playing a leadership role in development of a similar international system, urged the United States Government to seek the active cooperation of other countries in the enforcement of such statutes, urged the Secretary of the Treasury to negotiate with finance ministers of foreign countries to establish an international currency control agency to serve as a central source of information and database for international drug enforcement agencies to collect and analyze currency transaction reports filed by member countries, and encouraged the adoption, by member countries, of uniform cash transaction and money laundering statutes, was repealed by Pub.L. 102–583, § 6(e)(1), Nov. 2, 1992, 106 Stat. 4933.

Restrictions on Laundering of United States Currency

Pub.L. 100–690, Title IV, § 4702, Nov. 18, 1988, 102 Stat. 4291, as amended Pub.L. 103–447, Title I, § 103(b), Nov. 2, 1994, 108 Stat. 4693, provided that:

"(a) **Findings.**—The Congress finds that international currency transactions, especially in United States currency, that involve the proceeds of narcotics trafficking fuel trade in narcotics in the United States and worldwide and consequently are a threat to the national security of the United States.

"(b) **Purpose.**—The purpose of this section is to provide for international negotiations that would expand access to information on transactions involving large amounts of United States currency wherever those transactions occur worldwide.

"(c) **Negotiations.**—(1) The Secretary of the Treasury (hereinafter in this section referred to as the 'Secretary') shall enter into negotiations with the appropriate financial supervisory agencies and other officials of any foreign country the financial institutions of which do business in United States currency. Highest priority shall be attached to countries whose financial institutions the Secretary determines, in consultation with the Attorney General and the Director of National Drug Control Policy, may be engaging in currency transactions involving the proceeds of international narcotics trafficking, particularly United States currency derived from drug sales in the United States.

"(2) The purposes of negotiations under this subsection are—

"(A) to reach one or more international agreements to ensure that foreign banks and other financial institutions maintain adequate records of large United States currency transactions, and

"(B) to establish a mechanism whereby such records may be made available to United States law enforcement officials.

In carrying out such negotiations, the Secretary should seek to enter into and further cooperative efforts, voluntary information exchanges, the use of letters rogatory, and mutual legal assistance treaties.

"(d) **Reports.**—Not later than 1 year after the date of enactment of this Act [Nov. 18, 1988], the Secretary shall submit an interim report to the Committee on Banking, Finance and Urban Affairs of the House of Representatives and the Committee on Banking, Housing, and Urban Affairs of the Senate on progress in the negotiations under subsection (c). Not later than 2 years after such enactment [Nov. 18, 1988], the Secretary shall submit a final report to such Committees and the President on the outcome of those negotiations and shall identify, in consultation with the Attorney General and the Director of National Drug Control Policy, countries—

"(1) with respect to which the Secretary determines there is evidence that the financial institutions in such countries are engaging in currency transactions involving the proceeds of international narcotics trafficking; and

"(2) which have not reached agreement with United States authorities on a mechanism for exchanging adequate records on international currency transactions in connection with narcotics investigations and proceedings.

"**(e) Authority.**—If after receiving the advice of the Secretary and in any case at the time of receipt of the Secretary's report, the Secretary determines that a foreign country—

"(1) has jurisdiction over financial institutions that are substantially engaging in currency transactions that effect the United States involving the proceeds of international narcotics trafficking;

"(2) such country has not reached agreement on a mechanism for exchanging adequate records on international currency transactions in connection with narcotics investigations and proceedings; and

"(3) such country is not negotiating in good faith to reach such an agreement,

the President shall impose appropriate penalties and sanctions, including temporarily or permanently—

"(1) prohibiting such persons, institutions or other entities in such countries from participating in any United States dollar clearing or wire transfer system; and

"(2) prohibiting such persons, institutions or entities in such countries from maintaining an account with any bank or other financial institution chartered under the laws of the United States or any State.

Any penalties or sanctions so imposed may be delayed or waived upon certification of the President to the Congress that it is in the national interest to do so. Financial institutions in such countries that maintain adequate records shall be exempt from such penalties and sanctions.

"**(f) Definitions.**—For the purposes of this section—

"(1) The term 'United States currency' means Federal Reserve Notes and United States coins.

"(2) The term 'adequate records' means records of United States' currency transactions in excess of $10,000 including the identification of the person initiating the transaction, the person's business or occupation, and the account or accounts affected by the transaction, or other records of comparable effect.

"**(g) [Repealed.** Pub.L. 103–447, Title I, § 103(b), Nov. 2, 1994, 108 Stat. 4693]."

[Any reference in any provision of law enacted before Jan. 4, 1995, to the Committee on Banking, Finance and Urban Affairs of the House of Representatives treated as referring to the Committee on Banking and Financial Services of the House of Representatives, see section 1(a)(2) of Pub.L. 104–14, set out as a note preceding section 21 of Title 2, The Congress.]

International Information Exchange System: Study of Foreign Branches of Domestic Institutions

Pub.L. 99–570, Title I, § 1363, Oct. 27, 1986, 100 Stat. 3207–33, required the Secretary of the Treasury to initiate discussions with the central banks or other appropriate governmental authorities of other countries and propose that an information exchange system be established to reduce international flow of money derived from illicit drug operations and other criminal activities and to report to Congress before the end of the 9–month period beginning Oct. 27, 1986. The Secretary of the Treasury was also required to conduct a study of (1) the extent to which foreign branches of domestic institutions are used to facilitate illicit transfers of or to evade reporting requirements on transfers of coins, currency, and other monetary instruments into and out of the United States; (2) the extent to which the law of the United States is applicable to the activities of such foreign branches; and (3) methods for obtaining the cooperation of the country in which any such foreign branch is located for purposes of enforcing the law of the United States with respect to transfers, and reports on transfers, of such monetary instruments into and out of the United States and to report to Congress before the end of the 9–month period beginning Oct. 27, 1986.

§ 5312. Definitions and application

(a) In this subchapter—

(1) "financial agency" means a person acting for a person (except for a country, a monetary or financial authority acting as a monetary or financial authority, or an international financial institution of which the United States Government is a member) as a financial institution, bailee, depository trustee, or agent, or acting in a similar way related to money, credit, securities, gold, or a transaction in money, credit, securities, or gold.

(2) "financial institution" means—

(A) an insured bank (as defined in section 3(h) of the Federal Deposit Insurance Act (12 U.S.C. 1813(h)));

(B) a commercial bank or trust company;

(C) a private banker;

(D) an agency or branch of a foreign bank in the United States;

(E) any credit union;

(F) a thrift institution;

(G) a broker or dealer registered with the Securities and Exchange Commission under the Securities Exchange Act of 1934 (15 U.S.C. 78a et seq.);

(H) a broker or dealer in securities or commodities;

(I) an investment banker or investment company;

(J) a currency exchange;

(K) an issuer, redeemer, or cashier of travelers' checks, checks, money orders, or similar instruments;

(L) an operator of a credit card system;

(M) an insurance company;

(N) a dealer in precious metals, stones, or jewels;

(O) a pawnbroker;

(P) a loan or finance company;

(Q) a travel agency;

(R) a licensed sender of money or any other person who engages as a business in the transmission of funds, including any person who engages as a business in an informal money transfer system or any network of people who engage as a business in facilitating the transfer of money domestically or internationally outside of the conventional financial institutions system;

(S) a telegraph company;

(T) a business engaged in vehicle sales, including automobile, airplane, and boat sales;

(U) persons involved in real estate closings and settlements;

(V) the United States Postal Service;

(W) an agency of the United States Government or of a State or local government carrying out a duty or power of a business described in this paragraph;

(X) a casino, gambling casino, or gaming establishment with an annual gaming revenue of more than $1,000,000 which—

(i) is licensed as a casino, gambling casino, or gaming establishment under the laws of any State or any political subdivision of any State; or

(ii) is an Indian gaming operation conducted under or pursuant to the Indian Gaming Regulatory Act other than an operation which is limited to class I gaming (as defined in section 4(6) of such Act);

(Y) any business or agency which engages in any activity which the Secretary of the Treasury determines, by regulation, to be an activity which is similar to, related to, or a substitute for any activity in which any business described in this paragraph is authorized to engage; or

(Z) any other business designated by the Secretary whose cash transactions have a high degree of usefulness in criminal, tax, or regulatory matters.

(3) "monetary instruments" means—

(A) United States coins and currency;

(B) as the Secretary may prescribe by regulation, coins and currency of a foreign country, travelers' checks, bearer negotiable instruments, bearer investment securities, bearer securities, stock on which title is passed on delivery, and similar material; and

(C) as the Secretary of the Treasury shall provide by regulation for purposes of sections 5316 and 5331, checks, drafts, notes, money orders, and other similar instruments which are drawn on or by a foreign financial institution and are not in bearer form.

(4) Nonfinancial trade or business.—The term "nonfinancial trade or business" means any trade or business other than a financial institution that is subject to the reporting requirements of section 5313 and regulations prescribed under such section.

(5) "person", in addition to its meaning under section 1 of title 1, includes a trustee, a representative of an estate and, when the Secretary prescribes, a governmental entity.

(6) "United States" means the States of the United States, the District of Columbia, and, when the Secretary prescribes by regulation, the Commonwealth of Puerto Rico, the Virgin Islands, Guam, the Northern Mariana Islands, American Samoa, the Trust Territory of the Pacific Islands, a territory or possession of the United States, or a military or diplomatic establishment.

(b) In this subchapter—

(1) "domestic financial agency" and "domestic financial institution" apply to an action in the United States of a financial agency or institution.

(2) "foreign financial agency" and "foreign financial institution" apply to an action outside the United States of a financial agency or institution.

(c) Additional definitions.—For purposes of this subchapter, the following definitions shall apply:

(1) [1] **Certain institutions included in definition.**—The term "financial institution" (as defined in subsection (a)) includes the following:

(A) [2] Any futures commission merchant, commodity trading advisor, or commodity pool operator registered, or required to register, under the Commodity Exchange Act [7 U.S.C.A. § 1 et seq.].

(Pub.L. 97–258, Sept. 13, 1982, 96 Stat. 995; Pub.L. 99–570, Title I, § 1362, Oct. 27, 1986, 100 Stat. 3207–33; Pub.L. 100–690, Title VI, § 6185(a), (g)(1), Nov. 18, 1988, 102 Stat. 4354, 4357; Pub.L. 103–325, Title IV, §§ 405, 409, Sept. 23, 1994, 108 Stat. 2247, 2252; Pub.L. 107–56, Title III, §§ 321(a), (b), 359(a), 365(c)(1), (2)(A), Oct. 26, 2001, 115 Stat. 315, 328, 335; Pub.L. 108–458, Title VI, §§ 6202(g), 6203(b), Dec. 17, 2004, 118 Stat. 3746.)

[1] So in original. No par. (2) was enacted.

[2] So in original. No subpar. (B) was enacted.

HISTORICAL AND STATUTORY NOTES

References in Text

Section 3(h) of the Federal Deposit Insurance Act, referred to in subsec. (a)(2)(A), is § 3(h) of Act Sept. 21, 1950, c. 967, 64 Stat. 873, which is classified to § 1813(h) of Title 12, Banks and Banking.

The Securities Exchange Act of 1934, referred to in subsec. (a)(2)(G), is Act June 6, 1934, c. 404, 48 Stat. 881, as amended, which is classified principally to chapter 2B (§ 78a et seq.) of Title 15, Commerce and Trade. For complete classification of this Act to the Code, see § 78a of Title 15, and Tables.

The Indian Gaming Regulatory Act, referred to in subsec. (a)(2)(X), is Pub.L. 100–497, Oct. 17, 1988, 192 Stat. 2467, as amended, which is classified generally to chapter 29 (section 2701 et seq.) of Title 25, Indians. Section 4(6) of such Act is classified to section 2703(6) of Title 25. For complete classification of this Act to the Code, see Short Title note set out under section 2701 of Title 25 and Tables.

The Commodity Exchange Act, referred to in subsec. (c)(1)(A), is Act Sept. 21, 1922, c. 369, 42 Stat. 998, as amended, which is classified generally to chapter 1 of Title 7, 7 U.S.C.A. § 1 et seq. For complete classification, see 7 U.S.C.A. § 1 seq. and Tables.

Another section 365(c) of Pub.L. 107–56 amended the table of contents at the beginning of this chapter.

Effective and Applicability Provisions

2004 Acts. Amendments by Pub.L. 108–458, Title VI, Subtitle C, to Public Law 107–56, the United States Code, the Federal Deposit Insurance Act, and any other provision of law to take effect as if such amendments had been included in Public Law 107–56, as of Oct. 26, 2001, and no amendment made by such Public Law that is inconsistent with an amendment made by this subtitle to be deemed to have taken effect, see Pub.L. 108–458, § 6205, set out as a note under 12 U.S.C.A. § 1828.

4–Year Congressional Review; Expedited Consideration

Effective on and after the first day of fiscal year 2005, amendments by Title III (§§ 301 to 377) of Pub.L. 107–56 shall terminate if Congress enacts a joint resolution to that effect; such resolution shall be given expedited consideration, see Pub.L. 107–56, Title III, § 303, Oct. 26, 2001, 115 Stat. 298, set out as a note under 31 U.S.C.A. § 5311.

§ 5313. Reports on domestic coins and currency transactions

(a) When a domestic financial institution is involved in a transaction for the payment, receipt, or transfer of United States coins or currency (or other monetary instruments the Secretary of the Treasury prescribes), in an amount, denomination, or amount and denomination, or under circumstances the Secretary prescribes by regulation, the institution and any other participant in the transaction the Secretary may prescribe shall file a report on the transaction at the time and in the way the Secretary prescribes. A participant acting for another person shall make the report as the agent or bailee of the person and identify the person for whom the transaction is being made.

(b) The Secretary may designate a domestic financial institution as an agent of the United States Government to receive a report under this section. However, the Secretary may designate a domestic financial institution that is not insured, chartered, examined, or registered as a domestic financial institution only if the institution consents. The Secretary may suspend or revoke a designation for a violation of this subchapter or a regulation under this subchapter (except a violation of section 5315 of this title or a regulation prescribed under section 5315), section 411 of the National Housing Act (12 U.S.C. 1730d), or section 21 of the Federal Deposit Insurance Act (12 U.S.C. 1829b).

(c)(1) A person (except a domestic financial institution designated under subsection (b) of this section) required to file a report under this section shall file the report—

(A) with the institution involved in the transaction if the institution was designated;

(B) in the way the Secretary prescribes when the institution was not designated; or

(C) with the Secretary.

(2) The Secretary shall prescribe—

(A) the filing procedure for a domestic financial institution designated under subsection (b) of this section; and

(B) the way the institution shall submit reports filed with it.

(d) Mandatory exemptions from reporting requirements.—

(1) In general.—The Secretary of the Treasury shall exempt, pursuant to section 5318(a)(6), a depository institution from the reporting requirements of subsection (a) with respect to transactions between the depository institution and the following categories of entities:

(A) Another depository institution.

(B) A department or agency of the United States, any State, or any political subdivision of any State.

(C) Any entity established under the laws of the United States, any State, or any political subdivision of any State, or under an interstate compact between 2 or more States, which exercises governmental authority on behalf of the United States or any such State or political subdivision.

(D) Any business or category of business the reports on which have little or no value for law enforcement purposes.

(2) Notice of exemption.—The Secretary of the Treasury shall publish in the Federal Register at such times as the Secretary determines to be appropriate (but not less frequently than once each year) a list of all the entities whose transactions with a depository institution are exempt under this subsection from the reporting requirements of subsection (a).

(e) Discretionary exemptions from reporting requirements.—

(1) In general.—The Secretary of the Treasury may exempt, pursuant to section 5318(a)(6), a depository institution from the reporting requirements of subsection (a) with respect to transactions between the depository institution and a qualified business customer of the institution on the basis of information submitted to the Secretary by the institution in accordance with procedures which the Secretary shall establish.

(2) Qualified business customer defined.—For purposes of this subsection, the term "qualified business customer" means a business which—

(A) maintains a transaction account (as defined in section 19(b)(1)(C) of the Federal Reserve Act) at the depository institution;

(B) frequently engages in transactions with the depository institution which are subject to the reporting requirements of subsection (a); and

(C) meets criteria which the Secretary determines are sufficient to ensure that the purposes of this subchapter are carried out without requiring a report with respect to such transactions.

(3) Criteria for exemption.—The Secretary of the Treasury shall establish, by regulation, the criteria for granting and maintaining an exemption under paragraph (1).

(4) Guidelines.—

(A) In general.—The Secretary of the Treasury shall establish guidelines for depository institutions to follow in selecting customers for an exemption under this subsection.

(B) Contents.—The guidelines may include a description of the types of businesses or an itemization of specific businesses for which no exemption will be granted under this subsection to any depository institution.

(5) Annual review.—The Secretary of the Treasury shall prescribe regulations requiring each depository institution to—

(A) review, at least once each year, the qualified business customers of such institution with respect to whom an exemption has been granted under this subsection; and

(B) upon the completion of such review, resubmit information about such customers, with such modifications as the institution determines to be appropriate, to the Secretary for the Secretary's approval.

(6) 2–Year phase-in provision.—During the 2–year period beginning on the date of enactment of the Money Laundering Suppression Act of 1994, this subsection shall be applied by the Secretary on the basis of such criteria as the Secretary determines to be appropriate to achieve an orderly implementation of the requirements of this subsection.

(f) Provisions applicable to mandatory and discretionary exemptions.—

(1) Limitation on liability of depository institutions.—No depository institution shall be subject to any penalty which may be imposed under this subchapter for the failure of the institution to file a report with respect to a transaction with a customer for whom an exemption has been granted under subsection (d) or (e) unless the institution—

(A) knowingly files false or incomplete information to the Secretary with respect to the transaction or the customer engaging in the transaction; or

(B) has reason to believe at the time the exemption is granted or the transaction is entered into that the customer or the transaction does not meet the criteria established for granting such exemption.

(2) Coordination with other provisions.—Any exemption granted by the Secretary of the Treasury under section 5318(a) in accordance with this section, and any transaction which is subject to such exemption, shall be subject to any other provision of law applicable to such exemption, including—

(A) the authority of the Secretary, under section 5318(a)(6), to revoke such exemption at any time; and

(B) any requirement to report, or any authority to require a report on, any possible violation of any law or regulation or any suspected criminal activity.

(g) Depository institution defined.—For purposes of this section, the term "depository institution"—

(1) has the meaning given to such term in section 19(b)(1)(A) of the Federal Reserve Act; and

(2) includes—

(A) any branch, agency, or commercial lending company (as such terms are defined in section 1(b) of the International Banking Act of 1978);

(B) any corporation chartered under section 25A of the Federal Reserve Act; and

(C) any corporation having an agreement or undertaking with the Board of Governors of the Federal Reserve System under section 25 of the Federal Reserve Act.

(Pub.L. 97–258, Sept. 13, 1982, 96 Stat. 996; Pub.L. 103–325, Title IV, § 402(a), Sept. 23, 1994, 108 Stat. 2243.)

HISTORICAL AND STATUTORY NOTES

References in Text

Section 411 of the National Housing Act, referred to in subsec. (b), is § 411 of Act June 27, 1934, c. 847, Title IV, as added Oct. 26, 1970, Pub.L. 91–508, Title I, § 102, 84 Stat. 1116, which is classified to § 1730d of Title 12, Banks and Banking.

Section 21 of the Federal Deposit Insurance Act, referred to in subsec. (b), is § 2[21] of Act Sept. 21, 1950, c. 967, as added Oct. 26, 1970, Pub.L. 91–508, Title I, § 101, 84 Stat. 1114, which is classified to § 1829b of Title 12.

Section 19(b)(1)(C) of the Federal Reserve Act, referred to in subsec. (e)(2)(A), is section 19(b)(1)(C) of Act Dec. 23, 1913, c. 6, 38 Stat. 251, as amended, which is classified to section 461(b)(1)(C) of Title 12, Banks and Banking.

The date of enactment of the Money Laundering Suppression Act of 1994, referred to in subsec. (e)(6), means the date of enactment of Title IV of Pub.L. 103-325, 108 Stat. 2243, which was approved Sept. 23, 1994.

Section 19(b)(1)(A) of the Federal Reserve Act, referred to in subsec. (g)(1), is section 19(b)(1)(A) of Act Dec. 23, 1913, c. 6, 38 Stat. 251, as amended, which is classified to section 461(b)(1)(A) of Title 12.

Section 1(b) of the International Banking Act of 1978, referred to in subsec. (g)(2)(A), is section 1(b) of Pub.L. 95-369, Sept. 17, 1978, 92 Stat. 607, which is classified to section 3101 of Title 12.

Section 25A of the Federal Reserve Act, referred to in subsec. (g)(2)(B), is section 25A of Act Dec. 23, 1913, c. 6, as added by Act Dec. 24, 1919, c. 18, 41 Stat. 378, and renumbered by Pub.L. 102-242, Title I, § 142(e)(2), Dec. 19, 1991, 105 Stat. 2281, which is classified generally to subchapter II (section 611 et seq.) of Title 12.

Section 25 of the Federal Reserve Act, referred to in subsec. (g)(2)(C), is section 25 of Act Dec. 23, 1913, c. 6, 38 Stat. 273, which is classified generally to subchapter I (section 601 et seq.) of Title 12.

Efficient Use of Currency Transaction Report System

Pub.L. 107–56, Title III, § 366, Oct. 26, 2001, 115 Stat. 335, provided that:

"**(a) Findings.**—The Congress finds the following:

"(1) The Congress established the currency transaction reporting requirements in 1970 because the Congress found then that such reports have a high degree of usefulness in criminal, tax, and regulatory investigations and proceedings and the usefulness of such reports has only increased in the years since the requirements were established.

"(2) In 1994, in response to reports and testimony that excess amounts of currency transaction reports were interfering with effective law enforcement, the Congress reformed the currency transaction report exemption requirements to provide—

"(A) mandatory exemptions for certain reports that had little usefulness for law enforcement, such as cash transfers between depository institutions and cash deposits from government agencies; and

"(B) discretionary authority for the Secretary of the Treasury to provide exemptions, subject to criteria and guidelines established by the Secretary, for financial institutions with regard to regular business customers that maintain accounts at an institution into which frequent cash deposits are made.

"(3) Today there is evidence that some financial institutions are not utilizing the exemption system, or are filing reports even if there is an exemption in effect, with the result that the volume of currency transaction reports is once again interfering with effective law enforcement.

"**(b) Study and report.**—

"**(1) Study required.**—The Secretary shall conduct a study of—

"(A) the possible expansion of the statutory exemption system in effect under section 5313 of title 31, United States Code [this section]; and

"(B) methods for improving financial institution utilization of the statutory exemption provisions as a way of reducing the submission of currency transaction reports that have little or no value for law enforcement purposes, including improvements in the systems in effect at financial institutions for regular review of the exemption procedures used at the institution and the training of personnel in its effective use.

"**(2) Report required.**—The Secretary of the Treasury shall submit a report to the Congress before the end of the 1-year period beginning on the date of enactment of this Act [Oct. 26, 2001] containing the findings and conclusions of the Secretary with regard to the study required under subsection (a) [of this note], and such recommendations for legislative or administrative action as the Secretary determines to be appropriate."

[Effective on and after the first day of fiscal year 2005, amendments by Title III (§§ 301 to 377) of Pub.L. 107–56 shall terminate if Congress enacts a joint resolution to that effect; such resolution shall be given expedited consideration, see Pub.L. 107–56, Title III, § 303, Oct. 26, 2001, 115 Stat. 298, set out as a note under 31 U.S.C.A. § 5311.]

Report Reduction Goal; Reports

Section 402(b) of Pub.L. 103–325 provided that:

"**(1) In general.**—In implementing the amendment made by subsection (a) [amending this section], the Secretary of the Treasury shall seek to reduce, within a reasonable period of time, the number of reports required to be filed in the aggregate by depository institutions pursuant to section 5313(a) of title 31, United States Code [subsec. (a) of this section], by at least 30 percent of the number filed during the year preceding the date of enactment of this Act [Sept. 23, 1994].

"**(2) Interim report.**—The Secretary of the Treasury shall submit a report to the Congress not later than the end of the 180–day period beginning on the date of enactment of this Act [Sept. 23, 1994] on the progress made by the Secretary in implementing the amendment made by subsection (a).

"**(3) Annual report.**—The Secretary of the Treasury shall submit an annual report to the Congress after the end of each of the first 5 calendar years which begin after the date of enactment of this Act [Sept. 23, 1994] on the extent to which the Secretary has reduced the overall number of currency transaction reports filed with the Secretary pursuant to section 5313(a) of title 31, United States Code [subsec. (a) of this section], consistent with the purposes of such section and effective law enforcement."

Streamlined Currency Transaction Reports

Section 402(c) of Pub.L. 103–325 provided that: "The Secretary of the Treasury shall take such action as may be appropriate to—

"(1) redesign the format of reports required to be filed under section 5313(a) of title 31, United States Code [Subsec. (a) of this section], by any financial institution (as defined in section 5312(a)(2) of such title [section 5312 (a)(2) of this title]) to eliminate the need to report information which has little or no value for law enforcement purposes; and

"(2) reduce the time and effort required to prepare such report for filing by any such financial institution under such section."

§ 5314. Records and reports on foreign financial agency transactions

(a) Considering the need to avoid impeding or controlling the export or import of monetary instruments and the need to avoid burdening unreasonably a person making a transaction with a foreign financial agency, the Secretary of the Treasury shall require a resident or citizen of the United States or a person in, and doing business in, the United States, to keep records, file reports, or keep records and file reports, when the resident, citizen, or person makes a transaction or maintains a relation for any person with a foreign financial agency. The records and reports shall contain the following information in the way and to the extent the Secretary prescribes:

(1) the identity and address of participants in a transaction or relationship.

(2) the legal capacity in which a participant is acting.

(3) the identity of real parties in interest.

(4) a description of the transaction.

(b) The Secretary may prescribe—

(1) a reasonable classification of persons subject to or exempt from a requirement under this section or a regulation under this section;

(2) a foreign country to which a requirement or a regulation under this section applies if the Secretary decides applying the requirement or regulation to all foreign countries is unnecessary or undesirable;

(3) the magnitude of transactions subject to a requirement or a regulation under this section;

(4) the kind of transaction subject to or exempt from a requirement or a regulation under this section; and

(5) other matters the Secretary considers necessary to carry out this section or a regulation under this section.

(c) A person shall be required to disclose a record required to be kept under this section or under a regulation under this section only as required by law.

(Pub.L. 97–258, Sept. 13, 1982, 96 Stat. 997.)

HISTORICAL AND STATUTORY NOTES

Codifications

Pub.L. 102–550, Title XV, § 1517(b), Oct. 28, 1992, 106 Stat. 4059, which directed the amendment of this section was executed to section 5318 of this title to reflect the probable intent of Congress. See H. Report No. 102–1017, page 404.

Compliance with Reporting Requirements

Pub.L. 107–56, Title III, § 361(b), Oct. 26, 2001, 115 Stat. 332, provided that: "The Secretary of the Treasury shall study methods for improving compliance with the reporting requirements established in section 5314 of title 31, United States Code [this section], and shall submit a report on such study to the Congress by the end of the 6–month period beginning on the date of enactment of this Act [Oct. 26, 2001] and each 1–year period thereafter. The initial report shall include historical data on compliance with such reporting requirements."

[Effective on and after the first day of fiscal year 2005, amendments by Title III (§§ 301 to 377) of Pub.L. 107–56 shall terminate if Congress enacts a joint resolution to that effect; such resolution shall be given expedited consideration, see Pub.L. 107–56, Title III, § 303, Oct. 26, 2001, 115 Stat. 298, set out as a note under 31 U.S.C.A. § 5311.]

§ 5315. Reports on foreign currency transactions

(a) Congress finds that—

(1) moving mobile capital can have a significant impact on the proper functioning of the international monetary system;

(2) it is important to have the most feasible current and complete information on the kind and source of capital flows, including transactions by large United States businesses and their foreign affiliates; and

(3) additional authority should be provided to collect information on capital flows under section 5(b) of the Trading With the Enemy Act (50 App. U.S.C. 5(b)) and section 8 of the Bretton Woods Agreement Act (22 U.S.C. 286f).

(b) In this section, "United States person" and "foreign person controlled by a United States person" have the same meanings given those terms in section 7(f)(2)(A) and (C), respectively, of the Securities and Exchange Act of 1934 (15 U.S.C. 78g(f)(2)(A), (C)).

(c) The Secretary of the Treasury shall prescribe regulations consistent with subsection (a) of this section requiring reports on foreign currency transactions conducted by a United States person or a foreign person controlled by a United States person. The regulations shall require that a report contain information and be submitted at the time and in the way, with reasonable exceptions and classifications, necessary to carry out this section.

(Pub.L. 97–258, Sept. 13, 1982, 96 Stat. 997.)

HISTORICAL AND STATUTORY NOTES

References in Text

Section 5(b) of the Trading With the Enemy Act, referred to in subsec. (a)(3), is also classified to section 95a of Title 12, Banks and Banking.

Section 8 of the Bretton Woods Agreement Act, referred to in subsec. (a)(3), is § 8 of Act July 31, 1945, c. 339, 59 Stat. 515, which is classified to § 286f of Title 22, Foreign Relations and Intercourse.

Section 7(f)(2)(A) and (C) of the Securities and Exchange Act of 1934, referred to in subsec. (b), is § 7(f)(2)(A) and (C) of Act June 6, 1934, c. 404, Title I, 48 Stat. 886, which is classified to § 78g(f)(2)(A) and (C) of Title 15, Commerce and Trade.

§ 5316. Reports on exporting and importing monetary instruments

(a) Except as provided in subsection (c) of this section, a person or an agent or bailee of the person shall file a report under subsection (b) of this section when the person, agent, or bailee knowingly—

(1) transports, is about to transport, or has transported, monetary instruments of more than $10,000 at one time—

(A) from a place in the United States to or through a place outside the United States; or

(B) to a place in the United States from or through a place outside the United States; or

(2) receives monetary instruments of more than $10,000 at one time transported into the United States from or through a place outside the United States.

(b) A report under this section shall be filed at the time and place the Secretary of the Treasury prescribes. The report shall contain the following information to the extent the Secretary prescribes:

(1) the legal capacity in which the person filing the report is acting.

(2) the origin, destination, and route of the monetary instruments.

(3) when the monetary instruments are not legally and beneficially owned by the person transporting the instruments, or if the person transporting the instruments personally is not going to use them, the identity of the person that gave the instruments to the person transporting them, the identity of the person who is to receive them, or both.

(4) the amount and kind of monetary instruments transported.

(5) additional information.

(c) This section or a regulation under this section does not apply to a common carrier of passengers when a passenger possesses a monetary instrument, or to a common carrier of goods if the shipper does not declare the instrument.

(d) Cumulation of closely related events.—The Secretary of the Treasury may prescribe regulations under this section defining the term "at one time" for purposes of subsection (a). Such regulations may permit the cumulation of closely related events in order that such events may collectively be considered to occur at one time for the purposes of subsection (a).

(Pub.L. 97–258, Sept. 13, 1982, 96 Stat. 998; Pub.L. 98–473, Title II, § 901(c), Oct. 12, 1984, 98 Stat. 2135; Pub.L. 99–570, Title I, § 1358, Title III, § 3153, Oct. 27, 1986, 100 Stat. 3207–26, 3207–94.)

HISTORICAL AND STATUTORY NOTES

Effective Date of Regulations Prescribed by 1986 Amendment

Section 1364(d) of Pub.L. 99–570 provided that: "Any regulation prescribed under the amendments made by section 1358 [amending this section] shall apply with respect to transactions completed after the effective date of such regulation."

§ 5317. Search and forfeiture of monetary instruments

(a) The Secretary of the Treasury may apply to a court of competent jurisdiction for a search warrant when the Secretary reasonably believes a monetary instrument is being transported and a report on the instrument under section 5316 of this title has not been filed or contains a material omission or misstatement. The Secretary shall include a statement of information in support of the warrant. On a showing of probable cause, the court may issue a search warrant for a designated person or a designated or described place or physical object. This subsection does not affect the authority of the Secretary under another law.

(b) Searches at border.—For purposes of ensuring compliance with the requirements of section 5316, a customs officer may stop and search, at the border and without a search warrant, any vehicle, vessel, aircraft, or other conveyance, any envelope or other container, and any person entering or departing from the United States.

(c) Forfeiture.—

(1) Criminal forfeiture.—

(A) In general.—The court in imposing sentence for any violation of section 5313, 5316, or 5324 of this title, or any conspiracy to commit such violation, shall order the defendant to forfeit all property, real or personal, involved in the offense and any property traceable thereto.

(B) Procedure.—Forfeitures under this paragraph shall be governed by the procedures established in section 413 of the Controlled Substances Act.

(2) Civil forfeiture.—Any property involved in a violation of section 5313, 5316, or 5324 of this title, or any conspiracy to commit any such violation, and any property traceable to any such violation or conspiracy, may be seized and forfeited to the United States in accordance with the procedures governing civil forfeitures in money laundering cases pursuant to section 981(a)(1)(A) of title 18, United States Code.

(Pub.L. 97–258, Sept. 13, 1982, 96 Stat. 998; Pub.L. 98–473, Title II, § 901(d), Oct. 12, 1984, 98 Stat. 2135; Pub.L. 99–570, Title I, § 1355, Oct. 27, 1986, 100 Stat. 3207–22; Pub.L. 102–550, Title XV, § 1525(c)(2), Oct. 28, 1992, 106 Stat. 4065;

Pub.L. 107–56, Title III, §§ 365(b)(2)(B), 372(a), Oct. 26, 2001, 115 Stat. 335, 338.)

HISTORICAL AND STATUTORY NOTES

References in Text

Section 413 of the Controlled Substances Act, referred to in subsec. (c)(1)(B), is Pub.L. 91–513, Title IV, § 403, Oct. 27, 1970, 84 Stat. 1263, which is classified to 21 U.S.C.A. § 843.

Effective and Applicability Provisions

1992 Acts. Except as otherwise provided, amendment by Pub.L. 102–550 effective Oct. 28, 1992, see section 2 of Pub.L. 102–550, set out as a note under section 5301 of Title 42, The Public Health and Welfare.

1986 Acts. Section 1364(b) of Pub.L. 99–570 provided that: "The amendments made by sections 1355(b) [amending subsec. (c) of this section] and 1357(a) [amending section 5321(a) of this title by adding par. (4) thereto] shall apply with respect to violations committed after the end of the 3-month period beginning on the date of the enactment of this Act [Oct. 27, 1986]."

4-Year Congressional Review; Expedited Consideration

Effective on and after the first day of fiscal year 2005, amendments by Title III (§§ 301 to 377) of Pub.L. 107–56 shall terminate if Congress enacts a joint resolution to that effect; such resolution shall be given expedited consideration, see Pub.L. 107–56, Title III, § 303, Oct. 26, 2001, 115 Stat. 298, set out as a note under 31 U.S.C.A. § 5311.

§ 5318. Compliance, exemptions, and summons authority

(a) General powers of Secretary.—The Secretary of the Treasury may (except under section 5315 of this title and regulations prescribed under section 5315)—

(1) except as provided in subsection (b)(2), delegate duties and powers under this subchapter to an appropriate supervising agency and the United States Postal Service;

(2) require a class of domestic financial institutions or nonfinancial trades or businesses to maintain appropriate procedures to ensure compliance with this subchapter and regulations prescribed under this subchapter or to guard against money laundering;

(3) examine any books, papers, records, or other data of domestic financial institutions or nonfinancial trades or businesses relevant to the recordkeeping or reporting requirements of this subchapter;

(4) summon a financial institution or nonfinancial trade or business, an officer or employee of a financial institution or nonfinancial trade or business (including a former officer or employee), or any person having possession, custody, or care of the reports and records required under this subchapter, to appear before the Secretary of the Treasury or his delegate at a time and place named in the summons and to produce such books, papers, records, or other data, and to give testimony, under oath, as may be relevant or material to an investigation described in subsection (b);

(5) exempt from the requirements of this subchapter any class of transactions within any State if the Secretary determines that—

(A) under the laws of such State, that class of transactions is subject to requirements substantially similar to those imposed under this subchapter; and

(B) there is adequate provision for the enforcement of such requirements; and

(6) prescribe an appropriate exemption from a requirement under this subchapter and regulations prescribed under this subchapter. The Secretary may revoke an exemption under this paragraph or paragraph (5) by actually or constructively notifying the parties affected. A revocation is effective during judicial review.

(b) Limitations on summons power.—

(1) Scope of power.—The Secretary of the Treasury may take any action described in paragraph (3) or (4) of subsection (a) only in connection with investigations for the purpose of civil enforcement of violations of this subchapter, section 21 of the Federal Deposit Insurance Act, section 411 of the National Housing Act, or chapter 2 of Public Law 91–508 (12 U.S.C. 1951 et seq.) or any regulation under any such provision.

(2) Authority to issue.—A summons may be issued under subsection (a)(4) only by, or with the approval of, the Secretary of the Treasury or a supervisory level delegate of the Secretary of the Treasury.

(c) Administrative aspects of summons.—

(1) Production at designated site.—A summons issued pursuant to this section may require that books, papers, records, or other data stored or maintained at any place be produced at any designated location in any State or in any territory or other place subject to the jurisdiction of the United States not more than 500 miles distant from any place where the financial institution or nonfinancial trade or business operates or conducts business in the United States.

(2) Fees and travel expenses.—Persons summoned under this section shall be paid the same fees and mileage for travel in the United States that are paid witnesses in the courts of the United States.

(3) No liability for expenses.—The United States shall not be liable for any expense, other than an expense described in paragraph (2), incurred in connection with the production of books, papers, records, or other data under this section.

(d) Service of summons.—Service of a summons issued under this section may be by registered mail or in such other manner calculated to give actual notice as the Secretary may prescribe by regulation.

(e) Contumacy or refusal.—

(1) Referral to Attorney General.—In case of contumacy by a person issued a summons under paragraph (3) or (4) of subsection (a) or a refusal by such person to obey such summons, the Secretary of the Treasury shall refer the matter to the Attorney General.

(2) Jurisdiction of court.—The Attorney General may invoke the aid of any court of the United States within the jurisdiction of which—

(A) the investigation which gave rise to the summons is being or has been carried on;

(B) the person summoned is an inhabitant; or

(C) the person summoned carries on business or may be found,

to compel compliance with the summons.

(3) Court order.—The court may issue an order requiring the person summoned to appear before the Secretary or his delegate to produce books, papers, records, and other data, to give testimony as may be necessary to explain how such material was compiled and maintained, and to pay the costs of the proceeding.

(4) Failure to comply with order.—Any failure to obey the order of the court may be punished by the court as a contempt thereof.

(5) Service of process.—All process in any case under this subsection may be served in any judicial district in which such person may be found.

(f) Written and signed statement required.—No person shall qualify for an exemption under subsection (a)(5) unless the relevant financial institution or nonfinancial trade or business prepares and maintains a statement which—

(1) describes in detail the reasons why such person is qualified for such exemption; and

(2) contains the signature of such person.

(g) Reporting of suspicious transactions.—

(1) In general.—The Secretary may require any financial institution, and any director, officer, employee, or agent of any financial institution, to report any suspicious transaction relevant to a possible violation of law or regulation.

(2) Notification prohibited.—

(A) In general.—If a financial institution or any director, officer, employee, or agent of any financial institution, voluntarily or pursuant to this section or any other authority, reports a suspicious transaction to a government agency—

(i) the financial institution, director, officer, employee, or agent may not notify any person involved in the transaction that the transaction has been reported; and

(ii) no officer or employee of the Federal Government or of any State, local, tribal, or territorial government within the United States, who has any knowledge that such report was made may disclose to any person involved in the transaction that the transaction has been reported, other than as necessary to fulfill the official duties of such officer or employee.

(B) Disclosures in certain employment references.—

(i) Rule of construction.—Notwithstanding the application of subparagraph (A) in any other context, subparagraph (A) shall not be construed as prohibiting any financial institution, or any director, officer, employee, or agent of such institution, from including information that was included in a report to which subparagraph (A) applies—

(I) in a written employment reference that is provided in accordance with section 18(w) of the Federal Deposit Insurance Act in response to a request from another financial institution; or

(II) in a written termination notice or employment reference that is provided in accordance with the rules of a self-regulatory organization registered with the Securities and Exchange Commission or the Commodity Futures Trading Commission,

except that such written reference or notice may not disclose that such information was also included in any such report, or that such report was made.

(ii) Information not required.—Clause (i) shall not be construed, by itself, to create any affirmative duty to include any information described in clause (i) in any employment reference or termination notice referred to in clause (i).

(3) Liability for disclosures.—

(A) In general.—Any financial institution that makes a voluntary disclosure of any possible violation of law or regulation to a government agency or makes a disclosure pursuant to this subsection or any other authority, and any director, officer, employee, or agent of such institution who makes, or requires another to make any such disclosure, shall not be liable to any person under any law or regulation of the United States, any constitution, law, or regulation of any State or political subdivision of any State, or under any contract or other legally enforceable agreement (including any arbitration agreement), for such disclosure or for any failure to provide notice of such disclosure to the person who is the subject of such disclosure or any other person identified in the disclosure.

(B) Rule of construction.—Subparagraph (A) shall not be construed as creating—

(i) any inference that the term "person", as used in such subparagraph, may be construed more broadly than its ordinary usage so as to include any government or agency of government; or

(ii) any immunity against, or otherwise affecting, any civil or criminal action brought by any government or agency of government to enforce any constitution, law, or regulation of such government or agency.

(4) Single designee for reporting suspicious transactions.—

(A) In general.—In requiring reports under paragraph (1) of suspicious transactions, the Secretary of the Treasury shall designate, to the extent practicable and appropriate, a single officer or agency of the United States to whom such reports shall be made.

(B) Duty of designee.—The officer or agency of the United States designated by the Secretary of the Treasury pursuant to subparagraph (A) shall refer any report of a suspicious transaction to any appropriate law enforcement, supervisory agency, or United States intelligence agency for use in the conduct of intelligence or counterintelligence activities, including analysis, to protect against international terrorism.

(C) Coordination with other reporting requirements.—Subparagraph (A) shall not be construed as precluding any supervisory agency for any financial institution from requiring the financial institution to submit any information or report to the agency or another agency pursuant to any other applicable provision of law.

(h) Anti-money laundering programs.—

(1) In general.—In order to guard against money laundering through financial institutions, each financial institution shall establish anti-money laundering programs, including, at a minimum—

(A) the development of internal policies, procedures, and controls;

(B) the designation of a compliance officer;

(C) an ongoing employee training program; and

(D) an independent audit function to test programs.

(2) Regulations.—The Secretary of the Treasury, after consultation with the appropriate Federal functional regulator (as defined in section 509 of the Gramm-Leach-Bliley Act), may prescribe minimum standards for programs established under paragraph (1), and may exempt from the application of those standards any financial institution that is not subject to the provisions of the rules contained in part 103 of title 31, of the Code of Federal Regulations, or any successor rule thereto, for so long as such financial institution is not subject to the provisions of such rules.

(3) Concentration accounts.—The Secretary may prescribe regulations under this subsection that govern maintenance of concentration accounts by financial institutions, in order to ensure that such accounts are not used to prevent association of the identity of an individual customer with the movement of funds of which the customer is the direct or beneficial owner, which regulations shall, at a minimum—

(A) prohibit financial institutions from allowing clients to direct transactions that move their funds into, out of, or through the concentration accounts of the financial institution;

(B) prohibit financial institutions and their employees from informing customers of the existence of, or the means of identifying, the concentration accounts of the institution; and

(C) require each financial institution to establish written procedures governing the documentation of all transactions involving a concentration account, which procedures shall ensure that, any time a transaction involving a concentration account commingles funds belonging to 1 or more customers, the identity of, and specific amount belonging to, each customer is documented.

(i) Due diligence for United States private banking and correspondent bank accounts involving foreign persons.—

(1) In general.—Each financial institution that establishes, maintains, administers, or manages a private banking account or a correspondent account in the United States for a non-United States person, including a foreign individual visiting the United States, or a representative of a non-United States person shall establish appropriate, specific, and, where necessary, enhanced, due diligence policies, procedures, and controls that are reasonably designed to detect and report instances of money laundering through those accounts.

(2) Additional standards for certain correspondent accounts.—

(A) In general.—Subparagraph (B) shall apply if a correspondent account is requested or maintained by, or on behalf of, a foreign bank operating—

(i) under an offshore banking license; or

(ii) under a banking license issued by a foreign country that has been designated—

(I) as noncooperative with international anti-money laundering principles or procedures by an intergovernmental group or organization of which the United States is a member, with which designation the United States representative to the group or organization concurs; or

(II) by the Secretary of the Treasury as warranting special measures due to money laundering concerns.

(B) Policies, procedures, and controls.—The enhanced due diligence policies, procedures, and controls required under paragraph (1) shall, at a minimum, ensure that the financial institution in the United States takes reasonable steps—

(i) to ascertain for any such foreign bank, the shares of which are not publicly traded, the identity of each of the owners of the foreign bank, and the nature and extent of the ownership interest of each such owner;

(ii) to conduct enhanced scrutiny of such account to guard against money laundering and report any suspicious transactions under subsection (g); and

(iii) to ascertain whether such foreign bank provides correspondent accounts to other foreign banks and, if so, the identity of those foreign banks and related due diligence information, as appropriate under paragraph (1).

(3) Minimum standards for private banking accounts.—If a private banking account is requested or maintained by, or on behalf of, a non-United States person, then the due diligence policies, procedures, and controls required under paragraph (1) shall, at a minimum, ensure that the financial institution takes reasonable steps—

(A) to ascertain the identity of the nominal and beneficial owners of, and the source of funds deposited into, such account as needed to guard against money laundering and report any suspicious transactions under subsection (g); and

(B) to conduct enhanced scrutiny of any such account that is requested or maintained by, or on behalf of, a senior foreign political figure, or any immediate family member or close associate of a senior foreign political figure, that is reasonably designed to detect and report transactions that may involve the proceeds of foreign corruption.

(4) Definitions.—For purposes of this subsection, the following definitions shall apply:

(A) Offshore banking license.—The term "offshore banking license" means a license to conduct banking activities which, as a condition of the license, prohibits the licensed entity from conducting banking activities with the citizens of, or with the local currency of, the country which issued the license.

(B) Private banking account.—The term "private banking account" means an account (or any combination of accounts) that—

(i) requires a minimum aggregate deposits of funds or other assets of not less than $1,000,000;

(ii) is established on behalf of 1 or more individuals who have a direct or beneficial ownership interest in the account; and

(iii) is assigned to, or is administered or managed by, in whole or in part, an officer, employee, or agent of a financial institution acting as a liaison between the financial institution and the direct or beneficial owner of the account.

(j) Prohibition on United States correspondent accounts with foreign shell banks.—

(1) In general.—A financial institution described in subparagraphs (A) through (G) of section 5312(a)(2) (in this subsection referred to as a "covered financial institution") shall not establish, maintain, administer, or manage a correspondent account in the United States for, or on behalf of, a foreign bank that does not have a physical presence in any country.

(2) Prevention of indirect service to foreign shell banks.—A covered financial institution shall take reasonable steps to ensure that any correspondent account established, maintained, administered, or managed by that covered financial institution in the United States for a foreign bank is not being used by that foreign bank to indirectly provide banking services to another foreign bank that does not have a physical presence in any country. The Secretary of the Treasury shall, by regulation, delineate the reasonable steps necessary to comply with this paragraph.

(3) Exception.—Paragraphs (1) and (2) do not prohibit a covered financial institution from providing a correspondent account to a foreign bank, if the foreign bank—

(A) is an affiliate of a depository institution, credit union, or foreign bank that maintains a physical presence in the United States or a foreign country, as applicable; and

(B) is subject to supervision by a banking authority in the country regulating the affiliated depository institution, credit union, or foreign bank described in subparagraph (A), as applicable.

(4) Definitions.—For purposes of this subsection—

(A) the term "affiliate" means a foreign bank that is controlled by or is under common control with a depository institution, credit union, or foreign bank; and

(B) the term "physical presence" means a place of business that—

(i) is maintained by a foreign bank;

(ii) is located at a fixed address (other than solely an electronic address) in a country in which the foreign bank is authorized to conduct banking activities, at which location the foreign bank—

(I) employs 1 or more individuals on a full-time basis; and

(II) maintains operating records related to its banking activities; and

(iii) is subject to inspection by the banking authority which licensed the foreign bank to conduct banking activities.

(k) Bank records related to anti-money laundering programs.—

(1) Definitions.—For purposes of this subsection, the following definitions shall apply:

(A) Appropriate Federal banking agency.—The term "appropriate Federal banking agency" has the same meaning as in section 3 of the Federal Deposit Insurance Act (12 U.S.C. 1813).

(B) Incorporated term.—The term "correspondent account" has the same meaning as in section 5318A(e)(1)(B).

(2) 120-hour rule.—Not later than 120 hours after receiving a request by an appropriate Federal banking agency for information related to anti-money laundering compliance by a covered financial institution or a customer of such institution, a covered financial institution shall provide to the appropriate Federal banking agency, or make available at a location specified by the representative of the appropriate Federal banking agency, information and account documentation for any account opened, maintained, administered or managed in the United States by the covered financial institution.

(3) Foreign bank records.—

(A) Summons or subpoena of records.—

(i) In general.—The Secretary of the Treasury or the Attorney General may issue a summons or subpoena to any foreign bank that maintains a correspondent account in the United States and request records related to such correspondent account, including records maintained outside of the United States relating to the deposit of funds into the foreign bank.

(ii) Service of summons or subpoena.—A summons or subpoena referred to in clause (i) may be served on the foreign bank in the United States if the foreign bank has a representative in the United States, or in a foreign country pursuant to any mutual legal assistance treaty, multilateral agreement, or other request for international law enforcement assistance.

(B) Acceptance of service.—

(i) Maintaining records in the United States.—Any covered financial institution which maintains a correspondent account in the United States for a foreign bank shall maintain records in the United States identifying the owners of such foreign bank and the name and address of a person who resides in the United States and is authorized to accept service of legal process for records regarding the correspondent account.

(ii) Law enforcement request.—Upon receipt of a written request from a Federal law enforcement officer for information required to be maintained under this paragraph, the covered financial institution shall provide the information to the requesting officer not later than 7 days after receipt of the request.

(C) Termination of correspondent relationship.—

(i) Termination upon receipt of notice.—A covered financial institution shall terminate any correspondent relationship with a foreign bank not later than 10 business days after receipt of written notice from the Secretary or the Attorney General (in each case, after consultation with the other) that the foreign bank has failed—

(I) to comply with a summons or subpoena issued under subparagraph (A); or

(II) to initiate proceedings in a United States court contesting such summons or subpoena.

(ii) Limitation on liability.—A covered financial institution shall not be liable to any person in any court or arbitration proceeding for terminating a correspondent relationship in accordance with this subsection.

(iii) Failure to terminate relationship.—Failure to terminate a correspondent relationship in accordance with this subsection shall render the covered financial institution liable for a civil penalty of up to $10,000 per day until the correspondent relationship is so terminated.

***(l)* Identification and verification of accountholders.—**

(1) In general.—Subject to the requirements of this subsection, the Secretary of the Treasury shall prescribe regulations setting forth the minimum standards for financial institutions and their customers regarding the identity of the customer that shall apply in connection with the opening of an account at a financial institution.

(2) Minimum requirements.—The regulations shall, at a minimum, require financial institutions to implement, and customers (after being given adequate notice) to comply with, reasonable procedures for—

(A) verifying the identity of any person seeking to open an account to the extent reasonable and practicable;

(B) maintaining records of the information used to verify a person's identity, including name, address, and other identifying information; and

(C) consulting lists of known or suspected terrorists or terrorist organizations provided to the financial institution by any government agency to determine whether a person seeking to open an account appears on any such list.

(3) Factors to be considered.—In prescribing regulations under this subsection, the Secretary shall take into consideration the various types of accounts maintained by various types of financial institutions, the various methods of opening accounts, and the various types of identifying information available.

(4) Certain financial institutions.—In the case of any financial institution the business of which is engaging in financial activities described in section 4(k) of the Bank Holding Company Act of 1956 (including financial activities subject to the jurisdiction of the Commodity Futures Trading Commission), the regulations prescribed by the Secretary under paragraph (1) shall be prescribed jointly with each Federal functional regulator (as defined in section 509 of the Gramm-Leach-Bliley Act, including the Commodity Futures Trading Commission) appropriate for such financial institution.

(5) Exemptions.—The Secretary (and, in the case of any financial institution described in paragraph (4), any Federal agency described in such paragraph) may, by regulation or order, exempt any financial institution or type of account from the requirements of any regulation prescribed under this subsection in accordance with such standards and procedures as the Secretary may prescribe.

(6) Effective date.—Final regulations prescribed under this subsection shall take effect before the end of the 1-year period beginning on the date of enactment of the International Money Laundering Abatement and Financial Anti-Terrorism Act of 2001.

(m) Applicability of rules.—Any rules promulgated pursuant to the authority contained in section 21 of the Federal Deposit Insurance Act (12 U.S.C. 1829b) shall apply, in addition to any other financial institution to which such rules apply, to any person that engages as a business in the transmission of funds, including any person who engages as a business in an informal money transfer system or any network of people who engage as a business in facilitating the transfer of money domestically or internationally outside of the conventional financial institutions system.

(n) Reporting of certain cross-border transmittals of funds.—

(1) In general.—Subject to paragraphs (3) and (4), the Secretary shall prescribe regulations requiring such financial institutions as the Secretary determines to be appropriate to report to the Financial Crimes Enforcement Network certain cross-border electronic transmittals of funds, if the Secretary determines that reporting of such transmittals is reasonably necessary to conduct the efforts of the Secretary against money laundering and terrorist financing.

(2) Limitation on reporting requirements.—Information required to be reported by the regulations prescribed under paragraph (1) shall not exceed the information required to be retained by the reporting financial institution pursuant to section 21 of the Federal Deposit Insurance Act and the regulations promulgated thereunder, unless—

(A) the Board of Governors of the Federal Reserve System and the Secretary jointly determine that a particular item or items of information are not currently required to be retained under such section or such regulations; and

(B) the Secretary determines, after consultation with the Board of Governors of the Federal Reserve System, that the reporting of such information is reasonably necessary to conduct the efforts of the Secretary to identify cross-border money laundering and terrorist financing.

(3) Form and manner of reports.—In prescribing the regulations required under paragraph (1), the Secretary shall, subject to paragraph (2), determine the appropriate form, manner, content, and frequency of filing of the required reports.

(4) Feasibility report.—

(A) In general.—Before prescribing the regulations required under paragraph (1), and as soon as is practicable after the date of enactment of the Intelligence Reform and Terrorism Prevention Act of 2004, the Secretary shall submit a report to the Committee on Banking, Housing, and Urban Affairs of the Senate and the Committee on Financial Services of the House of Representatives that—

(i) identifies the information in cross-border electronic transmittals of funds that may be found in particular cases to be reasonably necessary to conduct the efforts of the Secretary to identify money laundering and terrorist financing, and outlines the criteria to be used by the Secretary to select the situations in which reporting under this subsection may be required;

(ii) outlines the appropriate form, manner, content, and frequency of filing of the reports that may be required under such regulations;

(iii) identifies the technology necessary for the Financial Crimes Enforcement Network to receive, keep, exploit, protect the security of, and disseminate information from reports of cross-border electronic transmittals of funds to law enforcement and other entities engaged in efforts against money laundering and terrorist financing; and

(iv) discusses the information security protections required by the exercise of the Secretary's authority under this subsection.

(B) Consultation.—In reporting the feasibility report under subparagraph (A), the Secretary may consult with the Bank Secrecy Act Advisory Group established by the Secretary, and any other group considered by the Secretary to be relevant.

(5) Regulations.—

(A) In general.—Subject to subparagraph (B), the regulations required by paragraph (1) shall be prescribed in final form by the Secretary, in consultation with the Board of Governors of the Federal Reserve System, before the end of the 3–year period beginning on the date of enactment of the National Intelligence Reform Act of 2004.

(B) Technological feasibility.—No regulations shall be prescribed under this subsection before the Secretary certifies to the Congress that the Financial Crimes Enforcement Network has the technological systems in place to effectively and efficiently receive, keep, exploit, protect the security of, and disseminate information from reports of cross-border electronic transmittals of funds to law enforcement and other entities engaged in efforts against money laundering and terrorist financing.

(Pub.L. 97–258, Sept. 13, 1982, 96 Stat. 999; Pub.L. 99–570, Title I, § 1356(a), (b), (c)(2), Oct. 27, 1986, 100 Stat. 3207–23, 3207–24; Pub.L. 100–690, Title VI, §§ 6185(e), 6469(c), Nov. 18, 1988, 102 Stat. 4357, 4377; Pub.L. 102–550, Title XV, §§ 1504(d)(1), 1513, 1517(b), Oct. 28, 1992, 106 Stat. 4055, 4058, 4059; Pub.L. 103–322, Title XXXIII, § 330017(b)(1), Sept. 13, 1994, 108 Stat. 2149; Pub.L. 103–325, Title IV, §§ 403(a), 410, 413(b)(1), Sept. 23, 1994, 108 Stat. 2245, 2252, 2254; Pub.L. 107–56, Title III, §§ 312(a), 313(a), 319(b), 325, 326(a), 351, 352(a), 358(b), 359(c), 365(c)(2)(B), Oct. 26, 2001, 115 Stat. 304, 306, 312, 317, 320, 322, 326, 328, 335; Pub.L. 108–159, Title VIII, § 811(g), Dec. 4, 2003, 117 Stat. 2012; Pub.L. 108–458, Title VI, §§ 6202(h), 6203(c), (d), 6302, Dec. 17, 2004, 118 Stat. 3746, 3748; Pub.L. 109–177, Title IV, § 407, Mar. 9, 2006, 120 Stat. 245.)

HISTORICAL AND STATUTORY NOTES

References in Text

Section 21 of the Federal Deposit Insurance Act, referred to in subsecs. (b)(1), (m), and (n)(2), is Sept. 21, 1950, c. 967, 2[21], as added Oct. 26, 1970, Pub.L. 91–508, Title I, § 101, 84 Stat. 1114, as amended, which is classified to 12 U.S.C.A. § 1829b.

Section 411 of the National Housing Act, referred to in subsec. (b)(1), is section 411 of Act June 27, 1934, c. 847, Title IV, as added Oct. 26, 1970, Pub.L. 91–508, Title I, § 102, 84 Stat. 1116, which is classified to section 1730d of Title 12.

Chapter 2 of Pub.L. 91–508 (12 U.S.C. 1951 et seq.), referred to in subsec. (b)(1), probably means Pub.L. 91–508, Title I, Chapter 2, § 121 et seq., Oct. 26, 1970, 84 Stat. 1116, which is classified to chapter 21 (section 1951 et seq.) of Title 12.

Subsection (a)(5), referred to in subsec. (f), was redesignated subsec. (a)(6) by section 410(a)(2) of Pub.L. 103–325.

Section 18(w) of the Federal Deposit Insurance Act, referred to in subsec. (g)(2)(B)(i)(I), is Act Sept. 21, 1950, c. 967, § 2[18(w)], 64 Stat. 891, as amended, which is classified to 12 U.S.C.A. § 1828(w).

Section 509 of the Gramm-Leach-Bliley Act, referred to in subsecs. (h)(2) and (*l*)(4), is the Financial Services Modernization Act of 1999, Pub.L. 106–102, Title V, § 509, Nov. 12, 1999, 113 Stat. 1443, which is classified to 15 U.S.C.A. § 6809. The term "Federal functional regulator" is defined in par. (2) of that section.

Section 3 of the Federal Deposit Insurance Act, referred to in subsec. (k)(1)(A), is Act Sept. 21, 1950, c. 967, § 2[3], 64 Stat. 873, as amended, which is classified to 12 U.S.C.A. § 1813.

Section 4(k) of the Bank Holding Company Act of 1956, or BHCA, referred to in subsec. (*l*)(4), is Act May 9, 1956, c. 240, § 4(k), 70 Stat. 135, which is classified to 12 U.S.C.A. § 1843(k).

The date of enactment of the International Money Laundering Abatement and Financial Anti-Terrorism Act of 2001, referred to in subsec. (*l*)(6), is the date of enactment of Pub.L. 107–56, Title III, Oct. 26, 2001, 115 Stat. 296, which enacted this subsection and was approved Oct. 26, 200. For complete classification, see Short Title note set out under 31 U.S.C.A. § 5301 and Tables.

The date of enactment of the Intelligence Reform and Terrorism Prevention Act of 2004, referred to in subsec. (n)(4)(A), is December 17, 2004, the date of enactment of Pub.L. 108–458, Dec. 17, 2004, 118 Stat. 3638, which was approved Dec. 17, 2004. For complete classification, see Short Title note set out under 50 U.S.C.A. § 401 and Tables.

The date of enactment of the National Intelligence Reform Act of 2004, referred to in subsec. (n)(5)(A), probably means December 17, 2004, the date of enactment of the National Security Intelligence Reform Act of 2004, Pub.L. 108–458, Title I, Dec. 17, 2004, 118 Stat. 3643. For complete classification, see Short Title note set out under 50 U.S.C.A. § 401 and Tables.

Codifications

Another section 365(c) of Pub.L. 107–56 amended the table of contents at the beginning of this chapter.

Effective and Applicability Provisions

2004 Acts. Amendments by Pub.L. 108–458, Title VI, Subtitle C, to Public Law 107–56, the United States Code, the Federal Deposit Insurance Act, and any other provision of law to take effect as if such amendments had been included in Public Law 107–56, as of Oct. 26, 2001, and no amendment made by such Public Law that is inconsistent with an amendment made by this subtitle to be deemed to have taken effect, see Pub.L. 108–458, § 6205, set out as a note under 12 U.S.C.A. § 1828.

2003 Acts. Unless otherwise specifically provided, amendments by Pub.L. 108–159 effective as established in final regulations jointly prescribed by the Board of Governors of the Federal Reserve System and the Federal Trade Commission, before the end of the 2–month period beginning on Dec. 4, 2003, with effective dates no later than 10 months after the date of issuance of the final regulations [see 16 C.F.R. § 602.1(c)(2)(vi) and 12 C.F.R. § 222.1(c)(2)(vi), providing effective date of March 31, 2004 for amendments made to subsecs. (*l*) and (m) of this section by Pub.L. 108–159, § 811], see Pub.L. 108–159, § 3, set out as an Effective and Applicability Provisions note under 15 U.S.C.A. § 1681.

2001 Acts. For effective date of subsec. (i), see Regulatory Authority and Effective Date note under this section.

Pub.L. 107–56, Title III, § 313(b), Oct. 26, 2001, 115 Stat. 307, provided that: "The amendment made by subsection (a) [enacting subsec. (j) of this section] shall take effect at the end of the 60–day period beginning on the date of enactment of this Act [Oct. 26, 2001]."

Pub.L. 107–56, Title III, § 352(b), Oct. 26, 2001, 115 Stat. 322, provided that: "The amendment made by subsection (a) [amending subsec. (h) of this section] shall take effect at the end of the 180–day period beginning on the date of enactment of this Act [Oct. 26, 2001]."

Amendments by section 358 of Pub.L. 107–56 applicable with respect to reports filed or records maintained on, before, or after Oct. 26, 2001, see section 358(h) of Pub.L. 107–56, set out as a note under 12 U.S.C.A. § 1829b.

4–Year Congressional Review; Expedited Consideration

Effective on and after the first day of fiscal year 2005, amendments by Title III (§§ 301 to 377) of Pub.L. 107–56 shall terminate if Congress enacts a joint resolution to that effect; such resolution shall be given expedited consideration, see Pub.L. 107–56, Title III, § 303, Oct. 26, 2001, 115 Stat. 298, set out as a note under 31 U.S.C.A. § 5311.

Regulatory Authority and Effective Date

Pub.L. 107–56, Title III, § 312(b), Oct. 26, 2001, 115 Stat. 305, provided that:

"(1) **Regulatory authority.**—Not later than 180 days after the date of enactment of this Act [Oct. 26, 2001], the Secretary, in consultation with the appropriate Federal functional regulators (as defined in section 509 of the Gramm-Leach-Bliley Act [15 U.S.C.A. § 6809(2)]) of the affected financial institutions, shall further delineate, by regulation, the due diligence policies, procedures, and controls required under section 5318(i)(1) of title 31, United States Code [subsec. (i)(1) of this section], as added by this section.

"(2) **Effective date.**—Section 5318(i) of title 31, United States Code [subsec. (i) of this section], as added by this section, shall take effect 270 days after the date of enactment of this Act [Oct. 26, 2001], whether or not final regulations are issued under paragraph (1), and the failure to issue such regulations shall in no way affect the enforceability of this section or the amendments made by this section. Section 5318(i) of title 31, United States Code [subsec. (i) of this section], as added by this section, shall apply with respect to accounts covered by that section 5318(i) [subsec. (i) of this section], that are opened before, on, or after the date of enactment of this Act [Oct. 26, 2001]."

Grace Period

Pub.L. 107–56, Title III, § 319(c), Oct. 26, 2001, 115 Stat. 314, provided that: "Financial institutions shall have 60 days from the date of enactment of this Act [Oct. 26, 2001] to comply with the provisions of section 5318(k) of title 31, United States Code [subsec. (k) of this section], as added by this section."

Federal Functional Regulator—Scope of Term

Pub.L. 107–56, Title III, § 321(c), Oct. 26, 2001, 115 Stat. 315, provided that: "For purposes of this Act and any amendment made by this Act [the Uniting and Strengthening America by Providing Appropriate Tools Required to Intercept and Obstruct Terrorism (USA PATRIOT ACT) Act of 2001, Pub.L. 107–56, Oct. 26, 2001, 115 Stat. 272; see Tables for classification] to any other provision of law, the term 'Federal functional regulator' includes the Commodity Futures Trading Commission."

Date of Application of Regulations; Factors to be Taken Into Account

Pub.L. 107–56, Title III, § 352(c), Oct. 26, 2001, 115 Stat. 322, provided that: "Before the end of the 180–day period beginning on the date of enactment of this Act [Oct. 26, 2001], the Secretary shall prescribe regulations that consider the extent to which the requirements imposed under this section [amending subsec. (h) of this section] are commensurate with the size, location, and activities of the financial institutions to which such regulations apply."

Reporting of Suspicious Activities by Securities Brokers and Dealers

Pub.L. 107–56, Title III, § 356(a), (b), Oct. 26, 2001, 115 Stat. 324, provided that:

"(a) **Deadline for suspicious activity reporting requirements for registered brokers and dealers.**—The Secretary, after consultation with the Securities and Exchange Commission and the Board of Governors of the Federal Reserve System, shall publish proposed regulations in the Federal Register before January 1, 2002, requiring brokers and dealers registered with the Securities and Exchange Commission under the Securities Exchange Act of 1934 to submit suspicious activity reports under section 5318(g) of title 31, United States Code [subsec. (g) of this section]. Such regulations shall be published in final form not later than July 1, 2002.

"(b) **Suspicious activity reporting requirements for futures Commission merchants, commodity trading advisors, and commodity pool operators.**—The Secretary, in consultation with the Commodity Futures Trading Commission, may prescribe regulations requiring futures commission merchants, commodity trading advisors, and commodity pool operators registered under the Commodity Exchange Act to submit suspicious activity reports under section 5318(g) of title 31, United States Code [subsec. (g) of this section]."

Reports

Section 403(b) of Pub.L. 103–325 provided that:

"(1) **Reports required.**—The Secretary of the Treasury shall submit an annual report to the Congress at the times required under paragraph (2) on the number of suspicious transactions reported to the officer or agency designated under section 5318(g)(4)(A) of title 31, United States Code [subsec. (g)(4)(A) of this section], during the period covered by the report and the disposition of such reports.

"(2) **Time for submitting reports.**—The 1st report required under paragraph (1) shall be filed before the end of the 1-year period beginning on the date of enactment of the Money Laundering Suppression Act of 1994 [Sept. 23, 1994] and each subsequent report shall be filed within 90 days after the end of each of the 5 calendar years which begin after such date of enactment."

Designation Required to be Made Expeditiously

Section 403(c) of Pub.L. 103-325 provided that: "The initial designation of an officer or agency of the United States pursuant to the amendment made by subsection (a) [amending this section] shall be made before the end of the 180-day period beginning on the date of enactment of this Act [Sept. 23, 1994]."

Improvement of Identification of Money Laundering Schemes

Section 404 of Pub.L. 103-325 provided that:

"(a) **Enhanced training, examinations, and referrals by banking agencies.**—Before the end of the 6-month period beginning on the date of enactment of this Act [Sept. 23, 1994], each appropriate Federal banking agency shall, in consultation with the Secretary of the Treasury and other appropriate law enforcement agencies—

"(1) review and enhance training and examination procedures to improve the identification of money laundering schemes involving depository institutions; and

"(2) review and enhance procedures for referring cases to any appropriate law enforcement agency.

"(b) **Improved reporting of criminal schemes by law enforcement agencies.**—The Secretary of the Treasury and each appropriate law enforcement agency shall provide, on a regular basis, information regarding money laundering schemes and activities involving depository institutions to each appropriate Federal banking agency in order to enhance each agency's ability to examine for and identify money laundering activity.

"(c) **Report to Congress.**—The Financial Institutions Examination Council shall submit a report on the progress made in carrying out subsection (a) and the usefulness of information received pursuant to subsection (b) to the Congress by the end of the 1-year period beginning on the date of enactment of this Act [Sept. 23, 1994].

"(d) **Definition.**—For purposes of this section, the term 'appropriate Federal banking agency' has the same meaning as in section 3 of the Federal Deposit Insurance Act [section 2[3] of Act Sept. 21, 1950, ch. 967, which is classified to section 1813 of Title 12, Banks and Banking]."

§ 5318A. Special measures for jurisdictions, financial institutions, international transactions, or types of accounts of primary money laundering concern

(a) International counter-money laundering requirements.—

(1) In general.—The Secretary of the Treasury may require domestic financial institutions and domestic financial agencies to take 1 or more of the special measures described in subsection (b) if the Secretary finds that reasonable grounds exist for concluding that a jurisdiction outside of the United States, 1 or more financial institutions operating outside of the United States, 1 or more classes of transactions within, or involving, a jurisdiction outside of the United States, or 1 or more types of accounts is of primary money laundering concern, in accordance with subsection (c).

(2) Form of requirement.—The special measures described in—

(A) subsection (b) may be imposed in such sequence or combination as the Secretary shall determine;

(B) paragraphs (1) through (4) of subsection (b) may be imposed by regulation, order, or otherwise as permitted by law; and

(C) subsection (b)(5) may be imposed only by regulation.

(3) Duration of orders; rulemaking.—Any order by which a special measure described in paragraphs (1) through (4) of subsection (b) is imposed (other than an order described in section 5326)—

(A) shall be issued together with a notice of proposed rulemaking relating to the imposition of such special measure; and

(B) may not remain in effect for more than 120 days, except pursuant to a rule promulgated on or before the end of the 120-day period beginning on the date of issuance of such order.

(4) Process for selecting special measures.—In selecting which special measure or measures to take under this subsection, the Secretary of the Treasury—

(A) shall consult with the Chairman of the Board of Governors of the Federal Reserve System, any other appropriate Federal banking agency (as defined in section 3 of the Federal Deposit Insurance Act) [1] the Secretary of State, the Securities and Exchange Commission, the Commodity Futures Trading Commission, the National Credit Union Administration Board, and in the sole discretion of the Secretary, such other agencies and interested parties as the Secretary may find to be appropriate; and

(B) shall consider—

(i) whether similar action has been or is being taken by other nations or multilateral groups;

(ii) whether the imposition of any particular special measure would create a significant competitive disadvantage, including any undue cost or burden associated with compliance, for financial institutions organized or licensed in the United States;

(iii) the extent to which the action or the timing of the action would have a significant adverse systemic impact on the international payment, clearance, and settlement system, or on legitimate business activities involving the particular jurisdiction, institution, class of transactions, or type of account; and

(iv) the effect of the action on United States national security and foreign policy.

(5) No limitation on other authority.—This section shall not be construed as superseding or otherwise restricting any other authority granted to the Secretary, or to any other agency, by this subchapter or otherwise.

(b) Special measures.—The special measures referred to in subsection (a), with respect to a jurisdiction outside of the United States, financial institution operating outside of the United States, class of transaction within, or involving, a jurisdiction outside of the United States, or 1 or more types of accounts are as follows:

(1) Recordkeeping and reporting of certain financial transactions.—

(A) In general.—The Secretary of the Treasury may require any domestic financial institution or domestic financial agency to maintain records, file reports, or both, concerning the aggregate amount of transactions, or concerning each transaction, with respect to a jurisdiction outside of the United States, 1 or more financial institutions operating outside of the United States, 1 or more classes of transactions within, or involving, a jurisdiction outside of the United States, or 1 or more types of accounts if the Secretary finds any such jurisdiction, institution, class of transactions, or type of account to be of primary money laundering concern.

(B) Form of records and reports.—Such records and reports shall be made and retained at such time, in such manner, and for such period of time, as the Secretary shall determine, and shall include such information as the Secretary may determine, including—

(i) the identity and address of the participants in a transaction or relationship, including the identity of the originator of any funds transfer;

(ii) the legal capacity in which a participant in any transaction is acting;

(iii) the identity of the beneficial owner of the funds involved in any transaction, in accordance with such procedures as the Secretary determines to be reasonable and practicable to obtain and retain the information; and

(iv) a description of any transaction.

(2) Information relating to beneficial ownership.—In addition to any other requirement under any other provision of law, the Secretary may require any domestic financial institution or domestic financial agency to take such steps as the Secretary may determine to be reasonable and practicable to obtain and retain information concerning the beneficial ownership of any account opened or maintained in the United States by a foreign person (other than a foreign entity whose shares are subject to public reporting requirements or are listed and traded on a regulated exchange or trading market), or a representative of such a foreign person, that involves a jurisdiction outside of the United States, 1 or more financial institutions operating outside of the United States, 1 or more classes of transactions within, or involving, a jurisdiction outside of the United States, or 1 or more types of accounts if the Secretary finds any such jurisdiction, institution, or transaction or type of account to be of primary money laundering concern.

(3) Information relating to certain payable-through accounts.—If the Secretary finds a jurisdiction outside of the United States, 1 or more financial institutions operating outside of the United States, or 1 or more classes of transactions within, or involving, a jurisdiction outside of the United States to be of primary money laundering concern, the Secretary may require any domestic financial institution or domestic financial agency that opens or maintains a payable-through account in the United States for a foreign financial institution involving any such jurisdiction or any such financial institution operating outside of the United States, or a payable through account through which any such transaction may be conducted, as a condition of opening or maintaining such account—

(A) to identify each customer (and representative of such customer) of such financial institution who is permitted to use, or whose transactions are routed through, such payable-through account; and

(B) to obtain, with respect to each such customer (and each such representative), information that is substantially comparable to that which the depository institution obtains in the ordinary course of business with respect to its customers residing in the United States.

(4) Information relating to certain correspondent accounts.—If the Secretary finds a jurisdiction outside of the United States, 1 or more financial institutions operating outside of the United States, or 1 or more classes of transactions within, or involving, a jurisdiction outside of the United States to be of primary money laundering concern, the Secretary may require any domestic financial institution or domestic financial agency that opens or maintains a correspondent account in the United States for a foreign financial institution involving any such jurisdiction or any such financial institution operating outside of the United States, or a correspondent account through which any such transaction may be conducted, as a condition of opening or maintaining such account—

(A) to identify each customer (and representative of such customer) of any such financial institution who is permitted to use, or whose transactions are routed through, such correspondent account; and

(B) to obtain, with respect to each such customer (and each such representative), information that is substantially comparable to that which the depository institution obtains in the ordinary course of business with respect to its customers residing in the United States.

(5) Prohibitions or conditions on opening or maintaining certain correspondent or payable-through accounts.—If the Secretary finds a jurisdiction outside of the United States, 1 or more financial institutions operating outside of the United States, or 1 or more classes of transactions within, or involving, a jurisdiction outside of the United States to be of primary money laundering concern, the Secretary, in consultation with the Secretary of State, the Attorney General, and the Chairman of the Board of Governors of the Federal Reserve System, may prohibit, or impose conditions upon, the opening or maintaining in the United States of a correspondent account or payable- through account by any domestic financial institution or domestic financial agency for or on behalf of a foreign banking institution, if such correspondent account or payable-through account involves any such jurisdiction or institution, or if any such transaction may be conducted through such correspondent account or payable-through account.

(c) Consultations and information to be considered in finding jurisdictions, institutions, types of accounts, or transactions to be of primary money laundering concern.—

(1) In general.—In making a finding that reasonable grounds exist for concluding that a jurisdiction outside of the United States, 1 or more financial institutions operating outside of the United States, 1 or more classes of transactions within, or involving, a jurisdiction outside of the United States, or 1 or more types of accounts is of primary money laundering concern so as to authorize the Secretary of the Treasury to take 1 or more of the special measures described in subsection (b), the Secretary shall consult with the Secretary of State and the Attorney General.

(2) Additional considerations.—In making a finding described in paragraph (1), the Secretary shall consider in addition such information as the Secretary determines to be relevant, including the following potentially relevant factors:

(A) Jurisdictional factors.—In the case of a particular jurisdiction—

(i) evidence that organized criminal groups, international terrorists, or entities involved in the proliferation of weapons of mass destruction or missiles have transacted business in that jurisdiction;

(ii) the extent to which that jurisdiction or financial institutions operating in that jurisdiction offer bank secrecy or special regulatory advantages to nonresidents or nondomiciliaries of that jurisdiction;

(iii) the substance and quality of administration of the bank supervisory and counter-money laundering laws of that jurisdiction;

(iv) the relationship between the volume of financial transactions occurring in that jurisdiction and the size of the economy of the jurisdiction;

(v) the extent to which that jurisdiction is characterized as an offshore banking or secrecy haven by credible international organizations or multilateral expert groups;

(vi) whether the United States has a mutual legal assistance treaty with that jurisdiction, and the experience of United States law enforcement officials and regulatory officials in obtaining information about transactions originating in or routed through or to such jurisdiction; and

(vii) the extent to which that jurisdiction is characterized by high levels of official or institutional corruption.

(B) Institutional factors.—In the case of a decision to apply 1 or more of the special measures described in subsection (b) only to a financial institution or institutions, or to a transaction or class of transactions, or to a type of account, or to all 3, within or involving a particular jurisdiction—

(i) the extent to which such financial institutions, transactions, or types of accounts are used to facilitate or promote money laundering in or through the jurisdiction, including any money laundering activity by organized criminal groups, international terrorists, or entities involved in the proliferation of weapons of mass destruction or missiles;

(ii) the extent to which such institutions, transactions, or types of accounts are used for legitimate business purposes in the jurisdiction; and

(iii) the extent to which such action is sufficient to ensure, with respect to transactions involving the jurisdiction and institutions operating in the jurisdiction, that the purposes of this subchapter continue to be fulfilled, and to guard against international money laundering and other financial crimes.

(d) Notification of special measures invoked by the Secretary.—Not later than 10 days after the date of any action taken by the Secretary of the Treasury under subsection (a)(1), the Secretary shall notify, in writing, the Committee on Financial Services of the House of Representatives and the Committee on Banking, Housing, and Urban Affairs of the Senate of any such action.

(e) Definitions.—Notwithstanding any other provision of this subchapter, for purposes of this section and subsections (i) and (j) of section 5318, the following definitions shall apply:

(1) Bank definitions.—The following definitions shall apply with respect to a bank:

(A) Account.—The term "account"—

(i) means a formal banking or business relationship established to provide regular services, dealings, and other financial transactions; and

(ii) includes a demand deposit, savings deposit, or other transaction or asset account and a credit account or other extension of credit.

(B) Correspondent account.—The term "correspondent account" means an account established to receive deposits from, make payments on behalf of a foreign financial institution, or handle other financial transactions related to such institution.

(C) Payable-through account.—The term "payable-through account" means an account, including a transaction account (as defined in section 19(b)(1)(C) of the Federal Reserve Act), opened at a depository institution by a foreign financial institution by means of which the foreign financial institution permits its customers to engage, either directly or through a subaccount, in banking activities usual in connection with the business of banking in the United States.

(2) Definitions applicable to institutions other than banks.—With respect to any financial institution other than a bank, the Secretary shall, after consultation with the appropriate Federal functional regulators (as defined in section 509 of the Gramm-Leach-Bliley Act), define by regulation the term "account", and shall include within the meaning of that term, to the extent, if any, that the Secretary deems appropriate, arrangements similar to payable-through and correspondent accounts.

(3) Regulatory definition of beneficial ownership.—The Secretary shall promulgate regulations defining beneficial ownership of an account for purposes of this section and subsections (i) and (j) of section 5318. Such regulations shall address issues related to an individual's authority to fund, direct, or manage the account (including, without limitation, the power to direct payments into or out of the account), and an individual's material interest in the income or corpus of the account, and shall ensure that the identification of individuals under this section or subsection (i) or (j) of section 5318 does not extend to any individual whose beneficial interest in the income or corpus of the account is immaterial.

(4) Other terms.—The Secretary may, by regulation, further define the terms in paragraphs (1), (2), and (3), and define other terms for the purposes of this section, as the Secretary deems appropriate.

(f) Classified information.—In any judicial review of a finding of the existence of a primary money laundering concern, or of the requirement for 1 or more special measures with respect to a primary money laundering concern, made under this section, if the designation or imposition, or both, were based on classified information (as defined in section 1(a) of the Classified Information Procedures Act (18 U.S.C. App.),[2] such information may be submitted by the Secretary to the reviewing court ex parte and in camera. This subsection does not confer or imply any right to judicial review of any finding made or any requirement imposed under this section.

(Added Pub.L. 107–56, Title III, § 311(a), Oct. 26, 2001, 115 Stat. 298, and amended Pub.L. 108–177, Title III, § 376, Dec. 13, 2003, 117 Stat. 2630; Pub.L. 108–458, Title VI, § 6203(e), (f), Dec. 17, 2004, 118 Stat. 3747; Pub.L. 109–293, Title V, § 501, Sept. 30, 2006, 120 Stat. 1350.)

1 So in original. Probably should be followed by a comma.

2 So in original. A second closing parenthesis probably should precede the comma.

HISTORICAL AND STATUTORY NOTES

References in Text

Section 3 of the Federal Deposit Insurance Act, referred to in subsec. (a)(4)(A), is Act Sept. 21, 1950, c. 967, § 3, 64 Stat. 894, as amended, which is classified to 18 U.S.C.A. § 709. For complete classification, see Tables.

Section 19(b)(1)(C) of the Federal Reserve Act, referred to in subsec. (e)(1)(C), is Act Dec. 23, 1913, c. 6, § 19(b)(1)(C), as amended, which is classified to 12 U.S.C.A. § 461(b)(1)(C).

Section 509 of the Gramm-Leach-Bliley Act, referred to in subsec. (e)(2), is the Financial Services Modernization Act of 1999, Pub.L. 106–102, Title V, § 509, Nov. 12, 1999, 113 Stat. 1443, as amended, which is classified to 15 U.S.C.A. § 6809. The term "Federal functional regulator" is defined in par. (2) of that section.

Effective and Applicability Provisions

2004 Acts. Amendments by Pub.L. 108–458, Title VI, Subtitle C, to Public Law 107–56, the United States Code, the Federal Deposit Insurance Act, and any other provision of law to take effect as if such amendments had been included in Public Law 107–56, as of Oct. 26, 2001, and no amendment made by such Public Law that is inconsistent with an amendment made by this subtitle to be deemed to have taken effect, see Pub.L. 108–458, § 6205, set out as a note under 12 U.S.C.A. § 1828.

4–Year Congressional Review; Expedited Consideration

Effective on and after the first day of fiscal year 2005, amendments by Title III (§§ 301 to 377) of Pub.L. 107–56 shall terminate if Congress enacts a joint resolution to that effect; such resolution shall be given expedited consideration, see Pub.L. 107–56, Title III, § 303, Oct. 26, 2001, 115 Stat. 298, set out as a note under 31 U.S.C.A. § 5311.

§ 5319. Availability of reports

The Secretary of the Treasury shall make information in a report filed under this subchapter available to an agency, including any State financial institutions supervisory agency, United States intelligence agency or self-regulatory organization registered with the Securities and Exchange Commission or the Commodity Futures Trading Commission, upon request of the head of the agency or organization. The report shall be available for a purpose that is consistent with this subchapter. The Secretary may only require reports on the use of such information by any State financial institutions supervisory agency for other than supervisory purposes or by United States intelligence agencies. However, a report and records of reports are exempt from disclosure under section 552 of title 5.

(Pub.L. 97–258, Sept. 13, 1982, 96 Stat. 999; Pub.L. 102–550, Title XV, § 1506, Oct. 28, 1992, 106 Stat. 4055; Pub.L. 107–56, Title III, § 358(c), Oct. 26, 2001, 115 Stat. 326.)

HISTORICAL AND STATUTORY NOTES

Effective and Applicability Provisions

2001 Acts. Amendments by section 358 of Pub.L. 107–56 applicable with respect to reports filed or records maintained on, before, or after Oct. 26, 2001, see section 358(h) of Pub.L. 107–56, set out as a note under 12 U.S.C.A. § 1829b.

1992 Acts. Except as otherwise provided, amendment by Pub.L. 102–550 effective Oct. 28, 1992, see section 2 of Pub.L. 102–550, set out as a note under section 5301 of Title 42, The Public Health and Welfare.

4–Year Congressional Review; Expedited Consideration

Effective on and after the first day of fiscal year 2005, amendments by Title III (§§ 301 to 377) of Pub.L. 107–56 shall terminate if Congress enacts a joint resolution to that effect; such resolution shall be given expedited consideration, see Pub.L. 107–56, Title III, § 303, Oct. 26, 2001, 115 Stat. 298, set out as a note under 31 U.S.C.A. § 5311.

§ 5320. Injunctions

When the Secretary of the Treasury believes a person has violated, is violating, or will violate this subchapter or a regulation prescribed or order issued under this subchapter, the Secretary may bring a civil action in the appropriate district court of the United States or appropriate United States court of a territory or possession of the United States to enjoin the violation or to enforce compliance with the subchapter, regulation, or order. An injunction or temporary restraining order shall be issued without bond.

(Pub.L. 97–258, Sept. 13, 1982, 96 Stat. 999.)

§ 5321. Civil penalties

(a)(1) A domestic financial institution or nonfinancial trade or business, and a partner, director, officer, or employee of a domestic financial institution or nonfinancial trade or business, willfully violating this subchapter or a regulation prescribed or order issued under this subchapter (except sections 5314 and 5315 of this title or a regulation prescribed under sections 5314 and 5315), or willfully violating a regulation prescribed under section 21 of the Federal Deposit Insurance Act or section 123 of Public Law 91–508, is liable to the United States Government for a civil penalty of not more than the greater of the amount (not to exceed $100,000) involved in the transaction (if any) or $25,000. For a violation of section 5318(a)(2) of this title or a regulation prescribed under section 5318(a)(2), a separate violation occurs for each day the violation continues and at each office, branch, or place of business at which a violation occurs or continues.

(2) The Secretary of the Treasury may impose an additional civil penalty on a person not filing a report, or filing a report containing a material omission or misstatement, under section 5316 of this title or a regulation prescribed under section 5316. A civil penalty under this paragraph may not be more than the amount of the monetary instrument for which the report was required. A civil penalty under this paragraph is reduced by an amount forfeited under section 5317(b) of this title.

(3) A person not filing a report under a regulation prescribed under section 5315 of this title or not complying with an injunction under section 5320 of this title enjoining a violation of, or enforcing compliance with, section 5315 or a regulation prescribed under section 5315, is liable to the Government for a civil penalty of not more than $10,000.

(4) Structured transaction violation.—

(A) Penalty authorized.—The Secretary of the Treasury may impose a civil money penalty on any person who violates any provision of section 5324.

(B) Maximum amount limitation.—The amount of any civil money penalty imposed under subparagraph (A) shall not exceed the amount of the coins and currency (or such other monetary instruments as the Secretary may prescribe) involved in the transaction with respect to which such penalty is imposed.

(C) Coordination with forfeiture provision.—The amount of any civil money penalty imposed by the Secretary under subparagraph (A) shall be reduced by the amount of any forfeiture to the United

States in connection with the transaction with respect to which such penalty is imposed.

(5) Foreign financial agency transaction violation.—

(A) Penalty authorized.—The Secretary of the Treasury may impose a civil money penalty on any person who violates, or causes any violation of, any provision of section 5314.

(B) Amount of penalty.—

(i) In general.—Except as provided in subparagraph (C), the amount of any civil penalty imposed under subparagraph (A) shall not exceed $10,000.

(ii) Reasonable cause exception.—No penalty shall be imposed under subparagraph (A) with respect to any violation if—

(I) such violation was due to reasonable cause, and

(II) the amount of the transaction or the balance in the account at the time of the transaction was properly reported.

(C) Willful violations.—In the case of any person willfully violating, or willfully causing any violation of, any provision of section 5314—

(i) the maximum penalty under subparagraph (B)(i) shall be increased to the greater of—

(I) $100,000, or

(II) 50 percent of the amount determined under subparagraph (D), and

(ii) subparagraph (B)(ii) shall not apply.

(D) Amount.—The amount determined under this subparagraph is—

(i) in the case of a violation involving a transaction, the amount of the transaction, or

(ii) in the case of a violation involving a failure to report the existence of an account or any identifying information required to be provided with respect to an account, the balance in the account at the time of the violation.

(6) Negligence.—

(A) In general.—The Secretary of the Treasury may impose a civil money penalty of not more than $500 on any financial institution or nonfinancial trade or business which negligently violates any provision of this subchapter or any regulation prescribed under this subchapter.

(B) Pattern of negligent activity.—If any financial institution or nonfinancial trade or business engages in a pattern of negligent violations of any provision of this subchapter or any regulation prescribed under this subchapter, the Secretary of the Treasury may, in addition to any penalty imposed under subparagraph (A) with respect to any such violation, impose a civil money penalty of not more than $50,000 on the financial institution or nonfinancial trade or business.

(7) Penalties for international counter money laundering violations.—The Secretary may impose a civil money penalty in an amount equal to not less than 2 times the amount of the transaction, but not more than $1,000,000, on any financial institution or agency that violates any provision of subsection (i) or (j) of section 5318 or any special measures imposed under section 5318A.

(b) Time limitations for assessments and commencement of civil actions.—

(1) Assessments.—The Secretary of the Treasury may assess a civil penalty under subsection (a) at any time before the end of the 6–year period beginning on the date of the transaction with respect to which the penalty is assessed.

(2) Civil actions.—The Secretary may commence a civil action to recover a civil penalty assessed under subsection (a) at any time before the end of the 2–year period beginning on the later of—

(A) the date the penalty was assessed; or

(B) the date any judgment becomes final in any criminal action under section 5322 in connection with the same transaction with respect to which the penalty is assessed.

(c) The Secretary may remit any part of a forfeiture under subsection (c) or (d) [1] of section 5317 of this title or civil penalty under subsection (a)(2) of this section.

(d) Criminal penalty not exclusive of civil penalty.—A civil money penalty may be imposed under subsection (a) with respect to any violation of this subchapter notwithstanding the fact that a criminal penalty is imposed with respect to the same violation.

(e) Delegation of assessment authority to banking agencies.—

(1) In general.—The Secretary of the Treasury shall delegate, in accordance with section 5318(a)(1) and subject to such terms and conditions as the Secretary may impose in accordance with paragraph (3), any authority of the Secretary to assess a civil money penalty under this section on depository institutions (as defined in section 3 of the Federal Deposit Insurance Act) to the appropriate Federal banking agencies (as defined in such section 3).

(2) Authority of agencies.—Subject to any term or condition imposed by the Secretary of the Treasury under paragraph (3), the provisions of this section shall apply to an appropriate Federal banking agency to which is delegated any authority of the Secretary under this section in the same manner such provisions apply to the Secretary.

(3) **Terms and conditions.**—

(A) **In general.**—The Secretary of the Treasury shall prescribe by regulation the terms and conditions which shall apply to any delegation under paragraph (1).

(B) **Maximum dollar amount.**—The terms and conditions authorized under subparagraph (A) may include, in the Secretary's sole discretion, a limitation on the amount of any civil penalty which may be assessed by an appropriate Federal banking agency pursuant to a delegation under paragraph (1).

(Pub.L. 97–258, Sept. 13, 1982, 96 Stat. 999; Pub.L. 98–473, Title II, § 901(a), Oct. 12, 1984, 98 Stat. 2135; Pub.L. 99–570, Title I, §§ 1356(c)(1), 1357(a)–(f), (h), Oct. 27, 1986, 100 Stat. 3207–24, 3207–25, 3207–26; Pub.L. 100–690, Title VI, § 6185(g)(2), Nov. 18, 1988, 102 Stat. 4357; Pub.L. 102–550, Title XV, §§ 1511(b), 1525(b), 1535(a)(2), 1561(a), Oct. 28, 1992, 106 Stat. 4057, 4065, 4066, 4071; Pub.L. 103–322, Title XXXIII, § 330017(a)(1), Sept. 13, 1994, 108 Stat. 2149; Pub.L. 103–325, Title IV, §§ 406, 411(b), 413(a)(1), Sept. 23, 1994, 108 Stat. 2247, 2253, 2254; Pub.L. 104–208, Div. A, Title II, § 2223(3), Sept. 30, 1996, 110 Stat. 3009–415; Pub.L. 107–56, Title III, §§ 353(a), 363(a), 365(c)(2)(B)(i), Oct. 26, 2001, 115 Stat. 322, 332, 335; Pub.L. 108–357, Title VIII, § 821(a), Oct. 22, 2004, 118 Stat. 1586.)

[1] So in original. Section 5317 does not contain a subsec. (d).

HISTORICAL AND STATUTORY NOTES

References in Text

Section 21 of the Federal Deposit Insurance Act, referred to in subsec. (a)(1), is Act Sept. 21, 1950, c. 967, § 2[21], as added Oct. 26, 1970, Pub.L. 91–508, Title I, § 101, 84 Stat. 1114, as amended, which is classified to 12 U.S.C.A. § 1829b.

Section 123 of Public Law 91–508, referred to in subsec. (a)(1), is Bank Secrecy Act, Pub.L. 91–508, Title I, § 123, Oct. 26, 1970, 84 Stat. 1116, as amended, which is classified to 12 U.S.C.A. § 1953.

Section 3 of the Federal Deposit Insurance Act referred to in subsec. (e)(1), is section 2[3] of Act Sept. 21, 1950, c. 967, 64 Stat. 873, as amended, which is classified to 12 U.S.C.A. § 1813.

Effective and Applicability Provisions

2004 Acts. Pub.L. 108–357, Title VIII, § 821(b), Oct. 22, 2004, 118 Stat. 1586, provided that: "The amendment made by this section [amending subsec. (a)(5) of this section] shall apply to violations occurring after the date of the enactment of this Act [Oct. 22, 2004]."

4–Year Congressional Review; Expedited Consideration

Effective on and after the first day of fiscal year 2005, amendments by Title III (§§ 301 to 377) of Pub.L. 107–56 shall terminate if Congress enacts a joint resolution to that effect; such resolution shall be given expedited consideration, see Pub.L. 107–56, Title III, § 303, Oct. 26, 2001, 115 Stat. 298, set out as a note under 31 U.S.C.A. § 5311.

§ 5322. Criminal penalties

(a) A person willfully violating this subchapter or a regulation prescribed or order issued under this subchapter (except section 5315 or 5324 of this title or a regulation prescribed under section 5315 or 5324), or willfully violating a regulation prescribed under section 21 of the Federal Deposit Insurance Act or section 123 of Public Law 91–508, shall be fined not more than $250,000, or imprisoned for not more than five years, or both.

(b) A person willfully violating this subchapter or a regulation prescribed or order issued under this subchapter (except section 5315 or 5324 of this title or a regulation prescribed under section 5315 or 5324), or willfully violating a regulation prescribed under section 21 of the Federal Deposit Insurance Act or section 123 of Public Law 91–508, while violating another law of the United States or as part of a pattern of any illegal activity involving more than $100,000 in a 12–month period, shall be fined not more than $500,000, imprisoned for not more than 10 years, or both.

(c) For a violation of section 5318(a)(2) of this title or a regulation prescribed under section 5318(a)(2), a separate violation occurs for each day the violation continues and at each office, branch, or place of business at which a violation occurs or continues.

(d) A financial institution or agency that violates any provision of subsection (i) or (j) of section 5318, or any special measures imposed under section 5318A, or any regulation prescribed under subsection (i) or (j) of section 5318 or section 5318A, shall be fined in an amount equal to not less than 2 times the amount of the transaction, but not more than $1, 000,000.

(Pub.L. 97–258, Sept. 13, 1982, 96 Stat. 1000; Pub.L. 98–473, Title II, § 901(b), Oct. 12, 1984, 98 Stat. 2135; Pub.L. 99–570, Title I, §§ 1356(c)(1), 1357(g), Oct. 27, 1986, 100 Stat. 3207–24, 3207–26; Pub.L. 102–550, Title XV, § 1504(d)(2), Oct. 28, 1992, 106 Stat. 4055; Pub.L. 103–325, Title IV, § 411(c)(1), Sept. 23, 1994, 108 Stat. 2253; Pub.L. 107–56, Title III, §§ 353(b), 363(b), Oct. 26, 2001, 115 Stat. 323, 332.)

HISTORICAL AND STATUTORY NOTES

References in Text

Section 21 of the Federal Deposit Insurance Act, referred to in subsecs. (a) and (b), is Act Sept. 21, 1950, c. 967, § 2[21], as added Oct. 26, 1970, Pub.L. 91–508, Title I, § 101, 84 Stat. 1114, as amended, which is classified to 12 U.S.C.A. § 1829b.

Section 123 of Public Law 91–508, referred to in subsecs. (a) and (b), is Bank Secrecy Act, Pub.L. 91–508, Title I, § 123, Oct. 26, 1970, 84 Stat. 1116, as amended, which is classified to 12 U.S.C.A. § 1953.

Effective and Applicability Provisions

1992 Amendments. Except as otherwise provided, amendment by Pub.L. 102–550 effective Oct. 28, 1992, see section 2 of Pub.L. 102–550, set out as a note under section 5301 of Title 42, The Public Health and Welfare.

1986 Amendments. Amendment to subsec. (b) of this section by section 1357(g) of Pub.L. 99–570 to apply with respect to violations committed after Oct. 27, 1986, see section 1364(c) of Pub.L. 99–570, set out as a note under section 5321 of this title.

4-Year Congressional Review; Expedited Consideration

Effective on and after the first day of fiscal year 2005, amendments by Title III (§§ 301 to 377) of Pub.L. 107–56 shall terminate if Congress enacts a joint resolution to that effect; such resolution shall be given expedited consideration, see Pub.L. 107–56, Title III, § 303, Oct. 26, 2001, 115 Stat. 298, set out as a note under 31 U.S.C.A. § 5311.

§ 5323. Rewards for informants

(a) The Secretary may pay a reward to an individual who provides original information which leads to a recovery of a criminal fine, civil penalty, or forfeiture, which exceeds $50,000, for a violation of this chapter.

(b) The Secretary shall determine the amount of a reward under this section. The Secretary may not award more than 25 per centum of the net amount of the fine, penalty, or forfeiture collected or $150,000, whichever is less.

(c) An officer or employee of the United States, a State, or a local government who provides information described in subsection (a) in the performance of official duties is not eligible for a reward under this section.

(d) There are authorized to be appropriated such sums as may be necessary to carry out the provisions of this section.

(Added Pub.L. 98–473, Title II, § 901(e), Oct. 12, 1984, 98 Stat. 2135.)

§ 5324. Structuring transactions to evade reporting requirement prohibited

(a) Domestic coin and currency transactions involving financial institutions.—No person shall, for the purpose of evading the reporting requirements of section 5313(a) or 5325 or any regulation prescribed under any such section, the reporting or recordkeeping requirements imposed by any order issued under section 5326, or the recordkeeping requirements imposed by any regulation prescribed under section 21 of the Federal Deposit Insurance Act or section 123 of Public Law 91–508—

(1) cause or attempt to cause a domestic financial institution to fail to file a report required under section 5313(a) or 5325 or any regulation prescribed under any such section, to file a report or to maintain a record required by an order issued under section 5326, or to maintain a record required pursuant to any regulation prescribed under section 21 of the Federal Deposit Insurance Act or section 123 of Public Law 91–508;

(2) cause or attempt to cause a domestic financial institution to file a report required under section 5313(a) or 5325 or any regulation prescribed under any such section, to file a report or to maintain a record required by any order issued under section 5326, or to maintain a record required pursuant to any regulation prescribed under section 5326, or to maintain a record required pursuant to any regulation prescribed under section 21 of the Federal Deposit Insurance Act or section 123 of Public Law 91–508, that contains a material omission or misstatement of fact; or

(3) structure or assist in structuring, or attempt to structure or assist in structuring, any transaction with one or more domestic financial institutions.

(b) Domestic coin and currency transactions involving nonfinancial trades or businesses.—No person shall, for the purpose of evading the report requirements of section 5331 or any regulation prescribed under such section—

(1) cause or attempt to cause a nonfinancial trade or business to fail to file a report required under section 5331 or any regulation prescribed under such section;

(2) cause or attempt to cause a nonfinancial trade or business to file a report required under section 5331 or any regulation prescribed under such section that contains a material omission or misstatement of fact; or

(3) structure or assist in structuring, or attempt to structure or assist in structuring, any transaction with 1 or more nonfinancial trades or businesses.

(c) International monetary instrument transactions.—No person shall, for the purpose of evading the reporting requirements of section 5316—

(1) fail to file a report required by section 5316, or cause or attempt to cause a person to fail to file such a report;

(2) file or cause or attempt to cause a person to file a report required under section 5316 that contains a material omission or misstatement of fact; or

(3) structure or assist in structuring, or attempt to structure or assist in structuring, any importation or exportation of monetary instruments.

(d) Criminal penalty.—

(1) In general.—Whoever violates this section shall be fined in accordance with title 18, United States Code, imprisoned for not more than 5 years, or both.

(2) Enhanced penalty for aggravated cases.—Whoever violates this section while violating another law of the United States or as part of a pattern of any illegal activity involving more than $100,000 in a 12-month period shall be fined twice the amount provided in subsection (b)(3) or (c)(3) (as the case may be) of section 3571 of title 18, United States Code, imprisoned for not more than 10 years, or both.

(Added Pub.L. 99–570, Title I, § 1354(a), Oct. 27, 1986, 100 Stat. 3207–22, and amended Pub.L. 102–550, Title XV,

§§ 1517(a), 1525(a), 1535(a)(1), Oct. 28, 1992, 106 Stat. 4059, 4064, 4066; Pub.L. 103–322, Title XXXIII, § 330017(a)(2), Sept. 13, 1994, 108 Stat. 2149; Pub.L. 103–325, Title IV, §§ 411(a), 413(a)(2), Sept. 23, 1994, 108 Stat. 2253, 2254; Pub.L. 107–56, Title III, §§ 353(c), 365(b)(1), (2)(A), Oct. 26, 2001, 115 Stat. 323, 334, 335; Pub.L. 108–458, Title VI, § 6203(g), Dec. 17, 2004, 118 Stat. 3747.)

HISTORICAL AND STATUTORY NOTES

References in Text

Section 21 of the Federal Deposit Insurance Act, referred to in subsec. (a), is Act Sept. 21, 1950, c. 967, § 2[21], as added Oct. 26, 1970, Pub.L. 91–508, Title I, § 101, 84 Stat. 1114, as amended, which is classified to 12 U.S.C.A. § 1829b.

Section 123 of Public Law 91–508, referred to in subsec. (a), is the Bank Secrecy Act, Pub.L. 91–508, Title I, § 123, Oct. 26, 1970, 84 Stat. 1116, as amended, which is classified to 12 U.S.C.A. § 1953.

Codifications

Section 413(a)(2) of Pub.L. 103–325, directing that subsec. (a) of this section be amended by substituting "section 5313(a) or 5325 or any regulation prescribed under any such section" for "section 5313(a), section 5325, or the regulations issued thereunder or section 5325 or regulations prescribed under such section 5325", wherever appearing, and by striking out "with respect to such transaction", was incapable of execution due to prior, identical amendment by section 330017(a)(2) of Pub.L. 103–322.

Effective and Applicability Provisions

2004 Acts. Amendments by Pub.L. 108–458, Title VI, Subtitle C, to Public Law 107–56, the United States Code, the Federal Deposit Insurance Act, and any other provision of law to take effect as if such amendments had been included in Public Law 107–56, as of Oct. 26, 2001, and no amendment made by such Public Law that is inconsistent with an amendment made by this subtitle to be deemed to have taken effect, see Pub.L. 108–458, § 6205, set out as a note under 12 U.S.C.A. § 1828.

1992 Acts. Except as otherwise provided, amendment by Pub.L. 102–550 effective Oct. 28, 1992, see section 2 of Pub.L. 102–550, set out as a note under section 5301 of Title 42, The Public Health and Welfare.

1986 Acts. Section 1364(a) of Pub.L. 99–570 provided that: "The amendment made by section 1354 [enacting this section] shall apply with respect to transactions for the payment, receipt, or transfer of United States coins or currency or other monetary instruments completed after the end of the 3–month period beginning on the date of the enactment of this Act [Oct. 27, 1986]."

4–Year Congressional Review; Expedited Consideration

Effective on and after the first day of fiscal year 2005, amendments by Title III (§§ 301 to 377) of Pub.L. 107–56 shall terminate if Congress enacts a joint resolution to that effect; such resolution shall be given expedited consideration, see Pub.L. 107–56, Title III, § 303, Oct. 26, 2001, 115 Stat. 298, set out as a note under 31 U.S.C.A. § 5311.

§ 5325. Identification required to purchase certain monetary instruments

(a) In general.—No financial institution may issue or sell a bank check, cashier's check, traveler's check, or money order to any individual in connection with a transaction or group of such contemporaneous transactions which involves United States coins or currency (or such other monetary instruments as the Secretary may prescribe) in amounts or denominations of $3,000 or more unless—

(1) the individual has a transaction account with such financial institution and the financial institution—

(A) verifies that fact through a signature card or other information maintained by such institution in connection with the account of such individual; and

(B) records the method of verification in accordance with regulations which the Secretary of the Treasury shall prescribe; or

(2) the individual furnishes the financial institution with such forms of identification as the Secretary of the Treasury may require in regulations which the Secretary shall prescribe and the financial institution verifies and records such information in accordance with regulations which such Secretary shall prescribe.

(b) Report to Secretary upon request.—Any information required to be recorded by any financial institution under paragraph (1) or (2) of subsection (a) shall be reported by such institution to the Secretary of the Treasury at the request of such Secretary.

(c) Transaction account defined.—For purposes of this section, the term "transaction account" has the meaning given to such term in section 19(b)(1)(C) of the Federal Reserve Act.

(Added Pub.L. 100–690, Title VI, § 6185(b), Nov. 18, 1988, 102 Stat. 4355.)

HISTORICAL AND STATUTORY NOTES

References in Text

Section 19(b)(1)(C) of the Federal Reserve Act, referred to in subsec. (c), is section 19(b)(1)(C) of Act Dec. 23, 1913, c. 6, 38 Stat. 270, as amended, which is classified to section 461(b)(1)(C) of Title 12, Banks and Banking.

§ 5326. Records of certain domestic coin and currency transactions

(a) In general.—If the Secretary of the Treasury finds, upon the Secretary's own initiative or at the request of an appropriate Federal or State law enforcement official, that reasonable grounds exist for concluding that additional recordkeeping and reporting requirements are necessary to carry out the purposes of this subtitle and prevent evasions thereof, the Secretary may issue an order requiring any domestic financial institution or nonfinancial trade or business or group of domestic financial institutions or nonfinancial trades or businesses in a geographic area—

(1) to obtain such information as the Secretary may describe in such order concerning—

(A) any transaction in which such financial institution or nonfinancial trade or business is involved for the payment, receipt, or transfer of United States coins or currency (or such other monetary instruments as the Secretary may describe in such order) the total amounts or denominations of which are equal to or greater than an amount which the Secretary may prescribe; and

(B) any other person participating in such transaction;

(2) to maintain a record of such information for such period of time as the Secretary may require; and

(3) to file a report with respect to any transaction described in paragraph (1)(A) in the manner and to the extent specified in the order.

(b) Authority to order depository institutions to obtain reports from customers.—

(1) In general.—The Secretary of the Treasury may, by regulation or order, require any depository institution (as defined in section 3(c) of the Federal Deposit Insurance Act)—

(A) to request any financial institution or nonfinancial trade or business (other than a depository institution) which engages in any reportable transaction with the depository institution to provide the depository institution with a copy of any report filed by the financial institution or nonfinancial trade or business under this subtitle with respect to any prior transaction (between such financial institution or nonfinancial trade or business and any other person) which involved any portion of the coins or currency (or monetary instruments) which are involved in the reportable transaction with the depository institution; and

(B) if no copy of any report described in subparagraph (A) is received by the depository institution in connection with any reportable transaction to which such subparagraph applies, to submit (in addition to any report required under this subtitle with respect to the reportable transaction) a written notice to the Secretary that the financial institution or nonfinancial trade or business failed to provide any copy of such report.

(2) Reportable transaction defined.—For purposes of this subsection, the term "reportable transaction" means any transaction involving coins or currency (or such other monetary instruments as the Secretary may describe in the regulation or order) the total amounts or denominations of which are equal to or greater than an amount which the Secretary may prescribe.

(c) Nondisclosure of orders.—No financial institution or nonfinancial trade or business or officer, director, employee or agent of a financial institution or nonfinancial trade or business subject to an order under this section may disclose the existence of, or terms of, the order to any person except as prescribed by the Secretary.

(d) Maximum effective period for order.—No order issued under subsection (a) shall be effective for more than 180 days unless renewed pursuant to the requirements of subsection (a).

(Added Pub.L. 100–690, Title VI, § 6185(c), Nov. 18, 1988, 102 Stat. 4355, and amended Pub.L. 102–550, Title XV, §§ 1514, 1562, Oct. 28, 1992, 106 Stat. 4058, 4072; Pub.L. 107–56, Title III, §§ 353(d), 365(c)(2)(B), Oct. 26, 2001, 115 Stat. 323, 335.)

HISTORICAL AND STATUTORY NOTES

References in Text

Section 3(c) of the Federal Deposit Insurance Act, referred to in subsec. (b)(1), is classified to section 1813(c) of Title 12, Banks and Banking.

Codifications

Another section 365(c) of Pub.L. 107–56 amended the table of contents at the beginning of this chapter.

Effective and Applicability Provisions

1992 Acts. Except as otherwise provided, amendment by Pub.L. 102–550 effective Oct. 28, 1992, see section 2 of Pub.L. 102–550, set out as a note under section 5301 of Title 42, The Public Health and Welfare.

4–Year Congressional Review; Expedited Consideration

Effective on and after the first day of fiscal year 2005, amendments by Title III (§§ 301 to 377) of Pub.L. 107–56 shall terminate if Congress enacts a joint resolution to that effect; such resolution shall be given expedited consideration, see Pub.L. 107–56, Title III, § 303, Oct. 26, 2001, 115 Stat. 298, set out as a note under 31 U.S.C.A. § 5311.

[§ 5327. Repealed. Pub.L. 104–208, Div. A, Title II, § 2223(1), Sept. 30, 1996, 110 Stat. 3009–415]

HISTORICAL AND STATUTORY NOTES

Section, added Pub.L. 102–550, Title XV, § 1511(a), Oct. 28, 1992, 106 Stat. 4056, required the Secretary to prescribe regulations requiring depository institutions to identify and report on financial institution customers.

§ 5328. Whistleblower protections

(a) Prohibition against discrimination.—No financial institution or nonfinancial trade or business may discharge or otherwise discriminate against any employee with respect to compensation, terms, conditions, or privileges of employment because the employee (or any person acting pursuant to the request of the employee) provided information to the Secretary of the Treasury, the Attorney General, or any Federal supervisory agency regarding a possible violation of any provision of this subchapter or section 1956, 1957, or 1960 of title 18, or any regulation under any such provision, by the financial institution or nonfinancial trade or business or any director, officer, or employee of the financial institution or nonfinancial trade or business.

(b) Enforcement.—Any employee or former employee who believes that such employee has been discharged or discriminated against in violation of subsection (a) may file a civil action in the appropriate United States district court before the end of the 2–year period beginning on the date of such discharge or discrimination.

(c) Remedies.—If the district court determines that a violation has occurred, the court may order the financial institution or nonfinancial trade or business which committed the violation to—

(1) reinstate the employee to the employee's former position;

(2) pay compensatory damages; or

(3) take other appropriate actions to remedy any past discrimination.

(d) Limitation.—The protections of this section shall not apply to any employee who—

(1) deliberately causes or participates in the alleged violation of law or regulation; or

(2) knowingly or recklessly provides substantially false information to the Secretary, the Attorney General, or any Federal supervisory agency.

(e) Coordination with other provisions of law.—This section shall not apply with respect to any financial institution or nonfinancial trade or business which is subject to section 33 of the Federal Deposit Insurance Act, section 213 of the Federal Credit Union Act, or section 21A(q) of the Home Owners' Loan Act (as added by section 251(c) of the Federal Deposit Insurance Corporation Improvement Act of 1991).

(Added Pub.L. 102–550, Title XV, § 1563(a), Oct. 28, 1992, 106 Stat. 4072, and amended Pub.L. 107–56, Title III, § 365(c)(2)(B)(i), Oct. 26, 2001, 115 Stat. 335.)

HISTORICAL AND STATUTORY NOTES

References in Text

The Federal Deposit Insurance Act, referred to in subsec. (e), is Act Sept. 21, 1950, c. 967, § 2, 64 Stat. 873, as amended, which is classified generally to chapter 16 (section 1811 et seq.) of Title 12, Banks and Banking. Section 33 of the Federal Deposit Insurance Act is classified to section 1831j of Title 12. For complete classification of this Act to the Code, see Short Title note set out under section 1811 of Title 12 and Tables.

The Federal Credit Union Act, referred to in subsec. (e), is Act June 26, 1934, c. 750, 48 Stat. 1216, as amended, which is classified generally to chapter 14 (section 1751 et seq.) of Title 12, Banks and Banking. Section 213 of the Federal Credit Union Act is classified to section 1790b of Title 12. For complete classification of this Act to the Code, see section 1751 of Title 12 and Tables.

The Home Owner's Loan Act, referred to in subsec. (e), is Act June 13, 1933, c. 64, 48 Stat. 128, as amended, which is classified generally to chapter 12 (section 1461 et seq.) of Title 12, Banks and Banking. Section 21A(q) of the Home Owner's Loan Act is classified to section 1441a(q) of Title 12. For complete classification of this Act to the Code, see section 1461 of Title 12 and Tables.

Codifications

Another section 365(c) of Pub.L. 107–56 amended the table of contents at the beginning of this chapter.

Effective and Applicability Provisions

1992 Acts. Except as otherwise provided, section effective Oct. 28, 1992, see section 2 of Pub.L. 102–550, set out as a note under section 5301 of Title 42, The Public Health and Welfare.

4–Year Congressional Review; Expedited Consideration

Effective on and after the first day of fiscal year 2005, amendments by Title III (§§ 301 to 377) of Pub.L. 107–56 shall terminate if Congress enacts a joint resolution to that effect; such resolution shall be given expedited consideration, see Pub.L. 107–56, Title III, § 303, Oct. 26, 2001, 115 Stat. 298, set out as a note under 31 U.S.C.A. § 5311.

§ 5329. Staff commentaries

The Secretary shall—

(1) publish all written rulings interpreting this subchapter; and

(2) annually issue a staff commentary on the regulations issued under this subchapter.

(Added Pub.L. 103–325, Title III, § 311(a), Sept. 23, 1994, 108 Stat. 2221.)

§ 5330. Registration of money transmitting businesses

(a) Registration with Secretary of the Treasury required.—

(1) In general.—Any person who owns or controls a money transmitting business shall register the business (whether or not the business is licensed as a money transmitting business in any State) with the Secretary of the Treasury not later than the end of the 180–day period beginning on the later of—

(A) the date of enactment of the Money Laundering Suppression Act of 1994; or

(B) the date on which the business is established.

(2) Form and manner of registration.—Subject to the requirements of subsection (b), the Secretary of the Treasury shall prescribe, by regulation, the form and manner for registering a money transmitting business pursuant to paragraph (1).

(3) Businesses remain subject to State law.—This section shall not be construed as superseding any requirement of State law relating to money transmitting businesses operating in such State.

(4) False and incomplete information.—The filing of false or materially incomplete information in connection with the registration of a money transmitting business shall be considered as a failure to comply with the requirements of this subchapter.

(b) Contents of registration.—The registration of a money transmitting business under subsection (a) shall include the following information:

(1) The name and location of the business.

(2) The name and address of each person who—

(A) owns or controls the business;

(B) is a director or officer of the business; or

(C) otherwise participates in the conduct of the affairs of the business.

(3) The name and address of any depository institution at which the business maintains a transaction account (as defined in section 19(b)(1)(C) of the Federal Reserve Act).

(4) An estimate of the volume of business in the coming year (which shall be reported annually to the Secretary).

(5) Such other information as the Secretary of the Treasury may require.

(c) Agents of money transmitting businesses.—

(1) Maintenance of lists of agents of money transmitting businesses.—Pursuant to regulations which the Secretary of the Treasury shall prescribe, each money transmitting business shall—

(A) maintain a list containing the names and addresses of all persons authorized to act as an agent for such business in connection with activities described in subsection (d)(1)(A) and such other information about such agents as the Secretary may require; and

(B) make the list and other information available on request to any appropriate law enforcement agency.

(2) Treatment of agent as money transmitting business.—The Secretary of the Treasury shall prescribe regulations establishing, on the basis of such criteria as the Secretary determines to be appropriate, a threshold point for treating an agent of a money transmitting business as a money transmitting business for purposes of this section.

(d) Definitions.—For purposes of this section, the following definitions shall apply:

(1) Money transmitting business.—The term "money transmitting business" means any business other than the United States Postal Service which—

(A) provides check cashing, currency exchange, or money transmitting or remittance services, or issues or redeems money orders, travelers' checks, and other similar instruments or any other person who engages as a business in the transmission of funds, including any person who engages as a business in an informal money transfer system or any network of people who engage as a business in facilitating the transfer of money domestically or internationally outside of the conventional financial institutions system;; [1]

(B) is required to file reports under section 5313; and

(C) is not a depository institution (as defined in section 5313(g)).

(2) Money transmitting service.—The term "money transmitting service" includes accepting currency or funds denominated in the currency of any country and transmitting the currency or funds, or the value of the currency or funds, by any means through a financial agency or institution, a Federal reserve bank or other facility of the Board of Governors of the Federal Reserve System, or an electronic funds transfer network.

(e) Civil penalty for failure to comply with registration requirements.—

(1) In general.—Any person who fails to comply with any requirement of this section or any regulation prescribed under this section shall be liable to the United States for a civil penalty of $5,000 for each such violation.

(2) Continuing violation.—Each day a violation described in paragraph (1) continues shall constitute a separate violation for purposes of such paragraph.

(3) Assessments.—Any penalty imposed under this subsection shall be assessed and collected by the Secretary of the Treasury in the manner provided in section 5321 and any such assessment shall be subject to the provisions of such section.

(Added Pub.L. 103–325, Title IV, § 408(b), Sept. 23, 1994, 108 Stat. 2250, and amended Pub.L. 107–56, Title III, § 359(b), Oct. 26, 2001, 115 Stat. 328.)

[1] So in original. The second semicolon probably should not appear.

HISTORICAL AND STATUTORY NOTES

References in Text

The date of enactment of the Money Laundering Suppression Act of 1994, referred to in subsec. (a)(1)(A), means the date of enactment of Title IV of Pub.L. 103–325, 108 Stat. 2160, which was approved Sept. 23, 1994.

Section 19(b)(1)(C) of the Federal Reserve Act, referred to in subsec. (b)(3), is section 19(b)(1)(C) of Act Dec. 23, 1913, c. 6, 38 Stat. 251, as amended, which is classified to section 461(b)(1)(C) of Title 12, Banks and Banking.

4-Year Congressional Review; Expedited Consideration

Effective on and after the first day of fiscal year 2005, amendments by Title III (§§ 301 to 377) of Pub.L. 107–56 shall terminate if Congress enacts a joint resolution to that effect; such resolution shall be given expedited consideration, see Pub.L. 107–56, Title III, § 303, Oct. 26, 2001, 115 Stat. 298, set out as a note under 31 U.S.C.A. § 5311.

Registration of Money Transmitting Businesses to Promote Effective Law Enforcement; Findings and Purposes

Section 408(a) of Pub.L. 103–325 provided that:

"(1) **Findings.**—The Congress hereby finds the following:

"(A) Money transmitting businesses are subject to the recordkeeping and reporting requirements of subchapter II of chapter 53 of title 31, United States Code [this subchapter].

"(B) Money transmitting businesses are largely unregulated businesses and are frequently used in sophisticated schemes to—

"(i) transfer large amounts of money which are the proceeds of unlawful enterprises; and

"(ii) evade the requirements of such subchapter II [this subchapter], the Internal Revenue Code of 1986 [Title 26, Internal Revenue Code], and other laws of the United States.

"(C) Information on the identity of money transmitting businesses and the names of the persons who own or control, or are officers or employees of, a money transmitting business would have a high degree of usefulness in criminal, tax, or regulatory investigations and proceedings.

"(2) **Purpose.**—It is the purpose of this section [enacting this section and amending section 1960 of Title 18, Crimes and Criminal Procedure] to establish a registration requirement for businesses engaged in providing check cashing, currency exchange, or money transmitting or remittance services, or issuing or redeeming money orders, travelers' checks, and other similar instruments to assist the Secretary of the Treasury, the Attorney General, and other supervisory and law enforcement agencies to effectively enforce the criminal tax, and regulatory laws and prevent such money transmitting businesses from engaging in illegal activities."

§ 5331. Reports relating to coins and currency received in nonfinancial trade or business

(a) Coin and currency receipts of more than $10,000.—Any person—

(1) who is engaged in a trade or business; and

(2) who, in the course of such trade or business, receives more than $10,000 in coins or currency in 1 transaction (or 2 or more related transactions),

shall file a report described in subsection (b) with respect to such transaction (or related transactions) with the Financial Crimes Enforcement Network at such time and in such manner as the Secretary may, by regulation, prescribe.

(b) Form and manner of reports.—A report is described in this subsection if such report—

(1) is in such form as the Secretary may prescribe;

(2) contains—

(A) the name and address, and such other identification information as the Secretary may require, of the person from whom the coins or currency was received;

(B) the amount of coins or currency received;

(C) the date and nature of the transaction; and

(D) such other information, including the identification of the person filing the report, as the Secretary may prescribe.

(c) Exceptions.—

(1) Amounts received by financial institutions.—Subsection (a) shall not apply to amounts received in a transaction reported under section 5313 and regulations prescribed under such section.

(2) Transactions occurring outside the United States.—Except to the extent provided in regulations prescribed by the Secretary, subsection (a) shall not apply to any transaction if the entire transaction occurs outside the United States.

(d) Currency includes foreign currency and certain monetary instruments.—

(1) In general.—For purposes of this section, the term "currency" includes—

(A) foreign currency; and

(B) to the extent provided in regulations prescribed by the Secretary, any monetary instrument (whether or not in bearer form) with a face amount of not more than $10,000.

(2) Scope of application.—Paragraph (1)(B) shall not apply to any check drawn on the account of the writer in a financial institution referred to in subparagraph (A), (B), (C), (D), (E), (F), (G), (J), (K), (R), or (S) of section 5312(a)(2).

(Added Pub.L. 107–56, Title III, § 365(a), Oct. 26, 2001, 115 Stat. 333.)

HISTORICAL AND STATUTORY NOTES

4–Year Congressional Review; Expedited Consideration

Effective on and after the first day of fiscal year 2005, amendments by Title III (§§ 301 to 377) of Pub.L. 107–56 shall terminate if Congress enacts a joint resolution to that effect; such resolution shall be given expedited consideration, see Pub.L. 107–56, Title III, § 303, Oct. 26, 2001, 115 Stat. 298, set out as a note under 31 U.S.C.A. § 5311.

Regulations

Pub.L. 107–56, Title III, § 365(e), formerly (f), Oct. 26, 2001, 115 Stat. 335, renumbered (e), Pub.L. 108–458, Title VI, § 6202(n)(2), Dec. 17, 2004, 118 Stat. 3746, provided that: "Regulations which the Secretary determines are necessary to implement this section [enacting this section and amending sections 5312, 5317, 5318, 5321, 5324, 5326, and 5328 of this title] shall be published in final form before the end of the 6–month period beginning on the date of enactment of this Act [Oct. 26, 2001]."

[Amendments by Pub.L. 108–458, Title VI, Subtitle C, to Public Law 107–56, the United States Code, the Federal

Deposit Insurance Act, and any other provision of law to take effect as if such amendments had been included in Public Law 107–56, as of Oct. 26, 2001, and no amendment made by such Public Law that is inconsistent with an amendment made by this subtitle to be deemed to have taken effect, see Pub.L. 108–458, § 6205, set out as a note under 12 U.S.C.A. § 1828.]

§ 5332. Bulk cash smuggling into or out of the United States

(a) Criminal offense.—

(1) In general.—Whoever, with the intent to evade a currency reporting requirement under section 5316, knowingly conceals more than $10,000 in currency or other monetary instruments on the person of such individual or in any conveyance, article of luggage, merchandise, or other container, and transports or transfers or attempts to transport or transfer such currency or monetary instruments from a place within the United States to a place outside of the United States, or from a place outside the United States to a place within the United States, shall be guilty of a currency smuggling offense and subject to punishment pursuant to subsection (b).

(2) Concealment on person.—For purposes of this section, the concealment of currency on the person of any individual includes concealment in any article of clothing worn by the individual or in any luggage, backpack, or other container worn or carried by such individual.

(b) Penalty.—

(1) Term of imprisonment.—A person convicted of a currency smuggling offense under subsection (a), or a conspiracy to commit such offense, shall be imprisoned for not more than 5 years.

(2) Forfeiture.—In addition, the court, in imposing sentence under paragraph (1), shall order that the defendant forfeit to the United States, any property, real or personal, involved in the offense, and any property traceable to such property.

(3) Procedure.—The seizure, restraint, and forfeiture of property under this section shall be governed by section 413 of the Controlled Substances Act.

(4) Personal money judgment.—If the property subject to forfeiture under paragraph (2) is unavailable, and the defendant has insufficient substitute property that may be forfeited pursuant to section 413(p) of the Controlled Substances Act, the court shall enter a personal money judgment against the defendant for the amount that would be subject to forfeiture.

(c) Civil forfeiture.—

(1) In general.—Any property involved in a violation of subsection (a), or a conspiracy to commit such violation, and any property traceable to such violation or conspiracy, may be seized and forfeited to the United States.

(2) Procedure.—The seizure and forfeiture shall be governed by the procedures governing civil forfeitures in money laundering cases pursuant to section 981(a)(1)(A) of title 18, United States Code.

(3) Treatment of certain property as involved in the offense.—For purposes of this subsection and subsection (b), any currency or other monetary instrument that is concealed or intended to be concealed in violation of subsection (a) or a conspiracy to commit such violation, any article, container, or conveyance used, or intended to be used, to conceal or transport the currency or other monetary instrument, and any other property used, or intended to be used, to facilitate the offense, shall be considered property involved in the offense.

(Added Pub.L. 107–56, Title III, § 371(c), Oct. 26, 2001, 115 Stat. 337, and amended Pub.L. 108–458, Title VI, § 6203(h), Dec. 17, 2004, 118 Stat. 3747.)

HISTORICAL AND STATUTORY NOTES

References in Text

Section 413 of the Controlled Substances Act, referred to in subsec. (b)(3), (4), is Pub.L. 91–513, Title IV, § 403, Oct. 27, 1970, 84 Stat. 1263, which is classified to 21 U.S.C.A. § 843.

Codifications

Another section 371(c) of Pub.L. 107–56 amended the table of contents at the beginning of this chapter.

Effective and Applicability Provisions

2004 Acts. Amendments by Pub.L. 108–458, Title VI, Subtitle C, to Public Law 107–56, the United States Code, the Federal Deposit Insurance Act, and any other provision of law to take effect as if such amendments had been included in Public Law 107–56, as of Oct. 26, 2001, and no amendment made by such Public Law that is inconsistent with an amendment made by this subtitle to be deemed to have taken effect, see Pub.L. 108–458, § 6205, set out as a note under 12 U.S.C.A. § 1828.

4–Year Congressional Review; Expedited Consideration

Effective on and after the first day of fiscal year 2005, amendments by Title III (§§ 301 to 377) of Pub.L. 107–56 shall terminate if Congress enacts a joint resolution to that effect; such resolution shall be given expedited consideration, see Pub.L. 107–56, Title III, § 303, Oct. 26, 2001, 115 Stat. 298, set out as a note under 31 U.S.C.A. § 5311.

Findings; Purposes

Pub.L. 107–56, Title III, § 371(a), (b), Oct. 26, 2001, 115 Stat. 336, 337, provided that:

"**(a) Findings.**—The Congress finds the following:

"(1) Effective enforcement of the currency reporting requirements of subchapter II of chapter 53 of title 31, United States Code [31 U.S.C.A. § 5311 et seq.], and the regulations prescribed under such subchapter, has forced drug dealers and other criminals engaged in cash-based businesses to avoid using traditional financial institutions.

"(2) In their effort to avoid using traditional financial institutions, drug dealers and other criminals are forced to move large quantities of currency in bulk form to and through the airports, border crossings, and other ports of entry where the currency can be smuggled out of the United States and placed in a foreign financial institution or sold on the black market.

"(3) The transportation and smuggling of cash in bulk form may now be the most common form of money laundering, and the movement of large sums of cash is one of the most reliable warning signs of drug trafficking, terrorism, money laundering, racketeering, tax evasion and similar crimes.

"(4) The intentional transportation into or out of the United States of large amounts of currency or monetary instruments, in a manner designed to circumvent the mandatory reporting provisions of subchapter II of chapter 53 of title 31, United States Code [31 U.S.C.A. § 5311 et seq.],,[sic] is the equivalent of, and creates the same harm as, the smuggling of goods.

"(5) The arrest and prosecution of bulk cash smugglers are important parts of law enforcement's effort to stop the laundering of criminal proceeds, but the couriers who attempt to smuggle the cash out of the United States are typically low-level employees of large criminal organizations, and thus are easily replaced. Accordingly, only the confiscation of the smuggled bulk cash can effectively break the cycle of criminal activity of which the laundering of the bulk cash is a critical part.

"(6) The current penalties for violations of the currency reporting requirements are insufficient to provide a deterrent to the laundering of criminal proceeds. In particular, in cases where the only criminal violation under current law is a reporting offense, the law does not adequately provide for the confiscation of smuggled currency. In contrast, if the smuggling of bulk cash were itself an offense, the cash could be confiscated as the corpus delicti of the smuggling offense.

"(b) **Purposes.**—The purposes of this section are—

"(1) to make the act of smuggling bulk cash itself a criminal offense;

"(2) to authorize forfeiture of any cash or instruments of the smuggling offense; and

"(3) to emphasize the seriousness of the act of bulk cash smuggling."

SUBCHAPTER III—MONEY LAUNDERING AND RELATED FINANCIAL CRIMES

§ 5340. Definitions

For purposes of this subchapter, the following definitions shall apply:

(1) Department of the treasury law enforcement organizations.—The term "Department of the Treasury law enforcement organizations" has the meaning given to such term in section 9703(p)(1).

(2) Money laundering and related financial crime.—The term "money laundering and related financial crime"—

(A) means the movement of illicit cash or cash equivalent proceeds into, out of, or through the United States, or into, out of, or through United States financial institutions, as defined in section 5312 of title 31, United States Code; or

(B) has the meaning given that term (or the term used for an equivalent offense) under State and local criminal statutes pertaining to the movement of illicit cash or cash equivalent proceeds.

(3) Secretary.—The term "Secretary" means the Secretary of the Treasury.

(4) Attorney general.—The term "Attorney General" means the Attorney General of the United States.

(Added Pub.L. 105–310, § 2(a), Oct. 30, 1998, 112 Stat. 2941.)

PART 1—NATIONAL MONEY LAUNDERING AND RELATED FINANCIAL CRIMES STRATEGY

§ 5341. National money laundering and related financial crimes strategy

(a) Development and transmittal to Congress.—

(1) Development.—The President, acting through the Secretary and in consultation with the Attorney General, shall develop a national strategy for combating money laundering and related financial crimes.

(2) Transmittal to Congress.—By August 1 of 1999, 2000, 2001, 2002, 2003, 2005, and 2007, the President shall submit a national strategy developed in accordance with paragraph (1) to the Congress.

(3) Separate presentation of classified material.—Any part of the strategy that involves information which is properly classified under criteria established by Executive Order shall be submitted to the Congress separately in classified form.

(b) Development of strategy.—The national strategy for combating money laundering and related financial crimes shall address any area the President, acting through the Secretary and in consultation with the Attorney General, considers appropriate, including the following:

(1) Goals, objectives, and priorities.—Comprehensive, research-based goals, objectives, and priorities for reducing money laundering and related financial crime in the United States.

(2) Prevention.—Coordination of regulatory and other efforts to prevent the exploitation of financial systems in the United States for money laundering and related financial crimes, including a requirement that the Secretary shall—

(A) regularly review enforcement efforts under this subchapter and other provisions of law and, when appropriate, modify existing regulations or prescribe new regulations for purposes of preventing such criminal activity; and

(B) coordinate prevention efforts and other enforcement action with the Board of Governors of the Federal Reserve System, the Securities and Exchange Commission, the Federal Trade Commission, other Federal banking agencies, the National Credit Union Administration Board, and such other Federal agencies as the Secretary, in consultation with the Attorney General, determines to be appropriate.

(3) Detection and prosecution initiatives.—A description of operational initiatives to improve detection and prosecution of money laundering and related financial crimes and the seizure and forfeiture of proceeds and instrumentalities derived from such crimes.

(4) Enhancement of the role of the private financial sector in prevention.—The enhancement of partnerships between the private financial sector and law enforcement agencies with regard to the prevention and detection of money laundering and related financial crimes, including providing incentives to strengthen internal controls and to adopt on an industrywide basis more effective policies.

(5) Enhancement of interGovernmental cooperation.—The enhancement of—

(A) cooperative efforts between the Federal Government and State and local officials, including State and local prosecutors and other law enforcement officials; and

(B) cooperative efforts among the several States and between State and local officials, including State and local prosecutors and other law enforcement officials,

for financial crimes control which could be utilized or should be encouraged.

(6) Project and budget priorities.—A 3-year projection for program and budget priorities and achievable projects for reductions in financial crimes.

(7) Assessment of funding.—A complete assessment of how the proposed budget is intended to implement the strategy and whether the funding levels contained in the proposed budget are sufficient to implement the strategy.

(8) Designated areas.—A description of geographical areas designated as "high-risk money laundering and related financial crime areas" in accordance with, but not limited to, section 5342.

(9) Persons consulted.—Persons or officers consulted by the Secretary pursuant to subsection (d).

(10) Data regarding trends in money laundering and related financial crimes.—The need for additional information necessary for the purpose of developing and analyzing data in order to ascertain financial crime trends.

(11) Improved communications systems.—A plan for enhancing the compatibility of automated information and facilitating access of the Federal Government and State and local governments to timely, accurate, and complete information.

(12) Data regarding funding of terrorism.—Data concerning money laundering efforts related to the funding of acts of international terrorism, and efforts directed at the prevention, detection, and prosecution of such funding.

(c) Effectiveness report.—At the time each national strategy for combating financial crimes is transmitted by the President to the Congress (other than the first transmission of any such strategy) pursuant to subsection (a), the Secretary shall submit a report containing an evaluation of the effectiveness of policies to combat money laundering and related financial crimes.

(d) Consultations.—In addition to the consultations required under this section with the Attorney General, in developing the national strategy for combating money laundering and related financial crimes, the Secretary shall consult with—

(1) the Board of Governors of the Federal Reserve System and other Federal banking agencies and the National Credit Union Administration Board;

(2) State and local officials, including State and local prosecutors;

(3) the Securities and Exchange Commission;

(4) the Commodities and Futures Trading Commission;

(5) the Director of the Office of National Drug Control Policy, with respect to money laundering and related financial crimes involving the proceeds of drug trafficking;

(6) the Chief of the United States Postal Inspection Service;

(7) to the extent appropriate, State and local officials responsible for financial institution and financial market regulation;

(8) any other State or local government authority, to the extent appropriate;

(9) any other Federal Government authority or instrumentality, to the extent appropriate; and

(10) representatives of the private financial services sector, to the extent appropriate.

(Added Pub.L. 105–310, § 2(a), Oct. 30, 1998, 112 Stat. 2942, and amended Pub.L. 107–56, Title III, § 354, Oct. 26, 2001, 115 Stat. 323; Pub.L. 108–458, Title VI, § 6102(a), Dec. 17, 2004, 118 Stat. 3744.)

HISTORICAL AND STATUTORY NOTES

4–Year Congressional Review; Expedited Consideration

Effective on and after the first day of fiscal year 2005, amendments by Title III (§§ 301 to 377) of Pub.L. 107–56 shall terminate if Congress enacts a joint resolution to that effect; such resolution shall be given expedited consideration, see Pub.L. 107–56, Title III, § 303, Oct. 26, 2001, 115 Stat. 298, set out as a note under 31 U.S.C.A. § 5311.

§ 5342. High-risk money laundering and related financial crime areas

(a) Findings and purpose.—

(1) Findings.—The Congress finds the following:

(A) Money laundering and related financial crimes frequently appear to be concentrated in particular geographic areas, financial systems, industry sectors, or financial institutions.

(B) While the Secretary has the responsibility to act with regard to Federal offenses which are being committed in a particular locality or are directed at a single institution, because modern financial systems and institutions are interconnected to a degree which was not possible until recently, money laundering and other related financial crimes are likely to have local, State, national, and international effects wherever they are committed.

(2) Purpose and objective.—It is the purpose of this section to provide a mechanism for designating any area where money laundering or a related financial crime appears to be occurring at a higher than average rate such that—

(A) a comprehensive approach to the problem of such crime in such area can be developed, in cooperation with State and local law enforcement agencies, which utilizes the authority of the Secretary to prevent such activity; or

(B) such area can be targeted for law enforcement action.

(b) Element of National strategy.—The designation of certain areas as areas in which money laundering and related financial crimes are extensive or present a substantial risk shall be an element of the national strategy developed pursuant to section 5341(b).

(c) Designation of areas.—

(1) Designation by Secretary.—The Secretary, after taking into consideration the factors specified in subsection (d), shall designate any geographical area, industry, sector, or institution in the United States in which money laundering and related financial crimes are extensive or present a substantial risk as a "high-risk money laundering and related financial crimes area".

(2) Case-by-case determination in consultation with the attorney general.—In addition to the factors specified in subsection (d), any designation of any area under paragraph (1) shall be made on the basis of a determination by the Secretary, in consultation with the Attorney General, that the particular area, industry, sector, or institution is being victimized by, or is particularly vulnerable to, money laundering and related financial crimes.

(3) Specific initiatives.—Any head of a department, bureau, or law enforcement agency, including any State or local prosecutor, involved in the detection, prevention, and suppression of money laundering and related financial crimes and any State or local official or prosecutor may submit—

(A) a written request for the designation of any area as a high-risk money laundering and related financial crimes area; or

(B) a written request for funding under section 5351 for a specific prevention or enforcement initiative, or to determine the extent of financial criminal activity, in an area.

(d) Factors.—In considering the designation of any area as a high-risk money laundering and related financial crimes area, the Secretary shall, to the extent appropriate and in consultation with the Attorney General, take into account the following factors:

(1) The population of the area.

(2) The number of bank and nonbank financial institution transactions which originate in such area or involve institutions located in such area.

(3) The number of stock or commodities transactions which originate in such area or involve institutions located in such area.

(4) Whether the area is a key transportation hub with any international ports or airports or an extensive highway system.

(5) Whether the area is an international center for banking or commerce.

(6) The extent to which financial crimes and financial crime-related activities in such area are having a harmful impact in other areas of the country.

(7) The number or nature of requests for information or analytical assistance which—

(A) are made to the analytical component of the Department of the Treasury; and

(B) originate from law enforcement or regulatory authorities located in such area or involve institutions or businesses located in such area or residents of such area.

(8) The volume or nature of suspicious activity reports originating in the area.

(9) The volume or nature of currency transaction reports or reports of cross-border movements of currency or monetary instruments originating in, or transported through, the area.

(10) Whether, and how often, the area has been the subject of a geographical targeting order.

(11) Observed changes in trends and patterns of money laundering activity.

(12) Unusual patterns, anomalies, growth, or other changes in the volume or nature of core economic statistics or indicators.

(13) Statistics or indicators of unusual or unexplained volumes of cash transactions.

(14) Unusual patterns, anomalies, or changes in the volume or nature of transactions conducted through financial institutions operating within or outside the United States.

(15) The extent to which State and local governments and State and local law enforcement agencies have committed resources to respond to the financial crime problem in the area and the degree to which the commitment of such resources reflects a determination by such government and agencies to address the problem aggressively.

(16) The extent to which a significant increase in the allocation of Federal resources to combat financial crimes in such area is necessary to provide an adequate State and local response to financial crimes and financial crime-related activities in such area.

(Added Pub.L. 105–310, § 2(a), Oct. 30, 1998, 112 Stat. 2944.)

HISTORICAL AND STATUTORY NOTES

Report and recommendations

Pub.L. 105–310, § 2(c), Oct. 30, 1998, 112 Stat. 2949, provided that: "Before the end of the 5–year period beginning on the date the first national strategy for combating money laundering and related financial crimes is submitted to the Congress pursuant to section 5341(a)(1) of title 31, United States Code (as added by section 2(a) of this Act [Money Laundering and Financial Crimes Strategy Act of 1998, Pub.L. 103–310, Oct. 30, 1998, 112 Stat. 2941. For complete classification of this Act to the Code, see Short Title note set out under section 5301 of this title, and Tables.]), the Secretary of the Treasury, in consultation with the Attorney General, shall submit a report to the Committee on Banking and Financial Services and the Committee on the Judiciary of the House of Representatives and the Committee on Banking, Housing, and Urban Affairs and the Committee on the Judiciary of the Senate on the effectiveness of and the need for the designation of areas, under section 5342 of title 31, United States Code (as added by such section 2(a)), as high-risk money laundering and related financial crime areas, together with recommendations for such legislation as the Secretary and the Attorney General may determine to be appropriate to carry out the purposes of such section."

PART 2—FINANCIAL CRIME-FREE COMMUNITIES SUPPORT PROGRAM

§ 5351. Establishment of financial crime-free communities support program

(a) Establishment.—The Secretary of the Treasury, in consultation with the Attorney General, shall establish a program to support local law enforcement efforts in the development and implementation of a program for the detection, prevention, and suppression of money laundering and related financial crimes.

(b) Program.—In carrying out the program, the Secretary of the Treasury, in consultation with the Attorney General, shall—

(1) make and track grants to grant recipients;

(2) provide for technical assistance and training, data collection, and dissemination of information on state-of-the-art practices that the Secretary determines to be effective in detecting, preventing, and suppressing money laundering and related financial crimes; and

(3) provide for the general administration of the program.

(c) Administration.—The Secretary shall appoint an administrator to carry out the program.

(d) Contracting.—The Secretary may employ any necessary staff and may enter into contracts or agreements with Federal and State law enforcement agencies to delegate authority for the execution of grants and for such other activities necessary to carry out this chapter.

(Added Pub.L. 105–310, § 2(a), Oct. 30, 1998, 112 Stat. 2946.)

§ 5352. Program authorization

(a) Grant eligibility.—To be eligible to receive an initial grant or a renewal grant under this part, a State or local law enforcement agency or prosecutor shall meet each of the following criteria:

(1) Application.—The State or local law enforcement agency or prosecutor shall submit an application to the Secretary in accordance with section 5353(a)(2).

(2) Accountability.—The State or local law enforcement agency or prosecutor shall—

(A) establish a system to measure and report outcomes—

(i) consistent with common indicators and evaluation protocols established by the Secretary, in consultation with the Attorney General; and

(ii) approved by the Secretary;

(B) conduct biennial surveys (or incorporate local surveys in existence at the time of the evaluation) to measure the progress and effectiveness of the coalition; and

(C) provide assurances that the entity conducting an evaluation under this paragraph, or from which the applicant receives information, has experience in gathering data related to money laundering and related financial crimes.

(b) Grant amounts.—

(1) Grants.—

(A) In general.—Subject to subparagraph (D), for a fiscal year, the Secretary of the Treasury, in consultation with the Attorney General, may grant to an eligible applicant under this section for that fiscal year, an amount determined by the Secretary of the Treasury, in consultation with the Attorney General, to be appropriate.

(B) Suspension of grants.—If such grant recipient fails to continue to meet the criteria specified in subsection (a), the Secretary may suspend the grant, after providing written notice to the grant recipient and an opportunity to appeal.

(C) Renewal grants.—Subject to subparagraph (D), the Secretary may award a renewal grant to a grant recipient under this subparagraph for each fiscal year following the fiscal year for which an initial grant is awarded.

(D) Limitation.—The amount of a grant award under this paragraph may not exceed $750,000 for a fiscal year.

(2) Grant awards.—

(A) In general.—Except as provided in subparagraph (B), the Secretary may, with respect to a community, make a grant to one eligible applicant that represents that community.

(B) Exception.—The Secretary may make a grant to more than one eligible applicant that represent [1] a community if—

(i) the eligible coalitions demonstrate that the coalitions are collaborating with one another; and

(ii) each of the coalitions has independently met the requirements set forth in subsection (a).

(c) Condition relating to proceeds of asset forfeitures.—

(1) In general.—No grant may be made or renewed under this part to any State or local law enforcement agency or prosecutor unless the agency or prosecutor agrees to donate to the Secretary of the Treasury for the program established under this part any amount received by such agency or prosecutor (after the grant is made) pursuant to any criminal or civil forfeiture under chapter 46 of title 18, United States Code, or any similar provision of State law.

(2) Scope of application.—Paragraph (1) shall not apply to any amount received by a State or local law enforcement agency or prosecutor pursuant to any criminal or civil forfeiture referred to in such paragraph in excess of the aggregate amount of grants received by such agency or prosecutor under this part.

(d) Rolling grant application periods.—In establishing the program under this part, the Secretary shall take such action as may be necessary to ensure, to the extent practicable, that—

(1) applications for grants under this part may be filed at any time during a fiscal year; and

(2) some portion of the funds appropriated under this part for any such fiscal year will remain available for grant applications filed later in the fiscal year.

(Added Pub.L. 105–310, § 2(a), Oct. 30, 1998, 112 Stat. 2946.)

[1] So in original. Probably should be "represents".

§ 5353. Information collection and dissemination with respect to grant recipients

(a) Applicant and grantee information.—

(1) Application process.—The Secretary shall issue requests for proposal, as necessary, regarding, with respect to the grants awarded under section 5352, the application process, grant renewal, and suspension or withholding of renewal grants. Each application under this paragraph shall be in writing and shall be subject to review by the Secretary.

(2) Reporting.—The Secretary shall, to the maximum extent practicable and in a manner consistent with applicable law, minimize reporting requirements by a grant recipient and expedite any application for a renewal grant made under this part.

(b) Activities of Secretary.—The Secretary may—

(1) evaluate the utility of specific initiatives relating to the purposes of the program;

(2) conduct an evaluation of the program; and

(3) disseminate information described in this subsection to—

(A) eligible State local law enforcement agencies or prosecutors; and

(B) the general public.

(Added Pub.L. 105–310, § 2(a), Oct. 30, 1998, 112 Stat. 2948.)

§ 5354. Grants for fighting money laundering and related financial crimes

(a) In general.—After the end of the 1-year period beginning on the date the first national strategy for combating money laundering and related financial crimes is submitted to the Congress in accordance with section 5341, and subject to subsection (b), the Secretary may review, select, and award grants for State or local law enforcement agencies and prosecutors to provide funding necessary to investigate and prosecute money laundering and related financial crimes in high-risk money laundering and related financial crime areas.

(b) Special preference.—Special preference shall be given to applications submitted to the Secretary which demonstrate collaborative efforts of two or more State and local law enforcement agencies or prosecutors who have a history of Federal, State, and local cooperative law enforcement and prosecutorial efforts in responding to such criminal activity.

(Added Pub.L. 105–310, § 2(a), Oct. 30, 1998, 112 Stat. 2948.)

§ 5355. Authorization of appropriations

There are authorized to be appropriated the following amounts for the following fiscal years to carry out the purposes of this subchapter:

For fiscal year:	The amount authorized is:
1999	$ 5,000,000.
2000	$ 7,500,000.
2001	$10,000,000.
2002	$12,500,000.
2003	$15,000,000.
2004	$15,000,000.
2005	$15,000,000.

(Added Pub.L. 105–310, § 2(a), Oct. 30, 1998, 112 Stat. 2948, and amended Pub.L. 108–458, Title VI, § 6102(b), Dec. 17, 2004, 118 Stat. 3745.)

TITLE 41
PUBLIC CONTRACTS

CHAPTER 1—GENERAL PROVISIONS

EXECUTIVE ORDERS

EXECUTIVE ORDER NO. 10925

Ex. Ord. No. 10925, Mar. 6, 1961, 26 F.R. 1977, which related to nondiscrimination provisions in Government contracts and established the President's Committee on Equal Employment Opportunity, was revoked by section 403 of Ex. Ord. No. 11246, Sept. 24, 1965, 30 F.R. 12319, set out as a note under section 2000e of Title 42, The Public Health and Welfare.

§ 51. Short title

Sections 51 to 58 of this title may be cited as the "Anti–Kickback Act of 1986".

(Mar. 8, 1946, c. 80, § 1, 60 Stat. 37; Sept. 2, 1960, Pub.L. 86–695, 74 Stat. 740; Nov. 7, 1986, Pub.L. 99–634, § 2(a), 100 Stat. 3523.)

HISTORICAL AND STATUTORY NOTES

Effective and Applicability Provisions

1986 Acts. Section 3 of Pub.L. 99–634 provided that:

"(a) Except as provided in subsection (b), the Anti–Kickback Act of 1986 (as set out in section 2(a)) [enacting sections 55, 56, 57(c), and 58 and amending sections 51 to 54 of this title] shall take effect with respect to conduct described in section 3 of such Act [section 53 of this title] which occurs on or after the date of the enactment of this Act [Nov. 7, 1986].

"(b) Subsections (a) and (b) of section 7 of the Anti–Kickback Act of 1986 (as set out in section 2(a)) [section 57(a) and (b) of this title] shall take effect with respect to contract solicitations issued by an agency, department, or other establishment of the Federal Government on or after the date which is 90 days after the date of the enactment of this Act [Nov. 7, 1986]."

Short Title

1986 Amendments. Section 1 of Pub.L. 99–634 provided: "That this Act [enacting sections 55 to 58, amending sections 51 to 54 of this title and enacting provision set out as a note under this section] may be cited as the 'Anti–Kickback Enforcement Act of 1986'."

§ 52. Definitions

As used in sections 51 to 58 of this title:

(1) The term "contracting agency", when used with respect to a prime contractor, means any department, agency, or establishment of the United States which enters into a prime contract with a prime contractor.

(2) The term "kickback" means any money, fee, commission, credit, gift, gratuity, thing of value, or compensation of any kind which is provided, directly or indirectly, to any prime contractor, prime contractor employee, subcontractor, or subcontractor employee for the purpose of improperly obtaining or rewarding favorable treatment in connection with a prime contract or in connection with a subcontract relating to a prime contract.

(3) The term "person" means a corporation, partnership, business association of any kind, trust, joint-stock company, or individual.

(4) The term "prime contract" means a contract or contractual action entered into by the United States for the purpose of obtaining supplies, materials, equipment, or services of any kind.

(5) The term "prime contractor" means a person who has entered into a prime contract with the United States.

(6) The term "prime contractor employee" means any officer, partner, employee, or agent of a prime contractor.

(7) The term "subcontract" means a contract or contractual action entered into by a prime contractor or subcontractor for the purpose of obtaining supplies, materials, equipment, or services of any kind under a prime contract.

(8) The term "subcontractor"—

(A) means any person, other than the prime contractor, who offers to furnish or furnishes any supplies, materials, equipment, or services of any kind under a prime contract or a subcontract entered into in connection with such prime contract; and

(B) includes any person who offers to furnish or furnishes general supplies to the prime contractor or a higher tier subcontractor.

(9) The term "subcontractor employee" means any officer, partner, employee, or agent of a subcontractor.

(Mar. 8, 1946, c. 80, § 2, 60 Stat. 38; Sept. 2, 1960, Pub.L. 86–695, 74 Stat. 740; Nov. 7, 1986, Pub.L. 99–634, § 2(a), 100 Stat. 3523.)

HISTORICAL AND STATUTORY NOTES

Effective and Applicability Provisions

1986 Acts. Amendment by Pub.L. 99–634 effective with respect to conduct described in section 53 of this title which occurs on or after Nov. 7, 1986, see section 3(a) of Pub.L. 99–634, set out as a note under section 51 of this title.

§ 53. Prohibited conduct

It is prohibited for any person—

(1) to provide, attempt to provide, or offer to provide any kickback;

(2) to solicit, accept, or attempt to accept any kickback; or

(3) to include, directly or indirectly, the amount of any kickback prohibited by clause (1) or (2) in the contract price charged by a subcontractor to a prime contractor or a higher tier subcontractor or in the contract price charged by a prime contractor to the United States.

(Mar. 8, 1946, c. 80, § 3, 60 Stat. 38; Sept. 2, 1960, Pub.L. 86–695, 74 Stat. 741; Nov. 7, 1986, Pub.L. 99–634, § 2(a), 100 Stat. 3524.)

HISTORICAL AND STATUTORY NOTES

Effective and Applicability Provisions

1986 Acts. Amendment by Pub.L. 99–634 effective with respect to conduct described in this section which occurs on or after Nov. 7, 1986, see section 3(a) of Pub.L. 99–634, set out as a note under section 51 of this title.

§ 54. Criminal penalties

Any person who knowingly and willfully engages in conduct prohibited by section 53 of this title shall be imprisoned for not more than 10 years or shall be subject to a fine in accordance with Title 18, or both.

(Mar. 8, 1946, c. 80, § 4, 60 Stat. 38; Sept. 2, 1960, Pub.L. 86–695, 74 Stat. 741; Nov. 7, 1986, Pub.L. 99–634, § 2(a), 100 Stat. 3524.)

HISTORICAL AND STATUTORY NOTES

Effective and Applicability Provisions

1986 Acts. Amendment by Pub.L. 99–634 effective with respect to conduct described in section 53 of this title which occurs on or after Nov. 7, 1986, see section 3(a) of Pub.L. 99–634, set out as a note under section 51 of this title.

§ 55. Civil actions

(a)(1) The United States may, in a civil action, recover a civil penalty from any person who knowingly engages in conduct prohibited by section 53 of this title. The amount of such civil penalty shall be—

(A) twice the amount of each kickback involved in the violation; and

(B) not more than $10,000 for each occurrence of prohibited conduct.

(2) The United States may, in a civil action, recover a civil penalty from any person whose employee, subcontractor or subcontractor employee violates section 53 of this title by providing, accepting, or charging a kickback. The amount of such civil penalty shall be the amount of that kickback.

(b) A civil action under this section shall be barred unless the action is commenced within 6 years after the later of (1) the date on which the prohibited conduct establishing the cause of action occurred, and (2) the date on which the United States first knew or should reasonably have known that the prohibited conduct had occurred.

(Mar. 8, 1946, c. 80, § 5, as added Nov. 7, 1986, Pub.L. 99–634, § 2(a), 100 Stat. 3524.)

HISTORICAL AND STATUTORY NOTES

Effective and Applicability Provisions

1986 Acts. Section effective with respect to conduct described in section 53 of this title which occurs on or after Nov. 7, 1986, see section 3(a) of Pub.L. 99–634, set out as a note under section 51 of this title.

§ 56. Administrative offsets

(a) Offset authority

A contracting officer of a contracting agency may offset the amount of a kickback provided, accepted, or charged in violation of section 53 of this title against any moneys owed by the United States to the prime contractor under the prime contract to which such kickback relates.

(b) Duties of prime contractor

(1) Upon direction of a contracting officer of a contracting agency with respect to a prime contract, the prime contractor shall withhold from any sums owed to a subcontractor under a subcontract of the prime contract the amount of any kickback which was or may be offset against that prime contractor under subsection (a) of this section.

(2) Such contracting officer may order that sums withheld under paragraph (1)—

(A) be paid over to the contracting agency; or

(B) if the United States has already offset the amount of such sums against that prime contractor, be retained by the prime contractor.

(3) The prime contractor shall notify the contracting officer when an amount is withheld and retained under paragraph (2)(B).

(c) Claim of Government

An offset under subsection (a) of this section or a direction or order of a contracting officer under subsection (b) of this section is a claim by the Government for the purposes of the Contract Disputes Act of 1978 [41 U.S.C.A. § 601 et seq.].

(d) "Contracting officer" defined

As used in this section, the term "contracting officer" has the meaning given that term for the purposes of the Contract Disputes Act of 1978 [41 U.S.C.A. § 601 et seq.].

(Mar. 8, 1946, c. 80, § 6, as added Nov. 7, 1986, Pub.L. 99–634, § 2(a), 100 Stat. 3524.)

HISTORICAL AND STATUTORY NOTES

References in Text

The Contract Disputes Act of 1978, referred to in subsecs. (c) and (d), is Pub.L. 95–563, Nov. 1, 1978, 92 Stat. 2383, which is classified principally to chapter 9 (section 601 et seq.) of this title. For complete classification of this Act to the Code, see Short Title note set out under section 601 of this title and Tables.

Effective and Applicability Provisions

1986 Acts. Section effective with respect to conduct described in section 53 of this title which occurs on or after Nov. 7, 1986, see section 3(a) of Pub.L. 99–634, set out as a note under section 51 of this title.

§ 57. Contractor responsibilities

(a) Procedural requirements for prevention and detection of violations

Each contracting agency shall include in each prime contract awarded by such agency a requirement that the prime contractor shall have in place and follow reasonable procedures designed to prevent and detect violations of section 53 of this title in its own operations and direct business relationships.

(b) Cooperation in investigations requirement

Each contracting agency shall include in each prime contract awarded by such agency a requirement that the prime contractor shall cooperate fully with any Federal Government agency investigating a violation of section 53 of this title.

(c) Reporting requirement; supplying information as favorable evidence of responsibility

(1)(A) Whenever a prime contractor or subcontractor has reasonable grounds to believe that a violation of section 53 of this title may have occurred, the prime contractor or subcontractor shall promptly report the possible violation in writing.

(B) A contractor shall make the reports required by subparagraph (A) to the inspector general of the contracting agency, the head of the contracting agency if the agency does not have an inspector general, or the Department of Justice.

(2) In the case of an administrative or contractual action to suspend or debar any person who is eligible to enter into contracts with the Federal Government, evidence that such person has supplied information to the United States pursuant to paragraph (1) shall be favorable evidence of such person's responsibility for the purposes of Federal procurement laws and regulations.

(d) Partial inapplicability to small contracts

Subsections (a) and (b) of this section do not apply to a prime contract that is not greater than $100,000 or to a prime contract for the acquisition of commercial items (as defined in section 403(12) of this title).

(e) Cooperation in investigations regardless of contract amount

Notwithstanding subsection (d) of this section, a prime contractor shall cooperate fully with any Federal Government agency investigating a violation of section 53 of this title.

(Mar. 8, 1946, c. 80, § 7, as added Nov. 7, 1986, Pub.L. 99–634, § 2(a), 100 Stat. 3525, and amended Oct. 13, 1994, Pub.L. 103–355, Title IV, § 4104(a), Title VIII, 8301(c)(1), 108 Stat. 3341, 3397; Feb. 10, 1996, Pub.L. 104–106, Div. D, Title XLIII, § 4321(g), 110 Stat. 675.)

HISTORICAL AND STATUTORY NOTES

Effective and Applicability Provisions

1996 Acts. Amendment by Pub.L. 104–106 effective Feb. 10, 1996, except as otherwise provided, see section 4401 of Pub.L. 104–106, set out as a note under section 251 of this title.

1994 Acts. Amendment by sections 4104(a) and 8301(c)(1) of Pub.L. 103–355 effective Oct. 13, 1994, except as otherwise provided, see section 10001 of Pub.L. 103–355, set out as a note under section 251 of this title.

1986 Acts. Subsecs. (a) and (b) effective with respect to contract solicitations issued by an agency, department, or other establishment of the Federal Government on or after the date which is 90 days after Nov. 7, 1986; and subsec. (c) effective with respect to conduct described in section 53 of this title which occurs on or after Nov. 7, 1986, see section 3 of Pub.L. 99–634, set out as a note under section 51 of this title.

§ 58. Inspection authority

For the purpose of ascertaining whether there has been a violation of section 53 of this title with respect to any prime contract, the Government Accountability Office and the inspector general of the contracting agency, or a representative of such contracting agency designated by the head of such agency if the agency does not have an inspector general, shall have access to and may inspect the facilities and audit the books and records, including any electronic data or records, of any prime contractor or subcontractor under a prime contract awarded by such agency. This section does not apply with respect to a prime contract for the acquisition of commercial items (as defined in section 403(12) of this title).

(Mar. 8, 1946, c. 80, § 8, as added Nov. 7, 1986, Pub.L. 99–634, § 2(a), 100 Stat. 3525, and amended Oct. 13, 1994, Pub.L. 103–355, Title VIII, § 8301(c)(2), 108 Stat. 3397; Pub.L. 108–271, § 8(b), July 7, 2004, 118 Stat. 814.)

HISTORICAL AND STATUTORY NOTES

Effective and Applicability Provisions

1994 Acts. Amendment by section 8301(c)(2) of Pub.L. 103–355 effective Oct. 13, 1994, except as otherwise provided, see section 10001 of Pub.L. 103–355, set out as a note under section 251 of this title.

1986 Acts. Section effective with respect to conduct described in section 53 of this title which occurs on or after Nov. 7, 1986, see section 3(a) of Pub.L. 99–634, set out as a note under section 51 of this title.

Change of Name

"Government Accountability Office" substituted for "General Accounting Office" in text on authority of Pub.L. 108–271, § 8(b), cited in the credit to this section and set out as a note under 31 U.S.C.A. § 702, which provided that any reference to the General Accounting Office in any law, rule, regulation, certificate, directive, instruction, or other official paper in force on July 17, 2004, to refer and apply to the Government Accountability Office.

TITLE 46
SHIPPING

CHAPTER 705—MARITIME DRUG LAW ENFORCEMENT

§ 70501. Findings and declarations

Congress finds and declares that trafficking in controlled substances aboard vessels is a serious international problem, is universally condemned, and presents a specific threat to the security and societal well-being of the United States.

(Pub.L. 109–304, § 10(2), Oct. 6, 2006, 120 Stat. 1685.)

§ 70502. Definitions

(a) Application of other definitions.—The definitions in section 102 of the Comprehensive Drug Abuse Prevention and Control Act of 1970 (21 U.S.C. 802) apply to this chapter.

(b) Vessel of the United States.—In this chapter, the term "vessel of the United States" means—

(1) a vessel documented under chapter 121 of this title or numbered as provided in chapter 123 of this title;

(2) a vessel owned in any part by an individual who is a citizen of the United States, the United States Government, the government of a State or political subdivision of a State, or a corporation incorporated under the laws of the United States or of a State, unless—

(A) the vessel has been granted the nationality of a foreign nation under article 5 of the 1958 Convention on the High Seas; and

(B) a claim of nationality or registry for the vessel is made by the master or individual in charge at the time of the enforcement action by an officer or employee of the United States who is authorized to enforce applicable provisions of United States law; and

(3) a vessel that was once documented under the laws of the United States and, in violation of the laws of the United States, was sold to a person not a citizen of the United States, placed under foreign registry, or operated under the authority of a foreign nation, whether or not the vessel has been granted the nationality of a foreign nation.

(c) Vessel subject to the jurisdiction of the United States.—

(1) In general.—In this chapter, the term "vessel subject to the jurisdiction of the United States" includes—

(A) a vessel without nationality;

(B) a vessel assimilated to a vessel without nationality under paragraph (2) of article 6 of the 1958 Convention on the High Seas;

(C) a vessel registered in a foreign nation if that nation has consented or waived objection to the enforcement of United States law by the United States;

(D) a vessel in the customs waters of the United States;

(E) a vessel in the territorial waters of a foreign nation if the nation consents to the enforcement of United States law by the United States; and

(F) a vessel in the contiguous zone of the United States, as defined in Presidential Proclamation 7219 of September 2, 1999 [1] (43 U.S.C. 1331 note), that—

(i) is entering the United States;

(ii) has departed the United States; or

(iii) is a hovering vessel as defined in section 401 of the Tariff Act of 1930 (19 U.S.C. 1401).

(2) Consent or waiver of objection.—Consent or waiver of objection by a foreign nation to the enforcement of United States law by the United States under paragraph (1)(C) or (E)—

(A) may be obtained by radio, telephone, or similar oral or electronic means; and

(B) is proved conclusively by certification of the Secretary of State or the Secretary's designee.

(d) Vessel without nationality.—

(1) In general.—In this chapter, the term "vessel without nationality" includes—

(A) a vessel aboard which the master or individual in charge makes a claim of registry that is denied by the nation whose registry is claimed;

(B) a vessel aboard which the master or individual in charge fails, on request of an officer of the United States authorized to enforce applicable provisions of United States law, to make a claim of nationality or registry for that vessel; and

(C) a vessel aboard which the master or individual in charge makes a claim of registry and for which the claimed nation of registry does not affirmatively and unequivocally assert that the vessel is of its nationality.

(2) Verification or denial.—A claim of registry under paragraph (1)(A) or (C) may be verified or denied by radio, telephone, or similar oral or electronic means. The denial of such a claim is proved conclusively by certification of the Secretary of State or the Secretary's designee.

(e) Claim of nationality or registry.—A claim of nationality or registry under this section includes only—

(1) possession on board the vessel and production of documents evidencing the vessel's nationality as provided in article 5 of the 1958 Convention on the High Seas;

(2) flying its nation's ensign or flag; or

(3) a verbal claim of nationality or registry by the master or individual in charge of the vessel.

(Pub.L. 109–304, § 10(2), Oct. 6, 2006, 120 Stat. 1685.)

[1] So in original. Probably should be "August 2, 1999".

HISTORICAL AND STATUTORY NOTES

References in Text

Section 102 of the Comprehensive Drug Abuse Prevention and Control Act of 1970, referred to in subsec. (a), is Pub.L. 91–513, Title II, § 102, Oct. 27, 1970, 84 Stat. 1242, as amended, which is classified to 21 U.S.C.A. § 802.

Chapter 121 of this title, referred to in subsec. (b)(1), is Documentation of Vessels, 46 U.S.C.A. § 12101 et seq.

Chapter 123 of this title, referred to in subsec. (b)(1), is Numbering Undocumented Vessels, 46 U.S.C.A. § 12301 et seq.

Presidential Proclamation 7219 of September 2, 1999, referred to in subsec. (c)(1)(F), probably means Proc. No. 7219, Aug. 2, 1999, 64 FR 48701, which is set out as a note under 43 U.S.C.A. § 1331.

Section 401 of the Tariff Act of 1930, referred to in subsec. (c)(1)(F)(iii), is Act June 17, 1930, c. 497, Title IV, § 401, 46 Stat. 708, which is classified to 19 U.S.C.A. § 1401.

§ 70503. Manufacture, distribution, or possession of controlled substances on vessels

(a) Prohibitions.—An individual may not knowingly or intentionally manufacture or distribute, or possess with intent to manufacture or distribute, a controlled substance on board—

(1) a vessel of the United States or a vessel subject to the jurisdiction of the United States; or

(2) any vessel if the individual is a citizen of the United States or a resident alien of the United States.

(b) Extension beyond territorial jurisdiction.—Subsection (a) applies even though the act is committed outside the territorial jurisdiction of the United States.

(c) Nonapplication.—

(1) In general.—Subject to paragraph (2), subsection (a) does not apply to—

(A) a common or contract carrier or an employee of the carrier who possesses or distributes a controlled substance in the lawful and usual course of the carrier's business; or

(B) a public vessel of the United States or an individual on board the vessel who possesses or distributes a controlled substance in the lawful course of the individual's duties.

(2) Entered in manifest.—Paragraph (1) applies only if the controlled substance is part of the cargo entered in the vessel's manifest and is intended to be imported lawfully into the country of destination for scientific, medical, or other lawful purposes.

(d) Burden of proof.—The United States Government is not required to negative a defense provided by subsection (c) in a complaint, information, indictment, or other pleading or in a trial or other proceeding. The burden of going forward with the evidence supporting the defense is on the person claiming its benefit.

(Pub.L. 109–304, § 10(2), Oct. 6, 2006, 120 Stat. 1687.)

§ 70504. Jurisdiction and venue

(a) Jurisdiction.—Jurisdiction of the United States with respect to a vessel subject to this chapter is not an element of an offense. Jurisdictional issues arising under this chapter are preliminary questions of law to be determined solely by the trial judge.

(b) Venue.—A person violating section 70503 of this title shall be tried in the district court of the United States for—

(1) the district at which the person enters the United States; or

(2) the District of Columbia.

(Pub.L. 109–304, § 10(2), Oct. 6, 2006, 120 Stat. 1688.)

§ 70505. Failure to comply with international law as a defense

A person charged with violating section 70503 of this title does not have standing to raise a claim of failure to comply with international law as a basis for a defense. A claim of failure to comply with international law in the enforcement of this chapter may be made only by a foreign nation. A failure to comply with international law does not divest a court of jurisdiction and is not a defense to a proceeding under this chapter.

(Pub.L. 109–304, § 10(2), Oct. 6, 2006, 120 Stat. 1688.)

§ 70506. Penalties

(a) Violations.—A person violating section 70503 of this title shall be punished as provided in section 1010 of the Comprehensive Drug Abuse Prevention and Control Act of 1970 (21 U.S.C. 960). However, if the offense is a second or subsequent offense as provided in section 1012(b) of that Act (21 U.S.C. 962(b)), the person shall be punished as provided in section 1012 of that Act (21 U.S.C. 962).

(b) Attempts and conspiracies.—A person attempting or conspiring to violate section 70503 of this title is subject to the same penalties as provided for violating section 70503.

(Pub.L. 109–304, § 10(2), Oct. 6, 2006, 120 Stat. 1688.)

§ 70507. Forfeitures

(a) In general.—Property described in section 511(a) of the Comprehensive Drug Abuse Prevention and Control Act of 1970 (21 U.S.C. 881(a)) that is used or intended for use to commit, or to facilitate the commission of, an offense under section 70503 of this title may be seized and forfeited in the same manner that similar property may be seized and forfeited under section 511 of that Act (21 U.S.C. 881).

(b) Prima facie evidence of violation.—Practices commonly recognized as smuggling tactics may provide prima facie evidence of intent to use a vessel to commit, or to facilitate the commission of, an offense under section 70503 of this title, and may support seizure and forfeiture of the vessel, even in the absence of controlled substances aboard the vessel. The following indicia, among others, may be considered, in the totality of the circumstances, to be prima facie evidence that a vessel is intended to be used to commit, or to facilitate the commission of, such an offense:

(1) The construction or adaptation of the vessel in a manner that facilitates smuggling, including—

(A) the configuration of the vessel to ride low in the water or present a low hull profile to avoid being detected visually or by radar;

(B) the presence of any compartment or equipment that is built or fitted out for smuggling, not including items such as a safe or lock-box reasonably used for the storage of personal valuables;

(C) the presence of an auxiliary tank not installed in accordance with applicable law or installed in such a manner as to enhance the vessel's smuggling capability;

(D) the presence of engines that are excessively over-powered in relation to the design and size of the vessel;

(E) the presence of materials used to reduce or alter the heat or radar signature of the vessel and avoid detection;

(F) the presence of a camouflaging paint scheme, or of materials used to camouflage the vessel, to avoid detection; or

(G) the display of false vessel registration numbers, false indicia of vessel nationality, false vessel name, or false vessel homeport.

(2) The presence or absence of equipment, personnel, or cargo inconsistent with the type or declared purpose of the vessel.

(3) The presence of excessive fuel, lube oil, food, water, or spare parts, inconsistent with legitimate vessel operation, inconsistent with the construction or equipment of the vessel, or inconsistent with the character of the vessel's stated purpose.

(4) The operation of the vessel without lights during times lights are required to be displayed under applicable law or regulation and in a manner of navigation consistent with smuggling tactics used to avoid detection by law enforcement authorities.

(5) The failure of the vessel to stop or respond or heave to when hailed by government authority, especially where the vessel conducts evasive maneuvering when hailed.

(6) The declaration to government authority of apparently false information about the vessel, crew, or voyage or the failure to identify the vessel by name or country of registration when requested to do so by government authority.

(7) The presence of controlled substance residue on the vessel, on an item aboard the vessel, or on an individual aboard the vessel, of a quantity or other nature that reasonably indicates manufacturing or distribution activity.

(8) The use of petroleum products or other substances on the vessel to foil the detection of controlled substance residue.

(9) The presence of a controlled substance in the water in the vicinity of the vessel, where given the currents, weather conditions, and course and speed of the vessel, the quantity or other nature is such that it reasonably indicates manufacturing or distribution activity.

(Pub.L. 109–304, § 10(2), Oct. 6, 2006, 120 Stat. 1688.)

TITLE 49

TRANSPORTATION

CHAPTER 11—NATIONAL TRANSPORTATION SAFETY BOARD

SUBCHAPTER IV—ENFORCEMENT AND PENALTIES

§ 1155. Aviation penalties

(a) Civil penalty.—(1) A person violating section 1132, section 1134(b), section 1134(f)(1), or section 1136(g) (related to an aircraft accident) of this title or a regulation prescribed or order issued under any of those sections is liable to the United States Government for a civil penalty of not more than $1,000. A separate violation occurs for each day a violation continues.

(2) This subsection does not apply to a member of the armed forces of the United States or an employee of the Department of Defense subject to the Uniform Code of Military Justice when the member or employee is performing official duties. The appropriate military authorities are responsible for taking necessary disciplinary action and submitting to the National Transportation Safety Board a timely report on action taken.

(3) The Board may compromise the amount of a civil penalty imposed under this subsection.

(4) The Government may deduct the amount of a civil penalty imposed or compromised under this subsection from amounts it owes the person liable for the penalty.

(5) A civil penalty under this subsection may be collected by bringing a civil action against the person liable for the penalty. The action shall conform as nearly as practicable to a civil action in admiralty.

(b) Criminal penalty.—A person that knowingly and without authority removes, conceals, or withholds a part of a civil aircraft involved in an accident, or property on the aircraft at the time of the accident, shall be fined under title 18, imprisoned for not more than 10 years, or both.

(Added Pub.L. 103–272, § 1(d), July 5, 1994, 108 Stat. 758, and amended Pub.L. 104–264, Title VII, § 702(b), Oct. 9, 1996, 110 Stat. 3267.)

HISTORICAL AND STATUTORY NOTES

References in Text

The Uniform Code of Military Justice, referred to in subsec. (a)(2), is classified generally to chapter 47 (section 801 et seq.) of Title 10, Armed Forces.

Effective and Applicability Provisions

1996 Acts. Except as otherwise specifically provided, amendment by Pub.L. 104–264 applicable only to fiscal years beginning after Sept. 30, 1996, and not to be construed as affecting funds made available for a fiscal year ending before Oct. 1, 1996, see section 3 of Pub.L. 104–264, set out as a note under section 106 of this title.

Prior Provisions

Prior chapter 31 (sections 3101 to 3104) of subtitle II redesignated and restated as chapter 315 (sections 31501 to 31504) of subtitle VI of this title by Pub.L. 103–272, § 1(c), (e).

Limitation on Statutory Construction

Nothing in Title VII of Pub.L. 104–264 to be construed as limiting the actions that an air carrier may take, or the obligations that an air carrier may have, in providing assistance to the families of passengers involved in an aircraft accident, see section 705 of Pub.L. 104–264, set out as a note under section 41113 of this title.

CHAPTER 463—PENALTIES

§ 46306. Registration violations involving aircraft not providing air transportation

(a) **Application.**—This section applies only to aircraft not used to provide air transportation.

(b) **General criminal penalty.**—Except as provided by subsection (c) of this section, a person shall be fined under title 18, imprisoned for not more than 3 years, or both, if the person—

(1) knowingly and willfully forges or alters a certificate authorized to be issued under this part;

(2) knowingly sells, uses, attempts to use, or possesses with the intent to use, such a certificate;

(3) knowingly and willfully displays or causes to be displayed on an aircraft a mark that is false or misleading about the nationality or registration of the aircraft;

(4) obtains a certificate authorized to be issued under this part by knowingly and willfully falsifying or concealing a material fact, making a false, fictitious, or fraudulent statement, or making or using a false document knowing it contains a false, fictitious, or fraudulent statement or entry;

(5) owns an aircraft eligible for registration under section 44102 of this title and knowingly and willfully operates, attempts to operate, or allows another person to operate the aircraft when—

(A) the aircraft is not registered under section 44103 of this title or the certificate of registration is suspended or revoked; or

(B) the owner knows or has reason to know that the other person does not have proper authorization to operate or navigate the aircraft without registration for a period of time after transfer of ownership;

(6) knowingly and willfully operates or attempts to operate an aircraft eligible for registration under section 44102 of this title knowing that—

(A) the aircraft is not registered under section 44103 of this title;

(B) the certificate of registration is suspended or revoked; or

(C) the person does not have proper authorization to operate or navigate the aircraft without registration for a period of time after transfer of ownership;

(7) knowingly and willfully serves or attempts to serve in any capacity as an airman without an airman's certificate authorizing the individual to serve in that capacity;

(8) knowingly and willfully employs for service or uses in any capacity as an airman an individual who does not have an airman's certificate authorizing the individual to serve in that capacity; or

(9) operates an aircraft with a fuel tank or fuel system that has been installed or modified knowing that the tank, system, installation, or modification does not comply with regulations and requirements of the Administrator of the Federal Aviation Administration.

(c) **Controlled substance criminal penalty.—(1)** In this subsection, "controlled substance" has the same meaning given that term in section 102 of the Comprehensive Drug Abuse Prevention and Control Act of 1970 (21 U.S.C. 802).

(2) A person violating subsection (b) of this section shall be fined under title 18, imprisoned for not more than 5 years, or both, if the violation is related to transporting a controlled substance by aircraft or aiding or facilitating a controlled substance violation and the transporting, aiding, or facilitating—

(A) is punishable by death or imprisonment of more than one year under a law of the United States or a State; or

(B) that is provided is related to an act punishable by death or imprisonment for more than one year under a law of the United States or a State related to a controlled substance (except a law related to simple possession of a controlled substance).

(3) A term of imprisonment imposed under paragraph (2) of this subsection shall be served in addition to, and not concurrently with, any other term of imprisonment imposed on the individual.

(d) **Seizure and forfeiture.—(1)** The Administrator of Drug Enforcement or the Commissioner of Customs may seize and forfeit under the customs laws an aircraft whose use is related to a violation of subsection (b) of this section, or to aid or facilitate a violation, regardless of whether a person is charged with the violation.

(2) An aircraft's use is presumed to have been related to a violation of, or to aid or facilitate a violation of—

(A) subsection (b)(1) of this section if the aircraft certificate of registration has been forged or altered;

(B) subsection (b)(3) of this section if there is an external display of false or misleading registration numbers or country of registration;

(C) subsection (b)(4) of this section if—

(i) the aircraft is registered to a false or fictitious person; or

(ii) the application form used to obtain the aircraft certificate of registration contains a material false statement;

(D) subsection (b)(5) of this section if the aircraft was operated when it was not registered under section 44103 of this title; or

(E) subsection (b)(9) of this section if the aircraft has a fuel tank or fuel system that was installed or altered—

(i) in violation of a regulation or requirement of the Administrator of the Federal Aviation Administration; or

(ii) if a certificate required to be issued for the installation or alteration is not carried on the aircraft.

(3) The Administrator of the Federal Aviation Administration, the Administrator of Drug Enforcement, and the Commissioner shall agree to a memorandum of understanding to establish procedures to carry out this subsection.

(e) Relationship to State laws.—This part does not prevent a State from establishing a criminal penalty, including providing for forfeiture and seizure of aircraft, for a person that—

(1) knowingly and willfully forges or alters an aircraft certificate of registration;

(2) knowingly sells, uses, attempts to use, or possesses with the intent to use, a fraudulent aircraft certificate of registration;

(3) knowingly and willfully displays or causes to be displayed on an aircraft a mark that is false or misleading about the nationality or registration of the aircraft; or

(4) obtains an aircraft certificate of registration from the Administrator of the Federal Aviation Administration by—

(A) knowingly and willfully falsifying or concealing a material fact;

(B) making a false, fictitious, or fraudulent statement; or

(C) making or using a false document knowing it contains a false, fictitious, or fraudulent statement or entry.

(Added Pub.L. 103–272, § 1(e), July 5, 1994, 108 Stat. 1235, and amended Pub.L. 104–287, § 5(78), Oct. 11, 1996, 110 Stat. 3397.)

HISTORICAL AND STATUTORY NOTES

Effective and Applicability Provisions

1996 Acts. Amendment by section 5(78) of Pub.L. 104–287 effective July 5, 1994, see section 8(1) of Pub.L. 104–287, set out as a note under section 5303 of this title.

Transfer of Functions

For transfer of functions, personnel, assets, and liabilities of the Transportation Security Administration (TSA) of the Department of Transportation, including the functions of the Secretary of Transportation, and of the Under Secretary of Transportation for Security, relating thereto, to the Secretary of Homeland Security, and for treatment of related references, see 6 U.S.C.A. §§ 203(2), 551(d), 552(d), and 557 of Title 6, Domestic Security, and the Department of Homeland Security Reorganization Plan of November 25, 2002, as modified, set out as a note under 6 U.S.C.A. § 542.

§ 46307. Violation of national defense airspace

A person that knowingly or willfully violates section 40103(b)(3) of this title or a regulation prescribed or order issued under section 40103(b)(3) shall be fined under title 18, imprisoned for not more than one year, or both.

(Added Pub.L. 103–272, § 1(e), July 5, 1994, 108 Stat. 1237.)

§ 46308. Interference with air navigation

A person shall be fined under title 18, imprisoned for not more than 5 years, or both, if the person—

(1) with intent to interfere with air navigation in the United States, exhibits in the United States a light or signal at a place or in a way likely to be mistaken for a true light or signal established under this part or for a true light or signal used at an air navigation facility;

(2) after a warning from the Administrator of the Federal Aviation Administration, continues to maintain a misleading light or signal; or

(3) knowingly interferes with the operation of a true light or signal.

(Added Pub.L. 103–272, § 1(e), July 5, 1994, 108 Stat. 1238.)

§ 46309. Concession and price violations

(a) Criminal penalty for offering, granting, giving, or helping to obtain concessions and lower prices.—An air carrier, foreign air carrier, ticket agent, or officer, agent, or employee of an air carrier, foreign air carrier, or ticket agent shall be fined under title 18 if the air carrier, foreign air carrier, ticket agent, officer, agent, or employee—

(1) knowingly and willfully offers, grants, or gives, or causes to be offered, granted, or given, a rebate or other concession in violation of this part; or

(2) by any means knowingly and willfully assists, or willingly allows, a person to obtain transportation or services subject to this part at less than the price lawfully in effect.

(b) Criminal penalty for receiving rebates, privileges, and facilities.—A person shall be fined under title 18 if the person by any means—

(1) knowingly and willfully solicits, accepts, or receives a rebate of a part of a price lawfully in effect for the foreign air transportation of property, or a service related to the foreign air transportation; or

(2) knowingly solicits, accepts, or receives a privilege or facility related to a matter the Secretary of Transportation requires be specified in a currently effective tariff applicable to the foreign air transportation of property.

(Added Pub.L. 103–272, § 1(e), July 5, 1994, 108 Stat. 1238.)

§ 46310. Reporting and recordkeeping violations

(a) General criminal penalty.—An air carrier or an officer, agent, or employee of an air carrier shall be fined under title 18 for intentionally—

(1) failing to make a report or keep a record under this part;

(2) falsifying, mutilating, or altering a report or record under this part; or

(3) filing a false report or record under this part.

(b) Safety regulation criminal penalty.—An air carrier or an officer, agent, or employee of an air carrier shall be fined under title 18, imprisoned for not more than 5 years, or both, for intentionally falsifying or concealing a material fact, or inducing reliance on a false statement of material fact, in a report or record under section 44701(a) or (b) or any of sections 44702–44716 of this title.

(Added Pub.L. 103–272, § 1(e), July 5, 1994, 108 Stat. 1238, and amended Pub.L. 103–429, § 6(56), Oct. 31, 1994, 108 Stat. 4385.)

HISTORICAL AND STATUTORY NOTES

Effective and Applicability Provisions

1994 Acts. Amendment by Pub.L. 103–429 effective July 5, 1994, see section 9 of Pub.L. 103–429, set out as a note under section 321 of this title.

§ 46311. Unlawful disclosure of information

(a) Criminal penalty.—The Secretary of Transportation, the Under Secretary of Transportation for Security with respect to security duties and powers designated to be carried out by the Under Secretary, the Administrator of the Federal Aviation Administration with respect to aviation safety duties and powers designated to be carried out by the Administrator, or an officer or employee of the Secretary, Under Secretary, or Administrator shall be fined under title 18, imprisoned for not more than 2 years, or both, if the Secretary, Under Secretary, Administrator, officer, or employee knowingly and willfully discloses information that—

(1) the Secretary, Under Secretary, Administrator, officer, or employee acquires when inspecting the records of an air carrier; or

(2) is withheld from public disclosure under section 40115 of this title.

(b) Nonapplication.—Subsection (a) of this section does not apply if—

(1) the officer or employee is directed by the Secretary, Under Secretary, or Administrator to disclose information that the Secretary, Under Secretary, or Administrator had ordered withheld; or

(2) the Secretary, Under Secretary, Administrator, officer, or employee is directed by a court of competent jurisdiction to disclose the information.

(c) Withholding information from Congress.—This section does not authorize the Secretary, Under Secretary, or Administrator to withhold information from a committee of Congress authorized to have the information.

(Added Pub.L. 103–272, § 1(e), July 5, 1994, 108 Stat. 1239, and amended Pub.L. 107–71, Title I, § 140(d)(6), Nov. 19, 2001, 115 Stat. 642.)

HISTORICAL AND STATUTORY NOTES

Transfer of Functions

For transfer of functions, personnel, assets, and liabilities of the Transportation Security Administration (TSA) of the Department of Transportation, including the functions of the Secretary of Transportation, and of the Under Secretary of Transportation for Security, relating thereto, to the Secretary of Homeland Security, and for treatment of related references, see 6 U.S.C.A. §§ 203(2), 551(d), 552(d), and 557 of Title 6, Domestic Security, and the Department of Homeland Security Reorganization Plan of November 25, 2002, as modified, set out as a note under 6 U.S.C.A. § 542.

§ 46312. Transporting hazardous material

(a) In general.—A person shall be fined under title 18, imprisoned for not more than 5 years, or both, if the person, in violation of a regulation or requirement related to the transportation of hazardous material prescribed by the Secretary of Transportation under this part or chapter 51—

(1) willfully delivers, or causes to be delivered, property containing hazardous material to an air carrier or to an operator of a civil aircraft for transportation in air commerce; or

(2) recklessly causes the transportation in air commerce of the property.

(b) Knowledge of regulations.—For purposes of subsection (a), knowledge by the person of the existence of a regulation or requirement related to the transportation of hazardous material prescribed by the Secretary under this part or chapter 51 is not an element of an offense under this section but shall be considered in mitigation of the penalty.

(Added Pub.L. 103–272, § 1(e), July 5, 1994, 108 Stat. 1239, and amended Pub.L. 106–181, Title V, § 507, Apr. 5, 2000, 114 Stat. 140; Pub.L. 109–59, Title VII, § 7128(a), Aug. 10, 2005, 119 Stat. 1909.)

HISTORICAL AND STATUTORY NOTES

References in Text

Chapter 51, referred to in subsecs. (a) and (b), is chapter 51 of this title, Transportation of Hazardous Material, 49 U.S.C.A. § 5101 et seq.

Effective and Applicability Provisions

2000 Acts. Amendment by Pub.L. 106–181 applicable only to fiscal years beginning after September 30, 1999, see section 3 of Pub.L. 106–181, set out as a note under section 106 of this title.

§ 46313. Refusing to appear or produce records

A person not obeying a subpena or requirement of the Secretary of Transportation (or the Under Secretary of Transportation for Security with respect to security duties and powers designated to be carried out by the Under Secretary or the Administrator of the Federal Aviation Administration with respect to aviation safety duties and powers designated to be carried out by the Administrator) to appear and testify or produce records shall be fined under title 18, imprisoned for not more than one year, or both.

(Added Pub.L. 103–272, § 1(e), July 5, 1994, 108 Stat. 1239, and amended Pub.L. 107–71, Title I, § 140(d)(7), Nov. 19, 2001, 115 Stat. 642.)

HISTORICAL AND STATUTORY NOTES

Transfer of Functions

For transfer of functions, personnel, assets, and liabilities of the Transportation Security Administration (TSA) of the Department of Transportation, including the functions of the Secretary of Transportation, and of the Under Secretary of Transportation for Security, relating thereto, to the Secretary of Homeland Security, and for treatment of related references, see 6 U.S.C.A. §§ 203(2), 551(d), 552(d), and 557 of Title 6, Domestic Security, and the Department of Homeland Security Reorganization Plan of November 25, 2002, as modified, set out as a note under 6 U.S.C.A. § 542.

§ 46314. Entering aircraft or airport area in violation of security requirements

(a) Prohibition.—A person may not knowingly and willfully enter, in violation of security requirements prescribed under section 44901, 44903(b) or (c), or 44906 of this title, an aircraft or an airport area that serves an air carrier or foreign air carrier.

(b) Criminal penalty.—(1) A person violating subsection (a) of this section shall be fined under title 18, imprisoned for not more than one year, or both.

(2) A person violating subsection (a) of this section with intent to commit, in the aircraft or airport area, a felony under a law of the United States or a State shall be fined under title 18, imprisoned for not more than 10 years, or both.

(Added Pub.L. 103–272, § 1(e), July 5, 1994, 108 Stat. 1239.)

§ 46315. Lighting violations involving transporting controlled substances by aircraft not providing air transportation

(a) Application.—This section applies only to aircraft not used to provide air transportation.

(b) Criminal penalty.—A person shall be fined under title 18, imprisoned for not more than 5 years, or both, if—

(1) the person knowingly and willfully operates an aircraft in violation of a regulation or requirement of the Administrator of the Federal Aviation Administration related to the display of navigation or anticollision lights;

(2) the person is knowingly transporting a controlled substance by aircraft or aiding or facilitating a controlled substance offense; and

(3) the transporting, aiding, or facilitating—

(A) is punishable by death or imprisonment for more than one year under a law of the United States or a State; or

(B) is provided in connection with an act punishable by death or imprisonment for more than one year under a law of the United States or a State related to a controlled substance (except a law related to simple possession of a controlled substance).

(Added Pub.L. 103–272, § 1(e), July 5, 1994, 108 Stat. 1240.)

§ 46316. General criminal penalty when specific penalty not provided

(a) Criminal penalty.—Except as provided by subsection (b) of this section, when another criminal penalty is not provided under this chapter, a person that knowingly and willfully violates this part, a regulation prescribed or order issued by the Secretary of Transportation (or the Under Secretary of Transportation for Security with respect to security duties and powers designated to be carried out by the Under Secretary or the Administrator of the Federal Aviation Administration with respect to aviation safety duties and powers designated to be carried out by the Administrator) under this part, or any term of a certificate or permit issued under section 41102, 41103, or 41302 of this title shall be fined under title 18. A separate violation occurs for each day the violation continues.

(b) Nonapplication.—Subsection (a) of this section does not apply to chapter 401 (except sections 40103(a) and (d), 40105, 40116, and 40117), chapter 441 (except section 44109), chapter 445, chapter 447 (except section 44718(a)), and chapter 449 (except sections 44902, 44903(d), 44904, and 44907–44909) of this title.

(Added Pub.L. 103–272, § 1(e), July 5, 1994, 108 Stat. 1240, and amended Pub.L. 104–287, § 5(79), Oct. 11, 1996, 110 Stat.

3397; Pub.L. 105–102, § 3(d)(1)(D), Nov. 20, 1997, 111 Stat. 2215; Pub.L. 107–71, Title I, § 140(d)(7), Nov. 19, 2001, 115 Stat. 642.)

HISTORICAL AND STATUTORY NOTES

Codifications

Pub.L. 105–102, § 3(d)(1)(D), amended Pub.L. 104–287, § 5(79), by substituting "section 44718(a)" for "sections 44717–44723" following "447 (except" thereby amending subsec. (b) of this section. Such amendment by section 3(d)(1)(D) of Pub.L. 105–102 effective as if included in 104–287 when enacted on October 11, 1996.

Effective and Applicability Provisions

1997 Acts. The amendment to this section by section 3(d) of Pub.L. 105–102 is effective Oct. 11, 1996.

Amendments by Pub.L. 105–102, § 3(a) to (d), effective as if included in the provisions of the Acts to which the amendments relate, see section 3(f) of Pub.L. 105–102, set out as a note under section 106 of this title.

1996 Acts. Amendment by section 5(79) of Pub.L. 104–287, effective July 5, 1994, see section 8(1) of Pub.L. 104–287, as amended by Pub.L. 105–102, § 3(d)(2)(A), set out as a note under section 5303 of this title.

Transfer of Functions

For transfer of functions, personnel, assets, and liabilities of the Transportation Security Administration (TSA) of the Department of Transportation, including the functions of the Secretary of Transportation, and of the Under Secretary of Transportation for Security, relating thereto, to the Secretary of Homeland Security, and for treatment of related references, see 6 U.S.C.A. §§ 203(2), 551(d), 552(d), and 557 of Title 6, Domestic Security, and the Department of Homeland Security Reorganization Plan of November 25, 2002, as modified, set out as a note under 6

§ 46317. Criminal penalty for pilots operating in air transportation without an airman's certificate

(a) General criminal penalty.—An individual shall be fined under title 18 or imprisoned for not more than 3 years, or both, if that individual—

(1) knowingly and willfully serves or attempts to serve in any capacity as an airman operating an aircraft in air transportation without an airman's certificate authorizing the individual to serve in that capacity; or

(2) knowingly and willfully employs for service or uses in any capacity as an airman to operate an aircraft in air transportation an individual who does not have an airman's certificate authorizing the individual to serve in that capacity.

(b) Controlled substance criminal penalty.—

(1) Controlled substances defined.—In this subsection, the term "controlled substance" has the meaning given that term in section 102 of the Comprehensive Drug Abuse Prevention and Control Act of 1970 (21 U.S.C. 802).

(2) Criminal penalty.—An individual violating subsection (a) shall be fined under title 18 or imprisoned for not more than 5 years, or both, if the violation is related to transporting a controlled substance by aircraft or aiding or facilitating a controlled substance violation and that transporting, aiding, or facilitating—

(A) is punishable by death or imprisonment of more than 1 year under a Federal or State law; or

(B) is related to an act punishable by death or imprisonment for more than 1 year under a Federal or State law related to a controlled substance (except a law related to simple possession (as that term is used in section 46306(c)) of a controlled substance).

(3) Terms of imprisonment.—A term of imprisonment imposed under paragraph (2) shall be served in addition to, and not concurrently with, any other term of imprisonment imposed on the individual subject to the imprisonment.

(Added Pub.L. 106–181, Title V, § 509(a), Apr. 5, 2000, 114 Stat. 141.)

HISTORICAL AND STATUTORY NOTES

Effective and Applicability Provisions

2000 Acts. Section applicable only to fiscal years beginning after September 30, 1999, see section 3 of Pub.L. 106–181, set out as a note under section 106 of this title.

§ 46318. Interference with cabin or flight crew

(a) General rule.—An individual who physically assaults or threatens to physically assault a member of the flight crew or cabin crew of a civil aircraft or any other individual on the aircraft, or takes any action that poses an imminent threat to the safety of the aircraft or other individuals on the aircraft is liable to the United States Government for a civil penalty of not more than $25,000.

(b) Compromise and setoff.—

(1) Compromise.—The Secretary may compromise the amount of a civil penalty imposed under this section.

(2) Setoff.—The United States Government may deduct the amount of a civil penalty imposed or compromised under this section from amounts the Government owes the person liable for the penalty.

(Added Pub.L. 106–181, Title V, § 511(a), Apr. 5, 2000, 114 Stat. 142.)

HISTORICAL AND STATUTORY NOTES

Effective and Applicability Provisions

2000 Acts. Section applicable only to fiscal years beginning after September 30, 1999, see section 3 of Pub.L. 106–181, set out as a note under section 106 of this title.

§ 46319. Permanent closure of an airport without providing sufficient notice

(a) Prohibition.—A public agency (as defined in section 47102) may not permanently close an airport listed in the national plan of integrated airport systems under section 47103 without providing written notice to the Administrator of the Federal Aviation Administration at least 30 days before the date of the closure.

(b) Publication of notice.—The Administrator shall publish each notice received under subsection (a) in the Federal Register.

(c) Civil penalty.—A public agency violating subsection (a) shall be liable for a civil penalty of $10,000 for each day that the airport remains closed without having given the notice required by this section.

(Added Pub.L. 108–176, Title I, § 185(a), Dec. 12, 2003, 117 Stat. 2517.)

HISTORICAL AND STATUTORY NOTES

Effective and Applicability Provisions

2003 Acts. Except as otherwise provided, amendments by Pub.L. 108–176 applicable to fiscal years beginning after Sept. 30, 2003, see Pub.L. 108–176, § 3, set out as a note under 49 U.S.C.A. § 106.

CHAPTER 465—SPECIAL AIRCRAFT JURISDICTION OF THE UNITED STATES

Sec.

[1] So in original. This item probably should not appear.

§ 46501. Definitions

In this chapter—

(1) "aircraft in flight" means an aircraft from the moment all external doors are closed following boarding—

(A) through the moment when one external door is opened to allow passengers to leave the aircraft; or

(B) until, if a forced landing, competent authorities take over responsibility for the aircraft and individuals and property on the aircraft.

(2) "special aircraft jurisdiction of the United States" includes any of the following aircraft in flight:

(A) a civil aircraft of the United States.

(B) an aircraft of the armed forces of the United States.

(C) another aircraft in the United States.

(D) another aircraft outside the United States—

(i) that has its next scheduled destination or last place of departure in the United States, if the aircraft next lands in the United States;

(ii) on which an individual commits an offense (as defined in the Convention for the Suppression of Unlawful Seizure of Aircraft) if the aircraft lands in the United States with the individual still on the aircraft; or

(iii) against which an individual commits an offense (as defined in subsection (d) or (e) of article I, section I of the Convention for the Suppression of Unlawful Acts against the Safety of Civil Aviation) if the aircraft lands in the United States with the individual still on the aircraft.

(E) any other aircraft leased without crew to a lessee whose principal place of business is in the United States or, if the lessee does not have a principal place of business, whose permanent residence is in the United States.

(3) an individual commits an offense (as defined in the Convention for the Suppression of Unlawful Seizure of Aircraft) when the individual, when on an aircraft in flight—

(A) by any form of intimidation, unlawfully seizes, exercises control of, or attempts to seize or exercise control of, the aircraft; or

(B) is an accomplice of an individual referred to in subclause (A) of this clause.

(Added Pub.L. 103–272, § 1(e), July 5, 1994, 108 Stat. 1240.)

§ 46502. Aircraft piracy

(a) In special aircraft jurisdiction.—(1) In this subsection—

(A) "aircraft piracy" means seizing or exercising control of an aircraft in the special aircraft jurisdiction of the United States by force, violence, threat of force or violence, or any form of intimidation, and with wrongful intent.

(B) an attempt to commit aircraft piracy is in the special aircraft jurisdiction of the United States although the aircraft is not in flight at the time of the attempt if the aircraft would have been in the special aircraft jurisdiction of the United States had the aircraft piracy been completed.

(2) An individual committing or attempting or conspiring to commit aircraft piracy—

(A) shall be imprisoned for at least 20 years; or

(B) notwithstanding section 3559(b) of title 18, if the death of another individual results from the commission or attempt, shall be put to death or imprisoned for life.

(b) Outside special aircraft jurisdiction.—(1) An individual committing or conspiring to commit an offense (as defined in the Convention for the Suppression of Unlawful Seizure of Aircraft) on an aircraft in flight outside the special aircraft jurisdiction of the United States—

(A) shall be imprisoned for at least 20 years; or

(B) notwithstanding section 3559(b) of title 18, if the death of another individual results from the commission or attempt, shall be put to death or imprisoned for life.

(2) There is jurisdiction over the offense in paragraph (1) if—

(A) a national of the United States was aboard the aircraft;

(B) an offender is a national of the United States; or

(C) an offender is afterwards found in the United States.

(3) For purposes of this subsection, the term "national of the United States" has the meaning prescribed in section 101(a)(22) of the Immigration and Nationality Act (8 U.S.C. 1101(a)(22)).

(Added Pub.L. 103–272, § 1(e), July 5, 1994, 108 Stat. 1241, and amended Pub.L. 103–429, § 6(61), Oct. 31, 1994, 108 Stat. 4385; Pub.L. 104–132, Title VII, §§ 721(a), 723(b), Apr. 24, 1996, 110 Stat. 1298, 1300.)

HISTORICAL AND STATUTORY NOTES

Effective and Applicability Provisions

1994 Acts. Amendment by Pub.L. 103–429 effective July 5, 1994, see section 9 of Pub.L. 103–429, set out as a note under section 321 of this title.

Death Penalty Procedures for Certain Air Piracy Cases Occurring Before Enactment of the Federal Death Penalty Act of 1994

Pub.L. 109–177, Title II, § 211, Mar. 9, 2006, 120 Stat. 230, provided that:

"**(a) In general.**—Section 60003 of the Violent Crime Control and Law Enforcement Act of 1994 (Public Law 103–322), is amended, as of the time of its enactment [Sept. 13, 1994], by adding at the end the following:

"'**(c) Death penalty procedures for certain previous aircraft piracy violations.**—[Pub.L. 103–322, Title VI, § 60003(c), as added Pub.L. 109–177, Title II, § 211(a), Mar. 9, 2006, 120 Stat. 230; set out as a note under this section.]

"**(b) Severability clause.**—If any provision of section 60003(b)(2) of the Violent Crime and Law Enforcement Act of 1994 (Public Law 103–322 [repealing former 49 U.S.C.A. § 46503]), or the application thereof to any person or any circumstance is held invalid, the remainder of such section and the application of such section to other persons or circumstances shall not be affected thereby."

Death Penalty Procedures for Certain Previous Aircraft Piracy Violations

Pub.L. 103–322, Title VI, § 60003(c), as added Pub.L. 109–177, Title II, § 211(a), Mar. 9, 2006, 120 Stat. 230, provided that: "An individual convicted of violating section 46502 of title 49, United States Code, or its predecessor, may be sentenced to death in accordance with the procedures established in chapter 228 of title 18, United States Code [18 U.S.C.A. § 3591 et seq.], if for any offense committed before the enactment of the Violent Crime Control and Law Enforcement Act of 1994 (Public Law 103–322) [Pub.L. 103–322, Sept. 13, 1994, 108 Stat. 1796], but after the enactment of the Antihijacking Act of 1974 (Public Law 93–366) [Pub.L. 93–366, Aug. 5, 1974, 88 Stat. 409], it is determined by the finder of fact, before consideration of the factors set forth in sections 3591(a)(2) and 3592(a) and (c) of title 18, United States Code, that one or more of the factors set forth in former section 46503(c)(2) of title 49, United States Code, or its predecessor, has been proven by the Government to exist, beyond a reasonable doubt, and that none of the factors set forth in former section 46503(c)(1) of title 49, United States Code, or its predecessor, has been proven by the defendant to exist, by a preponderance of the information. The meaning of the term 'especially heinous, cruel, or depraved', as used in the factor set forth in former section 46503(c)(2)(B)(iv) of title 49, United States Code, or its predecessor, shall be narrowed by adding the limiting language 'in that it involved torture or serious physical abuse to the victim', and shall be construed as when that term is used in section 3592(c)(6) of title 18, United States Code."

[Pub.L. 109–177, Title II, § 211(a), Mar. 9, 2006, 120 Stat. 230, provided in part that this note is effective as of the time of the enactment of Pub.L. 103–322, which was approved on Sept. 13, 1994.]

Aircraft Piracy

The United States is a party to the Convention for the Suppression of Unlawful Seizure of Aircraft, signed at The Hague, Dec. 16, 1970, entered into force as to the United States, Oct. 14, 1971, 22 UST 1641.

§ 46503. Interference with security screening personnel

An individual in an area within a commercial service airport in the United States who, by assaulting a Federal, airport, or air carrier employee who has security duties within the airport, interferes with the performance of the duties of the employee or lessens the ability of the employee to perform those duties, shall be fined under title 18, imprisoned for not more than 10 years, or both. If the individual used a dangerous weapon in committing the assault or interference, the individual may be imprisoned for any term of years or life imprisonment.

(Added Pub.L. 107–71, Title I, § 114(a), Nov. 19, 2001, 115 Stat. 623.)

HISTORICAL AND STATUTORY NOTES

Severability

If any provision of Pub.L. 103–322, § 60003(b)(2) [which repealed a prior version of this section], or the application thereof to any person or circumstance is held invalid, the remainder of such section and the application of such section to other persons or circumstances, shall not be affected, see Pub.L. 109–177, § 211(b), set out as a note under 49 U.S.C.A. § 46502.

Prior Provisions

A prior section 46503, added Pub.L. 103–272, § 1(e), July 5, 1994, 108 Stat. 1242, which related to death penalty sentencing procedure for individuals convicted of aircraft piracy, was repealed by Pub.L. 103–322, Title VI, § 60003(b)(2), Sept. 13, 1994, 108 Stat. 1970. See 18 U.S.C. 3591 et seq.

§ 46504. Interference with flight crew members and attendants

An individual on an aircraft in the special aircraft jurisdiction of the United States who, by assaulting or intimidating a flight crew member or flight attendant of the aircraft, interferes with the performance of the duties of the member or attendant or lessens the ability of the member or attendant to perform those duties, or attempts or conspires to do such an act, shall be fined under title 18, imprisoned for not more than 20 years, or both. However, if a dangerous weapon is used in assaulting or intimidating the member or attendant, the individual shall be imprisoned for any term of years or for life.

(Added Pub.L. 103–272, § 1(e), July 5, 1994, 108 Stat. 1244, and amended Pub.L. 107–56, Title VIII, § 811(i), Oct. 26, 2001, 115 Stat. 382.)

§ 46505. Carrying a weapon or explosive on an aircraft

(a) Definition.—In this section, "loaded firearm" means a starter gun or a weapon designed or converted to expel a projectile through an explosive, that has a cartridge, a detonator, or powder in the chamber, magazine, cylinder, or clip.

(b) General criminal penalty.—An individual shall be fined under title 18, imprisoned for not more than 10 years, or both, if the individual—

(1) when on, or attempting to get on, an aircraft in, or intended for operation in, air transportation or intrastate air transportation, has on or about the individual or the property of the individual a concealed dangerous weapon that is or would be accessible to the individual in flight;

(2) has placed, attempted to place, or attempted to have placed a loaded firearm on that aircraft in property not accessible to passengers in flight; or

(3) has on or about the individual, or has placed, attempted to place, or attempted to have placed on that aircraft, an explosive or incendiary device.

(c) Criminal penalty involving disregard for human life.—An individual who willfully and without regard for the safety of human life, or with reckless disregard for the safety of human life, violates subsection (b) of this section, shall be fined under title 18, imprisoned for not more than 20 years, or both, and, if death results to any person, shall be imprisoned for any term of years or for life.

(d) Nonapplication.—Subsection (b)(1) of this section does not apply to—

(1) a law enforcement officer of a State or political subdivision of a State, or an officer or employee of the United States Government, authorized to carry arms in an official capacity;

(2) another individual the Administrator of the Federal Aviation Administration or the Under Secretary of Transportation for Security by regulation authorizes to carry a dangerous weapon in air transportation or intrastate air transportation; or

(3) an individual transporting a weapon (except a loaded firearm) in baggage not accessible to a passenger in flight if the air carrier was informed of the presence of the weapon.

(e) Conspiracy.—If two or more persons conspire to violate subsection (b) or (c), and one or more of such persons do any act to effect the object of the conspiracy, each of the parties to such conspiracy shall be punished as provided in such subsection.

(Added Pub.L. 103–272, § 1(e), July 5, 1994, 108 Stat. 1244, and amended Pub.L. 104–132, Title VII, § 705(b), Apr. 24, 1996, 110 Stat. 1295; Pub.L. 107–56, Title VIII, §§ 810(g), 811(j), Oct. 26, 2001, 115 Stat. 381, 382; Pub.L. 107–71, Title I, § 140(d)(8), Nov. 19, 2001, 115 Stat. 642.)

HISTORICAL AND STATUTORY NOTES

Transfer of Functions

For transfer of functions, personnel, assets, and liabilities of the Transportation Security Administration (TSA) of the Department of Transportation, including the functions of the Secretary of Transportation, and of the Under Secretary of Transportation for Security, relating thereto, to the Secretary of Homeland Security, and for treatment of related references, see 6 U.S.C.A. §§ 203(2), 551(d), 552(d), and 557 of Title 6, Domestic Security, and the Department of Homeland Security Reorganization Plan of November 25, 2002, as modified, set out as a note under 6 U.S.C.A. § 542.

§ 46506. Application of certain criminal laws to acts on aircraft

An individual on an aircraft in the special aircraft jurisdiction of the United States who commits an act that—

(1) if committed in the special maritime and territorial jurisdiction of the United States (as defined in section 7 of title 18) would violate section 113, 114, 661, 662, 1111, 1112, 1113, or 2111 or chapter

109A of title 18, shall be fined under title 18, imprisoned under that section or chapter, or both; or

(2) if committed in the District of Columbia would violate section 9 of the Act of July 29, 1892 (D.C. Code § 22–1112), shall be fined under title 18, imprisoned under section 9 of the Act, or both.

(Added Pub.L. 103–272, § 1(e), July 5, 1994, 108 Stat. 1245.)

HISTORICAL AND STATUTORY NOTES

References in Text

Section 9 of the Act of July 29, 1892, referred to in par. (2), is section 9 of the Act entitled "An Act for the preservation of the public peace and the protection of property within the District of Columbia", 27 Stat. 324, c. 320, as amended. Section 9 of such Act, which relates to the imposition of fines and criminal penalties for obscene or indecent exposure and sexual solicitation, was not classified to the U.S. Code.

§ 46507. False information and threats

An individual shall be fined under title 18, imprisoned for not more than 5 years, or both, if the individual—

(1) knowing the information to be false, willfully and maliciously or with reckless disregard for the safety of human life, gives, or causes to be given, under circumstances in which the information reasonably may be believed, false information about an alleged attempt being made or to be made to do an act that would violate section 46502(a), 46504, 46505, or 46506 of this title; or

(2)(A) threatens to violate section 46502(a), 46504, 46505, or 46506 of this title, or causes a threat to violate any of those sections to be made; and

(B) has the apparent determination and will to carry out the threat.

(Added Pub.L. 103–272, § 1(e), July 5, 1994, 108 Stat. 1245.)

FEDERAL CRIMINAL CODE AND RULES INDEX

References are to United States Code Annotated unless otherwise noted.

Constitution of the United States (see text following Title 18 U.S. Code).

CITATION ABBREVIATIONS

FRCRP	**Federal Rules of Criminal Procedure**
HCR	**Rules Governing Cases Under Section 2254, 28 U.S.Code**
MAS	**Rules Governing Proceedings Under Section 2255, 28 U.S.Code**
ATRC	**Rules for the Alien Terrorist Removal Court**
FRE	**Federal Rules of Evidence**
FRAP	**Federal Rules of Appellate Procedure**
FRAP Form	**Federal Rules of Appellate Procedure Form**
SCR	**Rules of the Supreme Court of the United States**
EON	**Executive Order Number**
nt	**Note**

†